ThE STONE EdITION

TANACh

ArtScroll Series®

A PROJECT OF THE

Mesorah Heritage Foundation

Rabbi Nosson Scherman / Rabbi Meir Zlotowitz
General Editors

TANACH

תורה נביאים כתובים

The ArtScroll Series®

Published by

Mesorah Publications, ltd

THE
STONE
EDITION

THE TORAH / PROPHETS / WRITINGS:
THE TWENTY-FOUR BOOKS OF THE BIBLE
NEWLY TRANSLATED AND ANNOTATED

Edited by
Rabbi Nosson Scherman

Contributing Editors:
Rabbi Yaakov Blinder
Rabbi Avie Gold
Rabbi Meir Zlotowitz

Designed by
Rabbi Sheah Brander

FIRST FULL SIZE EDITION
First Impression ... December 1996

FIRST STUDENT SIZE EDITION
Seven Impressions ... August 1998 — October 2009

SECOND STUDENT SIZE EDITION
First Impression ... August 2011
Second Impression ... December 2012

Published and Distributed by
MESORAH PUBLICATIONS, Ltd.
4401 Second Avenue
Brooklyn, New York 11232

Distributed in Europe by
LEHMANNS
Unit E, Viking Business Park
Rolling Mill Road
Jarrow, Tyne & Wear NE32 3DP
England

Distributed in Australia & New Zealand by
GOLDS WORLD OF JUDAICA
3-13 William Street
Balaclava, Melbourne 3183
Victoria Australia

Distributed in Israel by
SIFRIATI / A. GITLER — BOOKS
6 Hayarkon Street
Bnei Brak 51127, Israel

Distributed in South Africa by
KOLLEL BOOKSHOP
Northfield Centre 17 Northfield Avenue
Glenhazel 2192, Johannesburg, South Africa

THE ARTSCROLL SERIES® / STONE EDITION
THE TANACH — STUDENT SIZE EDITION

[Hunter Green] — ISBN 10: 1-57819-109-2 / ISBN 13: 978-1-57819-109-3
[Ivory Parchment] — ISBN 10: 1-57819-110-6 / ISBN 13: 978-1-57819-110-9
[Deluxe Leather] — ISBN 10: 1-57819-111-4 / ISBN 13: 978-1-57819-111-6
[Black] — ISBN 10: 1-57819-112-2 / ISBN 13: 978-1-57819-112-3

Typography by CompuScribe at ArtScroll Studios, Ltd.
Printed in Canada. Custom bound by **Sefercraft, Inc.,** Brooklyn, N.Y.

The patron of the
STONE EDITION OF TANACH is

Mr. Irving I. Stone נ"י

*T*his is yet another milestone in a great career
that has propelled Jewish life, Torah study,
and Jewish education to height after height.

When Irving I. Stone began his work for
Jewish posterity, day schools were a rarity
and intensive Jewish education almost a relic.
To a man raised with the conviction that
"Jewish education means Jewish survival,"
this was intolerable.
To a man whose vocabulary
did not contain the word "impossible,"
the prevalent apathy was unacceptable.

Others moaned; he moved.

Today, the continent is crowded with Torah schools
and foundations put education on their urgent agenda.
In great measure this is thanks to Irving I. Stone.

This volume brings his illustrious career to a new plateau.
The STONE EDITION OF TANACH will open millions of
minds and hearts to Torah, for generations to come.

Table of Contents

תורה / Torah [Haftaros are listed at the end of each Sidra]

TORAH READING, MAFTIR AND HAFTARAH FOR FESTIVALS AND OTHER SPECIAL OCCASIONS

OCCASION	TORAH READING	PAGE	MAFTIR	PAGE	HAFTARAH	PAGE
ROSH CHODESH	Numbers 28:1-15	398				
SABBATH EREV ROSH CHODESH	Regular weekly *Parashah*		Regular weekly *Maftir*		*I Samuel* 20:18-42	696
SABBATH ROSH CHODESH	Regular weekly *Parashah*		Numbers 28:9-15	400	*Isaiah* 66:1-24	1066
FIRST DAY ROSH HASHANAH	Genesis Ch. 21	42	Numbers 29:1-6	400	*I Samuel* 1:1-2:10	646
SECOND DAY ROSH HASHANAH	Genesis Ch. 22	46	Numbers 29:1-6	400	*Jeremiah* 31:1-19	1142
FAST OF GEDALIAH[1]	Exodus 32:11-14;	216			*Isaiah* 55:6-56:8	1050
YOM KIPPUR—SHACHARIS	Leviticus Ch. 16	284	Numbers 29:7-11	402	*Isaiah* 57:14-58:14	1052
YOM KIPPUR—MINCHAH	Leviticus Ch. 18	290			*Book of Jonah*	1372
FIRST DAY SUCCOS	Leviticus 22:26-23:44	302	Numbers 29:12-16	402	*Zechariah* 14:1-21	1424
SECOND DAY SUCCOS	Leviticus 22:26-23:44	302	Numbers 29:12-16	402	*I Kings* 8:2-21	820
DAY 1 CHOL HAMOED SUCCOS	Numbers 29:17-25	402				
DAY 2 CHOL HAMOED SUCCOS	Numbers 29:20-28	402				
DAY 3 CHOL HAMOED SUCCOS	Numbers 29:23-31	402				
DAY 4 CHOL HAMOED SUCCOS	Numbers 29:26-34	402				
SABBATH CHOL HAMOED SUCCOS	Exodus 33:12-34:26	220	See note 2 below	402	*Ezekiel* 38:18-39:16	1298
HOSHANA RABBAH	Numbers 29:26-34	402				
SHEMINI ATZERES	Deuteronomy 14:22-16:17	462	Numbers 29:35-30:1	404	*I Kings* 8:54-9:1	826
SIMCHAS TORAH	Deuteronomy 33:1-34:12 Genesis 1:1-2:3	510 2	Numbers 29:35-30:1	404	*Joshua* 1:1-18	518
DAY 1 CHANUKAH	Numbers 7:1-17	340				
DAY 2 CHANUKAH	Numbers 7:18-29	342				
DAY 3 CHANUKAH	Numbers 7:24-35	342				
DAY 4 CHANUKAH	Numbers 7:30-41	342				
DAY 5 CHANUKAH	Numbers 7:36-47	344				
DAY 6 CHANUKAH [Rosh Chodesh]	Numbers 28:1-15 Numbers 7:42-47	398 344				
DAY 7 CHANUKAH	Numbers 7:48-59	344				
DAY 7 CHANUKAH [Rosh Chodesh]	Numbers 28:1-15 Numbers 7:42-47	398 344				
DAY 8 CHANUKAH	Numbers 7:54-8:4	344				
FIRST SABBATH OF CHANUKAH	Regular weekly *Parashah*		See note 3 below		*Zechariah* 2:14-4:7	1408
SECOND SABBATH OF CHANUKAH	Regular weekly *Parashah*		Numbers 7:54-8:4	344	*I Kings* 7:40-50	820

OCCASION	TORAH READING	PAGE	MAFTIR	PAGE	HAFTARAH	PAGE
TENTH OF TEVES[1]	Exodus 32:11-14; 34:1-10	216			Isaiah 55:6-56:8	1050
PARASHAS SHEKALIM	Regular weekly Parashah[4]		Exodus 30:11-16	212	II Kings 11:17-12:17	908
PARASHAS ZACHOR	Regular weekly Parashah		Deuteronomy 25:17-19	486	I Samuel 15:1-34	680
FAST OF ESTHER[1]	Exodus 32:11-14; 34:1-10	216			Isaiah 55:6-56:8	1050
PURIM	Exodus 17:8-16	176				
PARASHAS PARAH	Regular weekly Parashah		Numbers 19:1-22	376	Ezekiel 36:16-38	1292
PARASHAS HACHODESH	Regular weekly Parashah[4]		Exodus 12:1-20	160	Ezekiel 45:16-46:18	1320
SABBATH HAGADOL	Regular weekly Parashah		Regular weekly Maftir		Malachi 3:4-24	1430
FIRST DAY PESACH	Exodus 12:21-51	162	Numbers 28:16-25	400	Joshua 3:5-7; 5:2-6:1; 6:27	522
SECOND DAY PESACH	Leviticus 22:26-23:44	302	Numbers 28:16-25	400	II Kings 23:1-9, 21-25	940
DAY 1 CHOL HAMOED PESACH[5]	Exodus 13:1-16 Numbers 28:19-25	164 400				
DAY 2 CHOL HAMOED PESACH[5]	Exodus 22:24-23:19 Numbers 28:19-25	190 400				
DAY 3 CHOL HAMOED PESACH[5]	Exodus 34:1-26 Numbers 28:19-25	220 400				
DAY 4 CHOL HAMOED PESACH	Numbers 9:1-14 Numbers 28:19-25	348 400				
SABBATH CHOL HAMOED PESACH[5]	Exodus 33:12-34:26	220	Numbers 28:19-25	400	Ezekiel 37:1-14	1294
SEVENTH DAY PESACH	Exodus 13:17-15:26	166	Numbers 28:19-25	400	II Samuel 22:1-51	782
EIGHTH DAY PESACH (WEEKDAY)	Deuteronomy 15:19-16:17	466	Numbers 28:19-25	400	Isaiah 10:32-12:6	972
EIGHTH DAY PESACH (SABBATH)	Deuteronomy 14:22-16:17	462	Numbers 28:19-25	400	Isaiah 10:32-12:6	972
FIRST DAY SHAVUOS	Exodus 19:1-20:23	180	Numbers 28:26-31	400	Ezekiel 1:1-28; 3:12	1208
SECOND DAY SHAVUOS (WEEKDAY)	Deuteronomy 15:19-16:17	466	Numbers 28:26-31	400	Habakkuk 2:20-3:19	1392
SECOND DAY SHAVUOS (SABBATH)	Deuteronomy 14:22-16:17	462	Numbers 28:26-31	400	Habakkuk 2:20-3:19	1392
SEVENTEENTH OF TAMMUZ[1]	Exodus 32:11-14; 34:1-10	216			Isaiah 55:6-56:8	1050
TISHAH B'AV – SHACHARIS	Deuteronomy 4:25-40	438			Jeremiah 8:13-9:23	1092
TISHAH B'AV – MINCHAH	Exodus 32:11-14, 34:1-10	216			Isaiah 55:6-56:8	1050

1. On these days the Torah is read during both *Shacharis* and *Minchah*. The *Haftarah* is read during *Minchah* only.

2. If Sabbath Chol HaMoed is on day one — *Numbers* 29:17-22 (p. 402) day two — *Numbers* 29:20-25 (p. 402); day four — *Numbers* 29:26-31 (p. 402).

3. If the Sabbath of Chanukah is on day one — *Numbers* 7:1-17 (p. 340); day two — *Numbers* 7:18-23 (p. 342); day three — *Numbers* 7:24-29 (p. 342); day four — *Numbers* 7:30-35 (p. 342); day five — *Numbers* 7:36-41 (p. 344); day six — six *aliyos* are given from the regular weekly *Parashah*, then *Numbers* 28:9-15 (p. 400) is read as the seventh *aliyah*, then *Numbers* 7:42-47 (p. 344) is read as *maftir*; day seven — *Numbers* 7:48-53 (p. 344).

4. If *Parashas Shekalim* or *HaChodesh* falls on Rosh Chodesh, six *aliyos* are given from the regular weekly *Parashah*, then *Numbers* 28:9-15 (p. 400) is read as the seventh *aliyah*.

5. When the first day of Chol HaMoed Pesach occurs on the Sabbath, the readings of the first two days of Chol HaMoed are each postponed one day and the reading of the third day is omitted.

This personal-size offering of the Stone Edition of Tanach is further testimony to the resurgent interest in Torah as understood by classic commentators. It comes in the wake of the vastly popular full-size edition, which has achieved unprecedented popularity throughout the English-speaking world. Its goal, like that of all our work, is to help the people of the Torah come closer to the Giver of the Torah. The public's response to the work of the Mesorah Heritage Foundation and the various books of the ArtScroll Series — on Tanach, Mishnah, Talmud, liturgy, and so on — has demonstrated that there is a thirst for Torah knowledge, that people want it in their own language, and that they want it to be presented in a manner that is faithful to the interpretation of the Sages and the classic commentators. We are hopeful that, with God's help, this new Tanach will be equally useful and well received.

This volume is in response to countless requests from many sectors of the Jewish community for a one-volume Tanach that is accurate, graceful, clear, and, most of all, faithful to traditional Torah commentary. After years of preparation, we present it to the public with the prayer that it will become a fit vehicle to open the portals of the Written Torah to more and more Jews and that, having tasted the beauty of the Word of God, they will follow the Mishnah's exhortation: "Delve in [the Torah] and continue to delve in [the Torah], for everything is in it. Look deeply into it; grow old and gray over it, and do not stir from it, for you can have no better portion than it" (*Avos* 5:26).

TRANSLATION

THE FIRST GOAL OF A TRANSLATION MUST BE ACCURACY; no effort was spared in the successful quest of that goal. Scriptural Hebrew is laden with nuance and meaning. The language is replete with allusion. The scholars involved in this task were consumed with the sense of mission — that they were dealing with the sacred and eternal word of God, not mere "literature"; that their task was not to rewrite the text, but to convey its meaning faithfully. The translation balances the lofty beauty of the Hebrew with the need to provide a literate and comprehensible English rendering. Where a choice had to be made, we preferred fidelity to the text over inaccurate simplicity, but occasionally we had to stray from the literal translation or Hebrew syntax in order to capture the essence of a phrase or to make it intelligible in English. We feel that the translators have succeeded admirably.

The reader will note that this translation very often varies from other ArtScroll translations of Scripture. This was necessitated by the nature of this work. In standard ArtScroll works, wherever the Hebrew was obscure, the extensive commentary would clarify and give varying opinions on its meaning; consequently, the translation could remain close to the Hebrew and rely on the commentary. For this edition, however, the translation had to stand on its own and be clear without resort to the notes, wherever possible.

In the Chumash portion of this work, the translation follows *Rashi*, the "Father of Commentators," because the study of Chumash has been synonymous with Chumash-*Rashi* for nine centuries. In the Prophets and the Writings, however, following the guidance of our great mentors, we are more eclectic. The translation of these Books utilizes all the classic commentators, such as *Targum, Ramban, Radak, Ralbag, Ibn Ezra, Kara, Metzudos, Malbim* and others. While the translation always follows an authoritative opinion, we tried to choose the interpretation that would best fit the text and be as clear as possible to the reader.

We use the word "HASHEM," (literally "the Name") as the translation of the Tetragrammaton, the sacred Hebrew Four-letter Name of God. In the commentary we often refer to it as "the Four-letter Name." For the Hebrew *Elohim* and *El*, which are more general and less "personal" Names of the Deity, we use the translation God.

Prophecies and prayers are indented for prominence.

COMMENTARY

BECAUSE IT PROVIDES CLARITY AND PERSPECTIVE, the commentary is one of the most important features of this volume, despite its relative brevity. The commentary serves three major functions: to clarify the meaning of an obscure verse or phrase; to provide background information needed to understand a narrative or concept; to explain the halachic or philosophical basis of an event or course of action.

The comments are almost invariably drawn from Talmudic or rabbinic literature; in this sense, the commentary may be regarded as an anthology, but it is original in its choice and blend of material. Many attributed comments are shortened or given only in part, and unattributed comments often contain strands from several sources; all are grounded in traditional sources. An asterisk in the translation indicates a comment. A bibliography and brief description of the sources appear in the Stone Edition of the Chumash. For a more extensive commentary on Books of Scripture, the reader is directed to the ongoing ArtScroll Tanach Series.

The volume includes a generous selection of charts, illustrations, diagrams, and timelines, all of which assist in the comprehension of the text.

MARGINAL AIDS AND ANNOTATIONS

HELPFUL SERVICES TO THE READER may be found in the margins of the text. To aid in the understanding of the context, brief notes appear alongside the translation, to introduce topics, summarize the flow of the narrative, and identify speakers.

The place of Sabbath *aliyahs* is indicated at the right of the Hebrew text. Chapter and verse numbers are found next to both the Hebrew and English texts.

The location of the Haftarah, according to each of the various customs, is noted at the end of each Sidra, and also in a separate table. In addition, the Haftarah readings in the Prophets are indicated by arrows at the beginning and end, and also by gray bars alongside the text of the Hebrew Prophets.

TRANSLITERATION

CHOICE OF TRANSLITERATION PRESENTS A PROBLEM in all works of this sort. Ashkenazi, pure Sephardi, current Israeli, and generally accepted scholarly usages frequently diverge, and such familiar names as Isaac, Jacob, and Moses differ from them all. All ArtScroll commentaries use a cross between the Sephardi and Ashkenazi transliterations, using Sephardi vowels and Ashkenazi consonants. Thus, we use *Akeidas Yitzchak*, rather than *Akedat Izhak* or *Akeidas Yitzchok*. True, this blend may require some adjustment on the part of many readers, but it has proven successful. In the translation of the Text, however, we follow the traditionally accepted English versions, such as Moses, Methuselah, Isaac, and so on. This will surely ease the way for readers who have become familiar with standard English spellings; for those more familiar with the original Hebrew text, the transition will present little or no difficulty. Nevertheless, a table of Hebrew names with their English equivalents has been provided (p. 2049).

HEBREW TEXT

FOR THE HEBREW TEXT, WE FOLLOW THE TRADITIONAL EDITIONS that have been used for centuries. The texts that are read publicly (Chumash, Haftaros, and Five Megillos) are taken from the standard Chumashim, as they appear in the Stone Edition of the Chumash. For the balance of Scripture, we follow the traditional *Mikraos Gedolos* editions that have been used for centuries. In order to assure the accuracy of the text, including the vowelization, grammatical signs, and the cantillation (*trop*) — and to correct errors that have crept into the printed texts over the years — we have engaged many teams of proofreaders, in America and Israel, who have consulted the various editions.

❦ ❦ ❦

THE STONE EDITION

IT IS FITTING THAT THIS EDITION OF THE TANACH, which will bring a new appreciation of the Torah to multitudes, has been dedicated by a man who has been a lifelong pioneer in bringing new horizons to Jewish education. MR. IRVING I. STONE grew up in Cleveland, Ohio, a city where Torah education was scarce — as it was across the length and breadth of the continent in the first half of this century — but he lived in a home where Torah was precious. His parents, JACOB AND JENNIE SAPIRSTEIN, ע"ה, taught him by example to love learning, and imbued him with the conviction that superior teaching is the best way to communicate the infectious joy of Torah study to Jews in the Western world.

Irving I. Stone became a leader of his industry, and simultaneously he and his wife BEATRICE ע"ה became leaders in the uphill struggle for Jewish education. The first major tribute to their vision and generosity was the Hebrew Academy of Cleveland, the model day school that has been a partnership between its founder, RABBI NACHUM ZEV DESSLER, and the Stone family for over fifty years.

The Stone vision of Orthodox life was never narrow. Irving Stone was convinced that the way to bring Jews close to Torah was to bring Torah to Jews. Wherever he found a cause that was dedicated to that goal, he adopted it as his own. The people and institutions that have earned his friendship and support span the gamut of Jewish life. Diverse though they may be, they share his commitment to effective and inspired teaching and to building vibrant Jewish communities. The list of institutions and leaders who are beneficiaries of his support is a worldwide honor roll of Torah education and Jewish philanthropy.

Nor was he content with his own accomplishments. The increasing nationwide support of Jewish community federations for Torah education throughout the land, especially in Cleveland, is a tribute to Irving Stone's success in communicating his zeal to Jewish leaders around the country.

IRVING AND HELEN STONE are writing new chapters in the story of Jewish eternity — and one of those chapters is this edition of the Tanach. Joining them in the dedication of this momentous work are MORRY AND JUDY WEISS. Mr. Stone's son-in-law and colleague, Morry Weiss epitomizes the very finest of the next generation of Jewish leadership.

We pray that this great undertaking will be a source of merit for the entire Stone-Weiss family, including Mr. Stone's other children, HENSHA, NEIL and MYRNA, their families, and all his grandchildren and great-grandchildren.

This Tanach will, we pray, fill a need for countless thousands of people, providing them with a work that is faithful to tradition and accessible to intelligent readers.

For as long as English-speaking Jews of today and tomorrow are nourished by the wisdom of the Torah as presented in this volume, the Stone-Weiss family will earn their gratitude. A Jew can accomplish nothing more meaningful or lasting in his sojourn on earth.

❧ ❧ ❧

ACKNOWLEDGMENTS

THIS WORK COMBINES THE CONTRIBUTIONS of many people and was made possible by the guidance and encouragement of many others. Foremost among them are the Torah giants of the last generation, who, as our teachers and mentors, put their stamp on the ArtScroll Series, as they did on the new generations of Torah institutions and families in the Western Hemisphere. Their teachings remain, though they are no longer with us. There are no words to describe our gratitude to them, nor the gratitude that all of Jewry, present and future, must feel for their enormous contributions to the survival of Torah Judaism after the horrors of the Holocaust and the ravages of assimilation.

In the Stone Edition of the Chumash, we acknowledged our debt to the many authorities, leaders and teachers of Torah Jewry whose encouragement and support has helped make our work possible. Those sentiments apply, as well, to the Stone Edition of Tanach. May the Jewish people continue to enjoy their leadership in good health, for many years to come.

Words cannot express the editor's gratitude to RABBI MEIR ZLOTOWITZ. The concept of ArtScroll was his, and it is he who has made it into a powerful vehicle of service to the Jewish people. Significant portions of this volume are based on his works, and his guidance and advice have shaped the entire project. His friendship is one of the highlights of the editor's life, as it is to many, many others.

RABBI SHEAH BRANDER is one of the wonders of Judaica publishing. His skill as a graphics genius, his uncompromising zeal for perfection, his perceptive suggestions and illuminating comments — all these are indispensable to the quality and success of this volume.

RABBI AVIE GOLD, a scholar of unusual breadth and conscientiousness, has been an astute reader, editor, and critic. His contribution to this volume is enormous, as it has been to scores of other ArtScroll works.

SHMUEL BLITZ, director of the Foundation's activities in Israel, is a friend and counselor of the first order. With skill and perseverance, he coordinated the interaction between our scholars in Israel and our headquarters in New York. Reb Shmuel also compiled the book's index.

RABBI YAAKOV BLINDER is an important and very welcome addition to our staff. He wrote first drafts of many parts of this volume and provided extensive review and comment. As a brilliant scholar and incisive critic, he has been a major participant in the preparation of this book.

AVROHOM BIDERMAN has been tireless, dedicated, and perceptive in his many roles as coordinator of the preparation and flow of material. His learning and devotion were essential to the success of the project.

RABBI MOSHE ROSENBLUM is a fount of Torah knowledge and scholarship, whose meticulous reading and research was most valuable.

ELI KROEN has been involved in many aspects of the graphics of this volume. Much of its beauty and utility are thanks to him.

We are grateful also to RABBI CHAIM COHEN, an expert in his field, who proofread the Hebrew text; to RABBI ASHER MARGOLIOT, who contributed the first draft of Proverbs; and to RABBI MOSHE SHAPIRO, who contributed the first draft of Job.

We express our gratitude to MRS. JUDI DICK, MRS. MINDY STERN, and MRS. FAIGIE WEINBAUM, who proofread with diligence and judgment. We are grateful also to those who performed the often arduous and hectic task of typing and correcting the many drafts of the manuscript: MR. YEHUDAH GORDON, MRS. BASSIE GUTMAN, MRS. DEVOIRY BICK, MRS. MINDY BREIER, MRS. ESTIE DICKER, MRS. ESTHER FEIERSTEIN, MRS. CHAYA GITTY LOEVY, TOBY BRANDER, TOBY HEILBRUN, UDI HERSKOVITS, and MRS. LEAH BRACHAH STEINHARTER.

THE MESORAH HERITAGE FOUNDATION, which made possible the research and writing of this and other important works of Torah scholarship, has become a major source of Jewish learning. For this we are grateful to the Foundation's trustees and governors, who are listed above.

A major project of the Foundation is the monumental SCHOTTENSTEIN EDITION OF THE TALMUD, which was made possible by the vision and generosity of JEROME SCHOTTENSTEIN ע״ה and his wife GERALDINE, who carries on his resolve, and of SAUL AND SONIA SCHOTTENSTEIN. Jerome Schottenstein's legacy of dedication to Jewish eternity is carried on by JAY AND JEANIE SCHOTTENSTEIN in a host of worthy causes around the world, and by SUSIE AND JON DIAMOND, ANN AND ARI DESHE, and LORI SCHOTTENSTEIN. We treasure their friendship.

A huge investment of time and resources was required to turn this multi-year project from aspiration to reality. We are deeply grateful to the many friends whose generous support enable us to undertake such ambitious projects and make them available to the average family and institution. Prominently among them are MR. AND MRS. LAURENCE A. TISCH and family, MR. AND MRS. JAMES S. TISCH, MR. AND MRS. ELLIS A. SAFDEYE, MR. AND MRS. BENJAMIN C. FISHOFF, MR. AND MRS. HIRSCH WOLF, MR. AND MRS. MICHAEL M.H. GROSS, MR. AND MRS. ZVI RYZMAN, MR. AND MRS. REUVEN DESSLER, MR. SHLOMO SEGEV, MR. AND MRS. JOSEPH BERLINER, and RABBI AND MRS. YEHUDA LEVI.

RABBI RAPHAEL BUTLER has extended himself mightily to help bring the work of the Foundation to the attention of the masses of English-speaking Jews. RABBI MOSHE MENDEL GLUSTEIN has helped tirelessly to expand the work of the Foundation.

The editor acknowledges his eternal debt to his roshei yeshivah, RABBI YAAKOV KAMENETSKY and RABBI GEDALIAH SCHORR זצ״ל who were guides and role models as well as teachers; to his parents, ABRAHAM AND LUBA SCHERMAN ר׳ אברהם דב בן ר׳ שמואל נטע ורעיתו ליבא בת ר׳ זאב וואלף ע״ה to להבחל״ח and ע״ה; his father-in-law, החבר אפרים בן הרב רפאל ע״ה his mother-in-law ETTA GUGENHEIM, who succeeded in establishing truly Jewish homes in the New World, during years when it was exceedingly difficult to do so.

The editor expresses his gratitude to his wife CHANA תחי׳, who feels most comfortable in the background. To all who know her, she epitomizes nobility, kindness, dedication, and wisdom. May her efforts for others be rewarded with the blessing she wants most: that our children and grandchildren dwell in the tents of Torah, always.

Finally, my colleagues and I thank the Almighty for permitting us to be the quills that record His Torah. May He continue His blessings so that we may merit the privilege of helping place His word in every Jewish home and heart.

◆§ An Overview:
Tanach — Textbook of the Soul

Tanach — the word evokes images of the Revelation at Sinai.

TANACH — the word evokes images of the Revelation at Sinai, with thunder and lightning, shofar blast and pillar of cloud, an awestruck nation receiving the Ten Commandments and Moses ascending to heaven as its intermediary. And the same word evokes the image of King David, the Sweet Singer of Israel, whose quill recorded the longings and achievements, the heartbreak and inspiration of countless millions of people from shepherd tents in the desert to penthouse towers in teeming cities. It evokes the soaring visions of Isaiah, the anguish of Esther, the heroism of Daniel. It evokes the history of a nation that accepted upon itself the privileged burden of carrying out the mission that began when God created heaven and earth. It evokes the goal of bringing about the human manifestion of "let there be light."

It evokes the history of a nation that accepted upon itself the mission that began when God created heaven and earth.

Tanach is the Hebrew acronym for the three sections of Scripture: **T**orah, **N**eviim [i.e., Prophets], and **K**esuvim [i.e., Writings]. The Tanach has many faces. It is the compendium of God's commandments, the "constitution" of His People. It is a book of "history," although it is certainly not a "history book" in the ordinary sense of the word. It is filled with promises of the rewards that await those who do good and the punishments that will come in the wake of evil. It looks at life wisely and offers advice and guidance. It comforts the aggrieved and inspires the crestfallen. It illuminates events and helps place them in perspective. Let us try to understand these faces of the Tanach — not only as a book of law and surely not as a book of lore, but as the book of life.

Let us try to understand these faces of the Tanach — not only as a book of law and surely not as a book of lore, but as the book of life.

I. The Creator's Code

Code of Letter and Spirit

It was only logical for the Creator of the universe to provide man with a code of conduct; otherwise man would be like a helpless creature thrashing about in an impenetrable maze. The best proof of this, unfortunately, is found in history books and daily newspapers. The earth is filled with creeds — religious, political, economic, philosophical and intellectual; and so many oceans of blood have been spilled and mountains of treasure expended in the name of those beliefs. After all these centuries, man is still trapped in the maze, lashing out against those who stand in his often directionless path. Surely God's plan of Creation would have helped man answer the essential questions of existence. Where should he turn? For what should he strive? How should he behave? What will help him achieve his goal? What will hinder him? What does God expect, desire, demand, of him?

After all these centuries, man is still trapped in the maze, lashing out against those who stand in his often directionless path.

Although the commandments contained in the Five Books of Moses are the Jew's code of conduct, God wants more than strict adherence to the letter of His laws. The Torah is meant to shape *people* as well as deeds, because it is only human beings who are God's standard bearers and whose personal example can inspire others to serve Him.

So important is this concept that Genesis devotes much space to the conduct of the Patriarchal family — and even of its servants. God wants us to learn not merely from written texts; the most eloquent texts are of flesh and blood. No abstract sermon about compassion can surpass the story of how Abraham turned principle into practice when he appealed for the people of Sodom and Gomorrah. The inhabitants of those prosperous city-states were so incredibly evil that they have entered the language as paragons of perversion. And Abraham knew it. Yet he pleaded strenuously that God save them (*Genesis* 18:17-33).

God wants us to learn not merely from written texts; the most eloquent texts are of flesh and blood.

Qualifications for Jewish Greatness

Eliezer, Abraham's most trusted servant, was dispatched on one of history's momentous missions. In their advanced old age, after a lifetime of longing, God blessed Abraham and Sarah with a child, Isaac. The future shape of the nation of Israel — its very existence — depended on finding a proper mate for him, and it was for that purpose that Eliezer was sent to Abraham's ancestral home. How did Eliezer test Rebeccah's qualifications? Voluntary kindness to a stranger. Would she offer to draw hundreds of quarts of water for ten thirsty camels? If so, she could become a Matriarch of the Chosen People (ibid. 24:1-27).

Joseph's brothers betrayed him and sold him into slavery. When he revealed himself to them as the viceroy of Egypt who held their lives in the palm of his hand, they blanched in fear and trepidation. He pleaded with them, "And now, be not distressed, nor reproach yourselves for having sold me here, for it was to be a provider that God sent me ahead of you" (*Genesis* 45:5). Joseph demonstrated generosity of spirit to and sensitive sympathy for frightened, helpless people. He also taught that people should understand events as part of God's plan, not as haphazard, random, purposeless coincidences. When he was sold into slavery, he could not have known that he would become the instrument to save the world from famine, but in the perspective of

Joseph demonstrated generosity of spirit to and sensitive sympathy for frightened, helpless people.

events he understood his ordeal as Divinely ordained for the benefit of his family and others.

The experiences of the Patriarchs and Matriarchs show how God accepts the prayers of those who fear Him, how He protects them against their enemies, and how He tests them to bring out their innate greatness. The early life of Moses shows how an abandoned infant, a tongue-tied, reluctant exile, became the greatest of all prophets and the conduit of God's law. The Exodus from Egypt demonstrates that the forces of nature and the power of the state are merely tools or matchsticks in the hands of God. The wanderings of the Jews in the Wilderness proves that fears are groundless where there is Divine protection, but that foolish rebellion against God destroys people's paradise on earth. The point is that the narratives of the Torah must be read as lessons for eternity.

The early life of Moses shows how an abandoned infant, a tongue-tied, reluctant exile, became the greatest of all prophets.

Certainty and Subtlety

The Books of Tanach are replete with both certainty and subtlety. The Five Books of Moses emphasize that virtue brings blessing and sin brings curse. On the other hand, other Books show that God is often patient and that His ways are often hidden.

The Book of Esther records nine years of history with not a single mention of God's Name. Esther is a righteous Jewish woman forced to become queen of the Persian Empire, while her king conspires in history's first attempted genocide against the Jewish people. The events took place at a nadir of Jewish history, after the First Temple was destroyed and Israel seemed to have been toppled forever from its pedestal as the Chosen People. God's Presence was invisible. Esther is isolated in the palace. Israel is alone in the world. And then — in a dizzying confluence of events, Haman's plot is foiled and Esther's King Ahasuerus becomes the reluctant champion of the newly rejuvenated Jewish people. And the story ends in a flash of understanding that God's hand may be gloved, but it is never completely withdrawn.

God is Never Gone

This is a major principle in the understanding of history. God may *seem* to slumber, but He never abandons His master plan for Creation. It has been noted that the day after the Jews were expelled from Spain in 1492, Christopher Columbus set sail to discover the land that was to become a major refuge and source of support for the Jewish people in the future. It took centuries before this connection became apparent, but the descendants of the despised and tortured Jewish nation would follow in the wake of the explorer who had been commissioned by Ferdinand and Isabella, architects of the Inquisition.

The descendants of the despised and tortured Jewish nation would follow in the wake of the explorer who had been commissioned by Ferdinand and Isabella.

When Jacob's sons came back from Egypt with the bitter news that they must bring young Benjamin to Egypt, the distraught Patriarch exclaimed in despair, "Why did you treat me so ill?" (*Genesis* 43:6).

Joseph was gone. Simeon was gone. Jacob's land was gripped by famine, and God was not revealing Himself to him. Can we blame him for his outburst?

And yet the *Midrash* describes that moment as the only time Jacob ever said something pointless!

Like an embryo forming unseen in its mother's womb, Israel's destiny was being prepared in Egypt. There, Joseph was preparing the crucible in which Israel would be formed into a nation. Jacob's family would soon go down to Egypt, eventually to explode in a blaze of miracles and the Revelation at Sinai. It was an eternal lesson to future generations that God's plan moves forward, even when its progress is inscrutable.

Like an embryo forming unseen in its mother's womb, Israel's destiny was being prepared in Egypt.

II. Prophecy

Essential to an understanding of Tanach is the concept of prophecy. Colloquially, people think of prophets as predictors of the future or as spokesmen for an ideal. However, although prophets may perform these functions, they are not essential to prophecy. As defined by the classic Renaissance commentator, Rabbi Moshe Chaim Luzzatto:

The Essence of Prophecy

> Part of a prophet's function may include being sent on a mission by God, but this in itself is not the essence of prophecy, nor is it necessary that a prophet be sent on a mission to others . . . The essence of prophecy is that one be attached to God, and he experience His revelation (Derech Hashem 3:4:6).

The Talmud teaches that there were hundreds of thousands of prophets, but Scripture quotes only fifty-five. What did the rest of them do, and why are so few mentioned in Scripture?

By definition, prophets are people who had refined their minds and conduct sufficiently to deserve that God's spirit could rest upon them. It was not necessary for them to bring messages to the people; their greatness was personal. Indeed, prophets were also known as "seers" (*I Samuel* 9:9), because they were people whom God had given insight far beyond that of ordinary people. In a sense we may compare prophets to outstanding scholars, some of whom may write and teach, while others may devote themselves exclusively to study and personal growth. The way to compare their relative stature is certainly not by counting their published works.

By definition, prophets are people who had refined their minds and conduct sufficiently to deserve that God's spirit could rest upon them.

The prophets elevated the nation simply by being role models of holiness, scholarship and closeness to God. In modern times, civilized societies value artists and intellectuals for what they are and for the standards they set for the rest of the community. Governments and philanthropists support them because of the benefits they provide to society. How much more so the people who bring the spirit of God into their communities. Such were the prophets. Seeing them, their peers would know that God had rested His spirit upon Israel, and this itself would raise the level of national aspirations.

When Moses received the Ten Commandments at Mount Sinai, God taught him the future Books of the Prophets and Writings.

According to the Talmud, when Moses received the Ten Command-ments at Mount Sinai, God taught him the entire Torah, including the future Books of the Prophets and Writings (*Berachos* 5a). Strange. How could Moses have received books that would not be composed for hundreds of years?

The answer begins with an understanding of different perspectives. For example, if people were asked to describe their own hypothetical ideal person, the answers would be many and varied. Each respondent will know what *he* or *she* admires, but what one considers the ideal person may be a bizarre or even repulsive caricature to someone else.

The generation that stood at Sinai could hear the teachings of Moses and detect in them the holiness of Samuel.

So, too, people whose spiritual antennae are attuned to holiness can hear things that others do not. The generation that stood at Sinai, that saw and heard the Revelation, that experienced prophecy, that lived with daily miracles, that could feel the Divine Presence hovering above them — such people could hear the teachings of Moses and detect in them the holiness of Samuel, the inspiration of David, the wisdom of Solomon, the visions of Isaiah. They were so imbued with the lessons and perspectives of the Torah that the future teachings of the great prophets had become part of their nature, in the same way that someone who has mastered a field of knowledge knows the contents of elementary textbooks without ever having seen them. He knows them because he has mastered the subject perfectly.

Deaf to the Message

It was only later, when Moses and Joshua were gone and subsequent generations let themselves be seduced by the life-styles of their pagan neighbors, that the clarity of Moses' teaching began to fade, and the people failed to hear its sacred resonance.

The Book of Judges is like an introduction to Jewish history. The tribes of Israel had settled into a complacent coexistence with their Canaanite neighbors — the people they could not bring themselves to drive from the land. Inexplicably, it seemed, foreign invaders defeated the Jews. Why had God forsaken them? Had they not been promised that the land would be theirs and that their enemies would crumble before them?

Three hundred years after the period of the judges began, the prophet Samuel wrote the Book of Judges, which sets these events in perspec-tive. Israel had allowed pagan practices and beliefs to seep into their lives. Like a leak too long ignored, the seepage weakened the sacred foundations upon which Israel's existence had been based, and opened breaches through which enemies could swarm into the land. Then God would appoint leaders; the people would repent; the enemy would be subdued, and the land would have an extended period of tranquility — until the people sinned again and the cycle was repeated. The theme of the Book of Judges, therefore, was that obedience to the Torah earns God's protection and sin begets catastrophe.

The generation of Moses did not need a Book of Judges to teach them that; they saw it in the Torah. Succeeding generations needed Samuel to place "history" in the context of reality — the reality that events are determined not by geopolitics, but by virtue and sin.

In contemporary times, we *do* have both the Torah of Moses and the Book of Judges. Can we say that we have absorbed their message? Is it not true that we analyze events in terms of national ambitions and greed for resources, in terms of public image and political rivalry? The lessons are there in the Tanach, but we must open our eyes and ears to see and hear them — and to apply them.

A New Era

Until Samuel's time, the prophets tended to be only "seers" rather than "leaders." The leaders of the nation were the "judges," righteous people chosen by God. But in the days of Samuel, there was a turning point in Jewish history — the establishment of the monarchy. No longer would every national leader be picked by God. The succession would be hereditary, which meant that the heads of state would not necessarily be righteous. Some would be models of spiritual greatness, such as David, Solomon, and Hezekiah, but there would also be despicable kings like Jeroboam, Ahab, and Manasseh, who disgraced the nation and pushed it down the slippery slope to destruction and exile.

Since the political leaders of the nation failed to be its spiritual leaders, the Jewish people needed prophets who would lead and admonish, tasks that had once belonged exclusively to the judges.

In later years, the nation split into two kingdoms and the spiritual standing of the people began to erode. The nature of the prophecies began to turn from providing perspective and guidance to admonitions that tragedy and exile from their land would be inevitable unless the people repented and relearned the lessons of their past. Such were the courageous public demonstrations of Elijah and Elisha, the stirring poetry of Isaiah, the terrible personal ordeals of Hosea and Ezekiel, the dirges of Jeremiah.

Other prophecies were encouraging. They came to Israel during times of catastrophic downfall, when the people feared that their bright future was forever behind them, that they had forfeited their right to consider themselves God's Chosen People. At such times, God sent prophets to inspire the downtrodden people and assure them that the sun would shine again. As the Sages put it, "Had I not fallen, I could not have arisen; had I not sat in the darkness [God] would not have been a light for me " (*Midrash Tehillim* 22). This, too, was a message of the prophets.

The Hebrew word נָבִיא, *prophet*, comes from the term נִיב שְׂפָתַיִם, *fruit or expression of the lips*. This very title implies the mission of the prophet: he was given a message by God and commanded to *express* it, to *speak* to the people and tell them what God had revealed to him. For this reason, the Books containing such revelations are called *Prophets*, and, as the Sages explain, "Only such prophecy as was needed for future generations was written [in Scripture]" (*Yoma* 9b). Thus, there were surely untold numbers of prophets whose personal greatness was equal to those we know from Scripture, but whose messages were not relevant to us. On the other hand, every word of Scripture has something meaningful to tell "future generations," including our own.

This very title implies the mission of the prophet: he was given a message by God and commanded to express it, to speak to the people.

The Writings

Not all sacred teachings were meant as Divine messages to be conveyed to the people. Those are the Writings — so-called because they were to be *written*, rather than proclaimed as "prophecies," but God ordained that they be preserved as part of Scripture. The reasons vary. It may have been to provide perspectives on history, such as the Books of Chronicles, Ruth, and Esther. It may have been to provide wise perspective on the meaning and conduct of life, such as King Solomon's Proverbs and Ecclesiastes. It may have been to allude to the future Redemption, such as the Book of Daniel. Or it may have been to shed light on the eternally perplexing question of why the righteous may suffer while the wicked prosper, such as the heated disputations of the Book of Job.

Perhaps the best example of a non-prophetic work that has a profound effect on countless millions of people is the Book of Psalms.

Perhaps the best example of a non-prophetic work that has a profound effect on countless millions of people is the Book of Psalms. King David is more than the "Sweet Singer of Israel." He is a musician of the soul, who plucks at the heartstrings of every Jew and makes sacred music of every life experience. Whatever a Jew needs, he finds in his Book of Psalms — gratitude, hope, prayer, aspiration, courage, insight. Millions of *Tehillim'lech* (i.e., little Books of Psalms) have soaked up infinite numbers of tears — tears that God treasures in His own treasury.

Goal of Our Study

So let us open our Tanach and read from it with receptive minds and open hearts. Let us absorb its teachings as the great nineteenth century teacher and thinker Rabbi Samson Raphael Hirsch urged us to:

> The Tanach should be studied as the foundation of a new science. Let us look at nature as King David did. Let us listen to the march of history with the intent ear of the prophet Isaiah. And with eyes thus opened and ears thus

attuned, let us draw from Tanach our lessons about God, the world, mankind ... The books of Tanach should become the source of instruction for life, and [people] should learn to hear their message throughout their lives. Their eyes should be opened to see the world surrounding them as God's world, and themselves as God's servants in His world; their ears should be opened to perceive history as a process of educating all mankind toward the service of God.

With eyes thus opened and ears thus attuned, let us draw from Tanach our lessons about God, the world, mankind.

As we turn the page to begin our study of Tanach — of God's Torah, Prophets and Writings — let this be our goal. We are not studying "literature," though Tanach is surely prose and poetry of the highest order. We are not studying "history," though Tanach is surely an authoritative chronicle. We are studying God's word, as conveyed to us through the throats and quills of His emissaries. They spoke to their contemporaries and they still speak to us, for only the words of eternity were immortalized in the sacred Scriptures. Let us read with our eyes and listen with our souls. And let our lives be transformed to what God intended them to be.

Let us read with our eyes and listen with our souls.

Rabbi Nosson Scherman

December 1996 / Teves 5757

BLESSINGS OF THE TORAH / ברכות התורה

The reader shows the *oleh* (person called to the Torah) the place in the Torah.
The *oleh* touches the Torah with a corner of his *tallis*, or the belt or mantle of the Torah, and kisses it.
He then begins the blessing, bowing at בָּרְכוּ,'*Bless,' and straightening up at* ה', HASHEM.

Bless HASHEM, the blessed One.

בָּרְכוּ אֶת יהוה הַמְבֹרָךְ.

Congregation, followed by *oleh*, responds bowing at בָּרוּךְ, *'Blessed,'* and straightening up at HASHEM.

Blessed is HASHEM, the blessed One, for all eternity.

בָּרוּךְ יהוה הַמְבֹרָךְ לְעוֹלָם וָעֶד.

Oleh continues:

Blessed are You, HASHEM, our God, King of the universe, Who selected us from all the peoples and gave us His Torah. Blessed are You, HASHEM, Giver of the Torah. (Cong. – Amen.)

בָּרוּךְ אַתָּה יהוה אֱלֹהֵינוּ מֶלֶךְ הָעוֹלָם, אֲשֶׁר בָּחַר בָּנוּ מִכָּל הָעַמִּים, וְנָתַן לָנוּ אֶת תּוֹרָתוֹ. בָּרוּךְ אַתָּה יהוה, נוֹתֵן הַתּוֹרָה. (קהל – אָמֵן)

After his Torah portion has been read, the *oleh* recites:

Blessed are You, HASHEM, our God, King of the universe, Who gave us the Torah of truth and implanted eternal life within us. Blessed are You, HASHEM, Giver of the Torah. (Cong. – Amen.)

בָּרוּךְ אַתָּה יהוה אֱלֹהֵינוּ מֶלֶךְ הָעוֹלָם, אֲשֶׁר נָתַן לָנוּ תּוֹרַת אֱמֶת, וְחַיֵּי עוֹלָם נָטַע בְּתוֹכֵנוּ. בָּרוּךְ אַתָּה יהוה, נוֹתֵן הַתּוֹרָה. (קהל – אָמֵן)

Pronouncing the Names of God

The Four-Letter Name of HASHEM [י-ה-ו-ה] indicates that God is timeless and infinite, for the letters of this Name are those of the words הָיָה הֹוֶה וְיִהְיֶה, *He was, He is, and He will be.* This name appears in some editions with vowel points [יְ-ה-וִ-ה] and in others, such as the present edition, without vowels. In either case, this Name is *never* pronounced as it is spelled.

During prayer, or when a blessing is recited, or when a Torah verse is read, the Four-Letter Name should be pronounced as if it were spelled אֲדֹנָי, *ă dō nai'*, the Name that identifies God as the Master of All. At other times, it should be pronounced הַשֵּׁם, *Hashem,* literally, "the Name."

In this work, the Four-Letter Name of God is translated "HASHEM," the pronounciation traditionally used for the Name to avoid pronouncing it unnecessarily.

The following table gives the pronunciations of the Name when it appears with a prefix.

בַּי-ה-ו-ה	— *bă dō nai'*
הַי-ה-ו-ה	— *Hăă dō nǎi'*
וַי-ה-ו-ה	— *vă dō nai'*
כַּי-ה-ו-ה	— *kă dō nai'*
לַי-ה-ו-ה	— *lă dō nai'*
מֵי-ה-ו-ה	— *mă ä dō nai'*
שֶׁי-ה-ו-ה	— *she ä dō nai'*

Sometimes the Name appears with the vowelization יֱ-ה-וִ-ה. This version of the Name is pronounced as if it were spelled אֱלֹהִים, *e lō him'*, the Name that refers to God as the One Who is all-powerful. When it appears with a prefix לֵי-ה-וִ-ה, it is pronounced *lă lō him'*. We have translated this Name as HASHEM/ELOHIM to indicate that it refers to the aspects inherent in each of those Names.

BLESSINGS OF THE HAFTARAH / ברכות ההפטרה

After the Torah Scroll has been tied and covered, the *Maftir* recites the *Haftarah* blessings.

Blessed are You, HASHEM, our God, King of the universe, Who has chosen good prophets and was pleased with their words that were uttered with truth. Blessed are You, HASHEM, Who chooses the Torah; Moses, His servant; Israel, His nation; and the prophets of truth and righteousness. (Cong. — Amen.)

בָּרוּךְ אַתָּה יהוה אֱלֹהֵינוּ מֶלֶךְ הָעוֹלָם, אֲשֶׁר בָּחַר בִּנְבִיאִים טוֹבִים, וְרָצָה בְדִבְרֵיהֶם הַנֶּאֱמָרִים בֶּאֱמֶת, בָּרוּךְ אַתָּה יהוה, הַבּוֹחֵר בַּתּוֹרָה וּבְמֹשֶׁה עַבְדּוֹ, וּבְיִשְׂרָאֵל עַמּוֹ, וּבִנְבִיאֵי הָאֱמֶת וָצֶדֶק. (קהל – אָמֵן)

The *Haftarah* is read, after which the *Maftir* recites the following blessings.

Blessed are You, HASHEM, our God, King of the universe, Rock of all eternities, Righteous in all generations, the trustworthy God, Who says and does, Who speaks and fulfills, all of Whose words are true and righteous. Trustworthy are You, HASHEM, our God, and trustworthy are Your words, not one of Your words is turned back to its origin unfulfilled, for You are God, trustworthy (and compassionate) King. Blessed are You, HASHEM, the God Who is trustworthy in all His words. (Cong. — Amen.)

בָּרוּךְ אַתָּה יהוה אֱלֹהֵינוּ מֶלֶךְ הָעוֹלָם, צוּר כָּל הָעוֹלָמִים, צַדִּיק בְּכָל הַדּוֹרוֹת, הָאֵל הַנֶּאֱמָן הָאוֹמֵר וְעֹשֶׂה, הַמְדַבֵּר וּמְקַיֵּם, שֶׁכָּל דְּבָרָיו אֱמֶת וָצֶדֶק. נֶאֱמָן אַתָּה הוּא יהוה אֱלֹהֵינוּ, וְנֶאֱמָנִים דְּבָרֶיךָ, וְדָבָר אֶחָד מִדְּבָרֶיךָ אָחוֹר לֹא יָשׁוּב רֵיקָם, כִּי אֵל מֶלֶךְ נֶאֱמָן (וְרַחֲמָן) אָתָּה. בָּרוּךְ אַתָּה יהוה, הָאֵל הַנֶּאֱמָן בְּכָל דְּבָרָיו. (קהל – אָמֵן)

Have mercy on Zion for it is the source of our life; to the one who is deeply humiliated bring salvation speedily, in our days. Blessed are You, HASHEM, Who gladdens Zion through her children. (Cong. — Amen.)

רַחֵם עַל צִיּוֹן כִּי הִיא בֵּית חַיֵּינוּ, וְלַעֲלוּבַת נֶפֶשׁ תּוֹשִׁיעַ בִּמְהֵרָה בְיָמֵינוּ. בָּרוּךְ אַתָּה יהוה, מְשַׂמֵּחַ צִיּוֹן בְּבָנֶיהָ. (קהל – אָמֵן)

Gladden us, HASHEM, our God, with Elijah the prophet Your servant, and with the kingdom of the House of David, Your anointed, may he come speedily and cause our heart to exult. On his throne let no stranger sit nor let others continue to inherit his honor, for by Your holy Name You swore to him that his lamp will not be extinguished forever and ever. Blessed are You, HASHEM, Shield of David. (Cong. — Amen.)

שַׂמְּחֵנוּ יהוה אֱלֹהֵינוּ בְּאֵלִיָּהוּ הַנָּבִיא עַבְדֶּךָ, וּבְמַלְכוּת בֵּית דָּוִד מְשִׁיחֶךָ, בִּמְהֵרָה יָבֹא וְיָגֵל לִבֵּנוּ, עַל כִּסְאוֹ לֹא יֵשֶׁב זָר וְלֹא יִנְחֲלוּ עוֹד אֲחֵרִים אֶת כְּבוֹדוֹ, כִּי בְשֵׁם קָדְשְׁךָ נִשְׁבַּעְתָּ לּוֹ, שֶׁלֹּא יִכְבֶּה נֵרוֹ לְעוֹלָם וָעֶד. בָּרוּךְ אַתָּה יהוה, מָגֵן דָּוִד. (קהל – אָמֵן)

ON FAST DAYS THE BLESSINGS END HERE.

On an ordinary Sabbath (including the Sabbath of Chol HaMoed Pesach) continue:

For the Torah reading, for the prayer service, for the reading from the Prophets and for this Sabbath day that You, HASHEM, our God, have given us for holiness and contentment, for glory and splendor — for all this, HASHEM, our God, we gratefully thank You and bless You. May Your Name be blessed by the mouth of all the living always, for all eternity. Blessed are You, HASHEM, Who sanctifies the Sabbath. (Cong. — Amen.)

עַל הַתּוֹרָה, וְעַל הָעֲבוֹדָה, וְעַל הַנְּבִיאִים, וְעַל יוֹם הַשַּׁבָּת הַזֶּה, שֶׁנָּתַתָּ לָּנוּ יהוה אֱלֹהֵינוּ, לִקְדֻשָּׁה וְלִמְנוּחָה, לְכָבוֹד וּלְתִפְאָרֶת. עַל הַכֹּל יהוה אֱלֹהֵינוּ, אֲנַחְנוּ מוֹדִים לָךְ, וּמְבָרְכִים אוֹתָךְ, יִתְבָּרַךְ שִׁמְךָ בְּפִי כָּל חַי תָּמִיד לְעוֹלָם וָעֶד. בָּרוּךְ אַתָּה יהוה, מְקַדֵּשׁ הַשַּׁבָּת. (קהל – אָמֵן)

On a festival and on a Sabbath that coincides with a Festival (including the Sabbath of Chol HaMoed Succos) continue here [the words in brackets are inserted on the Sabbath]:

For the Torah reading, for the prayer service, for the reading from the Prophets and for this [Sabbath day and this] day of the

עַל הַתּוֹרָה, וְעַל הָעֲבוֹדָה, וְעַל הַנְּבִיאִים, וְעַל יוֹם [הַשַּׁבָּת הַזֶּה וְיוֹם]

On Pesach:

Festival of Matzos — חַג הַמַּצּוֹת

On Shavuos:

Shavuos Festival — חַג הַשָּׁבֻעוֹת

On Succos:

Succos Festival — חַג הַסֻּכּוֹת

On Shemini Atzeres and Simchas Torah:

Shemini Atzeres Festival — הַשְּׁמִינִי חַג הָעֲצֶרֶת (שְׁמִינִי עֲצֶרֶת הַחַג)

that You, HASHEM, our God, have given us [for holiness and contentment], for gladness and joy, for glory and splendor. For all this, HASHEM, our God, we gratefully thank You and bless You. May Your Name be blessed by the mouth of all the living, always, for all eternity. Blessed are You, HASHEM, Who sanctifies [the Sabbath], Israel and the festival seasons. *(Cong. — Amen.)*

הַזֶּה, שֶׁנָּתַתָּ לָנוּ יהוה אֱלֹהֵינוּ, [לִקְדֻשָּׁה וְלִמְנוּחָה,] לְשָׂשׂוֹן וּלְשִׂמְחָה, לְכָבוֹד וּלְתִפְאָרֶת. עַל הַכֹּל יהוה אֱלֹהֵינוּ, אֲנַחְנוּ מוֹדִים לָךְ, וּמְבָרְכִים אוֹתָךְ, יִתְבָּרַךְ שִׁמְךָ בְּפִי כָּל חַי תָּמִיד לְעוֹלָם וָעֶד. בָּרוּךְ אַתָּה יהוה, מְקַדֵּשׁ [הַשַּׁבָּת וְ]יִשְׂרָאֵל וְהַזְּמַנִּים. (קהל – אָמֵן)

On Rosh Hashanah continue here [the words in brackets are inserted on the Sabbath]:

For the Torah reading, for the prayer service, for the reading from the Prophets [and for this Sabbath day] and for this Day of Remembrance that You, HASHEM, our God, have given us [for holiness and contentment,] for glory and splendor — for all this, HASHEM, our God, we gratefully thank You and bless You. May Your Name be blessed by the mouth of all the living, always, for all eternity, for Your word is true and endures forever. Blessed are You, HASHEM, Who sanctifies [the Sabbath,] Israel and the Day of Remembrance. *(Cong. — Amen.)*

עַל הַתּוֹרָה, וְעַל הָעֲבוֹדָה, וְעַל הַנְּבִיאִים, וְעַל יוֹם [הַשַּׁבָּת הַזֶּה וְיוֹם] הַזִּכָּרוֹן הַזֶּה, שֶׁנָּתַתָּ לָנוּ יהוה אֱלֹהֵינוּ, [לִקְדֻשָּׁה וְלִמְנוּחָה,] לְכָבוֹד וּלְתִפְאָרֶת. עַל הַכֹּל יהוה אֱלֹהֵינוּ, אֲנַחְנוּ מוֹדִים לָךְ, וּמְבָרְכִים אוֹתָךְ, יִתְבָּרַךְ שִׁמְךָ בְּפִי כָּל חַי תָּמִיד לְעוֹלָם וָעֶד. וּדְבָרְךָ אֱמֶת וְקַיָּם לָעַד. בָּרוּךְ אַתָּה יהוה, מֶלֶךְ עַל כָּל הָאָרֶץ, מְקַדֵּשׁ [הַשַּׁבָּת וְ]יִשְׂרָאֵל וְיוֹם הַזִּכָּרוֹן. (קהל – אָמֵן)

On Yom Kippur continue here [the words in brackets are inserted on the Sabbath]:

For the Torah reading, for the prayer service, for the reading from the Prophets, [and for this Sabbath day] and for this Day of Atonement that You, HASHEM, our God, have given us [for holiness and contentment,] for pardon, forgiveness and atonement, for glory and splendor — for all this, HASHEM, our God, we gratefully thank You and bless You. May Your Name be blessed by the mouth of all the living, always, for all eternity, for Your word is true and endures forever. Blessed are You, HASHEM, the King Who pardons and forgives our iniquities and the iniquities of His people, the Family of Israel, and removes our sins every single year, King over all the world, Who sanctifies [the Sabbath,] Israel and the Day of Atonement. *(Cong. — Amen.)*

עַל הַתּוֹרָה, וְעַל הָעֲבוֹדָה, וְעַל הַנְּבִיאִים, וְעַל יוֹם [הַשַּׁבָּת הַזֶּה וְיוֹם] הַכִּפֻּרִים הַזֶּה שֶׁנָּתַתָּ לָנוּ יהוה אֱלֹהֵינוּ, [לִקְדֻשָּׁה וְלִמְנוּחָה,] לִמְחִילָה וְלִסְלִיחָה וּלְכַפָּרָה, לְכָבוֹד וּלְתִפְאָרֶת. עַל הַכֹּל יהוה אֱלֹהֵינוּ, אֲנַחְנוּ מוֹדִים לָךְ, וּמְבָרְכִים אוֹתָךְ, יִתְבָּרַךְ שִׁמְךָ בְּפִי כָּל חַי תָּמִיד לְעוֹלָם וָעֶד. וּדְבָרְךָ אֱמֶת וְקַיָּם לָעַד. בָּרוּךְ אַתָּה יהוה, מֶלֶךְ מוֹחֵל וְסוֹלֵחַ לַעֲוֹנוֹתֵינוּ וְלַעֲוֹנוֹת עַמּוֹ בֵּית יִשְׂרָאֵל, וּמַעֲבִיר אַשְׁמוֹתֵינוּ בְּכָל שָׁנָה וְשָׁנָה, מֶלֶךְ עַל כָּל הָאָרֶץ מְקַדֵּשׁ [הַשַּׁבָּת וְ]יִשְׂרָאֵל וְיוֹם הַכִּפֻּרִים. (קהל – אָמֵן)

Cantillation Marks / טעמי המקרא

פַּשְׁטָא֙ מֻנַּ֣ח זַרְקָ֮א מֻנַּ֣ח סֶגּ֖וֹל מֻנַּ֣ח ׀ מֻנַּ֣ח רְבִיעִ֑י מֻנַּ֣ח מַהְפַּ֤ךְ

פַּשְׁטָא֙ זָקֵף־קָטֹן זָקֵף־גָּד֔וֹל מֵרְכָ֥א טִפְחָ֖א מֻנַּ֣ח אֶתְנַחְתָּ֑א

פָּזֵ֡ר תְּלִישָׁא־קְטַנָּה֩ תְּלִישָׁא־גְדוֹלָה֠ קַדְמָ֨א וְאַזְלָ֝א

אַזְלָא־גֵּ֝רֵשׁ גֵּרְשַׁ֞יִם דַּרְגָּ֧א תְּבִ֛יר יְ֚תִיב פְּסִ֣יק ׀ סוֹף־פָּס֑וּק׃

שַׁלְשֶׁ֓לֶת קַרְנֵי־פָרָ֟ה מֵרְכָ֦א כְפוּלָ֦ה יֶ֫רַח־בֶּן־יוֹמ֗וֹ׃

טעמי אמ״ת (איוב משלי תהלים)
Cantillations of Psalms, Proverbs and Job

Kings (Dividers)[1] / מלכים (מפסיקים)

סִלּ֣וּק ע֜וֹלֶ֑ה וְיוֹרֵ֧ד אַתְנָ֣ח רְבִ֖יעַ גָּד֑וֹל רְבִ֖יעַ קָטֹ֖ן

רְבִ֖יעַ מֻגְרָ֣שׁ צִנּ֬וֹר שַׁלְשֶׁ֓לֶת גְּדוֹלָ֥ה ׀ דֶּ֛חִי פָּזֵ֡ר

לְגַרְמֵ֣הּ ׀

Servants (Connectors) / משרתים (מחברים)

מֵרְכָ֥א מֻנַּ֣ח עִלּ֬וּי טַרְחָ֖א גַּלְגַּ֪ל מַהְפַּ֤ךְ אַזְלָ֝א

שַׁלְשֶׁ֓לֶת קְטַנָּ֬ה צִנּוֹרִ֬ית

---

1. In addition to their musical functions, these marks also serve as punctuation marks similar to periods, colons and commas.

Torah תורה

Genesis בראשית

There are two kinds of creation. There is a creation of mountains and valleys, of solar systems and brain cells — and there is the creation of the people who give meaning and purpose to the universe they inhabit. The commentators refer to Genesis as the "Book of Creation," but the events of the six days when heaven and earth and all their fullness were brought into being occupy but a small fraction of the Book. Rather, the primary emphasis of the Book of Creation is how the Patriarchs fashioned a family into the nation that became the Chosen People. It is noteworthy that the Sages juxtapose three historical phenomena: "With ten utterances the world was created … "; "There were ten generations from Adam to Noah … "; and "There were ten generations from Noah to Abraham … until our forefather Abraham came and received the reward of them all" (Avos 5:1-3). The implication is plain — that although the physical work of creation had been completed with the ten utterances, it was not until Abraham that its human heir had come forward.

As Ramban and others point out in their commentaries on Genesis, the events in the lives of the Patriarchs were portents for the future history of their descendants. Consequently, when this Book tells how the seeds of man's spiritual history were sown, it is no less the story of Creation than the terse narrative of the first six days.

Choice, winnowing, and tests are primary themes of Genesis. The universe is a mixture of good and evil, and it is the responsibility of each individual, in his or her own life, to choose the good and spurn the evil. Thus, Noah stands out when humanity becomes corrupt; Abraham stands tall when everyone else fails; Isaac and Jacob prevail over Ishmael and Esau; and Jacob's family emerges unblemished to carry on the legacy of Abraham, Isaac, and Jacob; Sarah, Rebeccah, Rachel, and Leah.

Greatness must surmount adversity. This is why Abraham was tested. God is all-knowing; He did not become wiser after Abraham's successful performance than He was before. Rather, the tests were to give Abraham the opportunity to bring his spiritual potential to reality, and thereby to establish the precedents that remain with Israel to this day. Jewish tenacity in the service of God was forged in the tests of the Patriarchs and Matriarchs, and it remained impregnable throughout history. All this was "created" during the twenty-two centuries of the Book of Genesis.

The Book ends with the Patriarchal family having become a nation, purified and noble, ready to withstand a terrible exile in Egypt and follow Moses to Mount Sinai. Creation was complete.

פרשת בראשית

א־ב בְּרֵאשִׁ֖ית בָּרָ֣א אֱלֹהִ֑ים אֵ֥ת הַשָּׁמַ֖יִם וְאֵ֥ת הָאָֽרֶץ: וְהָאָ֗רֶץ הָיְתָ֥ה תֹ֨הוּ֙ וָבֹ֔הוּ

ג וְחֹ֖שֶׁךְ עַל־פְּנֵ֣י תְה֑וֹם וְר֣וּחַ אֱלֹהִ֔ים מְרַחֶ֖פֶת עַל־פְּנֵ֥י הַמָּֽיִם: וַיֹּ֥אמֶר

ד אֱלֹהִ֖ים יְהִ֣י א֑וֹר וַֽיְהִי־אֽוֹר: וַיַּ֧רְא אֱלֹהִ֛ים אֶת־הָא֖וֹר כִּי־ט֑וֹב וַיַּבְדֵּ֣ל

אֱלֹהִ֔ים בֵּ֥ין הָא֖וֹר וּבֵ֥ין הַחֹֽשֶׁךְ: וַיִּקְרָ֨א אֱלֹהִ֤ים ׀ לָאוֹר֙ י֔וֹם וְלַחֹ֖שֶׁךְ קָ֣רָא

לָ֑יְלָה וַֽיְהִי־עֶ֥רֶב וַֽיְהִי־בֹ֖קֶר י֥וֹם אֶחָֽד:

ה־ז וַיֹּ֣אמֶר אֱלֹהִ֗ים יְהִ֥י רָקִ֛יעַ בְּת֣וֹךְ הַמָּ֑יִם וִיהִ֣י מַבְדִּ֔יל בֵּ֥ין מַ֖יִם לָמָֽיִם: וַיַּ֣עַשׂ

אֱלֹהִים֮ אֶת־הָרָקִיעַ֒ וַיַּבְדֵּ֗ל בֵּ֤ין הַמַּ֨יִם֙ אֲשֶׁר֙ מִתַּ֣חַת לָֽרָקִ֔יעַ וּבֵ֣ין הַמַּ֔יִם

ח אֲשֶׁ֖ר מֵעַ֣ל לָרָקִ֑יעַ וַֽיְהִי־כֵֽן: וַיִּקְרָ֧א אֱלֹהִ֛ים לָֽרָקִ֖יעַ שָׁמָ֑יִם וַֽיְהִי־עֶ֥רֶב וַֽיְהִי־

בֹ֖קֶר י֥וֹם שֵׁנִֽי:

ט וַיֹּ֣אמֶר אֱלֹהִ֗ים יִקָּו֨וּ הַמַּ֜יִם מִתַּ֤חַת הַשָּׁמַ֨יִם֙ אֶל־מָק֣וֹם אֶחָ֔ד וְתֵרָאֶ֖ה

י הַיַּבָּשָׁ֑ה וַֽיְהִי־כֵֽן: וַיִּקְרָ֨א אֱלֹהִ֤ים ׀ לַיַּבָּשָׁה֙ אֶ֔רֶץ וּלְמִקְוֵ֥ה הַמַּ֖יִם קָרָ֣א יַמִּ֑ים

יא וַיַּ֥רְא אֱלֹהִ֖ים כִּי־טֽוֹב: וַיֹּ֣אמֶר אֱלֹהִ֗ים תַּֽדְשֵׁ֤א הָאָ֨רֶץ֙ דֶּ֔שֶׁא עֵ֚שֶׂב מַזְרִ֣יעַ

יב זֶ֔רַע עֵ֣ץ פְּרִ֞י עֹ֤שֶׂה פְּרִי֙ לְמִינ֔וֹ אֲשֶׁ֥ר זַרְעוֹ־ב֖וֹ עַל־הָאָ֑רֶץ וַֽיְהִי־כֵֽן: וַתּוֹצֵ֨א

הָאָ֜רֶץ דֶּ֠שֶׁא עֵ֣שֶׂב מַזְרִ֤יעַ זֶ֨רַע֙ לְמִינֵ֔הוּ וְעֵ֧ץ עֹֽשֶׂה־פְּרִ֛י אֲשֶׁ֥ר זַרְעוֹ־ב֖וֹ

יג לְמִינֵ֑הוּ וַיַּ֥רְא אֱלֹהִ֖ים כִּי־טֽוֹב: וַֽיְהִי־עֶ֥רֶב וַֽיְהִי־בֹ֖קֶר י֥וֹם שְׁלִישִֽׁי:

יד וַיֹּ֣אמֶר אֱלֹהִ֗ים יְהִ֤י מְאֹרֹת֙ בִּרְקִ֣יעַ הַשָּׁמַ֔יִם לְהַבְדִּ֕יל בֵּ֥ין הַיּ֖וֹם וּבֵ֣ין הַלָּ֑יְלָה

טו וְהָי֤וּ לְאֹתֹת֙ וּלְמ֣וֹעֲדִ֔ים וּלְיָמִ֖ים וְשָׁנִֽים: וְהָי֤וּ לִמְאוֹרֹת֙ בִּרְקִ֣יעַ הַשָּׁמַ֔יִם

טז לְהָאִ֖יר עַל־הָאָ֑רֶץ וַֽיְהִי־כֵֽן: וַיַּ֣עַשׂ אֱלֹהִ֔ים אֶת־שְׁנֵ֥י הַמְּאֹרֹ֖ת הַגְּדֹלִ֑ים

אֶת־הַמָּא֤וֹר הַגָּדֹל֙ לְמֶמְשֶׁ֣לֶת הַיּ֔וֹם וְאֶת־הַמָּא֤וֹר הַקָּטֹן֙ לְמֶמְשֶׁ֣לֶת

יז הַלַּ֔יְלָה וְאֵ֖ת הַכּֽוֹכָבִֽים: וַיִּתֵּ֥ן אֹתָ֛ם אֱלֹהִ֖ים בִּרְקִ֣יעַ הַשָּׁמָ֑יִם לְהָאִ֖יר עַל־

יח הָאָֽרֶץ: וְלִמְשֹׁל֙ בַּיּ֣וֹם וּבַלַּ֔יְלָה וּֽלְהַבְדִּ֔יל בֵּ֥ין הָא֖וֹר וּבֵ֣ין הַחֹ֑שֶׁךְ וַיַּ֥רְא

יט אֱלֹהִ֖ים כִּי־טֽוֹב: וַֽיְהִי־עֶ֥רֶב וַֽיְהִי־בֹ֖קֶר י֥וֹם רְבִיעִֽי:

כ וַיֹּ֣אמֶר אֱלֹהִ֔ים יִשְׁרְצ֣וּ הַמַּ֔יִם שֶׁ֖רֶץ נֶ֣פֶשׁ חַיָּ֑ה וְעוֹף֙ יְעוֹפֵ֣ף עַל־הָאָ֔רֶץ

כא עַל־פְּנֵ֖י רְקִ֥יעַ הַשָּׁמָֽיִם: וַיִּבְרָ֣א אֱלֹהִ֔ים אֶת־הַתַּנִּינִ֖ם הַגְּדֹלִ֑ים וְאֵ֣ת כָּל־

נֶ֣פֶשׁ הַֽחַיָּ֣ה ׀ הָֽרֹמֶ֡שֶׂת אֲשֶׁר֩ שָׁרְצ֨וּ הַמַּ֜יִם לְמִֽינֵהֶ֗ם וְאֵ֨ת כָּל־ע֤וֹף כָּנָף֙

כב לְמִינֵ֔הוּ וַיַּ֥רְא אֱלֹהִ֖ים כִּי־טֽוֹב: וַיְבָ֧רֶךְ אֹתָ֛ם אֱלֹהִ֖ים לֵאמֹ֑ר פְּר֣וּ וּרְב֗וּ

כג וּמִלְא֤וּ אֶת־הַמַּ֨יִם֙ בַּיַּמִּ֔ים וְהָע֖וֹף יִ֥רֶב בָּאָ֑רֶץ וַֽיְהִי־עֶ֥רֶב וַֽיְהִי־בֹ֖קֶר י֥וֹם

חֲמִישִֽׁי:

READING FOR SIMCHAS TORAH (CHASAN BEREISHIS)
1:1-2:3

⁕§ **Parashas Bereishis**

We begin the study of the Torah with the realization that the Torah is not a history book, but the charter of Man's mission in the universe. Thus, *Rashi* explains, the Torah's narrative of Creation establishes that God is the Sovereign of the universe.

The Torah relates the story of the six days of Creation *ex nihilo* to refute the theories that claim that the universe came into being through some massive coincidence or accident. The story of Creation speaks only in general terms, because its primary purpose is to state that nothing came into being except at God's command (*Ramban*).

1:1. The phrase בְּרֵאשִׁית בָּרָא אֱלֹהִים is commonly rendered *In the beginning God created,* which would indicate that the Torah is giving the sequence of Creation — that God

PARASHAS BEREISHIS

1

The beginning: First day

¹In the beginning of God's creating* the heavens and the earth — ² when the earth was astonishingly empty, with darkness upon the surface of the deep, and the Divine Presence hovered upon the surface of the waters — ³ God said, "Let there be light," and there was light. ⁴ God saw that the light was good,* and God separated between the light and the darkness. ⁵ God called to the light: "Day," and to the darkness He called: "Night." And there was evening and there was morning, one day.

Second day

⁶ God said, "Let there be a firmament in the midst of the waters, and let it separate between water and water." ⁷ So God made the firmament, and separated between the waters which were beneath the firmament and the waters which were above the firmament. And it was so. ⁸ God called to the firmament: "Heaven." And there was evening and there was morning, a second day.

Third day

⁹ God said, "Let the waters beneath the heaven be gathered into one area, and let the dry land appear." And it was so. ¹⁰ God called to the dry land: "Earth," and to the gathering of waters He called: "Seas." And God saw that it was good. ¹¹ God said, "Let the earth sprout vegetation: herbage yielding seed, fruit trees yielding fruit each after its kind, containing its own seed on the earth." And it was so. ¹² And the earth brought forth vegetation: herbage yielding seed after its kind, and trees yielding fruit, each containing its seed after its kind. And God saw that it was good. ¹³ And there was evening and there was morning, a third day.

Fourth day

¹⁴ God said, "Let there be luminaries in the firmament of the heaven to separate between the day and the night; and they shall serve as signs, and for festivals, and for days and years; ¹⁵ and they shall serve as luminaries in the firmament of the heaven to shine upon the earth." And it was so. ¹⁶ And God made the two great luminaries, the greater luminary to dominate the day and the lesser luminary to dominate the night; and the stars. ¹⁷ And God set them in the firmament of the heaven to give light upon the earth, ¹⁸ to dominate by day and by night, and to separate between the light and the darkness. And God saw that it was good. ¹⁹ And there was evening and there was morning, a fourth day.

Fifth day

²⁰ God said, "Let the waters teem with teeming living creatures, and fowl that fly about over the earth across the expanse of the heavens." ²¹ And God created the great sea-giants and every living being that creeps, with which the waters teemed after their kinds; and all winged fowl of every kind. And God saw that it was good. ²² God blessed them, saying, "Be fruitful and multiply, and fill the waters in the seas; but the fowl shall increase on the earth." ²³ And there was evening and there was morning, a fifth day.

---

created the heaven, the earth, darkness, water, light, and so on. However, *Rashi* and *Ibn Ezra* maintain that this verse cannot be chronological; our translation follows their view.

The name אֱלֹהִים denotes God in His Attribute of Justice [מִדַּת הַדִּין], as Ruler, Lawgiver, and Judge of the world.

1:4. Throughout the narrative, the term כִּי־טוֹב means that the creation of the item under discussion was completed.

1:6-8. Second day. The commentators generally agree that the term "firmament" refers to the atmosphere that encircles the world.

1:9-13. Third day. Up to now, the entire earth was submerged under water. On the third day, God decreed boundaries for the water, making way for the development of land, vegetation, animal life, and, ultimately, Man.

1:14-19. Fourth day. The luminaries, which had been created on the first day, were set in place on the fourth (*Chagigah* 12a). Indeed, all the potentials of heaven and earth were created on the first day but each was set in place on the day when it was so commanded (*Rashi*).

כד וַיֹּ֣אמֶר אֱלֹהִ֗ים תּוֹצֵ֤א הָאָ֙רֶץ֙ נֶ֣פֶשׁ חַיָּה֙ לְמִינָ֔הּ בְּהֵמָ֥ה וָרֶ֛מֶשׂ וְחַֽיְתוֹ־אֶ֖רֶץ

כה לְמִינָ֑הּ וַֽיְהִי־כֵֽן: וַיַּ֣עַשׂ אֱלֹהִים֩ אֶת־חַיַּ֨ת הָאָ֜רֶץ לְמִינָ֗הּ וְאֶת־הַבְּהֵמָה֙

כו לְמִינָ֔הּ וְאֵ֛ת כָּל־רֶ֥מֶשׂ הָֽאֲדָמָ֖ה לְמִינֵ֑הוּ וַיַּ֥רְא אֱלֹהִ֖ים כִּי־טֽוֹב: וַיֹּ֣אמֶר

אֱלֹהִ֔ים נַֽעֲשֶׂ֥ה אָדָ֛ם בְּצַלְמֵ֖נוּ כִּדְמוּתֵ֑נוּ וְיִרְדּוּ֩ בִדְגַ֨ת הַיָּ֜ם וּבְע֣וֹף הַשָּׁמַ֗יִם

כז וּבַבְּהֵמָה֙ וּבְכָל־הָאָ֔רֶץ וּבְכָל־הָרֶ֖מֶשׂ הָֽרֹמֵ֣שׂ עַל־הָאָֽרֶץ: וַיִּבְרָ֨א אֱלֹהִ֤ים ׀

אֶת־הָֽאָדָם֙ בְּצַלְמ֔וֹ בְּצֶ֥לֶם אֱלֹהִ֖ים בָּרָ֣א אֹת֑וֹ זָכָ֥ר וּנְקֵבָ֖ה בָּרָ֥א אֹתָֽם:

כח וַיְבָ֣רֶךְ אֹתָם֮ אֱלֹהִים֒ וַיֹּ֨אמֶר לָהֶ֜ם אֱלֹהִ֗ים פְּר֥וּ וּרְב֛וּ וּמִלְא֥וּ אֶת־הָאָ֖רֶץ

וְכִבְשֻׁ֑הָ וּרְד֞וּ בִּדְגַ֤ת הַיָּם֙ וּבְע֣וֹף הַשָּׁמַ֔יִם וּבְכָל־חַיָּ֖ה הָֽרֹמֶ֥שֶׂת עַל־הָאָֽרֶץ:

כט וַיֹּ֣אמֶר אֱלֹהִ֗ים הִנֵּה֩ נָתַ֨תִּי לָכֶ֜ם אֶת־כָּל־עֵ֣שֶׂב ׀ זֹרֵ֣עַ זֶ֗רַע אֲשֶׁר֙ עַל־פְּנֵ֣י

כָל־הָאָ֔רֶץ וְאֶת־כָּל־הָעֵ֛ץ אֲשֶׁר־בּ֥וֹ פְרִֽי־עֵ֖ץ זֹרֵ֣עַ זָ֑רַע לָכֶ֥ם יִֽהְיֶ֖ה לְאָכְלָֽה:

ל וּֽלְכָל־חַיַּ֣ת הָ֠אָרֶץ וּלְכָל־ע֨וֹף הַשָּׁמַ֜יִם וּלְכֹ֣ל ׀ רוֹמֵ֣שׂ עַל־הָאָ֗רֶץ אֲשֶׁר־בּוֹ֙

לא נֶ֣פֶשׁ חַיָּ֔ה אֶת־כָּל־יֶ֥רֶק עֵ֖שֶׂב לְאָכְלָ֑ה וַֽיְהִי־כֵֽן: וַיַּ֤רְא אֱלֹהִים֙ אֶת־כָּל־

אֲשֶׁ֣ר עָשָׂ֔ה וְהִנֵּה־ט֖וֹב מְאֹ֑ד וַֽיְהִי־עֶ֥רֶב וַֽיְהִי־בֹ֖קֶר י֥וֹם הַשִּׁשִּֽׁי:

ב א־ב וַיְכֻלּ֛וּ הַשָּׁמַ֥יִם וְהָאָ֖רֶץ וְכָל־צְבָאָֽם: וַיְכַ֤ל אֱלֹהִים֙ בַּיּ֣וֹם הַשְּׁבִיעִ֔י מְלַאכְתּ֖וֹ

ג אֲשֶׁ֣ר עָשָׂ֑ה וַיִּשְׁבֹּת֙ בַּיּ֣וֹם הַשְּׁבִיעִ֔י מִכָּל־מְלַאכְתּ֖וֹ אֲשֶׁ֥ר עָשָֽׂה: וַיְבָ֤רֶךְ

אֱלֹהִים֙ אֶת־י֣וֹם הַשְּׁבִיעִ֔י וַיְקַדֵּ֖שׁ אֹת֑וֹ כִּ֣י ב֤וֹ שָׁבַת֙ מִכָּל־מְלַאכְתּ֔וֹ אֲשֶׁר־

בָּרָ֥א אֱלֹהִ֖ים לַֽעֲשֽׂוֹת:

שני [יה זעירא] ד אֵ֣לֶּה תֽוֹלְד֧וֹת הַשָּׁמַ֛יִם וְהָאָ֖רֶץ בְּהִ֣בָּֽרְאָ֑ם בְּי֗וֹם עֲשׂ֛וֹת יְהֹוָ֥ה אֱלֹהִ֖ים אֶ֥רֶץ

ה וְשָׁמָֽיִם: וְכֹ֣ל ׀ שִׂ֣יחַ הַשָּׂדֶ֗ה טֶ֚רֶם יִֽהְיֶ֣ה בָאָ֔רֶץ וְכָל־עֵ֥שֶׂב הַשָּׂדֶ֖ה טֶ֣רֶם

יִצְמָ֑ח כִּי֩ לֹ֨א הִמְטִ֜יר יְהֹוָ֤ה אֱלֹהִים֙ עַל־הָאָ֔רֶץ וְאָדָ֣ם אַ֔יִן לַֽעֲבֹ֖ד אֶת־

ו־ז הָֽאֲדָמָֽה: וְאֵ֖ד יַֽעֲלֶ֣ה מִן־הָאָ֑רֶץ וְהִשְׁקָ֖ה אֶֽת־כָּל־פְּנֵֽי־הָֽאֲדָמָֽה: וַיִּ֩יצֶר֩ יְהֹוָ֨ה

אֱלֹהִ֜ים אֶת־הָֽאָדָ֗ם עָפָר֙ מִן־הָ֣אֲדָמָ֔ה וַיִּפַּ֥ח בְּאַפָּ֖יו נִשְׁמַ֣ת חַיִּ֑ים וַֽיְהִ֥י

ח הָֽאָדָ֖ם לְנֶ֥פֶשׁ חַיָּֽה: וַיִּטַּ֞ע יְהֹוָ֧ה אֱלֹהִ֛ים גַּן־בְּעֵ֖דֶן מִקֶּ֑דֶם וַיָּ֣שֶׂם שָׁ֔ם אֶת־

ט הָֽאָדָ֖ם אֲשֶׁ֥ר יָצָֽר: וַיַּצְמַ֞ח יְהֹוָ֤ה אֱלֹהִים֙ מִן־הָ֣אֲדָמָ֔ה כָּל־עֵ֛ץ נֶחְמָ֥ד

י לְמַרְאֶ֖ה וְט֣וֹב לְמַֽאֲכָ֑ל וְעֵ֤ץ הַֽחַיִּים֙ בְּת֣וֹךְ הַגָּ֔ן וְעֵ֕ץ הַדַּ֖עַת ט֥וֹב וָרָֽע: וְנָהָר֙

יֹצֵ֣א מֵעֵ֔דֶן לְהַשְׁק֖וֹת אֶת־הַגָּ֑ן וּמִשָּׁם֙ יִפָּרֵ֔ד וְהָיָ֖ה לְאַרְבָּעָ֥ה רָאשִֽׁים:

יא שֵׁ֥ם הָֽאֶחָ֖ד פִּישׁ֑וֹן ה֣וּא הַסֹּבֵ֗ב אֵ֚ת כָּל־אֶ֣רֶץ הַֽחֲוִילָ֔ה אֲשֶׁר־שָׁ֖ם הַזָּהָֽב:

יב־יג וּֽזֲהַ֛ב הָאָ֥רֶץ הַהִ֖וא ט֑וֹב שָׁ֥ם הַבְּדֹ֖לַח וְאֶ֥בֶן הַשֹּֽׁהַם: וְשֵֽׁם־הַנָּהָ֖ר הַשֵּׁנִ֣י

1:24-31. Sixth day. The climax of the physical creation is at hand. Animal life was created first, and then Man, the being whose performance for good or ill would determine the destiny of the universe. This sequence implies that God was telling Adam, in effect: The complete world is now placed in your hands; make it function properly.

1:26. *Targum Yonasan* paraphrases: "And God said to the ministering angels who had been created on the second day of Creation of the world, 'Let us make Man.'"

When Moses wrote the Torah and came to this verse (*let us make*), which is in the plural and implies חֵיל that there

is more than one Creator, he said: "Sovereign of the Universe! Why do You thus furnish a pretext for heretics to maintain that there is a plurality of divinities?" "Write!" God replied. "Whoever wishes to err will err . . . Instead, let them learn from their Creator Who created all, yet when He came to create Man He took counsel with the ministering angels" (*Midrash*).

1:27. Among all living creatures, Man alone is endowed — like his Creator — with morality, reason and free will. He can know and love God and can hold spiritual communion with Him; and Man alone can guide his actions

^{Sixth} ²⁴ *God said, "Let the earth bring forth living creatures, each according to its kind:*
^{day} *animal, and creeping thing, and beast of the land each according to its kind." And*
it was so. ²⁵ *God made the beast of the earth according to its kind, and the animal*
according to its kind, and every creeping being of the ground according to its kind.
And God saw that it was good.

²⁶ *And God said, "Let us make Man* * *in Our image, after Our likeness. They shall*
rule over the fish of the sea, the birds of the sky, and over the animal, the whole
earth, and every creeping thing that creeps upon the earth." ²⁷ *So God created Man*
in His image, in the image of God * *He created him; male and female He created*
them.

²⁸ *God blessed them and God said to them, "Be fruitful and multiply, fill the earth*
and subdue it; and rule over the fish of the sea, the bird of the sky, and every living
thing that moves on the earth."

²⁹ *God said, "Behold, I have given to you all herbage yielding seed that is on*
the surface of the entire earth, and every tree that has seed-yielding fruit; it shall
be yours for food. ³⁰ *And to every beast of the earth, to every bird of the sky, and*
to everything that moves on the earth, within which there is a living soul, every
green herb is for food." And it was so. ³¹ *And God saw all that He had made,*
and behold it was very good. And there was evening and there was morning,
the sixth day.

2   ¹ *Thus the heaven and the earth were finished, and all their array.* ² *By the*
Seventh day: *seventh day God completed His work which He had done, and He abstained*
The Sabbath   *on the seventh day from all His work which He had done.* ³ *God blessed the*
seventh day and sanctified it because on it He abstained from all His work which
God created to make.

⁴ *These are the products of the heaven and the earth when they were created*
on the day that HASHEM God made earth and heaven — ⁵ *now all the trees of the*
field were not yet on the earth and all the herb of the field had not yet sprouted,
for HASHEM God had not sent rain upon the earth and there was no man to work
the soil. ⁶ *A mist ascended from the earth and watered the whole surface of the*
soil. ⁷ *And HASHEM God formed the man of dust from the ground, and He blew into*
his nostrils the soul of life; and man became a living being.

The Garden   ⁸ *HASHEM God planted a garden in Eden, to the east, and placed there the man*
of Eden   *whom He had formed.* ⁹ *And HASHEM God caused to sprout from the ground every*
tree that was pleasing to the sight and good for food; also the Tree of Life in the
midst of the garden, and the Tree of Knowledge of Good and Bad.

¹⁰ *A river issues forth from Eden to water the garden, and from there it is divided*
and becomes four headwaters. ¹¹ *The name of the first is Pishon, the one that*
encircles the whole land of Havilah, where the gold is. ¹² *The gold of that land is*
good; the bedolach is there, and the shoham stone. ¹³ *The name of the second river*

---

through reason. It is in this sense that the Torah describes
Man as having been created in God's image and likeness
(*Rambam*).

2:1-3. The seventh day / the Sabbath. The Sabbath is
introduced with the declaration that the work of heaven
and earth were complete, and that they stand before us
in their final intended state of harmonious perfection.
Then, God proclaimed His Sabbath. This passage, the
first paragraph of the Sabbath *Kiddush*, proclaims that

God is the Creator Who brought the universe into being in
six days and rested on the seventh. Israel's observance
of the Sabbath laws constitutes devoted testimony to
this.

2:8-14. The Garden of Eden. God formed Adam outside
the garden so he would see the world of thorns and
thistles; only then did God lead him into the garden, so
that he would see the alternatives before he was given his
first commandment (*Chizkuni*).

יד גִּיחֹ֑ון ה֣וּא הַסּוֹבֵ֔ב אֵ֖ת כָּל־אֶ֥רֶץ כּֽוּשׁ׃ וְשֵׁ֨ם הַנָּהָ֤ר הַשְּׁלִישִׁי֙ חִדֶּ֔קֶל ה֥וּא

טו הַהֹלֵ֖ךְ קִדְמַ֣ת אַשּׁ֑וּר וְהַנָּהָ֥ר הָֽרְבִיעִ֖י ה֥וּא פְרָֽת׃ וַיִּקַּ֛ח יהו֥ה אֱלֹהִ֖ים אֶת־

טז הָֽאָדָ֑ם וַיַּנִּחֵ֣הוּ בְגַן־עֵ֔דֶן לְעָבְדָ֖הּ וּלְשָׁמְרָֽהּ׃ וַיְצַו֙ יהו֣ה אֱלֹהִ֔ים עַל־הָֽאָדָ֖ם

יז לֵאמֹ֑ר מִכֹּ֥ל עֵֽץ־הַגָּ֖ן אָכֹ֥ל תֹּאכֵֽל׃ וּמֵעֵ֗ץ הַדַּ֨עַת֙ ט֣וֹב וָרָ֔ע לֹ֥א תֹאכַ֖ל מִמֶּ֑נּוּ

יח כִּ֗י בְּי֛וֹם אֲכָלְךָ֥ מִמֶּ֖נּוּ מ֥וֹת תָּמֽוּת׃ וַיֹּ֨אמֶר֙ יהו֣ה אֱלֹהִ֔ים לֹא־ט֛וֹב הֱי֥וֹת

יט הָֽאָדָ֖ם לְבַדּ֑וֹ אֶֽעֱשֶׂהּ־לּ֥וֹ עֵ֖זֶר כְּנֶגְדּֽוֹ׃ וַיִּ֩צֶר֩ יהו֨ה אֱלֹהִ֜ים מִן־הָֽאֲדָמָ֗ה כָּל־

חַיַּ֤ת הַשָּׂדֶה֙ וְאֵת֙ כָּל־ע֣וֹף הַשָּׁמַ֔יִם וַיָּבֵא֙ אֶל־הָ֣אָדָ֔ם לִרְא֖וֹת מַה־יִּקְרָא־ל֑וֹ

כ וְכֹל֩ אֲשֶׁ֨ר יִקְרָא־ל֧וֹ הָֽאָדָ֛ם נֶ֥פֶשׁ חַיָּ֖ה ה֥וּא שְׁמֽוֹ׃ וַיִּקְרָ֣א הָֽאָדָ֗ם שֵׁמוֹת֙ לְכָל־

הַבְּהֵמָה֙ וּלְע֣וֹף הַשָּׁמַ֔יִם וּלְכֹ֖ל חַיַּ֣ת הַשָּׂדֶ֑ה וּלְאָדָ֕ם לֹֽא־מָצָ֥א עֵ֖זֶר כְּנֶגְדּֽוֹ׃

כא וַיַּפֵּל֩ יהו֨ה אֱלֹהִ֧ים ׀ תַּרְדֵּמָ֛ה עַל־הָֽאָדָ֖ם וַיִּישָׁ֑ן וַיִּקַּ֗ח אַחַת֙ מִצַּלְעֹתָ֔יו וַיִּסְגֹּ֥ר

כב בָּשָׂ֖ר תַּחְתֶּֽנָּה׃ וַיִּ֩בֶן֩ יהו֨ה אֱלֹהִ֧ים ׀ אֶֽת־הַצֵּלָ֛ע אֲשֶׁר־לָקַ֥ח מִן־הָֽאָדָ֖ם לְאִשָּׁ֑ה

כג וַיְבִאֶ֖הָ אֶל־הָֽאָדָֽם׃ וַיֹּאמֶר֮ הָֽאָדָם֒ זֹ֣את הַפַּ֗עַם עֶ֚צֶם מֵֽעֲצָמַ֔י וּבָשָׂ֖ר מִבְּשָׂרִ֑י

כד לְזֹאת֙ יִקָּרֵ֣א אִשָּׁ֔ה כִּ֥י מֵאִ֖ישׁ לֻֽקֳחָה־זֹּֽאת׃ עַל־כֵּן֙ יַֽעֲזָב־אִ֔ישׁ אֶת־אָבִ֖יו

כה וְאֶת־אִמּ֑וֹ וְדָבַ֣ק בְּאִשְׁתּ֔וֹ וְהָי֖וּ לְבָשָׂ֥ר אֶחָֽד׃ וַיִּֽהְי֤וּ שְׁנֵיהֶם֙ עֲרוּמִּ֔ים הָֽאָדָ֖ם

א וְאִשְׁתּ֑וֹ וְלֹ֖א יִתְבֹּשָֽׁשׁוּ׃ וְהַנָּחָשׁ֙ הָיָ֣ה עָר֔וּם מִכֹּל֙ חַיַּ֣ת הַשָּׂדֶ֔ה אֲשֶׁ֥ר עָשָׂ֖ה

יהו֣ה אֱלֹהִ֑ים וַיֹּ֨אמֶר֙ אֶל־הָ֣אִשָּׁ֔ה אַ֚ף כִּֽי־אָמַ֣ר אֱלֹהִ֔ים לֹ֣א תֹֽאכְל֔וּ מִכֹּ֖ל עֵ֥ץ

ב־ג הַגָּֽן׃ וַתֹּ֥אמֶר הָֽאִשָּׁ֖ה אֶל־הַנָּחָ֑שׁ מִפְּרִ֥י עֵֽץ־הַגָּ֖ן נֹאכֵֽל׃ וּמִפְּרִ֣י הָעֵץ֮ אֲשֶׁ֣ר

בְּתוֹךְ־הַגָּן֒ אָמַ֣ר אֱלֹהִ֗ים לֹ֤א תֹֽאכְלוּ֙ מִמֶּ֔נּוּ וְלֹ֥א תִגְּע֖וּ בּ֑וֹ פֶּן־תְּמֻתֽוּן׃ וַיֹּ֥אמֶר

ד־ה הַנָּחָ֖שׁ אֶל־הָֽאִשָּׁ֑ה לֹֽא־מ֖וֹת תְּמֻתֽוּן׃ כִּ֚י יֹדֵ֣עַ אֱלֹהִ֔ים כִּ֗י בְּיוֹם֙ אֲכָלְכֶ֣ם

מִמֶּ֔נּוּ וְנִפְקְח֖וּ עֵֽינֵיכֶ֑ם וִֽהְיִיתֶם֙ כֵּֽאלֹהִ֔ים יֹדְעֵ֖י ט֥וֹב וָרָֽע׃ וַתֵּ֣רֶא הָֽאִשָּׁ֡ה כִּ֣י

ו ט֣וֹב הָעֵץ֩ לְמַֽאֲכָ֨ל וְכִ֧י תַֽאֲוָה־ה֣וּא לָעֵינַ֗יִם וְנֶחְמָ֤ד הָעֵץ֙ לְהַשְׂכִּ֔יל וַתִּקַּ֥ח

מִפִּרְי֖וֹ וַתֹּאכַ֑ל וַתִּתֵּ֧ן גַּם־לְאִישָׁ֛הּ עִמָּ֖הּ וַיֹּאכַֽל׃ וַתִּפָּקַ֨חְנָה֙ עֵינֵ֣י שְׁנֵיהֶ֔ם

ז וַיֵּ֣דְע֔וּ כִּ֥י עֵֽירֻמִּ֖ם הֵ֑ם וַֽיִּתְפְּרוּ֙ עֲלֵ֣ה תְאֵנָ֔ה וַיַּֽעֲשׂ֥וּ לָהֶ֖ם חֲגֹרֹֽת׃ וַיִּשְׁמְע֡וּ אֶת־

ח ק֣וֹל יהו֨ה אֱלֹהִ֜ים מִתְהַלֵּ֤ךְ בַּגָּן֙ לְר֣וּחַ הַיּ֔וֹם וַיִּתְחַבֵּ֨א הָֽאָדָ֜ם וְאִשְׁתּ֗וֹ מִפְּנֵי֙

ט יהו֣ה אֱלֹהִ֔ים בְּת֖וֹךְ עֵ֣ץ הַגָּֽן׃ וַיִּקְרָ֛א יהו֥ה אֱלֹהִ֖ים אֶל־הָֽאָדָ֑ם וַיֹּ֥אמֶר ל֖וֹ

י־יא אַיֶּֽכָּה׃ וַיֹּ֕אמֶר אֶת־קֹֽלְךָ֥ שָׁמַ֖עְתִּי בַּגָּ֑ן וָֽאִירָ֛א כִּֽי־עֵירֹ֥ם אָנֹ֖כִי וָֽאֵחָבֵֽא׃ וַיֹּ֕אמֶר

מִ֚י הִגִּ֣יד לְךָ֔ כִּ֥י עֵירֹ֖ם אָ֑תָּה הֲמִן־הָעֵ֗ץ אֲשֶׁ֧ר צִוִּיתִ֛יךָ לְבִלְתִּ֥י אֲכָל־מִמֶּ֖נּוּ

יב אָכָֽלְתָּ׃ וַיֹּ֖אמֶר הָֽאָדָ֑ם הָֽאִשָּׁה֙ אֲשֶׁ֣ר נָתַ֣תָּה עִמָּדִ֔י הִ֛וא נָֽתְנָה־לִּ֥י מִן־הָעֵ֖ץ

יג וָֽאֹכֵֽל׃ וַיֹּ֨אמֶר יהו֧ה אֱלֹהִ֛ים לָֽאִשָּׁ֖ה מַה־זֹּ֣את עָשִׂ֑ית וַתֹּ֙אמֶר֙ הָֽאִשָּׁ֔ה

יד הַנָּחָ֥שׁ הִשִּׁיאַ֖נִי וָֽאֹכֵֽל׃ וַיֹּ֩אמֶר֩ יהו֨ה אֱלֹהִ֥ים ׀ אֶֽל־הַנָּחָשׁ֮ כִּ֣י עָשִׂ֣יתָ זֹּאת֒

שלישי

ג

2:17. Since Adam lived to the age of nine hundred and thirty, it is clear that he was not to die as soon as he ate the fruit. Rather, he would become *subject* to death.

2:18-25. This passage elaborates upon the making of the creatures mentioned in 1:25.

3:1-14. Adam had been given only one commandment: not to eat from the tree, and now his resolve would be tested to see if he could withstand temptation.

3:9. God knew where Adam was, of course. The question was meant to initiate a dialogue so Adam would not be too terrified to repent [or: reply]. But he did not confess. Instead, as verse 12 shows, he hurled against God the very kindness of the gift of Eve, by implying that God was at fault for giving him his wife (*Midrash Aggadah*).

is Gihon, the one that encircles the whole land of Cush. ¹⁴ The name of the third river is Hiddekel, the one that flows toward the east of Assyria; and the fourth river is the Euphrates.

Man in the garden   ¹⁵ HASHEM God took the man and placed him in the Garden of Eden, to work it and to guard it. ¹⁶ And HASHEM God commanded the man, saying, "Of every tree of the garden you may freely eat; ¹⁷ but of the Tree of Knowledge of Good and Bad, you must not eat thereof; for on the day you eat of it, you shall surely die."*

¹⁸ HASHEM God said, "It is not good that man be alone; I will make him a helper corresponding to him." ¹⁹ Now, HASHEM God had formed out of the ground every beast of the field and every bird of the sky, and brought them to the man to see what he would call each one; and whatever the man called each living creature, that remained its name. ²⁰ And the man assigned names to all the cattle and to the birds of the sky and to every beast of the field; but as for man, he did not find a helper corresponding to him.

²¹ So HASHEM God cast a deep sleep upon the man and he slept; and He took one of his sides and He filled in flesh in its place. ²² Then HASHEM God fashioned the side that He had taken from the man into a woman, and He brought her to the man. ²³ And the man said, "This time it is bone of my bones and flesh of my flesh. This shall be called Woman, for from man was she taken." ²⁴ Therefore a man shall leave his father and his mother and cling to his wife and they shall become one flesh.

²⁵ They were both naked, the man and his wife, and they were not ashamed.

3   **N**ow the serpent was cunning beyond any beast of the field that HASHEM God had made. He said to the woman, "Did, perhaps, God say: 'You shall not *The Serpent's enticement* eat of any tree of the garden'?"

² The woman said to the serpent, "Of the fruit of any tree of the garden we may eat. ³ Of the fruit of the tree which is in the center of the garden God has said: 'You shall neither eat of it nor touch it, lest you die.' "

⁴ The serpent said to the woman, "You will not surely die; ⁵ for God knows that on the day you eat of it your eyes will be opened and you will be like God, knowing good and bad."

⁶ And the woman perceived that the tree was good for eating and that it was a delight to the eyes, and that the tree was desirable as a means to wisdom, and she took of its fruit and ate; and she gave also to her husband with her and he ate. ⁷ Then the eyes of both of them were opened and they realized that they were naked; and they sewed together a fig leaf and made themselves aprons.

⁸ They heard the sound of HASHEM God manifesting Itself in the garden toward evening; and the man and his wife hid from HASHEM God among the trees of the garden. ⁹ HASHEM God called out to the man and said to him, "Where are you?"*

¹⁰ He said, "I heard the sound of You in the garden, and I was afraid because I am naked, so I hid."

¹¹ And He said, "Who told you that you are naked? Have you eaten of the tree from which I commanded you not to eat?"

¹² The man said, "The woman whom You gave to be with me — she gave me of the tree, and I ate."

¹³ And HASHEM God said to the woman, "What is this that you have done!" The woman said, "The serpent deceived me, and I ate."

¹⁴ And HASHEM God said to the serpent, "Because you have done this,

אָר֤וּר אַתָּה֙ מִכָּל־הַבְּהֵמָ֔ה וּמִכֹּ֖ל חַיַּ֣ת הַשָּׂדֶ֑ה עַל־גְּחֹֽנְךָ֣ תֵלֵ֔ךְ וְעָפָ֥ר תֹּאכַ֖ל

כָּל־יְמֵ֥י חַיֶּֽיךָ׃ וְאֵיבָ֣ה ׀ אָשִׁ֗ית בֵּֽינְךָ֙ וּבֵ֣ין הָֽאִשָּׁ֔ה וּבֵ֥ין זַרְעֲךָ֖ וּבֵ֣ין זַרְעָ֑הּ ה֚וּא   טו

יְשֽׁוּפְךָ֣ רֹ֔אשׁ וְאַתָּ֖ה תְּשׁוּפֶ֥נּוּ עָקֵֽב׃   אֶל־הָֽאִשָּׁ֣ה אָמַ֗ר הַרְבָּ֤ה   טז

אַרְבֶּה֙ עִצְּבוֹנֵ֣ךְ וְהֵֽרֹנֵ֔ךְ בְּעֶ֖צֶב תֵּֽלְדִ֣י בָנִ֑ים וְאֶל־אִישֵׁךְ֙ תְּשׁ֣וּקָתֵ֔ךְ וְה֖וּא

יִמְשָׁל־בָּֽךְ׃   וּלְאָדָ֣ם אָמַ֗ר כִּֽי־שָׁמַ֘עְתָּ֮ לְק֣וֹל אִשְׁתֶּךָ֒ וַתֹּ֙אכַל֙ מִן־הָעֵ֔ץ   יז

אֲשֶׁ֣ר צִוִּיתִ֗יךָ לֵאמֹר֙ לֹ֣א תֹאכַ֣ל מִמֶּ֔נּוּ אֲרוּרָ֤ה הָֽאֲדָמָה֙ בַּֽעֲבוּרֶ֔ךָ בְּעִצָּבוֹן֙

תֹּֽאכֲלֶ֔נָּה כֹּ֖ל יְמֵ֥י חַיֶּֽיךָ׃ וְק֥וֹץ וְדַרְדַּ֖ר תַּצְמִ֣יחַֽ לָ֑ךְ וְאָֽכַלְתָּ֖ אֶת־עֵ֥שֶׂב הַשָּׂדֶֽה׃   יח

בְּזֵעַ֤ת אַפֶּ֙יךָ֙ תֹּ֣אכַל לֶ֔חֶם עַ֤ד שֽׁוּבְךָ֙ אֶל־הָ֣אֲדָמָ֔ה כִּ֥י מִמֶּ֖נָּה לֻקָּ֑חְתָּ כִּֽי־עָפָ֣ר   יט

אַ֔תָּה וְאֶל־עָפָ֖ר תָּשֽׁוּב׃ וַיִּקְרָ֧א הָֽאָדָ֛ם שֵׁ֥ם אִשְׁתּ֖וֹ חַוָּ֑ה כִּ֛י הִ֥וא הָֽיְתָ֖ה אֵ֥ם   כ

כָּל־חָֽי׃ וַיַּעַשׂ֩ יְהֹוָ֨ה אֱלֹהִ֜ים לְאָדָ֧ם וּלְאִשְׁתּ֛וֹ כָּתְנ֥וֹת ע֖וֹר וַיַּלְבִּשֵֽׁם׃   כא

רביעי וַיֹּ֣אמֶר ׀ יְהֹוָ֣ה אֱלֹהִ֗ים הֵ֤ן הָֽאָדָם֙ הָיָה֙ כְּאַחַ֣ד מִמֶּ֔נּוּ לָדַ֖עַת ט֣וֹב וָרָ֑ע   כב

וְעַתָּ֣ה ׀ פֶּן־יִשְׁלַ֣ח יָד֗וֹ וְלָקַח֙ גַּ֚ם מֵעֵ֣ץ הַֽחַיִּ֔ים וְאָכַ֖ל וָחַ֥י לְעֹלָֽם׃ וַֽיְשַׁלְּחֵ֛הוּ   כג

יְהֹוָ֥ה אֱלֹהִ֖ים מִגַּן־עֵ֑דֶן לַֽעֲבֹד֙ אֶת־הָ֣אֲדָמָ֔ה אֲשֶׁ֥ר לֻקַּ֖ח מִשָּֽׁם׃ וַיְגָ֖רֶשׁ אֶת־   כד

הָֽאָדָ֑ם וַיַּשְׁכֵּן֩ מִקֶּ֨דֶם לְגַן־עֵ֜דֶן אֶת־הַכְּרֻבִ֗ים וְאֵ֨ת לַ֤הַט הַחֶ֙רֶב֙ הַמִּתְהַפֶּ֔כֶת

לִשְׁמֹ֕ר אֶת־דֶּ֖רֶךְ עֵ֥ץ הַֽחַיִּֽים׃   וְהָ֣אָדָ֔ם יָדַ֖ע אֶת־חַוָּ֣ה אִשְׁתּ֑וֹ   **א**   **ד**

וַתַּ֙הַר֙ וַתֵּ֣לֶד אֶת־קַ֔יִן וַתֹּ֕אמֶר קָנִ֥יתִי אִ֖ישׁ אֶת־יְהֹוָֽה׃ וַתֹּ֣סֶף לָלֶ֔דֶת   ב

אֶת־אָחִ֖יו אֶת־הָ֑בֶל וַֽיְהִי־הֶ֙בֶל֙ רֹ֣עֵה צֹ֔אן וְקַ֕יִן הָיָ֖ה עֹבֵ֥ד אֲדָמָֽה׃ וַֽיְהִ֖י   ג

מִקֵּ֣ץ יָמִ֑ים וַיָּבֵ֨א קַ֜יִן מִפְּרִ֧י הָֽאֲדָמָ֛ה מִנְחָ֖ה לַֽיהֹוָֽה׃ וְהֶ֨בֶל הֵבִ֥יא גַם־ה֛וּא   ד

מִבְּכֹר֥וֹת צֹאנ֖וֹ וּמֵֽחֶלְבֵהֶ֑ן וַיִּ֣שַׁע יְהֹוָ֔ה אֶל־הֶ֖בֶל וְאֶל־מִנְחָתֽוֹ׃ וְאֶל־קַ֥יִן   ה

וְאֶל־מִנְחָת֖וֹ לֹ֣א שָׁעָ֑ה וַיִּ֤חַר לְקַ֙יִן֙ מְאֹ֔ד וַֽיִּפְּל֖וּ פָּנָֽיו׃ וַיֹּ֥אמֶר יְהֹוָ֖ה אֶל־קָ֑יִן   ו

לָ֚מָּה חָ֣רָה לָ֔ךְ וְלָ֖מָּה נָֽפְל֥וּ פָנֶֽיךָ׃ הֲל֤וֹא אִם־תֵּיטִיב֙ שְׂאֵ֔ת וְאִם֙ לֹ֣א תֵיטִ֔יב   ז

לַפֶּ֖תַח חַטָּ֣את רֹבֵ֑ץ וְאֵלֶ֙יךָ֙ תְּשׁ֣וּקָת֔וֹ וְאַתָּ֖ה תִּמְשָׁל־בּֽוֹ׃ וַיֹּ֥אמֶר קַ֖יִן אֶל־   ח

הֶ֣בֶל אָחִ֑יו וַֽיְהִי֙ בִּֽהְיוֹתָ֣ם בַּשָּׂדֶ֔ה וַיָּ֥קָם קַ֛יִן אֶל־הֶ֥בֶל אָחִ֖יו וַיַּֽהַרְגֵֽהוּ׃

וַיֹּ֤אמֶר יְהֹוָה֙ אֶל־קַ֔יִן אֵ֖י הֶ֣בֶל אָחִ֑יךָ וַיֹּ֙אמֶר֙ לֹ֣א יָדַ֔עְתִּי הֲשֹׁמֵ֥ר אָחִ֖י אָנֹֽכִי׃   ט

וַיֹּ֖אמֶר מֶ֣ה עָשִׂ֑יתָ ק֚וֹל דְּמֵ֣י אָחִ֔יךָ צֹֽעֲקִ֥ים אֵלַ֖י מִן־הָֽאֲדָמָֽה׃ וְעַתָּ֖ה אָר֣וּר   יא

אָ֑תָּה מִן־הָֽאֲדָמָה֙ אֲשֶׁ֣ר פָּֽצְתָ֣ה אֶת־פִּ֔יהָ לָקַ֛חַת אֶת־דְּמֵ֥י אָחִ֖יךָ מִיָּדֶֽךָ׃

כִּ֤י תַֽעֲבֹד֙ אֶת־הָ֣אֲדָמָ֔ה לֹֽא־תֹסֵ֥ף תֵּת־כֹּחָ֖הּ לָ֑ךְ נָ֥ע וָנָ֖ד תִּֽהְיֶ֥ה בָאָֽרֶץ׃   יב

3:14-21. By assimilating into their nature an awareness of and a temptation to sin, Adam and Eve became unworthy of remaining in the spiritual paradise of Eden; as a result, life changed in virtually every conceivable way.

3:16. The new conditions of life that made sustenance the product of hard labor would naturally make women dependent on the physically stronger men. Obedience to the Torah, however, restores her to her former and proper status as the *crown of her husband* and *pearl of his life* [*Proverbs* 12:4, 31:10] (R' Hirsch).

4:3-5. From the subtle contrast between the simple description of Cain's offering and the more specific descrip-

tion of Abel's offering — *from the firstlings of his flock and from their choicest* — the Sages derive that Cain's offering was from the inferior portions of the crop, while Abel chose only the finest of his flock. Therefore, Abel's sacrifice was accepted, but not Cain's (*Ibn Ezra; Radak*).

4:7. If you succumb to your Evil Inclination, punishment and evil will be as ever present as if they lived in your doorway (*Sforno*).

4:9. The question was rhetorical, for God knew full well where he was. He engaged Cain in a gentle conversation to give him the opportunity to confess and repent (*Rashi; Radak; Sforno*).

The sinners are punished accursed are you beyond all the cattle and beyond all beasts of the field; upon your belly shall you go, and dust shall you eat all the days of your life. ¹⁵ I will put enmity between you and the woman, and between your offspring and her offspring. He will pound your head, and you will bite his heel."

¹⁶ To the woman He said, "I will greatly increase your suffering and your childbearing; in pain shall you bear children. Yet your craving shall be for your husband, and he shall rule over you."*

¹⁷ To Adam He said, "Because you listened to the voice of your wife and ate of the tree about which I commanded you saying, 'You shall not eat of it,' accursed is the ground because of you; through suffering shall you eat of it all the days of your life. ¹⁸ Thorns and thistles shall it sprout for you, and you shall eat the herb of the field. ¹⁹ By the sweat of your brow shall you eat bread until you return to the ground, from which you were taken: For you are dust, and to dust shall you return."

²⁰ The man called his wife's name Eve, because she had become the mother of all the living.

²¹ And HASHEM God made for Adam and his wife garments of skin, and He clothed them.

²² And HASHEM God said, "Behold Man has become like the Unique One among us, knowing good and bad; and now, lest he put forth his hand and take also of the Tree of Life, and eat and live forever!"

Man's expulsion from Eden ²³ So HASHEM God banished him from the Garden of Eden, to work the soil from which he was taken. ²⁴ And having driven out the man, He stationed at the east of the Garden of Eden the Cherubim and the flame of the ever-turning sword, to guard the way to the Tree of Life.

4

Cain and Abel ¹ Now the man had known his wife Eve, and she conceived and bore Cain, saying, "I have acquired a man with HASHEM." ² And additionally she bore his brother Abel. Abel became a shepherd, and Cain became a tiller of the ground.

³ After a period of time, Cain brought an offering to HASHEM of the fruit of the ground; ⁴ and as for Abel, he also brought of the firstlings of his flock and from their choicest. HASHEM turned to Abel and to his offering, ⁵ but to Cain and to his offering He did not turn. This annoyed Cain exceedingly, and his countenance fell.

⁶ And HASHEM said to Cain, "Why are you annoyed, and why has your countenance fallen? ⁷ Surely, if you improve yourself, you will be forgiven. But if you do not improve yourself, sin rests at the door.* Its desire is toward you, yet you can conquer it."

⁸ Cain spoke with his brother Abel. And it happened when they were in the field, that Cain rose up against his brother Abel and killed him.

⁹ HASHEM said to Cain, "Where is Abel your brother?"*

And he said, "I do not know. Am I my brother's keeper?"

¹⁰ Then He said, "What have you done? The voice of your brother's blood cries out to Me from the ground! ¹¹ Therefore, you are cursed more than the ground, which opened wide its mouth to receive your brother's blood from your hand. ¹² When you work the ground, it shall no longer yield its strength to you. You shall become a vagrant and a wanderer on earth."

יג-יד	וַיֹּאמֶר קַיִן אֶל־יהוה גָּדוֹל עֲוֺנִי מִנְּשֹׂא: הֵן גֵּרַשְׁתָּ אֹתִי הַיּוֹם מֵעַל פְּנֵי הָאֲדָמָה וּמִפָּנֶיךָ אֶסָּתֵר וְהָיִיתִי נָע וָנָד בָּאָרֶץ וְהָיָה כָל־מֹצְאִי יַהַרְגֵנִי:
טו	וַיֹּאמֶר לוֹ יהוה לָכֵן כָּל־הֹרֵג קַיִן שִׁבְעָתַיִם יֻקָּם וַיָּשֶׂם יהוה לְקַיִן אוֹת לְבִלְתִּי הַכּוֹת־אֹתוֹ כָּל־מֹצְאוֹ: וַיֵּצֵא קַיִן מִלִּפְנֵי יהוה וַיֵּשֶׁב בְּאֶרֶץ־נוֹד
טז	קִדְמַת־עֵדֶן: וַיֵּדַע קַיִן אֶת־אִשְׁתּוֹ וַתַּהַר וַתֵּלֶד אֶת־חֲנוֹךְ וַיְהִי בֹּנֶה עִיר
יז	וַיִּקְרָא שֵׁם הָעִיר כְּשֵׁם בְּנוֹ חֲנוֹךְ: וַיִּוָּלֵד לַחֲנוֹךְ אֶת־עִירָד וְעִירָד יָלַד אֶת־
יח	מְחוּיָאֵל וּמְחִיָּיאֵל יָלַד אֶת־מְתוּשָׁאֵל וּמְתוּשָׁאֵל יָלַד אֶת־לָמֶךְ: וַיִּקַּח־
חמישי / יט	לוֹ לֶמֶךְ שְׁתֵּי נָשִׁים שֵׁם הָאַחַת עָדָה וְשֵׁם הַשֵּׁנִית צִלָּה: וַתֵּלֶד עָדָה
כ	אֶת־יָבָל הוּא הָיָה אֲבִי יֹשֵׁב אֹהֶל וּמִקְנֶה: וְשֵׁם אָחִיו יוּבָל הוּא הָיָה אֲבִי
כא	כָּל־תֹּפֵשׂ כִּנּוֹר וְעוּגָב: וְצִלָּה גַם־הִוא יָלְדָה אֶת־תּוּבַל קַיִן לֹטֵשׁ כָּל־
כב	חֹרֵשׁ נְחֹשֶׁת וּבַרְזֶל וַאֲחוֹת תּוּבַל־קַיִן נַעֲמָה: וַיֹּאמֶר לֶמֶךְ לְנָשָׁיו עָדָה
ששי / כג	וְצִלָּה שְׁמַעַן קוֹלִי נְשֵׁי לֶמֶךְ הַאְזֵנָּה אִמְרָתִי כִּי אִישׁ הָרַגְתִּי לְפִצְעִי
כד-כה	וְיֶלֶד לְחַבֻּרָתִי: כִּי שִׁבְעָתַיִם יֻקַּם־קָיִן וְלֶמֶךְ שִׁבְעִים וְשִׁבְעָה: וַיֵּדַע אָדָם עוֹד אֶת־אִשְׁתּוֹ וַתֵּלֶד בֵּן וַתִּקְרָא אֶת־שְׁמוֹ שֵׁת כִּי שָׁת־לִי אֱלֹהִים
כו	זֶרַע אַחֵר תַּחַת הֶבֶל כִּי הֲרָגוֹ קָיִן: וּלְשֵׁת גַּם־הוּא יֻלַּד־בֵּן וַיִּקְרָא אֶת־
ה / א	שְׁמוֹ אֱנוֹשׁ אָז הוּחַל לִקְרֹא בְּשֵׁם יהוה: זֶה סֵפֶר תּוֹלְדֹת
ב	אָדָם בְּיוֹם בְּרֹא אֱלֹהִים אָדָם בִּדְמוּת אֱלֹהִים עָשָׂה אֹתוֹ: זָכָר וּנְקֵבָה
ג	בְּרָאָם וַיְבָרֶךְ אֹתָם וַיִּקְרָא אֶת־שְׁמָם אָדָם בְּיוֹם הִבָּרְאָם: וַיְחִי אָדָם שְׁלֹשִׁים וּמְאַת שָׁנָה וַיּוֹלֶד בִּדְמוּתוֹ כְּצַלְמוֹ וַיִּקְרָא אֶת־שְׁמוֹ שֵׁת:
ד	וַיִּהְיוּ יְמֵי־אָדָם אַחֲרֵי הוֹלִידוֹ אֶת־שֵׁת שְׁמֹנֶה מֵאֹת שָׁנָה וַיּוֹלֶד בָּנִים
ה	וּבָנוֹת: וַיִּהְיוּ כָּל־יְמֵי אָדָם אֲשֶׁר־חַי תְּשַׁע מֵאוֹת שָׁנָה וּשְׁלֹשִׁים שָׁנָה
ו	וַיָּמֹת: וַיְחִי־שֵׁת חָמֵשׁ שָׁנִים וּמְאַת שָׁנָה וַיּוֹלֶד אֶת־אֱנוֹשׁ:
ז	וַיְחִי־שֵׁת אַחֲרֵי הוֹלִידוֹ אֶת־אֱנוֹשׁ שֶׁבַע שָׁנִים וּשְׁמֹנֶה מֵאוֹת שָׁנָה
ח	וַיּוֹלֶד בָּנִים וּבָנוֹת: וַיִּהְיוּ כָּל־יְמֵי־שֵׁת שְׁתֵּים עֶשְׂרֵה שָׁנָה וּתְשַׁע מֵאוֹת
ט-י	שָׁנָה וַיָּמֹת: וַיְחִי אֱנוֹשׁ תִּשְׁעִים שָׁנָה וַיּוֹלֶד אֶת־קֵינָן: וַיְחִי
	אֱנוֹשׁ אַחֲרֵי הוֹלִידוֹ אֶת־קֵינָן חֲמֵשׁ עֶשְׂרֵה שָׁנָה וּשְׁמֹנֶה מֵאוֹת שָׁנָה
יא	וַיּוֹלֶד בָּנִים וּבָנוֹת: וַיִּהְיוּ כָּל־יְמֵי אֱנוֹשׁ חָמֵשׁ שָׁנִים וּתְשַׁע מֵאוֹת שָׁנָה
יב-יג	וַיָּמֹת: וַיְחִי קֵינָן שִׁבְעִים שָׁנָה וַיּוֹלֶד אֶת־מַהֲלַלְאֵל: וַיְחִי קֵינָן
	אַחֲרֵי הוֹלִידוֹ אֶת־מַהֲלַלְאֵל אַרְבָּעִים שָׁנָה וּשְׁמֹנֶה מֵאוֹת שָׁנָה וַיּוֹלֶד
יד	בָּנִים וּבָנוֹת: וַיִּהְיוּ כָּל־יְמֵי קֵינָן עֶשֶׂר שָׁנִים וּתְשַׁע מֵאוֹת שָׁנָה וַיָּמֹת:
טו-טז	וַיְחִי מַהֲלַלְאֵל חָמֵשׁ שָׁנִים וְשִׁשִּׁים שָׁנָה וַיּוֹלֶד אֶת־יָרֶד: וַיְחִי מַהֲלַלְאֵל

4:23-24. Lamech was blind and his son Tubal-cain would lead him. One day, Tubal-cain saw Cain and, mistaking him for an animal, he bade his father to shoot an arrow, which killed Cain. When Lamech realized he had killed Cain, he beat his hands together in grief, and accidentally killed his son. His wives were angered and refused to live with him. He tried to appease them: "If the punishment of Cain, an intentional murderer, was delayed until the seventh generation, surely my punishment will be deferred many times seven because I killed accidentally!" (*Rashi*).

¹³ Cain said to HASHEM, "Is my iniquity too great to be borne? ¹⁴ Behold, You have banished me this day from the face of the earth — can I be hidden from Your presence? I must become a vagrant and a wanderer on earth; whoever meets me will kill me!" ¹⁵ HASHEM said to him, "Therefore, whoever slays Cain, before seven generations have passed he will be punished." And HASHEM placed a mark upon Cain, so that none that meet him might kill him. ¹⁶ Cain left the presence of HASHEM and settled in the land of Nod, east of Eden.

The descendants of Cain ¹⁷ And Cain knew his wife, and she conceived and bore Enoch. He became a city-builder, and he named the city after his son Enoch. ¹⁸ To Enoch was born Irad, and Irad begot Mehujael, and Mehujael begot Methushael, and Methushael begot Lamech.

¹⁹ Lamech took to himself two wives: The name of one was Adah, and the name of the second was Zillah. ²⁰ And Adah bore Jabal; he was the first of those who dwell in tents and breed cattle. ²¹ The name of his brother was Jubal; he was the first of all who handle the harp and flute. ²² And Zillah, too — she bore Tubal-cain, who sharpened all cutting implements of copper and iron. And the sister of Tubal-cain was Naamah.

²³ And Lamech said to his wives, "Adah and Zillah, hear my voice; wives of Lemech, give ear to my speech: Have I slain a man by my wound and a child by my bruise? ²⁴ If Cain suffered vengeance at seven generations, then Lamech at seventy-seven!"

²⁵ Adam knew his wife again, and she bore a son and named him Seth, because: "God has provided me another child in place of Abel, for Cain had killed him." ²⁶ And as for Seth, to him also a son was born, and he named him Enosh. Then to call in the Name of HASHEM became profaned.

5

The genealogy of mankind ¹ This is the account of the descendants of Adam — on the day that God created Man, He made him in the likeness of God. ²He created them male and female. He blessed them and called their name Man on the day they were created — ³ when Adam had lived one hundred and thirty years, he begot in his *The ten generations from Adam to Noah* likeness and his image, and he named him Seth. ⁴ And the days of Adam after begetting Seth were eight hundred years, and he begot sons and daughters. ⁵ All the days that Adam lived were nine hundred and thirty years; and he died.

⁶ Seth lived one hundred and five years and begot Enosh. ⁷ And Seth lived eight hundred and seven years after begetting Enosh, and he begot sons and daughters. ⁸ All the days of Seth were nine hundred and twelve years; and he died.

⁹ Enosh lived ninety years, and begot Kenan. ¹⁰ And Enosh lived eight hundred and fifteen years after begetting Kenan, and he begot sons and daughters. ¹¹ All the days of Enosh were nine hundred and five years; and he died.

¹² Kenan lived seventy years, and begot Mahalalel. ¹³And Kenan lived eight hundred and forty years after begetting Mahalalel, and he begot sons and daughters. ¹⁴ All the days of Kenan were nine hundred and ten years; and he died.

¹⁵ Mahalalel lived sixty-five years, and begot Jared. ¹⁶ And Mahalalel lived

---

5:1. The genealogy of mankind. A new narrative begins, enumerating the generations from Adam to Noah. The genealogy begins with Seth, for it was through him that the human race survived. Abel died without issue, and Cain's descendants perished in the Flood (*Radak; Chizkuni*). (See Appendix A, timeline 1.)

אַחֲרֵי הוֹלִידוֹ אֶת־יֶרֶד שְׁלֹשִׁים שָׁנָה וּשְׁמֹנֶה מֵאוֹת שָׁנָה וַיּוֹלֶד בָּנִים

יז וּבָנוֹת: וַיִּהְיוּ כָּל־יְמֵי מַהֲלַלְאֵל חָמֵשׁ וְתִשְׁעִים שָׁנָה וּשְׁמֹנֶה מֵאוֹת שָׁנָה

יח וַיָּמֹת: וַיְחִי־יֶרֶד שְׁתַּיִם וְשִׁשִּׁים שָׁנָה וּמְאַת שָׁנָה וַיּוֹלֶד אֶת־

יט חֲנוֹךְ: וַיְחִי־יֶרֶד אַחֲרֵי הוֹלִידוֹ אֶת־חֲנוֹךְ שְׁמֹנֶה מֵאוֹת שָׁנָה וַיּוֹלֶד בָּנִים

כ וּבָנוֹת: וַיִּהְיוּ כָּל־יְמֵי־יֶרֶד שְׁתַּיִם וְשִׁשִּׁים שָׁנָה וּתְשַׁע מֵאוֹת שָׁנָה

כא וַיָּמֹת: וַיְחִי חֲנוֹךְ חָמֵשׁ וְשִׁשִּׁים שָׁנָה וַיּוֹלֶד אֶת־מְתוּשָׁלַח:

כב וַיִּתְהַלֵּךְ חֲנוֹךְ אֶת־הָאֱלֹהִים אַחֲרֵי הוֹלִידוֹ אֶת־מְתוּשֶׁלַח שְׁלֹשׁ מֵאוֹת

כג שָׁנָה וַיּוֹלֶד בָּנִים וּבָנוֹת: וַיְהִי כָּל־יְמֵי חֲנוֹךְ חָמֵשׁ וְשִׁשִּׁים שָׁנָה

כד וּשְׁלֹשׁ מֵאוֹת שָׁנָה: וַיִּתְהַלֵּךְ חֲנוֹךְ אֶת־הָאֱלֹהִים וְאֵינֶנּוּ כִּי־לָקַח אֹתוֹ

כה אֱלֹהִים: וַיְחִי מְתוּשֶׁלַח שֶׁבַע וּשְׁמֹנִים שָׁנָה וּמְאַת שָׁנָה וַיּוֹלֶד

כו אֶת־לָמֶךְ: וַיְחִי מְתוּשֶׁלַח אַחֲרֵי הוֹלִידוֹ אֶת־לֶמֶךְ שְׁתַּיִם וּשְׁמוֹנִים

כז שָׁנָה וּשְׁבַע מֵאוֹת שָׁנָה וַיּוֹלֶד בָּנִים וּבָנוֹת: וַיִּהְיוּ כָּל־יְמֵי מְתוּשֶׁלַח

כח תֵּשַׁע וְשִׁשִּׁים שָׁנָה וּתְשַׁע מֵאוֹת שָׁנָה וַיָּמֹת: וַיְחִי־לֶמֶךְ

כט שְׁתַּיִם וּשְׁמֹנִים שָׁנָה וּמְאַת שָׁנָה וַיּוֹלֶד בֵּן: וַיִּקְרָא אֶת־שְׁמוֹ נֹחַ לֵאמֹר

*זֶה יְנַחֲמֵנוּ מִמַּעֲשֵׂנוּ וּמֵעִצְּבוֹן יָדֵינוּ מִן־הָאֲדָמָה אֲשֶׁר אֵרְרָהּ יהוה:

ל וַיְחִי־לֶמֶךְ אַחֲרֵי הוֹלִידוֹ אֶת־נֹחַ חָמֵשׁ וְתִשְׁעִים שָׁנָה וַחֲמֵשׁ מֵאֹת שָׁנָה

לא וַיּוֹלֶד בָּנִים וּבָנוֹת: וַיְהִי כָּל־יְמֵי־לֶמֶךְ שֶׁבַע וְשִׁבְעִים שָׁנָה וּשְׁבַע מֵאוֹת

לב שָׁנָה וַיָּמֹת: וַיְהִי־נֹחַ בֶּן־חֲמֵשׁ מֵאוֹת שָׁנָה וַיּוֹלֶד נֹחַ אֶת־

א שֵׁם אֶת־חָם וְאֶת־יָפֶת: וַיְהִי כִּי־הֵחֵל הָאָדָם לָרֹב עַל־פְּנֵי הָאֲדָמָה וּבָנוֹת

ב יֻלְּדוּ לָהֶם: וַיִּרְאוּ בְנֵי־הָאֱלֹהִים אֶת־בְּנוֹת הָאָדָם כִּי טֹבֹת הֵנָּה וַיִּקְחוּ

ג לָהֶם נָשִׁים מִכֹּל אֲשֶׁר בָּחָרוּ: וַיֹּאמֶר יהוה לֹא־יָדוֹן רוּחִי בָאָדָם לְעֹלָם

ד בְּשַׁגַּם הוּא בָשָׂר וְהָיוּ יָמָיו מֵאָה וְעֶשְׂרִים שָׁנָה: הַנְּפִלִים הָיוּ בָאָרֶץ בַּיָּמִים

הָהֵם וְגַם אַחֲרֵי־כֵן אֲשֶׁר יָבֹאוּ בְּנֵי הָאֱלֹהִים אֶל־בְּנוֹת הָאָדָם וְיָלְדוּ לָהֶם

הֵמָּה הַגִּבֹּרִים אֲשֶׁר מֵעוֹלָם אַנְשֵׁי הַשֵּׁם:

ה וַיַּרְא יהוה כִּי רַבָּה רָעַת הָאָדָם בָּאָרֶץ וְכָל־יֵצֶר מַחְשְׁבֹת לִבּוֹ רַק רַע כָּל־

ו-ז הַיּוֹם: וַיִּנָּחֶם יהוה כִּי־עָשָׂה אֶת־הָאָדָם בָּאָרֶץ וַיִּתְעַצֵּב אֶל־לִבּוֹ: וַיֹּאמֶר

יהוה אֶמְחֶה אֶת־הָאָדָם אֲשֶׁר־בָּרָאתִי מֵעַל פְּנֵי הָאֲדָמָה מֵאָדָם עַד־

בְּהֵמָה עַד־רֶמֶשׂ וְעַד־עוֹף הַשָּׁמָיִם כִּי נִחַמְתִּי כִּי עֲשִׂיתִם: וְנֹחַ מָצָא חֵן

בְּעֵינֵי יהוה: פפפ   קמ"ו פסוקים. אמצי"ה סימן. יחזקיה"ו סימן.

'הקורא יטעים הגרשיים קדם התלישא

מפטיר

*Haftaras
Bereishis:*
p. 1026

For special
Sabbaths,
see pp. x-xi

ו

פרשת נח

ט אֵלֶּה תּוֹלְדֹת נֹחַ נֹחַ אִישׁ צַדִּיק תָּמִים הָיָה בְּדֹרֹתָיו אֶת־הָאֱלֹהִים

י הִתְהַלֶּךְ־נֹחַ: וַיּוֹלֶד נֹחַ שְׁלֹשָׁה בָנִים אֶת־שֵׁם אֶת־חָם וְאֶת־יָפֶת:

6:2. These were the sons of the princes and judges, for *elohim* always implies rulership (*Rashi*). *Daughters of man* refers to the general populace (*R' Saadiah Gaon*). **6:3.** God would wait 120 years before bringing the Flood, eight hundred and thirty years after begetting Jared, and he begot sons and daughters. [17] All the days of Mahalalel were eight hundred and ninety-five years; and he died.

[18] Jared lived one hundred and sixty-two years, and begot Enoch. [19] And Jared lived eight hundred years after begetting Enoch and he begot sons and daughters. [20] All the days of Jared came to nine hundred and sixty-two years; and he died.

[21] Enoch lived sixty-five years, and begot Methuselah. [22] Enoch walked with God for three hundred years after begetting Methuselah; and he begot sons and daughters. [23] All the days of Enoch were three hundred and sixty-five years. [24] And Enoch walked with God; then he was no more, for God had taken him.

[25] Methuselah lived one hundred and eighty-seven years, and begot Lamech. [26] And Methuselah lived seven hundred and eighty-two years after begetting Lamech, and he begot sons and daughters. [27] All the days of Methuselah were nine hundred and sixty-nine years; and he died.

[28] Lamech lived one hundred and eighty-two years, and begot a son. [29] And he called his name Noah, saying, "This one will bring us rest from our work and from the toil of our hands, from the ground which HASHEM had cursed." [30] Lamech lived five hundred and ninety-five years after begetting Noah, and he begot sons and daughters. [31] All the days of Lamech were seven hundred and seventy-seven years; and he died.

[32] When Noah was five hundred years old, Noah begot Shem, Ham, and Japheth.

6

Prelude to the Flood

[1] And it came to pass when Man began to increase upon the face of the ground and daughters were born to them, [2] the sons of the rulers * saw that the daughters of man were good and they took themselves wives from whomever they chose. [3] And HASHEM said, "My spirit shall not contend evermore concerning Man since he is but flesh; his days shall be a hundred and twenty years." *

[4] The Nephilim * were on the earth in those days — and also afterward when the sons of the rulers would consort with the daughters of man, who would bear to them. They were the mighty who, from old, were men of devastation.

[5] HASHEM saw that the wickedness of Man was great upon the earth, and that every product of the thoughts of his heart was but evil always. [6] And HASHEM reconsidered having made Man on earth, and He had heartfelt sadness. [7] And HASHEM said, "I will blot out Man whom I created from the face of the ground — from man to animal, to creeping things, and to birds of the sky; for I have reconsidered My having made them." [8] But Noah found grace in the eyes of HASHEM.

PARASHAS NOACH

Noah [9] These are the offspring of Noah — Noah was a righteous man, perfect in his generations; * Noah walked with God. — [10] Noah had begotten three sons: Shem, Ham, and Japheth.

---

to give mankind ample opportunity to repent (*Rashi, Ramban*).

6:4. The *Nephilim* were giants — see *Numbers* 13:33.

◄§ Parashas Noach

6:9. Some Sages maintain that the phrase **in his generations** is in Noah's praise — he was righteous even in his corrupt generation; how much more righteous would he have been if he had had the companionship and inspiration of Abraham! According to others, however, it is critical of him — only **in his generations,** by comparison with his extremely wicked contemporaries, did Noah stand out as a righteous man; but had he lived in the time of Abraham he would have been insignificant (*Rashi*).

יא-יב וַתִּשָּׁחֵת הָאָרֶץ לִפְנֵי הָאֱלֹהִים וַתִּמָּלֵא הָאָרֶץ חָמָס: וַיַּרְא אֱלֹהִים
אֶת־הָאָרֶץ וְהִנֵּה נִשְׁחָתָה כִּי־הִשְׁחִית כָּל־בָּשָׂר אֶת־דַּרְכּוֹ עַל־
יג הָאָרֶץ: וַיֹּאמֶר אֱלֹהִים לְנֹחַ קֵץ כָּל־בָּשָׂר
בָּא לְפָנַי כִּי־מָלְאָה הָאָרֶץ חָמָס מִפְּנֵיהֶם וְהִנְנִי מַשְׁחִיתָם אֶת־הָאָרֶץ:
יד עֲשֵׂה לְךָ תֵּבַת עֲצֵי־גֹפֶר קִנִּים תַּעֲשֶׂה אֶת־הַתֵּבָה וְכָפַרְתָּ אֹתָהּ מִבַּיִת
טו וּמִחוּץ בַּכֹּפֶר: וְזֶה אֲשֶׁר תַּעֲשֶׂה אֹתָהּ שְׁלֹשׁ מֵאוֹת אַמָּה אֹרֶךְ הַתֵּבָה
טז חֲמִשִּׁים אַמָּה רָחְבָּהּ וּשְׁלֹשִׁים אַמָּה קוֹמָתָהּ: צֹהַר ׀ תַּעֲשֶׂה לַתֵּבָה וְאֶל־
אַמָּה תְּכַלֶּנָּה מִלְמַעְלָה וּפֶתַח הַתֵּבָה בְּצִדָּהּ תָּשִׂים תַּחְתִּיִּם שְׁנִיִּם
יז וּשְׁלִשִׁים תַּעֲשֶׂהָ: וַאֲנִי הִנְנִי מֵבִיא אֶת־הַמַּבּוּל מַיִם עַל־הָאָרֶץ לְשַׁחֵת
כָּל־בָּשָׂר אֲשֶׁר־בּוֹ רוּחַ חַיִּים מִתַּחַת הַשָּׁמָיִם כֹּל אֲשֶׁר־בָּאָרֶץ יִגְוָע:
יח וַהֲקִמֹתִי אֶת־בְּרִיתִי אִתָּךְ וּבָאתָ אֶל־הַתֵּבָה אַתָּה וּבָנֶיךָ וְאִשְׁתְּךָ וּנְשֵׁי־
יט בָנֶיךָ אִתָּךְ: וּמִכָּל־הָחַי מִכָּל־בָּשָׂר שְׁנַיִם מִכֹּל תָּבִיא אֶל־הַתֵּבָה לְהַחֲיֹת
כ אִתָּךְ זָכָר וּנְקֵבָה יִהְיוּ: מֵהָעוֹף לְמִינֵהוּ וּמִן־הַבְּהֵמָה לְמִינָהּ מִכֹּל רֶמֶשׂ
כא הָאֲדָמָה לְמִינֵהוּ שְׁנַיִם מִכֹּל יָבֹאוּ אֵלֶיךָ לְהַחֲיוֹת: וְאַתָּה קַח־לְךָ מִכָּל־
כב מַאֲכָל אֲשֶׁר יֵאָכֵל וְאָסַפְתָּ אֵלֶיךָ וְהָיָה לְךָ וְלָהֶם לְאָכְלָה: וַיַּעַשׂ נֹחַ כְּכֹל

ז א אֲשֶׁר צִוָּה אֹתוֹ אֱלֹהִים כֵּן עָשָׂה: וַיֹּאמֶר יהוה לְנֹחַ בֹּא־אַתָּה וְכָל־בֵּיתְךָ **שני**
ב אֶל־הַתֵּבָה כִּי־אֹתְךָ רָאִיתִי צַדִּיק לְפָנַי בַּדּוֹר הַזֶּה: מִכֹּל ׀ הַבְּהֵמָה
הַטְּהוֹרָה תִּקַּח־לְךָ שִׁבְעָה שִׁבְעָה אִישׁ וְאִשְׁתּוֹ וּמִן־הַבְּהֵמָה אֲשֶׁר לֹא
ג טְהֹרָה הִוא שְׁנַיִם אִישׁ וְאִשְׁתּוֹ: גַּם מֵעוֹף הַשָּׁמַיִם שִׁבְעָה שִׁבְעָה זָכָר
ד וּנְקֵבָה לְחַיּוֹת זֶרַע עַל־פְּנֵי כָל־הָאָרֶץ: כִּי לְיָמִים עוֹד שִׁבְעָה אָנֹכִי מַמְטִיר
עַל־הָאָרֶץ אַרְבָּעִים יוֹם וְאַרְבָּעִים לָיְלָה וּמָחִיתִי אֶת־כָּל־הַיְקוּם
ה-ו אֲשֶׁר עָשִׂיתִי מֵעַל פְּנֵי הָאֲדָמָה: וַיַּעַשׂ נֹחַ כְּכֹל אֲשֶׁר־צִוָּהוּ יהוה: וְנֹחַ
ז בֶּן־שֵׁשׁ מֵאוֹת שָׁנָה וְהַמַּבּוּל הָיָה מַיִם עַל־הָאָרֶץ: וַיָּבֹא נֹחַ וּבָנָיו
ח וְאִשְׁתּוֹ וּנְשֵׁי־בָנָיו אִתּוֹ אֶל־הַתֵּבָה מִפְּנֵי מֵי הַמַּבּוּל: מִן־הַבְּהֵמָה
הַטְּהוֹרָה וּמִן־הַבְּהֵמָה אֲשֶׁר אֵינֶנָּה טְהֹרָה וּמִן־הָעוֹף וְכֹל אֲשֶׁר־רֹמֵשׂ
ט עַל־הָאֲדָמָה: שְׁנַיִם שְׁנַיִם בָּאוּ אֶל־נֹחַ אֶל־הַתֵּבָה זָכָר וּנְקֵבָה כַּאֲשֶׁר צִוָּה
י אֱלֹהִים אֶת־נֹחַ: וַיְהִי לְשִׁבְעַת הַיָּמִים וּמֵי הַמַּבּוּל הָיוּ עַל־הָאָרֶץ:
יא בִּשְׁנַת שֵׁשׁ־מֵאוֹת שָׁנָה לְחַיֵּי־נֹחַ בַּחֹדֶשׁ הַשֵּׁנִי בְּשִׁבְעָה־עָשָׂר יוֹם לַחֹדֶשׁ
יב בַּיּוֹם הַזֶּה נִבְקְעוּ כָּל־מַעְיְנֹת תְּהוֹם רַבָּה וַאֲרֻבֹּת הַשָּׁמַיִם נִפְתָּחוּ: וַיְהִי
יג הַגֶּשֶׁם עַל־הָאָרֶץ אַרְבָּעִים יוֹם וְאַרְבָּעִים לָיְלָה: בְּעֶצֶם הַיּוֹם הַזֶּה בָּא נֹחַ
וְשֵׁם־וְחָם וָיֶפֶת בְּנֵי־נֹחַ וְאֵשֶׁת נֹחַ וּשְׁלֹשֶׁת נְשֵׁי־בָנָיו אִתָּם אֶל־הַתֵּבָה:

6:15. Even according to the smallest estimate of 18 inches per cubit, the dimensions of the Ark were 450 × 75 × 45 feet = 1,518,750 cubit feet. Each of its three stories had 33,750 sq. feet of floor space for a total of 101,250 square feet.

7:1-10. Up to now, the *Sidrah* had spoken of *Elohim*,

indicating God's Attribute of Justice. Here He is called HASHEM, the God of Mercy, for He is saving Noah from the Flood, and, in addition, He is saving Noah's entire family and possessions, which, on their own merits, did not deserve to be saved (*Sforno*).

7:10-24. The Flood inundates the world. In the six

[11] *Now the earth had become corrupt before God; and the earth had become filled with robbery.* [12] *And God saw the earth and behold it was corrupted, for all flesh had corrupted its way upon the earth.*

The decree of the Flood

[13] *God said to Noah, "The end of all flesh has come before Me, for the earth is filled with robbery through them; and behold, I am about to destroy them from the earth.* [14] *Make for yourself an Ark of gopher wood; make the Ark with compartments, and cover it inside and out with pitch.* [15] *This is how you should make it — three hundred cubits the length of the Ark; fifty cubits its width; and thirty cubits its height.* [16] *A window shall you make for the Ark, and to a cubit finish it from above. Put the entrance of the Ark in its side; make it with bottom, second, and third decks.*

[17] *"And as for Me — Behold, I am about to bring the Flood-waters upon the earth to destroy all flesh, in which there is a breath of life, from under the heavens; everything that is in the earth shall expire.* [18] *But I will establish My covenant with you, and you shall enter the Ark — you, your sons, your wife, and your sons' wives with you.* [19] *And from all that lives, of all flesh, two of each shall you bring into the Ark to keep alive with you; they shall be male and female.* [20] *From each bird according to its kind, and from each animal according to its kind, and from each thing that creeps on the ground according to its kind, two of each shall come to you to keep alive.*

[21] *"And as for you, take yourself of every food that is eaten and gather it in to yourself, that it shall be as food for you and for them."* [22] *Noah did according to everything God commanded him, so he did.*

7

The final call

[1] *Then HASHEM said to Noah, "Come to the Ark, you and all your household, for it is you that I have seen to be righteous before Me in this generation.* [2] *Of every clean animal take unto you seven pairs, a male with its mate, and of the animal that is not clean, two, a male with its mate;* [3] *of the birds of the heavens also, seven pairs, male and female, to keep seed alive upon the face of all the earth.* [4] *For in seven more days' time I will send rain upon the earth, forty days and forty nights, and I will blot out all existence that I have made from upon the face of the ground."* [5] *And Noah did according to everything that HASHEM had commanded him.*

[6] *Noah was six hundred years old when the Flood was water upon the earth.* [7] *Noah, with his sons, his wife, and his sons' wives with him, went into the Ark because of the waters of the Flood.* [8] *Of the clean animal, of the animal that is not clean, of the birds, and of each thing that creeps upon the ground,* [9] *two by two they came to Noah into the Ark, male and female, as God had com-*

The Flood inundates the world

manded Noah. [10] *And it came to pass after the seven-day period that the waters of the Flood were upon the earth.*

[11] *In the six hundredth year of Noah's life, in the second month, on the seventeenth day of the month, on that day all the fountains of the great deep burst forth; and the windows of the heavens were opened.* [12] *And the rain was upon the earth forty days and forty nights.*

[13] *On that very day Noah came, with Shem, Ham, and Japheth, Noah's sons, with Noah's wife, and the three wives of his sons with them, into the Ark*

---

hundredth year of Noah's life — the year 1656 from Creation (*Seder Olam*) — the deluge began. Now Scripture gives the exact date and the details of the events as they happened. (See Appendix A, timeline 2.)

יד הֵ֡מָּה וְכָל־הַֽחַיָּ֣ה לְמִינָהּ֩ וְכָל־הַבְּהֵמָ֨ה לְמִינָ֜הּ וְכָל־הָרֶ֙מֶשׂ֙ הָרֹמֵ֣שׂ עַל־
טו הָאָ֖רֶץ לְמִינֵ֑הוּ וְכָל־הָע֖וֹף לְמִינֵ֑הוּ כֹּ֖ל צִפּ֥וֹר כָּל־כָּנָֽף: וַיָּבֹ֥אוּ אֶל־נֹ֖חַ
טז אֶל־הַתֵּבָ֑ה שְׁנַ֤יִם שְׁנַ֙יִם֙ מִכָּל־הַבָּשָׂ֔ר אֲשֶׁר־בּ֖וֹ ר֣וּחַ חַיִּֽים: וְהַבָּאִ֗ים זָכָ֨ר
שלישי יז וּנְקֵבָ֤ה מִכָּל־בָּשָׂר֙ בָּ֔אוּ כַּֽאֲשֶׁ֛ר צִוָּ֥ה אֹת֖וֹ אֱלֹהִ֑ים וַיִּסְגֹּ֥ר יְהֹוָ֖ה בַּֽעֲדֽוֹ: וַֽיְהִ֧י
הַמַּבּ֛וּל אַרְבָּעִ֥ים י֖וֹם עַל־הָאָ֑רֶץ וַיִּרְבּ֣וּ הַמַּ֗יִם וַיִּשְׂאוּ֙ אֶת־הַתֵּבָ֔ה וַתָּ֖רָם
יח מֵעַ֥ל הָאָֽרֶץ: וַיִּגְבְּר֥וּ הַמַּ֛יִם וַיִּרְבּ֥וּ מְאֹ֖ד עַל־הָאָ֑רֶץ וַתֵּ֥לֶךְ הַתֵּבָ֖ה עַל־פְּנֵ֥י
יט הַמָּֽיִם: וְהַמַּ֗יִם גָּבְר֛וּ מְאֹ֥ד מְאֹ֖ד עַל־הָאָ֑רֶץ וַיְכֻסּ֗וּ כָּל־הֶֽהָרִים֙ הַגְּבֹהִ֔ים
כ אֲשֶׁר־תַּ֖חַת כָּל־הַשָּׁמָֽיִם: חֲמֵ֨שׁ עֶשְׂרֵ֤ה אַמָּה֙ מִלְמַ֔עְלָה גָּבְר֖וּ הַמָּ֑יִם וַיְכֻסּ֖וּ
כא הֶהָרִֽים: וַיִּגְוַ֞ע כָּל־בָּשָׂ֣ר ׀ הָֽרֹמֵ֣שׂ עַל־הָאָ֗רֶץ בָּע֤וֹף וּבַבְּהֵמָה֙ וּבַ֣חַיָּ֔ה
כב וּבְכָל־הַשֶּׁ֖רֶץ הַשֹּׁרֵ֣ץ עַל־הָאָ֑רֶץ וְכֹ֖ל הָֽאָדָֽם: כֹּ֡ל אֲשֶׁר֩ נִשְׁמַת־ר֨וּחַ חַיִּ֜ים
כג בְּאַפָּ֗יו מִכֹּ֛ל אֲשֶׁ֥ר בֶּחָֽרָבָ֖ה מֵֽתוּ: וַיִּ֜מַח אֶת־כָּל־הַיְק֣וּם ׀ אֲשֶׁ֣ר ׀ עַל־פְּנֵ֣י
*מי רפה הָֽאֲדָמָ֗ה מֵֽאָדָ֤ם עַד־בְּהֵמָה֙ עַד־רֶ֙מֶשׂ֙ וְעַד־ע֣וֹף הַשָּׁמַ֔יִם וַיִּמָּח֖וּ מִן־הָאָ֑רֶץ
כד וַיִּשָּׁ֧אֶר אַךְ־נֹ֛חַ וַֽאֲשֶׁ֥ר אִתּ֖וֹ בַּתֵּבָֽה: וַיִּגְבְּר֥וּ הַמַּ֖יִם עַל־הָאָ֑רֶץ חֲמִשִּׁ֥ים
ח א וּמְאַ֖ת יֽוֹם: וַיִּזְכֹּ֣ר אֱלֹהִ֗ים אֶת־נֹ֙חַ֙ וְאֵ֤ת כָּל־הַֽחַיָּה֙ וְאֶת־כָּל־הַבְּהֵמָ֔ה אֲשֶׁ֣ר
ב אִתּ֖וֹ בַּתֵּבָ֑ה וַיַּֽעֲבֵ֨ר אֱלֹהִ֥ים ר֙וּחַ֙ עַל־הָאָ֔רֶץ וַיָּשֹׁ֖כּוּ הַמָּֽיִם: וַיִּסָּֽכְרוּ֙ מַעְיְנֹ֣ת
ג תְּה֔וֹם וַֽאֲרֻבֹּ֖ת הַשָּׁמָ֑יִם וַיִּכָּלֵ֥א הַגֶּ֖שֶׁם מִן־הַשָּׁמָֽיִם: וַיָּשֻׁ֧בוּ הַמַּ֛יִם מֵעַ֥ל
ד הָאָ֖רֶץ הָל֣וֹךְ וָשׁ֑וֹב וַיַּחְסְר֣וּ הַמַּ֔יִם מִקְצֵ֕ה חֲמִשִּׁ֥ים וּמְאַ֖ת יֽוֹם: וַתָּ֤נַח הַתֵּבָה֙
ה בַּחֹ֣דֶשׁ הַשְּׁבִיעִ֔י בְּשִׁבְעָה־עָשָׂ֥ר י֖וֹם לַחֹ֑דֶשׁ עַ֖ל הָרֵ֥י אֲרָרָֽט: וְהַמַּ֗יִם הָיוּ֙
הָל֣וֹךְ וְחָס֔וֹר עַ֖ד הַחֹ֣דֶשׁ הָֽעֲשִׂירִ֑י בָּֽעֲשִׂירִי֙ בְּאֶחָ֣ד לַחֹ֔דֶשׁ נִרְא֖וּ רָאשֵׁ֥י
ו הֶֽהָרִֽים: וַֽיְהִ֕י מִקֵּ֖ץ אַרְבָּעִ֣ים י֑וֹם וַיִּפְתַּ֣ח נֹ֔חַ אֶת־חַלּ֥וֹן הַתֵּבָ֖ה אֲשֶׁ֥ר עָשָֽׂה:
ז וַיְשַׁלַּ֖ח אֶת־הָֽעֹרֵ֑ב וַיֵּצֵ֤א יָצוֹא֙ וָשׁ֔וֹב עַד־יְבֹ֥שֶׁת הַמַּ֖יִם מֵעַ֥ל הָאָֽרֶץ:
ח וַיְשַׁלַּ֥ח אֶת־הַיּוֹנָ֖ה מֵֽאִתּ֑וֹ לִרְאוֹת֙ הֲקַ֣לּוּ הַמַּ֔יִם מֵעַ֖ל פְּנֵ֥י הָֽאֲדָמָֽה:
ט וְלֹֽא־מָֽצְאָה֩ הַיּוֹנָ֨ה מָנ֜וֹחַ לְכַף־רַגְלָ֗הּ וַתָּ֤שָׁב אֵלָיו֙ אֶל־הַתֵּבָ֔ה כִּי־מַ֖יִם
י עַל־פְּנֵ֣י כָל־הָאָ֑רֶץ וַיִּשְׁלַ֤ח יָדוֹ֙ וַיִּקָּחֶ֔הָ וַיָּבֵ֥א אֹתָ֛הּ אֵלָ֖יו אֶל־הַתֵּבָֽה: וַיָּ֣חֶל
יא ע֖וֹד שִׁבְעַ֣ת יָמִ֣ים אֲחֵרִ֑ים וַיֹּ֛סֶף שַׁלַּ֥ח אֶת־הַיּוֹנָ֖ה מִן־הַתֵּבָֽה: וַתָּבֹ֨א אֵלָ֤יו
הַיּוֹנָה֙ לְעֵ֣ת עֶ֔רֶב וְהִנֵּ֥ה עֲלֵה־זַ֖יִת טָרָ֣ף בְּפִ֑יהָ וַיֵּ֣דַע נֹ֔חַ כִּי־קַ֥לּוּ הַמַּ֖יִם מֵעַ֥ל
יב הָאָֽרֶץ: וַיִּיָּ֣חֶל ע֔וֹד שִׁבְעַ֥ת יָמִ֖ים אֲחֵרִ֑ים וַיְשַׁלַּח֙ אֶת־הַיּוֹנָ֔ה וְלֹֽא־יָֽסְפָ֥ה
יג שׁוּב־אֵלָ֖יו עֽוֹד: וַֽיְהִ֡י בְּאַחַת֩ וְשֵׁשׁ־מֵא֨וֹת שָׁנָ֜ה בָּֽרִאשׁוֹן֙ בְּאֶחָ֣ד לַחֹ֔דֶשׁ
חָֽרְב֥וּ הַמַּ֖יִם מֵעַ֣ל הָאָ֑רֶץ וַיָּ֤סַר נֹ֙חַ֙ אֶת־מִכְסֵ֣ה הַתֵּבָ֔ה וַיַּ֕רְא וְהִנֵּ֥ה
יד חָֽרְב֖וּ פְּנֵ֥י הָֽאֲדָמָֽה: וּבַחֹ֙דֶשׁ֙ הַשֵּׁנִ֔י בְּשִׁבְעָ֧ה וְעֶשְׂרִ֛ים י֖וֹם לַחֹ֑דֶשׁ יָֽבְשָׁ֖ה

7:20. *Haamek Davar* suggests that Mt. Ararat was the world's highest mountain at the time of the Flood. The numerous mountains that are now far higher than Ararat came into being or bulged up to their present height as a result of the upheavals of the Flood.

8:1-8. The waters recede. This chapter recounts the onset of God's mercy, as the water began to recede and

the earth slowly reached the stage where Noah could begin to resettle it and resume normal life again.

8:7. Sending forth the raven. Noah wanted to test whether the air was still too moist for the raven to tolerate. It was, for the raven kept circling back and forth (*Sforno*).

8:8-12. The dove. Seven days after sending the raven, Noah set the dove free; if it would find a resting place, it

¹⁴ they and every beast after its kind, every animal after its kind, every creeping thing that creeps on the earth after its kind, and every bird after its kind, and every bird of any kind of wing. ¹⁵ They came to Noah into the Ark; two by two of all flesh in which there was a breath of life. ¹⁶ Thus they that came, came male and female of all flesh, as God had commanded him. And HASHEM shut it on his behalf.

¹⁷ When the Flood was on the earth forty days, the waters increased and raised the Ark so that it was lifted above the earth. ¹⁸ The waters strengthened and increased greatly upon the earth, and the Ark drifted upon the surface of the waters. ¹⁹ The waters strengthened very much upon the earth, all the high mountains which are under the entire heavens were covered. ²⁰ Fifteen cubits upward did the waters strengthen, and the mountains were covered. ²¹ And all flesh that moves upon the earth expired — among the birds, the animals, the beasts, and all the creeping things that creep upon the earth, and all mankind. ²² All in whose nostrils was the breath of the spirit of life, of everything that was on dry land, died. ²³ And He blotted out all existence that was on the face of the ground — from man to animals to creeping things and to the bird of the heavens; and they were blotted out from the earth. Only Noah survived, and those with him in the Ark. ²⁴ And the waters strengthened on the earth a hundred and fifty days.

8

The waters recede

¹ **G**od remembered Noah and all the beasts and all the animals that were with him in the Ark, and God caused a spirit to pass over the earth, and the waters subsided. ² The fountains of the deep and the windows of the heavens were closed, and the rain from heaven was restrained. ³ The waters then receded from upon the earth, receding continuously, and the waters diminished at the end of a hundred and fifty days. ⁴ And the Ark came to rest in the seventh [month], on the seventeenth day of the month, upon the mountains of Ararat. ⁵ The waters were continuously diminishing until the tenth month. In the tenth month, on the first of the month, the tops of the mountains became visible.

Sending forth the raven

The dove

⁶ And it came to pass at the end of forty days, that Noah opened the window of the Ark which he had made. ⁷ He sent out the raven, and it kept going and returning until the waters dried from upon the earth. ⁸ Then he sent out the dove from him to see whether the waters had subsided from the face of the ground. ⁹ But the dove could not find a resting place for the sole of its foot, and it returned to him to the Ark, for water was upon the surface of all the earth. So he put forth his hand, and took it, and brought it to him to the Ark. ¹⁰ He waited again another seven days, and again sent out the dove from the Ark. ¹¹ The dove came back to him in the evening — and behold! an olive leaf* it had plucked with its bill! And Noah knew that the waters had subsided from upon the earth. ¹² Then he waited again another seven days and sent the dove forth; and it did not return to him any more.

¹³ And it came to pass in the six hundred and first year, in the first [month] on the first of the month, the waters dried from upon the earth; Noah removed the covering of the Ark, and looked — and behold! the surface of the ground had dried. ¹⁴ And in the second month, on the twenty-seventh day of the month, the earth was fully dried.

The earth dries

---

would not return to him (*Rashi*).
8:11. By bringing back a bitter leaf the dove was symbol-

izing, "Better that my food be bitter but from God's hand, than sweet as honey but dependent upon man" (*Rashi*).

רביעי
טו-טז וַיְדַבֵּר אֱלֹהִים אֶל־נֹחַ לֵאמֹר: צֵא מִן־הַתֵּבָה אַתָּה הָאָרֶץ:

יז וְאִשְׁתְּךָ וּבָנֶיךָ וּנְשֵׁי־בָנֶיךָ אִתָּךְ: כָּל־הַחַיָּה אֲשֶׁר־אִתְּךָ מִכָּל־בָּשָׂר בָּעוֹף וּבַבְּהֵמָה וּבְכָל־הָרֶמֶשׂ הָרֹמֵשׂ עַל־הָאָרֶץ הוֹצֵא [°הַיְצֵא ק] אִתָּךְ

יח-יט וְשָׁרְצוּ בָאָרֶץ וּפָרוּ וְרָבוּ עַל־הָאָרֶץ: וַיֵּצֵא־נֹחַ וּבָנָיו וְאִשְׁתּוֹ וּנְשֵׁי־בָנָיו אִתּוֹ: כָּל־הַחַיָּה כָּל־הָרֶמֶשׂ וְכָל־הָעוֹף כֹּל רוֹמֵשׂ עַל־הָאָרֶץ

כ לְמִשְׁפְּחֹתֵיהֶם יָצְאוּ מִן־הַתֵּבָה: וַיִּבֶן נֹחַ מִזְבֵּחַ לַיהוָה וַיִּקַּח מִכֹּל ׀ הַבְּהֵמָה

כא הַטְּהֹרָה וּמִכֹּל הָעוֹף הַטָּהוֹר וַיַּעַל עֹלֹת בַּמִּזְבֵּחַ: וַיָּרַח יהוה אֶת־רֵיחַ הַנִּיחֹחַ וַיֹּאמֶר יהוה אֶל־לִבּוֹ לֹא אֹסִף לְקַלֵּל עוֹד אֶת־הָאֲדָמָה בַּעֲבוּר

כב הָאָדָם כִּי יֵצֶר לֵב הָאָדָם רַע מִנְּעֻרָיו וְלֹא־אֹסִף עוֹד לְהַכּוֹת אֶת־כָּל־חַי כַּאֲשֶׁר עָשִׂיתִי: עֹד כָּל־יְמֵי הָאָרֶץ זֶרַע וְקָצִיר וְקֹר וָחֹם וְקַיִץ וָחֹרֶף וְיוֹם

ט
א וָלַיְלָה לֹא יִשְׁבֹּתוּ: וַיְבָרֶךְ אֱלֹהִים אֶת־נֹחַ וְאֶת־בָּנָיו וַיֹּאמֶר לָהֶם פְּרוּ וּרְבוּ

ב וּמִלְאוּ אֶת־הָאָרֶץ: וּמוֹרַאֲכֶם וְחִתְּכֶם יִהְיֶה עַל כָּל־חַיַּת הָאָרֶץ וְעַל כָּל־

ג עוֹף הַשָּׁמָיִם בְּכֹל אֲשֶׁר תִּרְמֹשׂ הָאֲדָמָה וּבְכָל־דְּגֵי הַיָּם בְּיֶדְכֶם נִתָּנוּ: כָּל־

ד רֶמֶשׂ אֲשֶׁר הוּא־חַי לָכֶם יִהְיֶה לְאָכְלָה כְּיֶרֶק עֵשֶׂב נָתַתִּי לָכֶם אֶת־כֹּל:

ה אַךְ־בָּשָׂר בְּנַפְשׁוֹ דָמוֹ לֹא תֹאכֵלוּ: וְאַךְ אֶת־דִּמְכֶם לְנַפְשֹׁתֵיכֶם אֶדְרֹשׁ

ו מִיַּד כָּל־חַיָּה אֶדְרְשֶׁנּוּ וּמִיַּד הָאָדָם מִיַּד אִישׁ אָחִיו אֶדְרֹשׁ אֶת־נֶפֶשׁ

ז הָאָדָם: שֹׁפֵךְ דַּם הָאָדָם בָּאָדָם דָּמוֹ יִשָּׁפֵךְ כִּי בְּצֶלֶם אֱלֹהִים עָשָׂה אֶת־

ח הָאָדָם: וְאַתֶּם פְּרוּ וּרְבוּ שִׁרְצוּ בָאָרֶץ וּרְבוּ־בָהּ: וַיֹּאמֶר אֱלֹהִים אֶל־נֹחַ

חמישי

ט וְאֶל־בָּנָיו אִתּוֹ לֵאמֹר: וַאֲנִי הִנְנִי מֵקִים אֶת־בְּרִיתִי אִתְּכֶם וְאֶת־זַרְעֲכֶם

י אַחֲרֵיכֶם: וְאֵת כָּל־נֶפֶשׁ הַחַיָּה אֲשֶׁר אִתְּכֶם בָּעוֹף בַּבְּהֵמָה וּבְכָל־חַיַּת

יא הָאָרֶץ אִתְּכֶם מִכֹּל יֹצְאֵי הַתֵּבָה לְכֹל חַיַּת הָאָרֶץ: וַהֲקִמֹתִי אֶת־בְּרִיתִי אִתְּכֶם וְלֹא־יִכָּרֵת כָּל־בָּשָׂר עוֹד מִמֵּי הַמַּבּוּל וְלֹא־יִהְיֶה עוֹד מַבּוּל

יב לְשַׁחֵת הָאָרֶץ: וַיֹּאמֶר אֱלֹהִים זֹאת אוֹת־הַבְּרִית אֲשֶׁר־אֲנִי נֹתֵן בֵּינִי

יג וּבֵינֵיכֶם וּבֵין כָּל־נֶפֶשׁ חַיָּה אֲשֶׁר אִתְּכֶם לְדֹרֹת עוֹלָם: אֶת־קַשְׁתִּי

יד נָתַתִּי בֶּעָנָן וְהָיְתָה לְאוֹת בְּרִית בֵּינִי וּבֵין הָאָרֶץ: וְהָיָה בְּעַנְנִי עָנָן עַל־הָאָרֶץ וְנִרְאֲתָה הַקֶּשֶׁת בֶּעָנָן: וְזָכַרְתִּי אֶת־בְּרִיתִי אֲשֶׁר בֵּינִי וּבֵינֵיכֶם וּבֵין

טו כָּל־נֶפֶשׁ חַיָּה בְּכָל־בָּשָׂר וְלֹא־יִהְיֶה עוֹד הַמַּיִם לְמַבּוּל לְשַׁחֵת כָּל־

טז בָּשָׂר: וְהָיְתָה הַקֶּשֶׁת בֶּעָנָן וּרְאִיתִיהָ לִזְכֹּר בְּרִית עוֹלָם בֵּין אֱלֹהִים וּבֵין

יז כָּל־נֶפֶשׁ חַיָּה בְּכָל־בָּשָׂר אֲשֶׁר עַל־הָאָרֶץ: וַיֹּאמֶר אֱלֹהִים אֶל־נֹחַ זֹאת אוֹת־הַבְּרִית אֲשֶׁר הֲקִמֹתִי בֵּינִי וּבֵין כָּל־בָּשָׂר אֲשֶׁר עַל־הָאָרֶץ:

8:15. In telling Noah that the Ark would save him, God used the Name *Hashem* (7:1), which denotes mercy. Here, in telling him to return to the world, He uses the Name *Elohim*, and this Name is used throughout the narrative. In addition to its familiar connotation of God as Judge, it also refers to Him as God Who dominates nature and uses it to carry out His ends. The Name *Elohim* has the con-

notation of "the Mighty One Who wields authority over the beings above and below" (*Tur Orach Chaim* 5).

8:17. The *k'siv* (Masoretic spelling) is הוצא, while the *k'ri* (Masoretic pronunciation) is הַיְצֵא. *Rashi* explains the duality: הַיְצֵא means *order them out*, i.e. tell them to leave on their own, while הוצא means *force them out*, in the event they refuse to leave.

The command to leave the Ark ¹⁵ God spoke to Noah, saying, ¹⁶ "Go forth from the Ark: you and your wife, your sons, and your sons' wives with you. ¹⁷ Every living being that is with you of all flesh, of birds, of animals, and all moving things that move on the earth — order them out* with you, and let them teem on the earth and be fruitful and multiply on the earth." ¹⁸ So Noah went forth, and his sons, his wife, and his sons' wives with him. ¹⁹ Every living being, every creeping thing, and every bird, everything that moves on earth came out of the Ark by their families.

Noah brings an offering ²⁰ Then Noah built an altar to HASHEM and took of every clean animal and of every clean bird, and offered burnt-offerings on the altar. ²¹ HASHEM smelled the pleasing aroma, and HASHEM said in His heart: "I will not continue to curse again the ground because of man, since the imagery of man's heart is evil from his youth; nor will I again continue to smite every living being, as I have done. ²² Continuously, all the days of the earth, seedtime and harvest, cold and heat, summer and winter, day and night, shall not cease."

9

Rebuilding a ruined world: God's covenant with Noah ¹ God blessed Noah and his sons, and He said to them, "Be fruitful and multiply* and fill the land. ² The fear of you and the dread of you shall be upon every beast of the earth and upon every bird of the heavens, in everything that moves on earth and in all the fish of the sea; in your hand they are given. ³ Every moving thing that lives shall be food for you; like the green herbage I have given you everything. * ⁴ But flesh; with its soul its blood you shall not eat. ⁵ However, your blood which belongs to your souls I will demand, of every beast will I demand it; but of man, of every man for that of his brother I will demand the soul of man. ⁶ Whoever sheds the blood of man, by man shall his blood be shed; for in the image of God He made man. ⁷ And you, be fruitful and multiply; teem on the earth and multiply on it."

⁸ And God said to Noah and to his sons with him saying: ⁹ "And as for Me, behold, I establish My covenant with you and with your offspring after you, ¹⁰ and with every living being that is with you — with the birds, with the animals, and with every beast of the land with you — of all that departed the Ark, to every beast of the land. ¹¹ And I will confirm My covenant with you: Never again shall all flesh be cut off by the waters of the flood, and never again shall there be a flood to destroy the earth."

The rainbow: An eternal covenant ¹² And God said, "This is the sign of the covenant that I give between Me and you, and every living being that is with you, to generations forever: ¹³ I have set My rainbow in the cloud, and it shall be a sign of the covenant between Me and the earth. ¹⁴ And it shall happen, when I place a cloud over the earth, and the bow will be seen in the cloud, ¹⁵ I will remember My covenant between Me and you and every living being among all flesh, and the water shall never again become a flood to destroy all flesh. ¹⁶ And the bow shall be in the cloud, and I will look upon it to remember the everlasting covenant between God and every living being, among all flesh that is on earth." ¹⁷ And God said to Noah, "This is the sign of the covenant that I have confirmed between Me and all flesh that is upon the earth."

9:1. The words *Be fruitful and multiply* will be repeated in verse 7. Here it is a blessing that the human race would be prolific; there it is a command to beget children (*Rashi*).

9:3. God gave Noah and his descendants what had never been given to Adam or his progeny: the right to eat meat.

9:5. The Torah places another limitation on man's right to take a life: God will demand an accounting from one who spills his *own* blood, for a human being's life belongs not to him but to God.

ששי
יח וַיִּהְיוּ בְנֵי־נֹחַ הַיֹּצְאִים מִן־הַתֵּבָה שֵׁם וְחָם וָיָפֶת וְחָם הוּא אֲבִי כְנָעַן:
יט־כב שְׁלֹשָׁה אֵלֶּה בְּנֵי־נֹחַ וּמֵאֵלֶּה נָפְצָה כָל־הָאָרֶץ: וַיָּחֶל נֹחַ אִישׁ הָאֲדָמָה
כא־כב וַיִּטַּע כָּרֶם: וַיֵּשְׁתְּ מִן־הַיַּיִן וַיִּשְׁכָּר וַיִּתְגַּל בְּתוֹךְ אָהֳלֹה: וַיַּרְא חָם אֲבִי כְנַעַן
כג אֵת עֶרְוַת אָבִיו וַיַּגֵּד לִשְׁנֵי־אֶחָיו בַּחוּץ: וַיִּקַּח שֵׁם וָיֶפֶת אֶת־הַשִּׂמְלָה
וַיָּשִׂימוּ עַל־שְׁכֶם שְׁנֵיהֶם וַיֵּלְכוּ אֲחֹרַנִּית וַיְכַסּוּ אֵת עֶרְוַת אֲבִיהֶם וּפְנֵיהֶם
כד אֲחֹרַנִּית וְעֶרְוַת אֲבִיהֶם לֹא רָאוּ: וַיִּיקֶץ נֹחַ מִיֵּינוֹ וַיֵּדַע אֵת אֲשֶׁר־עָשָׂה לוֹ
כה־כו בְּנוֹ הַקָּטָן: וַיֹּאמֶר אָרוּר כְּנָעַן עֶבֶד עֲבָדִים יִהְיֶה לְאֶחָיו: וַיֹּאמֶר בָּרוּךְ יְהֹוָה
כו אֱלֹהֵי שֵׁם וִיהִי כְנַעַן עֶבֶד לָמוֹ: יַפְתְּ אֱלֹהִים לְיֶפֶת וְיִשְׁכֹּן בְּאָהֳלֵי־שֵׁם וִיהִי
כח כְנַעַן עֶבֶד לָמוֹ: וַיְחִי־נֹחַ אַחַר הַמַּבּוּל שְׁלֹשׁ מֵאוֹת שָׁנָה וַחֲמִשִּׁים שָׁנָה:
כט וַיִּהְיוּ כָּל־יְמֵי־נֹחַ תְּשַׁע מֵאוֹת שָׁנָה וַחֲמִשִּׁים שָׁנָה וַיָּמֹת:

י
א וְאֵלֶּה תּוֹלְדֹת בְּנֵי־נֹחַ שֵׁם חָם וָיָפֶת וַיִּוָּלְדוּ לָהֶם בָּנִים אַחַר הַמַּבּוּל: בְּנֵי
ב יֶפֶת גֹּמֶר וּמָגוֹג וּמָדַי וְיָוָן וְתֻבָל וּמֶשֶׁךְ וְתִירָס: וּבְנֵי גֹמֶר אַשְׁכְּנַז וְרִיפַת
ד־ה וְתֹגַרְמָה: וּבְנֵי יָוָן אֱלִישָׁה וְתַרְשִׁישׁ כִּתִּים וְדֹדָנִים: מֵאֵלֶּה נִפְרְדוּ אִיֵּי
ו הַגּוֹיִם בְּאַרְצֹתָם אִישׁ לִלְשֹׁנוֹ לְמִשְׁפְּחֹתָם בְּגוֹיֵהֶם: וּבְנֵי חָם כּוּשׁ וּמִצְרַיִם
ז וּפוּט וּכְנָעַן: וּבְנֵי כוּשׁ סְבָא וַחֲוִילָה וְסַבְתָּה וְרַעְמָה וְסַבְתְּכָא וּבְנֵי רַעְמָה
ח־ט שְׁבָא וּדְדָן: וְכוּשׁ יָלַד אֶת־נִמְרֹד הוּא הֵחֵל לִהְיוֹת גִּבֹּר בָּאָרֶץ: הוּא־הָיָה
י גִּבֹּר־צַיִד לִפְנֵי יְהֹוָה עַל־כֵּן יֵאָמַר כְּנִמְרֹד גִּבּוֹר צַיִד לִפְנֵי יְהֹוָה: וַתְּהִי
ראשִׁית מַמְלַכְתּוֹ בָּבֶל וְאֶרֶךְ וְאַכַּד וְכַלְנֵה בְּאֶרֶץ שִׁנְעָר: מִן־הָאָרֶץ הַהִוא
יב יָצָא אַשּׁוּר וַיִּבֶן אֶת־נִינְוֵה וְאֶת־רְחֹבֹת עִיר וְאֶת־כָּלַח: וְאֶת־רֶסֶן בֵּין
יג נִינְוֵה וּבֵין כֶּלַח הִוא הָעִיר הַגְּדֹלָה: וּמִצְרַיִם יָלַד אֶת־לוּדִים וְאֶת־עֲנָמִים
יד וְאֶת־לְהָבִים וְאֶת־נַפְתֻּחִים: וְאֶת־פַּתְרֻסִים וְאֶת־כַּסְלֻחִים אֲשֶׁר יָצְאוּ
טו מִשָּׁם פְּלִשְׁתִּים וְאֶת־כַּפְתֹּרִים: וּכְנַעַן יָלַד אֶת־צִידֹן
טז־יז בְּכֹרוֹ וְאֶת־חֵת: וְאֶת־הַיְבוּסִי וְאֶת־הָאֱמֹרִי וְאֵת הַגִּרְגָּשִׁי: וְאֶת־הַחִוִּי
יח וְאֶת־הָעַרְקִי וְאֶת־הַסִּינִי: וְאֶת־הָאַרְוָדִי וְאֶת־הַצְּמָרִי וְאֶת־הַחֲמָתִי
יט וְאַחַר נָפֹצוּ מִשְׁפְּחוֹת הַכְּנַעֲנִי: וַיְהִי גְּבוּל הַכְּנַעֲנִי מִצִּידֹן בֹּאֲכָה גְרָרָה
כ עַד־עַזָּה בֹּאֲכָה סְדֹמָה וַעֲמֹרָה וְאַדְמָה וּצְבֹיִם עַד־לָשַׁע: אֵלֶּה בְנֵי־חָם
כא לְמִשְׁפְּחֹתָם לִלְשֹׁנֹתָם בְּאַרְצֹתָם בְּגוֹיֵהֶם: וּלְשֵׁם
כב יֻלַּד גַּם־הוּא אֲבִי כָּל־בְּנֵי־עֵבֶר אֲחִי יֶפֶת הַגָּדוֹל: בְּנֵי שֵׁם עֵילָם
כג וְאַשּׁוּר וְאַרְפַּכְשַׁד וְלוּד וַאֲרָם: וּבְנֵי אֲרָם עוּץ וְחוּל וְגֶתֶר וָמַשׁ:
כד־כה וְאַרְפַּכְשַׁד יָלַד אֶת־שָׁלַח וְשֶׁלַח יָלַד אֶת־עֵבֶר: וּלְעֵבֶר יֻלַּד שְׁנֵי בָנִים שֵׁם
כו הָאֶחָד פֶּלֶג כִּי בְיָמָיו נִפְלְגָה הָאָרֶץ וְשֵׁם אָחִיו יָקְטָן: וְיָקְטָן יָלַד אֶת־

9:18-27. The intoxication and shame of Noah. The Torah records a shameful event through which Noah was humiliated and which resulted in the blessings and curse that influence the trend of history to this very day. This experience demonstrates that even the greatest people

can become degraded if they lose control of themselves.

9:25-27. Noah foretells the destiny of his sons. R' Hirsch calls these verses the most far-reaching prophecy ever uttered, for in it Noah encapsulated the entire course of human history.

¹⁸ *The sons of Noah who came out of the Ark were Shem, Ham, and Japheth — Ham being the father of Canaan.* ¹⁹ *These three were the sons of Noah, and from these the whole world was spread out.*

The intoxication and shame of Noah

²⁰ *Noah, the man of the earth, debased himself and planted a vineyard.* ²¹ *He drank of the wine and became drunk, and he uncovered himself within his tent.* ²² *Ham, the father of Canaan, saw his father's nakedness and told his two brothers outside.* ²³ *And Shem and Japheth took a garment, laid it upon both their shoulders, and they walked backwards, and covered their father's nakedness; their faces were turned away, and they saw not their father's nakedness.*

²⁴ *Noah awoke from his wine and realized what his small son had done to him.*

Noah foretells the destiny of his sons

²⁵ *And he said, "Cursed is Canaan; a slave of slaves shall he be to his brothers."* ²⁶ *And he said, "Blessed is* HASHEM*, the God of Shem; and let Canaan be a slave to them.*

²⁷ *"May God extend Japheth, but he will dwell in the tents of Shem; may Canaan be a slave to them."*

²⁸ *Noah lived after the Flood three hundred fifty years.* ²⁹ *And all the days of Noah were nine hundred fifty years; and he died.*

10

¹ *These are the descendants of the sons of Noah: Shem, Ham, and Japheth; sons were born to them after the Flood.*

The descendants of Noah: The seventy nations

(See Appendix B, chart 1)

² *The sons of Japheth: Gomer, Magog, Madai, Javan, Tubal, Meshech, and Tiras.* ³ *The sons of Gomer: Ashkenaz, Riphath, and Togarmah.* ⁴ *The sons of Javan: Elishah and Tarshish, the Kittim and the Dodanim.* ⁵ *From these the islands of the nations were separated in their lands — each according to its language, by their families, in their nations.*

⁶ *The sons of Ham: Cush, Mizraim, Put, and Canaan.* ⁷ *The sons of Cush: Seba, Havilah, Sabtah, Raamah, and Sabteca. The sons of Raamah: Sheba and Dedan.*

Nimrod

⁸ *And Cush begot Nimrod. He was the first to be a mighty man on earth.* ⁹ *He was a mighty hunter before* HASHEM*; therefore it is said: "Like Nimrod a mighty hunter before* HASHEM*."* ¹⁰ *The beginning of his kingdom was Babel, Erech, Accad, and Calneh in the land of Shinar.* ¹¹ *From that land Asshur went forth and built Nineveh, Rehovoth-ir, Calah,* ¹² *and Resen between Nineveh and Calah, that is the great city.*

¹³ *And Mizraim begot Ludim, Anamim, Lehabim, Naphtuhim,* ¹⁴ *Pathrusim, and Casluhim, whence the Philistines came forth, and Caphtorim.*

¹⁵ *Canaan begot Zidon his firstborn, and Heth;* ¹⁶ *and the Jebusite, the Amorite, the Girgashite,* ¹⁷ *the Hivite, the Arkite, the Sinite,* ¹⁸ *the Arvadite, the Zemarite, and the Hamathite. Afterward, the families of the Canaanites branched out.* ¹⁹ *And the Canaanite boundary extended from Zidon going toward Gerar, as far as Gaza; going toward Sodom, Gomorrah, Admah, and Zeboiim, as far as Lasha.* ²⁰ *These are the descendants of Ham, by their families, by their languages, in their lands, in their nations.*

²¹ *And to Shem, also to him were born; he was the ancestor of all those who lived on the other side; the brother of Japheth the elder.* ²² *The sons of Shem: Elam, Asshur, Arpachshad, Lud, and Aram.* ²³ *The sons of Aram: Uz, Hul, Gether, and Mash.* ²⁴ *Arpachshad begot Shelah, and Shelah begot Eber.* ²⁵ *And to Eber were born two sons: The name of the first was Peleg, for in his days the earth was divided; and the name of his brother was Joktan.* ²⁶ *Joktan begot*

כז אַלְמוֹדָד וְאֶת־שֶׁלֶף וְאֶת־חֲצַרְמָוֶת וְאֶת־יָרַח: וְאֶת־הֲדוֹרָם וְאֶת־אוּזָל

כח-כט וְאֶת־דִּקְלָה: וְאֶת־עוֹבָל וְאֶת־אֲבִימָאֵל וְאֶת־שְׁבָא: וְאֶת־אוֹפִר וְאֶת־

ל חֲוִילָה וְאֶת־יוֹבָב כָּל־אֵלֶּה בְּנֵי יָקְטָן: וַיְהִי מוֹשָׁבָם מִמֵּשָׁא בֹּאֲכָה סְפָרָה

לא-לב הַר הַקֶּדֶם: אֵלֶּה בְנֵי־שֵׁם לְמִשְׁפְּחֹתָם לִלְשֹׁנֹתָם בְּאַרְצֹתָם לְגוֹיֵהֶם: אֵלֶּה

מִשְׁפְּחֹת בְּנֵי־נֹחַ לְתוֹלְדֹתָם בְּגוֹיֵהֶם וּמֵאֵלֶּה נִפְרְדוּ הַגּוֹיִם בָּאָרֶץ אַחַר

הַמַּבּוּל:

יא
שביעי
א-ב וַיְהִי כָל־הָאָרֶץ שָׂפָה אֶחָת וּדְבָרִים אֲחָדִים: וַיְהִי בְּנָסְעָם מִקֶּדֶם וַיִּמְצְאוּ

ג בִקְעָה בְּאֶרֶץ שִׁנְעָר וַיֵּשְׁבוּ שָׁם: וַיֹּאמְרוּ אִישׁ אֶל־רֵעֵהוּ הָבָה נִלְבְּנָה

לְבֵנִים וְנִשְׂרְפָה לִשְׂרֵפָה וַתְּהִי לָהֶם הַלְּבֵנָה לְאָבֶן וְהַחֵמָר הָיָה לָהֶם

ד לַחֹמֶר: וַיֹּאמְרוּ הָבָה ׀ נִבְנֶה־לָּנוּ עִיר וּמִגְדָּל וְרֹאשׁוֹ בַשָּׁמַיִם וְנַעֲשֶׂה־לָּנוּ

ה שֵׁם פֶּן־נָפוּץ עַל־פְּנֵי כָל־הָאָרֶץ: וַיֵּרֶד יְהוָה לִרְאֹת אֶת־הָעִיר וְאֶת־

ו הַמִּגְדָּל אֲשֶׁר בָּנוּ בְּנֵי הָאָדָם: וַיֹּאמֶר יְהוָה הֵן עַם אֶחָד וְשָׂפָה אַחַת

לְכֻלָּם וְזֶה הַחִלָּם לַעֲשׂוֹת וְעַתָּה לֹא־יִבָּצֵר מֵהֶם כֹּל אֲשֶׁר יָזְמוּ לַעֲשׂוֹת:

ז-ח הָבָה נֵרְדָה וְנָבְלָה שָׁם שְׂפָתָם אֲשֶׁר לֹא יִשְׁמְעוּ אִישׁ שְׂפַת רֵעֵהוּ: וַיָּפֶץ

ט יְהוָה אֹתָם מִשָּׁם עַל־פְּנֵי כָל־הָאָרֶץ וַיַּחְדְּלוּ לִבְנֹת הָעִיר: עַל־כֵּן קָרָא

שְׁמָהּ בָּבֶל כִּי־שָׁם בָּלַל יְהוָה שְׂפַת כָּל־הָאָרֶץ וּמִשָּׁם הֱפִיצָם יְהוָה עַל־

פְּנֵי כָּל־הָאָרֶץ:

י אֵלֶּה תּוֹלְדֹת שֵׁם שֵׁם בֶּן־מְאַת שָׁנָה וַיּוֹלֶד אֶת־אַרְפַּכְשָׁד שְׁנָתַיִם אַחַר

יא הַמַּבּוּל: וַיְחִי־שֵׁם אַחֲרֵי הוֹלִידוֹ אֶת־אַרְפַּכְשָׁד חֲמֵשׁ מֵאוֹת שָׁנָה

יב וַיּוֹלֶד בָּנִים וּבָנוֹת: וְאַרְפַּכְשַׁד חַי חָמֵשׁ וּשְׁלֹשִׁים שָׁנָה וַיּוֹלֶד

יג אֶת־שָׁלַח: וַיְחִי אַרְפַּכְשַׁד אַחֲרֵי הוֹלִידוֹ אֶת־שֶׁלַח שָׁלֹשׁ שָׁנִים וְאַרְבַּע

יד מֵאוֹת שָׁנָה וַיּוֹלֶד בָּנִים וּבָנוֹת: וְשֶׁלַח חַי שְׁלֹשִׁים שָׁנָה וַיּוֹלֶד

טו אֶת־עֵבֶר: וַיְחִי־שֶׁלַח אַחֲרֵי הוֹלִידוֹ אֶת־עֵבֶר שָׁלֹשׁ שָׁנִים וְאַרְבַּע מֵאוֹת

טז שָׁנָה וַיּוֹלֶד בָּנִים וּבָנוֹת: וַיְחִי־עֵבֶר אַרְבַּע וּשְׁלֹשִׁים שָׁנָה וַיּוֹלֶד

יז אֶת־פָּלֶג: וַיְחִי־עֵבֶר אַחֲרֵי הוֹלִידוֹ אֶת־פֶּלֶג שְׁלֹשִׁים שָׁנָה וְאַרְבַּע מֵאוֹת

יח שָׁנָה וַיּוֹלֶד בָּנִים וּבָנוֹת: וַיְחִי־פֶלֶג שְׁלֹשִׁים שָׁנָה וַיּוֹלֶד אֶת־רְעוּ:

יט וַיְחִי־פֶלֶג אַחֲרֵי הוֹלִידוֹ אֶת־רְעוּ תֵּשַׁע שָׁנִים וּמָאתַיִם שָׁנָה וַיּוֹלֶד בָּנִים

כ-כא וּבָנוֹת: וַיְחִי רְעוּ שְׁתַּיִם וּשְׁלֹשִׁים שָׁנָה וַיּוֹלֶד אֶת־שְׂרוּג: וַיְחִי

רְעוּ אַחֲרֵי הוֹלִידוֹ אֶת־שְׂרוּג שֶׁבַע שָׁנִים וּמָאתַיִם שָׁנָה וַיּוֹלֶד בָּנִים

כב-כג וּבָנוֹת: וַיְחִי שְׂרוּג שְׁלֹשִׁים שָׁנָה וַיּוֹלֶד אֶת־נָחוֹר: וַיְחִי שְׂרוּג

כד אַחֲרֵי הוֹלִידוֹ אֶת־נָחוֹר מָאתַיִם שָׁנָה וַיּוֹלֶד בָּנִים וּבָנוֹת: וַיְחִי

11:1-9. The Tower of Babel and the Dispersion. *Ram-bam* in *Moreh Nevuchim* states that a fundamental princi-ple of the Torah is that the universe was created *ex nihilo*, and Adam was the forerunner of all people. Since the human race was later dispersed over all the earth, and divided into different families speaking dissimilar lan-guages, people might come to doubt that they could all have originated from one person. Therefore the Torah records the genealogy of the nations, and explains why they were dispersed, and the reason God gave them

Almodad, Sheleph, Hazarmaveth, Jerah, ²⁷ Hadoram, Uzal, Diklah, ²⁸ Obal, Abimael, Sheba, ²⁹ Ophir, Havilah, and Jobab; all these were the sons of Joktan. ³⁰ Their dwelling place extended from Mesha going toward Sephar, the mountain to the east. ³¹ These are the descendants of Shem according to their families, by their languages, in their lands, by their nations.

³² These are the families of Noah's descendants, according to their generations, by their nations; and from these the nations were separated on the earth after the Flood.

11

The Tower of Babel and the dispersion

¹ The whole earth was of one language and of common purpose. ² And it came to pass, when they migrated from the east they found a valley in the land of Shinar and settled there. ³ They said to one another, "Come, let us* make bricks and burn them in fire." And the brick served them as stone, and the bitumen served them as mortar. ⁴ And they said, "Come, let us build us a city, and a tower with its top in the heavens, and let us make a name for ourselves, lest we be dispersed across the whole earth."

⁵ HASHEM descended to look at the city and tower which the sons of man built, ⁶ and HASHEM said, "Behold, they are one people with one language for all, and this they begin to do! And now, should it not be withheld from them all they proposed to do? ⁷ Come, let us* descend and there confuse their language, that they should not understand one another's language."

⁸ And HASHEM dispersed them from there over the face of the whole earth; and they stopped building the city. ⁹ That is why it was called Babel, because it was there that HASHEM confused the language of the whole earth, and from there HASHEM scattered them over the face of the whole earth.

The ten generations from Noah to Abraham
(See Appendix A, timeline 1)

¹⁰ These are the descendants of Shem: Shem was one hundred years old when he begot Arpachshad, two years after the Flood. ¹¹ And Shem lived five hundred years after begetting Arpachshad, and he begot sons and daughters. ¹² Arpachshad had lived thirty-five years when he begot Shelah. ¹³ And Arpachshad lived four hundred three years after begetting Shelah; and he begot sons and daughters.

¹⁴ Shelah had lived thirty years when he begot Eber. ¹⁵ And Shelah lived four hundred and three years after begetting Eber, and begot sons and daughters.

¹⁶ When Eber had lived thirty-four years, he begot Peleg. ¹⁷ And Eber lived four hundred and thirty years after begetting Peleg, and he begot sons and daughters.

¹⁸ When Peleg had lived thirty years, he begot Reu. ¹⁹ And Peleg lived two hundred and nine years after begetting Reu, and he begot sons and daughters.

²⁰When Reu had lived thirty-two years, he begot Serug. ²¹ And Reu lived two hundred and seven years after begetting Serug, and he begot sons and daughters.

²² When Serug had lived thirty years, he begot Nahor. ²³ And Serug lived two hundred years after begetting Nahor, and he begot sons and daughters.

---

different languages.

According to the Sages, Nimrod was the primary force behind this rebellion. The *Midrashim* explain his sinister motive. He planned to build a tower ascending to Heaven and, from it, wage war against God.

11:7. The plural *us* indicates that God deliberated with His Celestial Court (*Rashi*). God does not need the advice of the angels, of course, but He consulted with them, as it were, to set an example so that people should show courtesy to others by involving them in discussions.

כה נָח֗וֹר תֵּ֣שַׁע וְעֶשְׂרִ֤ים שָׁנָה֙ וַיּ֣וֹלֶד אֶת־תָּ֑רַח: וַֽיְחִ֣י נָח֗וֹר אַֽחֲרֵ֛י הֽוֹלִיד֥וֹ אֶת־

כו תֶּ֗רַח תֵּֽשַׁע־עֶשְׂרֵ֤ה שָׁנָה֙ וּמְאַ֣ת שָׁנָ֔ה וַיּ֥וֹלֶד בָּנִ֖ים וּבָנֽוֹת: וַֽיְחִ֣י־

כז תֶּ֖רַח שִׁבְעִ֣ים שָׁנָ֑ה וַיּ֨וֹלֶד֙ אֶת־אַבְרָ֔ם אֶת־נָח֖וֹר וְאֶת־הָרָֽן: וְאֵ֗לֶּה תּֽוֹלְדֹ֣ת

תֶּ֔רַח תֶּ֚רַח הוֹלִ֣יד אֶת־אַבְרָ֔ם אֶת־נָח֖וֹר וְאֶת־הָרָ֑ן וְהָרָ֖ן הוֹלִ֥יד אֶת־

כח ל֑וֹט: וַיָּ֣מָת הָרָ֗ן עַל־פְּנֵי֙ תֶּ֣רַח אָבִ֔יו בְּאֶ֥רֶץ מֽוֹלַדְתּ֖וֹ בְּא֥וּר כַּשְׂדִּֽים:

כט וַיִּקַּ֨ח אַבְרָ֧ם וְנָח֛וֹר לָהֶ֖ם נָשִׁ֑ים שֵׁ֣ם אֵֽשֶׁת־אַבְרָם֙ שָׂרָ֔י וְשֵׁ֤ם אֵֽשֶׁת־נָחוֹר֙

ל מִלְכָּ֔ה בַּת־הָרָ֥ן אֲבִֽי־מִלְכָּ֖ה וַֽאֲבִ֣י יִסְכָּֽה: וַתְּהִ֥י שָׂרַ֖י עֲקָרָ֑ה אֵ֥ין לָ֖הּ וָלָֽד:

לא וַיִּקַּ֨ח תֶּ֜רַח אֶת־אַבְרָ֣ם בְּנ֗וֹ וְאֶת־ל֤וֹט בֶּן־הָרָן֙ בֶּן־בְּנ֔וֹ וְאֵת֙ שָׂרַ֣י כַּלָּת֔וֹ

אֵ֖שֶׁת אַבְרָ֣ם בְּנ֑וֹ וַיֵּֽצְא֨וּ אִתָּ֜ם מֵא֣וּר כַּשְׂדִּ֗ים לָלֶ֨כֶת֙ אַ֣רְצָה כְּנַ֔עַן וַיָּבֹ֥אוּ עַד־

לב חָרָ֖ן וַיֵּ֥שְׁבוּ שָֽׁם: וַיִּֽהְי֣וּ יְמֵי־תֶ֔רַח חָמֵ֥שׁ שָׁנִ֖ים וּמָאתַ֣יִם שָׁנָ֑ה וַיָּ֥מָת תֶּ֖רַח

בְּחָרָֽן: פפפ   קנ"ג פסוקים. בצלא"ל סימן. אב"י יסכ"ה לו"ט סימן.

מפטיר

Haftaras
Noach:
p. 1048

For special
Sabbaths,
see pp. x-xi

פרשת לך לך

א וַיֹּ֤אמֶר יהוה֙ אֶל־אַבְרָ֔ם לֶךְ־לְךָ֛ מֵֽאַרְצְךָ֥ וּמִמּֽוֹלַדְתְּךָ֖ וּמִבֵּ֣ית אָבִ֑יךָ אֶל־

ב הָאָ֖רֶץ אֲשֶׁ֥ר אַרְאֶֽךָּ: וְאֶֽעֶשְׂךָ֙ לְג֣וֹי גָּד֔וֹל וַֽאֲבָ֣רֶכְךָ֔ וַֽאֲגַדְּלָ֖ה שְׁמֶ֑ךָ וֶֽהְיֵ֖ה

ג בְּרָכָֽה: וַֽאֲבָֽרְכָה֙ מְבָ֣רְכֶ֔יךָ וּמְקַלֶּלְךָ֖ אָאֹ֑ר וְנִבְרְכ֣וּ בְךָ֔ כֹּ֖ל מִשְׁפְּחֹ֥ת הָֽאֲדָמָֽה:

ד וַיֵּ֣לֶךְ אַבְרָ֗ם כַּֽאֲשֶׁ֨ר דִּבֶּ֤ר אֵלָיו֙ יהוה וַיֵּ֥לֶךְ אִתּ֖וֹ ל֑וֹט וְאַבְרָ֗ם בֶּן־חָמֵ֤שׁ שָׁנִים֙

ה וְשִׁבְעִ֣ים שָׁנָ֔ה בְּצֵאת֖וֹ מֵֽחָרָֽן: וַיִּקַּ֣ח אַבְרָ֡ם אֶת־שָׂרַ֣י אִשְׁתּוֹ֩ וְאֶת־ל֨וֹט בֶּן־

אָחִ֜יו וְאֶת־כָּל־רְכֽוּשָׁם֙ אֲשֶׁ֣ר רָכָ֔שׁוּ וְאֶת־הַנֶּ֖פֶשׁ אֲשֶׁר־עָשׂ֣וּ בְחָרָ֑ן וַיֵּֽצְא֗וּ

ו לָלֶ֨כֶת֙ אַ֣רְצָה כְּנַ֔עַן וַיָּבֹ֖אוּ אַ֣רְצָה כְּנָֽעַן: וַיַּֽעֲבֹ֤ר אַבְרָם֙ בָּאָ֔רֶץ עַ֚ד מְק֣וֹם

ז שְׁכֶ֔ם עַ֖ד אֵל֣וֹן מוֹרֶ֑ה וְהַֽכְּנַֽעֲנִ֖י אָ֥ז בָּאָֽרֶץ: וַיֵּרָ֤א יהוה֙ אֶל־אַבְרָ֔ם וַיֹּ֕אמֶר

ח לְזַ֨רְעֲךָ֔ אֶתֵּ֖ן אֶת־הָאָ֣רֶץ הַזֹּ֑את וַיִּ֤בֶן שָׁם֙ מִזְבֵּ֔חַ לַֽיהוה הַנִּרְאֶ֥ה אֵלָֽיו: וַיַּעְתֵּ֨ק

מִשָּׁ֜ם הָהָ֗רָה מִקֶּ֛דֶם לְבֵֽית־אֵ֖ל וַיֵּ֣ט אָֽהֳלֹ֑ה בֵּֽית־אֵ֤ל מִיָּם֙ וְהָעַ֣י מִקֶּ֔דֶם וַיִּֽבֶן־

ט שָׁ֤ם מִזְבֵּ֨חַ֙ לַֽיהוה וַיִּקְרָ֖א בְּשֵׁ֥ם יהוה: וַיִּסַּ֣ע אַבְרָ֔ם הָל֥וֹךְ וְנָס֖וֹעַ הַנֶּֽגְבָּה:

י וַיְהִ֥י רָעָ֖ב בָּאָ֑רֶץ וַיֵּ֨רֶד אַבְרָ֤ם מִצְרַ֨יְמָה֙ לָג֣וּר שָׁ֔ם כִּֽי־כָבֵ֥ד הָֽרָעָ֖ב בָּאָֽרֶץ:

יא וַיְהִ֕י כַּֽאֲשֶׁ֥ר הִקְרִ֖יב לָב֣וֹא מִצְרָ֑יְמָה וַיֹּ֨אמֶר֙ אֶל־שָׂרַ֣י אִשְׁתּ֔וֹ הִנֵּה־נָ֣א

יב יָדַ֔עְתִּי כִּ֛י אִשָּׁ֥ה יְפַת־מַרְאֶ֖ה אָֽתְּ: וְהָיָ֗ה כִּֽי־יִרְא֤וּ אֹתָךְ֙ הַמִּצְרִ֔ים וְאָֽמְר֖וּ

יג אִשְׁתּ֣וֹ זֹ֑את וְהָֽרְג֥וּ אֹתִ֖י וְאֹתָ֥ךְ יְחַיּֽוּ: אִמְרִי־נָ֖א אֲחֹ֣תִי אָ֑תְּ לְמַ֨עַן֙ יִֽיטַב־לִ֣י

11:29. Iscah was Sarah (*Rashi*).

11:32. Terah died in the year 2083; Isaac was thirty-five years old at the time (*Seder Olam*). The Torah's common practice is to record a person's death when he ceases to be involved in the narrative.

⊸§ Parashas Lech Lecha

This *Sidrah* begins the story of Abraham and his descendants. The first two thousand years from Creation were the Era of Desolation. Adam had fallen, Abel had been murdered, idolatry had been introduced to the world, ten dismal generations had been washed away by

the Deluge, and the ten generations from Noah had failed [see *Avos* 5:2]. Abraham was born in the year 1948 from Creation. In the year 2,000 — four years after the Dispersion and six years before the death of Noah — he started to influence disciples to serve God. With the emergence of Abraham, the Era of Desolation had come to an end and the Era of Torah had begun (*Avodah Zarah* 9a).

⊸§ **The concept of trial.** In order to win his new status Abraham had to prove his greatness by passing ten tests of faith (*Avos* 5:4; see Appendix B, chart 3). This *Sidrah* begins with the first trial mentioned in Scripture, the command that Abraham give up his entire past and follow

²⁴ *When Nahor had lived twenty-nine years, he begot Terah.* ²⁵ *And Nahor lived one hundred nineteen years after begetting Terah, and he begot sons and daughters.*

(See Appendix B, chart 2)

²⁶*When Terah had lived seventy years, he begot Abram, Nahor, and Haran.* ²⁷ *Now these are the chronicles of Terah: Terah begot Abram, Nahor, and Haran; and Haran begot Lot.* ²⁸ *Haran died in the lifetime of Terah his father, in his native land, in Ur Kasdim.* ²⁹ *And Abram and Nahor took themselves wives; the name of Abram's wife was Sarai, and the name of Nahor's wife was Milcah, the daughter of Haran, the father of Milcah and the father of Iscah.* * ³⁰ *And Sarai was barren, she had no child.*

³¹ *Terah took his son Abram, and Lot the son of Haran, his grandson, and his daughter-in-law Sarai, the wife of Abram his son, and they departed with them from Ur Kasdim to go to the land of Canaan; they arrived at Haran and they settled there.*

³² *The days of Terah were two hundred and five years, and Terah died in Haran.*

PARASHAS LECH LECHA

12

God's call to Abraham

¹H ASHEM said to Abram, "Go for yourself from your land, from your relatives, and from your father's house to the land that I will show you. ²And I will make of you a great nation; I will bless you, and make your name great, and you shall be a blessing. ³I will bless those who bless you, and him who curses you I will curse; and all the families of the earth shall bless themselves by you."

Abraham comes to Canaan

⁴ So Abram went as HASHEM had spoken to him, and Lot went with him; Abram was seventy-five years old when he left Haran. ⁵ Abram took his wife Sarai and Lot, his brother's son, and all their wealth that they had amassed, and the souls they made in Haran; and they left to go to the land of Canaan, and they came to the land of Canaan. ⁶ Abram passed into the land as far as the site of Shechem, until the Plain of Moreh. The Canaanite was then in the land.

⁷ HASHEM appeared to Abram and said, "To your offspring I will give this land." So he built an altar there to HASHEM Who appeared to him. ⁸ From there he relocated to the mountain east of Beth-el and pitched his tent, with Beth-el on the west and Ai on the east; and he built there an altar to HASHEM and invoked HASHEM by Name. ⁹ Then Abram journeyed on, journeying steadily toward the south.

Abraham and Sarah in Egypt

¹⁰ There was a famine in the land, and Abram descended to Egypt to sojourn there, for the famine was severe in the land. ¹¹ And it occurred, as he was about to enter Egypt, he said to his wife Sarai, "See now, I have known that you are a woman of beautiful appearance. ¹² And it shall occur, when the Egyptians will see you, they will say, 'This is his wife!'; then they will kill me, but you they will let live. ¹³ Please say that you are my sister, that it may go well with me

---

God's lead to a new land.

At this point in his life, the Patriarch's name was Abram and the Matriarch's was Sarai; their names were not changed to Abraham and Sarah until 17:5 and 15, twenty-four years after they left for Canaan. Nevertheless, in the notes we refer to them by their familiar names of Abraham and Sarah, as do the commentators.

12:6. Deeds of the Patriarchs, portents for the children. *Ramban* states a fundamental principle in understanding the Torah's narrative concerning the Patriarchs: מַה כָּל

שֶׁאֵירַע לְאָבוֹת סִימָן לַבָּנִים, *Whatever happened to the Patriarchs is a portent for the children,* meaning that the events of their lives symbolized the future. Thus, Abraham's trip to Egypt in the face of a famine portended the exile of Jacob and his family.

12:10-20. Abraham in Egypt. This is another test of Abraham's faith. Immediately after he settled in the new homeland where God had promised him every manner of blessing, there was a famine, whereupon God commanded him to leave the land for Egypt (*Midrash*).

שני

יד בַּעֲבוּרֵךְ וְחָיְתָה נַפְשִׁי בִּגְלָלֵךְ: וַיְהִי כְּבוֹא אַבְרָם מִצְרָיְמָה וַיִּרְאוּ

טו הַמִּצְרִים אֶת־הָאִשָּׁה כִּי־יָפָה הִוא מְאֹד: וַיִּרְאוּ אֹתָהּ שָׂרֵי פַרְעֹה וַיְהַלְלוּ

טז אֹתָהּ אֶל־פַּרְעֹה וַתֻּקַּח הָאִשָּׁה בֵּית פַּרְעֹה: וּלְאַבְרָם הֵיטִיב בַּעֲבוּרָהּ

יז וַיְהִי־לוֹ צֹאן־וּבָקָר וַחֲמֹרִים וַעֲבָדִים וּשְׁפָחֹת וַאֲתֹנֹת וּגְמַלִּים: וַיְנַגַּע

יהוה אֶת־פַּרְעֹה נְגָעִים גְּדֹלִים וְאֶת־בֵּיתוֹ עַל־דְּבַר שָׂרַי אֵשֶׁת אַבְרָם:

יח וַיִּקְרָא פַרְעֹה לְאַבְרָם וַיֹּאמֶר מַה־זֹּאת עָשִׂיתָ לִּי לָמָּה לֹא־הִגַּדְתָּ לִּי כִּי

יט אִשְׁתְּךָ הִוא: לָמָה אָמַרְתָּ אֲחֹתִי הִוא וָאֶקַּח אֹתָהּ לִי לְאִשָּׁה וְעַתָּה הִנֵּה

כ אִשְׁתְּךָ קַח וָלֵךְ: וַיְצַו עָלָיו פַּרְעֹה אֲנָשִׁים וַיְשַׁלְּחוּ אֹתוֹ וְאֶת־אִשְׁתּוֹ

יג א וְאֶת־כָּל־אֲשֶׁר־לוֹ: וַיַּעַל אַבְרָם מִמִּצְרַיִם הוּא וְאִשְׁתּוֹ וְכָל־אֲשֶׁר־לוֹ

ב־ג וְלוֹט עִמּוֹ הַנֶּגְבָּה: וְאַבְרָם כָּבֵד מְאֹד בַּמִּקְנֶה בַּכֶּסֶף וּבַזָּהָב: וַיֵּלֶךְ

לְמַסָּעָיו מִנֶּגֶב וְעַד־בֵּית־אֵל עַד־הַמָּקוֹם אֲשֶׁר־הָיָה שָׁם אָהֳלֹה בַּתְּחִלָּה

ד בֵּין בֵּית־אֵל וּבֵין הָעָי: אֶל־מְקוֹם הַמִּזְבֵּחַ אֲשֶׁר־עָשָׂה שָׁם בָּרִאשֹׁנָה

שלישי

ה וַיִּקְרָא שָׁם אַבְרָם בְּשֵׁם יהוה: וְגַם־לְלוֹט הַהֹלֵךְ אֶת־אַבְרָם הָיָה

ו צֹאן־וּבָקָר וְאֹהָלִים: וְלֹא־נָשָׂא אֹתָם הָאָרֶץ לָשֶׁבֶת יַחְדָּו כִּי־הָיָה

ז רְכוּשָׁם רָב וְלֹא יָכְלוּ לָשֶׁבֶת יַחְדָּו: וַיְהִי־רִיב בֵּין רֹעֵי מִקְנֵה־אַבְרָם וּבֵין

ח רֹעֵי מִקְנֵה־לוֹט וְהַכְּנַעֲנִי וְהַפְּרִזִּי אָז יֹשֵׁב בָּאָרֶץ: וַיֹּאמֶר אַבְרָם אֶל־לוֹט

אַל־נָא תְהִי מְרִיבָה בֵּינִי וּבֵינֶךָ וּבֵין רֹעַי וּבֵין רֹעֶיךָ כִּי־אֲנָשִׁים אַחִים

ט אֲנָחְנוּ: הֲלֹא כָל־הָאָרֶץ לְפָנֶיךָ הִפָּרֶד נָא מֵעָלָי אִם־הַשְּׂמֹאל וְאֵימִנָה

י וְאִם־הַיָּמִין וְאַשְׂמְאִילָה: וַיִּשָּׂא־לוֹט אֶת־עֵינָיו וַיַּרְא אֶת־כָּל־כִּכַּר הַיַּרְדֵּן

כִּי כֻלָּהּ מַשְׁקֶה לִפְנֵי שַׁחֵת יהוה אֶת־סְדֹם וְאֶת־עֲמֹרָה כְּגַן־יהוה

יא כְּאֶרֶץ מִצְרַיִם בֹּאֲכָה צֹעַר: וַיִּבְחַר־לוֹ לוֹט אֵת כָּל־כִּכַּר הַיַּרְדֵּן וַיִּסַּע

יב לוֹט מִקֶּדֶם וַיִּפָּרְדוּ אִישׁ מֵעַל אָחִיו: אַבְרָם יָשַׁב בְּאֶרֶץ־כְּנָעַן וְלוֹט יָשַׁב

יג בְּעָרֵי הַכִּכָּר וַיֶּאֱהַל עַד־סְדֹם: וְאַנְשֵׁי סְדֹם רָעִים וְחַטָּאִים לַיהוה

יד מְאֹד: וַיהוה אָמַר אֶל־אַבְרָם אַחֲרֵי הִפָּרֶד־לוֹט מֵעִמּוֹ שָׂא־נָא עֵינֶיךָ

טו וּרְאֵה מִן־הַמָּקוֹם אֲשֶׁר־אַתָּה שָׁם צָפֹנָה וָנֶגְבָּה וָקֵדְמָה וָיָמָּה: כִּי

אֶת־כָּל־הָאָרֶץ אֲשֶׁר־אַתָּה רֹאֶה לְךָ אֶתְּנֶנָּה וּלְזַרְעֲךָ עַד־עוֹלָם:

טז וְשַׂמְתִּי אֶת־זַרְעֲךָ כַּעֲפַר הָאָרֶץ אֲשֶׁר אִם־יוּכַל אִישׁ לִמְנוֹת אֶת־עֲפַר

יז הָאָרֶץ גַּם־זַרְעֲךָ יִמָּנֶה: קוּם הִתְהַלֵּךְ בָּאָרֶץ לְאָרְכָּהּ וּלְרָחְבָּהּ כִּי לְךָ

יח אֶתְּנֶנָּה: וַיֶּאֱהַל אַבְרָם וַיָּבֹא וַיֵּשֶׁב בְּאֵלֹנֵי מַמְרֵא אֲשֶׁר בְּחֶבְרוֹן וַיִּבֶן־שָׁם

מִזְבֵּחַ לַיהוה:

13:1. Although it is literally true that Abraham *went up*, because the terrain of *Eretz Yisrael* is higher than that of Egypt, the *Zohar* perceives in the verb the additional indication that Abraham *ascended spiritually*. He left a place of spiritual pollution and returned to his former, higher condition.

13:6-9. Abraham and Lot part ways.
    Wealth and the lust for more of it brings out the worst in people. Abraham resisted it completely, but Lot allowed it to warp his judgment until, as the succeeding passages indicate, it destroyed nearly all of his family.

for your sake, and that I may live on account of you."

[14] *But it occurred, with Abram's coming to Egypt, the Egyptians saw that the woman was very beautiful.* [15] *When the officials of Pharaoh saw her, they lauded her for Pharaoh, and the woman was taken to Pharaoh's house.* [16] *And he treated Abram well for her sake, and he acquired sheep, cattle, donkeys, slaves and maidservants, female donkeys, and camels.*

[17] *But HASHEM afflicted Pharaoh along with his household with severe plagues because of the matter of Sarai, the wife of Abram.* [18] *Pharaoh summoned Abram and said, "What is this you have done to me? Why did you not tell me that she is your wife?* [19] *Why did you say, 'She is my sister,' so that I would take her as my wife? Now, here is your wife; take her and go!"* [20] *So Pharaoh gave men orders concerning him, and they escorted him and his wife and all that was his.*

13

The return to Eretz Yisrael

[1] *So Abram went up* from Egypt, he with his wife and all that was his — and Lot with him — to the south.* [2] *Now Abram was very laden with livestock, silver, and gold.* [3] *He proceeded on his journeys from the south to Beth-el to the place where his tent had been at first, between Beth-el and Ai,* [4] *to the site of the altar which he had erected there at first; and there Abram invoked HASHEM by Name.*

Abraham and Lot part ways

[5] *Also Lot who went with Abram had flocks, cattle, and tents.* [6] *And the land could not support them dwelling together for their possessions were abundant and they were unable to dwell together.* [7] *And there was quarreling between the herdsmen of Abram's livestock and the herdsmen of Lot's livestock — and the Canaanite and the Perizzite were then dwelling in the land.*

[8] *So Abram said to Lot: "Please let there be no strife between me and you, and between my herdsmen and your herdsmen, for we are kinsmen.* [9] *Is not all the land before you? Please separate from me: If you go left then I will go right, and if you go right then I will go left."*

[10] *So Lot raised his eyes and saw the entire plain of the Jordan that it was well watered everywhere — before HASHEM destroyed Sodom and Gomorrah —like the garden of HASHEM, like the land of Egypt, going toward Zoar.* [11] *So Lot chose for himself the whole plain of the Jordan, and Lot journeyed from the east; thus they parted, one from his brother.*

[12] *Abram dwelled in the land of Canaan while Lot dwelled in the cities of the plain and pitched tents as far as Sodom.* [13] *Now the people of Sodom were wicked and sinful toward HASHEM, exceedingly.*

The repetition of the promise

[14] *HASHEM said to Abram after Lot had parted from him, "Raise now your eyes and look out from where you are: northward, southward, eastward and westward.* [15] *For all the land that you see, to you will I give it, and to your descendants forever.* [16] *I will make your offspring as the dust of the earth so that if one can count the dust of the earth, then your offspring, too, can be counted.* [17] *Arise, walk about the land through its length and breadth! For to you will I give it."* [18] *And Abram moved his tent and came and dwelled in the plains of Mamre which are in Hebron; and he built there an altar to HASHEM.*

יד רביעי א וַיְהִי בִּימֵי אַמְרָפֶל מֶלֶךְ־שִׁנְעָר אַרְיֹוךְ מֶלֶךְ אֶלָּסָר כְּדָרְלָעֹמֶר מֶלֶךְ עֵילָם וְתִדְעָל מֶלֶךְ גּוֹיִם: ב עָשׂוּ מִלְחָמָה אֶת־בֶּרַע מֶלֶךְ־סְדֹם וְאֶת־בִּרְשַׁע מֶלֶךְ עֲמֹרָה שִׁנְאָב ׀ מֶלֶךְ אַדְמָה וְשֶׁמְאֵבֶר מֶלֶךְ °צביים [צְבוֹיִם ק] וּמֶלֶךְ בֶּלַע

ג הִיא־צֹעַר: כָּל־אֵלֶּה חָבְרוּ אֶל־עֵמֶק הַשִּׂדִּים הוּא יָם הַמֶּלַח: ד שְׁתֵּים עֶשְׂרֵה שָׁנָה עָבְדוּ אֶת־כְּדָרְלָעֹמֶר וּשְׁלֹשׁ־עֶשְׂרֵה שָׁנָה מָרָדוּ: ה וּבְאַרְבַּע עֶשְׂרֵה שָׁנָה בָּא כְדָרְלָעֹמֶר וְהַמְּלָכִים אֲשֶׁר אִתּוֹ וַיַּכּוּ אֶת־רְפָאִים בְּעַשְׁתְּרֹת קַרְנַיִם וְאֶת־הַזּוּזִים בְּהָם וְאֵת הָאֵימִים בְּשָׁוֵה קִרְיָתָיִם: ו וְאֶת־ הַחֹרִי בְּהַרְרָם שֵׂעִיר עַד אֵיל פָּארָן אֲשֶׁר עַל־הַמִּדְבָּר: ז וַיָּשֻׁבוּ וַיָּבֹאוּ אֶל־ עֵין מִשְׁפָּט הִוא קָדֵשׁ וַיַּכּוּ אֶת־כָּל־שְׂדֵה הָעֲמָלֵקִי וְגַם אֶת־הָאֱמֹרִי הַיֹּשֵׁב בְּחַצְצֹן תָּמָר: ח וַיֵּצֵא מֶלֶךְ־סְדֹם וּמֶלֶךְ עֲמֹרָה וּמֶלֶךְ אַדְמָה וּמֶלֶךְ °צביים [צְבוֹיִם ק] וּמֶלֶךְ בֶּלַע הִוא־צֹעַר וַיַּעַרְכוּ אִתָּם מִלְחָמָה בְּעֵמֶק הַשִּׂדִּים: ט אֵת כְּדָרְלָעֹמֶר מֶלֶךְ עֵילָם וְתִדְעָל מֶלֶךְ גּוֹיִם וְאַמְרָפֶל מֶלֶךְ שִׁנְעָר וְאַרְיוֹךְ מֶלֶךְ אֶלָּסָר אַרְבָּעָה מְלָכִים אֶת־הַחֲמִשָּׁה: י וְעֵמֶק הַשִּׂדִּים בֶּאֱרֹת בֶּאֱרֹת חֵמָר וַיָּנֻסוּ מֶלֶךְ־סְדֹם וַעֲמֹרָה וַיִּפְּלוּ־שָׁמָּה וְהַנִּשְׁאָרִים הֶרָה נָּסוּ:

יא-יב וַיִּקְחוּ אֶת־כָּל־רְכֻשׁ סְדֹם וַעֲמֹרָה וְאֶת־כָּל־אָכְלָם וַיֵּלֵכוּ: וַיִּקְחוּ אֶת־ לוֹט וְאֶת־רְכֻשׁוֹ בֶּן־אֲחִי אַבְרָם וַיֵּלֵכוּ וְהוּא יֹשֵׁב בִּסְדֹם: יג וַיָּבֹא הַפָּלִיט וַיַּגֵּד לְאַבְרָם הָעִבְרִי וְהוּא שֹׁכֵן בְּאֵלֹנֵי מַמְרֵא הָאֱמֹרִי אֲחִי אֶשְׁכֹּל וַאֲחִי עָנֵר וְהֵם בַּעֲלֵי בְרִית־אַבְרָם: יד וַיִּשְׁמַע אַבְרָם כִּי נִשְׁבָּה אָחִיו וַיָּרֶק אֶת־חֲנִיכָיו יְלִידֵי בֵיתוֹ שְׁמֹנָה עָשָׂר וּשְׁלֹשׁ מֵאוֹת וַיִּרְדֹּף עַד־דָּן: טו וַיֵּחָלֵק עֲלֵיהֶם ׀ לַיְלָה הוּא וַעֲבָדָיו וַיַּכֵּם וַיִּרְדְּפֵם עַד־חוֹבָה אֲשֶׁר מִשְּׂמֹאל לְדַמָּשֶׂק: טז וַיָּשֶׁב אֵת כָּל־הָרְכֻשׁ וְגַם אֶת־לוֹט אָחִיו וּרְכֻשׁוֹ הֵשִׁיב וְגַם אֶת־הַנָּשִׁים וְאֶת־ הָעָם: יז וַיֵּצֵא מֶלֶךְ־סְדֹם לִקְרָאתוֹ אַחֲרֵי שׁוּבוֹ מֵהַכּוֹת אֶת־כְּדָרְלָעֹמֶר וְאֶת־הַמְּלָכִים אֲשֶׁר אִתּוֹ אֶל־עֵמֶק שָׁוֵה הוּא עֵמֶק הַמֶּלֶךְ: יח וּמַלְכִּי־צֶדֶק מֶלֶךְ שָׁלֵם הוֹצִיא לֶחֶם וָיָיִן וְהוּא כֹהֵן לְאֵל עֶלְיוֹן: יט וַיְבָרְכֵהוּ וַיֹּאמַר בָּרוּךְ אַבְרָם לְאֵל עֶלְיוֹן קֹנֵה שָׁמַיִם וָאָרֶץ: כ וּבָרוּךְ אֵל עֶלְיוֹן אֲשֶׁר־מִגֵּן צָרֶיךָ בְּיָדֶךָ וַיִּתֶּן־לוֹ מַעֲשֵׂר מִכֹּל:

חמישי כא וַיֹּאמֶר מֶלֶךְ־סְדֹם אֶל־אַבְרָם תֶּן־לִי הַנֶּפֶשׁ וְהָרְכֻשׁ קַח־לָךְ: כב וַיֹּאמֶר אַבְרָם אֶל־מֶלֶךְ סְדֹם הֲרִמֹתִי יָדִי אֶל־יהוה אֵל עֶלְיוֹן קֹנֵה שָׁמַיִם וָאָרֶץ: כג אִם־מִחוּט וְעַד שְׂרוֹךְ־נַעַל וְאִם־אֶקַּח מִכָּל־ אֲשֶׁר־לָךְ וְלֹא תֹאמַר אֲנִי הֶעֱשַׁרְתִּי אֶת־אַבְרָם: כד בִּלְעָדַי רַק אֲשֶׁר אָכְלוּ הַנְּעָרִים וְחֵלֶק הָאֲנָשִׁים אֲשֶׁר הָלְכוּ אִתִּי עָנֵר אֶשְׁכֹּל וּמַמְרֵא הֵם

◆§ **The war of the kings.** This chapter reveals a new side of Abraham's nature: his physical courage in battle.

14:13. Abraham was called the *Ivri* from the word עֵבֶר, *the other side.* Literally, this means that he came from the other side of the Euphrates. Figuratively, he was on the other side of a moral and spiritual divide from the rest of the world. Alternatively, the name means that he was a descendant of Eber. Only Abraham's descendants are called "Ivrim" for they alone spoke Hebrew, Eber's language. His other descendants spoke Aramaic, and are called Arameans (*Radak*).

14:18. After meeting Abraham at the Valley of Shaveh,

14

The war
of the kings

¹ A nd it happened in the days of Amraphel, king of Shinar; Arioch, king of Ellasar; Chedorlaomer, king of Elam, and Tidal, king of Goiim, ² that these made war on Bera, king of Sodom; Birsha, king of Gomorrah; Shinab, king of Admah; Shemeber, king of Zeboiim; and the king of Bela, which is Zoar. ³ All these had joined at the Valley of Siddim, now the Salt Sea. ⁴ Twelve years they served Chedorlaomer, and they rebelled thirteen years. ⁵ In the fourteenth year, Chedorlaomer and the kings who were with him came and struck the Rephaim at Ashteroth-karnaim, the Zuzim in Ham, the Emim at Shaveh-kiriathaim; ⁶ and the Horites in their mountains of Seir, as far as the Plain of Paran which is by the desert. ⁷ Then they turned back and came to En-mishpat, which is Kadesh; they struck all the territory of the Amalekites; and also the Amorites who dwell in Hazazon-tamar.

⁸ And the king of Sodom went forth with the king of Gomorrah, the king of Admah, the king of Zeboiim and the king of Bela, which is Zoar, and engaged them in battle in the Valley of Siddim: ⁹ With Chedorlaomer, king of Elam; Tidal, king of Goiim; Amraphel, king of Shinar; and Arioch, king of Ellasar — four kings against five.

Sodom is
defeated

¹⁰ The Valley of Siddim was full of bitumen wells. The kings of Sodom and Gomorrah fled and fell into them while the rest fled to a mountain. ¹¹ They seized all the wealth of Sodom and Gomorrah and all their food and they departed.

Lot taken
captive

¹² And they captured Lot and his possessions — Abram's nephew — and they left; for he was residing in Sodom.

¹³ Then there came the fugitive and told Abram, the Ivri, * who dwelt in the plains of Mamre, the Amorite, the brother of Eshcol and the brother of Aner, these being Abram's allies. ¹⁴ And when Abram heard that his kinsman was taken captive, he armed his disciples who had been born in his house — three hundred and eighteen — and he pursued them as far as Dan. ¹⁵ And he with his servants deployed against them at night and struck them; he pursued them as

Abraham
saves Lot

far as Hobah which is to the north of Damascus. ¹⁶ He brought back all the possessions; he also brought back his kinsman, Lot, with his possessions, as well as the women and the people.

¹⁷ The king of Sodom went out to meet him after his return from defeating Chedorlaomer and the kings that were with him, to the Valley of Shaveh which is the king's valley. ¹⁸ But Malchizedek, king of Salem, brought out bread and wine; he was a priest of God, the Most High. ¹⁹ He blessed him saying: "Blessed is Abram of God, the Most High, Maker of heaven and earth; ²⁰ and blessed be God, the Most High, Who has delivered your foes into your hand"; and he gave him a tenth of everything.

²¹ The king of Sodom said to Abram: "Give me the people and take the possessions for yourself."

Abraham
shuns
honors

²² Abram said to the king of Sodom: "I lift up my hand to HASHEM, God, the Most High, Maker of heaven and earth, ²³ if so much as a thread to a shoestrap; or if I shall take from anything of yours! So you shall not say, 'It is I who made Abram rich.' ²⁴ Far from me! Only what the young men have eaten, and the share of the men who accompanied me: Aner, Eshcol, and Mamre — they

---

the king of Sodom escorted him to the city of Salem [= Jerusalem] where they were met by King Malchizedek, whom the Sages identify as Shem, son of Noah. He is

called a *priest of God, the Most High,* because unlike priests of the other nations who served angels, Malchizedek served Hashem (*Ramban*).

טו אַחַר ׀ הַדְּבָרִים הָאֵלֶּה הָיָה דְבַר־יהוה אֶל־אַבְרָם בַּמַּחֲזֶה לֵאמֹר אַל־תִּירָא אַבְרָם אָנֹכִי מָגֵן לָךְ שְׂכָרְךָ הַרְבֵּה מְאֹד:

ב וַיֹּאמֶר אַבְרָם אֲדֹנָי יֱהוִה מַה־תִּתֶּן־לִי וְאָנֹכִי הוֹלֵךְ עֲרִירִי וּבֶן־מֶשֶׁק בֵּיתִי הוּא דַּמֶּשֶׂק אֱלִיעֶזֶר:

ג וַיֹּאמֶר אַבְרָם הֵן לִי לֹא נָתַתָּה זָרַע וְהִנֵּה בֶן־בֵּיתִי יוֹרֵשׁ אֹתִי:

ד וְהִנֵּה דְבַר־יהוה אֵלָיו לֵאמֹר לֹא יִירָשְׁךָ זֶה כִּי־אִם אֲשֶׁר יֵצֵא מִמֵּעֶיךָ הוּא יִירָשֶׁךָ:

ה וַיּוֹצֵא אֹתוֹ הַחוּצָה וַיֹּאמֶר הַבֶּט־נָא הַשָּׁמַיְמָה וּסְפֹר הַכּוֹכָבִים אִם־תּוּכַל לִסְפֹּר אֹתָם וַיֹּאמֶר לוֹ כֹּה יִהְיֶה זַרְעֶךָ:

ו וְהֶאֱמִן בַּיהוה וַיַּחְשְׁבֶהָ לּוֹ צְדָקָה:

ששי ז וַיֹּאמֶר אֵלָיו אֲנִי יהוה אֲשֶׁר הוֹצֵאתִיךָ מֵאוּר כַּשְׂדִּים לָתֶת לְךָ אֶת־הָאָרֶץ הַזֹּאת לְרִשְׁתָּהּ:

ח וַיֹּאמַר אֲדֹנָי יֱהוִה בַּמָּה אֵדַע כִּי אִירָשֶׁנָּה:

ט וַיֹּאמֶר אֵלָיו קְחָה לִי עֶגְלָה מְשֻׁלֶּשֶׁת וְעֵז מְשֻׁלֶּשֶׁת וְאַיִל מְשֻׁלָּשׁ וְתֹר וְגוֹזָל:

י וַיִּקַּח־לוֹ אֶת־כָּל־אֵלֶּה וַיְבַתֵּר אֹתָם בַּתָּוֶךְ וַיִּתֵּן אִישׁ־בִּתְרוֹ לִקְרַאת רֵעֵהוּ וְאֶת־הַצִּפֹּר לֹא בָתָר:

יא וַיֵּרֶד הָעַיִט עַל־הַפְּגָרִים וַיַּשֵּׁב אֹתָם אַבְרָם:

יב וַיְהִי הַשֶּׁמֶשׁ לָבוֹא וְתַרְדֵּמָה נָפְלָה עַל־אַבְרָם וְהִנֵּה אֵימָה חֲשֵׁכָה גְדֹלָה נֹפֶלֶת עָלָיו:

יג וַיֹּאמֶר לְאַבְרָם יָדֹעַ תֵּדַע כִּי־גֵר ׀ יִהְיֶה זַרְעֲךָ בְּאֶרֶץ לֹא לָהֶם וַעֲבָדוּם וְעִנּוּ אֹתָם אַרְבַּע מֵאוֹת שָׁנָה:

יד וְגַם אֶת־הַגּוֹי אֲשֶׁר יַעֲבֹדוּ דָּן אָנֹכִי וְאַחֲרֵי־כֵן יֵצְאוּ בִּרְכֻשׁ גָּדוֹל:

טו וְאַתָּה תָּבוֹא אֶל־אֲבֹתֶיךָ בְּשָׁלוֹם תִּקָּבֵר בְּשֵׂיבָה טוֹבָה:

טז וְדוֹר רְבִיעִי יָשׁוּבוּ הֵנָּה כִּי לֹא־שָׁלֵם עֲוֹן הָאֱמֹרִי עַד־הֵנָּה:

יז וַיְהִי הַשֶּׁמֶשׁ בָּאָה וַעֲלָטָה הָיָה וְהִנֵּה תַנּוּר עָשָׁן וְלַפִּיד אֵשׁ אֲשֶׁר עָבַר בֵּין הַגְּזָרִים הָאֵלֶּה:

יח בַּיּוֹם הַהוּא כָּרַת יהוה אֶת־אַבְרָם בְּרִית לֵאמֹר לְזַרְעֲךָ נָתַתִּי אֶת־הָאָרֶץ הַזֹּאת מִנְּהַר מִצְרַיִם עַד־הַנָּהָר הַגָּדֹל נְהַר־פְּרָת:

יט-כ אֶת־הַקֵּינִי וְאֶת־הַקְּנִזִּי וְאֵת הַקַּדְמֹנִי: וְאֶת־הַחִתִּי וְאֶת־הַפְּרִזִּי וְאֶת־הָרְפָאִים:

כא וְאֶת־הָאֱמֹרִי וְאֶת־הַכְּנַעֲנִי וְאֶת־הַגִּרְגָּשִׁי וְאֶת־הַיְבוּסִי:

טז א וְשָׂרַי אֵשֶׁת אַבְרָם לֹא יָלְדָה לוֹ וְלָהּ שִׁפְחָה מִצְרִית וּשְׁמָהּ הָגָר:

ב וַתֹּאמֶר שָׂרַי אֶל־אַבְרָם הִנֵּה־נָא עֲצָרַנִי יהוה מִלֶּדֶת בֹּא־נָא אֶל־שִׁפְחָתִי אוּלַי אִבָּנֶה מִמֶּנָּה וַיִּשְׁמַע אַבְרָם לְקוֹל שָׂרָי:

15:2. This is an unusual combination of Divine Names. Abraham addressed God as *my Lord,* indicating complete obedience and acknowledgment of His mastery, and the Sages comment that he was the first person ever to refer to God as *Adon* [*Master*] (*Berachos* 7b). The second Name in our verse, HASHEM/ELOHIM, is spelled like the Four-letter Name, but punctuated and pronounced *Elohim*. This usage combines the Names that refer respectively to mercy and judgment. By this combination, Abraham was saying that God is merciful even in judgment (*Rashi, Deuteronomy* 3:24, according to *Mizrachi*).

15:8. Abraham thought that the promise of the land was conditional on the righteousness of himself and his offspring, and he feared that he was not worthy to receive it and that his descendants might sin and become unwor-

thy to retain it (*Rashi; Mizrachi; Gur Aryeh, Maharzu*).

15:10. Abraham cut the animals into two parts and walked between them. In those days, the partners to a covenant passed between the severed parts to symbolize their acceptance of the new pact.

15:13. There would be a total of four hundred years of alien status, in which would be included the two hundred ten years of literal exile in Egypt, and also the twenty years that Jacob spent with Laban in Haran. The *servitude* mentioned in this prophecy took place during the last one hundred sixteen years of the Egyptian servitude, the last eighty-six years of which were a time of harsh *oppression*, when Pharaoh intensified the suffering of the Jews. The calculation of the four hundred years would begin thirty years after this vision, with the birth of *will take their portion."*

15

God's reassurance to Abraham

¹ **A**fter these events, the word of HASHEM came to Abram in a vision, saying, "Fear not, Abram, I am a shield for you; your reward is very great."
² And Abram said, "My Lord, HASHEM/ELOHIM:* What can You give me seeing that I go childless, and the steward of my house is the Damascene Eliezer?"

³ Then Abram said, "See, to me You have given no offspring; and see, my steward inherits me . . ."

⁴ Suddenly, the word of HASHEM came to him, saying: "That one will not inherit you. Only he that shall come forth from within you shall inherit you."
⁵ And He took him outside, and said, "Gaze, now, toward the Heavens, and count the stars if you are able to count them!" And He said to him, "So shall your offspring be!" ⁶ And he trusted in HASHEM, and He reckoned it to him as righteousness.

The Covenant Between the Parts: The promise of the land

⁷ He said to him, "I am HASHEM Who brought you out of Ur Kasdim to give you this land to inherit it."
⁸ He said, "My Lord, HASHEM/ELOHIM: Whereby shall I know that I am to inherit it?"*
⁹ And He said to him, "Take to Me three heifers, three goats, three rams, a turtledove, and a young dove." ¹⁰ He took all these to Him: he cut them in the center, and placed each piece opposite its counterpart. The birds, however, he did not cut up.

¹¹ Birds of prey descended upon the carcasses, and Abram drove them away.
¹² And it happened, as the sun was about to set, a deep sleep fell upon Abram; and behold — a dread! great darkness fell upon him.

Egyptian exile and redemption

¹³ And He said to Abram, "Know with certainty that your offspring shall be aliens* in a land not their own — and they will serve them, and they will oppress them — four hundred years. ¹⁴ But also the nation that they will serve, I shall judge, and afterwards they will leave with great wealth. ¹⁵ As for you: you shall come to your ancestors in peace; you shall be buried in a good old age. ¹⁶ And the fourth generation shall return here, for the iniquity of the Amorite shall not yet be full until then."

The ratification of the covenant

¹⁷ So it happened: The sun set, and it was very dark. Behold — there was a smoky furnace and a torch of fire which passed between these pieces. ¹⁸ On that day HASHEM made a covenant with Abram, saying, "To your descendants have I given this land, from the river of Egypt to the great river, the Euphrates River: ¹⁹ the Kennite, the Kenizzite, and the Kadmonite; ²⁰ the Hittite, the Perizzite, and the Rephaim; ²¹ the Amorite, the Canaanite, the Girgashite, and the Jebusite."

16

¹ **N**ow Sarai, Abram's wife, had borne him no children. She had an Egyptian maidservant whose name was Hagar. ² And Sarai said to Abram, "See, now, HASHEM has restrained me from bearing; consort, now, with my maidservant, perhaps I will be built up through her." And Abram heeded the voice of Sarai.

Isaac; since he never had the permanent home or the prestige and honor enjoyed by Abraham, he and his offspring were considered aliens, even during the years that they lived in *Eretz Yisrael*. After those four hundred years, Abraham's offspring would be able to take possession of the land.

ג וַתִּקַּ֞ח שָׂרַ֣י אֵֽשֶׁת־אַבְרָ֗ם אֶת־הָגָ֤ר הַמִּצְרִית֙ שִׁפְחָתָ֔הּ מִקֵּץ֙ עֶ֣שֶׂר שָׁנִ֔ים
ד לְשֶׁ֥בֶת אַבְרָ֖ם בְּאֶ֣רֶץ כְּנָ֑עַן וַתִּתֵּ֥ן אֹתָ֛הּ לְאַבְרָ֥ם אִישָׁ֖הּ ל֥וֹ לְאִשָּֽׁה: וַיָּבֹ֤א
ה אֶל־הָגָ֖ר וַתַּ֑הַר וַתֵּ֙רֶא֙ כִּ֣י הָרָ֔תָה וַתֵּקַ֥ל גְּבִרְתָּ֖הּ בְּעֵינֶֽיהָ: וַתֹּ֨אמֶר שָׂרַ֣י אֶל־
אַבְרָם֮ חֲמָסִ֣י עָלֶ֒יךָ֒ אָנֹכִ֗י נָתַ֤תִּי שִׁפְחָתִי֙ בְּחֵיקֶ֔ךָ וַתֵּ֙רֶא֙ כִּ֣י הָרָ֔תָה וָאֵקַ֖ל
ו בְּעֵינֶ֑יהָ יִשְׁפֹּ֥ט יְהוָֹ֖ה בֵּינִ֥י *וּבֵינֶֽיךָ: וַיֹּ֨אמֶר אַבְרָ֜ם אֶל־שָׂרַ֗י הִנֵּ֤ה שִׁפְחָתֵךְ֙

*נקוד על י
בתרא

ז בְּיָדֵ֔ךְ עֲשִׂי־לָ֖הּ הַטּ֣וֹב בְּעֵינָ֑יִךְ וַתְּעַנֶּ֣הָ שָׂרַ֔י וַתִּבְרַ֖ח מִפָּנֶֽיהָ: וַֽיִּמְצָאָ֞הּ מַלְאַ֧ךְ
ח יְהוָֹ֛ה עַל־עֵ֥ין הַמַּ֖יִם בַּמִּדְבָּ֑ר עַל־הָעַ֖יִן בְּדֶ֥רֶךְ שֽׁוּר: וַיֹּאמַ֗ר הָגָ֞ר שִׁפְחַ֥ת
שָׂרַ֛י אֵֽי־מִזֶּ֥ה בָ֖את וְאָ֣נָה תֵלֵ֑כִי וַתֹּ֕אמֶר מִפְּנֵי֙ שָׂרַ֣י גְּבִרְתִּ֔י אָנֹכִ֖י בֹּרַֽחַת:
ט וַיֹּ֤אמֶר לָהּ֙ מַלְאַ֣ךְ יְהוָֹ֔ה שׁ֖וּבִי אֶל־גְּבִרְתֵּ֑ךְ וְהִתְעַנִּ֖י תַּ֥חַת יָדֶֽיהָ: וַיֹּ֤אמֶר לָהּ֙
י מַלְאַ֣ךְ יְהוָֹ֔ה הַרְבָּ֥ה אַרְבֶּ֖ה אֶת־זַרְעֵ֑ךְ וְלֹ֥א יִסָּפֵ֖ר מֵרֹֽב: וַיֹּ֥אמֶר לָ֛הּ מַלְאַ֥ךְ
יא יְהוָֹ֖ה הִנָּ֣ךְ הָרָ֑ה וְיֹלַ֣דְתְּ בֵּ֔ן וְקָרָ֥את שְׁמוֹ֙ יִשְׁמָעֵ֔אל כִּֽי־שָׁמַ֥ע יְהוָֹ֖ה אֶל־עָנְיֵֽךְ:
יב-יג וְה֤וּא יִֽהְיֶה֙ פֶּ֣רֶא אָדָ֔ם יָד֣וֹ בַכֹּ֔ל וְיַ֥ד כֹּ֖ל בּ֑וֹ וְעַל־פְּנֵ֥י כָל־אֶחָ֖יו יִשְׁכֹּֽן: וַתִּקְרָ֤א
שֵׁם־יְהוָֹה֙ הַדֹּבֵ֣ר אֵלֶ֔יהָ אַתָּ֖ה אֵ֣ל רֳאִ֑י כִּ֣י אָֽמְרָ֗ה הֲגַ֥ם הֲלֹ֛ם רָאִ֖יתִי
יד אַחֲרֵ֥י רֹאִֽי: עַל־כֵּן֙ קָרָ֣א לַבְּאֵ֔ר בְּאֵ֥ר לַחַ֖י רֹאִ֑י הִנֵּ֥ה בֵֽין־קָדֵ֖שׁ וּבֵ֥ין
טו בָּֽרֶד: וַתֵּ֧לֶד הָגָ֛ר לְאַבְרָ֖ם בֵּ֑ן וַיִּקְרָ֨א אַבְרָ֧ם שֶׁם־בְּנ֛וֹ אֲשֶׁר־יָלְדָ֥ה הָגָ֖ר
טז יִשְׁמָעֵֽאל: וְאַבְרָ֕ם בֶּן־שְׁמֹנִ֥ים שָׁנָ֖ה וְשֵׁ֣שׁ שָׁנִ֑ים בְּלֶֽדֶת־הָגָ֥ר אֶת־יִשְׁמָעֵ֖אל
א לְאַבְרָֽם: וַיְהִ֣י אַבְרָ֔ם בֶּן־תִּשְׁעִ֥ים שָׁנָ֖ה וְתֵ֣שַׁע שָׁנִ֑ים וַיֵּרָ֨א

יז

יְהוָֹ֜ה אֶל־אַבְרָ֗ם וַיֹּ֤אמֶר אֵלָיו֙ אֲנִי־אֵ֣ל שַׁדַּ֔י הִתְהַלֵּ֥ךְ לְפָנַ֖י וֶהְיֵ֥ה תָמִֽים:
ב-ג וְאֶתְּנָ֥ה בְרִיתִ֖י בֵּינִ֣י וּבֵינֶ֑ךָ וְאַרְבֶּ֥ה אֽוֹתְךָ֖ בִּמְאֹ֥ד מְאֹֽד: וַיִּפֹּ֥ל אַבְרָ֖ם עַל־פָּנָ֑יו
ד וַיְדַבֵּ֥ר אִתּ֖וֹ אֱלֹהִ֥ים לֵאמֹֽר: אֲנִ֕י הִנֵּ֥ה בְרִיתִ֖י אִתָּ֑ךְ וְהָיִ֔יתָ לְאַ֖ב הֲמ֥וֹן גּוֹיִֽם:
ה וְלֹֽא־יִקָּרֵ֥א ע֛וֹד אֶת־שִׁמְךָ֖ אַבְרָ֑ם וְהָיָ֤ה שִׁמְךָ֙ אַבְרָהָ֔ם כִּ֛י אַב־הֲמ֥וֹן גּוֹיִ֖ם
ו נְתַתִּֽיךָ: וְהִפְרֵתִ֤י אֹֽתְךָ֙ בִּמְאֹ֣ד מְאֹ֔ד וּנְתַתִּ֖יךָ לְגוֹיִ֑ם וּמְלָכִ֖ים מִמְּךָ֥ יֵצֵֽאוּ:
ז וַהֲקִמֹתִ֨י אֶת־בְּרִיתִ֜י בֵּינִ֣י וּבֵינֶ֗ךָ וּבֵ֨ין זַרְעֲךָ֧ אַחֲרֶ֛יךָ לְדֹֽרֹתָ֖ם לִבְרִ֣ית עוֹלָ֑ם

שביעי

ח לִֽהְי֤וֹת לְךָ֙ לֵֽאלֹהִ֔ים וּֽלְזַרְעֲךָ֖ אַחֲרֶֽיךָ: וְנָתַתִּ֣י לְ֠ךָ וּלְזַרְעֲךָ֨ אַחֲרֶ֜יךָ אֵ֣ת |
אֶ֣רֶץ מְגֻרֶ֗יךָ אֵ֚ת כָּל־אֶ֣רֶץ כְּנַ֔עַן לַאֲחֻזַּ֖ת עוֹלָ֑ם וְהָיִ֥יתִי לָהֶ֖ם לֵֽאלֹהִֽים:
ט וַיֹּ֤אמֶר אֱלֹהִים֙ אֶל־אַבְרָהָ֔ם וְאַתָּ֖ה אֶת־בְּרִיתִ֣י תִשְׁמֹ֑ר אַתָּ֛ה וְזַרְעֲךָ֥
י אַֽחֲרֶ֖יךָ לְדֹֽרֹתָֽם: זֹ֣את בְּרִיתִ֞י אֲשֶׁ֣ר תִּשְׁמְר֗וּ בֵּינִי֙ וּבֵ֣ינֵיכֶ֔ם וּבֵ֥ין זַרְעֲךָ֖

⊰ঙ The birth of Ishmael. Hagar was a daughter of
Pharaoh. After seeing the miracles that were wrought on
Sarah's behalf when she was abducted and taken to his
palace, he gave Hagar to Sarah, saying, "Better that she
be a servant in their house than a princess in someone
else's." So it was that Hagar, an Egyptian princess, became Abraham's wife and bore him Ishmael (*Midrash;
Rashi*).

Recognizing that it was she who was infertile, Sarah
suggested that Abraham marry her maidservant Hagar,
and, if a son were born, Sarah would raise him, so that he
would be considered her adopted child.

⊰ঙ The covenant of circumcision: new names and a new

destiny. The year was 2047 from Creation; Abraham was
ninety-nine years old, Sarah eighty-nine, and Ishmael
thirteen. At this advanced age Abraham was given the
commandment of circumcision, one of his ten trials.
Despite his age and the difficulty of performing the hith-
erto unknown operation, he did not hesitate to comply.

17:5. God changed Abram's name to *Abraham,* a contraction representing his new status as *av hamon* —
father of a multitude — whereas the name Avram represented his former status as only *av Aram* — father of
Aram, his native country.

17:9-14. The covenant of circumcision. From the sequence of this chapter, it is clear that the blessings of

Hagar and Ishmael

³ So Sarai, Abram's wife, took Hagar the Egyptian, her maidservant — after ten years of Abram's dwelling in the land of Canaan — and gave her to Abram her husband, to him as a wife. ⁴ He consorted with Hagar and she conceived; and when she saw that she had conceived, her mistress was lowered in her esteem. ⁵ So Sarai said to Abram, "The outrage against me is due to you! It was I who gave my maidservant into your bosom, and when she saw that she had conceived, I became lowered in her esteem. Let HASHEM judge between me and you!"

⁶ Abram said to Sarai, "Behold! — your maidservant is in your hand; do to her as you see fit." And Sarai dealt harshly with her, so she fled from her.

⁷ An angel of HASHEM found her by the spring of water in the desert, at the spring on the road to Shur. ⁸ And he said, "Hagar, maidservant of Sarai, where have you come from and where are you going?" And she said, "I am running away from Sarai my mistress."

⁹ And an angel of HASHEM said to her, "Return to your mistress, and submit yourself to her domination."

¹⁰ And an angel of HASHEM said to her, "I will greatly increase your offspring, and they will not be counted for abundance."

¹¹ And an angel of HASHEM said to her, "Behold, you will conceive, and give birth to a son; you shall name him Ishmael, for HASHEM has heard your prayer. ¹² And he shall be a wild-ass of a man: his hand against everyone, and everyone's hand against him; and over all his brothers shall he dwell."

¹³ And she called the Name of HASHEM Who spoke to her "You are the God of Vision," for she said, "Could I have seen even here after having seen?" ¹⁴ Therefore the well was called "The Well of the Living One Appearing to Me." It is between Kadesh and Bered.

¹⁵ Hagar bore Abram a son and Abram called the name of his son that Hagar bore him Ishmael. ¹⁶ And Abram was eighty-six years old when Hagar bore Ishmael to Abram.

17

The covenant

¹ When Abram was ninety-nine years old, HASHEM appeared to Abram and said to him, "I am El Shaddai; walk before Me and be perfect. ² I will set My covenant between Me and you, and I will increase you most exceedingly."
³ Abram threw himself upon his face, and God spoke with him saying, ⁴ "As for Me, this is My covenant with you: You shall be a father of a multitude of nations;

New names and a new destiny

⁵ your name shall no longer be called Abram, but your name shall be Abraham, for I have made you the father of a multitude of nations; ⁶ I will make you most exceedingly fruitful, and make nations of you; and kings shall descend from you. ⁷ I will ratify My covenant between Me and you and between your offspring after you, throughout their generations, as an everlasting covenant, to be a God to you and to your offspring after you; ⁸ and I will give to you and to your offspring after you the land of your sojourns — the whole of the land of Canaan — as an everlasting possession; and I shall be a God to them."

⁹ God said to Abraham, "And as for you, you shall keep My covenant — you and your offspring after you throughout their generations. ¹⁰ This is My covenant which you shall keep between Me and you and your offspring

---

children and possession of the land depended on circumcision, a connection that is also implied in the second blessing of the Grace After Meals. Although this concept is beyond human understanding, circumcision is a means to help the Jew ennoble himself and return to the spiritual state of Adam before his sin.

יא אַחֲרֵיךֶ הִמּוֹל לָכֶם כָּל־זָכָר: וּנְמַלְתֶּם אֵת בְּשַׂר עָרְלַתְכֶם וְהָיָה לְאוֹת
יב בְּרִית בֵּינִי וּבֵינֵיכֶם: וּבֶן־שְׁמֹנַת יָמִים יִמּוֹל לָכֶם כָּל־זָכָר לְדֹרֹתֵיכֶם יְלִיד
יג בָּיִת וּמִקְנַת־כֶּסֶף מִכֹּל בֶּן־נֵכָר אֲשֶׁר לֹא מִזַּרְעֲךָ הוּא: הִמּוֹל ׀ יִמּוֹל יְלִיד
יד בֵּיתְךָ וּמִקְנַת כַּסְפֶּךָ וְהָיְתָה בְרִיתִי בִּבְשַׂרְכֶם לִבְרִית עוֹלָם: וְעָרֵל ׀ זָכָר
אֲשֶׁר לֹא־יִמּוֹל אֶת־בְּשַׂר עָרְלָתוֹ וְנִכְרְתָה הַנֶּפֶשׁ הַהִוא מֵעַמֶּיהָ אֶת־
טו בְּרִיתִי הֵפַר: וַיֹּאמֶר אֱלֹהִים אֶל־אַבְרָהָם שָׂרַי אִשְׁתְּךָ לֹא־
טז תִקְרָא אֶת־שְׁמָהּ שָׂרָי כִּי שָׂרָה שְׁמָהּ: וּבֵרַכְתִּי אֹתָהּ וְגַם נָתַתִּי מִמֶּנָּה לְךָ
יז בֵּן וּבֵרַכְתִּיהָ וְהָיְתָה לְגוֹיִם מַלְכֵי עַמִּים מִמֶּנָּה יִהְיוּ: וַיִּפֹּל אַבְרָהָם עַל־פָּנָיו
וַיִּצְחָק וַיֹּאמֶר בְּלִבּוֹ הַלְּבֶן מֵאָה־שָׁנָה יִוָּלֵד וְאִם־שָׂרָה הֲבַת־תִּשְׁעִים שָׁנָה
יח־יט תֵּלֵד: וַיֹּאמֶר אַבְרָהָם אֶל־הָאֱלֹהִים לוּ יִשְׁמָעֵאל יִחְיֶה לְפָנֶיךָ: וַיֹּאמֶר
אֱלֹהִים אֲבָל שָׂרָה אִשְׁתְּךָ יֹלֶדֶת לְךָ בֵּן וְקָרָאתָ אֶת־שְׁמוֹ יִצְחָק וַהֲקִמֹתִי
כ אֶת־בְּרִיתִי אִתּוֹ לִבְרִית עוֹלָם לְזַרְעוֹ אַחֲרָיו: וּלְיִשְׁמָעֵאל שְׁמַעְתִּיךָ
הִנֵּה ׀ בֵּרַכְתִּי אֹתוֹ וְהִפְרֵיתִי אֹתוֹ וְהִרְבֵּיתִי אֹתוֹ בִּמְאֹד מְאֹד שְׁנֵים־עָשָׂר
כא נְשִׂיאִם יוֹלִיד וּנְתַתִּיו לְגוֹי גָּדוֹל: וְאֶת־בְּרִיתִי אָקִים אֶת־יִצְחָק אֲשֶׁר תֵּלֵד
כב לְךָ שָׂרָה לַמּוֹעֵד הַזֶּה בַּשָּׁנָה הָאַחֶרֶת: וַיְכַל לְדַבֵּר אִתּוֹ וַיַּעַל אֱלֹהִים מֵעַל
כג אַבְרָהָם: וַיִּקַּח אַבְרָהָם אֶת־יִשְׁמָעֵאל בְּנוֹ וְאֵת כָּל־יְלִידֵי בֵיתוֹ וְאֵת כָּל־
מִקְנַת כַּסְפּוֹ כָּל־זָכָר בְּאַנְשֵׁי בֵּית אַבְרָהָם וַיָּמָל אֶת־בְּשַׂר עָרְלָתָם
כד בְּעֶצֶם הַיּוֹם הַזֶּה כַּאֲשֶׁר דִּבֶּר אִתּוֹ אֱלֹהִים: וְאַבְרָהָם בֶּן־תִּשְׁעִים וָתֵשַׁע
כה שָׁנָה בְּהִמֹּלוֹ בְּשַׂר עָרְלָתוֹ: וְיִשְׁמָעֵאל בְּנוֹ בֶּן־שְׁלֹשׁ עֶשְׂרֵה שָׁנָה בְּהִמֹּלוֹ
כו אֵת בְּשַׂר עָרְלָתוֹ: בְּעֶצֶם הַיּוֹם הַזֶּה נִמּוֹל אַבְרָהָם וְיִשְׁמָעֵאל בְּנוֹ:
כז וְכָל־אַנְשֵׁי בֵיתוֹ יְלִיד בָּיִת וּמִקְנַת־כֶּסֶף מֵאֵת בֶּן־נֵכָר נִמֹּלוּ אִתּוֹ: פפפ

קכ"ו פסוקים. נמל"ו סימן. מכנדב"י סימן.

פרשת וירא

יח א וַיֵּרָא אֵלָיו יהוה בְּאֵלֹנֵי מַמְרֵא וְהוּא יֹשֵׁב פֶּתַח־הָאֹהֶל כְּחֹם הַיּוֹם:
ב וַיִּשָּׂא עֵינָיו וַיַּרְא וְהִנֵּה שְׁלֹשָׁה אֲנָשִׁים נִצָּבִים עָלָיו וַיַּרְא וַיָּרָץ
לִקְרָאתָם מִפֶּתַח הָאֹהֶל וַיִּשְׁתַּחוּ אָרְצָה: וַיֹּאמַר אֲדֹנָי אִם־נָא מָצָאתִי
ג חֵן בְּעֵינֶיךָ אַל־נָא תַעֲבֹר מֵעַל עַבְדֶּךָ: יֻקַּח־נָא מְעַט־מַיִם וְרַחֲצוּ
ד רַגְלֵיכֶם וְהִשָּׁעֲנוּ תַּחַת הָעֵץ: וְאֶקְחָה פַת־לֶחֶם וְסַעֲדוּ לִבְּכֶם אַחַר
ה תַּעֲבֹרוּ כִּי־עַל־כֵּן עֲבַרְתֶּם עַל־עַבְדְּכֶם וַיֹּאמְרוּ כֵּן תַּעֲשֶׂה כַּאֲשֶׁר

מפטיר

Haftaras
Lech
Lecha:
p. 1022

17:14. An adult who intentionally remains uncircumcised suffers כָּרֵת, *spiritual excision,* meaning that the soul loses its share in the World to Come, and the violator may die childless and prematurely.

17:15. *Sarai, my* princess, implies that she owed her greatness to her status as Abraham's wife. Henceforth, she would be called *Sarah,* which signifies that she is a "*princess* to all the nations of the world." She was princess

"par excellence" — to all mankind (*Rashi; Berachos* 13a). **17:17.** Abraham's laughter was not skeptical but jubilant; it came from sheer joy at the news that Sarah would bear a son. *Onkelos* renders וַחֲדִי, *and he rejoiced.* In the case of Sarah, however [see 18:12], *Onkelos* rendered the verb וַתִּצְחָק as וְחַיְכָת, *she laughed,* a translation that is supported by the context of that passage. Abraham had faith and *rejoiced,* while Sarah was skeptical and *laughed;*

after you: Every male among you shall be circumcised. [11] You shall circumcise the flesh of your foreskin, and that shall be the sign of the covenant between Me and you. [12] At the age of eight days every male among you shall be circumcised, throughout your generations — he that is born in the household or purchased with money from any stranger who is not of your offspring. [13] He that is born in your household or purchased with your money shall surely be circumcised. Thus, My covenant shall be in your flesh for an everlasting covenant. [14] An uncircumcised male who will not circumcise the flesh of his foreskin — that soul shall be cut off from its people; * he has invalidated My covenant."

The promise to Sarah

[15] And God said to Abraham, "As for Sarai your wife — do not call her name Sarai, for Sarah is her name. * [16] I will bless her; indeed, I will give you a son through her; I will bless her and she shall give rise to nations; kings of peoples will rise from her."

[17] And Abraham threw himself upon his face and laughed; * and he thought, "Shall a child be born to a hundred-year-old man? And shall Sarah — a ninety-year-old woman — give birth?" [18] And Abraham said to God, "O that Ishmael might live before You!" [19] God said, "Nonetheless, your wife Sarah will bear you a son and you shall call his name Isaac; and I will fulfill My covenant with him as an everlasting covenant for his offspring after him. [20] But regarding Ishmael I have heard you: I have blessed him, will make him fruitful, and will increase him most exceedingly; he will beget twelve princes and I will make him into a great nation. [21] But I will maintain My covenant through Isaac whom Sarah will bear to you by this time next year." [22] And when He had finished speaking with him, God ascended from upon Abraham.

[23] Then Abraham took his son Ishmael and all those servants born in his household and all those he had purchased for money — all the male members of Abraham's house — and he circumcised the flesh of their foreskin on that very day as God had spoken with him. [24] Abraham was ninety-nine years old when he was circumcised on the flesh of his foreskin; [25] and his son Ishmael was thirteen years old when he was circumcised on the flesh of his foreskin. [26] On that very day was Abraham circumcised with Ishmael his son, [27] and all the people of his household, born in his household and purchased for money from a stranger, were circumcised with him.

PARASHAS VAYEIRA

18

Visiting the sick and hospitality to strangers

[1] HASHEM appeared to him in the plains of Mamre while he was sitting at the entrance of the tent in the heat of the day. [2] He lifted his eyes and saw: And behold! three men * were standing over him. He perceived, so he ran toward them from the entrance of the tent, and bowed toward the ground. [3] And he said, "My Lord, if I find favor in Your eyes, please pass not away from Your servant." [4] "Let some water be brought and wash your feet, and recline beneath the tree. [5] I will fetch a morsel of bread that you may sustain yourselves, then go on — inasmuch as you have passed your servant's way." They said, "Do so, just as

---

hence, God was angry only with Sarah (Rashi).

◈§ Parashas Vayeira

18:1-8. God visited Abraham to show him honor for having carried out the commandment and to acknowledge that he had thereby elevated himself to a new spiritual plateau. As if to show what it was about Abraham

that made him so uniquely worthy to be the spiritual father of all mankind, the Torah relates what he did on the third day after his circumcision, when the wound is most painful and the patient most weakened.

18:2. As is apparent from the rest of the narrative, these three men were actually angels in the "guise" of men.

ו דְּבָרְךָ: וַיְמַהֵר אַבְרָהָם הָאֹהֱלָה אֶל־שָׂרָה וַיֹּאמֶר מַהֲרִי שְׁלֹשׁ סְאִים

ז קֶמַח סֹלֶת לוּשִׁי וַעֲשִׂי עֻגוֹת: וְאֶל־הַבָּקָר רָץ אַבְרָהָם וַיִּקַּח בֶּן־בָּקָר

ח רַךְ וָטוֹב וַיִּתֵּן אֶל־הַנַּעַר וַיְמַהֵר לַעֲשׂוֹת אֹתוֹ: וַיִּקַּח חֶמְאָה וְחָלָב וּבֶן־
הַבָּקָר אֲשֶׁר עָשָׂה וַיִּתֵּן לִפְנֵיהֶם וְהוּא־עֹמֵד עֲלֵיהֶם תַּחַת הָעֵץ וַיֹּאכֵלוּ:

ט נקוד על איו* וַיֹּאמְרוּ *אֵלָיו אַיֵּה שָׂרָה אִשְׁתֶּךָ וַיֹּאמֶר הִנֵּה בָאֹהֶל: וַיֹּאמֶר שׁוֹב אָשׁוּב
אֵלֶיךָ כָּעֵת חַיָּה וְהִנֵּה־בֵן לְשָׂרָה אִשְׁתֶּךָ וְשָׂרָה שֹׁמַעַת פֶּתַח הָאֹהֶל

יא וְהוּא אַחֲרָיו: וְאַבְרָהָם וְשָׂרָה זְקֵנִים בָּאִים בַּיָּמִים חָדַל לִהְיוֹת לְשָׂרָה

יב אֹרַח כַּנָּשִׁים: וַתִּצְחַק שָׂרָה בְּקִרְבָּהּ לֵאמֹר אַחֲרֵי בְלֹתִי הָיְתָה־לִּי

יג עֶדְנָה וַאדֹנִי זָקֵן: וַיֹּאמֶר יְהוָה אֶל־אַבְרָהָם לָמָּה זֶּה צָחֲקָה שָׂרָה לֵאמֹר

יד הַאַף אֻמְנָם אֵלֵד וַאֲנִי זָקַנְתִּי: הֲיִפָּלֵא מֵיהוָה דָּבָר לַמּוֹעֵד אָשׁוּב אֵלֶיךָ

טו שני כָּעֵת חַיָּה וּלְשָׂרָה בֵן: וַתְּכַחֵשׁ שָׂרָה ׀ לֵאמֹר לֹא צָחַקְתִּי כִּי ׀ יָרֵאָה

טז וַיֹּאמֶר ׀ לֹא כִּי צָחָקְתְּ: וַיָּקֻמוּ מִשָּׁם הָאֲנָשִׁים וַיַּשְׁקִפוּ עַל־פְּנֵי סְדֹם
וְאַבְרָהָם הֹלֵךְ עִמָּם לְשַׁלְּחָם: וַיהוָה אָמָר הַמְכַסֶּה אֲנִי מֵאַבְרָהָם אֲשֶׁר

יח אֲנִי עֹשֶׂה: וְאַבְרָהָם הָיוֹ יִהְיֶה לְגוֹי גָּדוֹל וְעָצוּם וְנִבְרְכוּ־בוֹ כֹּל גּוֹיֵי

יט הָאָרֶץ: כִּי יְדַעְתִּיו לְמַעַן אֲשֶׁר יְצַוֶּה אֶת־בָּנָיו וְאֶת־בֵּיתוֹ אַחֲרָיו וְשָׁמְרוּ
דֶּרֶךְ יְהוָה לַעֲשׂוֹת צְדָקָה וּמִשְׁפָּט לְמַעַן הָבִיא יְהוָה עַל־אַבְרָהָם אֵת

כ אֲשֶׁר־דִּבֶּר עָלָיו: וַיֹּאמֶר יְהוָה זַעֲקַת סְדֹם וַעֲמֹרָה כִּי־רָבָּה וְחַטָּאתָם

כא כִּי כָבְדָה מְאֹד: אֵרֲדָה־נָּא וְאֶרְאֶה הַכְּצַעֲקָתָהּ הַבָּאָה אֵלַי ׀ עָשׂוּ ׀

כב כָּלָה וְאִם־לֹא אֵדָעָה: וַיִּפְנוּ מִשָּׁם הָאֲנָשִׁים וַיֵּלְכוּ סְדֹמָה וְאַבְרָהָם

כג עוֹדֶנּוּ עֹמֵד לִפְנֵי יְהוָה: וַיִּגַּשׁ אַבְרָהָם וַיֹּאמַר הַאַף תִּסְפֶּה צַדִּיק עִם־

כד רָשָׁע: אוּלַי יֵשׁ חֲמִשִּׁים צַדִּיקִם בְּתוֹךְ הָעִיר הַאַף תִּסְפֶּה וְלֹא־תִשָּׂא

כה לַמָּקוֹם לְמַעַן חֲמִשִּׁים הַצַּדִּיקִם אֲשֶׁר בְּקִרְבָּהּ: חָלִלָה לְּךָ ׀ מֵעֲשֹׂת ׀
כַּדָּבָר הַזֶּה לְהָמִית צַדִּיק עִם־רָשָׁע וְהָיָה כַצַּדִּיק כָּרָשָׁע חָלִלָה לָּךְ

כו הֲשֹׁפֵט כָּל־הָאָרֶץ לֹא יַעֲשֶׂה מִשְׁפָּט: וַיֹּאמֶר יְהוָה אִם־אֶמְצָא בִסְדֹם

כז חֲמִשִּׁים צַדִּיקִם בְּתוֹךְ הָעִיר וְנָשָׂאתִי לְכָל־הַמָּקוֹם בַּעֲבוּרָם: וַיַּעַן
אַבְרָהָם וַיֹּאמַר הִנֵּה־נָא הוֹאַלְתִּי לְדַבֵּר אֶל־אֲדֹנָי וְאָנֹכִי עָפָר וָאֵפֶר:

כח אוּלַי* יַחְסְרוּן חֲמִשִּׁים הַצַּדִּיקִם חֲמִשָּׁה הֲתַשְׁחִית בַּחֲמִשָּׁה אֶת־
כָּל־הָעִיר וַיֹּאמֶר לֹא אַשְׁחִית אִם־אֶמְצָא שָׁם אַרְבָּעִים וַחֲמִשָּׁה:

18:8. Angels do not eat in the human sense; they only appeared to do so. This teaches that one should not deviate from the local custom (*Rashi*).

18:11. They reached their old age with a rich harvest of days that truly mattered.

18:12. Sarah laughed in disbelief because she thought that the guest's statement was simply a courteous but meaningless blessing, not a prophecy from God (*Radak; Sforno*). Although she did not know this truly was a message from God Himself, He was angered at her reaction, for a person of her great stature should have had faith that the miracle of birth *could* happen. She should at least have said, "Amen, may it be so."

18:13. Her actual words in verse 12 were וַאדֹנִי זָקֵן, *my husband is old,* but for the sake of peace between husband and wife, Scripture [i.e., God] now changed the uncomplimentary reference from her husband to herself — וַאֲנִי זָקַנְתִּי (*Rashi*).

you have said."

⁶ So Abraham hastened to the tent to Sarah and said, "Hurry! Three se'ahs of meal, fine flour! Knead and make cakes!" ⁷ Then Abraham ran to the cattle, took a calf, tender and good, and gave it to the youth who hurried to prepare it. ⁸ He took cream and milk and the calf which he had prepared, and placed these before them; he stood over them beneath the tree and they ate. *

⁹ They said to him, "Where is Sarah your wife?" And he said, "Behold! — in the tent!"

The promise of a son is revealed to Sarah

¹⁰ And he said, "I will surely return to you at this time next year, and behold Sarah your wife will have a son." Now Sarah was listening at the entrance of the tent which was behind him.

¹¹ Now Abraham and Sarah were old, well on in years; * the manner of women had ceased to be with Sarah —

¹² And Sarah laughed* at herself, saying, "After I have withered shall I again have delicate skin? And my husband is old!"

¹³ Then HASHEM said to Abraham, "Why is it that Sarah laughed, saying: 'Shall I in truth bear a child, though I have aged?'* ¹⁴ — Is anything beyond HASHEM?! At the appointed time I will return to you at this time next year, and Sarah will have a son."

¹⁵ Sarah denied it, saying, "I did not laugh," for she was frightened. But he said, "No, you laughed indeed."

¹⁶ So the men got up from there, and gazed down toward Sodom, while Abraham walked with them to escort them.

¹⁷ And HASHEM said, "Shall I conceal from Abraham what I do, ¹⁸ now that Abraham is surely to become a great and mighty nation, and all the nations of the earth shall bless themselves by him? ¹⁹ For I have loved him, because he commands his children and his household after him that they keep the way of HASHEM, doing charity and justice, in order that HASHEM might then bring upon Abraham that which He had spoken of him."

God's love for Abraham

²⁰ So HASHEM said, "Because the outcry of Sodom and Gomorrah has become great, and because their sin has been very grave, ²¹ I will descend and see: If they act in accordance with its outcry which has come to Me — then destruction! And if not, I will know."

²² The men turned from there and went to Sodom, while Abraham was still standing before HASHEM.

Abraham intercedes for Sodom

²³ Abraham came forward and said, "Will You also stamp out the righteous along with the wicked? ²⁴ What if there should be fifty righteous people in the midst of the city? Would You still stamp it out rather than spare the place for the sake of the fifty righteous people within it? ²⁵ It would be sacrilege to You to do such a thing, to bring death upon the righteous along with the wicked; so the righteous will be like the wicked. It would be sacrilege to You! Shall the Judge of all the earth not do justice?"

²⁶ And HASHEM said, "If I find in Sodom fifty righteous people in the midst of the city, then I would spare the entire place on their account."

²⁷ Abraham responded and said, "Behold, now, I desired to speak to my Lord although I am but dust and ash. ²⁸ What if the fifty righteous people should lack five? Would You destroy the entire city because of the five?" And He said, "I will not destroy if I find there forty-five."

כח וַיֹּ֨סֶף ע֜וֹד לְדַבֵּ֣ר אֵלָיו֮ וַיֹּאמַר֒ אוּלַ֛י יִמָּצְא֥וּן שָׁ֖ם אַרְבָּעִ֑ים וַיֹּ֙אמֶר֙ לֹ֣א
אֶ֣עֱשֶׂ֔ה בַּעֲב֖וּר הָאַרְבָּעִֽים: כט וַיֹּ֣אמֶר אַל־נָ֞א יִ֤חַר לַֽאדֹנָי֙ וַאֲדַבֵּ֔רָה אוּלַ֛י
יִמָּצְא֥וּן שָׁ֖ם שְׁלֹשִׁ֑ים וַיֹּ֙אמֶר֙ לֹ֣א אֶֽעֱשֶׂ֔ה אִם־אֶמְצָ֥א שָׁ֖ם שְׁלֹשִֽׁים: ל וַיֹּ֗אמֶר
הִנֵּה־נָ֤א הוֹאַ֙לְתִּי֙ לְדַבֵּ֣ר אֶל־אֲדֹנָ֔י אוּלַ֛י יִמָּצְא֥וּן שָׁ֖ם עֶשְׂרִ֑ים וַיֹּ֙אמֶר֙ לֹ֣א
לא אַשְׁחִ֔ית בַּעֲב֖וּר הָֽעֶשְׂרִֽים: וַיֹּ֗אמֶר אַל־נָ֞א יִ֤חַר לַֽאדֹנָי֙ וַאֲדַבְּרָ֣ה אַךְ־
הַפַּ֔עַם אוּלַ֛י יִמָּצְא֥וּן שָׁ֖ם עֲשָׂרָ֑ה וַיֹּ֙אמֶר֙ לֹ֣א אַשְׁחִ֔ית בַּעֲב֖וּר הָעֲשָׂרָֽה:
לב וַיֵּ֣לֶךְ יְהֹוָ֔ה כַּאֲשֶׁ֣ר כִּלָּ֔ה לְדַבֵּ֖ר אֶל־אַבְרָהָ֑ם וְאַבְרָהָ֖ם שָׁ֥ב לִמְקֹמֽוֹ:

יט שלישי א וַ֠יָּבֹ֠אוּ שְׁנֵ֨י הַמַּלְאָכִ֤ים סְדֹ֙מָה֙ בָּעֶ֔רֶב וְל֖וֹט יֹשֵׁ֣ב בְּשַֽׁעַר־סְדֹ֑ם וַיַּרְא־לוֹט֙
ב וַיָּ֙קׇם֙ לִקְרָאתָ֔ם וַיִּשְׁתַּ֥חוּ אַפַּ֖יִם אָֽרְצָה: וַיֹּ֜אמֶר הִנֶּ֣ה נָּא־אֲדֹנַ֗י ס֤וּרוּ נָא֙ אֶל־
בֵּ֣ית עַבְדְּכֶם֮ וְלִ֣ינוּ וְרַחֲצ֣וּ רַגְלֵיכֶם֒ וְהִשְׁכַּמְתֶּ֖ם וַהֲלַכְתֶּ֣ם לְדַרְכְּכֶ֑ם וַיֹּאמְר֣וּ
* ל׳ דגושה ‏ ג ‏ לֹ֔א כִּ֥י בָרְח֖וֹב נָלִֽין: וַיִּפְצַר־בָּ֣ם מְאֹ֔ד וַיָּסֻ֣רוּ אֵלָ֔יו וַיָּבֹ֖אוּ אֶל־בֵּית֑וֹ וַיַּ֤עַשׂ
ד לָהֶם֙ מִשְׁתֶּ֔ה וּמַצּ֥וֹת אָפָ֖ה וַיֹּאכֵֽלוּ: טֶ֘רֶם֮ יִשְׁכָּבוּ֒ וְאַנְשֵׁ֨י הָעִ֜יר אַנְשֵׁ֤י סְדֹם֙
ה נָסַ֣בּוּ עַל־הַבַּ֔יִת מִנַּ֖עַר וְעַד־זָקֵ֑ן כׇּל־הָעָ֖ם מִקָּצֶֽה: וַיִּקְרְא֤וּ אֶל־לוֹט֙ וַיֹּ֣אמְרוּ
ל֔וֹ אַיֵּ֧ה הָאֲנָשִׁ֛ים אֲשֶׁר־בָּ֥אוּ אֵלֶ֖יךָ הַלָּ֑יְלָה הוֹצִיאֵ֣ם אֵלֵ֔ינוּ וְנֵדְעָ֖ה אֹתָֽם:
ו-ז וַיֵּצֵ֧א אֲלֵהֶ֛ם ל֖וֹט הַפֶּ֑תְחָה וְהַדֶּ֖לֶת סָגַ֥ר אַחֲרָֽיו: וַיֹּאמַ֑ר אַל־נָ֥א אַחַ֖י תָּרֵֽעוּ:
ח הִנֵּה־נָ֨א לִ֜י שְׁתֵּ֣י בָנ֗וֹת אֲשֶׁ֤ר לֹא־יָֽדְעוּ֙ אִ֔ישׁ אוֹצִֽיאָה־נָּ֤א אֶתְהֶן֙ אֲלֵיכֶ֔ם
וַעֲשׂ֣וּ לָהֶ֔ן כַּטּ֖וֹב בְּעֵינֵיכֶ֑ם רַ֠ק לָֽאֲנָשִׁ֤ים הָאֵל֙ אַל־תַּעֲשׂ֣וּ דָבָ֔ר כִּֽי־עַל־כֵּ֥ן
ט בָּ֖אוּ בְּצֵ֥ל קֹרָתִֽי: וַיֹּאמְר֣וּ ׀ גֶּשׁ־הָ֗לְאָה וַיֹּֽאמְרוּ֙ הָאֶחָ֤ד בָּֽא־לָגוּר֙ וַיִּשְׁפֹּ֣ט
שָׁפ֔וֹט עַתָּ֕ה נָרַ֥ע לְךָ֖ מֵהֶ֑ם וַיִּפְצְר֨וּ בָאִ֤ישׁ בְּלוֹט֙ מְאֹ֔ד וַֽיִּגְּשׁ֖וּ לִשְׁבֹּ֥ר הַדָּֽלֶת:
י וַיִּשְׁלְח֤וּ הָֽאֲנָשִׁים֙ אֶת־יָדָ֔ם וַיָּבִ֧יאוּ אֶת־ל֛וֹט אֲלֵיהֶ֖ם הַבָּ֑יְתָה וְאֶת־הַדֶּ֖לֶת
יא סָגָֽרוּ: וְֽאֶת־הָאֲנָשִׁ֞ים אֲשֶׁר־פֶּ֣תַח הַבַּ֗יִת הִכּוּ֙ בַּסַּנְוֵרִ֔ים מִקָּטֹ֖ן וְעַד־גָּד֑וֹל
יב וַיִּלְא֖וּ לִמְצֹ֥א הַפָּֽתַח: וַיֹּאמְר֨וּ הָאֲנָשִׁ֜ים אֶל־ל֗וֹט עֹ֚ד מִֽי־לְךָ֣ פֹ֔ה חָתָן֙ וּבָנֶ֣יךָ
וּבְנֹתֶ֔יךָ וְכֹ֥ל אֲשֶׁר־לְךָ֖ בָּעִ֑יר הוֹצֵ֖א מִן־הַמָּקֽוֹם: כִּֽי־מַשְׁחִתִ֣ים אֲנַ֔חְנוּ אֶת־
יג הַמָּק֖וֹם הַזֶּ֑ה כִּֽי־גָֽדְלָ֤ה צַעֲקָתָם֙ אֶת־פְּנֵ֣י יְהֹוָ֔ה וַיְשַׁלְּחֵ֥נוּ יְהֹוָ֖ה לְשַׁחֲתָֽהּ:
* צ׳ דגושה ‏ יד ‏ וַיֵּצֵ֨א ל֜וֹט וַיְדַבֵּ֣ר ׀ אֶל־חֲתָנָ֣יו ׀ לֹקְחֵ֣י בְנֹתָ֗יו וַיֹּ֙אמֶר֙ ק֤וּמוּ צְּאוּ֙ מִן־
הַמָּק֣וֹם הַזֶּ֔ה כִּֽי־מַשְׁחִ֥ית יְהֹוָ֖ה אֶת־הָעִ֑יר וַיְהִ֥י כִמְצַחֵ֖ק בְּעֵינֵ֥י חֲתָנָֽיו:
טו וּכְמוֹ֙ הַשַּׁ֣חַר עָלָ֔ה וַיָּאִ֥יצוּ הַמַּלְאָכִ֖ים בְּל֣וֹט לֵאמֹ֑ר קוּם֩ קַ֨ח אֶת־אִשְׁתְּךָ֜
טז וְאֶת־שְׁתֵּ֤י בְנֹתֶ֙יךָ֙ הַנִּמְצָאֹ֔ת פֶּן־תִּסָּפֶ֖ה בַּעֲוֺ֣ן הָעִֽיר: וַֽיִּתְמַהְמָ֓הּ ׀ וַיַּחֲזִ֨יקוּ
הָאֲנָשִׁ֜ים בְּיָד֣וֹ וּבְיַד־אִשְׁתּ֗וֹ וּבְיַד֙ שְׁתֵּ֣י בְנֹתָ֔יו בְּחֶמְלַ֥ת יְהֹוָ֖ה עָלָ֑יו וַיֹּצִאֻ֥הוּ

19:1-22. Sodom is destroyed and Lot is saved. The conduct of Sodom's populace more than justified the Divine
judgment of its corruption. Lot, however, showed that his
years with Abraham had ennobled him so much that, although Sodom had made a mark on him, he had remained righteous, even heroically so. Despite the mortal
danger of being hospitable to visitors in the cruel environment of Sodom, Lot took the "men" into his home.

19:5. When the Sodomites said that they wanted to know

them, they meant that they wanted to sodomize them
(Rashi, Ibn Ezra).

19:15-26. Lot is saved. By their impudence, Lot's
sons-in-law had lost their chance to be saved, so the
angels insisted that Lot hurry and take his wife and single
daughters, for if he delayed, the lethal downpour would
begin and it would be too late for him.

Moreover, Lot could be saved only before the upheaval
but not from its midst. Furthermore, neither he nor the

²⁹ He further continued to speak to Him and he said, "What if forty would be found there?" And He said, "I will not act on account of the forty."

³⁰ And he said, "Let not my Lord be annoyed and I will speak: What if thirty would be found there?" And He said, "I will not act if I find there thirty."

³¹ So he said, "Behold, now, I desired to speak to my Lord: What if twenty would be found there?" And He said, "I will not destroy on account of the twenty."

³² So he said, "Let not my Lord be annoyed and I will speak but this once: What if ten would be found there?" And He said, "I will not destroy on account of the ten."

³³ HASHEM departed when He had finished speaking to Abraham, and Abraham returned to his place.

19

Sodom is destroyed

¹ The two angels came to Sodom in the evening and Lot was sitting at the gate of Sodom; now Lot saw and stood up to meet them and he bowed, face to the ground. ² And he said, "Behold now, my lords; turn about, please, to your servant's house; spend the night and wash your feet, then wake up early and go your way!" And they said, "No, rather we will spend the night in the square."

³ And he urged them very much, so they turned toward him and came to his house; he made a feast for them and baked matzos, and they ate.

⁴ They had not yet lain down when the townspeople, Sodomites, converged upon the house, from young to old, all the people from every quarter. ⁵ And they called to Lot and said to him, "Where are the men who came to you tonight?

Lot — a perplexing hero

Bring them out to us that we may know them."* ⁶ Lot went out to them to the entrance, and shut the door behind him. ⁷ And he said, "I beg you, my brothers, do not act wickedly. ⁸ See, now, I have two daughters who have never known a man. I shall bring them out to you and do to them as you please; but to these men do nothing inasmuch as they have come under the shelter of my roof."

⁹ And they said, "Stand back!" Then they said, "This fellow came to sojourn and would act as a judge? Now we will treat you worse than them!" They pressed exceedingly upon the man, upon Lot, and they approached to break the door.

¹⁰ The men stretched out their hand and brought Lot into the house with them, and closed the door. ¹¹ And the men who were at the entrance of the house they struck with blindness, from small to great; and they tried vainly to find the entrance. ¹² Then the men said to Lot, "Whom else do you have here — a son-in-law, your sons, or your daughters? All that you have in the city remove from the place, ¹³ for we are about to destroy this place; for their outcry has become great before HASHEM, so HASHEM has sent us to destroy it."

¹⁴ So Lot went out and spoke to his sons-in-law, [and] the betrothed of his daughters, and he said, "Get up and leave this place, for HASHEM is about to destroy the city!" But he seemed like a jester in the eyes of his sons-in-law.

¹⁵ And just as dawn was breaking, the angels urged Lot on saying: "Get up — take your wife and your two daughters who are present, lest you be swept away because of the sin of the city!"

Lot is saved

¹⁶ Still he lingered — so the men grasped him by his hand, his wife's hand, and the hand of his two daughters in HASHEM's mercy on him; and they took him out

---

others in his entourage were entitled to witness the fate of the other Sodomites and still remain unscathed. Thus, when Lot's wife turned around to see the horrors that her fellows were suffering, she, too, died.

יז וַיְנַחֵהוּ מִחוּץ לָעִיר: וַיְהִי כְהוֹצִיאָם אֹתָם הַחוּצָה וַיֹּאמֶר הִמָּלֵט עַל־
נַפְשֶׁךָ אַל־תַּבִּיט אַחֲרֶיךָ וְאַל־תַּעֲמֹד בְּכָל־הַכִּכָּר הָהָרָה הִמָּלֵט פֶּן־
יח-יט תִּסָּפֶה: וַיֹּאמֶר לוֹט אֲלֵהֶם אַל־נָא אֲדֹנָי: הִנֵּה־נָא מָצָא עַבְדְּךָ חֵן בְּעֵינֶיךָ
וַתַּגְדֵּל חַסְדְּךָ אֲשֶׁר עָשִׂיתָ עִמָּדִי לְהַחֲיוֹת אֶת־נַפְשִׁי וְאָנֹכִי לֹא אוּכַל
כ לְהִמָּלֵט הָהָרָה פֶּן־תִּדְבָּקַנִי הָרָעָה וָמַתִּי: הִנֵּה־נָא הָעִיר הַזֹּאת קְרֹבָה לָנוּס
כא שָׁמָּה וְהִוא מִצְעָר אִמָּלְטָה נָּא שָׁמָּה הֲלֹא מִצְעָר הִוא וּתְחִי נַפְשִׁי: וַיֹּאמֶר

רביעי

אֵלָיו הִנֵּה נָשָׂאתִי פָנֶיךָ גַּם לַדָּבָר הַזֶּה לְבִלְתִּי הָפְכִּי אֶת־הָעִיר אֲשֶׁר
כב דִּבַּרְתָּ: מַהֵר הִמָּלֵט שָׁמָּה כִּי לֹא אוּכַל לַעֲשׂוֹת דָּבָר עַד־בֹּאֲךָ שָׁמָּה עַל־
כג-כד כֵּן קָרָא שֵׁם־הָעִיר צוֹעַר: הַשֶּׁמֶשׁ יָצָא עַל־הָאָרֶץ וְלוֹט בָּא צֹעֲרָה: וַיהוָה
הִמְטִיר עַל־סְדֹם וְעַל־עֲמֹרָה גָּפְרִית וָאֵשׁ מֵאֵת יהוה מִן־הַשָּׁמָיִם: וַיַּהֲפֹךְ
כה אֶת־הֶעָרִים הָאֵל וְאֵת כָּל־הַכִּכָּר וְאֵת כָּל־יֹשְׁבֵי הֶעָרִים וְצֶמַח הָאֲדָמָה:
כו-כז וַתַּבֵּט אִשְׁתּוֹ מֵאַחֲרָיו וַתְּהִי נְצִיב מֶלַח: וַיַּשְׁכֵּם אַבְרָהָם בַּבֹּקֶר אֶל־
כח הַמָּקוֹם אֲשֶׁר־עָמַד שָׁם אֶת־פְּנֵי יהוה: וַיַּשְׁקֵף עַל־פְּנֵי סְדֹם וַעֲמֹרָה וְעַל־
כט כָּל־פְּנֵי אֶרֶץ הַכִּכָּר וַיַּרְא וְהִנֵּה עָלָה קִיטֹר הָאָרֶץ כְּקִיטֹר הַכִּבְשָׁן: וַיְהִי
בְּשַׁחֵת אֱלֹהִים אֶת־עָרֵי הַכִּכָּר וַיִּזְכֹּר אֱלֹהִים אֶת־אַבְרָהָם וַיְשַׁלַּח אֶת־
ל לוֹט מִתּוֹךְ הַהֲפֵכָה בַּהֲפֹךְ אֶת־הֶעָרִים אֲשֶׁר־יָשַׁב בָּהֵן לוֹט: וַיַּעַל לוֹט
מִצּוֹעַר וַיֵּשֶׁב בָּהָר וּשְׁתֵּי בְנֹתָיו עִמּוֹ כִּי יָרֵא לָשֶׁבֶת בְּצוֹעַר וַיֵּשֶׁב בַּמְּעָרָה
לא הוּא וּשְׁתֵּי בְנֹתָיו: וַתֹּאמֶר הַבְּכִירָה אֶל־הַצְּעִירָה אָבִינוּ זָקֵן וְאִישׁ אֵין
לב בָּאָרֶץ לָבוֹא עָלֵינוּ כְּדֶרֶךְ כָּל־הָאָרֶץ: לְכָה נַשְׁקֶה אֶת־אָבִינוּ יַיִן וְנִשְׁכְּבָה
לג עִמּוֹ וּנְחַיֶּה מֵאָבִינוּ זָרַע: וַתַּשְׁקֶיןָ אֶת־אֲבִיהֶן יַיִן בַּלַּיְלָה הוּא וַתָּבֹא
לד הַבְּכִירָה וַתִּשְׁכַּב אֶת־אָבִיהָ וְלֹא־יָדַע בְּשִׁכְבָהּ *וּבְקוּמָהּ: וַיְהִי מִמָּחֳרָת

*נָקֹד עַל ו'
בַּתְרָא

וַתֹּאמֶר הַבְּכִירָה אֶל־הַצְּעִירָה הֵן־שָׁכַבְתִּי אֶמֶשׁ אֶת־אָבִי נַשְׁקֶנּוּ יַיִן גַּם־
לה הַלַּיְלָה וּבֹאִי שִׁכְבִי עִמּוֹ וּנְחַיֶּה מֵאָבִינוּ זָרַע: וַתַּשְׁקֶיןָ גַּם בַּלַּיְלָה הַהוּא
אֶת־אֲבִיהֶן יָיִן וַתָּקָם הַצְּעִירָה וַתִּשְׁכַּב עִמּוֹ וְלֹא־יָדַע בְּשִׁכְבָהּ וּבְקֻמָהּ:
לו-לז וַתַּהֲרֶיןָ שְׁתֵּי בְנוֹת־לוֹט מֵאֲבִיהֶן: וַתֵּלֶד הַבְּכִירָה בֵּן וַתִּקְרָא שְׁמוֹ מוֹאָב
לח הוּא אֲבִי־מוֹאָב עַד־הַיּוֹם: וְהַצְּעִירָה גַם־הִוא יָלְדָה בֵּן וַתִּקְרָא שְׁמוֹ בֶּן־

כ

א עַמִּי הוּא אֲבִי בְנֵי־עַמּוֹן עַד־הַיּוֹם: וַיִּסַּע מִשָּׁם אַבְרָהָם אַרְצָה
ב הַנֶּגֶב וַיֵּשֶׁב בֵּין־קָדֵשׁ וּבֵין שׁוּר וַיָּגָר בִּגְרָר: וַיֹּאמֶר אַבְרָהָם אֶל־שָׂרָה

19:24. The Torah uses *Hashem*, the Name that denotes mercy, and it speaks of *rain*, although what descended from heaven was hardly rain in the usual sense of the word. This is because nothing evil descends directly from heaven. First it descended as beneficent *rain*; only when it approached earth did it change to sulfur and fire (*Tanchuma*).

19:31-38. Lot's daughters: Moab and Ammon — the roots of Jewish monarchy. [This theme is treated at length in the *Overview* to the ArtScroll edition of *Ruth*.] Lot's daughters were modest, righteous women whose

actions were nobly motivated. Thinking that the rest of the world had been destroyed in the upheaval of Sodom — and that even Zoar had been spared only while they were there — they felt that it was their responsibility to save the human race by bearing children, even though the only living male was their own father: Because their intentions were pure, they merited that among their descendants would be Ruth, ancestress of David, and Naamah, queen of Solomon and mother of Rehoboam, his successor and the next link in the Davidic chain (*R' Bachya*). Lot, however, was different; his inten-

and left him outside the city. ¹⁷ *And it was as they took them out that one said: "Flee for your life! Do not look behind you nor stop anywhere in all the plain; flee to the mountain lest you be swept away."*

Lot begs for a concession

¹⁸ *Lot said to them: "Please, no! My Lord —* ¹⁹ *See, now, Your servant has found grace in Your eyes and Your kindness was great which You did with me to save my life; but I cannot escape to the mountain lest the evil attach itself to me and I die.* ²⁰ *Behold, please, this city is near enough to escape there and it is small; I shall flee there. Is it not small? — and I will live."*

²¹ *And He replied to him: "Behold, I have granted you consideration even regarding this, that I not overturn the city about which you have spoken.* ²² *Hurry, flee there, for I cannot do a thing until you arrive there." He therefore called the name of the city Zoar.*

²³ *The sun rose upon the earth and Lot arrived at Zoar.* ²⁴ *Now HASHEM* had caused sulfur and fire to rain upon Sodom and Gomorrah, from HASHEM, out of heaven.* ²⁵ *He overturned these cities and the entire plain, with all the inhabitants of the cities and the vegetation of the soil.* ²⁶ *His wife peered behind him and she became a pillar of salt.*

²⁷ *Abraham arose early in the morning to the place where he had stood before HASHEM.* ²⁸ *And he gazed down upon Sodom and Gomorrah and the entire surface of the land of the plain; and saw — and behold! the smoke of the earth rose like the smoke of a kiln.* ²⁹ *And so it was when God destroyed the cities of the plain that God remembered Abraham; so He sent Lot from amidst the upheaval when He overturned the cities in which Lot had lived.*

Lot's daughters and the birth of Moab and Ammon: The roots of Jewish monarchy

³⁰ *Now Lot went up from Zoar and settled on the mountain, his two daughters with him, for he was afraid to remain in Zoar; he dwelt in a cave, he with his two daughters.* ³¹ *The older one said to the younger, "Our father is old and there is no man in the land to marry us in the usual manner.* ³² *Come, let us ply our father with wine and lie with him that we may give life to offspring through our father."*

³³ *So they plied their father with wine on that night; and the older one came and lie with her father, and he was not aware of her lying down and of her getting up.*

³⁴ *And it was on the next day that the older one said to the younger, "Behold, I lay with my father last night; let us ply him with wine tonight as well, and you come lie with him that we may give life to offspring through our father."*

³⁵ *So they plied their father with wine that night also; and the younger one got up and lay with him, and he was not aware of her lying down and of her getting up.*

³⁶ *Thus, Lot's two daughters conceived from their father.*

³⁷ *The older bore a son and she called his name Moab; he is the ancestor of Moab until this day.* ³⁸ *And the younger one also bore a son and she called his name Ben-ammi; he is the ancestor of the children of Ammon until this day.*

20

¹ *A*braham journeyed from there to the region of the south and settled between Kadesh and Shur, and he sojourned in Gerar.* ² *Abraham said of Sarah*

---

tions were not at all sincere. Even though he was intoxicated and unaware of what he was doing the first night, he knew in the morning what had happened — but allowed himself to be intoxicated again, knowing

full well what the result would be (*Rashi*). Unlike his daughters, he knew from the angels that the upheaval was to affect only a limited group of cities, not the whole world.

ג אִשְׁתּוֹ אֲחוֹתִי הִוא וַיִּשְׁלַח אֲבִימֶלֶךְ מֶלֶךְ גְּרָר וַיִּקַּח אֶת־שָׂרָה: וַיָּבֹא
אֱלֹהִים אֶל־אֲבִימֶלֶךְ בַּחֲלוֹם הַלָּיְלָה וַיֹּאמֶר לוֹ הִנְּךָ מֵת עַל־הָאִשָּׁה
ד אֲשֶׁר־לָקַחְתָּ וְהִוא בְּעֻלַת בָּעַל: וַאֲבִימֶלֶךְ לֹא קָרַב אֵלֶיהָ וַיֹּאמַר אֲדֹנָי
ה הֲגוֹי גַּם־צַדִּיק תַּהֲרֹג: הֲלֹא הוּא אָמַר־לִי אֲחֹתִי הִוא וְהִיא־גַם־הִוא
ו אָמְרָה אָחִי הוּא בְּתָם־לְבָבִי וּבְנִקְיֹן כַּפַּי עָשִׂיתִי זֹאת: וַיֹּאמֶר אֵלָיו
הָאֱלֹהִים בַּחֲלֹם גַּם אָנֹכִי יָדַעְתִּי כִּי בְתָם־לְבָבְךָ עָשִׂיתָ זֹּאת וָאֶחְשֹׂךְ
ז גַּם־אָנֹכִי אוֹתְךָ מֵחֲטוֹ־לִי עַל־כֵּן לֹא־נְתַתִּיךָ לִנְגֹּעַ אֵלֶיהָ: וְעַתָּה הָשֵׁב
אֵשֶׁת־הָאִישׁ כִּי־נָבִיא הוּא וְיִתְפַּלֵּל בַּעַדְךָ וֶחְיֵה וְאִם־אֵינְךָ מֵשִׁיב דַּע
ח כִּי־מוֹת תָּמוּת אַתָּה וְכָל־אֲשֶׁר־לָךְ: וַיַּשְׁכֵּם אֲבִימֶלֶךְ בַּבֹּקֶר וַיִּקְרָא לְכָל־
עֲבָדָיו וַיְדַבֵּר אֶת־כָּל־הַדְּבָרִים הָאֵלֶּה בְּאָזְנֵיהֶם וַיִּירְאוּ הָאֲנָשִׁים מְאֹד:
ט וַיִּקְרָא אֲבִימֶלֶךְ לְאַבְרָהָם וַיֹּאמֶר לוֹ מֶה־עָשִׂיתָ לָּנוּ וּמֶה־חָטָאתִי לָךְ
כִּי־הֵבֵאתָ עָלַי וְעַל־מַמְלַכְתִּי חֲטָאָה גְדֹלָה מַעֲשִׂים אֲשֶׁר לֹא־יֵעָשׂוּ
י עָשִׂיתָ עִמָּדִי: וַיֹּאמֶר אֲבִימֶלֶךְ אֶל־אַבְרָהָם מָה רָאִיתָ כִּי עָשִׂיתָ אֶת־
יא הַדָּבָר הַזֶּה: וַיֹּאמֶר אַבְרָהָם כִּי אָמַרְתִּי רַק אֵין־יִרְאַת אֱלֹהִים בַּמָּקוֹם
הַזֶּה וַהֲרָגוּנִי עַל־דְּבַר אִשְׁתִּי: וְגַם־אָמְנָה אֲחֹתִי בַת־אָבִי הִוא אַךְ לֹא
יב בַת־אִמִּי וַתְּהִי־לִי לְאִשָּׁה: וַיְהִי כַּאֲשֶׁר הִתְעוּ אֹתִי אֱלֹהִים מִבֵּית אָבִי
יג וָאֹמַר לָהּ זֶה חַסְדֵּךְ אֲשֶׁר תַּעֲשִׂי עִמָּדִי אֶל כָּל־הַמָּקוֹם אֲשֶׁר נָבוֹא שָׁמָּה
אִמְרִי־לִי אָחִי הוּא: וַיִּקַּח אֲבִימֶלֶךְ צֹאן וּבָקָר וַעֲבָדִים וּשְׁפָחֹת וַיִּתֵּן
יד לְאַבְרָהָם וַיָּשֶׁב לוֹ אֵת שָׂרָה אִשְׁתּוֹ: וַיֹּאמֶר אֲבִימֶלֶךְ הִנֵּה אַרְצִי לְפָנֶיךָ
טו בַּטּוֹב בְּעֵינֶיךָ שֵׁב: וּלְשָׂרָה אָמַר הִנֵּה נָתַתִּי אֶלֶף כֶּסֶף לְאָחִיךְ הִנֵּה
טז הוּא־לָךְ כְּסוּת עֵינַיִם לְכֹל אֲשֶׁר אִתָּךְ וְאֵת כֹּל וְנֹכָחַת: וַיִּתְפַּלֵּל אַבְרָהָם
יז אֶל־הָאֱלֹהִים וַיִּרְפָּא אֱלֹהִים אֶת־אֲבִימֶלֶךְ וְאֶת־אִשְׁתּוֹ וְאַמְהֹתָיו
יח וַיֵּלֵדוּ: כִּי־עָצֹר עָצַר יְהוָֹה בְּעַד כָּל־רֶחֶם לְבֵית אֲבִימֶלֶךְ עַל־דְּבַר
שָׂרָה אֵשֶׁת אַבְרָהָם:

כא
א וַיהוָֹה פָּקַד אֶת־שָׂרָה כַּאֲשֶׁר אָמָר וַיַּעַשׂ יְהוָֹה לְשָׂרָה כַּאֲשֶׁר דִּבֵּר: וַתַּהַר וַתֵּלֶד שָׂרָה לְאַבְרָהָם בֵּן
ב לִזְקֻנָיו לַמּוֹעֵד אֲשֶׁר־דִּבֶּר אֹתוֹ אֱלֹהִים: וַיִּקְרָא אַבְרָהָם אֶת־שֶׁם־בְּנוֹ
ג הַנּוֹלַד־לוֹ אֲשֶׁר־יָלְדָה־לּוֹ שָׂרָה יִצְחָק: וַיָּמָל אַבְרָהָם אֶת־יִצְחָק בְּנוֹ בֶּן־
ד שְׁמֹנַת יָמִים כַּאֲשֶׁר צִוָּה אֹתוֹ אֱלֹהִים: וְאַבְרָהָם בֶּן־מְאַת שָׁנָה בְּהִוָּלֶד
ה לוֹ אֵת יִצְחָק בְּנוֹ: וַתֹּאמֶר שָׂרָה צְחֹק עָשָׂה לִי אֱלֹהִים כָּל־הַשֹּׁמֵעַ

READING FOR FIRST DAY ROSH HASHANAH 21:1-34

Maftir: p. 400
Haftarah: p. 646

חמישי

⦿**Sarah is abducted by Abimelech.** Although Abraham had once felt the bitter taste of an abduction of Sarah, he did not expect a repetition of that experience because, as the narrative will show, Abimelech was a righteous king (by the standards of the time) and Philistia was a more law-abiding country than Egypt. That Sarah was indeed abducted was one of Abraham's Ten Trials.

20:4-5. Abimelech felt that since his intentions were good, he was blameless. Judaism rejects this view. Good intentions do not purify a wrong deed. If it is wrong in God's eyes, then good intentions do not give it sanction. Moreover, lack of knowledge is itself sinful, for a person has the obligation to seek instruction. A person in Abimelech's position has the further obligation to set an example of appropriate behavior — is it right that even an unmarried woman must fear the whim of every

Abraham
in Gerar: his wife, "She is my sister"; so Abimelech, king of Gerar, sent, and took Sarah.
Sarah is ³ And God came to Abimelech in a dream by night and said to him, "Behold you
abducted are to die because of the woman you have taken; moreover she is a married
woman."

⁴ Now Abimelech had not approached her; so he said, "O my Lord, will You slay a nation even though it is righteous? ⁵ Did not he himself tell me: 'She is my sister'? And she, too, herself said: 'He is my brother!' In the innocence of my heart and integrity of my hands have I done this."

⁶ And God said to him in the dream, "I, too, knew that it was in the innocence of your heart that you did this, and I, too, prevented you from sinning against Me; that is why I did not permit you to touch her. ⁷ But now, return the man's wife for he is a prophet, and he will pray for you and you will live, but if you do not return her, be aware that you shall surely die: you and all that is yours."

⁸ Abimelech arose early next morning; he summoned all his servants and told them all of these things in their ears, and the people were very frightened. ⁹ Then Abimelech summoned Abraham and said to him, "What have you done to us? How have I sinned against you that you brought upon me and my kingdom such great sin? Deeds that ought not to be done have you done to me!" ¹⁰ And Abimelech said to Abraham, "What did you see that you did such a thing?"

¹¹ And Abraham said, "Because I said, 'There is but no fear of God in this place and they will slay me because of my wife.' ¹² Moreover, she is indeed my sister, my father's daughter, though not my mother's daughter; and she became my wife. ¹³ And so it was, when God caused me to wander from my father's house, I said to her, 'Let this be your kindness which you shall do for me — to whatever place we come, say of me: He is my brother.' "

Abimelech ¹⁴ So Abimelech took flocks and cattle and servants and maidservants and
appeases gave to Abraham; and he returned his wife Sarah to him.
Abraham
and Sarah ¹⁵ And Abimelech said, "Behold, my land is before you: settle wherever you see fit." ¹⁶ And to Sarah he said, "Behold, I have given your brother a thousand pieces of silver. Behold! Let it be for you an eye-covering for all who are with you; and to all you will be vindicated."

¹⁷ Abraham prayed to God, and God healed Abimelech, his wife, and his maids, and they were relieved; ¹⁸ for HASHEM had completely restrained every orifice of the household of Abimelech, because of Sarah, the wife of Abraham.

21 ¹ HASHEM had remembered Sarah as He had said; and HASHEM did for Sarah
The birth as He had spoken. ² Sarah conceived and bore a son unto Abraham in his
of Isaac old age, at the appointed time which God had spoken. ³ Abraham called the name of his son who was born to him — whom Sarah had borne him — Isaac. *

⁴ Abraham circumcised his son Isaac at the age of eight days as God had commanded him. ⁵ And Abraham was a hundred years old when his son Isaac was born to him. ⁶ Sarah said, "God has made laughter for me; whoever hears

---

prince? (*R' Hirsch*).

21:1-8. The birth of Isaac. The prophecies to Abraham and Sarah, and their joint longings to build the future for which God had created the world, finally found fulfillment with the birth of Sarah's son. According to tradition, Sarah conceived on the first day of Rosh Hashanah. Therefore, this narrative is the Torah reading of that day,

to inspire people to follow Sarah's example of righteousness and prayer.

21:3. The name יִצְחָק — which God had commanded Abraham to give (17:19) — is derived from the word צָחַק, *laughter*. The laughter memorialized in this name, however, is the joy of Abraham, not the original skepticism of Sarah (*R' Bachya*).

ז יִצְחָק־לִי: וַתֹּאמֶר מִי מִלֵּל לְאַבְרָהָם הֵינִיקָה בָנִים שָׂרָה כִּי־יָלַדְתִּי בֵן
ח לִזְקֻנָיו: וַיִּגְדַּל הַיֶּלֶד וַיִּגָּמַל וַיַּעַשׂ אַבְרָהָם מִשְׁתֶּה גָדוֹל בְּיוֹם הִגָּמֵל אֶת־
ט יִצְחָק: וַתֵּרֶא שָׂרָה אֶת־בֶּן־הָגָר הַמִּצְרִית אֲשֶׁר־יָלְדָה לְאַבְרָהָם מְצַחֵק:
י וַתֹּאמֶר לְאַבְרָהָם גָּרֵשׁ הָאָמָה הַזֹּאת וְאֶת־בְּנָהּ כִּי לֹא יִירַשׁ בֶּן־הָאָמָה
יא הַזֹּאת עִם־בְּנִי עִם־יִצְחָק: וַיֵּרַע הַדָּבָר מְאֹד בְּעֵינֵי אַבְרָהָם עַל אוֹדֹת
יב בְּנוֹ: וַיֹּאמֶר אֱלֹהִים אֶל־אַבְרָהָם אַל־יֵרַע בְּעֵינֶיךָ עַל־הַנַּעַר וְעַל־אֲמָתֶךָ
יג כֹּל אֲשֶׁר תֹּאמַר אֵלֶיךָ שָׂרָה שְׁמַע בְּקֹלָהּ כִּי בְיִצְחָק יִקָּרֵא לְךָ זָרַע: וְגַם
יד אֶת־בֶּן־הָאָמָה לְגוֹי אֲשִׂימֶנּוּ כִּי זַרְעֲךָ הוּא: וַיַּשְׁכֵּם אַבְרָהָם ׀ בַּבֹּקֶר
וַיִּקַּח־לֶחֶם וְחֵמַת מַיִם וַיִּתֵּן אֶל־הָגָר שָׂם עַל־שִׁכְמָהּ וְאֶת־הַיֶּלֶד
טו וַיְשַׁלְּחֶהָ וַתֵּלֶךְ וַתֵּתַע בְּמִדְבַּר בְּאֵר שָׁבַע: וַיִּכְלוּ הַמַּיִם מִן־הַחֵמֶת
טז וַתַּשְׁלֵךְ אֶת־הַיֶּלֶד תַּחַת אַחַד הַשִּׂיחִם: וַתֵּלֶךְ וַתֵּשֶׁב לָהּ מִנֶּגֶד הַרְחֵק
כִּמְטַחֲוֵי קֶשֶׁת כִּי אָמְרָה אַל־אֶרְאֶה בְּמוֹת הַיָּלֶד וַתֵּשֶׁב מִנֶּגֶד וַתִּשָּׂא
יז אֶת־קֹלָהּ וַתֵּבְךְּ: וַיִּשְׁמַע אֱלֹהִים אֶת־קוֹל הַנַּעַר וַיִּקְרָא מַלְאַךְ אֱלֹהִים ׀
אֶל־הָגָר מִן־הַשָּׁמַיִם וַיֹּאמֶר לָהּ מַה־לָּךְ הָגָר אַל־תִּירְאִי כִּי־שָׁמַע
יח אֱלֹהִים אֶל־קוֹל הַנַּעַר בַּאֲשֶׁר הוּא־שָׁם: קוּמִי שְׂאִי אֶת־הַנַּעַר וְהַחֲזִיקִי
יט אֶת־יָדֵךְ בּוֹ כִּי־לְגוֹי גָּדוֹל אֲשִׂימֶנּוּ: וַיִּפְקַח אֱלֹהִים אֶת־עֵינֶיהָ וַתֵּרֶא
כ בְּאֵר מָיִם וַתֵּלֶךְ וַתְּמַלֵּא אֶת־הַחֵמֶת מַיִם וַתַּשְׁקְ אֶת־הַנָּעַר: וַיְהִי אֱלֹהִים
כא אֶת־הַנַּעַר וַיִּגְדָּל וַיֵּשֶׁב בַּמִּדְבָּר וַיְהִי רֹבֶה קַשָּׁת: וַיֵּשֶׁב בְּמִדְבַּר פָּארָן
וַתִּקַּח־לוֹ אִמּוֹ אִשָּׁה מֵאֶרֶץ מִצְרָיִם:

ששי כב וַיְהִי בָּעֵת הַהִוא וַיֹּאמֶר אֲבִימֶלֶךְ וּפִיכֹל שַׂר־צְבָאוֹ אֶל־אַבְרָהָם לֵאמֹר
כג אֱלֹהִים עִמְּךָ בְּכֹל אֲשֶׁר־אַתָּה עֹשֶׂה: וְעַתָּה הִשָּׁבְעָה לִּי בֵאלֹהִים הֵנָּה
אִם־תִּשְׁקֹר לִי וּלְנִינִי וּלְנֶכְדִּי כַּחֶסֶד אֲשֶׁר־עָשִׂיתִי עִמְּךָ תַּעֲשֶׂה עִמָּדִי
כד-כה וְעִם־הָאָרֶץ אֲשֶׁר־גַּרְתָּה בָּהּ: וַיֹּאמֶר אַבְרָהָם אָנֹכִי אִשָּׁבֵעַ: וְהוֹכִחַ
אַבְרָהָם אֶת־אֲבִימֶלֶךְ עַל־אֹדוֹת בְּאֵר הַמַּיִם אֲשֶׁר גָּזְלוּ עַבְדֵי אֲבִימֶלֶךְ:
כו וַיֹּאמֶר אֲבִימֶלֶךְ לֹא יָדַעְתִּי מִי עָשָׂה אֶת־הַדָּבָר הַזֶּה וְגַם־אַתָּה
כז לֹא־הִגַּדְתָּ לִּי וְגַם אָנֹכִי לֹא שָׁמַעְתִּי בִּלְתִּי הַיּוֹם: וַיִּקַּח אַבְרָהָם צֹאן
כח וּבָקָר וַיִּתֵּן לַאֲבִימֶלֶךְ וַיִּכְרְתוּ שְׁנֵיהֶם בְּרִית: וַיַּצֵּב אַבְרָהָם אֶת־
כט שֶׁבַע כִּבְשֹׂת הַצֹּאן לְבַדְּהֶן: וַיֹּאמֶר אֲבִימֶלֶךְ אֶל־אַבְרָהָם מָה הֵנָּה
ל שֶׁבַע כְּבָשֹׂת הָאֵלֶּה אֲשֶׁר הִצַּבְתָּ לְבַדָּנָה: וַיֹּאמֶר כִּי אֶת־שֶׁבַע
כְּבָשֹׂת תִּקַּח מִיָּדִי בַּעֲבוּר תִּהְיֶה־לִּי לְעֵדָה כִּי חָפַרְתִּי אֶת־הַבְּאֵר
לא הַזֹּאת: עַל־כֵּן קָרָא לַמָּקוֹם הַהוּא בְּאֵר שָׁבַע כִּי שָׁם נִשְׁבְּעוּ שְׁנֵיהֶם:

21:8. According to *Tosafos* (*Shabbos* 130a), this feast took place at Isaac's *circumcision*.

21:9-14. Ishmael is expelled. In the ninth of Abraham's Ten Trials, God commanded him to banish Ishmael, because he was a menace to the spiritual health — and perhaps the very life — of Isaac.

21:9. Scripture uses the verb מְצַחֵק to denote the three cardinal sins: idolatry [*Exodus* 32:6]; adultery [39:17]; and murder [*II Samuel* 2:14]. Thus Ishmael's behavior proved to Sarah that he had become thor-will laugh for me." [7] And she said, "Who is the One Who said to Abraham, 'Sarah would nurse children'? For I have borne a son in his old age!"

[8] The child grew and was weaned. Abraham made a great feast* on the day Isaac was weaned.

Hagar and Ishmael are expelled   [9] Sarah saw the son of Hagar, the Egyptian, whom she had borne to Abraham, mocking. * [10] So she said to Abraham, "Drive out this slavewoman with her son, for the son of that slavewoman shall not inherit with my son, with Isaac!"

[11] The matter greatly distressed Abraham regarding his son. [12] So God said to Abraham, "Be not distressed over the youth or your slavewoman: Whatever Sarah tells you, heed her voice, since through Isaac will offspring be considered yours. [13] But the son of the slavewoman as well will I make into a nation for he is your offspring."

[14] So Abraham awoke early in the morning, took bread and a skin of water, and gave them to Hagar. He placed them on her shoulder along with the boy, and sent her off. She departed, and strayed in the desert of Beer-sheba.

[15] When the water of the skin was consumed, she cast off the boy beneath one of the trees. [16] She went and sat herself down at a distance, some bowshots away, for she said, "Let me not see the death of the child." And she sat at a distance, lifted her voice, and wept.

Ishmael is saved   [17] God heard the cry of the youth, and an angel of God called to Hagar from heaven and said to her, "What troubles you, Hagar? Fear not, for God has heeded the cry of the youth in his present state. * [18] Arise, lift up the youth and grasp your hand upon him, for I will make a great nation of him."

[19] Then God opened her eyes and she perceived a well of water; she went and filled the skin with water and gave the youth to drink.

[20] God was with the youth and he grew up; he dwelt in the desert and became an accomplished archer. [21] He lived in the desert of Paran, and his mother took a wife for him from the land of Egypt.

The alliance with Abimelech at Beer-sheba   [22] At that time, Abimelech and Phicol, general of his legion, said to Abraham, "God is with you in all that you do. [23] Now swear to me here by God that you will not deal falsely with me nor with my son nor with my grandson; according to the kindness that I have done with you, do with me, and with the land in which you have sojourned." [24] And Abraham said, "I will swear." [25] Then Abraham disputed with Abimelech regarding the well of water that Abimelech's servants had seized. [26] But Abimelech said, "I do not know who did this thing; furthermore, you have never told me, and moreover I myself have heard nothing of it except for today."

[27] So Abraham took flocks and cattle and gave them to Abimelech; and the two of them entered into a covenant. [28] Abraham set seven ewes of the flock by themselves. [29] And Abimelech said to Abraham, "What are these seven ewes which you have set by themselves?"

[30] And he replied, "Because you are to take these seven ewes from me, that it may serve me as testimony that I dug this well." [31] Therefore that place was called Beer-sheba because there the two of them took an oath.

---

oughly corrupt and evil, and he had to be sent away (*Rashi*).

21:17. According to the Midrash, the angels pleaded with God not to perform a miracle for Ishmael, because his offspring were destined to persecute and murder Jews, but God responded that He would judge Ishmael only according to his present deeds and not according to what would happen in the future (*Rashi*).

לב וַיִּכְרְת֥וּ בְרִ֖ית בִּבְאֵ֣ר שָׁ֑בַע וַיָּ֣קָם אֲבִימֶ֗לֶךְ וּפִיכֹל֙ שַׂר־צְבָא֔וֹ וַיָּשֻׁ֖בוּ אֶל־

לג אֶ֥רֶץ פְּלִשְׁתִּֽים: וַיִּטַּ֥ע אֶ֖שֶׁל בִּבְאֵ֣ר שָׁ֑בַע וַיִּ֨קְרָא־שָׁ֔ם בְּשֵׁ֥ם יהו֖ה אֵ֥ל

לד עוֹלָֽם: וַיָּ֧גָר אַבְרָהָ֛ם בְּאֶ֥רֶץ פְּלִשְׁתִּ֖ים יָמִ֥ים רַבִּֽים:

שביעי **כב** א
READING
FOR
SECOND
DAY ROSH
HASHANAH
22:1-24
Maftir:
p. 400
Haftarah:
p. 1142

א וַיְהִ֗י אַחַר֙ הַדְּבָרִ֣ים הָאֵ֔לֶּה וְהָ֣אֱלֹהִ֔ים נִסָּ֖ה אֶת־אַבְרָהָ֑ם וַיֹּ֣אמֶר אֵלָ֔יו

ב אַבְרָהָ֖ם וַיֹּ֥אמֶר הִנֵּֽנִי: וַיֹּ֡אמֶר קַח־נָ֠א אֶת־בִּנְךָ֨ אֶת־יְחִֽידְךָ֤ אֲשֶׁר־אָהַ֨בְתָּ֙ אֶת־יִצְחָ֔ק וְלֶ֨ךְ־לְךָ֔ אֶל־אֶ֖רֶץ הַמֹּרִיָּ֑ה וְהַעֲלֵ֤הוּ שָׁם֙ לְעֹלָ֔ה עַ֚ל אַחַ֣ד

ג הֶֽהָרִ֔ים אֲשֶׁ֖ר אֹמַ֥ר אֵלֶֽיךָ: וַיַּשְׁכֵּ֨ם אַבְרָהָ֜ם בַּבֹּ֗קֶר וַֽיַּחֲבֹשׁ֙ אֶת־חֲמֹר֔וֹ וַיִּקַּ֞ח אֶת־שְׁנֵ֤י נְעָרָיו֙ אִתּ֔וֹ וְאֵ֖ת יִצְחָ֣ק בְּנ֑וֹ וַיְבַקַּע֙ עֲצֵ֣י עֹלָ֔ה וַיָּ֣קָם וַיֵּ֔לֶךְ

ד אֶל־הַמָּק֖וֹם אֲשֶׁר־אָֽמַר־ל֥וֹ הָאֱלֹהִֽים: בַּיּ֣וֹם הַשְּׁלִישִׁ֗י וַיִּשָּׂ֨א אַבְרָהָ֧ם

ה אֶת־עֵינָ֛יו וַיַּ֥רְא אֶת־הַמָּק֖וֹם מֵֽרָחֹֽק: וַיֹּ֨אמֶר אַבְרָהָ֜ם אֶל־נְעָרָ֗יו שְׁבֽוּ־לָכֶ֥ם פֹּה֙ עִֽם־הַחֲמ֔וֹר וַאֲנִ֣י וְהַנַּ֔עַר נֵלְכָ֖ה עַד־כֹּ֑ה וְנִֽשְׁתַּחֲוֶ֖ה וְנָשׁ֥וּבָה

ו אֲלֵיכֶֽם: וַיִּקַּ֨ח אַבְרָהָ֜ם אֶת־עֲצֵ֣י הָעֹלָ֗ה וַיָּ֨שֶׂם֙ עַל־יִצְחָ֣ק בְּנ֔וֹ וַיִּקַּ֣ח בְּיָד֔וֹ

ז אֶת־הָאֵ֖שׁ וְאֶת־הַֽמַּאֲכֶ֑לֶת וַיֵּלְכ֥וּ שְׁנֵיהֶ֖ם יַחְדָּֽו: וַיֹּ֨אמֶר יִצְחָ֜ק אֶל־אַבְרָהָ֤ם אָבִיו֙ וַיֹּ֣אמֶר אָבִ֔י וַיֹּ֖אמֶר הִנֶּ֣נִּֽי בְנִ֑י וַיֹּ֗אמֶר הִנֵּ֤ה הָאֵשׁ֙ וְהָ֣עֵצִ֔ים

ח וְאַיֵּ֥ה הַשֶּׂ֖ה לְעֹלָֽה: וַיֹּ֨אמֶר֙ אַבְרָהָ֔ם אֱלֹהִ֞ים יִרְאֶה־לּ֥וֹ הַשֶּׂ֛ה לְעֹלָ֖ה בְּנִ֑י

ט וַיֵּלְכ֥וּ שְׁנֵיהֶ֖ם יַחְדָּֽו: וַיָּבֹ֗אוּ אֶֽל־הַמָּקוֹם֮ אֲשֶׁ֣ר אָֽמַר־ל֣וֹ הָאֱלֹהִים֒ וַיִּ֨בֶן שָׁ֤ם אַבְרָהָם֙ אֶת־הַמִּזְבֵּ֔חַ וַֽיַּעֲרֹ֖ךְ אֶת־הָעֵצִ֑ים וַֽיַּעֲקֹד֙ אֶת־יִצְחָ֣ק בְּנ֔וֹ

י וַיָּ֤שֶׂם אֹתוֹ֙ עַל־הַמִּזְבֵּ֔חַ מִמַּ֖עַל לָעֵצִֽים: וַיִּשְׁלַ֤ח אַבְרָהָם֙ אֶת־יָד֔וֹ וַיִּקַּ֖ח

יא אֶת־הַֽמַּאֲכֶ֑לֶת לִשְׁחֹ֖ט אֶת־בְּנֽוֹ: וַיִּקְרָ֨א אֵלָ֜יו מַלְאַ֤ךְ יהוה֙ מִן־הַשָּׁמַ֔יִם

יב וַיֹּ֖אמֶר אַבְרָהָ֣ם ׀ אַבְרָהָ֑ם וַיֹּ֖אמֶר הִנֵּֽנִי: וַיֹּ֗אמֶר אַל־תִּשְׁלַ֤ח יָֽדְךָ֙ אֶל־הַנַּ֔עַר וְאַל־תַּ֥עַשׂ ל֖וֹ מְא֑וּמָה כִּ֣י ׀ עַתָּ֣ה יָדַ֗עְתִּי כִּֽי־יְרֵ֤א אֱלֹהִים֙ אַ֔תָּה

יג וְלֹ֥א חָשַׂ֛כְתָּ אֶת־בִּנְךָ֥ אֶת־יְחִֽידְךָ֖ מִמֶּֽנִּי: וַיִּשָּׂ֨א אַבְרָהָ֜ם אֶת־עֵינָ֗יו וַיַּרְא֙ וְהִנֵּה־אַ֔יִל אַחַ֕ר נֶאֱחַ֥ז בַּסְּבַ֖ךְ בְּקַרְנָ֑יו וַיֵּ֣לֶךְ אַבְרָהָ֗ם וַיִּקַּ֤ח אֶת־הָאַ֨יִל֙

יד וַיַּעֲלֵ֥הוּ לְעֹלָ֖ה תַּ֣חַת בְּנֽוֹ: וַיִּקְרָ֧א אַבְרָהָ֛ם שֵֽׁם־הַמָּק֥וֹם הַה֖וּא יהו֣ה ׀ יִרְאֶ֑ה אֲשֶׁר֙ יֵֽאָמֵ֣ר הַיּ֔וֹם בְּהַ֥ר יהו֖ה יֵֽרָאֶֽה:

טו וַיִּקְרָ֛א מַלְאַ֥ךְ יהו֖ה אֶל־

טז אַבְרָהָ֑ם שֵׁנִ֖ית מִן־הַשָּׁמָֽיִם: וַיֹּ֕אמֶר בִּ֥י נִשְׁבַּ֖עְתִּי נְאֻם־יהו֑ה כִּ֗י יַ֚עַן אֲשֶׁ֣ר

⊸§ The tenth trial: The Akeidah/Binding of Isaac on the altar. This section epitomizes the Jew's determination to serve God no matter how difficult the circumstances, which is the very reason for Israel's existence (*Abarbanel*). This test was especially difficult because Abraham could not rationalize that Isaac deserved to die because he had somehow been found unworthy or that he had become evil. He knew this was not the case.

According to the accepted chronology, Isaac was thirty-seven at the *Akeidah*.

Pesikta Rabbasi teaches that the *Akeidah* took place on Rosh Hashanah. For that reason it is the Torah reading for the second day of Rosh Hashanah, and the prayers of that day are filled with references to this supreme act of devotion to God.

⊸§ Abraham's Ten Trials (according to *Rashi*)
1. Abraham hides for thirteen years from King Nimrod, who wants to kill him.
2. Nimrod throws him into a burning furnace.
3. God commands Abraham to leave his family and homeland.
4. A famine forces him to leave Canaan.
5. Pharaoh's officials kidnap Sarah.
6. Abraham goes to war to rescue Lot.
7. God tells him that his offspring will suffer under four kingdoms.
8. God commands him to circumcise himself and Ishmael.
9. God commands him to banish Hagar and Ishmael.
10. God commands him to offer Isaac on the altar.

³² Thus, they entered into a covenant at Beer-sheba; Abimelech then arose, with Phicol, his general, and they returned to the land of the Philistines.

³³ He planted an "eshel" in Beer-sheba, and there he proclaimed the Name of HASHEM, God of the Universe. ³⁴ And Abraham sojourned in the land of the Philistines many years.

22

The tenth trial: The Akeidah/ Binding of Isaac on the altar

¹ **A**nd it happened after these things that God tested* Abraham and said to him, "Abraham," and he replied, "Here I am."

² And He said, "Please take your son, your only one, whom you love — Isaac — and go to the land of Moriah; bring him up there as an offering upon one of the mountains which I shall tell you."

³ So Abraham woke up early in the morning and he saddled his donkey; he took his two young men with him and Isaac, his son; he split the wood for the offering, and stood up and went to the place of which God had spoken to him.

⁴ On the third day, Abraham raised his eyes and perceived the place from afar. ⁵ And Abraham said to his young men, "Stay here by yourselves with the donkey, while I and the lad will go yonder; we will worship and we will return to you."

⁶ And Abraham took the wood for the offering, and placed it on Isaac, his son. He took in his hand the fire and the knife, and the two of them went together. ⁷ Then Isaac spoke to Abraham his father and said, "Father — "

And he said, "Here I am, my son."

And he said, "Here are the fire and the wood, but where is the lamb for the offering?"

⁸ And Abraham said, "God will seek out for Himself the lamb for the offering, my son." And the two of them went together.

⁹ They arrived at the place of which God had spoken to him; Abraham built the altar there, and arranged the wood; he bound Isaac, his son, and he placed him on the altar atop the wood. ¹⁰ Abraham stretched out his hand, and took the knife to slaughter his son.

¹¹ And an angel of HASHEM called to him from heaven, and said, "Abraham! Abraham!"*

And he said, "Here I am."

¹² And he said, "Do not stretch out your hand against the lad nor do anything to him for now I know that you are a God-fearing man, since you have not withheld your son, your only one, from Me."

¹³ And Abraham raised his eyes and saw — behold, a ram! — afterwards, caught in the thicket by its horns; so Abraham went and took the ram and offered it up as an offering instead of his son. ¹⁴ And Abraham called the name of that site "HASHEM Yireh," * as it is said this day, on the mountain HASHEM will be seen.

¹⁵ The angel of HASHEM called to Abraham a second time from heaven. ¹⁶ And he said, "By Myself I swear — the word of HASHEM — that because

---

22:1. The Midrash derives נִסָּה, *tested*, from נֵס, a *banner*, that flies high above an army or ship. Hence the verse would be rendered: And God *elevated* Abraham, trial upon trial, greatness after greatness.

God did not say, "Slaughter him," because He did not intend for Isaac to be slaughtered, but only that he be *brought up* to the mountain and be *prepared* as an offering. Mount Moriah is the Temple Mount in Jerusalem.

22:11. This repetition expresses love (*Rashi*), and urgency (*Midrash*).

22:14. The original name of the place was *Shalem*, the name given it by Shem, son of Noah — whom the Sages identify with Malchizedek, king of Jerusalem. After the *Akeidah*, Abraham called it *Yireh*, i.e., HASHEM *will see*. In deference to both Shem and Abraham, God synthesized both names and called it *Yerushalayim* (*Midrash*).

יז עָשִׂיתָ אֶת־הַדָּבָר הַזֶּה וְלֹא חָשַׂכְתָּ אֶת־בִּנְךָ אֶת־יְחִידֶךָ: כִּי־בָרֵךְ
אֲבָרֶכְךָ וְהַרְבָּה אַרְבֶּה אֶת־זַרְעֲךָ כְּכוֹכְבֵי הַשָּׁמַיִם וְכַחוֹל אֲשֶׁר עַל־
יח שְׂפַת הַיָּם וְיִרַשׁ זַרְעֲךָ אֵת שַׁעַר אֹיְבָיו: וְהִתְבָּרְכוּ בְזַרְעֲךָ כֹּל גּוֹיֵי הָאָרֶץ
יט עֵקֶב אֲשֶׁר שָׁמַעְתָּ בְּקֹלִי: וַיָּשָׁב אַבְרָהָם אֶל־נְעָרָיו וַיָּקֻמוּ וַיֵּלְכוּ יַחְדָּו
אֶל־בְּאֵר שָׁבַע וַיֵּשֶׁב אַבְרָהָם בִּבְאֵר שָׁבַע:

מפטיר

כ וַיְהִי אַחֲרֵי הַדְּבָרִים הָאֵלֶּה וַיֻּגַּד לְאַבְרָהָם לֵאמֹר הִנֵּה יָלְדָה מִלְכָּה גַם־
כא הִוא בָּנִים לְנָחוֹר אָחִיךָ: אֶת־עוּץ בְּכֹרוֹ וְאֶת־בּוּז אָחִיו וְאֶת־קְמוּאֵל
כב אֲבִי אֲרָם: וְאֶת־כֶּשֶׂד וְאֶת־חֲזוֹ וְאֶת־פִּלְדָּשׁ וְאֶת־יִדְלָף וְאֵת בְּתוּאֵל:
כג וּבְתוּאֵל יָלַד אֶת־רִבְקָה שְׁמֹנָה אֵלֶּה יָלְדָה מִלְכָּה לְנָחוֹר אֲחִי אַבְרָהָם:
כד וּפִילַגְשׁוֹ וּשְׁמָהּ רְאוּמָה וַתֵּלֶד גַּם־הִוא אֶת־טֶבַח וְאֶת־גַּחַם וְאֶת־תַּחַשׁ
וְאֶת־מַעֲכָה: פפפ קמ"ז פסוקים. אמנו"ן סימן.

Haftaras
Vayeira:
p. 882
For special
Sabbaths,
see pp. x-xi

פרשת חיי שרה

כג א וַיִּהְיוּ חַיֵּי שָׂרָה מֵאָה שָׁנָה וְעֶשְׂרִים שָׁנָה וְשֶׁבַע שָׁנִים שְׁנֵי חַיֵּי שָׂרָה:
ב וַתָּמָת שָׂרָה בְּקִרְיַת אַרְבַּע הִוא חֶבְרוֹן בְּאֶרֶץ כְּנָעַן וַיָּבֹא אַבְרָהָם לִסְפֹּד
ג לְשָׂרָה וְלִבְכֹּתָהּ: וַיָּקָם אַבְרָהָם מֵעַל פְּנֵי מֵתוֹ וַיְדַבֵּר אֶל־בְּנֵי־חֵת לֵאמֹר:
ד גֵּר־וְתוֹשָׁב אָנֹכִי עִמָּכֶם תְּנוּ לִי אֲחֻזַּת־קֶבֶר עִמָּכֶם וְאֶקְבְּרָה מֵתִי מִלְּפָנָי:
ה-ו וַיַּעֲנוּ בְנֵי־חֵת אֶת־אַבְרָהָם לֵאמֹר לוֹ: שְׁמָעֵנוּ ׀ אֲדֹנִי נְשִׂיא אֱלֹהִים אַתָּה
בְּתוֹכֵנוּ בְּמִבְחַר קְבָרֵינוּ קְבֹר אֶת־מֵתֶךָ אִישׁ מִמֶּנּוּ אֶת־קִבְרוֹ לֹא־יִכְלֶה
ז-ח מִמְּךָ מִקְּבֹר מֵתֶךָ: וַיָּקָם אַבְרָהָם וַיִּשְׁתַּחוּ לְעַם־הָאָרֶץ לִבְנֵי־חֵת: וַיְדַבֵּר
אִתָּם לֵאמֹר אִם־יֵשׁ אֶת־נַפְשְׁכֶם לִקְבֹּר אֶת־מֵתִי מִלְּפָנַי שְׁמָעוּנִי
ט וּפִגְעוּ־לִי בְּעֶפְרוֹן בֶּן־צֹחַר: וְיִתֶּן־לִי אֶת־מְעָרַת הַמַּכְפֵּלָה אֲשֶׁר־לוֹ
אֲשֶׁר בִּקְצֵה שָׂדֵהוּ בְּכֶסֶף מָלֵא יִתְּנֶנָּה לִי בְּתוֹכְכֶם לַאֲחֻזַּת־קָבֶר:
י וְעֶפְרוֹן יֹשֵׁב בְּתוֹךְ בְּנֵי־חֵת וַיַּעַן עֶפְרוֹן הַחִתִּי אֶת־אַבְרָהָם בְּאָזְנֵי בְנֵי־
יא חֵת לְכֹל בָּאֵי שַׁעַר־עִירוֹ לֵאמֹר: לֹא־אֲדֹנִי שְׁמָעֵנִי הַשָּׂדֶה נָתַתִּי לָךְ
וְהַמְּעָרָה אֲשֶׁר־בּוֹ לְךָ נְתַתִּיהָ לְעֵינֵי בְנֵי־עַמִּי נְתַתִּיהָ לָּךְ קְבֹר מֵתֶךָ:
יב-יג וַיִּשְׁתַּחוּ אַבְרָהָם לִפְנֵי עַם־הָאָרֶץ: וַיְדַבֵּר אֶל־עֶפְרוֹן בְּאָזְנֵי עַם־הָאָרֶץ
לֵאמֹר אַךְ אִם־אַתָּה לוּ שְׁמָעֵנִי נָתַתִּי כֶּסֶף הַשָּׂדֶה קַח מִמֶּנִּי וְאֶקְבְּרָה
יד-טו אֶת־מֵתִי שָׁמָּה: וַיַּעַן עֶפְרוֹן אֶת־אַבְרָהָם לֵאמֹר לוֹ: אֲדֹנִי שְׁמָעֵנִי
אֶרֶץ אַרְבַּע מֵאֹת שֶׁקֶל־כֶּסֶף בֵּינִי וּבֵינְךָ מַה־הִוא וְאֶת־מֵתְךָ קְבֹר:

כג

* כ' זעירא

⊷ **Parashas Chayei Sarah.** The *Sidrah* shows Jewish respect for the dead and concern for the future. These are essential concepts in Judaism, for we neither reject what has gone before nor neglect what lies ahead.

⊷ **Sarah's life span, and purchase of a burial site.** The Sages teach that the narratives of Sarah's death and the *Akeidah* follow one another to indicate that she died as a result of that event. Told by Satan that Abraham had

actually slaughtered Isaac, she cried out in grief, and died (*Targum Yonasan*). This explains why Abraham and Isaac were not present at her death.

23:1. *Rashi* explains that the repetition of the word *years* divides Sarah's life into three periods, each with its own uniqueness [and each period shared the particular characteristic of its neighbor]. At a hundred she was as sinless as a twenty-year-old, for until the age of twenty, a person *you have done this thing, and have not withheld your son, your only one,* [17] *that I shall surely bless you and greatly increase your offspring like the stars of the heavens and like the sand on the seashore; and your offspring shall inherit the gate of its enemy.* [18] *And all the nations of the earth shall bless themselves by your offspring, because you have listened to My voice."*

[19] *Abraham returned to his young men, and they stood up and went together to Beer-sheba, and Abraham stayed at Beer-sheba.*

The birth of Rebecca [20] *It came to pass after these things, that Abraham was told, saying: Behold, Milcah too has borne children to Nahor, your brother:* [21] *Uz, his firstborn; Buz, his brother; Kemuel, the father of Aram;* [22] *and Chesed, Hazo, Pildash, Jidlaph, and Bethuel;* [23] *And Bethuel begot Rebecca. These eight Milcah bore to Nahor, Abraham's brother.* [24] *And his concubine, whose name was Reumah, also bore children: Tebah, Gaham, Tahash, and Maachah.*

PARASHAS CHAYEI SARAH

23

Sarah's death, and purchase of a burial site

[1] *S̲arah's lifetime was one hundred years, twenty years, and seven years; the years of Sarah's life.* [2] *Sarah died in Kiriath-arba which is Hebron in the land of Canaan; and Abraham came to eulogize Sarah and to weep for her.* [3] *Abraham rose up from the presence of his dead, and spoke to the children of Heth, saying:* [4] *"I am an alien and a resident among you; grant me an estate for a burial site with you, that I may bury my dead from before me."*

[5] *And the children of Heth answered Abraham, saying to him:* [6] *"Hear us, my lord: You are a prince of God in our midst; in the choicest of our burial places bury your dead, any of us will not withhold his burial place from you, from burying your dead."*

[7] *Then Abraham rose up and bowed down to the members of the council, to the children of Heth.* [8] *He spoke to them saying: "If it is truly your will to bury my dead from before me, heed me, and intercede for me with Ephron son of Zohar.* [9] *Let him grant me the Cave of Machpelah which is his, on the edge of his field; let him grant it to me for its full price, in your midst, as an estate for a burial site."*

[10] *Now, Ephron was sitting in the midst of the children of Heth; and Ephron the Hittite responded to Abraham in the hearing of the children of Heth, for all who come to the gate of his city, saying:* [11] *"No, my lord; heed me! I have given you the field, and as for the cave that is in it, I have given it to you; In the view of the children of my people have I given it to you; bury your dead."* [12] *So Abraham bowed down before the members of the council.* [13] *He spoke to Ephron in the hearing of the members of the council, saying: "Rather, if only you would heed me! I give the price of the field, accept it from me, that I may bury my dead there."*

[14] *And Ephron replied to Abraham, saying to him:* [15] *"My lord, heed me! Land worth four hundred silver shekels; between me and you — what is it? Bury your dead."*

---

does not suffer Heavenly punishment. And at twenty she still had the wholesome natural beauty of a seven-year-old, who does not use cosmetics (*Chizkuni*).

23:2. The word וְלִבְכֹּתָהּ, *and to bewail her,* is written with a small כ to suggest that although Abraham's grief was infinite, the full measure of his pain was concealed in his heart and the privacy of his home (*R' Hirsch*).

23:11. As the later verses reveal, Ephron's public generosity was a sham. Not only had he no intention of making a gift, he hypocritically implied to Abraham that he expected an outrageously high price. As the Sages put it, the righteous say little but do much [see 18:5], but the wicked promise much and perform not even a little. They would offer to anoint with oil from an empty flask.

טז וַיִּשְׁמַ֣ע אַבְרָהָם֮ אֶל־עֶפְרוֹן֒ וַיִּשְׁקֹ֤ל אַבְרָהָם֙ לְעֶפְרֹ֔ן אֶת־הַכֶּ֕סֶף אֲשֶׁ֥ר דִּבֶּ֖ר בְּאָזְנֵ֣י בְנֵי־חֵ֑ת אַרְבַּ֤ע מֵאוֹת֙ שֶׁ֣קֶל כֶּ֔סֶף עֹבֵ֖ר לַסֹּחֵֽר:

יז וַיָּ֣קָם ׀ שְׂדֵ֣ה עֶפְר֗וֹן אֲשֶׁר֙ בַּמַּכְפֵּלָ֔ה אֲשֶׁ֖ר לִפְנֵ֣י מַמְרֵ֑א הַשָּׂדֶה֙ וְהַמְּעָרָ֣ה אֲשֶׁר־בּ֔וֹ וְכָל־הָעֵץ֙ אֲשֶׁ֣ר בַּשָּׂדֶ֔ה אֲשֶׁ֥ר בְּכָל־גְּבֻל֖וֹ סָבִֽיב:

יח לְאַבְרָהָ֥ם לְמִקְנָ֖ה לְעֵינֵ֣י בְנֵי־חֵ֑ת בְּכֹ֖ל בָּאֵ֥י שַֽׁעַר־עִירֽוֹ:

יט וְאַחֲרֵי־כֵן֩ קָבַ֨ר אַבְרָהָ֜ם אֶת־שָׂרָ֣ה אִשְׁתּ֗וֹ אֶל־מְעָרַ֞ת שְׂדֵ֧ה הַמַּכְפֵּלָ֛ה עַל־פְּנֵ֥י מַמְרֵ֖א הִ֣וא חֶבְר֑וֹן בְּאֶ֖רֶץ כְּנָֽעַן:

כ וַיָּ֨קָם הַשָּׂדֶ֜ה וְהַמְּעָרָ֧ה אֲשֶׁר־בּ֛וֹ לְאַבְרָהָ֖ם לַאֲחֻזַּת־קָ֑בֶר מֵאֵ֖ת בְּנֵי־חֵֽת:

כד
א וְאַבְרָהָ֣ם זָקֵ֔ן בָּ֖א בַּיָּמִ֑ים וַֽיהוָ֛ה בֵּרַ֥ךְ אֶת־אַבְרָהָ֖ם בַּכֹּֽל:

ב וַיֹּ֣אמֶר אַבְרָהָ֗ם אֶל־עַבְדּוֹ֙ זְקַ֣ן בֵּית֔וֹ הַמֹּשֵׁ֖ל בְּכָל־אֲשֶׁר־ל֑וֹ שִֽׂים־נָ֥א יָדְךָ֖ תַּ֥חַת יְרֵכִֽי:

ג וְאַשְׁבִּ֣יעֲךָ֔ בַּֽיהוָה֙ אֱלֹהֵ֣י הַשָּׁמַ֔יִם וֵֽאלֹהֵ֖י הָאָ֑רֶץ אֲשֶׁ֨ר לֹֽא־תִקַּ֤ח אִשָּׁה֙ לִבְנִ֔י מִבְּנוֹת֙ הַֽכְּנַעֲנִ֔י אֲשֶׁ֥ר אָנֹכִ֖י יוֹשֵׁ֥ב בְּקִרְבּֽוֹ:

ד כִּ֧י אֶל־אַרְצִ֛י וְאֶל־מֽוֹלַדְתִּ֖י תֵּלֵ֑ךְ וְלָקַחְתָּ֥ אִשָּׁ֖ה לִבְנִ֥י לְיִצְחָֽק:

ה וַיֹּ֤אמֶר אֵלָיו֙ הָעֶ֔בֶד אוּלַי֙ לֹא־תֹאבֶ֣ה הָֽאִשָּׁ֔ה לָלֶ֥כֶת אַחֲרַ֖י אֶל־הָאָ֣רֶץ הַזֹּ֑את הֶֽהָשֵׁ֤ב אָשִׁיב֙ אֶת־בִּנְךָ֔ אֶל־הָאָ֖רֶץ אֲשֶׁר־יָצָ֥אתָ מִשָּֽׁם:

ו וַיֹּ֥אמֶר אֵלָ֖יו אַבְרָהָ֑ם הִשָּׁ֣מֶר לְךָ֔ פֶּן־תָּשִׁ֥יב אֶת־בְּנִ֖י שָֽׁמָּה:

ז יְהוָ֣ה ׀ אֱלֹהֵ֣י הַשָּׁמַ֗יִם אֲשֶׁ֤ר לְקָחַ֨נִי֙ מִבֵּ֣ית אָבִי֙ וּמֵאֶ֣רֶץ מֽוֹלַדְתִּ֔י וַאֲשֶׁ֨ר דִּבֶּר־לִ֜י וַאֲשֶׁ֤ר נִֽשְׁבַּֽע־לִי֙ לֵאמֹ֔ר לְזַ֨רְעֲךָ֔ אֶתֵּ֖ן אֶת־הָאָ֣רֶץ הַזֹּ֑את ה֗וּא יִשְׁלַ֤ח מַלְאָכוֹ֙ לְפָנֶ֔יךָ וְלָקַחְתָּ֥ אִשָּׁ֛ה לִבְנִ֖י מִשָּֽׁם:

ח וְאִם־לֹ֨א תֹאבֶ֤ה הָֽאִשָּׁה֙ לָלֶ֣כֶת אַחֲרֶ֔יךָ וְנִקִּ֕יתָ מִשְּׁבֻעָתִ֖י זֹ֑את רַ֧ק אֶת־בְּנִ֛י לֹ֥א תָשֵׁ֖ב שָֽׁמָּה:

ט וַיָּ֤שֶׂם הָעֶ֨בֶד֙ אֶת־יָד֔וֹ תַּ֛חַת יֶ֥רֶךְ אַבְרָהָ֖ם אֲדֹנָ֑יו וַיִּשָּׁ֣בַֽע ל֔וֹ עַל־הַדָּבָ֖ר הַזֶּֽה:

י וַיִּקַּ֣ח הָ֠עֶבֶד עֲשָׂרָ֨ה גְמַלִּ֜ים מִגְּמַלֵּ֤י אֲדֹנָיו֙ וַיֵּ֔לֶךְ וְכָל־ט֥וּב אֲדֹנָ֖יו בְּיָד֑וֹ וַיָּ֗קָם וַיֵּ֛לֶךְ אֶל־אֲרַ֥ם נַֽהֲרַ֖יִם אֶל־עִ֥יר נָחֽוֹר:

יא וַיַּבְרֵ֧ךְ הַגְּמַלִּ֛ים מִח֥וּץ לָעִ֖יר אֶל־בְּאֵ֣ר הַמָּ֑יִם לְעֵ֣ת עֶ֔רֶב לְעֵ֖ת צֵ֥את הַשֹּׁאֲבֹֽת:

יב וַיֹּאמַ֓ר ׀ יְהוָ֗ה אֱלֹהֵי֙ אֲדֹנִ֣י אַבְרָהָ֔ם הַקְרֵה־נָ֥א לְפָנַ֖י הַיּ֑וֹם וַֽעֲשֵׂה־חֶ֕סֶד עִ֖ם אֲדֹנִ֥י אַבְרָהָֽם:

יג הִנֵּ֛ה אָנֹכִ֥י נִצָּ֖ב עַל־עֵ֣ין הַמָּ֑יִם וּבְנוֹת֙ אַנְשֵׁ֣י הָעִ֔יר יֹצְאֹ֖ת לִשְׁאֹ֥ב מָֽיִם:

יד וְהָיָ֣ה הַֽנַּעֲרָ֗ אֲשֶׁ֨ר אֹמַ֤ר אֵלֶ֨יהָ֙ הַטִּי־נָ֤א כַדֵּךְ֙ וְאֶשְׁתֶּ֔ה וְאָמְרָ֣ה שְׁתֵ֔ה וְגַם־גְּמַלֶּ֖יךָ אַשְׁקֶ֑ה אֹתָ֤הּ הֹכַ֨חְתָּ֙ לְעַבְדְּךָ֣ לְיִצְחָ֔ק וּבָ֣הּ אֵדַ֔ע כִּי־עָשִׂ֥יתָ חֶ֖סֶד עִם־אֲדֹנִֽי:

טו וַֽיְהִי־ה֗וּא טֶרֶם֮ כִּלָּ֣ה לְדַבֵּר֒ וְהִנֵּ֧ה רִבְקָ֣ה יֹצֵ֗את אֲשֶׁ֤ר יֻלְּדָה֙ לִבְתוּאֵ֔ל בֶּן־מִלְכָּ֔ה אֵ֥שֶׁת נָח֖וֹר אֲחִ֣י אַבְרָהָ֑ם וְכַדָּ֖הּ עַל־שִׁכְמָֽהּ:

טז וְהַֽנַּעֲרָ֗ טֹבַ֤ת מַרְאֶה֙ מְאֹ֔ד בְּתוּלָ֕ה וְאִ֖ישׁ לֹ֣א יְדָעָ֑הּ

שני (verse 17)
שלישי (verse 10)

24:1-10. Finding a wife for Isaac. Abraham's own productive life was coming to an end. Isaac was thirty-seven years old when Sarah died and Abraham was troubled by the thought that had Isaac been slaughtered at the *Akeidah*, he would have left no worthy successor. Therefore, Abraham undertook to provide for the future by finding a wife for Isaac. But she had to be the next Sarah of the Jewish people, a woman who would be not only a wife and mother, but a Matriarch.

24:3. The rejection of the Canaanites could not have been based on their idol worship, because Abraham's family in Charan worshiped idols, as well. Rather, Abraham was motivated by the moral degeneracy of the Canaanites. Idolatry is an intellectual perversion, and as such it can be remedied, but a lack of morality, ethics, and modesty affects one's entire nature, and disqualifies a woman from being the mate of an Isaac (*R' Hirsch*, based on *Drashos HaRan*).

¹⁶ Abraham heeded Ephron, and Abraham weighed out to Ephron the price which he had mentioned in the hearing of the children of Heth, four hundred silver shekels in negotiable currency. ¹⁷ And Ephron's field, which was in Machpelah, facing Mamre, the field and the cave within it and all the trees in the field, within all its surrounding boundaries, was confirmed ¹⁸ as Abraham's as a purchase in the view of the children of Heth, among all who came to the gate of his city. ¹⁹ And afterwards Abraham buried Sarah his wife in the cave of the field of Machpelah facing Mamre, which is Hebron, in the land of Canaan. ²⁰ Thus, the field with the cave that was in it, was confirmed as Abraham's as an estate for a burial site, from the children of Heth.

24

Finding a wife for Isaac

¹ **N**ow Abraham was old, well on in years, and HASHEM had blessed Abraham with everything. ² And Abraham said to his servant, the elder of his household who controlled all that was his: "Place now your hand under my thigh. ³ And I will have you swear by HASHEM, God of heaven and God of earth, that you not take a wife for my son from the daughters of the Canaanites, * among whom I dwell. ⁴ Rather, to my land and to my kindred shall you go and take a wife for my son for Isaac."

⁵ The servant said to him: "Perhaps the woman shall not wish to follow me to this land; shall I take your son back to the land from which you departed?" ⁶ Abraham answered him, 'Beware not to return my son to there. ⁷ HASHEM, God of heaven, Who took me from the house of my father and from the land of my birth; Who spoke concerning me, and Who swore to me saying, 'To your offspring will I give this land,' He will send His angel before you, and you will take a wife for my son from there. ⁸ But if the woman will not wish to follow you, you shall then be absolved of this oath of mine. However, do not return my son to there."

⁹ So the servant placed his hand under the thigh of Abraham his master and swore to him regarding this matter. ¹⁰ Then the servant took ten camels of his master's camels and set out with all the bounty of his master in his hand and made his way to Aram Naharaim to the city of Nahor. ¹¹ He made the camels kneel down outside the city towards a well of water at evening time, the time when the women who draw water come out. ¹² And he said, "HASHEM, God of my master Abraham, may You so arrange it for me this day that You do kindness with my master Abraham. ¹³ Behold, I am standing here by the spring of water and the daughters of the townsmen come out to draw water. ¹⁴ Let it be that the maiden to whom I shall say, 'Please tip over your jug so I may drink,' and who replies, 'Drink, and I will even water your camels,'* her will You have designated for Your servant, for Isaac; and may I know through her that You have done kindness with my master."

Eliezer's criteria

¹⁵ And it was when he had not yet finished speaking that suddenly Rebecca was coming out — she who had been born to Bethuel the son of Milcah the wife of Nahor, brother of Abraham — with her jug upon her shoulder. ¹⁶ Now the maiden was very fair to look upon; a virgin whom no man had known.

24:14. Ordinarily it is forbidden to base one's actions on omens (see *Deuteronomy* 18:10). The prohibition, however, applies only to omens unrelated to the choice being made, such as saying, "If the sun shines tomorrow, it is a sign that I should marry this woman."

In Eliezer's case, his omen was appropriate to his mission: Since the Matriarch of Israel had to be a woman of kindness and sensitivity, Eliezer was looking, not for omens, but for proof of her qualifications (*Ran, Chullin* 95b).

יז וַתֵּרֶד הָעַיְנָה וַתְּמַלֵּא כַדָּהּ וַתָּעַל: וַיָּרָץ הָעֶבֶד לִקְרָאתָהּ וַיֹּאמֶר הַגְמִיאִינִי

יח נָא מְעַט־מַיִם מִכַּדֵּךְ: וַתֹּאמֶר שְׁתֵה אֲדֹנִי וַתְּמַהֵר וַתֹּרֶד כַּדָּהּ עַל־יָדָהּ

יט וַתַּשְׁקֵהוּ: וַתְּכַל לְהַשְׁקֹתוֹ וַתֹּאמֶר גַּם לִגְמַלֶּיךָ אֶשְׁאָב עַד אִם־כִּלּוּ

כ לִשְׁתֹּת: וַתְּמַהֵר וַתְּעַר כַּדָּהּ אֶל־הַשֹּׁקֶת וַתָּרָץ עוֹד אֶל־הַבְּאֵר לִשְׁאֹב

כא וַתִּשְׁאַב לְכָל־גְּמַלָּיו: וְהָאִישׁ מִשְׁתָּאֵה לָהּ מַחֲרִישׁ לָדַעַת הַהִצְלִיחַ יְהוָה

כב דַּרְכּוֹ אִם־לֹא: וַיְהִי כַּאֲשֶׁר כִּלּוּ הַגְּמַלִּים לִשְׁתּוֹת וַיִּקַּח הָאִישׁ נֶזֶם זָהָב

כג בֶּקַע מִשְׁקָלוֹ וּשְׁנֵי צְמִידִים עַל־יָדֶיהָ עֲשָׂרָה זָהָב מִשְׁקָלָם: וַיֹּאמֶר בַּת־מִי

כד אַתְּ הַגִּידִי נָא לִי הֲיֵשׁ בֵּית־אָבִיךְ מָקוֹם לָנוּ לָלִין: וַתֹּאמֶר אֵלָיו בַּת־

כה בְּתוּאֵל אָנֹכִי בֶּן־מִלְכָּה אֲשֶׁר יָלְדָה לְנָחוֹר: וַתֹּאמֶר אֵלָיו גַּם־תֶּבֶן

כו גַּם־מִסְפּוֹא רַב עִמָּנוּ גַּם־מָקוֹם לָלוּן: וַיִּקֹּד הָאִישׁ וַיִּשְׁתַּחוּ לַיהוָה:

רביעי

כז וַיֹּאמֶר בָּרוּךְ יְהוָה אֱלֹהֵי אֲדֹנִי אַבְרָהָם אֲשֶׁר לֹא־עָזַב חַסְדּוֹ וַאֲמִתּוֹ מֵעִם

כח אֲדֹנִי אָנֹכִי בַּדֶּרֶךְ נָחַנִי יְהוָה בֵּית אֲחֵי אֲדֹנִי: וַתָּרָץ הַנַּעֲרָ וַתַּגֵּד לְבֵית

כט אִמָּהּ כַּדְּבָרִים הָאֵלֶּה: וּלְרִבְקָה אָח וּשְׁמוֹ לָבָן וַיָּרָץ לָבָן אֶל־הָאִישׁ

ל הַחוּצָה אֶל־הָעָיִן: וַיְהִי ׀ כִּרְאֹת אֶת־הַנֶּזֶם וְאֶת־הַצְּמִדִים עַל־יְדֵי אֲחֹתוֹ

לא וּכְשָׁמְעוֹ אֶת־דִּבְרֵי רִבְקָה אֲחֹתוֹ לֵאמֹר כֹּה־דִבֶּר אֵלַי הָאִישׁ וַיָּבֹא אֶל־

הָאִישׁ וְהִנֵּה עֹמֵד עַל־הַגְּמַלִּים עַל־הָעָיִן: וַיֹּאמֶר בּוֹא בְּרוּךְ יְהוָה לָמָּה

לב תַעֲמֹד בַּחוּץ וְאָנֹכִי פִּנִּיתִי הַבַּיִת וּמָקוֹם לַגְּמַלִּים: וַיָּבֹא הָאִישׁ הַבַּיְתָה

וַיְפַתַּח הַגְּמַלִּים וַיִּתֵּן תֶּבֶן וּמִסְפּוֹא לַגְּמַלִּים וּמַיִם לִרְחֹץ רַגְלָיו וְרַגְלֵי

לג הָאֲנָשִׁים אֲשֶׁר אִתּוֹ: °וַיּישֶׂם [°וַיּוּשַׂם ק] לְפָנָיו לֶאֱכֹל וַיֹּאמֶר לֹא אֹכַל

לד-לה עַד אִם־דִּבַּרְתִּי דְּבָרָי וַיֹּאמֶר דַּבֵּר: וַיֹּאמַר עֶבֶד אַבְרָהָם אָנֹכִי: וַיהוָה בֵּרַךְ

אֶת־אֲדֹנִי מְאֹד וַיִּגְדָּל וַיִּתֶּן־לוֹ צֹאן וּבָקָר וְכֶסֶף וְזָהָב וַעֲבָדִם וּשְׁפָחֹת

לו וּגְמַלִּים וַחֲמֹרִים: וַתֵּלֶד שָׂרָה אֵשֶׁת אֲדֹנִי בֵן לַאדֹנִי אַחֲרֵי זִקְנָתָהּ וַיִּתֶּן־לוֹ

לז אֶת־כָּל־אֲשֶׁר־לוֹ: וַיַּשְׁבִּעֵנִי אֲדֹנִי לֵאמֹר לֹא־תִקַּח אִשָּׁה לִבְנִי מִבְּנוֹת

לח הַכְּנַעֲנִי אֲשֶׁר אָנֹכִי יֹשֵׁב בְּאַרְצוֹ: אִם־לֹא אֶל־בֵּית־אָבִי תֵּלֵךְ וְאֶל־

לט מִשְׁפַּחְתִּי וְלָקַחְתָּ אִשָּׁה לִבְנִי: וָאֹמַר אֶל־אֲדֹנִי אֻלַי לֹא־תֵלֵךְ הָאִשָּׁה

מ אַחֲרָי: וַיֹּאמֶר אֵלָי יְהוָה אֲשֶׁר־הִתְהַלַּכְתִּי לְפָנָיו יִשְׁלַח מַלְאָכוֹ אִתָּךְ

מא וְהִצְלִיחַ דַּרְכֶּךָ וְלָקַחְתָּ אִשָּׁה לִבְנִי מִמִּשְׁפַּחְתִּי וּמִבֵּית אָבִי: אָז תִּנָּקֶה

מֵאָלָתִי כִּי תָבוֹא אֶל־מִשְׁפַּחְתִּי וְאִם־לֹא יִתְּנוּ לָךְ וְהָיִיתָ נָקִי מֵאָלָתִי:

24:27. Eliezer's expression of gratitude revealed his own stature as Abraham's prime disciple and the master of his household. Everything that had happened he ascribed to the grace of God, and made clear that it was not in his merit, but in Abraham's.

24:28-31. Laban. The Torah introduces us to Rebecca's family, where it seems that her father played little role, and her brother, Laban, was dominant. From his profound influence in the household it would appear that he was either the only son or the oldest (R' Hoffmann).

24:32. Abraham's livestock were muzzled whenever they were away from home, so that they could not graze in other people's fields (Rashi; Midrash).

24:33-39. The recapitulation. Eliezer repeated the entire story in order to convince them that God willed this marriage, thus delicately suggesting that it was not in their power to prevent it (Radak). Why does the Torah, which is so sparing of words, record Eliezer's entire recapitulation? The Sages exclaimed: יָפָה שִׂיחָתָן שֶׁל עַבְדֵי אָבוֹת לִפְנֵי הַמָּקוֹם מִתּוֹרָתָן שֶׁל בְּנֵיהֶם, *The ordinary conversation of the Patriarchs' servants is more pleasing before God than even*

She descended to the spring, filled her jug and ascended. [17] *The servant ran towards her and said, "Let me sip, if you please, a little water from your jug."*

Rebecca is equal to the test [18] *She said, "Drink, my lord," and quickly she lowered her jug to her hand and gave him to drink.*

[19] *When she finished giving him to drink, she said, "I will draw water even for your camels until they have finished drinking."* [20] *So she hurried and emptied her jug into the trough and kept running to the well to draw water; and she drew for all his camels.* [21] *The man was astonished at her, reflecting silently to know whether HASHEM had made his journey successful or not.* [22] *And it was, when the camels had finished drinking, the man took a golden nose ring, its weight was a beka, and two bracelets on her arms, ten gold shekels was their weight.* [23] *And he said, "Whose daughter are you? Pray tell me. Is there room in your father's house for us to spend the night?"*

[24] *She said to him, "I am the daughter of Bethuel the son of Milcah whom she bore to Nahor."* [25] *And she said to him, "Even straw and feed is plentiful with us as well as place to lodge."*

[26] *So the man bowed low and prostrated himself to HASHEM.* [27] *He said, "Blessed is HASHEM, * God of my master Abraham, Who has not withheld His kindness and truth from my master. As for me, HASHEM has guided me on the way to the house of my master's brothers."*

[28] *The maiden ran and told her mother's household according to these events.*

Laban [29] *Rebecca had a brother whose name was Laban: Laban ran to the man, outside to the spring.* [30] *For upon seeing the nose ring, and the bracelets on his sister's hands, and upon his hearing his sister Rebecca's words, saying, "Thus has the man spoken to me," he approached the man, who was still standing by the camels by the spring.* [31] *He said, "Come, O blessed of HASHEM! Why should you stand outside when I have cleared the house, and place for the camels?"*

[32] *So the man entered the house, and unmuzzled the camels. * He gave straw and feed for the camels, and water to bathe his feet and the feet of the men who were with him.* [33] *Food was set before him, but he said, "I will not eat until I have spoken my piece."*

And he said, "Speak."

The recapitulation [34] *Then he said, "A servant of Abraham am I.* [35] *HASHEM has greatly blessed my master, and he prospered; He has given him flocks, cattle, silver and gold, servants and maidservants, camels and donkeys.* [36] *Sarah, my master's wife, bore my master a son after she had grown old, and he gave him all that he possesses.* [37] *And my master had me take an oath saying, 'Do not take a wife for my son from the daughters of the Canaanites in whose land I dwell.* [38] *Unless you go to my father's house and to my family and take a wife for my son.'* [39] *And I said to my master, 'Perhaps the woman will not follow me?'* [40] *He replied to me, 'HASHEM, before Whom I have walked, will send His angel with you and make your journey successful, and you will take a wife for my son from my family and my father's house.* [41] *Then will you be absolved from my oath when you have come to my family; and if they will not give her to you, then, you shall be absolved from my oath.'*

---

the teachings of their children, for Eliezer's full account of his journey is recorded in the Torah, whereas many important halachic principles are derived only from textual allusions. From Eliezer's subtle changes in recounting the episode, the expositors have perceived both great ethical messages and Eliezer's own wisdom.

מב וָאָבֹא הַיּוֹם אֶל־הָעָיִן וָאֹמַר יְהֹוָה אֱלֹהֵי אֲדֹנִי אַבְרָהָם אִם־יֶשְׁךָ־נָּא
מג מַצְלִיחַ דַּרְכִּי אֲשֶׁר אָנֹכִי הֹלֵךְ עָלֶיהָ: הִנֵּה אָנֹכִי נִצָּב עַל־עֵין הַמָּיִם וְהָיָה
הָעַלְמָה הַיֹּצֵאת לִשְׁאֹב וְאָמַרְתִּי אֵלֶיהָ הַשְׁקִינִי־נָא מְעַט־מַיִם מִכַּדֵּךְ:
מד וְאָמְרָה אֵלַי גַּם־אַתָּה שְׁתֵה וְגַם לִגְמַלֶּיךָ אֶשְׁאָב הִוא הָאִשָּׁה אֲשֶׁר־
מה הֹכִיחַ יְהֹוָה לְבֶן־אֲדֹנִי: אֲנִי טֶרֶם אֲכַלֶּה לְדַבֵּר אֶל־לִבִּי וְהִנֵּה רִבְקָה
יֹצֵאת וְכַדָּהּ עַל־שִׁכְמָהּ וַתֵּרֶד הָעַיְנָה וַתִּשְׁאָב וָאֹמַר אֵלֶיהָ הַשְׁקִינִי נָא:
מו וַתְּמַהֵר וַתּוֹרֶד כַּדָּהּ מֵעָלֶיהָ וַתֹּאמֶר שְׁתֵה וְגַם־גְּמַלֶּיךָ אַשְׁקֶה וָאֵשְׁתְּ וְגַם
מז הַגְּמַלִּים הִשְׁקָתָה: וָאֶשְׁאַל אֹתָהּ וָאֹמַר בַּת־מִי אַתְּ וַתֹּאמֶר בַּת־בְּתוּאֵל
בֶּן־נָחוֹר אֲשֶׁר יָלְדָה־לּוֹ מִלְכָּה וָאָשִׂם הַנֶּזֶם עַל־אַפָּהּ וְהַצְּמִידִים עַל־
מח יָדֶיהָ: וָאֶקֹּד וָאֶשְׁתַּחֲוֶה לַיהֹוָה וָאֲבָרֵךְ אֶת־יְהֹוָה אֱלֹהֵי אֲדֹנִי אַבְרָהָם
מט אֲשֶׁר הִנְחַנִי בְּדֶרֶךְ אֱמֶת לָקַחַת אֶת־בַּת־אֲחִי אֲדֹנִי לִבְנוֹ: וְעַתָּה אִם־
יֶשְׁכֶם עֹשִׂים חֶסֶד וֶאֱמֶת אֶת־אֲדֹנִי הַגִּידוּ לִי וְאִם־לֹא הַגִּידוּ לִי וְאֶפְנֶה
נ עַל־יָמִין אוֹ עַל־שְׂמֹאל: וַיַּעַן לָבָן וּבְתוּאֵל וַיֹּאמְרוּ מֵיְהֹוָה יָצָא הַדָּבָר לֹא
נא נוּכַל דַּבֵּר אֵלֶיךָ רַע אוֹ־טוֹב: הִנֵּה־רִבְקָה לְפָנֶיךָ קַח וָלֵךְ וּתְהִי אִשָּׁה לְבֶן־
נב אֲדֹנֶיךָ כַּאֲשֶׁר דִּבֶּר יְהֹוָה: וַיְהִי כַּאֲשֶׁר שָׁמַע עֶבֶד אַבְרָהָם אֶת־דִּבְרֵיהֶם
נג וַיִּשְׁתַּחוּ אַרְצָה לַיהֹוָה: וַיּוֹצֵא הָעֶבֶד כְּלֵי־כֶסֶף וּכְלֵי זָהָב וּבְגָדִים וַיִּתֵּן   חמישי
נד לְרִבְקָה וּמִגְדָּנֹת נָתַן לְאָחִיהָ וּלְאִמָּהּ: וַיֹּאכְלוּ וַיִּשְׁתּוּ הוּא וְהָאֲנָשִׁים
אֲשֶׁר־עִמּוֹ וַיָּלִינוּ וַיָּקוּמוּ בַבֹּקֶר וַיֹּאמֶר שַׁלְּחֻנִי לַאדֹנִי: וַיֹּאמֶר אָחִיהָ
נו וְאִמָּהּ תֵּשֵׁב הַנַּעֲרָ אִתָּנוּ יָמִים אוֹ עָשׂוֹר אַחַר תֵּלֵךְ: וַיֹּאמֶר אֲלֵהֶם אַל־
נז תְּאַחֲרוּ אֹתִי וַיהֹוָה הִצְלִיחַ דַּרְכִּי שַׁלְּחוּנִי וְאֵלְכָה לַאדֹנִי: וַיֹּאמְרוּ נִקְרָא
נח לַנַּעֲרָ וְנִשְׁאֲלָה אֶת־פִּיהָ: וַיִּקְרְאוּ לְרִבְקָה וַיֹּאמְרוּ אֵלֶיהָ הֲתֵלְכִי עִם־
נט הָאִישׁ הַזֶּה וַתֹּאמֶר אֵלֵךְ: וַיְשַׁלְּחוּ אֶת־רִבְקָה אֲחֹתָם וְאֶת־מֵנִקְתָּהּ
ס וְאֶת־עֶבֶד אַבְרָהָם וְאֶת־אֲנָשָׁיו: וַיְבָרֲכוּ אֶת־רִבְקָה וַיֹּאמְרוּ לָהּ אֲחֹתֵנוּ
סא אַתְּ הֲיִי לְאַלְפֵי רְבָבָה וְיִירַשׁ זַרְעֵךְ אֵת שַׁעַר שֹׂנְאָיו: וַתָּקָם רִבְקָה
וְנַעֲרֹתֶיהָ וַתִּרְכַּבְנָה עַל־הַגְּמַלִּים וַתֵּלַכְנָה אַחֲרֵי הָאִישׁ וַיִּקַּח הָעֶבֶד אֶת־
סב רִבְקָה וַיֵּלַךְ: וְיִצְחָק בָּא מִבּוֹא בְּאֵר לַחַי רֹאִי וְהוּא יוֹשֵׁב בְּאֶרֶץ הַנֶּגֶב:
סג וַיֵּצֵא יִצְחָק לָשׂוּחַ בַּשָּׂדֶה לִפְנוֹת עָרֶב וַיִּשָּׂא עֵינָיו וַיַּרְא וְהִנֵּה גְמַלִּים
סד בָּאִים: וַתִּשָּׂא רִבְקָה אֶת־עֵינֶיהָ וַתֵּרֶא אֶת־יִצְחָק וַתִּפֹּל מֵעַל הַגָּמָל:

24:50. The family's response is the best evidence of Eliezer's success in having carried out his mission.

The Sages see this response as a proof that God ordains a man's proper mate (*Moed Kattan* 18b).

24:62-67. Isaac and Rebecca. The brief passage describing the meeting and marriage of Isaac and Rebecca is touching and reflective of basic principles of Judaism and Jewish marriage. It begins with Isaac walking back home from praying at a place that recalled God's mercy to the previous generation, for Jews cleave

to their past and the God Who guided it. Isaac and Rebecca "met," but not by chance. She displayed the personal modesty that has always been one of the glories of Jewish women and she recognized intuitively that the stranger she had just encountered was a holy person. Finally, Isaac brought her to his mother's tent, and there it became apparent that she was a fitting successor to Sarah, for the holy presence of Sarah returned to the tent of her son. It was when he saw that holiness that Isaac loved her (v. 67), for the Jewish home is a temple and

[42] "I came today to the spring and said, 'HASHEM, God of my master Abraham, if You would graciously make successful the way on which I go. [43] Behold, I am standing by the spring of water; let it be that the young woman who comes out to draw and to whom I shall say, "Please give me some water to drink from your jug," [44] and who will answer, "You may also drink and I will draw water for your camels, too," she shall be the woman whom HASHEM has designated for my master's son.' [45] I had not yet finished meditating when suddenly Rebecca came out with a jug on her shoulder, and descended to the spring and drew water. Then I said to her, 'Please give me a drink.' [46] She hurried and lowered her jug from upon herself and said, 'Drink, and I will even water your camels.' So I drank and she watered the camels also.

[47] "Then I questioned her and said, 'Whose daughter are you?' And she said, 'The daughter of Bethuel, son of Nahor, whom Milcah bore to him.' And I placed the ring on her nose and the bracelets on her hands. [48] Then I bowed and prostrated myself to HASHEM and blessed HASHEM, God of my master Abraham, Who led me on a true path to take the daughter of my master's brother for his son. [49] And now, if you intend to do kindness and truth with my master, tell me; and if not, tell me, and I will turn to the right or to the left."

[50] Then Laban and Bethuel answered and said, "The matter stemmed from HASHEM!* We can say to you neither bad nor good. [51] Here, Rebecca is before you; take her and go, and let her be a wife to your master's son as HASHEM has spoken." [52] And it was, when Abraham's servant heard their words, he prostrated himself to the ground unto HASHEM. [53] The servant brought out objects of silver and gold, and garments, and gave them to Rebecca; and delicious fruits he gave to her brother and her mother. [54] They ate and drank, he and the men who were with him, and they spent the night; when they arose next morning, he said, "Send me to my master."

[55] Her brother and mother said, "Let the maiden remain with us a year or ten [months]; then she will go." [56] He said to them, "Do not delay me now that HASHEM had made my journey successful. Send me, and I will go to my master." [57] And they said, "Let us call the maiden and ask her decision."

[58] They called Rebecca and said to her, "Will you go with this man?" And she said, "I will go."

[59] So they escorted Rebecca their sister, and her nurse, as well as Abraham's servant and his men. [60] They blessed Rebecca and said to her, "Our sister, may you come to be thousands of myriads, and may your offspring inherit the gate of its foes."

[61] Then Rebecca arose with her maidens; they rode upon the camels and proceeded after the man; the servant took Rebecca and went.

Isaac and Rebecca [62] Now Isaac came from having gone to Beer-lahai-roi, for he dwelt in the south country. [63] Isaac went out to supplicate in the field towards evening* and he raised his eyes and saw, and behold! camels were coming. [64] And Rebecca raised her eyes and saw Isaac; she inclined while upon the camel.

---

its priestess is the wife and mother whose spirit infuses it.

24:63. From the fact that Isaac prayed before nightfall, the Talmud (*Berachos* 26b) and Midrash derive the tradi-

tion that Isaac instituted the *Minchah* [afternoon] prayer. That Abraham instituted the *Shacharis* [morning] prayer is derived from 19:27; and that Jacob instituted the *Maariv* [evening] prayer is derived from 28:11.

סה וַתֹּאמֶר אֶל־הָעֶבֶד מִי־הָאִישׁ הַלָּזֶה הַהֹלֵךְ בַּשָּׂדֶה לִקְרָאתֵנוּ וַיֹּאמֶר

סו הָעֶבֶד הוּא אֲדֹנִי וַתִּקַּח הַצָּעִיף וַתִּתְכָּס: וַיְסַפֵּר הָעֶבֶד לְיִצְחָק אֵת כָּל־

סז הַדְּבָרִים אֲשֶׁר עָשָׂה: וַיְבִאֶהָ יִצְחָק הָאֹהֱלָה שָׂרָה אִמּוֹ וַיִּקַּח אֶת־רִבְקָה וַתְּהִי־לוֹ לְאִשָּׁה וַיֶּאֱהָבֶהָ וַיִּנָּחֵם יִצְחָק אַחֲרֵי אִמּוֹ:

כה ששי א-ב וַיֹּסֶף אַבְרָהָם וַיִּקַּח אִשָּׁה וּשְׁמָהּ קְטוּרָה: וַתֵּלֶד לוֹ אֶת־זִמְרָן וְאֶת־יָקְשָׁן

ג וְאֶת־מְדָן וְאֶת־מִדְיָן וְאֶת־יִשְׁבָּק וְאֶת־שׁוּחַ: וְיָקְשָׁן יָלַד אֶת־שְׁבָא וְאֶת־

ד דְּדָן וּבְנֵי דְדָן הָיוּ אַשּׁוּרִם וּלְטוּשִׁם וּלְאֻמִּים: וּבְנֵי מִדְיָן עֵיפָה וָעֵפֶר וַחֲנֹךְ

ה וַאֲבִידָע וְאֶלְדָּעָה כָּל־אֵלֶּה בְּנֵי קְטוּרָה: וַיִּתֵּן אַבְרָהָם אֶת־כָּל־אֲשֶׁר־לוֹ

ו לְיִצְחָק: וְלִבְנֵי הַפִּילַגְשִׁים אֲשֶׁר לְאַבְרָהָם נָתַן אַבְרָהָם מַתָּנֹת וַיְשַׁלְּחֵם

ז מֵעַל יִצְחָק בְּנוֹ בְּעוֹדֶנּוּ חַי קֵדְמָה אֶל־אֶרֶץ קֶדֶם: וְאֵלֶּה יְמֵי שְׁנֵי־חַיֵּי

ח אַבְרָהָם אֲשֶׁר־חָי מְאַת שָׁנָה וְשִׁבְעִים שָׁנָה וְחָמֵשׁ שָׁנִים: וַיִּגְוַע וַיָּמָת

ט אַבְרָהָם בְּשֵׂיבָה טוֹבָה זָקֵן וְשָׂבֵעַ וַיֵּאָסֶף אֶל־עַמָּיו: וַיִּקְבְּרוּ אֹתוֹ יִצְחָק וְיִשְׁמָעֵאל בָּנָיו אֶל־מְעָרַת הַמַּכְפֵּלָה אֶל־שְׂדֵה עֶפְרֹן בֶּן־צֹחַר הַחִתִּי

י אֲשֶׁר עַל־פְּנֵי מַמְרֵא: הַשָּׂדֶה אֲשֶׁר־קָנָה אַבְרָהָם מֵאֵת בְּנֵי־חֵת שָׁמָּה

יא קֻבַּר אַבְרָהָם וְשָׂרָה אִשְׁתּוֹ: וַיְהִי אַחֲרֵי מוֹת אַבְרָהָם וַיְבָרֶךְ אֱלֹהִים אֶת־יִצְחָק בְּנוֹ וַיֵּשֶׁב יִצְחָק עִם־בְּאֵר לַחַי רֹאִי:

שביעי יב וְאֵלֶּה תֹּלְדֹת יִשְׁמָעֵאל בֶּן־אַבְרָהָם אֲשֶׁר יָלְדָה הָגָר הַמִּצְרִית שִׁפְחַת

יג שָׂרָה לְאַבְרָהָם: וְאֵלֶּה שְׁמוֹת בְּנֵי יִשְׁמָעֵאל בִּשְׁמֹתָם לְתוֹלְדֹתָם בְּכֹר

יד-טו יִשְׁמָעֵאל נְבָיֹת וְקֵדָר וְאַדְבְּאֵל וּמִבְשָׂם: וּמִשְׁמָע וְדוּמָה וּמַשָּׂא: חֲדַד

מפטיר טז וְתֵימָא יְטוּר נָפִישׁ וָקֵדְמָה: אֵלֶּה הֵם בְּנֵי יִשְׁמָעֵאל וְאֵלֶּה שְׁמֹתָם בְּחַצְרֵיהֶם וּבְטִירֹתָם שְׁנֵים־עָשָׂר נְשִׂיאִם לְאֻמֹּתָם: וְאֵלֶּה שְׁנֵי חַיֵּי

יז יִשְׁמָעֵאל מְאַת שָׁנָה וּשְׁלֹשִׁים שָׁנָה וְשֶׁבַע שָׁנִים וַיִּגְוַע וַיָּמָת וַיֵּאָסֶף אֶל־

יח עַמָּיו: וַיִּשְׁכְּנוּ מֵחֲוִילָה עַד־שׁוּר אֲשֶׁר עַל־פְּנֵי מִצְרַיִם בֹּאֲכָה אַשּׁוּרָה עַל־פְּנֵי כָל־אֶחָיו נָפָל: פפפ ק״ה פסוקים. יהויד״ע סימן.

Haftaras Chayei Sarah: p. 796

פרשת תולדות

יט-כ וְאֵלֶּה תּוֹלְדֹת יִצְחָק בֶּן־אַבְרָהָם אַבְרָהָם הוֹלִיד אֶת־יִצְחָק: וַיְהִי יִצְחָק בֶּן־אַרְבָּעִים שָׁנָה בְּקַחְתּוֹ אֶת־רִבְקָה בַּת־בְּתוּאֵל הָאֲרַמִּי מִפַּדַּן אֲרָם אֲחוֹת

כא לָבָן הָאֲרַמִּי לוֹ לְאִשָּׁה: וַיֶּעְתַּר יִצְחָק לַיהוה לְנֹכַח אִשְׁתּוֹ כִּי עֲקָרָה הִוא

⇤ Abraham's later years. As is customary in the Torah, when a person's role in the development of the narrative is completed, his life is summed up, even though he may have lived for many more years. Once Abraham, at the age of 140, had arranged for the marriage of Isaac, the destiny of the Jewish people moved on to the next generation, even though Abraham lived to the age of 175. The Torah now summarizes the rest of his life.

25:1. Abraham remarried Keturah [Hagar], who was given this name because her deeds were as beautiful as incense [ketores], and because she had remained chaste [keturah is Aramaic for restrained] from the time she was separated from Abraham (Midrash; Rashi).

25:7. Abraham had lived his life fully; not one day was wasted. He died in the year 2123 from Creation (Seder Olam).

In giving his life span, the Torah follows the pattern it used in giving Sarah's years (see above, 23:1), to indicate that at a hundred he was like seventy, and at seventy like five — without sin (Rashi).

⁶⁵ *And she said to the servant, "Who is that man walking in the field toward us?"*
And the servant said, "He is my master." She then took the veil and covered
herself. ⁶⁶ *The servant told Isaac all the things he had done.* ⁶⁷ *And Isaac brought*
her into the tent of Sarah his mother; he married Rebecca, she became his wife,
and he loved her; and thus was Isaac consoled after his mother.

25

(See Appendix B,
chart 2)

¹ **A**braham proceeded and took a wife whose name was Keturah. * ² She bore
him Zimran, Jokshan, Medan, Midian, Ishbak and Shuah.* ³ *Jokshan begot*
Sheba and Dedan, and the children of Dedan were Asshurim, Letushim, and
Leummim. ⁴ *And the children of Midian: Ephah [and] Epher, Hanoch, Abida,*
and Eldaah; all these were the descendants of Keturah. ⁵ *Abraham gave all that*
he had to Isaac. ⁶ *But to the concubine-children who were Abraham's, Abra-*
ham gave gifts; then he sent them away from Isaac his son, while he was still
alive, eastward to the land of the east.

⁷ *Now these are the days of the years of Abraham's life which he lived:* * *a*
hundred years, seventy years, and five years. ⁸ *And Abraham expired and died*
at a good old age, mature and content, and he was gathered to his people. ⁹ *His*
sons Isaac and Ishmael buried him in the cave of Machpelah, in the field of
Ephron the son of Zohar the Hittite, facing Mamre. ¹⁰ *The field that Abraham*
had bought from the children of Heth, there Abraham was buried, and Sarah his
wife. ¹¹ *And it was after the death of Abraham that God blessed Isaac his son,*
and Isaac settled near Beer-lahai-roi.

¹² *These are the descendants of Ishmael, Abraham's son, whom Hagar the*
Egyptian, Sarah's maidservant, bore to Abraham. ¹³ *These are the names of the*
sons of Ishmael by their names, in order of their birth: Ishmael's firstborn
Nebaioth, Kedar, Adbeel, and Mibsam, ¹⁴ *Mishma, Dumah, and Massa,*
¹⁵ *Hadad and Tema, Jetur, Naphish, and Kedem.* ¹⁶ *These are the sons of*
Ishmael, and these are their names by their open cities and by their strongholds,
twelve chieftains for their nations.

¹⁷ *These were the years of Ishmael's life: a hundred and thirty-seven years,*
when he expired and died, and was gathered to his people. ¹⁸ *They dwelt from*
Havilah to Shur — which is near Egypt — toward Assyria; over all his brothers
he dwelt.

PARASHAS TOLDOS

Rebecca's
barrenness
and
pregnancy

¹⁹ **A**nd these are the offspring of Isaac son of Abraham — Abraham begot
Isaac.* ²⁰ *Isaac was forty years old when he took Rebecca, daughter of Be-*
thuel the Aramean from Paddan-aram, sister of Laban the Aramean, as a wife
for himself. ²¹ *Isaac entreated HASHEM opposite his wife, because she was barren.*

⋖§ Parashas Toldos

The Torah devotes much less space to Isaac's life than to the lives of Abraham and Jacob. On the one hand, Isaac seems to be but a bridge between his father and his son; on the other hand, he had the task of drawing the line separating good from evil — as represented by Jacob and Esau — because the emerging nation of Israel could not be a mixture of good and evil. In contrast to Abraham whose primary characteristic was *chessed*, or kindness, Isaac's was *gevurah*, or strength. One requires strength to differentiate between good and evil — and then to purge the bad and nurture the good. Isaac and Rebecca produced two sons; one became the personification of

righteousness and the other the personification of wickedness, and the parents had to make the distinction so that the nation of Israel would be pure.

25:19-23. The Sages note that the Matriarchs Sarah, Rebecca, and Rachel were barren. The commentators explain that their experiences prove that the emergence of Israel is a miracle, for each new generation was a gift of God to a mother who could not have given birth naturally. Their experience is a demonstration of the dictum that God desires the prayers of the righteous (*Yevamos* 64a), whose pleas for Heavenly mercy and attempts at self-improvement show how human beings can raise themselves to spiritual heights.

כב וַיֶּעְתַּר לוֹ יהוה וַתַּהַר רִבְקָה אִשְׁתּוֹ: וַיִּתְרֹצֲצוּ הַבָּנִים בְּקִרְבָּהּ וַתֹּאמֶר
כג אִם־כֵּן לָמָּה זֶּה אָנֹכִי וַתֵּלֶךְ לִדְרֹשׁ אֶת־יהוה: וַיֹּאמֶר יהוה לָהּ שְׁנֵי °גיים [°גוֹיִם ק]
בְּבִטְנֵךְ וּשְׁנֵי לְאֻמִּים מִמֵּעַיִךְ יִפָּרֵדוּ וּלְאֹם מִלְאֹם יֶאֱמָץ וְרַב
כד-כה יַעֲבֹד צָעִיר: וַיִּמְלְאוּ יָמֶיהָ לָלֶדֶת וְהִנֵּה תוֹמִם בְּבִטְנָהּ: וַיֵּצֵא הָרִאשׁוֹן
כו אַדְמוֹנִי כֻּלּוֹ כְּאַדֶּרֶת שֵׂעָר וַיִּקְרְאוּ שְׁמוֹ עֵשָׂו: וְאַחֲרֵי־כֵן יָצָא אָחִיו וְיָדוֹ
אֹחֶזֶת בַּעֲקֵב עֵשָׂו וַיִּקְרָא שְׁמוֹ יַעֲקֹב וְיִצְחָק בֶּן־שִׁשִּׁים שָׁנָה בְּלֶדֶת אֹתָם:
כז וַיִּגְדְּלוּ הַנְּעָרִים וַיְהִי עֵשָׂו אִישׁ יֹדֵעַ צַיִד אִישׁ שָׂדֶה וְיַעֲקֹב אִישׁ תָּם יֹשֵׁב
כח אֹהָלִים: וַיֶּאֱהַב יִצְחָק אֶת־עֵשָׂו כִּי־צַיִד בְּפִיו וְרִבְקָה אֹהֶבֶת אֶת־יַעֲקֹב:
כט-ל וַיָּזֶד יַעֲקֹב נָזִיד וַיָּבֹא עֵשָׂו מִן־הַשָּׂדֶה וְהוּא עָיֵף: וַיֹּאמֶר עֵשָׂו אֶל־יַעֲקֹב
הַלְעִיטֵנִי נָא מִן־הָאָדֹם הָאָדֹם הַזֶּה כִּי עָיֵף אָנֹכִי עַל־כֵּן קָרָא־שְׁמוֹ
לא-לב אֱדוֹם: וַיֹּאמֶר יַעֲקֹב מִכְרָה כַיּוֹם אֶת־בְּכֹרָתְךָ לִי: וַיֹּאמֶר עֵשָׂו הִנֵּה אָנֹכִי
לג הוֹלֵךְ לָמוּת וְלָמָּה־זֶּה לִי בְּכֹרָה: וַיֹּאמֶר יַעֲקֹב הִשָּׁבְעָה לִּי כַּיּוֹם וַיִּשָּׁבַע
לד לוֹ וַיִּמְכֹּר אֶת־בְּכֹרָתוֹ לְיַעֲקֹב: וְיַעֲקֹב נָתַן לְעֵשָׂו לֶחֶם וּנְזִיד עֲדָשִׁים
וַיֹּאכַל וַיֵּשְׁתְּ וַיָּקָם וַיֵּלַךְ וַיִּבֶז עֵשָׂו אֶת־הַבְּכֹרָה:

כו
א וַיְהִי רָעָב בָּאָרֶץ מִלְּבַד הָרָעָב הָרִאשׁוֹן אֲשֶׁר הָיָה בִּימֵי אַבְרָהָם וַיֵּלֶךְ
ב יִצְחָק אֶל־אֲבִימֶלֶךְ מֶלֶךְ־פְּלִשְׁתִּים גְּרָרָה: וַיֵּרָא אֵלָיו יהוה וַיֹּאמֶר אַל־
ג תֵּרֵד מִצְרָיְמָה שְׁכֹן בָּאָרֶץ אֲשֶׁר אֹמַר אֵלֶיךָ: גּוּר בָּאָרֶץ הַזֹּאת וְאֶהְיֶה
עִמְּךָ וַאֲבָרְכֶךָּ כִּי־לְךָ וּלְזַרְעֲךָ אֶתֵּן אֶת־כָּל־הָאֲרָצֹת הָאֵל וַהֲקִמֹתִי אֶת־
ד הַשְּׁבֻעָה אֲשֶׁר נִשְׁבַּעְתִּי לְאַבְרָהָם אָבִיךָ: וְהִרְבֵּיתִי אֶת־זַרְעֲךָ כְּכוֹכְבֵי
הַשָּׁמַיִם וְנָתַתִּי לְזַרְעֲךָ אֵת כָּל־הָאֲרָצֹת הָאֵל וְהִתְבָּרֲכוּ בְזַרְעֲךָ כֹּל
ה גּוֹיֵי הָאָרֶץ: עֵקֶב אֲשֶׁר־שָׁמַע אַבְרָהָם בְּקֹלִי וַיִּשְׁמֹר מִשְׁמַרְתִּי מִצְוֹתַי
ו-ז חֻקּוֹתַי וְתוֹרֹתָי: וַיֵּשֶׁב יִצְחָק בִּגְרָר: וַיִּשְׁאֲלוּ אַנְשֵׁי הַמָּקוֹם לְאִשְׁתּוֹ
וַיֹּאמֶר אֲחֹתִי הִוא כִּי יָרֵא לֵאמֹר אִשְׁתִּי פֶּן־יַהַרְגֻנִי אַנְשֵׁי הַמָּקוֹם עַל־
ח רִבְקָה כִּי־טוֹבַת מַרְאֶה הִוא: וַיְהִי כִּי אָרְכוּ־לוֹ שָׁם הַיָּמִים וַיַּשְׁקֵף
אֲבִימֶלֶךְ מֶלֶךְ פְּלִשְׁתִּים בְּעַד הַחַלּוֹן וַיַּרְא וְהִנֵּה יִצְחָק מְצַחֵק אֵת
ט רִבְקָה אִשְׁתּוֹ: וַיִּקְרָא אֲבִימֶלֶךְ לְיִצְחָק וַיֹּאמֶר אַךְ הִנֵּה אִשְׁתְּךָ הִוא
וְאֵיךְ אָמַרְתָּ אֲחֹתִי הִוא וַיֹּאמֶר אֵלָיו יִצְחָק כִּי אָמַרְתִּי פֶּן־אָמוּת עָלֶיהָ:

שני
*

25:29-34. Sale of the birthright. Abraham died that day and Jacob was preparing the traditional mourner's meal for Isaac (*Bava Basra* 16b); on that very day, Esau's sinfulness became public knowledge. This made the birthright even more precious to Jacob, because the spiritual mission of Abraham's family was brought to mind, and it was blatantly obvious that Esau was unsuitable for it.

25:29. The great of all the nations stood in the mourner's row and lamented, "Woe to the world that has lost its leader; woe to the ship that has lost its pilot!" (*Bava Basra* 91b), but Esau went about his evil business as usual, uninvolved in his family's bereavement.

25:34. This sums up the transaction. Esau was neither duped nor defrauded. He sold the birthright because he held it in contempt.

26:1-12. A famine forces Isaac to Philistia. In a repetition of Abraham's experience, Isaac was faced with a famine that forced him to leave his home. In line with his famous principle that the experiences of the Patriarchs foreshadowed the future history of their descendants, *Ramban* comments that Isaac's sojourn in Philistia portended the Babylonian Exile, just as Abraham's descent to Egypt had portended the Egyptian Exile. In Babylonia, too, the Jews were treated relatively well and even rose to prominence, just as Isaac,

HASHEM allowed Himself to be entreated by him, and his wife Rebecca conceived.

²² The children agitated within her, and she said, "If so, why am I thus?" And she went to inquire of HASHEM.

²³ And HASHEM said to her: "Two nations are in your womb; two regimes from your insides shall be separated; the might shall pass from one regime to the other, and the elder shall serve the younger."

The birth of Jacob and Esau

²⁴ When her term to bear grew full, then behold! there were twins in her womb. ²⁵ The first one emerged red, entirely like a hairy mantle; so they named him Esau. ²⁶ After that his brother emerged with his hand grasping on to the heel of Esau; so he called his name Jacob; Isaac was sixty years old when she bore them.

The personalities emerge

²⁷ The lads grew up and Esau became one who knows hunting, a man of the field; but Jacob was a wholesome man, abiding in tents. ²⁸ Isaac loved Esau for game was in his mouth; but Rebecca loved Jacob.

Sale of the birthright

²⁹ Jacob simmered a stew, and Esau came in from the field, * and he was exhausted. ³⁰ Esau said to Jacob, "Pour into me, now, some of that very red stuff for I am exhausted." (He therefore called his name Edom.)

³¹ Jacob said, "Sell, as this day, your birthright to me."

³² And Esau said, "Look, I am going to die, so of what use to me is a birthright?"

³³ Jacob said, "Swear to me as this day"; he swore to him and sold his birthright to Jacob. ³⁴ Jacob gave Esau bread and lentil stew, and he ate and drank, got up and left; thus, Esau spurned the birthright. *

26

A famine forces Isaac to Philistia

¹ There was a famine in the land, aside from the first famine that was in the days of Abraham; and Isaac went to Abimelech king of the Philistines, to Gerar. ² HASHEM appeared to him and said, "Do not descend to Egypt; dwell in the land that I shall indicate to you. ³ Sojourn in this land and I will be with you and bless you; for to you and your offspring will I give all these lands, and establish the oath that I swore to Abraham your father: ⁴ 'I will increase your offspring like the stars of the heavens; and will give to your offspring all these lands'; and all the nations of the earth shall bless themselves by your offspring. ⁵ Because Abraham obeyed My voice, and observed My safeguards, My commandments, My decrees, and My Torahs."

Isaac in Gerar

⁶ So Isaac settled in Gerar. ⁷ When the men of the place asked about his wife, he said, "She is my sister" — for he was afraid to say "my wife" — "lest the men of the place kill me because of Rebecca for she is fair to look upon!"

⁸ And it came to pass, as his days there lengthened, that Abimelech king of the Philistines gazed down through the window and saw — behold! Isaac was jesting with his wife Rebecca. ⁹ Abimelech summoned Isaac and said, "But look! She is your wife! How could you say, 'She is my sister?' "

Isaac said to him, "Because I said that I would be killed because of her."

---

though imperiled, was not mistreated and was even honored by Abimelech. At the same time, in another episode that seems familiar in the light of Jewish history, when Isaac became *too* successful, he aroused the jealousy of the masses and was forced to leave the country.

26:5. The gift of the land is attributed to Abraham's loyalty in obeying the word of God. The consensus of Rabbinic opinion is that Abraham arrived at a knowledge of the *entire Torah* through Divine Inspiration and observed it voluntarily. This explains how Abraham observed Rabbinic ordinances (*Rambam*).

וַיֹּאמֶר אֲבִימֶלֶךְ מַה־זֹּאת עָשִׂיתָ לָּנוּ כִּמְעַט שָׁכַב אַחַד הָעָם אֶת־אִשְׁתֶּךָ י

וְהֵבֵאתָ עָלֵינוּ אָשָׁם: וַיְצַו אֲבִימֶלֶךְ אֶת־כָּל־הָעָם לֵאמֹר הַנֹּגֵעַ בָּאִישׁ יא

הַזֶּה וּבְאִשְׁתּוֹ מוֹת יוּמָת: וַיִּזְרַע יִצְחָק בָּאָרֶץ הַהִוא וַיִּמְצָא בַּשָּׁנָה הַהִוא יב

שְׁלִישִׁי   מֵאָה שְׁעָרִים וַיְבָרֲכֵהוּ יהוה: וַיִּגְדַּל הָאִישׁ וַיֵּלֶךְ הָלוֹךְ וְגָדֵל עַד כִּי־גָדַל יג

מְאֹד: וַיְהִי־לוֹ מִקְנֵה־צֹאן וּמִקְנֵה בָקָר וַעֲבֻדָּה רַבָּה וַיְקַנְאוּ אֹתוֹ יד

פְלִשְׁתִּים: וְכָל־הַבְּאֵרֹת אֲשֶׁר חָפְרוּ עַבְדֵי אָבִיו בִּימֵי אַבְרָהָם אָבִיו טו

סִתְּמוּם פְּלִשְׁתִּים וַיְמַלְאוּם עָפָר: וַיֹּאמֶר אֲבִימֶלֶךְ אֶל־יִצְחָק לֵךְ מֵעִמָּנוּ טז

כִּי־עָצַמְתָּ מִמֶּנּוּ מְאֹד: וַיֵּלֶךְ מִשָּׁם יִצְחָק וַיִּחַן בְּנַחַל־גְּרָר וַיֵּשֶׁב שָׁם: וַיָּשָׁב יז-יח

יִצְחָק וַיַּחְפֹּר | אֶת־בְּאֵרֹת הַמַּיִם אֲשֶׁר חָפְרוּ בִּימֵי אַבְרָהָם אָבִיו

וַיְסַתְּמוּם פְּלִשְׁתִּים אַחֲרֵי מוֹת אַבְרָהָם וַיִּקְרָא לָהֶן שֵׁמוֹת כַּשֵּׁמֹת אֲשֶׁר־

קָרָא לָהֶן אָבִיו: וַיַּחְפְּרוּ עַבְדֵי־יִצְחָק בַּנָּחַל וַיִּמְצְאוּ־שָׁם בְּאֵר מַיִם חַיִּים: יט

וַיָּרִיבוּ רֹעֵי גְרָר עִם־רֹעֵי יִצְחָק לֵאמֹר לָנוּ הַמָּיִם וַיִּקְרָא שֵׁם־הַבְּאֵר עֵשֶׂק כ

כִּי הִתְעַשְּׂקוּ עִמּוֹ: וַיַּחְפְּרוּ בְּאֵר אַחֶרֶת וַיָּרִיבוּ גַּם־עָלֶיהָ וַיִּקְרָא שְׁמָהּ כא

שִׂטְנָה: וַיַּעְתֵּק מִשָּׁם וַיַּחְפֹּר בְּאֵר אַחֶרֶת וְלֹא רָבוּ עָלֶיהָ וַיִּקְרָא שְׁמָהּ כב

רְחֹבוֹת וַיֹּאמֶר כִּי־עַתָּה הִרְחִיב יהוה לָנוּ וּפָרִינוּ בָאָרֶץ: וַיַּעַל מִשָּׁם בְּאֵר כג

רְבִיעִי   שָׁבַע: וַיֵּרָא אֵלָיו יהוה בַּלַּיְלָה הַהוּא וַיֹּאמֶר אָנֹכִי אֱלֹהֵי אַבְרָהָם כד

אָבִיךָ אַל־תִּירָא כִּי־אִתְּךָ אָנֹכִי וּבֵרַכְתִּיךָ וְהִרְבֵּיתִי אֶת־זַרְעֲךָ בַּעֲבוּר

אַבְרָהָם עַבְדִּי: וַיִּבֶן שָׁם מִזְבֵּחַ וַיִּקְרָא בְּשֵׁם יהוה וַיֶּט־שָׁם אָהֳלוֹ וַיִּכְרוּ־ כה

שָׁם עַבְדֵי־יִצְחָק בְּאֵר: וַאֲבִימֶלֶךְ הָלַךְ אֵלָיו מִגְּרָר וַאֲחֻזַּת מֵרֵעֵהוּ וּפִיכֹל כו

שַׂר־צְבָאוֹ: וַיֹּאמֶר אֲלֵהֶם יִצְחָק מַדּוּעַ בָּאתֶם אֵלָי וְאַתֶּם שְׂנֵאתֶם אֹתִי כז

וַתְּשַׁלְּחוּנִי מֵאִתְּכֶם: וַיֹּאמְרוּ רָאוֹ רָאִינוּ כִּי־הָיָה יהוה | עִמָּךְ וַנֹּאמֶר כח

תְּהִי נָא אָלָה בֵּינוֹתֵינוּ בֵּינֵינוּ וּבֵינֶךָ וְנִכְרְתָה בְרִית עִמָּךְ: אִם־תַּעֲשֵׂה כט

עִמָּנוּ רָעָה כַּאֲשֶׁר לֹא נְגַעֲנוּךָ וְכַאֲשֶׁר עָשִׂינוּ עִמְּךָ רַק־טוֹב וַנְּשַׁלֵּחֲךָ

חֲמִישִׁי   בְּשָׁלוֹם אַתָּה עַתָּה בְּרוּךְ יהוה: וַיַּעַשׂ לָהֶם מִשְׁתֶּה וַיֹּאכְלוּ וַיִּשְׁתּוּ: ל

וַיַּשְׁכִּימוּ בַבֹּקֶר וַיִּשָּׁבְעוּ אִישׁ לְאָחִיו וַיְשַׁלְּחֵם יִצְחָק וַיֵּלְכוּ מֵאִתּוֹ בְּשָׁלוֹם: לא

וַיְהִי | בַּיּוֹם הַהוּא וַיָּבֹאוּ עַבְדֵי יִצְחָק וַיַּגִּדוּ לוֹ עַל־אֹדוֹת הַבְּאֵר אֲשֶׁר לב

חָפָרוּ וַיֹּאמְרוּ לוֹ מָצָאנוּ מָיִם: וַיִּקְרָא אֹתָהּ שִׁבְעָה עַל־כֵּן שֵׁם־הָעִיר בְּאֵר לג

שֶׁבַע עַד הַיּוֹם הַזֶּה: וַיְהִי עֵשָׂו בֶּן־אַרְבָּעִים שָׁנָה וַיִּקַּח אִשָּׁה לד

אֶת־יְהוּדִית בַּת־בְּאֵרִי הַחִתִּי וְאֶת־בָּשְׂמַת בַּת־אֵילֹן הַחִתִּי: וַתִּהְיֶיןָ לה

26:6-16. Isaac in Gerar. Because of his covenant with Abraham, Abimelech showed Isaac no malice; it was the *residents* who inquired about the identity of Rebecca. Knowing that they could spirit a wife away from her husband and murder him on some pretext, Isaac used Abraham's ruse of identifying his wife as his sister (*Ramban* to v. 1 and 12:11).

26:20. They quibbled in the exact style that has been used against the Jews in Exile throughout the centuries: "Yes, *you* dug the well; the *hole* is yours, but the *water* is ours!" (*R' Hirsch*).

26:23-25. God assures Isaac. After the conflict, Isaac feared that the Philistines would kill him (*Ramban*), or that he would continue to lose assets because of their enmity (*Sforno*). In response, God promised him protection.

¹⁰ Abimelech said, "What is this that you have done to us? One of the people has nearly lain with your wife, and you would have brought guilt upon us!" ¹¹ Abimelech then warned all the people saying, "Whoever molests this man or his wife shall surely be put to death."

¹² Isaac sowed in that land, and in that year he reaped a hundredfold; thus had HASHEM blessed him. ¹³ The man became great and kept becoming greater until he was very great. ¹⁴ He had acquired flocks and herds and many enterprises; and the Philistines envied him.

¹⁵ All the wells that his father's servants had dug in the days of Abraham his father, the Philistines stopped up, and filled them with earth. ¹⁶ And Abimelech said to Isaac, "Go away from us for you have become much mightier than we!" ¹⁷ So Isaac departed from there and encamped in the valley of Gerar, and dwelled there. ¹⁸ And Isaac dug anew the wells of water which they had dug in the days of Abraham his father and the Philistines had stopped them up after Abraham's death; and he called them by the same names that his father had called them.

The prophetic dispute over the wells ¹⁹ Isaac's servants dug in the valley and found there a well of fresh water. ²⁰ The herdsmen of Gerar quarreled with Isaac's herdsmen saying, "The water is ours,"* so he called the name of that well Esek because they involved themselves with him. ²¹ Then they dug another well, and they quarreled over that also; so he called its name Sitnah. ²² He relocated from there and dug another well; they did not quarrel over it, so he called its name Rehoboth, and said, "For now HASHEM has granted us ample space, and we can be fruitful in the land."

God assures Isaac ²³ He went up from there to Beer-sheba. ²⁴ HASHEM appeared to him that night and said, "I am the God of your father Abraham: Fear not, for I am with you; I will bless you and increase your offspring because of Abraham my servant." ²⁵ He built an altar there, invoked HASHEM by Name, and there he pitched his tent; there Isaac's servants dug a well.

Abimelech reaffirms the treaty ²⁶ Abimelech went to him from Gerar with a group of his friends and Phicol, general of his legion. ²⁷ Isaac said to him, "Why have you come to me? You hate me and drove me away from you!"

²⁸ And they said, "We have indeed seen that HASHEM has been with you, so we said, 'Let the oath between ourselves now be between us and you, and let us make a covenant with you: ²⁹ If you do evil with us...! Just as we have not molested you, and just as we have done with you only good, and sent you away in peace — Now, you, O blessed of HASHEM!'"

³⁰ He made them a feast and they ate and drank. ³¹ They awoke early in the morning and swore to one another; then Isaac saw them off and they departed from him in peace. ³² And it was on that very day that Isaac's servants came and told him about the well they had dug, and they said to him, "We have found water!" ³³ And he named it Shibah; therefore, the name of the city is Beersheba* until this very day.*

Esau marries ³⁴ When Esau was forty years old, he took as a wife Judith daughter of Beeri the Hittite, and Basemath daughter of Elon the Hittite; ³⁵ and they were a source

---

26:33. The name of the city commemorates two occurrences; the בְּאֵר, *well*, and the שְׁבוּעָה, *oath* (*Ramban*).

26:33. *Until this very day,* i.e., the days of Moses, when the Torah was given. Throughout Scripture, *until this day* means until the time of the scribe who recorded the matter (*Rashbam* to 19:37).

כז א מֵרֵאֹת וַיִּקְרָא אֶת־עֵשָׂו ׀ בְּנוֹ הַגָּדֹל וַיֹּאמֶר אֵלָיו בְּנִי וַיֹּאמֶר אֵלָיו הִנֵּנִי:
מְרֹאֹת מְרֹת רוּחַ לְיִצְחָק וּלְרִבְקָה: וַיְהִי כִּי־זָקֵן יִצְחָק וַתִּכְהֶיןָ עֵינָיו
ב־ג וַיֹּאמֶר הִנֵּה־נָא זָקַנְתִּי לֹא יָדַעְתִּי יוֹם מוֹתִי: וְעַתָּה שָׂא־נָא כֵלֶיךָ תֶּלְיְךָ
ד וְקַשְׁתֶּךָ וְצֵא הַשָּׂדֶה וְצוּדָה לִּי °צידה [°צַיִד ק]: וַעֲשֵׂה־לִי מַטְעַמִּים
כַּאֲשֶׁר אָהַבְתִּי וְהָבִיאָה לִּי וְאֹכֵלָה בַּעֲבוּר תְּבָרֶכְךָ נַפְשִׁי בְּטֶרֶם אָמוּת:
ה וְרִבְקָה שֹׁמַעַת בְּדַבֵּר יִצְחָק אֶל־עֵשָׂו בְּנוֹ וַיֵּלֶךְ עֵשָׂו הַשָּׂדֶה לָצוּד צַיִד
ו לְהָבִיא: וְרִבְקָה אָמְרָה אֶל־יַעֲקֹב בְּנָהּ לֵאמֹר הִנֵּה שָׁמַעְתִּי אֶת־אָבִיךָ
ז מְדַבֵּר אֶל־עֵשָׂו אָחִיךָ לֵאמֹר: הָבִיאָה לִּי צַיִד וַעֲשֵׂה־לִי מַטְעַמִּים וְאֹכֵלָה
ח וַאֲבָרֶכְכָה לִפְנֵי יהוה לִפְנֵי מוֹתִי: וְעַתָּה בְנִי שְׁמַע בְּקֹלִי לַאֲשֶׁר אֲנִי מְצַוָּה
ט אֹתָךְ: לֶךְ־נָא אֶל־הַצֹּאן וְקַח־לִי מִשָּׁם שְׁנֵי גְּדָיֵי עִזִּים טֹבִים וְאֶעֱשֶׂה אֹתָם
י מַטְעַמִּים לְאָבִיךָ כַּאֲשֶׁר אָהֵב: וְהֵבֵאתָ לְאָבִיךָ וְאָכָל בַּעֲבֻר אֲשֶׁר יְבָרֶכְךָ
יא לִפְנֵי מוֹתוֹ: וַיֹּאמֶר יַעֲקֹב אֶל־רִבְקָה אִמּוֹ הֵן עֵשָׂו אָחִי אִישׁ שָׂעִר וְאָנֹכִי
יב אִישׁ חָלָק: אוּלַי יְמֻשֵּׁנִי אָבִי וְהָיִיתִי בְעֵינָיו כִּמְתַעְתֵּעַ וְהֵבֵאתִי עָלַי קְלָלָה
יג וְלֹא בְרָכָה: וַתֹּאמֶר לוֹ אִמּוֹ עָלַי קִלְלָתְךָ בְּנִי אַךְ שְׁמַע בְּקֹלִי וְלֵךְ קַח־לִי:
יד־טו וַיֵּלֶךְ וַיִּקַּח וַיָּבֵא לְאִמּוֹ וַתַּעַשׂ אִמּוֹ מַטְעַמִּים כַּאֲשֶׁר אָהֵב אָבִיו: וַתִּקַּח
רִבְקָה אֶת־בִּגְדֵי עֵשָׂו בְּנָהּ הַגָּדֹל הַחֲמֻדֹת אֲשֶׁר אִתָּהּ בַּבָּיִת וַתַּלְבֵּשׁ אֶת־
טז יַעֲקֹב בְּנָהּ הַקָּטָן: וְאֵת עֹרֹת גְּדָיֵי הָעִזִּים הִלְבִּישָׁה עַל־יָדָיו וְעַל חֶלְקַת
יז צַוָּארָיו: וַתִּתֵּן אֶת־הַמַּטְעַמִּים וְאֶת־הַלֶּחֶם אֲשֶׁר עָשָׂתָה בְּיַד יַעֲקֹב בְּנָהּ:
יח־יט וַיָּבֹא אֶל־אָבִיו וַיֹּאמֶר אָבִי וַיֹּאמֶר הִנֶּנִּי מִי אַתָּה בְּנִי: וַיֹּאמֶר יַעֲקֹב אֶל־
אָבִיו אָנֹכִי עֵשָׂו בְּכֹרֶךָ עָשִׂיתִי כַּאֲשֶׁר דִּבַּרְתָּ אֵלָי קוּם־נָא שְׁבָה וְאָכְלָה
כ מִצֵּידִי בַּעֲבוּר תְּבָרֲכַנִּי נַפְשֶׁךָ: וַיֹּאמֶר יִצְחָק אֶל־בְּנוֹ מַה־זֶּה מִהַרְתָּ לִמְצֹא
כא בְּנִי וַיֹּאמֶר כִּי הִקְרָה יהוה אֱלֹהֶיךָ לְפָנָי: וַיֹּאמֶר יִצְחָק אֶל־יַעֲקֹב גְּשָׁה־נָּא
כב וַאֲמֻשְׁךָ בְּנִי הַאַתָּה זֶה בְּנִי עֵשָׂו אִם־לֹא: וַיִּגַּשׁ יַעֲקֹב אֶל־יִצְחָק אָבִיו
כג וַיְמֻשֵּׁהוּ וַיֹּאמֶר הַקֹּל קוֹל יַעֲקֹב וְהַיָּדַיִם יְדֵי עֵשָׂו: וְלֹא הִכִּירוֹ כִּי־הָיוּ יָדָיו
כד כִּידֵי עֵשָׂו אָחִיו שְׂעִרֹת וַיְבָרֲכֵהוּ: וַיֹּאמֶר אַתָּה זֶה בְּנִי עֵשָׂו וַיֹּאמֶר אָנִי:

◆§ The Patriarchal blessings. This chapter is one of the most crucial and mystifying in the Torah — crucial because the decision about which son was to receive the Patriarchal blessings would determine which son would beget God's Chosen People, and mystifying because it is hard to fathom how Isaac could be so adamant in choosing Esau and why Rebecca would resort to such a blatant deception to secure the blessings for Jacob.

27:1-4. Isaac's decision to bless Esau. As the firstborn, Esau had the presumptive right to the blessings, and Isaac could not deny them to him without compelling cause. Clearly, Isaac was unaware of the *degree* of Esau's sinfulness, and Rebecca had not been authorized to tell him about the prophecy given her at the beginning of the *Sidrah*. Also, Isaac felt that it was Esau who needed blessings to arm him in his struggle against an inborn nature that tended toward bloodshed and other cardinal sins.

27:3-4. Isaac's wish for food was to satisfy his bodily appetite so that hunger would not interfere with his spiritual bliss. The prophetic spirit can rest only on someone who is in a state of joy (*Shabbos* 30b), which implies satisfaction of all one's needs (*Lekach Tov,* see *Ramban*).

27:5-17. Rebecca's scheme. Having been told that the younger one would be superior (25:23), Rebecca knew that the blessings had to go to Jacob. She also knew from that prophecy that when one would rise the other would fall — so that any plan Isaac might have to enlist them in joint service of God could not succeed — but she had not been authorized to convey this to Isaac. Her only alternative was to deceive Isaac into blessing Jacob.

For Jacob, this was his personal *Akeidah* — a test of awesome proportions — because, as the Sages derive from Scripture, Jacob personified truth and the blessings would be ratified by God, Whose very seal is "Truth." But *of spiritual rebellion to Isaac and to Rebecca.*

27

Isaac's decision to bless Esau

¹ **A**nd it came to pass, when Isaac had become old, and his eyes dimmed from seeing, that he summoned Esau, his older son, and said to him, "My son." And he said to him, "Here I am." ² And he said, "See, now, I have aged; I know not the day of my death. ³ Now sharpen, if you please, your gear — your sword and your bow — and go out to the field and hunt game for me. ⁴ Then make me delicacies such as I love and bring it to me and I will eat, so that my soul may bless you before I die."

Rebecca's scheme

⁵ Now Rebecca was listening as Isaac spoke to Esau his son; and Esau went to the field to hunt game to bring. ⁶ But Rebecca had said to Jacob her son, saying, "Behold I heard your father speaking to your brother Esau saying, ⁷ 'Bring me some game and make me delicacies to eat, and I will bless you in the presence of HASHEM before my death.' ⁸ So now, my son, heed my voice to that which I command you. ⁹ Go now to the flock and fetch me from there two choice young kids of the goats, and I will make of them delicacies for your father, as he loves. ¹⁰ Then bring it to your father and he shall eat, so that he may bless you before his death."

¹¹ Jacob replied to Rebecca, his mother, "But my brother Esau is a hairy man and I am a smooth-skinned man. ¹² Perhaps my father will feel me and I shall be as a mocker in his eyes; I will thus bring upon myself a curse rather than a blessing." ¹³ But his mother said to him, "Your curse be on me, * my son; only heed my voice and go fetch them for me." ¹⁴ So he went, fetched, and brought to his mother, and his mother made delicacies as his father loved. ¹⁵ Rebecca then took her older son Esau's clean garments * which were with her in the house, and clothed Jacob her young son. ¹⁶ With the skins of the goat-kids she covered his arms and his smooth-skinned neck. ¹⁷ She placed the delicacies and the bread which she had made into the hand of her son Jacob.

Jacob comes to Isaac

¹⁸ And he came to his father and said, "Father," and he said, "Here I am; who are you, my son?" ¹⁹ Jacob said to his father, "It is I, Esau your firstborn; * I have done as you told me; rise up, please, * sit and eat of my game that your soul may bless me."

²⁰ Isaac said to his son, "How is it that you were so quick to find, my son?" And he said, "Because HASHEM, your God, arranged it for me." ²¹ And Isaac said to Jacob, "Come close, if you please, * so I can feel you, my son; are you, indeed, my son Esau or not?"

²² So Jacob drew close to Isaac his father who felt him and said, "The voice is Jacob's voice, * but the hands are Esau's hands." ²³ But he did not recognize him because his hands were hairy like the hands of Esau his brother; so he blessed him. ²⁴ He said, "You are, indeed, my son Esau!" And he said, "I am."

---

his mother was commanding him to secure those blessings by deceiving his father! For Jacob to do so was totally foreign to his nature.

27:13. I take full responsibility. Rebecca had no fear that there would be a curse, for she had complete confidence in the prophecy that *the elder shall serve the younger* [25:23] (*Rashbam*).

27:15. This translation follows *Onkelos*. Alternatively: The *precious garments* that Esau stole from the great hunter Nimrod (*Rashi*).

27:18-27. Jacob comes to Isaac. With head bowed and

in tears, so unhappy was he that he had to use deception, even though it was to gain what was truly his (*Midrash*).

27:19. *Rashi* explains: אָנֹכִי, *It is I* who bring this to you; עֵשָׂו בְּכֹרֶךָ, *Esau,* (however), *is your firstborn.*

27:21. Jacob's mention of God's Name (v. 20) made Isaac suspicious, since it was not characteristic of Esau to speak that way (*Rashi*).

27:22. Isaac's statement that *the voice is Jacob's voice* refers to Jacob's manner of speaking, inasmuch as Jacob spoke gently and invoked the name of Heaven (*Rashi*).

כה וַיֹּאמֶר הַגִּשָׁה לִּי וְאֹכְלָה מִצֵּיד בְּנִי לְמַעַן תְּבָרֶכְךָ נַפְשִׁי וַיַּגֶּשׁ־לוֹ וַיֹּאכַל

כו־כז וַיָּבֵא לוֹ יַיִן וַיֵּשְׁתְּ: וַיֹּאמֶר אֵלָיו יִצְחָק אָבִיו גְּשָׁה־נָּא וּשְׁקָה־לִּי בְּנִי: וַיִּגַּשׁ

וַיִּשַּׁק־לוֹ וַיָּרַח אֶת־רֵיחַ בְּגָדָיו וַיְבָרֲכֵהוּ וַיֹּאמֶר רְאֵה רֵיחַ בְּנִי כְּרֵיחַ

כח שָׂדֶה אֲשֶׁר בֵּרֲכוֹ יְהֹוָה: וְיִתֶּן־לְךָ הָאֱלֹהִים מִטַּל הַשָּׁמַיִם וּמִשְׁמַנֵּי הָאָרֶץ שׁשׁי

כט וְרֹב דָּגָן וְתִירֹשׁ: יַעַבְדוּךָ עַמִּים °וְיִשְׁתַּחֲוּ °וְיִשְׁתַּחוּ] לְךָ לְאֻמִּים הֱוֵה

ל גְבִיר לְאַחֶיךָ וְיִשְׁתַּחֲוּ לְךָ בְּנֵי אִמֶּךָ אֹרֲרֶיךָ אָרוּר וּמְבָרֲכֶיךָ בָּרוּךְ: וַיְהִי

כַּאֲשֶׁר כִּלָּה יִצְחָק לְבָרֵךְ אֶת־יַעֲקֹב וַיְהִי אַךְ יָצֹא יָצָא יַעֲקֹב מֵאֵת פְּנֵי

לא יִצְחָק אָבִיו וְעֵשָׂו אָחִיו בָּא מִצֵּידוֹ: וַיַּעַשׂ גַּם־הוּא מַטְעַמִּים וַיָּבֵא לְאָבִיו

לב וַיֹּאמֶר לְאָבִיו יָקֻם אָבִי וְיֹאכַל מִצֵּיד בְּנוֹ בַּעֲבֻר תְּבָרֲכַנִּי נַפְשֶׁךָ: וַיֹּאמֶר

לג לוֹ יִצְחָק אָבִיו מִי־אָתָּה וַיֹּאמֶר אֲנִי בִּנְךָ בְכֹרְךָ עֵשָׂו: וַיֶּחֱרַד יִצְחָק חֲרָדָה

גְּדֹלָה עַד־מְאֹד וַיֹּאמֶר מִי־אֵפוֹא הוּא הַצָּד־צַיִד וַיָּבֵא לִי וָאֹכַל מִכֹּל

לד בְּטֶרֶם תָּבוֹא וָאֲבָרֲכֵהוּ גַּם־בָּרוּךְ יִהְיֶה: כִּשְׁמֹעַ עֵשָׂו אֶת־דִּבְרֵי אָבִיו

וַיִּצְעַק צְעָקָה גְּדֹלָה וּמָרָה עַד־מְאֹד וַיֹּאמֶר לְאָבִיו בָּרֲכֵנִי גַם־אָנִי אָבִי:

לה־לו וַיֹּאמֶר בָּא אָחִיךָ בְּמִרְמָה וַיִּקַּח בִּרְכָתֶךָ: וַיֹּאמֶר הֲכִי קָרָא שְׁמוֹ יַעֲקֹב

וַיַּעְקְבֵנִי זֶה פַעֲמַיִם אֶת־בְּכֹרָתִי לָקָח וְהִנֵּה עַתָּה לָקַח בִּרְכָתִי וַיֹּאמַר

לז הֲלֹא־אָצַלְתָּ לִּי בְּרָכָה: וַיַּעַן יִצְחָק וַיֹּאמֶר לְעֵשָׂו הֵן גְּבִיר שַׂמְתִּיו לָךְ

וְאֶת־כָּל־אֶחָיו נָתַתִּי לוֹ לַעֲבָדִים וְדָגָן וְתִירֹשׁ סְמַכְתִּיו וּלְכָה אֵפוֹא מָה

לח אֶעֱשֶׂה בְּנִי: וַיֹּאמֶר עֵשָׂו אֶל־אָבִיו הַבְרָכָה אַחַת הִוא־לְךָ אָבִי בָּרֲכֵנִי

לט גַם־אָנִי אָבִי וַיִּשָּׂא עֵשָׂו קֹלוֹ וַיֵּבְךְּ: וַיַּעַן יִצְחָק אָבִיו וַיֹּאמֶר אֵלָיו הִנֵּה

מ מִשְׁמַנֵּי הָאָרֶץ יִהְיֶה מוֹשָׁבֶךָ וּמִטַּל הַשָּׁמַיִם מֵעָל: וְעַל־חַרְבְּךָ תִחְיֶה

מא וְאֶת־אָחִיךָ תַּעֲבֹד וְהָיָה כַּאֲשֶׁר תָּרִיד וּפָרַקְתָּ עֻלּוֹ מֵעַל צַוָּארֶךָ: וַיִּשְׂטֹם

עֵשָׂו אֶת־יַעֲקֹב עַל־הַבְּרָכָה אֲשֶׁר בֵּרֲכוֹ אָבִיו וַיֹּאמֶר עֵשָׂו בְּלִבּוֹ

מב יִקְרְבוּ יְמֵי אֵבֶל אָבִי וְאַהַרְגָה אֶת־יַעֲקֹב אָחִי: וַיֻּגַּד לְרִבְקָה אֶת־דִּבְרֵי

עֵשָׂו בְּנָהּ הַגָּדֹל וַתִּשְׁלַח וַתִּקְרָא לְיַעֲקֹב בְּנָהּ הַקָּטָן וַתֹּאמֶר אֵלָיו

מג הִנֵּה עֵשָׂו אָחִיךָ מִתְנַחֵם לְךָ לְהָרְגֶךָ: וְעַתָּה בְנִי שְׁמַע בְּקֹלִי וְקוּם

מד בְּרַח־לְךָ אֶל־לָבָן אָחִי חָרָנָה: וְיָשַׁבְתָּ עִמּוֹ יָמִים אֲחָדִים עַד אֲשֶׁר־

מה תָּשׁוּב חֲמַת אָחִיךָ: עַד־שׁוּב אַף־אָחִיךָ מִמְּךָ וְשָׁכַח אֵת אֲשֶׁר־

עָשִׂיתָ לּוֹ וְשָׁלַחְתִּי וּלְקַחְתִּיךָ מִשָּׁם לָמָה אֶשְׁכַּל גַּם־שְׁנֵיכֶם יוֹם אֶחָד:

27:28-29. The blessing. Since the Divine Presence was resting upon him, Isaac knew that the person standing before him was worthy of the blessings.

27:29. According to the view that Isaac still thought he was blessing Esau, this verse says clearly that Isaac wanted Esau to be Esau's vassal, but it was for Jacob's benefit that Isaac blessed Esau with mastery. Isaac did not want Jacob to be encumbered by material responsibilities which would hinder his spiritual development, nor did he want him to have too much material wealth and power, lest he become corrupted by it. Thus Jacob would

have inherited *Eretz Yisrael* and been free to serve God, while Esau would rule the country and provide for its inhabitants. That Isaac meant for Jacob to inherit the land and have the spiritual blessings of Abraham is clear from 28:4, where he knew he was blessing Jacob and specified both the blessings and the land (*Sforno*).

27:31. The commentators compare Esau's tone and content as he addressed Isaac with Jacob's.

27:41-45. Esau's hatred of Jacob. The eternal rivalry between the brothers became intensified with Esau's determination to kill Jacob when the opportune time

²⁵ He said, "Serve me and let me eat of my son's game that my soul may bless you." So he served him and he ate, and he brought him wine and he drank.

²⁶ Then his father Isaac said to him, "Come close, if you please, and kiss me, my son." ²⁷ So he drew close and kissed him; he smelled the fragrance of his garments and blessed him; he said, "See, the fragrance of my son is like the fragrance of a field which HASHEM had blessed — ²⁸ And may God give you of the dew of the heavens and of the fatness of the earth, and abundant grain and wine. ²⁹ Peoples will serve you, and regimes will prostrate themselves to you; be a lord to your kinsmen, and your mother's sons will prostrate themselves to you; cursed be they who curse you, and blessed be they who bless you."

³⁰ And it was, when Isaac had finished blessing Jacob, and Jacob had scarcely left from the presence of Isaac his father, that Esau his brother came back from his hunt. ³¹ He, too, made delicacies, and brought them to his father; he said to his father, "Let my father rise and eat of his son's game, so that your soul will bless me."

³² Isaac his father said to him, "Who are you?" And he said, "I am your firstborn son Esau." ³³ Then Isaac trembled in very great perplexity, and said, "Who — where — is the one who hunted game, brought it to me, and I partook of all when you had not yet come, and I blessed him? Indeed, he shall remain blessed!"

³⁴ When Esau heard his father's words, he cried out an exceedingly great and bitter cry, and said to his father, "Bless me too, Father!"

³⁵ But he said, "Your brother came with cleverness and took your blessing."

³⁶ He said, "Is it because his name was called Jacob that he outwitted me these two times? — He took away my birthright and see, now he took away my blessing!" Then he said, "Have you not reserved a blessing for me?"

³⁷ Isaac answered, and said to Esau, "Behold, a lord have I made him over you, and all his kin have I given him as servants; with grain and wine have I supported him, and for you, where — what can I do, my son?"

³⁸ And Esau said to his father, "Have you but one blessing, Father? Bless me too, Father!" And Esau raised his voice and wept.

³⁹ So Isaac his father answered, and said to him: "Behold, of the fatness of the earth shall be your dwelling and of the dew of the heavens from above. ⁴⁰ By your sword you shall live, but your brother you shall serve; yet it shall be that when you are aggrieved, you may cast off his yoke from upon your neck."

⁴¹ Now Esau harbored hatred toward Jacob because of the blessing with which his father had blessed him; and Esau thought, "May the days of mourning for my father draw near, then I will kill my brother Jacob."

⁴² When Rebecca was told of the words of her older son Esau, she sent and summoned Jacob her younger son and said to him, "Behold, your brother Esau is consoling himself regarding you to kill you. ⁴³ So now, my son, heed my voice and arise; flee to my brother Laban, to Charan. ⁴⁴ And remain with him a short while until your brother's wrath subsides. ⁴⁵ Until your brother's anger against you subsides and he forgets what you have done to him; then I will send and bring you from there; why should I be bereaved of both of you on the same day?"

Jacob receives Isaac's blessing

Esau arrives for his blessings

Esau's hatred of Jacob

Jacob is told to flee to Laban

---

came. It was a resolve that his descendants would attempt to carry out time after time to this very day, but, as the Pesach *Haggadah* declares, the Holy One, Blessed is He, rescues us from their hand.

מו וַתֹּאמֶר רִבְקָה אֶל־יִצְחָק קַצְתִּי בְחַיַּי מִפְּנֵי בְּנוֹת חֵת אִם־לֹקֵחַ יַעֲקֹב

א אִשָּׁה מִבְּנוֹת־חֵת כָּאֵלֶּה מִבְּנוֹת הָאָרֶץ לָמָּה לִי חַיִּים: וַיִּקְרָא יִצְחָק אֶל־

ב יַעֲקֹב וַיְבָרֶךְ אֹתוֹ וַיְצַוֵּהוּ וַיֹּאמֶר לוֹ לֹא־תִקַּח אִשָּׁה מִבְּנוֹת כְּנָעַן: קוּם לֵךְ

פַּדֶּנָה אֲרָם בֵּיתָה בְתוּאֵל אֲבִי אִמֶּךָ וְקַח־לְךָ מִשָּׁם אִשָּׁה מִבְּנוֹת לָבָן אֲחִי

ג אִמֶּךָ: וְאֵל שַׁדַּי יְבָרֵךְ אֹתְךָ וְיַפְרְךָ וְיַרְבֶּךָ וְהָיִיתָ לִקְהַל עַמִּים: וְיִתֶּן־לְךָ

אֶת־בִּרְכַּת אַבְרָהָם לְךָ וּלְזַרְעֲךָ אִתָּךְ לְרִשְׁתְּךָ אֶת־אֶרֶץ מְגֻרֶיךָ אֲשֶׁר־

ה נָתַן אֱלֹהִים לְאַבְרָהָם: וַיִּשְׁלַח יִצְחָק אֶת־יַעֲקֹב וַיֵּלֶךְ פַּדֶּנָה אֲרָם אֶל־

ו לָבָן בֶּן־בְּתוּאֵל הָאֲרַמִּי אֲחִי רִבְקָה אֵם יַעֲקֹב וְעֵשָׂו: וַיַּרְא עֵשָׂו כִּי־בֵרַךְ

יִצְחָק אֶת־יַעֲקֹב וְשִׁלַּח אֹתוֹ פַּדֶּנָה אֲרָם לָקַחַת־לוֹ מִשָּׁם אִשָּׁה בְּבָרֲכוֹ

ז אֹתוֹ וַיְצַו עָלָיו לֵאמֹר לֹא־תִקַּח אִשָּׁה מִבְּנוֹת כְּנָעַן: וַיִּשְׁמַע יַעֲקֹב אֶל־

ח אָבִיו וְאֶל־אִמּוֹ וַיֵּלֶךְ פַּדֶּנָה אֲרָם: וַיַּרְא עֵשָׂו כִּי רָעוֹת בְּנוֹת כְּנָעַן בְּעֵינֵי

ט יִצְחָק אָבִיו: וַיֵּלֶךְ עֵשָׂו אֶל־יִשְׁמָעֵאל וַיִּקַּח אֶת־מָחֲלַת ׀ בַּת־יִשְׁמָעֵאל

בֶּן־אַבְרָהָם אֲחוֹת נְבָיוֹת עַל־נָשָׁיו לוֹ לְאִשָּׁה: ססס קי"ז פסוקים. על"ז סימן.

*ק' זעירא

Haftaras
Toldos:
p. 1428

For special
Sabbaths,
see pp. x-xi

פרשת ויצא

יא וַיֵּצֵא יַעֲקֹב מִבְּאֵר שָׁבַע וַיֵּלֶךְ חָרָנָה: וַיִּפְגַּע בַּמָּקוֹם וַיָּלֶן שָׁם כִּי־בָא

הַשֶּׁמֶשׁ וַיִּקַּח מֵאַבְנֵי הַמָּקוֹם וַיָּשֶׂם מְרַאֲשֹׁתָיו וַיִּשְׁכַּב בַּמָּקוֹם הַהוּא:

יב וַיַּחֲלֹם וְהִנֵּה סֻלָּם מֻצָּב אַרְצָה וְרֹאשׁוֹ מַגִּיעַ הַשָּׁמָיְמָה וְהִנֵּה מַלְאֲכֵי

יג אֱלֹהִים עֹלִים וְיֹרְדִים בּוֹ: וְהִנֵּה יהוה נִצָּב עָלָיו וַיֹּאמַר אֲנִי יהוה אֱלֹהֵי

אַבְרָהָם אָבִיךָ וֵאלֹהֵי יִצְחָק הָאָרֶץ אֲשֶׁר אַתָּה שֹׁכֵב עָלֶיהָ לְךָ אֶתְּנֶנָּה

יד וּלְזַרְעֶךָ: וְהָיָה זַרְעֲךָ כַּעֲפַר הָאָרֶץ וּפָרַצְתָּ יָמָּה וָקֵדְמָה וְצָפֹנָה וָנֶגְבָּה

טו וְנִבְרֲכוּ בְךָ כָּל־מִשְׁפְּחֹת הָאֲדָמָה וּבְזַרְעֶךָ: וְהִנֵּה אָנֹכִי עִמָּךְ וּשְׁמַרְתִּיךָ

בְּכֹל אֲשֶׁר־תֵּלֵךְ וַהֲשִׁבֹתִיךָ אֶל־הָאֲדָמָה הַזֹּאת כִּי לֹא אֶעֱזָבְךָ עַד אֲשֶׁר

טז אִם־עָשִׂיתִי אֵת אֲשֶׁר־דִּבַּרְתִּי לָךְ: וַיִּיקַץ יַעֲקֹב מִשְּׁנָתוֹ וַיֹּאמֶר אָכֵן יֵשׁ

יהוה בַּמָּקוֹם הַזֶּה וְאָנֹכִי לֹא יָדָעְתִּי: וַיִּירָא וַיֹּאמַר מַה־נּוֹרָא הַמָּקוֹם הַזֶּה

יח אֵין זֶה כִּי אִם־בֵּית אֱלֹהִים וְזֶה שַׁעַר הַשָּׁמָיִם: וַיַּשְׁכֵּם יַעֲקֹב בַּבֹּקֶר וַיִּקַּח

אֶת־הָאֶבֶן אֲשֶׁר־שָׂם מְרַאֲשֹׁתָיו וַיָּשֶׂם אֹתָהּ מַצֵּבָה וַיִּצֹק שֶׁמֶן עַל־

יט רֹאשָׁהּ: וַיִּקְרָא אֶת־שֵׁם־הַמָּקוֹם הַהוּא בֵּית־אֵל וְאוּלָם לוּז שֵׁם־הָעִיר

כ לָרִאשֹׁנָה: וַיִּדַּר יַעֲקֹב נֶדֶר לֵאמֹר אִם־יִהְיֶה אֱלֹהִים עִמָּדִי וּשְׁמָרַנִי

28:1. This *blessing* is the one given further in v. 3 (*Radak*). Earlier, Isaac had been tricked into blessing Jacob; now he ratified the blessing of his own free will.

⋅ঙ **Parashas Vayeitzi**

28:10-22. Jacob had left his parents to begin a personal exile that would include twenty years in the home of Laban, a mendacious rogue, who, as the Passover *Haggadah* says, attempted to uproot the Jewish people. Before going to Haran, Jacob spent fourteen years at the academy of Shem and Eber, a fact that the Sages deduce

from the chronology of the period. As great a man as Jacob did not need more years of study to become a scholar. He went to prepare spiritually for the rigors of exile.

28:10. "A righteous person's departure from a place leaves a void. As long as he lives in a city, he constitutes its glory, its splendor, and its beauty; when he departs, its glory, splendor, and beauty depart with him" (*Rashi*).

28:11. This place was Mount Moriah, the site where Abraham bound Isaac on the altar and where the Temple

⁴⁶ *Rebecca said to Isaac, "I am disgusted with my life on account of the daughters of Heth; if Jacob takes a wife of the daughters of Heth like these, of the daughters of the land, what is life to me?"*

28

The admonition against marrying a Canaanite; the Abrahamitic blessing is conveyed to Jacob

¹ **S**o Isaac summoned Jacob and blessed him;* he instructed him, and said to him, "Do not take a wife from the Canaanite women. ² Arise, go to Paddan-aram, to the house of Bethuel your mother's father, and take a wife from there from the daughters of Laban your mother's brother. ³ And may El Shaddai bless you, make you fruitful and make you numerous, and may you be a congregation of peoples. ⁴ May He grant you the blessing of Abraham to you and to your offspring with you, that you may possess the land of your sojourns which God gave to Abraham." ⁵ So Isaac sent away Jacob and he went toward Paddan-aram, to Laban the son of Bethuel the Aramean, brother of Rebecca, mother of Jacob and Esau.

⁶ When Esau saw that Isaac had blessed Jacob and sent him off to Paddan-aram to take himself a wife from there, as he blessed him he commanded him, saying, "You shall not take a wife from among the daughters of Canaan"; ⁷ and that Jacob obeyed his father and mother and went to Paddan-aram; ⁸ then Esau perceived that the daughters of Canaan were evil in the eyes of Isaac, his father. ⁹ So Esau went to Ishmael and took Mahalath, the daughter of Ishmael son of Abraham, sister of Nebaioth, in addition to his wives, as a wife for himself.

Esau marries the daughter of Ishmael

PARASHAS VAYEITZEI

Jacob's flight and his vision at Moriah

¹⁰ **J**acob departed* from Beer-sheba and went toward Haran. ¹¹ He encountered the place and spent the night there because the sun had set; he took from the stones of the place which he arranged around his head, and lay down in that place.* ¹² And he dreamt, and behold! A ladder was set earthward and its top reached heavenward; and behold! angels of God were ascending and descending on it.

¹³ And behold! H<small>ASHEM</small> was standing over him, and He said, "I am H<small>ASHEM</small>, God of Abraham your father and God of Isaac; the ground upon which you are lying, to you will I give it and to your descendants. ¹⁴ Your offspring shall be as the dust of the earth, and you shall spread out powerfully westward, eastward, northward and southward; and all the families of the earth shall bless themselves by you and by your offspring. ¹⁵ Behold, I am with you; I will guard you wherever you go, and I will return you to this soil; for I will not forsake you until I will have done what I have spoken about you."

¹⁶ Jacob awoke from his sleep and said, "Surely H<small>ASHEM</small> is present in this place* and I did not know!" ¹⁷ And he became frightened and said, "How awesome is this place! This is none other than the abode of God and this is the gate of the heavens!" ¹⁸ Jacob arose early in the morning and took the stone that he placed around his head and set it up as a pillar; and he poured oil on its top. ¹⁹ And he named that place Beth-el; however, Luz was the city's name originally.

²⁰ Then Jacob took a vow, saying, "If God will be with me, will guard me

---

would later stand.

28:12. Symbolism of Jacob's dream. The dreams mentioned in Scripture are vehicles of prophecy. Jacob's dream symbolized the future of the Jewish people and

man's ability to connect himself to God's master plan.

28:16. When prophets are shown a vision, they recognize it to be a communication from God (*Moreh Nevuchim*).

כא בַּדֶּרֶךְ הַזֶּה אֲשֶׁר אָנֹכִי הוֹלֵךְ וְנָתַן־לִי לֶחֶם לֶאֱכֹל וּבֶגֶד לִלְבֹּשׁ: וְשַׁבְתִּי
כב בְשָׁלוֹם אֶל־בֵּית אָבִי וְהָיָה יְהֹוָה לִי לֵאלֹהִים: וְהָאֶבֶן הַזֹּאת אֲשֶׁר־
שַׂמְתִּי מַצֵּבָה יִהְיֶה בֵּית אֱלֹהִים וְכֹל אֲשֶׁר תִּתֶּן־לִי עַשֵּׂר אֲעַשְּׂרֶנּוּ לָךְ:

כט שני א־ב וַיִּשָּׂא יַעֲקֹב רַגְלָיו וַיֵּלֶךְ אַרְצָה בְנֵי־קֶדֶם: וַיַּרְא וְהִנֵּה בְאֵר בַּשָּׂדֶה וְהִנֵּה־
שָׁם שְׁלֹשָׁה עֶדְרֵי־צֹאן רֹבְצִים עָלֶיהָ כִּי מִן־הַבְּאֵר הַהִוא יַשְׁקוּ
ג הָעֲדָרִים וְהָאֶבֶן גְּדֹלָה עַל־פִּי הַבְּאֵר: וְנֶאֶסְפוּ־שָׁמָּה כָל־הָעֲדָרִים וְגָלְלוּ
אֶת־הָאֶבֶן מֵעַל פִּי הַבְּאֵר וְהִשְׁקוּ אֶת־הַצֹּאן וְהֵשִׁיבוּ אֶת־הָאֶבֶן עַל־פִּי
ד הַבְּאֵר לִמְקֹמָהּ: וַיֹּאמֶר לָהֶם יַעֲקֹב אַחַי מֵאַיִן אַתֶּם וַיֹּאמְרוּ מֵחָרָן
ה־ו אֲנָחְנוּ: וַיֹּאמֶר לָהֶם הַיְדַעְתֶּם אֶת־לָבָן בֶּן־נָחוֹר וַיֹּאמְרוּ יָדָעְנוּ: וַיֹּאמֶר
ז לָהֶם הֲשָׁלוֹם לוֹ וַיֹּאמְרוּ שָׁלוֹם וְהִנֵּה רָחֵל בִּתּוֹ בָּאָה עִם־הַצֹּאן: וַיֹּאמֶר
הֵן עוֹד הַיּוֹם גָּדוֹל לֹא־עֵת הֵאָסֵף הַמִּקְנֶה הַשְׁקוּ הַצֹּאן וּלְכוּ רְעוּ:
ח וַיֹּאמְרוּ לֹא נוּכַל עַד אֲשֶׁר יֵאָסְפוּ כָּל־הָעֲדָרִים וְגָלְלוּ אֶת־הָאֶבֶן מֵעַל
ט פִּי הַבְּאֵר וְהִשְׁקִינוּ הַצֹּאן: עוֹדֶנּוּ מְדַבֵּר עִמָּם וְרָחֵל | בָּאָה עִם־הַצֹּאן
י אֲשֶׁר לְאָבִיהָ כִּי רֹעָה הִוא: וַיְהִי כַּאֲשֶׁר רָאָה יַעֲקֹב אֶת־רָחֵל בַּת־לָבָן
אֲחִי אִמּוֹ וְאֶת־צֹאן לָבָן אֲחִי אִמּוֹ וַיִּגַּשׁ יַעֲקֹב וַיָּגֶל אֶת־הָאֶבֶן מֵעַל פִּי
יא הַבְּאֵר וַיַּשְׁקְ אֶת־צֹאן לָבָן אֲחִי אִמּוֹ: וַיִּשַּׁק יַעֲקֹב לְרָחֵל וַיִּשָּׂא אֶת־קֹלוֹ
יב וַיֵּבְךְּ: וַיַּגֵּד יַעֲקֹב לְרָחֵל כִּי אֲחִי אָבִיהָ הוּא וְכִי בֶן־רִבְקָה הוּא וַתָּרָץ
יג וַתַּגֵּד לְאָבִיהָ: וַיְהִי כִשְׁמֹעַ לָבָן אֶת־שֵׁמַע | יַעֲקֹב בֶּן־אֲחֹתוֹ וַיָּרָץ
לִקְרָאתוֹ וַיְחַבֶּק־לוֹ וַיְנַשֶּׁק־לוֹ וַיְבִיאֵהוּ אֶל־בֵּיתוֹ וַיְסַפֵּר לְלָבָן אֵת כָּל־
יד הַדְּבָרִים הָאֵלֶּה: וַיֹּאמֶר לוֹ לָבָן אַךְ עַצְמִי וּבְשָׂרִי אָתָּה וַיֵּשֶׁב עִמּוֹ חֹדֶשׁ
טו יָמִים: וַיֹּאמֶר לָבָן לְיַעֲקֹב הֲכִי־אָחִי אַתָּה וַעֲבַדְתַּנִי חִנָּם הַגִּידָה לִּי מַה־
טז־יז מַּשְׂכֻּרְתֶּךָ: וּלְלָבָן שְׁתֵּי בָנוֹת שֵׁם הַגְּדֹלָה לֵאָה וְשֵׁם הַקְּטַנָּה רָחֵל: וְעֵינֵי
יח לֵאָה רַכּוֹת וְרָחֵל הָיְתָה יְפַת־תֹּאַר וִיפַת מַרְאֶה: וַיֶּאֱהַב יַעֲקֹב אֶת־ שלישי
יט רָחֵל וַיֹּאמֶר אֶעֱבָדְךָ שֶׁבַע שָׁנִים בְּרָחֵל בִּתְּךָ הַקְּטַנָּה: וַיֹּאמֶר לָבָן
כ טוֹב תִּתִּי אֹתָהּ לָךְ מִתִּתִּי אֹתָהּ לְאִישׁ אַחֵר שְׁבָה עִמָּדִי: וַיַּעֲבֹד
יַעֲקֹב בְּרָחֵל שֶׁבַע שָׁנִים וַיִּהְיוּ בְעֵינָיו כְּיָמִים אֲחָדִים בְּאַהֲבָתוֹ אֹתָהּ:
כא וַיֹּאמֶר יַעֲקֹב אֶל־לָבָן הָבָה אֶת־אִשְׁתִּי כִּי מָלְאוּ יָמָי וְאָבוֹאָה אֵלֶיהָ:

29:1-12. Jacob meets Rachel at the well. Again, a well is the place where a mate is found for a major figure in Jewish history. At a well, Eliezer found Rebecca, and later Moses met Zipporah at a well. Commentators note that wisdom is symbolized by the water below the ground; it is buried and hidden, but is accessible to those who put in the intense effort needed to bring it to the surface. Women, too, represent wisdom: *Wisdom of women builds her home* (Proverbs 14:1), as when Abraham hesitated to send away Hagar and Ishmael at Sarah's insistence and God told him to do everything she asked of him (21:12). It is understandable, therefore, that human symbols of wisdom were associated with earthly symbols of wisdom.

29:1. The reference is to Abraham's ancestral home — Aram and Ur Kasdim, the regions east of *Eretz Yisrael*.

29:13-30. Jacob is deceived. Jacob had come to Haran to find the woman with whom he would build the holy family that would change God's people from a family to a nation. She was ordained for this august calling, and for her sake ordinary materialistic considerations fell by the wayside. Rachel was that mate, and Jacob devoted seven years of hard physical toil to win the right to marry her. But he was dealing with Laban, whose name was synonymous with self-righteous dishonesty, and despite Jacob's best efforts to protect himself, Laban deceived him.

on this way that I am going; will give me bread to eat and clothes to wear; ²¹ *and I return in peace to my father's house, and HASHEM will be a God to me —* ²² *then this stone which I have set up as a pillar shall become a house of God, and whatever You will give me, I shall repeatedly tithe to You."*

29

Jacob meets Rachel

¹ **S**o Jacob lifted his feet, and went toward the land of the easterners. * ² *He looked, and behold — a well in the field! And behold! three flocks of sheep lay there beside it, for from that well they would water the flocks, and the stone over the mouth of the well was large.* ³ *When all the flocks would be assembled there they would roll the stone from the mouth of the well and water the sheep; then they would put back the stone over the mouth of the well, in its place.*

⁴ *Jacob said to them, "My brothers, where are you from?" And they said, "We are from Haran."* ⁵ *He said to them, "Do you know Laban the son of Nahor?" And they said, "We know."* ⁶ *Then he said to them, "Is it well with him?" They answered, "It is well; and see — his daughter Rachel is coming with the flock!"*

⁷ *He said, "Look, the day is still long; it is not yet time to bring the livestock in; water the flock and go on grazing."* ⁸ *But they said, "We will be unable to, until all the flocks will have been gathered and they will roll the stone off the mouth of the well; we will then water the flock."*

⁹ *While he was still speaking with them, Rachel had arrived with her father's flock, for she was a shepherdess.* ¹⁰ *And it was, when Jacob saw Rachel, daughter of Laban his mother's brother, and the flock of Laban his mother's brother, Jacob came forward and rolled the stone off the mouth of the well and watered the sheep of Laban his mother's brother.* ¹¹ *Then Jacob kissed Rachel; and he raised his voice and wept.* ¹² *Jacob told Rachel that he was her father's relative, and that he was Rebecca's son; then she ran and told her father.*

¹³ *And it was, when Laban heard the news of Jacob his sister's son, he ran toward him, embraced him, kissed him, and took him to his house; he re-*

Jacob contracts to marry, and is deceived

counted to Laban all these events. ¹⁴ *Then Laban said to him, "Nevertheless, you are my flesh and blood!" And he stayed with him a month's time.*

¹⁵ *Then Laban said to Jacob, "Just because you are my relative, should you serve me for nothing? Tell me: What are your wages?"*

¹⁶ *(Laban had two daughters. The name of the older one was Leah and the name of the younger one was Rachel.* ¹⁷ *Leah's eyes were tender, while Rachel was beautiful of form and beautiful of appearance.)*

¹⁸ *Jacob loved Rachel, so he said, "I will work for you seven years, for Rachel your younger daughter."*

¹⁹ *Laban said, "It is better that I give her to you than that I give her to another man; remain with me."* ²⁰ *So Jacob worked seven years for Rachel and they seemed to him a few days because of his love for her.*

²¹ *Jacob said to Laban, "Deliver my wife for my term is fulfilled, and I will consort with her."* *

◆§ **Jacob's voluntary separation from his parents.** Jacob was taken to task for voluntarily offering to remain in Laban's employ and not seeking to return home as soon as possible. He was away from his parents for a total of thirty-six years. For his fourteen years of study in the academy of Eber he was not considered negligent for not honoring his parents. For the next twenty-two years, however — twenty years with Laban and two years of

journeying — the Sages hold that Jacob was derelict in failing to return home. His punishment was that Joseph remained separated from him for a like number of years.

29:21. The expression *and I will consort with her* would have been vulgar in a lesser person. Jacob's only intent was that he was eighty-four years old and had to begin his mission of bringing the twelve tribes into the world. His only concern was to serve God (*Rashi*).

כב-כג וַיֶּאֱסֹף לָבָן אֶת־כָּל־אַנְשֵׁי הַמָּקוֹם וַיַּעַשׂ מִשְׁתֶּה: וַיְהִי בָעֶרֶב וַיִּקַּח אֶת־

כד לֵאָה בִתּוֹ וַיָּבֵא אֹתָהּ אֵלָיו וַיָּבֹא אֵלֶיהָ: וַיִּתֵּן לָבָן לָהּ אֶת־זִלְפָּה שִׁפְחָתוֹ

כה לְלֵאָה בִתּוֹ שִׁפְחָה: וַיְהִי בַבֹּקֶר וְהִנֵּה־הִוא לֵאָה וַיֹּאמֶר אֶל־לָבָן מַה־זֹּאת

כו עָשִׂיתָ לִּי הֲלֹא בְרָחֵל עָבַדְתִּי עִמָּךְ וְלָמָּה רִמִּיתָנִי: וַיֹּאמֶר לָבָן לֹא־

כז יֵעָשֶׂה כֵן בִּמְקוֹמֵנוּ לָתֵת הַצְּעִירָה לִפְנֵי הַבְּכִירָה: מַלֵּא שְׁבֻעַ זֹאת וְנִתְּנָה

לְךָ גַּם־אֶת־זֹאת בַּעֲבֹדָה אֲשֶׁר תַּעֲבֹד עִמָּדִי עוֹד שֶׁבַע־שָׁנִים אֲחֵרוֹת:

כח-כט וַיַּעַשׂ יַעֲקֹב כֵּן וַיְמַלֵּא שְׁבֻעַ זֹאת וַיִּתֶּן־לוֹ אֶת־רָחֵל בִּתּוֹ לוֹ לְאִשָּׁה: וַיִּתֵּן

ל לָבָן לְרָחֵל בִּתּוֹ אֶת־בִּלְהָה שִׁפְחָתוֹ לָהּ לְשִׁפְחָה: וַיָּבֹא גַּם אֶל־רָחֵל

לא וַיֶּאֱהַב גַּם־אֶת־רָחֵל מִלֵּאָה וַיַּעֲבֹד עִמּוֹ עוֹד שֶׁבַע־שָׁנִים אֲחֵרוֹת: וַיַּרְא

לב יהוה כִּי־שְׂנוּאָה לֵאָה וַיִּפְתַּח אֶת־רַחְמָהּ וְרָחֵל עֲקָרָה: וַתַּהַר לֵאָה וַתֵּלֶד

בֵּן וַתִּקְרָא שְׁמוֹ רְאוּבֵן כִּי אָמְרָה כִּי־רָאָה יהוה בְּעָנְיִי כִּי עַתָּה יֶאֱהָבַנִי

לג אִישִׁי: וַתַּהַר עוֹד וַתֵּלֶד בֵּן וַתֹּאמֶר כִּי־שָׁמַע יהוה כִּי־שְׂנוּאָה אָנֹכִי וַיִּתֶּן־

לד לִי גַּם־אֶת־זֶה וַתִּקְרָא שְׁמוֹ שִׁמְעוֹן: וַתַּהַר עוֹד וַתֵּלֶד בֵּן וַתֹּאמֶר עַתָּה

הַפַּעַם יִלָּוֶה אִישִׁי אֵלַי כִּי־יָלַדְתִּי לוֹ שְׁלֹשָׁה בָנִים עַל־כֵּן קָרָא־שְׁמוֹ

לה לֵוִי: וַתַּהַר עוֹד וַתֵּלֶד בֵּן וַתֹּאמֶר הַפַּעַם אוֹדֶה אֶת־יהוה עַל־כֵּן קָרְאָה

א שְׁמוֹ יְהוּדָה וַתַּעֲמֹד מִלֶּדֶת: וַתֵּרֶא רָחֵל כִּי לֹא יָלְדָה לְיַעֲקֹב וַתְּקַנֵּא

רָחֵל בַּאֲחֹתָהּ וַתֹּאמֶר אֶל־יַעֲקֹב הָבָה־לִּי בָנִים וְאִם־אַיִן מֵתָה אָנֹכִי:

ב וַיִּחַר־אַף יַעֲקֹב בְּרָחֵל וַיֹּאמֶר הֲתַחַת אֱלֹהִים אָנֹכִי אֲשֶׁר־מָנַע מִמֵּךְ

ג פְּרִי־בָטֶן: וַתֹּאמֶר הִנֵּה אֲמָתִי בִלְהָה בֹּא אֵלֶיהָ וְתֵלֵד עַל־בִּרְכַּי וְאִבָּנֶה

ד גַם־אָנֹכִי מִמֶּנָּה: וַתִּתֶּן־לוֹ אֶת־בִּלְהָה שִׁפְחָתָהּ לְאִשָּׁה וַיָּבֹא אֵלֶיהָ

ה-ו יַעֲקֹב: וַתַּהַר בִּלְהָה וַתֵּלֶד לְיַעֲקֹב בֵּן: וַתֹּאמֶר רָחֵל דָּנַנִּי אֱלֹהִים וְגַם

ז שָׁמַע בְּקֹלִי וַיִּתֶּן־לִי בֵּן עַל־כֵּן קָרְאָה שְׁמוֹ דָּן: וַתַּהַר עוֹד וַתֵּלֶד בִּלְהָה

ח שִׁפְחַת רָחֵל בֵּן שֵׁנִי לְיַעֲקֹב: וַתֹּאמֶר רָחֵל נַפְתּוּלֵי אֱלֹהִים ׀ נִפְתַּלְתִּי עִם־

ט אֲחֹתִי גַּם־יָכֹלְתִּי וַתִּקְרָא שְׁמוֹ נַפְתָּלִי: וַתֵּרֶא לֵאָה כִּי עָמְדָה מִלֶּדֶת

י וַתִּקַּח אֶת־זִלְפָּה שִׁפְחָתָהּ וַתִּתֵּן אֹתָהּ לְיַעֲקֹב לְאִשָּׁה: וַתֵּלֶד זִלְפָּה שִׁפְחַת

יא לֵאָה לְיַעֲקֹב בֵּן: וַתֹּאמֶר לֵאָה [°בָּא גָד ק] °בגד [כְּתִיב] וַתִּקְרָא אֶת־שְׁמוֹ גָּד:

ל

29:22-25. Laban substitutes Leah for Rachel. Living up to his reputation as a deceitful rogue, Laban substituted Leah for Rachel on the wedding night. Anticipating such a deception, Jacob arranged a secret signal with Rachel, but Rachel confided the sign to Leah so that she would not be put to shame (*Rashi* from *Megillah* 13b).

29:31. *Ramban* cites *Radak* that Jacob surely loved Leah, but that his greater love for Rachel made her seem unloved — or even hated — by comparison.

29:35. The word יְהוּדָה contains the letters of God's Four-letter Name, as well as the root that means "thankfulness" and "praise" (*Sforno*). Leah was especially grateful now, because, as the mother of four of Jacob's twelve sons, she had been granted more than her rightful share (*Rashi*).

30:1-8. Rachel is fulfilled through Bilhah. Rachel longed for children, but in vain. She begged Jacob to help her, to no avail. Finally, she followed the course of Sarah, who asked Abraham to marry her servant Hagar, in the expectation that she would be fulfilled vicariously by raising Hagar's children.

30:1. "If I remain childless I will be regarded as dead," or, alternatively, knowing how much Jacob loved her, Rachel sought to frighten him by saying she would die from grief.

30:11. The phrase בָּא גָד is written (כְּתִיב) in the Torah as a single word, בגד, but pronounced (קְרִי) as it were two words, בָּא גָד. *Rashi* interprets גָד as מַזָּל טוֹב, *good fortune*.

Laban
substitutes
Leah
for Rachel

²² So Laban gathered all the people of the place and made a feast. ²³ And it was in the evening, that he took Leah his daughter and brought her to him; and he consorted with her.

²⁴ — And Laban gave her Zilpah his maidservant — a maidservant to Leah his daughter.

²⁵ And it was, in the morning, that behold it was Leah! So he said to Laban, "What is this you have done to me? Was it not for Rachel that I worked for you? Why have you deceived me?"

²⁶ Laban said, "Such is not done in our place, to give the younger before the elder. ²⁷ Complete the week of this one and we will give you the other one too, for the work which you will perform for me yet another seven years."

²⁸ So Jacob did so and he completed the week for her; and he gave him Rachel his daughter to him as a wife. ²⁹ And Laban gave Rachel his daughter Bilhah his maidservant — to her as a maidservant. ³⁰ He consorted also with Rachel and loved Rachel even more than Leah; and he worked for him yet another seven years.

Leah bears
four sons
(See Appendix B,
chart 4)

³¹ HASHEM saw that Leah was unloved, * so He opened her womb; but Rachel remained barren.

³² Leah conceived and bore a son, and she called his name Reuben, as she had declared, "Because HASHEM has discerned my humiliation, for now my husband will love me."

³³ And she conceived again and bore a son and declared, "Because HASHEM has heard that I am unloved, He has given me this one also," and she called his name Simeon.

³⁴ Again she conceived, and bore a son and declared, "This time my husband will become attached to me for I have borne him three sons"; therefore He called his name Levi.

³⁵ She conceived again, and bore a son and declared, "This time let me gratefully praise HASHEM"; therefore she called his name Judah; * then she stopped giving birth.

30

Rachel is
fulfilled
through
Bilhah

¹ **R**achel saw that she had not borne children to Jacob, so Rachel became envious of her sister; she said to Jacob, "Give me children — otherwise I am dead."*

² Jacob's anger flared up at Rachel, and he said, "Am I instead of God Who has withheld from you fruit of the womb?"

³ She said, "Here is my maid Bilhah, consort with her, that she may bear upon my knees and I too may be built up through her."

⁴ So she gave him Bilhah her maidservant as a wife, and Jacob consorted with her. ⁵ Bilhah conceived and bore Jacob a son. ⁶ Then Rachel said, "God has judged me, He has also heard my voice and has given me a son." She therefore called his name Dan.

⁷ Bilhah, Rachel's maidservant, conceived again and bore Jacob a second son. ⁸ And Rachel said, "Sacred schemes have I maneuvered to equal my sister, and I have also prevailed!" And she called his name Naphtali.

⁹ When Leah saw that she had stopped giving birth, she took Zilpah her maidservant and gave her to Jacob as a wife. ¹⁰ Zilpah, Leah's maidservant, bore Jacob a son. ¹¹ And Leah declared, "Good luck has come!"* So she called his name Gad.

רביעי

יב־יג וַתֵּ֗לֶד זִלְפָּ֛ה שִׁפְחַ֥ת לֵאָ֖ה בֵּ֣ן שֵׁנִ֑י לְיַעֲקֹֽב: וַתֹּ֣אמֶר לֵאָ֗ה בְּאָשְׁרִ֔י כִּ֥י

יד אִשְּׁר֖וּנִי בָּנ֑וֹת וַתִּקְרָ֥א אֶת־שְׁמ֖וֹ אָשֵֽׁר: וַיֵּ֨לֶךְ רְאוּבֵ֜ן בִּימֵ֣י קְצִיר־חִטִּ֗ים

וַיִּמְצָ֤א דֽוּדָאִים֙ בַּשָּׂדֶ֔ה וַיָּבֵ֣א אֹתָ֔ם אֶל־לֵאָ֖ה אִמּ֑וֹ וַתֹּ֤אמֶר רָחֵל֙ אֶל־לֵאָ֔ה

טו תְּנִי־נָ֣א לִ֔י מִדּֽוּדָאֵ֖י בְּנֵֽךְ: וַתֹּ֣אמֶר לָ֗הּ הַמְעַט֙ קַחְתֵּ֣ךְ אֶת־אִישִׁ֔י וְלָקַ֕חַת גַּ֥ם

אֶת־דּֽוּדָאֵ֖י בְּנִ֑י וַתֹּ֣אמֶר רָחֵ֗ל לָכֵן֙ יִשְׁכַּ֤ב עִמָּךְ֙ הַלַּ֔יְלָה תַּ֖חַת דּֽוּדָאֵ֥י בְנֵֽךְ:

טז וַיָּבֹ֙א יַעֲקֹ֥ב מִן־הַשָּׂדֶה֮ בָּעֶ֒רֶב֒ וַתֵּצֵ֨א לֵאָ֜ה לִקְרָאת֗וֹ וַתֹּ֙אמֶר֙ אֵלַ֣י תָּב֔וֹא כִּ֣י

שָׂכֹ֤ר שְׂכַרְתִּ֙יךָ֙ בְּדֽוּדָאֵ֖י בְּנִ֑י וַיִּשְׁכַּ֥ב עִמָּ֖הּ בַּלַּ֥יְלָה הֽוּא: וַיִּשְׁמַ֥ע אֱלֹהִ֖ים

יז יח אֶל־לֵאָ֑ה וַתַּ֛הַר וַתֵּ֥לֶד לְיַעֲקֹ֖ב בֵּ֥ן חֲמִישִֽׁי: וַתֹּ֣אמֶר לֵאָ֗ה נָתַ֤ן אֱלֹהִים֙

יט שְׂכָרִ֔י אֲשֶׁר־נָתַ֥תִּי שִׁפְחָתִ֖י לְאִישִׁ֑י וַתִּקְרָ֥א שְׁמ֖וֹ יִשָּׂשכָֽר: וַתַּ֤הַר עוֹד֙ לֵאָ֔ה

כ וַתֵּ֥לֶד בֵּן־שִׁשִּׁ֖י לְיַעֲקֹֽב: וַתֹּ֣אמֶר לֵאָ֗ה זְבָדַ֨נִי אֱלֹהִ֥ים ׀ אֹתִי֮ זֵ֣בֶד טוֹב֒ הַפַּ֙עַם֙

יִזְבְּלֵ֣נִי אִישִׁ֔י כִּֽי־יָלַ֥דְתִּי ל֖וֹ שִׁשָּׁ֣ה בָנִ֑ים וַתִּקְרָ֥א אֶת־שְׁמ֖וֹ זְבֻלֽוּן: וְאַחַ֖ר

כא כב יָֽלְדָ֣ה בַּ֑ת וַתִּקְרָ֥א אֶת־שְׁמָ֖הּ דִּינָֽה: וַיִּזְכֹּ֥ר אֱלֹהִ֖ים אֶת־רָחֵ֑ל וַיִּשְׁמַ֤ע אֵלֶ֙יהָ֙

כג אֱלֹהִ֔ים וַיִּפְתַּ֖ח אֶת־רַחְמָֽהּ: וַתַּ֖הַר וַתֵּ֣לֶד בֵּ֑ן וַתֹּ֕אמֶר אָסַ֥ף אֱלֹהִ֖ים אֶת־

כד־כה חֶרְפָּתִֽי: וַתִּקְרָ֧א אֶת־שְׁמ֛וֹ יוֹסֵ֖ף לֵאמֹ֑ר יֹסֵ֧ף יְהֹוָ֛ה לִ֖י בֵּ֥ן אַחֵֽר: וַיְהִ֕י כַּאֲשֶׁ֛ר

יָֽלְדָ֥ה רָחֵ֖ל אֶת־יוֹסֵ֑ף וַיֹּ֤אמֶר יַעֲקֹב֙ אֶל־לָבָ֔ן שַׁלְּחֵ֙נִי֙ וְאֵ֣לְכָ֔ה אֶל־מְקוֹמִ֖י

כו וּלְאַרְצִֽי: תְּנָ֞ה אֶת־נָשַׁ֣י וְאֶת־יְלָדַ֗י אֲשֶׁ֨ר עָבַ֧דְתִּי אֹֽתְךָ֛ בָּהֵ֖ן וְאֵלֵ֑כָה כִּ֚י

כז אַתָּ֣ה יָדַ֔עְתָּ אֶת־עֲבֹֽדָתִ֖י אֲשֶׁ֥ר עֲבַדְתִּֽיךָ: וַיֹּ֤אמֶר אֵלָיו֙ לָבָ֔ן אִם־נָ֛א מָצָ֥אתִי

חמישי

חֵ֖ן בְּעֵינֶ֑יךָ נִחַ֕שְׁתִּי וַיְבָרֲכֵ֥נִי יְהֹוָ֖ה בִּגְלָלֶֽךָ: וַיֹּאמַ֑ר נָקְבָ֧ה שְׂכָרְךָ֛ עָלַ֖י

כח כט וְאֶתֵּֽנָה: וַיֹּ֣אמֶר אֵלָ֔יו אַתָּ֣ה יָדַ֔עְתָּ אֵ֥ת אֲשֶׁ֖ר עֲבַדְתִּ֑יךָ וְאֵ֛ת אֲשֶׁר־הָיָ֥ה

ל מִקְנְךָ֖ אִתִּֽי: כִּ֡י מְעַט֩ אֲשֶׁר־הָיָ֨ה לְךָ֤ לְפָנַי֙ וַיִּפְרֹ֣ץ לָרֹ֔ב וַיְבָ֧רֶךְ יְהֹוָ֛ה אֹֽתְךָ֖

לא לְרַגְלִ֑י וְעַתָּ֗ה מָתַ֛י אֶֽעֱשֶׂ֥ה גַם־אָנֹכִ֖י לְבֵיתִֽי: וַיֹּ֖אמֶר מָ֣ה אֶתֶּן־לָ֑ךְ וַיֹּ֣אמֶר

יַעֲקֹ֗ב לֹא־תִתֶּן־לִ֣י מְא֔וּמָה אִם־תַּֽעֲשֶׂה־לִּי֙ הַדָּבָ֣ר הַזֶּ֔ה אָשׁ֛וּבָה אֶרְעֶ֥ה

לב צֹֽאנְךָ֖ אֶשְׁמֹֽר: אֶֽעֱבֹ֨ר בְּכָל־צֹֽאנְךָ֜ הַיּ֗וֹם הָסֵ֨ר מִשָּׁ֜ם כָּל־שֶׂ֣ה ׀ נָקֹ֣ד וְטָל֗וּא

לג וְכָל־שֶׂה־חוּם֙ בַּכְּשָׂבִ֔ים וְטָל֥וּא וְנָקֹ֖ד בָּֽעִזִּ֑ים וְהָיָ֖ה שְׂכָרִֽי: וְעָֽנְתָה־בִּ֤י

צִדְקָתִי֙ בְּי֣וֹם מָחָ֔ר כִּֽי־תָב֥וֹא עַל־שְׂכָרִ֖י לְפָנֶ֑יךָ כֹּ֣ל אֲשֶׁר־אֵינֶ֩נּוּ֩ נָקֹ֨ד

לה וְטָל֜וּא בָּֽעִזִּ֗ים וְחוּם֙ בַּכְּשָׂבִ֔ים גָּנ֥וּב ה֖וּא אִתִּֽי: וַיֹּ֥אמֶר לָבָ֖ן הֵ֑ן ל֥וּ יְהִ֖י

לה כִדְבָרֶֽךָ: וַיָּ֣סַר בַּיּוֹם֩ הַה֨וּא אֶת־הַתְּיָשִׁ֜ים הָֽעֲקֻדִּ֣ים וְהַטְּלֻאִ֗ים וְאֵ֤ת כָּל־

30:14-16. The dudaim. The incident of the *dudaim* is most puzzling. What were they? Why were they so important to Rachel, Leah, and Reuben? Why does the Torah relate the puzzling episode? It is obvious that the episode is filled with mysteries of the Torah. Indeed, the Sages and commentators found many teachings in these cryptic verses, among them insights into the noble character of the people involved — and even the statements or deeds for which they were reprimanded are indicative of their greatness, for only people of very high stature can be held to such high standards.

Among the possible translations of this word are jasmine, violets, mandrakes, and baskets of figs. Some of these were reputed to induce fertility and others were fragrant and capable of inducing good feelings.

30:17. The Torah stresses that God responded to her prayers, not that there was some magical power in the *dudaim*. Children are a gift of God (*Radak*).

30:22-24. Rachel conceives; the birth of Joseph. God *remembered* Rachel in the sense that He took cognizance of her virtues. This auspicious event took place on Rosh Hashanah, the Day of Remembrance (*Rosh Hashanah* 11a).

30:31. From the flocks in Jacob's care, Laban would remove all animals of unusual color, leaving the nor-

¹² *Zilpah, Leah's maidservant, bore a second son to Jacob.* ¹³ *Leah declared, "In my good fortune! For women have deemed me fortunate!" So she called his name Asher.*

The dudaim   ¹⁴ *Reuben went out in the days of the wheat harvest; he found dudaim in the field and brought them to Leah his mother; Rachel said to Leah, "Please give me some of your son's dudaim." * ¹⁵ *But she said to her, "Was your taking my husband insignificant? — And now to take even my son's dudaim!" Rachel said, "Therefore, he shall lie with you tonight in return for your son's dudaim."*

¹⁶ *When Jacob came from the field in the evening, Leah went out to meet him and said, "It is to me that you must come for I have clearly hired you with my son's dudaim." So he lay with her that night.*

Leah's   ¹⁷ *God hearkened to Leah;* * and she conceived and bore Jacob a fifth son.*
last three   ¹⁸ *And Leah declared, "God has granted me my reward because I gave my*
children   *maidservant to my husband." So she called his name Issachar.*

¹⁹ *Then Leah conceived again and bore Jacob a sixth son.* ²⁰ *Leah said, "God has endowed me with a good endowment; now my husband will make his permanent home with me for I have borne him six sons." So she called his name Zebulun.* ²¹ *Afterwards, she bore a daughter and she called her name Dinah.*

Rachel   ²² *God remembered Rachel; God hearkened to her and He opened her womb.*
conceives;   ²³ *She conceived and bore a son, and said, "God has taken away my disgrace."*
the birth of   ²⁴ *So she called his name Joseph, saying, "May HASHEM add on for me another*
Joseph   *son."*

²⁵ *And it was, when Rachel had given birth to Joseph, Jacob said to Laban, "Grant me leave that I may go to my place and to my land.* ²⁶ *Give me my wives and my children for whom I have served you, and I will go; for you are aware of my service that I labored for you."*

Jacob   ²⁷ *But Laban said to him, "If I have found favor in your eyes! — I have learned*
wishes to   *by divination that HASHEM has blessed me on account of you."* ²⁸ *And he said,*
leave, but   *"Specify your wage to me and I will give it."* ²⁹ *But he said to him, "You*
concludes an   *know how I served you and what your livestock were with me.* ³⁰ *For the little*
employment   *that you had before I came has expanded substantially as HASHEM has blessed*
contract with   *you with my coming; and now, when will I also do something for my own*
Laban   *house?"*

³¹ *He said, "What shall I give you?" And Jacob said, "Do not give me anything; if you will do this thing for me, I will resume pasturing and guarding your flocks:* ³² *Let me pass through your whole flock today. Remove from there every speckled or spotted lamb, every brownish lamb among the sheep and the spotted or speckled among the goats — that will be my wage.* ³³ *Let my integrity testify for me in the future when it comes before you regarding my wage; any among the goats that is not speckled or spotted, or among the sheep that is not brownish, is stolen, if in my possession."*

³⁴ *And Laban said, "Agreed! If only it will be as you say."*

³⁵ *So he removed on that very day the ringed and spotted he-goats and all*

---

mally colored ones with Jacob. Of the animals to be born from the flocks he would be tending, Jacob would keep only the abnormally colored ones. Since such animals are freakish, and since the removal of such existing animals assured that heredity would not contribute to such future births, the arrangement was weighted in favor of Laban.

As Jacob later charged, Laban unilaterally changed the terms of the agreement a hundred times (31:41), all to Jacob's disadvantage.

הָעִזִּים הַנְּקֻדּוֹת וְהַטְּלֻאֹת כֹּל אֲשֶׁר־לָבָן בּוֹ וְכָל־חוּם בַּכְּשָׂבִים וַיִּתֵּן בְּיַד־

לו בָּנָיו: וַיָּשֶׂם דֶּרֶךְ שְׁלֹשֶׁת יָמִים בֵּינוֹ וּבֵין יַעֲקֹב וְיַעֲקֹב רֹעֶה אֶת־צֹאן לָבָן

לז הַנּוֹתָרֹת: וַיִּקַּח־לוֹ יַעֲקֹב מַקַּל לִבְנֶה לַח וְלוּז וְעַרְמוֹן וַיְפַצֵּל בָּהֵן פְּצָלוֹת

לח לְבָנוֹת מַחְשֹׂף הַלָּבָן אֲשֶׁר עַל־הַמַּקְלוֹת: וַיַּצֵּג אֶת־הַמַּקְלוֹת אֲשֶׁר פִּצֵּל

בָּרְהָטִים בְּשִׁקֲתוֹת הַמָּיִם אֲשֶׁר תָּבֹאןָ הַצֹּאן לִשְׁתּוֹת לְנֹכַח הַצֹּאן וַיֵּחַמְנָה

לט בְּבֹאָן לִשְׁתּוֹת: וַיֶּחֱמוּ הַצֹּאן אֶל־הַמַּקְלוֹת וַתֵּלַדְןָ הַצֹּאן עֲקֻדִּים נְקֻדִּים

מ וּטְלֻאִים: וְהַכְּשָׂבִים הִפְרִיד יַעֲקֹב וַיִּתֵּן פְּנֵי הַצֹּאן אֶל־עָקֹד וְכָל־חוּם

מא בְּצֹאן לָבָן וַיָּשֶׁת לוֹ עֲדָרִים לְבַדּוֹ וְלֹא שָׁתָם עַל־צֹאן לָבָן: וְהָיָה בְּכָל־יַחֵם

הַצֹּאן הַמְקֻשָּׁרוֹת וְשָׂם יַעֲקֹב אֶת־הַמַּקְלוֹת לְעֵינֵי הַצֹּאן בָּרְהָטִים

מב לְיַחְמֵנָּה בַּמַּקְלוֹת: וּבְהַעֲטִיף הַצֹּאן לֹא יָשִׂים וְהָיָה הָעֲטֻפִים לְלָבָן

מג וְהַקְּשֻׁרִים לְיַעֲקֹב: וַיִּפְרֹץ הָאִישׁ מְאֹד מְאֹד וַיְהִי־לוֹ צֹאן רַבּוֹת וּשְׁפָחוֹת

וַעֲבָדִים וּגְמַלִּים וַחֲמֹרִים: וַיִּשְׁמַע אֶת־דִּבְרֵי בְנֵי־לָבָן לֵאמֹר לָקַח יַעֲקֹב

לא א

ב אֵת כָּל־אֲשֶׁר לְאָבִינוּ וּמֵאֲשֶׁר לְאָבִינוּ עָשָׂה אֵת כָּל־הַכָּבֹד הַזֶּה: וַיַּרְא

ג יַעֲקֹב אֶת־פְּנֵי לָבָן וְהִנֵּה אֵינֶנּוּ עִמּוֹ כִּתְמוֹל שִׁלְשׁוֹם: וַיֹּאמֶר יהוה אֶל־

ד יַעֲקֹב שׁוּב אֶל־אֶרֶץ אֲבוֹתֶיךָ וּלְמוֹלַדְתֶּךָ וְאֶהְיֶה עִמָּךְ: וַיִּשְׁלַח יַעֲקֹב

ה וַיִּקְרָא לְרָחֵל וּלְלֵאָה הַשָּׂדֶה אֶל־צֹאנוֹ: וַיֹּאמֶר לָהֶן רֹאֶה אָנֹכִי אֶת־פְּנֵי

ו אֲבִיכֶן כִּי־אֵינֶנּוּ אֵלַי כִּתְמֹל שִׁלְשֹׁם וֵאלֹהֵי אָבִי הָיָה עִמָּדִי: וְאַתֵּנָה יְדַעְתֶּן

ז כִּי בְּכָל־כֹּחִי עָבַדְתִּי אֶת־אֲבִיכֶן: וַאֲבִיכֶן הֵתֶל בִּי וְהֶחֱלִף אֶת־מַשְׂכֻּרְתִּי

ח עֲשֶׂרֶת מֹנִים וְלֹא־נְתָנוֹ אֱלֹהִים לְהָרַע עִמָּדִי: אִם־כֹּה יֹאמַר נְקֻדִּים יִהְיֶה

שְׂכָרֶךָ וְיָלְדוּ כָל־הַצֹּאן נְקֻדִּים וְאִם־כֹּה יֹאמַר עֲקֻדִּים יִהְיֶה שְׂכָרֶךָ וְיָלְדוּ

ט-י כָל־הַצֹּאן עֲקֻדִּים: וַיַּצֵּל אֱלֹהִים אֶת־מִקְנֵה אֲבִיכֶם וַיִּתֶּן־לִי: וַיְהִי בְּעֵת

יַחֵם הַצֹּאן וָאֶשָּׂא עֵינַי וָאֵרֶא בַּחֲלוֹם וְהִנֵּה הָעַתֻּדִים הָעֹלִים עַל־הַצֹּאן

יא עֲקֻדִּים נְקֻדִּים וּבְרֻדִּים: וַיֹּאמֶר אֵלַי מַלְאַךְ הָאֱלֹהִים בַּחֲלוֹם יַעֲקֹב וָאֹמַר

יב הִנֵּנִי: וַיֹּאמֶר שָׂא־נָא עֵינֶיךָ וּרְאֵה כָּל־הָעַתֻּדִים הָעֹלִים עַל־הַצֹּאן עֲקֻדִּים

יג נְקֻדִּים וּבְרֻדִּים כִּי רָאִיתִי אֵת כָּל־אֲשֶׁר לָבָן עֹשֶׂה לָּךְ: אָנֹכִי הָאֵל בֵּית־

אֵל אֲשֶׁר מָשַׁחְתָּ שָּׁם מַצֵּבָה אֲשֶׁר נָדַרְתָּ לִּי שָׁם נֶדֶר עַתָּה קוּם צֵא

יד מִן־הָאָרֶץ הַזֹּאת וְשׁוּב אֶל־אֶרֶץ מוֹלַדְתֶּךָ: וַתַּעַן רָחֵל וְלֵאָה וַתֹּאמַרְנָה

טו לוֹ הַעוֹד לָנוּ חֵלֶק וְנַחֲלָה בְּבֵית אָבִינוּ: הֲלוֹא נָכְרִיּוֹת נֶחְשַׁבְנוּ לוֹ כִּי

טז מְכָרָנוּ וַיֹּאכַל גַּם־אָכוֹל אֶת־כַּסְפֵּנוּ: כִּי כָל־הָעֹשֶׁר אֲשֶׁר הִצִּיל אֱלֹהִים

מֵאָבִינוּ לָנוּ הוּא וּלְבָנֵינוּ וְעַתָּה כֹּל אֲשֶׁר אָמַר אֱלֹהִים אֵלֶיךָ עֲשֵׂה:

30:37-38. Citing *II Samuel* 22:27: *With the trustworthy, act trustingly; and with the crooked, act perversely,* the Talmud (*Megillah* 13b) teaches that while it is never permitted to steal or lie, one must protect oneself against thieves and connivers. Consequently, Jacob resorted to several devices to outwit his uncle and retain what was rightfully his, under the original terms of the arrangement.

31:1-3. The decision to flee. After twenty years, Jacob and his family returned to *Eretz Yisrael*. The decision was precipitated by the clear perception that Laban's family resented Jacob's success.

31:7. The Torah specifies only one example of Laban's deceit [see 30:35]; however, as *Ramban* emphasizes, there must have been many such instances that the Torah

Laban's new deceit the speckled and spotted goats — every one that contained white, as well as all the brownish ones among the sheep — and he left them in the charge of his sons. ³⁶ And he put a distance of three days between himself and Jacob; and Jacob tended Laban's remaining flock.

³⁷ Jacob then took himself fresh rods of poplar and hazel and chestnut. He peeled white streaks in them, laying bare the white of the rods. ³⁸ And he set up the rods which he had peeled, in the runnels — in the watering receptacles to which the flocks came to drink — facing the flocks, so they would become stimulated when they came to drink. ³⁹ Then the flocks became stimulated by the rods and the flocks gave birth to ringed ones, speckled ones, and spotted ones. ⁴⁰ Jacob segregated the lambs and he made the flocks face the ringed ones and all the brownish ones among Laban's flocks. He formed separate droves of his own and did not mingle them with Laban's flocks.

⁴¹ Whenever it was mating time for the early-bearing flocks, Jacob would place the rods in the runnels, in full view of the flock to stimulate them among the rods. ⁴² But when the sheep were late bearing, he would not emplace; thus, the late-bearing ones went to Laban and the early-bearing ones to Jacob.

⁴³ The man became exceedingly prosperous and he attained fecund flocks, maidservants and servants, camels and donkeys.

31

The decision to flee from Laban

Jacob wins the consent of his wives

¹ Then he heard the words of Laban's sons, saying, "Jacob has taken all that belonged to our father, and from that which belonged to our father he amassed all this wealth." ² Jacob also noticed Laban's disposition that, behold, it was not toward him as in earlier days. ³ And HASHEM said to Jacob, "Return to the land of your fathers and to your native land, and I will be with you."

⁴ Jacob sent and summoned Rachel and Leah to the field, to his flock, ⁵ and said to them, "I have noticed that your father's disposition is not toward me as in earlier days; but the God of my father was with me. ⁶ Now you have known that it was with all my might that I served your father, ⁷ yet your father mocked me and changed my wage a hundred times;* but God did not permit him to harm me. ⁸ If he would stipulate: 'Speckled ones shall be your wages,' then the entire flock bore speckled ones; and if he would stipulate: 'Ringed ones shall be your wages,' then the entire flock bore ringed ones. ⁹ Thus, God took away your father's livestock, and gave them to me. ¹⁰ It once happened at the mating time of the flock that I raised my eyes and saw in a dream — Behold! The he-goats that mounted the flock were ringed, speckled, and checkered. ¹¹ And an angel of God said to me in the dream, 'Jacob!' And I said, 'Here I am.' ¹² And he said, 'Raise your eyes, if you please, and see that all the he-goats mounting the flocks are ringed, speckled, and checkered, for I have seen all that Laban is doing to you. ¹³ I am the God of Beth-el where you anointed a pillar and where you made Me a vow. Now — arise, leave this land and return to your native land.' "

¹⁴ Then Rachel and Leah replied and said to him, "Have we then still a share and an inheritance in our father's house? ¹⁵ Are we not considered by him as strangers? For he has sold us and even totally consumed our money! ¹⁶ But, all the wealth that God has taken away from our father belongs to us and to our children; so now, whatever God has said to you, do."

---

does not enumerate. Laban did not deny Jacob's direct reproach regarding his pattern of constant duplic-   ity, as well as regular unilateral changes of his wage (vv. 36ff).

יז-יח   וַיָּ֣קָם יַעֲקֹ֔ב וַיִּשָּׂ֛א אֶת־בָּנָ֥יו וְאֶת־נָשָׁ֖יו עַל־הַגְּמַלִּֽים: וַיִּנְהַ֣ג אֶת־כָּל־

מִקְנֵ֗הוּ וְאֶת־כָּל־רְכֻשׁוֹ֙ אֲשֶׁ֣ר רָכָ֔שׁ מִקְנֵה֙ קִנְיָנ֔וֹ אֲשֶׁ֥ר רָכַ֖שׁ בְּפַדַּ֣ן אֲרָ֑ם

יט   לָב֛וֹא אֶל־יִצְחָ֥ק אָבִ֖יו אַ֣רְצָה כְּנָֽעַן: וְלָבָ֣ן הָלַ֔ךְ לִגְזֹ֖ז אֶת־צֹאנ֑וֹ וַתִּגְנֹ֣ב רָחֵ֔ל

כ   אֶת־הַתְּרָפִ֖ים אֲשֶׁ֥ר לְאָבִֽיהָ: וַיִּגְנֹ֣ב יַעֲקֹ֔ב אֶת־לֵ֥ב לָבָ֖ן הָאֲרַמִּ֑י עַל־בְּלִי־

כא   הִגִּ֣יד ל֔וֹ כִּ֥י בֹרֵ֖חַ הֽוּא: וַיִּבְרַ֣ח הוּא֙ וְכָל־אֲשֶׁר־ל֔וֹ וַיָּ֖קָם וַיַּעֲבֹ֣ר אֶת־הַנָּהָ֑ר

כב-כג   וַיָּ֥שֶׂם אֶת־פָּנָ֖יו הַ֥ר הַגִּלְעָֽד: וַיֻּגַּ֥ד לְלָבָ֖ן בַּיּ֣וֹם הַשְּׁלִישִׁ֑י כִּ֥י בָרַ֖ח יַעֲקֹֽב: וַיִּקַּ֤ח

אֶת־אֶחָיו֙ עִמּ֔וֹ וַיִּרְדֹּ֣ף אַחֲרָ֔יו דֶּ֖רֶךְ שִׁבְעַ֣ת יָמִ֑ים וַיַּדְבֵּ֥ק אֹת֖וֹ בְּהַ֥ר הַגִּלְעָֽד:

כד   וַיָּבֹ֧א אֱלֹהִ֛ים אֶל־לָבָ֥ן הָאֲרַמִּ֖י בַּחֲלֹ֣ם הַלָּ֑יְלָה וַיֹּ֣אמֶר ל֔וֹ הִשָּׁ֧מֶר לְךָ֛ פֶּן־

כה   תְּדַבֵּ֥ר עִֽם־יַעֲקֹ֖ב מִטּ֥וֹב עַד־רָֽע: וַיַּשֵּׂ֥ג לָבָ֖ן אֶת־יַעֲקֹ֑ב וְיַעֲקֹ֗ב תָּקַ֤ע אֶת־

כו   אָהֳלוֹ֙ בָּהָ֔ר וְלָבָ֛ן תָּקַ֥ע אֶת־אֶחָ֖יו בְּהַ֥ר הַגִּלְעָֽד: וַיֹּ֤אמֶר לָבָן֙ לְיַעֲקֹ֔ב מֶ֣ה

כז   עָשִׂ֔יתָ וַתִּגְנֹ֖ב אֶת־לְבָבִ֑י וַתְּנַהֵג֙ אֶת־בְּנֹתַ֔י כִּשְׁבֻי֖וֹת חָֽרֶב: לָ֤מָּה נַחְבֵּ֨אתָ֙

לִבְרֹ֔חַ וַתִּגְנֹ֖ב אֹתִ֑י וְלֹא־הִגַּ֣דְתָּ לִּ֔י וָֽאֲשַׁלֵּחֲךָ֛ בְּשִׂמְחָ֥ה וּבְשִׁרִ֖ים בְּתֹ֥ף

כח-כט   וּבְכִנּֽוֹר: וְלֹ֣א נְטַשְׁתַּ֔נִי לְנַשֵּׁ֥ק לְבָנַ֖י וְלִבְנֹתָ֑י עַתָּ֖ה הִסְכַּ֥לְתָּֽ עֲשֽׂוֹ: יֶשׁ־לְאֵ֣ל

יָדִ֔י לַעֲשׂ֥וֹת עִמָּכֶ֖ם רָ֑ע וֵֽאלֹהֵ֨י אֲבִיכֶ֜ם אֶ֗מֶשׁ ׀ אָמַ֤ר אֵלַי֙ לֵאמֹ֔ר הִשָּׁ֧מֶר לְךָ֛

ל   מִדַּבֵּ֥ר עִֽם־יַעֲקֹ֖ב מִטּ֥וֹב עַד־רָֽע: וְעַתָּה֙ הָלֹ֣ךְ הָלַ֔כְתָּ כִּֽי־נִכְסֹ֥ף נִכְסַ֖פְתָּה

לא   לְבֵ֣ית אָבִ֑יךָ לָ֥מָּה גָנַ֖בְתָּ אֶת־אֱלֹהָֽי: וַיַּ֥עַן יַעֲקֹ֖ב וַיֹּ֣אמֶר לְלָבָ֑ן כִּ֣י יָרֵ֔אתִי כִּ֣י

לב   אָמַ֔רְתִּי פֶּן־תִּגְזֹ֥ל אֶת־בְּנוֹתֶ֖יךָ מֵעִמִּֽי: עִם֩ אֲשֶׁ֨ר תִּמְצָ֤א אֶת־אֱלֹהֶ֨יךָ֙ לֹ֣א

יִֽחְיֶ֔ה נֶ֣גֶד אַחֵ֧ינוּ הַכֶּר־לְךָ֛ מָ֥ה עִמָּדִ֖י וְקַֽח־לָ֑ךְ וְלֹֽא־יָדַ֣ע יַעֲקֹ֔ב כִּ֥י רָחֵ֖ל

לג   גְּנָבָֽתַם: וַיָּבֹ֨א לָבָ֜ן בְּאֹ֥הֶל יַעֲקֹ֣ב ׀ וּבְאֹ֣הֶל לֵאָ֗ה וּבְאֹ֛הֶל שְׁתֵּ֥י הָאֲמָהֹ֖ת וְלֹ֣א

לד   מָצָ֑א וַיֵּצֵא֙ מֵאֹ֣הֶל לֵאָ֔ה וַיָּבֹ֖א בְּאֹ֣הֶל רָחֵֽל: וְרָחֵ֞ל לָקְחָ֣ה אֶת־הַתְּרָפִ֗ים

וַתְּשִׂמֵ֛ם בְּכַ֥ר הַגָּמָ֖ל וַתֵּ֣שֶׁב עֲלֵיהֶ֑ם וַיְמַשֵּׁ֥שׁ לָבָ֛ן אֶת־כָּל־הָאֹ֖הֶל וְלֹ֥א

לה   מָצָֽא: וַתֹּ֣אמֶר אֶל־אָבִ֗יהָ אַל־יִ֨חַר֙ בְּעֵינֵ֣י אֲדֹנִ֔י כִּ֣י ל֤וֹא אוּכַל֙ לָק֣וּם

מִפָּנֶ֔יךָ כִּי־דֶ֥רֶךְ נָשִׁ֖ים לִ֑י וַיְחַפֵּ֕שׂ וְלֹ֥א מָצָ֖א אֶת־הַתְּרָפִֽים: וַיִּ֥חַר לְיַעֲקֹ֖ב

לו   וַיָּ֣רֶב בְּלָבָ֑ן וַיַּ֤עַן יַעֲקֹב֙ וַיֹּ֣אמֶר לְלָבָ֔ן מַה־פִּשְׁעִי֙ מַ֣ה חַטָּאתִ֔י כִּ֥י דָלַ֖קְתָּ

לז   אַחֲרָֽי: כִּֽי־מִשַּׁ֣שְׁתָּ אֶת־כָּל־כֵּלַ֗י מַה־מָּצָ֨אתָ֙ מִכֹּ֣ל כְּלֵי־בֵיתֶ֔ךָ שִׂ֣ים כֹּ֗ה

לח   נֶ֚גֶד אַחַ֣י וְאַחֶ֔יךָ וְיוֹכִ֖יחוּ בֵּ֥ין שְׁנֵֽינוּ: זֶה֩ עֶשְׂרִ֨ים שָׁנָ֤ה אָנֹכִי֙ עִמָּ֔ךְ

לט   רְחֵלֶ֥יךָ וְעִזֶּ֖יךָ לֹ֣א שִׁכֵּ֑לוּ וְאֵילֵ֥י צֹאנְךָ֖ לֹ֥א אָכָֽלְתִּי: טְרֵפָה֙ לֹא־הֵבֵ֣אתִי

מ   אֵלֶ֔יךָ אָנֹכִ֣י אֲחַטֶּ֔נָּה מִיָּדִ֖י תְּבַקְשֶׁ֑נָּה גְּנֻֽבְתִ֣י י֔וֹם וּגְנֻֽבְתִ֖י לָֽיְלָה: הָיִ֧יתִי

מא   בַיּ֛וֹם אֲכָלַ֥נִי חֹ֖רֶב וְקֶ֣רַח בַּלָּ֑יְלָה וַתִּדַּ֥ד שְׁנָתִ֖י מֵֽעֵינָֽי: זֶה־לִּ֞י עֶשְׂרִ֣ים שָׁנָה֮

בְּבֵיתֶךָ֒ עֲבַדְתִּ֜יךָ אַרְבַּֽע־עֶשְׂרֵ֤ה שָׁנָה֙ בִּשְׁתֵּ֣י בְנֹתֶ֔יךָ וְשֵׁ֥שׁ שָׁנִ֖ים בְּצֹאנֶ֑ךָ

מב   וַתַּחֲלֵ֥ף אֶת־מַשְׂכֻּרְתִּ֖י עֲשֶׂ֥רֶת מֹנִֽים: לוּלֵ֡י אֱלֹהֵ֣י אָבִי֩ אֱלֹהֵ֨י אַבְרָהָ֜ם

31:19. The *teraphim* were idols, which Rachel took to keep her father from idol worship (*Rashi*). The Torah records this episode because her intentions were noble (*Midrash*).

31:32. This curse that Jacob pronounced came true with Rachel's premature death. For, as the Sages teach, even an unintentional curse that escapes the lips of the righteous comes about (*Rashi*).

Jacob's flight

¹⁷ Jacob arose and lifted his children and his wives onto the camels. ¹⁸ He led away all his livestock and all the wealth which he had amassed — his purchased property which he had amassed in Paddan-aram — to go to his father Isaac, to the land of Canaan.

¹⁹ Laban had gone to shear his sheep, and Rachel stole the teraphim that belonged to her father. * ²⁰ Jacob deceived Laban the Aramean by not telling him that he was fleeing. ²¹ Thus, he fled with all he had. He arose and crossed the river, and he set his direction toward Mount Gilead.

Laban's pursuit and God's warning

²² It was told to Laban on the third day that Jacob had fled. ²³ So he took his kinsmen with him and pursued him a distance of seven days, catching up with him on Mount Gilead. ²⁴ But God had come to Laban the Aramean in a dream by night and said to him, "Beware lest you speak with Jacob either good or bad."

The confrontation of Jacob and Laban

²⁵ Laban overtook Jacob. Jacob had pitched his tent on the mountain, while Laban had stationed his kinsmen on Mount Gilead. ²⁶ Laban said to Jacob, "What have you done that you have deceived me and led my daughters away like captives of the sword? ²⁷ Why have you fled so stealthily, and cheated me? Nor did you tell me — for I would have sent you off with gladness, with songs, with timbrel, and with lyre! ²⁸ And you did not even allow me to kiss my sons and daughters; now you have acted foolishly. ²⁹ It is in my power to do you all harm; but the God of your father addressed me last night, saying, 'Beware of speaking with Jacob either good or bad.' ³⁰ Now — you have left because you longed greatly for your father's house; but why did you steal my gods?"

³¹ Jacob answered and said to Laban, "Because I was afraid, for I thought, perhaps you might steal your daughters from me. ³² With whomever you find your gods, he shall not live; * in the presence of our kinsmen ascertain for yourself what is with me and take it back." (Now Jacob did not know that Rachel had stolen them.)

³³ Laban came into Jacob's tent, and into Leah's tent, and into the tent of the two maidservants, but he found nothing. When he had left Leah's tent, he came into Rachel's tent. ³⁴ Now Rachel had taken the teraphim, put them into the camel's packsaddle and sat on them. Laban rummaged through the whole tent, but found nothing. ³⁵ She said to her father, "Let not my lord be angered that I cannot rise up before you, for the way of women is upon me." Thus he searched but did not find the teraphim.

³⁶ Then Jacob became angered and he took up his grievance with Laban; Jacob spoke up and said to Laban, "What is my transgression? What is my sin that you have hotly pursued me? ³⁷ When you rummaged through all my things, what did you find of all your household objects? Set it here before my kinsmen and your kinsmen, and let them decide between the two of us.

³⁸ "These twenty years I have been with you, your ewes and she-goats never miscarried, nor did I eat rams of your flock. ³⁹ That which was mangled I never brought you — I myself would bear the loss, from me you would exact it, whether it was stolen by day or stolen by night. ⁴⁰ This is how I was: By day scorching heat consumed me, and frost by night; my sleep drifted from my eyes. ⁴¹ This is my twenty years in your household: I served you fourteen years for your two daughters, and six years for your flocks; and you changed my wage a hundred times. ⁴² Had not the God of my father — the God of Abraham

שביעי   וּפַ֣חַד יִצְחָ֔ק הָ֥יָה לִ֖י כִּ֣י עַתָּ֤ה רֵיקָ֣ם שִׁלַּחְתָּ֔נִי אֶת־עָנְיִ֞י וְאֶת־יְגִ֧יעַ כַּפַּ֛י רָאָ֥ה

מג   אֱלֹהִ֖ים וַיּ֥וֹכַח אָֽמֶשׁ: וַיַּ֨עַן לָבָ֜ן וַיֹּ֣אמֶר אֶֽל־יַעֲקֹ֗ב הַבָּנ֨וֹת בְּנֹתַ֜י וְהַבָּנִ֣ים בָּנַ֗י

וְהַצֹּ֣אן צֹאנִי֮ וְכֹ֣ל אֲשֶׁר־אַתָּ֣ה רֹאֶה֮ לִי־ה֒וּא וְלִבְנֹתַ֞י מָֽה־אֶעֱשֶׂ֤ה לָאֵ֨לֶּה֙

מד   הַיּ֔וֹם א֥וֹ לִבְנֵיהֶ֖ן אֲשֶׁ֥ר יָלָֽדוּ: וְעַתָּ֗ה לְכָ֛ה נִכְרְתָ֥ה בְרִ֖ית אֲנִ֣י וָאָ֑תָּה וְהָיָ֥ה

מה־מו   לְעֵ֖ד בֵּינִ֥י וּבֵינֶֽךָ: וַיִּקַּ֥ח יַעֲקֹ֖ב אָ֑בֶן וַיְרִימֶ֖הָ מַצֵּבָֽה: וַיֹּ֨אמֶר יַעֲקֹ֤ב לְאֶחָיו֙

מז   לִקְט֣וּ אֲבָנִ֔ים וַיִּקְח֥וּ אֲבָנִ֖ים וַיַּֽעֲשׂוּ־גָ֑ל וַיֹּ֥אכְלוּ שָׁ֖ם עַל־הַגָּֽל: וַיִּקְרָא־ל֣וֹ

מח   לָבָ֔ן יְגַ֖ר שָׂהֲדוּתָ֑א וְיַֽעֲקֹ֔ב קָ֥רָא ל֖וֹ גַּלְעֵֽד: וַיֹּ֣אמֶר לָבָ֔ן הַגַּ֨ל הַזֶּ֥ה עֵ֛ד בֵּינִ֥י

מט   וּבֵינְךָ֖ הַיּ֑וֹם עַל־כֵּ֥ן קָֽרָא־שְׁמ֖וֹ גַּלְעֵֽד: וְהַמִּצְפָּה֙ אֲשֶׁ֣ר אָמַ֔ר יִ֥צֶף יְהֹוָ֖ה בֵּינִ֣י

נ   וּבֵינֶ֑ךָ כִּ֥י נִסָּתֵ֖ר אִ֣ישׁ מֵֽרֵעֵֽהוּ: אִם־תְּעַנֶּ֣ה אֶת־בְּנֹתַ֗י וְאִם־תִּקַּ֤ח נָשִׁים֙

נא   עַל־בְּנֹתַ֔י אֵ֥ין אִ֖ישׁ עִמָּ֑נוּ רְאֵ֕ה אֱלֹהִ֥ים עֵ֖ד בֵּינִ֥י וּבֵינֶֽךָ: וַיֹּ֥אמֶר לָבָ֖ן לְיַֽעֲקֹ֑ב

נב   הִנֵּ֣ה ׀ הַגַּ֣ל הַזֶּ֗ה וְהִנֵּה֙ הַמַּצֵּבָ֔ה אֲשֶׁ֥ר יָרִ֖יתִי בֵּינִ֣י וּבֵינֶֽךָ: עֵ֚ד הַגַּ֣ל הַזֶּ֔ה וְעֵדָ֖ה

הַמַּצֵּבָ֑ה אִם־אָ֗נִי לֹֽא־אֶעֱבֹ֤ר אֵלֶ֨יךָ֙ אֶת־הַגַּ֣ל הַזֶּ֔ה וְאִם־אַ֠תָּה לֹא־תַֽעֲבֹ֨ר

חול   נג   אֵלַ֜י אֶת־הַגַּ֥ל הַזֶּ֛ה וְאֶת־הַמַּצֵּבָ֥ה הַזֹּ֖את לְרָעָֽה: אֱלֹהֵ֨י אַבְרָהָ֜ם וֵֽאלֹהֵ֤י*

חול   נָחוֹר֙ יִשְׁפְּט֣וּ בֵינֵ֔ינוּ אֱלֹהֵ֖י* אֲבִיהֶ֑ם וַיִּשָּׁבַ֣ע יַֽעֲקֹ֔ב בְּפַ֖חַד אָבִ֥יו יִצְחָֽק:

נד   וַיִּזְבַּ֨ח יַעֲקֹ֥ב זֶ֨בַח֙ בָּהָ֔ר וַיִּקְרָ֥א לְאֶחָ֖יו לֶֽאֱכָל־לָ֑חֶם וַיֹּ֣אכְלוּ לֶ֔חֶם וַיָּלִ֖ינוּ

לב   מפטיר   א   בָּהָֽר: וַיַּשְׁכֵּ֨ם לָבָ֜ן בַּבֹּ֗קֶר וַיְנַשֵּׁ֧ק לְבָנָ֛יו וְלִבְנוֹתָ֖יו וַיְבָ֣רֶךְ אֶתְהֶ֑ם וַיֵּ֛לֶךְ וַיָּ֥שָׁב

ב־ג   לָבָ֖ן לִמְקֹמֽוֹ: וְיַֽעֲקֹ֖ב הָלַ֣ךְ לְדַרְכּ֑וֹ וַיִּפְגְּעוּ־ב֖וֹ מַלְאֲכֵ֥י אֱלֹהִֽים: וַיֹּ֤אמֶר יַֽעֲקֹב֙

כַּֽאֲשֶׁ֣ר רָאָ֔ם מַֽחֲנֵ֥ה אֱלֹהִ֖ים זֶ֑ה וַיִּקְרָ֛א שֵֽׁם־הַמָּק֥וֹם הַה֖וּא מַֽחֲנָֽיִם: פפפ

Haftaras Vayeitzei: p. 1344

קמ"ח פסוקים. חלק"י סימן. מחני"ם סימן.

פרשת וישלח

ד   וַיִּשְׁלַ֨ח יַֽעֲקֹ֤ב מַלְאָכִים֙ לְפָנָ֔יו אֶל־עֵשָׂ֖ו אָחִ֑יו אַ֥רְצָה שֵׂעִ֖יר שְׂדֵ֥ה אֱדֽוֹם:

ה   וַיְצַ֤ו אֹתָם֙ לֵאמֹ֔ר כֹּ֣ה תֹֽאמְר֔וּן לַֽאדֹנִ֖י לְעֵשָׂ֑ו כֹּ֤ה אָמַר֙ עַבְדְּךָ֣ יַֽעֲקֹ֔ב עִם־

ו   לָבָ֣ן גַּ֔רְתִּי וָֽאֵחַ֖ר עַד־עָֽתָּה: וַֽיְהִי־לִי֙ שׁ֣וֹר וַֽחֲמ֔וֹר צֹ֖אן וְעֶ֣בֶד וְשִׁפְחָ֑ה

ז   וָֽאֶשְׁלְחָה֙ לְהַגִּ֣יד לַֽאדֹנִ֔י לִמְצֹא־חֵ֖ן בְּעֵינֶֽיךָ: וַיָּשֻׁ֨בוּ֙ הַמַּלְאָכִ֔ים אֶֽל־יַעֲקֹ֖ב

לֵאמֹ֑ר בָּ֤אנוּ אֶל־אָחִ֨יךָ֙ אֶל־עֵשָׂ֔ו וְגַם֙ הֹלֵ֣ךְ לִקְרָֽאתְךָ֔ וְאַרְבַּע־מֵא֥וֹת אִ֖ישׁ

ח   עִמּֽוֹ: וַיִּירָ֧א יַֽעֲקֹ֛ב מְאֹ֖ד וַיֵּ֣צֶר ל֑וֹ וַיַּ֣חַץ אֶת־הָעָ֣ם אֲשֶׁר־אִתּ֗וֹ וְאֶת־הַצֹּ֧אן

ט   וְאֶת־הַבָּקָ֛ר וְהַגְּמַלִּ֖ים לִשְׁנֵ֥י מַֽחֲנֽוֹת: וַיֹּ֕אמֶר אִם־יָב֥וֹא עֵשָׂ֛ו אֶל־הַֽמַּחֲנֶ֥ה

י   הָֽאַחַ֖ת וְהִכָּ֑הוּ וְהָיָ֛ה הַמַּֽחֲנֶ֥ה הַנִּשְׁאָ֖ר לִפְלֵיטָֽה: וַיֹּאמֶר֮ יַֽעֲקֹב֒ אֱלֹהֵי֙ אָבִ֣י

31:42. This appellation for God refers to the instinctive dread that Isaac felt at the *Akeidah* when the knife was on his throat. Isaac conquered the fear and dedicated himself to God, and Jacob credited this merit with defending him against Laban's machinations (*R' Hirsch*).

⇥ Parashas Vayishlach

32:4-7. The confrontation between the brothers is recorded to illustrate how God sent an angel to save His servant from the hand of a stronger enemy. Furthermore, it shows that Jacob did not rely on his own righteousness, but strove mightily to ensure his safety through *practical*

measures. Indeed, our Sages saw in this chapter the textbook of Jewish behavior in this exile, and, accordingly, we should follow his example by making a threefold preparation in our struggles with Esau's descendants: prayer, gifts [appeasement], and battle (*Ramban*).

32:4. He sent real angels (*Rashi*). According to another view, Jacob's emissaries were human — the word מַלְאָכִים can be rendered either as *angels* or *human emissaries*.

32:5. The verb גַּרְתִּי, *sojourned*, implies staying as a *stranger* [from גֵר = *alien*]. Thus Jacob implied, "I have not become a great prince nor have I achieved status . . . I and the Dread of Isaac* — been with me, you would surely have now sent me away empty handed; God saw my wretchedness and the toil of my hands, so He admonished you last night."

⁴³ Then Laban spoke up and said to Jacob, "The daughters are my daughters, the children are my children and the flock is my flock, and all that you see is mine. Yet to my daughters — what could I do to them this day? Or to their

Laban proposes a treaty children whom they have borne! ⁴⁴ So now, come, let us make a covenant, I and you, and He shall be a witness between me and you."

⁴⁵ Then Jacob took a stone and raised it up as a monument. ⁴⁶ And Jacob said to his brethren, "Gather stones!" So they took stones and made a mound, and they ate there on the mound. ⁴⁷ Laban called it Jegar-sahadutha, but Jacob called it Galeed.

⁴⁸ And Laban declared, "This mound is a witness between me and you today"; therefore he called its name Galeed. ⁴⁹ And as for the Mizpah — because he said, "May HASHEM keep watch between me and you when we are out of each other's sight. ⁵⁰ If you will ill-treat my daughters or if you will marry wives in addition to my daughters — though no man may be among us — but see! God is a witness between me and you." ⁵¹ And Laban said to Jacob, "Here is this mound, and here is the monument which I have cast between me and you. ⁵² This mound shall be witness and the monument shall be witness that I may not cross over to you past this mound, nor may you cross over to me past this mound and this monument for evil. ⁵³ May the God of Abraham and the god of Nahor judge between us — the god of their father." And Jacob swore by the Dread of his father Isaac. ⁵⁴ Then Jacob slaughtered for a feast on the mountain and summoned his kinsmen to break bread; and they broke bread and spent the night on the mountain.

32   ¹ And Laban awoke early in the morning; he kissed his sons and his daughters and blessed them; then Laban went and returned to his place. ² Jacob went on his way, and angels of God encountered him. ³ Jacob said when he saw them, "This is a Godly camp!" So he called the name of that place Mahanaim.

PARASHAS VAYISHLACH

⁴ Then Jacob sent angels* ahead of him to Esau his brother to the land of Seir,
Esau advances to attack Jacob the field of Edom. ⁵ He charged them, saying: "Thus shall you say, 'To my lord, to Esau, so said your servant Jacob: I have sojourned with Laban* and have lingered until now. ⁶ I have acquired oxen and donkeys, flocks, servants, and maidservants and I am sending to tell my lord to find favor in your eyes.' "

⁷ The angels returned to Jacob, saying, "We came to your brother, to Esau; moreover, he is heading toward you, and four hundred men are with him."

Military preparations ⁸ Jacob became very frightened, and it distressed him. So he divided the people with him, and the flocks, cattle, and camels, into two camps. ⁹ For he said, "If Esau comes to the one camp and strikes it down, then the *Prayer* remaining camp shall survive." ¹⁰ Then Jacob said, "God of my father

---

remained merely an alien. Therefore, you need not hate me for having received Father's blessing [27:29], since it has not been fulfilled."

The numerical value of גַרְתִּי equals תרי"ג, 613. Thus Jacob implied, "Though I have sojourned with Laban, I have observed the 613 Divine Commandments, and have

not learned from his evil ways" (Rashi). This was a message that Esau should not trifle with Jacob, for his righteousness was still intact.

32:10-13. Prayer. This was the second component of Jacob's three-pronged strategy, for he knew that without God's help, all of man's plans are in vain.

אַבְרָהָם וֵאלֹהֵי אָבִי יִצְחָק יְהֹוָה הָאֹמֵר אֵלַי שׁוּב לְאַרְצְךָ וּלְמוֹלַדְתְּךָ

יא וְאֵיטִיבָה עִמָּךְ: קָטֹנְתִּי מִכֹּל הַחֲסָדִים וּמִכָּל־הָאֱמֶת אֲשֶׁר עָשִׂיתָ אֶת־
עַבְדֶּךָ כִּי בְמַקְלִי עָבַרְתִּי אֶת־הַיַּרְדֵּן הַזֶּה וְעַתָּה הָיִיתִי לִשְׁנֵי מַחֲנוֹת:

יב הַצִּילֵנִי נָא מִיַּד אָחִי מִיַּד עֵשָׂו כִּי־יָרֵא אָנֹכִי אֹתוֹ פֶּן־יָבוֹא וְהִכַּנִי אֵם

יג עַל־בָּנִים: וְאַתָּה אָמַרְתָּ הֵיטֵב אֵיטִיב עִמָּךְ וְשַׂמְתִּי אֶת־זַרְעֲךָ כְּחוֹל הַיָּם

יד אֲשֶׁר לֹא־יִסָּפֵר מֵרֹב: וַיָּלֶן שָׁם בַּלַּיְלָה הַהוּא וַיִּקַּח מִן־הַבָּא בְיָדוֹ מִנְחָה

טו לְעֵשָׂו אָחִיו: עִזִּים מָאתַיִם וּתְיָשִׁים עֶשְׂרִים רְחֵלִים מָאתַיִם וְאֵילִים

טז עֶשְׂרִים: גְּמַלִּים מֵינִיקוֹת וּבְנֵיהֶם שְׁלֹשִׁים פָּרוֹת אַרְבָּעִים וּפָרִים עֲשָׂרָה

יז אֲתֹנֹת עֶשְׂרִים וַעְיָרִם עֲשָׂרָה: וַיִּתֵּן בְּיַד־עֲבָדָיו עֵדֶר עֵדֶר לְבַדּוֹ וַיֹּאמֶר

יח אֶל־עֲבָדָיו עִבְרוּ לְפָנַי וְרֶוַח תָּשִׂימוּ בֵּין עֵדֶר וּבֵין עֵדֶר: וַיְצַו אֶת־
הָרִאשׁוֹן לֵאמֹר כִּי יִפְגָּשְׁךָ עֵשָׂו אָחִי וִשְׁאֵלְךָ לֵאמֹר לְמִי־אַתָּה וְאָנָה

יט תֵלֵךְ וּלְמִי אֵלֶּה לְפָנֶיךָ: וְאָמַרְתָּ לְעַבְדְּךָ לְיַעֲקֹב מִנְחָה הִוא שְׁלוּחָה
לַאדֹנִי לְעֵשָׂו וְהִנֵּה גַם־הוּא אַחֲרֵינוּ: וַיְצַו גַּם אֶת־הַשֵּׁנִי גַּם אֶת־

כ הַשְּׁלִישִׁי גַּם אֶת־כָּל־הַהֹלְכִים אַחֲרֵי הָעֲדָרִים לֵאמֹר כַּדָּבָר הַזֶּה

כא תְּדַבְּרוּן אֶל־עֵשָׂו בְּמֹצַאֲכֶם אֹתוֹ: וַאֲמַרְתֶּם גַּם הִנֵּה עַבְדְּךָ יַעֲקֹב אַחֲרֵינוּ
כִּי־אָמַר אֲכַפְּרָה פָנָיו בַּמִּנְחָה הַהֹלֶכֶת לְפָנָי וְאַחֲרֵי־כֵן אֶרְאֶה פָנָיו

כב אוּלַי יִשָּׂא פָנָי: וַתַּעֲבֹר הַמִּנְחָה עַל־פָּנָיו וְהוּא לָן בַּלַּיְלָה־הַהוּא בַּמַּחֲנֶה:

כג וַיָּקָם ׀ בַּלַּיְלָה הוּא וַיִּקַּח אֶת־שְׁתֵּי נָשָׁיו וְאֶת־שְׁתֵּי שִׁפְחֹתָיו וְאֶת־אַחַד
עָשָׂר יְלָדָיו וַיַּעֲבֹר אֵת מַעֲבַר יַבֹּק: וַיִּקָּחֵם וַיַּעֲבִרֵם אֶת־הַנָּחַל וַיַּעֲבֵר

כד אֶת־אֲשֶׁר־לוֹ: וַיִּוָּתֵר יַעֲקֹב לְבַדּוֹ וַיֵּאָבֵק אִישׁ עִמּוֹ עַד עֲלוֹת הַשָּׁחַר:

כה וַיַּרְא כִּי לֹא יָכֹל לוֹ וַיִּגַּע בְּכַף־יְרֵכוֹ וַתֵּקַע כַּף־יֶרֶךְ יַעֲקֹב בְּהֵאָבְקוֹ

כו עִמּוֹ: וַיֹּאמֶר שַׁלְּחֵנִי כִּי עָלָה הַשָּׁחַר וַיֹּאמֶר לֹא אֲשַׁלֵּחֲךָ כִּי אִם־

כז-כח בֵּרַכְתָּנִי: וַיֹּאמֶר אֵלָיו מַה־שְּׁמֶךָ וַיֹּאמֶר יַעֲקֹב: וַיֹּאמֶר לֹא יַעֲקֹב יֵאָמֵר
עוֹד שִׁמְךָ כִּי אִם־יִשְׂרָאֵל כִּי־שָׂרִיתָ עִם־אֱלֹהִים וְעִם־אֲנָשִׁים וַתּוּכָל:

כט-ל וַיִּשְׁאַל יַעֲקֹב וַיֹּאמֶר הַגִּידָה־נָּא שְׁמֶךָ וַיֹּאמֶר לָמָּה זֶּה תִּשְׁאַל לִשְׁמִי

לא וַיְבָרֶךְ אֹתוֹ שָׁם: וַיִּקְרָא יַעֲקֹב שֵׁם הַמָּקוֹם פְּנִיאֵל כִּי־רָאִיתִי אֱלֹהִים

לב פָּנִים אֶל־פָּנִים וַתִּנָּצֵל נַפְשִׁי: וַיִּזְרַח־לוֹ הַשֶּׁמֶשׁ כַּאֲשֶׁר עָבַר אֶת־פְּנוּאֵל

לג וְהוּא צֹלֵעַ עַל־יְרֵכוֹ: עַל־כֵּן לֹא־יֹאכְלוּ בְנֵי־יִשְׂרָאֵל אֶת־גִּיד הַנָּשֶׁה
אֲשֶׁר עַל־כַּף הַיָּרֵךְ עַד הַיּוֹם הַזֶּה כִּי נָגַע בְּכַף־יֶרֶךְ יַעֲקֹב בְּגִיד הַנָּשֶׁה:

32:11. My merits have been diminished by all the *kindnesses* You have shown me; I may have become soiled by sin and not deserve to be saved from Esau (*Rashi*). According to *Ramban*, Jacob declared that he had never been worthy of all God's kindnesses.

32:25-32. The struggle with the angel. This confrontation was a cosmic event in Jewish history. The Rabbis explained that this "man" was the guardian angel of Esau (*Rashi*), in a human guise. The Sages teach that every

nation has an angel that guides its destiny as an "intermediary" between it and God. Two nations, however, are unique: Israel is God's own people and just as Esau epitomizes evil, so his angel is the prime spiritual force of evil — Satan himself. Thus, this battle was the eternal struggle between good and evil, between man's capacity to perfect himself and Satan's determination to destroy him spiritually.

32:29. The verse explains the name *Yisrael* as a com-

Abraham and God of my father Isaac; HASHEM Who said to me, 'Return to your land and to your relatives and I will do good with you' — ¹¹ I have been diminished by all the kindnesses * and by all the truth that You have done Your servant; for with my staff I crossed this Jordan and now I have become two camps. ¹² Rescue me, please, from the hand of my brother, from the hand of Esau, for I fear him lest he come and strike me down, mother and children. ¹³ And You had said, 'I will surely do good with you and I will make your offspring like the sand of the sea which is too numerous to count.' "

The tribute ¹⁴ He spent the night there, then he took, from that which had come in his hand, a tribute to Esau his brother: ¹⁵ Two hundred she-goats and twenty he-goats; two hundred ewes and twenty rams; ¹⁶ thirty nursing camels with their colts; forty cows and ten bulls; twenty she-donkeys and ten he-donkeys. ¹⁷ He put in his servants' charge each drove separately and said to his servants, "Pass on ahead of me and leave a space between drove and drove." ¹⁸ He instructed the first one, saying, "When my brother Esau meets you and asks you, saying, 'Whose are you, where are you going, and whose are these that are before you?' — ¹⁹ You shall say, 'Your servant Jacob's. It is a tribute sent to my lord, to Esau, and behold he himself is behind us.' "

²⁰ He similarly instructed the second, also the third, as well as all who followed the droves, saying, "In this manner shall you speak to Esau when you find him. ²¹ And you shall say, 'Moreover — behold your servant Jacob is behind us.' " (For he said, "I will appease him with the tribute that precedes me, and afterwards I will face him; perhaps he will forgive me.") ²² So the tribute passed on before him while he spent that night in the camp.

²³ But he got up that night and took his two wives, his two handmaids, and *The struggle* his eleven sons and crossed the ford of the Jabbok. ²⁴ And when he took them *with the* and had them cross over the stream, he sent over his possessions.
angel

²⁵ Jacob was left alone and a man wrestled with him until the break of dawn. ²⁶ When he perceived that he could not overcome him, he struck the socket of his hip; so Jacob's hip-socket was dislocated as he wrestled with him. ²⁷ Then he said, "Let me go, for dawn has broken."

And he said, "I will not let you go unless you bless me."

²⁸ He said to him, "What is your name?"

He replied, "Jacob."

²⁹ He said, "No longer will it be said that your name is Jacob, but Israel, * for you have striven with the Divine and with man and have overcome."

³⁰ Then Jacob inquired, and he said, "Divulge, if you please, your name."

And he said, "Why then do you inquire of my name?" And he blessed him there.

The ³¹ So Jacob called the name of the place Peniel — "For I have seen the Divine
prohibition face to face, yet my life was spared." ³² The sun rose for him as he passed
of eating Penuel and he was limping on his hip. ³³ Therefore the Children of Israel are not
the tendon to eat the displaced sinew on the hip-socket to this day, because he struck
of an ani- Jacob's hip-socket on the displaced sinew.
mal's thigh

---

bination of יִשְׂרָה, *to prevail,* over אֵל, *the Divine,* i.e., the angel.

32:33. The prohibition of eating the tendon of an animal's thigh. Two primary tissues are forbidden in the hindquarter: The inner sinew — the sciatic nerve — is forbidden by Torah law. The outer sinew — the common peroneal nerve — is forbidden by the Sages (*Chullin* 91a).

לג

א וַיִּשָּׂא יַעֲקֹב עֵינָיו וַיַּרְא וְהִנֵּה עֵשָׂו בָּא וְעִמּוֹ אַרְבַּע מֵאוֹת אִישׁ וַיַּחַץ
ב אֶת־הַיְלָדִים עַל־לֵאָה וְעַל־רָחֵל וְעַל שְׁתֵּי הַשְּׁפָחוֹת: וַיָּשֶׂם אֶת־
הַשְּׁפָחוֹת וְאֶת־יַלְדֵיהֶן רִאשֹׁנָה וְאֶת־לֵאָה וִילָדֶיהָ אַחֲרֹנִים וְאֶת־רָחֵל
ג וְאֶת־יוֹסֵף אַחֲרֹנִים: וְהוּא עָבַר לִפְנֵיהֶם וַיִּשְׁתַּחוּ אַרְצָה שֶׁבַע פְּעָמִים
ד עַד־גִּשְׁתּוֹ עַד־אָחִיו: וַיָּרָץ עֵשָׂו לִקְרָאתוֹ וַיְחַבְּקֵהוּ וַיִּפֹּל עַל־צַוָּארָו
ה וַיִּשָּׁקֵהוּ וַיִּבְכּוּ: וַיִּשָּׂא אֶת־עֵינָיו וַיַּרְא אֶת־הַנָּשִׁים וְאֶת־הַיְלָדִים וַיֹּאמֶר

*נקוד על
וישקהו

ו מִי־אֵלֶּה לָּךְ וַיֹּאמַר הַיְלָדִים אֲשֶׁר־חָנַן אֱלֹהִים אֶת־עַבְדֶּךָ: וַתִּגַּשְׁןָ
רביעי
ז הַשְּׁפָחוֹת הֵנָּה וְיַלְדֵיהֶן וַתִּשְׁתַּחֲוֶיןָ: וַתִּגַּשׁ גַּם־לֵאָה וִילָדֶיהָ וַיִּשְׁתַּחֲווּ
ח וְאַחַר נִגַּשׁ יוֹסֵף וְרָחֵל וַיִּשְׁתַּחֲווּ: וַיֹּאמֶר מִי לְךָ כָּל־הַמַּחֲנֶה הַזֶּה אֲשֶׁר
ט פָּגָשְׁתִּי וַיֹּאמֶר לִמְצֹא־חֵן בְּעֵינֵי אֲדֹנִי: וַיֹּאמֶר עֵשָׂו יֶשׁ־לִי רָב אָחִי יְהִי
י לְךָ אֲשֶׁר־לָךְ: וַיֹּאמֶר יַעֲקֹב אַל־נָא אִם־נָא מָצָאתִי חֵן בְּעֵינֶיךָ וְלָקַחְתָּ
יא מִנְחָתִי מִיָּדִי כִּי עַל־כֵּן רָאִיתִי פָנֶיךָ כִּרְאֹת פְּנֵי אֱלֹהִים וַתִּרְצֵנִי: קַח־נָא
אֶת־בִּרְכָתִי אֲשֶׁר הֻבָאת לָךְ כִּי־חַנַּנִי אֱלֹהִים וְכִי יֶשׁ־לִי־כֹל וַיִּפְצַר־בּוֹ
יב-יג וַיִּקָּח: וַיֹּאמֶר נִסְעָה וְנֵלֵכָה וְאֵלְכָה לְנֶגְדֶּךָ: וַיֹּאמֶר אֵלָיו אֲדֹנִי יֹדֵעַ כִּי־
הַיְלָדִים רַכִּים וְהַצֹּאן וְהַבָּקָר עָלוֹת עָלָי וּדְפָקוּם יוֹם אֶחָד וָמֵתוּ כָּל־
יד הַצֹּאן: יַעֲבָר־נָא אֲדֹנִי לִפְנֵי עַבְדּוֹ וַאֲנִי אֶתְנָהֲלָה לְאִטִּי לְרֶגֶל הַמְּלָאכָה
טו אֲשֶׁר־לְפָנַי וּלְרֶגֶל הַיְלָדִים עַד אֲשֶׁר־אָבֹא אֶל־אֲדֹנִי שֵׂעִירָה: וַיֹּאמֶר
עֵשָׂו אַצִּיגָה־נָּא עִמְּךָ מִן־הָעָם אֲשֶׁר אִתִּי וַיֹּאמֶר לָמָּה זֶּה אֶמְצָא־
טז-יז חֵן בְּעֵינֵי אֲדֹנִי: וַיָּשָׁב בַּיּוֹם הַהוּא עֵשָׂו לְדַרְכּוֹ שֵׂעִירָה: וְיַעֲקֹב נָסַע
סֻכֹּתָה וַיִּבֶן לוֹ בָּיִת וּלְמִקְנֵהוּ עָשָׂה סֻכֹּת עַל־כֵּן קָרָא שֵׁם־הַמָּקוֹם
יח סֻכּוֹת: וַיָּבֹא יַעֲקֹב שָׁלֵם עִיר שְׁכֶם אֲשֶׁר בְּאֶרֶץ כְּנַעַן בְּבֹאוֹ
יט מִפַּדַּן אֲרָם וַיִּחַן אֶת־פְּנֵי הָעִיר: וַיִּקֶן אֶת־חֶלְקַת הַשָּׂדֶה אֲשֶׁר נָטָה־שָׁם
כ אָהֳלוֹ מִיַּד בְּנֵי־חֲמוֹר אֲבִי שְׁכֶם בְּמֵאָה קְשִׂיטָה: וַיַּצֶּב־שָׁם מִזְבֵּחַ וַיִּקְרָא־
לוֹ אֵל אֱלֹהֵי יִשְׂרָאֵל:

לד   א   וַתֵּצֵא דִינָה בַּת־לֵאָה אֲשֶׁר יָלְדָה
חמישי
ב לְיַעֲקֹב לִרְאוֹת בִּבְנוֹת הָאָרֶץ: וַיַּרְא אֹתָהּ שְׁכֶם בֶּן־חֲמוֹר הַחִוִּי נְשִׂיא
ג הָאָרֶץ וַיִּקַּח אֹתָהּ וַיִּשְׁכַּב אֹתָהּ וַיְעַנֶּהָ: וַתִּדְבַּק נַפְשׁוֹ בְּדִינָה בַּת־יַעֲקֹב
ד וַיֶּאֱהַב אֶת־הַנַּעֲרָ וַיְדַבֵּר עַל־לֵב הַנַּעֲרָ: וַיֹּאמֶר שְׁכֶם אֶל־חֲמוֹר אָבִיו
ה לֵאמֹר קַח־לִי אֶת־הַיַּלְדָּה הַזֹּאת לְאִשָּׁה: וְיַעֲקֹב שָׁמַע כִּי טִמֵּא
אֶת־דִּינָה בִתּוֹ וּבָנָיו הָיוּ אֶת־מִקְנֵהוּ בַּשָּׂדֶה וְהֶחֱרִשׁ יַעֲקֹב עַד־בֹּאָם:

33:4. In the Torah Scroll, there are dots over each letter of the word וַיִּשָּׁקֵהוּ, an exegetical device that calls attention to hidden allusions. Some Sages hold that Esau's kisses were insincere; but R' Shimon bar Yochai says that at this moment his mercy was aroused and he kissed Jacob with all his heart (*Rashi*).

33:17. *Succoth*, literally, *huts; shelters*.

33:18. Literally, the word שָׁלֵם means *whole; perfect;*

unimpaired. Jacob arrived *intact* physically — having recovered from the injury to his hip; *intact* financially — although he had showered a lavish gift upon Esau; and *intact* in his learning — having forgotten nothing while in Laban's house (*Rashi* from *Shabbos* 33b).

33:20. By erecting the altar and giving it this name, Jacob fulfilled the vow he had made twenty-two years earlier, before leaving the land (*Alshich*).

33

The
encounter

¹ Jacob raised his eyes and saw — behold, Esau was coming, and with him were four hundred men — so he divided the children among Leah, Rachel, and the two handmaids. ² He put the handmaids and their children first, Leah and her children next, and Rachel and Joseph last. ³ Then he himself went on ahead of them and bowed earthward seven times until he reached his brother.

⁴ Esau ran toward him, embraced him, fell upon his neck, and kissed him; * then they wept. ⁵ He raised his eyes and saw the women and children, and he asked, "Who are these to you?"

He answered, "The children whom God has graciously given your servant."

⁶ Then the handmaids came forward — they and their children — and they bowed down. ⁷ Leah, too, came forward with her children and they bowed down; and afterwards, Joseph and Rachel came forward and bowed down.

⁸ And he asked, "What did you intend by that whole camp that I met?"

He answered, "To gain favor in my lord's eyes."

⁹ Esau said, "I have plenty. My brother, let what you have remain yours."

¹⁰ But Jacob said, "No, I beg of you! If I have now found favor in your eyes, then accept my tribute from me, inasmuch as I have seen your face, which is like seeing the face of a Divine being, and you were appeased by me. ¹¹ Please accept my gift which was brought to you, inasmuch as God has been gracious to me and inasmuch as I have everything." He urged him, and he accepted.

¹² And he said, "Travel on and let us go — I will proceed alongside you."

¹³ But he said to him, "My lord knows that the children are tender, and the nursing flocks and cattle are upon me; if they will be driven hard for a single day, then all the flocks will die. ¹⁴ Let my lord go ahead of his servant; I will make my way at my slow pace according to the gait of the drove before me and the gait of the children, until I come to my lord at Seir."

¹⁵ Then Esau said, "Let me assign to you some of the people who are with me."

And he said, "To what purpose? Let me just have favor in my lord's eyes!"

The parting

¹⁶ So Esau started back that day on his way toward Seir. ¹⁷ But Jacob journeyed to Succoth * and built himself a house, and for his livestock he made shelters; he therefore called the name of the place Succoth.

Jacob
arrives in
Shechem

¹⁸ Jacob arrived intact * at the city of Shechem which is in the land of Canaan, upon his arriving from Paddan-aram, and he encamped before the city. ¹⁹ He bought the parcel of land upon which he pitched his tent from the children of Hamor, Shechem's father, for one hundred kesitahs. ²⁰ He set up an altar there and proclaimed, "God, the God of Israel." *

34

Dinah's
abduction

¹ Now Dinah — the daughter of Leah, whom she had borne to Jacob — went out to look over the daughters of the land. ² Shechem, son of Hamor the Hivvite, the prince of the region, saw her; he took her, lay with her, and violated her. ³ He became deeply attached to Dinah, daughter of Jacob; he loved the maiden and appealed to the maiden's emotions. ⁴ So Shechem spoke to Hamor, his father, saying, "Take me this girl for a wife."

⁵ Now Jacob heard that he had defiled his daughter Dinah, while his sons were with his cattle in the field; so Jacob kept silent until their arrival.

34:1-4. Dinah's abduction. Jacob believed that at last he would find tranquility in *Eretz Yisrael*, but his family had to experience a moral outrage upon its own flesh and blood from its beginning. Its reaction to this ordeal would establish the sacred character of its purity: It could not tolerate what others might consider commonplace (*R' Hirsch*).

יז וַיֵּצֵא חֲמוֹר אֲבִי־שְׁכֶם אֶל־יַעֲקֹב לְדַבֵּר אִתּוֹ: וּבְנֵי יַעֲקֹב בָּאוּ מִן־הַשָּׂדֶה

כְּשָׁמְעָם וַיִּתְעַצְּבוּ הָאֲנָשִׁים וַיִּחַר לָהֶם מְאֹד כִּי־נְבָלָה עָשָׂה בְיִשְׂרָאֵל

ח לִשְׁכַּב אֶת־בַּת־יַעֲקֹב וְכֵן לֹא יֵעָשֶׂה: וַיְדַבֵּר חֲמוֹר אִתָּם לֵאמֹר שְׁכֶם

ט בְּנִי חָשְׁקָה נַפְשׁוֹ בְּבִתְּכֶם תְּנוּ נָא אֹתָהּ לוֹ לְאִשָּׁה: וְהִתְחַתְּנוּ אֹתָנוּ

י בְּנֹתֵיכֶם תִּתְּנוּ־לָנוּ וְאֶת־בְּנֹתֵינוּ תִּקְחוּ לָכֶם: וְאִתָּנוּ תֵּשֵׁבוּ וְהָאָרֶץ תִּהְיֶה

יא לִפְנֵיכֶם שְׁבוּ וּסְחָרוּהָ וְהֵאָחֲזוּ בָּהּ: וַיֹּאמֶר שְׁכֶם אֶל־אָבִיהָ וְאֶל־אַחֶיהָ

יב אֶמְצָא־חֵן בְּעֵינֵיכֶם וַאֲשֶׁר תֹּאמְרוּ אֵלַי אֶתֵּן: הַרְבּוּ עָלַי מְאֹד מֹהַר וּמַתָּן

יג וְאֶתְּנָה כַּאֲשֶׁר תֹּאמְרוּ אֵלָי וּתְנוּ־לִי אֶת־הַנַּעֲרָ לְאִשָּׁה: וַיַּעֲנוּ בְנֵי־יַעֲקֹב

אֶת־שְׁכֶם וְאֶת־חֲמוֹר אָבִיו בְּמִרְמָה וַיְדַבֵּרוּ אֲשֶׁר טִמֵּא אֵת דִּינָה

יד אֲחֹתָם: וַיֹּאמְרוּ אֲלֵיהֶם לֹא נוּכַל לַעֲשׂוֹת הַדָּבָר הַזֶּה לָתֵת אֶת־אֲחֹתֵנוּ

טו לְאִישׁ אֲשֶׁר־לוֹ עָרְלָה כִּי־חֶרְפָּה הִוא לָנוּ: אַךְ־בְּזֹאת נֵאוֹת לָכֶם אִם

טז תִּהְיוּ כָמֹנוּ לְהִמֹּל לָכֶם כָּל־זָכָר: וְנָתַנּוּ אֶת־בְּנֹתֵינוּ לָכֶם וְאֶת־בְּנֹתֵיכֶם

נִקַּח־לָנוּ וְיָשַׁבְנוּ אִתְּכֶם וְהָיִינוּ לְעַם אֶחָד: וְאִם־לֹא תִשְׁמְעוּ אֵלֵינוּ

יח לְהִמּוֹל וְלָקַחְנוּ אֶת־בִּתֵּנוּ וְהָלָכְנוּ: וַיִּיטְבוּ דִבְרֵיהֶם בְּעֵינֵי חֲמוֹר וּבְעֵינֵי

יט שְׁכֶם בֶּן־חֲמוֹר: וְלֹא־אֵחַר הַנַּעַר לַעֲשׂוֹת הַדָּבָר כִּי חָפֵץ בְּבַת־יַעֲקֹב

כ וְהוּא נִכְבָּד מִכֹּל בֵּית אָבִיו: וַיָּבֹא חֲמוֹר וּשְׁכֶם בְּנוֹ אֶל־שַׁעַר עִירָם

כא וַיְדַבְּרוּ אֶל־אַנְשֵׁי עִירָם לֵאמֹר: הָאֲנָשִׁים הָאֵלֶּה שְׁלֵמִים הֵם אִתָּנוּ

וְיֵשְׁבוּ בָאָרֶץ וְיִסְחֲרוּ אֹתָהּ וְהָאָרֶץ הִנֵּה רַחֲבַת־יָדַיִם לִפְנֵיהֶם אֶת־

כב בְּנֹתָם נִקַּח־לָנוּ לְנָשִׁים וְאֶת־בְּנֹתֵינוּ נִתֵּן לָהֶם: אַךְ־בְּזֹאת יֵאֹתוּ לָנוּ

הָאֲנָשִׁים לָשֶׁבֶת אִתָּנוּ לִהְיוֹת לְעַם אֶחָד בְּהִמּוֹל לָנוּ כָּל־זָכָר כַּאֲשֶׁר הֵם

כג נִמֹּלִים: מִקְנֵהֶם וְקִנְיָנָם וְכָל־בְּהֶמְתָּם הֲלוֹא לָנוּ הֵם אַךְ נֵאוֹתָה לָהֶם

כד וְיֵשְׁבוּ אִתָּנוּ: וַיִּשְׁמְעוּ אֶל־חֲמוֹר וְאֶל־שְׁכֶם בְּנוֹ כָּל־יֹצְאֵי שַׁעַר עִירוֹ

כה וַיִּמֹּלוּ כָּל־זָכָר כָּל־יֹצְאֵי שַׁעַר עִירוֹ: וַיְהִי בַיּוֹם הַשְּׁלִישִׁי בִּהְיוֹתָם

כֹּאֲבִים וַיִּקְחוּ שְׁנֵי־בְנֵי־יַעֲקֹב שִׁמְעוֹן וְלֵוִי אֲחֵי דִינָה אִישׁ חַרְבּוֹ וַיָּבֹאוּ

כו עַל־הָעִיר בֶּטַח וַיַּהַרְגוּ כָּל־זָכָר: וְאֶת־חֲמוֹר וְאֶת־שְׁכֶם בְּנוֹ הָרְגוּ לְפִי־

כז חָרֶב וַיִּקְחוּ אֶת־דִּינָה מִבֵּית שְׁכֶם וַיֵּצֵאוּ: בְּנֵי יַעֲקֹב בָּאוּ עַל־הַחֲלָלִים

כח וַיָּבֹזּוּ הָעִיר אֲשֶׁר טִמְּאוּ אֲחוֹתָם: אֶת־צֹאנָם וְאֶת־בְּקָרָם וְאֶת־חֲמֹרֵיהֶם

כט וְאֵת אֲשֶׁר־בָּעִיר וְאֶת־אֲשֶׁר בַּשָּׂדֶה לָקָחוּ: וְאֶת־כָּל־חֵילָם וְאֶת־כָּל־

טַפָּם וְאֶת־נְשֵׁיהֶם שָׁבוּ וַיָּבֹזּוּ וְאֵת כָּל־אֲשֶׁר בַּבָּיִת: וַיֹּאמֶר יַעֲקֹב אֶל־

ל שִׁמְעוֹן וְאֶל־לֵוִי עֲכַרְתֶּם אֹתִי לְהַבְאִישֵׁנִי בְּיֹשֵׁב הָאָרֶץ בַּכְּנַעֲנִי

וּבַפְּרִזִּי וַאֲנִי מְתֵי מִסְפָּר וְנֶאֶסְפוּ עָלַי וְהִכּוּנִי וְנִשְׁמַדְתִּי אֲנִי וּבֵיתִי:

34:25-31. Simeon and Levi decimate Shechem. As noted above, the brothers intended to rescue Dinah while the Shechemites were weak and ill, but Simeon and Levi acted on their own, and carried out a death sentence on all the males of the city. By what right they did so halachically is discussed by the major commentators. Whatever the interpretation of the legal status of the attack on the city, the other nine brothers apparently refused to take part in the attack, and Jacob was sharply critical of Simeon and Levi.

Jacob's family learns of the outrage

⁶ Hamor, Shechem's father, went out to Jacob to speak to him. ⁷ Jacob's sons arrived from the field, when they heard; the men were distressed, and were fired deeply with indignation, for he had committed an outrage in Israel by lying with a daughter of Jacob — such a thing may not be done!

⁸ Hamor spoke with them, saying, "Shechem, my son, longs deeply for your daughter — please give her to him as a wife. ⁹ And intermarry with us; give your daughters to us, and take our daughters for yourselves. ¹⁰ And among us you shall dwell; the land will be before you — settle and trade in it, and acquire property in it."

¹¹ Then Shechem said to her father and brothers, "Let me gain favor in your eyes; and whatever you tell me — I will give. ¹² Inflate exceedingly upon me the marriage settlement and gifts and I will give whatever you tell me; only give me the maiden for a wife."

The deception

¹³ Jacob's sons answered Shechem and his father Hamor cleverly and they spoke (because he had defiled their sister Dinah). ¹⁴ They said to them, "We cannot do this thing, to give our sister to a man who is uncircumcised, for that is a disgrace for us. ¹⁵ Only on this condition will we acquiesce to you: If you become like us by letting every male among you become circumcised. ¹⁶ Then we will give our daughters to you, and take your daughters to ourselves; we will dwell with you, and become a single people. ¹⁷ But if you will not listen to us to be circumcised, we will take our daughter and go."

¹⁸ Their proposal seemed good in the view of Hamor, and in the view of Shechem, Hamor's son. ¹⁹ The youth did not delay doing the thing, for he wanted Jacob's daughter. Now he was the most respected of all his father's household.

²⁰ Hamor — with his son Shechem — came to the gate of their city and spoke to the people of their city, saying, ²¹ "These people are peaceable with us; let them settle in the land and trade in it, for see, there is ample room in the land for them! Let us take their daughters for ourselves as wives and give our daughters to them. ²² Only on this condition will the people acquiesce with us to dwell with us to become a single people: that all our males become circumcised as they themselves are circumcised. ²³ Their livestock, their possessions, and all their animals — will they not be ours? Only let us acquiesce to them and they will settle with us."

²⁴ All the people who depart through the gate of his city listened to Hamor and his son Shechem, and all the males — all those who depart through the gate of his city — were circumcised.

Simeon and Levi decimate Shechem

²⁵ And it came to pass on the third day, when they were in pain, that two of Jacob's sons, Simeon and Levi, Dinah's brothers, each took his sword and they came upon the city confidently, and killed every male. ²⁶ And Hamor and Shechem his son they killed at the point of sword. Then they took Dinah from Shechem's house and left.

²⁷ The sons of Jacob came upon the slain, and they plundered the city which had defiled their sister. ²⁸ Their flocks, their cattle, their donkeys, whatever was in the town and whatever was in the field, they took. ²⁹ All their wealth, all their children and wives they took captive and they plundered, as well as everything in the house.

³⁰ Jacob said to Simeon and to Levi, "You have discomposed me, making me odious among the inhabitants of the land, among the Canaanite and among the Perizzite; I am few in number and should they band together and attack me, I will be annihilated — I and my household."

לא וַיֹּאמְרוּ הַכְזוֹנָה יַעֲשֶׂה אֶת־אֲחוֹתֵנוּ:

לה א וַיֹּאמֶר אֱלֹהִים אֶל־יַעֲקֹב קוּם עֲלֵה בֵית־אֵל וְשֶׁב־שָׁם וַעֲשֵׂה־שָׁם מִזְבֵּחַ
לָאֵל הַנִּרְאֶה אֵלֶיךָ בְּבָרְחֲךָ מִפְּנֵי עֵשָׂו אָחִיךָ: ב וַיֹּאמֶר יַעֲקֹב אֶל־בֵּיתוֹ וְאֶל
כָּל־אֲשֶׁר עִמּוֹ הָסִרוּ אֶת־אֱלֹהֵי הַנֵּכָר אֲשֶׁר בְּתֹכְכֶם וְהִטַּהֲרוּ וְהַחֲלִיפוּ
שִׂמְלֹתֵיכֶם: ג וְנָקוּמָה וְנַעֲלֶה בֵּית־אֵל וְאֶעֱשֶׂה־שָּׁם מִזְבֵּחַ לָאֵל הָעֹנֶה אֹתִי
בְּיוֹם צָרָתִי וַיְהִי עִמָּדִי בַּדֶּרֶךְ אֲשֶׁר הָלָכְתִּי: ד וַיִּתְּנוּ אֶל־יַעֲקֹב אֵת כָּל־
אֱלֹהֵי הַנֵּכָר אֲשֶׁר בְּיָדָם וְאֶת־הַנְּזָמִים אֲשֶׁר בְּאָזְנֵיהֶם וַיִּטְמֹן אֹתָם יַעֲקֹב
תַּחַת הָאֵלָה אֲשֶׁר עִם־שְׁכֶם: ה וַיִּסָּעוּ וַיְהִי ׀ חִתַּת אֱלֹהִים עַל־הֶעָרִים אֲשֶׁר
סְבִיבֹתֵיהֶם וְלֹא רָדְפוּ אַחֲרֵי בְּנֵי יַעֲקֹב: ו וַיָּבֹא יַעֲקֹב לוּזָה אֲשֶׁר בְּאֶרֶץ
כְּנַעַן הִוא בֵּית־אֵל הוּא וְכָל־הָעָם אֲשֶׁר עִמּוֹ: ז וַיִּבֶן שָׁם מִזְבֵּחַ וַיִּקְרָא
לַמָּקוֹם אֵל בֵּית־אֵל כִּי שָׁם נִגְלוּ אֵלָיו הָאֱלֹהִים בְּבָרְחוֹ מִפְּנֵי אָחִיו:
ח וַתָּמָת דְּבֹרָה מֵינֶקֶת רִבְקָה וַתִּקָּבֵר מִתַּחַת לְבֵית־אֵל תַּחַת הָאַלּוֹן וַיִּקְרָא
שְׁמוֹ אַלּוֹן בָּכוּת:

ט וַיֵּרָא אֱלֹהִים אֶל־יַעֲקֹב עוֹד בְּבֹאוֹ מִפַּדַּן אֲרָם וַיְבָרֶךְ אֹתוֹ: י וַיֹּאמֶר־לוֹ
אֱלֹהִים שִׁמְךָ יַעֲקֹב לֹא־יִקָּרֵא שִׁמְךָ עוֹד יַעֲקֹב כִּי אִם־יִשְׂרָאֵל יִהְיֶה
שְׁמֶךָ וַיִּקְרָא אֶת־שְׁמוֹ יִשְׂרָאֵל: יא וַיֹּאמֶר לוֹ אֱלֹהִים אֲנִי אֵל שַׁדַּי פְּרֵה וּרְבֵה
ששי גוֹי וּקְהַל גּוֹיִם יִהְיֶה מִמֶּךָּ וּמְלָכִים מֵחֲלָצֶיךָ יֵצֵאוּ: יב וְאֶת־הָאָרֶץ אֲשֶׁר
נָתַתִּי לְאַבְרָהָם וּלְיִצְחָק לְךָ אֶתְּנֶנָּה וּלְזַרְעֲךָ אַחֲרֶיךָ אֶתֵּן אֶת־הָאָרֶץ:
יג-יד וַיַּעַל מֵעָלָיו אֱלֹהִים בַּמָּקוֹם אֲשֶׁר־דִּבֶּר אִתּוֹ: וַיַּצֵּב יַעֲקֹב מַצֵּבָה בַּמָּקוֹם
אֲשֶׁר־דִּבֶּר אִתּוֹ מַצֶּבֶת אָבֶן וַיַּסֵּךְ עָלֶיהָ נֶסֶךְ וַיִּצֹק עָלֶיהָ שָׁמֶן: טו וַיִּקְרָא
יַעֲקֹב אֶת־שֵׁם הַמָּקוֹם אֲשֶׁר דִּבֶּר אִתּוֹ שָׁם אֱלֹהִים בֵּית־אֵל: טז וַיִּסְעוּ מִבֵּית
אֵל וַיְהִי־עוֹד כִּבְרַת־הָאָרֶץ לָבוֹא אֶפְרָתָה וַתֵּלֶד רָחֵל וַתְּקַשׁ בְּלִדְתָּהּ:
יז וַיְהִי בְהַקְשֹׁתָהּ בְּלִדְתָּהּ וַתֹּאמֶר לָהּ הַמְיַלֶּדֶת אַל־תִּירְאִי כִּי־גַם־זֶה לָךְ
בֵּן: יח וַיְהִי ׀ בְּצֵאת נַפְשָׁהּ כִּי מֵתָה וַתִּקְרָא שְׁמוֹ בֶּן־אוֹנִי וְאָבִיו קָרָא־לוֹ
יט-כ בִנְיָמִין: וַתָּמָת רָחֵל וַתִּקָּבֵר בְּדֶרֶךְ אֶפְרָתָה הִוא בֵּית לָחֶם: וַיַּצֵּב יַעֲקֹב
מַצֵּבָה עַל־קְבֻרָתָהּ הִוא מַצֶּבֶת קְבֻרַת־רָחֵל עַד־הַיּוֹם: כא וַיִּסַּע יִשְׂרָאֵל וַיֵּט
אָהֳלֹה מֵהָלְאָה לְמִגְדַּל־עֵדֶר: כב וַיְהִי בִּשְׁכֹּן יִשְׂרָאֵל בָּאָרֶץ הַהִוא וַיֵּלֶךְ
רְאוּבֵן וַיִּשְׁכַּב אֶת־בִּלְהָה פִּילֶגֶשׁ אָבִיו וַיִּשְׁמַע יִשְׂרָאֵל *

*פסקא באמצע פסוק

35:7. *El-beth-el*, i.e., God makes His Presence felt in Beth-el (*Rashi*).

35:8. The deaths of Rebecca and Deborah. There is a Midrashic tradition that this verse, which mentions only the death of Deborah, is an allusion also to the death of Rebecca which occurred at that time.

35:9. *And He blessed him*, upon Rebecca's death, with the blessing of consolation given to mourners (*Rashi*).

35:10. Although He was about to give Jacob the additional name of Israel, God told him that he would continue

to be called Jacob (*Ramban; Sforno*). From that time onward, the name Jacob would be used for matters pertaining to physical and mundane matters, while the name Israel would be used for matters reflecting the spiritual role of the Patriarch and his descendants (*R' Bachya*).

35:18. *Ben Oni*, literally, *Son of My Mourning*, as if to say: His birth caused my death (*Ibn Ezra; Ramban*).

Ramban comments that Jacob wanted to preserve the *form* of the name Rachel gave, but wished to give it an

³¹ *And they said, "Should he treat our sister like a harlot?"*

35

Jacob journeys to Beth-el

¹ **G**od said to Jacob, *"Arise — go up to Beth-el and dwell there, and make an altar there to God Who appeared to you when you fled from Esau your brother."* ² *So Jacob said to his household and to all who were with him, "Discard the alien gods that are in your midst; cleanse yourselves and change your clothes.* ³ *Then come, let us go up to Beth-el; I will make there an altar to God Who answered me in my time of distress, and was with me on the road that I traveled."* ⁴ *So they gave to Jacob all the alien gods that were in their possession, as well as the rings that were in their ears, and Jacob buried them underneath the terebinth near Shechem.* ⁵ *They set out, and there fell a Godly terror on the cities which were around them, so that they did not pursue Jacob's sons.*

The deaths of Rebecca and Deborah

⁶ *Thus Jacob came to Luz in the land of Canaan — it is Beth-el — he, and all the people who were with him.* ⁷ *And he built an altar there and called the place El-beth-el,* * *for it was there that God had been revealed to him during his flight from his brother.*

⁸ *Deborah, the wet nurse of Rebecca, died, and she was buried below Beth-el, below the plateau; and he named it Allon-bachuth.*

God blesses and renames Jacob

⁹ *And God appeared to Jacob again when he came from Paddan-aram, and He blessed him.* *

¹⁰ *Then God said to him, "Your name is Jacob.* * *Your name shall not always be called Jacob, but Israel shall be your name." Thus He called his name Israel.* ¹¹ *And God said to him, "I am El Shaddai. Be fruitful and multiply; a nation and a congregation of nations shall descend from you, and kings shall issue from your loins.* ¹² *The land that I gave to Abraham and to Isaac, I will give to you; and to your offspring after you I will give the land."* ¹³ *Then God ascended from upon him in the place where He had spoken with him.*

¹⁴ *Jacob had set up a pillar at the place where God had spoken with him — a pillar of stone — and he poured a libation upon it, and poured oil upon it.* ¹⁵ *Then Jacob called the name of the place where God had spoken with him Beth-el.*

The birth of Benjamin and death of Rachel

¹⁶ *They journeyed from Beth-el and there was still a stretch of land to go to Ephrath, when Rachel went into labor and had difficulty in her childbirth.* ¹⁷ *And it was when she had difficulty in her labor that the midwife said to her, "Have no fear, for this one, too, is a son for you."* ¹⁸ *And it came to pass, as her soul was departing — for she died — that she called his name Ben Oni,* * *but his father called him Benjamin.* ¹⁹ *Thus Rachel died,* * *and was buried on the road to Ephrath,* * *which is Bethlehem.* ²⁰ *Jacob set up a monument over her grave; it is the monument of Rachel's grave until today.*

Reuben's error

²¹ *Israel journeyed on, and he pitched his tent beyond Migdal-eder.* ²² *And it came to pass, while Israel dwelt in that land, that Reuben went and lay with Bilhah, his father's concubine, and Israel heard.*

---

optimistic connotation. Giving the homonym *Oni* its other translation of *strength* , he named the child *Benjamin* [lit., *son of the right*], a symbol of strength and success.

35:19. Rachel was born on the day Jacob received the blessings. Since he was sixty-three then, and ninety-nine when he entered the Land, Rachel died at thirty-six (*Seder Olam*).

Rachel's tomb was on the roadside outside of Bethle-

hem; in modern times, however, the city has grown until the tomb is now inside it. Jacob chose that site because he foresaw that his descendants would pass it on their way to the Babylonian exile, and Rachel would pray for them, as it is said concerning that tragic journey (*Jeremiah* 31:14): *Rachel weeping for her children* (*Midrash*). To this very day, it is a place where men and women shed tears and beg "Mother Rachel" to intercede with God on their behalf.

כג וַיִּהְי֥וּ בְנֵי־יַעֲקֹ֖ב שְׁנֵ֣ים עָשָׂ֑ר בְּנֵ֣י לֵאָ֗ה בְּכ֤וֹר יַעֲקֹב֙ רְאוּבֵ֔ן וְשִׁמְעוֹן֙ וְלֵוִ֣י

כד-כה וִֽיהוּדָ֔ה וְיִשָּׂשכָ֖ר וּזְבֻל֑וּן בְּנֵ֣י רָחֵ֔ל יוֹסֵ֖ף וּבִנְיָמִֽן: וּבְנֵ֤י בִלְהָה֙ שִׁפְחַ֣ת רָחֵ֔ל

כו דָּ֖ן וְנַפְתָּלִֽי: וּבְנֵ֤י זִלְפָּה֙ שִׁפְחַ֣ת לֵאָ֔ה גָּ֖ד וְאָשֵׁ֑ר אֵ֚לֶּה בְּנֵ֣י יַעֲקֹ֔ב אֲשֶׁ֥ר יֻלַּד־ל֖וֹ

כז בְּפַדַּ֥ן אֲרָֽם: וַיָּבֹ֤א יַעֲקֹב֙ אֶל־יִצְחָ֣ק אָבִ֔יו מַמְרֵ֖א קִרְיַ֣ת הָֽאַרְבַּ֑ע הִ֚וא חֶבְר֔וֹן

כח אֲשֶׁר־גָּֽר־שָׁ֥ם אַבְרָהָ֖ם וְיִצְחָֽק: וַיִּֽהְי֖וּ יְמֵ֣י יִצְחָ֑ק מְאַ֥ת שָׁנָ֖ה וּשְׁמֹנִ֥ים שָׁנָֽה:

כט וַיִּגְוַ֨ע יִצְחָ֜ק וַיָּ֗מָת וַיֵּאָ֙סֶף֙ אֶל־עַמָּ֔יו זָקֵ֖ן וּשְׂבַ֣ע יָמִ֑ים וַיִּקְבְּר֣וּ אֹת֔וֹ עֵשָׂ֖ו וְיַעֲקֹ֥ב בָּנָֽיו:

לו א-ב וְאֵ֛לֶּה תֹּלְד֥וֹת עֵשָׂ֖ו ה֥וּא אֱד֑וֹם: עֵשָׂ֗ו לָקַ֤ח אֶת־נָשָׁיו֙ מִבְּנ֣וֹת כְּנָ֔עַן אֶת־עָדָ֗ה

ג בַּת־אֵילוֹן֙ הַֽחִתִּ֔י וְאֶת־אׇהֳלִֽיבָמָה֙ בַּת־עֲנָ֔ה בַּת־צִבְע֖וֹן הַֽחִוִּֽי: וְאֶת־בָּ֣שְׂמַ֔ת

ד בַּת־יִשְׁמָעֵ֖אל אֲח֥וֹת נְבָיֽוֹת: וַתֵּ֧לֶד עָדָ֛ה לְעֵשָׂ֖ו אֶת־אֱלִיפָ֑ז וּבָ֣שְׂמַ֔ת יָֽלְדָ֖ה

ה אֶת־רְעוּאֵֽל: וְאׇהֳלִֽיבָמָה֙ יָֽלְדָ֔ה אֶת־[יעיש ק°] יְע֖וּשׁ וְאֶת־יַעְלָ֣ם וְאֶת־

ו קֹ֑רַח אֵ֚לֶּה בְּנֵ֣י עֵשָׂ֔ו אֲשֶׁ֥ר יֻלְּדוּ־ל֖וֹ בְּאֶ֥רֶץ כְּנָֽעַן: וַיִּקַּ֣ח עֵשָׂ֡ו אֶת־נָשָׁיו֩ וְאֶת־בָּנָ֨יו וְאֶת־בְּנֹתָ֜יו וְאֶת־כׇּל־נַפְשׁ֣וֹת בֵּית֗וֹ וְאֶת־מִקְנֵ֤הוּ וְאֶת־כׇּל־בְּהֶמְתּ֔וֹ וְאֵת֙ כׇּל־קִנְיָנ֔וֹ אֲשֶׁ֥ר רָכַ֖שׁ בְּאֶ֣רֶץ כְּנָ֑עַן וַיֵּ֣לֶךְ אֶל־אֶ֔רֶץ מִפְּנֵ֖י יַעֲקֹ֥ב אָחִֽיו:

ז כִּֽי־הָיָ֧ה רְכוּשָׁ֛ם רָ֖ב מִשֶּׁ֣בֶת יַחְדָּ֑ו וְלֹ֣א יָֽכְלָ֗ה אֶ֤רֶץ מְגֽוּרֵיהֶם֙ לָשֵׂ֣את אֹתָ֔ם

ח-ט מִפְּנֵ֖י מִקְנֵיהֶֽם: וַיֵּ֤שֶׁב עֵשָׂו֙ בְּהַ֣ר שֵׂעִ֔יר עֵשָׂ֖ו ה֥וּא אֱדֽוֹם: וְאֵ֛לֶּה תֹּלְד֥וֹת עֵשָׂ֖ו

י אֲבִ֣י אֱד֑וֹם בְּהַ֖ר שֵׂעִֽיר: אֵ֖לֶּה שְׁמ֣וֹת בְּנֵֽי־עֵשָׂ֑ו אֱלִיפַ֗ז בֶּן־עָדָה֙ אֵ֣שֶׁת עֵשָׂ֔ו

יא רְעוּאֵ֕ל בֶּן־בָּשְׂמַ֖ת אֵ֥שֶׁת עֵשָֽׂו: וַיִּֽהְי֖וּ בְּנֵ֣י אֱלִיפָ֑ז תֵּימָ֣ן אוֹמָ֔ר צְפ֥וֹ וְגַעְתָּ֖ם

יב וּקְנַֽז: וְתִמְנַ֣ע ׀ הָיְתָ֣ה פִילֶ֗גֶשׁ לֶֽאֱלִיפַז֙ בֶּן־עֵשָׂ֔ו וַתֵּ֥לֶד לֶאֱלִיפַ֖ז אֶת־עֲמָלֵ֑ק אֵ֕לֶּה

יג בְּנֵ֥י עָדָ֖ה אֵ֥שֶׁת עֵשָֽׂו: וְאֵ֙לֶּה֙ בְּנֵ֣י רְעוּאֵ֔ל נַ֥חַת וָזֶ֖רַח שַׁמָּ֣ה וּמִזָּ֑ה אֵ֣לֶּה

יד הָי֔וּ בְּנֵ֥י בָשְׂמַ֖ת אֵ֥שֶׁת עֵשָֽׂו: וְאֵ֣לֶּה הָי֗וּ בְּנֵ֤י אׇהֳלִֽיבָמָה֙ בַת־עֲנָ֔ה בַּת־צִבְע֖וֹן אֵ֣שֶׁת עֵשָׂ֑ו וַתֵּ֤לֶד לְעֵשָׂו֙ אֶת־[יעיש ק°] יְע֔וּשׁ וְאֶת־יַעְלָ֖ם וְאֶת־קֹֽרַח:

טו אֵ֖לֶּה אַלּוּפֵ֣י בְנֵֽי־עֵשָׂ֑ו בְּנֵ֤י אֱלִיפַז֙ בְּכ֣וֹר עֵשָׂ֔ו אַלּ֤וּף תֵּימָן֙ אַלּ֣וּף אוֹמָ֔ר אַלּ֥וּף

טז צְפ֖וֹ אַלּ֥וּף קְנַֽז: אַלּֽוּף־קֹ֛רַח אַלּ֥וּף גַּעְתָּ֖ם אַלּ֣וּף עֲמָלֵ֑ק אֵ֣לֶּה אַלּוּפֵ֤י אֱלִיפַז֙

יז בְּאֶ֣רֶץ אֱד֔וֹם אֵ֖לֶּה בְּנֵ֥י עָדָֽה: וְאֵ֗לֶּה בְּנֵ֤י רְעוּאֵל֙ בֶּן־עֵשָׂ֔ו אַלּ֥וּף נַ֙חַת֙ אַלּ֣וּף זֶ֔רַח אַלּ֥וּף שַׁמָּ֖ה אַלּ֣וּף מִזָּ֑ה אֵ֣לֶּה אַלּוּפֵ֤י רְעוּאֵל֙ בְּאֶ֣רֶץ אֱד֔וֹם

יח אֵ֕לֶּה בְּנֵ֥י בָשְׂמַ֖ת אֵ֥שֶׁת עֵשָֽׂו: וְאֵ֗לֶּה בְּנֵ֤י אׇהֳלִֽיבָמָה֙ אֵ֣שֶׁת עֵשָׂ֔ו אַלּ֥וּף יְע֛וּשׁ אַלּ֥וּף יַעְלָ֖ם אַלּ֣וּף קֹ֑רַח אֵ֣לֶּה אַלּוּפֵ֞י אׇהֳלִֽיבָמָ֛ה בַּת־עֲנָ֖ה אֵ֥שֶׁת עֵשָֽׂו:

שביעי יט-כ אֵ֧לֶּה בְנֵי־עֵשָׂ֛ו וְאֵ֥לֶּה אַלּוּפֵיהֶ֖ם ה֥וּא אֱדֽוֹם: אֵ֤לֶּה

35:22-26. Reuben's error and partial vindication. After Rachel's death, Jacob established his primary residence in the tent of Bilhah, Rachel's maidservant. Reuben considered this an affront to his mother Leah, so he moved Jacob's bed to her tent. This is all that transpired (*Shabbos* 55b). Scripture describes it as starkly as if Reuben had sinned grievously, because the conduct of great people is measured by an infinitely higher standard. See *Overview* to the ArtScroll edition of *Ruth* for a full explanation.

36:1-43. The Chronicles of Esau. The Torah would not have devoted an entire chapter to Esau's genealogy unless it contained vital teachings; indeed, a section of the *Zohar, Idra Rabbah*, is devoted to the mystical exposition of this chapter. From the literal sense of the verses and the parallel genealogies in *Chronicles*, it becomes clear that many of Esau's descendants were products of incest and illegitimacy. According to *Mizrachi*, this is reason enough for the chapter. There are other lessons, as well, some of

. . . and partial vindication	The sons of Jacob were twelve. ²³ The sons of Leah: Jacob's firstborn, Reuben; Simeon; Levi; Judah; Issachar; and Zebulun. ²⁴ The sons of Rachel: Joseph and Benjamin. ²⁵ The sons of Bilhah, maidservant of Rachel: Dan and Naphtali. ²⁶ And the sons of Zilpah, maidservant of Leah: Gad and Asher — these are the sons of Jacob, who were born to him in Paddan Aram.
Jacob and Isaac are reunited	²⁷ Jacob came to Isaac his father, at Mamre, Kiriath-arba; that is Hebron where Abraham and Isaac sojourned. ²⁸ Isaac's days were one hundred and eighty years. ²⁹ And Isaac expired and died, and he was gathered to his people,
Isaac's death	old and fulfilled of days; his sons, Esau and Jacob, buried him.

36

The chronicles of Esau
(See Appendix B, chart 5)

¹ **A**nd these are the descendants of Esau, he is Edom. ² Esau had taken his wives from among the Canaanite women: Adah, daughter of Elon the Hittite; and Oholibamah, daughter of Anah, daughter of Zibeon the Hivvite; ³ and Basemath, * daughter of Ishmael, sister of Nebaioth.

⁴ Adah bore to Esau Eliphaz; Basemath bore Reuel; ⁵ and Oholibamah bore Jeush, Jalam, and Korah; these are Esau's sons who were born to him in the land of Canaan.

Esau separates himself from Jacob

⁶ Esau took his wives, his sons, his daughters, and all the members of his household, and his livestock and all his animals, and all the wealth he had acquired in the land of Canaan, and went to a land because of his brother Jacob. ⁷ For their wealth was too abundant for them to dwell together, and the land of their sojourns could not support them because of their livestock. ⁸ So Esau settled on Mount Seir; Esau, he is Edom.

⁹ And these are the descendants of Esau, ancestor of Edom, on Mount Seir. ¹⁰ These are the names of Esau's sons: Eliphaz, son of Adah, Esau's wife; Reuel, son of Basemath, Esau's wife.

¹¹ The sons of Eliphaz were: Teman; Omar; Zepho; Gatam; and Kenaz. ¹² And Timna was a concubine of Eliphaz, son of Esau, and she bore Amalek to Eliphaz; these are the children of Adah, Esau's wife.

¹³ And these are the sons of Reuel: Nahath and Zerah; Shammah and Mizzah — these were the children of Basemath, Esau's wife.

¹⁴ And these were the sons of Oholibamah, daughter of Anah, daughter of Zibeon, Esau's wife: She bore to Esau Jeush, and Jalam, and Korah.

¹⁵ These are the chiefs of the children of Esau — the descendants of Esau's firstborn Eliphaz: Chief Teman, Chief Omar, Chief Zepho, Chief Kenaz; ¹⁶ Chief Korah, Chief Gatam, Chief Amalek; these are the chiefs of Eliphaz in the land of Edom — these are the descendants of Adah.

¹⁷ And these are the descendants of Reuel, Esau's son: Chief Nahath, Chief Zerah, Chief Shammah, Chief Mizzah; these are the chiefs of Reuel in the land of Edom — these are the descendants of Basemath, Esau's wife.

¹⁸ And these are the descendants of Ohlibamah, Esau's wife: Chief Jeush, Chief Jalam, Chief Korah — these are the chiefs of Ohlibamah, daughter of Anah, Esau's wife. ¹⁹ These are the children of Esau, and these are their chiefs; he is Edom. *

---

them halachic, which are discussed by the commentators. Furthermore, the Torah teaches us the honor that came to Esau because he was an offspring of Abraham.

36:3. In 28:9 *Basemath* is called Mahalath, which implies forgiveness, from the root מחל. The Sages derive that

one's sins are forgiven on the day of one's marriage (*Rashi*).

36:19. In this genealogy lay the roots of Edom, which evolved into Rome, the perpetual enemy of Israel (*Lekach Tov*).

כא בְּנֵי־שֵׂעִיר הַחֹרִי יֹשְׁבֵי הָאָרֶץ לוֹטָן וְשׁוֹבָל וְצִבְעוֹן וַעֲנָה: וְדִשׁוֹן וְאֵצֶר
כב וְדִישָׁן אֵלֶּה אַלּוּפֵי הַחֹרִי בְּנֵי שֵׂעִיר בְּאֶרֶץ אֱדוֹם: וַיִּהְיוּ בְנֵי־לוֹטָן חֹרִי
כג וְהֵימָם וַאֲחוֹת לוֹטָן תִּמְנָע: וְאֵלֶּה בְּנֵי שׁוֹבָל עַלְוָן וּמָנַחַת וְעֵיבָל שְׁפוֹ
כד וְאוֹנָם: וְאֵלֶּה בְנֵי־צִבְעוֹן וְאַיָּה וַעֲנָה הוּא עֲנָה אֲשֶׁר מָצָא אֶת־הַיֵּמִם
כה בַּמִּדְבָּר בִּרְעֹתוֹ אֶת־הַחֲמֹרִים לְצִבְעוֹן אָבִיו: וְאֵלֶּה בְנֵי־עֲנָה דִּשֹׁן
כו-כז וְאָהֳלִיבָמָה בַּת־עֲנָה: וְאֵלֶּה בְּנֵי דִישָׁן חֶמְדָּן וְאֶשְׁבָּן וְיִתְרָן וּכְרָן: אֵלֶּה
כח-כט בְּנֵי־אֵצֶר בִּלְהָן וְזַעֲוָן וַעֲקָן: אֵלֶּה בְּנֵי־דִישָׁן עוּץ וַאֲרָן: אֵלֶּה אַלּוּפֵי הַחֹרִי
ל אַלּוּף לוֹטָן אַלּוּף שׁוֹבָל אַלּוּף צִבְעוֹן אַלּוּף עֲנָה: אַלּוּף דִּשֹׁן אַלּוּף אֵצֶר
אַלּוּף דִּישָׁן אֵלֶּה אַלּוּפֵי הַחֹרִי לְאַלֻּפֵיהֶם בְּאֶרֶץ שֵׂעִיר:

לא וְאֵלֶּה הַמְּלָכִים אֲשֶׁר מָלְכוּ בְּאֶרֶץ אֱדוֹם לִפְנֵי מְלָךְ־מֶלֶךְ לִבְנֵי יִשְׂרָאֵל:
לב-לג וַיִּמְלֹךְ בֶּאֱדוֹם בֶּלַע בֶּן־בְּעוֹר וְשֵׁם עִירוֹ דִּנְהָבָה: וַיָּמָת בָּלַע וַיִּמְלֹךְ
לד תַּחְתָּיו יוֹבָב בֶּן־זֶרַח מִבָּצְרָה: וַיָּמָת יוֹבָב וַיִּמְלֹךְ תַּחְתָּיו חֻשָׁם מֵאֶרֶץ
לה הַתֵּימָנִי: וַיָּמָת חֻשָׁם וַיִּמְלֹךְ תַּחְתָּיו הֲדַד בֶּן־בְּדַד הַמַּכֶּה אֶת־מִדְיָן בִּשְׂדֵה
לו-לז מוֹאָב וְשֵׁם עִירוֹ עֲוִית: וַיָּמָת הֲדָד וַיִּמְלֹךְ תַּחְתָּיו שַׂמְלָה מִמַּשְׂרֵקָה: וַיָּמָת
לח שַׂמְלָה וַיִּמְלֹךְ תַּחְתָּיו שָׁאוּל מֵרְחֹבוֹת הַנָּהָר: וַיָּמָת שָׁאוּל וַיִּמְלֹךְ תַּחְתָּיו
לט בַּעַל חָנָן בֶּן־עַכְבּוֹר: וַיָּמָת בַּעַל חָנָן בֶּן־עַכְבּוֹר וַיִּמְלֹךְ תַּחְתָּיו הֲדַר וְשֵׁם
מ עִירוֹ פָּעוּ וְשֵׁם אִשְׁתּוֹ מְהֵיטַבְאֵל בַּת־מַטְרֵד בַּת מֵי זָהָב: וְאֵלֶּה שְׁמוֹת
אַלּוּפֵי עֵשָׂו לְמִשְׁפְּחֹתָם לִמְקֹמֹתָם בִּשְׁמֹתָם אַלּוּף תִּמְנָע אַלּוּף עַלְוָה
מא-מב אַלּוּף יְתֵת: אַלּוּף אָהֳלִיבָמָה אַלּוּף אֵלָה אַלּוּף פִּינֹן: אַלּוּף קְנַז אַלּוּף תֵּימָן
מג אַלּוּף מִבְצָר: אַלּוּף מַגְדִּיאֵל אַלּוּף עִירָם אֵלֶּה ׀ אַלּוּפֵי אֱדוֹם לְמֹשְׁבֹתָם
בְּאֶרֶץ אֲחֻזָּתָם הוּא עֵשָׂו אֲבִי אֱדוֹם: קנ״ד פסוקים.קליט״ה סימן. פפפ

פרשת וישב

לז א-ב וַיֵּשֶׁב יַעֲקֹב בְּאֶרֶץ מְגוּרֵי אָבִיו בְּאֶרֶץ כְּנָעַן: אֵלֶּה ׀ תֹּלְדוֹת יַעֲקֹב יוֹסֵף בֶּן־
שְׁבַע־עֶשְׂרֵה שָׁנָה הָיָה רֹעֶה אֶת־אֶחָיו בַּצֹּאן וְהוּא נַעַר אֶת־בְּנֵי בִלְהָה
וְאֶת־בְּנֵי זִלְפָּה נְשֵׁי אָבִיו וַיָּבֵא יוֹסֵף אֶת־דִּבָּתָם רָעָה אֶל־אֲבִיהֶם:
ג וְיִשְׂרָאֵל אָהַב אֶת־יוֹסֵף מִכָּל־בָּנָיו כִּי־בֶן־זְקֻנִים הוּא לוֹ וְעָשָׂה לוֹ כְּתֹנֶת
ד פַּסִּים: וַיִּרְאוּ אֶחָיו כִּי־אֹתוֹ אָהַב אֲבִיהֶם מִכָּל־אֶחָיו וַיִּשְׂנְאוּ אֹתוֹ וְלֹא
ה יָכְלוּ דַּבְּרוֹ לְשָׁלֹם: וַיַּחֲלֹם יוֹסֵף חֲלוֹם וַיַּגֵּד לְאֶחָיו וַיּוֹסִפוּ עוֹד שְׂנֹא אֹתוֹ:

36:31. The Edomite kings. The eight Edomite kings listed here reigned either before Moses, who had the status of a king, or who were destined to reign in *future* years, prior to Saul, the first Jewish king (*Ibn Ezra*).

⧽ Parashas Vayeishev

37:1. After his long exile and struggles, Jacob wished finally *לֵישֵׁב בְּשַׁלְוָה, to settle down in tranquility,* but the anguish of Joseph's kidnaping pounced upon him. God says, "Are the righteous not satisfied with what awaits them in the World to Come that they expect to live at

ease in This World, too?" (*Rashi*).

37:2. At this time Jacob was 108 years old; Isaac was 168 and lived for another twelve years. Leah died at about this time (see *Seder Olam* 2).

37:5-11. Joseph's dreams and the intensified hatred. Although the Sages leave it as an open question whether dreams have validity (*Berachos* 55a), it is clear from the Scriptural accounts of the dreams of Joseph, Pharaoh, and his officials that God used them to convey revelations of future events.

The Seirite genealogy

20 These are the sons of Seir the Horite who were settled in the land: Lotan and Shobal and Zibeon and Anah, 21 and Dishon and Ezer and Dishan — these are the chiefs of the Horite, the descendants of Seir in the land of Edom.

22 The sons of Lotan were: Hori and Hemam; Lotan's sister was Timna.

23 These are the sons of Shobal: Alvan and Manahath and Ebal; Shepho and Onam.

24 These are the sons of Zibeon: Aiah and Anah — the same Anah who discovered the mules in the desert while he was pasturing the donkeys for Zibeon, his father.

25 These are the children of Anah: Dishon and Oholibamah daughter of Anah.

26 These are the sons of Dishan: Hemdan and Eshban and Ithran and Cheran.

27 These are the sons of Ezer: Bilhan and Zaavan and Akan.

28 These are the sons of Dishan: Uz and Aran.

29 These are the chiefs of the Horite: Chief Lotan, Chief Shobal, Chief Zibeon, Chief Anah, 30 Chief Dishon, Chief Ezer, Chief Dishan — these are the chiefs of the Horite, according to their chiefs, in the land of Seir.

The Edomite kings

31 Now these are the kings who reigned in the land of Edom before a king reigned over the Children of Israel: 32 Bela, son of Beor, reigned in Edom, and the name of his city was Dinhabah. 33 And Bela died, and Jobab son of Zerah, from Bozrah, reigned after him. 34 And Jobab died and Husham, of the land of the Temanites, reigned after him. 35 And Husham died, and Hadad son of Bedad, who defeated the Midianites in the field of Moab, reigned after him, and the name of his city was Avith. 36 And Hadad died, and Samlah of Masrekah reigned after him. 37 And Samlah died, and Saul of Rehoboth-nahar reigned after him. 38 And Saul died, and Baal-hanan, son of Achbor, reigned after him. 39 Baal-hanan, son of Achbor, died, and Hadar reigned after him; the name of his city was Pau, and his wife's name was Mehetabel, daughter of Matred, daughter of Me-zahab.

40 Now these are the names of the chiefs of Esau, by their families, by their regions, by their names: the chief of Timna; the chief of Alvah; the chief of Jetheth; 41 the chief of Oholibamah; the chief of Elah; the chief of Pinon; 42 the chief of Kenaz; the chief of Teman; the chief of Mibzar; 43 the chief of Magdiel and the chief of Iram; these are the chiefs of Edom by their settlements, in the land of their possession — he is Esau, father of Edom.

PARASHAS VAYEISHEV

37

Jacob settled* in the land of his father's sojournings, in the land of Canaan.

The chronicles of Jacob and his offspring

2 These are the chronicles of Jacob: Joseph, at the age of seventeen years, * was a shepherd with his brothers by the flock, but he was a youth with the sons of Bilhah and the sons of Zilpah, his father's wives; and Joseph would bring evil reports about them to their father. 3 Now Israel loved Joseph more than all his sons since he was a child of his old age, and he made him a fine woolen tunic.

4 His brothers saw that it was he whom their father loved most of all his brothers so they hated him; and they could not speak to him peaceably.

Joseph's dreams

5 Joseph dreamt a dream which he told to his brothers, and they hated him

---

Joseph's dreams were Divine revelations that he was to be the leader of the family. As Sh'lah puts it, he was to be a spiritual bridge between the exalted level of the Patri- archs and the lesser one of the tribal ancestors. The bro- thers, however, understood his dreams to be reflections of his waking fantasies that he would dominate his peers.

ז וַיֹּאמֶר אֲלֵיהֶם שִׁמְעוּ־נָא הַחֲלוֹם הַזֶּה אֲשֶׁר חָלָמְתִּי: וְהִנֵּה אֲנַחְנוּ
מְאַלְּמִים אֲלֻמִּים בְּתוֹךְ הַשָּׂדֶה וְהִנֵּה קָמָה אֲלֻמָּתִי וְגַם־נִצָּבָה וְהִנֵּה
ח תְסֻבֶּינָה אֲלֻמֹּתֵיכֶם וַתִּשְׁתַּחֲוֶיןָ לַאֲלֻמָּתִי: וַיֹּאמְרוּ לוֹ אֶחָיו הֲמָלֹךְ תִּמְלֹךְ
עָלֵינוּ אִם־מָשׁוֹל תִּמְשֹׁל בָּנוּ וַיּוֹסִפוּ עוֹד שְׂנֹא אֹתוֹ עַל־חֲלֹמֹתָיו וְעַל־
ט דְּבָרָיו: וַיַּחֲלֹם עוֹד חֲלוֹם אַחֵר וַיְסַפֵּר אֹתוֹ לְאֶחָיו וַיֹּאמֶר הִנֵּה חָלַמְתִּי
חֲלוֹם עוֹד וְהִנֵּה הַשֶּׁמֶשׁ וְהַיָּרֵחַ וְאַחַד עָשָׂר כּוֹכָבִים מִשְׁתַּחֲוִים לִי:
י וַיְסַפֵּר אֶל־אָבִיו וְאֶל־אֶחָיו וַיִּגְעַר־בּוֹ אָבִיו וַיֹּאמֶר לוֹ מָה הַחֲלוֹם הַזֶּה
יא אֲשֶׁר חָלָמְתָּ הֲבוֹא נָבוֹא אֲנִי וְאִמְּךָ וְאַחֶיךָ לְהִשְׁתַּחֲוֹת לְךָ אָרְצָה: וַיְקַנְאוּ־
יב בוֹ אֶחָיו וְאָבִיו שָׁמַר אֶת־הַדָּבָר: וַיֵּלְכוּ אֶחָיו לִרְעוֹת אֶת־צֹאן אֲבִיהֶם
יג בִּשְׁכֶם: וַיֹּאמֶר יִשְׂרָאֵל אֶל־יוֹסֵף הֲלוֹא אַחֶיךָ רֹעִים בִּשְׁכֶם לְכָה
יד וְאֶשְׁלָחֲךָ אֲלֵיהֶם וַיֹּאמֶר לוֹ הִנֵּנִי: וַיֹּאמֶר לוֹ לֶךְ־נָא רְאֵה אֶת־שְׁלוֹם אַחֶיךָ
וְאֶת־שְׁלוֹם הַצֹּאן וַהֲשִׁבֵנִי דָּבָר וַיִּשְׁלָחֵהוּ מֵעֵמֶק חֶבְרוֹן וַיָּבֹא שְׁכֶמָה:
טו וַיִּמְצָאֵהוּ אִישׁ וְהִנֵּה תֹעֶה בַּשָּׂדֶה וַיִּשְׁאָלֵהוּ הָאִישׁ לֵאמֹר מַה־תְּבַקֵּשׁ:
טז-יז וַיֹּאמֶר אֶת־אַחַי אָנֹכִי מְבַקֵּשׁ הַגִּידָה־נָּא לִי אֵיפֹה הֵם רֹעִים: וַיֹּאמֶר
הָאִישׁ נָסְעוּ מִזֶּה כִּי שָׁמַעְתִּי אֹמְרִים נֵלְכָה דֹּתָיְנָה וַיֵּלֶךְ יוֹסֵף אַחַר אֶחָיו
יח וַיִּמְצָאֵם בְּדֹתָן: וַיִּרְאוּ אֹתוֹ מֵרָחֹק וּבְטֶרֶם יִקְרַב אֲלֵיהֶם וַיִּתְנַכְּלוּ אֹתוֹ
יט-כ לַהֲמִיתוֹ: וַיֹּאמְרוּ אִישׁ אֶל־אָחִיו הִנֵּה בַּעַל הַחֲלֹמוֹת הַלָּזֶה בָּא: וְעַתָּה ׀
לְכוּ וְנַהַרְגֵהוּ וְנַשְׁלִכֵהוּ בְּאַחַד הַבֹּרוֹת וְאָמַרְנוּ חַיָּה רָעָה אֲכָלָתְהוּ וְנִרְאֶה
כא מַה־יִּהְיוּ חֲלֹמֹתָיו: וַיִּשְׁמַע רְאוּבֵן וַיַּצִּלֵהוּ מִיָּדָם וַיֹּאמֶר לֹא נַכֶּנּוּ נָפֶשׁ:
כב וַיֹּאמֶר אֲלֵהֶם ׀ רְאוּבֵן אַל־תִּשְׁפְּכוּ־דָם הַשְׁלִיכוּ אֹתוֹ אֶל־הַבּוֹר הַזֶּה אֲשֶׁר
בַּמִּדְבָּר וְיָד אַל־תִּשְׁלְחוּ־בוֹ לְמַעַן הַצִּיל אֹתוֹ מִיָּדָם לַהֲשִׁיבוֹ אֶל־אָבִיו:
כג וַיְהִי כַּאֲשֶׁר־בָּא יוֹסֵף אֶל־אֶחָיו וַיַּפְשִׁיטוּ אֶת־יוֹסֵף אֶת־כֻּתָּנְתּוֹ אֶת־
כד כְּתֹנֶת הַפַּסִּים אֲשֶׁר עָלָיו: וַיִּקָּחֻהוּ וַיַּשְׁלִכוּ אֹתוֹ הַבֹּרָה וְהַבּוֹר רֵק אֵין בּוֹ
כה מָיִם: וַיֵּשְׁבוּ לֶאֱכָל־לֶחֶם וַיִּשְׂאוּ עֵינֵיהֶם וַיִּרְאוּ וְהִנֵּה אֹרְחַת יִשְׁמְעֵאלִים
בָּאָה מִגִּלְעָד וּגְמַלֵּיהֶם נֹשְׂאִים נְכֹאת וּצְרִי וָלֹט הוֹלְכִים לְהוֹרִיד
כו מִצְרָיְמָה: וַיֹּאמֶר יְהוּדָה אֶל־אֶחָיו מַה־בֶּצַע כִּי נַהֲרֹג אֶת־אָחִינוּ וְכִסִּינוּ

שלישי

37:12-28. Joseph is sent to visit his brothers; his sale into slavery. The stage now is set for one of the most perplexing events recorded in the Torah: the near killing of Joseph and his sale into slavery by his brothers. The story cannot be understood superficially, for we are not dealing with a band of robbers and murderers who would murder because of a coat. The brothers felt that Joseph was a threat not so much to them as to the family's destiny. They knew that the weeding-out process that banished Ishmael and Esau from the chosenness of Israel was to be over in their generation, so that the mission of the Patriarchs could go forward with them. But if Joseph were to bring dissension into the family, he would destroy this potential with untold consequences. If so, then he had to be judged as a traitor and a danger to them all.

⋙ Why were the brothers the ones who made Joseph suffer? The hand of Heaven was at work in the sale of Joseph. The brothers thought he was a menace to the unity and destiny of the family. They thought that they would kill him — and a dead man cannot reign. They thought that they would make him a slave — and a slave cannot reign. But God thought otherwise; Joseph *would* be king, no matter what they did. The Sages teach:

Our father Jacob would have had to descend to Egypt in chains and a collar. Said God, "He is My firstborn son, shall I bring him down there in disgrace? . . . Rather, I will lead his son before him and he will be forced to descend after him" (*Midrash Bereishis Rabbah* 86:2).

But why did his great and righteous brothers have to be the instruments of his mistreatment?

even more. ⁶He said to them, "Hear, if you please, this dream which I dreamt:
⁷ Behold! — we were binding sheaves in the middle of the field, when, behold!
— my sheaf arose and also remained standing; then behold! — your sheaves
gathered around and bowed down to my sheaf."

The intensi-
fied hatred
⁸ His brothers said to him, "Would you then reign over us? Would you then
dominate us?" And they hated him even more — because of his dreams and
because of his talk.

Joseph's
second
dream
⁹ He dreamt another dream, and related it to his brothers. And he said, "Look,
I dreamt another dream: Behold! the sun, the moon, and eleven stars were
bowing down to me."

¹⁰ And he related it to his father and to his brothers; his father scolded him, and
said to him, "What is this dream that you have dreamt! Are we to come — I and
your mother and your brothers — to bow down to you to the ground?" ¹¹ So his
brothers were jealous of him, but his father kept the matter in mind.

Joseph is
sent to visit
his brothers
¹² Now, his brothers went to pasture their father's flock in Shechem. ¹³ And
Israel said to Joseph, "Your brothers are pasturing in Shechem, are they not?
Come, I will send you to them." He said to him, "Here I am!" ¹⁴ And he said to
him, "Go now, look into the welfare of your brothers and the welfare of the flock,
and bring me back word." So he sent him from the depth of Hebron, and he
arrived at Shechem.

¹⁵A man discovered him, and behold! — he was blundering in the field; the
man asked him, saying, "What do you seek?" ¹⁶ And he said, "My brothers do
I seek; tell me, please, where they are pasturing." ¹⁷ The man said, "They have
journeyed on from here, for I heard them saying, 'Let us go to Dothan.' " So
Joseph went after his brothers and found them at Dothan.

¹⁸ They saw him from afar; and when he had not yet approached them they
conspired against him to kill him. ¹⁹ And they said to one another, "Look! That
dreamer is coming! ²⁰ So now, come and let us kill him, and throw him into one
of the pits; and we will say, 'A wild beast devoured him.' Then we shall see what
will become of his dreams."

Reuben
saves
Joseph from
the plot to
kill him
²¹ Reuben heard, and he rescued him from their hand; he said, "We will not
strike him mortally!" ²² And Reuben said to them: "Shed no blood! Throw him
into this pit in the wilderness, but lay no hand on him!" — intending to rescue
him from their hand, to return him to his father.

²³ And so it was, when Joseph came to his brothers they stripped Joseph of
his tunic, the fine woolen tunic that was on him. ²⁴ Then they took him, and cast
him into the pit; the pit was empty, no water was in it.

Joseph is
sold
²⁵ They sat to eat food; they raised their eyes and they saw, behold! — a
caravan of Ishmaelites was coming from Gilead, their camels bearing spices,
balsam, and lotus — on their way to bring them down to Egypt. ²⁶ Judah
said to his brothers, "What gain will there be if we kill our brother and cover up

---

It is true that the brothers had reason to dislike Joseph. According to their *own* evaluation of their mission and his deeds, they had reason even to hate him. But their verdict was tainted by jealousy, and because men of their stature had no right to be jealous, God made them the instruments to bring Joseph to Egypt in such a heartless manner, causing their father twenty-two years of grief. Since it was foreordained that Jacob and his family go to Egypt,

Joseph would have gone there anyway, but if his brothers had not fallen short of their ideal, Joseph's and Jacob's tears would not have been on their heads.

Nevertheless, because they truly wanted only to do the right thing, even their misdeed had a good outcome. Thanks to them, Joseph was in Egypt to save the world from famine and lay the foundations for the Exodus and the triumphant journey to Mount Sinai.

כז אֶת־דָּמֽוֹ: לְכֿוּ וְנִמְכְּרֶ֣נּוּ לַיִּשְׁמְעֵאלִ֗ים וְיָדֵ֙נוּ֙ אַל־תְּהִי־ב֔וֹ כִּֽי־אָחִ֥ינוּ בְשָׂרֵ֖נוּ

כח ה֑וּא וַיִּשְׁמְע֖וּ אֶחָֽיו: וַיַּֽעַבְרוּ֩ אֲנָשִׁ֨ים מִדְיָנִ֜ים סֹֽחֲרִ֗ים וַֽיִּמְשְׁכוּ֙ וַיַּֽעֲל֤וּ אֶת־יוֹסֵף֙ מִן־הַבּ֔וֹר וַיִּמְכְּר֧וּ אֶת־יוֹסֵ֛ף לַיִּשְׁמְעֵאלִ֖ים בְּעֶשְׂרִ֣ים כָּ֑סֶף וַיָּבִ֥יאוּ אֶת־

כט יוֹסֵ֖ף מִצְרָֽיְמָה: וַיָּ֤שָׁב רְאוּבֵן֙ אֶל־הַבּ֔וֹר וְהִנֵּ֥ה אֵין־יוֹסֵ֖ף בַּבּ֑וֹר וַיִּקְרַ֖ע אֶת־

ל-לא בְּגָדָֽיו: וַיָּ֥שָׁב אֶל־אֶחָ֖יו וַיֹּאמַ֑ר הַיֶּ֣לֶד אֵינֶ֔נּוּ וַֽאֲנִ֖י אָ֥נָה אֲנִי־בָֽא: וַיִּקְח֖וּ

לב אֶת־כְּתֹ֣נֶת יוֹסֵ֑ף וַֽיִּשְׁחֲטוּ֙ שְׂעִ֣יר עִזִּ֔ים וַיִּטְבְּל֥וּ אֶת־הַכֻּתֹּ֖נֶת בַּדָּֽם: וַֽיְשַׁלְּח֞וּ אֶת־כְּתֹ֣נֶת הַפַּסִּ֗ים וַיָּבִ֙יאוּ֙ אֶל־אֲבִיהֶ֔ם וַיֹּֽאמְר֖וּ זֹ֣את מָצָ֑אנוּ הַכֶּר־נָ֗א

לג הַכְּתֹ֧נֶת בִּנְךָ֛ הִ֖וא אִם־לֹֽא: וַיַּכִּירָ֤הּ וַיֹּ֨אמֶר֙ כְּתֹ֣נֶת בְּנִ֔י חַיָּ֥ה רָעָ֖ה אֲכָלָ֑תְהוּ

לד טָרֹ֥ף טֹרַ֖ף יוֹסֵֽף: וַיִּקְרַ֤ע יַֽעֲקֹב֙ שִׂמְלֹתָ֔יו וַיָּ֥שֶׂם שַׂ֖ק בְּמָתְנָ֑יו וַיִּתְאַבֵּ֥ל עַל־בְּנ֖וֹ

לה יָמִ֥ים רַבִּֽים: וַיָּקֻ֩מוּ֩ כָל־בָּנָ֨יו וְכָל־בְּנֹתָ֜יו לְנַֽחֲמ֗וֹ וַיְמָאֵן֙ לְהִתְנַחֵ֔ם וַיֹּ֕אמֶר כִּֽי־אֵרֵ֧ד אֶל־בְּנִ֛י אָבֵ֖ל שְׁאֹ֑לָה וַיֵּ֥בְךְּ אֹת֖וֹ אָבִֽיו: וְהַ֨מְּדָנִ֔ים מָכְר֥וּ אֹת֖וֹ אֶל־

לו מִצְרָ֑יִם לְפֽוֹטִיפַר֙ סְרִ֣יס פַּרְעֹ֔ה שַׂ֖ר הַטַּבָּחִֽים:

לח רביעי א וַֽיְהִי֙ בָּעֵ֣ת הַהִ֔וא וַיֵּ֥רֶד יְהוּדָ֖ה מֵאֵ֣ת אֶחָ֑יו וַיֵּ֛ט עַד־אִ֥ישׁ עֲדֻלָּמִ֖י וּשְׁמ֥וֹ

ב חִירָֽה: וַיַּרְא־שָׁ֧ם יְהוּדָ֛ה בַּת־אִ֥ישׁ כְּנַֽעֲנִ֖י וּשְׁמ֣וֹ שׁ֑וּעַ וַיִּקָּחֶ֖הָ וַיָּבֹ֥א אֵלֶֽיהָ:

ג-ד וַתַּ֖הַר וַתֵּ֣לֶד בֵּ֑ן וַיִּקְרָ֥א אֶת־שְׁמ֖וֹ עֵֽר: וַתַּ֥הַר ע֖וֹד וַתֵּ֣לֶד בֵּ֑ן וַתִּקְרָ֥א אֶת־

ה שְׁמ֖וֹ אוֹנָֽן: וַתֹּ֤סֶף עוֹד֙ וַתֵּ֣לֶד בֵּ֔ן וַתִּקְרָ֥א אֶת־שְׁמ֖וֹ שֵׁלָ֑ה וְהָיָ֥ה בִכְזִ֖יב

ו-ז בְּלִדְתָּ֥הּ אֹתֽוֹ: וַיִּקַּ֧ח יְהוּדָ֛ה אִשָּׁ֖ה לְעֵ֣ר בְּכוֹר֑וֹ וּשְׁמָ֖הּ תָּמָֽר: וַיְהִ֗י עֵ֚ר

ח בְּכ֣וֹר יְהוּדָ֔ה רַ֖ע בְּעֵינֵ֣י יְהֹוָ֑ה וַיְמִתֵ֖הוּ יְהֹוָֽה: וַיֹּ֤אמֶר יְהוּדָה֙ לְאוֹנָ֔ן בֹּ֛א אֶל־

ט אֵ֥שֶׁת אָחִ֖יךָ וְיַבֵּ֣ם אֹתָ֑הּ וְהָקֵ֥ם זֶ֖רַע לְאָחִֽיךָ: וַיֵּ֣דַע אוֹנָ֔ן כִּ֛י לֹּ֥א ל֖וֹ יִֽהְיֶ֣ה הַזָּ֑רַע וְהָיָ֞ה אִם־בָּ֨א אֶל־אֵ֤שֶׁת אָחִיו֙ וְשִׁחֵ֣ת אַ֔רְצָה לְבִלְתִּ֥י נְתָן־זֶ֖רַע

י-יא לְאָחִֽיו: וַיֵּ֛רַע בְּעֵינֵ֥י יְהֹוָ֖ה אֲשֶׁ֣ר עָשָׂ֑ה וַיָּ֖מֶת גַּם־אֹתֽוֹ: וַיֹּ֣אמֶר יְהוּדָ֣ה לְתָמָ֣ר כַּלָּת֡וֹ שְׁבִי֩ אַלְמָנָ֨ה בֵית־אָבִ֜יךְ עַד־יִגְדַּל֙ שֵׁלָ֣ה בְנִ֔י כִּ֣י אָמַ֗ר פֶּן־

יב יָמ֥וּת גַּם־ה֖וּא כְּאֶחָ֑יו וַתֵּ֣לֶךְ תָּמָ֔ר וַתֵּ֖שֶׁב בֵּ֥ית אָבִֽיהָ: וַיִּרְבּוּ֙ הַיָּמִ֔ים וַתָּ֖מָת בַּת־שׁ֣וּעַ אֵֽשֶׁת־יְהוּדָ֑ה וַיִּנָּ֣חֶם יְהוּדָ֗ה וַיַּ֜עַל עַל־גֹּֽזְזֵ֤י צֹאנוֹ֙ ה֣וּא

יג וְחִירָ֛ה רֵעֵ֥הוּ הָֽעֲדֻלָּמִ֖י תִּמְנָֽתָה: וַיֻּגַּ֥ד לְתָמָ֖ר לֵאמֹ֑ר הִנֵּ֥ה חָמִ֛יךְ עֹלֶ֥ה

יד תִמְנָ֖תָה לָגֹ֥ז צֹאנֽוֹ: וַתָּ֩סַר֩ בִּגְדֵ֨י אַלְמְנוּתָ֜הּ מֵֽעָלֶ֗יהָ וַתְּכַ֤ס בַּצָּעִיף֙ וַתִּתְעַלָּ֔ף וַתֵּ֙שֶׁב֙ בְּפֶ֣תַח עֵינַ֔יִם אֲשֶׁ֖ר עַל־דֶּ֣רֶךְ תִּמְנָ֑תָה כִּ֤י רָֽאֲתָה֙ כִּֽי־גָדַ֣ל שֵׁלָ֔ה

טו וְהִ֕וא לֹֽא־נִתְּנָ֥ה ל֖וֹ לְאִשָּֽׁה: וַיִּרְאֶ֣הָ יְהוּדָ֔ה וַיַּחְשְׁבֶ֖הָ לְזוֹנָ֑ה כִּ֥י כִסְּתָ֖ה

38:6-10. Judah's sons marry Tamar, but die for their sin. According to the Midrash, Tamar was the daughter of Noah's son Shem (*Bereishis Rabbah* 85:10), who resided in Canaan. Er was very young when he married, for all the events related in this chapter transpired in the twenty-two years between the sale of Joseph and Jacob's descent to Egypt (*Seder Olam*).

The nature of the sin of Er and Onan is given in verse 9. Er and Onan did not want Tamar's beauty to be marred by pregnancy, so they wasted their seed. For this grave sin they suffered death (*Rashi*).

38:14-19. The moral basis for the union of Tamar and Judah. At times when there is an enormous potential for a breakthrough of good, the forces of evil fight back furiously, just as an army with its back to the barricades will counterattack tenaciously. Tamar, a very righteous woman, was Divinely ordained to become the ancestress of the Davidic dynasty. But Judah's two oldest sons were unworthy, and Judah rebuffed her. In the normal course of events, therefore, she would not have been able to marry anyone from Judah's family, which would have made it impossible for her to carry out her spiritual his blood? ²⁷ Come, let us sell him to the Ishmaelites — but let our hand not be upon him, for he is our brother, our own flesh." His brothers agreed. ²⁸ Midianite men, traders, passed by; they drew Joseph up and lifted him out of the pit and sold Joseph to the Ishmaelites for twenty pieces of silver; then they brought Joseph to Egypt. ²⁹ Reuben returned to the pit — and behold! — Joseph was not in the pit! So he rent his garments. ³⁰ Returning to his brothers he said, "The boy is gone! And I — where can I go?" ³¹ They took Joseph's tunic, slaughtered a goatling, and dipped the tunic in the blood. ³² They dispatched the fine woolen tunic and they brought it to their father, and said, "We found this; identify, if you please: Is it your son's tunic or not?" ³³ He recognized it and he said, "My son's tunic! A savage beast devoured him! Joseph has surely been torn to bits!" ³⁴ Then Jacob rent his garments and placed sackcloth on his loins; he mourned for his son many days. ³⁵ All his sons and all his daughters arose to comfort him, but he refused to comfort himself, and said: "For I will go down to the grave mourning for my son." And his father bewailed him. ³⁶ Now the Medanites had sold him to Egypt, to Potiphar, a courtier of Pharaoh, the Chamberlain of the Butchers.

The version told to Jacob

38

Judah and Tamar: The roots of the Messiah and the Israelite monarchy

¹ It was at that time that Judah went down from his brothers and turned away towards an Adullamite man whose name was Hirah. ² There Judah saw the daughter of a prominent merchant whose name was Shua; he married her and consorted with her. ³ She conceived and bore a son and he called his name Er. ⁴ She conceived again and bore a son and she called his name Onan. ⁵ And yet again and she bore a son; and called his name Shelah; and it was in Chezib when she bore him.

⁶ Judah took a wife for Er his firstborn; her name was Tamar. ⁷ But Er, Judah's firstborn, was evil in the eyes of HASHEM, and HASHEM caused him to die. ⁸ Then Judah said to Onan, "Consort with your brother's wife and enter into levirate marriage with her, and establish offspring for your brother."

Judah's sons marry Tamar, but die for their sin

⁹ But Onan knew that the seed would not be his; so it was, that whenever he would consort with his brother's wife, he would let it go to waste on the ground so as not to provide offspring for his brother. ¹⁰ What he did was evil in the eyes of HASHEM, and He caused him to die also.

¹¹ Then Judah said to Tamar, his daughter-in-law, "Remain a widow in your father's house until my son Shelah grows up" — for he thought, "Lest he also die like his brothers." — So Tamar went and lived in her father's house.

¹² Many days passed and Shua's daughter, the wife of Judah, died; when Judah was consoled, he went up to oversee his sheepshearers — he and his Adullamite friend, Hirah — to Timnah.

The moral basis for the union of Tamar and Judah

¹³ And Tamar was told, as follows, "Behold your father-in-law is coming up to Timnah to shear his sheep." ¹⁴ So she removed her widow's garb from upon her, covered herself with a veil, and wrapped herself up; she then sat by the crossroads which is on the road toward Timnah, for she saw that Shelah had grown, and she had not been given to him as a wife.

¹⁵ When Judah saw her, he thought her to be a harlot since she had covered

---

destiny. Consequently, to bring about the union between herself and Judah, Tamar decided that she had to seek unconventional — even distasteful — means, by enticing Judah. But even that ruse would not have succeeded in the normal course of events, for the righteous Judah would never have lowered himself to immorality. The Midrash teaches that God pushed him, as it were, to cohabit with Tamar.

פָּנֶיהָ: וַיֵּט אֵלֶיהָ אֶל־הַדֶּרֶךְ וַיֹּאמֶר הָבָה־נָּא אָבוֹא אֵלַיִךְ כִּי לֹא יָדַע טז

כִּי כַלָּתוֹ הִוא וַתֹּאמֶר מַה־תִּתֶּן־לִי כִּי תָבוֹא אֵלָי: וַיֹּאמֶר אָנֹכִי אֲשַׁלַּח יז

גְּדִי־עִזִּים מִן־הַצֹּאן וַתֹּאמֶר אִם־תִּתֵּן עֵרָבוֹן עַד שָׁלְחֶךָ: וַיֹּאמֶר מָה יח

הָעֵרָבוֹן אֲשֶׁר אֶתֶּן־לָךְ וַתֹּאמֶר חֹתָמְךָ וּפְתִילֶךָ וּמַטְּךָ אֲשֶׁר בְּיָדֶךָ וַיִּתֶּן־

לָהּ וַיָּבֹא אֵלֶיהָ וַתַּהַר לוֹ: וַתָּקָם וַתֵּלֶךְ וַתָּסַר צְעִיפָהּ מֵעָלֶיהָ וַתִּלְבַּשׁ יט

בִּגְדֵי אַלְמְנוּתָהּ: וַיִּשְׁלַח יְהוּדָה אֶת־גְּדִי הָעִזִּים בְּיַד רֵעֵהוּ הָעֲדֻלָּמִי כ

לָקַחַת הָעֵרָבוֹן מִיַּד הָאִשָּׁה וְלֹא מְצָאָהּ: וַיִּשְׁאַל אֶת־אַנְשֵׁי מְקֹמָהּ כא

לֵאמֹר אַיֵּה הַקְּדֵשָׁה הִוא בָעֵינַיִם עַל־הַדָּרֶךְ וַיֹּאמְרוּ לֹא־הָיְתָה בָזֶה

קְדֵשָׁה: וַיָּשָׁב אֶל־יְהוּדָה וַיֹּאמֶר לֹא מְצָאתִיהָ וְגַם אַנְשֵׁי הַמָּקוֹם אָמְרוּ כב

לֹא־הָיְתָה בָזֶה קְדֵשָׁה: וַיֹּאמֶר יְהוּדָה תִּקַּח־לָהּ פֶּן נִהְיֶה לָבוּז הִנֵּה כג

שָׁלַחְתִּי הַגְּדִי הַזֶּה וְאַתָּה לֹא מְצָאתָהּ: וַיְהִי ׀ כְּמִשְׁלֹשׁ חֳדָשִׁים וַיֻּגַּד כד

לִיהוּדָה לֵאמֹר זָנְתָה תָּמָר כַּלָּתֶךָ וְגַם הִנֵּה הָרָה לִזְנוּנִים וַיֹּאמֶר יְהוּדָה

הוֹצִיאוּהָ וְתִשָּׂרֵף: הִוא מוּצֵאת וְהִיא שָׁלְחָה אֶל־חָמִיהָ לֵאמֹר לְאִישׁ כה

אֲשֶׁר־אֵלֶּה לּוֹ אָנֹכִי הָרָה וַתֹּאמֶר הַכֶּר־נָא לְמִי הַחֹתֶמֶת וְהַפְּתִילִים

וְהַמַּטֶּה הָאֵלֶּה: וַיַּכֵּר יְהוּדָה וַיֹּאמֶר צָדְקָה מִמֶּנִּי כִּי־עַל־כֵּן לֹא־נְתַתִּיהָ כו

לְשֵׁלָה בְנִי וְלֹא־יָסַף עוֹד לְדַעְתָּהּ: וַיְהִי בְּעֵת לִדְתָּהּ וְהִנֵּה תְאוֹמִים כז

בְּבִטְנָהּ: וַיְהִי בְלִדְתָּהּ וַיִּתֶּן־יָד וַתִּקַּח הַמְיַלֶּדֶת וַתִּקְשֹׁר עַל־יָדוֹ שָׁנִי כח

לֵאמֹר זֶה יָצָא רִאשֹׁנָה: וַיְהִי ׀ כְּמֵשִׁיב יָדוֹ וְהִנֵּה יָצָא אָחִיו וַתֹּאמֶר מַה־ כט

פָּרַצְתָּ עָלֶיךָ פָּרֶץ וַיִּקְרָא שְׁמוֹ פָּרֶץ: וְאַחַר יָצָא אָחִיו אֲשֶׁר עַל־יָדוֹ ל

הַשָּׁנִי וַיִּקְרָא שְׁמוֹ זָרַח:

לט חמישי וְיוֹסֵף הוּרַד מִצְרָיְמָה וַיִּקְנֵהוּ א

פּוֹטִיפַר סְרִיס פַּרְעֹה שַׂר הַטַּבָּחִים אִישׁ מִצְרִי מִיַּד הַיִּשְׁמְעֵאלִים אֲשֶׁר

הוֹרִדֻהוּ שָׁמָּה: וַיְהִי יְהוָה אֶת־יוֹסֵף וַיְהִי אִישׁ מַצְלִיחַ וַיְהִי בְּבֵית אֲדֹנָיו ב

הַמִּצְרִי: וַיַּרְא אֲדֹנָיו כִּי יְהוָה אִתּוֹ וְכֹל אֲשֶׁר־הוּא עֹשֶׂה יְהוָה מַצְלִיחַ ג

בְּיָדוֹ: וַיִּמְצָא יוֹסֵף חֵן בְּעֵינָיו וַיְשָׁרֶת אֹתוֹ וַיַּפְקִדֵהוּ עַל־בֵּיתוֹ וְכָל־יֶשׁ־לוֹ ד

נָתַן בְּיָדוֹ: וַיְהִי מֵאָז הִפְקִיד אֹתוֹ בְּבֵיתוֹ וְעַל כָּל־אֲשֶׁר יֶשׁ־לוֹ וַיְבָרֶךְ ה

יְהוָה אֶת־בֵּית הַמִּצְרִי בִּגְלַל יוֹסֵף וַיְהִי בִּרְכַּת יְהוָה בְּכָל־אֲשֶׁר יֶשׁ־לוֹ

בַּבַּיִת וּבַשָּׂדֶה: וַיַּעֲזֹב כָּל־אֲשֶׁר־לוֹ בְּיַד־יוֹסֵף וְלֹא־יָדַע אִתּוֹ מְאוּמָה כִּי ו

אִם־הַלֶּחֶם אֲשֶׁר־הוּא אוֹכֵל וַיְהִי יוֹסֵף יְפֵה־תֹאַר וִיפֵה מַרְאֶה: וַיְהִי ששי ז

אַחַר הַדְּבָרִים הָאֵלֶּה וַתִּשָּׂא אֵשֶׁת־אֲדֹנָיו אֶת־עֵינֶיהָ אֶל־יוֹסֵף וַתֹּאמֶר

38:25. Tamar did not name Judah publicly. She reasoned: "If he admits it voluntarily, well and good; if not, let them burn me, but let me not publicly disgrace him." Thus the Sages derived [*Sotah* 10b]: "One should let himself be thrown into a fiery furnace rather than expose his neighbor to public shame" (*Rashi*).

38:26. *She is right; it is from me.* The translation follows *Rashi*. Judah's response testifies to his moral integrity.

Though his public admission surely subjected him to the jibes of the populace, he did not hesitate to admit that he was the father.

Ramban and *Rashbam* render that Judah called out, "*She is more righteous than I!*"

39:1. Joseph in Egypt/Prelude to exile. Joseph's descent into Egypt was the prelude to the exile foretold to Abraham at the Covenant Between the Parts [15:13].

her face. ¹⁶ So he detoured to her by the road and said, "Come, if you please, let me consort with you," for he did not know that she was his daughter-in-law.

Judah's pledge   And she said, "What will you give me if you consort with me?"

¹⁷ He replied, "I will send you a kid of the goats from the flock."

And she said, "Provided you leave a pledge until you send it."

¹⁸ And he said, "What pledge shall I give you?"

She replied, "Your signet, your wrap, and your staff that is in your hand." And he gave them to her, and consorted with her, and she conceived by him.

¹⁹ Then she arose, left, and removed her veil from upon her, and she put on her widow's garb.

²⁰ Judah sent the kid of the goats through his friend the Adullamite to retrieve the pledge from the woman; but he did not find her. ²¹ He inquired of the people of her place, saying, "Where is the prostitute, the one at the crossroads by the road?"

And they said, "There was no prostitute here." ²² So he returned to Judah and said, "I did not find her; even the local men said, 'There was no prostitute here.'"

²³ So Judah said, "Let her keep them, lest we become a laughingstock; I really sent her this kid, but you could not find her."

Tamar's pregnancy   ²⁴ And it was when about three months had passed, that Judah was told, "Your daughter-in-law Tamar has committed harlotry, and moreover, she has conceived by harlotry."

Judah said, "Take her out and let her be burned!"

²⁵ As she was taken out, she sent word to her father-in-law, saying, "By the man to whom these belong I am with child." And she said, "Identify, if you please, whose are this signet, this wrap, and this staff."

²⁶ Judah recognized; and he said, "She is right; it is from me, * inasmuch as I did not give her to Shelah my son," and he was not intimate with her anymore.

Tamar bears twins   ²⁷ And it came to pass at the time she gave birth that behold! There were twins in her womb. ²⁸ And it happened that as she gave birth, one put out a hand; the midwife took a crimson thread and tied it on his hand saying, "This one emerged first!" ²⁹ And it was, as he drew back his hand, that behold! his brother emerged. And she said, "With what strength you asserted yourself!" And he called his name Perez. ³⁰ Afterwards his brother on whose hand was the crimson thread came out; and he called his name Zerah.

39   ¹ **A**nd Joseph had been brought down to Egypt.* Potiphar, a courtier of

Joseph in Egypt   Pharaoh, the Chamberlain of the Butchers, a prominent Egyptian, purchased him from the Ishmaelites who had brought him down there. ² HASHEM was with Joseph, and he became a successful man; and he remained in the house of his Egyptian master. ³ His master perceived that HASHEM was with him, and whatever he did HASHEM made succeed in his hand. ⁴ Joseph found favor in his eyes, and he attended him; he appointed him over his household, and whatever he had he placed in his custody.

⁵ And it happened, that from the time he appointed him in his house and over whatever he had, HASHEM blessed the Egyptian's house on Joseph's account, so that HASHEM's blessing was in whatever he owned, in the house and in the field. ⁶ He left all that he had in Joseph's custody and with him present he concerned himself with nothing except for the bread he ate. Now Joseph was handsome of form and handsome of appearance.

⁷ After these things, his master's wife cast her eyes upon Joseph and she said,

ח שִׁכְבָה עִמִּי: וַיְמָאֵן ׀ וַיֹּאמֶר אֶל־אֵשֶׁת אֲדֹנָיו הֵן אֲדֹנִי לֹא־יָדַע אִתִּי מַה־

ט בַּבָּיִת וְכֹל אֲשֶׁר־יֶשׁ־לוֹ נָתַן בְּיָדִי: אֵינֶנּוּ גָדוֹל בַּבַּיִת הַזֶּה מִמֶּנִּי וְלֹא־חָשַׂךְ

מִמֶּנִּי מְאוּמָה כִּי אִם־אוֹתָךְ בַּאֲשֶׁר אַתְּ־אִשְׁתּוֹ וְאֵיךְ אֶעֱשֶׂה הָרָעָה

י הַגְּדֹלָה הַזֹּאת וְחָטָאתִי לֵאלֹהִים: וַיְהִי כְּדַבְּרָהּ אֶל־יוֹסֵף יוֹם ׀ יוֹם וְלֹא־

יא שָׁמַע אֵלֶיהָ לִשְׁכַּב אֶצְלָהּ לִהְיוֹת עִמָּהּ: וַיְהִי כְּהַיּוֹם הַזֶּה וַיָּבֹא הַבַּיְתָה

יב לַעֲשׂוֹת מְלַאכְתּוֹ וְאֵין אִישׁ מֵאַנְשֵׁי הַבַּיִת שָׁם בַּבָּיִת: וַתִּתְפְּשֵׂהוּ בְּבִגְדוֹ

יג לֵאמֹר שִׁכְבָה עִמִּי וַיַּעֲזֹב בִּגְדוֹ בְּיָדָהּ וַיָּנָס וַיֵּצֵא הַחוּצָה: וַיְהִי כִּרְאוֹתָהּ

יד כִּי־עָזַב בִּגְדוֹ בְּיָדָהּ וַיָּנָס הַחוּצָה: וַתִּקְרָא לְאַנְשֵׁי בֵיתָהּ וַתֹּאמֶר לָהֶם

לֵאמֹר רְאוּ הֵבִיא לָנוּ אִישׁ עִבְרִי לְצַחֶק בָּנוּ בָּא אֵלַי לִשְׁכַּב עִמִּי וָאֶקְרָא

טו בְּקוֹל גָּדוֹל: וַיְהִי כְשָׁמְעוֹ כִּי־הֲרִימֹתִי קוֹלִי וָאֶקְרָא וַיַּעֲזֹב בִּגְדוֹ אֶצְלִי וַיָּנָס

טז־יז וַיֵּצֵא הַחוּצָה: וַתַּנַּח בִּגְדוֹ אֶצְלָהּ עַד־בּוֹא אֲדֹנָיו אֶל־בֵּיתוֹ: וַתְּדַבֵּר אֵלָיו

כַּדְּבָרִים הָאֵלֶּה לֵאמֹר בָּא אֵלַי הָעֶבֶד הָעִבְרִי אֲשֶׁר־הֵבֵאתָ לָּנוּ לְצַחֶק

יח־יט בִּי: וַיְהִי כַּהֲרִימִי קוֹלִי וָאֶקְרָא וַיַּעֲזֹב בִּגְדוֹ אֶצְלִי וַיָּנָס הַחוּצָה: וַיְהִי כִשְׁמֹעַ

אֲדֹנָיו אֶת־דִּבְרֵי אִשְׁתּוֹ אֲשֶׁר דִּבְּרָה אֵלָיו לֵאמֹר כַּדְּבָרִים הָאֵלֶּה עָשָׂה

כ לִי עַבְדֶּךָ וַיִּחַר אַפּוֹ: וַיִּקַּח אֲדֹנֵי יוֹסֵף אֹתוֹ וַיִּתְּנֵהוּ אֶל־בֵּית הַסֹּהַר מְקוֹם

כא אֲשֶׁר־°אסורי [°אֲסִירֵי ק׳] הַמֶּלֶךְ אֲסוּרִים וַיְהִי־שָׁם בְּבֵית הַסֹּהַר: וַיְהִי

כב יְהֹוָה אֶת־יוֹסֵף וַיֵּט אֵלָיו חָסֶד וַיִּתֵּן חִנּוֹ בְּעֵינֵי שַׂר בֵּית־הַסֹּהַר: וַיִּתֵּן שַׂר

בֵּית־הַסֹּהַר בְּיַד־יוֹסֵף אֵת כָּל־הָאֲסִירִם אֲשֶׁר בְּבֵית הַסֹּהַר וְאֵת כָּל־

כג אֲשֶׁר עֹשִׂים שָׁם הוּא הָיָה עֹשֶׂה: אֵין ׀ שַׂר בֵּית־הַסֹּהַר רֹאֶה אֶת־כָּל־

מְאוּמָה בְּיָדוֹ בַּאֲשֶׁר יְהֹוָה אִתּוֹ וַאֲשֶׁר־הוּא עֹשֶׂה יְהֹוָה מַצְלִיחַ:

מ א שביעי וַיְהִי אַחַר הַדְּבָרִים הָאֵלֶּה חָטְאוּ מַשְׁקֵה מֶלֶךְ־מִצְרַיִם וְהָאֹפֶה לַאֲדֹנֵיהֶם

ב לְמֶלֶךְ מִצְרָיִם: וַיִּקְצֹף פַּרְעֹה עַל שְׁנֵי סָרִיסָיו עַל שַׂר הַמַּשְׁקִים וְעַל שַׂר

ג הָאוֹפִים: וַיִּתֵּן אֹתָם בְּמִשְׁמַר בֵּית שַׂר הַטַּבָּחִים אֶל־בֵּית הַסֹּהַר מְקוֹם

ד אֲשֶׁר יוֹסֵף אָסוּר שָׁם: וַיִּפְקֹד שַׂר הַטַּבָּחִים אֶת־יוֹסֵף אִתָּם וַיְשָׁרֶת אֹתָם

ה וַיִּהְיוּ יָמִים בְּמִשְׁמָר: וַיַּחַלְמוּ חֲלוֹם שְׁנֵיהֶם אִישׁ חֲלֹמוֹ בְּלַיְלָה אֶחָד אִישׁ

כְּפִתְרוֹן חֲלֹמוֹ הַמַּשְׁקֶה וְהָאֹפֶה אֲשֶׁר לְמֶלֶךְ מִצְרַיִם אֲשֶׁר אֲסוּרִים בְּבֵית

ו־ז הַסֹּהַר: וַיָּבֹא אֲלֵיהֶם יוֹסֵף בַּבֹּקֶר וַיַּרְא אֹתָם וְהִנָּם זֹעֲפִים: וַיִּשְׁאַל אֶת־

סְרִיסֵי פַרְעֹה אֲשֶׁר אִתּוֹ בְמִשְׁמַר בֵּית אֲדֹנָיו לֵאמֹר מַדּוּעַ פְּנֵיכֶם רָעִים

ח הַיּוֹם: וַיֹּאמְרוּ אֵלָיו חֲלוֹם חָלַמְנוּ וּפֹתֵר אֵין אֹתוֹ וַיֹּאמֶר אֲלֵהֶם יוֹסֵף

39:8-9. His sense of right and wrong was so clear that he did not even consider her pleadings. To her, however, he gave an explanation, trying to convince her to stop pestering him.

39:19. That he did not have Joseph killed was because of his affection for Joseph; because God protected Joseph; or because — knowing Joseph's righteousness — he doubted his wife's story (*Ibn Ezra; Ramban*). According to the *Yalkut*, Potiphar's daughter Asenath swore to him that

Joseph was innocent and told him what really happened. In this merit, she was privileged to eventually marry Joseph [see 41:50].

40:1. In the case of the cupbearer, a fly was found in Pharaoh's goblet of wine, while in the case of the baker, a pebble was found in the king's bread (*Rashi* from *Midrash*). Eventually Pharaoh pardoned the cupbearer because the fly fell in accidentally, but not the baker, for had he sifted the flour properly, he would have discovered the pebble.

"Lie with me." [8] *But he adamantly refused;* * *he said to his master's wife, "Look — with me here, my master concerns himself about nothing in the house, and whatever he has he placed in my custody.* [9] *There is no one greater in this house than I, and he has denied me nothing but you, since you are his wife; how then can I perpetrate this great evil and have sinned against God!"*

[10] *And so it was — just as she coaxed Joseph day after day, so he would not listen to her to lie beside her, to be with her.* [11] *Then there was an opportune day when he entered the house to do his work — no man of the household staff being there in the house —* [12] *that she caught hold of him by his garment, saying, "Lie with me!" But he left his garment in her hand, and he fled, and went outside.*

Potiphar's wife slanders Joseph

[13] *When she saw that he had left his garment in her hand and fled outside,* [14] *she called out to the men of her household and spoke to them saying, "Look! He brought us a Hebrew man to sport with us! He came to lie with me but I called out with a loud scream.* [15] *And when he heard that I raised my voice and screamed, he left his garment beside me, fled, and went outside!"*

[16] *She kept his garment beside her until his master came home.* [17] *Then she told him a similar account saying, "The Hebrew slave whom you brought to us came to me to sport with me.* [18] *But it happened that when I raised my voice and screamed, he left his garment beside me, and ran outside."*

[19] *And it was, when his master heard his wife's words which she spoke to him, saying, "Your slave did things like these to me," his anger flared up.* * [20] *Then Joseph's master took him and placed him in the prison — the place where the king's prisoners were confined — and he remained there in prison.*

[21] HASHEM *was with Joseph, and He endowed him with charisma, and He put his favor in the eyes of the prison warden.* [22] *The prison warden placed all inmates of the prison in Joseph's custody, and everything that was done there, he would accomplish.* [23] *The prison warden did not scrutinize anything that was in his charge inasmuch as* HASHEM *was with him; and whatever he did* HASHEM *made successful.*

40

[1] *A*nd it happened after these things that the cupbearer of the king of Egypt and the baker transgressed against their master, against the king of Egypt.* [2] *Pharaoh was enraged at his two courtiers, the Chamberlain of the Cupbearers and the Chamberlain of the Bakers.* [3] *And he placed them in the ward of the house of the Chamberlain of the Butchers, into the prison, the place where Joseph was confined.* [4] *The Chamberlain of the Butchers appointed Joseph to be with them, and he attended them and they remained in the ward for a period of days.*

The cupbearer and the baker: Their dreams and Joseph's interpretations

[5] *The two of them dreamt a dream, each one had his dream on the same night, each one according to the interpretation of his dream — the cupbearer and the baker of the king of Egypt who were confined in the prison.*

[6] *Joseph came to them in the morning. He saw them and behold! they were aggrieved.*

[7] *And he asked Pharaoh's courtiers who were with him in the ward of his master's house, saying, "Why do you appear downcast today?"* [8] *And they said to him, "We dreamt a dream, but there is no interpreter for it." So Joseph said to*

ט הֲלוֹא לֵאלֹהִים פִּתְרֹנִים סַפְּרוּ־נָא לִי: וַיְסַפֵּר שַׂר־הַמַּשְׁקִים אֶת־חֲלֹמוֹ

י לְיוֹסֵף וַיֹּאמֶר לוֹ בַּחֲלוֹמִי וְהִנֵּה־גֶפֶן לְפָנָי: וּבַגֶּפֶן שְׁלֹשָׁה שָׂרִיגִם וְהִוא

יא כְפֹרַחַת עָלְתָה נִצָּהּ הִבְשִׁילוּ אַשְׁכְּלֹתֶיהָ עֲנָבִים: וְכוֹס פַּרְעֹה בְּיָדִי וָאֶקַּח אֶת־הָעֲנָבִים וָאֶשְׂחַט אֹתָם אֶל־כּוֹס פַּרְעֹה וָאֶתֵּן אֶת־הַכּוֹס עַל־כַּף

יב פַּרְעֹה: וַיֹּאמֶר לוֹ יוֹסֵף זֶה פִּתְרֹנוֹ שְׁלֹשֶׁת הַשָּׂרִגִים שְׁלֹשֶׁת יָמִים הֵם:

יג בְּעוֹד ׀ שְׁלֹשֶׁת יָמִים יִשָּׂא פַרְעֹה אֶת־רֹאשֶׁךָ וַהֲשִׁיבְךָ עַל־כַּנֶּךָ וְנָתַתָּ

יד כוֹס־פַּרְעֹה בְּיָדוֹ כַּמִּשְׁפָּט הָרִאשׁוֹן אֲשֶׁר הָיִיתָ מַשְׁקֵהוּ: כִּי אִם־זְכַרְתַּנִי אִתְּךָ כַּאֲשֶׁר יִיטַב לָךְ וְעָשִׂיתָ־נָּא עִמָּדִי חָסֶד וְהִזְכַּרְתַּנִי אֶל־פַּרְעֹה

טו וְהוֹצֵאתַנִי מִן־הַבַּיִת הַזֶּה: כִּי־גֻנֹּב גֻּנַּבְתִּי מֵאֶרֶץ הָעִבְרִים וְגַם־פֹּה לֹא־

טז עָשִׂיתִי מְאוּמָה כִּי־שָׂמוּ אֹתִי בַּבּוֹר: וַיַּרְא שַׂר־הָאֹפִים כִּי טוֹב פָּתָר וַיֹּאמֶר אֶל־יוֹסֵף אַף־אֲנִי בַּחֲלוֹמִי וְהִנֵּה שְׁלֹשָׁה סַלֵּי חֹרִי עַל־רֹאשִׁי:

יז וּבַסַּל הָעֶלְיוֹן מִכֹּל מַאֲכַל פַּרְעֹה מַעֲשֵׂה אֹפֶה וְהָעוֹף אֹכֵל אֹתָם מִן־הַסַּל

יח מֵעַל רֹאשִׁי: וַיַּעַן יוֹסֵף וַיֹּאמֶר זֶה פִּתְרֹנוֹ שְׁלֹשֶׁת הַסַּלִּים שְׁלֹשֶׁת יָמִים

יט הֵם: בְּעוֹד ׀ שְׁלֹשֶׁת יָמִים יִשָּׂא פַרְעֹה אֶת־רֹאשְׁךָ מֵעָלֶיךָ וְתָלָה אוֹתְךָ

כ עַל־עֵץ וְאָכַל הָעוֹף אֶת־בְּשָׂרְךָ מֵעָלֶיךָ: וַיְהִי ׀ בַּיּוֹם הַשְּׁלִישִׁי יוֹם הֻלֶּדֶת אֶת־פַּרְעֹה וַיַּעַשׂ מִשְׁתֶּה לְכָל־עֲבָדָיו וַיִּשָּׂא אֶת־רֹאשׁ ׀ שַׂר הַמַּשְׁקִים

כא וְאֶת־רֹאשׁ שַׂר הָאֹפִים בְּתוֹךְ עֲבָדָיו: וַיָּשֶׁב אֶת־שַׂר הַמַּשְׁקִים עַל־

כב מַשְׁקֵהוּ וַיִּתֵּן הַכּוֹס עַל־כַּף פַּרְעֹה: וְאֵת שַׂר הָאֹפִים תָּלָה כַּאֲשֶׁר פָּתַר

כג לָהֶם יוֹסֵף: וְלֹא־זָכַר שַׂר־הַמַּשְׁקִים אֶת־יוֹסֵף וַיִּשְׁכָּחֵהוּ: פפפ

קי"ב פסוקים. יב"ק סימן.

פרשת מקץ

מפטיר

Haftaras
Vayeishev:
p. 1358.
On
Chanukah
Maftir:
p. 340-342
Haftarah:
p. 1408

מא א־ב וַיְהִי מִקֵּץ שְׁנָתַיִם יָמִים וּפַרְעֹה חֹלֵם וְהִנֵּה עֹמֵד עַל־הַיְאֹר: וְהִנֵּה מִן־הַיְאֹר עֹלֹת שֶׁבַע פָּרוֹת יְפוֹת מַרְאֶה וּבְרִיאֹת בָּשָׂר וַתִּרְעֶינָה בָּאָחוּ:

ג וְהִנֵּה שֶׁבַע פָּרוֹת אֲחֵרוֹת עֹלוֹת אַחֲרֵיהֶן מִן־הַיְאֹר רָעוֹת מַרְאֶה

ד וְדַקּוֹת בָּשָׂר וַתַּעֲמֹדְנָה אֵצֶל הַפָּרוֹת עַל־שְׂפַת הַיְאֹר: וַתֹּאכַלְנָה הַפָּרוֹת רָעוֹת הַמַּרְאֶה וְדַקֹּת הַבָּשָׂר אֵת שֶׁבַע הַפָּרוֹת יְפֹת הַמַּרְאֶה וְהַבְּרִיאֹת

ה וַיִּיקַץ פַּרְעֹה: וַיִּישָׁן וַיַּחֲלֹם שֵׁנִית וְהִנֵּה ׀ שֶׁבַע שִׁבֳּלִים עֹלוֹת בְּקָנֶה

ו אֶחָד בְּרִיאוֹת וְטֹבוֹת: וְהִנֵּה שֶׁבַע שִׁבֳּלִים דַּקּוֹת וּשְׁדוּפֹת קָדִים צֹמְחוֹת

ז אַחֲרֵיהֶן: וַתִּבְלַעְנָה הַשִּׁבֳּלִים הַדַּקּוֹת אֵת שֶׁבַע הַשִּׁבֳּלִים הַבְּרִיאוֹת

ח וְהַמְּלֵאוֹת וַיִּיקַץ פַּרְעֹה וְהִנֵּה חֲלוֹם: וַיְהִי בַבֹּקֶר וַתִּפָּעֶם רוּחוֹ וַיִּשְׁלַח וַיִּקְרָא אֶת־כָּל־חַרְטֻמֵּי מִצְרַיִם וְאֶת־כָּל־חֲכָמֶיהָ וַיְסַפֵּר פַּרְעֹה

◄§ **Parashas Mikeitz**

41:1-7. The time had come to free Joseph and begin the chain of events that would bring Jacob and his family to Egypt to fulfill the last part of the prophecy to Abraham, that his offspring would be subjugated and persecuted

(15:13-16). The events of this *Sidrah* began two years to the day after the release of the Chamberlain of the Cupbearers — a total of twelve years since Joseph was imprisoned. At this point, Joseph was almost 30 years old, Jacob 120, and Isaac 180. Isaac died about this time.

them, "Do not interpretations belong to God? Relate it to me, if you please."

⁹ Then the Chamberlain of the Cupbearers recounted his dream to Joseph and said to him, "In my dream — behold! there was a grapevine in front of me! ¹⁰ On the grapevine were three tendrils; and it was as though it budded — its blossoms bloomed and its clusters ripened into grapes. ¹¹ And Pharaoh's cup was in my hand and I took the grapes, pressed them into Pharaoh's cup, and I placed the cup on Pharaoh's palm."

¹² Joseph said to him, "This is its interpretation: The three tendrils are three days. ¹³ In another three days Pharaoh will lift up your head and will restore you to your post, and you will place Pharaoh's cup in his hand as was the former practice when you were his cupbearer. ¹⁴ If only you would think of me with yourself when he benefits you, and you will do me a kindness, if you please, and mention me to Pharaoh, then you would take me out of this building. ¹⁵ For indeed I was kidnaped from the land of the Hebrews, and even here I have done nothing for them to have put me in the pit."

¹⁶ The Chamberlain of the Bakers saw that he had interpreted well, so he said to Joseph, "I, too! In my dream — behold! three wicker baskets were on my head. ¹⁷ And in the uppermost basket were all kinds of Pharaoh's food — baker's handiwork — and the birds were eating them from the basket above my head."

¹⁸ Joseph responded and said, "This is its interpretation: The three baskets are three days. ¹⁹ In three days Pharaoh will lift your head from you and hang you on a tree; birds will eat your flesh from you."

²⁰ And it was on the third day, Pharaoh's birthday, that he made a feast for all his servants and he counted the Chamberlain of the Cupbearers and the Chamberlain of the Bakers among his servants. ²¹ He restored the Chamberlain of the Cupbearers to his cupbearing and he placed the cup on Pharaoh's palm. ²² But he hanged the Chamberlain of the Bakers, just as Joseph had interpreted to them.

²³ Yet the Chamberlain of the Cupbearers did not remember Joseph, but he forgot him.

PARASHAS MIKEITZ

41

Pharaoh's dream

¹ It happened at the end of two years to the day: Pharaoh was dreaming that behold! — he was standing over the River, ² when behold! out of the River there emerged seven cows, of beautiful appearance and robust flesh, and they were grazing in the marshland. ³ Then behold! — seven other cows emerged after them out of the River — of ugly appearance and gaunt flesh; and they stood next to the cows on the bank of the River. ⁴ The cows of ugly appearance and gaunt flesh ate the seven cows of beautiful appearance and robust, and Pharaoh awoke. ⁵ He fell asleep and dreamt a second time, and behold! seven ears of grain were sprouting on a single stalk — healthy and good. ⁶ And behold! seven ears, thin, and scorched by the east wind, were growing after them. ⁷ Then the thin ears swallowed up the seven healthy and full ears; Pharaoh awoke and behold! — it had been a dream.

⁸ And it was in the morning: His spirit was agitated, so he sent and summoned all the necromancers of Egypt and all its wise men; Pharaoh related

---

41:2. The symbolism of Pharaoh's dream is clear: Since famine and abundance in Egypt depend on the overflow of the Nile, Pharaoh saw the cows coming up from the River. That the fat cows remained near the River symbol- ized that the ensuing prosperity would be limited to Egypt, but the lean cows, which alluded to years of famine, did not remain at the riverbank, suggesting that the famine would be very widespread (*Ramban*).

ט לָהֶם אֶת־חֲלֹמוֹ וְאֵין־פּוֹתֵר אוֹתָם לְפַרְעֹה: וַיְדַבֵּר שַׂר הַמַּשְׁקִים אֶת־

י פַּרְעֹה לֵאמֹר אֶת־חֲטָאַי אֲנִי מַזְכִּיר הַיּוֹם: פַּרְעֹה קָצַף עַל־עֲבָדָיו וַיִּתֵּן

יא אֹתִי בְּמִשְׁמַר בֵּית שַׂר הַטַּבָּחִים אֹתִי וְאֵת שַׂר הָאֹפִים: וַנַּחַלְמָה חֲלוֹם

יב בְּלַיְלָה אֶחָד אֲנִי וָהוּא אִישׁ כְּפִתְרוֹן חֲלֹמוֹ חָלָמְנוּ: וְשָׁם אִתָּנוּ נַעַר עִבְרִי

עֶבֶד לְשַׂר הַטַּבָּחִים וַנְּסַפֶּר־לוֹ וַיִּפְתָּר־לָנוּ אֶת־חֲלֹמֹתֵינוּ אִישׁ כַּחֲלֹמוֹ

יג פָּתָר: וַיְהִי כַּאֲשֶׁר פָּתַר־לָנוּ כֵּן הָיָה אֹתִי הֵשִׁיב עַל־כַּנִּי וְאֹתוֹ תָלָה:

יד וַיִּשְׁלַח פַּרְעֹה וַיִּקְרָא אֶת־יוֹסֵף וַיְרִיצֻהוּ מִן־הַבּוֹר וַיְגַלַּח וַיְחַלֵּף שִׂמְלֹתָיו

טו וַיָּבֹא אֶל־פַּרְעֹה: וַיֹּאמֶר פַּרְעֹה אֶל־יוֹסֵף חֲלוֹם חָלַמְתִּי וּפֹתֵר אֵין אֹתוֹ

שני

טז וַאֲנִי שָׁמַעְתִּי עָלֶיךָ לֵאמֹר תִּשְׁמַע חֲלוֹם לִפְתֹּר אֹתוֹ: וַיַּעַן יוֹסֵף אֶת־

יז פַּרְעֹה לֵאמֹר בִּלְעָדָי אֱלֹהִים יַעֲנֶה אֶת־שְׁלוֹם פַּרְעֹה: וַיְדַבֵּר פַּרְעֹה אֶל־

יח יוֹסֵף בַּחֲלֹמִי הִנְנִי עֹמֵד עַל־שְׂפַת הַיְאֹר: וְהִנֵּה מִן־הַיְאֹר עֹלֹת שֶׁבַע

יט פָּרוֹת בְּרִיאוֹת בָּשָׂר וִיפֹת תֹּאַר וַתִּרְעֶינָה בָּאָחוּ: וְהִנֵּה שֶׁבַע־פָּרוֹת

אֲחֵרוֹת עֹלוֹת אַחֲרֵיהֶן דַּלּוֹת וְרָעוֹת תֹּאַר מְאֹד וְרַקּוֹת בָּשָׂר לֹא־רָאִיתִי

כ כָהֵנָּה בְּכָל־אֶרֶץ מִצְרַיִם לָרֹעַ: וַתֹּאכַלְנָה הַפָּרוֹת הָרַקּוֹת וְהָרָעוֹת אֵת

כא שֶׁבַע הַפָּרוֹת הָרִאשֹׁנוֹת הַבְּרִיאֹת: וַתָּבֹאנָה אֶל־קִרְבֶּנָה וְלֹא נוֹדַע כִּי־

כב בָאוּ אֶל־קִרְבֶּנָה וּמַרְאֵיהֶן רַע כַּאֲשֶׁר בַּתְּחִלָּה וָאִיקָץ: וָאֵרֶא בַּחֲלֹמִי

כג וְהִנֵּה שֶׁבַע שִׁבֳּלִים עֹלֹת בְּקָנֶה אֶחָד מְלֵאֹת וְטֹבוֹת: וְהִנֵּה שֶׁבַע שִׁבֳּלִים

כד צְנֻמוֹת דַּקּוֹת שְׁדֻפוֹת קָדִים צֹמְחוֹת אַחֲרֵיהֶם: וַתִּבְלַעְןָ הַשִּׁבֳּלִים הַדַּקֹּת

כה אֵת שֶׁבַע הַשִּׁבֳּלִים הַטֹּבוֹת וָאֹמַר אֶל־הַחַרְטֻמִּים וְאֵין מַגִּיד לִי: וַיֹּאמֶר

יוֹסֵף אֶל־פַּרְעֹה חֲלוֹם פַּרְעֹה אֶחָד הוּא אֵת אֲשֶׁר הָאֱלֹהִים עֹשֶׂה הִגִּיד

כו לְפַרְעֹה: שֶׁבַע פָּרֹת הַטֹּבֹת שֶׁבַע שָׁנִים הֵנָּה וְשֶׁבַע הַשִּׁבֳּלִים הַטֹּבֹת

שֶׁבַע שָׁנִים הֵנָּה חֲלוֹם אֶחָד הוּא: וְשֶׁבַע הַפָּרוֹת הָרַקּוֹת וְהָרָעֹת הָעֹלֹת

כז אַחֲרֵיהֶן שֶׁבַע שָׁנִים הֵנָּה וְשֶׁבַע הַשִּׁבֳּלִים הָרֵקוֹת שְׁדֻפוֹת הַקָּדִים יִהְיוּ

כח שֶׁבַע שְׁנֵי רָעָב: הוּא הַדָּבָר אֲשֶׁר דִּבַּרְתִּי אֶל־פַּרְעֹה אֲשֶׁר הָאֱלֹהִים

כט עֹשֶׂה הֶרְאָה אֶת־פַּרְעֹה: הִנֵּה שֶׁבַע שָׁנִים בָּאוֹת שָׂבָע גָּדוֹל בְּכָל־אֶרֶץ

ל מִצְרָיִם: וְקָמוּ שֶׁבַע שְׁנֵי רָעָב אַחֲרֵיהֶן וְנִשְׁכַּח כָּל־הַשָּׂבָע בְּאֶרֶץ

לא מִצְרָיִם וְכִלָּה הָרָעָב אֶת־הָאָרֶץ: וְלֹא־יִוָּדַע הַשָּׂבָע בָּאָרֶץ מִפְּנֵי הָרָעָב

לב הַהוּא אַחֲרֵי־כֵן כִּי־כָבֵד הוּא מְאֹד: וְעַל הִשָּׁנוֹת הַחֲלוֹם אֶל־פַּרְעֹה

לג פַּעֲמָיִם כִּי־נָכוֹן הַדָּבָר מֵעִם הָאֱלֹהִים וּמְמַהֵר הָאֱלֹהִים לַעֲשֹׂתוֹ: וְעַתָּה

לד יֵרֶא פַרְעֹה אִישׁ נָבוֹן וְחָכָם וִישִׁיתֵהוּ עַל־אֶרֶץ מִצְרָיִם: יַעֲשֶׂה פַרְעֹה

וְיַפְקֵד פְּקִדִים עַל־הָאָרֶץ וְחִמֵּשׁ אֶת־אֶרֶץ מִצְרַיִם בְּשֶׁבַע שְׁנֵי הַשָּׂבָע:

41:14-16. Joseph is summoned, on Rosh Hashanah in the year 2230 from Creation (*Rosh Hashanah* 10b).

41:25-36. Joseph's interpretation is accepted. Joseph offered a dazzling interpretation and went so far as to tell Pharaoh that the dream itself indicated the course of

action to be taken. The result was unprecedented: A foreigner, a youth, a slave — everything derogatory that the cupbearer said about Joseph — became the ruler of the land. When God wills something, nature and politics alike yield to make the impossible possible.

his dream to them, but none could interpret them for Pharaoh.

The Chamberlain of the Cupbearers "remembers Joseph"

⁹ *Then the Chamberlain of the Cupbearers spoke up before Pharaoh, saying, "My transgressions do I mention today.* ¹⁰ *Pharaoh had become incensed at his servants and placed me in the ward of the house of the Chamberlain of the Butchers — me and the Chamberlain of the Bakers.* ¹¹ *We dreamt a dream on the same night, I and he; each one according to the interpretation of his dream did we dream.* ¹² *And there, with us, was a Hebrew youth, a slave of the Chamberlain of the Butchers; we related it to him, and he interpreted our dreams for us; he interpreted for each in accordance with his dream.* ¹³ *And it was that just as he interpreted for us so did it happen; me he restored to my post and him he hanged."*

Joseph is summoned

¹⁴ *So Pharaoh sent and summoned Joseph, and they rushed him from the dungeon. He shaved and changed his clothes, and he came to Pharaoh.* ¹⁵ *And Pharaoh said to Joseph, "I dreamt a dream, but no one can interpret it. Now I heard it said of you that you comprehend a dream to interpret it."*

¹⁶ *Joseph answered Pharaoh, saying, "That is beyond me; it is God Who will respond with Pharaoh's welfare."*

Pharaoh recapitulates his dream

¹⁷ *Then Pharaoh said to Joseph, "In my dream, behold! — I was standing upon the bank of the River.* ¹⁸ *And behold, out of the River there emerged seven cows, of robust flesh and beautiful form, and they were grazing in the marshland.* ¹⁹ *Suddenly, seven other cows emerged after them — scrawny and of very inferior form and of emaciated flesh; I have never seen inferiority like theirs in all the land of Egypt.* ²⁰ *And the emaciated and inferior cows ate up the first seven healthy cows.* ²¹ *They came inside them, but it was not apparent that they had come inside them, for their appearance remained as inferior as at first. Then I awoke.* ²² *I then saw in my dream: Behold! — seven ears of grain were sprouting on a single stalk — full and good.* ²³ *And suddenly! — seven ears of grain, withered, thin and scorched by the east wind were growing after them.* ²⁴ *Then the thin ears of grain swallowed up the seven good ears; I said this to the necromancers, but no one could explain it to me."*

Joseph's interpretation

²⁵ *Joseph said to Pharaoh, "The dream of Pharaoh is a single one; what God is about to do, He has told to Pharaoh:* ²⁶ *The seven good cows are seven years, and the seven good ears are seven years; it is a single dream.* ²⁷ *Now, the seven emaciated and bad cows who emerged after them — they are seven years; as are the seven emaciated ears scorched by the east wind. There shall be seven years of famine.* ²⁸ *It is this matter that I have spoken to Pharaoh: What God is about to do He has shown to Pharaoh.*

²⁹ *"Behold! — seven years are coming — a great abundance throughout all the land of Egypt.* ³⁰ *Then seven years of famine will arise after them and all the abundance in the land of Egypt will be forgotten; the famine will ravage the land.* ³¹ *And the abundance will be unknown in the land in the face of the subsequent famine — for it will be terribly severe.* ³² *As for the repetition of the dream to Pharaoh — two times — it is because the matter stands ready before God, and God is hastening to accomplish it.*

³³ *"Now let Pharaoh seek out a discerning and wise man and set him over the land of Egypt.* ³⁴ *Let Pharaoh proceed and let him appoint overseers on the land, and he shall prepare the land of Egypt during the seven years of abundance.*

לה וְיִקְבְּצוּ אֶת־כָּל־אֹכֶל הַשָּׁנִים הַטֹּבֹת הַבָּאֹת הָאֵלֶּה וְיִצְבְּרוּ־בָר תַּחַת
יַד־פַּרְעֹה אֹכֶל בֶּעָרִים וְשָׁמָרוּ: וְהָיָה הָאֹכֶל לְפִקָּדוֹן לָאָרֶץ לְשֶׁבַע
שְׁנֵי הָרָעָב אֲשֶׁר תִּהְיֶיןָ בְּאֶרֶץ מִצְרָיִם וְלֹא־תִכָּרֵת הָאָרֶץ בָּרָעָב:
לז-לח וַיִּיטַב הַדָּבָר בְּעֵינֵי פַרְעֹה וּבְעֵינֵי כָּל־עֲבָדָיו: וַיֹּאמֶר פַּרְעֹה אֶל־עֲבָדָיו
שלישי   הֲנִמְצָא כָזֶה אִישׁ אֲשֶׁר רוּחַ אֱלֹהִים בּוֹ: וַיֹּאמֶר פַּרְעֹה אֶל־יוֹסֵף אַחֲרֵי
מ הוֹדִיעַ אֱלֹהִים אוֹתְךָ אֶת־כָּל־זֹאת אֵין־נָבוֹן וְחָכָם כָּמוֹךָ: אַתָּה תִּהְיֶה
מא עַל־בֵּיתִי וְעַל־פִּיךָ יִשַּׁק כָּל־עַמִּי רַק הַכִּסֵּא אֶגְדַּל מִמֶּךָּ: וַיֹּאמֶר פַּרְעֹה
מב אֶל־יוֹסֵף רְאֵה נָתַתִּי אֹתְךָ עַל כָּל־אֶרֶץ מִצְרָיִם: וַיָּסַר פַּרְעֹה אֶת־
טַבַּעְתּוֹ מֵעַל יָדוֹ וַיִּתֵּן אֹתָהּ עַל־יַד יוֹסֵף וַיַּלְבֵּשׁ אֹתוֹ בִּגְדֵי־שֵׁשׁ וַיָּשֶׂם
מג רְבִד הַזָּהָב עַל־צַוָּארוֹ: וַיַּרְכֵּב אֹתוֹ בְּמִרְכֶּבֶת הַמִּשְׁנֶה אֲשֶׁר־לוֹ וַיִּקְרְאוּ
מד לְפָנָיו אַבְרֵךְ וְנָתוֹן אֹתוֹ עַל כָּל־אֶרֶץ מִצְרָיִם: וַיֹּאמֶר פַּרְעֹה אֶל־יוֹסֵף
אֲנִי פַרְעֹה וּבִלְעָדֶיךָ לֹא־יָרִים אִישׁ אֶת־יָדוֹ וְאֶת־רַגְלוֹ בְּכָל־אֶרֶץ
מה מִצְרָיִם: וַיִּקְרָא פַרְעֹה שֵׁם־יוֹסֵף צָפְנַת פַּעְנֵחַ וַיִּתֶּן־לוֹ אֶת־אָסְנַת בַּת־
מו פּוֹטִי פֶרַע כֹּהֵן אֹן לְאִשָּׁה וַיֵּצֵא יוֹסֵף עַל־אֶרֶץ מִצְרָיִם: וְיוֹסֵף בֶּן־
שְׁלֹשִׁים שָׁנָה בְּעָמְדוֹ לִפְנֵי פַּרְעֹה מֶלֶךְ־מִצְרָיִם וַיֵּצֵא יוֹסֵף מִלִּפְנֵי פַרְעֹה
מז וַיַּעֲבֹר בְּכָל־אֶרֶץ מִצְרָיִם: וַתַּעַשׂ הָאָרֶץ בְּשֶׁבַע שְׁנֵי הַשָּׂבָע לִקְמָצִים:
מח וַיִּקְבֹּץ אֶת־כָּל־אֹכֶל ׀ שֶׁבַע שָׁנִים אֲשֶׁר הָיוּ בְּאֶרֶץ מִצְרַיִם וַיִּתֶּן־אֹכֶל
מט בֶּעָרִים אֹכֶל שְׂדֵה־הָעִיר אֲשֶׁר סְבִיבֹתֶיהָ נָתַן בְּתוֹכָהּ: וַיִּצְבֹּר יוֹסֵף בָּר
כְּחוֹל הַיָּם הַרְבֵּה מְאֹד עַד כִּי־חָדַל לִסְפֹּר כִּי־אֵין מִסְפָּר: וּלְיוֹסֵף יֻלַּד
נ שְׁנֵי בָנִים בְּטֶרֶם תָּבוֹא שְׁנַת הָרָעָב אֲשֶׁר יָלְדָה־לּוֹ אָסְנַת בַּת־פּוֹטִי פֶרַע
נא כֹּהֵן אוֹן: וַיִּקְרָא יוֹסֵף אֶת־שֵׁם הַבְּכוֹר מְנַשֶּׁה כִּי־נַשַּׁנִי אֱלֹהִים אֶת־כָּל־
נב עֲמָלִי וְאֵת כָּל־בֵּית אָבִי: וְאֵת שֵׁם הַשֵּׁנִי קָרָא אֶפְרָיִם כִּי־הִפְרַנִי אֱלֹהִים
נג בְּאֶרֶץ עָנְיִי: וַתִּכְלֶינָה שֶׁבַע שְׁנֵי הַשָּׂבָע אֲשֶׁר הָיָה בְּאֶרֶץ מִצְרָיִם:
רביעי
נד וַתְּחִלֶּינָה שֶׁבַע שְׁנֵי הָרָעָב לָבוֹא כַּאֲשֶׁר אָמַר יוֹסֵף וַיְהִי רָעָב בְּכָל־
נה הָאֲרָצוֹת וּבְכָל־אֶרֶץ מִצְרַיִם הָיָה לָחֶם: וַתִּרְעַב כָּל־אֶרֶץ מִצְרַיִם וַיִּצְעַק
הָעָם אֶל־פַּרְעֹה לַלָּחֶם וַיֹּאמֶר פַּרְעֹה לְכָל־מִצְרַיִם לְכוּ אֶל־יוֹסֵף
נו אֲשֶׁר־יֹאמַר לָכֶם תַּעֲשׂוּ: וְהָרָעָב הָיָה עַל כָּל־פְּנֵי הָאָרֶץ וַיִּפְתַּח יוֹסֵף
אֶת־כָּל־אֲשֶׁר בָּהֶם וַיִּשְׁבֹּר לְמִצְרַיִם וַיֶּחֱזַק הָרָעָב בְּאֶרֶץ מִצְרָיִם:
נז וְכָל־הָאָרֶץ בָּאוּ מִצְרַיְמָה לִשְׁבֹּר אֶל־יוֹסֵף כִּי־חָזַק הָרָעָב בְּכָל־הָאָרֶץ:

41:43. As Joseph rode on the chariot, the servants called out before him *Avrech*, which is a composite of two words: אַב, *father* [i.e., counselor; mentor], to the *rach*, which means king in Aramaic (Rashi; Onkelos). Another interpretation is that the word is a composite of *av* (father) in wisdom, though *rach* (tender) in years (*Midrash*).

41:45. *Zaphenath-paneah*, i.e., מְפָרֵשׁ הַצְּפוּנוֹת, *he who explains what is hidden* (Rashi; Rashbam). Appointees to a high position were customarily assigned a name com-

mensurate with their new eminence.

Daughter of Poti-phera. Poti-phera is identical with Potiphar [see above 37:36], Joseph's former master. That he allowed his daughter to marry Joseph vindicated Joseph in the eyes of the Egyptians from the charge that he had assaulted Potiphar's wife (*Alshich*).

41:50-52. Joseph's children: Manasseh and Ephraim. As the daughter of aristocracy married to a foreign slave and former convict who owed his position to Pharaoh's

³⁵ And let them gather all the food of those approaching good years; let them amass grain under Pharaoh's authority for food in the cities, and safeguard it. ³⁶ The food will be a reserve for the land against the seven years of famine which will befall the land of Egypt, so that the land will not perish in the famine."

Joseph becomes Viceroy ³⁷ The matter appeared good in Pharaoh's eyes and in the eyes of all his servants. ³⁸ Pharaoh said to his servants, "Could we find another like him — a man in whom is the spirit of God?"

³⁹ Then Pharaoh said to Joseph, "Since God has informed you of all this, there can be no one so discerning and wise as you. ⁴⁰ You shall be in charge of my palace and by your command shall all my people be sustained; only by the throne shall I outrank you."

⁴¹ Then Pharaoh said to Joseph, "See! I have placed you in charge of all the land of Egypt." ⁴² And Pharaoh removed his ring from his hand and put it on Joseph's hand. He then had him dressed in garments of fine linen and he placed a gold chain upon his neck. ⁴³ He also had him ride in his second chariot and they proclaimed before him: "Avrech!"* Thus, he appointed him over all the land of Egypt.

⁴⁴ Pharaoh said to Joseph, "I am Pharaoh. And without you no man may lift up his hand or foot in all the land of Egypt." ⁴⁵ Pharaoh called Joseph's name Zaphenath-paneah* and he gave him Asenath daughter of Poti-phera,* Chief of On, for a wife. Thus, Joseph emerged in charge of the land of Egypt. ⁴⁶ Now Joseph was thirty years old when he stood before Pharaoh king of Egypt; Joseph left Pharaoh's presence and he passed through the entire land of Egypt.

Joseph's plan is implemented ⁴⁷ The earth produced during the seven years of abundance by the handfuls. ⁴⁸ He gathered all food of the seven years that came to pass in the land of Egypt, and he placed food in the cities; the food of the field around each city he placed within it. ⁴⁹ Joseph amassed grain like the sand of the sea in great abundance until he ceased counting, for there was no number.

Joseph's children: Manasseh and Ephraim ⁵⁰ Now to Joseph were born two sons — when the year of famine had not yet set in — whom Asenath daughter of Poti-phera, Chief of On, bore to him. ⁵¹ Joseph called the name of the firstborn Manasseh for, "God has made me forget all my hardship and all my father's household." ⁵² And the name of the second he called Ephraim for, "God has made me fruitful in the land of my suffering."

The famine devastates Egypt ⁵³ The seven years of abundance that came to pass in the land of Egypt ended. ⁵⁴ And the seven years of famine began approaching just as Joseph had said. There was famine in all the lands, but in all the land of Egypt there was bread. ⁵⁵ When all the land of Egypt hungered, the people cried out to Pharaoh for bread. So Pharaoh said to all of Egypt, "Go to Joseph. Whatever he tells you, you should do." ⁵⁶ When the famine spread over all the face of the earth, Joseph opened all the containers and sold provisions to Egypt; and the famine became severe in the land of Egypt. ⁵⁷ All the earth came to Egypt to Joseph to buy provisions, for the famine had become severe in all the earth.

---

whim, Asenath might well have dominated the home atmosphere, in which case the children would have been *hers*. The Torah tells us, therefore, that she bore children to *him*, i.e., she adopted Joseph's spiritual and moral outlook. To be the only Jew in Egypt, yet to raise children who remain the model after whom Jewish parents bless their children — *may God make you like Ephraim and Manasseh* (48:20) — is no small privilege (*R' Hirsch*).

א וַיַּ֣רְא יַעֲקֹ֔ב כִּ֥י יֶשׁ־שֶׁ֖בֶר בְּמִצְרָ֑יִם וַיֹּ֤אמֶר יַעֲקֹב֙ לְבָנָ֔יו לָ֖מָּה תִּתְרָאֽוּ:
ב וַיֹּ֕אמֶר הִנֵּ֣ה שָׁמַ֔עְתִּי כִּ֥י יֶשׁ־שֶׁ֖בֶר בְּמִצְרָ֑יִם רְדוּ־שָׁ֨מָּה֙ וְשִׁבְרוּ־לָ֣נוּ
ג מִשָּׁ֔ם וְנִֽחְיֶ֖ה וְלֹ֥א נָמֽוּת: וַיֵּֽרְד֥וּ אֲחֵֽי־יוֹסֵ֖ף עֲשָׂרָ֑ה לִשְׁבֹּ֥ר בָּ֖ר מִמִּצְרָֽיִם:
ד וְאֶת־בִּנְיָמִין֙ אֲחִ֣י יוֹסֵ֔ף לֹֽא־שָׁלַ֥ח יַעֲקֹ֖ב אֶת־אֶחָ֑יו כִּ֣י אָמַ֔ר פֶּן־יִקְרָאֶ֖נּוּ
ה אָסֽוֹן: וַיָּבֹ֨אוּ֙ בְּנֵ֣י יִשְׂרָאֵ֔ל לִשְׁבֹּ֖ר בְּת֣וֹךְ הַבָּאִ֑ים כִּֽי־הָיָ֥ה הָרָעָ֖ב בְּאֶ֥רֶץ
ו כְּנָֽעַן: וְיוֹסֵ֗ף ה֚וּא הַשַּׁלִּ֣יט עַל־הָאָ֔רֶץ ה֥וּא הַמַּשְׁבִּ֖יר לְכָל־עַ֣ם הָאָ֑רֶץ
ז וַיָּבֹ֨אוּ֙ אֲחֵ֣י יוֹסֵ֔ף וַיִּשְׁתַּֽחֲווּ־ל֥וֹ אַפַּ֖יִם אָֽרְצָה: וַיַּ֤רְא יוֹסֵף֙ אֶת־אֶחָ֔יו
וַיַּכִּרֵ֑ם וַיִּתְנַכֵּ֨ר אֲלֵיהֶ֜ם וַיְדַבֵּ֧ר אִתָּ֣ם קָשׁ֗וֹת וַיֹּ֤אמֶר אֲלֵהֶם֙ מֵאַ֣יִן בָּאתֶ֔ם
ח וַיֹּ֣אמְר֔וּ מֵאֶ֥רֶץ כְּנַ֖עַן לִשְׁבָּר־אֹֽכֶל: וַיַּכֵּ֥ר יוֹסֵ֖ף אֶת־אֶחָ֑יו וְהֵ֖ם לֹ֥א הִכִּרֻֽהוּ:
ט וַיִּזְכֹּ֣ר יוֹסֵ֔ף אֵ֚ת הַחֲלֹמ֔וֹת אֲשֶׁ֥ר חָלַ֖ם לָהֶ֑ם וַיֹּ֤אמֶר אֲלֵהֶם֙ מְרַגְּלִ֣ים אַתֶּ֔ם
י לִרְא֛וֹת אֶת־עֶרְוַ֥ת הָאָ֖רֶץ בָּאתֶֽם: וַיֹּאמְר֥וּ אֵלָ֖יו לֹ֣א אֲדֹנִ֑י וַעֲבָדֶ֖יךָ בָּ֥אוּ
יא לִשְׁבָּר־אֹֽכֶל: כֻּלָּ֕נוּ בְּנֵ֥י אִישׁ־אֶחָ֖ד נָ֑חְנוּ כֵּנִ֣ים אֲנַ֔חְנוּ לֹא־הָי֥וּ עֲבָדֶ֖יךָ
יב-יג מְרַגְּלִֽים: וַיֹּ֖אמֶר אֲלֵהֶ֑ם לֹ֕א כִּֽי־עֶרְוַ֥ת הָאָ֖רֶץ בָּאתֶ֥ם לִרְאֽוֹת: וַיֹּאמְר֗וּ
שְׁנֵ֣ים עָשָׂר֩ עֲבָדֶ֨יךָ אַחִ֧ים ׀ אֲנַ֛חְנוּ בְּנֵ֥י אִישׁ־אֶחָ֖ד בְּאֶ֣רֶץ כְּנָ֑עַן וְהִנֵּ֨ה
יד הַקָּטֹ֤ן אֶת־אָבִ֨ינוּ֙ הַיּ֔וֹם וְהָאֶחָ֖ד אֵינֶֽנּוּ: וַיֹּ֥אמֶר אֲלֵהֶ֖ם יוֹסֵ֑ף ה֚וּא אֲשֶׁ֣ר
טו דִּבַּ֣רְתִּי אֲלֵכֶ֔ם לֵאמֹ֖ר מְרַגְּלִ֥ים אַתֶּֽם: בְּזֹ֖את תִּבָּחֵ֑נוּ חֵ֤י פַרְעֹה֙ אִם־
טז תֵּצְא֣וּ מִזֶּ֔ה כִּ֧י אִם־בְּב֛וֹא אֲחִיכֶ֥ם הַקָּטֹ֖ן הֵֽנָּה: שִׁלְח֨וּ מִכֶּ֜ם אֶחָד֮ וְיִקַּ֣ח
אֶת־אֲחִיכֶם֒ וְאַתֶּם֙ הֵאָ֣סְר֔וּ וְיִבָּֽחֲנוּ֙ דִּבְרֵיכֶ֔ם הַאֱמֶ֖ת אִתְּכֶ֑ם וְאִם־לֹ֕א
יז חֵ֥י פַרְעֹ֖ה כִּ֥י מְרַגְּלִ֥ים אַתֶּֽם: וַיֶּאֱסֹ֥ף אֹתָ֛ם אֶל־מִשְׁמָ֖ר שְׁלֹ֥שֶׁת יָמִֽים:
יח וַיֹּ֨אמֶר אֲלֵהֶ֤ם יוֹסֵף֙ בַּיּ֣וֹם הַשְּׁלִישִׁ֔י זֹ֥את עֲשׂ֖וּ וִֽחְי֑וּ אֶת־הָאֱלֹהִ֖ים אֲנִ֥י
יט יָרֵֽא: אִם־כֵּנִ֣ים אַתֶּ֔ם אֲחִיכֶ֣ם אֶחָ֔ד יֵאָסֵ֖ר בְּבֵ֣ית מִשְׁמַרְכֶ֑ם וְאַתֶּם֙ לְכ֣וּ
כ הָבִ֔יאוּ שֶׁ֖בֶר רַעֲב֣וֹן בָּֽתֵּיכֶֽם: וְאֶת־אֲחִיכֶ֤ם הַקָּטֹן֙ תָּבִ֣יאוּ אֵלַ֔י וְיֵאָֽמְנ֥וּ
כא דִבְרֵיכֶ֖ם וְלֹ֣א תָמ֑וּתוּ וַיַּעֲשׂוּ־כֵֽן: וַיֹּאמְר֞וּ אִ֣ישׁ אֶל־אָחִ֗יו אֲבָל֮ אֲשֵׁמִ֣ים ׀
אֲנַחְנוּ֮ עַל־אָחִינוּ֒ אֲשֶׁ֨ר רָאִ֜ינוּ צָרַ֥ת נַפְשׁ֛וֹ בְּהִתְחַֽנְנ֥וֹ אֵלֵ֖ינוּ וְלֹ֣א שָׁמָ֑עְנוּ
כב עַל־כֵּן֙ בָּ֣אָה אֵלֵ֔ינוּ הַצָּרָ֖ה הַזֹּֽאת: וַיַּ֩עַן֩ רְאוּבֵ֨ן אֹתָ֜ם לֵאמֹ֗ר הֲלוֹא֩ אָמַ֨רְתִּי
אֲלֵיכֶ֧ם ׀ לֵאמֹ֛ר אַל־תֶּחֶטְא֥וּ בַיֶּ֖לֶד וְלֹ֣א שְׁמַעְתֶּ֑ם וְגַם־דָּמ֖וֹ הִנֵּ֥ה נִדְרָֽשׁ:

42:1-4. Jacob sends his sons to Egypt. It was the second year of the famine (*Seder Olam*), and although Jacob's family still had provisions, Jacob was concerned for the future and dispatched his sons to Egypt.

42:2. Jacob did not use the verb לְכוּ, go, but רְדוּ [*go down*], thereby alluding to the 210 years they would be exiled in Egypt. [The *gematria* (numerical value) of the word רְדוּ is 210: ר = 200; ד = 4; וּ = 6.] (*Rashi*).

⋙ **Joseph conceals his identity and persecutes his brothers.** Joseph knew that his dreams were prophecies that had to be fulfilled, and he knew that he had to do all in his power to bring about that result. That is why the Torah stresses that when he saw his brothers he remembered the dreams. He also knew that the two dreams had to be

fulfilled in sequence, the first and then the second. So far, *ten* brothers had bowed, but his first dream called for all *eleven*; therefore, he had to engineer Benjamin's appearance with the brothers, and only then could Jacob come, in fulfillment of the second dream.

R' Hirsch maintains that Joseph needed two tests before he could be reunited with his brothers: (a) Was their old rancor against him solely motivated by how they perceived the underlying motive of his dreams, or were they resentful of Rachel's special place in their father's affections? If the latter, then they could be as much of a menace to Benjamin as they had been to Joseph. And if Joseph had revealed himself now, when they were in his power, he would never know how much hatred lingered beneath the surface. Therefore, he wanted to put them

42

Jacob sends his sons to Egypt

¹ **J**acob perceived that there were provisions in Egypt; so Jacob said to his sons, "Why do you make yourselves conspicuous?" ² And he said, "Behold, I have heard that there are provisions in Egypt; go down* there and purchase for us from there, that we may live and not die." ³ So Joseph's brothers — ten of them — went down to buy grain from Egypt. ⁴ But Benjamin, Joseph's brother, Jacob did not send along with his brothers, for he said, "Lest disaster befall him." ⁵ So the sons of Israel came to buy provisions among the arrivals, for the famine was in the land of Canaan.

The brothers bow to Joseph

⁶ Now Joseph — he was the viceroy over the land, he was the provider to all the people of the land. Joseph's brothers came and they bowed to him, faces to the ground.

⁷ Joseph saw his brothers and he recognized them, but he acted like a stranger toward them and spoke with them harshly. He asked them, "From where have you come?" And they said, "From the land of Canaan to buy food." ⁸ Joseph recognized his brothers, but they did not recognize him.

⁹ Joseph recalled the dreams that he dreamed about them, so he said to them, "You are spies! To see the land's nakedness have you come!"

¹⁰ They answered him, "Not so, my lord! For your servants have come to buy food. ¹¹ All of us, sons of one man are we; we are truthful people; your servants have never been spies."

¹² And he said to them, "No! But the land's nakedness have you come to see."

¹³ And they replied, "We, your servants, are twelve brothers, the sons of one man in the land of Canaan. The youngest is now with our father and one is gone."

Joseph stands his ground, but offers his brothers a way out

¹⁴ But Joseph said to them, "It is just as I have declared to you saying, 'You are spies!' ¹⁵ By this shall you be tested: By Pharaoh's life you will not leave here unless your youngest brother comes here. ¹⁶ Send one of you, and let him fetch your brother while you shall remain imprisoned, so that your words may be tested whether truth is with you; but if not, by Pharaoh's life — surely you are spies!" ¹⁷ Then he herded them into a ward for a three-day period.

¹⁸ Joseph said to them on the third day, "Do this and live; I fear God:* ¹⁹ If you are truthful people, let one of your brothers be imprisoned in your place of confinement while you go and bring provisions for the hunger of your households. ²⁰ Then bring your youngest brother to me so your words will be verified and you will not die." And they did so.

The brothers' regret

²¹ They then said to one another, "Indeed we are guilty concerning our brother inasmuch as we saw his heartfelt anguish when he pleaded with us and we paid no heed; that is why this anguish has come upon us."

²² Reuben spoke up to them, saying, "Did I not speak to you saying, 'Do not sin against the boy,' but you would not listen! And his blood as well — behold! — is being avenged."

---

into a situation where they could gain their own freedom at the expense of Benjamin's, and see how they would react. (b) If they hated Joseph when he merely *dreamed* of being a king, how much more would they hate him now that he truly had the power of life and death over them? Therefore, he wanted to show them that, after the long chain of events, he truly loved them and had only their good interests at heart. This, he was sure, would melt their

long-standing resentment.

42:18. Accordingly, I will not keep *all* of you imprisoned while your families are starving. I will let you bring provisions home, and detain only one of you as a hostage (*Ramban*, *Sforno*).

42:21-22. The brothers' regret. The brothers became introspective and recognized their lot as a Divine punishment for their cruel treatment of Joseph.

כג-כד וְהֵם לֹא יָדְעוּ כִּי שֹׁמֵעַ יוֹסֵף כִּי הַמֵּלִיץ בֵּינֹתָם: וַיִּסֹּב מֵעֲלֵיהֶם וַיֵּבְךְּ
וַיָּשָׁב אֲלֵהֶם וַיְדַבֵּר אֲלֵהֶם וַיִּקַּח מֵאִתָּם אֶת־שִׁמְעוֹן וַיֶּאֱסֹר אֹתוֹ
כה לְעֵינֵיהֶם: וַיְצַו יוֹסֵף וַיְמַלְאוּ אֶת־כְּלֵיהֶם בָּר וּלְהָשִׁיב כַּסְפֵּיהֶם אִישׁ
כו אֶל־שַׂקּוֹ וְלָתֵת לָהֶם צֵדָה לַדָּרֶךְ וַיַּעַשׂ לָהֶם כֵּן: וַיִּשְׂאוּ אֶת־שִׁבְרָם
כז עַל־חֲמֹרֵיהֶם וַיֵּלְכוּ מִשָּׁם: וַיִּפְתַּח הָאֶחָד אֶת־שַׂקּוֹ לָתֵת מִסְפּוֹא
כח לַחֲמֹרוֹ בַּמָּלוֹן וַיַּרְא אֶת־כַּסְפּוֹ וְהִנֵּה־הוּא בְּפִי אַמְתַּחְתּוֹ: וַיֹּאמֶר אֶל־
אֶחָיו הוּשַׁב כַּסְפִּי וְגַם הִנֵּה בְאַמְתַּחְתִּי וַיֵּצֵא לִבָּם וַיֶּחֶרְדוּ אִישׁ אֶל־אָחִיו
כט לֵאמֹר מַה־זֹּאת עָשָׂה אֱלֹהִים לָנוּ: וַיָּבֹאוּ אֶל־יַעֲקֹב אֲבִיהֶם אַרְצָה
ל כְּנָעַן וַיַּגִּידוּ לוֹ אֵת כָּל־הַקֹּרֹת אֹתָם לֵאמֹר: דִּבֶּר הָאִישׁ אֲדֹנֵי הָאָרֶץ
לא אִתָּנוּ קָשׁוֹת וַיִּתֵּן אֹתָנוּ כִּמְרַגְּלִים אֶת־הָאָרֶץ: וַנֹּאמֶר אֵלָיו כֵּנִים אֲנָחְנוּ
לב לֹא הָיִינוּ מְרַגְּלִים: שְׁנֵים־עָשָׂר אֲנַחְנוּ אַחִים בְּנֵי אָבִינוּ הָאֶחָד אֵינֶנּוּ
לג וְהַקָּטֹן הַיּוֹם אֶת־אָבִינוּ בְּאֶרֶץ כְּנָעַן: וַיֹּאמֶר אֵלֵינוּ הָאִישׁ אֲדֹנֵי הָאָרֶץ
בְּזֹאת אֵדַע כִּי כֵנִים אַתֶּם אֲחִיכֶם הָאֶחָד הַנִּיחוּ אִתִּי וְאֶת־רַעֲבוֹן
לד בָּתֵּיכֶם קְחוּ וָלֵכוּ: וְהָבִיאוּ אֶת־אֲחִיכֶם הַקָּטֹן אֵלַי וְאֵדְעָה כִּי לֹא
מְרַגְּלִים אַתֶּם כִּי כֵנִים אַתֶּם אֶת־אֲחִיכֶם אֶתֵּן לָכֶם וְאֶת־הָאָרֶץ תִּסְחָרוּ:
לה וַיְהִי הֵם מְרִיקִים שַׂקֵּיהֶם וְהִנֵּה־אִישׁ צְרוֹר־כַּסְפּוֹ בְּשַׂקּוֹ וַיִּרְאוּ אֶת־
לו צְרֹרוֹת כַּסְפֵּיהֶם הֵמָּה וַאֲבִיהֶם וַיִּירָאוּ: וַיֹּאמֶר אֲלֵהֶם יַעֲקֹב אֲבִיהֶם
אֹתִי שִׁכַּלְתֶּם יוֹסֵף אֵינֶנּוּ וְשִׁמְעוֹן אֵינֶנּוּ וְאֶת־בִּנְיָמִן תִּקָּחוּ עָלַי הָיוּ
לז כֻלָּנָה: וַיֹּאמֶר רְאוּבֵן אֶל־אָבִיו לֵאמֹר אֶת־שְׁנֵי בָנַי תָּמִית אִם־לֹא
לח אֲבִיאֶנּוּ אֵלֶיךָ תְּנָה אֹתוֹ עַל־יָדִי וַאֲנִי אֲשִׁיבֶנּוּ אֵלֶיךָ: וַיֹּאמֶר לֹא־יֵרֵד בְּנִי
עִמָּכֶם כִּי־אָחִיו מֵת וְהוּא לְבַדּוֹ נִשְׁאָר וּקְרָאָהוּ אָסוֹן בַּדֶּרֶךְ אֲשֶׁר
מג א תֵּלְכוּ־בָהּ וְהוֹרַדְתֶּם אֶת־שֵׂיבָתִי בְּיָגוֹן שְׁאוֹלָה: וְהָרָעָב כָּבֵד בָּאָרֶץ:
ב וַיְהִי כַּאֲשֶׁר כִּלּוּ לֶאֱכֹל אֶת־הַשֶּׁבֶר אֲשֶׁר הֵבִיאוּ מִמִּצְרָיִם וַיֹּאמֶר
ג אֲלֵיהֶם אֲבִיהֶם שֻׁבוּ שִׁבְרוּ־לָנוּ מְעַט־אֹכֶל: וַיֹּאמֶר אֵלָיו יְהוּדָה
לֵאמֹר הָעֵד הֵעִד בָּנוּ הָאִישׁ לֵאמֹר לֹא־תִרְאוּ פָנַי בִּלְתִּי אֲחִיכֶם אִתְּכֶם:
ד-ה אִם־יֶשְׁךָ מְשַׁלֵּחַ אֶת־אָחִינוּ אִתָּנוּ נֵרְדָה וְנִשְׁבְּרָה לְךָ אֹכֶל: וְאִם־אֵינְךָ
מְשַׁלֵּחַ לֹא נֵרֵד כִּי־הָאִישׁ אָמַר אֵלֵינוּ לֹא־תִרְאוּ פָנַי בִּלְתִּי אֲחִיכֶם
ו אִתְּכֶם: וַיֹּאמֶר יִשְׂרָאֵל לָמָה הֲרֵעֹתֶם לִי לְהַגִּיד לָאִישׁ הַעוֹד לָכֶם אָח:
ז וַיֹּאמְרוּ שָׁאוֹל שָׁאַל־הָאִישׁ לָנוּ וּלְמוֹלַדְתֵּנוּ לֵאמֹר הַעוֹד אֲבִיכֶם חַי
הֲיֵשׁ לָכֶם אָח וַנַּגֶּד־לוֹ עַל־פִּי הַדְּבָרִים הָאֵלֶּה הֲיָדוֹעַ נֵדַע כִּי יֹאמַר
ח הוֹרִידוּ אֶת־אֲחִיכֶם: וַיֹּאמֶר יְהוּדָה אֶל־יִשְׂרָאֵל אָבִיו שִׁלְחָה הַנַּעַר
אִתִּי וְנָקוּמָה וְנֵלֵכָה וְנִחְיֶה וְלֹא נָמוּת גַּם־אֲנַחְנוּ גַם־אַתָּה גַם־טַפֵּנוּ:

42:35. They knew that money could have been left in one sack by a careless official, but the money in *all* their sacks could not possibly be an oversight. It was obvious that there was a plot against them (*Alshich*).

Joseph chooses his hostage

²³ Now they did not know that Joseph understood, for an interpreter was between them. ²⁴ He turned away from them and wept; he returned to them and spoke to them; he took Simeon from them and imprisoned him before their eyes.

Joseph sends them back — with their money

²⁵ Joseph commanded that they fill their vessels with grain, and to return their money, each one's to his sack, and to give them provisions for the journey. And so he did for them. ²⁶ Then they loaded their purchase onto their donkeys and departed from there.

²⁷ When the one of them opened his sack to give feed to his donkey at the inn, he saw his money, and behold! — it was in the mouth of his sack. ²⁸ So he said to his brothers, "My money has been returned and behold! it, too, is in my sack!" Their hearts sank, and they turned trembling one to another, saying, "What is this that God has done to us?"

The dialogue with Jacob

²⁹ They came to Jacob their father in the land of Canaan and they told him of all that had happened to them, saying: ³⁰ "The man, the lord of the land, spoke harshly to us and considered us as if we were spying out the land. ³¹ But we said to him, 'We are truthful men: We have never been spies! ³² We are twelve brothers, sons of our father. One is gone and the youngest is now with our father in the land of Canaan.' ³³ Then the man, the lord of the land, said to us, 'By this I will ascertain whether you are truthful people: One of your brothers, leave with me; and what is needed for the hunger of your households take and go. ³⁴ And bring your youngest brother to me so I will know that you are not spies, but truthful people. I will restore your brother to you and you will be free to circulate about the land.' "

³⁵ Then, as they were emptying their sacks, behold! — every man's bundle of money was in his sack. When they and their father saw their bundles of money, they were terrified. * ³⁶ Their father Jacob said to them, "I am the one whom you bereaved! Joseph is gone, Simeon is gone, and now you would take away Benjamin? Upon me has it all fallen!"

³⁷ Then Reuben told his father, saying, "You may slay my two sons if I fail to bring him back to you. Put him in my care and I will return him to you."

³⁸ But he said, "My son shall not go down with you, for his brother is dead and he alone is left. Should disaster befall him on the journey which you shall take, then you will have brought down my hoariness in sorrow to the grave."

43 ¹ The famine was severe in the land. ² When they had finished eating the provisions which they had brought from Egypt their father said to them, "Go back, buy us some food." ³ But Judah told him, saying, "The man sternly warned us saying, 'Do not see my face unless your brother is with you.' ⁴ If you are ready to send our brother with us, we will go down and buy you food. ⁵ But if you do not send, we will not go down, for the man said to us, 'Do not see my face unless your brother is with you.' "

The brothers request that Jacob send Benjamin to Egypt

⁶ Then Israel said, "Why did you treat me so ill by telling the man that you had another brother?"

⁷ And they said, "The man persistently asked about us and our relatives saying, 'Is your father still alive? Have you a brother?' and we responded to him according to these words; could we possibly have known that he would say, 'Bring your brother down'?"

Judah's guarantee

⁸ Then Judah said to Israel his father, "Send the lad with me, and let us arise and go, so we will live and not die, we as well as you as well as our children.

ט אָנֹכִי אֶעֶרְבֶנּוּ מִיָּדִי תְּבַקְשֶׁנּוּ אִם־לֹא הֲבִיאֹתִיו אֵלֶיךָ וְהִצַּגְתִּיו לְפָנֶיךָ
י וְחָטָאתִי לְךָ כָּל־הַיָּמִים: כִּי לוּלֵא הִתְמַהְמָהְנוּ כִּי־עַתָּה שַׁבְנוּ זֶה פַעֲמָיִם:
יא וַיֹּאמֶר אֲלֵהֶם יִשְׂרָאֵל אֲבִיהֶם אִם־כֵּן | אֵפוֹא זֹאת עֲשׂוּ קְחוּ מִזִּמְרַת הָאָרֶץ בִּכְלֵיכֶם וְהוֹרִידוּ לָאִישׁ מִנְחָה מְעַט צֳרִי וּמְעַט דְּבַשׁ נְכֹאת וָלֹט בָּטְנִים
יב וּשְׁקֵדִים: וְכֶסֶף מִשְׁנֶה קְחוּ בְיֶדְכֶם וְאֶת־הַכֶּסֶף הַמּוּשָׁב בְּפִי אַמְתְּחֹתֵיכֶם
יג תָּשִׁיבוּ בְיֶדְכֶם אוּלַי מִשְׁגֶּה הוּא: וְאֶת־אֲחִיכֶם קָחוּ וְקוּמוּ שׁוּבוּ אֶל־הָאִישׁ:
יד וְאֵל שַׁדַּי יִתֵּן לָכֶם רַחֲמִים לִפְנֵי הָאִישׁ וְשִׁלַּח לָכֶם אֶת־אֲחִיכֶם אַחֵר וְאֶת־
טו בִּנְיָמִין וַאֲנִי כַּאֲשֶׁר שָׁכֹלְתִּי שָׁכָלְתִּי: וַיִּקְחוּ הָאֲנָשִׁים אֶת־הַמִּנְחָה הַזֹּאת וּמִשְׁנֶה־כֶּסֶף לָקְחוּ בְיָדָם וְאֶת־בִּנְיָמִן וַיָּקֻמוּ וַיֵּרְדוּ מִצְרַיִם וַיַּעַמְדוּ לִפְנֵי
ששי טז יוֹסֵף: וַיַּרְא יוֹסֵף אִתָּם אֶת־בִּנְיָמִין וַיֹּאמֶר לַאֲשֶׁר עַל־בֵּיתוֹ הָבֵא אֶת־
יז הָאֲנָשִׁים הַבָּיְתָה וּטְבֹחַ טֶבַח וְהָכֵן כִּי אִתִּי יֹאכְלוּ הָאֲנָשִׁים בַּצָּהֳרָיִם: וַיַּעַשׂ
יח הָאִישׁ כַּאֲשֶׁר אָמַר יוֹסֵף וַיָּבֵא הָאִישׁ אֶת־הָאֲנָשִׁים בֵּיתָה יוֹסֵף: וַיִּירְאוּ הָאֲנָשִׁים כִּי הוּבְאוּ בֵּית יוֹסֵף וַיֹּאמְרוּ עַל־דְּבַר הַכֶּסֶף הַשָּׁב בְּאַמְתְּחֹתֵינוּ בַּתְּחִלָּה אֲנַחְנוּ מוּבָאִים לְהִתְגֹּלֵל עָלֵינוּ וּלְהִתְנַפֵּל עָלֵינוּ וְלָקַחַת אֹתָנוּ
יט לַעֲבָדִים וְאֶת־חֲמֹרֵינוּ: וַיִּגְּשׁוּ אֶל־הָאִישׁ אֲשֶׁר עַל־בֵּית יוֹסֵף וַיְדַבְּרוּ
כ אֵלָיו פֶּתַח הַבָּיִת: וַיֹּאמְרוּ בִּי אֲדֹנִי יָרֹד יָרַדְנוּ בַּתְּחִלָּה לִשְׁבָּר־אֹכֶל:
כא וַיְהִי כִּי־בָאנוּ אֶל־הַמָּלוֹן וַנִּפְתְּחָה אֶת־אַמְתְּחֹתֵינוּ וְהִנֵּה כֶסֶף־אִישׁ בְּפִי
כב אַמְתַּחְתּוֹ כַּסְפֵּנוּ בְּמִשְׁקָלוֹ וַנָּשֶׁב אֹתוֹ בְּיָדֵנוּ: וְכֶסֶף אַחֵר הוֹרַדְנוּ בְיָדֵנוּ
כג לִשְׁבָּר־אֹכֶל לֹא יָדַעְנוּ מִי־שָׂם כַּסְפֵּנוּ בְּאַמְתְּחֹתֵינוּ: וַיֹּאמֶר שָׁלוֹם לָכֶם אַל־תִּירָאוּ אֱלֹהֵיכֶם וֵאלֹהֵי אֲבִיכֶם נָתַן לָכֶם מַטְמוֹן בְּאַמְתְּחֹתֵיכֶם
כד כַּסְפְּכֶם בָּא אֵלָי וַיּוֹצֵא אֲלֵהֶם אֶת־שִׁמְעוֹן: וַיָּבֵא הָאִישׁ אֶת־הָאֲנָשִׁים
כה בֵּיתָה יוֹסֵף וַיִּתֶּן־מַיִם וַיִּרְחֲצוּ רַגְלֵיהֶם וַיִּתֵּן מִסְפּוֹא לַחֲמֹרֵיהֶם: וַיָּכִינוּ אֶת־הַמִּנְחָה עַד־בּוֹא יוֹסֵף בַּצָּהֳרָיִם כִּי שָׁמְעוּ כִּי־שָׁם יֹאכְלוּ לָחֶם:
כו וַיָּבֹא יוֹסֵף הַבַּיְתָה וַיָּבִיאוּ לוֹ אֶת־הַמִּנְחָה אֲשֶׁר־בְּיָדָם הַבָּיְתָה וַיִּשְׁתַּחֲווּ־
כז לוֹ אָרְצָה: וַיִּשְׁאַל לָהֶם לְשָׁלוֹם וַיֹּאמֶר הֲשָׁלוֹם אֲבִיכֶם הַזָּקֵן אֲשֶׁר אֲמַרְתֶּם
כח הַעוֹדֶנּוּ חָי: וַיֹּאמְרוּ שָׁלוֹם לְעַבְדְּךָ לְאָבִינוּ עוֹדֶנּוּ חָי וַיִּקְּדוּ °וַיִּשְׁתַּחוּ
כט [°וַיִּשְׁתַּחֲווּ ק׳]: וַיִּשָּׂא עֵינָיו וַיַּרְא אֶת־בִּנְיָמִין אָחִיו בֶּן־אִמּוֹ וַיֹּאמֶר הֲזֶה
שביעי ל אֲחִיכֶם הַקָּטֹן אֲשֶׁר אֲמַרְתֶּם אֵלָי וַיֹּאמַר אֱלֹהִים יָחְנְךָ בְּנִי: וַיְמַהֵר יוֹסֵף כִּי־נִכְמְרוּ רַחֲמָיו אֶל־אָחִיו וַיְבַקֵּשׁ לִבְכּוֹת וַיָּבֹא הַחַדְרָה וַיֵּבְךְ שָׁמָּה:

43:9. In his commentary to ArtScroll *Bereishis*, R' Meir Zlotowitz suggests why Judah's offer were more acceptable than Reuben's. Only a father could realize the magnitude of the loss of two of his children. Of all the brothers, only Judah who had lost two children (38:7,10) could appreciate his father's grief. Therefore, when Judah accepted responsibility for Benjamin's welfare, Jacob acquiesced.

43:14. See 17:1 for a discussion of this Divine Name. It is a conjunction of שֶׁ־דַּי, *Who is sufficient* or *enough*. He is sufficient in His mercies and His hand is sufficient to give you whatever you need. "May He Who said to the world, 'Enough,' now declare that my troubles are enough. I have had no rest since my youth; trouble with Laban, trouble with Esau, the troubles of Rachel, Dinah, Joseph, Simeon — and now Benjamin" (*Rashi*).

⁹ *I will personally guarantee him;* * *of my own hand you can demand him. If I do not bring him back to you and stand him before you, then I will have sinned to you for all time.* ¹⁰ *For had we not delayed, by now we could have returned twice."*

¹¹ *Israel their father said to them, "If it must be so, then do this: Take of the land's glory in your baggage and bring it down to the man as a tribute — a bit of balsam, a bit of honey, wax, lotus, pistachios, and almonds.* ¹² *And take with you double the money, and the money that was returned in the mouth of your sacks return in your hands; perhaps it was an oversight.* ¹³ *Take your brother, and arise, return to the man.* ¹⁴ *And may El Shaddai* * *grant you mercy before the man that he may release to you your other brother as well as Benjamin. And as for me, as I have been bereaved, so I am bereaved."*

¹⁵ *So the men took this tribute and they took double money in their hand, as well as Benjamin. They set out and went down to Egypt and stood before Joseph.*

Joseph sees Benjamin and tests his brothers' sincerity

¹⁶ *Joseph saw Benjamin with them; so he said to the one in charge of his house, "Bring the men into the house. Have meat slaughtered, and prepare it, for with me will these men dine at noon."* ¹⁷ *The man did as Joseph said, and the man brought the men to Joseph's house.* ¹⁸ *But the men became frightened when they were brought to Joseph's house, and they said, "Because of the money replaced in our sacks originally are we being brought, so that a charge can be fabricated against us, that it crash down on us, and that we be taken as slaves along with our donkeys."*

¹⁹ *They approached the man who was in charge of Joseph's house and spoke to him at the entrance of the house.* ²⁰ *And they said, "If you please, my lord: We had indeed come down originally to buy food.* ²¹ *But it happened, when we arrived at the inn and opened our sacks, that behold! each one's money was in the mouth of his sack; it was our own money in its full amount, so we have brought it back in our hand.* ²² *We have also brought other money down in our hand to buy food; we do not know who put our money in our sacks."*

²³ *He replied, "Peace with you, fear not. Your God and the God of your father has put a hidden treasure in your sacks. Your payment had reached me." And he brought Simeon out to them.*

²⁴ *Then the man brought the men into Joseph's house. He provided water and they washed their feet, and he gave feed to their donkeys.* ²⁵ *They prepared the tribute for when Joseph would come at noon, for they had heard that they were to eat a meal there.*

²⁶ *When Joseph came to the house they brought the tribute that was in their hands to him to the house, and they prostrated themselves to him toward the ground.* ²⁷ *He inquired after their welfare, and he said, "Is your aged father of whom you spoke at peace? Is he still alive?"*

²⁸ *They replied, "Your servant our father is at peace; he still lives," and they bowed and prostrated themselves.*

²⁹ *Then he lifted up his eyes and saw his brother Benjamin, his mother's son, so he said, "Is this your 'little' brother of whom you spoke to me?" And he said, "God be gracious to you, my son."*

³⁰ *Then Joseph rushed because his compassion for his brother had been stirred and he wanted to weep; so he went into the room and wept there.*

לא-לב וַיִּרְחַץ פָּנָיו וַיֵּצֵא וַיִּתְאַפַּק וַיֹּאמֶר שִׂימוּ לָחֶם: וַיָּשִׂימוּ לוֹ לְבַדּוֹ וְלָהֶם לְבַדָּם וְלַמִּצְרִים הָאֹכְלִים אִתּוֹ לְבַדָּם כִּי לֹא יוּכְלוּן הַמִּצְרִים לֶאֱכֹל

לג אֶת־הָעִבְרִים לֶחֶם כִּי־תוֹעֵבָה הִוא לְמִצְרָיִם: וַיֵּשְׁבוּ לְפָנָיו הַבְּכֹר

לד כִּבְכֹרָתוֹ וְהַצָּעִיר כִּצְעִרָתוֹ וַיִּתְמְהוּ הָאֲנָשִׁים אִישׁ אֶל־רֵעֵהוּ: וַיִּשָּׂא מַשְׂאֹת מֵאֵת פָּנָיו אֲלֵהֶם וַתֵּרֶב מַשְׂאַת בִּנְיָמִן מִמַּשְׂאֹת כֻּלָּם חָמֵשׁ יָדוֹת

מד א וַיִּשְׁתּוּ וַיִּשְׁכְּרוּ עִמּוֹ: וַיְצַו אֶת־אֲשֶׁר עַל־בֵּיתוֹ לֵאמֹר מַלֵּא אֶת־אַמְתְּחֹת הָאֲנָשִׁים אֹכֶל כַּאֲשֶׁר יוּכְלוּן שְׂאֵת וְשִׂים כֶּסֶף־אִישׁ בְּפִי אַמְתַּחְתּוֹ:

ב וְאֶת־גְּבִיעִי גְּבִיעַ הַכֶּסֶף תָּשִׂים בְּפִי אַמְתַּחַת הַקָּטֹן וְאֵת כֶּסֶף שִׁבְרוֹ

ג וַיַּעַשׂ כִּדְבַר יוֹסֵף אֲשֶׁר דִּבֵּר: הַבֹּקֶר אוֹר וְהָאֲנָשִׁים שֻׁלְּחוּ הֵמָּה

ד וַחֲמֹרֵיהֶם: הֵם יָצְאוּ אֶת־הָעִיר לֹא הִרְחִיקוּ וְיוֹסֵף אָמַר לַאֲשֶׁר עַל־בֵּיתוֹ קוּם רְדֹף אַחֲרֵי הָאֲנָשִׁים וְהִשַּׂגְתָּם וְאָמַרְתָּ אֲלֵהֶם לָמָּה שִׁלַּמְתֶּם

ה רָעָה תַּחַת טוֹבָה: הֲלוֹא זֶה אֲשֶׁר יִשְׁתֶּה אֲדֹנִי בּוֹ וְהוּא נַחֵשׁ יְנַחֵשׁ בּוֹ

ו הֲרֵעֹתֶם אֲשֶׁר עֲשִׂיתֶם: וַיַּשִּׂגֵם וַיְדַבֵּר אֲלֵהֶם אֶת־הַדְּבָרִים הָאֵלֶּה:

ז וַיֹּאמְרוּ אֵלָיו לָמָּה יְדַבֵּר אֲדֹנִי כַּדְּבָרִים הָאֵלֶּה חָלִילָה לַעֲבָדֶיךָ מֵעֲשׂוֹת

ח כַּדָּבָר הַזֶּה: הֵן כֶּסֶף אֲשֶׁר מָצָאנוּ בְּפִי אַמְתְּחֹתֵינוּ הֱשִׁיבֹנוּ אֵלֶיךָ מֵאֶרֶץ

ט כְּנָעַן וְאֵיךְ נִגְנֹב מִבֵּית אֲדֹנֶיךָ כֶּסֶף אוֹ זָהָב: אֲשֶׁר יִמָּצֵא אִתּוֹ מֵעֲבָדֶיךָ

י וָמֵת וְגַם־אֲנַחְנוּ נִהְיֶה לַאדֹנִי לַעֲבָדִים: וַיֹּאמֶר גַּם־עַתָּה כְדִבְרֵיכֶם כֶּן

יא הוּא אֲשֶׁר יִמָּצֵא אִתּוֹ יִהְיֶה־לִּי עָבֶד וְאַתֶּם תִּהְיוּ נְקִיִּם: וַיְמַהֲרוּ וַיּוֹרִדוּ

יב אִישׁ אֶת־אַמְתַּחְתּוֹ אָרְצָה וַיִּפְתְּחוּ אִישׁ אַמְתַּחְתּוֹ: וַיְחַפֵּשׂ בַּגָּדוֹל הֵחֵל וּבַקָּטֹן כִּלָּה וַיִּמָּצֵא הַגָּבִיעַ בְּאַמְתַּחַת בִּנְיָמִן: וַיִּקְרְעוּ שִׂמְלֹתָם וַיַּעֲמֹס

יג אִישׁ עַל־חֲמֹרוֹ וַיָּשֻׁבוּ הָעִירָה: וַיָּבֹא יְהוּדָה וְאֶחָיו בֵּיתָה יוֹסֵף וְהוּא

יד עוֹדֶנּוּ שָׁם וַיִּפְּלוּ לְפָנָיו אָרְצָה: וַיֹּאמֶר לָהֶם יוֹסֵף מָה־הַמַּעֲשֶׂה הַזֶּה אֲשֶׁר

טו עֲשִׂיתֶם הֲלוֹא יְדַעְתֶּם כִּי־נַחֵשׁ יְנַחֵשׁ אִישׁ אֲשֶׁר כָּמֹנִי: וַיֹּאמֶר יְהוּדָה מַה־נֹּאמַר לַאדֹנִי מַה־נְּדַבֵּר וּמַה־נִּצְטַדָּק הָאֱלֹהִים מָצָא אֶת־עֲוֹן

טז עֲבָדֶיךָ הִנֶּנּוּ עֲבָדִים לַאדֹנִי גַּם־אֲנַחְנוּ גַּם אֲשֶׁר־נִמְצָא הַגָּבִיעַ בְּיָדוֹ:

יז וַיֹּאמֶר חָלִילָה לִּי מֵעֲשׂוֹת זֹאת הָאִישׁ אֲשֶׁר נִמְצָא הַגָּבִיעַ בְּיָדוֹ הוּא יִהְיֶה־לִּי עָבֶד וְאַתֶּם עֲלוּ לְשָׁלוֹם אֶל־אֲבִיכֶם: ססס

מפטיר

*Haftaras
Mikeitz:*
p. 806.
On
Chanukah:
(on 6th day,
shevii: p. 400)
Maftir: pp.
342-344
Haftarah:
p. 1408;
(on 8th day,
Haftarah:
p. 820).

קמ״ו פסוקים. יחזקיה״ו סימן. אמצי״ה סימן. יהו״ה ל״י עב״ד סימן. ותיבות אלפים כ״ה.

43:16-34. Joseph sees Benjamin and tests his brothers' sincerity. That Joseph was deeply moved by the sight of Benjamin is clear from the next several verses. Nevertheless, he refrained from identifying himself because he still had vital questions: Had the brothers lost their jealousy of Rachel's children? How would they react when he showed favoritism to Benjamin? What would they do when he announced his intention to detain Benjamin as a slave? (*Akeidah*; R' Hirsch).

44:1-10. Benjamin is accused of thievery. The brothers' attitude toward his privileged treatment of Benjamin con-

vinced Joseph that they were no longer spiteful, but would they be ready to fight and sacrifice for the sake of a child of Rachel? To test them, he had Benjamin arrested for theft and sentenced to a lifetime of slavery. Possibly, too, there was enmity between them because Benjamin may have known or suspected what they had done to Joseph (*Ramban*). Thus, Joseph was about to create a situation that was parallel to his own. He had been carted off to slavery because of his brothers; would they now permit Benjamin to become a slave?

44:14. *They fell to the ground before him*, in obeisance.

[31] He washed his face and went out, fortified himself and said, "Serve food." [32] They served him separately and them separately and the Egyptians who ate with him separately, for the Egyptians could not bear to eat food with the Hebrews, it being loathsome to Egyptians. [33] They were seated before him, the firstborn according to his seniority and the youngest according to his youth. The men looked at one another in astonishment.

[34] He had portions that had been set before him served to them, and Benjamin's portion was five times as much as the portion of any of them. They drank and became intoxicated with him.

44

The final test: Benjamin is accused of thievery

[1] Then he instructed the one in charge of his house, saying, "Fill the men's sacks with as much food as they can carry and put each man's money in the mouth of his sack. [2] And my goblet — the silver goblet — place in the mouth of the youngest one's sack along with the money of his purchase." And he followed Joseph's word exactly.

[3] The day dawned and the men were sent off, they and their donkeys. [4] They had left the city, had not gone far, when Joseph said to the one in charge of his house, "Get up, chase after the men; when you overtake them, you are to say to them, 'Why do you repay evil for good? [5] Is this not the one from which my master drinks, and with which he regularly divines? You have done evil in how you acted!' "

[6] He overtook them and spoke those words to them. [7] And they said to him, "Why does my lord say such things? It would be sacrilegious for your servants to do such a thing! [8] Here, look: The money that we found in the mouth of our sacks we brought back to you from the land of Canaan. How then could we have stolen from your master's house any silver or gold? [9] Anyone among your servants with whom it is found shall die, and we also will become slaves to my lord."

[10] He replied, "What you say now is also correct. The one with whom it is found shall be my slave, but the rest of you shall be exonerated."

[11] Hurriedly, each one lowered his sack to the ground, and each one opened his sack. [12] He searched; he began with the oldest and ended with the youngest; and the goblet was found in Benjamin's sack. [13] They rent their garments. Each one reloaded his donkey and they returned to the city.

[14] When Judah arrived with his brothers to Joseph's house, he was still there. They fell to the ground before him. * [15] Joseph said to them, "What is this deed that you have done? Do you not realize that a man like me practices divination!"

Judah, the leader of the brothers, speaks on behalf of all

[16] So Judah said, "What can we say to my lord? How can we speak? And how can we justify ourselves? God has uncovered the sin of your servants. Here we are: We are ready to be slaves to my lord — both we and the one in whose hand the goblet was found."

[17] But he replied, "It would be sacrilegious for me to do this. * The man in whose possession the goblet was found, only he shall be my slave, and as for you — go up in peace to your father."

According to *Tanchuma*, Joseph's dream of the eleven bowing stars [37:9] was now fulfilled.

44:17. In response to Judah's contrite statement that God was punishing the brothers for an old sin, Joseph

replied that he would never punish people for a sin not committed against him. The only guilty party was Benjamin, and only he would be punished. The others would go free (*Sforno*).

פרשת ויגש

יח וַיִּגַּ֨שׁ אֵלָ֜יו יְהוּדָ֗ה וַיֹּ֨אמֶר֙ בִּ֣י אֲדֹנִ֔י יְדַבֶּר־נָ֨א עַבְדְּךָ֤ דָבָר֙ בְּאָזְנֵ֣י אֲדֹנִ֔י
יט וְאַל־יִ֥חַר אַפְּךָ֖ בְּעַבְדֶּ֑ךָ כִּ֥י כָמ֖וֹךָ כְּפַרְעֹֽה: אֲדֹנִ֣י שָׁאַ֔ל אֶת־עֲבָדָ֖יו לֵאמֹ֑ר
כ הֲיֵשׁ־לָכֶ֥ם אָ֖ב אוֹ־אָֽח: וַנֹּ֨אמֶר֙ אֶל־אֲדֹנִ֔י יֶשׁ־לָ֨נוּ֙ אָ֣ב זָקֵ֔ן וְיֶ֥לֶד זְקֻנִ֖ים קָטָ֑ן
כא וְאָחִ֣יו מֵ֗ת וַיִּוָּתֵ֨ר ה֧וּא לְבַדּ֛וֹ לְאִמּ֖וֹ וְאָבִ֥יו אֲהֵבֽוֹ: וַתֹּ֨אמֶר֙ אֶל־עֲבָדֶ֔יךָ
כב הוֹרִדֻ֖הוּ אֵלָ֑י וְאָשִׂ֥ימָה עֵינִ֖י עָלָֽיו: וַנֹּ֨אמֶר֙ אֶל־אֲדֹנִ֔י לֹא־יוּכַ֥ל הַנַּ֖עַר לַעֲזֹ֣ב
כג אֶת־אָבִ֑יו וְעָזַ֥ב אֶת־אָבִ֖יו וָמֵֽת: וַתֹּ֨אמֶר֙ אֶל־עֲבָדֶ֔יךָ אִם־לֹ֥א יֵרֵ֛ד אֲחִיכֶ֥ם
כד הַקָּטֹ֖ן אִתְּכֶ֑ם לֹ֥א תֹסִפ֖וּן לִרְא֥וֹת פָּנָֽי: וַֽיְהִי֙ כִּ֣י עָלִ֔ינוּ אֶל־עַבְדְּךָ֖ אָבִ֑י וַנַּ֨גֶּד־
כה־כו ל֕וֹ אֵ֖ת דִּבְרֵ֥י אֲדֹנִֽי: וַיֹּ֖אמֶר אָבִ֑ינוּ שֻׁ֖בוּ שִׁבְרוּ־לָ֥נוּ מְעַט־אֹֽכֶל: וַנֹּ֕אמֶר לֹ֥א
נוּכַ֖ל לָרֶ֑דֶת אִם־יֵ֩שׁ֩ אָחִ֨ינוּ הַקָּטֹ֤ן אִתָּ֨נוּ֙ וְיָרַ֔דְנוּ כִּי־לֹ֣א נוּכַ֗ל לִרְאוֹת֙ פְּנֵ֣י
כז הָאִ֔ישׁ וְאָחִ֥ינוּ הַקָּטֹ֖ן אֵינֶ֥נּוּ אִתָּֽנוּ: וַיֹּ֛אמֶר עַבְדְּךָ֥ אָבִ֖י אֵלֵ֑ינוּ אַתֶּ֣ם יְדַעְתֶּ֔ם
כח כִּ֥י שְׁנַ֖יִם יָֽלְדָה־לִּ֥י אִשְׁתִּֽי: וַיֵּצֵ֤א הָֽאֶחָד֙ מֵֽאִתִּ֔י וָאֹמַ֕ר אַ֖ךְ טָרֹ֣ף טֹרָ֑ף וְלֹ֥א
כט רְאִיתִ֖יו עַד־הֵֽנָּה: וּלְקַחְתֶּ֧ם גַּם־אֶת־זֶ֛ה מֵעִ֥ם פָּנַ֖י וְקָרָ֑הוּ אָ֕סוֹן וְהֽוֹרַדְתֶּ֧ם
ל אֶת־שֵׂיבָתִ֛י בְּרָעָ֖ה שְׁאֹֽלָה: וְעַתָּ֗ה כְּבֹאִי֙ אֶל־עַבְדְּךָ֣ אָבִ֔י וְהַנַּ֖עַר אֵינֶ֣נּוּ
שני
לא אִתָּ֑נוּ וְנַפְשׁ֖וֹ קְשׁוּרָ֥ה בְנַפְשֽׁוֹ: וְהָיָ֗ה כִּרְאוֹת֛וֹ כִּי־אֵ֥ין הַנַּ֖עַר וָמֵ֑ת וְהוֹרִ֨ידוּ
לב עֲבָדֶ֜יךָ אֶת־שֵׂיבַ֨ת עַבְדְּךָ֥ אָבִ֛ינוּ בְּיָג֖וֹן שְׁאֹֽלָה: כִּ֤י עַבְדְּךָ֙ עָרַ֣ב אֶת־הַנַּ֔עַר
מֵעִ֥ם אָבִ֖י לֵאמֹ֑ר אִם־לֹ֤א אֲבִיאֶ֨נּוּ֙ אֵלֶ֔יךָ וְחָטָ֥אתִי לְאָבִ֖י כָּל־הַיָּמִֽים:
לג וְעַתָּ֗ה יֵֽשֶׁב־נָ֤א עַבְדְּךָ֙ תַּ֣חַת הַנַּ֔עַר עֶ֖בֶד לַֽאדֹנִ֑י וְהַנַּ֖עַר יַ֥עַל עִם־אֶחָֽיו:
לד כִּי־אֵיךְ֙ אֶֽעֱלֶ֣ה אֶל־אָבִ֔י וְהַנַּ֖עַר אֵינֶ֣נּוּ אִתִּ֑י פֶּ֚ן אֶרְאֶ֣ה בָרָ֔ע אֲשֶׁ֥ר יִמְצָ֖א
מה א אֶת־אָבִֽי: וְלֹֽא־יָכֹ֨ל יוֹסֵ֜ף לְהִתְאַפֵּ֗ק לְכֹ֤ל הַנִּצָּבִים֙ עָלָ֔יו וַיִּקְרָ֕א הוֹצִ֥יאוּ
ב כָל־אִ֖ישׁ מֵֽעָלָ֑י וְלֹא־עָ֤מַד אִישׁ֙ אִתּ֔וֹ בְּהִתְוַדַּ֥ע יוֹסֵ֖ף אֶל־אֶחָֽיו: וַיִּתֵּ֥ן אֶת־
ג קֹל֖וֹ בִּבְכִ֑י וַיִּשְׁמְע֣וּ מִצְרַ֔יִם וַיִּשְׁמַ֖ע בֵּ֥ית פַּרְעֹֽה: וַיֹּ֨אמֶר יוֹסֵ֤ף אֶל־אֶחָיו֙
אֲנִ֣י יוֹסֵ֔ף הַע֥וֹד אָבִ֖י חָ֑י וְלֹֽא־יָֽכְל֤וּ אֶחָיו֙ לַֽעֲנ֣וֹת אֹת֔וֹ כִּ֥י נִבְהֲל֖וּ מִפָּנָֽיו:
ד וַיֹּ֨אמֶר יוֹסֵ֧ף אֶל־אֶחָ֛יו גְּשׁוּ־נָ֥א אֵלַ֖י וַיִּגָּ֑שׁוּ וַיֹּ֗אמֶר אֲנִי֙ יוֹסֵ֣ף אֲחִיכֶ֔ם
ה אֲשֶׁר־מְכַרְתֶּ֥ם אֹתִ֖י מִצְרָֽיְמָה: וְעַתָּ֣ה ׀ אַל־תֵּעָ֣צְב֗וּ וְאַל־יִ֨חַר֙ בְּעֵ֣ינֵיכֶ֔ם
ו כִּֽי־מְכַרְתֶּ֥ם אֹתִ֖י הֵ֑נָּה כִּ֣י לְמִֽחְיָ֔ה שְׁלָחַ֥נִי אֱלֹהִ֖ים לִפְנֵיכֶֽם: כִּי־זֶ֛ה
שְׁנָתַ֥יִם הָֽרָעָ֖ב בְּקֶ֣רֶב הָאָ֑רֶץ וְעוֹד֙ חָמֵ֣שׁ שָׁנִ֔ים אֲשֶׁ֥ר אֵֽין־חָרִ֖ישׁ וְקָצִֽיר:
ז וַיִּשְׁלָחֵ֣נִי אֱלֹהִ֗ים לִפְנֵיכֶ֔ם לָשׂ֥וּם לָכֶ֛ם שְׁאֵרִ֖ית בָּאָ֑רֶץ וּלְהַֽחֲי֣וֹת לָכֶ֗ם

⋖§ Parashas Vayigash

44:18-34. Benjamin had been caught with the viceroy's goblet, and the all-powerful Egyptian ruled that Benjamin would have to remain in Egypt as a slave. Only Judah risked his life to intercede. Simple yet eloquent, controlled yet emotional, respectful yet firm, Judah offered *himself* as a slave — not realizing that he was speaking to the very person whom he had once sold into slavery.

44:19. Implicit in Judah's extended recapitulation of the events is a suspicion that the affair of the goblet was a sinister conspiracy against Benjamin and the brothers.

44:24. *Your servant.* In punishment for remaining silent while his father was described in this degrading manner, Joseph lost ten years of his life (*Sotah* 13b).

44:27-28. This passage was not recorded in the original account (43:6-7), in keeping with the rule that the Torah is brief in one place and expansive in another, reserving details for wherever they would be more pertinent.

44:32. Judah explained why he was the only one of all the brothers pleading Benjamin's cause.

PARASHAS VAYIGASH

Judah steps forward

[18] **T**hen Judah approached him and said, "If you please, my lord, may your servant speak a word in my lord's ears and let not your anger flare up at your servant — for you are like Pharaoh. [19] My lord has asked his servants, saying, 'Have you a father or brother?' [20] And we said to my lord, 'We have an old father and a young child of [his] old age; his brother is dead, he alone is left from his mother, and his father loves him.' [21] Then you said to your servants, 'Bring him down to me, and I will set my eye on him.' [22] We said to my lord, 'The youth cannot leave his father, for should he leave his father he will die.' [23] But you said to your servants, 'If your youngest brother does not come down with you, you will not see my face again!'

[24] "And it was, when we went up to your servant my father, * we told him my lord's words; [25] and our father said, 'Go back, buy us some food.' [26] We said, 'We cannot go down; only if our youngest brother is with us, then we will go down, for we cannot see the man's face if our youngest brother is not with us.' [27] Then your servant my father said to us, 'You know that my wife bore me two [sons]. [28] One has left me and I presumed: Alas, he has surely been torn to pieces, for I have not seen him since! [29] So should you take this one, too, from my presence, and disaster befall him, then you will have brought down my hoariness in evil to the grave.'

[30] "And now, if I come to your servant my father and the youth is not with us — since his soul is so bound up with his soul — [31] it will happen that when he sees the youth is missing he will die, and your servants will have brought down the hoariness of your servant our father in sorrow to the grave. [32] For your servant took responsibility for the youth from my father saying, 'If I do not bring him back to you then I will have sinned to my father for all time.' [33] Now, therefore, please let your servant remain instead of the youth as a servant to my lord, and let the youth go up with his brothers. [34] For how can I go up to my father if the youth is not with me, lest I see the evil that will befall my father!"

45

Joseph identifies himself and conciliates his brothers

[1] **N**ow Joseph could not restrain himself in the presence of all who stood before him, so he called out, "Remove everyone from before me!" Thus no one remained with him when Joseph made himself known to his brothers.

[2] He cried in a loud voice. Egypt heard, and Pharaoh's household heard.

[3] And Joseph said to his brothers, "I am Joseph. * Is my father still alive?" But his brothers could not answer him because they were left disconcerted before him.

[4] Then Joseph said to his brothers, "Come close to me, if you please," and they came close. And he said, "I am Joseph your brother — it is me, whom you sold into Egypt. [5] And now, be not distressed, nor reproach yourselves for having sold me here, for it was to be a provider that God sent you ahead of you. [6] For this has been two of the hunger years in the midst of the land, and there are yet five years in which there shall be neither plowing nor harvest. [7] Thus God has sent me ahead of you to insure your survival in the land and to sustain you

---

45:2. It is indicative of Joseph's rank and the high esteem in which he was held that his weeping caused such universal concern (*R' Hirsch*).

45:3. When Joseph said, "I am Joseph," God's master plan became clear to the brothers; everything that had

happened for the last twenty-two years fell into perspective. So, too, will it be in the time to come when God will reveal Himself and announce, "I am HASHEM!" The veil will be lifted from our eyes and we will comprehend everything that transpired throughout history (*Chafetz Chaim*).

שלישי
ח לִפְלֵיטָ֣ה גְדֹלָֽה: וְעַתָּ֗ה לֹֽא־אַתֶּ֞ם שְׁלַחְתֶּ֤ם אֹתִי֙ הֵ֔נָּה כִּ֖י הָֽאֱלֹהִ֑ים וַיְשִׂימֵ֨נִי
ט לְאָ֜ב לְפַרְעֹ֗ה וּלְאָדוֹן֙ לְכָל־בֵּית֔וֹ וּמֹשֵׁ֖ל בְּכָל־אֶ֣רֶץ מִצְרָֽיִם: מַֽהֲרוּ֮ וַֽעֲל֣וּ
אֶל־אָבִי֒ וַֽאֲמַרְתֶּ֣ם אֵלָ֗יו כֹּ֤ה אָמַר֙ בִּנְךָ֣ יוֹסֵ֔ף שָׂמַ֧נִי אֱלֹהִ֛ים לְאָד֖וֹן לְכָל־
י מִצְרָ֑יִם רְדָ֥ה אֵלַ֖י אַל־תַּֽעֲמֹֽד: וְיָֽשַׁבְתָּ֣ בְאֶֽרֶץ־גֹּ֗שֶׁן וְהָיִ֤יתָ קָרוֹב֙ אֵלַ֔י אַתָּה֙
יא וּבָנֶ֣יךָ וּבְנֵ֣י בָנֶ֔יךָ וְצֹֽאנְךָ֥ וּבְקָֽרְךָ֖ וְכָל־אֲשֶׁר־לָֽךְ: וְכִלְכַּלְתִּ֤י אֹֽתְךָ֙ שָׁ֔ם כִּי־
יב ע֛וֹד חָמֵ֥שׁ שָׁנִ֖ים רָעָ֑ב פֶּן־תִּוָּרֵ֛שׁ אַתָּ֥ה וּבֵֽיתְךָ֖ וְכָל־אֲשֶׁר־לָֽךְ: וְהִנֵּ֤ה
יג עֵֽינֵיכֶם֙ רֹא֔וֹת וְעֵינֵ֖י אָחִ֣י בִנְיָמִ֑ין כִּי־פִ֖י הַֽמְדַבֵּ֥ר אֲלֵיכֶֽם: וְהִגַּדְתֶּ֣ם לְאָבִ֗י אֶת־
יד כָּל־כְּבוֹדִי֙ בְּמִצְרַ֔יִם וְאֵ֖ת כָּל־אֲשֶׁ֣ר רְאִיתֶ֑ם וּמִֽהַרְתֶּ֛ם וְהֽוֹרַדְתֶּ֥ם אֶת־
אָבִ֖י הֵֽנָּה: וַיִּפֹּ֛ל עַל־צַוְּארֵ֥י בִנְיָֽמִן־אָחִ֖יו וַיֵּ֑בְךְּ וּבִ֨נְיָמִ֔ן בָּכָ֖ה עַל־צַוָּארָֽיו:
טו-טז וַיְנַשֵּׁ֥ק לְכָל־אֶחָ֖יו וַיֵּ֣בְךְּ עֲלֵיהֶ֑ם וְאַֽחֲרֵי־כֵ֔ן דִּבְּר֥וּ אֶחָ֖יו אִתּֽוֹ: וְהַקֹּ֣ל נִשְׁמַ֗ע
בֵּ֤ית פַּרְעֹה֙ לֵאמֹ֔ר בָּ֖אוּ אֲחֵ֣י יוֹסֵ֑ף וַיִּיטַב֙ בְּעֵינֵ֣י פַרְעֹ֔ה וּבְעֵינֵ֖י עֲבָדָֽיו:
יז וַיֹּ֤אמֶר פַּרְעֹה֙ אֶל־יוֹסֵ֔ף אֱמֹ֥ר אֶל־אַחֶ֖יךָ זֹ֣את עֲשׂ֑וּ טַֽעֲנוּ֙ אֶת־בְּעִ֣ירְכֶ֔ם
יח וּלְכוּ־בֹ֖אוּ אַ֣רְצָה כְּנָֽעַן: וּקְח֧וּ אֶת־אֲבִיכֶ֛ם וְאֶת־בָּֽתֵּיכֶ֖ם וּבֹ֣אוּ אֵלָ֑י וְאֶתְּנָ֣ה
לָכֶ֗ם אֶת־טוּב֙ אֶ֣רֶץ מִצְרַ֔יִם וְאִכְל֖וּ אֶת־חֵ֥לֶב הָאָֽרֶץ: וְאַתָּ֥ה צֻוֵּ֖יתָה זֹ֣את
רביעי
יט עֲשׂ֑וּ קְחֽוּ־לָכֶם֩ מֵאֶ֨רֶץ מִצְרַ֜יִם עֲגָל֗וֹת לְטַפְּכֶם֙ וְלִנְשֵׁיכֶ֔ם וּנְשָׂאתֶ֥ם אֶת־
כ אֲבִיכֶ֖ם וּבָאתֶֽם: וְעֵ֣ינְכֶ֔ם אַל־תָּחֹ֖ס עַל־כְּלֵיכֶ֑ם כִּי־ט֛וּב כָּל־אֶ֥רֶץ מִצְרַ֖יִם
כא לָכֶ֥ם הֽוּא: וַיַּֽעֲשׂוּ־כֵן֙ בְּנֵ֣י יִשְׂרָאֵ֔ל וַיִּתֵּ֨ן לָהֶ֥ם יוֹסֵ֛ף עֲגָל֖וֹת עַל־פִּ֥י פַרְעֹ֑ה
כב וַיִּתֵּ֥ן לָהֶ֛ם צֵדָ֖ה לַדָּֽרֶךְ: לְכֻלָּ֥ם נָתַ֛ן לָאִ֖ישׁ חֲלִפ֣וֹת שְׂמָלֹ֑ת וּלְבִנְיָמִ֤ן נָתַן֙
כג שְׁלֹ֣שׁ מֵא֣וֹת כֶּ֔סֶף וְחָמֵ֖שׁ חֲלִפֹ֥ת שְׂמָלֹֽת: וּלְאָבִ֞יו שָׁלַ֤ח כְּזֹאת֙ עֲשָׂרָ֣ה
חֲמֹרִ֔ים נֹֽשְׂאִ֖ים מִטּ֣וּב מִצְרָ֑יִם וְעֶ֣שֶׂר אֲתֹנֹ֡ת נֹֽשְׂאֹת֩ בָּ֨ר וָלֶ֧חֶם וּמָז֛וֹן
כד לְאָבִ֖יו לַדָּֽרֶךְ: וַיְשַׁלַּ֥ח אֶת־אֶחָ֖יו וַיֵּלֵ֑כוּ וַיֹּ֣אמֶר אֲלֵהֶ֔ם אַל־תִּרְגְּז֖וּ בַּדָּֽרֶךְ:
כה-כו וַיַּֽעֲל֖וּ מִמִּצְרָ֑יִם וַיָּבֹ֨אוּ֙ אֶ֣רֶץ כְּנַ֔עַן אֶל־יַֽעֲקֹ֖ב אֲבִיהֶֽם: וַיַּגִּ֨דוּ ל֜וֹ לֵאמֹ֗ר
ע֤וֹד יוֹסֵ֣ף חַ֔י וְכִֽי־ה֥וּא מֹשֵׁ֖ל בְּכָל־אֶ֣רֶץ מִצְרָ֑יִם וַיָּ֣פָג לִבּ֔וֹ כִּ֥י לֹֽא־הֶֽאֱמִ֖ין
כז לָהֶֽם: וַיְדַבְּר֣וּ אֵלָ֗יו אֵ֣ת כָּל־דִּבְרֵ֤י יוֹסֵף֙ אֲשֶׁ֣ר דִּבֶּ֣ר אֲלֵהֶ֔ם וַיַּרְא֙ אֶת־
הָ֣עֲגָל֔וֹת אֲשֶׁר־שָׁלַ֥ח יוֹסֵ֖ף לָשֵׂ֣את אֹת֑וֹ וַתְּחִ֕י ר֖וּחַ יַֽעֲקֹ֥ב אֲבִיהֶֽם:
חמישי
כח וַיֹּ֨אמֶר֙ יִשְׂרָאֵ֔ל רַ֛ב עֽוֹד־יוֹסֵ֥ף בְּנִ֖י חָ֑י אֵֽלְכָ֥ה וְאֶרְאֶ֖נּוּ בְּטֶ֥רֶם אָמֽוּת:

45:10. Joseph had good reason to choose Goshen as the home of his family throughout their stay in Egypt: He wanted to keep them segregated from the mainstream of Egypt's idolatrous, immoral life, and to allow them to freely pursue their shepherding, an activity that was hateful to the Egyptians. Goshen was a fertile region in northeast Egypt, east of the Nile delta, which contained the country's most fertile soil and is described as *the best of the land* (47:6). Its major city was Rameses.

45:19-20. Since the export of wagons from Egypt was prohibited (*Abarbanel*), the unimpeachably honest Joseph might not send his father anything. Therefore Pharaoh specifically *commanded* him to send a generous supply of provisions and enough cargo space to bring back all their necessary belongings (*Ramban*).

45:25-28. Jacob receives the news. One can barely imagine the tremendous emotional impact upon Jacob of the news that Joseph was still alive and that, despite his long isolation from his family and the harmful influence of Egyptian society, he remained Jacob's loyal son. Fearing that a sudden announcement might shock and harm Jacob, his granddaughter, Serach daughter of Asher, was sent to prepare him for it. She played her harp and sang gently that Joseph was still alive and that he was the ruler of Egypt. Slowly, Jacob's long sadness evaporated and he blessed her for having lifted his spirits. As a result, she was still active centuries later, and eventually entered the Garden of Eden alive (*Pirkei d'R'Eliezer*).

for a momentous deliverance. [8] And now: It was not you who sent me here, but God; He has made me father to Pharaoh, master of his entire household, and ruler throughout the entire land of Egypt. [9] Hurry — go up to my father and say *Joseph* to him, 'So said your son Joseph: "God has made me master of all Egypt. *invites* Come down to me; do not delay. [10] You will reside in the land of Goshen* and *Jacob to* you will be near to me — you, your sons, your grandchildren, your flock and *Egypt* your cattle, and all that is yours. [11] And I will provide for you there — for there will be five more years of famine — so you do not become destitute, you, your household, and all that is yours. " '

[12] "Behold! Your eyes see as do the eyes of my brother Benjamin that it is my mouth that is speaking to you. [13] Therefore, tell my father of all my glory in Egypt and all that you saw; but you must hurry, and bring my father down here."

[14] Then he fell upon his brother Benjamin's neck and wept; and Benjamin wept upon his neck. [15] He then kissed all his brothers and wept upon them; afterwards his brothers conversed with him.

Pharaoh [16] The news was heard in Pharaoh's palace saying, "Joseph's brothers have *joins in the* come!" And it was pleasing in the eyes of Pharaoh and in the eyes of his *welcome* servants. [17] Pharaoh said to Joseph, "Say to your brothers, 'Do this: Load up your animals and go directly to the land of Canaan. [18] Bring your father and your households and come to me. I will give you the best of the land of Egypt and you will eat the fat of the land.' [19] And you are commanded [to say], 'Do this: Take for yourselves from the land of Egypt wagons for your small *Joseph* children and for your wives; transport your father and come. [20] And let your *dispenses* eye not take pity on your belongings, for the best of all the land of Egypt — it *gifts and* is yours.' "
sends his
brothers off [21] The sons of Israel did so, and Joseph gave them wagons by Pharaoh's word, and he gave them provisions for the journey. [22] To each of them he gave changes of clothing; but to Benjamin he gave three hundred pieces of silver and five changes of clothing. [23] And to his father he sent the following: ten he-donkeys laden with the best of Egypt and ten she-donkeys laden with grain, bread, and food for his father for the journey. [24] And he sent off his brothers, and they went. He said to them, "Do not become agitated on the way."

Jacob [25] They went up from Egypt and came to the land of Canaan to Jacob their *receives* father. [26] And they told him, saying, "Joseph is still alive," and that he is ruler *the news* over all the land of Egypt; but his heart rejected it, for he could not believe them. [27] However, when they related to him all the words that Joseph had spoken to them, and he saw the wagons that Joseph had sent* to transport him, then the spirit of their father Jacob was revived.

[28] And Israel said, "How great! My son Joseph still lives! I shall go and see him before I die."

45:27. To prove to Jacob that Joseph had sent these messages, Joseph directed his brothers to tell him that the last topic he and Jacob had studied together was that of *eglah arufah* [the ritual of expiation of an unsolved murder (see *Deut*. 21:1-9)]. The word עֲגָלוֹת, *wagons*, can also be translated *calves*, thus alluding to that topic. Therefore it is written [further in this verse], *And [Jacob]*

saw the agalos that **Joseph** *had sent*; it does not say . . . that *Pharaoh* had sent (*Rashi*).

45:28. Jacob defined life in spiritual terms. What resuscitated Jacob's — *Israel's* — spirit was the assurance that the viceroy of Egypt was the same Joseph who had left Canaan twenty-two years before, and that he even remembered the Torah he had studied with his father.

מו א וַיִּסַּע יִשְׂרָאֵל וְכָל־אֲשֶׁר־לוֹ וַיָּבֹא בְּאֵרָה שָּׁבַע וַיִּזְבַּח זְבָחִים לֵאלֹהֵי אָבִיו
ב יִצְחָק: וַיֹּאמֶר אֱלֹהִים ׀ לְיִשְׂרָאֵל בְּמַרְאֹת הַלַּיְלָה וַיֹּאמֶר יַעֲקֹב ׀ יַעֲקֹב
ג וַיֹּאמֶר הִנֵּנִי: וַיֹּאמֶר אָנֹכִי הָאֵל אֱלֹהֵי אָבִיךָ אַל־תִּירָא מֵרְדָה מִצְרַיְמָה
ד כִּי־לְגוֹי גָּדוֹל אֲשִׂימְךָ שָׁם: אָנֹכִי אֵרֵד עִמְּךָ מִצְרַיְמָה וְאָנֹכִי אַעַלְךָ גַם־
ה עָלֹה וְיוֹסֵף יָשִׁית יָדוֹ עַל־עֵינֶיךָ: וַיָּקָם יַעֲקֹב מִבְּאֵר שָׁבַע וַיִּשְׂאוּ בְנֵי־
יִשְׂרָאֵל אֶת־יַעֲקֹב אֲבִיהֶם וְאֶת־טַפָּם וְאֶת־נְשֵׁיהֶם בָּעֲגָלוֹת אֲשֶׁר־שָׁלַח
ו פַּרְעֹה לָשֵׂאת אֹתוֹ: וַיִּקְחוּ אֶת־מִקְנֵיהֶם וְאֶת־רְכוּשָׁם אֲשֶׁר רָכְשׁוּ בְּאֶרֶץ
ז כְּנַעַן וַיָּבֹאוּ מִצְרָיְמָה יַעֲקֹב וְכָל־זַרְעוֹ אִתּוֹ: בָּנָיו וּבְנֵי בָנָיו אִתּוֹ בְּנֹתָיו
ח וּבְנוֹת בָּנָיו וְכָל־זַרְעוֹ הֵבִיא אִתּוֹ מִצְרָיְמָה: וְאֵלֶּה
ט שְׁמוֹת בְּנֵי־יִשְׂרָאֵל הַבָּאִים מִצְרַיְמָה יַעֲקֹב וּבָנָיו בְּכֹר יַעֲקֹב רְאוּבֵן: וּבְנֵי
י רְאוּבֵן חֲנוֹךְ וּפַלּוּא וְחֶצְרֹן וְכַרְמִי: וּבְנֵי שִׁמְעוֹן יְמוּאֵל וְיָמִין וְאֹהַד וְיָכִין
יא-יב וְצֹחַר וְשָׁאוּל בֶּן־הַכְּנַעֲנִית: וּבְנֵי לֵוִי גֵּרְשׁוֹן קְהָת וּמְרָרִי: וּבְנֵי יְהוּדָה עֵר
וְאוֹנָן וְשֵׁלָה וָפֶרֶץ וָזָרַח וַיָּמָת עֵר וְאוֹנָן בְּאֶרֶץ כְּנַעַן וַיִּהְיוּ בְנֵי־פֶרֶץ חֶצְרֹן
יג-יד וְחָמוּל: וּבְנֵי יִשָּׂשכָר תּוֹלָע וּפֻוָּה וְיוֹב וְשִׁמְרֹן: וּבְנֵי זְבֻלוּן סֶרֶד וְאֵלוֹן
טו וְיַחְלְאֵל: אֵלֶּה ׀ בְּנֵי לֵאָה אֲשֶׁר יָלְדָה לְיַעֲקֹב בְּפַדַּן אֲרָם וְאֵת דִּינָה בִתּוֹ
טז כָּל־נֶפֶשׁ בָּנָיו וּבְנוֹתָיו שְׁלֹשִׁים וְשָׁלֹשׁ: וּבְנֵי גָד צִפְיוֹן וְחַגִּי שׁוּנִי וְאֶצְבֹּן
יז עֵרִי וַאֲרוֹדִי וְאַרְאֵלִי: וּבְנֵי אָשֵׁר יִמְנָה וְיִשְׁוָה וְיִשְׁוִי וּבְרִיעָה וְשֶׂרַח אֲחֹתָם
יח וּבְנֵי בְרִיעָה חֶבֶר וּמַלְכִּיאֵל: אֵלֶּה בְּנֵי זִלְפָּה אֲשֶׁר־נָתַן לָבָן לְלֵאָה בִתּוֹ
יט וַתֵּלֶד אֶת־אֵלֶּה לְיַעֲקֹב שֵׁשׁ עֶשְׂרֵה נָפֶשׁ: בְּנֵי רָחֵל אֵשֶׁת יַעֲקֹב יוֹסֵף
כ וּבִנְיָמִן: וַיִּוָּלֵד לְיוֹסֵף בְּאֶרֶץ מִצְרַיִם אֲשֶׁר יָלְדָה־לּוֹ אָסְנַת בַּת־פּוֹטִי פֶרַע
כא כֹּהֵן אֹן אֶת־מְנַשֶּׁה וְאֶת־אֶפְרָיִם: וּבְנֵי בִנְיָמִן בֶּלַע וָבֶכֶר וְאַשְׁבֵּל גֵּרָא
כב וְנַעֲמָן אֵחִי וָרֹאשׁ מֻפִּים וְחֻפִּים וָאָרְדְּ: אֵלֶּה בְּנֵי רָחֵל אֲשֶׁר יֻלַּד לְיַעֲקֹב
כג-כד כָּל־נֶפֶשׁ אַרְבָּעָה עָשָׂר: וּבְנֵי־דָן חֻשִׁים: וּבְנֵי נַפְתָּלִי יַחְצְאֵל וְגוּנִי וְיֵצֶר
כה וְשִׁלֵּם: אֵלֶּה בְּנֵי בִלְהָה אֲשֶׁר־נָתַן לָבָן לְרָחֵל בִּתּוֹ וַתֵּלֶד אֶת־אֵלֶּה
כו לְיַעֲקֹב כָּל־נֶפֶשׁ שִׁבְעָה: כָּל־הַנֶּפֶשׁ הַבָּאָה לְיַעֲקֹב מִצְרַיְמָה יֹצְאֵי
כז יְרֵכוֹ מִלְּבַד נְשֵׁי בְנֵי־יַעֲקֹב כָּל־נֶפֶשׁ שִׁשִּׁים וָשֵׁשׁ: וּבְנֵי יוֹסֵף אֲשֶׁר־
יֻלַּד־לוֹ בְמִצְרַיִם נֶפֶשׁ שְׁנָיִם כָּל־הַנֶּפֶשׁ לְבֵית־יַעֲקֹב הַבָּאָה מִצְרַיְמָה
כח שִׁבְעִים: וְאֶת־יְהוּדָה שָׁלַח לְפָנָיו אֶל־יוֹסֵף לְהוֹרֹת לְפָנָיו גֹּשְׁנָה שׁשׁי
כט וַיָּבֹאוּ אַרְצָה גֹּשֶׁן: וַיֶּאְסֹר יוֹסֵף מֶרְכַּבְתּוֹ וַיַּעַל לִקְרַאת־יִשְׂרָאֵל אָבִיו

46:3-4. When asked why he was afraid to go to Egypt, Jacob said, "I am afraid that my family will succumb there, that the *Shechinah* will no longer dwell among us, that I will not be buried with my ancestors, and that I will not see the redemption of my children." God reassured him on all counts (*Zohar*). Additionally, God promised Jacob that Joseph would not die in his lifetime (*Ibn Ezra*).

46:7. The Torah groups Jacob's offspring according to

their respective mothers.

46:15. The verse gives the total of Leah's offspring as thirty-three, but the foregoing list contains only thirty-*two* names. The thirty-third child was Jochebed, the future mother of Moses, who was born as they entered the gateway of the city. Although *Numbers* 26:59 states that she was born in Egypt, she had been conceived in Canaan (*Rashi*).

46

Jacob undertakes the journey to Joseph

¹ So Israel set out with all that he had and he came to Beer-sheba where he slaughtered sacrifices to the God of his father Isaac.

² God spoke to Israel in night visions and He said, "Jacob, Jacob." And he said, "Here I am."

³ And He said, "I am the God — God of your father. Have no fear* of descending to Egypt, for I shall establish you as a great nation there. ⁴ I shall descend with you to Egypt, and I shall also surely bring you up; and Joseph shall place his hand on your eyes."

⁵ So Jacob arose from Beer-sheba; the sons of Israel transported Jacob their father, as well as their young children and wives, in the wagons which Pharaoh had sent to transport him. ⁶ They took their livestock and their wealth which they had amassed in the land of Canaan and they came to Egypt — Jacob and all his offspring with him. ⁷ His sons and grandsons with him, his daughters and granddaughters and all his offspring he brought with him to Egypt.

(See Appendix B, chart 4)

⁸ Now these are the names of the children of Israel who were coming to Egypt — Jacob and his children: Jacob's firstborn, Reuben.

⁹ Reuben's sons: Hanoch, Pallu, Hezron, and Carmi.

¹⁰ Simeon's sons: Jemuel, Jamin, Ohad, Jachin, Zohar, and Shaul, son of the Canaanite woman.

¹¹ Levi's sons: Gershon, Kohath, and Merari.

¹² Judah's sons: Er, Onan, Shelah, Perez, and Zerah; but Er and Onan had died in the land of Canaan — and Perez's sons were Hezron and Hamul.

¹³ Issachar's sons: Tola, Puvah, Iov, and Shimron.

¹⁴ Zebulun's sons: Sered, Elon, and Jahleel. ¹⁵ These are the sons of Leah whom she bore to Jacob in Paddan-aram, in addition to Dinah his daughter. All the people — his sons and daughters — numbered thirty-three. *

¹⁶ Gad's sons: Ziphion, Haggi, Shuni, Ezbon, Eri, Arodi, and Areli.

¹⁷ Asher's sons: Imnah, Ishvah, Ishvi, Beriah, and their sister Serah; and Beriah's sons, Heber and Malchiel. ¹⁸ These are the sons of Zilpah whom Laban had given to Leah his daughter. These she bore to Jacob — sixteen people.

¹⁹ The sons of Rachel, Jacob's wife: Joseph and Benjamin.

²⁰ To Joseph were born in the land of Egypt — whom Asenath daughter of Poti-phera Chief of On bore to him — Manasseh and Ephraim.

²¹ Benjamin's sons: Bela, Becher, Ashbel, Gera, Naaman, Ehi, Rosh, Muppim, Huppim, and Ard. ²² These are the sons of Rachel who were born to Jacob — fourteen persons in all.

²³ Dan's sons: Hushim.

²⁴ Naphtali's sons: Jahzeel, Guni, Jezer, and Shillem. ²⁵ These are the sons of Bilhah whom Laban had given to Rachel his daughter. She bore these to Jacob — seven people in all.

²⁶ All the persons coming with Jacob to Egypt — his own descendants, aside from the wives of Jacob's sons — sixty-six persons in all.

The grand total of seventy descendants

²⁷ And Joseph's sons who were born to him in Egypt numbered two persons. All the people of Jacob's household who came to Egypt — seventy.

²⁸ He sent Judah ahead of him to Joseph, to prepare ahead of him in Goshen; and they arrived in the region of Goshen.

²⁹ Joseph harnessed his chariot and went up to meet Israel his father in

ל גְּשְׁנָה וַיֵּרָא אֵלָיו וַיִּפֹּל עַל־צַוָּארָיו וַיֵּבְךְּ עַל־צַוָּארָיו עוֹד: וַיֹּאמֶר יִשְׂרָאֵל

לא אֶל־יוֹסֵף אָמוּתָה הַפָּעַם אַחֲרֵי רְאוֹתִי אֶת־פָּנֶיךָ כִּי עוֹדְךָ חָי: וַיֹּאמֶר

יוֹסֵף אֶל־אֶחָיו וְאֶל־בֵּית אָבִיו אֶעֱלֶה וְאַגִּידָה לְפַרְעֹה וְאֹמְרָה אֵלָיו אַחַי

לב וּבֵית־אָבִי אֲשֶׁר בְּאֶרֶץ־כְּנַעַן בָּאוּ אֵלָי: וְהָאֲנָשִׁים רֹעֵי צֹאן כִּי־אַנְשֵׁי

לג מִקְנֶה הָיוּ וְצֹאנָם וּבְקָרָם וְכָל־אֲשֶׁר לָהֶם הֵבִיאוּ: וְהָיָה כִּי־יִקְרָא לָכֶם

לד פַּרְעֹה וְאָמַר מַה־מַּעֲשֵׂיכֶם: וַאֲמַרְתֶּם אַנְשֵׁי מִקְנֶה הָיוּ עֲבָדֶיךָ מִנְּעוּרֵינוּ

וְעַד־עַתָּה גַּם־אֲנַחְנוּ גַּם־אֲבֹתֵינוּ בַּעֲבוּר תֵּשְׁבוּ בְּאֶרֶץ גֹּשֶׁן כִּי־תוֹעֲבַת

מז א מִצְרַיִם כָּל־רֹעֵה צֹאן: וַיָּבֹא יוֹסֵף וַיַּגֵּד לְפַרְעֹה וַיֹּאמֶר אָבִי וְאַחַי וְצֹאנָם

ב וּבְקָרָם וְכָל־אֲשֶׁר לָהֶם בָּאוּ מֵאֶרֶץ כְּנָעַן וְהִנָּם בְּאֶרֶץ גֹּשֶׁן: וּמִקְצֵה אֶחָיו

ג לָקַח חֲמִשָּׁה אֲנָשִׁים וַיַּצִּגֵם לִפְנֵי פַרְעֹה: וַיֹּאמֶר פַּרְעֹה אֶל־אֶחָיו מַה־

מַּעֲשֵׂיכֶם וַיֹּאמְרוּ אֶל־פַּרְעֹה רֹעֵה צֹאן עֲבָדֶיךָ גַּם־אֲנַחְנוּ גַּם־אֲבוֹתֵינוּ:

ד וַיֹּאמְרוּ אֶל־פַּרְעֹה לָגוּר בָּאָרֶץ בָּאנוּ כִּי־אֵין מִרְעֶה לַצֹּאן אֲשֶׁר לַעֲבָדֶיךָ

ה כִּי־כָבֵד הָרָעָב בְּאֶרֶץ כְּנָעַן וְעַתָּה יֵשְׁבוּ־נָא עֲבָדֶיךָ בְּאֶרֶץ גֹּשֶׁן: וַיֹּאמֶר

ו פַּרְעֹה אֶל־יוֹסֵף לֵאמֹר אָבִיךָ וְאַחֶיךָ בָּאוּ אֵלֶיךָ: אֶרֶץ מִצְרַיִם לְפָנֶיךָ

הִוא בְּמֵיטַב הָאָרֶץ הוֹשֵׁב אֶת־אָבִיךָ וְאֶת־אַחֶיךָ יֵשְׁבוּ בְּאֶרֶץ גֹּשֶׁן

וְאִם־יָדַעְתָּ וְיֶשׁ־בָּם אַנְשֵׁי־חַיִל וְשַׂמְתָּם שָׂרֵי מִקְנֶה עַל־אֲשֶׁר־לִי:

ז וַיָּבֵא יוֹסֵף אֶת־יַעֲקֹב אָבִיו וַיַּעֲמִדֵהוּ לִפְנֵי פַרְעֹה וַיְבָרֶךְ יַעֲקֹב אֶת־

חט פַּרְעֹה: וַיֹּאמֶר פַּרְעֹה אֶל־יַעֲקֹב כַּמָּה יְמֵי שְׁנֵי חַיֶּיךָ: וַיֹּאמֶר יַעֲקֹב אֶל־

פַּרְעֹה יְמֵי שְׁנֵי מְגוּרַי שְׁלֹשִׁים וּמְאַת שָׁנָה מְעַט וְרָעִים הָיוּ יְמֵי שְׁנֵי חַיַּי

י וְלֹא הִשִּׂיגוּ אֶת־יְמֵי שְׁנֵי חַיֵּי אֲבֹתַי בִּימֵי מְגוּרֵיהֶם: וַיְבָרֶךְ יַעֲקֹב אֶת־

שביעי יא פַּרְעֹה וַיֵּצֵא מִלִּפְנֵי פַרְעֹה: וַיּוֹשֵׁב יוֹסֵף אֶת־אָבִיו וְאֶת־אֶחָיו וַיִּתֵּן לָהֶם

אֲחֻזָּה בְּאֶרֶץ מִצְרַיִם בְּמֵיטַב הָאָרֶץ בְּאֶרֶץ רַעְמְסֵס כַּאֲשֶׁר צִוָּה

יב פַרְעֹה: וַיְכַלְכֵּל יוֹסֵף אֶת־אָבִיו וְאֶת־אֶחָיו וְאֵת כָּל־בֵּית אָבִיו לֶחֶם לְפִי

יג הַטָּף: וְלֶחֶם אֵין בְּכָל־הָאָרֶץ כִּי־כָבֵד הָרָעָב מְאֹד וַתֵּלַהּ אֶרֶץ מִצְרַיִם

יד וְאֶרֶץ כְּנַעַן מִפְּנֵי הָרָעָב: וַיְלַקֵּט יוֹסֵף אֶת־כָּל־הַכֶּסֶף הַנִּמְצָא בְאֶרֶץ־

מִצְרַיִם וּבְאֶרֶץ כְּנַעַן בַּשֶּׁבֶר אֲשֶׁר־הֵם שֹׁבְרִים וַיָּבֵא יוֹסֵף אֶת־הַכֶּסֶף

טו בֵּיתָה פַרְעֹה: וַיִּתֹּם הַכֶּסֶף מֵאֶרֶץ מִצְרַיִם וּמֵאֶרֶץ כְּנַעַן וַיָּבֹאוּ כָל־

מִצְרַיִם אֶל־יוֹסֵף לֵאמֹר הָבָה־לָּנוּ לֶחֶם וְלָמָּה נָמוּת נֶגְדֶּךָ כִּי אָפֵס כָּסֶף:

46:29. Joseph wept contiuously. Jacob, however, did not fall upon Joseph's neck, nor did he kiss him, for, as the Sages say, Jacob was reciting the *Shema* at that moment (*Rashi*).

Ramban maintains that, in the literal sense, the subject of the verb *wept* is not Joseph but Jacob: "It is well known whose tears are more present, those of the aged parent who finds his long-lost son alive, after having despaired and mourned for him, or the young son who rules."

47:2. Afraid that if Pharaoh were introduced to powerful men, he would enlist them in his military, Joseph chose the five who were least impressive physically (*Rashi*).

47:5-6. Pharaoh responded as graciously as Joseph had hoped, giving Joseph full authority to provide his family with the best that Egypt had to offer.

47:10. As a result of Jacob's blessing, the famine ended after only two years, instead of the seven years foretold by Joseph (*Midrash*).

Jacob arrives in Egypt   Goshen. He appeared before him, fell on his neck, and he wept* on his neck excessively. [30] Then Israel said to Joseph, "Now I can die, after my having seen your face, because you are still alive."

Joseph ensures his family's settlement in Goshen   [31] And Joseph said to his brothers and to his father's household, "I will go up and tell Pharaoh, and I will say to him, 'My brothers and my father's household who were in the land of Canaan have come to me. [32] The men are shepherds, for they have been cattlemen; their flocks and cattle — and everything they own — they have brought.' [33] And it shall be, when Pharaoh summons you, and says, 'What is your occupation?' [34] Then you are to say, 'Your servants have been cattlemen from our youth till now, both we and our forefathers,' so that you may be able to settle on the region of Goshen, since all shepherds are abhorrent to Egyptians."

47   [1] Then Joseph came and told Pharaoh, and he said, "My father and my brothers, their flocks, their cattle, and everything they own, have arrived from the land of Canaan and they are now in the region of Goshen." [2] From the least of his brothers* he took five men and presented them to Pharaoh. [3] Pharaoh said to his brothers, "What is your occupation?" They answered Pharaoh, "Your servants are shepherds — we as well as our forefathers." [4] And they said to Pharaoh, "We have come to sojourn in the land, since there is no grazing for your servants' flocks, for the famine is severe in the land of Canaan; now, if you please, allow your servants to dwell in the region of Goshen."

[5] And Pharaoh said to Joseph saying, "Your father and your brothers have come to you. [6] The land of Egypt is before you — in the best part of the land settle your father and your brothers; let them settle in the region of Goshen, and if you know that there are capable men among them, appoint them as chamberlains over the livestock that belongs to me."

Jacob and Pharaoh meet   [7] Then Joseph brought Jacob, his father, and presented him to Pharaoh, and Jacob blessed Pharaoh. [8] Pharaoh said to Jacob, "How many are the days of the years of your life?"

[9] Jacob answered Pharaoh, "The days of the years of my sojourns have been a hundred and thirty years. Few and bad have been the days of the years of my life, and they have not reached the life spans of my forefathers in the days of their sojourns." [10] Then Jacob blessed Pharaoh, * and left Pharaoh's presence.

[11] So Joseph settled his father and his brothers and he gave them a possession in the land of Egypt in the best part of the land, in the region of Rameses, as Pharaoh had commanded. [12] Joseph sustained his father and his brothers and all of his father's household with food according to the children.

Joseph and the famine   [13] Now there was no bread in all the earth for the famine was very severe; the land of Egypt and the land of Canaan became weary from hunger. [14] Joseph gathered all the money that was to be found in the land of Egypt and in the land of Canaan through the provisions that they were purchasing, and Joseph brought the money into Pharaoh's palace. [15] And when the money was exhausted from the land of Egypt and from the land of Canaan, all the Egyptians came to Joseph, saying, "Give us bread; why should we die in your presence? — for the money is gone!"

47:13-27. The narrative reverts to the famine and describes how Joseph used his immense economic power to accumulate nearly all the wealth of Egypt and Canaan and nearly all Egyptian land for Pharaoh.

טז וַיֹּ֣אמֶר יוֹסֵ֩ף הָב֨וּ מִקְנֵיכֶ֜ם וְאֶתְּנָ֤ה לָכֶם֙ בְּמִקְנֵיכֶ֔ם אִם־אָפֵ֖ס כָּֽסֶף: וַיָּבִ֣יאוּ אֶת־מִקְנֵיהֶם֮ אֶל־יוֹסֵף֒ וַיִּתֵּ֣ן לָהֶם֩ יוֹסֵ֨ף לֶ֜חֶם בַּסּוּסִ֗ים וּבְמִקְנֵ֤ה הַצֹּאן֙ וּבְמִקְנֵ֣ה הַבָּקָ֔ר וּבַֽחֲמֹרִ֑ים וַיְנַֽהֲלֵ֤ם בַּלֶּ֨חֶם֙ בְּכָל־מִקְנֵהֶ֔ם בַּשָּׁנָ֖ה הַהִֽוא:

יז וַתִּתֹּ֣ם הַשָּׁנָ֣ה הַהִ֗וא וַיָּבֹ֨אוּ אֵלָ֜יו בַּשָּׁנָ֣ה הַשֵּׁנִ֗ית וַיֹּ֤אמְרוּ לוֹ֙ לֹֽא־נְכַחֵ֣ד מֵֽאֲדֹנִ֔י כִּ֚י אִם־תַּ֣ם הַכֶּ֔סֶף וּמִקְנֵ֥ה הַבְּהֵמָ֖ה אֶל־אֲדֹנִ֑י לֹ֤א נִשְׁאַר֙ לִפְנֵ֣י

יח אֲדֹנִ֔י בִּלְתִּ֖י אִם־גְּוִיָּתֵ֥נוּ וְאַדְמָתֵֽנוּ: לָ֧מָּה נָמ֣וּת לְעֵינֶ֗יךָ גַּם־אֲנַ֨חְנוּ֙ גַּם־אַדְמָתֵ֔נוּ קְנֵֽה־אֹתָ֥נוּ וְאֶת־אַדְמָתֵ֖נוּ בַּלָּ֑חֶם וְנִֽהְיֶ֞ה אֲנַ֤חְנוּ וְאַדְמָתֵ֨נוּ֙ עֲבָדִ֣ים

יט לְפַרְעֹ֔ה וְתֶן־זֶ֗רַע וְנִֽחְיֶה֙ וְלֹ֣א נָמ֔וּת וְהָֽאֲדָמָ֖ה לֹ֥א תֵשָֽׁם: וַיִּ֨קֶן יוֹסֵ֜ף אֶת־

כ כָּל־אַדְמַ֤ת מִצְרַ֨יִם֙ לְפַרְעֹ֔ה כִּֽי־מָֽכְר֤וּ מִצְרַ֨יִם֙ אִ֣ישׁ שָׂדֵ֔הוּ כִּֽי־חָזַ֥ק עֲלֵהֶ֖ם הָֽרָעָ֑ב וַתְּהִ֥י הָאָ֖רֶץ לְפַרְעֹֽה:

כא וְאֶ֨ת־הָעָ֔ם הֶֽעֱבִ֥יר אֹת֖וֹ לֶֽעָרִ֑ים מִקְצֵ֥ה גְבֽוּל־ מִצְרַ֖יִם וְעַד־קָצֵֽהוּ: רַ֛ק אַדְמַ֥ת הַכֹּֽהֲנִ֖ים לֹ֣א קָנָ֑ה כִּי֩ חֹ֨ק לַכֹּֽהֲנִ֜ים מֵאֵ֣ת

כב פַּרְעֹ֗ה וְאָֽכְל֤וּ אֶת־חֻקָּם֙ אֲשֶׁ֨ר נָתַ֤ן לָהֶם֙ פַּרְעֹ֔ה עַל־כֵּ֕ן לֹ֥א מָֽכְר֖וּ אֶת־

כג אַדְמָתָֽם: וַיֹּ֤אמֶר יוֹסֵף֙ אֶל־הָעָ֔ם הֵן֩ קָנִ֨יתִי אֶתְכֶ֥ם הַיּ֛וֹם וְאֶת־אַדְמַתְכֶ֖ם לְפַרְעֹ֑ה הֵֽא־לָכֶ֣ם זֶ֔רַע וּזְרַעְתֶּ֖ם אֶת־הָֽאֲדָמָֽה: וְהָיָה֙ בַּתְּבוּאֹ֔ת וּנְתַתֶּ֥ם

כד חֲמִישִׁ֖ית לְפַרְעֹ֑ה וְאַרְבַּ֣ע הַיָּדֹ֡ת יִֽהְיֶ֣ה לָכֶם֩ לְזֶ֨רַע הַשָּׂדֶ֧ה וּֽלְאָכְלְכֶ֛ם וְלַֽאֲשֶׁ֥ר בְּבָֽתֵּיכֶ֖ם וְלֶֽאֱכֹ֥ל לְטַפְּכֶֽם: וַיֹּֽאמְר֖וּ הֶֽחֱיִתָ֑נוּ נִמְצָא־חֵן֙ בְּעֵינֵ֣י אֲדֹנִ֔י

כה וְהָיִ֥ינוּ עֲבָדִ֖ים לְפַרְעֹֽה: וַיָּ֣שֶׂם אֹתָ֣הּ יוֹסֵ֗ף לְחֹ֨ק עַד־הַיּ֤וֹם הַזֶּה֙ עַל־אַדְמַ֣ת

כו מִצְרַ֔יִם לְפַרְעֹ֖ה לַחֹ֑מֶשׁ רַ֞ק אַדְמַ֤ת הַכֹּֽהֲנִים֙ לְבַדָּ֔ם לֹ֥א הָֽיְתָ֖ה לְפַרְעֹֽה:

כז וַיֵּ֧שֶׁב יִשְׂרָאֵ֛ל בְּאֶ֥רֶץ מִצְרַ֖יִם בְּאֶ֣רֶץ גֹּ֑שֶׁן וַיֵּאָֽחֲז֣וּ בָ֔הּ וַיִּפְר֥וּ וַיִּרְבּ֖וּ מְאֹֽד:

בס״ת אין כאן פיסקא אלא אות אחת. ק״ו פסוקים. יהללא״ל סימן.

מפטיר

Haftaras Vayigash: p. 1296

פרשת ויחי

כח וַיְחִ֤י יַֽעֲקֹב֙ בְּאֶ֣רֶץ מִצְרַ֔יִם שְׁבַ֥ע עֶשְׂרֵ֖ה שָׁנָ֑ה וַיְהִ֤י יְמֵֽי־יַֽעֲקֹב֙ שְׁנֵ֣י חַיָּ֔יו

כט שֶׁ֣בַע שָׁנִ֔ים וְאַרְבָּעִ֥ים וּמְאַ֖ת שָׁנָֽה: וַיִּקְרְב֣וּ יְמֵֽי־יִשְׂרָאֵל֮ לָמוּת֒ וַיִּקְרָ֣א ׀ לִבְנ֣וֹ לְיוֹסֵ֗ף וַיֹּ֤אמֶר לוֹ֙ אִם־נָ֨א מָצָ֤אתִי חֵן֙ בְּעֵינֶ֔יךָ שִֽׂים־נָ֥א יָֽדְךָ֖ תַּ֣חַת יְרֵכִ֑י

ל וְעָשִׂ֤יתָ עִמָּדִי֙ חֶ֣סֶד וֶֽאֱמֶ֔ת אַל־נָ֥א תִקְבְּרֵ֖נִי בְּמִצְרָֽיִם: וְשָֽׁכַבְתִּי֙ עִם־אֲבֹתַ֔י וּנְשָׂאתַ֨נִי֙ מִמִּצְרַ֔יִם וּקְבַרְתַּ֖נִי בִּקְבֻֽרָתָ֑ם וַיֹּאמַ֕ר אָֽנֹכִ֖י אֶֽעֱשֶׂ֥ה כִדְבָרֶֽךָ:

לא וַיֹּ֗אמֶר הִשָּֽׁבְעָה֙ לִ֔י וַיִּשָּׁבַ֖ע ל֑וֹ וַיִּשְׁתַּ֥חוּ יִשְׂרָאֵ֖ל עַל־רֹ֥אשׁ הַמִּטָּֽה:

47:16. Joseph's master plan was to impoverish the Egyptians and make them totally dependent upon the king.

47:21. *As for the nation, he resettled it by cities*, i.e. from city to city. Joseph transferred the population from one city to the other to establish the monarchy's undisputed ownership of the land, and to demonstrate that individuals no longer had claim to their former property.

47:22. The stress on the royal provision for the priests is a lesson for future generations of Israel never to be reluctant to give their tithes to the Kohanim, Levites, and the poor. God says: "If Pharaoh did not take the land of his

idol-worshiping priests and freed them from paying a fifth of their produce to the crown, then surely you, My children, whom I have given *Eretz Yisrael* as an outright gift, should graciously contribute a fifth" (*Moshav Zekeinim*).

⊸ **Parashas Vayechi: The "closed" section.** In the entire Torah Scroll, *Vayechi* is unique in that there is no extra space between it and the preceding *parashah*, in contrast to the general rule that a *Sidrah* begins on a new line or is separated from the previous one by at least a nine-letter space. *Rashi*, therefore, describes *Vayechi* as סְתוּמָה, *closed*. At the time of Jacob's death, his children's hearts

¹⁶ And Joseph said, "Bring your livestock and I will provide for you in return for your livestock if the money is gone." ¹⁷ So they brought their livestock to Joseph, and Joseph gave them bread in return for the horses, for the flocks of sheep, for the herds of cattle, and for the donkeys; thus he provided them with bread in exchange for all their livestock during that year.

¹⁸ And when that year ended, they came to him in the next year and said to him, "We will not withhold from my lord that with the money and flocks of cattle having been exhausted to my lord, nothing is left before my lord but our bodies and our land. ¹⁹ Why should we die before your eyes, both we and our land? Acquire us and our land for bread; and we — with our land — will become serfs to Pharaoh; and provide seed so that we may live and not die, and the land will not become desolate."

The Egyptians become Pharaoh's serfs   ²⁰ Thus Joseph acquired all the land of Egypt for Pharaoh, for every Egyptian sold his field because the famine had overwhelmed them; and the land became Pharaoh's. ²¹ As for the nation, he resettled it by cities, * from one end of Egypt's borders to the other. ²² Only the land of the priests he did not buy, since the priests had a stipend from Pharaoh, and they lived off their stipend that Pharaoh had given them; therefore they did not sell their land.

²³ Joseph said to the people, "Look — I have acquired you this day with your land for Pharaoh; here is seed for you — sow the land. ²⁴ At the ingathering of the harvests you will give a fifth to Pharaoh; the [other] four parts shall be yours — as seed for the field, and food for yourselves and for those in your household, and to feed your young ones."

²⁵ And they said, "You have saved our lives; may we find favor in your eyes, my lord, and we will be serfs to Pharaoh."

²⁶ So Joseph imposed it as a statute till this day regarding the land of Egypt: It was Pharaoh's for the fifth; only the priests' land alone did not become Pharaoh's.

²⁷ Thus Israel settled in the land of Egypt in the region of Goshen; they acquired property in it and they were fruitful and multiplied greatly.

PARASHAS VAYECHI

Jacob's end draws near; his request of Joseph   ²⁸ Jacob lived in the land of Egypt seventeen years; and the days of Jacob — the years of his life — were one hundred and forty-seven years. ²⁹ The time approached for Israel to die, so he called for his son, for Joseph, and said to him, "Please — if I have found favor in your eyes, please place your hand under my thigh * and do kindness and truth with me — please do not bury me in Egypt. ³⁰ For I will lie down with my fathers and you shall transport me out of Egypt and bury me in their tomb."

He said, "I personally will do as you have said."

³¹ He replied, "Swear to me," and he swore to him; then Israel prostrated himself towards the head of the bed.

---

were "closed" in expectation of the suffering and despair of the impending bondage. Alternatively, Jacob wanted to reveal to his children the time of the "End," i.e. the Messianic age when Israel's exiles would finally end, but he was prevented from doing so because his prophetic vision was *closed*, i.e., it was concealed from him.

47:28-31. Jacob's request of Joseph. Feeling that his death was drawing near, Jacob sent for Joseph — the only one of his sons who held power — and asked him to swear that he would bury him in the Cave of Machpelah, in Hebron.

47:29. This was the means of taking an oath; see 24:2.

מח

א וַיְהִ֗י אַחֲרֵי֙ הַדְּבָרִ֣ים הָאֵ֔לֶּה וַיֹּ֣אמֶר לְיוֹסֵ֔ף הִנֵּ֥ה אָבִ֖יךָ חֹלֶ֑ה וַיִּקַּ֞ח אֶת־שְׁנֵ֤י

ב בָנָיו֙ עִמּ֔וֹ אֶת־מְנַשֶּׁ֖ה וְאֶת־אֶפְרָ֑יִם: וַיַּגֵּ֣ד לְיַעֲקֹ֔ב וַיֹּ֕אמֶר הִנֵּ֛ה בִּנְךָ֥ יוֹסֵ֖ף

ג בָּ֣א אֵלֶ֑יךָ וַיִּתְחַזֵּק֙ יִשְׂרָאֵ֔ל וַיֵּ֖שֶׁב עַל־הַמִּטָּֽה: וַיֹּ֤אמֶר יַעֲקֹב֙ אֶל־יוֹסֵ֔ף אֵ֥ל

ד שַׁדַּ֛י נִרְאָֽה־אֵלַ֥י בְּל֖וּז בְּאֶ֣רֶץ כְּנָ֑עַן וַיְבָ֖רֶךְ אֹתִֽי: וַיֹּ֣אמֶר אֵלַ֗י הִנְנִ֤י מַפְרְךָ֙

וְהִרְבִּיתִ֔ךָ וּנְתַתִּ֖יךָ לִקְהַ֣ל עַמִּ֑ים וְנָ֨תַתִּ֜י אֶת־הָאָ֧רֶץ הַזֹּ֛את לְזַרְעֲךָ֥ אַחֲרֶ֖יךָ

ה אֲחֻזַּ֥ת עוֹלָֽם: וְעַתָּ֡ה שְׁנֵֽי־בָנֶיךָ֩ הַנּוֹלָדִ֨ים לְךָ֜ בְּאֶ֣רֶץ מִצְרַ֗יִם עַד־בֹּאִ֤י

אֵלֶ֨יךָ֙ מִצְרַ֔יְמָה לִי־הֵ֑ם אֶפְרַ֨יִם֙ וּמְנַשֶּׁ֔ה כִּרְאוּבֵ֥ן וְשִׁמְע֖וֹן יִֽהְיוּ־לִֽי:

ו וּמוֹלַדְתְּךָ֛ אֲשֶׁר־הוֹלַ֥דְתָּ אַחֲרֵיהֶ֖ם לְךָ֣ יִֽהְי֑וּ עַ֣ל שֵׁ֧ם אֲחֵיהֶ֛ם יִקָּרְא֖וּ

ז בְּנַחֲלָתָֽם: וַאֲנִ֣י | בְּבֹאִ֣י מִפַּדָּ֗ן מֵ֩תָה֩ עָלַ֨י רָחֵ֜ל בְּאֶ֤רֶץ כְּנַ֨עַן֙ בַּדֶּ֔רֶךְ בְּע֥וֹד

כִּבְרַת־אֶ֖רֶץ לָבֹ֣א אֶפְרָ֑תָה וָאֶקְבְּרֶ֤הָ שָּׁם֙ בְּדֶ֣רֶךְ אֶפְרָ֔ת הִ֖וא בֵּ֥ית לָֽחֶם:

ח-ט וַיַּ֥רְא יִשְׂרָאֵ֖ל אֶת־בְּנֵ֣י יוֹסֵ֑ף וַיֹּ֖אמֶר מִי־אֵֽלֶּה: וַיֹּ֤אמֶר יוֹסֵף֙ אֶל־אָבִ֔יו בָּנַ֣י

שני

הֵ֔ם אֲשֶׁר־נָֽתַן־לִ֥י אֱלֹהִ֖ים בָּזֶ֑ה וַיֹּאמַ֕ר קָֽחֶם־נָ֥א אֵלַ֖י וַאֲבָרֲכֵֽם: וְעֵינֵ֤י

י יִשְׂרָאֵל֙ כָּבְד֣וּ מִזֹּ֔קֶן לֹ֥א יוּכַ֖ל לִרְא֑וֹת וַיַּגֵּ֤שׁ אֹתָם֙ אֵלָ֔יו וַיִּשַּׁ֥ק לָהֶ֖ם וַיְחַבֵּ֥ק

יא לָהֶֽם: וַיֹּ֤אמֶר יִשְׂרָאֵל֙ אֶל־יוֹסֵ֔ף רְאֹ֥ה פָנֶ֖יךָ לֹ֣א פִלָּ֑לְתִּי וְהִנֵּ֨ה הֶרְאָ֥ה אֹתִ֛י

יב אֱלֹהִ֖ים גַּ֥ם אֶת־זַרְעֶֽךָ: וַיּוֹצֵ֥א יוֹסֵ֛ף אֹתָ֖ם מֵעִ֣ם בִּרְכָּ֑יו וַיִּשְׁתַּ֥חוּ לְאַפָּ֖יו

יג אָֽרְצָה: וַיִּקַּ֣ח יוֹסֵף֮ אֶת־שְׁנֵיהֶם֒ אֶת־אֶפְרַ֤יִם בִּֽימִינוֹ֙ מִשְּׂמֹ֣אל יִשְׂרָאֵ֔ל

יד וְאֶת־מְנַשֶּׁ֥ה בִשְׂמֹאל֖וֹ מִימִ֣ין יִשְׂרָאֵ֑ל וַיַּגֵּ֖שׁ אֵלָֽיו: וַיִּשְׁלַח֩ יִשְׂרָאֵ֨ל אֶת־

יְמִינ֜וֹ וַיָּ֣שֶׁת עַל־רֹ֣אשׁ אֶפְרַ֗יִם וְה֣וּא הַצָּעִ֔יר וְאֶת־שְׂמֹאל֖וֹ עַל־רֹ֣אשׁ

טו מְנַשֶּׁ֑ה שִׂכֵּל֙ אֶת־יָדָ֔יו כִּ֥י מְנַשֶּׁ֖ה הַבְּכֽוֹר: וַיְבָ֥רֶךְ אֶת־יוֹסֵ֖ף וַיֹּאמַ֑ר

הָֽאֱלֹהִ֡ים אֲשֶׁר֩ הִתְהַלְּכ֨וּ אֲבֹתַ֤י לְפָנָיו֙ אַבְרָהָ֣ם וְיִצְחָ֔ק הָֽאֱלֹהִים֙ הָרֹעֶ֣ה אֹתִ֔י

טז מֵעוֹדִ֖י עַד־הַיּ֥וֹם הַזֶּֽה: הַמַּלְאָךְ֩ הַגֹּאֵ֨ל אֹתִ֜י מִכָּל־רָ֗ע יְבָרֵךְ֮ אֶת־

הַנְּעָרִים֒ וְיִקָּרֵ֤א בָהֶם֙ שְׁמִ֔י וְשֵׁ֖ם אֲבֹתַ֣י אַבְרָהָ֣ם וְיִצְחָ֑ק וְיִדְגּ֥וּ לָרֹ֖ב בְּקֶ֥רֶב

יז הָאָֽרֶץ: וַיַּ֣רְא יוֹסֵ֗ף כִּֽי־יָשִׁ֨ית אָבִ֧יו יַד־יְמִינ֛וֹ עַל־רֹ֥אשׁ אֶפְרַ֖יִם וַיֵּ֣רַע

שלישי

בְּעֵינָ֑יו וַיִּתְמֹ֣ךְ יַד־אָבִ֗יו לְהָסִ֥יר אֹתָ֛הּ מֵעַ֥ל רֹאשׁ־אֶפְרַ֖יִם עַל־רֹ֥אשׁ

יח מְנַשֶּֽׁה: וַיֹּ֧אמֶר יוֹסֵ֛ף אֶל־אָבִ֖יו לֹא־כֵ֣ן אָבִ֑י כִּי־זֶ֣ה הַבְּכֹ֔ר שִׂ֥ים יְמִֽינְךָ֖ עַל־

יט רֹאשֽׁוֹ: וַיְמָאֵ֣ן אָבִ֗יו וַיֹּ֨אמֶר֙ יָדַ֤עְתִּֽי בְנִי֙ יָדַ֔עְתִּי גַּם־ה֥וּא יִֽהְיֶה־לְּעָ֖ם וְגַם־

ה֣וּא יִגְדָּ֑ל וְאוּלָ֗ם אָחִ֤יו הַקָּטֹן֙ יִגְדַּ֣ל מִמֶּ֔נּוּ וְזַרְע֖וֹ יִהְיֶ֥ה מְלֹֽא־הַגּוֹיִֽם:

48:1-7. Jacob's illness and Joseph's birthright. When Jacob became ill, Joseph brought his two sons for Jacob's blessing (*Ramban* 47:29). The blessing included a major change in the composition of the Jewish people, in that Jacob elevated Manasseh and Ephraim to the status of his own sons — in effect adopting them as his own — thereby removing the firstborn status from the tribe of Reuben and giving it to Joseph's offspring.

48:13. Traditionally, blessings are bestowed with the blesser laying his hands on the head of the blessed. Since the right hand has spiritual primacy and is the preferred one for the performance of *mitzvos*, if both sons were to

be blessed simultaneously, Jacob's right hand would be on the head of Manasseh, the firstborn, and his left on Ephraim's. Therefore, Joseph positioned Ephraim on his own right side, facing Jacob's left.

48:16. This is the essence of the prayer that began with the previous verse: May You, O God, assign Your "emissary" — the angel whom You always dispatched to redeem me from all evil — to bless the lads, etc. Jacob's prayer was certainly not addressed to the angel himself, for angels have no power to act except as agents of the Holy One, to Whom Jacob referred in the previous verse.

My name . . . and the names of my forefathers. May they

48

Jacob's illness

¹ **A**nd it came to pass after these things that someone said to Joseph, "Behold! — your father is ill." So he took his two sons, Manasseh and Ephraim, with him.

² Jacob was told, "Behold! — your son Joseph has come to you." So Israel exerted himself and sat up on the bed.

³ Jacob said to Joseph, "El Shaddai had appeared to me in Luz in the land of Canaan and He blessed me. ⁴ He said to me, 'Behold — I will make you fruitful and numerous; I will make you a congregation of nations, and I will give this land to your offspring after you as an eternal possession.' ⁵ And now, your two sons who were born to you in the land of Egypt before my coming to you in Egypt shall be mine; Ephraim and Manasseh shall be mine like Reuben and Simeon. ⁶ But progeny born to you after them shall be yours; they will be included under the name of their brothers with regard to their inheritance. ⁷ But as for me — when I came from Paddan, Rachel died on me in the land of Canaan on the road, while there was still a stretch of land to go to Ephrath; and I buried her there on the road to Ephrath, which is Bethlehem."

The blessing of Manasseh and Ephraim

⁸ Then Israel saw Joseph's sons and he said, "Who are these?"

⁹ And Joseph said to his father, "They are my sons whom God has given me here."

He said, "Bring them to me, if you please, and I will bless them."

¹⁰ Now Israel's eyes were heavy with age, he could not see; so he brought them near him and he kissed them and hugged them. ¹¹ Israel said to Joseph, "I dared not accept the thought that I would see your face, and here God has shown me even your offspring!"

¹² Joseph then removed them from his knees and he prostrated himself with his face toward the ground.

¹³ Joseph took the two of them — Ephraim with his right [hand], to Israel's left, and Manasseh with his left, to Israel's right — and he drew close to him. ¹⁴ But Israel extended his right hand and laid it on Ephraim's head though he was the younger and his left hand on Manasseh's head. He maneuvered his hands, for Manasseh was the firstborn. ¹⁵ He blessed Joseph and he said, "O God before Whom my forefathers Abraham and Isaac walked — God Who shepherds me from my inception until this day: ¹⁶ May the angel* who redeems me from all evil bless the lads, and may my name be declared upon them, and the names of my forefathers* Abraham and Isaac, and may they proliferate abundantly like fish* within the land."

¹⁷ Joseph saw that his father was placing his right hand on Ephraim's head and it displeased him; so he supported his father's hand to remove it from upon Ephraim's head to Manasseh's head. ¹⁸ And Joseph said to his father, "Not so, Father, for this is the firstborn; place your right hand on his head."

¹⁹ But his father refused, saying, "I know, my son, I know; he too will become a people, and he too will become great; yet his younger brother shall become greater than he, and his off-spring['s fame] will fill the nations."

---

deserve to have their names coupled with those of the Patriarchs (*Rashi*).

And may they proliferate abundantly like fish. Fish are

fruitful and multiply, and are not affected by the evil eye [since they live calmly, unseen by man (*Berachos* 20a)] (*Rashi*).

כ וַיְבָרֲכֵם בַּיּוֹם הַהוּא ⁎לֵאמוֹר בְּךָ יְבָרֵךְ יִשְׂרָאֵל לֵאמֹר יְשִׂמְךָ אֱלֹהִים

כא כְּאֶפְרַיִם וְכִמְנַשֶּׁה וַיָּשֶׂם אֶת־אֶפְרַיִם לִפְנֵי מְנַשֶּׁה: וַיֹּאמֶר יִשְׂרָאֵל אֶל־

יוֹסֵף הִנֵּה אָנֹכִי מֵת וְהָיָה אֱלֹהִים עִמָּכֶם וְהֵשִׁיב אֶתְכֶם אֶל־אֶרֶץ

כב אֲבֹתֵיכֶם: וַאֲנִי נָתַתִּי לְךָ שְׁכֶם אַחַד עַל־אַחֶיךָ אֲשֶׁר לָקַחְתִּי מִיַּד הָאֱמֹרִי

בְּחַרְבִּי וּבְקַשְׁתִּי:

מט א רביעי וַיִּקְרָא יַעֲקֹב אֶל־בָּנָיו וַיֹּאמֶר הֵאָסְפוּ וְאַגִּידָה לָכֶם אֵת אֲשֶׁר־יִקְרָא

ב אֶתְכֶם בְּאַחֲרִית הַיָּמִים: הִקָּבְצוּ וְשִׁמְעוּ בְּנֵי יַעֲקֹב וְשִׁמְעוּ אֶל־יִשְׂרָאֵל

ג-ד אֲבִיכֶם: רְאוּבֵן בְּכֹרִי אַתָּה כֹּחִי וְרֵאשִׁית אוֹנִי יֶתֶר שְׂאֵת וְיֶתֶר עָז: פַּחַז

כַּמַּיִם אַל־תּוֹתַר כִּי עָלִיתָ מִשְׁכְּבֵי אָבִיךָ אָז חִלַּלְתָּ יְצוּעִי עָלָה:

ה-ו שִׁמְעוֹן וְלֵוִי אַחִים כְּלֵי חָמָס מְכֵרֹתֵיהֶם: בְּסֹדָם אַל־תָּבֹא נַפְשִׁי בִּקְהָלָם

ז אַל־תֵּחַד כְּבֹדִי כִּי בְאַפָּם הָרְגוּ אִישׁ וּבִרְצֹנָם עִקְּרוּ־שׁוֹר: אָרוּר אַפָּם כִּי

עָז וְעֶבְרָתָם כִּי קָשָׁתָה אֲחַלְּקֵם בְּיַעֲקֹב וַאֲפִיצֵם בְּיִשְׂרָאֵל:

ח ⁎יְהוּדָה אַתָּה יוֹדוּךָ אַחֶיךָ יָדְךָ בְּעֹרֶף אֹיְבֶיךָ יִשְׁתַּחֲווּ לְךָ בְּנֵי אָבִיךָ:

ט גּוּר אַרְיֵה יְהוּדָה מִטֶּרֶף בְּנִי עָלִיתָ כָּרַע רָבַץ כְּאַרְיֵה וּכְלָבִיא מִי יְקִימֶנּוּ:

י לֹא־יָסוּר שֵׁבֶט מִיהוּדָה וּמְחֹקֵק מִבֵּין רַגְלָיו עַד כִּי־יָבֹא שִׁילֹה וְלוֹ יִקְּהַת

יא עַמִּים: אֹסְרִי לַגֶּפֶן עִירֹה וְלַשֹּׂרֵקָה בְּנִי אֲתֹנוֹ כִּבֵּס בַּיַּיִן לְבֻשׁוֹ וּבְדַם־

יב עֲנָבִים סוּתֹה: חַכְלִילִי עֵינַיִם מִיָּיִן וּלְבֶן־שִׁנַּיִם מֵחָלָב:

יג זְבוּלֻן לְחוֹף יַמִּים יִשְׁכֹּן וְהוּא לְחוֹף אֳנִיֹּת וְיַרְכָתוֹ עַל־צִידֹן:

יד-טו יִשָּׂשכָר חֲמֹר גָּרֶם רֹבֵץ בֵּין הַמִּשְׁפְּתָיִם: וַיַּרְא מְנֻחָה כִּי טוֹב וְאֶת־הָאָרֶץ

טז כִּי נָעֵמָה וַיֵּט שִׁכְמוֹ לִסְבֹּל וַיְהִי לְמַס־עֹבֵד: דָּן יָדִין עַמּוֹ

יז כְּאַחַד שִׁבְטֵי יִשְׂרָאֵל: יְהִי־דָן נָחָשׁ עֲלֵי־דֶרֶךְ שְׁפִיפֹן עֲלֵי־אֹרַח הַנֹּשֵׁךְ

יח-יט חמישי עִקְּבֵי־סוּס וַיִּפֹּל רֹכְבוֹ אָחוֹר: לִישׁוּעָתְךָ קִוִּיתִי יְהוָה: ⁎גָּד

כ גְּדוּד יְגוּדֶנּוּ וְהוּא יָגֻד עָקֵב: מֵאָשֵׁר

48:20. Jewish parents will always remember that Joseph's sons were elevated to the status of full-fledged tribal fathers. Additionally, Ephraim and Manasseh maintained their Jewishness in the face of the hostility and temptation of Egyptian culture. Jewish parents always hope that their children show comparable commitment to their heritage.

⇛ Jacob blesses his children. Jacob blessed the tribes individually, each in line with its own character and ability, so that they would be directed toward the paths for which God had suited them, for his blessings would make clear that each of the tribes has its own unique mission.

49:4. Reuben lost his right to national leadership because of the *impetuosity* with which he rushed to vent his anger [in the incident with Bilhah; see 35:22].

49:5-7. Simeon and Levi. Having explained why Reuben forfeited the prerogatives of the birthright, Jacob then explained why Simeon and Levi, the next oldest, were also unworthy to succeed him as rulers.

49:6. Simeon and Levi sought to disable Joseph, who is figuratively likened to an *ox;* see *Deuteronomy* 33:17 (Rashi).

49:7. Even when Jacob was chastising his sons, he did not curse *them*, but their *rage* (Rashi).

49:8-12. Judah. When Judah heard Jacob's rebuke of his brothers, he drew back, afraid that Jacob might chastise him over the affair of Tamar. So Jacob called him soothingly, "Judah — *you* [this word is emphatic] are not like *them*. *You*, your brothers shall acknowledge!" (Midrash; Rashi). Judah would be the source of Jewish leadership and royalty, of the Davidic dynasty and Messiah.

So admired will you be by all your brothers that Jews will not say, I am a Reubenite or a Simeonite, but I am a Yehudi [Judahite; Jew] (Midrash).

49:10. The privilege of providing Israel's sovereign ruler — symbolized by the royal scepter — shall not pass from the House of Judah (Onkelos).

Until Shiloh arrives, i.e., the Messiah, to whom the

²⁰ So he blessed them that day, saying, "By you shall Israel bless* saying, 'May God make you like Ephraim and like Manasseh' " — and he put Ephraim before Manasseh.

²¹ Then Israel said to Joseph, "Behold! — I am about to die; God will be with you and will bring you back to the land of your fathers. ²² And as for me, I have given you Shechem — one portion more than your brothers, which I took from the hand of the Amorite with my sword and with my bow."

49

¹Then Jacob called for his sons and said, "Assemble yourselves and I will tell you what will befall you in the End of Days. ² Gather yourselves and listen, O sons of Jacob, and listen to Israel your father.

Jacob's blessings:

Reuben

³ "Reuben, you are my firstborn, my strength and my initial vigor, foremost in rank and foremost in power. ⁴ Water-like impetuosity* — you cannot be foremost, because you mounted your father's bed; then you desecrated Him Who ascended my couch.

Simeon and Levi

⁵ "Simeon and Levi are comrades, their weaponry is a stolen craft. ⁶ Into their conspiracy, may my soul not enter! With their congregation, do not join, O my honor! For in their rage they murdered people and at their whim they hamstrung an ox.* ⁷ Accursed is their rage* for it is intense, and their wrath for it is harsh; I will separate them within Jacob, and I will disperse them in Israel.

Judah

⁸ "Judah — you, your brothers shall acknowledge; your hand will be at your enemies' nape; your father's sons will prostrate themselves to you. ⁹ A lion cub is Judah; from the prey, my son, you elevated yourself. He crouches, lies down like a lion, and like an awesome lion, who dares rouse him? ¹⁰ The scepter shall not depart from Judah* nor a scholar from among his descendants until Shiloh arrives* and his will be an assemblage of nations. ¹¹ He will tie his donkey to the vine; to the vine branch his donkey's foal; he will launder his garments in wine and his robe in the blood of grapes. ¹² Red-eyed from wine, and white-toothed from milk.

A tiny glimpse at the Messianic era

Zebulun

¹³ "Zebulun shall settle by seashores. He shall be at the ship's harbor, and his last border will reach Zidon.

Issachar

¹⁴ "Issachar is a strong-boned donkey; he rests between the boundaries. ¹⁵ He saw tranquility that it was good, and the land that it was pleasant, yet he bent his shoulder to bear and he became an indentured laborer.

Dan

¹⁶ "Dan will avenge his people, the tribes of Israel will be united as one. ¹⁷ Dan will be a serpent on the highway, a viper by the path, that bites a horse's heels so its rider falls backward. ¹⁸ For Your salvation do I long, O HASHEM!

Gad

¹⁹ "Gad will recruit a regiment and it will retreat on its heel.

---

kingdom belongs (Rashi). The word *until* does not mean that Judah's ascendancy will end with the coming of Messiah. To the contrary, the sense of the verse is that once Messiah begins to reign, Judah's blessing of kingship will become fully realized (Sh'lah), for all the nations will acknowledge him and pay homage to him.

49:13. Zebulun precedes Issachar. Although Issachar was older, Jacob gave precedence to Zebulun because [as Rashi notes] Zebulun engaged in commerce and supported Issachar (Tanchuma).

49:14-15. Issachar. The simile of a *strong-boned donkey* refers to Issachar's *spiritual* role as bearer of the yoke

of Torah and cultivator of the spiritual treasures of the people (Rashi).

49:16-18. Dan. Having concluded his blessings of Leah's six sons, Jacob went on to the older son of Bilhah, Rachel's maidservant. He left the sons of Rachel for last.

49:19. Gad. Jacob went from Bilhah's older son to Zilpah's. Although the Gadites' territory was on the east of the Jordan, they crossed the river to assist their brothers in conquering the land. Jacob prophesied that after the conquest, Gad would return safely *on its heel*, i.e., by the same roads and paths upon which it had initially traveled — and not one of the troops will be lost (Rashi).

כא שְׁמֵנָה לַחְמוֹ וְהוּא יִתֵּן מַעֲדַנֵּי־מֶלֶךְ: נַפְתָּלִי אַיָּלָה שְׁלֻחָה
כב הַנֹּתֵן אִמְרֵי־שָׁפֶר: בֵּן פֹּרָת יוֹסֵף בֵּן פֹּרָת עֲלֵי־עָיִן בָּנוֹת
כג-כד צָעֲדָה עֲלֵי־שׁוּר: וַיְמָרְרֻהוּ וָרֹבּוּ וַיִּשְׂטְמֻהוּ בַּעֲלֵי חִצִּים: וַתֵּשֶׁב בְּאֵיתָן
כה קַשְׁתּוֹ וַיָּפֹזּוּ זְרֹעֵי יָדָיו מִידֵי אֲבִיר יַעֲקֹב מִשָּׁם רֹעֶה אֶבֶן יִשְׂרָאֵל: מֵאֵל
אָבִיךָ וְיַעְזְרֶךָּ וְאֵת שַׁדַּי וִיבָרְכֶךָּ בִּרְכֹת שָׁמַיִם מֵעָל בִּרְכֹת תְּהוֹם רֹבֶצֶת
כו תָּחַת בִּרְכֹת שָׁדַיִם וָרָחַם: בִּרְכֹת אָבִיךָ גָּבְרוּ עַל־בִּרְכֹת הוֹרַי עַד־תַּאֲוַת
גִּבְעֹת עוֹלָם תִּהְיֶיןָ לְרֹאשׁ יוֹסֵף וּלְקָדְקֹד נְזִיר אֶחָיו:
ששי כז-כח בִּנְיָמִין זְאֵב יִטְרָף בַּבֹּקֶר יֹאכַל עַד וְלָעֶרֶב יְחַלֵּק שָׁלָל: כָּל־אֵלֶּה שִׁבְטֵי
יִשְׂרָאֵל שְׁנֵים עָשָׂר וְזֹאת אֲשֶׁר־דִּבֶּר לָהֶם אֲבִיהֶם וַיְבָרֶךְ אוֹתָם אִישׁ אֲשֶׁר
כט כְּבִרְכָתוֹ בֵּרַךְ אֹתָם: וַיְצַו אוֹתָם וַיֹּאמֶר אֲלֵהֶם אֲנִי נֶאֱסָף אֶל־עַמִּי קִבְרוּ
ל אֹתִי אֶל־אֲבֹתָי אֶל־הַמְּעָרָה אֲשֶׁר בִּשְׂדֵה עֶפְרוֹן הַחִתִּי: בַּמְּעָרָה אֲשֶׁר
בִּשְׂדֵה הַמַּכְפֵּלָה אֲשֶׁר־עַל־פְּנֵי מַמְרֵא בְּאֶרֶץ כְּנָעַן אֲשֶׁר קָנָה אַבְרָהָם
לא אֶת־הַשָּׂדֶה מֵאֵת עֶפְרֹן הַחִתִּי לַאֲחֻזַּת־קָבֶר: שָׁמָּה קָבְרוּ אֶת־אַבְרָהָם
וְאֵת שָׂרָה אִשְׁתּוֹ שָׁמָּה קָבְרוּ אֶת־יִצְחָק וְאֵת רִבְקָה אִשְׁתּוֹ וְשָׁמָּה קָבַרְתִּי
לב-לג אֶת־לֵאָה: מִקְנֵה הַשָּׂדֶה וְהַמְּעָרָה אֲשֶׁר־בּוֹ מֵאֵת בְּנֵי־חֵת: וַיְכַל יַעֲקֹב
נ א לְצַוֹּת אֶת־בָּנָיו וַיֶּאֱסֹף רַגְלָיו אֶל־הַמִּטָּה וַיִּגְוַע וַיֵּאָסֶף אֶל־עַמָּיו: וַיִּפֹּל
ב יוֹסֵף עַל־פְּנֵי אָבִיו וַיֵּבְךְּ עָלָיו וַיִּשַּׁק־לוֹ: וַיְצַו יוֹסֵף אֶת־עֲבָדָיו אֶת־הָרֹפְאִים
ג לַחֲנֹט אֶת־אָבִיו וַיַּחַנְטוּ הָרֹפְאִים אֶת־יִשְׂרָאֵל: וַיִּמְלְאוּ־לוֹ אַרְבָּעִים יוֹם
ד כִּי כֵּן יִמְלְאוּ יְמֵי הַחֲנֻטִים וַיִּבְכּוּ אֹתוֹ מִצְרַיִם שִׁבְעִים יוֹם: וַיַּעַבְרוּ יְמֵי
בְכִיתוֹ וַיְדַבֵּר יוֹסֵף אֶל־בֵּית פַּרְעֹה לֵאמֹר אִם־נָא מָצָאתִי חֵן בְּעֵינֵיכֶם
ה דַּבְּרוּ־נָא בְּאָזְנֵי פַרְעֹה לֵאמֹר: אָבִי הִשְׁבִּיעַנִי לֵאמֹר הִנֵּה אָנֹכִי מֵת בְּקִבְרִי
אֲשֶׁר כָּרִיתִי לִי בְּאֶרֶץ כְּנַעַן שָׁמָּה תִּקְבְּרֵנִי וְעַתָּה אֶעֱלֶה־נָּא וְאֶקְבְּרָה
ו אֶת־אָבִי וְאָשׁוּבָה: וַיֹּאמֶר פַּרְעֹה עֲלֵה וּקְבֹר אֶת־אָבִיךָ כַּאֲשֶׁר הִשְׁבִּיעֶךָ:

49:20. Asher. Asher's land will be so rich in olive groves that it will flow with oil like a fountain (*Rashi*); *and he will provide kingly delicacies,* i.e., his rich produce will be worthy of royal tables and will be sought by kings (*Radak*).

49:21. Naphtali. Having blessed Zilpah's sons, Jacob blessed Bilhah's younger son, and thus concluded the blessings of the sons of the maidservants.

49:22. Joseph. Jacob turns to Rachel's sons, who were born last and who were his comfort after the loss of his beloved wife. He begins with ecstatic praise of Joseph, whose talent and purity survived hatred and temptation.

49:23-24. According to *Rashi* (as understood by the commentaries), these two verses are linked: Joseph rose to prominence despite the hatred he suffered. His brothers and Potiphar and his wife all *embittered him and became antagonists.* People with arrow-like tongues — a Scriptural allusion to purveyors of malicious slander and gossip — dealt bitterly with Joseph, but, by the grace of God, he rose to prominence despite them (*Rashi*).

49:24. From his God-given position as viceroy, or from his position as the victim of slander, Joseph became *the shepherd* who provided sustenance for Jacob, *the stone of Israel.* The word *stone* denotes the primary personage of the nation, as it is used in *Zechariah* 4:7.

49:27. Benjamin. His descendants were likened to a wolf — they were mighty, fearless warriors, as depicted in the affair of the Concubine at Gibeah [*Judges* chapters 19-20] (*Radak*), as was King Saul, a Benjamite, who, in his short reign, defeated Moab, Edom, and Philistia.

49:29-32. Jacob's final request. Although Joseph had already sworn to bury Jacob in the Cave of Machpelah, Jacob now imposed this duty upon the rest of his sons as well, because he feared that Pharaoh might forbid Joseph to leave the country, but would let the others go (*Ramban*).

49:33. "Our father Jacob did not die" (*Taanis* 5b). R' Yochanan maintains that Jacob did not die, even though

Asher   20 "From Asher — his bread will have richness, and he will provide kingly delicacies.

Naphtali   21 "Naphtali is a hind let loose who delivers beautiful sayings.

Joseph   22 "A charming son is Joseph, a charming son to the eye; each of the daughters climbed heights to gaze. 23 They embittered him and became antagonists; the arrow-tongued men hated him. 24 But his bow was firmly emplaced and his arms were gilded, from the hands of the Mighty Power of Jacob — from there, he shepherded the stone of Israel. * 25 [That was] from the God of your father and He will help you, and with Shaddai — and He will bless you [with] blessings of heaven from above, blessings of the deep crouching below, blessings of the bosom and womb. 26 The blessings of your father surpassed the blessings of my parents to the endless bounds of the world's hills. Let them be upon Joseph's head and upon the head of the exile from his brothers.

Benjamin   27 "Benjamin is a predatory wolf; in the morning he will devour prey and in the evening he will distribute spoils."

28 All these are the tribes of Israel — twelve — and this is what their father spoke to them and he blessed them; he blessed each according to his appropriate blessing.

Jacob's final request   29 Then he instructed them; and he said to them, "I shall be gathered to my people; bury me with my fathers in the cave that is in the field of Ephron the Hittite. 30 In the cave that is in the field of Machpelah, which faces Mamre, in the land of Canaan, which Abraham bought with the field from Ephron the Hittite as a burial estate. 31 There they buried Abraham and Sarah his wife; there they buried Isaac and Rebecca his wife; and there I buried Leah. 32 Purchase of the field and the cave within it was from the sons of Heth."

33 When Jacob finished instructing his sons, he drew his feet onto the bed; he expired and was gathered to his people.

50   1 Then Joseph fell upon his father's face; he wept over him and kissed him. 2 Joseph ordered his servants, the physicians, to embalm his father; * so the physicians embalmed Israel.

3 His forty-day term was completed, for such is the term of the embalmed; and Egypt bewailed him for seventy days. 4 When his bewailing period passed,

Jacob is mourned by all Egypt   Joseph spoke to Pharaoh's household, saying, "If you please — if I have found favor in your eyes, speak now in the ears of Pharaoh, saying: 5 My father had adjured me, saying, 'Behold, I am about to die; in my grave, which I have hewn for myself in the land of Canaan — there you are to bury me.' Now, I will go up if you please, and bury my father; then I will return."

Permission for burial   6 And Pharaoh said, "Go up and bury your father as he adjured you." *

---

the Torah relates below that he was mourned, embalmed, and buried. Most commentators understand this statement to imply that Jacob lives on spiritually because his offspring maintain his heritage.

50:2. Embalming was an Egyptian custom based on the teachings of the nation's idolatrous beliefs. Under Torah law, however, it is strictly forbidden. The Torah requires that the body be permitted to decompose naturally, as quickly as possible and without impediment.

Or HaChaim comments that since the body of a completely righteous person never putrefies, Joseph was

afraid that the Egyptians, upon noting this phenomenon, would treat Jacob's body as an idol. In order to spare his father that awful indignity, Joseph had the body embalmed, so that the Egyptians would attribute its preservation to their own skill.

50:4-6. Permission for burial. As Egypt's ruler, Joseph could not leave for an extended period without his absence affecting the administration of government.

50:6. Pharaoh's implication was clear: Had Joseph not sworn to do so, he would not have been permitted to go (Rashi).

ז וַיַּעַל יוֹסֵף לִקְבֹּר אֶת־אָבִיו וַיַּעֲלוּ אִתּוֹ כָּל־עַבְדֵי פַרְעֹה זִקְנֵי בֵיתוֹ וְכֹל

ח זִקְנֵי אֶרֶץ־מִצְרָיִם: וְכֹל בֵּית יוֹסֵף וְאֶחָיו וּבֵית אָבִיו רַק טַפָּם וְצֹאנָם

ט וּבְקָרָם עָזְבוּ בְּאֶרֶץ גֹּשֶׁן: וַיַּעַל עִמּוֹ גַּם־רֶכֶב גַּם־פָּרָשִׁים וַיְהִי הַמַּחֲנֶה

י כָּבֵד מְאֹד: וַיָּבֹאוּ עַד־גֹּרֶן הָאָטָד אֲשֶׁר בְּעֵבֶר הַיַּרְדֵּן וַיִּסְפְּדוּ־שָׁם מִסְפֵּד

יא גָּדוֹל וְכָבֵד מְאֹד וַיַּעַשׂ לְאָבִיו אֵבֶל שִׁבְעַת יָמִים: וַיַּרְא יוֹשֵׁב הָאָרֶץ

הַכְּנַעֲנִי אֶת־הָאֵבֶל בְּגֹרֶן הָאָטָד וַיֹּאמְרוּ אֵבֶל־כָּבֵד זֶה לְמִצְרָיִם עַל־כֵּן

יב קָרָא שְׁמָהּ אָבֵל מִצְרַיִם אֲשֶׁר בְּעֵבֶר הַיַּרְדֵּן: וַיַּעֲשׂוּ בָנָיו לוֹ כֵּן כַּאֲשֶׁר

יג צִוָּם: וַיִּשְׂאוּ אֹתוֹ בָנָיו אַרְצָה כְּנַעַן וַיִּקְבְּרוּ אֹתוֹ בִּמְעָרַת שְׂדֵה הַמַּכְפֵּלָה

אֲשֶׁר קָנָה אַבְרָהָם אֶת־הַשָּׂדֶה לַאֲחֻזַּת־קֶבֶר מֵאֵת עֶפְרֹן הַחִתִּי עַל־פְּנֵי

יד מַמְרֵא: וַיָּשָׁב יוֹסֵף מִצְרַיְמָה הוּא וְאֶחָיו וְכָל־הָעֹלִים אִתּוֹ לִקְבֹּר אֶת־

טו אָבִיו אַחֲרֵי קָבְרוֹ אֶת־אָבִיו: וַיִּרְאוּ אֲחֵי־יוֹסֵף כִּי־מֵת אֲבִיהֶם וַיֹּאמְרוּ לוּ

טז יִשְׂטְמֵנוּ יוֹסֵף וְהָשֵׁב יָשִׁיב לָנוּ אֵת כָּל־הָרָעָה אֲשֶׁר גָּמַלְנוּ אֹתוֹ: וַיְצַוּוּ

יז אֶל־יוֹסֵף לֵאמֹר אָבִיךָ צִוָּה לִפְנֵי מוֹתוֹ לֵאמֹר: כֹּה־תֹאמְרוּ לְיוֹסֵף אָנָּא

שָׂא נָא פֶּשַׁע אַחֶיךָ וְחַטָּאתָם כִּי־רָעָה גְמָלוּךָ וְעַתָּה שָׂא נָא לְפֶשַׁע

יח עַבְדֵי אֱלֹהֵי אָבִיךָ וַיֵּבְךְּ יוֹסֵף בְּדַבְּרָם אֵלָיו: וַיֵּלְכוּ גַּם־אֶחָיו וַיִּפְּלוּ לְפָנָיו

יט וַיֹּאמְרוּ הִנֶּנּוּ לְךָ לַעֲבָדִים: וַיֹּאמֶר אֲלֵהֶם יוֹסֵף אַל־תִּירָאוּ כִּי הֲתַחַת

כ אֱלֹהִים אָנִי: וְאַתֶּם חֲשַׁבְתֶּם עָלַי רָעָה אֱלֹהִים חֲשָׁבָהּ לְטֹבָה לְמַעַן

כא עֲשֹׂה כַּיּוֹם הַזֶּה לְהַחֲיֹת עַם־רָב: וְעַתָּה אַל־תִּירָאוּ אָנֹכִי אֲכַלְכֵּל אֶתְכֶם שביעי

כב וְאֶת־טַפְּכֶם וַיְנַחֵם אוֹתָם וַיְדַבֵּר עַל־לִבָּם: וַיֵּשֶׁב יוֹסֵף בְּמִצְרַיִם הוּא

כג וּבֵית אָבִיו וַיְחִי יוֹסֵף מֵאָה וָעֶשֶׂר שָׁנִים: וַיַּרְא יוֹסֵף לְאֶפְרַיִם בְּנֵי שִׁלֵּשִׁים מפטיר

כד גַּם בְּנֵי מָכִיר בֶּן־מְנַשֶּׁה יֻלְּדוּ עַל־בִּרְכֵּי יוֹסֵף: וַיֹּאמֶר יוֹסֵף אֶל־אֶחָיו Haftaras
Vayechi:
p. 800

אָנֹכִי מֵת וֵאלֹהִים פָּקֹד יִפְקֹד אֶתְכֶם וְהֶעֱלָה אֶתְכֶם מִן־הָאָרֶץ הַזֹּאת

כה אֶל־הָאָרֶץ אֲשֶׁר נִשְׁבַּע לְאַבְרָהָם לְיִצְחָק וּלְיַעֲקֹב: וַיַּשְׁבַּע יוֹסֵף אֶת־בְּנֵי

יִשְׂרָאֵל לֵאמֹר פָּקֹד יִפְקֹד אֱלֹהִים אֶתְכֶם וְהַעֲלִתֶם אֶת־עַצְמֹתַי מִזֶּה:

כו וַיָּמָת יוֹסֵף בֶּן־מֵאָה וָעֶשֶׂר שָׁנִים וַיַּחַנְטוּ אֹתוֹ וַיִּישֶׂם בָּאָרוֹן בְּמִצְרָיִם:

It is customary for the congregation followed by the reader to proclaim:

חֲזַק! חֲזַק! וְנִתְחַזֵּק!

פ״ה פְּסוּקִים. פ״ה אל פ״ה סִימָן. סְכוּם פְּסוּקֵי דְּסֵפֶר בְּרֵאשִׁית אֶלֶף וְחָמֵשׁ מֵאוֹת וּשְׁלֹשִׁים וְאַרְבָּעָה. אך לד׳ סִימָן.

50:19-20. Joseph reassured his brothers, saying that he could not harm them even if he wanted to. If God would not permit them — a large group of righteous people — to harm him, how could he as an individual succeed in harming them? (*Rashi*).

50:23. Although Joseph was the first of the brothers to die, he lived to see Ephraim's children, grandchildren, and great-grandchildren.

50:24. Signs of the redemption. Joseph shared with his brothers a secret sign of the redemption that Jacob had confided to him in the last moments of his life. Some day

a redeemer would tell the enslaved Jews in Egypt that God had declared פָּקֹד פָּקַדְתִּי, *I have indeed remembered you* (*Exodus* 3:16), just as Joseph now promised his brothers, וֵאלֹהִים פָּקֹד יִפְקֹד אֶתְכֶם, *But God will surely remember you* (*Mizrachi*). The implication of the term is that after a long period of time during which it seemed as if God had "forgotten" His people, He would manifest His Presence, as if He had "remembered" them once more. This "password" was transmitted to the leaders of the people, and when Moses came and proclaimed these words, they knew that he was truly speaking in God's Name.

The burial procession   ⁷ So Joseph went up to bury his father, and with him went up all of Pharaoh's servants, the elders of his household, and all the elders of the land of Egypt, ⁸ and all of Joseph's household — his brothers, and his father's household; only their young children, their flocks, and their cattle did they leave in the region of Goshen. ⁹ And he brought up with him both chariots and horsemen; and the camp was very imposing. ¹⁰ They came to Goren HaAtad, which is across the Jordan, and there they held a very great and imposing eulogy; and he ordained a seven-day mourning period for his father. ¹¹ When the Canaanite inhabitants of the land saw the mourning in Goren HaAtad, they said, "This is a grievous mourning for Egypt." Therefore, it was named Avel Mizraim, which is across the Jordan.

¹² His sons did for him exactly as he had instructed them. ¹³ His sons carried him to the land of Canaan and they buried him in the cave of the Machpelah field, the field that Abraham had bought as a burial estate from Ephron the Hittite, facing Mamre. ¹⁴ Joseph returned to Egypt — he and his brothers, and all who had gone up with him to bury his father — after he buried his father.

Joseph reassures his brothers   ¹⁵ Joseph's brothers perceived that their father was dead, and they said, "Perhaps Joseph will nurse hatred against us and then he will surely repay us all the evil that we did him." ¹⁶ So they instructed that Joseph be told, "Your father gave orders before his death, saying: ¹⁷ 'Thus shall you say to Joseph: "O please, kindly forgive the flagrant offense of your brothers and their sin for they have done you evil" '; so now, please forgive the flagrant offense of the servants of your father's God." And Joseph wept when they spoke to him.

¹⁸ His brothers themselves also went and flung themselves before him and said, "We are ready to be your slaves."

¹⁹ But Joseph said to them, "Fear not, for am I instead of God? ²⁰ Although you intended me harm, God intended it for good: in order to accomplish — it is as clear as this day — that a vast people be kept alive. ²¹ So now, fear not — I will sustain you and your young ones." Thus he comforted them and spoke to their heart.

Joseph lives out his years   ²² Joseph dwelt in Egypt — he and his father's household — and Joseph lived one hundred and ten years. ²³ Joseph saw three generations* through Ephraim; even the sons of Machir son of Manasseh were raised on Joseph's knees.

Signs of the redemption   ²⁴ Joseph said to his brothers, "I am about to die, but God will surely remember you* and bring you up out of this land to the land that He swore to Abraham, to Isaac, and to Jacob."

²⁵ Then Joseph adjured the children of Israel saying, "When God will indeed remember you, then you must bring my bones up out of here."

²⁶ Joseph died at the age of one hundred and ten years; they embalmed him and he was placed in a coffin in Egypt.

It is customary for the congregation followed by the reader to proclaim:
"Chazak! Chazak! Venischazeik!
(Be strong! Be strong! And may we be strengthened!)"

50:25. Joseph knew that Pharaoh and his people would not have permitted his survivors to bury him in *Eretz Yisrael* — but he exacted this pledge that when the time came for the nation to leave the land of their servitude, they should take his remains with them.

Exodus שמות

*I*n the Book of Exodus, the nation takes shape and learns eternal lessons of faith. The Jews came to Egypt in a blaze of glory, as the family of the viceroy and the offspring of the Patriarch who inspired awe and respect even from Pharaoh. But as soon as Joseph and his generation had passed from the scene, Egypt resented the growth of this upstart immigrant people; Israel's very success proved to be its undoing — a phenomenon that has become very familiar in Jewish history. Lured into slavery and so powerless that it could not even prevent the murder of its infants, Israel's plight seemed hopeless, until God's mercy was aroused and He sent Moses as His emissary.

Israel's innate holiness had been buffeted but not destroyed; they believed Moses, because they knew that God would not forsake them. The legacy of the Patriarchs remained intact, despite the slavery that had driven Israel to the "forty-ninth level of spiritual impurity" — another portent for times when the Jewish spirit might appear to be extinguished. Like a firebrand that flickers before blazing anew, Israel has always confounded the prophets of its doom.

The miracles of the Exodus are well known. What is more important than the events themselves is that God demonstrated that He is the Master of nature and the Architect of history. To the Patriarchs, it had been a principle of faith that God would carry out His pledges to their offspring; to the Children of Israel watching themselves being liberated from Egypt, God's intervention was an established, visible fact, as was the indisputable proof that He controls nature.

Exodus' theme of liberation is carried forward at Mount Sinai, where it is made clear that true freedom is not merely the removal of an alien yoke. The Exodus would have been a farce if Israel had not declared unanimously, "Everything that HASHEM has said, we will do and we will obey" (Exodus 24:7). As the Sages express it, "You can have no freer person than one who engages in the study of the Torah" (Avos 6:2). Libertines live for pleasure; truly free people submit to a higher calling.

The climax of this Book of Redemption, as Ramban calls the Book of Exodus, is the construction of the Tabernacle. Built by human hands, of the generosity of human hearts, it became the resting place for God's Presence, a place of such overpowering holiness that even Moses could not enter; "Moses could not enter ... for the cloud rested upon it, and the glory of HASHEM filled the Tabernacle" (Exodus 40:35). Clearly, the Jewish vision of redemption is to create a home for holiness. When the nation accomplished that, its redemption was complete.

פרשת שמות

א וְאֵ֗לֶּה שְׁמוֹת֙ בְּנֵ֣י יִשְׂרָאֵ֔ל הַבָּאִ֖ים מִצְרָ֑יְמָה אֵ֣ת יַעֲקֹ֔ב אִ֥ישׁ וּבֵית֖וֹ בָּֽאוּ:

ב־ד רְאוּבֵ֣ן שִׁמְע֔וֹן לֵוִ֖י וִיהוּדָֽה: יִשָּׂשכָ֥ר זְבוּלֻ֖ן וּבְנְיָמִֽן: דָּ֥ן וְנַפְתָּלִ֖י גָּ֥ד וְאָשֵֽׁר:

ה־ו וַֽיְהִ֗י כָּל־נֶ֛פֶשׁ יֹצְאֵ֥י יֶֽרֶךְ־יַעֲקֹ֖ב שִׁבְעִ֣ים נָ֑פֶשׁ וְיוֹסֵ֖ף הָיָ֥ה בְמִצְרָֽיִם: וַיָּ֤מָת

ז יוֹסֵף֙ וְכָל־אֶחָ֔יו וְכֹ֖ל הַדּ֥וֹר הַהֽוּא: וּבְנֵ֣י יִשְׂרָאֵ֗ל פָּר֧וּ וַֽיִּשְׁרְצ֛וּ וַיִּרְבּ֥וּ וַיַּֽעַצְמ֖וּ בִּמְאֹ֣ד מְאֹ֑ד וַתִּמָּלֵ֥א הָאָ֖רֶץ אֹתָֽם:

ח־ט וַיָּ֥קָם מֶֽלֶךְ־חָדָ֖שׁ עַל־מִצְרָ֑יִם אֲשֶׁ֥ר לֹֽא־יָדַ֖ע אֶת־יוֹסֵֽף: וַיֹּ֖אמֶר אֶל־עַמּ֑וֹ

י הִנֵּ֗ה עַ֚ם בְּנֵ֣י יִשְׂרָאֵ֔ל רַ֥ב וְעָצ֖וּם מִמֶּֽנּוּ: הָ֣בָה נִּֽתְחַכְּמָ֖ה ל֑וֹ פֶּן־יִרְבֶּ֗ה וְהָיָ֞ה כִּֽי־תִקְרֶ֤אנָה מִלְחָמָה֙ וְנוֹסַ֤ף גַּם־הוּא֙ עַל־שֹֽׂנְאֵ֔ינוּ וְנִלְחַם־בָּ֖נוּ וְעָלָ֥ה מִן־

יא הָאָֽרֶץ: וַיָּשִׂ֤ימוּ עָלָיו֙ שָׂרֵ֣י מִסִּ֔ים לְמַ֥עַן עַנֹּת֖וֹ בְּסִבְלֹתָ֑ם וַיִּ֜בֶן עָרֵ֤י מִסְכְּנוֹת֙

יב לְפַרְעֹ֔ה אֶת־פִּתֹ֖ם וְאֶת־רַֽעַמְסֵֽס: וְכַֽאֲשֶׁר֙ יְעַנּ֣וּ אֹת֔וֹ כֵּ֥ן יִרְבֶּ֖ה וְכֵ֣ן יִפְרֹ֑ץ

יג־יד וַיָּקֻ֕צוּ מִפְּנֵ֖י בְּנֵ֥י יִשְׂרָאֵֽל: וַיַּעֲבִ֧דוּ מִצְרַ֛יִם אֶת־בְּנֵ֥י יִשְׂרָאֵ֖ל בְּפָֽרֶךְ: וַיְמָֽרְר֨וּ אֶת־חַיֵּיהֶ֜ם בַּעֲבֹדָ֣ה קָשָׁ֗ה בְּחֹ֙מֶר֙ וּבִלְבֵנִ֔ים וּבְכָל־עֲבֹדָ֖ה בַּשָּׂדֶ֑ה אֵ֖ת כָּל־

טו עֲבֹ֣דָתָ֔ם אֲשֶׁר־עָבְד֥וּ בָהֶ֖ם בְּפָֽרֶךְ: וַיֹּ֙אמֶר֙ מֶ֣לֶךְ מִצְרַ֔יִם לַֽמְיַלְּדֹ֖ת הָֽעִבְרִיֹּ֑ת

טז אֲשֶׁ֨ר שֵׁ֤ם הָֽאַחַת֙ שִׁפְרָ֔ה וְשֵׁ֥ם הַשֵּׁנִ֖ית פּוּעָֽה: וַיֹּ֗אמֶר בְּיַלֶּדְכֶן֙ אֶת־הָֽעִבְרִיּ֔וֹת וּרְאִיתֶ֖ן עַל־הָאָבְנָ֑יִם אִם־בֵּ֥ן הוּא֙ וַהֲמִתֶּ֣ן אֹת֔וֹ וְאִם־בַּ֥ת הִ֖וא

יז וָחָֽיָה: וַתִּירֶ֤אןָ הַֽמְיַלְּדֹת֙ אֶת־הָ֣אֱלֹהִ֔ים וְלֹ֣א עָשׂ֔וּ כַּאֲשֶׁ֛ר דִּבֶּ֥ר אֲלֵיהֶ֖ן מֶ֣לֶךְ

יח מִצְרָ֑יִם וַתְּחַיֶּ֖יןָ אֶת־הַיְלָדִֽים: וַיִּקְרָ֤א מֶֽלֶךְ־מִצְרַ֙יִם֙ לַֽמְיַלְּדֹ֔ת וַיֹּ֣אמֶר לָהֶ֔ן

יט מַדּ֥וּעַ עֲשִׂיתֶ֖ן הַדָּבָ֣ר הַזֶּ֑ה וַתְּחַיֶּ֖יןָ אֶת־הַיְלָדִֽים: וַתֹּאמַ֤רְןָ הַֽמְיַלְּדֹת֙ אֶל־פַּרְעֹ֔ה כִּ֣י לֹ֧א כַנָּשִׁ֛ים הַמִּצְרִיֹּ֖ת הָֽעִבְרִיֹּ֑ת כִּֽי־חָי֣וֹת הֵ֔נָּה בְּטֶ֨רֶם תָּב֧וֹא אֲלֵהֶ֛ן

כ־כא הַֽמְיַלֶּ֖דֶת וְיָלָֽדוּ: וַיֵּ֥יטֶב אֱלֹהִ֖ים לַֽמְיַלְּדֹ֑ת וַיִּ֧רֶב הָעָ֛ם וַיַּֽעַצְמ֖וּ מְאֹֽד: וַיְהִ֕י כִּֽי־

כב יָֽרְא֥וּ הַֽמְיַלְּדֹ֖ת אֶת־הָֽאֱלֹהִ֑ים וַיַּ֥עַשׂ לָהֶ֖ם בָּתִּֽים: וַיְצַ֣ו פַּרְעֹ֔ה לְכָל־עַמּ֖וֹ לֵאמֹ֑ר כָּל־הַבֵּ֣ן הַיִּלּ֗וֹד הַיְאֹ֙רָה֙ תַּשְׁלִיכֻ֔הוּ וְכָל־הַבַּ֖ת תְּחַיּֽוּן:

ב א־ב וַיֵּ֥לֶךְ אִ֖ישׁ מִבֵּ֣ית לֵוִ֑י וַיִּקַּ֖ח אֶת־בַּת־לֵוִֽי: וַתַּ֥הַר הָאִשָּׁ֖ה וַתֵּ֣לֶד בֵּ֑ן וַתֵּ֤רֶא

ג אֹתוֹ֙ כִּי־ט֣וֹב ה֔וּא וַֽתִּצְפְּנֵ֖הוּ שְׁלֹשָׁ֥ה יְרָחִֽים: וְלֹא־יָֽכְלָ֣ה עוֹד֮ הַצְּפִינוֹ֒ וַתִּֽקַּֽח־לוֹ֙ תֵּ֣בַת גֹּ֔מֶא וַתַּחְמְרָ֥ה בַחֵמָ֖ר וּבַזָּ֑פֶת וַתָּ֤שֶׂם בָּהּ֙ אֶת־הַיֶּ֔לֶד וַתָּ֥שֶׂם

ד בַּסּ֖וּף עַל־שְׂפַ֥ת הַיְאֹֽר: וַתֵּתַצַּ֥ב אֲחֹת֖וֹ מֵרָחֹ֑ק לְדֵעָ֕ה מַה־יֵּעָשֶׂ֖ה לֽוֹ:

◦⁄§ Parashas Shemos

1:1. The Book of *Exodus* begins with the conjunction *and* in order to relate it to the conclusion of *Genesis*. There, Jacob's family begins the process of exile by descending to Egypt, and here the narrative of the exile is developed until it ends with the blaze of miracles that culminated in the Exodus and the giving of the Torah at Sinai (*Ramban, R' Bachya*).

1:8-14. The Egyptians were frightened by Israel's growth. They might overwhelm the natives — but they were also too useful to be permitted to leave the country. It was the first instance in history of what has become the familiar pattern of anti-Semitism: The Jews are too dangerous to keep and they are too important to lose. So Pharaoh proposes a solution. He will harness the Jews by enslaving them, so that the state will benefit from their talents without fear that they will desert the country.

1:12. God thwarted the evil plot. The more the Jews were tormented, the more their population grew, and infuriated the Egyptians further (*Rashi*), thus leading to the next stage in persecution.

1:15-22. Having failed to stem Jewish growth through slavery, Pharaoh devised a more blatant, if secret, form of destruction. He ordered the Jewish midwives to kill the

PARASHAS SHEMOS

1

The generation passes

¹ **A**nd* these are the names of the Children of Israel who were coming to Egypt; with Jacob, each man and his household came. ² Reuben, Simeon, Levi, and Judah; ³ Issachar, Zebulun, and Benjamin; ⁴ Dan and Naphtali; Gad and Asher. ⁵ And all the persons who emerged from Jacob's loins were seventy souls, and Joseph was in Egypt. ⁶ Joseph died, and all his brothers and that entire generation. ⁷ The Children of Israel were fruitful, teemed, increased, and became strong — very, very much so; and the land became filled with them.

Pharaoh's plot

⁸ A new king arose over Egypt, * who did not know of Joseph. ⁹ He said to his people, "Behold! the people, the Children of Israel, are more numerous and stronger than we. ¹⁰ Come, let us outsmart it lest it become numerous and it may be that if a war will occur, it, too, may join our enemies, and wage war against us and go up from the land."

¹¹ So they appointed taskmasters over it in order to afflict it with their burdens; it built storage cities for Pharaoh, Pithom and Raamses. ¹² But as much as they would afflict it, so it would increase* and so it would spread out; and they became disgusted because of the Children of Israel. ¹³ Egypt enslaved the Children of Israel with crushing harshness. ¹⁴ They embittered their lives with hard work, with mortar and with bricks, and with every labor of the field; all their labors that they performed with them were with crushing harshness.

Infanticide

¹⁵ The king of Egypt said to the Hebrew midwives, * of whom the name of the first was Shifrah and the name of the second was Puah — ¹⁶ and he said, "When you deliver the Hebrew women, and you see them on the birthstool; if it is a son, you are to kill him, and if it is a daughter, she shall live." ¹⁷ But the midwives feared God and they did not do as the king of Egypt spoke to them, and they caused the boys to live.

¹⁸ The king of Egypt summoned the midwives and said to them, "Why have you done this thing, that you have caused the boys to live!"

¹⁹ The midwives said to Pharaoh, "Because the Hebrew women are unlike the Egyptian women, for they are experts; before the midwife comes to them, they have given birth."

²⁰ God benefited the midwives — and the people increased and became very strong. ²¹ And it was because the midwives feared God that He made them houses.

²² Pharaoh commanded his entire people, saying, "Every son that will be born — into the River shall you throw him! And every daughter shall you keep alive!"

2

The birth of Moses

¹ **A** man went from the house of Levi and he took a daughter of Levi. * ² The woman conceived and gave birth to a son. She saw that he was good and she hid him for three months. ³ She could not hide him any longer, so she took for him a wicker basket and smeared it with clay and pitch; she placed the child into it and placed it among the reeds at the bank of the River. ⁴ His sister stationed herself at a distance to know what would be done with him.

---

male babies; then the females would be forced to blend into Egypt. According to the Sages, the midwives Shifrah and Puah were Jochebed and Miriam, the mother and sister of Moses (*Sotah* 11b). Pharaoh had another reason for the infanticide. His astrologers told him that the savior of the Jews was about to be born, so Pharaoh ordered all

the *boys* to be killed (ibid. 12b). Indeed, Moses was born during the time this cruel order was in effect.

2:1. *A man . . . a daughter of Levi.* In 6:20 they are identified as Amram and Jochebed. He was a grandson of Levi, while she was literally a daughter; she gave birth miraculously at the age of 130 (*Rashi*).

ה וַתֵּרֶד בַּת־פַּרְעֹה לִרְחֹץ עַל־הַיְאֹר וְנַעֲרֹתֶיהָ הֹלְכֹת עַל־יַד הַיְאֹר וַתֵּרֶא
אֶת־הַתֵּבָה בְּתוֹךְ הַסּוּף וַתִּשְׁלַח אֶת־אֲמָתָהּ וַתִּקָּחֶהָ: ו וַתִּפְתַּח וַתִּרְאֵהוּ
אֶת־הַיֶּלֶד וְהִנֵּה־נַעַר בֹּכֶה וַתַּחְמֹל עָלָיו וַתֹּאמֶר מִיַּלְדֵי הָעִבְרִים זֶה:
ז וַתֹּאמֶר אֲחֹתוֹ אֶל־בַּת־פַּרְעֹה הַאֵלֵךְ וְקָרָאתִי לָךְ אִשָּׁה מֵינֶקֶת מִן
הָעִבְרִיֹּת וְתֵינִק לָךְ אֶת־הַיָּלֶד: ח וַתֹּאמֶר־לָהּ בַּת־פַּרְעֹה לֵכִי וַתֵּלֶךְ
הָעַלְמָה וַתִּקְרָא אֶת־אֵם הַיָּלֶד: ט וַתֹּאמֶר לָהּ בַּת־פַּרְעֹה הֵילִיכִי אֶת־
הַיֶּלֶד הַזֶּה וְהֵינִקִהוּ לִי וַאֲנִי אֶתֵּן אֶת־שְׂכָרֵךְ וַתִּקַּח הָאִשָּׁה הַיֶּלֶד
וַתְּנִיקֵהוּ: י וַיִּגְדַּל הַיֶּלֶד וַתְּבִאֵהוּ לְבַת־פַּרְעֹה וַיְהִי־לָהּ לְבֵן וַתִּקְרָא שְׁמוֹ
משֶׁה וַתֹּאמֶר כִּי מִן־הַמַּיִם מְשִׁיתִהוּ: יא וַיְהִי בַּיָּמִים הָהֵם וַיִּגְדַּל משֶׁה
וַיֵּצֵא אֶל־אֶחָיו וַיַּרְא בְּסִבְלֹתָם וַיַּרְא אִישׁ מִצְרִי מַכֶּה אִישׁ־עִבְרִי
מֵאֶחָיו: יב וַיִּפֶן כֹּה וָכֹה וַיַּרְא כִּי אֵין אִישׁ וַיַּךְ אֶת־הַמִּצְרִי וַיִּטְמְנֵהוּ בַּחוֹל:
יג וַיֵּצֵא בַּיּוֹם הַשֵּׁנִי וְהִנֵּה שְׁנֵי־אֲנָשִׁים עִבְרִים נִצִּים וַיֹּאמֶר לָרָשָׁע לָמָּה
תַכֶּה רֵעֶךָ: יד וַיֹּאמֶר מִי שָׂמְךָ לְאִישׁ שַׂר וְשֹׁפֵט עָלֵינוּ הַלְהָרְגֵנִי אַתָּה אֹמֵר
כַּאֲשֶׁר הָרַגְתָּ אֶת־הַמִּצְרִי וַיִּירָא משֶׁה וַיֹּאמַר אָכֵן נוֹדַע הַדָּבָר: טו וַיִּשְׁמַע
פַּרְעֹה אֶת־הַדָּבָר הַזֶּה וַיְבַקֵּשׁ לַהֲרֹג אֶת־משֶׁה וַיִּבְרַח משֶׁה מִפְּנֵי פַרְעֹה
וַיֵּשֶׁב בְּאֶרֶץ־מִדְיָן וַיֵּשֶׁב עַל־הַבְּאֵר: טז וּלְכֹהֵן מִדְיָן שֶׁבַע בָּנוֹת וַתָּבֹאנָה
וַתִּדְלֶנָה וַתְּמַלֶּאנָה אֶת־הָרְהָטִים לְהַשְׁקוֹת צֹאן אֲבִיהֶן: יז וַיָּבֹאוּ הָרֹעִים
וַיְגָרְשׁוּם וַיָּקָם משֶׁה וַיּוֹשִׁעָן וַיַּשְׁקְ אֶת־צֹאנָם: יח וַתָּבֹאנָה אֶל־רְעוּאֵל
אֲבִיהֶן וַיֹּאמֶר מַדּוּעַ מִהַרְתֶּן בֹּא הַיּוֹם: יט וַתֹּאמַרְןָ אִישׁ מִצְרִי הִצִּילָנוּ מִיַּד
הָרֹעִים וְגַם־דָּלֹה דָלָה לָנוּ וַיַּשְׁקְ אֶת־הַצֹּאן: כ וַיֹּאמֶר אֶל־בְּנֹתָיו וְאַיּוֹ
לָמָּה זֶּה עֲזַבְתֶּן אֶת־הָאִישׁ קִרְאֶן לוֹ וְיֹאכַל לָחֶם: כא וַיּוֹאֶל משֶׁה לָשֶׁבֶת
אֶת־הָאִישׁ וַיִּתֵּן אֶת־צִפֹּרָה בִתּוֹ לְמשֶׁה: כב וַתֵּלֶד בֵּן וַיִּקְרָא אֶת־שְׁמוֹ
גֵּרְשֹׁם כִּי אָמַר גֵּר הָיִיתִי בְּאֶרֶץ נָכְרִיָּה:
כג וַיְהִי בַיָּמִים הָרַבִּים הָהֵם וַיָּמָת מֶלֶךְ מִצְרַיִם וַיֵּאָנְחוּ בְנֵי־יִשְׂרָאֵל מִן
הָעֲבֹדָה וַיִּזְעָקוּ וַתַּעַל שַׁוְעָתָם אֶל־הָאֱלֹהִים מִן־הָעֲבֹדָה: כד וַיִּשְׁמַע אֱלֹהִים
אֶת־נַאֲקָתָם וַיִּזְכֹּר אֱלֹהִים אֶת־בְּרִיתוֹ אֶת־אַבְרָהָם אֶת־יִצְחָק וְאֶת־
יַעֲקֹב: כה וַיַּרְא אֱלֹהִים אֶת־בְּנֵי יִשְׂרָאֵל וַיֵּדַע אֱלֹהִים: ג וּמשֶׁה הָיָה
רֹעֶה אֶת־צֹאן יִתְרוֹ חֹתְנוֹ כֹּהֵן מִדְיָן וַיִּנְהַג אֶת־הַצֹּאן אַחַר הַמִּדְבָּר וַיָּבֹא

שלישי   רביעי

2:10. She gave him the Egyptian name Monios, which means that he was drawn from the water. Moses/Moshe is the Hebrew translation of that word (*Ibn Ezra*).

2:11-15. Though Moses had been raised in the splendor and anti-Semitism of the palace, he remained the son of Amram and Jochebed. Though his mother had had him for only the earliest years of his life, she had succeeded in imbuing him with love of and loyalty to his people; he remained not an Egyptian prince, but a Jew, and he displayed the compassion for the downtrodden that stamped him as the future redeemer of Israel.

2:16-22. Moses sought a wife, so he stationed himself at a well, following the example of Isaac and Jacob (*Shemos Rabbah* 1:32). There he again displayed his willingness to fight for the victims of superior force.

2:16. The unnamed leader is Jethro, who was a כֹּהֵן, *minister*, in both senses of the word, priest and leader. After serving as a priest to the Midianite deity, he renounced idolatry, whereupon he remained merely a prestigious leader (*Tanchuma*).

2:23-25. The narrative now leaves Moses and returns to the plight of the Jews in Egypt. Nearly 210 years had

⁵ *Pharaoh's daughter went down to bathe by the River and her maidens walked along the River. She saw the basket among the reeds and she sent her maidservant and she took it.* ⁶ *She opened it and saw him, the child, and behold! a youth was crying. She took pity on him and said, "This is one of the Hebrew boys."*

⁷ *His sister said to Pharaoh's daughter, "Shall I go and summon for you a wet nurse from the Hebrew women, who will nurse the boy for you?"*

⁸ *The daughter of Pharaoh said, "Go." The girl went and summoned the boy's mother.* ⁹ *Pharaoh's daughter said to her, "Take this boy and nurse him for me, and I will give your pay." So the woman took the boy and nursed him.* ¹⁰ *The boy grew up and she brought him to the daughter of Pharaoh and he was a son to her. She called his name Moses, * as she said, "For I drew him from the water."*

Moses identifies with his people

¹¹ *It happened in those days that Moses grew up and went out to his brethren * and observed their burdens; and he saw an Egyptian man striking a Hebrew man, of his brethren.* ¹² *He turned this way and that and saw that there was no man, so he struck down the Egyptian and hid him in the sand.*

¹³ *He went out the next day and behold! two Hebrew men were fighting. He said to the wicked one, "Why would you strike your fellow?"* ¹⁴ *He replied, "Who appointed you as a dignitary, a ruler, and a judge over us? Do you propose to murder me, as you murdered the Egyptian?" Moses was frightened and he thought, "Indeed, the matter is known!"* ¹⁵ *Pharaoh heard about this matter and sought to kill Moses; so Moses fled from before Pharaoh and settled in the land of Midian. He sat by a well.*

Moses marries

¹⁶ *The minister of Midian * had seven daughters; they came and drew water and filled the troughs to water their father's sheep.* ¹⁷ *The shepherds came and drove them away. Moses got up and saved them and watered their sheep.* ¹⁸ *They came to Reuel their father. He said, "How could you come so quickly today?"* ¹⁹ *They replied, "An Egyptian man saved us from the shepherds, and he even drew water for us and watered the sheep."* ²⁰ *He said to his daughters, "Then where is he? Why did you leave the man? Summon him and let him eat bread!"*

²¹ *Moses desired to dwell with the man; and he gave his daughter Zipporah to Moses.* ²² *She gave birth to a son and he named him Gershom, for he said, "I have been a stranger in a foreign land."*

God concludes that the time of salvation has arrived

²³ *During those many days, * it happened that the king of Egypt died, and the Children of Israel groaned because of the work and they cried out. Their outcry because of the work went up to God.* ²⁴ *God heard their moaning, and God remembered His covenant with Abraham, with Isaac, and with Jacob.* ²⁵ *God saw the Children of Israel; and God knew.*

3   ¹ M*oses was shepherding the sheep of Jethro, his father-in-law, * the priest of Midian; he guided the sheep far into the wilderness, and he arrived*

---

elapsed since Jacob's descent to Egypt, 116 since the beginning of servitude, and 86 since the beginning of the backbreaking oppression. The Jewish people groaned. God heard their outcry, looked at their degrading conditions, and determined that the time had come to begin the process of redemption. Thus the two threads of the previous narrative — the enslavement of Israel and the

growth of Moses to maturity — come together.

3:1-10. As shepherd of his father-in-law's sheep, Moses proved himself worthy to become the "shepherd" of the Children of Israel. The Midrash tells how he showed compassion for a thirsty sheep, whereupon God said that a person who pities even a helpless beast will surely show compassion for an entire nation.

ב אֶל־הַר הָאֱלֹהִים חֹרֵבָה: וַיֵּרָ֠א מַלְאַ֨ךְ יהוה אֵלָ֛יו בְּלַבַּת־אֵשׁ מִתּ֣וֹךְ
הַסְּנֶ֑ה וַיַּ֗רְא וְהִנֵּ֤ה הַסְּנֶה֙ בֹּעֵ֣ר בָּאֵ֔שׁ וְהַסְּנֶ֖ה אֵינֶ֣נּוּ אֻכָּ֑ל: וַיֹּ֣אמֶר מֹשֶׁ֗ה
ג אָסֻֽרָה־נָּ֣א וְאֶרְאֶ֔ה אֶת־הַמַּרְאֶ֥ה הַגָּדֹ֖ל הַזֶּ֑ה מַדּ֖וּעַ לֹא־יִבְעַ֥ר הַסְּנֶֽה: וַיַּ֥רְא
ד יהוה כִּ֣י סָ֣ר לִרְא֑וֹת וַיִּקְרָא֩ אֵלָ֨יו אֱלֹהִ֜ים מִתּ֣וֹךְ הַסְּנֶ֗ה וַיֹּ֛אמֶר מֹשֶׁ֥ה מֹשֶׁ֖ה
ה וַיֹּ֥אמֶר הִנֵּֽנִי: וַיֹּ֖אמֶר אַל־תִּקְרַ֣ב הֲלֹ֑ם שַׁל־נְעָלֶ֙יךָ֙ מֵעַ֣ל רַגְלֶ֔יךָ כִּ֣י הַמָּק֗וֹם
ו אֲשֶׁ֤ר אַתָּה֙ עוֹמֵ֣ד עָלָ֔יו אַדְמַת־קֹ֖דֶשׁ הֽוּא: וַיֹּ֗אמֶר אָֽנֹכִי֙ אֱלֹהֵ֣י אָבִ֔יךָ אֱלֹהֵ֧י
אַבְרָהָ֛ם אֱלֹהֵ֥י יִצְחָ֖ק וֵֽאלֹהֵ֣י יַֽעֲקֹ֑ב וַיַּסְתֵּ֤ר מֹשֶׁה֙ פָּנָ֔יו כִּ֣י יָרֵ֔א מֵֽהַבִּ֖יט אֶל־
ז הָֽאֱלֹהִֽים: וַיֹּ֣אמֶר יהוה רָאֹ֥ה רָאִ֛יתִי אֶת־עֳנִ֥י עַמִּ֖י אֲשֶׁ֣ר בְּמִצְרָ֑יִם וְאֶת־
ח צַֽעֲקָתָ֤ם שָׁמַ֙עְתִּי֙ מִפְּנֵ֣י נֹֽגְשָׂ֔יו כִּ֥י יָדַ֖עְתִּי אֶת־מַכְאֹבָֽיו: וָֽאֵרֵ֞ד לְהַצִּיל֣וֹ ׀ מִיַּ֣ד
מִצְרַ֗יִם וּֽלְהַֽעֲלֹתוֹ֮ מִן־הָאָ֣רֶץ הַהִוא֒ אֶל־אֶ֤רֶץ טוֹבָה֙ וּרְחָבָ֔ה אֶל־אֶ֛רֶץ זָבַ֥ת
חָלָ֖ב וּדְבָ֑שׁ אֶל־מְק֤וֹם הַֽכְּנַֽעֲנִי֙ וְהַ֣חִתִּ֔י וְהָֽאֱמֹרִי֙ וְהַפְּרִזִּ֔י וְהַֽחִוִּ֖י וְהַיְבוּסִֽי:
ט וְעַתָּ֕ה הִנֵּ֛ה צַֽעֲקַ֥ת בְּנֵֽי־יִשְׂרָאֵ֖ל בָּ֣אָה אֵלָ֑י וְגַם־רָאִ֙יתִי֙ אֶת־הַלַּ֔חַץ אֲשֶׁ֥ר
י מִצְרַ֖יִם לֹֽחֲצִ֥ים אֹתָֽם: וְעַתָּ֣ה לְכָ֔ה וְאֶשְׁלָֽחֲךָ֖ אֶל־פַּרְעֹ֑ה וְהוֹצֵ֛א אֶת־עַמִּ֥י בְנֵֽי־
יא יִשְׂרָאֵ֖ל מִמִּצְרָֽיִם: וַיֹּ֤אמֶר מֹשֶׁה֙ אֶל־הָ֣אֱלֹהִ֔ים מִ֣י אָנֹ֔כִי כִּ֥י אֵלֵ֖ךְ אֶל־
יב פַּרְעֹ֑ה וְכִ֥י אוֹצִ֛יא אֶת־בְּנֵ֥י יִשְׂרָאֵ֖ל מִמִּצְרָֽיִם: וַיֹּ֙אמֶר֙ כִּֽי־אֶֽהְיֶ֣ה עִמָּ֔ךְ וְזֶה־
לְּךָ֣ הָא֔וֹת כִּ֥י אָֽנֹכִ֖י שְׁלַחְתִּ֑יךָ בְּהוֹצִֽיאֲךָ֤ אֶת־הָעָם֙ מִמִּצְרַ֔יִם תַּֽעַבְדוּן֙ אֶת־
יג הָ֣אֱלֹהִ֔ים עַ֖ל הָהָ֥ר הַזֶּֽה: וַיֹּ֨אמֶר מֹשֶׁ֜ה אֶל־הָֽאֱלֹהִ֗ים הִנֵּ֣ה אָֽנֹכִי֮ בָא֮ אֶל־בְּנֵ֣י
יִשְׂרָאֵל֒ וְאָֽמַרְתִּ֣י לָהֶ֔ם אֱלֹהֵ֥י אֲבֽוֹתֵיכֶ֖ם שְׁלָחַ֣נִי אֲלֵיכֶ֑ם וְאָֽמְרוּ־לִ֣י מַה־
יד שְּׁמ֔וֹ מָ֥ה אֹמַ֖ר אֲלֵהֶֽם: וַיֹּ֤אמֶר אֱלֹהִים֙ אֶל־מֹשֶׁ֔ה אֶֽהְיֶ֖ה אֲשֶׁ֣ר אֶֽהְיֶ֑ה וַיֹּ֗אמֶר
כֹּ֤ה תֹאמַר֙ לִבְנֵ֣י יִשְׂרָאֵ֔ל אֶֽהְיֶ֖ה שְׁלָחַ֥נִי אֲלֵיכֶֽם: וַיֹּאמֶר֩ ע֨וֹד אֱלֹהִ֜ים אֶל־
טו מֹשֶׁ֗ה כֹּֽה־תֹאמַר֮ אֶל־בְּנֵ֣י יִשְׂרָאֵל֒ יהוה אֱלֹהֵ֣י אֲבֹֽתֵיכֶ֗ם אֱלֹהֵ֨י אַבְרָהָ֜ם
אֱלֹהֵ֥י יִצְחָ֛ק וֵֽאלֹהֵ֥י יַֽעֲקֹ֖ב שְׁלָחַ֣נִי אֲלֵיכֶ֑ם זֶה־שְּׁמִ֣י לְעֹלָ֔ם וְזֶ֥ה זִכְרִ֖י לְדֹ֥ר
טז דֹּֽר: לֵ֣ךְ וְאָֽסַפְתָּ֞ אֶת־זִקְנֵ֣י יִשְׂרָאֵ֗ל וְאָֽמַרְתָּ֤ אֲלֵהֶם֙ יהוה אֱלֹהֵ֤י אֲבֹֽתֵיכֶם֙
נִרְאָ֣ה אֵלַ֔י אֱלֹהֵ֧י אַבְרָהָ֛ם יִצְחָ֥ק וְיַֽעֲקֹ֖ב לֵאמֹ֑ר פָּקֹ֤ד פָּקַ֙דְתִּי֙ אֶתְכֶ֔ם וְאֶת־
הֶֽעָשׂ֥וּי לָכֶ֖ם בְּמִצְרָֽיִם: וָֽאֹמַ֗ר אַֽעֲלֶ֣ה אֶתְכֶם֮ מֵֽעֳנִ֣י מִצְרַ֒יִם֒ אֶל־אֶ֤רֶץ
יז הַֽכְּנַֽעֲנִי֙ וְהַ֣חִתִּ֔י וְהָֽאֱמֹרִי֙ וְהַפְּרִזִּ֔י וְהַֽחִוִּ֖י וְהַיְבוּסִ֑י אֶל־אֶ֛רֶץ זָבַ֥ת חָלָ֖ב וּדְבָֽשׁ:

3:2-5. Moses' first prophetic vision. The Torah describes Moses' vision in three different ways: a fire, an angel, and, finally, as God. Like someone in a dark room whose eyes cannot tolerate an immediate exposure to blinding sunlight, Moses had to be exposed to prophecy gradually. First, he was shown a fire that was strange because it did not consume the bush. Then it was revealed to him that an angel was in the fire, and once he had become accustomed to this new phenomenon, he was given the vision of God Himself (*R' Bachya*).

The preponderant Name of God in this chapter is *Elohim*, the Name that connotes strict justice, because God was about to judge Egypt for its excessive cruelty. In the three places where He reveals Himself to Moses (vv. 2,4,

and 7), however, He is called *Hashem*, the Name of mercy, to show that His primary intention is to save Israel in a historic demonstration of Divine mercy (see *Ramban* to v. 7).

3:5. God commanded him to remove his shoes because in places of exalted sanctity, such as the Temple, even Kohanim may not wear shoes (*Ramban*).

3:11. *Who am I . . . and that I should take . . . out.* These are two separate questions. How can I, who am so unqualified, influence Pharaoh? And what have the Jewish people done to deserve such a miracle? (*Rashi*).

3:13. Obviously the Jews knew the various Names of God, so that the question cannot be understood literally. Each of God's Names represents the way in which He

at the Mountain of God, toward Horeb. ² An angel of HASHEM appeared to him *
in a blaze of fire from amid the bush. He saw and behold! the bush was burning
in the fire but the bush was not consumed. ³ Moses thought, "I will turn aside now
and look at this great sight — why will the bush not be burned?"

The ⁴ HASHEM saw that he turned aside to see; and God called out to him from amid
burning the bush and said, "Moses, Moses," and he replied, "Here I am!" ⁵ He said, "Do
bush not come closer to here, remove your shoes from your feet, * for the place upon
which you stand is holy ground." ⁶ And He said, "I am the God of your father,
the God of Abraham, the God of Isaac, and the God of Jacob." Moses hid his
face, for he was afraid to gaze toward God.

⁷ HASHEM said, "I have indeed seen the affliction of My people that is in Egypt
and I have heard its outcry because of its taskmasters, for I have known of its
sufferings. ⁸ I shall descend to rescue it from the hand of Egypt and to bring it
up from that land to a good and spacious land, to a land flowing with milk and
honey, to the place of the Canaanite, the Hittite, the Amorite, the Perizzite, the
Hivvite, and the Jebusite. ⁹ And now, behold! the outcry of the Children of Israel
has come to Me, and I have also seen the oppression with which the Egyptians
Moses' oppress them. ¹⁰ And now, go and I shall dispatch you to Pharaoh and you shall
doubts take My people the Children of Israel out of Egypt."
and God's ¹¹ Moses replied to God, "Who am I that I should go to Pharaoh and that I
reassurance should take the Children of Israel out * of Egypt?"

¹² And He said, "For I shall be with you — and this is your sign that I have sent
you: When you take the people out of Egypt, you will serve God on this
mountain."

¹³ Moses said to God, "Behold, when I come to the Children of Israel and say
to them, 'The God of your forefathers has sent me to you,' and they say to me,
The Names 'What is His Name?'* — what shall I say to them?"
of God ¹⁴ God answered Moses, "I Shall Be As I Shall Be."* And He said, "So shall
you say to the Children of Israel, 'I Shall Be has sent me to you.'" ¹⁵ God said
further to Moses, "So shall you say to the Children of Israel, 'HASHEM, the God
of your forefathers, the God of Abraham, the God of Isaac, and the God of Jacob,
has dispatched me to you. This is My Name forever, * and this is My remembrance from generation to generation.' ¹⁶ Go and gather the elders of Israel and
say to them, 'HASHEM, the God of your forefathers, has appeared to me, the God
of Abraham, Isaac, and Jacob, saying, "I have surely remembered you and
what is done to you in Egypt." ' ¹⁷ And I have said, 'I shall bring you up from the
affliction of Egypt to the land of the Canaanite, the Hittite, the Amorite, the
Perizzite, the Hivvite, and the Jebusite, to a land flowing with milk and honey.'

---

reveals Himself through His behavior toward the world.
When He is merciful, He is called *Hashem* [יְ-ה-ו-ה]. When
He exercises strict judgment, He is called *Elohim*. When
He exercises His mastery over nature and performs hidden miracles — as He did for the Patriarchs — He is
called *Shaddai*, and so on. Thus Moses was saying that
once the Jews accepted him as God's emissary, they
would want to know which of God's attributes He would
manifest in the course of redeeming them from Egypt
(*Ramban*).

3:14. This is in itself a Divine Name. God said, *"I shall be
with them in this sorrow* as *I shall be* with them in other

sorrows." To this Moses replied, "An evil in its own time
is enough!" I.e., why should You imply to them that there
will be future exiles; is it not enough that they suffer now
in Egypt? Accepting Moses' argument, God instructed
him to say, "I Shall Be [with them in *this* sorrow] has sent
me to you" (*Rashi* from *Berachos* 9b).

3:15. Since לְעֹלָם is spelled without a *vav*, it can be pro-
nounced לְעַלֵּם, *to conceal.* This implies that the Divine
Name should not be pronounced as it is spelled. *"This is
My remembrance"* means that God taught Moses to pro-
nounce the Name as *Adonoy* (*Rashi* from *Pesachim* 50a,
Midrash).

יח וְשָׁמְע֖וּ לְקֹלֶ֑ךָ וּבָאתָ֡ אַתָּה֩ וְזִקְנֵ֨י יִשְׂרָאֵ֜ל אֶל־מֶ֣לֶךְ מִצְרַ֗יִם וַאֲמַרְתֶּ֤ם אֵלָיו֙
יהֹוָ֞ה אֱלֹהֵ֤י הָֽעִבְרִיִּים֙ נִקְרָ֣ה עָלֵ֔ינוּ וְעַתָּ֗ה נֵֽלְכָה־נָּ֞א דֶּ֣רֶךְ שְׁלֹ֤שֶׁת יָמִים֙
יט בַּמִּדְבָּ֔ר וְנִזְבְּחָ֖ה לַֽיהֹוָ֥ה אֱלֹהֵֽינוּ: וַאֲנִ֣י יָדַ֔עְתִּי כִּ֠י לֹֽא־יִתֵּ֥ן אֶתְכֶ֛ם מֶ֥לֶךְ
כ מִצְרַ֖יִם לַֽהֲלֹ֑ךְ וְלֹ֖א בְּיָ֥ד חֲזָקָֽה: וְשָׁלַחְתִּ֤י אֶת־יָדִי֙ וְהִכֵּיתִ֣י אֶת־מִצְרַ֔יִם
כא בְּכֹל֙ נִפְלְאֹתַ֔י אֲשֶׁ֥ר אֶֽעֱשֶׂ֖ה בְּקִרְבּ֑וֹ וְאַֽחֲרֵי־כֵ֖ן יְשַׁלַּ֥ח אֶתְכֶֽם: וְנָֽתַתִּ֛י אֶת־
כב חֵ֥ן הָֽעָם־הַזֶּ֖ה בְּעֵינֵ֣י מִצְרָ֑יִם וְהָיָה֙ כִּ֣י תֵֽלֵכ֔וּן לֹ֥א תֵֽלְכ֖וּ רֵיקָֽם: וְשָֽׁאֲלָ֨ה
אִשָּׁ֤ה מִשְּׁכֶנְתָּהּ֙ וּמִגָּרַ֣ת בֵּיתָ֔הּ כְּלֵי־כֶ֛סֶף וּכְלֵ֥י זָהָ֖ב וּשְׂמָלֹ֑ת וְשַׂמְתֶּ֗ם עַל־

ד א בְּנֵיכֶם֙ וְעַל־בְּנֹ֣תֵיכֶ֔ם וְנִצַּלְתֶּ֖ם אֶת־מִצְרָֽיִם: וַיַּ֤עַן מֹשֶׁה֙ וַיֹּ֔אמֶר וְהֵן֙ לֹא־
ב יַאֲמִ֣ינוּ לִ֔י וְלֹ֥א יִשְׁמְע֖וּ בְּקֹלִ֑י כִּ֣י יֹֽאמְר֔וּ לֹֽא־נִרְאָ֥ה אֵלֶ֖יךָ יְהֹוָֽה: וַיֹּ֧אמֶר
ג אֵלָ֛יו יְהֹוָ֖ה [מַזֶּ֥ה °מזה] בְיָדֶ֑ךָ וַיֹּ֖אמֶר מַטֶּֽה: וַיֹּ֨אמֶר֙ הַשְׁלִיכֵ֣הוּ אַ֔רְצָה
ד וַיַּשְׁלִכֵ֤הוּ אַ֨רְצָה֙ וַיְהִ֣י לְנָחָ֔שׁ וַיָּ֥נָס מֹשֶׁ֖ה מִפָּנָֽיו: וַיֹּ֤אמֶר יְהֹוָה֙ אֶל־מֹשֶׁ֔ה
ה שְׁלַח֙ יָ֣דְךָ֔ וֶֽאֱחֹ֖ז בִּזְנָב֑וֹ וַיִּשְׁלַ֤ח יָדוֹ֙ וַיַּ֣חֲזֶק־בּ֔וֹ וַיְהִ֥י לְמַטֶּ֖ה בְּכַפּֽוֹ: לְמַ֣עַן
יַאֲמִ֔ינוּ כִּֽי־נִרְאָ֥ה אֵלֶ֛יךָ יְהֹוָ֖ה אֱלֹהֵ֣י אֲבֹתָ֑ם אֱלֹהֵ֧י אַבְרָהָ֛ם אֱלֹהֵ֥י יִצְחָ֖ק
ו וֵֽאלֹהֵ֥י יַֽעֲקֹֽב: וַיֹּ֩אמֶר֩ יְהֹוָ֨ה ל֜וֹ ע֗וֹד הָֽבֵא־נָ֤א יָֽדְךָ֙ בְּחֵיקֶ֔ךָ וַיָּבֵ֥א יָד֖וֹ בְּחֵיק֑וֹ
ז וַיּ֣וֹצִאָ֔הּ וְהִנֵּ֥ה יָד֖וֹ מְצֹרַ֣עַת כַּשָּׁ֑לֶג: וַיֹּ֗אמֶר הָשֵׁ֤ב יָֽדְךָ֙ אֶל־חֵיקֶ֔ךָ וַיָּ֥שֶׁב יָד֖וֹ
ח אֶל־חֵיק֑וֹ וַיּֽוֹצִאָהּ֙ מֵֽחֵיק֔וֹ וְהִנֵּה־שָׁ֖בָה כִּבְשָׂר֑וֹ: וְהָיָה֙ אִם־לֹ֣א יַֽאֲמִ֣ינוּ לָ֔ךְ
ט וְלֹ֣א יִשְׁמְע֔וּ לְקֹל֙ הָאֹ֣ת הָֽרִאשׁ֔וֹן וְהֶֽאֱמִ֔ינוּ לְקֹ֖ל הָאֹ֣ת הָאַֽחֲר֑וֹן: וְהָיָ֡ה אִם־
לֹ֣א יַֽאֲמִ֡ינוּ גַּם֩ לִשְׁנֵ֨י הָֽאֹת֜וֹת הָאֵ֗לֶּה וְלֹ֤א יִשְׁמְעוּן֙ לְקֹלֶ֔ךָ וְלָֽקַחְתָּ֙ מִמֵּימֵ֣י
הַיְאֹ֔ר וְשָֽׁפַכְתָּ֖ הַיַּבָּשָׁ֑ה וְהָי֤וּ הַמַּ֨יִם֙ אֲשֶׁ֣ר תִּקַּ֣ח מִן־הַיְאֹ֔ר וְהָי֥וּ לְדָ֖ם בַּיַּבָּֽשֶׁת:
י וַיֹּ֨אמֶר מֹשֶׁ֣ה אֶל־יְהֹוָה֮ בִּ֣י אֲדֹנָי֒ לֹא֩ אִ֨ישׁ דְּבָרִ֜ים אָנֹ֗כִי גַּ֤ם מִתְּמוֹל֙ גַּ֣ם
משלשם גַּ֣ם מֵאָ֔ז דַּבֶּרְךָ֖ אֶל־עַבְדֶּ֑ךָ כִּ֧י כְבַד־פֶּ֛ה וּכְבַ֥ד לָשׁ֖וֹן אָנֹֽכִי: וַיֹּ֨אמֶר
יא יְהֹוָ֜ה אֵלָ֗יו מִ֣י שָׂ֣ם פֶּה֮ לָֽאָדָם֒ א֚וֹ מִֽי־יָשׂ֣וּם אִלֵּ֔ם א֤וֹ חֵרֵשׁ֙ א֣וֹ פִקֵּ֔חַ א֖וֹ עִוֵּ֑ר
יב הֲלֹ֥א אָֽנֹכִ֖י יְהֹוָֽה: וְעַתָּ֖ה לֵ֑ךְ וְאָֽנֹכִי֙ אֶֽהְיֶ֣ה עִם־פִּ֔יךָ וְהֽוֹרֵיתִ֖יךָ אֲשֶׁ֥ר תְּדַבֵּֽר:
יג-יד וַיֹּ֖אמֶר בִּ֣י אֲדֹנָ֑י שְׁלַֽח־נָ֖א בְּיַד־תִּשְׁלָֽח: וַיִּֽחַר־אַ֨ף יְהֹוָ֜ה בְּמֹשֶׁ֗ה וַיֹּ֨אמֶר֙
הֲלֹ֨א אַֽהֲרֹ֤ן אָחִ֨יךָ֙ הַלֵּוִ֔י יָדַ֕עְתִּי כִּֽי־דַבֵּ֥ר יְדַבֵּ֖ר ה֑וּא וְגַ֤ם הִנֵּה־הוּא֙ יֹצֵ֣א
טו לִקְרָאתֶ֔ךָ וְרָֽאֲךָ֖ וְשָׂמַ֥ח בְּלִבּֽוֹ: וְדִבַּרְתָּ֣ אֵלָ֗יו וְשַׂמְתָּ֛ אֶת־הַדְּבָרִ֖ים בְּפִ֑יו
טז וְאָֽנֹכִ֗י אֶֽהְיֶ֤ה עִם־פִּ֨יךָ֙ וְעִם־פִּ֔יהוּ וְהֽוֹרֵיתִ֣י אֶתְכֶ֔ם אֵ֖ת אֲשֶׁ֥ר תַּֽעֲשֽׂוּן: וְדִבֶּר־
ה֥וּא לְךָ֖ אֶל־הָעָ֑ם וְהָ֤יָה הוּא֙ יִֽהְיֶה־לְּךָ֣ לְפֶ֔ה וְאַתָּ֖ה תִּֽהְיֶה־לּ֥וֹ לֵֽאלֹהִֽים:
יז וְאֶת־הַמַּטֶּ֥ה הַזֶּ֖ה תִּקַּ֣ח בְּיָדֶ֑ךָ אֲשֶׁ֥ר תַּֽעֲשֶׂה־בּ֖וֹ אֶת־הָֽאֹתֹֽת:

3:18. The elders will heed Moses' call because of their tradition from Jacob and Joseph that the eventual redeemer would use the expression פָּקֹד פָּקַדְתִּי, *I have surely remembered* (Rashi). Even though the expression was surely no secret, this tradition was a prophecy that no one but God's chosen redeemer would ever use the term (Ramban).

Ramban, however, cites the Midrash that Moses would have been believed because he had fled Egypt at the age

of twelve, and would not have known the above tradition.

4:1-17. Even after God's assurances, Moses insists that the people will not believe him. God then shows him three miracles that he is to display to the people to win their confidence.

4:10. All his arguments having been refuted, Moses throws himself upon God's mercy — addressing Him as Hashem, the Name of mercy (*Or HaChaim*) — and begging to be relieved of the mission.

The
request
to the
Egyptians

¹⁸ *"They will heed your voice. * You and the elders of Israel shall come to the king of Egypt and say to him, 'HASHEM, the God of the Hebrews, happened upon us. And now, please let us go on a three-day journey in the Wilderness, and we shall bring offerings to HASHEM, our God.'* ¹⁹ *I know that the king of Egypt will not allow you to go, except through a strong hand.* ²⁰ *I shall stretch out My hand and I shall strike Egypt with all My wonders that I shall perform in its midst, and after that he will send you out.* ²¹ *I shall grant this people favor in the eyes of Egypt, so that it will happen that when you go, you will not go empty-handed.* ²² *Each woman shall request from her neighbor and from the one who lives in her house silver vessels, golden vessels, and garments; and you shall put them on your sons and daughters, and you shall empty out Egypt."*

4

Moses
doubts the
people's faith

¹ **M**oses responded and said, *"But they will not believe me * and they will not heed my voice, for they will say, 'HASHEM did not appear to you.'"* ² HASHEM *said to him, "What is that in your hand?" and he said, "A staff."* ³ He said, *"Cast it on the ground,"* and he cast it on the ground and it became a snake. Moses fled from it. ⁴ HASHEM *said to Moses, "Stretch out your hand and grasp its tail."* He stretched out his hand and grasped it tightly, and it became a staff in his palm. ⁵ *"So that they shall believe that HASHEM, the God of their forefathers, appeared to you, the God of Abraham, the God of Isaac, and the God of Jacob."* ⁶ HASHEM *said further to him, "Bring your hand to your bosom,"* and he brought his hand to his bosom; then he withdrew it and behold, his hand was leprous, like snow. ⁷ He said, *"Return your hand to your bosom,"* and he returned his hand to his bosom; then he removed it from his bosom and behold, it reverted to be like his flesh. ⁸ *"It shall be that if they do not believe you and do not heed the voice of the first sign, they will believe the voice of the latter sign.* ⁹ *And it shall be that if they do not believe even these two signs and do not heed your voice, then you shall take from the water of the River and pour it out on the dry land, and the water that you shall take from the River will become blood when it is on the dry land."*

Moses'
desperate
plea

¹⁰ Moses replied to HASHEM, *"Please, my Lord, I am not a man of words, * not since yesterday, nor since the day before yesterday, nor since You first spoke to Your servant, for I am heavy of mouth and heavy of speech."*

God's
response

¹¹ Then HASHEM said to him, *"Who makes a mouth for man, * or who makes one dumb or deaf, or sighted or blind? Is it not I, HASHEM?* ¹² *So now, go! I shall be with your mouth and teach you what you should say."*

¹³ He replied, *"Please, my Lord, send through whomever You will send!"*

Moses'
objections
are
overridden

¹⁴ The wrath of HASHEM burned against Moses * and He said, *"Is there not Aaron your brother, the Levite? I know that he will surely speak; moreover, behold, he is going out to meet you and when he sees you he will rejoice in his heart.* ¹⁵ *You shall speak to him and put the words in his mouth; and I shall be with your mouth and with his mouth, and teach you both what you are to do.* ¹⁶ *He shall speak for you to the people; and it will be that he will be your mouth and you will be his leader.* ¹⁷ *And this staff you shall take in your hand, with which you shall perform the signs."*

4:11-12. God refuted Moses on two counts: whatever communications skills he required are well within God's capacity to give, and He would provide whatever guidance and assistance Moses needed.

4:14-17. No longer did God seek Moses' acquiescence to be His emissary; He *commanded* him to go. But to ease his fears, God appointed Aaron to act as his spokesman to Pharaoh.

יח וַיֵּלֶךְ מֹשֶׁה וַיָּשָׁב ׀ אֶל־יֶתֶר חֹתְנוֹ וַיֹּאמֶר לוֹ אֵלְכָה נָּא וְאָשׁוּבָה אֶל־אַחַי אֲשֶׁר־בְּמִצְרַיִם וְאֶרְאֶה הַעוֹדָם חַיִּים וַיֹּאמֶר יִתְרוֹ לְמֹשֶׁה לֵךְ לְשָׁלוֹם:

יט וַיֹּאמֶר יהוה אֶל־מֹשֶׁה בְּמִדְיָן לֵךְ שֻׁב מִצְרָיִם כִּי־מֵתוּ כָּל־הָאֲנָשִׁים הַמְבַקְשִׁים אֶת־נַפְשֶׁךָ: כ וַיִּקַּח מֹשֶׁה אֶת־אִשְׁתּוֹ וְאֶת־בָּנָיו וַיַּרְכִּבֵם עַל־הַחֲמֹר וַיָּשָׁב אַרְצָה מִצְרָיִם וַיִּקַּח מֹשֶׁה אֶת־מַטֵּה הָאֱלֹהִים בְּיָדוֹ: כא וַיֹּאמֶר יהוה אֶל־מֹשֶׁה בְּלֶכְתְּךָ לָשׁוּב מִצְרַיְמָה רְאֵה כָּל־הַמֹּפְתִים אֲשֶׁר־שַׂמְתִּי בְיָדֶךָ וַעֲשִׂיתָם לִפְנֵי פַרְעֹה וַאֲנִי אֲחַזֵּק אֶת־לִבּוֹ וְלֹא יְשַׁלַּח אֶת־הָעָם:

כב-כג וְאָמַרְתָּ אֶל־פַּרְעֹה כֹּה אָמַר יהוה בְּנִי בְכֹרִי יִשְׂרָאֵל: וָאֹמַר אֵלֶיךָ שַׁלַּח אֶת־בְּנִי וְיַעַבְדֵנִי וַתְּמָאֵן לְשַׁלְּחוֹ הִנֵּה אָנֹכִי הֹרֵג אֶת־בִּנְךָ בְּכֹרֶךָ: כד וַיְהִי בַדֶּרֶךְ בַּמָּלוֹן וַיִּפְגְּשֵׁהוּ יהוה וַיְבַקֵּשׁ הֲמִיתוֹ: כה וַתִּקַּח צִפֹּרָה צֹר וַתִּכְרֹת אֶת־עָרְלַת בְּנָהּ וַתַּגַּע לְרַגְלָיו וַתֹּאמֶר כִּי חֲתַן־דָּמִים אַתָּה לִי: כו וַיִּרֶף מִמֶּנּוּ אָז אָמְרָה חֲתַן דָּמִים לַמּוּלֹת:

כז וַיֹּאמֶר יהוה אֶל־אַהֲרֹן לֵךְ לִקְרַאת מֹשֶׁה הַמִּדְבָּרָה וַיֵּלֶךְ וַיִּפְגְּשֵׁהוּ בְּהַר הָאֱלֹהִים וַיִּשַּׁק־לוֹ: כח וַיַּגֵּד מֹשֶׁה לְאַהֲרֹן אֵת כָּל־דִּבְרֵי יהוה אֲשֶׁר שְׁלָחוֹ וְאֵת כָּל־הָאֹתֹת אֲשֶׁר צִוָּהוּ: כט וַיֵּלֶךְ מֹשֶׁה וְאַהֲרֹן וַיַּאַסְפוּ אֶת־כָּל־זִקְנֵי בְּנֵי יִשְׂרָאֵל: ל וַיְדַבֵּר אַהֲרֹן אֵת כָּל־הַדְּבָרִים אֲשֶׁר־דִּבֶּר יהוה אֶל־מֹשֶׁה וַיַּעַשׂ הָאֹתֹת לְעֵינֵי הָעָם: לא וַיַּאֲמֵן הָעָם וַיִּשְׁמְעוּ כִּי־פָקַד יהוה אֶת־בְּנֵי יִשְׂרָאֵל

ה א וְכִי רָאָה אֶת־עָנְיָם וַיִּקְּדוּ וַיִּשְׁתַּחֲווּ: וְאַחַר בָּאוּ מֹשֶׁה וְאַהֲרֹן וַיֹּאמְרוּ אֶל־פַּרְעֹה כֹּה־אָמַר יהוה אֱלֹהֵי יִשְׂרָאֵל שַׁלַּח אֶת־עַמִּי וְיָחֹגּוּ לִי בַּמִּדְבָּר: ב וַיֹּאמֶר פַּרְעֹה מִי יהוה אֲשֶׁר אֶשְׁמַע בְּקֹלוֹ לְשַׁלַּח אֶת־יִשְׂרָאֵל לֹא יָדַעְתִּי אֶת־יהוה וְגַם אֶת־יִשְׂרָאֵל לֹא אֲשַׁלֵּחַ: ג וַיֹּאמְרוּ אֱלֹהֵי הָעִבְרִים נִקְרָא עָלֵינוּ נֵלְכָה נָּא דֶּרֶךְ שְׁלֹשֶׁת יָמִים בַּמִּדְבָּר וְנִזְבְּחָה לַיהוה אֱלֹהֵינוּ פֶּן־יִפְגָּעֵנוּ בַּדֶּבֶר אוֹ בֶחָרֶב: ד וַיֹּאמֶר אֲלֵהֶם מֶלֶךְ מִצְרַיִם לָמָּה מֹשֶׁה וְאַהֲרֹן תַּפְרִיעוּ אֶת־הָעָם מִמַּעֲשָׂיו לְכוּ לְסִבְלֹתֵיכֶם: ה וַיֹּאמֶר פַּרְעֹה הֵן־רַבִּים עַתָּה עַם הָאָרֶץ וְהִשְׁבַּתֶּם אֹתָם מִסִּבְלֹתָם: ו וַיְצַו פַּרְעֹה בַּיּוֹם הַהוּא אֶת־הַנֹּגְשִׂים בָּעָם וְאֶת־שֹׁטְרָיו לֵאמֹר: ז לֹא תֹאסִפוּן לָתֵת תֶּבֶן לָעָם לִלְבֹּן הַלְּבֵנִים כִּתְמוֹל שִׁלְשֹׁם הֵם יֵלְכוּ וְקֹשְׁשׁוּ לָהֶם תֶּבֶן: ח וְאֶת־מַתְכֹּנֶת הַלְּבֵנִים אֲשֶׁר הֵם עֹשִׂים תְּמוֹל שִׁלְשֹׁם תָּשִׂימוּ עֲלֵיהֶם לֹא תִגְרְעוּ מִמֶּנּוּ

4:18. Moses told God, "Jethro accepted me, opened his home to me, and treated me with honor. One owes his life to someone who opens his home to him. Therefore, I cannot go without his permission" (Midrash).

4:24-26. As Moses set out for Egypt with his family, he was faced with a dilemma. Should he perform the circumcision and then take the child with him? — but the infant would be in danger for the first three days after the circumcision! Should he perform the circumcision and delay the trip for three days? — but God had commanded him to go! He decided to travel immediately

[since the baby was already born when God commanded him to go]. Nevertheless, he was held culpable because, when they arrived at an inn, he began making arrangements for his lodging instead of performing the circumcision without delay (Rashi from Nedarim 31b-32a). Even though he would have to resume his trip to Egypt after the circumcision, the inn was close enough to Egypt that the short trip would not endanger the child's health (Ran, ibid.).

5:1-5. After gaining the allegiance of the Jewish elders, Moses and Aaron went to deliver God's message to

Moses embarks for Egypt — [18] So Moses went and returned to Jether, his father-in-law, and said to him, "Let me now go back* to my brethren who are in Egypt, and see if they are still alive." And Jethro said to Moses, "Go to peace."

[19] HASHEM said to Moses in Midian, "Go, return to Egypt, for all the people who seek your life have died."

[20] So Moses took his wife and sons, mounted them on the donkey, and returned to the land of Egypt; and Moses took the staff of God in his hand. [21] HASHEM said to Moses, "When you go to return to Egypt, see all the wonders that I have put in your hand and perform them before Pharaoh; but I shall strengthen his heart and he will not send out the people. [22] You shall say to Pharaoh, 'So said HASHEM, My firstborn son is Israel. [23] So I say to you, Send out My son that he may serve Me — but you have refused to send him out; behold, I shall kill your firstborn son.'"

Zipporah circumcises her son — [24] It was on the way, in the lodging,* that HASHEM encountered him and sought to kill him. [25] So Zipporah took a sharp stone and cut off the foreskin of her son and touched it to his feet; and she said, "You caused my bridegroom's bloodshed!" [26] So he released him; then she said, "A bridegroom's bloodshed was because of circumcision."

[27] HASHEM said to Aaron, "Go to meet Moses, to the Wilderness." So he went and encountered him at the mountain of God, and he kissed him. [28] Moses related to Aaron all the words of HASHEM, that He had dispatched him, and all the signs that He had commanded him.

[29] Moses and Aaron went and gathered all the elders of the Children of Israel. [30] Aaron spoke all the words that HASHEM had spoken to Moses; and he performed the signs in the sight of the people. [31] And the people believed, and they heard that HASHEM had remembered the Children of Israel and that He saw their affliction, and they bowed their heads and prostrated themselves.

5

[1] Afterwards* Moses and Aaron came and said to Pharaoh, "So said HASHEM, the God of Israel, 'Send out My people that they may celebrate for Me in the Wilderness.'"

Moses and Aaron come to Pharaoh — [2] Pharaoh replied, "Who is HASHEM that I should heed His voice to send out Israel? I do not know HASHEM, nor will I send out Israel!" [3] So they said, "The God of the Hebrews happened upon us. Let us now go for a three-day journey in the Wilderness and we shall bring offerings to HASHEM, our God, lest He strike us dead with the plague or the sword." [4] The king of Egypt said to them, "Moses and Aaron, why do you disturb the people from its work?* Go to your own burdens." [5] And Pharaoh said, "Behold! the people of the land are now numerous, and you would have them cease from their burdens!"

Pharaoh increases the burden on the people — [6] On that day Pharaoh ordered the taskmasters over the people and its foremen, saying, [7] "You shall no longer give straw to the people to manufacture the bricks as yesterday and before yesterday; let them go and gather straw for themselves. [8] But the quota of bricks that they were making yesterday and before yesterday you shall impose upon them — do not reduce it —

Pharaoh, but Pharaoh was not receptive, as God had predicted to Moses.

5:4-5. Pharaoh dismisses the two Jewish leaders curtly and chastises them for interfering with the Egyptian economy by causing the Jewish laborers to use fantasies of Godly service as an excuse for idleness. In verse 5 he implied a further criticism: The Jewish nation is too large for him even to consider a mass exodus for three days. Therefore, let Moses and Aaron cease making trouble and go back to their own personal chores.

ט כִּי־נִרְפִּים הֵם עַל־כֵּן הֵם צְעֲקִים לֵאמֹר נֵלְכָה נִזְבְּחָה לֵאלֹהֵינוּ: תִּכְבַּד

י הֵעֲבֹדָה עַל־הָאֲנָשִׁים וְיַעֲשׂוּ־בָהּ וְאַל־יִשְׁעוּ בְּדִבְרֵי־שָׁקֶר: וַיֵּצְאוּ נֹגְשֵׂי

הָעָם וְשֹׁטְרָיו וַיֹּאמְרוּ אֶל־הָעָם לֵאמֹר כֹּה אָמַר פַּרְעֹה אֵינֶנִּי נֹתֵן לָכֶם

יא תֶּבֶן: אַתֶּם לְכוּ קְחוּ לָכֶם תֶּבֶן מֵאֲשֶׁר תִּמְצָאוּ כִּי אֵין נִגְרָע מֵעֲבֹדַתְכֶם

יב־יג דָּבָר: וַיָּפֶץ הָעָם בְּכָל־אֶרֶץ מִצְרָיִם לְקֹשֵׁשׁ קַשׁ לַתֶּבֶן: וְהַנֹּגְשִׂים אָצִים

לֵאמֹר כַּלּוּ מַעֲשֵׂיכֶם דְּבַר־יוֹם בְּיוֹמוֹ כַּאֲשֶׁר בִּהְיוֹת הַתֶּבֶן: וַיֻּכּוּ שֹׁטְרֵי

יד בְּנֵי יִשְׂרָאֵל אֲשֶׁר־שָׂמוּ עֲלֵהֶם נֹגְשֵׂי פַרְעֹה לֵאמֹר מַדּוּעַ לֹא כִלִּיתֶם

טו חָקְכֶם לִלְבֹּן כִּתְמוֹל שִׁלְשֹׁם גַּם־תְּמוֹל גַּם־הַיּוֹם: וַיָּבֹאוּ שֹׁטְרֵי בְּנֵי

טז יִשְׂרָאֵל וַיִּצְעֲקוּ אֶל־פַּרְעֹה לֵאמֹר לָמָּה תַעֲשֶׂה כֹה לַעֲבָדֶיךָ: תֶּבֶן אֵין

נִתָּן לַעֲבָדֶיךָ וּלְבֵנִים אֹמְרִים לָנוּ עֲשׂוּ וְהִנֵּה עֲבָדֶיךָ מֻכִּים וְחָטָאת עַמֶּךָ:

יז וַיֹּאמֶר נִרְפִּים אַתֶּם נִרְפִּים עַל־כֵּן אַתֶּם אֹמְרִים נֵלְכָה נִזְבְּחָה לַיהוָה:

יח־יט וְעַתָּה לְכוּ עִבְדוּ וְתֶבֶן לֹא־יִנָּתֵן לָכֶם וְתֹכֶן לְבֵנִים תִּתֵּנוּ: וַיִּרְאוּ שֹׁטְרֵי

בְנֵי־יִשְׂרָאֵל אֹתָם בְּרָע לֵאמֹר לֹא־תִגְרְעוּ מִלִּבְנֵיכֶם דְּבַר־יוֹם בְּיוֹמוֹ:

כ וַיִּפְגְּעוּ אֶת־מֹשֶׁה וְאֶת־אַהֲרֹן נִצָּבִים לִקְרָאתָם בְּצֵאתָם מֵאֵת פַּרְעֹה:

כא וַיֹּאמְרוּ אֲלֵהֶם יֵרֶא יְהוָה עֲלֵיכֶם וְיִשְׁפֹּט אֲשֶׁר הִבְאַשְׁתֶּם אֶת־רֵיחֵנוּ

כב בְּעֵינֵי פַרְעֹה וּבְעֵינֵי עֲבָדָיו לָתֶת־חֶרֶב בְּיָדָם לְהָרְגֵנוּ: וַיָּשָׁב מֹשֶׁה אֶל־

כג יְהוָה וַיֹּאמַר אֲדֹנָי לָמָה הֲרֵעֹתָה לָעָם הַזֶּה לָמָּה זֶּה שְׁלַחְתָּנִי: וּמֵאָז

בָּאתִי אֶל־פַּרְעֹה לְדַבֵּר בִּשְׁמֶךָ הֵרַע לָעָם הַזֶּה וְהַצֵּל לֹא־הִצַּלְתָּ אֶת־

א עַמֶּךָ: וַיֹּאמֶר יהוה אֶל־מֹשֶׁה עַתָּה תִרְאֶה אֲשֶׁר אֶעֱשֶׂה לְפַרְעֹה כִּי בְיָד

חֲזָקָה יְשַׁלְּחֵם וּבְיָד חֲזָקָה יְגָרְשֵׁם מֵאַרְצוֹ: ססס   קכ״ד פסוקים. ויק״ח סימן. מעד״י סימן.

מפטיר

Haftaras
Shemos
Ashkenazim:
p. 996
Sephardim:
p. 1072

ו

פרשת וארא

ב־ג וַיְדַבֵּר אֱלֹהִים אֶל־מֹשֶׁה וַיֹּאמֶר אֵלָיו אֲנִי יְהוָה: וָאֵרָא אֶל־אַבְרָהָם

ד אֶל־יִצְחָק וְאֶל־יַעֲקֹב בְּאֵל שַׁדָּי וּשְׁמִי יהוה לֹא נוֹדַעְתִּי לָהֶם: וְגַם

הֲקִמֹתִי אֶת־בְּרִיתִי אִתָּם לָתֵת לָהֶם אֶת־אֶרֶץ כְּנָעַן אֵת אֶרֶץ מְגֻרֵיהֶם

ה אֲשֶׁר־גָּרוּ בָהּ: וְגַם | אֲנִי שָׁמַעְתִּי אֶת־נַאֲקַת בְּנֵי יִשְׂרָאֵל אֲשֶׁר

5:20-23. The Jewish foremen blamed Moses and Aaron for the new and worsening plight of the Jews. Feeling that he had indeed caused his brethren only harm, Moses questions God's conduct. In a sense, we see here the intense self-sacrifice of Moses where Israel's interests are involved. He dares to reproach God because he cannot bear to see his people suffer.

6:1. God may bring good fortune to the wicked in order to let their punishments accumulate for the future, and He may let the innocent suffer so that they will deserve greater reward later on. This is what God told Moses in response to his question: *Now you will see . . .* Pharaoh's invincibility is temporary; he is about to feel the might of God's anger. And Israel's pain is temporary; it is about to witness a redemption that will inspire its offspring throughout history. This should serve as a source of per-

spective and comfort for us in our present exile. As the redemption from Egypt was about to commence, the persecution became worse. So it is in our time. And so must we view the phenomena of history. Israel may suffer more and more, but it may well be the last darkness before the light of redemption, and it may well mean, as it did in Egypt, that God is increasing our suffering only to prepare the way for the dawn of the Messianic Era (R' Bachya).

⊷§ **Parashas Va'eira**

6:2. God rebukes Moses for his complaint and assures him that the redemption is at hand. Moses had complained that God had sent him in vain, for instead of helping the people, he had only made it worse for them. God now continues His response. He speaks harshly to for they are lazy; therefore they cry out saying, 'Let us go and bring offerings to our God.' ⁹ Let the work be heavier upon the men and let them engage in it; and let them not pay attention to false words."

¹⁰ The taskmasters of the people and its foremen went out and spoke to the people, saying, "So said Pharaoh, I am not giving you straw. ¹¹ Go yourselves and take yourselves straw from whatever you find, for nothing will be reduced from your work."

Egyptian taskmasters and Jewish foremen

¹² So the people spread out through the entire land of Egypt to gather gleanings for straw. ¹³ The taskmasters pressed, saying, "Complete your work, the daily matter each day, as when there was straw!" ¹⁴ The foremen of the Children of Israel, whom Pharaoh's taskmasters had appointed over them, were beaten, saying, "Why did you not complete your requirement to make bricks, as yesterday and before yesterday, even yesterday and even today?"

Protesting in vain

¹⁵ The foremen of the Children of Israel came and cried out to Pharaoh, saying, "Why do you this to your servants? ¹⁶ Straw is not given to your servants, yet they tell us, 'Make bricks!' Behold, your servants are being beaten, and it is a sin for your people."

¹⁷ He said, "You are lazy, lazy! Therefore you say, 'Let us go and bring offerings to HASHEM.' ¹⁸ Now go to work. Straw will not be given to you, but you must provide the quota of bricks!"

¹⁹ The foremen of the Children of Israel saw them in distress when they said, "Do not reduce your bricks, the daily matter each day."

The Jews complain to Moses and Aaron; Moses complains to God

²⁰ They encountered Moses and Aaron standing opposite them, * as they left Pharaoh's presence. ²¹ They said to them, "May HASHEM look upon you and judge, for you have made our very scent abhorrent in the eyes of Pharaoh and the eyes of his servants, to place a sword in their hands to murder us!"

²² Moses returned to HASHEM and said, "My Lord, why have You done evil to this people, why have You sent me? ²³ From the time I came to Pharaoh to speak in Your Name he did evil to this people, but You did not rescue Your people."

6

Portent for the future

¹ HASHEM said to Moses, "Now you will see what I shall do to Pharaoh, * for through a strong hand will he send them out, and with a strong hand will he drive them from his land."

PARASHAS VA'EIRA

God reassures Moses

² God spoke to Moses * and said to him, "I am HASHEM. ³ I appeared to Abraham, to Isaac, and to Jacob as El Shaddai, * but with My Name HASHEM I did not make Myself known to them. ⁴ Moreover, I established My covenant with them to give them the land of Canaan, the land of their sojourning, in which they sojourned. ⁵ Moreover, I have heard the groan of the Children of Israel whom

---

Moses, comparing him unfavorably to the Patriarchs, who maintained their faith without complaint, even though they were not privileged to see the fulfillment of God's oaths to them, while Moses, who had been told that the redemption was at hand, was so disillusioned that he could not wait for God to carry His plan to its conclusion.

6:3. God's Names. The Names used here represent differing ways in which God revealed Himself to the Patriarchs and to Moses. Moses had had the revelation of HASHEM, God's highest manifestation, yet he questioned

His ways, while the Patriarchs had maintained their strong faith even though God had revealed Himself to them only with His other Name El Shaddai. The latter Name derives from the word די, *sufficient*, and denotes God as the One Who sets limits on Creation by establishing the laws of nature, the limitations within which the universe functions, and also the One Who limits the success one enjoys and the suffering one must endure. By comparing the revelation of Moses with that of the Patriarchs, God was chastising him for his insufficient faith.

מִצְרַ֔יִם מֵעֲבֹדִ֖ים אֹתָ֑ם וָאֶזְכֹּ֖ר אֶת־בְּרִיתִֽי: לָכֵ֞ן אֱמֹ֥ר לִבְנֵֽי־יִשְׂרָאֵל֮ אֲנִ֣י   ו
יְהוָה֒ וְהוֹצֵאתִ֣י אֶתְכֶ֗ם מִתַּ֨חַת֙ סִבְלֹ֣ת מִצְרַ֔יִם וְהִצַּלְתִּ֥י אֶתְכֶ֖ם מֵעֲבֹֽדָתָ֑ם
וְגָאַלְתִּ֤י אֶתְכֶם֙ בִּזְר֣וֹעַ נְטוּיָ֔ה וּבִשְׁפָטִ֖ים גְּדֹלִֽים: וְלָקַחְתִּ֨י אֶתְכֶ֥ם לִי֙ לְעָ֔ם   ז
וְהָיִ֥יתִי לָכֶ֖ם לֵֽאלֹהִ֑ים וִֽידַעְתֶּ֗ם כִּ֣י אֲנִ֤י יְהוָה֙ אֱלֹ֣הֵיכֶ֔ם הַמּוֹצִ֣יא אֶתְכֶ֔ם
מִתַּ֖חַת סִבְל֥וֹת מִצְרָֽיִם: וְהֵבֵאתִ֤י אֶתְכֶם֙ אֶל־הָאָ֔רֶץ אֲשֶׁ֤ר נָשָׂ֨אתִי֙ אֶת־   ח
יָדִ֔י לָתֵ֣ת אֹתָ֔הּ לְאַבְרָהָ֥ם לְיִצְחָ֖ק וּֽלְיַעֲקֹ֑ב וְנָתַתִּ֨י אֹתָ֥הּ לָכֶ֛ם מֽוֹרָשָׁ֖ה אֲנִ֥י
יְהוָֽה: וַיְדַבֵּ֥ר מֹשֶׁ֛ה כֵּ֖ן אֶל־בְּנֵ֣י יִשְׂרָאֵ֑ל וְלֹ֤א שָֽׁמְעוּ֙ אֶל־מֹשֶׁ֔ה מִקֹּ֣צֶר ר֔וּחַ   ט
וּמֵעֲבֹדָ֖ה קָשָֽׁה:

וַיְדַבֵּ֥ר יְהוָ֖ה אֶל־מֹשֶׁ֥ה לֵּאמֹֽר: בֹּ֣א דַבֵּ֔ר אֶל־פַּרְעֹ֖ה מֶ֣לֶךְ מִצְרָ֑יִם וִֽישַׁלַּ֥ח   י־יא
אֶת־בְּנֵֽי־יִשְׂרָאֵ֖ל מֵֽאַרְצֽוֹ: וַיְדַבֵּ֣ר מֹשֶׁ֔ה לִפְנֵ֥י יְהוָ֖ה לֵאמֹ֑ר הֵ֤ן בְּנֵֽי־יִשְׂרָאֵל֙   יב
לֹֽא־שָֽׁמְע֣וּ אֵלַ֔י וְאֵיךְ֙ יִשְׁמָעֵ֣נִי פַרְעֹ֔ה וַאֲנִ֖י עֲרַ֥ל שְׂפָתָֽיִם:

וַיְדַבֵּ֣ר יְהוָה֘ אֶל־מֹשֶׁ֣ה וְאֶֽל־אַהֲרֹן֒ וַיְצַוֵּם֙ אֶל־בְּנֵ֣י יִשְׂרָאֵ֔ל וְאֶל־פַּרְעֹ֖ה   יג
מֶ֣לֶךְ מִצְרָ֑יִם לְהוֹצִ֥יא אֶת־בְּנֵֽי־יִשְׂרָאֵ֖ל מֵאֶ֥רֶץ מִצְרָֽיִם: אֵ֖לֶּה   יד   שני
רָאשֵׁ֣י בֵית־אֲבֹתָ֑ם בְּנֵ֨י רְאוּבֵ֜ן בְּכֹ֣ר יִשְׂרָאֵ֗ל חֲנ֤וֹךְ וּפַלּוּא֙ חֶצְרֹ֣ן וְכַרְמִ֔י
אֵ֖לֶּה מִשְׁפְּחֹ֥ת רְאוּבֵֽן: וּבְנֵ֣י שִׁמְע֗וֹן יְמוּאֵ֨ל וְיָמִ֤ין וְאֹ֨הַד֙ וְיָכִ֣ין וְצֹ֔חַר וְשָׁא֖וּל   טו
בֶּן־הַֽכְּנַעֲנִ֑ית אֵ֖לֶּה מִשְׁפְּחֹ֥ת שִׁמְעֽוֹן: וְאֵ֨לֶּה שְׁמ֤וֹת בְּנֵֽי־לֵוִי֙ לְתֹ֣לְדֹתָ֔ם   טז
גֵּֽרְשׁ֕וֹן וּקְהָ֖ת וּמְרָרִ֑י וּשְׁנֵי֙ חַיֵּ֣י לֵוִ֔י שֶׁ֧בַע וּשְׁלֹשִׁ֛ים וּמְאַ֖ת שָׁנָֽה: בְּנֵ֥י גֵֽרְשׁ֖וֹן   יז
לִבְנִ֥י וְשִׁמְעִ֖י לְמִשְׁפְּחֹתָֽם: וּבְנֵ֣י קְהָ֔ת עַמְרָ֣ם וְיִצְהָ֔ר וְחֶבְר֖וֹן וְעֻזִּיאֵ֑ל וּשְׁנֵי֙   יח
חַיֵּ֣י קְהָ֔ת שָׁלֹ֧שׁ וּשְׁלֹשִׁ֛ים וּמְאַ֖ת שָׁנָֽה: וּבְנֵ֥י מְרָרִ֖י מַחְלִ֣י וּמוּשִׁ֑י אֵ֛לֶּה   יט
מִשְׁפְּחֹ֥ת הַלֵּוִ֖י לְתֹלְדֹתָֽם: וַיִּקַּ֨ח עַמְרָ֜ם אֶת־יוֹכֶ֤בֶד דֹּֽדָתוֹ֙ ל֣וֹ לְאִשָּׁ֔ה וַתֵּ֣לֶד   כ
ל֔וֹ אֶֽת־אַהֲרֹ֖ן וְאֶת־מֹשֶׁ֑ה וּשְׁנֵי֙ חַיֵּ֣י עַמְרָ֔ם שֶׁ֧בַע וּשְׁלֹשִׁ֛ים וּמְאַ֖ת שָׁנָֽה:
וּבְנֵ֣י יִצְהָ֔ר קֹ֥רַח וָנֶ֖פֶג וְזִכְרִ֑י וּבְנֵ֖י עֻזִּיאֵ֑ל מִֽישָׁאֵ֥ל וְאֶלְצָפָ֖ן וְסִתְרִֽי: וַיִּקַּ֨ח   כא־כג
אַהֲרֹ֜ן אֶת־אֱלִישֶׁ֧בַע בַּת־עַמִּֽינָדָ֛ב אֲח֥וֹת נַחְשׁ֖וֹן ל֣וֹ לְאִשָּׁ֑ה וַתֵּ֣לֶד ל֗וֹ אֶת־
נָדָב֙ וְאֶת־אֲבִיה֔וּא אֶת־אֶלְעָזָ֖ר וְאֶת־אִֽיתָמָֽר: וּבְנֵ֣י קֹ֔רַח אַסִּ֥יר וְאֶלְקָנָ֖ה   כד
וַאֲבִֽיאָסָ֑ף אֵ֖לֶּה מִשְׁפְּחֹ֥ת הַקָּרְחִֽי: וְאֶלְעָזָ֨ר בֶּֽן־אַהֲרֹ֜ן לָֽקַח־ל֨וֹ מִבְּנ֤וֹת   כה
פּֽוּטִיאֵל֙ ל֣וֹ לְאִשָּׁ֔ה וַתֵּ֥לֶד ל֖וֹ אֶת־פִּֽינְחָ֑ס אֵ֗לֶּה רָאשֵׁ֛י אֲב֥וֹת הַלְוִיִּ֖ם
לְמִשְׁפְּחֹתָֽם: ה֥וּא אַהֲרֹ֖ן וּמֹשֶׁ֑ה אֲשֶׁ֨ר אָמַ֤ר יְהוָה֙ לָהֶ֔ם הוֹצִ֜יאוּ אֶת־   כו
בְּנֵ֧י יִשְׂרָאֵ֛ל מֵאֶ֥רֶץ מִצְרַ֖יִם עַל־צִבְאֹתָֽם: הֵ֗ם הַֽמְדַבְּרִים֙ אֶל־פַּרְעֹ֣ה   כז
מֶֽלֶךְ־מִצְרַ֔יִם לְהוֹצִ֥יא אֶת־בְּנֵֽי־יִשְׂרָאֵ֖ל מִמִּצְרָ֑יִם ה֥וּא מֹשֶׁ֖ה וְאַהֲרֹֽן:

6:6-7. The four expressions of redemption. Having told
Moses that the impending revelation would be greater
than that which was revealed to the Patriarchs, God
commands him to tell the Jews that He — as *Hashem* —
is about to redeem them. These two verses contain four
different expressions, representing progressive stages of
the redemption. These four stages are the basis for the
Rabbinic requirement of the Four Cups at the Pesach
Seder. The expressions, as explained by *R' Bachya*, are:

▫ וְהוֹצֵאתִי — *I shall take you out*. God would remove the
Jews from the burdens of slavery, even before they were
freed from the mastery of Egypt. The slavery ended in the
month of Tishrei, but they did not leave Egypt until six
months later.

▫ וְהִצַּלְתִּי — *I shall rescue you*. The subjugation to Egypt
will be formally ended.

▫ וְגָאַלְתִּי — *I shall redeem you*. This alludes to the Splitting
of the Sea, when God's *outstretched arm with great*

The four
expressions
of
redemption

Egypt enslaves and I have remembered My covenant. ⁶ Therefore, say to the Children of Israel: 'I am HASHEM, and I shall take you out* from under the burdens of Egypt; I shall rescue you* from their service; I shall redeem you* with an outstretched arm and with great judgments. ⁷ I shall take you* to Me for a people and I shall be a God to you; and you shall know that I am HASHEM your God, Who takes you out from under the burdens of Egypt. ⁸ I shall bring you to the land about which I raised My hand to give it to Abraham, Isaac, and Jacob; and I shall give it to you as a heritage — I am HASHEM.' "

⁹ So Moses spoke accordingly to the Children of Israel; but they did not heed Moses, because of shortness of breath and hard work.

¹⁰ HASHEM spoke to Moses, saying, ¹¹ "Come speak to Pharaoh, king of Egypt, that he send the Children of Israel from his land."

Moses
demurs

¹² Moses spoke before HASHEM, saying, "Behold, the Children of Israel have not listened to me, so how will Pharaoh listen to me? And I have sealed lips!"

The mission
and
its bearers

¹³ HASHEM spoke to Moses and Aaron and commanded them regarding the Children of Israel and regarding Pharaoh, king of Egypt, to take the Children of Israel out of the land of Egypt.

¹⁴ These were the heads of their fathers' houses: The sons of Reuben the firstborn of Israel: Hanoch and Pallu, Hezron and Carmi; these were the families of Reuben. ¹⁵ The sons of Simeon: Jemuel, Jamin, Ohad, Jachin, and Zohar; and Shaul the son of a Canaanite woman; these were the families of Simeon. ¹⁶ These are the names of the sons of Levi in order of their birth: Gershon, Kohath, and Merari; the years of Levi's life were one hundred and thirty-seven years. ¹⁷ The sons of Gershon: Livni and Shimei, according to their families. ¹⁸ The sons of Kohath: Amram, Izhar, Hebron, and Uzziel; the years of Kohath's life were one hundred and thirty-three years. ¹⁹ The sons of Merari: Mahli and Mushi; these were the Levite families, in order of their birth. ²⁰ Amram took his aunt Jochebed as a wife,* and she bore him Aaron and Moses; the years of Amram's life were one hundred and thirty-seven years. ²¹ The sons of Izhar: Korah, Nepheg, and Zichri. ²² The sons of Uzziel: Mishael, Elzaphan, and Sithri. ²³ Aaron took Elisheba daughter of Amminadab, sister of Nahshon, as a wife;* and she bore him Nadab and Abihu, Elazar and Ithamar. ²⁴ The sons of Korah: Assir, Elkanah, and Abiasaph; these were the Korahite families. ²⁵ Elazar son of Aaron took for himself from the daughters of Putiel as a wife,* and she bore to him Phinehas; these were the leaders of the fathers of the Levites, according to their families. ²⁶ This was the Aaron and Moses to whom HASHEM said: "Take the Children of Israel out of the land of Egypt according to their legions." ²⁷ They were the ones who spoke to Pharaoh, king of Egypt, to take the Children of Israel out of Egypt; this was the Moses and Aaron.

---

judgments crushed Egypt's power for good. Until then, the Jews feared that they would be pursued by their former masters and returned to slavery.

וְלָקַחְתִּי □ — *I shall take you.* God took the Jews as His people when He gave them the Torah at Sinai. That was the climax, the purpose, of the Exodus.

6:20,23,25. The wives. In only three cases does the Torah mention the wives of leaders; in all three cases the reason is to show that great people had to descend not only from distinguished fathers but from distinguished

mothers as well. Amram married Jochebed, a daughter of Levi. Aaron married Elisheba, from the royal tribe of Judah; she was a sister of the man who later became the most distinguished of the tribal princes. And Elazar, whose son Phineas became the only one who was granted priesthood as a result of his own merit [see *Numbers* 25:13], married a [grand] daughter of Putiel, a name that, the Sages teach, refers to both Joseph and Jethro (*Ramban*). [Moses' wife Zipporah is not mentioned in this context, because her identity is already known from ch. 4.]

כח-כט ‏ *שלישי‏ וַיְהִ֗י בְּי֨וֹם דִּבֶּ֧ר יהוֹה אֶל־מֹשֶׁ֛ה בְּאֶ֣רֶץ מִצְרָ֑יִם: ‏ * וַיְדַבֵּ֧ר יהוֹ֛ה
אֶל־מֹשֶׁ֥ה לֵּאמֹ֖ר אֲנִ֣י יהוֹ֑ה דַּבֵּ֗ר אֶל־פַּרְעֹה֙ מֶ֣לֶךְ מִצְרַ֔יִם אֵ֛ת כָּל־אֲשֶׁ֥ר
ל ‏ אֲנִ֖י דֹּבֵ֥ר אֵלֶֽיךָ: ‏ וַיֹּ֥אמֶר מֹשֶׁ֖ה לִפְנֵ֣י יהוֹ֑ה הֵ֤ן אֲנִי֙ עֲרַ֣ל שְׂפָתַ֔יִם וְאֵ֖יךְ יִשְׁמַ֥ע
אֵלַ֖י פַּרְעֹֽה:

ז א ‏ וַיֹּ֤אמֶר יהוֹה֙ אֶל־מֹשֶׁ֔ה רְאֵ֛ה נְתַתִּ֥יךָ אֱלֹהִ֖ים לְפַרְעֹ֑ה וְאַֽהֲרֹ֥ן אָחִ֖יךָ יִֽהְיֶ֥ה
ב ‏ נְבִיאֶֽךָ: ‏ אַתָּ֣ה תְדַבֵּ֔ר אֵ֖ת כָּל־אֲשֶׁ֣ר אֲצַוֶּ֑ךָּ וְאַֽהֲרֹ֤ן אָחִ֙יךָ֙ יְדַבֵּ֣ר אֶל־פַּרְעֹ֔ה
ג ‏ וְשִׁלַּ֥ח אֶת־בְּנֵֽי־יִשְׂרָאֵ֖ל מֵֽאַרְצֽוֹ: ‏ וַֽאֲנִ֥י אַקְשֶׁ֖ה אֶת־לֵ֣ב פַּרְעֹ֑ה וְהִרְבֵּיתִ֧י
ד ‏ אֶת־אֹֽתֹתַ֛י וְאֶת־מֽוֹפְתַ֖י בְּאֶ֥רֶץ מִצְרָֽיִם: ‏ וְלֹֽא־יִשְׁמַ֤ע אֲלֵכֶם֙ פַּרְעֹ֔ה וְנָֽתַתִּ֥י
אֶת־יָדִ֖י בְּמִצְרָ֑יִם וְהֽוֹצֵאתִ֨י אֶת־צִבְאֹתַ֜י אֶת־עַמִּ֤י בְנֵֽי־יִשְׂרָאֵל֙ מֵאֶ֣רֶץ
ה ‏ מִצְרַ֔יִם בִּשְׁפָטִ֖ים גְּדֹלִֽים: ‏ וְיָֽדְע֤וּ מִצְרַ֙יִם֙ כִּֽי־אֲנִ֣י יהוֹ֔ה בִּנְטֹתִ֥י אֶת־יָדִ֖י עַל־
ו ‏ מִצְרָ֑יִם וְהֽוֹצֵאתִ֥י אֶת־בְּנֵֽי־יִשְׂרָאֵ֖ל מִתּוֹכָֽם: ‏ וַיַּ֥עַשׂ מֹשֶׁ֖ה וְאַֽהֲרֹ֑ן כַּֽאֲשֶׁ֨ר
ז ‏ צִוָּ֧ה יהוֹ֛ה אֹתָ֖ם כֵּ֥ן עָשֽׂוּ: ‏ וּמֹשֶׁה֙ בֶּן־שְׁמֹנִ֣ים שָׁנָ֔ה וְאַֽהֲרֹ֕ן בֶּן־שָׁלֹ֥שׁ
וּשְׁמֹנִ֖ים שָׁנָ֑ה בְּדַבְּרָ֖ם אֶל־פַּרְעֹֽה:

ח-ט ‏ רביעי‏ וַיֹּ֣אמֶר יהוֹ֔ה אֶל־מֹשֶׁ֥ה וְאֶֽל־אַֽהֲרֹ֖ן לֵאמֹֽר: ‏ כִּי֩ יְדַבֵּ֨ר אֲלֵכֶ֤ם פַּרְעֹה֙ לֵאמֹ֔ר
תְּנ֥וּ לָכֶ֖ם מוֹפֵ֑ת וְאָֽמַרְתָּ֣ אֶל־אַֽהֲרֹ֗ן קַ֧ח אֶת־מַטְּךָ֛ וְהַשְׁלֵ֥ךְ לִפְנֵֽי־פַרְעֹ֖ה יְהִ֥י
י ‏ לְתַנִּֽין: ‏ וַיָּבֹ֨א מֹשֶׁ֤ה וְאַֽהֲרֹן֙ אֶל־פַּרְעֹ֔ה וַיַּ֣עֲשׂוּ כֵ֔ן כַּֽאֲשֶׁ֖ר צִוָּ֣ה יהוֹ֑ה וַיַּשְׁלֵ֨ךְ
יא ‏ אַֽהֲרֹ֜ן אֶת־מַטֵּ֗הוּ לִפְנֵ֥י פַרְעֹ֛ה וְלִפְנֵ֥י עֲבָדָ֖יו וַיְהִ֥י לְתַנִּֽין: ‏ וַיִּקְרָא֙ גַּם־פַּרְעֹ֔ה
לַֽחֲכָמִ֖ים וְלַֽמְכַשְּׁפִ֑ים וַיַּֽעֲשׂ֨וּ גַם־הֵ֜ם חַרְטֻמֵּ֥י מִצְרַ֛יִם בְּלַֽהֲטֵיהֶ֖ם כֵּֽן:
יב-יג ‏ וַיַּשְׁלִ֙יכוּ֙ אִ֣ישׁ מַטֵּ֔הוּ וַיִּֽהְי֖וּ לְתַנִּינִ֑ם וַיִּבְלַ֥ע מַטֵּֽה־אַֽהֲרֹ֖ן אֶת־מַטֹּתָֽם: ‏ וַיֶּֽחֱזַק֙
יד ‏ לֵ֣ב פַּרְעֹ֔ה וְלֹ֥א שָׁמַ֖ע אֲלֵהֶ֑ם כַּֽאֲשֶׁ֖ר דִּבֶּ֥ר יהוֹֽה: ‏ וַיֹּ֤אמֶר
טו ‏ יהוֹה֙ אֶל־מֹשֶׁ֔ה כָּבֵ֖ד לֵ֣ב פַּרְעֹ֑ה מֵאֵ֖ן לְשַׁלַּ֥ח הָעָֽם: ‏ לֵ֣ךְ אֶל־פַּרְעֹה֮ בַּבֹּ֒קֶר֒
הִנֵּה֙ יֹצֵ֣א הַמַּ֔יְמָה וְנִצַּבְתָּ֥ לִקְרָאת֖וֹ עַל־שְׂפַ֣ת הַיְאֹ֑ר וְהַמַּטֶּ֛ה אֲשֶׁר־נֶהְפַּ֥ךְ
טז ‏ לְנָחָ֖שׁ תִּקַּ֥ח בְּיָדֶֽךָ: ‏ וְאָֽמַרְתָּ֣ אֵלָ֗יו יהוֹ֞ה אֱלֹהֵ֤י הָֽעִבְרִים֙ שְׁלָחַ֣נִי אֵלֶ֣יךָ
יז ‏ לֵאמֹ֗ר שַׁלַּח֙ אֶת־עַמִּ֔י וְיַֽעַבְדֻ֖נִי בַּמִּדְבָּ֑ר וְהִנֵּ֥ה לֹֽא־שָׁמַ֖עְתָּ עַד־כֹּֽה: ‏ כֹּ֚ה
אָמַ֣ר יהוֹ֔ה בְּזֹ֣את תֵּדַ֔ע כִּ֖י אֲנִ֣י יהוֹ֑ה הִנֵּ֨ה אָֽנֹכִ֜י מַכֶּ֣ה | בַּמַּטֶּ֣ה אֲשֶׁר־בְּיָדִ֗י
יח ‏ עַל־הַמַּ֛יִם אֲשֶׁ֥ר בַּיְאֹ֖ר וְנֶהֶפְכ֥וּ לְדָֽם: ‏ וְהַדָּגָ֧ה אֲשֶׁר־בַּיְאֹ֛ר תָּמ֖וּת וּבָאַ֣שׁ
יט ‏ הַיְאֹ֑ר וְנִלְא֣וּ מִצְרַ֔יִם לִשְׁתּ֥וֹת מַ֖יִם מִן־הַיְאֹֽר: ‏ וַיֹּ֣אמֶר
יהוֹ֣ה אֶל־מֹשֶׁ֡ה אֱמֹ֣ר אֶֽל־אַֽהֲרֹ֡ן קַ֣ח מַטְּךָ֣ וּנְטֵֽה־יָֽדְךָ֩ עַל־מֵימֵ֨י
מִצְרַ֜יִם עַֽל־נַֽהֲרֹתָ֣ם | עַל־יְאֹֽרֵיהֶ֣ם וְעַל־אַגְמֵיהֶ֗ם וְעַ֛ל כָּל־מִקְוֵ֥ה
מֵֽימֵיהֶ֖ם וְיִֽהְיוּ־דָ֑ם וְהָ֤יָה דָם֙ בְּכָל־אֶ֣רֶץ מִצְרַ֔יִם וּבָֽעֵצִ֖ים וּבָֽאֲבָנִֽים:

7:3. Pharaoh and free choice. God tells Moses that He will *harden Pharaoh's heart*, thus preventing him from repenting, with the result that God will inflict a multitude of punishments upon Egypt. How could Pharaoh be punished for not releasing the Jews, when it was God Who prevented him from doing so? *Ramban* explains that Egypt was punished only for the sins that were committed before Pharaoh was coerced, such as the enslavement and the intense persecution. That God hardened his heart afterward was merely to prevent him from escaping the retribution he had richly earned.

7:14-12:36. The Ten Plagues: their general pattern. The Ten Plagues consisted of three sets of three plagues each, which were intended to establish three

²⁸ *It was on the day when* HASHEM *spoke to Moses in the land of Egypt.* ²⁹ HASHEM *spoke to Moses, saying, "I am* HASHEM. *Speak to Pharaoh, king of*

Second *Egypt, everything that I speak to you."* ³⁰ *Moses said before* HASHEM, *"Behold!*
demurral *I have sealed lips, so how shall Pharaoh heed me?"*

7   ¹H ASHEM *said to Moses, "See, I have made you a master over Pharaoh, and*
The   Aaron *your brother shall be your spokesman.* ² *You shall speak everything*
redemption *that I shall command you, and Aaron your brother shall speak to Pharaoh, that*
begins *he should send the Children of Israel from his land.* ³ *But I shall harden Pharaoh's heart* * *and I shall multiply My signs and My wonders in the land of Egypt.* ⁴ *Pharaoh will not heed you, and I shall put My hand upon Egypt; and I shall take out My legions — My people, the Children of Israel — from the land of Egypt, with great judgments.* ⁵ *And Egypt shall know that I am* HASHEM, *when I stretch out My hand over Egypt; and I shall take the Children of Israel out from among them."*

⁶ *Moses and Aaron did as* HASHEM *commanded them; so they did.* ⁷ *Moses was eighty years old and Aaron was eighty-three years old when they spoke to Pharaoh.*

⁸ HASHEM *said to Moses and Aaron, saying:* ⁹ *"When Pharaoh speaks to you, saying, 'Provide a wonder for yourselves,' you shall say to Aaron, 'Take your staff and cast it down before Pharaoh — it will become a snake!' "*

¹⁰ *Moses came with Aaron to Pharaoh and they did so, as* HASHEM *had commanded; Aaron cast down his staff before Pharaoh and before his servants, and it became a snake.* ¹¹ *Pharaoh, too, summoned his wise men and sorcerers, and they, too — the necromancers of Egypt — did so with their incantations.* ¹² *Each one cast down his staff and they became snakes; and the staff of Aaron swallowed their staffs.* ¹³ *The heart of Pharaoh was strong and he did not heed them, as* HASHEM *had spoken.*

The Ten   ¹⁴ HASHEM *said to Moses, "Pharaoh's heart is stubborn, he has refused to send*
Plagues* *the people.* ¹⁵ *Go to Pharaoh in the morning — behold! he goes out to the water — and you shall stand opposite him at the River's bank, and the staff that was turned into a snake you shall take in your hand.* ¹⁶ *You shall say to him, 'HASHEM, the God of the Hebrews, has sent me to you, saying: Send out My people that they may serve Me in the Wilderness — but behold, you have not*
The first *heeded up to now.'* ¹⁷ *So says* HASHEM, *'Through this shall you know that I am*
plague: HASHEM; * *behold, with the staff that is in my hand I shall strike the waters that*
Blood *are in the River, and they shall change to blood.* ¹⁸ *The fish-life that is in the River shall die and the River shall become foul. Egypt will grow weary of trying to drink water from the River.' "*

¹⁹ HASHEM *said to Moses, "Say to Aaron, 'Take your staff and stretch out your hand over the waters of Egypt: over their rivers, over their canals, over their reservoirs, and over all their gatherings of water, and they shall become blood; there shall be blood throughout the land of Egypt, even in the wooden and stone vessels.' "*

---

eternal principles for all time. The first three plagues proved the existence of God (7:17); the next three proved that His providence extends to earthly affairs and that He does not choose to be oblivious to material matters (8:18); and the next three proved that God is unmatched by any power (9:14). The tenth plague, the

Plague of the Firstborn, was meant to break down Pharaoh's resistance and bring the redemption from Egypt.

7:17. Because Pharaoh had proclaimed initially that he knew of no "Hashem," the first three plagues were intended to prove to him that *I am* HASHEM.

כ וַיַּעֲשׂוּ־כֵן מֹשֶׁה וְאַהֲרֹן כַּאֲשֶׁר ׀ צִוָּה יהוה וַיָּרֶם בַּמַּטֶּה וַיַּךְ אֶת־הַמַּיִם אֲשֶׁר בַּיְאֹר לְעֵינֵי פַרְעֹה וּלְעֵינֵי עֲבָדָיו וַיֵּהָפְכוּ כָּל־הַמַּיִם אֲשֶׁר־בַּיְאֹר

כא לְדָם: וְהַדָּגָה אֲשֶׁר־בַּיְאֹר מֵתָה וַיִּבְאַשׁ הַיְאֹר וְלֹא־יָכְלוּ מִצְרַיִם לִשְׁתּוֹת

כב מַיִם מִן־הַיְאֹר וַיְהִי הַדָּם בְּכָל־אֶרֶץ מִצְרָיִם: וַיַּעֲשׂוּ־כֵן חַרְטֻמֵּי מִצְרַיִם

כג בְּלָטֵיהֶם וַיֶּחֱזַק לֵב־פַּרְעֹה וְלֹא־שָׁמַע אֲלֵהֶם כַּאֲשֶׁר דִּבֶּר יהוה: וַיִּפֶן

כד פַּרְעֹה וַיָּבֹא אֶל־בֵּיתוֹ וְלֹא־שָׁת לִבּוֹ גַּם־לָזֹאת: וַיַּחְפְּרוּ כָל־מִצְרַיִם

כה סְבִיבֹת הַיְאֹר מַיִם לִשְׁתּוֹת כִּי לֹא יָכְלוּ לִשְׁתֹּת מִמֵּימֵי הַיְאֹר: וַיִּמָּלֵא שִׁבְעַת יָמִים אַחֲרֵי הַכּוֹת־יהוה אֶת־הַיְאֹר:

כו וַיֹּאמֶר יהוה אֶל־מֹשֶׁה בֹּא אֶל־פַּרְעֹה וְאָמַרְתָּ אֵלָיו כֹּה אָמַר יהוה שַׁלַּח

כז אֶת־עַמִּי וְיַעַבְדֻנִי: וְאִם־מָאֵן אַתָּה לְשַׁלֵּחַ הִנֵּה אָנֹכִי נֹגֵף אֶת־כָּל־גְּבוּלְךָ

כח בַּצְפַרְדְּעִים: וְשָׁרַץ הַיְאֹר צְפַרְדְּעִים וְעָלוּ וּבָאוּ בְּבֵיתֶךָ וּבַחֲדַר מִשְׁכָּבְךָ

כט וְעַל־מִטָּתֶךָ וּבְבֵית עֲבָדֶיךָ וּבְעַמֶּךָ וּבְתַנּוּרֶיךָ וּבְמִשְׁאֲרוֹתֶיךָ: וּבְכָה

ח א וּבְעַמְּךָ וּבְכָל־עֲבָדֶיךָ יַעֲלוּ הַצְפַרְדְּעִים: וַיֹּאמֶר יהוה אֶל־מֹשֶׁה אֱמֹר אֶל־אַהֲרֹן נְטֵה אֶת־יָדְךָ בְּמַטֶּךָ עַל־הַנְּהָרֹת עַל־הַיְאֹרִים וְעַל־הָאֲגַמִּים

ב וְהַעַל אֶת־הַצְפַרְדְּעִים עַל־אֶרֶץ מִצְרָיִם: וַיֵּט אַהֲרֹן אֶת־יָדוֹ עַל מֵימֵי

ג מִצְרָיִם וַתַּעַל הַצְפַרְדֵּעַ וַתְּכַס אֶת־אֶרֶץ מִצְרָיִם: וַיַּעֲשׂוּ־כֵן הַחַרְטֻמִּים

ד בְּלָטֵיהֶם וַיַּעֲלוּ אֶת־הַצְפַרְדְּעִים עַל־אֶרֶץ מִצְרָיִם: וַיִּקְרָא פַרְעֹה לְמֹשֶׁה וּלְאַהֲרֹן וַיֹּאמֶר הַעְתִּירוּ אֶל־יהוה וְיָסֵר הַצְפַרְדְּעִים מִמֶּנִּי וּמֵעַמִּי

ה וַאֲשַׁלְּחָה אֶת־הָעָם וְיִזְבְּחוּ לַיהוה: וַיֹּאמֶר מֹשֶׁה לְפַרְעֹה הִתְפָּאֵר עָלַי לְמָתַי ׀ אַעְתִּיר לְךָ וְלַעֲבָדֶיךָ וּלְעַמְּךָ לְהַכְרִית הַצְפַרְדְּעִים מִמְּךָ וּמִבָּתֶּיךָ

ו רַק בַּיְאֹר תִּשָּׁאַרְנָה: וַיֹּאמֶר לְמָחָר וַיֹּאמֶר כִּדְבָרְךָ לְמַעַן תֵּדַע כִּי־אֵין

ז כַּיהוה אֱלֹהֵינוּ: וְסָרוּ הַצְפַרְדְּעִים מִמְּךָ וּמִבָּתֶּיךָ וּמֵעֲבָדֶיךָ וּמֵעַמֶּךָ רַק חמישי

ח בַּיְאֹר תִּשָּׁאַרְנָה: וַיֵּצֵא מֹשֶׁה וְאַהֲרֹן מֵעִם פַּרְעֹה וַיִּצְעַק מֹשֶׁה אֶל־יהוה

ט עַל־דְּבַר הַצְפַרְדְּעִים אֲשֶׁר־שָׂם לְפַרְעֹה: וַיַּעַשׂ יהוה כִּדְבַר מֹשֶׁה וַיָּמֻתוּ

י הַצְפַרְדְּעִים מִן־הַבָּתִּים מִן־הַחֲצֵרֹת וּמִן־הַשָּׂדֹת: וַיִּצְבְּרוּ אֹתָם חֳמָרִם

יא חֳמָרִם וַתִּבְאַשׁ הָאָרֶץ: וַיַּרְא פַּרְעֹה כִּי הָיְתָה הָרְוָחָה וְהַכְבֵּד אֶת־לִבּוֹ

יב וְלֹא שָׁמַע אֲלֵהֶם כַּאֲשֶׁר דִּבֶּר יהוה: וַיֹּאמֶר יהוה אֶל־מֹשֶׁה אֱמֹר אֶל־אַהֲרֹן נְטֵה אֶת־מַטְּךָ וְהַךְ אֶת־עֲפַר הָאָרֶץ וְהָיָה

יג לְכִנִּם בְּכָל־אֶרֶץ מִצְרָיִם: וַיַּעֲשׂוּ־כֵן וַיֵּט אַהֲרֹן אֶת־יָדוֹ בְמַטֵּהוּ וַיַּךְ אֶת־עֲפַר הָאָרֶץ וַתְּהִי הַכִּנָּם בָּאָדָם וּבַבְּהֵמָה כָּל־עֲפַר הָאָרֶץ הָיָה כִנִּים

יד בְּכָל־אֶרֶץ מִצְרָיִם: וַיַּעֲשׂוּ־כֵן הַחַרְטֻמִּים בְּלָטֵיהֶם לְהוֹצִיא אֶת־הַכִּנִּים

טו וְלֹא יָכֹלוּ וַתְּהִי הַכִּנָּם בָּאָדָם וּבַבְּהֵמָה: וַיֹּאמְרוּ הַחַרְטֻמִּם אֶל־פַּרְעֹה

7:27. *Frogs.* This is Rashi's generally accepted translation of צְפַרְדְּעִים. Some commentaries render *crocodiles.*
8:5. Make a request that you feel I cannot fulfill, and if
you are right, you will be able to claim that I failed your
test! Tell me the moment when you want the frog-infesta-
tion to end (*Rashi*).

²⁰ *Moses and Aaron did so, as HASHEM had commanded. He held the staff aloft and struck the water that was in the River in the presence of Pharaoh and in the presence of his servants, and all the water that was in the River changed to blood.* ²¹ *The fish-life that was in the River died and the River became foul; Egypt could not drink water from the River, and the blood was throughout the land of Egypt.* ²² *The necromancers of Egypt did the same by means of their incantations; so Pharaoh's heart was strong and he did not heed them, as HASHEM had spoken.* ²³ *Pharaoh turned away and came to his palace. He did not take this to heart either.* ²⁴ *All of the Egyptians dug roundabout the River for water to drink, for they could not drink from the waters of the River.* ²⁵ *Seven days were completed after HASHEM struck the River.*

The second   ²⁶ *HASHEM said to Moses, "Come to Pharaoh and say to him, 'So said HASHEM:*
plague: *Send out My people that they may serve Me.* ²⁷ *But if you refuse to send out,*
Frogs   *behold, I shall strike your entire boundary with frogs.* * ²⁸ *The River shall swarm with frogs, and they shall ascend and come into your palace and your bedroom and your bed, and into the house of your servants and of your people, and into your ovens and into your kneading bowls.* ²⁹ *And into you and your people and all your servants will the frogs ascend.' "*

8   ¹ **H**ASHEM *said to Moses, "Say to Aaron, 'Stretch out your hand with your staff over the rivers, over the canals, and over the reservoirs, and raise up the frogs over the land of Egypt.' "*

    ² *Aaron stretched out his hand over the waters of Egypt, and the frog-infestation ascended and covered the land of Egypt.* ³ *The necromancers did the same through their incantations, and they brought up the frogs upon the land of Egypt.*

    ⁴ *Pharaoh summoned Moses and Aaron and said, "Entreat HASHEM that He remove the frogs from me and my people, and I shall send out the people that they may bring offerings to HASHEM."*

    ⁵ *Moses said to Pharaoh, "Glorify yourself over me* * — *for when should I entreat for you, for your servants, and for your people, to excise the frogs from you and from your houses? Only in the River shall they remain."* ⁶ *And he said, "For tomorrow." He said, "As you say — so that you will know that there is none like HASHEM, our God.* ⁷ *The frogs will depart from you and your houses, and from your servants and your people; only in the River shall they remain."*

    ⁸ *Moses and Aaron left Pharaoh's presence; Moses cried out to HASHEM concerning the frogs that he had inflicted upon Pharaoh.* ⁹ *HASHEM carried out the word of Moses, and the frogs died — from the houses, from the courtyards, and from the fields.* ¹⁰ *They piled them up into heaps and heaps, and the land stank.* ¹¹ *Pharaoh saw that there had been a relief, and kept making his heart stubborn. He did not heed them, as HASHEM had spoken.*

The third   ¹² *HASHEM said to Moses, "Say to Aaron, 'Stretch out your staff and strike*
plague: Lice   *the dust of the land; it shall become lice throughout the land of Egypt.' "*
    ¹³ *So they did: Aaron stretched out his hand with his staff and struck the dust of the land, and the lice-infestation was on man and beast; all the dust of the land became lice, throughout the land of Egypt.* ¹⁴ *The sorcerers did the same with their incantations to draw forth the lice, but they could not. And the lice-infestation was on man and beast.* ¹⁵ *The sorcerers said to Pharaoh,*

אֶצְבַּע אֱלֹהִים הִוא וַיֶּחֱזַק לֵב־פַּרְעֹה וְלֹא־שָׁמַע אֲלֵהֶם כַּאֲשֶׁר דִּבֶּר

יהוה: וַיֹּאמֶר יהוה אֶל־מֹשֶׁה הַשְׁכֵּם בַּבֹּקֶר וְהִתְיַצֵּב   טז

לִפְנֵי פַרְעֹה הִנֵּה יוֹצֵא הַמָּיְמָה וְאָמַרְתָּ אֵלָיו כֹּה אָמַר יהוה שַׁלַּח עַמִּי

וְיַעַבְדֻנִי: כִּי אִם־אֵינְךָ מְשַׁלֵּחַ אֶת־עַמִּי הִנְנִי מַשְׁלִיחַ בְּךָ וּבַעֲבָדֶיךָ   יז

וּבְעַמְּךָ וּבְבָתֶּיךָ אֶת־הֶעָרֹב וּמָלְאוּ בָּתֵּי מִצְרַיִם אֶת־הֶעָרֹב וְגַם הָאֲדָמָה

אֲשֶׁר־הֵם עָלֶיהָ: וְהִפְלֵיתִי בַיּוֹם הַהוּא אֶת־אֶרֶץ גֹּשֶׁן אֲשֶׁר עַמִּי עֹמֵד   יח

עָלֶיהָ לְבִלְתִּי הֱיוֹת־שָׁם עָרֹב לְמַעַן תֵּדַע כִּי אֲנִי יהוה בְּקֶרֶב הָאָרֶץ:

ששי   וְשַׂמְתִּי פְדֻת בֵּין עַמִּי וּבֵין עַמֶּךָ לְמָחָר יִהְיֶה הָאֹת הַזֶּה: וַיַּעַשׂ יהוה כֵּן   יט-כ

וַיָּבֹא עָרֹב כָּבֵד בֵּיתָה פַרְעֹה וּבֵית עֲבָדָיו וּבְכָל־אֶרֶץ מִצְרַיִם תִּשָּׁחֵת

הָאָרֶץ מִפְּנֵי הֶעָרֹב: וַיִּקְרָא פַרְעֹה אֶל־מֹשֶׁה וּלְאַהֲרֹן וַיֹּאמֶר לְכוּ זִבְחוּ   כא

לֵאלֹהֵיכֶם בָּאָרֶץ: וַיֹּאמֶר מֹשֶׁה לֹא נָכוֹן לַעֲשׂוֹת כֵּן כִּי תּוֹעֲבַת מִצְרַיִם   כב

נִזְבַּח לַיהוה אֱלֹהֵינוּ הֵן נִזְבַּח אֶת־תּוֹעֲבַת מִצְרַיִם לְעֵינֵיהֶם וְלֹא יִסְקְלֻנוּ:

דֶּרֶךְ שְׁלֹשֶׁת יָמִים נֵלֵךְ בַּמִּדְבָּר וְזָבַחְנוּ לַיהוה אֱלֹהֵינוּ כַּאֲשֶׁר יֹאמַר   כג

אֵלֵינוּ: וַיֹּאמֶר פַּרְעֹה אָנֹכִי אֲשַׁלַּח אֶתְכֶם וּזְבַחְתֶּם לַיהוה אֱלֹהֵיכֶם   כד

בַּמִּדְבָּר רַק הַרְחֵק לֹא־תַרְחִיקוּ לָלֶכֶת הַעְתִּירוּ בַּעֲדִי: וַיֹּאמֶר מֹשֶׁה הִנֵּה   כה

אָנֹכִי יוֹצֵא מֵעִמָּךְ וְהַעְתַּרְתִּי אֶל־יהוה וְסָר הֶעָרֹב מִפַּרְעֹה מֵעֲבָדָיו

וּמֵעַמּוֹ מָחָר רַק אַל־יֹסֵף פַּרְעֹה הָתֵל לְבִלְתִּי שַׁלַּח אֶת־הָעָם לִזְבֹּחַ

לַיהוה: וַיֵּצֵא מֹשֶׁה מֵעִם פַּרְעֹה וַיֶּעְתַּר אֶל־יהוה: וַיַּעַשׂ יהוה כִּדְבַר מֹשֶׁה   כו-כז

וַיָּסַר הֶעָרֹב מִפַּרְעֹה מֵעֲבָדָיו וּמֵעַמּוֹ לֹא נִשְׁאַר אֶחָד: וַיַּכְבֵּד פַּרְעֹה אֶת־   כח

לִבּוֹ גַּם בַּפַּעַם הַזֹּאת וְלֹא שִׁלַּח אֶת־הָעָם:

ט   וַיֹּאמֶר יהוה אֶל־מֹשֶׁה בֹּא אֶל־פַּרְעֹה וְדִבַּרְתָּ אֵלָיו כֹּה־אָמַר יהוה אֱלֹהֵי   א

הָעִבְרִים שַׁלַּח אֶת־עַמִּי וְיַעַבְדֻנִי: כִּי אִם־מָאֵן אַתָּה לְשַׁלֵּחַ וְעוֹדְךָ מַחֲזִיק   ב

בָּם: הִנֵּה יַד־יהוה הוֹיָה בְּמִקְנְךָ אֲשֶׁר בַּשָּׂדֶה בַּסּוּסִים בַּחֲמֹרִים בַּגְּמַלִּים   ג

בַּבָּקָר וּבַצֹּאן דֶּבֶר כָּבֵד מְאֹד: וְהִפְלָה יהוה בֵּין מִקְנֵה יִשְׂרָאֵל וּבֵין מִקְנֵה   ד

מִצְרָיִם וְלֹא יָמוּת מִכָּל־לִבְנֵי יִשְׂרָאֵל דָּבָר: וַיָּשֶׂם יהוה מוֹעֵד לֵאמֹר מָחָר   ה

יַעֲשֶׂה יהוה הַדָּבָר הַזֶּה בָּאָרֶץ: וַיַּעַשׂ יהוה אֶת־הַדָּבָר הַזֶּה מִמָּחֳרָת וַיָּמָת   ו

כֹּל מִקְנֵה מִצְרָיִם וּמִמִּקְנֵה בְנֵי־יִשְׂרָאֵל לֹא־מֵת אֶחָד: וַיִּשְׁלַח פַּרְעֹה   ז

8:15. Though they had no choice but to acknowledge that the plague was of Divine origin, the magicians attempted to minimize it. By calling it only a *finger*, they implied that it was not of major consequence.

They did not use the Name "*HASHEM*" — the God of Israel — of Whom Pharaoh had denied knowledge, for they would not acknowledge that the plague had come about for the sake of the Jewish people. Instead, they used the generic word for a deity, implying that it was a natural phenomenon, for even Pharaoh did not deny that there was a Creator of nature (*Ramban*).

8:18-9:12. The second series of three plagues. These were intended to prove that God is involved in the day-to-day affairs of the world, and differentiates between Jewish and Egyptian people and property.

8:22. *The deity* [lit. *abomination*] *of Egypt.* When speaking to Pharaoh, Moses surely used a more respectful term, but the Torah typically refers to all idols as abominations (*Rashi*).

8:24-25. Pharaoh concedes that it would be improper to slaughter sheep in Egypt, but he offers another condition: *Do not go far.* To escape the wrath of the Egyptian populace, the Jews need not travel for three days; it would be sufficient for them merely to leave the cities, and bring their offerings in the secluded countryside. Moses did not contest this request. He merely warned Pharaoh

"It is a finger of God!"* But Pharaoh's heart was strong and he did not heed them, as HASHEM had spoken.

^{The fourth plague: Swarm of wild beasts}

¹⁶ *HASHEM said to Moses, "Arise early in the morning and station yourself before Pharaoh — behold, he goes out to the water — and you shall say to him, 'So said HASHEM: Send out My people that they may serve Me.* ¹⁷ *For if you do not send out My people, behold, I shall incite against you, your servants, your people, and your houses, the swarm of wild beasts; and the houses of Egypt shall be filled with the swarm, and even the ground upon which they are.* ¹⁸ *And on that day I shall set apart the land of Goshen upon which My people stands, that there shall be no swarm there; so that you will know that I am HASHEM in the midst of the land.* * ¹⁹ *I shall make a distinction between My people and your people — tomorrow this sign will come about.'"*

²⁰ *HASHEM did so and a severe swarm of wild beasts came to the house of Pharaoh and the house of his servants; and throughout the land of Egypt the land was being ruined because of the swarm.*

²¹ *Pharaoh summoned Moses and Aaron and said, "Go — bring offerings to your God in the land."* ²² *Moses said, "It is not proper to do so, for we will offer the deity of Egypt* to HASHEM, our God — behold, if we were to slaughter the deity of Egypt in their sight, will they not stone us?* ²³ *We will go on a three-day journey in the Wilderness, and bring offerings to HASHEM, our God, as He will tell us."*

²⁴ *Pharaoh said, "I will send you* and you shall bring offerings to HASHEM, your God, in the Wilderness; only do not go far off — entreat for me!"*

²⁵ *Moses said, "Behold! I leave you and I shall entreat HASHEM — and the swarm will depart from Pharaoh, from his servants, and from his people — tomorrow. Only let Pharaoh not continue to mock, by not sending out the people to bring offerings to HASHEM."*

²⁶ *Moses left Pharaoh's presence and entreated HASHEM.* ²⁷ *HASHEM did in accordance with Moses' word and He removed the swarm of wild beasts from Pharaoh, from his servants, and from his people — not one remained.* ²⁸ *But Pharaoh made his heart stubborn even this time, and he did not send out the people.*

9

^{The fifth plague: Epidemic}

¹ *HASHEM said to Moses, "Come to Pharaoh and speak to him, 'So said HASHEM, the God of the Hebrews: Send out My people that they may serve Me.'* ² *For if you refuse to send out, and you continue to grip them;* ³ *behold, the hand of HASHEM is on your livestock that are in the field, on the horses, on the donkeys, on the camels, on the cattle, and on the flock — a very severe epidemic.* ⁴ *HASHEM shall distinguish* between the livestock of Israel and the livestock of Egypt, and not a thing that belongs to the Children of Israel will die.* ⁵ *HASHEM has set an appointed time, saying, 'Tomorrow HASHEM shall carry out this word in the land.'"*

⁶ *HASHEM carried out this word the next day, and all the livestock of Egypt died, and of the livestock of the Children of Israel not one died.* ⁷ *Pharaoh sent*

---

not to mock the people by going back on his word (*Or HaChaim*).

9:4. Since the Egyptians worshiped animals and detested sheep herders, they concentrated most of their own live-

stock in Goshen, where they mingled with the Jewish animals. Thus, the survival of Jewish flocks — which shared the pasture, water, and air of Egyptian livestock — was an undeniable miracle (*Ramban*).

וְהִנֵּה לֹא־מֵת מִמִּקְנֵה יִשְׂרָאֵל עַד־אֶחָד וַיִּכְבַּד לֵב פַּרְעֹה וְלֹא שִׁלַּח אֶת־הָעָם:

ח וַיֹּאמֶר יהוה אֶל־מֹשֶׁה וְאֶל־אַהֲרֹן קְחוּ לָכֶם מְלֹא חָפְנֵיכֶם פִּיחַ כִּבְשָׁן

ט וּזְרָקוֹ מֹשֶׁה הַשָּׁמַיְמָה לְעֵינֵי פַרְעֹה: וְהָיָה לְאָבָק עַל כָּל־אֶרֶץ מִצְרָיִם וְהָיָה עַל־הָאָדָם וְעַל־הַבְּהֵמָה לִשְׁחִין פֹּרֵחַ אֲבַעְבֻּעֹת בְּכָל־אֶרֶץ מִצְרָיִם:

י וַיִּקְחוּ אֶת־פִּיחַ הַכִּבְשָׁן וַיַּעַמְדוּ לִפְנֵי פַרְעֹה וַיִּזְרֹק אֹתוֹ מֹשֶׁה הַשָּׁמַיְמָה

יא וַיְהִי שְׁחִין אֲבַעְבֻּעֹת פֹּרֵחַ בָּאָדָם וּבַבְּהֵמָה: וְלֹא־יָכְלוּ הַחַרְטֻמִּים לַעֲמֹד לִפְנֵי מֹשֶׁה מִפְּנֵי הַשְּׁחִין כִּי־הָיָה הַשְּׁחִין בַּחַרְטֻמִּם וּבְכָל־מִצְרָיִם:

יב וַיְחַזֵּק יהוה אֶת־לֵב פַּרְעֹה וְלֹא שָׁמַע אֲלֵהֶם כַּאֲשֶׁר דִּבֶּר יהוה אֶל־מֹשֶׁה:

יג וַיֹּאמֶר יהוה אֶל־מֹשֶׁה הַשְׁכֵּם בַּבֹּקֶר וְהִתְיַצֵּב לִפְנֵי פַרְעֹה וְאָמַרְתָּ אֵלָיו כֹּה־אָמַר יהוה אֱלֹהֵי הָעִבְרִים שַׁלַּח אֶת־עַמִּי וְיַעַבְדֻנִי: כִּי ׀ בַּפַּעַם הַזֹּאת אֲנִי שֹׁלֵחַ אֶת־כָּל־מַגֵּפֹתַי אֶל־לִבְּךָ וּבַעֲבָדֶיךָ

יד וּבְעַמֶּךָ בַּעֲבוּר תֵּדַע כִּי אֵין כָּמֹנִי בְּכָל־הָאָרֶץ: כִּי עַתָּה שָׁלַחְתִּי אֶת־יָדִי

טו וָאַךְ אוֹתְךָ וְאֶת־עַמְּךָ בַּדָּבֶר וַתִּכָּחֵד מִן־הָאָרֶץ: וְאוּלָם בַּעֲבוּר זֹאת

טז הֶעֱמַדְתִּיךָ בַּעֲבוּר הַרְאֹתְךָ אֶת־כֹּחִי וּלְמַעַן סַפֵּר שְׁמִי בְּכָל־הָאָרֶץ: עוֹדְךָ

יז מִסְתּוֹלֵל בְּעַמִּי לְבִלְתִּי שַׁלְּחָם: הִנְנִי מַמְטִיר כָּעֵת מָחָר בָּרָד כָּבֵד מְאֹד

יח אֲשֶׁר לֹא־הָיָה כָמֹהוּ בְּמִצְרַיִם לְמִן־הַיּוֹם הִוָּסְדָה וְעַד־עָתָּה: וְעַתָּה שְׁלַח הָעֵז אֶת־מִקְנְךָ וְאֵת כָּל־אֲשֶׁר לְךָ בַּשָּׂדֶה כָּל־הָאָדָם וְהַבְּהֵמָה אֲשֶׁר־

יט יִמָּצֵא בַשָּׂדֶה וְלֹא יֵאָסֵף הַבַּיְתָה וְיָרַד עֲלֵהֶם הַבָּרָד וָמֵתוּ: הַיָּרֵא אֶת־דְּבַר

כ יהוה מֵעַבְדֵי פַּרְעֹה הֵנִיס אֶת־עֲבָדָיו וְאֶת־מִקְנֵהוּ אֶל־הַבָּתִּים: וַאֲשֶׁר לֹא־שָׂם לִבּוֹ אֶל־דְּבַר יהוה וַיַּעֲזֹב אֶת־עֲבָדָיו וְאֶת־מִקְנֵהוּ בַּשָּׂדֶה:

כא וַיֹּאמֶר יהוה אֶל־מֹשֶׁה נְטֵה אֶת־יָדְךָ עַל־הַשָּׁמַיִם וִיהִי בָרָד בְּכָל־אֶרֶץ מִצְרָיִם עַל־הָאָדָם וְעַל־הַבְּהֵמָה וְעַל כָּל־עֵשֶׂב הַשָּׂדֶה בְּאֶרֶץ מִצְרָיִם:

כב וַיֵּט מֹשֶׁה אֶת־מַטֵּהוּ עַל־הַשָּׁמַיִם וַיהוה נָתַן קֹלֹת וּבָרָד וַתִּהֲלַךְ־אֵשׁ

כג אָרְצָה וַיַּמְטֵר יהוה בָּרָד עַל־אֶרֶץ מִצְרָיִם: וַיְהִי בָרָד וְאֵשׁ מִתְלַקַּחַת בְּתוֹךְ הַבָּרָד כָּבֵד מְאֹד אֲשֶׁר לֹא־הָיָה כָמֹהוּ בְּכָל־אֶרֶץ מִצְרַיִם מֵאָז

כד הָיְתָה לְגוֹי: וַיַּךְ הַבָּרָד בְּכָל־אֶרֶץ מִצְרַיִם אֵת כָּל־אֲשֶׁר בַּשָּׂדֶה מֵאָדָם וְעַד־בְּהֵמָה וְאֵת כָּל־עֵשֶׂב הַשָּׂדֶה הִכָּה הַבָּרָד וְאֶת־כָּל־עֵץ הַשָּׂדֶה שִׁבֵּר:

כה-כו רַק בְּאֶרֶץ גֹּשֶׁן אֲשֶׁר־שָׁם בְּנֵי יִשְׂרָאֵל לֹא הָיָה בָּרָד: וַיִּשְׁלַח פַּרְעֹה וַיִּקְרָא לְמֹשֶׁה וּלְאַהֲרֹן וַיֹּאמֶר אֲלֵהֶם חָטָאתִי הַפָּעַם יהוה הַצַּדִּיק וַאֲנִי וְעַמִּי

9:8. With the sixth plague, a new phenomenon began. Pharaoh's personal stubbornness was broken and he would have freed the people, but God strengthened his resolve so that he could still be punished for his earlier sins.

9:13-10:23. The third series of plagues. With the hail, the final set of plagues began. Its purpose was to prove

that God has no equal in the entire world.

9:15-16. God now introduces a new dimension to the plagues and their purpose: the public sanctification of His Name. Moses is to inform Pharaoh that he deserved to be killed during the pestilence, but God allowed him to survive so that he would be forced to recognize God's greatness and proclaim it to the world.

and behold, of the livestock of Israel not even one had died — yet Pharaoh's heart became stubborn and he did not send out the people.

The sixth plague: Boils ⁸ HASHEM said to Moses and Aaron, "Take for yourselves handfuls of furnace soot, and let Moses hurl it heavenward before Pharaoh's eyes. ⁹ It will become dust over the entire land of Egypt, and it will become boils erupting into blisters on man and beast throughout the land of Egypt." ¹⁰ They took soot of the furnace, and stood before Pharaoh, and Moses threw it heavenward; and it became boils and blisters, erupting on man and beast. ¹¹ The necromancers could not stand before Moses because of the boils, because the boils were on the necromancers and on all of Egypt. ¹² HASHEM strengthened the heart of Pharaoh and he did not heed them, as HASHEM had spoken to Moses.

The seventh plague: Hail ¹³ HASHEM spoke to Moses, * "Arise early in the morning and station yourself before Pharaoh; say to him, 'So said HASHEM, the God of the Hebrews: Send out My people that they may serve Me. ¹⁴ For this time I shall send all My plagues against your heart, and upon your servants, and your people, so that you shall know that there is none like Me in all the world. * ¹⁵ For now I could have sent My hand and stricken you and your people with the pestilence and you would have been obliterated from the earth. ¹⁶ However, for this have I let you endure, in order to show you My strength and so that My Name may be declared throughout the world.

¹⁷ 'You still tread upon My people, not to send them out. ¹⁸ Behold, at this time tomorrow I shall rain a very heavy hail, such as there has never been in Egypt, from the day it was founded until now. ¹⁹ And now send, gather in your livestock and everything you have in the field; all the people and animals that are found in the field that are not gathered into the house — the hail shall descend upon them and they shall die.' "

²⁰ Whoever among the servants of Pharaoh feared the word of HASHEM chased his servants and his livestock to the houses. ²¹ And whoever did not take the word of HASHEM to heart — he left his servants and livestock in the field.

²² HASHEM said to Moses, "Stretch out your hand toward heaven and there will be hail in the entire land of Egypt, on man and beast, and on all the grass of the field in the land of Egypt."

²³ Moses stretched out his staff toward heaven, and HASHEM sent thunder and hail, and fire went earthward, and HASHEM rained hail upon the land of Egypt. ²⁴ There was hail, and fire flaming amid the hail* — very heavy such as had never been in the entire land of Egypt, from the time it became a nation. ²⁵ The hail struck in the entire land of Egypt, everything that was in the field from man to beast; all the grass of the field the hail struck and every tree of the field it smashed. ²⁶ Only in the land of Goshen, where the Children of Israel were, there was no hail.

²⁷ Pharaoh sent and summoned Moses and Aaron and said to them, "This time I have sinned;* HASHEM is the Righteous One, and I and my people are

---

9:24. It was a miracle within a miracle. [The first miracle was that fire shot downward, though fire usually rises, and the second miracle was that fire and water functioned in unison (*Mizrachi*).] To serve God, fire and water made peace with one another (*Rashi*).

9:27. Pharaoh contrasted his own actions with God's. God, the *Righteous One*, warned the Egyptians to bring the people and livestock indoors, but Pharaoh and his cohorts, *the wicked ones*, let people and animals remain in the fields where they were struck by the hail (*Midrash*).

כח הָרְשָׁעִים: הַעְתִּירוּ אֶל־יהוה וְרַב מִהְיֹת קֹלֹת אֱלֹהִים וּבָרָד וַאֲשַׁלְּחָה

כט אֶתְכֶם וְלֹא תֹסִפוּן לַעֲמֹד: וַיֹּאמֶר אֵלָיו מֹשֶׁה כְּצֵאתִי אֶת־הָעִיר אֶפְרֹשׂ אֶת־כַּפַּי אֶל־יהוה הַקֹּלוֹת יֶחְדָּלוּן וְהַבָּרָד לֹא יִהְיֶה־עוֹד לְמַעַן תֵּדַע כִּי

ל לַיהוה הָאָרֶץ: וְאַתָּה וַעֲבָדֶיךָ יָדַעְתִּי כִּי טֶרֶם תִּירְאוּן מִפְּנֵי יהוה אֱלֹהִים:

לא־לב וְהַפִּשְׁתָּה וְהַשְּׂעֹרָה נֻכָּתָה כִּי הַשְּׂעֹרָה אָבִיב וְהַפִּשְׁתָּה גִּבְעֹל: וְהַחִטָּה

לג וְהַכֻּסֶּמֶת לֹא נֻכּוּ כִּי אֲפִילֹת הֵנָּה: וַיֵּצֵא מֹשֶׁה מֵעִם פַּרְעֹה אֶת־הָעִיר וַיִּפְרֹשׂ כַּפָּיו אֶל־יהוה וַיַּחְדְּלוּ הַקֹּלוֹת וְהַבָּרָד וּמָטָר לֹא־נִתַּךְ אָרְצָה:

לד וַיַּרְא פַּרְעֹה כִּי־חָדַל הַמָּטָר וְהַבָּרָד וְהַקֹּלֹת וַיֹּסֶף לַחֲטֹא וַיַּכְבֵּד לִבּוֹ הוּא

לה וַעֲבָדָיו: וַיֶּחֱזַק לֵב פַּרְעֹה וְלֹא שִׁלַּח אֶת־בְּנֵי יִשְׂרָאֵל כַּאֲשֶׁר דִּבֶּר יהוה בְּיַד־מֹשֶׁה: פפפ קכ"א פסוקים. גיבעו"ל סימן. יעיא"ל סימן.

מפטיר

Haftaras
Va'eira
p. 1274

For special
Sabbaths,
see
pp. x-xi

פרשת בא

א וַיֹּאמֶר יהוה אֶל־מֹשֶׁה בֹּא אֶל־פַּרְעֹה כִּי־אֲנִי הִכְבַּדְתִּי אֶת־לִבּוֹ וְאֶת־

ב לֵב עֲבָדָיו לְמַעַן שִׁתִי אֹתֹתַי אֵלֶּה בְּקִרְבּוֹ: וּלְמַעַן תְּסַפֵּר בְּאָזְנֵי בִנְךָ וּבֶן־ בִּנְךָ אֵת אֲשֶׁר הִתְעַלַּלְתִּי בְּמִצְרַיִם וְאֶת־אֹתֹתַי אֲשֶׁר־שַׂמְתִּי בָם וִידַעְתֶּם

ג כִּי־אֲנִי יהוה: וַיָּבֹא מֹשֶׁה וְאַהֲרֹן אֶל־פַּרְעֹה וַיֹּאמְרוּ אֵלָיו כֹּה־אָמַר יהוה

ד אֱלֹהֵי הָעִבְרִים עַד־מָתַי מֵאַנְתָּ לֵעָנֹת מִפָּנָי שַׁלַּח עַמִּי וְיַעַבְדֻנִי: כִּי אִם־

ה מָאֵן אַתָּה לְשַׁלֵּחַ אֶת־עַמִּי הִנְנִי מֵבִיא מָחָר אַרְבֶּה בִּגְבֻלֶךָ: וְכִסָּה אֶת־ עֵין הָאָרֶץ וְלֹא יוּכַל לִרְאֹת אֶת־הָאָרֶץ וְאָכַל | אֶת־יֶתֶר הַפְּלֵטָה הַנִּשְׁאֶרֶת לָכֶם מִן־הַבָּרָד וְאָכַל אֶת־כָּל־הָעֵץ הַצֹּמֵחַ לָכֶם מִן־הַשָּׂדֶה:

ו וּמָלְאוּ בָתֶּיךָ וּבָתֵּי כָל־עֲבָדֶיךָ וּבָתֵּי כָל־מִצְרַיִם אֲשֶׁר לֹא־רָאוּ אֲבֹתֶיךָ וַאֲבוֹת אֲבֹתֶיךָ מִיּוֹם הֱיוֹתָם עַל־הָאֲדָמָה עַד הַיּוֹם הַזֶּה וַיִּפֶן וַיֵּצֵא מֵעִם

ז פַּרְעֹה: וַיֹּאמְרוּ עַבְדֵי פַרְעֹה אֵלָיו עַד־מָתַי יִהְיֶה זֶה לָנוּ לְמוֹקֵשׁ שַׁלַּח אֶת־הָאֲנָשִׁים וְיַעַבְדוּ אֶת־יהוה אֱלֹהֵיהֶם הֲטֶרֶם תֵּדַע כִּי אָבְדָה מִצְרָיִם:

ח וַיּוּשַׁב אֶת־מֹשֶׁה וְאֶת־אַהֲרֹן אֶל־פַּרְעֹה וַיֹּאמֶר אֲלֵהֶם לְכוּ עִבְדוּ אֶת־

ט יהוה אֱלֹהֵיכֶם מִי וָמִי הַהֹלְכִים: וַיֹּאמֶר מֹשֶׁה בִּנְעָרֵינוּ וּבִזְקֵנֵינוּ נֵלֵךְ

י בְּבָנֵינוּ וּבִבְנוֹתֵנוּ בְּצֹאנֵנוּ וּבִבְקָרֵנוּ נֵלֵךְ כִּי חַג־יהוה לָנוּ: וַיֹּאמֶר אֲלֵהֶם יְהִי כֵן יהוה עִמָּכֶם כַּאֲשֶׁר אֲשַׁלַּח אֶתְכֶם וְאֶת־טַפְּכֶם רְאוּ כִּי רָעָה

יא נֶגֶד פְּנֵיכֶם: לֹא כֵן לְכוּ־נָא הַגְּבָרִים וְעִבְדוּ אֶת־יהוה כִּי אֹתָהּ אַתֶּם

יב מְבַקְשִׁים וַיְגָרֶשׁ אֹתָם מֵאֵת פְּנֵי פַרְעֹה:

שני

וַיֹּאמֶר

⋙ Parashas Bo

The climax of Moses' mission is impending. The last three plagues, the commandment to sanctify the New Moon (which is the basis of the Jewish calendar and the festival cycle), the laws of Passover, and the sanctification of the firstborn are about to come in quick succession. Soon, Pharaoh's resistance will be completely destroyed

and he personally will dash through the streets of Goshen, urging his erstwhile slaves to leave their land of bondage as soon as possible.

10:1-20. The plague of locusts was "measure for measure": The Egyptians forced their Jewish slaves to grow crops; the locusts devoured the crops.

10:2. The Exodus was a seminal event in world history

the wicked ones. [28] Entreat HASHEM — there has been an overabundance of Godly thunder and hail; I shall send you out and you shall not continue to remain."

Not to pray in an idolatrous city
[29] Moses said to him, "When I leave the city I shall spread out my hands to HASHEM; the thunder will cease and the hail will no longer be, so that you shall know that the earth is HASHEM's. [30] And as for you and your servants, I know that you are not yet afraid of HASHEM, God." [31] The flax and the barley were struck, for the barley was ripe and the flax was in its stalk. [32] And the wheat and the spelt were not struck, for they ripen later.

[33] Moses went out from Pharaoh, from the city, and he stretched out his hands to HASHEM; the thunder and hail ceased and rain did not reach the earth. [34] Pharaoh saw that the rain, the hail, and the thunder ceased, and he continued to sin; and he made his heart stubborn, he and his servants. [35] Pharaoh's heart became strong and he did not send out the Children of Israel, as HASHEM had spoken through Moses.

PARASHAS BO

10
The eighth plague: Locusts*
[1] HASHEM said to Moses, "Come to Pharaoh, for I have made his heart and the heart of his servants stubborn so that I can put these signs of Mine in his midst; [2] and so that you may relate* in the ears of your son and your son's son that I made a mockery of Egypt and My signs that I placed among them — that you may know that I am HASHEM."

[3] Moses and Aaron came to Pharaoh and said to him, "So said HASHEM, God of the Hebrews: Until when will you refuse to be humbled before Me? Send out My people that they may serve Me! [4] For if you refuse to send forth My people, behold, tomorrow I shall bring a locust-swarm into your border. [5] It will cover the surface of the earth so that one will not be able to see the earth; and it will consume the remaining residue that was left to you by the hail, and it will consume all the trees that grow for you from the field. [6] They will fill your houses, the houses of all your servants, and the houses of all Egypt, such as your fathers and your grandfathers have not seen from the day they came onto the earth until this day." And he turned and left Pharaoh's presence.

Pharaoh's servants complain
[7] Pharaoh's servants said to him, "How long will this be a snare for us? Send out the men that they may serve HASHEM, their God! Do you not yet know that Egypt is lost?"

[8] So Moses and Aaron were returned to Pharaoh and he said to them, "Go and serve HASHEM, your God; which ones are going?"

[9] Moses said, "With our youngsters and with our elders shall we go; with our sons and with our daughters, with our flock and with our cattle shall we go, because it is a festival of HASHEM for us."*

[10] He said to them, "So be HASHEM with you as I will send you forth with your children! Look — the evil intent is opposite your faces. [11] Not so; let the men go now. Serve HASHEM, for that is what you seek!" And he drove them out from Pharaoh's presence.

---

because it demonstrated God's mastery over nature. Thus it became the textbook lesson for humanity of God not as an aloof Creator, but as the Master of the universe day-by-day and event-by-event. This verse contains the concept that God can toy with the most powerful king-

doms, and that this creates the perception that He is HASHEM, the Name that denotes וְיִהְיֶה הֹוֶה הָיָה, *He was, is, and will be*.

10:9. The Torah requires the same of every boy and girl as it does of the Patriarchs and Matriarchs.

יְהוָה אֶל־מֹשֶׁה נְטֵה יָדְךָ עַל־אֶרֶץ מִצְרַיִם בָּאַרְבֶּה וְיַעַל עַל־אֶרֶץ

יג מִצְרַיִם וְיֹאכַל אֶת־כָּל־עֵשֶׂב הָאָרֶץ אֵת כָּל־אֲשֶׁר הִשְׁאִיר הַבָּרָד: וַיֵּט

מֹשֶׁה אֶת־מַטֵּהוּ עַל־אֶרֶץ מִצְרַיִם וַיהוָה נִהַג רְוּחַ־קָדִים בָּאָרֶץ כָּל־הַיּוֹם

יד הַהוּא וְכָל־הַלָּיְלָה הַבֹּקֶר הָיָה וְרוּחַ הַקָּדִים נָשָׂא אֶת־הָאַרְבֶּה: וַיַּעַל

הָאַרְבֶּה עַל כָּל־אֶרֶץ מִצְרַיִם וַיָּנַח בְּכֹל גְּבוּל מִצְרָיִם כָּבֵד מְאֹד לְפָנָיו

טו לֹא־הָיָה כֵן אַרְבֶּה כָּמֹהוּ וְאַחֲרָיו לֹא יִהְיֶה־כֵּן: וַיְכַס אֶת־עֵין כָּל־הָאָרֶץ

וַתֶּחְשַׁךְ הָאָרֶץ וַיֹּאכַל אֶת־כָּל־עֵשֶׂב הָאָרֶץ וְאֵת כָּל־פְּרִי הָעֵץ אֲשֶׁר

הוֹתִיר הַבָּרָד וְלֹא־נוֹתַר כָּל־יֶרֶק בָּעֵץ וּבְעֵשֶׂב הַשָּׂדֶה בְּכָל־אֶרֶץ

טז מִצְרָיִם: וַיְמַהֵר פַּרְעֹה לִקְרֹא לְמֹשֶׁה וּלְאַהֲרֹן וַיֹּאמֶר חָטָאתִי לַיהוָה

יז אֱלֹהֵיכֶם וְלָכֶם: וְעַתָּה שָׂא נָא חַטָּאתִי אַךְ הַפַּעַם וְהַעְתִּירוּ לַיהוָה

יח אֱלֹהֵיכֶם וְיָסֵר מֵעָלַי רַק אֶת־הַמָּוֶת הַזֶּה: וַיֵּצֵא מֵעִם פַּרְעֹה וַיֶּעְתַּר אֶל־

יט יְהוָה: וַיַּהֲפֹךְ יְהוָה רוּחַ־יָם חָזָק מְאֹד וַיִּשָּׂא אֶת־הָאַרְבֶּה וַיִּתְקָעֵהוּ יָמָּה

כ סוּף לֹא נִשְׁאַר אַרְבֶּה אֶחָד בְּכֹל גְּבוּל מִצְרָיִם: וַיְחַזֵּק יְהוָה אֶת־לֵב

פַּרְעֹה וְלֹא שִׁלַּח אֶת־בְּנֵי יִשְׂרָאֵל:

כא וַיֹּאמֶר יְהוָה אֶל־מֹשֶׁה נְטֵה יָדְךָ עַל־הַשָּׁמַיִם וִיהִי חֹשֶׁךְ עַל־אֶרֶץ מִצְרָיִם

כב וְיָמֵשׁ חֹשֶׁךְ: וַיֵּט מֹשֶׁה אֶת־יָדוֹ עַל־הַשָּׁמָיִם וַיְהִי חֹשֶׁךְ־אֲפֵלָה בְּכָל־אֶרֶץ

כג מִצְרַיִם שְׁלֹשֶׁת יָמִים: לֹא־רָאוּ אִישׁ אֶת־אָחִיו וְלֹא־קָמוּ אִישׁ מִתַּחְתָּיו

שלישי שְׁלֹשֶׁת יָמִים וּלְכָל־בְּנֵי יִשְׂרָאֵל הָיָה אוֹר בְּמוֹשְׁבֹתָם: וַיִּקְרָא פַרְעֹה אֶל־

כד מֹשֶׁה וַיֹּאמֶר לְכוּ עִבְדוּ אֶת־יְהוָה רַק צֹאנְכֶם וּבְקַרְכֶם יֻצָּג גַּם־טַפְּכֶם

כה יֵלֵךְ עִמָּכֶם: וַיֹּאמֶר מֹשֶׁה גַּם־אַתָּה תִּתֵּן בְּיָדֵנוּ זְבָחִים וְעֹלֹת וְעָשִׂינוּ

כו לַיהוָה אֱלֹהֵינוּ: וְגַם־מִקְנֵנוּ יֵלֵךְ עִמָּנוּ לֹא תִשָּׁאֵר פַּרְסָה כִּי מִמֶּנּוּ נִקַּח

לַעֲבֹד אֶת־יְהוָה אֱלֹהֵינוּ וַאֲנַחְנוּ לֹא־נֵדַע מַה־נַּעֲבֹד אֶת־יְהוָה עַד־

כז-כח בֹּאֵנוּ שָׁמָּה: וַיְחַזֵּק יְהוָה אֶת־לֵב פַּרְעֹה וְלֹא אָבָה לְשַׁלְּחָם: וַיֹּאמֶר־לוֹ

פַרְעֹה לֵךְ מֵעָלָי הִשָּׁמֶר לְךָ אַל־תֹּסֶף רְאוֹת פָּנַי כִּי בְּיוֹם רְאֹתְךָ פָנַי

כט תָּמוּת: וַיֹּאמֶר מֹשֶׁה כֵּן דִּבַּרְתָּ לֹא־אֹסִף עוֹד רְאוֹת פָּנֶיךָ:

יא א וַיֹּאמֶר יְהוָה אֶל־מֹשֶׁה עוֹד נֶגַע אֶחָד אָבִיא עַל־פַּרְעֹה וְעַל־מִצְרַיִם

ב אַחֲרֵי־כֵן יְשַׁלַּח אֶתְכֶם מִזֶּה כְּשַׁלְּחוֹ כָּלָה גָּרֵשׁ יְגָרֵשׁ אֶתְכֶם מִזֶּה: דַּבֶּר־

נָא בְּאָזְנֵי הָעָם וְיִשְׁאֲלוּ אִישׁ ׀ מֵאֵת רֵעֵהוּ וְאִשָּׁה מֵאֵת רְעוּתָהּ כְּלֵי־כֶסֶף

ג וּכְלֵי זָהָב: וַיִּתֵּן יְהוָה אֶת־חֵן הָעָם בְּעֵינֵי מִצְרָיִם גַּם ׀ הָאִישׁ מֹשֶׁה גָּדוֹל

10:19-20. God changed the east wind, which brought the locusts, to a west wind that blew them away. Not a single locust remained, not even those that the Egyptians had preserved for food (*Midrash*).

10:23. *Ramban* comments that the darkness was not merely an absence of light, but an opaque, fog-like condition that extinguished all flames, so that the Egyptians could not even use lamps.

10:27-29. God strengthened the king's heart once again

and he became more defiant than ever: For the first time, he ejected Moses and threatened him with death if he dared appear again. Moses agrees, for there will be no need for him to seek out Pharaoh again. The next plague would kill the firstborn of Egypt, and bring Pharaoh groveling and begging the Jews to leave as soon as possible.

11:2. God asked Moses to make a special effort to prevail upon the Jews to request valuables from their Egyptian

¹² HASHEM said to Moses, "Stretch out your hand over the land of Egypt for the locust-swarm, and it will ascend upon the land of Egypt and eat all the grass of the land, everything that the hail had left." ¹³ Moses stretched his staff over the land of Egypt, and HASHEM guided an east wind through the land all that day and all the night. It became morning and the east wind carried the locust-swarm. ¹⁴ The locust-swarm ascended over the entire land of Egypt and it rested in the entire border of Egypt, very severely; before it there was never a locust-swarm like it and after it there will not be its equal. ¹⁵ It covered the surface of the entire land and the land was darkened; it ate all the grass of the land and all the fruit of the tree that the hail left over. No greenery remained on the trees or the grass of the field in the entire land of Egypt.

¹⁶ Pharaoh hastened to summon Moses and Aaron and he said, "I have sinned to HASHEM, your God, and to you. ¹⁷ And now, please forgive my sin just this time, and entreat HASHEM, your God, that He remove from me only this death."

¹⁸ He left Pharaoh and entreated HASHEM. ¹⁹ HASHEM turned back a very powerful west wind* and it carried the locust-swarm and hurled it toward the Sea of Reeds; not a single locust remained within the entire border of Egypt. ²⁰ But HASHEM strengthened the heart of Pharaoh, and he did not send out the Children of Israel.

The ninth plague: Darkness

²¹ HASHEM said to Moses, "Stretch forth your hand toward the heavens, and there shall be darkness upon the land of Egypt, and the darkness will be tangible." ²² Moses stretched forth his hand toward the heavens and there was a thick darkness throughout the land of Egypt for a three-day period. ²³ No man could see his brother* nor could anyone rise from his place for a three-day period; but for all the Children of Israel there was light in their dwellings.

²⁴ Pharaoh summoned Moses and said, "Go — serve HASHEM, only your flock and cattle shall remain behind; even your children may go with you."

Pharaoh's offerings . . .

²⁵ Moses said, "Even you will place in our hands feast-offerings and burnt-offerings, and we shall offer them to HASHEM, our God. ²⁶ And our livestock, as well, will go with us — not a hoof will be left — for from it shall we take to serve HASHEM, our God; and we will not know with what we are to serve HASHEM until our arrival there."

. . . and final intransigence

²⁷ HASHEM strengthened the heart of Pharaoh* and he did not wish to send them out. ²⁸ Pharaoh said to him, "Go from me! Beware — do not see my face any more, for on the day you see my face you shall die!"

²⁹ Moses said, "You have spoken correctly. I shall never see your face again."

11

Warning of the Plague of the Firstborn

¹ HASHEM said to Moses, "One more plague shall I bring upon Pharaoh and upon Egypt; after that he shall send you forth from here. When he sends forth, it shall be complete — he shall drive you out of here. ² Please speak* in the ears of the people: Let each man request of his fellow and each woman from her fellow silver vessels and gold vessels." ³ HASHEM granted the people favor in the eyes of Egypt; moreover, the man Moses was very great

---

neighbors. Unless they did so, "that righteous man" — Abraham — would have a grievance against God, saying, "You fulfilled with them [the prophecy that] they [the Jews] will serve them [the Egyptians] and they will oppress

them, but You did not fulfill with them [the prophecy] and afterwards they will go out with great possessions" (Genesis 15:14-15). God pleaded, as it were, with Moses to avoid Abraham's possible complaint (Rashi from Midrash).

רביעי מְאֹד בְּאֶרֶץ מִצְרַיִם בְּעֵינֵי עַבְדֵי־פַרְעֹה וּבְעֵינֵי הָעָם: וַיֹּאמֶר ד

ה מֹשֶׁה כֹּה אָמַר יהוה כַּחֲצֹת הַלַּיְלָה אֲנִי יוֹצֵא בְּתוֹךְ מִצְרָיִם: וּמֵת כָּל־

בְּכוֹר בְּאֶרֶץ מִצְרַיִם מִבְּכוֹר פַּרְעֹה הַיֹּשֵׁב עַל־כִּסְאוֹ עַד בְּכוֹר הַשִּׁפְחָה

ו אֲשֶׁר אַחַר הָרֵחָיִם וְכֹל בְּכוֹר בְּהֵמָה: וְהָיְתָה צְעָקָה גְדֹלָה בְּכָל־אֶרֶץ

ז מִצְרָיִם אֲשֶׁר כָּמֹהוּ לֹא נִהְיָתָה וְכָמֹהוּ לֹא תֹסִף: וּלְכֹל ׀ בְּנֵי יִשְׂרָאֵל לֹא

יֶחֱרַץ־כֶּלֶב לְשֹׁנוֹ לְמֵאִישׁ וְעַד־בְּהֵמָה לְמַעַן תֵּדְעוּן אֲשֶׁר יַפְלֶה יהוה

ח בֵּין מִצְרַיִם וּבֵין יִשְׂרָאֵל: וְיָרְדוּ כָל־עֲבָדֶיךָ אֵלֶּה אֵלַי וְהִשְׁתַּחֲווּ־לִי

לֵאמֹר צֵא אַתָּה וְכָל־הָעָם אֲשֶׁר־בְּרַגְלֶיךָ וְאַחֲרֵי־כֵן אֵצֵא וַיֵּצֵא מֵעִם־

ט פַּרְעֹה בָּחֳרִי־אָף: וַיֹּאמֶר יהוה אֶל־מֹשֶׁה לֹא־יִשְׁמַע אֲלֵיכֶם

י פַּרְעֹה לְמַעַן רְבוֹת מוֹפְתַי בְּאֶרֶץ מִצְרָיִם: וּמֹשֶׁה וְאַהֲרֹן עָשׂוּ אֶת־כָּל־

הַמֹּפְתִים הָאֵלֶּה לִפְנֵי פַרְעֹה וַיְחַזֵּק יהוה אֶת־לֵב פַּרְעֹה וְלֹא־שִׁלַּח אֶת־

יב בְּנֵי־יִשְׂרָאֵל מֵאַרְצוֹ: וַיֹּאמֶר יהוה אֶל־מֹשֶׁה וְאֶל־אַהֲרֹן א

MAFTIR FOR PARASHAS HACHODESH 12:1-20

Haftarah: p. 1320

בְּאֶרֶץ מִצְרַיִם לֵאמֹר: הַחֹדֶשׁ הַזֶּה לָכֶם רֹאשׁ חֳדָשִׁים רִאשׁוֹן הוּא

ב לָכֶם לְחָדְשֵׁי הַשָּׁנָה: דַּבְּרוּ אֶל־כָּל־עֲדַת יִשְׂרָאֵל לֵאמֹר בֶּעָשֹׂר לַחֹדֶשׁ ג

ד הַזֶּה וְיִקְחוּ לָהֶם אִישׁ שֶׂה לְבֵית־אָבֹת שֶׂה לַבָּיִת: וְאִם־יִמְעַט הַבַּיִת

מִהְיֹת מִשֶּׂה וְלָקַח הוּא וּשְׁכֵנוֹ הַקָּרֹב אֶל־בֵּיתוֹ בְּמִכְסַת נְפָשֹׁת אִישׁ לְפִי

ה אָכְלוֹ תָּכֹסּוּ עַל־הַשֶּׂה: שֶׂה תָמִים זָכָר בֶּן־שָׁנָה יִהְיֶה לָכֶם מִן־הַכְּבָשִׂים

ו וּמִן־הָעִזִּים תִּקָּחוּ: וְהָיָה לָכֶם לְמִשְׁמֶרֶת עַד אַרְבָּעָה עָשָׂר יוֹם לַחֹדֶשׁ

ז הַזֶּה וְשָׁחֲטוּ אֹתוֹ כֹּל קְהַל עֲדַת־יִשְׂרָאֵל בֵּין הָעַרְבָּיִם: וְלָקְחוּ מִן־הַדָּם

וְנָתְנוּ עַל־שְׁתֵּי הַמְּזוּזֹת וְעַל־הַמַּשְׁקוֹף עַל הַבָּתִּים אֲשֶׁר־יֹאכְלוּ אֹתוֹ

ח בָּהֶם: וְאָכְלוּ אֶת־הַבָּשָׂר בַּלַּיְלָה הַזֶּה צְלִי־אֵשׁ וּמַצּוֹת עַל־מְרֹרִים

ט יֹאכְלֻהוּ: אַל־תֹּאכְלוּ מִמֶּנּוּ נָא וּבָשֵׁל מְבֻשָּׁל בַּמָּיִם כִּי אִם־צְלִי־אֵשׁ

רֹאשׁוֹ עַל־כְּרָעָיו וְעַל־קִרְבּוֹ: וְלֹא־תוֹתִירוּ מִמֶּנּוּ עַד־בֹּקֶר וְהַנֹּתָר מִמֶּנּוּ י

יא עַד־בֹּקֶר בָּאֵשׁ תִּשְׂרֹפוּ: וְכָכָה תֹּאכְלוּ אֹתוֹ מָתְנֵיכֶם חֲגֻרִים נַעֲלֵיכֶם

בְּרַגְלֵיכֶם וּמַקֶּלְכֶם בְּיֶדְכֶם וַאֲכַלְתֶּם אֹתוֹ בְּחִפָּזוֹן פֶּסַח הוּא לַיהוה:

יב וְעָבַרְתִּי בְאֶרֶץ־מִצְרַיִם בַּלַּיְלָה הַזֶּה וְהִכֵּיתִי כָל־בְּכוֹר בְּאֶרֶץ מִצְרַיִם

מֵאָדָם וְעַד־בְּהֵמָה וּבְכָל־אֱלֹהֵי מִצְרַיִם אֶעֱשֶׂה שְׁפָטִים אֲנִי יהוה:

יג וְהָיָה הַדָּם לָכֶם לְאֹת עַל הַבָּתִּים אֲשֶׁר אַתֶּם שָׁם וְרָאִיתִי אֶת־הַדָּם

וּפָסַחְתִּי עֲלֵכֶם וְלֹא־יִהְיֶה בָכֶם נֶגֶף לְמַשְׁחִית בְּהַכֹּתִי בְּאֶרֶץ מִצְרָיִם:

11:4. Moses was not to say that the plague would occur exactly at midnight, because if Pharaoh's astrologers miscalculated and thought that the plague took place somewhat before or after midnight, they would claim that Moses was a charlatan for predicting the wrong time (*Rashi*).

12:2-28. The Torah here presents the commandments that commemorate the Exodus and whose merit made the nation worthy of their liberation from Egypt. These

include the New Moon, the *pesach*-offering and the Seder in the unique forms in which they were observed in Egypt, and the general laws of the Pesach festival.

12:2. Nissan, the month in which this commandment was given, is to be *the beginning of the months,* i.e., even though the new year begins with Tishrei, the months are to be numbered from the month of the Exodus. Thus, Nissan is the "first" month, while Tishrei is the "seventh" month (*Rashi*).

The new
status of the
Jews
in the land of Egypt, in the eyes of the servants of Pharaoh and in the eyes of the people.

⁴ Moses said, "So said HASHEM, 'At about midnight* I shall go out in the midst of Egypt. ⁵ Every firstborn in the land of Egypt shall die, from the firstborn of Pharaoh who sits on his throne to the firstborn of the maidservant who is behind the millstone and all the firstborn of beast. ⁶ There shall be a great outcry in the entire land of Egypt, such as there has never been and such as there shall never be again. ⁷ But against all the Children of Israel, no dog shall whet its tongue, against neither man nor beast, so that you shall know that HASHEM will have differentiated between Egypt and Israel.' ⁸ Then all these servants of yours will come down to me and bow to me, saying, 'Leave — you and the entire people that follows you.' After that, I will leave!" And he left Pharaoh's presence in a burning anger.

⁹ HASHEM said to Moses, "Pharaoh will not heed you, so that My wonders may be multiplied in the land of Egypt." ¹⁰ So Moses and Aaron performed all these wonders before Pharaoh, but HASHEM strengthened the heart of Pharaoh, and he did not send out the Children of Israel from his land.

12

Rosh
Chodesh
The pesach-
offering

¹ **H**ASHEM said to Moses and Aaron in the land of Egypt, saying, ² "This month* shall be for you the beginning of the months, it shall be for you the first of the months of the year.

³ "Speak to the entire assembly of Israel, saying: On the tenth of this month they shall take for themselves — each man — a lamb or kid for each father's house, a lamb or kid for the household.* ⁴ But if the household will be too small for a lamb or kid, then he and his neighbor who is near his house shall take according to the number of people; everyone according to what he eats shall be counted for the lamb or kid. ⁵ An unblemished lamb or kid, a male, within its first year shall it be for you; from the sheep or goats shall you take it. ⁶ It shall be yours for examination until the fourteenth day of this month; the entire congregation of the assembly of Israel shall slaughter it in the afternoon. ⁷ They shall take some of the blood and place it on the two doorposts and on the lintel of the houses in which they will eat it. ⁸ They shall eat the flesh on that night — roasted over the fire — and matzos; with bitter herbs shall they eat it.

⁹ "You shall not eat it partially roasted or cooked in water; only roasted over fire — its head, its legs, with its innards. ¹⁰ You shall not leave any of it until morning; any of it that is left until morning you shall burn in the fire.

¹¹ "So shall you eat it: your loins girded, your shoes on your feet, and your staff in your hand; you shall eat it in haste — it is a pesach-offering to HASHEM.

God Himself
will carry
out the
plague

¹² "I shall go through the land of Egypt on this night, and I shall strike* every firstborn in the land of Egypt, from man to beast; and against all the gods of Egypt I shall mete out punishment — I am HASHEM. ¹³ The blood shall be a sign for you upon the houses where you are; when I shall see the blood and I shall pass over you; there shall not be a plague of destruction upon you when I strike in the land of Egypt.

12:3-11. The *pesach*-offering. The word *pesach* means *pass over*, and it commemorates God's mercy toward the Jewish people on the night of Pesach in Egypt, for He took the lives of the Egyptian firstborn, but He *passed over* the homes where Jews were eating their *pesach*-offering [see vs. 12-13].

12:12. From this verse, which is familiar from the Pesach *Haggadah,* the Sages derive that God *personally* carried out the Plague of the Firstborn, and did not dispatch an angel or emissary to do so.

יד וְהָיָה הַיּוֹם הַזֶּה לָכֶם לְזִכָּרוֹן וְחַגֹּתֶם אֹתוֹ חַג לַיהוָה לְדֹרֹתֵיכֶם חֻקַּת
טו עוֹלָם תְּחָגֻּהוּ׃ שִׁבְעַת יָמִים מַצּוֹת תֹּאכֵלוּ אַךְ בַּיּוֹם הָרִאשׁוֹן תַּשְׁבִּיתוּ
שְּׂאֹר מִבָּתֵּיכֶם כִּי ׀ כָּל־אֹכֵל חָמֵץ וְנִכְרְתָה הַנֶּפֶשׁ הַהִוא מִיִּשְׂרָאֵל מִיּוֹם
טז הָרִאשֹׁן עַד־יוֹם הַשְּׁבִעִי׃ וּבַיּוֹם הָרִאשׁוֹן מִקְרָא־קֹדֶשׁ וּבַיּוֹם הַשְּׁבִיעִי
מִקְרָא־קֹדֶשׁ יִהְיֶה לָכֶם כָּל־מְלָאכָה לֹא־יֵעָשֶׂה בָהֶם אַךְ אֲשֶׁר יֵאָכֵל
יז לְכָל־נֶפֶשׁ הוּא לְבַדּוֹ יֵעָשֶׂה לָכֶם׃ וּשְׁמַרְתֶּם אֶת־הַמַּצּוֹת כִּי בְּעֶצֶם הַיּוֹם
הַזֶּה הוֹצֵאתִי אֶת־צִבְאוֹתֵיכֶם מֵאֶרֶץ מִצְרָיִם וּשְׁמַרְתֶּם אֶת־הַיּוֹם הַזֶּה
יח לְדֹרֹתֵיכֶם חֻקַּת עוֹלָם׃ בָּרִאשֹׁן בְּאַרְבָּעָה עָשָׂר יוֹם לַחֹדֶשׁ בָּעֶרֶב תֹּאכְלוּ
יט מַצֹּת עַד יוֹם הָאֶחָד וְעֶשְׂרִים לַחֹדֶשׁ בָּעָרֶב׃ שִׁבְעַת יָמִים שְׂאֹר לֹא
יִמָּצֵא בְּבָתֵּיכֶם כִּי ׀ כָּל־אֹכֵל מַחְמֶצֶת וְנִכְרְתָה הַנֶּפֶשׁ הַהִוא מֵעֲדַת
כ יִשְׂרָאֵל בַּגֵּר וּבְאֶזְרַח הָאָרֶץ׃ כָּל־מַחְמֶצֶת לֹא תֹאכֵלוּ בְּכֹל מוֹשְׁבֹתֵיכֶם
תֹּאכְלוּ מַצּוֹת׃
חמישי כא וַיִּקְרָא מֹשֶׁה לְכָל־זִקְנֵי יִשְׂרָאֵל וַיֹּאמֶר אֲלֵהֶם מִשְׁכוּ וּקְחוּ לָכֶם צֹאן
כב לְמִשְׁפְּחֹתֵיכֶם וְשַׁחֲטוּ הַפָּסַח׃ וּלְקַחְתֶּם אֲגֻדַּת אֵזוֹב וּטְבַלְתֶּם בַּדָּם
אֲשֶׁר־בַּסַּף וְהִגַּעְתֶּם אֶל־הַמַּשְׁקוֹף וְאֶל־שְׁתֵּי הַמְּזוּזֹת מִן־הַדָּם אֲשֶׁר
כג בַּסָּף וְאַתֶּם לֹא תֵצְאוּ אִישׁ מִפֶּתַח־בֵּיתוֹ עַד־בֹּקֶר׃ וְעָבַר יהוה לִנְגֹּף אֶת־
מִצְרַיִם וְרָאָה אֶת־הַדָּם עַל־הַמַּשְׁקוֹף וְעַל שְׁתֵּי הַמְּזוּזֹת וּפָסַח יהוה
כד עַל־הַפֶּתַח וְלֹא יִתֵּן הַמַּשְׁחִית לָבֹא אֶל־בָּתֵּיכֶם לִנְגֹּף׃ וּשְׁמַרְתֶּם אֶת־
כה הַדָּבָר הַזֶּה לְחָק־לְךָ וּלְבָנֶיךָ עַד־עוֹלָם׃ וְהָיָה כִּי־תָבֹאוּ אֶל־הָאָרֶץ אֲשֶׁר
כו יִתֵּן יהוה לָכֶם כַּאֲשֶׁר דִּבֵּר וּשְׁמַרְתֶּם אֶת־הָעֲבֹדָה הַזֹּאת׃ וְהָיָה כִּי־
כז יֹאמְרוּ אֲלֵיכֶם בְּנֵיכֶם מָה הָעֲבֹדָה הַזֹּאת לָכֶם׃ וַאֲמַרְתֶּם זֶבַח־פֶּסַח
הוּא לַיהוָה אֲשֶׁר פָּסַח עַל־בָּתֵּי בְנֵי־יִשְׂרָאֵל בְּמִצְרַיִם בְּנָגְפּוֹ אֶת־
כח מִצְרַיִם וְאֶת־בָּתֵּינוּ הִצִּיל וַיִּקֹּד הָעָם וַיִּשְׁתַּחֲווּ׃ וַיֵּלְכוּ וַיַּעֲשׂוּ בְּנֵי יִשְׂרָאֵל
ששי כט כַּאֲשֶׁר צִוָּה יהוה אֶת־מֹשֶׁה וְאַהֲרֹן כֵּן עָשׂוּ׃ וַיְהִי ׀ בַּחֲצִי
הַלַּיְלָה וַיהוה הִכָּה כָל־בְּכוֹר בְּאֶרֶץ מִצְרַיִם מִבְּכֹר פַּרְעֹה הַיֹּשֵׁב עַל־
ל כִּסְאוֹ עַד בְּכוֹר הַשְּׁבִי אֲשֶׁר בְּבֵית הַבּוֹר וְכֹל בְּכוֹר בְּהֵמָה׃ וַיָּקָם פַּרְעֹה
לַיְלָה הוּא וְכָל־עֲבָדָיו וְכָל־מִצְרַיִם וַתְּהִי צְעָקָה גְדֹלָה בְּמִצְרָיִם כִּי־אֵין
לא בַּיִת אֲשֶׁר אֵין־שָׁם מֵת׃ וַיִּקְרָא לְמֹשֶׁה וּלְאַהֲרֹן לַיְלָה וַיֹּאמֶר קוּמוּ *צְּאוּ
מִתּוֹךְ עַמִּי גַּם־אַתֶּם גַּם־בְּנֵי יִשְׂרָאֵל וּלְכוּ עִבְדוּ אֶת־יהוה כְּדַבֶּרְכֶם׃

READING FOR FIRST DAY PESACH 12:21-51
Maftir: p. 400
Haftarah: p. 522

*צ׳ דגושה

12:14-20. The Torah now sets forth the laws of Pesach, even though they would not be observed until the next year. This annual observance inscribes in the national consciousness the experiences of the Exodus so that the genesis of Jewish nationhood would always remain fresh and relevant. Even at times when the lot of Jewry seems even more bitter than it was in Egypt, the observance of the "festival of freedom" is *an eternal decree* (v. 14). As *Maharal* expresses it, the Exodus made the Jewish people eternally free; from that time on, any servitude or oppression would be a temporary phenomenon that could not change the pure essence of the nation.

12:15. Leaven must be removed the day before Pesach. The word ראשון here cannot have its usual meaning of *first* [day of Pesach] because it is stated clearly in 34:25 that the leaven must be removed before the *pesach*-offering may be offered, which is noon of the day before the festival (*Rashi*).

The Pesach festival

¹⁴ *"This day shall become a remembrance for you* and you shall celebrate it as a festival for HASHEM; for your generations, as an eternal decree shall you celebrate it.* ¹⁵ *For a seven-day period shall you eat matzos, but on the previous day* you shall nullify the leaven from your homes; for anyone who eats leavened food — that soul shall be cut off from Israel, from the first day to the seventh day.*

¹⁶ *"On the first day shall be a holy convocation and on the seventh day shall be a holy convocation for you, no work may be done on them, except for what must be eaten for any person — only that may be done for you.*

¹⁷ *"You shall safeguard the matzos, for on this very day I will have taken your legions out of the land of Egypt; you shall observe this day for your generations as an eternal decree.* ¹⁸ *In the first [month], on the fourteenth day of the month in the evening shall you eat matzos, until the twenty-first day of the month in the evening.*

¹⁹ *"For seven days, leaven may not be found in your houses, for anyone who eats leavening — that soul shall be cut off from the assembly of Israel, whether a convert or a native of the land.* ²⁰ *You shall not eat any leavening; in all your dwellings shall you eat matzos."*

The pesach-offering

²¹ *Moses called to all the elders of Israel and said to them, "Draw forth or buy for yourselves one of the flock for your families, and slaughter the pesach-offering.* ²² *You shall take a bundle of hyssop and dip it into the blood that is in the basin, and touch the lintel and the two doorposts with some of the blood that is in the basin, and as for you, no man shall leave the entrance of his house until morning.* ²³ *HASHEM will pass through to smite Egypt, and He will see the blood that is on the lintel and the two doorposts; and HASHEM will pass over the entrance and He will not permit the destroyer to enter your homes to smite.* ²⁴ *You shall observe this matter as a decree for yourself and for your children forever.*

²⁵ *"It shall be that when you come to the land that HASHEM will give you, as He has spoken, you shall observe this service.* ²⁶ *And it shall be that when your children say to you, 'What is this service to you?'** ²⁷ *You shall say, 'It is a pesach feast-offering to HASHEM, Who passed over the houses of the Children of Israel in Egypt when He smote the Egyptians, but He saved our households,'"* and the people bowed their heads and prostrated themselves. ²⁸ *The Children of Israel went and did as HASHEM commanded Moses and Aaron, so did they do.*

The tenth plague: Death of the Firstborn

²⁹ *It was at midnight that HASHEM smote every firstborn* in the land of Egypt, from the firstborn of Pharaoh sitting on his throne to the firstborn of the captive who was in the dungeon, and every firstborn animal.* ³⁰ *Pharaoh rose up at midnight, he and all his servants and all Egypt, and there was a great outcry in Egypt, for there was not a house where there was no corpse.* ³¹ *He called to*

Pharaoh's surrender

Moses and Aaron at night and said, "Rise up, go out from among my people, even you, even the Children of Israel; go and serve HASHEM as you have spoken!

12:26-27. The wicked son's question. As expounded by the *Haggadah*, this is the question of the Wicked Son, who removes himself from the community and does not wish to join in their service. In response, we are to say that this offering commemorates the salvation of our forefathers from Egypt, thereby implying that those who deny the service, like the Wicked Son, would not have

been saved.

12:29. The Egyptian firstborn died because they had persecuted the Jews; those of the captives died because they enjoyed Jewish suffering, or so that they would not be able to claim that their idols had protected them. Pharaoh, a firstborn, was spared, to tell all the world about God's greatness.

לב   גַּם־צֹאנְכֶ֨ם גַּם־בְּקַרְכֶ֜ם קְח֧וּ כַּאֲשֶׁ֛ר דִּבַּרְתֶּ֖ם וָלֵ֑כוּ וּבֵרַכְתֶּ֖ם גַּם־אֹתִֽי:

לג   וַתֶּחֱזַ֤ק מִצְרַ֨יִם֙ עַל־הָעָ֔ם לְמַהֵ֖ר לְשַׁלְּחָ֣ם מִן־הָאָ֑רֶץ כִּ֥י אָמְר֖וּ כֻּלָּ֥נוּ מֵתִֽים:

לד   וַיִּשָּׂ֥א הָעָ֛ם אֶת־בְּצֵק֖וֹ טֶ֣רֶם יֶחְמָ֑ץ מִשְׁאֲרֹתָ֛ם צְרֻרֹ֥ת בְּשִׂמְלֹתָ֖ם עַל־

לה   שִׁכְמָֽם: וּבְנֵֽי־יִשְׂרָאֵ֥ל עָשׂ֖וּ כִּדְבַ֣ר מֹשֶׁ֑ה וַֽיִּשְׁאֲלוּ֙ מִמִּצְרַ֔יִם כְּלֵי־כֶ֥סֶף וּכְלֵ֥י

לו   זָהָ֖ב וּשְׂמָלֹֽת: וַֽיהֹוָ֞ה נָתַ֨ן אֶת־חֵ֥ן הָעָ֛ם בְּעֵינֵ֥י מִצְרַ֖יִם וַיַּשְׁאִל֑וּם וַֽיְנַצְּל֖וּ אֶת־מִצְרָֽיִם:

לז   וַיִּסְע֧וּ בְנֵֽי־יִשְׂרָאֵ֛ל מֵרַעְמְסֵ֖ס סֻכֹּ֑תָה כְּשֵׁשׁ־מֵא֨וֹת אֶ֧לֶף רַגְלִ֛י הַגְּבָרִ֖ים

לח-לט   לְבַ֥ד מִטָּֽף: וְגַם־עֵ֥רֶב רַ֖ב עָלָ֣ה אִתָּ֑ם וְצֹ֣אן וּבָקָ֔ר מִקְנֶ֖ה כָּבֵ֥ד מְאֹֽד: וַיֹּאפ֨וּ אֶת־הַבָּצֵ֜ק אֲשֶׁ֨ר הוֹצִ֧יאוּ מִמִּצְרַ֛יִם עֻגֹ֥ת מַצּ֖וֹת כִּ֣י לֹ֣א חָמֵ֑ץ כִּֽי־גֹרְשׁ֣וּ

מ   מִמִּצְרַ֗יִם וְלֹ֤א יָֽכְלוּ֙ לְהִתְמַהְמֵ֔הַּ וְגַם־צֵדָ֖ה לֹא־עָשׂ֥וּ לָהֶֽם: וּמוֹשַׁב֙ בְּנֵ֣י

מא   יִשְׂרָאֵ֔ל אֲשֶׁ֥ר יָֽשְׁב֖וּ בְּמִצְרָ֑יִם שְׁלֹשִׁ֣ים שָׁנָ֔ה וְאַרְבַּ֥ע מֵא֖וֹת שָׁנָֽה: וַיְהִ֗י מִקֵּץ֙ שְׁלֹשִׁ֣ים שָׁנָ֔ה וְאַרְבַּ֖ע מֵא֣וֹת שָׁנָ֑ה וַיְהִ֗י בְּעֶ֨צֶם֙ הַיּ֣וֹם הַזֶּ֔ה יָ֥צְא֛וּ כָּל־צִבְא֥וֹת

מב   יְהֹוָ֖ה מֵאֶ֥רֶץ מִצְרָֽיִם: לֵ֣יל שִׁמֻּרִ֥ים הוּא֙ לַֽיהֹוָ֔ה לְהוֹצִיאָ֖ם מֵאֶ֣רֶץ מִצְרָ֑יִם הֽוּא־הַלַּ֤יְלָה הַזֶּה֙ לַֽיהֹוָ֔ה שִׁמֻּרִ֛ים לְכָל־בְּנֵ֥י יִשְׂרָאֵ֖ל לְדֹֽרֹתָֽם:

מג   וַיֹּ֤אמֶר יְהֹוָה֙ אֶל־מֹשֶׁ֣ה וְאַהֲרֹ֔ן זֹ֖את חֻקַּ֣ת הַפָּ֑סַח כָּל־בֶּן־נֵכָ֖ר לֹא־יֹ֥אכַל

מד-מה   בּֽוֹ: וְכָל־עֶ֥בֶד אִ֖ישׁ מִקְנַת־כָּ֑סֶף וּמַלְתָּ֣ה אֹת֔וֹ אָ֖ז יֹ֥אכַל בּֽוֹ: תּוֹשָׁ֥ב וְשָׂכִ֖יר

מו   לֹא־יֹ֥אכַל־בּֽוֹ: בְּבַ֤יִת אֶחָד֙ יֵֽאָכֵ֔ל לֹֽא־תוֹצִ֧יא מִן־הַבַּ֛יִת מִן־הַבָּשָׂ֖ר ח֑וּצָה

מז-מח   וְעֶ֖צֶם לֹ֥א תִשְׁבְּרוּ־בֽוֹ: כָּל־עֲדַ֥ת יִשְׂרָאֵ֖ל יַֽעֲשׂ֥וּ אֹתֽוֹ: וְכִֽי־יָג֨וּר אִתְּךָ֜ גֵּ֗ר וְעָ֣שָׂה פֶ֨סַח֙ לַֽיהֹוָ֔ה הִמּ֧וֹל ל֣וֹ כָל־זָכָ֗ר וְאָז֙ יִקְרַ֣ב לַֽעֲשֹׂת֔וֹ וְהָיָ֖ה כְּאֶזְרַ֣ח

מט   הָאָ֑רֶץ וְכָל־עָרֵ֖ל לֹֽא־יֹ֥אכַל בּֽוֹ: תּוֹרָ֣ה אַחַ֔ת יִֽהְיֶ֖ה לָֽאֶזְרָ֑ח וְלַגֵּ֖ר הַגָּ֥ר

נ   בְּתֽוֹכְכֶֽם: וַֽיַּעֲשׂ֖וּ כָּל־בְּנֵ֣י יִשְׂרָאֵ֑ל כַּאֲשֶׁ֨ר צִוָּ֧ה יְהֹוָ֛ה אֶת־מֹשֶׁ֥ה וְאֶֽת־אַהֲרֹ֖ן

נא   כֵּ֥ן עָשֽׂוּ: וַיְהִ֕י בְּעֶ֖צֶם הַיּ֣וֹם הַזֶּ֑ה הוֹצִ֨יא יְהֹוָ֜ה אֶת־בְּנֵ֧י יִשְׂרָאֵ֛ל מֵאֶ֥רֶץ מִצְרַ֖יִם עַל־צִבְאֹתָֽם:

יג   ^{שביעי א-ב}   וַיְדַבֵּ֥ר יְהֹוָ֖ה אֶל־מֹשֶׁ֥ה לֵּאמֹֽר: קַדֶּשׁ־לִ֨י כָל־בְּכ֜וֹר פֶּ֤טֶר כָּל־רֶ֨חֶם֙

ב   בִּבְנֵ֣י יִשְׂרָאֵ֔ל בָּֽאָדָ֖ם וּבַבְּהֵמָ֑ה לִ֖י הֽוּא: וַיֹּ֨אמֶר מֹשֶׁ֜ה אֶל־הָעָ֗ם זָכ֞וֹר

ג   אֶת־הַיּ֤וֹם הַזֶּה֙ אֲשֶׁ֨ר יְצָאתֶ֤ם מִמִּצְרַ֨יִם֙ מִבֵּ֣ית עֲבָדִ֔ים כִּ֚י בְּחֹ֣זֶק יָ֔ד

ד   הוֹצִ֧יא יְהֹוָ֛ה אֶתְכֶ֖ם מִזֶּ֑ה וְלֹ֥א יֵֽאָכֵ֖ל חָמֵֽץ: הַיּ֕וֹם אַתֶּ֖ם יֹֽצְאִ֑ים בְּחֹ֖דֶשׁ

ה   הָֽאָבִֽיב: וְהָיָ֣ה כִֽי־יְבִֽיאֲךָ֣ יְהֹוָ֡ה אֶל־אֶ֣רֶץ הַֽכְּנַעֲנִ֣י וְהַֽחִתִּ֡י וְהָֽאֱמֹרִי֩ וְהַֽחִוִּ֨י

READING
FOR FIRST
DAY CHOL
HAMOED
PESACH
13:1-16;

Revi'i/Maftir:
p. 400

12:37-42. The huge number of 600,000 adult males —
which, allowing for women, children, and elderly men,
indicates a total population of about three million —
gives some idea of the magnitude of the miracle. It also
indicates the nation's inspiring faith in God, for they
followed Moses into the Wilderness, where the lack of
food would have terrified anyone who was not prepared to
rely on God.

12:38. A multitude of people of various nationalities
converted to Judaism and accompanied the Jews out of
Egypt (*Rashi*).

12:40. The Covenant Between the Parts took place 430
years before the Exodus, and it is the period referred to in
our verse. God foretold to Abraham that his offspring
would endure 400 years during which there would be
exile, persecution, and servitude. Those 400 years began
with the birth of Isaac — 30 years after the Covenant
Between the Parts — since the prophecy referred to
Abraham's *offspring* (*Genesis* 15:13). The actual sojourn
in Egypt lasted 210 years (*Rashi*). According, the
verse's reference to 430 years as the time they *dwelled in
Egypt* means that the Egyptian exile had been decreed

³² Take even your sheep and even your cattle, as you have spoken, and go — and bless me as well!"

³³ Egypt imposed itself strongly upon the people to hasten to send them out of the land, for they said, "We are all dying!"

³⁴ The people picked up its dough before it could become leavened, their leftovers bound up in their garments upon their shoulders. ³⁵ The Children of Israel carried out the word of Moses; they requested from the Egyptians silver vessels, gold vessels, and garments. ³⁶ HASHEM gave the people favor in the eyes of the Egyptians and they granted their request — so they emptied Egypt.

The Exodus ³⁷ The Children of Israel journeyed from Rameses to Succoth, * about six hundred thousand men on foot, aside from children. ³⁸ Also a mixed multitude * went up with them, and flock and cattle, very much livestock. ³⁹ They baked the dough that they took out of Egypt into unleavened cakes, for they could not be leavened, for they were driven from Egypt for they could not delay, nor had they *The* made provisions for themselves. ⁴⁰ The habitation of the Children of Israel during *duration* which they dwelled in Egypt was four hundred and thirty years. * ⁴¹ It was at the *of the* end of four hundred and thirty years, and it was on that very day that all the *Egyptian* legions of HASHEM left the land of Egypt. ⁴² It is a night of anticipation for HASHEM *exile* to take them out of the land of Egypt, this was the night for HASHEM; a protection for all the Children of Israel for their generations.

Additional ⁴³ HASHEM said to Moses and Aaron, "This is the decree of the pesach-offering: *laws of the* no alienated person may eat from it. ⁴⁴ Every slave of a man, who was bought *pesach-* for money, you shall circumcise him; then he may eat of it. ⁴⁵ A sojourner and *offering* a hired laborer may not eat it. ⁴⁶ In one house shall it be eaten; you shall not remove any of the meat from the house to the outside, and you shall not break a bone in it. ⁴⁷ The entire assembly of Israel shall perform it.

⁴⁸ "When a proselyte * sojourns among you he shall make the pesach-offering for HASHEM, each of his males shall be circumcised, and then he may draw near to perform it and he shall be like the native of the land; no uncircumcised male may eat of it. ⁴⁹ One law shall there be for the native and the proselyte who lives among you." ⁵⁰ All the Children of Israel did as HASHEM had commanded Moses and Aaron, so did they do.

⁵¹ It happened on that very day: HASHEM took the Children of Israel out of the land of Egypt, in their legions.

13 ¹ HASHEM spoke to Moses, saying, ² "Sanctify to Me every firstborn, * the first issue of every womb among the Children of Israel, of man and beast, is Mine."

³ Moses said to the people, "Remember this day on which you departed from Egypt, from the house of bondage, for with a strong hand HASHEM removed *Remember* you from here, and therefore chametz may not be eaten. ⁴ Today you are *the Exodus* leaving, in the month of springtime. ⁵ And it shall come to pass when HASHEM shall bring you to the land of the Canaanite, the Hittite, the Amorite, the Hivvite,

---

430 years before the Exodus.

12:48. This is one of the many passages in which the Torah requires that converts be treated as equals. Even though their ancestors did not emerge from Egypt, they bring the offering along with all other Jews.

13:1-16. Firstborn, Pesach, and tefillin. The three top-

ics are related. The conclusion of the *Sidrah* consists of two passages, both of which refer to the holiness of the firstborn and the obligation to teach future generations about the miracles of the Exodus. Also, both of them conclude with the commandment of tefillin and are therefore included among the four Scriptural passages that are contained in the compartments of tefillin.

וְהַיְבוּסִ֑י אֲשֶׁ֨ר נִשְׁבַּ֤ע לַֽאֲבֹתֶ֙יךָ֙ לָ֣תֶת לָ֔ךְ אֶ֛רֶץ זָבַ֥ת חָלָ֖ב וּדְבָ֑שׁ וְעָבַדְתָּ֛

אֶת־הָֽעֲבֹדָ֥ה הַזֹּ֖את בַּחֹ֥דֶשׁ הַזֶּֽה: שִׁבְעַ֥ת יָמִ֖ים תֹּאכַ֣ל מַצֹּ֑ת וּבַיּוֹם֙ הַשְּׁבִיעִ֔י **ו**

חַ֖ג לַֽיהוָֹֽה: מַצּוֹת֙ יֵֽאָכֵ֔ל אֵ֖ת שִׁבְעַ֣ת הַיָּמִ֑ים וְלֹֽא־יֵֽרָאֶ֨ה לְךָ֜ חָמֵ֗ץ וְלֹֽא־ **ז**

יֵֽרָאֶ֥ה לְךָ֛ שְׂאֹ֖ר בְּכָל־גְּבֻלֶֽךָ: וְהִגַּדְתָּ֣ לְבִנְךָ֔ בַּיּ֥וֹם הַה֖וּא לֵאמֹ֑ר בַּֽעֲב֣וּר זֶ֗ה **ח**

עָשָׂ֤ה יְהוָֹה֙ לִ֔י בְּצֵאתִ֖י מִמִּצְרָֽיִם: וְהָיָה֩ לְךָ֨ לְא֜וֹת עַל־יָֽדְךָ֗ וּלְזִכָּרוֹן֙ בֵּ֣ין **ט**

עֵינֶ֔יךָ לְמַ֗עַן תִּֽהְיֶ֛ה תּוֹרַ֥ת יְהוָֹ֖ה בְּפִ֑יךָ כִּ֚י בְּיָ֣ד חֲזָקָ֔ה הֽוֹצִֽאֲךָ֥ יְהוָֹ֖ה

מִמִּצְרָֽיִם: וְשָֽׁמַרְתָּ֛ אֶת־הַֽחֻקָּ֥ה הַזֹּ֖את לְמֽוֹעֲדָ֑הּ מִיָּמִ֖ים יָמִֽימָה: **י**

וְהָיָ֞ה כִּֽי־יְבִֽאֲךָ֤ יְהוָֹה֙ אֶל־אֶ֣רֶץ הַֽכְּנַֽעֲנִ֔י כַּֽאֲשֶׁ֛ר נִשְׁבַּ֥ע לְךָ֖ וְלַֽאֲבֹתֶ֑יךָ וּנְתָנָ֖הּ **יא**

לָֽךְ: וְהַֽעֲבַרְתָּ֥ כָל־פֶּֽטֶר־רֶ֖חֶם לַֽיהוָֹ֑ה וְכָל־פֶּ֣טֶר ׀ שֶׁ֣גֶר בְּהֵמָ֗ה אֲשֶׁ֨ר יִֽהְיֶ֥ה **יב**

לְךָ֛ הַזְּכָרִ֖ים לַֽיהוָֹֽה: וְכָל־פֶּ֤טֶר חֲמֹר֙ תִּפְדֶּ֣ה בְשֶׂ֔ה וְאִם־לֹ֥א תִפְדֶּ֖ה וַֽעֲרַפְתּ֑וֹ **יג**

וְכֹ֨ל בְּכ֥וֹר אָדָ֛ם בְּבָנֶ֖יךָ תִּפְדֶּֽה: וְהָיָ֞ה כִּֽי־יִשְׁאָֽלְךָ֥ בִנְךָ֛ מָחָ֖ר לֵאמֹ֣ר מַה־ **יד** מפטיר

זֹּ֑את וְאָֽמַרְתָּ֣ אֵלָ֔יו בְּחֹ֣זֶק יָ֗ד הֽוֹצִיאָ֧נוּ יְהוָֹ֛ה מִמִּצְרַ֖יִם מִבֵּ֥ית עֲבָדִֽים: וַיְהִ֗י **טו**

כִּֽי־הִקְשָׁ֣ה פַרְעֹה֮ לְשַׁלְּחֵנוּ֒ וַיַּֽהֲרֹ֨ג יְהוָֹ֤ה כָּל־בְּכוֹר֙ בְּאֶ֣רֶץ מִצְרַ֔יִם מִבְּכֹ֥ר

אָדָ֖ם וְעַד־בְּכ֣וֹר בְּהֵמָ֑ה עַל־כֵּן֩ אֲנִ֨י זֹבֵ֜חַ לַֽיהוָֹ֗ה כָּל־פֶּ֤טֶר רֶ֨חֶם֙ הַזְּכָרִ֔ים

וְכָל־בְּכ֥וֹר בָּנַ֖י אֶפְדֶּֽה: וְהָיָ֤ה לְאוֹת֙ עַל־יָ֣דְכָ֔ה וּלְטֽוֹטָפֹ֖ת בֵּ֣ין עֵינֶ֑יךָ כִּ֚י **טז** *Haftaras Bo:* p. 1180

בְּחֹ֣זֶק יָ֔ד הֽוֹצִיאָ֥נוּ יְהוָֹ֖ה מִמִּצְרָֽיִם: ססס ק״ה פסוקים. ימנ״ה סימן.

פרשת בשלח

וַיְהִ֗י בְּשַׁלַּ֣ח פַּרְעֹה֮ אֶת־הָעָם֒ וְלֹֽא־נָחָ֣ם אֱלֹהִ֗ים דֶּ֚רֶךְ אֶ֣רֶץ פְּלִשְׁתִּ֔ים כִּ֥י **יז** READING FOR SEVENTH DAY PESACH 13:17-15:26

קָר֖וֹב ה֑וּא כִּ֣י ׀ אָמַ֣ר אֱלֹהִ֗ים פֶּֽן־יִנָּחֵ֥ם הָעָ֛ם בִּרְאֹתָ֥ם מִלְחָמָ֖ה וְשָׁ֥בוּ

מִצְרָֽיְמָה: וַיַּסֵּ֨ב אֱלֹהִ֧ים ׀ אֶת־הָעָ֛ם דֶּ֥רֶךְ הַמִּדְבָּ֖ר יַם־ס֑וּף וַֽחֲמֻשִׁ֛ים עָל֥וּ **יח** *Maftir:* p. 400

בְנֵֽי־יִשְׂרָאֵ֖ל מֵאֶ֥רֶץ מִצְרָֽיִם: וַיִּקַּ֥ח מֹשֶׁ֛ה אֶת־עַצְמ֥וֹת יוֹסֵ֖ף עִמּ֑וֹ כִּי֩ הַשְׁבֵּ֨עַ **יט** *Haftarah:* p. 782

הִשְׁבִּ֜יעַ אֶת־בְּנֵ֤י יִשְׂרָאֵל֙ לֵאמֹ֔ר פָּקֹ֨ד יִפְקֹ֤ד אֱלֹהִים֙ אֶתְכֶ֔ם וְהַֽעֲלִיתֶ֧ם

אֶת־עַצְמֹתַ֛י מִזֶּ֖ה אִתְּכֶֽם: וַיִּסְע֖וּ מִסֻּכֹּ֑ת וַיַּֽחֲנ֣וּ בְאֵתָ֔ם בִּקְצֵ֖ה הַמִּדְבָּֽר: **כ**

וַֽיהוָֹ֡ה הֹלֵךְ֩ לִפְנֵיהֶ֨ם יוֹמָ֜ם בְּעַמּ֤וּד עָנָן֙ לַנְחֹתָ֣ם הַדֶּ֔רֶךְ וְלַ֛יְלָה בְּעַמּ֥וּד אֵ֖שׁ **כא**

לְהָאִ֣יר לָהֶ֑ם לָלֶ֖כֶת יוֹמָ֥ם וָלָֽיְלָה: לֹֽא־יָמִ֞ישׁ עַמּ֤וּד הֶֽעָנָן֙ יוֹמָ֔ם וְעַמּ֥וּד **כב**

הָאֵ֖שׁ לָ֑יְלָה לִפְנֵ֖י הָעָֽם:

⚜ **The four passages of Tefillin.** The four Scriptural passages that are contained in tefillin — the first two passages of the *Shema* and the two passages of this chapter — are basic to Judaism. The two passages in this chapter speak of the Exodus, which is basic to the Jew's awareness of his responsibilities to God, Who liberated him and made Israel a nation. The first two passages of *Shema* express the concept that God is One and that we accept His Kingship, the concept of reward and punishment, and the responsibility to observe all the commandments. These principles must always be with us: upon the arm that symbolizes our capacity for action and is opposite the heart, the seat of emotion, and upon the head, the

abode of the intellectual soul and the power of memory, which enables us to be conscious of our antecedents and obligations to do His will.

⚜ **Parashas Beshalach**

13:17-18. The quickest and most direct route from Egypt to *Eretz Yisrael* is northeast, along the coast of the Mediterranean Sea, a route that goes through Philistia, which is on the west coast of the Holy Land. However, just as this was the easiest way to leave Egypt, it was also the easiest way to return there. Since the war-like Philistines were sure to fight the Jewish "invaders," God knew that the people would lose heart and return to Egypt. To avoid this, He led them on a roundabout path through the Sinai and the Jebusite, which He swore to your forefathers to give you — a land flowing with milk and honey — you shall perform this service in this month. ⁶ For a seven-day period shall you eat matzos, and on the seventh day there shall be a festival to HASHEM. ⁷ Matzos shall be eaten throughout the seven-day period; no chametz may be seen in your possession, nor may leaven be seen in your possession in all your borders. ⁸ And you shall tell your son on that day, saying, 'It is because of this that HASHEM acted on my behalf when I left Egypt.' ⁹ And it shall be for you a sign on your arm and a reminder between your eyes — so that HASHEM's Torah may be in your mouth — for with a strong hand HASHEM removed you from Egypt. ¹⁰ You shall observe this decree at its designated time from year to year.

The firstborn ¹¹ "It shall come to pass, when HASHEM will bring you to the land of the Canaanites, as He swore to you and your forefathers, and He will have given it to you; ¹² then you shall set apart every first issue of the womb to HASHEM, and of every first issue that is dropped by livestock that belong to you, the males are HASHEM's. ¹³ Every first-issue donkey you shall redeem with a lamb or kid; if you do not redeem it, you shall axe the back of its neck. And you shall redeem every human firstborn among your sons. ¹⁴ And it shall be when your son will ask you at some future time, 'What is this?' you shall say to him, 'With a strong hand HASHEM removed us from Egypt from the house of bondage. ¹⁵ And it happened when Pharaoh stubbornly refused to send us out, that HASHEM killed all the firstborn in the land of Egypt, from the firstborn of man to the firstborn of beast. Therefore I offer to HASHEM all male first issue of the womb, and I shall redeem all the firstborn of my sons. ¹⁶ And it shall be a sign upon your arm, and an *Tefillin and* ornament between your eyes, for with a strong hand HASHEM removed us from *the Exodus* Egypt.' "

PARASHAS BESHALACH

The route to Eretz Yisrael ¹⁷It happened when Pharaoh sent out the people that God did not lead them by way of the land of the Philistines, * because it was near, for God said, "Perhaps the people will reconsider when they see a war, and they will return to Egypt." ¹⁸ So God turned the people toward the way of the Wilderness to the Sea of Reeds. * The Children of Israel were armed when they went up from the land of Egypt. ¹⁹ Moses took the bones of Joseph with him, for he had firmly adjured the Children of Israel, saying, "God will surely remember you, and you shall bring up my bones from here with you."

²⁰ They journeyed from Succoth, and encamped in Etham, at the edge of the Wilderness. ²¹ HASHEM went before them by day in a pillar of cloud to lead them on the way, and by night in a pillar of fire to give them light, so that they could travel day and night. ²² He did not remove the pillar of cloud by day and the pillar of fire by night from before the people.

Desert, going east and then north, so that they would enter the land from the west. This would take them so far from Egypt that it would be difficult for them to return. Even so, there were times in the Wilderness when they complained and wanted to return to Egypt; had such a return been quick and easy, they would surely have attempted it.

13:18. *Sea of Reeds* [or: *Red Sea*]. This may have been the Gulf of Suez, which branches northward from the Red Sea and separates Egypt from the Sinai Desert; but what is known today as the Red Sea is south of the Sinai Peninsula and so far south of the populated area of Egypt that it is unlikely that the Exodus and the later Splitting of the Sea could have taken place there. It may be that the Sea of Reeds was the Great Bitter Lake, which is between the Gulf and the Mediterranean Sea; or the large delta at the mouth of the Nile, in the north of Egypt; or it may have been the southern Mediterranean.

יד

א-ב וַיְדַבֵּר יהוה אֶל־מֹשֶׁה לֵּאמֹר: דַּבֵּר אֶל־בְּנֵי יִשְׂרָאֵל וְיָשֻׁבוּ וְיַחֲנוּ לִפְנֵי פִּי
הַחִירֹת בֵּין מִגְדֹּל וּבֵין הַיָּם לִפְנֵי בַּעַל צְפֹן נִכְחוֹ תַחֲנוּ עַל־הַיָּם: וְאָמַר
ג-ד פַּרְעֹה לִבְנֵי יִשְׂרָאֵל נְבֻכִים הֵם בָּאָרֶץ סָגַר עֲלֵיהֶם הַמִּדְבָּר: וְחִזַּקְתִּי אֶת־
לֵב־פַּרְעֹה וְרָדַף אַחֲרֵיהֶם וְאִכָּבְדָה בְּפַרְעֹה וּבְכָל־חֵילוֹ וְיָדְעוּ מִצְרַיִם
ה כִּי־אֲנִי יהוה וַיַּעֲשׂוּ־כֵן: וַיֻּגַּד לְמֶלֶךְ מִצְרַיִם כִּי בָרַח הָעָם וַיֵּהָפֵךְ לְבַב
פַּרְעֹה וַעֲבָדָיו אֶל־הָעָם וַיֹּאמְרוּ מַה־זֹּאת עָשִׂינוּ כִּי־שִׁלַּחְנוּ אֶת־יִשְׂרָאֵל
ו-ז מֵעָבְדֵנוּ: וַיֶּאְסֹר אֶת־רִכְבּוֹ וְאֶת־עַמּוֹ לָקַח עִמּוֹ: וַיִּקַּח שֵׁשׁ־מֵאוֹת רֶכֶב
ח בָּחוּר וְכֹל רֶכֶב מִצְרָיִם וְשָׁלִשִׁם עַל־כֻּלּוֹ: וַיְחַזֵּק יהוה אֶת־לֵב פַּרְעֹה מֶלֶךְ
שני ט מִצְרַיִם וַיִּרְדֹּף אַחֲרֵי בְּנֵי יִשְׂרָאֵל וּבְנֵי יִשְׂרָאֵל יֹצְאִים בְּיָד רָמָה: וַיִּרְדְּפוּ
מִצְרַיִם אַחֲרֵיהֶם וַיַּשִּׂיגוּ אוֹתָם חֹנִים עַל־הַיָּם כָּל־סוּס רֶכֶב פַּרְעֹה
י וּפָרָשָׁיו וְחֵילוֹ עַל־פִּי הַחִירֹת לִפְנֵי בַּעַל צְפֹן: וּפַרְעֹה הִקְרִיב וַיִּשְׂאוּ בְנֵי־
יִשְׂרָאֵל אֶת־עֵינֵיהֶם וְהִנֵּה מִצְרַיִם נֹסֵעַ אַחֲרֵיהֶם וַיִּירְאוּ מְאֹד וַיִּצְעֲקוּ
יא בְנֵי־יִשְׂרָאֵל אֶל־יהוה: וַיֹּאמְרוּ אֶל־מֹשֶׁה הֲמִבְּלִי אֵין־קְבָרִים בְּמִצְרַיִם
יב לְקַחְתָּנוּ לָמוּת בַּמִּדְבָּר מַה־זֹּאת עָשִׂיתָ לָּנוּ לְהוֹצִיאָנוּ מִמִּצְרָיִם: הֲלֹא־
זֶה הַדָּבָר אֲשֶׁר דִּבַּרְנוּ אֵלֶיךָ בְמִצְרַיִם לֵאמֹר חֲדַל מִמֶּנּוּ וְנַעַבְדָה אֶת־
יג מִצְרָיִם כִּי טוֹב לָנוּ עֲבֹד אֶת־מִצְרַיִם מִמֻּתֵנוּ בַּמִּדְבָּר: וַיֹּאמֶר מֹשֶׁה אֶל־
הָעָם אַל־תִּירָאוּ הִתְיַצְּבוּ וּרְאוּ אֶת־יְשׁוּעַת יהוה אֲשֶׁר־יַעֲשֶׂה לָכֶם הַיּוֹם
כִּי אֲשֶׁר רְאִיתֶם אֶת־מִצְרַיִם הַיּוֹם לֹא תֹסִפוּ לִרְאֹתָם עוֹד עַד־עוֹלָם:
יד יהוה יִלָּחֵם לָכֶם וְאַתֶּם תַּחֲרִשׁוּן:
שלישי טו-טז וַיֹּאמֶר יהוה אֶל־מֹשֶׁה מַה־תִּצְעַק אֵלָי דַּבֵּר אֶל־בְּנֵי־יִשְׂרָאֵל וְיִסָּעוּ: וְאַתָּה
הָרֵם אֶת־מַטְּךָ וּנְטֵה אֶת־יָדְךָ עַל־הַיָּם וּבְקָעֵהוּ וְיָבֹאוּ בְנֵי־יִשְׂרָאֵל בְּתוֹךְ
יז הַיָּם בַּיַּבָּשָׁה: וַאֲנִי הִנְנִי מְחַזֵּק אֶת־לֵב מִצְרַיִם וְיָבֹאוּ אַחֲרֵיהֶם וְאִכָּבְדָה
יח בְּפַרְעֹה וּבְכָל־חֵילוֹ בְּרִכְבּוֹ וּבְפָרָשָׁיו: וְיָדְעוּ מִצְרַיִם כִּי־אֲנִי יהוה בְּהִכָּבְדִי
יט בְּפַרְעֹה בְּרִכְבּוֹ וּבְפָרָשָׁיו: וַיִּסַּע מַלְאַךְ הָאֱלֹהִים הַהֹלֵךְ לִפְנֵי מַחֲנֵה
יִשְׂרָאֵל וַיֵּלֶךְ מֵאַחֲרֵיהֶם וַיִּסַּע עַמּוּד הֶעָנָן מִפְּנֵיהֶם וַיַּעֲמֹד מֵאַחֲרֵיהֶם:
כ וַיָּבֹא בֵּין מַחֲנֵה מִצְרַיִם וּבֵין מַחֲנֵה יִשְׂרָאֵל וַיְהִי הֶעָנָן וְהַחֹשֶׁךְ וַיָּאֶר אֶת־
כא הַלָּיְלָה וְלֹא־קָרַב זֶה אֶל־זֶה כָּל־הַלָּיְלָה: וַיֵּט מֹשֶׁה אֶת־יָדוֹ עַל־הַיָּם
וַיּוֹלֶךְ יהוה אֶת־הַיָּם בְּרוּחַ קָדִים עַזָּה כָּל־הַלַּיְלָה וַיָּשֶׂם אֶת־הַיָּם לֶחָרָבָה
כב וַיִּבָּקְעוּ הַמָּיִם: וַיָּבֹאוּ בְנֵי־יִשְׂרָאֵל בְּתוֹךְ הַיָּם בַּיַּבָּשָׁה וְהַמַּיִם לָהֶם חוֹמָה

14:3-8. Although Pharaoh had demanded that the Jews leave the country as soon as possible, he thought that they were going only for a three-day trip. Even if they had no intention of returning, Pharaoh should have been so terrified by the plagues, and especially the Plague of the Firstborn, that it would have been sheer insanity for him to try to bring them back. However, God wished to demonstrate conclusively that He was the Master of all; for when the wicked are punished, God is glorified. For this to take place, three things had to happen: Pharaoh had to realize that the Jews were not returning, he had to regret his decision to let them go, and he had to overcome his terror at standing in their way. Our passage reveals the process through which God made this happen.

14:13-18. There were two responses to the Jewish fears: First, Moses assured the people that not only would God

14 ¹Hashem spoke to Moses, saying, ² "Speak to the Children of Israel and let them turn back and encamp before Pi-hahiroth, between Migdol and the sea, before Baal-zephon; you shall encamp opposite it, by the sea. ³ Pharaoh will say* of the Children of Israel, 'They are imprisoned in the land, the

Pharaoh's change of heart

Wilderness has locked them in.' ⁴ I shall strengthen the heart of Pharaoh and he will pursue them, and I will be glorified through Pharaoh and his entire army, and Egypt will know that I am Hashem." And so they did.

⁵ It was told to the king of Egypt that the people had fled; and the heart of Pharaoh and his servants became transformed regarding the people, and they said, "What is this that we have done that we have sent away Israel from serving us?"

⁶ He harnessed his chariot and attracted his people with him. ⁷ He took six hundred elite chariots and all the chariots of Egypt, with officers on them all. ⁸ Hashem strengthened the heart of Pharaoh, king of Egypt, and he pursued the Children of Israel — and the Children of Israel were going out with an upraised arm.

Israel panics

⁹ Egypt pursued them and overtook them, encamped by the sea — all the horses and chariots of Pharaoh, and his horsemen and army — by Pi-hahiroth before Baal-zephon. ¹⁰ Pharaoh approached; the Children of Israel raised their eyes and behold! — Egypt was journeying after them, and they were very frightened; the Children of Israel cried out to Hashem. ¹¹ They said to Moses, "Were there no graves in Egypt that you took us to die in the Wilderness? What is this that you have done to us to take us out of Egypt? ¹² Is this not the statement that we made to you in Egypt, saying, 'Let us be and we will serve Egypt'? — for it is better that we should serve Egypt than that we should die in the Wilderness!"

God's assurance

¹³ Moses said to the people, "Do not fear!* Stand fast and see the salvation of Hashem that He will perform for you today; for as you have seen Egypt today, you shall not see them ever again! ¹⁴ Hashem shall make war for you, and you shall remain silent."

¹⁵ Hashem said to Moses, "Why do you cry out to Me? Speak to the Children of Israel and let them journey forth! ¹⁶ And you — lift up your staff and stretch out your arm over the sea and split it; and the Children of Israel shall come into the midst of the sea on dry land. ¹⁷ And I — behold! — I shall strengthen the heart of Egypt and they will come after them; and I will be glorified through Pharaoh and through his entire army, through his chariots and through his horsemen. ¹⁸ Egypt will know that I am Hashem, when I am glorified through Pharaoh, his chariots, and his horsemen."

The sea splits

¹⁹ The angel of God who had been going in front of the camp of Israel moved and went behind them; and the pillar of cloud moved from in front of them and went behind them. ²⁰ It came between the camp of Egypt and the camp of Israel and there were cloud and darkness — while it illuminated the night — and one did not draw near the other all the night. ²¹ Moses stretched out his hand over the sea, and Hashem moved the sea with a strong east wind all the night, and He turned the sea to damp land and the water split. ²² The Children of Israel came within the sea on dry land; and the water was a wall for them,

wage their battle, He would eliminate Egypt as a threat to them. Second, God told Moses that the time for prayer was over; all that remained was for Israel to prove its faith by plunging into the sea.

כג מֵימִינָם וּמִשְּׂמֹאלָם: וַיִּרְדְּפוּ מִצְרַיִם וַיָּבֹאוּ אַחֲרֵיהֶם כֹּל סוּס פַּרְעֹה

כד רִכְבּוֹ וּפָרָשָׁיו אֶל־תּוֹךְ הַיָּם: וַיְהִי בְּאַשְׁמֹרֶת הַבֹּקֶר וַיַּשְׁקֵף יהוה אֶל־

כה מַחֲנֵה מִצְרַיִם בְּעַמּוּד אֵשׁ וְעָנָן וַיָּהָם אֵת מַחֲנֵה מִצְרָיִם: וַיָּסַר אֵת אֹפַן

מַרְכְּבֹתָיו וַיְנַהֲגֵהוּ בִּכְבֵדֻת וַיֹּאמֶר מִצְרַיִם אָנוּסָה מִפְּנֵי יִשְׂרָאֵל כִּי יהוה

נִלְחָם לָהֶם בְּמִצְרָיִם:

רביעי כו וַיֹּאמֶר יהוה אֶל־מֹשֶׁה נְטֵה אֶת־יָדְךָ עַל־הַיָּם וְיָשֻׁבוּ הַמַּיִם עַל־

כז מִצְרַיִם עַל־רִכְבּוֹ וְעַל־פָּרָשָׁיו: וַיֵּט מֹשֶׁה אֶת־יָדוֹ עַל־הַיָּם וַיָּשָׁב הַיָּם

לִפְנוֹת בֹּקֶר לְאֵיתָנוֹ וּמִצְרַיִם נָסִים לִקְרָאתוֹ וַיְנַעֵר יהוה אֶת־מִצְרַיִם

כח בְּתוֹךְ הַיָּם: וַיָּשֻׁבוּ הַמַּיִם וַיְכַסּוּ אֶת־הָרֶכֶב וְאֶת־הַפָּרָשִׁים לְכֹל חֵיל

כט פַּרְעֹה *הַבָּאִים אַחֲרֵיהֶם בַּיָּם לֹא־נִשְׁאַר בָּהֶם עַד־אֶחָד: וּבְנֵי יִשְׂרָאֵל

הָלְכוּ בַיַּבָּשָׁה בְּתוֹךְ הַיָּם וְהַמַּיִם לָהֶם חֹמָה מִימִינָם וּמִשְּׂמֹאלָם:

ל וַיּוֹשַׁע יהוה בַּיּוֹם הַהוּא אֶת־יִשְׂרָאֵל מִיַּד מִצְרָיִם וַיַּרְא יִשְׂרָאֵל אֶת־

לא מִצְרַיִם מֵת עַל־שְׂפַת הַיָּם: וַיַּרְא יִשְׂרָאֵל אֶת־הַיָּד הַגְּדֹלָה אֲשֶׁר עָשָׂה

יהוה בְּמִצְרַיִם וַיִּירְאוּ הָעָם אֶת־יהוה וַיַּאֲמִינוּ בַּיהוה וּבְמֹשֶׁה עַבְדּוֹ:

*בראש עמוד
בי"ה שמיר סימן

טו א אָז יָשִׁיר־מֹשֶׁה וּבְנֵי יִשְׂרָאֵל אֶת־הַשִּׁירָה הַזֹּאת לַיהוה וַיֹּאמְרוּ

לֵאמֹר אָשִׁירָה לַיהוה כִּי־גָאֹה גָּאָה סוּס

ב וְרֹכְבוֹ רָמָה בַיָּם: עָזִּי וְזִמְרָת יָהּ וַיְהִי־לִי

לִישׁוּעָה זֶה אֵלִי וְאַנְוֵהוּ אֱלֹהֵי

ג אָבִי וַאֲרֹמְמֶנְהוּ: יהוה אִישׁ מִלְחָמָה יהוה

ד שְׁמוֹ: מַרְכְּבֹת פַּרְעֹה וְחֵילוֹ יָרָה בַיָּם וּמִבְחַר

ה שָׁלִשָׁיו טֻבְּעוּ בְיַם־סוּף: תְּהֹמֹת יְכַסְיֻמוּ יָרְדוּ בִמְצוֹלֹת

ו כְּמוֹ־אָבֶן: יְמִינְךָ יהוה נֶאְדָּרִי בַּכֹּחַ יְמִינְךָ

ז יהוה תִּרְעַץ אוֹיֵב: וּבְרֹב גְּאוֹנְךָ תַּהֲרֹס

ח קָמֶיךָ תְּשַׁלַּח חֲרֹנְךָ יֹאכְלֵמוֹ כַּקַּשׁ: וּבְרוּחַ

אַפֶּיךָ נֶעֶרְמוּ מַיִם נִצְּבוּ כְמוֹ־נֵד

ט נֹזְלִים קָפְאוּ תְהֹמֹת בְּלֶב־יָם: אָמַר

אוֹיֵב אֶרְדֹּף אַשִּׂיג אֲחַלֵּק שָׁלָל תִּמְלָאֵמוֹ

י נַפְשִׁי אָרִיק חַרְבִּי תּוֹרִישֵׁמוֹ יָדִי: נָשַׁפְתָּ

בְרוּחֲךָ כִּסָּמוֹ יָם צָלֲלוּ כַּעוֹפֶרֶת בְּמַיִם

יא אַדִּירִים: מִי־כָמֹכָה בָּאֵלִם יהוה מִי

כָּמֹכָה נֶאְדָּר בַּקֹּדֶשׁ נוֹרָא תְהִלֹּת עֹשֵׂה

14:30-31. God wanted the Jews to see the full extent of the salvation, so He had the sea toss the bodies of the dead Egyptians onto the shore where the Jews had emerged. Otherwise, the Jews might think, "Just as we came out on this bank, so the Egyptians came up on the other side and will pursue us" (*Rashi*).

on their right and on their left.

²³ *Egypt pursued and came after them — every horse of Pharaoh, his chariots, and his horsemen — into the midst of the sea.* ²⁴ *It happened at the morning watch that* HASHEM *looked down at the camp of Egypt with a pillar of fire and cloud, and He confounded the camp of Egypt.* ²⁵ *He removed the wheels of their chariots and caused them to drive with difficulty. Egypt said, "I shall flee before Israel, for* HASHEM *is waging war for them against Egypt."*

²⁶ HASHEM *said to Moses, "Stretch out your hand over the sea, and the water will go back upon Egypt, upon its chariots and upon its horsemen."* ²⁷ *Moses stretched out his hand over the sea, and toward morning the water went back to its power as the Egyptians were fleeing toward it; and* HASHEM *churned Egypt*

The water crashes down upon Egypt

in the midst of the sea. ²⁸ *The water came back and covered the chariots and the horsemen of the entire army of Pharaoh, who were coming behind them in the sea — there remained not a one of them.* ²⁹ *The Children of Israel went on dry land in the midst of the sea; the water was a wall for them, on their right and on their left.*

The salvation

³⁰ *On that day,* HASHEM *saved Israel* from the hand of Egypt, and Israel saw the Egyptians dead on the seashore.* ³¹ *Israel saw the great hand that* HASHEM *inflicted upon Egypt; and the people revered* HASHEM, *and they had faith in* HASHEM *and in Moses, His servant.*

15

The Song by the Sea

¹ Then *Moses and the Children of Israel chose to sing this song* to* HASHEM, *and they said the following:*

I shall sing to HASHEM *for He is exalted above the arrogant, having hurled horse with its rider into the sea.*

² *The might and vengeance of God was salvation for me. This is my God* and I will build Him a Sanctuary; the God of my father and I will exalt Him.*

³ HASHEM *is Master of war — His name is* HASHEM.

⁴ *Pharaoh's chariots and army He threw in the sea, and the pick of his officers were mired in the Sea of Reeds.*

⁵ *Deep waters covered them; they descended in the depths like stone.*

⁶ *Your right hand,* HASHEM, *is glorified with strength; Your right hand,* HASHEM, *smashes the enemy.*

⁷ *In Your abundant grandeur You shatter Your opponents; You send forth Your wrath, it consumes them like straw.*

⁸ *At a blast from Your nostrils the waters were heaped up; straight as a wall stood the running water, the deep waters congealed in the heart of the sea.*

⁹ *The enemy declared, "I will pursue, I will overtake, I will divide plunder; I will satisfy my lust with them. I will unsheathe my sword, my hand will impoverish them."*

¹⁰ *You blew with Your wind — the sea enshrouded them; the mighty sank like lead in water.*

¹¹ *Who is like You among the heavenly powers,* HASHEM! *Who is like You, mighty in holiness, too awesome for praise, Doer of wonders!*

15:1. Moses *led* the song, but all the people sang responsively with him (*Sotah* 30b). The uniqueness of this Song was that an entire nation — not merely its prophets, scholars, and leaders — could rise to a state of prophecy.

15:2. So clear was the manifestation of Godliness that even the humblest Jew could literally point with his finger and say, "*This is my God!*" (*Rashi*).

נָטִיתָ יְמִינְךָ תִּבְלָעֵמוֹ אָרֶץ: יב-יג   פֶּלֶא: נָחִיתָ

בְחַסְדְּךָ עַם־זוּ גָּאָלְתָּ   נֵהַלְתָּ בְעָזְּךָ אֶל־נְוֵה

קָדְשֶׁךָ:   יד   שָׁמְעוּ עַמִּים יִרְגָּזוּן   חִיל

אָחַז יֹשְׁבֵי פְּלָשֶׁת: טו   אָז נִבְהֲלוּ אַלּוּפֵי

אֱדוֹם   אֵילֵי מוֹאָב יֹאחֲזֵמוֹ רָעַד   נָמֹגוּ

כֹּל יֹשְׁבֵי כְנָעַן: טז   תִּפֹּל עֲלֵיהֶם אֵימָתָה

וָפַחַד   בִּגְדֹל זְרוֹעֲךָ יִדְּמוּ כָּאָבֶן   עַד־

יַעֲבֹר עַמְּךָ יְהֹוָה   עַד־יַעֲבֹר עַם־זוּ

קָנִיתָ:   יז   תְּבִאֵמוֹ וְתִטָּעֵמוֹ בְּהַר נַחֲלָתְךָ   מָכוֹן

לְשִׁבְתְּךָ פָּעַלְתָּ יְהֹוָה   מִקְּדָשׁ אֲדֹנָי כּוֹנְנוּ

יָדֶיךָ:   יח-יט   יְהֹוָה ׀ יִמְלֹךְ לְעֹלָם וָעֶד: כִּי בָא

סוּס פַּרְעֹה בְּרִכְבּוֹ וּבְפָרָשָׁיו בַּיָּם   וַיָּשֶׁב יְהֹוָה עֲלֵהֶם אֶת־מֵי

הַיָּם   וּבְנֵי יִשְׂרָאֵל הָלְכוּ בַיַּבָּשָׁה בְּתוֹךְ

הַיָּם:

כ   וַתִּקַּח מִרְיָם הַנְּבִיאָה אֲחוֹת אַהֲרֹן אֶת־הַתֹּף בְּיָדָהּ   וַתֵּצֶאןָ כָל־הַנָּשִׁים

אַחֲרֶיהָ בְּתֻפִּים וּבִמְחֹלֹת: כא   וַתַּעַן לָהֶם מִרְיָם שִׁירוּ לַיהֹוָה כִּי־גָאֹה גָּאָה

סוּס וְרֹכְבוֹ רָמָה בַיָּם: כב   וַיַּסַּע מֹשֶׁה אֶת־יִשְׂרָאֵל מִיַּם־סוּף

וַיֵּצְאוּ אֶל־מִדְבַּר־שׁוּר וַיֵּלְכוּ שְׁלֹשֶׁת־יָמִים בַּמִּדְבָּר וְלֹא־מָצְאוּ מָיִם:

כג   וַיָּבֹאוּ מָרָתָה וְלֹא יָכְלוּ לִשְׁתֹּת מַיִם מִמָּרָה כִּי מָרִים הֵם עַל־כֵּן קָרָא־

שְׁמָהּ מָרָה: כד-כה   וַיִּלֹּנוּ הָעָם עַל־מֹשֶׁה לֵּאמֹר מַה־נִּשְׁתֶּה: וַיִּצְעַק אֶל־יְהֹוָה

וַיּוֹרֵהוּ יְהֹוָה עֵץ וַיַּשְׁלֵךְ אֶל־הַמַּיִם וַיִּמְתְּקוּ הַמָּיִם שָׁם שָׂם לוֹ חֹק וּמִשְׁפָּט

וְשָׁם נִסָּהוּ:   כו   וַיֹּאמֶר אִם־שָׁמוֹעַ תִּשְׁמַע לְקוֹל ׀ יְהֹוָה אֱלֹהֶיךָ וְהַיָּשָׁר בְּעֵינָיו

תַּעֲשֶׂה וְהַאֲזַנְתָּ לְמִצְוֹתָיו וְשָׁמַרְתָּ כָּל־חֻקָּיו כָּל־הַמַּחֲלָה אֲשֶׁר־שַׂמְתִּי

בְמִצְרַיִם לֹא־אָשִׂים עָלֶיךָ כִּי אֲנִי יְהֹוָה רֹפְאֶךָ:   כז   וַיָּבֹאוּ   חמישי

אֵילִמָה וְשָׁם שְׁתֵּים עֶשְׂרֵה עֵינֹת מַיִם וְשִׁבְעִים תְּמָרִים וַיַּחֲנוּ־שָׁם

עַל־הַמָּיִם: א   וַיִּסְעוּ מֵאֵילִם וַיָּבֹאוּ כָּל־עֲדַת בְּנֵי־יִשְׂרָאֵל אֶל־מִדְבַּר־סִין   טז

אֲשֶׁר בֵּין־אֵילִם וּבֵין סִינָי בַּחֲמִשָּׁה עָשָׂר יוֹם לַחֹדֶשׁ הַשֵּׁנִי לְצֵאתָם

מֵאֶרֶץ מִצְרָיִם: ב   °וַיִּלּוֹנוּ [°וַיִּלּוֹנוּ ק] כָּל־עֲדַת בְּנֵי־יִשְׂרָאֵל עַל־מֹשֶׁה

15:14-16. Nations will be unsettled by the coming of the Jews, but for different reasons. The Philistines had massacred large numbers of the tribe of Ephraim, who had left Egypt prematurely on the mistaken notion that the time of the redemption had arrived. Thus, the Philistines feared that they would be the objects of revenge. Ammon and Moab had no reason for fear, since their lands were not part of *Eretz Yisrael* — in fact, the Jews would later be commanded not to attack them — but their hatred of Israel was so great that they could not tolerate the idea that the nation would be independent in its own land. The

Canaanites had reason to *melt,* for they were about to be displaced. Those who were far away felt *fear* [אֵימָתָה]; but those who were closer were in greater danger and therefore felt *terror* [פַּחַד] (*Rashi*).

15:20-21. The Talmud (*Sotah* 11b) teaches, "In the merit of righteous women of that generation were the Children of Israel redeemed from Egypt." In addition to maintaining the spiritual vigor of the nation during the years of oppression, the women had greater faith than the men that there would be an eventual redemption, accompanied by miracles of great magnitude.

¹² You stretched out Your right hand — the earth swallowed them.

¹³ With Your kindness You guided this people that You redeemed; You led with Your might to Your holy abode.

¹⁴ Peoples heard* — they were agitated; terror gripped the dwellers of Philistia.

¹⁵ Then the chieftains of Edom were confounded, trembling gripped the powers of Moab, all the dwellers of Canaan dissolved.

¹⁶ May fear and terror befall them, at the greatness of Your arm may they be still as stone; until Your people passes through, HASHEM — until this people You have acquired passes through.

¹⁷ You will bring them and implant them on the mount of Your heritage, the foundation of Your dwelling-place that You, HASHEM, have made — the Sanctuary, my Lord, that Your hands established.

¹⁸ HASHEM shall reign for all eternity!

¹⁹ When Pharaoh's cavalry came with his chariots and horsemen into the sea and HASHEM turned back the waters of the sea upon them, the Children of Israel walked on the dry land amid the sea.

The women sing   ²⁰ Miriam the prophetess,* sister of Aaron, took the drum in her hand and all the women went forth after her with drums and with dances. ²¹ Miriam spoke up to them, "Sing to HASHEM for He is exalted above the arrogant, having hurled horse with its rider into the sea."

²² Moses caused Israel to journey from the Sea of Reeds and they went out to the Wilderness of Shur; they went for a three-day period in the Wilderness, but *Marah: Israel tests God* they did not find water.* ²³ They came to Marah,* but they could not drink the waters of Marah because they were bitter; therefore they named it Marah. ²⁴ The people complained against Moses, saying, "What shall we drink?"

²⁵ He cried out to HASHEM, and HASHEM showed him a tree; he threw it into the water and the water became sweet. There He established for [the nation] a decree and an ordinance, and there He tested it. ²⁶ He said, "If you hearken diligently to the voice of HASHEM, your God, and do what is just in His eyes, give ear to His commandments and observe all His decrees, then any of the diseases that I placed in Egypt, I will not bring upon you, for I am HASHEM, your Healer."*

²⁷ They arrived at Elim, where there were twelve springs of water and seventy date-palms; they encamped there by the water.

16 ¹ They journeyed from Elim, and the entire assembly of the Children of Israel arrived at the Wilderness of Sin, which is between Elim and Sinai, on the fifteenth day of the second month from their departure from the land of Egypt. ² The entire assembly of the Children of Israel complained against Moses

---

15:22-27. After the momentous miracles at the sea, how could they have doubted God's readiness to give them a necessity of life — water? *R' Hirsch* explains that the purpose of Israel's journey through the Wilderness was to show that God is involved in daily, "petty" human affairs, as well as in cosmic occurrences. It is easy to think, as many still do, that God creates worlds and splits seas, but is unconcerned with the water or food supply of communities and individuals. This is what frightened the Jews in the Wilderness. When there was no water, the nation

feared that it was being left to its own devices. The people were not wrong in asking for water — thirsty people surely have that right — but in protesting so vociferously.

15:23. The word מָרָה means *bitterness*, as in מָרוֹר, *maror*, the bitter herbs of the Seder.

15:26. Homiletically, *R' Tzaddok HaCohen* commented that even when God brings suffering upon Israel, His intention is *never* to destroy them, as He did to Egypt. Rather, God is Israel's Healer, and even exile and suffering are only to purge them of sin and influence them to repent.

ג וְעַל־אַהֲרֹן בַּמִּדְבָּר: וַיֹּאמְרוּ אֲלֵהֶם בְּנֵי יִשְׂרָאֵל מִי־יִתֵּן מוּתֵנוּ בְיַד־
יְהוָה בְּאֶרֶץ מִצְרַיִם בְּשִׁבְתֵּנוּ עַל־סִיר הַבָּשָׂר בְּאָכְלֵנוּ לֶחֶם לָשֹׂבַע
כִּי־הוֹצֵאתֶם אֹתָנוּ אֶל־הַמִּדְבָּר הַזֶּה לְהָמִית אֶת־כָּל־הַקָּהָל הַזֶּה
ד בָּרָעָב: וַיֹּאמֶר יְהוָה אֶל־מֹשֶׁה הִנְנִי מַמְטִיר לָכֶם לֶחֶם
מִן־הַשָּׁמָיִם וְיָצָא הָעָם וְלָקְטוּ דְּבַר־יוֹם בְּיוֹמוֹ לְמַעַן אֲנַסֶּנּוּ הֲיֵלֵךְ
בְּתוֹרָתִי אִם־לֹא: וְהָיָה בַּיּוֹם הַשִּׁשִּׁי וְהֵכִינוּ אֵת אֲשֶׁר־יָבִיאוּ וְהָיָה
ו מִשְׁנֶה עַל אֲשֶׁר־יִלְקְטוּ יוֹם ׀ יוֹם: וַיֹּאמֶר מֹשֶׁה וְאַהֲרֹן אֶל־כָּל־בְּנֵי
ז יִשְׂרָאֵל עֶרֶב וִידַעְתֶּם כִּי יְהוָה הוֹצִיא אֶתְכֶם מֵאֶרֶץ מִצְרָיִם: וּבֹקֶר
וּרְאִיתֶם אֶת־כְּבוֹד יְהוָה בְּשָׁמְעוֹ אֶת־תְּלֻנֹּתֵיכֶם עַל־יְהוָה וְנַחְנוּ מָה כִּי
ח תַלִּינוּ ⟨°תַלּוֹנוּ ק⟩ עָלֵינוּ: וַיֹּאמֶר מֹשֶׁה בְּתֵת יְהוָה לָכֶם בָּעֶרֶב בָּשָׂר
לֶאֱכֹל וְלֶחֶם בַּבֹּקֶר לִשְׂבֹּעַ בִּשְׁמֹעַ יְהוָה אֶת־תְּלֻנֹּתֵיכֶם אֲשֶׁר־אַתֶּם
ט מַלִּינִם עָלָיו וְנַחְנוּ מָה לֹא־עָלֵינוּ תְלֻנֹּתֵיכֶם כִּי עַל־יְהוָה: וַיֹּאמֶר מֹשֶׁה
אֶל־אַהֲרֹן אֱמֹר אֶל־כָּל־עֲדַת בְּנֵי יִשְׂרָאֵל קִרְבוּ לִפְנֵי יְהוָה כִּי שָׁמַע אֵת
י תְּלֻנֹּתֵיכֶם: וַיְהִי כְּדַבֵּר אַהֲרֹן אֶל־כָּל־עֲדַת בְּנֵי־יִשְׂרָאֵל וַיִּפְנוּ אֶל־
הַמִּדְבָּר וְהִנֵּה כְּבוֹד יְהוָה נִרְאָה בֶּעָנָן:

יא-יב וַיְדַבֵּר יְהוָה אֶל־מֹשֶׁה לֵּאמֹר: שָׁמַעְתִּי אֶת־תְּלוּנֹת בְּנֵי יִשְׂרָאֵל דַּבֵּר
אֲלֵהֶם לֵאמֹר בֵּין הָעַרְבַּיִם תֹּאכְלוּ בָשָׂר וּבַבֹּקֶר תִּשְׂבְּעוּ־לָחֶם וִידַעְתֶּם
יג כִּי אֲנִי יְהוָה אֱלֹהֵיכֶם: וַיְהִי בָעֶרֶב וַתַּעַל הַשְּׂלָו וַתְּכַס אֶת־הַמַּחֲנֶה וּבַבֹּקֶר
יד הָיְתָה שִׁכְבַת הַטַּל סָבִיב לַמַּחֲנֶה: וַתַּעַל שִׁכְבַת הַטָּל וְהִנֵּה עַל־פְּנֵי
טו הַמִּדְבָּר דַּק מְחֻסְפָּס דַּק כַּכְּפֹר עַל־הָאָרֶץ: וַיִּרְאוּ בְנֵי־יִשְׂרָאֵל וַיֹּאמְרוּ
אִישׁ אֶל־אָחִיו מָן הוּא כִּי לֹא יָדְעוּ מַה־הוּא וַיֹּאמֶר מֹשֶׁה אֲלֵהֶם הוּא
טז הַלֶּחֶם אֲשֶׁר נָתַן יְהוָה לָכֶם לְאָכְלָה: זֶה הַדָּבָר אֲשֶׁר צִוָּה יְהוָה לִקְטוּ
מִמֶּנּוּ אִישׁ לְפִי אָכְלוֹ עֹמֶר לַגֻּלְגֹּלֶת מִסְפַּר נַפְשֹׁתֵיכֶם אִישׁ לַאֲשֶׁר בְּאָהֳלוֹ
יז-יח תִּקָּחוּ: וַיַּעֲשׂוּ־כֵן בְּנֵי יִשְׂרָאֵל וַיִּלְקְטוּ הַמַּרְבֶּה וְהַמַּמְעִיט: וַיָּמֹדּוּ בָעֹמֶר
יט וְלֹא הֶעְדִּיף הַמַּרְבֶּה וְהַמַּמְעִיט לֹא הֶחְסִיר אִישׁ לְפִי־אָכְלוֹ לָקָטוּ: וַיֹּאמֶר
מֹשֶׁה אֲלֵהֶם אִישׁ אַל־יוֹתֵר מִמֶּנּוּ עַד־בֹּקֶר: וְלֹא־שָׁמְעוּ אֶל־מֹשֶׁה וַיּוֹתִרוּ
כ אֲנָשִׁים מִמֶּנּוּ עַד־בֹּקֶר וַיָּרֻם תּוֹלָעִים וַיִּבְאַשׁ וַיִּקְצֹף עֲלֵהֶם מֹשֶׁה: וַיִּלְקְטוּ
כא אֹתוֹ בַּבֹּקֶר בַּבֹּקֶר אִישׁ כְּפִי אָכְלוֹ וְחַם הַשֶּׁמֶשׁ וְנָמָס: וַיְהִי ׀ בַּיּוֹם הַשִּׁשִּׁי
כב לָקְטוּ לֶחֶם מִשְׁנֶה שְׁנֵי הָעֹמֶר לָאֶחָד וַיָּבֹאוּ כָּל־נְשִׂיאֵי הָעֵדָה וַיַּגִּידוּ

שׁשׁי

16:4-36. The lesson of the sweetened water of Marah had not yet been fully absorbed. When the people felt threatened by hunger, they protested even more vehemently than in Marah, going so far as to say that they were better off in Egypt than now.

This, too, was part of Israel's schooling for eternity, for God was about to give them manna, heavenly food, which proved that deserts cannot hamper God's infinite capacity to provide for His children. Often one hears that the observance of the Torah stands in the way of a livelihood; the blessing of the manna proves the opposite. When Israel neglected the Torah or lost faith, it was thirsty or hungry; when it recognized that God is its Healer and Provider, there was plenty in place of need.

16:22. The Jews gathered their normal daily portion, but when they came home they saw that they had two *omer* and Aaron in the Wilderness. [3] The Children of Israel said to them, "If only we had died by the hand of HASHEM in the land of Egypt, as we sat by the pot of meat, when we ate bread to satiety, for you have taken us out to this Wilderness to kill this entire congregation by famine."

<small>Manna:
Food from
heaven</small> [4] HASHEM said to Moses, "Behold! — I shall rain down for you food from heaven;* let the people go out and pick each day's portion on its day, so that I can test them, whether they will follow My teaching or not. [5] And it shall be that on the sixth day when they prepare what they bring, it will be double what they pick every day."

[6] Moses and Aaron said to all the Children of Israel, "In the evening, you shall know that HASHEM took you out of the land of Egypt. [7] And in the morning you will see the glory of HASHEM, that He has heard your complaints against HASHEM — for what are we that you should incite complaints against us?" — [8] and Moses said, "When, in the evening, HASHEM gives you meat to eat and bread to satiety in the morning, as HASHEM hears your complaints that you complain against Him — for what are we? — not against us are your complaints, but against HASHEM!"

[9] Moses said to Aaron, "Say to the entire assembly of the Children of Israel, 'Approach the presence of HASHEM, for He has heard your complaints.' " [10] When Aaron spoke to the entire assembly of the Children of Israel, they turned to the Wilderness and behold! — the glory of HASHEM appeared in a cloud.

[11] HASHEM spoke to Moses, saying, [12] "I have heard the complaints of the Children of Israel. Speak to them, saying, 'In the afternoon you shall eat meat and in the morning you shall be sated with bread, and you shall know that I am HASHEM, your God.' "

<small>Quail</small> [13] It was toward evening that the quail ascended and covered the camp, and in the morning there was a layer of dew around the camp. [14] The layer of dew ascended and behold! — upon the surface of the Wilderness was something thin, exposed — thin as frost on the earth. [15] The Children of Israel saw and said to one another, "It is food!" — for they did not know what it was. Moses said to them, "This is the food that HASHEM has given you for eating. [16] This is the thing that HASHEM has commanded, 'Gather from it, for every man according to what he eats — an omer per person — according to the number of your people, everyone according to whoever is in his tent shall you take.' "

<small>Equal
portions</small> [17] The Children of Israel did so and they gathered, whoever took more and whoever took less. [18] They measured in an omer and whoever took more had nothing extra and whoever took less was not lacking; everyone according to what he eats had they gathered.

[19] Moses said to them, "No man may leave over from it until morning." [20] But they did not obey Moses and people left over from it until morning and it became infested with worms and it stank; and Moses became angry with them. [21] They gathered it morning by morning, every man according to what he eats, and when the sun grew hot it melted.

[22] It happened on the sixth day that they gathered a double portion of food, * two omers for each; and all the princes of the assembly came and told

---

per capita. The princes reported this irregularity to Moses. Obviously, he had not instructed the people to   gather a double portion every Friday; this was a sin of omission on Moses' part (*Rashi*).

כג לְמֹשֶׁ֔ה וַיֹּ֣אמֶר אֲלֵהֶ֗ם ה֚וּא אֲשֶׁ֣ר דִּבֶּ֣ר יְהֹוָ֔ה שַׁבָּת֧וֹן שַׁבַּת־קֹ֛דֶשׁ לַֽיהֹוָ֖ה מָחָ֑ר אֵ֣ת אֲשֶׁר־תֹּאפ֞וּ אֵפ֗וּ וְאֵ֤ת אֲשֶֽׁר־תְּבַשְּׁלוּ֙ בַּשֵּׁ֔לוּ וְאֵת֙ כָּל־הָ֣עֹדֵ֔ף

כד הַנִּ֧יחוּ לָכֶ֛ם לְמִשְׁמֶ֖רֶת עַד־הַבֹּֽקֶר: וַיַּנִּ֤יחוּ אֹתוֹ֙ עַד־הַבֹּ֔קֶר כַּאֲשֶׁ֖ר צִוָּ֣ה

כה מֹשֶׁ֑ה וְלֹ֣א הִבְאִ֔ישׁ וְרִמָּ֖ה לֹא־הָ֥יְתָה בּֽוֹ: וַיֹּ֤אמֶר מֹשֶׁה֙ אִכְלֻ֣הוּ הַיּ֔וֹם כִּֽי־

כו שַׁבָּ֥ת הַיּ֖וֹם לַֽיהֹוָ֑ה הַיּ֕וֹם לֹ֥א תִמְצָאֻ֖הוּ בַּשָּׂדֶֽה: שֵׁ֣שֶׁת יָמִ֖ים תִּלְקְטֻ֑הוּ וּבַיּ֧וֹם

כז הַשְּׁבִיעִ֛י שַׁבָּ֖ת לֹ֥א יִֽהְיֶה־בּֽוֹ: וַֽיְהִי֙ בַּיּ֣וֹם הַשְּׁבִיעִ֔י יָצְא֥וּ מִן־הָעָ֖ם לִלְקֹ֑ט

כח וְלֹ֖א מָצָֽאוּ: וַיֹּ֥אמֶר יְהֹוָ֖ה אֶל־מֹשֶׁ֑ה עַד־אָ֙נָה֙ מֵֽאַנְתֶּ֔ם

כט לִשְׁמֹ֥ר מִצְוֺתַ֖י וְתֽוֹרֹתָֽי: רְא֗וּ כִּֽי־יְהֹוָה֮ נָתַ֣ן לָכֶ֣ם הַשַּׁבָּת֒ עַל־כֵּ֠ן ה֣וּא נֹתֵ֧ן לָכֶ֛ם בַּיּ֥וֹם הַשִּׁשִּׁ֖י לֶ֣חֶם יוֹמָ֑יִם שְׁב֣וּ ׀ אִ֣ישׁ תַּחְתָּ֗יו אַל־יֵ֥צֵא אִ֛ישׁ מִמְּקֹמ֖וֹ

ל-לא בַּיּ֥וֹם הַשְּׁבִיעִֽי: וַיִּשְׁבְּת֥וּ הָעָ֖ם בַּיּ֥וֹם הַשְּׁבִעִֽי: וַיִּקְרְא֧וּ בֵֽית־יִשְׂרָאֵ֛ל אֶת־

לב שְׁמ֖וֹ מָ֑ן וְה֗וּא כְּזֶ֤רַע גַּד֙ לָבָ֔ן וְטַעְמ֖וֹ כְּצַפִּיחִ֥ת בִּדְבָֽשׁ: וַיֹּ֣אמֶר מֹשֶׁ֗ה זֶ֤ה הַדָּבָר֙ אֲשֶׁ֣ר צִוָּ֣ה יְהֹוָ֔ה מְלֹ֤א הָעֹ֙מֶר֙ מִמֶּ֔נּוּ לְמִשְׁמֶ֖רֶת לְדֹרֹֽתֵיכֶ֑ם לְמַ֣עַן ׀ יִרְא֣וּ אֶת־הַלֶּ֗חֶם אֲשֶׁ֨ר הֶאֱכַ֤לְתִּי אֶתְכֶם֙ בַּמִּדְבָּ֔ר בְּהוֹצִיאִ֥י אֶתְכֶ֖ם מֵאֶ֥רֶץ

לג מִצְרָֽיִם: וַיֹּ֨אמֶר מֹשֶׁ֜ה אֶֽל־אַהֲרֹ֗ן קַ֚ח צִנְצֶ֣נֶת אַחַ֔ת וְתֶן־

לד שָׁ֥מָּה מְלֹֽא־הָעֹ֖מֶר מָ֑ן וְהַנַּ֤ח אֹתוֹ֙ לִפְנֵ֣י יְהֹוָ֔ה לְמִשְׁמֶ֖רֶת לְדֹרֹֽתֵיכֶֽם: כַּאֲשֶׁ֛ר צִוָּ֥ה יְהֹוָ֖ה

לה אֶל־מֹשֶׁ֑ה וַיַּנִּיחֵ֧הוּ אַהֲרֹ֛ן לִפְנֵ֥י הָעֵדֻ֖ת לְמִשְׁמָֽרֶת: וּבְנֵ֣י יִשְׂרָאֵ֗ל אָֽכְל֤וּ אֶת־הַמָּן֙ אַרְבָּעִ֣ים שָׁנָ֔ה עַד־בֹּאָ֖ם אֶל־אֶ֣רֶץ נוֹשָׁ֑בֶת אֶת־הַמָּן֙ אָֽכְל֔וּ עַד־

לו בֹּאָ֕ם אֶל־קְצֵ֖ה אֶ֥רֶץ כְּנָֽעַן: וְהָעֹ֕מֶר עֲשִׂרִ֥ית הָאֵיפָ֖ה הֽוּא:

יז שביעי א וַ֠יִּסְע֠וּ כָּל־עֲדַ֨ת בְּנֵֽי־יִשְׂרָאֵ֧ל מִמִּדְבַּר־סִ֛ין לְמַסְעֵיהֶ֖ם עַל־פִּ֣י יְהֹוָ֑ה וַֽיַּחֲנוּ֙

ב בִּרְפִידִ֔ים וְאֵ֥ין מַ֖יִם לִשְׁתֹּ֥ת הָעָֽם: וַיָּ֤רֶב הָעָם֙ עִם־מֹשֶׁ֔ה וַיֹּ֣אמְר֔וּ תְּנוּ־לָ֥נוּ מַ֖יִם וְנִשְׁתֶּ֑ה וַיֹּ֤אמֶר לָהֶם֙ מֹשֶׁ֔ה מַה־תְּרִיבוּן֙ עִמָּדִ֔י מַה־תְּנַסּ֖וּן אֶת־יְהֹוָֽה:

ג וַיִּצְמָ֨א שָׁ֤ם הָעָם֙ לַמַּ֔יִם וַיָּ֥לֶן הָעָ֖ם עַל־מֹשֶׁ֑ה וַיֹּ֗אמֶר לָ֤מָּה זֶּה֙ הֶעֱלִיתָ֣נוּ

ד מִמִּצְרַ֔יִם לְהָמִ֥ית אֹתִ֛י וְאֶת־בָּנַ֥י וְאֶת־מִקְנַ֖י בַּצָּמָֽא: וַיִּצְעַ֤ק מֹשֶׁה֙ אֶל־

ה יְהֹוָ֣ה לֵאמֹ֔ר מָ֥ה אֶעֱשֶׂ֖ה לָעָ֣ם הַזֶּ֑ה ע֥וֹד מְעַ֖ט וּסְקָלֻֽנִי: וַיֹּ֨אמֶר יְהֹוָ֜ה אֶל־מֹשֶׁ֗ה עֲבֹר֙ לִפְנֵ֣י הָעָ֔ם וְקַ֥ח אִתְּךָ֖ מִזִּקְנֵ֣י יִשְׂרָאֵ֑ל וּמַטְּךָ֗ אֲשֶׁ֨ר הִכִּ֤יתָ בּוֹ֙

ו אֶת־הַיְאֹ֔ר קַ֥ח בְּיָדְךָ֖ וְהָלָֽכְתָּ: הִנְנִ֣י עֹמֵד֩ לְפָנֶ֨יךָ שָּׁ֜ם ׀ עַל־הַצּוּר֮ בְּחֹרֵב֒ וְהִכִּ֣יתָ בַצּ֗וּר וְיָצְא֥וּ מִמֶּ֛נּוּ מַ֖יִם וְשָׁתָ֣ה הָעָ֑ם וַיַּ֤עַשׂ כֵּן֙ מֹשֶׁ֔ה לְעֵינֵ֖י זִקְנֵ֥י

ז יִשְׂרָאֵֽל: וַיִּקְרָא֙ שֵׁ֣ם הַמָּק֔וֹם מַסָּ֖ה וּמְרִיבָ֑ה עַל־רִ֣יב ׀ בְּנֵ֣י יִשְׂרָאֵ֗ל וְעַ֨ל נַסֹּתָ֤ם אֶת־יְהֹוָה֙ לֵאמֹ֔ר הֲיֵ֧שׁ יְהֹוָ֛ה בְּקִרְבֵּ֖נוּ אִם־אָֽיִן:

ח-ט וַיָּבֹ֖א עֲמָלֵ֑ק וַיִּלָּ֥חֶם עִם־יִשְׂרָאֵ֖ל בִּרְפִידִֽם: וַיֹּ֨אמֶר מֹשֶׁ֤ה אֶל־יְהוֹשֻׁ֙עַ֙

READING
FOR PURIM
17:8-16

16:35. The manna fell until the seventh of Adar, when Moses died, before the people had crossed the Jordan into *Eretz Yisrael*. From then on, remnants of manna remained in their vessels and they continued to eat it until the sixteenth of Nissan, when they were in the land and were able to eat its produce (*Kiddushin* 38a).

17:1-7. Test and contention. Again, the nation is with-

out a basic requirement of life and it complains bitterly.

God put them through this ordeal in order to train them to turn to Him in prayer when faced with deprivation. Instead of turning on Moses as if the water spigot was in his control, they should have prayed to God for water.

17:7. *Massah U'Meribah*, literally: *test and contention*. The people *tested* God to see if He was truly among them.

Preparation
for the
Sabbath Moses. [23] He said to them, "This is what HASHEM had spoken; tomorrow is a rest day, a holy Sabbath to HASHEM. Bake what you wish to bake and cook what you wish to cook; and whatever is left over, put away for yourselves as a safekeeping until the morning. [24] They put it away until morning, as Moses had commanded; it did not stink and there was no infestation in it.

[25] Moses said, "Eat it today, for today is a Sabbath for HASHEM; today you shall not find it in the field. [26] Six days shall you gather it, but the seventh day is a Sabbath, on it there will be none." [27] It happened on the seventh day that some of the people went out to gather, and they did not find.

[28] HASHEM said to Moses, "How long will you refuse to observe My command-ments and My teachings? [29] See that HASHEM has given you the Sabbath; that is why He gives you on the sixth day a two-day portion of bread. Let every man remain in his place; let no man leave his place on the seventh day." [30] The people rested on the seventh day.

[31] The House of Israel called it manna. It was like coriander seed, it was white, and it tasted like a cake fried in honey. [32] Moses said, "This is the thing that HASHEM has commanded: A full omer of it shall be a safekeeping for your generations, so that they will see the food with which I fed you in the Wilderness when I took you out of Egypt." [33] Moses said to Aaron, "Take one jar and put a full omer of manna into it; place it before HASHEM for a safekeeping for your generations." [34] As HASHEM had commanded Moses, Aaron placed it before the Ark of Testimony for a safekeeping. [35] The Children of Israel ate the manna for forty years, * until their arrival in an inhabited land; they ate the manna until their arrival at the border of the land of Canaan. [36] The omer is a tenth of an ephah.

17

Test and
contention:
water from
a rock

[1] **T**he entire assembly of the Children of Israel journeyed from the Wilderness of Sin to their journeys, according to the word of HASHEM. They encamped in Rephidim and there was no water for the people to drink. [2] The people contended with Moses and they said, "Give us water that we may drink!" Moses said to them, "Why do you contend with me? Why do you test HASHEM?" [3] The people thirsted there for water, and the people complained against Moses, and it said, "Why is this that you have brought us up from Egypt to kill me and my children and my livestock through thirst?"

[4] Moses cried out to HASHEM, saying, "What shall I do for this people? A bit more and they will stone me!"

[5] HASHEM said to Moses, "Pass before the people and take with you some of the elders of Israel; and in your hand take your staff with which you struck the River, and go. [6] Behold! — I shall stand before you by the rock in Horeb; you shall strike the rock and water will come forth from it and the people will drink." Moses did so in the sight of the elders of Israel. [7] He called the place Massah U'Meribah, * because of the contention of the Children of Israel and because of their test of HASHEM, saying, "Is HASHEM among us or not?"

Amalek   [8] Amalek* came and battled Israel in Rephidim. [9] Moses said to Joshua,

---

They contended with Him by putting their complaint in the form of a challenge. By naming the place for their behavior, Moses reminded the people for all time that God was indeed among them and that the way to express their needs is only through prayer.

17:8-16. Amalek's enmity against Israel stems not only

from its legacy as Esau's grandson, but from what it represents. The evil prophet Bilaam referred to Amalek as the first among nations (*Numbers* 24:20), i.e., the leading force of evil, just as Israel is the leading force of good. Consequently, their struggle is the eternal struggle of good versus evil.

בְּחַר־לָ֣נוּ אֲנָשִׁ֗ים וְצֵא֙ הִלָּחֵ֣ם בַּֽעֲמָלֵ֔ק מָחָ֗ר אָֽנֹכִ֤י נִצָּב֙ עַל־רֹ֣אשׁ הַגִּבְעָ֔ה
וּמַטֵּ֥ה הָֽאֱלֹהִ֖ים בְּיָדִֽי: וַיַּ֣עַשׂ יְהוֹשֻׁ֗עַ כַּֽאֲשֶׁ֤ר אָֽמַר־לוֹ֙ מֹשֶׁ֔ה לְהִלָּחֵ֖ם
י
בַּֽעֲמָלֵ֑ק וּמֹשֶׁה֙ אַֽהֲרֹ֣ן וְח֔וּר עָל֖וּ רֹ֣אשׁ הַגִּבְעָֽה: וְהָיָ֗ה כַּֽאֲשֶׁ֨ר יָרִ֥ים מֹשֶׁ֛ה
יא
יָד֖וֹ וְגָבַ֣ר יִשְׂרָאֵ֑ל וְכַֽאֲשֶׁ֥ר יָנִ֛יחַ יָד֖וֹ וְגָבַ֥ר עֲמָלֵֽק: וִידֵ֤י מֹשֶׁה֙ כְּבֵדִ֔ים וַיִּקְחוּ־
יב
אֶ֛בֶן וַיָּשִׂ֥ימוּ תַחְתָּ֖יו וַיֵּ֣שֶׁב עָלֶ֑יהָ וְאַֽהֲרֹ֨ן וְח֜וּר תָּֽמְכ֣וּ בְיָדָ֗יו מִזֶּ֤ה אֶחָד֙ וּמִזֶּ֣ה
אֶחָ֔ד וַיְהִ֥י יָדָ֛יו אֱמוּנָ֖ה עַד־בֹּ֥א הַשָּֽׁמֶשׁ: וַיַּֽחֲלֹ֧שׁ יְהוֹשֻׁ֛עַ אֶת־עֲמָלֵ֥ק וְאֶת־
יג
עַמּ֖וֹ לְפִי־חָֽרֶב:
וַיֹּ֨אמֶר יְהֹוָ֜ה אֶל־מֹשֶׁ֗ה כְּתֹ֨ב זֹ֤את זִכָּרוֹן֙ בַּסֵּ֔פֶר וְשִׂ֖ים בְּאָזְנֵ֣י יְהוֹשֻׁ֑עַ   מפטיר
יד
כִּֽי־מָחֹ֤ה אֶמְחֶה֙ אֶת־זֵ֣כֶר עֲמָלֵ֔ק מִתַּ֖חַת הַשָּׁמָֽיִם: וַיִּ֥בֶן מֹשֶׁ֖ה מִזְבֵּ֑חַ
טו

Haftaras
Beshalach:
Ashkenazim:
p. 590
Sephardim:
p. 592

וַיִּקְרָ֥א שְׁמ֖וֹ יְהֹוָ֥ה | נִסִּֽי: וַיֹּ֗אמֶר כִּֽי־יָד֙ עַל־כֵּ֣ס יָ֔הּ מִלְחָמָ֥ה לַֽיהֹוָ֖ה בַּֽעֲמָלֵ֑ק
טז
מִדֹּ֖ר דֹּֽר: פפפ קט״ז פסוקים. י״ד אמוז״ה סימן. סנא״ה סימן.

פרשת יתרו

וַיִּשְׁמַ֞ע יִתְר֨וֹ כֹהֵ֤ן מִדְיָן֙ חֹתֵ֣ן מֹשֶׁ֔ה אֵת֩ כָּל־אֲשֶׁ֨ר עָשָׂ֤ה אֱלֹהִים֙ לְמֹשֶׁ֔ה   **יח**
א
וּלְיִשְׂרָאֵ֖ל עַמּ֑וֹ כִּֽי־הוֹצִ֧יא יְהֹוָ֛ה אֶת־יִשְׂרָאֵ֖ל מִמִּצְרָֽיִם: וַיִּקַּ֗ח יִתְרוֹ֙ חֹתֵ֣ן
ב
מֹשֶׁ֔ה אֶת־צִפֹּרָ֖ה אֵ֣שֶׁת מֹשֶׁ֑ה אַחַ֖ר שִׁלּוּחֶֽיהָ: וְאֵ֖ת שְׁנֵ֣י בָנֶ֑יהָ אֲשֶׁ֨ר שֵׁ֤ם
ג
הָֽאֶחָד֙ גֵּֽרְשֹׁ֔ם כִּ֣י אָמַ֔ר גֵּ֣ר הָיִ֔יתִי בְּאֶ֖רֶץ נָכְרִיָּֽה: וְשֵׁ֥ם הָֽאֶחָ֖ד אֱלִיעֶ֑זֶר
ד
כִּֽי־אֱלֹהֵ֤י אָבִי֙ בְּעֶזְרִ֔י וַיַּצִּלֵ֖נִי מֵחֶ֥רֶב פַּרְעֹֽה: וַיָּבֹ֞א יִתְר֨וֹ חֹתֵ֥ן מֹשֶׁ֛ה
ה
וּבָנָ֥יו וְאִשְׁתּ֖וֹ אֶל־מֹשֶׁ֑ה אֶל־הַמִּדְבָּ֕ר אֲשֶׁר־ה֛וּא חֹנֶ֥ה שָׁ֖ם הַ֥ר הָֽאֱלֹהִֽים:
וַיֹּ֨אמֶר֙ אֶל־מֹשֶׁ֔ה אֲנִ֛י חֹתֶנְךָ֥ יִתְר֖וֹ בָּ֣א אֵלֶ֑יךָ וְאִ֨שְׁתְּךָ֔ וּשְׁנֵ֥י בָנֶ֖יהָ עִמָּֽהּ:
ו
וַיֵּצֵ֨א מֹשֶׁ֜ה לִקְרַ֣את חֹֽתְנ֗וֹ וַיִּשְׁתַּ֨חוּ֙ וַיִּשַּׁק־ל֔וֹ וַיִּשְׁאֲל֥וּ אִֽישׁ־לְרֵעֵ֖הוּ
ז
לְשָׁל֑וֹם וַיָּבֹ֖אוּ הָאֹֽהֱלָה: וַיְסַפֵּ֤ר מֹשֶׁה֙ לְחֹ֣תְנ֔וֹ אֵת֩ כָּל־אֲשֶׁ֨ר עָשָׂ֤ה יְהֹוָה֙
ח
לְפַרְעֹ֣ה וּלְמִצְרַ֔יִם עַ֖ל אוֹדֹ֣ת יִשְׂרָאֵ֑ל אֵ֤ת כָּל־הַתְּלָאָה֙ אֲשֶׁ֣ר מְצָאָ֣תַם
בַּדֶּ֔רֶךְ וַיַּצִּלֵ֖ם יְהֹוָֽה: וַיִּ֣חַדְּ יִתְר֔וֹ עַ֚ל כָּל־הַטּוֹבָ֔ה אֲשֶׁר־עָשָׂ֥ה יְהֹוָ֖ה
ט
לְיִשְׂרָאֵ֑ל אֲשֶׁ֥ר הִצִּיל֖וֹ מִיַּ֣ד מִצְרָֽיִם: וַיֹּ֘אמֶר֮ יִתְרוֹ֒ בָּר֣וּךְ יְהֹוָ֔ה אֲשֶׁ֨ר הִצִּ֥יל
י
אֶתְכֶ֛ם מִיַּ֥ד מִצְרַ֖יִם וּמִיַּ֣ד פַּרְעֹ֑ה אֲשֶׁ֤ר הִצִּיל֙ אֶת־הָעָ֔ם מִתַּ֖חַת יַד־
מִצְרָֽיִם: עַתָּ֣ה יָדַ֔עְתִּי כִּֽי־גָד֥וֹל יְהֹוָ֖ה מִכָּל־הָֽאֱלֹהִ֑ים כִּ֣י בַדָּבָ֔ר אֲשֶׁ֖ר
יא
זָד֖וּ עֲלֵיהֶֽם: וַיִּקַּ֞ח יִתְר֨וֹ חֹתֵ֤ן מֹשֶׁה֙ עֹלָ֣ה וּזְבָחִ֖ים לֵֽאלֹהִ֑ים וַיָּבֹ֨א אַֽהֲרֹ֜ן
יב
וְכֹ֣ל | זִקְנֵ֣י יִשְׂרָאֵ֗ל לֶֽאֱכָל־לֶ֛חֶם עִם־חֹתֵ֥ן מֹשֶׁ֖ה לִפְנֵ֥י הָֽאֱלֹהִֽים: וַיְהִי֙   שני
יג
מִֽמָּחֳרָ֔ת וַיֵּ֥שֶׁב מֹשֶׁ֖ה לִשְׁפֹּ֣ט אֶת־הָעָ֑ם וַיַּֽעֲמֹ֤ד הָעָם֙ עַל־מֹשֶׁ֔ה מִן־הַבֹּ֖קֶר
עַד־הָעָֽרֶב: וַיַּרְא֙ חֹתֵ֣ן מֹשֶׁ֔ה אֵ֛ת כָּל־אֲשֶׁר־ה֥וּא עֹשֶׂ֖ה לָעָ֑ם וַיֹּ֕אמֶר מָֽה־
יד

17:11. "Was it Moses' hands that won the battle or lost the battle? Rather [the Torah] teaches you: As long as Israel looked heavenward and subjected their hearts to their Father in Heaven, they would prevail. But when they did not, they would fall" (*Mishnah Rosh Hashanah* 3:8).

17:16. Moses declared that God swears, by placing His

hand on His throne, as it were, that He will continue the war against Amalek forever, until the memory of that evil nation is obliterated.

⇐ Parashas Yisro

18:1-12. Whereas Jethro had once been a distinguished priest of Midian and Moses was the homeless wanderer

"Choose people for us and go do battle with Amalek; tomorrow I will stand on top of the hill with the staff of God in my hand." [10] Joshua did as Moses said to him, to do battle with Amalek; and Moses, Aaron, and Hur ascended to the top of the hill. [11] It happened that when Moses raised his hand* Israel was stronger, and when he lowered his hand Amalek was stronger. [12] Moses' hands grew heavy, so they took a stone and put it under him and he sat on it, and Aaron and Hur supported his hands, one on this side and one on that side, and he remained with his hands in faithful prayer until sunset. [13] Joshua weakened Amalek and its people with the sword's blade.

The eternal struggle against Amalek
[14] HASHEM said to Moses, "Write this as a remembrance in the Book and recite it in the ears of Joshua, that I shall surely erase the memory of Amalek from under the heavens." [15] Moses built an altar and called its name "HASHEM Is My Miracle"; [16] and he said,* "For the hand is on the throne of God: HASHEM maintains a war against Amalek, from generation to generation."

PARASHAS YISRO

18

Jethro's arrival
[1] Jethro, the minister of Midian,* the father-in-law of Moses, heard everything that God did to Moses and to Israel, His people — that HASHEM had taken Israel out of Egypt. [2] Jethro, the father-in-law of Moses, took Zipporah, the wife of Moses, after she had been sent away; [3] and her two sons: of whom the name of one was Gershom, for he had said, "I was a sojourner in a strange land"; [4] and the name of the other was Eliezer, for "the God of my father came to my aid, and He saved me from the sword of Pharaoh."

[5] Jethro, the father-in-law of Moses, came to Moses with his sons and his wife, to the wilderness where he was encamped, by the Mountain of God. [6] He said to Moses, "I, your father-in-law Jethro, have come to you, with your wife and her two sons with her."

[7] Moses went out to meet his father-in-law, and he prostrated himself and kissed him, and each inquired about the other's well-being; then they came to the tent. [8] Moses told his father-in-law everything that HASHEM had done to Pharaoh and Egypt for Israel's sake — all the travail that had befallen them on the way — and that HASHEM had rescued them.

Jethro rejoices
[9] Jethro rejoiced* over all the good that HASHEM had done for Israel, that He had rescued it from the land of Egypt. [10] Jethro said, "Blessed is HASHEM, Who has rescued you from the hand of Egypt and from the hand of Pharaoh, Who has rescued the people from under the hand of Egypt. [11] Now I know that HASHEM is greater than all the gods, for in the very matter in which [the Egyptians] had conspired against them . . . !" [12] Jethro, the father-in-law of Moses, took a burnt-offering and feast-offerings for God; and Aaron and all the elders of Israel came to eat bread with the father-in-law of Moses before God.

[13] It was on the next day that Moses sat to judge the people, and the people stood by Moses from the morning until the evening. [14] The father-in-law of Moses saw everything that he was doing to the people, and he said, "What is

---

who married the dignitary's daughter, now the roles are reversed. Jethro brings Moses' family to rejoin him and introduces himself as Moses' *father-in-law*, his new claim to distinction. The entire nation receives him royally, and he later justifies the honor by offering counsel on how to organize the nation's system of providing halachic leader-

ship (vv. 13-23).

18:9-12. Jethro was truly grateful and happy over Israel's good fortune. The word וַיִּחַדְּ, [*Jethro*] *rejoiced*, however, alludes to the homonym חִדּוּדִים, *prickles* (*Or HaChaim*): Despite his happiness for Israel, he felt "prickles of unhappiness" over what had happened to the Egyptians (*Rashi*).

הַדָּבָר הַזֶּה אֲשֶׁר אַתָּה עֹשֶׂה לָעָם מַדּוּעַ אַתָּה יוֹשֵׁב לְבַדֶּךָ וְכָל־הָעָם

נִצָּב עָלֶיךָ מִן־בֹּקֶר עַד־עָרֶב: וַיֹּאמֶר מֹשֶׁה לְחֹתְנוֹ כִּי־יָבֹא אֵלַי הָעָם טו

לִדְרֹשׁ אֱלֹהִים: כִּי־יִהְיֶה לָהֶם דָּבָר בָּא אֵלַי וְשָׁפַטְתִּי בֵּין אִישׁ וּבֵין רֵעֵהוּ טז

וְהוֹדַעְתִּי אֶת־חֻקֵּי הָאֱלֹהִים וְאֶת־תּוֹרֹתָיו: וַיֹּאמֶר חֹתֵן מֹשֶׁה אֵלָיו לֹא־ יז

טוֹב הַדָּבָר אֲשֶׁר אַתָּה עֹשֶׂה: נָבֹל תִּבֹּל גַּם־אַתָּה גַּם־הָעָם הַזֶּה אֲשֶׁר יח

עִמָּךְ כִּי־כָבֵד מִמְּךָ הַדָּבָר לֹא־תוּכַל עֲשֹׂהוּ לְבַדֶּךָ: עַתָּה שְׁמַע בְּקֹלִי יט

אִיעָצְךָ וִיהִי אֱלֹהִים עִמָּךְ הֱיֵה אַתָּה לָעָם מוּל הָאֱלֹהִים וְהֵבֵאתָ אַתָּה

אֶת־הַדְּבָרִים אֶל־הָאֱלֹהִים: וְהִזְהַרְתָּה אֶתְהֶם אֶת־הַחֻקִּים וְאֶת־הַתּוֹרֹת כ

וְהוֹדַעְתָּ לָהֶם אֶת־הַדֶּרֶךְ יֵלְכוּ בָהּ וְאֶת־הַמַּעֲשֶׂה אֲשֶׁר יַעֲשׂוּן: וְאַתָּה כא

תֶחֱזֶה מִכָּל־הָעָם אַנְשֵׁי־חַיִל יִרְאֵי אֱלֹהִים אַנְשֵׁי אֱמֶת שֹׂנְאֵי בָצַע

וְשַׂמְתָּ עֲלֵהֶם שָׂרֵי אֲלָפִים שָׂרֵי מֵאוֹת שָׂרֵי חֲמִשִּׁים וְשָׂרֵי עֲשָׂרֹת: וְשָׁפְטוּ כב

אֶת־הָעָם בְּכָל־עֵת וְהָיָה כָּל־הַדָּבָר הַגָּדֹל יָבִיאוּ אֵלֶיךָ וְכָל־הַדָּבָר הַקָּטֹן

יִשְׁפְּטוּ־הֵם וְהָקֵל מֵעָלֶיךָ וְנָשְׂאוּ אִתָּךְ: אִם אֶת־הַדָּבָר הַזֶּה תַּעֲשֶׂה וְצִוְּךָ כג

אֱלֹהִים וְיָכָלְתָּ עֲמֹד וְגַם כָּל־הָעָם הַזֶּה עַל־מְקֹמוֹ יָבֹא בְשָׁלוֹם: וַיִּשְׁמַע כד   שלישי

מֹשֶׁה לְקוֹל חֹתְנוֹ וַיַּעַשׂ כֹּל אֲשֶׁר אָמָר: וַיִּבְחַר מֹשֶׁה אַנְשֵׁי־חַיִל מִכָּל־ כה

יִשְׂרָאֵל וַיִּתֵּן אֹתָם רָאשִׁים עַל־הָעָם שָׂרֵי אֲלָפִים שָׂרֵי מֵאוֹת שָׂרֵי

חֲמִשִּׁים וְשָׂרֵי עֲשָׂרֹת: וְשָׁפְטוּ אֶת־הָעָם בְּכָל־עֵת אֶת־הַדָּבָר הַקָּשֶׁה כו

יְבִיאוּן אֶל־מֹשֶׁה וְכָל־הַדָּבָר הַקָּטֹן יִשְׁפּוּטוּ הֵם: וַיְשַׁלַּח מֹשֶׁה אֶת־חֹתְנוֹ כז

וַיֵּלֶךְ לוֹ אֶל־אַרְצוֹ:

יט בַּחֹדֶשׁ הַשְּׁלִישִׁי לְצֵאת בְּנֵי־יִשְׂרָאֵל מֵאֶרֶץ מִצְרָיִם בַּיּוֹם הַזֶּה בָּאוּ א   רביעי

מִדְבַּר סִינָי: וַיִּסְעוּ מֵרְפִידִים וַיָּבֹאוּ מִדְבַּר סִינַי וַיַּחֲנוּ בַּמִּדְבָּר וַיִּחַן־ ב

שָׁם יִשְׂרָאֵל נֶגֶד הָהָר: וּמֹשֶׁה עָלָה אֶל־הָאֱלֹהִים וַיִּקְרָא אֵלָיו יהוה מִן־ ג

הָהָר לֵאמֹר כֹּה תֹאמַר לְבֵית יַעֲקֹב וְתַגֵּיד לִבְנֵי יִשְׂרָאֵל: אַתֶּם רְאִיתֶם ד

אֲשֶׁר עָשִׂיתִי לְמִצְרָיִם וָאֶשָּׂא אֶתְכֶם עַל־כַּנְפֵי נְשָׁרִים וָאָבִא אֶתְכֶם

אֵלָי: וְעַתָּה אִם־שָׁמוֹעַ תִּשְׁמְעוּ בְּקֹלִי וּשְׁמַרְתֶּם אֶת־בְּרִיתִי וִהְיִיתֶם לִי ה

סְגֻלָּה מִכָּל־הָעַמִּים כִּי־לִי כָּל־הָאָרֶץ: וְאַתֶּם תִּהְיוּ־לִי מַמְלֶכֶת כֹּהֲנִים ו

וְגוֹי קָדוֹשׁ אֵלֶּה הַדְּבָרִים אֲשֶׁר תְּדַבֵּר אֶל־בְּנֵי יִשְׂרָאֵל: וַיָּבֹא ז   חמישי

מֹשֶׁה וַיִּקְרָא לְזִקְנֵי הָעָם וַיָּשֶׂם לִפְנֵיהֶם אֵת כָּל־הַדְּבָרִים הָאֵלֶּה אֲשֶׁר

צִוָּהוּ יהוה: וַיַּעֲנוּ כָל־הָעָם יַחְדָּו וַיֹּאמְרוּ כֹּל אֲשֶׁר־דִּבֶּר יהוה נַעֲשֶׂה ח

READING FOR FIRST DAY SHAVUOS 19:1-20:23

Maftir: p. 400
Haftarah: p. 1208

18:19-22. New judicial system. Though conceding that only Moses could serve as the intermediary between God and Israel and teach them the general laws of the Torah, Jethro suggested a system of delegated authority for the adjudication of disputes.

19:1. The climax of the Exodus is now at hand. Moses' early doubts about Israel's worthiness to be redeemed are being answered by the nation's readiness to serve God at this mountain.

19:3. The word תֹאמַר, *say*, implies a mild form of speech. When Moses spoke to the *House of Jacob*, which refers to the women (*Mechilta*), he was to express the commandments in a manner suited to their compassionate, maternal nature. The word וְתַגֵּיד, *and relate*, implies firmness, for when Moses spoke *to the Children of Israel*, which refers to the men, he was to teach the commandments in a firm manner (*R' Bachya*).

19:5-6. Although the Creator, Who had delivered Israel

this thing that you do to the people? Why do you sit alone with all the people standing by you from morning to evening?"

¹⁵ Moses said to his father-in law, "Because the people come to me to seek God. ¹⁶ When they have a matter, one comes to me, and I judge between a man and his fellow, and I make known the decrees of God and His teachings."

Jethro's advice ¹⁷ The father-in-law of Moses said to him, "The thing that you do is not good. ¹⁸ You will surely become worn out — you as well as this people that is with you — for this matter is too hard for you, you will not be able to do it alone. ¹⁹ Now heed my voice, I shall advise you, and may God be with you. You be a *The list of require- ments for leadership* representative to God, * and you convey the matters to God. ²⁰ You shall caution them regarding the decrees and the teachings, and you shall make known to them the path in which they should go and the deeds that they should do. ²¹ And you shall discern from among the entire people, men of accomplishment, God-fearing people, men of truth, people who despise money, and it shall be that you shall appoint them leaders of thousands, leaders of hundreds, leaders of fifties, and leaders of tens. ²² They shall judge the people at all times, and they shall bring every major matter to you, and every minor matter they shall judge, and it will be eased for you, and they shall bear with you. ²³ If you do this thing — and God shall command you — then you will be able to endure, and this entire people, as well, shall arrive at its destination in peace."*

²⁴ Moses heeded the voice of his father-in-law, and did everything that he had said. ²⁵ Moses chose men of accomplishment from among all Israel and ap- pointed them heads of the people, leaders of thousands, leaders of hundreds, leaders of fifties, and leaders of tens. ²⁶ They judged the people at all times; the difficult thing they would bring to Moses and the minor thing they themselves *Jethro leaves* would judge.

²⁷ Moses sent off his father-in-law, and he went to his land.

19

Arrival at Sinai ¹ In the third month from the Exodus of the Children of Israel from Egypt, on this day, they arrived at the Wilderness of Sinai. * ² They journeyed from Rephidim and arrived at the Wilderness of Sinai and encamped in the Wilderness; and Israel encamped there, opposite the mountain.

God's proposal ³ Moses ascended to God, and HASHEM called to him from the mountain, say- ing, "So shall you say to the House of Jacob and relate* to the Children of Israel. ⁴ 'You have seen what I did to Egypt, and that I have borne you on the wings of eagles and brought you to Me. ⁵ And now, if you hearken well to My voice and observe My covenant, * you shall be to Me the most beloved treasure of all peoples, for Mine is the entire world. ⁶ You shall be to Me a kingdom of ministers * and a holy nation.' These are the words that you shall speak to the Children of Israel."*

⁷ Moses came and summoned the elders of the people, and put before them all these words that HASHEM had commanded him. ⁸ The entire people re- sponded together and said, "Everything that HASHEM has spoken we shall do!"*

---

from slavery, had the right to demand that they accept the Torah, such was not the Divine plan. As the familiar narra- tive of the Sages teaches (*Sifrei*, *Vezos Haberachah*): God offered the Torah to other nations but they all refused it. Esau's offspring would not tolerate a law that prohibited murder; Ishmael's could not live with a law that banned thievery; and Lot's would not accept a ban on adultery. Now it was Israel's turn. That Israel was willing to accept

the Torah without even inquiring as to its contents was because it had inherited the spiritual sublimity of the Patriarchs that its cousins had rejected.

19:6. *A kingdom of ministers* . . . Although usually trans- lated as *priests* , the word כֹּהֲנִים in the context of this verse means that the entire nation is to be dedicated to leading the world toward an understanding and acceptance of God's mission.

ט וַיֵּשֶׁב מֹשֶׁה אֶת־דִּבְרֵי הָעָם אֶל־יהוֹה: וַיֹּאמֶר יהוֹה אֶל־מֹשֶׁה הִנֵּה אֲנֹכִי
בָּא אֵלֶ֫יךָ֮ בְּעַב הֶעָנָ֒ן בַּעֲבוּר יִשְׁמַע הָעָם בְּדַבְּרִי עִמָּ֔ךְ וְגַם־בְּךָ֖ יַאֲמִינוּ
לְעוֹלָם וַיַּגֵּד מֹשֶׁה אֶת־דִּבְרֵי הָעָם אֶל־יהוֹה: וַיֹּאמֶר יהוֹה אֶל־מֹשֶׁה לֵךְ
יא אֶל־הָעָם וְקִדַּשְׁתָּם הַיּוֹם וּמָחָר וְכִבְּסוּ שִׂמְלֹתָם: וְהָיוּ נְכֹנִים לַיּוֹם הַשְּׁלִישִׁי
יב כִּי | בַּיּוֹם הַשְּׁלִשִׁי יֵרֵד יהוֹה לְעֵינֵי כָל־הָעָם עַל־הַר סִינָי: וְהִגְבַּלְתָּ אֶת־
הָעָם סָבִיב לֵאמֹר הִשָּׁמְרוּ לָכֶם עֲלוֹת בָּהָר וּנְגֹעַ בְּקָצֵהוּ כָּל־הַנֹּגֵעַ בָּהָר
יג מוֹת יוּמָת: לֹא־תִגַּע בּוֹ יָד כִּי־סָקוֹל יִסָּקֵל אוֹ־יָרֹה יִיָּרֶה אִם־בְּהֵמָה אִם־
יד אִישׁ לֹא יִחְיֶה בִּמְשֹׁךְ הַיֹּבֵל הֵמָּה יַעֲלוּ בָהָר: וַיֵּרֶד מֹשֶׁה מִן־הָהָר אֶל־הָעָם
טו וַיְקַדֵּשׁ אֶת־הָעָם וַיְכַבְּסוּ שִׂמְלֹתָם: וַיֹּאמֶר אֶל־הָעָם הֱיוּ נְכֹנִים לִשְׁלֹשֶׁת
טז יָמִים אַל־תִּגְּשׁוּ אֶל־אִשָּׁה: וַיְהִי בַיּוֹם הַשְּׁלִישִׁי בִּהְיֹת הַבֹּקֶר וַיְהִי קֹלֹת
וּבְרָקִים וְעָנָן כָּבֵד עַל־הָהָר וְקֹל שֹׁפָר חָזָק מְאֹד וַיֶּחֱרַד כָּל־הָעָם אֲשֶׁר
יז בַּמַּחֲנֶה: וַיּוֹצֵא מֹשֶׁה אֶת־הָעָם לִקְרַאת הָאֱלֹהִים מִן־הַמַּחֲנֶה וַיִּתְיַצְּבוּ
יח בְּתַחְתִּית הָהָר: וְהַר סִינַי עָשַׁן כֻּלּוֹ מִפְּנֵי אֲשֶׁר יָרַד עָלָיו יהוֹה בָּאֵשׁ וַיַּעַל
יט עֲשָׁנוֹ כְּעֶשֶׁן הַכִּבְשָׁן וַיֶּחֱרַד כָּל־הָהָר מְאֹד: וַיְהִי קוֹל הַשֹּׁפָר הוֹלֵךְ וְחָזֵק
כ מְאֹד מֹשֶׁה יְדַבֵּר וְהָאֱלֹהִים יַעֲנֶנּוּ בְקוֹל: וַיֵּרֶד יהוֹה עַל־הַר סִינַי אֶל־רֹאשׁ
כא הָהָר וַיִּקְרָא יהוֹה לְמֹשֶׁה אֶל־רֹאשׁ הָהָר וַיַּעַל מֹשֶׁה: וַיֹּאמֶר יהוֹה אֶל־
כב מֹשֶׁה רֵד הָעֵד בָּעָם פֶּן־יֶהֶרְסוּ אֶל־יהוֹה לִרְאוֹת וְנָפַל מִמֶּנּוּ רָב: וְגַם
כג הַכֹּהֲנִים הַנִּגָּשִׁים אֶל־יהוֹה יִתְקַדָּשׁוּ פֶּן־יִפְרֹץ בָּהֶם יהוֹה: וַיֹּאמֶר מֹשֶׁה
אֶל־יהוֹה לֹא־יוּכַל הָעָם לַעֲלֹת אֶל־הַר סִינָי כִּי־אַתָּה הַעֵדֹתָה בָּנוּ לֵאמֹר
כד הַגְבֵּל אֶת־הָהָר וְקִדַּשְׁתּוֹ: וַיֹּאמֶר אֵלָיו יהוֹה לֶךְ־רֵד וְעָלִיתָ אַתָּה וְאַהֲרֹן
כה עִמָּךְ וְהַכֹּהֲנִים וְהָעָם אַל־יֶהֶרְסוּ לַעֲלֹת אֶל־יהוֹה פֶּן־יִפְרָץ־בָּם: וַיֵּרֶד

ששי

כ א מֹשֶׁה אֶל־הָעָם וַיֹּאמֶר אֲלֵהֶם: וַיְדַבֵּר אֱלֹהִים אֵת כָּל־הַדְּבָרִים
ב הָאֵלֶּה לֵאמֹר: * אָנֹכִי יהוֹה אֱלֹהֶיךָ אֲשֶׁר הוֹצֵאתִיךָ מֵאֶרֶץ מִצְרַיִם
ג מִבֵּית עֲבָדִים: לֹא־יִהְיֶה לְךָ אֱלֹהִים אֲחֵרִים עַל־פָּנָי: לֹא־תַעֲשֶׂה לְךָ
ד פֶסֶל וְכָל־תְּמוּנָה אֲשֶׁר בַּשָּׁמַיִם מִמַּעַל וַאֲשֶׁר בָּאָרֶץ מִתַּחַת וַאֲשֶׁר בַּמַּיִם
ה מִתַּחַת לָאָרֶץ: לֹא־תִשְׁתַּחֲוֶה לָהֶם וְלֹא תָעָבְדֵם כִּי אָנֹכִי יהוֹה אֱלֹהֶיךָ
אֵל קַנָּא פֹּקֵד עֲוֹן אָבֹת עַל־בָּנִים עַל־שִׁלֵּשִׁים וְעַל־רִבֵּעִים לְשֹׂנְאָי:

כ

*See box
below

19:16-25. Heralded by an awesome display of thunder, lightning, smoke, shofar blasts, and fire, God's Presence descended upon Mount Sinai. Thus the stage was set for the most auspicious moment in history: God's declaration of the Ten Commandments.

20:1-14. When the Holy One, Blessed is He, presented the Torah at Sinai, not a bird chirped, not a fowl flew, not an ox lowed, not an angel ascended, not a seraph pro-

claimed, קָדוֹשׁ, *Holy*. The sea did not roll and no creature made a sound. All of the vast universe was silent and mute. It was then that the Voice went forth and proclaimed, *I am Hashem, your God!* (*Shemos Rabbah* 29:9).

20:2. First Commandment: Belief in God. This is the positive commandment to believe in the existence of Hashem as the only God.

20:3-6. Second Commandment: Prohibition of idolatry.

THE TEN COMMANDMENTS ARE READ WITH TWO DIFFERENT SETS OF *TROP* (CANTILLATION NOTES). THE VERSION PRESENTED IN THE TEXT IS USED BY THE INDIVIDUAL WHO IS REVIEWING THE WEEKLY *SIDRAH*. THE VERSION USED BY THE READER FOR THE PUBLIC TORAH READING ON THE SABBATH AND ON SHAVUOS APPEARS IN A BOX ON PAGE 242.

*Moses brought back the words of the people to H*ASHEM.

⁹ H*ASHEM said to Moses, "Behold! I come to you in the thickness of the cloud, so that the people will hear as I speak to you, and they will also believe in you forever." Moses related the words of the people to H*ASHEM.

Preparing for ¹⁰ H*ASHEM said to Moses, "Go to the people and sanctify them today and* *the Torah* tomorrow, and they shall wash their clothing. ¹¹ Let them be prepared for the third day, for on the third day H*ASHEM shall descend in the sight of the entire people on Mount Sinai. ¹² You shall set boundaries for the people roundabout, saying, 'Beware of ascending the mountain or touching its edge; whoever touches the mountain shall surely die. ¹³ A hand shall not touch it, for he shall surely be stoned or thrown down; whether animal or person he shall not live; upon an extended blast of the shofar, they may ascend the mountain.' "*

¹⁴ *Moses descended from the mountain to the people. He sanctified the people and they washed their clothing. ¹⁵ He said to the people, "Be prepared after a three-day period; do not draw near a woman."*

The day ¹⁶ *On the third day when it was morning, there was thunder and lightning* and* *of the* a heavy cloud on the mountain, and the sound of the shofar was very powerful,* *Revelation* and the entire people that was in the camp shuddered. ¹⁷ Moses brought the peo-*ple forth from the camp toward God, and they stood at the bottom of the moun-tain. ¹⁸ All of Mount Sinai was smoking because H*ASHEM had descended upon it in the fire; its smoke ascended like the smoke of the furnace, and the entire mountain shuddered exceedingly. ¹⁹ The sound of the shofar grew continually much stronger; Moses would speak and God would respond to him with a voice.*

²⁰ H*ASHEM descended upon Mount Sinai to the top of the mountain; H*ASHEM *summoned Moses to the top of the mountain, and Moses ascended. ²¹ H*ASHEM *said to Moses, "Descend, warn the people, lest they break through to H*ASHEM *to see, and a multitude of them will fall. ²² Even the Kohanim who approach* H*ASHEM should be prepared, lest H*ASHEM burst forth against them."*

²³ *Moses said to H*ASHEM, *"The people cannot ascend Mount Sinai, for You have warned us, saying, 'Bound the mountain and sanctify it.' "*

²⁴ H*ASHEM said to him, "Go, descend. Then you shall ascend, and Aaron with you, but the Kohanim, and the people — they shall not break through to ascend to H*ASHEM, lest He burst forth against them." ²⁵ Moses descended to the people and said [it] to them.*

20   ¹G*od spoke all these statements, * saying:*

The Ten ² *I am H*ASHEM, *your God, Who has taken you out of the land of Egypt,* *Command-* from the house of slavery.*
ments
³ *You shall not recognize the gods of others in My presence. ⁴ You shall not make yourself a carved image nor any likeness of that which is in the heavens above or on the earth below or in the water beneath the earth. ⁵ You shall not prostrate yourself to them nor worship them, for I am H*ASHEM, *your God — a jealous God, Who visits the sin of fathers upon children* to the third and fourth generations, for My enemies;*

This commandment comprises four negative injunc-tions: (1) It is forbidden to believe in idols; (2) it is forbidden to make or possess them; (3) it is forbidden to worship them through any of the four forms of Divine service [prostration, slaughter, offering upon an altar, libations of wine or other liquids upon an altar]; and (4) it

is forbidden to worship an idol by a means that is unique to it.

20:5. Children are punished only if they adopt and carry on the sinful legacy of their parents, or if it was in their power to protest, but they acquiesced to the life-style that was shown them (*Sanhedrin* 27b).

לֹא תִשָּׂא   ו וְעֹשֶׂה חֶסֶד לַאֲלָפִים לְאֹהֲבַי וּלְשֹׁמְרֵי מִצְוֹתָי:

ז אֶת־שֵׁם־יהוה אֱלֹהֶיךָ לַשָּׁוְא כִּי לֹא יְנַקֶּה יהוה אֵת אֲשֶׁר־יִשָּׂא אֶת־שְׁמוֹ לַשָּׁוְא:

ח־ט זָכוֹר אֶת־יוֹם הַשַּׁבָּת לְקַדְּשׁוֹ: שֵׁשֶׁת יָמִים תַּעֲבֹד וְעָשִׂיתָ כָּל־מְלַאכְתֶּךָ:

י וְיוֹם הַשְּׁבִיעִי שַׁבָּת לַיהוה אֱלֹהֶיךָ לֹא־תַעֲשֶׂה כָל־מְלָאכָה אַתָּה ׀ וּבִנְךָ

יא וּבִתֶּךָ עַבְדְּךָ וַאֲמָתְךָ וּבְהֶמְתֶּךָ וְגֵרְךָ אֲשֶׁר בִּשְׁעָרֶיךָ: כִּי שֵׁשֶׁת־יָמִים עָשָׂה יהוה אֶת־הַשָּׁמַיִם וְאֶת־הָאָרֶץ אֶת־הַיָּם וְאֶת־כָּל־אֲשֶׁר־בָּם וַיָּנַח בַּיּוֹם

יב הַשְּׁבִיעִי עַל־כֵּן בֵּרַךְ יהוה אֶת־יוֹם הַשַּׁבָּת וַיְקַדְּשֵׁהוּ: כַּבֵּד אֶת־אָבִיךָ וְאֶת־אִמֶּךָ לְמַעַן יַאֲרִכוּן יָמֶיךָ עַל הָאֲדָמָה אֲשֶׁר־יהוה אֱלֹהֶיךָ נֹתֵן

יג לָךְ: לֹא תִרְצָח   לֹא תִנְאָף   לֹא תִגְנֹב   לֹא־

יד תַעֲנֶה בְרֵעֲךָ עֵד שָׁקֶר: לֹא תַחְמֹד בֵּית רֵעֶךָ   לֹא־תַחְמֹד אֵשֶׁת רֵעֶךָ וְעַבְדּוֹ וַאֲמָתוֹ וְשׁוֹרוֹ וַחֲמֹרוֹ וְכֹל אֲשֶׁר לְרֵעֶךָ:

טו וְכָל־הָעָם רֹאִים אֶת־הַקּוֹלֹת וְאֶת־הַלַּפִּידִם וְאֵת קוֹל הַשֹּׁפָר וְאֶת־הָהָר

טז עָשֵׁן וַיַּרְא הָעָם וַיָּנֻעוּ וַיַּעַמְדוּ מֵרָחֹק: וַיֹּאמְרוּ אֶל־מֹשֶׁה דַּבֵּר־אַתָּה עִמָּנוּ

יז וְנִשְׁמָעָה וְאַל־יְדַבֵּר עִמָּנוּ אֱלֹהִים פֶּן־נָמוּת: וַיֹּאמֶר מֹשֶׁה אֶל־הָעָם אַל־תִּירָאוּ כִּי לְבַעֲבוּר נַסּוֹת אֶתְכֶם בָּא הָאֱלֹהִים וּבַעֲבוּר תִּהְיֶה יִרְאָתוֹ עַל־

יח פְּנֵיכֶם לְבִלְתִּי תֶחֱטָאוּ: וַיַּעֲמֹד הָעָם מֵרָחֹק וּמֹשֶׁה נִגַּשׁ אֶל־הָעֲרָפֶל

יט אֲשֶׁר־שָׁם הָאֱלֹהִים: וַיֹּאמֶר יהוה אֶל־מֹשֶׁה כֹּה תֹאמַר

כ אֶל־בְּנֵי יִשְׂרָאֵל אַתֶּם רְאִיתֶם כִּי מִן־הַשָּׁמַיִם דִּבַּרְתִּי עִמָּכֶם: לֹא תַעֲשׂוּן

Haftaras Yisro: p. 962

כא אִתִּי אֱלֹהֵי כֶסֶף וֵאלֹהֵי זָהָב לֹא תַעֲשׂוּ לָכֶם: מִזְבַּח אֲדָמָה תַּעֲשֶׂה־לִּי וְזָבַחְתָּ עָלָיו אֶת־עֹלֹתֶיךָ וְאֶת־שְׁלָמֶיךָ אֶת־צֹאנְךָ וְאֶת־בְּקָרֶךָ בְּכָל־

כב הַמָּקוֹם אֲשֶׁר אַזְכִּיר אֶת־שְׁמִי אָבוֹא אֵלֶיךָ וּבֵרַכְתִּיךָ: וְאִם־מִזְבַּח אֲבָנִים תַּעֲשֶׂה־לִּי לֹא־תִבְנֶה אֶתְהֶן גָּזִית כִּי חַרְבְּךָ הֵנַפְתָּ עָלֶיהָ וַתְּחַלְלֶהָ:

כג וְלֹא־תַעֲלֶה בְמַעֲלֹת עַל־מִזְבְּחִי אֲשֶׁר לֹא־תִגָּלֶה עֶרְוָתְךָ עָלָיו: פפפ

ע"ב פסוקים. יונד"ב סימן:

20:7. Third Commandment: Prohibition of vain oaths. Just as it is forbidden to show contempt for God by making an idol, so it is forbidden to disgrace His Name by using it for no valid purpose.

20:8-11. Fourth Commandment: The Sabbath. This day serves as a constant reminder that God is the Creator, Who created for six days and rested on the seventh. Sabbath observance bears testimony to this concept.

20:9-10. The commandment of the Sabbath includes not only deed, but attitude, for when the Sabbath arrives, one should feel that all his work is finished, even though his desk or workbench is still piled high. *Six days shall you work and accomplish all your work* means that no matter what is still left to be done, one should feel as much at ease as if everything was finished (*Rashi*).

20:12. Fifth Commandment: Honoring parents. The

Ten Commandments are inscribed on two tablets, five on each. The first tablet contains laws regarding Man's relationship with God while the second refers to relationships among people. This casts a revealing light on the significance God attaches to the honor He wants us to show parents. When people honor their parents, God regards it as if they honor Him.

20:13. Sixth Commandment: Prohibition against murder. *Mechilta* notes that the first commandment of the second tablet corresponds to the first of the other one, faith in God. Someone with true belief in God as the Creator and Sustainer of human life will not commit murder.

Seventh Commandment: Prohibition against adultery. By definition, this term refers only to cohabitation with a married woman, which is a capital offense. It is parallel to the second commandment, which forbids idolatry, for

⁶ but Who shows kindness for thousands [of generations] to those who love
Me and observe My commandments.
⁷ You shall not take the Name of HASHEM, your God, in vain, * for HASHEM
will not absolve anyone who takes His Name in vain.
⁸ Remember the Sabbath day * to sanctify it. ⁹ Six days shall you work *
and accomplish all your work; ¹⁰ but the seventh day is Sabbath to
HASHEM, your God; you shall not do any work — you, your son, your
daughter, your slave, your maidservant, your animal, and your convert
within your gates — ¹¹ for in six days HASHEM made the heavens and the
earth, the sea and all that is in them, and He rested on the seventh day.
Therefore, HASHEM blessed the Sabbath day and sanctified it.
¹² Honor your father and your mother, * so that your days will be
lengthened upon the land that HASHEM, your God, gives you.
¹³ You shall not kill; * you shall not commit adultery; * you shall not
steal; * you shall not bear false witness against your fellow. *
¹⁴ You shall not covet * your fellow's house. You shall not covet your
fellow's wife, his manservant, his maidservant, his ox, his donkey, nor
anything that belongs to your fellow.

¹⁵ The entire people saw the thunder and the flames, the sound of the shofar
and the smoking mountain; the people saw and trembled and stood from afar.
¹⁶ They said to Moses, "You speak to us and we shall hear; let God not speak
to us lest we die."
¹⁷ Moses said to the people, "Do not fear, for in order to elevate you has God
come; so that awe of Him shall be upon your faces, so that you shall not sin."
¹⁸ The people stood from afar and Moses approached the thick cloud where God
was.
¹⁹ HASHEM said to Moses, "So shall you say to the Children of Israel, 'You have
seen that I have spoken to you from heaven. ²⁰ You shall not make [images of
what is] with Me; gods of silver and gods of gold shall you not make for
yourselves.
²¹ " 'An Altar of earth shall you make for Me, and you shall slaughter near it
your burnt-offerings and your peace-offerings, your flock and your herd;
wherever I permit My Name to be mentioned I shall come to you and bless you.
²² And when you make for Me an Altar of stones, do not build them hewn, * for
you will have raised your sword over it and desecrated it. ²³ You shall not ascend
My Altar on steps, so that your nakedness will not be uncovered upon it.' "

---

someone who betrays the marital relationship can be
expected to betray God (Mechilta).

Eighth Commandment: Prohibition against kidnaping.
In this prohibition, "stealing" refers to kidnaping. A
kidnaper who forces his victim to work for him and then
sells him into slavery is liable to the death penalty (Sanhedrin 86a). The commandment against ordinary theft is
found in Leviticus 19:11. Mechilta compares stealing to
the third commandment because one who steals may
well seek to cover his tracks by swearing falsely.

**Ninth Commandment: Prohibition against bearing false
witness.** In addition to its literal meaning, this passage
prohibits gossip and slander (Sforno).

20:14. Tenth Commandment: Prohibition against cov-

eting. R' Hirsch notes that this last commandment is one
that only a Divine Lawgiver could have decreed. A mortal
ruler can legislate against murder and theft, but only God
can demand that people sanctify their thoughts and
attitudes to the point where they purge themselves of
such natural tendencies as jealousy and covetousness.

20:22-23. The last two verses of the Sidrah contain a
profound lesson in sensitivity. The Altar and steps are
inanimate objects; they would not be conscious of the
pounding of iron or the exposed anatomy of the Kohanim. If the Torah commands us to refrain from "shaming" objects, surely a person should be eternally vigilant
never to cause shame or embarrassment to living, breath-
ing human beings (Rashi).

פרשת משפטים

כא
א־ב וְאֵ֗לֶּה הַמִּשְׁפָּטִ֔ים אֲשֶׁ֥ר תָּשִׂ֖ים לִפְנֵיהֶֽם: כִּ֤י תִקְנֶה֙ עֶ֣בֶד עִבְרִ֔י שֵׁ֥שׁ שָׁנִ֖ים

ג יַעֲבֹ֑ד וּבַ֨שְּׁבִעִ֔ת יֵצֵ֥א לַֽחָפְשִׁ֖י חִנָּֽם: אִם־בְּגַפּ֣וֹ יָבֹ֔א בְּגַפּ֖וֹ יֵצֵ֑א אִם־בַּ֤עַל

ד אִשָּׁה֙ ה֔וּא וְיָצְאָ֥ה אִשְׁתּ֖וֹ עִמּֽוֹ: אִם־אֲדֹנָיו֙ יִתֶּן־ל֣וֹ אִשָּׁ֔ה וְיָלְדָה־ל֖וֹ בָנִ֣ים א֑וֹ

ה בָנ֔וֹת הָאִשָּׁ֣ה וִֽילָדֶ֔יהָ תִּֽהְיֶ֣ה לַֽאדֹנֶ֔יהָ וְה֖וּא יֵצֵ֥א בְגַפּֽוֹ: וְאִם־אָמֹ֤ר יֹאמַר֙

ו הָעֶ֔בֶד אָהַ֨בְתִּי֙ אֶת־אֲדֹנִ֔י אֶת־אִשְׁתִּ֖י וְאֶת־בָּנָ֑י לֹ֥א אֵצֵ֖א חָפְשִֽׁי: וְהִגִּישׁ֤וֹ

אֲדֹנָיו֙ אֶל־הָ֣אֱלֹהִ֔ים וְהִגִּישׁוֹ֙ אֶל־הַדֶּ֔לֶת א֖וֹ אֶל־הַמְּזוּזָ֑ה וְרָצַ֨ע אֲדֹנָ֤יו אֶת־

ז אָזְנוֹ֙ בַּמַּרְצֵ֔עַ וַעֲבָד֖וֹ לְעֹלָֽם: וְכִֽי־יִמְכֹּ֥ר אִ֛ישׁ אֶת־בִּתּ֖וֹ לְאָמָ֑ה

ח לֹ֥א תֵצֵ֖א כְּצֵ֥את הָעֲבָדִֽים: אִם־רָעָ֞ה בְּעֵינֵ֧י אֲדֹנֶ֛יהָ אֲשֶׁר־°ל֥א [ל֖וֹ ק] ֮

ט יְעָדָ֖הּ וְהֶפְדָּ֑הּ לְעַ֥ם נָכְרִ֛י לֹא־יִמְשֹׁ֥ל לְמָכְרָ֖הּ בְּבִגְדוֹ־בָֽהּ: וְאִם־לִבְנ֖וֹ

י יִֽיעָדֶ֑נָּה כְּמִשְׁפַּ֥ט הַבָּנ֖וֹת יַעֲשֶׂה־לָּֽהּ: אִם־אַחֶ֖רֶת יִֽקַּח־ל֑וֹ שְׁאֵרָ֛הּ כְּסוּתָ֥הּ

יא וְעֹנָתָ֖הּ לֹ֥א יִגְרָֽע: וְאִם־שְׁלָ֨שׁ־אֵ֔לֶּה לֹ֥א יַעֲשֶׂ֖ה לָ֑הּ וְיָצְאָ֥ה חִנָּ֖ם אֵ֥ין

יב־יג כָּֽסֶף: מַכֵּ֥ה אִ֛ישׁ וָמֵ֖ת מ֥וֹת יוּמָֽת: וַאֲשֶׁר֙ לֹ֣א צָדָ֔ה וְהָאֱלֹהִ֖ים אִנָּ֣ה

יד לְיָד֑וֹ וְשַׂמְתִּ֤י לְךָ֙ מָק֔וֹם אֲשֶׁ֥ר יָנ֖וּס שָֽׁמָּה: וְכִֽי־יָזִ֥ד אִ֛ישׁ עַל־רֵעֵ֖הוּ

טו לְהָרְג֣וֹ בְעָרְמָ֑ה מֵעִ֣ם מִזְבְּחִ֔י תִּקָּחֶ֖נּוּ לָמֽוּת: וּמַכֵּ֥ה אָבִ֛יו וְאִמּ֖וֹ מ֥וֹת

טז־יז יוּמָֽת: וְגֹנֵ֨ב אִ֧ישׁ וּמְכָר֛וֹ וְנִמְצָ֥א בְיָד֖וֹ מ֥וֹת יוּמָֽת: וּמְקַלֵּ֛ל

יח אָבִ֥יו וְאִמּ֖וֹ מ֥וֹת יוּמָֽת: וְכִֽי־יְרִיבֻ֣ן אֲנָשִׁ֔ים וְהִכָּה־אִישׁ֙ אֶת־

יט רֵעֵ֔הוּ בְּאֶ֖בֶן א֣וֹ בְאֶגְרֹ֑ף וְלֹ֥א יָמ֖וּת וְנָפַ֥ל לְמִשְׁכָּֽב: אִם־יָק֞וּם וְהִתְהַלֵּ֤ךְ בַּחוּץ֙

כ עַל־מִשְׁעַנְתּ֔וֹ וְנִקָּ֖ה הַמַּכֶּ֑ה רַ֥ק שִׁבְתּ֛וֹ יִתֵּ֖ן וְרַפֹּ֥א יְרַפֵּֽא: אַ֗ךְ

כא כִּֽי־יַכֶּה֩ אִ֨ישׁ אֶת־עַבְדּ֜וֹ א֤וֹ אֶת־אֲמָתוֹ֙ בַּשֵּׁ֔בֶט וּמֵ֖ת תַּ֣חַת יָד֑וֹ נָקֹ֖ם יִנָּקֵֽם: אַ֥ךְ

כב אִם־י֛וֹם א֥וֹ יוֹמַ֖יִם יַעֲמֹ֑ד לֹ֣א יֻקַּ֔ם כִּ֥י כַסְפּ֖וֹ הֽוּא: וְכִֽי־יִנָּצ֣וּ

אֲנָשִׁ֗ים וְנָ֨גְפ֜וּ אִשָּׁ֤ה הָרָה֙ וְיָצְא֣וּ יְלָדֶ֔יהָ וְלֹ֥א יִהְיֶ֖ה אָס֑וֹן עָנ֣וֹשׁ יֵעָנֵ֗שׁ

כג כַּֽאֲשֶׁ֨ר יָשִׁ֤ית עָלָיו֙ בַּ֣עַל הָֽאִשָּׁ֔ה וְנָתַ֖ן בִּפְלִלִֽים: וְאִם־אָס֖וֹן יִהְיֶ֑ה וְנָתַתָּ֥ה

כד נֶ֖פֶשׁ תַּ֥חַת נָֽפֶשׁ: עַ֚יִן תַּ֣חַת עַ֔יִן שֵׁ֖ן תַּ֣חַת שֵׁ֑ן יָ֚ד תַּ֣חַת יָ֔ד רֶ֖גֶל תַּ֥חַת רָֽגֶל:

‎⧏ Parashas Mishpatim

21:1. The juxtaposition of this *Sidrah* (dealing primarily with civil and tort law) with the Ten Commandments and the laws of the Altar provide a startling insight into Judaism. Religion is not limited to ritual and spirituality. To the contrary, all areas of life are intertwined and holiness derives from halachically correct business dealings no less than from piety in matters of ritual.

21:2-6. A Jew can become a bondsman either by selling himself as an escape from extreme poverty (*Leviticus* 25:39), or he may be a thief who is sold by the court to raise funds to pay his victims (22:2). This passage refers only to the latter case (*Rashi*).

21:6. The court sold him for six years, so it is involved in his decision to extend his term (*Rashi*). The court is called *Elohim* — which also means God — because the court carries out God's law on earth (*Ibn Ezra*), and because God's

Presence and influence rests upon the judges (*Ramban*). In this context, the word לְעֹלָם, *forever,* means until the Jubilee [fiftieth] Year.

21:7-11. Until a girl reaches puberty, the Torah gives her father the right to "sell" her as a bondswoman. However, the passage itself and the teachings of the Sages make it clear that the purpose of this right is for her benefit, not his. He is permitted to "sell" her in this case because the sale is expected to result in her marriage to either her master or his son. In fact, if neither of the two marries her, the Torah regards it as a betrayal of the girl (v. 8). Ordinarily, a father should not exercise his right of betrothal while his daughter is a child (*Kiddushin* 41a). He does so in the case of this passage because it is an opportunity to provide for her future that would otherwise not be available (*R' Hirsch*).

21:12-14. Murder and homicide. Only premeditated murder incurs the death penalty, in which case it is forbid-

PARASHAS MISHPATIM

21

The civil law

¹ **A**nd these are the ordinances* that you shall place before them: ² If you buy a Jewish bondsman,* he shall work for six years; and in the seventh he shall go free, for no charge. ³ If he shall arrive by himself, he shall leave by himself; if he is the husband of a woman, his wife shall leave with him.

Jewish bondsmen

⁴ If his master will give him a woman and she bears him sons or daughters, the wife and her children shall belong to her master, and he shall go out by himself. ⁵ But if the bondsman shall say, "I love my master, my wife, and my children — I shall not go free"; ⁶ then his master shall bring him to the court* and shall bring him to the door or to the doorpost, and his master shall bore through his ear with the awl, and he shall serve him forever.*

"Sale" of a daughter

⁷ If a man will sell his daughter* as a bondswoman, she shall not leave like the leavetaking of the slaves. ⁸ If she is displeasing in the eyes of her master, who should have designated her for himself, he shall assist in her redemption; he shall not have the power to sell her to a strange man, for he had betrayed her. ⁹ If he had designated her for his son, he shall deal with her according to the rights of the young women. ¹⁰ If he shall take another for himself, he shall not diminish her food, her clothing, or her marital relationship. ¹¹ If he does not perform these three for her, she shall leave free of charge, without payment.

Murder and manslaughter

¹² One who strikes a man, so that he dies,* shall surely be put to death. ¹³ But for one who had not lain in ambush and God had caused it to come to his hand, I shall provide you a place to which he shall flee.

¹⁴ If a man shall act intentionally against his fellow to murder him with guile, from My Altar shall you take him to die.

¹⁵ One who strikes his father or mother shall surely be put to death.

¹⁶ One who kidnaps a man and sells him, and he was found to have been in his power, shall surely be put to death.

¹⁷ One who curses his father or mother shall surely be put to death.

¹⁸ If men quarrel and one strikes his fellow with a stone or a fist, and he does not die but falls into bed: ¹⁹ If he gets up and goes about outside under his own power, the one who struck is absolved. Only for his lost time shall he pay, and he shall provide for healing.

Killing of a slave

²⁰ If a man shall strike his slave or his maidservant with the rod and he shall die under his hand, he shall surely be avenged. ²¹ But if he will survive for a day or two, he shall not be avenged, for he is his property.

Penalty for bodily injury

²² If men shall fight and they collide with a pregnant woman and she miscarries, but there will be no fatality, he shall surely be punished as the husband of the woman shall cause to be assessed against him, and he shall pay it by order of judges. ²³ But if there shall be a fatality, then you shall award a life for a life; ²⁴ an eye for an eye,* a tooth for a tooth, a hand for a hand, a foot for a foot;

---

den to spare the murderer. Even if he is a Kohen about to perform the service on the Altar, he must be removed to suffer his penalty. However, if someone killed through carelessness, but unintentionally — for example, he *had not lain in ambush* — he is not deserving of death. Such an offender is exiled in specially designated cities. The nature of the crime that incurs exile and the other related laws are found in *Numbers* 35 and *Deuteronomy* 19.

21:24. The term *an eye for an eye* means that the responsible party must pay the *monetary value* for an eye (*Bava Kamma* 83b-84a). The Torah uses the expression *an eye for an eye* because in the Heavenly scales the perpetrator *deserves* to lose his own eye — and for this reason cannot find atonement merely by making the required monetary payments; he must also beg his victim's forgiveness (*Rambam*).

כה-כו כְּוִיָּה֙ תַּ֣חַת כְּוִיָּ֔ה פֶּ֖צַע תַּ֣חַת פָּ֑צַע חַבּוּרָ֕ה תַּ֖חַת חַבּוּרָֽה׃ וְכִֽי־יַכֶּ֨ה אִ֜ישׁ אֶת־עֵ֥ין עַבְדּ֛וֹ אֽוֹ־אֶת־עֵ֥ין אֲמָת֖וֹ וְשִֽׁחֲתָ֑הּ לַֽחָפְשִׁ֥י יְשַׁלְּחֶ֖נּוּ תַּ֥חַת

כז עֵינֽוֹ׃ וְאִם־שֵׁ֥ן עַבְדּ֛וֹ אֽוֹ־שֵׁ֥ן אֲמָת֖וֹ יַפִּ֑יל לַֽחָפְשִׁ֥י יְשַׁלְּחֶ֖נּוּ תַּ֥חַת

כח שִׁנּֽוֹ׃ וְכִֽי־יִגַּ֨ח שׁ֜וֹר אֶת־אִ֥ישׁ א֤וֹ אֶת־אִשָּׁה֙ וָמֵ֔ת סָק֤וֹל יִסָּקֵל֙ הַשּׁ֔וֹר וְלֹ֥א יֵֽאָכֵ֖ל

כט אֶת־בְּשָׂר֑וֹ וּבַ֥עַל הַשּׁ֖וֹר נָקִֽי׃ וְאִ֡ם שׁוֹר֩ נַגָּ֨ח ה֜וּא מִתְּמֹ֣ל שִׁלְשֹׁ֗ם וְהוּעַ֤ד בִּבְעָלָיו֙ וְלֹ֣א יִשְׁמְרֶ֔נּוּ וְהֵמִ֥ית אִ֖ישׁ א֣וֹ אִשָּׁ֑ה הַשּׁוֹר֙ יִסָּקֵ֔ל וְגַם־בְּעָלָ֖יו יוּמָֽת׃

ל-לא אִם־כֹּ֖פֶר יוּשַׁ֣ת עָלָ֑יו וְנָתַן֙ פִּדְיֹ֣ן נַפְשׁ֔וֹ כְּכֹ֥ל אֲשֶׁר־יוּשַׁ֖ת עָלָֽיו׃ אוֹ־בֵ֥ן יִגָּ֖ח

לב אוֹ־בַ֣ת יִגָּ֑ח כַּמִּשְׁפָּ֥ט הַזֶּ֖ה יֵעָ֥שֶׂה לּֽוֹ׃ אִם־עֶ֛בֶד יִגַּ֥ח הַשּׁ֖וֹר א֣וֹ אָמָ֑ה כֶּ֣סֶף ׀ שְׁלֹשִׁ֣ים שְׁקָלִ֗ים יִתֵּן֙ לַֽאדֹנָ֔יו וְהַשּׁ֖וֹר יִסָּקֵֽל׃

לג וְכִֽי־יִפְתַּ֨ח אִ֜ישׁ בּ֗וֹר אוֹ כִּֽי־יִכְרֶ֥ה אִ֛ישׁ בֹּ֖ר וְלֹ֣א יְכַסֶּ֑נּוּ וְנָֽפַל־שָׁ֥מָּה שּׁ֖וֹר א֥וֹ חֲמֽוֹר׃

לד בַּ֤עַל הַבּוֹר֙ יְשַׁלֵּ֔ם כֶּ֖סֶף יָשִׁ֣יב לִבְעָלָ֑יו וְהַמֵּ֖ת יִֽהְיֶה־לּֽוֹ׃ וְכִֽי־יִגֹּ֧ף

לה שֽׁוֹר־אִ֛ישׁ אֶת־שׁ֥וֹר רֵעֵ֖הוּ וָמֵ֑ת וּמָ֨כְר֜וּ אֶת־הַשּׁ֤וֹר הַחַי֙ וְחָצ֣וּ אֶת־כַּסְפּ֔וֹ

לו וְגַ֥ם אֶת־הַמֵּ֖ת יֶֽחֱצֽוּן׃ א֣וֹ נוֹדַ֗ע כִּ֠י שׁ֣וֹר נַגָּ֥ח הוּא֙ מִתְּמ֣וֹל שִׁלְשֹׁ֔ם וְלֹ֥א יִשְׁמְרֶ֖נּוּ בְּעָלָ֑יו שַׁלֵּ֨ם יְשַׁלֵּ֥ם שׁוֹר֙ תַּ֣חַת הַשּׁ֔וֹר וְהַמֵּ֖ת יִֽהְיֶה־לּֽוֹ׃ כִּ֤י יִגְנֹֽב־

כב א אִישׁ֙ שׁ֣וֹר אוֹ־שֶׂ֔ה וּטְבָח֖וֹ א֣וֹ מְכָר֑וֹ חֲמִשָּׁ֣ה בָקָ֗ר יְשַׁלֵּם֙ תַּ֣חַת הַשּׁ֔וֹר וְאַרְבַּע־צֹ֖אן תַּ֥חַת הַשֶּֽׂה׃ אִם־בַּמַּחְתֶּ֛רֶת יִמָּצֵ֥א הַגַּנָּ֖ב וְהֻכָּ֣ה וָמֵ֑ת אֵ֥ין ל֖וֹ

ב דָּמִֽים׃ אִם־זָֽרְחָ֥ה הַשֶּׁ֛מֶשׁ עָלָ֖יו דָּמִ֣ים ל֑וֹ שַׁלֵּ֣ם יְשַׁלֵּ֔ם אִם־אֵ֣ין ל֔וֹ וְנִמְכַּ֖ר

ג בִּגְנֵבָתֽוֹ׃ אִֽם־הִמָּצֵא֩ תִמָּצֵ֨א בְיָד֜וֹ הַגְּנֵבָ֗ה מִשּׁ֧וֹר עַד־חֲמ֛וֹר עַד־שֶׂ֖ה חַיִּ֑ים

ד שְׁנַ֖יִם יְשַׁלֵּֽם׃ כִּ֤י יַבְעֶר־אִישׁ֙ שָׂדֶ֣ה אוֹ־כֶ֔רֶם וְשִׁלַּח֙ אֶת־בְּעִיר֔וֹה וּבִעֵ֖ר בִּשְׂדֵ֣ה אַחֵ֑ר מֵיטַ֥ב שָׂדֵ֛הוּ וּמֵיטַ֥ב כַּרְמ֖וֹ יְשַׁלֵּֽם׃ כִּֽי־

ה תֵצֵ֨א אֵ֜שׁ וּמָצְאָ֤ה קֹצִים֙ וְנֶֽאֱכַ֣ל גָּדִ֔ישׁ א֥וֹ הַקָּמָ֖ה א֣וֹ הַשָּׂדֶ֑ה שַׁלֵּ֣ם

ו יְשַׁלֵּ֔ם הַמַּבְעִ֖ר אֶת־הַבְּעֵרָֽה׃ כִּֽי־יִתֵּן֩ אִ֨ישׁ אֶל־רֵעֵ֜הוּ כֶּ֤סֶף אֽוֹ־כֵלִים֙ לִשְׁמֹ֔ר וְגֻנַּ֖ב מִבֵּ֣ית הָאִ֑ישׁ אִם־יִמָּצֵ֥א הַגַּנָּ֖ב יְשַׁלֵּ֥ם שְׁנָֽיִם׃

ז אִם־לֹ֤א יִמָּצֵא֙ הַגַּנָּ֔ב וְנִקְרַ֥ב בַּֽעַל־הַבַּ֖יִת אֶל־הָֽאֱלֹהִ֑ים אִם־לֹ֥א שָׁלַ֛ח

ח יָד֖וֹ בִּמְלֶ֥אכֶת רֵעֵֽהוּ׃ עַֽל־כָּל־דְּבַר־פֶּ֡שַׁע עַל־שׁ֡וֹר עַל־חֲ֠מוֹר עַל־שֶׂ֨ה עַל־שַׂלְמָ֜ה עַל־כָּל־אֲבֵדָ֗ה אֲשֶׁ֤ר יֹאמַר֙ כִּי־ה֣וּא זֶ֔ה עַ֚ד הָֽאֱלֹהִ֔ים יָבֹ֖א

ט דְּבַר־שְׁנֵיהֶ֑ם אֲשֶׁ֤ר יַרְשִׁיעֻן֙ אֱלֹהִ֔ים יְשַׁלֵּ֥ם שְׁנַ֖יִם לְרֵעֵֽהוּ׃

21:28. This is an expression of the sanctity of human life: A beast cannot be permitted to remain alive if it caused the death of a human being, who was created in the image of God (see Ibn Ezra, R' Hirsch).

21:35-36. Once it has become established that the animal is aggressive, the owner's responsibility and liability grow.

22:1. The fact that all editions of *Tanach* list this as a new chapter illustrates a problem that came into being many centuries ago. The division of the Torah into the commonly used chapters is a Christian device introduced into printed editions of the Torah by non-Jewish Italian printers, who did not take into account the Jewish

interpretations of the Torah. This "chapter" is a continuation of the previous one, which discusses the laws of thieves and their penalties. This is especially obvious from verse 1, which speaks of *the thief*. Clearly, the reference is to the same thief who has been discussed in the earlier verse.

22:1-3. One may kill his attacker to save his own life but not to save his property. The Torah illustrates this law with the case of a thief tunneling into a home. Since the thief is aware that the householder will protect his property, we assume that the thief is ready to overpower him and kill, if need be.

22:2. *If the sun shone,* i.e., if it is as clear that the

²⁵ *a burn for a burn, a wound for a wound, a bruise for a bruise.*

²⁶ *If a man shall strike the eye of his slave or the eye of his maidservant and destroy it, he shall set him free in return for his eye.* ²⁷ *And if he knocks out the tooth of his slave or the tooth of his maidservant, he shall set him free in return for his tooth.*

Death caused by an animal ²⁸ *If an ox shall gore a man or woman and he shall die, the ox shall surely be stoned;* * *its flesh may not be eaten and the owner of the ox shall be innocent.* ²⁹ *But if it was an ox that gores habitually from yesterday and the day before yesterday, and its owner had been warned but did not guard it, and it killed a man or woman, the ox shall be stoned and even its owner shall die.* ³⁰ *When an atonement-payment shall be assessed against him, he shall pay as a redemption for his life whatever shall be assessed against him.* ³¹ *Whether it gores a boy or it gores a girl, in accordance with this judgment shall be done to him.* ³² *If the ox shall gore a slave or a maidservant, thirty silver shekels shall he give to his master, and the ox shall be stoned.*

A pit ³³ *If a man shall uncover a pit, or if a man shall dig a pit and not cover it, and an ox or a donkey fall into it,* ³⁴ *the owner of the pit shall make restitution. He shall return money to its owner, and the carcass shall be his.*

An animal damaging property ³⁵ *If one man's ox shall strike his fellow's ox* * *which dies, they shall sell the living ox and divide its money, and the carcass, too, shall they divide.* ³⁶ *But if it becomes known that it was an ox that had gored habitually, from yesterday and before yesterday, but its owner did not guard it, he shall surely pay an ox in place of the ox, and the carcass shall be his.*

Stealing livestock ³⁷ *If a man shall steal an ox, or a sheep or goat, and slaughter it or sell it, he shall pay five cattle in place of the ox, and four sheep in place of the sheep.*

22

Self-defense; payment for theft ¹ *If the thief* * *is discovered while tunneling in, and he is struck and dies,* * *there is no blood-guilt on his account.* ² *If the sun shone* * *upon him, there is blood-guilt on his account. He shall make restitution; if he has nothing, he shall be sold for his theft.* ³ *If the theft shall be found in his possession — whether a live ox or donkey or sheep or goat — he shall pay double.*

Damages caused by livestock ⁴ *If a man permits livestock to devour a field or vineyard — whether he set loose his livestock or he grazed it in another's field — from the best of his field and the best of his vineyard shall he pay.*

⁵ *If a fire shall go forth and find thorns, and a stack of grain or a standing crop or a field is consumed, the one who kindled the fire shall make restitution.*

Laws of custodians ⁶ *If a man shall give money* * *or vessels to his fellow to safeguard, and it is stolen from the house of the man, if the thief is found he shall pay double.* ⁷ *If the thief is not found, then the householder* * *shall approach the court that he had not laid his hand upon his fellow's property.* ⁸ *For every item of liability — whether an ox, a donkey, a sheep, or a garment — regarding any lost item about which he says, "This is it!" to the court shall come both their claims. Whomever the court finds guilty shall pay double to his fellow.*

---

intruder means no physical harm as it is clear that the shining sun brings healing to the world, then it is forbidden for the householder to kill. An example of such clarity is the case of a father burglarizing his son, for one may be certain that a parent will not murder his child.

22:6-14. The passage discusses the laws of people who

are entrusted to safeguard someone else's property. If the charge [*pikadon*] is lost, stolen, or damaged, the liability of the custodian varies according to whether and how he may have been compensated for the task.

22:7. The unpaid custodian who claims innocence swears in court that he has not made unauthorized personal use of the item (*Rashi*).

יִתֵּ֨ן אִ֜ישׁ אֶל־רֵעֵ֗הוּ חֲמ֨וֹר אוֹ־שׁ֥וֹר אוֹ־שֶׂ֛ה וְכָל־בְּהֵמָ֖ה לִשְׁמֹ֑ר וּמֵ֣ת אוֹ־

י נִשְׁבַּ֤ר אוֹ־נִשְׁבָּ֙ה אֵ֣ין רֹאֶֽה: שְׁבֻעַ֣ת יְהֹוָ֗ה תִּֽהְיֶה֙ בֵּ֣ין שְׁנֵיהֶ֔ם אִם־לֹ֥א שָׁלַ֛ח

יא יָד֖וֹ בִּמְלֶ֣אכֶת רֵעֵ֑הוּ וְלָקַ֥ח בְּעָלָ֖יו וְלֹ֣א יְשַׁלֵּֽם: וְאִם־גָּנֹ֥ב יִגָּנֵ֖ב מֵֽעִמּ֑וֹ יְשַׁלֵּ֖ם

יב לִבְעָלָֽיו: אִם־טָרֹ֣ף יִטָּרֵ֔ף יְבִאֵ֖הוּ עֵ֑ד הַטְּרֵפָ֖ה לֹ֥א יְשַׁלֵּֽם:

יג וְכִֽי־יִשְׁאַ֥ל אִ֛ישׁ מֵעִ֥ם רֵעֵ֖הוּ וְנִשְׁבַּ֣ר אוֹ־מֵ֑ת בְּעָלָ֥יו אֵין־עִמּ֖וֹ שַׁלֵּ֥ם יְשַׁלֵּֽם:

יד־טו אִם־בְּעָלָ֥יו עִמּ֖וֹ לֹ֣א יְשַׁלֵּ֑ם אִם־שָׂכִ֣יר ה֔וּא בָּ֖א בִּשְׂכָרֽוֹ: וְכִֽי־יְפַתֶּ֣ה

טז אִ֗ישׁ בְּתוּלָ֛ה אֲשֶׁ֥ר לֹא־אֹרָ֖שָׂה וְשָׁכַ֣ב עִמָּ֑הּ מָהֹ֛ר יִמְהָרֶ֥נָּה לּ֖וֹ לְאִשָּֽׁה: אִם־

יז מָאֵ֧ן יְמָאֵ֛ן אָבִ֖יהָ לְתִתָּ֣הּ ל֑וֹ כֶּ֣סֶף יִשְׁקֹ֔ל כְּמֹ֖הַר הַבְּתוּלֹֽת: מְכַשֵּׁפָ֖ה

יח־יט לֹ֥א תְחַיֶּֽה: כָּל־שֹׁכֵ֥ב עִם־בְּהֵמָ֖ה מ֣וֹת יוּמָֽת: זֹבֵ֥חַ לָֽאֱלֹהִ֖ים

כ יָֽחֳרָ֑ם בִּלְתִּ֥י לַֽיהֹוָ֖ה לְבַדּֽוֹ: וְגֵ֥ר לֹֽא־תוֹנֶ֖ה וְלֹ֣א תִלְחָצֶ֑נּוּ כִּֽי־גֵרִ֥ים הֱיִיתֶ֖ם

כא־כב בְּאֶ֥רֶץ מִצְרָֽיִם: כָּל־אַלְמָנָ֥ה וְיָת֖וֹם לֹ֥א תְעַנּֽוּן: אִם־עַנֵּ֤ה תְעַנֶּה֙ אֹת֔וֹ כִּ֣י אִם־

כג צָעֹ֤ק יִצְעַק֙ אֵלַ֔י שָׁמֹ֥עַ אֶשְׁמַ֖ע צַֽעֲקָתֽוֹ: וְחָרָ֣ה אַפִּ֔י וְהָרַגְתִּ֥י אֶתְכֶ֖ם בֶּחָ֑רֶב וְהָי֤וּ נְשֵׁיכֶם֙ אַלְמָנ֔וֹת וּבְנֵיכֶ֖ם יְתֹמִֽים:

כד אִם־כֶּ֣סֶף ׀ תַּלְוֶ֣ה אֶת־עַמִּ֗י אֶת־הֶֽעָנִי֙ עִמָּ֔ךְ לֹא־תִֽהְיֶ֥ה ל֖וֹ כְּנֹשֶׁ֑ה לֹֽא־

כה תְשִׂימ֥וּן עָלָ֖יו נֶֽשֶׁךְ: אִם־חָבֹ֥ל תַּחְבֹּ֖ל שַׂלְמַ֣ת רֵעֶ֑ךָ עַד־בֹּ֥א הַשֶּׁ֖מֶשׁ תְּשִׁיבֶ֥נּוּ

כו לֽוֹ: כִּ֣י הִ֤וא כְסוּתֹה֙ לְבַדָּ֔הּ הִ֥וא שִׂמְלָת֖וֹ לְעֹר֑וֹ בַּמֶּ֣ה יִשְׁכָּ֔ב וְהָיָה֙ כִּֽי־יִצְעַ֣ק

כז אֵלַ֔י וְשָֽׁמַעְתִּ֖י כִּֽי־חַנּ֥וּן אָֽנִי: אֱלֹהִ֖ים לֹ֣א תְקַלֵּ֑ל וְנָשִׂ֥יא

כח־כט בְעַמְּךָ֖ לֹ֣א תָאֹֽר: מְלֵֽאָתְךָ֥ וְדִמְעֲךָ֖ לֹ֣א תְאַחֵ֑ר בְּכ֥וֹר בָּנֶ֖יךָ תִּתֶּן־לִֽי: כֵּֽן־

ל תַּֽעֲשֶׂ֥ה לְשֹֽׁרְךָ֖ לְצֹאנֶ֑ךָ שִׁבְעַ֤ת יָמִים֙ יִֽהְיֶ֣ה עִם־אִמּ֔וֹ בַּיּ֥וֹם הַשְּׁמִינִ֖י תִּתְּנוֹ־לִֽי: וְאַנְשֵׁי־קֹ֨דֶשׁ֙ תִּֽהְי֣וּן לִ֔י וּבָשָׂ֧ר בַּשָּׂדֶ֛ה טְרֵפָ֖ה לֹ֣א תֹאכֵ֑לוּ לַכֶּ֖לֶב תַּשְׁלִכ֥וּן

א אֹתֽוֹ: כג לֹ֥א תִשָּׂ֖א שֵׁ֣מַע שָׁ֑וְא אַל־תָּ֤שֶׁת יָֽדְךָ֙ עִם־רָשָׁ֔ע לִֽהְיֹ֖ת

ב עֵ֥ד חָמָֽס: לֹֽא־תִהְיֶ֥ה אַֽחֲרֵֽי־רַבִּ֖ים לְרָעֹ֑ת וְלֹא־תַֽעֲנֶ֣ה עַל־רִ֗ב לִנְטֹ֛ת

ג־ד אַֽחֲרֵ֥י רַבִּ֖ים לְהַטֹּֽת: וְדָ֕ל לֹ֥א תֶהְדַּ֖ר בְּרִיבֽוֹ: כִּ֤י תִפְגַּע֙ שׁ֣וֹר

ה אֹֽיִבְךָ֔ א֖וֹ חֲמֹר֑וֹ תָּעֶ֖ה הָשֵׁ֥ב תְּשִׁיבֶ֖נּוּ לֽוֹ: כִּֽי־תִרְאֶ֞ה חֲמ֣וֹר

ו שֹֽׂנַֽאֲךָ֗ רֹבֵץ֙ תַּ֣חַת מַשָּׂא֔וֹ וְחָֽדַלְתָּ֖ מֵֽעֲזֹ֣ב ל֑וֹ עָזֹ֥ב תַּֽעֲזֹ֖ב עִמּֽוֹ: לֹ֣א

READING
SECOND
DAY CHOL
HAMOED
PESACH
22:24-23:19
Revi'i/Maftir:
p. 400

רביעי

חמישי

22:20-23. Although it is forbidden to abuse anyone, this prohibition is framed specifically with reference to the disadvantaged because they are most vulnerable to such mistreatment.

22:22. The Torah implies that anyone who dares cause a widow or orphan to suffer should expect severe retaliation from the Father of orphans and the Judge of widows (Rashi).

22:24-26. A loan is one of the highest forms of charity, because it preserves the self-respect of the borrower and allows him to rebuild his own independent financial stability.

22:24. This is one of three cases in Scripture where the word אם means when, and not if [cf. 20:22 and Leviticus 2:14]. To assist the poor with a loan is not optional, but

obligatory (Rashi).

22:28. Your fullness-offering, i.e., bikkurim, the first fruits, which are picked when they become full and ripe, and are presented to the Kohanim (Rashi).

22:30. The Torah mentions holiness in introducing the prohibition against a certain forbidden food to put it in perspective: The forbidden foods deter the Jew from the attainment of holiness, the goal which God sets for His people (Ramban).

23:2. Several laws are derived from this verse by means of Talmudic exegesis. Our translation of the plain meaning follows Rashi: A judge must voice his opinion according to his understanding of the law and the evidence. Even if he is heavily outnumbered by others, he must not change his opinion to agree with them, if he considers

⁹ *If a man shall give his fellow a donkey or an ox or a sheep or any animal to safeguard, and it died or was broken or was looted, without an eyewitness;* ¹⁰ *an oath of HASHEM shall be between them both that he did not lay his hand upon the property of his fellow; the owner shall accept it and he shall not pay.* ¹¹ *If it shall be stolen from him, he shall pay to its owner.* ¹² *If it shall be torn to death, he shall produce a witness; for a torn animal he does not pay.*

A borrower   ¹³ *If a man shall borrow from his fellow and it shall become broken or shall die — provided its owner is not with him — he shall surely make restitution.* ¹⁴ *If its owner is with him, he shall not make restitution. If he was a renter, it came in return for his rental.*

Seduction   ¹⁵ *If a man shall seduce a virgin who was not betrothed and lie with her, he shall provide her with a marriage contract as his wife.* ¹⁶ *If her father refuses to give her to him, he shall weigh out silver according to the marriage contract of the virgins.*

¹⁷ *You shall not permit a sorceress to live.*

¹⁸ *Anyone who lies with an animal shall surely be put to death.*

¹⁹ *One who brings offerings to the gods shall be destroyed — only to HASHEM alone!*

Sensitivity   ²⁰ *You shall not taunt or oppress a stranger,* * *for you were strangers in the*
to the   *land of Egypt.* ²¹ *You shall not cause pain to any widow or orphan.* ²² *If you [dare*
helpless and   *to] cause him pain . . . !* * *— for if he shall cry out to Me, I shall surely hear his*
abandoned   *outcry.* ²³ *My wrath shall blaze and I shall kill you by the sword, and your wives will be widows and your children orphans.*

The   ²⁴ *When* * *you lend money* * *to My people, to the poor person who is with you,*
command-   *do not act toward him as a creditor; do not lay interest upon him.* ²⁵ *If you take*
ment   *your fellow's garment as security, until sunset shall you return it to him.* ²⁶ *For*
to extend   *it alone is his clothing, it is his garment for his skin — in what should he lie down?*
free loans   *— so it will be that if he cries out to Me, I shall listen, for I am compassionate.*

²⁷ *You shall not revile God, and you shall not curse a leader among your people.*

²⁸ *Do not delay your fullness-offering* * *or your priestly heave-offering; the firstborn of your sons shall you present to Me.* ²⁹ *So shall you do to your ox, to your flock; for a seven-day period shall it be with its mother, on the eighth day you may present it to Me.* ³⁰ *People of holiness* * *shall you be to Me; you shall not eat flesh of an animal that was torn in the field; to the dog shall you throw it.*

23   ¹ **D**o *not accept a false report, do not extend your hand with the wicked to be*
Integrity of   *a venal witness.* ² *Do not be a follower of the majority for evil;* * *and do not*
the judicial   *respond to a grievance by yielding to the majority to pervert [the law].* ³ *Do not*
process   *glorify* * *a destitute person in his grievance.*

⁴ *If you encounter an ox of your enemy or his donkey wandering, you shall return it to him repeatedly.*

Fair   ⁵ *If you see the donkey of someone you hate crouching under its burden,*
dispensation   *would you refrain from helping him? — you shall help repeatedly with him.*
of justice

---

them to be mistaken or intentionally perverting the law.   poor, it is forbidden to pervert the law, no matter how
23:3. Despite the temptation to ease the plight of the   noble the intention.

ז   תִּתֵּה מִשְׁפַּט אֶבְיֹנְךָ בְּרִיבוֹ: מִדְּבַר־שֶׁקֶר תִּרְחָק וְנָקִי וְצַדִּיק אַל־תַּהֲרֹג כִּי

ח   לֹא־אַצְדִּיק רָשָׁע: וְשֹׁחַד לֹא תִקָּח כִּי הַשֹּׁחַד יְעַוֵּר פִּקְחִים וִיסַלֵּף דִּבְרֵי

ט   צַדִּיקִים: וְגֵר לֹא תִלְחָץ וְאַתֶּם יְדַעְתֶּם אֶת־נֶפֶשׁ הַגֵּר כִּי־גֵרִים הֱיִיתֶם

י   בְּאֶרֶץ מִצְרָיִם: וְשֵׁשׁ שָׁנִים תִּזְרַע אֶת־אַרְצֶךָ וְאָסַפְתָּ אֶת־תְּבוּאָתָהּ:

יא   וְהַשְּׁבִיעִת תִּשְׁמְטֶנָּה וּנְטַשְׁתָּהּ וְאָכְלוּ אֶבְיֹנֵי עַמֶּךָ וְיִתְרָם תֹּאכַל חַיַּת

יב   הַשָּׂדֶה כֵּן־תַּעֲשֶׂה לְכַרְמְךָ לְזֵיתֶךָ: שֵׁשֶׁת יָמִים תַּעֲשֶׂה מַעֲשֶׂיךָ וּבַיּוֹם

יג   הַשְּׁבִיעִי תִּשְׁבֹּת לְמַעַן יָנוּחַ שׁוֹרְךָ וַחֲמֹרֶךָ וְיִנָּפֵשׁ בֶּן־אֲמָתְךָ וְהַגֵּר: וּבְכֹל

אֲשֶׁר־אָמַרְתִּי אֲלֵיכֶם תִּשָּׁמֵרוּ וְשֵׁם אֱלֹהִים אֲחֵרִים לֹא תַזְכִּירוּ לֹא

יד-טו   יִשָּׁמַע עַל־פִּיךָ: שָׁלֹשׁ רְגָלִים תָּחֹג לִי בַּשָּׁנָה: אֶת־חַג הַמַּצּוֹת תִּשְׁמֹר

שִׁבְעַת יָמִים תֹּאכַל מַצּוֹת כַּאֲשֶׁר צִוִּיתִךָ לְמוֹעֵד חֹדֶשׁ הָאָבִיב כִּי־בוֹ

טז   יָצָאתָ מִמִּצְרָיִם וְלֹא־יֵרָאוּ פָנַי רֵיקָם: וְחַג הַקָּצִיר בִּכּוּרֵי מַעֲשֶׂיךָ אֲשֶׁר

תִּזְרַע בַּשָּׂדֶה וְחַג הָאָסִף בְּצֵאת הַשָּׁנָה בְּאָסְפְּךָ אֶת־מַעֲשֶׂיךָ מִן־הַשָּׂדֶה:

יז-יח   שָׁלֹשׁ פְּעָמִים בַּשָּׁנָה יֵרָאֶה כָּל־זְכוּרְךָ אֶל־פְּנֵי הָאָדֹן | יהוה: לֹא־תִזְבַּח

יט   עַל־חָמֵץ דַּם־זִבְחִי וְלֹא־יָלִין חֵלֶב־חַגִּי עַד־בֹּקֶר: רֵאשִׁית בִּכּוּרֵי

אַדְמָתְךָ תָּבִיא בֵּית יהוה אֱלֹהֶיךָ לֹא־תְבַשֵּׁל גְּדִי בַּחֲלֵב אִמּוֹ:

  כ   הִנֵּה אָנֹכִי שֹׁלֵחַ מַלְאָךְ לְפָנֶיךָ לִשְׁמָרְךָ בַּדָּרֶךְ וְלַהֲבִיאֲךָ אֶל־הַמָּקוֹם

כא   אֲשֶׁר הֲכִנֹתִי: הִשָּׁמֶר מִפָּנָיו וּשְׁמַע בְּקֹלוֹ אַל־תַּמֵּר בּוֹ כִּי לֹא יִשָּׂא

כב   לְפִשְׁעֲכֶם כִּי שְׁמִי בְּקִרְבּוֹ: כִּי אִם־שָׁמֹעַ תִּשְׁמַע בְּקֹלוֹ וְעָשִׂיתָ כֹּל אֲשֶׁר

כג   אֲדַבֵּר וְאָיַבְתִּי אֶת־אֹיְבֶיךָ וְצַרְתִּי אֶת־צֹרְרֶיךָ: כִּי־יֵלֵךְ מַלְאָכִי לְפָנֶיךָ

וֶהֱבִיאֲךָ אֶל־הָאֱמֹרִי וְהַחִתִּי וְהַפְּרִזִּי וְהַכְּנַעֲנִי הַחִוִּי וְהַיְבוּסִי וְהִכְחַדְתִּיו:

כד   לֹא־תִשְׁתַּחֲוֶה לֵאלֹהֵיהֶם וְלֹא תָעָבְדֵם וְלֹא תַעֲשֶׂה כְּמַעֲשֵׂיהֶם כִּי הָרֵס

כה   תְּהָרְסֵם וְשַׁבֵּר תְּשַׁבֵּר מַצֵּבֹתֵיהֶם: וַעֲבַדְתֶּם אֵת יהוה אֱלֹהֵיכֶם וּבֵרַךְ

  כו   אֶת־לַחְמְךָ וְאֶת־מֵימֶיךָ וַהֲסִרֹתִי מַחֲלָה מִקִּרְבֶּךָ: לֹא תִהְיֶה

מְשַׁכֵּלָה וַעֲקָרָה בְּאַרְצֶךָ אֶת־מִסְפַּר יָמֶיךָ אֲמַלֵּא: אֶת־אֵימָתִי אֲשַׁלַּח

כז   לְפָנֶיךָ וְהַמֹּתִי אֶת־כָּל־הָעָם אֲשֶׁר תָּבֹא בָּהֶם וְנָתַתִּי אֶת־כָּל־אֹיְבֶיךָ

כח   אֵלֶיךָ עֹרֶף: וְשָׁלַחְתִּי אֶת־הַצִּרְעָה לְפָנֶיךָ וְגֵרְשָׁה אֶת־הַחִוִּי אֶת־הַכְּנַעֲנִי

כט   וְאֶת־הַחִתִּי מִלְּפָנֶיךָ: לֹא אֲגָרְשֶׁנּוּ מִפָּנֶיךָ בְּשָׁנָה אֶחָת פֶּן־תִּהְיֶה הָאָרֶץ

23:7. Regarding no other transgression does the Torah say that one should *distance* himself. So much does God abhor falsehood that we are commanded to stay far even from an appearance of a lie (*R' Bunam of P'schis'cha*).

23:14-19. The concepts symbolized by these festivals — freedom, the seasons, and prosperity — are at the root of human existence and happiness. By celebrating them in Jerusalem at the resting place of God's Presence and by bringing offerings to mark the occasions, we acknowledge Him as the Lord (v. 17), Who controls all aspects of life (*Sforno*).

23:19. The commandment of the first fruits [*bikkurim*]

applies to the seven species for which *Eretz Yisrael* is known: wheat, barley, figs, grapes, pomegranates, olives, and dates. Because *bikkurim* symbolize the Jew's devotion of the first fruits of his labors to the service of God, the trip to Jerusalem was celebrated in every town along the way with music and parades.

The prohibition against cooking meat and milk applies to all ages and species of sheep [and cattle; Rabbinic law extended it to all kosher meat and fowl]. The Torah mentions this prohibition three times, from which the Sages derive that there are three elements of the prohibition. It is forbidden to cook the mixture, to eat it, and even to benefit from it (*Rashi*).

⁶ *Do not pervert the judgment of your destitute person in his grievance.* ⁷ *Distance yourself* from a false word; do not execute the innocent or the righteous, for I shall not exonerate the wicked.* ⁸ *Do not accept a bribe, for the bribe will blind those who see and corrupt words that are just.* ⁹ *Do not oppress a stranger; you know the feelings of a stranger, for you were strangers in the*

The Sabbaths of the land and the week

land of Egypt. ¹⁰ *Six years shall you sow your land and gather in its produce.* ¹¹ *And in the seventh, you shall leave it untended and unharvested, and the destitute of your people shall eat, and the wildlife of the field shall eat what is left; so shall you do to your vineyard and your olive grove.* ¹² *Six days shall you accomplish your activities, and on the seventh day you shall desist, so that your ox and donkey may be content and your maidservant's son and the sojourner may be refreshed.* ¹³ *Be careful regarding everything I have said to you. The name of the gods of others you shall not mention, nor shall your mouth cause it to be heard.*

The Three Pilgrimage Festivals

¹⁴ *Three pilgrimage festivals* shall you celebrate for Me during the year.* ¹⁵ *You shall observe the Festival of Matzos; seven days shall you eat matzos, as I have commanded you, at the appointed time of the month of springtime, for in it you left Egypt; you shall not be seen before Me empty-handed.* ¹⁶ *And the Festival of the Harvest of the first fruits of your labor that you sow in the field; and the Festival of the Ingathering at the close of the year, when you gather in your work from the field.* ¹⁷ *Three times during the year shall all your menfolk appear before the Lord, HASHEM.* ¹⁸ *You shall not offer the blood of My feast-offering upon leavened bread; nor may the fat of My festive-offering remain overnight until morning.* ¹⁹ *The choicest* first fruit of your land shall you bring to the House of HASHEM, your God; you shall not cook* a kid in the milk of its mother.*

The promise of swift passage to, and conquest of, the land

²⁰ *Behold! I send an angel before you to protect you on the way, and to bring you to the place that I have made ready.* ²¹ *Beware of him — hearken to his voice, do not rebel against him, for he will not forgive your willful sin — for My Name is within him.* ²² *For if you hearken to his voice and carry out all that I shall speak, then I shall be the enemy of your enemies and persecute your persecutors.* ²³ *For My angel shall go before you and bring you to the Amorite, the Hittite, the Perizzite, the Canaanite, the Hivvite, and the Jebusite, and I will annihilate them.* ²⁴ *Do not prostrate yourself to their gods, do not worship them, and do not act according to their practices; rather, you shall tear them apart, and you shall smash their pillars.* ²⁵ *You shall worship HASHEM,* your God, and He shall bless your bread and your water, and I shall remove illness from your midst.*

²⁶ *There shall be no woman who loses her young or is infertile in your land; I shall fill the number of your days.* ²⁷ *I shall send My fear before you and I shall confound the entire people among whom you shall come; and I shall make all your enemies turn the back of the neck to you.* ²⁸ *I shall send the hornet-swarm before you and it will drive away the Hivvite, the Canaanite, and the Hittite before you.* ²⁹ *I shall not drive them away from you in a single year, lest the Land become*

23:25. The more "enlightened" idol worshipers held that by honoring God's ministers, such as the sun and the power of vegetation, they would be blessed. The Torah promises, therefore, that no such intermediaries are needed or permitted. *Worship HASHEM,* and *He* will provide all the blessings you need (*Ramban*).

שְׁמָמָ֔ה וְרַבָּ֥ה עָלֶ֖יךָ חַיַּ֣ת הַשָּׂדֶֽה: מְעַ֤ט מְעַט֙ אֲגָרְשֶׁ֔נּוּ מִפָּנֶ֑יךָ עַ֚ד אֲשֶׁ֣ר ל

תִּפְרֶ֔ה וְנָחַלְתָּ֖ אֶת־הָאָֽרֶץ: וְשַׁתִּ֣י אֶת־גְּבֻלְךָ֗ מִיַּם־סוּף֙ וְעַד־יָ֣ם פְּלִשְׁתִּ֔ים לא

וּמִמִּדְבָּ֖ר עַד־הַנָּהָ֑ר כִּ֣י ׀ אֶתֵּ֣ן בְּיֶדְכֶ֗ם אֵ֚ת יֹֽשְׁבֵ֣י הָאָ֔רֶץ וְגֵרַשְׁתָּ֖מוֹ מִפָּנֶֽיךָ:

לֹֽא־תִכְרֹ֥ת לָהֶ֛ם וְלֵֽאלֹֽהֵיהֶ֖ם בְּרִֽית: לֹ֤א יֵֽשְׁבוּ֙ בְּאַרְצְךָ֔ פֶּן־יַֽחֲטִ֥יאוּ אֹֽתְךָ֖ לב-לג

לִ֑י כִּ֤י תַֽעֲבֹד֙ אֶת־אֱלֹ֣הֵיהֶ֔ם כִּֽי־יִֽהְיֶ֥ה לְךָ֖ לְמוֹקֵֽשׁ:

כד וְאֶל־מֹשֶׁ֨ה אָמַ֜ר עֲלֵ֣ה אֶל־יהוה֗ אַתָּה֙ וְאַֽהֲרֹן֙ נָדָ֣ב וַֽאֲבִיה֔וּא וְשִׁבְעִ֖ים א

מִזִּקְנֵ֣י יִשְׂרָאֵ֑ל וְהִשְׁתַּֽחֲוִיתֶ֖ם מֵֽרָחֹֽק: וְנִגַּ֨שׁ מֹשֶׁ֤ה לְבַדּוֹ֙ אֶל־יהוה֔ וְהֵ֖ם ב

לֹ֣א יִגָּ֑שׁוּ וְהָעָ֕ם לֹ֥א יַֽעֲל֖וּ עִמּֽוֹ: וַיָּבֹ֣א מֹשֶׁ֗ה וַיְסַפֵּ֤ר לָעָם֙ אֵ֚ת כָּל־דִּבְרֵ֣י ג

יהוה֔ וְאֵ֖ת כָּל־הַמִּשְׁפָּטִ֑ים וַיַּ֨עַן כָּל־הָעָ֜ם ק֤וֹל אֶחָד֙ וַיֹּ֣אמְר֔וּ כָּל־הַדְּבָרִ֛ים

אֲשֶׁר־דִּבֶּ֥ר יהוה֖ נַֽעֲשֶֽׂה: וַיִּכְתֹּ֣ב מֹשֶׁ֗ה אֵ֚ת כָּל־דִּבְרֵ֣י יהוה֔ וַיַּשְׁכֵּ֣ם בַּבֹּ֔קֶר ד

וַיִּ֥בֶן מִזְבֵּ֖חַ תַּ֣חַת הָהָ֑ר וּשְׁתֵּ֤ים עֶשְׂרֵה֙ מַצֵּבָ֔ה לִשְׁנֵ֖ים עָשָׂ֥ר שִׁבְטֵ֥י

יִשְׂרָאֵֽל: וַיִּשְׁלַ֗ח אֶֽת־נַֽעֲרֵי֙ בְּנֵ֣י יִשְׂרָאֵ֔ל וַיַּֽעֲל֖וּ עֹלֹ֑ת וַֽיִּזְבְּח֞וּ זְבָחִ֧ים ה

שְׁלָמִ֛ים לַֽיהוה֖ פָּרִ֑ים וַיִּקַּ֤ח מֹשֶׁה֙ חֲצִ֣י הַדָּ֔ם וַיָּ֖שֶׂם בָּֽאַגָּנֹ֑ת וַֽחֲצִ֣י הַדָּ֔ם ו

זָרַ֖ק עַל־הַמִּזְבֵּֽחַ: וַיִּקַּח֙ סֵ֣פֶר הַבְּרִ֔ית וַיִּקְרָ֖א בְּאָזְנֵ֣י הָעָ֑ם וַיֹּ֣אמְר֔וּ כֹּ֛ל ז

אֲשֶׁר־דִּבֶּ֥ר יהוה֖ נַֽעֲשֶׂ֥ה וְנִשְׁמָֽע: וַיִּקַּ֤ח מֹשֶׁה֙ אֶת־הַדָּ֔ם וַיִּזְרֹ֖ק עַל־הָעָ֑ם ח

וַיֹּ֕אמֶר הִנֵּ֤ה דַם־הַבְּרִית֙ אֲשֶׁ֨ר כָּרַ֤ת יהוה֙ עִמָּכֶ֔ם עַ֥ל כָּל־הַדְּבָרִ֖ים

הָאֵֽלֶּה: וַיַּ֥עַל מֹשֶׁ֖ה וְאַֽהֲרֹ֑ן נָדָב֙ וַֽאֲבִיה֔וּא וְשִׁבְעִ֖ים מִזִּקְנֵ֥י יִשְׂרָאֵֽל: וַיִּרְא֕וּ ט

אֵ֖ת אֱלֹהֵ֣י יִשְׂרָאֵ֑ל וְתַ֣חַת רַגְלָ֗יו כְּמַֽעֲשֵׂה֙ לִבְנַ֣ת הַסַּפִּ֔יר וּכְעֶ֥צֶם הַשָּׁמַ֖יִם

לָטֹֽהַר: וְאֶל־אֲצִילֵי֙ בְּנֵ֣י יִשְׂרָאֵ֔ל לֹ֥א שָׁלַ֖ח יָד֑וֹ וַֽיֶּֽחֱזוּ֙ אֶת־הָ֣אֱלֹהִ֔ים יא

וַיֹּֽאכְל֖וּ וַיִּשְׁתּֽוּ: וַיֹּ֨אמֶר יהוה֜ אֶל־מֹשֶׁ֗ה עֲלֵ֥ה אֵלַ֛י יב

הָהָ֖רָה וֶֽהְיֵה־שָׁ֑ם וְאֶתְּנָ֨ה לְךָ֜ אֶת־לֻחֹ֣ת הָאֶ֗בֶן וְהַתּוֹרָה֙ וְהַמִּצְוָ֔ה אֲשֶׁ֥ר

כָּתַ֖בְתִּי לְהֽוֹרֹתָֽם: וַיָּ֣קָם מֹשֶׁ֔ה וִֽיהוֹשֻׁ֖עַ מְשָֽׁרְת֑וֹ וַיַּ֥עַל מֹשֶׁ֖ה אֶל־ יג

הַ֥ר הָֽאֱלֹהִֽים: וְאֶל־הַזְּקֵנִ֤ים אָמַר֙ שְׁבוּ־לָ֣נוּ בָזֶ֔ה עַ֥ד אֲשֶׁר־נָשׁ֖וּב אֲלֵיכֶ֑ם יד

וְהִנֵּ֨ה אַֽהֲרֹ֤ן וְחוּר֙ עִמָּכֶ֔ם מִי־בַ֥עַל דְּבָרִ֖ים יִגַּ֥שׁ אֲלֵהֶֽם: וַיַּ֥עַל מֹשֶׁ֖ה אֶל־ טו

הָהָ֑ר וַיְכַ֥ס הֶֽעָנָ֖ן אֶת־הָהָֽר: וַיִּשְׁכֹּ֤ן כְּבֽוֹד־יהוה֙ עַל־הַ֣ר סִינַ֔י וַיְכַסֵּ֥הוּ טז

מפטיר

הֶֽעָנָ֖ן שֵׁ֣שֶׁת יָמִ֑ים וַיִּקְרָ֧א אֶל־מֹשֶׁ֛ה בַּיּ֥וֹם הַשְּׁבִיעִ֖י מִתּ֥וֹךְ הֶֽעָנָֽן: וּמַרְאֵה֙ יז

Haftaras
Mishpatim:
p. 1154

כְּב֣וֹד יהוה֔ כְּאֵ֥שׁ אֹכֶ֖לֶת בְּרֹ֣אשׁ הָהָ֑ר לְעֵינֵ֖י בְּנֵ֣י יִשְׂרָאֵֽל: וַיָּבֹ֥א יח

For special
Sabbaths,
see pp. x-xi

מֹשֶׁ֛ה בְּת֥וֹךְ הֶֽעָנָ֖ן וַיַּ֣עַל אֶל־הָהָ֑ר וַיְהִ֤י מֹשֶׁה֙ בָּהָ֔ר אַרְבָּעִ֣ים יוֹם֙ וְאַרְבָּעִ֖ים

לָֽיְלָה: **פפפ** קי״ז פסוקים. עזיא״ל סימן. חנו״יי סימן.

23:31. *The Sea of the Philistines* is the Mediterranean, and the *River* is the Euphrates. *Ibn Ezra* comments that this verse, which describes the great extent of the land, explains why it would have to be conquered gradually.

24:1. This chapter shifts back to the Revelation at Sinai. Moses is instructed regarding his ascent up the mountain for forty days to be taught the Torah in its entirety, and regarding the covenant that the Jewish people will seal

with God, signifying their acceptance of the Torah and their eternal responsibility to study and uphold it.

24:4. The *twelve pillars* were to symbolize that all twelve components of the nation accepted the covenant (*Rashbam*). By setting up twelve separate monuments, Moses alluded to this and showed that each tribe accepted its own unique responsibility as part of God's nation.

24:7. The Jews declared their resolve to "*do and obey*" *desolate and the wildlife of the field multiply against you.* [30] *Little by little shall I drive them away from you, until you become fruitful and make the Land your heritage.*

[31] *I shall set your border from the Sea of Reeds to the Sea of the Philistines,* * *and from the Wilderness until the River, for I shall deliver the inhabitants of the Land into your hands and you shall drive them away from before you.* [32] *You shall not seal a covenant with them or their gods.* [33] *They shall not dwell in your Land lest they cause you to sin against Me, that you will worship their gods, for it will be a trap for you.*

24 [1] To Moses He said,* *"Go up to HASHEM, you, Aaron, Nadab and Abihu, and seventy of the elders of Israel, and you shall prostrate yourselves from a distance.* [2] *And Moses alone shall approach HASHEM, but they shall not approach, and the people shall not go up with him."*

[3] *Moses came and told the people all the words of HASHEM and all the ordinances, and the entire people responded with one voice and they said, "All the words that HASHEM has spoken, we will do."*

[4] *Moses wrote all the words of HASHEM. He arose early in the morning and built an altar at the foot of the mountain, and twelve pillars* * *for the twelve tribes of Israel.* [5] *He sent the youths of the Children of Israel and they brought up burnt-offerings, and they slaughtered bulls to HASHEM as feast peace-offerings to HASHEM.* [6] *Moses took half the blood and placed it in basins, and half the blood he threw upon the altar.* [7] *He took the Book of the Covenant and read it*

"We will do and we will obey!"

in earshot of the people, and they said, "Everything that HASHEM has said, we will do and we will obey!" * [8] *Moses took the blood and threw it upon the people, and he said, "Behold the blood of the covenant that HASHEM sealed with you concerning all these matters."*

Prophecy at the mountain

[9] *Moses, Aaron, Nadab and Abihu, and seventy of the elders of Israel ascended.* [10] *They saw the God of Israel, and under His feet was the likeness of sapphire brickwork, and it was like the essence of the heaven in purity.* [11] *Against the great men of the Children of Israel, He did not stretch out His hand — they gazed at God, yet they ate and drank.*

[12] *HASHEM said to Moses, "Ascend to Me to the mountain and remain there, and I shall give you the stone Tablets and the teaching and the commandment that I have written, to teach them."* [13] *Moses stood up with Joshua, his servant; and Moses ascended to the Mountain of God.* [14] *To the elders he said, "Wait for us here until we return to you. Behold! Aaron and Hur are with you; whoever has a grievance should approach them."*

[15] *Moses ascended the mountain, and the cloud covered the mountain.* [16] *The glory of HASHEM rested upon Mount Sinai, and the cloud covered it for a six-day period. He called to Moses on the seventh day from the midst of the cloud.* [17] *The appearance of the glory of HASHEM was like a consuming fire on the mountaintop before the eyes of the Children of Israel.* [18] *Moses arrived in the midst of the cloud and ascended the mountain; and Moses was on the mountain for forty days and forty nights.*

---

whatever God would command — even before the commandments were issued. This declaration has remained for all time the anthem of Israel's faith in God and devotion to His word.

פרשת תרומה

כה א-ב וַיְדַבֵּר יהוָה אֶל־מֹשֶׁה לֵּאמְר: דַּבֵּר אֶל־בְּנֵי יִשְׂרָאֵל וְיִקְחוּ־לִי תְּרוּמָה

ג מֵאֵת כָּל־אִישׁ אֲשֶׁר יִדְּבֶנּוּ לִבּוֹ תִּקְחוּ אֶת־תְּרוּמָתִי: וְזֹאת הַתְּרוּמָה

ד אֲשֶׁר תִּקְחוּ מֵאִתָּם זָהָב וָכֶסֶף וּנְחְשֶׁת: וּתְכֵלֶת וְאַרְגָּמָן וְתוֹלַעַת שָׁנִי

ה וְשֵׁשׁ וְעִזִּים: וְעֹרֹת אֵילִם מְאָדָּמִים וְעֹרֹת תְּחָשִׁים וַעֲצֵי שִׁטִּים:

ו-ז שֶׁמֶן לַמָּאֹר בְּשָׂמִים לְשֶׁמֶן הַמִּשְׁחָה וְלִקְטֹרֶת הַסַּמִּים: אַבְנֵי־שֹׁהַם

ח-ט וְאַבְנֵי מִלֻּאִים לָאֵפֹד וְלַחֹשֶׁן: וְעָשׂוּ לִי מִקְדָּשׁ וְשָׁכַנְתִּי בְּתוֹכָם: כְּכֹל

אֲשֶׁר אֲנִי מַרְאֶה אוֹתְךָ אֵת תַּבְנִית הַמִּשְׁכָּן וְאֵת תַּבְנִית כָּל־כֵּלָיו וְכֵן

י תַּעֲשׂוּ: וְעָשׂוּ אֲרוֹן עֲצֵי שִׁטִּים אַמָּתַיִם וָחֵצִי אָרְכּוֹ וְאַמָּה

יא וָחֵצִי רָחְבּוֹ וְאַמָּה וָחֵצִי קֹמָתוֹ: וְצִפִּיתָ אֹתוֹ זָהָב טָהוֹר מִבַּיִת וּמִחוּץ

יב תְּצַפֶּנּוּ וְעָשִׂיתָ עָלָיו זֵר זָהָב סָבִיב: וְיָצַקְתָּ לּוֹ אַרְבַּע טַבְּעֹת זָהָב וְנָתַתָּה עַל־

אַרְבַּע פַּעֲמֹתָיו וּשְׁתֵּי טַבָּעֹת עַל־צַלְעוֹ הָאֶחָת וּשְׁתֵּי טַבָּעֹת עַל־

יג-יד צַלְעוֹ הַשֵּׁנִית: וְעָשִׂיתָ בַדֵּי עֲצֵי שִׁטִּים וְצִפִּיתָ אֹתָם זָהָב: וְהֵבֵאתָ אֶת־

הַבַּדִּים בַּטַּבָּעֹת עַל צַלְעֹת הָאָרֹן לָשֵׂאת אֶת־הָאָרֹן בָּהֶם: בְּטַבְּעֹת

טו-טז הָאָרֹן יִהְיוּ הַבַּדִּים לֹא יָסֻרוּ מִמֶּנּוּ: וְנָתַתָּ אֶל־הָאָרֹן אֵת הָעֵדֻת אֲשֶׁר

יז אֶתֵּן אֵלֶיךָ: וְעָשִׂיתָ כַפֹּרֶת זָהָב טָהוֹר אַמָּתַיִם וָחֵצִי אָרְכָּהּ וְאַמָּה וָחֵצִי

יח רָחְבָּהּ: וְעָשִׂיתָ שְׁנַיִם כְּרֻבִים זָהָב מִקְשָׁה תַּעֲשֶׂה אֹתָם מִשְּׁנֵי קְצוֹת

יט הַכַּפֹּרֶת: וַעֲשֵׂה כְּרוּב אֶחָד מִקָּצָה מִזֶּה וּכְרוּב־אֶחָד מִקָּצָה מִזֶּה מִן־

כ הַכַּפֹּרֶת תַּעֲשׂוּ אֶת־הַכְּרֻבִים עַל־שְׁנֵי קְצוֹתָיו: וְהָיוּ הַכְּרֻבִים פֹּרְשֵׂי

כְנָפַיִם לְמַעְלָה סֹכְכִים בְּכַנְפֵיהֶם עַל־הַכַּפֹּרֶת וּפְנֵיהֶם אִישׁ אֶל־אָחִיו

כא אֶל־הַכַּפֹּרֶת יִהְיוּ פְּנֵי הַכְּרֻבִים: וְנָתַתָּ אֶת־הַכַּפֹּרֶת עַל־הָאָרֹן מִלְמָעְלָה

כב וְאֶל־הָאָרֹן תִּתֵּן אֶת־הָעֵדֻת אֲשֶׁר אֶתֵּן אֵלֶיךָ: וְנוֹעַדְתִּי לְךָ שָׁם וְדִבַּרְתִּי

אִתְּךָ מֵעַל הַכַּפֹּרֶת מִבֵּין שְׁנֵי הַכְּרֻבִים אֲשֶׁר עַל־אֲרוֹן הָעֵדֻת אֵת כָּל־

אֲשֶׁר אֲצַוֶּה אוֹתְךָ אֶל־בְּנֵי יִשְׂרָאֵל:

כג וְעָשִׂיתָ שֻׁלְחָן עֲצֵי שִׁטִּים אַמָּתַיִם אָרְכּוֹ וְאַמָּה רָחְבּוֹ וְאַמָּה וָחֵצִי קֹמָתוֹ:

כד-כה וְצִפִּיתָ אֹתוֹ זָהָב טָהוֹר וְעָשִׂיתָ לּוֹ זֵר זָהָב סָבִיב: וְעָשִׂיתָ לּוֹ מִסְגֶּרֶת

שני (marginal note at verse 17)

◄§ Parashas Terumah

With the exception of the tragic incident of the Golden Calf (chs. 32-33), the entire balance of the Book of *Exodus* is devoted to the preparations for and the construction of the מִשְׁכָּן, *Mishkan* [lit., *dwelling place*] or *Tabernacle*.

Ramban explains that the redemption from Egypt was not complete until the heights that the nation had achieved temporarily at Sinai were made a permanent part of existence by means of the Tabernacle.

In this light, the Tabernacle, and later the Temple in Jerusalem, was intended to be the central rallying point of the nation, ringed by the tribes, topped by the cloud of God's Presence, and the place to which every Jew would bring his offerings. Throughout the long and bitter exile

— which alternates between grinding oppression and spiritually debilitating affluence — the centrality of God's Presence is represented by the *miniature sanctuaries* of synagogues and study halls (*Ezekiel* 11:16), for it is in them and through them that Jews hark back to the sounds of Sinai and the radiance of the Temple.

25:1-7. Contributions for the Tabernacle. The Tabernacle, its vessels, and the priestly garments were made from the thirteen types of raw materials listed here. So anxious were the people to have a share in creating a resting place for the *Shechinah*, and so enthusiastic was their free-willed response, that Moses had to order a halt to the contributions (36:3-6).

25:8. The Sanctuary was to be a structure *for Me*, i.e.,

PARASHAS TERUMAH

25   ¹ Hashem spoke to Moses, saying: ² Speak to the Children of Israel and let them take for Me a portion, * from every man whose heart motivates him you shall take My portion.

The Tabernacle: A resting place for God's presence   ³ This is the portion that you shall take from them: gold, silver, and copper; ⁴ and turquoise, purple, and scarlet wool; linen and goat hair; ⁵ red-dyed ram skins, tachash skins, acacia wood; ⁶ oil for illumination, spices for the anointment oil and the aromatic incense; ⁷ shoham stones and stones for the settings, for the Ephod and the Breastplate.

⁸ They shall make a Sanctuary for Me * — so that I may dwell among them — ⁹ like everything that I show you, the form of the Tabernacle and the form of all its vessels; and so shall you do.

The Ark   ¹⁰ They shall make an Ark * of acacia wood, two and a half cubits its length; *(See Appendix C, illustration 1)* a cubit and a half its width; and a cubit and a half its height. ¹¹ You shall cover it with pure gold, from within and from without shall you cover it, and you shall make on it a gold crown all around. ¹² You shall cast for it four rings of gold and place them on its four corners, two rings on its one side and two rings on its second side. ¹³ You shall make staves of acacia wood and cover them with gold; ¹⁴ and insert the staves in the rings on the sides of the Ark, with which to carry the Ark. ¹⁵ The staves shall remain in the rings of the Ark; they may not be removed from it. ¹⁶ You shall place in the Ark the Testimonial-tablets * that I shall give you.

The Cover   ¹⁷ You shall make a Cover of pure gold, two and a half cubits its length; and a cubit and a half its width. ¹⁸ You shall make two Cherubim * of gold — hammered out shall you make them — from both ends of the Cover. ¹⁹ You shall make one Cherub from the end at one side and one Cherub from the end at the other; from the Cover shall you make the Cherubim at its two ends. ²⁰ The Cherubim shall be with wings spread upward, sheltering the Cover with their wings with their faces toward one another; toward the Cover shall be the faces of the Cherubim. ²¹ You shall place the Cover on the Ark from above, and into the Ark shall you place the Testimonial-tablets that I shall give you. ²² It is there that I will set My meetings with you, and I shall speak with you * from atop the Cover, from between the two Cherubim that are on the Ark of the Testimonial-tablets, everything that I shall command you to the Children of Israel.

The Table   ²³ You shall make a Table * of acacia wood, two cubits its length, a cubit its *(See Appendix C, illustration 2)* width, and a cubit and a half its height. ²⁴ You shall cover it with pure gold and you shall make for it a gold crown all around. ²⁵ You shall make for it a molding

---

dedicated to God's service (*Rashi*). Elegant synagogues are meaningless unless they are built for the sake of God.

25:10-22. The Ark and its Cover. The central feature of the Tabernacle was the Ark, which housed the Tablets of the Law. This is easily understood because, in the memorable expression of R' Saadiah Gaon, Israel is a nation only by virtue of the Torah.

25:16. The Tablets of the Law (הָעֵדֻת) testify that God has commanded Israel to keep the commandments of the Torah (*Rashi*).

25:18-20. The Cherubim had large wings, and the faces of young children, like the angels Isaiah (ch. 6) and Ezekiel (chs. 1 and 10) saw in their vision of the Heavenly Court.

The entire Cover, including the Cherubim, had to be מִקְשָׁה, *hammered out*, of one large ingot of gold (*Rashi*).

25:22. When God spoke to Moses, the Voice would come from heaven to the top of the Cover, and from between the Cherubim it would emanate to where Moses stood, in the outer chamber of the Tabernacle (*Rashi*).

25:23-30. The Table was placed along the north wall of the Tabernacle's outer chamber, and twelve specially baked loaves of "show-bread" were on it at all times, in two columns of six loaves each. They were baked on Friday and put on the Table on the Sabbath, when the old loaves were removed and divided among the Kohanim. [The bread is described in *Leviticus* 24:5-9.]

כו טֹפַח סָבִ֔יב וְעָשִׂ֧יתָ זֵר־זָהָ֛ב לְמִסְגַּרְתּ֖וֹ סָבִֽיב: וְעָשִׂ֣יתָ לּ֔וֹ אַרְבַּ֖ע טַבְּעֹ֣ת

כז זָהָ֑ב וְנָֽתַתָּ֙ אֶת־הַטַּבָּעֹ֔ת עַ֚ל אַרְבַּ֣ע הַפֵּאֹ֔ת אֲשֶׁ֖ר לְאַרְבַּ֥ע רַגְלָֽיו: לְעֻמַּת֙

כח הַמִּסְגֶּ֔רֶת תִּֽהְיֶ֖יןָ הַטַּבָּעֹ֑ת לְבָתִּ֣ים לְבַדִּ֔ים לָשֵׂ֖את אֶת־הַשֻּׁלְחָֽן: וְעָשִׂ֧יתָ

כט אֶת־הַבַּדִּ֗ים עֲצֵ֣י שִׁטִּ֔ים וְצִפִּיתָ֥ אֹתָ֖ם זָהָ֑ב וְנִשָּׂא־בָ֖ם אֶת־הַשֻּׁלְחָֽן: וְעָשִׂ֨יתָ

קְּעָרֹתָ֜יו וְכַפֹּתָ֗יו וּקְשׂוֹתָיו֙ וּמְנַקִּיֹּתָ֔יו אֲשֶׁ֥ר יֻסַּ֖ךְ בָּהֵ֑ן זָהָ֥ב טָה֖וֹר תַּעֲשֶׂ֥ה

ל אֹתָֽם: וְנָֽתַתָּ֧ עַל־הַשֻּׁלְחָ֛ן לֶ֥חֶם פָּנִ֖ים לְפָנַ֥י תָּמִֽיד:

לא **שלישי** וְעָשִׂ֥יתָ מְנֹרַ֖ת זָהָ֣ב טָה֑וֹר מִקְשָׁ֞ה תֵּעָשֶׂ֤ה הַמְּנוֹרָה֙ יְרֵכָ֣הּ וְקָנָ֔הּ גְּבִיעֶ֛יהָ

לב כַּפְתֹּרֶ֥יהָ וּפְרָחֶ֖יהָ מִמֶּ֥נָּה יִהְיֽוּ: וְשִׁשָּׁ֣ה קָנִ֔ים יֹֽצְאִ֖ים מִצִּדֶּ֑יהָ שְׁלֹשָׁ֣ה | קְנֵ֣י

לג מְנֹרָ֗ה מִצִּדָּהּ֙ הָֽאֶחָ֔ד וּשְׁלֹשָׁה֙ קְנֵ֣י מְנֹרָ֔ה מִצִּדָּ֖הּ הַשֵּׁנִֽי: שְׁלֹשָׁ֣ה גְ֠בִעִ֠ים

מְשֻׁקָּדִ֜ים בַּקָּנֶ֣ה הָֽאֶחָד֮ כַּפְתֹּ֣ר וָפֶ֒רַח֒ וּשְׁלֹשָׁ֣ה גְבִעִ֗ים מְשֻׁקָּדִ֛ים בַּקָּנֶ֥ה

לד הָֽאֶחָ֖ד כַּפְתֹּ֣ר וָפָ֑רַח כֵּ֚ן לְשֵׁ֣שֶׁת הַקָּנִ֔ים הַיֹּֽצְאִ֖ים מִן־הַמְּנֹרָֽה: וּבַמְּנֹרָ֖ה

לה אַרְבָּעָ֣ה גְבִעִ֑ים מְשֻׁקָּדִ֔ים כַּפְתֹּרֶ֖יהָ וּפְרָחֶֽיהָ: וְכַפְתֹּ֡ר תַּ֣חַת שְׁנֵי֩ הַקָּנִ֨ים

מִמֶּ֜נָּה וְכַפְתֹּ֗ר תַּ֚חַת שְׁנֵ֣י הַקָּנִ֔ים מִמֶּ֔נָּה וְכַפְתֹּ֕ר תַּֽחַת־שְׁנֵ֥י הַקָּנִ֖ים מִמֶּ֑נָּה

לו לְשֵׁ֨שֶׁת֙ הַקָּנִ֔ים הַיֹּֽצְאִ֖ים מִן־הַמְּנֹרָֽה: כַּפְתֹּֽרֵיהֶ֥ם וּקְנֹתָ֖ם מִמֶּ֣נָּה יִהְי֑וּ כֻּלָּ֛הּ

לז מִקְשָׁ֥ה אַחַ֖ת זָהָ֥ב טָהֽוֹר: וְעָשִׂ֥יתָ אֶת־נֵֽרֹתֶ֖יהָ שִׁבְעָ֑ה וְהֶֽעֱלָה֙ אֶת־נֵ֣רֹתֶ֔יהָ

לח־לט וְהֵאִ֖יר עַל־עֵ֥בֶר פָּנֶֽיהָ: וּמַלְקָחֶ֥יהָ וּמַחְתֹּתֶ֖יהָ זָהָ֣ב טָה֑וֹר: כִּכָּ֛ר זָהָ֥ב טָה֖וֹר

מ יַֽעֲשֶׂ֣ה אֹתָ֔הּ אֵ֥ת כָּל־הַכֵּלִ֖ים הָאֵֽלֶּה: וּרְאֵ֖ה וַֽעֲשֵׂ֑ה בְּתַ֨בְנִיתָ֔ם אֲשֶׁר־אַתָּ֥ה

מָרְאֶ֖ה בָּהָֽר:

כו א וְאֶת־הַמִּשְׁכָּ֥ן תַּֽעֲשֶׂ֖ה עֶ֣שֶׂר יְרִיעֹ֑ת שֵׁ֣שׁ מָשְׁזָ֗ר

ב וּתְכֵ֤לֶת וְאַרְגָּמָן֙ וְתֹלַ֣עַת שָׁנִ֔י כְּרֻבִ֛ים מַֽעֲשֵׂ֥ה חֹשֵׁ֖ב תַּֽעֲשֶׂ֥ה אֹתָֽם: אֹ֣רֶךְ |

הַיְרִיעָ֣ה הָֽאַחַ֗ת שְׁמֹנֶ֤ה וְעֶשְׂרִים֙ בָּֽאַמָּ֔ה וְרֹ֨חַב֙ אַרְבַּ֣ע בָּֽאַמָּ֔ה הַיְרִיעָ֖ה

ג הָֽאֶחָ֑ת מִדָּ֥ה אַחַ֖ת לְכָל־הַיְרִיעֹֽת: חֲמֵ֣שׁ הַיְרִיעֹ֗ת תִּֽהְיֶ֨יןָ֙ חֹֽבְרֹ֔ת אִשָּׁ֖ה אֶל־

ד אֲחֹתָ֑הּ וְחָמֵ֤שׁ יְרִיעֹת֙ חֹֽבְרֹ֔ת אִשָּׁ֖ה אֶל־אֲחֹתָֽהּ: וְעָשִׂ֜יתָ לֻֽלְאֹ֣ת תְּכֵ֗לֶת עַ֣ל

שְׂפַ֤ת הַיְרִיעָה֙ הָֽאֶחָ֔ת מִקָּצָ֖ה בַּֽחֹבָ֑רֶת וְכֵ֤ן תַּֽעֲשֶׂה֙ בִּשְׂפַ֣ת הַיְרִיעָ֔ה

ה הַקִּ֣יצוֹנָ֔ה בַּמַּחְבֶּ֖רֶת הַשֵּׁנִֽית: חֲמִשִּׁ֣ים לֻֽלָאֹ֗ת תַּֽעֲשֶׂה֮ בַּיְרִיעָ֣ה הָֽאֶחָת֒

וַֽחֲמִשִּׁ֣ים לֻֽלָאֹ֗ת תַּֽעֲשֶׂה֙ בִּקְצֵ֣ה הַיְרִיעָ֔ה אֲשֶׁ֖ר בַּמַּחְבֶּ֣רֶת הַשֵּׁנִ֑ית מַקְבִּילֹת֙

ו הַלֻּ֣לָאֹ֔ת אִשָּׁ֖ה אֶל־אֲחֹתָֽהּ: וְעָשִׂ֕יתָ חֲמִשִּׁ֖ים קַרְסֵ֣י זָהָ֑ב וְחִבַּרְתָּ֙ אֶת־

ז הַיְרִיעֹ֜ת אִשָּׁ֤ה אֶל־אֲחֹתָהּ֙ בַּקְּרָסִ֔ים וְהָיָ֥ה הַמִּשְׁכָּ֖ן אֶחָֽד: וְעָשִׂ֨יתָ֙ יְרִיעֹ֣ת

ח עִזִּ֔ים לְאֹ֖הֶל עַל־הַמִּשְׁכָּ֑ן עַשְׁתֵּֽי־עֶשְׂרֵ֥ה יְרִיעֹ֖ת תַּֽעֲשֶׂ֥ה אֹתָֽם: אֹ֣רֶךְ |

הַיְרִיעָ֣ה הָֽאַחַ֗ת שְׁלֹשִׁים֙ בָּֽאַמָּ֔ה וְרֹ֨חַב֙ אַרְבַּ֣ע בָּֽאַמָּ֔ה הַיְרִיעָ֖ה הָֽאֶחָ֑ת

ט מִדָּ֣ה אַחַ֔ת לְעַשְׁתֵּ֥י עֶשְׂרֵ֖ה יְרִיעֹֽת: וְחִבַּרְתָּ֞ אֶת־חֲמֵ֤שׁ הַיְרִיעֹת֙ לְבָ֔ד וְאֶת־

שֵׁ֥שׁ הַיְרִיעֹ֖ת לְבָ֑ד וְכָֽפַלְתָּ֙ אֶת־הַיְרִיעָ֣ה הַשִּׁשִּׁ֔ית אֶל־מ֖וּל פְּנֵ֥י הָאֹֽהֶל:

25:31-40. The symbolic and esoteric interpretations attached to the Menorah are virtually endless. In its simple sense, the Menorah served to demonstrate the majesty of the Tabernacle. It was placed in the outer chamber, so that it would be visible — and inspirational — to every-

one, and it was outside of the Holy of Holies to show that the Ark and all that it represented did not require light; the Torah is its own light (*R' Bachya*).

25:31. Although the Menorah consisted of many shapes and forms, all of them had been hammered from the same of one handbreadth all around, and you shall make a gold crown on the molding all around. ²⁶ You shall make for it four rings of gold and place the rings upon the four corners of its four legs. ²⁷ The rings shall be opposite the molding as housings for the staves, to carry the Table. ²⁸ You shall make the staves of acacia wood and cover them with gold, and the Table shall be carried through them. ²⁹ You shall make its dishes, its spoons, its shelving-tubes, and its pillars, with which it shall be covered; of pure gold shall you make them. ³⁰ On the Table shall you place show-bread before Me, always.

The Menorah
(See Appendix C, illustration 3)

³¹ You shall make a Menorah of pure gold, hammered out* shall the Menorah be made, its base, its shaft, its cups, its knobs, and its blossoms shall be [hammered] from it. ³² Six branches shall emerge from its sides, three branches of the Menorah from its one side and three branches of the Menorah from its second side; ³³ three cups engraved like almonds on the one branch, a knob and a flower; and three cups engraved like almonds on the next branch, a knob and a flower — so for the six branches that emerge from the Menorah. ³⁴ And on the Menorah shall be four cups, engraved like almonds, its knobs and its flowers. ³⁵ A knob shall be under two of the branches from it, a knob under two of the branches from it, and a knob under two of the branches from it — for the six branches emerging from the Menorah. ³⁶ Their knobs and branches shall be of it; all of it a single hammered piece of pure gold. ³⁷ You shall make its lamps seven; he shall kindle its lamps so as to give light toward its face. ³⁸ Its tongs and its spoons shall be of pure gold. ³⁹ Of a talent of pure gold shall he make it, with all these vessels. ⁴⁰ See and make, according to their form that you are shown on the mountain.

26

Covers of the Tabernacle

¹ **Y**ou shall make the Tabernacle of ten curtains* — linen, twisted, with turquoise, purple, and scarlet wool — with a woven design of cherubim shall you make them. ² The length of a single curtain twenty-eight cubits, and the width four cubits for each curtain, the same measure for all the curtains. ³ Five curtains shall be attached to one another, and five curtains attached to one another. ⁴ You shall make loops of turquoise wool at the edge of the single curtain at the end of one set, and you shall make the same on the edge of the outermost curtain on the second set. ⁵ Fifty loops shall you make on the first curtain and fifty loops shall you make on the end of the curtain that is on the second set; the loops shall correspond to one another. ⁶ You shall make fifty hooks of gold, and you shall attach the curtains to one another with the hooks, so that the Tabernacle shall become one.

⁷ You shall make curtains of goat hair for a Tent over the Tabernacle; eleven curtains shall you make them. ⁸ The length of a single curtain thirty cubits, and the width of a single curtain four cubits; the same measure for the eleven curtains. ⁹ You shall attach five of the curtains separately and six of the curtains separately, and you shall fold the sixth curtain over the front of the Tent.

---

ingot; nothing could be made separately and then attached. *Midrash Tanchuma* teaches that so difficult was this feat that Moses could not visualize how the Menorah should look, whereupon God showed him a menorah of fire. Even then, Moses despaired of actually being able to make it properly, so God instructed him to throw the ingot into a fire — and the completed Menorah emerged (*Rashi*).

26:1-14. The Tabernacle had three or four covers one on top of the other, two of them made of fabric and the other(s) of animal hide. By covering the walls and air space of the building, these covers unified everything that was inside the Tabernacle, meaning that the Ark, Table, Menorah, and Golden Altar were not unrelated vessels, each performing its own designated task, but parts of a united whole.

י וְעָשִׂ֜יתָ חֲמִשִּׁ֣ים לֻלָאֹ֗ת עַ֣ל שְׂפַ֤ת הַיְרִיעָה֙ הָֽאֶחָ֔ת הַקִּיצֹנָ֖ה בַּֽחֹבָ֑רֶת

יא וַֽחֲמִשִּׁ֣ים לֻֽלָאֹ֗ת תַּֽעֲשֶׂה֙ עַל־שְׂפַ֣ת הַיְרִיעָ֔ה הַֽחֹבֶ֖רֶת הַשֵּׁנִ֑ית וְעָשִׂ֛יתָ קַרְסֵ֥י נְחֹ֖שֶׁת חֲמִשִּׁ֑ים וְהֵֽבֵאתָ֤ אֶת־הַקְּרָסִים֙ בַּלֻּ֣לָאֹ֔ת וְחִבַּרְתָּ֥ אֶת־הָאֹ֖הֶל וְהָיָ֥ה אֶחָֽד:

יב וְסֶ֨רַח֙ הָֽעֹדֵ֔ף בִּֽירִיעֹ֖ת הָאֹ֑הֶל חֲצִ֤י הַיְרִיעָה֙ הָֽעֹדֶ֔פֶת תִּסְרַ֕ח עַ֖ל אֲחֹרֵ֥י הַמִּשְׁכָּֽן:

יג וְהָֽאַמָּ֨ה מִזֶּ֜ה וְהָֽאַמָּ֤ה מִזֶּה֙ בָּֽעֹדֵ֔ף בְּאֹ֖רֶךְ יְרִיעֹ֣ת הָאֹ֑הֶל יִֽהְיֶ֨ה

יד סָר֜וּחַ עַל־צִדֵּ֧י הַמִּשְׁכָּ֛ן מִזֶּ֥ה וּמִזֶּ֖ה לְכַסֹּתֽוֹ: וְעָשִׂ֤יתָ מִכְסֶה֙ לָאֹ֔הֶל עֹרֹ֥ת אֵלִ֖ם מְאׇדָּמִ֑ים וּמִכְסֵ֛ה עֹרֹ֥ת תְּחָשִׁ֖ים מִלְמָֽעְלָה:

טו-טז רביעי וְעָשִׂ֥יתָ אֶת־הַקְּרָשִׁ֖ים לַמִּשְׁכָּ֑ן עֲצֵ֥י שִׁטִּ֖ים עֹֽמְדִֽים: עֶ֥שֶׂר אַמּ֖וֹת אֹ֣רֶךְ הַקָּ֑רֶשׁ וְאַמָּה֙ וַֽחֲצִ֣י הָֽאַמָּ֔ה רֹ֖חַב הַקֶּ֥רֶשׁ הָֽאֶחָֽד: שְׁתֵּ֣י יָד֗וֹת לַקֶּ֨רֶשׁ֙

יז-יח הָֽאֶחָ֔ד מְשֻׁ֨לָּבֹ֔ת אִשָּׁ֖ה אֶל־אֲחֹתָ֑הּ כֵּ֣ן תַּֽעֲשֶׂ֔ה לְכֹ֖ל קַרְשֵׁ֥י הַמִּשְׁכָּֽן: וְעָשִׂ֥יתָ אֶת־הַקְּרָשִׁ֖ים לַמִּשְׁכָּ֑ן עֶשְׂרִ֣ים קֶ֔רֶשׁ לִפְאַ֖ת נֶ֥גְבָּה תֵימָֽנָה:

יט וְאַרְבָּעִים֙ אַדְנֵי־כֶ֔סֶף תַּֽעֲשֶׂ֕ה תַּ֖חַת עֶשְׂרִ֣ים הַקָּ֑רֶשׁ שְׁנֵ֣י אֲדָנִ֗ים תַּֽחַת־הַקֶּ֤רֶשׁ הָֽאֶחָד֙

כ לִשְׁתֵּ֣י יְדֹתָ֔יו וּשְׁנֵ֣י אֲדָנִ֗ים תַּֽחַת־הַקֶּ֥רֶשׁ הָֽאֶחָ֖ד לִשְׁתֵּ֥י יְדֹתָֽיו: וּלְצֶ֧לַע

כא הַמִּשְׁכָּ֛ן הַשֵּׁנִ֖ית לִפְאַ֣ת צָפ֑וֹן עֶשְׂרִ֖ים קָ֑רֶשׁ: וְאַרְבָּעִ֥ים אַדְנֵיהֶ֖ם כָּ֑סֶף שְׁנֵ֣י

כב אֲדָנִ֗ים תַּ֚חַת הַקֶּ֣רֶשׁ הָֽאֶחָ֔ד וּשְׁנֵ֣י אֲדָנִ֔ים תַּ֖חַת הַקֶּ֥רֶשׁ הָֽאֶחָֽד: וּלְיַרְכְּתֵ֥י

כג הַמִּשְׁכָּ֖ן יָ֑מָּה תַּֽעֲשֶׂ֖ה שִׁשָּׁ֥ה קְרָשִֽׁים: וּשְׁנֵ֤י קְרָשִׁים֙ תַּֽעֲשֶׂ֔ה לִמְקֻצְעֹ֖ת

כד הַמִּשְׁכָּ֖ן בַּיַּרְכָתָֽיִם: וְיִֽהְי֣וּ תֹֽאֲמִם֮ מִלְּמַ֒טָּה֒ וְיַחְדָּ֗ו יִֽהְי֤וּ תַמִּים֙ עַל־רֹאשׁ֔וֹ

כה אֶל־הַטַּבַּ֖עַת הָֽאֶחָ֑ת כֵּ֚ן יִֽהְיֶ֣ה לִשְׁנֵיהֶ֔ם לִשְׁנֵ֥י הַמִּקְצֹעֹ֖ת יִֽהְיֽוּ: וְהָיוּ֙ שְׁמֹנָ֣ה

כו קְרָשִׁ֔ים וְאַדְנֵיהֶ֣ם כֶּ֔סֶף שִׁשָּׁ֥ה עָשָׂ֖ר אֲדָנִ֑ים שְׁנֵ֣י אֲדָנִ֗ים תַּ֚חַת הַקֶּ֣רֶשׁ

הָֽאֶחָ֔ד וּשְׁנֵ֣י אֲדָנִ֔ים תַּ֖חַת הַקֶּ֥רֶשׁ הָֽאֶחָֽד: וְעָשִׂ֥יתָ בְרִיחִ֖ם עֲצֵ֣י שִׁטִּ֑ים

כז חֲמִשָּׁ֕ה לְקַרְשֵׁ֥י צֶֽלַע־הַמִּשְׁכָּ֖ן הָֽאֶחָֽד: וַֽחֲמִשָּׁ֣ה בְרִיחִ֗ם לְקַרְשֵׁ֤י צֶֽלַע־הַמִּשְׁכָּן֙ הַשֵּׁנִ֔ית וַֽחֲמִשָּׁ֣ה בְרִיחִ֗ם לְקַרְשֵׁי֙ צֶ֣לַע הַמִּשְׁכָּ֔ן לַיַּרְכָתַ֖יִם יָֽמָּה:

כח-כט וְהַבְּרִ֥יחַ הַתִּיכֹ֖ן בְּת֣וֹךְ הַקְּרָשִׁ֑ים מַבְרִ֕חַ מִן־הַקָּצֶ֖ה אֶל־הַקָּצֶֽה: וְֽאֶת־הַקְּרָשִׁ֞ים תְּצַפֶּ֣ה זָהָ֗ב וְאֶת־טַבְּעֹֽתֵיהֶם֙ תַּֽעֲשֶׂ֣ה זָהָ֔ב בָּתִּ֖ים לַבְּרִיחִ֑ם

ל וְצִפִּיתָ֥ אֶת־הַבְּרִיחִ֖ם זָהָֽב: וַֽהֲקֵֽמֹתָ֖ אֶת־הַמִּשְׁכָּ֑ן כְּמִ֨שְׁפָּט֔וֹ אֲשֶׁ֥ר הׇרְאֵ֖יתָ

לא חמישי בָּהָֽר: וְעָשִׂ֣יתָ פָרֹ֗כֶת תְּכֵ֧לֶת וְאַרְגָּמָ֛ן וְתוֹלַ֥עַת שָׁנִ֖י וְשֵׁ֣שׁ

לב מׇשְׁזָ֑ר מַֽעֲשֵׂ֥ה חֹשֵׁ֛ב יַֽעֲשֶׂ֥ה אֹתָ֖הּ כְּרֻבִֽים: וְנָֽתַתָּ֣ה אֹתָ֗הּ עַל־אַרְבָּעָה֙

לג עַמּוּדֵ֣י שִׁטִּ֔ים מְצֻפִּ֣ים זָהָ֗ב וָֽוֵיהֶ֣ם זָהָ֔ב עַל־אַרְבָּעָ֖ה אַדְנֵי־כָֽסֶף: וְנָֽתַתָּ֣ה אֶת־הַפָּרֹ֘כֶת֮ תַּ֣חַת הַקְּרָסִים֒ וְהֵֽבֵאתָ֥ שָׁ֨מָּה֙ מִבֵּ֣ית לַפָּרֹ֔כֶת אֵ֖ת אֲר֣וֹן הָֽעֵד֑וּת וְהִבְדִּילָ֤ה הַפָּרֹ֨כֶת֙ לָכֶ֔ם בֵּ֣ין הַקֹּ֔דֶשׁ וּבֵ֖ין קֹ֥דֶשׁ הַקֳּדָשִֽׁים: וְנָֽתַתָּ֤

לד אֶת־הַכַּפֹּ֨רֶת֙ עַ֚ל אֲר֣וֹן הָֽעֵדֻ֔ת בְּקֹ֖דֶשׁ הַקֳּדָשִֽׁים: וְשַׂמְתָּ֤ אֶת־הַשֻּׁלְחָן֙ מִח֣וּץ

לה לַפָּרֹ֔כֶת וְאֶת־הַמְּנֹרָה֙ נֹ֣כַח הַשֻּׁלְחָ֔ן עַ֛ל צֶ֥לַע הַמִּשְׁכָּ֖ן תֵּימָ֑נָה וְהַשֻּׁלְחָ֕ן

26:15-30. The walls were made of huge planks of acacia wood. According to *Midrash Tanchuma* cited by *Rashi* (v. 15), the Patriarch Jacob anticipated the need for such lumber in the Wilderness. He planted these trees in Egypt and instructed his children to take the wood with them when they left their exile.

¹⁰ *You shall make fifty loops on the edge of the first curtain at the end of one set, and fifty loops on the edge of the curtain of the second set.* ¹¹ *You shall make fifty hooks of copper; you shall bring the hooks into the loops and attach the Tent, so that it shall become one.* ¹² *As for the extra overhang of the curtains of the Tent — half of the extra curtain shall hang over the back of the Tabernacle.* ¹³ *And the cubit on one side and the cubit on the other side, that are extra in the length of the curtains of the Tent, shall hang over the sides of the Tabernacle on one side and the other, to cover it.*

¹⁴ *You shall make a Cover for the Tent of red-dyed ram skins, and a Cover of tachash skins above.*

Walls of the Tabernacle
(See Appendix C, illustration 4)

¹⁵ *You shall make the planks* of the Tabernacle of acacia wood, standing erect.* ¹⁶ *Ten cubits the length of each plank, and a cubit and a half the width of each plank.* ¹⁷ *Each plank should have two tenons, parallel to one another — so shall you do for all the planks of the Tabernacle.*

¹⁸ *You shall make planks for the Tabernacle, twenty planks for the south side.* ¹⁹ *You shall make forty silver sockets under the twenty planks; two sockets under one plank for its two tenons, and two sockets under the next plank for its two tenons.* ²⁰ *For the second wall of the Tabernacle on the north side — twenty planks.* ²¹ *Their forty silver sockets: two sockets under one plank and two sockets under the next plank.* ²² *For the back of the Tabernacle on the west, you shall make six planks.* ²³ *You shall make two planks for the corners of the Tabernacle, in the back.* ²⁴ *They shall be even at the bottom, and together shall they match at its top, for a single ring, so shall it be for them both, for the two corners shall they be.* ²⁵ *There shall be eight planks and their silver sockets, sixteen sockets — two sockets under one plank and two sockets under the next plank.*

²⁶ *You shall make bars of acacia wood; five for the planks of one side of the Tabernacle,* ²⁷ *and five bars for the planks of the second wall of the Tabernacle, and five bars for the planks of the Tabernacle wall at the back, on the west.* ²⁸ *The middle bar inside the planks shall extend from end to end.*

²⁹ *You shall cover the planks with gold, and their rings shall you make of gold as housing for the bars, and you shall cover the bars with gold.* ³⁰ *You shall erect the Tabernacle according to its manner, as you will have been shown on the mountain.*

The Paroches/ Partition

³¹ *You shall make a Partition* of turquoise, purple, and scarlet wool, and linen, twisted; a weaver's craft he shall make it, [with a woven design of] cherubim.* ³² *You shall place it upon four pillars of acacia wood, plated with gold with hooks of gold, upon four silver sockets.* ³³ *You shall put the Partition under the hooks. You shall bring there, inside the Partition, the Ark of the Testimonial-tablets, and the Partition shall separate for you between the Holy and the Holy of Holies.*

³⁴ *You shall put the Cover upon the Ark of the Testimonial-tablets in the Holy of Holies.* ³⁵ *You shall place the Table outside the Partition, and the Menorah opposite the Table on the south side of the Tabernacle, and the Table*

26:31-33. The Tabernacle was divided into two chambers, the Holy of Holies, which no one may ever enter except for the Kohen Gadol on Yom Kippur, and the Holy, which may be entered by any Kohen who is not in a state of spiritual contamination. The Partition, which was hung from a bar draped over the pillars described here, divided the two domains.

לו תִּתֵּן עַל־צֶלַע צָפוֹן: וְעָשִׂיתָ מָסָךְ לְפֶתַח הָאֹהֶל תְּכֵלֶת וְאַרְגָּמָן וְתוֹלַעַת

לז שָׁנִי וְשֵׁשׁ מָשְׁזָר מַעֲשֵׂה רֹקֵם: וְעָשִׂיתָ לַמָּסָךְ חֲמִשָּׁה עַמּוּדֵי שִׁטִּים וְצִפִּיתָ

כז שׁשׁ א אֹתָם זָהָב וָוֵיהֶם זָהָב וְיָצַקְתָּ לָהֶם חֲמִשָּׁה אַדְנֵי נְחֹשֶׁת: וְעָשִׂיתָ

אֶת־הַמִּזְבֵּחַ עֲצֵי שִׁטִּים חָמֵשׁ אַמּוֹת אֹרֶךְ וְחָמֵשׁ אַמּוֹת רֹחַב רָבוּעַ יִהְיֶה

ב הַמִּזְבֵּחַ וְשָׁלֹשׁ אַמּוֹת קֹמָתוֹ: וְעָשִׂיתָ קַרְנֹתָיו עַל אַרְבַּע פִּנֹּתָיו מִמֶּנּוּ

ג תִּהְיֶיןָ קַרְנֹתָיו וְצִפִּיתָ אֹתוֹ נְחֹשֶׁת: וְעָשִׂיתָ סִּירֹתָיו לְדַשְּׁנוֹ וְיָעָיו וּמִזְרְקֹתָיו

ד וּמִזְלְגֹתָיו וּמַחְתֹּתָיו לְכָל־כֵּלָיו תַּעֲשֶׂה נְחֹשֶׁת: וְעָשִׂיתָ לּוֹ מִכְבָּר מַעֲשֵׂה

רֶשֶׁת נְחֹשֶׁת וְעָשִׂיתָ עַל־הָרֶשֶׁת אַרְבַּע טַבְּעֹת נְחֹשֶׁת עַל אַרְבַּע קְצוֹתָיו:

ה וְנָתַתָּה אֹתָהּ תַּחַת כַּרְכֹּב הַמִּזְבֵּחַ מִלְּמָטָּה וְהָיְתָה הָרֶשֶׁת עַד חֲצִי

ו הַמִּזְבֵּחַ: וְעָשִׂיתָ בַדִּים לַמִּזְבֵּחַ בַּדֵּי עֲצֵי שִׁטִּים וְצִפִּיתָ אֹתָם נְחֹשֶׁת:

ז וְהוּבָא אֶת־בַּדָּיו בַּטַּבָּעֹת וְהָיוּ הַבַּדִּים עַל־שְׁתֵּי צַלְעֹת הַמִּזְבֵּחַ

ח בִּשְׂאֵת אֹתוֹ: נְבוּב לֻחֹת תַּעֲשֶׂה אֹתוֹ כַּאֲשֶׁר הֶרְאָה אֹתְךָ בָּהָר כֵּן

ט יַעֲשׂוּ:   וְעָשִׂיתָ אֵת חֲצַר הַמִּשְׁכָּן לִפְאַת נֶגֶב־תֵּימָנָה קְלָעִים

שביעי

י לֶחָצֵר שֵׁשׁ מָשְׁזָר מֵאָה בָאַמָּה אֹרֶךְ לַפֵּאָה הָאֶחָת: וְעַמֻּדָיו עֶשְׂרִים

יא וְאַדְנֵיהֶם עֶשְׂרִים נְחֹשֶׁת וָוֵי הָעַמֻּדִים וַחֲשֻׁקֵיהֶם כָּסֶף: וְכֵן לִפְאַת צָפוֹן

בָּאֹרֶךְ קְלָעִים מֵאָה אֹרֶךְ וְעַמְדָו עֶשְׂרִים וְאַדְנֵיהֶם עֶשְׂרִים נְחֹשֶׁת וָוֵי

יב הָעַמֻּדִים וַחֲשֻׁקֵיהֶם כָּסֶף: וְרֹחַב הֶחָצֵר לִפְאַת־יָם קְלָעִים חֲמִשִּׁים אַמָּה

יג עַמֻּדֵיהֶם עֲשָׂרָה וְאַדְנֵיהֶם עֲשָׂרָה: וְרֹחַב הֶחָצֵר לִפְאַת קֵדְמָה מִזְרָחָה

יד חֲמִשִּׁים אַמָּה: וַחֲמֵשׁ עֶשְׂרֵה אַמָּה קְלָעִים לַכָּתֵף עַמֻּדֵיהֶם שְׁלֹשָׁה

טו וְאַדְנֵיהֶם שְׁלֹשָׁה: וְלַכָּתֵף הַשֵּׁנִית חֲמֵשׁ עֶשְׂרֵה קְלָעִים עַמֻּדֵיהֶם שְׁלֹשָׁה

טז וְאַדְנֵיהֶם שְׁלֹשָׁה: וּלְשַׁעַר הֶחָצֵר מָסָךְ | עֶשְׂרִים אַמָּה תְּכֵלֶת וְאַרְגָּמָן

וְתוֹלַעַת שָׁנִי וְשֵׁשׁ מָשְׁזָר מַעֲשֵׂה רֹקֵם עַמֻּדֵיהֶם אַרְבָּעָה וְאַדְנֵיהֶם

יז אַרְבָּעָה: כָּל־עַמּוּדֵי הֶחָצֵר סָבִיב מְחֻשָּׁקִים כֶּסֶף וָוֵיהֶם כָּסֶף וְאַדְנֵיהֶם

מפטיר

יח נְחֹשֶׁת: אֹרֶךְ הֶחָצֵר מֵאָה בָאַמָּה וְרֹחַב | חֲמִשִּׁים בַּחֲמִשִּׁים וְקֹמָה חָמֵשׁ

*Haftaras
Terumah:
p. 812*

יט אַמּוֹת שֵׁשׁ מָשְׁזָר וְאַדְנֵיהֶם נְחֹשֶׁת: לְכֹל כְּלֵי הַמִּשְׁכָּן בְּכֹל עֲבֹדָתוֹ וְכָל־

For special
Sabbaths,
see pp. x-xi

יְתֵדֹתָיו וְכָל־יִתְדֹת הֶחָצֵר נְחֹשֶׁת: ססס   צ"ו פסוקים. יער"ז סימן. סל"ו סימן:

פרשת תצוה

כ וְאַתָּה תְּצַוֶּה | אֶת־בְּנֵי יִשְׂרָאֵל וְיִקְחוּ אֵלֶיךָ שֶׁמֶן זַיִת זָךְ כָּתִית

כא לַמָּאוֹר לְהַעֲלֹת נֵר תָּמִיד: בְּאֹהֶל מוֹעֵד מִחוּץ לַפָּרֹכֶת אֲשֶׁר עַל־

הָעֵדֻת יַעֲרֹךְ אֹתוֹ אַהֲרֹן וּבָנָיו מֵעֶרֶב עַד־בֹּקֶר לִפְנֵי יהוה חֻקַּת עוֹלָם

כח א לְדֹרֹתָם מֵאֵת בְּנֵי יִשְׂרָאֵל: וְאַתָּה

27:1-8. This Altar, located in the Tabernacle Courtyard, was known as the מִזְבֵּחַ, *Altar.* It had three other names: מִזְבֵּחַ הָעֹלָה, *Altar of the Elevation-offering* , because the sacrificial parts were burned on it; מִזְבַּח הַנְּחֹשֶׁת, *the Copper*

Altar, because it was coated with copper (v. 2); and מִזְבֵּחַ הַחִיצוֹן, *the Outer Altar,* because it was outside of the Tabernacle. There was another Altar (30:1-7) which was located inside the Tabernacle.

you shall place on the north side. ³⁶ *You shall make a Screen for the entrance of the Tent, of turquoise, purple, and scarlet wool, and twisted linen; an embroiderer's craft.* ³⁷ *You shall make for the Screen five pillars of acacia wood and cover them with gold, and their hooks shall be gold; and you shall cast for them five sockets of copper.*

27

The Altar
(See Appendix C, illustration 5)

¹ **Y**ou shall make the Altar* of acacia wood, five cubits in length and five cubits in width — the Altar shall be square — and three cubits its height. ² You shall make its horns on its four corners, from it shall its horns be; and you shall cover it with copper. ³ You shall make its pots to clear its ashes, its shovels, its basins, its forks, and its fire-pans; you shall make all its vessels of copper. ⁴ You shall make for it a netting of copper meshwork and make upon the meshwork four copper rings at its four edges. ⁵ You shall place it under the surrounding border of the Altar from below, and the meshwork shall go to the midpoint of the Altar. ⁶ You shall make staves for the Altar, staves of acacia wood, and you shall plate them with copper. ⁷ Its staves shall be brought into the rings, and the staves shall be on two sides of the Altar when it is carried. ⁸ Hollow, of boards, shall you make it; as you were shown on the mountain, so shall they do.*

The Courtyard
(See Appendix C, illustration 6)

⁹ *You shall make the Courtyard of the Tabernacle: On the south side lace-hangings of the Courtyard, of twisted linen, a hundred cubits long for one side;* ¹⁰ *and its pillars twenty and their sockets twenty, of copper, the hooks of the pillars and their bands silver.* ¹¹ *So, too, for the north side in length, lace-hangings a hundred long: its pillars twenty; and their sockets twenty, of copper; the hooks of the pillars and their bands, silver.* ¹² *The width of the Courtyard on the west side, lace-hangings of fifty cubits, their pillars ten; and their sockets ten.* ¹³ *The width of the Courtyard on the eastern side, fifty cubits;* ¹⁴ *and fifteen cubits of lace-hangings on a shoulder, their pillars three; and their sockets three.* ¹⁵ *And the second shoulder, fifteen of lace-hangings; their pillars three; and their sockets three.* ¹⁶ *At the gate of the Courtyard, a Screen of twenty cubits: turquoise, purple, and scarlet wool, and twisted linen, an embroiderer's craft; their pillars four and their sockets four.*

¹⁷ *All the pillars of the Courtyard, all around, banded with silver; their hooks of silver, and their sockets of copper.* ¹⁸ *The length of the Courtyard a hundred cubits; the width fifty by fifty; and the height five cubits of twisted linen; and their sockets of copper.* ¹⁹ *All the vessels of the Tabernacle for all its labor, all its pegs and all the pegs of the Courtyard — copper.*

PARASHAS TETZAVEH

The oil

²⁰ **N**ow you shall command the Children of Israel that they shall take for you clear olive oil*, crushed, for illumination, to kindle a lamp continually. ²¹ In the Tent of Meeting, outside the Partition that is near the Testimonial-tablets, Aaron and his sons shall arrange it from evening until morning, before HASHEM, an eternal decree for their generations, from the Children of Israel.*

⇥ Parashas Tetzaveh.

The *Sidrah* deals almost exclusively with the Kohanim: their selection, their vestments, and the inauguration service by which they and their offspring would become confirmed for all time as the special ministers of God.

27:20-21. The Torah now turns to those who will perform the service within the Tabernacle. It begins by teaching that the oil for the Menorah must be absolutely pure, a fitting prelude to the selection of Aaron and his sons as Kohanim, for they, too, must remain pure and separate from the rest of the nation (*Ibn Ezra*).

הַקְרֵב אֵלֶיךָ אֶת־אַהֲרֹן אָחִיךָ וְאֶת־בָּנָיו אִתּוֹ מִתּוֹךְ בְּנֵי יִשְׂרָאֵל לְכַהֲנוֹ־

ב לִי אַהֲרֹן נָדָב וַאֲבִיהוּא אֶלְעָזָר וְאִיתָמָר בְּנֵי אַהֲרֹן: וְעָשִׂיתָ בִגְדֵי־קֹדֶשׁ

ג לְאַהֲרֹן אָחִיךָ לְכָבוֹד וּלְתִפְאָרֶת: וְאַתָּה תְּדַבֵּר אֶל־כָּל־חַכְמֵי־לֵב אֲשֶׁר

ד מִלֵּאתִיו רוּחַ חָכְמָה וְעָשׂוּ אֶת־בִּגְדֵי אַהֲרֹן לְקַדְּשׁוֹ לְכַהֲנוֹ־לִי: וְאֵלֶּה

הַבְּגָדִים אֲשֶׁר יַעֲשׂוּ חֹשֶׁן וְאֵפוֹד וּמְעִיל וּכְתֹנֶת תַּשְׁבֵּץ מִצְנֶפֶת וְאַבְנֵט

ה וְעָשׂוּ בִגְדֵי־קֹדֶשׁ לְאַהֲרֹן אָחִיךָ וּלְבָנָיו לְכַהֲנוֹ־לִי: וְהֵם יִקְחוּ אֶת־הַזָּהָב

וְאֶת־הַתְּכֵלֶת וְאֶת־הָאַרְגָּמָן וְאֶת־תּוֹלַעַת הַשָּׁנִי וְאֶת־הַשֵּׁשׁ:

ו וְעָשׂוּ אֶת־הָאֵפֹד זָהָב תְּכֵלֶת וְאַרְגָּמָן תּוֹלַעַת שָׁנִי וְשֵׁשׁ מָשְׁזָר מַעֲשֵׂה

ז־ח חֹשֵׁב: שְׁתֵּי כְתֵפֹת חֹבְרֹת יִהְיֶה־לּוֹ אֶל־שְׁנֵי קְצוֹתָיו וְחֻבָּר: וְחֵשֶׁב אֲפֻדָּתוֹ

אֲשֶׁר עָלָיו כְּמַעֲשֵׂהוּ מִמֶּנּוּ יִהְיֶה זָהָב תְּכֵלֶת וְאַרְגָּמָן וְתוֹלַעַת שָׁנִי וְשֵׁשׁ

ט מָשְׁזָר: וְלָקַחְתָּ אֶת־שְׁתֵּי אַבְנֵי־שֹׁהַם וּפִתַּחְתָּ עֲלֵיהֶם שְׁמוֹת בְּנֵי יִשְׂרָאֵל:

י שִׁשָּׁה מִשְּׁמֹתָם עַל הָאֶבֶן הָאֶחָת וְאֶת־שְׁמוֹת הַשִּׁשָּׁה הַנּוֹתָרִים עַל־הָאֶבֶן

יא הַשֵּׁנִית כְּתוֹלְדֹתָם: מַעֲשֵׂה חָרַשׁ אֶבֶן פִּתּוּחֵי חֹתָם תְּפַתַּח אֶת־שְׁתֵּי

יב הָאֲבָנִים עַל־שְׁמֹת בְּנֵי יִשְׂרָאֵל מֻסַבֹּת מִשְׁבְּצוֹת זָהָב תַּעֲשֶׂה אֹתָם: וְשַׂמְתָּ

אֶת־שְׁתֵּי הָאֲבָנִים עַל כִּתְפֹת הָאֵפֹד אַבְנֵי זִכָּרֹן לִבְנֵי יִשְׂרָאֵל וְנָשָׂא אַהֲרֹן

יג אֶת־שְׁמוֹתָם לִפְנֵי יהוה עַל־שְׁתֵּי כְתֵפָיו לְזִכָּרֹן: שני   וְעָשִׂיתָ

יד מִשְׁבְּצֹת זָהָב: וּשְׁתֵּי שַׁרְשְׁרֹת זָהָב טָהוֹר מִגְבָּלֹת תַּעֲשֶׂה אֹתָם מַעֲשֵׂה

טו עֲבֹת וְנָתַתָּה אֶת־שַׁרְשְׁרֹת הָעֲבֹתֹת עַל־הַמִּשְׁבְּצֹת: וְעָשִׂיתָ

חֹשֶׁן מִשְׁפָּט מַעֲשֵׂה חֹשֵׁב כְּמַעֲשֵׂה אֵפֹד תַּעֲשֶׂנּוּ זָהָב תְּכֵלֶת וְאַרְגָּמָן

טז וְתוֹלַעַת שָׁנִי וְשֵׁשׁ מָשְׁזָר תַּעֲשֶׂה אֹתוֹ: רָבוּעַ יִהְיֶה כָּפוּל זֶרֶת אָרְכּוֹ

יז וְזֶרֶת רָחְבּוֹ: וּמִלֵּאתָ בוֹ מִלֻּאַת אֶבֶן אַרְבָּעָה טוּרִים אָבֶן טוּר אֹדֶם

יח־יט פִּטְדָה וּבָרֶקֶת הַטּוּר הָאֶחָד: וְהַטּוּר הַשֵּׁנִי נֹפֶךְ סַפִּיר וְיָהֲלֹם: וְהַטּוּר

כ הַשְּׁלִישִׁי לֶשֶׁם שְׁבוֹ וְאַחְלָמָה: וְהַטּוּר הָרְבִיעִי תַּרְשִׁישׁ וְשֹׁהַם וְיָשְׁפֵה

מְשֻׁבָּצִים זָהָב יִהְיוּ בְּמִלּוּאֹתָם: וְהָאֲבָנִים תִּהְיֶיןָ עַל־שְׁמֹת בְּנֵי־יִשְׂרָאֵל

כא שְׁתֵּים עֶשְׂרֵה עַל־שְׁמֹתָם פִּתּוּחֵי חוֹתָם אִישׁ עַל־שְׁמוֹ תִּהְיֶיןָ לִשְׁנֵי

כב עָשָׂר שָׁבֶט: וְעָשִׂיתָ עַל־הַחֹשֶׁן שַׁרְשֹׁת גַּבְלֻת מַעֲשֵׂה עֲבֹת זָהָב טָהוֹר:

כג וְעָשִׂיתָ עַל־הַחֹשֶׁן שְׁתֵּי טַבְּעוֹת זָהָב וְנָתַתָּ אֶת־שְׁתֵּי הַטַּבָּעוֹת עַל־

כד שְׁנֵי קְצוֹת הַחֹשֶׁן: וְנָתַתָּה אֶת־שְׁתֵּי עֲבֹתֹת הַזָּהָב עַל־שְׁתֵּי הַטַּבָּעֹת אֶל־

כה קְצוֹת הַחֹשֶׁן: וְאֵת שְׁתֵּי קְצוֹת שְׁתֵּי הָעֲבֹתֹת תִּתֵּן עַל־שְׁתֵּי הַמִּשְׁבְּצוֹת

28:1. Aaron's four sons are specified by name, because only he and they were to be anointed as Kohanim. Thus, any children born to them later would be Kohanim automatically. However, any of Aaron's already living grandsons, such as Phinehas, were not included in this appointment; they would remain Levites (*Ramban*). Later, God appointed Phinehas as a Kohen in his own right (*Numbers* 25:13).

28:4-43. While performing the Temple service, a Kohen

had to wear the vestments; otherwise, any service he performed was invalid.

The Kohen Gadol usually wore eight vestments, which were called the שְׁמֹנָה בְּגָדִים, *Eight Vestments*, or the בִּגְדֵי זָהָב, *Gold Vestments* (since some of them contained gold). The כֹּהֵן הֶדְיוֹט, *ordinary Kohen*, wore four vestments at all times during the service. (See Appendix C, illustrations 7-14.)

28:6-12. Aaron wore this garment — which was similar

28

The Kohanim and their vestments

[1] **N**ow you, bring near to yourself Aaron your brother, and his sons * with him, from among the Children of Israel — Aaron, Nadab and Abihu, Elazar and Ithamar, the sons of Aaron — to minister to Me. [2] You shall make vestments of sanctity for Aaron your brother, for glory and splendor. [3] And you shall speak to all the wise-hearted people whom I have invested with a spirit of wisdom, and they shall make the vestments of Aaron, to sanctify him to minister to Me.

The vestments

[4] These are the vestments * that they shall make: a Breastplate, an Ephod, a Robe, a Tunic of a box-like knit, a Turban, and a Sash. They shall make vestments of sanctity for Aaron your brother and his sons, to minister to Me. [5] They shall take the gold, the turquoise, purple, and scarlet wool, and the linen.

The Ephod
(See Appendix C, illustration 9)

[6] They shall make the Ephod * of gold, turquoise, purple, and scarlet wool, and twisted linen, a weaver's craft. [7] It shall have two shoulder straps attached to its two ends, and it shall be attached. [8] The belt with which it is emplaced, which is on it, shall be of the same workmanship, it shall be made of it, of gold; turquoise, purple, and scarlet wool, and twisted linen. [9] You shall take the two shoham stones and engrave upon them the names of the sons of Israel; [10] six of their names on one stone, and the names of the six remaining ones on the second stone, according to the order of their birth. [11] A jeweler's craft, like the engraving of a signet ring, shall you engrave the two stones with the names of the sons of Israel; encircled with gold settings shall you make them. [12] You shall place both stones on the shoulder straps of the Ephod, remembrance stones for the sons of Israel. Aaron shall carry their names before HASHEM on both his shoulders as a remembrance.

The settings

[13] You shall make settings of gold; [14] and two chains of pure gold — make them at the edges, of braided craftsmanship — and place the braided chains on the settings.

The Breastplate of Judgment
(See Appendix C, illustrations 10-11)

[15] You shall make a Breastplate of Judgment of a woven design, like the craftsmanship of the Ephod shall you make it, of gold, turquoise, purple, and scarlet wool; and twisted linen shall you make it. [16] Square shall it be, folded, its length a half-cubit and its width a half-cubit. [17] You shall fill it with stone mounting, four rows of stone: a row of odem, pitdah, and barekes — the one row; [18] the second row: nophech, sapir, and yahalom; [19] the third row: leshem, shevo, and achlamah; [20] and the fourth row: tarshish, shoham, and yashfeh; set in gold shall they be in their mountings. [21] The stones shall be according to the names of the sons of Israel, twelve according to their names, engraved like a signet ring, each according to its name shall they be, for the twelve tribes.

[22] For the Breastplate you shall make chains at the edges, of braided craftsmanship, of pure gold. [23] For the Breastplate you shall make two rings of gold, and you shall place the two rings on the two ends of the Breastplate. [24] You shall place the two golden ropes on the two rings, at the ends of the Breastplate. [25] And the two ends of the two ropes, you shall place on the two settings,

---

to an apron — over his tunic and robe. The *Ephod* and *Cheishev* — its sash-like belt atop the *Ephod* — were a single woven piece of material. The *Ephod*'s two shoulder straps were sewn to the top of the belt at Aaron's back, and extended upward, just covering his shoulders in front. On the tops of the straps, on Aaron's shoulders,

were two gold settings, into which precious stones, known as the *avnei shoham*, were set. Attached to the tops and bottoms of the two shoulder straps was the Breastplate, or Choshen Mishpat (vs. 15-30), which was held in place by means of rings, gold chains, and linen cords, as described below.

כו וְנָתַתָּ֗ה עַל־כִּתְפ֣וֹת הָאֵפֹ֔ד אֶל־מ֖וּל פָּנָ֑יו: וְעָשִׂ֗יתָ שְׁתֵּי֙ טַבְּע֣וֹת זָהָ֔ב וְשַׂמְתָּ֣ אֹתָ֗ם עַל־שְׁנֵי֙ קְצ֣וֹת הַחֹ֔שֶׁן עַל־שְׂפָת֕וֹ אֲשֶׁ֛ר אֶל־עֵ֥בֶר הָאֵפֹ֖ד בָּֽיְתָה:

כז וְעָשִׂ֗יתָ שְׁתֵּי֙ טַבְּע֣וֹת זָהָ֔ב וְנָתַתָּ֣ה אֹתָ֗ם עַל־שְׁתֵּ֣י כִתְפ֣וֹת הָאֵפ֜וֹד מִלְּמַ֗טָּה

כח מִמּ֣וּל פָּנָ֗יו לְעֻמַּת֙ מַחְבַּרְתּ֔וֹ מִמַּ֕עַל לְחֵ֖שֶׁב הָאֵפֹ֑ד: וְיִרְכְּס֣וּ אֶת־הַחֹ֡שֶׁן מִטַּבְּעֹתָו֩ אֶל־טַבְּעֹ֨ת הָאֵפ֜וֹד בִּפְתִ֣יל תְּכֵ֗לֶת לִֽהְי֖וֹת עַל־חֵ֣שֶׁב הָאֵפֹ֑ד

כט וְלֹֽא־יִזַּ֣ח הַחֹ֔שֶׁן מֵעַ֖ל הָאֵפֹֽד: וְנָשָׂ֣א אַ֠הֲרֹן אֶת־שְׁמ֨וֹת בְּנֵֽי־יִשְׂרָאֵ֜ל בְּחֹ֧שֶׁן הַמִּשְׁפָּ֛ט עַל־לִבּ֖וֹ בְּבֹא֣וֹ אֶל־הַקֹּ֑דֶשׁ לְזִכָּרֹ֥ן לִפְנֵֽי־יְהֹוָ֖ה תָּמִֽיד:

ל וְנָתַתָּ֞ אֶל־חֹ֣שֶׁן הַמִּשְׁפָּ֗ט אֶת־הָֽאוּרִים֙ וְאֶת־הַתֻּמִּ֔ים וְהָיוּ֙ עַל־לֵ֣ב אַֽהֲרֹ֔ן בְּבֹא֖וֹ לִפְנֵ֣י יְהֹוָ֑ה וְנָשָׂ֣א אַ֠הֲרֹן אֶת־מִשְׁפַּ֨ט בְּנֵֽי־יִשְׂרָאֵ֧ל עַל־לִבּ֛וֹ לִפְנֵ֥י יְהֹוָ֖ה תָּמִֽיד:

שלישי לא וְעָשִׂ֛יתָ אֶת־מְעִ֥יל הָאֵפ֖וֹד כְּלִ֥יל תְּכֵֽלֶת:

לב וְהָיָ֥ה פִֽי־רֹאשׁ֖וֹ בְּתוֹכ֑וֹ שָׂפָ֡ה יִֽהְיֶה֩ לְפִ֨יו סָבִ֜יב מַֽעֲשֵׂ֣ה אֹרֵ֗ג כְּפִ֥י תַֽחְרָ֛א יִֽהְיֶה־לּ֖וֹ לֹ֥א יִקָּרֵֽעַ:

לג וְעָשִׂ֣יתָ עַל־שׁוּלָ֗יו רִמֹּנֵי֙ תְּכֵ֤לֶת וְאַרְגָּמָן֙ וְתוֹלַ֣עַת שָׁנִ֔י עַל־שׁוּלָ֖יו סָבִ֑יב וּפַֽעֲמֹנֵ֥י זָהָ֛ב בְּתוֹכָ֖ם סָבִֽיב:

לד פַּֽעֲמֹ֤ן זָהָב֙ וְרִמּ֔וֹן פַּֽעֲמֹ֥ן זָהָ֖ב וְרִמּ֑וֹן עַל־שׁוּלֵ֥י הַמְּעִ֖יל סָבִֽיב:

לה וְהָיָ֥ה עַל־אַֽהֲרֹ֖ן לְשָׁרֵ֑ת וְנִשְׁמַ֣ע ק֠וֹל֠וֹ בְּבֹא֨וֹ אֶל־הַקֹּ֜דֶשׁ לִפְנֵ֧י יְהֹוָ֛ה וּבְצֵאת֖וֹ וְלֹ֥א יָמֽוּת:

לו וְעָשִׂ֥יתָ צִּ֖יץ זָהָ֣ב טָה֑וֹר וּפִתַּחְתָּ֤ עָלָיו֙ פִּתּוּחֵ֣י חֹתָ֔ם קֹ֖דֶשׁ לַֽיהֹוָֽה:

לז וְשַׂמְתָּ֤ אֹתוֹ֙ עַל־פְּתִ֣יל תְּכֵ֔לֶת וְהָיָ֖ה עַל־הַמִּצְנָ֑פֶת אֶל־מ֥וּל פְּנֵֽי־הַמִּצְנֶ֖פֶת יִֽהְיֶֽה:

לח וְהָיָה֮ עַל־מֵ֣צַח אַֽהֲרֹן֒ וְנָשָׂ֨א אַֽהֲרֹ֜ן אֶת־עֲוֺ֣ן הַקֳּדָשִׁ֗ים אֲשֶׁ֤ר יַקְדִּ֨ישׁוּ֙ בְּנֵ֣י יִשְׂרָאֵ֔ל לְכָל־מַתְּנֹ֖ת קָדְשֵׁיהֶ֑ם וְהָיָ֤ה עַל־מִצְחוֹ֙ תָּמִ֔יד לְרָצ֥וֹן לָהֶ֖ם לִפְנֵ֥י יְהֹוָֽה:

לט וְשִׁבַּצְתָּ֙ הַכְּתֹ֣נֶת שֵׁ֔שׁ וְעָשִׂ֖יתָ מִצְנֶ֣פֶת שֵׁ֑שׁ וְאַבְנֵ֥ט תַּֽעֲשֶׂ֖ה מַֽעֲשֵׂ֥ה רֹקֵֽם:

מ וְלִבְנֵ֤י אַֽהֲרֹן֙ תַּֽעֲשֶׂ֣ה כֻתֳּנֹ֔ת וְעָשִׂ֥יתָ לָהֶ֖ם אַבְנֵטִ֑ים וּמִגְבָּעוֹת֙ תַּֽעֲשֶׂ֣ה לָהֶ֔ם לְכָב֖וֹד וּלְתִפְאָֽרֶת:

מא וְהִלְבַּשְׁתָּ֣ אֹתָ֗ם אֶת־אַֽהֲרֹ֤ן אָחִ֨יךָ֙ וְאֶת־בָּנָ֣יו אִתּ֔וֹ וּמָֽשַׁחְתָּ֣ אֹתָ֗ם וּמִלֵּאתָ֧ אֶת־יָדָ֛ם וְקִדַּשְׁתָּ֥ אֹתָ֖ם וְכִֽהֲנוּ־לִֽי:

מב וַֽעֲשֵׂ֤ה לָהֶם֙ מִכְנְסֵי־בָ֔ד לְכַסּ֖וֹת בְּשַׂ֣ר עֶרְוָ֑ה מִמָּתְנַ֥יִם וְעַד־יְרֵכַ֖יִם יִֽהְיֽוּ:

מג וְהָיוּ֩ עַל־אַֽהֲרֹ֨ן וְעַל־בָּנָ֜יו בְּבֹאָ֣ם | אֶל־אֹ֣הֶל מוֹעֵ֗ד א֚וֹ בְגִשְׁתָּ֣ם אֶל־הַמִּזְבֵּ֔חַ לְשָׁרֵ֖ת בַּקֹּ֑דֶשׁ וְלֹֽא־יִשְׂא֥וּ עָוֺ֛ן וָמֵ֖תוּ חֻקַּ֥ת עוֹלָ֛ם ל֖וֹ וּלְזַרְע֥וֹ אַֽחֲרָֽיו:

כט רביעי א וְזֶ֨ה הַדָּבָ֜ר אֲשֶׁ֥ר תַּֽעֲשֶׂ֛ה לָהֶ֖ם לְקַדֵּ֣שׁ אֹתָ֑ם לְכַהֵ֖ן לִ֑י לְ֠קַ֠ח פַּ֣ר אֶחָ֧ד בֶּן־

ב בָּקָ֛ר וְאֵילִ֥ם שְׁנַ֖יִם תְּמִימִ֑ם וְלֶ֣חֶם מַצּ֗וֹת וְחַלֹּ֤ת מַצֹּת֙ בְּלוּלֹ֣ת בַּשֶּׁ֔מֶן

ג וּרְקִיקֵ֥י מַצּ֖וֹת מְשֻׁחִ֣ים בַּשָּׁ֑מֶן סֹ֣לֶת חִטִּ֔ים תַּֽעֲשֶׂ֖ה אֹתָֽם: וְנָתַתָּ֣ אוֹתָם֮ עַל־

28:30. The Breastplate was folded in half to form a pouch-like pocket. Into it Moses was to insert a slip of parchment containing the Ineffable Name [according to *Ramban*, there was more than one Name]. This Name was called *Urim*, from the word אוֹר, *light*, because it would cause individual letters of the tribal names on the Breastplate to light up; and it was called *Tumim*, from the word תַּמִּים, *completeness*, because, if read properly, these letters presented complete and true answers to the ques-

tions of national import that the Kohen Gadol would ask of God (*Rashi* from *Yoma* 73b).

28:36-38. On his forehead the Kohen Gadol wore a narrow gold plate upon which were inscribed the words קֹדֶשׁ לַה׳, *Holy to HASHEM*. It served to gain favor for blood or sacrificial parts that were offered on the Altar in a state of contamination (*Pesachim* 16b).

28:41. For Aaron and his sons to become Kohanim, they had to be inaugurated by Moses, just as the Tabernacle *which you shall place on the shoulder straps of the Ephod, toward its front.* ²⁶ *You shall make two rings of gold and place them on the two ends of the Breastplate at its bottom, on its inner side, toward the Ephod.* ²⁷ *You shall make two rings of gold and place them at the bottom of the two shoulder straps of the Ephod toward its front, opposite its seam, above the belt of the Ephod.* ²⁸ *They shall attach the Breastplate from its rings to the rings of the Ephod with a turquoise woolen cord so that it will remain above the belt of the Ephod, and the Breastplate will not be loosened from upon the Ephod.* ²⁹ *Aaron shall bear the names of the sons of Israel on the Breastplate of Judgment on his heart when he enters the Sanctuary, as a constant remembrance before HASHEM.* ³⁰ *Into the Breastplate of Judgment shall you place the Urim and the Tumim,* * and they shall be on Aaron's heart when he comes before HASHEM; and Aaron shall bear the judgment of the Children of Israel on his heart constantly before HASHEM.*

The Urim and the Tumim

³¹ *You shall make the Robe of the Ephod entirely of turquoise wool.* ³² *Its head-opening shall be folded over within it, its opening shall have a border all around of weaver's work — it shall be for it like the opening of a coat of mail — it may not be torn.* ³³ *You shall make on its hem pomegranates of turquoise, purple, and scarlet wool, on its hem all around, and gold bells between them, all around;* ³⁴ *a gold bell and a pomegranate, a gold bell and a pomegranate on the hem of the robe, all around.* ³⁵ *It must be on Aaron in order to minister. Its sound shall be heard when he enters the Sanctuary before HASHEM and when he leaves, so that he not die.*

Robe of the Ephod
(See Appendix C, illustrations 12-13)

³⁶ *You shall make a Headplate* * of pure gold, and you shall engrave upon it, engraved like a signet ring, "HOLY TO HASHEM."* ³⁷ *You shall place it on a cord of turquoise wool and it shall be on the Turban, opposite the front of the Turban shall it be.* ³⁸ *It shall be on Aaron's forehead so that Aaron shall bring forgiveness for a sin regarding the sacred offerings that the Children of Israel consecrate for any gifts of their sacred offerings; and it shall be on his forehead always, to bring them favor before HASHEM.*

Headplate
(See Appendix C, illustration 14)

³⁹ *You shall make a linen Tunic of a box-like knit. You shall make a linen Turban and you shall make a Sash of embroiderer's work.*

Tunic

⁴⁰ *For the sons of Aaron you shall make Tunics and make them Sashes; and you shall make them Headdresses for glory and splendor.* ⁴¹ *With them you shall dress Aaron your brother and his sons with him.* * *You shall anoint them, inaugurate them and sanctify them, and they shall minister to Me.* ⁴² *You shall make them linen breeches to cover the flesh of nakedness, from the hips to the thighs shall they be.* ⁴³ *They shall be on Aaron and his sons when they enter the Tent of Meeting or when they approach the Altar to serve in holiness, and they should not bear a sin and die; it is an eternal decree for him and his offspring after him.*

Vestments of the ordinary Kohanim

29

Inauguration ritual

¹ **T**his is the matter that you shall do for them to sanctify them to minister for Me: Take one young bull and two rams, unblemished;* ² *with unleavened breads, unleavened loaves mixed with oil, and unleavened wafers smeared with oil; of fine wheat flour shall you make them.* ³ *You shall place them in*

---

itself had to be inaugurated and sanctified by being erected and anointed. As the next chapter sets forth, there was a seven-day sacrificial service that was performed only by Moses. The anointment of ordinary

Kohanim did not have to be done ever again; henceforth their newborn children would automatically be Kohanim simply by virtue of their descent from the priestly family. In the future only a Kohen Gadol would be anointed.

ד סַל אֶחָד וְהִקְרַבְתָּ אֹתָם בַּסָּל וְאֶת־הַפָּר וְאֵת שְׁנֵי הָאֵילִם: וְאֶת־אַהֲרֹן

ה וְאֶת־בָּנָיו תַּקְרִיב אֶל־פֶּתַח אֹהֶל מוֹעֵד וְרָחַצְתָּ אֹתָם בַּמָּיִם: וְלָקַחְתָּ אֶת־הַבְּגָדִים וְהִלְבַּשְׁתָּ אֶת־אַהֲרֹן אֶת־הַכֻּתֹּנֶת וְאֵת מְעִיל הָאֵפֹד וְאֶת־

ו הָאֵפֹד וְאֶת־הַחֹשֶׁן וְאָפַדְתָּ לוֹ בְּחֵשֶׁב הָאֵפֹד: וְשַׂמְתָּ הַמִּצְנֶפֶת עַל־רֹאשׁוֹ

ז וְנָתַתָּ אֶת־נֵזֶר הַקֹּדֶשׁ עַל־הַמִּצְנָפֶת: וְלָקַחְתָּ אֶת־שֶׁמֶן הַמִּשְׁחָה וְיָצַקְתָּ

ח-ט עַל־רֹאשׁוֹ וּמָשַׁחְתָּ אֹתוֹ: וְאֶת־בָּנָיו תַּקְרִיב וְהִלְבַּשְׁתָּם כֻּתֳּנֹת: וְחָגַרְתָּ אֹתָם אַבְנֵט אַהֲרֹן וּבָנָיו וְחָבַשְׁתָּ לָהֶם מִגְבָּעֹת וְהָיְתָה לָהֶם כְּהֻנָּה לְחֻקַּת

י עוֹלָם וּמִלֵּאתָ יַד־אַהֲרֹן וְיַד־בָּנָיו: וְהִקְרַבְתָּ אֶת־הַפָּר לִפְנֵי אֹהֶל מוֹעֵד

יא וְסָמַךְ אַהֲרֹן וּבָנָיו אֶת־יְדֵיהֶם עַל־רֹאשׁ הַפָּר: וְשָׁחַטְתָּ אֶת־הַפָּר לִפְנֵי יהוה

יב פֶּתַח אֹהֶל מוֹעֵד: וְלָקַחְתָּ מִדַּם הַפָּר וְנָתַתָּה עַל־קַרְנֹת הַמִּזְבֵּחַ בְּאֶצְבָּעֶךָ

יג וְאֶת־כָּל־הַדָּם תִּשְׁפֹּךְ אֶל־יְסוֹד הַמִּזְבֵּחַ: וְלָקַחְתָּ אֶת־כָּל־הַחֵלֶב הַמְכַסֶּה אֶת־הַקֶּרֶב וְאֵת הַיֹּתֶרֶת עַל־הַכָּבֵד וְאֵת שְׁתֵּי הַכְּלָיֹת וְאֶת־הַחֵלֶב אֲשֶׁר

יד עֲלֵיהֶן וְהִקְטַרְתָּ הַמִּזְבֵּחָה: וְאֶת־בְּשַׂר הַפָּר וְאֶת־עֹרוֹ וְאֶת־פִּרְשׁוֹ תִּשְׂרֹף

טו בָּאֵשׁ מִחוּץ לַמַּחֲנֶה חַטָּאת הוּא: וְאֵת־הָאַיִל הָאֶחָד תִּקָּח וְסָמְכוּ אַהֲרֹן

טז וּבָנָיו אֶת־יְדֵיהֶם עַל־רֹאשׁ הָאָיִל: וְשָׁחַטְתָּ אֶת־הָאָיִל וְלָקַחְתָּ אֶת־דָּמוֹ

יז וְזָרַקְתָּ עַל־הַמִּזְבֵּחַ סָבִיב: וְאֶת־הָאַיִל תְּנַתֵּחַ לִנְתָחָיו וְרָחַצְתָּ קִרְבּוֹ

יח וּכְרָעָיו וְנָתַתָּ עַל־נְתָחָיו וְעַל־רֹאשׁוֹ: וְהִקְטַרְתָּ אֶת־כָּל־הָאַיִל הַמִּזְבֵּחָה עֹלָה הוּא לַיהוה רֵיחַ נִיחוֹחַ אִשֶּׁה לַיהוה הוּא: וְלָקַחְתָּ אֵת הָאַיִל הַשֵּׁנִי   חמישי

כ וְסָמַךְ אַהֲרֹן וּבָנָיו אֶת־יְדֵיהֶם עַל־רֹאשׁ הָאָיִל: וְשָׁחַטְתָּ אֶת־הָאַיִל וְלָקַחְתָּ מִדָּמוֹ וְנָתַתָּה עַל־תְּנוּךְ אֹזֶן אַהֲרֹן וְעַל־תְּנוּךְ אֹזֶן בָּנָיו הַיְמָנִית וְעַל־בֹּהֶן יָדָם הַיְמָנִית וְעַל־בֹּהֶן רַגְלָם הַיְמָנִית וְזָרַקְתָּ אֶת־הַדָּם עַל־הַמִּזְבֵּחַ סָבִיב:

כא וְלָקַחְתָּ מִן־הַדָּם אֲשֶׁר עַל־הַמִּזְבֵּחַ וּמִשֶּׁמֶן הַמִּשְׁחָה וְהִזֵּיתָ עַל־אַהֲרֹן וְעַל־בְּגָדָיו וְעַל־בָּנָיו וְעַל־בִּגְדֵי בָנָיו אִתּוֹ וְקָדַשׁ הוּא וּבְגָדָיו וּבָנָיו וּבִגְדֵי

כב בָנָיו אִתּוֹ: וְלָקַחְתָּ מִן־הָאַיִל הַחֵלֶב וְהָאַלְיָה וְאֶת־הַחֵלֶב ׀ הַמְכַסֶּה אֶת־הַקֶּרֶב וְאֵת יֹתֶרֶת הַכָּבֵד וְאֵת ׀ שְׁתֵּי הַכְּלָיֹת וְאֶת־הַחֵלֶב אֲשֶׁר עֲלֵיהֶן

כג וְאֵת שׁוֹק הַיָּמִין כִּי אֵיל מִלֻּאִים הוּא: וְכִכַּר לֶחֶם אַחַת וְחַלַּת לֶחֶם שֶׁמֶן אַחַת וְרָקִיק אֶחָד מִסַּל הַמַּצּוֹת אֲשֶׁר לִפְנֵי יהוה: וְשַׂמְתָּ הַכֹּל עַל כַּפֵּי

כה אַהֲרֹן וְעַל כַּפֵּי בָנָיו וְהֵנַפְתָּ אֹתָם תְּנוּפָה לִפְנֵי יהוה: וְלָקַחְתָּ אֹתָם מִיָּדָם וְהִקְטַרְתָּ הַמִּזְבֵּחָה עַל־הָעֹלָה לְרֵיחַ נִיחוֹחַ לִפְנֵי יהוה אִשֶּׁה הוּא לַיהוה:

כו וְלָקַחְתָּ אֶת־הֶחָזֶה מֵאֵיל הַמִּלֻּאִים אֲשֶׁר לְאַהֲרֹן וְהֵנַפְתָּ אֹתוֹ תְּנוּפָה

כז לִפְנֵי יהוה וְהָיָה לְךָ לְמָנָה: וְקִדַּשְׁתָּ אֵת ׀ חֲזֵה הַתְּנוּפָה וְאֵת שׁוֹק הַתְּרוּמָה אֲשֶׁר הוּנַף וַאֲשֶׁר הוּרָם מֵאֵיל הַמִּלֻּאִים מֵאֲשֶׁר לְאַהֲרֹן וּמֵאֲשֶׁר לְבָנָיו:

29:20. Through the ear, one hears and understands; through the hand, one acts; through the feet, one moves about. All three are consecrated to show that the Kohen dedicates all his faculties to God's service (R' Hirsch).

29:24. Moses and the Kohanim acted together in waving these sacrificial parts in all four directions, acknowledging God's mastery everywhere (*Rashi*).

a single basket and bring them near in the basket, with the bull and the two rams. ⁴ Aaron and his sons you shall bring near to the entrance of the Tent of Meeting, and you shall immerse them in the water. ⁵ You shall take the vestments and dress Aaron with the Tunic, the Robe of the Ephod, the Ephod, and the Breastplate, and you shall girdle him with the belt of the Ephod. ⁶ You shall place the Turban on his head and place the crown of sanctity over the Turban. ⁷ You shall take the anointment oil and pour it on his head, and anoint him.

Immersing, vestments, anointment

⁸ You shall cause his sons to come near, and dress them in Tunics. ⁹ You shall girdle them with a Sash — Aaron and his sons — and you shall wrap the Headdresses on them. The priesthood shall be an eternal duty for them, and you shall inaugurate Aaron and his sons.

The bull ¹⁰ You shall bring the bull near before the Tent of Meeting; Aaron and his sons shall lean their hands upon the head of the bull. ¹¹ You shall slaughter the bull before HASHEM, before the entrance of the Tent of Meeting. ¹² You shall take some blood of the bull and place it with your finger on the horns of the Altar, and you shall pour all the blood on the base of the Altar. ¹³ You shall take all the fat that covers the innards, the diaphragm with the liver, the two kidneys and the fat that is upon them; and you shall cause them to go up in smoke upon the Altar. ¹⁴ The flesh of the bull, its hide, and its waste you shall burn in fire outside the camp — it is a sin-offering.

The first ram ¹⁵ You shall take the first ram. Aaron and his sons shall lean their hands on the head of the ram. ¹⁶ You shall slaughter the ram, and take its blood and throw it on the Altar all around. ¹⁷ You shall cut the ram into its pieces; wash its innards and feet, and place [them] with its pieces and its head. ¹⁸ You shall cause the entire ram to go up in smoke upon the Altar — it is a burnt-offering to HASHEM; it is a satisfying aroma, a fire-offering to HASHEM.

The second ram ¹⁹ You shall take the second ram. Aaron and his sons shall lean their hands on the head of the ram. ²⁰ You shall slaughter the ram. You shall take some of its blood and place it on the middle part of the ear* of Aaron and on the middle part of the ear of his sons — the right one — and on the thumb of their right hand and the big toe of their right foot, and you shall throw the blood upon the Altar, all around. ²¹ You shall take some of the blood that is on the Altar and some of the anointment oil and sprinkle on Aaron and on his vestments, and on his sons and the vestments of his sons with him; he and his vestments, and his sons and his sons' vestments with him, shall become holy.

²² From the ram you shall take the fat, the tail, the fat that covers the innards, the diaphragm with the liver, the two kidneys and the fat that is on them, and the right thigh — it is a ram of perfection — ²³ one cake of bread, one oily loaf, and one wafer from the basket of unleavened loaves that is before HASHEM. ²⁴ You shall place it all on the palms of Aaron and on the palms of his sons, and you shall wave them as a waving* before HASHEM. ²⁵ You shall take them from their hands and cause it to go up in smoke on the Altar, on the burnt-offering, as a satisfying aroma before HASHEM; it is a fire-offering to HASHEM. ²⁶ You shall take the breast of the inauguration ram that is Aaron's, and you shall wave it as a waving before HASHEM. Then it shall be your portion. ²⁷ You shall sanctify the breast of the waving and the thigh of the raising-up, that was waved and that was raised up, from the inauguration ram that was for Aaron and for his sons.

כח וְהָיָה לְאַהֲרֹן וּלְבָנָיו לְחָק־עוֹלָם מֵאֵת בְּנֵי יִשְׂרָאֵל כִּי תְרוּמָה הוּא
כט וּתְרוּמָה יִהְיֶה מֵאֵת בְּנֵי־יִשְׂרָאֵל מִזִּבְחֵי שַׁלְמֵיהֶם תְּרוּמָתָם לַיהוָה: וּבִגְדֵי
הַקֹּדֶשׁ אֲשֶׁר לְאַהֲרֹן יִהְיוּ לְבָנָיו אַחֲרָיו לְמָשְׁחָה בָהֶם וּלְמַלֵּא־בָם אֶת־
ל יָדָם: שִׁבְעַת יָמִים יִלְבָּשָׁם הַכֹּהֵן תַּחְתָּיו מִבָּנָיו אֲשֶׁר יָבֹא אֶל־אֹהֶל מוֹעֵד
לא לְשָׁרֵת בַּקֹּדֶשׁ: וְאֵת אֵיל הַמִּלֻּאִים תִּקָּח וּבִשַּׁלְתָּ אֶת־בְּשָׂרוֹ בְּמָקֹם קָדֹשׁ:
לב וְאָכַל אַהֲרֹן וּבָנָיו אֶת־בְּשַׂר הָאַיִל וְאֶת־הַלֶּחֶם אֲשֶׁר בַּסָּל פֶּתַח אֹהֶל
לג מוֹעֵד: וְאָכְלוּ אֹתָם אֲשֶׁר כֻּפַּר בָּהֶם לְמַלֵּא אֶת־יָדָם לְקַדֵּשׁ אֹתָם וְזָר לֹא־
לד יֹאכַל כִּי־קֹדֶשׁ הֵם: וְאִם־יִוָּתֵר מִבְּשַׂר הַמִּלֻּאִים וּמִן־הַלֶּחֶם עַד־הַבֹּקֶר
לה וְשָׂרַפְתָּ אֶת־הַנּוֹתָר בָּאֵשׁ לֹא יֵאָכֵל כִּי־קֹדֶשׁ הוּא: וְעָשִׂיתָ לְאַהֲרֹן וּלְבָנָיו
לו כָּכָה כְּכֹל אֲשֶׁר־צִוִּיתִי אֹתָכָה שִׁבְעַת יָמִים תְּמַלֵּא יָדָם: וּפַר חַטָּאת
תַּעֲשֶׂה לַיּוֹם עַל־הַכִּפֻּרִים וְחִטֵּאתָ עַל־הַמִּזְבֵּחַ בְּכַפֶּרְךָ עָלָיו וּמָשַׁחְתָּ
לז אֹתוֹ לְקַדְּשׁוֹ: שִׁבְעַת יָמִים תְּכַפֵּר עַל־הַמִּזְבֵּחַ וְקִדַּשְׁתָּ אֹתוֹ וְהָיָה הַמִּזְבֵּחַ
לח קֹדֶשׁ קָדָשִׁים כָּל־הַנֹּגֵעַ בַּמִּזְבֵּחַ יִקְדָּשׁ:　　וְזֶה אֲשֶׁר תַּעֲשֶׂה עַל־

ששי

לט הַמִּזְבֵּחַ כְּבָשִׂים בְּנֵי־שָׁנָה שְׁנַיִם לַיּוֹם תָּמִיד: אֶת־הַכֶּבֶשׂ הָאֶחָד תַּעֲשֶׂה
מ בַבֹּקֶר וְאֵת הַכֶּבֶשׂ הַשֵּׁנִי תַּעֲשֶׂה בֵּין הָעַרְבָּיִם: וְעִשָּׂרֹן סֹלֶת בָּלוּל בְּשֶׁמֶן
מא כָּתִית רֶבַע הַהִין וְנֵסֶךְ רְבִיעִת הַהִין יָיִן לַכֶּבֶשׂ הָאֶחָד: וְאֵת הַכֶּבֶשׂ הַשֵּׁנִי
תַּעֲשֶׂה בֵּין הָעַרְבָּיִם כְּמִנְחַת הַבֹּקֶר וּכְנִסְכָּהּ תַּעֲשֶׂה־לָּהּ לְרֵיחַ נִיחֹחַ
מב אִשֶּׁה לַיהוָה: עֹלַת תָּמִיד לְדֹרֹתֵיכֶם פֶּתַח אֹהֶל־מוֹעֵד לִפְנֵי יהוָה אֲשֶׁר
מג אִוָּעֵד לָכֶם שָׁמָּה לְדַבֵּר אֵלֶיךָ שָׁם: וְנֹעַדְתִּי שָׁמָּה לִבְנֵי יִשְׂרָאֵל וְנִקְדַּשׁ
מד בִּכְבֹדִי: וְקִדַּשְׁתִּי אֶת־אֹהֶל מוֹעֵד וְאֶת־הַמִּזְבֵּחַ וְאֶת־אַהֲרֹן וְאֶת־בָּנָיו
מה-מו אֲקַדֵּשׁ לְכַהֵן לִי: וְשָׁכַנְתִּי בְּתוֹךְ בְּנֵי יִשְׂרָאֵל וְהָיִיתִי לָהֶם לֵאלֹהִים: וְיָדְעוּ
כִּי אֲנִי יהוָה אֱלֹהֵיהֶם אֲשֶׁר הוֹצֵאתִי אֹתָם מֵאֶרֶץ מִצְרַיִם לְשָׁכְנִי בְתוֹכָם
אֲנִי יהוָה אֱלֹהֵיהֶם:

ל שביעי א-ב וְעָשִׂיתָ מִזְבֵּחַ מִקְטַר קְטֹרֶת עֲצֵי שִׁטִּים תַּעֲשֶׂה אֹתוֹ: אַמָּה אָרְכּוֹ וְאַמָּה
ג רָחְבּוֹ רָבוּעַ יִהְיֶה וְאַמָּתַיִם קֹמָתוֹ מִמֶּנּוּ קַרְנֹתָיו: וְצִפִּיתָ אֹתוֹ זָהָב
טָהוֹר אֶת־גַּגּוֹ וְאֶת־קִירֹתָיו סָבִיב וְאֶת־קַרְנֹתָיו וְעָשִׂיתָ לּוֹ זֵר זָהָב
ד סָבִיב: וּשְׁתֵּי טַבְּעֹת זָהָב תַּעֲשֶׂה־לּוֹ | מִתַּחַת לְזֵרוֹ עַל שְׁתֵּי צַלְעֹתָיו
ה תַּעֲשֶׂה עַל־שְׁנֵי צִדָּיו וְהָיָה לְבָתִּים לְבַדִּים לָשֵׂאת אֹתוֹ בָּהֵמָּה: וְעָשִׂיתָ
ו אֶת־הַבַּדִּים עֲצֵי שִׁטִּים וְצִפִּיתָ אֹתָם זָהָב: וְנָתַתָּה אֹתוֹ לִפְנֵי הַפָּרֹכֶת אֲשֶׁר
עַל־אֲרֹן הָעֵדֻת לִפְנֵי הַכַּפֹּרֶת אֲשֶׁר עַל־הָעֵדֻת אֲשֶׁר אִוָּעֵד לְךָ שָׁמָּה:

29:38-46. The offering outlined in this passage was offered every day, seven days a week, and was totally unrelated to the Inauguration ritual. The Torah mentions it here to tell us that it was offered even before the Tabernacle assumed its full sanctity. *Ibn Ezra* and *Chizkuni* note that the *tamid,* like the other offerings of the inauguration week, was offered by Moses, and the

Kohanim assumed their responsibility for it on the first of Nissan.

30:1-10. The last of the Tabernacle's vessels is the Altar upon which incense was burned, morning and evening. It was known as מִזְבַּח הַקְּטֹרֶת, *the Incense Altar*; מִזְבַּח הַזָּהָב, *the Golden Altar*; and מִזְבֵּחַ הַפְּנִימִי, *the Inner Altar*.

²⁸ It shall be for Aaron and his sons as an eternal portion from the Children of Israel, for it is a portion and it shall remain a portion from the Children of Israel from their peace-offering feasts, their portion to HASHEM.

Succession of High Priesthood

²⁹ The holy vestments of Aaron shall belong to his sons after him to become elevated through them, to become inaugurated through them. ³⁰ For a seven-day period, the Kohen who succeeds him from his sons, who shall enter the Tent of Meeting to serve in the Sanctuary, shall don them.

³¹ You shall take the inauguration ram and cook its flesh in a holy place. ³² Aaron and his sons shall eat the flesh of the ram and the bread that is in the basket before the entrance of the Tent of Meeting. ³³ They — who received atonement through them, to inaugurate them, to sanctify them — shall eat them; an alien shall not eat for they are holy. ³⁴ If anything shall be left over from the flesh of the inauguration-offering or from the bread until the morning, you shall burn the leftover in the fire. It may not be eaten, for it is holy.

³⁵ You shall do thus for Aaron and his sons, like everything that I have commanded you; for a seven-day period shall you inaugurate them. ³⁶ A bull sin-offering shall you make for each day for the atonements; you shall purify the Altar by bringing atonement for it and you shall anoint it to sanctify it. ³⁷ For a seven-day period shall you bring atonement for the Altar and sanctify it. The Altar shall be holy of holies; whatever touches the Altar shall become sanctified.

The tamid-offering

³⁸ This is what you shall offer* upon the Altar: two sheep within their first year every day, continually. ³⁹ You shall offer the one sheep in the morning, and the second sheep shall you offer in the afternoon; ⁴⁰ and a tenth-ephah of fine flour mixed with a quarter-hin of beaten oil, and a libation of a quarter-hin of wine for each sheep. ⁴¹ You shall offer the second sheep in the afternoon, like the meal-offering of the morning and its libation shall you offer for it, for a satisfying aroma, a fire-offering to HASHEM; ⁴² as a continual burnt-offering for your generations, at the entrance of the Tent of Meeting, before HASHEM; where I shall set My meeting with you to speak to you there.

⁴³ I shall set My meeting there with the Children of Israel, and it shall be sanctified with My glory. ⁴⁴ I shall sanctify the Tent of Meeting and the Altar; and Aaron and his sons shall I sanctify to minister to Me. ⁴⁵ I shall rest My Presence among the Children of Israel, and I shall be their God. ⁴⁶ They shall know that I am HASHEM, their God, Who took them out of the land of Egypt to rest My Presence among them. I am HASHEM, their God.

30

The Incense Altar
(See Appendix C, illustration 15)

¹ You shall make an Altar* on which to bring incense up in smoke, of acacia wood shall you make it. ² Its length a cubit; and its width a cubit — it shall be square — and its height two cubits; from it shall its horns be. ³ You shall cover it with pure gold, its roof and its walls all around, and its horns, and you shall make for it a gold crown, all around. ⁴ You shall make for it two gold rings under its crown on its two corners, you shall make on its two sides; and it shall be for housings for the staves, with which to carry it. ⁵ You shall make the staves of acacia wood and cover them with gold. ⁶ You shall place it before the Partition that is by the Ark of the Testimonial-tablets, in front of the Cover that is on the Testimonial-tablets, where I shall set My meetings with you.

ז וְהִקְטִיר עָלָיו אַהֲרֹן קְטֹרֶת סַמִּים בַּבֹּקֶר בַּבֹּקֶר בְּהֵיטִיבוֹ אֶת־הַנֵּרֹת

ח יַקְטִירֶנָּה: וּבְהַעֲלֹת אַהֲרֹן אֶת־הַנֵּרֹת בֵּין הָעַרְבַּיִם יַקְטִירֶנָּה קְטֹרֶת תָּמִיד

ט לִפְנֵי יהוה לְדֹרֹתֵיכֶם: לֹא־תַעֲלוּ עָלָיו קְטֹרֶת זָרָה וְעֹלָה וּמִנְחָה וְנֵסֶךְ לֹא

י תִסְּכוּ עָלָיו: וְכִפֶּר אַהֲרֹן עַל־קַרְנֹתָיו אַחַת בַּשָּׁנָה מִדַּם חַטַּאת הַכִּפֻּרִים אַחַת בַּשָּׁנָה יְכַפֵּר עָלָיו לְדֹרֹתֵיכֶם קֹדֶשׁ־קָדָשִׁים הוּא לַיהוה: פפפ

מפטיר

Haftaras
Tetzaveh:
p. 1312

For special
Sabbaths,
see pp. x-xi

ק"א פסוקים. מיכא"ל סימן.

פרשת כי תשא

יא־יב וַיְדַבֵּר יהוה אֶל־מֹשֶׁה לֵּאמֹר: כִּי תִשָּׂא אֶת־רֹאשׁ בְּנֵי־יִשְׂרָאֵל לִפְקֻדֵיהֶם וְנָתְנוּ אִישׁ כֹּפֶר נַפְשׁוֹ לַיהוה בִּפְקֹד אֹתָם וְלֹא־יִהְיֶה בָהֶם נֶגֶף בִּפְקֹד אֹתָם:

יג זֶה ׀ יִתְּנוּ כָּל־הָעֹבֵר עַל־הַפְּקֻדִים מַחֲצִית הַשֶּׁקֶל בְּשֶׁקֶל הַקֹּדֶשׁ עֶשְׂרִים

יד גֵּרָה הַשֶּׁקֶל מַחֲצִית הַשֶּׁקֶל תְּרוּמָה לַיהוה: כֹּל הָעֹבֵר עַל־הַפְּקֻדִים מִבֶּן

טו עֶשְׂרִים שָׁנָה וָמָעְלָה יִתֵּן תְּרוּמַת יהוה: הֶעָשִׁיר לֹא־יַרְבֶּה וְהַדַּל לֹא יַמְעִיט מִמַּחֲצִית הַשָּׁקֶל לָתֵת אֶת־תְּרוּמַת יהוה לְכַפֵּר עַל־נַפְשֹׁתֵיכֶם:

טז וְלָקַחְתָּ אֶת־כֶּסֶף הַכִּפֻּרִים מֵאֵת בְּנֵי יִשְׂרָאֵל וְנָתַתָּ אֹתוֹ עַל־עֲבֹדַת אֹהֶל מוֹעֵד וְהָיָה לִבְנֵי יִשְׂרָאֵל לְזִכָּרוֹן לִפְנֵי יהוה לְכַפֵּר עַל־נַפְשֹׁתֵיכֶם:

יז־יח וַיְדַבֵּר יהוה אֶל־מֹשֶׁה לֵּאמֹר: וְעָשִׂיתָ כִּיּוֹר נְחֹשֶׁת וְכַנּוֹ נְחֹשֶׁת לְרָחְצָה

יט וְנָתַתָּ אֹתוֹ בֵּין־אֹהֶל מוֹעֵד וּבֵין הַמִּזְבֵּחַ וְנָתַתָּ שָׁמָּה מָיִם: וְרָחֲצוּ אַהֲרֹן

כ וּבָנָיו מִמֶּנּוּ אֶת־יְדֵיהֶם וְאֶת־רַגְלֵיהֶם: בְּבֹאָם אֶל־אֹהֶל מוֹעֵד יִרְחֲצוּ־מַיִם וְלֹא יָמֻתוּ אוֹ בְגִשְׁתָּם אֶל־הַמִּזְבֵּחַ לְשָׁרֵת לְהַקְטִיר אִשֶּׁה לַיהוה:

כא וְרָחֲצוּ יְדֵיהֶם וְרַגְלֵיהֶם וְלֹא יָמֻתוּ וְהָיְתָה לָהֶם חָק־עוֹלָם לוֹ וּלְזַרְעוֹ לְדֹרֹתָם:

כב־כג וַיְדַבֵּר יהוה אֶל־מֹשֶׁה לֵּאמֹר: וְאַתָּה קַח־לְךָ בְּשָׂמִים רֹאשׁ מָר־דְּרוֹר חֲמֵשׁ מֵאוֹת וְקִנְּמָן־בֶּשֶׂם מַחֲצִיתוֹ חֲמִשִּׁים וּמָאתָיִם וּקְנֵה־בֹשֶׂם חֲמִשִּׁים

כד־כה וּמָאתָיִם: וְקִדָּה חֲמֵשׁ מֵאוֹת בְּשֶׁקֶל הַקֹּדֶשׁ וְשֶׁמֶן זַיִת הִין: וְעָשִׂיתָ אֹתוֹ שֶׁמֶן מִשְׁחַת־קֹדֶשׁ רֹקַח מִרְקַחַת מַעֲשֵׂה רֹקֵחַ שֶׁמֶן מִשְׁחַת־קֹדֶשׁ יִהְיֶה:

כו־כז וּמָשַׁחְתָּ בוֹ אֶת־אֹהֶל מוֹעֵד וְאֵת אֲרוֹן הָעֵדֻת: וְאֶת־הַשֻּׁלְחָן וְאֶת־כָּל־ כֵּלָיו וְאֶת־הַמְּנֹרָה וְאֶת־כֵּלֶיהָ וְאֵת מִזְבַּח הַקְּטֹרֶת: וְאֶת־מִזְבַּח הָעֹלָה

כח וְאֶת־כָּל־כֵּלָיו וְאֶת־הַכִּיֹּר וְאֶת־כַּנּוֹ: וְקִדַּשְׁתָּ אֹתָם וְהָיוּ קֹדֶשׁ קָדָשִׁים כָּל־

כט

ל הַנֹּגֵעַ בָּהֶם יִקְדָּשׁ: וְאֶת־אַהֲרֹן וְאֶת־בָּנָיו תִּמְשָׁח וְקִדַּשְׁתָּ אֹתָם לְכַהֵן לִי:

MAFTIR
FOR
PARASHAS
SHEKALIM
30:11-16

Haftarah:
p. 908

⌇ **Parashas Ki Sisa**

30:11-16. When it is necessary to conduct a census of Jews, it must be done by having the people contribute items, which would then be counted.

30:13. God showed Moses a coin of fire and said to him, "Like *this shall they give*" (*Tanchuma*; *Rashi*). The commentators find homiletic insights in this Midrash. Among them are:

☐ Money, like fire, can be either beneficial or destructive, depending on how it is used (*Noam Elimelech*).
☐ One seeking atonement through charity should do the good deed with fiery enthusiasm (*R' Mendel of Kotzk*).

30:13. The shekel was a specific weight of silver that Moses instituted as the standard coinage. In contemporary weights, *Chazon Ish* calculates this shekel as 16 grams, or .51 troy ounces, of pure silver.

⁷ *Upon it shall Aaron bring the spice incense up in smoke, every morning, when he cleans the lamps he shall bring it up in smoke.* ⁸ *And when Aaron kindles the lamps in the afternoon he shall bring it up in smoke, continual incense before HASHEM, for your generations.* ⁹ *You shall not bring upon it alien incense, or a burnt-offering or meal-offering; nor may you pour a libation upon it.* ¹⁰ *Aaron shall bring atonement upon its horns once a year, from the blood of the sin-offering of the atonements, once a year, shall he bring atonement upon it for your generations; it is holy of holies to HASHEM.*

PARASHAS KI SISA

The census ¹¹ **H**ASHEM *spoke to Moses, saying:* ¹² *"When you take a census* of the Children of Israel according to their numbers, every man shall give HASHEM an atonement for his soul when counting them, so that there will not be a plague among them when counting them.* ¹³ *This shall they give* — everyone who passes through the census — a half shekel of the sacred shekel,* the shekel is twenty geras, half a shekel as a portion to HASHEM.* ¹⁴ *Everyone who passes through the census, from twenty years of age and up, shall give the portion of HASHEM.* ¹⁵ *The wealthy shall not increase and the destitute shall not decrease from half a shekel — to give the portion of HASHEM, to atone for your souls.* ¹⁶ *You shall take the silver of the atonements from the Children of Israel and give it for the work of the Tent of Meeting; and it shall be a remembrance before HASHEM for the Children of Israel, to atone for your souls."*

The Laver ¹⁷ *HASHEM spoke to Moses, saying:* ¹⁸ *"You shall make a copper Laver* and its base of copper, for washing; place it between the Tent of Meeting and the Altar, and put water there.* ¹⁹ *From it, Aaron and his sons shall wash their hands together with their feet.* ²⁰ *Whenever they come to the Tent of Meeting, they shall wash with water and not die, or when they approach the Altar to serve, to raise up in smoke a fire-offering to HASHEM.* ²¹ *They shall wash their hands and feet and not die. It shall be for them an eternal decree, for him and his offspring for their generations."*

Anointment ²² *HASHEM spoke to Moses, saying:* ²³ *"Now you, take for yourself choice* oil *spices:* five hundred shekel-weights of pure myrrh; fragrant cinnamon, half of which shall be two hundred fifty; two hundred fifty of fragrant cane;* ²⁴ *five hundred of cassia — in the sacred shekel-weight, and a hin of olive oil.* ²⁵ *Of it you shall make oil of sacred anointment, a blended compound, the handiwork of a perfumer; it shall remain oil of sacred anointment.* ²⁶ *With it you shall anoint the Tent of Meeting and the Ark of Testimonial-tablets;* ²⁷ *the Table and all its utensils, the Menorah and its utensils, and the Incense Altar;* ²⁸ *the Burnt-offering Altar and all its utensils; and the Laver and its base.* ²⁹ *You shall sanctify them and they shall remain holy of holies; whatever touches them shall become holy.*

³⁰ *"You shall anoint Aaron and his sons and sanctify them to minister to Me.*

Homiletically, the requirement of *half* a coin alludes to the concept that no Jew is complete unless he joins with others; alone, he is only a "half" of his full potential.

30:17-21. In the Courtyard of the Tabernacle stood a large copper utensil from which the Kohanim were required to wash their hands and feet before performing the service. The purpose of this washing was for sanctity rather than cleanliness.

30:22-33. Moses was commanded to compound a mixture of oil and spices that would be used to anoint and consecrate all the vessels of the Tabernacle, and also Aaron and his sons, for their tasks. In the future, this same oil would be used to anoint the kings of the Davidic dynasty and Kohanim Gedolim.

לא וְאֶל־בְּנֵי יִשְׂרָאֵל תְּדַבֵּר לֵאמֹר שֶׁמֶן מִשְׁחַת־קֹדֶשׁ יִהְיֶה זֶה לִי לְדֹרֹתֵיכֶם:

לב עַל־בְּשַׂר אָדָם לֹא יִיסָךְ וּבְמַתְכֻּנְתּוֹ לֹא תַעֲשׂוּ כָּמֹהוּ קֹדֶשׁ הוּא קֹדֶשׁ

לג יִהְיֶה לָכֶם: אִישׁ אֲשֶׁר יִרְקַח כָּמֹהוּ וַאֲשֶׁר יִתֵּן מִמֶּנּוּ עַל־זָר וְנִכְרַת

לד מֵעַמָּיו: וַיֹּאמֶר יהוה אֶל־מֹשֶׁה קַח־לְךָ סַמִּים נָטָף ׀ וּשְׁחֵלֶת

לה וְחֶלְבְּנָה סַמִּים וּלְבֹנָה זַכָּה בַּד בְּבַד יִהְיֶה: וְעָשִׂיתָ אֹתָהּ קְטֹרֶת רֹקַח

לו מַעֲשֵׂה רוֹקֵחַ מְמֻלָּח טָהוֹר קֹדֶשׁ: וְשָׁחַקְתָּ מִמֶּנָּה הָדֵק וְנָתַתָּה מִמֶּנָּה לִפְנֵי
הָעֵדֻת בְּאֹהֶל מוֹעֵד אֲשֶׁר אִוָּעֵד לְךָ שָׁמָּה קֹדֶשׁ קָדָשִׁים תִּהְיֶה לָכֶם:

לז וְהַקְּטֹרֶת אֲשֶׁר תַּעֲשֶׂה בְּמַתְכֻּנְתָּהּ לֹא תַעֲשׂוּ לָכֶם קֹדֶשׁ תִּהְיֶה לְךָ לַיהוה:

לא לח-א אִישׁ אֲשֶׁר־יַעֲשֶׂה כָמוֹהָ לְהָרִיחַ בָּהּ וְנִכְרַת מֵעַמָּיו: וַיְדַבֵּר

ב יהוה אֶל־מֹשֶׁה לֵּאמֹר: רְאֵה קָרָאתִי בְשֵׁם בְּצַלְאֵל בֶּן־אוּרִי בֶן־חוּר

ג לְמַטֵּה יְהוּדָה: וָאֲמַלֵּא אֹתוֹ רוּחַ אֱלֹהִים בְּחָכְמָה וּבִתְבוּנָה וּבְדַעַת וּבְכָל־

ד-ה מְלָאכָה: לַחְשֹׁב מַחֲשָׁבֹת לַעֲשׂוֹת בַּזָּהָב וּבַכֶּסֶף וּבַנְּחֹשֶׁת: וּבַחֲרֹשֶׁת אֶבֶן

ו לְמַלֹּאת וּבַחֲרֹשֶׁת עֵץ לַעֲשׂוֹת בְּכָל־מְלָאכָה: וַאֲנִי הִנֵּה נָתַתִּי אִתּוֹ אֵת
אָהֳלִיאָב בֶּן־אֲחִיסָמָךְ לְמַטֵּה־דָן וּבְלֵב כָּל־חֲכַם־לֵב נָתַתִּי חָכְמָה וְעָשׂוּ

ז אֵת כָּל־אֲשֶׁר צִוִּיתִךָ: אֵת ׀ אֹהֶל מוֹעֵד וְאֶת־הָאָרֹן לָעֵדֻת וְאֶת־הַכַּפֹּרֶת

ח אֲשֶׁר עָלָיו וְאֵת כָּל־כְּלֵי הָאֹהֶל: וְאֶת־הַשֻּׁלְחָן וְאֶת־כֵּלָיו וְאֶת־הַמְּנֹרָה

ט הַטְּהֹרָה וְאֶת־כָּל־כֵּלֶיהָ וְאֵת מִזְבַּח הַקְּטֹרֶת: וְאֶת־מִזְבַּח הָעֹלָה וְאֶת־

י כָּל־כֵּלָיו וְאֶת־הַכִּיּוֹר וְאֶת־כַּנּוֹ: וְאֵת בִּגְדֵי הַשְּׂרָד וְאֶת־בִּגְדֵי הַקֹּדֶשׁ

יא לְאַהֲרֹן הַכֹּהֵן וְאֶת־בִּגְדֵי בָנָיו לְכַהֵן: וְאֵת שֶׁמֶן הַמִּשְׁחָה וְאֶת־קְטֹרֶת
הַסַּמִּים לַקֹּדֶשׁ כְּכֹל אֲשֶׁר־צִוִּיתִךָ יַעֲשׂוּ:

יב-יג וַיֹּאמֶר יהוה אֶל־מֹשֶׁה לֵּאמֹר: וְאַתָּה דַּבֵּר אֶל־בְּנֵי יִשְׂרָאֵל לֵאמֹר אַךְ
אֶת־שַׁבְּתֹתַי תִּשְׁמֹרוּ כִּי אוֹת הִוא בֵּינִי וּבֵינֵיכֶם לְדֹרֹתֵיכֶם לָדַעַת כִּי אֲנִי

יד יהוה מְקַדִּשְׁכֶם: וּשְׁמַרְתֶּם אֶת־הַשַּׁבָּת כִּי קֹדֶשׁ הִוא לָכֶם מְחַלְלֶיהָ מוֹת
יוּמָת כִּי כָּל־הָעֹשֶׂה בָהּ מְלָאכָה וְנִכְרְתָה הַנֶּפֶשׁ הַהִוא מִקֶּרֶב עַמֶּיהָ:

טו שֵׁשֶׁת יָמִים יֵעָשֶׂה מְלָאכָה וּבַיּוֹם הַשְּׁבִיעִי שַׁבַּת שַׁבָּתוֹן קֹדֶשׁ לַיהוה כָּל־

טז הָעֹשֶׂה מְלָאכָה בְּיוֹם הַשַּׁבָּת מוֹת יוּמָת: וְשָׁמְרוּ בְנֵי־יִשְׂרָאֵל אֶת־הַשַּׁבָּת

יז לַעֲשׂוֹת אֶת־הַשַּׁבָּת לְדֹרֹתָם בְּרִית עוֹלָם: בֵּינִי וּבֵין בְּנֵי יִשְׂרָאֵל אוֹת
הִוא לְעֹלָם כִּי־שֵׁשֶׁת יָמִים עָשָׂה יהוה אֶת־הַשָּׁמַיִם וְאֶת־הָאָרֶץ וּבַיּוֹם

יח הַשְּׁבִיעִי שָׁבַת וַיִּנָּפַשׁ: וַיִּתֵּן אֶל־מֹשֶׁה כְּכַלֹּתוֹ לְדַבֵּר
אִתּוֹ בְּהַר סִינַי שְׁנֵי לֻחֹת הָעֵדֻת לֻחֹת אֶבֶן כְּתֻבִים בְּאֶצְבַּע אֱלֹהִים:

שני

30:34-38. The fragrance of the incense, which was offered twice a day, represented Israel's responsibility and desire to serve God in a manner pleasing to Him. One of the spices, galbanum, had a foul aroma, from which the Sages (Kereisos 6b) derive that non-observant people should be included in our prayers (Rashi) — thus, the incense expresses the idea of Jewish unity.

31:1-11. That Bezalel — who was thirteen years old at this time (Sanhedrin 69b) — mastered the wide array of crafts needed to build the Tabernacle was remarkable, if not miraculous. By filling him with a Godly spirit, with wisdom, insight, and knowledge . . . (v. 3), God showed that He had not merely redeemed Israel from slavery, He had endowed them with the capacity to serve Him

³¹ "You shall speak to the Children of Israel, saying: 'This shall remain for Me oil of sacred anointment for your generations. ³² It shall not be smeared on human flesh and you shall not duplicate it in its formulation; it is holy, it shall remain holy for you. ³³ Anyone who shall compound its like or who shall put it upon an alien shall be cut off from his people.' "

Incense ³⁴ HASHEM said to Moses: "Take yourself spices* — stacte, onycha and galbanum — spices and pure frankincense: These shall all be of equal weight. ³⁵ You shall make it into incense, a spice-compound, the handiwork of a perfumer, thoroughly mixed, pure and holy. ³⁶ You shall grind some of it finely and place some of it before the Testimonial-tablets in the Tent of Meeting, where I shall designate a time to meet you; it shall remain holy of holies to you. ³⁷ The incense that you shall make — in its proportion you shall not make for yourselves; it shall remain holy to you, for HASHEM. ³⁸ Whoever makes its like to smell it shall be cut off from his people."

31 ¹ HASHEM spoke to Moses, saying: ² "See, I have called by the name: Bezalel* *Designation* son of Uri, son of Hur, of the tribe of Judah. ³ I have filled him with a Godly *of Bezalel* spirit, with wisdom, insight, and knowledge, and with every craft; ⁴ to weave *and Oholiab* designs, to work with gold, silver, and copper; ⁵ stone-cutting for setting, and wood-carving — to perform every craft.

⁶ "And I, behold, I have assigned with him Oholiab son of Ahisamach of the tribe of Dan, and I have endowed the heart of every wise-hearted person with wisdom, and they shall make all that I have commanded you: ⁷ the Tent of Meeting, the Ark of the Testimonial-tablets and the Cover that is upon it, and all the utensils of the Tent; ⁸ the Table and its utensils, the pure Menorah and all its utensils, and the Incense Altar; ⁹ the Burnt-offering Altar and all its utensils, the Laver and its base; ¹⁰ the knit vestments, the sacred vestments of Aaron the Kohen and the vestments of his sons, to minister; ¹¹ the anointment oil and the incense-spices of the Sanctuary. Like everything that I have commanded you shall they make."

The ¹² HASHEM said to Moses, saying: ¹³ "Now you speak to the Children of Israel, *Sabbath* saying: 'However, you must observe My Sabbaths, * for it is a sign between Me and you for your generations, to know that I am HASHEM, Who makes you holy. ¹⁴ You shall observe the Sabbath, for it is holy to you; its desecrators shall be put to death, for whoever does work on it, that soul shall be cut off from among its people. ¹⁵ For six days work may be done and the seventh day is a day of complete rest, it is sacred to HASHEM; whoever does work on the Sabbath day shall be put to death.'

¹⁶ "The Children of Israel shall observe the Sabbath, to make the Sabbath an eternal covenant for their generations. ¹⁷ Between Me and the Children of Israel it is a sign forever that in a six-day period HASHEM made heaven and earth, and on the seventh day He rested and was refreshed."

Moses ¹⁸ When He finished speaking to him on Mount Sinai, He gave Moses the two *receives* Tablets of Testimony, * stone tablets inscribed by the finger of God. *the Tablets*

---

beyond their ordinary human potential.

31:12-17. The Torah teaches that the construction of the Sanctuary does not override the Sabbath. This contradicts those who claim that Sabbath law must be pliable enough to permit its relaxation for what they

regard as valid "spiritual" considerations.

31:18. Having completed the instructions regarding the Tabernacle and the Kohanim, the Torah goes back to the narrative of the Giving of the Law at Mount Sinai.

לב

א וַיַּרְא הָעָם כִּי־בֹשֵׁשׁ מֹשֶׁה לָרֶדֶת מִן־הָהָר וַיִּקָּהֵל הָעָם עַל־אַהֲרֹן וַיֹּאמְרוּ
אֵלָיו קוּם ׀ עֲשֵׂה־לָנוּ אֱלֹהִים אֲשֶׁר יֵלְכוּ לְפָנֵינוּ כִּי־זֶה ׀ מֹשֶׁה הָאִישׁ
ב אֲשֶׁר הֶעֱלָנוּ מֵאֶרֶץ מִצְרַיִם לֹא יָדַעְנוּ מֶה־הָיָה לוֹ: וַיֹּאמֶר אֲלֵהֶם אַהֲרֹן
פָּרְקוּ נִזְמֵי הַזָּהָב אֲשֶׁר בְּאָזְנֵי נְשֵׁיכֶם בְּנֵיכֶם וּבְנֹתֵיכֶם וְהָבִיאוּ אֵלָי:
ג וַיִּתְפָּרְקוּ כָּל־הָעָם אֶת־נִזְמֵי הַזָּהָב אֲשֶׁר בְּאָזְנֵיהֶם וַיָּבִיאוּ אֶל־אַהֲרֹן:
ד וַיִּקַּח מִיָּדָם וַיָּצַר אֹתוֹ בַּחֶרֶט וַיַּעֲשֵׂהוּ עֵגֶל מַסֵּכָה וַיֹּאמְרוּ אֵלֶּה אֱלֹהֶיךָ
ה יִשְׂרָאֵל אֲשֶׁר הֶעֱלוּךָ מֵאֶרֶץ מִצְרָיִם: וַיַּרְא אַהֲרֹן וַיִּבֶן מִזְבֵּחַ לְפָנָיו וַיִּקְרָא
ו אַהֲרֹן וַיֹּאמַר חַג לַיהוָה מָחָר: וַיַּשְׁכִּימוּ מִמָּחֳרָת וַיַּעֲלוּ עֹלֹת וַיַּגִּשׁוּ
שְׁלָמִים וַיֵּשֶׁב הָעָם לֶאֱכֹל וְשָׁתוֹ וַיָּקֻמוּ לְצַחֵק:
ז וַיְדַבֵּר יהוָה אֶל־מֹשֶׁה לֶךְ־רֵד כִּי שִׁחֵת עַמְּךָ אֲשֶׁר הֶעֱלֵיתָ מֵאֶרֶץ מִצְרָיִם:
ח סָרוּ מַהֵר מִן־הַדֶּרֶךְ אֲשֶׁר צִוִּיתִם עָשׂוּ לָהֶם עֵגֶל מַסֵּכָה וַיִּשְׁתַּחֲווּ־לוֹ
וַיִּזְבְּחוּ־לוֹ וַיֹּאמְרוּ אֵלֶּה אֱלֹהֶיךָ יִשְׂרָאֵל אֲשֶׁר הֶעֱלוּךָ מֵאֶרֶץ מִצְרָיִם:
ט וַיֹּאמֶר יהוָה אֶל־מֹשֶׁה רָאִיתִי אֶת־הָעָם הַזֶּה וְהִנֵּה עַם־קְשֵׁה־עֹרֶף
י הוּא: וְעַתָּה הַנִּיחָה לִּי וְיִחַר־אַפִּי בָהֶם וַאֲכַלֵּם וְאֶעֱשֶׂה אוֹתְךָ לְגוֹי גָּדוֹל:
יא וַיְחַל מֹשֶׁה אֶת־פְּנֵי יהוָה אֱלֹהָיו וַיֹּאמֶר לָמָה יהוָה יֶחֱרֶה אַפְּךָ בְּעַמֶּךָ
יב אֲשֶׁר הוֹצֵאתָ מֵאֶרֶץ מִצְרַיִם בְּכֹחַ גָּדוֹל וּבְיָד חֲזָקָה: לָמָּה יֹאמְרוּ מִצְרַיִם
לֵאמֹר בְּרָעָה הוֹצִיאָם לַהֲרֹג אֹתָם בֶּהָרִים וּלְכַלֹּתָם מֵעַל פְּנֵי הָאֲדָמָה
יג שׁוּב מֵחֲרוֹן אַפֶּךָ וְהִנָּחֵם עַל־הָרָעָה לְעַמֶּךָ: זְכֹר לְאַבְרָהָם לְיִצְחָק
וּלְיִשְׂרָאֵל עֲבָדֶיךָ אֲשֶׁר נִשְׁבַּעְתָּ לָהֶם בָּךְ וַתְּדַבֵּר אֲלֵהֶם אַרְבֶּה אֶת־
זַרְעֲכֶם כְּכוֹכְבֵי הַשָּׁמָיִם וְכָל־הָאָרֶץ הַזֹּאת אֲשֶׁר אָמַרְתִּי אֶתֵּן לְזַרְעֲכֶם
יד וְנָחֲלוּ לְעֹלָם: וַיִּנָּחֶם יהוָה עַל־הָרָעָה אֲשֶׁר דִּבֶּר לַעֲשׂוֹת לְעַמּוֹ:
טו וַיִּפֶן וַיֵּרֶד מֹשֶׁה מִן־הָהָר וּשְׁנֵי לֻחֹת הָעֵדֻת בְּיָדוֹ לֻחֹת כְּתֻבִים
טז מִשְּׁנֵי עֶבְרֵיהֶם מִזֶּה וּמִזֶּה הֵם כְּתֻבִים: וְהַלֻּחֹת מַעֲשֵׂה אֱלֹהִים הֵמָּה
יז וְהַמִּכְתָּב מִכְתַּב אֱלֹהִים הוּא חָרוּת עַל־הַלֻּחֹת: וַיִּשְׁמַע יְהוֹשֻׁעַ
יח אֶת־קוֹל הָעָם בְּרֵעֹה וַיֹּאמֶר אֶל־מֹשֶׁה קוֹל מִלְחָמָה בַּמַּחֲנֶה: וַיֹּאמֶר
אֵין קוֹל עֲנוֹת גְּבוּרָה וְאֵין קוֹל עֲנוֹת חֲלוּשָׁה קוֹל עַנּוֹת אָנֹכִי שֹׁמֵעַ:

READING
FOR
FAST DAY
32:11-14;
34:1-10

Haftarah at
Minchah:
p. 1050

32:1-6. If the sin of the Golden Calf was one of mass idol worship, the entire affair is incomprehensible, both from the standpoint of Aaron, who fashioned it, and Israel, which demanded and worshiped it. Indeed, the consensus of commentators agrees on an entirely different interpretation.

What began with an error of fact mushroomed into a grievous misunderstanding of Israel's relationship with God. Thinking that Moses was dead (v. 1), the people felt that they needed a tangible presence to take his place as intermediary between themselves and God. This was not a denial of God. Aaron acquiesced to them because he felt that it would be best for him to appear to yield until he could wean them from their error.

Bais Halevi asserts that such errors are not uncommon

even today. The people thought that they had a right to design their own "tabernacle," but Jews cannot customtailor their religion. The Tabernacle's specifications are based on Divine mysteries; no human being can use the Tabernacle or any of the Torah's commandments as the prototype for a man-made religious practice.

32:6. The term לְצַחֵק implies the three cardinal sins of idolatry, licentiousness, and murder. In addition to their worship of the Golden Calf, they committed immoral acts and they had murdered Hur, who attempted to restrain them (*Rashi*).

32:7-10. With Israel's spiritual downfall, Moses was dismissed from his lofty perch (*Rashi*). It is a general rule of Jewish leadership that the community's merit is indispensable to the success of those who serve it.

32

The Golden Calf

[1] T he people saw that Moses had delayed in descending the mountain, and the people gathered around Aaron and said to him, "Rise up, make for us gods* that will go before us, for this man Moses who brought us up from the land of Egypt — we do not know what became of him!"

[2] Aaron said to them, "Remove the rings of gold that are in the ears of your wives, sons, and daughters, and bring them to me."

[3] The entire people removed the gold rings that were in their ears, and brought them to Aaron. [4] He took it from their hands and bound it up in a cloth, and fashioned it into a molten calf. They said, "This is your god, O Israel, which brought you up from the land of Egypt."

[5] Aaron saw and built an altar before him. Aaron called out and said, "A festival for HASHEM tomorrow!"

[6] They arose early the next day and offered up burnt-offerings and brought peace-offerings. The people sat to eat and drink, and they got up to revel. *

God's anger

[7] HASHEM spoke to Moses: "Go, descend* — for your people that you brought up from the land of Egypt has become corrupt. [8] They have strayed quickly from the way that I have commanded them. They have made themselves a molten calf, prostrated themselves to it and sacrificed to it, and they said, 'This is your god, O Israel, which brought you up from the land of Egypt.' " [9] HASHEM said to Moses, "I have seen this people, and behold! it is a stiff-necked* people. [10] And now, desist from Me. Let My anger flare up against them and I shall annihilate them; and I shall make you a great nation."

Moses' successful prayer

[11] Moses pleaded before HASHEM, his God, and said, "Why, HASHEM, should Your anger flare up against Your people, whom You have taken out of the land of Egypt, with great power and a strong hand? [12] Why should Egypt say the following: 'With evil intent did He take them out, to kill them in the mountains and to annihilate them from the face of the earth'? Relent from Your flaring anger and reconsider regarding the evil against Your people. [13] Remember for the sake of Abraham, Isaac, and Israel, Your servants, to whom You swore by Yourself, and You told them, 'I shall increase your offspring like the stars of heaven, and this entire land of which I spoke, I shall give to your offspring and it shall be their heritage forever.' "

[14] HASHEM reconsidered* regarding the evil that He declared He would do to His people.

Moses descends

[15] Moses turned* and descended from the mountain, with the two Tablets of the Testimony in his hand, Tablets inscribed on both their sides; they were inscribed on one side and the other. [16] The Tablets were God's handiwork, and the script was the script of God, engraved on the Tablets.

[17] Joshua heard the sound of the people in its shouting, and he said to Moses, "The sound of battle is in the camp!"

[18] He said, "Not a sound shouting strength nor a sound shouting weakness; a sound of distress do I hear!"

32:9. Stiff-necked is the familiar simile for stubbornness, because a stiff-necked person never looks back once he has embarked on a course (*Ibn Ezra*).

32:14. God reconsidered His intention to destroy the nation immediately and replace it with Moses; however, the sin of the Golden Calf was not forgotten. Moses led the people in repentance, and went back to Mount Sinai to pray on their behalf for forty days. Nevertheless, the residue of that sin remains with us.

32:15-19. Moses smashed the incomparably sacred physical embodiment of the word of God in the sight of a people that had shown itself unworthy of receiving it. This spectacle shocked them into recognition of the enormity of their sin.

יט וַיְהִ֗י כַּאֲשֶׁ֤ר קָרַב֙ אֶל־הַֽמַּחֲנֶ֔ה וַיַּ֥רְא אֶת־הָעֵ֖גֶל וּמְחֹלֹ֑ת וַיִּֽחַר־אַ֣ף מֹשֶׁ֗ה

כ וַיַּשְׁלֵ֤ךְ מִיָּדָו֙ אֶת־הַלֻּחֹ֔ת וַיְשַׁבֵּ֥ר אֹתָ֖ם תַּ֣חַת הָהָֽר: וַיִּקַּ֞ח אֶת־הָעֵ֣גֶל אֲשֶׁ֣ר עָשׂ֗וּ וַיִּשְׂרֹ֤ף בָּאֵשׁ֙ וַיִּטְחַ֣ן עַ֣ד אֲשֶׁר־דָּ֔ק וַיִּ֙זֶר֙ עַל־פְּנֵ֣י הַמַּ֔יִם וַיַּ֖שְׁקְ אֶת־בְּנֵ֥י

כא יִשְׂרָאֵֽל: וַיֹּ֤אמֶר מֹשֶׁה֙ אֶֽל־אַהֲרֹ֔ן מֶֽה־עָשָׂ֥ה לְךָ֖ הָעָ֣ם הַזֶּ֑ה כִּֽי־הֵבֵ֥אתָ עָלָ֖יו

כב חֲטָאָ֥ה גְדֹלָֽה: וַיֹּ֣אמֶר אַהֲרֹ֔ן אַל־יִ֥חַר אַ֖ף אֲדֹנִ֑י אַתָּה֙ יָדַ֣עְתָּ אֶת־הָעָ֔ם כִּ֥י

כג בְרָ֖ע הֽוּא: וַיֹּ֣אמְרוּ לִ֔י עֲשֵׂה־לָ֣נוּ אֱלֹהִ֔ים אֲשֶׁ֥ר יֵֽלְכ֖וּ לְפָנֵ֑ינוּ כִּי־זֶ֣ה ׀ מֹשֶׁ֣ה

כד הָאִ֗ישׁ אֲשֶׁ֤ר הֶֽעֱלָ֙נוּ֙ מֵאֶ֣רֶץ מִצְרַ֔יִם לֹ֥א יָדַ֖עְנוּ מֶה־הָ֥יָה לֽוֹ: וָאֹמַ֤ר לָהֶם֙

כה לְמִ֣י זָהָ֔ב הִתְפָּרָ֖קוּ וַיִּתְּנוּ־לִ֑י וָאַשְׁלִכֵ֣הוּ בָאֵ֔שׁ וַיֵּצֵ֖א הָעֵ֥גֶל הַזֶּֽה: וַיַּ֣רְא מֹשֶׁ֤ה

כו אֶת־הָעָם֙ כִּ֣י פָרֻ֣עַ ה֔וּא כִּֽי־פְרָעֹ֣ה אַהֲרֹ֔ן לְשִׁמְצָ֖ה בְּקָֽמֵיהֶֽם: וַיַּעֲמֹ֤ד מֹשֶׁה֙

כז בְּשַׁ֣עַר הַֽמַּחֲנֶ֔ה וַיֹּ֕אמֶר מִ֥י לַֽיהֹוָ֖ה אֵלָ֑י וַיֵּאָֽסְפ֥וּ אֵלָ֖יו כָּל־בְּנֵ֥י לֵוִֽי: וַיֹּ֣אמֶר

לָהֶ֗ם כֹּֽה־אָמַ֤ר יְהֹוָה֙ אֱלֹהֵ֣י יִשְׂרָאֵ֔ל שִׂ֥ימוּ אִישׁ־חַרְבּ֖וֹ עַל־יְרֵכ֑וֹ עִבְר֨וּ

וָשׁ֜וּבוּ מִשַּׁ֤עַר לָשַׁ֙עַר֙ בַּֽמַּחֲנֶ֔ה וְהִרְג֧וּ אִֽישׁ־אֶת־אָחִ֛יו וְאִ֥ישׁ אֶת־רֵעֵ֖הוּ

כח וְאִ֥ישׁ אֶת־קְרֹבֽוֹ: וַיַּֽעֲשׂ֥וּ בְנֵֽי־לֵוִ֖י כִּדְבַ֣ר מֹשֶׁ֑ה וַיִּפֹּ֤ל מִן־הָעָם֙ בַּיּ֣וֹם הַה֔וּא

כט כִּשְׁלֹ֥שֶׁת אַלְפֵ֖י אִֽישׁ: וַיֹּ֣אמֶר מֹשֶׁ֗ה מִלְא֨וּ יֶדְכֶ֤ם הַיּוֹם֙ לַֽיהֹוָ֔ה כִּ֛י אִ֥ישׁ בִּבְנ֖וֹ

ל וּבְאָחִ֑יו וְלָתֵ֧ת עֲלֵיכֶ֛ם הַיּ֖וֹם בְּרָכָֽה: וַֽיְהִי֙ מִמָּ֣חֳרָ֔ת וַיֹּ֤אמֶר מֹשֶׁה֙ אֶל־הָעָ֔ם

אַתֶּ֥ם חֲטָאתֶ֖ם חֲטָאָ֣ה גְדֹלָ֑ה וְעַתָּה֙ אֶֽעֱלֶ֣ה אֶל־יְהֹוָ֔ה אוּלַ֥י אֲכַפְּרָ֖ה בְּעַ֥ד

לא חַטַּאתְכֶֽם: וַיָּ֧שָׁב מֹשֶׁ֛ה אֶל־יְהֹוָ֖ה וַיֹּאמַ֑ר *אָ֣נָּ֗א חָטָ֞א הָעָ֤ם הַזֶּה֙ חֲטָאָ֣ה

לב גְדֹלָ֔ה וַיַּֽעֲשׂ֥וּ לָהֶ֖ם אֱלֹהֵ֣י זָהָֽב: וְעַתָּ֖ה אִם־תִּשָּׂ֣א חַטָּאתָ֑ם וְאִם־אַ֕יִן מְחֵ֣נִי

לג נָ֕א מִֽסִּפְרְךָ֖ אֲשֶׁ֥ר כָּתָֽבְתָּ: וַיֹּ֥אמֶר יְהֹוָ֖ה אֶל־מֹשֶׁ֑ה מִ֣י אֲשֶׁ֤ר חָֽטָא־לִ֔י

לד אֶמְחֶ֖נּוּ מִסִּפְרִֽי: וְעַתָּ֞ה לֵ֣ךְ ׀ נְחֵ֣ה אֶת־הָעָ֗ם אֶ֤ל אֲשֶׁר־דִּבַּ֙רְתִּי֙ לָ֔ךְ הִנֵּ֥ה

לה מַלְאָכִ֖י יֵלֵ֣ךְ לְפָנֶ֑יךָ וּבְי֣וֹם פָּקְדִ֔י וּפָֽקַדְתִּ֥י עֲלֵהֶ֖ם חַטָּאתָֽם: וַיִּגֹּ֥ף יְהֹוָ֖ה אֶת־

א הָעָ֑ם עַ֚ל אֲשֶׁ֣ר עָשׂ֣וּ אֶת־הָעֵ֔גֶל אֲשֶׁ֥ר עָשָׂ֖ה אַהֲרֹֽן: וַיְדַבֵּ֨ר יְהֹוָ֜ה

לג

אֶל־מֹשֶׁ֗ה לֵ֣ךְ עֲלֵ֣ה מִזֶּ֔ה אַתָּ֣ה וְהָעָ֔ם אֲשֶׁ֥ר הֶֽעֱלִ֖יתָ מֵאֶ֣רֶץ מִצְרָ֑יִם אֶל־

הָאָ֗רֶץ אֲשֶׁ֣ר נִ֠שְׁבַּ֠עְתִּי לְאַבְרָהָ֨ם לְיִצְחָ֤ק וּֽלְיַעֲקֹב֙ לֵאמֹ֔ר לְזַרְעֲךָ֖ אֶתְּנֶֽנָּה:

ב וְשָׁלַחְתִּ֥י לְפָנֶ֖יךָ מַלְאָ֑ךְ וְגֵֽרַשְׁתִּ֗י אֶת־הַֽכְּנַעֲנִי֙ הָֽאֱמֹרִ֔י וְהַֽחִתִּי֙ וְהַפְּרִזִּ֔י הַֽחִוִּ֖י

ג וְהַיְבוּסִֽי: אֶל־אֶ֛רֶץ זָבַ֥ת חָלָ֖ב וּדְבָ֑שׁ כִּי֩ לֹ֨א אֶֽעֱלֶ֜ה בְּקִרְבְּךָ֗ כִּ֤י עַם־קְשֵׁה־

ד עֹ֙רֶף֙ אַ֔תָּה פֶּן־אֲכֶלְךָ֖ בַּדָּֽרֶךְ: וַיִּשְׁמַ֣ע הָעָ֗ם אֶת־הַדָּבָ֥ר הָרָ֛ע הַזֶּ֖ה וַיִּתְאַבָּ֑לוּ

ה וְלֹא־שָׁ֛תוּ אִ֥ישׁ עֶדְי֖וֹ עָלָֽיו: וַיֹּ֨אמֶר יְהֹוָ֜ה אֶל־מֹשֶׁ֗ה אֱמֹ֤ר אֶל־בְּנֵֽי־

יִשְׂרָאֵל֙ אַתֶּ֣ם עַם־קְשֵׁה־עֹ֔רֶף רֶ֧גַע אֶחָ֛ד אֶֽעֱלֶ֥ה בְקִרְבְּךָ֖ וְכִלִּיתִ֑יךָ וְעַתָּ֗ה

32:20-29. Before Moses could plead that the Jews regain the Tablets and the spiritual role they had forfeited, he had to purge the nation of the idolaters.

32:26. The people's response showed the depth of their spiritual fall, for only the Levites stepped forward.

32:29. By their loyalty, the Levites earned the right to replace the firstborn and be designated as God's chosen tribe, which would serve Him in the Temple (Rashi).

32:34. Whenever Israel would sin in the future, they would suffer some of the punishment that they should have received in retribution for the sin of the Golden Calf (Rashi). The sin of the Golden Calf left an indelible stigma on the people. Thus, all future national sins are due in part to the spiritual residue of the Golden Calf. Sin does not take place in a vacuum; we are heirs of our history.

33:3. Because you are a stiff-necked people, in constant danger of sinning and incurring My wrath, I cannot remain in your midst. Therefore I must send My angel with you.

Moses
smashes
the Tablets

¹⁹ It happened as he drew near the camp and saw the calf and the dances, that Moses' anger flared up. He threw down the Tablets from his hands and shattered them at the foot of the mountain. ²⁰ He took the calf that they had made and burned it in fire. He ground it to a fine powder and sprinkled it over the water. He made the Children of Israel drink. *

²¹ Moses said to Aaron, "What did this people do to you that you brought a grievous sin upon it?"

Aaron
explains

²² Aaron said, "Let not my master's anger flare up. You know that the people is disposed toward evil. ²³ They said to me, 'Make us a god that will go before us, for this man Moses who brought us up from the land of Egypt — we do not know what became of him.' ²⁴ So I said to them, 'Who has gold?' They removed it and gave it to me. I threw it into the fire, and this calf emerged."

²⁵ Moses saw the people, that it was exposed, for Aaron had exposed them to disgrace among those who rise up against them.

²⁶ Moses stood at the gateway of the camp, and said, "Whoever is for HASHEM, join me!" — and all the Levites gathered around him. * ²⁷ He said to them, "So said HASHEM the God of Israel, 'Every man, put his sword on his thigh and pass back and forth from gate to gate in the camp. Let every man kill his brother, every man his fellow, and every man his near one.' "

²⁸ The Levites did as Moses said, and about three thousand men of the people fell that day. ²⁹ Moses said, "Dedicate yourselves* this day to HASHEM — for each has opposed his son and his brother — that He may bestow upon you a blessing, this day."

Moses
prays

³⁰ On the next day, Moses said to the people, "You have committed a grievous sin! And now I shall ascend to HASHEM — perhaps I can win atonement in the face of your sin." ³¹ Moses returned to HASHEM and said, "I implore! This people has committed a grievous sin and made themselves a god of gold. ³² And now if You would but forgive their sin! — but if not, erase me now from Your book that You have written."

³³ HASHEM said to Moses, "Whoever has sinned against Me, I shall erase him from My book. ³⁴ Now, go and lead the people to where I have told you. Behold! My angel shall go before you, and on the day that I make My account,* I shall bring their sin to account against them."

³⁵ Then HASHEM struck the people with a plague, because they had made the calf that Aaron had made.

33

¹H ASHEM spoke to Moses, "Go, ascend from here, you and the people whom you brought up from the land of Egypt, to the land about which I swore to Abraham, to Isaac, and to Jacob, saying, 'I shall give it to your offspring.' ² I shall send an angel ahead of you, and I shall drive out the Canaanite, the Amorite, the Hittite, the Perizzite, the Hivvite, and the Jebusite — ³ to a land that flows with milk and honey, because I shall not ascend among you,* for you are a stiff-necked people, lest I annihilate you on the way."

Aftermath
of the
Golden Calf

⁴ The people heard this bad tiding and they became grief-stricken, and no one donned his jewelry.

⁵ HASHEM said to Moses, "Say to the Children of Israel, 'You are a stiff-necked people. If I ascend among you, I may annihilate you in an instant. And now

ו הוֹרֵד עֶדְיְךָ מֵעָלֶיךָ וְאֵדְעָה מָה אֶעֱשֶׂה־לָּךְ: וַיִּתְנַצְּלוּ בְנֵי־יִשְׂרָאֵל אֶת־עֶדְיָם
ז מֵהַר חוֹרֵב: וּמֹשֶׁה יִקַּח אֶת־הָאֹהֶל וְנָטָה־לוֹ ׀ מִחוּץ לַמַּחֲנֶה הַרְחֵק מִן־
הַמַּחֲנֶה וְקָרָא לוֹ אֹהֶל מוֹעֵד וְהָיָה כָּל־מְבַקֵּשׁ יהוה יֵצֵא אֶל־אֹהֶל מוֹעֵד
ח אֲשֶׁר מִחוּץ לַמַּחֲנֶה: וְהָיָה כְּצֵאת מֹשֶׁה אֶל־הָאֹהֶל יָקוּמוּ כָּל־הָעָם וְנִצְּבוּ
ט אִישׁ פֶּתַח אָהֳלוֹ וְהִבִּיטוּ אַחֲרֵי מֹשֶׁה עַד־בֹּאוֹ הָאֹהֱלָה: וְהָיָה כְּבֹא מֹשֶׁה
י הָאֹהֱלָה יֵרֵד עַמּוּד הֶעָנָן וְעָמַד פֶּתַח הָאֹהֶל וְדִבֶּר עִם־מֹשֶׁה: וְרָאָה כָל־
הָעָם אֶת־עַמּוּד הֶעָנָן עֹמֵד פֶּתַח הָאֹהֶל וְקָם כָּל־הָעָם וְהִשְׁתַּחֲווּ אִישׁ פֶּתַח
יא אָהֳלוֹ: וְדִבֶּר יהוה אֶל־מֹשֶׁה פָּנִים אֶל־פָּנִים כַּאֲשֶׁר יְדַבֵּר אִישׁ אֶל־רֵעֵהוּ
וְשָׁב אֶל־הַמַּחֲנֶה וּמְשָׁרְתוֹ יְהוֹשֻׁעַ בִּן־נוּן נַעַר לֹא יָמִישׁ מִתּוֹךְ הָאֹהֶל:

שלישי
SABBATH
OF CHOL
HAMOED
33:12-34:26

Pesach:
Maftir: p. 400
Haftarah:
p. 1294
Succos:
Maftir: p. 402
Haftarah:
p. 1298

יב וַיֹּאמֶר מֹשֶׁה אֶל־יהוה רְאֵה אַתָּה אֹמֵר אֵלַי הַעַל אֶת־הָעָם הַזֶּה וְאַתָּה
לֹא הוֹדַעְתַּנִי אֵת אֲשֶׁר־תִּשְׁלַח עִמִּי וְאַתָּה אָמַרְתָּ יְדַעְתִּיךָ בְשֵׁם וְגַם־
יג מָצָאתָ חֵן בְּעֵינָי: וְעַתָּה אִם־נָא מָצָאתִי חֵן בְּעֵינֶיךָ הוֹדִעֵנִי נָא אֶת־דְּרָכֶךָ
וְאֵדָעֲךָ לְמַעַן אֶמְצָא־חֵן בְּעֵינֶיךָ וּרְאֵה כִּי עַמְּךָ הַגּוֹי הַזֶּה: וַיֹּאמַר פָּנַי יֵלֵכוּ
יד-טו וַהֲנִחֹתִי לָךְ: וַיֹּאמֶר אֵלָיו אִם־אֵין פָּנֶיךָ הֹלְכִים אַל־תַּעֲלֵנוּ מִזֶּה: וּבַמֶּה ׀
טז יִוָּדַע אֵפוֹא כִּי־מָצָאתִי חֵן בְּעֵינֶיךָ אֲנִי וְעַמֶּךָ הֲלוֹא בְּלֶכְתְּךָ עִמָּנוּ וְנִפְלִינוּ
אֲנִי וְעַמְּךָ מִכָּל־הָעָם אֲשֶׁר עַל־פְּנֵי הָאֲדָמָה:

רביעי

יז וַיֹּאמֶר יהוה אֶל־מֹשֶׁה גַּם אֶת־הַדָּבָר הַזֶּה אֲשֶׁר דִּבַּרְתָּ אֶעֱשֶׂה כִּי־מָצָאתָ
יח-יט חֵן בְּעֵינַי וָאֵדָעֲךָ בְּשֵׁם: וַיֹּאמַר הַרְאֵנִי נָא אֶת־כְּבֹדֶךָ: וַיֹּאמֶר אֲנִי אַעֲבִיר
כָּל־טוּבִי עַל־פָּנֶיךָ וְקָרָאתִי בְשֵׁם יהוה לְפָנֶיךָ וְחַנֹּתִי אֶת־אֲשֶׁר אָחֹן
כ וְרִחַמְתִּי אֶת־אֲשֶׁר אֲרַחֵם: וַיֹּאמֶר לֹא תוּכַל לִרְאֹת אֶת־פָּנָי כִּי לֹא־יִרְאַנִי
כא-כב הָאָדָם וָחָי: וַיֹּאמֶר יהוה הִנֵּה מָקוֹם אִתִּי וְנִצַּבְתָּ עַל־הַצּוּר: וְהָיָה בַּעֲבֹר
כג כְּבֹדִי וְשַׂמְתִּיךָ בְּנִקְרַת הַצּוּר וְשַׂכֹּתִי כַפִּי עָלֶיךָ עַד־עָבְרִי: וַהֲסִרֹתִי אֶת־
כַּפִּי וְרָאִיתָ אֶת־אֲחֹרָי וּפָנַי לֹא יֵרָאוּ:

לד חמישי
THIRD DAY
CHOL
HAMOED
PESACH
34:1-26

Revi'i: p. 400

לד א וַיֹּאמֶר יהוה אֶל־מֹשֶׁה פְּסָל־לְךָ שְׁנֵי־לֻחֹת אֲבָנִים כָּרִאשֹׁנִים וְכָתַבְתִּי
עַל־הַלֻּחֹת אֶת־הַדְּבָרִים אֲשֶׁר הָיוּ עַל־הַלֻּחֹת הָרִאשֹׁנִים אֲשֶׁר שִׁבַּרְתָּ:
ב וְהָיֵה נָכוֹן לַבֹּקֶר וְעָלִיתָ בַבֹּקֶר אֶל־הַר סִינַי וְנִצַּבְתָּ לִי שָׁם עַל־רֹאשׁ
ג הָהָר: וְאִישׁ לֹא־יַעֲלֶה עִמָּךְ וְגַם־אִישׁ אַל־יֵרָא בְּכָל־הָהָר גַּם־הַצֹּאן

33:7-11. Since God had announced to Moses that His Presence would not reside among them, God's prophet set up his Tent in isolation, where God would speak to him. However, Moses remained available to any Jew who sought the word of God.

33:11. Unlike other prophets, Moses needed no intermediary (*R' Bachya*) and he was fully conscious (*Sforno*) when God spoke to him.

33:12-19. There are various interpretations of the mystical dialogue between God and Moses, but all agree on the general theme: Israel had fallen precipitously from its high spiritual standing, and Moses wanted it restored, as much as possible. Furthermore, he sought to increase his own understanding of God's essence and ways.

33:13. Moses was seeking an answer to the age-old question of why the righteous suffer while the wicked prosper (*Rashi* to *Berachos* 7a).

33:14. God acceded to Moses' first request, and stated that His Presence, not an angel, would accompany Israel.

33:18. Seeing that it was a time of favor, Moses was emboldened to request a greater degree of perception than any person had ever experienced (*Ramban*), so that he could understand the full extent of Godliness (*Or HaChaim*), and so that he could grasp how God conveys His influence to every part of the universe (*Sforno*).

33:19. God promised to teach Moses the Thirteen At-

remove your jewelry from yourself, and I shall know what I shall do to you.'" ⁶ *So the Children of Israel were stripped of their jewelry from Mount Horeb.*

Moses' Tent   ⁷ *Moses would take the Tent* and pitch it outside the camp, far from the camp, and call it the Tent of Meeting. So it was that whoever sought HASHEM would go out to the Tent of Meeting, which was outside the camp.* ⁸ *Whenever Moses would go out to the Tent, the entire people would stand up and remain standing, everyone at the entrance of his tent, and they would gaze after Moses until he arrived at the Tent.* ⁹ *When Moses would arrive at the Tent, a pillar of cloud would descend and stand at the entrance of the Tent, and He would speak with Moses.* ¹⁰ *The entire people would see the pillar of cloud standing at the entrance of the Tent, and the entire people would rise and prostrate themselves, everyone at the entrance of his tent.* ¹¹ *HASHEM would speak to Moses face to face,* as a man would speak with his fellow; then he would return to the camp. His servant, Joshua son of Nun, a lad, would not depart from within the Tent.*

Moses pleads for God's nearness   ¹² *Moses said* to HASHEM, "See, You say to me, 'Take this people onward,' but You did not inform me whom You will send with me; and You had said, 'I shall know you by name, and you have also found favor in My eyes.'* ¹³ *And now, if I have indeed found favor in Your eyes, make Your way known to me,* so that I know You, so that I may find favor in Your eyes. And see that this nation is Your people."*

¹⁴ *He said, "My Presence will go* and provide you rest."*

¹⁵ *He said to Him, "If Your Presence does not go along, do not bring us forward from here.* ¹⁶ *How, then, will it be known that I have found favor in Your eyes — I and Your people — unless You accompany us, and I and Your people will be made distinct from every people on the face of the earth!"*

¹⁷ *HASHEM said to Moses, "Even this thing of which you spoke I shall do, for you have found favor in My eyes, and I have known you by name."*

¹⁸ *He said, "Show me now Your glory."**

The limits of Moses' vision   ¹⁹ *He said, "I shall make all My goodness pass before you, and I shall call out with the Name HASHEM* before you; I shall show favor when I choose to show favor, and I shall show mercy when I choose to show mercy."*

²⁰ *He said, "You will not be able to see My face,* for no human can see Me and live."* ²¹ *HASHEM said, "Behold! there is a place near Me; you may stand on the rock.* ²² *When My glory passes by, I shall place you in a cleft of the rock; I shall shield you with My hand until I have passed.* ²³ *Then I shall remove My hand and you will see My back, but My face may not be seen."*

34

The second Tablets   ¹ H*ASHEM said to Moses, "Carve for yourself two stone Tablets* like the first ones, and I shall inscribe on the Tablets the words that were on the first Tablets, which you shattered.* ² *Be prepared in the morning; ascend Mount Sinai in the morning and stand by Me there on the mountaintop.* ³ *No man may ascend with you nor may anyone be seen on the entire mountain. Even the flock*

---

tributes, which begin with the Name HASHEM (Rashi).

33:20. This simile refers to a complete and unadulterated perception of God. To achieve such a perception was impossible, but God would allow Moses to see *His back* (v. 23), i.e., a vague degree of knowledge.

34:1-4. At the end of Moses' second forty-day period on Mount Sinai, God agreed to give a second set of Tablets to Israel. This time, however, the stone Tablets them-

selves would not be the handiwork of God; instead, Moses was commanded to carve out the stone cubes and bring them to the mountain, whereupon God would inscribe the Ten Commandments on them. This change was a reflection of the lowered status of the nation, but it also had a very positive aspect. Just as the word of God could be engraved on Tablets fashioned by man, so mortal human beings can sanctify themselves.

ד וְהַבֹּקֶר אַל־יֵרֶעוּ אֶל־מוּל הָהָר הַהוּא: וַיִּפְסֹל שְׁנֵי־לֻחֹת אֲבָנִים
כָּרִאשֹׁנִים וַיַּשְׁכֵּם מֹשֶׁה בַבֹּקֶר וַיַּעַל אֶל־הַר סִינַי כַּאֲשֶׁר צִוָּה יהוה אֹתוֹ

ה וַיִּקַּח בְּיָדוֹ שְׁנֵי לֻחֹת אֲבָנִים: וַיֵּרֶד יהוה בֶּעָנָן וַיִּתְיַצֵּב עִמּוֹ שָׁם וַיִּקְרָא
בְשֵׁם יהוה:

ו וַיַּעֲבֹר יהוה ׀ עַל־פָּנָיו וַיִּקְרָא יהוה ׀ יהוה אֵל רַחוּם וְחַנּוּן

ז אֶרֶךְ אַפַּיִם וְרַב־חֶסֶד וֶאֱמֶת: *נֹצֵר חֶסֶד לָאֲלָפִים נֹשֵׂא עָוֹן וָפֶשַׁע
וְחַטָּאָה וְנַקֵּה לֹא יְנַקֶּה פֹּקֵד ׀ עֲוֹן אָבוֹת עַל־בָּנִים וְעַל־בְּנֵי בָנִים עַל־

ח־ט שִׁלֵּשִׁים וְעַל־רִבֵּעִים: וַיְמַהֵר מֹשֶׁה וַיִּקֹּד אַרְצָה וַיִּשְׁתָּחוּ: וַיֹּאמֶר אִם־נָא
מָצָאתִי חֵן בְּעֵינֶיךָ אֲדֹנָי יֵלֶךְ־נָא אֲדֹנָי בְּקִרְבֵּנוּ כִּי עַם־קְשֵׁה־עֹרֶף

י הוּא וְסָלַחְתָּ לַעֲוֹנֵנוּ וּלְחַטָּאתֵנוּ וּנְחַלְתָּנוּ: וַיֹּאמֶר הִנֵּה אָנֹכִי כֹּרֵת בְּרִית
נֶגֶד כָּל־עַמְּךָ אֶעֱשֶׂה נִפְלָאֹת אֲשֶׁר לֹא־נִבְרְאוּ בְכָל־הָאָרֶץ וּבְכָל־
הַגּוֹיִם וְרָאָה כָל־הָעָם אֲשֶׁר־אַתָּה בְקִרְבּוֹ אֶת־מַעֲשֵׂה יהוה כִּי־נוֹרָא

יא הוּא אֲשֶׁר אֲנִי עֹשֶׂה עִמָּךְ: *שְׁמָר־לְךָ אֵת אֲשֶׁר אָנֹכִי מְצַוְּךָ הַיּוֹם הִנְנִי

יב גֹרֵשׁ מִפָּנֶיךָ אֶת־הָאֱמֹרִי וְהַכְּנַעֲנִי וְהַחִתִּי וְהַפְּרִזִּי וְהַחִוִּי וְהַיְבוּסִי: הִשָּׁמֶר
לְךָ פֶּן־תִּכְרֹת בְּרִית לְיוֹשֵׁב הָאָרֶץ אֲשֶׁר אַתָּה בָּא עָלֶיהָ פֶּן־יִהְיֶה

יג לְמוֹקֵשׁ בְּקִרְבֶּךָ: כִּי אֶת־מִזְבְּחֹתָם תִּתֹּצוּן וְאֶת־מַצֵּבֹתָם תְּשַׁבֵּרוּן וְאֶת־

יד אֲשֵׁרָיו תִּכְרֹתוּן: כִּי לֹא תִשְׁתַּחֲוֶה לְאֵל אַחֵר* כִּי יהוה קַנָּא שְׁמוֹ אֵל

טו קַנָּא הוּא: פֶּן־תִּכְרֹת בְּרִית לְיוֹשֵׁב הָאָרֶץ וְזָנוּ ׀ אַחֲרֵי אֱלֹהֵיהֶם וְזָבְחוּ

טז לֵאלֹהֵיהֶם וְקָרָא לְךָ וְאָכַלְתָּ מִזִּבְחוֹ: וְלָקַחְתָּ מִבְּנֹתָיו לְבָנֶיךָ וְזָנוּ בְנֹתָיו
אַחֲרֵי אֱלֹהֵיהֶן וְהִזְנוּ אֶת־בָּנֶיךָ אַחֲרֵי אֱלֹהֵיהֶן: אֱלֹהֵי מַסֵּכָה לֹא

יז־יח תַעֲשֶׂה־לָּךְ: אֶת־חַג הַמַּצּוֹת תִּשְׁמֹר שִׁבְעַת יָמִים תֹּאכַל מַצּוֹת אֲשֶׁר

יט צִוִּיתִךָ לְמוֹעֵד חֹדֶשׁ הָאָבִיב כִּי בְּחֹדֶשׁ הָאָבִיב יָצָאתָ מִמִּצְרָיִם: כָּל־

כ פֶּטֶר רֶחֶם לִי וְכָל־מִקְנְךָ תִּזָּכָר פֶּטֶר שׁוֹר וָשֶׂה: וּפֶטֶר חֲמוֹר תִּפְדֶּה בְשֶׂה
וְאִם־לֹא תִפְדֶּה וַעֲרַפְתּוֹ כֹּל בְּכוֹר בָּנֶיךָ תִּפְדֶּה וְלֹא־יֵרָאוּ פָנַי רֵיקָם:

כא שֵׁשֶׁת יָמִים תַּעֲבֹד וּבַיּוֹם הַשְּׁבִיעִי תִּשְׁבֹּת בֶּחָרִישׁ וּבַקָּצִיר תִּשְׁבֹּת:

כב וְחַג שָׁבֻעֹת תַּעֲשֶׂה לְךָ בִּכּוּרֵי קְצִיר חִטִּים וְחַג הָאָסִיף תְּקוּפַת הַשָּׁנָה:

כג שָׁלֹשׁ פְּעָמִים בַּשָּׁנָה יֵרָאֶה כָּל־זְכוּרְךָ אֶת־פְּנֵי הָאָדֹן ׀ יהוה אֱלֹהֵי

כד יִשְׂרָאֵל: כִּי־אוֹרִישׁ גּוֹיִם מִפָּנֶיךָ וְהִרְחַבְתִּי אֶת־גְּבֻלֶךָ וְלֹא־יַחְמֹד אִישׁ
אֶת־אַרְצְךָ בַּעֲלֹתְךָ לֵרָאוֹת אֶת־פְּנֵי יהוה אֱלֹהֶיךָ שָׁלֹשׁ פְּעָמִים בַּשָּׁנָה:

נ' רבתי

ששי

*"בראש עמוד
ברי"ה שמ"ץ סימן*

ר' רבתי

34:5-7. R' Yochanan said: Were it not written in Scripture, it would be impossible [for us] to say it. This passage teaches that God wrapped Himself [in a *tallis*] like one leading the congregation in prayer, and showed Moses the order of prayer. He said, "Whenever Israel sins, let them perform before Me this order [of prayer], and I shall forgive them" (*Rosh Hashanah* 17b).

34:11-26. Despite the covenant, Israel could jeopardize its position by sinning. God tells Moses what sins are particularly threatening and what commandments are especially propitious for safeguarding Israel's spiritual greatness. He begins by reiterating His promise to drive out the Canaanite nations, but then cautions Israel that it must avoid the temptations that would await them in the Land.

34:19. See 13:2, 12-13. No miracle was greater proof of God's involvement in the most minute affairs of this world than His pinpoint selection of the Egyptian firstborn.

34:24. This is one of the great hidden miracles of the Torah. There is no other way that a vast territory can be left undefended and virtually unpopulated without inviting the aggression of alien predators.

and the cattle may not graze facing that mountain."

⁴ So he carved out two stone Tablets like the first ones. Moses arose early in the morning and ascended to Mount Sinai, as HASHEM had commanded him, and he took two stone Tablets in his hand.

⁵ HASHEM descended in a cloud and stood with him there, and He called out
God reveals with the Name HASHEM. ⁶ HASHEM passed before him and proclaimed: *
His Thirteen HASHEM, HASHEM, God, Compassionate and Gracious, Slow to Anger, and
Attributes Abundant in Kindness and Truth; ⁷ Preserver of Kindness for thousands of
of Mercy generations, Forgiver of Iniquity, Willful Sin, and Error, and Who Cleanses — but does not cleanse completely, recalling the iniquity of parents upon children and grandchildren, to the third and fourth generations.

⁸ Moses hastened to bow his head toward the ground and prostrate himself.
Moses' ⁹ He said, "If I have now found favor in Your eyes, my Lord, let my Lord go
request among us — for it is a stiff-necked people, and You shall forgive our iniquity and error, and make us Your heritage."

¹⁰ He said, "Behold! I seal a covenant: Before your entire people I shall make distinctions such as have never been created in the entire world and among all the nations; and the entire people among whom you are will see the work of HASHEM — which is awesome — that I am about to do with you.

¹¹ "Beware * of what I command you today: Behold I drive out before you the
Safeguarding Amorite, the Canaanite, the Hittite, the Perizzite, the Hivvite, and the Jebusite.
the promise ¹² Be vigilant lest you seal a covenant with an inhabitant of the land to which you come, lest it be a snare among you. ¹³ Rather you shall break apart their altars, smash their pillars, and cut down its sacred trees. ¹⁴ For you shall not prostrate yourselves to an alien god, for the very Name of HASHEM is 'Jealous One,' He is a jealous God. ¹⁵ Lest you seal a covenant with an inhabitant of the land, and they will stray after their gods and slaughter to their gods; and he will invite you and you will eat from his slaughter. ¹⁶ And you will take their daughters for your sons, and their daughters will stray after their gods and entice your sons to stray after their gods!

¹⁷ "You shall not make for yourselves molten gods.

¹⁸ "You shall observe the Festival of Matzos: For a seven-day period you shall eat matzos, as I commanded you, at the appointed time in the month of spring, for in the month of spring you went forth from Egypt.

¹⁹ "Every first issue of a womb is Mine; * as well as any of your livestock that produces a male, the first issue of an ox or a sheep. ²⁰ The first issue of a donkey you shall redeem with a lamb or kid, and if you do not redeem it you shall axe the back of its neck. You shall redeem every firstborn of your sons. They shall not appear before Me emptyhanded.

²¹ "Six days shall you work and on the seventh day you shall desist; you shall desist from plowing and harvesting. ²² You shall make the Festival of Weeks with the first offering of the wheat harvest; and the Festival of the Harvest shall be at the changing of the year. ²³ Three times a year all your males shall appear before the Lord HASHEM, the God of Israel. ²⁴ For I shall banish nations before you and broaden your boundary; no man will covet * your land when you go up to appear before HASHEM, your God, three times a year.

כה לֹא־תִשְׁחַט עַל־חָמֵץ דַּם־זִבְחִי וְלֹא־יָלִין לַבֹּקֶר זֶבַח חַג הַפָּסַח:

כו רֵאשִׁית בִּכּוּרֵי אַדְמָתְךָ תָּבִיא בֵּית יהוה אֱלֹהֶיךָ לֹא־תְבַשֵּׁל גְּדִי בַּחֲלֵב אִמּוֹ:

שביעי כז וַיֹּאמֶר יהוה אֶל־מֹשֶׁה כְּתָב־לְךָ אֶת־הַדְּבָרִים הָאֵלֶּה כִּי עַל־פִּי ׀

כח הַדְּבָרִים הָאֵלֶּה כָּרַתִּי אִתְּךָ בְּרִית וְאֶת־יִשְׂרָאֵל: וַיְהִי־שָׁם עִם־יהוה אַרְבָּעִים יוֹם וְאַרְבָּעִים לַיְלָה לֶחֶם לֹא אָכַל וּמַיִם לֹא שָׁתָה וַיִּכְתֹּב עַל־

כט הַלֻּחֹת אֵת דִּבְרֵי הַבְּרִית עֲשֶׂרֶת הַדְּבָרִים: וַיְהִי בְּרֶדֶת מֹשֶׁה מֵהַר סִינַי וּשְׁנֵי לֻחֹת הָעֵדֻת בְּיַד־מֹשֶׁה בְּרִדְתּוֹ מִן־הָהָר וּמֹשֶׁה לֹא־יָדַע כִּי קָרַן

ל עוֹר פָּנָיו בְּדַבְּרוֹ אִתּוֹ: וַיַּרְא אַהֲרֹן וְכָל־בְּנֵי יִשְׂרָאֵל אֶת־מֹשֶׁה וְהִנֵּה קָרַן

לא עוֹר פָּנָיו וַיִּירְאוּ מִגֶּשֶׁת אֵלָיו: וַיִּקְרָא אֲלֵהֶם מֹשֶׁה וַיָּשֻׁבוּ אֵלָיו אַהֲרֹן

לב וְכָל־הַנְּשִׂאִים בָּעֵדָה וַיְדַבֵּר מֹשֶׁה אֲלֵהֶם: וְאַחֲרֵי־כֵן נִגְּשׁוּ כָּל־בְּנֵי

לג יִשְׂרָאֵל וַיְצַוֵּם אֵת כָּל־אֲשֶׁר דִּבֶּר יהוה אִתּוֹ בְּהַר סִינָי: וַיְכַל מֹשֶׁה מִדַּבֵּר

מפטיר לד אִתָּם וַיִּתֵּן עַל־פָּנָיו מַסְוֶה: וּבְבֹא מֹשֶׁה לִפְנֵי יהוה לְדַבֵּר אִתּוֹ יָסִיר אֶת־

Haftaras
Ki Sisa
Ashkenazim:
p. 854
Sephardim:
p. 856

For special
Sabbaths,
see pp. x-xi

לה הַמַּסְוֶה עַד־צֵאתוֹ וְיָצָא וְדִבֶּר אֶל־בְּנֵי יִשְׂרָאֵל אֵת אֲשֶׁר יְצֻוֶּה: וְרָאוּ בְנֵי־יִשְׂרָאֵל אֶת־פְּנֵי מֹשֶׁה כִּי קָרַן עוֹר פְּנֵי מֹשֶׁה וְהֵשִׁיב מֹשֶׁה אֶת־הַמַּסְוֶה עַל־פָּנָיו עַד־בֹּאוֹ לְדַבֵּר אִתּוֹ: ססס קט"ל פסוקים. חננט"ל סימן.

פרשת ויקהל

לה א וַיַּקְהֵל מֹשֶׁה אֶת־כָּל־עֲדַת בְּנֵי יִשְׂרָאֵל וַיֹּאמֶר אֲלֵהֶם אֵלֶּה הַדְּבָרִים

ב אֲשֶׁר־צִוָּה יהוה לַעֲשֹׂת אֹתָם: שֵׁשֶׁת יָמִים תֵּעָשֶׂה מְלָאכָה וּבַיּוֹם הַשְּׁבִיעִי יִהְיֶה לָכֶם קֹדֶשׁ שַׁבַּת שַׁבָּתוֹן לַיהוה כָּל־הָעֹשֶׂה בוֹ מְלָאכָה

ג יוּמָת: לֹא־תְבַעֲרוּ אֵשׁ בְּכֹל מֹשְׁבֹתֵיכֶם בְּיוֹם הַשַּׁבָּת:

ד וַיֹּאמֶר מֹשֶׁה אֶל־כָּל־עֲדַת בְּנֵי־יִשְׂרָאֵל לֵאמֹר זֶה הַדָּבָר אֲשֶׁר־צִוָּה

ה יהוה לֵאמֹר: קְחוּ מֵאִתְּכֶם תְּרוּמָה לַיהוה כֹּל נְדִיב לִבּוֹ יְבִיאֶהָ אֵת

ו תְּרוּמַת יהוה זָהָב וָכֶסֶף וּנְחֹשֶׁת: וּתְכֵלֶת וְאַרְגָּמָן וְתוֹלַעַת שָׁנִי וְשֵׁשׁ

ז-ח וְעִזִּים: וְעֹרֹת אֵילִם מְאָדָּמִים וְעֹרֹת תְּחָשִׁים וַעֲצֵי שִׁטִּים: שֶׁמֶן

ט לַמָּאוֹר וּבְשָׂמִים לְשֶׁמֶן הַמִּשְׁחָה וְלִקְטֹרֶת הַסַּמִּים: וְאַבְנֵי־שֹׁהַם

י וְאַבְנֵי מִלֻּאִים לָאֵפוֹד וְלַחֹשֶׁן: וְכָל־חֲכַם־לֵב בָּכֶם יָבֹאוּ וְיַעֲשׂוּ אֵת כָּל־

יא אֲשֶׁר צִוָּה יהוה: אֶת־הַמִּשְׁכָּן אֶת־אָהֳלוֹ וְאֶת־מִכְסֵהוּ אֶת־קְרָסָיו

יב וְאֶת־קְרָשָׁיו אֶת־בְּרִיחָו אֶת־עַמֻּדָיו וְאֶת־אֲדָנָיו: אֶת־הָאָרֹן וְאֶת־בַּדָּיו

34:27-35. God instructs Moses to write a new covenant, which the people would accept, as they had accepted the original one, by saying, "We will do and we will obey," and God, too, would ratify it in the form of a promise not to destroy them (*Ramban*). God taught Moses the entire Torah anew and gave him the second Tablets. A further result of the nation's fall from its earlier spiritual plateau was that they could not tolerate the holy glow that shone from Moses' face as a result of his new exposure to God's glory.

34:35. When Moses taught the word of God he did not wear the mask, so that nothing would interpose between God's teaching and Israel. Then, he would put the mask back on and wear it until God spoke to him again.

²⁵ "You shall not slaughter My blood-offering while in the possession of leavened food, nor may the feast-offering of the Pesach festival be left overnight until morning. ²⁶ The first of your land's early produce you shall bring to the Temple of HASHEM, your God. Do not cook a kid in its mother's milk."

Renewal of the covenant

²⁷ HASHEM said to Moses, "Write these words for yourself,* for according to these words have I sealed a covenant with you and Israel." ²⁸ He remained there with HASHEM for forty days and forty nights — he did not eat bread and he did not drink water — and He wrote on the Tablets the words of the covenant, the Ten Commandments.

²⁹ When Moses descended from Mount Sinai — with the two Tablets of the Testimony in the hand of Moses as he descended from the mountain — Moses did not know that the skin of his face had become radiant when He had spoken to him. ³⁰ Aaron and all the Children of Israel saw Moses, and behold! — the skin of his face had become radiant; and they feared to approach him. ³¹ Moses called to them, and Aaron and all the leaders of the assembly returned to him, and Moses would speak to them. ³² After that, all the Children of Israel would approach; he would command them regarding everything that HASHEM had spoken to him on Mount Sinai.

The radiance of Moses

³³ Moses finished speaking with them and placed a mask on his face. ³⁴ When Moses would come before HASHEM to speak with Him, he would remove the mask* until his departure; then he would leave and tell the Children of Israel whatever he had been commanded. ³⁵ When the Children of Israel saw Moses' face, that the skin of Moses' face had become radiant, Moses put the mask back on his face, until he came to speak with Him.

PARASHAS VAYAKHEL

35

¹ Moses assembled* the entire assembly of the Children of Israel and said to them: "These are the things that HASHEM commanded, to do them:

The Sabbath

² " 'On six days, work may be done, but the seventh day shall be holy for you, a day of complete rest for HASHEM; whoever does work on it shall be put to death. ³ You shall not kindle fire* in any of your dwellings on the Sabbath day.' "

Contributions for the Tabernacle

⁴ Moses said to the entire assembly of the Children of Israel, saying: "This is the word that HASHEM has commanded, saying: ⁵ 'Take from yourselves a portion for HASHEM, everyone whose heart motivates him shall bring it, as the gift for HASHEM: gold, silver, copper; ⁶ turquoise, purple, and scarlet wool; linen, goat hair; ⁷ red-dyed ram skins, tachash skins, acacia wood; ⁸ oil for illumination, spices for the anointment oil and the aromatic incense; ⁹ shoham stones and stones for the settings, for the Ephod and the Breastplate.

The construction of the Tabernacle

¹⁰ " 'Every wise-hearted person among you shall come and make everything that HASHEM has commanded: ¹¹ the Tabernacle, its Tent, and its Cover, its hooks, its planks, its bars, its pillars, and its sockets; ¹² the Ark and its staves,

⋅§ **Parashas Vayakhel.**
35:1. Moses assembled the entire nation and charged them with the privilege of building the Tabernacle. That much of the text is virtually a repetition of the instructions of the three previous *Sidrahs* is indicative of the great significance of the Tabernacle. Israel's ability to create a setting for God's Presence is a measure of its greatness and, indeed, a primary reason for its very existence.

35:3. The Torah can be understood only as it is interpreted by the Oral Law, which God taught to Moses, and which He transmitted to the nation. The Oral Law makes clear that only the *creation* of a fire and such use of it as cooking and baking are forbidden, but there is no prohibition against enjoying its light and heat. Deviant sects that denied the teachings of the Sages misinterpreted this passage, so they would sit in the dark throughout the Sabbath, just as they sat in spiritual darkness all their lives.

יג אֶת־הַכַּפֹּ֜רֶת וְאֵ֨ת פָּרֹ֤כֶת הַמָּסָ֑ךְ: אֶת־הַשֻּׁלְחָ֥ן וְאֶת־בַּדָּ֖יו וְאֶת־כָּל־כֵּלָֽיו

יד וְאֵ֖ת לֶ֣חֶם הַפָּנִֽים: וְאֶת־מְנֹרַ֧ת הַמָּא֛וֹר וְאֶת־כֵּלֶ֖יהָ וְאֶת־נֵרֹתֶ֑יהָ וְאֵ֖ת שֶׁ֥מֶן

טו הַמָּאֽוֹר: וְאֶת־מִזְבַּ֤ח הַקְּטֹ֙רֶת֙ וְאֶת־בַּדָּ֔יו וְאֵת֙ שֶׁ֣מֶן הַמִּשְׁחָ֔ה וְאֵ֖ת קְטֹ֥רֶת

טז הַסַּמִּ֑ים וְאֶת־מָסַ֥ךְ הַפֶּ֖תַח לְפֶ֥תַח הַמִּשְׁכָּֽן: אֵ֣ת ׀ מִזְבַּ֣ח הָעֹלָ֗ה וְאֶת־מִכְבַּ֤ר

יז הַנְּחֹ֙שֶׁת֙ אֲשֶׁר־ל֔וֹ אֶת־בַּדָּ֖יו וְאֶת־כָּל־כֵּלָ֑יו אֶת־הַכִּיֹּ֖ר וְאֶת־כַּנּֽוֹ: אֵ֚ת

יח קַלְעֵ֣י הֶֽחָצֵ֔ר אֶת־עַמֻּדָ֖יו וְאֶת־אֲדָנֶ֑יהָ וְאֵ֕ת מָסַ֖ךְ שַׁ֥עַר הֶחָצֵֽר: אֶת־יִתְדֹ֧ת

יט הַמִּשְׁכָּ֛ן וְאֶת־יִתְדֹ֥ת הֶחָצֵ֖ר וְאֶת־מֵֽיתְרֵיהֶֽם: אֶת־בִּגְדֵ֥י הַשְּׂרָ֖ד לְשָׁרֵ֣ת

כ בַּקֹּ֑דֶשׁ אֶת־בִּגְדֵ֤י הַקֹּ֙דֶשׁ֙ לְאַֽהֲרֹ֣ן הַכֹּהֵ֔ן וְאֶת־בִּגְדֵ֥י בָנָ֖יו לְכַהֵֽן: וַיֵּ֥צְא֛וּ כָּל־

כא עֲדַ֥ת בְּנֵֽי־יִשְׂרָאֵ֖ל מִלִּפְנֵ֥י מֹשֶֽׁה: וַיָּבֹ֕אוּ כָּל־אִ֖ישׁ אֲשֶׁר־נְשָׂא֣וֹ לִבּ֑וֹ וְכֹ֡ל

אֲשֶׁר֩ נָֽדְבָ֨ה רוּח֜וֹ אֹת֗וֹ הֵ֠בִ֠יאוּ אֶת־תְּרוּמַ֨ת יְהֹוָ֜ה לִמְלֶ֣אכֶת אֹ֤הֶל מוֹעֵד֙

כב וּלְכָל־עֲבֹ֣דָת֔וֹ וּלְבִגְדֵ֖י הַקֹּֽדֶשׁ: וַיָּבֹ֥אוּ הָֽאֲנָשִׁ֖ים עַל־הַנָּשִׁ֑ים כֹּ֣ל ׀ נְדִ֣יב לֵ֗ב

הֵ֠בִ֠יאוּ חָ֣ח וָנֶ֜זֶם וְטַבַּ֤עַת וְכוּמָז֙ כָּל־כְּלִ֣י זָהָ֔ב וְכָל־אִ֕ישׁ אֲשֶׁ֥ר הֵנִ֛יף תְּנוּפַ֥ת

כג זָהָ֖ב לַֽיהֹוָֽה: וְכָל־אִ֞ישׁ אֲשֶׁר־נִמְצָ֣א אִתּ֗וֹ תְּכֵ֧לֶת וְאַרְגָּמָ֛ן וְתוֹלַ֥עַת שָׁנִ֖י

כד וְשֵׁ֣שׁ וְעִזִּ֑ים וְעֹרֹ֨ת אֵילִ֧ם מְאָדָּמִ֛ים וְעֹרֹ֥ת תְּחָשִׁ֖ים הֵבִֽיאוּ: כָּל־מֵרִ֗ים

תְּרוּמַ֤ת כֶּ֙סֶף֙ וּנְחֹ֔שֶׁת הֵבִ֕יאוּ אֵ֖ת תְּרוּמַ֣ת יְהֹוָ֑ה וְכֹ֡ל אֲשֶׁר֩ נִמְצָ֨א אִתּ֜וֹ עֲצֵ֥י

כה שִׁטִּ֛ים לְכָל־מְלֶ֥אכֶת הָֽעֲבֹדָ֖ה הֵבִֽיאוּ: וְכָל־אִשָּׁ֥ה חַכְמַת־לֵ֖ב בְּיָדֶ֣יהָ טָו֑וּ

וַיָּבִ֣יאוּ מַטְוֶ֗ה אֶֽת־הַתְּכֵ֙לֶת֙ וְאֶת־הָ֣אַרְגָּמָ֔ן אֶת־תּוֹלַ֥עַת הַשָּׁנִ֖י וְאֶת־הַשֵּֽׁשׁ:

כו-כז וְכָ֨ל־הַנָּשִׁ֔ים אֲשֶׁ֨ר נָשָׂ֥א לִבָּ֛ן אֹתָ֖נָה בְּחָכְמָ֑ה טָו֖וּ אֶת־הָֽעִזִּֽים: וְהַנְּשִׂאִ֣ם

כח הֵבִ֔יאוּ אֵ֚ת אַבְנֵ֣י הַשֹּׁ֔הַם וְאֵ֖ת אַבְנֵ֣י הַמִּלֻּאִ֑ים לָֽאֵפ֖וֹד וְלַחֹֽשֶׁן: וְאֶת־הַבֹּ֖שֶׂם

כט וְאֶת־הַשָּׁ֑מֶן לְמָא֕וֹר וּלְשֶׁ֙מֶן֙ הַמִּשְׁחָ֔ה וְלִקְטֹ֖רֶת הַסַּמִּֽים: כָּל־אִ֣ישׁ וְאִשָּׁ֗ה

אֲשֶׁ֨ר נָדַ֣ב לִבָּם֮ אֹתָם֒ לְהָבִיא֙ לְכָל־הַמְּלָאכָ֔ה אֲשֶׁ֨ר צִוָּ֧ה יְהֹוָ֛ה לַֽעֲשׂ֖וֹת

בְּיַד־מֹשֶׁ֑ה הֵבִ֧יאוּ בְנֵֽי־יִשְׂרָאֵ֛ל נְדָבָ֖ה לַֽיהֹוָֽה:

ל שלישי [שני] וַיֹּ֤אמֶר מֹשֶׁה֙ אֶל־בְּנֵ֣י יִשְׂרָאֵ֔ל רְא֛וּ קָרָ֥א יְהֹוָ֖ה בְּשֵׁ֑ם בְּצַלְאֵ֛ל בֶּן־אוּרִ֥י בֶן־

לא ח֖וּר לְמַטֵּ֥ה יְהוּדָֽה: וַיְמַלֵּ֥א אֹת֖וֹ ר֣וּחַ אֱלֹהִ֑ים בְּחָכְמָ֛ה בִּתְבוּנָ֥ה וּבְדַ֖עַת

לב וּבְכָל־מְלָאכָֽה: וְלַחְשֹׁ֖ב מַֽחֲשָׁבֹ֑ת לַֽעֲשֹׂ֛ת בַּזָּהָ֥ב וּבַכֶּ֖סֶף וּבַנְּחֹֽשֶׁת:

לג וּבַֽחֲרֹ֤שֶׁת אֶ֙בֶן֙ לְמַלֹּ֔את וּבַֽחֲרֹ֖שֶׁת עֵ֑ץ לַֽעֲשׂ֖וֹת בְּכָל־מְלֶ֥אכֶת מַֽחֲשָֽׁבֶת:

לד-לה וּלְהוֹרֹ֖ת נָתַ֣ן בְּלִבּ֑וֹ ה֕וּא וְאָֽהֳלִיאָ֥ב בֶּן־אֲחִֽיסָמָ֖ךְ לְמַטֵּה־דָֽן: מִלֵּ֨א אֹתָ֜ם

חָכְמַת־לֵ֗ב לַֽעֲשׂוֹת֮ כָּל־מְלֶ֣אכֶת חָרָ֣שׁ ׀ וְחֹשֵׁב֒ וְרֹקֵ֞ם בַּתְּכֵ֣לֶת וּבָֽאַרְגָּמָ֗ן

בְּתוֹלַ֧עַת הַשָּׁנִ֛י וּבַשֵּׁ֖שׁ וְאֹרֵ֑ג עֹשֵׂי֙ כָּל־מְלָאכָ֔ה וְחֹֽשְׁבֵ֖י מַֽחֲשָׁבֹֽת:

לו א וְעָשָׂה֩ בְצַלְאֵ֨ל וְאָֽהֳלִיאָ֜ב וְכֹ֣ל ׀ אִ֣ישׁ חֲכַם־לֵ֗ב אֲשֶׁר֩ נָתַ֨ן יְהֹוָ֜ה חָכְמָ֤ה

וּתְבוּנָה֙ בָּהֵ֔מָּה לָדַ֣עַת לַֽעֲשֹׂ֔ת אֶֽת־כָּל־מְלֶ֖אכֶת עֲבֹדַ֣ת הַקֹּ֑דֶשׁ לְכֹ֥ל

ב אֲשֶׁר־צִוָּ֖ה יְהֹוָֽה: וַיִּקְרָ֣א מֹשֶׁ֗ה אֶל־בְּצַלְאֵל֙ וְאֶל־אָ֣הֳלִיאָ֔ב וְאֶל֙ כָּל־אִ֣ישׁ

חֲכַם־לֵ֔ב אֲשֶׁ֨ר נָתַ֧ן יְהֹוָ֛ה חָכְמָ֖ה בְּלִבּ֑וֹ כֹּ֚ל אֲשֶׁ֣ר נְשָׂא֣וֹ לִבּ֔וֹ לְקָרְבָ֖ה אֶל־

ג הַמְּלָאכָ֖ה לַֽעֲשֹׂ֥ת אֹתָֽהּ: וַיִּקְח֞וּ מִלִּפְנֵ֣י מֹשֶׁ֗ה אֵ֤ת כָּל־הַתְּרוּמָה֙ אֲשֶׁ֣ר

the Cover, the Partition-curtain; [13] the Table, its staves, and all its utensils, and the show-bread; [14] the Menorah of illumination, its utensils, and its lamps, and oil for the illumination; [15] the Incense Altar and its staves, the anointment oil and the incense spices, and the entrance-screen for the entrance of the Tabernacle; [16] the Burnt-offering Altar and the copper netting for it, its staves, and all its utensils, the Laver and its base; [17] the curtains of the Courtyard, its pillars, and its sockets, and the screen of the gate of the Courtyard; [18] the pegs of the Tabernacle, the pegs of the Courtyard, and their cords; [19] the knit vestments to serve in the Sanctuary, the sacred vestments for Aaron the Kohen and the vestments of his sons to minister.' "

[20] The entire assembly of the Children of Israel left Moses' presence.

Inspiration from the heart; motivation from the spirit

[21] Every man whose heart inspired him came; and everyone whose spirit motivated him brought the portion of HASHEM for the work of the Tent of Meeting, for all its labor and for the sacred vestments. [22] The men came with the women; * everyone whose heart motivated him brought bracelets, nose-rings, rings, body ornaments — all sorts of gold ornaments — every man who raised up an offering of gold to HASHEM. [23] Every man with whom was found turquoise, purple, and scarlet wool, linen, and goat hair, red-dyed ram skins, and tachash skins brought them. [24] Every man who separated a portion of silver or copper brought it as a portion for HASHEM; and everyone with whom there was acacia wood for any work of the labor brought it. [25] Every wise-hearted woman spun with her hands; and they brought the spun yarn of turquoise, purple, and scarlet wool, and the linen. [26] All the women whose hearts inspired them with wisdom spun the goat hair. [27] The leaders brought the shoham stones and the stones for the settings for the Ephod and the Breastplate; [28] the spice and the oil, for illumination and for the anointment oil and the incense spices. [29] Every man and woman whose heart motivated them to bring for any of the work that HASHEM had commanded to make, through Moses — the Children of Israel brought a free-willed offering to HASHEM.

The craftsmen are selected

[30] Moses said to the Children of Israel, "See, HASHEM has proclaimed by name, Bezalel, son of Uri son of Hur, of the tribe of Judah. [31] He filled him with Godly spirit, with wisdom, insight, and knowledge, and with every craft — [32] to weave designs, to work with gold, silver, and copper; [33] stone-cutting for setting, and wood-carving — to perform every craft of design. [34] He gave him the ability to teach, him and Oholiab, son of Ahisamach, of the tribe of Dan. [35] He filled them with a wise heart to do every craft of the carver, weaver of designs, and embroiderer — with the turquoise, purple, and scarlet wool, and the linen — and the weaver; the artisans of every craft and makers of designs.

36

The mandate

[1] Bezalel shall carry out — with Oholiab and every wise-hearted man within whom HASHEM had endowed wisdom and insight to know and to do all the work for the labor of the Sanctuary — everything that HASHEM had commanded." [2] Moses summoned Bezalel, Oholiab, and every wise-hearted man whose heart HASHEM endowed with wisdom, everyone whose heart inspired him, to approach the work, to do it. [3] From Moses' presence they took the entire gift that

---

35:22. Since the jewelry enumerated in this verse was worn mainly by women, the Torah pays tribute to them, for as soon as they heard that precious metals were needed, they immediately rushed to bring their most precious possessions (*Ramban*).

הֵבִיאוּ בְּנֵי יִשְׂרָאֵל לִמְלֶאכֶת עֲבֹדַת הַקֹּדֶשׁ לַעֲשֹׂת אֹתָהּ וְהֵם הֵבִיאוּ אֵלָיו

ד   עוֹד נְדָבָה בַּבֹּקֶר בַּבֹּקֶר: וַיָּבֹאוּ כָּל־הַחֲכָמִים הָעֹשִׂים אֵת כָּל־מְלֶאכֶת

ה   הַקֹּדֶשׁ אִישׁ־אִישׁ מִמְּלַאכְתּוֹ אֲשֶׁר־הֵמָּה עֹשִׂים: וַיֹּאמְרוּ אֶל־מֹשֶׁה

לֵאמֹר מַרְבִּים הָעָם לְהָבִיא מִדֵּי הָעֲבֹדָה לַמְּלָאכָה אֲשֶׁר־צִוָּה יהוה

ו   לַעֲשֹׂת אֹתָהּ: וַיְצַו מֹשֶׁה וַיַּעֲבִירוּ קוֹל בַּמַּחֲנֶה לֵאמֹר אִישׁ וְאִשָּׁה אַל־

ז   יַעֲשׂוּ־עוֹד מְלָאכָה לִתְרוּמַת הַקֹּדֶשׁ וַיִּכָּלֵא הָעָם מֵהָבִיא: וְהַמְּלָאכָה

ח   הָיְתָה דַיָּם לְכָל־הַמְּלָאכָה לַעֲשׂוֹת אֹתָהּ וְהוֹתֵר: רביעי   וַיַּעֲשׂוּ כָל־

חֲכַם־לֵב בְּעֹשֵׂי הַמְּלָאכָה אֶת־הַמִּשְׁכָּן עֶשֶׂר יְרִיעֹת שֵׁשׁ מָשְׁזָר וּתְכֵלֶת

ט   וְאַרְגָּמָן וְתוֹלַעַת שָׁנִי כְּרֻבִים מַעֲשֵׂה חֹשֵׁב עָשָׂה אֹתָם: אֹרֶךְ הַיְרִיעָה

הָאַחַת שְׁמֹנֶה וְעֶשְׂרִים בָּאַמָּה וְרֹחַב אַרְבַּע בָּאַמָּה הַיְרִיעָה הָאֶחָת מִדָּה

י   אַחַת לְכָל־הַיְרִיעֹת: וַיְחַבֵּר אֶת־חֲמֵשׁ הַיְרִיעֹת אַחַת אֶל־אֶחָת וְחָמֵשׁ

יא   יְרִיעֹת חִבַּר אַחַת אֶל־אֶחָת: וַיַּעַשׂ לֻלְאֹת תְּכֵלֶת עַל שְׂפַת הַיְרִיעָה

הָאֶחָת מִקָּצָה בַּמַּחְבָּרֶת כֵּן עָשָׂה בִּשְׂפַת הַיְרִיעָה הַקִּיצוֹנָה בַּמַּחְבֶּרֶת

יב   הַשֵּׁנִית: חֲמִשִּׁים לֻלָאֹת עָשָׂה בַּיְרִיעָה הָאֶחָת וַחֲמִשִּׁים לֻלָאֹת עָשָׂה

בִּקְצֵה הַיְרִיעָה אֲשֶׁר בַּמַּחְבֶּרֶת הַשֵּׁנִית מַקְבִּילֹת הַלֻּלָאֹת אַחַת אֶל־

יג   אֶחָת: וַיַּעַשׂ חֲמִשִּׁים קַרְסֵי זָהָב וַיְחַבֵּר אֶת־הַיְרִיעֹת אַחַת אֶל־אַחַת

בַּקְּרָסִים וַיְהִי הַמִּשְׁכָּן אֶחָד:

יד   וַיַּעַשׂ יְרִיעֹת עִזִּים לְאֹהֶל עַל־הַמִּשְׁכָּן עַשְׁתֵּי־עֶשְׂרֵה יְרִיעֹת עָשָׂה אֹתָם:

טו   אֹרֶךְ הַיְרִיעָה הָאַחַת שְׁלֹשִׁים בָּאַמָּה וְאַרְבַּע אַמּוֹת רֹחַב הַיְרִיעָה הָאֶחָת

טז   מִדָּה אַחַת לְעַשְׁתֵּי עֶשְׂרֵה יְרִיעֹת: וַיְחַבֵּר אֶת־חֲמֵשׁ הַיְרִיעֹת לְבָד וְאֶת־

יז   שֵׁשׁ הַיְרִיעֹת לְבָד: וַיַּעַשׂ לֻלָאֹת חֲמִשִּׁים עַל שְׂפַת הַיְרִיעָה הַקִּיצֹנָה

בַּמַּחְבָּרֶת וַחֲמִשִּׁים לֻלָאֹת עָשָׂה עַל־שְׂפַת הַיְרִיעָה הַחֹבֶרֶת הַשֵּׁנִית:

יח-יט   וַיַּעַשׂ קַרְסֵי נְחֹשֶׁת חֲמִשִּׁים לְחַבֵּר אֶת־הָאֹהֶל לִהְיֹת אֶחָד: וַיַּעַשׂ מִכְסֶה

כ   לָאֹהֶל עֹרֹת אֵילִם מְאָדָּמִים וּמִכְסֵה עֹרֹת תְּחָשִׁים מִלְמָעְלָה: חמישי   וַיַּעַשׂ

כא   אֶת־הַקְּרָשִׁים לַמִּשְׁכָּן עֲצֵי שִׁטִּים עֹמְדִים: עֶשֶׂר אַמֹּת אֹרֶךְ הַקָּרֶשׁ וְאַמָּה

כב   וַחֲצִי הָאַמָּה רֹחַב הַקֶּרֶשׁ הָאֶחָד: שְׁתֵּי יָדֹת לַקֶּרֶשׁ הָאֶחָד מְשֻׁלָּבֹת אַחַת

כג   אֶל־אֶחָת כֵּן עָשָׂה לְכֹל קַרְשֵׁי הַמִּשְׁכָּן: וַיַּעַשׂ אֶת־הַקְּרָשִׁים לַמִּשְׁכָּן

כד   עֶשְׂרִים קְרָשִׁים לִפְאַת נֶגֶב תֵּימָנָה: וְאַרְבָּעִים אַדְנֵי־כֶסֶף עָשָׂה תַּחַת

עֶשְׂרִים הַקְּרָשִׁים שְׁנֵי אֲדָנִים תַּחַת־הַקֶּרֶשׁ הָאֶחָד לִשְׁתֵּי יְדֹתָיו וּשְׁנֵי

כה   אֲדָנִים תַּחַת־הַקֶּרֶשׁ הָאֶחָד לִשְׁתֵּי יְדֹתָיו: וּלְצֶלַע הַמִּשְׁכָּן הַשֵּׁנִית לִפְאַת

כו   צָפוֹן עָשָׂה עֶשְׂרִים קְרָשִׁים: וְאַרְבָּעִים אַדְנֵיהֶם כָּסֶף שְׁנֵי אֲדָנִים תַּחַת

כז   הַקֶּרֶשׁ הָאֶחָד וּשְׁנֵי אֲדָנִים תַּחַת הַקֶּרֶשׁ הָאֶחָד: וּלְיַרְכְּתֵי הַמִּשְׁכָּן יָמָּה

כח-כט   עָשָׂה שִׁשָּׁה קְרָשִׁים: וּשְׁנֵי קְרָשִׁים עָשָׂה לִמְקֻצְעֹת הַמִּשְׁכָּן בַּיַּרְכָתָיִם: וְהָיוּ

תוֹאֲמִם מִלְּמַטָּה וְיַחְדָּו יִהְיוּ תַמִּים אֶל־רֹאשׁוֹ אֶל־הַטַּבַּעַת הָאֶחָת כֵּן

the Children of Israel had brought for the work for the labor of the Sanctuary, to do it. But they continued to bring him free-willed gifts morning after morning.

⁴ All the wise people came — those performing all the sacred work, each of them from his work that they were doing — ⁵ and they said to Moses, as follows, "The people are bringing more than enough for the labor of the work that HASHEM has commanded to perform."

⁶ Moses commanded that they proclaim throughout the camp, saying, "Man and woman shall not do more work toward the gift for the Sanctuary!" And the people were restrained from bringing. ⁷ But the work had been enough for all the work, to do it — and there was extra.

The work begins: The curtains ⁸ The wise-hearted among those doing the work made the Tabernacle: ten curtains of linen, twisted with turquoise, purple, and scarlet wool; they made them with a woven design of cherubs. ⁹ The length of each curtain was twenty-eight cubits, and the width of each curtain was four cubits, the same measure for all the curtains. ¹⁰ He attached five curtains to one another, and five curtains he attached to one another. ¹¹ He made loops of turquoise wool on the edge of a single curtain at the end of one set; so he did at the edge of the outermost curtain on the second set. ¹² He made fifty loops on the one curtain and he made fifty loops at the end of the curtain that was on the second set, the loops corresponding to one another. ¹³ He made fifty clasps of gold and attached the curtains to one another with the clasps — so the Tabernacle became one.

¹⁴ He made curtains of goat hair for a Tent over the Tabernacle; he made them eleven curtains. ¹⁵ The length of each curtain was thirty cubits, and the width of each curtain was four cubits; the same measure for the eleven curtains. ¹⁶ He attached five curtains separately and six curtains separately. ¹⁷ He made fifty loops on the edge of the outermost curtain of the set, and he made fifty loops on the edge of the curtain of the second set. ¹⁸ He made fifty clasps of copper to attach the Tent so that it would become one.

The Cover ¹⁹ He made a Cover for the Tent of red-dyed ram hides, and a Cover of tachash hides on top.

The planks (See Appendix C, illustration 4) ²⁰ He made the planks for the Tabernacle of acacia wood, standing erect. ²¹ Ten cubits was the height of the plank, and a cubit and a half was the width of each plank. ²² Each plank shall have two tenons, parallel to one another, so he did for all the planks of the Tabernacle. ²³ He made the planks for the Tabernacle, twenty planks for the south side. ²⁴ He made forty silver sockets under the twenty planks, two sockets under one plank for its two tenons, and two sockets under the next plank for its two tenons. ²⁵ And for the second wall of the Tabernacle on its north side, he made twenty planks. ²⁶ Their forty sockets of silver, two sockets under one plank and two sockets under the next plank. ²⁷ For the back of the Tabernacle on the west, he made six planks. ²⁸ He made two planks for the corners of the Tabernacle, in the back. ²⁹ They were even at the bottom and together they were matching at the top, to a single ring, so

ל עָשָׂה לִשְׁנֵיהֶם לִשְׁנֵי הַמִּקְצֹעֹת: וְהָיוּ שְׁמֹנָה קְרָשִׁים וְאַדְנֵיהֶם כֶּסֶף שִׁשָּׁה

לא עָשָׂר אֲדָנִים שְׁנֵי אֲדָנִים שְׁנֵי אֲדָנִים תַּחַת הַקֶּרֶשׁ הָאֶחָד: וַיַּעַשׂ בְּרִיחֵי

לב עֲצֵי שִׁטִּים חֲמִשָּׁה לְקַרְשֵׁי צֶלַע־הַמִּשְׁכָּן הָאֶחָת: וַחֲמִשָּׁה בְרִיחִם לְקַרְשֵׁי

צֶלַע־הַמִּשְׁכָּן הַשֵּׁנִית וַחֲמִשָּׁה בְרִיחִם לְקַרְשֵׁי הַמִּשְׁכָּן לַיַּרְכָתַיִם יָמָּה:

לג וַיַּעַשׂ אֶת־הַבְּרִיחַ הַתִּיכֹן לִבְרֹחַ בְּתוֹךְ הַקְּרָשִׁים מִן־הַקָּצֶה אֶל־הַקָּצֶה:

לד וְאֶת־הַקְּרָשִׁים צִפָּה זָהָב וְאֶת־טַבְּעֹתָם עָשָׂה זָהָב בָּתִּים לַבְּרִיחִם וַיְצַף

אֶת־הַבְּרִיחִם זָהָב: וַיַּעַשׂ אֶת־הַפָּרֹכֶת תְּכֵלֶת וְאַרְגָּמָן וְתוֹלַעַת שָׁנִי וְשֵׁשׁ לה

לו מָשְׁזָר מַעֲשֵׂה חֹשֵׁב עָשָׂה אֹתָהּ כְּרֻבִים: וַיַּעַשׂ לָהּ אַרְבָּעָה עַמּוּדֵי שִׁטִּים

לז וַיְצַפֵּם זָהָב וָוֵיהֶם זָהָב וַיִּצֹק לָהֶם אַרְבָּעָה אַדְנֵי־כָסֶף: וַיַּעַשׂ מָסָךְ לְפֶתַח

לח הָאֹהֶל תְּכֵלֶת וְאַרְגָּמָן וְתוֹלַעַת שָׁנִי וְשֵׁשׁ מָשְׁזָר מַעֲשֵׂה רֹקֵם: וְאֶת־

עַמּוּדָיו חֲמִשָּׁה וְאֶת־וָוֵיהֶם וְצִפָּה רָאשֵׁיהֶם וַחֲשֻׁקֵיהֶם זָהָב וְאַדְנֵיהֶם

חֲמִשָּׁה נְחֹשֶׁת:

לז א וַיַּעַשׂ בְּצַלְאֵל אֶת־הָאָרֹן עֲצֵי שִׁטִּים אַמָּתַיִם וָחֵצִי אָרְכּוֹ וְאַמָּה וָחֵצִי

ב רָחְבּוֹ וְאַמָּה וָחֵצִי קֹמָתוֹ: וַיְצַפֵּהוּ זָהָב טָהוֹר מִבַּיִת וּמִחוּץ וַיַּעַשׂ לוֹ זֵר זָהָב

ג סָבִיב: וַיִּצֹק לוֹ אַרְבַּע טַבְּעֹת זָהָב עַל אַרְבַּע פַּעֲמֹתָיו וּשְׁתֵּי טַבָּעֹת עַל־

ד צַלְעוֹ הָאֶחָת וּשְׁתֵּי טַבָּעֹת עַל־צַלְעוֹ הַשֵּׁנִית: וַיַּעַשׂ בַּדֵּי עֲצֵי שִׁטִּים וַיְצַף

ה אֹתָם זָהָב: וַיָּבֵא אֶת־הַבַּדִּים בַּטַּבָּעֹת עַל צַלְעֹת הָאָרֹן לָשֵׂאת אֶת־הָאָרֹן:

ו-ז וַיַּעַשׂ כַּפֹּרֶת זָהָב טָהוֹר אַמָּתַיִם וָחֵצִי אָרְכָּהּ וְאַמָּה וָחֵצִי רָחְבָּהּ: וַיַּעַשׂ

ח שְׁנֵי כְרֻבִים זָהָב מִקְשָׁה עָשָׂה אֹתָם מִשְּׁנֵי קְצוֹת הַכַּפֹּרֶת: כְּרוּב־אֶחָד

מִקָּצָה מִזֶּה וּכְרוּב־אֶחָד מִקָּצָה מִזֶּה מִן־הַכַּפֹּרֶת עָשָׂה אֶת־הַכְּרֻבִים

ט מִשְּׁנֵי °קִצְוֹותוֹ [קְצוֹתָיו ק]: וַיִּהְיוּ הַכְּרֻבִים פֹּרְשֵׂי כְנָפַיִם לְמַעְלָה סֹכְכִים

בְּכַנְפֵיהֶם עַל־הַכַּפֹּרֶת וּפְנֵיהֶם אִישׁ אֶל־אָחִיו אֶל־הַכַּפֹּרֶת הָיוּ פְּנֵי

הַכְּרֻבִים:

י וַיַּעַשׂ אֶת־הַשֻּׁלְחָן עֲצֵי שִׁטִּים אַמָּתַיִם אָרְכּוֹ וְאַמָּה רָחְבּוֹ וְאַמָּה וָחֵצִי

יא-יב קֹמָתוֹ: וַיְצַף אֹתוֹ זָהָב טָהוֹר וַיַּעַשׂ לוֹ זֵר זָהָב סָבִיב: וַיַּעַשׂ לוֹ מִסְגֶּרֶת טֹפַח

יג סָבִיב וַיַּעַשׂ זֵר־זָהָב לְמִסְגַּרְתּוֹ סָבִיב: וַיִּצֹק לוֹ אַרְבַּע טַבְּעֹת זָהָב וַיִּתֵּן אֶת־

יד הַטַּבָּעֹת עַל אַרְבַּע הַפֵּאֹת אֲשֶׁר לְאַרְבַּע רַגְלָיו: לְעֻמַּת הַמִּסְגֶּרֶת הָיוּ

טו הַטַּבָּעֹת בָּתִּים לַבַּדִּים לָשֵׂאת אֶת־הַשֻּׁלְחָן: וַיַּעַשׂ אֶת־הַבַּדִּים עֲצֵי שִׁטִּים

טז וַיְצַף אֹתָם זָהָב לָשֵׂאת אֶת־הַשֻּׁלְחָן: וַיַּעַשׂ אֶת־הַכֵּלִים ׀ אֲשֶׁר עַל־

הַשֻּׁלְחָן אֶת־קְעָרֹתָיו וְאֶת־כַּפֹּתָיו וְאֵת מְנַקִּיֹּתָיו וְאֶת־הַקְּשָׂוֹת אֲשֶׁר יֻסַּךְ

בָּהֵן זָהָב טָהוֹר:

ששי [שלישי] יז וַיַּעַשׂ אֶת־הַמְּנֹרָה זָהָב טָהוֹר מִקְשָׁה עָשָׂה אֶת־הַמְּנֹרָה יְרֵכָהּ וְקָנָהּ

יח גְּבִיעֶיהָ כַּפְתֹּרֶיהָ וּפְרָחֶיהָ מִמֶּנָּה הָיוּ: וְשִׁשָּׁה קָנִים יֹצְאִים מִצִּדֶּיהָ שְׁלֹשָׁה ׀

יט קְנֵי מְנֹרָה מִצִּדָּהּ הָאֶחָד וּשְׁלֹשָׁה קְנֵי מְנֹרָה מִצִּדָּהּ הַשֵּׁנִי: שְׁלֹשָׁה גְבִעִים

he did to them both, at the two corners. ³⁰ There were eight planks and their silver sockets, sixteen sockets, two sockets, two sockets, under each plank. ³¹ He made bars of acacia wood, five for the planks of one side of the Tabernacle; ³² and five bars for the planks of the second side, and five bars for the planks of the Tabernacle at the back, on the west. ³³ He made the middle bar to extend within the planks from end to end.

³⁴ He covered the planks with gold and made their rings of gold as housings for the bars, and he covered the bars with gold.

The Partitions   ³⁵ He made the Partition of turquoise, purple, and scarlet wool, and linen, twisted; he made it with a woven design of cherubs. ³⁶ He made for it four pillars of acacia wood and plated them with gold, their hooks were gold; and he cast for them four sockets of silver.

The Screen   ³⁷ For the entrance of the Tent he made a Screen of turquoise, purple, and scarlet wool, and linen, twisted; work of an embroiderer. ³⁸ Its pillars were five, with their hooks, and he plated their tops and their bands with gold; and their sockets were five, of copper.

37

The Ark
(See Appendix C, illustration 1)

¹ Bezalel made the Ark of acacia wood, two and a half cubits its length; a cubit and a half its width; and a cubit and a half its height. ² He covered it with pure gold, within and without, and he made for it a gold crown all around. ³ He cast for it four rings of gold on its four corners; two rings on its one side and two rings on its second side. ⁴ He made staves of acacia wood and covered them with gold. ⁵ He inserted the staves in the rings on the sides of the Ark, to carry the Ark.

The Cover   ⁶ He made a Cover of pure gold, two and a half cubits its length, and a cubit and a half its width. ⁷ He made two Cherubs of gold — hammered out did he make them — from the two ends of the Cover: ⁸ one Cherub from the end at one side and one Cherub from the end at the other; from the Cover did he make the Cherubs, from its two ends. ⁹ The Cherubs were with wings spread upward sheltering the Cover with their wings, with their faces toward one another; toward the Cover were the faces of the Cherubs.

The Table
(See Appendix C, illustration 2)

¹⁰ He made the Table of acacia wood; two cubits its length; a cubit its width; and a cubit and a half its height. ¹¹ He covered it with pure gold and made for it a gold crown all around. ¹² He made for it a molding of one handbreadth all around, and he made a gold crown for its molding all around. ¹³ He cast for it four rings of gold and placed the rings on the four corners of its four legs. ¹⁴ The rings were opposite the molding as housings for the staves, to carry the Table. ¹⁵ He made the staves of acacia wood and covered them with gold, to carry the Table. ¹⁶ He made the utensils that were on the Table, its dishes, its spoons, its pillars, and its shelving-tubes, with which it was covered, of pure gold.

The Menorah
(See Appendix C, illustration 3)

¹⁷ He made the Menorah of pure gold, hammered out did he make the Menorah, its base and its shaft, its cups, its knobs, and its flowers were from it. ¹⁸ Six branches emerged from its sides, three branches of the Menorah from its side and three branches of the Menorah from its second side; ¹⁹ three cups

---

37:1. The account of the Tabernacle's construction ends with the vessels that represent the essence of the Sanctuary's teaching. These vessels, contained in the Tabernacle structure, symbolize the innermost of human ideals: the Ark contains God's teachings; the Table reflects man's struggle to sustain his physical being by fighting for his daily bread; and finally, the Menorah reflects man's obligation to spread the light of Torah beyond himself. The Ark that is in the Holy of Holies radiates its holiness to the Table and Menorah, and through them to the entire world.

מְשֻׁקָּדִים בַּקָּנֶה הָאֶחָד כַּפְתֹּר וָפֶרַח וּשְׁלֹשָׁה גְבִעִים מְשֻׁקָּדִים בְּקָנֶה אֶחָד

כ כַּפְתֹּר וָפֶרַח כֵּן לְשֵׁשֶׁת הַקָּנִים הַיֹּצְאִים מִן-הַמְּנֹרָה: וּבַמְּנֹרָה אַרְבָּעָה

כא גְבִעִים מְשֻׁקָּדִים כַּפְתֹּרֶיהָ וּפְרָחֶיהָ: וְכַפְתֹּר תַּחַת שְׁנֵי הַקָּנִים מִמֶּנָּה

וְכַפְתֹּר תַּחַת שְׁנֵי הַקָּנִים מִמֶּנָּה וְכַפְתֹּר תַּחַת-שְׁנֵי הַקָּנִים מִמֶּנָּה לְשֵׁשֶׁת

כב הַקָּנִים הַיֹּצְאִים מִמֶּנָּה: כַּפְתֹּרֵיהֶם וּקְנֹתָם מִמֶּנָּה הָיוּ כֻּלָּהּ מִקְשָׁה אַחַת

כג זָהָב טָהוֹר: וַיַּעַשׂ אֶת-נֵרֹתֶיהָ שִׁבְעָה וּמַלְקָחֶיהָ וּמַחְתֹּתֶיהָ זָהָב טָהוֹר:

כד כִּכָּר זָהָב טָהוֹר עָשָׂה אֹתָהּ וְאֵת כָּל-כֵּלֶיהָ:

כה וַיַּעַשׂ אֶת-מִזְבַּח הַקְּטֹרֶת עֲצֵי שִׁטִּים אַמָּה אָרְכּוֹ וְאַמָּה רָחְבּוֹ רָבוּעַ

כו וְאַמָּתַיִם קֹמָתוֹ מִמֶּנּוּ הָיוּ קַרְנֹתָיו: וַיְצַף אֹתוֹ זָהָב טָהוֹר אֶת-גַּגּוֹ וְאֶת-

כז קִירֹתָיו סָבִיב וְאֶת-קַרְנֹתָיו וַיַּעַשׂ לוֹ זֵר זָהָב סָבִיב: וּשְׁתֵּי טַבְּעֹת

זָהָב עָשָׂה-לוֹ ׀ מִתַּחַת לְזֵרוֹ עַל שְׁתֵּי צַלְעֹתָיו עַל שְׁנֵי צִדָּיו לְבָתִּים

כח לְבַדִּים לָשֵׂאת אֹתוֹ בָּהֶם: וַיַּעַשׂ אֶת-הַבַּדִּים עֲצֵי שִׁטִּים וַיְצַף אֹתָם

כט זָהָב: וַיַּעַשׂ אֶת-שֶׁמֶן הַמִּשְׁחָה קֹדֶשׁ וְאֶת-קְטֹרֶת הַסַּמִּים טָהוֹר מַעֲשֵׂה

רֹקֵחַ: **לח** שביעי א   וַיַּעַשׂ אֶת-מִזְבַּח הָעֹלָה עֲצֵי שִׁטִּים חָמֵשׁ אַמּוֹת אָרְכּוֹ

ב וְחָמֵשׁ-אַמּוֹת רָחְבּוֹ רָבוּעַ וְשָׁלֹשׁ אַמּוֹת קֹמָתוֹ: וַיַּעַשׂ קַרְנֹתָיו עַל אַרְבַּע

ג פִּנֹּתָיו מִמֶּנּוּ הָיוּ קַרְנֹתָיו וַיְצַף אֹתוֹ נְחֹשֶׁת: וַיַּעַשׂ אֶת-כָּל-כְּלֵי הַמִּזְבֵּחַ

אֶת-הַסִּירֹת וְאֶת-הַיָּעִים וְאֶת-הַמִּזְרָקֹת אֶת-הַמִּזְלָגֹת וְאֶת-הַמַּחְתֹּת

ד כָּל-כֵּלָיו עָשָׂה נְחֹשֶׁת: וַיַּעַשׂ לַמִּזְבֵּחַ מִכְבָּר מַעֲשֵׂה רֶשֶׁת נְחֹשֶׁת תַּחַת

כַּרְכֻּבּוֹ מִלְמַטָּה עַד-חֶצְיוֹ: וַיִּצֹק אַרְבַּע טַבָּעֹת בְּאַרְבַּע הַקְּצָוֹת לְמִכְבַּר

ו הַנְּחֹשֶׁת בָּתִּים לַבַּדִּים: וַיַּעַשׂ אֶת-הַבַּדִּים עֲצֵי שִׁטִּים וַיְצַף אֹתָם נְחֹשֶׁת:

ז וַיָּבֵא אֶת-הַבַּדִּים בַּטַּבָּעֹת עַל צַלְעֹת הַמִּזְבֵּחַ לָשֵׂאת אֹתוֹ בָּהֶם נְבוּב

ח לֻחֹת עָשָׂה אֹתוֹ:   וַיַּעַשׂ אֵת הַכִּיּוֹר נְחֹשֶׁת וְאֵת כַּנּוֹ נְחֹשֶׁת

ט בְּמַרְאֹת הַצֹּבְאֹת אֲשֶׁר צָבְאוּ פֶּתַח אֹהֶל מוֹעֵד: וַיַּעַשׂ

אֶת-הֶחָצֵר לִפְאַת ׀ נֶגֶב תֵּימָנָה קַלְעֵי הֶחָצֵר שֵׁשׁ מָשְׁזָר מֵאָה בָּאַמָּה:

י עַמּוּדֵיהֶם עֶשְׂרִים וְאַדְנֵיהֶם עֶשְׂרִים נְחֹשֶׁת וָוֵי הָעַמֻּדִים וַחֲשֻׁקֵיהֶם כָּסֶף:

יא וְלִפְאַת צָפוֹן מֵאָה בָאַמָּה עַמּוּדֵיהֶם עֶשְׂרִים וְאַדְנֵיהֶם עֶשְׂרִים נְחֹשֶׁת וָוֵי

יב הָעַמּוּדִים וַחֲשֻׁקֵיהֶם כָּסֶף: וְלִפְאַת-יָם קְלָעִים חֲמִשִּׁים בָּאַמָּה עַמּוּדֵיהֶם

יג עֲשָׂרָה וְאַדְנֵיהֶם עֲשָׂרָה וָוֵי הָעַמֻּדִים וַחֲשׁוּקֵיהֶם כָּסֶף: וְלִפְאַת קֵדְמָה

יד מִזְרָחָה חֲמִשִּׁים אַמָּה: קְלָעִים חֲמֵשׁ-עֶשְׂרֵה אַמָּה אֶל-הַכָּתֵף עַמֻּדֵיהֶם

טו שְׁלֹשָׁה וְאַדְנֵיהֶם שְׁלֹשָׁה: וְלַכָּתֵף הַשֵּׁנִית מִזֶּה וּמִזֶּה לְשַׁעַר הֶחָצֵר קְלָעִים

טז חֲמֵשׁ עֶשְׂרֵה אַמָּה עַמֻּדֵיהֶם שְׁלֹשָׁה וְאַדְנֵיהֶם שְׁלֹשָׁה: כָּל-קַלְעֵי הֶחָצֵר

יז סָבִיב שֵׁשׁ מָשְׁזָר: וְהָאֲדָנִים לָעַמֻּדִים נְחֹשֶׁת וָוֵי הָעַמּוּדִים וַחֲשׁוּקֵיהֶם

כֶּסֶף וְצִפּוּי רָאשֵׁיהֶם כָּסֶף וְהֵם מְחֻשָּׁקִים כֶּסֶף כֹּל עַמֻּדֵי הֶחָצֵר:

38:8. The Laver was a very large basin in the Tabernacle Courtyard from which the Kohanim were required to wash their hands and feet before performing the service. It was made entirely of copper mirrors. The mirrors used engraved like almonds on one branch, a knob and a flower; and three cups engraved like almonds, a knob and a flower on the next branch — so for the six branches that emerge from the Menorah. ²⁰ And on the Menorah were four cups, engraved like almonds, its knobs and its blossoms. ²¹ A knob was under two of the branches from it, a knob was under two of the branches from it, and a knob was under two of the branches from it — for the six branches emerging from it. ²² Their knobs and branches were of it, all of a single hammered piece of pure gold. ²³ He made its lamps seven, and its tongs and spoons of pure gold. ²⁴ Of a talent of pure gold did he make it and all its utensils.

The Incense Altar
(See Appendix C, illustration 15)

²⁵ He made the Incense Altar of acacia wood; a cubit its length, and a cubit its width — square — and two cubits its height, from it were its horns. ²⁶ He covered it with pure gold, its roof and its walls all around and its horns, and he made for it a gold crown all around. ²⁷ He made for it two gold rings under its crown on its two corners, on its two sides, as housings for staves, with which to carry it. ²⁸ He made the staves of acacia wood, and covered them with gold. ²⁹ He made the anointment oil holy; and the incense spices, pure; a perfumer's handiwork.

38

The Burnt-Offering Altar
(See Appendix C, illustration 5)

¹He made the Burnt-offering Altar of acacia wood; five cubits its length, and five cubits its width — square — and three cubits its height. ² He made its horns on its four corners, from it were its horns, and he covered it with copper. ³ He made all the utensils of the Altar — the pots, the shovels, the basins, the forks, and the fire-pans — he made all its utensils of copper. ⁴ He made for the Altar a netting of copper meshwork, below its surrounding border downwards until its midpoint. ⁵ He cast four rings on the four edges of the copper netting, as housings for the staves. ⁶ He made the staves of acacia wood and covered them with copper. ⁷ He inserted the staves in the rings on the sides of the Altar, with which to carry it; hollow, of boards, did he make it.

The Laver

⁸ He made the Laver of copper and its base of copper, from the mirrors of the legions* who massed at the entrance of the Tent of Meeting.

The Courtyard

⁹ He made the Courtyard: on the south side, the lace-hangings of the Courtyard, of twisted linen, a hundred cubits. ¹⁰ Their pillars twenty, and their sockets twenty, of copper; the hooks of the pillars and their bands of silver. ¹¹ On the north side, a hundred cubits, their pillars twenty and their sockets twenty, of copper; the hooks of the pillars and their bands of silver. ¹² On the west side, lace-hangings of fifty cubits; their pillars ten and their sockets ten; the hooks of the pillars and their bands of silver. ¹³ And on the eastern side, fifty cubits; ¹⁴ fifteen-cubit lace-hangings at the shoulder, their pillars three and their sockets three; ¹⁵ and at the second shoulder — on either side of the gate of the Courtyard — fifteen-cubit lace-hangings; their pillars three and their sockets three. ¹⁶ All the lace-hangings of the Courtyard all around were of twisted linen. ¹⁷ The sockets of the pillars were copper, the hooks of the pillars and their bands were silver, and the plating of their tops was silver. They were banded with silver, all the pillars of the Courtyard.

---

by women in those days were brightly polished sheets of copper. When the call went out for contributions, the women came with their copper mirrors and piled them up at the *Tent of Meeting*, which, until the erection of the Tabernacle, was the name given to Moses' tent (33:7).

מפטיר

Haftaras
Vayakhel
Ashkenazim:
p. 820
Sephardim:
p. 816

For special
Sabbaths,
see pp. x-xi

יח וּמָסַךְ שַׁעַר הֶחָצֵר מַעֲשֵׂה רֹקֵם תְּכֵלֶת וְאַרְגָּמָן וְתוֹלַעַת שָׁנִי וְשֵׁשׁ מָשְׁזָר וְעֶשְׂרִים אַמָּה אֹרֶךְ וְקוֹמָה בְרֹחַב חָמֵשׁ אַמּוֹת לְעֻמַּת קַלְעֵי הֶחָצֵר:

יט וְעַמֻּדֵיהֶם אַרְבָּעָה וְאַדְנֵיהֶם אַרְבָּעָה נְחֹשֶׁת וָוֵיהֶם כֶּסֶף וְצִפּוּי רָאשֵׁיהֶם וַחֲשֻׁקֵיהֶם כָּסֶף:

כ וְכָל־הַיְתֵדֹת לַמִּשְׁכָּן וְלֶחָצֵר סָבִיב נְחֹשֶׁת: ססס

קכ״ב פסוקים. סנואֻ״ה סימן.

פרשת פקודי

כא אֵלֶּה פְקוּדֵי הַמִּשְׁכָּן מִשְׁכַּן הָעֵדֻת אֲשֶׁר פֻּקַּד עַל־פִּי מֹשֶׁה עֲבֹדַת הַלְוִיִּם בְּיַד אִיתָמָר בֶּן־אַהֲרֹן הַכֹּהֵן:

כב וּבְצַלְאֵל בֶּן־אוּרִי בֶן־חוּר לְמַטֵּה יְהוּדָה עָשָׂה אֵת כָּל־אֲשֶׁר־צִוָּה יהוה אֶת־מֹשֶׁה:

כג וְאִתּוֹ אָהֳלִיאָב בֶּן־אֲחִיסָמָךְ לְמַטֵּה־דָן חָרָשׁ וְחֹשֵׁב וְרֹקֵם בַּתְּכֵלֶת וּבָאַרְגָּמָן וּבְתוֹלַעַת הַשָּׁנִי וּבַשֵּׁשׁ:

כד כָּל־הַזָּהָב הֶעָשׂוּי לַמְּלָאכָה בְּכֹל מְלֶאכֶת הַקֹּדֶשׁ וַיְהִי | זְהַב הַתְּנוּפָה תֵּשַׁע וְעֶשְׂרִים כִּכָּר וּשְׁבַע מֵאוֹת וּשְׁלֹשִׁים שֶׁקֶל בְּשֶׁקֶל הַקֹּדֶשׁ:

כה וְכֶסֶף פְּקוּדֵי הָעֵדָה מְאַת כִּכָּר וְאֶלֶף וּשְׁבַע מֵאוֹת וַחֲמִשָּׁה וְשִׁבְעִים שֶׁקֶל בְּשֶׁקֶל הַקֹּדֶשׁ:

כו בֶּקַע לַגֻּלְגֹּלֶת מַחֲצִית הַשֶּׁקֶל בְּשֶׁקֶל הַקֹּדֶשׁ לְכֹל הָעֹבֵר עַל־הַפְּקֻדִים מִבֶּן עֶשְׂרִים שָׁנָה וָמַעְלָה לְשֵׁשׁ־מֵאוֹת אֶלֶף וּשְׁלֹשֶׁת אֲלָפִים וַחֲמֵשׁ מֵאוֹת וַחֲמִשִּׁים:

כז וַיְהִי מְאַת כִּכַּר הַכֶּסֶף לָצֶקֶת אֵת אַדְנֵי הַקֹּדֶשׁ וְאֵת אַדְנֵי הַפָּרֹכֶת מְאַת אֲדָנִים לִמְאַת הַכִּכָּר כִּכָּר לָאָדֶן:

כח וְאֶת־הָאֶלֶף וּשְׁבַע הַמֵּאוֹת וַחֲמִשָּׁה וְשִׁבְעִים עָשָׂה וָוִים לָעַמּוּדִים וְצִפָּה רָאשֵׁיהֶם וְחִשַּׁק אֹתָם:

כט וּנְחֹשֶׁת הַתְּנוּפָה שִׁבְעִים כִּכָּר וְאַלְפַּיִם וְאַרְבַּע־מֵאוֹת שָׁקֶל:

ל וַיַּעַשׂ בָּהּ אֶת־אַדְנֵי פֶּתַח אֹהֶל מוֹעֵד וְאֵת מִזְבַּח הַנְּחֹשֶׁת וְאֶת־מִכְבַּר הַנְּחֹשֶׁת אֲשֶׁר־לוֹ וְאֵת כָּל־כְּלֵי הַמִּזְבֵּחַ:

לא וְאֶת־אַדְנֵי הֶחָצֵר סָבִיב וְאֶת־אַדְנֵי שַׁעַר הֶחָצֵר וְאֵת כָּל־יִתְדֹת הַמִּשְׁכָּן וְאֶת־כָּל־יִתְדֹת הֶחָצֵר סָבִיב:

לט א וּמִן־הַתְּכֵלֶת וְהָאַרְגָּמָן וְתוֹלַעַת הַשָּׁנִי עָשׂוּ בִגְדֵי־שְׂרָד לְשָׁרֵת בַּקֹּדֶשׁ וַיַּעֲשׂוּ אֶת־בִּגְדֵי הַקֹּדֶשׁ אֲשֶׁר לְאַהֲרֹן כַּאֲשֶׁר צִוָּה יהוה אֶת־מֹשֶׁה:

שני [חמישי] ב וַיַּעַשׂ אֶת־הָאֵפֹד זָהָב תְּכֵלֶת וְאַרְגָּמָן וְתוֹלַעַת שָׁנִי וְשֵׁשׁ מָשְׁזָר:

ג וַיְרַקְּעוּ אֶת־פַּחֵי הַזָּהָב וְקִצֵּץ פְּתִילִם לַעֲשׂוֹת בְּתוֹךְ הַתְּכֵלֶת וּבְתוֹךְ הָאַרְגָּמָן וּבְתוֹךְ תּוֹלַעַת הַשָּׁנִי וּבְתוֹךְ הַשֵּׁשׁ מַעֲשֵׂה חֹשֵׁב:

ד כְּתֵפֹת עָשׂוּ־לוֹ חֹבְרֹת עַל־שְׁנֵי °קצוותו [°קְצוֹתָיו ק] חֻבָּר:

ה וְחֵשֶׁב אֲפֻדָּתוֹ אֲשֶׁר עָלָיו מִמֶּנּוּ הוּא כְּמַעֲשֵׂהוּ זָהָב תְּכֵלֶת וְאַרְגָּמָן וְתוֹלַעַת שָׁנִי וְשֵׁשׁ מָשְׁזָר כַּאֲשֶׁר צִוָּה יהוה אֶת־מֹשֶׁה:

ו וַיַּעֲשׂוּ אֶת־אַבְנֵי הַשֹּׁהַם מֻסַבֹּת מִשְׁבְּצֹת זָהָב מְפֻתָּחֹת פִּתּוּחֵי חוֹתָם עַל־שְׁמוֹת בְּנֵי יִשְׂרָאֵל:

ז וַיָּשֶׂם אֹתָם עַל כִּתְפֹת הָאֵפֹד אַבְנֵי זִכָּרוֹן לִבְנֵי יִשְׂרָאֵל כַּאֲשֶׁר צִוָּה יהוה אֶת־מֹשֶׁה:

⮡ **Parashas Pekudei.** The *Sidrah* begins with a detailed listing of the amounts of gold, silver, and copper that were contributed for the construction of the Tabernacle. Despite the fact that the metals were deposited with

The Screen   ¹⁸ The Screen of the gate of the Courtyard was embroiderer's work, of turquoise, purple, and scarlet wool, and twisted linen; twenty cubits in length and the height, in width, was five cubits, corresponding to the lace-hangings of the Courtyard. ¹⁹ Their pillars four and their sockets four, of copper; their hooks silver, and the plating of their tops and their bands silver. ²⁰ All the pegs of the Tabernacle and the Courtyard all around were copper.

PARASHAS PEKUDEI

The reckonings   ²¹ These are the reckonings * of the Tabernacle, the Tabernacle of Testimony, which were reckoned at Moses' bidding. The labor of the Levites was under the authority of Issamar, son of Aaron the Kohen. ²² Bezalel, son of Uri son of Hur, of the tribe of Judah, did everything that HASHEM commanded Moses. ²³ With him was Oholiab, son of Ahisamach, of the tribe of Dan, a carver, weaver, and embroiderer, with turquoise, purple, and scarlet wool, and with linen.

The materials used for the work   ²⁴ All the gold that was used for the work — for all the holy work — the offered-up gold was twenty-nine talents and seven hundred thirty shekels, in the sacred shekel.

²⁵ The silver of the census of the community was one hundred talents, one thousand seven hundred seventy-five shekels, in the sacred shekel; ²⁶ a beka for every head, a half-shekel in the sacred shekel for everyone who passed through the census takers, from twenty years of age and up, for the six hundred three thousand, five hundred fifty. ²⁷ The hundred talents of silver were to cast the sockets of the Sanctuary and the sockets of the Partition; a hundred sockets for a hundred talents, a talent per socket. ²⁸ And from the one thousand seven hundred seventy-five he made hooks for the pillars, covered their tops and banded them.

²⁹ The offered-up copper was seventy talents and two thousand four hundred shekels. ³⁰ With it he made the sockets of the entrance to the Tent of Meeting, the Copper Altar, the copper meshwork that was on it, and all the vessels of the Altar; ³¹ the sockets of the Courtyard all around, the sockets of the gate of the Courtyard, all the pegs of the Tabernacle, and all the pegs of the Courtyard, all around.

39

Aaron's vestments   ¹ From the turquoise, purple, and scarlet wool they made knit vestments to serve in the Sanctuary, and they made the holy vestments for Aaron, as HASHEM had commanded Moses.

The Ephod   ² He made the Ephod of gold, turquoise, purple, and scarlet wool, and twisted (See Appendix C, illustration 9)   linen. ³ They hammered out the thin sheets of gold and cut threads to work the weaver's craft into the turquoise, into the purple, and into the scarlet wool, and into the linen. ⁴ They made attached shoulder straps for it, attached to its two ends. ⁵ The belt with which it was emplaced, which was on it, was made from it, of the same workmanship, of gold, turquoise, purple, and scarlet wool, and linen, twisted, as HASHEM had commanded Moses.

⁶ They fashioned the shoham stones, encircled with gold settings, engraved like the engraving of a signet ring, according to the names of the sons of Israel. ⁷ He placed them on the shoulder straps of the Ephod as remembrance stones for the sons of Israel, as HASHEM had commanded Moses.

Moses and were under the supervision of Bezalel — people whose greatness and integrity were indisputable, known to the people, and attested to by God — Moses would not rely on assumptions. Leaders must be beyond reproach and must keep accounts of the funds that pass through their hands.

ח וַיַּעַשׂ אֶת־הַחֹשֶׁן מַעֲשֵׂה חֹשֵׁב כְּמַעֲשֵׂה אֵפֹד זָהָב תְּכֵלֶת וְאַרְגָּמָן

ט וְתוֹלַעַת שָׁנִי וְשֵׁשׁ מָשְׁזָר: רָבוּעַ הָיָה כָּפוּל עָשׂוּ אֶת־הַחֹשֶׁן זֶרֶת אָרְכּוֹ

י וְזֶרֶת רָחְבּוֹ כָּפוּל: וַיְמַלְאוּ־בוֹ אַרְבָּעָה טוּרֵי אָבֶן טוּר אֹדֶם פִּטְדָה וּבָרֶקֶת

יא־יב הַטּוּר הָאֶחָד: וְהַטּוּר הַשֵּׁנִי נֹפֶךְ סַפִּיר וְיָהֲלֹם: וְהַטּוּר הַשְּׁלִישִׁי לֶשֶׁם שְׁבוֹ

יג וְאַחְלָמָה: וְהַטּוּר הָרְבִיעִי תַּרְשִׁישׁ שֹׁהַם וְיָשְׁפֵה מוּסַבֹּת מִשְׁבְּצֹת זָהָב

יד בְּמִלֻּאֹתָם: וְהָאֲבָנִים עַל־שְׁמֹת בְּנֵי־יִשְׂרָאֵל הֵנָּה שְׁתֵּים עֶשְׂרֵה עַל־

טו שְׁמֹתָם פִּתּוּחֵי חֹתָם אִישׁ עַל־שְׁמוֹ לִשְׁנֵים עָשָׂר שָׁבֶט: וַיַּעֲשׂוּ עַל־הַחֹשֶׁן

טז שַׁרְשְׁרֹת גַּבְלֻת מַעֲשֵׂה עֲבֹת זָהָב טָהוֹר: וַיַּעֲשׂוּ שְׁתֵּי מִשְׁבְּצֹת זָהָב וּשְׁתֵּי

יז טַבְּעֹת זָהָב וַיִּתְּנוּ אֶת־שְׁתֵּי הַטַּבָּעֹת עַל־שְׁנֵי קְצוֹת הַחֹשֶׁן: וַיִּתְּנוּ שְׁתֵּי

יח הָעֲבֹתֹת הַזָּהָב עַל־שְׁתֵּי הַטַּבָּעֹת עַל־קְצוֹת הַחֹשֶׁן: וְאֵת שְׁתֵּי קְצוֹת שְׁתֵּי

יט הָעֲבֹתֹת נָתְנוּ עַל־שְׁתֵּי הַמִּשְׁבְּצֹת וַיִּתְּנֻם עַל־כִּתְפֹת הָאֵפֹד אֶל־מוּל פָּנָיו:

וַיַּעֲשׂוּ שְׁתֵּי טַבְּעֹת זָהָב וַיָּשִׂימוּ עַל־שְׁנֵי קְצוֹת הַחֹשֶׁן עַל־שְׂפָתוֹ אֲשֶׁר

כ אֶל־עֵבֶר הָאֵפֹד בָּיְתָה: וַיַּעֲשׂוּ שְׁתֵּי טַבְּעֹת זָהָב וַיִּתְּנֻם עַל־שְׁתֵּי כִתְפֹת

כא הָאֵפֹד מִלְּמַטָּה מִמּוּל פָּנָיו לְעֻמַּת מַחְבַּרְתּוֹ מִמַּעַל לְחֵשֶׁב הָאֵפֹד: וַיִּרְכְּסוּ

אֶת־הַחֹשֶׁן מִטַּבְּעֹתָיו אֶל־טַבְּעֹת הָאֵפֹד בִּפְתִיל תְּכֵלֶת לִהְיֹת עַל־חֵשֶׁב

הָאֵפֹד וְלֹא־יִזַּח הַחֹשֶׁן מֵעַל הָאֵפֹד כַּאֲשֶׁר צִוָּה יְהוָה אֶת־מֹשֶׁה:

כב־כג **שלישי** וַיַּעַשׂ אֶת־מְעִיל הָאֵפֹד מַעֲשֵׂה אֹרֵג כְּלִיל תְּכֵלֶת: וּפִי־הַמְּעִיל בְּתוֹכוֹ כְּפִי

[ששי]

כד תַחְרָא שָׂפָה לְפִיו סָבִיב לֹא יִקָּרֵעַ: וַיַּעֲשׂוּ עַל־שׁוּלֵי הַמְּעִיל רִמּוֹנֵי תְּכֵלֶת

כה וְאַרְגָּמָן וְתוֹלַעַת שָׁנִי מָשְׁזָר: וַיַּעֲשׂוּ פַעֲמֹנֵי זָהָב טָהוֹר וַיִּתְּנוּ אֶת־

כו הַפַּעֲמֹנִים בְּתוֹךְ הָרִמֹּנִים עַל־שׁוּלֵי הַמְּעִיל סָבִיב בְּתוֹךְ הָרִמֹּנִים: פַּעֲמֹן

וְרִמֹּן פַּעֲמֹן וְרִמֹּן עַל־שׁוּלֵי הַמְּעִיל סָבִיב לְשָׁרֵת כַּאֲשֶׁר צִוָּה יְהוָה אֶת־

כז מֹשֶׁה: וַיַּעֲשׂוּ אֶת־הַכֻּתֳּנֹת שֵׁשׁ מַעֲשֵׂה אֹרֵג לְאַהֲרֹן

כח וּלְבָנָיו: וְאֵת הַמִּצְנֶפֶת שֵׁשׁ וְאֶת־פַּאֲרֵי הַמִּגְבָּעֹת שֵׁשׁ וְאֶת־מִכְנְסֵי הַבָּד

כט שֵׁשׁ מָשְׁזָר: וְאֶת־הָאַבְנֵט שֵׁשׁ מָשְׁזָר וּתְכֵלֶת וְאַרְגָּמָן וְתוֹלַעַת שָׁנִי מַעֲשֵׂה

ל רֹקֵם כַּאֲשֶׁר צִוָּה יְהוָה אֶת־מֹשֶׁה: וַיַּעֲשׂוּ אֶת־צִיץ

נֵזֶר־הַקֹּדֶשׁ זָהָב טָהוֹר וַיִּכְתְּבוּ עָלָיו מִכְתַּב פִּתּוּחֵי חֹתָם קֹדֶשׁ לַיהוָה:

לא וַיִּתְּנוּ עָלָיו פְּתִיל תְּכֵלֶת לָתֵת עַל־הַמִּצְנֶפֶת מִלְמָעְלָה כַּאֲשֶׁר צִוָּה יְהוָה

לב אֶת־מֹשֶׁה: וַתֵּכֶל כָּל־עֲבֹדַת מִשְׁכַּן אֹהֶל מוֹעֵד וַיַּעֲשׂוּ

בְּנֵי יִשְׂרָאֵל כְּכֹל אֲשֶׁר צִוָּה יְהוָה אֶת־מֹשֶׁה כֵּן עָשׂוּ:

לג **רביעי** וַיָּבִיאוּ אֶת־הַמִּשְׁכָּן אֶל־מֹשֶׁה אֶת־הָאֹהֶל וְאֶת־כָּל־כֵּלָיו קְרָסָיו קְרָשָׁיו

לד בְּרִיחָו וְעַמֻּדָיו וַאֲדָנָיו: וְאֶת־מִכְסֵה עוֹרֹת הָאֵילִם הַמְאָדָּמִים וְאֶת־מִכְסֵה

לה עֹרֹת הַתְּחָשִׁים וְאֵת פָּרֹכֶת הַמָּסָךְ: אֶת־אֲרוֹן הָעֵדֻת וְאֶת־בַּדָּיו וְאֵת

לו־לז הַכַּפֹּרֶת: אֶת־הַשֻּׁלְחָן אֶת־כָּל־כֵּלָיו וְאֵת לֶחֶם הַפָּנִים: אֶת־הַמְּנֹרָה

הַטְּהֹרָה אֶת־נֵרֹתֶיהָ נֵרֹת הַמַּעֲרָכָה וְאֶת־כָּל־כֵּלֶיהָ וְאֵת שֶׁמֶן הַמָּאוֹר:

The
Breastplate
(See Appendix C,
illustrations 10-11)

⁸ He made the Breastplate of a weaver's craft, like the workmanship of the Ephod, of gold, turquoise, purple, and scarlet wool, and linen, twisted. ⁹ It was square, folded over did they make the Breastplate; its length was a half-cubit and its width was a half-cubit, folded over. ¹⁰ They filled it with four rows of stones: a row of odem, pitdah, and barekes — one row; ¹¹ the second row: nofech, sapir, and yahalom; ¹² the third row: leshem, shevo, and achlamah; ¹³ the fourth row: tarshish, shoham, and yashfeh; encircled with gold settings in their mountings. ¹⁴ The stones were according to the names of the sons of Israel, twelve according to their names, like the engraving of a signet ring, each man according to his name, for the twelve tribes.

¹⁵ For the Breastplate they made chains at the edges, of braided craftsmanship, of pure gold. ¹⁶ They made two gold settings and two gold rings, and they placed the two rings on the two ends of the Breastplate. ¹⁷ They placed the two gold ropes on the two rings, on the ends of the Breastplate. ¹⁸ The two ends of the two ropes they placed on the two settings, and placed them on the shoulder straps of the Ephod, toward its front. ¹⁹ They made two gold rings and placed them on the two ends of the Breastplate, at its edge, which is on its inner side, toward the Ephod. ²⁰ They made two gold rings and placed them at the bottom of the two shoulder straps, toward the front, opposite its seam, above the belt of the Ephod. ²¹ They attached the Breastplate from its rings to the rings of the Ephod with a turquoise woolen cord, so that it would remain above the belt of the Ephod, and the Breastplate would not be loosened from above the Ephod, as HASHEM had commanded Moses.

Robe of
the Ephod
(See Appendix C,
illustration 12)

²² He made the Robe of the Ephod of a weaver's craft, entirely of turquoise wool. ²³ Its head-opening was folded over within, like the opening of a coat of mail; its opening had a border all around, so that it would not tear. ²⁴ On the Robe's hem they made pomegranates of turquoise, purple, and scarlet wool, twisted. ²⁵ They made bells of pure gold, and they placed the bells amid the pomegranates on the hem of the Robe, all around, amid the pomegranates. ²⁶ A bell and a pomegranate, a bell and a pomegranate on the hem of the Robe all around, to minister, as HASHEM commanded Moses.

Tunics
of linen
(See Appendix C,
illustration 8)

²⁷ They made the Tunics of linen, of a weaver's craft, for Aaron and his sons; ²⁸ and the Turban of linen, and the splendid Headdresses of linen, and the linen Breeches of twisted linen; ²⁹ the Sash of twisted linen, turquoise, purple, and scarlet wool, of an embroiderer's work, as HASHEM had commanded Moses.

Headplate
(See Appendix C,
illustration 14)

³⁰ They made the Headplate, the holy crown, of pure gold, and they inscribed on it with script like that of a signet ring, "HOLY TO HASHEM." ³¹ They placed on it a cord of turquoise wool, to put over the Turban from above, as HASHEM commanded Moses.

³² All the work of the Tabernacle, the Tent of Meeting, was completed, and the Children of Israel had done everything that HASHEM commanded Moses, so did they do.

Moses
inspects the
Tabernacle

³³ They brought the Tabernacle to Moses, the Tent and all its utensils: its hooks, its planks, its bars, its pillars, and its sockets; ³⁴ the Cover of red-dyed ram hides, and the Cover of tachash skins, and the Partition-curtain; ³⁵ the Ark of Testimony and its staves, and the Cover; ³⁶ the Table and all its utensils, and the show-bread; ³⁷ the pure Menorah, its lamps — the lamps of the prescribed order — and all its utensils, and the oil of illumination;

לח וְאֵת֙ מִזְבַּ֣ח הַזָּהָ֔ב וְאֵת֙ שֶׁ֣מֶן הַמִּשְׁחָ֔ה וְאֵ֖ת קְטֹ֣רֶת הַסַּמִּ֑ים וְאֵ֕ת מָסַ֖ךְ

לט פֶּ֥תַח הָאֹֽהֶל: אֵ֣ת ׀ מִזְבַּ֣ח הַנְּחֹ֗שֶׁת וְאֶת־מִכְבַּ֤ר הַנְּחֹ֙שֶׁת֙ אֲשֶׁר־ל֔וֹ אֶת־

מ בַּדָּ֖יו וְאֶת־כָּל־כֵּלָ֑יו אֶת־הַכִּיֹּ֖ר וְאֶת־כַּנּֽוֹ: אֵ֣ת קַלְעֵ֣י הֶֽחָצֵ֗ר אֶת־עַמֻּדֶ֙יהָ֙ וְאֶת־אֲדָנֶ֔יהָ וְאֶת־הַמָּסָךְ֙ לְשַׁ֣עַר הֶֽחָצֵ֔ר אֶת־מֵֽיתָרָ֖יו וִיתֵֽדֹתֶ֑יהָ וְאֵ֗ת

מא כָּל־כְּלֵ֛י עֲבֹדַ֥ת הַמִּשְׁכָּ֖ן לְאֹ֥הֶל מוֹעֵֽד: אֶת־בִּגְדֵ֥י הַשְּׂרָ֖ד לְשָׁרֵ֣ת בַּקֹּ֑דֶשׁ

מב אֶת־בִּגְדֵ֤י הַקֹּ֙דֶשׁ֙ לְאַֽהֲרֹ֣ן הַכֹּהֵ֔ן וְאֶת־בִּגְדֵ֥י בָנָ֖יו לְכַהֵֽן: כְּכֹ֛ל אֲשֶׁר־

מג צִוָּ֥ה יהו֖ה אֶת־מֹשֶׁ֑ה כֵּ֤ן עָשׂוּ֙ בְּנֵ֣י יִשְׂרָאֵ֔ל אֵ֖ת כָּל־הָעֲבֹדָֽה: וַיַּ֨רְא מֹשֶׁ֜ה אֶת־כָּל־הַמְּלָאכָ֗ה וְהִנֵּה֙ עָשׂ֣וּ אֹתָ֔הּ כַּאֲשֶׁ֛ר צִוָּ֥ה יהו֖ה כֵּ֣ן עָשׂ֑וּ וַיְבָ֥רֶךְ אֹתָ֖ם מֹשֶֽׁה:

מ חמישי א-ב וַיְדַבֵּ֥ר יהו֖ה אֶל־מֹשֶׁ֥ה לֵּאמֹֽר: בְּיוֹם־הַחֹ֥דֶשׁ הָרִאשׁ֖וֹן בְּאֶחָ֣ד לַחֹ֑דֶשׁ תָּקִ֕ים
[שביעי]

ג אֶת־מִשְׁכַּ֖ן אֹ֥הֶל מוֹעֵֽד: וְשַׂמְתָּ֣ שָׁ֔ם אֵ֖ת אֲר֣וֹן הָעֵד֑וּת וְסַכֹּתָ֥ עַל־הָאָרֹ֖ן

ד אֶת־הַפָּרֹֽכֶת: וְהֵבֵאתָ֣ אֶת־הַשֻּׁלְחָ֔ן וְעָרַכְתָּ֖ אֶת־עֶרְכּ֑וֹ וְהֵבֵאתָ֙ אֶת־

ה הַמְּנֹרָ֔ה וְהַעֲלֵיתָ֖ אֶת־נֵרֹתֶֽיהָ: וְנָתַתָּ֞ה אֶת־מִזְבַּ֤ח הַזָּהָב֙ לִקְטֹ֔רֶת לִפְנֵ֖י אֲר֣וֹן

ו הָעֵדֻ֑ת וְשַׂמְתָּ֛ אֶת־מָסַ֥ךְ הַפֶּ֖תַח לַמִּשְׁכָּֽן: וְנָ֣תַתָּ֔ה אֵ֖ת מִזְבַּ֣ח הָעֹלָ֑ה לִפְנֵ֕י

ז פֶּ֖תַח מִשְׁכַּ֥ן אֹֽהֶל־מוֹעֵֽד: וְנָֽתַתָּ֙ אֶת־הַכִּיֹּ֔ר בֵּֽין־אֹ֥הֶל מוֹעֵ֖ד וּבֵ֣ין הַמִּזְבֵּ֑חַ

ח וְנָתַתָּ֥ שָׁ֖ם מָֽיִם: וְשַׂמְתָּ֥ אֶת־הֶחָצֵ֖ר סָבִ֑יב וְנָ֣תַתָּ֔ אֶת־מָסַ֖ךְ שַׁ֥עַר הֶחָצֵֽר:

ט וְלָקַחְתָּ֙ אֶת־שֶׁ֣מֶן הַמִּשְׁחָ֔ה וּמָשַׁחְתָּ֥ אֶת־הַמִּשְׁכָּ֖ן וְאֶת־כָּל־אֲשֶׁר־בּ֑וֹ

י וְקִדַּשְׁתָּ֥ אֹת֛וֹ וְאֶת־כָּל־כֵּלָ֖יו וְהָ֥יָה קֹֽדֶשׁ: וּמָֽשַׁחְתָּ֛ אֶת־מִזְבַּ֥ח הָעֹלָ֖ה וְאֶת־

יא כָּל־כֵּלָ֑יו וְקִדַּשְׁתָּ֙ אֶת־הַמִּזְבֵּ֔חַ וְהָיָ֥ה הַמִּזְבֵּ֖חַ קֹ֣דֶשׁ קָֽדָשִׁ֑ים: וּמָשַׁחְתָּ֥ אֶת־

יב הַכִּיֹּ֖ר וְאֶת־כַּנּ֑וֹ וְקִדַּשְׁתָּ֖ אֹתֽוֹ: וְהִקְרַבְתָּ֤ אֶֽת־אַֽהֲרֹן֙ וְאֶת־בָּנָ֔יו אֶל־פֶּ֖תַח

יג אֹ֣הֶל מוֹעֵ֑ד וְרָחַצְתָּ֥ אֹתָ֖ם בַּמָּֽיִם: וְהִלְבַּשְׁתָּ֙ אֶֽת־אַֽהֲרֹ֔ן אֵ֖ת בִּגְדֵ֣י הַקֹּ֑דֶשׁ

יד וּמָשַׁחְתָּ֥ אֹת֛וֹ וְקִדַּשְׁתָּ֥ אֹת֖וֹ וְכִהֵ֣ן לִ֑י: וְאֶת־בָּנָ֖יו תַּקְרִ֑יב וְהִלְבַּשְׁתָּ֥ אֹתָ֖ם

טו כֻּתֳּנֹֽת: וּמָשַׁחְתָּ֣ אֹתָ֗ם כַּאֲשֶׁ֤ר מָשַׁ֙חְתָּ֙ אֶת־אֲבִיהֶ֔ם וְכִהֲנ֖וּ לִ֑י וְ֠הָיְתָ֞ה לִֽהְיֹ֙ת

טז לָהֶ֧ם מָשְׁחָתָ֛ם לִכְהֻנַּ֥ת עוֹלָ֖ם לְדֹֽרֹתָֽם: וַיַּ֖עַשׂ מֹשֶׁ֑ה כְּ֠כֹל אֲשֶׁ֨ר צִוָּ֧ה יהו֛ה אֹת֖וֹ כֵּ֥ן עָשָֽׂה:

ששי יז וַיְהִ֞י בַּחֹ֧דֶשׁ הָרִאשׁ֛וֹן בַּשָּׁנָ֥ה הַשֵּׁנִ֖ית בְּאֶחָ֣ד לַחֹ֑דֶשׁ הוּקַ֖ם הַמִּשְׁכָּֽן: וַיָּ֨קֶם מֹשֶׁ֜ה אֶת־הַמִּשְׁכָּ֗ן וַיִּתֵּן֙ אֶת־אֲדָנָ֔יו וַיָּ֙שֶׂם֙

יט אֶת־קְרָשָׁ֔יו וַיִּתֵּ֖ן אֶת־בְּרִיחָ֑יו וַיָּ֖קֶם אֶת־עַמּוּדָֽיו: וַיִּפְרֹ֤שׂ אֶת־הָאֹ֙הֶל֙ עַל־הַמִּשְׁכָּ֔ן וַיָּ֜שֶׂם אֶת־מִכְסֵ֤ה הָאֹ֙הֶל֙ עָלָ֖יו מִלְמָ֑עְלָה כַּאֲשֶׁ֛ר צִוָּ֥ה יהו֖ה אֶת־

כ מֹשֶֽׁה: וַיִּקַּ֞ח וַיִּתֵּ֤ן אֶת־הָֽעֵדֻת֙ אֶל־הָ֣אָרֹ֔ן וַיָּ֥שֶׂם אֶת־הַבַּדִּ֖ים

39:43. He said, "May it be God's will that the *Shechinah* rest upon Your handiwork," and the verse "May the pleasantness of my Lord, our God, be upon us — may He establish our handiwork for us; our handiwork may He establish" (*Psalms* 90:17), from the psalm which he [Moses] had composed (*Rashi*).

40:2. Rosh Chodesh Nissan was the day when the Tabernacle was erected permanently. From then on, it would be disassembled only when the nation traveled. Before

that day, however, Moses performed the procedure of sanctification, during which he erected and dismantled the Tabernacle every day for the seven days before the first of Nissan. During that week, Moses served as the Kohen Gadol, performing the entire inauguration service.

40:17-38. The Tabernacle assumes its holiness. Until every part of the Tabernacle was in place, no individual part had the status of a Tabernacle. For example, until

³⁸ the Gold Altar, the anointment oil, and the incense spices; and the Partition of the entrance of the Tent; ³⁹ the Copper Altar and its copper meshwork, its staves, and all its utensils, the Laver and its base; ⁴⁰ the curtains of the Courtyard, its pillars and its sockets, the Partition of the gate of the Courtyard, its ropes and its pegs, and all the utensils for the service of the Tabernacle of the Tent of Meeting; ⁴¹ the knitted vestments to serve in the Sanctuary, the sacred vestments of Aaron the Kohen, and the vestments of his sons to minister.

Moses approves ⁴² Like everything that HASHEM commanded Moses, so did the Children of Israel perform all the labor. ⁴³ Moses saw the entire work, and behold! — they had done it as HASHEM had commanded, so had they done! And Moses blessed them. *

40

The command to set up the Tabernacle ¹ HASHEM spoke to Moses, saying: ² "On the day of the first new moon, on the first of the month, * you shall erect the Tabernacle, the Tent of Meeting. ³ There you shall place the Ark of Testimony and screen the Ark with the Partition. ⁴ You shall bring the Table and prepare its setting, bring the Menorah and kindle its lamps. ⁵ You shall place the Gold Altar for incense in front of the Ark of Testimony, and emplace the Curtain of the entrance of the Tabernacle. ⁶ You shall place the Burnt-offering Altar in front of the entrance of the Tabernacle, the Tent of Meeting. ⁷ You shall place the Laver between the Tent of Meeting and the Altar, and you shall put water there. ⁸ You shall emplace the Courtyard all around, and emplace the Curtain at the gate of the Courtyard. ⁹ You shall take the anointment oil and anoint the Tabernacle and everything that is in it, sanctify it and all its utensils, and it shall become holy. ¹⁰ You shall anoint the Burnt-offering Altar and all its utensils; you shall sanctify the Altar, and the Altar shall become holy of holies. ¹¹ You shall anoint the Laver and its stand, and sanctify it.

¹² "You shall bring Aaron and his sons near to the entrance of the Tent of Meeting, and immerse them in water. ¹³ You shall dress Aaron in the sacred vestments and anoint him; you shall sanctify him and he shall minister to Me. ¹⁴ And his sons you shall bring near and dress them in tunics. ¹⁵ You shall anoint them as you had anointed their father and they shall minister to Me, and so it shall be that their anointment shall be for eternal priesthood for their generations." ¹⁶ Moses did according to everything that HASHEM commanded him, so he did.

The Tabernacle is erected ¹⁷ It was in the first month of the second year on the first of the month that the Tabernacle was erected. ¹⁸ Moses erected the Tabernacle; he put down its sockets and emplaced its planks and inserted its bars, and erected its pillars. ¹⁹ He spread the Tent over the Tabernacle and put the Cover of the Tent on it from above, as HASHEM had commanded Moses.

²⁰ He took and placed the Testimony into the Ark and inserted the staves

---

the curtains enclosing the Courtyard were in place, offerings could not be brought on the Altar. This passage, therefore, describes how Moses actually erected the Tabernacle and put all of its parts in place.

The process was climaxed by as phenomenal an occurrence as human beings have ever been able to bring about: The glory of God rested upon the handiwork of Man, in full sight of every Jewish man, woman, and child. Now, they would see *their* Tabernacle enveloped in holiness, the Tabernacle that was built with *their* gifts, made by *their* hands, erected by *their* prophet, made possible by *their* repentance, assuring them that God's Presence would forever remain in *their* midst — if they would but continue to make it welcome.

כא עַל־הָאָרֹן וַיִּתֵּן אֶת־הַכַּפֹּרֶת עַל־הָאָרֹן מִלְמָעְלָה: וַיָּבֵא אֶת־הָאָרֹן אֶל־הַמִּשְׁכָּן וַיָּשֶׂם אֵת פָּרֹכֶת הַמָּסָךְ וַיָּסֶךְ עַל אֲרוֹן הָעֵדוּת כַּאֲשֶׁר צִוָּה יהוה כב אֶת־מֹשֶׁה: וַיִּתֵּן אֶת־הַשֻּׁלְחָן בְּאֹהֶל מוֹעֵד עַל יֶרֶךְ כג הַמִּשְׁכָּן צָפֹנָה מִחוּץ לַפָּרֹכֶת: וַיַּעֲרֹךְ עָלָיו עֵרֶךְ לֶחֶם לִפְנֵי יהוה כַּאֲשֶׁר כד צִוָּה יהוה אֶת־מֹשֶׁה: וַיָּשֶׂם אֶת־הַמְּנֹרָה בְּאֹהֶל כה מוֹעֵד נֹכַח הַשֻּׁלְחָן עַל יֶרֶךְ הַמִּשְׁכָּן נֶגְבָּה: וַיַּעַל הַנֵּרֹת לִפְנֵי יהוה כַּאֲשֶׁר כו צִוָּה יהוה אֶת־מֹשֶׁה: וַיָּשֶׂם אֶת־מִזְבַּח הַזָּהָב כז בְּאֹהֶל מוֹעֵד לִפְנֵי הַפָּרֹכֶת: וַיַּקְטֵר עָלָיו קְטֹרֶת סַמִּים כַּאֲשֶׁר צִוָּה יהוה כח אֶת־מֹשֶׁה: וַיָּשֶׂם אֶת־מָסַךְ הַפֶּתַח לַמִּשְׁכָּן:

כט וְאֵת מִזְבַּח הָעֹלָה שָׂם פֶּתַח מִשְׁכַּן אֹהֶל־מוֹעֵד וַיַּעַל עָלָיו אֶת־הָעֹלָה ל וְאֶת־הַמִּנְחָה כַּאֲשֶׁר צִוָּה יהוה אֶת־מֹשֶׁה: וַיָּשֶׂם אֶת־הַכִּיֹּר בֵּין־אֹהֶל מוֹעֵד וּבֵין הַמִּזְבֵּחַ וַיִּתֵּן שָׁמָּה מַיִם לְרָחְצָה: לא-לב וְרָחֲצוּ מִמֶּנּוּ מֹשֶׁה וְאַהֲרֹן וּבָנָיו אֶת־יְדֵיהֶם וְאֶת־רַגְלֵיהֶם: בְּבֹאָם אֶל־אֹהֶל מוֹעֵד וּבְקָרְבָתָם אֶל־הַמִּזְבֵּחַ יִרְחָצוּ כַּאֲשֶׁר צִוָּה יהוה אֶת־ לג מֹשֶׁה: וַיָּקֶם אֶת־הֶחָצֵר סָבִיב לַמִּשְׁכָּן וְלַמִּזְבֵּחַ וַיִּתֵּן אֶת־מָסַךְ שַׁעַר הֶחָצֵר וַיְכַל מֹשֶׁה אֶת־הַמְּלָאכָה:

לד-לה וַיְכַס הֶעָנָן אֶת־אֹהֶל מוֹעֵד וּכְבוֹד יהוה מָלֵא אֶת־הַמִּשְׁכָּן: וְלֹא־יָכֹל מֹשֶׁה לָבוֹא אֶל־אֹהֶל מוֹעֵד כִּי־שָׁכַן עָלָיו הֶעָנָן וּכְבוֹד יהוה מָלֵא אֶת־ לו הַמִּשְׁכָּן: וּבְהֵעָלוֹת הֶעָנָן מֵעַל הַמִּשְׁכָּן יִסְעוּ בְּנֵי יִשְׂרָאֵל בְּכֹל מַסְעֵיהֶם: לז-לח וְאִם־לֹא יֵעָלֶה הֶעָנָן וְלֹא יִסְעוּ עַד־יוֹם הֵעָלֹתוֹ: כִּי עֲנַן יהוה עַל־ הַמִּשְׁכָּן יוֹמָם וְאֵשׁ תִּהְיֶה לַיְלָה בּוֹ לְעֵינֵי כָל־בֵּית־יִשְׂרָאֵל בְּכָל־ מַסְעֵיהֶם:

Haftaras
Pekudei:
p. 820

For
special
Sabbaths,
see
pp. x-xi

It is customary for the congregation followed by the reader to proclaim:

חֲזַק! חֲזַק! וְנִתְחַזֵּק!

סְכוּם פְּסוּקֵי דְּסֵפֶר וְאֵלֶּה שְׁמוֹת אֶלֶף מָאתַיִם וְתִשְׁעָה. אַרְ״ט סִימָן.

40:35. The glory of God was so intense that Moses could not enter, but a later verse (*Numbers* 7:89) states that he would regularly enter the Tent of Meeting. The second half of this verse resolves the contradiction: *for the cloud rested upon it* . . . Thus, when the cloud rested upon the Tabernacle, Moses *could not enter,* but when the cloud on the Ark, and he placed the Cover on the Ark from above. [21] He brought the Ark into the Tabernacle and emplaced the Partition sheltering the Ark of Testimony, as HASHEM had commanded Moses.

[22] He put the Table in the Tent of Meeting on the north side of the Tabernacle, outside the Partition. [23] He prepared on it the setting of bread before HASHEM, as HASHEM had commanded Moses.

[24] He placed the Menorah in the Tent of Meeting, opposite the Table, on the south side of the Tabernacle. [25] He kindled the lamps before HASHEM, as HASHEM had commanded Moses.

[26] He placed the Gold Altar in the Tent of Meeting, in front of the Partition. [27] Upon it he caused incense spices to go up in smoke, as HASHEM had commanded Moses.

[28] He emplaced the Curtain of the entrance of the Tabernacle. [29] He placed the Burnt-offering Altar at the entrance of the Tent of Meeting, and brought up upon it the elevation-offering and the meal-offering, as HASHEM had commanded Moses.

[30] He emplaced the Laver between the Tent of Meeting and the Altar, and there he put water for washing. [31] Moses, Aaron, and his sons washed their hands and feet from it. [32] When they came to the Tent of Meeting and when they approached the Altar they would wash, as HASHEM had commanded Moses.

[33] He erected the Courtyard all around the Tabernacle and the Altar, and he emplaced the curtain of the gate of the Courtyard. So Moses completed the work.

God's glory
fills the
Tabernacle
[34] The cloud covered the Tent of Meeting, and the glory of HASHEM filled the Tabernacle. [35] Moses could not enter* the Tent of Meeting, for the cloud rested upon it, and the glory of HASHEM filled the Tabernacle. [36] When the cloud was raised up from upon the Tabernacle, the Children of Israel would embark on all their journeys. [37] If the cloud did not rise up, they would not embark, until the day it rose up. [38] For the cloud of HASHEM would be on the Tabernacle by day, and fire would be on it at night, before the eyes of all of the House of Israel throughout their journeys.

It is customary for the congregation followed by the reader to proclaim:
"Chazak! Chazak! Venischazeik!
(Be strong! Be strong! And may we be strengthened!)"

---

lifted, he could enter to speak to God (*Rashi,* from *Toras Kohanim*). In the plain meaning of the verses, however, when God wished to speak to Moses, He summoned him and Moses stood outside the Tent of Meeting, so that he did not enter the place that was filled with God's glory (*Ramban*).

THE TEN COMMANDMENTS WITH THE *TROP* (CANTILLATION NOTES) USED BY THE READER FOR THE PUBLIC TORAH READING ON THE SABBATH AND ON SHAVUOS (see page 182).

אָנֹכִי יהוָה אֱלֹהֶיךָ אֲשֶׁר הוֹצֵאתִיךָ מֵאֶרֶץ מִצְרַיִם מִבֵּית עֲבָדִים לֹא
יִהְיֶה־לְךָ אֱלֹהִים אֲחֵרִים עַל־פָּנָי לֹא תַעֲשֶׂה־לְךָ פֶסֶל ׀ וְכָל־תְּמוּנָה
אֲשֶׁר בַּשָּׁמַיִם ׀ מִמַּעַל וַאֲשֶׁר בָּאָרֶץ מִתָּחַת וַאֲשֶׁר בַּמַּיִם ׀ מִתַּחַת
לָאָרֶץ לֹא־תִשְׁתַּחֲוֶה לָהֶם וְלֹא תָעָבְדֵם כִּי אָנֹכִי יהוָה אֱלֹהֶיךָ אֵל
קַנָּא פֹּקֵד עֲוֺן אָבֹת עַל־בָּנִים עַל־שִׁלֵּשִׁים וְעַל־רִבֵּעִים לְשֹׂנְאָי וְעֹשֶׂה
חֶסֶד לַאֲלָפִים לְאֹהֲבַי וּלְשֹׁמְרֵי מִצְוֺתָי: לֹא תִשָּׂא
אֶת־שֵׁם־יהוָה אֱלֹהֶיךָ לַשָּׁוְא כִּי לֹא יְנַקֶּה יהוָה אֵת אֲשֶׁר־יִשָּׂא אֶת־
שְׁמוֹ לַשָּׁוְא:
זָכוֹר אֶת־יוֹם הַשַּׁבָּת לְקַדְּשׁוֹ שֵׁשֶׁת יָמִים תַּעֲבֹד וְעָשִׂיתָ כָּל־
מְלַאכְתֶּךָ וְיוֹם הַשְּׁבִיעִי שַׁבָּת ׀ לַיהוָה אֱלֹהֶיךָ לֹא תַעֲשֶׂה כָל־
מְלָאכָה אַתָּה וּבִנְךָ־וּבִתֶּךָ עַבְדְּךָ וַאֲמָתְךָ וּבְהֶמְתֶּךָ וְגֵרְךָ אֲשֶׁר
בִּשְׁעָרֶיךָ כִּי שֵׁשֶׁת־יָמִים עָשָׂה יהוה אֶת־הַשָּׁמַיִם וְאֶת־הָאָרֶץ אֶת־
הַיָּם וְאֶת־כָּל־אֲשֶׁר־בָּם וַיָּנַח בַּיּוֹם הַשְּׁבִיעִי עַל־כֵּן בֵּרַךְ יהוָה אֶת־
יוֹם הַשַּׁבָּת וַיְקַדְּשֵׁהוּ:   כַּבֵּד אֶת־אָבִיךָ וְאֶת־אִמֶּךָ לְמַעַן
יַאֲרִכוּן יָמֶיךָ עַל הָאֲדָמָה אֲשֶׁר־יהוָה אֱלֹהֶיךָ נֹתֵן לָךְ:   לֹא
תִּרְצָח: לֹא תִּנְאָף: לֹא תִּגְנֹב: לֹא־תַעֲנֶה
בְרֵעֲךָ עֵד שָׁקֶר: לֹא תַחְמֹד בֵּית רֵעֶךָ   לֹא־תַחְמֹד
אֵשֶׁת רֵעֶךָ וְעַבְדּוֹ וַאֲמָתוֹ וְשׁוֹרוֹ וַחֲמֹרוֹ וְכֹל אֲשֶׁר לְרֵעֶךָ:

Leviticus ויקרא

*I*n the lexicon of the Talmudic Sages, the Book of Leviticus is called *Toras Kohanim,* the Torah of the Kohanim, or priests, because most of the Book deals with the laws of the Temple service and other laws relating to the priests and their responsibilities.

The opening chapters of the Book deal almost exclusively with animal *"korbanos,"* a word that is commonly translated as either sacrifices or offerings, but the truth is that the English language does not have a word that accurately expresses the concept of a korban. The word *"sacrifice"* implies that the person bringing it is expected to deprive himself of something valuable — but God finds no joy in His children's anguish or deprivation. *"Offering"* is more positive and closer to the mark — indeed, we use it in our translation — but it too falls far short of the Hebrew korban. Does God require our gifts to appease Him or assuage His anger? And if He did, of what significance is a bull or lamb to Him? *"If you have acted righteously, what have you given Him?"* (Job 35:7); God does not become enriched by man's largess.

The root of the word korban is קרב, to come near. The person bringing an offering comes closer to God; he elevates his level of spirituality. That is the true meaning of the word and the significance of the act. For modern man — who has been weaned on the delusion that anything not measurable or replicable is unworthy of serious consideration, and who, after all, is the product of over nineteen centuries without the Temple — the notion of animal offerings seems bizarre, even primitive. However, let us imagine ourselves among our ancestors when the first Kohanim brought their first offerings in their newly-built Tabernacle. There was a palpable recognition of God's glory resting upon their handiwork, and a miraculous Heavenly fire descending to consume the offerings. Could they have doubted the efficacy of the service? Would we have felt otherwise if we had been there too?

The commentators offer various rational and meta-rational explanations for the offerings (see Overview to ArtScroll Vayikra/ Leviticus). Without attempting to more than barely scratch the surface, we briefly summarize one thought: Wherever the Torah speaks of the offerings, it uses the Four-letter Name of God that signifies His mercy. The offerings are the means He gives us to rejuvenate ourselves, to provide us a means to bring elevation and purity into our lives. It is when man serves God this way that He finds the offering to be *"a satisfying aroma,"* meaning, as the Sages explain, that God says, as it were, *"I have commanded and My will has been done."*

פרשת ויקרא

א   א־ב וַיִּקְרָא* אֶל־מֹשֶׁה וַיְדַבֵּר יהוה אֵלָיו מֵאֹהֶל מוֹעֵד לֵאמֹר: דַּבֵּר אֶל־בְּנֵי
יִשְׂרָאֵל וְאָמַרְתָּ אֲלֵהֶם אָדָם כִּי־יַקְרִיב מִכֶּם קָרְבָּן לַיהוה מִן־הַבְּהֵמָה
ג מִן־הַבָּקָר וּמִן־הַצֹּאן תַּקְרִיבוּ אֶת־קָרְבַּנְכֶם: אִם־עֹלָה קָרְבָּנוֹ מִן־הַבָּקָר
זָכָר תָּמִים יַקְרִיבֶנּוּ אֶל־פֶּתַח אֹהֶל מוֹעֵד יַקְרִיב אֹתוֹ לִרְצֹנוֹ לִפְנֵי יהוה:
ד־ה וְסָמַךְ יָדוֹ עַל רֹאשׁ הָעֹלָה וְנִרְצָה לוֹ לְכַפֵּר עָלָיו: וְשָׁחַט אֶת־בֶּן הַבָּקָר
לִפְנֵי יהוה וְהִקְרִיבוּ בְּנֵי אַהֲרֹן הַכֹּהֲנִים אֶת־הַדָּם וְזָרְקוּ אֶת־הַדָּם עַל־
ו הַמִּזְבֵּחַ סָבִיב אֲשֶׁר־פֶּתַח אֹהֶל מוֹעֵד: וְהִפְשִׁיט אֶת־הָעֹלָה וְנִתַּח אֹתָהּ
ז לִנְתָחֶיהָ: וְנָתְנוּ בְּנֵי אַהֲרֹן הַכֹּהֵן אֵשׁ עַל־הַמִּזְבֵּחַ וְעָרְכוּ עֵצִים עַל־
ח הָאֵשׁ: וְעָרְכוּ בְּנֵי אַהֲרֹן הַכֹּהֲנִים אֵת הַנְּתָחִים אֶת־הָרֹאשׁ וְאֶת־הַפָּדֶר
ט עַל־הָעֵצִים אֲשֶׁר עַל־הָאֵשׁ אֲשֶׁר עַל־הַמִּזְבֵּחַ: וְקִרְבּוֹ וּכְרָעָיו יִרְחַץ
בַּמָּיִם וְהִקְטִיר הַכֹּהֵן אֶת־הַכֹּל הַמִּזְבֵּחָה עֹלָה אִשֵּׁה רֵיחַ־נִיחֹחַ
י לַיהוה: וְאִם־מִן־הַצֹּאן קָרְבָּנוֹ מִן־הַכְּשָׂבִים אוֹ מִן־הָעִזִּים
יא לְעֹלָה זָכָר תָּמִים יַקְרִיבֶנּוּ: וְשָׁחַט אֹתוֹ עַל יֶרֶךְ הַמִּזְבֵּחַ צָפֹנָה לִפְנֵי יהוה
יב וְזָרְקוּ בְּנֵי אַהֲרֹן הַכֹּהֲנִים אֶת־דָּמוֹ עַל־הַמִּזְבֵּחַ סָבִיב: וְנִתַּח אֹתוֹ לִנְתָחָיו
וְאֶת־רֹאשׁוֹ וְאֶת־פִּדְרוֹ וְעָרַךְ הַכֹּהֵן אֹתָם עַל־הָעֵצִים אֲשֶׁר עַל־הָאֵשׁ
יג אֲשֶׁר עַל־הַמִּזְבֵּחַ: וְהַקֶּרֶב וְהַכְּרָעַיִם יִרְחַץ בַּמָּיִם וְהִקְרִיב הַכֹּהֵן אֶת־
הַכֹּל וְהִקְטִיר הַמִּזְבֵּחָה עֹלָה הוּא אִשֵּׁה רֵיחַ נִיחֹחַ לַיהוה:
יד   וְאִם מִן־הָעוֹף עֹלָה קָרְבָּנוֹ לַיהוה וְהִקְרִיב מִן־הַתֹּרִים אוֹ מִן־בְּנֵי הַיּוֹנָה
טו אֶת־קָרְבָּנוֹ: וְהִקְרִיבוֹ הַכֹּהֵן אֶל־הַמִּזְבֵּחַ וּמָלַק אֶת־רֹאשׁוֹ וְהִקְטִיר
טז הַמִּזְבֵּחָה וְנִמְצָה דָמוֹ עַל קִיר הַמִּזְבֵּחַ: וְהֵסִיר אֶת־מֻרְאָתוֹ בְּנֹצָתָהּ
יז וְהִשְׁלִיךְ אֹתָהּ אֵצֶל הַמִּזְבֵּחַ קֵדְמָה אֶל־מְקוֹם הַדָּשֶׁן: וְשִׁסַּע אֹתוֹ בִכְנָפָיו
לֹא יַבְדִּיל וְהִקְטִיר אֹתוֹ הַכֹּהֵן הַמִּזְבֵּחָה עַל־הָעֵצִים אֲשֶׁר עַל־הָאֵשׁ
עֹלָה הוּא אִשֵּׁה רֵיחַ נִיחֹחַ לַיהוה: וְנֶפֶשׁ כִּי־תַקְרִיב קָרְבַּן
ב   א מִנְחָה לַיהוה סֹלֶת יִהְיֶה קָרְבָּנוֹ וְיָצַק עָלֶיהָ שֶׁמֶן וְנָתַן עָלֶיהָ לְבֹנָה:
ב וֶהֱבִיאָהּ אֶל־בְּנֵי אַהֲרֹן הַכֹּהֲנִים וְקָמַץ מִשָּׁם מְלֹא קֻמְצוֹ מִסָּלְתָּהּ
וּמִשַּׁמְנָהּ עַל כָּל־לְבֹנָתָהּ וְהִקְטִיר הַכֹּהֵן אֶת־אַזְכָּרָתָהּ הַמִּזְבֵּחָה אִשֵּׁה
ג רֵיחַ נִיחֹחַ לַיהוה: וְהַנּוֹתֶרֶת מִן־הַמִּנְחָה לְאַהֲרֹן וּלְבָנָיו קֹדֶשׁ קָדָשִׁים

⋗ **Parashas Vayikra**

1:1. So great and awesome was the glory of God that covered the new Tabernacle that even Moses was afraid to enter until God "called" [to reassure him that the Tabernacle had been built to benefit Israel] (*Ramban*, et al.).

1:2. From this introduction to the subject of animal-offerings, the Sages derive many laws regarding animals that are ineligible for the Altar (see *Rashi* and *Sifra*).

    The common translation, *sacrifice*, does not capture the essence of the word קָרְבָּן, *offering*, whose root is קרב,

coming near, because an offering is the means to bring us closer to God and to elevate ourselves (*R' Hirsch*).

1:3. A burnt-offering may be brought by one who has intentionally committed a sin for which the Torah does not prescribe a punishment, one who failed to perform a positive commandment, one who had sinful thoughts, and by everyone who comes to Jerusalem for the Three Pilgrimage Festivals. Similarly, it may be brought by anyone who wishes to raise his spiritual level.

1:7. Even though a Heavenly fire was always on the Altar

PARASHAS VAYIKRA

1

*General rules
of offerings*

(See Appendix B,
charts 6-7)

¹ **H**e called to Moses, * and HASHEM spoke to him from the Tent of Meeting, saying: ² Speak to the Children of Israel and say to them: When a man among you brings an offering to HASHEM: from animals — from the cattle or from the flock shall you bring your offering. *

³ If one's offering is a burnt-offering from the cattle, he shall offer an unblemished male; he shall bring it to the entrance of the Tent of Meeting, voluntarily, before HASHEM. ⁴ He shall lean his hands upon the head of the burnt-offering; and it shall become acceptable for him, to atone for him. ⁵ He shall slaughter the bull before HASHEM; the sons of Aaron, the Kohanim, shall bring the blood and throw the blood on the Altar, all around — which is at the entrance of the Tent of Meeting. ⁶ He shall skin the burnt-offering and cut it into its pieces. ⁷ The sons of Aaron the Kohen shall place fire on the Altar, * and arrange wood on the fire. ⁸ The sons of Aaron, the Kohanim, shall arrange the pieces, the head and the fats, on the wood that is on the fire, that is on the Altar. ⁹ He shall wash its innards and its feet with water; and the Kohen shall cause it all to go up in smoke on the Altar — a burnt-offering, a fire-offering, a satisfying aroma to HASHEM.

*Burnt-
offerings
from sheep
and goats*

¹⁰ And if one's offering is from the flock, from the sheep or from the goats, for a burnt-offering: he shall offer an unblemished male. ¹¹ He shall slaughter it at the northern side of the Altar before HASHEM; and the sons of Aaron, the Kohanim, shall throw its blood on the Altar, all around. ¹² He shall cut it into its pieces, its head, and its fats. The Kohen shall arrange them on the wood that is on the fire that is on the Altar. ¹³ He shall wash the innards and the feet in water; the Kohen shall bring it all and cause it to go up in smoke on the Altar — it is a burnt-offering, a fire-offering, a satisfying aroma to HASHEM.

*Burnt-
offering
from fowl*
(See Appendix B,
chart 8)

¹⁴ If one's offering to HASHEM is a burnt-offering of fowl, * he shall bring his offering from turtledoves or from young doves. ¹⁵ The Kohen shall bring it to the Altar, nip * its head, and cause it to go up in smoke on the Altar, having pressed out its blood on the Altar's wall. ¹⁶ He shall remove its crop with its feathers, and he shall throw it near the Altar toward the east, to the place of the ashes. ¹⁷ He shall split it — with its feathers — he need not sever it; the Kohen shall cause it to go up in smoke on the Altar, on the wood that is on the fire — it is a burnt-offering, a fire-offering, a satisfying aroma to HASHEM.

2

*Fine flour
offering*
(See Appendix B,
chart 9)

¹ **W**hen a person offers a meal-offering * to HASHEM, his offering shall be of fine flour; he shall pour oil upon it and place frankincense upon it. ² He shall bring it to the sons of Aaron, the Kohanim, one of whom shall scoop his threefingersful from it, from its fine flour and from its oil, as well as all its frankincense; and the Kohen shall cause its memorial portion to go up in smoke upon the Altar — a fire-offering, a satisfying aroma to HASHEM. ³ The remnant of the meal-offering is for Aaron and his sons; most holy,

---

(9:24), the Kohanim are commanded to add fire of secular origin (*Rashi; Sifra*).

1:14. As long as one serves God according to his ability, his offering — even an inexpensive bird — is appreciated and rewarded.

1:15. "Nipping" refers to a unique method of slaughter performed on fowl-offerings with the Kohen's fingernail

instead of a knife. Ordinary fowl slaughtered by this method are forbidden as food.

2:1-10. A meal-offering consists of nothing more than *flour, oil, and frankincense* (with water added in most cases) and is most likely brought by a very poor person. Because he extends himself to bring an offering despite his poverty, it is as if he had given his own נֶפֶשׁ, soul.

ד מֵאִשֵּׁי יְהוָה: וְכִי תַקְרִב קָרְבַּן מִנְחָה מַאֲפֵה תַנּוּר סֹלֶת חַלּוֹת

ה מַצֹּת בְּלוּלֹת בַּשֶּׁמֶן וּרְקִיקֵי מַצּוֹת מְשֻׁחִים בַּשָּׁמֶן: וְאִם־

ו מִנְחָה עַל־הַמַּחֲבַת קָרְבָּנֶךָ סֹלֶת בְּלוּלָה בַשֶּׁמֶן מַצָּה תִהְיֶה: פָּתוֹת אֹתָהּ

ז פִּתִּים וְיָצַקְתָּ עָלֶיהָ שָׁמֶן מִנְחָה הִוא: וְאִם־מִנְחַת מַרְחֶשֶׁת   *שלישי*

ח קָרְבָּנֶךָ סֹלֶת בַּשֶּׁמֶן תֵּעָשֶׂה: וְהֵבֵאתָ אֶת־הַמִּנְחָה אֲשֶׁר יֵעָשֶׂה מֵאֵלֶּה

ט לַיהוָה וְהִקְרִיבָהּ אֶל־הַכֹּהֵן וְהִגִּישָׁהּ אֶל־הַמִּזְבֵּחַ: וְהֵרִים הַכֹּהֵן מִן־

הַמִּנְחָה אֶת־אַזְכָּרָתָהּ וְהִקְטִיר הַמִּזְבֵּחָה אִשֵּׁה רֵיחַ נִיחֹחַ לַיהוָה:

יא וְהַנּוֹתֶרֶת מִן־הַמִּנְחָה לְאַהֲרֹן וּלְבָנָיו קֹדֶשׁ קָדָשִׁים מֵאִשֵּׁי יְהוָה: כָּל־

הַמִּנְחָה אֲשֶׁר תַּקְרִיבוּ לַיהוָה לֹא תֵעָשֶׂה חָמֵץ כִּי כָל־שְׂאֹר וְכָל־דְּבַשׁ

יב לֹא־תַקְטִירוּ מִמֶּנּוּ אִשֶּׁה לַיהוָה: קָרְבַּן רֵאשִׁית תַּקְרִיבוּ אֹתָם לַיהוָה

יג וְאֶל־הַמִּזְבֵּחַ לֹא־יַעֲלוּ לְרֵיחַ נִיחֹחַ: וְכָל־קָרְבַּן מִנְחָתְךָ בַּמֶּלַח תִּמְלָח

וְלֹא תַשְׁבִּית מֶלַח בְּרִית אֱלֹהֶיךָ מֵעַל מִנְחָתֶךָ עַל כָּל־קָרְבָּנְךָ תַּקְרִיב

יד מֶלַח: וְאִם־תַּקְרִיב מִנְחַת בִּכּוּרִים לַיהוָה אָבִיב קָלוּי

טו בָּאֵשׁ גֶּרֶשׂ כַּרְמֶל תַּקְרִיב אֵת מִנְחַת בִּכּוּרֶיךָ: וְנָתַתָּ עָלֶיהָ שֶׁמֶן וְשַׂמְתָּ

טז עָלֶיהָ לְבֹנָה מִנְחָה הִוא: וְהִקְטִיר הַכֹּהֵן אֶת־אַזְכָּרָתָהּ מִגִּרְשָׂהּ וּמִשַּׁמְנָהּ

עַל כָּל־לְבֹנָתָהּ אִשֶּׁה לַיהוָה:

ג א וְאִם־זֶבַח שְׁלָמִים קָרְבָּנוֹ אִם מִן־הַבָּקָר הוּא מַקְרִיב אִם־זָכָר אִם־נְקֵבָה   *רביעי*   **ג**

ב תָּמִים יַקְרִיבֶנּוּ לִפְנֵי יְהוָה: וְסָמַךְ יָדוֹ עַל־רֹאשׁ קָרְבָּנוֹ וּשְׁחָטוֹ פֶּתַח אֹהֶל

ג מוֹעֵד וְזָרְקוּ בְּנֵי אַהֲרֹן הַכֹּהֲנִים אֶת־הַדָּם עַל־הַמִּזְבֵּחַ סָבִיב: וְהִקְרִיב

מִזֶּבַח הַשְּׁלָמִים אִשֶּׁה לַיהוָה אֶת־הַחֵלֶב הַמְכַסֶּה אֶת־הַקֶּרֶב וְאֵת כָּל־

ד הַחֵלֶב אֲשֶׁר עַל־הַקֶּרֶב: וְאֵת שְׁתֵּי הַכְּלָיֹת וְאֶת־הַחֵלֶב אֲשֶׁר עֲלֵהֶן אֲשֶׁר

ה עַל־הַכְּסָלִים וְאֶת־הַיֹּתֶרֶת עַל־הַכָּבֵד עַל־הַכְּלָיוֹת יְסִירֶנָּה: וְהִקְטִירוּ

אֹתוֹ בְנֵי־אַהֲרֹן הַמִּזְבֵּחָה עַל־הָעֹלָה אֲשֶׁר עַל־הָעֵצִים אֲשֶׁר עַל־הָאֵשׁ

אִשֵּׁה רֵיחַ נִיחֹחַ לַיהוָה:

ו וְאִם־מִן־הַצֹּאן קָרְבָּנוֹ לְזֶבַח שְׁלָמִים לַיהוָה זָכָר אוֹ נְקֵבָה תָּמִים

ז יַקְרִיבֶנּוּ: אִם־כֶּשֶׂב הוּא־מַקְרִיב אֶת־קָרְבָּנוֹ וְהִקְרִיב אֹתוֹ לִפְנֵי יְהוָה:

ח וְסָמַךְ אֶת־יָדוֹ עַל־רֹאשׁ קָרְבָּנוֹ וְשָׁחַט אֹתוֹ לִפְנֵי אֹהֶל מוֹעֵד וְזָרְקוּ

ט בְּנֵי אַהֲרֹן אֶת־דָּמוֹ עַל־הַמִּזְבֵּחַ סָבִיב: וְהִקְרִיב מִזֶּבַח הַשְּׁלָמִים אִשֶּׁה

לַיהוָה חֶלְבּוֹ הָאַלְיָה תְמִימָה לְעֻמַּת הֶעָצֶה יְסִירֶנָּה וְאֶת־הַחֵלֶב

י הַמְכַסֶּה אֶת־הַקֶּרֶב וְאֵת כָּל־הַחֵלֶב אֲשֶׁר עַל־הַקֶּרֶב: וְאֵת שְׁתֵּי הַכְּלָיֹת

וְאֶת־הַחֵלֶב אֲשֶׁר עֲלֵהֶן אֲשֶׁר עַל־הַכְּסָלִים וְאֶת־הַיֹּתֶרֶת עַל־הַכָּבֵד

2:14-16. This passage refers to the *Omer*, which was brought from the new barley crop and burned on the Altar on the second day of Pesach. Before this offering, no grain of the new crops could be eaten (see 23:9-14).

3:1-17. Peace-offerings are brought voluntarily by a

person or a group of people who are moved to express their love of God and their gratitude for His goodness, and to enhance their closeness to Him. The name is derived from *shalom*, peace, because this offering has the spiritual capacity of increasing peace in the world. Alterna-

from the fire-offerings of HASHEM.

Oven-baked offering   [4] *When you offer a meal-offering that is baked in an oven, it shall be of fine flour: unleavened loaves mixed with oil, or unleavened wafers smeared with oil.*

Pan-baked offering   [5] *If your offering is a meal-offering on the pan, it shall be of fine flour mixed with oil, it shall be unleavened.* [6] *You shall break it into pieces and pour oil upon it — it is a meal-offering.*

Deep-pan offering   [7] *If your offering is a meal-offering in a deep pan, it shall be made of fine flour with oil.* [8] *You shall present to* HASHEM *the meal-offering that will be prepared from these; he shall bring it to the Kohen who shall bring it close to the Altar.*

[9] *The Kohen shall lift up its memorial portion from the meal-offering and cause it to go up in smoke on the Altar — a fire-offering, a satisfying aroma to* HASHEM. [10] *The remnant of the meal-offering is for Aaron and his sons — most holy, from the fire-offerings of* HASHEM.

[11] *Any meal-offering that you offer to* HASHEM *shall not be prepared leavened, for you shall not cause to go up in smoke from any leavening or fruit-honey as a fire-offering to* HASHEM. [12] *You shall offer them as a first-fruit offering to* HASHEM, *but they may not go up upon the Altar for a satisfying aroma.*

Covenant of salt   [13] *You shall salt your every meal-offering with salt; you may not discontinue the salt of your God's covenant from upon your meal-offering — on your every offering shall you offer salt.*

[14] *When you bring a meal-offering of the first grain* * *to* HASHEM: *from ripe ears, parched over fire, ground from plump kernels, shall you offer the meal-offering of your first grain.* [15] *You shall put oil on it and place frankincense on it — a meal-offering.* [16] *The Kohen shall cause its memorial portion to go up in smoke — from its flour and its oil, as well as its frankincense — a fire-offering to* HASHEM.

3

Peace-offering
(See Appendix B, charts 6-7)

[1] *I f his offering is a feast peace-offering,* * *if he offers it from the cattle — whether male or female — unblemished shall he offer it before* HASHEM. [2] *He shall lean his hands upon the head of his offering and slaughter it at the entrance of the Tent of Meeting; the sons of Aaron, the Kohanim, shall throw the blood upon the Altar, all around.* [3] *From the feast peace-offering he shall offer as a fire-offering to* HASHEM: *the fat that covers the innards, and all the fat that is upon the innards;* [4] *and the two kidneys with the fat that is upon them, that is upon the flanks, and he shall remove the diaphragm with the liver, with the kidneys.* [5] *The sons of Aaron shall cause it to go up in smoke on the Altar, besides the burnt-offering that is on the wood that is on the fire — a fire-offering, a satisfying aroma to* HASHEM.

[6] *If his offering to* HASHEM *is a feast peace-offering from the flock — male or female — unblemished shall he offer it.* [7] *If he offers a sheep as his offering, he shall bring it before* HASHEM. [8] *He shall lean his hands upon the head of his offering and slaughter it before the Tent of Meeting; and the sons of Aaron shall throw its blood upon the Altar, all around.* [9] *From the feast peace-offering he shall offer as a fire-offering to* HASHEM *its choicest part — the entire tail — he shall remove it above the kidneys; and the fat that covers the innards and all the fat that is upon the innards;* [10] *and the two kidneys and the fat that is upon them, that is upon the flanks; and he shall remove the diaphragm with the liver,*

---

tively, since the peace-offering has portions for the Altar, the Kohanim, and the owners, its name symbolizes the

peace that results when the legitimate needs of all groups are satisfied.

יא עַל־הַכְּלָיֹ֖ת יְסִירֶ֑נָּה וְהִקְטִירָ֤ם הַכֹּהֵן֙ הַמִּזְבֵּ֔חָה לֶ֥חֶם אִשֶּׁ֖ה לַֽיהֹוָֽה:

יב-יג וְאִם־עֵ֖ז קָרְבָּנ֑וֹ וְהִקְרִיב֖וֹ לִפְנֵ֥י יְהֹוָֽה: וְסָמַ֤ךְ אֶת־יָדוֹ֙ עַל־רֹאשׁ֔וֹ וְשָׁחַ֣ט אֹת֔וֹ

יד לִפְנֵי֙ אֹ֣הֶל מוֹעֵ֔ד וְ֠זָרְק֠וּ בְּנֵ֨י אַֽהֲרֹ֧ן אֶת־דָּמ֛וֹ עַל־הַמִּזְבֵּ֖חַ סָבִֽיב: וְהִקְרִ֤יב

מִמֶּ֨נּוּ֙ קָרְבָּנ֔וֹ אִשֶּׁ֖ה לַֽיהֹוָ֑ה אֶת־הַחֵ֙לֶב֙ הַֽמְכַסֶּ֣ה אֶת־הַקֶּ֔רֶב וְאֵת֙ כָּל־

טו הַחֵ֔לֶב אֲשֶׁ֖ר עַל־הַקֶּ֑רֶב וְאֵת֙ שְׁתֵּ֣י הַכְּלָיֹ֔ת וְאֶת־הַחֵ֙לֶב֙ אֲשֶׁ֣ר עֲלֵהֶ֔ן אֲשֶׁ֖ר

טז עַל־הַכְּסָלִ֑ים וְאֶת־הַיֹּתֶ֙רֶת֙ עַל־הַכָּבֵ֔ד עַל־הַכְּלָיֹ֖ת יְסִירֶֽנָּה: וְהִקְטִירָ֤ם

יז הַכֹּהֵן֙ הַמִּזְבֵּ֔חָה לֶ֤חֶם אִשֶּׁה֙ לְרֵ֣יחַ נִיחֹ֔חַ כָּל־חֵ֖לֶב לַֽיהֹוָֽה: חֻקַּ֤ת עוֹלָם֙

לְדֹרֹ֣תֵיכֶ֔ם בְּכֹ֖ל מֽוֹשְׁבֹֽתֵיכֶ֑ם כָּל־חֵ֥לֶב וְכָל־דָּ֖ם לֹ֥א תֹאכֵֽלוּ:

ד חמישי א-ב וַיְדַבֵּ֥ר יְהֹוָ֖ה אֶל־מֹשֶׁ֥ה לֵּאמֹֽר: דַּבֵּ֞ר אֶל־בְּנֵ֤י יִשְׂרָאֵל֙ לֵאמֹ֔ר נֶ֗פֶשׁ כִּֽי־

תֶחֱטָ֤א בִשְׁגָגָה֙ מִכֹּל֙ מִצְוֺ֣ת יְהֹוָ֔ה אֲשֶׁ֖ר לֹ֣א תֵֽעָשֶׂ֑ינָה וְעָשָׂ֕ה מֵֽאַחַ֖ת

ג מֵהֵֽנָּה: אִ֣ם הַכֹּהֵ֧ן הַמָּשִׁ֛יחַ יֶֽחֱטָ֖א לְאַשְׁמַ֣ת הָעָ֑ם וְהִקְרִ֡יב עַ֣ל חַטָּאתוֹ֩ אֲשֶׁ֨ר

ד חָטָ֜א פַּ֣ר בֶּן־בָּקָ֥ר תָּמִ֛ים לַֽיהֹוָ֖ה לְחַטָּֽאת: וְהֵבִ֣יא אֶת־הַפָּ֗ר אֶל־פֶּ֛תַח אֹ֥הֶל

מוֹעֵ֖ד לִפְנֵ֣י יְהֹוָ֑ה וְסָמַ֤ךְ אֶת־יָדוֹ֙ עַל־רֹ֣אשׁ הַפָּ֔ר וְשָׁחַ֥ט אֶת־הַפָּ֖ר לִפְנֵ֥י

ה יְהֹוָֽה: וְלָקַ֛ח הַכֹּהֵ֥ן הַמָּשִׁ֖יחַ מִדַּ֣ם הַפָּ֑ר וְהֵבִ֥יא אֹת֖וֹ אֶל־אֹ֥הֶל מוֹעֵֽד: וְטָבַ֧ל

הַכֹּהֵ֛ן אֶת־אֶצְבָּע֖וֹ בַּדָּ֑ם וְהִזָּ֨ה מִן־הַדָּ֜ם שֶׁ֤בַע פְּעָמִים֙ לִפְנֵ֣י יְהֹוָ֔ה אֶת־פְּנֵ֖י

ו פָּרֹ֥כֶת הַקֹּֽדֶשׁ: וְנָתַן֩ הַכֹּהֵ֨ן מִן־הַדָּ֜ם עַל־קַ֠רְנ֠וֹת מִזְבַּ֨ח קְטֹ֤רֶת הַסַּמִּים֙ לִפְנֵ֣י

יְהֹוָ֔ה אֲשֶׁ֖ר בְּאֹ֣הֶל מוֹעֵ֑ד וְאֵ֣ת ׀ כָּל־דַּ֣ם הַפָּ֗ר יִשְׁפֹּךְ֙ אֶל־יְסוֹד֙ מִזְבַּ֣ח

ז הָֽעֹלָ֔ה אֲשֶׁר־פֶּ֖תַח אֹ֣הֶל מוֹעֵֽד: וְאֶת־כָּל־חֵ֛לֶב פַּ֥ר הַֽחַטָּ֖את יָרִ֣ים מִמֶּ֑נּוּ

אֶת־הַחֵ֙לֶב֙ הַֽמְכַסֶּ֣ה עַל־הַקֶּ֔רֶב וְאֵת֙ כָּל־הַחֵ֔לֶב אֲשֶׁ֖ר עַל־הַקֶּֽרֶב: וְאֵת֙

ח שְׁתֵּ֣י הַכְּלָיֹ֔ת וְאֶת־הַחֵ֙לֶב֙ אֲשֶׁ֣ר עֲלֵיהֶ֔ן אֲשֶׁ֖ר עַל־הַכְּסָלִ֑ים וְאֶת־הַיֹּתֶ֙רֶת֙

ט עַל־הַכָּבֵ֔ד עַל־הַכְּלָיֹ֖ות יְסִירֶֽנָּה: כַּֽאֲשֶׁ֣ר יוּרַ֔ם מִשּׁ֖וֹר זֶ֣בַח הַשְּׁלָמִ֑ים

י וְהִקְטִירָם֙ הַכֹּהֵ֔ן עַ֖ל מִזְבַּ֣ח הָֽעֹלָֽה: וְאֶת־ע֤וֹר הַפָּר֙ וְאֶת־כָּל־בְּשָׂרוֹ֙ עַל־

יא רֹאשׁ֔וֹ וְעַל־כְּרָעָ֖יו וְקִרְבּ֥וֹ וּפִרְשֽׁוֹ: וְהוֹצִ֣יא אֶת־כָּל־הַ֠פָּ֠ר אֶל־מִח֨וּץ

יב לַֽמַּחֲנֶ֜ה אֶל־מָק֤וֹם טָהוֹר֙ אֶל־שֶׁ֣פֶךְ הַדֶּ֔שֶׁן וְשָׂרַ֥ף אֹת֛וֹ עַל־עֵצִ֖ים בָּאֵ֑שׁ

עַל־שֶׁ֥פֶךְ הַדֶּ֖שֶׁן יִשָּׂרֵֽף:

יג וְאִ֤ם כָּל־עֲדַ֤ת יִשְׂרָאֵל֙ יִשְׁגּ֔וּ וְנֶעְלַ֣ם דָּבָ֔ר מֵֽעֵינֵ֖י הַקָּהָ֑ל וְ֠עָשׂ֠וּ אַחַ֨ת

יד מִכָּל־מִצְוֺ֧ת יְהֹוָ֛ה אֲשֶׁ֥ר לֹֽא־תֵֽעָשֶׂ֖ינָה וְאָשֵֽׁמוּ: וְנֽוֹדְעָה֙ הַֽחַטָּ֔את

אֲשֶׁ֥ר חָֽטְא֖וּ עָלֶ֑יהָ וְהִקְרִ֡יבוּ הַקָּהָל֩ פַּ֨ר בֶּן־בָּקָ֤ר לְחַטָּאת֙ וְהֵבִ֣יאוּ אֹת֔וֹ

טו לִפְנֵ֖י אֹ֣הֶל מוֹעֵֽד: וְ֠סָֽמְכ֠וּ זִקְנֵ֨י הָֽעֵדָ֧ה אֶת־יְדֵיהֶ֛ם עַל־רֹ֥אשׁ הַפָּ֖ר

4:1-5:26. The Torah now lists offerings that are *required* in order to atone for sins, in contrast to the offerings of the previous three chapters that one brings *voluntarily* in order to elevate oneself spiritually.

Sin-offerings atone for deeds that were committed בְּשׁוֹגֵג, *inadvertently*, as a result of *carelessness;* intentional sins require sincere repentance and accidental sins do not require an offering. As *Ramban* (v. 2) points out, even though they were unintentional, such deeds blemish the

soul; for if the sinner had regarded them with the proper gravity, the violations would not have occurred.

4:3-12. The Kohen Gadol, who has been elevated to his office through anointment (*Horayos* 11b), has special responsibility for the spiritual well-being of the nation, so that his sin is treated more gravely than that of others.

4:4. Here, and in the case of the next offering, that of the Sanhedrin (High Court), the bull is brought to the front of the Sanctuary, because it is a source of pride that the *with the kidneys.* [11] *The Kohen shall cause it to go up in smoke on the Altar; it is the food of the fire — for HASHEM.*

[12] *If his offering is a goat, he shall bring it before HASHEM.* [13] *He shall lean his hands upon its head and slaughter it before the Tent of Meeting; and the sons of Aaron shall throw its blood upon the Altar, all around.* [14] *He shall bring his offering from it as a fire-offering to HASHEM: the fat that covers the innards and all the fat that is upon the innards;* [15] *and the two kidneys and the fat that is upon them, that is upon the flanks; and he shall remove the diaphragm with the liver, with the kidneys.* [16] *The Kohen shall cause them to go up in smoke on the Altar — the food of the fire for a satisfying aroma, all the choice parts for HASHEM.* [17] *An eternal decree for your generations in all your dwelling places; you may not consume any fat or any blood.*

4

*Sin-offering
(See Appendix B,
charts 6-7)*

[1] **H**ASHEM *spoke to Moses, saying:* [2] *Speak to the Children of Israel, saying: When a person will sin unintentionally from among all the commandments of HASHEM that may not be done, and he commits one of them.*

*The bull
of the
anointed
Kohen*

[3] *If the anointed Kohen* * will sin, bringing guilt upon the people; for his sin that he committed he shall offer a young bull, unblemished, to HASHEM as a sin-offering.* [4] *He shall bring the bull to the entrance of the Tent of Meeting* * before HASHEM; he shall lean his hands upon the head of the bull, and he shall slaughter the bull before HASHEM.* [5] *The anointed Kohen shall take from the blood of the bull and bring it to the Tent of Meeting.* [6] *The Kohen shall dip his forefinger into the blood; he shall sprinkle some of the blood seven times before HASHEM toward the Curtain of the Holy.* [7] *The Kohen shall put some of the blood on the horns of the Altar where incense is caused to go up in smoke before HASHEM, which is in the Tent of Meeting; and all the [remaining] blood of the bull he shall pour onto the base of the Burnt-offering Altar, which is at the entrance of the Tent of Meeting.* [8] *He shall separate all the fats of the sin-offering bull from it: the fat that covers the innards and all the fat that is upon the innards;* [9] *and the two kidneys and the fat that is upon them, which is upon the flanks; and he shall remove the diaphragm with the liver, with the kidneys —* [10] *just as it would be removed from the feast peace-offering bull; and the Kohen shall cause them to go up in smoke on the Burnt-offering Altar.* [11] *But the hide of the bull and all its flesh with its head and with its feet, and its innards and its waste —* [12] *the entire bull shall he remove to the outside of the camp, to a pure place, to where the ash is poured, and he shall burn it on wood in fire; on the place where the ash is poured shall it be burned.*

*The bull
for a matter
that was
hidden
from the
congregation*

[13] *If the entire assembly of Israel shall err,* * and a matter became obscured from the eyes of the congregation;* * and they commit one from among all the commandments of HASHEM that may not be done, and they become guilty;* [14] *when the sin regarding which they committed becomes known, the congregation shall offer a young bull as a sin-offering, and they shall bring it before the Tent of Meeting.* [15] *The elders of the assembly shall lean their hands upon the head of the bull*

---

nation's most august personages do not hesitate to seek atonement for their sins. This shows that the law applies to the privileged and the common people alike.

4:13-21. This offering applies only if the Great Sanhedrin of seventy-one judges issued a mistaken ruling, as a result of which the majority of the nation unintention-

ally transgressed a serious negative commandment.

4:13. *Sifra* derives hermeneutically that the term כָּל־עֲדַת יִשְׂרָאֵל, *the entire assembly of Israel,* refers to the Great Sanhedrin. Additionally, as the group that charts the lives of the nation through the map of Halachah, the Sanhedrin is the *"eyes" of the congregation.*

טז לִפְנֵי יְהֹוָה וְשָׁחַט אֶת־הַפָּר לִפְנֵי יְהֹוָה: וְהֵבִיא הַכֹּהֵן הַמָּשִׁיחַ מִדַּם הַפָּר

יז אֶל־אֹהֶל מוֹעֵד: וְטָבַל הַכֹּהֵן אֶצְבָּעוֹ מִן־הַדָּם וְהִזָּה שֶׁבַע פְּעָמִים לִפְנֵי

יח יְהֹוָה אֵת פְּנֵי הַפָּרֹכֶת: וּמִן־הַדָּם יִתֵּן ׀ עַל־קַרְנֹת הַמִּזְבֵּחַ אֲשֶׁר לִפְנֵי יְהֹוָה אֲשֶׁר בְּאֹהֶל מוֹעֵד וְאֵת כָּל־הַדָּם יִשְׁפֹּךְ אֶל־יְסוֹד מִזְבַּח הָעֹלָה אֲשֶׁר־

יט-כ פֶּתַח אֹהֶל מוֹעֵד: וְאֵת כָּל־חֶלְבּוֹ יָרִים מִמֶּנּוּ וְהִקְטִיר הַמִּזְבֵּחָה: וְעָשָׂה לַפָּר כַּאֲשֶׁר עָשָׂה לְפַר הַחַטָּאת כֵּן יַעֲשֶׂה־לּוֹ וְכִפֶּר עֲלֵהֶם הַכֹּהֵן וְנִסְלַח

כא לָהֶם: וְהוֹצִיא אֶת־הַפָּר אֶל־מִחוּץ לַמַּחֲנֶה וְשָׂרַף אֹתוֹ כַּאֲשֶׁר שָׂרַף אֵת הַפָּר הָרִאשׁוֹן חַטַּאת הַקָּהָל הוּא:

כב אֲשֶׁר נָשִׂיא יֶחֱטָא וְעָשָׂה אַחַת מִכָּל־מִצְוֹת יְהֹוָה אֱלֹהָיו אֲשֶׁר לֹא־

כג תֵעָשֶׂינָה בִּשְׁגָגָה וְאָשֵׁם: אוֹ־הוֹדַע אֵלָיו חַטָּאתוֹ אֲשֶׁר חָטָא בָּהּ וְהֵבִיא

כד אֶת־קָרְבָּנוֹ שְׂעִיר עִזִּים זָכָר תָּמִים: וְסָמַךְ יָדוֹ עַל־רֹאשׁ הַשָּׂעִיר וְשָׁחַט

כה אֹתוֹ בִּמְקוֹם אֲשֶׁר־יִשְׁחַט אֶת־הָעֹלָה לִפְנֵי יְהֹוָה חַטָּאת הוּא: וְלָקַח הַכֹּהֵן מִדַּם הַחַטָּאת בְּאֶצְבָּעוֹ וְנָתַן עַל־קַרְנֹת מִזְבַּח הָעֹלָה וְאֶת־דָּמוֹ

כו יִשְׁפֹּךְ אֶל־יְסוֹד מִזְבַּח הָעֹלָה: וְאֶת־כָּל־חֶלְבּוֹ יַקְטִיר הַמִּזְבֵּחָה כְּחֵלֶב זֶבַח הַשְּׁלָמִים וְכִפֶּר עָלָיו הַכֹּהֵן מֵחַטָּאתוֹ וְנִסְלַח לוֹ:

ששי

כז וְאִם־נֶפֶשׁ אַחַת תֶּחֱטָא בִשְׁגָגָה מֵעַם הָאָרֶץ בַּעֲשֹׂתָהּ אַחַת מִמִּצְוֹת

כח יְהֹוָה אֲשֶׁר לֹא־תֵעָשֶׂינָה וְאָשֵׁם: אוֹ הוֹדַע אֵלָיו חַטָּאתוֹ אֲשֶׁר חָטָא

כט וְהֵבִיא קָרְבָּנוֹ שְׂעִירַת עִזִּים תְּמִימָה נְקֵבָה עַל־חַטָּאתוֹ אֲשֶׁר חָטָא: וְסָמַךְ

ל אֶת־יָדוֹ עַל רֹאשׁ הַחַטָּאת וְשָׁחַט אֶת־הַחַטָּאת בִּמְקוֹם הָעֹלָה: וְלָקַח הַכֹּהֵן מִדָּמָהּ בְּאֶצְבָּעוֹ וְנָתַן עַל־קַרְנֹת מִזְבַּח הָעֹלָה וְאֶת־כָּל־דָּמָהּ יִשְׁפֹּךְ

לא אֶל־יְסוֹד הַמִּזְבֵּחַ: וְאֶת־כָּל־חֶלְבָּהּ יָסִיר כַּאֲשֶׁר הוּסַר חֵלֶב מֵעַל זֶבַח הַשְּׁלָמִים וְהִקְטִיר הַכֹּהֵן הַמִּזְבֵּחָה לְרֵיחַ נִיחֹחַ לַיהֹוָה וְכִפֶּר עָלָיו הַכֹּהֵן וְנִסְלַח לוֹ:

לב-לג וְאִם־כֶּבֶשׂ יָבִיא קָרְבָּנוֹ לְחַטָּאת נְקֵבָה תְמִימָה יְבִיאֶנָּה: וְסָמַךְ אֶת־יָדוֹ עַל רֹאשׁ הַחַטָּאת וְשָׁחַט אֹתָהּ לְחַטָּאת בִּמְקוֹם אֲשֶׁר יִשְׁחַט אֶת־הָעֹלָה:

לד וְלָקַח הַכֹּהֵן מִדַּם הַחַטָּאת בְּאֶצְבָּעוֹ וְנָתַן עַל־קַרְנֹת מִזְבַּח הָעֹלָה וְאֶת־

לה כָּל־דָּמָהּ יִשְׁפֹּךְ אֶל־יְסוֹד הַמִּזְבֵּחַ: וְאֶת־כָּל־חֶלְבָּהּ יָסִיר כַּאֲשֶׁר יוּסַר חֵלֶב־הַכֶּשֶׂב מִזֶּבַח הַשְּׁלָמִים וְהִקְטִיר הַכֹּהֵן אֹתָם הַמִּזְבֵּחָה עַל אִשֵּׁי יְהֹוָה וְכִפֶּר עָלָיו הַכֹּהֵן עַל־חַטָּאתוֹ אֲשֶׁר־חָטָא וְנִסְלַח לוֹ:

ה

א וְנֶפֶשׁ כִּי־תֶחֱטָא וְשָׁמְעָה קוֹל אָלָה וְהוּא עֵד אוֹ רָאָה אוֹ יָדָע

ב אִם־לוֹא יַגִּיד וְנָשָׂא עֲוֹנוֹ: אוֹ נֶפֶשׁ אֲשֶׁר תִּגַּע בְּכָל־דָּבָר טָמֵא אוֹ

4:22-26. This sin-offering applies only to the king. He must be as subservient as any commoner to the teachings of the nation's Torah authorities.

5:1-13. This passage introduces an offering which varies with the sinner's financial resources. Because of this

variable aspect of the offering, the Sages called it: קָרְבָּן עוֹלֶה וְיוֹרֵד, *an offering that goes up or down.*

5:1. This witness had taken an oath denying knowledge of a case, and then admitted his lie.

5:2-3. Our passage speaks of someone who knew of his

before HASHEM, and someone shall slaughter the bull before HASHEM. ¹⁶ The anointed Kohen shall bring part of the bull's blood to the Tent of Meeting. ¹⁷ The Kohen shall dip his finger from the blood; and he shall sprinkle seven times before HASHEM, toward the Curtain. ¹⁸ He shall put some of the blood upon the horns of the Altar that is before HASHEM, which is in the Tent of Meeting; and all the remaining blood he shall pour onto the base of the Burnt-offering Altar, which is at the entrance of the Tent of Meeting. ¹⁹ He shall separate all its fats from it and cause it to go up in smoke on the Altar. ²⁰ He shall do to the bull as he had done to the sin-offering bull, so shall he do to it; thus shall the Kohen provide them atonement and it shall be forgiven them. ²¹ He shall remove the bull to the outside of the camp and burn it, as he had burned the first bull; it is a sin-offering of the congregation.

He-goat of a ruler
(See Appendix B, charts 6-7)

²² When a ruler* sins, and commits one from among all the commandments of HASHEM, his God, that may not be done — unintentionally — and becomes guilty: ²³ If the sin that he committed becomes known to him, he shall bring his offering, a male goat, unblemished. ²⁴ He shall lean his hands on the head of the goat and he shall slaughter it in the place he would slaughter the burnt-offering before HASHEM; it is a sin-offering. ²⁵ The Kohen shall take from the blood of the sin-offering with his forefinger and place it upon the horns of the Burnt-offering Altar; and he shall pour its [remaining] blood upon the base of the Burnt-offering Altar. ²⁶ And he shall cause all its fats to go up in smoke on the Altar, like the fats of the feast peace-offering; thus shall the Kohen provide him atonement for his sin, and it shall be forgiven him.

Sin-offering of an individual

²⁷ If an individual person from among the people of the land shall sin unintentionally, by committing one of the commandments of HASHEM that may not be done, and he becomes guilty: ²⁸ If his sin that he committed becomes known to him, he shall bring as his offering a she-goat, unblemished, for the sin that he committed. ²⁹ He shall lean his hands upon the head of the sin-offering; and he shall slaughter the sin-offering in the place of the burnt-offering. ³⁰ The Kohen shall take from its blood with his forefinger and place it on the horns of the Burnt-offering Altar; and he shall pour all of its [remaining] blood upon the base of the Altar. ³¹ He shall remove all of its fat, as the fat had been removed from upon the feast peace-offering, and the Kohen shall cause it to go up in smoke on the Altar as a satisfying aroma to HASHEM; and the Kohen shall provide him atonement, and it shall be forgiven him.

³² If he shall bring a sheep as his offering for a sin-offering, he shall bring a female, unblemished. ³³ He shall lean his hands upon the head of the sin-offering; he shall slaughter it for a sin-offering in the place where he would slaughter the burnt-offering. ³⁴ The Kohen shall take from the blood of the sin-offering with his forefinger and place it upon the horns of the Burnt-offering Altar; and he shall pour all its [remaining] blood upon the base of the Altar. ³⁵ And he shall remove all its fat as the fat would be removed from the feast peace-offering sheep, and the Kohen shall cause them to go up in smoke on the Altar, on the fires of HASHEM; and the Kohen shall provide him atonement for his sin that he committed, and it shall be forgiven him.

5

The variable-offering

¹ If a person will sin: If he accepted a demand for an oath, and he is a witness* — either he saw or he knew — if he does not testify, he shall bear his iniquity; ² or if a person will have touched any contaminated object — whether

בְּנִבְלַת חַיָּה טְמֵאָה אוֹ בְּנִבְלַת בְּהֵמָה טְמֵאָה אוֹ בְּנִבְלַת שֶׁרֶץ טָמֵא

ג וְנֶעְלַם מִמֶּנּוּ וְהוּא טָמֵא וְאָשֵׁם: אוֹ כִי יִגַּע בְּטֻמְאַת אָדָם לְכֹל טֻמְאָתוֹ

ד אֲשֶׁר יִטְמָא בָּהּ וְנֶעְלַם מִמֶּנּוּ וְהוּא יָדָע וְאָשֵׁם: אוֹ נֶפֶשׁ כִּי תִשָּׁבַע לְבַטֵּא

בִשְׂפָתַיִם לְהָרַע ׀ אוֹ לְהֵיטִיב לְכֹל אֲשֶׁר יְבַטֵּא הָאָדָם בִּשְׁבֻעָה וְנֶעְלַם

ה מִמֶּנּוּ וְהוּא־יָדָע וְאָשֵׁם לְאַחַת מֵאֵלֶּה: וְהָיָה כִי־יֶאְשַׁם לְאַחַת מֵאֵלֶּה

ו וְהִתְוַדָּה אֲשֶׁר חָטָא עָלֶיהָ: וְהֵבִיא אֶת־אֲשָׁמוֹ לַיהוָה עַל חַטָּאתוֹ אֲשֶׁר

חָטָא נְקֵבָה מִן־הַצֹּאן כִּשְׂבָּה אוֹ־שְׂעִירַת עִזִּים לְחַטָּאת וְכִפֶּר עָלָיו הַכֹּהֵן

ז מֵחַטָּאתוֹ: וְאִם־לֹא תַגִּיעַ יָדוֹ דֵּי שֶׂה וְהֵבִיא אֶת־אֲשָׁמוֹ אֲשֶׁר חָטָא שְׁתֵּי

ח תֹרִים אוֹ־שְׁנֵי בְנֵי־יוֹנָה לַיהוָה אֶחָד לְחַטָּאת וְאֶחָד לְעֹלָה: וְהֵבִיא אֹתָם

אֶל־הַכֹּהֵן וְהִקְרִיב אֶת־אֲשֶׁר לַחַטָּאת רִאשׁוֹנָה וּמָלַק אֶת־רֹאשׁוֹ מִמּוּל

ט עָרְפּוֹ וְלֹא יַבְדִּיל: וְהִזָּה מִדַּם הַחַטָּאת עַל־קִיר הַמִּזְבֵּחַ וְהַנִּשְׁאָר בַּדָּם

י יִמָּצֵה אֶל־יְסוֹד הַמִּזְבֵּחַ חַטָּאת הוּא: וְאֶת־הַשֵּׁנִי יַעֲשֶׂה עֹלָה כַּמִּשְׁפָּט

יא וְכִפֶּר עָלָיו הַכֹּהֵן מֵחַטָּאתוֹ אֲשֶׁר־חָטָא וְנִסְלַח לוֹ: וְאִם־

לֹא תַשִּׂיג יָדוֹ לִשְׁתֵּי תֹרִים אוֹ לִשְׁנֵי בְנֵי־יוֹנָה וְהֵבִיא אֶת־קָרְבָּנוֹ אֲשֶׁר

חָטָא עֲשִׂירִת הָאֵפָה סֹלֶת לְחַטָּאת לֹא־יָשִׂים עָלֶיהָ שֶׁמֶן וְלֹא־יִתֵּן עָלֶיהָ

יב לְבֹנָה כִּי חַטָּאת הִוא: וֶהֱבִיאָהּ אֶל־הַכֹּהֵן וְקָמַץ הַכֹּהֵן ׀ מִמֶּנָּה מְלוֹא

יג קֻמְצוֹ אֶת־אַזְכָּרָתָהּ וְהִקְטִיר הַמִּזְבֵּחָה עַל אִשֵּׁי יהוה חַטָּאת הִוא: וְכִפֶּר

עָלָיו הַכֹּהֵן עַל־חַטָּאתוֹ אֲשֶׁר־חָטָא מֵאַחַת מֵאֵלֶּה וְנִסְלַח לוֹ וְהָיְתָה

יד-טו לַכֹּהֵן כַּמִּנְחָה: וַיְדַבֵּר יהוה אֶל־מֹשֶׁה לֵּאמֹר: נֶפֶשׁ כִּי־

תִמְעֹל מַעַל וְחָטְאָה בִּשְׁגָגָה מִקָּדְשֵׁי יהוה וְהֵבִיא אֶת־אֲשָׁמוֹ לַיהוָה אַיִל

טז תָּמִים מִן־הַצֹּאן בְּעֶרְכְּךָ כֶּסֶף־שְׁקָלִים בְּשֶׁקֶל־הַקֹּדֶשׁ לְאָשָׁם: וְאֵת אֲשֶׁר

חָטָא מִן־הַקֹּדֶשׁ יְשַׁלֵּם וְאֶת־חֲמִישִׁתוֹ יוֹסֵף עָלָיו וְנָתַן אֹתוֹ לַכֹּהֵן וְהַכֹּהֵן

יז יְכַפֵּר עָלָיו בְּאֵיל הָאָשָׁם וְנִסְלַח לוֹ: וְאִם־נֶפֶשׁ כִּי תֶחֱטָא וְעָשְׂתָה אַחַת מִכָּל־מִצְוֹת יהוה אֲשֶׁר לֹא תֵעָשֶׂינָה

יח וְלֹא־יָדַע וְאָשֵׁם וְנָשָׂא עֲוֹנוֹ: וְהֵבִיא אַיִל תָּמִים מִן־הַצֹּאן בְּעֶרְכְּךָ לְאָשָׁם

אֶל־הַכֹּהֵן וְכִפֶּר עָלָיו הַכֹּהֵן עַל שִׁגְגָתוֹ אֲשֶׁר־שָׁגָג וְהוּא לֹא־יָדַע וְנִסְלַח

יט לוֹ: אָשָׁם הוּא אָשֹׁם אָשַׁם לַיהוָה:

כ-כא וַיְדַבֵּר יהוה אֶל־מֹשֶׁה לֵּאמֹר: נֶפֶשׁ כִּי תֶחֱטָא וּמָעֲלָה מַעַל בַּיהוָה וְכִחֵשׁ

כב בַּעֲמִיתוֹ בְּפִקָּדוֹן אוֹ־בִתְשׂוּמֶת יָד אוֹ בְגָזֵל אוֹ עָשַׁק אֶת־עֲמִיתוֹ: אוֹ־מָצָא

---

contamination, but during a temporary lapse in which he forgot about his contamination or the holiness of the Sanctuary or the food, he either entered the Sanctuary or ate the food, and then realized what he had done.

5:14-26. The word חַטָּאת implies *error*; one brings a sin-offering because he "missed the mark" by sinning inadvertently. This is not a matter of the utmost gravity. The term אָשָׁם, however, implies *guilt*. In this passage, the sins are robbery, misappropriation of Temple property, and

the *asham* of one whose liability to bring a sin-offering is in doubt. The latter is serious because the possible sinner is unlikely to feel contrite and repent (*Ramban*).

5:17-19. One who is not sure whether he has committed a sin requiring a sin-offering brings this guilt-offering, which protects him from punishment as long as the doubt remains. If he then learns that he had indeed sinned, he must bring a *chatas* (*Rashi; Kereisos* 26b).

5:20-26. This passage refers to someone who unlawfully

Contamination of the Sanctuary and its sancities

the contaminating* carcass of a beast, the contaminating carcass of an animal, or the contaminating carcass of a creeping animal — but it was concealed from him, and he is contaminated and became guilty; ³ or if he will touch a human contamination in any manner of its contamination through which he can become contaminated but it was concealed from him — and then he knew — and he became guilty; ⁴ or if a person will swear, expressing with his lips to do harm or to do good, anything that a person will express in an oath, but it was concealed from him, and then he knew — and he became guilty regarding one of these matters. ⁵ When one shall become guilty regarding one of these matters, he shall confess what he had sinned. ⁶ He shall bring as his guilt-offering to HASHEM, for his sin that he committed, a female from the flock — a sheep or a goat — for a sin-offering; and the Kohen shall provide him atonement for his sin.

A spoken oath
(See Appendix B, chart 8)

⁷ But if his means are insufficient for a sheep or goat, then he shall bring as his guilt-offering for that which he sinned: two turtledoves or two young doves to HASHEM, one for a sin-offering and one for a burnt-offering. ⁸ He shall bring them to the Kohen, who shall offer first the one that is for a sin-offering; he shall nip its head at its nape, but not separate it. ⁹ He shall sprinkle from the blood of the sin-offering upon the wall of the Altar, and the remainder of the blood he shall press out toward the base of the Altar; it is a sin-offering. ¹⁰ And he shall make the second one a burnt-offering according to [its] law; and the Kohen shall provide him atonement for his sin that he committed, and it shall be forgiven him.

¹¹ But if his means are insufficient for two turtledoves or for two young doves, then he shall bring, as his guilt-offering for that which he sinned, a tenth-ephah of fine flour for a sin-offering; he shall not place oil on it nor shall he put frankincense on it, for it is a sin-offering. ¹² He shall bring it to the Kohen, and the Kohen shall scoop from it his threefingersful as its memorial portion and cause it to go up in smoke on the Altar, on the fires of HASHEM; it is a sin-offering. ¹³ The Kohen shall provide him atonement for the sin that he committed regarding any of these, and it will be forgiven him; and it shall belong to the Kohen, like the meal-offering.

Guilt-offering
(See Appendix B, charts 6-7)

¹⁴ HASHEM spoke* to Moses, saying: ¹⁵ If a person commits treachery and sins unintentionally against HASHEM's holies, he shall bring his guilt-offering to HASHEM, an unblemished ram from the flock, with a value of silver shekels, according to the sacred shekel, for a guilt-offering. ¹⁶ For what he has deprived the Sanctuary he shall make restitution, and add a fifth to it, and give it to the Kohen; then the Kohen shall provide him atonement with the ram of the guilt-offering and it shall be forgiven him.

Guilt-offering in case of doubt

¹⁷ If a person will sin and will commit one of all the commandments of HASHEM that may not be done, but did not know* and became guilty, he shall bear his iniquity; ¹⁸ he shall bring an unblemished ram from the flock, of the proper value, as a guilt-offering — to the Kohen; and the Kohen shall provide him atonement for the inadvertence that he committed unintentionally and he did not know, and it shall be forgiven him. ¹⁹ It is a guilt-offering; he has become guilty before HASHEM.

²⁰ HASHEM spoke* to Moses, saying: ²¹ If a person will sin and commit a treachery against HASHEM by lying to his fellow regarding a pledge or a loan or a robbery; or by defrauding his fellow; ²² or he found a

אַבֵדָה וְכִחֶשׁ בָּהּ וְנִשְׁבַּע עַל־שָׁקֶר עַל־אַחַת מִכֹּל אֲשֶׁר־יַעֲשֶׂה הָאָדָם

כג לַחֲטֹא בָהֵנָּה: וְהָיָה כִּי־יֶחֱטָא וְאָשֵׁם וְהֵשִׁיב אֶת־הַגְּזֵלָה אֲשֶׁר גָּזָל אוֹ אֶת־

הָעֹשֶׁק אֲשֶׁר עָשָׁק אוֹ אֶת־הַפִּקָּדוֹן אֲשֶׁר הָפְקַד אִתּוֹ אוֹ אֶת־הָאֲבֵדָה אֲשֶׁר

כד מָצָא: אוֹ מִכֹּל אֲשֶׁר־יִשָּׁבַע עָלָיו לַשֶּׁקֶר וְשִׁלַּם אֹתוֹ בְּרֹאשׁוֹ וַחֲמִשִׁתָיו

כה יֹסֵף עָלָיו לַאֲשֶׁר הוּא לוֹ יִתְּנֶנּוּ בְּיוֹם אַשְׁמָתוֹ: וְאֶת־אֲשָׁמוֹ יָבִיא לַיהוָה אַיִל

כו תָּמִים מִן־הַצֹּאן בְּעֶרְכְּךָ לְאָשָׁם אֶל־הַכֹּהֵן: וְכִפֶּר עָלָיו הַכֹּהֵן לִפְנֵי יהוה

וְנִסְלַח לוֹ עַל־אַחַת מִכֹּל אֲשֶׁר־יַעֲשֶׂה לְאַשְׁמָה בָהּ: פפפ

מפטיר

Haftaras
Vayikra:
p. 1030

For special
Sabbaths,
see pp. x–xi

קי״ג פסוקים. דעוא״ל סימן. ציו״ה סימן.

פרשת צו

ו

א־ב וַיְדַבֵּר יהוה אֶל־מֹשֶׁה לֵּאמֹר: צַו אֶת־אַהֲרֹן וְאֶת־בָּנָיו לֵאמֹר זֹאת תּוֹרַת

הָעֹלָה הִוא הָעֹלָה עַל מוֹקְדָה עַל־הַמִּזְבֵּחַ כָּל־הַלַּיְלָה עַד־הַבֹּקֶר וְאֵשׁ

ג הַמִּזְבֵּחַ תּוּקַד בּוֹ: וְלָבַשׁ הַכֹּהֵן מִדּוֹ בַד וּמִכְנְסֵי־בַד יִלְבַּשׁ עַל־בְּשָׂרוֹ

וְהֵרִים אֶת־הַדֶּשֶׁן אֲשֶׁר תֹּאכַל הָאֵשׁ אֶת־הָעֹלָה עַל־הַמִּזְבֵּחַ וְשָׂמוֹ אֵצֶל

ד הַמִּזְבֵּחַ: וּפָשַׁט אֶת־בְּגָדָיו וְלָבַשׁ בְּגָדִים אֲחֵרִים וְהוֹצִיא אֶת־הַדֶּשֶׁן אֶל־

ה מִחוּץ לַמַּחֲנֶה אֶל־מָקוֹם טָהוֹר: וְהָאֵשׁ עַל־הַמִּזְבֵּחַ תּוּקַד־בּוֹ לֹא תִכְבֶּה

וּבִעֵר עָלֶיהָ הַכֹּהֵן עֵצִים בַּבֹּקֶר בַּבֹּקֶר וְעָרַךְ עָלֶיהָ הָעֹלָה וְהִקְטִיר עָלֶיהָ

ו־ז חֶלְבֵי הַשְּׁלָמִים: אֵשׁ תָּמִיד תּוּקַד עַל־הַמִּזְבֵּחַ לֹא תִכְבֶּה: וְזֹאת

ח תּוֹרַת הַמִּנְחָה הַקְרֵב אֹתָהּ בְּנֵי־אַהֲרֹן לִפְנֵי יהוה אֶל־פְּנֵי הַמִּזְבֵּחַ: וְהֵרִים

מִמֶּנּוּ בְּקֻמְצוֹ מִסֹּלֶת הַמִּנְחָה וּמִשַּׁמְנָהּ וְאֵת כָּל־הַלְּבֹנָה אֲשֶׁר עַל־

ט הַמִּנְחָה וְהִקְטִיר הַמִּזְבֵּחַ רֵיחַ נִיחֹחַ אַזְכָּרָתָהּ לַיהוה: וְהַנּוֹתֶרֶת מִמֶּנָּה

יֹאכְלוּ אַהֲרֹן וּבָנָיו מַצּוֹת תֵּאָכֵל בְּמָקוֹם קָדֹשׁ בַּחֲצַר אֹהֶל־מוֹעֵד

י יֹאכְלוּהָ: לֹא תֵאָפֶה חָמֵץ חֶלְקָם נָתַתִּי אֹתָהּ מֵאִשָּׁי קֹדֶשׁ קָדָשִׁים הִוא

יא כַּחַטָּאת וְכָאָשָׁם: כָּל־זָכָר בִּבְנֵי אַהֲרֹן יֹאכְלֶנָּה חָק־עוֹלָם לְדֹרֹתֵיכֶם

מֵאִשֵּׁי יהוה כֹּל אֲשֶׁר־יִגַּע בָּהֶם יִקְדָּשׁ:

יב־יג וַיְדַבֵּר יהוה אֶל־מֹשֶׁה לֵּאמֹר: זֶה קָרְבַּן אַהֲרֹן וּבָנָיו אֲשֶׁר־יַקְרִיבוּ לַיהוה

בְּיוֹם הִמָּשַׁח אֹתוֹ עֲשִׂירִת הָאֵפָה סֹלֶת מִנְחָה תָּמִיד מַחֲצִיתָהּ בַּבֹּקֶר

יד וּמַחֲצִיתָהּ בָּעָרֶב: עַל־מַחֲבַת בַּשֶּׁמֶן תֵּעָשֶׂה מֻרְבֶּכֶת תְּבִיאֶנָּה תֻּפִינֵי

טו מִנְחַת פִּתִּים תַּקְרִיב רֵיחַ־נִיחֹחַ לַיהוה: וְהַכֹּהֵן הַמָּשִׁיחַ תַּחְתָּיו מִבָּנָיו

טז יַעֲשֶׂה אֹתָהּ חָק־עוֹלָם לַיהוה כָּלִיל תָּקְטָר: וְכָל־מִנְחַת כֹּהֵן כָּלִיל תִּהְיֶה

לֹא תֵאָכֵל:

---

holds his fellow Jew's money but cannot be required to
pay because the plaintiff lacks proof. If he swears falsely
that he is not liable, he must pay what he owes plus
one-fifth and must bring a guilt-offering.

◆§ **Parashas Tzav**

Chapters 6 and 7 discuss offerings that have been
mentioned above: *olah* [burnt-offering], *minchah* [meal-
offering], *shelamim* [peace-offering], *chatas* [sin-offering],

and *asham* [guilt-offering]. Here, the Torah teaches *Aaron
and his sons* (v. 2) additional laws that relate to their
sacrificial service (*Ramban*).

6:3. The first two Temple services of the day were
תְּרוּמַת הַדֶּשֶׁן, *separating the ash,* removing a portion of
the previous day's ashes from the Altar [see below],
and then placing two logs of wood on the main Altar
fire.

lost item and denied it — and he swore falsely about any of all the things that a person can do and sin thereby — ²³ *so it shall be that when he will sin and become guilty, he shall return the robbed item that he robbed, or the proceeds of his fraud, or the pledge that was left with him, or the lost item that he found,* ²⁴ *or anything about which he had sworn falsely — he shall repay its principal and add its fifth to it; he shall give it to its owner on the day he admits his guilt.*

Guilt-offering for thefts
(See Appendix B, charts 6-7)

²⁵ *And he shall bring his guilt-offering to HASHEM — an unblemished ram from the flock, of the proper value, as a guilt-offering — to the Kohen.* ²⁶ *The Kohen shall provide him atonement before HASHEM, and it shall be forgiven him for any of all the things he might do to incur guilt.*

PARASHAS TZAV

6

The taking of the ash and the Altar fire

¹ Hᴀsʜᴇᴍ *spoke to Moses, saying:* ² *Command Aaron and his sons, saying: This is the law of the burnt-offering: It is the burnt-offering [that stays] on the flame, on the Altar, all night until the morning, and the fire of the Altar should be kept aflame on it.* ³ *The Kohen shall don his fitted linen Tunic, and he shall don linen Breeches on his flesh; he shall separate the ash* of what the fire consumed of the burnt-offering on the Altar, and place it next to the Altar.* ⁴ *He shall remove his garments and don other garments, and he shall remove the ash*

The three Altar fires

to the outside of the camp, to a pure place. ⁵ *The fire on the Altar shall be kept burning on it, it shall not be extinguished;* and the Kohen shall kindle wood upon it every morning; he shall prepare the burnt-offering upon it and shall cause the fats of the peace-offerings to go up in smoke upon it.* ⁶ *A permanent fire shall remain aflame on the Altar; it shall not be extinguished.*

Meal-offering
(See Appendix B, chart 9)

⁷ *This is the law of the meal-offering: The sons of Aaron shall bring it before* Hᴀsʜᴇᴍ, *to the front of the Altar.* ⁸ *He shall separate from it with his threefingersful some of the fine flour of the meal-offering and some of its oil, and all the frankincense that is on the meal-offering; and he shall cause them to go up in smoke on the Altar for a satisfying aroma — its memorial portion unto* Hᴀsʜᴇᴍ. ⁹ *Aaron and his sons shall eat what is left of it; it shall be eaten unleavened in a holy place, in the Courtyard of the Tent of Meeting shall they eat it.* ¹⁰ *It shall not be baked leavened, I have presented it as their share from My fire-offerings; it is most holy, like the sin-offering and like the guilt-offering.* ¹¹ *Every male of the children of Aaron shall eat it, an eternal portion for your generations, from the fire-offerings of* Hᴀsʜᴇᴍ; *whatever touches them shall become holy.*

¹² Hᴀsʜᴇᴍ *spoke to Moses, saying:* ¹³ *This is the offering of Aaron and his sons,* which each shall offer to* Hᴀsʜᴇᴍ *on the day he is inaugurated: a tenth-ephah of fine flour as a continual meal-offering; half of it in the morning and half of it in the afternoon.* ¹⁴ *It should be made on a pan with oil, scalded shall you bring it; a repeatedly baked meal-offering, broken into pieces, you shall offer it as a satisfying aroma to* Hᴀsʜᴇᴍ. ¹⁵ *The Kohen from among his sons who is anointed in his place shall perform it; [it is] an eternal decree for* Hᴀsʜᴇᴍ; *it shall be caused to go up in smoke in its entirety.* ¹⁶ *Every meal-offering of a Kohen is to be entirely [caused to go up in smoke]; it shall not be eaten.*

6:5. The Altar of Moses' Tabernacle was used for about 116 years, during which the fire burned continuously, yet the Altar's thin copper layer never melted and its wooden structure was never charred (*Vayikra Rabbah* 7:5).

6:13. Every Kohen must offer this meal-offering the first time he performs the Temple service; the Kohen Gadol must offer it when he assumes office and every day thereafter (see v. 15).

יז-יח וַיְדַבֵּ֥ר יְהוָ֖ה אֶל־מֹשֶׁ֥ה לֵּאמֹֽר: דַּבֵּ֤ר אֶֽל־אַהֲרֹן֙ וְאֶל־בָּנָ֣יו לֵאמֹר֒ זֹ֚את תּוֹרַ֣ת הַֽחַטָּ֔את בִּמְק֗וֹם אֲשֶׁ֤ר תִּשָּׁחֵט֙ הָֽעֹלָ֔ה תִּשָּׁחֵ֤ט הַֽחַטָּאת֙ לִפְנֵ֣י יְהוָ֔ה

יט קֹ֥דֶשׁ קָֽדָשִׁ֖ים הִֽוא: הַכֹּהֵ֛ן הַֽמְחַטֵּ֥א אֹתָ֖הּ יֹֽאכְלֶ֑נָּה בְּמָק֤וֹם קָדֹשׁ֙ תֵּ֣אָכֵ֔ל

כ בַּֽחֲצַ֖ר אֹ֥הֶל מוֹעֵֽד: כֹּ֛ל אֲשֶׁר־יִגַּ֥ע בִּבְשָׂרָ֖הּ יִקְדָּ֑שׁ וַֽאֲשֶׁ֨ר יִזֶּ֤ה מִדָּמָהּ֙ עַל־

כא הַבֶּ֔גֶד אֲשֶׁר֙ יִזֶּ֣ה עָלֶ֔יהָ תְּכַבֵּ֖ס בְּמָק֣וֹם קָדֹ֑שׁ: וּכְלִי־חֶ֛רֶשׂ אֲשֶׁ֥ר תְּבֻשַּׁל־בּ֖וֹ

כב יִשָּׁבֵ֑ר וְאִם־בִּכְלִ֤י נְחֹ֨שֶׁת֙ בֻּשָּׁ֔לָה וּמֹרַ֥ק וְשֻׁטַּ֖ף בַּמָּֽיִם: כָּל־זָכָ֥ר בַּֽכֹּֽהֲנִ֖ים

כג יֹאכַ֣ל אֹתָ֑הּ קֹ֥דֶשׁ קָֽדָשִׁ֖ים הִֽוא: וְכָל־חַטָּ֡את אֲשֶׁר֩ יוּבָ֨א מִדָּמָ֜הּ אֶל־אֹ֧הֶל מוֹעֵ֛ד לְכַפֵּ֥ר בַּקֹּ֖דֶשׁ לֹ֣א תֵֽאָכֵ֑ל בָּאֵ֖שׁ תִּשָּׂרֵֽף:

ז

א-ב וְזֹ֥את תּוֹרַ֖ת הָֽאָשָׁ֑ם קֹ֥דֶשׁ קָֽדָשִׁ֖ים הֽוּא: בִּמְק֗וֹם אֲשֶׁ֤ר יִשְׁחֲטוּ֙ אֶת־הָ֣עֹלָ֔ה

ג יִשְׁחֲט֖וּ אֶת־הָֽאָשָׁ֑ם וְאֶת־דָּמ֛וֹ יִזְרֹ֥ק עַל־הַמִּזְבֵּ֖חַ סָבִֽיב: וְאֵ֥ת כָּל־חֶלְבּ֖וֹ

ד יַקְרִ֣יב מִמֶּ֑נּוּ אֵ֚ת הָֽאַלְיָ֔ה וְאֶת־הַחֵ֖לֶב הַֽמְכַסֶּ֥ה אֶת־הַקֶּֽרֶב: וְאֵת֙ שְׁתֵּ֣י הַכְּלָיֹ֔ת וְאֶת־הַחֵ֨לֶב֙ אֲשֶׁ֣ר עֲלֵיהֶ֔ן אֲשֶׁ֖ר עַל־הַכְּסָלִ֑ים וְאֶת־הַיֹּתֶ֨רֶת֙ עַל־

ה הַכָּבֵ֔ד עַל־הַכְּלָיֹ֖ת יְסִירֶֽנָּה: וְהִקְטִ֨יר אֹתָ֤ם הַכֹּהֵן֙ הַמִּזְבֵּ֔חָה אִשֶּׁ֖ה לַֽיהוָ֑ה

ו אָשָׁ֖ם הֽוּא: כָּל־זָכָ֥ר בַּֽכֹּֽהֲנִ֖ים יֹֽאכְלֶ֑נּוּ בְּמָק֤וֹם קָדוֹשׁ֙ יֵֽאָכֵ֔ל קֹ֥דֶשׁ קָֽדָשִׁ֖ים

ז הֽוּא: כַּֽחַטָּאת֙ כָּֽאָשָׁ֔ם תּוֹרָ֥ה אַחַ֖ת לָהֶ֑ם הַכֹּהֵ֛ן אֲשֶׁ֥ר יְכַפֶּר־בּ֖וֹ ל֥וֹ יִֽהְיֶֽה:

ח וְהַ֨כֹּהֵ֔ן הַמַּקְרִ֖יב אֶת־עֹ֣לַת אִ֑ישׁ ע֤וֹר הָֽעֹלָה֙ אֲשֶׁ֣ר הִקְרִ֔יב לַכֹּהֵ֖ן ל֥וֹ יִֽהְיֶֽה:

ט וְכָל־מִנְחָ֗ה אֲשֶׁ֤ר תֵּֽאָפֶה֙ בַּתַּנּ֔וּר וְכָל־נַֽעֲשָׂ֥ה בַמַּרְחֶ֖שֶׁת וְעַל־מַֽחֲבַ֑ת

י לַכֹּהֵ֛ן הַמַּקְרִ֥יב אֹתָ֖הּ ל֥וֹ תִֽהְיֶֽה: וְכָל־מִנְחָ֥ה בְלוּלָֽה־בַשֶּׁ֖מֶן וַֽחֲרֵבָ֑ה לְכָל־בְּנֵ֧י אַֽהֲרֹ֛ן תִּֽהְיֶ֖ה אִ֥ישׁ כְּאָחִֽיו:

יא-יב וְזֹ֥את תּוֹרַ֖ת זֶ֣בַח הַשְּׁלָמִ֑ים אֲשֶׁ֥ר יַקְרִ֖יב לַֽיהוָֽה: אִ֣ם עַל־תּוֹדָה֮ יַקְרִיבֶ֒נּוּ֒ וְהִקְרִ֣יב ׀ עַל־זֶ֣בַח הַתּוֹדָ֗ה חַלּ֤וֹת מַצּוֹת֙ בְּלוּלֹ֣ת בַּשֶּׁ֔מֶן וּרְקִיקֵ֥י מַצּ֖וֹת

יג מְשֻׁחִ֣ים בַּשָּׁ֑מֶן וְסֹ֣לֶת מֻרְבֶּ֔כֶת חַלֹּ֖ת בְּלוּלֹ֥ת בַּשָּֽׁמֶן: עַל־חַלֹּת֙ לֶ֔חֶם

יד חָמֵ֔ץ יַקְרִ֖יב קָרְבָּנ֑וֹ עַל־זֶ֖בַח תּוֹדַ֥ת שְׁלָמָֽיו: וְהִקְרִ֨יב מִמֶּ֤נּוּ אֶחָד֙ מִכָּל־

טו קָרְבָּ֔ן תְּרוּמָ֖ה לַֽיהוָ֑ה לַכֹּהֵ֗ן הַזֹּרֵ֛ק אֶת־דַּ֥ם הַשְּׁלָמִ֖ים ל֥וֹ יִֽהְיֶֽה: וּבְשַׂ֗ר

טז זֶ֚בַח תּוֹדַ֣ת שְׁלָמָ֔יו בְּי֥וֹם קָרְבָּנ֖וֹ יֵֽאָכֵ֑ל לֹֽא־יַנִּ֥יחַ מִמֶּ֖נּוּ עַד־בֹּֽקֶר: וְאִם־נֶ֣דֶר ׀ א֣וֹ נְדָבָ֗ה זֶ֚בַח קָרְבָּנ֔וֹ בְּי֛וֹם הַקְרִיב֥וֹ אֶת־זִבְח֖וֹ יֵֽאָכֵ֑ל וּמִמָּ֣חֳרָ֔ת

יז וְהַנּוֹתָ֥ר מִמֶּ֖נּוּ יֵֽאָכֵֽל: וְהַנּוֹתָ֖ר מִבְּשַׂ֣ר הַזָּ֑בַח בַּיּוֹם֙ הַשְּׁלִישִׁ֔י בָּאֵ֖שׁ יִשָּׂרֵֽף:

יח וְאִ֣ם הֵֽאָכֹ֣ל יֵֽ֠אָכֵ֠ל מִבְּשַׂר־זֶ֨בַח שְׁלָמָ֜יו בַּיּ֣וֹם הַשְּׁלִישִׁי֮ לֹ֣א יֵֽרָצֶה֒ הַמַּקְרִ֣יב אֹת֗וֹ לֹ֧א יֵֽחָשֵׁ֛ב ל֖וֹ פִּגּ֣וּל יִֽהְיֶ֑ה וְהַנֶּ֛פֶשׁ הָֽאֹכֶ֥לֶת מִמֶּ֖נּוּ עֲוֺנָ֥הּ תִּשָּֽׂא:

6:17-23. This passage adds to the laws of sin-offerings that were given in Chapter 4.

6:21. A vessel assumes the halachic status of the food whose taste it absorbed. Metal vessels *can* be purged of their absorbed taste. However, earthenware cannot be purged; consequently, there is no way to make its use permissible if it had absorbed the taste of non-kosher food.

7:8-10. The parts of the offerings that go to the Kohanim are divided among all who were at the Temple and

were *eligible* to perform the service, not only those who actually did so.

7:12. Someone who survives a life-threatening crisis brings a תוֹדָה, *thanksgiving-offering*, to express his gratitude to God. From Psalm 107, David's hymn of gratitude, the Sages (*Berachos* 54b) derive that survivors of four categories of danger are required to bring the offering: a desert [or other potentially hazardous] journey, dangerous imprisonment, serious illness, or a sea vogage.

Sin-offering
(See Appendix B,
charts 6-7)

[17] HASHEM spoke to Moses, saying: [18] Speak to Aaron and his sons, saying: This is the law of the sin-offering; in the place where the burnt-offering is slaughtered shall the sin-offering be slaughtered, before HASHEM — it is most holy. [19] The Kohen who performs its sin-offering service shall eat it; it shall be eaten in a holy place: in the Courtyard of the Tent of Meeting.

Koshering

[20] Whatever touches its flesh becomes holy; and if its blood is sprinkled upon a garment, whatever it has been sprinkled upon you shall wash in a holy place. [21] An earthenware vessel in which it was cooked shall be broken; but if it was cooked in a copper vessel, that should be purged and rinsed in water. * [22] Every male among the Kohanim may eat it; it is most holy. [23] Any sin-offering from which some blood has been brought to the Tent of Meeting, to effect atonement within the Holy, shall not be eaten; it shall be burned in fire.

7

Guilt-offering

[1] This is the teaching of the guilt-offering; it is most holy. [2] In the place where they shall slaughter the burnt-offering shall they slaughter the guilt-offering; and he shall throw its blood upon the Altar, all around. [3] All of its fat shall he offer of it; the tail and the fat that covers the innards; [4] and the two kidneys and the fat that covers them, which is on the flanks; and he shall remove the diaphragm as well as the liver, as well as the kidneys. [5] The Kohen shall cause them to go up in smoke on the Altar, a fire-offering to HASHEM; it is a guilt-offering.

[6] Every male among the Kohanim may eat it; it shall be eaten in a holy place, it is most holy. [7] Like the sin-offering is the guilt-offering, there is one law for them; it shall belong to a Kohen who performs its atonement

Miscella-neous gifts to the Kohen

service. [8] And the Kohen who offers* a person's burnt-offering — the hide of the burnt-offering that he offered shall belong to that Kohen, it shall be his.

[9] Any meal-offering that is baked in the oven and any that is made in a deep pan or upon a shallow pan — it shall belong to the Kohen who offers it; it shall be his. [10] And any meal-offering that is mixed with oil or that is dry, it shall belong to all the sons of Aaron, every man alike.

Thanks-giving-offering
(See Appendix B,
chart 10)

[11] This is the law of the feast peace-offering that one will offer to HASHEM: [12] If he shall offer it for a thanksgiving-offering, * he shall offer with the feast thanksgiving-offering unleavened loaves mixed with oil, unleavened wafers smeared with oil, and loaves of scalded fine flour mixed with oil. [13] With loaves of leavened bread shall he bring his offering, with his feast thanksgiving peace-offering. [14] From it he shall offer one from each as an offering, a portion to HASHEM; it shall belong to the Kohen who throws the blood of the peace-offering. [15] And the flesh of his feast thanksgiving peace-offering must be eaten on the day of its offering; he shall not leave any of it until morning.

Piggul/ Rejected

[16] If his feast-offering is for a vow or a donation, it must be eaten on the day he offered his feast-offering; and on the next day, what is left over may be eaten. [17] What is left over from the flesh of the feast-offering shall be burned in the fire on the third day. [18] And if some of the flesh of his feast thanksgiving peace-offering was intended to be eaten on the third day, it is not acceptable, the one who offers it may not intend this — it remains rejected; and the soul that eats it shall bear its iniquity.

יט וְהַבָּשָׂר אֲשֶׁר־יִגַּע בְּכָל־טָמֵא לֹא יֵאָכֵל בָּאֵשׁ יִשָּׂרֵף וְהַבָּשָׂר כָּל־טָהוֹר

כ יֹאכַל בָּשָׂר: וְהַנֶּפֶשׁ אֲשֶׁר־תֹּאכַל בָּשָׂר מִזֶּבַח הַשְּׁלָמִים אֲשֶׁר לַיהוה

כא וְטֻמְאָתוֹ עָלָיו וְנִכְרְתָה הַנֶּפֶשׁ הַהִוא מֵעַמֶּיהָ: וְנֶפֶשׁ כִּי־תִגַּע בְּכָל־טָמֵא בְּטֻמְאַת אָדָם אוֹ ׀ בִּבְהֵמָה טְמֵאָה אוֹ בְּכָל־שֶׁקֶץ טָמֵא וְאָכַל מִבְּשַׂר־

כב זֶבַח הַשְּׁלָמִים אֲשֶׁר לַיהוה וְנִכְרְתָה הַנֶּפֶשׁ הַהִוא מֵעַמֶּיהָ: וַיְדַבֵּר יהוה

כג אֶל־מֹשֶׁה לֵּאמֹר: דַּבֵּר אֶל־בְּנֵי יִשְׂרָאֵל לֵאמֹר כָּל־חֵלֶב שׁוֹר וְכֶשֶׂב וָעֵז

כד לֹא תֹאכֵלוּ: וְחֵלֶב נְבֵלָה וְחֵלֶב טְרֵפָה יֵעָשֶׂה לְכָל־מְלָאכָה וְאָכֹל לֹא

כה תֹאכְלֻהוּ: כִּי כָּל־אֹכֵל חֵלֶב מִן־הַבְּהֵמָה אֲשֶׁר יַקְרִיב מִמֶּנָּה אִשֶּׁה

כו לַיהוה וְנִכְרְתָה הַנֶּפֶשׁ הָאֹכֶלֶת מֵעַמֶּיהָ: וְכָל־דָּם לֹא תֹאכְלוּ בְּכֹל

כז מוֹשְׁבֹתֵיכֶם לָעוֹף וְלַבְּהֵמָה: כָּל־נֶפֶשׁ אֲשֶׁר־תֹּאכַל כָּל־דָּם וְנִכְרְתָה הַנֶּפֶשׁ הַהִוא מֵעַמֶּיהָ:

כח-כט וַיְדַבֵּר יהוה אֶל־מֹשֶׁה לֵּאמֹר: דַּבֵּר אֶל־בְּנֵי יִשְׂרָאֵל לֵאמֹר הַמַּקְרִיב

ל אֶת־זֶבַח שְׁלָמָיו לַיהוה יָבִיא אֶת־קָרְבָּנוֹ לַיהוה מִזֶּבַח שְׁלָמָיו: יָדָיו תְּבִיאֶינָה אֵת אִשֵּׁי יהוה אֶת־הַחֵלֶב עַל־הֶחָזֶה יְבִיאֶנּוּ אֵת הֶחָזֶה לְהָנִיף

לא אֹתוֹ תְּנוּפָה לִפְנֵי יהוה: וְהִקְטִיר הַכֹּהֵן אֶת־הַחֵלֶב הַמִּזְבֵּחָה וְהָיָה הֶחָזֶה

לב לְאַהֲרֹן וּלְבָנָיו: וְאֵת שׁוֹק הַיָּמִין תִּתְּנוּ תְרוּמָה לַכֹּהֵן מִזִּבְחֵי שַׁלְמֵיכֶם:

לג הַמַּקְרִיב אֶת־דַּם הַשְּׁלָמִים וְאֶת־הַחֵלֶב מִבְּנֵי אַהֲרֹן לוֹ תִהְיֶה שׁוֹק הַיָּמִין

לד לְמָנָה: כִּי אֶת־חֲזֵה הַתְּנוּפָה וְאֵת ׀ שׁוֹק הַתְּרוּמָה לָקַחְתִּי מֵאֵת בְּנֵי־ יִשְׂרָאֵל מִזִּבְחֵי שַׁלְמֵיהֶם וָאֶתֵּן אֹתָם לְאַהֲרֹן הַכֹּהֵן וּלְבָנָיו לְחָק־עוֹלָם

לה מֵאֵת בְּנֵי יִשְׂרָאֵל: זֹאת מִשְׁחַת אַהֲרֹן וּמִשְׁחַת בָּנָיו מֵאִשֵּׁי יהוה בְּיוֹם

לו הִקְרִיב אֹתָם לְכַהֵן לַיהוה: אֲשֶׁר צִוָּה יהוה לָתֵת לָהֶם בְּיוֹם מָשְׁחוֹ אֹתָם

לז מֵאֵת בְּנֵי יִשְׂרָאֵל חֻקַּת עוֹלָם לְדֹרֹתָם: זֹאת הַתּוֹרָה לָעֹלָה לַמִּנְחָה

לח וְלַחַטָּאת וְלָאָשָׁם וְלַמִּלּוּאִים וּלְזֶבַח הַשְּׁלָמִים: אֲשֶׁר צִוָּה יהוה אֶת־ מֹשֶׁה בְּהַר סִינָי בְּיוֹם צַוֹּתוֹ אֶת־בְּנֵי יִשְׂרָאֵל לְהַקְרִיב אֶת־קָרְבְּנֵיהֶם לַיהוה בְּמִדְבַּר סִינָי:

ח רביעי א-ב וַיְדַבֵּר יהוה אֶל־מֹשֶׁה לֵּאמֹר: קַח אֶת־אַהֲרֹן וְאֶת־בָּנָיו אִתּוֹ וְאֵת הַבְּגָדִים וְאֵת שֶׁמֶן הַמִּשְׁחָה וְאֵת ׀ פַּר הַחַטָּאת וְאֵת שְׁנֵי הָאֵילִים וְאֵת

ג-ד סַל הַמַּצּוֹת: וְאֵת כָּל־הָעֵדָה הַקְהֵל אֶל־פֶּתַח אֹהֶל מוֹעֵד: וַיַּעַשׂ מֹשֶׁה

ה כַּאֲשֶׁר צִוָּה יהוה אֹתוֹ וַתִּקָּהֵל הָעֵדָה אֶל־פֶּתַח אֹהֶל מוֹעֵד: וַיֹּאמֶר מֹשֶׁה

7:19-21. The meat of offerings must be eaten in a state of טָהֳרָה, *spiritual purity*, on the part of both the meat and the eater. This passage sets forth the prohibitions and the penalties for *intentional* violation of this requirement.

7:20, 21, 27. The term נִכְרְתָה הַנֶּפֶשׁ, *that soul will be cut off*, refers to the punishment of *kares*, which includes excision of the soul and premature death.

7:22-27. In terms of this prohibition, "fat" means only the fatty tissue of sheep, goats, and cattle that would be placed on the Altar in the case of offerings.

7:30. This waving ritual is performed with the parts of the peace-offering that will be placed upon the Altar, and with the parts that will be presented as a gift to the Kohanim. They are *waved* in all four directions, and then lifted up and lowered. These motions signify that God controls existence everywhere, in all four directions, as well as above and below (*R' Hirsch*).

Eating in **19** *The flesh that touches any contaminated thing* may not be eaten, it shall*
a state of *be burned in fire; but of the [uncontaminated] flesh, any uncontaminated*
contamina- *person may eat the flesh.* **20** *A person who eats flesh from the feast peace-*
tion *offering that is HASHEM's while his contamination is upon him, that soul will*
be cut off* from its people. **21** *If a person touches any contamination —*
whether human contamination or a contaminated animal [carcass] or any
contaminated detestable [carcass] — and he eats from the flesh of a feast
peace-offering that is HASHEM's, then that soul will be cut off from its
people.

Fat and **22** *HASHEM spoke to Moses, saying:* **23** *Speak to the Children of Israel, saying:*
blood *Any fat* of oxen, sheep, or goats — you shall not eat.* **24** *The fat of an animal*
that died and the fat of an animal that had been torn to death may be put to any
use; but you shall not eat it. **25** *For anyone who eats the fat of animal species*
from which one may bring a fire-offering to HASHEM — the soul that eats will be
cut off from its people. **26** *You shall not consume any blood, in any of your*
dwelling places, whether from fowl or from animals. **27** *Any person who con-*
sumes any blood — that soul will be cut off from its people.

The parts **28** *HASHEM spoke to Moses, saying:* **29** *Speak to the Children of Israel, saying:*
and their *When one brings his feast peace-offering to HASHEM, he shall deliver his offering*
order *to HASHEM from his feast peace-offering.* **30** *With his own hands shall he bring*
the fire-offerings of HASHEM: the fat atop the breast shall he bring; the breast, in
order to wave it as a wave-service* before HASHEM. **31** *The Kohen shall cause*
the fat to go up in smoke on the Altar; and the breast shall be for Aaron and his
sons. **32** *You shall give the right thigh as a raised-up gift to the Kohen, from your*
feast peace-offerings. **33** *Anyone from among the sons of Aaron who shall offer*
the blood of the peace-offering and the fat — the right thigh shall be his as a
portion. **34** *For the breast of the waving and the thigh of the raising-up have I*
taken from the Children of Israel, from their feast peace-offering, and I have
given them to Aaron the Kohen and his sons as an eternal stipend from the
Children of Israel.

35 *This is the anointment [portion] of Aaron and the anointment [portion] of*
his sons from the fire-offerings of HASHEM, on the day He brought them near to
minister to HASHEM; **36** *that HASHEM commanded to be given them on the day He*
anointed them from among the Children of Israel; it is an eternal decree for their
generations.

37 *This is the law of the burnt-offering, the meal-offering, the sin-offering, and*
the guilt-offering; and the inauguration-offerings, and the feast peace-offering;
38 *which HASHEM commanded Moses on Mount Sinai, on the day He com-*
manded the Children of Israel to bring their offerings to HASHEM, in the
Wilderness of Sinai.

8

Consecration
of the
Kohanim

1 *H*ASHEM *spoke to Moses, saying:* **2** *Take* Aaron and his sons with him, and*
the garments and the oil of anointment, and the bull of the sin-offering, and
the two rams, and the basket of matzos. **3** *Gather the entire assembly to the*
entrance of the Tent of Meeting. **4** *Moses did as HASHEM commanded him; and*
the assembly was gathered to the entrance of the Tent of Meeting. **5** *Moses said*

8:2. The word נק signifies "win Aaron over with words," because Aaron felt unworthy for this task.

א אֶל־הָעֵדָה זֶה הַדָּבָר אֲשֶׁר־צִוָּה יהוה לַעֲשֽׂוֹת: וַיַּקְרֵב מֹשֶׁה אֶת־אַהֲרֹן

ו וְאֶת־בָּנָיו וַיִּרְחַץ אֹתָם בַּמָּיִם: וַיִּתֵּן עָלָיו אֶת־הַכֻּתֹּנֶת וַיַּחְגֹּר אֹתוֹ בָּאַבְנֵט

ז וַיַּלְבֵּשׁ אֹתוֹ אֶת־הַמְּעִיל וַיִּתֵּן עָלָיו אֶת־הָאֵפֹד וַיַּחְגֹּר אֹתוֹ בְּחֵשֶׁב הָאֵפֹד

ח וַיֶּאְפֹּד לוֹ בּֽוֹ: * וַיָּשֶׂם עָלָיו אֶת־הַחֹשֶׁן וַיִּתֵּן אֶל־הַחֹשֶׁן אֶת־הָאוּרִים

* חצי התורה בפסוקים

ט וְאֶת־הַתֻּמִּים: וַיָּשֶׂם אֶת־הַמִּצְנֶפֶת עַל־רֹאשׁוֹ וַיָּשֶׂם עַל־הַמִּצְנֶפֶת אֶל־

י מוּל פָּנָיו אֵת צִיץ הַזָּהָב נֵזֶר הַקֹּדֶשׁ כַּאֲשֶׁר צִוָּה יהוה אֶת־מֹשֶׁה: וַיִּקַּח

מֹשֶׁה אֶת־שֶׁמֶן הַמִּשְׁחָה וַיִּמְשַׁח אֶת־הַמִּשְׁכָּן וְאֶת־כָּל־אֲשֶׁר־בּוֹ וַיְקַדֵּשׁ

יא אֹתָם: וַיַּז מִמֶּנּוּ עַל־הַמִּזְבֵּחַ שֶׁבַע פְּעָמִים וַיִּמְשַׁח אֶת־הַמִּזְבֵּחַ וְאֶת־כָּל־

יב כֵּלָיו וְאֶת־הַכִּיֹּר וְאֶת־כַּנּוֹ לְקַדְּשָׁם: וַיִּצֹק מִשֶּׁמֶן הַמִּשְׁחָה עַל רֹאשׁ אַהֲרֹן

יג וַיִּמְשַׁח אֹתוֹ לְקַדְּשׁוֹ: וַיַּקְרֵב מֹשֶׁה אֶת־בְּנֵי אַהֲרֹן וַיַּלְבִּשֵׁם כֻּתֳּנֹת וַיַּחְגֹּר

חמישי

יד אֹתָם אַבְנֵט וַיַּחֲבֹשׁ לָהֶם מִגְבָּעוֹת כַּאֲשֶׁר צִוָּה יהוה אֶת־מֹשֶׁה: וַיַּגֵּשׁ אֵת

פַּר הַחַטָּאת וַיִּסְמֹךְ אַהֲרֹן וּבָנָיו אֶת־יְדֵיהֶם עַל־רֹאשׁ פַּר הַחַטָּאת:

טו וַיִּשְׁחָט וַיִּקַּח מֹשֶׁה אֶת־הַדָּם וַיִּתֵּן עַל־קַרְנוֹת הַמִּזְבֵּחַ סָבִיב בְּאֶצְבָּעוֹ

וַיְחַטֵּא אֶת־הַמִּזְבֵּחַ וְאֶת־הַדָּם יָצַק אֶל־יְסוֹד הַמִּזְבֵּחַ וַיְקַדְּשֵׁהוּ לְכַפֵּר

טז עָלָיו: וַיִּקַּח אֶת־כָּל־הַחֵלֶב אֲשֶׁר עַל־הַקֶּרֶב וְאֵת יֹתֶרֶת הַכָּבֵד וְאֶת־שְׁתֵּי

יז הַכְּלָיֹת וְאֶת־חֶלְבְּהֶן וַיַּקְטֵר מֹשֶׁה הַמִּזְבֵּחָה: וְאֶת־הַפָּר וְאֶת־עֹרוֹ וְאֶת־

בְּשָׂרוֹ וְאֶת־פִּרְשׁוֹ שָׂרַף בָּאֵשׁ מִחוּץ לַמַּחֲנֶה כַּאֲשֶׁר צִוָּה יהוה אֶת־

יח מֹשֶׁה: וַיַּקְרֵב אֵת אֵיל הָעֹלָה וַיִּסְמְכוּ אַהֲרֹן וּבָנָיו אֶת־יְדֵיהֶם עַל־רֹאשׁ

יט-כ הָאָיִל: וַיִּשְׁחָט וַיִּזְרֹק מֹשֶׁה אֶת־הַדָּם עַל־הַמִּזְבֵּחַ סָבִיב: וְאֶת־הָאַיִל נִתַּח

כא לִנְתָחָיו וַיַּקְטֵר מֹשֶׁה אֶת־הָרֹאשׁ וְאֶת־הַנְּתָחִים וְאֶת־הַפָּדֶר: וְאֶת־

הַקֶּרֶב וְאֶת־הַכְּרָעַיִם רָחַץ בַּמָּיִם וַיַּקְטֵר מֹשֶׁה אֶת־כָּל־הָאַיִל הַמִּזְבֵּחָה

עֹלָה הוּא לְרֵיחַ־נִיחֹחַ אִשֶּׁה הוּא לַיהוה כַּאֲשֶׁר צִוָּה יהוה אֶת־מֹשֶׁה:

כב וַיַּקְרֵב אֶת־הָאַיִל הַשֵּׁנִי אֵיל הַמִּלֻּאִים וַיִּסְמְכוּ אַהֲרֹן וּבָנָיו אֶת־יְדֵיהֶם

ששי

כג עַל־רֹאשׁ הָאָיִל: וַיִּשְׁחָט וַיִּקַּח מֹשֶׁה מִדָּמוֹ וַיִּתֵּן עַל־תְּנוּךְ אֹזֶן־אַהֲרֹן

כד הַיְמָנִית וְעַל־בֹּהֶן יָדוֹ הַיְמָנִית וְעַל־בֹּהֶן רַגְלוֹ הַיְמָנִית: וַיַּקְרֵב אֶת־בְּנֵי

אַהֲרֹן וַיִּתֵּן מֹשֶׁה מִן־הַדָּם עַל־תְּנוּךְ אָזְנָם הַיְמָנִית וְעַל־בֹּהֶן יָדָם הַיְמָנִית

וְעַל־בֹּהֶן רַגְלָם הַיְמָנִית וַיִּזְרֹק מֹשֶׁה אֶת־הַדָּם עַל־הַמִּזְבֵּחַ סָבִיב:

כה וַיִּקַּח אֶת־הַחֵלֶב וְאֶת־הָאַלְיָה וְאֶת־כָּל־הַחֵלֶב אֲשֶׁר עַל־הַקֶּרֶב וְאֵת

כו יֹתֶרֶת הַכָּבֵד וְאֶת־שְׁתֵּי הַכְּלָיֹת וְאֶת־חֶלְבְּהֶן וְאֵת שׁוֹק הַיָּמִין: וּמִסַּל

הַמַּצּוֹת אֲשֶׁר | לִפְנֵי יהוה לָקַח חַלַּת מַצָּה אַחַת וְחַלַּת לֶחֶם שֶׁמֶן

כז אַחַת וְרָקִיק אֶחָד וַיָּשֶׂם עַל־הַחֲלָבִים וְעַל שׁוֹק הַיָּמִין: וַיִּתֵּן אֶת־הַכֹּל

כח עַל כַּפֵּי אַהֲרֹן וְעַל כַּפֵּי בָנָיו וַיָּנֶף אֹתָם תְּנוּפָה לִפְנֵי יהוה: וַיִּקַּח מֹשֶׁה

אֹתָם מֵעַל כַּפֵּיהֶם וַיַּקְטֵר הַמִּזְבֵּחָה עַל־הָעֹלָה מִלֻּאִים הֵם לְרֵיחַ נִיחֹחַ

8:12. There are two kinds of anointment. A king is anointed to invest him with a spirit of power — but a   Kohen Gadol is anointed to elevate him to a station of holiness (*Haamek Davar*).

to the assembly: "This is the thing that HASHEM commanded to be done."

Aaron's immersion, investiture and anointment

(See Appendix C, illustration 7)

6 Moses brought Aaron and his sons forward and he immersed them in water. 7 He placed the Tunic upon him and girdled him with the Sash; he dressed him in the Robe and placed the Ephod on him; he girdled him with the belt of the Ephod and adorned him with it. 8 He placed the Breastplate upon him; and in the Breastplate he placed the Urim and the Tumim. 9 He put the Turban upon his head; and upon the Turban, toward his face, he placed the golden Head-plate, the sacred diadem, as HASHEM had commanded Moses.

10 Moses took the oil of anointment and anointed the Tabernacle and everything within it; thus he sanctified them. 11 He sprinkled from it seven times upon the Altar; he anointed the Altar and all its utensils, and the Laver and its base, in order to sanctify them. 12 He poured from the oil of anointment upon Aaron's head, and he anointed him to sanctify him. *

13 Moses brought the sons of Aaron forward, he dressed them in Tunics and girdled [each of] them with a Sash and wrapped the Headdresses upon them, as HASHEM had commanded Moses.

The sin-offering bull

14 He brought forward the sin-offering bull; Aaron and his sons leaned their hands upon the head of the sin-offering bull. 15 He slaughtered it, and Moses took the blood and placed it on the horns of the Altar, all around, with his forefinger, and he purified the Altar; he poured the [remaining] blood upon the base of the Altar and he sanctified it to provide atonement for it.

16 Then he took all the fat that is upon the innards, and the diaphragm of the liver, and the two kidneys with their fat; and Moses caused them to go up in smoke on the Altar. 17 And the bull, with its hide, flesh and waste, he burned in fire outside the camp, as HASHEM had commanded Moses. 18 Then he brought near the ram for the burnt-offering, and Aaron and his sons leaned their hands upon the head of the ram. 19 He slaughtered it, and Moses threw its blood upon the Altar, all around. 20 He cut the ram into its parts; Moses caused the head, the parts, and the fats to go up in smoke. 21 He washed the innards and the feet with water; Moses caused the entire ram to go up in smoke on the Altar — it was a burnt-offering, for a satisfying aroma; it was a fire-offering to HASHEM, as HASHEM had commanded Moses.

The inauguration ram

22 Then he brought near the second ram, the inauguration ram, and Aaron and his sons leaned their hands upon the head of the ram. 23 He slaughtered it, and Moses took some of its blood and placed it upon the middle part of Aaron's right ear, upon the thumb of his right hand, and upon the big toe of his right foot. 24 He brought the sons of Aaron forward, and Moses put some of the blood upon the middle part of their right ear, upon the thumb of their right hand and upon the big toe of their right foot; and Moses threw the [remaining] blood upon the Altar, all around. 25 He took the fat, and the tail, and all the fat that was upon the innards, and the diaphragm of the liver, and the two kidneys and their fat, and the right thigh. 26 And from the basket of matzos that was before HASHEM he took one matzah loaf, one oily bread loaf, and one wafer, and placed them on the fats and on the right thigh. 27 He put it all on Aaron's palms and on the palms of his sons; and he waved them as a wave-service before HASHEM. 28 Then Moses took them from on their palms and caused them to go up in smoke on the Altar after the burnt-offering; they were inauguration offerings, for a satisfying aroma;

כט אִשֶּׁה הוּא לַיהוָה: וַיִּקַּח מֹשֶׁה אֶת־הֶחָזֶה וַיְנִיפֵהוּ תְנוּפָה לִפְנֵי יהוָה מֵאֵיל

שביעי

ל הַמִּלֻּאִים לְמֹשֶׁה הָיָה לְמָנָה כַּאֲשֶׁר צִוָּה יהוָה אֶת־מֹשֶׁה: וַיִּקַּח מֹשֶׁה
מִשֶּׁמֶן הַמִּשְׁחָה וּמִן־הַדָּם אֲשֶׁר עַל־הַמִּזְבֵּחַ וַיַּז עַל־אַהֲרֹן עַל־בְּגָדָיו וְעַל־
בָּנָיו וְעַל־בִּגְדֵי בָנָיו אִתּוֹ וַיְקַדֵּשׁ אֶת־אַהֲרֹן אֶת־בְּגָדָיו וְאֶת־בָּנָיו וְאֶת־בִּגְדֵי

לא בָנָיו אִתּוֹ: וַיֹּאמֶר מֹשֶׁה אֶל־אַהֲרֹן וְאֶל־בָּנָיו בַּשְּׁלוּ אֶת־הַבָּשָׂר פֶּתַח אֹהֶל
מוֹעֵד וְשָׁם תֹּאכְלוּ אֹתוֹ וְאֶת־הַלֶּחֶם אֲשֶׁר בְּסַל הַמִּלֻּאִים כַּאֲשֶׁר צִוֵּיתִי

לב לֵאמֹר אַהֲרֹן וּבָנָיו יֹאכְלֻהוּ: וְהַנּוֹתָר בַּבָּשָׂר וּבַלָּחֶם בָּאֵשׁ תִּשְׂרֹפוּ: וּמִפֶּתַח

מפטיר

לג אֹהֶל מוֹעֵד לֹא תֵצְאוּ שִׁבְעַת יָמִים עַד יוֹם מְלֹאת יְמֵי מִלֻּאֵיכֶם כִּי שִׁבְעַת

Haftaras
Tzav:
p. 1088

לד יָמִים יְמַלֵּא אֶת־יֶדְכֶם: כַּאֲשֶׁר עָשָׂה בַּיּוֹם הַזֶּה צִוָּה יהוָה לַעֲשֹׂת לְכַפֵּר

לה עֲלֵיכֶם: וּפֶתַח אֹהֶל מוֹעֵד תֵּשְׁבוּ יוֹמָם וָלַיְלָה שִׁבְעַת יָמִים וּשְׁמַרְתֶּם אֶת־

For special
Sabbaths,
see
pp. x-xi

מִשְׁמֶרֶת יהוָה וְלֹא תָמוּתוּ כִּי־כֵן צֻוֵּיתִי: וַיַּעַשׂ אַהֲרֹן וּבָנָיו אֵת כָּל־

לו הַדְּבָרִים אֲשֶׁר־צִוָּה יהוָה בְּיַד־מֹשֶׁה: ססס   צ״ז פסוקים. צ״ז סימן.

פרשת שמיני

ט א-ב וַיְהִי בַּיּוֹם הַשְּׁמִינִי קָרָא מֹשֶׁה לְאַהֲרֹן וּלְבָנָיו וּלְזִקְנֵי יִשְׂרָאֵל: וַיֹּאמֶר
אֶל־אַהֲרֹן קַח־לְךָ עֵגֶל בֶּן־בָּקָר לְחַטָּאת וְאַיִל לְעֹלָה תְּמִימִם וְהַקְרֵב לִפְנֵי

ג יהוָה: וְאֶל־בְּנֵי יִשְׂרָאֵל תְּדַבֵּר לֵאמֹר קְחוּ שְׂעִיר־עִזִּים לְחַטָּאת וְעֵגֶל

ד וָכֶבֶשׂ בְּנֵי־שָׁנָה תְּמִימִם לְעֹלָה: וְשׁוֹר וָאַיִל לִשְׁלָמִים לִזְבֹּחַ לִפְנֵי יהוָה

ה וּמִנְחָה בְלוּלָה בַשָּׁמֶן כִּי הַיּוֹם יהוָה נִרְאָה אֲלֵיכֶם: וַיִּקְחוּ אֵת
אֲשֶׁר צִוָּה מֹשֶׁה אֶל־פְּנֵי אֹהֶל מוֹעֵד וַיִּקְרְבוּ כָּל־הָעֵדָה וַיַּעַמְדוּ לִפְנֵי יהוָה:

ו וַיֹּאמֶר מֹשֶׁה זֶה הַדָּבָר אֲשֶׁר־צִוָּה יהוָה תַּעֲשׂוּ וְיֵרָא אֲלֵיכֶם כְּבוֹד יהוָה:

ז וַיֹּאמֶר מֹשֶׁה אֶל־אַהֲרֹן קְרַב אֶל־הַמִּזְבֵּחַ וַעֲשֵׂה אֶת־חַטָּאתְךָ וְאֶת־עֹלָתֶךָ
וְכַפֵּר בַּעַדְךָ וּבְעַד הָעָם וַעֲשֵׂה אֶת־קָרְבַּן הָעָם וְכַפֵּר בַּעֲדָם כַּאֲשֶׁר צִוָּה יהוָה:

ח וַיִּקְרַב אַהֲרֹן אֶל־הַמִּזְבֵּחַ וַיִּשְׁחַט אֶת־עֵגֶל

ט הַחַטָּאת אֲשֶׁר־לוֹ: וַיַּקְרִבוּ בְּנֵי אַהֲרֹן אֶת־הַדָּם אֵלָיו וַיִּטְבֹּל אֶצְבָּעוֹ בַּדָּם

י וַיִּתֵּן עַל־קַרְנוֹת הַמִּזְבֵּחַ וְאֶת־הַדָּם יָצַק אֶל־יְסוֹד הַמִּזְבֵּחַ: וְאֶת־הַחֵלֶב
וְאֶת־הַכְּלָיֹת וְאֶת־הַיֹּתֶרֶת מִן־הַכָּבֵד מִן־הַחַטָּאת הִקְטִיר הַמִּזְבֵּחָה כַּאֲשֶׁר

יא צִוָּה יהוָה אֶת־מֹשֶׁה: וְאֶת־הַבָּשָׂר וְאֶת־הָעוֹר שָׂרַף בָּאֵשׁ

יב מִחוּץ לַמַּחֲנֶה: וַיִּשְׁחַט אֶת־הָעֹלָה וַיַּמְצִאוּ בְּנֵי אַהֲרֹן אֵלָיו אֶת־הַדָּם

יג וַיִּזְרְקֵהוּ עַל־הַמִּזְבֵּחַ סָבִיב: וְאֶת־הָעֹלָה הִמְצִיאוּ אֵלָיו לִנְתָחֶיהָ וְאֶת־

8:35. The Kohanim must remain at the Tent as long as there is a sacrificial service to be done; once the service is completed, they were free to leave (*Ramban, Sifra*).

◆§ **Parashas Shemini**

9:1. Each day for seven days Moses erected the Tabernacle, performed the entire service himself, and disassembled the Tabernacle when the service was done. The inauguration period climaxed with the consecration of

Aaron and his sons as Kohanim on the eighth day. From then on only Kohanim were eligible to perform the Tabernacle service. This *Sidrah* describes the special service that the newly consecrated Kohanim performed on the day they achieved their new status.

9:4. Their offerings would bring about the descent of a Heavenly fire, which represented God's appearance among the people (v. 24, *Rashbam*).

it was a fire-offering to HASHEM. ²⁹ Moses took the breast and waved it as a wave-service before HASHEM; from the inauguration ram it was a portion for Moses, as HASHEM had commanded Moses.

³⁰ Moses took from the oil of anointment and some of the blood that was on the Altar, and he sprinkled it upon Aaron and his vestments, and upon his sons and upon the vestments of his sons who were with him; thus he sanctified Aaron and his vestments, and his sons, and the vestments of his sons with him.

Seven days of inauguration ³¹ Moses said to Aaron and to his sons: Cook the flesh at the entrance of the Tent of Meeting and there you shall eat it and the bread that is in the basket of the inauguration offerings, as I have commanded, saying: "Aaron and his sons shall eat it." ³² And whatever is left over of the flesh and of the bread, you shall burn in the fire. ³³ You shall not leave the entrance of the Tent of Meeting for seven days, until the day when your days of inauguration are completed; for you shall be inaugurated for a seven-day period.

³⁴ As he did on this day, so HASHEM had commanded to be done to provide atonement for you. ³⁵ At the entrance of the Tent of Meeting shall you dwell * day and night for a seven-day period, and you shall protect HASHEM's charge so that you will not die; for so have I been commanded.

³⁶ Aaron and his sons carried out all the matters that HASHEM commanded through Moses.

PARASHAS SHEMINI

9

The Priestly service begins ¹ It was on the eighth day, * Moses summoned Aaron and his sons, and the elders of Israel. ² He said to Aaron: Take for yourself a young bull for a sin-offering and a ram for a burnt-offering — unblemished; and offer [them] before HASHEM. ³ And to the Children of Israel speak as follows: Take a he-goat for a sin-offering, and a calf and a sheep in their first year — unblemished — for a burnt-offering. ⁴ And a bull and a ram for a peace-offering to slaughter before HASHEM, and a meal-offering mixed with oil; for today HASHEM appears to you. *

⁵ They took what Moses had commanded to the front of the Tent of Meeting; and the entire assembly approached and stood before HASHEM. ⁶ Moses said: This is the thing that HASHEM has commanded you to do; then the glory of HASHEM will appear to you.

⁷ Moses said to Aaron: Come near to the Altar and perform the service of your sin-offering and your burnt-offering and provide atonement for yourself and for the people; then perform the service of the people's offering and provide atonement for them, as HASHEM has commanded.

⁸ Aaron came near to the Altar, and slaughtered the sin-offering calf that was his. ⁹ The sons of Aaron brought the blood to him. He dipped his finger into the blood and placed it upon the horns of the Altar, and he poured the [remaining] blood upon the foundation of the Altar. ¹⁰ And the fats, and the kidneys, and the diaphragm with the liver of the sin-offering, he caused to go up in smoke on the Altar, as HASHEM had commanded Moses. ¹¹ And the flesh and the hide he burned in fire outside the camp. ¹² He slaughtered the burnt-offering; the sons of Aaron presented the blood to him and he threw it upon the Altar, all around. ¹³ They presented the burnt-offering to him in its pieces with

יד הָרֹאשׁ וַיַּקְטֵר עַל־הַמִּזְבֵּחַ: וַיִּרְחַץ אֶת־הַקֶּרֶב וְאֶת־הַכְּרָעַיִם וַיַּקְטֵר עַל־

טו הָעֹלָה הַמִּזְבֵּחָה: וַיַּקְרֵב אֵת קָרְבַּן הָעָם וַיִּקַּח אֶת־שְׂעִיר הַחַטָּאת אֲשֶׁר

טז לָעָם וַיִּשְׁחָטֵהוּ וַיְחַטְּאֵהוּ כָּרִאשֹׁן: וַיַּקְרֵב אֶת־הָעֹלָה וַיַּעֲשֶׂהָ כַּמִּשְׁפָּט:

יז וַיַּקְרֵב אֶת־הַמִּנְחָה וַיְמַלֵּא כַפּוֹ מִמֶּנָּה וַיַּקְטֵר עַל־הַמִּזְבֵּחַ מִלְּבַד עֹלַת

יח הַבֹּקֶר: וַיִּשְׁחַט אֶת־הַשּׁוֹר וְאֶת־הָאַיִל זֶבַח הַשְּׁלָמִים אֲשֶׁר לָעָם וַיַּמְצִאוּ

יט בְּנֵי אַהֲרֹן אֶת־הַדָּם אֵלָיו וַיִּזְרְקֵהוּ עַל־הַמִּזְבֵּחַ סָבִיב: וְאֶת־הַחֲלָבִים מִן־

כ הַשּׁוֹר וּמִן־הָאַיִל הָאַלְיָה וְהַמְכַסֶּה וְהַכְּלָיֹת וְיֹתֶרֶת הַכָּבֵד: וַיָּשִׂימוּ אֶת־

כא הַחֲלָבִים עַל־הֶחָזוֹת וַיַּקְטֵר הַחֲלָבִים הַמִּזְבֵּחָה: וְאֵת הֶחָזוֹת וְאֵת שׁוֹק

כב הַיָּמִין הֵנִיף אַהֲרֹן תְּנוּפָה לִפְנֵי יהוה כַּאֲשֶׁר צִוָּה מֹשֶׁה: וַיִּשָּׂא אַהֲרֹן אֶת־

כג יָדָו אֶל־הָעָם וַיְבָרְכֵם וַיֵּרֶד מֵעֲשֹׂת הַחַטָּאת וְהָעֹלָה וְהַשְּׁלָמִים: וַיָּבֹא

מֹשֶׁה וְאַהֲרֹן אֶל־אֹהֶל מוֹעֵד וַיֵּצְאוּ וַיְבָרְכוּ אֶת־הָעָם וַיֵּרָא כְבוֹד־יהוה

כד אֶל־כָּל־הָעָם: וַתֵּצֵא אֵשׁ מִלִּפְנֵי יהוה וַתֹּאכַל עַל־הַמִּזְבֵּחַ אֶת־הָעֹלָה

א וְאֶת־הַחֲלָבִים וַיַּרְא כָּל־הָעָם וַיָּרֹנּוּ וַיִּפְּלוּ עַל־פְּנֵיהֶם: וַיִּקְחוּ בְנֵי־אַהֲרֹן

נָדָב וַאֲבִיהוּא אִישׁ מַחְתָּתוֹ וַיִּתְּנוּ בָהֵן אֵשׁ וַיָּשִׂימוּ עָלֶיהָ קְטֹרֶת וַיַּקְרִיבוּ

ב לִפְנֵי יהוה אֵשׁ זָרָה אֲשֶׁר לֹא צִוָּה אֹתָם: וַתֵּצֵא אֵשׁ מִלִּפְנֵי יהוה וַתֹּאכַל

ג אוֹתָם וַיָּמֻתוּ לִפְנֵי יהוה: וַיֹּאמֶר מֹשֶׁה אֶל־אַהֲרֹן הוּא אֲשֶׁר־דִּבֶּר יהוה |

לֵאמֹר בִּקְרֹבַי אֶקָּדֵשׁ וְעַל־פְּנֵי כָל־הָעָם אֶכָּבֵד וַיִּדֹּם אַהֲרֹן: וַיִּקְרָא מֹשֶׁה

ד אֶל־מִישָׁאֵל וְאֶל אֶלְצָפָן בְּנֵי עֻזִּיאֵל דֹּד אַהֲרֹן וַיֹּאמֶר אֲלֵהֶם *קִרְבוּ שְׂאוּ

ה אֶת־אֲחֵיכֶם מֵאֵת פְּנֵי־הַקֹּדֶשׁ אֶל־מִחוּץ לַמַּחֲנֶה: וַיִּקְרְבוּ וַיִּשָּׂאֻם

ו בְּכֻתֳּנֹתָם אֶל־מִחוּץ לַמַּחֲנֶה כַּאֲשֶׁר דִּבֶּר מֹשֶׁה: וַיֹּאמֶר מֹשֶׁה אֶל־אַהֲרֹן

וּלְאֶלְעָזָר וּלְאִיתָמָר | בָּנָיו רָאשֵׁיכֶם אַל־תִּפְרָעוּ | וּבִגְדֵיכֶם לֹא־תִפְרֹמוּ

וְלֹא תָמֻתוּ וְעַל כָּל־הָעֵדָה יִקְצֹף וַאֲחֵיכֶם כָּל־בֵּית יִשְׂרָאֵל יִבְכּוּ אֶת־

ז הַשְּׂרֵפָה אֲשֶׁר שָׂרַף יהוה: וּמִפֶּתַח אֹהֶל מוֹעֵד לֹא תֵצְאוּ פֶּן־תָּמֻתוּ כִּי־

שֶׁמֶן מִשְׁחַת יהוה עֲלֵיכֶם וַיַּעֲשׂוּ כִּדְבַר מֹשֶׁה:

ח-ט וַיְדַבֵּר יהוה אֶל־אַהֲרֹן לֵאמֹר: יַיִן וְשֵׁכָר אַל־תֵּשְׁתְּ | אַתָּה | וּבָנֶיךָ אִתָּךְ

בְּבֹאֲכֶם אֶל־אֹהֶל מוֹעֵד וְלֹא תָמֻתוּ חֻקַּת עוֹלָם לְדֹרֹתֵיכֶם: וּלֲהַבְדִּיל בֵּין

יא הַקֹּדֶשׁ וּבֵין הַחֹל וּבֵין הַטָּמֵא וּבֵין הַטָּהוֹר: וּלְהוֹרֹת אֶת־בְּנֵי יִשְׂרָאֵל אֵת

כָּל־הַחֻקִּים אֲשֶׁר דִּבֶּר יהוה אֲלֵיהֶם בְּיַד־מֹשֶׁה:

שני   (marginal notes, right column)
שלישי
י

* הַקּוֹרֵא יִטְעַם
הַגֵּרְשַׁיִם קֹדֶם
הַתְּלִישָׁא

9:22-24. Having completed his first day of sacrificial service, Aaron joyously blessed the people, for the first time. Aaron had an overpowering desire to bless the people, for such is the generous and loving nature of Aaron and his descendants. In reward, God gave the Kohanim the eternal commandment of conferring the Priestly Blessing upon the Jewish people (*Sfas Emes*).

10:1-7. Just as the joy of the inauguration ritual reached its peak, tragedy struck. Aaron's two oldest sons performed an unauthorized incense service and lost their

lives. The behavior of Moses and Aaron in the face of this grievous loss gave further testimony to their own greatness and brought about a new sanctification of God's Name.

10:5. The Heavenly fire entered their nostrils and burned their souls, as it were, but did not affect their bodies or clothing (*Rashi; Sanhedrin* 52a).

True, a Jew should try to accept God's justice with faith that it is for the best — as Aaron did — but should mourn over the misfortunes of a fellow Jew (*R' Shlomo Kluger*).

the head; and he caused it to go up in smoke on the Altar. ¹⁴ He washed the innards and the feet, and caused them to go up in smoke on the burnt-offering on the Altar.

¹⁵ He brought near the offering of the people: He took the sin-offering goat that was for the people, and slaughtered it and performed the sin-offering service, as for the first one. ¹⁶ He brought near the burnt-offering and performed its service according to the law. ¹⁷ He brought near the meal-offering, filled his palm from it, and caused it to go up in smoke on the Altar; aside from the morning burnt-offering. ¹⁸ He slaughtered the bull and the ram — the people's feast peace-offering; the sons of Aaron presented the blood to him, and he threw it upon the Altar, all around. ¹⁹ As for the fats from the bull and from the ram, and the tail, the covering fats, the kidneys, and the diaphragm with the liver, ²⁰ they placed the fats upon the breasts, and caused the fats to go up in smoke on the Altar. ²¹ Aaron had lifted up the breasts and the right thigh as a wave-service before HASHEM, as Moses had commanded.

Aaron's blessing and the Divine Presence. ²² Aaron raised his hands* toward the people and blessed them; then he descended from having performed the sin-offering, the burnt-offering, and the peace-offering. ²³ Moses and Aaron came to the Tent of Meeting, and they went out and they blessed the people — and the glory of HASHEM appeared to the entire people!

²⁴ A fire went forth from before HASHEM and consumed upon the Altar the burnt-offering and the fats; all the people saw and sang glad song and fell upon their faces.

10

The death of Nadab and Abihu ¹ The sons of Aaron, * Nadab and Abihu, each took his fire pan, they put fire in them and placed incense upon it; and they brought before HASHEM an alien fire that He had not commanded them. ² A fire came forth from before HASHEM and consumed them, and they died before HASHEM.

³ Moses said to Aaron: Of this did HASHEM speak, saying: "I will be sanctified through those who are nearest Me, thus I will be honored before the entire people"; and Aaron was silent.

⁴ Moses summoned Mishael and Elzaphan, sons of Aaron's uncle Uzziel, and said to them, "Approach, carry your brothers out of the Sanctuary to the outside of the camp." ⁵ They approached and carried them by their Tunics* to the outside of the camp, as Moses had spoken.

⁶ Moses said to Aaron and to his sons Elazar and Ithamar, "Do not leave your heads unshorn and do not rend your garments that you not die and He become wrathful with the entire assembly; and your brethren the entire House of Israel shall bewail the conflagration that HASHEM ignited. ⁷ Do not leave the entrance of the Tent of Meeting lest you die, for the oil of HASHEM's anointment is upon you"; and they carried out Moses' bidding. *

The commandments to Aaron against intoxicants ⁸ HASHEM spoke to Aaron saying: ⁹ Do not drink intoxicating wine, you and your sons with you, when you come to the Tent of Meeting, that you not die — this is an eternal decree for your generations. ¹⁰ In order to distinguish between the sacred and the profane, and between the contaminated and the pure, ¹¹ and to teach the Children of Israel all the decrees that HASHEM had spoken to them through Moses.

רביעי

יב וַיְדַבֵּ֨ר מֹשֶׁ֜ה אֶֽל־אַהֲרֹ֗ן וְאֶ֣ל אֶ֠לְעָזָ֠ר וְאֶל־אִֽיתָמָ֤ר ׀ בָּנָיו֙ הַנּֽוֹתָרִ֔ים קְח֣וּ אֶת־הַמִּנְחָ֗ה הַנּוֹתֶ֨רֶת֙ מֵאִשֵּׁ֣י יהו֔ה וְאִכְל֥וּהָ מַצּ֖וֹת אֵ֣צֶל הַמִּזְבֵּ֑חַ כִּ֥י קֹ֖דֶשׁ

יג קָֽדָשִׁ֥ים הִֽוא: וַאֲכַלְתֶּ֤ם אֹתָהּ֙ בְּמָק֣וֹם קָד֔וֹשׁ כִּ֣י חָקְךָ֤ וְחָק־בָּנֶ֨יךָ֙ הִ֔וא

יד מֵאִשֵּׁ֖י יהו֑ה כִּי־כֵ֖ן צֻוֵּֽיתִי: וְאֵת֩ חֲזֵ֨ה הַתְּנוּפָ֜ה וְאֵ֣ת ׀ שׁ֣וֹק הַתְּרוּמָ֗ה תֹּֽאכְלוּ֙ בְּמָק֣וֹם טָה֔וֹר אַתָּ֕ה וּבָנֶ֥יךָ וּבְנֹתֶ֖יךָ אִתָּ֑ךְ כִּֽי־חָקְךָ֤ וְחָק־בָּנֶ֨יךָ֙ נִתְּנ֔וּ מִזִּבְחֵ֥י

טו שַׁלְמֵ֖י בְּנֵ֥י יִשְׂרָאֵֽל: שׁ֣וֹק הַתְּרוּמָ֞ה וַחֲזֵ֣ה הַתְּנוּפָ֗ה עַ֣ל אִשֵּׁ֤י הַֽחֲלָבִים֙ יָבִ֔יאוּ לְהָנִ֥יף תְּנוּפָ֖ה לִפְנֵ֣י יהו֑ה וְהָיָ֨ה לְךָ֜ וּלְבָנֶ֤יךָ אִתְּךָ֙ לְחָק־עוֹלָ֔ם כַּאֲשֶׁ֖ר צִוָּ֥ה

טז יהוֽה: וְאֵ֣ת ׀ שְׂעִ֣יר הַֽחַטָּ֗את דָּרֹ֥שׁ ֿ דָּרַ֛שׁ מֹשֶׁ֖ה וְהִנֵּ֣ה שֹׂרָ֑ף וַיִּקְצֹ֥ף עַל־

חמישי

אֶלְעָזָ֤ר וְעַל־אִֽיתָמָר֙ בְּנֵ֣י אַהֲרֹ֔ן הַנּֽוֹתָרִ֖ם לֵאמֹֽר: מַדּ֗וּעַ לֹֽא־אֲכַלְתֶּ֤ם אֶת־

*חצי התורה
בתיבת דרש
מכא ומכא

יז הַֽחַטָּאת֙ בִּמְק֣וֹם הַקֹּ֔דֶשׁ כִּ֛י קֹ֥דֶשׁ קָֽדָשִׁ֖ים הִ֑וא וְאֹתָ֣הּ ׀ נָתַ֣ן לָכֶ֔ם לָשֵׂ֗את אֶת־עֲוֺ֣ן הָֽעֵדָ֔ה לְכַפֵּ֥ר עֲלֵיהֶ֖ם לִפְנֵ֣י יהוֽה: הֵ֚ן לֹֽא־הוּבָ֤א אֶת־דָּמָהּ֙ אֶל־

יח הַקֹּ֣דֶשׁ פְּנִ֑ימָה אָכ֨וֹל תֹּאכְל֥וּ אֹתָ֛הּ בַּקֹּ֖דֶשׁ כַּאֲשֶׁ֥ר צִוֵּֽיתִי: וַיְדַבֵּ֨ר אַהֲרֹ֜ן

יט אֶל־מֹשֶׁ֗ה הֵ֣ן הַ֠יּ֠וֹם הִקְרִ֨יבוּ אֶת־חַטָּאתָ֜ם וְאֶת־עֹֽלָתָם֙ לִפְנֵ֣י יהו֔ה

כ וַתִּקְרֶ֥אנָה אֹתִ֖י כָּאֵ֑לֶּה וְאָכַ֤לְתִּי חַטָּאת֙ הַיּ֔וֹם הַיִּיטַ֖ב בְּעֵינֵ֣י יהוֽה: וַיִּשְׁמַ֣ע מֹשֶׁ֔ה וַיִּיטַ֖ב בְּעֵינָֽיו:

יא

ששי

א וַיְדַבֵּ֧ר יהו֛ה אֶל־מֹשֶׁ֥ה וְאֶֽל־אַהֲרֹ֖ן לֵאמֹ֥ר אֲלֵהֶֽם: דַּבְּר֛וּ אֶל־בְּנֵ֥י יִשְׂרָאֵ֖ל

ב לֵאמֹ֑ר זֹ֤את הַֽחַיָּה֙ אֲשֶׁ֣ר תֹּֽאכְל֔וּ מִכָּל־הַבְּהֵמָ֖ה אֲשֶׁ֥ר עַל־הָאָֽרֶץ: כֹּ֣ל ׀

ג מַפְרֶ֣סֶת פַּרְסָ֗ה וְשֹׁסַ֤עַת שֶׁ֨סַע֙ פְּרָסֹ֔ת מַעֲלַ֥ת גֵּרָ֖ה בַּבְּהֵמָ֑ה אֹתָ֖הּ תֹּאכֵֽלוּ:

ד אַ֣ךְ אֶת־זֶ֞ה לֹ֤א תֹֽאכְלוּ֙ מִֽמַּעֲלֵ֣י הַגֵּרָ֔ה וּמִמַּפְרִסֵ֖י הַפַּרְסָ֑ה אֶֽת־הַ֠גָּמָ֠ל

ה כִּֽי־מַעֲלֵ֨ה גֵרָ֜ה ה֗וּא וּפַרְסָה֙ אֵינֶ֣נּוּ מַפְרִ֔יס טָמֵ֥א ה֖וּא לָכֶֽם: וְאֶת־הַשָּׁפָ֗ן

ו כִּֽי־מַעֲלֵ֤ה גֵרָה֙ ה֔וּא וּפַרְסָ֖ה לֹ֣א יַפְרִ֑יס טָמֵ֥א ה֖וּא לָכֶֽם: וְאֶת־הָֽאַרְנֶ֗בֶת

ז כִּֽי־מַעֲלַ֤ת גֵּרָה֙ הִ֔וא וּפַרְסָ֖ה לֹ֣א הִפְרִ֑יסָה טְמֵאָ֥ה הִ֖וא לָכֶֽם: וְאֶת־

הַ֠חֲזִ֠יר כִּֽי־מַפְרִ֨יס פַּרְסָ֜ה ה֗וּא וְשֹׁסַ֥ע שֶׁ֨סַע֙ פַּרְסָ֔ה וְה֖וּא גֵּרָ֣ה לֹֽא־יִגָּ֑ר

ח טָמֵ֥א ה֖וּא לָכֶֽם: מִבְּשָׂרָם֙ לֹ֣א תֹאכֵ֔לוּ וּבְנִבְלָתָ֖ם לֹ֣א תִגָּ֑עוּ טְמֵאִ֥ים הֵ֖ם

ט לָכֶֽם: אֶת־זֶה֙ תֹּֽאכְל֔וּ מִכֹּ֖ל אֲשֶׁ֣ר בַּמָּ֑יִם כֹּ֣ל אֲשֶׁר־לוֹ֩ סְנַפִּ֨יר וְקַשְׂקֶ֜שֶׂת

י בַּמַּ֗יִם בַּיַּמִּ֛ים וּבַנְּחָלִ֖ים אֹתָ֥ם תֹּאכֵֽלוּ: וְכֹל֩ אֲשֶׁ֨ר אֵֽין־ל֜וֹ סְנַפִּ֣יר וְקַשְׂקֶ֗שֶׂת בַּיַּמִּים֙ וּבַנְּחָלִ֔ים מִכֹּל֙ שֶׁ֣רֶץ הַמַּ֔יִם וּמִכֹּ֛ל נֶ֥פֶשׁ הַֽחַיָּ֖ה אֲשֶׁ֣ר בַּמָּ֑יִם

יא שֶׁ֥קֶץ הֵ֖ם לָכֶֽם: וְשֶׁ֖קֶץ יִֽהְי֣וּ לָכֶ֑ם מִבְּשָׂרָם֙ לֹ֣א תֹאכֵ֔לוּ וְאֶת־נִבְלָתָ֖ם

יב תְּשַׁקֵּֽצוּ: כֹּ֣ל אֲשֶׁ֥ר אֵֽין־ל֛וֹ סְנַפִּ֥יר וְקַשְׂקֶ֖שֶׂת בַּמָּ֑יִם שֶׁ֥קֶץ ה֖וּא לָכֶֽם:

10:16. דָּרֹשׁ דָּרַשׁ — *Inquired insistently* [lit., *inquire he inquired*]. This is the exact halfway mark of the words of the Torah. This teaches us that one must always *inquire*; one must never stop seeking an ever deeper and broader understanding of the Torah (*Degel Machaneh Ephraim*).

11:1-23. At the end of this chapter (vv. 43-45) the Torah stresses the reason for *kashrus* very clearly: By observing these laws the Jew pulls himself up the ladder of holiness; by ignoring them, he contaminates himself and

builds a barrier that blocks out his comprehension of holiness. Just as someone who is constantly exposed to loud music and harsh noise slowly and imperceptibly loses his ability to hear fine sounds and detect subtle modulations, so too consumption of non-kosher food deadens a Jew's spiritual capacities and lessens his opportunity to become holy. And worst of all, it renders him incapable of even perceiving his loss. For this reason, *Rema* (*Yoreh Deah* 81:7) cautions that even small

Disposition of the day's offerings
¹² *Moses spoke to Aaron and to Elazar and Ithamar, his remaining sons, "Take the meal-offering that is left from the fire-offerings of HASHEM, and eat it unleavened near the Altar; for it is the most holy.* ¹³ *You shall eat it in a holy place, for it is your portion and the portion of your sons from the fire-offerings of HASHEM, for so have I been commanded.* ¹⁴ *And the breast of the waving and the thigh of the raising-up you shall eat in a pure place, you and your sons and daughters with you; for they have been given as your portion and the portion of your sons from the feast peace-offerings of the Children of Israel.* ¹⁵ *They are to bring the thigh of the raising-up and the breast of the waving upon the fire-offering fats to wave as a wave-service before HASHEM; and it shall be for you and your sons with you for an eternal portion, as HASHEM has commanded."*

The dispute between Moses and Aaron
¹⁶ *Moses inquired insistently** about the he-goat of the sin-offering, for behold, it had been burned! — and he was wrathful with Elazar and Ithamar, Aaron's remaining sons, saying:* ¹⁷ *"Why did you not eat the sin-offering in a holy place, for it is most holy; and He gave it to you to gain forgiveness for the sin of the assembly and to atone for them before HASHEM?* ¹⁸ *Behold, its blood was not brought into the Sanctuary within; you should have eaten it in the Holy, as I had commanded!"*

¹⁹ *Aaron spoke to Moses: "Was it they who this day offered their sin-offering and their burnt-offering before HASHEM? Now that such things befell me — were I to eat this day's sin-offering, would HASHEM approve?"*

²⁰ *Moses heard and he approved.*

11
*Laws of kashrus**
(See Appendix C, illustration 16-17)
¹ H ASHEM *spoke to Moses and to Aaron, saying to them.* ² *Speak to the Children of Israel, saying: These are the creatures that you may eat from among all the animals that are upon the earth.* ³ *Everything among the animals that has a split hoof, which is completely separated into double hooves, and that brings up its cud — that one you may eat.* ⁴ *But this is what you shall not eat from among those that bring up their cud or that have split hooves: the camel, for it brings up its cud, but its hoof is not split — it is unclean to you;** ⁵ and the hyrax, for it brings up its cud, but its hoof is not split — it is*

Land animals
unclean to you; ⁶ *and the hare, for it brings up its cud, but its hoof is not split — it is unclean to you;* ⁷ *and the pig, for its hoof is split and its hoof is completely separated, but it does not chew its cud — it is unclean to you.* ⁸ *You shall not eat of their flesh nor shall you touch their carcass — they are unclean to you.*

Fish
(See Appendix C, illustration 18)
⁹ *This may you eat from everything that is in the water: everything that has fins and scales** in the water, in the seas, and in the streams, those may you eat.* ¹⁰ *And everything that does not have fins and scales in the seas and in the streams — from all that teems in the water, and from all living creatures in the water — they are an abomination to you.* ¹¹ *And they shall remain an abomination to you; you shall not eat of their flesh and you shall abominate their carcass.* ¹² *Everything that does not have fins and scales in the water — it is an abomination to you.*

---

children should be prevented from eating forbidden foods.

11:4. With regard to food, the term *tumah* means that it is forbidden for consumption.

11:9. The scales that are indicative of a kosher fish are only those that can be scraped off easily with a knife (*Ramban*). This excludes fish whose scales are not clearly defined, such as shellfish and amphibians.

יג וְאֶת־אֵלֶּה תְּשַׁקְּצוּ מִן־הָעוֹף לֹא יֵאָכְלוּ שֶׁקֶץ הֵם אֶת־הַנֶּשֶׁר וְאֶת־הַפֶּרֶס וְאֵת הָעָזְנִיָּה: וְאֶת־הַדָּאָה וְאֶת־הָאַיָּה לְמִינָהּ: אֵת כָּל־עֹרֵב לְמִינוֹ: וְאֵת

יד-טו בַּת הַיַּעֲנָה וְאֶת־הַתַּחְמָס וְאֶת־הַשָּׁחַף וְאֶת־הַנֵּץ לְמִינֵהוּ: וְאֶת־הַכּוֹס

יז וְאֶת־הַשָּׁלָךְ וְאֶת־הַיַּנְשׁוּף: וְאֶת־הַתִּנְשֶׁמֶת וְאֶת־הַקָּאָת וְאֶת־הָרָחָם:

יח וְאֵת הַחֲסִידָה הָאֲנָפָה לְמִינָהּ וְאֶת־הַדּוּכִיפַת וְאֶת־הָעֲטַלֵּף: כֹּל שֶׁרֶץ

יט-כ הָעוֹף הַהֹלֵךְ עַל־אַרְבַּע שֶׁקֶץ הוּא לָכֶם: אַךְ אֶת־זֶה תֹּאכְלוּ מִכֹּל שֶׁרֶץ

כא הָעוֹף הַהֹלֵךְ עַל־אַרְבַּע אֲשֶׁר־°לֹא [לוֹ ק] כְרָעַיִם מִמַּעַל לְרַגְלָיו לְנַתֵּר

כב בָּהֵן עַל־הָאָרֶץ: אֶת־אֵלֶּה מֵהֶם תֹּאכֵלוּ אֶת־הָאַרְבֶּה לְמִינוֹ וְאֶת־הַסָּלְעָם

כג לְמִינֵהוּ וְאֶת־הַחַרְגֹּל לְמִינֵהוּ וְאֶת־הֶחָגָב לְמִינֵהוּ: וְכֹל שֶׁרֶץ הָעוֹף אֲשֶׁר־

כד לוֹ אַרְבַּע רַגְלָיִם שֶׁקֶץ הוּא לָכֶם: וּלְאֵלֶּה תִּטַּמָּאוּ כָּל־הַנֹּגֵעַ בְּנִבְלָתָם

כה יִטְמָא עַד־הָעָרֶב: וְכָל־הַנֹּשֵׂא מִנִּבְלָתָם יְכַבֵּס בְּגָדָיו וְטָמֵא עַד־הָעָרֶב:

כו לְכָל־הַבְּהֵמָה אֲשֶׁר הִוא מַפְרֶסֶת פַּרְסָה וְשֶׁסַע | אֵינֶנָּה שֹׁסַעַת וְגֵרָה

כז אֵינֶנָּה מַעֲלָה טְמֵאִים הֵם לָכֶם כָּל־הַנֹּגֵעַ בָּהֶם יִטְמָא: וְכֹל | הוֹלֵךְ עַל־

כח כַּפָּיו בְּכָל־הַחַיָּה הַהֹלֶכֶת עַל־אַרְבַּע טְמֵאִים הֵם לָכֶם כָּל־הַנֹּגֵעַ בְּנִבְלָתָם יִטְמָא עַד־הָעָרֶב: וְהַנֹּשֵׂא אֶת־נִבְלָתָם יְכַבֵּס בְּגָדָיו וְטָמֵא עַד־

כט הָעָרֶב טְמֵאִים הֵמָּה לָכֶם: וְזֶה לָכֶם הַטָּמֵא

ל בַּשֶּׁרֶץ הַשֹּׁרֵץ עַל־הָאָרֶץ הַחֹלֶד וְהָעַכְבָּר וְהַצָּב לְמִינֵהוּ: וְהָאֲנָקָה וְהַכֹּחַ

לא וְהַלְּטָאָה וְהַחֹמֶט וְהַתִּנְשָׁמֶת: אֵלֶּה הַטְּמֵאִים לָכֶם בְּכָל־הַשָּׁרֶץ כָּל־הַנֹּגֵעַ

לב בָּהֶם בְּמֹתָם יִטְמָא עַד־הָעָרֶב: וְכֹל אֲשֶׁר־יִפֹּל־עָלָיו מֵהֶם | בְּמֹתָם יִטְמָא מִכָּל־כְּלִי־עֵץ אוֹ בֶגֶד אוֹ־עוֹר אוֹ שָׂק כָּל־כְּלִי אֲשֶׁר־יֵעָשֶׂה מְלָאכָה

לג בָּהֶם בַּמַּיִם יוּבָא וְטָמֵא עַד־הָעֶרֶב וְטָהֵר: וְכָל־כְּלִי־חֶרֶשׂ אֲשֶׁר־יִפֹּל

לד מֵהֶם אֶל־תּוֹכוֹ כֹּל אֲשֶׁר בְּתוֹכוֹ יִטְמָא וְאֹתוֹ תִשְׁבֹּרוּ: מִכָּל־הָאֹכֶל אֲשֶׁר

שביעי

11:13-19. The Torah names the twenty non-kosher species of birds, but as a result of the various exiles and dispersions, the language of the Torah fell into relative disuse, and the exact identities of the non-kosher birds became doubtful. Therefore, the *Shulchan Aruch* (*Yoreh Deah* 82:2) rules that it is forbidden to eat any species of bird unless there is a well-established tradition that it is kosher. We follow the lead of R' Hirsch in transliterating the names, but the commentary offers possible translations.

11:13. Most commentators agree that the *nesher* is the eagle or bald eagle.

The *peres* is identified as the bearded vulture (*R' Saadiah Gaon*).

11:14. According to R' D.Z. Hoffmann's translation of R' Saadiah, the *daah* is the kite. *Ralbag* translates it as a species of vulture.

11:15. The *orev* is generally assumed to be the raven.

11:16. The *bas hayaanah* is identified as the ostrich (*R' Saadiah; Chizkuni*).

The *netz* is identified as the sparrow hawk (*Rashi; Ramban; Ralbag*).

11:17. Both the *kos* and the *yanshuf* are birds which howl at night and have cheeks that are similar to those of humans, i.e., the owl and the great horned owl (*Rashi*). According to *Ralbag*, *kos* is the falcon.

The *shalach* is a bird that draws fish from the water (*Rashi*), apparently a pelican, heron, or cormorant.

11:18. The *tinshemes* is identified as the bat (*Rashi; Chizkuni*), or the owl (*Ralbag*).

11:19. The *chasidah* is called by that name because it displays kindness [חֶסֶד] by sharing food with others of its species (*Rashi; Chullin* 63a). It is, however, not kosher because it directs its kindness exclusively towards its fellows, but will not help other species (*Rizhiner Rebbe*).

The *anafah* is identified as the heron (*Rashi*).

Rashi (*Chullin* 63a) identifies the *duchifas* as the wild hen whose comb is doubled over. *Rashi* here identifies it as the hoopoe.

The *atalef* is identified as the bat (*R' Saadiah*).

The forbidden birds * ¹³ These shall you abominate from among the birds, they may not be eaten — they are an abomination: the nesher, * the peres, * the ozniah; ¹⁴ the daah* and the ayah according to its kind; ¹⁵ every orev* according to its kind; ¹⁶ the bas hayaanah, * the tachmos, the shachaf, and the netz* according to its kind; ¹⁷ the kos, * the shalach, * and the yanshuf; * ¹⁸ the tinshemes, * the ka'as, and the racham; ¹⁹ the chasidah, * the anafah* according to its kind, the duchifas, * and the atalef. *

Forbidden and permissible insects ²⁰ Every flying teeming creature that walks on four legs — it is an abomination to you. ²¹ Only this may you eat from among all flying teeming creatures that walk on four legs: one that has jumping legs above its legs, with which to spring upon the earth. ²² You may eat these from among them: the arbeh according to its kind, the sal'am according to its kind, the chargol according to its kind, and the chagav according to its kind. ²³ Every flying teeming thing that has four legs — it is an abomination to you.

²⁴ You become contaminated* through the following — anyone who touches their carcass becomes contaminated until the evening; ²⁵ and anyone who carries part of their carcass shall immerse his clothing and be contaminated until *The non-kosher creatures that transmit contamination* the evening — ²⁶ every animal that has split hooves that are not completely split, or does not chew its cud, they are contaminated to you; whoever touches them becomes contaminated. ²⁷ And every one that walks on its paws, among all animals that walk on four legs, they are contaminated to you; whoever touches their carcass shall be contaminated until the evening. ²⁸ One who carries their carcass shall immerse his clothing and be contaminated until evening; they are contaminated to you.

The small creeping animals ²⁹ These are the contaminated ones* to you among the teeming animals that teem upon the earth: the choled, * the achbar, * and the tzav* according to its kind; ³⁰ the anakah, * the koach, * and the letaah; * and the chomet* and the tinshemes. * ³¹ Only these are contaminated to you among all the teeming animals; anyone who touches them when they are dead shall be contaminated *Objects receiving contamination* until evening; ³² and when they are dead, anything upon which part of them will fall shall become contaminated, * whether it is a wooden utensil, a garment, leather, or sackcloth — any utensil with which work is done — shall be brought into the water, and remain contaminated until evening, and then become cleansed.

³³ Any earthenware utensil into whose interior one of them will fall, everything in it shall become contaminated — and you shall break it — ³⁴ of any food that

---

11:24-47. The rest of the chapter discusses the transmission of טֻמְאָה, contamination.

11:29-31. This passage lists the eight small animals whose carcasses convey their contamination to people and objects.

11:29. According to Rashi and others, the choled is identified as a weasel. R' Saadiah identifies it as a mole.

It is generally agreed that the achbar is a mouse, and it may include similar rodents.

Rashi notes that the tzav resembles a frog, thus it is presumably a toad.

11:30. The anakah is identified as the hedgehog or porcupine (Rashi). According to Radak, it is a viper.

According to R' Saadiah, the koach is a species of lizard.

Rashi identifies the letaah as the lizard.

The chomet is identified as the snail (Rashi), or the chameleon (Radak).

The tinshemes is not the bird of the same name in verse 18 (Chullin 63a). According to Rashi, it is a mole; according to R' Saadiah, a type of lizard.

11:32-38. The Torah now turns to objects and how they receive contamination through coming in contact with any of the carcasses mentioned above.

יֹאכֵל אֲשֶׁר יָב֣וֹא עָלָ֧יו מַ֛יִם יִטְמָ֖א וְכָל־מַשְׁקֶה֙ אֲשֶׁ֣ר יִשָּׁתֶ֔ה בְּכָל־

לה כְּלִ֖י יִטְמָֽא: וְכֹ֣ל אֲשֶׁר־יִפֹּ֨ל מִנִּבְלָתָ֥ם ׀ עָלָיו֮ יִטְמָא֒ תַּנּ֧וּר וְכִירַ֛יִם יֻתָּ֖ץ

לו טְמֵאִ֥ים הֵ֖ם וּטְמֵאִ֥ים יִהְי֥וּ לָכֶֽם: אַ֣ךְ מַעְיָ֣ן וּב֗וֹר מִקְוֵה־מַ֛יִם יִהְיֶ֣ה

לז טָה֑וֹר וְנֹגֵ֥עַ בְּנִבְלָתָ֖ם יִטְמָֽא: וְכִ֣י יִפֹּל֮ מִנִּבְלָתָם֮ עַל־כָּל־זֶ֣רַע זֵר֖וּעַ אֲשֶׁ֣ר

לח יִזָּרֵ֑עַ טָה֖וֹר הֽוּא: וְכִ֤י יֻתַּן־מַ֙יִם֙ עַל־זֶ֔רַע וְנָפַ֥ל מִנִּבְלָתָ֖ם עָלָ֑יו טָמֵ֥א

לט ה֖וּא לָכֶֽם: וְכִ֤י יָמוּת֙ מִן־הַבְּהֵמָ֔ה אֲשֶׁר־הִ֥יא לָכֶ֖ם

מ לְאָכְלָ֑ה הַנֹּגֵ֥עַ בְּנִבְלָתָ֖הּ יִטְמָ֥א עַד־הָעָֽרֶב: וְהָ֣אֹכֵל֙ מִנִּבְלָתָ֔הּ יְכַבֵּ֥ס בְּגָדָ֖יו

    וְטָמֵ֣א עַד־הָעָ֑רֶב וְהַנֹּשֵׂא֙ אֶת־נִבְלָתָ֔הּ יְכַבֵּ֥ס בְּגָדָ֖יו וְטָמֵ֥א עַד־הָעָֽרֶב:

מא-מב וְכָל־הַשֶּׁ֖רֶץ הַשֹּׁרֵ֣ץ עַל־הָאָ֑רֶץ שֶׁ֥קֶץ ה֖וּא לֹ֥א יֵֽאָכֵֽל: כֹּל֩ הוֹלֵ֨ךְ עַל־

    *גָּח֜וֹן וְכֹ֣ל ׀ הוֹלֵ֣ךְ עַל־אַרְבַּ֗ע עַ֚ד כָּל־מַרְבֵּ֣ה רַגְלַ֔יִם לְכָל־הַשֶּׁ֖רֶץ הַשֹּׁרֵ֣ץ

מג עַל־הָאָ֑רֶץ לֹ֥א תֹֽאכְל֖וּם כִּי־שֶׁ֥קֶץ הֵֽם: אַל־תְּשַׁקְּצוּ֙ אֶת־נַפְשֹׁ֣תֵיכֶ֔ם

מד בְּכָל־הַשֶּׁ֖רֶץ הַשֹּׁרֵ֑ץ וְלֹ֤א תִֽטַּמְּאוּ֙ בָּהֶ֔ם וְנִטְמֵתֶ֖ם בָּֽם: כִּ֣י אֲנִ֣י יְהֹוָה֮

    אֱלֹֽהֵיכֶם֒ וְהִתְקַדִּשְׁתֶּם֙ וִהְיִיתֶ֣ם קְדֹשִׁ֔ים כִּ֥י קָד֖וֹשׁ אָ֑נִי וְלֹ֤א תְטַמְּאוּ֙ אֶת־

מה נַפְשֹׁ֣תֵיכֶ֔ם בְּכָל־הַשֶּׁ֖רֶץ הָרֹמֵ֥שׂ עַל־הָאָֽרֶץ: כִּ֣י ׀ אֲנִ֣י יְהֹוָ֗ה הַמַּעֲלֶ֤ה אֶתְכֶם֙

מו מֵאֶ֣רֶץ מִצְרַ֔יִם לִהְיֹ֥ת לָכֶ֖ם לֵֽאלֹהִ֑ים וִהְיִיתֶ֣ם קְדֹשִׁ֔ים כִּ֥י קָד֖וֹשׁ אָֽנִי: זֹ֣את

    תּוֹרַ֤ת הַבְּהֵמָה֙ וְהָע֔וֹף וְכֹל֙ נֶ֣פֶשׁ הַֽחַיָּ֔ה הָרֹמֶ֖שֶׂת בַּמָּ֑יִם וּלְכָל־נֶ֖פֶשׁ

מז הַשֹּׁרֶ֥צֶת עַל־הָאָֽרֶץ: לְהַבְדִּ֕יל בֵּ֥ין הַטָּמֵ֖א וּבֵ֣ין הַטָּהֹ֑ר וּבֵ֤ין הַֽחַיָּה֙

    הַנֶּֽאֱכֶ֔לֶת וּבֵין֙ הַֽחַיָּ֔ה אֲשֶׁ֖ר לֹ֥א תֵֽאָכֵֽל: פפפ   צ"א פסוקים. עבדי"ה סימן.

*ד׳ דגשון רבתי
וזיא חצי התורה
באותיות

מפטיר

Haftaras
Shemini:
p. 736

For special
Sabbaths,
see
pp. x-xi

פרשת תזריע

יב א-ב וַיְדַבֵּ֥ר יְהֹוָ֖ה אֶל־מֹשֶׁ֥ה לֵּאמֹֽר: דַּבֵּ֞ר אֶל־בְּנֵ֤י יִשְׂרָאֵל֙ לֵאמֹ֔ר אִשָּׁה֙ כִּ֣י

ג תַזְרִ֔יעַ וְיָלְדָ֖ה זָכָ֑ר וְטָֽמְאָה֙ שִׁבְעַ֣ת יָמִ֔ים כִּימֵ֛י נִדַּ֥ת דְּוֺתָ֖הּ תִּטְמָֽא: וּבַיּ֖וֹם

ד הַשְּׁמִינִ֑י יִמּ֖וֹל בְּשַׂ֥ר עָרְלָתֽוֹ: וּשְׁלֹשִׁ֥ים יוֹם֙ וּשְׁלֹ֣שֶׁת יָמִ֔ים תֵּשֵׁ֖ב בִּדְמֵ֣י

    טׇהֳרָ֑ה בְּכָל־קֹ֣דֶשׁ לֹֽא־תִגָּ֗ע וְאֶל־הַמִּקְדָּשׁ֙ לֹ֣א תָבֹ֔א עַד־מְלֹ֖את יְמֵ֥י

ה טׇהֳרָֽהּ: וְאִם־נְקֵבָ֣ה תֵלֵ֔ד וְטָֽמְאָ֥ה שְׁבֻעַ֖יִם כְּנִדָּתָ֑הּ וְשִׁשִּׁ֥ים יוֹם֙ וְשֵׁ֣שֶׁת

ו יָמִ֔ים תֵּשֵׁ֖ב עַל־דְּמֵ֥י טׇהֳרָֽה: וּבִמְלֹ֣את ׀ יְמֵ֣י טׇהֳרָ֗הּ לְבֵן֮ א֣וֹ לְבַת֒ תָּבִ֞יא

    כֶּ֤בֶשׂ בֶּן־שְׁנָתוֹ֙ לְעֹלָ֔ה וּבֶן־יוֹנָ֥ה אוֹ־תֹ֖ר לְחַטָּ֑את אֶל־פֶּ֥תַח אֹֽהֶל־מוֹעֵ֖ד

ז אֶל־הַכֹּהֵֽן: וְהִקְרִיב֞וֹ לִפְנֵ֤י יְהֹוָה֙ וְכִפֶּ֣ר עָלֶ֔יהָ וְטָהֲרָ֖ה מִמְּקֹ֣ר דָּמֶ֑יהָ זֹ֤את

ח תּוֹרַת֙ הַיֹּלֶ֔דֶת לַזָּכָ֖ר א֣וֹ לַנְּקֵבָֽה: וְאִם־לֹ֨א תִמְצָ֣א יָדָהּ֮ דֵּ֣י שֶׂה֒ וְלָקְחָ֣ה

    שְׁתֵּֽי־תֹרִ֗ים א֤וֹ שְׁנֵי֙ בְּנֵ֣י יוֹנָ֔ה אֶחָ֥ד לְעֹלָ֖ה וְאֶחָ֣ד לְחַטָּ֑את וְכִפֶּ֥ר עָלֶ֛יהָ

    הַכֹּהֵ֖ן וְטָהֵֽרָה:

◆§ Parashas Tazria. The Torah now turns to *tumah* that
emanates from human beings (Chs. 12-15).

12:4. Seven days after giving birth to a boy, the mother
immerses herself to remove the *niddah* contamination,

following which she assumes a new status for the next
thirty-three days. She remains in a partial state of contamination, until she brings her offering at the end of the
thirty-three-day period.

is edible, upon which water comes, shall become contaminated; and any bever-age that can be drunk, in any vessel, shall become contaminated. ³⁵ *Anything upon which part of their carcass may fall shall be contaminated — an oven or a stove shall be smashed — they are contaminated and they shall remain contam-inated to you —* ³⁶ *only a spring or a cistern, a gathering of water, shall remain pure — but one who touches their carcass shall become contaminated.* ³⁷ *And if its carcass will fall upon any edible seed that has been planted, it remains pure.* ³⁸ *But if water had been placed upon a seed and then their carcass falls upon it, it is contaminated to you.*

Contamin-ation of kosher animals

³⁹ *If an animal that you may eat has died, one who touches its carcass shall become contaminated until evening.* ⁴⁰ *And one who eats from its carcass shall immerse his clothing and remain contaminated until evening; and one who car-ries its carcass shall immerse his clothing and remain contaminated until evening.*

Prohibition of eating creeping creatures

⁴¹ *Every teeming creature that teems upon the ground — it is an abomination, it shall not be eaten.* ⁴² *Everything that creeps on its belly, and everything that walks on four legs, up to those with numerous legs, among all the teeming things that teem upon the earth, you may not eat them, for they are an abomination.* ⁴³ *Do not make yourselves abominable by means of any teeming thing; do not contaminate yourselves through them lest you become contaminated through them.*

⁴⁴ *For I am* HASHEM *your God — you are to sanctify yourselves and you shall be holy, for I am holy; and you shall not contaminate yourselves through any teeming thing that creeps on the earth.* ⁴⁵ *For I am* HASHEM *Who elevates you from the land of Egypt to be a God unto you; you shall be holy, for I am holy.*

⁴⁶ *This is the law of the animal, the bird, every living creature that swarms in the water, and for every creature that teems on the ground;* ⁴⁷ *to distinguish between the contaminated and the pure, and between the creature that may be eaten and the creature that may not be eaten.*

PARASHAS TAZRIA

12

¹ **H**ASHEM *spoke to Moses, saying:* ² *Speak to the Children of Israel, saying: When a woman conceives and gives birth to a male, she shall be contami-nated for a seven-day period, as during the days of her separation infirmity shall*

Human contamina-tion

she be contaminated. ³ *On the eighth day, the flesh of his foreskin shall be circumcised.* ⁴ *For thirty-three days she shall remain in blood of purity; she may not touch anything sacred and she may not enter the Sanctuary, until the*

Childbirth and purification
(See Appendix B, charts 6-8)

completion of her days of purity. * ⁵ *If she gives birth to a female, she shall be contaminated for two weeks, as during her separation; and for sixty-six days she shall remain in blood of purity.*

⁶ *Upon the completion of the days of her purity for a son or for a daughter, she shall bring a sheep within its first year for a burnt-offering, and a young dove or a turtledove for a sin-offering, to the entrance of the Tent of Meeting, to the Kohen.* ⁷ *He shall offer it before* HASHEM *and atone for her, and she becomes purified from the source of her blood; this is the law of one who gives birth to a male or to a female.* ⁸ *But if she cannot afford a sheep, then she shall take two turtledoves or two young doves, one for a burnt-offering and one for a sin-offering; and the Kohen shall provide atonement for her and she shall become purified.*

יג

א־ב וַיְדַבֵּ֣ר יהוה אֶל־מֹשֶׁ֥ה וְאֶֽל־אַהֲרֹ֖ן לֵאמֹֽר: אָדָ֗ם כִּֽי־יִהְיֶ֤ה בְעוֹר־בְּשָׂרוֹ֙ שְׂאֵ֤ת אֽוֹ־סַפַּ֙חַת֙ א֣וֹ בַהֶ֔רֶת וְהָיָ֥ה בְעוֹר־בְּשָׂר֖וֹ לְנֶ֣גַע צָרָ֑עַת וְהוּבָא֙

ג אֶל־אַהֲרֹ֣ן הַכֹּהֵ֔ן א֛וֹ אֶל־אַחַ֥ד מִבָּנָ֖יו הַכֹּהֲנִֽים: וְרָאָ֣ה הַכֹּהֵ֣ן אֶת־הַנֶּ֣גַע בְּעֽוֹר־הַבָּשָׂ֡ר וְשֵׂעָר֩ בַּנֶּ֨גַע הָפַ֣ךְ ׀ לָבָ֗ן וּמַרְאֵ֤ה הַנֶּ֙גַע֙ עָמֹק֙ מֵע֣וֹר בְּשָׂר֔וֹ נֶ֥גַע

ד צָרַ֖עַת ה֑וּא וְרָאָ֥הוּ הַכֹּהֵ֖ן וְטִמֵּ֥א אֹתֽוֹ: וְאִם־בַּהֶ֩רֶת֩ לְבָנָ֨ה הִ֜וא בְּע֣וֹר בְּשָׂר֗וֹ וְעָמֹק֙ אֵין־מַרְאֶ֣הָ מִן־הָע֔וֹר וּשְׂעָרָ֖הֿ לֹא־הָפַ֣ךְ לָבָ֑ן וְהִסְגִּ֧יר הַכֹּהֵ֛ן אֶת־ *וֹ רפה

ה הַנֶּ֖גַע שִׁבְעַ֥ת יָמִֽים: וְרָאָ֣הוּ הַכֹּהֵן֮ בַּיּ֣וֹם הַשְּׁבִיעִי֒ וְהִנֵּ֤ה הַנֶּ֙גַע֙ עָמַ֣ד בְּעֵינָ֔יו

ו לֹֽא־פָשָׂ֥ה הַנֶּ֖גַע בָּע֑וֹר וְהִסְגִּיר֧וֹ הַכֹּהֵ֛ן שִׁבְעַ֥ת יָמִ֖ים שֵׁנִֽית: וְרָאָה֩ הַכֹּהֵ֨ן אֹת֜וֹ בַּיּ֣וֹם הַשְּׁבִיעִי֮ שֵׁנִית֒ וְהִנֵּה֙ כֵּהָ֣ה הַנֶּ֔גַע וְלֹא־פָשָׂ֥ה הַנֶּ֖גַע בָּע֑וֹר וְטִהֲר֤וֹ שֵׁנִי

ז הַכֹּהֵן֙ מִסְפַּ֣חַת הִ֔וא וְכִבֶּ֥ס בְּגָדָ֖יו וְטָהֵֽר: וְאִם־פָּשֹׂ֨ה תִפְשֶׂ֤ה הַמִּסְפַּ֙חַת֙

ח בָּע֔וֹר אַחֲרֵ֧י הֵרָאֹת֛וֹ אֶל־הַכֹּהֵ֖ן לְטָהֳרָת֑וֹ וְנִרְאָ֥ה שֵׁנִ֖ית אֶל־הַכֹּהֵֽן: וְרָאָה֙ הַכֹּהֵ֔ן וְהִנֵּ֛ה פָּשְׂתָ֥ה הַמִּסְפַּ֖חַת בָּע֑וֹר וְטִמְּא֥וֹ הַכֹּהֵ֖ן צָרַ֥עַת הִֽוא:

ט נֶ֣גַע צָרַ֔עַת כִּ֥י תִהְיֶ֖ה בְּאָדָ֑ם וְהוּבָ֖א אֶל־הַכֹּהֵֽן: וְרָאָ֣ה הַכֹּהֵ֗ן וְהִנֵּ֤ה שְׂאֵת־

י לְבָנָה֙ בָּע֔וֹר וְהִ֕יא הָפְכָ֖ה שֵׂעָ֣ר לָבָ֑ן וּמִֽחְיַ֛ת בָּשָׂ֥ר חַ֖י בַּשְׂאֵֽת: צָרַ֨עַת נוֹשֶׁ֤נֶת

יא הִוא֙ בְּע֣וֹר בְּשָׂר֔וֹ וְטִמְּא֖וֹ הַכֹּהֵ֑ן לֹ֣א יַסְגִּרֶ֔נּוּ כִּ֥י טָמֵ֖א הֽוּא: וְאִם־פָּר֨וֹחַ

יב תִּפְרַ֤ח הַצָּרַ֙עַת֙ בָּע֔וֹר וְכִסְּתָ֣ה הַצָּרַ֗עַת אֵ֚ת כָּל־ע֣וֹר הַנֶּ֔גַע מֵרֹאשׁ֖וֹ וְעַד־כָּל־

יג רַגְלָ֑יו לְכָל־מַרְאֵ֖ה עֵינֵ֥י הַכֹּהֵֽן: וְרָאָ֣ה הַכֹּהֵ֗ן וְהִנֵּ֨ה כִסְּתָ֤ה הַצָּרַ֙עַת֙ אֶת־כָּל־

יד בְּשָׂר֔וֹ וְטִהַ֖ר אֶת־הַנָּ֑גַע כֻּלּ֛וֹ הָפַ֥ךְ לָבָ֖ן טָה֥וֹר הֽוּא: וּבְי֨וֹם הֵרָא֥וֹת בּ֛וֹ בָּשָׂ֥ר

טו חַ֖י יִטְמָֽא: וְרָאָ֤ה הַכֹּהֵן֙ אֶת־הַבָּשָׂ֣ר הַחַ֔י וְטִמְּא֑וֹ הַבָּשָׂ֥ר הַחַ֛י טָמֵ֥א ה֖וּא

טז־יז צָרַ֥עַת הֽוּא: א֣וֹ כִ֣י יָשׁ֞וּב הַבָּשָׂ֧ר הַחַ֛י וְנֶהְפַּ֥ךְ לְלָבָ֖ן וּבָ֥א אֶל־הַכֹּהֵֽן: וְרָאָ֙הוּ֙ הַכֹּהֵ֔ן וְהִנֵּ֛ה נֶהְפַּ֥ךְ הַנֶּ֖גַע לְלָבָ֑ן וְטִהַ֧ר הַכֹּהֵ֛ן אֶת־הַנֶּ֖גַע טָה֥וֹר הֽוּא:

יח־יט וּבָשָׂ֕ר כִּֽי־יִהְיֶ֥ה בֽוֹ־בְעֹר֖וֹ שְׁחִ֑ין וְנִרְפָּֽא: וְהָיָ֞ה בִּמְק֤וֹם הַשְּׁחִין֙ שְׂאֵ֣ת לְבָנָ֔ה שלישי

כ א֥וֹ בַהֶ֖רֶת לְבָנָ֣ה אֲדַמְדָּ֑מֶת וְנִרְאָ֖ה אֶל־הַכֹּהֵֽן: וְרָאָ֣ה הַכֹּהֵ֗ן וְהִנֵּ֤ה מַרְאֶ֙הָ֙ שָׁפָ֣ל מִן־הָע֔וֹר וּשְׂעָרָ֖הּ הָפַ֣ךְ לָבָ֑ן וְטִמְּא֧וֹ הַכֹּהֵ֛ן נֶֽגַע־צָרַ֥עַת הִ֖וא בַּשְּׁחִ֥ין

כא פָּרָֽחָה: וְאִ֣ם ׀ יִרְאֶ֣נָּה הַכֹּהֵ֗ן וְהִנֵּ֤ה אֵֽין־בָּהּ֙ שֵׂעָ֣ר לָבָ֔ן וּשְׁפָלָ֥ה אֵינֶ֖נָּה מִן־

כב הָע֛וֹר וְהִ֥יא כֵהָ֖ה וְהִסְגִּיר֥וֹ הַכֹּהֵ֖ן שִׁבְעַ֥ת יָמִֽים: וְאִם־פָּשֹׂ֥ה תִפְשֶׂ֖ה בָּע֑וֹר

כג וְטִמֵּ֧א הַכֹּהֵ֛ן אֹת֖וֹ נֶ֣גַע הִֽוא: וְאִם־תַּחְתֶּ֜יהָ תַּעֲמֹ֤ד הַבַּהֶ֙רֶת֙ לֹ֣א פָשָׂ֔תָה

כד צָרֶ֥בֶת הַשְּׁחִ֖ין הִ֑וא וְטִהֲר֖וֹ הַכֹּהֵֽן: רביעי [שני]

⮜§ **Chapter 13: The laws of tzaraas.**

13:2. The popular translation of צָרַעַת [tzaraas] has been "leprosy," and it was commonly accepted that prevention of the disease's spread was the reason for the quarantine of a person smitten with the malady. However, R' Hirsch demonstrates at length that these notions are completely erroneous.

Tzaraas is the physical manifestation of a spiritual malaise. The primary cause of tzaraas is the sin of slander. Similarly, it is a punishment for the sins of blood-shed, false oaths, sexual immorality, pride, robbery, and selfishness (Arachin 16a, Midrash). Thus tzaraas is a Divine retribution for the offender's failure to feel the needs and share the hurt of others. God isolates him from society, so that he can experience the pain he has imposed on others — and heal himself through repentance.

We transliterate the Hebrew, since there is no accurate translation of either the word tzaraas or its subdivisions. The forms of tzaraas mentioned here are all white patches on the skin.

13

The basic tzaraas and the procedure for verification

¹ HASHEM spoke to Moses and to Aaron, saying: ² If a person will have on the skin of his flesh a s'eis, or a sapachas, or a baheres, and it will become a tzaraas* affliction on the skin of his flesh; he shall be brought to Aaron the Kohen, or to one of his sons the Kohanim. ³ The Kohen shall look at the affliction on the skin of his flesh: If hair in the affliction has changed to white, and the affliction's appearance is deeper than the skin of his flesh — it is a tzaraas affliction; the Kohen shall look at it and declare him contaminated.

Baheres

⁴ If it is a white baheres on the skin of his flesh, and its appearance is not deeper than the skin, and the hair has not changed to white, then the Kohen shall quarantine the affliction for a seven-day period. ⁵ The Kohen shall look at it on the seventh day, and behold! — the affliction retained its color, and the affliction did not spread on the skin, then the Kohen shall quarantine it for a second seven-day period. ⁶ The Kohen shall look at it again on the seventh day, and behold! — if the affliction has dimmed and the affliction has not spread on the skin, then the Kohen shall declare him pure, it is a mispachas; he shall immerse his garments and become pure. ⁷ But if the mispachas should spread on the skin after it had been shown to the Kohen for its purification, it should be shown to the Kohen again. ⁸ The Kohen shall look, and behold! — the mispachas has spread on the skin; the Kohen shall declare him contaminated; it is tzaraas.

⁹ If a tzaraas affliction will be in a person, he shall be brought to the Kohen.

S'eis

¹⁰ The Kohen shall look, and behold! — it is a white s'eis on the skin, and it has changed hair to white, or there is healthy, live flesh within the s'eis: ¹¹ It is an old tzaraas on the skin of his flesh and the Kohen shall declare him contaminated; he shall not quarantine it for it is contaminated.

¹² If the tzaraas will erupt on the skin, and the tzaraas will cover the entire skin of the tzaraas from his head to his feet, wherever the eyes of the Kohen can see — ¹³ the Kohen shall look, and behold! — the affliction has covered his entire flesh, then he shall declare the affliction to be pure; having turned completely white, it is pure. ¹⁴ On the day healthy flesh appears in it, it shall be contaminated. ¹⁵ The Kohen shall look at the healthy flesh and declare him contaminated; the healthy flesh is contaminated, it is tzaraas. ¹⁶ But if the healthy flesh changes again and turns white, he shall come to the Kohen. ¹⁷ The Kohen shall look at it, and behold! — the affliction has changed to white, the Kohen shall declare the affliction pure; it is pure.

Inflammations

¹⁸ If flesh will have had an inflammation* on its skin, and it will have healed, ¹⁹ and on the place of the inflammation there will be a white s'eis or a white baheres, streaked with red; it shall be shown to the Kohen. ²⁰ The Kohen shall look, and behold! — its appearance is lower than the skin, and its hair has turned white: The Kohen shall declare him contaminated; it is a tzaraas affliction that erupted on the inflammation. ²¹ But if the Kohen looks at it, and behold! — there is no white hair in it, and it is not lower than the skin, and it is dim; the Kohen shall quarantine it for a seven-day period. ²² If it spreads on the skin, the Kohen shall declare him contaminated; it is an affliction. ²³ But if the baheres remains in its place without spreading, it is the scarring of the inflammation; the Kohen shall declare him pure. *

13:18-23. Any wound to the flesh, whether due to illness or a blow, is called *inflammation*. Only after it is completely healed is it treated like the afflictions described above. The verses below discuss a wound that has begun to heal and has a thin layer of skin over it.

כה כִּי־יִהְיֶה בְעֹרוֹ מִכְוַת־אֵשׁ וְהָיְתָה מִחְיַת הַמִּכְוָה בַּהֶרֶת לְבָנָה אֲדַמְדֶּמֶת אוֹ לְבָנָה: וְרָאָה אֹתָהּ הַכֹּהֵן וְהִנֵּה נֶהְפַּךְ שֵׂעָר לָבָן בַּבַּהֶרֶת וּמַרְאֶהָ עָמֹק מִן־הָעוֹר צָרַעַת הִוא בַּמִּכְוָה פָּרָחָה וְטִמֵּא אֹתוֹ הַכֹּהֵן נֶגַע צָרַעַת הִוא:

כו וְאִם ׀ יִרְאֶנָּה הַכֹּהֵן וְהִנֵּה אֵין־בַּבַּהֶרֶת שֵׂעָר לָבָן וּשְׁפָלָה אֵינֶנָּה מִן־הָעוֹר כז וְהִוא כֵהָה וְהִסְגִּירוֹ הַכֹּהֵן שִׁבְעַת יָמִים: וְרָאָהוּ הַכֹּהֵן בַּיּוֹם הַשְּׁבִיעִי אִם־ כח פָּשֹׂה תִפְשֶׂה בָּעוֹר וְטִמֵּא הַכֹּהֵן אֹתוֹ נֶגַע צָרַעַת הִוא: וְאִם־תַּחְתֶּיהָ תַעֲמֹד הַבַּהֶרֶת לֹא־פָשְׂתָה בָעוֹר וְהִוא כֵהָה שְׂאֵת הַמִּכְוָה הִוא וְטִהֲרוֹ הַכֹּהֵן כִּי־צָרֶבֶת הַמִּכְוָה הִוא:

חמישי כט וְאִישׁ אוֹ אִשָּׁה כִּי־יִהְיֶה בוֹ נָגַע בְּרֹאשׁ אוֹ בְזָקָן: וְרָאָה הַכֹּהֵן אֶת־הַנֶּגַע ל וְהִנֵּה מַרְאֵהוּ עָמֹק מִן־הָעוֹר וּבוֹ שֵׂעָר צָהֹב דָּק וְטִמֵּא אֹתוֹ הַכֹּהֵן נֶתֶק לא הוּא צָרַעַת הָרֹאשׁ אוֹ הַזָּקָן הוּא: וְכִי־יִרְאֶה הַכֹּהֵן אֶת־נֶגַע הַנֶּתֶק וְהִנֵּה אֵין־מַרְאֵהוּ עָמֹק מִן־הָעוֹר וְשֵׂעָר שָׁחֹר אֵין בּוֹ וְהִסְגִּיר הַכֹּהֵן אֶת־ לב נֶגַע הַנֶּתֶק שִׁבְעַת יָמִים: וְרָאָה הַכֹּהֵן אֶת־הַנֶּגַע בַּיּוֹם הַשְּׁבִיעִי וְהִנֵּה לֹא־פָשָׂה הַנֶּתֶק וְלֹא־הָיָה בוֹ שֵׂעָר צָהֹב וּמַרְאֵה הַנֶּתֶק אֵין עָמֹק מִן־

יג רבתי לג הָעוֹר: וְהִתְגַּלָּח וְאֶת־הַנֶּתֶק לֹא יְגַלֵּחַ וְהִסְגִּיר הַכֹּהֵן אֶת־הַנֶּתֶק שִׁבְעַת לד יָמִים שֵׁנִית: וְרָאָה הַכֹּהֵן אֶת־הַנֶּתֶק בַּיּוֹם הַשְּׁבִיעִי וְהִנֵּה לֹא־פָשָׂה הַנֶּתֶק בָּעוֹר וּמַרְאֵהוּ אֵינֶנּוּ עָמֹק מִן־הָעוֹר וְטִהַר אֹתוֹ הַכֹּהֵן וְכִבֶּס בְּגָדָיו לה-לו וְטָהֵר: וְאִם־פָּשֹׂה יִפְשֶׂה הַנֶּתֶק בָּעוֹר אַחֲרֵי טָהֳרָתוֹ: וְרָאָהוּ הַכֹּהֵן לז וְהִנֵּה פָּשָׂה הַנֶּתֶק בָּעוֹר לֹא־יְבַקֵּר הַכֹּהֵן לַשֵּׂעָר הַצָּהֹב טָמֵא הוּא: וְאִם־ בְּעֵינָיו עָמַד הַנֶּתֶק וְשֵׂעָר שָׁחֹר צָמַח־בּוֹ נִרְפָּא הַנֶּתֶק טָהוֹר הוּא וְטִהֲרוֹ לח הַכֹּהֵן: וְאִישׁ אוֹ־אִשָּׁה כִּי־יִהְיֶה בְעוֹר־בְּשָׂרָם בֶּהָרֹת לט בֶּהָרֹת לְבָנֹת: וְרָאָה הַכֹּהֵן וְהִנֵּה בְעוֹר־בְּשָׂרָם בֶּהָרֹת כֵּהוֹת לְבָנֹת בֹּהַק הוּא פָּרַח בָּעוֹר טָהוֹר הוּא:

ששי [שלישי] מ וְאִישׁ כִּי יִמָּרֵט רֹאשׁוֹ קֵרֵחַ הוּא טָהוֹר הוּא: וְאִם מִפְּאַת פָּנָיו יִמָּרֵט מא רֹאשׁוֹ גִּבֵּחַ הוּא טָהוֹר הוּא: מב וְכִי־יִהְיֶה בַקָּרַחַת אוֹ בַגַּבַּחַת נֶגַע לָבָן אֲדַמְדָּם צָרַעַת פֹּרַחַת הִוא מג בְּקָרַחְתּוֹ אוֹ בְגַבַּחְתּוֹ: וְרָאָה אֹתוֹ הַכֹּהֵן וְהִנֵּה שְׂאֵת־הַנֶּגַע לְבָנָה מד אֲדַמְדֶּמֶת בְּקָרַחְתּוֹ אוֹ בְגַבַּחְתּוֹ כְּמַרְאֵה צָרַעַת עוֹר בָּשָׂר: אִישׁ־צָרוּעַ מה הוּא טָמֵא הוּא טַמֵּא יְטַמְּאֶנּוּ הַכֹּהֵן בְּרֹאשׁוֹ נִגְעוֹ: וְהַצָּרוּעַ אֲשֶׁר־בּוֹ הַנֶּגַע בְּגָדָיו יִהְיוּ פְרֻמִים וְרֹאשׁוֹ יִהְיֶה פָרוּעַ וְעַל־שָׂפָם יַעְטֶה וְטָמֵא ׀ טָמֵא מו יִקְרָא: כָּל־יְמֵי אֲשֶׁר הַנֶּגַע בּוֹ יִטְמָא טָמֵא הוּא בָּדָד יֵשֵׁב מִחוּץ לַמַּחֲנֶה

13:30. A *nesek* is the name of *tzaraas* of the scalp or beard area (*Rashi*). It is the *tzaraas* affliction that caused the hair loss (*Sforno*).

13:40-44. In case someone loses *all* the hair of the back half of his head [*karachas*], of the front half of his head [*gabachas*], or of his beard, the newly bald skin is treated like skin anywhere else on his body.

13:45-46. The list of human *tzaraas* afflictions has been concluded and the Torah goes on to the laws relating to the *metzora's* required behavior. The rules of his isolation from the community are given in these two verses, and they apply to all the cases in this chapter. The procedure of his cleansing ritual once his affliction has healed is given in the next *Sidrah*.

Burns   ²⁴ If a person will have a burn from fire on his skin, and the healed skin of the burn is a white baheres that is streaked with red or is all white; ²⁵ the Kohen shall look, and behold! — hair has turned white in the baheres, and its appearance is deeper than the skin, it is tzaraas that erupted on the burn, the Kohen shall declare him contaminated; it is a tzaraas affliction. ²⁶ And if the Kohen looks at it and behold! — there is no white hair in the baheres, and it is not lower than the skin, and it is dim; the Kohen shall quarantine him for a seven-day period. ²⁷ The Kohen shall look at it on the seventh day: If it has spread on the skin, the Kohen shall declare him contaminated; it is a tzaraas affliction. ²⁸ But if the baheres remains in its place, not spreading on the skin, and it is dim, it is a s'eis of the burn; the Kohen shall declare him pure, for it is the scarring of the burn.

Tzaraas of the head or face   ²⁹ A man or a woman in whom there will be an affliction, on the scalp or in the beard: ³⁰ The Kohen shall look at the affliction, and behold! — its appearance is deeper than the skin, and within it is weak, golden hair; the Kohen shall declare him contaminated; it is a nesek, * a tzaraas of the head or the beard.

³¹ But if the Kohen looks at the nesek affliction, and behold! — its appearance is not deeper than the skin, but there is no dark hair within it; the Kohen shall quarantine the nesek affliction for a seven-day period. ³² The Kohen shall look at the affliction on the seventh day and behold! — the nesek had not spread and no golden hair was in it, and the appearance of the nesek is not deeper than the skin — ³³ then he shall shave himself, but he shall not shave the nesek; and the Kohen shall quarantine the nesek for a second seven-day period. ³⁴ The Kohen shall look at the nesek on the seventh day, and behold! — the nesek had not spread on the skin, and its appearance is not deeper than the skin; the Kohen shall declare him pure, and he shall immerse his clothing and he is pure.

³⁵ But if the nesek shall spread on the skin after he has been declared pure, ³⁶ the Kohen shall look at it, and behold! — the nesek has spread on the skin: The Kohen need not examine it for a golden hair, it is contaminated. ³⁷ But if the nesek has retained its appearance, and dark hair has sprouted in it, the nesek has healed — it is pure; the Kohen shall declare it pure.

³⁸ If a man or woman has spots in the skin of their flesh, white spots; ³⁹ the Kohen shall look, and behold! — on the skin of their flesh are dim white spots, it is a bohak that has erupted on the skin, it is pure.

Baldness at the front and back of the head   ⁴⁰ If the hair of a man's head falls out: He is bald at the back of the head, * he is pure. ⁴¹ And if his hair falls out toward the front of his head, he is frontally bald, he is pure. ⁴² And if in the posterior or frontal baldness there shall be a white affliction streaked with red: It is an eruption of tzaraas on his posterior or frontal baldness. ⁴³ The Kohen shall look at it, and behold! — there is a s'eis affliction that is white streaked with red, in his posterior or frontal baldness, like the appearance of tzaraas on the skin of the flesh. ⁴⁴ He is a person with tzaraas, he is contaminated; the Kohen shall declare him contaminated; his affliction is upon his head.

The metzora's isolation   ⁴⁵ And the person with tzaraas in whom there is the affliction * — his garments shall be rent, the hair of his head shall be unshorn, and he shall cloak himself up to his lips; he is to call out: "Contaminated, contaminated!" ⁴⁶ All the days that the affliction is upon him he shall remain contaminated; he is contaminated. He shall dwell in isolation; his dwelling shall be outside the camp.

מז מוֹשָׁבֽוֹ׃ וְהַבֶּ֣גֶד כִּֽי־יִהְיֶ֧ה ב֣וֹ נֶ֣גַע צָרָ֑עַת בְּבֶ֣גֶד צֶ֔מֶר א֖וֹ בְּבֶ֥גֶד

מח פִּשְׁתִּֽים׃ א֤וֹ בִשְׁתִי֙ א֣וֹ בְעֵ֔רֶב לַפִּשְׁתִּ֖ים וְלַצָּ֑מֶר א֣וֹ בְע֔וֹר א֖וֹ בְּכָל־מְלֶ֥אכֶת

מט עֽוֹר׃ וְהָיָ֣ה הַנֶּ֡גַע יְרַקְרַ֣ק ׀ א֣וֹ אֲדַמְדָּ֗ם בַּבֶּ֩גֶד֩ א֨וֹ בָע֜וֹר אֽוֹ־בַשְּׁתִ֤י אֽוֹ־בָעֵ֙רֶב֙

נ א֣וֹ בְכָל־כְּלִי־ע֔וֹר נֶ֥גַע צָרַ֖עַת ה֑וּא וְהָרְאָ֖ה אֶת־הַכֹּהֵֽן׃ וְרָאָ֥ה הַכֹּהֵ֖ן אֶת־

נא הַנָּ֑גַע וְהִסְגִּ֥יר אֶת־הַנֶּ֖גַע שִׁבְעַ֥ת יָמִֽים׃ וְרָאָ֣ה אֶת־הַנֶּ֗גַע בַּיּוֹם֙ הַשְּׁבִיעִי֙ כִּֽי־

נב פָשָׂ֤ה הַנֶּ֙גַע֙ בַּ֠בֶּ֠גֶד אֽוֹ־בַשְּׁתִ֤י אֽוֹ־בָעֵ֙רֶב֙ א֣וֹ בָע֔וֹר לְכֹ֛ל אֲשֶׁר־יֵעָשֶׂ֥ה הָע֖וֹר

נג לִמְלָאכָ֑ה צָרַ֨עַת מַמְאֶ֤רֶת הַנֶּ֙גַע֙ ה֔וּא בָּאֵ֖שׁ תִּשָּׂרֵֽף׃ וְשָׂרַ֣ף אֶת־הַבֶּ֗גֶד א֤וֹ אֶת־

נד הַשְּׁתִי֙ ׀ א֣וֹ אֶת־הָעֵ֔רֶב בַּצֶּ֙מֶר֙ א֣וֹ בַפִּשְׁתִּ֔ים א֚וֹ אֶת־כָּל־כְּלִ֣י הָע֔וֹר אֲשֶׁר־

נה יִהְיֶ֥ה ב֖וֹ הַנָּ֑גַע כִּֽי־צָרַ֤עַת מַמְאֶ֙רֶת֙ ה֔וּא בָּאֵ֖שׁ תִּשָּׂרֵֽף׃ וְאִם֮ יִרְאֶ֣ה הַכֹּהֵן֒

נו וְהִנֵּה֙ לֹֽא־פָשָׂ֤ה הַנֶּ֙גַע֙ בַּבֶּ֔גֶד א֥וֹ בַשְּׁתִ֖י א֣וֹ בָעֵ֑רֶב א֖וֹ בְכָל־כְּלִי־ע֔וֹר׃ וְצִוָּה֙

הַכֹּהֵ֗ן וְכִבְּס֗וּ אֵ֤ת אֲשֶׁר־בּוֹ֙ הַנָּ֔גַע וְהִסְגִּיר֥וֹ שִׁבְעַת־יָמִ֖ים שֵׁנִֽית׃ וְרָאָ֣ה הַכֹּהֵ֣ן

אַֽחֲרֵ֣י ׀ הֻכַּבֵּ֣ס אֶת־הַנֶּ֡גַע וְ֠הִנֵּ֠ה לֹֽא־הָפַ֨ךְ הַנֶּ֤גַע אֶת־עֵינוֹ֙ וְהַנֶּ֣גַע לֹֽא־פָשָׂ֔ה

טָמֵ֣א ה֔וּא בָּאֵ֖שׁ תִּשְׂרְפֶ֑נּוּ פְּחֶ֣תֶת הִ֔וא בְּקָרַחְתּ֖וֹ א֥וֹ בְגַבַּחְתּֽוֹ׃ וְאִם֩ רָאָ֨ה

נו הַכֹּהֵ֜ן וְהִנֵּ֣ה כֵּהָ֣ה הַנֶּ֗גַע אַֽחֲרֵי֙ הֻכַּבֵּ֣ס אֹת֔וֹ וְקָרַ֣ע אֹת֔וֹ מִן־הַבֶּ֙גֶד֙ א֣וֹ מִן־

נז הָע֔וֹר א֥וֹ מִן־הַשְּׁתִ֖י א֣וֹ מִן־הָעֵ֑רֶב וְאִם־תֵּֽרָאֶ֨ה ע֜וֹד בַּבֶּ֤גֶד אֽוֹ־בַשְּׁתִ֤י אֽוֹ־

בָעֵ֙רֶב֙ א֣וֹ בְכָל־כְּלִי־ע֔וֹר פֹּרַ֖חַת הִ֑וא בָּאֵ֣שׁ תִּשְׂרְפֶ֔נּוּ אֵ֥ת אֲשֶׁר־בּ֖וֹ הַנָּֽגַע׃

נח וְהַבֶּ֡גֶד אֽוֹ־הַשְּׁתִ֨י אֽוֹ־הָעֵ֜רֶב אֽוֹ־כָל־כְּלִ֣י הָע֗וֹר אֲשֶׁ֣ר תְּכַבֵּ֔ס וְסָ֥ר מֵהֶ֖ם הַנָּ֑גַע

נט וְכֻבַּ֖ס שֵׁנִ֥ית וְטָהֵֽר׃ זֹ֠את תּוֹרַ֨ת נֶֽגַע־צָרַ֜עַת בֶּ֥גֶד הַצֶּ֣מֶר ׀ א֣וֹ הַפִּשְׁתִּ֗ים א֤וֹ

הַשְּׁתִי֙ א֣וֹ הָעֵ֔רֶב א֖וֹ כָּל־כְּלִי־ע֑וֹר לְטַֽהֲר֖וֹ א֥וֹ לְטַמְּאֽוֹ׃ **פפפ** ס"ז פסוקים. בנ"י"ה סימן.

שביעי [רביעי]

מפטיר

Haftaras Tazria: p. 886

For special Sabbaths, see pp. x-xi

פרשת מצורע

א-ב יד וַיְדַבֵּ֥ר יְהֹוָ֖ה אֶל־מֹשֶׁ֥ה לֵּאמֹֽר׃ זֹ֤את תִּֽהְיֶה֙ תּוֹרַ֣ת הַמְּצֹרָ֔ע בְּי֖וֹם טָֽהֳרָת֑וֹ

ג וְהוּבָ֖א אֶל־הַכֹּהֵֽן׃ וְיָצָא֙ הַכֹּהֵ֔ן אֶל־מִח֖וּץ לַמַּֽחֲנֶ֑ה וְרָאָה֙ הַכֹּהֵ֔ן וְהִנֵּ֛ה נִרְפָּ֥א

ד נֶֽגַע־הַצָּרַ֖עַת מִן־הַצָּרֽוּעַ׃ וְצִוָּה֙ הַכֹּהֵ֔ן וְלָקַ֧ח לַמִּטַּהֵ֛ר שְׁתֵּֽי־צִפֳּרִ֥ים חַיּ֖וֹת

ה טְהֹר֑וֹת וְעֵ֣ץ אֶ֔רֶז וּשְׁנִ֥י תוֹלַ֖עַת וְאֵזֹֽב׃ וְצִוָּה֙ הַכֹּהֵ֔ן וְשָׁחַ֖ט אֶת־הַצִּפּ֣וֹר הָֽאֶחָ֑ת

ו אֶל־כְּלִי־חֶ֖רֶשׂ עַל־מַ֥יִם חַיִּֽים׃ אֶת־הַצִּפֹּ֤ר הַֽחַיָּה֙ יִקַּ֣ח אֹתָ֔הּ וְאֶת־עֵ֥ץ הָאֶ֖רֶז וְאֶת־שְׁנִ֤י

הַתּוֹלַ֙עַת֙ וְאֶת־הָ֣אֵזֹ֔ב וְטָבַ֣ל אוֹתָ֗ם וְאֵ֣ת ׀ הַצִּפֹּ֣ר

ז הַֽחַיָּ֔ה בְּדַם֙ הַצִּפֹּ֣ר הַשְּׁחֻטָ֔ה עַ֖ל הַמַּ֥יִם הַֽחַיִּֽים׃ וְהִזָּ֗ה עַ֧ל הַמִּטַּהֵ֛ר

מִן־הַצָּרַ֖עַת שֶׁ֣בַע פְּעָמִ֑ים וְטִ֣הֲר֔וֹ וְשִׁלַּ֛ח אֶת־הַצִּפֹּ֥ר הַֽחַיָּ֖ה עַל־פְּנֵ֥י הַשָּׂדֶֽה׃

ח וְכִבֶּס֩ הַמִּטַּהֵ֨ר אֶת־בְּגָדָ֜יו וְגִלַּ֣ח אֶת־כָּל־שְׂעָר֗וֹ וְרָחַ֤ץ בַּמַּ֙יִם֙ וְטָהֵ֔ר וְאַחַ֖ר

יָב֣וֹא אֶל־הַמַּֽחֲנֶ֑ה וְיָשַׁ֛ב מִח֥וּץ לְאָֽהֳל֖וֹ שִׁבְעַ֥ת יָמִֽים׃

13:47-58. Supernatural afflictions on garments and houses appeared only when the Jewish nation was generally in perfect accord with God and was a fitting host to His Presence. When an individual broke ranks with this role and was no longer worthy of this exalted rank, his possessions would be afflicted (*Ramban; Sforno*).

◆§ **Parashas Metzora**

14:1-32. Being alone outside the camp lets a *metzora* reflect on his spiritual deficiencies, causing him to repent. Then God removes the mark of his degradation and he can begin the process of returning to his people (*R' Hirsch*).

Afflictions of garments ⁴⁷ *If there shall be a tzaraas affliction in a garment,* * *in a woolen garment or a linen garment,* ⁴⁸ *or in the warp or the woof of the linen or the wool; or in leather or in anything fashioned of leather;* ⁴⁹ *and the affliction shall be deep green or deep red, in the garment or the leather, or the warp or the woof, or in any leather utensil: It is a tzaraas affliction, and it shall be shown to the Kohen.* ⁵⁰ *The Kohen shall look at the affliction; and he shall quarantine the affliction for a seven-day period.* ⁵¹ *He shall look at the affliction on the seventh day: If the affliction has spread in the garment or in the warp or in the woof or in the leather — for whatever purpose the leather has been fashioned — the affliction is a malignant tzaraas; it is contaminated.* ⁵² *He shall burn the garment, or the warp or the woof, of the wool or of the linen, or any leather utensil in which the affliction may be; for it is a malignant tzaraas, it shall be burned in fire.*

⁵³ *But if the Kohen shall look, and behold! — the affliction had not spread in the garment, or the warp or the woof; or in any leather utensil,* ⁵⁴ *the Kohen shall command; and they shall wash the area of the affliction; and he shall quarantine it for a second seven-day period.* ⁵⁵ *The Kohen shall look after the affliction has been washed, and behold! — the affliction has not changed its color and the affliction has not spread, it is contaminated, you shall burn it in fire; it is a penetrating affliction in his worn garment or in his new garment.* ⁵⁶ *But if the Kohen shall look, and behold! — the affliction grew dimmer after it was washed, he shall rip it from the garment or from the leather, or from the warp or from the woof.* ⁵⁷ *If it appears again in the garment or in the warp or in the woof, or in any leather utensil, it is an eruption; you shall burn in fire that which contains the affliction.* ⁵⁸ *But if the garment or the warp or the woof or any leather utensil had been washed and then the affliction left them, it shall be immersed again and it shall become pure.*

⁵⁹ *This is the law of the tzaraas affliction, a garment of wool or linen, or the warp or the woof, or any leather utensil; to declare it pure or to declare it contaminated.*

PARASHAS METZORA

14

The first stage of the metzora's purification *

¹ H*ASHEM spoke to Moses, saying:* ² *This shall be the law of the metzora on the day of his purification: He shall be brought to the Kohen.* ³ *The Kohen shall go forth to the outside of the camp; the Kohen shall look, and behold! — the tzaraas affliction had been healed from the metzora.* ⁴ *The Kohen shall command; and for the person being purified there shall be taken two live, clean birds, cedar wood, crimson thread, and hyssop.* ⁵ *The Kohen shall command; and the one bird shall be slaughtered into an earthenware vessel over spring water.* ⁶ *As for the live bird: He shall take it with the cedar wood and the crimson thread and the hyssop, and he shall dip them and the live bird into the blood of the bird that was slaughtered over the spring water.* ⁷ *Then he shall sprinkle seven times upon the person being purified from the tzaraas; he shall purify him, and he shall set the live bird free upon the open field.* ⁸ *The person being purified shall immerse his clothing, shave off all his hair, and immerse himself in the water and become pure. Thereafter he may enter the camp; but he shall dwell outside of his tent for seven days.*

From arrogance to humility

ט וְהָיָה֩ בַיּ֨וֹם הַשְּׁבִיעִ֜י יְגַלַּ֣ח אֶת־כָּל־שְׂעָר֗וֹ אֶת־רֹאשׁ֤וֹ וְאֶת־זְקָנוֹ֙ וְאֵת֙ גַּבֹּ֣ת עֵינָ֔יו וְאֶת־כָּל־שְׂעָר֖וֹ יְגַלֵּ֑חַ וְכִבֶּ֣ס אֶת־בְּגָדָ֗יו וְרָחַ֧ץ אֶת־בְּשָׂר֛וֹ

י בַּמַּ֖יִם וְטָהֵֽר: וּבַיּ֣וֹם הַשְּׁמִינִ֗י יִקַּ֤ח שְׁנֵֽי־כְבָשִׂים֙ תְּמִימִ֔ם וְכַבְשָׂ֥ה אַחַ֛ת בַּת־שְׁנָתָ֖הּ תְּמִימָ֑ה וּשְׁלֹשָׁ֣ה עֶשְׂרֹנִ֗ים סֹ֤לֶת מִנְחָה֙ בְּלוּלָ֣ה בַשֶּׁ֔מֶן וְלֹ֥ג

יא שָֽׁמֶן: וְהֶעֱמִ֞יד הַכֹּהֵ֣ן הַֽמְטַהֵ֗ר אֵ֛ת הָאִ֥ישׁ הַמִּטַּהֵ֖ר וְאֹתָ֑ם לִפְנֵ֥י יְהוָֹ֖ה

יב פֶּ֖תַח אֹ֥הֶל מוֹעֵֽד: וְלָקַ֨ח הַכֹּהֵ֜ן אֶת־הַכֶּ֤בֶשׂ הָֽאֶחָד֙ וְהִקְרִ֣יב אֹת֣וֹ לְאָשָׁ֔ם

שני   יג וְאֶת־לֹ֖ג הַשָּׁ֑מֶן וְהֵנִ֥יף אֹתָ֛ם תְּנוּפָ֖ה לִפְנֵ֥י יְהוָֹֽה: וְשָׁחַ֣ט אֶת־הַכֶּ֗בֶשׂ בִּ֠מְקוֹם אֲשֶׁ֨ר יִשְׁחַ֧ט אֶת־הַֽחַטָּ֛את וְאֶת־הָֽעֹלָ֖ה בִּמְק֣וֹם הַקֹּ֑דֶשׁ כִּ֡י

יד כַּֽ֠חַטָּאת הָֽאָשָׁ֥ם הוּא֙ לַכֹּהֵ֔ן קֹ֥דֶשׁ קָֽדָשִׁ֖ים הֽוּא: וְלָקַ֣ח הַכֹּהֵן֮ מִדַּ֣ם הָֽאָשָׁם֒ וְנָתַ֣ן הַכֹּהֵ֗ן עַל־תְּנ֛וּךְ אֹ֥זֶן הַמִּטַּהֵ֖ר הַיְמָנִ֑ית וְעַל־בֹּ֤הֶן יָדוֹ֙ הַיְמָנִ֔ית

טו וְעַל־בֹּ֥הֶן רַגְל֖וֹ הַיְמָנִֽית: וְלָקַ֥ח הַכֹּהֵ֖ן מִלֹּ֣ג הַשָּׁ֑מֶן וְיָצַ֛ק עַל־כַּ֥ף הַכֹּהֵ֖ן

טז הַשְּׂמָאלִֽית: וְטָבַ֤ל הַכֹּהֵן֙ אֶת־אֶצְבָּע֣וֹ הַיְמָנִ֔ית מִן־הַשֶּׁ֕מֶן אֲשֶׁ֥ר עַל־כַּפּ֖וֹ

יז הַשְּׂמָאלִ֑ית וְהִזָּ֨ה מִן־הַשֶּׁ֧מֶן בְּאֶצְבָּע֛וֹ שֶׁ֥בַע פְּעָמִ֖ים לִפְנֵ֥י יְהוָֹֽה: וּמִיֶּ֨תֶר הַשֶּׁ֜מֶן אֲשֶׁ֣ר עַל־כַּפּ֗וֹ יִתֵּ֣ן הַכֹּהֵ֡ן עַל־תְּנוּךְ֩ אֹ֨זֶן הַמִּטַּהֵ֤ר הַיְמָנִית֙ וְעַל־בֹּ֣הֶן

יח יָדוֹ֙ הַיְמָנִ֔ית וְעַל־בֹּ֥הֶן רַגְל֖וֹ הַיְמָנִ֑ית עַ֖ל דַּ֣ם הָֽאָשָֽׁם: וְהַנּוֹתָ֗ר בַּשֶּׁ֙מֶן֙ אֲשֶׁר֙ עַל־כַּ֣ף הַכֹּהֵ֔ן יִתֵּ֖ן עַל־רֹ֣אשׁ הַמִּטַּהֵ֑ר וְכִפֶּ֥ר עָלָ֛יו הַכֹּהֵ֖ן לִפְנֵ֥י יְהוָֹֽה:

יט וְעָשָׂ֤ה הַכֹּהֵן֙ אֶת־הַ֣חַטָּ֔את וְכִפֶּ֕ר עַל־הַמִּטַּהֵ֖ר מִטֻּמְאָת֑וֹ וְאַחַ֖ר יִשְׁחַ֥ט

כ אֶת־הָֽעֹלָֽה: וְהֶעֱלָ֧ה הַכֹּהֵ֛ן אֶת־הָֽעֹלָ֥ה וְאֶת־הַמִּנְחָ֖ה הַמִּזְבֵּ֑חָה וְכִפֶּ֥ר

שלישי   כא עָלָ֛יו הַכֹּהֵ֖ן וְטָהֵֽר: וְאִם־דַּ֣ל ה֗וּא וְאֵ֣ין יָדוֹ֮ מַשֶּׂ֒גֶת֒
[חמישי]

וְלָקַ֣ח כֶּ֣בֶשׂ אֶחָ֠ד אָשָׁ֥ם לִתְנוּפָ֛ה לְכַפֵּ֥ר עָלָ֖יו וְעִשָּׂר֨וֹן סֹ֧לֶת אֶחָ֛ד בָּל֥וּל

כב בַשֶּׁ֖מֶן לְמִנְחָ֑ה וְלֹ֥ג שָֽׁמֶן: וּשְׁתֵּ֣י תֹרִ֗ים א֤וֹ שְׁנֵי֙ בְּנֵ֣י יוֹנָ֔ה אֲשֶׁ֥ר תַּשִּׂ֖יג יָד֑וֹ

כג וְהָיָ֤ה אֶחָד֙ חַטָּ֔את וְהָֽאֶחָ֖ד עֹלָֽה: וְהֵבִ֨יא אֹתָ֜ם בַּיּ֧וֹם הַשְּׁמִינִ֛י לְטָֽהֳרָת֖וֹ

כד אֶל־הַכֹּהֵ֑ן אֶל־פֶּ֥תַח אֹֽהֶל־מוֹעֵ֖ד לִפְנֵ֥י יְהוָֹֽה: וְלָקַ֧ח הַכֹּהֵ֛ן אֶת־כֶּ֥בֶשׂ

כה הָֽאָשָׁ֖ם וְאֶת־לֹ֣ג הַשָּׁ֑מֶן וְהֵנִ֨יף אֹתָ֧ם הַכֹּהֵ֛ן תְּנוּפָ֖ה לִפְנֵ֥י יְהוָֹֽה: וְשָׁחַט֮ אֶת־כֶּ֣בֶשׂ הָֽאָשָׁם֒ וְלָקַ֤ח הַכֹּהֵן֙ מִדַּ֣ם הָֽאָשָׁ֔ם וְנָתַ֛ן עַל־תְּנ֥וּךְ אֹֽזֶן־הַמִּטַּהֵ֖ר

כו הַיְמָנִ֑ית וְעַל־בֹּ֤הֶן יָדוֹ֙ הַיְמָנִ֔ית וְעַל־בֹּ֥הֶן רַגְל֖וֹ הַיְמָנִֽית: וּמִן־הַשֶּׁ֖מֶן יִצֹ֣ק

כז הַכֹּהֵ֑ן עַל־כַּ֥ף הַכֹּהֵ֖ן הַשְּׂמָאלִֽית: וְהִזָּ֤ה הַכֹּהֵן֙ בְּאֶצְבָּע֣וֹ הַיְמָנִ֔ית מִן־הַשֶּׁ֕מֶן

כח אֲשֶׁ֥ר עַל־כַּפּ֖וֹ הַשְּׂמָאלִ֑ית שֶׁ֥בַע פְּעָמִ֖ים לִפְנֵ֥י יְהוָֹֽה: וְנָתַ֨ן הַכֹּהֵ֜ן מִן־הַשֶּׁ֗מֶן ׀ אֲשֶׁ֣ר עַל־כַּפּוֹ֮ עַל־תְּנ֣וּךְ אֹ֣זֶן הַמִּטַּהֵר֮ הַיְמָנִית֒ וְעַל־בֹּ֤הֶן יָדוֹ֙

כט הַיְמָנִ֔ית וְעַל־בֹּ֥הֶן רַגְל֖וֹ הַיְמָנִ֑ית עַל־מְק֖וֹם דַּ֥ם הָֽאָשָֽׁם: וְהַנּוֹתָ֗ר מִן־הַשֶּׁ֙מֶן֙ אֲשֶׁר֙ עַל־כַּ֣ף הַכֹּהֵ֔ן יִתֵּ֖ן עַל־רֹ֣אשׁ הַמִּטַּהֵ֑ר לְכַפֵּ֥ר עָלָ֖יו לִפְנֵ֥י

ל יְהוָֹֽה: וְעָשָׂ֤ה אֶת־הָֽאֶחָד֙ מִן־הַתֹּרִ֔ים א֥וֹ מִן־בְּנֵ֥י הַיּוֹנָ֖ה מֵֽאֲשֶׁ֥ר תַּשִּׂ֖יג

לא יָד֑וֹ: אֵ֣ת אֲשֶׁר־תַּשִּׂ֣יג יָד֗וֹ אֶת־הָֽאֶחָ֤ד חַטָּאת֙ וְאֶת־הָֽאֶחָ֣ד עֹלָ֔ה עַל־

The second stage: Shaving

⁹ On the seventh day he shall shave off all his hair — his head, his beard, his eyebrows, and all his hair shall he shave off; he shall immerse his clothing and immerse his flesh in water, and become pure.

The final stage of purification: Offerings
(See Appendix B, charts 6-7)

¹⁰ On the eighth day, he shall take two unblemished male lambs and one unblemished ewe in its first year, three tenth-ephah of fine flour mixed with oil, and one log* of oil. ¹¹ The Kohen who purifies shall place the person being purified along with them before HASHEM at the entrance of the Tent of Meeting. ¹² The Kohen shall take the one lamb and bring it near for a guilt-offering, with the log of oil; and he shall wave them as a wave-service before HASHEM.

¹³ He shall slaughter the lamb in the place where he would slaughter the sin-offering and the burnt-offering, in the holy place; for like the sin-offering, the guilt-offering is the Kohen's, it is most holy. ¹⁴ The Kohen shall take from the blood of the guilt-offering, and the Kohen shall place it on the middle part of the right ear of the person being purified and on the thumb of his right hand and the big toe of his right foot. ¹⁵ The Kohen shall take from the log of oil and he shall pour it upon another Kohen's left palm. ¹⁶ The Kohen shall dip his right forefinger into the oil that is in his left palm; and he shall sprinkle from the oil with his finger seven times before HASHEM. ¹⁷ Some of the oil remaining on his palm, the Kohen shall put on the middle part of the right ear of the man being purified, on the thumb of his right hand and on the big toe of his right foot; on the blood of the guilt-offering. ¹⁸ And the rest of the oil that is on the Kohen's palm, he shall place upon the head of the person being purified; and the Kohen shall provide him atonement before HASHEM. ¹⁹ The Kohen shall perform the sin-offering service and provide atonement for the person being purified from his contamination; after that he shall slaughter the burnt-offering. ²⁰ The Kohen shall bring the burnt-offering and the meal-offering up to the Altar; and the Kohen shall provide him atonement, and he becomes pure.

The offering of the poor metzora
(See Appendix B, chart 8)

²¹ If he is poor and his means are not sufficient, then he shall take one male lamb as a guilt-offering for a wave-service to provide atonement for him; and one tenth-ephah of fine flour mixed with oil for a meal-offering, and a log of oil. ²² And two turtledoves or two young doves — for whichever his means are sufficient — one shall be a sin-offering and one a burnt-offering. ²³ He shall bring them to the Kohen, on the eighth day of his purification, to the entrance of the Tent of Meeting, before HASHEM. ²⁴ The Kohen shall take the guilt-offering lamb and the log of oil; and the Kohen shall wave them as a wave-service before HASHEM. ²⁵ He shall slaughter the guilt-offering lamb and the Kohen shall take some of the guilt-offering's blood and place it on the middle part of the right ear of the man being purified and on the thumb of his right hand and on the big toe of his right foot. ²⁶ From the oil, the Kohen shall pour upon the Kohen's left palm. ²⁷ The Kohen shall sprinkle with his right forefinger some of the oil that is in his left palm seven times before HASHEM. ²⁸ The Kohen shall place some of the oil that is on his palm upon the middle of the right ear of the person being purified, on the thumb of his right hand and on the big toe of his right foot — on the place of the guilt-offering's blood. ²⁹ And the rest of the oil that is on the Kohen's palm, he shall place upon the head of the person being purified; to provide him atonement before HASHEM.

³⁰ He shall then perform the service of one of the turtledoves or of the young doves, for whichever his means are sufficient. ³¹ Of whichever his means are sufficient — one is a sin-offering and one is a burnt-offering — along with

לב הַמִּנְחָה וְכִפֶּר הַכֹּהֵן עַל הַמִּטַּהֵר לִפְנֵי יהוָה: זֹאת תּוֹרַת אֲשֶׁר־בּוֹ נֶגַע צָרָעַת אֲשֶׁר לֹא־תַשִּׂיג יָדוֹ בְּטָהֳרָתוֹ:

רביעי
[ששי]
לג-לד וַיְדַבֵּר יהוָה אֶל־מֹשֶׁה וְאֶל־אַהֲרֹן לֵאמֹר: כִּי תָבֹאוּ אֶל־אֶרֶץ כְּנַעַן אֲשֶׁר אֲנִי נֹתֵן לָכֶם לַאֲחֻזָּה וְנָתַתִּי נֶגַע צָרַעַת בְּבֵית אֶרֶץ אֲחֻזַּתְכֶם: וּבָא

לה אֲשֶׁר־לוֹ הַבַּיִת וְהִגִּיד לַכֹּהֵן לֵאמֹר כְּנֶגַע נִרְאָה לִי בַּבָּיִת: וְצִוָּה הַכֹּהֵן
לו וּפִנּוּ אֶת־הַבַּיִת בְּטֶרֶם יָבֹא הַכֹּהֵן לִרְאוֹת אֶת־הַנֶּגַע וְלֹא יִטְמָא כָּל־אֲשֶׁר בַּבָּיִת וְאַחַר כֵּן יָבֹא הַכֹּהֵן לִרְאוֹת אֶת־הַבָּיִת: וְרָאָה אֶת־הַנֶּגַע וְהִנֵּה

לז הַנֶּגַע בְּקִירֹת הַבַּיִת שְׁקַעֲרוּרֹת יְרַקְרַקֹּת אוֹ אֲדַמְדַּמֹּת וּמַרְאֵיהֶן שָׁפָל מִן־הַקִּיר: וְיָצָא הַכֹּהֵן מִן־הַבַּיִת אֶל־פֶּתַח הַבָּיִת וְהִסְגִּיר אֶת־הַבַּיִת

לח שִׁבְעַת יָמִים: וְשָׁב הַכֹּהֵן בַּיּוֹם הַשְּׁבִיעִי וְרָאָה וְהִנֵּה פָּשָׂה הַנֶּגַע בְּקִירֹת
לט הַבָּיִת: וְצִוָּה הַכֹּהֵן וְחִלְּצוּ אֶת־הָאֲבָנִים אֲשֶׁר בָּהֵן הַנָּגַע וְהִשְׁלִיכוּ אֶתְהֶן
מ אֶל־מִחוּץ לָעִיר אֶל־מָקוֹם טָמֵא: וְאֶת־הַבַּיִת יַקְצִעַ מִבַּיִת סָבִיב וְשָׁפְכוּ
מא אֶת־הֶעָפָר אֲשֶׁר הִקְצוּ אֶל־מִחוּץ לָעִיר אֶל־מָקוֹם טָמֵא: וְלָקְחוּ אֲבָנִים אֲחֵרוֹת וְהֵבִיאוּ אֶל־תַּחַת הָאֲבָנִים וְעָפָר אַחֵר יִקַּח וְטָח אֶת־הַבָּיִת:

מב וְאִם־יָשׁוּב הַנֶּגַע וּפָרַח בַּבַּיִת אַחַר חִלֵּץ אֶת־הָאֲבָנִים וְאַחֲרֵי הִקְצוֹת
מג אֶת־הַבַּיִת וְאַחֲרֵי הִטּוֹחַ: וּבָא הַכֹּהֵן וְרָאָה וְהִנֵּה פָּשָׂה הַנֶּגַע בַּבָּיִת צָרַעַת
מד מַמְאֶרֶת הִוא בַּבַּיִת טָמֵא הוּא: וְנָתַץ אֶת־הַבַּיִת אֶת־אֲבָנָיו וְאֶת־עֵצָיו
מה וְאֵת כָּל־עֲפַר הַבָּיִת וְהוֹצִיא אֶל־מִחוּץ לָעִיר אֶל־מָקוֹם טָמֵא: וְהַבָּא אֶל־הַבַּיִת כָּל־יְמֵי הִסְגִּיר אֹתוֹ יִטְמָא עַד־הָעָרֶב: וְהַשֹּׁכֵב בַּבַּיִת יְכַבֵּס

מו אֶת־בְּגָדָיו וְהָאֹכֵל בַּבַּיִת יְכַבֵּס אֶת־בְּגָדָיו: וְאִם־בֹּא יָבֹא הַכֹּהֵן וְרָאָה
מז וְהִנֵּה לֹא־פָשָׂה הַנֶּגַע בַּבַּיִת אַחֲרֵי הִטֹּחַ אֶת־הַבָּיִת וְטִהַר הַכֹּהֵן אֶת־
מח הַבַּיִת כִּי נִרְפָּא הַנָּגַע: וְלָקַח לְחַטֵּא אֶת־הַבַּיִת שְׁתֵּי צִפֳּרִים וְעֵץ אֶרֶז
מט וּשְׁנִי תוֹלַעַת וְאֵזֹב: וְשָׁחַט אֶת־הַצִּפֹּר הָאֶחָת אֶל־כְּלִי־חֶרֶשׂ עַל־מַיִם חַיִּים: וְלָקַח אֶת־עֵץ־הָאֶרֶז וְאֶת־הָאֵזֹב וְאֵת ׀ שְׁנִי הַתּוֹלַעַת וְאֵת הַצִּפֹּר

נ הַחַיָּה וְטָבַל אֹתָם בְּדַם הַצִּפֹּר הַשְּׁחוּטָה וּבַמַּיִם הַחַיִּים וְהִזָּה אֶל־הַבַּיִת
נא שֶׁבַע פְּעָמִים: וְחִטֵּא אֶת־הַבַּיִת בְּדַם הַצִּפּוֹר וּבַמַּיִם הַחַיִּים וּבַצִּפֹּר הַחַיָּה
נב וּבְעֵץ הָאֶרֶז וּבָאֵזֹב וּבִשְׁנִי הַתּוֹלָעַת: וְשִׁלַּח אֶת־הַצִּפֹּר הַחַיָּה אֶל־מִחוּץ

חמישי
נג לָעִיר אֶל־פְּנֵי הַשָּׂדֶה וְכִפֶּר עַל־הַבַּיִת וְטָהֵר: זֹאת הַתּוֹרָה לְכָל־נֶגַע

נד *ש רפה
נה-נד הַצָּרַעַת וְלַנָּתֶק: וּלְצָרַעַת הַבֶּגֶד וְלַבָּיִת: וְלַשְׂאֵת וְלַסַּפַּחַת וְלַבֶּהָרֶת:
נו לְהוֹרֹת בְּיוֹם הַטָּמֵא וּבְיוֹם הַטָּהֹר זֹאת תּוֹרַת הַצָּרָעַת:

14:33-57. *Tzaraas*-type afflictions on houses are clearly supernatural occurrences. Two very different explanations are given. According to *Sifra* and *Vayikra Rabbah*, the Canaanites hid their valuables in the walls of their homes. For the sake of the new Jewish homeowners, God placed an affliction on the wall so that the offending stones had to be cut away, revealing the treasure.

According to *Rambam* (Hil. *Tumas Tzaraas* 16:10), these *tzaraas* afflictions are Divine punishments for selfish behavior and gossip. He adds that God mercifully begins by afflicting property before striking the person's body. The Talmud (*Yoma* 11b) derives this from verse 35, which describes the owner of the house as *the one to whom the house belongs*; he felt that the house is *his* and *the meal-offering; and the Kohen shall provide atonement for the one being purified, before HASHEM.* [32] *This is the law of one in whom there is a tzaraas affliction — whose means are not sufficient — for his purification.*

Tzaraas on houses [33] *HASHEM spoke to Moses and Aaron, saying:* [34] *When you arrive in the land of Canaan that I give you as a possession, and I will place a tzaraas affliction upon a house in the land of your possession;* [35] *the one to whom the house belongs shall come and declare to the Kohen, saying: Something like an affliction has appeared to me in the house.* [36] *The Kohen shall command; and they shall clear the house before the Kohen comes to look at the affliction, so that everything in the house should not become contaminated; and afterward shall the Kohen come to look at the house.* [37] *He shall look at the affliction and behold! — the affliction is in the walls of the house, depressed, deep greens or deep reds; and their appearance is lower than the wall.* [38] *The Kohen shall exit from the house to the entrance of the house; and he shall quarantine the house for a seven-day period.* [39] *The Kohen shall return on the seventh day; he shall look and behold! — the affliction had spread in the walls of the house.* [40] *The Kohen shall command, and they shall remove the stones that contain the affliction, and they shall cast them outside the city onto a contaminated place.* [41] *And the house shall be scraped on the inside, all around; the mortar that they have scraped they are to pour outside the city onto a contaminated place.* [42] *They shall take other stones and bring them in place of the stones; and they shall take other mortar and plaster the house.*

[43] *If the affliction returns and erupts in the house after he has removed the stones, after he has scraped the house and after plastering;* [44] *then the Kohen shall come and look, and behold! — the affliction had spread in the house: It is a malignant tzaraas in the house, it is contaminated.* [45] *He shall demolish the house — its stones, its timber, and all the mortar of the house; they shall take it to the outside of the city, to a contaminated place.* [46] *Anyone who comes into the house during all the days he had quarantined it shall be contaminated until evening.* [47] *But one who reclines in the house shall immerse his garments; and one who eats in the house shall immerse his garments.*

[48] *If the Kohen is to come and look and behold! — the affliction has not spread in the house after the plastering of the house; then the Kohen shall declare the* Purification of the house *house to be pure, for the affliction has healed.* [49] *To purify the house, he shall take two birds, cedar wood, crimson thread, and hyssop.* [50] *He shall slaughter the one bird into an earthenware vessel over spring water.* [51] *He shall take the cedar wood, the hyssop, the crimson thread, and the live bird, and he shall dip them into the blood of the slaughtered bird and into the spring water; and he shall sprinkle upon the house seven times.* [52] *He shall cleanse the house with the blood of the bird and with the spring water; and with the live bird, with the cedar wood, with the hyssop, and with the crimson thread.* [53] *He shall set the live bird free toward the outside of the city upon the open field; thus he shall provide atonement for the house, and it shall become purified.*

[54] *This is the law for every tzaraas affliction and the nesek;* [55] *and tzaraas of the garment and of the house;* [56] *and of the s'eis, of the sapachas, and of the baheres;* [57] *to rule on which day it is contaminated and on which day it is purified; this is the law of tzaraas.*

---

he need not share his blessings with anyone else. But God, Who gave him what he has, wants him to share with others, and God can easily give him more or take away what he is misusing (*Tzror HaMor*).

א־ב וַיְדַבֵּ֣ר יהוה֮ אֶל־מֹשֶׁ֣ה וְאֶֽל־אַהֲרֹ֣ן לֵאמֹֽר: דַּבְּרוּ֙ אֶל־בְּנֵ֣י יִשְׂרָאֵ֔ל

ג וַאֲמַרְתֶּ֖ם אֲלֵהֶ֑ם אִ֣ישׁ אִ֗ישׁ כִּ֤י יִהְיֶה֙ זָ֣ב מִבְּשָׂר֔וֹ זוֹב֖וֹ טָמֵ֥א הֽוּא: וְזֹ֛את

תִּהְיֶ֥ה טֻמְאָת֖וֹ בְּזוֹב֑וֹ רָ֣ר בְּשָׂר֞וֹ אֶת־זוֹב֗וֹ אֽוֹ־הֶחְתִּ֤ים בְּשָׂרוֹ֙ מִזּוֹב֔וֹ

ד טֻמְאָת֖וֹ הִֽוא: כׇּל־הַמִּשְׁכָּ֗ב אֲשֶׁ֨ר יִשְׁכַּ֥ב עָלָ֛יו הַזָּ֖ב יִטְמָ֑א וְכׇֽל־הַכְּלִ֛י

ה אֲשֶׁר־יֵשֵׁ֥ב עָלָ֖יו יִטְמָֽא: וְאִ֕ישׁ אֲשֶׁ֥ר יִגַּ֖ע בְּמִשְׁכָּב֑וֹ יְכַבֵּ֧ס בְּגָדָ֛יו וְרָחַ֥ץ

ו בַּמַּ֖יִם וְטָמֵ֥א עַד־הָעָֽרֶב: וְהַיֹּשֵׁב֙ עַֽל־הַכְּלִ֔י אֲשֶׁר־יֵשֵׁ֥ב עָלָ֖יו הַזָּ֑ב יְכַבֵּ֣ס

ז בְּגָדָ֗יו וְרָחַ֥ץ בַּמַּ֖יִם וְטָמֵ֥א עַד־הָעָֽרֶב: וְהַנֹּגֵ֙עַ֙ בִּבְשַׂ֣ר הַזָּ֔ב יְכַבֵּ֧ס בְּגָדָ֛יו

ח וְרָחַ֥ץ בַּמַּ֖יִם וְטָמֵ֥א עַד־הָעָֽרֶב: וְכִֽי־יָרֹ֥ק הַזָּ֖ב בַּטָּה֑וֹר וְכִבֶּ֧ס בְּגָדָ֛יו

ט וְרָחַ֥ץ בַּמַּ֖יִם וְטָמֵ֥א עַד־הָעָֽרֶב: וְכׇל־הַמֶּרְכָּ֗ב אֲשֶׁ֨ר יִרְכַּ֥ב עָלָ֛יו הַזָּ֖ב יִטְמָֽא:

י וְכׇל־הַנֹּגֵ֗עַ בְּכֹל֙ אֲשֶׁ֣ר יִהְיֶ֣ה תַחְתָּ֔יו יִטְמָ֖א עַד־הָעָ֑רֶב וְהַנּוֹשֵׂ֣א אוֹתָ֔ם

יא יְכַבֵּ֧ס בְּגָדָ֛יו וְרָחַ֥ץ בַּמַּ֖יִם וְטָמֵ֥א עַד־הָעָֽרֶב: וְכֹ֨ל אֲשֶׁ֤ר יִגַּע־בּוֹ֙ הַזָּ֔ב

יב וְיָדָ֖יו לֹא־שָׁטַ֣ף בַּמָּ֑יִם וְכִבֶּ֧ס בְּגָדָ֛יו וְרָחַ֥ץ בַּמַּ֖יִם וְטָמֵ֥א עַד־הָעָֽרֶב: וּכְלִי־

יג חֶ֛רֶשׂ אֲשֶׁר־יִגַּע־בּ֥וֹ הַזָּ֖ב יִשָּׁבֵ֑ר וְכׇל־כְּלִי־עֵ֔ץ יִשָּׁטֵ֖ף בַּמָּֽיִם: וְכִֽי־יִטְהַ֤ר

הַזָּב֙ מִזּוֹב֔וֹ וְסָ֧פַר ל֛וֹ שִׁבְעַ֥ת יָמִ֖ים לְטׇהֳרָת֑וֹ וְכִבֶּ֣ס בְּגָדָ֔יו וְרָחַ֧ץ בְּשָׂר֛וֹ

יד בְּמַ֥יִם חַיִּ֖ים וְטָהֵֽר: וּבַיּ֣וֹם הַשְּׁמִינִ֗י יִקַּֽח־לוֹ֙ שְׁתֵּ֣י תֹרִ֔ים א֖וֹ שְׁנֵ֣י בְּנֵ֣י

טו יוֹנָ֑ה וּבָ֣א ׀ לִפְנֵ֣י יהוה֗ אֶל־פֶּ֙תַח֙ אֹ֣הֶל מוֹעֵ֔ד וּנְתָנָ֖ם אֶל־הַכֹּהֵֽן: וְעָשָׂ֤ה

אֹתָם֙ הַכֹּהֵ֔ן אֶחָ֣ד חַטָּ֔את וְהָאֶחָ֖ד עֹלָ֑ה וְכִפֶּ֨ר עָלָ֧יו הַכֹּהֵ֛ן לִפְנֵ֥י יהוה

מִזּוֹבֽוֹ: וְאִ֗ישׁ כִּֽי־תֵצֵ֤א מִמֶּ֙נּוּ֙ שִׁכְבַת־זָ֔רַע וְרָחַ֥ץ בַּמַּ֖יִם

יו אֶת־כׇּל־בְּשָׂר֖וֹ וְטָמֵ֥א עַד־הָעָֽרֶב: וְכׇל־בֶּ֤גֶד וְכׇל־עוֹר֙ אֲשֶׁר־יִהְיֶ֥ה עָלָ֛יו

יז שִׁכְבַת־זָ֖רַע וְכֻבַּ֣ס בַּמַּ֖יִם וְטָמֵ֥א עַד־הָעָֽרֶב: וְאִשָּׁ֕ה אֲשֶׁ֨ר יִשְׁכַּ֥ב אִ֛ישׁ

יח אֹתָ֖הּ שִׁכְבַת־זָ֑רַע וְרָחֲצ֣וּ בַמַּ֔יִם וְטָמְא֖וּ עַד־הָעָֽרֶב:

יט וְאִשָּׁה֙ כִּֽי־תִהְיֶ֣ה זָבָ֔ה דָּ֛ם יִהְיֶ֥ה זֹבָ֖הּ בִּבְשָׂרָ֑הּ שִׁבְעַ֤ת יָמִים֙ תִּהְיֶ֣ה

כ בְנִדָּתָ֔הּ וְכׇל־הַנֹּגֵ֥עַ בָּ֖הּ יִטְמָ֥א עַד־הָעָֽרֶב: וְכֹל֩ אֲשֶׁ֨ר תִּשְׁכַּ֤ב עָלָיו֙

כא בְּנִדָּתָ֣הּ יִטְמָ֔א וְכֹ֛ל אֲשֶׁר־תֵּשֵׁ֥ב עָלָ֖יו יִטְמָֽא: וְכׇל־הַנֹּגֵ֖עַ בְּמִשְׁכָּבָ֑הּ

יְכַבֵּ֧ס בְּגָדָ֛יו וְרָחַ֥ץ בַּמַּ֖יִם וְטָמֵ֥א עַד־הָעָֽרֶב: וְכׇ֨ל־הַנֹּגֵ֔עַ בְּכׇל־כְּלִ֖י

כב אֲשֶׁר־תֵּשֵׁ֣ב עָלָ֑יו יְכַבֵּ֧ס בְּגָדָ֛יו וְרָחַ֥ץ בַּמַּ֖יִם וְטָמֵ֥א עַד־הָעָֽרֶב: וְאִ֨ם עַֽל־

כג הַמִּשְׁכָּ֜ב ה֗וּא א֧וֹ עַֽל־הַכְּלִ֛י אֲשֶׁר־הִ֥וא יֹשֶֽׁבֶת־עָלָ֖יו בְּנׇגְעוֹ־ב֑וֹ יִטְמָ֖א

כד עַד־הָעָֽרֶב: וְאִ֡ם שָׁכֹב֩ יִשְׁכַּ֨ב אִ֜ישׁ אֹתָ֗הּ וּתְהִ֤י נִדָּתָהּ֙ עָלָ֔יו וְטָמֵ֖א שִׁבְעַ֣ת

⌁§ Chapter 15

This entire chapter deals with the kinds of discharges from the human body that are contaminated to various degrees, and which may require offerings as part of the person's purification process.

15:2. Semen or a *zav*-emission (which is slightly different from semen) that is discharged from a Jewish male is contaminated in itself; in addition, it causes contamination to the one who emitted it and to others who come in contact with it. There are three degrees of such contamination, depending on the frequency and type of the discharge.

15:19. This passage contains the laws of the monthly period when husband and wife may not cohabit. This *mitzvah* is known as טׇהֳרַת הַמִּשְׁפָּחָה, *purity of the family*, for the sanctity of marriage depends on the constant purity of the family and the partners who create it.

15

Zav and baal keri/ male discharges

[1] HASHEM spoke to Moses and Aaron, saying: [2] Speak to the Children of Israel and say to them: Any man who will have a discharge from his flesh, * his discharge is contaminated. [3] Thus shall be his contamination when he discharges: whether his flesh runs with his discharge or it becomes stopped up because of his discharge, that is his contamination. [4] Any bedding upon which the person with the discharge will recline shall be contaminated, and any vessel upon which he will sit shall become contaminated. [5] A person who will touch his bedding shall immerse his garments and immerse himself in the water, and he remains contaminated until the evening. [6] And one who sits upon a vessel upon which the man with the discharge will sit, shall immerse his garments and immerse himself in the water, and he remains contaminated until the evening. [7] One who touches the flesh of the man with the discharge shall immerse his garments and immerse himself in the water, and he remains contaminated until the evening. [8] If the person with the discharge will spit upon a pure person, he shall immerse his garments and immerse himself in the water, and he remains contaminated until the evening. [9] Any riding equipment upon which the person with the discharge will ride shall become contaminated. [10] And whoever touches anything that will be beneath him shall become contaminated until evening; and whoever carries them shall immerse his garments and immerse himself in the water, and he remains contaminated until the evening. [11] Whomever the man with the discharge touches without having rinsed his hands in the water shall immerse his garments and immerse himself in the water, and he remains contaminated until the evening. [12] Pottery that the man with the discharge will touch shall be broken; and any wooden utensil shall be rinsed in water.

(See Appendix B, chart 8)

[13] When the man with the discharge ceases his discharge, he shall count for himself seven days from his cessation, immerse his garments and immerse his flesh in spring water, and become purified. [14] On the eighth day he shall take for himself two turtledoves or two young doves; he shall come before HASHEM to the entrance of the Tent of Meeting, and give them to the Kohen. [15] The Kohen shall make them one as a sin-offering and one as a burnt-offering — thus the Kohen shall provide him atonement before HASHEM from his discharge.

[16] A man from whom there is a discharge of semen shall immerse his entire flesh in the water and remain contaminated until evening. [17] Any garment or anything of leather, upon which there shall be semen, shall be immersed in the water and remain contaminated until evening. [18] A woman with whom a man will have carnal relations, they shall immerse themselves in the water and remain contaminated until evening.

Niddah and zavah/ female discharges

[19] When a woman has a discharge* — her discharge from her flesh being blood — she shall be in her state of separation for a seven-day period and anyone who touches her shall remain contaminated until the evening. [20] Anything upon which she may recline during her state of separation shall become contaminated; and anything upon which she sits shall become contaminated. [21] Anyone who touches her bedding shall immerse his garments and immerse himself in the water, and he remains contaminated until evening. [22] Anyone who touches any utensil upon which she will sit shall immerse his garments and immerse himself in the water, and he remains contaminated until evening. [23] Or if someone is upon the bedding or the utensil upon which she is sitting, when he touches it, he becomes contaminated until evening. [24] If a man lies with her, then her state of separation will be upon him and he becomes contaminated for a seven-

כה וְאִשָּׁה כָּל־יְמֵי זוֹב דָּמָהּ הַמִּשְׁכָּב אֲשֶׁר־יִשְׁכַּב עָלָיו יִטְמָא:
כִּי־יָזוּב זוֹב דָּמָהּ יָמִים רַבִּים בְּלֹא עֶת־נִדָּתָהּ אוֹ כִי־תָזוּב עַל־נִדָּתָהּ כָּל־
כו יְמֵי זוֹב טֻמְאָתָהּ כִּימֵי נִדָּתָהּ תִּהְיֶה טְמֵאָה הִוא: כָּל־הַמִּשְׁכָּב אֲשֶׁר־
תִּשְׁכַּב עָלָיו כָּל־יְמֵי זוֹבָהּ כְּמִשְׁכַּב נִדָּתָהּ יִהְיֶה־לָּהּ וְכָל־הַכְּלִי אֲשֶׁר תֵּשֵׁב
כז עָלָיו טָמֵא יִהְיֶה כְּטֻמְאַת נִדָּתָהּ: וְכָל־הַנּוֹגֵעַ בָּם יִטְמָא וְכִבֶּס בְּגָדָיו וְרָחַץ
כח בַּמַּיִם וְטָמֵא עַד־הָעָרֶב: וְאִם־טָהֲרָה מִזּוֹבָהּ וְסָפְרָה לָּהּ שִׁבְעַת יָמִים
כט וְאַחַר תִּטְהָר: וּבַיּוֹם הַשְּׁמִינִי תִּקַּח־לָהּ שְׁתֵּי תֹרִים אוֹ שְׁנֵי בְּנֵי יוֹנָה
ל וְהֵבִיאָה אוֹתָם אֶל־הַכֹּהֵן אֶל־פֶּתַח אֹהֶל מוֹעֵד: וְעָשָׂה הַכֹּהֵן אֶת־הָאֶחָד
חַטָּאת וְאֶת־הָאֶחָד עֹלָה וְכִפֶּר עָלֶיהָ הַכֹּהֵן לִפְנֵי יהוה מִזּוֹב טֻמְאָתָהּ:
לא וְהִזַּרְתֶּם אֶת־בְּנֵי־יִשְׂרָאֵל מִטֻּמְאָתָם וְלֹא יָמֻתוּ בְּטֻמְאָתָם בְּטַמְּאָם אֶת־
לב מִשְׁכָּנִי אֲשֶׁר בְּתוֹכָם: זֹאת תּוֹרַת הַזָּב וַאֲשֶׁר תֵּצֵא מִמֶּנּוּ שִׁכְבַת־זֶרַע
לג לְטָמְאָה־בָהּ: וְהַדָּוָה בְּנִדָּתָהּ וְהַזָּב אֶת־זוֹבוֹ לַזָּכָר וְלַנְּקֵבָה וּלְאִישׁ אֲשֶׁר
יִשְׁכַּב עִם־טְמֵאָה: פפפ צ׳ פסוקים. עד״ו סימן.

שביעי

מפטיר

Haftaras Metzora:
p. 892

For special Sabbaths, see pp. x-xi

פרשת אחרי

טז א וַיְדַבֵּר יהוה אֶל־מֹשֶׁה אַחֲרֵי מוֹת שְׁנֵי בְּנֵי אַהֲרֹן בְּקָרְבָתָם לִפְנֵי־יהוה
ב וַיָּמֻתוּ: וַיֹּאמֶר יהוה אֶל־מֹשֶׁה דַּבֵּר אֶל־אַהֲרֹן אָחִיךָ וְאַל־יָבֹא בְכָל־עֵת
אֶל־הַקֹּדֶשׁ מִבֵּית לַפָּרֹכֶת אֶל־פְּנֵי הַכַּפֹּרֶת אֲשֶׁר עַל־הָאָרֹן וְלֹא יָמוּת כִּי
ג בֶּעָנָן אֵרָאֶה עַל־הַכַּפֹּרֶת: בְּזֹאת יָבֹא אַהֲרֹן אֶל־הַקֹּדֶשׁ בְּפַר בֶּן־בָּקָר
ד לְחַטָּאת וְאַיִל לְעֹלָה: כְּתֹנֶת־בַּד קֹדֶשׁ יִלְבָּשׁ וּמִכְנְסֵי־בַד יִהְיוּ עַל־בְּשָׂרוֹ
וּבְאַבְנֵט בַּד יַחְגֹּר וּבְמִצְנֶפֶת בַּד יִצְנֹף בִּגְדֵי־קֹדֶשׁ הֵם וְרָחַץ בַּמַּיִם אֶת־
ה בְּשָׂרוֹ וּלְבֵשָׁם: וּמֵאֵת עֲדַת בְּנֵי יִשְׂרָאֵל יִקַּח שְׁנֵי־שְׂעִירֵי עִזִּים לְחַטָּאת
ו וְאַיִל אֶחָד לְעֹלָה: וְהִקְרִיב אַהֲרֹן אֶת־פַּר הַחַטָּאת אֲשֶׁר־לוֹ וְכִפֶּר בַּעֲדוֹ
ז וּבְעַד בֵּיתוֹ: וְלָקַח אֶת־שְׁנֵי הַשְּׂעִירִם וְהֶעֱמִיד אֹתָם לִפְנֵי יהוה פֶּתַח אֹהֶל
ח מוֹעֵד: וְנָתַן אַהֲרֹן עַל־שְׁנֵי הַשְּׂעִירִם גֹּרָלוֹת גּוֹרָל אֶחָד לַיהוה וְגוֹרָל אֶחָד
ט לַעֲזָאזֵל: וְהִקְרִיב אַהֲרֹן אֶת־הַשָּׂעִיר אֲשֶׁר עָלָה עָלָיו הַגּוֹרָל לַיהוה וְעָשָׂהוּ
י חַטָּאת: וְהַשָּׂעִיר אֲשֶׁר עָלָה עָלָיו הַגּוֹרָל לַעֲזָאזֵל יָעֳמַד־חַי לִפְנֵי יהוה
יא לְכַפֵּר עָלָיו לְשַׁלַּח אֹתוֹ לַעֲזָאזֵל הַמִּדְבָּרָה: וְהִקְרִיב אַהֲרֹן אֶת־פַּר
הַחַטָּאת אֲשֶׁר־לוֹ וְכִפֶּר בַּעֲדוֹ וּבְעַד בֵּיתוֹ וְשָׁחַט אֶת־פַּר הַחַטָּאת אֲשֶׁר־לוֹ:

טז

READING FOR YOM KIPPUR SHACHARIS 16:1-34

Maftir: p. 402

Haftarah: p. 1052

⁌ **Parashas Acharei**

16:2-34. The Yom Kippur service. Moses' long process of seeking forgiveness for the sin of the Golden Calf ended on the tenth of Tishrei, the day he came back from Sinai with the second Tablets of the Law. That day became ordained as Yom Kippur, the eternal day of forgiveness. In the Temple, the highlight of the day was the special service performed by the Kohen Gadol, as related in this chapter.

16:3. Only *with this,* i.e., the entire sacrificial service listed below, may the Kohen Gadol enter the Holy of Holies on Yom Kippur.

16:6. That is, he shall confess his sins and his household's. An essential part of repentance and hence of atonement (1:4; *Yoma* 5a), confession is one of God's greatest gifts. He permits a person to erase his past so that he can begin a life unhampered by the corrosive effects of past sins.

day period; any bedding upon which he may recline shall become contaminated.
²⁵ If a woman's blood flows for many days outside of her period of separa-tion, or if she has a flow after her separation, all the days of her contaminated flow shall be like the days of her separation; she is contaminated. ²⁶ Any bedding upon which she may lie throughout the days of her flow shall be to her like the bedding of her state of separation; any vessel upon which she may sit shall be contaminated, like the contamination of her state of separation. ²⁷ Anyone who touches them shall become contaminated; he shall immerse his garments and immerse himself in the water, and he remains contaminated until evening. ²⁸ If she ceases her flow, she must count seven days for herself, and afterwards she can be purified.

(See Appendix B, chart 8)
²⁹ On the eighth day she shall take for herself two turtledoves or two young doves; she shall bring them to the Kohen, to the entrance of the Tent of Meeting. ³⁰ The Kohen shall make one a sin-offering and one a burnt-offering; the Kohen shall provide atonement for her before HASHEM from her contami-nating flow.

³¹ You shall separate the Children of Israel from their contamination; and they shall not die as a result of their contamination if they contaminate My Tabernacle that is among them. ³² This is the law of the man with a discharge, and from whom there is a seminal discharge, through which he becomes contaminated; ³³ and concerning a woman who suffers through her separa-tion, and concerning a person who has his flow, whether male or female, and concerning a man who lies with a contaminated woman.

PARASHAS ACHAREI

16
The death of Aaron's sons and the Yom Kippur service

(See Appendix B, charts 6-7)

The lots

¹ Hᴀsʜᴇᴍ spoke to Moses after the death of Aaron's two sons, when they approached before HASHEM, and they died. ² And HASHEM said to Moses: Speak to Aaron, your brother — he shall not come at all times into the Sanc-tuary, within the Curtain, in front of the Cover that is upon the Ark, so that he should not die; for in a cloud will I appear upon the Ark-cover. ³ With this * shall Aaron come into the Sanctuary: with a young bull for a sin-offering and a ram for a burnt-offering. ⁴ He shall don a sacred linen Tunic; linen Breeches shall be upon his flesh, he shall gird himself with a linen Sash, and cover his head with a linen Turban; they are sacred vestments — he shall immerse himself in water and then don them. ⁵ From the assembly of the Children of Israel he shall take two he-goats for a sin-offering and one ram for a burnt-offering.

⁶ Aaron shall bring near his own sin-offering bull, and provide atonement * for himself and for his household. ⁷ He shall take the two he-goats and stand them before HASHEM, at the entrance of the Tent of Meeting. ⁸ Aaron shall place lots * upon the two he-goats: one lot "for HASHEM" and one lot "for Azazel." ⁹ Aaron shall bring near the he-goat designated by lot for HASHEM, and make it a sin-offering. ¹⁰ And the he-goat designated by lot for Azazel shall be stood alive before HASHEM, to provide atonement through it, to send it to Azazel to the Wilderness. ¹¹ Aaron shall bring near his own sin-offering bull and he shall provide atonement for himself and for his household; then he shall slaughter his own sin-offering bull.

16:8. The next step in the service was to select two he-goats: one that would become a national sin-offering and a second that would become the bearer of all the people's sins, as it were.

יב וְלָקַח מְלֹא־הַמַּחְתָּה גַּחֲלֵי־אֵשׁ מֵעַל הַמִּזְבֵּחַ מִלִּפְנֵי יהוֹה וּמְלֹא חָפְנָיו

יג קְטֹרֶת סַמִּים דַּקָּה וְהֵבִיא מִבֵּית לַפָּרֹכֶת: וְנָתַן אֶת־הַקְּטֹרֶת עַל־הָאֵשׁ לִפְנֵי יהוֹה וְכִסָּה | עֲנַן הַקְּטֹרֶת אֶת־הַכַּפֹּרֶת אֲשֶׁר עַל־הָעֵדוּת וְלֹא

יד יָמוּת: וְלָקַח מִדַּם הַפָּר וְהִזָּה בְאֶצְבָּעוֹ עַל־פְּנֵי הַכַּפֹּרֶת קֵדְמָה וְלִפְנֵי

טו הַכַּפֹּרֶת יַזֶּה שֶׁבַע־פְּעָמִים מִן־הַדָּם בְּאֶצְבָּעוֹ: וְשָׁחַט אֶת־שְׂעִיר הַחַטָּאת אֲשֶׁר לָעָם וְהֵבִיא אֶת־דָּמוֹ אֶל־מִבֵּית לַפָּרֹכֶת וְעָשָׂה אֶת־דָּמוֹ כַּאֲשֶׁר

טז עָשָׂה לְדַם הַפָּר וְהִזָּה אֹתוֹ עַל־הַכַּפֹּרֶת וְלִפְנֵי הַכַּפֹּרֶת: וְכִפֶּר עַל־הַקֹּדֶשׁ מִטֻּמְאֹת בְּנֵי יִשְׂרָאֵל וּמִפִּשְׁעֵיהֶם לְכָל־חַטֹּאתָם וְכֵן יַעֲשֶׂה לְאֹהֶל מוֹעֵד

יז הַשֹּׁכֵן אִתָּם בְּתוֹךְ טֻמְאֹתָם: וְכָל־אָדָם לֹא־יִהְיֶה | בְּאֹהֶל מוֹעֵד בְּבֹאוֹ לְכַפֵּר בַּקֹּדֶשׁ עַד־צֵאתוֹ וְכִפֶּר בַּעֲדוֹ וּבְעַד בֵּיתוֹ וּבְעַד כָּל־קְהַל יִשְׂרָאֵל:

יח וְיָצָא אֶל־הַמִּזְבֵּחַ אֲשֶׁר לִפְנֵי־יהוֹה וְכִפֶּר עָלָיו וְלָקַח מִדַּם הַפָּר וּמִדַּם

יט הַשָּׂעִיר וְנָתַן עַל־קַרְנוֹת הַמִּזְבֵּחַ סָבִיב: וְהִזָּה עָלָיו מִן־הַדָּם בְּאֶצְבָּעוֹ שֶׁבַע פְּעָמִים וְטִהֲרוֹ וְקִדְּשׁוֹ מִטֻּמְאֹת בְּנֵי יִשְׂרָאֵל: וְכִלָּה מִכַּפֵּר אֶת־

כ הַקֹּדֶשׁ וְאֶת־אֹהֶל מוֹעֵד וְאֶת־הַמִּזְבֵּחַ וְהִקְרִיב אֶת־הַשָּׂעִיר הֶחָי: וְסָמַךְ

כא אַהֲרֹן אֶת־שְׁתֵּי יָדָו עַל־רֹאשׁ הַשָּׂעִיר הַחַי וְהִתְוַדָּה עָלָיו אֶת־כָּל־עֲוֹנֹת בְּנֵי יִשְׂרָאֵל וְאֶת־כָּל־פִּשְׁעֵיהֶם לְכָל־חַטֹּאתָם וְנָתַן אֹתָם עַל־רֹאשׁ

כב הַשָּׂעִיר וְשִׁלַּח בְּיַד־אִישׁ עִתִּי הַמִּדְבָּרָה: וְנָשָׂא הַשָּׂעִיר עָלָיו אֶת־כָּל־

כג עֲוֹנֹתָם אֶל־אֶרֶץ גְּזֵרָה וְשִׁלַּח אֶת־הַשָּׂעִיר בַּמִּדְבָּר: וּבָא אַהֲרֹן אֶל־אֹהֶל מוֹעֵד וּפָשַׁט אֶת־בִּגְדֵי הַבָּד אֲשֶׁר לָבַשׁ בְּבֹאוֹ אֶל־הַקֹּדֶשׁ וְהִנִּיחָם שָׁם:

כד וְרָחַץ אֶת־בְּשָׂרוֹ בַמַּיִם בְּמָקוֹם קָדוֹשׁ וְלָבַשׁ אֶת־בְּגָדָיו וְיָצָא וְעָשָׂה

כה אֶת־עֹלָתוֹ וְאֶת־עֹלַת הָעָם וְכִפֶּר בַּעֲדוֹ וּבְעַד הָעָם: וְאֵת חֵלֶב הַחַטָּאת

כו יַקְטִיר הַמִּזְבֵּחָה: וְהַמְשַׁלֵּחַ אֶת־הַשָּׂעִיר לַעֲזָאזֵל יְכַבֵּס בְּגָדָיו וְרָחַץ אֶת־

כז בְּשָׂרוֹ בַּמָּיִם וְאַחֲרֵי־כֵן יָבוֹא אֶל־הַמַּחֲנֶה: וְאֵת פַּר הַחַטָּאת וְאֵת | שְׂעִיר הַחַטָּאת אֲשֶׁר הוּבָא אֶת־דָּמָם לְכַפֵּר בַּקֹּדֶשׁ יוֹצִיא אֶל־מִחוּץ

כח לַמַּחֲנֶה וְשָׂרְפוּ בָאֵשׁ אֶת־עֹרֹתָם וְאֶת־בְּשָׂרָם וְאֶת־פִּרְשָׁם: וְהַשֹּׂרֵף אֹתָם יְכַבֵּס בְּגָדָיו וְרָחַץ אֶת־בְּשָׂרוֹ בַּמָּיִם וְאַחֲרֵי־כֵן יָבוֹא אֶל־הַמַּחֲנֶה:

כט וְהָיְתָה לָכֶם לְחֻקַּת עוֹלָם בַּחֹדֶשׁ הַשְּׁבִיעִי בֶּעָשׂוֹר לַחֹדֶשׁ תְּעַנּוּ אֶת־נַפְשֹׁתֵיכֶם וְכָל־מְלָאכָה לֹא תַעֲשׂוּ הָאֶזְרָח וְהַגֵּר הַגָּר בְּתוֹכְכֶם:

שני (right margin)
שלישי [שני] (right margin)

16:12-13. The Kohen Gadol would bring burning coals from the outer Altar and specially ground incense to the Holy of Holies. There he would pour the incense onto the fire and wait until the incense cloud rose and covered the Ark.

16:14-28. Special blood service. The special blood service of the Kohen Gadol's own bull and the people's he-goat is performed in the Holy of Holies.

16:17. *Recanati* and *R' Bachya* explain that on Yom Kippur the Kohen Gadol had to approach God, as it were, without any intermediary between them.

16:20-22. Though the commandment to send a "scapegoat" to Azazel is a חק, *a decree* that is beyond human intelligence, commentators have attempted to offer rationales:

(a) The ritual of the scapegoat inspires the Jews to repent, for it symbolizes that people can remove from themselves the burden of past sins.

(b) The two identical he-goats symbolize that every person must choose between good and evil; those who do not choose holiness are inevitably pushing themselves toward a wasteland of spiritual destruction (*R' Hirsch*).

The incense
service

[12] He shall take a shovelful of fiery coals* from atop the Altar that is before HASHEM, and his cupped handsful of finely ground incense-spices, and bring it within the Curtain. [13] He shall place the incense upon the fire before HASHEM — so that the cloud of the incense shall blanket the Ark-cover that is atop the [Tablets of the] Testimony — so that he shall not die.

[14] He shall take some of the blood* of the bull and sprinkle with his forefinger upon the eastern front of the Ark-cover; and in front of the Ark-cover he shall sprinkle seven times from the blood with his forefinger. [15] He shall slaughter the sin-offering he-goat of the people, and bring its blood within the Curtain; he shall do with its blood as he had done with the blood of the bull, and sprinkle it upon the Ark-cover and in front of the Ark-cover. [16] Thus shall he provide atonement upon the Sanctuary for the contaminations of the Children of Israel, even for their rebellious sins among all their sins; and so shall he do for the Tent of Meeting that dwells with them amid their contamination. [17] Any person shall not be in the Tent of Meeting when he comes to provide atonement in the Sanctuary until his departure;* he shall provide atonement for himself, for his household, and for the entire congregation of Israel.

[18] He shall go out to the Altar that is before HASHEM, and make atonement upon it: He shall take some blood of the bull and some blood of the he-goat and place it on the horns of the Altar all around. [19] He shall sprinkle upon it from the blood with his forefinger seven times; thus shall he cleanse it and sanctify it from the contaminations of the Children of Israel.

The he-goat
to Azazel

[20] When he is finished atoning for the Sanctuary, the Tent of Meeting, and the Altar, he shall bring the living he-goat near.* [21] Aaron shall lean his two hands upon the head of the living he-goat and confess upon it all the iniquities of the Children of Israel, and all their rebellious sins among all their sins, and place them upon the head of the he-goat, and send it with a designated man to the desert. [22] The he-goat will bear upon itself all their iniquities to an uninhabited land, and he should send the he-goat to the desert.

Removal of
the shovel
and ladle

[23] Aaron shall come to the Tent of Meeting — he shall remove the linen vestments that he had worn when he entered the Sanctuary, and he shall leave them there. [24] He shall immerse himself in the water in a sacred place and don

Conclusion
of the
service

his vestments; he shall go out and perform his own burnt-offering and the burnt-offering of the people, and shall provide atonement for himself and for the people.

[25] And the fat of the sin-offering he shall cause to go up in smoke upon the Altar. [26] The one who dispatched the he-goat to Azazel shall immerse his clothing and immerse himself in the water; thereafter he may enter the camp. [27] The sin-offering bull and the sin-offering he-goat, whose blood had been brought to provide atonement in the Sanctuary, someone shall remove to the outside of the camp; and they shall burn in fire their hides, their flesh, and their dung. [28] The one who burns them shall immerse his clothing and immerse himself in the water; thereafter he may enter the camp.

The eternal
command-
ment of
Yom Kippur

[29] This shall remain for you an eternal decree: In the seventh month, on the tenth of the month, you shall afflict yourselves and you shall not do any work, neither the native nor the proselyte who dwells among you.

ל כִּי־בַיּוֹם הַזֶּה יְכַפֵּר עֲלֵיכֶם לְטַהֵר אֶתְכֶם מִכֹּל חַטֹּאתֵיכֶם לִפְנֵי יהוה
לא-לב תִּטְהָרוּ: שַׁבַּת שַׁבָּתוֹן הִיא לָכֶם וְעִנִּיתֶם אֶת־נַפְשֹׁתֵיכֶם חֻקַּת עוֹלָם: וְכִפֶּר
הַכֹּהֵן אֲשֶׁר־יִמְשַׁח אֹתוֹ וַאֲשֶׁר יְמַלֵּא אֶת־יָדוֹ לְכַהֵן תַּחַת אָבִיו וְלָבַשׁ
לג אֶת־בִּגְדֵי הַבָּד בִּגְדֵי הַקֹּדֶשׁ: וְכִפֶּר אֶת־מִקְדַּשׁ הַקֹּדֶשׁ וְאֶת־אֹהֶל מוֹעֵד
לד וְאֶת־הַמִּזְבֵּחַ יְכַפֵּר וְעַל הַכֹּהֲנִים וְעַל־כָּל־עַם הַקָּהָל יְכַפֵּר: וְהָיְתָה־זֹּאת
לָכֶם לְחֻקַּת עוֹלָם לְכַפֵּר עַל־בְּנֵי יִשְׂרָאֵל מִכָּל־חַטֹּאתָם אַחַת בַּשָּׁנָה
וַיַּעַשׂ כַּאֲשֶׁר צִוָּה יהוה אֶת־מֹשֶׁה:

יז רביעי א-ב וַיְדַבֵּר יהוה אֶל־מֹשֶׁה לֵּאמֹר: דַּבֵּר אֶל־אַהֲרֹן וְאֶל־בָּנָיו וְאֶל כָּל־בְּנֵי
ג יִשְׂרָאֵל וְאָמַרְתָּ אֲלֵיהֶם זֶה הַדָּבָר אֲשֶׁר־צִוָּה יהוה לֵאמֹר: אִישׁ אִישׁ
מִבֵּית יִשְׂרָאֵל אֲשֶׁר יִשְׁחַט שׁוֹר אוֹ־כֶשֶׂב אוֹ־עֵז בַּמַּחֲנֶה אוֹ אֲשֶׁר יִשְׁחָט
ד מִחוּץ לַמַּחֲנֶה: וְאֶל־פֶּתַח אֹהֶל מוֹעֵד לֹא הֱבִיאוֹ לְהַקְרִיב קָרְבָּן לַיהוה
לִפְנֵי מִשְׁכַּן יהוה דָּם יֵחָשֵׁב לָאִישׁ הַהוּא דָּם שָׁפָךְ וְנִכְרַת הָאִישׁ הַהוּא
ה מִקֶּרֶב עַמּוֹ: לְמַעַן אֲשֶׁר יָבִיאוּ בְּנֵי יִשְׂרָאֵל אֶת־זִבְחֵיהֶם אֲשֶׁר הֵם זֹבְחִים
עַל־פְּנֵי הַשָּׂדֶה וֶהֱבִיאֻם לַיהוה אֶל־פֶּתַח אֹהֶל מוֹעֵד אֶל־הַכֹּהֵן וְזָבְחוּ
ו זִבְחֵי שְׁלָמִים לַיהוה אוֹתָם: וְזָרַק הַכֹּהֵן אֶת־הַדָּם עַל־מִזְבַּח יהוה פֶּתַח
ז אֹהֶל מוֹעֵד וְהִקְטִיר הַחֵלֶב לְרֵיחַ נִיחֹחַ לַיהוה: וְלֹא־יִזְבְּחוּ עוֹד אֶת־
זִבְחֵיהֶם לַשְּׂעִירִם אֲשֶׁר הֵם זֹנִים אַחֲרֵיהֶם חֻקַּת עוֹלָם תִּהְיֶה־זֹּאת לָהֶם
ח לְדֹרֹתָם: וַאֲלֵהֶם תֹּאמַר אִישׁ אִישׁ מִבֵּית יִשְׂרָאֵל וּמִן־הַגֵּר אֲשֶׁר־יָגוּר
ט בְּתוֹכָם אֲשֶׁר־יַעֲלֶה עֹלָה אוֹ־זָבַח: וְאֶל־פֶּתַח אֹהֶל מוֹעֵד לֹא יְבִיאֶנּוּ
י לַעֲשׂוֹת אֹתוֹ לַיהוה וְנִכְרַת הָאִישׁ הַהוּא מֵעַמָּיו: וְאִישׁ אִישׁ מִבֵּית
יִשְׂרָאֵל וּמִן־הַגֵּר הַגָּר בְּתוֹכָם אֲשֶׁר יֹאכַל כָּל־דָּם וְנָתַתִּי פָנַי בַּנֶּפֶשׁ
יא הָאֹכֶלֶת אֶת־הַדָּם וְהִכְרַתִּי אֹתָהּ מִקֶּרֶב עַמָּהּ: כִּי־נֶפֶשׁ הַבָּשָׂר בַּדָּם הִוא
וַאֲנִי נְתַתִּיו לָכֶם עַל־הַמִּזְבֵּחַ לְכַפֵּר עַל־נַפְשֹׁתֵיכֶם כִּי־הַדָּם הוּא בַּנֶּפֶשׁ
יב יְכַפֵּר: עַל־כֵּן אָמַרְתִּי לִבְנֵי יִשְׂרָאֵל כָּל־נֶפֶשׁ מִכֶּם לֹא־תֹאכַל דָּם וְהַגֵּר
יג הַגָּר בְּתוֹכְכֶם לֹא־יֹאכַל דָּם: וְאִישׁ אִישׁ מִבְּנֵי יִשְׂרָאֵל וּמִן־הַגֵּר הַגָּר
בְּתוֹכָם אֲשֶׁר יָצוּד צֵיד חַיָּה אוֹ־עוֹף אֲשֶׁר יֵאָכֵל וְשָׁפַךְ אֶת־דָּמוֹ וְכִסָּהוּ
יד בֶּעָפָר: כִּי־נֶפֶשׁ כָּל־בָּשָׂר דָּמוֹ בְנַפְשׁוֹ הוּא וָאֹמַר לִבְנֵי יִשְׂרָאֵל דַּם כָּל־
בָּשָׂר לֹא תֹאכֵלוּ כִּי נֶפֶשׁ כָּל־בָּשָׂר דָּמוֹ הִוא כָּל־אֹכְלָיו יִכָּרֵת: וְכָל־נֶפֶשׁ
טו אֲשֶׁר תֹּאכַל נְבֵלָה וּטְרֵפָה בָּאֶזְרָח וּבַגֵּר וְכִבֶּס בְּגָדָיו וְרָחַץ בַּמַּיִם וְטָמֵא
טז עַד־הָעֶרֶב וְטָהֵר: וְאִם לֹא יְכַבֵּס וּבְשָׂרוֹ לֹא יִרְחָץ וְנָשָׂא עֲוֹנוֹ:

חמישי
[שלישי]

16:30. Sacrificial service can serve only to make God receptive to one's personal repentance — then the sinner must make himself worthy of God's forgiveness. Only through personal repentance and self-cleansing can a person "be cleansed of all his sins before God" (*Sforno*).

R' Elazar ben Azariah expounds that repentance and the Yom Kippur service can effect atonement only for sins

before HASHEM, i.e., against God; one who sinned against his fellow must first appease his fellow (*Sifra, Yoma* 85b).

17:11-12. Because life is dependent upon blood, God designated blood as the medium that goes upon the Altar for atonement, as if to say, "Let one life be offered to atone for another." Consequently, it is not appropriate for blood to be eaten (*Rashi; Sifra*).

³⁰ For on this day he shall provide atonement for you to cleanse you; from all your sins before HASHEM shall you be cleansed. *

³¹ It is a Sabbath of complete rest for you, and you shall afflict yourselves; an eternal decree. ³² The Kohen, who has been anointed or who has been given the authority to serve in place of his father, shall provide atonement; he shall don the linen vestments, the sacred vestments. ³³ He shall bring atonement upon the Holy of Holies, and he shall bring atonement upon the Tent of Meeting and the Altar; and upon the Kohanim and upon all the people of the congregation shall he bring atonement. ³⁴ This shall be to you an eternal decree to bring atonement upon the Children of Israel for all their sins once a year; and [Aaron] did as HASHEM commanded Moses.

17

Service outside the Tabernacle

¹ HASHEM spoke to Moses, saying: ² Speak to Aaron and to his sons and to all the Children of Israel, and say to them: This is the matter that HASHEM has commanded, saying: ³ Any man from the House of Israel who will slaughter an ox, a sheep, or a goat in the camp, or who will slaughter outside the camp, ⁴ and he has not brought it to the entrance of the Tent of Meeting to bring it as an offering to HASHEM before the Tabernacle of HASHEM — it shall be considered as bloodshed for that man, he has shed blood, and that man shall be cut off from the midst of his people. ⁵ So that the Children of Israel will bring their feast-offerings that they have been slaughtering on the open field, and they shall bring them to HASHEM to the entrance of the Tent of Meeting to the Kohen; and they shall slaughter them as feast peace-offerings to HASHEM. ⁶ The Kohen shall throw the blood upon the Altar of HASHEM, at the entrance of the Tent of Meeting; and he shall cause the fats to go up in smoke for a satisfying aroma to HASHEM. ⁷ They shall no longer slaughter their offerings to the demons after whom they stray; this shall be an eternal decree to them for their generations.

⁸ And to them you shall say: Any man of the House of Israel and of the proselyte who shall dwell among you who will offer up a burnt-offering or a feast-offering, ⁹ and he will not bring it to the entrance of the Tent of Meeting to perform its service to HASHEM — that man shall be cut off from the midst of his people.

Prohibition against eating blood

¹⁰ Any man of the House of Israel and of the proselyte who dwells among them who will consume any blood — I shall concentrate My attention upon the soul consuming the blood, and I will cut it off from its people. ¹¹For the soul of the flesh is in the blood* and I have assigned it for you upon the Altar to provide atonement for your souls; for it is the blood that atones for the soul. ¹² Therefore I have said to the Children of Israel: "Any person among you may not consume blood; and the proselyte who dwells among you may not consume blood."

Covering blood

¹³ Any man of the Children of Israel and of the proselyte who dwells among them who will trap a beast or bird that may be eaten, he shall pour out its blood and cover it with earth. ¹⁴ For the life of any creature — its blood represents its life, so I say to the Children of Israel, "You shall not consume the blood of any creature; for the life of any creature is its blood, whoever consumes it will be cut off."

¹⁵ Any person who will eat a [bird] that died or was torn — the native or the proselyte — he shall immerse his garments and immerse himself in the water; he shall remain contaminated until evening and then become pure. ¹⁶ But if he does not immerse [his garments] and does not immerse his flesh, he shall bear his iniquity.

יח

READING
FOR YOM
KIPPUR
MINCHAH
18:1-30
Haftarah:
p. 1372

ששי

א־ב וַיְדַבֵּר יְהֹוָה אֶל־מֹשֶׁה לֵּאמֹר: דַּבֵּר אֶל־בְּנֵי יִשְׂרָאֵל וְאָמַרְתָּ אֲלֵהֶם אֲנִי

ג יְהֹוָה אֱלֹהֵיכֶם: כְּמַעֲשֵׂה אֶרֶץ־מִצְרַיִם אֲשֶׁר יְשַׁבְתֶּם־בָּהּ לֹא תַעֲשׂוּ

וּכְמַעֲשֵׂה אֶרֶץ־כְּנַעַן אֲשֶׁר אֲנִי מֵבִיא אֶתְכֶם שָׁמָּה לֹא תַעֲשׂוּ וּבְחֻקֹּתֵיהֶם

ד לֹא תֵלֵכוּ: אֶת־מִשְׁפָּטַי תַּעֲשׂוּ וְאֶת־חֻקֹּתַי תִּשְׁמְרוּ לָלֶכֶת בָּהֶם אֲנִי יְהֹוָה

ה אֱלֹהֵיכֶם: וּשְׁמַרְתֶּם אֶת־חֻקֹּתַי וְאֶת־מִשְׁפָּטַי אֲשֶׁר יַעֲשֶׂה אֹתָם הָאָדָם

ו וָחַי בָּהֶם אֲנִי יְהֹוָה: אִישׁ אִישׁ אֶל־כָּל־שְׁאֵר בְּשָׂרוֹ לֹא תִקְרְבוּ

ז לְגַלּוֹת עֶרְוָה אֲנִי יְהֹוָה: עֶרְוַת אָבִיךָ וְעֶרְוַת אִמְּךָ לֹא תְגַלֵּה

ח אִמְּךָ הִוא לֹא תְגַלֶּה עֶרְוָתָהּ: עֶרְוַת אֵשֶׁת־אָבִיךָ לֹא תְגַלֵּה

ט עֶרְוַת אָבִיךָ הִוא: עֶרְוַת אֲחוֹתְךָ בַת־אָבִיךָ אוֹ בַת־אִמְּךָ מוֹלֶדֶת

י בַּיִת אוֹ מוֹלֶדֶת חוּץ לֹא תְגַלֶּה עֶרְוָתָן: עֶרְוַת בַּת־בִּנְךָ אוֹ

יא בַת־בִּתְּךָ לֹא תְגַלֶּה עֶרְוָתָן כִּי עֶרְוָתְךָ הֵנָּה: עֶרְוַת בַּת־אֵשֶׁת

יב אָבִיךָ מוֹלֶדֶת אָבִיךָ אֲחוֹתְךָ הִוא לֹא תְגַלֶּה עֶרְוָתָהּ: עֶרְוַת

יג אֲחוֹת־אָבִיךָ לֹא תְגַלֵּה שְׁאֵר אָבִיךָ הִוא: עֶרְוַת אֲחוֹת־אִמְּךָ

יד לֹא תְגַלֵּה כִּי־שְׁאֵר אִמְּךָ הִוא: עֶרְוַת אֲחִי־אָבִיךָ לֹא תְגַלֵּה

טו אֶל־אִשְׁתּוֹ לֹא תִקְרָב דֹּדָתְךָ הִוא: עֶרְוַת כַּלָּתְךָ לֹא תְגַלֵּה אֵשֶׁת

טז בִּנְךָ הִוא לֹא תְגַלֶּה עֶרְוָתָהּ: עֶרְוַת אֵשֶׁת־אָחִיךָ לֹא תְגַלֵּה

יז עֶרְוַת אָחִיךָ הִוא: עֶרְוַת אִשָּׁה וּבִתָּהּ לֹא תְגַלֵּה אֶת־בַּת־בְּנָהּ

יח וְאֶת־בַּת־בִּתָּהּ לֹא תִקַּח לְגַלּוֹת עֶרְוָתָהּ שַׁאֲרָה הֵנָּה זִמָּה הִוא: וְאִשָּׁה

יט אֶל־אֲחֹתָהּ לֹא תִקָּח לִצְרֹר לְגַלּוֹת עֶרְוָתָהּ עָלֶיהָ בְּחַיֶּיהָ: וְאֶל־אִשָּׁה

כ בְּנִדַּת טֻמְאָתָהּ לֹא תִקְרַב לְגַלּוֹת עֶרְוָתָהּ: וְאֶל־אֵשֶׁת עֲמִיתְךָ לֹא־תִתֵּן

כא שְׁכָבְתְּךָ לְזָרַע לְטָמְאָה־בָהּ: וּמִזַּרְעֲךָ לֹא־תִתֵּן לְהַעֲבִיר לַמֹּלֶךְ וְלֹא תְחַלֵּל

כב אֶת־שֵׁם אֱלֹהֶיךָ אֲנִי יְהֹוָה: וְאֶת־זָכָר לֹא תִשְׁכַּב מִשְׁכְּבֵי אִשָּׁה תּוֹעֵבָה

שביעי
[רביעי]

כג הִוא: וּבְכָל־בְּהֵמָה לֹא־תִתֵּן שְׁכָבְתְּךָ לְטָמְאָה־בָהּ וְאִשָּׁה לֹא־תַעֲמֹד

כד לִפְנֵי בְהֵמָה לְרִבְעָהּ תֶּבֶל הִוא: אַל־תִּטַּמְּאוּ בְּכָל־אֵלֶּה כִּי בְכָל־אֵלֶּה

כה נִטְמְאוּ הַגּוֹיִם אֲשֶׁר־אֲנִי מְשַׁלֵּחַ מִפְּנֵיכֶם: וַתִּטְמָא הָאָרֶץ וָאֶפְקֹד עֲוֹנָהּ

כו עָלֶיהָ וַתָּקִא הָאָרֶץ אֶת־יֹשְׁבֶיהָ: וּשְׁמַרְתֶּם אַתֶּם אֶת־חֻקֹּתַי וְאֶת־מִשְׁפָּטַי

18:4-5. Laws . . . decrees. *Laws* are practices that would
be dictated by reason even if they were not commanded
by the Torah. *Decrees* are beyond human intelligence,
such as the prohibitions against the consumption of
certain foods. The verse ends with *I am Hashem, Your God,*
i.e., it is not for you to decide whether God's decrees are
worthy of your approval (*Rashi; Sifra*).

18:6-20. The laws governing sexual relationships are the
key to Jewish holiness. As the Sages state, wherever one
finds safeguards of chastity, there one finds holiness
(*Vayikra Rabbah* 24:6).

18:9. Half sisters have the same status as full sisters
(*Yevamos* 54b), as do sisters born out of wedlock. The
same applies to the *brother* of verse 16 (*Rambam*).

18:21. In the worship of Molech, a popular idol in
Canaan, parents hand their child to the priests, who walk
the child between two bonfires (*Rashi*). *Ramban* comments that it is included here because, like immorality, its
practice contaminated the land and led directly to the
Divine expulsion of the Canaanites (vv. 24-28).

18:22-23. The harshness with which the Torah describes
these perversions testifies to the repugnance in which
God holds their practitioners.

18:22. None of the relationships forbidden earlier are
described with this term, *an abomination,* a term of
disgust, because they involve normal activity, though
with prohibited mates. Homosexuality, however, is unnatural and therefore abominable.

18

Forbidden practices and traditions

¹ HASHEM spoke to Moses, saying: ² Speak to the Children of Israel and say to them: I am HASHEM, your God. ³ Do not perform the practice of the land of Egypt in which you dwelled; and do not perform the practice of the land of Canaan to which I bring you, and do not follow their traditions. ⁴ Carry out My laws* and safeguard My decrees to follow them; I am HASHEM, your God. ⁵ You shall observe My decrees* and My laws, which man shall carry out and by which he shall live — I am HASHEM.

*Forbidden relationships**

⁶ Any man shall not approach his close relative to uncover nakedness; I am HASHEM.

⁷ The nakedness of your father and the nakedness of your mother you shall not uncover; she is your mother, you shall not uncover her nakedness.

⁸ The nakedness of your father's wife you shall not uncover; it is your father's shame.

⁹ The nakedness of your sister* — whether your father's daughter or your mother's daughter, whether born to one who may remain in the home or born to one who must remain outside of it — you shall not uncover their nakedness.

¹⁰ The nakedness of your son's daughter or your daughter's daughter — you shall not uncover their nakedness; for they are your own shame.

¹¹ The nakedness of your father's wife's daughter who was born to your father — she is your sister; you shall not uncover her nakedness.

¹² The nakedness of your father's sister you shall not uncover; she is your father's flesh.

¹³ The nakedness of your mother's sister you shall not uncover; for she is your mother's flesh.

¹⁴ The nakedness of your father's brother you shall not uncover; do not approach his wife, she is your aunt.

¹⁵ The nakedness of your daughter-in-law you shall not uncover; she is your son's wife, you shall not uncover her nakedness.

¹⁶ The nakedness of your brother's wife you shall not uncover; it is your brother's shame.

¹⁷ The nakedness of a woman and her daughter you shall not uncover; you shall not take her son's daughter or her daughter's daughter to uncover her nakedness — they are close relatives, it is a depraved plot. ¹⁸ You shall not take a woman in addition to her sister, to make them rivals, to uncover the nakedness of one upon the other in her lifetime.

¹⁹ You shall not approach a woman in her time of unclean separation, to uncover her nakedness. ²⁰ You shall not lie carnally with your fellow's wife, to contaminate yourself with her.

Molech

²¹ You shall not present any of your children to pass through for Molech, * and do not profane the Name of your God — I am HASHEM.

Sodomy and bestiality

²² You shall not lie with a man* as one lies with a woman, it is an abomination. * ²³ Do not lie with any animal to be contaminated with it; a woman shall not stand before an animal for mating, it is a perversion. *

The holiness of the land

²⁴ Do not become contaminated through any of these; for through all of these the nations that I expel before you became contaminated. ²⁵ The land became contaminated and I recalled its iniquity upon it; and the land disgorged its inhabitants. ²⁶ But you shall safeguard My decrees and My judgments,

כז וְלֹא תַעֲשׂוּ מִכֹּל הַתּוֹעֵבֹת הָאֵלֶּה הָאֶזְרָח וְהַגֵּר הַגָּר בְּתוֹכְכֶם: כִּי אֶת־
כָּל־הַתּוֹעֵבֹת הָאֵל עָשׂוּ אַנְשֵׁי־הָאָרֶץ אֲשֶׁר לִפְנֵיכֶם וַתִּטְמָא הָאָרֶץ:

כח וְלֹא־תָקִיא הָאָרֶץ אֶתְכֶם בְּטַמַּאֲכֶם אֹתָהּ כַּאֲשֶׁר קָאָה אֶת־הַגּוֹי אֲשֶׁר

מפטיר

Haftaras
Acharei
Ashkenazim:
p. 1368
Sephardim:
p. 1256

For special
Sabbaths,
see pp. x-xi

כט לִפְנֵיכֶם: כִּי כָּל־אֲשֶׁר יַעֲשֶׂה מִכֹּל הַתּוֹעֵבֹת הָאֵלֶּה וְנִכְרְתוּ הַנְּפָשׁוֹת
ל הָעֹשֹׂת מִקֶּרֶב עַמָּם: וּשְׁמַרְתֶּם אֶת־מִשְׁמַרְתִּי לְבִלְתִּי עֲשׂוֹת מֵחֻקּוֹת
הַתּוֹעֵבֹת אֲשֶׁר נַעֲשׂוּ לִפְנֵיכֶם וְלֹא תִטַּמְּאוּ בָּהֶם אֲנִי יְהוָה אֱלֹהֵיכֶם: פפפ

פ׳ פְּסוּקִים. כ״י כ״ל סִימָן. עד״ו סִימָן

פרשת קדושים

יט א־ב וַיְדַבֵּר יְהוָה אֶל־מֹשֶׁה לֵּאמֹר: דַּבֵּר אֶל־כָּל־עֲדַת בְּנֵי־יִשְׂרָאֵל וְאָמַרְתָּ
ג אֲלֵהֶם קְדֹשִׁים תִּהְיוּ כִּי קָדוֹשׁ אֲנִי יְהוָה אֱלֹהֵיכֶם: אִישׁ אִמּוֹ וְאָבִיו תִּירָאוּ
ד וְאֶת־שַׁבְּתֹתַי תִּשְׁמֹרוּ אֲנִי יְהוָה אֱלֹהֵיכֶם: אַל־תִּפְנוּ אֶל־הָאֱלִילִים וֵאלֹהֵי
ה מַסֵּכָה לֹא תַעֲשׂוּ לָכֶם אֲנִי יְהוָה אֱלֹהֵיכֶם: וְכִי תִזְבְּחוּ זֶבַח שְׁלָמִים לַיהוָה
ו לִרְצֹנְכֶם תִּזְבָּחֻהוּ: בְּיוֹם זִבְחֲכֶם יֵאָכֵל וּמִמָּחֳרָת וְהַנּוֹתָר עַד־יוֹם
ז הַשְּׁלִישִׁי בָּאֵשׁ יִשָּׂרֵף: וְאִם הֵאָכֹל יֵאָכֵל בַּיּוֹם הַשְּׁלִישִׁי פִּגּוּל הוּא לֹא
ח יֵרָצֶה: וְאֹכְלָיו עֲוֺנוֹ יִשָּׂא כִּי־אֶת־קֹדֶשׁ יְהוָה חִלֵּל וְנִכְרְתָה הַנֶּפֶשׁ הַהִוא
ט מֵעַמֶּיהָ: וּבְקֻצְרְכֶם אֶת־קְצִיר אַרְצְכֶם לֹא תְכַלֶּה פְּאַת שָׂדְךָ לִקְצֹר וְלֶקֶט
י קְצִירְךָ לֹא תְלַקֵּט: וְכַרְמְךָ לֹא תְעוֹלֵל וּפֶרֶט כַּרְמְךָ לֹא תְלַקֵּט לֶעָנִי וְלַגֵּר
יא תַּעֲזֹב אֹתָם אֲנִי יְהוָה אֱלֹהֵיכֶם: לֹא תִּגְנֹבוּ וְלֹא־תְכַחֲשׁוּ וְלֹא־תְשַׁקְּרוּ
יב אִישׁ בַּעֲמִיתוֹ: וְלֹא־תִשָּׁבְעוּ בִשְׁמִי לַשָּׁקֶר וְחִלַּלְתָּ אֶת־שֵׁם אֱלֹהֶיךָ אֲנִי
יג יְהוָה: לֹא־תַעֲשֹׁק אֶת־רֵעֲךָ וְלֹא תִגְזֹל לֹא־תָלִין פְּעֻלַּת שָׂכִיר אִתְּךָ עַד־
יד בֹּקֶר: לֹא־תְקַלֵּל חֵרֵשׁ וְלִפְנֵי עִוֵּר לֹא תִתֵּן מִכְשֹׁל וְיָרֵאתָ מֵּאֱלֹהֶיךָ

שני [חמישי]

טו אֲנִי יְהוָה: לֹא־תַעֲשׂוּ עָוֶל בַּמִּשְׁפָּט לֹא־תִשָּׂא פְנֵי־דָל וְלֹא תֶהְדַּר פְּנֵי
טז גָדוֹל בְּצֶדֶק תִּשְׁפֹּט עֲמִיתֶךָ: לֹא־תֵלֵךְ רָכִיל בְּעַמֶּיךָ לֹא תַעֲמֹד עַל־
יז דַּם רֵעֶךָ אֲנִי יְהוָה: לֹא־תִשְׂנָא אֶת־אָחִיךָ בִּלְבָבֶךָ הוֹכֵחַ תּוֹכִיחַ אֶת־
יח עֲמִיתֶךָ וְלֹא־תִשָּׂא עָלָיו חֵטְא: לֹא־תִקֹּם וְלֹא־תִטֹּר אֶת־בְּנֵי עַמֶּךָ
יט וְאָהַבְתָּ לְרֵעֲךָ כָּמוֹךָ אֲנִי יְהוָה: אֶת־חֻקֹּתַי תִּשְׁמֹרוּ בְּהֶמְתְּךָ לֹא־תַרְבִּיעַ
כִּלְאַיִם שָׂדְךָ לֹא־תִזְרַע כִּלְאָיִם וּבֶגֶד כִּלְאַיִם שַׁעַטְנֵז לֹא יַעֲלֶה עָלֶיךָ:

18:28. The land's holiness cannot tolerate the sort of sins described in this chapter, and it was about to vomit out its Canaanite inhabitants because they persisted in these activities. When the Jews themselves began to indulge in such behavior, they, too, were disgorged.

⊷§ Parashas Kedoshim

19:2. This *Sidrah* begins by instructing the nation to become holy by emulating God as much as possible; this will elevate their lives in this world. *"You shall be holy"* is a general admonition that one's approach to all aspects of life be governed by moderation.

19:5-8. Offerings can be disqualified by improper inten-

tions at the time of the service. It is not enough to carry out the commandments mechanically; one must perform them with the right intentions as well (*Sforno*).

19:13. If a worker was hired by the day, his employer has until morning to pay him; if he was hired for the night, he must be paid by the next evening (*Rashi; Sifra*).

19:14. *Before the blind.* [In addition to the literal meaning,] one may not give bad advice to an unsuspecting person (*Rashi; Sifra*), or cause someone to sin (*Rambam*).

19:15. It is improper for a judge to rule in favor of the poor litigant so that he will be supported in dignity; justice must be rendered honestly (*Rashi; Sifra*).

and not commit any of these abominations — the native or the proselyte who lives among you. ²⁷ For the inhabitants of the land who are before you committed all these abominations, and the land became contaminated. ²⁸ Let not the land disgorge you for having contaminated it, as it disgorged the nation that was before you. * ²⁹ For if anyone commits any of these abominations, the people doing so will be cut off from among their people.

³⁰ You shall safeguard My charge not to do any of the abominable traditions that were done before you and not contaminate yourselves through them; I am HASHEM, your God.

PARASHAS KEDOSHIM

19

Holiness

¹ Hashem spoke to Moses, saying: ² Speak to the entire assembly of the Children of Israel and say to them: You shall be holy, for holy am I, HASHEM, your God. *

³ Every man: Your mother and father shall you revere and My Sabbaths shall you observe — I am HASHEM, your God. ⁴ Do not turn to the idols, and molten gods shall you not make for yourselves — I am HASHEM, your God.

Piggul/ Rejected offerings

⁵ When you slaughter a feast peace-offering to HASHEM, you shall slaughter it to find favor for yourselves. * ⁶ On the day of your slaughter shall it be eaten and on the next day, and whatever remains until the third day shall be burned in fire. ⁷ But if it shall be eaten on the third day, it is rejected — it shall not be accepted. ⁸ Each of those who eat it will bear his iniquity, for what is sacred to HASHEM has he desecrated; and that soul will be cut off from its people.

Gifts to the poor

⁹ When you reap the harvest of your land, you shall not complete your reaping to the corner of your field, and the gleanings of your harvest you shall not take. ¹⁰ You shall not pick the undeveloped twigs of your vineyard; and the fallen fruit of your vineyard you shall not gather; for the poor and the proselyte shall you leave them — I am HASHEM, your God.

Honest dealings with others

¹¹ You shall not steal, you shall not deny falsely, and you shall not lie one man to his fellow. ¹² You shall not swear falsely by My Name, thereby desecrating the Name of your God — I am HASHEM. ¹³ You shall not cheat your fellow and you shall not rob; a worker's wage shall not remain with you overnight until morning. * ¹⁴ You shall not curse the deaf, and you shall not place a stumbling block before the blind; * you shall fear your God — I am HASHEM.

¹⁵ You shall not commit a perversion of justice; you shall not favor the poor and you shall not honor the great; with righteousness shall you judge your fellow. *

Love your fellow

¹⁶ You shall not be a gossipmonger among your people, you shall not stand aside while your fellow's blood is shed — I am HASHEM. ¹⁷ You shall not hate your brother in your heart; you shall reprove your fellow and do not bear a sin because of him. ¹⁸ You shall not take revenge and you shall not bear a grudge against the members of your people; you shall love your fellow as yourself * — I am HASHEM.

Kil'ayim/ Forbidden mixtures

¹⁹ You shall observe My decrees: you shall not mate your animal into another species, you shall not plant your field with mixed seed; and a garment that is a mixture of combined fibers shall not come upon you.

19:18. R' Akiva said that this is the fundamental rule of the Torah (Rashi; Sifra). Hillel paraphrased: "What is hateful to you, do not do to others" (Shabbos 31a). We must wish upon others the same degree of success and prosperity we wish upon ourselves and we must treat others with the utmost respect and consideration (Ramban).

כ וְאִישׁ כִּי־יִשְׁכַּב אֶת־אִשָּׁה שִׁכְבַת־זֶרַע וְהִוא שִׁפְחָה נֶחֱרֶפֶת לְאִישׁ וְהָפְדֵּה לֹא נִפְדָּתָה אוֹ חֻפְשָׁה לֹא נִתַּן־לָהּ בִּקֹּרֶת תִּהְיֶה לֹא יוּמְתוּ כִּי־לֹא חֻפָּשָׁה:

כא-כב וְהֵבִיא אֶת־אֲשָׁמוֹ לַיהוָה אֶל־פֶּתַח אֹהֶל מוֹעֵד אֵיל אָשָׁם: וְכִפֶּר עָלָיו הַכֹּהֵן בְּאֵיל הָאָשָׁם לִפְנֵי יהוה עַל־חַטָּאתוֹ אֲשֶׁר חָטָא וְנִסְלַח לוֹ מֵחַטָּאתוֹ אֲשֶׁר חָטָא:

כג שלישי וְכִי־תָבֹאוּ אֶל־הָאָרֶץ וּנְטַעְתֶּם כָּל־עֵץ מַאֲכָל וַעֲרַלְתֶּם עָרְלָתוֹ אֶת־פִּרְיוֹ

כד שָׁלֹשׁ שָׁנִים יִהְיֶה לָכֶם עֲרֵלִים לֹא יֵאָכֵל: וּבַשָּׁנָה הָרְבִיעִת יִהְיֶה כָּל־פִּרְיוֹ

כה קֹדֶשׁ הִלּוּלִים לַיהוָה: וּבַשָּׁנָה הַחֲמִישִׁת תֹּאכְלוּ אֶת־פִּרְיוֹ לְהוֹסִיף לָכֶם

כו תְּבוּאָתוֹ אֲנִי יהוה אֱלֹהֵיכֶם: לֹא תֹאכְלוּ עַל־הַדָּם לֹא תְנַחֲשׁוּ וְלֹא

כז-כח תְעוֹנֵנוּ: לֹא תַקִּפוּ פְּאַת רֹאשְׁכֶם וְלֹא תַשְׁחִית אֵת פְּאַת זְקָנֶךָ: וְשֶׂרֶט לָנֶפֶשׁ לֹא תִתְּנוּ בִּבְשַׂרְכֶם וּכְתֹבֶת קַעֲקַע לֹא תִתְּנוּ בָּכֶם אֲנִי יהוה: אַל־

כט תְּחַלֵּל אֶת־בִּתְּךָ לְהַזְנוֹתָהּ וְלֹא־תִזְנֶה הָאָרֶץ וּמָלְאָה הָאָרֶץ זִמָּה: אֶת־

ל שַׁבְּתֹתַי תִּשְׁמֹרוּ וּמִקְדָּשִׁי תִּירָאוּ אֲנִי יהוה: אַל־תִּפְנוּ אֶל־הָאֹבֹת וְאֶל־

לא מי דגושה הַיִּדְּעֹנִים אַל־תְּבַקְשׁוּ לְטָמְאָה בָהֶם אֲנִי יהוה אֱלֹהֵיכֶם: מִפְּנֵי שֵׂיבָה

לב רביעי [ששי] תָּקוּם וְהָדַרְתָּ פְּנֵי זָקֵן וְיָרֵאתָ מֵּאֱלֹהֶיךָ אֲנִי יהוה: וְכִי־יָגוּר

לג אִתְּךָ גֵּר בְּאַרְצְכֶם לֹא תוֹנוּ אֹתוֹ: כְּאֶזְרָח מִכֶּם יִהְיֶה לָכֶם הַגֵּר הַגָּר

לד אִתְּכֶם וְאָהַבְתָּ לוֹ כָּמוֹךָ כִּי־גֵרִים הֱיִיתֶם בְּאֶרֶץ מִצְרָיִם אֲנִי יהוה אֱלֹהֵיכֶם: לֹא־תַעֲשׂוּ עָוֶל בַּמִּשְׁפָּט בַּמִּדָּה בַּמִּשְׁקָל וּבַמְּשׂוּרָה: מֹאזְנֵי

לה-לו צֶדֶק אַבְנֵי־צֶדֶק אֵיפַת צֶדֶק וְהִין צֶדֶק יִהְיֶה לָכֶם אֲנִי יהוה אֱלֹהֵיכֶם

לז אֲשֶׁר־הוֹצֵאתִי אֶתְכֶם מֵאֶרֶץ מִצְרָיִם: וּשְׁמַרְתֶּם אֶת־כָּל־חֻקֹּתַי וְאֶת־ כָּל־מִשְׁפָּטַי וַעֲשִׂיתֶם אֹתָם אֲנִי יהוה:

כ א-ב חמישי וַיְדַבֵּר יהוה אֶל־מֹשֶׁה לֵּאמֹר: וְאֶל־בְּנֵי יִשְׂרָאֵל תֹּאמַר אִישׁ אִישׁ מִבְּנֵי יִשְׂרָאֵל וּמִן־הַגֵּר הַגָּר בְּיִשְׂרָאֵל אֲשֶׁר יִתֵּן מִזַּרְעוֹ לַמֹּלֶךְ מוֹת יוּמָת

ג עַם הָאָרֶץ יִרְגְּמֻהוּ בָאָבֶן: וַאֲנִי אֶתֵּן אֶת־פָּנַי בָּאִישׁ הַהוּא וְהִכְרַתִּי אֹתוֹ מִקֶּרֶב עַמּוֹ כִּי מִזַּרְעוֹ נָתַן לַמֹּלֶךְ לְמַעַן טַמֵּא אֶת־מִקְדָּשִׁי וּלְחַלֵּל

ד אֶת־שֵׁם קָדְשִׁי: וְאִם הַעְלֵם יַעְלִימוּ עַם הָאָרֶץ אֶת־עֵינֵיהֶם מִן־הָאִישׁ

ה הַהוּא בְּתִתּוֹ מִזַּרְעוֹ לַמֹּלֶךְ לְבִלְתִּי הָמִית אֹתוֹ: וְשַׂמְתִּי אֲנִי אֶת־פָּנַי בָּאִישׁ הַהוּא וּבְמִשְׁפַּחְתּוֹ וְהִכְרַתִּי אֹתוֹ וְאֵת ׀ כָּל־הַזֹּנִים אַחֲרָיו לִזְנוֹת

ו אַחֲרֵי הַמֹּלֶךְ מִקֶּרֶב עַמָּם: וְהַנֶּפֶשׁ אֲשֶׁר תִּפְנֶה אֶל־הָאֹבֹת וְאֶל־הַיִּדְּעֹנִים לִזְנוֹת אַחֲרֵיהֶם וְנָתַתִּי אֶת־פָּנַי בַּנֶּפֶשׁ הַהוּא וְהִכְרַתִּי אֹתוֹ מִקֶּרֶב עַמּוֹ:

19:23-25. All fruits from the first three years of a newly planted tree or its grafted shoots are forbidden for any conceivable use, and those of the fourth year are holy and are to be eaten in Jerusalem.

19:27. It is forbidden to remove the sideburns even by means of scissors. Regarding the beard, however, the Torah forbids removing it only by means of a razor.

19:31. Magical practices purport to foretell the future.

19:32. One can easily violate this commandment by pretending not to have noticed. Therefore, the Torah cautions us to revere God, Who knows our true intentions (*Rashi*; *Sifra*).

19:35-36. A businessman who falsifies weights and measures is likened to a judge who perverts judgment.

Shifchah
charufah/
Designated
maidservant

²⁰ *If a man lies carnally with a woman, and she is a slavewoman who has been designated for another man, and who has not been redeemed, or freedom has not been granted her; there shall be an investigation — they shall not be put to death, for she has not been freed.* ²¹ *He shall bring his guilt-offering to* HASHEM, *to the entrance of the Tent of Meeting, a ram guilt-offering.* ²² *The Kohen shall provide him atonement with the ram guilt-offering before* HASHEM *for the sin that he had committed; and the sin that he had committed shall be forgiven him.*

Fruit trees

²³ *When you shall come to the land and you shall plant any food tree, * you shall treat its fruit as forbidden; for three years they shall be forbidden to you, they shall not be eaten.* ²⁴ *In the fourth year, all its fruit shall be sanctified to laud* HASHEM. ²⁵ *And in the fifth year you may eat its fruit — so that it will increase its crop for you — I am* HASHEM, *your God.*

²⁶ *You shall not eat over the blood; you shall not indulge in sorcery and you shall not believe in lucky times.* ²⁷ *You shall not round off the edge of your scalp and you shall not destroy the edge of your beard. ** ²⁸ *You shall not make a cut in your flesh for the dead, and a tattoo shall you not place upon yourselves — I am* HASHEM.

²⁹ *Do not profane your daughter to make her a harlot, lest the land become lewd, and the land become filled with depravity.*

³⁰ *My Sabbaths shall you observe and My Sanctuary shall you revere — I am* HASHEM. ³¹ *Do not turn to [the sorcery of] the Ovos and Yid'onim*; do not seek to be contaminated through them — I am* HASHEM, *your God.*

³² *In the presence of an old person shall you rise and you shall honor the presence of a sage and you shall revere your God — I am* HASHEM. *

³³*When a proselyte dwells among you in your land, do not taunt him.* ³⁴ *The proselyte who dwells with you shall be like a native among you, and you shall love him like yourself, for you were aliens in the land of Egypt — I am* HASHEM, *your God.*

Weights and
measures

³⁵ *You shall not commit a perversion in justice, * in measures of length, weight, or volume.* ³⁶ *You shall have correct scales, correct weights, correct dry measures, and correct liquid measures — I am* HASHEM, *your God, Who brought you forth from the land of Egypt.* ³⁷ *You shall observe all My decrees and all My ordinances, and you shall perform them — I am* HASHEM.

20

Punishments

Molech

¹ HASHEM *spoke to Moses, saying:* ² *Say to the Children of Israel: Any man from the Children of Israel and from the proselyte who lives with Israel, who shall give of his seed to Molech, shall be put to death; the people of the land shall pelt him with stones.* ³ *I shall concentrate My attention upon that man, and I shall cut him off from among his people, for he had given from his offspring to Molech in order to defile My Sanctuary and to desecrate My holy Name.* ⁴ *But if the people of the land avert their eyes from that man when he gives from his offspring to Molech, not to put him to death —* ⁵ *then I shall concentrate My attention upon that man and upon his family; I will cut off from among their people, him and all who stray after him to stray after the Molech.* ⁶ *And the person who shall turn to the sorcery of the Ovos and the Yid'onim to stray after them — I shall concentrate My attention upon that person and cut him off from among his people.*

ז-ח וְהִתְקַדִּשְׁתֶּם וִהְיִיתֶם קְדֹשִׁים כִּי אֲנִי יהוה אֱלֹהֵיכֶם: * וּשְׁמַרְתֶּם אֶת־
חֻקֹּתַי וַעֲשִׂיתֶם אֹתָם אֲנִי יהוה מְקַדִּשְׁכֶם: ט כִּי־אִישׁ אִישׁ אֲשֶׁר יְקַלֵּל אֶת־
י אָבִיו וְאֶת־אִמּוֹ מוֹת יוּמָת אָבִיו וְאִמּוֹ קִלֵּל דָּמָיו בּוֹ: וְאִישׁ אֲשֶׁר יִנְאַף
אֶת־אֵשֶׁת אִישׁ אֲשֶׁר יִנְאַף אֶת־אֵשֶׁת רֵעֵהוּ מוֹת־יוּמַת הַנֹּאֵף וְהַנֹּאָפֶת:
יא וְאִישׁ אֲשֶׁר יִשְׁכַּב אֶת־אֵשֶׁת אָבִיו עֶרְוַת אָבִיו גִּלָּה מוֹת־יוּמְתוּ שְׁנֵיהֶם
יב דְּמֵיהֶם בָּם: וְאִישׁ אֲשֶׁר יִשְׁכַּב אֶת־כַּלָּתוֹ מוֹת יוּמְתוּ שְׁנֵיהֶם תֶּבֶל עָשׂוּ
יג דְּמֵיהֶם בָּם: וְאִישׁ אֲשֶׁר יִשְׁכַּב אֶת־זָכָר מִשְׁכְּבֵי אִשָּׁה תּוֹעֵבָה עָשׂוּ
יד שְׁנֵיהֶם מוֹת יוּמָתוּ דְּמֵיהֶם בָּם: וְאִישׁ אֲשֶׁר יִקַּח אֶת־אִשָּׁה וְאֶת־אִמָּהּ
טו זִמָּה הִוא בָּאֵשׁ יִשְׂרְפוּ אֹתוֹ וְאֶתְהֶן וְלֹא־תִהְיֶה זִמָּה בְּתוֹכְכֶם: וְאִישׁ
טז אֲשֶׁר יִתֵּן שְׁכָבְתּוֹ בִּבְהֵמָה מוֹת יוּמָת וְאֶת־הַבְּהֵמָה תַּהֲרֹגוּ: וְאִשָּׁה אֲשֶׁר
תִּקְרַב אֶל־כָּל־בְּהֵמָה לְרִבְעָה אֹתָהּ וְהָרַגְתָּ אֶת־הָאִשָּׁה וְאֶת־הַבְּהֵמָה
יז מוֹת יוּמָתוּ דְּמֵיהֶם בָּם: וְאִישׁ אֲשֶׁר־יִקַּח אֶת־אֲחֹתוֹ בַּת־אָבִיו אוֹ בַת־
אִמּוֹ וְרָאָה אֶת־עֶרְוָתָהּ וְהִיא־תִרְאֶה אֶת־עֶרְוָתוֹ חֶסֶד הוּא וְנִכְרְתוּ
יח לְעֵינֵי בְּנֵי עַמָּם עֶרְוַת אֲחֹתוֹ גִּלָּה עֲוֹנוֹ יִשָּׂא: וְאִישׁ אֲשֶׁר־יִשְׁכַּב אֶת־
אִשָּׁה דָּוָה וְגִלָּה אֶת־עֶרְוָתָהּ אֶת־מְקֹרָהּ הֶעֱרָה וְהִוא גִּלְּתָה אֶת־מְקוֹר
יט דָּמֶיהָ וְנִכְרְתוּ שְׁנֵיהֶם מִקֶּרֶב עַמָּם: וְעֶרְוַת אֲחוֹת אִמְּךָ וַאֲחוֹת אָבִיךָ לֹא
כ תְגַלֵּה כִּי אֶת־שְׁאֵרוֹ הֶעֱרָה עֲוֹנָם יִשָּׂאוּ: וְאִישׁ אֲשֶׁר יִשְׁכַּב אֶת־דֹּדָתוֹ
עֶרְוַת דֹּדוֹ גִּלָּה חֶטְאָם יִשָּׂאוּ עֲרִירִים יָמֻתוּ: כא וְאִישׁ אֲשֶׁר יִקַּח אֶת־אֵשֶׁת
כב אָחִיו נִדָּה הִוא עֶרְוַת אָחִיו גִּלָּה עֲרִירִים יִהְיוּ: וּשְׁמַרְתֶּם אֶת־כָּל־חֻקֹּתַי
וְאֶת־כָּל־מִשְׁפָּטַי וַעֲשִׂיתֶם אֹתָם וְלֹא־תָקִיא אֶתְכֶם הָאָרֶץ אֲשֶׁר אֲנִי
כג מֵבִיא אֶתְכֶם שָׁמָּה לָשֶׁבֶת בָּהּ: וְלֹא תֵלְכוּ בְּחֻקֹּת הַגּוֹי אֲשֶׁר־אֲנִי מְשַׁלֵּחַ
כד מִפְּנֵיכֶם כִּי אֶת־כָּל־אֵלֶּה עָשׂוּ וָאָקֻץ בָּם: וָאֹמַר לָכֶם אַתֶּם תִּירְשׁוּ אֶת־
אַדְמָתָם וַאֲנִי אֶתְּנֶנָּה לָכֶם לָרֶשֶׁת אֹתָהּ אֶרֶץ זָבַת חָלָב וּדְבָשׁ אֲנִי יהוה
כה אֱלֹהֵיכֶם אֲשֶׁר־הִבְדַּלְתִּי אֶתְכֶם מִן־הָעַמִּים: וְהִבְדַּלְתֶּם בֵּין־הַבְּהֵמָה
הַטְּהֹרָה לַטְּמֵאָה וּבֵין־הָעוֹף הַטָּמֵא לַטָּהֹר וְלֹא־תְשַׁקְּצוּ אֶת־נַפְשֹׁתֵיכֶם
בַּבְּהֵמָה וּבָעוֹף וּבְכֹל אֲשֶׁר תִּרְמֹשׂ הָאֲדָמָה אֲשֶׁר־הִבְדַּלְתִּי לָכֶם לְטַמֵּא:
כו וִהְיִיתֶם לִי קְדֹשִׁים כִּי קָדוֹשׁ אֲנִי יהוה וָאַבְדִּל אֶתְכֶם מִן־הָעַמִּים לִהְיוֹת
כז לִי: וְאִישׁ אוֹ־אִשָּׁה כִּי־יִהְיֶה בָהֶם אוֹב אוֹ יִדְּעֹנִי מוֹת יוּמָתוּ בָּאֶבֶן יִרְגְּמוּ
אֹתָם דְּמֵיהֶם בָּם: פפפ   ס"ד פסוקים. וגו"ה סימן. מ"י זה"ב סימן.

*ששי
[שביעי]

שביעי

מפטיר

*Haftaras
Kedoshim
Ashkenazim:*
p. 1256
Sephardim:
p. 1248

For special
Sabbaths, see
pp. x-xi

When *Acharei-Kedoshim* are read together, *Ashkenazim* read the *Haftarah* of *Acharei* (p. 1368).

20:9. The repetition אִישׁ אִישׁ teaches that one is liable for cursing his parents even if he does so after their death (*Rashi*).

20:10-21. The following passage sets forth the punishments for the transgressions that were given in 18:6-23.

20:17. The word חֶסֶד has two meanings: *kindness* and *disgrace*. The two are related, because the disgrace of immorality is the product of overindulgence (*Radak*).

20:25-26. The chapter concludes with an exhortation to avoid forbidden foods, as a prerequisite of holiness, as set forth in 11:44.

20:27. *Ov* and *Yid'oni* were magical means of foretelling the future. The chapter ends with this sin because it symbolizes the difference between Israel and the nations: If Israel serves God properly, it will deserve to have prophets and have no need for magic (*Baal HaTurim*).

⁷ You shall sanctify yourselves and you will be holy, for I am HASHEM, your God.

⁸ You shall observe My decrees and perform them — I am HASHEM, Who sanctifies you. ⁹ For any man * who will curse his father or his mother shall be put to death; his father or his mother has he cursed, his blood is upon himself.

Penalties for forbidden relationships * ¹⁰ A man who will commit adultery with a man's wife, who will commit adultery with his fellow's wife; the adulterer and the adulteress shall be put to death.

¹¹ A man who shall lie with his father's wife will have uncovered his father's shame; the two of them shall be put to death, their blood is upon themselves.

¹² A man who shall lie with his daughter-in-law, the two of them shall be put to death; they have committed a perversion, their blood is upon themselves.

¹³ A man who lies with a man as one lies with a woman, they have both done an abomination; they shall be put to death, their blood is upon themselves.

¹⁴ A man who shall take a woman and her mother, it is a depraved plot; they shall burn him and them in fire, and there shall not be depravity among you.

¹⁵ A man who shall lie with an animal shall be put to death; and you shall kill the animal. ¹⁶ And a woman who approaches any animal for it to mate with her, you shall kill the woman and the animal; they shall be put to death, their blood is upon them.

¹⁷ A man who shall take his sister, the daughter of his father or the daughter of his mother, and he shall see her nakedness and she shall see his nakedness, it is a disgrace * and they shall be cut off in the sight of the members of their people; he will have uncovered the nakedness of his sister, he shall bear his iniquity.

¹⁸ A man who shall lie with a woman in her affliction and has uncovered her nakedness, he will have bared her source and she has bared the source of her blood; the two of them will be cut off from the midst of their people.

¹⁹ The nakedness of your mother's sister or your father's sister shall you not uncover, for that is baring one's own flesh; they shall bear their iniquity. ²⁰ And a man who shall lie with his aunt will have uncovered the nakedness of his uncle; they shall bear their sin, they shall die childless. ²¹ A man who shall take his brother's wife, it is loathsome; he will have uncovered his brother's shame, they shall be childless.

The land and immorality ²² You shall observe all My decrees and all My ordinances and perform them; then the Land to which I bring you to dwell will not disgorge you. ²³ Do not follow the traditions of the nation that I expel from before you, for they did all of these and I was disgusted with them. ²⁴ So I said to you: You shall inherit their land, and I will give it to you to inherit it, a land flowing with milk and honey — **Holiness and kashrus** I am HASHEM, your God, Who has separated you from the peoples. ²⁵ You shall distinguish between the clean animal and the unclean, * and between the clean bird and the unclean; and you shall not render your souls abominable through such animals and birds, and through anything that creeps on the ground, which I have set apart for you to render unclean.

²⁶ You shall be holy for Me, for I HASHEM am holy; and I have separated you from the peoples to be Mine. ²⁷ Any man or woman in whom there shall be the sorcery of Ov or of Yid'oni, * they shall be put to death; they shall pelt them with stones, their blood is upon themselves.

פרשת אמור

א וַיֹּאמֶר יְהֹוָה אֶל־מֹשֶׁה אֱמֹר אֶל־הַכֹּהֲנִים בְּנֵי אַהֲרֹן וְאָמַרְתָּ אֲלֵהֶם

ב לְנֶפֶשׁ לֹא־יִטַּמָּא בְּעַמָּיו: כִּי אִם־לִשְׁאֵרוֹ הַקָּרֹב אֵלָיו לְאִמּוֹ וּלְאָבִיו

ג וְלִבְנוֹ וּלְבִתּוֹ וּלְאָחִיו: וְלַאֲחֹתוֹ הַבְּתוּלָה הַקְּרוֹבָה אֵלָיו אֲשֶׁר לֹא־

ד-ה הָיְתָה לְאִישׁ לָהּ יִטַּמָּא: לֹא יִטַּמָּא בַּעַל בְּעַמָּיו לְהֵחַלּוֹ: לֹא־°יִקְרְחָה

[°יִקְרְחוּ ק] קָרְחָה בְּרֹאשָׁם וּפְאַת זְקָנָם לֹא יְגַלֵּחוּ וּבִבְשָׂרָם לֹא יִשְׂרְטוּ

ו שָׂרָטֶת: קְדֹשִׁים יִהְיוּ לֵאלֹהֵיהֶם וְלֹא יְחַלְּלוּ שֵׁם אֱלֹהֵיהֶם כִּי אֶת־אִשֵּׁי

ז יְהֹוָה לֶחֶם אֱלֹהֵיהֶם הֵם מַקְרִיבִם וְהָיוּ קֹדֶשׁ: אִשָּׁה זֹנָה וַחֲלָלָה לֹא יִקָּחוּ

ח וְאִשָּׁה גְּרוּשָׁה מֵאִישָׁהּ לֹא יִקָּחוּ כִּי־קָדֹשׁ הוּא לֵאלֹהָיו: וְקִדַּשְׁתּוֹ כִּי־אֶת־

לֶחֶם אֱלֹהֶיךָ הוּא מַקְרִיב קָדֹשׁ יִהְיֶה־לָּךְ כִּי קָדוֹשׁ אֲנִי יְהֹוָה מְקַדִּשְׁכֶם:

ט וּבַת אִישׁ כֹּהֵן כִּי תֵחֵל לִזְנוֹת אֶת־אָבִיהָ הִיא מְחַלֶּלֶת בָּאֵשׁ

י תִּשָּׂרֵף: וְהַכֹּהֵן הַגָּדוֹל מֵאֶחָיו אֲשֶׁר־יוּצַק עַל־רֹאשׁוֹ ׀

שֶׁמֶן הַמִּשְׁחָה וּמִלֵּא אֶת־יָדוֹ לִלְבֹּשׁ אֶת־הַבְּגָדִים אֶת־רֹאשׁוֹ לֹא יִפְרָע

יא וּבְגָדָיו לֹא יִפְרֹם: וְעַל כָּל־נַפְשֹׁת מֵת לֹא יָבֹא לְאָבִיו וּלְאִמּוֹ לֹא יִטַּמָּא:

יב וּמִן־הַמִּקְדָּשׁ לֹא יֵצֵא וְלֹא יְחַלֵּל אֵת מִקְדַּשׁ אֱלֹהָיו כִּי נֵזֶר שֶׁמֶן מִשְׁחַת

יג-יד אֱלֹהָיו עָלָיו אֲנִי יְהֹוָה: וְהוּא אִשָּׁה בִבְתוּלֶיהָ יִקָּח: אַלְמָנָה וּגְרוּשָׁה

טו וַחֲלָלָה זֹנָה אֶת־אֵלֶּה לֹא יִקָּח כִּי אִם־בְּתוּלָה מֵעַמָּיו יִקַּח אִשָּׁה: וְלֹא־

יְחַלֵּל זַרְעוֹ בְּעַמָּיו כִּי אֲנִי יְהֹוָה מְקַדְּשׁוֹ:

טז וַיְדַבֵּר יְהֹוָה

יז אֶל־מֹשֶׁה לֵּאמֹר: דַּבֵּר אֶל־אַהֲרֹן לֵאמֹר אִישׁ מִזַּרְעֲךָ לְדֹרֹתָם אֲשֶׁר יִהְיֶה

יח בוֹ מוּם לֹא יִקְרַב לְהַקְרִיב לֶחֶם אֱלֹהָיו: כִּי כָל־אִישׁ אֲשֶׁר־בּוֹ

יט מוּם לֹא יִקְרָב אִישׁ עִוֵּר אוֹ פִסֵּחַ אוֹ חָרֻם אוֹ שָׂרוּעַ: אוֹ אִישׁ אֲשֶׁר־

כ יִהְיֶה בוֹ שֶׁבֶר רָגֶל אוֹ שֶׁבֶר יָד: אוֹ־גִבֵּן אוֹ־דַק אוֹ תְּבַלֻּל בְּעֵינוֹ אוֹ

כא גָרָב אוֹ יַלֶּפֶת אוֹ מְרוֹחַ אָשֶׁךְ: כָּל־אִישׁ אֲשֶׁר־בּוֹ מוּם מִזֶּרַע אַהֲרֹן הַכֹּהֵן

לֹא יִגַּשׁ לְהַקְרִיב אֶת־אִשֵּׁי יְהֹוָה מוּם בּוֹ אֵת לֶחֶם אֱלֹהָיו לֹא יִגַּשׁ

כב-כג לְהַקְרִיב: לֶחֶם אֱלֹהָיו מִקָּדְשֵׁי הַקֳּדָשִׁים וּמִן־הַקֳּדָשִׁים יֹאכֵל: אַךְ אֶל־

הַפָּרֹכֶת לֹא יָבֹא וְאֶל־הַמִּזְבֵּחַ לֹא יִגַּשׁ כִּי־מוּם בּוֹ וְלֹא יְחַלֵּל אֶת־

כד מִקְדָּשַׁי כִּי אֲנִי יְהֹוָה מְקַדְּשָׁם: וַיְדַבֵּר מֹשֶׁה אֶל־אַהֲרֹן וְאֶל־בָּנָיו וְאֶל־כָּל־

בְּנֵי יִשְׂרָאֵל:

⊸§ Parashas Emor

21:1-9. The previous *Sidrah* dealt with the commandment that the entire nation should strive to become holy. Now the Torah turns to the Kohanim, who have a particular responsibility to maintain higher standards of behavior and purity (*Ibn Ezra*).

21:2. *For the relative who is closest to him*, i.e., his wife (*Rashi; Sifra*).

21:3. As long as a sister is unmarried, she is still part of the Kohen's immediate family and he is required to participate in her funeral.

21:7. The *harlot* who is prohibited to a Kohen is a woman who has lived with any man who is not permitted to her because of a negative commandment.

The term *desecrated* refers to any woman who is forbidden to marry a Kohen or a Kohen Gadol, but lives with him, i.e., a divorcee, or a widow with a Kohen Gadol (v. 14) (*Rashi*).

PARASHAS EMOR

21

Laws of a Kohen

[1] HASHEM said to Moses: Say to the Kohanim, * the sons of Aaron, and tell them: Each of you shall not contaminate himself to a [dead] person among his people; [2] except for the relative who is closest to him, * to his mother and to his father, to his son, to his daughter, and to his brother; [3] and to his virgin sister who is close to him, who has not been wed to a man; to her shall he contaminate himself. * [4] A husband among his people shall not contaminate himself to one who desecrates him.

[5] They shall not make a bald spot on their heads, and they shall not shave an edge of their beard; and in their flesh they shall not cut a gash. [6] They shall be holy to their God and they shall not desecrate the Name of their God; for the fire-offerings of HASHEM, the food of their God, they offer, so they must remain holy.

[7] They shall not marry a woman who is a harlot or has been desecrated, * and they shall not marry a woman who has been divorced by her husband; for each one is holy to his God.

[8] You shall sanctify him, for he offers the food of your God; he shall remain holy to you, for holy am I, HASHEM, Who sanctifies you. [9] If the daughter of a Kohen will be desecrated through adultery, she desecrates her father — she shall be consumed by the fire.

Laws of the Kohen Gadol

[10] The Kohen who is exalted above his brethren — upon whose head the anointment oil has been poured or who has been inaugurated to don the vestments — shall not leave his head unshorn and shall not rend his garments. [11] He shall not come near any dead person; he shall not contaminate himself to his father or his mother. [12] He shall not leave the Sanctuary and he shall not desecrate the Sanctuary of his God; for a crown — the oil of his God's anointment — is upon him; I am HASHEM. [13] He shall marry a woman in her virginity. [14] A widow, a divorcee, a desecrated woman, a harlot — he shall not marry these; only a virgin of his people shall he take as a wife. [15] Thus shall he not desecrate his offspring among his people; for I am HASHEM Who sanctifies him.

Disqualifying blemishes

[16] HASHEM spoke to Moses, saying: [17] Speak to Aaron, saying: Any man of your offspring throughout their generations in whom there will be a blemish shall not come near to offer the food of his God. [18] For any man in whom there is a blemish shall not approach: a man who is blind or lame or whose nose has no bridge, or who has one limb longer than the other; [19] or in whom there will be a broken leg or a broken arm; [20] or who has abnormally long eyebrows, or a membrane on his eye, or a blemish in his eye, or a dry skin eruption, or a moist skin eruption, or has crushed testicles. [21] Any man from among the offspring of Aaron the Kohen who has a blemish shall not approach to offer the fire-offerings of HASHEM; he has a blemish — the food of his God he shall not approach to offer.

[22] The food of his God from the most holy and from the holy may he eat. [23] But he shall not come to the Curtain, and he shall not approach the Altar, for he has a blemish; and he shall not desecrate My sacred offerings, for I am HASHEM, Who sanctifies them. [24] Moses spoke to Aaron and to his sons, and to all the Children of Israel.

א-ב וַיְדַבֵּ֥ר יְהוָ֖ה אֶל־מֹשֶׁ֥ה לֵּאמֹֽר: דַּבֵּ֨ר אֶֽל־אַהֲרֹ֜ן וְאֶל־בָּנָ֗יו וְיִנָּֽזְרוּ֙ מִקָּדְשֵׁ֣י
בְנֵֽי־יִשְׂרָאֵ֔ל וְלֹ֥א יְחַלְּל֖וּ אֶת־שֵׁ֣ם קָדְשִׁ֑י אֲשֶׁ֨ר הֵ֧ם מַקְדִּשִׁ֛ים לִ֖י אֲנִ֥י יְהוָֽה:

ג אֱמֹ֣ר אֲלֵהֶ֗ם לְדֹרֹ֣תֵיכֶ֔ם כָּל־אִ֣ישׁ ׀ אֲשֶׁר־יִקְרַ֣ב מִכָּל־זַרְעֲכֶ֣ם אֶל־
הַקֳּדָשִׁ֗ים אֲשֶׁ֨ר יַקְדִּ֤ישׁוּ בְנֵֽי־יִשְׂרָאֵל֙ לַֽיהוָ֔ה וְטֻמְאָת֖וֹ עָלָ֑יו וְנִכְרְתָ֞ה

ד הַנֶּ֤פֶשׁ הַהִוא֙ מִלְּפָנַ֣י אֲנִ֣י יְהוָֽה: אִ֣ישׁ אִ֞ישׁ מִזֶּ֤רַע אַהֲרֹן֙ וְה֣וּא צָר֔וּעַ א֣וֹ זָ֔ב
בַּקֳּדָשִׁים֙ לֹ֣א יֹאכַ֔ל עַ֖ד אֲשֶׁ֣ר יִטְהָ֑ר וְהַנֹּגֵ֙עַ֙ בְּכָל־טְמֵא־נֶ֔פֶשׁ א֣וֹ אִ֔ישׁ

ה אֲשֶׁר־תֵּצֵ֥א מִמֶּ֖נּוּ שִׁכְבַת־זָֽרַע: אוֹ־אִישׁ֙ אֲשֶׁ֣ר יִגַּ֔ע בְּכָל־שֶׁ֖רֶץ אֲשֶׁ֣ר

ו יִטְמָא־ל֑וֹ א֤וֹ בְאָדָם֙ אֲשֶׁ֣ר יִטְמָא־ל֔וֹ לְכֹ֖ל טֻמְאָתֽוֹ: נֶ֚פֶשׁ אֲשֶׁ֣ר תִּגַּע־בּ֔וֹ
וְטָמְאָ֖ה עַד־הָעָ֑רֶב וְלֹ֤א יֹאכַל֙ מִן־הַקֳּדָשִׁ֔ים כִּ֥י אִם־רָחַ֥ץ בְּשָׂר֖וֹ בַּמָּֽיִם:

ז-ח וּבָ֣א הַשֶּׁ֔מֶשׁ וְטָהֵ֑ר וְאַחַר֙ יֹאכַ֣ל מִן־הַקֳּדָשִׁ֔ים כִּ֥י לַחְמ֖וֹ הֽוּא: נְבֵלָ֤ה
וּטְרֵפָה֙ לֹ֣א יֹאכַ֔ל לְטָמְאָה־בָ֑הּ אֲנִ֖י יְהוָֽה: וְשָׁמְר֣וּ אֶת־מִשְׁמַרְתִּ֗י וְלֹֽא־

ט-י יִשְׂא֤וּ עָלָיו֙ חֵ֔טְא וּמֵ֥תוּ ב֖וֹ כִּ֣י יְחַלְּלֻ֑הוּ אֲנִ֥י יְהוָ֖ה מְקַדְּשָֽׁם: וְכָל־זָ֖ר לֹא־
יֹ֣אכַל קֹ֑דֶשׁ תּוֹשַׁ֥ב כֹּהֵ֛ן וְשָׂכִ֖יר לֹא־יֹ֥אכַל קֹֽדֶשׁ: וְכֹהֵ֗ן כִּֽי־יִקְנֶ֥ה נֶ֙פֶשׁ֙ קִנְיַ֣ן

יא כַּסְפּ֔וֹ ה֖וּא יֹ֣אכַל בּ֑וֹ וִילִ֣יד בֵּית֔וֹ הֵ֖ם יֹֽאכְל֥וּ בְלַחְמֽוֹ: וּבַת־כֹּהֵ֔ן כִּ֥י תִֽהְיֶ֖ה

יב-יג לְאִ֣ישׁ זָ֑ר הִ֕וא בִּתְרוּמַ֥ת הַקֳּדָשִׁ֖ים לֹ֥א תֹאכֵֽל: וּבַת־כֹּהֵן֙ כִּ֣י תִֽהְיֶ֣ה אַלְמָנָ֣ה
וּגְרוּשָׁ֗ה וְזֶ֘רַע֘ אֵ֣ין לָהּ֒ וְשָׁבָ֞ה אֶל־בֵּ֤ית אָבִ֙יהָ֙ כִּנְעוּרֶ֔יהָ מִלֶּ֥חֶם אָבִ֖יהָ

יד תֹּאכֵ֑ל וְכָל־זָ֖ר לֹא־יֹ֥אכַל בּֽוֹ: וְאִ֕ישׁ כִּֽי־יֹאכַ֥ל קֹ֖דֶשׁ בִּשְׁגָגָ֑ה וְיָסַ֤ף

טו חֲמִֽשִׁיתוֹ֙ עָלָ֔יו וְנָתַ֥ן לַכֹּהֵ֖ן אֶת־הַקֹּֽדֶשׁ: וְלֹ֣א יְחַלְּל֔וּ אֶת־קָדְשֵׁ֖י בְּנֵ֣י

טז יִשְׂרָאֵ֑ל אֵ֥ת אֲשֶׁר־יָרִ֖ימוּ לַֽיהוָֽה: וְהִשִּׂ֤יאוּ אוֹתָם֙ עֲוֹ֣ן אַשְׁמָ֔ה בְּאָכְלָ֖ם אֶת־
קָדְשֵׁיהֶ֑ם כִּ֛י אֲנִ֥י יְהוָ֖ה מְקַדְּשָֽׁם:

שלישי יז-יח וַיְדַבֵּ֥ר יְהוָ֖ה אֶל־מֹשֶׁ֥ה לֵּאמֹֽר: דַּבֵּ֨ר אֶֽל־אַהֲרֹ֜ן וְאֶל־בָּנָ֗יו וְאֶל֙ כָּל־בְּנֵ֣י
יִשְׂרָאֵ֔ל וְאָמַרְתָּ֖ אֲלֵהֶ֑ם אִ֣ישׁ אִישׁ֩ מִבֵּ֨ית יִשְׂרָאֵ֜ל וּמִן־הַגֵּ֣ר בְּיִשְׂרָאֵ֗ל אֲשֶׁ֨ר
יַקְרִ֤יב קָרְבָּנוֹ֙ לְכָל־נִדְרֵיהֶ֔ם וּלְכָל־נִדְבוֹתָ֔ם אֲשֶׁר־יַקְרִ֥יבוּ לַֽיהוָ֖ה לְעֹלָֽה:

יט-כ לִֽרְצֹנְכֶ֑ם תָּמִ֣ים זָכָ֔ר בַּבָּקָ֕ר בַּכְּשָׂבִ֖ים וּבָֽעִזִּֽים: כֹּ֛ל אֲשֶׁר־בּ֥וֹ מ֖וּם לֹ֣א תַקְרִ֑יבוּ

כא כִּי־לֹ֥א לְרָצ֖וֹן יִהְיֶ֥ה לָכֶֽם: וְאִ֗ישׁ כִּֽי־יַקְרִ֥יב זֶֽבַח־שְׁלָמִים֮ לַֽיהוָה֒ לְפַלֵּא־נֶ֙דֶר֙
א֣וֹ לִנְדָבָ֔ה בַּבָּקָ֖ר א֣וֹ בַצֹּ֑אן תָּמִ֤ים יִהְיֶה֙ לְרָצ֔וֹן כָּל־מ֖וּם לֹ֥א יִהְיֶה־בּֽוֹ: עַוֶּרֶת֩

כב א֨וֹ שָׁב֜וּר אוֹ־חָר֤וּץ אֽוֹ־יַבֶּ֙לֶת֙ א֤וֹ גָרָב֙ א֣וֹ יַלֶּ֔פֶת לֹא־תַקְרִ֥יבוּ אֵ֖לֶּה לַֽיהוָ֑ה

כג וְאִשֶּׁ֗ה לֹֽא־תִתְּנ֥וּ מֵהֶ֛ם עַל־הַמִּזְבֵּ֖חַ לַֽיהוָֽה: וְשׁ֥וֹר וָשֶׂ֖ה שָׂר֣וּעַ וְקָל֑וּט נְדָבָה֙

כד תַּעֲשֶׂ֣ה אֹת֔וֹ וּלְנֵ֖דֶר לֹ֥א יֵֽרָצֶֽה: וּמָע֤וּךְ וְכָתוּת֙ וְנָת֣וּק וְכָר֔וּת לֹ֥א תַקְרִ֖יבוּ

כה לַֽיהוָ֑ה וּבְאַרְצְכֶ֖ם לֹ֥א תַעֲשֽׂוּ: וּמִיַּ֣ד בֶּן־נֵכָ֗ר לֹ֥א תַקְרִ֛יבוּ
אֶת־לֶ֥חֶם אֱלֹֽהֵיכֶ֖ם מִכָּל־אֵ֑לֶּה כִּ֣י מָשְׁחָתָ֤ם בָּהֶם֙ מ֣וּם בָּ֔ם לֹ֥א יֵרָצ֖וּ

22:2. People in a state of *tumah, ritual contamination,* are enjoined to *withdraw* from sacrificial meat and *terumah.*

22:20. Just as Kohanim with bodily blemishes are not permitted to perform the Divine service, so blemished animals are invalid as offerings.

22

Safeguarding the sanctity of offerings and terumah

¹ HASHEM spoke to Moses, saying: ² Speak to Aaron and his sons, that they shall withdraw * from the holies of the Children of Israel — that which they sanctify to Me — so as not to desecrate My holy Name, I am HASHEM. ³ Say to them: Throughout your generations, any man from among any of your off-spring who shall come near the holies that the Children of Israel may sanctify to HASHEM with his contamination upon him — that person shall be cut off from before Me, I am HASHEM. ⁴ Any man from the offspring of Aaron who is a metzora or a zav shall not eat from the holies until he becomes purified; and one who touches anyone contaminated by a corpse, or a man from whom there is a seminal emission; ⁵ or a man who touches any swarming thing through which he can become contaminated, or a person through whom he can become contaminated, whatever his contamination. ⁶ The person who touches it shall be contaminated until evening; he shall not eat from the holies unless he has immersed his body in the water. ⁷ After the sun has set he shall become purified; thereafter he may eat from the holies, for it is his food. ⁸ He shall not eat from a carcass or from a torn animal, to be contaminated through it — I am HASHEM.

⁹ They shall protect My charge and not bear a sin thereby and die because of it, for they will have desecrated it — I am HASHEM, Who sanctifies them.

Terumah

¹⁰ No layman shall eat of the holy; one who resides with a Kohen or his laborer shall not eat of the holy. ¹¹ If a Kohen shall acquire a person, an acquisition of his money, he may eat of it; and someone born in his home — they may eat of his food. ¹² If a Kohen's daughter shall be married to a layman, she may not eat of the separated holies. ¹³ And a Kohen's daughter who will become a widow or a divorcee, and not have offspring, she may return to her father's home, as in her youth, she may eat from her father's food; but no layman may eat of it. ¹⁴ If a man will eat of the holy inadvertently, he shall add its fifth to it and shall repay the holy to the Kohen. ¹⁵ They shall not desecrate the holies of the Children of Israel, which they set aside to HASHEM; ¹⁶ and they will cause themselves to bear the sin of guilt when they eat their holies — for I am HASHEM Who sanctifies them.

Blemished animals

¹⁷ HASHEM spoke to Moses, saying: ¹⁸ Speak to Aaron and to his sons and to all the Children of Israel and say to them: Any man of the House of Israel and of the proselytes among Israel who will bring his offering for any of their vows or their free-will offerings that they will bring to HASHEM for a burnt-offering; ¹⁹ to be favorable for you: [it must be] unblemished, male, from the cattle, the sheep, or the goats. ²⁰ Any in which there is a blemish you shall not offer, for it will not be favorable for you. * ²¹ And a man who will bring a feast peace-offering to HASHEM because of an articulated vow or as a free-will offering from the cattle or the flock, it shall be unblemished to find favor, there shall not be any blemish in it. ²² One that is blind or broken or with a split eyelid or a wart or a dry skin eruption or a moist skin eruption —you shall not offer these to HASHEM, and you shall not place any of them as a fire-offering on the Altar for HASHEM. ²³ An ox or a sheep that has one limb longer than the other or unsplit hooves — you may make it a donation, but it is not acceptable for a vow-offering. ²⁴ One whose testicles are squeezed, crushed, torn, or cut, you shall not offer to HASHEM, nor shall you do these in your Land. ²⁵ From the hand of a stranger you may not offer the food of your God from any of these, for their corruption is in them, a blemish is in them, they will not find favor for you.

2ND DAY
PESACH
AND FIRST
TWO DAYS
SUCCOS
22:26-23:44

PESACH
Maftir: p. 400
Haftarah:
p. 940

SUCCOS
Maftir: p. 402
Haftarah:
day 1: p. 1424
day 2: p. 820

כו-כז וַיְדַבֵּ֥ר יְהֹוָ֖ה אֶל־מֹשֶׁ֥ה לֵּאמֹֽר: שׁ֣וֹר אוֹ־כֶ֤שֶׂב אוֹ־עֵז֙ כִּ֣י יִוָּלֵ֔ד לָכֶֽם:

כח וְהָיָ֛ה שִׁבְעַ֥ת יָמִ֖ים תַּ֣חַת אִמּ֑וֹ וּמִיּ֤וֹם הַשְּׁמִינִי֙ וָהָ֔לְאָה יֵרָצֶ֕ה לְקָרְבַּ֥ן אִשֶּׁ֖ה לַֽיהֹוָֽה: וְשׁ֖וֹר אוֹ־שֶׂ֑ה אֹת֣וֹ וְאֶת־בְּנ֗וֹ לֹ֥א תִשְׁחֲט֛וּ בְּי֥וֹם אֶחָֽד: וְכִֽי־תִזְבְּח֥וּ

ל זֶֽבַח־תּוֹדָ֖ה לַֽיהֹוָ֑ה לִֽרְצֹנְכֶ֖ם תִּזְבָּֽחוּ: בַּיּ֤וֹם הַהוּא֙ יֵֽאָכֵ֔ל לֹֽא־תוֹתִ֥ירוּ מִמֶּ֖נּוּ

לא-לב עַד־בֹּ֑קֶר אֲנִ֖י יְהֹוָֽה: וּשְׁמַרְתֶּם֙ מִצְוֺתַ֔י וַֽעֲשִׂיתֶ֖ם אֹתָ֑ם אֲנִ֖י יְהֹוָֽה: וְלֹ֣א

לג תְחַלְּל֗וּ אֶת־שֵׁ֣ם קָדְשִׁ֔י וְנִ֨קְדַּשְׁתִּ֔י בְּת֖וֹךְ בְּנֵ֣י יִשְׂרָאֵ֑ל אֲנִ֥י יְהֹוָ֖ה מְקַדִּשְׁכֶֽם: הַמּוֹצִ֤יא אֶתְכֶם֙ מֵאֶ֣רֶץ מִצְרַ֔יִם לִֽהְי֥וֹת לָכֶ֖ם לֵֽאלֹהִ֑ים אֲנִ֖י יְהֹוָֽה:

כג רביעי א־ב וַיְדַבֵּ֥ר יְהֹוָ֖ה אֶל־מֹשֶׁ֥ה לֵּאמֹֽר: דַּבֵּ֞ר אֶל־בְּנֵ֤י יִשְׂרָאֵל֙ וְאָֽמַרְתָּ֣ אֲלֵהֶ֔ם מֽוֹעֲדֵ֣י יְהֹוָ֗ה אֲשֶׁר־תִּקְרְא֥וּ אֹתָ֖ם מִקְרָאֵ֣י קֹ֑דֶשׁ אֵ֥לֶּה הֵ֖ם מֽוֹעֲדָֽי: שֵׁ֣שֶׁת

ג יָמִים֮ תֵּֽעָשֶׂ֣ה מְלָאכָה֒ וּבַיּ֣וֹם הַשְּׁבִיעִ֗י שַׁבַּ֤ת שַׁבָּתוֹן֙ מִקְרָא־קֹ֔דֶשׁ כָּל־מְלָאכָ֖ה לֹ֣א תַֽעֲשׂ֑וּ שַׁבָּ֥ת הִוא֙ לַֽיהֹוָ֔ה בְּכֹ֖ל מֽוֹשְׁבֹֽתֵיכֶֽם:

ד־ה אֵ֚לֶּה מֽוֹעֲדֵ֣י יְהֹוָ֔ה מִקְרָאֵ֖י קֹ֑דֶשׁ אֲשֶׁר־תִּקְרְא֥וּ אֹתָ֖ם בְּמֽוֹעֲדָֽם: בַּחֹ֣דֶשׁ הָֽרִאשׁ֗וֹן בְּאַרְבָּעָ֥ה עָשָׂ֛ר לַחֹ֖דֶשׁ בֵּ֣ין הָֽעַרְבָּ֑יִם פֶּ֖סַח לַֽיהֹוָֽה: וּבַֽחֲמִשָּׁ֨ה

ו עָשָׂ֥ר יוֹם֙ לַחֹ֣דֶשׁ הַזֶּ֔ה חַ֥ג הַמַּצּ֖וֹת לַֽיהֹוָ֑ה שִׁבְעַ֥ת יָמִ֖ים מַצּ֥וֹת תֹּאכֵֽלוּ:

ז בַּיּוֹם֙ הָֽרִאשׁ֔וֹן מִקְרָא־קֹ֖דֶשׁ יִֽהְיֶ֣ה לָכֶ֑ם כָּל־מְלֶ֥אכֶת עֲבֹדָ֖ה לֹ֥א תַֽעֲשֽׂוּ:

ח וְהִקְרַבְתֶּ֥ם אִשֶּׁ֛ה לַֽיהֹוָ֖ה שִׁבְעַ֣ת יָמִ֑ים בַּיּ֤וֹם הַשְּׁבִיעִי֙ מִקְרָא־קֹ֔דֶשׁ כָּל־מְלֶ֥אכֶת עֲבֹדָ֖ה לֹ֥א תַֽעֲשֽׂוּ:

ט־י וַיְדַבֵּ֥ר יְהֹוָ֖ה אֶל־מֹשֶׁ֥ה לֵּאמֹֽר: דַּבֵּ֞ר אֶל־בְּנֵ֤י יִשְׂרָאֵל֙ וְאָֽמַרְתָּ֣ אֲלֵהֶ֔ם כִּֽי־תָבֹ֣אוּ אֶל־הָאָ֗רֶץ אֲשֶׁ֤ר אֲנִי֙ נֹתֵ֣ן לָכֶ֔ם וּקְצַרְתֶּ֖ם אֶת־קְצִירָ֑הּ וַֽהֲבֵאתֶ֥ם

יא אֶת־עֹ֛מֶר רֵאשִׁ֥ית קְצִֽירְכֶ֖ם אֶל־הַכֹּהֵֽן: וְהֵנִ֧יף אֶת־הָעֹ֛מֶר לִפְנֵ֥י יְהֹוָ֖ה לִֽרְצֹֽנְכֶ֑ם מִֽמׇּחֳרַת֙ הַשַּׁבָּ֔ת יְנִיפֶ֖נּוּ הַכֹּהֵֽן: וַֽעֲשִׂיתֶ֗ם בְּי֤וֹם הֲנִֽיפְכֶם֙ אֶת־

יב הָעֹ֔מֶר כֶּ֧בֶשׂ תָּמִ֛ים בֶּן־שְׁנָת֖וֹ לְעֹלָ֣ה לַֽיהֹוָֽה: וּמִנְחָתוֹ֩ שְׁנֵ֨י עֶשְׂרֹנִ֜ים סֹ֣לֶת

יג בְּלוּלָ֥ה בַשֶּׁ֛מֶן אִשֶּׁ֥ה לַֽיהֹוָ֖ה רֵ֣יחַ נִיחֹ֑חַ וְנִסְכֹּ֥ה יַּ֖יִן רְבִיעִ֥ת הַהִֽין: וְלֶ֩חֶם֩

יד וְקָלִ֨י וְכַרְמֶ֜ל לֹ֣א תֹֽאכְל֗וּ עַד־עֶ֙צֶם֙ הַיּ֣וֹם הַזֶּ֔ה עַ֚ד הֲבִ֣יאֲכֶ֔ם אֶת־קָרְבַּ֖ן אֱלֹֽהֵיכֶ֑ם חֻקַּ֤ת עוֹלָם֙ לְדֹרֹ֣תֵיכֶ֔ם בְּכֹ֖ל מֹֽשְׁבֹֽתֵיכֶֽם: וּסְפַרְתֶּ֤ם

טו לָכֶם֙ מִמׇּחֳרַ֣ת הַשַּׁבָּ֔ת מִיּוֹם֙ הֲבִ֣יאֲכֶ֔ם אֶת־עֹ֖מֶר הַתְּנוּפָ֑ה שֶׁ֥בַע שַׁבָּת֖וֹת

טז תְּמִימֹ֥ת תִּֽהְיֶֽינָה: עַ֣ד מִֽמׇּחֳרַ֤ת הַשַּׁבָּת֙ הַשְּׁבִיעִ֔ת תִּסְפְּר֖וּ חֲמִשִּׁ֣ים י֑וֹם

יז וְהִקְרַבְתֶּ֛ם מִנְחָ֥ה חֲדָשָׁ֖ה לַֽיהֹוָֽה: מִמּֽוֹשְׁבֹ֨תֵיכֶ֜ם תָּבִ֣יאּוּ ׀ לֶ֣חֶם תְּנוּפָ֗ה שְׁתַּ֙יִם֙ שְׁנֵ֣י עֶשְׂרֹנִ֔ים סֹ֣לֶת תִּֽהְיֶ֔ינָה חָמֵ֖ץ תֵּֽאָפֶ֑ינָה בִּכּוּרִ֖ים לַֽיהֹוָֽה:

יח וְהִקְרַבְתֶּ֣ם עַל־הַלֶּ֗חֶם שִׁבְעַ֤ת כְּבָשִׂים֙ תְּמִימִם֙ בְּנֵ֣י שָׁנָ֔ה וּפַ֧ר בֶּן־בָּקָ֛ר אֶחָ֖ד וְאֵילִ֣ם שְׁנָ֑יִם יִֽהְי֤וּ עֹלָה֙ לַֽיהֹוָ֔ה וּמִנְחָתָם֙ וְנִסְכֵּיהֶ֔ם אִשֵּׁ֥ה רֵֽיחַ־נִיחֹ֖חַ

*א׳ דגושה

22:32. A Jew's primary privilege and responsibility is to sanctify God's Name through his behavior, so that people say of him, "Fortunate are the parents and teachers who raised such a person." Conversely, there is no greater degradation for a Jew than to act in a way that will make people say the opposite (*Yoma* 86a).

23:2. The festivals, including the Sabbath, are called מֽוֹעֲדִים, *appointed times*, because they are special days when Jews "meet" with God, as it were. Just as *moed* in space refers to the locality which people have as their appointed place of assembly [e.g. the *Ohel Moed*, the Tent of Meeting], so *moed* in time is a point in time which

[26] HASHEM spoke to Moses, saying: [27] When an ox or a sheep or a goat is born, it shall remain under its mother for seven days; and from the eighth day on, it is acceptable for a fire-offering to HASHEM. [28] But an ox or a sheep or goat, you may

Desecration and sanctification of God's Name

not slaughter it and its offspring on the same day. [29] When you slaughter a feast thanksgiving-offering to HASHEM, you shall slaughter it to gain favor for yourselves. [30] It must be eaten on that same day, you shall not leave any of it until morning; I am HASHEM. [31] You shall observe My commandments and perform them; I am HASHEM. [32] You shall not desecrate My holy Name, rather I should be sanctified among the Children of Israel;* I am HASHEM Who sanctifies you, [33] Who took you out of the land of Egypt to be a God unto you; I am HASHEM.

23

Festivals

[1] HASHEM spoke to Moses, saying: [2] Speak to the Children of Israel and say to them: HASHEM's appointed festivals* that you are to designate as holy convocations — these are My appointed festivals. [3] For six days labor may be done, and the seventh day is a day of complete rest, a holy convocation, you shall not do any work; it is a Sabbath for HASHEM in all your dwelling places.

Pesach

[4] These are the appointed festivals of HASHEM, the holy convocations, which you shall designate in their appropriate time. [5] In the first month* on the fourteenth of the month in the afternoon is the time of the pesach-offering to HASHEM. [6] And on the fifteenth day of this month is the Festival of Matzos to HASHEM; you shall eat matzos for a seven-day period. [7] On the first day there shall be a holy convocation for you; you shall do no laborious work. [8] You shall bring a fire-offering to HASHEM for a seven-day period; on the seventh day shall be a holy convocation; you shall do no laborious work.

The Omer
(See Appendix B, charts 6,7,9)

[9] HASHEM spoke to Moses, saying: [10] Speak to the Children of Israel and say to them: When you shall enter the Land that I give you and you reap its harvest, you shall bring an Omer from your first harvest to the Kohen. [11] He shall wave the Omer before HASHEM to gain favor for you; on the morrow of the rest day the Kohen shall wave it. [12] On the day you wave the Omer, you shall perform the service of an unblemished lamb in its first year as a burnt-offering to HASHEM. [13] Its meal-offering shall be two tenth-ephah of fine flour mixed with oil, a fire-offering to HASHEM, a satisfying aroma; and its libation shall be wine, a quarter-hin. [14] You shall not eat bread or roasted kernels or plump kernels until this very day, until you bring the offering of your God; it is an eternal decree for your generations in all your dwelling places.

The Omer count and Shavuos
(See Appendix B, charts 6,7,10)

[15] You shall count for yourselves — from the morrow of the rest day, from the day when you bring the Omer of the waving — seven weeks, they shall be complete. [16] Until the morrow of the seventh week you shall count, fifty days*; and you shall offer a new meal-offering to HASHEM. [17] From your dwelling places you shall bring bread that shall be waved, two loaves made of two tenth-ephah, they shall be fine flour, they shall be baked leavened; first-offerings to HASHEM. [18] With the bread you shall offer seven unblemished lambs in their first year, one young bull, and two rams; they shall be a burnt-offering to HASHEM, with their meal-offering and their libations — a fire-offering, a satisfying aroma

---

summons us communally to an appointed activity — in this case an inner activity (R' *Hirsch*).

23:5. Although the new year begins in Tishrei with Rosh Hashanah, the months are counted from Nissan (*Exodus* 12:2), as a constant reminder of the Exodus.

23:16. Shavuos is not identified as a specific day in the calendar, but as the fiftieth day after the Omer-offering, recalling the days after the Exodus, when the Jews excitedly counted the days, each day elevating themselves, so that they would be worthy of receiving the Torah.

יט לַיהוָה: וַעֲשִׂיתֶם שְׂעִיר־עִזִּים אֶחָד לְחַטָּאת וּשְׁנֵי כְבָשִׂים בְּנֵי שָׁנָה לְזֶבַח
כ שְׁלָמִים: וְהֵנִיף הַכֹּהֵן ׀ אֹתָם עַל לֶחֶם הַבִּכּוּרִים תְּנוּפָה לִפְנֵי יהוָה עַל־שְׁנֵי
כא כְבָשִׂים קֹדֶשׁ יִהְיוּ לַיהוָה לַכֹּהֵן: וּקְרָאתֶם בְּעֶצֶם ׀ הַיּוֹם הַזֶּה מִקְרָא־קֹדֶשׁ
יִהְיֶה לָכֶם כָּל־מְלֶאכֶת עֲבֹדָה לֹא תַעֲשׂוּ חֻקַּת עוֹלָם בְּכָל־מוֹשְׁבֹתֵיכֶם
כב לְדֹרֹתֵיכֶם: וּבְקֻצְרְכֶם אֶת־קְצִיר אַרְצְכֶם לֹא־תְכַלֶּה פְּאַת שָׂדְךָ בְּקֻצְרֶךָ
וְלֶקֶט קְצִירְךָ לֹא תְלַקֵּט לֶעָנִי וְלַגֵּר תַּעֲזֹב אֹתָם אֲנִי יהוָה אֱלֹהֵיכֶם:

חמישי
כג-כד וַיְדַבֵּר יהוָה אֶל־מֹשֶׁה לֵּאמֹר: דַּבֵּר אֶל־בְּנֵי יִשְׂרָאֵל לֵאמֹר בַּחֹדֶשׁ הַשְּׁבִיעִי
כה בְּאֶחָד לַחֹדֶשׁ יִהְיֶה לָכֶם שַׁבָּתוֹן זִכְרוֹן תְּרוּעָה מִקְרָא־קֹדֶשׁ: כָּל־מְלֶאכֶת
כו עֲבֹדָה לֹא תַעֲשׂוּ וְהִקְרַבְתֶּם אִשֶּׁה לַיהוָה: וַיְדַבֵּר
כז יהוָה אֶל־מֹשֶׁה לֵּאמֹר: אַךְ בֶּעָשׂוֹר לַחֹדֶשׁ הַשְּׁבִיעִי הַזֶּה יוֹם הַכִּפֻּרִים
הוּא מִקְרָא־קֹדֶשׁ יִהְיֶה לָכֶם וְעִנִּיתֶם אֶת־נַפְשֹׁתֵיכֶם וְהִקְרַבְתֶּם אִשֶּׁה
כח לַיהוָה: וְכָל־מְלָאכָה לֹא תַעֲשׂוּ בְּעֶצֶם הַיּוֹם הַזֶּה כִּי יוֹם כִּפֻּרִים הוּא
כט לְכַפֵּר עֲלֵיכֶם לִפְנֵי יהוָה אֱלֹהֵיכֶם: כִּי כָל־הַנֶּפֶשׁ אֲשֶׁר לֹא־תְעֻנֶּה בְּעֶצֶם
ל הַיּוֹם הַזֶּה וְנִכְרְתָה מֵעַמֶּיהָ: וְכָל־הַנֶּפֶשׁ אֲשֶׁר תַּעֲשֶׂה כָּל־מְלָאכָה בְּעֶצֶם
לא הַיּוֹם הַזֶּה וְהַאֲבַדְתִּי אֶת־הַנֶּפֶשׁ הַהִוא מִקֶּרֶב עַמָּהּ: כָּל־מְלָאכָה לֹא
לב תַעֲשׂוּ חֻקַּת עוֹלָם לְדֹרֹתֵיכֶם בְּכֹל מֹשְׁבֹתֵיכֶם: שַׁבַּת שַׁבָּתוֹן הוּא לָכֶם
וְעִנִּיתֶם אֶת־נַפְשֹׁתֵיכֶם בְּתִשְׁעָה לַחֹדֶשׁ בָּעֶרֶב מֵעֶרֶב עַד־עֶרֶב תִּשְׁבְּתוּ
שַׁבַּתְּכֶם:

ששי
לג-לד וַיְדַבֵּר יהוָה אֶל־מֹשֶׁה לֵּאמֹר: דַּבֵּר אֶל־בְּנֵי יִשְׂרָאֵל לֵאמֹר בַּחֲמִשָּׁה
לה עָשָׂר יוֹם לַחֹדֶשׁ הַשְּׁבִיעִי הַזֶּה חַג הַסֻּכּוֹת שִׁבְעַת יָמִים לַיהוָה: בַּיּוֹם
לו הָרִאשׁוֹן מִקְרָא־קֹדֶשׁ כָּל־מְלֶאכֶת עֲבֹדָה לֹא תַעֲשׂוּ: שִׁבְעַת יָמִים
תַּקְרִיבוּ אִשֶּׁה לַיהוָה בַּיּוֹם הַשְּׁמִינִי מִקְרָא־קֹדֶשׁ יִהְיֶה לָכֶם וְהִקְרַבְתֶּם
לז אִשֶּׁה לַיהוָה עֲצֶרֶת הִוא כָּל־מְלֶאכֶת עֲבֹדָה לֹא תַעֲשׂוּ: אֵלֶּה מוֹעֲדֵי
יהוָה אֲשֶׁר־תִּקְרְאוּ אֹתָם מִקְרָאֵי קֹדֶשׁ לְהַקְרִיב אִשֶּׁה לַיהוָה עֹלָה
לח וּמִנְחָה זֶבַח וּנְסָכִים דְּבַר־יוֹם בְּיוֹמוֹ: מִלְּבַד שַׁבְּתֹת יהוָה וּמִלְּבַד
מַתְּנוֹתֵיכֶם וּמִלְּבַד כָּל־נִדְרֵיכֶם וּמִלְּבַד כָּל־נִדְבֹתֵיכֶם אֲשֶׁר תִּתְּנוּ לַיהוָה:
לט אַךְ בַּחֲמִשָּׁה עָשָׂר יוֹם לַחֹדֶשׁ הַשְּׁבִיעִי בְּאָסְפְּכֶם אֶת־תְּבוּאַת הָאָרֶץ
תָּחֹגּוּ אֶת־חַג־יהוָה שִׁבְעַת יָמִים בַּיּוֹם הָרִאשׁוֹן שַׁבָּתוֹן וּבַיּוֹם הַשְּׁמִינִי
מ שַׁבָּתוֹן: וּלְקַחְתֶּם לָכֶם בַּיּוֹם הָרִאשׁוֹן פְּרִי עֵץ הָדָר כַּפֹּת תְּמָרִים וַעֲנַף
עֵץ־עָבֹת וְעַרְבֵי־נָחַל וּשְׂמַחְתֶּם לִפְנֵי יהוָה אֱלֹהֵיכֶם שִׁבְעַת יָמִים:
מא וְחַגֹּתֶם אֹתוֹ חַג לַיהוָה שִׁבְעַת יָמִים בַּשָּׁנָה חֻקַּת עוֹלָם לְדֹרֹתֵיכֶם

23:24. The shofar is a call to repentance. As *Rambam* puts it, the shofar calls out: "Awake, you sleepers, from your sleep! Arise, you slumberers, from your slumber!" (*Hil. Teshuvah* 3:4).

23:27. The word אַךְ, *but,* always implies a limitation. Atonement is available to those who repent, but not to those who ignore this opportunity to earn forgiveness (*Rashi*). *You shall afflict* is the Torah's term for fasting.

to HASHEM. ¹⁹ You shall make one he-goat as a sin-offering, and two lambs in their first year as feast peace-offerings. ²⁰ The Kohen shall wave them upon the first-offering breads as a wave-service before HASHEM — upon the two sheep — they shall be holy, for HASHEM and for the Kohen. ²¹ You shall convoke on this very day — there shall be a holy convocation for yourselves — you shall do no laborious work; it is an eternal decree in your dwelling places for your generations.
²² When you reap the harvest of your land, you shall not remove completely the corners of your field as you reap and you shall not gather the gleanings of your harvest; for the poor and the proselyte shall you leave them; I am HASHEM, your God.

Rosh
Hashanah
²³ HASHEM spoke to Moses, saying: ²⁴ Speak to the Children of Israel, saying: In the seventh month, on the first of the month, there shall be a rest day for you, a remembrance with shofar blasts, * a holy convocation. ²⁵ You shall not do any laborious work, and you shall offer a fire-offering to HASHEM.

Yom Kippur
²⁶ HASHEM spoke to Moses, saying: ²⁷ But* on the tenth day of this seventh month it is the Day of Atonement; there shall be a holy convocation for you, and you shall afflict* yourselves; you shall offer a fire-offering to HASHEM. ²⁸ You shall not do any work on this very day, for it is the Day of Atonement to provide you atonement before HASHEM, your God. ²⁹ For any soul who will not be afflicted on this very day will be cut off from its people. ³⁰ And any soul who will do any work on this very day, I will destroy that soul from among its people. ³¹ You shall not do any work; it is an eternal decree throughout your generations in all your dwelling places. ³² It is a day of complete rest for you and you shall afflict yourselves; on the ninth of the month in the evening — from evening to evening — shall you rest on your rest day.

Succos and
Shemini
Atzeres
³³ HASHEM spoke to Moses, saying: ³⁴ Speak to the Children of Israel, saying: On the fifteenth day of this seventh month is the Festival of Succos, a seven-day period for HASHEM. ³⁵ On the first day is a holy convocation, you shall not do any laborious work. ³⁶ For a seven-day period you shall offer a fire-offering to HASHEM; on the eighth day there shall be a holy convocation for you and you shall offer a fire-offering to HASHEM, it is an assembly, you shall not do any laborious work.
³⁷ These are the appointed festivals of HASHEM that you shall proclaim as holy convocations, to offer a fire-offering to HASHEM: a burnt-offering and its meal-offering, a feast-offering and its libation, each day's requirement on its day. ³⁸ Aside from HASHEM's Sabbaths, and aside from your gifts, aside from all your vows, and aside from all your free-will offerings, which you will present to HASHEM.
³⁹ But on the fifteenth day of the seventh month, when you gather in the crop of the land, you shall celebrate HASHEM's festival for a seven-day period; the first day is a rest day and the eighth day is a rest day. ⁴⁰ You shall take for yourselves on the first day the fruit of a citron tree, the branches of date palms, twigs of a plaited tree, and brook willows;* and you shall rejoice before HASHEM, your God, for a seven-day period. ⁴¹ You shall celebrate it as a festival for HASHEM, a seven-day period in the year, an eternal decree for your generations;

23:40. The Four Species. The *esrog* (citron) resembles the heart; the *lulav* (palm branch), the spine; the *hadasim* (myrtle leaves), the eyes; and the *aravos* (willow branches), the lips. By holding all four together, we symbolize the need for a person to utilize all his faculties in the service of God.

מב בַּחֹ֨דֶשׁ הַשְּׁבִיעִ֜י תָּחֹ֣גּוּ אֹת֗וֹ בַּסֻּכֹּ֛ת תֵּשְׁב֖וּ שִׁבְעַ֣ת יָמִ֑ים כָּל־הָ֣אֶזְרָ֔ח
מג בְּיִשְׂרָאֵ֖ל יֵשְׁב֥וּ בַּסֻּכֹּֽת: לְמַ֘עַן֮ יֵדְע֣וּ דֹרֹֽתֵיכֶם֒ כִּ֣י בַסֻּכּ֗וֹת הוֹשַׁ֙בְתִּי֙ אֶת־בְּנֵ֣י
מד יִשְׂרָאֵ֔ל בְּהוֹצִיאִ֥י אוֹתָ֖ם מֵאֶ֣רֶץ מִצְרָ֑יִם אֲנִ֖י יְהֹוָ֥ה אֱלֹהֵיכֶֽם: וַיְדַבֵּ֣ר מֹשֶׁ֔ה
אֶת־מֹעֲדֵ֖י יְהֹוָ֑ה אֶל־בְּנֵ֖י יִשְׂרָאֵֽל:

כד שביעי א-ב וַיְדַבֵּ֥ר יְהֹוָ֖ה אֶל־מֹשֶׁ֥ה לֵּאמֹֽר: צַ֣ו אֶת־בְּנֵ֣י יִשְׂרָאֵ֗ל וְיִקְח֨וּ אֵלֶ֜יךָ שֶׁ֣מֶן זַ֣יִת
ג זָ֥ךְ כָּתִ֖ית לַמָּא֑וֹר לְהַעֲלֹ֥ת נֵ֖ר תָּמִֽיד: מִחוּץ֩ לְפָרֹ֨כֶת הָעֵדֻ֜ת בְּאֹ֣הֶל מוֹעֵ֗ד
יַעֲרֹךְ֩ אֹת֨וֹ אַהֲרֹ֜ן מֵעֶ֧רֶב עַד־בֹּ֛קֶר לִפְנֵ֥י יְהֹוָ֖ה תָּמִ֑יד חֻקַּ֥ת עוֹלָ֖ם לְדֹרֹֽתֵיכֶֽם:
ד עַ֚ל הַמְּנֹרָ֣ה הַטְּהֹרָ֔ה יַעֲרֹ֖ךְ אֶת־הַנֵּר֑וֹת לִפְנֵ֥י יְהֹוָ֖ה תָּמִֽיד:
ה וְלָקַחְתָּ֣ סֹ֔לֶת וְאָפִיתָ֣ אֹתָ֔הּ שְׁתֵּ֥ים עֶשְׂרֵ֖ה חַלּ֑וֹת שְׁנֵי֙ עֶשְׂרֹנִ֔ים יִֽהְיֶ֖ה הַֽחַלָּ֥ה
ו הָֽאֶחָֽת: וְשַׂמְתָּ֥ אוֹתָ֛ם שְׁתַּ֥יִם מַֽעֲרָכ֖וֹת שֵׁ֣שׁ הַֽמַּעֲרָ֑כֶת עַ֛ל הַשֻּׁלְחָ֥ן הַטָּהֹ֖ר
ז לִפְנֵ֥י יְהֹוָֽה: וְנָתַתָּ֥ עַל־הַֽמַּעֲרֶ֖כֶת לְבֹנָ֣ה זַכָּ֑ה וְהָֽיְתָ֤ה לַלֶּ֙חֶם֙ לְאַזְכָּרָ֔ה אִשֶּׁ֖ה
ח לַֽיהֹוָֽה: בְּי֨וֹם הַשַּׁבָּ֜ת בְּי֣וֹם הַשַּׁבָּ֗ת יַֽעַרְכֶ֛נּוּ לִפְנֵ֥י יְהֹוָ֖ה תָּמִ֑יד מֵאֵ֥ת בְּנֵֽי־
ט יִשְׂרָאֵ֖ל בְּרִ֥ית עוֹלָֽם: וְהָֽיְתָה֙ לְאַֽהֲרֹ֣ן וּלְבָנָ֔יו וַאֲכָלֻ֖הוּ בְּמָק֣וֹם קָדֹ֑שׁ כִּ֡י קֹ֩דֶשׁ
י קָֽדָשִׁ֨ים ה֥וּא ל֛וֹ מֵאִשֵּׁ֥י יְהֹוָ֖ה חָק־עוֹלָֽם: וַיֵּצֵא֙ בֶּן־אִשָּׁ֣ה
יִשְׂרְאֵלִ֔ית וְהוּא֙ בֶּן־אִ֣ישׁ מִצְרִ֔י בְּת֖וֹךְ בְּנֵ֣י יִשְׂרָאֵ֑ל וַיִּנָּצוּ֙ בַּֽמַּחֲנֶ֔ה בֶּ֚ן
יא הַיִּשְׂרְאֵלִ֔ית וְאִ֖ישׁ הַיִּשְׂרְאֵלִֽי: וַ֠יִּקֹּ֠ב בֶּן־הָֽאִשָּׁ֨ה הַיִּשְׂרְאֵלִ֤ית אֶת־הַשֵּׁם֙
וַיְקַלֵּ֔ל וַיָּבִ֥יאוּ אֹת֖וֹ אֶל־מֹשֶׁ֑ה וְשֵׁ֥ם אִמּ֛וֹ שְׁלֹמִ֥ית בַּת־דִּבְרִ֖י לְמַטֵּה־דָֽן:
יב וַיַּנִּיחֻ֖הוּ בַּמִּשְׁמָ֑ר לִפְרֹ֥שׁ לָהֶ֖ם עַל־פִּ֥י יְהֹוָֽה:

יג-יד וַיְדַבֵּ֥ר יְהֹוָ֖ה אֶל־מֹשֶׁ֥ה לֵּאמֹֽר: הוֹצֵ֣א אֶת־הַֽמְקַלֵּ֗ל אֶל־מִחוּץ֙ לַֽמַּחֲנֶ֔ה
וְסָמְכ֧וּ כָל־הַשֹּֽׁמְעִ֛ים אֶת־יְדֵיהֶ֖ם עַל־רֹאשׁ֑וֹ וְרָֽגְמ֥וּ אֹת֖וֹ כָּל־הָֽעֵדָֽה: וְאֶל־
טו בְּנֵ֥י יִשְׂרָאֵ֖ל תְּדַבֵּ֣ר לֵאמֹ֑ר אִ֥ישׁ אִ֛ישׁ כִּֽי־יְקַלֵּ֥ל אֱלֹהָ֖יו וְנָשָׂ֥א חֶטְאֽוֹ: וְנֹקֵ֤ב
טז שֵֽׁם־יְהֹוָה֙ מ֣וֹת יוּמָ֔ת רָג֥וֹם יִרְגְּמוּ־ב֖וֹ כָּל־הָֽעֵדָ֑ה כַּגֵּר֙ כָּֽאֶזְרָ֔ח בְּנָקְב֥וֹ שֵׁ֖ם
יז-יח יוּמָֽת: וְאִ֕ישׁ כִּ֥י יַכֶּ֖ה כָּל־נֶ֣פֶשׁ אָדָ֑ם מ֖וֹת יוּמָֽת: וּמַכֵּ֥ה נֶֽפֶשׁ־בְּהֵמָ֖ה יְשַׁלְּמֶ֑נָּה
יט נֶ֖פֶשׁ תַּ֥חַת נָֽפֶשׁ: וְאִ֕ישׁ כִּֽי־יִתֵּ֥ן מ֖וּם בַּֽעֲמִית֑וֹ כַּֽאֲשֶׁ֣ר עָשָׂ֔ה כֵּ֖ן יֵעָ֥שֶׂה לּֽוֹ:
כ שֶׁ֚בֶר תַּ֣חַת שֶׁ֔בֶר עַ֚יִן תַּ֣חַת עַ֔יִן שֵׁ֖ן תַּ֣חַת שֵׁ֑ן כַּֽאֲשֶׁ֨ר יִתֵּ֥ן מוּם֙ בָּֽאָדָ֔ם כֵּ֖ן

מפטיר כא-כב יִנָּ֥תֶן בּֽוֹ: * וּמַכֵּ֥ה בְהֵמָ֖ה יְשַׁלְּמֶ֑נָּה וּמַכֵּ֥ה אָדָ֖ם יוּמָֽת: מִשְׁפַּ֤ט אֶחָד֙ יִהְיֶ֣ה לָכֶ֔ם
כג כַּגֵּ֥ר כָּֽאֶזְרָ֖ח יִהְיֶ֑ה כִּ֛י אֲנִ֥י יְהֹוָ֖ה אֱלֹהֵיכֶֽם: וַיְדַבֵּ֣ר מֹשֶׁ֘ה אֶל־בְּנֵ֣י יִשְׂרָאֵל֒
וַיּוֹצִ֣יאוּ אֶת־הַֽמְקַלֵּ֗ל אֶל־מִחוּץ֙ לַֽמַּחֲנֶ֔ה וַיִּרְגְּמ֥וּ אֹת֖וֹ אָ֑בֶן וּבְנֵֽי־יִשְׂרָאֵ֣ל
עָשׂ֔וּ כַּֽאֲשֶׁ֛ר צִוָּ֥ה יְהֹוָ֖ה אֶת־מֹשֶֽׁה: פפפ קכ"ד פסוקים. עוזיא"ל סימן.

24:5-9. The Table and the breads are described in *Exodus* 25:23-30. Every Friday, twelve large loaves were baked and they were placed on the Table on the Sabbath.

24:10-16. The Torah now proceeds to a narrative that seems to be out of place: the story of a Jew who committed the atrocious sin of blaspheming the Name of God, Heaven forbid. The following Midrash gives a historical reason for the connection of this incident to the previous passage.

R' Berechiah taught that the "son of the Israelite woman" went about in the camp scoffing about the show-bread: "A king normally eats warm, freshly baked bread. Why should God have old, cold bread in the Tabernacle?" An Israelite rebuked him. The two came to blows, whereupon the son of the Israelite woman uttered the curse.

24:18. One who killed an animal must pay its market value.

Haftaras Emor: p. 1316

in the seventh month shall you celebrate it. [42] You shall dwell in booths for a seven-day period; every native in Israel shall dwell in booths. [43] So that your generations will know that I caused the Children of Israel to dwell in booths when I took them from the land of Egypt; I am HASHEM, your God.

[44] And Moses declared the appointed festivals of HASHEM to the Children of Israel.

24

The Menorah

[1] HASHEM spoke to Moses, saying: [2] Command the Children of Israel that they shall take for you pure olive oil, pressed, for illumination, to kindle a continual lamp. [3] Outside the Partition of the Testimony, in the Tent of Meeting, Aaron shall arrange it, from evening to morning, before HASHEM, continually; an eternal decree for your generations. [4] On the pure Menorah shall he arrange the lamps, before HASHEM, continually.

Show-bread
(See Appendix B, chart 10; Appendix C, illustration 2)

[5] You shall take fine flour and bake it into twelve loaves; * each loaf shall be two tenth-ephah. [6] You shall place them in two stacks, six in each stack, upon the pure Table, before HASHEM. [7] You shall put pure frankincense on each stack and it shall be a remembrance for the bread, a fire-offering for HASHEM. [8] Each and every Sabbath he shall arrange them before HASHEM continually, from the Children of Israel as an eternal covenant. [9] It shall belong to Aaron and his sons, and they shall eat it in a holy place; for it is most holy for him, from the fire-offerings of HASHEM, an eternal decree.

The blasphemer

[10] The son of an Israelite woman went out* — and he was the son of an Egyptian man — among the Children of Israel; they fought in the camp, the son of the Israelite woman and an Israelite man. [11] The son of the Israelite woman pronounced the Name and blasphemed — so they brought him to Moses; the name of his mother was Shelomis daughter of Divri, of the tribe of Dan. [12] They placed him in custody to clarify for themselves through HASHEM.

[13] HASHEM spoke to Moses, saying: [14] Remove the blasphemer to the outside of the camp, and all those who heard shall lean their hands upon his head: The entire assembly shall stone him. [15] And to the Children of Israel you shall speak, saying: Any man who will blaspheme his God shall bear his sin; [16] and one who pronounces blasphemously the Name of HASHEM shall be put to death, the entire assembly shall surely stone him; proselyte and native alike, when he blasphemes the Name, he shall be put to death.

[17] And a man — if he strikes mortally any human life, he shall be put to death. [18] And a man who strikes mortally an animal life shall make restitution, a life for a life. * [19] And if a man inflicts a wound in his fellow, as he did, so shall be done to him: [20] a break for a break, an eye for an eye, a tooth for a tooth; just as he will have inflicted a wound on a person, so shall be inflicted upon him. [21] One who strikes an animal shall make restitution, and one who strikes a person shall be put to death. [22] There shall be one law for you, it shall be for proselyte and native alike, for I, HASHEM, am your God.

[23] Moses spoke to the Children of Israel, and they took the blasphemer to the outside of the camp, and they stoned him to death; and the Children of Israel did as HASHEM had commanded Moses.

פרשת בהר

כה

א־ב וַיְדַבֵּר יהוה אֶל־מֹשֶׁה בְּהַר סִינַי לֵאמֹר: דַּבֵּר אֶל־בְּנֵי יִשְׂרָאֵל וְאָמַרְתָּ
אֲלֵהֶם כִּי תָבֹאוּ אֶל־הָאָרֶץ אֲשֶׁר אֲנִי נֹתֵן לָכֶם וְשָׁבְתָה הָאָרֶץ שַׁבָּת
ג לַיהוה: שֵׁשׁ שָׁנִים תִּזְרַע שָׂדֶךָ וְשֵׁשׁ שָׁנִים תִּזְמֹר כַּרְמֶךָ וְאָסַפְתָּ אֶת־
ד תְּבוּאָתָהּ: וּבַשָּׁנָה הַשְּׁבִיעִת שַׁבַּת שַׁבָּתוֹן יִהְיֶה לָאָרֶץ שַׁבָּת לַיהוה
ה שָׂדְךָ לֹא תִזְרָע וְכַרְמְךָ לֹא תִזְמֹר: אֵת סְפִיחַ קְצִירְךָ לֹא תִקְצוֹר וְאֶת־
ו עִנְּבֵי נְזִירֶךָ לֹא תִבְצֹר שְׁנַת שַׁבָּתוֹן יִהְיֶה לָאָרֶץ: וְהָיְתָה שַׁבַּת
הָאָרֶץ לָכֶם לְאָכְלָה לְךָ וּלְעַבְדְּךָ וְלַאֲמָתֶךָ וְלִשְׂכִירְךָ וּלְתוֹשָׁבְךָ
ז הַגָּרִים עִמָּךְ: וְלִבְהֶמְתְּךָ וְלַחַיָּה אֲשֶׁר בְּאַרְצֶךָ תִּהְיֶה כָל־תְּבוּאָתָהּ
ח לֶאֱכֹל: וְסָפַרְתָּ לְךָ שֶׁבַע שַׁבְּתֹת שָׁנִים שֶׁבַע שָׁנִים שֶׁבַע
פְּעָמִים וְהָיוּ לְךָ יְמֵי שֶׁבַע שַׁבְּתֹת הַשָּׁנִים תֵּשַׁע וְאַרְבָּעִים שָׁנָה: וְהַעֲבַרְתָּ
ט שׁוֹפַר תְּרוּעָה בַּחֹדֶשׁ הַשְּׁבִעִי בֶּעָשׂוֹר לַחֹדֶשׁ בְּיוֹם הַכִּפֻּרִים תַּעֲבִירוּ
י שׁוֹפָר בְּכָל־אַרְצְכֶם: וְקִדַּשְׁתֶּם אֵת שְׁנַת הַחֲמִשִּׁים שָׁנָה וּקְרָאתֶם דְּרוֹר
בָּאָרֶץ לְכָל־יֹשְׁבֶיהָ יוֹבֵל הִוא תִּהְיֶה לָכֶם וְשַׁבְתֶּם אִישׁ אֶל־אֲחֻזָּתוֹ
יא וְאִישׁ אֶל־מִשְׁפַּחְתּוֹ תָּשֻׁבוּ: יוֹבֵל הִוא שְׁנַת הַחֲמִשִּׁים שָׁנָה תִּהְיֶה לָכֶם
לֹא תִזְרָעוּ וְלֹא תִקְצְרוּ אֶת־סְפִיחֶיהָ וְלֹא תִבְצְרוּ אֶת־נְזִרֶיהָ: כִּי יוֹבֵל
יב הִוא קֹדֶשׁ תִּהְיֶה לָכֶם מִן־הַשָּׂדֶה תֹּאכְלוּ אֶת־תְּבוּאָתָהּ: בִּשְׁנַת הַיּוֹבֵל
יג הַזֹּאת תָּשֻׁבוּ אִישׁ אֶל־אֲחֻזָּתוֹ: וְכִי־תִמְכְּרוּ מִמְכָּר לַעֲמִיתֶךָ אוֹ קָנֹה מִיַּד

שני

יד עֲמִיתֶךָ אַל־תּוֹנוּ אִישׁ אֶת־אָחִיו: בְּמִסְפַּר שָׁנִים אַחַר הַיּוֹבֵל תִּקְנֶה מֵאֵת
טו עֲמִיתֶךָ בְּמִסְפַּר שְׁנֵי־תְבוּאֹת יִמְכָּר־לָךְ: לְפִי | רֹב הַשָּׁנִים תַּרְבֶּה מִקְנָתוֹ
טז וּלְפִי מְעֹט הַשָּׁנִים תַּמְעִיט מִקְנָתוֹ כִּי מִסְפַּר תְּבוּאֹת הוּא מֹכֵר לָךְ: וְלֹא
יז תוֹנוּ אִישׁ אֶת־עֲמִיתוֹ וְיָרֵאתָ מֵאֱלֹהֶיךָ כִּי אֲנִי יהוה אֱלֹהֵיכֶם: וַעֲשִׂיתֶם
יח אֶת־חֻקֹּתַי וְאֶת־מִשְׁפָּטַי תִּשְׁמְרוּ וַעֲשִׂיתֶם אֹתָם וִישַׁבְתֶּם עַל־הָאָרֶץ

שלישי [שני] יט לָבֶטַח: וְנָתְנָה הָאָרֶץ פִּרְיָהּ וַאֲכַלְתֶּם לָשֹׂבַע וִישַׁבְתֶּם לָבֶטַח עָלֶיהָ:
כ וְכִי תֹאמְרוּ מַה־נֹּאכַל בַּשָּׁנָה הַשְּׁבִיעִת הֵן לֹא נִזְרָע וְלֹא נֶאֱסֹף אֶת־
כא תְּבוּאָתֵנוּ: וְצִוִּיתִי אֶת־בִּרְכָתִי לָכֶם בַּשָּׁנָה הַשִּׁשִּׁית וְעָשָׂת אֶת־הַתְּבוּאָה
כב לִשְׁלֹשׁ הַשָּׁנִים: וּזְרַעְתֶּם אֵת הַשָּׁנָה הַשְּׁמִינִת וַאֲכַלְתֶּם מִן־הַתְּבוּאָה
כג יָשָׁן עַד | הַשָּׁנָה הַתְּשִׁיעִת עַד־בּוֹא תְּבוּאָתָהּ תֹּאכְלוּ יָשָׁן: וְהָאָרֶץ לֹא
תִמָּכֵר לִצְמִתֻת כִּי־לִי הָאָרֶץ כִּי־גֵרִים וְתוֹשָׁבִים אַתֶּם עִמָּדִי: וּבְכֹל אֶרֶץ
כה אֲחֻזַּתְכֶם גְּאֻלָּה תִּתְּנוּ לָאָרֶץ: כִּי־יָמוּךְ אָחִיךָ וּמָכַר מֵאֲחֻזָּתוֹ

רביעי

כו וּבָא גֹאֲלוֹ הַקָּרֹב אֵלָיו וְגָאַל אֵת מִמְכַּר אָחִיו: וְאִישׁ כִּי לֹא יִהְיֶה־לּוֹ גֹּאֵל

◆§ Parashas Behar

25:2. *Shemittah,* the Sabbatical Year, is likened to the Sabbath because both bear testimony to God's creation of the universe in six days and His rest on the seventh.

25:8-22. The laws of *Yovel,* the Jubilee Year, teach that the land and freedom are Divine gifts and that ownership reverts to those to whom He wills it (*Chinuch*).

25:17. *You shall not aggrieve* refers to not hurting people with words in personal relationships (*Rashi*).

PARASHAS BEHAR

25

Shemittah/ Sabbatical Year

¹ Hᴀsʜᴇᴍ spoke to Moses on Mount Sinai, saying: ² Speak to the Children of Israel and say to them: When you come into the land that I give you, the land shall observe a Sabbath* rest for Hᴀsʜᴇᴍ. ³ For six years you may sow your field and for six years you may prune your vineyard; and you may gather in its crop. ⁴ But the seventh year shall be a complete rest for the land, a Sabbath for Hᴀsʜᴇᴍ; your field you shall not sow and your vineyard you shall not prune. ⁵ The aftergrowth of your harvest you shall not reap and the grapes you had set aside for yourself you shall not pick; it shall be a year of rest for the land. ⁶ The Sabbath produce of the land shall be yours to eat, for you, for your slave, and for your maidservant; and for your laborer and for your resident who dwell with you. ⁷ And for your animal and for the beast that is in your land shall all its crop be to eat.

Yovel/ Jubilee Year

⁸ You shall count for yourself seven cycles of sabbatical years,* seven years seven times; the years of the seven cycles of sabbatical years shall be for you forty-nine years. ⁹ You shall sound a broken blast on the shofar, in the seventh month, on the tenth of the month; on the Day of Atonement you shall sound the shofar throughout your land. ¹⁰ You shall sanctify the fiftieth year and proclaim freedom throughout the land for all its inhabitants; it shall be the Jubilee Year for you, you shall return each man to his ancestral heritage and you shall return each man to his family. ¹¹ It shall be a Jubilee Year for you — this fiftieth year — you shall not sow, you shall not harvest its aftergrowth and you shall not pick what was set aside of it for yourself. ¹² For it is a Jubilee Year, it shall be holy to you; from the field you may eat its crop. ¹³ In this Jubilee Year you shall return each man to his ancestral heritage.

Sequence of the passages

¹⁴ When you make a sale to your fellow or make a purchase from the hand of your fellow, do not aggrieve one another. ¹⁵ According to the number of years after the Jubilee Year shall you buy from your fellow; according to the number of crop-years shall he sell to you. ¹⁶ According to the greater number of years shall you increase its price, and according to the lesser number of years shall you decrease its price; for he is selling you the number of crops.

¹⁷ Each of you shall not aggrieve* his fellow, and you shall fear your God; for I am Hᴀsʜᴇᴍ, your God.

¹⁸ You shall perform My decrees, and observe My ordinances and perform them; then you shall dwell securely on the land.

¹⁹ The land will give its fruit and you will eat your fill; you will dwell securely upon it. ²⁰ If you will say: What will we eat in the seventh year? — behold! we will not sow and not gather in our crops! ²¹ I will ordain My blessing for you in the sixth year and it will yield a crop sufficient for the three-year period. ²² You will sow in the eighth year, but you will eat from the old crop; until the ninth year, until the arrival of its crop, you will eat the old.

Redemption of land

²³ The land shall not be sold in perpetuity, for the land is Mine; for you are sojourners and residents with Me. ²⁴ In the entire land of your ancestral heritage you shall provide redemption for the land. ²⁵ If your brother becomes impoverished and sells part of his ancestral heritage, his redeemer who is closest to him shall come and redeem his brother's sale. ²⁶ If a man will have no redeemer,

כז וְהִשִּׂיגָה יָדוֹ וּמָצָא כְּדֵי גְאֻלָּתוֹ: וְחִשַּׁב אֶת־שְׁנֵי מִמְכָּרוֹ וְהֵשִׁיב אֶת־

כח הָעֹדֵף לָאִישׁ אֲשֶׁר מָכַר־לוֹ וְשָׁב לַאֲחֻזָּתוֹ: וְאִם לֹא־מָצְאָה יָדוֹ דֵּי הָשִׁיב לוֹ וְהָיָה מִמְכָּרוֹ בְּיַד הַקֹּנֶה אֹתוֹ עַד שְׁנַת הַיּוֹבֵל וְיָצָא בַּיֹּבֵל

כט וְשָׁב לַאֲחֻזָּתוֹ:   וְאִישׁ כִּי־יִמְכֹּר בֵּית־מוֹשַׁב עִיר

חמישי
[שלישי]

ל חוֹמָה וְהָיְתָה גְּאֻלָּתוֹ עַד־תֹּם שְׁנַת מִמְכָּרוֹ יָמִים תִּהְיֶה גְאֻלָּתוֹ: וְאִם לֹא־יִגָּאֵל עַד־מְלֹאת לוֹ שָׁנָה תְמִימָה וְקָם הַבַּיִת אֲשֶׁר־בָּעִיר אֲשֶׁר־

לא °לֹא [לוֹ ק] חֹמָה לַצְּמִיתֻת לַקֹּנֶה אֹתוֹ לְדֹרֹתָיו לֹא יֵצֵא בַּיֹּבֵל: וּבָתֵּי הַחֲצֵרִים אֲשֶׁר אֵין־לָהֶם חֹמָה סָבִיב עַל־שְׂדֵה הָאָרֶץ יֵחָשֵׁב גְּאֻלָּה

לב תִּהְיֶה־לּוֹ וּבַיֹּבֵל יֵצֵא: וְעָרֵי הַלְוִיִּם בָּתֵּי עָרֵי אֲחֻזָּתָם גְּאֻלַּת עוֹלָם תִּהְיֶה

לג לַלְוִיִּם: וַאֲשֶׁר יִגְאַל מִן־הַלְוִיִּם וְיָצָא מִמְכַּר־בַּיִת וְעִיר אֲחֻזָּתוֹ בַּיֹּבֵל כִּי

לד בָתֵּי עָרֵי הַלְוִיִּם הִוא אֲחֻזָּתָם בְּתוֹךְ בְּנֵי יִשְׂרָאֵל: וּשְׂדֵה מִגְרַשׁ עָרֵיהֶם

לה לֹא יִמָּכֵר כִּי־אֲחֻזַּת עוֹלָם הוּא לָהֶם: וְכִי־יָמוּךְ אָחִיךָ וּמָטָה יָדוֹ עִמָּךְ וְהֶחֱזַקְתָּ בּוֹ גֵּר וְתוֹשָׁב וָחַי עִמָּךְ: אַל־תִּקַּח

לו מֵאִתּוֹ נֶשֶׁךְ וְתַרְבִּית וְיָרֵאתָ מֵאֱלֹהֶיךָ וְחֵי אָחִיךָ עִמָּךְ: אֶת־כַּסְפְּךָ לֹא־

לז תִתֵּן לוֹ בְּנֶשֶׁךְ וּבְמַרְבִּית לֹא־תִתֵּן אָכְלֶךָ: אֲנִי יהוה אֱלֹהֵיכֶם אֲשֶׁר־

לח הוֹצֵאתִי אֶתְכֶם מֵאֶרֶץ מִצְרָיִם לָתֵת לָכֶם אֶת־אֶרֶץ כְּנַעַן לִהְיוֹת לָכֶם לֵאלֹהִים: וְכִי־יָמוּךְ אָחִיךָ עִמָּךְ וְנִמְכַּר־לָךְ לֹא־

ששי
[רביעי]

לט תַעֲבֹד בּוֹ עֲבֹדַת עָבֶד: כְּשָׂכִיר כְּתוֹשָׁב יִהְיֶה עִמָּךְ עַד־שְׁנַת הַיֹּבֵל יַעֲבֹד

מ עִמָּךְ: וְיָצָא מֵעִמָּךְ הוּא וּבָנָיו עִמּוֹ וְשָׁב אֶל־מִשְׁפַּחְתּוֹ וְאֶל־אֲחֻזַּת

מא אֲבֹתָיו יָשׁוּב: כִּי־עֲבָדַי הֵם אֲשֶׁר־הוֹצֵאתִי אֹתָם מֵאֶרֶץ מִצְרָיִם לֹא

מב יִמָּכְרוּ מִמְכֶּרֶת עָבֶד: לֹא־תִרְדֶּה בוֹ בְּפָרֶךְ וְיָרֵאתָ מֵאֱלֹהֶיךָ: וְעַבְדְּךָ

מג-מד וַאֲמָתְךָ אֲשֶׁר יִהְיוּ־לָךְ מֵאֵת הַגּוֹיִם אֲשֶׁר סְבִיבֹתֵיכֶם מֵהֶם תִּקְנוּ עֶבֶד

מה וְאָמָה: וְגַם מִבְּנֵי הַתּוֹשָׁבִים הַגָּרִים עִמָּכֶם מֵהֶם תִּקְנוּ וּמִמִּשְׁפַּחְתָּם

מו אֲשֶׁר עִמָּכֶם אֲשֶׁר הוֹלִידוּ בְּאַרְצְכֶם וְהָיוּ לָכֶם לַאֲחֻזָּה: וְהִתְנַחַלְתֶּם אֹתָם לִבְנֵיכֶם אַחֲרֵיכֶם לָרֶשֶׁת אֲחֻזָּה לְעֹלָם בָּהֶם תַּעֲבֹדוּ *וּבְאַחֵיכֶם

°ב' טעמים

מז בְּנֵי־יִשְׂרָאֵל אִישׁ בְּאָחִיו לֹא־תִרְדֶּה בוֹ בְּפָרֶךְ:   וְכִי

שביעי

תַשִּׂיג יַד גֵּר וְתוֹשָׁב עִמָּךְ וּמָךְ אָחִיךָ עִמּוֹ וְנִמְכַּר לְגֵר תּוֹשָׁב עִמָּךְ אוֹ

מח לְעֵקֶר מִשְׁפַּחַת גֵּר: אַחֲרֵי נִמְכַּר גְּאֻלָּה תִּהְיֶה־לּוֹ אֶחָד מֵאֶחָיו יִגְאָלֶנּוּ:

מט אוֹ־דֹדוֹ אוֹ בֶן־דֹּדוֹ יִגְאָלֶנּוּ אוֹ־מִשְּׁאֵר בְּשָׂרוֹ מִמִּשְׁפַּחְתּוֹ יִגְאָלֶנּוּ אוֹ־

נ הִשִּׂיגָה יָדוֹ וְנִגְאָל: וְחִשַּׁב עִם־קֹנֵהוּ מִשְּׁנַת הִמָּכְרוֹ לוֹ עַד שְׁנַת הַיֹּבֵל

נא וְהָיָה כֶּסֶף מִמְכָּרוֹ בְּמִסְפַּר שָׁנִים כִּימֵי שָׂכִיר יִהְיֶה עִמּוֹ: אִם־עוֹד

25:35-38. The highest form of charity is to prevent a person from becoming poor, by offering a loan or employment, investing in his business, or any other form of assistance that will avoid poverty (*Rambam*).

25:47-53. A Jew's ultimate degradation is to be sold as a slave to a non-Jewish resident of *Eretz Yisrael*. The Torah enjoins his kinsmen to redeem him, but without depriving the owner of his legitimate property rights.

but his means suffice and he acquires enough for its redemption, ²⁷ then he shall reckon the years of his sale and return the remainder to the man to whom he had sold it; and he shall return to his ancestral heritage. ²⁸ But if he does not acquire sufficient means to repay him, then his sale shall remain in possession of its purchaser until the Jubilee Year; in the Jubilee Year it shall leave, and he shall return to his ancestral heritage.

²⁹ If a man shall sell a residence house in a walled city, its redemption can take place until the end of the year of its sale; its period of redemption shall be a year. ³⁰ But if it is not redeemed until its full year has elapsed, then the home that is in a city that has a wall shall pass in perpetuity to the one who purchased it, for his generations; it shall not go out in the Jubilee Year. ³¹ But homes in the open towns, which have no surrounding wall, shall be considered like the land's open field; it shall have redemption, and shall go out in the Jubilee Year. ³² As for the cities of the Levites, the homes in the cities of their ancestral heritage, the Levites shall have an eternal right of redemption. ³³ And what one will buy from the Levites — a home that has been sold or the city of its ancestral heritage — shall go out in the Jubilee year; for the homes of the Levite cities, that is their ancestral heritage among the Children of Israel! ³⁴ But the fields of the open land of their cities may not be sold; for it is an eternal heritage for them.

Levite cities

³⁵ If your brother becomes impoverished* and his means falter in your proximity, you shall strengthen him — proselyte or resident — so that he can live with you. ³⁶ Do not take from him interest and increase; and you shall fear your God — and let your brother live with you. ³⁷ Do not give him your money for interest, and do not give your food for increase. ³⁸ I am HASHEM, your God, Who took you out of the land of Egypt, to give you the land of Canaan, to be God unto you.

Preventing poverty

³⁹ If your brother becomes impoverished with you and is sold to you; you shall not work him with slave labor. ⁴⁰ Like a laborer or a resident shall he be with you; until the Jubilee Year shall he work with you. ⁴¹ Then he shall leave you, he and his children with him; he shall return to his family, and to his ancestral heritage shall he return. ⁴² For they are My servants, whom I have taken out of the land of Egypt; they shall not be sold in the manner of a slave. ⁴³ You shall not subjugate him through hard labor — you shall fear your God.

A Jew's Jewish "slave"

⁴⁴ Your slave or your maidservant whom you may own, from the gentiles who surround you, from among them you may purchase a slave or a maidservant. ⁴⁵ Also from among the children of the residents who live with you, from them you may purchase, from their family that is with you, whom they begot in your land; and they shall remain yours as an ancestral heritage. ⁴⁶ You shall hold them as a heritage for your children after you to inherit as a possession, you shall work with them forever; but with your brethren, the Children of Israel — a man with his brother — you shall not subjugate him through hard labor.

Jewish slave of an idolater

⁴⁷ If the means of a sojourner who resides with you shall become sufficient, and your brother becomes impoverished with him, and he is sold to an alien* who resides with you, or to an idol of a sojourner's family; ⁴⁸ after he has been sold, he shall have a redemption; one of his brothers shall redeem him; ⁴⁹ or his uncle, or his cousin shall redeem him, or a relative from his family shall redeem him; or if his own means become sufficient, he shall be redeemed. ⁵⁰ He shall make a reckoning with his purchaser from the year he was sold to him until the Jubilee Year; the money of his purchase shall be divided by the number of years, he shall be regarded with him like the years of a laborer. ⁵¹If there are yet

נב רַבּוֹת בַּשָּׁנִים לְפִיהֶן יָשִׁיב גְּאֻלָּתוֹ מִכֶּסֶף מִקְנָתוֹ: וְאִם־מְעַט נִשְׁאַר בַּשָּׁנִים

נג עַד־שְׁנַת הַיֹּבֵל וְחִשַּׁב־לוֹ כְּפִי שָׁנָיו יָשִׁיב אֶת־גְּאֻלָּתוֹ: כִּשְׂכִיר שָׁנָה

נד בְּשָׁנָה יִהְיֶה עִמּוֹ לֹא־יִרְדֶּנּוּ בְּפֶרֶךְ לְעֵינֶיךָ: וְאִם־לֹא יִגָּאֵל בְּאֵלֶּה וְיָצָא

מפטיר נה בִּשְׁנַת הַיֹּבֵל הוּא וּבָנָיו עִמּוֹ: כִּי־לִי בְנֵי־יִשְׂרָאֵל עֲבָדִים עֲבָדַי הֵם אֲשֶׁר־

כו א הוֹצֵאתִי אוֹתָם מֵאֶרֶץ מִצְרַיִם אֲנִי יהוה אֱלֹהֵיכֶם: לֹא־תַעֲשׂוּ לָכֶם

אֱלִילִם וּפֶסֶל וּמַצֵּבָה לֹא־תָקִימוּ לָכֶם וְאֶבֶן מַשְׂכִּית לֹא תִתְּנוּ בְּאַרְצְכֶם

Haftaras
Behar:
p. 1146

ב לְהִשְׁתַּחֲוֺת עָלֶיהָ כִּי אֲנִי יהוה אֱלֹהֵיכֶם: אֶת־שַׁבְּתֹתַי תִּשְׁמֹרוּ וּמִקְדָּשִׁי

תִּירָאוּ אֲנִי יהוה: פפפ נ"ז פסוקים. חטי"ל סימן. לאחינ"ה סימן.

פרשת בחקתי

ג־ד אִם־בְּחֻקֹּתַי תֵּלֵכוּ וְאֶת־מִצְוֺתַי תִּשְׁמְרוּ וַעֲשִׂיתֶם אֹתָם: וְנָתַתִּי גִשְׁמֵיכֶם

ה בְּעִתָּם וְנָתְנָה הָאָרֶץ יְבוּלָהּ וְעֵץ הַשָּׂדֶה יִתֵּן פִּרְיוֹ: וְהִשִּׂיג לָכֶם דַּיִשׁ אֶת־

בָּצִיר וּבָצִיר יַשִּׂיג אֶת־זָרַע וַאֲכַלְתֶּם לַחְמְכֶם לָשֹׂבַע וִישַׁבְתֶּם לָבֶטַח

ו בְּאַרְצְכֶם: וְנָתַתִּי שָׁלוֹם בָּאָרֶץ וּשְׁכַבְתֶּם וְאֵין מַחֲרִיד וְהִשְׁבַּתִּי חַיָּה רָעָה

ז מִן־הָאָרֶץ וְחֶרֶב לֹא־תַעֲבֹר בְּאַרְצְכֶם: וּרְדַפְתֶּם אֶת־אֹיְבֵיכֶם וְנָפְלוּ

ח לִפְנֵיכֶם לֶחָרֶב: וְרָדְפוּ מִכֶּם חֲמִשָּׁה מֵאָה וּמֵאָה מִכֶּם רְבָבָה יִרְדֹּפוּ וְנָפְלוּ

ט אֹיְבֵיכֶם לִפְנֵיכֶם לֶחָרֶב: וּפָנִיתִי אֲלֵיכֶם וְהִפְרֵיתִי אֶתְכֶם וְהִרְבֵּיתִי אֶתְכֶם

שני

שלישי
[חמישי] י וַהֲקִימֹתִי אֶת־בְּרִיתִי אִתְּכֶם: וַאֲכַלְתֶּם יָשָׁן נוֹשָׁן וְיָשָׁן מִפְּנֵי חָדָשׁ תּוֹצִיאוּ:

יא־יב וְנָתַתִּי מִשְׁכָּנִי בְּתוֹכְכֶם וְלֹא־תִגְעַל נַפְשִׁי אֶתְכֶם: וְהִתְהַלַּכְתִּי בְּתוֹכְכֶם

יג וְהָיִיתִי לָכֶם לֵאלֹהִים וְאַתֶּם תִּהְיוּ־לִי לְעָם: אֲנִי יהוה אֱלֹהֵיכֶם אֲשֶׁר

הוֹצֵאתִי אֶתְכֶם מֵאֶרֶץ מִצְרַיִם מִהְיֹת לָהֶם עֲבָדִים וָאֶשְׁבֹּר מֹטֹת עֻלְּכֶם

וָאוֹלֵךְ אֶתְכֶם קוֹמְמִיּוּת:

יד־טו וְאִם־לֹא תִשְׁמְעוּ לִי וְלֹא תַעֲשׂוּ אֵת כָּל־הַמִּצְוֺת הָאֵלֶּה: וְאִם־בְּחֻקֹּתַי

תִּמְאָסוּ וְאִם אֶת־מִשְׁפָּטַי תִּגְעַל נַפְשְׁכֶם לְבִלְתִּי עֲשׂוֹת אֶת־כָּל־מִצְוֺתַי

טז לְהַפְרְכֶם אֶת־בְּרִיתִי: אַף־אֲנִי אֶעֱשֶׂה־זֹּאת לָכֶם וְהִפְקַדְתִּי עֲלֵיכֶם בֶּהָלָה

אֶת־הַשַּׁחֶפֶת וְאֶת־הַקַּדַּחַת מְכַלּוֹת עֵינַיִם וּמְדִיבֹת נָפֶשׁ וּזְרַעְתֶּם לָרִיק

יז זַרְעֲכֶם וַאֲכָלֻהוּ אֹיְבֵיכֶם: וְנָתַתִּי פָנַי בָּכֶם וְנִגַּפְתֶּם לִפְנֵי אֹיְבֵיכֶם וְרָדוּ בָכֶם

יח שֹׂנְאֵיכֶם וְנַסְתֶּם וְאֵין־רֹדֵף אֶתְכֶם: וְאִם־עַד־אֵלֶּה לֹא תִשְׁמְעוּ לִי וְיָסַפְתִּי

יט לְיַסְּרָה אֶתְכֶם שֶׁבַע עַל־חַטֹּאתֵיכֶם: וְשָׁבַרְתִּי אֶת־גְּאוֹן עֻזְּכֶם וְנָתַתִּי אֶת־

26:1-2. Through adherence to these commandments (avoidance of idolatry, observance of the Sabbath, and reverence for the Temple), a Jew will find the strength to observe all the others, thereby preserving his faith in the most adverse circumstances (*Ramban*).

◆§ **Parashas Bechukosai.** This *Sidrah* begins with the idyllic blessings that await the Jewish people if they live up to their covenant with God, and then proceeds to the תוֹכֵחָה, *Admonition,* a sobering account of punishments, frustrations, and curses that will result from attempts to

destroy the covenant. Indeed, though God's underlying mercy prevents all of these curses from befalling Israel in any one unbearable instant, a careful reading of Jewish history — and perhaps the twentieth century in particular — shows that they *have* taken place at various intervals, before and during the exiles.

The blessings are given in general terms; the curses, however, are given in great detail, because they are intended to awe the people into obedience to God's will (*Ibn Ezra* v. 13).

many years, he shall repay his redemption accordingly from the money of his purchase. [52] And if there are few years left until the Jubilee Year, he shall reckon that with him; according to his years shall he repay his redemption. [53] He shall be with him like a laborer hired by the year; he shall not subjugate him through hard labor in your sight.

[54] If he has not been redeemed by these means, then he shall go out in the Jubilee Year, he and his children with him.

[55] For the Children of Israel are servants to Me, they are My servants, whom I have taken out of the land of Egypt — I am HASHEM, your God.

26 ¹ **Y**ou shall not make idols* for yourselves, and you shall not erect for your-selves a statue or a pillar, and in your land you shall not emplace a flooring stone upon which to prostrate oneself — for I am HASHEM, your God. ² My Sab-baths shall you observe and My Sanctuary shall you revere — I am HASHEM.

PARASHAS BECHUKOSAI

Miracles of blessing and curse ³ **I**f you will follow My decrees and observe My commandments and perform them; ⁴ then I will provide your rains in their time, and the land will give its produce and the tree of the field will give its fruit. ⁵ Your threshing will last until the vintage, and the vintage will last until the sowing; you will eat your bread to satiety and you will dwell securely in your land.

⁶ I will provide peace* in the land, and you will lie down with none to frighten you; I will cause wild beasts to withdraw from the land, and a sword will not cross your land. ⁷ You will pursue your enemies; and they will fall before you by the sword. ⁸ Five of you will pursue a hundred, and a hundred of you will pursue ten thousand; and your enemies will fall before you by the sword. ⁹ I will turn My attention to you, I will make you fruitful and increase you; and I will establish My covenant with you.

¹⁰ You will eat very old grain and remove the old to make way for the new. ¹¹ I will place My Sanctuary among you; and My Spirit will not reject you. ¹² I will walk among you, I will be God unto you and you will be a people unto Me. ¹³ I am HASHEM, your God, Who took you out of the land of Egypt from being their slaves; I broke the staves of your yoke and I led you erect.

The Tochachah/ Admonition ¹⁴ But if you will not listen* to Me and will not perform all of these command-ments; ¹⁵ if you consider My decrees loathsome, and if your being rejects My ordinances, so as not to perform all My commandments, so that you annul My *The first series of punishments* covenant — ¹⁶ then I will do the same to you; I will assign upon you panic, swelling lesions, and burning fever, which cause eyes to long and souls to suffer; you will sow your seeds in vain, for your enemies will eat it. ¹⁷ I will turn My attention against you, you will be struck down before your enemies; those who hate you will subjugate you — you will flee with no one pursuing you. *The second series* ¹⁸ If despite this you do not heed Me, then I shall punish you further, seven ways for your sins. ¹⁹ I will break the pride of your might; I will make your

---

26:6. By climaxing the above blessings with that of peace, the Torah teaches that peace is equivalent to all the other blessings combined (*Rashi*; *Sifra*).

26:14-43. These horrendous punishments are meant not as revenge, but to influence people to repent, and for

that reason they are inflicted in stages of increasing severity. If the first stage comes and Israel does not derive the desired lesson, the next and more severe stage of punishment will befall them, until repentance and God's mercy finally come.

כ שְׁמֵיכֶם כַּבַּרְזֶל וְאֶת־אַרְצְכֶם כַּנְּחֻשָׁה: וְתַם לָרִיק כֹּחֲכֶם וְלֹא־תִתֵּן

כא אַרְצְכֶם אֶת־יְבוּלָהּ וְעֵץ הָאָרֶץ לֹא יִתֵּן פִּרְיוֹ: וְאִם־תֵּלְכוּ עִמִּי קֶרִי וְלֹא

כב תֹאבוּ לִשְׁמֹעַ לִי וְיָסַפְתִּי עֲלֵיכֶם מַכָּה שֶׁבַע כְּחַטֹּאתֵיכֶם: וְהִשְׁלַחְתִּי

בָכֶם אֶת־חַיַּת הַשָּׂדֶה וְשִׁכְּלָה אֶתְכֶם וְהִכְרִיתָה אֶת־בְּהֶמְתְּכֶם

כג וְהִמְעִיטָה אֶתְכֶם וְנָשַׁמּוּ דַּרְכֵיכֶם: וְאִם־בְּאֵלֶּה לֹא תִוָּסְרוּ לִי וַהֲלַכְתֶּם

כד עִמִּי קֶרִי: וְהָלַכְתִּי אַף־אֲנִי עִמָּכֶם בְּקֶרִי וְהִכֵּיתִי אֶתְכֶם גַּם־אָנִי שֶׁבַע

כה עַל־חַטֹּאתֵיכֶם: וְהֵבֵאתִי עֲלֵיכֶם חֶרֶב נֹקֶמֶת נְקַם־בְּרִית וְנֶאֱסַפְתֶּם אֶל־

כו עָרֵיכֶם וְשִׁלַּחְתִּי דֶבֶר בְּתוֹכְכֶם וְנִתַּתֶּם בְּיַד־אוֹיֵב: בְּשִׁבְרִי לָכֶם מַטֵּה־

לֶחֶם וְאָפוּ עֶשֶׂר נָשִׁים לַחְמְכֶם בְּתַנּוּר אֶחָד וְהֵשִׁיבוּ לַחְמְכֶם בַּמִּשְׁקָל

כז וַאֲכַלְתֶּם וְלֹא תִשְׂבָּעוּ: וְאִם־בְּזֹאת לֹא תִשְׁמְעוּ

כח לִי וַהֲלַכְתֶּם עִמִּי בְּקֶרִי: וְהָלַכְתִּי עִמָּכֶם בַּחֲמַת־קֶרִי וְיִסַּרְתִּי אֶתְכֶם אַף־

כט אָנִי שֶׁבַע עַל־חַטֹּאתֵיכֶם: וַאֲכַלְתֶּם בְּשַׂר בְּנֵיכֶם וּבְשַׂר בְּנֹתֵיכֶם תֹּאכֵלוּ:

ל וְהִשְׁמַדְתִּי אֶת־בָּמֹתֵיכֶם וְהִכְרַתִּי אֶת־חַמָּנֵיכֶם וְנָתַתִּי אֶת־פִּגְרֵיכֶם עַל־

לא פִּגְרֵי גִּלּוּלֵיכֶם וְגָעֲלָה נַפְשִׁי אֶתְכֶם: וְנָתַתִּי אֶת־עָרֵיכֶם חָרְבָּה וַהֲשִׁמּוֹתִי

לב אֶת־מִקְדְּשֵׁיכֶם וְלֹא אָרִיחַ בְּרֵיחַ נִיחֹחֲכֶם: וַהֲשִׁמֹּתִי אֲנִי אֶת־הָאָרֶץ

לג וְשָׁמְמוּ עָלֶיהָ אֹיְבֵיכֶם הַיֹּשְׁבִים בָּהּ: וְאֶתְכֶם אֱזָרֶה בַגּוֹיִם וַהֲרִיקֹתִי

לד אַחֲרֵיכֶם חָרֶב וְהָיְתָה אַרְצְכֶם שְׁמָמָה וְעָרֵיכֶם יִהְיוּ חָרְבָּה: אָז תִּרְצֶה

הָאָרֶץ אֶת־שַׁבְּתֹתֶיהָ כֹּל יְמֵי הָשַּׁמָּה וְאַתֶּם בְּאֶרֶץ אֹיְבֵיכֶם אָז תִּשְׁבַּת   *שי דגושה

לה הָאָרֶץ וְהִרְצָת אֶת־שַׁבְּתֹתֶיהָ: כָּל־יְמֵי הָשַּׁמָּה תִּשְׁבֹּת אֵת אֲשֶׁר לֹא־   *שי דגושה

לו שָׁבְתָה בְּשַׁבְּתֹתֵיכֶם בְּשִׁבְתְּכֶם עָלֶיהָ: וְהַנִּשְׁאָרִים בָּכֶם וְהֵבֵאתִי מֹרֶךְ

בִּלְבָבָם בְּאַרְצֹת אֹיְבֵיהֶם וְרָדַף אֹתָם קוֹל עָלֶה נִדָּף וְנָסוּ מְנֻסַת־חֶרֶב

לז וְנָפְלוּ וְאֵין רֹדֵף: וְכָשְׁלוּ אִישׁ־בְּאָחִיו כְּמִפְּנֵי־חֶרֶב וְרֹדֵף אָיִן וְלֹא־תִהְיֶה

לח לָכֶם תְּקוּמָה לִפְנֵי אֹיְבֵיכֶם: וַאֲבַדְתֶּם בַּגּוֹיִם וְאָכְלָה אֶתְכֶם אֶרֶץ

לט אֹיְבֵיכֶם: וְהַנִּשְׁאָרִים בָּכֶם יִמַּקּוּ בַּעֲוֹנָם בְּאַרְצֹת אֹיְבֵיכֶם וְאַף בַּעֲוֹנֹת

אֲבֹתָם אִתָּם יִמָּקּוּ: וְהִתְוַדּוּ אֶת־עֲוֹנָם וְאֶת־עֲוֹן אֲבֹתָם בְּמַעֲלָם אֲשֶׁר

מ מָעֲלוּ־בִי וְאַף אֲשֶׁר־הָלְכוּ עִמִּי בְּקֶרִי: אַף־אֲנִי אֵלֵךְ עִמָּם בְּקֶרִי וְהֵבֵאתִי

מא אֹתָם בְּאֶרֶץ אֹיְבֵיהֶם אוֹ־אָז יִכָּנַע לְבָבָם הֶעָרֵל וְאָז יִרְצוּ אֶת־עֲוֹנָם:

מב וְזָכַרְתִּי אֶת־בְּרִיתִי יַעֲקוֹב וְאַף אֶת־בְּרִיתִי יִצְחָק וְאַף אֶת־בְּרִיתִי   *מלא ו

מג אַבְרָהָם אֶזְכֹּר וְהָאָרֶץ אֶזְכֹּר: וְהָאָרֶץ תֵּעָזֵב מֵהֶם וְתִרֶץ אֶת־שַׁבְּתֹתֶיהָ

בָּהְשַׁמָּה מֵהֶם וְהֵם יִרְצוּ אֶת־עֲוֹנָם יַעַן וּבְיַעַן בְּמִשְׁפָּטַי מָאָסוּ

מד וְאֶת־חֻקֹּתַי גָּעֲלָה נַפְשָׁם: וְאַף־גַּם־זֹאת בִּהְיוֹתָם בְּאֶרֶץ אֹיְבֵיהֶם לֹא־

26:42. The order of the Patriarchs' names is reversed. This indicates that Jacob alone should be worthy of bringing redemption to his children; and even if his merit is insufficient, there is Isaac's merit. If even that is not enough, there is Abraham, whose merit will surely be sufficient (*Rashi*).

heaven like iron and your land like copper. ²⁰ Your strength will be spent in vain; your land will not give its produce and the tree of the land will not give its fruit.

The third series   ²¹ If you behave casually with Me and refuse to heed Me, then I shall lay a further blow upon you — seven ways, like your sins. ²² I will incite the wildlife of the field against you and it will leave you bereft of your children, decimate your livestock, and diminish you; and your roads will become desolate.

The fourth series   ²³ If despite these you will not be chastised toward Me, and you behave casually with Me, ²⁴ then I, too, will behave toward you with casualness; and I will strike you, even I, seven ways for your sins. ²⁵ I will bring upon you a sword, avenging the vengeance of a covenant, you will be gathered into your cities; then I will send a pestilence among you and you will be delivered into the hand of your enemy. ²⁶ When I break for you the staff of bread, ten women will bake your bread in one oven, and they will bring back your bread by weight; you will eat and not be sated.

The fifth series   ²⁷ If despite this you will not heed Me, and you behave toward Me with casualness, ²⁸ I will behave toward you with a fury of casualness; I will chastise you, even I, seven ways for your sins. ²⁹ You will eat the flesh of your sons; and the flesh of your daughters will you eat. ³⁰ I will destroy your lofty buildings and decimate your sun-idols, I will cast your carcasses upon the carcasses of your idols, and My Spirit will reject you. ³¹ I will lay your cities in ruin and I will make your sanctuaries desolate; I will not savor your satisfying aromas. ³² I will make the land desolate; and your foes who dwell upon it will be desolate. ³³ And you, I will scatter among the nations, I will unsheathe the sword after you; your land will be desolate and your cities will be a ruin.

³⁴ Then the land will be appeased for its sabbaticals during all the years of its desolation, while you are in the land of your foes; then the land will rest and it will appease for its sabbaticals. ³⁵ All the years of its desolation it will rest, whatever it did not rest during your sabbaticals when you dwelled upon her.

³⁶ The survivors among you — I will bring weakness into their hearts in the lands of their foes; the sound of a rustling leaf will pursue them, they will flee as one flees the sword, and they will fall, but without a pursuer. ³⁷ They will stumble over one another as in flight from the sword, but there is no pursuer; you will not have the power to withstand your foes. ³⁸ You will become lost among the nations; the land of your foes will devour you. ³⁹ Because of their iniquity, your remnant will disintegrate in the lands of your foes; and because the iniquities of their forefathers are with them as well, they will disintegrate.

⁴⁰ Then they will confess their sin and the sin of their forefathers, for the treachery with which they betrayed Me, and also for having behaved toward Me with casualness. ⁴¹ I, too, will behave toward them with casualness and I will bring them into the land of their enemies — perhaps then their unfeeling heart will be humbled and then they will gain appeasement for their sin. ⁴² I will remember My covenant with Jacob and also My covenant with Isaac, and also My covenant with Abraham* will I remember, and I will remember the Land.

The conclusion of the Admonition   ⁴³ The Land will be bereft of them; and it will be appeased for its sabbaticals having become desolate of them; and they must gain appeasement for their iniquity; because they were revolted by My ordinances and because their spirit rejected My decrees.

⁴⁴ But despite all this, while they will be in the land of their enemies, I will not

מְאַסְתִּים וְלֹא־גְעַלְתִּים לְכַלֹּתָם לְהָפֵר בְּרִיתִי אִתָּם כִּי אֲנִי יהוה

מה אֱלֹהֵיהֶם: וְזָכַרְתִּי לָהֶם בְּרִית רִאשֹׁנִים אֲשֶׁר הוֹצֵאתִי־אֹתָם מֵאֶרֶץ

מו מִצְרַיִם לְעֵינֵי הַגּוֹיִם לִהְיוֹת לָהֶם לֵאלֹהִים אֲנִי יהוה: אֵלֶּה הַחֻקִּים

וְהַמִּשְׁפָּטִים וְהַתּוֹרֹת אֲשֶׁר נָתַן יהוה בֵּינוֹ וּבֵין בְּנֵי יִשְׂרָאֵל בְּהַר סִינַי

בְּיַד־מֹשֶׁה:

כז
רביעי
[ששי]

א-ב וַיְדַבֵּר יהוה אֶל־מֹשֶׁה לֵּאמֹר: דַּבֵּר אֶל־בְּנֵי יִשְׂרָאֵל וְאָמַרְתָּ אֲלֵהֶם אִישׁ

ג כִּי יַפְלִא נֶדֶר בְּעֶרְכְּךָ נְפָשֹׁת לַיהוה: וְהָיָה עֶרְכְּךָ הַזָּכָר מִבֶּן עֶשְׂרִים שָׁנָה

ד וְעַד בֶּן־שִׁשִּׁים שָׁנָה וְהָיָה עֶרְכְּךָ חֲמִשִּׁים שֶׁקֶל כֶּסֶף בְּשֶׁקֶל הַקֹּדֶשׁ: וְאִם־

ה נְקֵבָה הִוא וְהָיָה עֶרְכְּךָ שְׁלֹשִׁים שָׁקֶל: וְאִם מִבֶּן־חָמֵשׁ שָׁנִים וְעַד בֶּן־

עֶשְׂרִים שָׁנָה וְהָיָה עֶרְכְּךָ הַזָּכָר עֶשְׂרִים שְׁקָלִים וְלַנְּקֵבָה עֲשֶׂרֶת שְׁקָלִים:

ו וְאִם מִבֶּן־חֹדֶשׁ וְעַד בֶּן־חָמֵשׁ שָׁנִים וְהָיָה עֶרְכְּךָ הַזָּכָר חֲמִשָּׁה שְׁקָלִים

ז כָּסֶף וְלַנְּקֵבָה עֶרְכְּךָ שְׁלֹשֶׁת שְׁקָלִים כָּסֶף: וְאִם מִבֶּן־שִׁשִּׁים שָׁנָה וָמַעְלָה

ח אִם־זָכָר וְהָיָה עֶרְכְּךָ חֲמִשָּׁה עָשָׂר שָׁקֶל וְלַנְּקֵבָה עֲשָׂרָה שְׁקָלִים: וְאִם־מָךְ

הוּא מֵעֶרְכֶּךָ וְהֶעֱמִידוֹ לִפְנֵי הַכֹּהֵן וְהֶעֱרִיךְ אֹתוֹ הַכֹּהֵן עַל־פִּי אֲשֶׁר תַּשִּׂיג

ט יַד הַנֹּדֵר יַעֲרִיכֶנּוּ הַכֹּהֵן: וְאִם־בְּהֵמָה אֲשֶׁר יַקְרִיבוּ מִמֶּנָּה

י קָרְבָּן לַיהוה כֹּל אֲשֶׁר יִתֵּן מִמֶּנּוּ לַיהוה יִהְיֶה־קֹּדֶשׁ: לֹא יַחֲלִיפֶנּוּ וְלֹא־

יָמִיר אֹתוֹ טוֹב בְּרָע אוֹ־רַע בְּטוֹב וְאִם־הָמֵר יָמִיר בְּהֵמָה בִּבְהֵמָה וְהָיָה־

יא הוּא וּתְמוּרָתוֹ יִהְיֶה־קֹּדֶשׁ: וְאִם כָּל־בְּהֵמָה טְמֵאָה אֲשֶׁר לֹא־יַקְרִיבוּ

יב מִמֶּנָּה קָרְבָּן לַיהוה וְהֶעֱמִיד אֶת־הַבְּהֵמָה לִפְנֵי הַכֹּהֵן: וְהֶעֱרִיךְ הַכֹּהֵן

יג אֹתָהּ בֵּין טוֹב וּבֵין רָע כְּעֶרְכְּךָ הַכֹּהֵן כֵּן יִהְיֶה: וְאִם־גָּאֹל יִגְאָלֶנָּה וְיָסַף

יד חֲמִישִׁתוֹ עַל־עֶרְכֶּךָ: וְאִישׁ כִּי־יַקְדִּשׁ אֶת־בֵּיתוֹ קֹּדֶשׁ לַיהוה וְהֶעֱרִיכוֹ

טו הַכֹּהֵן בֵּין טוֹב וּבֵין רָע כַּאֲשֶׁר יַעֲרִיךְ אֹתוֹ הַכֹּהֵן כֵּן יָקוּם: וְאִם־הַמַּקְדִּישׁ
חמישי
[שביעי]

טז יִגְאַל אֶת־בֵּיתוֹ וְיָסַף חֲמִישִׁית כֶּסֶף־עֶרְכְּךָ עָלָיו וְהָיָה לוֹ: וְאִם | מִשְּׂדֵה

אֲחֻזָּתוֹ יַקְדִּישׁ אִישׁ לַיהוה וְהָיָה עֶרְכְּךָ לְפִי זַרְעוֹ זֶרַע חֹמֶר שְׂעֹרִים

יז-יח בַּחֲמִשִּׁים שֶׁקֶל כָּסֶף: אִם־מִשְּׁנַת הַיֹּבֵל יַקְדִּישׁ שָׂדֵהוּ כְּעֶרְכְּךָ יָקוּם: וְאִם־

אַחַר הַיֹּבֵל יַקְדִּישׁ שָׂדֵהוּ וְחִשַּׁב־לוֹ הַכֹּהֵן אֶת־הַכֶּסֶף עַל־פִּי הַשָּׁנִים

יט הַנּוֹתָרֹת עַד שְׁנַת הַיֹּבֵל וְנִגְרַע מֵעֶרְכֶּךָ: וְאִם־גָּאֹל יִגְאַל אֶת־הַשָּׂדֶה

כ הַמַּקְדִּישׁ אֹתוֹ וְיָסַף חֲמִשִׁית כֶּסֶף־עֶרְכְּךָ עָלָיו וְקָם לוֹ: וְאִם־לֹא יִגְאַל

כא אֶת־הַשָּׂדֶה וְאִם־מָכַר אֶת־הַשָּׂדֶה לְאִישׁ אַחֵר לֹא־יִגָּאֵל עוֹד: וְהָיָה

הַשָּׂדֶה בְּצֵאתוֹ בַיֹּבֵל קֹדֶשׁ לַיהוה כִּשְׂדֵה הַחֵרֶם לַכֹּהֵן תִּהְיֶה אֲחֻזָּתוֹ: וְאִם

כב-כג אֶת־שְׂדֵה מִקְנָתוֹ אֲשֶׁר לֹא מִשְּׂדֵה אֲחֻזָּתוֹ יַקְדִּישׁ לַיהוה: וְחִשַּׁב־לוֹ הַכֹּהֵן
ששי

26:46. The word וְהַתּוֹרֹת is in the plural because it refers to the two Torahs: the Written Torah and the Oral Torah. This verse emphasizes that both were given at Sinai (*Rashi; Sifra*).

27:1-8. One may vow to contribute the "value" of oneself or of another person or thing. Here the Torah speaks of a specific form of vow known as עֵרֶךְ, which, for lack of an exact English equivalent, we translate as *valuation*.

have been revolted by them nor will I have rejected them to obliterate them, to annul My covenant with them — for I am HASHEM, their God. ⁴⁵ I will remember for them the covenant of the ancients, those whom I have taken out of the land of Egypt before the eyes of the nations, to be God unto them — I am HASHEM.

⁴⁶ These are the decrees, the ordinances, and the teachings* that HASHEM gave, between Himself and the Children of Israel, at Mount Sinai, through Moses.

27

*Gifts to the Temple: Valuations**

¹ H ASHEM spoke to Moses, saying: ² Speak to the Children of Israel and say to them: If a man articulates a vow to HASHEM regarding a valuation of living beings, ³ the valuation of a male shall be: for someone twenty years to sixty years of age, the valuation shall be fifty silver shekels, of the sacred shekel. ⁴ If she is female, the valuation shall be thirty shekels. ⁵ And if from five to twenty years of age, the valuation of a male shall be twenty shekels and of a female ten shekels. ⁶ And if from one month to five years of age, the valuation of a male shall be five silver shekels; and for a female, the valuation shall be three silver shekels. ⁷ And if from sixty years and up, if for a male, the valuation shall be fifteen shekels; and for a female, ten shekels. ⁸ But if he is too poor for the valuation, then he should cause him to stand before the Kohen, and the Kohen should evaluate him; according to what the person making the vow can afford should the Kohen evaluate him. *

Sanctification and redemption of animals

⁹ If it is the kind of animal that one can bring as an offering to HASHEM, * whatever part of it he may give to HASHEM shall be holy. ¹⁰ He shall not exchange it nor substitute it, whether good for bad or bad for good; but if he does substitute one animal for another animal, then it and its substitute shall be holy. ¹¹ And if it is any disqualified animal from which they may not bring an offering to HASHEM, then he shall stand the animal before the Kohen. ¹² The Kohen shall evaluate it, whether good or bad; like the Kohen's valuation so shall it be. ¹³ If he redeems it, he must add a fifth to the valuation. *

Redemption of houses and fields

¹⁴ If a man consecrates his house to be holy to HASHEM, the Kohen shall evaluate it, whether good or bad; as the Kohen shall evaluate it, so shall it remain. ¹⁵ If the one who sanctified it will redeem his house, he shall add a fifth of the money-valuation to it, and it shall be his.

¹⁶ If a man consecrates a field from his ancestral heritage to HASHEM, the valuation shall be according to its seeding: an area seeded by a chomer of barley for fifty silver shekels. ¹⁷ If he consecrates his field from the Jubilee Year, it shall remain at its valuation. ¹⁸ And if he consecrates his field after the Jubilee, the Kohen shall calculate the money for him according to the remaining years until the Jubilee Year, and it shall be subtracted from its valuation. ¹⁹ If the one who consecrated the field will redeem it, he shall add a fifth of the money-valuation to it, and it shall be his. ²⁰ But if he does not redeem the field, or if he had sold the field to another man — it cannot be redeemed anymore. ²¹ Then, when the field goes out in the Jubilee, it will be holy to HASHEM, like a segregated field; his ancestral heritage shall become the Kohen's.

²² But if he will consecrate to HASHEM a field that he acquired, that is not of the field of his ancestral heritage, ²³ then the Kohen shall calculate for him

---

27:9-13. If an animal is sanctified for use as an offering, and it is not suitable — blemished, for example — it is   redeemed and its value used for the offering for which the animal was originally dedicated.

אֶת מִכְסַ֣ת הָֽעֶרְכְּךָ֗ עַ֚ד שְׁנַ֣ת הַיֹּבֵ֔ל וְנָתַ֤ן אֶת־הָעֶרְכְּךָ֙ בַּיּ֥וֹם הַה֖וּא קֹ֥דֶשׁ

כד לַֽיהוָֽה: בִּשְׁנַ֤ת הַיּוֹבֵל֙ יָשׁ֣וּב הַשָּׂדֶ֔ה לַֽאֲשֶׁ֥ר קָנָ֖הוּ מֵֽאִתּ֑וֹ לַֽאֲשֶׁר־ל֖וֹ אֲחֻזַּ֥ת

כה-כו הָאָֽרֶץ: וְכָל־עֶרְכְּךָ֔ יִֽהְיֶ֖ה בְּשֶׁ֣קֶל הַקֹּ֑דֶשׁ עֶשְׂרִ֥ים גֵּרָ֖ה יִֽהְיֶ֥ה הַשָּֽׁקֶל: אַךְ־

בְּכ֡וֹר אֲשֶׁר־יְבֻכַּ֨ר לַֽיהוָה֙ בִּבְהֵמָ֔ה לֹֽא־יַקְדִּ֥ישׁ אִ֖ישׁ אֹת֑וֹ אִם־שׁ֣וֹר אִם־

כז שֶׂ֔ה לַֽיהוָ֖ה הֽוּא: וְאִ֨ם בַּבְּהֵמָ֤ה הַטְּמֵאָה֙ וּפָדָ֣ה בְעֶרְכֶּ֔ךָ וְיָסַ֥ף חֲמִֽשִׁת֖וֹ

עָלָ֑יו וְאִם־לֹ֥א יִגָּאֵ֖ל וְנִמְכַּ֥ר בְּעֶרְכֶּֽךָ: **כח** אַ֣ךְ כָּל־חֵ֡רֶם אֲשֶׁ֣ר יַֽחֲרִם֩ אִ֨ישׁ

לַֽיהוָ֜ה מִכָּל־אֲשֶׁר־ל֗וֹ מֵֽאָדָ֤ם וּבְהֵמָה֙ וּמִשְּׂדֵ֣ה אֲחֻזָּת֔וֹ לֹ֥א יִמָּכֵ֖ר וְלֹ֣א

כט יִגָּאֵ֑ל כָּל־חֵ֕רֶם קֹֽדֶשׁ־קָֽדָשִׁ֥ים ה֖וּא לַֽיהוָֽה: כָּל־חֵ֗רֶם אֲשֶׁ֧ר יָֽחֳרַ֛ם מִן־

ל הָֽאָדָ֖ם לֹ֣א יִפָּדֶ֑ה מ֖וֹת יוּמָֽת: וְכָל־מַעְשַׂ֨ר הָאָ֜רֶץ מִזֶּ֤רַע הָאָ֨רֶץ֙ מִפְּרִ֣י הָעֵ֔ץ

לא לַֽיהוָ֖ה ה֑וּא קֹ֖דֶשׁ לַֽיהוָֽה: וְאִם־גָּאֹ֥ל יִגְאַ֛ל אִ֖ישׁ מִמַּֽעַשְׂר֑וֹ חֲמִֽשִׁית֖וֹ יֹסֵ֥ף

לב עָלָֽיו: וְכָל־מַעְשַׂ֤ר בָּקָר֙ וָצֹ֔אן כֹּ֥ל אֲשֶׁר־יַֽעֲבֹ֖ר תַּ֣חַת הַשָּׁ֑בֶט הָֽעֲשִׂירִ֕י

לג יִֽהְיֶה־קֹּ֖דֶשׁ לַֽיהוָֽה: לֹ֧א יְבַקֵּ֛ר בֵּֽין־ט֥וֹב לָרַ֖ע וְלֹ֣א יְמִירֶ֑נּוּ וְאִם־הָמֵ֣ר

לד יְמִירֶ֔נּוּ וְהָֽיָה־ה֧וּא וּתְמֽוּרָת֛וֹ יִֽהְיֶה־קֹּ֖דֶשׁ לֹ֣א יִגָּאֵ֑ל: אֵ֣לֶּה הַמִּצְוֺ֗ת אֲשֶׁ֨ר

צִוָּ֧ה יְהוָ֛ה אֶת־מֹשֶׁ֖ה אֶל־בְּנֵ֣י יִשְׂרָאֵ֑ל בְּהַ֖ר סִינָֽי:

שביעי / מפטיר

Haftaras Bechukosai: p. 1110

It is customary for the congregation followed by the reader to proclaim:

חֲזַק! חֲזַק! וְנִתְחַזֵּק!

סכום פסוקי דספר ויקרא שמונה מאות וחמשים ותשעה. נט"ף סימן.

27:28-29. Cherem/Segregated property. In the context of this passage, the word *cherem* refers to a person's expressed resolution to consecrate an object and thus make it forbidden for personal use (*Ralbag*).

27:30-31. The second tithe. During the first, second, fourth, and fifth years of the seven-year *Shemittah* cycle, a farmer sets aside one-tenth of his produce, which he must take to Jerusalem to be eaten. It is known as מַעֲשֵׂר שֵׁנִי, *second tithe*, because it is separated from the crop only after the first tithe is separated for the Levite. The Torah permits the owner to redeem the tithe for coins, which he must take to the Holy City and use to purchase food or offerings that may be eaten. [See also *Deuteronomy* 14:22-27.]

the sum of the valuation until the Jubilee Year; and he shall pay the valuation of that day, it is holy to HASHEM. ²⁴ In the Jubilee Year the field shall return to the one from whom he acquired it; whose ancestral heritage of the land it was. ²⁵ Every valuation shall be in the sacred shekel; that shekel shall be twenty gera.

²⁶ However, a firstborn that will become a firstling for HASHEM among livestock, a man shall not consecrate it; whether it is of oxen or of the flock, it is HASHEM's. ²⁷ If among the unclean animals, he shall redeem it according to the valuation and add a fifth to it; and if it is not redeemed it shall be sold for its valuation.

Cherem/
Segregated
property

²⁸ However, any segregated property that a man will segregate for the sake of HASHEM, from anything that is his — whether human, animal, or the field of his ancestral heritage — may not be sold and may not be redeemed, any segregated item may be most holy to HASHEM.

²⁹ Any condemned person who has been banned from mankind shall not be redeemed; he shall be put to death.

The
second title

³⁰ Any tithe of the land, of the seed of the land, of the fruit of the tree, belongs to HASHEM; it is holy to HASHEM. ³¹ If a person shall redeem some of his tithe, he shall add his fifth to it.

The tithe
of animals
(See Appendix B,
charts 6-7)

³² Any tithe of cattle or of the flock, any that passes under the staff, the tenth one shall be holy to HASHEM. ³³ He shall not distinguish between good and bad and he should not substitute for it; and if he does substitute for it, then it and its substitute shall be holy, it may not be redeemed.

³⁴ These are the commandments that HASHEM commanded Moses to the Children of Israel on Mount Sinai.

It is customary for the congregation followed by the reader to proclaim:

"Chazak! Chazak! Venischazeik!
(Be strong! Be strong! And may we be strengthened!)"

27:32-33. The tithe of animals. The newborn herd or flock is put into a corral with a narrow opening, and the animals are allowed to leave one by one. The owner or his designee touches each tenth one with a paint-daubed stick, marking it as *maaser*, or the tithe (*Rashi; Bechoros* 58b).

Numbers במדבר

*T*he Book of Numbers begins and ends with Israel on the verge of entering its Land — but the thirty-eight intervening years of wandering in the Wilderness were a low point in Jewish history. This Book contains the episode of the spies, who poisoned the minds of the people, the rebellion of Korah and his assembly, and the error of Moses and Aaron that cost them the privilege of entering the land. But it also ends with the first step in the conquest of the Land of Israel.

In Talmudic and Rabbinic literature, the Book is known as Chumash HaPekudim, the Book of Numbers, because one of its major themes is the census of the people. At its outset, the members of the tribes were counted individually, as every Jew passed in front of Moses and Aaron and presented proof of his tribal descent. What an awesome experience it must have been for even the humblest Jew to stand before his two leaders — the greatest prophet who ever lived and God's holy servant — to identify himself and to receive their blessing and guidance! Once counted, the tribes were arrayed around the Tabernacle, demonstrating that the Presence of God was their rallying point, the central focus of the nation, then and always. For Jews are a nation by virtue of the Torah; it is their raison d'etre. By accepting it they became a people, and by following it they remain a people. There in the Wilderness, the people were to encamp around the Tabernacle which contained the Tablets of the Law, and march with it wherever God led them. That leitmotif of Jewish nationhood would continue throughout its history. As it has been aptly said, "More than the Jews have preserved the Sabbath, the Sabbath has preserved the Jews."

Rashi notes at the beginning of the Book that God counted the nation at every significant turn because He loves it. So, too, the fact that the people were counted as individuals proves the infinite worth of every Jew. Certainly it would have been easier and quicker to count the people en masse, and that would have been the proper course if all that mattered was sheer numbers. But that would have caused the individual to be an insignificant member of the total community and it would have obscured his personal responsibility to grow and contribute. Each tribe had its own uniqueness to contribute to the national well-being and each individual was precious in his own right.

True, this Book tells how the nation slid and an entire generation had to remain in the Wilderness and expire. But their children emerged strong and courageous, still gathered around the Tabernacle and ready to claim its destiny as the heirs to the blessings of Abraham, Isaac, and Jacob.

פרשת במדבר

א א וַיְדַבֵּ֨ר יהוָ֧ה אֶל־מֹשֶׁ֛ה בְּמִדְבַּ֥ר סִינַ֖י בְּאֹ֣הֶל מוֹעֵ֑ד בְּאֶחָד֩ לַחֹ֨דֶשׁ הַשֵּׁנִ֜י
ב בַּשָּׁנָ֣ה הַשֵּׁנִ֗ית לְצֵאתָ֛ם מֵאֶ֥רֶץ מִצְרַ֖יִם לֵאמֹֽר: שְׂא֗וּ אֶת־רֹאשׁ֙ כָּל־עֲדַ֣ת
בְּנֵֽי־יִשְׂרָאֵ֔ל לְמִשְׁפְּחֹתָ֖ם לְבֵ֣ית אֲבֹתָ֑ם בְּמִסְפַּ֣ר שֵׁמ֔וֹת כָּל־זָכָ֖ר
ג לְגֻלְגְּלֹתָֽם: מִבֶּ֨ן עֶשְׂרִ֤ים שָׁנָה֙ וָמַ֔עְלָה כָּל־יֹצֵ֥א צָבָ֖א בְּיִשְׂרָאֵ֑ל תִּפְקְד֥וּ
ד אֹתָ֛ם לְצִבְאֹתָ֖ם אַתָּ֥ה וְאַֽהֲרֹֽן: וְאִתְּכֶ֣ם יִֽהְי֔וּ אִ֥ישׁ אִ֖ישׁ לַמַּטֶּ֑ה אִ֛ישׁ רֹ֥אשׁ
ה לְבֵית־אֲבֹתָ֖יו הֽוּא: וְאֵ֨לֶּה֙ שְׁמ֣וֹת הָֽאֲנָשִׁ֔ים אֲשֶׁ֥ר יַֽעַמְד֖וּ אִתְּכֶ֑ם לִרְאוּבֵ֕ן
ו אֱלִיצ֖וּר בֶּן־שְׁדֵיאֽוּר: לְשִׁמְע֕וֹן שְׁלֻֽמִיאֵ֖ל בֶּן־צוּרִֽישַׁדָּֽי: לִֽיהוּדָ֕ה נַחְשׁ֖וֹן
ז בֶּן־עַמִּֽינָדָֽב: לְיִ֨שָּׂשכָ֔ר נְתַנְאֵ֖ל בֶּן־צוּעָֽר: לִזְבוּלֻ֕ן אֱלִיאָ֖ב בֶּן־חֵלֹֽן: לִבְנֵ֣י
ח יוֹסֵ֔ף לְאֶפְרַ֕יִם אֱלִֽישָׁמָ֖ע בֶּן־עַמִּיה֑וּד לִמְנַשֶּׁ֕ה גַּמְלִיאֵ֖ל בֶּן־פְּדָהצֽוּר:
י לְבִ֨נְיָמִ֔ן אֲבִידָ֖ן בֶּן־גִּדְעֹנִֽי: לְדָ֕ן אֲחִיעֶ֖זֶר בֶּן־עַמִּֽישַׁדָּֽי: לְאָשֵׁ֕ר פַּגְעִיאֵ֖ל בֶּן־
יא-יג עָכְרָ֑ן לְגָ֕ד אֶלְיָסָ֖ף בֶּן־דְּעוּאֵֽל: לְנַ֨פְתָּלִ֔י אֲחִירַ֖ע בֶּן־עֵינָֽן: אֵ֚לֶּה °קְרִיאֵ֣י
יד-טו [קְרוּאֵ֣י ק] הָֽעֵדָ֔ה נְשִׂיאֵ֖י מַטּ֣וֹת אֲבוֹתָ֑ם רָאשֵׁ֛י אַלְפֵ֥י יִשְׂרָאֵ֖ל הֵֽם: וַיִּקַּ֣ח
טז מֹשֶׁ֖ה וְאַֽהֲרֹ֑ן אֵ֚ת הָֽאֲנָשִׁ֣ים הָאֵ֔לֶּה אֲשֶׁ֥ר נִקְּב֖וּ בְּשֵׁמֽוֹת: וְאֵ֣ת כָּל־הָֽעֵדָ֗ה
יז הִקְהִ֨ילוּ֙ בְּאֶחָ֣ד לַחֹ֣דֶשׁ הַשֵּׁנִ֔י וַיִּֽתְיַֽלְד֥וּ עַל־מִשְׁפְּחֹתָ֖ם לְבֵ֣ית אֲבֹתָ֑ם
יח בְּמִסְפַּ֣ר שֵׁמ֗וֹת מִבֶּ֨ן עֶשְׂרִ֥ים שָׁנָ֛ה וָמַ֖עְלָה לְגֻלְגְּלֹתָֽם: כַּֽאֲשֶׁ֛ר צִוָּ֥ה יהוָ֖ה

שני
יט אֶת־מֹשֶׁ֑ה וַֽיִּפְקְדֵ֖ם בְּמִדְבַּ֥ר סִינָֽי: וַיִּֽהְי֤וּ בְנֵֽי־רְאוּבֵן֙ בְּכֹ֣ר
כ יִשְׂרָאֵ֔ל תּֽוֹלְדֹתָ֥ם לְמִשְׁפְּחֹתָ֖ם לְבֵ֣ית אֲבֹתָ֑ם בְּמִסְפַּ֤ר שֵׁמוֹת֙ לְגֻלְגְּלֹתָ֔ם
כא כָּל־זָכָ֗ר מִבֶּ֨ן עֶשְׂרִ֤ים שָׁנָה֙ וָמַ֔עְלָה כֹּ֖ל יֹצֵ֣א צָבָֽא: פְּקֻֽדֵיהֶ֖ם לְמַטֵּ֣ה רְאוּבֵ֑ן
שִׁשָּׁ֧ה וְאַרְבָּעִ֛ים אֶ֖לֶף וַֽחֲמֵ֥שׁ מֵאֽוֹת:
כב לִבְנֵ֣י שִׁמְע֗וֹן תּֽוֹלְדֹתָ֤ם לְמִשְׁפְּחֹתָם֙ לְבֵ֣ית אֲבֹתָ֔ם פְּקֻדָ֕יו בְּמִסְפַּ֣ר שֵׁמ֔וֹת
כג לְגֻלְגְּלֹתָ֔ם כָּל־זָכָ֗ר מִבֶּ֨ן עֶשְׂרִ֤ים שָׁנָה֙ וָמַ֔עְלָה כֹּ֖ל יֹצֵ֣א צָבָֽא: פְּקֻֽדֵיהֶ֖ם
לְמַטֵּ֣ה שִׁמְע֑וֹן תִּשְׁעָ֧ה וַֽחֲמִשִּׁ֛ים אֶ֖לֶף וּשְׁלֹ֥שׁ מֵאֽוֹת:
כד לִבְנֵ֣י גָ֔ד תּֽוֹלְדֹתָ֥ם לְמִשְׁפְּחֹתָ֖ם לְבֵ֣ית אֲבֹתָ֑ם בְּמִסְפַּ֣ר שֵׁמ֔וֹת מִבֶּ֨ן עֶשְׂרִ֤ים
כה שָׁנָה֙ וָמַ֔עְלָה כֹּ֖ל יֹצֵ֥א צָבָֽא: פְּקֻֽדֵיהֶ֖ם לְמַטֵּ֣ה גָ֑ד חֲמִשָּׁ֤ה וְאַרְבָּעִים֙ אֶ֔לֶף
וְשֵׁ֥שׁ מֵא֖וֹת וַֽחֲמִשִּֽׁים:
כו לִבְנֵ֣י יְהוּדָ֔ה תּֽוֹלְדֹתָ֥ם לְמִשְׁפְּחֹתָ֖ם לְבֵ֣ית אֲבֹתָ֑ם בְּמִסְפַּ֣ר שֵׁמֹ֔ת מִבֶּ֨ן

◈§ Parashas Bamidbar

The Book of *Bamidbar/Numbers* deals in great measure with the laws and history of the Tabernacle during Israel's years in the Wilderness. *Ramban* notes striking parallels between the Tabernacle, as seen through the light of these laws, and the Revelation at Sinai. These comparisons suggest that the Tabernacle — and later the Temple and the synagogue — was to serve as a permanent substitute for the Heavenly Presence that rested upon Israel at Sinai. By making the Tabernacle central to the nation, not only geographically but conceptually, the people would keep "Mount Sinai" among themselves always. Just as they had surrounded the mountain, longing for closeness to God, they would encamp around the Tabernacle symbolizing that their very existence was predicated on their closeness to the Torah.

Accordingly, the Book contains the commandments to safeguard the Tabernacle, for the tribes to be arrayed around it, and for the conduct of the Kohanim and the Levites when it was dismantled and transported. All of this enhances the glory and prestige of the Sanctuary, as illustrated by the parable of the Sages, "A royal palace that is not safeguarded is unlike one that is safeguarded" (*Sifrei Zuta, Korach* 8:14).

PARASHAS BAMIDBAR

1

Census in the Wilderness*
(See Appendix B, chart 11)

The tribal leaders

¹ HASHEM spoke to Moses in the Wilderness of Sinai, in the Tent of Meeting, on the first of the second month, in the second year after their exodus from the land of Egypt, saying:

² "Take a census of the entire assembly of the Children of Israel according to their families, according to their fathers' household, * by number of the names, every male according to their head count. ³ From twenty years of age and up — everyone who goes out to the legion in Israel — you shall count them according to their legions, you and Aaron. ⁴ And with you shall be one man from each tribe; a man who is a leader* of his fathers' household.

⁵ "These are the names of the men who shall stand with you: For Reuben, Elizur son of Shedeur. ⁶ For Simeon, Shelumiel son of Zurishaddai. ⁷ For Judah, Nahshon son of Amminadab. ⁸ For Issachar, Nethanel son of Zuar. ⁹ For Zebulun, Eliab son of Helon. ¹⁰ For the children of Joseph — for Ephraim, Elishama son of Ammihud; for Manasseh, Gamaliel son of Pedahzur. ¹¹ For Benjamin, Abidan son of Gideoni. ¹² For Dan, Ahiezer son of Ammishaddai. ¹³ For Asher, Pagiel son of Ochran. ¹⁴ For Gad, Eliasaph son of Deuel. ¹⁵ For Naphtali, Ahira son of Enan."

¹⁶ These were the ones summoned by the assembly, the leaders of their fathers' tribes, they are the heads of Israel's thousands. ¹⁷ Moses and Aaron took these men who had been designated by [their] names.

¹⁸ They gathered together the entire assembly on the first of the second month, and they established their genealogy according to their families, according to their fathers' household, by number of the names, from twenty years of age and up, according to their head count. ¹⁹ As HASHEM had commanded Moses, he counted them in the Wilderness of Sinai.

Reuben

²⁰ These were the sons of Reuben, firstborn of Israel, their offspring according to their families, according to their fathers' household, by number of the names according to their head count, every male from twenty years of age and up, everyone who goes out to the legion.²¹ Their count, for the tribe of Reuben: forty-six thousand, five hundred.

Simeon

²² For the sons of Simeon, their offspring according to their families, according to their fathers' household, its numbers, by number of the names according to their head count, every male from twenty years of age and up, everyone who goes out to the legion. ²³ Their count, for the tribe of Simeon: fifty-nine thousand, three hundred.

Gad

²⁴ For the sons of Gad, their offspring according to their families, according to their fathers' household, by number of the names, from twenty years of age and up, everyone who goes out to the legion. ²⁵ Their count, for the tribe of Gad: forty-five thousand, six hundred and fifty.

Judah

²⁶ For the sons of Judah, their offspring according to their families, according to their fathers' household, by number of the names, from

---

1:1-19. God commanded Moses and Aaron to take a tribe-by-tribe census of all males above the age of twenty.

1:2. A person's tribal affiliation is patrilineal. Thus, for example, a Jew with a father from Judah and a mother from Asher belonged to the tribe of Judah (*Rashi*).

Nationality, however, is matrilineal, so that the child of a Jewish father and a gentile mother is a gentile.

1:4-15. Moses and Aaron would count each tribe with the participation of its own leader (*Rashi*), who would be knowledgeable concerning the lineage of his tribe's members (*Sforno*).

כז עֶשְׂרִים שָׁנָה וָמַעְלָה כָּל יֹצֵא צָבָא: פְּקֻדֵיהֶם לְמַטֵּה יְהוּדָה אַרְבָּעָה
וְשִׁבְעִים אֶלֶף וְשֵׁשׁ מֵאוֹת:

כח לִבְנֵי יִשָּׂשכָר תּוֹלְדֹתָם לְמִשְׁפְּחֹתָם לְבֵית אֲבֹתָם בְּמִסְפַּר שֵׁמֹת מִבֶּן
כט עֶשְׂרִים שָׁנָה וָמַעְלָה כָּל יֹצֵא צָבָא: פְּקֻדֵיהֶם לְמַטֵּה יִשָּׂשכָר אַרְבָּעָה
וַחֲמִשִּׁים אֶלֶף וְאַרְבַּע מֵאוֹת:

ל לִבְנֵי זְבוּלֻן תּוֹלְדֹתָם לְמִשְׁפְּחֹתָם לְבֵית אֲבֹתָם בְּמִסְפַּר שֵׁמֹת מִבֶּן
לא עֶשְׂרִים שָׁנָה וָמַעְלָה כָּל יֹצֵא צָבָא: פְּקֻדֵיהֶם לְמַטֵּה זְבוּלֻן שִׁבְעָה
וַחֲמִשִּׁים אֶלֶף וְאַרְבַּע מֵאוֹת:

לב לִבְנֵי יוֹסֵף לִבְנֵי אֶפְרַיִם תּוֹלְדֹתָם לְמִשְׁפְּחֹתָם לְבֵית אֲבֹתָם בְּמִסְפַּר
לג שֵׁמֹת מִבֶּן עֶשְׂרִים שָׁנָה וָמַעְלָה כָּל יֹצֵא צָבָא: פְּקֻדֵיהֶם לְמַטֵּה אֶפְרַיִם
אַרְבָּעִים אֶלֶף וַחֲמֵשׁ מֵאוֹת:

לד לִבְנֵי מְנַשֶּׁה תּוֹלְדֹתָם לְמִשְׁפְּחֹתָם לְבֵית אֲבֹתָם בְּמִסְפַּר שֵׁמוֹת מִבֶּן
לה עֶשְׂרִים שָׁנָה וָמַעְלָה כָּל יֹצֵא צָבָא: פְּקֻדֵיהֶם לְמַטֵּה מְנַשֶּׁה שְׁנַיִם
וּשְׁלֹשִׁים אֶלֶף וּמָאתָיִם:

לו לִבְנֵי בִנְיָמִן תּוֹלְדֹתָם לְמִשְׁפְּחֹתָם לְבֵית אֲבֹתָם בְּמִסְפַּר שֵׁמֹת מִבֶּן
לז עֶשְׂרִים שָׁנָה וָמַעְלָה כָּל יֹצֵא צָבָא: פְּקֻדֵיהֶם לְמַטֵּה בִנְיָמִן חֲמִשָּׁה
וּשְׁלֹשִׁים אֶלֶף וְאַרְבַּע מֵאוֹת:

לח לִבְנֵי דָן תּוֹלְדֹתָם לְמִשְׁפְּחֹתָם לְבֵית אֲבֹתָם בְּמִסְפַּר שֵׁמֹת מִבֶּן עֶשְׂרִים
לט שָׁנָה וָמַעְלָה כָּל יֹצֵא צָבָא: פְּקֻדֵיהֶם לְמַטֵּה דָן שְׁנַיִם וְשִׁשִּׁים אֶלֶף וּשְׁבַע
מֵאוֹת:

מ לִבְנֵי אָשֵׁר תּוֹלְדֹתָם לְמִשְׁפְּחֹתָם לְבֵית אֲבֹתָם בְּמִסְפַּר שֵׁמֹת מִבֶּן
מא עֶשְׂרִים שָׁנָה וָמַעְלָה כָּל יֹצֵא צָבָא: פְּקֻדֵיהֶם לְמַטֵּה אָשֵׁר אֶחָד
וְאַרְבָּעִים אֶלֶף וַחֲמֵשׁ מֵאוֹת:

מב בְּנֵי נַפְתָּלִי תּוֹלְדֹתָם לְמִשְׁפְּחֹתָם לְבֵית אֲבֹתָם בְּמִסְפַּר שֵׁמֹת מִבֶּן
מג עֶשְׂרִים שָׁנָה וָמַעְלָה כָּל יֹצֵא צָבָא: פְּקֻדֵיהֶם לְמַטֵּה נַפְתָּלִי שְׁלֹשָׁה
וַחֲמִשִּׁים אֶלֶף וְאַרְבַּע מֵאוֹת:

מד אֵלֶּה הַפְּקֻדִים אֲשֶׁר פָּקַד מֹשֶׁה וְאַהֲרֹן וּנְשִׂיאֵי יִשְׂרָאֵל שְׁנֵים עָשָׂר אִישׁ
מה אִישׁ אֶחָד לְבֵית אֲבֹתָיו הָיוּ: וַיִּהְיוּ כָּל פְּקוּדֵי בְנֵי יִשְׂרָאֵל לְבֵית אֲבֹתָם
מו מִבֶּן עֶשְׂרִים שָׁנָה וָמַעְלָה כָּל יֹצֵא צָבָא בְּיִשְׂרָאֵל: וַיִּהְיוּ כָּל הַפְּקֻדִים
מז שֵׁשׁ מֵאוֹת אֶלֶף וּשְׁלֹשֶׁת אֲלָפִים וַחֲמֵשׁ מֵאוֹת וַחֲמִשִּׁים: וְהַלְוִיִּם לְמַטֵּה
אֲבֹתָם לֹא הָתְפָּקְדוּ בְּתוֹכָם:

מח-מט וַיְדַבֵּר יְהוָה אֶל מֹשֶׁה לֵּאמֹר: אַךְ אֶת מַטֵּה לֵוִי לֹא תִפְקֹד וְאֶת רֹאשָׁם
נ לֹא תִשָּׂא בְּתוֹךְ בְּנֵי יִשְׂרָאֵל: וְאַתָּה הַפְקֵד אֶת הַלְוִיִּם עַל מִשְׁכַּן הָעֵדֻת

1:47-54. Having shown their loyalty to God in the aftermath of the Golden Calf (*Exodus* 32: 26-29), the

Levites were now to be elevated to the status of God's own legion. This new status was given expression in twenty years of age and up, everyone who goes out to the legion. [27] Their count, for the tribe of Judah: seventy-four thousand, six hundred.

Issachar   [28] For the sons of Issachar, their offspring according to their families, according to their fathers' household, by number of the names, from twenty years of age and up, everyone who goes out to the legion. [29] Their count, for the tribe of Issachar: fifty-four thousand, four hundred.

Zebulun   [30] For the sons of Zebulun, their offspring according to their families, according to their fathers' household, by number of the names, from twenty years of age and up, everyone who goes out to the legion. [31] Their count, for the tribe of Zebulun: fifty-seven thousand, four hundred.

Ephraim   [32] For the sons of Joseph: for the sons of Ephraim, their offspring according to their families, according to their fathers' household, by number of the names, from twenty years of age and up, everyone who goes out to the legion. [33] Their count, for the tribe of Ephraim: forty thousand, five hundred.

Manasseh   [34] For the sons of Manasseh, their offspring according to their families, according to their fathers' household, by number of the names, from twenty years of age and up, everyone who goes out to the legion. [35] Their count, for the tribe of Manasseh: thirty-two thousand, two hundred.

Benjamin   [36] For the sons of Benjamin, their offspring according to their families, according to their fathers' household, by number of the names, from twenty years of age and up, everyone who goes out to the legion. [37] Their count, for the tribe of Benjamin: thirty-five thousand, four hundred.

Dan   [38] For the sons of Dan, their offspring according to their families, according to their fathers' household, by number of the names, from twenty years of age and up, everyone who goes out to the legion. [39] Their count, for the tribe of Dan: sixty-two thousand, seven hundred.

Asher   [40] For the sons of Asher, their offspring according to their families, according to their fathers' household, by numbers of the names, from twenty years of age and up, everyone who goes out to the legion. [41] Their count, for the tribe of Asher: forty-one thousand, five hundred.

Naphtali   [42] The sons of Naphtali, their offspring according to their families, according to their fathers' household, by number of the names, from twenty years of age and up, everyone who goes out to the legion. [43] Their count, for the tribe of Naphtali: fifty-three thousand, four hundred.

The total   [44] These are the countings that Moses, Aaron, and the leaders of Israel counted — twelve men, one man for his father's household, were they — [45] these were all the countings of the Children of Israel, according to their fathers' households, from twenty years of age and up, everyone who goes out to the legion in Israel: [46] All their countings were six hundred and three thousand, five hundred and fifty.

The Levites: [47] The Levites* according to their fathers' tribe were not counted among them.

The legion of   [48] HASHEM spoke to Moses, saying, [49] "But you shall not count the tribe
God   of Levi, and you shall not take a census of them among the Children of Israel. [50] Now you, appoint the Levites over the Tabernacle of the Testimony,

---

three ways: (a) The Levites would be counted separately and differently from the rest of the population (see ch. 3); (b) they would be assigned to guard the Tabernacle and its Courtyard, and to dismantle and transport the Tabernacle during the nation's travels (see ch. 4); and (c) the Levite camp would surround the Tabernacle, with the rest of the nation around their camp.

וְעַל כָּל־כֵּלָיו וְעַל כָּל־אֲשֶׁר־לוֹ הֵמָּה יִשְׂאוּ אֶת־הַמִּשְׁכָּן וְאֶת־כָּל־כֵּלָיו

נא וְהֵם יְשָׁרְתֻהוּ וְסָבִיב לַמִּשְׁכָּן יַחֲנוּ: וּבִנְסֹעַ הַמִּשְׁכָּן יוֹרִידוּ אֹתוֹ הַלְוִיִּם

נב וּבַחֲנֹת הַמִּשְׁכָּן יָקִימוּ אֹתוֹ הַלְוִיִּם וְהַזָּר הַקָּרֵב יוּמָת: וְחָנוּ בְּנֵי יִשְׂרָאֵל

נג אִישׁ עַל־מַחֲנֵהוּ וְאִישׁ עַל־דִּגְלוֹ לְצִבְאֹתָם: וְהַלְוִיִּם יַחֲנוּ סָבִיב לְמִשְׁכַּן הָעֵדֻת וְלֹא־יִהְיֶה קֶצֶף עַל־עֲדַת בְּנֵי יִשְׂרָאֵל וְשָׁמְרוּ הַלְוִיִּם אֶת־

נד מִשְׁמֶרֶת מִשְׁכַּן הָעֵדוּת: וַיַּעֲשׂוּ בְּנֵי יִשְׂרָאֵל כְּכֹל אֲשֶׁר צִוָּה יהוה אֶת־מֹשֶׁה כֵּן עָשׂוּ:

ב שלישי א־ב וַיְדַבֵּר יהוה אֶל־מֹשֶׁה וְאֶל־אַהֲרֹן לֵאמֹר: אִישׁ עַל־דִּגְלוֹ בְאֹתֹת לְבֵית

ג אֲבֹתָם יַחֲנוּ בְּנֵי יִשְׂרָאֵל מִנֶּגֶד סָבִיב לְאֹהֶל־מוֹעֵד יַחֲנוּ: וְהַחֹנִים קֵדְמָה מִזְרָחָה דֶּגֶל מַחֲנֵה יְהוּדָה לְצִבְאֹתָם וְנָשִׂיא לִבְנֵי יְהוּדָה נַחְשׁוֹן בֶּן־

ד־ה עַמִּינָדָב: וּצְבָאוֹ וּפְקֻדֵיהֶם אַרְבָּעָה וְשִׁבְעִים אֶלֶף וְשֵׁשׁ מֵאוֹת: וְהַחֹנִים

ו עָלָיו מַטֵּה יִשָּׂשכָר וְנָשִׂיא לִבְנֵי יִשָּׂשכָר נְתַנְאֵל בֶּן־צוּעָר: וּצְבָאוֹ וּפְקֻדָיו

ז אַרְבָּעָה וַחֲמִשִּׁים אֶלֶף וְאַרְבַּע מֵאוֹת: מַטֵּה זְבוּלֻן וְנָשִׂיא לִבְנֵי זְבוּלֻן

ח אֱלִיאָב בֶּן־חֵלֹן: וּצְבָאוֹ וּפְקֻדָיו שִׁבְעָה וַחֲמִשִּׁים אֶלֶף וְאַרְבַּע מֵאוֹת:

ט כָּל־הַפְּקֻדִים לְמַחֲנֵה יְהוּדָה מְאַת אֶלֶף וּשְׁמֹנִים אֶלֶף וְשֵׁשֶׁת־אֲלָפִים וְאַרְבַּע־מֵאוֹת לְצִבְאֹתָם רִאשֹׁנָה יִסָּעוּ: דֶּגֶל מַחֲנֵה

י רְאוּבֵן תֵּימָנָה לְצִבְאֹתָם וְנָשִׂיא לִבְנֵי רְאוּבֵן אֱלִיצוּר בֶּן־שְׁדֵיאוּר:

יא־יב וּצְבָאוֹ וּפְקֻדָיו שִׁשָּׁה וְאַרְבָּעִים אֶלֶף וַחֲמֵשׁ מֵאוֹת: וְהַחוֹנִם עָלָיו מַטֵּה

יג שִׁמְעוֹן וְנָשִׂיא לִבְנֵי שִׁמְעוֹן שְׁלֻמִיאֵל בֶּן־צוּרִישַׁדָּי: וּצְבָאוֹ וּפְקֻדֵיהֶם

יד תִּשְׁעָה וַחֲמִשִּׁים אֶלֶף וּשְׁלֹשׁ מֵאוֹת: וּמַטֵּה גָּד וְנָשִׂיא לִבְנֵי גָד אֶלְיָסָף

טו בֶּן־רְעוּאֵל: וּצְבָאוֹ וּפְקֻדֵיהֶם חֲמִשָּׁה וְאַרְבָּעִים אֶלֶף וְשֵׁשׁ מֵאוֹת

טז וַחֲמִשִּׁים: כָּל־הַפְּקֻדִים לְמַחֲנֵה רְאוּבֵן מְאַת אֶלֶף וְאֶחָד וַחֲמִשִּׁים אֶלֶף וְאַרְבַּע־מֵאוֹת וַחֲמִשִּׁים לְצִבְאֹתָם וּשְׁנִיִּם יִסָּעוּ: וְנָסַע

יז אֹהֶל־מוֹעֵד מַחֲנֵה הַלְוִיִּם בְּתוֹךְ הַמַּחֲנֹת כַּאֲשֶׁר יַחֲנוּ כֵּן יִסָּעוּ אִישׁ עַל־יָדוֹ לְדִגְלֵיהֶם: דֶּגֶל מַחֲנֵה אֶפְרַיִם לְצִבְאֹתָם יָמָּה

יח־יט וְנָשִׂיא לִבְנֵי אֶפְרַיִם אֱלִישָׁמָע בֶּן־עַמִּיהוּד: וּצְבָאוֹ וּפְקֻדֵיהֶם אַרְבָּעִים

כ אֶלֶף וַחֲמֵשׁ מֵאוֹת: וְעָלָיו מַטֵּה מְנַשֶּׁה וְנָשִׂיא לִבְנֵי מְנַשֶּׁה גַּמְלִיאֵל

כא־כב בֶּן־פְּדָהצוּר: וּצְבָאוֹ וּפְקֻדֵיהֶם שְׁנַיִם וּשְׁלֹשִׁים אֶלֶף וּמָאתָיִם: וּמַטֵּה

כג בִנְיָמִן וְנָשִׂיא לִבְנֵי בִנְיָמִן אֲבִידָן בֶּן־גִּדְעֹנִי: וּצְבָאוֹ וּפְקֻדֵיהֶם חֲמִשָּׁה

כד וּשְׁלֹשִׁים אֶלֶף וְאַרְבַּע מֵאוֹת: כָּל־הַפְּקֻדִים לְמַחֲנֵה אֶפְרַיִם מְאַת אֶלֶף

כה וּשְׁמֹנַת־אֲלָפִים וּמֵאָה לְצִבְאֹתָם וּשְׁלִשִׁים יִסָּעוּ: דֶּגֶל

2:1-34. The central position of the Tabernacle and the Levites having been given briefly above, the Torah now turns to the twelve tribes. They were to be organized into formations of three tribes each — known as דְּגָלִים, *banners* — with each "banner" led by a designated tribe

(*Rashi* from *Tanchuma*).

2:3. As the progenitor of the Davidic monarchy whom Jacob called *lion* [symbolizing kingship (*Genesis* 49:9-10)], Judah was awarded the place of honor (*Kli Yakar*).

2:14. Above, in 1:14, he is called רְעוּאֵל, *Deuel*.

over all of its utensils and over everything that belongs to it. They shall carry the Tabernacle and all its utensils and they shall minister to it; and they shall encamp around the Tabernacle. ⁵¹ When the Tabernacle journeys, the Levites shall take it down, and when the Tabernacle encamps, the Levites shall erect it, and an alien who approaches shall die. ⁵² The Children of Israel shall encamp, every man at his camp and every man at his banner, according to their legions. ⁵³ The Levites shall encamp around the Tabernacle of the Testimony so that there shall be no wrath upon the assembly of the Children of Israel, and the Levites shall safeguard the watch of the Tabernacle of the Testimony."

⁵⁴ The Children of Israel did everything that HASHEM commanded Moses, so did they do.

2 ¹ H ASHEM spoke to Moses and Aaron, saying, ² "The Children of Israel shall encamp, * each man by his banner according to the insignias of their fathers' household, at a distance surrounding the Tent of Meeting shall they encamp. ³ Those who encamp to the front, at the east, shall be the banner of the camp of Judah * according to their legions — and the leader of the children of Judah is Nahshon son of Amminadab — ⁴ its legion and their count are seventy-four thousand, six hundred. ⁵ Those encamping near him are: the tribe of Issachar — and the leader of the children of Issachar is Nethanel son of Zuar — ⁶ its legion and their count are fifty-four thousand, four hundred; ⁷ the tribe of Zebulun — and the leader of the children of Zebulun is Eliab son of Helon — ⁸ its legion and their count are fifty-seven thousand, four hundred. ⁹ All those counted for the camp of Judah are one hundred and eighty-six thousand, four hundred, according to their legions; they shall be the first to journey.

The four formations: Judah's encampment — to the east

¹⁰ "The banner of the camp of Reuben shall be to the south, according to their legions — and the leader of the children of Reuben is Elizur son of Shedeur — ¹¹ its legion and their count are forty-six thousand, five hundred. ¹² Those encamping near him are: the tribe of Simeon — and the leader of the children of Simeon is Shelumiel son of Zurishaddai — ¹³ its legion and their count are fifty-nine thousand, three hundred; ¹⁴ and the tribe of Gad — and the leader of the children of Gad is Eliasaph son of Reuel * — ¹⁵ its legion and their count are forty-five thousand, six hundred and fifty. ¹⁶ All those counted for the camp of Reuben are one hundred and fifty-one thousand, four hundred and fifty, according to their legions, they shall be the second to journey.

Reuben's encampment — to the south

¹⁷ "The Tent of Meeting, the camp of the Levites, shall journey in the middle of the camps; as they encamp so shall they journey, everyone at his place according to their banners.

¹⁸ "The banner of the camp of Ephraim according to their legions shall be to the west — and the leader of the children of Ephraim is Elishama son of Ammihud — ¹⁹ its legion and their count are forty thousand, five hundred. ²⁰ Those [encamping] near him are: the tribe of Manasseh — and the leader of the children of Manasseh is Gamaliel son of Pedahzur — ²¹ its legion and their count are thirty-two thousand, two hundred; ²² and the tribe of Benjamin — and the leader of the children of Benjamin is Abidan son of Gideoni — ²³ its legion and their count are thirty-five thousand, four hundred. ²⁴ All those counted for the camp of Ephraim are one hundred and eight thousand, one hundred, according to their legions; they shall be the third to journey.

Ephraim's encampment — to the west

כו מַחֲנֵה דָן צָפֹ֑נָה וְנָשִׂיא לִבְנֵי דָ֔ן אֲחִיעֶ֖זֶר בֶּן־עַמִּֽישַׁדָּֽי: וּצְבָא֖וֹ

כז וּפְקֻדֵיהֶ֑ם שְׁנַ֤יִם וְשִׁשִּׁים֙ אֶ֣לֶף וּשְׁבַ֣ע מֵא֑וֹת: וְהַחֹנִ֥ים עָלָ֖יו מַטֵּ֣ה אָשֵׁ֑ר

כח וְנָשִׂיא֙ לִבְנֵ֣י אָשֵׁ֔ר פַּגְעִיאֵ֖ל בֶּן־עָכְרָֽן: וּצְבָא֖וֹ וּפְקֻדֵיהֶ֑ם אֶחָ֥ד וְאַרְבָּעִ֖ים

כט אֶ֖לֶף וַחֲמֵ֥שׁ מֵאֽוֹת: וּמַטֵּ֖ה נַפְתָּלִ֑י וְנָשִׂיא֙ לִבְנֵ֣י נַפְתָּלִ֔י אֲחִירַ֖ע בֶּן־עֵינָֽן:

ל-לא וּצְבָא֖וֹ וּפְקֻדֵיהֶ֑ם שְׁלֹשָׁ֥ה וַחֲמִשִּׁ֖ים אֶ֥לֶף וְאַרְבַּ֥ע מֵאֽוֹת: כָּל־הַפְּקֻדִ֣ים

לְמַחֲנֵ֣ה דָ֗ן מְאַ֤ת אֶ֙לֶף֙ וְשִׁבְעָ֤ה וַחֲמִשִּׁים֙ אֶ֔לֶף וְשֵׁ֥שׁ מֵא֑וֹת לָאַחֲרֹנָ֥ה יִסְע֖וּ

לִדְגְלֵיהֶֽם:

לב אֵ֣לֶּה פְּקוּדֵ֤י בְנֵֽי־יִשְׂרָאֵל֙ לְבֵ֣ית אֲבֹתָ֔ם כָּל־פְּקוּדֵ֥י הַֽמַּחֲנֹ֖ת לְצִבְאֹתָ֑ם

לג שֵׁשׁ־מֵא֥וֹת אֶ֙לֶף֙ וּשְׁלֹ֣שֶׁת אֲלָפִ֔ים וַחֲמֵ֥שׁ מֵא֖וֹת וַחֲמִשִּׁ֑ים: וְהַ֨לְוִיִּ֔ם לֹ֣א

לד הָתְפָּֽקְד֔וּ בְּת֖וֹךְ בְּנֵ֣י יִשְׂרָאֵ֑ל כַּאֲשֶׁ֛ר צִוָּ֥ה יְהֹוָ֖ה אֶת־מֹשֶֽׁה: וַיַּֽעֲשׂ֖וּ בְּנֵ֣י

יִשְׂרָאֵ֑ל כְּ֠כֹ֠ל אֲשֶׁר־צִוָּ֤ה יְהֹוָה֙ אֶת־מֹשֶׁ֔ה כֵּֽן־חָנ֥וּ לְדִגְלֵיהֶ֖ם וְכֵ֣ן נָסָ֑עוּ

אִ֥ישׁ לְמִשְׁפְּחֹתָ֖יו עַל־בֵּ֥ית אֲבֹתָֽיו:

ג רביעי א-ב וְאֵ֛לֶּה תּוֹלְדֹ֥ת אַהֲרֹ֖ן וּמֹשֶׁ֑ה בְּי֗וֹם דִּבֶּ֧ר יְהֹוָ֛ה אֶת־מֹשֶׁ֖ה בְּהַ֥ר סִינָֽי: וְאֵ֨לֶּה

ג שְׁמ֤וֹת בְּנֵֽי־אַהֲרֹן֙ הַבְּכ֣וֹר ׀ נָדָ֔ב וַאֲבִיה֖וּא אֶלְעָזָ֥ר וְאִיתָמָֽר: אֵ֗לֶּה שְׁמוֹת֙

ד בְּנֵ֤י אַהֲרֹן֙ הַכֹּהֲנִ֣ים הַמְּשֻׁחִ֔ים אֲשֶׁר־מִלֵּ֥א יָדָ֖ם לְכַהֵֽן: וַיָּ֣מָת נָדָ֣ב

וַאֲבִיה֡וּא לִפְנֵ֣י יְהֹוָ֡ה בְּֽהַקְרִבָם֩ אֵ֨שׁ זָרָ֜ה לִפְנֵ֤י יְהֹוָה֙ בְּמִדְבַּ֣ר סִינַ֔י וּבָנִ֖ים

לֹא־הָי֣וּ לָהֶ֑ם וַיְכַהֵ֤ן אֶלְעָזָר֙ וְאִ֣יתָמָ֔ר עַל־פְּנֵ֖י אַהֲרֹ֥ן אֲבִיהֶֽם:

ה-ו וַיְדַבֵּ֥ר יְהֹוָ֖ה אֶל־מֹשֶׁ֥ה לֵּאמֹֽר: הַקְרֵב֙ אֶת־מַטֵּ֣ה לֵוִ֔י וְהַֽעֲמַדְתָּ֣ אֹת֔וֹ לִפְנֵ֖י

ז אַהֲרֹ֣ן הַכֹּהֵ֑ן וְשֵׁרְת֖וּ אֹתֽוֹ: וְשָׁמְר֣וּ אֶת־מִשְׁמַרְתּ֗וֹ וְאֶת־מִשְׁמֶ֙רֶת֙ כָּל־

ח הָ֣עֵדָ֔ה לִפְנֵ֖י אֹ֣הֶל מוֹעֵ֑ד לַעֲבֹ֖ד אֶת־עֲבֹדַ֥ת הַמִּשְׁכָּֽן: וְשָׁמְר֗וּ אֶת־כָּל־כְּלֵי֙

אֹ֣הֶל מוֹעֵ֔ד וְאֶת־מִשְׁמֶ֖רֶת בְּנֵ֣י יִשְׂרָאֵ֑ל לַעֲבֹ֖ד אֶת־עֲבֹדַ֥ת הַמִּשְׁכָּֽן:

ט וְנָתַתָּה֙ אֶת־הַלְוִיִּ֔ם לְאַהֲרֹ֖ן וּלְבָנָ֑יו נְתוּנִ֨ם נְתוּנִ֥ם הֵ֙מָּה֙ ל֔וֹ מֵאֵ֖ת בְּנֵ֥י

י יִשְׂרָאֵֽל: וְאֶת־אַהֲרֹ֤ן וְאֶת־בָּנָיו֙ תִּפְקֹ֔ד וְשָׁמְר֖וּ אֶת־כְּהֻנָּתָ֑ם וְהַזָּ֥ר הַקָּרֵ֖ב

יוּמָֽת:

יא-יב וַיְדַבֵּ֥ר יְהֹוָ֖ה אֶל־מֹשֶׁ֥ה לֵּאמֹֽר: וַאֲנִ֞י הִנֵּ֧ה לָקַ֣חְתִּי אֶת־הַלְוִיִּ֗ם מִתּוֹךְ֙ בְּנֵ֣י

יג יִשְׂרָאֵ֔ל תַּ֥חַת כָּל־בְּכ֛וֹר פֶּ֥טֶר רֶ֖חֶם מִבְּנֵ֣י יִשְׂרָאֵ֑ל וְהָ֥יוּ לִ֖י הַלְוִיִּֽם: כִּ֣י לִ֞י

כָּל־בְּכוֹר֒ בְּיוֹם֩ הַכֹּתִ֨י כָל־בְּכוֹר֙ בְּאֶ֣רֶץ מִצְרַ֔יִם הִקְדַּ֥שְׁתִּי לִ֛י כָל־בְּכ֖וֹר

בְּיִשְׂרָאֵ֑ל מֵאָדָ֖ם עַד־בְּהֵמָ֑ה לִ֥י יִהְי֖וּ אֲנִ֥י יְהֹוָֽה:

חמישי יד-טו וַיְדַבֵּ֤ר יְהֹוָה֙ אֶל־מֹשֶׁ֔ה בְּמִדְבַּ֥ר סִינַ֖י לֵאמֹֽר: פְּקֹד֙ אֶת־בְּנֵ֣י לֵוִ֔י לְבֵ֥ית

טז אֲבֹתָ֖ם לְמִשְׁפְּחֹתָ֑ם כָּל־זָכָ֛ר מִבֶּן־חֹ֥דֶשׁ וָמַ֖עְלָה תִּפְקְדֵֽם: וַיִּפְקֹ֤ד אֹתָם֙

יז מֹשֶׁ֔ה עַל־פִּ֥י יְהֹוָ֖ה כַּאֲשֶׁ֥ר צֻוָּֽה: וַיִּֽהְיוּ־אֵ֥לֶּה בְנֵֽי־לֵוִ֖י בִּשְׁמֹתָ֑ם

יח גֵּרְשׁ֕וֹן וּקְהָ֖ת וּמְרָרִֽי: וְאֵ֛לֶּה שְׁמ֥וֹת בְּנֵֽי־גֵרְשׁ֖וֹן לְמִשְׁפְּחֹתָ֑ם לִבְנִ֥י

3:6. Moses was to place the Levites before Aaron to symbolize that they would henceforth be consecrated to assist the Kohanim (Rashi).

3:11-49. In their new status, the Levites replaced the firstborn, who had performed the service heretofore.

Dan's encampment — to the north ²⁵ "The banner of the camp of Dan shall be to the north, according to their legions — and the leader of the children of Dan is Ahiezer son of Ammishaddai — ²⁶ its legion and their count are sixty-two thousand, seven hundred. ²⁷ Those encamping near him are: the tribe of Asher — and the leader of the children of Asher is Pagiel son of Ochran — ²⁸ its legion and their count are forty-one thousand, five hundred; ²⁹ and the tribe of Naphtali — and the leader of the children of Naphtali is Ahira son of Enan — ³⁰ its legion and their count are fifty-three thousand, four hundred. ³¹ All those counted for the camp of Dan are one hundred and fifty-seven thousand, six hundred; they shall be the last to journey according to their banners."

The total ³² These are the countings of the Children of Israel according to their fathers' households; all the countings of the camps according to their legions, six hundred and three thousand, five hundred and fifty.

³³ The Levites were not counted among the Children of Israel, as HASHEM had commanded Moses. ³⁴ The Children of Israel did everything that HASHEM had commanded Moses — so they encamped according to their banners and so they journeyed; every man according to his families, by his fathers' household.

3

The progeny of Moses and Aaron ¹ These are the offspring of Aaron and Moses on the day HASHEM spoke with Moses at Mount Sinai: ² These are the names of the sons of Aaron, the firstborn was Nadab, and Abihu, Elazar, and Ithamar. ³ These were the names of the sons of Aaron, the anointed Kohanim, whom he inaugurated to minister. ⁴ Nadab and Abihu died before HASHEM when they offered an alien fire before HASHEM in the Wilderness of Sinai, and they had no children; but Elazar and Ithamar ministered during the lifetime of Aaron, their father.

Appointment of the Levites ⁵ HASHEM spoke to Moses, saying, ⁶ "Bring near the tribe of Levi and have it stand before Aaron the Kohen, and they shall serve him. * ⁷ They shall safeguard his charge and the charge of the entire assembly before the Tent of Meeting, to perform the service of the Tabernacle. ⁸ They shall safeguard all the utensils of the Tent of Meeting and the charge of the Children of Israel, to perform the service of the Tabernacle. ⁹ You shall present the Levites to Aaron and his sons — presented, presented are they to him — from the Children of Israel. ¹⁰ You shall appoint Aaron and his sons and they shall safeguard their priesthood; and the alien who approaches will die."

The Levites replace the firstborn ¹¹ HASHEM spoke to Moses, saying, ¹² "Behold! I have taken the Levites from among the Children of Israel, in place of every firstborn, * the first issue of a womb among the Children of Israel, and the Levites shall be Mine. ¹³ For every firstborn is Mine: On the day I struck down every firstborn in the land of Egypt I sanctified every firstborn in Israel for Myself, from man to beast; they shall be Mine — I am HASHEM."

Census of the Levites (See Appendix B, chart 12) ¹⁴ HASHEM spoke to Moses in the Wilderness of Sinai, saying, ¹⁵ "Count the sons of Levi* according to their fathers' household, according to their families, every male from one month of age and up shall you count them." ¹⁶ Moses counted them according to the word of HASHEM, as he had been commanded.

¹⁷ These were the sons of Levi, by their names: Gershon, Kohath, and Merari. ¹⁸ These were the names of the sons of Gershon according to their families: Libni

---

3:15. Whereas the other tribes were counted once, from the ages of twenty to sixty, the Levites would be counted twice. In this chapter, they would be counted from the age of one month and up, with no upper age-limit. They would be counted again from the ages of thirty to fifty (4:29).

יט-כ וְשִׁמְעִי: וּבְנֵי קְהָת לְמִשְׁפְּחֹתָם עַמְרָם וְיִצְהָר חֶבְרוֹן וְעֻזִּיאֵל: וּבְנֵי מְרָרִי

כא לְמִשְׁפְּחֹתָם מַחְלִי וּמוּשִׁי אֵלֶּה הֵם מִשְׁפְּחֹת הַלֵּוִי לְבֵית אֲבֹתָם: לְגֵרְשׁוֹן

כב מִשְׁפַּחַת הַלִּבְנִי וּמִשְׁפַּחַת הַשִּׁמְעִי אֵלֶּה הֵם מִשְׁפְּחֹת הַגֵּרְשֻׁנִּי: פְּקֻדֵיהֶם

בְּמִסְפַּר כָּל־זָכָר מִבֶּן־חֹדֶשׁ וָמָעְלָה פְּקֻדֵיהֶם שִׁבְעַת אֲלָפִים וַחֲמֵשׁ

כג-כד מֵאוֹת: מִשְׁפְּחֹת הַגֵּרְשֻׁנִּי אַחֲרֵי הַמִּשְׁכָּן יַחֲנוּ יָמָּה: וּנְשִׂיא בֵית־אָב

כה לַגֵּרְשֻׁנִּי אֶלְיָסָף בֶּן־לָאֵל: וּמִשְׁמֶרֶת בְּנֵי־גֵרְשׁוֹן בְּאֹהֶל מוֹעֵד הַמִּשְׁכָּן

כו וְהָאֹהֶל מִכְסֵהוּ וּמָסַךְ פֶּתַח אֹהֶל מוֹעֵד: וְקַלְעֵי הֶחָצֵר וְאֶת־מָסַךְ

פֶּתַח הֶחָצֵר אֲשֶׁר עַל־הַמִּשְׁכָּן וְעַל־הַמִּזְבֵּחַ סָבִיב וְאֵת מֵיתָרָיו לְכֹל

כז עֲבֹדָתוֹ: וְלִקְהָת מִשְׁפַּחַת הָעַמְרָמִי וּמִשְׁפַּחַת הַיִּצְהָרִי

וּמִשְׁפַּחַת הַחֶבְרֹנִי וּמִשְׁפַּחַת הָעָזִּיאֵלִי אֵלֶּה הֵם מִשְׁפְּחֹת הַקְּהָתִי:

כח בְּמִסְפַּר כָּל־זָכָר מִבֶּן־חֹדֶשׁ וָמָעְלָה שְׁמֹנַת אֲלָפִים וְשֵׁשׁ מֵאוֹת שֹׁמְרֵי

כט-ל מִשְׁמֶרֶת הַקֹּדֶשׁ: מִשְׁפְּחֹת בְּנֵי־קְהָת יַחֲנוּ עַל יֶרֶךְ הַמִּשְׁכָּן תֵּימָנָה: וּנְשִׂיא

לא בֵית־אָב לְמִשְׁפְּחֹת הַקְּהָתִי אֱלִיצָפָן בֶּן־עֻזִּיאֵל: וּמִשְׁמַרְתָּם הָאָרֹן

וְהַשֻּׁלְחָן וְהַמְּנֹרָה וְהַמִּזְבְּחֹת וּכְלֵי הַקֹּדֶשׁ אֲשֶׁר יְשָׁרְתוּ בָּהֶם וְהַמָּסָךְ וְכֹל

לב עֲבֹדָתוֹ: וּנְשִׂיא נְשִׂיאֵי הַלֵּוִי אֶלְעָזָר בֶּן־אַהֲרֹן הַכֹּהֵן פְּקֻדַּת שֹׁמְרֵי

לג מִשְׁמֶרֶת הַקֹּדֶשׁ: לִמְרָרִי מִשְׁפַּחַת הַמַּחְלִי וּמִשְׁפַּחַת הַמּוּשִׁי אֵלֶּה הֵם

לד מִשְׁפְּחֹת מְרָרִי: וּפְקֻדֵיהֶם בְּמִסְפַּר כָּל־זָכָר מִבֶּן־חֹדֶשׁ וָמָעְלָה שֵׁשֶׁת

לה אֲלָפִים וּמָאתָיִם: וּנְשִׂיא בֵית־אָב לְמִשְׁפְּחֹת מְרָרִי צוּרִיאֵל בֶּן־אֲבִיחָיִל

לו עַל יֶרֶךְ הַמִּשְׁכָּן יַחֲנוּ צָפֹנָה: וּפְקֻדַּת מִשְׁמֶרֶת בְּנֵי מְרָרִי קַרְשֵׁי הַמִּשְׁכָּן

לז וּבְרִיחָיו וְעַמֻּדָיו וַאֲדָנָיו וְכָל־כֵּלָיו וְכֹל עֲבֹדָתוֹ: וְעַמֻּדֵי הֶחָצֵר סָבִיב

לח וְאַדְנֵיהֶם וִיתֵדֹתָם וּמֵיתְרֵיהֶם: וְהַחֹנִים לִפְנֵי הַמִּשְׁכָּן קֵדְמָה לִפְנֵי אֹהֶל־

מוֹעֵד ׀ מִזְרָחָה מֹשֶׁה ׀ וְאַהֲרֹן וּבָנָיו שֹׁמְרִים מִשְׁמֶרֶת הַמִּקְדָּשׁ לְמִשְׁמֶרֶת

לט בְּנֵי יִשְׂרָאֵל וְהַזָּר הַקָּרֵב יוּמָת: כָּל־פְּקוּדֵי הַלְוִיִּם אֲשֶׁר פָּקַד מֹשֶׁה *וְאַהֲרֹן   *נקוד על
ואהרן

עַל־פִּי יהוה לְמִשְׁפְּחֹתָם כָּל־זָכָר מִבֶּן־חֹדֶשׁ וָמַעְלָה שְׁנַיִם וְעֶשְׂרִים

מ אָלֶף: וַיֹּאמֶר יהוה אֶל־מֹשֶׁה פְּקֹד כָּל־בְּכֹר זָכָר לִבְנֵי   ששי

מא יִשְׂרָאֵל מִבֶּן־חֹדֶשׁ וָמָעְלָה וְשָׂא אֵת מִסְפַּר שְׁמֹתָם: וְלָקַחְתָּ אֶת־הַלְוִיִּם

לִי אֲנִי יהוה תַּחַת כָּל־בְּכֹר בִּבְנֵי יִשְׂרָאֵל וְאֵת בֶּהֱמַת הַלְוִיִּם תַּחַת כָּל־

מב בְּכוֹר בְּבֶהֱמַת בְּנֵי יִשְׂרָאֵל: וַיִּפְקֹד מֹשֶׁה כַּאֲשֶׁר צִוָּה יהוה אֹתוֹ אֶת־כָּל־

מג בְּכוֹר בִּבְנֵי יִשְׂרָאֵל: וַיְהִי כָל־בְּכוֹר זָכָר בְּמִסְפַּר שֵׁמֹת מִבֶּן־חֹדֶשׁ וָמָעְלָה

לִפְקֻדֵיהֶם שְׁנַיִם וְעֶשְׂרִים אֶלֶף שְׁלֹשָׁה וְשִׁבְעִים וּמָאתָיִם:

3:38. "Fortunate is a righteous person and fortunate is his neighbor" (*Tanchuma* 12). Because the tribes of Judah, Issachar, and Zebulun encamped to the east near Moses, who was engaged in Torah study, they became great in Torah. Conversely, "Woe to the wicked and woe to his neighbor." The tribe of Reuben encamped to the south near the Kohathites, which included the family of Korah; therefore many of the Reubenites became enmeshed in his rebellion (*Rashi* here and to 16:1).

3:40-51. The Levites themselves took the place of Israelite firstborn. The 273 more Israelite firstborn than Levites were redeemed for five shekels each, the same amount that the Torah would ordain as the redemption for all firstborn.

and Shimei. [19] *The sons of Kohath according to their families were Amram and Izhar, Hebron and Uzziel.* [20] *The sons of Merari according to their families were Mahli and Mushi. These were the families of the Levites, according to their fathers' household.*

Gershon   [21] *Gershon had the family of the Libnites and the family of the Shimeites; these were the Gershonite families.* [22] *Their count according to the number of every male, from one month of age and up: their count was seven thousand, five hundred.* [23] *The Gershonite families would encamp behind the Tabernacle, to the west.* [24] *The leader of the father's household of the Gershonites was Eliasaph son of Lael.* [25] *The charge of the sons of Gershon in the Tent of Meeting was the Tabernacle, the Tent, its Cover, the Screen of the entrance of the Tent of Meeting;* [26] *the curtains of the Courtyard, the Screen of the entrance of the Courtyard that surrounded the Tabernacle and the Altar, and its ropes — for all its labor.*

Kohath   [27] *Kohath had the family of the Amramites, the family of the Izharites, the family of the Hebronites, and the family of the Uzzielites; these were the Kohathite families.* [28] *The number of every male from one month of age and up was eight thousand, six hundred; the guardians of the charge of the sanctity.* [29] *The families of the children of Kohath would encamp on the side of the Tabernacle, to the south.* [30] *The leader of the father's household of the Kohathite families was Elizaphan son of Uzziel.* [31] *Their charge was the Ark, the Table, the Menorah, the Altars and the sacred utensils with which they would minister, the Partition and all its accessories.*

[32] *The leader of the Levite leaders was Elazar son of Aaron the Kohen, the assignment of the guardians of the charge of the sanctity.*

Merari   [33] *Merari had the family of the Mahlites and the family of the Mushites; these were the Merarite families.* [34] *Their count according to the number of every male from one month of age and up was six thousand, two hundred.* [35] *The leader of the father's household of the Merarite families was Zuriel son of Abihail; they would encamp on the side of the Tabernacle, to the north.* [36] *The assignment of the charge of the sons of Merari was the planks of the Tabernacle, its bars, its pillars, its sockets and all its utensils, and all its accessories.* [37] *The pillars of the Courtyard all around and their sockets, their pegs and their ropes.*

[38] *Those who encamped before the Tabernacle to the front, before the Tent of Meeting to the east, were Moses and Aaron and his sons,* * *guardians of the charge of the Sanctuary, for the charge of the Children of Israel; any alien who approaches shall die.*

[39] *All the countings of the Levites, which Moses and Aaron counted by the word of* HASHEM *according to their families, every male from one month of age and up, were twenty-two thousand.*

The Israelite   [40] HASHEM *said to Moses, "Count every firstborn* * *male of the Children of Israel* firstborn are   *from one month of age and up, and take a census of their names.* [41] *You shall* redeemed   *take the Levites for Me — I,* HASHEM *— in place of every firstborn of the Children of Israel, and the livestock of the Levites in place of every firstborn of the animals of the Children of Israel."* [42] *Moses counted — as* HASHEM *had commanded him — every firstborn of the Children of Israel.* [43] *Every firstborn male according to the number of their names, from one month of age and up, according to their numbers, was twenty-two thousand, two hundred and seventy-three.*

מד-מה וַיְדַבֵּ֣ר יְהוָ֔ה אֶל־מֹשֶׁ֥ה לֵּאמֹֽר׃ קַ֣ח אֶת־הַלְוִיִּ֗ם תַּ֤חַת כָּל־בְּכוֹר֙ בִּבְנֵ֣י

מו יִשְׂרָאֵ֔ל וְאֶת־בֶּהֱמַ֥ת הַלְוִיִּ֖ם תַּ֣חַת בְּהֶמְתָּ֑ם וְהָֽיוּ־לִ֥י הַלְוִיִּ֖ם אֲנִ֣י יְהוָֽה׃ וְאֵת֙

מז פְּדוּיֵ֣י הַשְּׁלֹשָׁ֗ה וְהַשִּׁבְעִ֛ים וְהַמָּאתָ֖יִם הָעֹֽדְפִ֑ים עַל־הַלְוִיִּ֖ם מִבְּכ֥וֹר בְּנֵ֥י

יִשְׂרָאֵֽל׃ וְלָֽקַחְתָּ֗ חֲמֵ֧שֶׁת חֲמֵ֛שֶׁת שְׁקָלִ֖ים לַגֻּלְגֹּ֑לֶת בְּשֶׁ֤קֶל הַקֹּ֙דֶשׁ֙ תִּקָּ֔ח

מח עֶשְׂרִ֥ים גֵּרָ֖ה הַשָּֽׁקֶל׃ וְנָֽתַתָּ֣ה הַכֶּ֔סֶף לְאַֽהֲרֹ֖ן וּלְבָנָ֑יו פְּדוּיֵ֕י הָעֹֽדְפִ֖ים בָּהֶֽם׃

מט וַיִּקַּ֣ח מֹשֶׁ֗ה אֵ֚ת כֶּ֣סֶף הַפִּדְי֔וֹם מֵאֵת֙ הָעֹ֣דְפִ֔ים עַ֖ל פְּדוּיֵ֥י הַלְוִיִּֽם׃ מֵאֵ֗ת

נ בְּכ֛וֹר בְּנֵ֥י יִשְׂרָאֵ֖ל לָקַ֣ח אֶת־הַכָּ֑סֶף חֲמִשָּׁ֣ה וְשִׁשִּׁ֗ים וּשְׁלֹ֧שׁ מֵא֛וֹת וָאֶ֖לֶף

נא בְּשֶׁ֥קֶל הַקֹּֽדֶשׁ׃ וַיִּתֵּ֨ן מֹשֶׁ֜ה אֶת־כֶּ֧סֶף הַפְּדֻיִ֛ם לְאַֽהֲרֹ֥ן וּלְבָנָ֖יו עַל־פִּ֣י יְהוָ֑ה

כַּֽאֲשֶׁ֛ר צִוָּ֥ה יְהוָ֖ה אֶת־מֹשֶֽׁה׃

ד שביעי א-ב וַיְדַבֵּ֣ר יְהוָ֔ה אֶל־מֹשֶׁ֥ה וְאֶֽל־אַֽהֲרֹ֖ן לֵאמֹֽר׃ נָשֹׂ֗א אֶת־רֹאשׁ֙ בְּנֵ֣י קְהָ֔ת

ג מִתּ֖וֹךְ בְּנֵ֣י לֵוִ֑י לְמִשְׁפְּחֹתָ֖ם לְבֵ֥ית אֲבֹתָֽם׃ מִבֶּ֨ן שְׁלֹשִׁ֤ים שָׁנָה֙ וָמַ֔עְלָה וְעַ֕ד

ד בֶּן־חֲמִשִּׁ֖ים שָׁנָ֑ה כָּל־בָּא֙ לַצָּבָ֔א לַֽעֲשׂ֥וֹת מְלָאכָ֖ה בְּאֹ֥הֶל מוֹעֵֽד׃ זֹ֛את

ה עֲבֹדַ֥ת בְּנֵֽי־קְהָ֖ת בְּאֹ֣הֶל מוֹעֵ֑ד קֹ֖דֶשׁ הַקֳּדָשִֽׁים׃ וּבָ֨א אַֽהֲרֹ֤ן וּבָנָיו֙ בִּנְסֹ֣עַ

ו הַֽמַּחֲנֶ֔ה וְהוֹרִ֕דוּ אֵ֖ת פָּרֹ֣כֶת הַמָּסָ֑ךְ וְכִ֨סּוּ־בָ֔הּ אֵ֖ת אֲרֹ֥ן הָֽעֵדֻֽת׃ וְנָֽתְנ֣וּ עָלָ֗יו

ז כְּסוּי֙ ע֣וֹר תַּ֔חַשׁ וּפָֽרְשׂ֧וּ בֶֽגֶד־כְּלִ֛יל תְּכֵ֖לֶת מִלְמָ֑עְלָה וְשָׂמ֖וּ בַּדָּֽיו׃ וְעַ֣ל ׀

שֻׁלְחַ֣ן הַפָּנִ֗ים יִפְרְשׂוּ֮ בֶּ֣גֶד תְּכֵ֒לֶת֒ וְנָֽתְנ֣וּ עָ֠לָ֠יו אֶת־הַקְּעָרֹ֤ת וְאֶת־הַכַּפֹּת֙

ח וְאֶת־הַמְּנַקִּיֹּ֔ת וְאֵ֖ת קְשׂ֣וֹת הַנָּ֑סֶךְ וְלֶ֥חֶם הַתָּמִ֖יד עָלָ֥יו יִֽהְיֶֽה׃ וּפָֽרְשׂ֣וּ

עֲלֵיהֶ֗ם בֶּ֚גֶד תּוֹלַ֣עַת שָׁנִ֔י וְכִסּ֣וּ אֹת֔וֹ בְּמִכְסֵ֖ה ע֣וֹר תָּ֑חַשׁ וְשָׂמ֖וּ אֶת־בַּדָּֽיו׃

ט וְלָֽקְח֣וּ ׀ בֶּ֣גֶד תְּכֵ֗לֶת וְכִסּ֞וּ אֶת־מְנֹרַ֤ת הַמָּאוֹר֙ וְאֶת־נֵ֣רֹתֶ֔יהָ וְאֶת־מַלְקָחֶ֖יהָ

י וְאֶת־מַחְתֹּתֶ֑יהָ וְאֵת֙ כָּל־כְּלֵ֣י שַׁמְנָ֔הּ אֲשֶׁ֥ר יְשָֽׁרְתוּ־לָ֖הּ בָּהֶֽם׃ וְנָֽתְנ֤וּ אֹתָהּ֙

יא וְאֶת־כָּל־כֵּלֶ֔יהָ אֶל־מִכְסֵ֖ה ע֣וֹר תָּ֑חַשׁ וְנָֽתְנ֖וּ עַל־הַמּֽוֹט׃ וְעַ֣ל ׀ מִזְבַּ֣ח

הַזָּהָ֗ב יִפְרְשׂוּ֙ בֶּ֣גֶד תְּכֵ֔לֶת וְכִסּ֣וּ אֹת֔וֹ בְּמִכְסֵ֖ה ע֣וֹר תָּ֑חַשׁ וְשָׂמ֖וּ אֶת־בַּדָּֽיו׃

יב וְלָֽקְחוּ֩ אֶת־כָּל־כְּלֵ֨י הַשָּׁרֵ֜ת אֲשֶׁ֧ר יְשָֽׁרְתוּ־בָ֣ם בַּקֹּ֗דֶשׁ וְנָֽתְנוּ֙ אֶל־בֶּ֣גֶד

יג תְּכֵ֔לֶת וְכִסּ֣וּ אוֹתָ֔ם בְּמִכְסֵ֖ה ע֣וֹר תָּ֑חַשׁ וְנָֽתְנ֖וּ עַל־הַמּֽוֹט׃ וְדִשְּׁנ֖וּ אֶת־

יד הַמִּזְבֵּ֑חַ וּפָֽרְשׂ֣וּ עָלָ֔יו בֶּ֖גֶד אַרְגָּמָֽן׃ וְנָֽתְנ֣וּ עָ֠לָ֠יו אֶֽת־כָּל־כֵּלָ֞יו אֲשֶׁ֣ר יְשָֽׁרְת֧וּ

עָלָ֣יו בָּהֶ֗ם אֶת־הַמַּחְתֹּ֤ת אֶת־הַמִּזְלָגֹת֙ וְאֶת־הַיָּעִ֣ים וְאֶת־הַמִּזְרָקֹ֔ת כֹּ֖ל

טו כְּלֵ֣י הַמִּזְבֵּ֑חַ וּפָֽרְשׂ֣וּ עָלָ֗יו כְּס֛וּי ע֥וֹר תַּ֖חַשׁ וְשָׂמ֥וּ בַדָּֽיו׃ וְכִלָּ֣ה אַֽהֲרֹן־וּ֠בָנָ֠יו

לְכַסֹּ֨ת אֶת־הַקֹּ֜דֶשׁ וְאֶת־כָּל־כְּלֵ֣י הַקֹּדֶשׁ֮ בִּנְסֹ֣עַ הַֽמַּחֲנֶה֒ וְאַֽחֲרֵי־כֵ֗ן יָבֹ֤אוּ

בְנֵֽי־קְהָת֙ לָשֵׂ֔את וְלֹֽא־יִגְּע֥וּ אֶל־הַקֹּ֖דֶשׁ וָמֵ֑תוּ אֵ֛לֶּה מַשָּׂ֥א בְנֵֽי־קְהָ֖ת

טז בְּאֹ֥הֶל מוֹעֵֽד׃ וּפְקֻדַּ֞ת אֶלְעָזָ֣ר ׀ בֶּן־אַֽהֲרֹ֣ן הַכֹּהֵ֗ן שֶׁ֤מֶן הַמָּאוֹר֙ וּקְטֹ֣רֶת

הַסַּמִּ֔ים וּמִנְחַ֥ת הַתָּמִ֖יד וְשֶׁ֣מֶן הַמִּשְׁחָ֑ה פְּקֻדַּ֗ת כָּל־הַמִּשְׁכָּן֙ וְכָל־אֲשֶׁר־

בּ֔וֹ בְּקֹ֖דֶשׁ וּבְכֵלָֽיו׃

4:4. *The most holy.* The term usually refers to the chamber that contained the Ark, but in the context of this passage, it refers to the holiest components of the Tabernacle (*Rashi*).

⁴⁴ *HASHEM spoke to Moses, saying,* ⁴⁵ *"Take the Levites in place of every firstborn of the Children of Israel, and the livestock of the Levites in place of their livestock, and the Levites shall be Mine, I am HASHEM.* ⁴⁶ *And as for the redemptions of the two hundred and seventy-three of the firstborn of the Children of Israel who are in excess of the Levites;* ⁴⁷ *you shall take five shekels each according to the head count, in the sacred shekel shall you take; the shekel is twenty geras.* ⁴⁸ *You shall give the money to Aaron and his sons, as redemptions of the additional ones among them."*

⁴⁹ *Moses took the money of the redemption from those who were in excess of the redemptions of the Levites;* ⁵⁰ *from the firstborn of the Children of Israel he took the money: one thousand, three hundred and sixty-five in the sacred shekels.* ⁵¹ *Moses gave the money of the redemptions to Aaron and his sons according to the word of HASHEM, as HASHEM had commanded Moses.*

4

The
Kohathites'
responsibilities

¹ Hᴀꜱʜᴇᴍ *spoke to Moses and Aaron, saying:* ² *"Take a census of the sons of Kohath from among the sons of Levi, according to their families, according to their fathers' household;* ³ *from thirty years of age and up, until fifty years of age, everyone who comes to the legion to perform work in the Tent of Meeting.*

⁴ *"This is the work of the sons of Kohath in the Tent of Meeting: the most holy.* * ⁵ *When the camp is to journey, Aaron and his sons shall come and take down the Partition-curtain and cover the Ark of the Testimony with it.* ⁶ *They shall place upon it a tachash-hide covering, and spread a cloth entirely of turquoise wool over it, and adjust its staves.* ⁷ *Upon the Table of the show-bread they shall spread a cloth of turquoise wool and place upon it the dishes, the spoons, the pillars, and the shelving-tubes; and the constant bread shall remain on it.* ⁸ *They shall spread over them a cloth of scarlet wool and cover it with a cover of tachash hide, and emplace its staves.* ⁹ *They shall take a cloth of turquoise wool and cover the Menorah of illumination, and its lamps, and its tongs, and its spoons, and all the vessels of its oil, with which they minister to it.* ¹⁰ *They shall place it and all its utensils into a cover of tachash-hide, and place it on the pole.* ¹¹ *Upon the Gold Altar they shall spread a cloth of turquoise wool, and cover it with a covering of tachash-hide, and emplace its staves.* ¹² *They shall take all the utensils of service with which they serve in the Sanctuary and place them on a cloth of turquoise wool, and cover them with a covering of tachash-hide, and place them on the pole.* ¹³ *They shall clear the ash from the Altar and spread a cloth of purple wool over it,* ¹⁴ *they shall place upon it all the utensils with which they minister upon it: the fire-pans, the forks, the shovels, and the basins — all the utensils of the Altar — and spread over it a covering of tachash hide, and emplace its staves.*

¹⁵ *"Aaron and his sons shall finish covering the holy and all the holy utensils when the camp journeys, and then the sons of Kohath shall come to carry, so that they not touch the Sanctuary and die. These are the burden of the sons of Kohath in the Tent of Meeting.*

¹⁶ *"The charge of Elazar son of Aaron the Kohen is the oil of illumination, the incense spices, the meal-offering of the continual offering, and the anointment oil — the charge of the entire Tabernacle and everything in it — of the Sanctuary and its utensils."*

מפטיר   יז־יח וַיְדַבֵּר יהוה אֶל־מֹשֶׁה וְאֶל־אַהֲרֹן לֵאמֹר: אַל־תַּכְרִיתוּ אֶת־שֵׁבֶט מִשְׁפְּחֹת

הַקְּהָתִי מִתּוֹךְ הַלְוִיִּם: וְזֹאת | עֲשׂוּ לָהֶם וְחָיוּ וְלֹא יָמֻתוּ בְּגִשְׁתָּם אֶת־קֹדֶשׁ יט

הַקֳּדָשִׁים אַהֲרֹן וּבָנָיו יָבֹאוּ וְשָׂמוּ אוֹתָם אִישׁ אִישׁ עַל־עֲבֹדָתוֹ וְאֶל־מַשָּׂאוֹ:

כ וְלֹא־יָבֹאוּ לִרְאוֹת כְּבַלַּע אֶת־הַקֹּדֶשׁ וָמֵתוּ: פפפ קנ"ט פסוקים. חלקיה"ו סימן.

פרשת נשא

Haftaras
Bamidbar:
p. 1332

For special
Sabbaths,
see pp. x-xi

כא־כב וַיְדַבֵּר יהוה אֶל־מֹשֶׁה לֵּאמֹר: נָשֹׂא אֶת־רֹאשׁ בְּנֵי גֵרְשׁוֹן גַּם־הֵם לְבֵית

כג אֲבֹתָם לְמִשְׁפְּחֹתָם: מִבֶּן שְׁלֹשִׁים שָׁנָה וָמַעְלָה עַד בֶּן־חֲמִשִּׁים שָׁנָה תִּפְקֹד

כד אוֹתָם כָּל־הַבָּא לִצְבֹא צָבָא לַעֲבֹד עֲבֹדָה בְּאֹהֶל מוֹעֵד: זֹאת עֲבֹדַת

כה מִשְׁפְּחֹת הַגֵּרְשֻׁנִּי לַעֲבֹד וּלְמַשָּׂא: וְנָשְׂאוּ אֶת־יְרִיעֹת הַמִּשְׁכָּן וְאֶת־אֹהֶל

מוֹעֵד מִכְסֵהוּ וּמִכְסֵה הַתַּחַשׁ אֲשֶׁר־עָלָיו מִלְמָעְלָה וְאֶת־מָסַךְ פֶּתַח אֹהֶל

כו מוֹעֵד: וְאֵת קַלְעֵי הֶחָצֵר וְאֶת־מָסַךְ | פֶּתַח | שַׁעַר הֶחָצֵר אֲשֶׁר עַל־הַמִּשְׁכָּן

וְעַל־הַמִּזְבֵּחַ סָבִיב וְאֵת מֵיתְרֵיהֶם וְאֶת־כָּל־כְּלֵי עֲבֹדָתָם וְאֵת כָּל־אֲשֶׁר

כז יֵעָשֶׂה לָהֶם וְעָבָדוּ: עַל־פִּי אַהֲרֹן וּבָנָיו תִּהְיֶה כָּל־עֲבֹדַת בְּנֵי הַגֵּרְשֻׁנִּי לְכָל־

מַשָּׂאָם וּלְכֹל עֲבֹדָתָם וּפְקַדְתֶּם עֲלֵהֶם בְּמִשְׁמֶרֶת אֵת כָּל־מַשָּׂאָם: זֹאת

כח עֲבֹדַת מִשְׁפְּחֹת בְּנֵי הַגֵּרְשֻׁנִּי בְּאֹהֶל מוֹעֵד וּמִשְׁמַרְתָּם בְּיַד אִיתָמָר בֶּן־

כט אַהֲרֹן הַכֹּהֵן: בְּנֵי מְרָרִי לְמִשְׁפְּחֹתָם לְבֵית־

ל אֲבֹתָם תִּפְקֹד אֹתָם: מִבֶּן שְׁלֹשִׁים שָׁנָה וָמַעְלָה וְעַד בֶּן־חֲמִשִּׁים שָׁנָה

לא תִּפְקְדֵם כָּל־הַבָּא לַצָּבָא לַעֲבֹד אֶת־עֲבֹדַת אֹהֶל מוֹעֵד: וְזֹאת מִשְׁמֶרֶת

מַשָּׂאָם לְכָל־עֲבֹדָתָם בְּאֹהֶל מוֹעֵד קַרְשֵׁי הַמִּשְׁכָּן וּבְרִיחָיו וְעַמּוּדָיו וַאֲדָנָיו:

לב וְעַמּוּדֵי הֶחָצֵר סָבִיב וְאַדְנֵיהֶם וִיתֵדֹתָם וּמֵיתְרֵיהֶם לְכָל־כְּלֵיהֶם וּלְכֹל

עֲבֹדָתָם וּבְשֵׁמֹת תִּפְקְדוּ אֶת־כְּלֵי מִשְׁמֶרֶת מַשָּׂאָם: זֹאת עֲבֹדַת מִשְׁפְּחֹת

לג בְּנֵי מְרָרִי לְכָל־עֲבֹדָתָם בְּאֹהֶל מוֹעֵד בְּיַד אִיתָמָר בֶּן־אַהֲרֹן הַכֹּהֵן: וַיִּפְקֹד

לד מֹשֶׁה וְאַהֲרֹן וּנְשִׂיאֵי הָעֵדָה אֶת־בְּנֵי הַקְּהָתִי לְמִשְׁפְּחֹתָם וּלְבֵית אֲבֹתָם:

לה מִבֶּן שְׁלֹשִׁים שָׁנָה וָמַעְלָה וְעַד בֶּן־חֲמִשִּׁים שָׁנָה כָּל־הַבָּא לַצָּבָא לַעֲבֹדָה

לו בְּאֹהֶל מוֹעֵד: וַיִּהְיוּ פְקֻדֵיהֶם לְמִשְׁפְּחֹתָם אַלְפַּיִם שְׁבַע מֵאוֹת וַחֲמִשִּׁים:

לז אֵלֶּה פְקוּדֵי מִשְׁפְּחֹת הַקְּהָתִי כָּל־הָעֹבֵד בְּאֹהֶל מוֹעֵד אֲשֶׁר פָּקַד מֹשֶׁה

שני   לח וְאַהֲרֹן עַל־פִּי יהוה בְּיַד־מֹשֶׁה: וּפְקוּדֵי

לט בְּנֵי גֵרְשׁוֹן לְמִשְׁפְּחוֹתָם וּלְבֵית אֲבֹתָם: מִבֶּן שְׁלֹשִׁים שָׁנָה וָמַעְלָה

מ וְעַד בֶּן־חֲמִשִּׁים שָׁנָה כָּל־הַבָּא לַצָּבָא לַעֲבֹדָה בְּאֹהֶל מוֹעֵד: וַיִּהְיוּ פְּקֻדֵיהֶם

לְמִשְׁפְּחֹתָם לְבֵית אֲבֹתָם אַלְפַּיִם וְשֵׁשׁ מֵאוֹת וּשְׁלֹשִׁים:

מא אֵלֶּה פְקוּדֵי מִשְׁפְּחֹת בְּנֵי גֵרְשׁוֹן כָּל־הָעֹבֵד בְּאֹהֶל מוֹעֵד אֲשֶׁר פָּקַד

מב מֹשֶׁה וְאַהֲרֹן עַל־פִּי יהוה: וּפְקוּדֵי מִשְׁפְּחֹת בְּנֵי מְרָרִי לְמִשְׁפְּחֹתָם

◄§ **Parashas Nasso**

4:23. *To perform work.* Part of Gershon's responsibility
was to participate in the musical accompaniment of

some of the communal offerings (*Bamidbar Rabbah* 6:5),
a duty that the Talmud (*Arachin* 11a) characterizes as
work.

Special
precautions
for the
Kohathites

¹⁷ HASHEM spoke to Moses and Aaron, saying: ¹⁸ "Do not let the tribe of the Kohathite families be cut off from among the Levites. ¹⁹ Thus shall you do for them so that they shall live and not die: when they approach the Holy of Holies, Aaron and his sons shall come and assign them, every man to his work and his burden. ²⁰ But they shall not come and look as the holy is inserted, lest they die."

PARASHAS NASSO

The
Gershonites'
responsibilities

²¹ HASHEM spoke to Moses, saying, ²² "Take a census of the sons of Gershon, as well, according to their fathers' household, according to their families. ²³ From thirty years of age and up, until fifty years of age shall you count them, everyone who comes to join the legion to perform work* in the Tent of Meeting. ²⁴ This is the work of the Gershonite families: to work and to carry. ²⁵ They shall carry the curtains of the Tabernacle and the Tent of Meeting, its Cover and the tachash cover that is over it from above. And the Screen of the entrance of the Tent of Meeting, ²⁶ the lace-hangings of the Courtyard and the Screen of the entrance of the gate of the Courtyard that were around the Tabernacle and the Altar, their ropes and all the utensils of their service, and everything that is made for them, and they shall serve. ²⁷ According to the word of Aaron and his sons shall be all the work of the sons of Gershonites, their entire burden and their entire work; you shall appoint their entire burden as their charge. ²⁸ This is the work of the families of the sons of the Gershonites in the Tent of Meeting; and their charge shall be under the authority of Ithamar, the son of Aaron the Kohen.

The
Merarites'
responsibilities

²⁹ "The sons of Merari — according to their families, according to their fathers' household shall you count them. ³⁰ From thirty years of age and up, until fifty years of age shall you count them, everyone who comes to the legion to perform the work of the Tent of Meeting. ³¹ This is the charge of their burden for all of their work in the Tent of Meeting: the planks of the Tabernacle, its bars, its pillars, and its sockets; ³² the pillars of the Courtyard all around and their sockets, their pegs and their ropes for all of their utensils and for all of their work. You shall appoint them by name to the utensils they are to carry on their watch. ³³ This is the work of the families of the sons of Merari according to all their work in the Tent of Meeting, under the authority of Ithamar, son of Aaron the Kohen."

³⁴ Moses and Aaron and the leaders of the assembly counted the sons of the Kohathites, according to their families, according to their fathers' household. ³⁵ From thirty years of age and up, until fifty years of age, everyone who comes to the legion for the work in the Tent of Meeting. ³⁶ Their countings according to their families were two thousand, seven hundred and fifty. ³⁷ These are the countings of the Kohathite families, all who work in the Tent of Meeting, whom Moses and Aaron counted, at the word of HASHEM, under the authority of Moses.

The totals

³⁸ The countings of the sons of Gershon according to their families, and according to their fathers' household; ³⁹ from thirty years of age and up, until fifty years of age, everyone who comes to the legion for the work in the Tent of Meeting. ⁴⁰ Their countings according to their families, according to their fathers household were two thousand, six hundred and thirty. ⁴¹ These are the countings of the families of the sons of Gershon, all who work in the Tent of Meeting, whom Moses and Aaron counted, at the word of HASHEM.

⁴² The countings of the families of the sons of Merari, according to their families,

מג לְבֵית אֲבֹתָם: מִבֶּן שְׁלֹשִׁים שָׁנָה וָמַעְלָה וְעַד בֶּן־חֲמִשִּׁים שָׁנָה כָּל־הַבָּא

מד לַצָּבָא לַעֲבֹדָה בְּאֹהֶל מוֹעֵד: וַיִּהְיוּ פְקֻדֵיהֶם לְמִשְׁפְּחֹתָם שְׁלֹשֶׁת אֲלָפִים

מה וּמָאתָיִם: אֵלֶּה פְקוּדֵי מִשְׁפְּחֹת בְּנֵי מְרָרִי אֲשֶׁר פָּקַד מֹשֶׁה וְאַהֲרֹן עַל־פִּי

מו יהוה בְּיַד־מֹשֶׁה: כָּל־הַפְּקֻדִים אֲשֶׁר פָּקַד מֹשֶׁה וְאַהֲרֹן וּנְשִׂיאֵי יִשְׂרָאֵל

מז אֶת־הַלְוִיִּם לְמִשְׁפְּחֹתָם וּלְבֵית אֲבֹתָם: מִבֶּן שְׁלֹשִׁים שָׁנָה וָמַעְלָה וְעַד

בֶּן־חֲמִשִּׁים שָׁנָה כָּל־הַבָּא לַעֲבֹד עֲבֹדַת עֲבֹדָה וַעֲבֹדַת מַשָּׂא בְּאֹהֶל

מח-מט מוֹעֵד: וַיִּהְיוּ פְּקֻדֵיהֶם שְׁמֹנַת אֲלָפִים וַחֲמֵשׁ מֵאוֹת וּשְׁמֹנִים: עַל־פִּי יהוה

פָּקַד אוֹתָם בְּיַד־מֹשֶׁה אִישׁ אִישׁ עַל־עֲבֹדָתוֹ וְעַל־מַשָּׂאוֹ וּפְקֻדָיו אֲשֶׁר־

צִוָּה יהוה אֶת־מֹשֶׁה:

ה שלישי א-ב וַיְדַבֵּר יהוה אֶל־מֹשֶׁה לֵּאמֹר: צַו אֶת־בְּנֵי יִשְׂרָאֵל וִישַׁלְּחוּ מִן־הַמַּחֲנֶה

ג כָּל־צָרוּעַ וְכָל־זָב וְכֹל טָמֵא לָנָפֶשׁ: מִזָּכָר עַד־נְקֵבָה תְּשַׁלֵּחוּ אֶל־מִחוּץ

לַמַּחֲנֶה תְּשַׁלְּחוּם וְלֹא יְטַמְּאוּ אֶת־מַחֲנֵיהֶם אֲשֶׁר אֲנִי שֹׁכֵן בְּתוֹכָם:

ד וַיַּעֲשׂוּ־כֵן בְּנֵי יִשְׂרָאֵל וַיְשַׁלְּחוּ אוֹתָם אֶל־מִחוּץ לַמַּחֲנֶה כַּאֲשֶׁר דִּבֶּר

יהוה אֶל־מֹשֶׁה כֵּן עָשׂוּ בְּנֵי יִשְׂרָאֵל:

ה-ו וַיְדַבֵּר יהוה אֶל־מֹשֶׁה לֵּאמֹר: דַּבֵּר אֶל־בְּנֵי יִשְׂרָאֵל אִישׁ אוֹ־אִשָּׁה כִּי

יַעֲשׂוּ מִכָּל־חַטֹּאת הָאָדָם לִמְעֹל מַעַל בַּיהוה וְאָשְׁמָה הַנֶּפֶשׁ הַהִוא:

ז וְהִתְוַדּוּ אֶת־חַטָּאתָם אֲשֶׁר עָשׂוּ וְהֵשִׁיב אֶת־אֲשָׁמוֹ בְּרֹאשׁוֹ וַחֲמִישִׁתוֹ

ח יֹסֵף עָלָיו וְנָתַן לַאֲשֶׁר אָשַׁם לוֹ: וְאִם־אֵין לָאִישׁ גֹּאֵל לְהָשִׁיב הָאָשָׁם אֵלָיו

הָאָשָׁם הַמּוּשָׁב לַיהוה לַכֹּהֵן מִלְּבַד אֵיל הַכִּפֻּרִים אֲשֶׁר יְכַפֶּר־בּוֹ עָלָיו:

ט וְכָל־תְּרוּמָה לְכָל־קָדְשֵׁי בְנֵי־יִשְׂרָאֵל אֲשֶׁר־יַקְרִיבוּ לַכֹּהֵן לוֹ יִהְיֶה: וְאִישׁ

אֶת־קֳדָשָׁיו לוֹ יִהְיוּ אִישׁ אֲשֶׁר־יִתֵּן לַכֹּהֵן לוֹ יִהְיֶה:

רביעי יא-יב וַיְדַבֵּר יהוה אֶל־מֹשֶׁה לֵּאמֹר: דַּבֵּר אֶל־בְּנֵי יִשְׂרָאֵל וְאָמַרְתָּ אֲלֵהֶם אִישׁ

יג אִישׁ כִּי־תִשְׂטֶה אִשְׁתּוֹ וּמָעֲלָה בוֹ מָעַל: וְשָׁכַב אִישׁ אֹתָהּ שִׁכְבַת־זֶרַע

וְנֶעְלַם מֵעֵינֵי אִישָׁהּ וְנִסְתְּרָה וְהִיא נִטְמָאָה וְעֵד אֵין בָּהּ וְהִוא לֹא נִתְפָּשָׂה:

יד וְעָבַר עָלָיו רוּחַ־קִנְאָה וְקִנֵּא אֶת־אִשְׁתּוֹ וְהִוא נִטְמָאָה אוֹ־עָבַר עָלָיו רוּחַ־

טו קִנְאָה וְקִנֵּא אֶת־אִשְׁתּוֹ וְהִיא לֹא נִטְמָאָה: וְהֵבִיא הָאִישׁ אֶת־אִשְׁתּוֹ אֶל־

הַכֹּהֵן וְהֵבִיא אֶת־קָרְבָּנָהּ עָלֶיהָ עֲשִׂירִת הָאֵיפָה קֶמַח שְׂעֹרִים לֹא־יִצֹק

עָלָיו שֶׁמֶן וְלֹא־יִתֵּן עָלָיו לְבֹנָה כִּי־מִנְחַת קְנָאֹת הוּא מִנְחַת זִכָּרוֹן מַזְכֶּרֶת

טז-יז עָוֹן: וְהִקְרִיב אֹתָהּ הַכֹּהֵן וְהֶעֱמִדָהּ לִפְנֵי יהוה: וְלָקַח הַכֹּהֵן מַיִם קְדֹשִׁים

בִּכְלִי־חָרֶשׂ וּמִן־הֶעָפָר אֲשֶׁר יִהְיֶה בְּקַרְקַע הַמִּשְׁכָּן יִקַּח הַכֹּהֵן וְנָתַן אֶל־

5:3. To make their camp a worthy home for the Divine Presence [*Shechinah*], the Jews were cautioned to free their camp of ritual contamination [*tumah*] (*Ramban*).

5:11-31. This woman behaved in an unseemly manner, giving her husband good reason to suspect her of adultery, but there is no proof of either guilt or innocence. The Torah provides a miraculous process that

will either prove that she sinned or show that she was faithful and thereby restore trust and love to the marriage. If her fear of imminent death induces her to confess, the marriage would end in divorce, but without any penalty to her.

The ordeal of bitter waters described in this passage is the only halachic procedure in the Torah that depends on *according to their fathers' household;* ⁴³ *from thirty years of age and up, until fifty years of age, everyone who comes to the legion, for the work in the Tent of Meeting.* ⁴⁴ *Their countings according to their families were three thousand, two hundred.* ⁴⁵ *These were the countings of the families of the sons of Merari, whom Moses and Aaron counted, at the word of* HASHEM, *through Moses.*

⁴⁶ *All those counted of the Levites, whom Moses and Aaron and the leaders of Israel counted, according to their families and according to their fathers' household;* ⁴⁷ *from thirty years of age and up, until fifty years of age, everyone who comes to perform the work of service and the work of burden in the Tent of Meeting.* ⁴⁸ *Their countings were eight thousand, five hundred and eighty.* ⁴⁹ *He counted them at the word of* HASHEM, *through Moses, every man over his work and over his burden; and his count [was] as* HASHEM *had commanded Moses.*

5

Purification of the camp

¹ Hashem *spoke to Moses, saying,* ² *"Command the Children of Israel that they shall expel from the camp everyone with tzaraas, everyone who has had a zav-emission, and everyone contaminated by a human corpse.* ³ *Male and female alike shall you expel, to the outside of the camp shall you expel them, so that they should not contaminate their camps, among which I dwell."* * ⁴ *The Children of Israel did so: They expelled them to the outside of the camp, as* HASHEM *had spoken to Moses — so did the Children of Israel do.*

Theft from a Jew and from a proselyte

⁵ Hashem *spoke to Moses, saying,* ⁶ *"Speak to the Children of Israel: A man or woman who commits any of man's sins, by committing treachery toward* HASHEM, *and that person shall become guilty —* ⁷ *they shall confess their sin that they committed; he shall make restitution for his guilt in its principal amount and add its fifth to it, and give it to the one to whom he is indebted.* ⁸ *If the man has no kinsman to whom the debt can be returned, the returned debt is for* HASHEM, *for the Kohen, aside from the ram of atonement with which he shall provide him atonement.* ⁹ *And every portion from any of the holies that the Children of Israel bring to the Kohen shall be his.* ¹⁰ *A man's holies shall be his, and what a man gives to the Kohen shall be his."*

Sotah/the wayward wife

¹¹ Hashem *spoke to Moses, saying,* ¹² *"Speak to the Children of Israel and say to them: Any man whose wife shall go astray and commit treachery against him;* ¹³ *and a man could have lain with her carnally, but it was hidden from the eyes of her husband, and she became secluded and could have been defiled — but there was no witness against her — and she had not been forced;* ¹⁴ *and a spirit of jealousy had passed over him and he had warned his wife, and she had become defiled, or a spirit of jealousy had passed over him and he had warned his wife and she had not become defiled.* ¹⁵ *The man shall bring his wife to the Kohen and he shall bring her offering for her, a tenth-ephah of barley flour; he shall not pour oil over it and shall not put frankincense upon it, for it is a meal-offering of jealousies, a meal-offering of remembrance, a reminder of iniquity.*

The meal-offering of jealousies
(See Appendix B, chart 9)

Confession

¹⁶ *"The Kohen shall bring her near and have her stand before* HASHEM. ¹⁷ *The Kohen shall take sacred water in an earthenware vessel, and the Kohen shall take from the earth that is on the floor of the Tabernacle and put it in*

---

supernatural intervention. It is a psychological reality that once a husband has come to suspect his wife, he will
not trust her even if a court rules that he is wrong; only God's own testimony would be convincing enough.

יח הַמָּיִם: וְהֶעֱמִיד הַכֹּהֵן אֶת־הָאִשָּׁה לִפְנֵי יהוה וּפָרַע אֶת־רֹאשׁ הָאִשָּׁה וְנָתַן עַל־כַּפֶּיהָ אֵת מִנְחַת הַזִּכָּרוֹן מִנְחַת קְנָאֹת הִוא וּבְיַד הַכֹּהֵן יִהְיוּ מֵי

יט הַמַּיִם הַמְאָרֲרִים: וְהִשְׁבִּיעַ אֹתָהּ הַכֹּהֵן וְאָמַר אֶל־הָאִשָּׁה אִם־לֹא שָׁכַב אִישׁ אֹתָךְ וְאִם־לֹא שָׂטִית טֻמְאָה תַּחַת אִישֵׁךְ הִנָּקִי מִמֵּי הַמָּרִים

כ הַמְאָרֲרִים הָאֵלֶּה: וְאַתְּ כִּי שָׂטִית תַּחַת אִישֵׁךְ וְכִי נִטְמֵאת וַיִּתֵּן אִישׁ בָּךְ אֶת־שְׁכָבְתּוֹ מִבַּלְעֲדֵי אִישֵׁךְ: וְהִשְׁבִּיעַ הַכֹּהֵן אֶת־הָאִשָּׁה בִּשְׁבֻעַת הָאָלָה

כא וְאָמַר הַכֹּהֵן לָאִשָּׁה יִתֵּן יהוה אוֹתָךְ לְאָלָה וְלִשְׁבֻעָה בְּתוֹךְ עַמֵּךְ בְּתֵת

כב יהוה אֶת־יְרֵכֵךְ נֹפֶלֶת וְאֶת־בִּטְנֵךְ צָבָה: וּבָאוּ הַמַּיִם הַמְאָרֲרִים הָאֵלֶּה בְּמֵעַיִךְ לַצְבּוֹת בֶּטֶן וְלַנְפִּל יָרֵךְ וְאָמְרָה הָאִשָּׁה אָמֵן ׀ אָמֵן: וְכָתַב אֶת־

כג הָאָלֹת הָאֵלֶּה הַכֹּהֵן בַּסֵּפֶר וּמָחָה אֶל־מֵי הַמָּרִים: וְהִשְׁקָה אֶת־הָאִשָּׁה

כד אֶת־מֵי הַמָּרִים הַמְאָרֲרִים וּבָאוּ בָהּ הַמַּיִם הַמְאָרֲרִים לְמָרִים: וְלָקַח

כה הַכֹּהֵן מִיַּד הָאִשָּׁה אֵת מִנְחַת הַקְּנָאֹת וְהֵנִיף אֶת־הַמִּנְחָה לִפְנֵי יהוה

כו וְהִקְרִיב אֹתָהּ אֶל־הַמִּזְבֵּחַ: וְקָמַץ הַכֹּהֵן מִן־הַמִּנְחָה אֶת־אַזְכָּרָתָהּ

כז וְהִקְטִיר הַמִּזְבֵּחָה וְאַחַר יַשְׁקֶה אֶת־הָאִשָּׁה אֶת־הַמָּיִם: וְהִשְׁקָהּ אֶת־הַמַּיִם וְהָיְתָה אִם־נִטְמְאָה וַתִּמְעֹל מַעַל בְּאִישָׁהּ וּבָאוּ בָהּ הַמַּיִם הַמְאָרֲרִים לְמָרִים וְצָבְתָה בִטְנָהּ וְנָפְלָה יְרֵכָהּ וְהָיְתָה הָאִשָּׁה לְאָלָה

כח בְּקֶרֶב עַמָּהּ: וְאִם־לֹא נִטְמְאָה הָאִשָּׁה וּטְהֹרָה הִוא וְנִקְּתָה וְנִזְרְעָה זָרַע:

כט-ל זֹאת תּוֹרַת הַקְּנָאֹת אֲשֶׁר תִּשְׂטֶה אִשָּׁה תַּחַת אִישָׁהּ וְנִטְמָאָה: אוֹ אִישׁ אֲשֶׁר תַּעֲבֹר עָלָיו רוּחַ קִנְאָה וְקִנֵּא אֶת־אִשְׁתּוֹ וְהֶעֱמִיד אֶת־הָאִשָּׁה לִפְנֵי

לא יהוה וְעָשָׂה לָהּ הַכֹּהֵן אֵת כָּל־הַתּוֹרָה הַזֹּאת: וְנִקָּה הָאִישׁ מֵעָוֺן וְהָאִשָּׁה הַהִוא תִּשָּׂא אֶת־עֲוֺנָהּ:

א-ב וַיְדַבֵּר יהוה אֶל־מֹשֶׁה לֵּאמֹר: דַּבֵּר אֶל־בְּנֵי יִשְׂרָאֵל וְאָמַרְתָּ אֲלֵהֶם אִישׁ

ו

ג אוֹ־אִשָּׁה כִּי יַפְלִא לִנְדֹּר נֶדֶר נָזִיר לְהַזִּיר לַיהוֹה: מִיַּיִן וְשֵׁכָר יַזִּיר חֹמֶץ יַיִן וְחֹמֶץ שֵׁכָר לֹא יִשְׁתֶּה וְכָל־מִשְׁרַת עֲנָבִים לֹא יִשְׁתֶּה וַעֲנָבִים לַחִים

ד וִיבֵשִׁים לֹא יֹאכֵל: כֹּל יְמֵי נִזְרוֹ מִכֹּל אֲשֶׁר יֵעָשֶׂה מִגֶּפֶן הַיַּיִן מֵחַרְצַנִּים

ה וְעַד־זָג לֹא יֹאכֵל: כָּל־יְמֵי נֶדֶר נִזְרוֹ תַּעַר לֹא־יַעֲבֹר עַל־רֹאשׁוֹ עַד־מְלֹאת הַיָּמִם אֲשֶׁר־יַזִּיר לַיהוֹה קָדֹשׁ יִהְיֶה גַּדֵּל פֶּרַע שְׂעַר רֹאשׁוֹ: כָּל־יְמֵי הַזִּירוֹ

ו-ז לַיהוֹה עַל־נֶפֶשׁ מֵת לֹא יָבֹא: לְאָבִיו וּלְאִמּוֹ לְאָחִיו וּלְאַחֹתוֹ לֹא־יִטַּמָּא

ח לָהֶם בְּמֹתָם כִּי נֵזֶר אֱלֹהָיו עַל־רֹאשׁוֹ: כֹּל יְמֵי נִזְרוֹ קָדֹשׁ הוּא לַיהוֹה:

5:18. The water is not literally bitter; rather, its effect upon a guilty party is bitter, for it causes her to die in the manner detailed below (*Rashi*).

5:19. The text begins with the alternative of innocence, because, in capital cases, a court must always begin with arguments for acquittal (*Rashi*).

5:23. Ordinarily, it is forbidden to erase God's sacred Name, but here God commanded that His Name be erased in order to bring peace between man and wife (*Yerushalmi Sotah* 1:4).

6:2. The Nazirite's heightened state of holiness is incompatible with the activities the Torah forbids him to engage in (*She'eilos U'Teshuvos Maharit* 1:543).

the water. ¹⁸ *The Kohen shall have the woman stand before* HASHEM *and uncover the woman's head, and upon her palms he shall put the meal-offering of remembrance — it is a meal-offering of jealousies, and in the hand of the Kohen shall be the bitter waters* that cause curse.*

The oath   ¹⁹ *"The Kohen shall adjure her and say to the woman, 'If a man has not lain with you, * and you have not strayed in defilement with someone other than your husband, then be proven innocent of these bitter waters that cause curse.* ²⁰ *But if you have strayed with someone other than your husband, and if you have become defiled, and a man other than your husband has lain with you —!'*

²¹ *"The Kohen shall adjure the woman with the oath of the curse, and the Kohen shall say to the woman, 'May* HASHEM *render you as a curse and as an oath amid your people, when* HASHEM *causes your thigh to collapse and your stomach to distend.* ²² *These waters that cause curse shall enter your innards to cause stomach to distend and thigh to collapse!' And the woman shall respond, 'Amen, amen.'*

The scroll   ²³ *"The Kohen shall inscribe these curses on a scroll* and erase it into the bitter waters.* ²⁴ *When he shall cause the woman to drink the bitter waters that cause curse, then the waters that cause curse shall come into her for bitterness.*

²⁵ *"The Kohen shall take the meal-offering of jealousies from the hand of the woman; he shall wave the meal-offering before* HASHEM, *and he shall bring it near the Altar.* ²⁶ *The Kohen shall scoop up from the meal-offering its remembrance and cause it to go up in smoke on the Altar; after which he shall cause the woman to drink the water.* ²⁷ *He shall cause her to drink the water, and it shall be that if she had become defiled and had committed treachery against her husband, the waters that cause curse shall come into her for bitterness, and her stomach shall be distended and her thigh shall collapse, and the woman shall become a curse amid her people.* ²⁸ *But if the woman had not become defiled, and she is pure, then she shall be proven innocent and she shall bear seed.*

²⁹ *"This is the law of the jealousies, when a woman shall go astray with someone other than her husband and become defiled;* ³⁰ *or of a man over whom passes a spirit of jealousy and he warns his wife, and he causes his wife to stand before* HASHEM, *then the Kohen shall carry out for her this entire law.* ³¹ *The man will be innocent of iniquity, but that woman shall bear her iniquity."*

6

The Nazirite

¹ H ASHEM *spoke to Moses, saying,* ² *"Speak to the Children of Israel and say to them: A man or woman who shall dissociate himself by taking a Nazirite vow of abstinence* for the sake of* HASHEM; ³ *from new or aged wine shall he abstain, and he shall not drink vinegar of wine or vinegar of aged wine; anything in which grapes have been steeped shall he not drink, and fresh and dried grapes shall he not eat.* ⁴ *All the days of his abstinence, anything made from wine grapes, even the pips or skin, he shall not eat.* ⁵ *All the days of his Nazirite vow, a razor shall not pass over his head; until the completion of the days that he will be a Nazirite for the sake of* HASHEM, *holy shall he be, the growth of hair on his head shall grow.* ⁶ *All the days of his abstinence for the sake of* HASHEM *he shall not come near a dead person.* ⁷ *To his father or to his mother, to his brother or to his sister — he shall not contaminate himself to them upon their death, for the crown of his God is upon his head.* ⁸ *All the days of his abstinence he is holy to* HASHEM.

ט וְכִי־יָמוּת מֵת עָלָיו בְּפֶתַע פִּתְאֹם וְטִמֵּא רֹאשׁ נִזְרוֹ וְגִלַּח רֹאשׁוֹ בְּיוֹם

י טָהֳרָתוֹ בַּיּוֹם הַשְּׁבִיעִי יְגַלְּחֶנּוּ: וּבַיּוֹם הַשְּׁמִינִי יָבִא שְׁתֵּי תֹרִים אוֹ שְׁנֵי בְּנֵי

יא יוֹנָה אֶל־הַכֹּהֵן אֶל־פֶּתַח אֹהֶל מוֹעֵד: וְעָשָׂה הַכֹּהֵן אֶחָד לְחַטָּאת וְאֶחָד לְעֹלָה וְכִפֶּר עָלָיו מֵאֲשֶׁר חָטָא עַל־הַנָּפֶשׁ וְקִדַּשׁ אֶת־רֹאשׁוֹ בַּיּוֹם הַהוּא:

יב וְהִזִּיר לַיהוָה אֶת־יְמֵי נִזְרוֹ וְהֵבִיא כֶּבֶשׂ בֶּן־שְׁנָתוֹ לְאָשָׁם וְהַיָּמִים

יג הָרִאשֹׁנִים יִפְּלוּ כִּי טָמֵא נִזְרוֹ: וְזֹאת תּוֹרַת הַנָּזִיר בְּיוֹם מְלֹאת יְמֵי נִזְרוֹ

יד יָבִיא אֹתוֹ אֶל־פֶּתַח אֹהֶל מוֹעֵד: וְהִקְרִיב אֶת־קָרְבָּנוֹ לַיהוָה כֶּבֶשׂ בֶּן־שְׁנָתוֹ תָמִים אֶחָד לְעֹלָה וְכַבְשָׂה אַחַת בַּת־שְׁנָתָהּ תְּמִימָה לְחַטָּאת

טו וְאַיִל־אֶחָד תָּמִים לִשְׁלָמִים: וְסַל מַצּוֹת סֹלֶת חַלֹּת בְּלוּלֹת בַּשֶּׁמֶן וּרְקִיקֵי

טז מַצּוֹת מְשֻׁחִים בַּשָּׁמֶן וּמִנְחָתָם וְנִסְכֵּיהֶם: וְהִקְרִיב הַכֹּהֵן לִפְנֵי יהוה וְעָשָׂה

יז אֶת־חַטָּאתוֹ וְאֶת־עֹלָתוֹ: וְאֶת־הָאַיִל יַעֲשֶׂה זֶבַח שְׁלָמִים לַיהוָה עַל סַל

יח הַמַּצּוֹת וְעָשָׂה הַכֹּהֵן אֶת־מִנְחָתוֹ וְאֶת־נִסְכּוֹ: וְגִלַּח הַנָּזִיר פֶּתַח אֹהֶל מוֹעֵד אֶת־רֹאשׁ נִזְרוֹ וְלָקַח אֶת־שְׂעַר רֹאשׁ נִזְרוֹ וְנָתַן עַל־הָאֵשׁ אֲשֶׁר־

יט תַּחַת זֶבַח הַשְּׁלָמִים: וְלָקַח הַכֹּהֵן אֶת־הַזְּרֹעַ בְּשֵׁלָה מִן־הָאַיִל וְחַלַּת מַצָּה אַחַת מִן־הַסַּל וּרְקִיק מַצָּה אֶחָד וְנָתַן עַל־כַּפֵּי הַנָּזִיר אַחַר הִתְגַּלְּחוֹ

כ אֶת־נִזְרוֹ: וְהֵנִיף אוֹתָם הַכֹּהֵן תְּנוּפָה לִפְנֵי יהוה קֹדֶשׁ הוּא לַכֹּהֵן עַל חֲזֵה הַתְּנוּפָה וְעַל שׁוֹק הַתְּרוּמָה וְאַחַר יִשְׁתֶּה הַנָּזִיר יָיִן:

כא זֹאת תּוֹרַת הַנָּזִיר אֲשֶׁר יִדֹּר קָרְבָּנוֹ לַיהוָה עַל־נִזְרוֹ מִלְּבַד אֲשֶׁר־תַּשִּׂיג יָדוֹ כְּפִי נִדְרוֹ אֲשֶׁר יִדֹּר כֵּן יַעֲשֶׂה עַל תּוֹרַת נִזְרוֹ:

כב-כג וַיְדַבֵּר יהוה אֶל־מֹשֶׁה לֵּאמֹר: דַּבֵּר אֶל־אַהֲרֹן וְאֶל־בָּנָיו לֵאמֹר כֹּה תְבָרְכוּ

כד-כה אֶת־בְּנֵי יִשְׂרָאֵל אָמוֹר לָהֶם: יְבָרֶכְךָ יהוה וְיִשְׁמְרֶךָ: יָאֵר

כו יהוה פָּנָיו אֵלֶיךָ וִיחֻנֶּךָּ: יִשָּׂא יהוה פָּנָיו אֵלֶיךָ וְיָשֵׂם לְךָ

כז שָׁלוֹם: וְשָׂמוּ אֶת־שְׁמִי עַל־בְּנֵי יִשְׂרָאֵל וַאֲנִי אֲבָרֲכֵם:

ז א וַיְהִי בְּיוֹם כַּלּוֹת מֹשֶׁה לְהָקִים אֶת־הַמִּשְׁכָּן וַיִּמְשַׁח אֹתוֹ וַיְקַדֵּשׁ אֹתוֹ וְאֶת־כָּל־כֵּלָיו וְאֶת־הַמִּזְבֵּחַ וְאֶת־כָּל־כֵּלָיו וַיִּמְשָׁחֵם וַיְקַדֵּשׁ אֹתָם:

ב וַיַּקְרִיבוּ נְשִׂיאֵי יִשְׂרָאֵל רָאשֵׁי בֵּית אֲבֹתָם הֵם נְשִׂיאֵי הַמַּטֹּת הֵם

ג הָעֹמְדִים עַל־הַפְּקֻדִים: וַיָּבִיאוּ אֶת־קָרְבָּנָם לִפְנֵי יהוה שֵׁשׁ־עֶגְלֹת צָב וּשְׁנֵי עָשָׂר בָּקָר עֲגָלָה עַל־שְׁנֵי הַנְּשִׂאִים וְשׁוֹר לְאֶחָד וַיַּקְרִיבוּ אוֹתָם

ד-ה לִפְנֵי הַמִּשְׁכָּן: וַיֹּאמֶר יהוה אֶל־מֹשֶׁה לֵּאמֹר: קַח מֵאִתָּם וְהָיוּ לַעֲבֹד אֶת־עֲבֹדַת אֹהֶל מוֹעֵד וְנָתַתָּה אוֹתָם אֶל־הַלְוִיִּם אִישׁ כְּפִי עֲבֹדָתוֹ:

חמישי ז

FIRST DAY
CHANUKAH
Weekday
reading and
Sabbath
Maftir:
7:1-17
(some begin
at 6:22)

6:24. The First Blessing. May God give you the many blessings that are specified in the Torah (Sifre), and protect your newly gained blessing of prosperity so that bandits cannot take it away from you (Rashi).

6:25. The Second Blessing. May God enable you to perceive the wondrous wisdom of the Torah (Sforno).

6:26. The Third Blessing. One may have prosperity,

health, food and drink, but if there is no peace it is all worthless (Sifra, Bechukosai).

6:27. The Kohanim do not have any independent power to confer or withhold blessings; rather, they are the conduit through which God's blessings would be pronounced upon His people.

7:2. The Midrash relates that, at first, Moses was

Sudden contamination
⁹ *"If a person should die near him with quick suddenness and contaminate his Nazirite head, he shall shave his head on the day he becomes purified; on the seventh day shall he shave it.* ¹⁰ *On the eighth day he shall bring two turtledoves or two young doves to the Kohen, to the entrance of the Tent of Meeting.* ¹¹ *The Kohen shall make one as a sin-offering and one as a burnt-offering, and he shall provide him atonement for having sinned regarding the person; and he shall sanctify his head on that day.* ¹² *He shall dedicate to HASHEM the days of his abstinence, and he shall bring a sheep in its first year for a guilt-offering; the first days shall fall aside, for his abstinence had been contaminated.*

Completion of the term
(See Appendix B, charts 8,10)
¹³ *"This shall be the law of the Nazirite: on the day his abstinence is completed, he shall bring himself to the entrance of the Tent of Meeting.* ¹⁴ *He shall bring his offering to HASHEM: one unblemished sheep in its first year as a burnt-offering, one unblemished ewe in its first year as a sin-offering, and one unblemished ram as a peace-offering;* ¹⁵ *a basket of unleavened loaves: loaves of fine flour mixed with oil and unleavened wafers smeared with oil; and their meal-offerings and their libations.* ¹⁶ *The Kohen shall approach before HASHEM and perform the service of his sin-offering and his burnt-offering.* ¹⁷ *He shall make the ram a feast peace-offering for HASHEM with the basket of unleavened loaves, and the Kohen shall make its meal-offering and its libation.* ¹⁸ *At the entrance of the Tent of Meeting the Nazirite shall shave his Nazirite head; he shall take the hair of his Nazirite head and put it on the fire that is under the feast peace-offering.* ¹⁹ *The Kohen shall take the cooked foreleg of the ram and one unleavened loaf from the basket and one unleavened wafer, and place them on the palms of the Nazirite after he has shaved his Nazirite hair.* ²⁰ *The Kohen shall wave them as a wave-service before HASHEM; it shall be holy for the Kohen, aside from the breast of the waving and the thigh of the raising-up — afterward the Nazirite may drink wine.*

²¹ *"This is the law of the Nazirite who shall pledge his offering to HASHEM for his abstinence — aside from what he can afford, according to his vow that he shall pledge, so shall he do in addition to the law of his abstinence."*

The Priestly Blessings
²² *HASHEM spoke to Moses, saying,* ²³ *"Speak to Aaron and his sons, saying: So shall you bless the Children of Israel, saying to them:* ²⁴ *'May HASHEM bless you and safeguard you.* * ²⁵ *May HASHEM illuminate His countenance for you and be gracious to you.* * ²⁶ *May HASHEM lift His countenance to you and establish peace for you.'* * ²⁷ *Let them place My Name upon the Children of Israel, and I shall bless them."* *

7
¹ *It was on the day that Moses finished erecting the Tabernacle that he anointed it, sanctified it and all its utensils, and the Altar and all its utensils, and he had anointed and sanctified them.* ² *The leaders of Israel, the heads of their fathers' household, brought offerings;* * *they were the leaders of the tribes, they were those who stand at the countings.* ³ *They brought their offering before HASHEM: six covered wagons and twelve oxen — a wagon for each two leaders and an ox for each — and they brought them before the Tabernacle.* ⁴ *HASHEM said to Moses, saying,* ⁵ *"Take from them, and they shall be to perform the work of the Tent of Meeting; you shall give them to the Levites, each man according to his work."*

The offerings of the tribal leaders

---

reluctant to accept the leaders' offerings, since God had not commanded that these offerings be brought. The experience of Nadab and Abihu, who died when they brought unauthorized incense, was a frightening prece-

ו-ז וַיִּקַּ֣ח מֹשֶׁ֗ה אֶת־הָעֲגָלֹ֖ת וְאֶת־הַבָּקָ֑ר וַיִּתֵּ֥ן אוֹתָ֖ם אֶל־הַלְוִיִּֽם: אֵ֣ת ׀ שְׁתֵּ֣י

ח הָעֲגָלֹ֗ת וְאֵת֙ אַרְבַּ֣עַת הַבָּקָ֔ר נָתַ֕ן לִבְנֵ֥י גֵרְשׁ֖וֹן כְּפִ֥י עֲבֹֽדָתָֽם: וְאֵ֣ת ׀ אַרְבַּ֣ע

הָעֲגָלֹ֗ת וְאֵת֙ שְׁמֹנַ֣ת הַבָּקָ֔ר נָתַ֕ן לִבְנֵ֣י מְרָרִ֑י כְּפִי֙ עֲבֹ֣דָתָ֔ם בְּיַד֙ אִֽיתָמָ֔ר בֶּֽן־

ט אַהֲרֹ֥ן הַכֹּהֵֽן: וְלִבְנֵ֥י קְהָ֖ת לֹ֣א נָתָ֑ן כִּֽי־עֲבֹדַ֤ת הַקֹּ֙דֶשׁ֙ עֲלֵהֶ֔ם בַּכָּתֵ֖ף יִשָּֽׂאוּ:

י וַיַּקְרִ֣יבוּ הַנְּשִׂאִ֗ים אֵ֚ת חֲנֻכַּ֣ת הַמִּזְבֵּ֔חַ בְּי֖וֹם הִמָּשַׁ֣ח אֹת֑וֹ וַיַּקְרִ֧יבוּ הַנְּשִׂיאִ֛ם

יא אֶת־קׇרְבָּנָ֖ם לִפְנֵ֥י הַמִּזְבֵּֽחַ: וַיֹּ֥אמֶר יְהֹוָ֖ה אֶל־מֹשֶׁ֑ה נָשִׂ֨יא אֶחָ֜ד לַיּ֗וֹם נָשִׂ֤יא

יב אֶחָד֙ לַיּ֔וֹם יַקְרִ֙יבוּ֙ אֶת־קׇרְבָּנָ֔ם לַחֲנֻכַּ֖ת הַמִּזְבֵּֽחַ: וַֽיְהִ֗י

הַמַּקְרִ֛יב בַּיּ֥וֹם הָרִאשׁ֖וֹן אֶת־קׇרְבָּנ֑וֹ נַחְשׁ֥וֹן בֶּן־עַמִּינָדָ֖ב לְמַטֵּ֥ה יְהוּדָֽה:

יג וְקׇרְבָּנ֞וֹ קַֽעֲרַת־כֶּ֣סֶף אַחַ֗ת שְׁלֹשִׁ֣ים וּמֵאָה֮ מִשְׁקָלָהּ֒ מִזְרָ֤ק אֶחָד֙ כֶּ֔סֶף

שִׁבְעִ֥ים שֶׁ֖קֶל בְּשֶׁ֣קֶל הַקֹּ֑דֶשׁ שְׁנֵיהֶ֣ם ׀ מְלֵאִ֗ים סֹ֛לֶת בְּלוּלָ֥ה בַשֶּׁ֖מֶן לְמִנְחָֽה:

יד-טו כַּ֣ף אַחַ֧ת עֲשָׂרָ֛ה זָהָ֖ב מְלֵאָ֥ה קְטֹֽרֶת: פַּ֣ר אֶחָ֞ד בֶּן־בָּקָ֗ר אַ֧יִל אֶחָ֛ד כֶּֽבֶשׂ־

טז-יז אֶחָ֥ד בֶּן־שְׁנָת֖וֹ לְעֹלָֽה: שְׂעִיר־עִזִּ֥ים אֶחָ֖ד לְחַטָּֽאת: וּלְזֶ֣בַח הַשְּׁלָמִים֮ בָּקָ֣ר

שְׁנַ֒יִם֒ אֵילִ֤ם חֲמִשָּׁה֙ עַתּוּדִ֣ים חֲמִשָּׁ֔ה כְּבָשִׂ֥ים בְּנֵֽי־שָׁנָ֖ה חֲמִשָּׁ֑ה זֶ֛ה קׇרְבַּ֥ן

נַחְשׁ֖וֹן בֶּן־עַמִּינָדָֽב:

SECOND DAY CHANUKAH Weekday reading: 7:18-29; Sabbath Maftir: 7:18-23

יח-יט בַּיּוֹם֙ הַשֵּׁנִ֔י הִקְרִ֖יב נְתַנְאֵ֣ל בֶּן־צוּעָ֑ר נְשִׂ֖יא יִשָּׂשכָֽר: הִקְרִ֨ב אֶת־קׇרְבָּנ֜וֹ

כ קַעֲרַת־כֶּ֣סֶף אַחַ֗ת שְׁלֹשִׁ֣ים וּמֵאָה֮ מִשְׁקָלָהּ֒ מִזְרָ֤ק אֶחָד֙ כֶּ֔סֶף שִׁבְעִ֥ים שֶׁ֖קֶל

בְּשֶׁ֣קֶל הַקֹּ֑דֶשׁ שְׁנֵיהֶ֣ם ׀ מְלֵאִ֗ים סֹ֛לֶת בְּלוּלָ֥ה בַשֶּׁ֖מֶן לְמִנְחָֽה: כַּ֚ף אַחַ֣ת

כא עֲשָׂרָ֣ה זָהָ֔ב מְלֵאָ֖ה קְטֹֽרֶת: פַּ֣ר אֶחָ֞ד בֶּן־בָּקָ֗ר אַ֧יִל אֶחָ֛ד כֶּֽבֶשׂ־אֶחָ֥ד בֶּן־

כב-כג שְׁנָת֖וֹ לְעֹלָֽה: שְׂעִיר־עִזִּ֥ים אֶחָ֖ד לְחַטָּֽאת: וּלְזֶ֣בַח הַשְּׁלָמִים֮ בָּקָ֣ר שְׁנַ֒יִם֒

אֵילִ֤ם חֲמִשָּׁה֙ עַתֻּדִ֣ים חֲמִשָּׁ֔ה כְּבָשִׂ֥ים בְּנֵי־שָׁנָ֖ה חֲמִשָּׁ֑ה זֶ֛ה קׇרְבַּ֥ן נְתַנְאֵ֖ל

בֶּן־צוּעָֽר:

THIRD DAY CHANUKAH Weekday reading: 7:24-35; Sabbath Maftir: 7:24-29

כד-כה בַּיּוֹם֙ הַשְּׁלִישִׁ֔י נָשִׂ֖יא לִבְנֵ֣י זְבוּלֻ֑ן אֱלִיאָ֖ב בֶּן־חֵלֹֽן: קׇרְבָּנ֞וֹ קַֽעֲרַת־כֶּ֣סֶף

אַחַ֗ת שְׁלֹשִׁ֣ים וּמֵאָה֮ מִשְׁקָלָהּ֒ מִזְרָ֤ק אֶחָד֙ כֶּ֔סֶף שִׁבְעִ֥ים שֶׁ֖קֶל בְּשֶׁ֣קֶל

כו הַקֹּ֑דֶשׁ שְׁנֵיהֶ֣ם ׀ מְלֵאִ֗ים סֹ֛לֶת בְּלוּלָ֥ה בַשֶּׁ֖מֶן לְמִנְחָֽה: כַּ֣ף אַחַ֧ת עֲשָׂרָ֛ה זָהָ֖ב

כז מְלֵאָ֥ה קְטֹֽרֶת: פַּ֣ר אֶחָ֞ד בֶּן־בָּקָ֗ר אַ֧יִל אֶחָ֛ד כֶּֽבֶשׂ־אֶחָ֥ד בֶּן־שְׁנָת֖וֹ לְעֹלָֽה:

כח-כט שְׂעִיר־עִזִּ֥ים אֶחָ֖ד לְחַטָּֽאת: וּלְזֶ֣בַח הַשְּׁלָמִים֮ בָּקָ֣ר שְׁנַ֒יִם֒ אֵילִ֤ם חֲמִשָּׁה֙

עַתֻּדִ֣ים חֲמִשָּׁ֔ה כְּבָשִׂ֥ים בְּנֵֽי־שָׁנָ֖ה חֲמִשָּׁ֑ה זֶ֛ה קׇרְבַּ֥ן אֱלִיאָ֖ב בֶּן־חֵלֹֽן:

FOURTH DAY CHANUKAH Weekday reading: 7:30-41; Sabbath Maftir: 7:30-35

ל-לא בַּיּוֹם֙ הָרְבִיעִ֔י נָשִׂ֖יא לִבְנֵ֣י רְאוּבֵ֑ן אֱלִיצ֖וּר בֶּן־שְׁדֵיאֽוּר: קׇרְבָּנ֞וֹ קַֽעֲרַת־

כֶּ֣סֶף אַחַ֗ת שְׁלֹשִׁ֣ים וּמֵאָה֮ מִשְׁקָלָהּ֒ מִזְרָ֤ק אֶחָד֙ כֶּ֔סֶף שִׁבְעִ֥ים שֶׁ֖קֶל

לב בְּשֶׁ֣קֶל הַקֹּ֑דֶשׁ שְׁנֵיהֶ֣ם ׀ מְלֵאִ֗ים סֹ֛לֶת בְּלוּלָ֥ה בַשֶּׁ֖מֶן לְמִנְחָֽה: כַּ֚ף אַחַ֣ת

לג עֲשָׂרָ֣ה זָהָ֔ב מְלֵאָ֖ה קְטֹֽרֶת: פַּ֣ר אֶחָ֞ד בֶּן־בָּקָ֗ר אַ֧יִל אֶחָ֛ד כֶּֽבֶשׂ־אֶחָ֥ד בֶּן־

לד-לה שְׁנָת֖וֹ לְעֹלָֽה: שְׂעִיר־עִזִּ֥ים אֶחָ֖ד לְחַטָּֽאת: וּלְזֶ֣בַח הַשְּׁלָמִים֮ בָּקָ֣ר שְׁנַ֒יִם֒

אֵילִ֤ם חֲמִשָּׁה֙ עַתֻּדִ֣ים חֲמִשָּׁ֔ה כְּבָשִׂ֥ים בְּנֵֽי־שָׁנָ֖ה חֲמִשָּׁ֑ה זֶ֛ה קׇרְבַּ֥ן אֱלִיצ֖וּר

בֶּן־שְׁדֵיאֽוּר:

⁶ *So Moses took the wagons and the oxen and gave them to the Levites.* ⁷ *Two of the wagons and four of the oxen he gave to the sons of Gershon, in accordance with their work.* ⁸ *And four of the wagons and eight of the oxen he gave to the sons of Merari, in accordance with their work, under the authority of Ithamar, son of Aaron the Kohen.* ⁹ *And to the sons of Kohath he did not give; since the sacred service was upon them, they carried on the shoulder.* ¹⁰ *Then the leaders brought forward offerings for the dedication of the Altar on the day it was anointed, and the leaders brought their offering before the Altar.* ¹¹ *HASHEM said to Moses, "One leader each day, one leader each day shall they bring their offering for the dedication of the Altar."*

One each day:

Judah ¹² *The one who brought his offering on the first day was Nahshon son of Amminadab, of the tribe of Judah.* ¹³ *His offering was: one silver bowl, its weight a hundred and thirty [shekels]; and one silver basin of seventy shekels in the sacred shekel; both of them filled with fine flour mixed with oil for a meal-offering;* ¹⁴ *one gold ladle of ten [shekels] filled with incense;* ¹⁵ *one young bull, one ram, one sheep in its first year for a burnt-offering;* ¹⁶ *one he-goat for a sin-offering;* ¹⁷ *and for a feast peace-offering: two cattle, five rams, five he-goats, five sheep in their first year — this is the offering of Nachshon son of Amminadab.*

Issachar ¹⁸ *On the second day, Nethanel son of Zuar offered, the leader of Issachar.* ¹⁹ *He brought his offering: one silver bowl, its weight a hundred and thirty [shekels]; and one silver basin of seventy shekels in the sacred shekel; both of them filled with fine flour mixed with oil for a meal-offering;* ²⁰ *one gold ladle of ten [shekels] filled with incense;* ²¹ *one young bull, one ram, one sheep in its first year for a burnt-offering;* ²² *one he-goat for a sin-offering;* ²³ *and for a feast peace-offering: two cattle, five rams, five he-goats, five sheep in their first year — this is the offering of Nethanel son of Zuar.*

Zebulun ²⁴ *On the third day, the leader of the children of Zebulun, Eliab son of Helon.* ²⁵ *His offering was: one silver bowl, its weight a hundred and thirty [shekels]; and one silver basin of seventy shekels in the sacred shekel; both of them filled with fine flour mixed with oil for a meal-offering;* ²⁶ *one gold ladle of ten [shekels] filled with incense;* ²⁷ *one young bull, one ram, one sheep in its first year for a burnt-offering;* ²⁸ *one he-goat for a sin-offering;* ²⁹ *and for a feast peace-offering: two cattle, five rams, five he-goats, five sheep in their first year — this is the offering of Eliab son of Helon.*

Reuben ³⁰ *On the fourth day, the leader of the children of Reuben, Elizur son of Shedeur.* ³¹ *His offering was: one silver bowl, its weight a hundred and thirty [shekels]; and one silver basin of seventy shekels in the sacred shekel; both of them filled with fine flour mixed with oil for a meal-offering;* ³² *one gold ladle of ten [shekels] filled with incense;* ³³ *one young bull, one ram, one sheep in its first year for a burnt-offering;* ³⁴ *one he-goat for a sin-offering;* ³⁵ *and for a feast peace-offering: two cattle, five rams, five he-goats, five sheep in their first year — this is the offering of Elizur son of Shedeur.*

---

dent (*Leviticus* 10:1-2). But God told him that the intention of the leaders was pure and their offerings were worthy of acceptance.

Although their offerings were identical, each one is mentioned separately because each was brought to represent a different set of symbols (see *Midrash*).

לו־לז בַּיּוֹם֙ הַֽחֲמִישִׁ֔י נָשִׂ֖יא לִבְנֵ֣י שִׁמְע֑וֹן שְׁלֻֽמִיאֵ֖ל בֶּן־צוּרִֽישַׁדָּֽי: קָרְבָּנ֞וֹ קַֽעֲרַת־כֶּ֣סֶף אַחַ֗ת שְׁלֹשִׁ֣ים וּמֵאָה֮ מִשְׁקָלָהּ֒ מִזְרָ֤ק אֶחָד֙ כֶּ֔סֶף שִׁבְעִ֥ים שֶׁ֖קֶל בְּשֶׁ֣קֶל הַקֹּ֑דֶשׁ

לח שְׁנֵיהֶ֣ם ׀ מְלֵאִ֗ים סֹ֛לֶת בְּלוּלָ֥ה בַשֶּׁ֖מֶן לְמִנְחָֽה: כַּ֥ף אַחַ֛ת עֲשָׂרָ֥ה זָהָ֖ב מְלֵאָ֥ה קְטֹֽרֶת:

לט פַּ֣ר אֶחָ֞ד בֶּן־בָּקָ֗ר אַ֧יִל אֶחָ֛ד כֶּֽבֶשׂ־אֶחָ֥ד בֶּן־שְׁנָת֖וֹ לְעֹלָֽה:

מ־מא שְׂעִיר־עִזִּ֥ים אֶחָ֖ד לְחַטָּֽאת: וּלְזֶ֣בַח הַשְּׁלָמִים֮ בָּקָ֣ר שְׁנַ֒יִם֒ אֵילִ֤ם חֲמִשָּׁה֙ עַתּוּדִ֣ים חֲמִשָּׁ֔ה כְּבָשִׂ֥ים בְּנֵֽי־שָׁנָ֖ה חֲמִשָּׁ֑ה זֶ֛ה קָרְבַּ֥ן שְׁלֻֽמִיאֵ֖ל בֶּן־צוּרִֽישַׁדָּֽי:

מב־מג בַּיּוֹם֙ הַשִּׁשִּׁ֔י נָשִׂ֖יא לִבְנֵ֣י גָ֑ד אֶלְיָסָ֖ף בֶּן־דְּעוּאֵֽל: קָרְבָּנ֞וֹ קַֽעֲרַת־כֶּ֣סֶף אַחַ֗ת שְׁלֹשִׁ֣ים וּמֵאָה֮ מִשְׁקָלָהּ֒ מִזְרָ֤ק אֶחָד֙ כֶּ֔סֶף שִׁבְעִ֥ים שֶׁ֖קֶל בְּשֶׁ֣קֶל הַקֹּ֑דֶשׁ

SIXTH DAY CHANUKAH
Weekday,
aliyos 1-3:
28:1-15;
4th aliyah:
7:42-47;
Sabbath
7th aliyah:
28:9-15;
Maftir:
7:42-47

מד שְׁנֵיהֶ֣ם ׀ מְלֵאִ֗ים סֹ֛לֶת בְּלוּלָ֥ה בַשֶּׁ֖מֶן לְמִנְחָֽה: כַּ֥ף אַחַ֛ת עֲשָׂרָ֥ה זָהָ֖ב מְלֵאָ֥ה קְטֹֽרֶת:

מה־מו פַּ֣ר אֶחָ֞ד בֶּן־בָּקָ֗ר אַ֧יִל אֶחָ֛ד כֶּֽבֶשׂ־אֶחָ֥ד בֶּן־שְׁנָת֖וֹ לְעֹלָֽה: שְׂעִיר־עִזִּ֥ים אֶחָ֖ד לְחַטָּֽאת:

מז וּלְזֶ֣בַח הַשְּׁלָמִים֮ בָּקָ֣ר שְׁנַ֒יִם֒ אֵילִ֤ם חֲמִשָּׁה֙ עַתּוּדִ֣ים חֲמִשָּׁ֔ה כְּבָשִׂ֥ים בְּנֵֽי־שָׁנָ֖ה חֲמִשָּׁ֑ה זֶ֛ה קָרְבַּ֥ן אֶלְיָסָ֖ף בֶּן־דְּעוּאֵֽל:

מח־מט בַּיּוֹם֙ הַשְּׁבִיעִ֔י נָשִׂ֖יא לִבְנֵ֣י אֶפְרָ֑יִם אֱלִֽישָׁמָ֖ע בֶּן־עַמִּיהֽוּד: קָרְבָּנ֞וֹ קַֽעֲרַת־כֶּ֣סֶף אַחַ֗ת שְׁלֹשִׁ֣ים וּמֵאָה֮ מִשְׁקָלָהּ֒ מִזְרָ֤ק אֶחָד֙ כֶּ֔סֶף שִׁבְעִ֥ים שֶׁ֖קֶל בְּשֶׁ֣קֶל הַקֹּ֑דֶשׁ שְׁנֵיהֶ֣ם ׀ מְלֵאִ֗ים

SEVENTH DAY CHANUKAH
7:48-59
(on Rosh
Chodesh,
aliyos 1-3:
28:1-15;
4th aliyah:
7:48-53)

סֹ֛לֶת בְּלוּלָ֥ה בַשֶּׁ֖מֶן לְמִנְחָֽה: כַּ֥ף אַחַ֛ת

נ עֲשָׂרָ֥ה זָהָ֖ב מְלֵאָ֥ה קְטֹֽרֶת: פַּ֣ר אֶחָ֞ד בֶּן־בָּקָ֗ר אַ֧יִל אֶחָ֛ד כֶּֽבֶשׂ־אֶחָ֥ד בֶּן־

נא שְׁנָת֖וֹ לְעֹלָֽה: שְׂעִיר־עִזִּ֥ים אֶחָ֖ד לְחַטָּֽאת: וּלְזֶ֣בַח הַשְּׁלָמִים֮ בָּקָ֣ר שְׁנַ֒יִם֒

נב־נג אֵילִ֤ם חֲמִשָּׁה֙ עַתּוּדִ֣ים חֲמִשָּׁ֔ה כְּבָשִׂ֥ים בְּנֵֽי־שָׁנָ֖ה חֲמִשָּׁ֑ה זֶ֛ה קָרְבַּ֥ן אֱלִֽישָׁמָ֖ע בֶּן־עַמִּיהֽוּד:

נד־נה בַּיּוֹם֙ הַשְּׁמִינִ֔י נָשִׂ֖יא לִבְנֵ֣י מְנַשֶּׁ֑ה גַּמְלִיאֵ֖ל בֶּן־פְּדָהצֽוּר: קָרְבָּנ֞וֹ קַֽעֲרַת־כֶּ֣סֶף אַחַ֗ת שְׁלֹשִׁ֣ים וּמֵאָה֮ מִשְׁקָלָהּ֒ מִזְרָ֤ק אֶחָד֙ כֶּ֔סֶף שִׁבְעִ֥ים שֶׁ֖קֶל בְּשֶׁ֣קֶל

נו הַקֹּ֑דֶשׁ שְׁנֵיהֶ֣ם ׀ מְלֵאִ֗ים סֹ֛לֶת בְּלוּלָ֥ה בַשֶּׁ֖מֶן לְמִנְחָֽה: כַּ֥ף אַחַ֛ת עֲשָׂרָ֥ה זָהָ֖ב מְלֵאָ֥ה קְטֹֽרֶת: פַּ֣ר אֶחָ֞ד בֶּן־בָּקָ֗ר אַ֧יִל אֶחָ֛ד כֶּֽבֶשׂ־אֶחָ֥ד בֶּן־שְׁנָת֖וֹ

נז לְעֹלָֽה: שְׂעִיר־עִזִּ֥ים אֶחָ֖ד לְחַטָּֽאת: וּלְזֶ֣בַח הַשְּׁלָמִים֮ בָּקָ֣ר שְׁנַ֒יִם֒ אֵילִ֤ם

נח־נט חֲמִשָּׁה֙ עַתּוּדִ֣ים חֲמִשָּׁ֔ה כְּבָשִׂ֥ים בְּנֵֽי־שָׁנָ֖ה חֲמִשָּׁ֑ה זֶ֛ה קָרְבַּ֥ן גַּמְלִיאֵ֖ל בֶּן־פְּדָהצֽוּר:

ס־סא בַּיּוֹם֙ הַתְּשִׁיעִ֔י נָשִׂ֖יא לִבְנֵ֣י בִנְיָמִ֑ן אֲבִידָ֖ן בֶּן־גִּדְעֹנִֽי: קָרְבָּנ֞וֹ קַֽעֲרַת־כֶּ֣סֶף אַחַ֗ת שְׁלֹשִׁ֣ים וּמֵאָה֮ מִשְׁקָלָהּ֒ מִזְרָ֤ק אֶחָד֙ כֶּ֔סֶף שִׁבְעִ֥ים שֶׁ֖קֶל בְּשֶׁ֣קֶל

סב הַקֹּ֑דֶשׁ שְׁנֵיהֶ֣ם ׀ מְלֵאִ֗ים סֹ֛לֶת בְּלוּלָ֥ה בַשֶּׁ֖מֶן לְמִנְחָֽה: כַּ֥ף אַחַ֛ת עֲשָׂרָ֥ה זָהָ֖ב

סג מְלֵאָ֥ה קְטֹֽרֶת: פַּ֣ר אֶחָ֞ד בֶּן־בָּקָ֗ר אַ֧יִל אֶחָ֛ד כֶּֽבֶשׂ־אֶחָ֥ד בֶּן־שְׁנָת֖וֹ לְעֹלָֽה:

סד־סה שְׂעִיר־עִזִּ֥ים אֶחָ֖ד לְחַטָּֽאת: וּלְזֶ֣בַח הַשְּׁלָמִים֮ בָּקָ֣ר שְׁנַ֒יִם֒ אֵילִ֤ם חֲמִשָּׁה֙ עַתּוּדִ֣ים חֲמִשָּׁ֔ה כְּבָשִׂ֥ים בְּנֵֽי־שָׁנָ֖ה חֲמִשָּׁ֑ה זֶ֛ה קָרְבַּ֥ן אֲבִידָ֖ן בֶּן־גִּדְעֹנִֽי:

סו־סז בַּיּוֹם֙ הָֽעֲשִׂירִ֔י נָשִׂ֖יא לִבְנֵ֣י דָ֑ן אֲחִיעֶ֖זֶר בֶּן־עַמִּֽישַׁדָּֽי: קָרְבָּנ֞וֹ קַֽעֲרַת־כֶּ֣סֶף אַחַ֗ת שְׁלֹשִׁ֣ים וּמֵאָה֮ מִשְׁקָלָהּ֒ מִזְרָ֤ק אֶחָד֙ כֶּ֔סֶף שִׁבְעִ֥ים שֶׁ֖קֶל בְּשֶׁ֣קֶל הַקֹּ֑דֶשׁ

Simeon   ³⁶ On the fifth day, the leader of the children of Simeon, Shelumiel son of Zurishaddai. ³⁷ His offering was: one silver bowl, its weight a hundred and thirty [shekels]; and one silver basin of seventy shekels in the sacred shekel; both of them filled with fine flour mixed with oil for a meal-offering; ³⁸ one gold ladle of ten [shekels] filled with incense; ³⁹ one young bull, one ram, one sheep in its first year for a burnt-offering; ⁴⁰ one he-goat for a sin-offering; ⁴¹ and for a feast peace-offering: two cattle, five rams, five he-goats, five sheep in their first year — this is the offering of Shelumiel son of Zurishaddai.

Gad   ⁴² On the sixth day, the leader of the children of Gad, Eliasaph son of Deuel. ⁴³ His offering was: one silver bowl, its weight a hundred and thirty [shekels]; and one silver basin of seventy shekels in the sacred shekel; both of them filled with fine flour mixed with oil for a meal-offering; ⁴⁴ one gold ladle of ten [shekels] filled with incense; ⁴⁵ one young bull, one ram, one sheep in its first year for a burnt-offering; ⁴⁶ one he-goat for a sin-offering; ⁴⁷ and for a feast peace-offering: two cattle, five rams, five he-goats, five sheep in their first year — this is the offering of Eliasaph son of Deuel.

Ephraim   ⁴⁸ On the seventh day, the leader of the children of Ephraim, Elishama son of Ammihud. ⁴⁹ His offering was: one silver bowl, its weight a hundred and thirty [shekels]; and one silver basin of seventy shekels in the sacred shekel; both of them filled with fine flour mixed with oil for a meal-offering; ⁵⁰ one gold ladle of ten [shekels] filled with incense; ⁵¹ one young bull, one ram, one sheep in its first year for a burnt-offering; ⁵² one he-goat for a sin-offering; ⁵³ and for a feast peace-offering: two cattle, five rams, five he-goats, five sheep in their first year — this is the offering of Elishama son of Ammihud.

Manasseh   ⁵⁴ On the eighth day, the leader of the children of Manasseh, Gamaliel son of Pedahzur. ⁵⁵ His offering was: one silver bowl, its weight a hundred and thirty [shekels]; and one silver basin of seventy shekels in the sacred shekel; both of them filled with fine flour mixed with oil for a meal-offering; ⁵⁶ one gold ladle of ten [shekels] filled with incense; ⁵⁷ one young bull, one ram, one sheep in its first year for a burnt-offering; ⁵⁸ one he-goat for a sin-offering; ⁵⁹ and for a feast peace-offering: two cattle, five rams, five he-goats, five sheep in their first year — this is the offering of Gamaliel son of Pedahzur.

Benjamin   ⁶⁰ On the ninth day, the leader of the children of Benjamin, Abidan son of Gideoni. ⁶¹ His offering was: one silver bowl, its weight a hundred and thirty [shekels]; and one silver basin of seventy shekels in the sacred shekel; both of them filled with fine flour mixed with oil for a meal-offering; ⁶² one gold ladle of ten [shekels] filled with incense; ⁶³ one young bull, one ram, one sheep in its first year for a burnt-offering; ⁶⁴ one he-goat for a sin-offering; ⁶⁵ and for a feast peace-offering: two cattle, five rams, five he-goats, five sheep in their first year — this is the offering of Abidan son of Gideoni.

Dan   ⁶⁶ On the tenth day, the leader of the children of Dan, Ahiezer son of Ammishaddai. ⁶⁷ His offering was: one silver bowl, its weight a hundred and thirty [shekels]; and one silver basin of seventy shekels in the sacred shekel;

סח   שְׁנֵיהֶ֣ם ׀ מְלֵאִ֗ים סֹ֛לֶת בְּלוּלָ֥ה בַשֶּׁ֖מֶן לְמִנְחָֽה: כַּ֣ף אַחַ֧ת עֲשָׂרָ֛ה זָהָ֖ב מְלֵאָ֥ה

סט־ע   קְטֹֽרֶת: פַּ֣ר אֶחָ֞ד בֶּן־בָּקָ֗ר אַ֧יִל אֶחָ֛ד כֶּֽבֶשׂ־אֶחָ֥ד בֶּן־שְׁנָת֖וֹ לְעֹלָֽה: שְׂעִיר־

עא   עִזִּ֥ים אֶחָ֖ד לְחַטָּֽאת: וּלְזֶ֣בַח הַשְּׁלָמִים֮ בָּקָ֣ר שְׁנַיִם֒ אֵילִ֤ם חֲמִשָּׁה֙ עַתֻּדִ֣ים

חֲמִשָּׁ֔ה כְּבָשִׂ֥ים בְּנֵֽי־שָׁנָ֖ה חֲמִשָּׁ֑ה זֶ֚ה קָרְבַּ֣ן אֲחִיעֶ֔זֶר בֶּן־עַמִּֽישַׁדָּֽי:

שביעי   עב־עג   בְּיוֹם֙ עַשְׁתֵּ֣י עָשָׂ֣ר י֔וֹם נָשִׂ֖יא לִבְנֵ֣י אָשֵׁ֑ר פַּגְעִיאֵ֖ל בֶּן־עָכְרָֽן: קָרְבָּנ֞וֹ קַֽעֲרַת־

כֶּ֣סֶף אַחַ֗ת שְׁלֹשִׁ֣ים וּמֵאָה֮ מִשְׁקָלָהּ֒ מִזְרָ֤ק אֶחָד֙ כֶּ֔סֶף שִׁבְעִ֥ים שֶׁ֖קֶל בְּשֶׁ֣קֶל

עד   הַקֹּ֑דֶשׁ שְׁנֵיהֶ֣ם ׀ מְלֵאִ֗ים סֹ֛לֶת בְּלוּלָ֥ה בַשֶּׁ֖מֶן לְמִנְחָֽה: כַּ֣ף אַחַ֧ת עֲשָׂרָ֛ה זָהָ֖ב

עה   מְלֵאָ֥ה קְטֹֽרֶת: פַּ֣ר אֶחָ֞ד בֶּן־בָּקָ֗ר אַ֧יִל אֶחָ֛ד כֶּֽבֶשׂ־אֶחָ֥ד בֶּן־שְׁנָת֖וֹ לְעֹלָֽה:

עו־עז   שְׂעִיר־עִזִּ֥ים אֶחָ֖ד לְחַטָּֽאת: וּלְזֶ֣בַח הַשְּׁלָמִים֮ בָּקָ֣ר שְׁנַיִם֒ אֵילִ֤ם חֲמִשָּׁה֙

עַתֻּדִ֣ים חֲמִשָּׁ֔ה כְּבָשִׂ֥ים בְּנֵֽי־שָׁנָ֖ה חֲמִשָּׁ֑ה זֶ֚ה קָרְבַּ֣ן פַּגְעִיאֵ֔ל בֶּן־עָכְרָֽן:

עח־עט   בְּיוֹם֙ שְׁנֵ֣ים עָשָׂ֣ר י֔וֹם נָשִׂ֖יא לִבְנֵ֣י נַפְתָּלִ֑י אֲחִירַ֖ע בֶּן־עֵינָֽן: קָרְבָּנ֞וֹ קַֽעֲרַת־

כֶּ֣סֶף אַחַ֗ת שְׁלֹשִׁ֣ים וּמֵאָה֮ מִשְׁקָלָהּ֒ מִזְרָ֤ק אֶחָד֙ כֶּ֔סֶף שִׁבְעִ֥ים שֶׁ֖קֶל בְּשֶׁ֣קֶל

פ   הַקֹּ֑דֶשׁ שְׁנֵיהֶ֣ם ׀ מְלֵאִ֗ים סֹ֛לֶת בְּלוּלָ֥ה בַשֶּׁ֖מֶן לְמִנְחָֽה: כַּ֣ף אַחַ֧ת עֲשָׂרָ֛ה זָהָ֖ב

פא   מְלֵאָ֥ה קְטֹֽרֶת: פַּ֣ר אֶחָ֞ד בֶּן־בָּקָ֗ר אַ֧יִל אֶחָ֛ד כֶּֽבֶשׂ־אֶחָ֥ד בֶּן־שְׁנָת֖וֹ לְעֹלָֽה:

פב־פג   שְׂעִיר־עִזִּ֥ים אֶחָ֖ד לְחַטָּֽאת: וּלְזֶ֣בַח הַשְּׁלָמִים֮ בָּקָ֣ר שְׁנַיִם֒ אֵילִ֤ם חֲמִשָּׁה֙

עַתֻּדִ֣ים חֲמִשָּׁ֔ה כְּבָשִׂ֥ים בְּנֵֽי־שָׁנָ֖ה חֲמִשָּׁ֑ה זֶ֚ה קָרְבַּ֣ן אֲחִירַ֔ע בֶּן־עֵינָֽן:

פד   זֹ֣את ׀ חֲנֻכַּ֣ת הַמִּזְבֵּ֗חַ בְּיוֹם֙ הִמָּשַׁ֣ח אֹת֔וֹ מֵאֵ֖ת נְשִׂיאֵ֣י יִשְׂרָאֵ֑ל קַֽעֲרֹ֨ת כֶּ֜סֶף

פה   שְׁתֵּ֣ים עֶשְׂרֵ֗ה מִֽזְרְקֵי־כֶ֨סֶף֙ שְׁנֵ֣ים עָשָׂ֔ר כַּפּ֥וֹת זָהָ֖ב שְׁתֵּ֥ים עֶשְׂרֵֽה: שְׁלֹשִׁ֣ים

וּמֵאָ֗ה הַקְּעָרָ֤ה הָֽאַחַת֙ כֶּ֔סֶף וְשִׁבְעִ֖ים הַמִּזְרָ֣ק הָֽאֶחָ֑ד כֹּ֚ל כֶּ֣סֶף הַכֵּלִ֔ים

אַלְפַּ֛יִם וְאַרְבַּע־מֵא֖וֹת בְּשֶׁ֥קֶל הַקֹּֽדֶשׁ: כַּפּ֨וֹת זָהָ֜ב שְׁתֵּים־עֶשְׂרֵ֣ה מְלֵאֹ֣ת

פו   קְטֹ֗רֶת עֲשָׂרָ֨ה עֲשָׂרָ֤ה הַכַּף֙ בְּשֶׁ֣קֶל הַקֹּ֔דֶשׁ כָּל־זְהַ֥ב הַכַּפּ֖וֹת עֶשְׂרִ֥ים וּמֵאָֽה:

מפטיר   פז   כָּל־הַבָּקָ֨ר לָֽעֹלָ֜ה שְׁנֵ֧ים עָשָׂ֣ר פָּרִ֗ים אֵילִ֤ם שְׁנֵים־עָשָׂר֙ כְּבָשִׂ֧ים בְּנֵֽי־שָׁנָ֛ה

Haftaras Nasso: p. 618   פח   שְׁנֵ֥ים עָשָׂ֖ר וּמִנְחָתָ֑ם וּשְׂעִירֵ֥י עִזִּ֛ים שְׁנֵ֥ים עָשָׂ֖ר לְחַטָּֽאת: וְכֹ֞ל בְּקַ֣ר ׀

זֶ֣בַח הַשְּׁלָמִ֗ים עֶשְׂרִ֣ים וְאַרְבָּעָה֙ פָּרִ֔ים אֵילִ֤ם שִׁשִּׁים֙ עַתֻּדִ֣ים שִׁשִּׁ֔ים

פט   כְּבָשִׂ֥ים בְּנֵֽי־שָׁנָ֖ה שִׁשִּׁ֑ים זֹ֚את חֲנֻכַּ֣ת הַמִּזְבֵּ֔חַ אַֽחֲרֵ֖י הִמָּשַׁ֥ח אֹתֽוֹ: וּבְבֹ֨א

מֹשֶׁ֜ה אֶל־אֹ֣הֶל מוֹעֵד֮ לְדַבֵּ֣ר אִתּוֹ֒ וַיִּשְׁמַ֨ע אֶת־הַקּ֜וֹל מִדַּבֵּ֤ר אֵלָיו֙ מֵעַ֣ל

הַכַּפֹּ֗רֶת אֲשֶׁר֙ עַל־אֲרֹ֣ן הָֽעֵדֻ֔ת מִבֵּ֖ין שְׁנֵ֣י הַכְּרֻבִ֑ים וַיְדַבֵּ֖ר אֵלָֽיו: פפפ

קע״ו פסוקים. עמו״ס סימן. עמינד״ב סימן.

פרשת בהעלותך

ח   א־ב   וַיְדַבֵּ֥ר יְהֹוָ֖ה אֶל־מֹשֶׁ֥ה לֵּאמֹֽר: דַּבֵּר֙ אֶֽל־אַֽהֲרֹ֔ן וְאָֽמַרְתָּ֖ אֵלָ֑יו בְּהַֽעֲלֹֽתְךָ֙

ג   אֶת־הַנֵּרֹ֔ת אֶל־מוּל֙ פְּנֵ֣י הַמְּנוֹרָ֔ה יָאִ֖ירוּ שִׁבְעַ֥ת הַנֵּרֽוֹת: וַיַּ֤עַשׂ כֵּן֙ אַֽהֲרֹ֔ן

ד   אֶל־מוּל֙ פְּנֵ֣י הַמְּנוֹרָ֔ה הֶֽעֱלָ֖ה נֵֽרֹתֶ֑יהָ כַּֽאֲשֶׁ֛ר צִוָּ֥ה יְהֹוָ֖ה אֶת־מֹשֶֽׁה: וְזֶ֨ה

מַֽעֲשֵׂ֤ה הַמְּנֹרָה֙ מִקְשָׁ֣ה זָהָ֔ב עַד־יְרֵכָ֥הּ עַד־פִּרְחָ֖הּ מִקְשָׁ֣ה הִ֑וא כַּמַּרְאֶ֗ה

אֲשֶׁ֨ר הֶרְאָ֤ה יְהֹוָה֙ אֶת־מֹשֶׁ֔ה כֵּ֥ן עָשָׂ֖ה אֶת־הַמְּנֹרָֽה:

both of them filled with fine flour mixed with oil for a meal-offering; [68] one gold ladle of ten [shekels] filled with incense; [69] one young bull, one ram, one sheep in its first year for a burnt-offering; [70] one he-goat for a sin-offering; [71] and for a feast peace-offering: two cattle, five rams, five he-goats, five sheep in their first year — this is the offering of Ahiezer son of Ammishaddai.

Asher   [72] On the eleventh day, the leader of the children of Asher, Pagiel son of Ochran. [73] His offering was: one silver bowl, its weight a hundred and thirty [shekels]; and one silver basin of seventy shekels in the sacred shekel; both of them filled with fine flour mixed with oil for a meal-offering; [74] one gold ladle of ten [shekels] filled with incense; [75] one young bull, one ram, one sheep in its first year for a burnt-offering; [76] one he-goat for a sin-offering; [77] and for a feast peace-offering: two cattle, five rams, five he-goats, five sheep in their first year — this is the offering of Pagiel son of Ochran.

Naphtali   [78] On the twelfth day, the leader of the children of Naphtali, Ahira son of Enan. [79] His offering was: one silver bowl, its weight a hundred and thirty [shekels]; and one silver basin of seventy shekels in the sacred shekel; both of them filled with fine flour mixed with oil for a meal-offering; [80] one gold ladle of ten [shekels] filled with incense; [81] one young bull, one ram, one sheep in its first year for a burnt-offering; [82] one he-goat for a sin-offering; [83] and for a feast peace-offering: two cattle, five rams, five he-goats, five sheep in their first year — this is the offering of Ahira son of Enan.

The total   [84] This was the dedication of the Altar, on the day it was anointed, from the leaders of Israel: twelve silver bowls, twelve silver basins, twelve gold ladles; [85] each bowl was one hundred and thirty silver [shekels] and each basin was seventy; all the silver of the vessels was two thousand, four hundred in the sacred shekel. [86] Twelve gold ladles filled with incense, each ladle was ten of the sacred shekels; all the gold of the ladles was one hundred and twenty [shekels]. [87] All the livestock for the burnt-offering: twelve bulls, twelve rams, twelve sheep in their first year, and their meal-offerings; and twelve he-goats for a sin-offering. [88] All the livestock for the feast peace-offering: twenty-four bulls, sixty rams, sixty he-goats, sixty sheep in their first year — this was the dedication of the Altar after it was anointed.

Moses enters   [89] When Moses arrived at the Tent of Meeting to speak with Him, he heard the
the   Voice speaking to him from atop the Cover that was upon the Ark of the
Tabernacle   Testimony, from between the two Cherubim, and He spoke to him.

PARASHAS BEHA'ALOSCHA

8   [1] HASHEM spoke to Moses, saying, [2] "Speak to Aaron* and say to him: When
The   you kindle the lamps, toward the face of the Menorah shall the seven
Menorah lamps cast light."

[3] Aaron did so; toward the face of the Menorah he kindled its lamps, as HASHEM had commanded Moses. [4] This is the workmanship of the Menorah, hammered-out gold, from its base to its flower it is hammered out; according to the vision that HASHEM showed Moses, so did he make the Menorah.

◄§ **Parashas Beha'aloscha**

8:2. Aaron was chagrined that every tribal leader had a role in dedicating the new Tabernacle, while he and his tribe of Levi were excluded. God comforted him, saying that his service was greater than theirs because he would

prepare and kindle the Menorah (*Rashi*).

Ramban comments that the kindling here alludes to a later Menorah, that of the miracle of Chanukah. Thus God comforted Aaron by telling him that his family would one day save the nation; his contribution would be eternal.

הה וַיְדַבֵּ֥ר יהוה אֶל־מֹשֶׁ֖ה לֵּאמֹֽר׃ קַ֣ח אֶת־הַלְוִיִּ֗ם מִתּ֙וֹךְ֙ בְּנֵ֣י יִשְׂרָאֵ֔ל וְטִֽהַרְתָּ֖

ז אֹתָֽם׃ וְכֹֽה־תַֽעֲשֶׂ֤ה לָהֶם֙ לְטַֽהֲרָ֔ם הַזֵּ֥ה עֲלֵיהֶ֖ם מֵ֣י חַטָּ֑את וְהֶֽעֱבִ֤ירוּ תַ֙עַר֙

ח עַל־כָּל־בְּשָׂרָ֔ם וְכִבְּס֥וּ בִגְדֵיהֶ֖ם וְהִטֶּהָֽרוּ׃ וְלָֽקְחוּ֙ פַּ֣ר בֶּן־בָּקָ֔ר וּמִנְחָת֖וֹ

ט סֹ֣לֶת בְּלוּלָ֣ה בַשָּׁ֑מֶן וּפַר־שֵׁנִ֥י בֶן־בָּקָ֖ר תִּקַּ֥ח לְחַטָּֽאת׃ וְהִקְרַבְתָּ֙ אֶת־

י הַ֣לְוִיִּ֔ם לִפְנֵ֖י אֹ֣הֶל מוֹעֵ֑ד וְהִ֨קְהַלְתָּ֔ אֶת־כָּל־עֲדַ֖ת בְּנֵ֥י יִשְׂרָאֵֽל׃ וְהִקְרַבְתָּ֥

יא אֶת־הַלְוִיִּ֖ם לִפְנֵ֣י יהוה וְסָֽמְכ֧וּ בְנֵֽי־יִשְׂרָאֵ֛ל אֶת־יְדֵיהֶ֖ם עַל־הַלְוִיִּֽם׃ וְהֵנִיף֩

אַֽהֲרֹ֨ן אֶת־הַלְוִיִּ֤ם תְּנוּפָה֙ לִפְנֵ֣י יהוה מֵאֵ֖ת בְּנֵ֣י יִשְׂרָאֵ֑ל וְהָי֕וּ לַֽעֲבֹ֖ד אֶת־

יב עֲבֹדַ֥ת יהוה׃ וְהַ֨לְוִיִּ֔ם יִסְמְכ֣וּ אֶת־יְדֵיהֶ֔ם עַ֖ל רֹ֣אשׁ הַפָּרִ֑ים וַ֠עֲשֵׂ֠ה אֶת־

יג הָֽאֶחָ֨ד חַטָּ֜את וְאֶת־הָֽאֶחָ֤ד עֹלָה֙ לַֽיהוה לְכַפֵּ֖ר עַל־הַלְוִיִּֽם׃ וְהַֽעֲמַדְתָּ֙ אֶת־

יד הַ֣לְוִיִּ֔ם לִפְנֵ֥י אַֽהֲרֹ֖ן וְלִפְנֵ֣י בָנָ֑יו וְהֵֽנַפְתָּ֥ אֹתָ֛ם תְּנוּפָ֖ה לַֽיהוה׃ וְהִבְדַּלְתָּ֙

טו אֶת־הַלְוִיִּ֔ם מִתּ֖וֹךְ בְּנֵ֣י יִשְׂרָאֵ֑ל וְהָ֥יוּ לִ֖י הַלְוִיִּֽם׃ וְאַֽחֲרֵי־כֵן֙ יָבֹ֣אוּ הַלְוִיִּ֔ם

טז לַֽעֲבֹ֖ד אֶת־אֹ֣הֶל מוֹעֵ֑ד וְטִֽהַרְתָּ֣ אֹתָ֔ם וְהֵֽנַפְתָּ֥ אֹתָ֖ם תְּנוּפָֽה׃ כִּי֩ נְתֻנִ֨ים

נְתֻנִ֥ים הֵ֙מָּה֙ לִ֔י מִתּ֖וֹךְ בְּנֵ֣י יִשְׂרָאֵ֑ל תַּ֩חַת֩ פִּטְרַ֨ת כָּל־רֶ֜חֶם בְּכ֣וֹר כֹּ֗ל מִבְּנֵ֤י

יז יִשְׂרָאֵל֙ לָקַ֣חְתִּי אֹתָ֖ם לִֽי׃ כִּ֣י לִ֤י כָל־בְּכוֹר֙ בִּבְנֵ֣י יִשְׂרָאֵ֔ל בָּֽאָדָ֖ם וּבַבְּהֵמָ֑ה

יח בְּי֗וֹם הַכֹּתִ֤י כָל־בְּכוֹר֙ בְּאֶ֣רֶץ מִצְרַ֔יִם הִקְדַּ֥שְׁתִּי אֹתָ֖ם לִֽי׃ וָֽאֶקַּח֙ אֶת־הַלְוִיִּ֔ם

יט תַּ֥חַת כָּל־בְּכ֖וֹר בִּבְנֵ֣י יִשְׂרָאֵֽל׃ וָֽאֶתְּנָ֨ה אֶת־הַלְוִיִּ֜ם נְתֻנִ֣ים ׀ לְאַֽהֲרֹ֣ן וּלְבָנָ֗יו

מִתּוֹךְ֮ בְּנֵ֣י יִשְׂרָאֵל֒ לַֽעֲבֹ֞ד אֶת־עֲבֹדַ֤ת בְּנֵֽי־יִשְׂרָאֵל֙ בְּאֹ֣הֶל מוֹעֵ֔ד וּלְכַפֵּ֖ר

עַל־בְּנֵ֣י יִשְׂרָאֵ֑ל וְלֹ֨א יִֽהְיֶ֜ה בִּבְנֵ֤י יִשְׂרָאֵל֙ נֶ֔גֶף בְּגֶ֥שֶׁת בְּנֵֽי־יִשְׂרָאֵ֖ל אֶל־

כ הַקֹּֽדֶשׁ׃ וַיַּ֨עַשׂ מֹשֶׁ֧ה וְאַֽהֲרֹ֛ן וְכָל־עֲדַ֥ת בְּנֵֽי־יִשְׂרָאֵ֖ל לַֽלְוִיִּ֑ם כְּ֠כֹ֠ל אֲשֶׁר־צִוָּ֨ה

כא יהוה אֶת־מֹשֶׁ֣ה לַֽלְוִיִּ֗ם כֵּֽן־עָשׂ֥וּ לָהֶ֖ם בְּנֵ֣י יִשְׂרָאֵֽל׃ וַיִּֽתְחַטְּא֣וּ הַלְוִיִּ֗ם

וַיְכַבְּסוּ֙ בִּגְדֵיהֶ֔ם וַיָּ֨נֶף אַֽהֲרֹ֧ן אֹתָ֛ם תְּנוּפָ֖ה לִפְנֵ֣י יהוה וַיְכַפֵּ֧ר עֲלֵיהֶ֛ם

כב אַֽהֲרֹ֖ן לְטַֽהֲרָֽם׃ וְאַֽחֲרֵי־כֵ֞ן בָּ֣אוּ הַלְוִיִּ֗ם לַֽעֲבֹ֤ד אֶת־עֲבֹֽדָתָם֙ בְּאֹ֣הֶל מוֹעֵ֔ד

לִפְנֵ֥י אַֽהֲרֹ֖ן וְלִפְנֵ֣י בָנָ֑יו כַּֽאֲשֶׁר֩ צִוָּ֨ה יהוה אֶת־מֹשֶׁ֜ה עַל־הַלְוִיִּ֔ם כֵּ֥ן עָשׂ֖וּ

כג-כד לָהֶֽם׃ וַיְדַבֵּ֥ר יהוה אֶל־מֹשֶׁ֖ה לֵּאמֹֽר׃ זֹ֖את אֲשֶׁ֣ר לַֽלְוִיִּ֑ם

מִבֶּן֩ חָמֵ֨שׁ וְעֶשְׂרִ֤ים שָׁנָה֙ וָמַ֔עְלָה יָבוֹא֙ לִצְבֹ֣א צָבָ֔א בַּֽעֲבֹדַ֖ת אֹ֥הֶל מוֹעֵֽד׃

כה-כו וּמִבֶּן֙ חֲמִשִּׁ֣ים שָׁנָ֔ה יָשׁ֖וּב מִצְּבָ֣א הָֽעֲבֹדָ֑ה וְלֹ֥א יַֽעֲבֹ֖ד עֽוֹד׃ וְשֵׁרֵ֨ת אֶת־

אֶחָ֜יו בְּאֹ֤הֶל מוֹעֵד֙ לִשְׁמֹ֣ר מִשְׁמֶ֔רֶת וַֽעֲבֹדָ֖ה לֹ֣א יַֽעֲבֹ֑ד כָּ֛כָה תַּֽעֲשֶׂ֥ה לַֽלְוִיִּ֖ם

בְּמִשְׁמְרֹתָֽם׃

ט א וַיְדַבֵּ֣ר יהוה אֶל־מֹשֶׁ֣ה בְמִדְבַּר־סִינַ֗י בַּשָּׁנָ֤ה הַשֵּׁנִית֙ לְצֵאתָ֞ם מֵאֶ֤רֶץ מִצְרַ֙יִם֙

ב בַּחֹ֥דֶשׁ הָֽרִאשׁ֖וֹן לֵאמֹֽר׃ וְיַֽעֲשׂ֧וּ בְנֵֽי־יִשְׂרָאֵ֛ל אֶת־הַפָּ֖סַח בְּמֽוֹעֲדֽוֹ׃

ג בְּאַרְבָּעָ֣ה עָשָׂר־י֠וֹם בַּחֹ֨דֶשׁ הַזֶּ֜ה בֵּ֧ין הָֽעַרְבַּ֛יִם תַּֽעֲשׂ֥וּ אֹת֖וֹ בְּמֹֽעֲד֑וֹ כְּכָל־חֻקֹּתָ֛יו

וּכְכָל־מִשְׁפָּטָ֖יו תַּֽעֲשׂ֥וּ אֹתֽוֹ׃ וַיְדַבֵּ֥ר מֹשֶׁ֛ה אֶל־בְּנֵ֥י יִשְׂרָאֵ֖ל לַֽעֲשֹׂ֥ת הַפָּֽסַח׃

שני

שלישי

ט

FOURTH DAY
CHOL
HAMOED
PESACH
9:1-14;
28:19-25

8:6. To assume their new status as the servants of God, the Levites required a sacrificial ritual as did the consecration of the Kohanim (*Leviticus* ch. 8).

8:24. *From twenty-five years of age.* They began to serve at thirty; our verse refers to a five-year period of apprenticeship beginning at the age of twenty-five (*Rashi*).

Consecration
of the
Levites

⁵ HASHEM spoke to Moses, saying, ⁶ "Take the Levites* from among the Children of Israel and purify them. ⁷ So shall you do to them to purify them: Sprinkle upon them water of purification, and let them pass a razor over their entire flesh, and let them immerse their garments, and they shall become pure. ⁸ They shall take a young bull and its meal-offering, fine flour mixed with oil, and a second young bull shall you take as a sin-offering. ⁹ You shall bring the Levites before the Tent of Meeting, and you shall gather together the entire assembly of the Children of Israel. ¹⁰ You shall bring the Levites before HASHEM, and the Children of Israel shall lean their hands upon the Levites. ¹¹ Aaron shall wave the Levites as a wave-service before HASHEM from the Children of Israel, and they shall remain to perform the service of HASHEM. ¹² The Levites shall lean their hands upon the head of the bulls; you shall make one a sin-offering and one a burnt-offering to HASHEM, to provide atonement for the Levites. ¹³ You shall stand the Levites before Aaron and before his sons, and wave them as a wave-service for HASHEM. ¹⁴ So shall you separate the Levites from among the Children of Israel, and the Levites shall remain Mine.

¹⁵ "Thereafter the Levites shall come to serve the Tent of Meeting; you shall purify them and you shall wave them as a wave-service. ¹⁶ For presented, presented are they to Me from among the Children of Israel; in place of the first issue of every womb, the firstborn of everyone of the Children of Israel, have I taken them to Myself. ¹⁷ For every firstborn of the Children of Israel became Mine, of man and livestock; on the day I struck every firstborn in the land of Egypt I sanctified them for Myself. ¹⁸ I took the Levites in place of every firstborn among the Children of Israel. ¹⁹ Then I assigned the Levites to be presented to Aaron and his sons from among the Children of Israel to perform the service of the Children of Israel in the Tent of Meeting and to provide atonement for the Children of Israel, so that there will not be a plague among the Children of Israel when the Children of Israel approach the Sanctuary."

²⁰ Moses, Aaron, and the entire assembly of the Children of Israel did to the Levites according to everything that HASHEM had commanded Moses about the Levites, so did the Children of Israel do to them. ²¹ The Levites purified themselves and immersed their garments; and Aaron waved them as a wave-service before HASHEM, and Aaron provided atonement for them to purify them. ²² Afterwards the Levites came to perform their service in the Tent of Meeting, before Aaron and before his sons, as HASHEM had commanded Moses concerning the Levites; so they did for them.

Apprentice-
ship and
responsibility

²³ HASHEM spoke to Moses, saying, ²⁴ "This shall apply to the Levites: From twenty-five years of age* and up, he shall join the legion of the service of the Tent of Meeting. ²⁵ From fifty years of age, he shall withdraw from the legion of work and no longer work. ²⁶ He shall minister with his brethren in the Tent of Meeting to safeguard the charge, but work shall he not perform. So shall you do to the Levites concerning their charge."

9

The pesach-
offering
in the
Wilderness

¹ HASHEM spoke to Moses, in the Wilderness of Sinai, in the second year from their exodus from the land of Egypt, in the first month, saying: ² "The Children of Israel shall make the pesach-offering in its appointed time. ³ On the fourteenth day of this month in the afternoon shall you make it, in its appointed time; according to all its decrees and laws shall you make it."

⁴ Moses spoke to the Children of Israel to make the pesach-offering.

ה וַיַּעֲשׂוּ אֶת־הַפֶּסַח בָּרִאשׁוֹן בְּאַרְבָּעָה עָשָׂר יוֹם לַחֹדֶשׁ בֵּין הָעַרְבַּיִם
בְּמִדְבַּר סִינָי כְּכֹל אֲשֶׁר צִוָּה יהוה אֶת־מֹשֶׁה כֵּן עָשׂוּ בְּנֵי יִשְׂרָאֵל: ו וַיְהִי
אֲנָשִׁים אֲשֶׁר הָיוּ טְמֵאִים לְנֶפֶשׁ אָדָם וְלֹא־יָכְלוּ לַעֲשֹׂת־הַפֶּסַח בַּיּוֹם
הַהוּא וַיִּקְרְבוּ לִפְנֵי מֹשֶׁה וְלִפְנֵי אַהֲרֹן בַּיּוֹם הַהוּא: ז וַיֹּאמְרוּ הָאֲנָשִׁים
הָהֵמָּה אֵלָיו אֲנַחְנוּ טְמֵאִים לְנֶפֶשׁ אָדָם לָמָּה נִגָּרַע לְבִלְתִּי הַקְרִיב אֶת־
קָרְבַּן יהוה בְּמֹעֲדוֹ בְּתוֹךְ בְּנֵי יִשְׂרָאֵל: ח וַיֹּאמֶר אֲלֵהֶם מֹשֶׁה עִמְדוּ
וְאֶשְׁמְעָה מַה־יְצַוֶּה יהוה לָכֶם:

ט־י וַיְדַבֵּר יהוה אֶל־מֹשֶׁה לֵּאמֹר: דַּבֵּר אֶל־בְּנֵי יִשְׂרָאֵל לֵאמֹר אִישׁ אִישׁ
כִּי־יִהְיֶה טָמֵא | לָנֶפֶשׁ אוֹ בְדֶרֶךְ ׳רְחֹקָה לָכֶם אוֹ לְדֹרֹתֵיכֶם וְעָשָׂה
פֶסַח לַיהוָה: יא בַּחֹדֶשׁ הַשֵּׁנִי בְּאַרְבָּעָה עָשָׂר יוֹם בֵּין הָעַרְבַּיִם יַעֲשׂוּ אֹתוֹ
עַל־מַצּוֹת וּמְרֹרִים יֹאכְלֻהוּ: יב לֹא־יַשְׁאִירוּ מִמֶּנּוּ עַד־בֹּקֶר וְעֶצֶם לֹא
יִשְׁבְּרוּ־בוֹ כְּכָל־חֻקַּת הַפֶּסַח יַעֲשׂוּ אֹתוֹ: יג וְהָאִישׁ אֲשֶׁר־הוּא טָהוֹר
וּבְדֶרֶךְ לֹא־הָיָה וְחָדַל לַעֲשׂוֹת הַפֶּסַח וְנִכְרְתָה הַנֶּפֶשׁ הַהִוא מֵעַמֶּיהָ
כִּי | קָרְבַּן יהוה לֹא הִקְרִיב בְּמֹעֲדוֹ חֶטְאוֹ יִשָּׂא הָאִישׁ הַהוּא: יד וְכִי־יָגוּר
אִתְּכֶם גֵּר וְעָשָׂה פֶסַח לַיהוָה כְּחֻקַּת הַפֶּסַח וּכְמִשְׁפָּטוֹ כֵּן יַעֲשֶׂה חֻקָּה
אַחַת יִהְיֶה לָכֶם וְלַגֵּר וּלְאֶזְרַח הָאָרֶץ:

טו וּבְיוֹם הָקִים אֶת־הַמִּשְׁכָּן כִּסָּה הֶעָנָן אֶת־הַמִּשְׁכָּן לְאֹהֶל הָעֵדֻת וּבָעֶרֶב יִהְיֶה
עַל־הַמִּשְׁכָּן כְּמַרְאֵה־אֵשׁ עַד־בֹּקֶר: טז כֵּן יִהְיֶה תָמִיד הֶעָנָן יְכַסֶּנּוּ
וּמַרְאֵה־אֵשׁ לָיְלָה: יז וּלְפִי הֵעָלוֹת הֶעָנָן מֵעַל הָאֹהֶל וְאַחֲרֵי כֵן יִסְעוּ בְּנֵי
יִשְׂרָאֵל וּבִמְקוֹם אֲשֶׁר יִשְׁכָּן־שָׁם הֶעָנָן שָׁם יַחֲנוּ בְּנֵי יִשְׂרָאֵל: יח עַל־פִּי
יהוה יִסְעוּ בְּנֵי יִשְׂרָאֵל וְעַל־פִּי יהוה יַחֲנוּ כָּל־יְמֵי אֲשֶׁר יִשְׁכֹּן הֶעָנָן עַל־
הַמִּשְׁכָּן יַחֲנוּ: יט וּבְהַאֲרִיךְ הֶעָנָן עַל־הַמִּשְׁכָּן יָמִים רַבִּים וְשָׁמְרוּ בְנֵי
יִשְׂרָאֵל אֶת־מִשְׁמֶרֶת יהוה וְלֹא יִסָּעוּ: כ וְיֵשׁ אֲשֶׁר יִהְיֶה הֶעָנָן יָמִים
מִסְפָּר עַל־הַמִּשְׁכָּן עַל־פִּי יהוה יַחֲנוּ וְעַל־פִּי יהוה יִסָּעוּ: כא וְיֵשׁ אֲשֶׁר
יִהְיֶה הֶעָנָן מֵעֶרֶב עַד־בֹּקֶר וְנַעֲלָה הֶעָנָן בַּבֹּקֶר וְנָסָעוּ אוֹ יוֹמָם וָלַיְלָה
וְנַעֲלָה הֶעָנָן וְנָסָעוּ: כב אוֹ־יֹמַיִם אוֹ־חֹדֶשׁ אוֹ־יָמִים בְּהַאֲרִיךְ הֶעָנָן עַל־
הַמִּשְׁכָּן לִשְׁכֹּן עָלָיו יַחֲנוּ בְנֵי־יִשְׂרָאֵל וְלֹא יִסָּעוּ וּבְהֵעָלֹתוֹ יִסָּעוּ: כג עַל־פִּי
יהוה יַחֲנוּ וְעַל־פִּי יהוה יִסָּעוּ אֶת־מִשְׁמֶרֶת יהוה שָׁמָרוּ עַל־פִּי יהוה
בְּיַד־מֹשֶׁה:

נקוד על ה׳

רביעי

9:6. A group of people were ineligible to bring the *pesach* offering. Having an intense desire to participate in the great spiritual experience, they appealed to Moses. God revealed the new commandment of *pesach sheni*, which would be brought a month after the appointed time for the *pesach*. Because of the sincere desire of these people for spiritual elevation, God gave them the honor of bringing about the giving of this new commandment.

The second *pesach* differs from the first in that there is no festival associated with it. Furthermore, although leavened food [*chametz*] may not be eaten with the offering (v. 11), they may eat *chametz* on that day (*Rashi; Pesachim* 95a).

⁵ They made the pesach-offering in the first [month], on the fourteenth day of the month, in the afternoon, in the Wilderness of Sinai; according to everything that HASHEM had commanded Moses, so the Children of Israel did.

Pesach sheni/ The second pesach-offering

⁶ There were men who had been contaminated by a human corpse and could not make the pesach-offering* on that day; so they approached Moses and Aaron on that day. ⁷ Those men said to him, "We are contaminated through a human corpse; why should we be diminished by not offering HASHEM's offering in its appointed time among the Children of Israel?"

⁸ Moses said to them, "Stand by and I will hear what HASHEM will command you."

⁹ HASHEM spoke to Moses, saying, ¹⁰ "Speak to the Children of Israel, saying: If any man will become contaminated through a human corpse or [will be] on a distant road, whether you or your generations, he shall make the pesach-offering for HASHEM, ¹¹ in the second month, on the fourteenth day, in the afternoon, shall they make it; with matzos and bitter herbs shall they eat it. ¹² They shall not leave over from it until morning nor shall they break a bone of it; like all the decrees of the pesach-offering shall they make it. ¹³ But a man who is pure and was not on the road and had refrained from making the pesach-offering, that soul shall be cut off from its people, for he had not offered HASHEM's offering in its appointed time; that man will bear his sin. ¹⁴ When a convert shall dwell with you, and he shall make a pesach-offering to HASHEM, according to the decree of the pesach-offering and its law, so shall he do; one decree shall be for you, for the proselyte and the native of the Land."

Divine signs of the Israelites' travels

¹⁵ On the day the Tabernacle was set up, the cloud covered the Tabernacle that was a tent for the Testimony, and in the evening there would be upon the Tabernacle like a fiery appearance until morning. ¹⁶ So it would always be: The cloud would cover it, and an appearance of fire at night. ¹⁷ And whenever the cloud was lifted from atop the Tent, afterwards the Children of Israel would journey, and in the place where the cloud would rest, there the Children of Israel would encamp. ¹⁸ According to the word of HASHEM would the Children of Israel journey, and according to the word of HASHEM would they encamp; all the days that the cloud would rest upon the Tabernacle they would encamp. ¹⁹ When the cloud lingered upon the Tabernacle many days, the Children of Israel would maintain the charge of HASHEM and would not journey. ²⁰ Sometimes the cloud would be upon the Tabernacle for a number of days; according to the word of HASHEM would they encamp and according to the word of HASHEM would they journey. ²¹ And sometimes the cloud would remain from evening until morning, and the cloud would be lifted in the morning and they would journey; or for a day and a night, and the cloud would be lifted and they would journey. ²² Or for two days, or a month, or a year, when the cloud would linger over the Tabernacle, resting upon it, the Children of Israel would encamp and would not journey, but when it was lifted they would journey. ²³ According to the word of HASHEM would they encamp, and according to the word of HASHEM would they journey; the charge of HASHEM would they safeguard, according to the word of HASHEM through Moses.

י

א-ב וַיְדַבֵּר יהוה אֶל־מֹשֶׁה לֵּאמֹר: עֲשֵׂה לְךָ שְׁתֵּי חֲצוֹצְרֹת כֶּסֶף מִקְשָׁה

ג תַּעֲשֶׂה אֹתָם וְהָיוּ לְךָ לְמִקְרָא הָעֵדָה וּלְמַסַּע אֶת־הַמַּחֲנוֹת: וְתָקְעוּ בָּהֵן

ד וְנוֹעֲדוּ אֵלֶיךָ כָּל־הָעֵדָה אֶל־פֶּתַח אֹהֶל מוֹעֵד: וְאִם־בְּאַחַת יִתְקָעוּ

ה וְנוֹעֲדוּ אֵלֶיךָ הַנְּשִׂיאִים רָאשֵׁי אַלְפֵי יִשְׂרָאֵל: וּתְקַעְתֶּם תְּרוּעָה וְנָסְעוּ

ו הַמַּחֲנוֹת הַחֹנִים קֵדְמָה: וּתְקַעְתֶּם תְּרוּעָה שֵׁנִית וְנָסְעוּ הַמַּחֲנוֹת הַחֹנִים

ז תֵּימָנָה תְּרוּעָה יִתְקְעוּ לְמַסְעֵיהֶם: וּבְהַקְהִיל אֶת־הַקָּהָל תִּתְקְעוּ וְלֹא

ח תָרִיעוּ: וּבְנֵי אַהֲרֹן הַכֹּהֲנִים יִתְקְעוּ בַּחֲצֹצְרוֹת וְהָיוּ לָכֶם לְחֻקַּת עוֹלָם

ט לְדֹרֹתֵיכֶם: וְכִי־תָבֹאוּ מִלְחָמָה בְּאַרְצְכֶם עַל־הַצַּר הַצֹּרֵר אֶתְכֶם

וַהֲרֵעֹתֶם בַּחֲצֹצְרֹת וְנִזְכַּרְתֶּם לִפְנֵי יהוה אֱלֹהֵיכֶם וְנוֹשַׁעְתֶּם מֵאֹיְבֵיכֶם:

י וּבְיוֹם שִׂמְחַתְכֶם וּבְמוֹעֲדֵיכֶם וּבְרָאשֵׁי חָדְשֵׁכֶם וּתְקַעְתֶּם בַּחֲצֹצְרֹת

עַל עֹלֹתֵיכֶם וְעַל זִבְחֵי שַׁלְמֵיכֶם וְהָיוּ לָכֶם לְזִכָּרוֹן לִפְנֵי אֱלֹהֵיכֶם אֲנִי

יהוה אֱלֹהֵיכֶם:

חמישי   יא וַיְהִי בַּשָּׁנָה הַשֵּׁנִית בַּחֹדֶשׁ הַשֵּׁנִי בְּעֶשְׂרִים בַּחֹדֶשׁ נַעֲלָה הֶעָנָן מֵעַל

יב מִשְׁכַּן הָעֵדֻת: וַיִּסְעוּ בְנֵי־יִשְׂרָאֵל לְמַסְעֵיהֶם מִמִּדְבַּר סִינָי וַיִּשְׁכֹּן

יג-יד הֶעָנָן בְּמִדְבַּר פָּארָן: וַיִּסְעוּ בָּרִאשֹׁנָה עַל־פִּי יהוה בְּיַד־מֹשֶׁה: וַיִּסַּע

דֶּגֶל מַחֲנֵה בְנֵי־יְהוּדָה בָּרִאשֹׁנָה לְצִבְאֹתָם וְעַל־צְבָאוֹ נַחְשׁוֹן בֶּן־

טו-טז עַמִּינָדָב: וְעַל־צְבָא מַטֵּה בְּנֵי יִשָּׂשכָר נְתַנְאֵל בֶּן־צוּעָר: וְעַל־צְבָא

יז מַטֵּה בְּנֵי זְבוּלֻן אֱלִיאָב בֶּן־חֵלֹן: וְהוּרַד הַמִּשְׁכָּן וְנָסְעוּ בְנֵי־גֵרְשׁוֹן

יח וּבְנֵי מְרָרִי נֹשְׂאֵי הַמִּשְׁכָּן: וְנָסַע דֶּגֶל מַחֲנֵה רְאוּבֵן לְצִבְאֹתָם וְעַל־

יט צְבָאוֹ אֱלִיצוּר בֶּן־שְׁדֵיאוּר: וְעַל־צְבָא מַטֵּה בְּנֵי שִׁמְעוֹן שְׁלֻמִיאֵל

כ-כא בֶּן־צוּרִישַׁדָּי: וְעַל־צְבָא מַטֵּה בְנֵי־גָד אֶלְיָסָף בֶּן־דְּעוּאֵל: וְנָסְעוּ

כב הַקְּהָתִים נֹשְׂאֵי הַמִּקְדָּשׁ וְהֵקִימוּ אֶת־הַמִּשְׁכָּן עַד־בֹּאָם: וְנָסַע דֶּגֶל

כג מַחֲנֵה בְנֵי־אֶפְרַיִם לְצִבְאֹתָם וְעַל־צְבָאוֹ אֱלִישָׁמָע בֶּן־עַמִּיהוּד: וְעַל־

כד צְבָא מַטֵּה בְּנֵי מְנַשֶּׁה גַּמְלִיאֵל בֶּן־פְּדָהצוּר: וְעַל־צְבָא מַטֵּה בְּנֵי

כה בִנְיָמִן אֲבִידָן בֶּן־גִּדְעוֹנִי: וְנָסַע דֶּגֶל מַחֲנֵה בְנֵי־דָן מְאַסֵּף לְכָל־הַמַּחֲנֹת

כו לְצִבְאֹתָם וְעַל־צְבָאוֹ אֲחִיעֶזֶר בֶּן־עַמִּישַׁדָּי: וְעַל־צְבָא מַטֵּה בְּנֵי אָשֵׁר

כז-כח פַּגְעִיאֵל בֶּן־עָכְרָן: וְעַל־צְבָא מַטֵּה בְּנֵי נַפְתָּלִי אֲחִירַע בֶּן־עֵינָן: אֵלֶּה

כט מַסְעֵי בְנֵי־יִשְׂרָאֵל לְצִבְאֹתָם וַיִּסָּעוּ:

וַיֹּאמֶר מֹשֶׁה לְחֹבָב בֶּן־רְעוּאֵל הַמִּדְיָנִי חֹתֵן מֹשֶׁה נֹסְעִים אֲנַחְנוּ אֶל־הַמָּקוֹם אֲשֶׁר

אָמַר יהוה אֹתוֹ אֶתֵּן לָכֶם לְכָה אִתָּנוּ וְהֵטַבְנוּ לָךְ כִּי־יהוה דִּבֶּר־טוֹב עַל־

10:10. The trumpets were sounded by Kohanim in conjunction with the communal burnt- and peace-offerings of the Sabbath and festive days.

10:12. The Torah now records in detail the order in which the four tribal formations and the Levite families began their journeys.

10:21. *The sanctuary.* This refers not to the building but

to its most sacred parts, such as the Ark, the Menorah, etc. (*Rashi*).

10:29-32. Israel would have been in the Holy Land in three days, had it not been for the sins described in the succeeding passages. Moses asked his father-in-law, who had arrived from Midian nearly a year before, to become part of the nation and accompany them to *Eretz Yisrael*.

10

The trumpets

¹ HASHEM spoke to Moses, saying, ² "Make for yourself two silver trumpets — make them hammered out, and they shall be yours for the summoning of the assembly and to cause the camps to journey. ³ When they sound a long blast with them, the entire assembly shall assemble to you, to the entrance of the Tent of Meeting. ⁴ If they sound a long blast with one, the leaders shall assemble to you, the heads of Israel's thousands. ⁵ When you sound short blasts, the camps resting to the east shall journey. ⁶ When you sound short blasts a second time, the camps resting to the south shall journey; short blasts shall they sound for their journeys. ⁷ When you gather together the congregation, you shall sound a long blast, but not a short blast. ⁸ The sons of Aaron, the Kohanim, shall sound the trumpets, and it shall be for you an eternal decree for your generations.

⁹ "When you go to wage war in your Land against an enemy who oppresses you, you shall sound short blasts of the trumpets, and you shall be recalled before HASHEM, your God, and you shall be saved from your foes.

¹⁰ "On a day of your gladness, and on your festivals, and on your new moons, you shall sound the trumpets over your burnt-offerings and over your feast peace-offerings; * and they shall be a remembrance for you before your God; I am HASHEM, your God."

The order of breaking camp

¹¹ It was in the second year, in the second month, on the twentieth of the month, the cloud was lifted from upon the Tabernacle of the Testimony. ¹² The Children of Israel journeyed* on their journeys from the Wilderness of Sinai, and the cloud rested in the Wilderness of Paran.

¹³ They journeyed for the first time at the bidding of HASHEM through Moses. ¹⁴ The banner of the camp of the children of Judah journeyed first according to their legions, and over its legion was Nahshon son of Amminadab; ¹⁵ over the legion of the tribe of the children of Issachar was Nethanel son of Zuar; ¹⁶ and over the legion of the tribe of the children of Zebulun was Eliab son of Helon.

¹⁷ The Tabernacle was taken down, then journeyed the sons of Gershon and the sons of Merari, the bearers of the Tabernacle.

¹⁸ Then journeyed the banner of the camp of Reuben according to their legions; and over its legion was Elizur son of Shedeur; ¹⁹ over the legion of the tribe of the children of Simeon was Shelumiel son of Zurishaddai; ²⁰ and over the legion of the tribe of the children of Gad was Eliasaph son of Deuel. ²¹ Then journeyed the Kohathites, bearers of the sanctuary; * and they would erect the Tabernacle before their arrival.

²² Then journeyed the banner of the camp of the children of Ephraim according to their legions, and over its legion was Elishama son of Ammihud; ²³ over the legion of the tribe of the children of Manasseh was Gamliel son of Pedahzur; ²⁴ and over the legion of the tribe of the children of Benjamin was Abidan son of Gideoni.

²⁵ Then journeyed the banner of the camp of the children of Dan, the rear guard of all the camps, according to their legions, and over its legion was Ahiezer son of Ammishaddai; ²⁶ over the legion of the tribe of the children of Asher was Pagiel son of Ochran; ²⁷ and over the legion of the tribe of the children of Naphtali was Ahira son of Enan. ²⁸ These were the journeys of the Children of Israel according to their legions, and they journeyed.

²⁹ Moses said to Hobab son of Reuel, * the Midianite, the father-in-law of Moses, "We are journeying to the place of which HASHEM has said, 'I shall give it to you.' Go with us and we shall treat you well, for HASHEM has spoken of good for

ל יִשְׂרָאֵל: וַיֹּאמֶר אֵלָיו לֹא אֵלֵךְ כִּי אִם־אֶל־אַרְצִי וְאֶל־מוֹלַדְתִּי אֵלֵךְ:

לא וַיֹּאמֶר אַל־נָא תַּעֲזֹב אֹתָנוּ כִּי ׀ עַל־כֵּן יָדַעְתָּ חֲנֹתֵנוּ בַּמִּדְבָּר וְהָיִיתָ לָּנוּ

לב לְעֵינָיִם: וְהָיָה כִּי־תֵלֵךְ עִמָּנוּ וְהָיָה ׀ הַטּוֹב הַהוּא אֲשֶׁר יֵיטִיב יְהֹוָה עִמָּנוּ

לג וְהֵטַבְנוּ לָךְ: וַיִּסְעוּ מֵהַר יְהֹוָה דֶּרֶךְ שְׁלֹשֶׁת יָמִים וַאֲרוֹן בְּרִית־יְהֹוָה נֹסֵעַ

לד לִפְנֵיהֶם דֶּרֶךְ שְׁלֹשֶׁת יָמִים לָתוּר לָהֶם מְנוּחָה: וַעֲנַן יְהֹוָה עֲלֵיהֶם יוֹמָם

לה בְּנָסְעָם מִן־הַמַּחֲנֶה: ׆   וַיְהִי בִּנְסֹעַ הָאָרֹן וַיֹּאמֶר מֹשֶׁה

לו קוּמָה ׀ יְהֹוָה וְיָפֻצוּ אֹיְבֶיךָ וְיָנֻסוּ מְשַׂנְאֶיךָ מִפָּנֶיךָ: וּבְנֻחֹה יֹאמַר שׁוּבָה

יא א יְהֹוָה רִבְבוֹת אַלְפֵי יִשְׂרָאֵל: ׆   וַיְהִי הָעָם כְּמִתְאֹנְנִים רַע

בְּאָזְנֵי יְהֹוָה וַיִּשְׁמַע יְהֹוָה וַיִּחַר אַפּוֹ וַתִּבְעַר־בָּם אֵשׁ יְהֹוָה וַתֹּאכַל בִּקְצֵה

ב הַמַּחֲנֶה: וַיִּצְעַק הָעָם אֶל־מֹשֶׁה וַיִּתְפַּלֵּל מֹשֶׁה אֶל־יְהֹוָה וַתִּשְׁקַע הָאֵשׁ:

ג וַיִּקְרָא שֵׁם־הַמָּקוֹם הַהוּא תַּבְעֵרָה כִּי־בָעֲרָה בָם אֵשׁ יְהֹוָה: וְהָאסַפְסֻף

ד אֲשֶׁר בְּקִרְבּוֹ הִתְאַוּוּ תַּאֲוָה וַיָּשֻׁבוּ וַיִּבְכּוּ גַּם בְּנֵי יִשְׂרָאֵל וַיֹּאמְרוּ מִי

ה יַאֲכִלֵנוּ בָּשָׂר: זָכַרְנוּ אֶת־הַדָּגָה אֲשֶׁר־נֹאכַל בְּמִצְרַיִם חִנָּם אֵת הַקִּשֻּׁאִים

ו וְאֵת הָאֲבַטִּחִים וְאֶת־הֶחָצִיר וְאֶת־הַבְּצָלִים וְאֶת־הַשּׁוּמִים: וְעַתָּה נַפְשֵׁנוּ

ז יְבֵשָׁה אֵין כֹּל בִּלְתִּי אֶל־הַמָּן עֵינֵינוּ: וְהַמָּן כִּזְרַע־גַּד הוּא וְעֵינוֹ כְּעֵין

ח הַבְּדֹלַח: שָׁטוּ הָעָם וְלָקְטוּ וְטָחֲנוּ בָרֵחַיִם אוֹ דָכוּ בַּמְּדֹכָה וּבִשְּׁלוּ בַּפָּרוּר

ט וְעָשׂוּ אֹתוֹ עֻגוֹת וְהָיָה טַעְמוֹ כְּטַעַם לְשַׁד הַשָּׁמֶן: וּבְרֶדֶת הַטַּל עַל־

י הַמַּחֲנֶה לָיְלָה יֵרֵד הַמָּן עָלָיו: וַיִּשְׁמַע מֹשֶׁה אֶת־הָעָם בֹּכֶה לְמִשְׁפְּחֹתָיו

יא אִישׁ לְפֶתַח אָהֳלוֹ וַיִּחַר־אַף יְהֹוָה מְאֹד וּבְעֵינֵי מֹשֶׁה רָע: וַיֹּאמֶר מֹשֶׁה

אֶל־יְהֹוָה לָמָה הֲרֵעֹתָ לְעַבְדֶּךָ וְלָמָּה לֹא־מָצָתִי חֵן בְּעֵינֶיךָ לָשׂוּם אֶת־   *חסר א

יב מַשָּׂא כָּל־הָעָם הַזֶּה עָלָי: הֶאָנֹכִי הָרִיתִי אֵת כָּל־הָעָם הַזֶּה אִם־אָנֹכִי

יְלִדְתִּיהוּ כִּי־תֹאמַר אֵלַי שָׂאֵהוּ בְחֵיקֶךָ כַּאֲשֶׁר יִשָּׂא הָאֹמֵן אֶת־הַיֹּנֵק עַל

יג הָאֲדָמָה אֲשֶׁר נִשְׁבַּעְתָּ לַאֲבֹתָיו: מֵאַיִן לִי בָּשָׂר לָתֵת לְכָל־הָעָם הַזֶּה כִּי־

יד יִבְכּוּ עָלַי לֵאמֹר תְּנָה־לָּנוּ בָשָׂר וְנֹאכֵלָה: לֹא־אוּכַל אָנֹכִי לְבַדִּי לָשֵׂאת

טו אֶת־כָּל־הָעָם הַזֶּה כִּי כָבֵד מִמֶּנִּי: וְאִם־כָּכָה ׀ אַתְּ־עֹשֶׂה לִּי הָרְגֵנִי נָא הָרֹג

אִם־מָצָאתִי חֵן בְּעֵינֶיךָ וְאַל־אֶרְאֶה בְּרָעָתִי:

טז וַיֹּאמֶר יְהֹוָה אֶל־מֹשֶׁה אֶסְפָה־לִּי שִׁבְעִים אִישׁ מִזִּקְנֵי יִשְׂרָאֵל אֲשֶׁר

יָדַעְתָּ כִּי־הֵם זִקְנֵי הָעָם וְשֹׁטְרָיו וְלָקַחְתָּ אֹתָם אֶל־אֹהֶל מוֹעֵד וְהִתְיַצְּבוּ

יז שָׁם עִמָּךְ: וְיָרַדְתִּי וְדִבַּרְתִּי עִמְּךָ שָׁם וְאָצַלְתִּי מִן־הָרוּחַ אֲשֶׁר עָלֶיךָ

וְשַׂמְתִּי עֲלֵיהֶם וְנָשְׂאוּ אִתְּךָ בְּמַשָּׂא הָעָם וְלֹא־תִשָּׂא אַתָּה לְבַדֶּךָ:

10:35-36. These two verses are set off from the rest of the Torah by means of an inverted letter נ, so that the Talmud (*Shabbos* 115b-116a) calls these verses a separate "book," indicating that it has it own message. In it, Moses speaks not of the *people's* journey, but of the Ark's progress, for the ultimate mission of the Jew is to bring the Torah and its teachings into every aspect of temporal life.

11:4. *The rabble,* i.e., the Egyptians who had joined Israel, influenced *the Children of Israel* to complain again (*Rashi*), going so far as to say that they preferred Egyptian slavery to the Presence of God (v. 20).

11:16. In response to Moses' complaint that he could not carry on alone, God commanded him to select seventy elders who would constitute a Sanhedrin.

Israel." ³⁰ He said to him, "I shall not go; only to my land and my family shall I go." ³¹ He said, "Please do not forsake us, inasmuch as you know our encampments in the Wilderness, and you have been as eyes for us. ³² And it shall be that if you come with us, then with the goodness with which HASHEM will benefit us, we will do good to you."

The first journey ³³ They journeyed from the Mountain of HASHEM a three-day distance, and the Ark of the covenant of HASHEM journeyed before them a three-day distance to search out for them a resting place. ³⁴ The cloud of HASHEM was over them by day when they journeyed from the camp.

The Ark goes forth ³⁵ When* the Ark would journey, Moses said, "Arise, HASHEM, and let Your foes be scattered, let those who hate You flee from before You." ³⁶ And when it rested, he would say, "Reside tranquilly, O, HASHEM, among the myriad thousands of Israel."

11

The complainers ¹ The people took to seeking complaints; it was evil in the ears of HASHEM, and HASHEM heard and His wrath flared, and a fire of HASHEM burned against them, and it consumed at the edge of the camp. ² The people cried out to Moses; Moses prayed to HASHEM, and the fire died down. ³ He named that place Taberah [Conflagration], for the fire of HASHEM had burned against them.

Dissatisfaction with the manna ⁴ The rabble* that was among them cultivated a craving, and the Children of Israel also wept once more, and said, "Who will feed us meat? ⁵ We remember the fish that we ate in Egypt free of charge; the cucumbers, melons, leeks, onions, and garlic. ⁶ But now, our life is parched, there is nothing; we have nothing to anticipate but the manna!"

⁷ Now the manna was like coriander seed and its color was like the color of the bedolach. ⁸ The people would stroll and gather it, and grind it in a mill or pound it in a mortar and cook it in a pot or make it into cakes, and its taste was like the taste of dough kneaded with oil. ⁹ When the dew descended upon the camp at night, the manna would descend upon it.

¹⁰ Moses heard the people weeping in their family groups, each one at the entrance of his tent, and the wrath of HASHEM flared greatly; and in the eyes of Moses it was bad.

Moses' despair ¹¹ Moses said to HASHEM, "Why have You done evil to Your servant; why have I not found favor in Your eyes, that You place the burden of this entire people upon me? ¹² Did I conceive this entire people or did I give birth to it, that You say to me, 'Carry them in your bosom, as a nurse carries a suckling, to the Land that You swore to its forefathers?' ¹³ Where shall I get meat to give to this entire people when they weep to me, saying, 'Give us meat that we may eat'? ¹⁴ I alone cannot carry this entire nation, for it is too heavy for me! ¹⁵ And if this is how You deal with me, then kill me now, if I have found favor in Your eyes, and let me not see my evil!"

The Sanhedrin ¹⁶ HASHEM said to Moses, "Gather to Me seventy men from the elders of Israel, whom you know to be the elders of the people and its officers; take them to the Tent of Meeting and have them stand there with you.* ¹⁷ I will descend and speak with you there, and I will increase some of the spirit that is upon you and place it upon them, and they shall bear the burden of the people with you, and you shall not bear alone.

יח וְאֶל־הָעָם תֹּאמַר הִתְקַדְּשׁוּ לְמָחָר וַאֲכַלְתֶּם בָּשָׂר כִּי בְּכִיתֶם בְּאָזְנֵי יהוה
לֵאמֹר מִי יַאֲכִלֵנוּ בָּשָׂר כִּי־טוֹב לָנוּ בְּמִצְרָיִם וְנָתַן יהוה לָכֶם בָּשָׂר
יט וַאֲכַלְתֶּם: לֹא יוֹם אֶחָד תֹּאכְלוּן וְלֹא יוֹמָיִם וְלֹא ׀ חֲמִשָּׁה יָמִים וְלֹא
כ עֲשָׂרָה יָמִים וְלֹא עֶשְׂרִים יוֹם: עַד ׀ חֹדֶשׁ יָמִים עַד אֲשֶׁר־יֵצֵא מֵאַפְּכֶם
וְהָיָה לָכֶם לְזָרָא יַעַן כִּי־מְאַסְתֶּם אֶת־יהוה אֲשֶׁר בְּקִרְבְּכֶם וַתִּבְכּוּ לְפָנָיו
כא לֵאמֹר לָמָּה זֶּה יָצָאנוּ מִמִּצְרָיִם: וַיֹּאמֶר מֹשֶׁה שֵׁשׁ־מֵאוֹת אֶלֶף רַגְלִי
הָעָם אֲשֶׁר אָנֹכִי בְּקִרְבּוֹ וְאַתָּה אָמַרְתָּ בָּשָׂר אֶתֵּן לָהֶם וְאָכְלוּ חֹדֶשׁ
כב יָמִים: הֲצֹאן וּבָקָר יִשָּׁחֵט לָהֶם וּמָצָא לָהֶם אִם אֶת־כָּל־דְּגֵי הַיָּם יֵאָסֵף
לָהֶם וּמָצָא לָהֶם:
כג וַיֹּאמֶר יהוה אֶל־מֹשֶׁה הֲיַד יהוה תִּקְצָר עַתָּה תִרְאֶה הֲיִקְרְךָ דְבָרִי
כד אִם־לֹא: וַיֵּצֵא מֹשֶׁה וַיְדַבֵּר אֶל־הָעָם אֵת דִּבְרֵי יהוה וַיֶּאֱסֹף שִׁבְעִים
כה אִישׁ מִזִּקְנֵי הָעָם וַיַּעֲמֵד אֹתָם סְבִיבֹת הָאֹהֶל: וַיֵּרֶד יהוה ׀ בֶּעָנָן וַיְדַבֵּר
אֵלָיו וַיָּאצֶל מִן־הָרוּחַ אֲשֶׁר עָלָיו וַיִּתֵּן עַל־שִׁבְעִים אִישׁ הַזְּקֵנִים וַיְהִי
כו כְּנוֹחַ עֲלֵיהֶם הָרוּחַ וַיִּתְנַבְּאוּ וְלֹא יָסָפוּ: וַיִּשָּׁאֲרוּ שְׁנֵי־אֲנָשִׁים ׀ בַּמַּחֲנֶה
שֵׁם הָאֶחָד ׀ אֶלְדָּד וְשֵׁם הַשֵּׁנִי מֵידָד וַתָּנַח עֲלֵהֶם הָרוּחַ וְהֵמָּה בַּכְּתֻבִים
כז וְלֹא יָצְאוּ הָאֹהֱלָה וַיִּתְנַבְּאוּ בַּמַּחֲנֶה: וַיָּרָץ הַנַּעַר וַיַּגֵּד לְמֹשֶׁה וַיֹּאמַר
כח אֶלְדָּד וּמֵידָד מִתְנַבְּאִים בַּמַּחֲנֶה: וַיַּעַן יְהוֹשֻׁעַ בִּן־נוּן מְשָׁרֵת מֹשֶׁה
כט מִבְּחֻרָיו וַיֹּאמַר אֲדֹנִי מֹשֶׁה כְּלָאֵם: וַיֹּאמֶר לוֹ מֹשֶׁה הַמְקַנֵּא אַתָּה לִי וּמִי
ל יִתֵּן כָּל־עַם יהוה נְבִיאִים כִּי־יִתֵּן יהוה אֶת־רוּחוֹ עֲלֵיהֶם: וַיֵּאָסֵף מֹשֶׁה
שביעי
לא אֶל־הַמַּחֲנֶה הוּא וְזִקְנֵי יִשְׂרָאֵל: וְרוּחַ נָסַע ׀ מֵאֵת יהוה וַיָּגָז שַׂלְוִים
מִן־הַיָּם וַיִּטֹּשׁ עַל־הַמַּחֲנֶה כְּדֶרֶךְ יוֹם כֹּה וּכְדֶרֶךְ יוֹם כֹּה סְבִיבוֹת
לב הַמַּחֲנֶה וּכְאַמָּתַיִם עַל־פְּנֵי הָאָרֶץ: וַיָּקָם הָעָם כָּל־הַיּוֹם הַהוּא וְכָל־
הַלַּיְלָה וְכֹל ׀ יוֹם הַמָּחֳרָת וַיַּאַסְפוּ אֶת־הַשְּׂלָו הַמַּמְעִיט אָסַף עֲשָׂרָה
לג חֳמָרִים וַיִּשְׁטְחוּ לָהֶם שָׁטוֹחַ סְבִיבוֹת הַמַּחֲנֶה: הַבָּשָׂר עוֹדֶנּוּ בֵּין שִׁנֵּיהֶם
לד טֶרֶם יִכָּרֵת וְאַף יהוה חָרָה בָעָם וַיַּךְ יהוה בָּעָם מַכָּה רַבָּה מְאֹד: וַיִּקְרָא
לה אֶת־שֵׁם־הַמָּקוֹם הַהוּא קִבְרוֹת הַתַּאֲוָה כִּי־שָׁם קָבְרוּ אֶת־הָעָם
הַמִּתְאַוִּים: מִקִּבְרוֹת הַתַּאֲוָה נָסְעוּ הָעָם חֲצֵרוֹת וַיִּהְיוּ בַּחֲצֵרוֹת:

יב א וַתְּדַבֵּר מִרְיָם וְאַהֲרֹן בְּמֹשֶׁה עַל־אֹדוֹת הָאִשָּׁה הַכֻּשִׁית אֲשֶׁר לָקָח
ב כִּי־אִשָּׁה כֻשִׁית לָקָח: וַיֹּאמְרוּ הֲרַק אַךְ־בְּמֹשֶׁה דִּבֶּר יהוה הֲלֹא גַּם־בָּנוּ
ג דִבֵּר וַיִּשְׁמַע יהוה: וְהָאִישׁ מֹשֶׁה עָנָו מְאֹד מִכֹּל הָאָדָם אֲשֶׁר עַל־פְּנֵי
ד הָאֲדָמָה: וַיֹּאמֶר יהוה פִּתְאֹם אֶל־מֹשֶׁה וְאֶל־אַהֲרֹן וְאֶל־מִרְיָם צְאוּ

12:1-16. Moses had to refrain from marital relations with his wife Zipporah, in order to be ritually pure at all times, since God could speak to him at any moment. Miriam disparagingly reported this to Aaron, who was critical as well. Because she instigated the slander, she was punished with *tzaraas*. Thus her mistake became an eternal teaching to the Jewish people of the gravity of the sin of slander.

God
responds to
the people

¹⁸ "To the people you shall say, 'Prepare yourselves for tomorrow and you shall eat meat, for you have wept in the ears of HASHEM, saying: "Who will feed us meat? for it was better for us in Egypt!" So HASHEM will give you meat and you will eat. ¹⁹ Not for one day shall you eat, nor two days, nor five days, nor ten days, nor twenty days. ²⁰ Until an entire month of days, until it comes out of your nose, and becomes nauseating to you, because you have rejected HASHEM Who is in your midst, and you have wept before Him, saying: "Why did we leave Egypt?" ' "

²¹ Moses said, "Six hundred thousand footsoldiers are the people in whose midst I am, yet You say I shall give them meat, and they shall eat for a month of days! ²² Can sheep and cattle be slaughtered for them and suffice for them? Or if all the fish of the sea will be gathered for them, would it suffice for them?"

²³ HASHEM said to Moses, "Is the hand of HASHEM limited? Now you will see whether My word comes to pass or not!"

New
prophets

²⁴ Moses left and spoke the words of HASHEM to the people; and he gathered seventy men from among the elders of the people and had them stand around the Tent.

²⁵ HASHEM descended in a cloud and spoke to him, and He increased some of the spirit that was upon him and gave it to the seventy men, the elders; when the spirit rested upon them, they prophesied, but did not do so again.

²⁶ Two men remained behind in the camp, the name of one was Eldad and the name of the second was Medad, and the spirit rested upon them; they had been among the recorded ones, but they had not gone out to the Tent, and they prophesied in the camp. ²⁷ The youth ran and told Moses, and he said, "Eldad and Medad are prophesying in the camp."

²⁸ Joshua son of Nun, the servant of Moses since his youth, spoke up and said, "My lord Moses, incarcerate them!"

²⁹ Moses said to him, "Are you being zealous for my sake? Would that the entire people of HASHEM could be prophets, if HASHEM would but place His spirit upon them!"

The quail

³⁰ Moses was brought into the camp, he and the elders of Israel. ³¹ A wind went forth from HASHEM and blew quail from the sea and spread them over the camp, a day's journey this way and a day's journey that way, all around the camp, and two cubits above the face of the earth. ³² The people rose up all that day and all the night and all the next day and gathered up the quail — the one with the least gathered in ten chomers — and they spread them out all around the camp. ³³ The meat was still between their teeth, not yet chewed, when the wrath of HASHEM flared against the people, and HASHEM struck a very mighty blow against the people. ³⁴ He named that place Kibroth-hattaavah, because there they buried the people who had been craving.

³⁵ From Kibroth-hattaavah the people journeyed to Hazeroth, and they remained in Hazeroth.

12

Moses'
uniqueness
is challenged
and affirmed

¹ Miriam and Aaron spoke against Moses* regarding the Cushite woman he had married, for he had married a Cushite woman. ² They said, "Was it only to Moses that HASHEM spoke? Did He not speak to us, as well?" And HASHEM heard. ³ Now the man Moses was exceedingly humble, more than any person on the face of the earth!

⁴ HASHEM said suddenly to Moses, to Aaron, and to Miriam, "You three,

ה שְׁלָשְׁתְּכֶם אֶל־אֹהֶל מוֹעֵד וַיֵּצְאוּ שְׁלָשְׁתָּם: וַיֵּרֶד יהוה בְּעַמּוּד עָנָן וַיַּעֲמֹד

ו פֶּתַח הָאֹהֶל וַיִּקְרָא אַהֲרֹן וּמִרְיָם וַיֵּצְאוּ שְׁנֵיהֶם: וַיֹּאמֶר שִׁמְעוּ־נָא דְבָרָי

ז אִם־יִהְיֶה נְבִיאֲכֶם יהוה בַּמַּרְאָה אֵלָיו אֶתְוַדָּע בַּחֲלוֹם אֲדַבֶּר־בּוֹ: לֹא־כֵן

ח עַבְדִּי מֹשֶׁה בְּכָל־בֵּיתִי נֶאֱמָן הוּא: פֶּה אֶל־פֶּה אֲדַבֶּר־בּוֹ וּמַרְאֶה וְלֹא

בְחִידֹת וּתְמֻנַת יהוה יַבִּיט וּמַדּוּעַ לֹא יְרֵאתֶם לְדַבֵּר בְּעַבְדִּי בְמֹשֶׁה:

ט וַיִּחַר־אַף יהוה בָּם וַיֵּלַךְ: וְהֶעָנָן סָר מֵעַל הָאֹהֶל וְהִנֵּה מִרְיָם מְצֹרַעַת

יא כַּשָּׁלֶג וַיִּפֶן אַהֲרֹן אֶל־מִרְיָם וְהִנֵּה מְצֹרָעַת: וַיֹּאמֶר אַהֲרֹן אֶל־מֹשֶׁה בִּי

יב אֲדֹנִי אַל־נָא תָשֵׁת עָלֵינוּ חַטָּאת אֲשֶׁר נוֹאַלְנוּ וַאֲשֶׁר חָטָאנוּ: אַל־נָא תְהִי

יג כַּמֵּת אֲשֶׁר בְּצֵאתוֹ מֵרֶחֶם אִמּוֹ וַיֵּאָכֵל חֲצִי בְשָׂרוֹ: וַיִּצְעַק מֹשֶׁה אֶל־יהוה

לֵאמֹר אֵל נָא רְפָא נָא לָהּ:

מפטיר

יד וַיֹּאמֶר יהוה אֶל־מֹשֶׁה וְאָבִיהָ יָרֹק יָרַק בְּפָנֶיהָ הֲלֹא תִכָּלֵם שִׁבְעַת יָמִים

טו תִּסָּגֵר שִׁבְעַת יָמִים מִחוּץ לַמַּחֲנֶה וְאַחַר תֵּאָסֵף: וַתִּסָּגֵר מִרְיָם מִחוּץ

Haftaras
Beha'aloscha:
p. 1408

טז לַמַּחֲנֶה שִׁבְעַת יָמִים וְהָעָם לֹא נָסַע עַד הֵאָסֵף מִרְיָם: וְאַחַר נָסְעוּ הָעָם

מֵחֲצֵרוֹת וַיַּחֲנוּ בְּמִדְבַּר פָּארָן: פפפ קל"ו פסוקים. מהלל"ל סימן.

פרשת שלח

יג

א־ב וַיְדַבֵּר יהוה אֶל־מֹשֶׁה לֵּאמֹר: שְׁלַח־לְךָ אֲנָשִׁים וְיָתֻרוּ אֶת־אֶרֶץ כְּנַעַן

אֲשֶׁר־אֲנִי נֹתֵן לִבְנֵי יִשְׂרָאֵל אִישׁ אֶחָד אִישׁ אֶחָד לְמַטֵּה אֲבֹתָיו תִּשְׁלָחוּ

ג כֹּל נָשִׂיא בָהֶם: וַיִּשְׁלַח אֹתָם מֹשֶׁה מִמִּדְבַּר פָּארָן עַל־פִּי יהוה כֻּלָּם

ד אֲנָשִׁים רָאשֵׁי בְנֵי־יִשְׂרָאֵל הֵמָּה: וְאֵלֶּה שְׁמוֹתָם לְמַטֵּה רְאוּבֵן שַׁמּוּעַ בֶּן־

ה־ו זַכּוּר: לְמַטֵּה שִׁמְעוֹן שָׁפָט בֶּן־חוֹרִי: לְמַטֵּה יְהוּדָה כָּלֵב בֶּן־יְפֻנֶּה: לְמַטֵּה

ח־ט יִשָּׂשכָר יִגְאָל בֶּן־יוֹסֵף: לְמַטֵּה אֶפְרָיִם הוֹשֵׁעַ בִּן־נוּן: לְמַטֵּה בִנְיָמִן פַּלְטִי

יא בֶּן־רָפוּא: לְמַטֵּה זְבוּלֻן גַּדִּיאֵל בֶּן־סוֹדִי: לְמַטֵּה יוֹסֵף לְמַטֵּה מְנַשֶּׁה גַּדִּי בֶּן־

יב־יד סוּסִי: לְמַטֵּה דָן עַמִּיאֵל בֶּן־גְּמַלִּי: לְמַטֵּה אָשֵׁר סְתוּר בֶּן־מִיכָאֵל: לְמַטֵּה

טו־טז נַפְתָּלִי נַחְבִּי בֶּן־וָפְסִי: לְמַטֵּה גָד גְּאוּאֵל בֶּן־מָכִי: אֵלֶּה שְׁמוֹת הָאֲנָשִׁים

אֲשֶׁר־שָׁלַח מֹשֶׁה לָתוּר אֶת־הָאָרֶץ וַיִּקְרָא מֹשֶׁה לְהוֹשֵׁעַ בִּן־נוּן

יז יְהוֹשֻׁעַ: וַיִּשְׁלַח אֹתָם מֹשֶׁה לָתוּר אֶת־אֶרֶץ כְּנָעַן וַיֹּאמֶר אֲלֵהֶם עֲלוּ זֶה

יח בַּנֶּגֶב וַעֲלִיתֶם אֶת־הָהָר: וּרְאִיתֶם אֶת־הָאָרֶץ מַה־הִוא וְאֶת־הָעָם

יט הַיֹּשֵׁב עָלֶיהָ הֶחָזָק הוּא הֲרָפֶה הַמְעַט הוּא אִם־רָב: וּמָה הָאָרֶץ אֲשֶׁר־

הוּא יֹשֵׁב בָּהּ הֲטוֹבָה הִוא אִם־רָעָה וּמָה הֶעָרִים אֲשֶׁר־הוּא יוֹשֵׁב בָּהֵנָּה

כ הַבְּמַחֲנִים אִם בְּמִבְצָרִים: וּמָה הָאָרֶץ הַשְּׁמֵנָה הִוא אִם־רָזָה הֲיֵשׁ־בָּהּ עֵץ

אִם־אַיִן וְהִתְחַזַּקְתֶּם וּלְקַחְתֶּם מִפְּרִי הָאָרֶץ וְהַיָּמִים יְמֵי בִּכּוּרֵי עֲנָבִים:

⇜ Parashas Shelach

13:16. Moses added the letter י to Hoshea's name, so
that his name would begin with the letters of God's

Name [י–ה]. This signifies that Moses prayed, "May God
[יָ–הּ] save [הושע] you from the conspiracy of the spies"
(Rashi).

go out to the Tent of Meeting." And the three of them went out. [5] HASHEM descended in a pillar of cloud and stood at the entrance to the Tent, and He summoned Aaron and Miriam; the two of them went out. [6] He said, "Hear now My words. If there shall be prophets among you, in a vision shall I, HASHEM, make Myself known to him; in a dream shall I speak with him. [7] Not so is My servant Moses; in My entire house he is the trusted one. [8] Mouth to mouth do I speak to him, in a clear vision and not in riddles, at the image of HASHEM does he gaze. Why did you not fear to speak against My servant Moses?"

[9] The wrath of HASHEM flared up against them, and He left.

[10] The cloud had departed from atop the Tent, and behold! Miriam was afflicted with tzaraas, like snow! Aaron turned to Miriam and behold! she was afflicted with tzaraas.

[11] Aaron said to Moses, "I beg you, my lord, do not cast a sin upon us, for we have been foolish and we have sinned. [12] Let her not be like a corpse, like one who leaves his mother's womb with half his flesh having been consumed!"

[13] Moses cried out to HASHEM, saying, "Please, God, heal her now."

Miriam is quarantined [14] HASHEM said to Moses, "Were her father to spit in her face, would she not be humiliated for seven days? Let her be quarantined outside the camp for seven days, and then she may be brought in." [15] So Miriam was quarantined outside the camp for seven days, and the people did not journey until Miriam was brought in. [16] Then the people journeyed from Hazeroth, and they encamped in the Wilderness of Paran.

PARASHAS SHELACH

13

The command to send spies to Eretz Yisrael

[1] HASHEM spoke to Moses, saying, [2] "Send forth men, if you please, and let them spy out the Land of Canaan that I give to the Children of Israel; one man each from his father's tribe shall you send, every one a leader among them." [3] Moses sent them forth from the Wilderness of Paran at HASHEM's command; they were all distinguished men; heads of the Children of Israel were they.

[4] These are their names: For the tribe of Reuben, Shammua son of Zaccur. [5] For the tribe of Simeon, Shaphat son of Hori. [6] For the tribe of Judah, Caleb son of Jephunneh. [7] For the tribe of Issachar, Yigal son of Joseph. [8] For the tribe of Ephraim, Hoshea son of Nun. [9] For the tribe of Benjamin, Palti son of Raphu. [10] For the tribe of Zebulun, Gaddiel son of Sodi. [11] For the tribe of Joseph for the tribe of Manasseh, Gaddi son of Susi. [12] For the tribe of Dan, Ammiel son of Gemalli. [13] For the tribe of Asher, Sethur son of Michael. [14] For the tribe of Naphtali, Nahbi son of Vophsi. [15] For the tribe of Gad, Geuel son of Machi.

Moses prays for Joshua [16] These are the names of the men whom Moses sent to spy out the Land. Moses called Hoshea son of Nun "Joshua."*

[17] Moses sent them to spy out the Land of Canaan, and he said to them, "Ascend here in the south and climb the mountain. [18] See the Land — how is it? and the people that dwells in it — is it strong or weak? is it few or numerous? [19] And how is the Land in which it dwells — is it good or is it bad? And how are the cities in which it dwells — are they open or are they fortified? [20] And how is the land — is it fertile or is it lean? are there trees in it or not? You shall strengthen yourselves and take from the fruit of the Land." The days were the season of the first ripe grapes.

שני

כא-כב וַיַּעֲלוּ וַיָּתֻרוּ אֶת־הָאָרֶץ מִמִּדְבַּר־צִן עַד־רְחֹב לְבֹא חֲמָת: וַיַּעֲלוּ בַנֶּגֶב
וַיָּבֹא עַד־חֶבְרוֹן וְשָׁם אֲחִימַן שֵׁשַׁי וְתַלְמַי יְלִידֵי הָעֲנָק וְחֶבְרוֹן שֶׁבַע שָׁנִים
כג נִבְנְתָה לִפְנֵי צֹעַן מִצְרָיִם: וַיָּבֹאוּ עַד־נַחַל אֶשְׁכֹּל וַיִּכְרְתוּ מִשָּׁם זְמוֹרָה
וְאֶשְׁכּוֹל עֲנָבִים אֶחָד וַיִּשָּׂאֻהוּ בַמּוֹט בִּשְׁנָיִם וּמִן־הָרִמֹּנִים וּמִן־הַתְּאֵנִים:
כד לַמָּקוֹם הַהוּא קָרָא נַחַל אֶשְׁכּוֹל עַל אֹדוֹת הָאֶשְׁכּוֹל אֲשֶׁר־כָּרְתוּ מִשָּׁם
כה-כו בְּנֵי יִשְׂרָאֵל: וַיָּשֻׁבוּ מִתּוּר הָאָרֶץ מִקֵּץ אַרְבָּעִים יוֹם: וַיֵּלְכוּ וַיָּבֹאוּ אֶל־
מֹשֶׁה וְאֶל־אַהֲרֹן וְאֶל־כָּל־עֲדַת בְּנֵי־יִשְׂרָאֵל אֶל־מִדְבַּר פָּארָן קָדֵשָׁה
כז וַיָּשִׁיבוּ אֹתָם דָּבָר וְאֶת־כָּל־הָעֵדָה וַיַּרְאוּם אֶת־פְּרִי הָאָרֶץ: וַיְסַפְּרוּ־לוֹ
וַיֹּאמְרוּ בָּאנוּ אֶל־הָאָרֶץ אֲשֶׁר שְׁלַחְתָּנוּ וְגַם זָבַת חָלָב וּדְבַשׁ הִוא וְזֶה
כח פִּרְיָהּ: אֶפֶס כִּי־עַז הָעָם הַיֹּשֵׁב בָּאָרֶץ וְהֶעָרִים בְּצֻרוֹת גְּדֹלֹת מְאֹד וְגַם
כט יְלִדֵי הָעֲנָק רָאִינוּ שָׁם: עֲמָלֵק יוֹשֵׁב בְּאֶרֶץ הַנֶּגֶב וְהַחִתִּי וְהַיְבוּסִי וְהָאֱמֹרִי
ל יוֹשֵׁב בָּהָר וְהַכְּנַעֲנִי יוֹשֵׁב עַל־הַיָּם וְעַל יַד הַיַּרְדֵּן: וַיַּהַס כָּלֵב אֶת־הָעָם
לא אֶל־מֹשֶׁה וַיֹּאמֶר עָלֹה נַעֲלֶה וְיָרַשְׁנוּ אֹתָהּ כִּי־יָכוֹל נוּכַל לָהּ: וְהָאֲנָשִׁים
אֲשֶׁר־עָלוּ עִמּוֹ אָמְרוּ לֹא נוּכַל לַעֲלוֹת אֶל־הָעָם כִּי־חָזָק הוּא מִמֶּנּוּ:
לב וַיֹּצִיאוּ דִּבַּת הָאָרֶץ אֲשֶׁר תָּרוּ אֹתָהּ אֶל־בְּנֵי יִשְׂרָאֵל לֵאמֹר הָאָרֶץ אֲשֶׁר
עָבַרְנוּ בָהּ לָתוּר אֹתָהּ אֶרֶץ אֹכֶלֶת יוֹשְׁבֶיהָ הִוא וְכָל־הָעָם אֲשֶׁר־רָאִינוּ
לג בְתוֹכָהּ אַנְשֵׁי מִדּוֹת: וְשָׁם רָאִינוּ אֶת־הַנְּפִילִים בְּנֵי עֲנָק מִן־הַנְּפִלִים וַנְּהִי
יד א בְעֵינֵינוּ כַּחֲגָבִים וְכֵן הָיִינוּ בְּעֵינֵיהֶם: וַתִּשָּׂא כָּל־הָעֵדָה וַיִּתְּנוּ אֶת־קוֹלָם
ב וַיִּבְכּוּ הָעָם בַּלַּיְלָה הַהוּא: וַיִּלֹּנוּ עַל־מֹשֶׁה וְעַל־אַהֲרֹן כֹּל בְּנֵי יִשְׂרָאֵל
וַיֹּאמְרוּ אֲלֵהֶם כָּל־הָעֵדָה לוּ־מַתְנוּ בְּאֶרֶץ מִצְרַיִם אוֹ בַּמִּדְבָּר הַזֶּה לוּ־
ג מָתְנוּ: וְלָמָה יְהוָֹה מֵבִיא אֹתָנוּ אֶל־הָאָרֶץ הַזֹּאת לִנְפֹּל בַּחֶרֶב נָשֵׁינוּ וְטַפֵּנוּ
ד יִהְיוּ לָבַז הֲלוֹא טוֹב לָנוּ שׁוּב מִצְרָיְמָה: וַיֹּאמְרוּ אִישׁ אֶל־אָחִיו נִתְּנָה רֹאשׁ
ה וְנָשׁוּבָה מִצְרָיְמָה: וַיִּפֹּל מֹשֶׁה וְאַהֲרֹן עַל־פְּנֵיהֶם לִפְנֵי כָּל־קְהַל עֲדַת בְּנֵי
ו יִשְׂרָאֵל: וִיהוֹשֻׁעַ בִּן־נוּן וְכָלֵב בֶּן־יְפֻנֶּה מִן־הַתָּרִים אֶת־הָאָרֶץ קָרְעוּ
ז בִּגְדֵיהֶם: וַיֹּאמְרוּ אֶל־כָּל־עֲדַת בְּנֵי־יִשְׂרָאֵל לֵאמֹר הָאָרֶץ אֲשֶׁר עָבַרְנוּ
ח בָהּ לָתוּר אֹתָהּ טוֹבָה הָאָרֶץ מְאֹד מְאֹד: אִם־חָפֵץ בָּנוּ יְהוָֹה וְהֵבִיא אֹתָנוּ

שלישי

ט אֶל־הָאָרֶץ הַזֹּאת וּנְתָנָהּ לָנוּ אֶרֶץ אֲשֶׁר־הִוא זָבַת חָלָב וּדְבָשׁ: אַךְ בַּיהוָֹה
אַל־תִּמְרֹדוּ וְאַתֶּם אַל־תִּירְאוּ אֶת־עַם הָאָרֶץ כִּי לַחְמֵנוּ הֵם סָר צִלָּם
י מֵעֲלֵיהֶם וַיהוָֹה אִתָּנוּ אַל־תִּירָאֻם: וַיֹּאמְרוּ כָּל־הָעֵדָה לִרְגּוֹם אֹתָם
בָּאֲבָנִים וּכְבוֹד יְהוָֹה נִרְאָה בְּאֹהֶל מוֹעֵד אֶל־כָּל־בְּנֵי יִשְׂרָאֵל:

13:22. *He* (in the singular) *arrived at Hebron.* Only Caleb went there to pray at the tomb of the Patriarchs for the strength to resist the conspiracy of his comrades (*Rashi*).

13:27-29. Instead of reporting privately to Moses, they made a loud public declaration.

14:1. God declared, "They indulged in weeping without a cause; I will establish [this night] for them [as a time of]

weeping throughout the generations." That night, Tishah B'Av [the Ninth of Av], is the date when both Temples were destroyed and many other tragedies took place throughout Jewish history (*Rashi* to *Psalms* 106:27).

14:6. They tore their clothing in mourning, because the loss of faith in God and the repudiation of Moses and Aaron were tantamount to the death of dear ones.

²¹ They ascended and spied out the Land, from the Wilderness of Zin to the expanse at the approach to Hamath. ²² They ascended in the south and he arrived at Hebron, * where there were Ahiman, Sheshai, and Talmai, the off-spring of the giant. Hebron had been built seven years before Zoan of Egypt. ²³ They arrived at the Valley of Eshcol and cut from there a vine with one cluster of grapes, and bore it on a double pole, and of the pomegranates and of the figs. ²⁴ They named that place the Valley of Eshcol because of the cluster that the Children of Israel cut from there.

²⁵ They returned from spying out the Land at the end of forty days. ²⁶ They went and came to Moses and to Aaron and to the entire assembly of the Children of Israel, to the Wilderness of Paran at Kadesh, and brought back the report to them and the entire assembly, and they showed them the fruit of the Land.

The spies' report ²⁷ They reported * to him and said, "We arrived at the Land to which you sent us, and indeed it flows with milk and honey, and this is its fruit. ²⁸ But — the people that dwells in the Land is powerful, the cities are fortified and very great, and we also saw there the offspring of the giant. ²⁹ Amalek dwells in the area of the south; the Hittite, the Jebusite, and the Amorite dwell on the mountain; and the Canaanite dwells by the Sea and on the bank of the Jordan."

³⁰ Caleb silenced the people toward Moses and said, "We shall surely ascend and conquer it, for we can surely do it!"

Caleb is shouted down ³¹ But the men who had ascended with him said, "We cannot ascend to that people for it is too strong for us!" ³² They brought forth to the Children of Israel an evil report on the Land that they had spied out, saying, "The Land through which we have passed, to spy it out, is a land that devours its inhabitants! All the people that we saw in it were huge! ³³ There we saw the Nephilim, the sons of the giant from among the Nephilim; we were like grasshoppers in our eyes, and so we were in their eyes!"

14

National hysteria ¹ The entire assembly raised up and issued its voice; the people wept that night. * ² All the Children of Israel murmured against Moses and Aaron, and the entire assembly said to them, "If only we had died in the land of Egypt, or if only we had died in this Wilderness! ³ Why is HASHEM bringing us to this Land to die by the sword? Our wives and young children will be taken captive! Is it not better for us to return to Egypt?"

⁴ So they said to one another, "Let us appoint a leader and let us return to Egypt!"

⁵ Moses and Aaron fell on their faces before the entire congregation of the assembly of the Children of Israel.

The people could not be placated ⁶ Joshua son of Nun and Caleb son of Jephunneh, of the spies of the Land, tore their garments. * ⁷ They spoke to the entire assembly of the Children of Israel, saying, "The Land that we passed through, to spy it out — the Land is very, very good! ⁸ If HASHEM desires us, He will bring us to this Land and give it to us, a Land that flows with milk and honey. ⁹ But do not rebel against HASHEM! You should not fear the people of the Land, for they are our bread. Their protection has departed from them; HASHEM is with us. Do not fear them!"

¹⁰ But the entire assembly said to pelt them with stones — and the glory of HASHEM appeared in the Tent of Meeting to all the Children of Israel.

יא וַיֹּאמֶר יהוה אֶל־מֹשֶׁה עַד־אָנָה יְנַאֲצֻנִי הָעָם הַזֶּה וְעַד־אָנָה לֹא־יַאֲמִינוּ

יב בִּי בְּכֹל הָאֹתוֹת אֲשֶׁר עָשִׂיתִי בְּקִרְבּוֹ: אַכֶּנּוּ בַדֶּבֶר וְאוֹרִשֶׁנּוּ וְאֶעֱשֶׂה

יג אֹתְךָ לְגוֹי־גָּדוֹל וְעָצוּם מִמֶּנּוּ: וַיֹּאמֶר מֹשֶׁה אֶל־יהוה וְשָׁמְעוּ מִצְרַיִם כִּי־

יד הֶעֱלִיתָ בְכֹחֲךָ אֶת־הָעָם הַזֶּה מִקִּרְבּוֹ: וְאָמְרוּ אֶל־יוֹשֵׁב הָאָרֶץ הַזֹּאת

שָׁמְעוּ כִּי־אַתָּה יהוה בְּקֶרֶב הָעָם הַזֶּה אֲשֶׁר־עַיִן בְּעַיִן נִרְאָה ׀ אַתָּה יהוה

וַעֲנָנְךָ עֹמֵד עֲלֵהֶם וּבְעַמֻּד עָנָן אַתָּה הֹלֵךְ לִפְנֵיהֶם יוֹמָם וּבְעַמּוּד אֵשׁ

טו לָיְלָה: וְהֵמַתָּה אֶת־הָעָם הַזֶּה כְּאִישׁ אֶחָד וְאָמְרוּ הַגּוֹיִם אֲשֶׁר־שָׁמְעוּ

טז אֶת־שִׁמְעֲךָ לֵאמֹר: מִבִּלְתִּי יְכֹלֶת יהוה לְהָבִיא אֶת־הָעָם הַזֶּה אֶל־

הָאָרֶץ אֲשֶׁר־נִשְׁבַּע לָהֶם וַיִּשְׁחָטֵם בַּמִּדְבָּר: וְעַתָּה *יִגְדַּל־נָא כֹּחַ אֲדֹנָי ⟨יי רבתי⟩

יח כַּאֲשֶׁר דִּבַּרְתָּ לֵאמֹר: יהוה אֶרֶךְ אַפַּיִם וְרַב־חֶסֶד נֹשֵׂא עָוֹן וָפָשַׁע וְנַקֵּה

יט לֹא יְנַקֶּה פֹּקֵד עֲוֹן אָבוֹת עַל־בָּנִים עַל־שִׁלֵּשִׁים וְעַל־רִבֵּעִים: סְלַח־נָא

לַעֲוֹן הָעָם הַזֶּה כְּגֹדֶל חַסְדֶּךָ וְכַאֲשֶׁר נָשָׂאתָה לָעָם הַזֶּה מִמִּצְרַיִם וְעַד־

כ-כא הֵנָּה: וַיֹּאמֶר יהוה סָלַחְתִּי כִּדְבָרֶךָ: וְאוּלָם חַי־אָנִי וְיִמָּלֵא כְבוֹד־יהוה

כב אֶת־כָּל־הָאָרֶץ: כִּי כָל־הָאֲנָשִׁים הָרֹאִים אֶת־כְּבֹדִי וְאֶת־אֹתֹתַי אֲשֶׁר־

עָשִׂיתִי בְמִצְרַיִם וּבַמִּדְבָּר וַיְנַסּוּ אֹתִי זֶה עֶשֶׂר פְּעָמִים וְלֹא שָׁמְעוּ בְּקוֹלִי:

כג אִם־יִרְאוּ אֶת־הָאָרֶץ אֲשֶׁר נִשְׁבַּעְתִּי לַאֲבֹתָם וְכָל־מְנַאֲצַי לֹא יִרְאוּהָ:

כד וְעַבְדִּי כָלֵב עֵקֶב הָיְתָה רוּחַ אַחֶרֶת עִמּוֹ וַיְמַלֵּא אַחֲרָי וַהֲבִיאֹתִיו אֶל־

כה הָאָרֶץ אֲשֶׁר־בָּא שָׁמָּה וְזַרְעוֹ יוֹרִשֶׁנָּה: וְהָעֲמָלֵקִי וְהַכְּנַעֲנִי יוֹשֵׁב בָּעֵמֶק

מָחָר פְּנוּ וּסְעוּ לָכֶם הַמִּדְבָּר דֶּרֶךְ יַם־סוּף:

רביעי

כו-כז וַיְדַבֵּר יהוה אֶל־מֹשֶׁה וְאֶל־אַהֲרֹן לֵאמֹר: עַד־מָתַי לָעֵדָה הָרָעָה

הַזֹּאת אֲשֶׁר הֵמָּה מַלִּינִים עָלָי אֶת־תְּלֻנּוֹת בְּנֵי יִשְׂרָאֵל אֲשֶׁר הֵמָּה

כח מַלִּינִים עָלַי שָׁמָעְתִּי: אֱמֹר אֲלֵהֶם חַי־אָנִי נְאֻם־יהוה אִם־לֹא כַּאֲשֶׁר

כט דִּבַּרְתֶּם בְּאָזְנָי כֵּן אֶעֱשֶׂה לָכֶם: בַּמִּדְבָּר הַזֶּה יִפְּלוּ פִגְרֵיכֶם וְכָל־פְּקֻדֵיכֶם

ל לְכָל־מִסְפַּרְכֶם מִבֶּן עֶשְׂרִים שָׁנָה וָמָעְלָה אֲשֶׁר הֲלִינֹתֶם עָלָי: אִם־

אַתֶּם תָּבֹאוּ אֶל־הָאָרֶץ אֲשֶׁר נָשָׂאתִי אֶת־יָדִי לְשַׁכֵּן אֶתְכֶם בָּהּ כִּי

לא אִם־כָּלֵב בֶּן־יְפֻנֶּה וִיהוֹשֻׁעַ בִּן־נוּן: וְטַפְּכֶם אֲשֶׁר אֲמַרְתֶּם לָבַז יִהְיֶה

לב וְהֵבֵיאתִי אֹתָם וְיָדְעוּ אֶת־הָאָרֶץ אֲשֶׁר מְאַסְתֶּם בָּהּ: וּפִגְרֵיכֶם אַתֶּם

לג יִפְּלוּ בַּמִּדְבָּר הַזֶּה: וּבְנֵיכֶם יִהְיוּ רֹעִים בַּמִּדְבָּר אַרְבָּעִים שָׁנָה וְנָשְׂאוּ

אֶת־זְנוּתֵיכֶם עַד־תֹּם פִּגְרֵיכֶם בַּמִּדְבָּר: בְּמִסְפַּר הַיָּמִים אֲשֶׁר־תַּרְתֶּם

לד אֶת־הָאָרֶץ אַרְבָּעִים יוֹם יוֹם לַשָּׁנָה יוֹם לַשָּׁנָה תִּשְׂאוּ אֶת־עֲוֹנֹתֵיכֶם

אַרְבָּעִים שָׁנָה וִידַעְתֶּם אֶת־תְּנוּאָתִי: אֲנִי יהוה דִּבַּרְתִּי אִם־לֹא ׀ זֹאת

לה אֶעֱשֶׂה לְכָל־הָעֵדָה הָרָעָה הַזֹּאת הַנּוֹעָדִים עָלָי בַּמִּדְבָּר הַזֶּה יִתַּמּוּ

לו וְשָׁם יָמֻתוּ: וְהָאֲנָשִׁים אֲשֶׁר־שָׁלַח מֹשֶׁה לָתוּר אֶת־הָאָרֶץ וַיָּשֻׁבוּ

14:13-19. As Isaiah (43:7) said, the purpose of Creation is to bring glory to God; therefore, Moses contended, God should once again forgive Israel to protect His own honor.

Israel is threatened with extermination

¹¹ HASHEM said to Moses, "How long will this people provoke Me, and how long will they not have faith in Me, despite all the signs that I have performed in their midst? ¹² I will smite them with the plague and annihilate them, and I shall make you a greater and more powerful nation than they."

Moses' successful plea

¹³ Moses said to HASHEM, "Then Egypt — from whose midst You brought up this nation with Your power — will hear,* ¹⁴ and they will say about the inhabitants of this Land, 'They have heard that You, HASHEM, are in the midst of this people — that You, HASHEM, appeared eye to eye and Your cloud stands over them, and that in a pillar of cloud You go before them by day and in a pillar of fire at night — ¹⁵ yet You killed this people like a single man!' Then the nations that heard of Your fame will say, ¹⁶ 'Because HASHEM lacked the ability to bring this people to the Land that He had sworn to give them, He slaughtered them in the Wilderness.' ¹⁷ And now — may the strength of my Lord be magnified as You have spoken, saying, ¹⁸ 'HASHEM, Slow to Anger, Abundant in Kindness, Forgiver of Iniquity and Willful Sin, and Who cleanses — but does not cleanse completely, recalling the iniquity of parents upon children to the third and fourth generations' — ¹⁹ forgive now the iniquity of this people according to the greatness of Your kindness and as You have forgiven this people from Egypt until now."

God forgives, and decrees forty years of wandering

²⁰ And HASHEM said, "I have forgiven because of your word. ²¹ But as I live — and the glory of HASHEM shall fill the entire world — ²² that all the men who have seen My glory and My signs that I performed in Egypt and in the Wilderness, and have tested Me these ten times and have not heeded My voice, ²³ if they will see the Land that I have sworn to give their forefathers! — and all who anger Me shall not see it. ²⁴ But My servant Caleb, because a different spirit was with him and he followed Me wholeheartedly, I shall bring him to the Land to which he came, and his offspring shall possess it. ²⁵ The Amalekite and the Canaanite dwell in the valley — tomorrow, turn and journey toward the Wilderness in the direction of the Sea of Reeds."

God spells out the decree

²⁶ HASHEM spoke to Moses and Aaron, saying, ²⁷ "How long for this evil assembly that provokes complaints against Me!? I have heard the complaints of the Children of Israel whom they provoke against Me. ²⁸ Say to them: As I live — the word of HASHEM — if I shall not do to you as you have spoken in My ears. ²⁹ In this Wilderness shall your carcasses drop; all of you who were counted in any of your numberings, from twenty years of age and above, whom you provoked against Me; ³⁰ if you shall come to the Land about which I have raised My hand in an oath to settle you there, except for Caleb son of Jephunneh and Joshua son of Nun. ³¹ And your young children of whom you said they will be taken captive, I shall bring them; they shall know the Land that you have despised. ³² But your carcasses shall drop in this Wilderness. ³³ Your children will roam in the Wilderness for forty years and bear your guilt, until the last of your carcasses in the Wilderness. ³⁴ Like the number of the days that you spied out the Land, forty days, a day for a year, a day for a year, shall you bear your iniquities — forty years — and you shall comprehend straying from Me. ³⁵ I HASHEM have spoken — if I shall not do this to this entire evil assembly that gathers against Me! In this Wilderness shall they cease to be, and there shall they die!"

³⁶ But as for the men whom Moses sent to spy out the Land, and who returned

לז וַיִּלֹּ֨נוּ [°וַיִּלּ֤וֹנוּ כ] עָלָיו֙ אֶת־כָּל־הָ֣עֵדָ֔ה לְהוֹצִ֥יא דִבָּ֖ה עַל־הָאָ֑רֶץ וַיָּמֻ֨תוּ֙

לח הָאֲנָשִׁ֔ים מוֹצִאֵ֥י דִבַּת־הָאָ֖רֶץ רָעָ֑ה בַּמַּגֵּפָ֖ה לִפְנֵ֥י יְהוָֹֽה: וִיהוֹשֻׁ֣עַ בִּן־נ֗וּן

לט וְכָלֵב֙ בֶּן־יְפֻנֶּ֔ה חָי֗וּ מִן־הָאֲנָשִׁ֣ים הָהֵ֔ם הַהֹֽלְכִ֖ים לָת֣וּר אֶת־הָאָֽרֶץ: וַיְדַבֵּ֤ר

מ מֹשֶׁה֙ אֶת־הַדְּבָרִ֣ים הָאֵ֔לֶּה אֶֽל־כָּל־בְּנֵ֖י יִשְׂרָאֵ֑ל וַיִּֽתְאַבְּל֥וּ הָעָ֖ם מְאֹֽד: וַיַּשְׁכִּ֣מוּ בַבֹּ֔קֶר וַיַּֽעֲל֥וּ אֶל־רֹאשׁ־הָהָ֖ר לֵאמֹ֑ר הִנֶּ֗נּוּ וְעָלִ֛ינוּ אֶל־הַמָּק֛וֹם

מא אֲשֶׁר־אָמַ֥ר יְהוָֹ֖ה כִּ֣י חָטָ֑אנוּ: וַיֹּ֣אמֶר מֹשֶׁ֗ה לָ֤מָּה זֶּה֙ אַתֶּ֣ם עֹֽבְרִ֔ים אֶת־פִּ֣י

מב יְהוָֹ֑ה וְהִ֖וא לֹ֥א תִצְלָֽח: אַֽל־תַּֽעֲל֔וּ כִּ֛י אֵ֥ין יְהוָֹ֖ה בְּקִרְבְּכֶ֑ם וְלֹא֙ תִּנָּ֣גְפ֔וּ לִפְנֵ֖י

מג אֹֽיְבֵיכֶֽם: כִּי֩ הָֽעֲמָלֵקִ֨י וְהַֽכְּנַֽעֲנִ֥י שָׁם֙ לִפְנֵיכֶ֔ם וּנְפַלְתֶּ֖ם בֶּחָ֑רֶב כִּֽי־עַל־כֵּ֤ן

מד שַׁבְתֶּם֙ מֵֽאַחֲרֵ֣י יְהוָֹ֔ה וְלֹֽא־יִהְיֶ֥ה יְהוָֹ֖ה עִמָּכֶֽם: וַיַּעְפִּ֕לוּ לַֽעֲל֖וֹת אֶל־רֹ֣אשׁ

מה הָהָ֑ר וַֽאֲר֨וֹן בְּרִית־יְהוָֹ֧ה וּמֹשֶׁ֛ה לֹא־מָ֖שׁוּ מִקֶּ֥רֶב הַֽמַּחֲנֶֽה: וַיֵּ֤רֶד הָֽעֲמָלֵקִי֙

וְהַֽכְּנַֽעֲנִ֔י הַיֹּשֵׁ֖ב בָּהָ֣ר הַה֑וּא וַיַּכּ֥וּם וַֽיַּכְּת֖וּם עַד־הַֽחָרְמָֽה:

טו א-ב וַיְדַבֵּ֥ר יְהוָֹ֖ה אֶל־מֹשֶׁ֥ה לֵּאמֹֽר: דַּבֵּר֙ אֶל־בְּנֵ֣י יִשְׂרָאֵ֔ל וְאָֽמַרְתָּ֖ אֲלֵהֶ֑ם כִּ֣י

ג תָבֹ֗אוּ אֶל־אֶ֨רֶץ֙ מֽוֹשְׁבֹ֣תֵיכֶ֔ם אֲשֶׁ֥ר אֲנִ֖י נֹתֵ֥ן לָכֶֽם: וַֽעֲשִׂיתֶ֨ם אִשֶּׁ֤ה לַֽיהוָֹה֙

עֹלָ֣ה אֽוֹ־זֶ֗בַח לְפַלֵּא־נֶ֨דֶר֙ א֣וֹ בִנְדָבָ֔ה א֖וֹ בְּמֹֽעֲדֵיכֶ֑ם לַֽעֲשׂ֞וֹת רֵ֤יחַ נִיחֹ֨חַ֙

ד לַֽיהוָֹ֔ה מִן־הַבָּקָ֖ר א֥וֹ מִן־הַצֹּֽאן: וְהִקְרִ֛יב הַמַּקְרִ֥יב קָרְבָּנ֖וֹ לַֽיהוָֹ֑ה מִנְחָה֙

ה סֹ֣לֶת עִשָּׂר֔וֹן בָּל֕וּל בִּרְבִעִ֥ית הַהִ֖ין שָׁ֑מֶן וְיַ֤יִן לַנֶּ֨סֶךְ֙ רְבִיעִ֣ית הַהִ֔ין תַּֽעֲשֶׂ֥ה

ו עַל־הָֽעֹלָ֖ה א֣וֹ לַזָּ֑בַח לַכֶּ֖בֶשׂ הָֽאֶחָֽד: א֤וֹ לָאַ֨יִל֙ תַּֽעֲשֶׂ֣ה מִנְחָ֔ה סֹ֖לֶת שְׁנֵ֣י

ז עֶשְׂרֹנִ֑ים בְּלוּלָ֥ה בַשֶּׁ֖מֶן שְׁלִשִׁ֥ית הַהִֽין: וְיַ֥יִן לַנֶּ֖סֶךְ שְׁלִשִׁ֣ית הַהִ֑ין תַּקְרִ֥יב

ח רֵֽיחַ־נִיחֹ֖חַ לַֽיהוָֹֽה: וְכִֽי־תַֽעֲשֶׂ֥ה בֶן־בָּקָ֖ר עֹלָ֣ה אוֹ־זָ֑בַח לְפַלֵּא־נֶ֨דֶר֙ א֣וֹ

ט שְׁלָמִ֖ים לַֽיהוָֹֽה: וְהִקְרִ֤יב עַל־בֶּן־הַבָּקָר֙ מִנְחָ֔ה סֹ֖לֶת שְׁלֹשָׁ֣ה עֶשְׂרֹנִ֑ים

י בָּל֥וּל בַּשֶּׁ֖מֶן חֲצִ֣י הַהִֽין: וְיַ֛יִן תַּקְרִ֥יב לַנֶּ֖סֶךְ חֲצִ֣י הַהִ֑ין אִשֵּׁ֥ה רֵֽיחַ־נִיחֹ֖חַ

יא לַֽיהוָֹֽה: כָּ֣כָה יֵֽעָשֶׂ֗ה לַשּׁוֹר֙ הָֽאֶחָ֔ד א֖וֹ לָאַ֣יִל הָֽאֶחָ֑ד אֽוֹ־לַשֶּׂ֥ה בַכְּבָשִׂ֖ים א֥וֹ

יב-יג בָֽעִזִּֽים: כַּמִּסְפָּ֖ר אֲשֶׁ֣ר תַּֽעֲשׂ֑וּ כָּ֣כָה תַּֽעֲשׂ֔וּ לָֽאֶחָ֖ד כְּמִסְפָּרָֽם: כָּל־הָֽאֶזְרָ֥ח

יד יַֽעֲשֶׂה־כָּ֖כָה אֶת־אֵ֑לֶּה לְהַקְרִ֛יב אִשֵּׁ֥ה רֵֽיחַ־נִיחֹ֖חַ לַֽיהוָֹֽה: וְכִֽי־יָג֨וּר אִתְּכֶ֜ם

גֵּ֗ר א֤וֹ אֲשֶׁר־בְּתֽוֹכְכֶם֙ לְדֹרֹ֣תֵיכֶ֔ם וְעָשָׂ֛ה אִשֵּׁ֥ה רֵֽיחַ־נִיחֹ֖חַ לַֽיהוָֹ֑ה כַּֽאֲשֶׁ֥ר

טו תַּֽעֲשׂ֖וּ כֵּ֣ן יַֽעֲשֶֽׂה: הַקָּהָ֕ל חֻקָּ֥ה אַחַ֛ת לָכֶ֖ם וְלַגֵּ֣ר הַגָּ֑ר חֻקַּ֤ת עוֹלָם֙ לְדֹרֹ֣תֵיכֶ֔ם

טז כָּכֶ֛ם כַּגֵּ֥ר יִֽהְיֶ֖ה לִפְנֵ֥י יְהוָֹֽה: תּוֹרָ֥ה אַחַ֛ת וּמִשְׁפָּ֥ט אֶחָ֖ד יִֽהְיֶ֣ה לָכֶ֑ם וְלַגֵּ֖ר הַגָּ֥ר

אִתְּכֶֽם:

ששי יז-יח וַיְדַבֵּ֥ר יְהוָֹ֖ה אֶל־מֹשֶׁ֥ה לֵּאמֹֽר: דַּבֵּר֙ אֶל־בְּנֵ֣י יִשְׂרָאֵ֔ל וְאָֽמַרְתָּ֖ אֲלֵהֶ֑ם בְּבֹֽאֲכֶם֙

יט אֶל־הָאָ֕רֶץ אֲשֶׁ֥ר אֲנִ֛י מֵבִ֥יא אֶתְכֶ֖ם שָׁ֑מָּה: וְהָיָ֕ה בַּֽאֲכָלְכֶ֖ם מִלֶּ֣חֶם הָאָ֑רֶץ

14:37. Although God would stretch out the punishment of the nation over a period of forty years, the spies themselves would die immediately.

14:40-45. The people awakened too late from their spiritual stupor; as is all too common, people refuse to move when they can, but are ready when it is too late.

15:2-16. Though this passage would not apply until thirty-nine years later, it was pronounced now to reassure the younger generation that God still intended to give them the Land (*Ibn Ezra; Ramban*).

15:19. By making the servants of God dependent on the gifts of the nation, God connects those who give with those who devote themselves to matters of the spirit.

and provoked the entire assembly against him by spreading a report against the Land — [37] the people who spread the evil report about the Land died in a plague before HASHEM. * [38] But Joshua son of Nun and Caleb son of Jephunneh lived from among those men who were going to spy out the Land.

[39] Moses spoke these words to all of the Children of Israel, and the people mourned exceedingly.

A chastened nation realizes too late
[40] They awoke early in the morning* and ascended toward the mountaintop saying, "We are ready, and we shall ascend to the place of which HASHEM has spoken, for we have sinned!"

[41] Moses said, "Why do you transgress the word of HASHEM? It will not succeed. [42] Do not ascend, for HASHEM is not in your midst! And do not be smitten before your enemies. [43] For the Amalekite and the Canaanite are there before you, and you will fall by the sword, because you have turned away from HASHEM, and HASHEM will not be with you."

[44] But they defiantly ascended to the mountaintop, while the Ark of HASHEM's covenant and Moses did not move from the midst of the camp. [45] The Amalekite and the Canaanite who dwelled on that mountain descended; they struck them and pounded them until Hormah.

15

The libations
(See Appendix B, chart 9)
[1] HASHEM spoke to Moses, saying, [2] "Speak to the Children of Israel and say to them: When you will come to the Land of your dwelling places* that I give you, [3] and you perform a fire-offering to HASHEM — a burnt-offering or a feast-offering because of an articulated vow or as a free-will offering, or on your festivals, to produce a satisfying aroma to HASHEM, from the cattle or from the flock — [4] the one who brings his offering to HASHEM shall bring a meal-offering of a tenth[-ephah] fine flour, mixed with a quarter-hin of oil; [5] and a quarter-hin of wine for a libation shall you prepare for the burnt-offering or the feast-offering for each sheep. [6] Or for a ram — you shall prepare a meal-offering, two tenth[-ephah] fine flour mixed with a third-hin of oil; [7] and a third-hin of wine for a libation shall you bring as a satisfying aroma to HASHEM. [8] When you prepare a young bull as a burnt-offering or feast-offering, because of an articulated vow, or a peace-offering to HASHEM, [9] one shall bring with the young bull a meal-offering: three tenth[-ephah] fine flour mixed with a half-hin of oil. [10] You shall bring a half-hin of wine for a libation, a fire-offering, a satisfying aroma to HASHEM.

[11] "So shall be done for each bull or for each ram, or for a lamb or kid among the sheep or goats. [12] According to the number that you prepare, so shall you do for each one, according to their number. [13] Every native shall do so with them, to bring a fire-offering, a satisfying aroma to HASHEM.

[14] "When a proselyte sojourns with you or one who is among you throughout your generations and he shall prepare a fire-offering, a satisfying aroma to HASHEM — as you do, so shall he do. [15] For the congregation — the same decree shall be for you and for the proselyte who sojourns, an eternal decree for your generations; like you like the proselyte shall it be before HASHEM. [16] One teaching and one judgment shall be for you and for the proselyte who sojourns among you."

[17] HASHEM spoke to Moses, saying, [18] "Speak to the Children of Israel and say to them: When you come to the Land to which I bring you, [19] it *Challah* shall be that when you will eat of the bread of the Land, you shall set aside*

כ תָּרִימוּ תְרוּמָה לַיהוֹה: רֵאשִׁית עֲרִסֹתֵכֶם חַלָּה תָּרִימוּ תְרוּמָה כִּתְרוּמַת

כא גֹּרֶן כֵּן תָּרִימוּ אֹתָהּ: מֵרֵאשִׁית עֲרִסֹתֵיכֶם תִּתְּנוּ לַיהוֹה תְּרוּמָה

כב לְדֹרֹתֵיכֶם: וְכִי תִשְׁגּוּ וְלֹא תַעֲשׂוּ אֵת כָּל־הַמִּצְוֹת

כג הָאֵלֶּה אֲשֶׁר־דִּבֶּר יְהוֹה אֶל־מֹשֶׁה: אֵת כָּל־אֲשֶׁר צִוָּה יְהוֹה אֲלֵיכֶם

כד בְּיַד־מֹשֶׁה מִן־הַיּוֹם אֲשֶׁר צִוָּה יְהוֹה וָהָלְאָה לְדֹרֹתֵיכֶם: וְהָיָה אִם

מֵעֵינֵי הָעֵדָה נֶעֶשְׂתָה לִשְׁגָגָה וְעָשׂוּ כָל־הָעֵדָה פַּר בֶּן־בָּקָר אֶחָד לְעֹלָה

לְרֵיחַ נִיחֹחַ לַיהוֹה וּמִנְחָתוֹ וְנִסְכּוֹ כַּמִּשְׁפָּט וּשְׂעִיר־עִזִּים אֶחָד לְחַטָּת:

כה וְכִפֶּר הַכֹּהֵן עַל־כָּל־עֲדַת בְּנֵי יִשְׂרָאֵל וְנִסְלַח לָהֶם כִּי־שְׁגָגָה הִוא

וְהֵם הֵבִיאוּ אֶת־קָרְבָּנָם אִשֶּׁה לַיהוֹה וְחַטָּאתָם לִפְנֵי יְהוֹה עַל־

כו שִׁגְגָתָם: וְנִסְלַח לְכָל־עֲדַת בְּנֵי יִשְׂרָאֵל וְלַגֵּר הַגָּר בְּתוֹכָם כִּי לְכָל־הָעָם

כז בִּשְׁגָגָה: וְאִם־נֶפֶשׁ אַחַת תֶּחֱטָא בִשְׁגָגָה   שביעי

כח וְהִקְרִיבָה עֵז בַּת־שְׁנָתָהּ לְחַטָּאת: וְכִפֶּר הַכֹּהֵן עַל־הַנֶּפֶשׁ הַשֹּׁגֶגֶת בְּחֶטְאָה* בִשְׁגָגָה   *ה רפה

כט לִפְנֵי יְהוֹה לְכַפֵּר עָלָיו וְנִסְלַח לוֹ: הָאֶזְרָח בִּבְנֵי יִשְׂרָאֵל וְלַגֵּר הַגָּר

ל בְּתוֹכָם תּוֹרָה אַחַת יִהְיֶה לָכֶם לָעֹשֶׂה בִּשְׁגָגָה: וְהַנֶּפֶשׁ אֲשֶׁר־תַּעֲשֶׂה ׀

בְּיָד רָמָה מִן־הָאֶזְרָח וּמִן־הַגֵּר אֶת־יְהוֹה הוּא מְגַדֵּף וְנִכְרְתָה הַנֶּפֶשׁ

לא הַהִוא מִקֶּרֶב עַמָּהּ: כִּי דְבַר־יְהוֹה בָּזָה וְאֶת־מִצְוָתוֹ הֵפַר הִכָּרֵת ׀ תִּכָּרֵת

הַנֶּפֶשׁ הַהִוא עֲוֹנָה* בָהּ:   *ה רפה

לב וַיִּהְיוּ בְנֵי־יִשְׂרָאֵל בַּמִּדְבָּר וַיִּמְצְאוּ אִישׁ מְקֹשֵׁשׁ עֵצִים בְּיוֹם הַשַּׁבָּת: וַיַּקְרִיבוּ

לג אֹתוֹ הַמֹּצְאִים אֹתוֹ מְקֹשֵׁשׁ עֵצִים אֶל־מֹשֶׁה וְאֶל־אַהֲרֹן וְאֶל כָּל־הָעֵדָה:

לד־לה וַיַּנִּיחוּ אֹתוֹ בַּמִּשְׁמָר כִּי לֹא פֹרַשׁ מַה־יֵּעָשֶׂה לוֹ: וַיֹּאמֶר

יְהוֹה אֶל־מֹשֶׁה מוֹת יוּמַת הָאִישׁ רָגוֹם אֹתוֹ בָאֲבָנִים כָּל־הָעֵדָה מִחוּץ

לו לַמַּחֲנֶה: וַיֹּצִיאוּ אֹתוֹ כָּל־הָעֵדָה אֶל־מִחוּץ לַמַּחֲנֶה וַיִּרְגְּמוּ אֹתוֹ בָּאֲבָנִים

וַיָּמֹת כַּאֲשֶׁר צִוָּה יְהוֹה אֶת־מֹשֶׁה:

לז־לח וַיֹּאמֶר יְהוֹה אֶל־מֹשֶׁה לֵּאמֹר: דַּבֵּר אֶל־בְּנֵי יִשְׂרָאֵל וְאָמַרְתָּ אֲלֵהֶם   מפטיר

וְעָשׂוּ לָהֶם צִיצִת עַל־כַּנְפֵי בִגְדֵיהֶם לְדֹרֹתָם וְנָתְנוּ עַל־צִיצִת הַכָּנָף פְּתִיל   *Haftaras*

לט תְּכֵלֶת: וְהָיָה לָכֶם לְצִיצִת וּרְאִיתֶם אֹתוֹ וּזְכַרְתֶּם אֶת־כָּל־מִצְוֹת יְהוֹה   *Shelach:*

וַעֲשִׂיתֶם אֹתָם וְלֹא־תָתוּרוּ אַחֲרֵי לְבַבְכֶם וְאַחֲרֵי עֵינֵיכֶם אֲשֶׁר־אַתֶּם זֹנִים   p. 518

מ אַחֲרֵיהֶם: לְמַעַן תִּזְכְּרוּ וַעֲשִׂיתֶם אֶת־כָּל־מִצְוֹתָי וִהְיִיתֶם קְדֹשִׁים

מא לֵאלֹהֵיכֶם: אֲנִי יְהוֹה אֱלֹהֵיכֶם אֲשֶׁר הוֹצֵאתִי אֶתְכֶם מֵאֶרֶץ מִצְרַיִם לִהְיוֹת

לָכֶם לֵאלֹהִים אֲנִי יְהוֹה אֱלֹהֵיכֶם: פפפ   קט"ו פסוקים. פל"ט סימן.

15:34. The nature and procedure of the death penalty had not been clarified, but they knew, as stated in *Exodus* 31:14, that Sabbath desecration incurs the death penalty (*Rashi*).

15:38. One of the strings of each fringe is to be dyed turquoise with the blood of an aquatic creature known as *chilazon* (*Rashi*). The exact identity of the creature that is

the source of this blue dye is unknown nowadays.

The *techeiles* thread helps its wearer focus on his duty to God because, as the Sages put it: *Techeiles* is similar to [the color of] the sea, the sea to the sky, and the sky to [God's] Throne of Glory (*Menachos* 43b).

15:41. The Torah commands that we remember the Exodus every day (*Deuteronomy* 16:3). The Sages instia portion for HASHEM. ²⁰ As the first of your kneading you shall set aside a loaf as a portion, like the portion of the threshing-floor, so shall you set it aside. ²¹ From the first of your kneading shall you give a portion to HASHEM, for your generations.

²² "If you err and do not perform all of these commandments, which HASHEM has spoken to Moses, ²³ everything that HASHEM commanded you through Moses, from the day that HASHEM commanded and onward, throughout your generations. ²⁴ If because of the eyes of the assembly it was done unintentionally, the entire assembly shall prepare one young bull as a burnt-offering for a satisfying aroma to HASHEM, and its meal-offering and its libation according to the rule, and one he-goat as a sin-offering. ²⁵ The Kohen shall atone for the entire assembly of the Children of Israel and it shall be forgiven them, for it was unintentional, and they have brought their offering, a fire-offering to HASHEM, and their sin-offering before HASHEM for their unintentional sin. ²⁶ And it shall be forgiven to the entire assembly of the Children of Israel and to the proselyte who sojourns among them, for it happened to the entire people unintentionally.

The atonement for public, unintentional idol worship (See Appendix B, charts 6-7)

²⁷ "If one person sins unintentionally, he shall offer a she-goat within its first year as a sin-offering. ²⁸ The Kohen shall atone for the erring person when he sins unintentionally before HASHEM, to atone for him; and it shall be forgiven him. ²⁹ The native among the Children of Israel and the proselyte who sojourns among them — there shall be a single teaching for you, for one who does unintentionally.

Individual idol worship

³⁰ "A person who shall act high-handedly, whether native or proselyte, he blasphemed HASHEM! — that person shall be cut off from among his people, ³¹ for he scorned the word of HASHEM and broke His commandment; that person will surely be cut off, his sin is upon him."

Intentional Idolatry

³² The Children of Israel were in the Wilderness and they found a man gathering wood on the Sabbath day. ³³ Those who found him gathering wood brought him to Moses and Aaron, and to the entire assembly. ³⁴ They placed him in custody, for it had not been clarified what should be done to him. *

Sabbath desecration in the Wilderness

³⁵ HASHEM said to Moses: "The man shall be put to death; the entire assembly shall pelt him with stones outside of the camp."

³⁶ The entire assembly removed him to the outside of the camp; they pelted him with stones and he died, as HASHEM had commanded Moses.

³⁷ HASHEM said to Moses, saying: ³⁸ "Speak to the Children of Israel and say to them that they shall make themselves tzitzis on the corners of their garments, throughout their generations. And they shall place upon the tzitzis of each corner a thread of turquoise wool. * ³⁹ It shall constitute tzitzis for you, that you may see it and remember all the commandments of HASHEM and perform them; and not explore after your heart and after your eyes after which you stray. ⁴⁰ So that you may remember and perform all My commandments and be holy to your God. ⁴¹ I am HASHEM, your God, Who has removed you from the land of Egypt to be a God unto you; I am HASHEM your God."*

Tzitzis and all the commandments

---

tuted that it should be fulfilled through the recitation of this paragraph because, in addition to the mention of the Exodus, it contains several other basic precepts (*Berachos* 12b).

פרשת קרח

טז א וַיִּקַּח קֹרַח בֶּן־יִצְהָר בֶּן־קְהָת בֶּן־לֵוִי וְדָתָן וַאֲבִירָם בְּנֵי אֱלִיאָב וְאוֹן בֶּן־

ב פֶּלֶת בְּנֵי רְאוּבֵן: וַיָּקֻמוּ לִפְנֵי מֹשֶׁה וַאֲנָשִׁים מִבְּנֵי־יִשְׂרָאֵל חֲמִשִּׁים

ג וּמָאתָיִם נְשִׂיאֵי עֵדָה קְרִאֵי מוֹעֵד אַנְשֵׁי־שֵׁם: וַיִּקָּהֲלוּ עַל־מֹשֶׁה וְעַל־

אַהֲרֹן וַיֹּאמְרוּ אֲלֵהֶם רַב־לָכֶם כִּי כָל־הָעֵדָה כֻּלָּם קְדֹשִׁים וּבְתוֹכָם יְהֹוָה

ד־ה וּמַדּוּעַ תִּתְנַשְּׂאוּ עַל־קְהַל יְהֹוָה: וַיִּשְׁמַע מֹשֶׁה וַיִּפֹּל עַל־פָּנָיו: וַיְדַבֵּר אֶל־

קֹרַח וְאֶל־כָּל־עֲדָתוֹ לֵאמֹר בֹּקֶר וְיֹדַע יְהֹוָה אֶת־אֲשֶׁר־לוֹ וְאֶת־הַקָּדוֹשׁ

ו וְהִקְרִיב אֵלָיו וְאֵת אֲשֶׁר יִבְחַר־בּוֹ יַקְרִיב אֵלָיו: זֹאת עֲשׂוּ קְחוּ־לָכֶם

ז מַחְתּוֹת קֹרַח וְכָל־עֲדָתוֹ: וּתְנוּ־בָהֶן ׀ אֵשׁ וְשִׂימוּ עֲלֵיהֶן ׀ קְטֹרֶת לִפְנֵי

יְהֹוָה מָחָר וְהָיָה הָאִישׁ אֲשֶׁר־יִבְחַר יְהֹוָה הוּא הַקָּדוֹשׁ רַב־לָכֶם בְּנֵי לֵוִי:

ח־ט וַיֹּאמֶר מֹשֶׁה אֶל־קֹרַח שִׁמְעוּ־נָא בְּנֵי לֵוִי: הַמְעַט מִכֶּם כִּי־הִבְדִּיל אֱלֹהֵי

יִשְׂרָאֵל אֶתְכֶם מֵעֲדַת יִשְׂרָאֵל לְהַקְרִיב אֶתְכֶם אֵלָיו לַעֲבֹד אֶת־עֲבֹדַת

י מִשְׁכַּן יְהֹוָה וְלַעֲמֹד לִפְנֵי הָעֵדָה לְשָׁרְתָם: וַיַּקְרֵב אֹתְךָ וְאֶת־כָּל־אַחֶיךָ

יא בְנֵי־לֵוִי אִתָּךְ וּבִקַּשְׁתֶּם גַּם־כְּהֻנָּה: לָכֵן אַתָּה וְכָל־עֲדָתְךָ הַנֹּעָדִים עַל־

יב יְהֹוָה וְאַהֲרֹן מַה־הוּא כִּי °תַלִּינוּ [¹תַלּוֹנוּ כ] עָלָיו: וַיִּשְׁלַח מֹשֶׁה לִקְרֹא

יג לְדָתָן וְלַאֲבִירָם בְּנֵי אֱלִיאָב וַיֹּאמְרוּ לֹא נַעֲלֶה: הַמְעַט כִּי הֶעֱלִיתָנוּ

מֵאֶרֶץ זָבַת חָלָב וּדְבַשׁ לַהֲמִיתֵנוּ בַּמִּדְבָּר כִּי־תִשְׂתָּרֵר עָלֵינוּ גַּם־

יד הִשְׂתָּרֵר: אַף לֹא אֶל־אֶרֶץ זָבַת חָלָב וּדְבַשׁ הֲבִיאֹתָנוּ וַתִּתֶּן־לָנוּ נַחֲלַת

טו שָׂדֶה וָכָרֶם הַעֵינֵי הָאֲנָשִׁים הָהֵם תְּנַקֵּר לֹא נַעֲלֶה: וַיִּחַר לְמֹשֶׁה מְאֹד

וַיֹּאמֶר אֶל־יְהֹוָה אַל־תֵּפֶן אֶל־מִנְחָתָם לֹא חֲמוֹר אֶחָד מֵהֶם נָשָׂאתִי

טז וְלֹא הֲרֵעֹתִי אֶת־אַחַד מֵהֶם: וַיֹּאמֶר מֹשֶׁה אֶל־קֹרַח אַתָּה וְכָל־עֲדָתְךָ

הֱיוּ לִפְנֵי יְהֹוָה אַתָּה וָהֵם וְאַהֲרֹן מָחָר: וּקְחוּ ׀ אִישׁ מַחְתָּתוֹ וּנְתַתֶּם

יז עֲלֵיהֶם קְטֹרֶת וְהִקְרַבְתֶּם לִפְנֵי יְהֹוָה אִישׁ מַחְתָּתוֹ חֲמִשִּׁים וּמָאתַיִם

יח מַחְתֹּת וְאַתָּה וְאַהֲרֹן אִישׁ מַחְתָּתוֹ: וַיִּקְחוּ אִישׁ מַחְתָּתוֹ וַיִּתְּנוּ עֲלֵיהֶם

יט אֵשׁ וַיָּשִׂימוּ עֲלֵיהֶם קְטֹרֶת וַיַּעַמְדוּ פֶּתַח אֹהֶל מוֹעֵד וּמֹשֶׁה וְאַהֲרֹן: וַיַּקְהֵל

עֲלֵיהֶם קֹרַח אֶת־כָּל־הָעֵדָה אֶל־פֶּתַח אֹהֶל מוֹעֵד וַיֵּרָא כְבוֹד־יְהֹוָה

כ אֶל־כָּל־הָעֵדָה: וַיְדַבֵּר יְהֹוָה אֶל־מֹשֶׁה וְאֶל־אַהֲרֹן לֵאמֹר:

כא־כב הִבָּדְלוּ מִתּוֹךְ הָעֵדָה הַזֹּאת וַאֲכַלֶּה אֹתָם כְּרָגַע: וַיִּפְּלוּ עַל־פְּנֵיהֶם

וַיֹּאמְרוּ אֵל אֱלֹהֵי הָרוּחֹת לְכָל־בָּשָׂר הָאִישׁ אֶחָד יֶחֱטָא וְעַל כָּל־הָעֵדָה

כג־כד תִּקְצֹף: וַיְדַבֵּר יְהֹוָה אֶל־מֹשֶׁה לֵּאמֹר: דַּבֵּר אֶל־הָעֵדָה לֵאמֹר

טז

שני

שלישי

◈§ Parashas Korach

16:1. Korah's genealogy stops with Levi, and omits the name of Jacob, because the Patriarch prayed on his deathbed (*Genesis* 49:6) that his name not be associated with Korah's assembly (*Rashi*).

16:2. The presence of such a respected delegation naturally lent credence to Korah's grievances.

16:3. Korah began his tirade by accusing Moses and Aaron of selfishly taking power and prestige for themselves at the expense of the rest of the nation, which was just as qualified as they.

16:13-14. They had the gall to describe the land of their servitude with the same words God had used to praise the Promised Land!

PARASHAS KORACH

16

*Rebellion
in the
Wilderness*

¹ Korah son of Izhar son of Kohath son of Levi* separated himself, with Dathan and Abiram, sons of Eliab, and On son of Peleth, the offspring of Reuben. ² They stood before Moses with two hundred and fifty men from the Children of Israel, leaders of the assembly, those summoned for meeting, men of renown.* ³ They gathered together against Moses and against Aaron and said to them, "It is too much for you! For the entire assembly — all of them — are holy and HASHEM is among them; why do you exalt yourselves over the congregation of HASHEM?"*

⁴ Moses heard and fell on his face.

⁵ He spoke to Korah and to his entire assembly, saying, "In the morning Hashem will make known the one who is His own and the holy one, and He will draw him close to Himself, and whomever He will choose, He will draw close to Himself. ⁶ Do this: Take for yourselves fire-pans — Korah and his entire assembly — ⁷ and put fire in them and place incense upon them before HASHEM tomorrow. Then the man whom HASHEM will choose — he is the holy one. It is too much for you, O offspring of Levi!"

⁸ Moses said to Korah, "Hear now, O offspring of Levi: ⁹ Is it not enough for you that the God of Israel has segregated you from the assembly of Israel to draw you near to Himself, to perform the service of the Tabernacle of HASHEM, and to stand before the assembly to minister to them? ¹⁰ And He drew you near, and all your brethren, the offspring of Levi, with you — yet you seek priesthood, as well! ¹¹ Therefore, you and your entire assembly that are joining together are against HASHEM! And as for Aaron — what is he that you protest against him?"

*Moses
summons
Dathan and
Abiram*

¹² Moses sent to summon Dathan and Abiram, the sons of Eliab, but they said, "We shall not go up! ¹³ Is it not enough that you have brought us up from a land flowing with milk and honey* to cause us to die in the Wilderness, yet you seek to dominate us, even to dominate further? ¹⁴ Moreover, you did not bring us to a land flowing with milk and honey nor give us a heritage of field and vineyard! Even if you would gouge out the eyes of those men, we shall not go up!"

¹⁵ This distressed Moses greatly, and he said to HASHEM, "Do not turn to their gift-offering! I have not taken even a single donkey of theirs, nor have I wronged even one of them."

¹⁶ Moses said to Korah, "You and your entire assembly, be before HASHEM — you, they, and Aaron — tomorrow. ¹⁷ Let each man take his fire-pan and you shall place incense on them and you shall bring before HASHEM each man with his fire-pan — two hundred and fifty fire-pans; and you and Aaron, each man with his fire-pan."

¹⁸ So they took — each man his fire-pan — and they placed fire on them and put incense on them; and they stood at the entrance of the Tent of Meeting, with Moses and Aaron. ¹⁹ Korah gathered the entire assembly against them to the entrance of the Tent of Meeting, and the glory of HASHEM appeared to the entire assembly.

*God
responds*

²⁰ HASHEM spoke to Moses and Aaron, saying, ²¹ "Separate yourselves from amid this assembly, and I shall destroy them in an instant!"

²² They fell on their faces and said, "O God, God of the spirits of all flesh, shall one man sin, and You be angry with the entire assembly?"

²³ HASHEM spoke to Moses saying, ²⁴ "Speak to the assembly, saying,

כה הֵעָלוּ מִסָּבִיב לְמִשְׁכַּן־קֹרַח דָּתָן וַאֲבִירָם: וַיָּקָם מֹשֶׁה וַיֵּלֶךְ אֶל־דָּתָן

כו וַאֲבִירָם וַיֵּלְכוּ אַחֲרָיו זִקְנֵי יִשְׂרָאֵל: וַיְדַבֵּר אֶל־הָעֵדָה לֵאמֹר סוּרוּ נָא

מֵעַל אָהֳלֵי הָאֲנָשִׁים הָרְשָׁעִים הָאֵלֶּה וְאַל־תִּגְּעוּ בְּכָל־אֲשֶׁר לָהֶם פֶּן־

כז תִּסָּפוּ בְּכָל־חַטֹּאתָם: וַיֵּעָלוּ מֵעַל מִשְׁכַּן־קֹרַח דָּתָן וַאֲבִירָם מִסָּבִיב וְדָתָן

כח וַאֲבִירָם יָצְאוּ נִצָּבִים פֶּתַח אָהֳלֵיהֶם וּנְשֵׁיהֶם וּבְנֵיהֶם וְטַפָּם: וַיֹּאמֶר מֹשֶׁה

בְּזֹאת תֵּדְעוּן כִּי־יהוה שְׁלָחַנִי לַעֲשׂוֹת אֵת כָּל־הַמַּעֲשִׂים הָאֵלֶּה כִּי־לֹא

כט מִלִּבִּי: אִם־כְּמוֹת כָּל־הָאָדָם יְמֻתוּן אֵלֶּה וּפְקֻדַּת כָּל־הָאָדָם יִפָּקֵד

ל עֲלֵיהֶם לֹא יהוה שְׁלָחָנִי: וְאִם־בְּרִיאָה יִבְרָא יהוה וּפָצְתָה הָאֲדָמָה אֶת־

פִּיהָ וּבָלְעָה אֹתָם וְאֶת־כָּל־אֲשֶׁר לָהֶם וְיָרְדוּ חַיִּים שְׁאֹלָה וִידַעְתֶּם כִּי

לא נִאֲצוּ הָאֲנָשִׁים הָאֵלֶּה אֶת־יהוה: וַיְהִי כְּכַלֹּתוֹ לְדַבֵּר אֵת כָּל־הַדְּבָרִים

לב הָאֵלֶּה וַתִּבָּקַע הָאֲדָמָה אֲשֶׁר תַּחְתֵּיהֶם: וַתִּפְתַּח הָאָרֶץ אֶת־פִּיהָ וַתִּבְלַע

לג אֹתָם וְאֶת־בָּתֵּיהֶם וְאֵת כָּל־הָאָדָם אֲשֶׁר לְקֹרַח וְאֵת כָּל־הָרְכוּשׁ: וַיֵּרְדוּ

הֵם וְכָל־אֲשֶׁר לָהֶם חַיִּים שְׁאֹלָה וַתְּכַס עֲלֵיהֶם הָאָרֶץ וַיֹּאבְדוּ מִתּוֹךְ

לד הַקָּהָל: וְכָל־יִשְׂרָאֵל אֲשֶׁר סְבִיבֹתֵיהֶם נָסוּ לְקֹלָם כִּי אָמְרוּ פֶּן־תִּבְלָעֵנוּ

לה הָאָרֶץ: וְאֵשׁ יָצְאָה מֵאֵת יהוה וַתֹּאכַל אֵת הַחֲמִשִּׁים וּמָאתַיִם אִישׁ

מַקְרִיבֵי הַקְּטֹרֶת: וַיְדַבֵּר יהוה אֶל־מֹשֶׁה לֵּאמֹר: **יז** א

ב אֱמֹר אֶל־אֶלְעָזָר בֶּן־אַהֲרֹן הַכֹּהֵן וְיָרֵם אֶת־הַמַּחְתֹּת מִבֵּין הַשְּׂרֵפָה

ג וְאֶת־הָאֵשׁ זְרֵה־הָלְאָה כִּי קָדֵשׁוּ: אֵת מַחְתּוֹת הַחַטָּאִים הָאֵלֶּה

בְּנַפְשֹׁתָם וְעָשׂוּ אֹתָם רִקֻּעֵי פַחִים צִפּוּי לַמִּזְבֵּחַ כִּי־הִקְרִיבֻם לִפְנֵי־יהוה

ד וַיִּקְדָּשׁוּ וְיִהְיוּ לְאוֹת לִבְנֵי יִשְׂרָאֵל: וַיִּקַּח אֶלְעָזָר הַכֹּהֵן אֵת מַחְתּוֹת

ה הַנְּחֹשֶׁת אֲשֶׁר הִקְרִיבוּ הַשְּׂרֻפִים וַיְרַקְּעוּם צִפּוּי לַמִּזְבֵּחַ: זִכָּרוֹן לִבְנֵי

יִשְׂרָאֵל לְמַעַן אֲשֶׁר לֹא־יִקְרַב אִישׁ זָר אֲשֶׁר לֹא מִזֶּרַע אַהֲרֹן הוּא

לְהַקְטִיר קְטֹרֶת לִפְנֵי יהוה וְלֹא־יִהְיֶה כְקֹרַח וְכַעֲדָתוֹ כַּאֲשֶׁר דִּבֶּר יהוה

בְּיַד־מֹשֶׁה לוֹ:

ו וַיִּלֹּנוּ כָּל־עֲדַת בְּנֵי־יִשְׂרָאֵל מִמָּחֳרָת עַל־מֹשֶׁה וְעַל־אַהֲרֹן לֵאמֹר אַתֶּם

ז הֲמִתֶּם אֶת־עַם יהוה: וַיְהִי בְּהִקָּהֵל הָעֵדָה עַל־מֹשֶׁה וְעַל־אַהֲרֹן וַיִּפְנוּ אֶל־

ח אֹהֶל מוֹעֵד וְהִנֵּה כִסָּהוּ הֶעָנָן וַיֵּרָא כְּבוֹד יהוה: וַיָּבֹא מֹשֶׁה וְאַהֲרֹן אֶל־פְּנֵי

ט אֹהֶל מוֹעֵד: וַיְדַבֵּר יהוה אֶל־מֹשֶׁה לֵּאמֹר: הֵרֹמּוּ מִתּוֹךְ | רביעי

י הָעֵדָה הַזֹּאת וַאֲכַלֶּה אֹתָם כְּרָגַע וַיִּפְּלוּ עַל־פְּנֵיהֶם: וַיֹּאמֶר מֹשֶׁה אֶל־אַהֲרֹן

יא קַח אֶת־הַמַּחְתָּה וְתֶן־עָלֶיהָ אֵשׁ מֵעַל הַמִּזְבֵּחַ וְשִׂים קְטֹרֶת וְהוֹלֵךְ מְהֵרָה

אֶל־הָעֵדָה וְכַפֵּר עֲלֵיהֶם כִּי־יָצָא הַקֶּצֶף מִלִּפְנֵי יהוה הֵחֵל הַנָּגֶף:

16:25. Having failed to persuade Korah, Moses made a final plea to Dathan and Abiram. The nation heeded his warning, but the rebels remained stubborn.

16:28-30. Moses proclaims a test. Moses wanted his veracity to be established so conclusively that no one

could doubt that he had acted only at God's command.

16:34. *At their sound,* i.e., they screamed from the deep, "God is righteous, His verdict is true, and the words of His servant Moses are true. We are evil because we rebelled against him" (*Targum Yonasan*).

'Get yourselves up from all around the dwelling places of Korah, Dathan, and Abiram.' "

²⁵ So Moses stood up and went to Dathan and Abiram, * and the elders of Israel followed him. ²⁶ He spoke to the assembly, saying, "Turn away now from near the tents of these wicked men, and do not touch anything of theirs, lest you perish because of all their sins." ²⁷ So they got themselves up from near the dwelling of Korah, Dathan, and Abiram, from all around. Dathan and Abiram went out erect at the entrance of their tents, with their wives, children, and infants.

²⁸ Moses said, "Through this shall you know* that HASHEM sent me to perform all these acts, that it was not from my heart. ²⁹ If these die like the death of all men, and the destiny of all men is visited upon them, then it is not HASHEM Who has sent me. ³⁰ But if HASHEM will create a phenomenon, and the earth opens its mouth and swallows them and all that is theirs, and they will descend alive to the pit — then you shall know that these men have provoked HASHEM!"

God creates a phenomenon ³¹ When he finished speaking all these words, the ground that was under them split open. ³² The earth opened its mouth and swallowed them and their households, and all the people who were with Korah, and the entire wealth. ³³ They and all that was theirs descended alive to the pit; the earth covered them over and they were lost from among the congregation. ³⁴ All Israel that were around them fled at their sound, * for they said, "Lest the earth swallow us!"

³⁵ A flame came forth from HASHEM and consumed the two hundred and fifty men who were offering the incense.

17 ¹ HASHEM spoke to Moses, saying, ² "Say to Elazar son of Aaron the Kohen and let him pick up the fire-pans from amid the fire — and he should throw away the flame — for they have become holy. ³ As for the fire-pans of these sinners against their souls — they shall make them hammered-out sheets as a covering for the Altar, for they offered them before HASHEM, so they became holy; they shall be for a sign to the Children of Israel." ⁴ Elazar the Kohen took the copper fire-pans that the consumed ones had offered and hammered them out as a covering for the Altar, ⁵ as a reminder to the Children of Israel, so that no alien who is not of the offspring of Aaron shall draw near to bring up the smoke of incense before HASHEM, that he not be like Korah and his assembly, as HASHEM spoke about him through Moses.

Protest and confirmation

⁶ The entire assembly of the Children of Israel complained on the morrow against Moses and Aaron, saying, "You have killed the people of HASHEM!" ⁷ And it was when the assembly gathered against Moses and Aaron, they turned to the Tent of Meeting and behold! the cloud had covered it, and the glory of HASHEM appeared. ⁸ Moses and Aaron came before the Tent of Meeting.

Moses intervenes again ⁹ HASHEM spoke to Moses, saying, ¹⁰ "Remove yourselves from among this assembly and I shall destroy them in an instant!" They fell on their faces.

¹¹ Moses said to Aaron, "Take the fire-pan and put on it fire from upon the Altar and place incense — and convey it quickly to the assembly and provide atonement for them, for the fury has gone forth from the presence of HASHEM; the plague has begun!"

יב וַיִּקַּ֨ח אַהֲרֹ֜ן כַּאֲשֶׁ֣ר ׀ דִּבֶּ֣ר מֹשֶׁ֗ה וַיָּ֨רׇץ֙ אֶל־תּ֣וֹךְ הַקָּהָ֔ל וְהִנֵּ֛ה הֵחֵ֥ל הַנֶּ֖גֶף

יג בָּעָ֑ם וַיִּתֵּן֙ אֶֽת־הַקְּטֹ֔רֶת וַיְכַפֵּ֖ר עַל־הָעָֽם: וַיַּעֲמֹ֥ד בֵּֽין־הַמֵּתִ֖ים וּבֵ֣ין הַֽחַיִּ֑ים

יד וַתֵּעָצַ֖ר הַמַּגֵּפָֽה: וַיִּהְי֗וּ הַמֵּתִים֙ בַּמַּגֵּפָ֔ה אַרְבָּעָ֥ה עָשָׂ֛ר אֶ֖לֶף וּשְׁבַ֣ע מֵא֑וֹת

טו מִלְּבַ֥ד הַמֵּתִ֖ים עַל־דְּבַר־קֹֽרַח: וַיָּ֤שׇׁב אַהֲרֹן֙ אֶל־מֹשֶׁ֔ה אֶל־פֶּ֖תַח אֹ֣הֶל

מוֹעֵ֑ד וְהַמַּגֵּפָ֖ה נֶעֱצָֽרָה:

טז-יז וַיְדַבֵּ֥ר יְהֹוָ֖ה אֶל־מֹשֶׁ֥ה לֵּאמֹֽר: דַּבֵּ֣ר ׀ אֶל־בְּנֵ֣י יִשְׂרָאֵ֗ל וְקַ֣ח מֵֽאִתָּ֡ם מַטֶּ֣ה

מַטֶּה֩ לְבֵ֨ית אָ֜ב מֵאֵ֤ת כׇּל־נְשִֽׂיאֵהֶם֙ לְבֵ֣ית אֲבֹתָ֔ם שְׁנֵ֥ים עָשָׂ֖ר מַטּ֑וֹת אִ֣ישׁ

יח אֶת־שְׁמ֗וֹ תִּכְתֹּ֖ב עַל־מַטֵּֽהוּ: וְאֵת֙ שֵׁ֣ם אַהֲרֹ֔ן תִּכְתֹּ֖ב עַל־מַטֵּ֣ה לֵוִ֑י כִּ֚י מַטֶּ֣ה

יט אֶחָ֔ד לְרֹ֖אשׁ בֵּ֥ית אֲבוֹתָֽם: וְהִנַּחְתָּ֖ם בְּאֹ֣הֶל מוֹעֵ֑ד לִפְנֵי֙ הָֽעֵד֔וּת אֲשֶׁ֛ר

אִוָּעֵ֥ד לָכֶ֖ם שָֽׁמָּה: * וְהָיָ֗ה הָאִ֛ישׁ אֲשֶׁ֥ר אֶבְחַר־בּ֖וֹ מַטֵּ֣הוּ יִפְרָ֑ח וַהֲשִׁכֹּתִ֣י

כא מֵֽעָלַ֗י אֶת־תְּלֻנּוֹת֙ בְּנֵ֣י יִשְׂרָאֵ֔ל אֲשֶׁ֛ר הֵ֥ם מַלִּינִ֖ם עֲלֵיכֶֽם: וַיְדַבֵּ֤ר מֹשֶׁה֙ אֶל־

בְּנֵ֣י יִשְׂרָאֵ֔ל וַיִּתְּנ֣וּ אֵלָ֣יו ׀ כׇּל־נְשִֽׂיאֵיהֶ֡ם מַטֶּה֩ לְנָשִׂ֨יא אֶחָ֜ד מַטֶּ֣ה לְנָשִׂ֗יא

כב לְבֵית֙ אֲבֹתָ֔ם שְׁנֵ֥ים עָשָׂ֖ר מַטּ֑וֹת וּמַטֵּ֥ה אַהֲרֹ֖ן בְּת֥וֹךְ מַטּוֹתָֽם: וַיַּנַּ֨ח

כג מֹשֶׁ֧ה אֶת־הַמַּטֹּ֛ת לִפְנֵ֥י יְהֹוָ֖ה בְּאֹ֣הֶל הָעֵדֻֽת: וַיְהִ֣י מִֽמׇּחֳרָ֗ת וַיָּבֹ֤א מֹשֶׁה֙

אֶל־אֹ֣הֶל הָעֵד֔וּת וְהִנֵּ֛ה פָּרַ֥ח מַטֵּֽה־אַהֲרֹ֖ן לְבֵ֣ית לֵוִ֑י וַיֹּ֤צֵא פֶ֙רַח֙ וַיָּ֣צֵֽץ צִ֔יץ

כד וַיִּגְמֹ֖ל שְׁקֵדִֽים: וַיֹּצֵ֨א מֹשֶׁ֤ה אֶת־כׇּל־הַמַּטֹּת֙ מִלִּפְנֵ֣י יְהֹוָ֔ה אֶֽל־כׇּל־בְּנֵ֣י

יִשְׂרָאֵ֑ל וַיִּרְא֥וּ וַיִּקְח֖וּ אִ֥ישׁ מַטֵּֽהוּ:

כה וַיֹּ֨אמֶר יְהֹוָ֜ה אֶל־מֹשֶׁ֗ה הָשֵׁ֞ב אֶת־מַטֵּ֤ה אַהֲרֹן֙ לִפְנֵ֣י הָעֵד֔וּת לְמִשְׁמֶ֥רֶת

כו לְא֖וֹת לִבְנֵי־מֶ֑רִי וּתְכַ֧ל תְּלוּנֹתָ֛ם מֵעָלַ֖י וְלֹ֥א יָמֻֽתוּ: וַיַּ֖עַשׂ מֹשֶׁ֑ה כַּאֲשֶׁ֨ר

צִוָּ֧ה יְהֹוָ֛ה אֹת֖וֹ כֵּ֥ן עָשָֽׂה:

כז-כח וַיֹּֽאמְרוּ֙ בְּנֵ֣י יִשְׂרָאֵ֔ל אֶל־מֹשֶׁ֖ה לֵאמֹ֑ר הֵ֥ן גָּוַ֛עְנוּ אָבַ֖דְנוּ כֻּלָּ֥נוּ אָבָֽדְנוּ: כֹּ֡ל

א הַקָּרֵ֣ב ׀ הַקָּרֵ֗ב אֶל־מִשְׁכַּ֤ן יְהֹוָה֙ יָמ֔וּת הַאִ֥ם תַּ֖מְנוּ לִגְוֺֽעַ: וַיֹּ֤אמֶר

יְהֹוָה֙ אֶֽל־אַהֲרֹ֔ן אַתָּ֗ה וּבָנֶ֤יךָ וּבֵית־אָבִ֙יךָ֙ אִתָּ֔ךְ תִּשְׂא֖וּ אֶת־עֲוֺ֣ן הַמִּקְדָּ֑שׁ

ב וְאַתָּ֗ה וּבָנֶ֤יךָ אִתְּךָ֙ תִּשְׂא֔וּ אֶת־עֲוֺ֖ן כְּהֻנַּתְכֶֽם: וְגַ֣ם אֶת־אַחֶ֩יךָ֩ מַטֵּ֨ה לֵוִ֜י

שֵׁ֤בֶט אָבִ֙יךָ֙ הַקְרֵ֣ב אִתָּ֔ךְ וְיִלָּו֥וּ עָלֶ֖יךָ וִֽישָׁרְת֑וּךָ וְאַתָּה֙ וּבָנֶ֣יךָ אִתָּ֔ךְ לִפְנֵ֖י

ג אֹ֥הֶל הָעֵדֻֽת: וְשָֽׁמְרוּ֙ מִֽשְׁמַרְתְּךָ֔ וּמִשְׁמֶ֖רֶת כׇּל־הָאֹ֑הֶל אַ֣ךְ אֶל־כְּלֵ֤י הַקֹּ֙דֶשׁ֙

ד וְאֶל־הַמִּזְבֵּ֙חַ֙ לֹ֣א יִקְרָ֔בוּ וְלֹֽא־יָמֻ֥תוּ גַם־הֵ֖ם גַּם־אַתֶּֽם: וְנִלְו֣וּ עָלֶ֔יךָ וְשָֽׁמְר֗וּ

אֶת־מִשְׁמֶ֙רֶת֙ אֹ֣הֶל מוֹעֵ֔ד לְכֹ֖ל עֲבֹדַ֣ת הָאֹ֑הֶל וְזָ֖ר לֹא־יִקְרַ֥ב אֲלֵיכֶֽם:

ה וּשְׁמַרְתֶּ֗ם אֵ֚ת מִשְׁמֶ֣רֶת הַקֹּ֔דֶשׁ וְאֵ֖ת מִשְׁמֶ֣רֶת הַמִּזְבֵּ֑חַ וְלֹא־יִהְיֶ֥ה ע֛וֹד

ו קֶ֖צֶף עַל־בְּנֵ֥י יִשְׂרָאֵֽל: וַאֲנִ֗י הִנֵּ֤ה לָקַ֙חְתִּי֙ אֶת־אֲחֵיכֶ֣ם הַלְוִיִּ֔ם מִתּ֖וֹךְ בְּנֵ֣י

ז יִשְׂרָאֵ֑ל לָכֶ֞ם מַתָּנָ֤ה נְתֻנִים֙ לַֽיהֹוָ֔ה לַעֲבֹ֕ד אֶת־עֲבֹדַ֖ת אֹ֣הֶל מוֹעֵֽד: וְאַתָּ֣ה

וּבָנֶ֣יךָ אִ֠תְּךָ֠ תִּשְׁמְר֨וּ אֶת־כְּהֻנַּתְכֶ֜ם לְכׇל־דְּבַ֧ר הַמִּזְבֵּ֛חַ וּלְמִבֵּ֥ית לַפָּרֹ֖כֶת

וַעֲבַדְתֶּ֑ם עֲבֹדַ֣ת מַתָּנָ֗ה אֶתֵּן֙ אֶת־כְּהֻנַּתְכֶ֔ם וְהַזָּ֥ר הַקָּרֵ֖ב יוּמָֽת:

18:1-7. God addressed the people's fear that proximity to the Tabernacle would gradually decimate them. He reiterated that Aaron, assisted by the Levites, were responsible to safeguard the Tabernacle against trespass.

¹² *Aaron took as Moses had spoken and ran to the midst of the congregation, and behold! the plague had begun among the people. He placed the incense and provided atonement for the people.* ¹³ *He stood between the dead and the living, and the plague was checked.* ¹⁴ *Those who died in the plague were fourteen thousand, seven hundred, aside from those who died because of the affair of Korah.* ¹⁵ *Aaron returned to Moses at the entrance of the Tent of Assembly, and the plague had been checked.*

A new proof of Aaron's greatness

¹⁶ HASHEM *spoke to Moses, saying:* ¹⁷ *"Speak to the Children of Israel and take from them one staff for each father's house, from all their leaders according to their fathers' house, twelve staffs; each man's name shall you inscribe on his staff.* ¹⁸ *And the name of Aaron shall you inscribe on the staff of Levi, for there shall be one staff for the head of their fathers' house.* ¹⁹ *You shall lay them in the Tent of Meeting before the Testimony, where I meet with you.* ²⁰ *It shall be that the man whom I shall choose — his staff will blossom; thus I shall cause to subside from upon Me the complaints of the Children of Israel, which they complain against you."*

²¹ *Moses spoke to the Children of Israel, and all their leaders gave him a staff for each leader, a staff for each leader, according to their fathers' house, twelve staffs; and Aaron's staff was among their staffs.* ²² *Moses laid the staffs before* HASHEM *in the Tent of the Testimony.* ²³ *On the next day, Moses came to the Tent of the Testimony and behold! the staff of Aaron of the house of Levi had blossomed; it brought forth a blossom, sprouted a bud and almonds ripened.* ²⁴ *Moses brought out all the staffs from before* HASHEM *to all the Children of Israel; they saw and they took, each man his staff.*

²⁵ HASHEM *said to Moses: "Bring back the staff of Aaron before the Testimony as a safekeeping, as a sign for rebellious ones; let their complaints cease from Me that they not die."* ²⁶ *Moses did as* HASHEM *had commanded him, so he did.*

The fears remain

²⁷ *The Children of Israel said to Moses, saying, "Behold! we perish, we are lost, we are all lost.* ²⁸ *Everyone who approaches closer to the Tabernacle of* HASHEM *will die. Will we ever stop perishing?"*

18

Aaron's duty reiterated

¹ **H**ASHEM *said to Aaron, "You, your sons, and your father's household with you shall bear the iniquity of the Sanctuary;* * *and you and your sons with you shall bear the iniquity of your priesthood.* ² *Also your brethren the tribe of Levi, the tribe of your father, shall you draw near with you, and they shall be joined to you and minister to you. You and your sons with you shall be before the Tent of the Testimony.* ³ *They shall safeguard your charge and the charge of the entire tent — but to the holy vessels and to the Altar they shall not approach, that they not die — they as well as you.* ⁴ *They shall be joined to you and safeguard the charge of the Tent of Meeting for the entire service of the Tent, and an alien shall not approach you.* ⁵ *You shall safeguard the charge of the Holy and the charge of the Altar, and there shall be no more wrath against the Children of Israel.* ⁶ *And I — behold! I have taken your brethren the Levites from among the Children of Israel; to you they are presented as a gift for* HASHEM, *to perform the service of the Tent of Meeting.* ⁷ *You and your sons with you shall safeguard your priesthood regarding every matter of the Altar and within the Curtain, and you shall serve; I have presented your priesthood as a service that is a gift, and any alien who approaches shall die."*

ח וַיְדַבֵּ֣ר יְהוָה֮ אֶֽל־אַהֲרֹן֒ וַאֲנִי֙ הִנֵּ֣ה נָתַ֣תִּי לְךָ֔ אֶת־מִשְׁמֶ֖רֶת תְּרֽוּמֹתָ֑י לְכָל־

ט קָדְשֵׁ֣י בְנֵֽי־יִ֠שְׂרָאֵל לְךָ֨ נְתַתִּ֧ים לְמָשְׁחָ֛ה וּלְבָנֶ֖יךָ לְחָק־עוֹלָֽם: זֶ֣ה יִהְיֶ֥ה לְךָ֛
מִקֹּ֥דֶשׁ הַקֳּדָשִׁ֖ים מִן־הָאֵ֑שׁ כָּל־קָ֠רְבָּנָם לְֽכָל־מִנְחָתָ֞ם וּלְכָל־חַטָּאתָ֗ם

י וּלְכָל־אֲשָׁמָם֙ אֲשֶׁ֣ר יָשִׁ֣יבוּ לִ֔י קֹ֥דֶשׁ קָֽדָשִׁ֛ים לְךָ֥ ה֖וּא וּלְבָנֶֽיךָ: בְּקֹ֣דֶשׁ

יא הַקֳּדָשִׁ֖ים תֹּֽאכְלֶ֑נּוּ כָּל־זָכָר֙ יֹאכַ֣ל אֹת֔וֹ קֹ֖דֶשׁ יִֽהְיֶה־לָּֽךְ: וְזֶה־לְּךָ֞ תְּרוּמַ֣ת
מַתָּנָ֗ם לְכָל־תְּנוּפֹת֮ בְּנֵ֣י יִשְׂרָאֵל֒ לְךָ֣ נְתַתִּ֗ים וּלְבָנֶ֧יךָ וְלִבְנֹתֶ֛יךָ אִתְּךָ֖ לְחָק־

יב עוֹלָ֑ם כָּל־טָה֥וֹר בְּבֵֽיתְךָ֖ יֹאכַ֥ל אֹתֽוֹ: כֹּ֣ל חֵ֣לֶב יִצְהָ֗ר וְכָל־חֵ֛לֶב תִּיר֥וֹשׁ וְדָגָ֖ן

יג רֵֽאשִׁיתָ֛ם אֲשֶׁר־יִתְּנ֥וּ לַֽיהוָ֖ה לְךָ֥ נְתַתִּֽים: בִּכּוּרֵ֞י כָּל־אֲשֶׁ֧ר בְּאַרְצָ֛ם אֲשֶׁר־

יד יָבִ֥יאוּ לַֽיהוָ֖ה לְךָ֣ יִהְיֶ֑ה כָּל־טָה֥וֹר בְּבֵיתְךָ֖ יֹאכְלֶֽנּוּ: כָּל־חֵ֥רֶם בְּיִשְׂרָאֵ֖ל לְךָ֥

טו יִהְיֶֽה: כָּל־פֶּ֣טֶר רֶ֠חֶם לְֽכָל־בָּשָׂ֞ר אֲשֶׁר־יַקְרִ֧יבוּ לַֽיהוָ֛ה בָּאָדָ֥ם וּבַבְּהֵמָ֖ה
יִֽהְיֶה־לָּ֑ךְ אַ֣ךְ ׀ פָּדֹ֣ה תִפְדֶּ֗ה אֵ֚ת בְּכ֣וֹר הָֽאָדָ֔ם וְאֵ֛ת בְּכֽוֹר־הַבְּהֵמָ֥ה הַטְּמֵאָ֖ה

טז תִּפְדֶּֽה: וּפְדוּיָו֙ מִבֶּן־חֹ֣דֶשׁ תִּפְדֶּ֔ה בְּעֶ֨רְכְּךָ֔ כֶּ֛סֶף חֲמֵ֥שֶׁת שְׁקָלִ֖ים בְּשֶׁ֣קֶל

יז הַקֹּ֑דֶשׁ עֶשְׂרִ֥ים גֵּרָ֖ה הֽוּא: אַ֣ךְ בְּכֽוֹר־שׁ֡וֹר אֽוֹ־בְכ֨וֹר כֶּ֜שֶׂב אֽוֹ־בְכ֥וֹר עֵ֛ז לֹ֥א
תִפְדֶּ֖ה קֹ֣דֶשׁ הֵ֑ם אֶת־דָּמָ֞ם תִּזְרֹ֤ק עַל־הַמִּזְבֵּ֙חַ֙ וְאֶת־חֶלְבָּ֣ם תַּקְטִ֔יר אִשֶּׁ֛ה

יח לְרֵ֥יחַ נִיחֹ֖חַ לַֽיהוָֽה: וּבְשָׂרָ֖ם יִֽהְיֶה־לָּ֑ךְ כַּחֲזֵ֧ה הַתְּנוּפָ֛ה וּכְשׁ֥וֹק הַיָּמִ֖ין לְךָ֥

יט יִהְיֶֽה: כֹּ֣ל ׀ תְּרוּמֹ֣ת הַקֳּדָשִׁ֗ים אֲשֶׁ֨ר יָרִ֥ימוּ בְנֵֽי־יִשְׂרָאֵל֮ לַֽיהוָה֒ נָתַ֣תִּי לְךָ֗
וּלְבָנֶ֧יךָ וְלִבְנֹתֶ֛יךָ אִתְּךָ֖ לְחָק־עוֹלָ֑ם בְּרִית֩ מֶ֨לַח עוֹלָ֥ם הִוא֙ לִפְנֵ֣י יְהוָ֔ה לְךָ֖

כ וּלְזַרְעֲךָ֥ אִתָּֽךְ: וַיֹּ֨אמֶר יְהוָ֜ה אֶֽל־אַהֲרֹ֗ן בְּאַרְצָם֙ לֹ֣א תִנְחָ֔ל וְחֵ֕לֶק לֹא־יִֽהְיֶ֥ה

שביעי

לְךָ֖ בְּתוֹכָ֑ם אֲנִ֤י חֶלְקְךָ֙ וְנַחֲלָ֣תְךָ֔ בְּת֖וֹךְ בְּנֵ֥י יִשְׂרָאֵֽל: וְלִבְנֵ֣י

כא לֵוִ֔י הִנֵּ֥ה נָתַ֛תִּי כָּל־מַֽעֲשֵׂ֥ר בְּיִשְׂרָאֵ֖ל לְנַחֲלָ֑ה חֵ֤לֶף עֲבֹֽדָתָם֙ אֲשֶׁר־הֵ֣ם
עֹֽבְדִ֔ים אֶת־עֲבֹדַ֖ת אֹ֥הֶל מוֹעֵֽד: וְלֹא־יִקְרְב֥וּ ע֖וֹד בְּנֵ֣י יִשְׂרָאֵ֑ל אֶל־אֹ֥הֶל

כב מוֹעֵ֖ד לָשֵׂ֥את חֵ֖טְא לָמֽוּת: וְעָבַ֨ד הַלֵּוִ֜י ה֗וּא אֶת־עֲבֹדַת֙ אֹ֣הֶל מוֹעֵ֔ד וְהֵ֖ם

כג יִשְׂא֣וּ עֲוֹנָ֑ם חֻקַּ֤ת עוֹלָם֙ לְדֹרֹ֣תֵיכֶ֔ם וּבְתוֹךְ֙ בְּנֵ֣י יִשְׂרָאֵ֔ל לֹ֥א יִנְחֲל֖וּ נַחֲלָֽה:

כד כִּ֞י אֶת־מַעְשַׂ֣ר בְּנֵֽי־יִשְׂרָאֵ֗ל אֲשֶׁ֨ר יָרִ֤ימוּ לַֽיהוָה֙ תְּרוּמָ֔ה נָתַ֥תִּי לַלְוִיִּ֖ם
לְנַחֲלָ֑ה עַל־כֵּן֙ אָמַ֣רְתִּי לָהֶ֔ם בְּתוֹךְ֙ בְּנֵ֣י יִשְׂרָאֵ֔ל לֹ֥א יִנְחֲל֖וּ נַחֲלָֽה:

כה-כו וַיְדַבֵּ֥ר יְהוָ֖ה אֶל־מֹשֶׁ֥ה לֵּאמֹֽר: וְאֶל־הַלְוִיִּ֣ם תְּדַבֵּר֮ וְאָמַרְתָּ֣ אֲלֵהֶם֒
כִּֽי־תִ֠קְחוּ מֵאֵ֨ת בְּנֵֽי־יִשְׂרָאֵ֜ל אֶת־הַֽמַּעֲשֵׂ֗ר אֲשֶׁ֨ר נָתַ֧תִּי לָכֶ֛ם מֵֽאִתָּ֖ם

כז בְּנַחֲלַתְכֶ֑ם וַהֲרֵמֹתֶ֤ם מִמֶּ֙נּוּ֙ תְּרוּמַ֣ת יְהוָ֔ה מַעֲשֵׂ֖ר מִן־הַֽמַּעֲשֵֽׂר: וְנֶחְשַׁ֥ב

כח לָכֶ֖ם תְּרוּמַתְכֶ֑ם כַּדָּגָן֙ מִן־הַגֹּ֔רֶן וְכַֽמְלֵאָ֖ה מִן־הַיָּֽקֶב: כֵּ֣ן תָּרִ֤ימוּ
גַם־אַתֶּם֙ תְּרוּמַ֣ת יְהוָ֔ה מִכֹּל֙ מַעְשְׂרֹ֣תֵיכֶ֔ם אֲשֶׁ֣ר תִּקְח֔וּ מֵאֵ֖ת בְּנֵ֣י

כט יִשְׂרָאֵ֑ל וּנְתַתֶּ֤ם מִמֶּ֙נּוּ֙ אֶת־תְּרוּמַ֣ת יְהוָ֔ה לְאַהֲרֹ֖ן הַכֹּהֵֽן: מִכֹּל֙
מַתְּנֹ֣תֵיכֶ֔ם תָּרִ֕ימוּ אֵ֖ת כָּל־תְּרוּמַ֣ת יְהוָ֑ה מִכָּל־חֶלְבּ֔וֹ אֶֽת־מִקְדְּשׁ֖וֹ מִמֶּֽנּוּ:

18:11. *The wavings* are the parts of peace-, thanksgiving-, and nazirite-offerings that are separated, waved, and presented to the Kohanim, as in *Leviticus* 7:33-34.

18:19. God's covenant with the Kohanim is eternal, as if sealed with salt, which is indestructible (*Rashi*).

18:21-29. The Levites, too, are rewarded for their dedication to the service of God, by receiving one-tenth of crops. They, in turn, give one-tenth of their share to a Kohen.

Gifts to the Kohanim

⁸ HASHEM spoke to Aaron: "And I — behold! I have given you the safeguard of My heave-offerings, of all the sanctities of the Children of Israel; I have given them to you for distinction and to your sons as an eternal portion. ⁹ This shall be yours from the most holy, from the fire: their every offering, their every meal-offering, their every sin-offering, their every guilt-offering, that which they return to Me — as most holy it shall be yours and your sons. ¹⁰ In the most holy shall you eat it, every male may eat it, it shall be holy for you. ¹¹ And this shall be yours: what is set aside from their gift, from all the wavings* of the Children of Israel, have I presented them to you and to your sons and daughters with you as an eternal portion; every pure person in your household may eat it. ¹² All the best of your oil and the best of your wine and grain, their first, which they give to HASHEM, to you have I given them. ¹³ The first fruits of everything that is in their land, which they bring to HASHEM, shall be yours, every pure person in your household may eat it. ¹⁴ Every segregated property in Israel shall be yours.

(See Appendix B, charts 6-7)

¹⁵ "Every first issue of a womb of any flesh that they offer to HASHEM, whether man or beast, shall be yours; but you shall surely redeem the firstborn of man, and the firstborn of an impure beast shall you redeem. ¹⁶ Those that are to be redeemed — from one month shall you redeem according to the valuation, five silver shekels by the sacred shekel; it is twenty gera. ¹⁷ But the firstborn of an ox or the firstborn of a sheep or the firstborn of a goat you shall not redeem; they are holy; their blood shall you throw upon the Altar and their fat shall you cause to go up in smoke, a fire-offering, a satisfying aroma to HASHEM. ¹⁸ Their flesh shall be yours; like the breast of the waving and the right thigh shall it be yours.

¹⁹ "Everything that is set aside from the sanctities that the Children of Israel raise up to HASHEM have I given to you and your sons and daughters with you as an eternal portion; it is an eternal salt-like covenant* before HASHEM, for you and your offspring with you."

²⁰ HASHEM said to Aaron, "In their Land you shall have no heritage, and a share shall you not have among them; I am your share and your heritage among the Children of Israel.

Tithes to the Levites

²¹ "To the sons of Levi, behold! I have given every tithe* in Israel as a heritage in exchange for the service that they perform, the service of the Tent of Meeting — ²² so that the Children of Israel shall not again approach the Tent of Meeting to bear a sin to die. ²³ The Levite himself shall perform the service of the Tent of Meeting, and they shall bear their iniquity, an eternal decree for your generations; and among the Children of Israel they shall not inherit a heritage. ²⁴ For the tithe of the Children of Israel that they raise up to HASHEM as a gift have I given to the Levites as a heritage; therefore have I said to them: Among the Children of Israel they shall not inherit a heritage."

²⁵ HASHEM spoke to Moses, saying, ²⁶ "To the Levites shall you speak and you shall say to them, 'When you accept from the Children of Israel the tithe that I have given you from them as your heritage, you shall raise up from it a gift to HASHEM, a tithe from the tithe. ²⁷ Your gift shall be reckoned for you like grain from the threshing-floor and like the ripeness of the vat. ²⁸ So shall you, too, raise up the gift of HASHEM from all your tithes that you accept from the Children of Israel, and you shall give from it a gift of HASHEM to Aaron the Kohen. ²⁹ From all your gifts you shall raise up every gift of HASHEM, from all its best part, its sacred part from it.'

מפטיר

Haftaras
Korach:
p. 668

For special
Sabbaths,
see pp. x-xi

יט

MAFTIR
FOR
PARASHAS
PARAH
19:1-22

Haftarah:
p. 1292

שני

ל וַאֲמַרְתָּ֣ אֲלֵהֶ֔ם בַּהֲרִֽימְכֶ֤ם אֶת־חֶלְבּוֹ֙ מִמֶּ֔נּוּ וְנֶחְשַׁב֙ לַלְוִיִּ֔ם כִּתְבוּאַ֥ת גֹּ֖רֶן

לא וְכִתְבוּאַ֥ת יָֽקֶב: וַֽאֲכַלְתֶּ֤ם אֹתוֹ֙ בְּכָל־מָק֔וֹם אַתֶּ֖ם וּבֵֽיתְכֶ֑ם כִּֽי־שָׂכָ֥ר הוּא֙

לב לָכֶ֔ם חֵ֖לֶף עֲבֹֽדַתְכֶ֑ם בְּאֹ֖הֶל מוֹעֵֽד: וְלֹֽא־תִשְׂא֤וּ עָלָיו֙ חֵ֔טְא בַּהֲרִֽימְכֶ֥ם אֶת־חֶלְבּ֖וֹ מִמֶּ֑נּוּ וְאֶת־קָדְשֵׁ֧י בְנֵֽי־יִשְׂרָאֵ֛ל לֹ֥א תְחַלְּל֖וּ וְלֹ֥א תָמֽוּתוּ: פפפ

צ״ה פסוקים. דניא״ל סימן.

פרשת חקת

א־ב וַיְדַבֵּ֣ר יְהֹוָ֗ה אֶל־מֹשֶׁ֧ה וְאֶֽל־אַהֲרֹ֖ן לֵאמֹֽר: זֹ֚את חֻקַּ֣ת הַתּוֹרָ֔ה אֲשֶׁר־צִוָּ֖ה יְהֹוָ֣ה לֵאמֹ֑ר דַּבֵּ֣ר ׀ אֶל־בְּנֵ֣י יִשְׂרָאֵ֗ל וְיִקְח֣וּ אֵלֶ֩יךָ֩ פָרָ֨ה אֲדֻמָּ֜ה תְּמִימָ֗ה

ג אֲשֶׁ֤ר אֵֽין־בָּהּ֙ מ֔וּם אֲשֶׁ֛ר לֹֽא־עָלָ֥ה עָלֶ֖יהָ עֹֽל: וּנְתַתֶּ֣ם אֹתָ֔הּ אֶל־אֶלְעָזָ֣ר

ד הַכֹּהֵ֑ן וְהוֹצִ֤יא אֹתָהּ֙ אֶל־מִח֣וּץ לַֽמַּחֲנֶ֔ה וְשָׁחַ֥ט אֹתָ֖הּ לְפָנָֽיו: וְלָקַ֞ח אֶלְעָזָ֧ר הַכֹּהֵ֛ן מִדָּמָ֖הּ בְּאֶצְבָּע֑וֹ וְהִזָּ֞ה אֶל־נֹ֨כַח פְּנֵ֧י אֹֽהֶל־מוֹעֵ֛ד מִדָּמָ֖הּ

ה שֶׁ֥בַע פְּעָמִֽים: וְשָׂרַ֥ף אֶת־הַפָּרָ֖ה לְעֵינָ֑יו אֶת־עֹרָ֤הּ וְאֶת־בְּשָׂרָהּ֙ וְאֶת־דָּמָ֔הּ

ו עַל־פִּרְשָׁ֖הּ יִשְׂרֹֽף: וְלָקַ֣ח הַכֹּהֵ֗ן עֵ֥ץ אֶ֛רֶז וְאֵז֖וֹב וּשְׁנִ֣י תוֹלָ֑עַת וְהִשְׁלִ֕יךְ אֶל־

ז תּ֖וֹךְ שְׂרֵפַ֥ת הַפָּרָֽה: וְכִבֶּ֨ס בְּגָדָ֜יו הַכֹּהֵ֗ן וְרָחַ֤ץ בְּשָׂרוֹ֙ בַּמַּ֔יִם וְאַחַ֖ר יָבֹ֣א

ח אֶל־הַֽמַּחֲנֶ֑ה וְטָמֵ֥א הַכֹּהֵ֖ן עַד־הָעָֽרֶב: וְהַשֹּׂרֵ֣ף אֹתָ֔הּ יְכַבֵּ֤ס בְּגָדָיו֙ בַּמַּ֔יִם

ט וְרָחַ֥ץ בְּשָׂר֖וֹ בַּמָּ֑יִם וְטָמֵ֖א עַד־הָעָֽרֶב: וְאָסַ֣ף ׀ אִ֣ישׁ טָה֗וֹר אֵ֚ת אֵ֣פֶר הַפָּרָ֔ה וְהִנִּ֛יחַ מִח֥וּץ לַֽמַּחֲנֶ֖ה בְּמָק֣וֹם טָה֑וֹר וְ֠הָיְתָ֠ה לַֽעֲדַ֨ת בְּנֵֽי־יִשְׂרָאֵ֧ל

י לְמִשְׁמֶ֛רֶת לְמֵ֥י נִדָּ֖ה חַטָּ֥את הִֽוא: וְ֠כִבֶּ֠ס הָֽאֹסֵ֨ף אֶת־אֵ֤פֶר הַפָּרָה֙ אֶת־בְּגָדָ֔יו וְטָמֵ֖א עַד־הָעָ֑רֶב וְֽהָיְתָ֞ה לִבְנֵ֣י יִשְׂרָאֵ֗ל וְלַגֵּ֛ר הַגָּ֥ר בְּתוֹכָ֖ם לְחֻקַּ֥ת

יא־יב עוֹלָֽם: הַנֹּגֵ֥עַ בְּמֵ֖ת לְכָל־נֶ֣פֶשׁ אָדָ֑ם וְטָמֵ֖א שִׁבְעַ֥ת יָמִֽים: ה֣וּא יִתְחַטָּא־ב֞וֹ בַּיּ֧וֹם הַשְּׁלִישִׁ֛י וּבַיּ֥וֹם הַשְּׁבִיעִ֖י יִטְהָ֑ר וְאִם־לֹ֨א יִתְחַטָּ֜א בַּיּ֧וֹם הַשְּׁלִישִׁ֛י

יג וּבַיּ֥וֹם הַשְּׁבִיעִ֖י לֹ֣א יִטְהָֽר: כָּֽל־הַנֹּגֵ֡עַ בְּמֵ֣ת בְּנֶ֩פֶשׁ֩ הָאָדָ֨ם אֲשֶׁר־יָמ֜וּת וְלֹ֣א יִתְחַטָּ֗א אֶת־מִשְׁכַּ֤ן יְהֹוָה֙ טִמֵּ֔א וְנִכְרְתָ֛ה הַנֶּ֥פֶשׁ הַהִ֖וא מִיִּשְׂרָאֵ֑ל כִּי֩ מֵ֨י

יד נִדָּ֜ה לֹֽא־זֹרַ֤ק עָלָיו֙ טָמֵ֣א יִֽהְיֶ֔ה ע֖וֹד טֻמְאָת֥וֹ בֽוֹ: זֹ֚את הַתּוֹרָ֔ה אָדָ֖ם כִּֽי־יָמ֣וּת בְּאֹ֑הֶל כָּל־הַבָּ֤א אֶל־הָאֹ֨הֶל֙ וְכָל־אֲשֶׁ֣ר בָּאֹ֔הֶל יִטְמָ֖א שִׁבְעַ֥ת יָמִֽים:

טו־טז וְכֹל֙ כְּלִ֣י פָת֔וּחַ אֲשֶׁ֛ר אֵֽין־צָמִ֥יד פָּתִ֖יל עָלָ֑יו טָמֵ֖א הֽוּא: וְכֹ֠ל אֲשֶׁר־יִגַּ֨ע עַל־פְּנֵ֤י הַשָּׂדֶה֙ בַּֽחֲלַל־חֶ֔רֶב א֣וֹ בְמֵ֔ת אֽוֹ־בְעֶ֥צֶם אָדָ֖ם א֣וֹ בְקָ֑בֶר יִטְמָ֖א

יז שִׁבְעַ֥ת יָמִֽים: וְלָֽקְחוּ֙ לַטָּמֵ֔א מֵֽעֲפַ֖ר שְׂרֵפַ֣ת הַֽחַטָּ֑את וְנָתַ֥ן עָלָ֛יו מַ֥יִם חַיִּ֖ים

יח אֶל־כֶּֽלִי: וְלָקַ֨ח אֵז֜וֹב וְטָבַ֣ל בַּמַּיִם֮ אִ֣ישׁ טָהוֹר֒ וְהִזָּ֤ה עַל־הָאֹ֨הֶל֙ וְעַל־כָּל־הַ֣כֵּלִ֔ים וְעַל־הַנְּפָשׁ֖וֹת אֲשֶׁ֣ר הָֽיוּ־שָׁ֑ם וְעַל־הַנֹּגֵ֗עַ בַּעֶ֨צֶם֙ א֣וֹ בֶֽחָלָ֔ל א֥וֹ

יט בַמֵּ֖ת א֣וֹ בַקָּֽבֶר: וְהִזָּ֤ה הַטָּהֹר֙ עַל־הַטָּמֵ֔א בַּיּ֥וֹם הַשְּׁלִישִׁ֖י וּבַיּ֣וֹם הַשְּׁבִיעִ֑י

⊷ Parashas Chukas

19:2. The law of the Red Cow is described by the Sages as the quintessential חֻקַּת הַתּוֹרָה, *decree of the Torah* (v. 2), meaning that it is beyond human understanding. It is axiomatic, however, that human inability to comprehend such decrees indicates the limitation of the student, not the Teacher (*Rambam*).

19:13. If a contaminated person intentionally enters the Sanctuary or Courtyard, his soul is cut off from the Jewish people (*Rashi; Ramban*).

³⁰ "You shall say to them: 'When you have raised up its best from it, it shall be considered for the Levites like the produce of the threshing-floor and the produce of the vat. ³¹ You may eat it everywhere, you and your household, for it is a wage for you in exchange for your service in the Tent of Meeting. ³² You shall not bear a sin because of it when you raise up its best from it; and the sanctities of the Children of Israel you shall not desecrate, so that you shall not die.'"

PARASHAS CHUKAS

19

¹ HASHEM spoke to Moses and to Aaron, saying: ² This is the decree of the Torah, which HASHEM has commanded, saying: Speak to the Children of Israel, and they shall take to you a completely red cow,* which is without blemish, and upon which a yoke has not come. ³ You shall give it to Elazar the Kohen; he shall take it out to the outside of the camp and someone shall slaughter it in his presence. ⁴ Elazar the Kohen shall take some of its blood with his forefinger, and sprinkle some of its blood toward the front of the Tent of Meeting seven times. ⁵ Someone shall burn the cow before his eyes — its hide, and its flesh, and its blood, with its dung, shall he burn. ⁶ The Kohen shall take cedar wood, hyssop, and crimson thread, and he shall throw [them] into the burning of the cow.

The Red Cow

⁷ The Kohen shall immerse his clothing and immerse himself in water, and afterwards he may enter the camp; and the Kohen shall remain contaminated until evening. ⁸ The one who burns it shall immerse his clothing in water and immerse himself in water; and he shall remain contaminated until evening. ⁹ A pure man shall gather the ash of the cow and place [it] outside the camp in a pure place. For the assembly of Israel it shall remain as a safekeeping, for water of sprinkling; it is for purification. ¹⁰ The one who gathers the ash of the cow shall immerse his clothing and remain contaminated until evening. It shall be for the Children of Israel and for the proselyte who dwells among them as an eternal decree.

¹¹ Whoever touches the corpse of any human being shall be contaminated for seven days. ¹² He shall purify himself with it on the third day and on the seventh day, then he shall become pure; but if he will not purify himself on the third day and on the seventh day he will not become pure. ¹³ Whoever touches the dead body of a human being who will have died, and will not have purified himself — if he shall have contaminated the Tabernacle of HASHEM, that person shall be cut off from Israel;* because the water of sprinkling has not been thrown upon him, he shall remain contaminated; his contamination is still upon him.

¹⁴ This is the teaching regarding a man who would die in a tent: Anything that enters the tent and anything that is in the tent shall be contaminated for seven days. ¹⁵ Any open vessel that has no cover fastened to it is contaminated. ¹⁶ On the open field: Anyone who touches one slain by the sword, or one that died, or a human bone, or a grave, shall be contaminated for seven days. ¹⁷ They shall take for the contaminated person some of the ashes of the burning of the purification [animal], and put upon it spring water in a vessel. ¹⁸ A pure man shall take hyssop and dip it in the water, and sprinkle upon the tent, upon all the vessels, upon the people who were there, and upon the one who touched the bone, or the slain one, or the one that died, or the grave. ¹⁹ The pure person shall sprinkle upon the contaminated person on the third day and on the seventh day,

כ וְחָטְא֞וֹ בַּיּ֣וֹם הַשְּׁבִיעִ֗י וְכִבֶּ֤ס בְּגָדָיו֙ וְרָחַ֣ץ בַּמַּ֔יִם וְטָהֵ֖ר בָּעָֽרֶב: וְאִ֣ישׁ אֲשֶׁר־
יִטְמָ֞א וְלֹ֣א יִתְחַטָּ֗א וְנִכְרְתָ֞ה הַנֶּ֤פֶשׁ הַהִוא֙ מִתּ֣וֹךְ הַקָּהָ֔ל כִּ֛י אֶת־מִקְדַּ֥שׁ
כא יְהֹוָ֖ה טִמֵּ֑א מֵ֧י נִדָּ֛ה לֹא־זֹרַ֥ק עָלָ֖יו טָמֵ֥א הֽוּא: וְהָיְתָ֥ה לָהֶ֖ם לְחֻקַּ֣ת עוֹלָ֑ם
כב וּמַזֵּ֤ה מֵֽי־הַנִּדָּה֙ יְכַבֵּ֣ס בְּגָדָ֔יו וְהַנֹּגֵ֨עַ֙ בְּמֵ֣י הַנִּדָּ֔ה יִטְמָ֖א עַד־הָעָֽרֶב: וְכֹ֛ל
אֲשֶׁר־יִגַּע־בּ֥וֹ הַטָּמֵ֖א יִטְמָ֑א וְהַנֶּ֥פֶשׁ הַנֹּגַ֖עַת תִּטְמָ֥א עַד־הָעָֽרֶב:

כ א וַיָּבֹ֣אוּ בְנֵֽי־יִ֠שְׂרָאֵ֠ל כָּל־הָ֨עֵדָ֤ה מִדְבַּר־צִן֙ בַּחֹ֣דֶשׁ הָֽרִאשׁ֔וֹן וַיֵּ֥שֶׁב הָעָ֖ם   *כ"ב טעמים
ב בְּקָדֵ֑שׁ וַתָּ֤מָת שָׁם֙ מִרְיָ֔ם וַתִּקָּבֵ֖ר שָֽׁם: וְלֹא־הָ֥יָה מַ֖יִם לָֽעֵדָ֑ה וַיִּקָּ֣הֲל֔וּ עַל־
ג מֹשֶׁ֖ה וְעַֽל־אַֽהֲרֹֽן: וַיָּ֥רֶב הָעָ֖ם עִם־מֹשֶׁ֑ה וַיֹּֽאמְר֣וּ לֵאמֹ֔ר וְל֥וּ גָוַ֛עְנוּ בִּגְוַ֥ע
ד אַחֵ֖ינוּ לִפְנֵ֥י יְהֹוָֽה: וְלָמָ֤ה הֲבֵאתֶם֙ אֶת־קְהַ֣ל יְהֹוָ֔ה אֶל־הַמִּדְבָּ֖ר הַזֶּ֑ה לָמ֣וּת
ה שָׁ֔ם אֲנַ֖חְנוּ וּבְעִירֵֽנוּ: וְלָמָ֤ה הֶֽעֱלִיתֻ֨נוּ֙ מִמִּצְרַ֔יִם לְהָבִ֣יא אֹתָ֔נוּ אֶל־הַמָּק֥וֹם
ו הָרָ֖ע הַזֶּ֑ה לֹ֣א ׀ מְק֣וֹם זֶ֗רַע וּתְאֵנָ֤ה וְגֶ֨פֶן֙ וְרִמּ֔וֹן וּמַ֥יִם אַ֖יִן לִשְׁתּֽוֹת: וַיָּבֹא֩
מֹשֶׁ֨ה וְאַֽהֲרֹ֜ן מִפְּנֵ֣י הַקָּהָ֗ל אֶל־פֶּ֨תַח֙ אֹ֣הֶל מוֹעֵ֔ד וַֽיִּפְּל֖וּ עַל־פְּנֵיהֶ֑ם וַיֵּרָ֥א
כְבֽוֹד־יְהֹוָ֖ה אֲלֵיהֶֽם:

ז-ח וַיְדַבֵּ֥ר יְהֹוָ֖ה אֶל־מֹשֶׁ֥ה לֵּאמֹֽר: קַ֣ח אֶת־הַמַּטֶּ֗ה וְהַקְהֵ֤ל אֶת־הָֽעֵדָה֙ אַתָּה֙   שלישי
וְאַֽהֲרֹ֣ן אָחִ֔יךָ וְדִבַּרְתֶּ֧ם אֶל־הַסֶּ֛לַע לְעֵֽינֵיהֶ֖ם וְנָתַ֣ן מֵימָ֑יו וְהֽוֹצֵאתָ֨ לָהֶ֤ם   [שני]
ט מַ֨יִם֙ מִן־הַסֶּ֔לַע וְהִשְׁקִיתָ֥ אֶת־הָֽעֵדָ֖ה וְאֶת־בְּעִירָֽם: וַיִּקַּ֥ח מֹשֶׁ֛ה אֶת־
י הַמַּטֶּ֖ה מִלִּפְנֵ֣י יְהֹוָ֑ה כַּֽאֲשֶׁ֖ר צִוָּֽהוּ: וַיַּקְהִ֜לוּ מֹשֶׁ֧ה וְאַֽהֲרֹ֛ן אֶת־הַקָּהָ֖ל אֶל־
פְּנֵ֣י הַסָּ֑לַע וַיֹּ֣אמֶר לָהֶ֗ם שִׁמְעוּ־נָא֙ הַמֹּרִ֔ים הֲמִן־הַסֶּ֣לַע הַזֶּ֔ה נוֹצִ֥יא לָכֶ֖ם
יא מָֽיִם: וַיָּ֨רֶם מֹשֶׁ֜ה אֶת־יָד֗וֹ וַיַּ֧ךְ אֶת־הַסֶּ֛לַע בְּמַטֵּ֖הוּ פַּֽעֲמָ֑יִם וַיֵּֽצְאוּ֙ מַ֣יִם רַבִּ֔ים
יב וַתֵּ֥שְׁתְּ הָֽעֵדָ֖ה וּבְעִירָֽם: וַיֹּ֣אמֶר יְהֹוָה֘ אֶל־מֹשֶׁ֣ה וְאֶֽל־
אַֽהֲרֹן֒ יַ֚עַן לֹֽא־הֶֽאֱמַנְתֶּ֣ם בִּ֔י לְהַ֨קְדִּישֵׁ֔נִי לְעֵינֵ֖י בְּנֵ֣י יִשְׂרָאֵ֑ל לָכֵ֗ן לֹ֤א
יג תָבִ֨יאוּ֙ אֶת־הַקָּהָ֣ל הַזֶּ֔ה אֶל־הָאָ֖רֶץ אֲשֶׁר־נָתַ֣תִּי לָהֶֽם: הֵ֚מָּה מֵ֣י מְרִיבָ֔ה
יד אֲשֶׁר־רָב֥וּ בְנֵֽי־יִשְׂרָאֵ֖ל אֶת־יְהֹוָ֑ה וַיִּקָּדֵ֖שׁ בָּֽם: וַיִּשְׁלַ֨ח   רביעי
מֹשֶׁ֧ה מַלְאָכִ֛ים מִקָּדֵ֖שׁ אֶל־מֶ֣לֶךְ אֱד֑וֹם כֹּ֤ה אָמַר֙ אָחִ֣יךָ יִשְׂרָאֵ֔ל אַתָּ֣ה
טו יָדַ֔עְתָּ אֵ֥ת כָּל־הַתְּלָאָ֖ה אֲשֶׁ֥ר מְצָאָֽתְנוּ: וַיֵּֽרְד֤וּ אֲבֹתֵ֨ינוּ֙ מִצְרַ֔יְמָה וַנֵּ֥שֶׁב
טז בְּמִצְרַ֖יִם יָמִ֣ים רַבִּ֑ים וַיָּרֵ֥עוּ לָ֛נוּ מִצְרַ֖יִם וְלַֽאֲבֹתֵֽינוּ: וַנִּצְעַ֤ק אֶל־יְהֹוָה֙
וַיִּשְׁמַ֣ע קֹלֵ֔נוּ וַיִּשְׁלַ֣ח מַלְאָ֔ךְ וַיֹּֽצִאֵ֖נוּ מִמִּצְרָ֑יִם וְהִנֵּה֙ אֲנַ֣חְנוּ בְקָדֵ֔שׁ עִ֖יר
יז קְצֵ֥ה גְבוּלֶֽךָ: נַעְבְּרָה־נָּ֣א בְאַרְצֶ֗ךָ לֹ֤א נַֽעֲבֹר֙ בְּשָׂדֶ֣ה וּבְכֶ֔רֶם וְלֹ֥א נִשְׁתֶּ֖ה מֵ֣י   *יתיר ר
בְאֵ֑ר דֶּ֧רֶךְ הַמֶּ֣לֶךְ נֵלֵ֗ךְ לֹ֤א נִטֶּה֙ יָמִ֣ין וּשְׂמֹ֔אול עַ֥ד אֲשֶֽׁר־נַֽעֲבֹ֖ר גְּבֻלֶֽךָ:

20:1. From this point on, the Torah records the events of the last year in the Wilderness and the commandments transmitted by Moses during that time.

20:1-2. The fact that there was no water after Miriam died shows that it was in her merit that the miraculous well followed the people throughout their wanderings (*Rashi*).

20:12. The commentators grapple with the question of defining the nature of the sin. According to *Rashi*, Moses was commanded to *speak* to the rock, not strike it.

Rambam holds that Moses spoke angrily (v. 10), thus implying that God was angry; but we do not see any indication that God was angered. *R' Chananel* and *Ramban* hold that Moses implied that it was in his and Aaron's power to produce water (v. 10).

20:14-21. Although they could easily have invaded Edom, as they would do to Sihon and Og, God did not want the Jews to provoke their Edomite cousins (*Deuteronomy* 2:4-5).

and shall purify him on the seventh day; then he shall immerse his clothing and immerse himself in water and become purified in the evening. ²⁰ *But a man who becomes contaminated and does not purify himself, that person shall be cut off from the midst of the congregation, if he shall have contaminated the Sanctuary of HASHEM; because the water of sprinkling has not been thrown upon him, he is contaminated.*

²¹ *This shall be for them an eternal decree. And the one who sprinkles the water of sprinkling shall immerse his clothing, and one who touches water of sprinkling shall be contaminated until evening.* ²² *Anything that the contaminated one may touch shall become contaminated, and the person who touches him shall become contaminated until evening.*

20

¹ *The Children of Israel, the whole assembly, arrived at the Wilderness of Zin * in the first month and the people settled in Kadesh. Miriam died there and she was buried there.* ² *There was no water for the assembly, * and they gathered against Moses and Aaron.* ³ *The people quarreled with Moses and spoke up, saying, "If only we had perished as our brethren perished before HASHEM!* ⁴ *Why have you brought the congregation of HASHEM to this wilderness to die there, we and our animals?* ⁵ *And why did you bring us up from Egypt to bring us to this evil place? — not a place of seed, or fig, or grape, or pomegranate; and there is no water to drink!"*

⁶ *Moses and Aaron went from the presence of the congregation to the entrance of the Tent of Meeting and fell on their faces. The glory of HASHEM appeared to them.*

⁷ *HASHEM spoke to Moses, saying,* ⁸ *"Take the staff and gather together the assembly, you and Aaron your brother, and speak to the rock before their eyes that it shall give its waters. You shall bring forth for them water from the rock and give drink to the assembly and to their animals."*

⁹ *Moses took the staff from before HASHEM, as He had commanded him.* ¹⁰ *Moses and Aaron gathered the congregation before the rock and he said to them, "Listen now, O rebels, shall we bring forth water for you from this rock?"* ¹¹ *Then Moses raised his arm and struck the rock with his staff twice; abundant water came forth and the assembly and their animals drank.*

¹² *HASHEM said to Moses and to Aaron, "Because you did not believe in Me to sanctify Me in the eyes of the Children of Israel, * therefore you will not bring this congregation to the Land that I have given them."* ¹³ *They are the waters of strife, where the Children of Israel contended with HASHEM, and He was sanctified through them.*

¹⁴ *Moses sent emissaries from Kadesh to the king of Edom: * "So said your brother Israel: You know all the hardship that has befallen us.* ¹⁵ *Our forefathers descended to Egypt and we dwelled in Egypt many years, and the Egyptians did evil to us and to our forefathers.* ¹⁶ *We cried out to HASHEM and He heard our voice; He sent an emissary and took us out of Egypt. Now behold! we are in Kadesh, a city at the edge of your border.* ¹⁷ *Let us pass through your land; we shall not pass through field or vineyard, and we shall not drink well water; * on the king's road shall we travel — we shall not veer right or left — until we pass through your border."*

Side notes

Miriam's death and the lack of water

The people protest

God commands Moses to bring water

Moses and Aaron err ...

... and are punished

20:17. A guest in a hotel should buy food from his host in order to assist him in earning his livelihood. Here, too, Moses said that the Jews would purchase water from the Edomites, instead of using their own well (*Tanchuma*).

יח־יט וַיֹּ֤אמֶר אֵלָיו֙ אֱד֔וֹם לֹ֥א תַעֲבֹ֖ר בִּ֑י פֶּן־בַּחֶ֖רֶב אֵצֵ֥א לִקְרָאתֶֽךָ: וַיֹּאמְר֨וּ אֵלָ֥יו בְּנֵֽי־יִשְׂרָאֵל֮ בַּֽמְסִלָּ֣ה נַעֲלֶה֒ וְאִם־מֵימֶ֤יךָ נִשְׁתֶּה֙ אֲנִ֣י וּמִקְנַ֔י וְנָתַתִּ֖י

כ מִכְרָ֑ם רַ֥ק אֵין־דָּבָ֖ר בְּרַגְלַ֣י אֶֽעֱבֹֽרָה: וַיֹּ֖אמֶר לֹ֣א תַעֲבֹ֑ר וַיֵּצֵ֤א אֱדוֹם֙

כא לִקְרָאת֔וֹ בְּעַ֥ם כָּבֵ֖ד וּבְיָ֥ד חֲזָקָֽה: וַיְמָאֵ֣ן ׀ אֱד֗וֹם נְתֹן֙ אֶת־יִשְׂרָאֵ֔ל עֲבֹ֖ר בִּגְבֻל֑וֹ וַיֵּ֥ט יִשְׂרָאֵ֖ל מֵעָלָֽיו:

חמישי [שלישי] כב־כג וַיִּסְע֖וּ מִקָּדֵ֑שׁ וַיָּבֹ֧אוּ בְנֵֽי־יִשְׂרָאֵ֛ל כָּל־הָעֵדָ֖ה הֹ֥ר הָהָֽר: וַיֹּ֧אמֶר יְהֹוָ֛ה אֶל־

כד מֹשֶׁ֥ה וְאֶֽל־אַהֲרֹ֖ן בְּהֹ֣ר הָהָ֑ר עַל־גְּב֥וּל אֶֽרֶץ־אֱד֖וֹם לֵאמֹֽר: יֵאָסֵ֤ף אַהֲרֹן֙ אֶל־עַמָּ֔יו כִּ֣י לֹ֤א יָבֹא֙ אֶל־הָאָ֔רֶץ אֲשֶׁ֥ר נָתַ֖תִּי לִבְנֵ֣י יִשְׂרָאֵ֑ל עַ֛ל אֲשֶׁר־

כה מְרִיתֶ֥ם אֶת־פִּ֖י לְמֵ֥י מְרִיבָֽה: קַ֚ח אֶֽת־אַהֲרֹ֔ן וְאֶת־אֶלְעָזָ֖ר בְּנ֑וֹ וְהַ֥עַל

כו אֹתָ֖ם הֹ֥ר הָהָֽר: וְהַפְשֵׁ֤ט אֶֽת־אַהֲרֹן֙ אֶת־בְּגָדָ֔יו וְהִלְבַּשְׁתָּ֖ם אֶת־אֶלְעָזָ֣ר

כז בְּנ֑וֹ וְאַהֲרֹ֥ן יֵאָסֵ֖ף וּמֵ֥ת שָֽׁם: וַיַּ֣עַשׂ מֹשֶׁ֔ה כַּאֲשֶׁ֖ר צִוָּ֣ה יְהֹוָ֑ה וַיַּֽעֲלוּ֙ אֶל־הֹ֣ר

כח הָהָ֔ר לְעֵינֵ֖י כָּל־הָעֵדָֽה: וַיַּפְשֵׁט֩ מֹשֶׁ֨ה אֶֽת־אַהֲרֹ֜ן אֶת־בְּגָדָ֗יו וַיַּלְבֵּ֤שׁ אֹתָם֙ אֶת־אֶלְעָזָ֣ר בְּנ֔וֹ וַיָּ֧מָת אַהֲרֹ֛ן שָׁ֖ם בְּרֹ֣אשׁ הָהָ֑ר וַיֵּ֧רֶד מֹשֶׁ֛ה וְאֶלְעָזָ֖ר מִן־

כט הָהָֽר: וַיִּרְאוּ֙ כָּל־הָ֣עֵדָ֔ה כִּ֥י גָוַ֖ע אַהֲרֹ֑ן וַיִּבְכּ֤וּ אֶֽת־אַהֲרֹן֙ שְׁלֹשִׁ֣ים י֔וֹם כֹּ֖ל

כא א בֵּ֥ית יִשְׂרָאֵֽל: וַיִּשְׁמַ֞ע הַכְּנַעֲנִ֤י מֶֽלֶךְ־עֲרָד֙ יֹשֵׁ֣ב הַנֶּ֔גֶב

ב כִּ֚י בָּ֣א יִשְׂרָאֵ֔ל דֶּ֖רֶךְ הָאֲתָרִ֑ים וַיִּלָּ֙חֶם֙ בְּיִשְׂרָאֵ֔ל וַיִּ֥שְׁבְּ ׀ מִמֶּ֖נּוּ שֶֽׁבִי: וַיִּדַּ֨ר יִשְׂרָאֵ֥ל נֶ֛דֶר לַֽיהֹוָ֖ה וַיֹּאמַ֑ר אִם־נָתֹ֨ן תִּתֵּ֜ן אֶת־הָעָ֤ם הַזֶּה֙ בְּיָדִ֔י וְהַֽחֲרַמְתִּ֖י

ג אֶת־עָרֵיהֶֽם: וַיִּשְׁמַ֨ע יְהֹוָ֜ה בְּק֣וֹל יִשְׂרָאֵ֗ל וַיִּתֵּן֙ אֶת־הַֽכְּנַעֲנִ֔י וַיַּחֲרֵ֥ם אֶתְהֶ֖ם וְאֶת־עָרֵיהֶ֑ם וַיִּקְרָ֥א שֵׁם־הַמָּק֖וֹם חָרְמָֽה:

ד וַיִּסְע֞וּ מֵהֹ֤ר הָהָר֙ דֶּ֣רֶךְ יַם־ס֔וּף לִסְבֹ֖ב אֶת־אֶ֣רֶץ אֱד֑וֹם וַתִּקְצַ֥ר נֶֽפֶשׁ־הָעָ֖ם

ה בַּדָּֽרֶךְ: וַיְדַבֵּ֣ר הָעָ֗ם בֵּֽאלֹהִים֘ וּבְמֹשֶׁה֒ לָמָ֤ה הֶֽעֱלִיתֻ֙נוּ֙ מִמִּצְרַ֔יִם לָמ֖וּת

ו בַּמִּדְבָּ֑ר כִּ֣י אֵ֥ין לֶ֙חֶם֙ וְאֵ֣ין מַ֔יִם וְנַפְשֵׁ֣נוּ קָ֔צָה בַּלֶּ֖חֶם הַקְּלֹקֵֽל: וַיְשַׁלַּ֨ח יְהֹוָ֜ה בָּעָ֗ם אֵ֚ת הַנְּחָשִׁ֣ים הַשְּׂרָפִ֔ים וַֽיְנַשְּׁכ֖וּ אֶת־הָעָ֑ם וַיָּ֥מָת עַם־רָ֖ב מִיִּשְׂרָאֵֽל:

ז וַיָּבֹא֩ הָעָ֨ם אֶל־מֹשֶׁ֜ה וַיֹּאמְר֣וּ חָטָ֗אנוּ כִּֽי־דִבַּ֤רְנוּ בַֽיהֹוָה֙ וָבָ֔ךְ הִתְפַּלֵּל֙ אֶל־

ח יְהֹוָ֔ה וְיָסֵ֥ר מֵעָלֵ֖ינוּ אֶת־הַנָּחָ֑שׁ וַיִּתְפַּלֵּ֥ל מֹשֶׁ֖ה בְּעַ֥ד הָעָֽם: וַיֹּ֨אמֶר יְהֹוָ֜ה אֶל־מֹשֶׁ֗ה עֲשֵׂ֤ה לְךָ֙ שָׂרָ֔ף וְשִׂ֥ים אֹת֖וֹ עַל־נֵ֑ס וְהָיָה֙ כָּל־הַנָּשׁ֔וּךְ וְרָאָ֥ה

ט אֹת֖וֹ וָחָֽי: וַיַּ֤עַשׂ מֹשֶׁה֙ נְחַ֣שׁ נְחֹ֔שֶׁת וַיְשִׂמֵ֖הוּ עַל־הַנֵּ֑ס וְהָיָ֗ה אִם־נָשַׁ֤ךְ

ששי י הַנָּחָשׁ֙ אֶת־אִ֔ישׁ וְהִבִּ֛יט אֶל־נְחַ֥שׁ הַנְּחֹ֖שֶׁת וָחָֽי: וַיִּסְע֖וּ בְּנֵ֣י יִשְׂרָאֵ֑ל וַיַּֽחֲנ֖וּ

יא בְּאֹבֹֽת: וַיִּסְע֖וּ מֵֽאֹבֹ֑ת וַֽיַּחֲנ֞וּ בְּעִיֵּ֣י הָֽעֲבָרִ֗ים בַּמִּדְבָּר֙ אֲשֶׁר֙ עַל־פְּנֵ֣י

יב־יג מוֹאָ֔ב מִמִּזְרַ֖ח הַשָּֽׁמֶשׁ: מִשָּׁ֖ם נָסָ֑עוּ וַֽיַּחֲנ֖וּ בְּנַ֣חַל זָ֑רֶד: מִשָּׁם֘ נָסָ֒עוּ֒ וַֽיַּחֲנ֗וּ

20:26. Aaron had the satisfaction of seeing Elazar clothed in the vestments of the Kohen Gadol, thus seeing how a great father was succeeded by a great son.

20:29. Aaron was mourned by *the entire House of Israel* — men and women alike — because Aaron pursued peace and extended himself to bring harmony between adversaries and between man and wife (*Rashi*).

21:1. The Sages (*Rosh Hashanah* 3a) teach that after Aaron died, the pillar of cloud, which had guided and protected the nation, left them. Assuming that Israel was now vulnerable, one of the Canaanite kings launched a foray against them.

¹⁸ Edom said to him, "You shall not pass through me — lest I come against you with the sword!"

¹⁹ The Children of Israel said to him, "We shall go up on the highway, and if we drink your water — I or my flock — I shall pay their price. Only nothing will happen; let me pass through on foot."

²⁰ He said, "You shall not pass through!" Then Edom went out against him with a massive throng and a strong hand. ²¹ So Edom refused to permit Israel to pass through his border, and Israel turned away from near him.

²² They journeyed from Kadesh and the Children of Israel arrived — the entire assembly — at Mount Hor. ²³ HASHEM said to Moses and Aaron at Mount Hor by the border of the land of Edom, saying, ²⁴ "Aaron shall be gathered to his people, for he shall not enter the Land that I have given to the Children of Israel, because you defied My word at the waters of strife. ²⁵ Take Aaron and Elazar his son and bring them up to Mount Hor. ²⁶ Strip Aaron of his vestments and dress Elazar his son in them; * Aaron shall be gathered in and die there."

²⁷ Moses did as HASHEM commanded, and they ascended Mount Hor before the eyes of the entire assembly. ²⁸ Moses stripped Aaron's garments from him and dressed Elazar his son in them; then Aaron died there on the top of the mountain, and Moses and Elazar descended from the mountain. ²⁹ When the entire assembly saw that Aaron had perished, they wept for Aaron thirty days, the entire House of Israel. *

21

Amalek attacks

¹ The Canaanite king of Arad, who dwelled in the south, heard that Israel had come by the route of the spies, and he warred against Israel and took a captive from it. * ² Israel made a vow to HASHEM and said, "If You will deliver this people into my hand, I will consecrate their cities." ³ HASHEM heard the voice of Israel, and He delivered the Canaanite, and it consecrated them and their cities. It named the place Hormah.

A new challenge

⁴ They journeyed from Mount Hor by way of the Sea of Reeds to go around the land of Edom, and the spirit of the people grew short on the way. ⁵ The people spoke against God and Moses: "Why did you bring us up from Egypt to die in the Wilderness, for there is no food and no water, and our soul is disgusted with the insubstantial food?"

⁶ God sent the fiery serpents against the people and they bit the people. A large multitude of Israel died. ⁷ The people came to Moses and said, "We have sinned, for we have spoken against HASHEM and against you! Pray to HASHEM that He remove from us the serpent." Moses prayed for the people.

⁸ HASHEM said to Moses, "Make for yourself a fiery [serpent] and place it on a pole, and it will be that anyone who was bitten will look at it and live." * ⁹ Moses made a serpent of copper and placed it on the pole; so it was that if the serpent bit a man, he would stare at the copper serpent and live.

¹⁰ The Children of Israel journeyed and encamped at Oboth. ¹¹ They journeyed from Oboth and encamped in the ruins of the passes in the wilderness facing Moab, towards the rising sun. ¹² From there they journeyed and encamped in the valley of Zered. ¹³ From there they journeyed and encamped

---

21:8. "Does a serpent cause death or life? Rather, when they looked upward and subjected their hearts to their   Father in Heaven they were healed, but if not, they died" (*Rosh Hashanah* 29a).

מֵעֵבֶר אַרְנוֹן אֲשֶׁר בַּמִּדְבָּר הַיֹּצֵא מִגְּבֻל הָאֱמֹרִי כִּי אַרְנוֹן גְּבוּל מוֹאָב

יד בֵּין מוֹאָב וּבֵין הָאֱמֹרִי: עַל־כֵּן יֵאָמַר בְּסֵפֶר מִלְחֲמֹת יְהוָֹה אֶת־וָהֵב

טו בְּסוּפָה וְאֶת־הַנְּחָלִים אַרְנוֹן: וְאֶשֶׁד הַנְּחָלִים אֲשֶׁר נָטָה לְשֶׁבֶת עָר

טז וְנִשְׁעַן לִגְבוּל מוֹאָב: וּמִשָּׁם בְּאֵרָה הִוא הַבְּאֵר אֲשֶׁר אָמַר יְהוָֹה

יז לְמֹשֶׁה אֱסֹף אֶת־הָעָם וְאֶתְּנָה לָהֶם מָיִם: אָז יָשִׁיר יִשְׂרָאֵל

יח אֶת־הַשִּׁירָה הַזֹּאת עֲלִי בְאֵר עֱנוּ־לָהּ: בְּאֵר חֲפָרוּהָ שָׂרִים כָּרוּהָ נְדִיבֵי

יט הָעָם בִּמְחֹקֵק בְּמִשְׁעֲנֹתָם וּמִמִּדְבָּר מַתָּנָה: וּמִמַּתָּנָה נַחֲלִיאֵל וּמִנַּחֲלִיאֵל

כ בָּמוֹת: וּמִבָּמוֹת הַגַּיְא אֲשֶׁר בִּשְׂדֵה מוֹאָב רֹאשׁ הַפִּסְגָּה וְנִשְׁקָפָה עַל־פְּנֵי

הַיְשִׁימֹן:

שביעי כא:כב [רביעי]

כא-כב וַיִּשְׁלַח יִשְׂרָאֵל מַלְאָכִים אֶל־סִיחֹן מֶלֶךְ־הָאֱמֹרִי לֵאמֹר: אֶעְבְּרָה

בְאַרְצֶךָ לֹא נִטֶּה בְּשָׂדֶה וּבְכֶרֶם לֹא נִשְׁתֶּה מֵי בְאֵר בְּדֶרֶךְ הַמֶּלֶךְ

כג נֵלֵךְ עַד אֲשֶׁר־נַעֲבֹר גְּבֻלֶךָ: וְלֹא־נָתַן סִיחֹן אֶת־יִשְׂרָאֵל עֲבֹר בִּגְבֻלוֹ

וַיֶּאֱסֹף סִיחֹן אֶת־כָּל־עַמּוֹ וַיֵּצֵא לִקְרַאת יִשְׂרָאֵל הַמִּדְבָּרָה וַיָּבֹא

כד יָהְצָה וַיִּלָּחֶם בְּיִשְׂרָאֵל: וַיַּכֵּהוּ יִשְׂרָאֵל לְפִי־חָרֶב וַיִּירַשׁ אֶת־אַרְצוֹ

כה מֵאַרְנֹן עַד־יַבֹּק עַד־בְּנֵי עַמּוֹן כִּי עַז גְּבוּל בְּנֵי עַמּוֹן: וַיִּקַּח יִשְׂרָאֵל אֵת

כָּל־הֶעָרִים הָאֵלֶּה וַיֵּשֶׁב יִשְׂרָאֵל בְּכָל־עָרֵי הָאֱמֹרִי בְּחֶשְׁבּוֹן וּבְכָל־

כו בְּנֹתֶיהָ: כִּי חֶשְׁבּוֹן עִיר סִיחֹן מֶלֶךְ הָאֱמֹרִי הִוא וְהוּא נִלְחַם בְּמֶלֶךְ

כז מוֹאָב הָרִאשׁוֹן וַיִּקַּח אֶת־כָּל־אַרְצוֹ מִיָּדוֹ עַד־אַרְנֹן: עַל־כֵּן יֹאמְרוּ

הַמֹּשְׁלִים בֹּאוּ חֶשְׁבּוֹן תִּבָּנֶה וְתִכּוֹנֵן עִיר סִיחוֹן: כִּי־אֵשׁ יָצְאָה מֵחֶשְׁבּוֹן

כח-כט לֶהָבָה מִקִּרְיַת סִיחֹן אָכְלָה עָר מוֹאָב בַּעֲלֵי בָּמוֹת אַרְנֹן: אוֹי־לְךָ מוֹאָב

אָבַדְתָּ עַם־כְּמוֹשׁ נָתַן בָּנָיו פְּלֵיטִם וּבְנֹתָיו בַּשְּׁבִית לְמֶלֶךְ אֱמֹרִי סִיחוֹן:

*נקֻד על ר'

ל וַנִּירָם אָבַד חֶשְׁבּוֹן עַד־דִּיבֹן וַנַּשִּׁים עַד־נֹפַח *אֲשֶׁר עַד־מֵידְבָא:

לא-לב וַיֵּשֶׁב יִשְׂרָאֵל בְּאֶרֶץ הָאֱמֹרִי: וַיִּשְׁלַח מֹשֶׁה לְרַגֵּל אֶת־יַעְזֵר וַיִּלְכְּדוּ

לג בְּנֹתֶיהָ [וַיִּירֶשׁ °וַיּוֹרֶשׁ ק] אֶת־הָאֱמֹרִי אֲשֶׁר־שָׁם: וַיִּפְנוּ וַיַּעֲלוּ דֶּרֶךְ

הַבָּשָׁן וַיֵּצֵא עוֹג מֶלֶךְ־הַבָּשָׁן לִקְרָאתָם הוּא וְכָל־עַמּוֹ לַמִּלְחָמָה

מפטיר

לד אֶדְרֶעִי: וַיֹּאמֶר יְהוָֹה אֶל־מֹשֶׁה אַל־תִּירָא אֹתוֹ כִּי בְיָדְךָ נָתַתִּי אֹתוֹ

Haftaras Chukas: p. 612

וְאֶת־כָּל־עַמּוֹ וְאֶת־אַרְצוֹ וְעָשִׂיתָ לּוֹ כַּאֲשֶׁר עָשִׂיתָ לְסִיחֹן מֶלֶךְ הָאֱמֹרִי

לה אֲשֶׁר יוֹשֵׁב בְּחֶשְׁבּוֹן: וַיַּכּוּ אֹתוֹ וְאֶת־בָּנָיו וְאֶת־כָּל־עַמּוֹ עַד־בִּלְתִּי

א הִשְׁאִיר־לוֹ שָׂרִיד וַיִּירְשׁוּ אֶת־אַרְצוֹ: וַיִּסְעוּ בְּנֵי יִשְׂרָאֵל וַיַּחֲנוּ בְּעַרְבוֹת

כב

For special Sabbaths, see pp. x-xi

מוֹאָב מֵעֵבֶר לְיַרְדֵּן יְרֵחוֹ: סס פ"ז פסוקים. למדב"א סימן. ימוא"ל סימן. עז"י סימן.

21:14. The wars of that era were recorded in the book of this name (*Ramban*). That book is no longer extant (*Ibn Ezra*).

21:18. The well was *a gift* to the people *from the Wilderness* where there was no natural source of water, thus accentuating the greatness of the miracle.

21:29. *Woe to you, O Moab*, was the curse that led to Moab's defeat. Chemosh was the Moabite deity (*Rashi*).

21:33. Og was the last survivor of the huge giants of the generation of the Flood (see *Deuteronomy* 3:11), a man whose very appearance inspired terror.

on the other side of Arnon — which is in the wilderness — that juts out from the border of the Amorite; for Arnon is the border of Moab, between Moab and the Amorite. ¹⁴ Therefore it is said in the Book of the Wars of HASHEM: *

The song in the Book of the Wars of HASHEM

The gift of [the Sea of] Reeds and the rivers of Arnon;
¹⁵ the outpouring of the rivers when it veered to dwell at Ar,
and leaned against the border of Moab.

¹⁶ And from there to the well — it is the well of which HASHEM said to Moses, "Assemble the people and I shall give them water."

¹⁷ Then Israel sang this song:

Come up, O well! Call out to it!
¹⁸ Well that the princes dug, that the nobles of the people excavated,
through a lawgiver, with their staffs. A gift from the Wilderness — *
¹⁹ the gift went to the valley, and from the valley to the heights,
²⁰ and from the heights to the valley in the field of Moab,
at the top of the peak, overlooking the surface of the wilderness.

The battle with Sihon (See Appendix D, map 1)

²¹ Israel sent emissaries to Sihon, king of the Amorite, saying, ²² "Let me pass through your land; we shall not turn off to field or vineyard; we shall not drink well water; on the king's road shall we travel, until we pass through your border."

²³ But Sihon did not permit Israel to pass through his border, and Sihon assembled his entire people and went out against Israel to the Wilderness. He arrived at Jahaz and waged war against Israel. ²⁴ Israel smote him with the edge of the sword and took possession of his land, from Arnon to Jabbok to the children of Ammon — for the border of the children of Ammon was powerful. ²⁵ Israel took all these cities, and Israel settled in all the Amorite cities, in Heshbon and all its suburbs. ²⁶ For Heshbon — it was the city of Sihon, king of the Amorite; and he had warred against the first king of Moab and took all his land from his control, until Arnon. ²⁷ Regarding this the poets would say:

Come to Heshbon — let it be built and established as the city of Sihon.
²⁸ For a fire has come forth from Heshbon, a flame from the city of Sihon.
It consumed Ar of Moab, the masters of Arnon's heights.
²⁹ Woe to you, O Moab, * you are lost, O people of Chemosh!
He made his sons fugitives and his daughters captives
of the king of the Amorite, Sihon.
³⁰ Their sovereignty over Heshbon was lost, it was removed from Dibon,
and we laid waste to Nophah, which reaches up to Medeba.

³¹ Israel settled in the land of the Amorite. ³² Moses sent to spy out Jazer and they conquered its suburbs; and he drove away the Amorite that was there.

Og does battle

³³ They turned and ascended by way of Bashan; Og, * king of Bashan, went out against them, he and his entire people, to do battle at Edrei. ³⁴ HASHEM said to Moses, "Do not fear him, for into your hand have I given him, his entire people, and his land; you shall do to him as you did to Sihon, king of the Amorite, who dwells in Heshbon." ³⁵ They smote him, his sons, and all his people, until there was no survivor left of him, and they took possession of his land.

22 ¹ The Children of Israel journeyed and encamped in the plains of Moab, on the bank of the Jordan, opposite Jericho.

פרשת בלק

ב-ג וַיַּ֧רְא בָּלָ֛ק בֶּן־צִפּ֖וֹר אֵ֣ת כָּל־אֲשֶׁר־עָשָׂ֥ה יִשְׂרָאֵ֖ל לָאֱמֹרִֽי: וַיָּ֨גָר מוֹאָ֜ב

ד מִפְּנֵ֤י הָעָם֙ מְאֹ֔ד כִּ֥י רַב־ה֑וּא וַיָּ֣קָץ מוֹאָ֔ב מִפְּנֵ֖י בְּנֵ֥י יִשְׂרָאֵֽל: וַיֹּ֨אמֶר מוֹאָ֜ב

אֶל־זִקְנֵ֣י מִדְיָ֗ן עַתָּ֞ה יְלַחֲכ֤וּ הַקָּהָל֙ אֶת־כָּל־סְבִ֣יבֹתֵ֔ינוּ כִּלְחֹ֣ךְ הַשּׁ֔וֹר אֵ֖ת

ה יֶ֣רֶק הַשָּׂדֶ֑ה וּבָלָ֧ק בֶּן־צִפּ֛וֹר מֶ֖לֶךְ לְמוֹאָ֑ב בָּעֵ֖ת הַהִֽוא: וַיִּשְׁלַ֨ח מַלְאָכִ֜ים

אֶל־בִּלְעָ֣ם בֶּן־בְּע֗וֹר פְּת֠וֹרָה אֲשֶׁ֧ר עַל־הַנָּהָ֛ר אֶ֥רֶץ בְּנֵי־עַמּ֖וֹ לִקְרֹא־ל֑וֹ

לֵאמֹ֗ר הִ֠נֵּה עַ֣ם יָצָ֤א מִמִּצְרַ֨יִם֙ הִנֵּ֤ה כִסָּה֙ אֶת־עֵ֣ין הָאָ֔רֶץ וְה֥וּא יֹשֵׁ֖ב מִמֻּלִֽי:

ו וְעַתָּה֩ לְכָה־נָּ֨א אָֽרָה־לִּ֜י אֶת־הָעָ֣ם הַזֶּ֗ה כִּֽי־עָצ֥וּם הוּא֙ מִמֶּ֔נִּי אוּלַ֤י אוּכַל֙

נַכֶּה־בּ֔וֹ וַאֲגָרְשֶׁ֖נּוּ מִן־הָאָ֑רֶץ כִּ֣י יָדַ֗עְתִּי אֵ֤ת אֲשֶׁר־תְּבָרֵךְ֙ מְבֹרָ֔ךְ וַאֲשֶׁ֥ר

ז תָּאֹ֖ר יוּאָֽר: וַיֵּ֨לְכ֜וּ זִקְנֵ֤י מוֹאָב֙ וְזִקְנֵ֣י מִדְיָ֔ן וּקְסָמִ֖ים בְּיָדָ֑ם וַיָּבֹ֨אוּ֙ אֶל־בִּלְעָ֔ם

ח וַיְדַבְּר֥וּ אֵלָ֖יו דִּבְרֵ֥י בָלָֽק: וַיֹּ֣אמֶר אֲלֵיהֶ֗ם לִ֤ינוּ פֹה֙ הַלַּ֔יְלָה וַהֲשִׁבֹתִ֤י אֶתְכֶם֙

ט דָּבָ֔ר כַּאֲשֶׁ֛ר יְדַבֵּ֥ר יְהֹוָ֖ה אֵלָ֑י וַיֵּשְׁב֥וּ שָׂרֵֽי־מוֹאָ֖ב עִם־בִּלְעָֽם: וַיָּבֹ֥א אֱלֹהִ֖ים

י אֶל־בִּלְעָ֑ם וַיֹּ֕אמֶר מִ֛י הָאֲנָשִׁ֥ים הָאֵ֖לֶּה עִמָּֽךְ: וַיֹּ֥אמֶר בִּלְעָ֖ם אֶל־הָאֱלֹהִ֑ים

יא בָּלָ֧ק בֶּן־צִפֹּ֛ר מֶ֥לֶךְ מוֹאָ֖ב שָׁלַ֥ח אֵלָֽי: הִנֵּ֤ה הָעָם֙ הַיֹּצֵ֣א מִמִּצְרַ֔יִם וַיְכַ֖ס אֶת־

עֵ֣ין הָאָ֑רֶץ עַתָּ֗ה לְכָ֤ה קָֽבָה־לִּי֙ אֹת֔וֹ אוּלַ֥י אוּכַ֛ל לְהִלָּ֥חֶם בּ֖וֹ וְגֵרַשְׁתִּֽיו:

יב וַיֹּ֤אמֶר אֱלֹהִים֙ אֶל־בִּלְעָ֔ם לֹ֥א תֵלֵ֖ךְ עִמָּהֶ֑ם לֹ֤א תָאֹר֙ אֶת־הָעָ֔ם כִּ֥י בָר֖וּךְ

יג ה֥וּא: וַיָּ֤קָם בִּלְעָם֙ בַּבֹּ֔קֶר וַיֹּ֨אמֶר֙ אֶל־שָׂרֵ֣י בָלָ֔ק לְכ֖וּ אֶל־אַרְצְכֶ֑ם כִּ֚י מֵאֵ֣ן   שני [חמישי]

יד יְהֹוָ֔ה לְתִתִּ֖י לַהֲלֹ֥ךְ עִמָּכֶֽם: וַיָּק֨וּמוּ֙ שָׂרֵ֣י מוֹאָ֔ב וַיָּבֹ֖אוּ אֶל־בָּלָ֑ק וַיֹּ֣אמְר֔וּ מֵאֵ֥ן

טו בִּלְעָ֖ם הֲלֹ֥ךְ עִמָּֽנוּ: וַיֹּ֥סֶף ע֖וֹד בָּלָ֑ק שְׁלֹ֣חַ שָׂרִ֔ים רַבִּ֥ים וְנִכְבָּדִ֖ים מֵאֵֽלֶּה:

טז וַיָּבֹ֖אוּ אֶל־בִּלְעָ֑ם וַיֹּ֣אמְרוּ ל֗וֹ כֹּ֤ה אָמַר֙ בָּלָ֣ק בֶּן־צִפּ֔וֹר אַל־נָ֥א תִמָּנַ֖ע

יז מֵהֲלֹ֣ךְ אֵלָֽי: כִּֽי־כַבֵּ֤ד אֲכַבֶּדְךָ֙ מְאֹ֔ד וְכֹ֛ל אֲשֶׁר־תֹּאמַ֥ר אֵלַ֖י אֶֽעֱשֶׂ֑ה וּלְכָה־

יח נָּא֙ קָֽבָה־לִּ֔י אֵ֖ת הָעָ֥ם הַזֶּֽה: וַיַּ֣עַן בִּלְעָ֗ם וַיֹּ֨אמֶר֙ אֶל־עַבְדֵ֣י בָלָ֔ק אִם־יִתֶּן־לִ֤י

בָלָק֙ מְלֹ֣א בֵית֔וֹ כֶּ֖סֶף וְזָהָ֑ב לֹ֣א אוּכַ֗ל לַעֲבֹר֙ אֶת־פִּי֙ יְהֹוָ֣ה אֱלֹהָ֔י לַעֲשׂ֥וֹת   *קמץ בד"ק
באות ה

יט קְטַנָּ֖ה א֥וֹ גְדוֹלָֽה: וְעַתָּ֗ה שְׁב֨וּ נָ֥א בָזֶ֛ה גַּם־אַתֶּ֖ם הַלָּ֑יְלָה וְאֵ֣דְעָ֔ה מַה־יֹּסֵ֥ף

כ יְהֹוָ֖ה דַּבֵּ֥ר עִמִּֽי: וַיָּבֹ֨א אֱלֹהִ֥ים ׀ אֶל־בִּלְעָם֮ לַיְלָה֒ וַיֹּ֣אמֶר ל֗וֹ אִם־לִקְרֹ֤א לְךָ֙

בָּ֣אוּ הָאֲנָשִׁ֔ים ק֖וּם לֵ֣ךְ אִתָּ֑ם וְאַ֗ךְ אֶת־הַדָּבָ֛ר אֲשֶׁר־אֲדַבֵּ֥ר אֵלֶ֖יךָ אֹת֥וֹ

כא תַעֲשֶֽׂה: וַיָּ֤קָם בִּלְעָם֙ בַּבֹּ֔קֶר וַיַּחֲבֹ֖שׁ אֶת־אֲתֹנ֑וֹ וַיֵּ֖לֶךְ עִם־שָׂרֵ֥י מוֹאָֽב: שלישי

כב וַיִּֽחַר־אַ֣ף אֱלֹהִים֮ כִּֽי־הוֹלֵ֣ךְ הוּא֒ וַיִּתְיַצֵּ֞ב מַלְאַ֧ךְ יְהֹוָ֛ה בַּדֶּ֖רֶךְ לְשָׂטָ֣ן ל֑וֹ

כג וְהוּא֙ רֹכֵ֣ב עַל־אֲתֹנ֔וֹ וּשְׁנֵ֥י נְעָרָ֖יו עִמּֽוֹ: וַתֵּ֣רֶא הָאָתוֹן֩ אֶת־מַלְאַ֨ךְ יְהֹוָ֜ה

נִצָּ֣ב בַּדֶּ֗רֶךְ וְחַרְבּ֤וֹ שְׁלוּפָה֙ בְּיָד֔וֹ וַתֵּ֤ט הָֽאָתוֹן֙ מִן־הַדֶּ֔רֶךְ וַתֵּ֖לֶךְ בַּשָּׂדֶ֑ה

כד וַיַּ֤ךְ בִּלְעָם֙ אֶת־הָ֣אָת֔וֹן לְהַטֹּתָ֖הּ הַדָּֽרֶךְ: וַיַּֽעֲמֹד֙ מַלְאַ֣ךְ יְהֹוָ֔ה בְּמִשְׁע֖וֹל

◆§ Parashas Balak

22:5. God ordained that the gentile nations should have a prophet, so that they would not be able to contend that if only they had had someone who could communicate to them the will of God, they would have been as righteous as Israel (see *Ramban* cited in notes to *Deuteronomy* 34:10). Balaam was that prophet.

22:20. God gave the greedy Balaam permission to go if he felt that it was to his financial advantage to do so. However, he could say only what God instructed him.

PARASHAS BALAK

² **B**alak son of Zippor saw all that Israel had done to the Amorite. ³ *Moab became very frightened of the people, because it was numerous, and Moab was disgusted in the face of the Children of Israel.* ⁴ *Moab said to the elders of Midian, "Now the congregation will lick up our entire surroundings, as an ox licks up the greenery of the field." Balak son of Zippor was king of Moab at that time.*

Balaam, prophet of the nations ⁵ *He sent messengers to Balaam* son of Beor to Pethor, which is by the River, the land of the members of his people, to summon him, saying, "Behold! a people has come out of Egypt, behold! it has covered the surface of the earth and it sits opposite me.* ⁶ *So now — please come and curse this people for me, for it is too powerful for me; perhaps I will be able to strike it and drive it away from the land. For I know that whomever you bless is blessed and whomever you curse is accursed."*

⁷ *The elders of Moab and the elders of Midian went with charms in their hand; they came to Balaam and spoke to him the words of Balak.* ⁸ *He said to them, "Spend the night here and I shall give you a response, as HASHEM shall speak to me." So the officers of Moab stayed with Balaam.*

⁹ *God came to Balaam and said, "Who are these men with you?"* ¹⁰ *Balaam said to God, "Balak son of Zippor, king of Moab, sent to me:* ¹¹ *'Behold! the people coming out of Egypt has covered the surface of the earth. Now go and curse it for me; perhaps I will be able to make war against it and drive it away.'"* ¹² *God said to Balaam, "You shall not go with them! You shall not curse the people, for it is blessed!"*

¹³ *Balaam arose in the morning and said to the officers of Balak, "Go to your land, for HASHEM refuses to let me go with you."* ¹⁴ *The officers of Moab arose and came to Balak and said, "Balaam refused to go with us."*

¹⁵ *Balak kept on sending officers — more, and higher ranking than these.* ¹⁶ *They came to Balaam and said to him, "So said Balak son of Zippor, 'Do not refrain from going to me,* ¹⁷ *for I shall honor you greatly, and everything that you say to me I shall do; so go now and curse this people for me.'"* ¹⁸ *Balaam answered and said to the servants of Balak, "If Balak will give me his houseful of silver and gold, I cannot transgress the word of HASHEM, my God, to do anything small or great.* ¹⁹ *And now, you, too, stay here for the night, and I will know what more HASHEM will speak with me."*

God's ambiguous permission ²⁰ *God came to Balaam at night and said to him, "If the men came to summon you, arise and go with them, but only the thing that I shall speak to you — that shall you do."**

²¹ *Balaam arose in the morning and saddled his she-donkey* and went with the officers of Moab.* ²² *God's wrath flared because he was going, and an angel of HASHEM stood on the road to impede him. He was riding on his she-donkey and his two young men were with him.* ²³ *The she-donkey saw the angel of HASHEM*

God impedes Balaam's path *standing on the road with his sword drawn in his hand, so the she-donkey turned away from the road and went into the field; then Balaam struck the she-donkey to turn it back onto the road.* ²⁴ *The angel of HASHEM stood in the path of*

22:21. Surely it was not fitting for a man of Balaam's stature to saddle his own donkey, but he hated Israel so much that he did not let dignity stand in his way (*Rashi*).

כה הַכְּרָמִים גָּדֵר מִזֶּה וְגָדֵר מִזֶּה: וַתֵּרֶא הָאָתוֹן אֶת־מַלְאַךְ יהוה וַתִּלָּחֵץ

כו אֶל־הַקִּיר וַתִּלְחַץ אֶת־רֶגֶל בִּלְעָם אֶל־הַקִּיר וַיֹּסֶף לְהַכֹּתָהּ: וַיּוֹסֶף

מַלְאַךְ־יהוה עֲבוֹר וַיַּעֲמֹד בְּמָקוֹם צָר אֲשֶׁר אֵין־דֶּרֶךְ לִנְטוֹת יָמִין

כז וּשְׂמֹאול*: וַתֵּרֶא הָאָתוֹן אֶת־מַלְאַךְ יהוה וַתִּרְבַּץ תַּחַת בִּלְעָם וַיִּחַר־אַף

כח בִּלְעָם וַיַּךְ אֶת־הָאָתוֹן בַּמַּקֵּל: וַיִּפְתַּח יהוה אֶת־פִּי הָאָתוֹן וַתֹּאמֶר

כט לְבִלְעָם מֶה־עָשִׂיתִי לְךָ כִּי הִכִּיתַנִי זֶה שָׁלֹשׁ רְגָלִים: וַיֹּאמֶר בִּלְעָם

ל לָאָתוֹן כִּי הִתְעַלַּלְתְּ בִּי לוּ יֶשׁ־חֶרֶב בְּיָדִי כִּי עַתָּה הֲרַגְתִּיךְ: וַתֹּאמֶר

הָאָתוֹן אֶל־בִּלְעָם הֲלוֹא אָנֹכִי אֲתֹנְךָ אֲשֶׁר־רָכַבְתָּ עָלַי מֵעוֹדְךָ עַד־הַיּוֹם

לא הַזֶּה הַהַסְכֵּן הִסְכַּנְתִּי לַעֲשׂוֹת לְךָ כֹּה וַיֹּאמֶר לֹא: וַיְגַל יהוה אֶת־עֵינֵי

בִלְעָם וַיַּרְא אֶת־מַלְאַךְ יהוה נִצָּב בַּדֶּרֶךְ וְחַרְבּוֹ שְׁלֻפָה בְּיָדוֹ וַיִּקֹּד

לב וַיִּשְׁתַּחוּ לְאַפָּיו: וַיֹּאמֶר אֵלָיו מַלְאַךְ יהוה עַל־מָה הִכִּיתָ אֶת־אֲתֹנְךָ זֶה

לג שָׁלוֹשׁ רְגָלִים הִנֵּה אָנֹכִי יָצָאתִי לְשָׂטָן כִּי־יָרַט הַדֶּרֶךְ לְנֶגְדִּי: וַתִּרְאַנִי

הָאָתוֹן וַתֵּט לְפָנַי זֶה שָׁלֹשׁ רְגָלִים אוּלַי נָטְתָה מִפָּנַי כִּי עַתָּה גַּם־אֹתְכָה

לד הָרַגְתִּי וְאוֹתָהּ הֶחֱיֵיתִי: וַיֹּאמֶר בִּלְעָם אֶל־מַלְאַךְ יהוה חָטָאתִי כִּי לֹא

יָדַעְתִּי כִּי אַתָּה נִצָּב לִקְרָאתִי בַּדָּרֶךְ וְעַתָּה אִם־רַע בְּעֵינֶיךָ אָשׁוּבָה לִּי:

לה וַיֹּאמֶר מַלְאַךְ יהוה אֶל־בִּלְעָם לֵךְ עִם־הָאֲנָשִׁים וְאֶפֶס אֶת־הַדָּבָר

אֲשֶׁר־אֲדַבֵּר אֵלֶיךָ אֹתוֹ תְדַבֵּר וַיֵּלֶךְ בִּלְעָם עִם־שָׂרֵי בָלָק: וַיִּשְׁמַע

לו בָּלָק כִּי בָא בִלְעָם וַיֵּצֵא לִקְרָאתוֹ אֶל־עִיר מוֹאָב אֲשֶׁר עַל־גְּבוּל אַרְנֹן

לז אֲשֶׁר בִּקְצֵה הַגְּבוּל: וַיֹּאמֶר בָּלָק אֶל־בִּלְעָם הֲלֹא שָׁלֹחַ שָׁלַחְתִּי אֵלֶיךָ

לח לִקְרֹא־לָךְ לָמָּה לֹא־הָלַכְתָּ אֵלָי הַאֻמְנָם לֹא אוּכַל כַּבְּדֶךָ: וַיֹּאמֶר בִּלְעָם

אֶל־בָּלָק הִנֵּה־בָאתִי אֵלֶיךָ עַתָּה הֲיָכֹל אוּכַל דַּבֵּר מְאוּמָה הַדָּבָר

לט אֲשֶׁר יָשִׂים אֱלֹהִים בְּפִי אֹתוֹ אֲדַבֵּר: וַיֵּלֶךְ בִּלְעָם עִם־בָּלָק וַיָּבֹאוּ

מ קִרְיַת חֻצוֹת: וַיִּזְבַּח בָּלָק בָּקָר וָצֹאן וַיְשַׁלַּח לְבִלְעָם וְלַשָּׂרִים אֲשֶׁר אִתּוֹ:

מא וַיְהִי בַבֹּקֶר וַיִּקַּח בָּלָק אֶת־בִּלְעָם וַיַּעֲלֵהוּ בָּמוֹת בָּעַל וַיַּרְא מִשָּׁם קְצֵה

כג א הָעָם: וַיֹּאמֶר בִּלְעָם אֶל־בָּלָק בְּנֵה־לִי בָזֶה שִׁבְעָה מִזְבְּחֹת וְהָכֵן לִי

ב בָּזֶה שִׁבְעָה פָרִים וְשִׁבְעָה אֵילִים: וַיַּעַשׂ בָּלָק כַּאֲשֶׁר דִּבֶּר בִּלְעָם

ג וַיַּעַל בָּלָק וּבִלְעָם פָּר וָאַיִל בַּמִּזְבֵּחַ: וַיֹּאמֶר בִּלְעָם לְבָלָק הִתְיַצֵּב עַל־

עֹלָתֶךָ וְאֵלְכָה אוּלַי יִקָּרֵה יהוה לִקְרָאתִי וּדְבַר מַה־יַּרְאֵנִי וְהִגַּדְתִּי

ד לָךְ וַיֵּלֶךְ שֶׁפִי: וַיִּקָּר אֱלֹהִים אֶל־בִּלְעָם וַיֹּאמֶר אֵלָיו אֶת־שִׁבְעַת

ה הַמִּזְבְּחֹת עָרַכְתִּי וָאַעַל פָּר וָאַיִל בַּמִּזְבֵּחַ: וַיָּשֶׂם יהוה דָּבָר בְּפִי בִלְעָם

ו וַיֹּאמֶר שׁוּב אֶל־בָּלָק וְכֹה תְדַבֵּר: וַיָּשָׁב אֵלָיו וְהִנֵּה נִצָּב עַל־עֹלָתוֹ הוּא

*יתיר ו

רביעי
[ששי]

22:28. The purpose of the miracle was to show Balaam that if a beast could speak intelligently, then surely Balaam could be forced to say what God wanted him to (*Ramban*).

22:37. Balak was convinced that Balaam was his only hope, yet he accused him, in effect, of being interested only in personal honor. And he did not even invite Balaam to dine with him.

the vineyards, a fence on this side and a fence on that side. ²⁵ The she-donkey saw the angel of HASHEM and pressed against the wall, and it pressed Balaam's leg against the wall — and he continued to strike it. ²⁶ The angel of HASHEM went further and stood in a narrow place, where there was no room to turn right or left. ²⁷ The she-donkey saw the angel of HASHEM and crouched beneath Balaam. Balaam's anger flared and he struck the she-donkey with the staff.

Balaam's she-donkey speaks

²⁸ HASHEM opened the mouth of the she-donkey* and it said to Balaam, "What have I done to you that you struck me these three times?"

²⁹ Balaam said to the she-donkey, "Because you mocked me! If only there were a sword in my hand I would now have killed you!"

³⁰ The she-donkey said to Balaam, "Am I not your she-donkey that you have ridden upon me all your life until this day? Have I been accustomed to do such a thing to you?"

He said, "No."

Balaam sees the angel

³¹ Then HASHEM uncovered Balaam's eyes and he saw the angel of HASHEM standing on the road with his sword drawn in his hand. He bowed his head and prostrated himself on his face.

³² The angel of HASHEM said to him, "For what reason did you strike your she-donkey these three times? Behold! I went out to impede, for you hastened on a road to oppose me. ³³ The she-donkey saw me and turned away from me these three times. Had it not turned away from me, I would now even have killed you and let it live!"

³⁴ Balaam said to the angel of HASHEM, " I have sinned, for I did not know that you were standing opposite me on the road. And now, if it is evil in your eyes, I shall return."

³⁵ The angel of HASHEM said to Balaam, "Go with the men, but only the word that I shall speak to you — that shall you speak." So Balaam went with the officers of Balak.

Balak's rebuke

³⁶ Balak heard that Balaam had come, so he went out toward him to the city of Moab, which is on the border of Arnon, which is at the edge of the border. ³⁷ Balak said to Balaam, "Did I not urgently send to you to summon you? Why did you not go to me? Am I not capable of honoring you?"*

³⁸ Balaam said to Balak, "Behold! now I have come to you — am I empowered to say anything? Whatever word God puts into my mouth, that shall I speak!"

³⁹ Balaam went with Balak and they came to Kiriath-huzoth. ⁴⁰ Balak slaughtered cattle and sheep and sent to Balaam and to the officers who were with him. ⁴¹ And it was in the morning: Balak took Balaam and brought him up to the heights of Baal, and from there he saw the edge of the people.

23

Balaam's altar offerings

¹ Balaam said to Balak, "Build for me here seven altars and prepare for me here seven bulls and seven rams."

² Balak did as Balaam had spoken, and Balak and Balaam brought up a bull and a ram on each altar. ³ Balaam said to Balak, "Stand by your burnt-offering while I go; perhaps HASHEM will happen toward me and show me something that I can tell you." He went alone.

⁴ God happened upon Balaam and he said to Him, "I have prepared the seven altars and brought up a bull and ram on each altar."

⁵ HASHEM put an utterance in Balaam's mouth, and said, "Go back to Balak, and thus shall you say."

⁶ He returned to him and behold! he was standing by his burnt-offering, he and

וְכָל־שָׂרֵי מוֹאָב: וַיִּשָּׂא מְשָׁלוֹ וַיֹּאמַר מִן־אֲרָם יַנְחֵנִי בָלָק מֶלֶךְ־ ז

מוֹאָב מֵהַרְרֵי־קֶדֶם לְכָה אָרָה־לִּי יַעֲקֹב וּלְכָה זֹעֲמָה יִשְׂרָאֵל: מָה אֶקֹּב ח

לֹא קַבֹּה אֵל וּמָה אֶזְעֹם לֹא זָעַם יהוה: כִּי־מֵרֹאשׁ צֻרִים אֶרְאֶנּוּ ט

וּמִגְּבָעוֹת אֲשׁוּרֶנּוּ הֶן־עָם לְבָדָד יִשְׁכֹּן וּבַגּוֹיִם לֹא יִתְחַשָּׁב: מִי מָנָה י

עֲפַר יַעֲקֹב וּמִסְפָּר אֶת־רֹבַע יִשְׂרָאֵל תָּמֹת נַפְשִׁי מוֹת יְשָׁרִים וּתְהִי

אַחֲרִיתִי כָּמֹהוּ: וַיֹּאמֶר בָּלָק אֶל־בִּלְעָם מֶה עָשִׂיתָ לִי לָקֹב אֹיְבַי יא

לְקַחְתִּיךָ וְהִנֵּה בֵּרַכְתָּ בָרֵךְ: וַיַּעַן וַיֹּאמַר הֲלֹא אֵת אֲשֶׁר יָשִׂים יהוה בְּפִי יב

אֹתוֹ אֶשְׁמֹר לְדַבֵּר: וַיֹּאמֶר אֵלָיו בָּלָק לך־נָא אִתִּי אֶל־מָקוֹם אַחֵר יג

אֲשֶׁר תִּרְאֶנּוּ מִשָּׁם אֶפֶס קָצֵהוּ תִרְאֶה וְכֻלּוֹ לֹא תִרְאֶה וְקָבְנוֹ־לִי מִשָּׁם:

וַיִּקָּחֵהוּ שְׂדֵה צֹפִים אֶל־רֹאשׁ הַפִּסְגָּה וַיִּבֶן שִׁבְעָה מִזְבְּחֹת וַיַּעַל פָּר יד

וָאַיִל בַּמִּזְבֵּחַ: וַיֹּאמֶר אֶל־בָּלָק הִתְיַצֵּב כֹּה עַל־עֹלָתֶךָ וְאָנֹכִי אִקָּרֶה טו

כֹּה: וַיִּקָּר יהוה אֶל־בִּלְעָם וַיָּשֶׂם דָּבָר בְּפִיו וַיֹּאמֶר שׁוּב אֶל־בָּלָק טז

וְכֹה תְדַבֵּר: וַיָּבֹא אֵלָיו וְהִנּוֹ נִצָּב עַל־עֹלָתוֹ וְשָׂרֵי מוֹאָב אִתּוֹ וַיֹּאמֶר לוֹ יז

בָּלָק מַה־דִּבֶּר יהוה: וַיִּשָּׂא מְשָׁלוֹ וַיֹּאמַר קוּם בָּלָק וּשֲׁמָע הַאֲזִינָה יח

עָדַי בְּנוֹ צִפֹּר: לֹא אִישׁ אֵל וִיכַזֵּב וּבֶן־אָדָם וְיִתְנֶחָם הַהוּא אָמַר וְלֹא יט

יַעֲשֶׂה וְדִבֶּר וְלֹא יְקִימֶנָּה: הִנֵּה בָרֵךְ לָקָחְתִּי וּבֵרֵךְ וְלֹא אֲשִׁיבֶנָּה: לֹא־ כ-כא

הִבִּיט אָוֶן בְּיַעֲקֹב וְלֹא־רָאָה עָמָל בְּיִשְׂרָאֵל יהוה אֱלֹהָיו עִמּוֹ וּתְרוּעַת

מֶלֶךְ בּוֹ: אֵל מוֹצִיאָם מִמִּצְרָיִם כְּתוֹעֲפֹת רְאֵם לוֹ: כִּי לֹא־נַחַשׁ בְּיַעֲקֹב כב-כג

וְלֹא־קֶסֶם בְּיִשְׂרָאֵל כָּעֵת יֵאָמֵר לְיַעֲקֹב וּלְיִשְׂרָאֵל מַה־פָּעַל אֵל: הֶן־ כד

עָם כְּלָבִיא יָקוּם וְכַאֲרִי יִתְנַשָּׂא לֹא יִשְׁכַּב עַד־יֹאכַל טֶרֶף וְדַם־חֲלָלִים

יִשְׁתֶּה: וַיֹּאמֶר בָּלָק אֶל־בִּלְעָם גַּם־קֹב לֹא תִקֳּבֶנּוּ גַּם־בָּרֵךְ לֹא כה

תְבָרֲכֶנּוּ: וַיַּעַן בִּלְעָם וַיֹּאמֶר אֶל־בָּלָק הֲלֹא דִּבַּרְתִּי אֵלֶיךָ לֵאמֹר כו

כֹּל אֲשֶׁר־יְדַבֵּר יהוה אֹתוֹ אֶעֱשֶׂה: וַיֹּאמֶר בָּלָק אֶל־בִּלְעָם לְכָה־נָּא כז

אֶקָּחֲךָ אֶל־מָקוֹם אַחֵר אוּלַי יִישַׁר בְּעֵינֵי הָאֱלֹהִים וְקַבֹּתוֹ לִי מִשָּׁם: וַיִּקַּח כח-כט

בָּלָק אֶת־בִּלְעָם רֹאשׁ הַפְּעוֹר הַנִּשְׁקָף עַל־פְּנֵי הַיְשִׁימֹן: וַיֹּאמֶר

בִּלְעָם אֶל־בָּלָק בְּנֵה־לִי בָזֶה שִׁבְעָה מִזְבְּחֹת וְהָכֵן לִי בָּזֶה שִׁבְעָה פָרִים

וְשִׁבְעָה אֵילִם: וַיַּעַשׂ בָּלָק כַּאֲשֶׁר אָמַר בִּלְעָם וַיַּעַל פָּר וָאַיִל בַּמִּזְבֵּחַ: ל

23:7. In spite of his exertions and against his hopes, Balaam was forced to pronounce blessings upon Israel.

23:18. Balaam responded to Balak's sarcasm by saying that, indeed, he had received a message from God, and that it behooved Balak to stand erect out of respect.

23:23. God redeemed Israel from Egypt with an awesome display of power because Jews rely on him, instead of seeking magical means of foretelling the future or affecting events (*Rashi*). One can only imagine the effect of this pronouncement on Balaam and Balak, for this prophecy made a sham of Balaam's mission. He and Balak, the sorcerers, were trying to curse a nation that was blessed because it repudiated sorcery.

23:24. Balaam foretold that Israel would begin its conquest of the Land and, like a young lion cub maturing to full strength, grow ever more powerful. It would not finish its work until it conquered and plundered all the Canaanite kings (*Onkelos*).

all the officers of Moab. [7] He declaimed his parable* and said:

"From Aram, Balak, king of Moab, led me, from the mountains of the east, 'Come curse Jacob for me, come bring anger upon Israel.'

[8] "How can I curse? — God has not cursed. How can I anger? — HASHEM is not angry.

[9] "For from its origins, I see it rock-like, and from hills do I see it. Behold! it is a nation that will dwell in solitude and not be reckoned among the nations.

[10] "Who has counted the dust of Jacob or numbered a quarter of Israel? May my soul die the death of the upright, and may my end be like his!"

[11] Balak said to Balaam, "What have you done to me! To curse my enemy have I brought you — but behold! you have even blessed!"

[12] He spoke up and said, "Is it not so that whatever HASHEM puts in my mouth, that I must take heed to speak?"

[13] Balak said to him, "Go now with me to a different place from which you will see them; however, you will see its edge but not see all of it — and you will curse it for me from there." [14] He took him to the field of the lookouts, to the top of the peak, and he built seven altars and brought up a bull and a ram on each altar. [15] He said to Balak, "Stand here by your burnt-offering, and I will be happened upon here."

[16] HASHEM happened upon Balaam and put an utterance in his mouth; and said, "Go back to Balak and so shall you say."

[17] He came to him and — behold! he was standing by his burnt-offering and the officers of Moab were with him. Balak said to him, "What did HASHEM speak?"

[18] He declaimed his parable and said: "Stand erect,* O Balak, and hear; give ear to me, O son of Zippor.

[19] "God is not a man that He should be deceitful, nor a son of man that He should relent.

Would He say and not do, or speak and not confirm it?

[20] "Behold! to bless have I received — He has blessed, and I shall not contradict it.

[21] "He perceived no iniquity in Jacob, and saw no perversity in Israel. HASHEM, his God, is with him, and the friendship of the King is in him.

[22] "It is God Who brought them out of Egypt according to the power of His loftiness,

[23] "for there is no divination in Jacob and no sorcery in Israel.* Even now it is said to Jacob and Israel what God has wrought.

[24] "Behold! the people will arise like a lion cub and raise itself like a lion*; it will not lie down until it consumes prey, and drinks the blood of the slain."

[25] Balak said to Balaam, "Neither shall you curse them at all, nor shall you bless them at all!"

[26] Balaam answered and said to Balak, "Have I not spoken to you, saying, 'Whatever HASHEM shall speak, that I shall do'?"

[27] Balak said to Balaam, "Go, now, I shall take you to a different place, perhaps it will be proper in God's eyes that you will curse them for me from there." [28] Balak took Balaam to the summit of the height that overlooks the face of the wasteland.

[29] Balaam said to Balak, "Build for me here seven altars and prepare for me here seven bulls and seven rams." [30] Balak did as Balaam said, and he brought up a bull and a ram on each altar.

כד

א וַיַּרְא בִּלְעָם כִּי טוֹב בְּעֵינֵי יהוה לְבָרֵךְ אֶת־יִשְׂרָאֵל וְלֹא־הָלַךְ
ב כְּפַעַם־בְּפַעַם לִקְרַאת נְחָשִׁים וַיָּשֶׁת אֶל־הַמִּדְבָּר פָּנָיו: וַיִּשָּׂא בִלְעָם
אֶת־עֵינָיו וַיַּרְא אֶת־יִשְׂרָאֵל שֹׁכֵן לִשְׁבָטָיו וַתְּהִי עָלָיו רוּחַ אֱלֹהִים:
ג וַיִּשָּׂא מְשָׁלוֹ וַיֹּאמַר נְאֻם בִּלְעָם בְּנוֹ בְעֹר וּנְאֻם הַגֶּבֶר שְׁתֻם הָעָיִן:
ד נְאֻם שֹׁמֵעַ אִמְרֵי־אֵל אֲשֶׁר מַחֲזֵה שַׁדַּי יֶחֱזֶה נֹפֵל וּגְלוּי עֵינָיִם:

*בראש עמוד
בי"ה שמיר סימן

ה-ו *מַה־טֹּבוּ אֹהָלֶיךָ יַעֲקֹב מִשְׁכְּנֹתֶיךָ יִשְׂרָאֵל: כִּנְחָלִים נִטָּיוּ כְּגַנֹּת עֲלֵי
ז נָהָר כַּאֲהָלִים נָטַע יהוה כַּאֲרָזִים עֲלֵי־מָיִם: יִזַּל־מַיִם מִדָּלְיָו וְזַרְעוֹ
ח בְּמַיִם רַבִּים וְיָרֹם מֵאֲגַג מַלְכּוֹ וְתִנַּשֵּׂא מַלְכֻתוֹ: אֵל מוֹצִיאוֹ מִמִּצְרַיִם
כְּתוֹעֲפֹת רְאֵם לוֹ יֹאכַל גּוֹיִם צָרָיו וְעַצְמֹתֵיהֶם יְגָרֵם וְחִצָּיו יִמְחָץ:

*הב' רפה

ט כָּרַע שָׁכַב כַּאֲרִי וּכְלָבִיא מִי יְקִימֶנּוּ מְבָרְכֶיךָ בָרוּךְ וְאֹרְרֶיךָ אָרוּר:
י וַיִּחַר־אַף בָּלָק אֶל־בִּלְעָם וַיִּסְפֹּק אֶת־כַּפָּיו וַיֹּאמֶר בָּלָק אֶל־בִּלְעָם
יא לָקֹב אֹיְבַי קְרָאתִיךָ וְהִנֵּה בֵּרַכְתָּ בָרֵךְ זֶה שָׁלֹשׁ פְּעָמִים: וְעַתָּה בְּרַח־
לְךָ אֶל־מְקוֹמֶךָ אָמַרְתִּי כַּבֵּד אֲכַבֶּדְךָ וְהִנֵּה מְנָעֲךָ יהוה מִכָּבוֹד:
יב וַיֹּאמֶר בִּלְעָם אֶל־בָּלָק הֲלֹא גַּם אֶל־מַלְאָכֶיךָ אֲשֶׁר־שָׁלַחְתָּ אֵלַי
יג דִּבַּרְתִּי לֵאמֹר: אִם־יִתֶּן־לִי בָלָק מְלֹא בֵיתוֹ כֶּסֶף וְזָהָב לֹא אוּכַל
לַעֲבֹר אֶת־פִּי יהוה לַעֲשׂוֹת טוֹבָה אוֹ רָעָה מִלִּבִּי אֲשֶׁר־יְדַבֵּר יהוה
יד אֹתוֹ אֲדַבֵּר: וְעַתָּה הִנְנִי הוֹלֵךְ לְעַמִּי לְכָה אִיעָצְךָ אֲשֶׁר יַעֲשֶׂה הָעָם הַזֶּה

שביעי

לְעַמְּךָ בְּאַחֲרִית הַיָּמִים: וַיִּשָּׂא מְשָׁלוֹ וַיֹּאמַר נְאֻם בִּלְעָם בְּנוֹ
טו בְעֹר וּנְאֻם הַגֶּבֶר שְׁתֻם הָעָיִן: נְאֻם שֹׁמֵעַ אִמְרֵי־אֵל וְיֹדֵעַ דַּעַת עֶלְיוֹן
טז מַחֲזֵה שַׁדַּי יֶחֱזֶה נֹפֵל וּגְלוּי עֵינָיִם: אֶרְאֶנּוּ וְלֹא עַתָּה אֲשׁוּרֶנּוּ וְלֹא
יז קָרוֹב דָּרַךְ כּוֹכָב מִיַּעֲקֹב וְקָם שֵׁבֶט מִיִּשְׂרָאֵל וּמָחַץ פַּאֲתֵי מוֹאָב
וְקַרְקַר כָּל־בְּנֵי־שֵׁת: וְהָיָה אֱדוֹם יְרֵשָׁה וְהָיָה יְרֵשָׁה שֵׂעִיר אֹיְבָיו
יח וְיִשְׂרָאֵל עֹשֶׂה חָיִל: וְיֵרְדְּ מִיַּעֲקֹב וְהֶאֱבִיד שָׂרִיד מֵעִיר: וַיַּרְא אֶת־
יט-כ עֲמָלֵק וַיִּשָּׂא מְשָׁלוֹ וַיֹּאמַר רֵאשִׁית גּוֹיִם עֲמָלֵק וְאַחֲרִיתוֹ עֲדֵי אֹבֵד:
כא וַיַּרְא אֶת־הַקֵּינִי וַיִּשָּׂא מְשָׁלוֹ וַיֹּאמַר אֵיתָן מוֹשָׁבֶךָ וְשִׂים בַּסֶּלַע
כב-כג קִנֶּךָ: כִּי אִם־יִהְיֶה לְבָעֵר קָיִן עַד־מָה אַשּׁוּר תִּשְׁבֶּךָ: וַיִּשָּׂא מְשָׁלוֹ
כד וַיֹּאמַר אוֹי מִי יִחְיֶה מִשֻּׂמוֹ אֵל: וְצִים מִיַּד כִּתִּים וְעִנּוּ אַשּׁוּר וְעִנּוּ
כה עֵבֶר וְגַם־הוּא עֲדֵי אֹבֵד: וַיָּקָם בִּלְעָם וַיֵּלֶךְ וַיָּשָׁב לִמְקֹמוֹ וְגַם־בָּלָק
הָלַךְ לְדַרְכּוֹ:

24:1. Now Balaam adopted an entirely new approach to his attempt to draw prophecy to himself. Previously, he had hoped to divine the moment of God's anger and utilize it to bring a curse upon Israel, but he finally realized that this was not to be. Having been told *there is no divination in Jacob* (23:23), he realized that his sorcery had no chance of success, so *he set his face*

toward the Wilderness (24:1) to open himself to the prophecy God wished to impart: His blessing of Israel. For the first time in his life, God did not merely "happen" upon him; for the sake of Israel, God appeared to Balaam in the fullness of His glory (v. 2), and Balaam experienced the height of true prophecy (*Ramban*).

24

Balaam's third blessing

¹ Balaam saw that it was good in HASHEM'S eyes to bless Israel, so he did not go as every other time* toward divinations, but he set his face toward the Wilderness. ² Balaam raised his eyes and saw Israel dwelling according to its tribes, and the spirit of God was upon him. ³ He declaimed his parable and said:

"The words of Balaam son of Beor, the words of the man with the open eye;

⁴ "the words of the one who hears the sayings of God, who sees the vision of Shaddai, while fallen and with uncovered eyes:

⁵ "How goodly are your tents, O Jacob, your dwelling places, O Israel;

⁶ "stretching out like brooks, like gardens by a river, like aloes planted by HASHEM, like cedars by water.

⁷ "Water shall flow from his wells, and his seed shall be by abundant waters. His king shall be exalted over Agag, and his kingdom shall be upraised.

⁸ "It is God Who brought him out of Egypt according to the power of His loftiness. He will consume the nations that oppress him and crush their bones, and his arrows shall pierce them.

⁹ "He crouched and lay down like a lion, and, like a lion cub — who can stand him up? Those who bless you are blessed and those who curse you are accursed."

Balak's renewed anger

¹⁰ Balak's anger flared against Balaam and he clapped his hands. Balak said to Balaam, "To curse my enemies did I summon you, and behold! you have continually blessed them these three times! ¹¹ Now, flee to your place. I said I would honor you, but — behold! HASHEM has withheld you from honor."

¹² Balaam said to Balak, "Did I not speak to your emissaries whom you sent to me, saying, ¹³ 'If Balak were to give me his houseful of silver and gold, I cannot transgress the word of HASHEM to do good or bad on my own. Whatever HASHEM speaks, that shall I speak.' ¹⁴ And now, behold! I go to my people. Come, I shall advise you what this people will do to your people in the End of Days." ¹⁵ He declaimed his parable and said:

Balaam's last prophecy . . .

"The words of Balaam son of Beor, the words of the man with the open eye.

¹⁶ "The words of one who hears the sayings of God, and knows the knowledge of the Supreme One, who sees the vision of Shaddai, while fallen and with uncovered eyes.

to Israel . . .

¹⁷ "I shall see him, but not now, I shall look at him, but it is not near. A star has issued from Jacob and a scepter-bearer has risen from Israel, and he shall pierce the nobles of Moab and undermine the children of Seth.

to Edom . . .

¹⁸ "Edom shall be a conquest and Seir shall be the conquest of his enemies — and Israel will attain success.

¹⁹ "One from Jacob shall rule and destroy the remnant of the city."

to Amalek . . .

²⁰ He saw Amalek and declaimed his parable and said: "Amalek is the first among nations, but its end will be eternal destruction."

and to the Kenite

²¹ He saw the Kenite and declaimed his parable and said: "Strong is your dwelling, and set in a rock is your nest.

²² "For if the Kenite should be laid waste, till where can Assyria take you captive?"

²³ He declaimed his parable and said: "Oh! Who will survive when He imposes these!

²⁴ "Big ships from the coast of Kittim will afflict Assyria and afflict the other bank — but it, too, will be forever destroyed."

²⁵ Then Balaam rose up and went and returned to his place, and Balak also went on his way.

כה

א־ב וַיֵּשֶׁב יִשְׂרָאֵל בַּשִּׁטִּים וַיָּחֶל הָעָם לִזְנוֹת אֶל־בְּנוֹת מוֹאָב: וַתִּקְרֶאןָ

ג לָעָם לְזִבְחֵי אֱלֹהֵיהֶן וַיֹּאכַל הָעָם וַיִּשְׁתַּחֲוּוּ לֵאלֹהֵיהֶן: וַיִּצָּמֶד יִשְׂרָאֵל

ד לְבַעַל פְּעוֹר וַיִּחַר־אַף־יהוה בְּיִשְׂרָאֵל: וַיֹּאמֶר יהוה אֶל־מֹשֶׁה קַח אֶת־כָּל־רָאשֵׁי הָעָם וְהוֹקַע אוֹתָם לַיהוה נֶגֶד הַשָּׁמֶשׁ וְיָשֹׁב חֲרוֹן אַף־

ה יהוה מִיִּשְׂרָאֵל: וַיֹּאמֶר מֹשֶׁה אֶל־שֹׁפְטֵי יִשְׂרָאֵל הִרְגוּ אִישׁ אֲנָשָׁיו

ו הַנִּצְמָדִים לְבַעַל פְּעוֹר: וְהִנֵּה אִישׁ מִבְּנֵי יִשְׂרָאֵל בָּא וַיַּקְרֵב אֶל־אֶחָיו אֶת־הַמִּדְיָנִית לְעֵינֵי מֹשֶׁה וּלְעֵינֵי כָּל־עֲדַת בְּנֵי־יִשְׂרָאֵל וְהֵמָּה בֹכִים

ז פֶּתַח אֹהֶל מוֹעֵד: וַיַּרְא פִּינְחָס בֶּן־אֶלְעָזָר בֶּן־אַהֲרֹן הַכֹּהֵן וַיָּקָם

מפטיר

ח מִתּוֹךְ הָעֵדָה וַיִּקַּח רֹמַח בְּיָדוֹ: וַיָּבֹא אַחַר אִישׁ־יִשְׂרָאֵל אֶל־הַקֻּבָּה וַיִּדְקֹר אֶת־שְׁנֵיהֶם אֵת אִישׁ יִשְׂרָאֵל וְאֶת־הָאִשָּׁה אֶל־קֳבָתָהּ וַתֵּעָצַר

Haftaras
Balak:
p. 1380

ט הַמַּגֵּפָה מֵעַל בְּנֵי יִשְׂרָאֵל: וַיִּהְיוּ הַמֵּתִים בַּמַּגֵּפָה אַרְבָּעָה וְעֶשְׂרִים
אָלֶף: פפפ ק״ד פסוקים. מנו״ח סימן.

פרשת פינחס

י־יא וַיְדַבֵּר יהוה אֶל־מֹשֶׁה לֵּאמֹר: פִּינְחָס בֶּן־אֶלְעָזָר בֶּן־אַהֲרֹן הַכֹּהֵן הֵשִׁיב אֶת־חֲמָתִי מֵעַל בְּנֵי־יִשְׂרָאֵל בְּקַנְאוֹ אֶת־קִנְאָתִי בְּתוֹכָם וְלֹא־כִלִּיתִי

*י׳ זעירא

יב אֶת־בְּנֵי־יִשְׂרָאֵל בְּקִנְאָתִי: לָכֵן אֱמֹר הִנְנִי נֹתֵן לוֹ אֶת־בְּרִיתִי שָׁלוֹם:

*י׳ קטיעא

יג וְהָיְתָה לּוֹ וּלְזַרְעוֹ אַחֲרָיו בְּרִית כְּהֻנַּת עוֹלָם תַּחַת אֲשֶׁר קִנֵּא לֵאלֹהָיו

יד וַיְכַפֵּר עַל־בְּנֵי יִשְׂרָאֵל: וְשֵׁם אִישׁ יִשְׂרָאֵל הַמֻּכֶּה אֲשֶׁר הֻכָּה אֶת־

טו הַמִּדְיָנִית זִמְרִי בֶּן־סָלוּא נְשִׂיא בֵית־אָב לַשִּׁמְעֹנִי: וְשֵׁם הָאִשָּׁה הַמֻּכָּה הַמִּדְיָנִית כָּזְבִּי בַת־צוּר רֹאשׁ אֻמּוֹת בֵּית־אָב בְּמִדְיָן הוּא:

טז־יח וַיְדַבֵּר יהוה אֶל־מֹשֶׁה לֵּאמֹר: צָרוֹר אֶת־הַמִּדְיָנִים וְהִכִּיתֶם אוֹתָם: כִּי צֹרְרִים הֵם לָכֶם בְּנִכְלֵיהֶם אֲשֶׁר־נִכְּלוּ לָכֶם עַל־דְּבַר־פְּעוֹר וְעַל־דְּבַר

כו

א כָּזְבִּי בַת־נְשִׂיא מִדְיָן אֲחֹתָם הַמֻּכָּה בְיוֹם־הַמַּגֵּפָה עַל־דְּבַר־פְּעוֹר: וַיְהִי אַחֲרֵי הַמַּגֵּפָה

*פסקא באמצע פסוק

ב וַיֹּאמֶר יהוה אֶל־מֹשֶׁה וְאֶל אֶלְעָזָר בֶּן־אַהֲרֹן הַכֹּהֵן לֵאמֹר: שְׂאוּ אֶת־רֹאשׁ ׀ כָּל־עֲדַת בְּנֵי־יִשְׂרָאֵל מִבֶּן עֶשְׂרִים שָׁנָה וָמַעְלָה לְבֵית אֲבֹתָם

ג כָּל־יֹצֵא צָבָא בְּיִשְׂרָאֵל: וַיְדַבֵּר מֹשֶׁה וְאֶלְעָזָר הַכֹּהֵן אֹתָם בְּעַרְבֹת מוֹאָב

ד עַל־יַרְדֵּן יְרֵחוֹ לֵאמֹר: מִבֶּן עֶשְׂרִים שָׁנָה וָמָעְלָה כַּאֲשֶׁר צִוָּה יהוה אֶת־

ה מֹשֶׁה וּבְנֵי יִשְׂרָאֵל הַיֹּצְאִים מֵאֶרֶץ מִצְרָיִם: רְאוּבֵן בְּכוֹר יִשְׂרָאֵל בְּנֵי

ו רְאוּבֵן חֲנוֹךְ מִשְׁפַּחַת הַחֲנֹכִי לְפַלּוּא מִשְׁפַּחַת הַפַּלֻּאִי: לְחֶצְרֹן מִשְׁפַּחַת

שני

25:1. Knowing that sexual morality is a foundation of Jewish holiness and that God does not tolerate immorality, Balaam counseled Balak to entice Jewish men to debauchery (see *Sanhedrin* 106a).

25:6. In a shocking exhibit of brazenness, a Jew brought his paramour directly to Moses and sinned in public view.

◆§ **Parashas Pinchas**

25:11. Instead of applauding Phinehas, the people accused him of wanton murder. In response, God declared that, far from murder, Phinehas' act had saved countless

25

Baalam's plot

¹Israel settled in the Shittim and the people began to commit harlotry* with the daughters of Moab. ² They invited the people to the feasts of their gods; the people ate and prostrated themselves to their gods. ³ Israel became attached to Baal-peor, and the wrath of HASHEM flared up against Israel.

⁴ HASHEM said to Moses, "Take all the leaders of the people. Hang them before HASHEM against the sun — and the flaring wrath of HASHEM will withdraw from Israel."

⁵ Moses said to the judges of Israel, "Let each man kill his men who were attached to Baal-peor."

⁶ Behold! a man of the Children of Israel came and brought a Midianite woman near to his brothers in the sight of Moses and in the sight of the entire assembly of the Children of Israel; and they were weeping at the entrance of the Tent of Meeting.*

Phinehas' zealotry

⁷ Phinehas son of Elazar son of Aaron the Kohen saw, and he stood up from amid the assembly and took a spear in his hand. ⁸ He followed the Israelite man into the tent and pierced them both, the Israelite man and the woman into her stomach — and the plague was halted from upon the Children of Israel. ⁹ Those who died in the plague were twenty-four thousand.

PARASHAS PINCHAS

¹⁰ HASHEM spoke to Moses, saying: ¹¹ "Phinehas son of Elazar son of Aaron the Kohen turned back My wrath from upon the Children of Israel, when he zealously avenged My vengeance among them, so I did not consume the Children of Israel in My vengeance.* ¹² Therefore, say: Behold! I give him My covenant of peace. ¹³ And it shall be for him and his offspring after him a covenant of eternal priesthood, because he took vengeance for his God, and he atoned for the Children of Israel."

¹⁴ The name of the slain Israelite man who was slain with the Midianite woman was Zimri son of Salu, leader of a father's house of the Simeonites. ¹⁵ And the name of the slain Midianite woman was Cozbi daughter of Zur, who was head of the peoples of a father's house in Midian.

A new attitude toward Midian

¹⁶ HASHEM spoke to Moses, saying: ¹⁷ "Harass the Midianites and smite them; ¹⁸ for they harassed you through their conspiracy that they conspired against you in the matter of Peor, and in the matter of Cozbi, daughter of a leader of Midian, their sister, who was slain on the day of the plague, in the matter of Peor."

26

The new census

(See Appendix B, chart 11)

¹ It was after the plague — HASHEM spoke to Moses and to Elazar son of Aaron the Kohen, saying: ² "Take a census of the entire assembly of the Children of Israel, from twenty years of age and up, according to their fathers' houses, all who go out to the legion in Israel."

³ Moses and Elazar the Kohen spoke to them in the plains of Moab, by the Jordan near Jericho, saying: ⁴ "From twenty years of age and up, as HASHEM had commanded Moses and the Children of Israel, who were coming out of the land of Egypt."

⁵ Reuben the firstborn of Israel — the sons of Reuben: of Hanoch, the Hanochite family; of Pallu, the Palluite family; ⁶ of Hezron, the Hezronite family;

---

lives. Indeed, God called him a descendant of Aaron (*Rashi*).

ז הַחֶצְרוֹנִי לְכַרְמִי מִשְׁפַּחַת הַכַּרְמִי: אֵלֶּה מִשְׁפְּחֹת הָרֽאוּבֵנִי וַיִּהְיוּ פְקֻדֵיהֶם

ח-ט שְׁלֹשָׁה וְאַרְבָּעִים אֶלֶף וּשְׁבַע מֵאוֹת וּשְׁלֹשִׁים: וּבְנֵי פַלּוּא אֱלִיאָב: וּבְנֵי

אֱלִיאָב נְמוּאֵל וְדָתָן וַאֲבִירָם הֽוּא־דָתָן וַאֲבִירָם °קְרוּאֵי [°קְרִיאֵי ק]

הָֽעֵדָה אֲשֶׁר הִצּוּ עַל־מֹשֶׁה וְעַל־אַהֲרֹן בַּֽעֲדַת־קֹרַח בְּהַצֹּתָם עַל־יְהוֹה:

י וַתִּפְתַּח הָאָרֶץ אֶת־פִּיהָ וַתִּבְלַע אֹתָם וְאֶת־קֹרַח בְּמוֹת הָֽעֵדָה בַּֽאֲכֹל הָאֵשׁ

יא-יב אֵת חֲמִשִּׁים וּמָאתַיִם אִישׁ וַיִּֽהְיוּ לְנֵס: וּבְנֵֽי־קֹרַח לֹא־מֵתוּ: בְּנֵי

שִׁמְעוֹן לְמִשְׁפְּחֹתָם לִנְמוּאֵל מִשְׁפַּחַת הַנְּמֽוּאֵלִי לְיָמִין מִשְׁפַּחַת הַיָּֽמִינִי

יג לְיָכִין מִשְׁפַּחַת הַיָּֽכִינִי: לְזֶרַח מִשְׁפַּחַת הַזַּרְחִי לְשָׁאוּל מִשְׁפַּחַת הַשָּׁאוּלִי:

יד-טו אֵלֶּה מִשְׁפְּחֹת הַשִּׁמְעֹנִי שְׁנַיִם וְעֶשְׂרִים אֶלֶף וּמָאתָֽיִם: בְּנֵי גָד

לְמִשְׁפְּחֹתָם לִצְפוֹן מִשְׁפַּחַת הַצְּפוֹנִי לְחַגִּי מִשְׁפַּחַת הַֽחַגִּי לְשׁוּנִי

טז-יז מִשְׁפַּחַת הַשּׁוּנִי: לְאָזְנִי מִשְׁפַּחַת הָֽאָזְנִי לְעֵרִי מִשְׁפַּחַת הָֽעֵרִי: לַֽאֲרוֹד

יח מִשְׁפַּחַת הָֽאֲרוֹדִי לְאַרְאֵלִי מִשְׁפַּחַת הָֽאַרְאֵלִי: אֵלֶּה מִשְׁפְּחֹת בְּנֵי־גָד

יט לִפְקֻֽדֵיהֶם אַרְבָּעִים אֶלֶף וַֽחֲמֵשׁ מֵאֽוֹת: בְּנֵי יְהוּדָה עֵר וְאוֹנָן

כ וַיָּמָת עֵר וְאוֹנָן בְּאֶרֶץ כְּנָעַן: וַיִּֽהְיוּ בְנֵֽי־יְהוּדָה לְמִשְׁפְּחֹתָם לְשֵׁלָה

כא מִשְׁפַּחַת הַשֵּׁלָנִי לְפֶרֶץ מִשְׁפַּחַת הַפַּרְצִי לְזֶרַח מִשְׁפַּחַת הַזַּרְחִי: וַיִּֽהְיוּ

כב בְנֵֽי־פֶרֶץ לְחֶצְרֹן מִשְׁפַּחַת הַֽחֶצְרֹנִי לְחָמוּל מִשְׁפַּחַת הֶֽחָמוּלִי: אֵלֶּה

כג מִשְׁפְּחֹת יְהוּדָה לִפְקֻֽדֵיהֶם שִׁשָּׁה וְשִׁבְעִים אֶלֶף וַֽחֲמֵשׁ מֵאֽוֹת: בְּנֵי

יִשָּׂשכָר לְמִשְׁפְּחֹתָם תּוֹלָע מִשְׁפַּחַת הַתּֽוֹלָעִי לְפֻוָּה מִשְׁפַּחַת הַפּוּנִי:

כד-כה לְיָשׁוּב מִשְׁפַּחַת הַיָּֽשֻׁבִי לְשִׁמְרֹן מִשְׁפַּחַת הַשִּׁמְרֹנִי: אֵלֶּה מִשְׁפְּחֹת

כו יִשָּׂשכָר לִפְקֻֽדֵיהֶם אַרְבָּעָה וְשִׁשִּׁים אֶלֶף וּשְׁלֹשׁ מֵאֽוֹת: בְּנֵי

זְבוּלֻן לְמִשְׁפְּחֹתָם לְסֶרֶד מִשְׁפַּחַת הַסַּרְדִּי לְאֵלוֹן מִשְׁפַּחַת הָֽאֵלֹנִי

כז לְיַחְלְאֵל מִשְׁפַּחַת הַיַּחְלְאֵלִי: אֵלֶּה מִשְׁפְּחֹת הַזְּבֽוּלֹנִי לִפְקֻֽדֵיהֶם שִׁשִּׁים

כח אֶלֶף וַֽחֲמֵשׁ מֵאֽוֹת: בְּנֵי יוֹסֵף לְמִשְׁפְּחֹתָם מְנַשֶּׁה וְאֶפְרָֽיִם:

כט בְּנֵי מְנַשֶּׁה לְמָכִיר מִשְׁפַּחַת הַמָּכִירִי וּמָכִיר הוֹלִיד אֶת־גִּלְעָד לְגִלְעָד

ל מִשְׁפַּחַת הַגִּלְעָדִי: אֵלֶּה בְּנֵי גִלְעָד אִיעֶזֶר מִשְׁפַּחַת הָאִֽיעֶזְרִי לְחֵלֶק

לא מִשְׁפַּחַת הַֽחֶלְקִי: וְאַשְׂרִיאֵל מִשְׁפַּחַת הָֽאַשְׂרִֽאֵלִי וְשֶׁכֶם מִשְׁפַּחַת

לב-לג הַשִּׁכְמִי: וּשְׁמִידָע מִשְׁפַּחַת הַשְּׁמִידָעִי וְחֵפֶר מִשְׁפַּחַת הַֽחֶפְרִי: וּצְלָפְחָד

בֶּן־חֵפֶר לֹא־הָיוּ לוֹ בָּנִים כִּי אִם־בָּנוֹת וְשֵׁם בְּנוֹת צְלָפְחָד מַחְלָה

לד וְנֹעָה חָגְלָה מִלְכָּה וְתִרְצָה: אֵלֶּה מִשְׁפְּחֹת מְנַשֶּׁה וּפְקֻדֵיהֶם שְׁנַיִם

לה וַֽחֲמִשִּׁים אֶלֶף וּשְׁבַע מֵאֽוֹת: אֵלֶּה בְנֵֽי־אֶפְרַיִם לְמִשְׁפְּחֹתָם

לְשׁוּתֶלַח מִשְׁפַּחַת הַשֻּׁתַלְחִי לְבֶכֶר מִשְׁפַּחַת הַבַּכְרִי לְתַחַן מִשְׁפַּחַת

לו-לז הַֽתַּחֲנִי: וְאֵלֶּה בְּנֵי שׁוּתָלַח לְעֵרָן מִשְׁפַּחַת הָעֵרָנִי: אֵלֶּה מִשְׁפְּחֹת בְּנֵֽי־

אֶפְרַיִם לִפְקֻֽדֵיהֶם שְׁנַיִם וּשְׁלֹשִׁים אֶלֶף וַֽחֲמֵשׁ מֵאוֹת אֵלֶּה בְנֵֽי־יוֹסֵף

לח לְמִשְׁפְּחֹתָֽם: בְּנֵי בִנְיָמִן לְמִשְׁפְּחֹתָם לְבֶלַע מִשְׁפַּחַת הַבַּלְעִי

of Carmi, the Carmite family. [7] *These are the families of the Reubenite; their count was forty-three thousand, seven hundred and thirty.* [8] *The sons of Pallu: Eliab.* [9] *And the sons of Eliab: Nemuel and Dathan and Abiram, the same Dathan and Abiram who were summoned by the assembly, who contended against Moses and Aaron among the assembly of Korah, when they contended against* HASHEM. [10] *Then the earth opened its mouth and swallowed them and Korah with the death of the assembly, when the fire consumed two hundred and fifty men — and they became a sign.* [11] *But the sons of Korah did not die.*

[12] *The sons of Simeon according to their families: of Nemuel, the Nemuelite family; of Jamin, the Jaminite family; of Jachin, the Jachinite family;* [13] *of Zerah, the Zerahite family; of Shaul, the Shaulite family.* [14] *These are the families of the Simeonite: twenty-two thousand, two hundred.*

[15] *The sons of Gad according to their families: of Zephon, the Zephonite family; of Haggi, the Haggite family; of Shuni, the Shunite family;* [16] *of Ozni, the Oznite family; of Eri, the Erite family;* [17] *of Arod, the Arodite family; of Areli, the Arelite family.* [18] *These are the families of the sons of Gad according to their count forty thousand, five hundred.*

[19] *The sons of Judah, Er and Onan; Er and Onan died in the land of Canaan.* [20] *The sons of Judah according to their families were: of Shelah, the Shelanite family; of Perez, the Perezite family; of Zerah, the Zerahite family.* [21] *The sons of Perez were: of Hezron, the Hezronite family; of Hamul, the Hamulite family.* [22] *These are the families of Judah according to their count: seventy-six thousand, five hundred.*

[23] *The sons of Issachar according to their families were: Tola, the Tolaite family; of Puvah, the Punite family;* [24] *of Jashub, the Jashubite family; of Shimron, the Shimronite family.* [25] *These are the families of Issachar according to their count: sixty-four thousand, three hundred.*

[26] *The sons of Zebulun according to their families: of Sered, the Seredite family; of Elon, the Elonite family; of Jahleel, the Jahleelite family.* [27] *These are the families of the Zebulunite according to their count: sixty thousand, five hundred.*

[28] *The sons of Joseph according to their families: Manasseh and Ephraim.* [29] *The sons of Manasseh: of Machir, the Machirite family, and Machir begat Gilead; of Gilead, the Gileadite family.* [30] *These are the sons of Gilead: of Iezer, the Iezerite family; of Helek, the Helekite family;* [31] *of Asriel, the Asrielite family; of Shechem, the Shechemite family;* [32] *of Shemida, the Shemidaite family; of Hepher, the Hepherite family.* [33] *Zelophehad son of Hepher had no sons, only daughters; and the names of Zelophehad's daughters: Mahlah, Noah, Hoglah, Milcah, and Tirzah.* [34] *These are the families of Manasseh, and their count: fifty-two thousand, seven hundred.*

[35] *These are the sons of Ephraim according to their families: of Shuthelah, the Shuthelahite family; of Becher, the Becherite family; of Tahan, the Tahanite family.* [36] *And these are the sons of Shuthelah: of Eran, the Eranite family.* [37] *These are the families of the sons of Ephraim according to their count: thirty-two thousand, five hundred. These are the sons of Joseph according to their families.*

[38] *The sons of Benjamin according to their families: of Bela, the Belaite family;*

לט לְאַשְׁבֵּ֕ל מִשְׁפַּ֖חַת הָאַשְׁבֵּלִ֑י לַאֲחִירָ֕ם מִשְׁפַּ֖חַת הָאֲחִירָמִֽי:
מ לִשְׁפוּפָ֕ם מִשְׁפַּ֖חַת הַשּׁוּפָמִ֑י לְחוּפָ֕ם מִשְׁפַּ֖חַת הַחוּפָמִֽי: מא וַיִּהְי֣וּ בְנֵי־בֶ֗לַע אַ֣רְדְּ וְנַעֲמָ֔ן
מִשְׁפַּ֙חַת֙ הָֽאַרְדִּ֔י לְנַ֣עֲמָ֔ן מִשְׁפַּ֖חַת הַנַּעֲמִֽי: מב אֵ֥לֶּה בְנֵֽי־בִנְיָמִ֖ן לְמִשְׁפְּחֹתָ֑ם וּפְקֻ֣דֵיהֶ֔ם חֲמִשָּׁ֧ה וְאַרְבָּעִ֛ים אֶ֖לֶף וְשֵׁ֥שׁ מֵאֽוֹת: אֵ֣לֶּה
מג בְנֵי־דָ֖ן לְמִשְׁפְּחֹתָ֑ם לְשׁוּחָ֕ם מִשְׁפַּ֖חַת הַשּׁוּחָמִ֑י אֵ֥לֶּה מִשְׁפְּחֹ֥ת דָּ֖ן
לְמִשְׁפְּחֹתָֽם: כָּל־מִשְׁפְּחֹ֣ת הַשּׁוּחָמִ֗י לִפְקֻ֣דֵיהֶ֔ם אַרְבָּעָ֧ה וְשִׁשִּׁ֛ים אֶ֖לֶף
מד וְאַרְבַּ֥ע מֵאֽוֹת: בְּנֵ֣י אָשֵׁר֮ לְמִשְׁפְּחֹתָם֒ לְיִמְנָ֗ה מִשְׁפַּ֙חַת֙
הַיִּמְנָ֔ה לְיִשְׁוִ֕י מִשְׁפַּ֖חַת הַיִּשְׁוִ֑י לִבְרִיעָ֕ה מִשְׁפַּ֖חַת הַבְּרִיעִֽי:
מה לִבְרִ֗יעָ֕ה לְחֶ֕בֶר מִשְׁפַּ֖חַת הַחֶבְרִ֑י לְמַ֨לְכִּיאֵ֔ל מִשְׁפַּ֖חַת הַמַּלְכִּיאֵלִֽי: וְשֵׁ֥ם בַּת־אָשֵׁ֖ר
מו שָֽׂרַח: מז אֵ֛לֶּה מִשְׁפְּחֹ֥ת בְּנֵֽי־אָשֵׁ֖ר לִפְקֻֽדֵיהֶ֑ם שְׁלֹשָׁ֧ה וַחֲמִשִּׁ֛ים אֶ֖לֶף וְאַרְבַּ֥ע
מח מֵאֽוֹת: בְּנֵ֤י נַפְתָּלִי֙ לְמִשְׁפְּחֹתָ֔ם לְיַ֨חְצְאֵ֔ל מִשְׁפַּ֖חַת
מט הַיַּחְצְאֵלִ֑י לְגוּנִ֕י מִשְׁפַּ֖חַת הַגּוּנִֽי: לְיֵ֕צֶר מִשְׁפַּ֖חַת הַיִּצְרִ֑י לְשִׁלֵּ֕ם מִשְׁפַּ֖חַת
נ הַשִּׁלֵּמִֽי: אֵ֛לֶּה מִשְׁפְּחֹ֥ת נַפְתָּלִ֖י לְמִשְׁפְּחֹתָ֑ם וּפְקֻ֣דֵיהֶ֔ם חֲמִשָּׁ֥ה וְאַרְבָּעִ֖ים
נא אֶ֖לֶף וְאַרְבַּ֥ע מֵאֽוֹת: אֵ֗לֶּה פְּקוּדֵי֙ בְּנֵ֣י יִשְׂרָאֵ֔ל שֵׁשׁ־מֵא֥וֹת אֶ֖לֶף וָאָ֑לֶף שְׁבַ֥ע
מֵא֖וֹת וּשְׁלֹשִֽׁים:

נב־נג **שלישי** וַיְדַבֵּ֥ר יְהוָ֖ה אֶל־מֹשֶׁ֥ה לֵּאמֹֽר: לָאֵ֗לֶּה תֵּחָלֵ֥ק הָאָ֛רֶץ בְּנַחֲלָ֖ה בְּמִסְפַּ֥ר
נד שֵׁמֽוֹת: לָרַ֗ב תַּרְבֶּה֙ נַחֲלָת֔וֹ וְלַמְעַ֖ט תַּמְעִ֣יט נַחֲלָת֑וֹ אִ֗ישׁ לְפִ֤י פְקֻדָיו֙ יֻתַּ֣ן
נה־נו נַחֲלָתֽוֹ: אַ֤ךְ בְּגוֹרָל֙ יֵֽחָלֵ֣ק אֶת־הָאָ֔רֶץ לִשְׁמ֖וֹת מַטּוֹת־אֲבֹתָ֥ם יִנְחָֽלוּ: עַל־
פִּ֣י הַגּוֹרָ֔ל תֵּֽחָלֵ֖ק נַחֲלָת֑וֹ בֵּ֥ין רַ֖ב לִמְעָֽט: וְאֵ֛לֶּה פְּקוּדֵ֥י הַלֵּוִ֖י
נז לְמִשְׁפְּחֹתָ֑ם לְגֵרְשׁ֗וֹן מִשְׁפַּ֙חַת֙ הַגֵּ֣רְשֻׁנִּ֔י לִקְהָ֕ת מִשְׁפַּ֖חַת הַקְּהָתִ֑י לִמְרָרִ֕י
נח מִשְׁפַּ֖חַת הַמְּרָרִֽי: אֵ֣לֶּה ׀ מִשְׁפְּחֹ֣ת לֵוִ֗י מִשְׁפַּ֤חַת הַלִּבְנִי֙ מִשְׁפַּ֣חַת הַחֶבְרֹנִ֔י
מִשְׁפַּ֤חַת הַמַּחְלִי֙ מִשְׁפַּ֣חַת הַמּוּשִׁ֔י מִשְׁפַּ֖חַת הַקָּרְחִ֑י וּקְהָ֖ת הוֹלִ֥ד אֶת־
נט עַמְרָֽם: וְשֵׁ֣ם ׀ אֵ֣שֶׁת עַמְרָ֗ם יוֹכֶ֙בֶד֙ בַּת־לֵוִ֔י אֲשֶׁ֨ר יָלְדָ֥ה אֹתָ֛הּ לְלֵוִ֖י בְּמִצְרָ֑יִם
ס וַתֵּ֣לֶד לְעַמְרָ֗ם אֶת־אַהֲרֹן֙ וְאֶת־מֹשֶׁ֔ה וְאֵ֖ת מִרְיָ֣ם אֲחֹתָֽם: וַיִּוָּלֵ֣ד לְאַהֲרֹ֔ן
סא אֶת־נָדָב֙ וְאֶת־אֲבִיה֔וּא אֶת־אֶלְעָזָ֖ר וְאֶת־אִֽיתָמָֽר: וַיָּ֥מָת נָדָ֖ב וַאֲבִיה֑וּא
סב בְּהַקְרִיבָ֥ם אֵשׁ־זָרָ֖ה לִפְנֵ֥י יְהוָֽה: וַיִּהְי֣וּ פְקֻדֵיהֶ֗ם שְׁלֹשָׁ֤ה וְעֶשְׂרִים֙ אֶ֔לֶף כָּל־
זָכָ֖ר מִבֶּן־חֹ֣דֶשׁ וָמָ֑עְלָה כִּ֣י ׀ לֹ֣א הָתְפָּ֗קְדוּ בְּתוֹךְ֙ בְּנֵ֣י יִשְׂרָאֵ֔ל כִּ֠י לֹא־נִתַּ֤ן
סג לָהֶם֙ נַֽחֲלָ֔ה בְּת֖וֹךְ בְּנֵ֥י יִשְׂרָאֵֽל: אֵ֚לֶּה פְּקוּדֵ֣י מֹשֶׁ֔ה וְאֶלְעָזָ֖ר הַכֹּהֵ֑ן אֲשֶׁ֨ר
סד פָּֽקְד֜וּ אֶת־בְּנֵ֤י יִשְׂרָאֵל֙ בְּעַֽרְבֹ֣ת מוֹאָ֔ב עַ֖ל יַרְדֵּ֥ן יְרֵחֽוֹ: וּבְאֵ֙לֶּה֙ לֹא־הָ֣יָה
אִ֔ישׁ מִפְּקוּדֵ֣י מֹשֶׁ֔ה וְאַהֲרֹ֖ן הַכֹּהֵ֑ן אֲשֶׁ֥ר פָּֽקְד֛וּ אֶת־בְּנֵ֥י יִשְׂרָאֵ֖ל בְּמִדְבַּ֥ר
סה סִינָֽי: כִּֽי־אָמַ֤ר יְהוָה֙ לָהֶ֔ם מ֥וֹת יָמֻ֖תוּ בַּמִּדְבָּ֑ר וְלֹא־נוֹתַ֤ר מֵהֶם֙ אִ֔ישׁ כִּ֚י

כז א אִם־כָּלֵ֣ב בֶּן־יְפֻנֶּ֔ה וִיהוֹשֻׁ֖עַ בִּן־נֽוּן: וַתִּקְרַ֜בְנָה בְּנ֣וֹת
צְלָפְחָ֡ד בֶּן־חֵ֩פֶר֩ בֶּן־גִּלְעָ֨ד בֶּן־מָכִ֜יר בֶּן־מְנַשֶּׁ֗ה לְמִשְׁפְּחֹ֖ת מְנַשֶּׁ֣ה בֶן־יוֹסֵ֑ף

27:1-5. In recognition of the righteousness of Zelophehad's daughters and their love for the Land, God gave them the honor of being the catalyst for the pronouncement of this chapter in the Torah (*Rashi; Sifre*).

of Ashbel, the Ashbelite family; of Ahiram, the Ahiramite family; ³⁹ of She-phupham, the Shuphamite family; of Hupham, the Huphamite family. ⁴⁰ And the sons of Bela were Ard and Naaman: the Ardite family; of Naaman, the Naamanite family. ⁴¹ These are the sons of Benjamin according to their families, and their count: forty-five thousand, six hundred.

⁴² These are the sons of Dan according to their families: of Shuham, the Shuhamite family. These are the families of Dan according to their families. ⁴³ All the Shuhamite families according to their count: sixty-four thousand, four hundred.

⁴⁴ The sons of Asher according to their families: of Imnah, the Imnite family; of Ishvi, the Ishvite family; of Beriah, the Beriite family; ⁴⁵ of the sons of Beriah: of Heber, the Heberite family; of Malchiel, the Malchielite family. ⁴⁶ The name of Asher's daughter: Serah. ⁴⁷ These are the families of the sons of Asher according to their count: fifty-three thousand, four hundred.

⁴⁸ The sons of Naphtali according to their families: of Jahzeel, the Jahzeelite family; of Guni, the Gunite family; ⁴⁹ of Jezer, the Jezerite family; of Shillem, the Shillemite family. ⁵⁰ These are the families of Naphtali according to their families, and their count: forty-five thousand, four hundred.

The census total ⁵¹ These are the countings of the sons of Israel: six hundred and one thousand, seven hundred and thirty.

⁵² HASHEM spoke to Moses, saying: ⁵³ "To these shall the Land be divided as an inheritance, according to the number of names. ⁵⁴ For the numerous one you shall increase its inheritance, and for the fewer one you shall lessen its inheritance; each one according to his count shall his inheritance be given. ⁵⁵ Only by lot shall the Land be divided, according to the names of their fathers' tribes shall they inherit. ⁵⁶ According to the lot shall one's inheritance be divided, between the numerous and the few."

The count of the Levites ⁵⁷ These are the countings of the Levites, according to their families: of Gershon, the Gershonite family; of Kohath, the Kohathite family; of Merari, the Merarite family. ⁵⁸ These are the Levite families: the Libnite family; the Hebronite family; the Mahlite family; the Mushite family; the Korahite family; and Kohath begat Amram. ⁵⁹ The name of Amram's wife was Jochebed, daughter of Levi, who was born to Levi in Egypt; and she bore to Amram Aaron, Moses, and their sister Miriam. ⁶⁰ To Aaron were born Nadab and Abihu, Elazar and Ithamar. ⁶¹ Nadab and Abihu died when they brought an alien fire before HASHEM. ⁶² Their counts were twenty-three thousand, every male from one month of age and above, for they were not counted among the Children of Israel, for an inheritance was not given them among the Children of Israel.

⁶³ These are the ones counted by Moses and Elazar the Kohen, who counted the Children of Israel in the plains of Moab, by the Jordan, near Jericho. ⁶⁴ And of these, there was no man of those counted by Moses and Aaron the Kohen, who counted the Children of Israel in the Wilderness of Sinai. ⁶⁵ For HASHEM had said of them, "They will surely die in the Wilderness," and not a man was left of them, except for Caleb son of Jephunneh, and Joshua son of Nun.

27 ¹ The daughters of Zelophehad, * son of Hepher, son of Gilead, son of Machir, son of Manasseh, of the families of Manasseh son of Joseph drew near —

ב וְאֵ֣לֶּה שְׁמ֣וֹת בְּנֹתָ֗יו מַחְלָ֤ה נֹעָה֙ וְחָגְלָ֣ה וּמִלְכָּ֔ה וְתִרְצָֽה: וַֽתַּעֲמֹ֜דְנָה לִפְנֵ֣י מֹשֶׁ֗ה וְלִפְנֵי֙ אֶלְעָזָ֣ר הַכֹּהֵ֔ן וְלִפְנֵ֥י הַנְּשִׂיאִ֖ם וְכָל־הָעֵדָ֑ה פֶּ֥תַח אֹֽהֶל־מוֹעֵ֖ד

ג לֵאמֹֽר: אָבִ֘ינוּ֮ מֵ֣ת בַּמִּדְבָּר֒ וְה֕וּא לֹֽא־הָיָ֣ה בְּת֣וֹךְ הָעֵדָ֗ה הַנּֽוֹעָדִ֛ים עַל־

ד יְהֹוָ֖ה בַּעֲדַת־קֹ֑רַח כִּֽי־בְחֶטְא֣וֹ מֵ֔ת וּבָנִ֖ים לֹא־הָ֣יוּ לֽוֹ: לָ֣מָּה יִגָּרַ֤ע שֵׁם־אָבִ֨ינוּ֙ מִתּ֣וֹךְ מִשְׁפַּחְתּ֔וֹ כִּ֛י אֵ֥ין ל֖וֹ בֵּ֑ן תְּנָה־לָּ֣נוּ אֲחֻזָּ֔ה בְּת֖וֹךְ אֲחֵ֥י אָבִֽינוּ:

ה וַיַּקְרֵ֥ב מֹשֶׁ֛ה אֶת־מִשְׁפָּטָ֖ן* לִפְנֵ֥י יְהֹוָֽה: ‏‏*נ׳ רבתי

רביעי ו-ז וַיֹּ֥אמֶר יְהֹוָ֖ה אֶל־מֹשֶׁ֥ה לֵּאמֹֽר: כֵּ֗ן בְּנ֣וֹת צְלָפְחָד֮ דֹּֽבְרֹת֒ נָתֹ֨ן תִּתֵּ֤ן לָהֶם֙

ח אֲחֻזַּ֣ת נַחֲלָ֔ה בְּת֖וֹךְ אֲחֵ֣י אֲבִיהֶ֑ם וְהַֽעֲבַרְתָּ֛ אֶת־נַחֲלַ֥ת אֲבִיהֶ֖ן לָהֶֽן: וְאֶל־בְּנֵ֥י יִשְׂרָאֵ֖ל תְּדַבֵּ֣ר לֵאמֹ֑ר אִ֣ישׁ כִּֽי־יָמ֗וּת וּבֵן֙ אֵ֣ין ל֔וֹ וְהַֽעֲבַרְתֶּ֥ם אֶת־

ט-י נַֽחֲלָת֖וֹ לְבִתּֽוֹ: וְאִם־אֵ֥ין ל֖וֹ בַּ֑ת וּנְתַתֶּ֥ם אֶת־נַחֲלָת֖וֹ לְאֶחָֽיו: וְאִם־אֵ֥ין ל֖וֹ

יא אַחִ֑ים וּנְתַתֶּ֥ם אֶת־נַחֲלָת֖וֹ לַֽאֲחֵ֣י אָבִֽיו: וְאִם־אֵ֣ין אַחִים֮ לְאָבִיו֒ וּנְתַתֶּ֣ם אֶת־נַֽחֲלָת֗וֹ לִשְׁאֵר֞וֹ הַקָּרֹ֥ב אֵלָ֛יו מִמִּשְׁפַּחְתּ֖וֹ וְיָרַ֣שׁ אֹתָ֑הּ וְהָ֨יְתָ֜ה לִבְנֵ֤י יִשְׂרָאֵל֙ לְחֻקַּ֣ת מִשְׁפָּ֔ט כַּֽאֲשֶׁ֛ר צִוָּ֥ה יְהֹוָ֖ה אֶת־מֹשֶֽׁה:

יב וַיֹּ֤אמֶר יְהֹוָה֙ אֶל־מֹשֶׁ֔ה עֲלֵ֛ה אֶל־הַ֥ר הָֽעֲבָרִ֖ים הַזֶּ֑ה וּרְאֵה֙ אֶת־הָאָ֔רֶץ

יג אֲשֶׁ֥ר נָתַ֖תִּי לִבְנֵ֥י יִשְׂרָאֵֽל: וְרָאִ֣יתָה אֹתָ֔הּ וְנֶֽאֱסַפְתָּ֥ אֶל־עַמֶּ֖יךָ גַּם־אָ֑תָּה

יד כַּֽאֲשֶׁ֥ר נֶֽאֱסַ֖ף אַֽהֲרֹ֥ן אָחִֽיךָ: כַּֽאֲשֶׁר֩ מְרִיתֶ֨ם פִּ֜י בְּמִדְבַּר־צִ֗ן בִּמְרִיבַת֙ הָֽעֵדָ֔ה לְהַקְדִּישֵׁ֥נִי בַמַּ֖יִם לְעֵֽינֵיהֶ֑ם הֵ֛ם מֵֽי־מְרִיבַ֥ת קָדֵ֖שׁ מִדְבַּר־

טו-טז צִֽן: וַיְדַבֵּ֣ר מֹשֶׁ֔ה אֶל־יְהֹוָ֖ה לֵאמֹֽר: יִפְקֹ֣ד יְהֹוָ֔ה אֱלֹהֵ֥י

יז הָֽרוּחֹ֖ת לְכָל־בָּשָׂ֑ר אִ֖ישׁ עַל־הָֽעֵדָֽה: אֲשֶׁר־יֵצֵ֣א לִפְנֵיהֶ֗ם וַֽאֲשֶׁ֤ר יָבֹא֙ לִפְנֵיהֶ֔ם וַֽאֲשֶׁ֥ר יֽוֹצִיאֵ֖ם וַֽאֲשֶׁ֣ר יְבִיאֵ֑ם וְלֹ֤א תִֽהְיֶה֙ עֲדַ֣ת יְהֹוָ֔ה כַּצֹּ֕אן אֲשֶׁ֥ר

יח אֵֽין־לָהֶ֖ם רֹעֶֽה: וַיֹּ֨אמֶר יְהֹוָ֜ה אֶל־מֹשֶׁ֗ה קַח־לְךָ֙ אֶת־יְהוֹשֻׁ֣עַ בִּן־נ֔וּן אִ֖ישׁ

יט אֲשֶׁר־ר֣וּחַ בּ֑וֹ וְסָֽמַכְתָּ֥ אֶת־יָֽדְךָ֖ עָלָֽיו: וְהַֽעֲמַדְתָּ֣ אֹת֗וֹ לִפְנֵי֙ אֶלְעָזָ֣ר הַכֹּהֵ֔ן וְלִפְנֵ֖י כָּל־הָֽעֵדָ֑ה וְצִוִּיתָ֥ה אֹת֖וֹ לְעֵֽינֵיהֶֽם: וְנָֽתַתָּ֥ה מֵהֽוֹדְךָ֖ עָלָ֑יו לְמַ֣עַן

כ-כא יִשְׁמְע֔וּ כָּל־עֲדַ֖ת בְּנֵ֥י יִשְׂרָאֵֽל: וְלִפְנֵ֨י אֶלְעָזָ֣ר הַכֹּהֵן֮ יַֽעֲמֹד֒ וְשָׁ֣אַל ל֗וֹ בְּמִשְׁפַּ֤ט הָֽאוּרִים֙ לִפְנֵ֣י יְהֹוָ֔ה עַל־פִּ֨יו יֵֽצְא֜וּ וְעַל־פִּ֣יו יָבֹ֗אוּ ה֛וּא וְכָל־בְּנֵֽי־

כב יִשְׂרָאֵ֥ל אִתּ֖וֹ וְכָל־הָֽעֵדָֽה: וַיַּ֣עַשׂ מֹשֶׁ֔ה כַּֽאֲשֶׁ֛ר צִוָּ֥ה יְהֹוָ֖ה אֹת֑וֹ וַיִּקַּ֣ח אֶת־

כג יְהוֹשֻׁ֗עַ וַיַּֽעֲמִדֵ֨הוּ֙ לִפְנֵי֙ אֶלְעָזָ֣ר הַכֹּהֵ֔ן וְלִפְנֵ֖י כָּל־הָֽעֵדָֽה: וַיִּסְמֹ֧ךְ אֶת־יָדָ֛יו עָלָ֖יו וַיְצַוֵּ֑הוּ כַּֽאֲשֶׁ֛ר דִּבֶּ֥ר יְהֹוָ֖ה בְּיַד־מֹשֶֽׁה:

כח **חמישי א-ב** וַיְדַבֵּ֥ר יְהֹוָ֖ה אֶל־מֹשֶׁ֥ה לֵּאמֹֽר: צַ֚ו אֶת־בְּנֵ֣י יִשְׂרָאֵ֔ל וְאָֽמַרְתָּ֖ אֲלֵהֶ֑ם אֶת־

ג קָרְבָּנִ֨י לַחְמִ֜י לְאִשַּׁ֗י רֵ֚יחַ נִֽיחֹחִ֔י תִּשְׁמְר֕וּ לְהַקְרִ֥יב לִ֖י בְּמֹֽועֲדֽוֹ: וְאָֽמַרְתָּ֣ לָהֶ֗ם זֶ֣ה הָֽאִשֶּׁ֔ה אֲשֶׁ֥ר תַּקְרִ֖יבוּ לַֽיהֹוָ֑ה כְּבָשִׂ֨ים בְּנֵֽי־שָׁנָ֧ה תְמִימִ֛ם שְׁנַ֥יִם

ד לַיּ֖וֹם עֹלָ֥ה תָמִֽיד: אֶת־הַכֶּ֥בֶשׂ אֶחָ֖ד תַּֽעֲשֶׂ֣ה בַבֹּ֑קֶר וְאֵת֙ הַכֶּ֣בֶשׂ הַשֵּׁנִ֔י

READING
FOR
ROSH
CHODESH
28:1-15

27:13. *You shall see it*, i.e., you will gain a deeper vision, a grasp of its inner, spiritual essence (*Or HaChaim*).

27:17. It is clear from Moses' description of the leader's qualifications that his primary concern was for the needs of the people.

27:18. "Joshua who has never departed from [your] tent (*Exodus* 33:11) deserves to be rewarded" (*Rashi*).

27:20. *"Some"* of your majesty. Joshua was a reflection

The grievance of Zelophehad's daughters

and these are the names of his daughters: Mahlah, Noah, Hoglah, Milcah, and Tirzah — ² *and they stood before Moses, before Elazar the Kohen, and before the leaders and the entire assembly at the entrance to the Tent of Meeting, saying:* ³ *"Our father died in the Wilderness, but he was not among the assembly that was gathering against HASHEM in the assembly of Korah, but he died of his own sin; and he had no sons.* ⁴ *Why should the name of our father be omitted from among his family because he had no son? Give us a possession among our father's brothers."* ⁵ *And Moses brought their claim before HASHEM.*

Laws of inheritance

⁶ *HASHEM said to Moses, saying,* ⁷ *"The daughters of Zelophehad speak properly. You shall surely give them a possession of inheritance among the brothers of their father, and you shall cause the inheritance of their father to pass over to them.* ⁸ *And to the Children of Israel you shall speak, saying: If a man will die and he has no son, you shall cause his inheritance to pass over to his daughter.* ⁹ *If he has no daughter, you shall give his inheritance to his brothers.* ¹⁰ *If he has no brothers, you shall give his inheritance to the brothers of his father.* ¹¹ *If there are no brothers of his father, you shall give his inheritance to his relative who is closest to him of his family, and he shall inherit it. This shall be for the Children of Israel as a decree of justice, as HASHEM commanded Moses."*

God shows Moses the Land

¹² *HASHEM said to Moses, "Go up to this mountain of Abarim and see the Land that I have given to the Children of Israel.* ¹³ *You shall see it* and you shall be gathered unto your people, you, too, as Aaron your brother was gathered in;* ¹⁴ *because you rebelled against My word in the Wilderness of Zin, in the assembly's strife, to sanctify Me at the water before their eyes. They were the waters of strife at Kadesh, in the Wilderness of Zin."*

Moses asks for a successor

¹⁵ *Moses spoke to HASHEM, saying,* ¹⁶ *"May HASHEM, God of the spirits of all flesh, appoint a man over the assembly,* ¹⁷ *who shall go out before them and come in before them, who shall take them out and bring them in;* and let the assembly of HASHEM not be like sheep that have no shepherd."*

¹⁸ *HASHEM said to Moses, "Take to yourself Joshua son of Nun, a man in whom there is spirit, and lean your hand upon him.** ¹⁹ *You shall stand him before Elazar the Kohen and before the entire assembly, and command him before their eyes.* ²⁰ *You shall place some of your majesty* upon him, so that the entire assembly of the Children of Israel will pay heed.* ²¹ *Before Elazar the Kohen shall he stand, who shall inquire for him of the judgment of the Urim before HASHEM; at his word shall they go out and at his word shall they come in, he and all the Children of Israel with him, and the entire assembly.*

²² *Moses did as HASHEM had commanded him. He took Joshua and stood him before Elazar the Kohen and before the entire assembly.* ²³ *He leaned his hands upon him and commanded him, as HASHEM had spoken through Moses.*

28

The Tamid — Continual daily offering

(See Appendix B, charts 6-7)

¹ HASHEM *spoke to Moses, saying:* ² *Command the Children of Israel and say to them: My offering,* My food for My fires, My satisfying aroma, shall you be scrupulous to offer to Me in its appointed time.* ³ *And you shall say to them: This is the fire-offering that you are to offer to HASHEM: male lambs in their first year, unblemished, two a day, as a continual burnt-offering.* ⁴ *The one lamb shall you make in the morning and the second lamb*

---

of Moses' greatness, but not his equal *(Rashi; Sifre)*.
28:2. The Torah begins this chapter by describing the *tamid*, the daily continual offering, then continues,

through Chapter 29, with the description of the *mussaf*, additional offerings, that were brought in the Temple on the Sabbath, the New Moon, and the festivals.

ה תַּעֲשֶׂה בֵּין הָעַרְבָּיִם: וַעֲשִׂירִית הָאֵיפָה סֹלֶת לְמִנְחָה בְּלוּלָה בְּשֶׁמֶן

ו כְּתִית רְבִיעַת הַהִין: עֹלַת תָּמִיד הָעֲשֻׂיָה בְּהַר סִינַי לְרֵיחַ נִיחֹחַ אִשֶּׁה

ז לַיהוָה: וְנִסְכּוֹ רְבִיעִת הַהִין לַכֶּבֶשׂ הָאֶחָד בַּקֹּדֶשׁ הַסֵּךְ נֶסֶךְ שֵׁכָר לַיהוָה:

ח וְאֵת הַכֶּבֶשׂ הַשֵּׁנִי תַּעֲשֶׂה בֵּין הָעַרְבָּיִם כְּמִנְחַת הַבֹּקֶר וּכְנִסְכּוֹ תַּעֲשֶׂה אִשֵּׁה רֵיחַ נִיחֹחַ לַיהוָה:

MAFTIR
SABBATH
ROSH
CHODESH
28:9-15
Haftarah:
p. 1066

ט וּבְיוֹם הַשַּׁבָּת שְׁנֵי־כְבָשִׂים בְּנֵי־שָׁנָה תְּמִימִם וּשְׁנֵי עֶשְׂרֹנִים סֹלֶת מִנְחָה

י בְּלוּלָה בַשֶּׁמֶן וְנִסְכּוֹ: עֹלַת שַׁבַּת בְּשַׁבַּתּוֹ עַל־עֹלַת הַתָּמִיד וְנִסְכָּהּ:

יא וּבְרָאשֵׁי חָדְשֵׁיכֶם תַּקְרִיבוּ עֹלָה לַיהוָה פָּרִים בְּנֵי־בָקָר שְׁנַיִם וְאַיִל אֶחָד

יב כְּבָשִׂים בְּנֵי־שָׁנָה שִׁבְעָה תְּמִימִם: וּשְׁלֹשָׁה עֶשְׂרֹנִים סֹלֶת מִנְחָה בְּלוּלָה

בַשֶּׁמֶן לַפָּר הָאֶחָד וּשְׁנֵי עֶשְׂרֹנִים סֹלֶת מִנְחָה בְּלוּלָה בַשֶּׁמֶן לָאַיִל

יג הָאֶחָד: וְעִשָּׂרֹן עִשָּׂרוֹן סֹלֶת מִנְחָה בְּלוּלָה בַשֶּׁמֶן לַכֶּבֶשׂ הָאֶחָד עֹלָה

יד רֵיחַ נִיחֹחַ אִשֶּׁה לַיהוָה: וְנִסְכֵּיהֶם חֲצִי הַהִין יִהְיֶה לַפָּר וּשְׁלִישִׁת

הַהִין לָאַיִל וּרְבִיעִת הַהִין לַכֶּבֶשׂ יָיִן זֹאת עֹלַת חֹדֶשׁ בְּחָדְשׁוֹ לְחָדְשֵׁי

טו הַשָּׁנָה: וּשְׂעִיר עִזִּים אֶחָד לְחַטָּאת לַיהוָה עַל־עֹלַת הַתָּמִיד יֵעָשֶׂה

טז וְנִסְכּוֹ:

ששי

וּבַחֹדֶשׁ הָרִאשׁוֹן בְּאַרְבָּעָה עָשָׂר יוֹם לַחֹדֶשׁ פֶּסַח

יז לַיהוָה: וּבַחֲמִשָּׁה עָשָׂר יוֹם לַחֹדֶשׁ הַזֶּה חָג שִׁבְעַת יָמִים מַצּוֹת יֵאָכֵל:

PESACH
Maftir
for first
two days:
28:16-25;
4th *aliyah*
for Chol
HaMoed,
Maftir for
Sabbath
Chol
HaMoed
and last
two days:
28:19-25

יח־יט בַּיּוֹם הָרִאשׁוֹן מִקְרָא־קֹדֶשׁ כָּל־מְלֶאכֶת עֲבֹדָה לֹא תַעֲשׂוּ: וְהִקְרַבְתֶּם

אִשֶּׁה עֹלָה לַיהוָה פָּרִים בְּנֵי־בָקָר שְׁנַיִם וְאַיִל אֶחָד וְשִׁבְעָה כְבָשִׂים בְּנֵי

כ שָׁנָה תְּמִימִם יִהְיוּ לָכֶם: וּמִנְחָתָם סֹלֶת בְּלוּלָה בַשָּׁמֶן שְׁלֹשָׁה עֶשְׂרֹנִים

כא לַפָּר וּשְׁנֵי עֶשְׂרֹנִים לָאַיִל תַּעֲשׂוּ: עִשָּׂרוֹן עִשָּׂרוֹן תַּעֲשֶׂה לַכֶּבֶשׂ הָאֶחָד

כב־כג לְשִׁבְעַת הַכְּבָשִׂים: וּשְׂעִיר חַטָּאת אֶחָד לְכַפֵּר עֲלֵיכֶם: מִלְּבַד עֹלַת

כד הַבֹּקֶר אֲשֶׁר לְעֹלַת הַתָּמִיד תַּעֲשׂוּ אֶת־אֵלֶּה: כָּאֵלֶּה תַּעֲשׂוּ לַיּוֹם שִׁבְעַת

יָמִים לֶחֶם אִשֵּׁה רֵיחַ־נִיחֹחַ לַיהוָה עַל־עוֹלַת הַתָּמִיד יֵעָשֶׂה וְנִסְכּוֹ:

כה וּבַיּוֹם הַשְּׁבִיעִי מִקְרָא־קֹדֶשׁ יִהְיֶה לָכֶם כָּל־מְלֶאכֶת עֲבֹדָה לֹא תַעֲשׂוּ:

MAFTIR
SHAVUOS
28:26-31
ב׳ טעמים

כו וּבְיוֹם הַבִּכּוּרִים בְּהַקְרִיבְכֶם מִנְחָה חֲדָשָׁה לַיהוָה

בְּשָׁבֻעֹתֵיכֶם מִקְרָא־קֹדֶשׁ יִהְיֶה לָכֶם כָּל־מְלֶאכֶת עֲבֹדָה לֹא תַעֲשׂוּ:

כז וְהִקְרַבְתֶּם עוֹלָה לְרֵיחַ נִיחֹחַ לַיהוָה פָּרִים בְּנֵי־בָקָר שְׁנַיִם אַיִל אֶחָד

כח שִׁבְעָה כְבָשִׂים בְּנֵי שָׁנָה: וּמִנְחָתָם סֹלֶת בְּלוּלָה בַשָּׁמֶן שְׁלֹשָׁה עֶשְׂרֹנִים

כט לַפָּר הָאֶחָד שְׁנֵי עֶשְׂרֹנִים לָאַיִל הָאֶחָד: עִשָּׂרוֹן עִשָּׂרוֹן לַכֶּבֶשׂ הָאֶחָד

ל־לא לְשִׁבְעַת הַכְּבָשִׂים: שְׂעִיר עִזִּים אֶחָד לְכַפֵּר עֲלֵיכֶם: מִלְּבַד עֹלַת הַתָּמִיד

וּמִנְחָתוֹ תַּעֲשׂוּ תְּמִימִם יִהְיוּ־לָכֶם וְנִסְכֵּיהֶם:

כט

א וּבַחֹדֶשׁ הַשְּׁבִיעִי בְּאֶחָד לַחֹדֶשׁ מִקְרָא־קֹדֶשׁ יִהְיֶה לָכֶם כָּל־מְלֶאכֶת

MAFTIR
ROSH
HASHANAH
29:1-6

ב עֲבֹדָה לֹא תַעֲשׂוּ יוֹם תְּרוּעָה יִהְיֶה לָכֶם: וַעֲשִׂיתֶם עֹלָה לְרֵיחַ נִיחֹחַ

לַיהוָה פַּר בֶּן־בָּקָר אֶחָד אַיִל אֶחָד כְּבָשִׂים בְּנֵי־שָׁנָה שִׁבְעָה תְּמִימִם:

shall you make in the afternoon, ⁵ with a tenth-ephah of fine flour as a meal-offering, mixed with a quarter-hin of crushed oil. ⁶ It is the continual burnt-offering that was done at Mount Sinai, for a satisfying aroma, a fire-offering to HASHEM. ⁷ And its libation is a quarter-hin for the one lamb, to be poured on the holy [Altar], an intoxicating libation for HASHEM. ⁸ The second lamb you shall make in the afternoon; like the meal-offering of the morning and like its libation shall you make, a fire-offering for a satisfying aroma to HASHEM.

The mussaf offerings:
(See Appendix B, chart 13)
Sabbath

⁹ And on the Sabbath day: two male lambs in their first year, unblemished, two tenth-ephah of fine flour for a meal offering, mixed with oil, and its libation. ¹⁰ The burnt-offering of each Sabbath on its own Sabbath, in addition to the continual burnt-offering and its libation.

Rosh Chodesh/ The New Moon

¹¹ On your New Moons, you shall bring a burnt-offering to HASHEM: two young bulls, one ram, seven male lambs in their first year, unblemished. ¹² And three tenth-ephah of fine flour for a meal-offering mixed with oil, for each bull; and two tenth-ephah of fine flour for a meal-offering mixed with oil, for the one ram; ¹³ and a tenth-ephah of fine flour for a meal-offering, mixed with oil, for each lamb — a burnt-offering, a satisfying aroma, a fire-offering to HASHEM. ¹⁴ And their libations: a half-hin for each bull, a third-hin for the ram, a quarter-hin for each lamb — of wine. This is the burnt-offering of each month in its own month for the months of the year. ¹⁵ And one male of the goats for a sin-offering to HASHEM. In addition to the continual burnt-offering shall it be made, and its libation.

Pesach

¹⁶ In the first month, on the fourteenth day of the month, shall be a pesach-offering to HASHEM. ¹⁷ And on the fifteenth day of this month is a festival; for a seven-day period matzos shall be eaten. ¹⁸ On the first day is a holy convocation; you shall not do any laborious work. ¹⁹ You shall offer a fire-offering, a burnt-offering to HASHEM: two young bulls, one ram, seven male lambs within their first year, unblemished shall they be for you. ²⁰ And their meal-offering: fine flour mixed with oil; you shall make three tenth-ephah for each bull and two tenth-ephah for the ram. ²¹ One tenth-ephah shall you make for each lamb of the seven lambs. ²² And one he-goat for a sin-offering, to atone for you. ²³ Aside from the burnt-offering of the morning that is for the continual burnt-offering shall you make these. ²⁴ Like these shall you make each day of the seven-day period: food, a fire-offering, a satisfying aroma to HASHEM; in addition to the continual burnt-offering shall it be made, and its libation. ²⁵ The seventh day shall be a holy convocation for you; you shall not do any laborious work.

Shavuos

²⁶ On the day of the first-fruits, when you offer a new meal-offering to HASHEM on your Festival of Weeks, it shall be a holy convocation to you; you shall not do any laborious work. ²⁷ You shall offer a burnt-offering for a satisfying aroma to HASHEM: two young bulls, one ram, seven lambs within their first year. ²⁸ And their meal-offering: fine flour mixed with oil — three tenth-ephah for each bull; two tenth-ephah for the one ram; ²⁹ one tenth-ephah for each lamb of the seven lambs. ³⁰ One male of the goats to atone for you. ³¹ Aside from the continual burnt-offering and its meal-offering shall you offer [them] — unblemished shall they be for you — and their libations.

29

Rosh Hashanah

¹ In the seventh month, on the first day of the month, there shall be a holy convocation for you; you shall do no laborious work, it shall be a day of shofar-sounding for you. ² You shall make a burnt-offering for a satisfying aroma to HASHEM: one young bull, one ram, seven male lambs in their first year, unblem-

ג וּמִנְחָתָם סֹלֶת בְּלוּלָה בַשֶּׁמֶן שְׁלֹשָׁה עֶשְׂרֹנִים לַפָּר שְׁנֵי עֶשְׂרֹנִים לָאָיִל:

ד-ה וְעִשָּׂרוֹן אֶחָד לַכֶּבֶשׂ הָאֶחָד לְשִׁבְעַת הַכְּבָשִׂים: וּשְׂעִיר־עִזִּים אֶחָד חַטָּאת

ו לְכַפֵּר עֲלֵיכֶם: מִלְּבַד עֹלַת הַחֹדֶשׁ וּמִנְחָתָהּ וְעֹלַת הַתָּמִיד וּמִנְחָתָהּ

ז וְנִסְכֵּיהֶם כְּמִשְׁפָּטָם לְרֵיחַ נִיחֹחַ אִשֶּׁה לַיהוָה: וּבֶעָשׂוֹר

MAFTIR
YOM
KIPPUR
29:7-11

לַחֹדֶשׁ הַשְּׁבִיעִי הַזֶּה מִקְרָא־קֹדֶשׁ יִהְיֶה לָכֶם וְעִנִּיתֶם אֶת־נַפְשֹׁתֵיכֶם כָּל־

ח מְלָאכָה לֹא תַעֲשׂוּ: וְהִקְרַבְתֶּם עֹלָה לַיהוָה רֵיחַ נִיחֹחַ פַּר בֶּן־בָּקָר אֶחָד

ט אַיִל אֶחָד כְּבָשִׂים בְּנֵי־שָׁנָה שִׁבְעָה תְּמִימִם יִהְיוּ לָכֶם: וּמִנְחָתָם סֹלֶת

י בְּלוּלָה בַשֶּׁמֶן שְׁלֹשָׁה עֶשְׂרֹנִים לַפָּר שְׁנֵי עֶשְׂרֹנִים לָאַיִל הָאֶחָד: עִשָּׂרוֹן

יא עִשָּׂרוֹן לַכֶּבֶשׂ הָאֶחָד לְשִׁבְעַת הַכְּבָשִׂים: שְׂעִיר־עִזִּים אֶחָד חַטָּאת מִלְּבַד

יב חַטַּאת הַכִּפֻּרִים וְעֹלַת הַתָּמִיד וּמִנְחָתָהּ וְנִסְכֵּיהֶם: וּבַחֲמִשָּׁה

שביעי

עָשָׂר יוֹם לַחֹדֶשׁ הַשְּׁבִיעִי מִקְרָא־קֹדֶשׁ יִהְיֶה לָכֶם כָּל־מְלֶאכֶת עֲבֹדָה לֹא

MAFTIR
FIRST
TWO DAYS
SUCCOS
29:12-16;

תַעֲשׂוּ וְחַגֹּתֶם חַג לַיהוָה שִׁבְעַת יָמִים: וְהִקְרַבְתֶּם עֹלָה אִשֶּׁה רֵיחַ נִיחֹחַ

ליהוָה פָּרִים בְּנֵי־בָקָר שְׁלֹשָׁה עָשָׂר אֵילִם שְׁנָיִם כְּבָשִׂים בְּנֵי־שָׁנָה

יד אַרְבָּעָה עָשָׂר תְּמִימִם יִהְיוּ: וּמִנְחָתָם סֹלֶת בְּלוּלָה בַשֶּׁמֶן שְׁלֹשָׁה עֶשְׂרֹנִים

לַפָּר הָאֶחָד לִשְׁלֹשָׁה עָשָׂר פָּרִים שְׁנֵי עֶשְׂרֹנִים לָאַיִל הָאֶחָד לִשְׁנֵי

טו-טז הָאֵילִם: וְעִשָּׂרוֹן עִשָּׂרוֹן לַכֶּבֶשׂ הָאֶחָד לְאַרְבָּעָה עָשָׂר כְּבָשִׂים: וּשְׂעִיר־

נקוד על
ר בתרא
של עשרון

עִזִּים אֶחָד חַטָּאת מִלְּבַד עֹלַת הַתָּמִיד מִנְחָתָהּ וְנִסְכָּהּ: וּבַיּוֹם

יז-יח הַשֵּׁנִי פָּרִים בְּנֵי־בָקָר שְׁנֵים עָשָׂר אֵילִם שְׁנָיִם כְּבָשִׂים בְּנֵי־שָׁנָה אַרְבָּעָה

עָשָׂר תְּמִימִם: וּמִנְחָתָם וְנִסְכֵּיהֶם לַפָּרִים לָאֵילִם וְלַכְּבָשִׂים בְּמִסְפָּרָם

CHOL
HAMOED
SUCCOS
Reading for
weekdays:
1st day:
29:17-25;
2nd day:
29:20-28;
3rd day:
29:23-31;
4th day:
29:26-34;
Hoshana
Rabbah:
29:26-34

Maftir for
Sabbath:
1st day:
29:17-22;
3rd day:
29:23-28;
4th day:
29:26-31

יט כַּמִּשְׁפָּט: וּשְׂעִיר־עִזִּים אֶחָד חַטָּאת מִלְּבַד עֹלַת הַתָּמִיד וּמִנְחָתָהּ

כ וְנִסְכֵּיהֶם: וּבַיּוֹם הַשְּׁלִישִׁי פָּרִים עַשְׁתֵּי־עָשָׂר אֵילִם שְׁנָיִם

כא כְּבָשִׂים בְּנֵי־שָׁנָה אַרְבָּעָה עָשָׂר תְּמִימִם: וּמִנְחָתָם וְנִסְכֵּיהֶם לַפָּרִים

כב לָאֵילִם וְלַכְּבָשִׂים בְּמִסְפָּרָם כַּמִּשְׁפָּט: וּשְׂעִיר חַטָּאת אֶחָד מִלְּבַד עֹלַת

כג הַתָּמִיד וּמִנְחָתָהּ וְנִסְכָּהּ: וּבַיּוֹם הָרְבִיעִי פָּרִים עֲשָׂרָה אֵילִם

כד שְׁנַיִם כְּבָשִׂים בְּנֵי־שָׁנָה אַרְבָּעָה עָשָׂר תְּמִימִם: מִנְחָתָם וְנִסְכֵּיהֶם לַפָּרִים

כה לָאֵילִם וְלַכְּבָשִׂים בְּמִסְפָּרָם כַּמִּשְׁפָּט: וּשְׂעִיר־עִזִּים אֶחָד חַטָּאת מִלְּבַד

כו עֹלַת הַתָּמִיד מִנְחָתָהּ וְנִסְכָּהּ: וּבַיּוֹם הַחֲמִישִׁי פָּרִים תִּשְׁעָה

אֵילִם שְׁנַיִם כְּבָשִׂים בְּנֵי־שָׁנָה אַרְבָּעָה עָשָׂר תְּמִימִם: וּמִנְחָתָם וְנִסְכֵּיהֶם

כז-כח לַפָּרִים לָאֵילִם וְלַכְּבָשִׂים בְּמִסְפָּרָם כַּמִּשְׁפָּט: וּשְׂעִיר חַטָּאת אֶחָד מִלְּבַד

כט עֹלַת הַתָּמִיד וּמִנְחָתָהּ וְנִסְכָּהּ: וּבַיּוֹם הַשִּׁשִּׁי פָּרִים שְׁמֹנָה

ל אֵילִם שְׁנַיִם כְּבָשִׂים בְּנֵי־שָׁנָה אַרְבָּעָה עָשָׂר תְּמִימִם: וּמִנְחָתָם וְנִסְכֵּיהֶם

29:13. The offerings of Succos are unique in three ways: (a) They include a total of seventy bulls, to invoke protection for the seventy gentile nations; (b) the number of bulls is different for each day of the festival; and (c) there is a special water libation, which was performed every morning of Succos.

ished. ³ And their meal-offering: fine flour mixed with oil — three tenth-ephah for the bull; two tenth-ephah for the ram; ⁴ and one tenth-ephah for each lamb of the seven lambs. ⁵ One male of the goats for a sin-offering to provide you atonement. ⁶ Aside from the burnt-offering of the New Moon and its meal-offering, the continual burnt-offering and its meal-offering, and their libations according to their law — for a satisfying aroma, a fire-offering to HASHEM.

Yom Kippur   ⁷ On the tenth day of this seventh month there shall be a holy convocation for you and you shall afflict yourselves; you shall not do any work. ⁸ You shall offer a burnt-offering to HASHEM for a satisfying aroma — one young bull, one ram, seven male lambs in their first year; unblemished shall they be for you. ⁹ And their meal-offering: fine flour mixed with oil — three tenth-ephah for the bull; two tenth-ephah for the one ram; ¹⁰ and one tenth-ephah for each lamb of the seven lambs. ¹¹ One male of the goats for a sin-offering, aside from the sin-offering of the atonement and the continual burnt-offering, with its meal-offering, and their libations.

Succos   ¹² On the fifteenth day of the seventh month, there shall be a holy convocation for you; you shall do no laborious work; you shall celebrate a festival to HASHEM for a seven-day period. ¹³ You shall offer a burnt-offering, a fire-offering, a satisfying aroma to HASHEM: thirteen young bulls, * two rams, fourteen male lambs in their first year; they shall be unblemished. ¹⁴ And their meal-offering: fine flour mixed with oil — three tenth-ephah for each bull of the thirteen bulls; two tenth-ephah for each ram of the two rams; ¹⁵ and one tenth-ephah for each lamb of the fourteen lambs. ¹⁶ One male of the goats for a sin-offering, aside from the continual burnt-offering with its meal-offering and its libation.

¹⁷ And on the second day: twelve young bulls, two rams, fourteen male lambs within their first year, unblemished. ¹⁸ And their meal-offering and their libations for the bulls, the rams, and the lambs, in their proper numbers, as required. ¹⁹ One male of the goats for a sin-offering; aside from the continual burnt-offering, its meal-offering and their libations.

²⁰ And on the third day: eleven bulls, two rams, fourteen male lambs within their first year, unblemished. ²¹ And their meal-offering and their libations for the bulls, the rams, and the lambs, in their proper numbers, as required. ²² One he-goat for a sin-offering; aside from the continual burnt-offering, its meal-offering and its libation.

²³ And on the fourth day: ten bulls, two rams, fourteen male lambs within their first year, unblemished. ²⁴ And their meal-offering and their libations for the bulls, the rams, and the lambs, in their proper numbers, as required. ²⁵ One male of the goats for a sin-offering; aside from the continual burnt-offering, its meal-offering and its libation.

²⁶ And on the fifth day: nine bulls, two rams, fourteen male lambs within their first year, unblemished. ²⁷ And their meal-offering and their libations for the bulls, the rams, and the lambs, in their proper numbers, as required. ²⁸ One he-goat for a sin-offering; aside from the continual burnt-offering, its meal-offering and its libation.

²⁹ And on the sixth day: eight bulls, two rams, fourteen male lambs within their first year, unblemished. ³⁰ And their meal-offering and their libations

Haftaras
Pinchas:
before 17
Tammuz:
p. 860;
after 17
Tammuz
(most years):
p. 1072

מפטיר

MAFTIR
SHEMINI
ATZERES
AND
SIMCHAS
TORAH
29:35-30:1

לא לַפָּרִים לָאֵילִם וְלַכְּבָשִׂים בְּמִסְפָּרָם כַּמִּשְׁפָּט: וּשְׂעִיר חַטָּאת אֶחָד
לב מִלְּבַד עֹלַת הַתָּמִיד מִנְחָתָהּ וְנִסְכָּהּ: וּבַיּוֹם הַשְּׁבִיעִי
לג פָרִים שִׁבְעָה אֵילִם שְׁנָיִם כְּבָשִׂים בְּנֵי־שָׁנָה אַרְבָּעָה עָשָׂר תְּמִימִם:
לד וּמִנְחָתָם וְנִסְכֵּהֶם לַפָּרִים לָאֵילִם וְלַכְּבָשִׂים בְּמִסְפָּרָם כַּמִּשְׁפָּטָם: וּשְׂעִיר
לה חַטָּאת אֶחָד מִלְּבַד עֹלַת הַתָּמִיד מִנְחָתָהּ וְנִסְכָּהּ: בַּיּוֹם
לו הַשְּׁמִינִי עֲצֶרֶת תִּהְיֶה לָכֶם כָּל־מְלֶאכֶת עֲבֹדָה לֹא תַעֲשׂוּ: וְהִקְרַבְתֶּם
עֹלָה אִשֵּׁה רֵיחַ נִיחֹחַ לַיהוָה פַּר אֶחָד אַיִל אֶחָד כְּבָשִׂים בְּנֵי־שָׁנָה
לז שִׁבְעָה תְּמִימִם: מִנְחָתָם וְנִסְכֵּיהֶם לַפָּר לָאַיִל וְלַכְּבָשִׂים בְּמִסְפָּרָם
לח כַּמִּשְׁפָּט: וּשְׂעִיר חַטָּאת אֶחָד מִלְּבַד עֹלַת הַתָּמִיד וּמִנְחָתָהּ וְנִסְכָּהּ:
לט אֵלֶּה תַּעֲשׂוּ לַיהוָה בְּמוֹעֲדֵיכֶם לְבַד מִנִּדְרֵיכֶם וְנִדְבֹתֵיכֶם לְעֹלֹתֵיכֶם
א וּלְמִנְחֹתֵיכֶם וּלְנִסְכֵּיכֶם וּלְשַׁלְמֵיכֶם: וַיֹּאמֶר מֹשֶׁה אֶל־בְּנֵי יִשְׂרָאֵל כְּכֹל
אֲשֶׁר־צִוָּה יהוה אֶת־מֹשֶׁה: פפפ קט״ח פסוקים. לחל״ק סימן. ואל״ף פלה״ו סימן.

פָּרָשַׁת מַטּוֹת

ב וַיְדַבֵּר מֹשֶׁה אֶל־רָאשֵׁי הַמַּטּוֹת לִבְנֵי יִשְׂרָאֵל לֵאמֹר זֶה הַדָּבָר אֲשֶׁר
ג צִוָּה יהוה: אִישׁ כִּי־יִדֹּר נֶדֶר לַיהוָה אוֹ־הִשָּׁבַע שְׁבֻעָה לֶאְסֹר אִסָּר עַל־
ד נַפְשׁוֹ לֹא יַחֵל דְּבָרוֹ כְּכָל־הַיֹּצֵא מִפִּיו יַעֲשֶׂה: וְאִשָּׁה כִּי־תִדֹּר נֶדֶר לַיהוָה
ה וְאָסְרָה אִסָּר בְּבֵית אָבִיהָ בִּנְעֻרֶיהָ: וְשָׁמַע אָבִיהָ אֶת־נִדְרָהּ וֶאֱסָרָהּ
אֲשֶׁר אָסְרָה עַל־נַפְשָׁהּ וְהֶחֱרִישׁ לָהּ אָבִיהָ וְקָמוּ כָּל־נְדָרֶיהָ וְכָל־אִסָּר
ו אֲשֶׁר־אָסְרָה עַל־נַפְשָׁהּ יָקוּם: וְאִם־הֵנִיא אָבִיהָ אֹתָהּ בְּיוֹם שָׁמְעוֹ כָּל־
נְדָרֶיהָ וֶאֱסָרֶיהָ אֲשֶׁר־אָסְרָה עַל־נַפְשָׁהּ לֹא יָקוּם וַיהוָה יִסְלַח־לָהּ כִּי־
ז הֵנִיא אָבִיהָ אֹתָהּ: וְאִם־הָיוֹ תִהְיֶה לְאִישׁ וּנְדָרֶיהָ עָלֶיהָ
ח אוֹ מִבְטָא שְׂפָתֶיהָ אֲשֶׁר אָסְרָה עַל־נַפְשָׁהּ: וְשָׁמַע אִישָׁהּ בְּיוֹם
שָׁמְעוֹ וְהֶחֱרִישׁ לָהּ וְקָמוּ נְדָרֶיהָ וֶאֱסָרֶהָ אֲשֶׁר־אָסְרָה עַל־נַפְשָׁהּ יָקֻמוּ:
ט וְאִם בְּיוֹם שְׁמֹעַ אִישָׁהּ יָנִיא אוֹתָהּ וְהֵפֵר אֶת־נִדְרָהּ אֲשֶׁר עָלֶיהָ וְאֵת
י מִבְטָא שְׂפָתֶיהָ אֲשֶׁר אָסְרָה עַל־נַפְשָׁהּ וַיהוָה יִסְלַח־לָהּ: וְנֵדֶר אַלְמָנָה
יא וּגְרוּשָׁה כֹּל אֲשֶׁר־אָסְרָה עַל־נַפְשָׁהּ יָקוּם עָלֶיהָ: וְאִם־בֵּית אִישָׁהּ
יב נָדָרָה אוֹ־אָסְרָה אִסָּר עַל־נַפְשָׁהּ בִּשְׁבֻעָה: וְשָׁמַע אִישָׁהּ וְהֶחֱרִשׁ לָהּ
לֹא הֵנִיא אֹתָהּ וְקָמוּ כָּל־נְדָרֶיהָ וְכָל־אִסָּר אֲשֶׁר־אָסְרָה עַל־נַפְשָׁהּ
יג יָקוּם: וְאִם־הָפֵר יָפֵר אֹתָם | אִישָׁהּ בְּיוֹם שָׁמְעוֹ כָּל־מוֹצָא שְׂפָתֶיהָ

29:35-38. Shemini Atzeres, the last day of the Succos festival, which is combined with Simchas Torah, the celebration of the completion of the year's Torah reading, is in certain ways an independent festival. Thus, its *mussaf*-offering is drastically different from that of the seven days of Succos.

29:39. *These*, i.e., all the *mussaf*-offerings listed in the two previous chapters (*Rashi*).

◆§ **Parashas Mattos**

30:3. A person is given the power to invoke a *neder*, i.e., a vow or oath, thereby placing upon himself or others, or upon objects of his choice, a status equivalent to that of a commandment of the Torah.

The second type of this passage is שְׁבֻעָה, *an oath*. By means of an oath, one may either prohibit oneself or require oneself to perform an act.

for the bulls, the rams, and the lambs, in their proper numbers, as required. ³¹ *One he-goat for a sin-offering; aside from the continual burnt-offering, its meal-offering and its libations.*

³² *And on the seventh day: seven bulls, two rams, fourteen lambs within their first year, unblemished.* ³³ *And their meal-offering and their libations for the bulls, the rams, and the lambs, in their proper numbers, in their requirements.* ³⁴ *One he-goat for a sin-offering; aside from the continual burnt-offering, its meal-offering and its libation.*

Shemini ³⁵ *The eighth day* shall be a restriction for you; you shall not do any labor-*
Atzeres *ious work.* ³⁶ *You shall offer a burnt-offering, a fire-offering, a satisfying aroma to HASHEM; one bull, one ram, seven lambs within their first year, unblemished.* ³⁷ *Their meal-offering and libations for the bull, the ram, and the lambs shall be in their proper numbers, as required.* ³⁸ *One he-goat for a sin-offering; aside from the continual burnt-offering, its meal-offering and its libation.*

³⁹ *These* are what you shall make for HASHEM on your appointed festivals, aside from your vows and your free-will offerings for your burnt-offerings, your meal-offerings, your libations, and your peace-offerings.*

30 ¹ M*oses said to the Children of Israel according to everything that HASHEM had commanded Moses.*

PARASHAS MATTOS

Vows and ² M*oses spoke to the heads of the tribes of the Children of Israel, saying: This*
oaths *is the thing that HASHEM has commanded:* ³ *If a man takes a vow* to HASHEM or swears an oath to establish a prohibition upon himself, he shall not desecrate his word; according to whatever comes from his mouth shall he do.*

⁴ *But if a woman will take a vow to HASHEM or establish a prohibition in her father's home in her youth;** ⁵ *and her father heard of her vow or her prohibition that she established upon herself, and her father was silent about her, then all her vows shall stand, and any prohibition that she established upon herself shall stand.* ⁶ *But if her father restrained her on the day of his hearing, all her vows or prohibitions that she established upon herself shall not stand; and HASHEM will forgive her, for her father had restrained her.*

⁷ *If she shall be married to a man and her vows were upon her, or an utterance of her lips by which she had prohibited something upon herself,* ⁸ *and her husband heard, and on the day of his hearing he was silent about her — then her vows shall stand and her prohibition that she established upon herself shall stand.* ⁹ *But if on the day of her husband's hearing he shall restrain her and he shall revoke the vow that is upon her or the utterance of her lips by which she had prohibited something upon herself — then HASHEM will forgive her.*

¹⁰ *The vow of a widow or a divorcee — anything she had prohibited upon herself — shall remain upon her.*

¹¹ *But if she vowed in her husband's home, or she established a prohibition upon herself through an oath,* ¹² *and her husband heard and was silent about her — he did not restrain her — then all her vows shall stand and any prohibition she established upon herself shall stand.* ¹³ *But if her husband shall revoke them on the day of his hearing, anything that came out of her mouth*

30:4. If a girl makes a *neder* while she is under her father's jurisdiction, he may approve it, even tacitly (vv. 4-5); he may revoke it (v. 6); or she may have married before her father did either of the above (vv. 7-9).

יד לִנְדָרֶיהָ וּלְאִסֵּר נַפְשָׁהּ לֹא יָקוּם אִישָׁהּ הֵפֵרָם וַיהוָה יִסְלַח־לָהּ: כָּל־נֶדֶר וְכָל־שְׁבֻעַת אִסָּר לְעַנֹּת נָפֶשׁ אִישָׁהּ יְקִימֶנּוּ וְאִישָׁהּ יְפֵרֶנּוּ:

טו וְאִם־הַחֲרֵשׁ יַחֲרִישׁ לָהּ אִישָׁהּ מִיּוֹם אֶל־יוֹם וְהֵקִים אֶת־כָּל־נְדָרֶיהָ אוֹ אֶת־כָּל־אֱסָרֶיהָ אֲשֶׁר עָלֶיהָ הֵקִים אֹתָם כִּי־הֶחֱרִשׁ לָהּ בְּיוֹם

טז-יז שָׁמְעוֹ: וְאִם־הָפֵר יָפֵר אֹתָם אַחֲרֵי שָׁמְעוֹ וְנָשָׂא אֶת־עֲוֹנָהּ: אֵלֶּה הַחֻקִּים אֲשֶׁר צִוָּה יְהוָה אֶת־מֹשֶׁה בֵּין אִישׁ לְאִשְׁתּוֹ בֵּין־אָב לְבִתּוֹ בִּנְעֻרֶיהָ בֵּית אָבִיהָ:

לא א־ב וַיְדַבֵּר יְהוָה אֶל־מֹשֶׁה לֵּאמֹר: נְקֹם נִקְמַת בְּנֵי יִשְׂרָאֵל מֵאֵת הַמִּדְיָנִים אַחַר תֵּאָסֵף אֶל־עַמֶּיךָ: ג וַיְדַבֵּר מֹשֶׁה אֶל־הָעָם לֵאמֹר הֵחָלְצוּ מֵאִתְּכֶם אֲנָשִׁים לַצָּבָא וְיִהְיוּ עַל־מִדְיָן לָתֵת נִקְמַת־יְהוָה בְּמִדְיָן: ד אֶלֶף לַמַּטֶּה אֶלֶף לַמַּטֶּה לְכֹל מַטּוֹת יִשְׂרָאֵל תִּשְׁלְחוּ לַצָּבָא: ה וַיִּמָּסְרוּ מֵאַלְפֵי יִשְׂרָאֵל אֶלֶף לַמַּטֶּה שְׁנֵים־עָשָׂר אֶלֶף חֲלוּצֵי צָבָא: ו וַיִּשְׁלַח אֹתָם מֹשֶׁה אֶלֶף לַמַּטֶּה לַצָּבָא אֹתָם וְאֶת־פִּינְחָס בֶּן־אֶלְעָזָר הַכֹּהֵן לַצָּבָא וּכְלֵי הַקֹּדֶשׁ וַחֲצֹצְרוֹת הַתְּרוּעָה בְּיָדוֹ: ז וַיִּצְבְּאוּ עַל־מִדְיָן כַּאֲשֶׁר צִוָּה יְהוָה אֶת־מֹשֶׁה וַיַּהַרְגוּ כָּל־זָכָר: ח וְאֶת־מַלְכֵי מִדְיָן הָרְגוּ עַל־חַלְלֵיהֶם אֶת־אֱוִי וְאֶת־רֶקֶם וְאֶת־צוּר וְאֶת־חוּר וְאֶת־רֶבַע חֲמֵשֶׁת מַלְכֵי מִדְיָן וְאֵת בִּלְעָם בֶּן־בְּעוֹר הָרְגוּ בֶּחָרֶב: ט וַיִּשְׁבּוּ בְנֵי־יִשְׂרָאֵל אֶת־נְשֵׁי מִדְיָן וְאֶת־טַפָּם וְאֵת כָּל־בְּהֶמְתָּם וְאֶת־כָּל־מִקְנֵהֶם וְאֶת־כָּל־חֵילָם בָּזָזוּ: י וְאֵת כָּל־עָרֵיהֶם בְּמוֹשְׁבֹתָם וְאֵת כָּל־טִירֹתָם שָׂרְפוּ בָּאֵשׁ: יא־יב וַיִּקְחוּ אֶת־כָּל־הַשָּׁלָל וְאֵת כָּל־הַמַּלְקוֹחַ בָּאָדָם וּבַבְּהֵמָה: וַיָּבִאוּ אֶל־מֹשֶׁה וְאֶל־אֶלְעָזָר הַכֹּהֵן וְאֶל־עֲדַת בְּנֵי־יִשְׂרָאֵל אֶת־הַשְּׁבִי וְאֶת־הַמַּלְקוֹחַ וְאֶת־הַשָּׁלָל אֶל־הַמַּחֲנֶה אֶל־עַרְבֹת מוֹאָב אֲשֶׁר עַל־יַרְדֵּן יְרֵחוֹ:

יג וַיֵּצְאוּ מֹשֶׁה וְאֶלְעָזָר הַכֹּהֵן וְכָל־נְשִׂיאֵי הָעֵדָה לִקְרָאתָם אֶל־מִחוּץ לַמַּחֲנֶה: יד וַיִּקְצֹף מֹשֶׁה עַל פְּקוּדֵי הֶחָיִל שָׂרֵי הָאֲלָפִים וְשָׂרֵי הַמֵּאוֹת הַבָּאִים מִצְּבָא הַמִּלְחָמָה: טו וַיֹּאמֶר אֲלֵיהֶם מֹשֶׁה הַחִיִּיתֶם כָּל־נְקֵבָה: טז הֵן הֵנָּה הָיוּ לִבְנֵי יִשְׂרָאֵל בִּדְבַר בִּלְעָם לִמְסָר־מַעַל בַּיהוָה עַל־דְּבַר־פְּעוֹר וַתְּהִי הַמַּגֵּפָה בַּעֲדַת יְהוָה: יז וְעַתָּה הִרְגוּ כָל־זָכָר בַּטָּף וְכָל־אִשָּׁה יֹדַעַת אִישׁ לְמִשְׁכַּב זָכָר הֲרֹגוּ: יח וְכֹל הַטַּף בַּנָּשִׁים אֲשֶׁר לֹא־יָדְעוּ מִשְׁכַּב זָכָר הַחֲיוּ לָכֶם: יט וְאַתֶּם חֲנוּ מִחוּץ לַמַּחֲנֶה שִׁבְעַת יָמִים כֹּל הֹרֵג נֶפֶשׁ וְכֹל נֹגֵעַ בֶּחָלָל תִּתְחַטְּאוּ בַּיּוֹם הַשְּׁלִישִׁי וּבַיּוֹם הַשְּׁבִיעִי אַתֶּם וּשְׁבִיכֶם: כ וְכָל־בֶּגֶד וְכָל־כְּלִי־עוֹר וְכָל־מַעֲשֵׂה עִזִּים וְכָל־כְּלִי־עֵץ תִּתְחַטָּאוּ: כא וַיֹּאמֶר

31:2. This was the retribution that had been promised against the Midianites (25:17) because of their responsibility for the Jewish sins of immorality and idolatry.

31:14. Moses was angry because the officers had allowed their troops to spare women who were known to have participated in the orgies (*Rashi* to v. 16).

regarding her vows or the prohibition upon herself shall not stand; her husband had revoked them and HASHEM will forgive her. ¹⁴ Any vow and any oath-prohibition to cause personal affliction, her husband may let it stand and her husband may revoke it. ¹⁵ If her husband shall be silent about her from day to day — he will have let stand all her vows; or all the prohibitions that are upon her, he will have let them stand, for he was silent about her on the day of his hearing. ¹⁶ But if he shall revoke them after his having heard, he shall bear her iniquity.

¹⁷ These are the decrees that HASHEM commanded Moses, between a man and his wife, between a father and his daughter in her youth, in her father's house.

31

The battle against Midian

¹ HASHEM spoke to Moses, saying, ² "Take vengeance for the Children of Israel against the Midianites;* afterward you will be gathered unto your people."

³ Moses spoke to the people, saying, "Arm men from among yourselves for the legion that they may be against Midian to inflict HASHEM's vengeance against Midian. ⁴ A thousand from a tribe, a thousand from a tribe, for all the tribes of Israel shall you send to the legion."

⁵ So there were delivered from the thousands of Israel, a thousand from each tribe, twelve thousand armed for the legion. ⁶ Moses sent them — a thousand from each tribe for the legion — them and Phinehas son of Elazar the Kohen to the legion, and the sacred vessels and the trumpets for sounding in his hand. ⁷ They massed against Midian, as HASHEM had commanded Moses, and they killed every male. ⁸ They killed the kings of Midian along with their slain ones: Evi, Rekem, Zur, Hur, and Reba, the five kings of Midian; and Balaam son of Beor they slew with the sword. ⁹ The Children of Israel took captive the women of Midian and their young children; and all their cattle and flocks and all their wealth they took as spoils. ¹⁰ All the cities of their habitations and all their palaces they burned in fire. ¹¹ They took all the booty and all the captives of people and animals. ¹² They brought to Moses, to Elazar the Kohen, and to the assembly of the Children of Israel the captives, the animals, and the booty to the camp, at the plains of Moab, which was by the Jordan near Jericho.

Moses rebukes the officers

¹³ Moses, Elazar the Kohen, and all the leaders of the assembly went out to meet them outside the camp. ¹⁴ Moses was angry with the commanders of the army,* the officers of the thousands and the officers of the hundreds, who came from the legion of the battle.

¹⁵ Moses said to them, "Did you let every female live? ¹⁶ Behold! — it was they who caused the Children of Israel, by the word of Balaam, to commit a betrayal against HASHEM regarding the matter of Peor; and the plague occurred in the assembly of HASHEM. ¹⁷ So now, kill every male among the young children, and every woman fit to know a man by lying with a male, you shall kill. ¹⁸ But all the young children among the women who have not known lying with a male, you may keep alive for yourselves. ¹⁹ And as for you, encamp outside the camp for a seven-day period; whoever killed a person or touched a corpse shall purify yourselves on the third day and on the seventh day — you and your captives. ²⁰ And every garment, every vessel of hide, everything made of that which comes from goats, and every vessel of wood, you shall purify."

אֶלְעָזָ֣ר הַכֹּהֵ֗ן אֶל־אַנְשֵׁ֤י הַצָּבָא֙ הַבָּאִ֣ים לַמִּלְחָמָ֔ה זֹ֚את חֻקַּ֣ת הַתּוֹרָ֔ה

כב אֲשֶׁר־צִוָּ֥ה יְהוָ֖ה אֶת־מֹשֶֽׁה: אַ֤ךְ אֶת־הַזָּהָב֙ וְאֶת־הַכֶּ֔סֶף אֶֽת־הַנְּחֹ֖שֶׁת

כג אֶת־הַבַּרְזֶ֕ל אֶֽת־הַבְּדִ֖יל וְאֶת־הָֽעֹפָֽרֶת: כָּל־דָּבָ֞ר אֲשֶׁר־יָבֹ֣א בָאֵ֗שׁ

תַּעֲבִ֤ירוּ בָאֵשׁ֙ וְטָהֵ֔ר אַ֕ךְ בְּמֵ֥י נִדָּ֖ה יִתְחַטָּ֑א וְכֹ֨ל אֲשֶׁ֧ר לֹֽא־יָבֹ֛א בָּאֵ֖שׁ

כד תַּעֲבִ֥ירוּ בַמָּֽיִם: וְכִבַּסְתֶּ֧ם בִּגְדֵיכֶ֛ם בַּיּ֥וֹם הַשְּׁבִיעִ֖י וּטְהַרְתֶּ֑ם וְאַחַ֖ר תָּבֹ֥אוּ

כה-כו אֶל־הַֽמַּחֲנֶֽה: וַיֹּ֥אמֶר יְהוָ֖ה אֶל־מֹשֶׁ֥ה לֵּאמֹֽר: שָׂ֗א אֵ֚ת   **רביעי**

רֹ֤אשׁ מַלְק֙וֹחַ֙ הַשְּׁבִ֔י בָּֽאָדָ֖ם וּבַבְּהֵמָ֑ה אַתָּה֙ וְאֶלְעָזָ֣ר הַכֹּהֵ֔ן וְרָאשֵׁ֖י אֲב֥וֹת

כז הָעֵדָֽה: וְחָצִ֙יתָ֙ אֶת־הַמַּלְק֔וֹחַ בֵּ֚ין תֹּפְשֵׂ֣י הַמִּלְחָמָ֔ה הַיֹּצְאִ֖ים לַצָּבָ֑א וּבֵ֖ין

כח כָּל־הָעֵדָֽה: וַהֲרֵמֹתָ֨ מֶ֜כֶס לַֽיהוָ֗ה מֵאֵ֞ת אַנְשֵׁ֤י הַמִּלְחָמָה֙ הַיֹּצְאִ֣ים לַצָּבָ֔א

אֶחָ֣ד נֶ֔פֶשׁ מֵחֲמֵ֖שׁ הַמֵּא֑וֹת מִן־הָֽאָדָ֣ם וּמִן־הַבָּקָ֔ר וּמִן־הַחֲמֹרִ֖ים וּמִן־

כט-ל הַצֹּֽאן: מִמַּֽחֲצִיתָ֖ם תִּקָּ֑חוּ וְנָתַתָּ֛ה לְאֶלְעָזָ֥ר הַכֹּהֵ֖ן תְּרוּמַ֥ת יְהוָֽה: וּמִמַּֽחֲצִ֨ת

בְּנֵֽי־יִשְׂרָאֵ֜ל תִּקַּ֣ח ׀ אֶחָ֣ד ׀ אָחֻ֣ז מִן־הַחֲמִשִּׁ֗ים מִן־הָֽאָדָם֙ מִן־הַבָּקָ֤ר מִן־

הַֽחֲמֹרִים֙ וּמִן־הַצֹּ֔אן מִכָּל־הַבְּהֵמָ֑ה וְנָתַתָּ֤ה אֹתָם֙ לַלְוִיִּ֔ם שֹׁמְרֵ֖י מִשְׁמֶ֥רֶת

לא-לב מִשְׁכַּ֥ן יְהוָֽה: וַיַּ֣עַשׂ מֹשֶׁ֗ה וְאֶלְעָזָ֣ר הַכֹּהֵ֔ן כַּֽאֲשֶׁ֛ר צִוָּ֥ה יְהוָ֖ה אֶת־מֹשֶֽׁה: וַיְהִי֙

הַמַּלְק֔וֹחַ יֶ֣תֶר הַבָּ֔ז אֲשֶׁ֥ר בָּזְז֖וּ עַ֣ם הַצָּבָ֑א צֹ֗אן שֵׁשׁ־מֵא֥וֹת אֶ֛לֶף וְשִׁבְעִ֥ים

לג-לד אֶ֖לֶף וַֽחֲמֵ֥שֶׁת אֲלָפִֽים: וּבָקָ֕ר שְׁנַ֥יִם וְשִׁבְעִ֖ים אָ֑לֶף: וַחֲמֹרִ֕ים אֶחָ֥ד וְשִׁשִּׁ֖ים

לה אָֽלֶף: וְנֶ֣פֶשׁ אָדָ֔ם מִן־הַנָּשִׁ֔ים אֲשֶׁ֥ר לֹֽא־יָדְע֖וּ מִשְׁכַּ֣ב זָכָ֑ר כָּל־נֶ֕פֶשׁ שְׁנַ֥יִם

לו וּשְׁלֹשִׁ֖ים אָֽלֶף: וַתְּהִי֙ הַֽמֶּחֱצָ֔ה חֵ֕לֶק הַיֹּצְאִ֖ים בַּצָּבָ֑א מִסְפַּ֣ר הַצֹּ֔אן שְׁלֹשׁ־

לז מֵא֥וֹת אֶ֙לֶף֙ וּשְׁלֹשִׁ֣ים אֶ֔לֶף וְשִׁבְעַ֥ת אֲלָפִ֖ים וַחֲמֵ֣שׁ מֵאֽוֹת: וַיְהִ֛י הַמֶּ֥כֶס

לח לַֽיהוָ֖ה מִן־הַצֹּ֑אן שֵׁ֥שׁ מֵא֖וֹת חָמֵ֥שׁ וְשִׁבְעִֽים: וְהַבָּקָ֕ר שִׁשָּׁ֥ה וּשְׁלֹשִׁ֖ים אֶ֑לֶף

לט וּמִכְסָ֥ם לַֽיהוָ֖ה שְׁנַ֥יִם וְשִׁבְעִֽים: וַחֲמֹרִ֕ים שְׁלֹשִׁ֥ים אֶ֖לֶף וַחֲמֵ֣שׁ מֵא֑וֹת

מ וּמִכְסָ֥ם לַֽיהוָ֖ה אֶחָ֥ד וְשִׁשִּֽׁים: וְנֶ֣פֶשׁ אָדָ֔ם שִׁשָּׁ֥ה עָשָׂ֖ר אָ֑לֶף וּמִכְסָם֙ לַֽיהוָ֔ה

מא שְׁנַ֥יִם וּשְׁלֹשִׁ֖ים נָֽפֶשׁ: וַיִּתֵּ֣ן מֹשֶׁ֗ה אֶת־מֶ֙כֶס֙ תְּרוּמַ֣ת יְהוָ֔ה לְאֶלְעָזָ֖ר הַכֹּהֵ֑ן

מב כַּֽאֲשֶׁ֛ר צִוָּ֥ה יְהוָ֖ה אֶת־מֹשֶֽׁה: וּמִֽמַּחֲצִ֖ית בְּנֵ֣י יִשְׂרָאֵ֑ל אֲשֶׁר֙ חָצָ֣ה מֹשֶׁ֔ה   **חמישי**

מג מִן־הָֽאֲנָשִׁ֖ים הַצֹּבְאִֽים: וַתְּהִ֛י מֶחֱצַ֥ת הָעֵדָ֖ה מִן־הַצֹּ֑אן שְׁלֹשׁ־מֵא֥וֹת אֶ֛לֶף

מד וּשְׁלֹשִׁ֥ים אֶ֖לֶף שִׁבְעַ֣ת אֲלָפִ֗ים וַחֲמֵ֥שׁ מֵאֽוֹת: וּבָקָ֕ר שִׁשָּׁ֥ה וּשְׁלֹשִׁ֖ים אָֽלֶף:

מה-מו וַחֲמֹרִ֕ים שְׁלֹשִׁ֥ים אֶ֖לֶף וַחֲמֵ֥שׁ מֵאֽוֹת: וְנֶ֣פֶשׁ אָדָ֔ם שִׁשָּׁ֥ה עָשָׂ֖ר אָ֑לֶף: וַיִּקַּ֨ח

מֹשֶׁ֜ה מִמַּֽחֲצִ֣ת בְּנֵֽי־יִשְׂרָאֵ֗ל אֶת־הָֽאָחֻז֙ אֶחָ֣ד מִן־הַחֲמִשִּׁ֔ים מִן־הָֽאָדָ֖ם

וּמִן־הַבְּהֵמָ֑ה וַיִּתֵּ֨ן אֹתָ֜ם לַלְוִיִּ֗ם שֹֽׁמְרֵי֙ מִשְׁמֶ֙רֶת֙ מִשְׁכַּ֣ן יְהוָ֔ה כַּֽאֲשֶׁ֥ר צִוָּ֛ה

מח יְהוָ֖ה אֶת־מֹשֶֽׁה: וַיִּקְרְבוּ֙ אֶל־מֹשֶׁ֔ה הַפְּקֻדִ֕ים אֲשֶׁ֖ר לְאַלְפֵ֣י הַצָּבָ֑א שָׂרֵ֥י

מט הָֽאֲלָפִ֖ים וְשָׂרֵ֣י הַמֵּא֑וֹת: וַיֹּֽאמְרוּ֙ אֶל־מֹשֶׁ֔ה עֲבָדֶ֣יךָ נָֽשְׂא֗וּ אֶת־רֹ֛אשׁ אַנְשֵׁ֥י

נ הַמִּלְחָמָ֖ה אֲשֶׁ֣ר בְּיָדֵ֑נוּ וְלֹא־נִפְקַ֥ד מִמֶּ֖נּוּ אִֽישׁ: וַנַּקְרֵ֞ב אֶת־קָרְבַּ֣ן יְהוָה֒

31:21-24. This passage teaches the methods by which the utensils taken or bought from non-Jews can be made kosher. If the vessels have no problem other than ritual contamination, immersion in a *mikveh* is sufficient, but

utensils used in cooking and eating must be purged (*kashered*) of any absorbed taste or non-kosher residue still on their surface.

31:23. Heat causes the pores of metal to expand so that

Laws of koshering utensils   [21] *Elazar the Kohen said to the men of the legion who came to the battle, "This is the decree of the Torah,* * *which HASHEM commanded Moses:* [22] *Only the gold and the silver, the copper, the iron, the tin, and the lead —* [23] *everything that comes into the fire — you shall pass through the fire and it will be purified;* * *but it must be purified with the water of sprinkling; and everything that would not come in the fire, you shall pass through the water.* [24] *You shall immerse your garments on the seventh day and become purified; afterward you may enter the camp.*

Division of the spoils   [25] *HASHEM said to Moses, saying:* [26] *Calculate the total of the captured spoils, of people and animals, you, Elazar the Kohen, and the heads of the fathers of the assembly.* [27] *Divide the spoils in half, between those who undertook the battle, who go out to the legion, and the entire assembly.* * [28] *You shall raise up a tribute to HASHEM from the men of war who go out to the legion, one living being of five hundred, from the people, from the cattle, from the donkeys, and* *Kohanim and Levites*   *from the flock.* [29] *You shall take it from their half and give it to Elazar the Kohen, as a portion of HASHEM.* [30] *And from the half of the Children of Israel you shall take one drawn from fifty, from the people, from the cattle, from the donkeys, from the flock — from all the animals — and you shall give them to the Levites, the guardians of the charge of HASHEM's Tabernacle.*

[31] *Moses and Elazar the Kohen did as HASHEM had commanded Moses.* [32] *The animal booty, beyond the spoils that the people of the legion looted: the flock, six hundred and seventy-five thousand;* [33] *and cattle, seventy-two thousand;* [34] *and donkeys, sixty-one thousand;* [35] *and human beings, the women who had* *The soldiers' share*   *not known lying with a male, all the souls, thirty-two thousand.* [36] *The half, which was the share of those who went out to the legion, was: the count of the flock, three hundred and thirty-seven thousand, five hundred —* [37] *the tribute to HASHEM from the flock, six hundred and seventy-five;* [38] *and the cattle, thirty-six thousand — and their tribute to HASHEM, seventy-two;* [39] *and the donkeys, thirty thousand, five hundred — and their tribute to HASHEM, sixty-one;* [40] *and the human beings, sixteen thousand — and their tribute to HASHEM, thirty-two people.* [41] *Moses gave the tribute that was raised up for HASHEM to Elazar the Kohen, as HASHEM had commanded Moses.*

The people's share   [42] *From the half of the Children of Israel that Moses had divided from the men of the legions,* [43] *the half of the assembly was: of the flock, three hundred and thirty-seven thousand, five hundred —* [44] *and the cattle, thirty-six thousand;* [45] *and the donkeys, thirty thousand, five hundred;* [46] *and the human beings, sixteen thousand.* [47] *Moses took from the half of the Children of Israel the one drawn from the fifty, from the people and the animals, and gave them to the Levites, the guardians of the charge of HASHEM's Tabernacle, as HASHEM had commanded Moses.*

The commanders   [48] *The commanders of the thousands in the legions, the officers of the thousands and the officers of the hundreds, approached Moses.* [49] *They said to Moses, "Your servants took a census of the men of war under our command, and not a man of us is missing.* [50] *So we have brought an offering for HASHEM:*

---

it absorbs the taste of foods that have come in contact with it. To remove what has been absorbed, the utensil must be heated in the same way as it was during its use.

31:27. The greatest share of the spoils went to those who actually fought. The rest of the nation received smaller shares, and a specified portion was to be contributed to the Tabernacle treasury and to the Levites.

אִישׁ אֲשֶׁר מָצָא כְלִי־זָהָב אֶצְעָדָה וְצָמִיד טַבַּעַת עָגִיל וְכוּמָז לְכַפֵּר עַל־

נא נַפְשֹׁתֵינוּ לִפְנֵי יְהֹוָה: וַיִּקַּח מֹשֶׁה וְאֶלְעָזָר הַכֹּהֵן אֶת־הַזָּהָב מֵאִתָּם כֹּל

נב כְּלִי מַעֲשֶׂה: וַיְהִי ׀ כׇּל־זְהַב הַתְּרוּמָה אֲשֶׁר הֵרִימוּ לַיהֹוָה שִׁשָּׁה עָשָׂר

אֶלֶף שְׁבַע־מֵאוֹת וַחֲמִשִּׁים שָׁקֶל מֵאֵת שָׂרֵי הָאֲלָפִים וּמֵאֵת שָׂרֵי

נג־נד הַמֵּאוֹת: אַנְשֵׁי הַצָּבָא בָּזְזוּ אִישׁ לוֹ: וַיִּקַּח מֹשֶׁה וְאֶלְעָזָר הַכֹּהֵן אֶת־הַזָּהָב

מֵאֵת שָׂרֵי הָאֲלָפִים וְהַמֵּאוֹת וַיָּבִאוּ אֹתוֹ אֶל־אֹהֶל מוֹעֵד זִכָּרוֹן לִבְנֵי־

יִשְׂרָאֵל לִפְנֵי יְהֹוָה:

לב ששי א וּמִקְנֶה ׀ רַב הָיָה לִבְנֵי רְאוּבֵן וְלִבְנֵי־גָד עָצוּם מְאֹד וַיִּרְאוּ אֶת־אֶרֶץ

[שלישי]

ב יַעְזֵר וְאֶת־אֶרֶץ גִּלְעָד וְהִנֵּה הַמָּקוֹם מְקוֹם מִקְנֶה: וַיָּבֹאוּ בְנֵי־גָד וּבְנֵי

רְאוּבֵן וַיֹּאמְרוּ אֶל־מֹשֶׁה וְאֶל־אֶלְעָזָר הַכֹּהֵן וְאֶל־נְשִׂיאֵי הָעֵדָה

ג לֵאמֹר: עֲטָרוֹת וְדִיבֹן וְיַעְזֵר וְנִמְרָה וְחֶשְׁבּוֹן וְאֶלְעָלֵה וּשְׂבָם וּנְבוֹ וּבְעֹן:

ד הָאָרֶץ אֲשֶׁר הִכָּה יְהֹוָה לִפְנֵי עֲדַת יִשְׂרָאֵל אֶרֶץ מִקְנֶה הִוא וְלַעֲבָדֶיךָ

ה מִקְנֶה: וַיֹּאמְרוּ אִם־מָצָאנוּ חֵן בְּעֵינֶיךָ יֻתַּן אֶת־הָאָרֶץ

הַזֹּאת לַעֲבָדֶיךָ לַאֲחֻזָּה אַל־תַּעֲבִרֵנוּ אֶת־הַיַּרְדֵּן: וַיֹּאמֶר מֹשֶׁה לִבְנֵי־גָד

ז וְלִבְנֵי רְאוּבֵן הַאַחֵיכֶם יָבֹאוּ לַמִּלְחָמָה וְאַתֶּם תֵּשְׁבוּ פֹה: וְלָמָּה °תְנִיאוּן

[תְנִיאוּן ק] אֶת־לֵב בְּנֵי יִשְׂרָאֵל מֵעֲבֹר אֶל־הָאָרֶץ אֲשֶׁר־נָתַן לָהֶם

ח יְהֹוָה: כֹּה עָשׂוּ אֲבֹתֵיכֶם בְּשׇׁלְחִי אֹתָם מִקָּדֵשׁ בַּרְנֵעַ לִרְאוֹת אֶת־הָאָרֶץ:

ט וַיַּעֲלוּ עַד־נַחַל אֶשְׁכּוֹל וַיִּרְאוּ אֶת־הָאָרֶץ וַיָּנִיאוּ אֶת־לֵב בְּנֵי יִשְׂרָאֵל

י לְבִלְתִּי־בֹא אֶל־הָאָרֶץ אֲשֶׁר־נָתַן לָהֶם יְהֹוָה: וַיִּחַר־אַף יְהֹוָה בַּיּוֹם

הַהוּא וַיִּשָּׁבַע לֵאמֹר: אִם־יִרְאוּ הָאֲנָשִׁים הָעֹלִים מִמִּצְרַיִם מִבֶּן עֶשְׂרִים

יא שָׁנָה וָמַעְלָה אֵת הָאֲדָמָה אֲשֶׁר נִשְׁבַּעְתִּי לְאַבְרָהָם לְיִצְחָק וּלְיַעֲקֹב כִּי

יב לֹא־מִלְאוּ אַחֲרָי: בִּלְתִּי כָּלֵב בֶּן־יְפֻנֶּה הַקְּנִזִּי וִיהוֹשֻׁעַ בִּן־נוּן כִּי מִלְאוּ

יג אַחֲרֵי יְהֹוָה: וַיִּחַר־אַף יְהֹוָה בְּיִשְׂרָאֵל וַיְנִעֵם בַּמִּדְבָּר אַרְבָּעִים שָׁנָה

עַד־תֹּם כׇּל־הַדּוֹר הָעֹשֶׂה הָרַע בְּעֵינֵי יְהֹוָה: וְהִנֵּה קַמְתֶּם תַּחַת אֲבֹתֵיכֶם

יד תַּרְבּוּת אֲנָשִׁים חַטָּאִים לִסְפּוֹת עוֹד עַל חֲרוֹן אַף־יְהֹוָה אֶל־יִשְׂרָאֵל:

טו כִּי תְשׁוּבֻן מֵאַחֲרָיו וְיָסַף עוֹד לְהַנִּיחוֹ בַּמִּדְבָּר וְשִׁחַתֶּם לְכׇל־הָעָם

טז הַזֶּה: וַיִּגְּשׁוּ אֵלָיו וַיֹּאמְרוּ גִּדְרֹת צֹאן נִבְנֶה לְמִקְנֵנוּ פֹּה וְעָרִים

יז לְטַפֵּנוּ: וַאֲנַחְנוּ נֵחָלֵץ חֻשִׁים לִפְנֵי בְּנֵי יִשְׂרָאֵל עַד אֲשֶׁר אִם־הֲבִיאֹנֻם

אֶל־מְקוֹמָם וְיָשַׁב טַפֵּנוּ בְּעָרֵי הַמִּבְצָר מִפְּנֵי יֹשְׁבֵי הָאָרֶץ: לֹא נָשׁוּב אֶל־

יח בָּתֵּינוּ עַד הִתְנַחֵל בְּנֵי יִשְׂרָאֵל אִישׁ נַחֲלָתוֹ: כִּי לֹא נִנְחַל אִתָּם מֵעֵבֶר

יט לַיַּרְדֵּן וָהָלְאָה כִּי בָאָה נַחֲלָתֵנוּ אֵלֵינוּ מֵעֵבֶר הַיַּרְדֵּן מִזְרָחָה:

כ שביעי וַיֹּאמֶר אֲלֵיהֶם מֹשֶׁה אִם־תַּעֲשׂוּן אֶת־הַדָּבָר הַזֶּה אִם־תֵּחָלְצוּ לִפְנֵי

[רביעי] יְהֹוָה לַמִּלְחָמָה: וְעָבַר לָכֶם כׇּל־חָלוּץ אֶת־הַיַּרְדֵּן לִפְנֵי יְהֹוָה עַד הוֹרִישׁוֹ

כא אֶת־אֹיְבָיו מִפָּנָיו: וְנִכְבְּשָׁה הָאָרֶץ לִפְנֵי יְהֹוָה וְאַחַר תָּשֻׁבוּ וִהְיִיתֶם

כב

what any man found of gold vessels, anklet and bracelet, ring, earring, and clasp, to atone for our souls before HASHEM." [51] *Moses and Elazar the Kohen took the gold from them, every fashioned vessel.* [52] *All the gold that was raised up, which they set apart for HASHEM, was sixteen thousand, seven hundred and fifty shekel, from the officers of the thousands and the officers of the hundreds.* [53] *As for the men of the legion, each man looted for himself.* [54] *Moses and Elazar the Kohen took the gold from the officers of the thousands and the hundreds and brought it to the Tent of Meeting, a remembrance for the Children of Israel before HASHEM.*

32

The request of Reuben and Gad
(See Appendix D, map 1)

[1] **T**he children of Reuben and the children of Gad had abundant livestock — very great. They saw the land of Jazer and the land of Gilead, and behold! — the place was a place for livestock. [2] *The children of Gad and the children of Reuben came and said to Moses, to Elazar the Kohen, and to the leaders of the assembly, saying,* [3] *"Ataroth, and Dibon, and Jazer, and Nimrah, and Heshbon, and Elealeh, and Sebam, and Nebo, and Beon —* [4] *the land that HASHEM smote before the assembly of Israel — it is a land for livestock, and your servants have livestock."*

[5] *They said, "If we have found favor in your eyes, let this land be given to your servants as a heritage; do not bring us across the Jordan."*

Moses' objection

[6] *Moses said to the children of Gad and the children of Reuben, "Shall your brothers go out to battle while you settle here?* [7] *Why do you dissuade the heart of the Children of Israel from crossing to the Land that HASHEM has given them?* [8] *This is what your fathers did, when I sent them from Kadesh-barnea to see the Land.* [9] *They went up to the valley of Eshcol and saw the Land and they dissuaded the heart of the Children of Israel, not to come to the Land that HASHEM has given them.* [10] *The wrath of HASHEM burned on that day, and He swore saying,* [11] *'If these men who came up from Egypt — from the age of twenty years and above — will see the ground that I swore to Abraham, to Isaac, and to Jacob for they have not followed Me fully,* [12] *except for Caleb son of Jephunneh, the Kenizzite, * and Joshua son of Nun, for they followed HASHEM fully.'* [13] *The wrath of HASHEM burned against Israel and He made them wander in the Wilderness for forty years, until the end of the entire generation that did evil in the eyes of HASHEM.* [14] *Behold! — you have risen up in place of your fathers, a brood of sinful people, to add more to the burning wrath of HASHEM against Israel.* [15] *For if you will turn away from after Him, He will again let it rest in the Wilderness, and you will destroy this entire people."*

The request is clarified

[16] *They approached him and said, "Pens for the flock shall we build here for our livestock and cities for our small children.* [17] *We shall arm ourselves swiftly in the vanguard of the Children of Israel until we will have brought them to their place, and our small children will dwell in the fortified cities before the inhabitants of the land.* [18] *We shall not return to our homes until the Children of Israel will have inherited — every man his inheritance —* [19] *for we shall not inherit with them across the Jordan and beyond, for our inheritance has come to us on the east bank of the Jordan."*

Moses' conditionf

[20] *Moses said to them, "If you do this thing, if you arm yourselves before HASHEM for the battle,* [21] *and every armed man among you shall cross the Jordan before HASHEM, until He drives out His enemies before Him,* [22] *and the Land shall be conquered before HASHEM, and then you shall return — then you shall be*

32:12. *The Kenizzite,* i.e., Caleb, because Kenaz was his stepfather (see *I Chronicles* 4:13).

נְקִיִּם מֵיהוָה וּמִיִּשְׂרָאֵל וְהָיְתָה הָאָרֶץ הַזֹּאת לָכֶם לַאֲחֻזָּה לִפְנֵי יהוָה:

כג וְאִם־לֹא תַעֲשׂוּן כֵּן הִנֵּה חֲטָאתֶם לַיהוָה וּדְעוּ חַטַּאתְכֶם אֲשֶׁר תִּמְצָא

אֶתְכֶם: כד בְּנוּ־לָכֶם עָרִים לְטַפְּכֶם וּגְדֵרֹת לְצֹנַאֲכֶם וְהַיֹּצֵא מִפִּיכֶם תַּעֲשֽׂוּ:

כה וַיֹּאמֶר בְּנֵי־גָד וּבְנֵי רְאוּבֵן אֶל־מֹשֶׁה לֵאמֹר עֲבָדֶיךָ יַעֲשׂוּ כַּאֲשֶׁר אֲדֹנִי

מְצַוֶּה: כו-כז טַפֵּנוּ נָשֵׁינוּ מִקְנֵנוּ וְכָל־בְּהֶמְתֵּנוּ יִהְיוּ־שָׁם בְּעָרֵי הַגִּלְעָד: וַעֲבָדֶיךָ

כח יַעַבְרוּ כָּל־חֲלוּץ צָבָא לִפְנֵי יהוָה לַמִּלְחָמָה כַּאֲשֶׁר אֲדֹנִי דֹּבֵר: וַיְצַו

לָהֶם מֹשֶׁה אֵת אֶלְעָזָר הַכֹּהֵן וְאֵת יְהוֹשֻׁעַ בִּן־נוּן וְאֶת־רָאשֵׁי אֲבוֹת

כט הַמַּטּוֹת לִבְנֵי יִשְׂרָאֵל: וַיֹּאמֶר מֹשֶׁה אֲלֵהֶם אִם־יַעַבְרוּ בְנֵי־גָד וּבְנֵי־

רְאוּבֵן | אִתְּכֶם אֶת־הַיַּרְדֵּן כָּל־חָלוּץ לַמִּלְחָמָה לִפְנֵי יהוָה וְנִכְבְּשָׁה

ל הָאָרֶץ לִפְנֵיכֶם וּנְתַתֶּם לָהֶם אֶת־אֶרֶץ הַגִּלְעָד לַאֲחֻזָּה: וְאִם־לֹא יַעַבְרוּ

חֲלוּצִים אִתְּכֶם וְנֹאחֲזוּ בְתֹכְכֶם בְּאֶרֶץ כְּנָעַן: לא וַיַּעֲנוּ בְנֵי־גָד וּבְנֵי רְאוּבֵן

לב לֵאמֹר אֵת אֲשֶׁר דִּבֶּר יהוָה אֶל־עֲבָדֶיךָ כֵּן נַעֲשֶׂה: נַחְנוּ נַעֲבֹר חֲלוּצִים

לג לִפְנֵי יהוָה אֶרֶץ כְּנָעַן וְאִתָּנוּ אֲחֻזַּת נַחֲלָתֵנוּ מֵעֵבֶר לַיַּרְדֵּן: וַיִּתֵּן לָהֶם |

מֹשֶׁה לִבְנֵי־גָד וְלִבְנֵי רְאוּבֵן וְלַחֲצִי | שֵׁבֶט | מְנַשֶּׁה בֶן־יוֹסֵף אֶת־מַמְלֶכֶת

סִיחֹן מֶלֶךְ הָאֱמֹרִי וְאֶת־מַמְלֶכֶת עוֹג מֶלֶךְ הַבָּשָׁן הָאָרֶץ לְעָרֶיהָ בִּגְבֻלֹת

לד-לה עָרֵי הָאָרֶץ סָבִיב: וַיִּבְנוּ בְנֵי־גָד אֶת־דִּיבֹן וְאֶת־עֲטָרֹת וְאֵת עֲרֹעֵר: וְאֶת־

לו עֲטְרֹת שׁוֹפָן וְאֶת־יַעְזֵר וְיָגְבְּהָה: וְאֶת־בֵּית נִמְרָה וְאֶת־בֵּית הָרָן עָרֵי

לז מִבְצָר וְגִדְרֹת צֹאן: וּבְנֵי רְאוּבֵן בָּנוּ אֶת־חֶשְׁבּוֹן וְאֶת־אֶלְעָלֵא וְאֶת

לח קִרְיָתָיִם: וְאֶת־נְבוֹ וְאֶת־בַּעַל מְעוֹן מוּסַבֹּת שֵׁם וְאֶת־שִׂבְמָה וַיִּקְרְאוּ

לט בְשֵׁמֹת אֶת־שְׁמוֹת הֶעָרִים אֲשֶׁר בָּנֽוּ: וַיֵּלְכוּ בְּנֵי מָכִיר בֶּן־מְנַשֶּׁה גִּלְעָדָה

מ וַיִּלְכְּדֻהָ וַיּוֹרֶשׁ אֶת־הָאֱמֹרִי אֲשֶׁר־בָּהּ: וַיִּתֵּן מֹשֶׁה אֶת־הַגִּלְעָד לְמָכִיר

מא בֶּן־מְנַשֶּׁה וַיֵּשֶׁב בָּהּ: וְיָאִיר בֶּן־מְנַשֶּׁה הָלַךְ וַיִּלְכֹּד אֶת־חַוֺּתֵיהֶם וַיִּקְרָא

מב אֶתְהֶן חַוֺּת יָאִיר: וְנֹבַח הָלַךְ וַיִּלְכֹּד אֶת־קְנָת וְאֶת־בְּנֹתֶיהָ וַיִּקְרָא

לָהּ נֹבַח בִּשְׁמֽוֹ: פפפ קי״ב פסוקים. בק״י סימן. יק״ב סימן. עי״ב״ל סימן.

**מְה רפה

פרשת מסעי

לג א אֵלֶּה מַסְעֵי בְנֵי־יִשְׂרָאֵל אֲשֶׁר יָצְאוּ מֵאֶרֶץ מִצְרַיִם לְצִבְאֹתָם בְּיַד־

ב מֹשֶׁה וְאַהֲרֹן: וַיִּכְתֹּב מֹשֶׁה אֶת־מוֹצָאֵיהֶם לְמַסְעֵיהֶם עַל־פִּי יהוָה

ג וְאֵלֶּה מַסְעֵיהֶם לְמוֹצָאֵיהֶם: וַיִּסְעוּ מֵרַעְמְסֵס בַּחֹדֶשׁ הָרִאשׁוֹן בַּחֲמִשָּׁה

עָשָׂר יוֹם לַחֹדֶשׁ הָרִאשׁוֹן מִמָּחֳרַת הַפֶּסַח יָצְאוּ בְנֵי־יִשְׂרָאֵל בְּיָד

ד רָמָה לְעֵינֵי כָּל־מִצְרָיִם: וּמִצְרַיִם מְקַבְּרִים אֵת אֲשֶׁר הִכָּה יהוָה בָּהֶם

כָּל־בְּכוֹר וּבֵאלֹהֵיהֶם עָשָׂה יהוָה שְׁפָטִים: ה וַיִּסְעוּ בְנֵי־יִשְׂרָאֵל

32:22. It is not enough for one to know that one's actions are proper in God's eyes. One must also act in such a way as not to engender suspicion on the part of human beings (*Yoma* 38a).

32:24. Moses accepted their proposal, but made a few subtle changes. One of them was the order of priorities. They spoke first of their livestock (v. 16); Moses insisted that the children come first.

vindicated from HASHEM and from Israel, * *and this Land shall be a heritage for you before HASHEM.* ²³ *But if you do not do so, behold! — you will have sinned to HASHEM; know your sin that will encounter you.* ²⁴ *Build for yourselves cities for your small children and pens for your flock,* * *and what has come from your mouth shall you do."*

²⁵ *The children of Gad and the children of Reuben said to Moses, saying, "Your servants shall do as my lord commands.* ²⁶ *Our small children, our wives, our livestock, and all our animals will be there in the cities of the Gilead.* ²⁷ *And your servants shall cross over — every armed person of the legion — before HASHEM, to do battle, as my lord speaks."*

²⁸ *Concerning them, Moses commanded Elazar the Kohen, Joshua son of Nun, and the heads of the fathers of the tribes of the Children of Israel.* ²⁹ *Moses said to them, "If the children of Gad and the children of Reuben will cross the Jordan with you — everyone armed for battle before HASHEM, and the Land is conquered before you — you shall give them the land of Gilead as a heritage.* ³⁰ *But if they do not cross over, armed, with you, then they will take [their] heritage among you in the land of Canaan."*

³¹ *The children of Gad and the children of Reuben spoke up, saying, "As HASHEM has spoken to your servants, so shall we do.* ³² *We shall cross over, armed, before HASHEM to the land of Canaan, and ours shall be the heritage of our inheritance across the Jordan."*

(See Appendix D, maps 1-2)
³³ *So Moses gave to them — to the children of Gad, and the children of Reuben, and half the tribe of Manasseh* * *son of Joseph — the kingdom of Sihon king of the Amorite, and the kingdom of Og king of the Bashan; the land with its cities in the boundaries, and the cities of the surrounding land.*

³⁴ *The children of Gad built Dibon, and Ataroth, and Aroer;* ³⁵ *and Atroth-shophan, and Jazer, and Jogbehah;* ³⁶ *and Beth-nimrah, and Beth-haran — fortified cities and pens for the flock.* ³⁷ *The children of Reuben built Heshbon, and Elealeh, and Kiriathaim;* ³⁸ *and Nebo and Baal-meon with altered names, and Sibmah; and they called [them] by [other] names [instead of] the names of the cities that they built.* ³⁹ *The children of Machir son of Manasseh went to Gilead and captured it, and drove out the Amorite who were in it.* ⁴⁰ *Moses gave the Gilead to Machir son of Manasseh and he settled in it.* ⁴¹ *Jair son of Manasseh went and captured their villages, and called them Havvoth-jair.* ⁴² *Nobah went and captured Kenath and her suburbs, and called it Nobah, after his name.*

PARASHAS MASEI

33

Summary of the journey

¹ *These are the journeys of the Children of Israel, who went forth from the land of Egypt according to their legions, under the hand of Moses and Aaron.* ² *Moses wrote their goings forth according to their journeys at the bidding of HASHEM, and these were their journeys according to their goings forth:* ³ *They journeyed from Rameses in the first month, on the fifteenth day of the first month — on the day after the pesach-offering — the Children of Israel went forth with an upraised hand, before the eyes of all Egypt.* ⁴ *And the Egyptians were burying those among them whom HASHEM had struck, every firstborn; and on their gods HASHEM had inflicted punishments.* ⁵ *The Children of Israel journeyed*

32:33. They had not joined originally. Moses, however, wanted outstanding Torah authorities to dwell with the relatively isolated two tribes and guide them. This set a precedent for Jewish continuity (*Haamek Davar*).

ו   מֵרַעְמְסֵס וַיַּחֲנוּ בְּסֻכֹּת: וַיִּסְעוּ מִסֻּכֹּת וַיַּחֲנוּ בְאֵתָם אֲשֶׁר בִּקְצֵה הַמִּדְבָּר:

ז   וַיִּסְעוּ מֵאֵתָם וַיָּשָׁב עַל־פִּי הַחִירֹת אֲשֶׁר עַל־פְּנֵי בַּעַל צְפוֹן וַיַּחֲנוּ

ח   לִפְנֵי מִגְדֹּל: וַיִּסְעוּ מִפְּנֵי הַחִירֹת וַיַּעַבְרוּ בְתוֹךְ־הַיָּם הַמִּדְבָּרָה וַיֵּלְכוּ

ט   דֶּרֶךְ שְׁלֹשֶׁת יָמִים בְּמִדְבַּר אֵתָם וַיַּחֲנוּ בְּמָרָה: וַיִּסְעוּ מִמָּרָה וַיָּבֹאוּ אֵילִמָה וּבְאֵילִם שְׁתֵּים עֶשְׂרֵה עֵינֹת מַיִם וְשִׁבְעִים תְּמָרִים וַיַּחֲנוּ־שָׁם:

יא   וַיִּסְעוּ מֵאֵילִם וַיַּחֲנוּ עַל־יַם־סוּף: * וַיִּסְעוּ מִיַּם־סוּף וַיַּחֲנוּ בְּמִדְבַּר־סִין:

יב־יד   וַיִּסְעוּ מִמִּדְבַּר־סִין וַיַּחֲנוּ בְּדָפְקָה: וַיִּסְעוּ מִדָּפְקָה וַיַּחֲנוּ בְּאָלוּשׁ: וַיִּסְעוּ

טו   מֵאָלוּשׁ וַיַּחֲנוּ בִּרְפִידִם וְלֹא־הָיָה שָׁם מַיִם לָעָם לִשְׁתּוֹת: וַיִּסְעוּ מֵרְפִידִם

טז־יז   וַיַּחֲנוּ בְּמִדְבַּר סִינָי: וַיִּסְעוּ מִמִּדְבַּר סִינָי וַיַּחֲנוּ בְּקִבְרֹת הַתַּאֲוָה: וַיִּסְעוּ

יח־יט   מִקִּבְרֹת הַתַּאֲוָה וַיַּחֲנוּ בַּחֲצֵרֹת: וַיִּסְעוּ מֵחֲצֵרֹת וַיַּחֲנוּ בְּרִתְמָה: וַיִּסְעוּ

כ־כא   מֵרִתְמָה וַיַּחֲנוּ בְּרִמֹּן פָּרֶץ: וַיִּסְעוּ מֵרִמֹּן פָּרֶץ וַיַּחֲנוּ בְּלִבְנָה: וַיִּסְעוּ

כב־כג   מִלִּבְנָה וַיַּחֲנוּ בְּרִסָּה: וַיִּסְעוּ מֵרִסָּה וַיַּחֲנוּ בִּקְהֵלָתָה: וַיִּסְעוּ מִקְּהֵלָתָה

כד־כה   וַיַּחֲנוּ בְּהַר־שָׁפֶר: וַיִּסְעוּ מֵהַר־שָׁפֶר וַיַּחֲנוּ בַּחֲרָדָה: וַיִּסְעוּ מֵחֲרָדָה וַיַּחֲנוּ

כו־כז   בְּמַקְהֵלֹת: וַיִּסְעוּ מִמַּקְהֵלֹת וַיַּחֲנוּ בְּתָחַת: וַיִּסְעוּ מִתָּחַת וַיַּחֲנוּ בְּתָרַח:

כח־ל   וַיִּסְעוּ מִתָּרַח וַיַּחֲנוּ בְּמִתְקָה: וַיִּסְעוּ מִמִּתְקָה וַיַּחֲנוּ בְּחַשְׁמֹנָה: וַיִּסְעוּ

לא־לב   מֵחַשְׁמֹנָה וַיַּחֲנוּ בְּמֹסֵרוֹת: וַיִּסְעוּ מִמֹּסֵרוֹת וַיַּחֲנוּ בִּבְנֵי יַעֲקָן: וַיִּסְעוּ מִבְּנֵי

לג־לד   יַעֲקָן וַיַּחֲנוּ בְּחֹר הַגִּדְגָּד: וַיִּסְעוּ מֵחֹר הַגִּדְגָּד וַיַּחֲנוּ בְּיָטְבָתָה: וַיִּסְעוּ

לה־לו   מִיָּטְבָתָה וַיַּחֲנוּ בְּעַבְרֹנָה: וַיִּסְעוּ מֵעַבְרֹנָה וַיַּחֲנוּ בְּעֶצְיֹן גָּבֶר: וַיִּסְעוּ

לו   מֵעֶצְיֹן גָּבֶר וַיַּחֲנוּ בְמִדְבַּר־צִן הִוא קָדֵשׁ: וַיִּסְעוּ מִקָּדֵשׁ וַיַּחֲנוּ בְּהֹר הָהָר

לח   בִּקְצֵה אֶרֶץ אֱדוֹם: וַיַּעַל אַהֲרֹן הַכֹּהֵן אֶל־הֹר הָהָר עַל־פִּי יהוה וַיָּמָת שָׁם בִּשְׁנַת הָאַרְבָּעִים לְצֵאת בְּנֵי־יִשְׂרָאֵל מֵאֶרֶץ מִצְרַיִם בַּחֹדֶשׁ

לט   הַחֲמִישִׁי בְּאֶחָד לַחֹדֶשׁ: וְאַהֲרֹן בֶּן־שָׁלֹשׁ וְעֶשְׂרִים וּמְאַת שָׁנָה בְּמֹתוֹ

מ   בְּהֹר הָהָר: וַיִּשְׁמַע הַכְּנַעֲנִי מֶלֶךְ עֲרָד וְהוּא־יֹשֵׁב בַּנֶּגֶב

מא־מב   בְּאֶרֶץ כְּנָעַן בְּבֹא בְּנֵי יִשְׂרָאֵל: וַיִּסְעוּ מֵהֹר הָהָר וַיַּחֲנוּ בְּצַלְמֹנָה: וַיִּסְעוּ

מג־מד   מִצַּלְמֹנָה וַיַּחֲנוּ בְּפוּנֹן: וַיִּסְעוּ מִפּוּנֹן וַיַּחֲנוּ בְּאֹבֹת: וַיִּסְעוּ מֵאֹבֹת וַיַּחֲנוּ

מה־מו   בְּעִיֵּי הָעֲבָרִים בִּגְבוּל מוֹאָב: וַיִּסְעוּ מֵעִיִּים וַיַּחֲנוּ בְּדִיבֹן גָּד: וַיִּסְעוּ מִדִּיבֹן

מז   גָּד וַיַּחֲנוּ בְּעַלְמֹן דִּבְלָתָיְמָה: וַיִּסְעוּ מֵעַלְמֹן דִּבְלָתָיְמָה וַיַּחֲנוּ בְּהָרֵי

מח   הָעֲבָרִים לִפְנֵי נְבוֹ: וַיִּסְעוּ מֵהָרֵי הָעֲבָרִים וַיַּחֲנוּ בְּעַרְבֹת מוֹאָב עַל

מט   יַרְדֵּן יְרֵחוֹ: וַיַּחֲנוּ עַל־הַיַּרְדֵּן מִבֵּית הַיְשִׁמֹת עַד אָבֵל הַשִּׁטִּים בְּעַרְבֹת

נ   מוֹאָב: וַיְדַבֵּר יהוה אֶל־מֹשֶׁה בְּעַרְבֹת מוֹאָב עַל־יַרְדֵּן

נא   יְרֵחוֹ לֵאמֹר: דַּבֵּר אֶל־בְּנֵי יִשְׂרָאֵל וְאָמַרְתָּ אֲלֵהֶם כִּי אַתֶּם עֹבְרִים אֶת־

*שני ... שלישי [חמישי]

◄§ Parashas Masei

33:36. *Kadesh.* This is not the Kadesh of the spies, for that was in the Wilderness of Paran, and is referred to here as Rithmah (v. 18). The arrival at the Kadesh of this

verse occurred on Rosh Chodesh Nissan of the fortieth year from the Exodus. It was here that Miriam died and where it was decreed that Moses and Aaron would not enter the Land (20:13).

from Rameses and encamped in Succoth. ⁶ They journeyed from Succoth and encamped in Etham, which is on the edge of the Wilderness. ⁷ They journeyed from Etham and it turned back to Pi-hahiroth, which is before Baal-zephon, and they encamped before Migdol. ⁸ They journeyed from before Hahiroth and passed through the midst of the Sea toward the Wilderness; they went on a three-day trip in the Wilderness of Etham, and they encamped in Marah. ⁹ They journeyed from Marah and arrived at Elim; in Elim were twelve springs of water and seventy date palms, and they encamped there. ¹⁰ They journeyed from Elim and encamped by the Sea of Reeds. ¹¹ They journeyed from the Sea of Reeds and encamped in the Wilderness of Sin. ¹² They journeyed from the Wilderness of Sin and encamped in Dophkah. ¹³ They journeyed from Dophkah and encamped in Alush. ¹⁴ They journeyed from Alush and encamped in Rephidim, and there was no water there for the people to drink. ¹⁵ They journeyed from Rephidim and encamped in the Wilderness of Sinai. ¹⁶ They journeyed from the Wilderness of Sinai and encamped in Kibroth-hattaavah. ¹⁷ They journeyed from Kibroth-hattaavah and encamped in Hazeroth. ¹⁸ They journeyed from Hazeroth and encamped in Rithmah. ¹⁹ They journeyed from Rithmah and encamped in Rimmon-perez. ²⁰ They journeyed from Rimmon-perez and encamped in Libnah. ²¹ They journeyed from Libnah and encamped in Rissah. ²² They journeyed from Rissah and encamped in Kehelathah. ²³ They journeyed from Kehelathah and encamped in Mount Shepher. ²⁴ They journeyed from Mount Shepher and encamped in Haradah. ²⁵ They journeyed from Haradah and encamped in Makheloth. ²⁶ They journeyed from Makheloth and encamped in Tahath. ²⁷ They journeyed from Tahath and encamped in Terah. ²⁸ They journeyed from Terah and encamped in Mithkah. ²⁹ They journeyed from Mithkah and encamped in Hashmonah. ³⁰ They journeyed from Hashmonah and encamped in Moseroth. ³¹ They journeyed from Moseroth and encamped in Bene-jaakan. ³² They journeyed from Bene-jaakan and encamped in Hor-hag-gidgad. ³³ They journeyed from Hor-haggidgad and encamped in Jotbathah. ³⁴ They journeyed from Jotbathah and encamped in Abronah. ³⁵ They journeyed from Abronah and encamped in Ezion-geber. ³⁶ They journeyed from Ezion-geber and encamped in the Wilderness of Zin, which is Kadesh. * ³⁷ They journeyed from Kadesh and encamped in Mount Hor, at the edge of the land of Edom. ³⁸ Then Aaron the Kohen went up to Mount Hor at the word of Hashem and died there, in the fortieth year after the Children of Israel went forth from the land of Egypt, in the fifth month on the first of the month. ³⁹ Aaron was one hundred and twenty-three years old at his death on Mount Hor.

⁴⁰ The Canaanite king of Arad heard — he was dwelling in the south, in the land of Canaan — of the approach of the Children of Israel. ⁴¹ They journeyed from Mount Hor and encamped in Zalmonah. ⁴² They journeyed from Zalmonah and encamped in Punon. ⁴³ They journeyed from Punon and encamped in Oboth. ⁴⁴ They journeyed from Oboth and encamped in the ruins of the passes, at the border of Moab. ⁴⁵ They journeyed from the ruins and encamped in Dibon-gad. ⁴⁶ They journeyed from Dibon-gad and encamped in Almon-diblathaimah. ⁴⁷ They journeyed from Almon-diblathaimah and encamped in the mountains of the passes before Nebo. ⁴⁸ They journeyed from the mountains of the passes and encamped in the plains of Moab by the Jordan, at Jericho. ⁴⁹ They encamped by the Jordan, from Beth-jeshimoth until Avel Shittim, in the plains of Moab.

Occupying the Land   ⁵⁰ Hashem spoke to Moses in the plains of Moab, by the Jordan, at Jericho, saying: ⁵¹ Speak to the Children of Israel and say to them: When you cross the

נב הַיַּרְדֵּן אֶל־אֶרֶץ כְּנָעַן: וְהוֹרַשְׁתֶּם אֶת־כָּל־יֹשְׁבֵי הָאָרֶץ מִפְּנֵיכֶם
וְאִבַּדְתֶּם אֵת כָּל־מַשְׂכִּיֹּתָם וְאֵת כָּל־צַלְמֵי מַסֵּכֹתָם תְּאַבֵּדוּ וְאֵת כָּל־
נג בָּמוֹתָם תַּשְׁמִידוּ: וְהוֹרַשְׁתֶּם אֶת־הָאָרֶץ וִישַׁבְתֶּם־בָּהּ כִּי לָכֶם נָתַתִּי אֶת־
נד הָאָרֶץ לָרֶשֶׁת אֹתָהּ: וְהִתְנַחַלְתֶּם אֶת־הָאָרֶץ בְּגוֹרָל לְמִשְׁפְּחֹתֵיכֶם לָרַב
תַּרְבּוּ אֶת־נַחֲלָתוֹ וְלַמְעַט תַּמְעִיט אֶת־נַחֲלָתוֹ אֶל אֲשֶׁר־יֵצֵא לוֹ שָׁמָּה
נה הַגּוֹרָל לוֹ יִהְיֶה לְמַטּוֹת אֲבֹתֵיכֶם תִּתְנֶחָלוּ: וְאִם־לֹא תוֹרִישׁוּ אֶת־יֹשְׁבֵי
הָאָרֶץ מִפְּנֵיכֶם וְהָיָה אֲשֶׁר תּוֹתִירוּ מֵהֶם לְשִׂכִּים בְּעֵינֵיכֶם וְלִצְנִינִם
נו בְּצִדֵּיכֶם וְצָרְרוּ אֶתְכֶם עַל־הָאָרֶץ אֲשֶׁר אַתֶּם יֹשְׁבִים בָּהּ: וְהָיָה כַּאֲשֶׁר
דִּמִּיתִי לַעֲשׂוֹת לָהֶם אֶעֱשֶׂה לָכֶם:

לד

א־ב וַיְדַבֵּר יְהֹוָה אֶל־מֹשֶׁה לֵּאמֹר: צַו אֶת־בְּנֵי יִשְׂרָאֵל וְאָמַרְתָּ אֲלֵהֶם כִּי־
אַתֶּם בָּאִים אֶל־הָאָרֶץ כְּנָעַן זֹאת הָאָרֶץ אֲשֶׁר תִּפֹּל לָכֶם בְּנַחֲלָה אֶרֶץ
ג כְּנַעַן לִגְבֻלֹתֶיהָ: וְהָיָה לָכֶם פְּאַת־נֶגֶב מִמִּדְבַּר־צִן עַל־יְדֵי אֱדוֹם וְהָיָה
ד לָכֶם גְּבוּל נֶגֶב מִקְצֵה יָם־הַמֶּלַח קֵדְמָה: וְנָסַב לָכֶם הַגְּבוּל מִנֶּגֶב לְמַעֲלֵה
עַקְרַבִּים וְעָבַר צִנָה וְהָיָה °וּהֲיָה [°וְהָיוּ ק] תּוֹצְאֹתָיו מִנֶּגֶב לְקָדֵשׁ בַּרְנֵעַ וְיָצָא
ה חֲצַר־אַדָּר וְעָבַר עַצְמֹנָה: וְנָסַב הַגְּבוּל מֵעַצְמוֹן נַחְלָה מִצְרָיִם וְהָיוּ
ו תוֹצְאֹתָיו הַיָּמָּה: וּגְבוּל יָם וְהָיָה לָכֶם הַיָּם הַגָּדוֹל וּגְבוּל זֶה־יִהְיֶה לָכֶם
ז גְּבוּל יָם: וְזֶה־יִהְיֶה לָכֶם גְּבוּל צָפוֹן מִן־הַיָּם הַגָּדֹל תְּתָאוּ לָכֶם הֹר הָהָר:
ח־ט מֵהֹר הָהָר תְּתָאוּ לְבֹא חֲמָת וְהָיוּ תּוֹצְאֹת הַגְּבֻל צְדָדָה: וְיָצָא הַגְּבֻל
זִפְרֹנָה וְהָיוּ תוֹצְאֹתָיו חֲצַר עֵינָן זֶה־יִהְיֶה לָכֶם גְּבוּל צָפוֹן: וְהִתְאַוִּיתֶם
י לָכֶם לִגְבוּל קֵדְמָה מֵחֲצַר עֵינָן שְׁפָמָה: וְיָרַד הַגְּבֻל מִשְּׁפָם הָרִבְלָה
יא מִקֶּדֶם לָעָיִן וְיָרַד הַגְּבֻל וּמָחָה עַל־כֶּתֶף יָם־כִּנֶּרֶת קֵדְמָה: וְיָרַד הַגְּבוּל
יב הַיַּרְדֵּנָה וְהָיוּ תוֹצְאֹתָיו יָם הַמֶּלַח זֹאת תִּהְיֶה לָכֶם הָאָרֶץ לִגְבֻלֹתֶיהָ
יג סָבִיב: וַיְצַו מֹשֶׁה אֶת־בְּנֵי יִשְׂרָאֵל לֵאמֹר זֹאת הָאָרֶץ אֲשֶׁר תִּתְנַחֲלוּ
יד אֹתָהּ בְּגוֹרָל אֲשֶׁר צִוָּה יְהֹוָה לָתֵת לְתִשְׁעַת הַמַּטּוֹת וַחֲצִי הַמַּטֶּה: כִּי
לָקְחוּ מַטֵּה בְנֵי הָרֽאוּבֵנִי לְבֵית אֲבֹתָם וּמַטֵּה בְנֵי־הַגָּדִי לְבֵית אֲבֹתָם
טו וַחֲצִי מַטֵּה מְנַשֶּׁה לָקְחוּ נַחֲלָתָם: שְׁנֵי הַמַּטּוֹת וַחֲצִי הַמַּטֶּה לָקְחוּ
נַחֲלָתָם מֵעֵבֶר לְיַרְדֵּן יְרֵחוֹ קֵדְמָה מִזְרָחָה:

רביעי
[ששי]
טז־יז וַיְדַבֵּר יְהֹוָה אֶל־מֹשֶׁה לֵּאמֹר: אֵלֶּה שְׁמוֹת הָאֲנָשִׁים אֲשֶׁר־יִנְחֲלוּ לָכֶם
יח אֶת־הָאָרֶץ אֶלְעָזָר הַכֹּהֵן וִיהוֹשֻׁעַ בִּן־נוּן: וְנָשִׂיא אֶחָד נָשִׂיא אֶחָד
יט מִמַּטֶּה תִּקְחוּ לִנְחֹל אֶת־הָאָרֶץ: וְאֵלֶּה שְׁמוֹת הָאֲנָשִׁים לְמַטֵּה
כ־כא יְהוּדָה כָּלֵב בֶּן־יְפֻנֶּה: וּלְמַטֵּה בְּנֵי שִׁמְעוֹן שְׁמוּאֵל בֶּן־עַמִּיהוּד: לְמַטֵּה

33:56. A necessary command. No human ruler has the right to decree that an entire population is to be exterminated or exiled, but God revealed that the Canaanite presence was incompatible with both the Land's holiness and Israel's mission on earth. History is the most conclu- sive proof of this, for the fact was that the Jews could not bring themselves to eliminate all the Canaanites, with the result that the Jews were drawn to idolatry and debauch- ery, and were in turn periodically oppressed and finally exiled.

(See Appendix D,   *Jordan to the land of Canaan, ⁵² you shall drive out all the inhabitants of the*
map 3)   *Land before you; and you shall destroy all their prostration stones; all their
molten images shall you destroy; and all their high places shall you demolish.
⁵³ You shall possess the Land and you shall settle in it, for to you have I given
the Land to possess it. ⁵⁴ You shall give the Land as an inheritance by lot to your
families; to the many you shall increase its inheritance and to the few shall you
decrease its inheritance; wherever its lot shall fall, his shall it be, according to the
tribes of your fathers shall you inherit. ⁵⁵ But if you do not drive out the
inhabitants of the Land before you, those of them whom you leave shall be pins
in your eyes and thorns in your sides, and they will harass you upon the Land
in which you dwell. ⁵⁶ And it shall be that what I had meant to do to them, I shall
do to you.* **

34   ¹ HASHEM spoke to Moses, saying: ² Command the Children of Israel and say
The   to them: When you come to the land of Canaan, this is the land that
boundaries shall fall to you as an inheritance, the land of Canaan according to its borders. *
of   ³ Your southern side shall be from the Wilderness of Zin at the side of Edom, and
Eretz Yisrael your southern border shall be from the edge of the Salt Sea to the east. * ⁴ The
(See Appendix D, border shall go around south of Maaleh-akrabbim, and shall pass toward Zin;
map 4)   and its outskirts shall be south of Kadesh-barnea; then it shall go out to
Hazar-addar and pass to Azmon. ⁵ The border shall go around from Azmon to
the stream of Egypt, and its outskirts shall be toward the Sea. ⁶ The western
border: It shall be for you the Great Sea and the district; this shall be for you the
western border.*

   *⁷ This shall be for you the northern border: from the Great Sea you shall turn
to Mount Hor. ⁸ From Mount Hor you shall turn to the approach to Hamath, and
the outskirts of the border shall be toward Zedad. ⁹ The border shall go forth
toward Zifron and its outskirts shall be Hazar-enan; this shall be for you the
northern border. ¹⁰ You shall draw yourselves as the eastern border from
Hazar-enan to Shefam. ¹¹ The border shall descend from Shefam to Riblah, east
of Ain; the border shall descend and extend to the bank of the Kinnereth Sea to
the east. ¹² The border shall descend to the Jordan, and its outskirts shall be the
Salt Sea; this shall be the Land for you, according to its borders all around.*

   *¹³ Moses commanded the Children of Israel, saying: This is the Land that you
shall divide as an inheritance by lot, which HASHEM has commanded to give to
the nine-and-a-half tribes. ¹⁴ For the tribe of the children of Reuben have taken
according to their fathers' house, and the tribe of the children of Gad according
to their fathers' house, and half the tribe of Manasseh have taken their inheritance. ¹⁵ Two-and-a-half tribes have taken their inheritance on the bank of the
Jordan by Jericho, eastward toward the sunrise.*

The   *¹⁶ HASHEM spoke to Moses, saying, ¹⁷ These are names of the men who are to
leadership take possession of the Land for you: Elazar the Kohen and Joshua son of Nun,
<CF   ¹⁸ and one leader from each tribe shall you take to possess the Land. ¹⁹ These
are the names of the men: for the tribe of Judah, Caleb son of Jephunneh; ²⁰ and
for the tribe of the children of Simeon, Shemuel son of Ammihud; ²¹ for the tribe*

34:2. The Torah delineates the boundaries of *Eretz
Yisrael* because of the many commandments that are
obligatory only within the Land (*Rashi*).

34:3. The border begins at the extreme southeast, and
goes from there to the west, then northward, eastward,
and, finally, southward.

כב-כג בְנְיָמִן אֱלִידָד בֶּן־כִּסְלוֹן: וּלְמַטֵּה בְנֵי־דָן נָשִׂיא בֻּקִּי בֶּן־יָגְלִי: לִבְנֵי יוֹסֵף

כד לְמַטֵּה בְנֵי־מְנַשֶּׁה נָשִׂיא חַנִּיאֵל בֶּן־אֵפֹד: וּלְמַטֵּה בְנֵי־אֶפְרַיִם נָשִׂיא

כה-כו קְמוּאֵל בֶּן־שִׁפְטָן: וּלְמַטֵּה בְנֵי־זְבוּלֻן נָשִׂיא אֱלִיצָפָן בֶּן־פַּרְנָךְ: וּלְמַטֵּה
בְנֵי־יִשָּׂשכָר נָשִׂיא פַּלְטִיאֵל בֶּן־עַזָּן: וּלְמַטֵּה בְנֵי־אָשֵׁר נָשִׂיא אֲחִיהוּד

כז-כט בֶּן־שְׁלֹמִי: וּלְמַטֵּה בְנֵי־נַפְתָּלִי נָשִׂיא פְּדַהְאֵל בֶּן־עַמִּיהוּד: אֵלֶּה אֲשֶׁר
צִוָּה יְהוָה לְנַחֵל אֶת־בְּנֵי־יִשְׂרָאֵל בְּאֶרֶץ כְּנָעַן:

לה א-ב חמישי וַיְדַבֵּר יְהוָה אֶל־מֹשֶׁה בְּעַרְבֹת מוֹאָב עַל־יַרְדֵּן יְרֵחוֹ לֵאמֹר: צַו אֶת־בְּנֵי
יִשְׂרָאֵל וְנָתְנוּ לַלְוִיִּם מִנַּחֲלַת אֲחֻזָּתָם עָרִים לָשָׁבֶת וּמִגְרָשׁ לֶעָרִים

ג סְבִיבֹתֵיהֶם תִּתְּנוּ לַלְוִיִּם: וְהָיוּ הֶעָרִים לָהֶם לָשָׁבֶת וּמִגְרְשֵׁיהֶם יִהְיוּ

ד לִבְהֶמְתָּם וְלִרְכֻשָׁם וּלְכֹל חַיָּתָם: וּמִגְרְשֵׁי הֶעָרִים אֲשֶׁר תִּתְּנוּ לַלְוִיִּם

ה מִקִּיר הָעִיר וָחוּצָה אֶלֶף אַמָּה סָבִיב: וּמַדֹּתֶם מִחוּץ לָעִיר אֶת־פְּאַת־
קֵדְמָה אַלְפַּיִם בָּאַמָּה וְאֶת־פְּאַת־נֶגֶב אַלְפַּיִם בָּאַמָּה וְאֶת־פְּאַת־יָם |
אַלְפַּיִם בָּאַמָּה וְאֵת פְּאַת צָפוֹן אַלְפַּיִם בָּאַמָּה וְהָעִיר בַּתָּוֶךְ זֶה יִהְיֶה לָהֶם

ו מִגְרְשֵׁי הֶעָרִים: וְאֵת הֶעָרִים אֲשֶׁר תִּתְּנוּ לַלְוִיִּם אֵת שֵׁשׁ־עָרֵי הַמִּקְלָט
אֲשֶׁר תִּתְּנוּ לָנֻס שָׁמָּה הָרֹצֵחַ וַעֲלֵיהֶם תִּתְּנוּ אַרְבָּעִים וּשְׁתַּיִם עִיר: כָּל־

ז הֶעָרִים אֲשֶׁר תִּתְּנוּ לַלְוִיִּם אַרְבָּעִים וּשְׁמֹנֶה עִיר אֶתְהֶן וְאֶת־מִגְרְשֵׁיהֶן:

ח וְהֶעָרִים אֲשֶׁר תִּתְּנוּ מֵאֲחֻזַּת בְּנֵי־יִשְׂרָאֵל מֵאֵת הָרַב תַּרְבּוּ וּמֵאֵת הַמְעַט
תַּמְעִיטוּ אִישׁ כְּפִי נַחֲלָתוֹ אֲשֶׁר יִנְחָלוּ יִתֵּן מֵעָרָיו לַלְוִיִּם:

ט-י שביעי [ששי] וַיְדַבֵּר יְהוָה אֶל־מֹשֶׁה לֵּאמֹר: דַּבֵּר אֶל־בְּנֵי יִשְׂרָאֵל וְאָמַרְתָּ אֲלֵהֶם

יא כִּי אַתֶּם עֹבְרִים אֶת־הַיַּרְדֵּן אַרְצָה כְּנָעַן: וְהִקְרִיתֶם לָכֶם עָרִים עָרֵי

יב מִקְלָט תִּהְיֶינָה לָכֶם וְנָס שָׁמָּה רֹצֵחַ מַכֵּה־נֶפֶשׁ בִּשְׁגָגָה: וְהָיוּ לָכֶם
הֶעָרִים לְמִקְלָט מִגֹּאֵל וְלֹא יָמוּת הָרֹצֵחַ עַד־עָמְדוֹ לִפְנֵי הָעֵדָה

יג-יד לַמִּשְׁפָּט: וְהֶעָרִים אֲשֶׁר תִּתֵּנוּ שֵׁשׁ־עָרֵי מִקְלָט תִּהְיֶינָה לָכֶם: אֵת |
שְׁלֹשׁ הֶעָרִים תִּתְּנוּ מֵעֵבֶר לַיַּרְדֵּן וְאֵת שְׁלֹשׁ הֶעָרִים תִּתְּנוּ בְּאֶרֶץ

טו כְּנָעַן עָרֵי מִקְלָט תִּהְיֶינָה: לִבְנֵי יִשְׂרָאֵל וְלַגֵּר וְלַתּוֹשָׁב בְּתוֹכָם תִּהְיֶינָה
שֵׁשׁ־הֶעָרִים הָאֵלֶּה לְמִקְלָט לָנוּס שָׁמָּה כָּל־מַכֵּה־נֶפֶשׁ בִּשְׁגָגָה:

טז-יז וְאִם־בִּכְלִי בַרְזֶל | הִכָּהוּ וַיָּמֹת רֹצֵחַ הוּא מוֹת יוּמַת הָרֹצֵחַ: וְאִם
בְּאֶבֶן יָד אֲשֶׁר־יָמוּת בָּהּ הִכָּהוּ וַיָּמֹת רֹצֵחַ הוּא מוֹת יוּמַת הָרֹצֵחַ: אוֹ

יח בִּכְלִי עֵץ־יָד אֲשֶׁר־יָמוּת בּוֹ הִכָּהוּ וַיָּמֹת רֹצֵחַ הוּא מוֹת יוּמַת

יט-כ הָרֹצֵחַ: גֹּאֵל הַדָּם הוּא יָמִית אֶת־הָרֹצֵחַ בְּפִגְעוֹ־בוֹ הוּא יְמִיתֶנּוּ: וְאִם־

35:2. The tribes were commanded to set aside forty-eight cities for the Levites, who were not to receive a regular portion of the Land. These scattered cities permitted all parts of the nation to be exposed to the "legion of God," thereby enabling them and their children to learn from the example of the Levites.

35:4-5. Two thousand cubits were allocated in all direc-

tions around each city, of which the inner thousand was to remain undeveloped and beautiful, while the outer thousand was for agriculture (*Rashi*).

35:11. Whenever someone takes a life, there are four general possibilities: (a) If the act was completely accidental, the perpetrator is absolved of responsibility; (b) if the act was unintentional, but careless, the perpetrator is of Benjamin, Elidad son of Chislon; [22] and for the tribe of the children of Dan, as leader, Bukki son of Jogli; [23] for the children of Joseph, for the tribe of the children of Manasseh, as leader, Hanniel son of Ephod; [24] and for the tribe of the children of Ephraim, as leader, Kemuel son of Shiftan; [25] and for the tribe of the children of Zebulun, as leader, Elizaphan son of Parnach; [26] and for the tribe of the children of Issachar, as leader, Paltiel son of Azzan; [27] and for the tribe of the children of Asher, as leader, Ahihud son of Shelomi; [28] and for the tribe of the children of Naphtali, as leader, Pedahel son of Ammihud. [29] These are the ones whom HASHEM commanded to apportion to the Children of Israel in the land of Canaan.

35

Cities for the Levites

[1] HASHEM spoke to Moses in the plains of Moab, by the Jordan, at Jericho, saying: [2] Command the Children of Israel that they shall give to the Levites, from the heritage of their possession, cities for dwelling, * and open space for the cities all around them shall you give to the Levites. [3] The cities shall be theirs for dwelling, and their open space shall be for their animals, for their wealth, and for all their needs. [4] The open spaces * of the cities that you shall give to the Levites, from the wall of the city outward: a thousand cubits all around. [5] You shall measure from outside the city on the eastern side two thousand cubits; on the southern side two thousand cubits; on the western side two thousand cubits; and on the northern side two thousand cubits, with the city in the middle; this shall be for them the open spaces of the cities. [6] The cities that you shall give to the Levites: the six cities of refuge that you shall provide for a murderer to flee there, and in addition to them you shall give forty-two cities. [7] All the cities that you shall give to the Levites: forty-eight cities, them and their open spaces. [8] The cities that you shall give from the possession of the Children of Israel, from the many you shall increase and from the few you shall decrease, each according to his inheritance that they shall inherit shall he give of his cities to the Levites.

(See Appendix D, map 5)

Cities of refuge for unintentional murder

[9] HASHEM spoke to Moses, saying: [10] Speak to the Children of Israel and say to them: When you cross the Jordan to the land of Canaan, [11] you shall designate cities for yourselves, cities of refuge shall they be for you, and a murderer shall flee there — one who takes a life unintentionally. * [12] The cities shall be for you a refuge from the avenger, so that the murderer will not die until he stands before the assembly for judgment. [13] As to the cities that you shall designate, there shall be six cities of refuge for you. [14] Three cities shall you designate on the other side of the Jordan, and three cities shall you designate in the land of Canaan; they shall be cities of refuge. [15] For the Children of Israel and the proselyte and resident among them shall these six cities be a refuge, for anyone who kills a person unintentionally to flee there.

Intentional murder

[16] If he had struck him with an iron implement and he died, he is a murderer; the murderer shall surely be put to death. [17] Or if with a hand-sized stone by which one could die did he strike him, and he died, he is a murderer; the murderer shall surely be put to death. [18] Or if he struck him with a hand-sized wood implement through which one could die, and he died, he is a murderer; the murderer shall surely be put to death. [19] The avenger of the blood, * he shall kill the murderer; when he encounters him, he shall kill him. [20] If

---

exiled to a city of refuge; (c) if it was intentional but the court cannot carry out the death penalty, or if there was a high degree of negligence, the sin is too grave to be absolved by exile; (d) if killing was intentional, and the

murderer was properly warned and his act was witnessed, he is liable to execution.

35:19. *The avenger* [lit., *redeemer*] *of the blood,* i.e., a close relative of the victim.

כא בְּשִׂנְאָה יֶהְדָּפֶנּוּ אוֹ־הִשְׁלִיךְ עָלָיו בִּצְדִיָּה וַיָּמֹת: אוֹ בְאֵיבָ֠ה הִכָּהוּ בְיָדוֹ
וַיָּמֹת מוֹת־יוּמַת הַמַּכֶּה רֹצֵחַ הוּא גֹּאֵל הַדָּם יָמִית אֶת־הָרֹצֵחַ בְּפִגְעוֹ־
כב בוֹ: וְאִם־בְּפֶתַע בְּלֹא־אֵיבָה הֲדָפוֹ אוֹ־הִשְׁלִיךְ עָלָיו כָּל־כְּלִי בְּלֹא
כג צְדִיָּה: אוֹ בְכָל־אֶבֶן אֲשֶׁר־יָמוּת בָּהּ בְּלֹא רְאוֹת וַיַּפֵּל עָלָיו וַיָּמֹת
כד וְהוּא לֹא־אוֹיֵב לוֹ וְלֹא מְבַקֵּשׁ רָעָתוֹ: וְשָׁפְטוּ הָעֵדָה בֵּין הַמַּכֶּה וּבֵין
כה גֹּאֵל הַדָּם עַל הַמִּשְׁפָּטִים הָאֵלֶּה: וְהִצִּילוּ הָעֵדָה אֶת־הָרֹצֵחַ מִיַּד גֹּאֵל
הַדָּם וְהֵשִׁיבוּ אֹתוֹ הָעֵדָה אֶל־עִיר מִקְלָטוֹ אֲשֶׁר־נָס שָׁמָּה וְיָשַׁב בָּהּ
כו עַד־מוֹת הַכֹּהֵן הַגָּדֹל אֲשֶׁר־מָשַׁח אֹתוֹ בְּשֶׁמֶן הַקֹּדֶשׁ: וְאִם־יָצֹא
כז יֵצֵא הָרֹצֵחַ אֶת־גְּבוּל עִיר מִקְלָטוֹ אֲשֶׁר יָנוּס שָׁמָּה: וּמָצָא אֹתוֹ גֹּאֵל
הַדָּם מִחוּץ לִגְבוּל עִיר מִקְלָטוֹ וְרָצַח גֹּאֵל הַדָּם אֶת־הָרֹצֵחַ אֵין לוֹ
כח דָּם: כִּי בְעִיר מִקְלָטוֹ יֵשֵׁב עַד־מוֹת הַכֹּהֵן הַגָּדֹל וְאַחֲרֵי מוֹת הַכֹּהֵן
כט הַגָּדֹל יָשׁוּב הָרֹצֵחַ אֶל־אֶרֶץ אֲחֻזָּתוֹ: וְהָיוּ אֵלֶּה לָכֶם לְחֻקַּת מִשְׁפָּט
ל לְדֹרֹתֵיכֶם בְּכֹל מוֹשְׁבֹתֵיכֶם: כָּל־מַכֵּה־נֶפֶשׁ לְפִי עֵדִים יִרְצַח אֶת־
לא הָרֹצֵחַ וְעֵד אֶחָד לֹא־יַעֲנֶה בְנֶפֶשׁ לָמוּת: וְלֹא־תִקְחוּ כֹפֶר לְנֶפֶשׁ רֹצֵחַ
לב אֲשֶׁר־הוּא רָשָׁע לָמוּת כִּי־מוֹת יוּמָת: וְלֹא־תִקְחוּ כֹפֶר לָנוּס אֶל־
לג עִיר מִקְלָטוֹ לָשׁוּב לָשֶׁבֶת בָּאָרֶץ עַד־מוֹת הַכֹּהֵן: וְלֹא־תַחֲנִיפוּ אֶת־
הָאָרֶץ אֲשֶׁר אַתֶּם בָּהּ כִּי הַדָּם הוּא יַחֲנִיף אֶת־הָאָרֶץ וְלָאָרֶץ לֹא־יְכֻפַּר
לד לַדָּם אֲשֶׁר שֻׁפַּךְ־בָּהּ כִּי־אִם בְּדַם שֹׁפְכוֹ: וְלֹא תְטַמֵּא אֶת־הָאָרֶץ אֲשֶׁר
אַתֶּם יֹשְׁבִים בָּהּ אֲשֶׁר אֲנִי שֹׁכֵן בְּתוֹכָהּ כִּי אֲנִי יהוה שֹׁכֵן בְּתוֹךְ בְּנֵי
יִשְׂרָאֵל:

לו שביעי א וַיִּקְרְבוּ רָאשֵׁי הָאָבוֹת לְמִשְׁפַּחַת בְּנֵי־גִלְעָד בֶּן־מָכִיר בֶּן־מְנַשֶּׁה
מִמִּשְׁפְּחֹת בְּנֵי יוֹסֵף וַיְדַבְּרוּ לִפְנֵי מֹשֶׁה וְלִפְנֵי הַנְּשִׂאִים רָאשֵׁי אָבוֹת לִבְנֵי
ב יִשְׂרָאֵל: וַיֹּאמְרוּ אֶת־אֲדֹנִי צִוָּה יהוה לָתֵת אֶת־הָאָרֶץ בְּנַחֲלָה בְּגוֹרָל
לִבְנֵי יִשְׂרָאֵל וַאדֹנִי צֻוָּה בַיהוה לָתֵת אֶת־נַחֲלַת צְלָפְחָד אָחִינוּ לִבְנֹתָיו:
ג וְהָיוּ לְאֶחָד מִבְּנֵי שִׁבְטֵי בְנֵי־יִשְׂרָאֵל לְנָשִׁים וְנִגְרְעָה נַחֲלָתָן מִנַּחֲלַת
אֲבֹתֵינוּ וְנוֹסַף עַל נַחֲלַת הַמַּטֶּה אֲשֶׁר תִּהְיֶינָה לָהֶם וּמִגֹּרַל נַחֲלָתֵנוּ יִגָּרֵעַ:
ד וְאִם־יִהְיֶה הַיֹּבֵל לִבְנֵי יִשְׂרָאֵל וְנוֹסְפָה נַחֲלָתָן עַל נַחֲלַת הַמַּטֶּה אֲשֶׁר
תִּהְיֶינָה לָהֶם וּמִנַּחֲלַת מַטֵּה אֲבֹתֵינוּ יִגָּרַע נַחֲלָתָן: וַיְצַו מֹשֶׁה אֶת־
ה בְּנֵי יִשְׂרָאֵל עַל־פִּי יהוה לֵאמֹר כֵּן מַטֵּה בְנֵי־יוֹסֵף דֹּבְרִים: זֶה הַדָּבָר
ו אֲשֶׁר־צִוָּה יהוה לִבְנוֹת צְלָפְחָד לֵאמֹר לַטּוֹב בְּעֵינֵיהֶם תִּהְיֶינָה לְנָשִׁים

35:25. The Kohen Gadol bears some responsibility for the death, because he should have prayed that fatal accidents would not occur during his tenure (*Rashi*).

35:33. The sin of murder and of condoning it is much worse in *Eretz Yisrael* than elsewhere, because of the Land's great holiness.

35:34. Since God rests among His people even when they are contaminated (see *Leviticus 16:16*), those who contaminate the Land cause God, as it were, to dwell amid their contamination, a grievous sin (*Rashi*).

he pushed him out of hatred or hurled upon him from ambush, and he died; [21] or in enmity struck him with his hand and he died, the assailant shall surely be put to death, he is a murderer; the avenger of the blood shall kill the murderer when he encounters him.

Unintentional murder [22] But if with suddenness, without enmity, did he push him, or he hurled any implement upon him without ambush; [23] or with any stone through which one could die, without having seen, and caused it to fall upon him and he died — but he was not his enemy and did not seek his harm — [24] then the assembly shall judge between the assailant and the avenger of the blood, according to these laws. [25] The assembly shall rescue the murderer from the hand of the avenger of the blood, and the assembly shall return him to his city of refuge where he had fled; he shall dwell in it until the death of the Kohen Gadol, * whom one had anointed with the sacred oil. [26] But if the murderer will ever leave the border of the city of refuge to which he had fled, [27] and the avenger of the blood shall find him outside of the border of his city of refuge, and the avenger of the blood will kill the murderer — he has no blood-guilt. [28] For he must dwell in his city of refuge until the death of the Kohen Gadol, and after the death of the Kohen Gadol the murderer shall return to the land of his possession.

[29] These shall be for you a decree of justice for your generations, in all your dwelling places. [30] Whoever smites a person, according to the testimony of witnesses shall one kill the murderer, but a single witness shall not testify against a person regarding death.

[31] You shall not accept ransom for the life of a murderer who is worthy of death, for he shall surely be put to death. [32] You shall not accept ransom for one who fled to his city of refuge to return to dwell in the land, before the death of the Kohen.

[33] You shall not bring guilt upon the land in which you are, for the blood will bring guilt upon the Land; the Land will not have atonement for the blood that was spilled in it, except through the blood of the one who spilled it. * [34] You shall not contaminate the Land in which you dwell, in whose midst I rest, for I am HASHEM Who rests among the Children of Israel. *

36

Tribal intermarriage [1] The heads of the fathers of the family of the children of Gilead, son of Machir son of Manasseh, of the families of the children of Joseph, approached and spoke before Moses and before the leaders, the heads of the fathers of the Children of Israel. [2] They said, "HASHEM has commanded my master to give the Land as an inheritance by lot to the Children of Israel, and my master has been commanded by HASHEM to give the inheritance of Zelophehad our brother to his daughters. [3] If they become wives of one of the sons of the tribes of the Children of Israel, then their inheritance will be subtracted from the inheritance of our fathers and be added to the inheritance of the tribe into which they will marry, and it will be subtracted from the lot of our inheritance. [4] And when the Jubilee will arrive for the Children of Israel, their inheritance will be added to the inheritance of the tribe into which they will marry; and from the inheritance of the tribe of our fathers will their inheritance be subtracted."

[5] Moses commanded the Children of Israel according to the word of HASHEM, saying, "Correctly does the tribe of the children of Joseph speak. [6] This is the word that HASHEM has commanded regarding the daughters of Zelophehad, saying: Let them be wives to whomever is good in their eyes,

ז אַ֣ךְ לְמִשְׁפַּ֣חַת מַטֵּ֣ה אֲבִיהֶ֔ם תִּֽהְיֶ֖ינָה לְנָשִׁ֑ים וְלֹֽא־תִסֹּ֤ב נַחֲלָה֙ לִבְנֵ֣י

יִשְׂרָאֵ֔ל מִמַּטֶּ֖ה אֶל־מַטֶּ֑ה כִּ֣י אִ֗ישׁ בְּנַחֲלַת֙ מַטֵּ֣ה אֲבֹתָ֔יו יִדְבְּק֖וּ בְּנֵ֥י

ח יִשְׂרָאֵֽל: וְכָל־בַּ֞ת יֹרֶ֣שֶׁת נַחֲלָ֗ה מִמַּטּוֹת֙ בְּנֵ֣י יִשְׂרָאֵ֔ל לְאֶחָ֣ד מִמִּשְׁפַּ֗חַת

מַטֵּ֤ה אָבִ֨יהָ֙ תִּֽהְיֶ֣ה לְאִשָּׁ֔ה לְמַ֗עַן יִֽירְשׁוּ֙ בְּנֵ֣י יִשְׂרָאֵ֔ל אִ֖ישׁ נַחֲלַ֥ת אֲבֹתָֽיו:

ט וְלֹֽא־תִסֹּ֤ב נַחֲלָה֙ מִמַּטֶּ֖ה לְמַטֶּ֣ה אַחֵ֑ר כִּי־אִ֗ישׁ בְּנַחֲלָת֔וֹ יִדְבְּק֖וּ מַטּ֥וֹת

י בְּנֵ֥י יִשְׂרָאֵֽל: כַּאֲשֶׁ֛ר צִוָּ֥ה יהוה אֶת־מֹשֶׁ֑ה כֵּ֥ן עָשׂ֖וּ בְּנ֥וֹת צְלָפְחָֽד:

יא וַתִּהְיֶ֜ינָה מַחְלָ֣ה תִרְצָ֗ה וְחָגְלָ֤ה וּמִלְכָּה֙ וְנֹעָ֔ה בְּנ֖וֹת צְלָפְחָ֑ד לִבְנֵ֥י דֹֽדֵיהֶ֖ן

יב לְנָשִֽׁים: מִֽמִּשְׁפְּחֹ֛ת בְּנֵֽי־מְנַשֶּׁ֥ה בֶן־יוֹסֵ֖ף הָי֣וּ לְנָשִׁ֑ים וַתְּהִי֙ נַ֣חֲלָתָ֔ן עַל־

יג מַטֵּ֖ה מִשְׁפַּ֥חַת אֲבִיהֶֽן: אֵ֣לֶּה הַמִּצְוֺ֞ת וְהַמִּשְׁפָּטִ֗ים אֲשֶׁ֨ר צִוָּ֤ה יהוה בְּיַד־

מֹשֶׁ֖ה אֶל־בְּנֵ֣י יִשְׂרָאֵ֑ל בְּעַֽרְבֹ֣ת מוֹאָ֔ב עַ֖ל יַרְדֵּ֥ן יְרֵחֽוֹ:

מפטיר

*Haftaras
Masei:*
p. 1072

(Most
congregations
read this
Haftarah even
on Rosh
Chodesh.)

It is customary for the congregation followed by the reader to proclaim:

חֲזַק! חֲזַק! וְנִתְחַזֵּק!

קל״ב פסוקים. מחל״ה חול״ה סימן. סכום פסוקי דספר במדבר אלף ומאתים ושמנים ושמנה. ארפ״ח (אפר״ח) סימן.

36:6. Even though the women were to marry within the tribe, no one had the right to dictate to them; the choice | of mate would be theirs alone.

After the Land was apportioned, the prohibition was

but only to the family of their father's tribe shall they become wives. * ⁷ An inheritance of the Children of Israel shall not make rounds from tribe to tribe; rather the Children of Israel shall cleave every man to the inheritance of the tribe of his fathers. ⁸ Every daughter who inherits an inheritance of the tribes of the Children of Israel shall become the wife of someone from a family of her father's tribe, so that everyone of the Children of Israel will inherit the inheritance of his fathers. ⁹ An inheritance shall not make rounds from a tribe to another tribe, for the tribes of the Children of Israel shall cleave every man to his own inheritance.

¹⁰ As HASHEM commanded Moses, so did the daughters of Zelophehad do. ¹¹ Mahlah, Tirzah, Hoglah, Milcah, and Noah, the daughters of Zelophehad, became wives to sons of their uncles. ¹² [To cousins] from the families of the children of Manasseh son of Joseph did they become wives, and their inheritance remained with the tribe of the family of their father.

¹³ These are the commandments and the ordinances that HASHEM commanded through Moses to the Children of Israel in the Plains of Moab, at the Jordan, by Jericho.

It is customary for the congregation followed by the reader to proclaim:

"Chazak! Chazak! Venischazeik!
(Be strong! Be strong! And may we be strengthened!)"

---

lifted, to universal rejoicing that a barrier to the nation's unity no longer existed. The anniversary of that event, the fifteenth of Av, became a time of great celebration (*Taanis* 30a).

Deuteronomy דברים

The Talmud refers to Deuteronomy as Mishneh Torah, commonly translated "Repetition (or Review) of the Torah," or "Explanation of the Torah." The entire Book was said by Moses to the nation during the last five weeks of his life; in effect, it was the prophet's last will and testament to his beloved people, in which he warned them of potential pitfalls and inspired them to rise to their calling. Since Deuteronomy does not review all the commandments and narratives of the preceding forty years, the question arises on what basis the commandments and narratives contained in this Book were chosen.

Rabbi Samson Raphael Hirsch explains that the Book of Deuteronomy was Israel's introduction to the new life they would have to forge in Eretz Yisrael. They would plow, plant, and harvest. They would establish courts and a government. They would forge social relationships and the means to provide for and protect the needy and helpless. They would need strong faith and self-discipline to avoid the snares and temptations of pagan neighbors and false prophets. To stress these laws and values, and to exhort Israel to be strong, was the function of this Book, with its laws and Moses' appeals to the conscience of the people. Deuteronomy is not merely a "review" of the previous four books of the Torah. True, Moses spent the final weeks of his life reviewing and teaching all the laws and the entire history of Israel, but the text of the Book of Deuteronomy records only those that were relevant for Israel's new life in its land.

Deuteronomy is unique in another way. As explained by the Vilna Gaon:

> The first four Books were heard directly from the mouth of the Holy One, Blessed is He, through the throat of Moses. Not so Deuteronomy. Israel heard the words of this Book the same way they heard the words of the prophets who came after Moses. God would speak to the prophet on one day, and on a later day he would go and make the vision known to Israel. Accordingly, at the time the prophet spoke to the people, the word of God had already been removed from him, [i.e., they did not hear God's word directly; they heard the prophet's comprehensoin of it]. So, too, the Book of Deuteronomy was heard from the mouth of Moses.

Moses teaches and guides. He chastises and admonishes. He reminds the people of their shortcomings and inspires them with their potential. Never has there been such a teacher or a prophet. But though Moses bid farewell in this Book, he is not gone. His teachings are here and his presence remains embodied in all his students, for the thousands of years since he lived.

פרשת דברים

א אֵ֣לֶּה הַדְּבָרִ֗ים אֲשֶׁ֨ר דִּבֶּ֤ר מֹשֶׁה֙ אֶל־כָּל־יִשְׂרָאֵ֔ל בְּעֵ֖בֶר הַיַּרְדֵּ֑ן בַּמִּדְבָּ֡ר

ב בָּֽעֲרָבָה֩ מ֨וֹל ס֜וּף בֵּֽין־פָּארָ֤ן וּבֵֽין־תֹּ֨פֶל֙ וְלָבָ֣ן וַֽחֲצֵרֹ֔ת וְדִ֖י זָהָֽב: אַחַ֨ד עָשָׂ֥ר

ג י֜וֹם מֵֽחֹרֵ֗ב דֶּ֛רֶךְ הַר־שֵׂעִ֖יר עַ֣ד קָדֵ֣שׁ בַּרְנֵ֑עַ: וַיְהִי֙ בְּאַרְבָּעִ֣ים שָׁנָ֔ה בְּעַשְׁתֵּֽי־

עָשָׂ֥ר חֹ֛דֶשׁ בְּאֶחָ֖ד לַחֹ֑דֶשׁ דִּבֶּ֤ר מֹשֶׁה֙ אֶל־בְּנֵ֣י יִשְׂרָאֵ֔ל כְּכֹ֛ל אֲשֶׁ֨ר צִוָּ֧ה

ד יְהֹוָ֛ה אֹת֖וֹ אֲלֵהֶֽם: אַֽחֲרֵ֣י הַכֹּת֗וֹ אֵ֚ת סִיחֹן֙ מֶ֣לֶךְ הָֽאֱמֹרִ֔י אֲשֶׁ֥ר יוֹשֵׁ֖ב

ה בְּחֶשְׁבּ֑וֹן וְאֵ֗ת ע֚וֹג מֶ֣לֶךְ הַבָּשָׁ֔ן אֲשֶׁר־יוֹשֵׁ֥ב בְּעַשְׁתָּרֹ֖ת בְּאֶדְרֶֽעִי: בְּעֵ֥בֶר

ו הַיַּרְדֵּ֖ן בְּאֶ֣רֶץ מוֹאָ֑ב הוֹאִ֣יל מֹשֶׁ֔ה בֵּאֵ֛ר אֶת־הַתּוֹרָ֥ה הַזֹּ֖את לֵאמֹֽר: יְהֹוָ֧ה

אֱלֹהֵ֛ינוּ דִּבֶּ֥ר אֵלֵ֖ינוּ בְּחֹרֵ֣ב לֵאמֹ֑ר רַב־לָכֶ֥ם שֶׁ֖בֶת בָּהָ֥ר הַזֶּֽה: פְּנ֣וּ | וּסְע֣וּ

ז לָכֶ֗ם וּבֹ֨אוּ הַ֤ר הָֽאֱמֹרִי֙ וְאֶל־כָּל־שְׁכֵנָ֔יו בָּֽעֲרָבָ֥ה בָהָ֖ר וּבַשְּׁפֵלָ֣ה וּבַנֶּ֑גֶב

ח וּבְח֣וֹף הַיָּ֗ם אֶ֤רֶץ הַֽכְּנַֽעֲנִי֙ וְהַלְּבָנ֔וֹן עַד־הַנָּהָ֥ר הַגָּדֹ֖ל נְהַר־פְּרָ֑ת: רְאֵ֛ה

נָתַ֥תִּי לִפְנֵיכֶ֖ם אֶת־הָאָ֑רֶץ בֹּ֚אוּ וּרְשׁ֣וּ אֶת־הָאָ֔רֶץ אֲשֶׁ֣ר נִשְׁבַּ֣ע יְהֹוָ֡ה

לַֽאֲבֹֽתֵיכֶ֡ם לְאַבְרָהָ֣ם לְיִצְחָ֣ק וּלְיַֽעֲקֹב֙ לָתֵ֣ת לָהֶ֔ם וּלְזַרְעָ֖ם אַֽחֲרֵיהֶֽם:

ט וָֽאֹמַ֣ר אֲלֵכֶ֔ם בָּעֵ֥ת הַהִ֖וא לֵאמֹ֑ר לֹֽא־אוּכַ֥ל לְבַדִּ֖י שְׂאֵ֥ת אֶתְכֶֽם: יְהֹוָ֣ה

יא אֱלֹֽהֵיכֶ֔ם הִרְבָּ֣ה אֶתְכֶ֑ם וְהִנְּכֶ֣ם הַיּ֔וֹם כְּכֽוֹכְבֵ֥י הַשָּׁמַ֖יִם לָרֹֽב: יְהֹוָ֞ה אֱלֹהֵ֣י

אֲבֽוֹתֵכֶ֗ם יֹסֵ֧ף עֲלֵיכֶ֛ם כָּכֶ֖ם אֶ֣לֶף פְּעָמִ֑ים וִיבָרֵ֣ךְ אֶתְכֶ֔ם כַּֽאֲשֶׁ֖ר דִּבֶּ֥ר לָכֶֽם:

יב־יג אֵיכָ֥ה אֶשָּׂ֖א לְבַדִּ֑י טָרְחֲכֶ֥ם וּמַֽשַּׂאֲכֶ֖ם וְרִֽיבְכֶֽם: הָב֣וּ לָ֠כֶ֠ם אֲנָשִׁ֨ים חֲכָמִ֤ים

יד וּנְבֹנִים֙ וִֽידֻעִ֔ים לְשִׁבְטֵיכֶ֑ם וַֽאֲשִׂימֵ֖ם בְּרָֽאשֵׁיכֶֽם: וַתַּֽעֲנ֖וּ אֹתִ֑י וַתֹּ֣אמְר֔וּ

טו טֽוֹב־הַדָּבָ֥ר אֲשֶׁר־דִּבַּ֖רְתָּ לַֽעֲשֽׂוֹת: וָֽאֶקַּ֞ח אֶת־רָאשֵׁ֣י שִׁבְטֵיכֶ֗ם אֲנָשִׁ֤ים

חֲכָמִים֙ וִֽידֻעִ֔ים וָֽאֶתֵּ֥ן אֹתָ֖ם רָאשִׁ֣ים עֲלֵיכֶ֑ם שָׂרֵ֨י אֲלָפִ֜ים וְשָׂרֵ֣י מֵא֗וֹת

טז וְשָׂרֵ֤י חֲמִשִּׁים֙ וְשָׂרֵ֣י עֲשָׂרֹ֔ת וְשֹֽׁטְרִ֖ים לְשִׁבְטֵיכֶֽם: וָֽאֲצַוֶּה֙ אֶת־שֹֽׁפְטֵיכֶ֔ם

בָּעֵ֥ת הַהִ֖וא לֵאמֹ֑ר שָׁמֹ֤עַ בֵּין־אֲחֵיכֶם֙ וּשְׁפַטְתֶּ֣ם צֶ֔דֶק בֵּֽין־אִ֥ישׁ וּבֵֽין־אָחִ֖יו

יז וּבֵ֥ין גֵּרֽוֹ: לֹֽא־תַכִּ֨ירוּ פָנִ֜ים בַּמִּשְׁפָּ֗ט כַּקָּטֹ֤ן כַּגָּדֹל֙ תִּשְׁמָע֔וּן לֹ֤א תָג֨וּרוּ֙

מִפְּנֵי־אִ֔ישׁ כִּ֥י הַמִּשְׁפָּ֖ט לֵֽאלֹהִ֣ים ה֑וּא וְהַדָּבָר֙ אֲשֶׁ֣ר יִקְשֶׁ֣ה מִכֶּ֔ם תַּקְרִב֥וּן

יח אֵלַ֖י וּשְׁמַעְתִּֽיו: וָֽאֲצַוֶּ֥ה אֶתְכֶ֖ם בָּעֵ֣ת הַהִ֑וא אֵ֥ת כָּל־הַדְּבָרִ֖ים אֲשֶׁ֥ר תַּֽעֲשֽׂוּן:

יט וַנִּסַּ֣ע מֵֽחֹרֵ֗ב וַנֵּ֡לֶךְ אֵ֣ת כָּל־הַמִּדְבָּ֣ר הַגָּד֣וֹל וְהַנּוֹרָ֣א הַה֗וּא אֲשֶׁ֤ר רְאִיתֶם֙

דֶּ֜רֶךְ הַ֤ר הָֽאֱמֹרִי֙ כַּֽאֲשֶׁ֥ר צִוָּ֛ה יְהֹוָ֥ה אֱלֹהֵ֖ינוּ אֹתָ֑נוּ וַנָּבֹ֕א עַ֖ד קָדֵ֥שׁ בַּרְנֵֽעַ:

⊷§ Parashas Devarim

In this Book, Moses was the speaker. This is indicated by the fact that in *Deuteronomy*, Moses says, "Hashem spoke to *me*" (1:42,2:9;3:2), whereas the constant refrain in the rest of the Torah is "Hashem spoke *to Moses."* In *Deuteronomy*, Moses chose the words and conveyed the commandments as he understood them.

1:1. The combination of דְּבָרִים, *words*, with דִּבֶּר, *he spoke*, instead of the more common אָמַר, *he said,* implies strong words of rebuke. Lest the people become over-confident that they would not succumb to the influences

of Canaan, Moses reminded them of their many sins and rebellions since the Exodus; if the people could sin when they were surrounded by miracles, surely they would be in greater danger without constant reminders of God's Presence. But in order not to embarrass and offend his listeners, he alluded to the sins by using place names or other veiled references. Moreover, as the Midrash cites: Rabbi Yochanan said, "We have reviewed the entirety of Scripture, but we have not found any place with the name Tophel or Laban!" And, as *Ramban* explains, it is unlikely that these are all descriptions of where Moses spoke, for if so, the Torah would be giving "more signs

PARASHAS DEVARIM

1

Veiled rebuke

¹ These are the words that Moses spoke to all Israel, on the other side of the Jordan, concerning the Wilderness, concerning the Arabah, opposite the Sea of Reeds, between Paran and Tophel, and Laban, and Hazeroth, and Di-zahab; ² eleven days from Horeb, by way of Mount Seir to Kadesh-barnea. ³ It was in the fortieth year, in the eleventh month, on the first of the month, when Moses spoke to the Children of Israel, according to everything that HASHEM commanded him to them, ⁴ after he had smitten Sihon, king of the Amorite, who dwelt in Heshbon, and Og, king of Bashan, who dwelt in Ashtaroth, in Edrei. ⁵ On the other side of the Jordan in the land of Moab, Moses began explaining this Torah, saying: *

⁶ HASHEM, our God, spoke to us in Horeb, saying: Enough of your dwelling by this mountain. ⁷ Turn yourselves around and journey, and come to the Amorite mountain and all its neighbors, in the Arabah, * on the mountain, and in the lowland, and in the south, and at the seacoast; the land of the Canaanite and the Lebanon, until the great river, the Euphrates River. ⁸ See! I have given the Land before you; come and possess the Land that HASHEM swore to your forefathers, to Abraham, to Isaac, and to Jacob, to give them and their children after them.

⁹ I said to you at that time, saying, "I cannot carry you alone. ¹⁰ HASHEM, your God, has multiplied you and behold! you are today like the stars of heaven in abundance. ¹¹ May HASHEM, the God of your forefathers, add to you a thousand times yourselves, and bless you as He has spoken of you. ¹² How can I alone

The appointment of judges

carry your contentiousness, your burdens, and your quarrels? ¹³ Provide for yourselves distinguished men, who are wise, understanding, and well known to your tribes, and I shall appoint them as your heads."

¹⁴ You answered me and said, "The thing that you have proposed to do is good."

¹⁵ So I took the heads of your tribes, distinguished men, who were wise and well known, and I appointed them as heads over you, leaders of thousands, leaders of hundreds, leaders of fifties, and leaders of tens, and officers for your tribes. ¹⁶ I instructed your judges at that time, saying, "Listen among your brethren and judge righteously between a man and his brother or his litigant. ¹⁷ You shall not show favoritism in judgment, small and great alike shall you hear; you shall not tremble before any man, for the judgment is God's; any matter that is too difficult for you, you shall bring to me and I shall hear it." ¹⁸ I commanded you at that time all the things that you should do.

The mission of the spies

¹⁹ We journeyed from Horeb and we went through that entire great and awesome Wilderness that you saw, by way of the Amorite mountain, as HASHEM, our God, commanded us, and we came until Kadesh-barnea.

---

and boundaries than one who sells a field."

Thus, for example, *Onkelos* and *Sifre* interpret the term *the Wilderness* as an allusion to the Wilderness of Sin, where the people complained that they had been led into a desert to starve (*Exodus* 16:1-3); and *Di-zahab*, literally, "abundance of gold," recalls that when God blessed the people with an abundance of gold when they

left Egypt, they used His gift to make the Golden Calf.
1:5. Moses explained the Torah in many languages (*Rashi*), to symbolize that wherever Jews would be in the future, they would study the Torah in their language (*Sfas Emes*).

1:7. *In the Arabah*, i.e., a forested plain (*Rashi*).
The great river, i.e., the Euphrates (*Rashi*).

וָאֹמַ֖ר אֲלֵכֶ֑ם בָּאתֶם֙ עַד־הַ֣ר הָאֱמֹרִ֔י אֲשֶׁר־יְהֹוָ֥ה אֱלֹהֵ֖ינוּ נֹתֵ֥ן לָֽנוּ: רְאֵ֠ה כ־כא

נָתַ֨ן יְהֹוָ֧ה אֱלֹהֶ֛יךָ לְפָנֶ֖יךָ אֶת־הָאָ֑רֶץ עֲלֵ֣ה רֵ֗שׁ כַּֽאֲשֶׁר֩ דִּבֶּ֨ר יְהֹוָ֜ה אֱלֹהֵ֤י

אֲבֹתֶ֨יךָ֙ לָ֔ךְ אַל־תִּירָ֖א וְאַל־תֵּחָֽת: וַתִּקְרְב֣וּן אֵלַי֮ כֻּלְּכֶם֒ וַתֹּֽאמְר֗וּ נִשְׁלְחָ֤ה כב   שלישי

אֲנָשִׁים֙ לְפָנֵ֔ינוּ וְיַחְפְּרוּ־לָ֖נוּ אֶת־הָאָ֑רֶץ וְיָשִׁ֤בוּ אֹתָ֨נוּ֙ דָּבָ֔ר אֶת־הַדֶּ֨רֶךְ֙

אֲשֶׁ֣ר נַֽעֲלֶה־בָּ֔הּ וְאֵת֙ הֶֽעָרִ֔ים אֲשֶׁ֥ר נָבֹ֖א אֲלֵיהֶֽן: וַיִּיטַ֥ב בְּעֵינַ֖י הַדָּבָ֑ר כג

וָֽאֶקַּ֤ח מִכֶּם֙ שְׁנֵ֣ים עָשָׂ֣ר אֲנָשִׁ֔ים אִ֥ישׁ אֶחָ֖ד לַשָּֽׁבֶט: וַיִּפְנוּ֙ וַיַּֽעֲל֣וּ הָהָ֔רָה כד

וַיָּבֹ֖אוּ עַד־נַ֣חַל אֶשְׁכֹּ֑ל וַֽיְרַגְּל֖וּ אֹתָֽהּ: וַיִּקְח֤וּ בְיָדָם֙ מִפְּרִ֣י הָאָ֔רֶץ וַיּוֹרִ֖דוּ כה

אֵלֵ֑ינוּ וַיָּשִׁ֨בוּ אֹתָ֤נוּ דָבָר֙ וַיֹּ֣אמְר֔וּ טוֹבָ֣ה הָאָ֔רֶץ אֲשֶׁר־יְהֹוָ֥ה אֱלֹהֵ֖ינוּ נֹתֵ֥ן

לָֽנוּ: וְלֹ֥א אֲבִיתֶ֖ם לַֽעֲלֹ֑ת וַתַּמְר֕וּ אֶת־פִּ֥י יְהֹוָ֖ה אֱלֹֽהֵיכֶֽם: וַתֵּרָֽגְנ֣וּ כו־כז

בְאָֽהֳלֵיכֶ֗ם וַתֹּֽאמְרוּ֙ בְּשִׂנְאַ֤ת יְהֹוָה֙ אֹתָ֔נוּ הֽוֹצִיאָ֖נוּ מֵאֶ֣רֶץ מִצְרָ֑יִם לָתֵ֥ת

אֹתָ֛נוּ בְּיַ֥ד הָֽאֱמֹרִ֖י לְהַשְׁמִידֵֽנוּ: אָנָ֣ה ׀ אֲנַ֣חְנוּ עֹלִ֗ים אַחֵ֩ינוּ֩ הֵמַ֨סּוּ כח

אֶת־לְבָבֵ֜נוּ לֵאמֹ֗ר עַ֣ם גָּד֤וֹל וָרָם֙ מִמֶּ֔נּוּ עָרִ֛ים גְּדֹלֹ֥ת וּבְצוּרֹ֖ת בַּשָּׁמָ֑יִם

וְגַם־בְּנֵ֥י עֲנָקִ֖ים רָאִ֥ינוּ שָֽׁם: וָֽאֹמַ֖ר אֲלֵכֶ֑ם לֹֽא־תַֽעַרְצ֥וּן וְלֹֽא־תִֽירְא֖וּן כט

מֵהֶֽם: יְהֹוָ֤ה אֱלֹֽהֵיכֶם֙ הַֽהֹלֵ֣ךְ לִפְנֵיכֶ֔ם ה֖וּא יִלָּחֵ֣ם לָכֶ֑ם כְּ֠כֹ֠ל אֲשֶׁ֨ר עָשָׂ֧ה ל

אִתְּכֶ֛ם בְּמִצְרַ֖יִם לְעֵֽינֵיכֶֽם: וּבַמִּדְבָּר֙ אֲשֶׁ֣ר רָאִ֔יתָ אֲשֶׁ֤ר נְשָֽׂאֲךָ֙ יְהֹוָ֣ה לא

אֱלֹהֶ֔יךָ כַּֽאֲשֶׁ֥ר יִשָּׂא־אִ֖ישׁ אֶת־בְּנ֑וֹ בְּכָל־הַדֶּ֨רֶךְ֙ אֲשֶׁ֣ר הֲלַכְתֶּ֔ם עַד־בֹּֽאֲכֶ֖ם

עַד־הַמָּק֥וֹם הַזֶּֽה: וּבַדָּבָ֖ר הַזֶּ֑ה אֵֽינְכֶם֙ מַֽאֲמִינִ֔ם בַּֽיהֹוָ֖ה אֱלֹֽהֵיכֶֽם: הַֽהֹלֵ֨ךְ לב־לג

לִפְנֵיכֶ֜ם בַּדֶּ֗רֶךְ לָת֤וּר לָכֶם֙ מָק֔וֹם לַֽחֲנֹֽתְכֶ֑ם בָּאֵ֣שׁ ׀ לַ֗יְלָה לַרְאֹֽתְכֶם֙ בַּדֶּ֨רֶךְ֙

אֲשֶׁ֣ר תֵּֽלְכוּ־בָ֔הּ וּבֶֽעָנָ֖ן יוֹמָֽם: וַיִּשְׁמַ֥ע יְהֹוָ֖ה אֶת־ק֣וֹל דִּבְרֵיכֶ֑ם וַיִּקְצֹ֖ף לד

וַיִּשָּׁבַ֣ע לֵאמֹֽר: אִם־יִרְאֶ֥ה אִישׁ֙ בָּֽאֲנָשִׁ֣ים הָאֵ֔לֶּה הַדּ֥וֹר הָרָ֖ע הַזֶּ֑ה אֵ֚ת לה

הָאָ֣רֶץ הַטּוֹבָ֔ה אֲשֶׁ֣ר נִשְׁבַּ֔עְתִּי לָתֵ֖ת לַֽאֲבֹֽתֵיכֶֽם: זֽוּלָתִ֞י כָּלֵ֤ב בֶּן־יְפֻנֶּה֙ ה֣וּא לו

יִרְאֶ֔נָּה וְלֽוֹ־אֶתֵּ֧ן אֶת־הָאָ֛רֶץ אֲשֶׁ֥ר דָּֽרַךְ־בָּ֖הּ וּלְבָנָ֑יו יַ֕עַן אֲשֶׁ֥ר מִלֵּ֖א אַֽחֲרֵ֥י

יְהֹוָֽה: גַּם־בִּי֙ הִתְאַנַּ֣ף יְהֹוָ֔ה בִּגְלַלְכֶ֖ם לֵאמֹ֑ר גַּם־אַתָּ֖ה לֹֽא־תָבֹ֥א שָֽׁם: לז

יְהוֹשֻׁ֤עַ בִּן־נוּן֙ הָֽעֹמֵ֣ד לְפָנֶ֔יךָ ה֖וּא יָ֣בֹא שָׁ֑מָּה אֹת֣וֹ חַזֵּ֔ק כִּי־ה֖וּא יַנְחִלֶ֥נָּה לח

אֶת־יִשְׂרָאֵֽל: וְטַפְּכֶ֡ם אֲשֶׁר֩ אֲמַרְתֶּ֨ם לָבַ֜ז יִֽהְיֶ֗ה וּבְנֵיכֶ֡ם אֲשֶׁ֣ר לֹֽא־יָֽדְע֣וּ לט   רביעי

הַיּוֹם֙ ט֣וֹב וָרָ֔ע הֵ֥מָּה יָבֹ֖אוּ שָׁ֑מָּה וְלָהֶ֣ם אֶתְּנֶ֔נָּה וְהֵ֖ם יִֽירָשֽׁוּהָ: וְאַתֶּ֖ם פְּנ֣וּ מ

לָכֶ֑ם וּסְע֥וּ הַמִּדְבָּ֖רָה דֶּ֥רֶךְ יַם־סֽוּף: וַתַּֽעֲנ֣וּ ׀ וַתֹּֽאמְר֣וּ אֵלַ֗י חָטָ֨אנוּ֙ לַֽיהֹוָ֔ה מא

אֲנַ֤חְנוּ נַֽעֲלֶה֙ וְנִלְחַ֔מְנוּ כְּכֹ֥ל אֲשֶׁר־צִוָּ֖נוּ יְהֹוָ֣ה אֱלֹהֵ֑ינוּ וַֽתַּחְגְּר֗וּ אִ֚ישׁ

אֶת־כְּלֵ֣י מִלְחַמְתּ֔וֹ וַתָּהִ֖ינוּ לַֽעֲלֹ֥ת הָהָֽרָה: וַיֹּ֨אמֶר יְהֹוָ֜ה אֵלַ֗י אֱמֹ֤ר לָהֶם֙ מב

לֹ֤א תַֽעֲלוּ֙ וְלֹֽא־תִלָּ֣חֲמ֔וּ כִּ֥י אֵינֶ֖נִּי בְּקִרְבְּכֶ֑ם וְלֹא֙ תִּנָּ֣גְפ֔וּ לִפְנֵ֖י אֹֽיְבֵיכֶֽם:

וָֽאֲדַבֵּ֥ר אֲלֵיכֶ֖ם וְלֹ֣א שְׁמַעְתֶּ֑ם וַתַּמְרוּ֙ אֶת־פִּ֣י יְהֹוָ֔ה וַתָּזִ֖דוּ וַתַּֽעֲל֥וּ הָהָֽרָה: מג

וַיֵּצֵ֨א הָֽאֱמֹרִ֜י הַיֹּשֵׁ֨ב בָּהָ֤ר הַהוּא֙ לִקְרַאתְכֶ֔ם וַיִּרְדְּפ֣וּ אֶתְכֶ֔ם כַּֽאֲשֶׁ֥ר מד

תַּֽעֲשֶׂ֖ינָה הַדְּבֹרִ֑ים וַיַּכְּת֥וּ אֶתְכֶ֛ם בְּשֵׂעִ֖יר עַד־חָרְמָֽה: וַתָּשֻׁ֥בוּ וַתִּבְכּ֖וּ לִפְנֵ֥י מה

1:29-33. Moses pleaded with the people to realize the foolishness of their charges.

²⁰ Then I said to you, "You have come until the Amorite mountain that HASHEM, our God, gives us. ²¹ See — HASHEM, your God, has placed the Land before you; go up and possess, as HASHEM, God of your forefathers, has spoken to you. Do not fear and do not lose resolve."

²² All of you approached me and said, "Let us send men ahead of us and let them spy out the Land for us, and bring word back to us: the road on which we should ascend and the cities to which we should come."

²³ The idea was good in my eyes, so I took from you twelve men, one man for each tribe. ²⁴ They turned and ascended the mountain and came until the Valley of Eshcol, and spied it out. ²⁵ They took in their hands from the fruit of the Land and brought it down to us; they brought back word to us and said, "Good is the Land that HASHEM, our God, gives us!"

²⁶ But you did not wish to ascend, and you rebelled against the word of HASHEM, your God. ²⁷ You slandered in your tents and said, "Because of HASHEM's hatred for us did He take us out of the land of Egypt, to deliver us into the hand of the Amorite to destroy us. ²⁸ To where shall we ascend? Our brothers have melted our hearts, saying, 'A people greater and taller than we, cities great and fortified to the heavens, and even children of giants have we seen there!'"

²⁹ *Then I said to you, "Do not be broken and do not fear them! ³⁰ HASHEM, your God, Who goes before you — He shall make war for you, like everything He did for you in Egypt, before your eyes. ³¹ And in the Wilderness, as you have seen, that HASHEM, your God, bore you, as a man carries his son, on the entire way that you traveled, until you arrived at this place. ³² Yet in this matter you do not believe in HASHEM, your God, ³³ Who goes before you on the way to seek out for you a place for you to encamp, with fire by night to show you the road that you should travel and with a cloud by day!"

³⁴ HASHEM heard the sound of your words, and He was incensed and He swore, saying, ³⁵ "If even a man of these people, this evil generation, shall see the good Land that I swore to give to your forefathers. ³⁶ Except for Caleb son of Jephunneh: He shall see it, and to him shall I give the Land on which he walked, and to his children, because he followed HASHEM wholeheartedly."

³⁷ With me, as well, HASHEM became angry because of you, saying: You, too, shall not come there. ³⁸ Joshua son of Nun, who stands before you, he shall come there; strengthen him, for he shall cause Israel to inherit it. ³⁹ And as for your small children, of whom you said, "They will be taken captive," and your children who did not know good from evil this day — they will come there; to them shall I give it and they shall possess it. ⁴⁰ And as for you, turn yourselves around and journey to the Wilderness, by way of the Sea of Reeds.

⁴¹ Then you spoke up and said to me, "We have sinned to HASHEM! We shall go up and do battle according to everything that HASHEM, our God, has commanded us!" Every man of you girded his weapons of war, and you were ready to ascend the mountain!

⁴² HASHEM said to me: Tell them, "Do not ascend and do not do battle, for I am not among you; so that you not be struck down before your enemies."

⁴³ So I spoke to you, but you did not listen. You rebelled against the word of HASHEM, and you were willful and climbed the mountain. ⁴⁴ The Amorite who dwell on that mountain went out against you and pursued you as the bees would do; they struck you in Seir until Hormah. ⁴⁵ Then you retreated and wept before

מו יְהוָֹה וְלֹא־שָׁמַע יהוה בְּקֹלְכֶם וְלֹא הֶאֱזִין אֲלֵיכֶם: וַתֵּשְׁבוּ בְקָדֵשׁ יָמִים
א רַבִּים כַּיָּמִים אֲשֶׁר יְשַׁבְתֶּם: וַנֵּפֶן וַנִּסַּע הַמִּדְבָּ֫רָה דֶּרֶךְ יַם־סוּף כַּאֲשֶׁר

ב דִּבֶּר יהוה אֵלָי וַנָּסָב אֶת־הַר־שֵׂעִיר יָמִים רַבִּים: וַיֹּאמֶר

ג־ד יהוה אֵלַי לֵאמֹר: רַב־לָכֶם סֹב אֶת־הָהָר הַזֶּה פְּנוּ לָכֶם צָפֹנָה: וְאֶת־
הָעָם צַו לֵאמֹר אַתֶּם עֹבְרִים בִּגְבוּל אֲחֵיכֶם בְּנֵי־עֵשָׂו הַיֹּשְׁבִים בְּשֵׂעִיר

ה וְיִירְאוּ מִכֶּם וְנִשְׁמַרְתֶּם מְאֹד: אַל־תִּתְגָּרוּ בָם כִּי לֹא־אֶתֵּן לָכֶם

ו מֵאַרְצָם עַד מִדְרַךְ כַּף־רָגֶל כִּי־יְרֻשָּׁה לְעֵשָׂו נָתַתִּי אֶת־הַר שֵׂעִיר: אֹכֶל
תִּשְׁבְּרוּ מֵאִתָּם בַּכֶּסֶף וַאֲכַלְתֶּם וְגַם־מַיִם תִּכְרוּ מֵאִתָּם בַּכֶּסֶף וּשְׁתִיתֶם:

ז כִּי יהוה אֱלֹהֶיךָ בֵּרַכְךָ בְּכֹל מַעֲשֵׂה יָדֶךָ יָדַע לֶכְתְּךָ אֶת־הַמִּדְבָּר הַגָּדֹל

ח הַזֶּה זֶה | אַרְבָּעִים שָׁנָה יהוה אֱלֹהֶיךָ עִמָּךְ לֹא חָסַרְתָּ דָּבָר: וַנַּעֲבֹר
מֵאֵת אַחֵינוּ בְנֵי־עֵשָׂו הַיֹּשְׁבִים בְּשֵׂעִיר מִדֶּרֶךְ הָעֲרָבָה מֵאֵילַת וּמֵעֶצְיֹן

ט גָּבֶר   וַנֵּפֶן וַנַּעֲבֹר דֶּרֶךְ מִדְבַּר מוֹאָב: וַיֹּאמֶר יהוה אֵלַי
אַל־תָּצַר אֶת־מוֹאָב וְאַל־תִּתְגָּר בָּם מִלְחָמָה כִּי לֹא־אֶתֵּן לְךָ מֵאַרְצוֹ

י יְרֻשָּׁה כִּי לִבְנֵי־לוֹט נָתַתִּי אֶת־עָר יְרֻשָּׁה: הָאֵמִים לְפָנִים יָשְׁבוּ בָהּ עַם

יא גָּדוֹל וְרַב וָרָם כָּעֲנָקִים: רְפָאִים יֵחָשְׁבוּ אַף־הֵם כָּעֲנָקִים וְהַמֹּאָבִים

יב יִקְרְאוּ לָהֶם אֵמִים: וּבְשֵׂעִיר יָשְׁבוּ הַחֹרִים לְפָנִים וּבְנֵי עֵשָׂו יִירָשׁוּם
וַיַּשְׁמִידוּם מִפְּנֵיהֶם וַיֵּשְׁבוּ תַּחְתָּם כַּאֲשֶׁר עָשָׂה יִשְׂרָאֵל לְאֶרֶץ יְרֻשָּׁתוֹ

יג אֲשֶׁר־נָתַן יהוה לָהֶם: עַתָּה קֻמוּ וְעִבְרוּ לָכֶם אֶת־נַחַל זָרֶד וַנַּעֲבֹר אֶת־

יד נַחַל זָרֶד: וְהַיָּמִים אֲשֶׁר־הָלַכְנוּ | מִקָּדֵשׁ בַּרְנֵעַ עַד אֲשֶׁר־עָבַרְנוּ אֶת־נַחַל
זֶרֶד שְׁלֹשִׁים וּשְׁמֹנֶה שָׁנָה עַד־תֹּם כָּל־הַדּוֹר אַנְשֵׁי הַמִּלְחָמָה מִקֶּרֶב

טו הַמַּחֲנֶה כַּאֲשֶׁר נִשְׁבַּע יהוה לָהֶם: וְגַם יַד־יהוה הָיְתָה בָּם לְהֻמָּם

טז מִקֶּרֶב הַמַּחֲנֶה עַד תֻּמָּם: וַיְהִי כַאֲשֶׁר־תַּמּוּ כָּל־אַנְשֵׁי הַמִּלְחָמָה לָמוּת

יז־יח מִקֶּרֶב הָעָם: וַיְדַבֵּר יהוה אֵלַי לֵאמֹר: אַתָּה עֹבֵר הַיּוֹם

יט אֶת־גְּבוּל מוֹאָב אֶת־עָר: וְקָרַבְתָּ מוּל בְּנֵי עַמּוֹן אַל־תְּצֻרֵם וְאַל־תִּתְגָּר
בָּם כִּי לֹא־אֶתֵּן מֵאֶרֶץ בְּנֵי־עַמּוֹן לְךָ יְרֻשָּׁה כִּי לִבְנֵי־לוֹט נְתַתִּיהָ יְרֻשָּׁה:

כ אֶרֶץ־רְפָאִים תֵּחָשֵׁב אַף־הִוא רְפָאִים יָשְׁבוּ־בָהּ לְפָנִים וְהָעַמֹּנִים יִקְרְאוּ

כא לָהֶם זַמְזֻמִּים: עַם גָּדוֹל וְרַב וָרָם כָּעֲנָקִים וַיַּשְׁמִידֵם יהוה מִפְּנֵיהֶם

כב וַיִּירָשֻׁם וַיֵּשְׁבוּ תַחְתָּם: כַּאֲשֶׁר עָשָׂה לִבְנֵי עֵשָׂו הַיֹּשְׁבִים בְּשֵׂעִיר
אֲשֶׁר הִשְׁמִיד אֶת־הַחֹרִי מִפְּנֵיהֶם וַיִּירָשֻׁם וַיֵּשְׁבוּ תַחְתָּם עַד הַיּוֹם הַזֶּה:

כג וְהָעַוִּים הַיֹּשְׁבִים בַּחֲצֵרִים עַד־עַזָּה כַּפְתֹּרִים הַיֹּצְאִים מִכַּפְתֹּר הִשְׁמִידֻם

כד וַיֵּשְׁבוּ תַחְתָּם: קוּמוּ סְּעוּ וְעִבְרוּ אֶת־נַחַל אַרְנֹן רְאֵה נָתַתִּי בְיָדְךָ אֶת־
סִיחֹן מֶלֶךְ־חֶשְׁבּוֹן הָאֱמֹרִי וְאֶת־אַרְצוֹ הָחֵל רָשׁ וְהִתְגָּר בּוֹ מִלְחָמָה:

2:1. This verse telescopes thirty-eight years, from the sin of the spies until the new generation was ready to enter the Land.

2:9. The Torah forbade Israel only from provoking *war* with Moab, but they were permitted to harass them short of war. As for Ammon, however, God forbade Israel from

HASHEM, but HASHEM did not listen to your voice and He did not hearken to you. [46] You dwelt in Kadesh for many days, as many days as you dwelt.

2

[1] **W**e turned and journeyed to the Wilderness toward the Sea of Reeds, as HASHEM spoke to me, and we circled Mount Seir for many days. *

[2] HASHEM said to me, saying: [3] Enough of your circling this mountain; turn yourselves northward. [4] You shall command the people, saying, "You are passing through the boundary of your brothers the children of Esau, who dwell in Seir; they will fear you, but you should be very careful. [5] You shall not provoke them, for I shall not give you of their land even the right to set foot, for as an inheritance to the children of Esau have I given Mount Seir. [6] You shall purchase food from them for money so that you may eat; also water shall you buy from them for money so that you may drink. [7] For HASHEM, your God, has blessed you in all your handiwork; He knew your way in this great Wilderness; this forty-year period HASHEM, your God, was with you; you did not lack a thing." [8] So we passed from our brothers, the children of Esau who dwell in Seir, from the way of the Arabah, from Elath and from Ezion-geber and we turned and passed on the way of the Moabite desert.

Esau/Seir (See Appendix D, map 1)

Moab — [9] HASHEM said to me: You shall not distress Moab * and you shall not provoke war with them, for I shall not give you an inheritance from their land, for to the children of Lot have I given Ar as an inheritance. [10] The Emim dwelled there previously, a great and populous people, and tall as the giants. [11] They, too, were considered Rephaim, like the giants; and the Moabites called them Emim. [12] And in Seir the Horites dwelled previously, and the children of Esau drove them away and destroyed them from before themselves and dwelled in their place, as Israel did to the Land of its inheritance, which HASHEM gave them. [13] Now, rise up and get yourselves across Zered Brook — so we crossed Zered Brook.

[14] The days that we traveled from Kadesh-barnea until we crossed Zered Brook were thirty-eight years, until the end of the entire generation, the men of war, from the midst of the camp, as HASHEM swore to them. [15] Even the hand of HASHEM was on them to confound them from the midst of the camp, until their end. [16] So it was that the men of war finished dying from amidst the people . . .

God commands Israel to march toward the Land — [17] HASHEM spoke to me, saying: [18] This day you shall cross the border of Moab, at Ar, [19] and you shall approach opposite the children of Ammon; you shall not distress them and you shall not provoke them, for I shall not give any of the land of the children of Ammon to you as an inheritance, for to the children of Lot have I given it as an inheritance. [20] It, too, is considered the land of the Rephaim; the Rephaim dwelled in it previously, and the Ammonites called them Zamzumim. [21] A great and populous people, and tall as giants, and HASHEM destroyed them before them, and they drove them out and dwelled in their place, [22] just as He did for the children of Esau who dwell in Seir, that He destroyed the Horite before them; they drove them out and dwelled in their place until this day. [23] As for the Avvim who dwell in open cities until Gaza, the Caphtorim who went out of Caphtor destroyed them, and dwelled in their place. [24] Rise up and cross Arnon Brook; see! into your hand have I delivered Sihon king of Heshbon, the Amorite, and his land; begin to drive [him] out, and provoke war with him.

---

any form of provocation [v. 19] (Rashi).

כה הַיּוֹם הַזֶּה אָחֵל תֵּת פַּחְדְּךָ וְיִרְאָתְךָ עַל־פְּנֵי הָעַמִּים תַּחַת כָּל־הַשָּׁמָיִם

כו אֲשֶׁר יִשְׁמְעוּן שִׁמְעֲךָ וְרָגְזוּ וְחָלוּ מִפָּנֶיךָ: וָאֶשְׁלַח מַלְאָכִים מִמִּדְבַּר

כז קְדֵמוֹת אֶל־סִיחוֹן מֶלֶךְ חֶשְׁבּוֹן דִּבְרֵי שָׁלוֹם לֵאמֹר: אֶעְבְּרָה בְאַרְצֶךָ

כח בַּדֶּרֶךְ בַּדֶּרֶךְ אֵלֵךְ לֹא אָסוּר יָמִין וּשְׂמֹאול: אֹכֶל בַּכֶּסֶף תַּשְׁבִּרֵנִי וְאָכַלְתִּי   * מלא ו

כט וּמַיִם בַּכֶּסֶף תִּתֶּן־לִי וְשָׁתִיתִי רַק אֶעְבְּרָה בְרַגְלָי: כַּאֲשֶׁר עָשׂוּ־לִי בְּנֵי

עֵשָׂו הַיֹּשְׁבִים בְּשֵׂעִיר וְהַמּוֹאָבִים הַיֹּשְׁבִים בְּעָר עַד אֲשֶׁר־אֶעֱבֹר אֶת־

ל הַיַּרְדֵּן אֶל־הָאָרֶץ אֲשֶׁר־יְהֹוָה אֱלֹהֵינוּ נֹתֵן לָנוּ: וְלֹא אָבָה סִיחֹן מֶלֶךְ

חֶשְׁבּוֹן הַעֲבִרֵנוּ בּוֹ כִּי־הִקְשָׁה יְהֹוָה אֱלֹהֶיךָ אֶת־רוּחוֹ וְאִמֵּץ אֶת־לְבָבוֹ

לא לְמַעַן תִּתּוֹ בְיָדְךָ כַּיּוֹם הַזֶּה: וַיֹּאמֶר יְהֹוָה אֵלַי רְאֵה   ששי

הַחִלֹּתִי תֵּת לְפָנֶיךָ אֶת־סִיחֹן וְאֶת־אַרְצוֹ הָחֵל רָשׁ לָרֶשֶׁת אֶת־אַרְצוֹ:

לב-לג וַיֵּצֵא סִיחֹן לִקְרָאתֵנוּ הוּא וְכָל־עַמּוֹ לַמִּלְחָמָה יָהְצָה: וַיִּתְּנֵהוּ יְהֹוָה

לד אֱלֹהֵינוּ לְפָנֵינוּ וַנַּךְ אֹתוֹ וְאֶת־בָּנָו וְאֶת־כָּל־עַמּוֹ: וַנִּלְכֹּד אֶת־כָּל־עָרָיו

בָּעֵת הַהִוא וַנַּחֲרֵם אֶת־כָּל־עִיר מְתִם וְהַנָּשִׁים וְהַטָּף לֹא הִשְׁאַרְנוּ שָׂרִיד:

לה-לו רַק הַבְּהֵמָה בָּזַזְנוּ לָנוּ וּשְׁלַל הֶעָרִים אֲשֶׁר לָכָדְנוּ: מֵעֲרֹעֵר אֲשֶׁר עַל־

שְׂפַת־נַחַל אַרְנֹן וְהָעִיר אֲשֶׁר בַּנַּחַל וְעַד־הַגִּלְעָד לֹא הָיְתָה קִרְיָה אֲשֶׁר

לז שָׂגְבָה מִמֶּנּוּ אֶת־הַכֹּל נָתַן יְהֹוָה אֱלֹהֵינוּ לְפָנֵינוּ: רַק אֶל־אֶרֶץ בְּנֵי־עַמּוֹן

א לֹא קָרָבְתָּ כָּל־יַד נַחַל יַבֹּק וְעָרֵי הָהָר וְכֹל אֲשֶׁר־צִוָּה יְהֹוָה אֱלֹהֵינוּ: וַנֵּפֶן   ג

וַנַּעַל דֶּרֶךְ הַבָּשָׁן וַיֵּצֵא עוֹג מֶלֶךְ־הַבָּשָׁן לִקְרָאתֵנוּ הוּא וְכָל־עַמּוֹ

ב לַמִּלְחָמָה אֶדְרֶעִי: וַיֹּאמֶר יְהֹוָה אֵלַי אַל־תִּירָא אֹתוֹ כִּי בְיָדְךָ נָתַתִּי אֹתוֹ

וְאֶת־כָּל־עַמּוֹ וְאֶת־אַרְצוֹ וְעָשִׂיתָ לּוֹ כַּאֲשֶׁר עָשִׂיתָ לְסִיחֹן מֶלֶךְ הָאֱמֹרִי

ג אֲשֶׁר יוֹשֵׁב בְּחֶשְׁבּוֹן: וַיִּתֵּן יְהֹוָה אֱלֹהֵינוּ בְּיָדֵנוּ גַּם אֶת־עוֹג מֶלֶךְ־הַבָּשָׁן

ד וְאֶת־כָּל־עַמּוֹ וַנַּכֵּהוּ עַד־בִּלְתִּי הִשְׁאִיר־לוֹ שָׂרִיד: וַנִּלְכֹּד אֶת־כָּל־עָרָיו

בָּעֵת הַהִוא לֹא הָיְתָה קִרְיָה אֲשֶׁר לֹא־לָקַחְנוּ מֵאִתָּם שִׁשִּׁים עִיר

ה כָּל־חֶבֶל אַרְגֹּב מַמְלֶכֶת עוֹג בַּבָּשָׁן: כָּל־אֵלֶּה עָרִים בְּצֻרֹת חוֹמָה גְבֹהָה

דְּלָתַיִם וּבְרִיחַ לְבַד מֵעָרֵי הַפְּרָזִי הַרְבֵּה מְאֹד: וַנַּחֲרֵם אוֹתָם כַּאֲשֶׁר

ז עָשִׂינוּ לְסִיחֹן מֶלֶךְ חֶשְׁבּוֹן הַחֲרֵם כָּל־עִיר מְתִם הַנָּשִׁים וְהַטָּף: וְכָל־

ח הַבְּהֵמָה וּשְׁלַל הֶעָרִים בַּזּוֹנוּ לָנוּ: וַנִּקַּח בָּעֵת הַהִוא אֶת־הָאָרֶץ מִיַּד שְׁנֵי

ט מַלְכֵי הָאֱמֹרִי אֲשֶׁר בְּעֵבֶר הַיַּרְדֵּן מִנַּחַל אַרְנֹן עַד־הַר חֶרְמוֹן: צִידֹנִים

י יִקְרְאוּ לְחֶרְמוֹן שִׂרְיֹן וְהָאֱמֹרִי יִקְרְאוּ־לוֹ שְׂנִיר: כֹּל עָרֵי הַמִּישֹׁר וְכָל־

יא הַגִּלְעָד וְכָל־הַבָּשָׁן עַד־סַלְכָה וְאֶדְרֶעִי עָרֵי מַמְלֶכֶת עוֹג בַּבָּשָׁן: כִּי רַק

עוֹג מֶלֶךְ הַבָּשָׁן נִשְׁאַר מִיֶּתֶר הָרְפָאִים הִנֵּה עַרְשׂוֹ עֶרֶשׂ בַּרְזֶל הֲלֹה הִוא

בְּרַבַּת בְּנֵי עַמּוֹן תֵּשַׁע אַמּוֹת אָרְכָּהּ וְאַרְבַּע אַמּוֹת רָחְבָּהּ בְּאַמַּת־אִישׁ:

2:31-37. See *Numbers* 21:21-26.   2:36. The mountainous region east of the Jordan.

²⁵ This day I shall begin to place dread and fear of you on the peoples under the entire heaven, when they hear of your reputation, and they will tremble and be anxious before you.

²⁶ I sent messengers from the Wilderness of Kedemoth to Sihon king of Heshbon, words of peace, saying, ²⁷ "Let me pass through your land; only on the road shall I go; I will not stray right or left. ²⁸ Food you will sell to me for money, and I shall eat; and you will give me water for money, and I shall drink — only let me pass through on foot; ²⁹ as the children of Esau who dwell in Seir did for me, and the Moabites who dwell in Ar — until I cross the Jordan to the Land that HASHEM, our God, gives us." ³⁰ But Sihon king of Heshbon was not willing to let us pass through it, for HASHEM, your God, hardened his spirit and made his heart stubborn, in order to give him into your hand, like this very day.

The first conquest: Sihon
³¹ HASHEM said to me: See, I have begun to deliver before you Sihon and his land; * begin to drive out, to possess his land.

³² Sihon went out toward us — he and his entire people — for battle, to Jahaz. ³³ HASHEM, our God, gave him before us, and we smote him and his sons and his entire people. ³⁴ We captured all his cities at that time, and we destroyed every populated city, with the women and small children; we did not leave a survivor. ³⁵ Only the animals did we loot for ourselves, and the booty of the cities that we captured: ³⁶ from Aroer, which is by the shore of Arnon Brook, and the city that is by the brook, and until Gilead* — there was no city that was too strong for us; HASHEM, our God, gave everything before us. ³⁷ Only to the land of the children of Ammon did you not draw near, everywhere near Jabbok Brook and the cities of the mountain, and everywhere that HASHEM, our God, commanded us.

3

The conquest of Og
¹ We turned and ascended by way of the Bashan, and Og king of Bashan went out toward us, he and his entire people, for war at Edrei. ² HASHEM said to me: Do not fear him, for in your hand have I given him and his entire people and his land, and you shall do to him as you did to Sihon king of the Amorite, who dwells in Heshbon. ³ HASHEM, our God, gave into our hand also Og king of the Bashan and his entire people, and we smote him until no survivor was left of him. ⁴ We captured all his cities at that time; there was no city that we did not take from them — sixty cities, the entire region of Argob — the kingdom of Og in the Bashan. ⁵ All these were fortified cities, with a high wall, doors and bar, aside from open cities, very many. ⁶ We destroyed them, as we did to Sihon king of Heshbon, destroying every populated city, the women and small children. ⁷ And all the animals and the booty of the cities we looted for ourselves. ⁸ At that time we took the land from the hand of the two kings of the Amorite that were on the other side of the Jordan, from Arnon Brook to Mount Hermon — ⁹ Sidonians would refer to Hermon as Sirion, and the Amorites would call it Senir — ¹⁰ all the cities of the plain, the entire Gilead, and the entire Bashan until Salcah and Edrei, the cities of the kingdom of Og in the Bashan. ¹¹ For only Og king of the Bashan was left of the remaining Rephaim — behold! his bed was an iron bed, it is in Rabbah of the children of Ammon — nine cubits was its length and four cubits its width, by the cubit of that man.

יב וְאֶת־הָאָ֨רֶץ הַזֹּ֜את יָרַ֣שְׁנוּ בָּעֵ֣ת הַהִ֗וא מֵעֲרֹעֵ֞ר אֲשֶׁר־עַל־נַ֤חַל אַרְנֹן֙ וַחֲצִ֤י

יג הַר־הַגִּלְעָד֙ וְעָרָ֔יו נָתַ֕תִּי לָרֻֽאוּבֵנִ֖י וְלַגָּדִ֑י וְיֶ֨תֶר הַגִּלְעָ֜ד וְכָל־הַבָּשָׁ֤ן מַמְלֶ֨כֶת עוֹג֙ נָתַ֨תִּי֙ לַחֲצִ֣י שֵׁ֣בֶט הַֽמְנַשֶּׁ֔ה כֹּ֚ל חֶ֣בֶל הָֽאַרְגֹּ֔ב לְכָל־הַבָּשָׁ֖ן

יד הַה֥וּא יִקָּרֵ֖א אֶ֥רֶץ רְפָאִֽים: יָאִ֣יר בֶּן־מְנַשֶּׁ֗ה לָקַח֙ אֶת־כָּל־חֶ֣בֶל אַרְגֹּ֔ב עַד־גְּב֥וּל הַגְּשׁוּרִ֖י וְהַמַּֽעֲכָתִ֑י וַיִּקְרָא֩ אֹתָ֨ם עַל־שְׁמ֤וֹ אֶת־הַבָּשָׁן֙ חַוֺּ֣ת יָאִ֔יר

טו עַ֖ד הַיּ֥וֹם הַזֶּֽה: וּלְמָכִ֖יר נָתַ֥תִּי אֶת־הַגִּלְעָֽד: טז וְלָרֻֽאוּבֵנִ֣י וְלַגָּדִ֗י נָתַ֤תִּי מִן־הַגִּלְעָד֙ וְעַד־נַ֣חַל אַרְנֹ֔ן תּ֥וֹךְ הַנַּ֖חַל וּגְבֻ֑ל וְעַד֙ יַבֹּ֣ק הַנַּ֔חַל גְּב֖וּל בְּנֵ֥י עַמּֽוֹן:

יז וְהָֽעֲרָבָ֖ה וְהַיַּרְדֵּ֣ן וּגְבֻ֑ל מִכִּנֶּ֗רֶת וְעַ֨ד יָ֤ם הָֽעֲרָבָה֙ יָ֣ם הַמֶּ֔לַח תַּ֛חַת אַשְׁדֹּ֥ת

יח הַפִּסְגָּ֖ה מִזְרָֽחָה: וָֽאֲצַ֣ו אֶתְכֶ֔ם בָּעֵ֥ת הַהִ֖וא לֵאמֹ֑ר יְהֹוָ֣ה אֱלֹֽהֵיכֶ֗ם נָתַ֨ן לָכֶ֜ם אֶת־הָאָ֤רֶץ הַזֹּאת֙ לְרִשְׁתָּ֔הּ חֲלוּצִ֣ים תַּֽעַבְר֗וּ לִפְנֵ֛י אֲחֵיכֶ֥ם בְּנֵֽי־יִשְׂרָאֵ֖ל

יט כָּל־בְּנֵי־חָֽיִל: רַ֠ק נְשֵׁיכֶ֤ם וְטַפְּכֶם֙ וּמִקְנֵכֶ֔ם יָדַ֕עְתִּי כִּֽי־מִקְנֶ֥ה רַ֖ב לָכֶ֑ם יֵֽשְׁבוּ֙

כ בְּעָ֣רֵיכֶ֔ם אֲשֶׁ֥ר נָתַ֖תִּי לָכֶֽם: עַ֠ד אֲשֶׁר־יָנִ֨יחַ יְהֹוָ֥ה ׀ לַֽאֲחֵיכֶם֮ כָּכֶם֒ וְיָֽרְשׁ֣וּ גַם־הֵ֔ם אֶת־הָאָ֕רֶץ אֲשֶׁ֨ר יְהֹוָ֧ה אֱלֹֽהֵיכֶ֛ם נֹתֵ֥ן לָהֶ֖ם בְּעֵ֣בֶר הַיַּרְדֵּ֑ן וְשַׁבְתֶּ֗ם

כא אִ֚ישׁ לִֽירֻשָּׁת֔וֹ אֲשֶׁ֥ר נָתַ֖תִּי לָכֶֽם: וְאֶת־יְהוֹשׁ֣וּעַ צִוֵּ֔יתִי בָּעֵ֥ת הַהִ֖וא לֵאמֹ֑ר עֵינֶ֣יךָ הָֽרֹאֹ֗ת אֵת֩ כָּל־אֲשֶׁ֨ר עָשָׂ֜ה יְהֹוָ֤ה אֱלֹֽהֵיכֶם֙ לִשְׁנֵי֙ הַמְּלָכִ֣ים הָאֵ֔לֶּה

כב כֵּֽן־יַֽעֲשֶׂ֤ה יְהֹוָה֙ לְכָל־הַמַּמְלָכ֔וֹת אֲשֶׁ֥ר אַתָּ֖ה עֹבֵ֥ר שָֽׁמָּה: לֹ֖א תִּֽירָא֑וּם כִּ֚י יְהֹוָ֣ה אֱלֹֽהֵיכֶ֔ם ה֖וּא הַנִּלְחָ֥ם לָכֶֽם: ססס

ק״ה פסוקים. מלכי״ה סימן.

פרשת ואתחנן

כג וָֽאֶתְחַנַּ֖ן אֶל־יְהֹוָ֑ה בָּעֵ֥ת הַהִ֖וא לֵאמֹֽר: כד אֲדֹנָ֣י יֱהֹוִ֗ה אַתָּ֤ה הַֽחִלּ֨וֹתָ֙ לְהַרְא֣וֹת אֶֽת־עַבְדְּךָ֔ אֶ֨ת־גָּדְלְךָ֔ וְאֶת־יָֽדְךָ֖ הַֽחֲזָקָ֑ה אֲשֶׁ֤ר מִי־אֵל֙ בַּשָּׁמַ֣יִם וּבָאָ֔רֶץ

כה אֲשֶׁר־יַֽעֲשֶׂ֥ה כְמַֽעֲשֶׂ֖יךָ וְכִגְבֽוּרֹתֶֽךָ: אֶעְבְּרָה־נָּ֗א וְאֶרְאֶה֙ אֶת־הָאָ֣רֶץ

כו הַטּוֹבָ֔ה אֲשֶׁ֖ר בְּעֵ֣בֶר הַיַּרְדֵּ֑ן הָהָ֥ר הַטּ֛וֹב הַזֶּ֖ה וְהַלְּבָנֹֽן: וַיִּתְעַבֵּ֨ר יְהֹוָ֥ה בִּי֙ לְמַ֣עַנְכֶ֔ם וְלֹ֥א שָׁמַ֖ע אֵלָ֑י וַיֹּ֨אמֶר יְהֹוָ֤ה אֵלַי֙ רַב־לָ֔ךְ אַל־תּ֗וֹסֶף דַּבֵּ֥ר אֵלַ֛י

כז ע֖וֹד בַּדָּבָ֥ר הַזֶּֽה: עֲלֵ֣ה ׀ רֹ֣אשׁ הַפִּסְגָּ֗ה וְשָׂ֥א עֵינֶ֛יךָ יָ֧מָּה וְצָפֹ֛נָה וְתֵימָ֥נָה

כח וּמִזְרָ֖חָה וּרְאֵ֣ה בְעֵינֶ֑יךָ כִּי־לֹ֥א תַֽעֲבֹ֖ר אֶת־הַיַּרְדֵּ֥ן הַזֶּֽה: וְצַ֥ו אֶת־יְהוֹשֻׁ֖עַ וְחַזְּקֵ֣הוּ וְאַמְּצֵ֑הוּ כִּי־ה֣וּא יַֽעֲבֹ֗ר לִפְנֵי֙ הָעָ֣ם הַזֶּ֔ה וְהוּא֙ יַנְחִ֣יל אוֹתָ֔ם

כט אֶת־הָאָ֖רֶץ אֲשֶׁ֥ר תִּרְאֶֽה: וַנֵּ֣שֶׁב בַּגָּ֔יְא מ֖וּל בֵּ֥ית פְּעֽוֹר:

ד א וְעַתָּ֣ה יִשְׂרָאֵ֗ל שְׁמַ֤ע אֶל־הַֽחֻקִּים֙ וְאֶל־הַמִּשְׁפָּטִ֔ים אֲשֶׁ֧ר אָֽנֹכִ֛י מְלַמֵּ֥ד אֶתְכֶ֖ם לַֽעֲשׂ֑וֹת לְמַ֣עַן תִּֽחְי֗וּ וּבָאתֶם֙ וִֽירִשְׁתֶּ֣ם אֶת־הָאָ֔רֶץ אֲשֶׁ֧ר יְהֹוָ֛ה אֱלֹהֵ֥י

ב אֲבֹֽתֵיכֶ֖ם נֹתֵ֥ן לָכֶֽם: לֹ֣א תֹסִ֗פוּ עַל־הַדָּבָר֙ אֲשֶׁ֤ר אָֽנֹכִי֙ מְצַוֶּ֣ה אֶתְכֶ֔ם וְלֹ֥א תִגְרְע֖וּ מִמֶּ֑נּוּ לִשְׁמֹ֕ר אֶת־מִצְוֺת֙ יְהֹוָ֣ה אֱלֹֽהֵיכֶ֔ם אֲשֶׁ֥ר אָֽנֹכִ֖י מְצַוֶּ֥ה אֶתְכֶֽם:

שביעי (טו-טז)

מפטיר

Haftaras Devarim: p. 954

3:12-20. See *Numbers* ch. 32.

◆§ **Parashas Va'eschanan**

3:23. Having conquered Sihon and Og, whose lands

were given to Israel, Moses hoped that perhaps he might indeed be permitted to enter the rest of the land as well, so he prayed for the right to cross the Jordan (*Rashi*).

The inheritance of Reuben, Gad, and half of Manasseh

¹² *And we possessed that land at that time; from Aroer, which is by Arnon Brook, and half of the mountain of Gilead and its cities did I give to the Reubenite and the Gadite.* * ¹³ *The rest of the Gilead and the entire Bashan, the kingdom of Og, did I give to half the tribe of Manasseh, the entire region of the Argov of the entire Bashan, that is called the land of Rephaim.* ¹⁴ *Jair son of Manasseh took the entire region of Argov until the border of the Geshurite and the Maacathite, and he named them, the Bashan, after himself, "Havvoth-jair," until this day.* ¹⁵ *To Machir I gave the Gilead.* ¹⁶ *To the Reubenite and the Gadite I gave from the Gilead until Arnon Brook, the midst of the brook and the border, until Jabbok Brook, the border of the children of Ammon,* ¹⁷ *and the Arabah and the Jordan and its border, from Kinnereth to the Arabah Sea, the Salt Sea, below the waterfalls from the mountaintop, eastward.*

¹⁸ *I commanded you at that time, saying, "HASHEM, your God, gave you this Land for a possession, armed shall you cross over before your brethren, the Children of Israel, all the men of accomplishment.* ¹⁹ *Only your wives, small children, and livestock — I know that you have abundant livestock — shall dwell in your cities that I have given you.* ²⁰ *Until HASHEM shall give rest to your brethren like yourselves, and they, too, shall possess the Land that HASHEM, your God, gives them on the other side of the Jordan; then you shall return, every man to his inheritance that I have given you."*

²¹ *I commanded Joshua at that time, saying, "Your eyes have seen everything that HASHEM, your God, has done to these two kings; so will HASHEM do to all the kingdoms where you cross over.* ²² *You shall not fear them, for HASHEM, your God — He shall wage war for you."*

PARASHAS VA'ESCHANAN

Moses prays again

²³ I *implored HASHEM at that time,* * *saying,* ²⁴ *"My Lord, HASHEM/ELOHIM, You have begun to show Your servant Your greatness and Your strong hand, for what power is there in the heaven or on the earth that can perform according to Your deeds and according to Your mighty acts?* ²⁵ *Let me now cross and see the good Land that is on the other side of the Jordan, this good mountain and the Lebanon."*

²⁶ *But HASHEM became angry with me because of you, and He did not listen to me; HASHEM said to me, "It is too much for you! Do not continue to speak to Me further about this matter.* ²⁷ *Ascend to the top of the cliff and raise your eyes westward, northward, southward, and eastward, and see with your eyes, for you shall not cross this Jordan.* ²⁸ *But you shall command Joshua, and strengthen him and give him resolve, for he shall cross before this people and he shall cause them to inherit the Land that you will see."*

²⁹ *So we remained in the valley, opposite Beth-peor.*

4

¹ **N**ow, *O Israel, listen to the decrees and to the ordinances that I teach you to perform, so that you may live, and you will come and possess the Land that HASHEM, the God of your forefathers, gives you.* ² *You shall not add to the word that I command you, nor shall you subtract from it, to observe the commandments of HASHEM, your God, that I command you.*

ג עֵינֵיכֶם הָרֹאֹת אֵת אֲשֶׁר־עָשָׂה יהוה בְּבַעַל פְּעוֹר כִּי כָל־הָאִישׁ אֲשֶׁר
ד הָלַךְ אַחֲרֵי בַעַל־פְּעוֹר הִשְׁמִידוֹ יהוה אֱלֹהֶיךָ מִקִּרְבֶּךָ: וְאַתֶּם הַדְּבֵקִים

שני ה בַּיהוה אֱלֹהֵיכֶם חַיִּים כֻּלְּכֶם הַיּוֹם: רְאֵה | לִמַּדְתִּי אֶתְכֶם חֻקִּים
וּמִשְׁפָּטִים כַּאֲשֶׁר צִוַּנִי יהוה אֱלֹהָי לַעֲשׂוֹת כֵּן בְּקֶרֶב הָאָרֶץ אֲשֶׁר אַתֶּם
ו בָּאִים שָׁמָּה לְרִשְׁתָּהּ: וּשְׁמַרְתֶּם וַעֲשִׂיתֶם כִּי הִוא חָכְמַתְכֶם וּבִינַתְכֶם
לְעֵינֵי הָעַמִּים אֲשֶׁר יִשְׁמְעוּן אֵת כָּל־הַחֻקִּים הָאֵלֶּה וְאָמְרוּ רַק עַם־
ז חָכָם וְנָבוֹן הַגּוֹי הַגָּדוֹל הַזֶּה: כִּי מִי־גוֹי גָּדוֹל אֲשֶׁר־לוֹ אֱלֹהִים קְרֹבִים
ח אֵלָיו כַּיהוה אֱלֹהֵינוּ בְּכָל־קָרְאֵנוּ אֵלָיו: וּמִי גּוֹי גָּדוֹל אֲשֶׁר־לוֹ חֻקִּים
ט וּמִשְׁפָּטִים צַדִּיקִם כְּכֹל הַתּוֹרָה הַזֹּאת אֲשֶׁר אָנֹכִי נֹתֵן לִפְנֵיכֶם הַיּוֹם: רַק
הִשָּׁמֶר לְךָ וּשְׁמֹר נַפְשְׁךָ מְאֹד פֶּן־תִּשְׁכַּח אֶת־הַדְּבָרִים אֲשֶׁר־רָאוּ עֵינֶיךָ
י וּפֶן־יָסוּרוּ מִלְּבָבְךָ כֹּל יְמֵי חַיֶּיךָ וְהוֹדַעְתָּם לְבָנֶיךָ וְלִבְנֵי בָנֶיךָ: יוֹם אֲשֶׁר
עָמַדְתָּ לִפְנֵי יהוה אֱלֹהֶיךָ בְּחֹרֵב בֶּאֱמֹר יהוה אֵלַי הַקְהֶל־לִי אֶת־הָעָם
וְאַשְׁמִעֵם אֶת־דְּבָרָי אֲשֶׁר יִלְמְדוּן לְיִרְאָה אֹתִי כָּל־הַיָּמִים אֲשֶׁר הֵם
יא חַיִּים עַל־הָאֲדָמָה וְאֶת־בְּנֵיהֶם יְלַמֵּדוּן: וַתִּקְרְבוּן וַתַּעַמְדוּן תַּחַת הָהָר
יב וְהָהָר בֹּעֵר בָּאֵשׁ עַד־לֵב הַשָּׁמַיִם חֹשֶׁךְ עָנָן וַעֲרָפֶל: וַיְדַבֵּר יהוה אֲלֵיכֶם
מִתּוֹךְ הָאֵשׁ קוֹל דְּבָרִים אַתֶּם שֹׁמְעִים וּתְמוּנָה אֵינְכֶם רֹאִים זוּלָתִי קוֹל:
יג וַיַּגֵּד לָכֶם אֶת־בְּרִיתוֹ אֲשֶׁר צִוָּה אֶתְכֶם לַעֲשׂוֹת עֲשֶׂרֶת הַדְּבָרִים וַיִּכְתְּבֵם
יד עַל־שְׁנֵי לֻחוֹת אֲבָנִים: וְאֹתִי צִוָּה יהוה בָּעֵת הַהִוא לְלַמֵּד אֶתְכֶם חֻקִּים
וּמִשְׁפָּטִים לַעֲשֹׂתְכֶם אֹתָם בָּאָרֶץ אֲשֶׁר אַתֶּם עֹבְרִים שָׁמָּה לְרִשְׁתָּהּ:
טו וְנִשְׁמַרְתֶּם מְאֹד לְנַפְשֹׁתֵיכֶם כִּי לֹא רְאִיתֶם כָּל־תְּמוּנָה בְּיוֹם דִּבֶּר יהוה
טז אֲלֵיכֶם בְּחֹרֵב מִתּוֹךְ הָאֵשׁ: פֶּן־תַּשְׁחִתוּן וַעֲשִׂיתֶם לָכֶם פֶּסֶל תְּמוּנַת כָּל־
יז סָמֶל תַּבְנִית זָכָר אוֹ נְקֵבָה: תַּבְנִית כָּל־בְּהֵמָה אֲשֶׁר בָּאָרֶץ תַּבְנִית כָּל־
יח צִפּוֹר כָּנָף אֲשֶׁר תָּעוּף בַּשָּׁמָיִם: תַּבְנִית כָּל־רֹמֵשׂ בָּאֲדָמָה תַּבְנִית כָּל־
יט דָּגָה אֲשֶׁר־בַּמַּיִם מִתַּחַת לָאָרֶץ: וּפֶן־תִּשָּׂא עֵינֶיךָ הַשָּׁמַיְמָה וְרָאִיתָ
אֶת־הַשֶּׁמֶשׁ וְאֶת־הַיָּרֵחַ וְאֶת־הַכּוֹכָבִים כֹּל צְבָא הַשָּׁמַיִם וְנִדַּחְתָּ
וְהִשְׁתַּחֲוִיתָ לָהֶם וַעֲבַדְתָּם אֲשֶׁר חָלַק יהוה אֱלֹהֶיךָ אֹתָם לְכֹל הָעַמִּים
כ תַּחַת כָּל־הַשָּׁמָיִם: וְאֶתְכֶם לָקַח יהוה וַיּוֹצִא אֶתְכֶם מִכּוּר הַבַּרְזֶל
כא מִמִּצְרָיִם לִהְיוֹת לוֹ לְעַם נַחֲלָה כַּיּוֹם הַזֶּה: וַיהוה הִתְאַנַּף־בִּי עַל־
דִּבְרֵיכֶם וַיִּשָּׁבַע לְבִלְתִּי עָבְרִי אֶת־הַיַּרְדֵּן וּלְבִלְתִּי־בֹא אֶל־הָאָרֶץ
כב הַטּוֹבָה אֲשֶׁר יהוה אֱלֹהֶיךָ נֹתֵן לְךָ נַחֲלָה: כִּי אָנֹכִי מֵת בָּאָרֶץ הַזֹּאת
אֵינֶנִּי עֹבֵר אֶת־הַיַּרְדֵּן וְאַתֶּם עֹבְרִים וִירִשְׁתֶּם אֶת־הָאָרֶץ הַטּוֹבָה
כג הַזֹּאת: הִשָּׁמְרוּ לָכֶם פֶּן־תִּשְׁכְּחוּ אֶת־בְּרִית יהוה אֱלֹהֵיכֶם אֲשֶׁר כָּרַת
כד עִמָּכֶם וַעֲשִׂיתֶם לָכֶם פֶּסֶל תְּמוּנַת כֹּל אֲשֶׁר צִוְּךָ יהוה אֱלֹהֶיךָ: כִּי יהוה

4:9. Moses exhorted the people to remember the Revelation at Sinai — that had been seen and heard by millions of people. Thus, the entire nation could testify to what they had witnessed, and share it with their

³ *Your eyes have seen what HASHEM did with Baal-peor, for every man that followed Baal-peor — HASHEM, your God, destroyed him from your midst.* ⁴ *But you who cling to HASHEM, your God — you are all alive today.*

Decrees and ordinances ⁵ *See, I have taught you decrees and ordinances, as HASHEM, my God, has commanded me, to do so in the midst of the Land to which you come, to possess it.* ⁶ *You shall safeguard and perform them, for it is your wisdom and discernment in the eyes of the peoples, who shall hear all these decrees and who shall say, "Surely a wise and discerning people is this great nation!"* ⁷ *For which is a great nation that has a God Who is close to it, as is HASHEM, our God, whenever we call to Him?* ⁸ *And which is a great nation that has righteous decrees and ordinances, such as this entire Torah that I place before you this day?* ⁹ *Only beware for yourself and greatly beware for your soul, lest you forget the things that your eyes have beheld and lest you remove them from your heart all the days of your life, and make them known to your children and your children's children** — ¹⁰ *the day that you stood before HASHEM, your God, at Horeb, when HASHEM said to me, "Gather the people to Me and I shall let them hear My words, so that they shall learn to fear Me all the days that they live on the earth, and they shall teach their children."*

¹¹ *So you approached and stood at the foot of the mountain, and the mountain was burning with fire up to the heart of heaven, darkness, cloud, and thick cloud.*

From the midst of the fire ¹² *HASHEM spoke to you from the midst of the fire; you were hearing the sound of words, but you were not seeing a likeness, only a sound.* ¹³ *He told you of His covenant that He commanded you to observe, the Ten Declarations, and He inscribed them on two stone Tablets.* ¹⁴ *HASHEM commanded me at that time to teach you decrees and ordinances, that you shall perform them in the Land to which you cross, to possess it.* ¹⁵ *But you shall greatly beware for your souls, for you did not see any likeness on the day HASHEM spoke to you at Horeb, from the midst of the fire,* ¹⁶ *lest you act corruptly and make for yourselves a carved image, a likeness of any shape; a form of a male or a female;* ¹⁷ *a form of any animal that is on the earth; a form of any winged bird that flies in the heaven;* ¹⁸ *a form of anything that creeps on the ground; a form of any fish that is in the water under the earth;* ¹⁹ *and lest you raise your eyes to the heaven and you see the sun, and the moon, and the stars — the entire legion of heaven — and you be drawn astray and bow to them and worship them, which HASHEM, your God, has apportioned to all the peoples under the entire heaven!* ²⁰ *But HASHEM has taken you and withdrawn you from the iron crucible, from Egypt, to be a nation of heritage for Him, as this very day.*

Moses would not enter the Land ²¹ *HASHEM became angry with me because of your deeds, and He swore that I would not cross the Jordan and not come to the good Land that HASHEM, your God, gives you as a heritage.* ²² *For I will die in this land; I am not crossing the Jordan — but you are crossing and you shall possess this good Land.* ²³ *Beware for yourselves lest you forget the covenant of HASHEM, your God, that He has sealed with you, and you make for yourselves a carved image, a likeness of anything, as HASHEM, your God, has commanded you.* ²⁴ *For HASHEM,*

---

posterity (*Ramban; Rambam, Hil. Yesodei HaTorah* 5:3).

אֱלֹהֶ֔יךָ אֵ֥שׁ אֹכְלָ֖ה ה֑וּא אֵ֖ל קַנָּֽא׃

כה כִּֽי־תוֹלִ֤יד בָּנִים֙ וּבְנֵ֣י בָנִ֔ים וְנְוֹשַׁנְתֶּ֖ם בָּאָ֑רֶץ וְהִשְׁחַתֶּ֗ם וַעֲשִׂ֤יתֶם פֶּ֨סֶל֙

כו תְּמ֣וּנַת כֹּ֔ל וַעֲשִׂיתֶ֥ם הָרַ֛ע בְּעֵינֵֽי־יהו֥ה אֱלֹהֶ֖יךָ לְהַכְעִיסֽוֹ׃ הַעִידֹ֩תִי֩ בָכֶ֨ם

הַיּ֜וֹם אֶת־הַשָּׁמַ֣יִם וְאֶת־הָאָ֗רֶץ כִּֽי־אָבֹ֣ד תֹּאבֵדוּן֮ מַהֵר֒ מֵעַ֣ל הָאָ֔רֶץ אֲשֶׁ֨ר

אַתֶּ֜ם עֹבְרִ֧ים אֶת־הַיַּרְדֵּ֛ן שָׁ֖מָּה לְרִשְׁתָּ֑הּ לֹֽא־תַאֲרִיכֻ֤ן יָמִים֙ עָלֶ֔יהָ כִּֽי

כז הִשָּׁמֵ֖ד תִּשָּׁמֵדֽוּן׃ וְהֵפִ֧יץ יהו֛ה אֶתְכֶ֖ם בָּֽעַמִּ֑ים וְנִשְׁאַרְתֶּם֙ מְתֵ֣י מִסְפָּ֔ר

כח בַּגּוֹיִ֕ם אֲשֶׁ֨ר יְנַהֵ֧ג יהו֛ה אֶתְכֶ֖ם שָֽׁמָּה׃ וַעֲבַדְתֶּם־שָׁ֣ם אֱלֹהִ֔ים מַעֲשֵׂ֖ה יְדֵ֣י

אָדָ֑ם עֵ֣ץ וָאֶ֔בֶן אֲשֶׁ֤ר לֹֽא־יִרְאוּן֙ וְלֹ֣א יִשְׁמְע֔וּן וְלֹ֥א יֹֽאכְל֖וּן וְלֹ֥א יְרִיחֻֽן׃

כט וּבִקַּשְׁתֶּ֥ם מִשָּׁ֛ם אֶת־יהו֥ה אֱלֹהֶ֖יךָ וּמָצָ֑אתָ כִּ֤י תִדְרְשֶׁ֨נּוּ֙ בְּכׇל־לְבָ֣בְךָ֔

ל וּבְכׇל־נַפְשֶֽׁךָ׃ בַּצַּ֣ר לְךָ֔ וּמְצָא֕וּךָ כֹּ֖ל הַדְּבָרִ֣ים הָאֵ֑לֶּה בְּאַחֲרִית֙ הַיָּמִ֔ים

לא וְשַׁבְתָּ֙ עַד־יהו֣ה אֱלֹהֶ֔יךָ וְשָׁמַעְתָּ֖ בְּקֹלֽוֹ׃ כִּ֣י אֵ֤ל רַחוּם֙ יהו֣ה אֱלֹהֶ֔יךָ לֹ֥א

לב יַרְפְּךָ֖ וְלֹ֣א יַשְׁחִיתֶ֑ךָ וְלֹ֤א יִשְׁכַּח֙ אֶת־בְּרִ֣ית אֲבֹתֶ֔יךָ אֲשֶׁ֥ר נִשְׁבַּ֖ע לָהֶֽם׃ כִּ֣י

שְׁאַל־נָא֩ לְיָמִ֨ים רִֽאשֹׁנִ֜ים אֲשֶׁר־הָי֣וּ לְפָנֶ֗יךָ לְמִן־הַיּוֹם֙ אֲשֶׁר֩ בָּרָ֨א

אֱלֹהִ֤ים ׀ אָדָם֙ עַל־הָאָ֔רֶץ וּלְמִקְצֵ֥ה הַשָּׁמַ֖יִם וְעַד־קְצֵ֣ה הַשָּׁמָ֑יִם הֲנִֽהְיָ֗ה

לג כַּדָּבָ֤ר הַגָּדוֹל֙ הַזֶּ֔ה א֖וֹ הֲנִשְׁמַ֥ע כָּמֹֽהוּ׃ הֲשָׁ֣מַֽע עָם֩ ק֨וֹל אֱלֹהִ֜ים מְדַבֵּ֤ר

לד מִתּוֹךְ־הָאֵ֨שׁ֙ כַּאֲשֶׁר־שָׁמַ֥עְתָּ אַתָּ֖ה וַיֶּֽחִי׃ א֣וֹ ׀ הֲנִסָּ֣ה אֱלֹהִ֗ים לָ֠בוֹא לָקַ֨חַת

ל֣וֹ גוֹי֮ מִקֶּ֣רֶב גּוֹי֒ בְּמַסֹּת֩ בְּאֹתֹ֨ת וּבְמוֹפְתִ֜ים וּבְמִלְחָמָ֗ה וּבְיָ֤ד חֲזָקָה֙ וּבִזְר֣וֹעַ

נְטוּיָ֔ה וּבְמוֹרָאִ֖ים גְּדֹלִ֑ים כְּ֠כֹ֠ל אֲשֶׁר־עָשָׂ֨ה לָכֶ֜ם יהו֧ה אֱלֹהֵיכֶ֛ם בְּמִצְרַ֖יִם

לה לְעֵינֶֽיךָ׃ אַתָּה֙ הׇרְאֵ֣תָ לָדַ֔עַת כִּ֥י יהו֖ה ה֣וּא הָאֱלֹהִ֑ים אֵ֥ין ע֖וֹד מִלְּבַדּֽוֹ׃

לו מִן־הַשָּׁמַ֛יִם הִשְׁמִֽיעֲךָ֥ אֶת־קֹל֖וֹ לְיַסְּרֶ֑ךָּ וְעַל־הָאָ֗רֶץ הֶרְאֲךָ֙ אֶת־אִשּׁ֣וֹ

לז הַגְּדוֹלָ֔ה וּדְבָרָ֥יו שָׁמַ֖עְתָּ מִתּ֥וֹךְ הָאֵֽשׁ׃ וְתַ֗חַת כִּ֤י אָהַב֙ אֶת־אֲבֹתֶ֔יךָ וַיִּבְחַ֥ר

לח בְּזַרְע֖וֹ אַחֲרָ֑יו וַיּוֹצִֽאֲךָ֧ בְּפָנָ֛יו בְּכֹח֥וֹ הַגָּדֹ֖ל מִמִּצְרָֽיִם׃ לְהוֹרִ֗ישׁ גּוֹיִ֛ם גְּדֹלִ֧ים

וַעֲצֻמִ֛ים מִמְּךָ֖ מִפָּנֶ֑יךָ לַהֲבִֽיאֲךָ֗ לָֽתֶת־לְךָ֧ אֶת־אַרְצָ֛ם נַחֲלָ֖ה כַּיּ֥וֹם הַזֶּֽה׃

לט וְיָדַעְתָּ֣ הַיּ֗וֹם וַהֲשֵׁבֹתָ֮ אֶל־לְבָבֶךָ֒ כִּ֤י יהו֙ה ה֣וּא הָֽאֱלֹהִ֔ים בַּשָּׁמַ֣יִם מִמַּ֔עַל

מ וְעַל־הָאָ֖רֶץ מִתָּ֑חַת אֵ֖ין עֽוֹד׃ וְשָׁמַרְתָּ֞ אֶת־חֻקָּ֣יו וְאֶת־מִצְוֺתָ֗יו אֲשֶׁ֤ר אָנֹכִי֙

מְצַוְּךָ֣ הַיּ֔וֹם אֲשֶׁר֙ יִיטַ֣ב לְךָ֔ וּלְבָנֶ֖יךָ אַחֲרֶ֑יךָ וּלְמַ֨עַן֙ תַּאֲרִ֣יךְ יָמִ֔ים

עַל־הָ֣אֲדָמָ֔ה אֲשֶׁ֨ר יהו֧ה אֱלֹהֶ֛יךָ נֹתֵ֥ן לְךָ֖ כׇּל־הַיָּמִֽים׃

מא-מב אָ֣ז יַבְדִּ֤יל מֹשֶׁה֙ שָׁלֹ֣שׁ עָרִ֔ים בְּעֵ֖בֶר הַיַּרְדֵּ֑ן מִזְרְחָ֖ה שָֽׁמֶשׁ׃ לָנֻ֨ס

שָׁ֜מָּה רוֹצֵ֗חַ אֲשֶׁ֨ר יִרְצַ֤ח אֶת־רֵעֵ֨הוּ֙ בִּבְלִי־דַ֔עַת וְה֛וּא לֹֽא־שֹׂנֵ֥א ל֖וֹ

מג מִתְּמֹ֣ל שִׁלְשֹׁ֑ם וְנָ֗ס אֶל־אַחַ֛ת מִן־הֶעָרִ֥ים הָאֵ֖ל וָחָֽי׃ אֶת־בֶּ֧צֶר בַּמִּדְבָּ֣ר

בְּאֶ֣רֶץ הַמִּישֹׁ֗ר לָרֽאוּבֵנִ֑י וְאֶת־רָאמֹ֤ת בַּגִּלְעָד֙ לַגָּדִ֔י וְאֶת־גּוֹלָ֥ן

מד-מה בַּבָּשָׁ֖ן לַֽמְנַשִּֽׁי׃ וְזֹ֖את הַתּוֹרָ֑ה אֲשֶׁר־שָׂ֣ם מֹשֶׁ֔ה לִפְנֵ֖י בְּנֵ֥י יִשְׂרָאֵֽל׃ אֵ֚לֶּה

TISHAH
B'AV
SHACHARIS
4:25:40

Haftarah:
p. 1092

שלישי

4:24. *Jealous.* See *Exodus* 20:5.

4:25-40. This passage is read on Tishah B'Av, because it tells how Israel will lapse into exile — and find its way back.

4:41. Moses knew that these three cities would not assume the status of cities of refuge until the three cities on the other side of the Jordan were designated after his your God — He is a consuming fire, a jealous.* God.

Exile and return*

²⁵ When you beget children and grandchildren and will have been long in the Land, you will grow corrupt and make a carved image, a likeness of anything, and you will do evil in the eyes of HASHEM, your God, to anger Him. ²⁶ I appoint heaven and earth this day to bear witness against you that you will surely perish quickly from the Land to which you are crossing the Jordan to possess; you shall not have lengthy days upon it, for you will be destroyed. ²⁷ HASHEM will scatter you among the peoples, and you will be left few in number among the nations where HASHEM will lead you. ²⁸ There you will serve gods, the handiwork of man, of wood and stone, which do not see, and do not hear, and do not eat, and do not smell.

²⁹ From there you will seek HASHEM, your God, and you will find Him, if you search for Him with all your heart and all your soul. ³⁰ When you are in distress and all these things have befallen you, at the end of days, you will return unto HASHEM, your God, and hearken to His voice. ³¹ For HASHEM, your God, is a

He will not abandon you

merciful God, He will not abandon you nor destroy you, and He will not forget the covenant of your forefathers that He swore to them. ³² For inquire now regarding the early days that preceded you, from the day when God created man on the earth, and from one end of heaven to the other end of heaven: Has there ever been anything like this great thing or has anything like it been heard? ³³ Has a people ever heard the voice of God speaking from the midst of the fire as you have heard, and survived? ³⁴ Or has any god ever miraculously come to take for himself a nation from amidst a nation, with challenges, with signs, and with wonders, and with war, and with a strong hand, and with an outstretched arm, and with greatly awesome deeds, such as everything that HASHEM, your God, did for you in Egypt before your eyes? ³⁵ You have been shown in order to know that HASHEM, He is the God! There is none beside Him!

You heard His voice

³⁶ From heaven He caused you to hear His voice in order to teach you, and on earth He showed you His great fire, and you heard His words from the midst of the fire, ³⁷ because He loved your forefathers, and He chose his offspring after him, and took you out before Himself with His great strength from Egypt; ³⁸ to drive away from before you nations that are greater and mightier than you, to bring you, to give you their land as an inheritance, as this very day. ³⁹ You shall know this day and take to your heart that HASHEM, He is the God — in heaven above and on the earth below — there is none other. ⁴⁰ You shall observe His decrees and His commandments that I command you this day, so that He will do good to you and to your children after you, and so that you will prolong your days on the Land that HASHEM, your God, gives you, for all the days.

Setting aside the cities of refuge
(See Appendix D, map 5)

⁴¹ Then Moses set aside three cities* on the bank of the Jordan, toward the rising sun, ⁴² for a killer to flee there, who will have killed his fellow without knowledge, but who was not an enemy of his from yesterday and before yesterday — then he shall flee to one of these cities and live: ⁴³ Bezer in the wilderness, in the land of the plain, of the Reubenite; Ramoth in the Gilead, of the Gadite; and Golan in the Bashan, of the Manassite.

⁴⁴ This is the teaching that Moses placed before the Children of Israel. ⁴⁵ These

---

death; nevertheless, his love of the commandments was so great that he wished to fulfill as many as he possibly   could (Rashi).
See Numbers 35:22-28 and Deuteronomy 19:1-10.

הָעֵדֹת וְהָחֻקִּים וְהַמִּשְׁפָּטִים אֲשֶׁר דִּבֶּר מֹשֶׁה אֶל־בְּנֵי יִשְׂרָאֵל בְּצֵאתָם

מו מִמִּצְרָיִם: בְּעֵבֶר הַיַּרְדֵּן בַּגַּיְא מוּל בֵּית פְּעוֹר בְּאֶרֶץ סִיחֹן מֶלֶךְ הָאֱמֹרִי

אֲשֶׁר יוֹשֵׁב בְּחֶשְׁבּוֹן אֲשֶׁר הִכָּה מֹשֶׁה וּבְנֵי יִשְׂרָאֵל בְּצֵאתָם מִמִּצְרָיִם:

מז וַיִּירְשׁוּ אֶת־אַרְצוֹ וְאֶת־אֶרֶץ ׀ עוֹג מֶלֶךְ־הַבָּשָׁן שְׁנֵי מַלְכֵי הָאֱמֹרִי אֲשֶׁר

מח בְּעֵבֶר הַיַּרְדֵּן מִזְרַח שָׁמֶשׁ: מֵעֲרֹעֵר אֲשֶׁר עַל־שְׂפַת־נַחַל אַרְנֹן וְעַד־הַר

מט שִׂיאֹן הוּא חֶרְמוֹן: וְכָל־הָעֲרָבָה עֵבֶר הַיַּרְדֵּן מִזְרָחָה וְעַד יָם הָעֲרָבָה תַּחַת

אַשְׁדֹּת הַפִּסְגָּה:

ה רביעי א וַיִּקְרָא מֹשֶׁה אֶל־כָּל־יִשְׂרָאֵל וַיֹּאמֶר אֲלֵהֶם שְׁמַע יִשְׂרָאֵל אֶת־הַחֻקִּים

וְאֶת־הַמִּשְׁפָּטִים אֲשֶׁר אָנֹכִי דֹּבֵר בְּאָזְנֵיכֶם הַיּוֹם וּלְמַדְתֶּם אֹתָם וּשְׁמַרְתֶּם

ב-ג לַעֲשֹׂתָם: יהוה אֱלֹהֵינוּ כָּרַת עִמָּנוּ בְּרִית בְּחֹרֵב: לֹא אֶת־אֲבֹתֵינוּ כָּרַת

ד יהוה אֶת־הַבְּרִית הַזֹּאת כִּי אִתָּנוּ אֲנַחְנוּ אֵלֶּה פֹה הַיּוֹם כֻּלָּנוּ חַיִּים: פָּנִים ׀

ה בְּפָנִים דִּבֶּר יהוה עִמָּכֶם בָּהָר מִתּוֹךְ הָאֵשׁ: אָנֹכִי עֹמֵד בֵּין־יהוה וּבֵינֵיכֶם

בָּעֵת הַהִוא לְהַגִּיד לָכֶם אֶת־דְּבַר יהוה כִּי יְרֵאתֶם מִפְּנֵי הָאֵשׁ וְלֹא־עֲלִיתֶם

ו בָּהָר לֵאמֹר: *אָנֹכִי יהוה אֱלֹהֶיךָ אֲשֶׁר הוֹצֵאתִיךָ מֵאֶרֶץ מִצְרַיִם

מִבֵּית עֲבָדִים: לֹא־יִהְיֶה לְךָ אֱלֹהִים אֲחֵרִים עַל־פָּנָי: לֹא־תַעֲשֶׂה לְךָ

ז-ח פֶסֶל ׀ כָּל־תְּמוּנָה אֲשֶׁר בַּשָּׁמַיִם ׀ מִמַּעַל וַאֲשֶׁר בָּאָרֶץ מִתָּחַת וַאֲשֶׁר בַּמַּיִם ׀

ט מִתַּחַת לָאָרֶץ: לֹא־תִשְׁתַּחֲוֶה לָהֶם וְלֹא תָעָבְדֵם כִּי אָנֹכִי יהוה אֱלֹהֶיךָ

י אֵל קַנָּא פֹּקֵד עֲוֹן אָבֹת עַל־בָּנִים וְעַל־שִׁלֵּשִׁים וְעַל־רִבֵּעִים לְשֹׂנְאָי: וְעֹשֶׂה

יא חֶסֶד לַאֲלָפִים לְאֹהֲבַי וּלְשֹׁמְרֵי °מִצְוֹתוֹ [°מִצְוֹתָי ק]:   לֹא תִשָּׂא אֶת־

שֵׁם־יהוה אֱלֹהֶיךָ לַשָּׁוְא כִּי לֹא יְנַקֶּה יהוה אֵת אֲשֶׁר־יִשָּׂא אֶת־שְׁמוֹ

יב לַשָּׁוְא: שָׁמוֹר אֶת־יוֹם הַשַּׁבָּת לְקַדְּשׁוֹ כַּאֲשֶׁר צִוְּךָ יהוה אֱלֹהֶיךָ:

יג-יד שֵׁשֶׁת יָמִים תַּעֲבֹד וְעָשִׂיתָ כָּל־מְלַאכְתֶּךָ: וְיוֹם הַשְּׁבִיעִי שַׁבָּת ׀ לַיהוה

אֱלֹהֶיךָ לֹא־תַעֲשֶׂה כָל־מְלָאכָה אַתָּה ׀ וּבִנְךָ־וּבִתֶּךָ וְעַבְדְּךָ־וַאֲמָתֶךָ

וְשׁוֹרְךָ וַחֲמֹרְךָ וְכָל־בְּהֶמְתֶּךָ וְגֵרְךָ אֲשֶׁר בִּשְׁעָרֶיךָ לְמַעַן יָנוּחַ עַבְדְּךָ

טו וַאֲמָתְךָ כָּמוֹךָ: וְזָכַרְתָּ כִּי־עֶבֶד הָיִיתָ ׀ בְּאֶרֶץ מִצְרַיִם וַיֹּצִאֲךָ יהוה אֱלֹהֶיךָ

מִשָּׁם בְּיָד חֲזָקָה וּבִזְרֹעַ נְטוּיָה עַל־כֵּן צִוְּךָ יהוה אֱלֹהֶיךָ לַעֲשׂוֹת אֶת־יוֹם

טז הַשַּׁבָּת: כַּבֵּד אֶת־אָבִיךָ וְאֶת־אִמֶּךָ כַּאֲשֶׁר צִוְּךָ יהוה אֱלֹהֶיךָ

לְמַעַן ׀ יַאֲרִיכֻן יָמֶיךָ וּלְמַעַן יִיטַב לָךְ עַל הָאֲדָמָה אֲשֶׁר־יהוה אֱלֹהֶיךָ נֹתֵן

יז לָךְ:   לֹא תִּרְצָח   וְלֹא תִּנְאָף   וְלֹא תִּגְנֹב   וְלֹא־

יח תַעֲנֶה בְרֵעֲךָ עֵד שָׁוְא: וְלֹא תַחְמֹד אֵשֶׁת רֵעֶךָ:   וְלֹא תִתְאַוֶּה

יט חמישי בֵּית רֵעֶךָ שָׂדֵהוּ וְעַבְדּוֹ וַאֲמָתוֹ שׁוֹרוֹ וַחֲמֹרוֹ וְכֹל אֲשֶׁר לְרֵעֶךָ:   אֶת־

*See box
below

THE TEN COMMANDMENTS ARE READ WITH TWO DIFFERENT SETS OF *TROP* (CANTILLATION NOTES). THE VERSION PRESENTED
IN THE TEXT IS USED BY THE INDIVIDUAL WHO IS REVIEWING THE WEEKLY *SIDRAH*. THE VERSION USED BY THE READER FOR THE
PUBLIC TORAH READING ON THE SABBATH APPEARS IN A BOX ON PAGE 514.

are the testimonies, the decrees, and the ordinances that Moses spoke to the Children of Israel, when they left Egypt, [46] on the bank of the Jordan, in the valley, opposite Beth-peor, in the land of Sihon, king of the Amorite, who dwells in Heshbon, whom Moses and the Children of Israel smote when they went out of Egypt. [47] They possessed his land and the land of Og the king of Bashan, two kings of the Amorite, which are on the bank of the Jordan, where the sun rises; [48] from Aroer that is by the shore of Arnon Brook until Mount Sion, which is Hermon, [49] and the entire Arabah, the eastern bank of the Jordan until the Sea of the Arabah, under the waterfalls of the cliffs.

5

[1] **M**oses called all of Israel and said to them: Hear, O Israel, the decrees and the ordinances that I speak in your ears today; learn them, and be careful to perform them. [2] HASHEM, our God, sealed a covenant with us at Horeb. [3] Not with our forefathers did HASHEM seal this covenant, but with us — we who are here, all of us alive today. [4] Face to face did HASHEM speak with you on the mountain, from amid the fire. [5] I was standing between HASHEM and you at that time, to relate the word of HASHEM to you — for you were afraid of the fire and you did not ascend the mountain — saying:

*The Ten Command-ments** [6] I am HASHEM, your God, Who has taken you out of the land of Egypt, from the house of slavery.

[7] You shall not recognize the gods of others in My Presence.

[8] You shall not make for yourself a carved image of any likeness of that which is in the heavens above or on the earth below or in the water beneath the earth. [9] You shall not prostrate yourself to them nor worship them, for I am HASHEM, your God — a jealous God, Who visits the sin of fathers upon children to the third and fourth generations, for My enemies; [10] but Who shows kindness for thousands [of generations], to those who love Me and observe My commandments.

[11] You shall not take the Name of HASHEM, your God, in vain, for HASHEM will not absolve anyone who takes His Name in vain.

[12] Safeguard the Sabbath day to sanctify it, as HASHEM, your God, has commanded you. [13] Six days shall you labor and accomplish all your work; [14] but the seventh day is Sabbath to HASHEM, your God; you shall not do any work — you, your son, your daughter, your slave, your maidservant, your ox, your donkey, and your every animal, and your convert within your gates, in order that your slave and your maidservant may rest like you. [15] And you shall remember that you were a slave in the land of Egypt, and HASHEM, your God, has taken you out from there with a strong hand and an outstretched arm; therefore HASHEM, your God, has commanded you to make the Sabbath day.

[16] Honor your father and your mother, as HASHEM, your God, commanded you, so that your days will be lengthened and so that it will be good for you, upon the land that HASHEM, your God, gives you.

[17] You shall not kill; and you shall not commit adultery; and you shall not steal; and you shall not bear vain witness against your fellow.

[18] And you shall not covet your fellow's wife, you shall not desire your fellow's house, his field, his slave, his maidservant, his ox, his donkey, or anything that belongs to your fellow.

5:6-18. See *Exodus* 20:2-14 for an interpretation of the Ten Commandments.

הַדְּבָרִים הָאֵלֶּה דִּבֶּר יהוה אֶל־כָּל־קְהַלְכֶם בָּהָר מִתּוֹךְ הָאֵשׁ הֶעָנָן
וְהָעֲרָפֶל קוֹל גָּדוֹל וְלֹא יָסָף וַיִּכְתְּבֵם עַל־שְׁנֵי לֻחֹת אֲבָנִים וַיִּתְּנֵם אֵלָי:

כ וַיְהִי כְּשָׁמְעֲכֶם אֶת־הַקּוֹל מִתּוֹךְ הַחֹשֶׁךְ וְהָהָר בֹּעֵר בָּאֵשׁ וַתִּקְרְבוּן אֵלַי
כא כָּל־רָאשֵׁי שִׁבְטֵיכֶם וְזִקְנֵיכֶם: וַתֹּאמְרוּ הֵן הֶרְאָנוּ יהוה אֱלֹהֵינוּ
אֶת־כְּבֹדוֹ וְאֶת־גָּדְלוֹ וְאֶת־קֹלוֹ שָׁמַעְנוּ מִתּוֹךְ הָאֵשׁ הַיּוֹם הַזֶּה רָאִינוּ
כב כִּי־יְדַבֵּר אֱלֹהִים אֶת־הָאָדָם וָחָי: וְעַתָּה לָמָּה נָמוּת כִּי תֹאכְלֵנוּ הָאֵשׁ
הַגְּדֹלָה הַזֹּאת אִם־יֹסְפִים ׀ אֲנַחְנוּ לִשְׁמֹעַ אֶת־קוֹל יהוה אֱלֹהֵינוּ עוֹד
כג וָמָתְנוּ: כִּי מִי כָל־בָּשָׂר אֲשֶׁר שָׁמַע קוֹל אֱלֹהִים חַיִּים מְדַבֵּר
כד מִתּוֹךְ־הָאֵשׁ כָּמֹנוּ וַיֶּחִי: קְרַב אַתָּה וּשְׁמָע אֵת כָּל־אֲשֶׁר יֹאמַר יהוה
אֱלֹהֵינוּ וְאַתְּ ׀ תְּדַבֵּר אֵלֵינוּ אֵת כָּל־אֲשֶׁר יְדַבֵּר יהוה אֱלֹהֵינוּ אֵלֶיךָ
כה וְשָׁמַעְנוּ וְעָשִׂינוּ: וַיִּשְׁמַע יהוה אֶת־קוֹל דִּבְרֵיכֶם בְּדַבֶּרְכֶם אֵלָי וַיֹּאמֶר
יהוה אֵלַי שָׁמַעְתִּי אֶת־קוֹל דִּבְרֵי הָעָם הַזֶּה אֲשֶׁר דִּבְּרוּ אֵלֶיךָ הֵיטִיבוּ
כו כָּל־אֲשֶׁר דִּבֵּרוּ: מִי־יִתֵּן וְהָיָה לְבָבָם זֶה לָהֶם לְיִרְאָה אֹתִי וְלִשְׁמֹר
כז אֶת־כָּל־מִצְוֹתַי כָּל־הַיָּמִים לְמַעַן יִיטַב לָהֶם וְלִבְנֵיהֶם לְעֹלָם: לֵךְ אֱמֹר
כח לָהֶם שׁוּבוּ לָכֶם לְאָהֳלֵיכֶם: וְאַתָּה פֹּה עֲמֹד עִמָּדִי וַאֲדַבְּרָה אֵלֶיךָ אֵת
כָּל־הַמִּצְוָה וְהַחֻקִּים וְהַמִּשְׁפָּטִים אֲשֶׁר תְּלַמְּדֵם וְעָשׂוּ בָאָרֶץ אֲשֶׁר אָנֹכִי
כט נֹתֵן לָהֶם לְרִשְׁתָּהּ: וּשְׁמַרְתֶּם לַעֲשׂוֹת כַּאֲשֶׁר צִוָּה יהוה אֱלֹהֵיכֶם אֶתְכֶם
ל לֹא תָסֻרוּ יָמִין וּשְׂמֹאל: בְּכָל־הַדֶּרֶךְ אֲשֶׁר צִוָּה יהוה אֱלֹהֵיכֶם אֶתְכֶם
תֵּלֵכוּ לְמַעַן תִּחְיוּן וְטוֹב לָכֶם וְהַאֲרַכְתֶּם יָמִים בָּאָרֶץ אֲשֶׁר תִּירָשׁוּן:

ו א וְזֹאת הַמִּצְוָה הַחֻקִּים וְהַמִּשְׁפָּטִים אֲשֶׁר צִוָּה יהוה אֱלֹהֵיכֶם לְלַמֵּד
ב אֶתְכֶם לַעֲשׂוֹת בָּאָרֶץ אֲשֶׁר אַתֶּם עֹבְרִים שָׁמָּה לְרִשְׁתָּהּ: לְמַעַן תִּירָא
אֶת־יהוה אֱלֹהֶיךָ לִשְׁמֹר אֶת־כָּל־חֻקֹּתָיו וּמִצְוֹתָיו אֲשֶׁר אָנֹכִי מְצַוֶּךָ
ג אַתָּה וּבִנְךָ וּבֶן־בִּנְךָ כֹּל יְמֵי חַיֶּיךָ וּלְמַעַן יַאֲרִכֻן יָמֶיךָ: וְשָׁמַעְתָּ יִשְׂרָאֵל
וְשָׁמַרְתָּ לַעֲשׂוֹת אֲשֶׁר יִיטַב לְךָ וַאֲשֶׁר תִּרְבּוּן מְאֹד כַּאֲשֶׁר דִּבֶּר יהוה
אֱלֹהֵי אֲבֹתֶיךָ לָךְ אֶרֶץ זָבַת חָלָב וּדְבָשׁ:

ששי ד־ה שְׁמַע יִשְׂרָאֵל יהוה אֱלֹהֵינוּ יהוה ׀ אֶחָד: וְאָהַבְתָּ אֵת יהוה אֱלֹהֶיךָ * ע' וד' רבתי
ו בְּכָל־לְבָבְךָ וּבְכָל־נַפְשְׁךָ וּבְכָל־מְאֹדֶךָ: וְהָיוּ הַדְּבָרִים הָאֵלֶּה אֲשֶׁר אָנֹכִי
ז מְצַוְּךָ הַיּוֹם עַל־לְבָבֶךָ: וְשִׁנַּנְתָּם לְבָנֶיךָ וְדִבַּרְתָּ בָּם בְּשִׁבְתְּךָ בְּבֵיתֶךָ
ח וּבְלֶכְתְּךָ בַדֶּרֶךְ וּבְשָׁכְבְּךָ וּבְקוּמֶךָ: וּקְשַׁרְתָּם לְאוֹת עַל־יָדֶךָ וְהָיוּ לְטֹטָפֹת
ט בֵּין עֵינֶיךָ: וּכְתַבְתָּם עַל־מְזֻזוֹת בֵּיתֶךָ וּבִשְׁעָרֶיךָ: וְהָיָה

6:4-5. The first two verses of the *Shema* command Israel to acknowledge God's Oneness and to love Him.

In today's world only Israel recognizes Hashem as the *One* and *Only*, thus He is *our God*; but after the final Redemption, all the world will acknowledge that HASHEM *is One* (*Rashi*).

6:5. One expresses love of God by performing His commandments lovingly.

With all your soul, i.e., even if your devotion to God requires that you forfeit your life (*Rashi*).

And with all your resources, i.e., even if love of God causes you to lose all your money.

Fire, cloud,   ¹⁹ *These words HASHEM spoke to your entire congregation on the mountain,*
thick smoke *from the midst of the fire, the cloud, and the thick cloud — a great voice, never*
to be repeated — and He inscribed them on two stone Tablets and gave them
to me. ²⁰ *It happened that when you heard the voice from the midst of the*
darkness and the mountain was burning in fire, that you — all the heads of your
tribes and your elders — approached me.

    ²¹ *You said, "Behold! HASHEM, our God, has shown us His glory and His*
greatness, and we have heard His voice from the midst of the fire; this day we
saw that HASHEM will speak to a person and he can live. ²² *But now, why should*
we die when this great fire consumes us? If we continue to hear the voice of
HASHEM, our God, any longer, we will die! ²³ *For is there any human that has*
heard the voice of the Living God speaking from the midst of the fire, as we
have, and lived? ²⁴ *You should approach and hear whatever HASHEM, our God,*
will say, and you should speak to us whatever HASHEM, our God, will speak to
you — then we shall hear and we shall do."

    ²⁵ *HASHEM heard the sound of your words when you spoke to me, and*
HASHEM said to me, "I heard the sound of the words of this people, that they
have spoken to you; they did well in all that they spoke. ²⁶ *Who can assure that*
this heart should remain theirs, to fear Me and observe all My commandments
all the days, so that it should be good for them and for their children forever?
"Return to ²⁷ *Go say to them, 'Return to your tents.'* ²⁸ *But as for you, stand here with Me*
your tents" *and I shall speak to you the entire commandment, and the decrees, and the*
ordinances that you shall teach them and they shall perform in the Land that I
give them, to possess it."

    ²⁹ *You shall be careful to act as HASHEM, your God, commanded you,*
you shall not stray to the right or left. ³⁰ *On the entire way that HASHEM,*
your God, commanded you shall you go, so that you shall live and it will be
good for you, and you shall prolong your days in the Land that you shall
possess.

6   ¹ T*his is the commandment, and the decrees, and the ordinances that*
HASHEM, your God, commanded to teach you, to perform in the Land to
which you are crossing, to possess it, ² *so that you will fear HASHEM, your*
God, to observe all His decrees and commandments that I command you —
you, your child, and your grandchild — all the days of your life, so that your
days will be lengthened. ³ *You shall hearken, O Israel, and beware to perform,*
so that it will be good for you, and so that you will increase very much, as
HASHEM, the God of your forefathers, spoke for you — a land flowing with milk
and honey.

The   ⁴ *Hear, O Israel: HASHEM is our God, HASHEM is the One and Only.* * ⁵ *You shall*
Shema *love HASHEM, your God, with all your heart, with all your soul,* * *and with all*
your resources. * ⁶ *And these matters that I command you today shall be upon*
your heart. ⁷ *You shall teach them thoroughly to your children and you shall*
speak of them while you sit in your home, while you walk on the way, when you
retire and when you arise. ⁸ *Bind them as a sign upon your arm and let them be*
ornaments between your eyes. ⁹ *And write them on the doorposts of your house*
and upon your gates.

כִּי יְבִיאֲךָ ׀ יהוה אֱלֹהֶיךָ אֶל־הָאָרֶץ אֲשֶׁר נִשְׁבַּע לַאֲבֹתֶיךָ לְאַבְרָהָם

יא לְיִצְחָק וּלְיַעֲקֹב לָתֶת לָךְ עָרִים גְּדֹלֹת וְטֹבֹת אֲשֶׁר לֹא־בָנִיתָ: וּבָתִּים
מְלֵאִים כָּל־טוּב אֲשֶׁר לֹא־מִלֵּאתָ וּבֹרֹת חֲצוּבִים אֲשֶׁר לֹא־חָצַבְתָּ

יב כְּרָמִים וְזֵיתִים אֲשֶׁר לֹא־נָטָעְתָּ וְאָכַלְתָּ וְשָׂבָעְתָּ: הִשָּׁמֶר לְךָ פֶּן־

יג תִּשְׁכַּח אֶת־יהוה אֲשֶׁר הוֹצִיאֲךָ מֵאֶרֶץ מִצְרַיִם מִבֵּית עֲבָדִים: אֶת־

יד יהוה אֱלֹהֶיךָ תִּירָא וְאֹתוֹ תַעֲבֹד וּבִשְׁמוֹ תִּשָּׁבֵעַ: לֹא תֵלְכוּן אַחֲרֵי

טו אֱלֹהִים אֲחֵרִים מֵאֱלֹהֵי הָעַמִּים אֲשֶׁר סְבִיבוֹתֵיכֶם: כִּי אֵל קַנָּא יהוה
אֱלֹהֶיךָ בְּקִרְבֶּךָ פֶּן־יֶחֱרֶה אַף־יהוה אֱלֹהֶיךָ בָּךְ וְהִשְׁמִידְךָ מֵעַל פְּנֵי

טז הָאֲדָמָה: לֹא תְנַסּוּ אֶת־יהוה אֱלֹהֵיכֶם כַּאֲשֶׁר נִסִּיתֶם בַּמַּסָּה:

יז שָׁמוֹר תִּשְׁמְרוּן אֶת־מִצְוֹת יהוה אֱלֹהֵיכֶם וְעֵדֹתָיו וְחֻקָּיו אֲשֶׁר צִוָּךְ:

יח וְעָשִׂיתָ הַיָּשָׁר וְהַטּוֹב בְּעֵינֵי יהוה לְמַעַן יִיטַב לָךְ וּבָאתָ וְיָרַשְׁתָּ אֶת־הָאָרֶץ

יט הַטֹּבָה אֲשֶׁר־נִשְׁבַּע יהוה לַאֲבֹתֶיךָ: לַהֲדֹף אֶת־כָּל־אֹיְבֶיךָ מִפָּנֶיךָ כַּאֲשֶׁר

כ דִּבֶּר יהוה: כִּי־יִשְׁאָלְךָ בִנְךָ מָחָר לֵאמֹר מָה הָעֵדֹת וְהַחֻקִּים

כא וְהַמִּשְׁפָּטִים אֲשֶׁר צִוָּה יהוה אֱלֹהֵינוּ אֶתְכֶם: וְאָמַרְתָּ לְבִנְךָ עֲבָדִים הָיִינוּ

כב לְפַרְעֹה בְּמִצְרָיִם וַיֹּצִיאֵנוּ יהוה מִמִּצְרַיִם בְּיָד חֲזָקָה: וַיִּתֵּן יהוה אוֹתֹת

כג וּמֹפְתִים גְּדֹלִים וְרָעִים ׀ בְּמִצְרַיִם בְּפַרְעֹה וּבְכָל־בֵּיתוֹ לְעֵינֵינוּ: וְאוֹתָנוּ
הוֹצִיא מִשָּׁם לְמַעַן הָבִיא אֹתָנוּ לָתֶת לָנוּ אֶת־הָאָרֶץ אֲשֶׁר נִשְׁבַּע

כד לַאֲבֹתֵינוּ: וַיְצַוֵּנוּ יהוה לַעֲשׂוֹת אֶת־כָּל־הַחֻקִּים הָאֵלֶּה לְיִרְאָה אֶת־יהוה

כה אֱלֹהֵינוּ לְטוֹב לָנוּ כָּל־הַיָּמִים לְחַיֹּתֵנוּ כְּהַיּוֹם הַזֶּה: וּצְדָקָה תִּהְיֶה־לָּנוּ
כִּי־נִשְׁמֹר לַעֲשׂוֹת אֶת־כָּל־הַמִּצְוָה הַזֹּאת לִפְנֵי יהוה אֱלֹהֵינוּ כַּאֲשֶׁר
צִוָּנוּ: ‎ ‎ כִּי יְבִיאֲךָ יהוה אֱלֹהֶיךָ אֶל־הָאָרֶץ אֲשֶׁר־אַתָּה בָא־ ‎ **ז** שביעי א

שָׁמָּה לְרִשְׁתָּהּ וְנָשַׁל גּוֹיִם־רַבִּים ׀ מִפָּנֶיךָ הַחִתִּי וְהַגִּרְגָּשִׁי וְהָאֱמֹרִי

ב וְהַכְּנַעֲנִי וְהַפְּרִזִּי וְהַחִוִּי וְהַיְבוּסִי שִׁבְעָה גוֹיִם רַבִּים וַעֲצוּמִים מִמֶּךָּ: וּנְתָנָם
יהוה אֱלֹהֶיךָ לְפָנֶיךָ וְהִכִּיתָם הַחֲרֵם תַּחֲרִים אֹתָם לֹא־תִכְרֹת לָהֶם בְּרִית

ג וְלֹא תְחָנֵּם: וְלֹא תִתְחַתֵּן בָּם בִּתְּךָ לֹא־תִתֵּן לִבְנוֹ וּבִתּוֹ לֹא־תִקַּח לִבְנֶךָ:

ד כִּי־יָסִיר אֶת־בִּנְךָ מֵאַחֲרַי וְעָבְדוּ אֱלֹהִים אֲחֵרִים וְחָרָה אַף־יהוה בָּכֶם

ה וְהִשְׁמִידְךָ מַהֵר: כִּי־אִם־כֹּה תַעֲשׂוּ לָהֶם מִזְבְּחֹתֵיהֶם תִּתֹּצוּ וּמַצֵּבֹתָם

ו תְּשַׁבֵּרוּ וַאֲשֵׁירֵהֶם תְּגַדֵּעוּן וּפְסִילֵיהֶם תִּשְׂרְפוּן בָּאֵשׁ: כִּי עַם קָדוֹשׁ אַתָּה
לַיהוה אֱלֹהֶיךָ בְּךָ בָּחַר ׀ יהוה אֱלֹהֶיךָ לִהְיוֹת לוֹ לְעַם סְגֻלָּה מִכֹּל הָעַמִּים

ז אֲשֶׁר עַל־פְּנֵי הָאֲדָמָה: לֹא מֵרֻבְּכֶם מִכָּל־הָעַמִּים חָשַׁק יהוה בָּכֶם וַיִּבְחַר

ח בָּכֶם כִּי־אַתֶּם הַמְעַט מִכָּל־הָעַמִּים: כִּי מֵאַהֲבַת יהוה אֶתְכֶם וּמִשָּׁמְרוֹ
אֶת־הַשְּׁבֻעָה אֲשֶׁר נִשְׁבַּע לַאֲבֹתֵיכֶם הוֹצִיא יהוה אֶתְכֶם בְּיָד חֲזָקָה

7:1. Moses returns to a recurring theme of his final words to Israel — the preparation of his people for their new life in the Land.

7:8. Moses gives two reasons for God's choice of Israel: (a) He found them worthy of His love; and (b) because of His oath to the Patriarchs (*Ramban*).

Not succumbing to prosperity ¹⁰ *It shall be that when HASHEM, your God, brings you to the Land that HASHEM swore to your forefathers, to Abraham, to Isaac, and to Jacob, to give you — great and good cities that you did not build,* ¹¹ *houses filled with every good thing that you did not fill, chiseled cisterns that you did not chisel, orchards and olive trees that you did not plant — and you shall eat and be satisfied —* ¹² *beware for yourself lest you forget HASHEM Who took you out of the land of Egypt, from the house of slavery.* ¹³ *HASHEM, your God, shall you fear, Him shall you serve, and in His Name shall you swear.* ¹⁴ *You shall not follow after gods of others, of the gods of the peoples that are around you.* ¹⁵ *For a jealous God is HASHEM, your God, among you — lest the wrath of HASHEM, your God, will flare against you and He destroy you from upon the face of the earth.*

Further trust in God

¹⁶ *You shall not test HASHEM, your God, as you tested Him at Massah.* ¹⁷ *You shall surely observe the commandments of HASHEM, your God, and His testimonies and His decrees that He commanded you.* ¹⁸ *You shall do what is fair and good in the eyes of HASHEM, so that it will be good for you, and you shall come and possess the good Land that HASHEM swore to your forefathers,* ¹⁹ *to thrust away all your enemies from before you, as HASHEM spoke.*

Teaching the tradition to children

²⁰ *If your child asks you tomorrow, saying, "What are the testimonies and the decrees and the ordinances that HASHEM, our God, commanded you?"*

²¹ *You shall say to your child, "We were slaves to Pharaoh in Egypt, and HASHEM took us out of Egypt with a strong hand.* ²² *HASHEM placed signs and wonders, great and harmful, against Egypt, against Pharaoh and against his entire household, before our eyes.* ²³ *And He took us out of there in order to bring us, to give us the Land that He swore to our forefathers.* ²⁴ *HASHEM commanded us to perform all these decrees, to fear HASHEM, our God, for our good, all the days, to give us life, as this very day.* ²⁵ *And it will be a merit for us if we are careful to perform this entire commandment before HASHEM, our God, as He commanded us.*

7

¹ **W**hen *HASHEM, your God, will bring you to the Land to which you come to possess it, and He will thrust away many nations from before you — the Hittite, the Girgashite, the Amorite, the Canaanite, the Perizzite, the Hivvite, and the Jebusite — seven nations greater and mightier than you,* ² *and HASHEM, your God, will deliver them before you, and you will smite them — you shall utterly destroy them; you shall not seal a covenant with them nor shall you show them favor.* ³ *You shall not intermarry with them; you shall not give your daughter to his son, and you shall not take his daughter for your son,* ⁴ *for he will cause your child to turn away from after Me and they will worship the gods of others; then HASHEM's wrath will burn against you, and He will destroy you quickly.* ⁵ *Rather, so shall you do to them: Their altars shall you break apart; their pillars shall you smash; their sacred trees shall you cut down; and their carved images shall you burn in fire.*

⁶ *For you are a holy people to HASHEM, your God; HASHEM, your God, has chosen you to be for Him a treasured people above all the peoples that are on the face of the earth.* ⁷ *Not because you are more numerous than all the peoples did HASHEM desire you and choose you, for you are the fewest of all the peoples.* ⁸ *Rather, because of HASHEM's love for you and because He observes the oath that He swore to your forefathers* * *did He take you out with a strong hand*

ט וַיִּפְדְּךָ מִבֵּית עֲבָדִים מִיַּד פַּרְעֹה מֶלֶךְ־מִצְרָיִם: וְיָדַעְתָּ כִּי־יהוה אֱלֹהֶיךָ הוּא הָאֱלֹהִים הָאֵל הַנֶּאֱמָן שֹׁמֵר הַבְּרִית וְהַחֶסֶד לְאֹהֲבָיו וּלְשֹׁמְרֵי מִצְוֺתָו לְאֶלֶף דּוֹר: וּמְשַׁלֵּם לְשֹׂנְאָיו אֶל־פָּנָיו לְהַאֲבִידוֹ לֹא יְאַחֵר לְשֹׂנְאוֹ

י אֶל־פָּנָיו יְשַׁלֶּם־לוֹ: וְשָׁמַרְתָּ אֶת־הַמִּצְוָה וְאֶת־הַחֻקִּים וְאֶת־הַמִּשְׁפָּטִים

יא אֲשֶׁר אָנֹכִי מְצַוְּךָ הַיּוֹם לַעֲשׂוֹתָם: פפפ קי״ח פסוקים. עזיא״ל סימן.

פרשת עקב

יב וְהָיָה | עֵקֶב תִּשְׁמְעוּן אֵת הַמִּשְׁפָּטִים הָאֵלֶּה וּשְׁמַרְתֶּם וַעֲשִׂיתֶם אֹתָם וְשָׁמַר יהוה אֱלֹהֶיךָ לְךָ אֶת־הַבְּרִית וְאֶת־הַחֶסֶד אֲשֶׁר נִשְׁבַּע לַאֲבֹתֶיךָ:

יג וַאֲהֵבְךָ וּבֵרַכְךָ וְהִרְבֶּךָ וּבֵרַךְ פְּרִי־בִטְנְךָ וּפְרִי־אַדְמָתֶךָ דְּגָנְךָ וְתִירֹשְׁךָ וְיִצְהָרֶךָ שְׁגַר־אֲלָפֶיךָ וְעַשְׁתְּרֹת צֹאנֶךָ עַל הָאֲדָמָה אֲשֶׁר־נִשְׁבַּע לַאֲבֹתֶיךָ

יד לָתֶת לָךְ: בָּרוּךְ תִּהְיֶה מִכָּל־הָעַמִּים לֹא־יִהְיֶה בְךָ עָקָר וַעֲקָרָה וּבִבְהֶמְתֶּךָ:

טו וְהֵסִיר יהוה מִמְּךָ כָּל־חֹלִי וְכָל־מַדְוֵי מִצְרַיִם הָרָעִים אֲשֶׁר יָדַעְתָּ לֹא יְשִׂימָם בָּךְ וּנְתָנָם בְּכָל־שֹׂנְאֶיךָ: וְאָכַלְתָּ אֶת־כָּל־הָעַמִּים אֲשֶׁר יהוה

טז אֱלֹהֶיךָ נֹתֵן לָךְ לֹא־תָחוֹס עֵינְךָ עֲלֵיהֶם וְלֹא תַעֲבֹד אֶת־אֱלֹהֵיהֶם כִּי־

יז מוֹקֵשׁ הוּא לָךְ: כִּי תֹאמַר בִּלְבָבְךָ רַבִּים הַגּוֹיִם הָאֵלֶּה

יח מִמֶּנִּי אֵיכָה אוּכַל לְהוֹרִישָׁם: לֹא תִירָא מֵהֶם זָכֹר תִּזְכֹּר אֵת אֲשֶׁר־עָשָׂה

יט יהוה אֱלֹהֶיךָ לְפַרְעֹה וּלְכָל־מִצְרָיִם: הַמַּסֹּת הַגְּדֹלֹת אֲשֶׁר־רָאוּ עֵינֶיךָ וְהָאֹתֹת וְהַמֹּפְתִים וְהַיָּד הַחֲזָקָה וְהַזְּרֹעַ הַנְּטוּיָה אֲשֶׁר הוֹצִאֲךָ יהוה אֱלֹהֶיךָ כֵּן־יַעֲשֶׂה יהוה אֱלֹהֶיךָ לְכָל־הָעַמִּים אֲשֶׁר־אַתָּה יָרֵא מִפְּנֵיהֶם:

כ וְגַם אֶת־הַצִּרְעָה יְשַׁלַּח יהוה אֱלֹהֶיךָ בָּם עַד־אֲבֹד הַנִּשְׁאָרִים וְהַנִּסְתָּרִים

כא מִפָּנֶיךָ: לֹא תַעֲרֹץ מִפְּנֵיהֶם כִּי־יהוה אֱלֹהֶיךָ בְּקִרְבֶּךָ אֵל גָּדוֹל וְנוֹרָא:

כב וְנָשַׁל יהוה אֱלֹהֶיךָ אֶת־הַגּוֹיִם הָאֵל מִפָּנֶיךָ מְעַט מְעָט לֹא תוּכַל כַּלֹּתָם

כג מַהֵר פֶּן־תִּרְבֶּה עָלֶיךָ חַיַּת הַשָּׂדֶה: וּנְתָנָם יהוה אֱלֹהֶיךָ לְפָנֶיךָ וְהָמָם

כד מְהוּמָה גְדֹלָה עַד הִשָּׁמְדָם: וְנָתַן מַלְכֵיהֶם בְּיָדֶךָ וְהַאֲבַדְתָּ אֶת־שְׁמָם מִתַּחַת הַשָּׁמָיִם לֹא־יִתְיַצֵּב אִישׁ בְּפָנֶיךָ עַד הִשְׁמִדְךָ אֹתָם: פְּסִילֵי

כה אֱלֹהֵיהֶם תִּשְׂרְפוּן בָּאֵשׁ לֹא־תַחְמֹד כֶּסֶף וְזָהָב עֲלֵיהֶם וְלָקַחְתָּ לָךְ פֶּן

כו תִּוָּקֵשׁ בּוֹ כִּי תוֹעֲבַת יהוה אֱלֹהֶיךָ הוּא: וְלֹא־תָבִיא תוֹעֵבָה אֶל־בֵּיתֶךָ וְהָיִיתָ חֵרֶם כָּמֹהוּ שַׁקֵּץ | תְּשַׁקְּצֶנּוּ וְתַעֵב | תְּתַעֲבֶנּוּ כִּי־חֵרֶם הוּא:

ח א כָּל־הַמִּצְוָה אֲשֶׁר אָנֹכִי מְצַוְּךָ הַיּוֹם תִּשְׁמְרוּן לַעֲשׂוֹת לְמַעַן תִּחְיוּן וּרְבִיתֶם וּבָאתֶם וִירִשְׁתֶּם אֶת־הָאָרֶץ אֲשֶׁר־נִשְׁבַּע יהוה לַאֲבֹתֵיכֶם:

ב וְזָכַרְתָּ אֶת־כָּל־הַדֶּרֶךְ אֲשֶׁר הֹלִיכֲךָ יהוה אֱלֹהֶיךָ זֶה אַרְבָּעִים שָׁנָה

≈§ **Parashas Eikev**

7:22-24. God assured the people of an overwhelming victory, but not so quickly that vast stretches of the land would be unpopulated and open to wild beasts.

8:1. *The entire commandment,* i.e., no Jew may pick and choose among the commandments; God's blessings were contingent on Israel's acceptance of the *entire* Torah.

and redeem you from the house of slavery, from the hand of Pharaoh, king of Egypt. ⁹ You must know that HASHEM, your God — He is the God, the faithful God, Who safeguards the covenant and the kindness for those who love Him and for those who observe His commandments, for a thousand generations. ¹⁰ And He repays His enemies in his lifetime to make him perish; He shall not delay for His enemy — in his lifetime He shall repay him. ¹¹ You shall observe the commandment, and the decrees and the ordinances that I command you today, to perform them.

PARASHAS EIKEV

The reward ¹² This shall be the reward when you hearken to these ordinances, and you observe and perform them; HASHEM, your God, will safeguard for you the covenant and the kindness that He swore to your forefathers. ¹³ He will love you, bless you and multiply you, and He will bless the fruit of your womb and the fruit of your Land; your grain, your wine, and your oil; the offspring of your cattle and the flocks of your sheep and goats; on the Land that He swore to your fore-fathers to give you. ¹⁴ You will be the most blessed of all the peoples; there will be no infertile male or infertile female among you or among your animals. ¹⁵ HASHEM will remove from you every illness; and all the bad maladies of Egypt that you knew — He will not put them upon you, but will put them upon all your foes. ¹⁶ You will devour all the peoples that HASHEM, your God, will deliver to you; your eye shall not pity them; you shall not worship their gods, for it is a snare for you.

¹⁷ Perhaps you will say in your heart, "These nations are more numerous than I; how will I be able to drive them out?"

The assurance ¹⁸ Do not fear them! You shall remember what HASHEM, your God, did to Pharaoh and to all of Egypt. ¹⁹ The great tests that your eyes saw, and the signs, the wonders, the strong hand, and the outstretched arm with which HASHEM, your God, took you out — so shall HASHEM, your God, do to all the peoples before whom you fear. ²⁰ Also the hornet-swarm will HASHEM, your God, send among them, until the survivors and hidden ones perish before you. ²¹ You shall not be broken before them, for HASHEM, your God is among you, a great and awesome God.

²² HASHEM, your God, will thrust these nations from before you little by little; * you will not be able to annihilate them quickly, lest the beasts of the field increase against you. ²³ HASHEM, your God, will deliver them before you, and will confound them with great confusion, until their destruction. ²⁴ He will deliver their kings into your hand and you shall cause their name to perish from under the heaven; no man will stand up against you until you have destroyed them. ²⁵ The carved images of their gods you shall burn in the fire; you shall not covet and take for yourself the silver and gold that is on them, lest you be ensnared by it, for it is an abomination of HASHEM, your God. ²⁶ And you shall not bring an abomination into your home and become banned like it; you shall surely loathe it and you shall surely abominate it, for it is banned.

8

The lesson of food ¹ The entire commandment * that I command you today you shall observe to perform, so that you may live and increase, and come and possess the Land that HASHEM swore to your forefathers. ² You shall remember the entire road on which HASHEM, your God, led you these forty years in the

בַּמִּדְבָּ֗ר לְמַ֣עַן עַנֹּֽתְךָ֮ לְנַסֹּֽתְךָ֒ לָדַ֙עַת֙ אֶת־אֲשֶׁ֣ר בִּלְבָֽבְךָ֔ הֲתִשְׁמֹ֥ר מִצְוֺתָ֖ו

ג אִם־לֹֽא: וַיְעַנְּךָ֮ וַיַּרְעִבֶ֒ךָ֒ וַיַּֽאֲכִֽלְךָ֤ אֶת־הַמָּן֙ אֲשֶׁ֣ר לֹֽא־יָדַ֔עְתָּ וְלֹ֥א יָֽדְע֖וּן

אֲבֹתֶ֑יךָ לְמַ֣עַן הוֹדִֽיעֲךָ֗ כִּ֠י לֹ֣א עַל־הַלֶּ֤חֶם לְבַדּוֹ֙ יִֽחְיֶ֣ה הָֽאָדָ֔ם כִּ֛י

ד עַל־כׇּל־מוֹצָ֥א פִֽי־יְהֹוָ֖ה יִֽחְיֶ֣ה הָֽאָדָ֑ם: שִׂמְלָֽתְךָ֗ לֹ֤א בָֽלְתָה֙ מֵֽעָלֶ֔יךָ וְרַגְלְךָ֖

ה לֹ֣א בָצֵ֑קָה זֶ֖ה אַרְבָּעִ֥ים שָׁנָֽה: וְיָֽדַעְתָּ֖ עִם־לְבָבֶ֑ךָ כִּ֗י כַּֽאֲשֶׁ֨ר יְיַסֵּ֥ר אִישׁ֙

אֶת־בְּנ֔וֹ יְהֹוָ֥ה אֱלֹהֶ֖יךָ מְיַסְּרֶֽךָּ: וְשָׁ֣מַרְתָּ֔ אֶת־מִצְוֺ֖ת יְהֹוָ֣ה אֱלֹהֶ֑יךָ לָלֶ֥כֶת

ז בִּדְרָכָ֖יו וּלְיִרְאָ֥ה אֹתֽוֹ: כִּ֚י יְהֹוָ֣ה אֱלֹהֶ֔יךָ מְבִֽיאֲךָ֖ אֶל־אֶ֣רֶץ טוֹבָ֑ה אֶ֚רֶץ

ח נַ֣חֲלֵי מָ֔יִם עֲיָנֹת֙ וּתְהֹמֹ֔ת יֹֽצְאִ֥ים בַּבִּקְעָ֖ה וּבָהָֽר: אֶ֤רֶץ חִטָּה֙ וּשְׂעֹרָ֔ה וְגֶ֥פֶן

ט וּתְאֵנָ֖ה וְרִמּ֑וֹן אֶֽרֶץ־זֵ֥ית שֶׁ֖מֶן וּדְבָֽשׁ: אֶ֗רֶץ אֲשֶׁ֨ר לֹ֤א בְמִסְכֵּנֻת֙ תֹּֽאכַל־בָּ֣הּ

לֶ֔חֶם לֹֽא־תֶחְסַ֥ר כֹּ֖ל בָּ֑הּ אֶ֚רֶץ אֲשֶׁ֣ר אֲבָנֶ֣יהָ בַרְזֶ֔ל וּמֵֽהֲרָרֶ֖יהָ תַּחְצֹ֥ב

י נְחֹֽשֶׁת: וְאָֽכַלְתָּ֖ וְשָׂבָ֑עְתָּ וּבֵֽרַכְתָּ֙ אֶת־יְהֹוָ֣ה אֱלֹהֶ֔יךָ עַל־הָאָ֥רֶץ הַטֹּבָ֖ה

יא אֲשֶׁ֥ר נָֽתַן־לָֽךְ: הִשָּׁ֣מֶר לְךָ֔ פֶּן־תִּשְׁכַּ֖ח אֶת־יְהֹוָ֣ה אֱלֹהֶ֑יךָ לְבִלְתִּ֣י שְׁמֹ֤ר

יב מִצְוֺתָיו֙ וּמִשְׁפָּטָ֣יו וְחֻקֹּתָ֔יו אֲשֶׁ֛ר אָֽנֹכִ֥י מְצַוְּךָ֖ הַיּֽוֹם: פֶּן־תֹּאכַ֖ל וְשָׂבָ֑עְתָּ

יג וּבָתִּ֥ים טֹבִ֛ים תִּבְנֶ֖ה וְיָשָֽׁבְתָּ: וּבְקָֽרְךָ֤ וְצֹֽאנְךָ֙ יִרְבְּיֻ֔ן וְכֶ֥סֶף וְזָהָ֖ב יִרְבֶּה־לָּ֑ךְ

יד וְכֹ֥ל אֲשֶׁר־לְךָ֖ יִרְבֶּֽה: וְרָ֖ם לְבָבֶ֑ךָ וְשָֽׁכַחְתָּ֙ אֶת־יְהֹוָ֣ה אֱלֹהֶ֔יךָ הַמּֽוֹצִֽיאֲךָ֛

טו מֵאֶ֥רֶץ מִצְרַ֖יִם מִבֵּ֣ית עֲבָדִֽים: הַמּוֹלִֽיכֲךָ֗ בַּמִּדְבָּ֣ר ׀ הַגָּדֹ֣ל וְהַנּוֹרָ֗א נָחָ֤שׁ ׀

שָׂרָף֙ וְעַקְרָ֔ב וְצִמָּא֖וֹן אֲשֶׁ֣ר אֵֽין־מָ֑יִם הַמּוֹצִ֤יא לְךָ֙ מַ֔יִם מִצּ֖וּר הַֽחַלָּמִֽישׁ:

טז הַמַּֽאֲכִֽלְךָ֥ מָן֙ בַּמִּדְבָּ֔ר אֲשֶׁ֥ר לֹֽא־יָֽדְע֖וּן אֲבֹתֶ֑יךָ לְמַ֣עַן עַנֹּֽתְךָ֗ וּלְמַ֙עַן֙

יז נַסֹּתֶ֔ךָ לְהֵיטִֽבְךָ֖ בְּאַֽחֲרִיתֶֽךָ: וְאָֽמַרְתָּ֖ בִּלְבָבֶ֑ךָ כֹּחִי֙ וְעֹ֣צֶם יָדִ֔י עָ֥שָׂה לִ֖י

יח אֶת־הַחַ֥יִל הַזֶּֽה: וְזָֽכַרְתָּ֙ אֶת־יְהֹוָ֣ה אֱלֹהֶ֔יךָ כִּ֣י ה֗וּא הַנֹּתֵ֥ן לְךָ֛ כֹּ֖חַ לַֽעֲשׂ֣וֹת

חָ֑יִל לְמַ֨עַן הָקִ֧ים אֶת־בְּרִית֛וֹ אֲשֶׁר־נִשְׁבַּ֥ע לַֽאֲבֹתֶ֖יךָ כַּיּ֥וֹם הַזֶּֽה:

יט וְהָיָ֗ה אִם־שָׁכֹ֤חַ תִּשְׁכַּח֙ אֶת־יְהֹוָ֣ה אֱלֹהֶ֔יךָ וְהָֽלַכְתָּ֗ אַֽחֲרֵי֙ אֱלֹהִ֣ים אֲחֵרִ֔ים

כ וַֽעֲבַדְתָּ֖ם וְהִשְׁתַּֽחֲוִ֣יתָ לָהֶ֑ם הַֽעִדֹ֤תִי בָכֶם֙ הַיּ֔וֹם כִּ֥י אָבֹ֖ד תֹּאבֵדֽוּן: כַּגּוֹיִ֗ם

אֲשֶׁ֤ר יְהֹוָה֙ מַֽאֲבִ֣יד מִפְּנֵיכֶ֔ם כֵּ֖ן תֹּֽאבֵד֑וּן עֵ֚קֶב לֹ֣א תִשְׁמְע֔וּן בְּק֖וֹל יְהֹוָ֥ה

אֱלֹֽהֵיכֶֽם:

א שְׁמַ֣ע יִשְׂרָאֵ֗ל אַתָּ֨ה עֹבֵ֤ר הַיּוֹם֙ אֶת־הַיַּרְדֵּ֔ן לָבֹא֙ לָרֶ֣שֶׁת גּוֹיִ֔ם גְּדֹלִ֥ים

ב וַֽעֲצֻמִ֖ים מִמֶּ֑ךָּ עָרִ֛ים גְּדֹלֹ֥ת וּבְצֻרֹ֖ת בַּשָּׁמָֽיִם: עַם־גָּד֥וֹל וָרָ֖ם בְּנֵ֥י עֲנָקִ֑ים

ג אֲשֶׁ֨ר אַתָּ֤ה יָדַ֙עְתָּ֙ וְאַתָּ֣ה שָׁמַ֔עְתָּ מִ֣י יִתְיַצֵּ֔ב לִפְנֵ֖י בְּנֵ֣י עֲנָ֑ק: וְיָֽדַעְתָּ֣ הַיּ֗וֹם כִּי֩

יְהֹוָ֨ה אֱלֹהֶ֜יךָ הֽוּא־הָֽעֹבֵ֤ר לְפָנֶ֙יךָ֙ אֵ֣שׁ אֹֽכְלָ֔ה ה֧וּא יַשְׁמִידֵ֛ם וְה֥וּא יַכְנִיעֵ֖ם

ד לְפָנֶ֑יךָ וְהֽוֹרַשְׁתָּ֤ם וְהַֽאֲבַדְתָּם֙ מַהֵ֔ר כַּֽאֲשֶׁ֛ר דִּבֶּ֥ר יְהֹוָ֖ה לָֽךְ: אַל־תֹּאמַ֣ר

בִּלְבָֽבְךָ֗ בַּֽהֲדֹ֣ף יְהֹוָה֩ אֱלֹהֶ֨יךָ אֹתָ֥ם ׀ מִלְּפָנֶ֘יךָ֘ לֵאמֹר֒ בְּצִדְקָתִי֙ הֱבִיאַ֣נִי

יְהֹוָ֔ה לָרֶ֖שֶׁת אֶת־הָאָ֣רֶץ הַזֹּ֑את וּבְרִשְׁעַת֙ הַגּוֹיִ֣ם הָאֵ֔לֶּה יְהֹוָ֖ה מֽוֹרִישָׁ֥ם

8:8. This verse lists the seven foods for which the Land was praised.

8:10. *And bless,* i.e., recite the Grace After Meals.

Wilderness so as to afflict you, to test you, to know what is in your heart, whether you would observe His commandments or not. ³ *He afflicted you and let you hunger, then He fed you the manna that you did not know, nor did your forefathers know, in order to make you know that not by bread alone does man live, rather by everything that emanates from the mouth of God does man live.* ⁴ *Your garment did not wear out upon you and your feet did not swell, these forty years.* ⁵ *You should know in your heart that just as a father will chastise his son, so* HASHEM, *your God, chastises you.* ⁶ *You shall observe the commandments of* HASHEM, *your God, to go in His ways and fear Him.* ⁷ *For* HASHEM, *your God, is bringing you to a good Land: a Land with streams of water, of springs and underground water coming forth in valley and mountain;* ⁸ *a Land of wheat, barley, grape, fig, and pomegranate; a Land of oil-olives and date-honey;* * ⁹ *a Land where you will eat bread without poverty — you will lack nothing there; a Land whose stones are iron and from whose mountains you will mine copper.* ¹⁰ *You will eat and you will be satisfied, and bless* * HASHEM, *your God, for the good Land that He gave you.*

A warning against the lure of prosperity

¹¹ *Take care lest you forget* HASHEM, *your God, by not observing His commandments, His ordinances, and His decrees, which I command you today,* ¹² *lest you eat and be satisfied, and you build good houses and settle,* ¹³ *and your cattle and sheep and goats increase, and you increase silver and gold for yourselves, and everything that you have will increase —* ¹⁴ *and your heart will become haughty and you will forget* HASHEM, *your God, Who took you out of the land of Egypt from the house of slavery,* ¹⁵ *Who leads you through the great and awesome Wilderness — of snake, fiery serpent, and scorpion, and thirst where there was no water — Who brings forth water for you from the rock of flint,* ¹⁶ *Who feeds you manna in the Wilderness, which your forefathers knew not, in order to afflict you and in order to test you, to do good for you in your end.* ¹⁷ *And you may say in your heart, "My strength and the might of my hand made me all this wealth!"* ¹⁸ *Then you shall remember* HASHEM, *your God: that it is He Who gives you strength to make wealth, in order to establish His covenant that He swore to your forefathers, as this day.*

¹⁹ *It shall be that if you forget* HASHEM, *your God, and go after the gods of others, and worship them and prostrate yourself to them — I testify against you today that you will surely perish,* ²⁰ *like the nations that* HASHEM *causes to perish before you, so will you perish because you will not have hearkened to the voice of* HASHEM, *your God.*

9

Remembering the Exodus and the tribulations in the Wilderness

¹ **H**ear, O Israel, today you cross the Jordan, to come and drive out nations *that are greater and mightier than you, cities that are great and fortified up to the heavens,* ² *a great and lofty people, children of giants, that you knew and of whom you have heard, "Who can stand up against the children of the giant?"* ³ *But you know today that* HASHEM, *your God — He crosses before you, a consuming fire; He will destroy them and He will subjugate them before you; you will drive them out and cause them to perish quickly, as* HASHEM *spoke to you.*

⁴ *Do not say in your heart, when* HASHEM *pushes them away from before you, saying, "Because of my righteousness did* HASHEM *bring me to possess this Land and because of the wickedness of these nations did* HASHEM *drive them*

ה מִפָּנֶיךָ: לֹא בְצִדְקָתְךָ וּבְיֹשֶׁר לְבָבְךָ אַתָּה בָא לָרֶשֶׁת אֶת־אַרְצָם כִּי
בְּרִשְׁעַת ׀ הַגּוֹיִם הָאֵלֶּה יהוה אֱלֹהֶיךָ מוֹרִישָׁם מִפָּנֶיךָ וּלְמַעַן הָקִים
ו אֶת־הַדָּבָר אֲשֶׁר נִשְׁבַּע יהוה לַאֲבֹתֶיךָ לְאַבְרָהָם לְיִצְחָק וּלְיַעֲקֹב: וְיָדַעְתָּ
כִּי לֹא בְצִדְקָתְךָ יהוה אֱלֹהֶיךָ נֹתֵן לְךָ אֶת־הָאָרֶץ הַטּוֹבָה הַזֹּאת לְרִשְׁתָּהּ
ז כִּי עַם־קְשֵׁה־עֹרֶף אָתָּה: זְכֹר אַל־תִּשְׁכַּח אֵת אֲשֶׁר־הִקְצַפְתָּ אֶת־יהוה
אֱלֹהֶיךָ בַּמִּדְבָּר לְמִן־הַיּוֹם אֲשֶׁר־יָצָאתָ ׀ מֵאֶרֶץ מִצְרַיִם עַד־בֹּאֲכֶם
ח עַד־הַמָּקוֹם הַזֶּה מַמְרִים הֱיִיתֶם עִם־יהוה: וּבְחֹרֵב הִקְצַפְתֶּם אֶת־יהוה
ט וַיִּתְאַנַּף יהוה בָּכֶם לְהַשְׁמִיד אֶתְכֶם: בַּעֲלֹתִי הָהָרָה לָקַחַת לוּחֹת הָאֲבָנִים
לוּחֹת הַבְּרִית אֲשֶׁר־כָּרַת יהוה עִמָּכֶם וָאֵשֵׁב בָּהָר אַרְבָּעִים יוֹם
י וְאַרְבָּעִים לַיְלָה לֶחֶם לֹא אָכַלְתִּי וּמַיִם לֹא שָׁתִיתִי: וַיִּתֵּן יהוה אֵלַי
אֶת־שְׁנֵי לוּחֹת הָאֲבָנִים כְּתֻבִים בְּאֶצְבַּע אֱלֹהִים וַעֲלֵיהֶם כְּכָל־הַדְּבָרִים
יא אֲשֶׁר דִּבֶּר יהוה עִמָּכֶם בָּהָר מִתּוֹךְ הָאֵשׁ בְּיוֹם הַקָּהָל: וַיְהִי מִקֵּץ אַרְבָּעִים
יוֹם וְאַרְבָּעִים לָיְלָה נָתַן יהוה אֵלַי אֶת־שְׁנֵי לֻחֹת הָאֲבָנִים לֻחוֹת הַבְּרִית:
יב וַיֹּאמֶר יהוה אֵלַי קוּם רֵד מַהֵר מִזֶּה כִּי שִׁחֵת עַמְּךָ אֲשֶׁר הוֹצֵאתָ מִמִּצְרָיִם
יג סָרוּ מַהֵר מִן־הַדֶּרֶךְ אֲשֶׁר צִוִּיתִם עָשׂוּ לָהֶם מַסֵּכָה: וַיֹּאמֶר יהוה אֵלַי
יד לֵאמֹר רָאִיתִי אֶת־הָעָם הַזֶּה וְהִנֵּה עַם־קְשֵׁה־עֹרֶף הוּא: הֶרֶף מִמֶּנִּי
וְאַשְׁמִידֵם וְאֶמְחֶה אֶת־שְׁמָם מִתַּחַת הַשָּׁמָיִם וְאֶעֱשֶׂה אוֹתְךָ לְגוֹי־עָצוּם
טו וָרָב מִמֶּנּוּ: וָאֵפֶן וָאֵרֵד מִן־הָהָר וְהָהָר בֹּעֵר בָּאֵשׁ וּשְׁנֵי לוּחֹת הַבְּרִית עַל
טז שְׁתֵּי יָדָי: וָאֵרֶא וְהִנֵּה חֲטָאתֶם לַיהוה אֱלֹהֵיכֶם עֲשִׂיתֶם לָכֶם עֵגֶל מַסֵּכָה
יז סַרְתֶּם מַהֵר מִן־הַדֶּרֶךְ אֲשֶׁר צִוָּה יהוה אֶתְכֶם: וָאֶתְפֹּשׂ בִּשְׁנֵי הַלֻּחֹת
יח וָאַשְׁלִכֵם מֵעַל שְׁתֵּי יָדָי וָאֲשַׁבְּרֵם לְעֵינֵיכֶם: וָאֶתְנַפַּל לִפְנֵי יהוה כָּרִאשֹׁנָה
אַרְבָּעִים יוֹם וְאַרְבָּעִים לַיְלָה לֶחֶם לֹא אָכַלְתִּי וּמַיִם לֹא שָׁתִיתִי עַל
יט כָּל־חַטַּאתְכֶם אֲשֶׁר חֲטָאתֶם לַעֲשׂוֹת הָרַע בְּעֵינֵי יהוה לְהַכְעִיסוֹ: כִּי
יָגֹרְתִּי מִפְּנֵי הָאַף וְהַחֵמָה אֲשֶׁר קָצַף יהוה עֲלֵיכֶם לְהַשְׁמִיד אֶתְכֶם וַיִּשְׁמַע
כ יהוה אֵלַי גַּם בַּפַּעַם הַהִוא: וּבְאַהֲרֹן הִתְאַנַּף יהוה מְאֹד לְהַשְׁמִידוֹ
כא וָאֶתְפַּלֵּל גַּם־בְּעַד אַהֲרֹן בָּעֵת הַהִוא: וְאֶת־חַטַּאתְכֶם אֲשֶׁר־עֲשִׂיתֶם
אֶת־הָעֵגֶל לָקַחְתִּי וָאֶשְׂרֹף אֹתוֹ ׀ בָּאֵשׁ וָאֶכֹּת אֹתוֹ טָחוֹן הֵיטֵב עַד
כב אֲשֶׁר־דַּק לְעָפָר וָאַשְׁלִךְ אֶת־עֲפָרוֹ אֶל־הַנַּחַל הַיֹּרֵד מִן־הָהָר: וּבְתַבְעֵרָה
כג וּבְמַסָּה וּבְקִבְרֹת הַתַּאֲוָה מַקְצִפִים הֱיִיתֶם אֶת־יהוה: וּבִשְׁלֹחַ יהוה אֶתְכֶם
מִקָּדֵשׁ בַּרְנֵעַ לֵאמֹר עֲלוּ וּרְשׁוּ אֶת־הָאָרֶץ אֲשֶׁר נָתַתִּי לָכֶם וַתַּמְרוּ אֶת־פִּי
כד יהוה אֱלֹהֵיכֶם וְלֹא הֶאֱמַנְתֶּם לוֹ וְלֹא שְׁמַעְתֶּם בְּקֹלוֹ: מַמְרִים הֱיִיתֶם
כה עִם־יהוה מִיּוֹם דַּעְתִּי אֶתְכֶם: וָאֶתְנַפַּל לִפְנֵי יהוה אֵת אַרְבָּעִים הַיּוֹם
וְאֶת־אַרְבָּעִים הַלַּיְלָה אֲשֶׁר הִתְנַפָּלְתִּי כִּי־אָמַר יהוה לְהַשְׁמִיד אֶתְכֶם:

9:7-29. Moses listed some of their sins in order to caution them not to take their responsibilities lightly.

away from before you." ⁵ Not because of your righteousness and the uprightness of your heart are you coming to possess their Land, but because of the wickedness of these nations does HASHEM, your God, drive them away from before you, and in order to establish the word that HASHEM swore to your forefathers, to Abraham, to Isaac, and to Jacob. ⁶ And you should know that not because of your righteousness does HASHEM, your God, give you this good Land to possess it, for you are a stiff-necked people.

Receiving the Tablets ⁷ Remember, do not forget, that you provoked HASHEM, * your God, in the Wilderness; from the day you left the land of Egypt until your arrival at this place, you have been rebels against HASHEM. ⁸ And in Horeb you provoked HASHEM, and HASHEM became angry with you to destroy you. ⁹ When I ascended the mountain to receive the Tablets of stone, the Tablets of the covenant that HASHEM sealed with you, and I remained on the mountain for forty days and forty nights; bread I did not eat, and water I did not drink. ¹⁰ And HASHEM gave me the two stone Tablets, inscribed with the finger of HASHEM, and on them were all the words that HASHEM spoke with you on the mountain from the midst of the fire, on the day of the congregation.

¹¹ It was at the end of forty days and forty nights that HASHEM gave me the two stone Tablets, the Tablets of the covenant. ¹² Then HASHEM said to me, "Arise, descend quickly from here, for your people that you took out of Egypt has become corrupt; they have strayed quickly from the way that I commanded them; they have made themselves a molten image."

A stiff-necked people ¹³ HASHEM said to me, saying, "I have seen this people, and behold! it is a stiff-necked people. ¹⁴ Release Me, and I shall destroy them and erase their name from under the heavens, and I shall make you a mightier, more numerous nation than they!" ¹⁵ So I turned and descended from the mountain as the mountain was burning in fire, and the two Tablets of the covenant were in my two hands.

¹⁶ Then I saw and behold! you had sinned to HASHEM, your God; you made yourselves a molten calf; you strayed quickly from the way that HASHEM commanded you. ¹⁷ I grasped the two Tablets and threw them from my two hands, and I smashed them before your eyes. ¹⁸ Then I threw myself down before HASHEM as the first time — forty days and forty nights — bread I did not eat and water I did not drink, because of your entire sin that you committed, to do that which is evil in the eyes of HASHEM, to anger Him, ¹⁹ for I was terrified of the wrath and blazing anger with which HASHEM had been provoked against you to destroy you; and HASHEM hearkened to me that time, as well. ²⁰ HASHEM became very angry with Aaron to destroy him, so I prayed also for Aaron at that time. ²¹ Your sin that you committed — the calf — I took and burned it in fire, and I pounded it, grinding it well, until it was fine as dust, and I threw its dust into the brook that descended from the mountain.

Repeated rebelliousness ²² And in Taberah, in Massah, and in Kibroth-hattaavah you were provoking HASHEM, ²³ and when HASHEM sent you from Kadesh-barnea, saying, "Go up and possess the Land that I gave you" — then you rebelled against the word of HASHEM, your God; you did not believe Him and you did not hearken to His voice. ²⁴ You have been rebels against HASHEM from the day that I knew you! ²⁵ I threw myself down before HASHEM for the forty days and the forty nights that I threw myself down, for HASHEM had intended to destroy you.

כו וָאֶתְפַּלֵּל אֶל־יְהוָה וָאֹמַר אֲדֹנָי יֱהֹוִה אַל־תַּשְׁחֵת עַמְּךָ וְנַחֲלָתְךָ אֲשֶׁר

כז פָּדִיתָ בְּגָדְלֶךָ אֲשֶׁר־הוֹצֵאתָ מִמִּצְרַיִם בְּיָד חֲזָקָה: זְכֹר לַעֲבָדֶיךָ לְאַבְרָהָם

לְיִצְחָק וּלְיַעֲקֹב אַל־תֵּפֶן אֶל־קְשִׁי הָעָם הַזֶּה וְאֶל־רִשְׁעוֹ וְאֶל־חַטָּאתוֹ:

כח פֶּן־יֹאמְרוּ הָאָרֶץ אֲשֶׁר הוֹצֵאתָנוּ מִשָּׁם מִבְּלִי יְכֹלֶת יְהוָה לַהֲבִיאָם אֶל־

כט הָאָרֶץ אֲשֶׁר־דִּבֶּר לָהֶם וּמִשִּׂנְאָתוֹ אוֹתָם הוֹצִיאָם לַהֲמִתָם בַּמִּדְבָּר: וְהֵם

עַמְּךָ וְנַחֲלָתֶךָ אֲשֶׁר הוֹצֵאתָ בְּכֹחֲךָ הַגָּדֹל וּבִזְרֹעֲךָ הַנְּטוּיָה:

רביעי   י א בָּעֵת הַהִוא אָמַר יְהוָה אֵלַי פְּסָל־לְךָ שְׁנֵי־לוּחֹת אֲבָנִים כָּרִאשֹׁנִים וַעֲלֵה

ב אֵלַי הָהָרָה וְעָשִׂיתָ לְּךָ אֲרוֹן עֵץ: וְאֶכְתֹּב עַל־הַלֻּחֹת אֶת־הַדְּבָרִים אֲשֶׁר

ג הָיוּ עַל־הַלֻּחֹת הָרִאשֹׁנִים אֲשֶׁר שִׁבַּרְתָּ וְשַׂמְתָּם בָּאָרוֹן: וָאַעַשׂ אֲרוֹן עֲצֵי

שִׁטִּים וָאֶפְסֹל שְׁנֵי־לֻחֹת אֲבָנִים כָּרִאשֹׁנִים וָאַעַל הָהָרָה וּשְׁנֵי הַלֻּחֹת בְּיָדִי:

ד וַיִּכְתֹּב עַל־הַלֻּחֹת כַּמִּכְתָּב הָרִאשׁוֹן אֵת עֲשֶׂרֶת הַדְּבָרִים אֲשֶׁר דִּבֶּר יְהוָה

אֲלֵיכֶם בָּהָר מִתּוֹךְ הָאֵשׁ בְּיוֹם הַקָּהָל וַיִּתְּנֵם יְהוָה אֵלָי: וָאֵפֶן וָאֵרֵד

ה מִן־הָהָר וָאָשִׂם אֶת־הַלֻּחֹת בָּאָרוֹן אֲשֶׁר עָשִׂיתִי וַיִּהְיוּ שָׁם כַּאֲשֶׁר צִוַּנִי

ו יְהוָה: וּבְנֵי יִשְׂרָאֵל נָסְעוּ מִבְּאֵרֹת בְּנֵי־יַעֲקָן מוֹסֵרָה שָׁם מֵת אַהֲרֹן וַיִּקָּבֵר

ז שָׁם וַיְכַהֵן אֶלְעָזָר בְּנוֹ תַּחְתָּיו: מִשָּׁם נָסְעוּ הַגֻּדְגֹּדָה וּמִן־הַגֻּדְגֹּדָה יָטְבָתָה

ח אֶרֶץ נַחֲלֵי מָיִם: בָּעֵת הַהִוא הִבְדִּיל יְהוָה אֶת־שֵׁבֶט הַלֵּוִי לָשֵׂאת

אֶת־אֲרוֹן בְּרִית־יְהוָה לַעֲמֹד לִפְנֵי יְהוָה לְשָׁרְתוֹ וּלְבָרֵךְ בִּשְׁמוֹ עַד הַיּוֹם

ט הַזֶּה: עַל־כֵּן לֹא־הָיָה לְלֵוִי חֵלֶק וְנַחֲלָה עִם־אֶחָיו יְהוָה הוּא נַחֲלָתוֹ

י כַּאֲשֶׁר דִּבֶּר יְהוָה אֱלֹהֶיךָ לוֹ: וְאָנֹכִי עָמַדְתִּי בָהָר כַּיָּמִים הָרִאשֹׁנִים

אַרְבָּעִים יוֹם וְאַרְבָּעִים לָיְלָה וַיִּשְׁמַע יְהוָה אֵלַי גַּם בַּפַּעַם הַהִוא לֹא־אָבָה

יא יְהוָה הַשְׁחִיתֶךָ: וַיֹּאמֶר יְהוָה אֵלַי קוּם לֵךְ לְמַסַּע לִפְנֵי הָעָם וְיָבֹאוּ וְיִירְשׁוּ

אֶת־הָאָרֶץ אֲשֶׁר־נִשְׁבַּעְתִּי לַאֲבֹתָם לָתֵת לָהֶם:

חמישי   יב וְעַתָּה יִשְׂרָאֵל מָה יְהוָה אֱלֹהֶיךָ שֹׁאֵל מֵעִמָּךְ כִּי אִם־לְיִרְאָה אֶת־יְהוָה

אֱלֹהֶיךָ לָלֶכֶת בְּכָל־דְּרָכָיו וּלְאַהֲבָה אֹתוֹ וְלַעֲבֹד אֶת־יְהוָה אֱלֹהֶיךָ

יג בְּכָל־לְבָבְךָ וּבְכָל־נַפְשֶׁךָ: לִשְׁמֹר אֶת־מִצְוֹת יְהוָה וְאֶת־חֻקֹּתָיו אֲשֶׁר אָנֹכִי

יד מְצַוְּךָ הַיּוֹם לְטוֹב לָךְ: הֵן לַיהוָה אֱלֹהֶיךָ הַשָּׁמַיִם וּשְׁמֵי הַשָּׁמָיִם הָאָרֶץ

טו וְכָל־אֲשֶׁר־בָּהּ: רַק בַּאֲבֹתֶיךָ חָשַׁק יְהוָה לְאַהֲבָה אוֹתָם וַיִּבְחַר בְּזַרְעָם

טז אַחֲרֵיהֶם בָּכֶם מִכָּל־הָעַמִּים כַּיּוֹם הַזֶּה: וּמַלְתֶּם אֵת עָרְלַת לְבַבְכֶם

יז וְעָרְפְּכֶם לֹא תַקְשׁוּ עוֹד: כִּי יְהוָה אֱלֹהֵיכֶם הוּא אֱלֹהֵי הָאֱלֹהִים וַאֲדֹנֵי

הָאֲדֹנִים הָאֵל הַגָּדֹל הַגִּבֹּר וְהַנּוֹרָא אֲשֶׁר לֹא־יִשָּׂא

יח פָנִים וְלֹא יִקַּח שֹׁחַד: עֹשֶׂה מִשְׁפַּט יָתוֹם וְאַלְמָנָה וְאֹהֵב גֵּר לָתֶת

יט לוֹ לֶחֶם וְשִׂמְלָה: וַאֲהַבְתֶּם אֶת־הַגֵּר כִּי־גֵרִים הֱיִיתֶם בְּאֶרֶץ מִצְרָיִם:

10:8-9. The Levites deserve to be God's legion because they remained loyal to God and Moses (*Exodus* 32:26).

10:17. *Who does not show favor*, i.e., the greater a person's status and opportunities to do good, the more demanding God is of him.

²⁶ I prayed to HASHEM and said, "My Lord, HASHEM/ELOHIM, do not destroy Your people and Your heritage that You redeemed in Your greatness, that You took out of Egypt with a strong hand. ²⁷ Remember for the sake of Your servants, for Abraham, for Isaac, and for Jacob; do not turn to the stubbornness of this people, and to its wickedness and to its sin, ²⁸ lest the land from which You took us out will say, 'For lack of HASHEM's ability to bring them to the Land of which He spoke to them, and because of His hatred of them did He take them out to let them die in the Wilderness.' ²⁹ Yet they are Your people and Your heritage, whom You took out with Your great strength and Your outstretched arm."

10

¹ At that time HASHEM said to me, "Carve for yourself two stone Tablets like the first ones, and ascend to Me to the mountain, and make a wooden Ark for yourself. ² And I shall inscribe on the Tablets the words that were on the first Tablets that you smashed, and you shall place them in the Ark."

A temporary Ark and the second Tablets

³ So I made an Ark of cedarwood and I carved out two stone Tablets like the first ones; then I ascended the mountain with the two Tablets in my hand. ⁴ He inscribed on the Tablets according to the first script, the Ten Statements that HASHEM spoke to you on the mountain from the midst of the fire, on the day of the congregation, and HASHEM gave them to me. ⁵ I turned and descended from the mountain, and I placed the Tablets in the Ark that I had made, and they remained there as HASHEM had commanded me.

Aaron's death

⁶ The Children of Israel journeyed from Beeroth-bene-jaakan to Moserah; there Aaron died and he was buried there, and Elazar his son ministered in his place. ⁷ From there they journeyed to Gudgod, and from Gudgod to Jotbah, a land of brooks of water. ⁸ At that time, HASHEM set apart the tribe of Levi* to carry the Ark of the covenant of HASHEM, to stand before HASHEM to minister to Him and to bless in His Name until this day. ⁹ Therefore, Levi did not have a share and a heritage with his brethren; HASHEM is his heritage, as HASHEM, your God, had spoken of him.

Elevation of the Levites

¹⁰ I remained on the mountain as on the first days — forty days and forty nights — and HASHEM listened to me this time, as well, and HASHEM did not wish to destroy you. ¹¹ HASHEM said to me, "Arise, go on the journey before the people; let them come and possess the Land that I swore to their forefathers to give them."

God's reconciliation

¹² Now, O Israel, what does HASHEM, your God, ask of you? Only to fear HASHEM, your God, to go in all His ways and to love Him, and to serve HASHEM, your God, with all your heart and with all your soul, ¹³ to observe the commandments of HASHEM and His decrees, which I command you today, for your benefit. ¹⁴ Behold! To HASHEM, your God, are the heaven and highest heaven, the earth and everything that is in it. ¹⁵ Only your forefathers did HASHEM cherish to love them, and He chose their offspring after them — you — from among all the peoples, as this day. ¹⁶ You shall cut away the barrier of your heart and no longer stiffen your neck. ¹⁷ For HASHEM, your God — He is the God of the powers and the Lord of the lords, the great, mighty, and awesome God, Who does not show favor* and Who does not accept a bribe. ¹⁸ He carries out the judgment of orphan and widow, and loves the proselyte to give him bread and garment. ¹⁹ You shall love the proselyte for you were strangers in the land of Egypt.

כ־כא אֶת־יהוֹה אֱלֹהֶיךָ תִּירָא אֹתוֹ תַעֲבֹד וּבוֹ תִדְבָּק וּבִשְׁמוֹ תִּשָּׁבֵעַ: הוּא תְהִלָּתְךָ וְהוּא אֱלֹהֶיךָ אֲשֶׁר־עָשָׂה אִתְּךָ אֶת־הַגְּדֹלֹת וְאֶת־הַנּוֹרָאֹת

כב הָאֵלֶּה אֲשֶׁר רָאוּ עֵינֶיךָ: בְּשִׁבְעִים נֶפֶשׁ יָרְדוּ אֲבֹתֶיךָ מִצְרָיְמָה וְעַתָּה

א שָׂמְךָ יהוֹה אֱלֹהֶיךָ כְּכוֹכְבֵי הַשָּׁמַיִם לָרֹב: וְאָהַבְתָּ אֵת יהוֹה אֱלֹהֶיךָ יא

ב וְשָׁמַרְתָּ מִשְׁמַרְתּוֹ וְחֻקֹּתָיו וּמִשְׁפָּטָיו וּמִצְוֹתָיו כָּל־הַיָּמִים: וִידַעְתֶּם הַיּוֹם כִּי | לֹא אֶת־בְּנֵיכֶם אֲשֶׁר לֹא־יָדְעוּ וַאֲשֶׁר לֹא־רָאוּ אֶת־מוּסַר יהוֹה

ג אֱלֹהֵיכֶם אֶת־גָּדְלוֹ אֶת־יָדוֹ הַחֲזָקָה וּזְרֹעוֹ הַנְּטוּיָה: וְאֶת־אֹתֹתָיו וְאֶת־מַעֲשָׂיו אֲשֶׁר עָשָׂה בְּתוֹךְ מִצְרָיִם לְפַרְעֹה מֶלֶךְ־מִצְרַיִם וּלְכָל־

ד אַרְצוֹ: וַאֲשֶׁר עָשָׂה לְחֵיל מִצְרַיִם לְסוּסָיו וּלְרִכְבּוֹ אֲשֶׁר הֵצִיף אֶת־מֵי־

ה יַם־סוּף עַל־פְּנֵיהֶם בְּרָדְפָם אַחֲרֵיכֶם וַיְאַבְּדֵם יהוֹה עַד הַיּוֹם הַזֶּה: וַאֲשֶׁר

ו עָשָׂה לָכֶם בַּמִּדְבָּר עַד־בֹּאֲכֶם עַד־הַמָּקוֹם הַזֶּה: וַאֲשֶׁר עָשָׂה לְדָתָן וְלַאֲבִירָם בְּנֵי אֱלִיאָב בֶּן־רְאוּבֵן אֲשֶׁר פָּצְתָה הָאָרֶץ אֶת־פִּיהָ וַתִּבְלָעֵם וְאֶת־בָּתֵּיהֶם וְאֶת־אָהֳלֵיהֶם וְאֵת כָּל־הַיְקוּם אֲשֶׁר בְּרַגְלֵיהֶם בְּקֶרֶב

ז כָּל־יִשְׂרָאֵל: כִּי עֵינֵיכֶם הָרֹאֹת אֵת כָּל־מַעֲשֵׂה יהוֹה הַגָּדֹל אֲשֶׁר עָשָׂה:

ח וּשְׁמַרְתֶּם אֶת־כָּל־הַמִּצְוָה אֲשֶׁר אָנֹכִי מְצַוְּךָ הַיּוֹם לְמַעַן תֶּחֶזְקוּ וּבָאתֶם

ט וִירִשְׁתֶּם אֶת־הָאָרֶץ אֲשֶׁר אַתֶּם עֹבְרִים שָׁמָּה לְרִשְׁתָּהּ: וּלְמַעַן תַּאֲרִיכוּ יָמִים עַל־הָאֲדָמָה אֲשֶׁר נִשְׁבַּע יהוֹה לַאֲבֹתֵיכֶם לָתֵת לָהֶם וּלְזַרְעָם אֶרֶץ

י זָבַת חָלָב וּדְבָשׁ: כִּי הָאָרֶץ אֲשֶׁר אַתָּה בָא־שָׁמָּה ששי

לְרִשְׁתָּהּ לֹא כְאֶרֶץ מִצְרַיִם הִוא אֲשֶׁר יְצָאתֶם מִשָּׁם אֲשֶׁר תִּזְרַע

יא אֶת־זַרְעֲךָ וְהִשְׁקִיתָ בְרַגְלְךָ כְּגַן הַיָּרָק: וְהָאָרֶץ אֲשֶׁר אַתֶּם עֹבְרִים שָׁמָּה

יב לְרִשְׁתָּהּ אֶרֶץ הָרִים וּבְקָעֹת לִמְטַר הַשָּׁמַיִם תִּשְׁתֶּה־מָּיִם: אֶרֶץ אֲשֶׁר־ יהוֹה אֱלֹהֶיךָ דֹּרֵשׁ אֹתָהּ תָּמִיד עֵינֵי יהוֹה אֱלֹהֶיךָ בָּהּ מֵרֵשִׁית הַשָּׁנָה וְעַד

יג אַחֲרִית שָׁנָה: וְהָיָה אִם־שָׁמֹעַ תִּשְׁמְעוּ אֶל־מִצְוֹתַי אֲשֶׁר אָנֹכִי מְצַוֶּה אֶתְכֶם הַיּוֹם לְאַהֲבָה אֶת־יהוֹה אֱלֹהֵיכֶם וּלְעָבְדוֹ

יד בְּכָל־לְבַבְכֶם וּבְכָל־נַפְשְׁכֶם: וְנָתַתִּי מְטַר־אַרְצְכֶם בְּעִתּוֹ יוֹרֶה וּמַלְקוֹשׁ

טו וְאָסַפְתָּ דְגָנֶךָ וְתִירֹשְׁךָ וְיִצְהָרֶךָ: וְנָתַתִּי עֵשֶׂב בְּשָׂדְךָ לִבְהֶמְתֶּךָ וְאָכַלְתָּ

טז וְשָׂבָעְתָּ: הִשָּׁמְרוּ לָכֶם פֶּן־יִפְתֶּה לְבַבְכֶם וְסַרְתֶּם וַעֲבַדְתֶּם אֱלֹהִים

יז אֲחֵרִים וְהִשְׁתַּחֲוִיתֶם לָהֶם: וְחָרָה אַף־יהוֹה בָּכֶם וְעָצַר אֶת־הַשָּׁמַיִם וְלֹא־יִהְיֶה מָטָר וְהָאֲדָמָה לֹא תִתֵּן אֶת־יְבוּלָהּ וַאֲבַדְתֶּם מְהֵרָה מֵעַל

יח הָאָרֶץ הַטֹּבָה אֲשֶׁר יהוֹה נֹתֵן לָכֶם: וְשַׂמְתֶּם אֶת־דְּבָרַי אֵלֶּה עַל־לְבַבְכֶם וְעַל־נַפְשְׁכֶם וּקְשַׁרְתֶּם אֹתָם לְאוֹת עַל־יֶדְכֶם וְהָיוּ לְטוֹטָפֹת בֵּין עֵינֵיכֶם:

11:1-7. Moses continued to exhort his people, telling them that they had a special responsibility to be loyal to God, because they had experienced His greatness and mercy firsthand.

11:12. God's principal attention is focused on *Eretz Yisrael;* only afterwards does He bless the rest of the world (*Rashi*).

11:13-21. These verse are recited daily as the second

²⁰ HASHEM, your God, shall you fear, Him shall you serve, to Him shall you cleave, and in His Name shall you swear. ²¹ He is your praise and He is your God, Who did for you these great and awesome things that your eyes saw. ²² With seventy souls did your ancestors descend to Egypt, and now HASHEM, your God, has made you like the stars of heaven for abundance.

11

Firsthand knowledge of God's miracles

¹ **Y**ou shall love HASHEM, your God, and you shall safeguard His charge, His decrees, His ordinances, and His commandments, all the days. ² You should know today that it is not your children who did not know and who did not see the chastisement of HASHEM, your God, His greatness, His strong hand, and His outstretched arm; ³ His signs and His deeds that He performed in the midst of Egypt, to Pharaoh, king of Egypt, and to all his land; ⁴ and what He did to the army of Egypt, to its horses and its chariots, over whom He swept the waters of the Sea of Reeds when they pursued you, and HASHEM caused them to perish until this day; ⁵ and what He did for you in the Wilderness, until you came to this place; ⁶ and what He did to Dathan and Abiram the sons of Eliab son of Reuben, when the earth opened its mouth wide and swallowed them, and their households, and their tents, and all the fortunes at their feet, in the midst of all Israel. ⁷ Rather it is your own eyes that see all the great work of HASHEM, which He did.

⁸ So you shall observe the entire commandment that I command you today, so that you will be strong, and you will come and possess the Land to which you are crossing, to possess it, ⁹ and so that you will prolong your days on the Land that HASHEM swore to your forefathers to give them and to their offspring — a land flowing with milk and honey.

The great virtues of the Land

¹⁰ For the Land to which you come, to possess it — it is not like the land of Egypt that you left, where you would plant your seed and water it on foot like a vegetable garden. ¹¹ But the Land to which you cross over to possess it is a Land of mountains and valleys; from the rain of heaven it drinks water; ¹² a Land that HASHEM, your God, seeks out; the eyes of HASHEM, your God, are always upon it, from the beginning of the year to year's end. *

*The second portion of the Shema **

¹³ It will be that if you hearken to My commandments that I command you today, to love* HASHEM, your God, and to serve Him with all your heart and with all your soul, ¹⁴ then I shall provide rain for your Land in its proper time, the early and the late rains, that you may gather in your grain, your wine, and your oil. ¹⁵ I shall provide grass in your field for your cattle and you will eat and you will be satisfied. ¹⁶ Beware for yourselves, * lest your heart be seduced and you turn astray and serve gods of others and prostrate yourselves to them. ¹⁷ Then the wrath of HASHEM will blaze against you; He will restrain the heaven so there will be no rain, and the ground will not yield its produce; and you will be swiftly banished from the goodly Land that HASHEM gives you. ¹⁸ You shall place these words of Mine upon your heart and upon your soul; you shall bind them for a sign upon your arm and let them be an ornament between your eyes.

---

portion of the *Shema*. They contain the acceptance of God's sovereignty, which is characterized by the Sages as קַבָּלַת עֹל הַמִּצְוֹת, *acceptance of the yoke of the commandments* (*Berachos* 13a).

11:13. *To love,* i.e., perform the commandments purely out of love, and the honor will come ultimately (*Rashi*).
11:16. People who are rich in wealth but poor in sophistication often succumb to temptation.

יט וְלִמַּדְתֶּ֥ם אֹתָ֛ם אֶת־בְּנֵיכֶ֖ם לְדַבֵּ֣ר בָּ֑ם בְּשִׁבְתְּךָ֤ בְּבֵיתֶ֙ךָ֙ וּבְלֶכְתְּךָ֣ בַדֶּ֔רֶךְ

כ־כא וּֽבְשָׁכְבְּךָ֖ וּבְקוּמֶֽךָ׃ וּכְתַבְתָּ֛ם עַל־מְזוּזֹ֥ות בֵּיתֶ֖ךָ וּבִשְׁעָרֶֽיךָ׃ לְמַ֨עַן יִרְבּ֤וּ יְמֵיכֶם֙ וִימֵ֣י בְנֵיכֶ֔ם עַ֚ל הָ֣אֲדָמָ֔ה אֲשֶׁ֨ר נִשְׁבַּ֧ע יְהֹוָ֛ה לַאֲבֹתֵיכֶ֖ם לָתֵ֣ת

כב לָהֶ֑ם כִּימֵ֥י הַשָּׁמַ֖יִם עַל־הָאָֽרֶץ׃   כִּי֩ אִם־שָׁמֹ֨ר תִּשְׁמְר֜וּן אֶת־כׇּל־הַמִּצְוָ֣ה הַזֹּ֗את אֲשֶׁ֧ר אָנֹכִ֛י מְצַוֶּ֥ה אֶתְכֶ֖ם לַעֲשֹׂתָ֑הּ לְאַהֲבָ֞ה

כג אֶת־יְהֹוָ֤ה אֱלֹֽהֵיכֶם֙ לָלֶ֣כֶת בְּכׇל־דְּרָכָ֔יו וּלְדׇבְקָה־בֽוֹ׃ וְהוֹרִ֧ישׁ יְהֹוָ֛ה אֶת־כׇּל־הַגּוֹיִ֥ם הָאֵ֖לֶּה מִלִּפְנֵיכֶ֑ם וִֽירִשְׁתֶּ֣ם גּוֹיִ֔ם גְּדֹלִ֥ים וַעֲצֻמִ֖ים מִכֶּֽם׃

כד כׇּל־הַמָּק֗וֹם אֲשֶׁ֨ר תִּדְרֹ֧ךְ כַּֽף־רַגְלְכֶ֛ם בּ֖וֹ לָכֶ֣ם יִהְיֶ֑ה מִן־הַמִּדְבָּ֨ר וְהַלְּבָנ֜וֹן

כה מִן־הַנָּהָ֣ר נְהַר־פְּרָ֗ת וְעַד֙ הַיָּ֣ם הָאַֽחֲר֔וֹן יִהְיֶ֖ה גְּבֻלְכֶֽם׃ לֹא־יִתְיַצֵּ֥ב אִ֖ישׁ בִּפְנֵיכֶ֑ם פַּחְדְּכֶ֤ם וּמֽוֹרַאֲכֶם֙ יִתֵּ֣ן ׀ יְהֹוָ֣ה אֱלֹֽהֵיכֶ֔ם עַל־פְּנֵ֥י כׇל־הָאָ֖רֶץ אֲשֶׁ֣ר תִּדְרְכוּ־בָ֑הּ כַּאֲשֶׁ֖ר דִּבֶּ֥ר לָכֶֽם׃   <small>קי״א פסוקים. ססס אי״ק סימן. יעל״א סימן.</small>

שביעי ומפטיר

Haftaras
Eikev:
p. 1040

פרשת ראה

כו־כז רְאֵ֗ה אָנֹכִ֛י נֹתֵ֥ן לִפְנֵיכֶ֖ם הַיּ֑וֹם בְּרָכָ֖ה וּקְלָלָֽה׃ אֶֽת־הַבְּרָכָ֑ה אֲשֶׁ֣ר תִּשְׁמְע֔וּ

כח אֶל־מִצְוֺת֙ יְהֹוָ֣ה אֱלֹֽהֵיכֶ֔ם אֲשֶׁ֧ר אָנֹכִ֛י מְצַוֶּ֥ה אֶתְכֶ֖ם הַיּֽוֹם׃ וְהַקְּלָלָ֗ה אִם־לֹ֤א תִשְׁמְעוּ֙ אֶל־מִצְוֺת֙ יְהֹוָ֣ה אֱלֹֽהֵיכֶ֔ם וְסַרְתֶּ֣ם מִן־הַדֶּ֔רֶךְ אֲשֶׁ֧ר אָנֹכִ֛י מְצַוֶּ֥ה אֶתְכֶ֖ם הַיּ֑וֹם לָלֶ֗כֶת אַחֲרֵ֛י אֱלֹהִ֥ים אֲחֵרִ֖ים אֲשֶׁ֥ר לֹֽא־

כט יְדַעְתֶּֽם׃   וְהָיָ֗ה כִּ֤י יְבִֽיאֲךָ֙ יְהֹוָ֣ה אֱלֹהֶ֔יךָ אֶל־הָאָ֖רֶץ אֲשֶׁר־אַתָּ֥ה בָא־שָׁ֖מָּה לְרִשְׁתָּ֑הּ וְנָתַתָּ֤ה אֶת־הַבְּרָכָה֙ עַל־הַ֣ר גְּרִזִ֔ים וְאֶת־

ל הַקְּלָלָ֖ה עַל־הַ֥ר עֵיבָֽל׃ הֲלֹא־הֵ֜מָּה בְּעֵ֣בֶר הַיַּרְדֵּ֗ן אַֽחֲרֵי֙ דֶּ֚רֶךְ מְב֣וֹא הַשֶּׁ֔מֶשׁ בְּאֶ֙רֶץ֙ הַֽכְּנַעֲנִ֔י הַיֹּשֵׁ֖ב בָּעֲרָבָ֑ה מ֚וּל הַגִּלְגָּ֔ל אֵ֖צֶל אֵלוֹנֵ֥י מֹרֶֽה׃

לא כִּ֤י אַתֶּם֙ עֹבְרִ֣ים אֶת־הַיַּרְדֵּ֔ן לָבֹא֙ לָרֶ֣שֶׁת אֶת־הָאָ֔רֶץ אֲשֶׁר־יְהֹוָ֥ה

לב אֱלֹהֵיכֶ֖ם נֹתֵ֣ן לָכֶ֑ם וִֽירִשְׁתֶּ֥ם אֹתָ֖הּ וִֽישַׁבְתֶּם־בָּֽהּ׃ וּשְׁמַרְתֶּ֣ם לַעֲשׂ֔וֹת אֵ֥ת כׇּל־הַֽחֻקִּ֖ים וְאֶת־הַמִּשְׁפָּטִ֑ים אֲשֶׁ֧ר אָנֹכִ֛י נֹתֵ֥ן לִפְנֵיכֶ֖ם הַיּֽוֹם׃

יב א אֵ֣לֶּה הַֽחֻקִּ֣ים וְהַמִּשְׁפָּטִים֮ אֲשֶׁ֣ר תִּשְׁמְר֣וּן לַעֲשׂוֹת֒ בָּאָ֕רֶץ אֲשֶׁר֩ נָתַ֨ן יְהֹוָ֜ה אֱלֹהֵ֧י אֲבֹתֶ֛יךָ לְךָ֖ לְרִשְׁתָּ֑הּ כׇּל־הַ֨יָּמִ֔ים אֲשֶׁר־אַתֶּ֥ם חַיִּ֖ים עַל־הָאֲדָמָֽה׃

ב אַבֵּ֣ד תְּ֠אַבְּד֠וּן אֶֽת־כׇּל־הַמְּקֹמ֞וֹת אֲשֶׁ֧ר עָֽבְדוּ־שָׁ֣ם הַגּוֹיִ֗ם אֲשֶׁ֥ר אַתֶּ֛ם יֹרְשִׁ֥ים אֹתָ֖ם אֶת־אֱלֹהֵיהֶ֑ם עַל־הֶהָרִ֤ים הָֽרָמִים֙ וְעַל־הַגְּבָע֔וֹת וְתַ֖חַת

ג כׇּל־עֵ֥ץ רַעֲנָֽן׃ וְנִתַּצְתֶּ֣ם אֶת־מִזְבְּחֹתָ֗ם וְשִׁבַּרְתֶּם֙ אֶת־מַצֵּ֣בֹתָ֔ם וַאֲשֵֽׁרֵיהֶם֙ תִּשְׂרְפ֣וּן בָּאֵ֔שׁ וּפְסִילֵ֥י אֱלֹהֵיהֶ֖ם תְּגַדֵּע֑וּן וְאִבַּדְתֶּ֣ם אֶת־

ד־ה שְׁמָ֔ם מִן־הַמָּק֖וֹם הַהֽוּא׃ לֹֽא־תַעֲשׂ֣וּן כֵּ֔ן לַיהֹוָ֖ה אֱלֹהֵיכֶֽם׃ כִּ֠י אִֽם־אֶל־הַמָּק֞וֹם אֲשֶׁר־יִבְחַ֨ר יְהֹוָ֤ה אֱלֹֽהֵיכֶם֙ מִכׇּל־שִׁבְטֵיכֶ֔ם לָשׂ֥וּם אֶת־שְׁמ֖וֹ

ו שָׁ֑ם לְשִׁכְנ֥וֹ תִדְרְשׁ֖וּ וּבָ֥אתָ שָּֽׁמָּה׃ וַהֲבֵאתֶ֣ם שָׁ֗מָּה עֹלֹתֵיכֶם֙ וְזִבְחֵיכֶ֔ם וְאֵת֙ מַעְשְׂרֹ֣תֵיכֶ֔ם וְאֵ֖ת תְּרוּמַ֣ת יֶדְכֶ֑ם וְנִדְרֵיכֶם֙ וְנִדְבֹ֣תֵיכֶ֔ם וּבְכֹרֹ֥ת

¹⁹ *You shall teach them to your children to discuss them, while you sit in your home, while you walk on the way, when you retire and when you arise.* ²⁰ *And you shall write them on the doorposts of your house and upon your gates.* ²¹ *In order to prolong your days and the days of your children upon the Land that* HASHEM *has sworn to your forefathers to give them, like the days of the heaven over the earth.*

²² *For if you will observe this entire commandment that I command you, to perform it, to love* HASHEM*, your God, to walk in all His ways and to cleave to*

(See Appendix D, map 4) *Him,* ²³ HASHEM *will drive out all these nations from before you, and you will drive out greater and mightier nations than yourselves.* ²⁴ *Every place where the sole of your foot will tread shall be yours— from the Wilderness and the Lebanon, from the river, the Euphrates River, until the Western Sea* shall be your boundary.* ²⁵ *No man will stand up against you;* HASHEM*, your God, will set your terror and fear on the entire face of the earth where you will tread, as He spoke to you.*

PARASHAS RE'EH

Blessing and curse

²⁶ **S**ee, *I present before you today a blessing and a curse.* ²⁷ *The blessing: that you hearken to the commandments of* HASHEM*, your God, that I command you today.* ²⁸ *And the curse: if you do not hearken to the commandments of* HASHEM*, your God, and you stray from the path that I command you today, to follow gods of others, that you did not know.*

²⁹ *It shall be that when* HASHEM*, your God, brings you to the Land to which you come, to possess it, then you shall deliver the blessing on Mount Gerizim and the curse on Mount Ebal.* ³⁰ *Are they not on the other side of the Jordan, far, in the direction of the sunset, in the land of the Canaanite, that dwells in the plain, far from Gilgal, near the plains of Moreh?* ³¹ *For you are crossing the Jordan to come and possess the Land that* HASHEM*, your God, gives you; you shall possess it and you shall settle in it.* ³² *You shall be careful to perform all the decrees and the ordinances that I present before you today.*

12

Sanctity of the Land

¹ **T**hese *are the decrees and the ordinances that you shall observe to perform in the Land that* HASHEM*, the God of your forefathers, has given you, to possess it, all the days that you live on the Land.* ² *You shall utterly destroy all the places where the nations that you are driving away worshiped their gods: on the high mountains and on the hills, and under every leafy tree.* ³ *You shall break apart their altars; you shall smash their pillars; and their sacred trees shall you burn in the fire; their carved images shall you cut down; and you shall obliterate their names from that place.*

⁴ *You shall not do this to* HASHEM*, your God.* ⁵ *Rather, only at the place that* HASHEM*, your God, will choose from among all your tribes to place His Name there shall you seek out His Presence and come there.* ⁶ *And there shall you bring your burnt-offerings and feast-offerings, your tithes and what you raise up with your hand, your vow offerings and your free-will offerings, and the firstborn of*

11:24. *The Western* [lit., *the rear*] *Sea*, i.e., the Mediterranean Sea.

⋖ Parashas Re'eh

The next three *Sidros* (*Re'eh, Shoftim,* and *Ki Seitzei*)

contain the bulk of the commandments found in *Deuteronomy.* Moses began by putting the commandments into perspective, saying that the choice of whether or not to accept the Torah is nothing less than the choice between blessing and curse.

ז בְּקַרְכֶ֖ם וְצֹאנְכֶ֑ם וַאֲכַלְתֶּם־שָׁ֗ם לִפְנֵי֙ יהוה אֱלֹֽהֵיכֶ֔ם וּשְׂמַחְתֶּם֙ בְּכֹל֙

ח מִשְׁלַ֣ח יֶדְכֶ֔ם אַתֶּ֖ם וּבָתֵּיכֶ֑ם אֲשֶׁ֥ר בֵּרַכְךָ֖ יהוה אֱלֹהֶֽיךָ: לֹ֣א תַעֲשׂ֔וּן כְּכֹ֗ל

ט אֲשֶׁ֨ר אֲנַ֧חְנוּ עֹשִׂ֛ים פֹּ֖ה הַיּ֑וֹם אִ֖ישׁ כָּל־הַיָּשָׁ֥ר בְּעֵינָֽיו: כִּ֥י לֹא־בָאתֶ֖ם

עַד־עָ֑תָּה אֶל־הַמְּנוּחָ֙ה וְאֶל־הַנַּחֲלָ֔ה אֲשֶׁר־יהוה אֱלֹהֶ֖יךָ נֹתֵ֥ן לָֽךְ:

י וַעֲבַרְתֶּם֮ אֶת־הַיַּרְדֵּן֒ וִֽישַׁבְתֶּ֣ם בָּאָ֔רֶץ אֲשֶׁר־יהוה אֱלֹהֵיכֶ֖ם מַנְחִ֣יל אֶתְכֶ֑ם

יא וְהֵנִ֨יחַ לָכֶ֧ם מִכָּל־אֹיְבֵיכֶ֛ם מִסָּבִ֖יב וִֽישַׁבְתֶּם־בֶּֽטַח: וְהָיָ֣ה הַמָּק֗וֹם אֲשֶׁר־

יִבְחַ֣ר יהוה אֱלֹֽהֵיכֶם֮ בּוֹ֒ לְשַׁכֵּ֤ן שְׁמוֹ֙ שָׁ֔ם שָׁ֣מָּה תָבִ֔יאוּ אֵ֛ת כָּל־אֲשֶׁ֥ר

אָנֹכִ֖י מְצַוֶּ֣ה אֶתְכֶ֑ם עוֹלֹֽתֵיכֶ֣ם וְזִבְחֵיכֶ֗ם מַעְשְׂרֹֽתֵיכֶם֙ וּתְרֻמַ֣ת יֶדְכֶ֔ם

יב וְכֹל֙ מִבְחַ֣ר נִדְרֵיכֶ֔ם אֲשֶׁ֥ר תִּדְּר֖וּ לַֽיהוה: וּשְׂמַחְתֶּ֗ם לִפְנֵי֙ יהוה אֱלֹֽהֵיכֶ֔ם

אַתֶּ֗ם וּבְנֵיכֶם֙ וּבְנֹ֣תֵיכֶ֔ם וְעַבְדֵיכֶ֖ם וְאַמְהֹֽתֵיכֶ֑ם וְהַלֵּוִי֙ אֲשֶׁ֣ר בְּשַֽׁעֲרֵיכֶ֔ם כִּ֣י

יג אֵ֥ין ל֛וֹ חֵ֥לֶק וְנַחֲלָ֖ה אִתְּכֶֽם: הִשָּׁ֣מֶר לְךָ֔ פֶּֽן־תַּעֲלֶ֖ה עֹֽלֹתֶ֑יךָ בְּכָל־מָק֖וֹם

יד אֲשֶׁ֥ר תִּרְאֶֽה: כִּ֣י אִם־בַּמָּק֞וֹם אֲשֶׁר־יִבְחַ֤ר יהוה בְּאַחַ֣ד שְׁבָטֶ֔יךָ שָׁ֖ם

תַּעֲלֶ֣ה עֹֽלֹתֶ֑יךָ וְשָׁ֣ם תַּעֲשֶׂ֔ה כֹּ֛ל אֲשֶׁ֥ר אָנֹכִ֖י מְצַוֶּֽךָּ: רַק֩ בְּכָל־אַוַּ֨ת נַפְשְׁךָ֜

טו תִּזְבַּ֣ח ׀ וְאָכַלְתָּ֣ בָשָׂ֗ר כְּבִרְכַּ֨ת יהוה אֱלֹהֶ֛יךָ אֲשֶׁ֥ר נָֽתַן־לְךָ֖ בְּכָל־שְׁעָרֶ֑יךָ

הַטָּמֵ֤א וְהַטָּהוֹר֙ יֹאכְלֶ֔נּוּ כַּצְּבִ֖י וְכָאַיָּֽל: רַ֥ק הַדָּ֖ם לֹ֣א תֹאכֵ֑לוּ עַל־הָאָ֛רֶץ

טז תִּשְׁפְּכֶ֖נּוּ כַּמָּֽיִם: לֹֽא־תוּכַ֞ל לֶאֱכֹ֣ל בִּשְׁעָרֶ֗יךָ מַעְשַׂ֤ר דְּגָֽנְךָ֙ וְתִירֹֽשְׁךָ֣

יז וְיִצְהָרֶ֔ךָ וּבְכֹרֹ֥ת בְּקָרְךָ֖ וְצֹאנֶ֑ךָ וְכָל־נְדָרֶ֨יךָ֙ אֲשֶׁ֣ר תִּדֹּ֔ר וְנִדְבֹתֶ֖יךָ וּתְרוּמַ֥ת

יח יָדֶֽךָ: כִּ֡י אִם־לִפְנֵי֩ יהוה אֱלֹהֶ֜יךָ תֹּאכְלֶ֗נּוּ בַּמָּקוֹם֙ אֲשֶׁ֨ר יִבְחַ֜ר יהוה

אֱלֹהֶ֣יךָ בּ֗וֹ אַתָּ֨ה וּבִנְךָ֤ וּבִתֶּ֨ךָ֙ וְעַבְדְּךָ֣ וַאֲמָתֶ֔ךָ וְהַלֵּוִ֖י אֲשֶׁ֣ר בִּשְׁעָרֶ֑יךָ

יט וְשָׂמַחְתָּ֗ לִפְנֵי֙ יהוה אֱלֹהֶ֔יךָ בְּכֹ֖ל מִשְׁלַ֣ח יָדֶֽךָ: הִשָּׁ֣מֶר לְךָ֔ פֶּֽן־תַּעֲזֹ֖ב

כ אֶת־הַלֵּוִ֑י כָּל־יָמֶ֖יךָ עַל־אַדְמָתֶֽךָ: כִּֽי־יַרְחִ֣יב יהוה

אֱלֹהֶיךָ֮ אֶֽת־גְּבֻֽלְךָ֒ כַּאֲשֶׁ֣ר דִּבֶּר־לָ֔ךְ וְאָמַרְתָּ֙ אֹכְלָ֣ה בָשָׂ֔ר כִּֽי־תְאַוֶּ֥ה נַפְשְׁךָ֖

כא לֶאֱכֹ֣ל בָּשָׂ֑ר בְּכָל־אַוַּ֥ת נַפְשְׁךָ֖ תֹּאכַ֥ל בָּשָֽׂר: כִּֽי־יִרְחַ֨ק מִמְּךָ֜ הַמָּק֗וֹם אֲשֶׁ֨ר

יִבְחַ֜ר יהוה אֱלֹהֶ֨יךָ֙ לָשׂ֣וּם שְׁמ֣וֹ שָׁ֔ם וְזָבַחְתָּ֞ מִבְּקָרְךָ֣ וּמִצֹּֽאנְךָ֗ אֲשֶׁ֨ר נָתַ֤ן

כב יהוה לְךָ֙ כַּאֲשֶׁ֣ר צִוִּיתִ֔ךָ וְאָ֣כַלְתָּ֔ בִּשְׁעָרֶ֖יךָ בְּכֹ֥ל אַוַּ֥ת נַפְשֶֽׁךָ: אַ֗ךְ כַּאֲשֶׁ֨ר

יֵאָכֵ֤ל אֶֽת־הַצְּבִי֙ וְאֶת־הָ֣אַיָּ֔ל כֵּ֖ן תֹּאכְלֶ֑נּוּ הַטָּמֵא֙ וְהַטָּה֔וֹר יַחְדָּ֖ו יֹאכְלֶֽנּוּ:

כג רַ֣ק חֲזַ֗ק לְבִלְתִּי֙ אֲכֹ֣ל הַדָּ֔ם כִּ֥י הַדָּ֖ם ה֣וּא הַנָּ֑פֶשׁ וְלֹא־תֹאכַ֥ל הַנֶּ֖פֶשׁ

כד-כה עִם־הַבָּשָֽׂר: לֹ֖א תֹּאכְלֶ֑נּוּ עַל־הָאָ֛רֶץ תִּשְׁפְּכֶ֖נּוּ כַּמָּֽיִם: לֹ֣א תֹּאכְלֶ֗נּוּ לְמַ֨עַן

יִיטַ֤ב לְךָ֙ וּלְבָנֶ֣יךָ אַחֲרֶ֔יךָ כִּֽי־תַעֲשֶׂ֥ה הַיָּשָׁ֖ר בְּעֵינֵ֣י יהוה: רַ֧ק קָֽדָשֶׁ֛יךָ אֲשֶׁר־

כז יִהְי֥וּ לְךָ֖ וּנְדָרֶ֑יךָ תִּשָּׂ֣א וּבָ֔אתָ אֶל־הַמָּק֖וֹם אֲשֶׁר־יִבְחַ֣ר יהוה: וְעָשִׂ֤יתָ

שני

12:7. The extent of your offerings should be commensurate with the prosperity God has given you (*Rashi*). This applies as well to charity, time for Torah study, and so on.

12:15-16. These verses refer to a consecrated animal that developed a blemish disqualifying it as an offering. It may be redeemed and slaughtered anywhere.

12:17-19. Sacred foods may be eaten only in Jerusalem

or, in the case of the Tabernacle at Shiloh, in the environs of the Sanctuary.

12:20-25. After Israel arrives in its land, animals may be slaughtered for their meat, even without bringing them as offerings.

12:23. *The life with the meat*, i.e., you may not eat meat that was torn from a living animal (*Rashi*).

your cattle and your flocks. ⁷ You shall eat there before HASHEM, your God, and you shall rejoice with your every undertaking, you and your households, as HASHEM, your God, has blessed you. *

Private altars   ⁸ You shall not do like everything that we do here today — [rather,] every man what is proper in his eyes — ⁹ for you will not yet have come to the resting place or to the heritage that HASHEM, your God, gives you.

¹⁰ You shall cross the Jordan and settle in the Land that HASHEM, your God, causes you to inherit, and He will give you rest from all your enemies all around, and you will dwell securely. ¹¹ It shall be that the place where HASHEM, your God, will choose to rest His Name — there shall you bring everything that I command you: your burnt-offerings and your feast-offerings, your tithes and what you raise up with your hands, and the choicest of your vow offerings that you will vow to HASHEM. ¹² You shall rejoice before HASHEM, your God — you, your sons and your daughters, your slaves and your maidservants, and the Levite who is in your cities, for he has no share and inheritance with you. ¹³ Beware for yourself lest you bring up your burnt-offerings in any place that you see. ¹⁴ Rather, only in the place that HASHEM will choose, among one of your tribes, there shall you bring up your burnt-offerings, and there shall you do all that I command you.

Permission to eat redeemed offerings   ¹⁵ However, in your soul's desire you may slaughter and eat* meat, according to the blessing that HASHEM, your God, will have given you in all your cities; the contaminated one and the pure one may eat it, like the deer and the hart. ¹⁶ But you shall not eat the blood; you shall pour it onto the earth, like water.

Sacred foods consumed only in Jerusalem   ¹⁷ In your [outlying] cities, you may not eat:* the tithe of your grain, and your wine, and your oil; the firstborn of your cattle and your flocks; all your vow offerings that you vow and your free-will offerings; and what you raise up with your hands. ¹⁸ Rather you shall eat them before HASHEM, your God, in the place that HASHEM, your God, will choose — you, your son, your daughter, your slave, your maidservant, and the Levite who is in your cities — and you shall rejoice before HASHEM, your God, in your every undertaking. ¹⁹ Beware for yourself lest you forsake the Levite, all your days on your Land.

Permission to eat unconsecrated meat   ²⁰ When HASHEM, your God, will broaden your boundary* as He spoke to you, and you say, "I would eat meat," for you will have a desire to eat meat, to your heart's entire desire may you eat meat. ²¹ If the place where HASHEM, your God, will choose to place His Name will be far from you, you may slaughter from your cattle and your flocks that HASHEM has given you, as I have commanded you, and you may eat in your cities according to your heart's entire desire. ²² Even as the deer and the hart are eaten, so may you eat it, the contaminated one and the pure one may eat it together. ²³ Only be strong not to eat the blood — for the blood, it is the life — and you shall not eat the life with the meat. * ²⁴ You shall not eat it, you shall pour it onto the ground like water. ²⁵ You shall not eat it, in order that it be well with you and your children after you, when you do what is right in the eyes of HASHEM.

²⁶ Only your sanctities that you will have and your vow offerings shall you carry, and come to the place that HASHEM will choose. ²⁷ You shall perform

עַל־תֵּרֶיךָ הַבָּשָׂר וְהַדָּם עַל־מִזְבַּח יהוה אֱלֹהֶיךָ וְדַם־זְבָחֶיךָ יִשָּׁפֵךְ עַל־

כח מִזְבַּח יהוה אֱלֹהֶיךָ וְהַבָּשָׂר תֹּאכֵל: שְׁמֹר וְשָׁמַעְתָּ אֵת כָּל־הַדְּבָרִים
הָאֵלֶּה אֲשֶׁר אָנֹכִי מְצַוֶּךָּ לְמַעַן יִיטַב לְךָ וּלְבָנֶיךָ אַחֲרֶיךָ עַד־עוֹלָם כִּי

שלישי כט תַעֲשֶׂה הַטּוֹב וְהַיָּשָׁר בְּעֵינֵי יהוה אֱלֹהֶיךָ: כִּי־יַכְרִית יהוה אֱלֹהֶיךָ אֶת־
הַגּוֹיִם אֲשֶׁר אַתָּה בָא־שָׁמָּה לָרֶשֶׁת אוֹתָם מִפָּנֶיךָ וְיָרַשְׁתָּ אֹתָם וְיָשַׁבְתָּ

ל בְּאַרְצָם: הִשָּׁמֶר לְךָ פֶּן־תִּנָּקֵשׁ אַחֲרֵיהֶם אַחֲרֵי הִשָּׁמְדָם מִפָּנֶיךָ וּפֶן־
תִּדְרֹשׁ לֵאלֹהֵיהֶם לֵאמֹר אֵיכָה יַעַבְדוּ הַגּוֹיִם הָאֵלֶּה אֶת־אֱלֹהֵיהֶם

לא וְאֶעֱשֶׂה־כֵּן גַּם־אָנִי: לֹא־תַעֲשֶׂה כֵן לַיהוה אֱלֹהֶיךָ כִּי כָל־תּוֹעֲבַת יהוה
אֲשֶׁר שָׂנֵא עָשׂוּ לֵאלֹהֵיהֶם כִּי גַם אֶת־בְּנֵיהֶם וְאֶת־בְּנֹתֵיהֶם יִשְׂרְפוּ בָאֵשׁ

יג א לֵאלֹהֵיהֶם: אֵת כָּל־הַדָּבָר אֲשֶׁר אָנֹכִי מְצַוֶּה אֶתְכֶם אֹתוֹ תִשְׁמְרוּ לַעֲשׂוֹת
לֹא־תֹסֵף עָלָיו וְלֹא תִגְרַע מִמֶּנּוּ:

ב־ג כִּי־יָקוּם בְּקִרְבְּךָ נָבִיא אוֹ חֹלֵם חֲלוֹם וְנָתַן אֵלֶיךָ אוֹת אוֹ מוֹפֵת: וּבָא
הָאוֹת וְהַמּוֹפֵת אֲשֶׁר־דִּבֶּר אֵלֶיךָ לֵאמֹר נֵלְכָה אַחֲרֵי אֱלֹהִים אֲחֵרִים

ד אֲשֶׁר לֹא־יְדַעְתָּם וְנָעָבְדֵם: לֹא תִשְׁמַע אֶל־דִּבְרֵי הַנָּבִיא הַהוּא אוֹ אֶל־
חוֹלֵם הַחֲלוֹם הַהוּא כִּי מְנַסֶּה יהוה אֱלֹהֵיכֶם אֶתְכֶם לָדַעַת הֲיִשְׁכֶם

ה אֹהֲבִים אֶת־יהוה אֱלֹהֵיכֶם בְּכָל־לְבַבְכֶם וּבְכָל־נַפְשְׁכֶם: אַחֲרֵי יהוה
אֱלֹהֵיכֶם תֵּלֵכוּ וְאֹתוֹ תִירָאוּ וְאֶת־מִצְוֹתָיו תִּשְׁמֹרוּ וּבְקֹלוֹ תִשְׁמָעוּ וְאֹתוֹ

ו תַעֲבֹדוּ וּבוֹ תִדְבָּקוּן: וְהַנָּבִיא הַהוּא אוֹ חֹלֵם הַחֲלוֹם הַהוּא יוּמָת כִּי דִבֶּר־
סָרָה עַל־יהוה אֱלֹהֵיכֶם הַמּוֹצִיא אֶתְכֶם | מֵאֶרֶץ מִצְרַיִם וְהַפֹּדְךָ מִבֵּית
עֲבָדִים לְהַדִּיחֲךָ מִן־הַדֶּרֶךְ אֲשֶׁר צִוְּךָ יהוה אֱלֹהֶיךָ לָלֶכֶת בָּהּ וּבִעַרְתָּ

ז הָרָע מִקִּרְבֶּךָ: כִּי יְסִיתְךָ אָחִיךָ בֶן־אִמֶּךָ אוֹ־בִנְךָ אוֹ־בִתְּךָ אוֹ |
אֵשֶׁת חֵיקֶךָ אוֹ רֵעֲךָ אֲשֶׁר כְּנַפְשְׁךָ בַּסֵּתֶר לֵאמֹר נֵלְכָה וְנַעַבְדָה אֱלֹהִים

ח אֲחֵרִים אֲשֶׁר לֹא יָדַעְתָּ אַתָּה וַאֲבֹתֶיךָ: מֵאֱלֹהֵי הָעַמִּים אֲשֶׁר סְבִיבֹתֵיכֶם

ט הַקְּרֹבִים אֵלֶיךָ אוֹ הָרְחֹקִים מִמֶּךָּ מִקְצֵה הָאָרֶץ וְעַד־קְצֵה הָאָרֶץ: לֹא־
תֹאבֶה לוֹ וְלֹא תִשְׁמַע אֵלָיו וְלֹא־תָחוֹס עֵינְךָ עָלָיו וְלֹא־תַחְמֹל וְלֹא־

י תְכַסֶּה עָלָיו: כִּי הָרֹג תַּהַרְגֶנּוּ יָדְךָ תִּהְיֶה־בּוֹ בָרִאשׁוֹנָה לַהֲמִיתוֹ וְיַד כָּל־

יא הָעָם בָּאַחֲרֹנָה: וּסְקַלְתּוֹ בָאֲבָנִים וָמֵת כִּי בִקֵּשׁ לְהַדִּיחֲךָ מֵעַל יהוה

יב אֱלֹהֶיךָ הַמּוֹצִיאֲךָ מֵאֶרֶץ מִצְרַיִם מִבֵּית עֲבָדִים: וְכָל־יִשְׂרָאֵל יִשְׁמְעוּ

יג וְיִרָאוּן וְלֹא־יוֹסִפוּ לַעֲשׂוֹת כַּדָּבָר הָרָע הַזֶּה בְּקִרְבֶּךָ: כִּי־
תִשְׁמַע בְּאַחַת עָרֶיךָ אֲשֶׁר יהוה אֱלֹהֶיךָ נֹתֵן לְךָ לָשֶׁבֶת שָׁם לֵאמֹר:

יד יָצְאוּ אֲנָשִׁים בְּנֵי־בְלִיַּעַל מִקִּרְבֶּךָ וַיַּדִּיחוּ אֶת־יֹשְׁבֵי עִירָם לֵאמֹר נֵלְכָה

13:1. One may not "improve" the Torah by adding new commandments; what human intelligence considers an honor to God may be an abomination in His eyes.

13:2-6. Even an acknowledged prophet is automatically proven false if he claims to have been sent by God to advocate any form of idolatry (*Rambam, Hil. Yesodei*

HaTorah 9:3), or if he claims that any precept of the Torah should be abrogated permanently (*Sanhedrin* 89a).

13:13-19. "The wayward city" is so spiritually corrupt that all or most of its citizens worshiped idols. Even after the court has established the city's guilt, it sends two Torah scholars there in an attempt to

General principles of observance

your burnt-offerings, the flesh and the blood, upon the Altar of HASHEM, your God; and the blood of your feast-offerings shall be poured upon the Altar of HASHEM, your God, and you shall eat the flesh.

²⁸ Safeguard and hearken to all these words that I command you, in order that it be well with you and your children after you forever, when you do what is good and right in the eyes of HASHEM, your God.

The prohibition against copying the rites of the Canaanites

²⁹ When HASHEM, your God, will cut down the nations, to which you come to take possession from them, before you, and you will take possession from them and settle in their land, ³⁰ beware for yourself lest you be attracted after them after they have been destroyed before you, and lest you seek out their gods, saying, "How did these nations worship their gods, and even I will do the same." ³¹ You shall not do so to HASHEM, your God, for everything that is an abomination of HASHEM, that He hates, have they done to their gods; for even their sons and their daughters have they burned in the fire for their gods.

13

¹ The entire word that I command you, that shall you observe to do; you shall not add to it and you shall not subtract from it. *

A false prophet

² If there should stand up in your midst a prophet * or a dreamer of a dream, and he will produce to you a sign or a wonder, ³ and the sign or the wonder comes about, of which he spoke to you, saying, "Let us follow gods of others that you did not know and we shall worship them!" — ⁴ do not hearken to the words of that prophet or to that dreamer of a dream, for HASHEM, your God, is testing you to know whether you love HASHEM, your God, with all your heart and with all your soul. ⁵ HASHEM, your God, shall you follow and Him shall you fear; His commandments shall you observe and to His voice shall you hearken; Him shall you serve and to Him shall you cleave. ⁶ And that prophet and that dreamer of a dream shall be put to death, for he had spoken perversion against HASHEM, your God — Who takes you out of the land of Egypt, and Who redeems you from the house of slavery — to make you stray from the path on which HASHEM, your God, has commanded you to go; and you shall destroy the evil from your midst.

One who entices others to go astray

⁷ If your brother, the son of your mother, or your son or your daughter, or the wife of your bosom, or your friend who is like your own soul will entice you secretly, saying, "Let us go and worship the gods of others" — that you did not know, you or your forefathers, ⁸ from the gods of the peoples that are all around you, those near to you or those far from you, from one end of the earth to the other end of the earth — ⁹ you shall not accede to him and not hearken to him; your eye shall not take pity on him, you shall not be compassionate nor conceal him. ¹⁰ Rather, you shall surely kill him; your hand shall be the first against him to kill him, and the hand of the entire people afterwards. ¹¹ You shall pelt him with stones and he shall die, for he sought to make you stray from near HASHEM, your God, Who takes you out of Egypt, from the house of slavery. ¹² All Israel shall hear and fear, and they shall not again do such an evil thing in your midst.

*The wayward city **

¹³ If, in one of your cities that HASHEM, your God, gives you in which to dwell, you hear, saying, ¹⁴ "Lawless men have emerged from your midst, and they have caused the dwellers of their city to go astray, saying, 'Let us go

influence the people to repent.

טו וְנַעַבְדָה אֱלֹהִים אֲחֵרִים אֲשֶׁר לֹא־יְדַעְתֶּם: וְדָרַשְׁתָּ וְחָקַרְתָּ וְשָׁאַלְתָּ

טז הֵיטֵב וְהִנֵּה אֱמֶת נָכוֹן הַדָּבָר נֶעֶשְׂתָה הַתּוֹעֵבָה הַזֹּאת בְּקִרְבֶּךָ: הַכֵּה תַכֶּה אֶת־יֹשְׁבֵי הָעִיר הַהִוא לְפִי־חָרֶב הַחֲרֵם אֹתָהּ וְאֶת־כָּל־אֲשֶׁר־בָּהּ וְאֶת־

יז בְּהֶמְתָּהּ לְפִי־חָרֶב: וְאֶת־כָּל־שְׁלָלָהּ תִּקְבֹּץ אֶל־תּוֹךְ רְחֹבָהּ וְשָׂרַפְתָּ בָאֵשׁ אֶת־הָעִיר וְאֶת־כָּל־שְׁלָלָהּ כָּלִיל לַיהוָה אֱלֹהֶיךָ וְהָיְתָה תֵּל עוֹלָם

יח לֹא תִבָּנֶה עוֹד: וְלֹא־יִדְבַּק בְּיָדְךָ מְאוּמָה מִן־הַחֵרֶם לְמַעַן יָשׁוּב יְהוָה

יט מֵחֲרוֹן אַפּוֹ וְנָתַן־לְךָ רַחֲמִים וְרִחַמְךָ וְהִרְבֶּךָ כַּאֲשֶׁר נִשְׁבַּע לַאֲבֹתֶיךָ: כִּי תִשְׁמַע בְּקוֹל יְהוָה אֱלֹהֶיךָ לִשְׁמֹר אֶת־כָּל־מִצְוֹתָיו אֲשֶׁר אָנֹכִי מְצַוְּךָ הַיּוֹם לַעֲשׂוֹת הַיָּשָׁר בְּעֵינֵי יְהוָה אֱלֹהֶיךָ:

יד א רביעי   בָּנִים אַתֶּם לַיהוָה אֱלֹהֵיכֶם לֹא תִתְגֹּדְדוּ וְלֹא־תָשִׂימוּ קָרְחָה בֵּין עֵינֵיכֶם לָמֵת: כִּי עַם קָדוֹשׁ

ב אַתָּה לַיהוָה אֱלֹהֶיךָ וּבְךָ בָּחַר יְהוָה לִהְיוֹת לוֹ לְעַם סְגֻלָּה מִכֹּל הָעַמִּים

ג-ד אֲשֶׁר עַל־פְּנֵי הָאֲדָמָה: לֹא תֹאכַל כָּל־תּוֹעֵבָה: זֹאת הַבְּהֵמָה אֲשֶׁר תֹּאכֵלוּ שׁוֹר שֵׂה כְשָׂבִים וְשֵׂה עִזִּים: אַיָּל וּצְבִי וְיַחְמוּר וְאַקּוֹ וְדִישֹׁן

ה וּתְאוֹ וָזָמֶר: וְכָל־בְּהֵמָה מַפְרֶסֶת פַּרְסָה וְשֹׁסַעַת שֶׁסַע שְׁתֵּי פְרָסוֹת מַעֲלַת

ו גֵּרָה בַּבְּהֵמָה אֹתָהּ תֹּאכֵלוּ: אַךְ אֶת־זֶה לֹא תֹאכְלוּ מִמַּעֲלֵי הַגֵּרָה

ז וּמִמַּפְרִיסֵי הַפַּרְסָה הַשְּׁסוּעָה אֶת־הַגָּמָל וְאֶת־הָאַרְנֶבֶת וְאֶת־הַשָּׁפָן כִּי מַעֲלֵה גֵרָה הֵמָּה וּפַרְסָה לֹא הִפְרִיסוּ טְמֵאִים הֵם לָכֶם: וְאֶת־הַחֲזִיר כִּי

ח מַפְרִיס פַּרְסָה הוּא וְלֹא גֵרָה טָמֵא הוּא לָכֶם מִבְּשָׂרָם לֹא תֹאכֵלוּ וּבְנִבְלָתָם לֹא תִגָּעוּ: אֶת־זֶה תֹּאכְלוּ מִכֹּל אֲשֶׁר בַּמָּיִם כֹּל

ט אֲשֶׁר־לוֹ סְנַפִּיר וְקַשְׂקֶשֶׂת תֹּאכֵלוּ: וְכֹל אֲשֶׁר אֵין־לוֹ סְנַפִּיר וְקַשְׂקֶשֶׂת לֹא

י תֹאכֵלוּ טָמֵא הוּא לָכֶם: כָּל־צִפּוֹר טְהֹרָה תֹּאכֵלוּ: וְזֶה אֲשֶׁר

יא-יב לֹא־תֹאכְלוּ מֵהֶם הַנֶּשֶׁר וְהַפֶּרֶס וְהָעָזְנִיָּה: וְהָרָאָה וְאֶת־הָאַיָּה וְהַדַּיָּה

יג למִינָהּ: וְאֵת כָּל־עֹרֵב לְמִינוֹ: וְאֵת בַּת הַיַּעֲנָה וְאֶת־הַתַּחְמָס וְאֶת־הַשָּׁחַף

יד-טו וְאֶת־הַנֵּץ לְמִינֵהוּ: אֶת־הַכּוֹס וְאֶת־הַיַּנְשׁוּף וְהַתִּנְשָׁמֶת: וְהַקָּאָת וְאֶת־

טז-יז הָרָחָמָה וְאֶת־הַשָּׁלָךְ: וְהַחֲסִידָה וְהָאֲנָפָה לְמִינָהּ וְהַדּוּכִיפַת וְהָעֲטַלֵּף:

יט-כ וְכֹל שֶׁרֶץ הָעוֹף טָמֵא הוּא לָכֶם לֹא יֵאָכֵלוּ: כָּל־עוֹף טָהוֹר תֹּאכֵלוּ:

כא לֹא תֹאכְלוּ כָל־נְבֵלָה לַגֵּר אֲשֶׁר־בִּשְׁעָרֶיךָ תִּתְּנֶנָּה וַאֲכָלָהּ אוֹ מָכֹר לְנָכְרִי כִּי עַם קָדוֹשׁ אַתָּה לַיהוָה אֱלֹהֶיךָ לֹא־תְבַשֵּׁל גְּדִי בַּחֲלֵב אִמּוֹ:

כב-כג חמישי   עַשֵּׂר תְּעַשֵּׂר אֵת כָּל־תְּבוּאַת זַרְעֶךָ הַיֹּצֵא הַשָּׂדֶה שָׁנָה שָׁנָה: וְאָכַלְתָּ לִפְנֵי יְהוָה אֱלֹהֶיךָ בַּמָּקוֹם אֲשֶׁר־יִבְחַר לְשַׁכֵּן שְׁמוֹ שָׁם מַעְשַׂר דְּגָנְךָ תִּירֹשְׁךָ וְיִצְהָרֶךָ וּבְכֹרֹת בְּקָרְךָ וְצֹאנֶךָ לְמַעַן תִּלְמַד לְיִרְאָה

**READING FOR
FESTIVALS**
(see next page)

14:1-21. Since the Jewish people are the "children of God," the laws given here are reflections of that special status. First, they must not engage in self-mutilation or eat forbidden foods, for they are an abomination and are destructive to the spirit and soul of a Jew. For transla-tions of transliterated words, see *Leviticus*, Chapter 11.

14:20. See *Exodus* 23:19.

14:22. The second part of the compound verb עַשֵּׂר תְּעַשֵּׂר, *you shall tithe*, can be read תְּעַשֵּׂר, *you will become rich*.

and worship the gods of others, that you have not known' " — ¹⁵ *you shall seek out and investigate, and inquire well, and behold! it is true, the word is correct, this abomination was committed in your midst.* ¹⁶ *You shall surely smite the inhabitants of that city with the edge of the sword; lay it waste and everything that is in it, and its animals, with the edge of the sword.* ¹⁷ *You shall gather together all its booty to the midst of its open square, and you shall burn in fire completely the city and all its booty to HASHEM, your God, and it shall be an eternal heap, it shall not be rebuilt.* ¹⁸ *No part of the banned property may adhere to your hand, so that HASHEM will turn back from His burning wrath; and He will give you mercy and be merciful to you and multiply you, as He swore to your forefathers,* ¹⁹ *when you hearken to the voice of HASHEM, your God, to observe all His commandments that I command you today, to do what is right in the eyes of HASHEM, your God.*

14   ¹ **Y**ou are children to HASHEM, your God* — *you shall not cut yourselves and you shall not make a bald spot between your eyes for a dead person.* ² *For*
A treasured *you are a holy people to HASHEM, your God, and HASHEM has chosen you for*
people *Himself to be a treasured people, from among all the peoples on the face of the earth.*

³ *You shall not eat any abomination.* ⁴ *These are the animals that you may*
Permitted *eat: the ox, sheep, and goat;* ⁵ *the hart, deer, and the yachmur, the akko,*
and *dishon, the teo, and the zamer.* ⁶ *And every animal that has a split hoof, which*
forbidden *is completely separated in two hooves, that brings up its cud among animals*
food *— it may you eat.* ⁷ *But this shall you not eat from among those that bring up*
(See Appendix C, *their cud or have a completely separated split hoof: the camel, the hare, and the*
illustrations 16-18) *hyrax, for they bring up their cud, but their hoof is not split — they are unclean to you;* ⁸ *and the pig, for it has a split hoof, but not the cud — it is unclean to you; from their flesh you shall not eat and you shall not touch their carcasses.*

⁹ *This you may eat of everything that is in the water: anything that has fins and scales you may eat.* ¹⁰ *And anything that does not have fins or scales you shall not eat; it is unclean to you.*

¹¹ *Every clean bird, you may eat.* ¹² *This is what you shall not eat from among them: the nesher, the peres, the ozniah;* ¹³ *the raah, the ayah, and the dayah according to its kind;* ¹⁴ *and every oreiv according to its kind;* ¹⁵ *the bas hayaanah, the tachmos, the shachaf, and the netz, according to its kind;* ¹⁶ *the kos, the yanshuf, and the tinshemes;* ¹⁷ *the kaas, the rachamah, and the shalach;* ¹⁸ *the chasidah, and the anafah according to its kind, the duchifas and the atalef.* ¹⁹ *And every flying swarming creature is unclean to you; they shall not be eaten.* ²⁰ *Every clean bird may you eat.* * ²¹ *You shall not eat any carcass; to the stranger who is in your cities shall you give it that he may eat it, or sell it to a gentile, for you are a holy people to HASHEM, your God; you shall not cook a kid in its mother's milk.*

The second ²² *You shall tithe* * *the entire crop of your planting, the produce of the field, year*
tithe *by year.* ²³ *And you shall eat before HASHEM, your God, in the place that He will choose to rest His Name there — the tithe of your grain, your wine, and your oil, and the firstborn of your cattle and your flocks, so that you will learn to fear*

The Torah teaches that if you give tithes, you will become rich, in complete contradiction to those who claim that they cannot contribute to charity because they are afraid of becoming poor (*Tanchuma*).

8th DAY PESACH
(Sabbath),
2nd DAY SHAVUOS
(Sabbath),
SHEMINI ATZERES
14:22-16:17

*Pesach:
Maftir: p. 400
Haftarah:
p. 972;
Shavuos:
Maftir: p. 400
Haftarah:
p. 1392;
Shemini
Atzeres:
Maftir: p. 404
Haftarah:
p. 826*

כד אֶת־יהוה אֱלֹהֶיךָ כָּל־הַיָּמִים: וְכִי־יִרְבֶּה מִמְּךָ הַדֶּרֶךְ כִּי לֹא תוּכַל שְׂאֵתוֹ כִּי־יִרְחַק מִמְּךָ הַמָּקוֹם אֲשֶׁר יִבְחַר יהוה אֱלֹהֶיךָ לָשׂוּם שְׁמוֹ שָׁם כִּי כה יְבָרֶכְךָ יהוה אֱלֹהֶיךָ: וְנָתַתָּה בַּכָּסֶף וְצַרְתָּ הַכֶּסֶף בְּיָדְךָ וְהָלַכְתָּ אֶל־ כו הַמָּקוֹם אֲשֶׁר יִבְחַר יהוה אֱלֹהֶיךָ בּוֹ: וְנָתַתָּה הַכֶּסֶף בְּכֹל אֲשֶׁר־תְּאַוֶּה נַפְשְׁךָ בַּבָּקָר וּבַצֹּאן וּבַיַּיִן וּבַשֵּׁכָר וּבְכֹל אֲשֶׁר תִּשְׁאָלְךָ נַפְשֶׁךָ וְאָכַלְתָּ כז שָׁם לִפְנֵי יהוה אֱלֹהֶיךָ וְשָׂמַחְתָּ אַתָּה וּבֵיתֶךָ: וְהַלֵּוִי אֲשֶׁר־בִּשְׁעָרֶיךָ לֹא כח תַעַזְבֶנּוּ כִּי אֵין לוֹ חֵלֶק וְנַחֲלָה עִמָּךְ: מִקְצֵה | שָׁלֹשׁ שָׁנִים כט תּוֹצִיא אֶת־כָּל־מַעְשַׂר תְּבוּאָתְךָ בַּשָּׁנָה הַהִוא וְהִנַּחְתָּ בִּשְׁעָרֶיךָ: וּבָא הַלֵּוִי כִּי אֵין־לוֹ חֵלֶק וְנַחֲלָה עִמָּךְ וְהַגֵּר וְהַיָּתוֹם וְהָאַלְמָנָה אֲשֶׁר בִּשְׁעָרֶיךָ וְאָכְלוּ וְשָׂבֵעוּ לְמַעַן יְבָרֶכְךָ יהוה אֱלֹהֶיךָ בְּכָל־מַעֲשֵׂה יָדְךָ אֲשֶׁר תַּעֲשֶׂה:

טו ששי א־ב מִקֵּץ שֶׁבַע־שָׁנִים תַּעֲשֶׂה שְׁמִטָּה: וְזֶה דְּבַר הַשְּׁמִטָּה שָׁמוֹט כָּל־בַּעַל מַשֵּׁה יָדוֹ אֲשֶׁר יַשֶּׁה בְּרֵעֵהוּ לֹא־יִגֹּשׂ אֶת־ ג רֵעֵהוּ וְאֶת־אָחִיו כִּי־קָרָא שְׁמִטָּה לַיהוה: אֶת־הַנָּכְרִי תִּגֹּשׂ וַאֲשֶׁר יִהְיֶה ד לְךָ אֶת־אָחִיךָ תַּשְׁמֵט יָדֶךָ: אֶפֶס כִּי לֹא יִהְיֶה־בְּךָ אֶבְיוֹן כִּי־בָרֵךְ יְבָרֶכְךָ ה יהוה בָּאָרֶץ אֲשֶׁר יהוה אֱלֹהֶיךָ נֹתֵן־לְךָ נַחֲלָה לְרִשְׁתָּהּ: רַק אִם־ שָׁמוֹעַ תִּשְׁמַע בְּקוֹל יהוה אֱלֹהֶיךָ לִשְׁמֹר לַעֲשׂוֹת אֶת־כָּל־הַמִּצְוָה ו הַזֹּאת אֲשֶׁר אָנֹכִי מְצַוְּךָ הַיּוֹם: כִּי־יהוה אֱלֹהֶיךָ בֵּרַכְךָ כַּאֲשֶׁר דִּבֶּר־לָךְ וְהַעֲבַטְתָּ גּוֹיִם רַבִּים וְאַתָּה לֹא תַעֲבֹט וּמָשַׁלְתָּ בְּגוֹיִם רַבִּים וּבְךָ לֹא ז יִמְשֹׁלוּ: כִּי־יִהְיֶה בְךָ אֶבְיוֹן מֵאַחַד אַחֶיךָ בְּאַחַד שְׁעָרֶיךָ בְּאַרְצְךָ אֲשֶׁר־יהוה אֱלֹהֶיךָ נֹתֵן לָךְ לֹא תְאַמֵּץ אֶת־לְבָבְךָ וְלֹא תִקְפֹּץ ח אֶת־יָדְךָ מֵאָחִיךָ הָאֶבְיוֹן: כִּי־פָתֹחַ תִּפְתַּח אֶת־יָדְךָ לוֹ וְהַעֲבֵט תַּעֲבִיטֶנּוּ ט דֵּי מַחְסֹרוֹ אֲשֶׁר יֶחְסַר לוֹ: הִשָּׁמֶר לְךָ פֶּן־יִהְיֶה דָבָר עִם־לְבָבְךָ בְלִיַּעַל לֵאמֹר קָרְבָה שְׁנַת־הַשֶּׁבַע שְׁנַת הַשְּׁמִטָּה וְרָעָה עֵינְךָ בְּאָחִיךָ הָאֶבְיוֹן י וְלֹא תִתֵּן לוֹ וְקָרָא עָלֶיךָ אֶל־יהוה וְהָיָה בְךָ חֵטְא: נָתוֹן תִּתֵּן לוֹ וְלֹא־יֵרַע לְבָבְךָ בְּתִתְּךָ לוֹ כִּי בִּגְלַל | הַדָּבָר הַזֶּה יְבָרֶכְךָ יהוה אֱלֹהֶיךָ יא בְּכָל־מַעֲשֶׂךָ וּבְכֹל מִשְׁלַח יָדֶךָ: כִּי לֹא־יֶחְדַּל אֶבְיוֹן מִקֶּרֶב הָאָרֶץ עַל־ כֵּן אָנֹכִי מְצַוְּךָ לֵאמֹר פָּתֹחַ תִּפְתַּח אֶת־יָדְךָ לְאָחִיךָ לַעֲנִיֶּךָ וּלְאֶבְיֹנְךָ יב בְּאַרְצֶךָ: כִּי־יִמָּכֵר לְךָ אָחִיךָ הָעִבְרִי אוֹ הָעִבְרִיָּה וַעֲבָדְךָ יג שֵׁשׁ שָׁנִים וּבַשָּׁנָה הַשְּׁבִיעִת תְּשַׁלְּחֶנּוּ חָפְשִׁי מֵעִמָּךְ: וְכִי־תְשַׁלְּחֶנּוּ יד חָפְשִׁי מֵעִמָּךְ לֹא תְשַׁלְּחֶנּוּ רֵיקָם: הַעֲנֵיק תַּעֲנִיק לוֹ מִצֹּאנְךָ וּמִגָּרְנְךָ טו וּמִיִּקְבֶךָ אֲשֶׁר בֵּרַכְךָ יהוה אֱלֹהֶיךָ תִּתֶּן־לוֹ: וְזָכַרְתָּ כִּי עֶבֶד הָיִיתָ בְּאֶרֶץ מִצְרַיִם וַיִּפְדְּךָ יהוה אֱלֹהֶיךָ עַל־כֵּן אָנֹכִי מְצַוְּךָ אֶת־הַדָּבָר הַזֶּה הַיּוֹם:

15:1. Loans are automatically canceled at *the end of seven years* as a special act of kindness to fellow Jews. **15:8.** The compound verb תִּפְתַּח פָּתֹחַ, *you shall open . . . ,* tells us to give again and again. If the needy person is too

proud to accept charity, lend him what he needs (*Rashi*). **15:14.** *Adorn* implies that the master should be very generous, to elevate the former slave's self-esteem and enhance his reputation (see *Ibn Ezra; R' Bachya*).

HASHEM, your God, all the days. [24] If the road will be too long for you, so that you cannot carry it, because the place that HASHEM, your God, will choose to place His Name there is far from you, for HASHEM, your God, will have blessed you — [25] then you may exchange it for money, wrap up the money in your hand, and go to the place that HASHEM, your God, will choose. [26] You may spend the money for whatever your soul desires — for cattle, for flocks, for wine, or for alcoholic beverage, or anything that your soul wishes; you shall eat it there before HASHEM, your God, and rejoice — you and your household. [27] You shall not forsake the Levite who is in your cities, for he has no portion or inheritance with you.

[28] At the end of three years you shall take out every tithe of your crop in that year and set it down within your cities. [29] Then the Levite can come — for he has no portion or inheritance with you — and the proselyte, the orphan, and the widow who are in your cities, so they may eat and be satisfied, in order that HASHEM, your God, will bless you in all your handiwork that you may undertake.

15

Remission of loans

[1] At the end of seven years * you shall institute a remission. [2] This is the matter of the remission: Every creditor shall remit his authority over what he has lent his fellow; he shall not press his fellow or his brother, for He has proclaimed a remission for HASHEM. [3] You may press the gentile; but over what you have with your brother, you shall remit your authority. [4] However, may there be no destitute among you; rather, HASHEM will surely bless you in the Land that HASHEM, your God, will give you as an inheritance, to possess it, [5] only if you will hearken to the voice of HASHEM, your God, to observe, to perform this entire commandment that I command you today. [6] For HASHEM, your God, has blessed you as He has told you; you will lend to many nations, but you will not borrow; and you will dominate many nations, but they will not dominate you.

To be warmhearted and openhanded to our brethren

[7] If there shall be a destitute person among you, any of your brethren in any of your cities, in your Land that HASHEM, your God, gives you, you shall not harden your heart or close your hand against your destitute brother. [8] Rather, you shall open * your hand to him; you shall lend him his requirement, whatever is lacking to him. [9] Beware lest there be a lawless thought in your heart, saying, "The seventh year approaches, the remission year," and you will look malevolently upon your destitute brother and refuse to give him — then he may appeal against you to HASHEM, and it will be a sin upon you. [10] You shall surely give him, and let your heart not feel bad when you give him, for in return for this matter, HASHEM, your God, will bless you in all your deeds and in your every undertaking. [11] For destitute people will not cease to exist within the Land; therefore I command you, saying, "You shall surely open your hand to your brother, to your poor, and to your destitute in your Land."

A Jewish bondsman

[12] If your brother, a Hebrew man or a Hebrew woman, will be sold to you, he shall serve you for six years, and in the seventh year you shall send him away from you free. [13] But when you send him away from you free, you shall not send him away empty handed. [14] Adorn * him generously from your flocks, from your threshing floor, and from your wine cellar; as HASHEM, your God, has blessed you, so shall you give him. [15] You shall remember that you were a slave in the land of Egypt, and HASHEM, your God, redeemed you; therefore, I command you regarding this matter today.

טז וְהָיָה כִּי־יֹאמַר אֵלֶיךָ לֹא אֵצֵא מֵעִמָּךְ כִּי אֲהֵבְךָ וְאֶת־בֵּיתֶךָ כִּי־טוֹב לוֹ

עִמָּךְ: וְלָקַחְתָּ אֶת־הַמַּרְצֵעַ וְנָתַתָּה בְאָזְנוֹ וּבַדֶּלֶת וְהָיָה לְךָ עֶבֶד עוֹלָם

יח וְאַף לַאֲמָתְךָ תַּעֲשֶׂה־כֵּן: לֹא־יִקְשֶׁה בְעֵינֶךָ בְּשַׁלֵּחֲךָ אֹתוֹ חָפְשִׁי מֵעִמָּךְ כִּי

מִשְׁנֶה שְׂכַר שָׂכִיר עֲבָדְךָ שֵׁשׁ שָׁנִים וּבֵרַכְךָ יהוה אֱלֹהֶיךָ בְּכֹל אֲשֶׁר

תַּעֲשֶׂה:

שביעי

יט כָּל־הַבְּכוֹר אֲשֶׁר יִוָּלֵד בִּבְקָרְךָ וּבְצֹאנְךָ הַזָּכָר תַּקְדִּישׁ לַיהוה אֱלֹהֶיךָ לֹא

כ תַעֲבֹד בִּבְכֹר שׁוֹרֶךָ וְלֹא תָגֹז בְּכוֹר צֹאנֶךָ: לִפְנֵי יהוה אֱלֹהֶיךָ תֹאכְלֶנּוּ

כא שָׁנָה בְשָׁנָה בַּמָּקוֹם אֲשֶׁר־יִבְחַר יהוה אַתָּה וּבֵיתֶךָ: וְכִי־יִהְיֶה בוֹ מוּם

כב פִּסֵּחַ אוֹ עִוֵּר כֹּל מוּם רָע לֹא תִזְבָּחֶנּוּ לַיהוה אֱלֹהֶיךָ: בִּשְׁעָרֶיךָ תֹּאכְלֶנּוּ

כג הַטָּמֵא וְהַטָּהוֹר יַחְדָּו כַּצְּבִי וְכָאַיָּל: רַק אֶת־דָּמוֹ לֹא תֹאכֵל עַל־הָאָרֶץ

תִּשְׁפְּכֶנּוּ כַּמָּיִם:

8th DAY
PESACH
(weekday),
2nd DAY
SHAVUOS
(weekday)
15:19-16:17

Pesach:
Maftir:
p. 400
Haftarah:
p. 972;
Shavuos:
Maftir:
p. 400
Haftarah:
p. 1392

טז א שָׁמוֹר אֶת־חֹדֶשׁ הָאָבִיב וְעָשִׂיתָ פֶּסַח לַיהוה אֱלֹהֶיךָ כִּי בְּחֹדֶשׁ הָאָבִיב

ב הוֹצִיאֲךָ יהוה אֱלֹהֶיךָ מִמִּצְרַיִם לָיְלָה: וְזָבַחְתָּ פֶּסַח לַיהוה אֱלֹהֶיךָ צֹאן

ג וּבָקָר בַּמָּקוֹם אֲשֶׁר יִבְחַר יהוה לְשַׁכֵּן שְׁמוֹ שָׁם: לֹא־תֹאכַל עָלָיו חָמֵץ

שִׁבְעַת יָמִים תֹּאכַל־עָלָיו מַצּוֹת לֶחֶם עֹנִי כִּי בְחִפָּזוֹן יָצָאתָ מֵאֶרֶץ

ד מִצְרַיִם לְמַעַן תִּזְכֹּר אֶת־יוֹם צֵאתְךָ מֵאֶרֶץ מִצְרַיִם כֹּל יְמֵי חַיֶּיךָ: וְלֹא־

יֵרָאֶה לְךָ שְׂאֹר בְּכָל־גְּבֻלְךָ שִׁבְעַת יָמִים וְלֹא־יָלִין מִן־הַבָּשָׂר אֲשֶׁר תִּזְבַּח

ה בָּעֶרֶב בַּיּוֹם הָרִאשׁוֹן לַבֹּקֶר: לֹא תוּכַל לִזְבֹּחַ אֶת־הַפָּסַח בְּאַחַד שְׁעָרֶיךָ

ו אֲשֶׁר־יהוה אֱלֹהֶיךָ נֹתֵן לָךְ: כִּי אִם־אֶל־הַמָּקוֹם אֲשֶׁר־יִבְחַר יהוה

אֱלֹהֶיךָ לְשַׁכֵּן שְׁמוֹ שָׁם תִּזְבַּח אֶת־הַפֶּסַח בָּעָרֶב כְּבוֹא הַשֶּׁמֶשׁ מוֹעֵד

ז צֵאתְךָ מִמִּצְרָיִם: וּבִשַּׁלְתָּ וְאָכַלְתָּ בַּמָּקוֹם אֲשֶׁר יִבְחַר יהוה אֱלֹהֶיךָ בּוֹ

ח וּפָנִיתָ בַבֹּקֶר וְהָלַכְתָּ לְאֹהָלֶיךָ: שֵׁשֶׁת יָמִים תֹּאכַל מַצּוֹת וּבַיּוֹם הַשְּׁבִיעִי

ט עֲצֶרֶת לַיהוה אֱלֹהֶיךָ לֹא תַעֲשֶׂה מְלָאכָה: שִׁבְעָה שָׁבֻעֹת

תִּסְפָּר־לָךְ מֵהָחֵל חֶרְמֵשׁ בַּקָּמָה תָּחֵל לִסְפֹּר שִׁבְעָה שָׁבֻעוֹת: וְעָשִׂיתָ חַג

י שָׁבֻעוֹת לַיהוה אֱלֹהֶיךָ מִסַּת נִדְבַת יָדְךָ אֲשֶׁר תִּתֵּן כַּאֲשֶׁר יְבָרֶכְךָ יהוה

יא אֱלֹהֶיךָ: וְשָׂמַחְתָּ לִפְנֵי | יהוה אֱלֹהֶיךָ אַתָּה וּבִנְךָ וּבִתֶּךָ וְעַבְדְּךָ וַאֲמָתֶךָ

וְהַלֵּוִי אֲשֶׁר בִּשְׁעָרֶיךָ וְהַגֵּר וְהַיָּתוֹם וְהָאַלְמָנָה אֲשֶׁר בְּקִרְבֶּךָ בַּמָּקוֹם אֲשֶׁר

יב יִבְחַר יהוה אֱלֹהֶיךָ לְשַׁכֵּן שְׁמוֹ שָׁם: וְזָכַרְתָּ כִּי־עֶבֶד הָיִיתָ בְּמִצְרָיִם

וְשָׁמַרְתָּ וְעָשִׂיתָ אֶת־הַחֻקִּים הָאֵלֶּה:

*מפטיר

יג-יד *חַג הַסֻּכֹּת תַּעֲשֶׂה לְךָ שִׁבְעַת יָמִים בְּאָסְפְּךָ מִגָּרְנְךָ וּמִיִּקְבֶךָ: וְשָׂמַחְתָּ

בְּחַגֶּךָ אַתָּה וּבִנְךָ וּבִתֶּךָ וְעַבְדְּךָ וַאֲמָתֶךָ וְהַלֵּוִי וְהַגֵּר וְהַיָּתוֹם וְהָאַלְמָנָה

16:1. Since Pesach is the *month of springtime*, implying that Nissan must fall in the spring, the Sanhedrin adds a thirteenth month to the year from time to time to assure that Nissan does not fall in the winter (*Rashi*).

16:8. *For a six-day period*, i.e., since the new grain crop may not be eaten until the Omer-offering is brought on the second day of Pesach, matzos from the *new* crop may be eaten for only six days (*Rashi*).

¹⁶ In the event he will say to you, "I will not leave you," for he loves you and your household, for it is good for him with you, ¹⁷ then you shall take the awl and put it through his ear and the door, and he shall be for you an eternal slave; even to your maidservant shall you do the same. ¹⁸ It shall not be difficult in your eyes when you send him away free from you, for twice the wage of a hired hand — six years — has he served you; and HASHEM, your God, will bless you in all that you do.

¹⁹ Every firstborn male that is born in your cattle and in your flock, you shall sanctify to HASHEM, your God; you shall not work with the firstborn of your ox nor shall you shear the firstborn of your flock. ²⁰ Before HASHEM, your God, shall you eat it, year by year, in the place that HASHEM will choose, you and your household. ²¹ If it shall have a blemish — lameness or blindness or any serious blemish — you shall not slaughter it to HASHEM, your God. ²² In your cities shall you eat it, the contaminated one and the pure one alike, like the deer and the hart. ²³ However you shall not eat its blood; you shall pour it onto the ground like water.

16

Three pilgrimage festivals

Pesach

¹ **Y**ou shall observe the month of springtime* and perform the pesach-offering for HASHEM, your God, for in the month of springtime HASHEM, your God, took you out of Egypt at night. ² You shall slaughter the pesach-offering to HASHEM, your God, from the flock, and [also offer] cattle, in the place where HASHEM will choose to rest His Name. ³ You shall not eat leavened bread with it, for seven days you shall eat matzos because of it, bread of affliction, for you departed from the land of Egypt in haste — so that you will remember the day of your departure from the land of Egypt all the days of your life.

⁴ No leaven of yours shall be seen throughout your boundary for seven days, nor shall any of the flesh that you slaughter on the afternoon before the first day remain overnight until morning. ⁵ You may not slaughter the pesach-offering in one of your cities that HASHEM, your God, gives you; ⁶ except at the place that HASHEM, your God, will choose to rest His Name, there shall you slaughter the pesach-offering in the afternoon, when the sun descends, the appointed time of your departure from Egypt. ⁷ You shall roast it and eat it in the place that HASHEM, your God, will choose, and in the morning you may turn back and go to your tents. ⁸ For a six-day period* you shall eat matzos and on the seventh day shall be an assembly to HASHEM, your God; you shall not perform labor.

Shavuos

⁹ You shall count seven weeks for yourselves; from when the sickle is first put to the standing crop shall you begin counting seven weeks. ¹⁰ Then you shall observe the festival of Shavuos for HASHEM, your God; the voluntary offerings that you give should be commensurate with how much HASHEM, your God, will have blessed you. ¹¹ You shall rejoice before HASHEM, your God — you, your son, your daughter, your slave, your maidservant, the Levite who is in your cities, the proselyte, the orphan, and the widow who are among you — in the place that HASHEM, your God, will choose to rest His Name. ¹² You shall remember that you were a slave in Egypt, and you shall observe and perform these decrees.

Succos

¹³ You shall make the festival of Succos for a seven-day period, when you gather in from your threshing floor and from your wine cellar. ¹⁴ You shall rejoice on your festival — you, your son, your daughter, your slave, your maidservant, the Levite, the proselyte, the orphan, and the widow who are

*Haftaras
Re'eh:
p. 1048*

(Most
congrega-
tions
read this
Haftarah
even on
Rosh
Chodesh.)

טו אֲשֶׁ֣ר בִּשְׁעָרֶ֑יךָ שִׁבְעַ֣ת יָמִ֗ים תָּחֹג֙ לַֽיהֹוָ֣ה אֱלֹהֶ֔יךָ בַּמָּק֖וֹם אֲשֶׁר־יִבְחַ֣ר יְהֹוָ֑ה כִּ֣י יְבָרֶכְךָ֞ יְהֹוָ֣ה אֱלֹהֶ֗יךָ בְּכֹ֤ל תְּבוּאָֽתְךָ֙ וּבְכֹל֙ מַעֲשֵׂ֣ה יָדֶ֔יךָ וְהָיִ֖יתָ

טז אַ֖ךְ שָׂמֵֽחַ: שָׁל֣וֹשׁ פְּעָמִ֣ים ׀ בַּשָּׁנָ֡ה יֵרָאֶ֨ה כָל־זְכֽוּרְךָ֜ אֶת־פְּנֵ֣י ׀ יְהֹוָ֣ה אֱלֹהֶ֗יךָ בַּמָּקוֹם֙ אֲשֶׁ֣ר יִבְחָ֔ר בְּחַ֧ג הַמַּצּ֛וֹת וּבְחַ֥ג הַשָּׁבֻע֖וֹת וּבְחַ֣ג הַסֻּכּ֑וֹת

יז וְלֹ֧א יֵרָאֶ֛ה אֶת־פְּנֵ֥י יְהֹוָ֖ה רֵיקָֽם: אִ֖ישׁ כְּמַתְּנַ֣ת יָד֑וֹ כְּבִרְכַּ֛ת יְהֹוָ֥ה אֱלֹהֶ֖יךָ אֲשֶׁ֥ר נָֽתַן־לָֽךְ: ססס קֹ"ו פסוקים. פֱליא"ה סימן.

פָּרָשַׁת שׁוֹפְטִים

יח שֹׁפְטִ֣ים וְשֹֽׁטְרִ֗ים תִּֽתֶּן־לְךָ֙ בְּכָל־שְׁעָרֶ֔יךָ אֲשֶׁ֨ר יְהֹוָ֧ה אֱלֹהֶ֛יךָ נֹתֵ֥ן לְךָ֖ לִשְׁבָטֶ֑יךָ וְשָֽׁפְט֥וּ אֶת־הָעָ֖ם מִשְׁפַּט־צֶֽדֶק:

יט לֹֽא־תַטֶּ֣ה מִשְׁפָּ֔ט לֹ֥א תַכִּ֖יר פָּנִ֑ים וְלֹֽא־תִקַּ֣ח שֹׁ֔חַד כִּ֣י הַשֹּׁ֗חַד יְעַוֵּר֙ עֵינֵ֣י חֲכָמִ֔ים וִֽיסַלֵּ֖ף דִּבְרֵ֥י צַדִּיקִֽם:

כ צֶ֥דֶק צֶ֖דֶק תִּרְדֹּ֑ף לְמַ֤עַן תִּֽחְיֶה֙ וְיָֽרַשְׁתָּ֣ אֶת־הָאָ֔רֶץ אֲשֶׁר־יְהֹוָ֥ה אֱלֹהֶ֖יךָ נֹתֵ֥ן לָֽךְ:

כא לֹֽא־תִטַּ֥ע לְךָ֛ אֲשֵׁרָ֖ה כָּל־עֵ֑ץ אֵ֗צֶל מִזְבַּ֛ח

כב יְהֹוָ֥ה אֱלֹהֶ֖יךָ אֲשֶׁ֥ר תַּֽעֲשֶׂה־לָּֽךְ: וְלֹֽא־תָקִ֤ים לְךָ֙ מַצֵּבָ֔ה אֲשֶׁ֥ר שָׂנֵ֖א יְהֹוָ֥ה

יז א אֱלֹהֶֽיךָ: לֹֽא־תִזְבַּח֩ לַֽיהֹוָ֨ה אֱלֹהֶ֜יךָ שׁ֣וֹר וָשֶׂ֗ה אֲשֶׁ֨ר

ב יִֽהְיֶ֥ה בוֹ֙ מ֔וּם כֹּ֖ל דָּבָ֣ר רָ֑ע כִּ֧י תֽוֹעֲבַ֛ת יְהֹוָ֥ה אֱלֹהֶ֖יךָ הֽוּא: כִּֽי־יִמָּצֵ֤א בְקִרְבְּךָ֙ בְּאַחַ֣ד שְׁעָרֶ֔יךָ אֲשֶׁר־יְהֹוָ֥ה אֱלֹהֶ֖יךָ נֹתֵ֣ן לָ֑ךְ אִ֣ישׁ אוֹ־אִשָּׁ֗ה

ג אֲשֶׁ֨ר יַֽעֲשֶׂ֧ה אֶת־הָרַ֛ע בְּעֵינֵ֥י יְהֹוָֽה־אֱלֹהֶ֖יךָ לַֽעֲבֹ֣ר בְּרִיתֽוֹ: וַיֵּ֗לֶךְ וַֽיַּעֲבֹד֙ אֱלֹהִ֣ים אֲחֵרִ֔ים וַיִּשְׁתַּ֖חוּ לָהֶ֑ם וְלַשֶּׁ֣מֶשׁ ׀ א֣וֹ לַיָּרֵ֗חַ א֛וֹ לְכָל־צְבָ֥א

ד הַשָּׁמַ֖יִם אֲשֶׁ֥ר לֹֽא־צִוִּֽיתִי: וְהֻגַּד־לְךָ֖ וְשָׁמָ֑עְתָּ וְדָֽרַשְׁתָּ֣ הֵיטֵ֔ב וְהִנֵּ֤ה אֱמֶת֙

ה נָכ֣וֹן הַדָּבָ֔ר נֶֽעֶשְׂתָ֛ה הַתּֽוֹעֵבָ֥ה הַזֹּ֖את בְּיִשְׂרָאֵֽל: וְהֽוֹצֵאתָ֣ אֶת־הָאִ֣ישׁ הַה֡וּא א֣וֹ אֶת־הָֽאִשָּׁ֣ה הַהִ֡וא אֲשֶׁ֣ר עָשׂוּ֩ אֶת־הַדָּבָ֨ר הָרָ֤ע הַזֶּה֙ אֶל־

ו שְׁעָרֶ֔יךָ אֶת־הָאִ֕ישׁ א֖וֹ אֶת־הָֽאִשָּׁ֑ה וּסְקַלְתָּ֥ם בָּֽאֲבָנִ֖ים וָמֵֽתוּ: עַל־פִּ֣י ׀ שְׁנַ֣יִם עֵדִ֗ים א֛וֹ שְׁלֹשָׁ֥ה עֵדִ֖ים יוּמַ֣ת הַמֵּ֑ת לֹ֣א יוּמַ֔ת עַל־פִּ֖י עֵ֥ד אֶחָֽד:

ז יַ֣ד הָֽעֵדִ֞ים תִּֽהְיֶה־בּ֤וֹ בָרִֽאשֹׁנָה֙ לַֽהֲמִית֔וֹ וְיַ֥ד כָּל־הָעָ֖ם בָּאַֽחֲרֹנָ֑ה וּבִֽעַרְתָּ֥ הָרָ֖ע מִקִּרְבֶּֽךָ:

ח כִּֽי־יִפָּלֵא֩ מִמְּךָ֨ דָבָ֜ר לַמִּשְׁפָּ֗ט בֵּֽין־דָּ֨ם ׀ לְדָ֜ם בֵּֽין־דִּ֣ין לְדִ֗ין וּבֵ֥ין נֶ֨גַע֙ לָנֶ֔גַע דִּבְרֵ֥י רִיבֹ֖ת בִּשְׁעָרֶ֑יךָ וְקַמְתָּ֣ וְעָלִ֔יתָ אֶל־הַמָּק֔וֹם אֲשֶׁ֥ר יִבְחַ֛ר יְהֹוָ֥ה אֱלֹהֶ֖יךָ בּֽוֹ:

ט וּבָאתָ֗ אֶל־הַכֹּֽהֲנִים֙ הַֽלְוִיִּ֔ם וְאֶל־הַשֹּׁפֵ֔ט אֲשֶׁ֥ר יִֽהְיֶ֖ה בַּיָּמִ֣ים הָהֵ֑ם וְדָֽרַשְׁתָּ֙

י וְהִגִּ֣ידוּ לְךָ֔ אֵ֖ת דְּבַ֥ר הַמִּשְׁפָּֽט: וְעָשִׂ֗יתָ עַל־פִּ֤י הַדָּבָר֙ אֲשֶׁ֣ר יַגִּ֣ידוּ לְךָ֔

16:15. This is God's assurance that Succos will be a time of undiluted joy (*Rashi*).

16:16-17. Jews must come to celebrate the pilgrimage festivals with offerings in honor of the occasion, commensurate with the prosperity with which God has blessed them.

◄§ Parashas Shoftim

16:18-20. In addition to judges, the Torah requires the appointment of officers of the court, who would have the responsibility to enforce the decisions of the judges, and would circulate in the marketplace and streets to enforce standards of honesty.

in your cities. [15] *A seven-day period shall you celebrate to* HASHEM, *your God, in the place that* HASHEM *will choose, for* HASHEM, *your God, will have blessed you in all your crop and in all your handiwork, and you will be completely joyous.* *

To come to Jerusalem with offerings [16] *Three times a year* * *all your males should appear before* HASHEM, *your God, in the place that He will choose: on the Festival of Matzos, the Festival of Shavuos, and the Festival of Succos; and he shall not appear before* HASHEM *empty handed,* [17] *everyone according to what he can give, according to the blessing that* HASHEM, *your God, gives you.*

PARASHAS SHOFTIM

Establishment of just courts [18] **J**udges *and officers* * *shall you appoint in all your cities — which* HASHEM, *your God, gives you — for your tribes; and they shall judge the people with righteous judgment.* [19] *You shall not pervert judgment, you shall not respect someone's presence, and you shall not accept a bribe, for the bribe will blind the eyes of the wise and make just words crooked.* [20] *Righteousness, righteousness shall you pursue, so that you will live and possess the Land that* HASHEM, *your God, gives you.*

Blemished sacrifice [21] *You shall not plant for yourselves an idolatrous tree — any tree — near the Altar of* HASHEM, *your God, that you shall make for yourself.* [22] *And you shall not erect for yourselves a pillar, which* HASHEM, *your God, hates.*

17 [1] **Y**ou *shall not slaughter for* HASHEM, *your God, an ox or a lamb or kid in which there will be a blemish, any bad thing, because that is an abomination of* HASHEM, *your God.*

The death penalty for an idol worshiper [2] *If there will be found among you in one of your cities, which* HASHEM, *your God, gives you, a man or woman who commits what is evil in the eyes of* HASHEM, *your God, to violate His covenant,* [3] *and he will go and serve gods of others and prostrate himself to them, or to the sun or to the moon or to any host of heaven, which I have not commanded,* [4] *and it will be told to you and you will hear; then you shall investigate well, and behold! it is true, the testimony is correct — this abomination was done in Israel —* [5] *then you shall remove that man or that woman who did this evil thing, to your cities — the man or the woman — and you shall pelt them with stones, so that they will die.* [6] *By the testimony of two witnesses or three witnesses shall the condemned person be put to death; he shall not be put to death by the testimony of a single witness.* [7] *The hand of the witnesses shall be upon him first to put him to death, and the hand of the entire people afterward, and you shall destroy the evil from your midst.* *

The rebellious elder [8] *If a matter of judgment is hidden from you, between blood and blood,* * *between verdict and verdict, between plague and plague, matters of dispute in your cities — you shall rise up and ascend to the place that* HASHEM, *your God, shall choose.* [9] *You shall come to the Kohanim, the Levites, and to the judge who will be in those days;* * *you shall inquire and they will tell you the word of judgment.* [10] *You shall do according to the word that they will tell you,*

17:7. In Judaism there is no professional "executioner" to shield society from unpleasantness.

17:8-13. Though differences of opinion are inevitable, it is so important to establish the authority of the Sages

that the Torah imposed the death penalty on a judge who rules against the decision of the Great Sanhedrin.

17:9. Even if he is not equal to the judges of previous days, you must obey him (*Rashi*).

מִן־הַמָּקוֹם הַהוּא אֲשֶׁר יִבְחַר יהוה וְשָׁמַרְתָּ לַעֲשׂוֹת כְּכֹל אֲשֶׁר יוֹרוּךָ:

יא עַל־פִּי הַתּוֹרָה אֲשֶׁר יוֹרוּךָ וְעַל־הַמִּשְׁפָּט אֲשֶׁר־יֹאמְרוּ לְךָ תַּעֲשֶׂה לֹא

תָסוּר מִן־הַדָּבָר אֲשֶׁר־יַגִּידוּ לְךָ יָמִין וּשְׂמֹאל: וְהָאִישׁ אֲשֶׁר־יַעֲשֶׂה בְזָדוֹן

לְבִלְתִּי שְׁמֹעַ אֶל־הַכֹּהֵן הָעֹמֵד לְשָׁרֶת שָׁם אֶת־יהוה אֱלֹהֶיךָ אוֹ אֶל־

הַשֹּׁפֵט וּמֵת הָאִישׁ הַהוּא וּבִעַרְתָּ הָרָע מִיִּשְׂרָאֵל: וְכָל־הָעָם יִשְׁמְעוּ וְיִרָאוּ

יג וְלֹא יְזִידוּן עוֹד: כִּי־תָבֹא אֶל־הָאָרֶץ אֲשֶׁר יהוה אֱלֹהֶיךָ

נֹתֵן לָךְ וִירִשְׁתָּהּ וְיָשַׁבְתָּה בָּהּ וְאָמַרְתָּ אָשִׂימָה עָלַי מֶלֶךְ כְּכָל־הַגּוֹיִם

טו אֲשֶׁר סְבִיבֹתָי: שׂוֹם תָּשִׂים עָלֶיךָ מֶלֶךְ אֲשֶׁר יִבְחַר יהוה אֱלֹהֶיךָ בּוֹ מִקֶּרֶב

אַחֶיךָ תָּשִׂים עָלֶיךָ מֶלֶךְ לֹא תוּכַל לָתֵת עָלֶיךָ אִישׁ נָכְרִי אֲשֶׁר לֹא־אָחִיךָ

טז הוּא: רַק לֹא־יַרְבֶּה־לּוֹ סוּסִים וְלֹא־יָשִׁיב אֶת־הָעָם מִצְרַיְמָה לְמַעַן

הַרְבּוֹת סוּס וַיהוה אָמַר לָכֶם לֹא תֹסִפוּן לָשׁוּב בַּדֶּרֶךְ הַזֶּה עוֹד: וְלֹא

יז יַרְבֶּה־לּוֹ נָשִׁים וְלֹא יָסוּר לְבָבוֹ וְכֶסֶף וְזָהָב לֹא יַרְבֶּה־לּוֹ מְאֹד: וְהָיָה

כְשִׁבְתּוֹ עַל כִּסֵּא מַמְלַכְתּוֹ וְכָתַב לוֹ אֶת־מִשְׁנֵה הַתּוֹרָה הַזֹּאת עַל־סֵפֶר

מִלִּפְנֵי הַכֹּהֲנִים הַלְוִיִּם: וְהָיְתָה עִמּוֹ וְקָרָא בוֹ כָּל־יְמֵי חַיָּיו לְמַעַן יִלְמַד

יט לְיִרְאָה אֶת־יהוה אֱלֹהָיו לִשְׁמֹר אֶת־כָּל־דִּבְרֵי הַתּוֹרָה הַזֹּאת וְאֶת־

הַחֻקִּים הָאֵלֶּה לַעֲשֹׂתָם: לְבִלְתִּי רוּם־לְבָבוֹ מֵאֶחָיו וּלְבִלְתִּי סוּר מִן־

הַמִּצְוָה יָמִין וּשְׂמֹאול לְמַעַן יַאֲרִיךְ יָמִים עַל־מַמְלַכְתּוֹ הוּא וּבָנָיו בְּקֶרֶב

* מלא ו

יח שלישי א יִשְׂרָאֵל: לֹא־יִהְיֶה לַכֹּהֲנִים הַלְוִיִּם כָּל־שֵׁבֶט לֵוִי חֵלֶק וְנַחֲלָה

ב עִם־יִשְׂרָאֵל אִשֵּׁי יהוה וְנַחֲלָתוֹ יֹאכֵלוּן: וְנַחֲלָה לֹא־יִהְיֶה־לּוֹ בְּקֶרֶב אֶחָיו

ג יהוה הוּא נַחֲלָתוֹ כַּאֲשֶׁר דִּבֶּר־לוֹ: וְזֶה יִהְיֶה מִשְׁפַּט הַכֹּהֲנִים

מֵאֵת הָעָם מֵאֵת זֹבְחֵי הַזֶּבַח אִם־שׁוֹר אִם־שֶׂה וְנָתַן לַכֹּהֵן הַזְּרֹעַ

ד וְהַלְּחָיַיִם וְהַקֵּבָה: רֵאשִׁית דְּגָנְךָ תִּירֹשְׁךָ וְיִצְהָרֶךָ וְרֵאשִׁית גֵּז צֹאנְךָ תִּתֶּן־

ה לּוֹ: כִּי בוֹ בָּחַר יהוה אֱלֹהֶיךָ מִכָּל־שְׁבָטֶיךָ לַעֲמֹד לְשָׁרֵת בְּשֵׁם־יהוה הוּא

ו וּבָנָיו כָּל־הַיָּמִים: וְכִי־יָבֹא הַלֵּוִי מֵאַחַד שְׁעָרֶיךָ מִכָּל־יִשְׂרָאֵל

רביעי אֲשֶׁר־הוּא גָּר שָׁם וּבָא בְּכָל־אַוַּת נַפְשׁוֹ אֶל־הַמָּקוֹם אֲשֶׁר־יִבְחַר יהוה:

ז-ח וְשֵׁרֵת בְּשֵׁם יהוה אֱלֹהָיו כְּכָל־אֶחָיו הַלְוִיִּם הָעֹמְדִים שָׁם לִפְנֵי יהוה: חֵלֶק

ט כְּחֵלֶק יֹאכֵלוּ לְבַד מִמְכָּרָיו עַל־הָאָבוֹת: כִּי אַתָּה בָּא אֶל־

הָאָרֶץ אֲשֶׁר־יהוה אֱלֹהֶיךָ נֹתֵן לָךְ לֹא־תִלְמַד לַעֲשׂוֹת כְּתוֹעֲבֹת הַגּוֹיִם

י הָהֵם: לֹא־יִמָּצֵא בְךָ מַעֲבִיר בְּנוֹ־וּבִתּוֹ בָּאֵשׁ קֹסֵם קְסָמִים מְעוֹנֵן וּמְנַחֵשׁ

יא-יב וּמְכַשֵּׁף: וְחֹבֵר חָבֶר וְשֹׁאֵל אוֹב וְיִדְּעֹנִי וְדֹרֵשׁ אֶל־הַמֵּתִים: כִּי־תוֹעֲבַת

יהוה כָּל־עֹשֵׂה אֵלֶּה וּבִגְלַל הַתּוֹעֵבֹת הָאֵלֶּה יהוה אֱלֹהֶיךָ מוֹרִישׁ אוֹתָם

17:14-20. Israel as a nation had three commandments once it was established in its land: (a) to request a king; (b) to eliminate the offspring of Amalek; and (c) to build the Temple (Sanhedrin 20b).

17:18. The king is to keep one copy of the Torah in his treasury, and the other one with him at all times (Rashi).

These Scrolls remind the king that, august though his position may be, he is a servant of the Torah.

18:8. What was transacted by the forefathers? Families were assigned specific weeks of the year to be in the Temple and perform the service. They had priority during those weeks. (See Appendix B, chart 12.)

from that place that HASHEM will choose, and you shall be careful to do according to everything that they will teach you. [11] According to the teaching that they will teach you and according to the judgment that they will say to you, shall you do; you shall not deviate from the word that they will tell you, right or left. [12] And the man who will act with willfulness, not listening to the Kohen who stands there to serve HASHEM, your God, or to the judge, that man shall die, and you shall destroy the evil from among Israel. [13] The entire nation shall listen and fear, and they shall not act willfully any more.

A king in Israel [14] When you come to the Land* that HASHEM, your God, gives you, and possess it, and settle in it, and you will say, "I will set a king over myself, like all the nations that are around me." [15] You shall surely set over yourself a king whom HASHEM, your God, shall choose; from among your brethren shall you set a king over yourself; you cannot place over yourself a foreign man, who is not your brother. [16] Only he shall not have too many horses for himself, so that he will not return the people to Egypt in order to increase horses, for HASHEM has said to you, "You shall no longer return on this road again." [17] And he shall not have too many wives, so that his heart not turn astray; and he shall not greatly increase silver and gold for himself. [18] It shall be that when he sits on the throne of his kingdom, he shall write for himself two copies of this Torah in a book,* from before the Kohanim, the Levites. [19] It shall be with him, and he shall read from it all the days of his life, so that he will learn to fear HASHEM, his God, to observe all the words of this Torah and these decrees, to perform them, [20] so that his heart does not become haughty over his brethren and not turn from the commandment right or left, so that he will prolong years over his kingdom, he and his sons amid Israel.

18 [1] There shall not be for the Kohanim, the Levites — the entire tribe of Levi — *Priestly* a portion and an inheritance with Israel; the fire-offerings of HASHEM and *gifts* His inheritance shall they eat. [2] He shall not have an inheritance among his brethren; HASHEM is his inheritance, as He spoke to him.

[3] This shall be the due of the Kohanim from the people, from those who perform a slaughter, whether of an ox or of the flock: he shall give the Kohen the foreleg, the jaw, and the maw. [4] The first of your grain, wine, and oil, and the first of the shearing of your flock shall you give him. [5] For him has HASHEM chosen from among all your tribes, to stand and minister in the Name of HASHEM, him and his sons, all the days.

[6] When the Levite will come from one of your cities, from all of Israel, where he sojourns, and he comes with all the desire of his soul to the place that HASHEM will choose, [7] then he shall minister in the Name of HASHEM, his God, like all of his brethren, the Levites, who stand there before HASHEM. [8] Portion for portion shall they eat, except for what was transacted by the forefathers. *

Prophecy [9] When you come to the Land that HASHEM, your God, gives you, you shall not learn to act according to the abominations of those nations. [10] There shall not be found among you one who causes his son or daughter to pass through the fire, one who practices divinations, an astrologer, one who reads omens, a sorcerer; [11] or an animal charmer, one who inquires of Ov or Yidoni, or one who consults the dead. [12] For anyone who does these is an abomination of HASHEM, and because of these abominations HASHEM, your God, banishes [the nations]

מִפָּנֶיךָ: תָּמִים תִּהְיֶה עִם יהוה אֱלֹהֶיךָ: כִּי ׀ הַגּוֹיִם הָאֵלֶּה אֲשֶׁר אַתָּה יוֹרֵשׁ   יג־יד

אוֹתָם אֶל־מְעֹנְנִים וְאֶל־קֹסְמִים יִשְׁמָעוּ וְאַתָּה לֹא כֵן נָתַן לְךָ יהוה

אֱלֹהֶיךָ: נָבִיא מִקִּרְבְּךָ מֵאַחֶיךָ כָּמֹנִי יָקִים לְךָ יהוה אֱלֹהֶיךָ אֵלָיו תִּשְׁמָעוּן: טו

כְּכֹל אֲשֶׁר־שָׁאַלְתָּ מֵעִם יהוה אֱלֹהֶיךָ בְּחֹרֵב בְּיוֹם הַקָּהָל לֵאמֹר לֹא אֹסֵף   טז

לִשְׁמֹעַ אֶת־קוֹל יהוה אֱלֹהָי וְאֶת־הָאֵשׁ הַגְּדֹלָה הַזֹּאת לֹא־אֶרְאֶה עוֹד

וְלֹא אָמוּת: וַיֹּאמֶר יהוה אֵלָי הֵיטִיבוּ אֲשֶׁר דִּבֵּרוּ: נָבִיא אָקִים לָהֶם מִקֶּרֶב   יז־יח

אֲחֵיהֶם כָּמוֹךָ וְנָתַתִּי דְבָרַי בְּפִיו וְדִבֶּר אֲלֵיהֶם אֵת כָּל־אֲשֶׁר אֲצַוֶּנּוּ: וְהָיָה   יט

הָאִישׁ אֲשֶׁר לֹא־יִשְׁמַע אֶל־דְּבָרַי אֲשֶׁר יְדַבֵּר בִּשְׁמִי אָנֹכִי אֶדְרֹשׁ מֵעִמּוֹ:

אַךְ הַנָּבִיא אֲשֶׁר יָזִיד לְדַבֵּר דָּבָר בִּשְׁמִי אֵת אֲשֶׁר לֹא־צִוִּיתִיו לְדַבֵּר   כ

וַאֲשֶׁר יְדַבֵּר בְּשֵׁם אֱלֹהִים אֲחֵרִים וּמֵת הַנָּבִיא הַהוּא: וְכִי תֹאמַר בִּלְבָבֶךָ   כא

אֵיכָה נֵדַע אֶת־הַדָּבָר אֲשֶׁר לֹא־דִבְּרוֹ יהוה: אֲשֶׁר יְדַבֵּר הַנָּבִיא בְּשֵׁם   כב

יהוה וְלֹא־יִהְיֶה הַדָּבָר וְלֹא יָבֹא הוּא הַדָּבָר אֲשֶׁר לֹא־דִבְּרוֹ יהוה בְּזָדוֹן

דִּבְּרוֹ הַנָּבִיא לֹא תָגוּר מִמֶּנּוּ:   כִּי־יַכְרִית יהוה אֱלֹהֶיךָ אֶת־   יט   א

הַגּוֹיִם אֲשֶׁר יהוה אֱלֹהֶיךָ נֹתֵן לְךָ אֶת־אַרְצָם וִירִשְׁתָּם וְיָשַׁבְתָּ בְעָרֵיהֶם

וּבְבָתֵּיהֶם: שָׁלוֹשׁ עָרִים תַּבְדִּיל לָךְ בְּתוֹךְ אַרְצְךָ אֲשֶׁר יהוה אֱלֹהֶיךָ נֹתֵן   ב

לְךָ לְרִשְׁתָּהּ: תָּכִין לְךָ הַדֶּרֶךְ וְשִׁלַּשְׁתָּ אֶת־גְּבוּל אַרְצְךָ אֲשֶׁר יַנְחִילְךָ יהוה   ג

אֱלֹהֶיךָ וְהָיָה לָנוּס שָׁמָּה כָּל־רֹצֵחַ: וְזֶה דְּבַר הָרֹצֵחַ אֲשֶׁר־יָנוּס שָׁמָּה וָחָי   ד

אֲשֶׁר יַכֶּה אֶת־רֵעֵהוּ בִּבְלִי־דַעַת וְהוּא לֹא־שֹׂנֵא לוֹ מִתְּמֹל שִׁלְשֹׁם: וַאֲשֶׁר   ה

יָבֹא אֶת־רֵעֵהוּ בַיַּעַר לַחְטֹב עֵצִים וְנִדְּחָה יָדוֹ בַגַּרְזֶן לִכְרֹת הָעֵץ וְנָשַׁל

הַבַּרְזֶל מִן־הָעֵץ וּמָצָא אֶת־רֵעֵהוּ וָמֵת הוּא יָנוּס אֶל־אַחַת הֶעָרִים־

הָאֵלֶּה וָחָי: פֶּן־יִרְדֹּף גֹּאֵל הַדָּם אַחֲרֵי הָרֹצֵחַ כִּי יֵחַם לְבָבוֹ וְהִשִּׂיגוֹ כִּי־   ו

יִרְבֶּה הַדֶּרֶךְ וְהִכָּהוּ נָפֶשׁ וְלוֹ אֵין מִשְׁפַּט־מָוֶת כִּי לֹא שֹׂנֵא הוּא לוֹ מִתְּמוֹל

שִׁלְשׁוֹם: עַל־כֵּן אָנֹכִי מְצַוְּךָ לֵאמֹר שָׁלֹשׁ עָרִים תַּבְדִּיל לָךְ: וְאִם־יַרְחִיב   ז־ח

יהוה אֱלֹהֶיךָ אֶת־גְּבֻלְךָ כַּאֲשֶׁר נִשְׁבַּע לַאֲבֹתֶיךָ וְנָתַן לְךָ אֶת־כָּל־הָאָרֶץ

אֲשֶׁר דִּבֶּר לָתֵת לַאֲבֹתֶיךָ: כִּי־תִשְׁמֹר אֶת־כָּל־הַמִּצְוָה הַזֹּאת לַעֲשֹׂתָהּ   ט

אֲשֶׁר אָנֹכִי מְצַוְּךָ הַיּוֹם לְאַהֲבָה אֶת־יהוה אֱלֹהֶיךָ וְלָלֶכֶת בִּדְרָכָיו כָּל־

הַיָּמִים וְיָסַפְתָּ לְךָ עוֹד שָׁלֹשׁ עָרִים עַל הַשָּׁלֹשׁ הָאֵלֶּה: וְלֹא יִשָּׁפֵךְ דָּם נָקִי   י

בְּקֶרֶב אַרְצְךָ אֲשֶׁר יהוה אֱלֹהֶיךָ נֹתֵן לְךָ נַחֲלָה וְהָיָה עָלֶיךָ דָּמִים:

וְכִי־יִהְיֶה אִישׁ שֹׂנֵא לְרֵעֵהוּ וְאָרַב לוֹ וְקָם עָלָיו וְהִכָּהוּ נֶפֶשׁ וָמֵת וְנָס   יא

אֶל־אַחַת הֶעָרִים הָאֵל: וְשָׁלְחוּ זִקְנֵי עִירוֹ וְלָקְחוּ אֹתוֹ מִשָּׁם וְנָתְנוּ אֹתוֹ   יב

בְּיַד גֹּאֵל הַדָּם וָמֵת: לֹא־תָחוֹס עֵינְךָ עָלָיו וּבִעַרְתָּ דַם־הַנָּקִי מִיִּשְׂרָאֵל   יג

*חמישי

18:13. You should follow God with perfect faith, without feeling a need to know what will happen (*Rashi*).

18:14-22. Israel need not fear the efforts of sorcerers, because Israel's destiny is far above anyone's ability to harm them (*Sforno*).

19:6. See *Numbers* 35:24. Since the redeemer's *heart will be hot*, the Torah commands that the path for the killer's escape should be eased.

from before you. [13] You shall be wholehearted* with HASHEM, your God. [14] For these nations that you are possessing — they hearken to astrologers and diviners; but as for you — not so has HASHEM, your God, given for you.

God sends His prophets to Israel

[15] A prophet from your midst,* from your brethren, like me, shall HASHEM, your God, establish for you — to him shall you hearken. [16] According to all that you asked of HASHEM, your God, in Horeb on the day of the congregation, saying, "I can no longer hear the voice of HASHEM, my God, and this great fire I can no longer see, so that I shall not die."

[17] Then HASHEM said to me: They have done well in what they have said. [18] I will establish a prophet for them from among their brethren, like you, and I will place My words in his mouth; He shall speak to them everything that I will command him. [19] And it shall be that the man who will not hearken to My words that he shall speak in My Name, I will exact from him. [20] But the prophet who willfully shall speak a word in My Name, that which I have not commanded him to speak, or who shall speak in the name of the gods of others — that prophet shall die. [21] When you say in your heart, "How can we know the word that HASHEM has not spoken?" [22] If the prophet will speak in the Name of HASHEM and that thing will not occur and not come about — that is the word that HASHEM has not spoken; with willfulness has the prophet spoken it, you should not fear him. *

19

Cities of refuge

(See Appendix D, map 5)

[1] When HASHEM, your God, will cut down the nations whose Land HASHEM, your God, gives you, and you will possess them, and you will settle in their cities and in their houses, [2] you shall separate three cities for yourselves in the midst of your Land, which HASHEM, your God, gives you to possess it. [3] Prepare the way for yourself, and divide into three parts the boundary of your Land that HASHEM, your God, causes you to inherit; and it shall be for any killer to flee there. [4] This is the matter of the killer who shall flee there and live: One who will strike his fellow without knowledge, and he did not hate him from yesterday or before yesterday; [5] or who will come with his fellow into the forest to hew trees, and his hand swings the axe to cut the tree, and the iron slips from the wood and finds his fellow and he dies, he shall flee to one of these cities and live, [6] lest the redeemer of the blood* will chase after the killer, for his heart will be hot, and he will overtake him for the way was long, and he shall strike him mortally — and there is no judgment of death upon him, for he did not hate him from yesterday and before yesterday. [7] Therefore I command you, saying: You shall separate three cities for yourselves.

[8] When HASHEM will broaden your boundary, as He swore to your forefathers, and He will give you the entire Land that He spoke to your forefathers to give, [9] when you observe this entire commandment to perform it — which I command you today — to love HASHEM, your God, and to walk in His ways all the years, then you shall add three more cities to these three. [10] Innocent blood shall not be shed in the midst of your Land that HASHEM, your God, gives as an inheritance, for then blood will be upon you.

[11] But if there will be a man who hates his fellow, and ambushes him and rises up against him, and strikes him mortally and he dies, and he flees to one of these cities — [12] then the elders of his city shall send and take him from there and place him in the hand of the redeemer of the blood, and he shall die. [13] Your eye shall not pity him; you shall remove the innocent blood from Israel;

ששי   וְטוֹב לָךְ:   לֹא תַסִּיג גְּבוּל רֵעֲךָ אֲשֶׁר גָּבְלוּ רִאשֹׁנִים בְּנַחֲלָתְךָ

טו אֲשֶׁר תִּנְחַל בָּאָרֶץ אֲשֶׁר יהוה אֱלֹהֶיךָ נֹתֵן לְךָ לְרִשְׁתָּהּ: לֹא־

יָקוּם עֵד אֶחָד בְּאִישׁ לְכָל־עָוֹן וּלְכָל־חַטָּאת בְּכָל־חֵטְא אֲשֶׁר יֶחֱטָא עַל־

טז פִּי | שְׁנֵי עֵדִים אוֹ עַל־פִּי שְׁלֹשָׁה־עֵדִים יָקוּם דָּבָר: כִּי־יָקוּם עֵד־חָמָס

בְּאִישׁ לַעֲנוֹת בּוֹ סָרָה: וְעָמְדוּ שְׁנֵי־הָאֲנָשִׁים אֲשֶׁר־לָהֶם הָרִיב לִפְנֵי יהוה

יח לִפְנֵי הַכֹּהֲנִים וְהַשֹּׁפְטִים אֲשֶׁר יִהְיוּ בַּיָּמִים הָהֵם: וְדָרְשׁוּ הַשֹּׁפְטִים הֵיטֵב

יט וְהִנֵּה עֵד־שֶׁקֶר הָעֵד שֶׁקֶר עָנָה בְאָחִיו: וַעֲשִׂיתֶם לוֹ כַּאֲשֶׁר זָמַם לַעֲשׂוֹת

כ לְאָחִיו וּבִעַרְתָּ הָרָע מִקִּרְבֶּךָ: וְהַנִּשְׁאָרִים יִשְׁמְעוּ וְיִרָאוּ וְלֹא־יֹסִפוּ לַעֲשׂוֹת

כא עוֹד כַּדָּבָר הָרָע הַזֶּה בְּקִרְבֶּךָ: וְלֹא תָחוֹס עֵינֶךָ נֶפֶשׁ בְּנֶפֶשׁ עַיִן בְּעַיִן שֵׁן

כ   א בְּשֵׁן יָד בְּיָד רֶגֶל בְּרָגֶל: כִּי־תֵצֵא לַמִּלְחָמָה עַל־אֹיְבֶךָ וְרָאִיתָ

סוּס וָרֶכֶב עַם רַב מִמְּךָ לֹא תִירָא מֵהֶם כִּי־יהוה אֱלֹהֶיךָ עִמָּךְ הַמַּעַלְךָ

ב מֵאֶרֶץ מִצְרָיִם: וְהָיָה כְּקָרָבְכֶם אֶל־הַמִּלְחָמָה וְנִגַּשׁ הַכֹּהֵן וְדִבֶּר אֶל־הָעָם:

ג וְאָמַר אֲלֵהֶם שְׁמַע יִשְׂרָאֵל אַתֶּם קְרֵבִים הַיּוֹם לַמִּלְחָמָה עַל־אֹיְבֵיכֶם

ד אַל־יֵרַךְ לְבַבְכֶם אַל־תִּירְאוּ וְאַל־תַּחְפְּזוּ וְאַל־תַּעַרְצוּ מִפְּנֵיהֶם: כִּי יהוה

ה אֱלֹהֵיכֶם הַהֹלֵךְ עִמָּכֶם לְהִלָּחֵם לָכֶם עִם־אֹיְבֵיכֶם לְהוֹשִׁיעַ אֶתְכֶם: וְדִבְּרוּ

הַשֹּׁטְרִים אֶל־הָעָם לֵאמֹר מִי־הָאִישׁ אֲשֶׁר בָּנָה בַיִת־חָדָשׁ וְלֹא חֲנָכוֹ

ו יֵלֵךְ וְיָשֹׁב לְבֵיתוֹ פֶּן־יָמוּת בַּמִּלְחָמָה וְאִישׁ אַחֵר יַחְנְכֶנּוּ: וּמִי־הָאִישׁ אֲשֶׁר

נָטַע כֶּרֶם וְלֹא חִלְּלוֹ יֵלֵךְ וְיָשֹׁב לְבֵיתוֹ פֶּן־יָמוּת בַּמִּלְחָמָה וְאִישׁ אַחֵר

ז יְחַלְּלֶנּוּ: וּמִי־הָאִישׁ אֲשֶׁר אֵרַשׂ אִשָּׁה וְלֹא לְקָחָהּ יֵלֵךְ וְיָשֹׁב לְבֵיתוֹ פֶּן־

ח יָמוּת בַּמִּלְחָמָה וְאִישׁ אַחֵר יִקָּחֶנָּה: וְיָסְפוּ הַשֹּׁטְרִים לְדַבֵּר אֶל־הָעָם

וְאָמְרוּ מִי־הָאִישׁ הַיָּרֵא וְרַךְ הַלֵּבָב יֵלֵךְ וְיָשֹׁב לְבֵיתוֹ וְלֹא יִמַּס אֶת־לְבַב

ט אֶחָיו כִּלְבָבוֹ: וְהָיָה כְּכַלֹּת הַשֹּׁטְרִים לְדַבֵּר אֶל־הָעָם וּפָקְדוּ שָׂרֵי צְבָאוֹת

שביעי   בְּרֹאשׁ הָעָם: כִּי־תִקְרַב אֶל־עִיר לְהִלָּחֵם עָלֶיהָ וְקָרָאתָ אֵלֶיהָ

יא לְשָׁלוֹם: וְהָיָה אִם־שָׁלוֹם תַּעַנְךָ וּפָתְחָה לָךְ וְהָיָה כָּל־הָעָם הַנִּמְצָא־בָהּ

יב יִהְיוּ לְךָ לָמַס וַעֲבָדוּךָ: וְאִם־לֹא תַשְׁלִים עִמָּךְ וְעָשְׂתָה עִמְּךָ מִלְחָמָה

יג וְצַרְתָּ עָלֶיהָ: וּנְתָנָהּ יהוה אֱלֹהֶיךָ בְּיָדֶךָ וְהִכִּיתָ אֶת־כָּל־זְכוּרָהּ לְפִי־חָרֶב:

יד רַק הַנָּשִׁים וְהַטַּף וְהַבְּהֵמָה וְכֹל אֲשֶׁר יִהְיֶה בָעִיר כָּל־שְׁלָלָהּ תָּבֹז לָךְ

טו וְאָכַלְתָּ אֶת־שְׁלַל אֹיְבֶיךָ אֲשֶׁר נָתַן יהוה אֱלֹהֶיךָ לָךְ: כֵּן תַּעֲשֶׂה לְכָל־

טז הֶעָרִים הָרְחֹקֹת מִמְּךָ מְאֹד אֲשֶׁר לֹא־מֵעָרֵי הַגּוֹיִם־הָאֵלֶּה הֵנָּה: רַק מֵעָרֵי

19:19. If the testimony of two witnesses results in a judgment against a defendant, but two other witnesses testify that the first pair could not have seen the event because, "You were with us at that very same time in a different place," the Torah states that the same penalty the first witnesses conspired to have imposed on their intended victim should be imposed on them.

20:5. Those excused from combat in this passage were responsible to assist the army by supplying food and water (*Rambam*).

20:10-18. Israel must give its enemy an opportunity to make peace. Those who accepted this offer were required to pay taxes, perform national service, and, if they were going to live in the Land, to accept the Seven Noahide Laws.

and it shall be good for you.

Preserving boundaries ¹⁴ You shall not move a boundary of your fellow, which the early ones marked out, in your inheritance that you shall inherit, in the Land that HASHEM, your God, gives you to possess it.

Conspiring witnesses ¹⁵ A single witness shall not stand up against any man for any iniquity or for any error, regarding any sin that he may commit; according to two witnesses or according to three witnesses shall a matter be confirmed. ¹⁶ If a false witness stands against a man to speak up spuriously against him, ¹⁷ then the two men [and those] who have the grievance shall stand before HASHEM, before the Kohanim and the judges who will be in those days. ¹⁸ The judges shall inquire thoroughly, and behold! the testimony was false testimony; he testified falsely against his fellow. ¹⁹ You shall do to him as he conspired to do to his fellow, * and you shall destroy the evil from your midst. ²⁰ And those who remain shall hearken and fear; and they shall not continue again to do such an evil thing in your midst. ²¹ Your eye shall not pity; life for life, eye for eye, tooth for tooth, hand for hand, foot for foot.

20

When Israel goes to war ¹ **W**hen you go out to the battle against your enemy, and you see horse and chariot — a people more numerous than you — you shall not fear them, for HASHEM, your God, is with you, Who brought you up from the land of Egypt. ² It shall be that when you draw near to the war, the Kohen shall approach and speak to the people.

The Kohen anointed for battle speaks to the people ³ He shall say to them, "Hear, O Israel, you are coming near to the battle against your enemies; let your heart not be faint; do not be afraid, do not panic, and do not be broken before them. ⁴ For HASHEM, your God, is the One Who goes with you, to fight for you with your enemies, to save you."

Those unqualified to fight ⁵ Then the officers shall speak to the people, saying, "Who is the man who has built a new house and has not inaugurated it? Let him go and return to his house, * lest he die in the war and another man will inaugurate it. ⁶ And who is the man who has planted a vineyard and not redeemed it? Let him go and return to his house, lest he die in the war and another man will redeem it. ⁷ And who is the man who has betrothed a woman and not married her? Let him go and return to his house, lest he die in the war and another man will marry her."

⁸ The officers shall continue speaking to the people and say, "Who is the man who is fearful and fainthearted? Let him go and return to his house, and let him not melt the heart of his fellows, like his heart." ⁹ When the officers have finished speaking to the people, the leaders of the legions shall take command at the head of the people.

Overtures for peace ¹⁰ When you draw near to a city to wage war against it, you shall call out to it for peace. * ¹¹ It shall be that if it responds to you in peace and opens for you, then the entire people found within it shall be as tribute for you, and they shall serve you. ¹² But if it does not make peace with you, but makes war with you, you shall besiege it. ¹³ HASHEM shall deliver it into your hand, and you shall smite all its males by the blade of the sword. ¹⁴ Only the women, the small children, the animals, and everything that will be in the city — all its booty — may you plunder for yourselves; you shall eat the booty of your enemies, which HASHEM, your God, gave you. ¹⁵ So shall you do to all the cities that are very distant from you, which are not of the cities of these nations. ¹⁶ But from the cities

הָעַמִּים הָאֵלֶּה אֲשֶׁר יְהוָה אֱלֹהֶיךָ נֹתֵן לְךָ נַחֲלָה לֹא תְחַיֶּה כָּל־נְשָׁמָה:

יז כִּי־הַחֲרֵם תַּחֲרִימֵם הַחִתִּי וְהָאֱמֹרִי הַכְּנַעֲנִי וְהַפְּרִזִּי הַחִוִּי וְהַיְבוּסִי כַּאֲשֶׁר

יח צִוְּךָ יְהוָה אֱלֹהֶיךָ: לְמַעַן אֲשֶׁר לֹא־יְלַמְּדוּ אֶתְכֶם לַעֲשׂוֹת כְּכֹל תּוֹעֲבֹתָם

יט אֲשֶׁר עָשׂוּ לֵאלֹהֵיהֶם וַחֲטָאתֶם לַיהוָה אֱלֹהֵיכֶם: כִּי־תָצוּר אֶל־עִיר יָמִים רַבִּים לְהִלָּחֵם עָלֶיהָ לְתָפְשָׂהּ לֹא־תַשְׁחִית אֶת־עֵצָהּ לִנְדֹּחַ עָלָיו גַּרְזֶן כִּי מִמֶּנּוּ תֹאכֵל וְאֹתוֹ לֹא תִכְרֹת כִּי הָאָדָם עֵץ הַשָּׂדֶה לָבֹא מִפָּנֶיךָ בַּמָּצוֹר: רַק עֵץ אֲשֶׁר־תֵּדַע כִּי־לֹא־עֵץ מַאֲכָל הוּא אֹתוֹ

כ תַשְׁחִית וְכָרָתָּ וּבָנִיתָ מָצוֹר עַל־הָעִיר אֲשֶׁר־הִוא עֹשָׂה עִמְּךָ מִלְחָמָה עַד רִדְתָּהּ:

כא א כִּי־יִמָּצֵא חָלָל בָּאֲדָמָה אֲשֶׁר יְהוָה אֱלֹהֶיךָ נֹתֵן לְךָ לְרִשְׁתָּהּ נֹפֵל בַּשָּׂדֶה

ב לֹא נוֹדַע מִי הִכָּהוּ: וְיָצְאוּ זְקֵנֶיךָ וְשֹׁפְטֶיךָ וּמָדְדוּ אֶל־הֶעָרִים אֲשֶׁר סְבִיבֹת

ג הֶחָלָל: וְהָיָה הָעִיר הַקְּרֹבָה אֶל־הֶחָלָל וְלָקְחוּ זִקְנֵי הָעִיר הַהִוא עֶגְלַת

ד בָּקָר אֲשֶׁר לֹא־עֻבַּד בָּהּ אֲשֶׁר לֹא־מָשְׁכָה בְּעֹל: וְהוֹרִדוּ זִקְנֵי הָעִיר הַהִוא אֶת־הָעֶגְלָה אֶל־נַחַל אֵיתָן אֲשֶׁר לֹא־יֵעָבֵד בּוֹ וְלֹא יִזָּרֵעַ וְעָרְפוּ־שָׁם

ה אֶת־הָעֶגְלָה בַּנָּחַל: וְנִגְּשׁוּ הַכֹּהֲנִים בְּנֵי לֵוִי כִּי בָם בָּחַר יְהוָה אֱלֹהֶיךָ לְשָׁרְתוֹ וּלְבָרֵךְ בְּשֵׁם יְהוָה וְעַל־פִּיהֶם יִהְיֶה כָּל־רִיב וְכָל־נָגַע: וְכֹל זִקְנֵי

ו הָעִיר הַהִוא הַקְּרֹבִים אֶל־הֶחָלָל יִרְחֲצוּ אֶת־יְדֵיהֶם עַל־הָעֶגְלָה הָעֲרוּפָה

ז בַנָּחַל: וְעָנוּ וְאָמְרוּ יָדֵינוּ לֹא *שָׁפְכָה [°שָׁפְכוּ ק] אֶת־הַדָּם הַזֶּה וְעֵינֵינוּ

ח לֹא רָאוּ: כַּפֵּר לְעַמְּךָ יִשְׂרָאֵל אֲשֶׁר־פָּדִיתָ יְהוָה וְאַל־תִּתֵּן דָּם נָקִי בְּקֶרֶב

ט עַמְּךָ יִשְׂרָאֵל וְנִכַּפֵּר לָהֶם הַדָּם: וְאַתָּה תְּבַעֵר הַדָּם הַנָּקִי מִקִּרְבֶּךָ כִּי־תַעֲשֶׂה הַיָּשָׁר בְּעֵינֵי יְהוָה: ססס צ״ו פסוקים. סלי״א סימן.

מפטיר

Haftaras
Shoftim:
p. 1044

פרשת כי תצא

י כִּי־תֵצֵא לַמִּלְחָמָה עַל־אֹיְבֶיךָ וּנְתָנוֹ יְהוָה אֱלֹהֶיךָ בְּיָדֶךָ וְשָׁבִיתָ שִׁבְיוֹ:

יא־יב וְרָאִיתָ בַּשִּׁבְיָה אֵשֶׁת יְפַת־תֹּאַר וְחָשַׁקְתָּ בָהּ וְלָקַחְתָּ לְךָ לְאִשָּׁה: וַהֲבֵאתָהּ אֶל־תּוֹךְ בֵּיתֶךָ וְגִלְּחָה אֶת־רֹאשָׁהּ וְעָשְׂתָה אֶת־צִפָּרְנֶיהָ: וְהֵסִירָה אֶת־

יג שִׂמְלַת שִׁבְיָהּ מֵעָלֶיהָ וְיָשְׁבָה בְּבֵיתֶךָ וּבָכְתָה אֶת־אָבִיהָ וְאֶת־אִמָּהּ יֶרַח

יד יָמִים וְאַחַר כֵּן תָּבוֹא אֵלֶיהָ וּבְעַלְתָּהּ וְהָיְתָה לְךָ לְאִשָּׁה: וְהָיָה אִם־לֹא חָפַצְתָּ בָּהּ וְשִׁלַּחְתָּהּ לְנַפְשָׁהּ וּמָכֹר לֹא־תִמְכְּרֶנָּה בַּכָּסֶף לֹא־תִתְעַמֵּר בָּהּ

טו תַּחַת אֲשֶׁר עִנִּיתָהּ: כִּי־תִהְיֶיןָ לְאִישׁ שְׁתֵּי נָשִׁים הָאַחַת אֲהוּבָה וְהָאַחַת שְׂנוּאָה וְיָלְדוּ־לוֹ בָנִים הָאֲהוּבָה וְהַשְּׂנוּאָה וְהָיָה הַבֵּן הַבְּכֹר

21:7. Did anyone suspect the elders of murder? They meant to say that they had no part in allowing him to go on his lonely way without food or escort (*Rashi*).

◆§ **Parashas Ki Seitzei**

21:11. The Torah responds to the often inflamed passion of a soldier in battle. Rather than risk sin, the Torah provides an avenue for the lustful soldier to satisfy his desire, so that it will cool before it causes more harm. After the laws of the captive woman, the Torah speaks of a hated wife, and then an incorrigibly rebellious child. The implication is that improper infatuation with a captive woman will lead to one family tragedy after another (*Rashi*).

of these peoples that HASHEM, your God, gives you as an inheritance, you shall not allow any person to live. ¹⁷ Rather you shall utterly destroy them: the Hittite, the Amorite, the Canaanite, the Perizzite, the Hivvite, and the Jebusite, as HASHEM, your God, has commanded you, ¹⁸ so that they will not teach you to act according to all their abominations that they performed for their gods, so that you will sin to HASHEM, your God.

Preservation of fruit trees ¹⁹ When you besiege a city for many days to wage war against it to seize it, do not destroy its trees by swinging an axe against them, for from it you will eat, and you shall not cut it down; is the tree of the field a man that it should enter the siege before you? ²⁰ Only a tree that you know is not a food tree, it you may destroy and cut down, and build a bulwark against the city that makes war with you, until it is conquered.

21

Unsolved murder: the axed heifer

¹ If a corpse will be found on the land that HASHEM, your God, gives you to possess it, fallen in the field, it was not known who smote him, ² your elders and judges shall go out and measure toward the cities that are around the corpse. ³ It shall be that the city nearest the corpse, the elders of that city shall take a heifer, with which no work has been done, which has not pulled with a yoke. ⁴ The elders of that city shall bring the heifer down to a harsh valley, which cannot be worked and cannot be sown, and they shall axe the back of its neck in the valley. ⁵ The Kohanim, the offspring of Levi, shall approach, for them has HASHEM, your God, chosen to minister to Him and to bless with the Name of HASHEM, and according to their word shall be every grievance and every plague.

⁶ All the elders of that city, who are closest to the corpse, shall wash their hands over the heifer that was axed in the valley. ⁷ They shall speak up and say, "Our hands have not spilled this blood, * and our eyes did not see. ⁸ Atone for Your people Israel that You have redeemed, O HASHEM: Do not place innocent blood in the midst of Your people Israel!" Then the blood shall be atoned for them.

⁹ But you shall remove the innocent blood from your midst when you do what is upright in the eyes of HASHEM.

PARASHAS KI SEITZEI

The woman of beautiful form ¹⁰ When you will go out to war against your enemies, and HASHEM, your God, will deliver him into your hand, and you will capture his captivity; ¹¹ and you will see among its captivity a woman who is beautiful of form, * and you will desire her, you may take her to yourself for a wife. ¹² You shall bring her to the midst of your house; she shall shave her head and let her nails grow. ¹³ She shall remove the garment of her captivity from upon herself and sit in your house and she shall weep for her father and her mother for a full month; thereafter you may come to her and live with her, and she shall be a wife to you. ¹⁴ But it shall be that if you do not desire her, then you shall send her on her own, but you may not sell her for money; you shall not enslave her, **The** because you have afflicted her.

firstborn's inviolable right ¹⁵ If a man will have two wives, one beloved and one hated, and they bear him sons, the beloved one and the hated one, and the firstborn son is

טז לַשְּׂנִיאָה: וְהָיָה בְּיוֹם הַנְחִילוֹ אֶת־בָּנָיו אֵת אֲשֶׁר־יִהְיֶה לוֹ לֹא יוּכַל לְבַכֵּר

יז אֶת־בֶּן־הָאֲהוּבָה עַל־פְּנֵי בֶן־הַשְּׂנוּאָה הַבְּכֹר: כִּי אֶת־הַבְּכֹר בֶּן־הַשְּׂנוּאָה יַכִּיר לָתֶת לוֹ פִּי שְׁנַיִם בְּכֹל אֲשֶׁר־יִמָּצֵא לוֹ כִּי־הוּא רֵאשִׁית אֹנוֹ לוֹ מִשְׁפַּט הַבְּכֹרָה:

יח כִּי־יִהְיֶה לְאִישׁ בֵּן סוֹרֵר וּמוֹרֶה אֵינֶנּוּ שֹׁמֵעַ בְּקוֹל אָבִיו וּבְקוֹל אִמּוֹ וְיִסְּרוּ אֹתוֹ וְלֹא יִשְׁמַע אֲלֵיהֶם: וְתָפְשׂוּ בוֹ

יט אָבִיו וְאִמּוֹ וְהוֹצִיאוּ אֹתוֹ אֶל־זִקְנֵי עִירוֹ וְאֶל־שַׁעַר מְקֹמוֹ: וְאָמְרוּ אֶל־זִקְנֵי

כ עִירוֹ בְּנֵנוּ זֶה סוֹרֵר וּמֹרֶה אֵינֶנּוּ שֹׁמֵעַ בְּקֹלֵנוּ זוֹלֵל וְסֹבֵא: וּרְגָמֻהוּ כָּל־

כא אַנְשֵׁי עִירוֹ בָאֲבָנִים וָמֵת וּבִעַרְתָּ הָרָע מִקִּרְבֶּךָ וְכָל־יִשְׂרָאֵל יִשְׁמְעוּ

שני   כב וְיִרָאוּ: וְכִי־יִהְיֶה בְאִישׁ חֵטְא מִשְׁפַּט־מָוֶת וְהוּמָת וְתָלִיתָ

כג אֹתוֹ עַל־עֵץ: לֹא־תָלִין נִבְלָתוֹ עַל־הָעֵץ כִּי־קָבוֹר תִּקְבְּרֶנּוּ בַּיּוֹם הַהוּא כִּי־קִלְלַת אֱלֹהִים תָּלוּי וְלֹא תְטַמֵּא אֶת־אַדְמָתְךָ אֲשֶׁר יהוה אֱלֹהֶיךָ נֹתֵן

כב   א לְךָ נַחֲלָה: לֹא־תִרְאֶה אֶת־שׁוֹר אָחִיךָ אוֹ אֶת־שֵׂיוֹ נִדָּחִים

ב וְהִתְעַלַּמְתָּ מֵהֶם הָשֵׁב תְּשִׁיבֵם לְאָחִיךָ: וְאִם־לֹא קָרוֹב אָחִיךָ אֵלֶיךָ וְלֹא יְדַעְתּוֹ וַאֲסַפְתּוֹ אֶל־תּוֹךְ בֵּיתֶךָ וְהָיָה עִמְּךָ עַד דְּרֹשׁ אָחִיךָ אֹתוֹ וַהֲשֵׁבֹתוֹ

ג לוֹ: וְכֵן תַּעֲשֶׂה לַחֲמֹרוֹ וְכֵן תַּעֲשֶׂה לְשִׂמְלָתוֹ וְכֵן תַּעֲשֶׂה לְכָל־אֲבֵדַת אָחִיךָ אֲשֶׁר־תֹּאבַד מִמֶּנּוּ וּמְצָאתָהּ לֹא תוּכַל לְהִתְעַלֵּם: לֹא־

ד תִרְאֶה אֶת־חֲמוֹר אָחִיךָ אוֹ שׁוֹרוֹ נֹפְלִים בַּדֶּרֶךְ וְהִתְעַלַּמְתָּ מֵהֶם הָקֵם תָּקִים עִמּוֹ:

ה לֹא־יִהְיֶה כְלִי־גֶבֶר עַל־אִשָּׁה וְלֹא־יִלְבַּשׁ גֶּבֶר שִׂמְלַת אִשָּׁה כִּי תוֹעֲבַת יהוה אֱלֹהֶיךָ כָּל־עֹשֵׂה אֵלֶּה:

ו כִּי יִקָּרֵא קַן־צִפּוֹר לְפָנֶיךָ בַּדֶּרֶךְ בְּכָל־עֵץ אוֹ עַל־הָאָרֶץ אֶפְרֹחִים אוֹ בֵיצִים וְהָאֵם רֹבֶצֶת עַל־הָאֶפְרֹחִים אוֹ עַל־הַבֵּיצִים לֹא־תִקַּח הָאֵם

ז עַל־הַבָּנִים: שַׁלֵּחַ תְּשַׁלַּח אֶת־הָאֵם וְאֶת־הַבָּנִים תִּקַּח־לָךְ לְמַעַן יִיטַב לָךְ וְהַאֲרַכְתָּ יָמִים: כִּי תִבְנֶה בַּיִת חָדָשׁ וְעָשִׂיתָ

שלישי   ח מַעֲקֶה לְגַגֶּךָ וְלֹא־תָשִׂים דָּמִים בְּבֵיתֶךָ כִּי־יִפֹּל הַנֹּפֵל מִמֶּנּוּ: לֹא־

ט תִזְרַע כַּרְמְךָ כִּלְאָיִם פֶּן־תִּקְדַּשׁ הַמְלֵאָה הַזֶּרַע אֲשֶׁר תִּזְרָע וּתְבוּאַת

י הַכָּרֶם: לֹא־תַחֲרֹשׁ בְּשׁוֹר־וּבַחֲמֹר יַחְדָּו: לֹא תִלְבַּשׁ

יא-יב שַׁעַטְנֵז צֶמֶר וּפִשְׁתִּים יַחְדָּו: גְּדִלִים תַּעֲשֶׂה־לָּךְ עַל־

יג אַרְבַּע כַּנְפוֹת כְּסוּתְךָ אֲשֶׁר תְּכַסֶּה־בָּהּ: כִּי־יִקַּח אִישׁ אִשָּׁה

יד וּבָא אֵלֶיהָ וּשְׂנֵאָהּ: וְשָׂם לָהּ עֲלִילֹת דְּבָרִים וְהוֹצִיא עָלֶיהָ שֵׁם רָע וְאָמַר

21:18-21. The death penalty is imposed only in very specific circumstances which make it clear that the youngster will degenerate into a monstrous human being, but the Sages state that there never was and never will be a capital case involving such a son (Sanhedrin 71a, 72a). The passage must be understood as an implied primer for parents on how to inculcate values into their children.

21:20. The boy must have stolen from his parents enough money to buy and consume a substantial amount of meat and alcoholic beverages (Sanhedrin 70a).

22:2. This applies to every case where one's physical or verbal intervention can help someone avoid a loss.

22:7. We are commanded to send the mother bird from the nest because animals instinctively care for their young and suffer when they see them slaughtered or taken away (Rambam).

22:8. The Torah requires a Jew to erect a fence or other the hated one's; [16] then it shall be that on the day that he causes his sons to inherit whatever will be his, he cannot give the right of the firstborn to the son of the beloved one ahead of the son of the hated one, the firstborn. [17] Rather, he must recognize the firstborn, the son of the hated one, to give him the double portion in all that is found with him; for he is his initial vigor, to him is the right of the firstborn.

[18] If a man will have a wayward and rebellious son, * who does not hearken to the voice of his father and the voice of his mother, and they discipline him, but he does not hearken to them; [19] then his father and mother shall grasp him and take him out to the elders of his city and the gate of his place. [20] They shall say to the elders of his city, "This son of ours is wayward and rebellious; he does not hearken to our voice; he is a glutton and a drunkard."* [21] All the men of his city shall pelt him with stones and he shall die; and you shall remove the evil from your midst; and all Israel shall hear and they shall fear.

The wayward and rebellious son

[22] If a man shall have committed a sin whose judgment is death, he shall be put to death, and you shall hang him on a gallows. [23] His body shall not remain for the night on the gallows, rather you shall surely bury him on that day, for a hanging person is a curse of God, and you shall not contaminate your Land, which HASHEM, your God, gives you as an inheritance.

Hanging and burial

22

[1] **Y**ou shall not see the ox of your brother or his sheep or goat cast off, and hide yourself from them; you shall surely return them to your brother. [2] If your brother is not near you and you do not know him, then gather it inside your house, and it shall remain with you until your brother inquires after it, and you return it to him. * [3] So shall you do for his donkey, so shall you do for his garment, and so shall you do for any lost article of your brother that may become lost from him and you find it; you shall not hide yourself.

Concern for the property of another

[4] You shall not see the donkey of your brother or his ox falling on the road and hide yourself from them; you shall surely stand them up, with him. *

[5] Male garb shall not be on a woman, and a man shall not wear a woman's garment, for anyone who does so is an abomination of HASHEM.

Male and female garb

[6] If a bird's nest happens to be before you on the road, on any tree or on the ground — young birds or eggs — and the mother is roosting on the young birds or on the eggs, you shall not take the mother with the young. [7] You shall surely send away the mother* and take the young for yourself, so that it will be good for you and will prolong your days.

Sending the mother bird from the nest

[8] If you build a new house, you shall make a fence for your roof, so that you will not place blood in your house if a fallen one falls from it. *

Protective fence

[9] You shall not sow your vineyard with a mixture, lest the growth of the seed that you plant and the produce of the vineyard become forbidden.

[10] You shall not plow with an ox and a donkey together. [11] You shall not wear combined fibers, wool and linen together.

[12] You shall make for yourselves twisted threads on the four corners of your garment with which you cover yourself.

Tzitzis

[13] If a man marries a wife, * and comes to her and hates her, [14] and he makes a wanton accusation against her, spreading a bad name against her, and he said,

---

form of barrier around his roof. This applies also to any dangerous situation, such as a swimming pool or a tall stairway.

22:13-19. The husband accuses his new wife of not being a virgin. If it can be proven that she had committed adultery after *kiddushin*, the first stage of marriage, she

טו אֶת־הָאִשָּׁה הַזֹּאת לָקַחְתִּי וָאֶקְרַב אֵלֶיהָ וְלֹא־מָצָאתִי לָהּ בְּתוּלִים: וְלָקַח אֲבִי הַנַּעֲרָ וְאִמָּהּ וְהוֹצִיאוּ אֶת־בְּתוּלֵי הַנַּעֲרָ אֶל־זִקְנֵי הָעִיר הַשָּׁעְרָה:

טז וְאָמַר אֲבִי הַנַּעֲרָ אֶל־הַזְּקֵנִים אֶת־בִּתִּי נָתַתִּי לָאִישׁ הַזֶּה לְאִשָּׁה וַיִּשְׂנָאֶהָ:

יז וְהִנֵּה־הוּא שָׂם עֲלִילֹת דְּבָרִים לֵאמֹר לֹא־מָצָאתִי לְבִתְּךָ בְּתוּלִים וְאֵלֶּה בְּתוּלֵי בִתִּי וּפָרְשׂוּ הַשִּׂמְלָה לִפְנֵי זִקְנֵי הָעִיר: וְלָקְחוּ זִקְנֵי הָעִיר־הַהִוא

יח אֶת־הָאִישׁ וְיִסְּרוּ אֹתוֹ:

יט וְעָנְשׁוּ אֹתוֹ מֵאָה כֶסֶף וְנָתְנוּ לַאֲבִי הַנַּעֲרָה כִּי הוֹצִיא שֵׁם רָע עַל בְּתוּלַת יִשְׂרָאֵל וְלוֹ־תִהְיֶה לְאִשָּׁה לֹא־יוּכַל לְשַׁלְּחָהּ כָּל־יָמָיו:

כ וְאִם־אֱמֶת הָיָה הַדָּבָר הַזֶּה לֹא־נִמְצְאוּ בְתוּלִים לַנַּעֲרָ:

כא וְהוֹצִיאוּ אֶת־הַנַּעֲרָ אֶל־פֶּתַח בֵּית־אָבִיהָ וּסְקָלוּהָ אַנְשֵׁי עִירָהּ בָּאֲבָנִים וָמֵתָה כִּי־עָשְׂתָה נְבָלָה בְּיִשְׂרָאֵל לִזְנוֹת בֵּית אָבִיהָ וּבִעַרְתָּ הָרָע מִקִּרְבֶּךָ:

כב כִּי־יִמָּצֵא אִישׁ שֹׁכֵב ׀ עִם־אִשָּׁה בְעֻלַת־בַּעַל וּמֵתוּ גַּם־שְׁנֵיהֶם הָאִישׁ הַשֹּׁכֵב עִם־הָאִשָּׁה וְהָאִשָּׁה וּבִעַרְתָּ הָרָע מִיִּשְׂרָאֵל:

כג כִּי יִהְיֶה נַעֲרָ בְתוּלָה מְאֹרָשָׂה לְאִישׁ וּמְצָאָהּ אִישׁ בָּעִיר וְשָׁכַב עִמָּהּ: וְהוֹצֵאתֶם אֶת־שְׁנֵיהֶם אֶל־שַׁעַר ׀ הָעִיר הַהִוא

כד וּסְקַלְתֶּם אֹתָם בָּאֲבָנִים וָמֵתוּ אֶת־הַנַּעֲרָ עַל־דְּבַר אֲשֶׁר לֹא־צָעֲקָה בָעִיר וְאֶת־הָאִישׁ עַל־דְּבַר אֲשֶׁר־עִנָּה אֶת־אֵשֶׁת רֵעֵהוּ וּבִעַרְתָּ הָרָע מִקִּרְבֶּךָ:

כה וְאִם־בַּשָּׂדֶה יִמְצָא הָאִישׁ אֶת־הַנַּעֲרָ הַמְאֹרָשָׂה וְהֶחֱזִיק־בָּהּ הָאִישׁ וְשָׁכַב עִמָּהּ וּמֵת הָאִישׁ אֲשֶׁר־שָׁכַב עִמָּהּ לְבַדּוֹ:

כו וְלַנַּעֲרָ לֹא־תַעֲשֶׂה דָבָר אֵין לַנַּעֲרָ חֵטְא מָוֶת כִּי כַּאֲשֶׁר יָקוּם אִישׁ עַל־רֵעֵהוּ וּרְצָחוֹ נֶפֶשׁ כֵּן הַדָּבָר הַזֶּה: כִּי בַשָּׂדֶה מְצָאָהּ צָעֲקָה הַנַּעֲרָ

כז הַמְאֹרָשָׂה וְאֵין מוֹשִׁיעַ לָהּ:

כח כִּי־יִמְצָא אִישׁ נַעֲרָ בְתוּלָה אֲשֶׁר לֹא־אֹרָשָׂה וּתְפָשָׂהּ וְשָׁכַב עִמָּהּ וְנִמְצָאוּ: וְנָתַן הָאִישׁ הַשֹּׁכֵב

כט עִמָּהּ לַאֲבִי הַנַּעֲרָ חֲמִשִּׁים כָּסֶף וְלוֹ־תִהְיֶה לְאִשָּׁה תַּחַת אֲשֶׁר עִנָּהּ לֹא־יוּכַל שַׁלְּחָהּ כָּל־יָמָיו:

כג א לֹא־יִקַּח אִישׁ אֶת־אֵשֶׁת אָבִיו וְלֹא יְגַלֶּה כְּנַף אָבִיו:

ב לֹא־יָבֹא פְצוּעַ־דַּכָּה וּכְרוּת שָׁפְכָה בִּקְהַל יהוה:

ג לֹא־יָבֹא מַמְזֵר בִּקְהַל יהוה גַּם דּוֹר עֲשִׂירִי לֹא־יָבֹא לוֹ בִּקְהַל יהוה:

ד לֹא־יָבֹא עַמּוֹנִי וּמוֹאָבִי בִּקְהַל יהוה גַּם דּוֹר עֲשִׂירִי לֹא־יָבֹא לָהֶם בִּקְהַל יהוה עַד־עוֹלָם:

ה עַל־דְּבַר אֲשֶׁר לֹא־קִדְּמוּ אֶתְכֶם בַּלֶּחֶם וּבַמַּיִם בַּדֶּרֶךְ בְּצֵאתְכֶם מִמִּצְרָיִם וַאֲשֶׁר שָׂכַר עָלֶיךָ אֶת־בִּלְעָם בֶּן־בְּעוֹר מִפְּתוֹר אֲרַם נַהֲרַיִם לְקַלְלֶךָּ:

ו וְלֹא־אָבָה יהוה אֱלֹהֶיךָ לִשְׁמֹעַ אֶל־בִּלְעָם וַיַּהֲפֹךְ יהוה אֱלֹהֶיךָ לְּךָ אֶת־הַקְּלָלָה לִבְרָכָה

---

would be subject to the death penalty. Otherwise, the slanderous husband is punished. Even if it is true that she was not a virgin, she is not liable to any punishment by the court, because she may have lived with a man *before* the marriage.

23:3. A *mamzer* is someone born of a union between a man and woman whose marriage could never be valid, such as a union between brother and sister or other such forms of incest, or from a married woman who bore another man's child.

Defamation of a married woman *"I married this woman, and I came near to her and I did not find signs of virginity on her."* [15] Then the father of the girl and her mother should take and bring proofs of the girl's virginity to the elders of the city, to the gate. [16] The father of the girl should say to the elders, "I gave my daughter to this man as a wife, and he hated her. [17] Now, behold! he made a wanton accusation against her, saying, 'I did not find signs of virginity on your daughter' — but these are the signs of virginity of my daughter!" And they should spread out the sheet before the elders of the city.

[18] The elders of the city shall take that man and punish him. [19] And they shall fine him one hundred silver [shekels] and give them to the father of the girl, for he had issued a slander against a virgin of Israel, and she shall remain with him as a wife; he cannot divorce her all his days.

If the accusation was true [20] But if this matter was true — signs of virginity were not found on the girl — [21] then they shall take the girl to the entrance of her father's house and the people of her city shall pelt her with stones and she shall die, for she had committed an outrage in Israel, to commit adultery in her father's house, and you shall remove the evil from your midst.

Adultery [22] If a man will be found lying with a woman who is married to a husband, then both of them shall die, the man who lay with the woman and the woman; and you shall remove the evil from Israel.

Betrothed maiden [23] If there will be a virgin girl who is betrothed to a man, and a man finds her in the city and lies with her, [24] then you shall take them both to the gate of that city and pelt them with stones and they shall die: the girl because of the fact that she did not cry out in the city, and the man because of the fact that he afflicted the wife of his fellow; and you shall remove the evil from your midst.

[25] But if it is in the field that the man will find the betrothed girl, and the man will seize her and lie with her, only the man who lies with her shall die. [26] But you shall do nothing to the girl, for the girl has committed no capital sin, for like a man who rises up against his fellow and murders him, so is this thing; [27] for he found her in the field, the betrothed girl cried out, but she had no savior.

[28] If a man will find a virgin maiden who was not betrothed, and takes hold of her and lies with her, and they are discovered, [29] then the man who lay with her shall give the father of the girl fifty silver [shekels], and she shall become his wife, because he had afflicted her; he cannot divorce her all his life.

23

Forbidden and restricted marriages [1] **A** man shall not marry the wife of his father; and he shall not uncover the robe of his father. [2] A man with crushed testicles or a severed organ shall not enter the congregation of HASHEM.

[3] A mamzer* shall not enter the congregation of HASHEM, even his tenth generation shall not enter the congregation of HASHEM.

[4] An Ammonite or Moabite* shall not enter the congregation of HASHEM, even their tenth generation shall not enter the congregation of HASHEM, to eternity, [5] because of the fact that they did not greet you with bread and water on the road when you were leaving Egypt, and because he hired against you Balaam son of Beor, of Pethor, Aram Naharaim, to curse you. [6] But HASHEM, your God, refused to listen to Balaam, and HASHEM, your God, reversed the curse to a blessing for

---

23:4-5. Ammon refused even to sell them bread and water, and Moab — which sold them food and water (see 2:28-29) — sinned by hiring Balaam to curse them

(*Ramban*). This was indicative of an ingrained selfishness and mean-spirited character that has no place in Israel.

ז כִּי אֲהֵבְךָ יְהוָה אֱלֹהֶיךָ: לֹא־תִדְרֹשׁ שְׁלֹמָם וְטֹבָתָם כָּל־יָמֶיךָ
ח לְעוֹלָם: לֹא־תְתַעֵב אֲדֹמִי כִּי אָחִיךָ הוּא לֹא־תְתַעֵב מִצְרִי

ט כִּי־גֵר הָיִיתָ בְאַרְצוֹ: בָּנִים אֲשֶׁר־יִוָּלְדוּ לָהֶם דּוֹר שְׁלִישִׁי יָבֹא לָהֶם בִּקְהַל
י יְהוָה: כִּי־תֵצֵא מַחֲנֶה עַל־אֹיְבֶיךָ וְנִשְׁמַרְתָּ מִכֹּל דָּבָר רָע:

יא כִּי־יִהְיֶה בְךָ אִישׁ אֲשֶׁר לֹא־יִהְיֶה טָהוֹר מִקְּרֵה־לָיְלָה וְיָצָא אֶל־מִחוּץ
יב לַמַּחֲנֶה לֹא יָבֹא אֶל־תּוֹךְ הַמַּחֲנֶה: וְהָיָה לִפְנוֹת־עֶרֶב יִרְחַץ בַּמָּיִם וּכְבֹא
יג הַשֶּׁמֶשׁ יָבֹא אֶל־תּוֹךְ הַמַּחֲנֶה: וְיָד תִּהְיֶה לְךָ מִחוּץ לַמַּחֲנֶה וְיָצָאתָ שָּׁמָּה
יד חוּץ: וְיָתֵד תִּהְיֶה לְךָ עַל־אֲזֵנֶךָ וְהָיָה בְּשִׁבְתְּךָ חוּץ וְחָפַרְתָּה בָהּ וְשַׁבְתָּ
טו וְכִסִּיתָ אֶת־צֵאָתֶךָ: כִּי יְהוָה אֱלֹהֶיךָ מִתְהַלֵּךְ ׀ בְּקֶרֶב מַחֲנֶךָ לְהַצִּילְךָ
וְלָתֵת אֹיְבֶיךָ לְפָנֶיךָ וְהָיָה מַחֲנֶיךָ קָדוֹשׁ וְלֹא־יִרְאֶה בְךָ עֶרְוַת דָּבָר וְשָׁב
טז מֵאַחֲרֶיךָ: לֹא־תַסְגִּיר עֶבֶד אֶל־אֲדֹנָיו אֲשֶׁר־יִנָּצֵל אֵלֶיךָ
יז מֵעִם אֲדֹנָיו: עִמְּךָ יֵשֵׁב בְּקִרְבְּךָ בַּמָּקוֹם אֲשֶׁר־יִבְחַר בְּאַחַד שְׁעָרֶיךָ בַּטּוֹב
יח לוֹ לֹא תּוֹנֶנּוּ: לֹא־תִהְיֶה קְדֵשָׁה מִבְּנוֹת יִשְׂרָאֵל וְלֹא־יִהְיֶה
יט קָדֵשׁ מִבְּנֵי יִשְׂרָאֵל: לֹא־תָבִיא אֶתְנַן זוֹנָה וּמְחִיר כֶּלֶב בֵּית יְהוָה אֱלֹהֶיךָ
כ לְכָל־נֶדֶר כִּי תוֹעֲבַת יְהוָה אֱלֹהֶיךָ גַּם־שְׁנֵיהֶם: לֹא־
כא תַשִּׁיךְ לְאָחִיךָ נֶשֶׁךְ כֶּסֶף נֶשֶׁךְ אֹכֶל נֶשֶׁךְ כָּל־דָּבָר אֲשֶׁר יִשָּׁךְ: לַנָּכְרִי תַשִּׁיךְ
וּלְאָחִיךָ לֹא תַשִּׁיךְ לְמַעַן יְבָרֶכְךָ יְהוָה אֱלֹהֶיךָ בְּכֹל מִשְׁלַח יָדֶךָ עַל־
כב הָאָרֶץ אֲשֶׁר־אַתָּה בָא־שָׁמָּה לְרִשְׁתָּהּ: כִּי־תִדֹּר נֶדֶר
לַיהוָה אֱלֹהֶיךָ לֹא תְאַחֵר לְשַׁלְּמוֹ כִּי־דָרֹשׁ יִדְרְשֶׁנּוּ יְהוָה אֱלֹהֶיךָ
כג-כד מֵעִמָּךְ וְהָיָה בְךָ חֵטְא: וְכִי תֶחְדַּל לִנְדֹּר לֹא־יִהְיֶה בְךָ חֵטְא: מוֹצָא
שְׂפָתֶיךָ תִּשְׁמֹר וְעָשִׂיתָ כַּאֲשֶׁר נָדַרְתָּ לַיהוָה אֱלֹהֶיךָ נְדָבָה אֲשֶׁר דִּבַּרְתָּ
כה בְּפִיךָ: כִּי תָבֹא בְּכֶרֶם רֵעֶךָ וְאָכַלְתָּ עֲנָבִים כְּנַפְשְׁךָ שָׂבְעֶךָ
כו וְאֶל־כֶּלְיְךָ לֹא תִתֵּן: כִּי תָבֹא בְּקָמַת רֵעֶךָ וְקָטַפְתָּ מְלִילֹת
כד א בְּיָדֶךָ וְחֶרְמֵשׁ לֹא תָנִיף עַל קָמַת רֵעֶךָ: כִּי־יִקַּח אִישׁ אִשָּׁה
וּבְעָלָהּ וְהָיָה אִם־לֹא תִמְצָא־חֵן בְּעֵינָיו כִּי־מָצָא בָהּ עֶרְוַת דָּבָר וְכָתַב לָהּ
ב סֵפֶר כְּרִיתֻת וְנָתַן בְּיָדָהּ וְשִׁלְּחָהּ מִבֵּיתוֹ: וְיָצְאָה מִבֵּיתוֹ וְהָלְכָה וְהָיְתָה
ג לְאִישׁ־אַחֵר: וּשְׂנֵאָהּ הָאִישׁ הָאַחֲרוֹן וְכָתַב לָהּ סֵפֶר כְּרִיתֻת וְנָתַן בְּיָדָהּ
ד וְשִׁלְּחָהּ מִבֵּיתוֹ אוֹ כִי יָמוּת הָאִישׁ הָאַחֲרוֹן אֲשֶׁר־לְקָחָהּ לוֹ לְאִשָּׁה: לֹא־
יוּכַל בַּעְלָהּ הָרִאשׁוֹן אֲשֶׁר־שִׁלְּחָהּ לָשׁוּב לְקַחְתָּהּ לִהְיוֹת לוֹ לְאִשָּׁה
אַחֲרֵי אֲשֶׁר הֻטַּמָּאָה כִּי־תוֹעֵבָה הִוא לִפְנֵי יְהוָה וְלֹא תַחֲטִיא אֶת־הָאָרֶץ
ה אֲשֶׁר יְהוָה אֱלֹהֶיךָ נֹתֵן לְךָ נַחֲלָה: כִּי־יִקַּח

רביעי

חמישי

כד

ששי

23:10-15. Sanctity of the camp. Other armies triumph by force of numbers and arms, but Israel's success is in the hands of God, and, therefore, sins that God might overlook in ordinary times become significant during wartime or other crises.

23:20-21. A borrower may not pay interest (*Rashi*).
23:22. This refers to vows to bring offerings, give charity, or perform other good deeds.
23:25-26. The passage refers to a laborer engaged in harvesting crops.

you, because HASHEM, your God, loved you. ⁷ You shall not seek their peace or their welfare, all your days, forever.

⁸ You shall not reject an Edomite, for he is your brother; you shall not reject an Egyptian, for you were a sojourner in his land. ⁹ Children who are born to them in the third generation may enter the congregation of HASHEM.

Sanctity of the camp ¹⁰ When a camp goes out against your enemies, you shall guard against anything evil. * ¹¹ If there will be among you a man who will not be clean because of a nocturnal occurrence, he shall go outside the camp; he shall not enter the midst of the camp. ¹² When it will be toward evening, he shall immerse himself in the water, and when the sun sets, he may enter the midst of the camp. ¹³ You shall have a place outside the camp, and to it you shall go out. ¹⁴ You shall have a shovel in addition to your weapons, and it will be that when you sit outside, you shall dig with it; you shall go back and cover your excrement. ¹⁵ For HASHEM, your God, walks in the midst of your camp to rescue you and to deliver your enemies before you; so your camp shall be holy, so that He will not see a shameful thing among you and turn away from behind you.

An escaped slave ¹⁶ You shall not turn over to his master a slave who is rescued from his master to you. ¹⁷ He shall dwell with you in your midst, in whatever place he will choose in one of your cities, which is beneficial to him; you shall not taunt him.

Sexual purity ¹⁸ There shall not be a promiscuous woman among the daughters of Israel, and there shall not be a promiscuous man among the sons of Israel. ¹⁹ You shall not bring a harlot's hire or the exchange for a dog to the House of HASHEM, your God, for any vow, for both of them are an abomination of HASHEM, your God.

Interest ²⁰ You shall not cause your brother to take interest, * interest of money or interest of food, interest of anything that he may take as interest. ²¹ You may cause a gentile to take interest, but you may not cause your brother to take interest, so that HASHEM, your God, will bless you in your every undertaking on the Land to which you are coming, to possess it.

Vows to God ²² When you make a vow to HASHEM, * your God, you shall not be late in paying it, for HASHEM, your God, will demand it of you, and there will be a sin in you. ²³ If you refrain from vowing, there will be no sin in you. ²⁴ You shall observe and carry out what emerges from your lips, just as you vowed a voluntary gift to HASHEM, your God, whatever you spoke with your mouth.

A worker's right to eat ²⁵ When you come into the vineyard of your fellow, * you may eat grapes as is your desire, to your fill, but you may not put into your vessel.

²⁶ When you come into the standing grain of your fellow, you may pluck ears with your hand, but you may not lift a sickle against the standing grain of your fellow.

24

Divorce and remarriage ¹ If a man marries a woman and lives with her, and it will be that she will not find favor in his eyes, for he found in her a matter of immorality, and he wrote her a bill of divorce and presented it into her hand, and sent her from his house, ² and she left his house and went and married another man, ³ and the latter man hated her and wrote her a bill of divorce and presented it into her hand and sent her from his house, or the latter man who married her to himself will die — ⁴ her first husband who divorced her shall not again take her to become his wife, after she had been defiled, for it is an abomination before HASHEM. You shall not bring sin upon the Land that HASHEM, your God, gives you as an inheritance.

אִישׁ אִשָּׁה חֲדָשָׁה לֹא יֵצֵא בַּצָּבָא וְלֹא־יַעֲבֹר עָלָיו לְכָל־דָּבָר נָקִי יִהְיֶה

ו לְבֵיתוֹ שָׁנָה אֶחָת וְשִׂמַּח אֶת־אִשְׁתּוֹ אֲשֶׁר־לָקָח: לֹא־יַחֲבֹל רֵחַיִם וָרָכֶב

ז כִּי־נֶפֶשׁ הוּא חֹבֵל: כִּי־יִמָּצֵא אִישׁ גֹּנֵב נֶפֶשׁ

מֵאֶחָיו מִבְּנֵי יִשְׂרָאֵל וְהִתְעַמֶּר־בּוֹ וּמְכָרוֹ וּמֵת הַגַּנָּב הַהוּא וּבִעַרְתָּ הָרָע

ח מִקִּרְבֶּךָ: הִשָּׁמֶר בְּנֶגַע־הַצָּרַעַת לִשְׁמֹר מְאֹד

וְלַעֲשׂוֹת כְּכֹל אֲשֶׁר־יוֹרוּ אֶתְכֶם הַכֹּהֲנִים הַלְוִיִּם כַּאֲשֶׁר צִוִּיתִם תִּשְׁמְרוּ

ט לַעֲשׂוֹת: זָכוֹר אֵת אֲשֶׁר־עָשָׂה יְהוָה אֱלֹהֶיךָ לְמִרְיָם בַּדֶּרֶךְ בְּצֵאתְכֶם

י מִמִּצְרָיִם: כִּי־תַשֶּׁה בְרֵעֲךָ מַשַּׁאת מְאוּמָה

יא לֹא־תָבֹא אֶל־בֵּיתוֹ לַעֲבֹט עֲבֹטוֹ: בַּחוּץ תַּעֲמֹד וְהָאִישׁ אֲשֶׁר אַתָּה נֹשֶׁה

יב בוֹ יוֹצִיא אֵלֶיךָ אֶת־הָעֲבוֹט הַחוּצָה: וְאִם־אִישׁ עָנִי הוּא לֹא תִשְׁכַּב

יג בַּעֲבֹטוֹ: הָשֵׁב תָּשִׁיב לוֹ אֶת־הָעֲבוֹט כְּבוֹא הַשֶּׁמֶשׁ וְשָׁכַב בְּשַׂלְמָתוֹ

שביעי וּבֵרֲכֶךָ וּלְךָ תִּהְיֶה צְדָקָה לִפְנֵי יְהוָה אֱלֹהֶיךָ: לֹא־

יד תַעֲשֹׁק שָׂכִיר עָנִי וְאֶבְיוֹן מֵאַחֶיךָ אוֹ מִגֵּרְךָ אֲשֶׁר בְּאַרְצְךָ בִּשְׁעָרֶיךָ:

טו בְּיוֹמוֹ תִתֵּן שְׂכָרוֹ וְלֹא־תָבוֹא עָלָיו הַשֶּׁמֶשׁ כִּי עָנִי הוּא וְאֵלָיו הוּא נֹשֵׂא

טז אֶת־נַפְשׁוֹ וְלֹא־יִקְרָא עָלֶיךָ אֶל־יְהוָה וְהָיָה בְךָ חֵטְא: לֹא־

יוּמְתוּ אָבוֹת עַל־בָּנִים וּבָנִים לֹא־יוּמְתוּ עַל־אָבוֹת אִישׁ בְּחֶטְאוֹ

יז יוּמָתוּ: לֹא תַטֶּה מִשְׁפַּט גֵּר יָתוֹם וְלֹא תַחֲבֹל בֶּגֶד

יח אַלְמָנָה: וְזָכַרְתָּ כִּי עֶבֶד הָיִיתָ בְּמִצְרַיִם וַיִּפְדְּךָ יְהוָה אֱלֹהֶיךָ מִשָּׁם

יט עַל־כֵּן אָנֹכִי מְצַוְּךָ לַעֲשׂוֹת אֶת־הַדָּבָר הַזֶּה: כִּי

תִקְצֹר קְצִירְךָ בְשָׂדֶךָ וְשָׁכַחְתָּ עֹמֶר בַּשָּׂדֶה לֹא תָשׁוּב לְקַחְתּוֹ לַגֵּר

לַיָּתוֹם וְלָאַלְמָנָה יִהְיֶה לְמַעַן יְבָרֶכְךָ יְהוָה אֱלֹהֶיךָ בְּכֹל מַעֲשֵׂה

כ יָדֶיךָ: כִּי תַחְבֹּט זֵיתְךָ לֹא תְפַאֵר אַחֲרֶיךָ לַגֵּר

כא לַיָּתוֹם וְלָאַלְמָנָה יִהְיֶה: כִּי תִבְצֹר כַּרְמְךָ לֹא תְעוֹלֵל אַחֲרֶיךָ לַגֵּר לַיָּתוֹם

כב וְלָאַלְמָנָה יִהְיֶה: וְזָכַרְתָּ כִּי־עֶבֶד הָיִיתָ בְּאֶרֶץ מִצְרָיִם עַל־כֵּן אָנֹכִי מְצַוְּךָ

כה א לַעֲשׂוֹת אֶת־הַדָּבָר הַזֶּה: כִּי־יִהְיֶה רִיב בֵּין אֲנָשִׁים

וְנִגְּשׁוּ אֶל־הַמִּשְׁפָּט וּשְׁפָטוּם וְהִצְדִּיקוּ אֶת־הַצַּדִּיק וְהִרְשִׁיעוּ אֶת־

ב הָרָשָׁע: וְהָיָה אִם־בִּן הַכּוֹת הָרָשָׁע וְהִפִּילוֹ הַשֹּׁפֵט וְהִכָּהוּ לְפָנָיו כְּדֵי

ג רִשְׁעָתוֹ בְּמִסְפָּר: אַרְבָּעִים יַכֶּנּוּ לֹא יֹסִיף פֶּן־יֹסִיף לְהַכֹּתוֹ עַל־אֵלֶּה מַכָּה

ד-ה רַבָּה וְנִקְלָה אָחִיךָ לְעֵינֶיךָ: לֹא־תַחְסֹם שׁוֹר בְּדִישׁוֹ: כִּי־

יֵשְׁבוּ אַחִים יַחְדָּו וּמֵת אַחַד מֵהֶם וּבֵן אֵין־לוֹ לֹא־תִהְיֶה אֵשֶׁת־

הַמֵּת הַחוּצָה לְאִישׁ זָר יְבָמָהּ יָבֹא עָלֶיהָ וּלְקָחָהּ לוֹ לְאִשָּׁה וְיִבְּמָהּ:

24:6. The Torah forbids a creditor to takes as collateral anything that the debtor needs for his livelihood, for to deprive a person of his means of making a living is tantamount to taking his life.

24:8-9. See introduction to *Leviticus* 13.

25:5-10. If a husband dies childless, his widow should marry one of his brothers. In case the brother does not wish to go through with the marriage, the *chalitzah* ritual severs the bond between them.

⁵ When a man marries a new wife, he shall not go out to the army, nor shall it obligate him for any matter; he shall be free for his home for one year, and he shall gladden his wife whom he has married.

Millstone   ⁶ One shall not take a lower or upper millstone as a pledge, * for he would be taking a life as a pledge.

Kidnaping   ⁷ If a man is found kidnaping a person of his brethren among the Children of Israel, and he enslaves him and sells him, that kidnaper shall die, and you shall remove the evil from your midst.

Tzaraas and slander   ⁸ Beware of a tzaraas affliction, * to be very careful and to act; according to everything that the Kohanim, the Levites, shall teach you — as I have commanded them — you shall be careful to perform. ⁹ Remember what HASHEM, your God, did to Miriam on the way, when you were leaving Egypt.

Dignity of a debtor   ¹⁰ When you make your fellow a loan of any amount, you shall not enter his home to take security for it. ¹¹ You shall stand outside; and the man to whom you lend shall bring the security to you outside. ¹² If that man is poor, you shall not sleep with his security. ¹³ You shall return the security to him when the sun sets, and he will sleep in his garment and bless you, and for you it will be an act of righteousness before HASHEM, your God.

Timely payment of workers   ¹⁴ You shall not cheat a poor or destitute hired person among your brethren, or a proselyte who is in your Land, or one who is in your cities. ¹⁵ On that day shall you pay his hire; the sun shall not set upon him, for he is poor, and his life depends on it; let him not call out against you to HASHEM, for it shall be a sin in you.

Individual responsibility   ¹⁶ Fathers shall not be put to death because of sons, and sons shall not be put to death because of fathers; a man should be put to death for his own sin.

Consideration for the orphan and widow   ¹⁷ You shall not pervert the judgment of a proselyte or orphan, and you shall not take the garment of a widow as a pledge. ¹⁸ You shall remember that you were a slave in Egypt, and HASHEM, your God, redeemed you from there; therefore I command you to do this thing.

Gifts to the poor from the harvest   ¹⁹ When you reap your harvest in your field, and you forget a bundle in the field, you shall not turn back to take it; it shall be for the proselyte, the orphan, and the widow, so that HASHEM, your God, will bless you in all your handiwork.

²⁰ When you beat your olive tree, do not remove all the splendor behind you; it shall be for the proselyte, the orphan, and the widow. ²¹ When you harvest your vineyard, you shall not glean behind you; it shall be for the proselyte, the orphan, and the widow. ²² You shall remember that you were a slave in the land of Egypt, therefore I command you to do this thing.

25   ¹ When there will be a grievance between people, and they approach the court, and they judge them, and they vindicate the righteous one and find the wicked one guilty; ² it will be that if the wicked one is liable to lashes,

Lashes   the judge shall cast him down and strike him, before him, according to his wickedness, by a count. ³ Forty shall he strike him, he shall not add; lest he strike him an additional blow beyond these, and your brother will be degraded in your eyes. ⁴ You shall not muzzle an ox in its threshing.

Levirate marriage and releasing the obligation   ⁵ When brothers dwell together and one of them dies, * and he has no child, the wife of the deceased shall not marry outside to a strange man; her brother-in-law shall come to her, and take her to himself as a wife, and perform levirate marriage.

וְהָיָה הַבְּכוֹר אֲשֶׁר תֵּלֵד יָקוּם עַל־שֵׁם אָחִיו הַמֵּת וְלֹא־יִמָּחֶה שְׁמוֹ
מִיִּשְׂרָאֵל: וְאִם־לֹא יַחְפֹּץ הָאִישׁ לָקַחַת אֶת־יְבִמְתּוֹ וְעָלְתָה יְבִמְתּוֹ
הַשַּׁעְרָה אֶל־הַזְּקֵנִים וְאָמְרָה מֵאֵן יְבָמִי לְהָקִים לְאָחִיו שֵׁם בְּיִשְׂרָאֵל לֹא
אָבָה יַבְּמִי: וְקָרְאוּ־לוֹ זִקְנֵי־עִירוֹ וְדִבְּרוּ אֵלָיו וְעָמַד וְאָמַר לֹא חָפַצְתִּי
לְקַחְתָּהּ: וְנִגְּשָׁה יְבִמְתּוֹ אֵלָיו לְעֵינֵי הַזְּקֵנִים וְחָלְצָה נַעֲלוֹ מֵעַל רַגְלוֹ
וְיָרְקָה בְּפָנָיו וְעָנְתָה וְאָמְרָה כָּכָה יֵעָשֶׂה לָאִישׁ אֲשֶׁר לֹא־יִבְנֶה אֶת־בֵּית
אָחִיו: וְנִקְרָא שְׁמוֹ בְּיִשְׂרָאֵל בֵּית חֲלוּץ הַנָּעַל: כִּי־יִנָּצוּ
אֲנָשִׁים יַחְדָּו אִישׁ וְאָחִיו וְקָרְבָה אֵשֶׁת הָאֶחָד לְהַצִּיל אֶת־אִישָׁהּ
מִיַּד מַכֵּהוּ וְשָׁלְחָה יָדָהּ וְהֶחֱזִיקָה בִּמְבֻשָׁיו: וְקַצֹּתָה אֶת־כַּפָּהּ לֹא תָחוֹס
עֵינֶךְ:   לֹא־יִהְיֶה לְךָ בְּכִיסְךָ אֶבֶן וָאָבֶן גְּדוֹלָה וּקְטַנָּה:
לֹא־יִהְיֶה לְךָ בְּבֵיתְךָ אֵיפָה וְאֵיפָה גְּדוֹלָה וּקְטַנָּה: אֶבֶן שְׁלֵמָה וָצֶדֶק
יִהְיֶה־לָּךְ אֵיפָה שְׁלֵמָה וָצֶדֶק יִהְיֶה־לָּךְ לְמַעַן יַאֲרִיכוּ יָמֶיךָ עַל הָאֲדָמָה
אֲשֶׁר־יְהוָה אֱלֹהֶיךָ נֹתֵן לָךְ: כִּי תוֹעֲבַת יְהוָה אֱלֹהֶיךָ כָּל־עֹשֵׂה אֵלֶּה כֹּל
עֹשֵׂה עָוֶל:

   * זָכוֹר אֵת אֲשֶׁר־עָשָׂה לְךָ עֲמָלֵק בַּדֶּרֶךְ בְּצֵאתְכֶם מִמִּצְרָיִם: אֲשֶׁר קָרְךָ
בַּדֶּרֶךְ וַיְזַנֵּב בְּךָ כָּל־הַנֶּחֱשָׁלִים אַחֲרֶיךָ וְאַתָּה עָיֵף וְיָגֵעַ וְלֹא יָרֵא
אֱלֹהִים: וְהָיָה בְּהָנִיחַ יְהוָה אֱלֹהֶיךָ ׀ לְךָ מִכָּל־אֹיְבֶיךָ מִסָּבִיב בָּאָרֶץ
אֲשֶׁר יְהוָה־אֱלֹהֶיךָ נֹתֵן לְךָ נַחֲלָה לְרִשְׁתָּהּ תִּמְחֶה אֶת־זֵכֶר עֲמָלֵק
מִתַּחַת הַשָּׁמָיִם לֹא תִּשְׁכָּח: פפפ   קי"ו פסוקים. על"י סימן.

פרשת כי תבוא

וְהָיָה כִּי־תָבוֹא אֶל־הָאָרֶץ אֲשֶׁר יְהוָה אֱלֹהֶיךָ נֹתֵן לְךָ נַחֲלָה וִירִשְׁתָּהּ   כו
וְיָשַׁבְתָּ בָּהּ: וְלָקַחְתָּ מֵרֵאשִׁית ׀ כָּל־פְּרִי הָאֲדָמָה אֲשֶׁר תָּבִיא מֵאַרְצְךָ
אֲשֶׁר יְהוָה אֱלֹהֶיךָ נֹתֵן לָךְ וְשַׂמְתָּ בַטֶּנֶא וְהָלַכְתָּ אֶל־הַמָּקוֹם אֲשֶׁר
יִבְחַר יְהוָה אֱלֹהֶיךָ לְשַׁכֵּן שְׁמוֹ שָׁם: וּבָאתָ אֶל־הַכֹּהֵן אֲשֶׁר יִהְיֶה בַּיָּמִים
הָהֵם וְאָמַרְתָּ אֵלָיו הִגַּדְתִּי הַיּוֹם לַיהוָה אֱלֹהֶיךָ כִּי־בָאתִי אֶל־הָאָרֶץ
אֲשֶׁר נִשְׁבַּע יְהוָה לַאֲבֹתֵינוּ לָתֶת לָנוּ: וְלָקַח הַכֹּהֵן הַטֶּנֶא מִיָּדֶךָ וְהִנִּיחוֹ
לִפְנֵי מִזְבַּח יְהוָה אֱלֹהֶיךָ: וְעָנִיתָ וְאָמַרְתָּ לִפְנֵי ׀ יְהוָה אֱלֹהֶיךָ אֲרַמִּי
אֹבֵד אָבִי וַיֵּרֶד מִצְרַיְמָה וַיָּגָר שָׁם בִּמְתֵי מְעָט וַיְהִי־שָׁם לְגוֹי גָּדוֹל
עָצוּם וָרָב: וַיָּרֵעוּ אֹתָנוּ הַמִּצְרִים וַיְעַנּוּנוּ וַיִּתְּנוּ עָלֵינוּ עֲבֹדָה קָשָׁה:

Haftaras
Ki Seitzei:
p. 1048

*מפטיר

MAFTIR
PARASHAS
ZACHOR
25:17-19

Haftarah:
p. 680

25:11-12. If a woman tries to help her husband by embarrassing someone else, she must pay a financial penalty to the victim (*Sforno*), and all assailants are fined for the embarrassment that they cause.

25:17-19. It is a positive commandment to erase the memory of Amalek and a positive commandment always to remember their treachery (see *Exodus* 17:7-16), in order to inspire hatred of them.

   Parashas Ki Savo

26:1-11. The Jew's gift of his first fruits, or *Bikkurim*, to the Kohen symbolizes that he dedicates everything he has to the service of God.

26:5. This declaration (until v. 10) is a brief sketch of Jewish history, which shows that the Land could never have been given to Israel without God's loving intervention.

The *Aramean* is the deceitful Laban, who deceived and

⁶ It shall be that the firstborn — if she can bear — shall succeed to the name of his dead brother, so that his name not be blotted out from Israel. ⁷ But if the man will not wish to marry his sister-in-law, then his sister-in-law shall ascend to the gate, to the elders, and she shall say, "My brother-in-law has refused to establish a name for his brother in Israel, he did not consent to perform levirate marriage with me."

⁸ Then the elders of his city shall summon him and speak to him, and he shall stand and say, "I do not wish to marry her."

⁹ Then his sister-in-law shall approach him before the eyes of the elders; she shall remove his shoe from on his foot and spit before him; she shall speak up and say, "So is done to the man who will not build the house of his brother." ¹⁰ Then his name shall be proclaimed in Israel, "The house of the one whose shoe was removed!"

Penalty for embarrassing another ¹¹ If men fight with one another, a man and his brother, and the wife of one of them approaches to rescue her husband from the hand of the one who is striking him, and she stretches out her hand and grasps his embarrassing place, * ¹² you shall cut off her hand; your eye shall not show pity.

Honest weights and measures ¹³ You shall not have in your pouch a weight and a weight — a large one and a small one. ¹⁴ You shall not have in your house a measure and a measure — a large one and a small one. ¹⁵ A perfect and honest weight shall you have, a perfect and honest measure shall you have, so that your days shall be lengthened on the Land that HASHEM, your God, gives you. ¹⁶ For an abomination of HASHEM, your God, are all who do this, all who act corruptly.

Remembering Amalek ¹⁷ Remember what Amalek did to you, * on the way, when you were leaving Egypt, ¹⁸ that he happened upon you on the way, and he struck those of you who were hindmost, all the weaklings at your rear, when you were faint and exhausted, and he did not fear God. ¹⁹ It shall be that when HASHEM, your God, gives you rest from all your enemies all around, in the Land that HASHEM, your God, gives you as an inheritance to possess it, you shall wipe out the memory of Amalek from under the heaven — you shall not forget!

PARASHAS KI SAVO

26

First fruits * ¹ It will be when you enter the Land that HASHEM, your God, gives you as an inheritance, and you possess it, and dwell in it, ² that you shall take of the first of every fruit of the ground that you bring in from your Land that HASHEM, your God, gives you, and you shall put it in a basket and go to the place that HASHEM, your God, will choose, to make His Name rest there.

³ You shall come to whoever will be the Kohen in those days, and you shall say to him, "I declare today to HASHEM, your God, that I have come to the Land that HASHEM swore to our forefathers to give us." ⁴ The Kohen shall take the basket from your hand, and lay it before the Altar of HASHEM, your God.

Declaration ⁵ Then you shall call out and say * before HASHEM, your God, "An Aramean tried to destroy my forefather. * He descended to Egypt and sojourned there, few in number, and there he became a nation — great, strong, and numerous. ⁶ The Egyptians mistreated us and afflicted us, and placed hard work upon us.

pursued our *forefather* Jacob (*Rashi*).

ז וַנִּצְעַק אֶל־יְהוָה אֱלֹהֵי אֲבֹתֵינוּ וַיִּשְׁמַע יְהוָה אֶת־קֹלֵנוּ וַיַּרְא אֶת־עָנְיֵנוּ

ח וְאֶת־עֲמָלֵנוּ וְאֶת־לַחֲצֵנוּ: וַיּוֹצִאֵנוּ יְהוָה מִמִּצְרַיִם בְּיָד חֲזָקָה וּבִזְרֹעַ

ט נְטוּיָה וּבְמֹרָא גָּדֹל וּבְאֹתוֹת וּבְמֹפְתִים: וַיְבִאֵנוּ אֶל־הַמָּקוֹם הַזֶּה וַיִּתֶּן־

י לָנוּ אֶת־הָאָרֶץ הַזֹּאת אֶרֶץ זָבַת חָלָב וּדְבָשׁ: וְעַתָּה הִנֵּה הֵבֵאתִי אֶת־

רֵאשִׁית פְּרִי הָאֲדָמָה אֲשֶׁר־נָתַתָּה לִּי יְהוָה וְהִנַּחְתּוֹ לִפְנֵי יְהוָה אֱלֹהֶיךָ

יא וְהִשְׁתַּחֲוִיתָ לִפְנֵי יְהוָה אֱלֹהֶיךָ: וְשָׂמַחְתָּ בְכָל־הַטּוֹב אֲשֶׁר נָתַן־לְךָ יְהוָה

שני אֱלֹהֶיךָ וּלְבֵיתֶךָ אַתָּה וְהַלֵּוִי וְהַגֵּר אֲשֶׁר בְּקִרְבֶּךָ: כִּי תְכַלֶּה

יב לַעְשֵׂר אֶת־כָּל־מַעְשַׂר תְּבוּאָתְךָ בַּשָּׁנָה הַשְּׁלִישִׁת שְׁנַת הַמַּעֲשֵׂר וְנָתַתָּה

יג לַלֵּוִי לַגֵּר לַיָּתוֹם וְלָאַלְמָנָה וְאָכְלוּ בִשְׁעָרֶיךָ וְשָׂבֵעוּ: וְאָמַרְתָּ לִפְנֵי יְהוָה

אֱלֹהֶיךָ בִּעַרְתִּי הַקֹּדֶשׁ מִן־הַבַּיִת וְגַם נְתַתִּיו לַלֵּוִי וְלַגֵּר לַיָּתוֹם וְלָאַלְמָנָה

יד כְּכָל־מִצְוָתְךָ אֲשֶׁר צִוִּיתָנִי לֹא־עָבַרְתִּי מִמִּצְוֹתֶיךָ וְלֹא שָׁכָחְתִּי: לֹא־

אָכַלְתִּי בְאֹנִי מִמֶּנּוּ וְלֹא־בִעַרְתִּי מִמֶּנּוּ בְּטָמֵא וְלֹא־נָתַתִּי מִמֶּנּוּ לְמֵת

טו שָׁמַעְתִּי בְּקוֹל יְהוָה אֱלֹהָי עָשִׂיתִי כְּכֹל אֲשֶׁר צִוִּיתָנִי: הַשְׁקִיפָה מִמְּעוֹן

קָדְשְׁךָ מִן־הַשָּׁמַיִם וּבָרֵךְ אֶת־עַמְּךָ אֶת־יִשְׂרָאֵל וְאֵת הָאֲדָמָה אֲשֶׁר

טז נָתַתָּה לָנוּ כַּאֲשֶׁר נִשְׁבַּעְתָּ לַאֲבֹתֵינוּ אֶרֶץ זָבַת חָלָב וּדְבָשׁ: הַיּוֹם

שלישי הַזֶּה יְהוָה אֱלֹהֶיךָ מְצַוְּךָ לַעֲשׂוֹת אֶת־הַחֻקִּים הָאֵלֶּה וְאֶת־הַמִּשְׁפָּטִים

יז וְשָׁמַרְתָּ וְעָשִׂיתָ אוֹתָם בְּכָל־לְבָבְךָ וּבְכָל־נַפְשֶׁךָ: אֶת־יְהוָה הֶאֱמַרְתָּ הַיּוֹם

לִהְיוֹת לְךָ לֵאלֹהִים וְלָלֶכֶת בִּדְרָכָיו וְלִשְׁמֹר חֻקָּיו וּמִצְוֹתָיו וּמִשְׁפָּטָיו

יח וְלִשְׁמֹעַ בְּקֹלוֹ: וַיהוָה הֶאֱמִירְךָ הַיּוֹם לִהְיוֹת לוֹ לְעַם סְגֻלָּה כַּאֲשֶׁר דִּבֶּר־

יט לָךְ וְלִשְׁמֹר כָּל־מִצְוֹתָיו: וּלְתִתְּךָ עֶלְיוֹן עַל כָּל־הַגּוֹיִם אֲשֶׁר עָשָׂה לִתְהִלָּה

וּלְשֵׁם וּלְתִפְאָרֶת וְלִהְיֹתְךָ עַם־קָדֹשׁ לַיהוָה אֱלֹהֶיךָ כַּאֲשֶׁר דִּבֵּר:

כז רביעי א וַיְצַו מֹשֶׁה וְזִקְנֵי יִשְׂרָאֵל אֶת־הָעָם לֵאמֹר שָׁמֹר אֶת־כָּל־הַמִּצְוָה

ב אֲשֶׁר אָנֹכִי מְצַוֶּה אֶתְכֶם הַיּוֹם: וְהָיָה בַּיּוֹם אֲשֶׁר תַּעַבְרוּ אֶת־הַיַּרְדֵּן

אֶל־הָאָרֶץ אֲשֶׁר־יְהוָה אֱלֹהֶיךָ נֹתֵן לָךְ וַהֲקֵמֹתָ לְךָ אֲבָנִים גְּדֹלוֹת וְשַׂדְתָּ

ג אֹתָם בַּשִּׂיד: וְכָתַבְתָּ עֲלֵיהֶן אֶת־כָּל־דִּבְרֵי הַתּוֹרָה הַזֹּאת בְּעָבְרֶךָ

לְמַעַן אֲשֶׁר תָּבֹא אֶל־הָאָרֶץ אֲשֶׁר־יְהוָה אֱלֹהֶיךָ ׀ נֹתֵן לְךָ אֶרֶץ זָבַת

ד חָלָב וּדְבַשׁ כַּאֲשֶׁר דִּבֶּר יְהוָה אֱלֹהֵי־אֲבֹתֶיךָ לָךְ: וְהָיָה בְּעָבְרְכֶם אֶת־

הַיַּרְדֵּן תָּקִימוּ אֶת־הָאֲבָנִים הָאֵלֶּה אֲשֶׁר אָנֹכִי מְצַוֶּה אֶתְכֶם הַיּוֹם

ה בְּהַר עֵיבָל וְשַׂדְתָּ אוֹתָם בַּשִּׂיד: וּבָנִיתָ שָּׁם מִזְבֵּחַ לַיהוָה אֱלֹהֶיךָ מִזְבַּח

ו אֲבָנִים לֹא־תָנִיף עֲלֵיהֶם בַּרְזֶל: אֲבָנִים שְׁלֵמוֹת תִּבְנֶה אֶת־מִזְבַּח יְהוָה

ז אֱלֹהֶיךָ וְהַעֲלִיתָ עָלָיו עוֹלֹת לַיהוָה אֱלֹהֶיךָ: וְזָבַחְתָּ שְׁלָמִים וְאָכַלְתָּ

ח שָּׁם וְשָׂמַחְתָּ לִפְנֵי יְהוָה אֱלֹהֶיךָ: וְכָתַבְתָּ עַל־הָאֲבָנִים אֶת־כָּל־דִּבְרֵי

27:1-11. Upon entering the Land, the people were to commit themselves anew to God and the Torah, by inscribing the entire Torah on twelve huge stones, by bringing offerings, and by gathering at two mountains to affirm their allegiance.

⁷ Then we cried out to HASHEM, the God of our forefathers, and HASHEM heard our voice and saw our affliction, our travail, and our oppression. ⁸ HASHEM took us out of Egypt with a strong hand and with an outstretched arm, with great awesomeness, and with signs and with wonders. ⁹ He brought us to this place, and He gave us this Land, a Land flowing with milk and honey. ¹⁰ And now, behold! I have brought the first fruit of the ground that You have given me, O HASHEM!" And you shall lay it before HASHEM, your God, and you shall prostrate yourself before HASHEM, your God.

¹¹ You shall rejoice with all the goodness that HASHEM, your God, has given you and your household — you and the Levite and the proselyte who is in your midst.

Confession of the tithes ¹² When you have finished tithing every tithe of your produce in the third year, the year of the tithe, you shall give to the Levite, to the proselyte, to the orphan, and to the widow, and they shall eat in your cities and be satisfied. ¹³ Then you shall say before HASHEM, your God, "I have removed the holy things from the house, and I have also given it to the Levite, to the proselyte, to the orphan, and to the widow, according to whatever commandment You commanded me; I have not transgressed any of Your commandments, and I have not forgotten. ¹⁴ I have not eaten of it in my intense mourning, I did not consume it in a state of contamination, and I did not give of it for the needs of the dead; I have hearkened to the voice of HASHEM, my God; I have acted according to everything You commanded me. ¹⁵ Gaze down from Your holy abode, from the heavens, and bless Your people Israel, and the ground that You gave us, as You swore to our forefathers, a Land flowing with milk and honey."

God and Israel are inseparable ¹⁶ This day, HASHEM, your God, commands you to perform these decrees and the statutes, and you shall observe and perform them with all your heart and with all your soul. ¹⁷ You have distinguished HASHEM today to be a God for you, and to walk in His ways, and to observe His decrees, His commandments, and His statutes, and to hearken to His voice. ¹⁸ And HASHEM has distinguished you today to be for Him a treasured people, as He spoke to you, and to observe all His commandments, ¹⁹ and to make you supreme over all the nations that He made, for praise, for renown, and for splendor, and so that you will be a holy people to HASHEM, your God, as He spoke.

27

The new commitment ¹ Moses and the elders of Israel commanded the people, saying, "Observe the entire commandment* that I command you this day. ² It shall be on the day that you cross the Jordan to the Land that HASHEM, your God, gives you, you shall set up great stones and you shall coat them with plaster. ³ You shall inscribe on them all the words of this Torah, when you cross over, so that you may enter the Land that HASHEM, your God, gives you, a Land flowing with milk and honey, as HASHEM, the God of your forefathers, spoke about you. ⁴ It shall be that when you cross the Jordan, you shall erect these stones, of which I command you today, on Mount Ebal, and you shall coat them with plaster. ⁵ There you shall build an altar for HASHEM, your God, an altar of stones; you shall not raise iron upon them. ⁶ Of whole stones shall you build the altar of HASHEM, your God, and you shall bring upon it burnt-offerings to HASHEM, your God. ⁷ You shall slaughter peace-offerings and eat there, and you shall rejoice before HASHEM, your God. ⁸ You shall inscribe on the stones all the words

ט וַיְדַבֵּ֤ר מֹשֶׁה֙ וְהַכֹּהֲנִ֣ים הַלְוִיִּ֔ם אֶֽל־כָּל־יִשְׂרָאֵ֖ל לֵאמֹ֑ר הַסְכֵּ֣ת ׀ וּשְׁמַ֣ע יִשְׂרָאֵ֔ל הַיּ֤וֹם הַזֶּה֙ הַתּוֹרָ֥ה הַזֹּ֖את בַּאֵ֥ר הֵיטֵֽב:

י נִהְיֵ֣יתָֽ לְעָ֔ם לַיהוָ֖ה אֱלֹהֶ֑יךָ: וְשָׁמַעְתָּ֗ בְּק֨וֹל֙ יְהוָ֣ה אֱלֹהֶ֔יךָ וְעָשִׂ֤יתָ אֶת־

יא מִצְוֺתָו֙ וְאֶת־חֻקָּ֔יו אֲשֶׁ֛ר אָנֹכִ֥י מְצַוְּךָ֖ הַיּֽוֹם: וַיְצַ֤ו מֹשֶׁה֙ חמישי

יב אֶת־הָעָ֔ם בַּיּ֥וֹם הַה֖וּא לֵאמֹֽר: אֵ֠לֶּה יַֽעַמְד֞וּ לְבָרֵ֤ךְ אֶת־הָעָם֙ עַל־הַ֣ר גְּרִזִ֔ים בְּעָבְרְכֶ֖ם אֶת־הַיַּרְדֵּ֑ן שִׁמְעוֹן֙ וְלֵוִ֣י וִֽיהוּדָ֔ה וְיִשָּׂשכָ֖ר וְיוֹסֵ֥ף וּבִנְיָמִֽן:

יג וְאֵ֛לֶּה יַֽעַמְד֥וּ עַל־הַקְּלָלָ֖ה בְּהַ֣ר עֵיבָ֑ל רְאוּבֵן֙ גָּ֣ד וְאָשֵׁ֔ר וּזְבוּלֻ֖ן דָּ֥ן וְנַפְתָּלִֽי:

יד־טו וְעָנ֣וּ הַלְוִיִּ֔ם וְאָֽמְר֛וּ אֶל־כָּל־אִ֥ישׁ יִשְׂרָאֵ֖ל ק֣וֹל רָֽם: אָר֣וּר הָאִ֡ישׁ אֲשֶׁ֣ר יַֽעֲשֶׂה֩ פֶ֨סֶל וּמַסֵּכָ֜ה תּֽוֹעֲבַ֣ת יְהוָ֗ה מַעֲשֵׂ֛ה יְדֵ֥י חָרָ֖שׁ וְשָׂ֣ם

טז בַּסָּ֑תֶר וְעָנ֧וּ כָל־הָעָ֛ם וְאָמְר֖וּ אָמֵֽן: אָר֕וּר מַקְלֶ֥ה אָבִ֖יו וְאִמּ֑וֹ וְאָמַ֥ר כָּל־הָעָ֖ם אָמֵֽן:

יז אָר֕וּר מַסִּ֖יג גְּב֣וּל רֵעֵ֑הוּ וְאָמַ֥ר כָּל־הָעָ֖ם אָמֵֽן:

יח אָר֕וּר מַשְׁגֶּ֥ה עִוֵּ֖ר בַּדָּ֑רֶךְ וְאָמַ֥ר כָּל־הָעָ֖ם אָמֵֽן:

יט אָר֗וּר מַטֶּ֛ה מִשְׁפַּ֥ט גֵּר־יָת֖וֹם וְאַלְמָנָ֑ה וְאָמַ֥ר כָּל־הָעָ֖ם אָמֵֽן:

כ אָר֗וּר שֹׁכֵב֙ עִם־אֵ֣שֶׁת אָבִ֔יו כִּ֥י גִלָּ֖ה כְּנַ֣ף אָבִ֑יו וְאָמַ֥ר כָּל־הָעָ֖ם אָמֵֽן:

כא אָר֕וּר שֹׁכֵ֖ב עִם־כָּל־בְּהֵמָ֑ה וְאָמַ֥ר כָּל־הָעָ֖ם אָמֵֽן:

כב אָר֗וּר שֹׁכֵב֙ עִם־אֲחֹת֔וֹ בַּת־אָבִ֖יו א֣וֹ בַת־אִמּ֑וֹ וְאָמַ֥ר כָּל־הָעָ֖ם אָמֵֽן:

כג אָר֕וּר שֹׁכֵ֖ב עִם־חֹֽתַנְתּ֑וֹ וְאָמַ֥ר כָּל־הָעָ֖ם אָמֵֽן:

כד אָר֕וּר מַכֵּ֥ה רֵעֵ֖הוּ בַּסָּ֑תֶר וְאָמַ֥ר כָּל־הָעָ֖ם אָמֵֽן:

כה אָר֗וּר לֹקֵ֣חַ שֹׁ֔חַד לְהַכּ֥וֹת נֶ֖פֶשׁ דָּ֣ם נָקִ֑י וְאָמַ֥ר כָּל־הָעָ֖ם אָמֵֽן:

כו אָר֗וּר אֲשֶׁ֤ר לֹֽא־יָקִים֙ אֶת־דִּבְרֵ֣י הַתּוֹרָֽה־הַזֹּ֖את לַעֲשׂ֣וֹת אוֹתָ֑ם וְאָמַ֥ר כָּל־הָעָ֖ם אָמֵֽן:

כח א וְהָיָ֗ה אִם־שָׁמ֤וֹעַ תִּשְׁמַע֙ בְּקוֹל֙ יְהוָ֣ה אֱלֹהֶ֔יךָ לִשְׁמֹ֤ר לַעֲשׂוֹת֙ אֶת־כָּל־מִצְוֺתָ֔יו אֲשֶׁ֛ר אָנֹכִ֥י מְצַוְּךָ֖ הַיּ֑וֹם וּנְתָ֨נְךָ֜ יְהוָ֤ה אֱלֹהֶ֙יךָ֙ עֶלְי֔וֹן עַ֖ל כָּל־גּוֹיֵ֥י

ב הָאָֽרֶץ: וּבָ֧אוּ עָלֶ֛יךָ כָּל־הַבְּרָכ֥וֹת הָאֵ֖לֶּה וְהִשִּׂיגֻ֑ךָ כִּ֣י תִשְׁמַ֔ע בְּק֖וֹל יְהוָ֥ה

ג־ד אֱלֹהֶֽיךָ: בָּר֥וּךְ אַתָּ֖ה בָּעִ֑יר וּבָר֥וּךְ אַתָּ֖ה בַּשָּׂדֶֽה: בָּר֧וּךְ פְּרִֽי־בִטְנְךָ֛ וּפְרִ֥י

ה אַדְמָֽתְךָ֖ וּפְרִ֣י בְהֶמְתֶּ֑ךָ שְׁגַ֥ר אֲלָפֶ֖יךָ וְעַשְׁתְּר֥וֹת צֹאנֶֽךָ: בָּר֥וּךְ טַנְאֲךָ֖

ו־ז וּמִשְׁאַרְתֶּֽךָ: בָּר֥וּךְ אַתָּ֖ה בְּבֹאֶ֑ךָ וּבָר֥וּךְ אַתָּ֖ה בְּצֵאתֶֽךָ: *יִתֵּ֨ן יְהוָ֤ה אֶת־ ששי אֹיְבֶ֙יךָ֙ הַקָּמִ֤ים עָלֶ֙יךָ֙ נִגָּפִ֖ים לְפָנֶ֑יךָ בְּדֶ֤רֶךְ אֶחָד֙ יֵצְא֣וּ אֵלֶ֔יךָ וּבְשִׁבְעָ֥ה

27:11-26. Six tribes were to stand on Mount Gerizim and six tribes on Mount Ebal, with the Ark, the Kohanim, and the elders of the Levites in the valley between. The Levite elders would turn to Mount Gerizim and call out, "Blessed is the man who . . .," and everyone would answer, "Amen!" Then they would turn to Mount Ebal and call out "Accursed is the man . . .," and everyone would answer, "Amen!" (*Rashi*).

•§ **Chapter 28. Blessing and admonition.**

Just before his death, Moses gave the people a chilling prophecy of the horrors that would befall them if they spurned God and the Torah.

28:1-14. The blessing. If loyalty to the commandments can cause one's business and family life to prosper, surely it can yield infinite spiritual bliss.

of this Torah, well clarified."

⁹ Moses and the Kohanim, the Levites, spoke to all Israel, saying, "Be attentive and hear, O Israel: This day you have become a people to HASHEM, your God. ¹⁰ You shall hearken to the voice of HASHEM, your God, and you shall perform all His commandments and His decrees, which I command you today."

Blessings and curses * ¹¹ Moses commanded the people on that day, saying, ¹² "These shall stand to bless the people on Mount Gerizim, when you have crossed the Jordan: Simeon, Levi, Judah, Issachar, Joseph, and Benjamin. ¹³ And these shall stand for the curse on Mount Ebal: Reuben, Gad, Asher, Zebulun, Dan, and Naphtali. ¹⁴ The Levites shall speak up and say to every man of Israel, in a loud voice:

¹⁵ 'Accursed is the man who will make a graven or molten image, an abomination of HASHEM, a craftsman's handiwork, and emplace it in secret.' And the entire people shall speak up and say, 'Amen.'

¹⁶ 'Accursed is one who degrades his father or mother.' And the entire people shall say, 'Amen.'

¹⁷ 'Accursed is one who moves the boundary of his fellow.' And the entire people shall say, 'Amen.'

¹⁸ 'Accursed is one who causes a blind person to go astray on the road.' And the entire people shall say, 'Amen.'

¹⁹ 'Accursed is one who perverts a judgment of a proselyte, orphan, or widow.' And the entire people shall say, 'Amen.'

²⁰ 'Accursed is one who lies with the wife of his father, for he will have uncovered the robe of his father.' And the entire people shall say, 'Amen.'

²¹ 'Accursed is one who lies with any animal.' And the entire people shall say, 'Amen.'

²² 'Accursed is one who lies with his sister, the daughter of his father or the daughter of his mother.' And the entire people shall say, 'Amen.'

²³ 'Accursed is one who lies with his mother-in-law.' And the entire people shall say, 'Amen.'

²⁴ 'Accursed is one who strikes his fellow stealthily.' And the entire people shall say, 'Amen.'

²⁵ 'Accursed is one who takes a bribe to kill a person of innocent blood.' And the entire people shall say, 'Amen.'

²⁶ 'Accursed is one who will not uphold the words of this Torah, to perform them.' And the entire people shall say, 'Amen.'"

28

The blessing for fulfilling the commandments ¹ It shall be that if you hearken to the voice of HASHEM, your God, * to observe, to perform all of His commandments that I command you this day, then HASHEM, your God, will make you supreme over all the nations of the earth. ² All these blessings will come upon you and overtake you, if you hearken to the voice of HASHEM, your God:

³ Blessed shall you be in the city and blessed shall you be in the field. ⁴ Blessed shall be the fruit of your womb, and the fruit of your ground, and the fruit of your animals; the offspring of your cattle and the flocks of your sheep and goats. ⁵ Blessed shall be your fruit basket and your kneading bowl. ⁶ Blessed shall you be when you come in and blessed shall you be when you go out. ⁷ HASHEM shall cause your enemies who rise up against you to be struck down before you; on one road will they go out toward you and on seven

ח דְּרָכִים יָנֻסוּ לְפָנֶיךָ: יְצַו יהוה אִתְּךָ אֶת־הַבְּרָכָה בַּאֲסָמֶיךָ וּבְכֹל מִשְׁלַח

ט יָדֶךָ וּבֵרַכְךָ בָּאָרֶץ אֲשֶׁר־יהוה אֱלֹהֶיךָ נֹתֵן לָךְ: יְקִימְךָ יהוה לוֹ לְעַם

קָדוֹשׁ כַּאֲשֶׁר נִשְׁבַּע־לָךְ כִּי תִשְׁמֹר אֶת־מִצְוֺת יהוה אֱלֹהֶיךָ וְהָלַכְתָּ

י בִּדְרָכָיו: וְרָאוּ כָּל־עַמֵּי הָאָרֶץ כִּי שֵׁם יהוה נִקְרָא עָלֶיךָ וְיָרְאוּ מִמֶּךָּ:

יא וְהוֹתִרְךָ יהוה לְטוֹבָה בִּפְרִי בִטְנְךָ וּבִפְרִי בְהֶמְתְּךָ וּבִפְרִי אַדְמָתֶךָ עַל

יב הָאֲדָמָה אֲשֶׁר נִשְׁבַּע יהוה לַאֲבֹתֶיךָ לָתֶת לָךְ: יִפְתַּח יהוה ׀ לְךָ

אֶת־אוֹצָרוֹ הַטּוֹב אֶת־הַשָּׁמַיִם לָתֵת מְטַר־אַרְצְךָ בְּעִתּוֹ וּלְבָרֵךְ אֵת

יג כָּל־מַעֲשֵׂה יָדֶךָ וְהִלְוִיתָ גּוֹיִם רַבִּים וְאַתָּה לֹא תִלְוֶה: וּנְתָנְךָ יהוה לְרֹאשׁ

וְלֹא לְזָנָב וְהָיִיתָ רַק לְמַעְלָה וְלֹא תִהְיֶה לְמָטָּה כִּי־תִשְׁמַע ׀ אֶל־מִצְוֺת

יד יהוה אֱלֹהֶיךָ אֲשֶׁר אָנֹכִי מְצַוְּךָ הַיּוֹם לִשְׁמֹר וְלַעֲשׂוֹת: וְלֹא תָסוּר

מִכָּל־הַדְּבָרִים אֲשֶׁר אָנֹכִי מְצַוֶּה אֶתְכֶם הַיּוֹם יָמִין וּשְׂמֹאול לָלֶכֶת

אַחֲרֵי אֱלֹהִים אֲחֵרִים לְעָבְדָם:

טו וְהָיָה אִם־לֹא תִשְׁמַע בְּקוֹל יהוה אֱלֹהֶיךָ לִשְׁמֹר לַעֲשׂוֹת אֶת־כָּל־

מִצְוֺתָיו וְחֻקֹּתָיו אֲשֶׁר אָנֹכִי מְצַוְּךָ הַיּוֹם וּבָאוּ עָלֶיךָ כָּל־הַקְּלָלוֹת הָאֵלֶּה

טז-יז וְהִשִּׂיגוּךָ: אָרוּר אַתָּה בָּעִיר וְאָרוּר אַתָּה בַּשָּׂדֶה: אָרוּר טַנְאֲךָ

יח וּמִשְׁאַרְתֶּךָ: אָרוּר פְּרִי־בִטְנְךָ וּפְרִי אַדְמָתֶךָ שְׁגַר אֲלָפֶיךָ וְעַשְׁתְּרֹת

יט-כ צֹאנֶךָ: אָרוּר אַתָּה בְּבֹאֶךָ וְאָרוּר אַתָּה בְּצֵאתֶךָ: יְשַׁלַּח יהוה ׀ בְּךָ

אֶת־הַמְּאֵרָה אֶת־הַמְּהוּמָה וְאֶת־הַמִּגְעֶרֶת בְּכָל־מִשְׁלַח יָדְךָ אֲשֶׁר

תַּעֲשֶׂה עַד הִשָּׁמֶדְךָ וְעַד־אֲבָדְךָ מַהֵר מִפְּנֵי רֹעַ מַעֲלָלֶיךָ אֲשֶׁר עֲזַבְתָּנִי:

כא יַדְבֵּק יהוה בְּךָ אֶת־הַדָּבֶר עַד כַּלֹּתוֹ אֹתְךָ מֵעַל הָאֲדָמָה אֲשֶׁר־אַתָּה

כב בָא־שָׁמָּה לְרִשְׁתָּהּ: יַכְּכָה יהוה בַּשַּׁחֶפֶת וּבַקַּדַּחַת וּבַדַּלֶּקֶת וּבַחַרְחֻר

כג וּבַחֶרֶב וּבַשִּׁדָּפוֹן וּבַיֵּרָקוֹן וּרְדָפוּךָ עַד אָבְדֶךָ: וְהָיוּ שָׁמֶיךָ אֲשֶׁר

כד עַל־רֹאשְׁךָ נְחֹשֶׁת וְהָאָרֶץ אֲשֶׁר־תַּחְתֶּיךָ בַּרְזֶל: יִתֵּן יהוה אֶת־מְטַר

כה אַרְצְךָ אָבָק וְעָפָר מִן־הַשָּׁמַיִם יֵרֵד עָלֶיךָ עַד הִשָּׁמְדָךְ: יִתֶּנְךָ יהוה ׀

נִגָּף לִפְנֵי אֹיְבֶיךָ בְּדֶרֶךְ אֶחָד תֵּצֵא אֵלָיו וּבְשִׁבְעָה דְרָכִים תָּנוּס

כו לְפָנָיו וְהָיִיתָ לְזַעֲוָה לְכֹל מַמְלְכוֹת הָאָרֶץ: וְהָיְתָה נִבְלָתְךָ לְמַאֲכָל

כז לְכָל־עוֹף הַשָּׁמַיִם וּלְבֶהֱמַת הָאָרֶץ וְאֵין מַחֲרִיד: יַכְּכָה יהוה בִּשְׁחִין

מִצְרַיִם °וּבעפלים [וּבַטְּחֹרִים ק] וּבַגָּרָב וּבֶחָרֶס אֲשֶׁר לֹא־תוּכַל

כח-כט לְהֵרָפֵא: יַכְּכָה יהוה בְּשִׁגָּעוֹן וּבְעִוָּרוֹן וּבְתִמְהוֹן לֵבָב: וְהָיִיתָ מְמַשֵּׁשׁ

בַּצׇּהֳרַיִם כַּאֲשֶׁר יְמַשֵּׁשׁ הָעִוֵּר בָּאֲפֵלָה וְלֹא תַצְלִיחַ אֶת־דְּרָכֶיךָ

ל וְהָיִיתָ אַךְ עָשׁוּק וְגָזוּל כָּל־הַיָּמִים וְאֵין מוֹשִׁיעַ: אִשָּׁה תְאָרֵשׂ וְאִישׁ

אַחֵר °ישגלנה [יִשְׁכָּבֶנָּה ק] בַּיִת תִּבְנֶה וְלֹא־תֵשֵׁב בּוֹ כֶּרֶם תִּטַּע וְלֹא

לא תְחַלְּלֶנּוּ: שׁוֹרְךָ טָבוּחַ לְעֵינֶיךָ וְלֹא תֹאכַל מִמֶּנּוּ חֲמֹרְךָ גָּזוּל מִלְּפָנֶיךָ

לב וְלֹא יָשׁוּב לָךְ צֹאנְךָ נְתֻנוֹת לְאֹיְבֶיךָ וְאֵין לְךָ מוֹשִׁיעַ: בָּנֶיךָ וּבְנֹתֶיךָ

roads will they flee before you. ⁸ HASHEM will command the blessing for you in your storehouses and your every undertaking; and He will bless you in the Land that HASHEM, your God, gives you. ⁹ HASHEM will confirm you for Himself as a holy people, as He swore to you — if you observe the commandments of HASHEM, your God, and you go in His ways. ¹⁰ Then all the peoples of the earth will see that the Name of HASHEM is proclaimed over you, and they will revere you. ¹¹ HASHEM shall give you bountiful goodness, in the fruit of your womb and the fruit of your animals and the fruit of your ground, on the ground that HASHEM swore to your forefathers to give you. ¹² HASHEM shall open for you His storehouse of goodness, the heavens, to provide rain for your Land in its time, and to bless all your handiwork; you shall lend to many nations, but you shall not borrow. ¹³ HASHEM shall place you as a head and not as a tail; you shall be only above and you shall not be below — if you hearken to the commandments of HASHEM, your God, that I command you today, to observe and to perform; ¹⁴ and you do not turn away from any of the words that I command you this day, right or left, to follow gods of others, to worship them.

The admonition for disobedience ¹⁵ But it will be that if you do not hearken to the voice of HASHEM, your God, to observe, to perform all His commandments and all His decrees that I command you today, then all these curses will come upon you and overtake you:

¹⁶ Accursed will you be in the city and accursed will you be in the field. ¹⁷ Accursed will be your fruit basket and your kneading bowl. ¹⁸ Accursed will be the fruit of your womb and the fruit of your ground, the offspring of your cattle and the flocks of your sheep and goats. ¹⁹ Accursed will you be when you come in and accursed will you be when you go out. ²⁰ HASHEM will send in your midst attrition, confusion, and worry, in your every undertaking that you will do, until you are destroyed, and until you are quickly annihilated, because of the evil of your deeds, for having forsaken Me. ²¹ HASHEM will attach the plague to you, until it consumes you from upon the ground to which you are coming, to possess it. ²² HASHEM will strike you with swelling lesions, with fever, with burning heat, with thirst, and with sword; and with wind blasts and with withering — and they will pursue you until your destruction. ²³ Your heavens over your head will be copper and the land beneath you will be iron. ²⁴ HASHEM will make the rain of your Land dust and dirt; from the heaven it will descend upon you until you are destroyed. ²⁵ HASHEM will cause you to be struck down before your enemies; on one road you will go out against him, but on seven roads will you flee before him; and you will be a cause of terror to all the kingdoms of the earth. ²⁶ Your carcass will be food for every bird of the sky and animal of the earth, and nothing will frighten them. ²⁷ HASHEM will strike you with the boils of Egypt, with hemorrhoids, with wet boils and dry boils, of which you cannot be cured. ²⁸ HASHEM will strike you with madness and with blindness, and with confounding of the heart. ²⁹ You will grope at noontime as a blind man gropes in the darkness, but you will not succeed on your way; you will be only cheated and robbed all the days, and there will be no savior. ³⁰ You will betroth a woman, but another man will lie with her; you will build a house, but you will not dwell in it; you will plant a vineyard, but you will not redeem it. ³¹ Your ox will be slaughtered before your eyes, but you will not eat from it; your donkey will be robbed from before you, but it will not return to you; your flocks will be given to your enemies, and you will have no savior. ³² Your sons and daughters

נְתֻנִ֞ים לְעַ֤ם אַחֵר֙ וְעֵינֶ֣יךָ רֹא֔וֹת וְכָל֖וֹת אֲלֵיהֶ֑ם כָּל־הַיּ֑וֹם וְאֵ֥ין לְאֵ֖ל יָדֶֽךָ׃

לג פְּרִ֤י אַדְמָֽתְךָ֙ וְכָל־יְגִ֣יעֲךָ֔ יֹאכַ֥ל עַ֖ם אֲשֶׁ֣ר לֹא־יָדָ֑עְתָּ וְהָיִ֗יתָ רַ֥ק עָשׁ֖וּק

לד-לה וְרָצ֖וּץ כָּל־הַיָּמִֽים׃ וְהָיִ֣יתָ מְשֻׁגָּ֔ע מִמַּרְאֵ֥ה עֵינֶ֖יךָ אֲשֶׁ֣ר תִּרְאֶֽה׃ יַכְּכָ֨ה יְהֹוָ֜ה בִּשְׁחִ֣ין רָ֗ע עַל־הַבִּרְכַּ֙יִם֙ וְעַל־הַשֹּׁקַ֔יִם אֲשֶׁ֥ר לֹא־תוּכַ֖ל לְהֵרָפֵ֑א מִכַּ֥ף

לו רַגְלְךָ֖ וְעַ֥ד קׇדְקֳדֶֽךָ׃ יוֹלֵ֨ךְ יְהֹוָ֜ה אֹֽתְךָ֗ וְאֶֽת־מַלְכְּךָ֙ אֲשֶׁ֣ר תָּקִ֣ים עָלֶ֔יךָ אֶל־גּ֕וֹי אֲשֶׁ֥ר לֹא־יָדַ֖עְתָּ אַתָּ֣ה וַאֲבֹתֶ֑יךָ וְעָבַ֥דְתָּ שָּׁ֛ם אֱלֹהִ֥ים אֲחֵרִ֖ים עֵ֥ץ וָאָֽבֶן׃

לז וְהָיִ֣יתָ לְשַׁמָּ֔ה לְמָשָׁ֖ל וְלִשְׁנִינָ֑ה בְּכֹל֙ הָֽעַמִּ֔ים אֲשֶׁר־יְנַהֶגְךָ֥ יְהֹוָ֖ה שָֽׁמָּה׃

לח-לט זֶ֥רַע רַ֖ב תּוֹצִ֣יא הַשָּׂדֶ֑ה וּמְעַ֣ט תֶּאֱסֹ֔ף כִּ֥י יַחְסְלֶ֖נּוּ הָאַרְבֶּֽה׃ כְּרָמִ֥ים תִּטַּ֖ע וְעָבָ֑דְתָּ וְיַ֤יִן לֹֽא־תִשְׁתֶּה֙ וְלֹ֣א תֶאֱגֹ֔ר כִּ֥י תֹאכְלֶ֖נּוּ הַתֹּלָֽעַת׃ זֵיתִ֛ים יִהְי֥וּ לְךָ֖

מ בְּכָל־גְּבוּלֶ֑ךָ וְשֶׁ֙מֶן֙ לֹ֣א תָס֔וּךְ כִּ֥י יִשַּׁ֖ל זֵיתֶֽךָ׃ בָּנִ֥ים וּבָנ֖וֹת תּוֹלִ֑יד וְלֹא־יִהְי֣וּ

מא לָ֔ךְ כִּ֥י יֵלְכ֖וּ בַּשֶּֽׁבִי׃ כָּל־עֵ֣צְךָ֔ וּפְרִ֖י אַדְמָתֶ֑ךָ יְיָרֵ֖שׁ הַצְּלָצַֽל׃ הַגֵּ֙ר֙ אֲשֶׁ֣ר

מב-מג בְּקִרְבְּךָ֔ יַעֲלֶ֥ה עָלֶ֖יךָ מַ֣עְלָה מָּ֑עְלָה וְאַתָּ֥ה תֵרֵ֖ד מַ֥טָּה מָּֽטָּה׃ ה֣וּא יַלְוְךָ֔

מד וְאַתָּ֖ה לֹ֣א תַלְוֶ֑נּוּ ה֚וּא יִהְיֶ֣ה לְרֹ֔אשׁ וְאַתָּ֖ה תִּהְיֶ֥ה לְזָנָֽב׃ וּבָ֨אוּ עָלֶ֜יךָ כָּל־

מה הַקְּלָל֣וֹת הָאֵ֗לֶּה וּרְדָפ֙וּךָ֙ וְהִשִּׂיג֔וּךָ עַ֖ד הִשָּֽׁמְדָ֑ךְ כִּי־לֹ֣א שָׁמַ֔עְתָּ בְּק֖וֹל

מו יְהֹוָ֣ה אֱלֹהֶ֑יךָ לִשְׁמֹ֧ר מִצְוֺתָ֛יו וְחֻקֹּתָ֖יו אֲשֶׁ֣ר צִוָּ֑ךְ׃ וְהָי֣וּ בְךָ֔ לְא֖וֹת וּלְמוֹפֵ֑ת

מז וּֽבְזַרְעֲךָ֖ עַד־עוֹלָֽם׃ תַּ֗חַת אֲשֶׁ֤ר לֹא־עָבַ֙דְתָּ֙ אֶת־יְהֹוָ֣ה אֱלֹהֶ֔יךָ בְּשִׂמְחָ֖ה

מח וּבְט֣וּב לֵבָ֑ב מֵרֹ֖ב כֹּֽל׃ וְעָבַדְתָּ֣ אֶת־אֹיְבֶ֗יךָ אֲשֶׁ֨ר יְשַׁלְּחֶ֤נּוּ יְהֹוָה֙ בָּ֔ךְ בְּרָעָ֧ב וּבְצָמָ֛א וּבְעֵירֹ֖ם וּבְחֹ֣סֶר כֹּ֑ל וְנָתַ֞ן עֹ֤ל בַּרְזֶל֙ עַל־צַוָּארֶ֔ךָ עַ֥ד הִשְׁמִיד֖וֹ

מט אֹתָֽךְ׃ יִשָּׂ֣א יְהֹוָה֩ עָלֶ֨יךָ גּ֤וֹי מֵרָחֹק֙ מִקְצֵ֣ה הָאָ֔רֶץ כַּאֲשֶׁ֖ר יִדְאֶ֣ה הַנָּ֑שֶׁר גּ֕וֹי

נ אֲשֶׁ֥ר לֹא־תִשְׁמַ֖ע לְשֹׁנֽוֹ׃ גּ֖וֹי עַ֣ז פָּנִ֑ים אֲשֶׁ֨ר לֹא־יִשָּׂ֤א פָנִים֙ לְזָקֵ֔ן וְנַ֖עַר לֹ֥א

נא יָחֹֽן׃ וְ֠אָכַ֠ל פְּרִ֨י בְהֶמְתְּךָ֥ וּפְרִֽי־אַדְמָתְךָ֮ עַ֣ד הִשָּׁמְדָךְ֒ אֲשֶׁ֣ר לֹֽא־יַשְׁאִ֣יר לְ֠ךָ֠ דָּגָ֞ן תִּיר֣וֹשׁ וְיִצְהָ֗ר שְׁגַ֤ר אֲלָפֶ֙יךָ֙ וְעַשְׁתְּרֹ֣ת צֹאנֶ֔ךָ עַ֥ד הַאֲבִיד֖וֹ אֹתָֽךְ׃

נב וְהֵצַ֨ר לְךָ֜ בְּכָל־שְׁעָרֶ֗יךָ עַ֣ד רֶ֤דֶת חֹמֹתֶ֙יךָ֙ הַגְּבֹה֣וֹת וְהַבְּצֻר֔וֹת אֲשֶׁ֥ר אַתָּ֛ה בֹּטֵ֥חַ בָּהֵ֖ן בְּכָל־אַרְצֶ֑ךָ וְהֵצַ֤ר לְךָ֙ בְּכָל־שְׁעָרֶ֔יךָ בְּכָ֨ל־אַרְצְךָ֔ אֲשֶׁ֥ר נָתַ֖ן

נג יְהֹוָ֥ה אֱלֹהֶ֖יךָ לָֽךְ׃ וְאָכַלְתָּ֣ פְרִֽי־בִטְנְךָ֗ בְּשַׂ֤ר בָּנֶ֙יךָ֙ וּבְנֹתֶ֔יךָ אֲשֶׁ֥ר נָֽתַן־לְךָ֖

נד יְהֹוָ֣ה אֱלֹהֶ֑יךָ בְּמָצוֹר֙ וּבְמָצ֔וֹק אֲשֶׁר־יָצִ֥יק לְךָ֖ אֹיְבֶֽךָ׃ הָאִישׁ֙ הָרַ֣ךְ בְּךָ֔ וְהֶעָנֹ֖ג מְאֹ֑ד תֵּרַ֨ע עֵינ֤וֹ בְאָחִיו֙ וּבְאֵ֣שֶׁת חֵיק֔וֹ וּבְיֶ֥תֶר בָּנָ֖יו אֲשֶׁ֥ר יוֹתִֽיר׃

נה מִתֵּ֣ת ׀ לְאַחַ֣ד מֵהֶ֗ם מִבְּשַׂ֤ר בָּנָיו֙ אֲשֶׁ֣ר יֹאכֵ֔ל מִבְּלִ֥י הִשְׁאִֽיר־ל֖וֹ כֹּ֑ל בְּמָצוֹר֙

נו וּבְמָצ֔וֹק אֲשֶׁ֨ר יָצִ֥יק לְךָ֛ אֹיִבְךָ֖ בְּכָל־שְׁעָרֶֽיךָ׃ הָרַכָּ֨ה בְךָ֜ וְהָעֲנֻגָּ֗ה אֲשֶׁ֨ר לֹא־נִסְּתָ֤ה כַף־רַגְלָהּ֙ הַצֵּ֣ג עַל־הָאָ֔רֶץ מֵהִתְעַנֵּ֖ג וּמֵרֹ֑ךְ תֵּרַ֤ע עֵינָהּ֙ בְּאִ֣ישׁ

נז חֵיקָ֔הּ וּבִבְנָ֖הּ וּבְבִתָּֽהּ׃ וּֽבְשִׁלְיָתָ֞הּ הַיּוֹצֵ֣ת ׀ מִבֵּ֣ין רַגְלֶ֗יהָ וּבְבָנֶ֙יהָ֙ אֲשֶׁ֣ר תֵּלֵ֔ד

28:47. The Torah once more stresses a contrast. Israel had happy times, prosperity, and everything it could have fairly desired, but it did not serve God. In return, it will become subservient to its enemies, amid humiliation, hunger, and disease.

Chasam Sofer interprets homiletically that God's anger is aroused when Israel's *failure* to serve God [לֹא עָבַדְתָּ] is done with gladness and goodness of heart.

will be given to another people — and your eyes will see and pine in vain for them all day long, but your hand will be powerless. ³³ *A nation unknown to you will devour the fruit of your ground and all your labor, and you will be only cheated and downtrodden all the days.* ³⁴ *You will go mad from the sight of your eyes that you will see.* ³⁵ HASHEM *will strike you with a foul boil, on the knees and on the legs, that cannot be cured, from the sole of your foot to your crown.* ³⁶ HASHEM *will lead you and your king whom you will set up over yourself to a nation you never knew — neither you nor your forefathers — and there you will work for the gods of others — of wood and of stone.* ³⁷ *You will be a source of astonishment, a parable, and a conversation piece, among all the peoples where* HASHEM *will lead you.* ³⁸ *You will take abundant seed out to the field, but you will harvest little, for the locust will devour it.* ³⁹ *You will plant vineyards and work them, but wine you will not drink and you will not gather in, for the worm will eat it.* ⁴⁰ *You will have olive trees throughout your boundaries, but you will not anoint with oil, for your olives will drop.* ⁴¹ *You will bear sons and daughters, but they will not be yours, for they will go into captivity.* ⁴² *All your trees and the fruits of your ground, the chirping locust will impoverish.* ⁴³ *The stranger who is among you will ascend above you higher and higher, while you will descend lower and lower.* ⁴⁴ *He will lend to you, but you will not lend to him; he will be a head, but you will be a tail.* ⁴⁵ *All these curses will come upon you and pursue you and overtake you, until you are destroyed, because you will not have hearkened to the voice of* HASHEM, *your God, to observe His commandments and decrees that He commanded you.* ⁴⁶ *They will be a sign and a wonder, in you and in your offspring, forever,* ⁴⁷ *because you did not serve* HASHEM, *your God, amid gladness and goodness of heart, when everything was abundant.* * ⁴⁸ *So you will serve your enemies whom* HASHEM *will send against you, in hunger and in thirst, in nakedness and without anything; and he will put an iron yoke on your neck, until he destroys you.* ⁴⁹ HASHEM *will carry against you a nation from afar, from the end of the earth, as an eagle will swoop, a nation whose language you will not understand,* ⁵⁰ *a brazen nation that will not be respectful to the old nor gracious to the young.* ⁵¹ *It will devour the fruit of your animals and the fruit of your ground, until you are destroyed — it will not leave you grain, wine, or oil, offspring of your cattle or flocks of your sheep and goats — until it causes you to perish.* ⁵² *It will besiege you in all your cities, until the collapse of your high and fortified walls in which you trusted throughout your Land; it will besiege you in all your cities, in all your Land, which* HASHEM, *your God, has given you.* ⁵³ *You will eat the fruit of your womb — the flesh of your sons and daughters, which* HASHEM, *your God, had given you — in the siege and distress that your enemy will distress you.* ⁵⁴ *The man among you who is tender and very delicate will turn selfish against his brother and the wife of his bosom, and against the remaining children that he has let survive,* ⁵⁵ *not to give even one of them of the flesh of his children that he will eat, not leaving anything for him, in the siege and distress that your enemy will distress you in all your cities.* ⁵⁶ *The tender and delicate woman among you, who had never tried to set the sole of her foot on the ground, because of delicacy and tenderness, will turn selfish against the husband of her bosom, and against her son and daughter,* ⁵⁷ *And against her afterbirth that emerges from between her legs, and against her children whom she will bear —*

כִּי־תֹאכְלֵם בְּחֹסֶר־כֹּל בַּסֵּתֶר בְּמָצוֹר וּבְמָצוֹק אֲשֶׁר יָצִיק לְךָ אֹיִבְךָ

נח בִּשְׁעָרֶיךָ: אִם־לֹא תִשְׁמֹר לַעֲשׂוֹת אֶת־כָּל־דִּבְרֵי הַתּוֹרָה הַזֹּאת הַכְּתוּבִים בַּסֵּפֶר הַזֶּה לְיִרְאָה אֶת־הַשֵּׁם הַנִּכְבָּד וְהַנּוֹרָא הַזֶּה אֵת יְהֹוָה

נט אֱלֹהֶיךָ: וְהִפְלָא יְהֹוָה אֶת־מַכֹּתְךָ וְאֵת מַכּוֹת זַרְעֶךָ מַכּוֹת גְּדֹלֹת

ס וְנֶאֱמָנוֹת וָחֳלָיִם רָעִים וְנֶאֱמָנִים: וְהֵשִׁיב בְּךָ אֵת כָּל־מַדְוֵה מִצְרַיִם אֲשֶׁר

סא יָגֹרְתָּ מִפְּנֵיהֶם וְדָבְקוּ בָּךְ: גַּם כָּל־חֳלִי וְכָל־מַכָּה אֲשֶׁר לֹא כָתוּב בְּסֵפֶר

סב הַתּוֹרָה הַזֹּאת יַעְלֵם יְהֹוָה עָלֶיךָ עַד הִשָּׁמְדָךְ: וְנִשְׁאַרְתֶּם בִּמְתֵי מְעָט תַּחַת אֲשֶׁר הֱיִיתֶם כְּכוֹכְבֵי הַשָּׁמַיִם לָרֹב כִּי־לֹא שָׁמַעְתָּ בְּקוֹל יְהֹוָה

סג אֱלֹהֶיךָ: וְהָיָה כַּאֲשֶׁר־שָׂשׂ יְהֹוָה עֲלֵיכֶם לְהֵיטִיב אֶתְכֶם וּלְהַרְבּוֹת אֶתְכֶם כֵּן יָשִׂישׂ יְהֹוָה עֲלֵיכֶם לְהַאֲבִיד אֶתְכֶם וּלְהַשְׁמִיד אֶתְכֶם וְנִסַּחְתֶּם

סד מֵעַל הָאֲדָמָה אֲשֶׁר־אַתָּה בָא־שָׁמָּה לְרִשְׁתָּהּ: וֶהֱפִיצְךָ יְהֹוָה בְּכָל־הָעַמִּים מִקְצֵה הָאָרֶץ וְעַד־קְצֵה הָאָרֶץ וְעָבַדְתָּ שָּׁם אֱלֹהִים אֲחֵרִים

סה אֲשֶׁר לֹא־יָדַעְתָּ אַתָּה וַאֲבֹתֶיךָ עֵץ וָאָבֶן: וּבַגּוֹיִם הָהֵם לֹא תַרְגִּיעַ וְלֹא־יִהְיֶה מָנוֹחַ לְכַף־רַגְלֶךָ וְנָתַן יְהֹוָה לְךָ שָׁם לֵב רַגָּז וְכִלְיוֹן עֵינַיִם וְדַאֲבוֹן

סו נָפֶשׁ: וְהָיוּ חַיֶּיךָ תְּלֻאִים לְךָ מִנֶּגֶד וּפָחַדְתָּ לַיְלָה וְיוֹמָם וְלֹא תַאֲמִין

סז בְּחַיֶּיךָ: בַּבֹּקֶר תֹּאמַר מִי־יִתֵּן עֶרֶב וּבָעֶרֶב תֹּאמַר מִי־יִתֵּן בֹּקֶר מִפַּחַד

סח לְבָבְךָ אֲשֶׁר תִּפְחָד וּמִמַּרְאֵה עֵינֶיךָ אֲשֶׁר תִּרְאֶה: וֶהֱשִׁיבְךָ יְהֹוָה מִצְרַיִם בָּאֳנִיּוֹת בַּדֶּרֶךְ אֲשֶׁר אָמַרְתִּי לְךָ לֹא־תֹסִיף עוֹד לִרְאֹתָהּ וְהִתְמַכַּרְתֶּם

סט שָׁם לְאֹיְבֶיךָ לַעֲבָדִים וְלִשְׁפָחוֹת וְאֵין קֹנֶה: אֵלֶּה דִבְרֵי הַבְּרִית אֲשֶׁר־צִוָּה יְהֹוָה אֶת־מֹשֶׁה לִכְרֹת אֶת־בְּנֵי יִשְׂרָאֵל בְּאֶרֶץ מוֹאָב מִלְּבַד הַבְּרִית אֲשֶׁר־כָּרַת אִתָּם בְּחֹרֵב:

כט א שביעי וַיִּקְרָא מֹשֶׁה אֶל־כָּל־יִשְׂרָאֵל וַיֹּאמֶר אֲלֵהֶם אַתֶּם רְאִיתֶם אֵת כָּל־אֲשֶׁר עָשָׂה יְהֹוָה לְעֵינֵיכֶם בְּאֶרֶץ מִצְרַיִם לְפַרְעֹה וּלְכָל־עֲבָדָיו וּלְכָל־אַרְצוֹ:

ב-ג הַמַּסּוֹת הַגְּדֹלֹת אֲשֶׁר רָאוּ עֵינֶיךָ הָאֹתֹת וְהַמֹּפְתִים הַגְּדֹלִים הָהֵם: וְלֹא־נָתַן יְהֹוָה לָכֶם לֵב לָדַעַת וְעֵינַיִם לִרְאוֹת וְאָזְנַיִם לִשְׁמֹעַ עַד הַיּוֹם הַזֶּה:

ד וָאוֹלֵךְ אֶתְכֶם אַרְבָּעִים שָׁנָה בַּמִּדְבָּר לֹא־בָלוּ שַׂלְמֹתֵיכֶם מֵעֲלֵיכֶם

ה וְנַעַלְךָ לֹא־בָלְתָה מֵעַל רַגְלֶךָ: לֶחֶם לֹא אֲכַלְתֶּם וְיַיִן וְשֵׁכָר לֹא שְׁתִיתֶם

ו לְמַעַן תֵּדְעוּ כִּי אֲנִי יְהֹוָה אֱלֹהֵיכֶם: וַתָּבֹאוּ אֶל־הַמָּקוֹם הַזֶּה וַיֵּצֵא סִיחֹן

ז מֶלֶךְ־חֶשְׁבּוֹן וְעוֹג מֶלֶךְ־הַבָּשָׁן לִקְרָאתֵנוּ לַמִּלְחָמָה וַנַּכֵּם: וַנִּקַּח אֶת־

ח אַרְצָם וַנִּתְּנָהּ לְנַחֲלָה לָראוּבֵנִי וְלַגָּדִי וְלַחֲצִי שֵׁבֶט הַמְנַשִּׁי: וּשְׁמַרְתֶּם אֶת־דִּבְרֵי הַבְּרִית הַזֹּאת וַעֲשִׂיתֶם אֹתָם לְמַעַן תַּשְׂכִּילוּ אֵת כָּל־אֲשֶׁר תַּעֲשׂוּן: פפפ קכ״ב פסוקים. לעבדיי״ו סימן.

מפטיר

Haftaras
Ki Savo:
p. 1056

28:63. When the verse speaks of the good that God does to Israel, it says that *He* rejoices, but it does not say that God Himself rejoices at the suffering of Israel. He only causes the enemy to triumph and rejoice (*Rashi*).

for she will eat them in secret for lack of anything, in the siege and distress that your enemy will distress you in your cities. [58] *If you will not be careful to perform all the words of this Torah that are written in this Book, to fear this honored and awesome Name: HASHEM, your God,* [59] *then HASHEM will make extraordinary your blows and the blows of your offspring — great and faithful blows, and evil and faithful illnesses.* [60] *He will bring back upon you all the sufferings of Egypt, of which you were terrified, and they will cleave to you.* [61] *Even any illness and any blow that is not written in this Book of the Torah, HASHEM will bring upon you, until you are destroyed.* [62] *You will be left few in number, instead of having been like the stars of heaven in abundance, for you will not have hearkened to the voice of HASHEM, your God.* [63] *And it will be that just as HASHEM rejoiced over you to benefit you and multiply you, so HASHEM will cause them to rejoice* * *over you to make you perish and to destroy you; and you will be torn from upon the ground to which you come to possess it.* [64] *HASHEM will scatter you among all the peoples, from the end of the earth to the end of the earth, and there you will work for gods of others, whom you did not know — you or your forefathers — of wood and of stone.* [65] *And among those nations you will not be tranquil, there will be no rest for the sole of your foot; there HASHEM will give you a trembling heart, longing of eyes, and suffering of soul.* [66] *Your life will hang in the balance, and you will be frightened night and day, and you will not be sure of your livelihood.* [67] *In the morning you will say, "Who can give back last night!" And in the evening you will say, "Who can give back this morning!" — for the fright of your heart that you will fear and the sight of your eyes that you will see.* * [68] *HASHEM will return you to Egypt in ships, on the road of which I said to you, "You shall never again see it!" And there you will offer yourselves for sale to your enemies as slaves and maidservants — but there will be no buyer!*

[69] *These are the words of the covenant that HASHEM commanded Moses to seal with the Children of Israel in the land of Moab, besides the covenant that He sealed with them in Horeb.*

29

Moses' final charge to the people

[1] **M**oses summoned all of Israel and said to them,* *"You have seen everything that HASHEM did before your eyes in the land of Egypt, to Pharaoh and to all his servants and to all his land —* [2] *the great trials that your eyes beheld, those great signs and wonders.* [3] *But HASHEM did not give you a heart to know, or eyes to see, or ears to hear until this day.* [4] *I led you for forty years in the Wilderness, your garment did not wear out from on you, and your shoe did not wear out from on your foot.* [5] *Bread you did not eat and wine or intoxicant you did not drink, so that you would know that I am HASHEM, your God.* [6] *Then you arrived at this place, and Sihon, king of Heshbon, and Og, king of Bashan, went out toward us to battle, and we smote them.* [7] *We took their land and gave it as an inheritance to the Reubenite, the Gadite, and to half the tribe of the Manassite.* [8] *You shall observe the words of this covenant, so that you will succeed in all that you do."*

28:67. Conditions will become worse and worse, until even the anguish of yesterday will seem preferable to the suffering of today (*Rashi*).

29:1. Moses was about to deliver his final charge to the people. Only after forty years of miraculous survival and the beginning of the conquest could the people fully appreciate the awesome degree of gratitude and allegiance they owed God.

פרשת נצבים

ט אַתֶּם נִצָּבִים הַיּוֹם כֻּלְּכֶם לִפְנֵי יהוה אֱלֹהֵיכֶם רָאשֵׁיכֶם שִׁבְטֵיכֶם זִקְנֵיכֶם
י וְשֹׁטְרֵיכֶם כֹּל אִישׁ יִשְׂרָאֵל: טַפְּכֶם נְשֵׁיכֶם וְגֵרְךָ אֲשֶׁר בְּקֶרֶב מַחֲנֶיךָ
יא מֵחֹטֵב עֵצֶיךָ עַד שֹׁאֵב מֵימֶיךָ: לְעָבְרְךָ בִּבְרִית יהוה אֱלֹהֶיךָ וּבְאָלָתוֹ
יב אֲשֶׁר יהוה אֱלֹהֶיךָ כֹּרֵת עִמְּךָ הַיּוֹם: לְמַעַן הָקִים־אֹתְךָ הַיּוֹם לוֹ לְעָם וְהוּא
יִהְיֶה־לְּךָ לֵאלֹהִים כַּאֲשֶׁר דִּבֶּר־לָךְ וְכַאֲשֶׁר נִשְׁבַּע לַאֲבֹתֶיךָ לְאַבְרָהָם
יג לְיִצְחָק וּלְיַעֲקֹב: וְלֹא אִתְּכֶם לְבַדְּכֶם אָנֹכִי כֹּרֵת אֶת־הַבְּרִית הַזֹּאת וְאֶת־
יד הָאָלָה הַזֹּאת: כִּי אֶת־אֲשֶׁר יֶשְׁנוֹ פֹּה עִמָּנוּ עֹמֵד הַיּוֹם לִפְנֵי יהוה אֱלֹהֵינוּ
טו וְאֵת אֲשֶׁר אֵינֶנּוּ פֹּה עִמָּנוּ הַיּוֹם: כִּי־אַתֶּם יְדַעְתֶּם אֵת אֲשֶׁר־יָשַׁבְנוּ בְּאֶרֶץ
טז מִצְרָיִם וְאֵת אֲשֶׁר־עָבַרְנוּ בְּקֶרֶב הַגּוֹיִם אֲשֶׁר עֲבַרְתֶּם: וַתִּרְאוּ אֶת־
יז שִׁקּוּצֵיהֶם וְאֵת גִּלֻּלֵיהֶם עֵץ וָאֶבֶן כֶּסֶף וְזָהָב אֲשֶׁר עִמָּהֶם: פֶּן־יֵשׁ בָּכֶם
אִישׁ אוֹ־אִשָּׁה אוֹ מִשְׁפָּחָה אוֹ־שֵׁבֶט אֲשֶׁר לְבָבוֹ פֹנֶה הַיּוֹם מֵעִם יהוה
אֱלֹהֵינוּ לָלֶכֶת לַעֲבֹד אֶת־אֱלֹהֵי הַגּוֹיִם הָהֵם פֶּן־יֵשׁ בָּכֶם שֹׁרֶשׁ פֹּרֶה
יח רֹאשׁ וְלַעֲנָה: וְהָיָה בְּשָׁמְעוֹ אֶת־דִּבְרֵי הָאָלָה הַזֹּאת וְהִתְבָּרֵךְ בִּלְבָבוֹ
לֵאמֹר שָׁלוֹם יִהְיֶה־לִּי כִּי בִּשְׁרִרוּת לִבִּי אֵלֵךְ לְמַעַן סְפוֹת הָרָוָה אֶת־
יט הַצְּמֵאָה: לֹא־יֹאבֶה יהוה סְלֹחַ לוֹ כִּי אָז יֶעְשַׁן אַף־יהוה וְקִנְאָתוֹ בָּאִישׁ
הַהוּא וְרָבְצָה בּוֹ כָּל־הָאָלָה הַכְּתוּבָה בַּסֵּפֶר הַזֶּה וּמָחָה יהוה אֶת־שְׁמוֹ
כ מִתַּחַת הַשָּׁמָיִם: וְהִבְדִּילוֹ יהוה לְרָעָה מִכֹּל שִׁבְטֵי יִשְׂרָאֵל כְּכֹל אָלוֹת
כא הַבְּרִית הַכְּתוּבָה בְּסֵפֶר הַתּוֹרָה הַזֶּה: וְאָמַר הַדּוֹר הָאַחֲרוֹן בְּנֵיכֶם אֲשֶׁר
יָקוּמוּ מֵאַחֲרֵיכֶם וְהַנָּכְרִי אֲשֶׁר יָבֹא מֵאֶרֶץ רְחוֹקָה וְרָאוּ אֶת־מַכּוֹת
כב הָאָרֶץ הַהִוא וְאֶת־תַּחֲלֻאֶיהָ אֲשֶׁר־חִלָּה יהוה בָּהּ: גָּפְרִית וָמֶלַח שְׂרֵפָה
כָל־אַרְצָהּ לֹא תִזָּרַע וְלֹא תַצְמִחַ וְלֹא־יַעֲלֶה בָהּ כָּל־עֵשֶׂב כְּמַהְפֵּכַת
סְדֹם וַעֲמֹרָה אַדְמָה °וּצְבֹיִים [וּצְבוֹיִם ק] אֲשֶׁר הָפַךְ יהוה בְּאַפּוֹ וּבַחֲמָתוֹ:
כג וְאָמְרוּ כָּל־הַגּוֹיִם עַל־מֶה עָשָׂה יהוה כָּכָה לָאָרֶץ הַזֹּאת מֶה חֳרִי הָאַף
כד הַגָּדוֹל הַזֶּה: וְאָמְרוּ עַל אֲשֶׁר עָזְבוּ אֶת־בְּרִית יהוה אֱלֹהֵי אֲבֹתָם אֲשֶׁר
כה כָּרַת עִמָּם בְּהוֹצִיאוֹ אֹתָם מֵאֶרֶץ מִצְרָיִם: וַיֵּלְכוּ וַיַּעַבְדוּ אֱלֹהִים אֲחֵרִים
כו וַיִּשְׁתַּחֲווּ לָהֶם אֱלֹהִים אֲשֶׁר לֹא־יְדָעוּם וְלֹא חָלַק לָהֶם: וַיִּחַר־אַף
יהוה בָּאָרֶץ הַהִוא לְהָבִיא עָלֶיהָ אֶת־כָּל־הַקְּלָלָה הַכְּתוּבָה בַּסֵּפֶר הַזֶּה:
כז וַיִּתְּשֵׁם יהוה מֵעַל אַדְמָתָם בְּאַף וּבְחֵמָה וּבְקֶצֶף גָּדוֹל וַיַּשְׁלִכֵם אֶל־אֶרֶץ
כח אַחֶרֶת כַּיּוֹם הַזֶּה: הַנִּסְתָּרֹת לַיהוה אֱלֹהֵינוּ וְהַנִּגְלֹת °לָנוּ וּלְבָנֵינוּ עַד־
ל א עוֹלָם לַעֲשׂוֹת אֶת־כָּל־דִּבְרֵי הַתּוֹרָה הַזֹּאת: וְהָיָה

שני
שלישי

*ל רבתי
**י"א נקודות על לנו ולבנינו עד

רביעי [שני]

◆§ Parashas Nitzavim

On the last day of his life, Moses initiated the entire nation for the last time into the covenant of God. This gathering introduced the concept of עֲרֵבוּת, *responsibility* for one another, under which every Jew is obligated to help others observe the Torah (see v. 28).

29:24-25. Seeing the incredible change in the Land from a country flowing with milk and honey to a wasteland from which the Jews were driven away, onlookers will conclude that only one thing could have caused such

PARASHAS NITZAVIM

Renewal of ⁹ **Y**ou are standing today, all of you, before HASHEM, your God: the heads of
the covenant   your tribes, your elders, and your officers — all the men of Israel; ¹⁰ your
small children, your women, and your proselyte who is in the midst of your
camp, from the hewer of your wood to the drawer of your water, ¹¹ for you to
pass into the covenant of HASHEM, your God, and into His imprecation that
HASHEM, your God, seals with you today, ¹² in order to establish you today as
a people to Him and that He be a God to you, as He spoke to you and as He
swore to your forefathers, to Abraham, to Isaac, and to Jacob. ¹³ Not with you
alone do I seal this covenant and this imprecation, ¹⁴ but with whoever is here,
standing with us today before HASHEM, our God, and with whoever is not here
with us today.

Warning   ¹⁵ For you know how we dwelled in the land of Egypt and how we passed
against through the midst of the nations through whom you passed. ¹⁶ And you saw
idolatry their abominations and their detestable idols — of wood and stone, of silver and
gold that were with them. ¹⁷ Perhaps there is among you a man or woman, or
a family or tribe, whose heart turns away today from being with HASHEM, our
God, to go and serve the gods of those nations; perhaps there is among you a
root flourishing with gall and wormwood. ¹⁸ And it will be that when he hears
the words of this imprecation, he will bless himself in his heart, saying, "Peace
will be with me, though I walk as my heart sees fit" — thereby adding the
watered upon the thirsty.

¹⁹ HASHEM will not be willing to forgive him, for then HASHEM's anger and
jealousy will smoke against that man, and the entire imprecation written in this
Book will come down upon him, and HASHEM will erase his name from under
heaven. ²⁰ HASHEM will set him aside for evil from among all the tribes of Israel,
like all the imprecations of the covenant that is written in this Book of the Torah.

²¹ The later generation will say — your children who will arise after you and
the foreigner who will come from a distant land — when they will see the
plagues of that Land and its illnesses with which HASHEM has afflicted it:
²² "Sulphur and salt, a conflagration of the entire Land, it cannot be sown and
it cannot sprout, and no grass shall rise up on it; like the upheaval of Sodom and
Gomorrah, Admah and Zeboiim, which HASHEM overturned in His anger and
wrath." ²³ And all the nations will say, "For what reason did HASHEM do so to
this Land; why this wrathfulness of great anger?"

²⁴ And they will say, "Because they forsook* the covenant of HASHEM, the
God of their forefathers, that He sealed with them when He took them out of the
land of Egypt; ²⁵ and they went and served the gods of others and prostrated
themselves to them — gods that they knew not and He did not apportion to
them. ²⁶ So God's anger flared against that Land, to bring upon it the entire curse
that is written in this Book; ²⁷ and HASHEM removed them from upon their soil,
with anger, with wrath, and with great fury, and He cast them to another land,
as this very day!"

²⁸ The hidden [sins] are for HASHEM, our God, but the revealed [sins] are for us
and our children forever, to carry out all the words of this Torah. *

---

desolation: The Jews forsook their proven, all-powerful   **29:28.** Everyone is obligated to safeguard the integrity
God to worship vain deities.   of Israel against openly committed sins (*Rashi*).

כִּי־יָבֹ֣אוּ עָלֶ֗יךָ כׇּל־הַדְּבָרִ֤ים הָאֵ֙לֶּה֙ הַבְּרָכָ֣ה וְהַקְּלָלָ֔ה אֲשֶׁ֥ר נָתַ֖תִּי לְפָנֶ֑יךָ

ב וַהֲשֵׁבֹתָ֙ אֶל־לְבָבֶ֔ךָ בְּכׇ֨ל־הַגּוֹיִ֔ם אֲשֶׁ֣ר הִדִּיחֲךָ֛ יְהֹוָ֥ה אֱלֹהֶ֖יךָ שָֽׁמָּה: וְשַׁבְתָּ֞
עַד־יְהֹוָ֤ה אֱלֹהֶ֙יךָ֙ וְשָׁמַעְתָּ֣ בְקֹל֔וֹ כְּכֹ֛ל אֲשֶׁר־אָנֹכִ֥י מְצַוְּךָ֖ הַיּ֑וֹם אַתָּ֣ה וּבָנֶ֔יךָ

ג בְּכׇל־לְבָבְךָ֖ וּבְכׇל־נַפְשֶֽׁךָ: וְשָׁ֨ב יְהֹוָ֧ה אֱלֹהֶ֛יךָ אֶת־שְׁבוּתְךָ֖ וְרִֽחֲמֶ֑ךָ וְשָׁ֗ב
וְקִבֶּצְךָ֙ מִכׇּל־הָ֣עַמִּ֔ים אֲשֶׁ֧ר הֱפִֽיצְךָ֛ יְהֹוָ֥ה אֱלֹהֶ֖יךָ שָֽׁמָּה: אִם־יִֽהְיֶ֥ה נִֽדַּחֲךָ֖

ד בִּקְצֵ֣ה הַשָּׁמָ֑יִם מִשָּׁ֗ם יְקַבֶּצְךָ֙ יְהֹוָ֣ה אֱלֹהֶ֔יךָ וּמִשָּׁ֖ם יִקָּחֶֽךָ: וֶהֱבִֽיאֲךָ֞ יְהֹוָ֣ה

ה אֱלֹהֶ֗יךָ אֶל־הָאָ֛רֶץ אֲשֶׁר־יָֽרְשׁ֥וּ אֲבֹתֶ֖יךָ וִֽירִשְׁתָּ֑הּ וְהֵיטִֽבְךָ֥ וְהִרְבְּךָ֖
מֵֽאֲבֹתֶֽיךָ: וּמָ֨ל יְהֹוָ֧ה אֱלֹהֶ֛יךָ אֶת־לְבָבְךָ֖ וְאֶת־לְבַ֣ב זַרְעֶ֑ךָ לְאַהֲבָ֞ה אֶת־

ו חמישי [שלישי] יְהֹוָ֧ה אֱלֹהֶ֛יךָ בְּכׇל־לְבָבְךָ֥ וּבְכׇל־נַפְשְׁךָ֖ לְמַ֥עַן חַיֶּֽיךָ: וְנָתַ֞ן יְהֹוָ֣ה אֱלֹהֶ֗יךָ אֵ֚ת

ז כׇּל־הָֽאָל֣וֹת הָאֵ֔לֶּה עַל־אֹֽיְבֶ֖יךָ וְעַל־שֹֽׂנְאֶ֑יךָ אֲשֶׁ֖ר רְדָפֽוּךָ: וְאַתָּ֣ה תָשׁ֔וּב

ח וְשָֽׁמַעְתָּ֖ בְּק֣וֹל יְהֹוָ֑ה וְעָשִׂ֙יתָ֙ אֶת־כׇּל־מִצְוֺתָ֔יו אֲשֶׁ֛ר אָנֹכִ֥י מְצַוְּךָ֖ הַיּֽוֹם:
וְהוֹתִֽירְךָ֩ יְהֹוָ֨ה אֱלֹהֶ֜יךָ בְּכֹ֣ל ׀ מַעֲשֵׂ֣ה יָדֶ֗ךָ בִּפְרִ֨י בִטְנְךָ֜ וּבִפְרִ֧י בְהֶמְתְּךָ֛

ט וּבִפְרִ֥י אַדְמָֽתְךָ֖ לְטֹבָ֑ה כִּ֣י ׀ יָשׁ֣וּב יְהֹוָ֗ה לָשׂ֤וּשׂ עָלֶ֙יךָ֙ לְט֔וֹב כַּֽאֲשֶׁר־שָׂ֖שׂ עַל־
אֲבֹתֶֽיךָ: כִּ֣י תִשְׁמַ֗ע בְּקוֹל֙ יְהֹוָ֣ה אֱלֹהֶ֔יךָ לִשְׁמֹ֤ר מִצְוֺתָיו֙ וְחֻקֹּתָ֔יו הַכְּתוּבָ֕ה

י בְּסֵ֖פֶר הַתּוֹרָ֣ה הַזֶּ֑ה כִּ֤י תָשׁוּב֙ אֶל־יְהֹוָ֣ה אֱלֹהֶ֔יךָ בְּכׇל־לְבָבְךָ֖ וּבְכׇל־

יא ששי נַפְשֶֽׁךָ: כִּ֚י הַמִּצְוָ֣ה הַזֹּ֔את אֲשֶׁ֛ר אָנֹכִ֥י מְצַוְּךָ֖ הַיּ֑וֹם לֹֽא־נִפְלֵ֥את
הִוא֙ מִמְּךָ֔ וְלֹ֥א רְחֹקָ֖ה הִֽוא: לֹ֣א בַשָּׁמַ֣יִם הִ֑וא לֵאמֹ֗ר מִ֣י יַֽעֲלֶה־לָּ֤נוּ

יב הַשָּׁמַ֙יְמָה֙ וְיִקָּחֶ֣הָ לָּ֔נוּ וְיַשְׁמִעֵ֥נוּ אֹתָ֖הּ וְנַֽעֲשֶֽׂנָּה: וְלֹֽא־מֵעֵ֥בֶר לַיָּ֖ם הִ֑וא לֵאמֹ֗ר

יג מִ֣י יַֽעֲבׇר־לָ֜נוּ אֶל־עֵ֤בֶר הַיָּם֙ וְיִקָּחֶ֣הָ לָּ֔נוּ וְיַשְׁמִעֵ֥נוּ אֹתָ֖הּ וְנַֽעֲשֶֽׂנָּה: כִּֽי־

יד שביעי ומפטיר [רביעי] קָר֥וֹב אֵלֶ֛יךָ הַדָּבָ֖ר מְאֹ֑ד בְּפִ֥יךָ וּבִֽלְבָבְךָ֖ לַֽעֲשֹׂתֽוֹ: רְאֵ֨ה נָתַ֤תִּי

טו לְפָנֶ֙יךָ֙ הַיּ֔וֹם אֶת־הַֽחַיִּ֖ים וְאֶת־הַטּ֑וֹב וְאֶת־הַמָּ֖וֶת וְאֶת־הָרָֽע: אֲשֶׁ֣ר אָֽנֹכִ֣י

טז מְצַוְּךָ֮ הַיּוֹם֒ לְאַהֲבָ֞ה אֶת־יְהֹוָ֤ה אֱלֹהֶ֙יךָ֙ לָלֶ֣כֶת בִּדְרָכָ֔יו וְלִשְׁמֹ֛ר מִצְוֺתָ֥יו
וְחֻקֹּתָ֖יו וּמִשְׁפָּטָ֑יו וְחָיִ֣יתָ וְרָבִ֔יתָ וּבֵֽרַכְךָ֙ יְהֹוָ֣ה אֱלֹהֶ֔יךָ בָּאָ֕רֶץ אֲשֶׁר־אַתָּ֥ה

Haftaras Nitzavim: p. 1060

יז בָא־שָׁ֖מָּה לְרִשְׁתָּֽהּ: וְאִם־יִפְנֶ֤ה לְבָֽבְךָ֙ וְלֹ֣א תִשְׁמָ֔ע וְנִדַּחְתָּ֖ וְהִֽשְׁתַּחֲוִ֥יתָ
לֵֽאלֹהִ֥ים אֲחֵרִ֖ים וַעֲבַדְתָּֽם: הִגַּ֤דְתִּי לָכֶם֙ הַיּ֔וֹם כִּ֥י אָבֹ֖ד תֹּֽאבֵד֑וּן לֹֽא־

יח תַּֽאֲרִיכֻ֤ן יָמִים֙ עַל־הָ֣אֲדָמָ֔ה אֲשֶׁ֨ר אַתָּ֤ה עֹבֵר֙ אֶת־הַיַּרְדֵּ֔ן לָב֥וֹא שָׁ֖מָּה

יט לְרִשְׁתָּֽהּ: הַעִדֹ֨תִי בָכֶ֣ם הַיּוֹם֮ אֶת־הַשָּׁמַ֣יִם וְאֶת־הָאָ֒רֶץ֒ הַֽחַיִּ֤ים וְהַמָּ֙וֶת֙
נָתַ֣תִּי לְפָנֶ֔יךָ הַבְּרָכָ֖ה וְהַקְּלָלָ֑ה וּבָֽחַרְתָּ֙ בַּֽחַיִּ֔ים לְמַ֥עַן תִּֽחְיֶ֖ה אַתָּ֥ה וְזַרְעֶֽךָ:

כ לְאַֽהֲבָה֙ אֶת־יְהֹוָ֣ה אֱלֹהֶ֔יךָ לִשְׁמֹ֥עַ בְּקֹל֖וֹ וּלְדׇבְקָה־ב֑וֹ כִּ֣י ה֤וּא חַיֶּ֙יךָ֙ וְאֹ֣רֶךְ
יָמֶ֔יךָ לָשֶׁ֣בֶת עַל־הָֽאֲדָמָ֗ה אֲשֶׁר֩ נִשְׁבַּ֨ע יְהֹוָ֧ה לַֽאֲבֹתֶ֛יךָ לְאַבְרָהָ֛ם לְיִצְחָ֥ק
וּֽלְיַֽעֲקֹ֖ב לָתֵ֥ת לָהֶֽם: פפפ מ פסוקים. לבב״ו סימן.

30:1-10. This passage is a commandment to repent, but it is phrased in the ordinary future tense, because God wanted to assure beleaguered Jews that sooner or later they *will* repent and be redeemed.

30:6. Once you repent, God will help you by "circumcising your heart," meaning that He will help you overcome the hurdles that the Evil Inclination always places in the way.

30   ¹ It will be that when all these things come upon you — the blessing and the
The   curse that I have presented before you — then you will take it to your heart *
eventual among all the nations where HASHEM, your God, has dispersed you; ² and you
repentance will return unto HASHEM, your God, and listen to His voice, according to
and everything that I command you today, you and your children, with all your
redemption heart and all your soul. ³ Then Hashem, your God, will bring back your captivity and have mercy upon you, and He will gather you in from all the peoples to
which HASHEM, your God, has scattered you. ⁴ If your dispersed will be at the
ends of heaven, from there HASHEM, your God, will gather you in and from
there He will take you. ⁵ HASHEM, your God, will bring you to the Land that your
forefathers possessed and you shall possess it; He will do good to you and
make you more numerous than your forefathers. ⁶ HASHEM, your God, will
circumcise your heart * and the heart of your offspring, to love HASHEM, your
God, with all your heart and with all your soul, that you may live.

⁷ HASHEM, your God, will place all these imprecations upon your enemies and
those who hate you, who pursued you. ⁸ You shall return and listen to the voice
of HASHEM, and perform all His commandments that I command you today.
⁹ HASHEM will make you abundant in all your handiwork — in the fruit of your
womb, the fruit of your animals, and the fruit of your Land — for good, when
HASHEM will return to rejoice over you for good, as He rejoiced over your
forefathers, ¹⁰ when you listen to the voice of HASHEM, your God, to observe His
commandments and His decrees, that are written in this Book of the Torah,
when you shall return to HASHEM, your God, with all your heart and all in your
soul.

The Torah is   ¹¹ For this commandment that I command you today — it is not hidden from
accessible you and it is not distant. * ¹² It is not in heaven, [for you] to say, "Who can
ascend to the heaven for us and take it for us, so that we can listen to it and
perform it?" ¹³ Nor is it across the sea, [for you] to say, "Who can cross to the
other side of the sea for us and take it for us, so that we can listen to it and
perform it?" ¹⁴ Rather, the matter is very near to you — in your mouth and in
your heart — to perform it.

Choose life   ¹⁵ See — I have placed before you today the life and the good, and the death
and the evil, ¹⁶ that which I command you today, to love HASHEM, your God, to
walk in His ways, to observe His commandments, His decrees, and His ordinances; then you will live and you will multiply, and HASHEM, your God, will
bless you in the Land to which you come, to possess it. ¹⁷ But if your heart will
stray and you will not listen, and you are led astray, and you prostrate yourself
to the gods of others and serve them, ¹⁸ I tell you today that you will surely be
lost; you will not lengthen your days upon the Land that you cross the Jordan
to come there, to possess it. ¹⁹ I call heaven and earth today to bear witness
against you: I have placed life and death before you, blessing and curse; and
you shall choose life, so that you will live, you and your offspring — ²⁰ to love
HASHEM, your God, to listen to His voice and to cleave to Him, for He is your life
and the length of your days, to dwell upon the land that HASHEM swore to your
forefathers, to Abraham, to Isaac, and to Jacob, to give them.

30:11-14. Far from requiring superhuman efforts or   tions, that goal is very much within reach — if people but
supernatural revelations to be equal to God's expecta-   make a sincere effort to grasp it.

פרשת וילך

לא

א־ב וַיֵּלֶךְ מֹשֶׁה וַיְדַבֵּר אֶת־הַדְּבָרִים הָאֵלֶּה אֶל־כָּל־יִשְׂרָאֵל: וַיֹּאמֶר אֲלֵהֶם בֶּן־מֵאָה וְעֶשְׂרִים שָׁנָה אָנֹכִי הַיּוֹם לֹא־אוּכַל עוֹד לָצֵאת וְלָבוֹא וַיהוָה אָמַר אֵלַי לֹא תַעֲבֹר אֶת־הַיַּרְדֵּן הַזֶּה: יְהוָה אֱלֹהֶיךָ הוּא ׀ עֹבֵר לְפָנֶיךָ

ג הוּא־יַשְׁמִיד אֶת־הַגּוֹיִם הָאֵלֶּה מִלְּפָנֶיךָ וִירִשְׁתָּם יְהוֹשֻׁעַ הוּא עֹבֵר לְפָנֶיךָ

ד כַּאֲשֶׁר דִּבֶּר יְהוָה: וְעָשָׂה יְהוָה לָהֶם כַּאֲשֶׁר עָשָׂה לְסִיחוֹן וּלְעוֹג מַלְכֵי הָאֱמֹרִי וּלְאַרְצָם אֲשֶׁר הִשְׁמִיד אֹתָם: וּנְתָנָם יְהוָה לִפְנֵיכֶם וַעֲשִׂיתֶם

ה לָהֶם כְּכָל־הַמִּצְוָה אֲשֶׁר צִוִּיתִי אֶתְכֶם: חִזְקוּ וְאִמְצוּ אַל־תִּירְאוּ וְאַל־

ו תַּעַרְצוּ מִפְּנֵיהֶם כִּי ׀ יְהוָה אֱלֹהֶיךָ הוּא הַהֹלֵךְ עִמָּךְ לֹא יַרְפְּךָ וְלֹא

ז יַעַזְבֶךָּ: וַיִּקְרָא מֹשֶׁה לִיהוֹשֻׁעַ וַיֹּאמֶר אֵלָיו לְעֵינֵי כָל־יִשְׂרָאֵל חֲזַק וֶאֱמָץ כִּי אַתָּה תָּבוֹא אֶת־הָעָם הַזֶּה אֶל־הָאָרֶץ אֲשֶׁר נִשְׁבַּע יְהוָה

ח לַאֲבֹתָם לָתֵת לָהֶם וְאַתָּה תַּנְחִילֶנָּה אוֹתָם: וַיהוָה הוּא ׀ הַהֹלֵךְ לְפָנֶיךָ

ט הוּא יִהְיֶה עִמָּךְ לֹא יַרְפְּךָ וְלֹא יַעַזְבֶךָּ לֹא תִירָא וְלֹא תֵחָת: וַיִּכְתֹּב מֹשֶׁה אֶת־הַתּוֹרָה הַזֹּאת וַיִּתְּנָהּ אֶל־הַכֹּהֲנִים בְּנֵי לֵוִי הַנֹּשְׂאִים אֶת־אֲרוֹן בְּרִית

י יְהוָה וְאֶל־כָּל־זִקְנֵי יִשְׂרָאֵל: וַיְצַו מֹשֶׁה אוֹתָם לֵאמֹר מִקֵּץ ׀ שֶׁבַע שָׁנִים

יא בְּמֹעֵד שְׁנַת הַשְּׁמִטָּה בְּחַג הַסֻּכּוֹת: בְּבוֹא כָל־יִשְׂרָאֵל לֵרָאוֹת אֶת־פְּנֵי יְהוָה אֱלֹהֶיךָ בַּמָּקוֹם אֲשֶׁר יִבְחָר תִּקְרָא אֶת־הַתּוֹרָה הַזֹּאת נֶגֶד כָּל־

יב יִשְׂרָאֵל בְּאָזְנֵיהֶם: הַקְהֵל אֶת־הָעָם הָאֲנָשִׁים וְהַנָּשִׁים וְהַטַּף וְגֵרְךָ אֲשֶׁר בִּשְׁעָרֶיךָ לְמַעַן יִשְׁמְעוּ וּלְמַעַן יִלְמְדוּ וְיָרְאוּ אֶת־יְהוָה אֱלֹהֵיכֶם וְשָׁמְרוּ

יג לַעֲשׂוֹת אֶת־כָּל־דִּבְרֵי הַתּוֹרָה הַזֹּאת: וּבְנֵיהֶם אֲשֶׁר לֹא־יָדְעוּ יִשְׁמְעוּ וְלָמְדוּ לְיִרְאָה אֶת־יְהוָה אֱלֹהֵיכֶם כָּל־הַיָּמִים אֲשֶׁר אַתֶּם חַיִּים עַל־הָאֲדָמָה אֲשֶׁר אַתֶּם עֹבְרִים אֶת־הַיַּרְדֵּן שָׁמָּה לְרִשְׁתָּהּ:

יד וַיֹּאמֶר יְהוָה אֶל־מֹשֶׁה הֵן קָרְבוּ יָמֶיךָ לָמוּת קְרָא אֶת־יְהוֹשֻׁעַ וְהִתְיַצְּבוּ בְּאֹהֶל מוֹעֵד וַאֲצַוֶּנּוּ וַיֵּלֶךְ מֹשֶׁה וִיהוֹשֻׁעַ וַיִּתְיַצְּבוּ בְּאֹהֶל מוֹעֵד: וַיֵּרָא

טו יְהוָה בָּאֹהֶל בְּעַמּוּד עָנָן וַיַּעֲמֹד עַמּוּד הֶעָנָן עַל־פֶּתַח הָאֹהֶל: וַיֹּאמֶר

טז יְהוָה אֶל־מֹשֶׁה הִנְּךָ שֹׁכֵב עִם־אֲבֹתֶיךָ וְקָם הָעָם הַזֶּה וְזָנָה ׀ אַחֲרֵי ׀ אֱלֹהֵי נֵכַר־הָאָרֶץ אֲשֶׁר הוּא בָא־שָׁמָּה בְּקִרְבּוֹ וַעֲזָבַנִי וְהֵפֵר אֶת־בְּרִיתִי אֲשֶׁר

יז כָּרַתִּי אִתּוֹ: וְחָרָה אַפִּי בוֹ בַיּוֹם־הַהוּא וַעֲזַבְתִּים וְהִסְתַּרְתִּי פָנַי מֵהֶם וְהָיָה לֶאֱכֹל וּמְצָאֻהוּ רָעוֹת רַבּוֹת וְצָרוֹת וְאָמַר בַּיּוֹם הַהוּא הֲלֹא עַל כִּי־אֵין

יח אֱלֹהַי בְּקִרְבִּי מְצָאוּנִי הָרָעוֹת הָאֵלֶּה: וְאָנֹכִי הַסְתֵּר אַסְתִּיר פָּנַי בַּיּוֹם

יט הַהוּא עַל כָּל־הָרָעָה אֲשֶׁר עָשָׂה כִּי פָנָה אֶל־אֱלֹהִים אֲחֵרִים: וְעַתָּה כִּתְבוּ לָכֶם אֶת־הַשִּׁירָה הַזֹּאת וְלַמְּדָהּ אֶת־בְּנֵי־יִשְׂרָאֵל שִׂימָהּ בְּפִיהֶם

שני

שלישי
[חמישי]

רביעי

חמישי
[ששי]

◄§ Parashas Vayeilech

31:2. On his last day, Moses urged Israel to trust in God's help, for they would triumph even without him.

31:7-8. To add to Joshua's prestige, Moses charged him in the presence of the nation.

31:10-13. Once every seven years the entire nation

PARASHAS VAYEILECH

31

Moses takes leave

¹ Moses went and spoke these words to all of Israel. ² He said to them, "I am a hundred and twenty years old today; * I can no longer go out and come in, for HASHEM has said to me, 'You shall not cross this Jordan.' ³ HASHEM, your God — He will cross before you; He will destroy these nations from before you, and you shall possess them; Joshua — he shall cross over before you, as HASHEM has spoken. ⁴ HASHEM will do to them as He did to Sihon and Og, the kings of the Amorite, and their land, which He destroyed, ⁵ and HASHEM gave them before you; and you shall do to them according to the entire command- ment that I have commanded you. ⁶ Be strong and courageous, do not be afraid and do not be broken before them, for HASHEM, your God — it is He Who goes before you, He will not release you nor will He forsake you."

Joshua

⁷ Moses summoned Joshua and said to him before the eyes of all Israel, * "Be strong and courageous, for you shall come with this people to the Land that HASHEM swore to their forefathers to give them, and you shall cause them to inherit it. ⁸ HASHEM — it is He Who goes before you; He will be with you; He will not release you nor will He forsake you; do not be afraid and do not be dismayed."

Hakhel/The king reads Deuteron- omy

⁹ Moses wrote this Torah and gave it to the Kohanim, the sons of Levi, the bearers of the Ark of the covenant of HASHEM, and to all the elders of Israel. ¹⁰ Moses commanded them, saying, "At the end of seven years, * at the time of the Sabbatical year, during the Succos festival, ¹¹ when all Israel comes to appear before HASHEM, your God, in the place that He will choose, you shall read this Torah before all Israel, in their ears, ¹² Gather together the people — the men, the women, and the small children, and your stranger who is in your cities — so that they will hear and so that they will learn, and they shall fear HASHEM, your God, and be careful to perform all the words of this Torah. ¹³ And their children who do not know — they shall hear and they shall learn to fear HASHEM, your God, all the days that you live on the land to which you are crossing the Jordan, to possess it."

Moses' end draws near

¹⁴ HASHEM spoke to Moses, "Behold, your days are drawing near to die; summon Joshua, and both of you shall stand in the Tent of Meeting, and I shall instruct him." So Moses and Joshua went and stood in the Tent of Meeting. ¹⁵ HASHEM appeared in the Tent, in a pillar of cloud, and the pillar of cloud stood by the entrance of the Tent. ¹⁶ HASHEM said to Moses, "Behold, you will lie with your forefathers, but this people will rise up and stray after the gods of the foreigners of the Land, in whose midst it is coming, and it will forsake Me and annul My covenant that I have sealed with it. ¹⁷ My anger will flare against it on that day and I will forsake them; and I will conceal My face from them and they will become prey, and many evils and distresses will encounter it. It will say on that day, 'Is it not because my God is not in my midst that these evils have come upon me?' ¹⁸ But I will surely have concealed My face on that day because of all the evil that it did, for it had turned to gods of others. ¹⁹ So now, write this song * for yourselves, and teach it to the Children of Israel, place it in their mouth,

---

came together at the Temple to hear the king read from *Deuteronomy.*

31:19. God commanded Moses and Joshua to write the Torah and place the Scroll at the side of the Ark. It would remain as a constant reminder of Israel's roots and the

unchanging focus of its devotion.

The Sages derive from this verse that every Jew is commanded to write a Torah Scroll, a commandment that can be fulfilled by writing a single letter of a com- plete scroll.

ששי
[שביעי]

כ לְמַעַן תִּֽהְיֶה־לִּי הַשִּׁירָה הַזֹּאת לְעֵד בִּבְנֵי יִשְׂרָאֵל: כִּי־אֲבִיאֶ֫נּוּ אֶל־הָאֲדָמָה | אֲשֶׁר־נִשְׁבַּ֫עְתִּי לַֽאֲבֹתָיו זָבַת חָלָב וּדְבַשׁ וְאָכַל וְשָׂבַע וְדָשֵׁן וּפָנָ֫ה אֶל־אֱלֹהִים אֲחֵרִים וַֽעֲבָדוּם וְנִֽאֲצוּנִי וְהֵפֵר אֶת־בְּרִיתִי: וְהָיָה כִּי־תִמְצֶ֫אןָ אֹתוֹ רָעוֹת רַבּוֹת וְצָרוֹת וְ֫עָנְתָה הַשִּׁירָה הַזֹּאת לְפָנָיו לְעֵד כִּי לֹא תִשָּׁכַח מִפִּי זַרְעוֹ כִּי יָדַעְתִּי אֶת־יִצְרוֹ אֲשֶׁר הוּא עֹשֶׂה הַיּוֹם בְּטֶרֶם אֲבִיאֶ֫נּוּ אֶל־הָאָרֶץ אֲשֶׁר נִשְׁבָּעְתִּי: וַיִּכְתֹּב מֹשֶׁה אֶת־הַשִּׁירָה הַזֹּאת בַּיּוֹם הַהוּא וַֽיְלַמְּדָהּ אֶת־בְּנֵי יִשְׂרָאֵל: וַיְצַו אֶת־יְהוֹשֻׁעַ בִּן־נוּן וַיֹּאמֶר חֲזַק וֶֽאֱמָץ כִּי אַתָּה תָּבִיא אֶת־בְּנֵי יִשְׂרָאֵל אֶל־הָאָרֶץ אֲשֶׁר־נִשְׁבַּ֫עְתִּי לָהֶם וְאָֽנֹכִי אֶֽהְיֶה עִמָּךְ: וַיְהִי | כְּכַלּוֹת מֹשֶׁה לִכְתֹּב אֶת־דִּבְרֵי הַתּוֹרָה־הַזֹּאת עַל־סֵפֶר עַד תֻּמָּם: וַיְצַו מֹשֶׁה אֶת־הַֽלְוִיִּם נֹֽשְׂאֵי אֲרוֹן בְּרִית־יהוה לֵאמֹר: לָקֹחַ אֵת סֵפֶר הַתּוֹרָה הַזֶּה וְשַׂמְתֶּם אֹתוֹ מִצַּד אֲרוֹן בְּרִית־יהוה אֱלֹֽהֵיכֶם וְהָֽיָה־שָׁם בְּךָ לְעֵד: כִּי אָֽנֹכִי יָדַעְתִּי אֶת־מֶרְיְךָ וְאֶת־עָרְפְּךָ הַקָּשֶׁה הֵן בְּעוֹדֶ֫נִּי חַי עִמָּכֶם הַיּוֹם מַמְרִים הֱיִתֶם עִם־יהוה וְאַף כִּֽי־אַֽחֲרֵי מוֹתִי: הַקְהִ֫ילוּ אֵלַי אֶת־כָּל־זִקְנֵי שִׁבְטֵיכֶם וְשֹֽׁטְרֵיכֶם וַֽאֲדַבְּרָה בְאָזְנֵיהֶם אֵת הַדְּבָרִים הָאֵלֶּה *וְאָעִ֫ידָה בָּם אֶת־הַשָּׁמַיִם וְאֶת־הָאָרֶץ: כִּי יָדַעְתִּי אַֽחֲרֵי מוֹתִי כִּֽי־הַשְׁחֵת תַּשְׁחִתוּן וְסַרְתֶּם מִן־הַדֶּרֶךְ אֲשֶׁר צִוִּ֫יתִי אֶתְכֶם וְקָרָאת אֶתְכֶם הָֽרָעָה בְּאַֽחֲרִית הַיָּמִים כִּֽי־תַֽעֲשׂוּ אֶת־הָרַע בְּעֵינֵי יהוה לְהַכְעִיסוֹ בְּמַֽעֲשֵׂה יְדֵיכֶם: וַיְדַבֵּר מֹשֶׁה בְּאָזְנֵי כָּל־קְהַל יִשְׂרָאֵל אֶת־דִּבְרֵי הַשִּׁירָה הַזֹּאת עַד תֻּמָּם: פפפ ע' פסוקים. אדני־ה סימן.

כא

כב

כג

כד

שביעי

כה

כו

כז

מפטיר

"בראש עמוד
בר"ה שמ"ר סימן

Haftaras
Vayeilech:
p. 1348;
when it is
read with
Nitzavim:
p. 1060

כח

כט

ל

פרשת האזינו

לב

א הַֽאֲזִינוּ הַשָּׁמַיִם וַֽאֲדַבֵּרָה   וְתִשְׁמַע הָאָרֶץ אִמְרֵי־פִי:
ב יַֽעֲרֹף כַּמָּטָר לִקְחִי   תִּזַּל כַּטַּל אִמְרָתִי
כִּשְׂעִירִם עֲלֵי־דֶשֶׁא   וְכִרְבִיבִים עֲלֵי־עֵשֶׂב:
ג כִּי שֵׁם יהוה אֶקְרָא   הָבוּ גֹדֶל לֵֽאלֹהֵינוּ:
ד הַצּוּר תָּמִים פָּֽעֳלוֹ   כִּי כָל־דְּרָכָיו מִשְׁפָּט
אֵל אֱמוּנָה וְאֵין עָוֶל   צַדִּיק וְיָשָׁר הוּא:
ה שִׁחֵת לוֹ לֹא בָּנָיו מוּמָם   דּוֹר עִקֵּשׁ וּפְתַלְתֹּל:
ו הֲ־לַֽיהוה תִּגְמְלוּ־זֹאת   עַם נָבָל וְלֹא חָכָם
הֲלוֹא־הוּא אָבִיךָ קָּנֶךָ   הוּא עָֽשְׂךָ וַֽיְכֹנְנֶךָ:
ז זְכֹר יְמוֹת עוֹלָם   בִּינוּ שְׁנוֹת דֹּר־וָדֹר
שְׁאַל אָבִיךָ וְיַגֵּדְךָ   זְקֵנֶיךָ וְיֹֽאמְרוּ לָךְ:
ח בְּהַנְחֵל עֶלְיוֹן גּוֹיִם   בְּהַפְרִידוֹ בְּנֵי אָדָם

"ה רבתי והיא
תיבה לעצמה

שני

◄§ Parashas Haazinu. To testify that he was warning Israel, Moses wanted witnesses that would outlive his and later generations. Therefore he appointed heaven and earth, which are eternal. Furthermore, if Israel were to be found guilty of violating the covenant, these witnesses would take the lead in administering the appropriate pun-

The Torah as testimony

so that this song shall be for Me a witness against the Children of Israel. ²⁰ "For I shall bring them to the Land that I swore to their forefathers, which flows with milk and honey, but it will eat, be sated, and grow fat, and turn to gods of others and serve them, it will provoke Me and annul My covenant. ²¹ It shall be that when many evils and distresses come upon it, then this song shall speak up before it as a witness, for it shall not be forgotten from the mouth of its offspring, for I know its inclination, what it does today, before I bring them to the Land that I have sworn."

²² Moses wrote this song on that day, and he taught it to the Children of Israel. ²³ He commanded Joshua son of Nun, and said, "Be strong and courageous, for you shall bring the Children of Israel to the Land that I have sworn to them, and I shall be with you."

²⁴ So it was that when Moses finished writing the words of this Torah onto a book, until their conclusion: ²⁵ Moses commanded the Levites, the bearers of the Ark of the Covenant of HASHEM, saying, ²⁶ "Take this book of the Torah and place it at the side of the Ark of the Covenant of HASHEM, your God, and it shall be there for you as a witness. ²⁷ For I know your rebelliousness and your stiff neck; behold! while I am still alive with you today, you have been rebels against HASHEM — and surely after my death. ²⁸ Gather to me all the elders of your tribes and your officers, and I shall speak these words into their ears, and call heaven and earth to bear witness against them. ²⁹ For I know that after my death you will surely act corruptly, and you will stray from the path that I have commanded you, and evil will befall you at the end of days, if you do what is evil in the eyes of HASHEM, to anger Him through your handiwork."

³⁰ Moses spoke the words of this song into the ears of the entire congregation of Israel, until their conclusion.

PARASHAS HAAZINU

32

The Song of Moses

¹ Give ear, O heavens, and I will speak;
and may the earth hear the words of my mouth.
² May my teaching drop like the rain, may my utterance flow like the dew;
like storm winds upon vegetation and like raindrops upon blades of grass.
³ When I call out the Name of HASHEM, ascribe greatness to our God.
⁴ The Rock! — perfect is His work, for all His paths are justice;
a God of faith without iniquity, righteous and fair is He. *
⁵ Corruption is not His — the blemish is His children's,
a perverse and twisted generation.
⁶ Is it to HASHEM that you do this, O vile and unwise people?
Is He not your Father, your Master? Has He not created you and firmed you? *
⁷ Remember the days of yore,
understand the years of generation after generation.
Ask your father and he will relate it to you, your elders and they will tell you.
⁸ When the Supreme One gave the nations their inheritance,
when He separated the children of man,

---

ishment, for the heaven would withhold its rain and the earth would withhold its produce (*Rashi; Ibn Ezra*).

32:4. God's judgment is exact and fair. He rewards the righteous, even though their reward may be slow in coming, and He rewards even the wicked for whatever good

they may do (*Rashi*).

32:7-9. Moses urges them to reflect upon the past, to inquire of people who remember and understand history, who know how God regulated the course of the world according to the needs of the Jewish people (*Ramban*).

יַצֵּב֙ גְּבֻלֹ֣ת עַמִּ֔ים לְמִסְפַּ֖ר בְּנֵ֥י יִשְׂרָאֵֽל׃

ט כִּ֛י חֵ֥לֶק יְהֹוָ֖ה עַמּ֑וֹ יַעֲקֹ֖ב חֶ֥בֶל נַחֲלָתֽוֹ׃

י יִמְצָאֵ֙הוּ֙ בְּאֶ֣רֶץ מִדְבָּ֔ר וּבְתֹ֖הוּ יְלֵ֣ל יְשִׁמֹ֑ן יְסֹֽבְבֶ֙נְהוּ֙ יְב֣וֹנְנֵ֔הוּ יִצְּרֶ֖נְהוּ כְּאִישׁ֥וֹן עֵינֽוֹ׃

יא כְּנֶ֙שֶׁר֙ יָעִ֣יר קִנּ֔וֹ עַל־גּוֹזָלָ֖יו יְרַחֵ֑ף יִפְרֹ֤שׂ כְּנָפָיו֙ יִקָּחֵ֔הוּ יִשָּׂאֵ֖הוּ עַל־אֶבְרָתֽוֹ׃

יב יְהֹוָ֖ה בָּדָ֣ד יַנְחֶ֑נּוּ וְאֵ֥ין עִמּ֖וֹ אֵ֥ל נֵכָֽר׃

[שלישי] יג יַרְכִּבֵ֙הוּ֙ עַל־°במותי [°בָּמֳתֵ֣י קרי] אָ֔רֶץ וַיֹּאכַ֖ל תְּנוּבֹ֣ת שָׂדָ֑י וַיֵּנִקֵ֤הֽוּ דְבַשׁ֙ מִסֶּ֔לַע וְשֶׁ֖מֶן מֵחַלְמִ֥ישׁ צֽוּר׃

יד חֶמְאַ֨ת בָּקָ֜ר וַחֲלֵ֣ב צֹ֗אן עִם־חֵ֤לֶב כָּרִים֙ וְאֵילִ֣ים בְּנֵֽי־בָשָׁן֮ וְעַתּוּדִים֒ עִם־חֵ֖לֶב כִּלְי֣וֹת חִטָּ֑ה

טו וַיִּשְׁמַ֤ן יְשֻׁרוּן֙ וַיִּבְעָ֔ט וְדַ֖ם עֵנָ֥ב תִּשְׁתֶּה־חָֽמֶר׃ שָׁמַ֙נְתָּ֙ עָבִ֣יתָ כָּשִׂ֔יתָ וַֽיִּטֹּשׁ֙ אֱל֣וֹהַּ עָשָׂ֔הוּ וַיְנַבֵּ֖ל צ֥וּר יְשֻׁעָתֽוֹ׃

טז יַקְנִאֻ֖הוּ בְּזָרִ֑ים בְּתוֹעֵבֹ֖ת יַכְעִיסֻֽהוּ׃

יז יִזְבְּח֗וּ לַשֵּׁדִים֙ לֹ֣א אֱלֹ֔הַּ אֱלֹהִ֖ים לֹ֣א יְדָע֑וּם חֲדָשִׁים֙ מִקָּרֹ֣ב בָּ֔אוּ לֹ֥א שְׂעָר֖וּם אֲבֹתֵיכֶֽם׃

[י זעירא] יח צ֥וּר יְלָדְךָ֖ תֶּ֑שִׁי וַתִּשְׁכַּ֖ח אֵ֥ל מְחֹלְלֶֽךָ׃

[רביעי] יט וַיַּ֥רְא יְהֹוָ֖ה וַיִּנְאָ֑ץ מִכַּ֥עַס בָּנָ֖יו וּבְנֹתָֽיו׃

כ וַיֹּ֗אמֶר אַסְתִּ֤ירָה פָנַי֙ מֵהֶ֔ם אֶרְאֶ֖ה מָ֣ה אַחֲרִיתָ֑ם כִּ֣י ד֤וֹר תַּהְפֻּכֹת֙ הֵ֔מָּה בָּנִ֖ים לֹא־אֵמֻ֥ן בָּֽם׃

[חול] כא הֵ֚ם קִנְא֣וּנִי בְלֹא־אֵ֔ל כִּעֲס֖וּנִי בְּהַבְלֵיהֶ֑ם וַאֲנִי֙ אַקְנִיאֵ֣ם בְּלֹא־עָ֔ם בְּג֥וֹי נָבָ֖ל אַכְעִיסֵֽם׃

כב כִּי־אֵשׁ֙ קָדְחָ֣ה בְאַפִּ֔י וַתִּיקַ֖ד עַד־שְׁא֣וֹל תַּחְתִּ֑ית וַתֹּ֤אכַל אֶ֙רֶץ֙ וִֽיבֻלָ֔הּ וַתְּלַהֵ֖ט מוֹסְדֵ֥י הָרִֽים׃

כג אַסְפֶּ֥ה עָלֵ֖ימוֹ רָע֑וֹת חִצַּ֖י אֲכַלֶּה־בָּֽם׃

כד מְזֵ֥י רָעָ֛ב וּלְחֻ֥מֵי רֶ֖שֶׁף וְקֶ֣טֶב מְרִירִ֑י וְשֶׁן־בְּהֵמֹת֙ אֲשַׁלַּח־בָּ֔ם עִם־חֲמַ֖ת זֹחֲלֵ֥י עָפָֽר׃

כה מִחוּץ֙ תְּשַׁכֶּל־חֶ֔רֶב וּמֵחֲדָרִ֖ים אֵימָ֑ה גַּם־בָּחוּר֙ גַּם־בְּתוּלָ֔ה יוֹנֵ֖ק עִם־אִ֥ישׁ שֵׂיבָֽה׃

כו אָמַ֖רְתִּי אַפְאֵיהֶ֑ם אַשְׁבִּ֥יתָה מֵאֱנ֖וֹשׁ זִכְרָֽם׃

כז לוּלֵ֗י כַּ֤עַס אוֹיֵב֙ אָג֔וּר פֶּֽן־יְנַכְּר֖וּ צָרֵ֑ימוֹ

32:15. The august title *Jeshurun*, from יָשָׁר, *upright, just, straight,* describes Israel when it does not deviate from the high standards demanded by God — but even Jeshurun is in danger if it succumbs to its desires (*R' Hirsch*).

32:19-25. If we use God's blessings to anger Him, He will remove them and cast us to the mercies of our enemies.

He set the borders of the peoples
   according to the number of the Children of Israel.
   ⁹ For HASHEM's portion is His people; Jacob is the measure of His inheritance.

God's ¹⁰ He discovered him in a desert land, in desolation, a howling wilderness;
kindness He encircled him, He granted him discernment,
to Israel   He preserved him like the pupil of His eye.
   ¹¹ He was like an eagle arousing its nest, hovering over its young,
      spreading its wings and taking them, carrying them on its pinions.
   ¹² HASHEM alone guided them, and no other power was with them.
   ¹³ He would make him ride on the heights of the Land
      and have him eat the ripe fruits of My fields;
   He would suckle him with honey from a stone, and oil from a flinty rock;
   ¹⁴ Butter of cattle and milk of sheep with fat of lambs,
      rams born in Bashan and he-goats, with wheat as fat as kidneys;
      and you would drink blood of grapes like delicious wine.

Prosperity ¹⁵ Jeshurun* became fat and kicked.
brings You became fat, you became thick, you became corpulent —
dissolution   and it deserted God its Maker,
      and was contemptuous of the Rock of its salvation.

The descent ¹⁶ They would provoke His jealousy with strangers;
worsens   they would anger Him with abominations.
   ¹⁷ They would slaughter to demons without power, gods whom they knew not,
   newcomers recently arrived, whom your ancestors did not dread.
   ¹⁸ You ignored the Rock Who gave birth to you,
      and forgot God Who brought you forth.

God's wrath ¹⁹ HASHEM will see and be provoked by the anger* of His sons and daughters,
   ²⁰ and He will say,
   "I shall hide My face from them and see what their end will be —
   for they are a generation of reversals,
   children whose upbringing is not in them.
   ²¹ They provoked Me with a non-god, angered Me with their vanities;
      so shall I provoke them with a non-people,
      with a vile nation shall I anger them.
   ²² For fire will have been kindled in My nostrils and blazed to the lowest depths.
   It shall consume the earth and its produce,
      and set ablaze what is founded on mountains.
   ²³ I shall accumulate evils against them, My arrows shall I use up against them;
   ²⁴ bloating of famine, battles of flaming demons,
      cutting down by the noontime demon,
   and the teeth of beasts shall I dispatch against them,
      with the venom of those that creep on the earth.
   ²⁵ On the outside, the sword will bereave, while indoors there will be dread —
   even a young man, even a virgin, a suckling with the gray-haired man.
   ²⁶ I had said, 'I will scatter them,
      I will cause their memory to cease from man' —
   ²⁷ were it not that the anger of the enemy was pent up,
      lest his tormenters misinterpret;
   lest they say, 'Our hand was raised in triumph,

כח וְלֹא יְהוָֹה פָּעַל כָּל־זֹאת: כִּי־גוֹי אֹבַד עֵצוֹת הֵמָּה

חמישי

כט וְאֵין בָּהֶם תְּבוּנָה: לוּ חָכְמוּ יַשְׂכִּילוּ זֹאת

ל יָבִינוּ לְאַחֲרִיתָם: אֵיכָה יִרְדֹּף אֶחָד אֶלֶף

וּשְׁנַיִם יָנִיסוּ רְבָבָה   אִם־לֹא כִּי־צוּרָם מְכָרָם

לא וַיהוָֹה הִסְגִּירָם: כִּי לֹא כְצוּרֵנוּ צוּרָם

לב וְאֹיְבֵינוּ פְּלִילִים: כִּי־מִגֶּפֶן סְדֹם גַּפְנָם

וּמִשַּׁדְמֹת עֲמֹרָה   עֲנָבֵמוֹ עִנְּבֵי־רוֹשׁ

אַשְׁכְּלֹת מְרֹרֹת לָמוֹ:   חֲמַת תַּנִּינִם יֵינָם

לג וְרֹאשׁ פְּתָנִים אַכְזָר: הֲלֹא־הוּא כָּמֻס עִמָּדִי

לד חָתוּם בְּאוֹצְרֹתָי: לִי נָקָם וְשִׁלֵּם

לה לְעֵת תָּמוּט רַגְלָם   כִּי קָרוֹב יוֹם אֵידָם

וְחָשׁ עֲתִדֹת לָמוֹ:   כִּי־יָדִין יְהוָֹה עַמּוֹ

לו וְעַל־עֲבָדָיו יִתְנֶחָם   כִּי יִרְאֶה כִּי־אָזְלַת יָד

וְאֶפֶס עָצוּר וְעָזוּב: וְאָמַר אֵי אֱלֹהֵימוֹ

לז צוּר חָסָיוּ בוֹ:   אֲשֶׁר חֵלֶב זְבָחֵימוֹ יֹאכֵלוּ

לח יִשְׁתּוּ יֵין נְסִיכָם   יָקוּמוּ וְיַעְזְרֻכֶם

יְהִי עֲלֵיכֶם סִתְרָה: רְאוּ | עַתָּה כִּי אֲנִי אֲנִי הוּא

לט וְאֵין אֱלֹהִים עִמָּדִי   אֲנִי אָמִית וַאֲחַיֶּה

מָחַצְתִּי וַאֲנִי אֶרְפָּא   וְאֵין מִיָּדִי מַצִּיל:

כִּי־אֶשָּׂא אֶל־שָׁמַיִם יָדִי   וְאָמַרְתִּי חַי אָנֹכִי לְעֹלָם:

מ אִם־שַׁנּוֹתִי בְּרַק חַרְבִּי   וְתֹאחֵז בְּמִשְׁפָּט יָדִי

ששי

מא אָשִׁיב נָקָם לְצָרָי   וְלִמְשַׂנְאַי אֲשַׁלֵּם:

מב אַשְׁכִּיר חִצַּי מִדָּם   וְחַרְבִּי תֹּאכַל בָּשָׂר

מִדַּם חָלָל וְשִׁבְיָה   מֵרֹאשׁ פַּרְעוֹת אוֹיֵב:

מג הַרְנִינוּ גוֹיִם עַמּוֹ   כִּי דַם־עֲבָדָיו יִקּוֹם

וְנָקָם יָשִׁיב לְצָרָיו   וְכִפֶּר אַדְמָתוֹ עַמּוֹ:

מד וַיָּבֹא מֹשֶׁה וַיְדַבֵּר אֶת־כָּל־דִּבְרֵי הַשִּׁירָה־הַזֹּאת בְּאָזְנֵי הָעָם הוּא וְהוֹשֵׁעַ

שביעי

מה בִּן־נוּן: וַיְכַל מֹשֶׁה לְדַבֵּר אֶת־כָּל־הַדְּבָרִים הָאֵלֶּה אֶל־כָּל־יִשְׂרָאֵל:

מו וַיֹּאמֶר אֲלֵהֶם שִׂימוּ לְבַבְכֶם לְכָל־הַדְּבָרִים אֲשֶׁר אָנֹכִי מֵעִיד בָּכֶם הַיּוֹם

מז אֲשֶׁר תְּצַוֻּם אֶת־בְּנֵיכֶם לִשְׁמֹר לַעֲשׂוֹת אֶת־כָּל־דִּבְרֵי הַתּוֹרָה הַזֹּאת: כִּי לֹא־דָבָר רֵק הוּא מִכֶּם כִּי־הוּא חַיֵּיכֶם וּבַדָּבָר הַזֶּה תַּאֲרִיכוּ יָמִים עַל־הָאֲדָמָה אֲשֶׁר אַתֶּם עֹבְרִים אֶת־הַיַּרְדֵּן שָׁמָּה לְרִשְׁתָּהּ:

32:28-31. Israel's defeat, the victors thought, was due to their own strength and that of their gods.

32:32-35. The Torah now reverts to Israel, explaining why they were deserving of such a crushing defeat.

and it was not HASHEM Who accomplished all this!'

The enemy's foolish conceit
³⁸ *For they are a nation bereft of counsel, * and there is no discernment in them.*
²⁹ *Were they wise they would comprehend this,*
     they would discern it from their end.
³⁰ *For how could one pursue a thousand, and two cause a myriad to flee,*
     if not that their Rock had sold them out, and HASHEM had delivered them?
³¹ *— for not like our Rock is their rock — yet our enemies judge us!*

Source of Israel's suffering
³² *For their vineyard is from the vineyard of Sodom, **
     and from the fields of Gomorrah;
   their grapes are grapes of gall, so clusters of bitterness were given them.
³³ *Serpents' venom is their wine, the poison of cruel vipers.*
³⁴ *Is it not revealed with Me, sealed in My treasuries?*

Israel is comforted
³⁵ *Mine is vengeance and retribution at the time their foot will falter,*
     for the day of their catastrophe is near, and future events are rushing at them."
³⁶ *When HASHEM will have judged His people, **
     He shall relent regarding His servants,
   when He sees that enemy power progresses, and none is saved or assisted.
³⁷ *He will say, "Where is their god, * the rock in whom they sought refuge,*
³⁸ *the fat of whose offerings they would eat,*
     they would drink the wine of their libations?
   Let them stand and help you! Let them be a shelter for you!
³⁹ *See, now, that I, I am He — and no god is with Me.*
     I put to death and I bring to life, I struck down and I will heal,
     and there is no rescuer from My hand.
⁴⁰ *For I shall raise My hand to heaven and say, 'As I live forever,*
⁴¹ *if I sharpen My flashing sword and My hand grasps judgment,*
   I shall return vengeance upon My enemies
     and upon those that hate Me shall I bring retribution.
⁴² *I shall intoxicate My arrows with blood and My sword shall devour flesh,*
     because of the blood of corpse and captive,
     because of the earliest depredations of the enemy.' "
⁴³ *O nations — sing the praises of His people,*
     for He will avenge the blood of His servants; *
   He will bring retribution upon His foes,
     and He will appease His Land and His people.

⁴⁴ *Moses came and spoke all the words of this Song in the ears of the people, he and Hoshea* son of Nun.* ⁴⁵ *Moses concluded speaking all these words to all Israel.* ⁴⁶ *He said to them, "Apply your hearts to all the words that I testify against you today, with which you are to instruct your children, to be careful to perform all the words of this Torah,* ⁴⁷ *for it is not an empty thing for you, for it is your life, and through this matter shall you prolong your days on the Land to which you cross the Jordan, to possess it."*

32:36-43. Nothing can sever the bond between Israel and God; eventually, the closeness will be restored.

32:37-38. God exhorts Israel to recognize that none of a multitude of gods — in the form of an idol, money, or privileged position — can repulse enemies or provide the antidote to the venom of sin; over the centuries, Israel has adopted the full panoply of such gods.

32:43. Though Israel's rebelliousness and disloyalty to God brought it terrible consequences, as described earlier in the Song, here the Song guarantees Israel's survival and the downfall of its enemies.

32:44. Here Joshua is called with his original name *Hoshea*, to imply that he was still as modest as he was before his name was enhanced (*Rashi*).

מפטיר מח־מט   וַיְדַבֵּ֤ר יְהֹוָה֙ אֶל־מֹשֶׁ֔ה בְּעֶ֛צֶם הַיּ֥וֹם הַזֶּ֖ה לֵאמֹֽר: עֲלֵ֡ה אֶל־הַר֩ הָעֲבָרִ֨ים הַזֶּ֜ה
הַר־נְב֗וֹ אֲשֶׁר֙ בְּאֶ֣רֶץ מוֹאָ֔ב אֲשֶׁ֖ר עַל־פְּנֵ֣י יְרֵח֑וֹ וּרְאֵה֙ אֶת־אֶ֣רֶץ כְּנַ֔עַן אֲשֶׁ֨ר
נ   אֲנִ֥י נֹתֵ֛ן לִבְנֵ֥י יִשְׂרָאֵ֖ל לַאֲחֻזָּֽה: וּמֻ֗ת בָּהָר֙ אֲשֶׁ֤ר אַתָּה֙ עֹלֶ֣ה שָׁ֔מָּה וְהֵאָסֵ֖ף
נא   אֶל־עַמֶּ֑יךָ כַּאֲשֶׁר־מֵ֞ת אַהֲרֹ֤ן אָחִ֙יךָ֙ בְּהֹ֣ר הָהָ֔ר וַיֵּאָ֖סֶף אֶל־עַמָּֽיו: עַ֡ל אֲשֶׁר֩
מְעַלְתֶּ֨ם בִּ֜י בְּת֣וֹךְ בְּנֵ֣י יִשְׂרָאֵ֗ל בְּמֵֽי־מְרִיבַ֥ת קָדֵ֖שׁ מִדְבַּר־צִ֑ן עַ֣ל אֲשֶׁ֤ר לֹֽא־
נב   קִדַּשְׁתֶּ֣ם אוֹתִ֔י בְּת֖וֹךְ בְּנֵ֥י יִשְׂרָאֵֽל: כִּ֥י מִנֶּ֖גֶד תִּרְאֶ֣ה אֶת־הָאָ֑רֶץ וְשָׁ֙מָּה֙ לֹ֣א
תָב֔וֹא אֶל־הָאָ֕רֶץ אֲשֶׁר־אֲנִ֥י נֹתֵ֖ן לִבְנֵ֥י יִשְׂרָאֵֽל: פפפ   נ"ב פסוקים. כל"ב סימן.

פרשת וזאת הברכה

לג   א   וְזֹ֣את הַבְּרָכָ֗ה אֲשֶׁ֨ר בֵּרַ֥ךְ מֹשֶׁ֛ה אִ֥ישׁ הָאֱלֹהִ֖ים אֶת־בְּנֵ֣י יִשְׂרָאֵ֑ל לִפְנֵ֖י מוֹתֽוֹ:
ב   וַיֹּאמַ֗ר יְהֹוָ֞ה מִסִּינַ֥י בָּא֙ וְזָרַ֤ח מִשֵּׂעִיר֙ לָ֔מוֹ הוֹפִ֙יעַ֙ מֵהַ֣ר פָּארָ֔ן וְאָתָ֖ה מֵרִבְבֹ֣ת
ג   קֹ֑דֶשׁ מִֽימִינ֕וֹ °אשדת [אֵ֥שׁ דָּ֖ת ק] לָֽמוֹ: אַ֚ף חֹבֵ֣ב עַמִּ֔ים כׇּל־קְדֹשָׁ֖יו בְּיָדֶ֑ךָ
ד   וְהֵם֙ תֻּכּ֣וּ לְרַגְלֶ֔ךָ יִשָּׂ֖א מִדַּבְּרֹתֶֽיךָ: תּוֹרָ֥ה צִוָּה־לָ֖נוּ מֹשֶׁ֑ה מוֹרָשָׁ֖ה קְהִלַּ֥ת
ה־ז   יַעֲקֹֽב: וַיְהִ֥י בִישֻׁר֖וּן מֶ֑לֶךְ בְּהִתְאַסֵּף֙ רָ֣אשֵׁי עָ֔ם יַ֖חַד שִׁבְטֵ֥י יִשְׂרָאֵֽל: יְחִ֤י
רְאוּבֵן֙ וְאַל־יָמֹ֔ת וִיהִ֥י מְתָ֖יו מִסְפָּֽר: וְזֹ֣את לִֽיהוּדָה֮ וַיֹּאמַר֒ שְׁמַ֤ע
יְהֹוָה֙ ק֣וֹל יְהוּדָ֔ה וְאֶל־עַמּ֖וֹ תְּבִיאֶ֑נּוּ יָדָיו֙ רָ֣ב ל֔וֹ וְעֵ֥זֶר מִצָּרָ֖יו תִּהְיֶֽה:
ח   וּלְלֵוִ֣י אָמַ֔ר תֻּמֶּ֥יךָ וְאוּרֶ֖יךָ לְאִ֣ישׁ חֲסִידֶ֑ךָ אֲשֶׁ֤ר נִסִּיתוֹ֙ בְּמַסָּ֔ה תְּרִיבֵ֖הוּ עַל־
ט   מֵ֣י מְרִיבָֽה: הָאֹמֵ֞ר לְאָבִ֤יו וּלְאִמּוֹ֙ לֹ֣א רְאִיתִ֔יו וְאֶת־אֶחָיו֙ לֹ֣א הִכִּ֔יר וְאֶת־
י   בָּנָ֖ו לֹ֣א יָדָ֑ע כִּ֤י שָׁמְרוּ֙ אִמְרָתֶ֔ךָ וּבְרִֽיתְךָ֖ יִנְצֹֽרוּ: יוֹר֤וּ מִשְׁפָּטֶ֙יךָ֙ לְיַעֲקֹ֔ב
יא   וְתוֹרָֽתְךָ֖ לְיִשְׂרָאֵ֑ל יָשִׂ֤ימוּ קְטוֹרָה֙ בְּאַפֶּ֔ךָ וְכָלִ֖יל עַל־מִזְבְּחֶֽךָ: בָּרֵ֤ךְ יְהֹוָה֙ חֵיל֔וֹ
וּפֹ֥עַל יָדָ֖יו תִּרְצֶ֑ה מְחַ֨ץ מׇתְנַ֧יִם קָמָ֛יו וּמְשַׂנְאָ֖יו מִן־יְקוּמֽוּן: לְבִנְיָמִ֣ן
שני   אָמַ֔ר יְדִ֣יד יְהֹוָ֔ה יִשְׁכֹּ֥ן לָבֶ֖טַח עָלָ֑יו חֹפֵ֤ף עָלָיו֙ כׇּל־הַיּ֔וֹם וּבֵ֥ין כְּתֵפָ֖יו
יג   שָׁכֵֽן: וּלְיוֹסֵ֣ף אָמַ֔ר מְבֹרֶ֥כֶת יְהֹוָ֖ה אַרְצ֑וֹ מִמֶּ֤גֶד שָׁמַ֙יִם֙ מִטָּ֔ל
שלישי   וּמִתְּה֖וֹם רֹבֶ֥צֶת תָּֽחַת: וּמִמֶּ֖גֶד תְּבוּאֹ֣ת שָׁ֑מֶשׁ וּמִמֶּ֖גֶד גֶּ֥רֶשׁ יְרָחִֽים:
יד־טו   וּמֵרֹ֖אשׁ הַרְרֵי־קֶ֑דֶם וּמִמֶּ֖גֶד גִּבְע֥וֹת עוֹלָֽם: וּמִמֶּ֗גֶד אֶ֚רֶץ וּמְלֹאָ֔הּ וּרְצ֥וֹן
שֹׁכְנִ֣י סְנֶ֑ה תָּב֙וֹאתָה֙ לְרֹ֣אשׁ יוֹסֵ֔ף וּלְקׇדְקֹ֖ד נְזִ֥יר אֶחָֽיו: בְּכ֨וֹר שׁוֹר֜וֹ הָדָ֣ר ל֗וֹ
וְקַרְנֵ֤י רְאֵם֙ קַרְנָ֔יו בָּהֶ֛ם עַמִּ֥ים יְנַגַּ֖ח יַחְדָּ֣ו אַפְסֵי־אָ֑רֶץ וְהֵם֙ רִבְב֣וֹת אֶפְרַ֔יִם
רביעי   וְהֵ֖ם אַלְפֵ֥י מְנַשֶּֽׁה: וְלִזְבוּלֻ֣ן אָמַ֔ר שְׂמַ֥ח זְבוּלֻ֖ן בְּצֵאתֶ֑ךָ וְיִשָּׂשכָ֖ר
בְּאֹהָלֶֽיךָ: עַמִּים֙ הַר־יִקְרָ֔אוּ שָׁ֖ם יִזְבְּח֣וּ זִבְחֵי־צֶ֑דֶק כִּ֣י שֶׁ֤פַע יַמִּים֙ יִינָ֔קוּ

Haftaras
Haazinu:
Between
Rosh
HaShanah
and Yom
Kippur:
p. 1348;
after Yom
Kippur:
p. 782

SIMCHAS
TORAH
33:1–
34:12;
Genesis
1:1-2:3

Maftir:
p. 404
Haftarah:
p. 518

◆§ **Parashas Vezos Haberachah**

Moses' final words are a combination of blessing and prophecy, in which he blesses each tribe according to its national responsibilities and individual greatness.

33:5. Once Israel declared its eternal loyalty to the Torah (vs. 3-4), God became "King of Jeshurun," because it is only among those who grasp and diligently involve themselves in the study of Torah that God is truly King (Sforno).

◆§ **Omission of Simeon.** Simeon is omitted because

Jacob had castigated him [see Genesis 49:5], and because the sinners in the terrible affair of Baal-peor were Simeonites [see Numbers 25:3] (Ibn Ezra).

33:8-11. Moses praised the steadfast loyalty and bravery of the Levites in the Wilderness, and blessed them as the teachers of the nation.

33:18-19. Issachar and Zebulun had a unique and inspiring partnership: Zebulun engaged successfully in maritime commerce and supported Issachar who devoted his time to Torah study (see I Chronicles 12:33).

God's last
command-
ment
to Moses

⁴⁸ HASHEM spoke to Moses on that very day, saying, ⁴⁹ "Ascend to this mount of Abarim, Mount Nebo, which is in the land of Moab, which is before Jericho, and see the Land of Canaan that I give to the Children of Israel as an inheritance, ⁵⁰ and die on the mountain where you will ascend, and be gathered to your people, as Aaron your brother died on Mount Hor, and was gathered to his people, ⁵¹ because you trespassed against Me among the Children of Israel at the waters of strife at Kadesh, in the Wilderness of Zin; because you did not sancti- fy Me among the Children of Israel. ⁵² For from a distance shall you see the Land, but you shall not enter there, into the Land that I give to the Children of Israel."

PARASHAS VEZOS HABERACHAH

33

The
Blessing of
Moses

¹ And this is the blessing that Moses, the man of God, bestowed upon the Children of Israel before his death. ² He said: HASHEM came from Sinai — having shone forth to them from Seir, having appeared from Mount Paran, and then approached with some of the holy myriads — from His right hand He presented the fiery Torah to them. ³ Indeed, You loved the tribes greatly, all its holy ones were in Your hands; for they planted themselves at Your feet, bearing [the yoke] of Your utterances: ⁴ "The Torah that Moses commanded us is the heritage of the Congregation of Jacob." ⁵ He became King over Jeshurun * when the numbers of the nation gathered — the tribes of Israel in unity.

Reuben
Judah

⁶ May Reuben live and not die, and may his population be included in the count.

⁷ And this to Judah, and he said: Hearken, O HASHEM, to Judah's voice, and return him to his people; may his hands fight his grievance and may You be a Helper against his enemies.

Levi

⁸ Of Levi he said: Your Tumim and Your Urim befit Your devout one, whom You tested at Massah, and whom You challenged at the waters of Meribah. * ⁹ The one who said of his father and mother, "I have not favored him"; his brothers he did not give recognition and his children he did not know; for they [the Levites] have observed Your word and Your covenant they preserved. ¹⁰ They shall teach Your ordinances to Jacob and Your Torah to Israel; they shall place incense before Your presence, and burnt offerings on Your Altar. ¹¹ Bless, O HASHEM, his resources, and favor the work of his hands; smash the loins of his foes and his enemies, that they may not rise.

Benjamin

¹² Of Benjamin he said: May HASHEM's beloved dwell securely by Him; He hovers over him all day long; and rests between his shoulders.

Joseph

¹³ Of Joseph he said: Blessed by HASHEM is his land — with the heavenly bounty of dew, and with the deep waters crouching below; ¹⁴ with the bounty of the sun's crops, and with the bounty of the moon's yield; ¹⁵ with the quick- ripening crops of the early mountains, and with the bounty of eternal hills; ¹⁶ with the bounty of the land and its fullness, and by the favor of He Who rested upon the thornbush; may this blessing rest upon Joseph's head, and upon the crown of he who was separated from his brothers. ¹⁷ A sovereignty is his ox-like one — majesty is his, and his glory will be like the horns of a re'eim; with them shall he gore nations together, to the ends of the Land; they are the myriads of Ephraim, and the thousands of Manasseh.

Zebulun and
Issachar

¹⁸ Of Zebulun he said: Rejoice, O Zebulun, in your excursions, * and Issachar in your tents. ¹⁹ The tribes will assemble at the mount, there they will slaughter offerings of righteousness, for by the riches of the sea they will be nourished,

כ וּלְגָד אָמַר בָּרוּךְ מַרְחִיב גָּד כְּלָבִיא שָׁכֵן וְשָׁרַף טְמוֹנֵי חוֹל:

כא וְטָרַף זְרוֹעַ אַף־קָדְקֹד: וַיַּרְא רֵאשִׁית לוֹ כִּי־שָׁם חֶלְקַת מְחֹקֵק סָפוּן וַיֵּתֵא רָאשֵׁי עָם צִדְקַת יהוה עָשָׂה וּמִשְׁפָּטָיו עִם־יִשְׂרָאֵל:

חמישי

כג וּלְנַפְתָּלִי אָמַר נַפְתָּלִי שְׂבַע רָצוֹן אָמַר דָּן גּוּר אַרְיֵה יְזַנֵּק מִן־הַבָּשָׁן:

כד וּלְאָשֵׁר אָמַר בָּרוּךְ וּמָלֵא בִּרְכַּת יהוה יָם וְדָרוֹם יְרָשָׁה:

כה מִבָּנִים אָשֵׁר יְהִי רְצוּי אֶחָיו וְטֹבֵל בַּשֶּׁמֶן רַגְלוֹ: בַּרְזֶל וּנְחֹשֶׁת מִנְעָלֶךָ

כו וּכְיָמֶיךָ דָּבְאֶךָ: אֵין כָּאֵל יְשֻׁרוּן רֹכֵב שָׁמַיִם בְּעֶזְרֶךָ וּבְגַאֲוָתוֹ שְׁחָקִים:

חתן התורה
(בארץ ישראל
בשבת: ששי)

כז מְעֹנָה אֱלֹהֵי קֶדֶם וּמִתַּחַת זְרֹעֹת עוֹלָם וַיְגָרֶשׁ מִפָּנֶיךָ אוֹיֵב וַיֹּאמֶר הַשְׁמֵד:

כח וַיִּשְׁכֹּן יִשְׂרָאֵל בֶּטַח בָּדָד עֵין יַעֲקֹב אֶל־אֶרֶץ דָּגָן וְתִירוֹשׁ אַף־שָׁמָיו יַעַרְפוּ

כט טָל: אַשְׁרֶיךָ יִשְׂרָאֵל מִי כָמוֹךָ עַם נוֹשַׁע בַּיהוה מָגֵן עֶזְרֶךָ וַאֲשֶׁר־חֶרֶב גַּאֲוָתֶךָ וְיִכָּחֲשׁוּ אֹיְבֶיךָ לָךְ וְאַתָּה עַל־בָּמוֹתֵימוֹ תִדְרֹךְ: וַיַּעַל

לד

בארץ ישראל
בשבת: שביעי

מֹשֶׁה מֵעַרְבֹת מוֹאָב אֶל־הַר נְבוֹ רֹאשׁ הַפִּסְגָּה אֲשֶׁר עַל־פְּנֵי יְרֵחוֹ

ב וַיַּרְאֵהוּ יהוה אֶת־כָּל־הָאָרֶץ אֶת־הַגִּלְעָד עַד־דָּן: וְאֵת כָּל־נַפְתָּלִי וְאֶת־

ג אֶרֶץ אֶפְרַיִם וּמְנַשֶּׁה וְאֵת כָּל־אֶרֶץ יְהוּדָה עַד הַיָּם הָאַחֲרוֹן: וְאֶת־הַנֶּגֶב

ד וְאֶת־הַכִּכָּר בִּקְעַת יְרֵחוֹ עִיר הַתְּמָרִים עַד־צֹעַר: וַיֹּאמֶר יהוה אֵלָיו זֹאת הָאָרֶץ אֲשֶׁר נִשְׁבַּעְתִּי לְאַבְרָהָם לְיִצְחָק וּלְיַעֲקֹב לֵאמֹר לְזַרְעֲךָ אֶתְּנֶנָּה

ה הֶרְאִיתִיךָ בְעֵינֶיךָ וְשָׁמָּה לֹא תַעֲבֹר: וַיָּמָת שָׁם מֹשֶׁה עֶבֶד־יהוה בְּאֶרֶץ

ו מוֹאָב עַל־פִּי יהוה: וַיִּקְבֹּר אֹתוֹ בַגַּי בְּאֶרֶץ מוֹאָב מוּל בֵּית פְּעוֹר וְלֹא־יָדַע

ז אִישׁ אֶת־קְבֻרָתוֹ עַד הַיּוֹם הַזֶּה: וּמֹשֶׁה בֶּן־מֵאָה וְעֶשְׂרִים שָׁנָה בְּמֹתוֹ לֹא־

ח כָהֲתָה עֵינוֹ וְלֹא־נָס לֵחֹה: וַיִּבְכּוּ בְנֵי יִשְׂרָאֵל אֶת־מֹשֶׁה בְּעַרְבֹת מוֹאָב

ט שְׁלֹשִׁים יוֹם וַיִּתְּמוּ יְמֵי בְכִי אֵבֶל מֹשֶׁה: וִיהוֹשֻׁעַ בִּן־נוּן מָלֵא רוּחַ חָכְמָה כִּי־סָמַךְ מֹשֶׁה אֶת־יָדָיו עָלָיו וַיִּשְׁמְעוּ אֵלָיו בְּנֵי־יִשְׂרָאֵל וַיַּעֲשׂוּ

י כַּאֲשֶׁר צִוָּה יהוה אֶת־מֹשֶׁה: וְלֹא־קָם נָבִיא עוֹד בְּיִשְׂרָאֵל כְּמֹשֶׁה אֲשֶׁר

יא יְדָעוֹ יהוה פָּנִים אֶל־פָּנִים: לְכָל־הָאֹתֹת וְהַמּוֹפְתִים אֲשֶׁר שְׁלָחוֹ יהוה

יב לַעֲשׂוֹת בְּאֶרֶץ מִצְרָיִם לְפַרְעֹה וּלְכָל־עֲבָדָיו וּלְכָל־אַרְצוֹ: וּלְכֹל הַיָּד הַחֲזָקָה וּלְכֹל הַמּוֹרָא הַגָּדוֹל אֲשֶׁר עָשָׂה מֹשֶׁה לְעֵינֵי כָּל־יִשְׂרָאֵל:

It is customary for the congregation followed by the reader to proclaim:

חֲזַק! חֲזַק! וְנִתְחַזֵּק!

סְכוּם פְּסוּקֵי דְּסֵפֶר דְּבָרִים תְּשַׁע מֵאוֹת וַחֲמִשִּׁים וַחֲמִשָּׁה. הנ״ץ סִימָן. סְכוּם פְּסוּקִים שֶׁל כָּל הַתּוֹרָה חֲמֵשֶׁת אֲלָפִים וּשְׁמֹנֶה מֵאוֹת וְאַרְבָּעִים וַחֲמִשָּׁה. וְאוֹר **הַחַמָּ״ה** יִהְיֶה שִׁבְעָתַיִם סִימָן.

33:22. Dan's province being on the Mediterranean coast, he was the first to encounter sea-borne marauders.

33:23. Naphtali's territory was blessed with riches.

33:24. Moses focused on the fertility of Asher's territory and the fruitfulness of his progeny.

33:25-26. This blessing is for the entire nation.

33:27-29. Moses took leave of his people with a remark-

able mixture of love and praise. Unlike his previous threats of a frightening array of punishments, his last words contain blessing and reassurance — for ultimately Israel will fulfill its promise and be showered with Divine rewards that will eclipse by far the horrors it has endured.

34:6. Moses' grave remained concealed, so that his tomb might not become a shrine of pilgrimage for those who deify national heroes.

and by the treasures concealed in the sand.

Gad ²⁰ *Of Gad he said: Blessed is He Who broadens Gad; he dwells like a lion, tearing off arm and even head.* ²¹ *He chose the first portion for himself, for that is where the lawgiver's plot is hidden; he came at the head of the nation, carrying out HASHEM's justice and His ordinances with Israel.*

Dan ²² *Of Dan he said: Dan is a lion cub, leaping forth from the Bashan.* *

Naphtali ²³ *Of Naphtali he said: Naphtali, satiated with favor, and filled with HASHEM's blessing;* * *go possess the sea and its south shore.*

Asher ²⁴ *Of Asher he said: The most blessed of children is Asher; he shall be pleasing to his brothers, and dip his feet in oil.* *

Epilogue: ²⁵ *May your borders be sealed like iron and copper,* * *and like the days of your*
Moses *prime, so may your old age be.* ²⁶ *There is none like God, O Jeshurun; He rides*
blesses
all of Israel *across heaven to help you, and in His majesty through the upper heights.*

²⁷ *That is the abode of God immemorial,* * *and below are the world's mighty ones; He drove the enemy away from before you, and He said, "Destroy!"* ²⁸ *Thus Israel shall dwell secure, solitary, in the likeness of Jacob, in a land of grain and wine; even his heavens shall drip with dew.*

²⁹ *Fortunate are you, O Israel: Who is like you! O people delivered by HASHEM, the Shield of your help, Who is the Sword of your grandeur; your foes will try to deceive you, but you will trample their haughty ones.*

34 ¹**M**oses *ascended from the plains of Moab to Mount Nebo, to the summit of*
Death of *the cliff that faces Jericho, and HASHEM showed him the entire Land: the*
Moses *Gilead as far as Dan;* ² *all of Naphtali, and the land of Ephraim and Manasseh;*
(See Appendix D, *the entire land of Judah as far as the western sea;* ³ *the Negev and the Plain —*
map 4) *the valley of Jericho, city of date palms — as far as Zoar.*

⁴ *And HASHEM said to him, "This is the land which I swore to Abraham, to Isaac, and to Jacob, saying, 'I will give it to your offspring.' I have let you see it with your own eyes, but you shall not cross over to there."*

⁵ *So Moses, servant of HASHEM, died there, in the land of Moab, by the mouth of HASHEM.* ⁶ *He buried him in the depression, in the land of Moab, opposite Beth-peor, and no one knows his burial place to this day.* * ⁷ *Moses was one hundred and twenty years old when he died; his eye had not dimmed, and his vigor had not diminished.* ⁸ *The Children of Israel bewailed Moses in the plains of Moab for thirty days; then the days of tearful mourning for Moses ended.*

⁹ *Joshua son of Nun was filled with the spirit of wisdom, because Moses had laid his hands upon him, so the Children of Israel obeyed him and did as HASHEM had commanded Moses.*

The quality ¹⁰ *Never again has there arisen in Israel a prophet like Moses, whom HASHEM*
of Moses' *had known face to face,* ¹¹ *as evidenced by all the signs and wonders that*
prophecy *HASHEM sent him to perform in the land of Egypt, against Pharaoh and all his courtiers and all his land,* ¹² *and by all the strong hand and awesome power that Moses performed before the eyes of all Israel.* *

It is customary for the congregation followed by the reader to proclaim:

"Chazak! Chazak! Venischazeik!
(Be strong! Be strong! And may we be strengthened!)"

34:10-12. Moses' prophetic prowess and signs did not have to be accepted on faith; his great acts were fully visible to the entire nation.

THE TEN COMMANDMENTS WITH THE *TROP* (CANTILLATION NOTES) USED BY THE READER FOR THE PUBLIC TORAH READING ON THE SABBATH (see page 440).

אָנֹכִי֙ יְהוָ֣ה אֱלֹהֶ֔יךָ אֲשֶׁ֧ר הוֹצֵאתִ֛יךָ מֵאֶ֥רֶץ מִצְרַ֖יִם מִבֵּ֣ית עֲבָדִ֑ים לֹֽא

יִהְיֶ֥ה לְךָ֛ אֱלֹהִ֥ים אֲחֵרִ֖ים עַל־פָּנָֽ֢י לֹֽא־תַעֲשֶׂ֨ה־לְךָ֥ פֶ֣סֶל ׀ כָּל־תְּמוּנָ֡ה

אֲשֶׁ֣ר בַּשָּׁמַ֣יִם ׀ מִמַּ֡עַל וַֽאֲשֶׁ֣ר בָּאָ֩רֶץ֩ מִתַּ֨חַת וַֽאֲשֶׁ֥ר בַּמַּ֣יִם ׀ מִתַּ֣חַת

לָאָ֑רֶץ לֹֽא־תִשְׁתַּחֲוֶ֥ה לָהֶ֖ם וְלֹ֣א תָֽעָבְדֵ֑ם כִּ֣י אָנֹכִ֞י יְהוָ֤ה אֱלֹהֶ֨יךָ֙ אֵ֣ל

קַנָּ֔א פֹּ֠קֵ֠ד עֲוֺ֨ן אָבֹ֧ת עַל־בָּנִ֛ים וְעַל־שִׁלֵּשִׁ֥ים וְעַל־רִבֵּעִ֖ים לְשֹׂנְאָֽ֢י

וְעֹ֥שֶׂה חֶ֖סֶד לַֽאֲלָפִ֑ים לְאֹהֲבַ֖י וּלְשֹׁמְרֵ֥י מִצְוֺתָֽי׃   לֹ֥א תִשָּׂ֛א

אֶת־שֵֽׁם־יְהוָ֥ה אֱלֹהֶ֖יךָ לַשָּׁ֑וְא כִּ֣י לֹ֤א יְנַקֶּה֙ יְהוָ֔ה אֵ֛ת אֲשֶׁר־יִשָּׂ֥א אֶת־

שְׁמ֖וֹ לַשָּֽׁוְא׃   שָׁמ֣וֹר אֶת־י֧וֹם הַשַּׁבָּ֛ת לְקַדְּשׁ֖וֹ כַּֽאֲשֶׁ֣ר צִוְּךָ֣ ׀

יְהוָ֣ה אֱלֹהֶ֑יךָ שֵׁ֣שֶׁת יָמִ֣ים תַּֽעֲבֹד֮ וְעָשִׂ֣יתָ כָּֽל־מְלַאכְתֶּךָ֒ וְי֙וֹם֙ הַשְּׁבִיעִ֔י

שַׁבָּ֖ת ׀ לַֽיהוָ֣ה אֱלֹהֶ֑יךָ לֹ֣א תַֽעֲשֶׂ֣ה כָל־מְלָאכָ֡ה אַתָּ֣ה וּבִנְךָֽ־וּבִתֶּ֣ךָ

וְעַבְדְּךָ֣ וַֽ֠אֲמָתֶ֨ךָ וְשֽׁוֹרְךָ֤ וַֽחֲמֹֽרְךָ֙ וְכָל־בְּהֶמְתֶּ֔ךָ וְגֵֽרְךָ֖ אֲשֶׁ֣ר בִּשְׁעָרֶ֑יךָ

לְמַ֗עַן יָנ֛וּחַ עַבְדְּךָ֥ וַֽאֲמָֽתְךָ֖ כָּמ֑וֹךָ וְזָֽכַרְתָּ֗ כִּ֣י עֶ֤בֶד הָיִ֨יתָ֙ ׀ בְּאֶ֣רֶץ מִצְרַ֔יִם

וַיֹּצִֽאֲךָ֩ יְהוָ֨ה אֱלֹהֶ֤יךָ מִשָּׁם֙ בְּיָ֣ד חֲזָקָ֔ה וּבִזְרֹ֖עַ נְטוּיָ֑ה עַל־כֵּ֗ן צִוְּךָ֙

יְהוָ֣ה אֱלֹהֶ֔יךָ לַֽעֲשׂ֖וֹת אֶת־י֥וֹם הַשַּׁבָּֽת׃   כַּבֵּ֥ד אֶת־אָבִ֖יךָ

וְאֶת־אִמֶּ֗ךָ כַּֽאֲשֶׁ֤ר צִוְּךָ֙ יְהוָ֣ה אֱלֹהֶ֔יךָ לְמַ֣עַן ׀ יַֽאֲרִיכֻ֣ן יָמֶ֗יךָ וּלְמַ֨עַן֙

יִ֣יטַב לָ֔ךְ עַ֚ל הָֽאֲדָמָ֔ה אֲשֶׁר־יְהוָ֥ה אֱלֹהֶ֖יךָ נֹתֵ֥ן לָֽךְ׃   לֹ֥א

תִרְצָֽח׃   וְלֹ֖א תִּנְאָֽף׃   וְלֹ֖א תִּגְנֹֽב׃   וְלֹֽא־תַעֲנֶ֥ה

בְרֵֽעֲךָ֖ עֵ֥ד שָֽׁוְא׃   וְלֹ֥א תַחְמֹ֖ד אֵ֣שֶׁת רֵעֶ֑ךָ   וְלֹ֨א

תִתְאַוֶּ֜ה בֵּ֣ית רֵעֶ֗ךָ שָׂדֵ֜הוּ וְעַבְדּ֤וֹ וַֽאֲמָתוֹ֙ שׁוֹר֣וֹ וַֽחֲמֹר֔וֹ וְכֹ֖ל אֲשֶׁ֥ר

לְרֵעֶֽךָ׃

נביאים
The Prophets

יהושע	❖	*Joshua / Yehoshua*
שופטים	❖	*Judges / Shoftim*
שמואל	❖	*Samuel / Shmuel*
מלכים	❖	*Kings / Melachim*
ישעיה	❖	*Isaiah / Yeshayah*
ירמיה	❖	*Jeremiah / Yirmiyah*
יחזקאל	❖	*Ezekiel / Yechezkel*
תרי עשר	❖	*The Twelve Prophets*
הושע	◦	◦ *Hosea / Hoshea*
יואל	◦	◦ *Joel / Yoel*
עמוס	◦	◦ *Amos / Amos*
עובדיה	◦	◦ *Obadiah / Ovadiah*
יונה	◦	◦ *Jonah / Yonah*
מיכה	◦	◦ *Micah / Michah*
נחום	◦	◦ *Nahum / Nachum*
חבקוק	◦	◦ *Habakkuk / Chavakkuk*
צפניה	◦	◦ *Zephaniah / Tzefaniah*
חגי	◦	◦ *Haggai / Chaggai*
זכריה	◦	◦ *Zechariah / Zechariah*
מלאכי	◦	◦ *Malachi / Malachi*

Joshua יהושע

A
s the Sages express it, the face of Moses was like the sun and the face of Joshua was like the moon. This is not a criticism of Joshua; neither he nor anyone else could approach Moses' level of prophecy. Rather, it is a compliment to Moses' primary disciple and Divinely designated successor that he was a faithful reflection of his master's teachings.

It was Joshua's mission to plant the seeds of Torah in the Land of Israel, and to mold the entirely new existence in which the people found themselves. In the Wilderness, they had been nestled in a cocoon of miracles. Their food, water, and protection from attack was provided by God. Now, upon entering the land, they would have to plow and plant, dig wells and irrigate fields, in addition to fighting wars of conquest and defense. If they maintained their allegiance to God and His Torah, He would give them victory and prosperity; if not, their future would be in peril.

Joshua had to inculcate the people with this fundamental truth. He had to gain their confidence and loyalty. He had to lead them in battle and imbue them with the conviction that Jewish warriors may not neglect their religious and moral responsibilities. He had to fulfill the commandment that the Canaanites who refused to make peace could not be allowed to survive, difficult though this was for a nation that was weaned on mercy. He had to divide the land among the tribes and establish the eternal borders of the land and its individual provinces. He had to assure that there would be national unity amid tribal diversity, especially in the case of the two-and-a-half tribes that had chosen to remain on the east bank of the Jordan. He succeeded to an astounding degree.

Interspersed in the successes were hints of a failure of national will, which mushroomed into the tragedies that marred the succeeding centuries. Despite Joshua's urgings that the tribes strengthen their resolve and complete the conquest of the land, most of them allowed pockets of Canaanites to remain in the country. They had been warned that this would lead to a seepage of idolatry into Israel, but they held back from further warfare; bloodshed was not in their spritual genes. The results of their weakness emerged later, primarily in the Book of Judges, and that distressing history would prove how necessary it was for them to remove every trace of Canaanite influence.

The Book of Joshua closes with the moving valedictory of Joshua, the "moon," who proved to his last breath that he radiated the wisdom and holiness of Moses.

א

HAFTARAS
VEZOS HA-
BERACHAH
Ashkenazim:
1:1-18
Sephardim:
1:1-9

א וַיְהִי אַחֲרֵי מוֹת מֹשֶׁה עֶבֶד יְהוָה וַיֹּאמֶר יְהוָה אֶל־יְהוֹשֻׁעַ בִּן־נ֔וּן

ב מְשָׁרֵ֥ת מֹשֶׁ֖ה לֵאמֹֽר: מֹשֶׁ֥ה עַבְדִּ֖י מֵ֑ת וְעַתָּה֩ ק֨וּם עֲבֹ֜ר אֶת־הַיַּרְדֵּ֣ן הַזֶּ֗ה

ג אַתָּה֙ וְכָל־הָעָ֣ם הַזֶּ֔ה אֶל־הָאָ֕רֶץ אֲשֶׁ֧ר אָנֹכִ֛י נֹתֵ֥ן לָהֶ֖ם לִבְנֵ֥י יִשְׂרָאֵֽל: כָּל־

מָק֗וֹם אֲשֶׁ֨ר תִּדְרֹ֧ךְ כַּף־רַגְלְכֶ֛ם בּ֖וֹ לָכֶ֣ם נְתַתִּ֑יו כַּאֲשֶׁ֥ר דִּבַּ֖רְתִּי אֶל־מֹשֶֽׁה:

ד מֵהַמִּדְבָּ֨ר וְהַלְּבָנ֜וֹן הַזֶּ֗ה וְעַד־הַנָּהָ֤ר הַגָּדוֹל֙ נְהַר־פְּרָ֔ת כֹּ֖ל אֶ֣רֶץ הַֽחִתִּ֑ים

ה וְעַד־הַיָּ֥ם הַגָּד֖וֹל מְב֣וֹא הַשָּׁ֑מֶשׁ יִהְיֶ֖ה גְּבֽוּלְכֶֽם: לֹֽא־יִתְיַצֵּ֥ב אִישׁ֙ לְפָנֶ֔יךָ

כֹּ֖ל יְמֵ֣י חַיֶּ֑יךָ כַּאֲשֶׁ֨ר הָיִ֤יתִי עִם־מֹשֶׁה֙ אֶֽהְיֶ֣ה עִמָּ֔ךְ לֹ֥א אַרְפְּךָ֖ וְלֹ֥א

ו אֶֽעֶזְבֶֽךָּ: חֲזַ֖ק וֶֽאֱמָ֑ץ כִּ֣י אַתָּ֗ה תַּנְחִיל֙ אֶת־הָעָ֣ם הַזֶּ֔ה אֶת־הָאָ֕רֶץ אֲשֶׁר־

ז נִשְׁבַּ֥עְתִּי לַאֲבוֹתָ֖ם לָתֵ֣ת לָהֶֽם: רַ֣ק חֲזַ֣ק וֶֽאֱמַ֣ץ מְאֹ֗ד לִשְׁמֹ֤ר לַעֲשׂוֹת֙ כְּכָל־

הַתּוֹרָ֗ה אֲשֶׁ֤ר צִוְּךָ֙ מֹשֶׁ֣ה עַבְדִּ֔י אַל־תָּס֥וּר מִמֶּ֖נּוּ יָמִ֣ין וּשְׂמֹ֑אול לְמַ֣עַן

ח תַּשְׂכִּ֔יל בְּכֹ֖ל אֲשֶׁ֥ר תֵּלֵֽךְ: לֹֽא־יָמ֡וּשׁ סֵפֶר֩ הַתּוֹרָ֨ה הַזֶּ֜ה מִפִּ֗יךָ וְהָגִ֤יתָ בּוֹ֙

יוֹמָ֣ם וָלַ֔יְלָה לְמַ֙עַן֙ תִּשְׁמֹ֣ר לַעֲשׂ֔וֹת כְּכָל־הַכָּת֣וּב בּ֑וֹ כִּי־אָ֛ז תַּצְלִ֥יחַ אֶת־

ט דְּרָכֶ֖ךָ וְאָ֥ז תַּשְׂכִּֽיל: הֲל֤וֹא צִוִּיתִ֙יךָ֙ חֲזַ֣ק וֶֽאֱמָ֔ץ אַֽל־תַּעֲרֹ֖ץ וְאַל־תֵּחָ֑ת

כִּ֤י עִמְּךָ֙ יְהוָ֣ה אֱלֹהֶ֔יךָ בְּכֹ֖ל אֲשֶׁ֥ר תֵּלֵֽךְ: ▸   וַיְצַ֤ו

י יְהוֹשֻׁ֙עַ֙ אֶת־שֹׁטְרֵ֣י הָעָ֔ם לֵאמֹֽר: עִבְר֣וּ ׀ בְּקֶ֣רֶב הַֽמַּחֲנֶ֗ה וְצַוּ֤וּ אֶת־

יא הָעָם֙ לֵאמֹ֔ר הָכִ֥ינוּ לָכֶ֖ם צֵידָ֑ה כִּ֞י בְּע֣וֹד ׀ שְׁלֹ֣שֶׁת יָמִ֗ים אַתֶּם֙ עֹבְרִים֙ אֶת־

הַיַּרְדֵּ֣ן הַזֶּ֔ה לָבוֹא֙ לָרֶ֣שֶׁת אֶת־הָאָ֔רֶץ אֲשֶׁר֙ יְהוָ֣ה אֱלֹֽהֵיכֶ֔ם נֹתֵ֥ן לָכֶ֖ם

יב לְרִשְׁתָּֽהּ: ▸   וְלָרֽאוּבֵנִ֣י וְלַגָּדִ֗י וְלַחֲצִי֙ שֵׁ֣בֶט הַֽמְנַשֶּׁ֔ה אָמַ֥ר

יג יְהוֹשֻׁ֖עַ לֵאמֹֽר: זָכוֹר֙ אֶת־הַדָּבָ֔ר אֲשֶׁ֨ר צִוָּ֥ה אֶתְכֶ֛ם מֹשֶׁ֥ה עֶבֶד־יְהוָ֖ה

יד לֵאמֹ֑ר יְהוָ֤ה אֱלֹֽהֵיכֶם֙ מֵנִ֣יחַ לָכֶ֔ם וְנָתַ֥ן לָכֶ֖ם אֶת־הָאָ֣רֶץ הַזֹּֽאת: נְשֵׁיכֶ֣ם

טַפְּכֶם֮ וּמִקְנֵיכֶם֒ יֵשְׁב֗וּ בָּאָ֙רֶץ֙ אֲשֶׁ֨ר נָתַ֤ן לָכֶם֙ מֹשֶׁ֔ה בְּעֵ֖בֶר הַיַּרְדֵּ֑ן וְאַתֶּם֩

טו תַּעַבְר֨וּ חֲמֻשִׁ֜ים לִפְנֵ֣י אֲחֵיכֶ֗ם כֹּ֚ל גִּבּוֹרֵ֣י הַחַ֔יִל וַעֲזַרְתֶּ֖ם אוֹתָֽם: עַ֠ד

אֲשֶׁר־יָנִ֨יחַ יְהוָ֥ה ׀ לַֽאֲחֵיכֶם֮ כָּכֶם֒ וְיָרְשׁ֣וּ גַם־הֵ֔מָּה אֶת־הָאָ֕רֶץ אֲשֶׁר־יְהוָ֥ה

אֱלֹֽהֵיכֶ֖ם נֹתֵ֣ן לָהֶ֑ם וְשַׁבְתֶּ֞ם לְאֶ֤רֶץ יְרֻשַּׁתְכֶם֙ וִֽירִשְׁתֶּ֣ם אוֹתָ֔הּ אֲשֶׁ֣ר ׀ נָתַ֣ן

טז לָכֶ֗ם מֹשֶׁה֙ עֶ֣בֶד יְהוָ֔ה בְּעֵ֥בֶר הַיַּרְדֵּ֖ן מִזְרַ֣ח הַשָּֽׁמֶשׁ: וַֽיַּעֲנ֔וּ אֶת־יְהוֹשֻׁ֖עַ

יז לֵאמֹ֑ר כֹּ֤ל אֲשֶׁר־צִוִּיתָ֙נוּ֙ נַֽעֲשֶׂ֔ה וְאֶֽל־כָּל־אֲשֶׁ֥ר תִּשְׁלָחֵ֖נוּ נֵלֵֽךְ: כְּכֹ֤ל

אֲשֶׁר־שָׁמַ֙עְנוּ֙ אֶל־מֹשֶׁ֔ה כֵּ֖ן נִשְׁמַ֣ע אֵלֶ֑יךָ רַ֠ק יִֽהְיֶ֞ה יְהוָ֤ה אֱלֹהֶ֙יךָ֙ עִמָּ֔ךְ

יח כַּאֲשֶׁ֥ר הָיָ֖ה עִם־מֹשֶֽׁה: כָּל־אִ֞ישׁ אֲשֶׁר־יַמְרֶ֣ה אֶת־פִּ֗יךָ וְלֹֽא־יִשְׁמַ֧ע אֶת־

דְּבָרֶ֛יךָ לְכֹ֥ל אֲשֶׁר־תְּצַוֶּ֖נּוּ יוּמָ֑ת רַ֖ק חֲזַ֥ק וֶאֱמָֽץ: ▸

א וַיִּשְׁלַ֣ח יְהוֹשֻֽׁעַ־בִּן־נ֠וּן מִֽן־הַשִּׁטִּ֞ים שְׁנַֽיִם־אֲנָשִׁ֤ים מְרַגְּלִים֙ חֶ֣רֶשׁ לֵאמֹ֔ר

לְכ֛וּ רְא֥וּ אֶת־הָאָ֖רֶץ וְאֶת־יְרִיח֑וֹ וַיֵּ֨לְכ֜וּ וַ֠יָּבֹ֜אוּ בֵּֽית־אִשָּׁ֥ה זוֹנָ֛ה וּשְׁמָ֥הּ רָחָ֖ב

ב וַיִּשְׁכְּבוּ־שָֽׁמָּה: וַיֵּ֣אָמַ֔ר לְמֶ֥לֶךְ יְרִיח֖וֹ לֵאמֹ֑ר הִנֵּ֣ה אֲ֠נָשִׁ֜ים בָּ֧אוּ הֵ֣נָּה

1:6. This exhortation, repeated in vv. 7 and 9, refers to Joshua's three major responsibilities: division of the land, Torah observance, and war. He was to exert himself completely in these essential areas of his mission (*Rashi*).

1:13. *Deuteronomy* 3:18.

1:18. The people echoed God's exhortation, urging Joshua to guide them only in the way of the Torah. Alternatively, they emphasized that a nation needs firm

1

ENTERING
THE LAND:
PREPARA-
TION AND
ENTRY
1:1-5:15

God
exhorts
Joshua

Constant
Torah study

¹ It happened after the death of Moses, servant of HASHEM, that HASHEM said to Joshua son of Nun, Moses' attendant, saying, ² "Moses My servant has died. Now, arise, cross this Jordan, you and this entire people, to the land that I give to them, to the Children of Israel. ³ Every place upon which the sole of your foot will tread I have given to you, as I spoke to Moses. ⁴ From the desert and this Lebanon until the great river, the Euphrates River, all the land of the Hittites until the Great Sea toward the setting of the sun will be your boundary. ⁵ No man will stand up to you all the days of your life; as I was with Moses so will I be with you; I will not release you nor will I forsake you. ⁶ Be strong and courageous* for it is you who will cause this people to inherit the Land that I have sworn to their fathers to give them. ⁷ Only be very strong and courageous, to observe, to do, according to the entire Torah that Moses My servant commanded you; do not deviate from it to the right or to the left, in order that you may succeed wherever you will go. ⁸ This Book of the Torah shall not depart from your mouth; rather you should contemplate it day and night in order that you observe to do according to all that is written in it; for then you will make your way successful, and then you will act wisely. ⁹ Behold, I have commanded you, 'Be strong and courageous,' do not fear and do not lose resolve, for HASHEM, your God, is with you wherever you will go."

Joshua
prepares the
nation . . .

¹⁰ Joshua then ordered the marshals of the people, saying, ¹¹ "Circulate in the midst of the camp and command the people, saying, 'Prepare provisions for yourselves, because in another three days you will be crossing this Jordan to come to take possession of the land that HASHEM, your God, is giving you, to inherit it.' "

. . . and
reinforces
the promise
of Reuben,
Gad, and
Manasseh

¹² To the Reubenite, to the Gadite, and to half the tribe of Manasseh, Joshua spoke, saying: ¹³ "Remember the matter that Moses, servant of HASHEM, commanded you, saying, 'HASHEM, your God, gives you rest and He will give you this land.'* ¹⁴ Your wives, your children, and your cattle will settle in the land that Moses had given you across the Jordan; then you — all the mighty warriors — will cross over, armed, before your brothers and help them, ¹⁵ until HASHEM gives your brothers rest, like you, and they too take possession of the land that HASHEM, your God, gives them. Then you will return to the land of your inheritance and possess it — that which Moses, servant of HASHEM, gave you across the Jordan, toward the rising of the sun."

They affirm
their loyalty
to him

¹⁶ They answered Joshua, saying, "All that you have commanded us we will do, and wherever you send us we will go. ¹⁷ As fully as we heeded Moses, so shall we heed you, provided that HASHEM, your God, is with you as He was with Moses! ¹⁸ Any man who will rebel against your utterance or will not listen to your words, in whatever you may command him, will be put to death. Only be strong and courageous!"*

2

The recon-
naissance
mission

¹ Joshua son of Nun dispatched two men — spies — from Shittim, secret-ly saying, "Go, observe the land and Jericho."* So they went and arrived at the house of a woman innkeeper* whose name was Rahab, and slept there. ² It was told to the king of Jericho, saying, "Behold, men have come here

---

leadership, and they wanted Joshua to provide it (*Ralbag*).
2:1. In order to avoid the sort of catastrophe that resulted
from Moses' spy mission (*Numbers* 13-14), Joshua chose
his spies carefully; according to the Talmud, they were

Caleb and Phinehas. He knew that they would return with
an encouraging report.
    The word זוֹנָה means both "harlot" and "grocer." Rahab
ran a brothel, disguised as an inn (*Abarbanel*).

ג הַלַּ֗יְלָה מִבְּנֵ֤י יִשְׂרָאֵל֙ לַחְפֹּ֣ר אֶת־הָאָ֔רֶץ: וַיִּשְׁלַ֞ח מֶ֤לֶךְ יְרִיחוֹ֙ אֶל־רָחָ֣ב
לֵאמֹ֔ר הוֹצִ֙יאִי֙ הָאֲנָשִׁ֣ים הַבָּאִ֣ים אֵלַ֔יִךְ אֲשֶׁר־בָּ֖אוּ לְבֵיתֵ֑ךְ כִּ֛י לַחְפֹּ֥ר אֶת־

ד כָּל־הָאָ֖רֶץ בָּֽאוּ: וַתִּקַּ֧ח הָאִשָּׁ֛ה אֶת־שְׁנֵ֥י הָאֲנָשִׁ֖ים וַֽתִּצְפְּנ֑וֹ וַתֹּ֣אמֶר ׀ כֵּ֣ן בָּ֤אוּ

ה אֵלַי֙ הָֽאֲנָשִׁ֔ים וְלֹ֥א יָדַ֖עְתִּי מֵאַ֣יִן הֵֽמָּה: וַיְהִ֣י הַשַּׁ֗עַר לִסְגּוֹר֙ בַּחֹ֔שֶׁךְ
וְהָֽאֲנָשִׁ֖ים יָצָ֑אוּ לֹ֣א יָדַ֔עְתִּי אָ֥נָה הָלְכ֖וּ הָֽאֲנָשִׁ֑ים רִדְפ֥וּ מַהֵ֛ר אַֽחֲרֵיהֶ֖ם כִּ֥י

ו תַשִּׂיגֽוּם: וְהִ֖יא הֶֽעֱלָ֣תַם הַגָּ֑גָה וַֽתִּטְמְנֵם֙ בְּפִשְׁתֵּ֣י הָעֵ֔ץ הָֽעֲרֻכ֥וֹת לָ֖הּ עַל־

ז הַגָּֽג: וְהָֽאֲנָשִׁ֗ים רָֽדְפ֤וּ אַֽחֲרֵיהֶם֙ דֶּ֣רֶךְ הַיַּרְדֵּ֔ן עַ֖ל הַֽמַּעְבְּר֑וֹת וְהַשַּׁ֣עַר סָגָ֔רוּ

ח אַֽחֲרֵ֕י כַּֽאֲשֶׁ֛ר יָצְא֥וּ הָרֹֽדְפִ֖ים אַֽחֲרֵיהֶֽם: וְהֵ֖מָּה טֶ֣רֶם יִשְׁכָּב֑וּן וְהִ֛יא עָֽלְתָ֥ה

ט עֲלֵיהֶ֖ם עַל־הַגָּֽג: וַתֹּ֙אמֶר֙ אֶל־הָ֣אֲנָשִׁ֔ים יָדַ֕עְתִּי כִּֽי־נָתַ֧ן יְהֹוָ֛ה לָכֶ֖ם אֶת־

י הָאָ֑רֶץ וְכִֽי־נָֽפְלָ֤ה אֵֽימַתְכֶם֙ עָלֵ֔ינוּ וְכִ֥י נָמֹ֛גוּ כָּל־יֹֽשְׁבֵ֥י הָאָ֖רֶץ מִפְּנֵיכֶֽם: כִּ֣י
שָׁמַ֗עְנוּ אֵ֠ת אֲשֶׁר־הוֹבִ֨ישׁ יְהֹוָ֜ה אֶת־מֵ֤י יַם־סוּף֙ מִפְּנֵיכֶ֔ם בְּצֵֽאתְכֶ֖ם
מִמִּצְרָ֑יִם וַֽאֲשֶׁ֣ר עֲשִׂיתֶ֡ם לִשְׁנֵי֩ מַלְכֵ֨י הָֽאֱמֹרִ֜י אֲשֶׁ֨ר בְּעֵ֤בֶר הַיַּרְדֵּן֙ לְסִיחֹ֣ן

יא וּלְע֔וֹג אֲשֶׁ֥ר הֶֽחֱרַמְתֶּ֖ם אוֹתָֽם: וַנִּשְׁמַע֙ וַיִּמַּ֣ס לְבָבֵ֔נוּ וְלֹא־קָ֨מָה ע֥וֹד ר֛וּחַ
בְּאִ֖ישׁ מִפְּנֵיכֶ֑ם כִּ֚י יְהֹוָ֣ה אֱלֹֽהֵיכֶ֔ם ה֤וּא אֱלֹהִים֙ בַּשָּׁמַ֣יִם מִמַּ֔עַל וְעַל־

יב הָאָ֖רֶץ מִתָּֽחַת: וְעַתָּ֗ה הִשָּֽׁבְעוּ־נָ֥א לִי֙ בַּֽיהֹוָ֔ה כִּֽי־עָשִׂ֥יתִי עִמָּכֶ֖ם חָ֑סֶד

יג וַֽעֲשִׂיתֶ֨ם גַּם־אַתֶּ֜ם עִם־בֵּ֤ית אָבִי֙ חֶ֔סֶד וּנְתַתֶּ֥ם לִ֖י א֣וֹת אֱמֶֽת: וְהַֽחֲיִתֶ֞ם
אֶת־אָבִ֣י וְאֶת־אִמִּ֗י וְאֶת־אַחַי֙ וְאֶת־[אַחְיוֹתַ֔י ק׳]°אחותי וְאֵ֖ת כָּל־

יד אֲשֶׁ֣ר לָהֶ֑ם וְהִצַּלְתֶּ֥ם אֶת־נַפְשֹׁתֵ֖ינוּ מִמָּֽוֶת: וַיֹּ֧אמְרוּ לָ֣הּ הָֽאֲנָשִׁ֗ים נַפְשֵׁ֤נוּ
תַחְתֵּיכֶם֙ לָמ֔וּת אִ֚ם לֹ֣א תַגִּ֔ידוּ אֶת־דְּבָרֵ֖נוּ זֶ֑ה וְהָיָ֗ה בְּתֵת־יְהֹוָ֥ה לָ֙נוּ֙ אֶת־

טו הָאָ֔רֶץ וְעָשִׂ֥ינוּ עִמָּ֖ךְ חֶ֥סֶד וֶֽאֱמֶֽת: וַתּֽוֹרִדֵ֥ם בַּחֶ֖בֶל בְּעַ֣ד הַֽחַלּ֑וֹן כִּ֤י בֵיתָהּ֙

טז בְּקִ֣יר הַֽחוֹמָ֔ה וּבַֽחוֹמָ֖ה הִ֥יא יוֹשָֽׁבֶת: וַתֹּ֤אמֶר לָהֶם֙ הָהָ֣רָה לֵּ֔כוּ פֶּֽן־יִפְגְּע֥וּ
בָכֶ֖ם הָרֹֽדְפִ֑ים וְנַחְבֵּתֶ֨ם שָׁ֜מָּה שְׁלֹ֣שֶׁת יָמִ֗ים עַ֚ד שׁ֣וֹב הָרֹֽדְפִ֔ים וְאַחַ֖ר תֵּֽלְכ֥וּ

יז לְדַרְכְּכֶֽם: וַיֹּֽאמְר֥וּ אֵלֶ֖יהָ הָֽאֲנָשִׁ֑ים נְקִיִּ֣ם אֲנַ֔חְנוּ מִשְּׁבֻֽעָתֵ֥ךְ הַזֶּ֖ה אֲשֶׁ֥ר

יח הִשְׁבַּעְתָּֽנוּ: הִנֵּ֛ה אֲנַ֥חְנוּ בָאִ֖ים בָּאָ֑רֶץ אֶת־תִּקְוַ֡ת חוּט֩ הַשָּׁנִ֨י הַזֶּ֜ה תִּקְשְׁרִ֗י
בַּֽחַלּוֹן֙ אֲשֶׁ֣ר הֽוֹרַדְתֵּ֣נוּ ב֔וֹ וְאֶת־אָבִ֨יךְ וְאֶת־אִמֵּ֜ךְ וְאֶת־אַחַ֗יִךְ וְאֵת֙ כָּל־

יט בֵּ֣ית אָבִ֔יךְ תַּֽאַסְפִ֥י אֵלַ֖יִךְ הַבָּֽיְתָה: וְהָיָ֡ה כֹּ֣ל אֲשֶׁר־יֵצֵא֩ מִדַּלְתֵ֨י בֵיתֵ֧ךְ ׀
הַח֛וּצָה דָּמ֥וֹ בְרֹאשׁ֖וֹ וַֽאֲנַ֣חְנוּ נְקִיִּ֑ם וְ֠כֹל אֲשֶׁ֨ר יִֽהְיֶ֤ה אִתָּךְ֙ בַּבַּ֔יִת דָּמ֣וֹ

כ בְרֹאשֵׁ֔נוּ אִם־יָ֖ד תִּֽהְיֶה־בּֽוֹ: וְאִם־תַּגִּ֖ידִי אֶת־דְּבָרֵ֣נוּ זֶ֑ה וְהָיִ֣ינוּ נְקִיִּ֔ם

כא מִשְּׁבֻֽעָתֵ֖ךְ אֲשֶׁ֣ר הִשְׁבַּעְתָּֽנוּ: וַתֹּ֙אמֶר֙ כְּדִבְרֵיכֶ֣ם כֶּן־ה֔וּא וַתְּשַׁלְּחֵ֖ם וַיֵּלֵ֑כוּ

כב וַתִּקְשֹׁ֛ר אֶת־תִּקְוַ֥ת הַשָּׁנִ֖י בַּֽחַלּֽוֹן: וַיֵּֽלְכוּ֙ וַיָּבֹ֣אוּ הָהָ֔רָה וַיֵּ֤שְׁבוּ שָׁם֙ שְׁלֹ֣שֶׁת
יָמִ֔ים עַד־שָׁ֖בוּ הָרֹֽדְפִ֑ים וַיְבַקְשׁ֧וּ הָרֹֽדְפִ֛ים בְּכָל־הַדֶּ֖רֶךְ וְלֹ֥א מָצָֽאוּ: וַיָּשֻׁ֜בוּ

כג שְׁנֵ֤י הָֽאֲנָשִׁים֙ וַיֵּֽרְד֣וּ מֵֽהָהָ֔ר וַיַּֽעַבְרוּ֙ וַיָּבֹ֔אוּ אֶל־יְהוֹשֻׁ֖עַ בִּן־נ֑וּן וַיְסַפְּרוּ־ל֔וֹ

2:7. The king's men locked the gates in case the spies were still in hiding inside the city (*Metzudos*).

2:9. Rahab's behavior was not an act of treason. She acted out of the sincere conviction that the Jewish conquest was Divinely ordained.

2:14. The men promised that they would protect Rahab's family with their own lives, if need be, but only if she would agree to the conditions they were about to set forth.

this night from the Children of Israel to spy out the land."

^{The king
discovers
the spies . . .} ³ *The king of Jericho sent to Rahab, saying, "Bring out the men who have come to you, who have come to your house, for they have come to spy out the entire land."* ⁴ *The woman had taken the two men and had hidden them. She* ^{. . . but
Rahab
protects
them} *said, "It is true; the men did come to me, but I do not know from where they are.* ⁵ *When the city gate was about to close at dark, the men went out; I do not know where the men went. Pursue them quickly, for you can overtake them!"* ⁶ *But she had brought them up to the roof and hidden them in the stalks of flax that had been arranged for her on the roof.*

⁷ *So the men pursued them in the direction of the Jordan to the crossings; and they closed the gate soon after the pursuers had gone out after them.* *

^{Rahab's
plea} ⁸ *They had not yet gone to sleep when she came up to them on the roof.* ⁹ *She said to the men, "I know that HASHEM has given you the land,* * *and that fear of you has fallen upon us, and all the inhabitants of the land have dissolved because of you;* ¹⁰ *for we have heard how HASHEM dried up the waters of the Sea of Reeds for you when you went forth from Egypt and what you did to the two kings of the Amorites who were across the Jordan — to Sihon and to Og — whom you utterly destroyed.* ¹¹ *We heard and our hearts melted — no spirit remained in any man because of you — for HASHEM, your God, He is God in the heavens above and on the earth below.* ¹² *Now, I beseech you, swear to me by HASHEM, since I have done kindness with you, that you too will do kindness with my father's household and give me a trustworthy countersign,* ¹³ *that you will keep alive my father, my mother, my brothers, and my sisters, and all that is theirs, and that you will save our souls from death."*

^{The spies'
conditional
promise} ¹⁴ *Then the men said to her, "Our souls will die instead of yours,* * *if you do not relate this discussion of ours. And it will be when HASHEM gives us the land that we will do kindness and truth with you."*

¹⁵ *She lowered them by the rope through the window, for her house was in a wall of the fortification, and she lived in the fortification.* ¹⁶ *She said to them, "Go to the mountain, lest the pursuers encounter you. Conceal yourselves there for three days until the pursuers turn back; then you may continue on your way."*

¹⁷ *The men said to her, "We are absolved from this oath of yours which you made us swear [unless]:* ¹⁸ *Behold, when we come into the land, you shall tie this cord of scarlet thread in the window through which you lowered us; and your father and your mother and your brothers and your father's entire household you shall bring in to you, into the house.* ¹⁹ *Then it shall be that anyone who leaves the doors of your house for the outside, his blood will be on his head, and we will be absolved. But regarding anyone who will be with you inside the house, his blood will be on our head, if a hand will be [laid] upon him.* ²⁰ *But if you relate this discussion of ours, we will be absolved of your oath that you have made us swear."* ²¹ *She said, "As you say, so it is." She sent them forth, and they went; and she tied the cord of scarlet thread in the window.*

²² *They went and arrived at the mountain and stayed there three days until the pursuers turned back; the pursuers searched along the entire way but they did not find [them].*

^{The spies
return
to Joshua} ²³ *The two men then returned and descended from the mountain; they crossed [the Jordan] and came to Joshua son of Nun and told him*

כד אֵת כָּל־הַמֹּצְאוֹת אוֹתָם: וַיֹּאמְרוּ אֶל־יְהוֹשֻׁעַ כִּי־נָתַן יהוה בְּיָדֵנוּ אֶת־

ג א כָּל־הָאָרֶץ וְגַם־נָמֹגוּ כָּל־יֹשְׁבֵי הָאָרֶץ מִפָּנֵינוּ: ◀ וַיַּשְׁכֵּם יְהוֹשֻׁעַ בַּבֹּקֶר וַיִּסְעוּ מֵהַשִּׁטִּים וַיָּבֹאוּ עַד־הַיַּרְדֵּן הוּא וְכָל־בְּנֵי יִשְׂרָאֵל ב וַיָּלִנוּ שָׁם טֶרֶם יַעֲבֹרוּ: וַיְהִי מִקְצֵה שְׁלֹשֶׁת יָמִים וַיַּעַבְרוּ הַשֹּׁטְרִים בְּקֶרֶב ג הַמַּחֲנֶה: וַיְצַוּוּ אֶת־הָעָם לֵאמֹר כִּרְאֽוֹתְכֶם אֵת אֲרוֹן בְּרִית־יהוה אֱלֹהֵיכֶם וְהַכֹּהֲנִים הַלְוִיִּם נֹשְׂאִים אֹתוֹ וְאַתֶּם תִּסְעוּ מִמְּקוֹמְכֶם וַהֲלַכְתֶּם ד אַחֲרָיו: אַךְ ׀ רָחוֹק יִהְיֶה בֵּינֵיכֶם °וּבֵינוֹ [°וּבֵינָיו ק] כְּאַלְפַּיִם אַמָּה בַּמִּדָּה אַל־תִּקְרְבוּ אֵלָיו לְמַעַן אֲשֶׁר־תֵּדְעוּ אֶת־הַדֶּרֶךְ אֲשֶׁר תֵּלְכוּ־בָהּ ה כִּי לֹא עֲבַרְתֶּם בַּדֶּרֶךְ מִתְּמוֹל שִׁלְשׁוֹם: ◀ וַיֹּאמֶר יְהוֹשֻׁעַ אֶל־הָעָם הִתְקַדָּשׁוּ כִּי מָחָר יַעֲשֶׂה יהוה בְּקִרְבְּכֶם נִפְלָאוֹת: ו וַיֹּאמֶר יְהוֹשֻׁעַ אֶל־הַכֹּהֲנִים לֵאמֹר שְׂאוּ אֶת־אֲרוֹן הַבְּרִית וְעִבְרוּ לִפְנֵי הָעָם וַיִּשְׂאוּ אֶת־אֲרוֹן הַבְּרִית וַיֵּלְכוּ לִפְנֵי הָעָם: ז וַיֹּאמֶר יהוה אֶל־יְהוֹשֻׁעַ הַיּוֹם הַזֶּה אָחֵל גַּדֶּלְךָ בְּעֵינֵי כָּל־יִשְׂרָאֵל אֲשֶׁר ח יֵדְעוּן כִּי כַּאֲשֶׁר הָיִיתִי עִם־מֹשֶׁה אֶהְיֶה עִמָּךְ: ◀ וְאַתָּה תְּצַוֶּה אֶת־הַכֹּהֲנִים נֹשְׂאֵי אֲרוֹן־הַבְּרִית לֵאמֹר כְּבֹאֲכֶם עַד־קְצֵה מֵי הַיַּרְדֵּן ט בַּיַּרְדֵּן תַּעֲמֹדוּ: וַיֹּאמֶר יְהוֹשֻׁעַ אֶל־בְּנֵי יִשְׂרָאֵל גֹּשׁוּ הֵנָּה וְשִׁמְעוּ אֶת־ י דִּבְרֵי יהוה אֱלֹהֵיכֶם: וַיֹּאמֶר יְהוֹשֻׁעַ בְּזֹאת תֵּדְעוּן כִּי אֵל חַי בְּקִרְבְּכֶם וְהוֹרֵשׁ יוֹרִישׁ מִפְּנֵיכֶם אֶת־הַכְּנַעֲנִי וְאֶת־הַחִתִּי וְאֶת־הַחִוִּי וְאֶת־הַפְּרִזִּי יא וְאֶת־הַגִּרְגָּשִׁי וְהָאֱמֹרִי וְהַיְבוּסִי: הִנֵּה אֲרוֹן הַבְּרִית אֲדוֹן כָּל־הָאָרֶץ עֹבֵר יב לִפְנֵיכֶם בַּיַּרְדֵּן: וְעַתָּה קְחוּ לָכֶם שְׁנֵי עָשָׂר אִישׁ מִשִּׁבְטֵי יִשְׂרָאֵל אִישׁ־ יג אֶחָד אִישׁ־אֶחָד לַשָּׁבֶט: וְהָיָה כְּנוֹחַ כַּפּוֹת רַגְלֵי הַכֹּהֲנִים נֹשְׂאֵי אֲרוֹן יהוה אֲדוֹן כָּל־הָאָרֶץ בְּמֵי הַיַּרְדֵּן מֵי הַיַּרְדֵּן יִכָּרֵתוּן הַמַּיִם הַיֹּרְדִים יד מִלְמָעְלָה וְיַעַמְדוּ נֵד אֶחָד: וַיְהִי בִּנְסֹעַ הָעָם מֵאָהֳלֵיהֶם לַעֲבֹר אֶת־ טו הַיַּרְדֵּן וְהַכֹּהֲנִים נֹשְׂאֵי הָאָרוֹן הַבְּרִית לִפְנֵי הָעָם: וּכְבוֹא נֹשְׂאֵי הָאָרוֹן עַד־הַיַּרְדֵּן וְרַגְלֵי הַכֹּהֲנִים נֹשְׂאֵי הָאָרוֹן נִטְבְּלוּ בִּקְצֵה הַמָּיִם וְהַיַּרְדֵּן טז מָלֵא עַל־כָּל־גְּדוֹתָיו כֹּל יְמֵי קָצִיר: וַיַּעַמְדוּ הַמַּיִם הַיֹּרְדִים מִלְמַעְלָה קָמוּ נֵד־אֶחָד הַרְחֵק מְאֹד °בָּאָדָם [°מֵאָדָם ק] הָעִיר אֲשֶׁר מִצַּד צָרְתָן וְהַיֹּרְדִים עַל יָם הָעֲרָבָה יָם־הַמֶּלַח תַּמּוּ נִכְרָתוּ וְהָעָם עָבְרוּ נֶגֶד יְרִיחוֹ: יז וַיַּעַמְדוּ הַכֹּהֲנִים נֹשְׂאֵי הָאָרוֹן בְּרִית־יהוה בֶּחָרָבָה בְּתוֹךְ הַיַּרְדֵּן הָכֵן וְכָל־יִשְׂרָאֵל עֹבְרִים בֶּחָרָבָה עַד אֲשֶׁר־תַּמּוּ כָּל־הַגּוֹי לַעֲבֹר אֶת־הַיַּרְדֵּן:

HAFTARAH
FIRST DAY
PESACH
3:5-7;
5:2-6:1;
6:27

*Haftarah
continues
on p. 526*

3:3. The Ark, containing the Tablets of the Ten Commandments, symbolized the covenant between God and Israel: God would guide and protect His people, and Israel would be loyal to Him and His Torah. On the threshold of the land, God admonished Joshua regarding this covenant (1:8). In the Wilderness, the Ark had led the nation's journeys; now it would guide them in their occupation of the land.

3:4. This is the reason that you are to follow the Ark (*Rashi*).

3:12. The mission of these tribal representatives is given below, 4:5.

3:16. Although the flow of the water was interrupted, the *all that had happened to them.* ²⁴ *They said to Joshua, "HASHEM has given the land into our hands; and all the inhabitants of the land have even melted because of us."*

3

The Ark leads the way

¹ Joshua arose early in the morning, and they journeyed from Shittim and arrived at the Jordan, he and all the Children of Israel, and they lodged there before they crossed.

Joshua's directives

² *It was at the end of three days that the marshals circulated in the midst of the camp.* ³ *They commanded the people, saying, "When you see the Ark of the Covenant of HASHEM,* * *your God, and the Kohanim, the Levites, carrying it, then you shall move from your place and follow it.* ⁴ *But there shall be a distance between yourselves and it — a measure of two thousand cubits — do not approach [closer to] it, so that you may know the way in which you should go,* * *for you have not passed this way yesterday or before yesterday."*

⁵ *Joshua said to the people, "Prepare yourselves, for tomorrow HASHEM will do wonders in your midst."* ⁶ *Joshua then spoke to the Kohanim, saying, "Carry the Ark of the Covenant and pass before the people"; so they carried the Ark of the Covenant and went before the people.*

⁷ *HASHEM said to Joshua, "This day I will begin to exalt you in the eyes of all Israel, that they may know that just as I was with Moses, so will I be with you.* ⁸ *You shall command the Kohanim, bearers of the Ark of the Covenant, saying, 'When you come to the edge of the waters of the Jordan, you shall stand in the Jordan.' "*

Testimony for the miracle

⁹ *Joshua said to the Children of Israel, "Come here and hear the words of HASHEM, your God."* ¹⁰ *Joshua said, "Through this you will know that the Living God is in your midst and He will surely drive away from before you the Canaanite and the Hittite and the Hivvite and the Perizzite and the Girgashite and the Amorite and the Jebusite.* ¹¹ *Behold, the Ark of the Covenant of the Master of all the earth is passing before you in the Jordan.* ¹² *Now, take for yourselves twelve men from the tribes of Israel, one man for each tribe.* * ¹³ *It*

The Kohanim in the overflowing river

shall happen, just as the soles of the feet of the Kohanim, the bearers of the Ark of HASHEM, Master of the entire earth, rest in the waters of the Jordan, the waters of the Jordan will be cut off — the waters that descend from upstream — and they will stand as one column.

¹⁴ *It happened when the people moved from their tents to cross the Jordan, and the Kohanim, the bearers of the Ark of the Covenant, were in front of the people:* ¹⁵ *When the bearers of the Ark arrived at the Jordan, and the feet of the Kohanim, the bearers of the Ark, were immersed in the edge of the water — and the Jordan was overflowing all its banks all the days of the harvest season —*

The waters part

¹⁶ *the waters descending from upstream stood still and they rose up in one column,* * *very far from Adam, the city that is near Zarethan; and [the water] that descends to the sea of the plain, the Dead Sea,* * *ceased, and was cut off; and the people crossed opposite Jericho.* ¹⁷ *The Kohanim, the bearers of the Ark of the Covenant of HASHEM, stood firmly on dry ground, in the middle of the Jordan, all Israel crossing on dry ground until the entire nation finished crossing the Jordan.*

---

water did not spill over and flood the adjacent area; rather it formed a large "pillar" and retained its original distance

from the city of Adam *(Radak).*

The Hebrew name of the Dead Sea means the Salt Sea.

ד א וַיְהִי כַּאֲשֶׁר־תַּמּוּ כָל־הַגּוֹי לַעֲבוֹר אֶת־הַיַּרְדֵּן וַיֹּאמֶר יהוה

ב אֶל־יְהוֹשֻׁעַ לֵאמֹר: קְחוּ לָכֶם מִן־הָעָם שְׁנֵים עָשָׂר אֲנָשִׁים אִישׁ־אֶחָד

ג אִישׁ־אֶחָד מִשָּׁבֶט: וְצַוּוּ אוֹתָם לֵאמֹר שְׂאוּ־לָכֶם מִזֶּה מִתּוֹךְ הַיַּרְדֵּן מִמַּצַּב

רַגְלֵי הַכֹּהֲנִים הָכִין שְׁתֵּים־עֶשְׂרֵה אֲבָנִים וְהַעֲבַרְתֶּם אוֹתָם עִמָּכֶם

ד וְהִנַּחְתֶּם אוֹתָם בַּמָּלוֹן אֲשֶׁר־תָּלִינוּ בוֹ הַלָּיְלָה: וַיִּקְרָא

יְהוֹשֻׁעַ אֶל־שְׁנֵים הֶעָשָׂר אִישׁ אֲשֶׁר הֵכִין מִבְּנֵי יִשְׂרָאֵל אִישׁ־אֶחָד

ה אִישׁ־אֶחָד מִשָּׁבֶט: וַיֹּאמֶר לָהֶם יְהוֹשֻׁעַ עִבְרוּ לִפְנֵי אֲרוֹן יהוה אֱלֹהֵיכֶם

אֶל־תּוֹךְ הַיַּרְדֵּן וְהָרִימוּ לָכֶם אִישׁ אֶבֶן אַחַת עַל־שִׁכְמוֹ לְמִסְפַּר

ו שִׁבְטֵי בְנֵי־יִשְׂרָאֵל: לְמַעַן תִּהְיֶה זֹאת אוֹת בְּקִרְבְּכֶם כִּי־יִשְׁאָלוּן בְּנֵיכֶם

ז מָחָר לֵאמֹר מָה הָאֲבָנִים הָאֵלֶּה לָכֶם: וַאֲמַרְתֶּם לָהֶם אֲשֶׁר נִכְרְתוּ

מֵימֵי הַיַּרְדֵּן מִפְּנֵי אֲרוֹן בְּרִית־יהוה בְּעָבְרוֹ בַּיַּרְדֵּן נִכְרְתוּ מֵי הַיַּרְדֵּן

ח וְהָיוּ הָאֲבָנִים הָאֵלֶּה לְזִכָּרוֹן לִבְנֵי יִשְׂרָאֵל עַד־עוֹלָם: וַיַּעֲשׂוּ־כֵן בְּנֵי־

יִשְׂרָאֵל כַּאֲשֶׁר צִוָּה יְהוֹשֻׁעַ וַיִּשְׂאוּ שְׁתֵּי־עֶשְׂרֵה אֲבָנִים מִתּוֹךְ הַיַּרְדֵּן

כַּאֲשֶׁר דִּבֶּר יהוה אֶל־יְהוֹשֻׁעַ לְמִסְפַּר שִׁבְטֵי בְנֵי־יִשְׂרָאֵל וַיַּעֲבִרוּם עִמָּם

ט אֶל־הַמָּלוֹן וַיַּנִּחוּם שָׁם: וּשְׁתֵּים עֶשְׂרֵה אֲבָנִים הֵקִים יְהוֹשֻׁעַ בְּתוֹךְ

הַיַּרְדֵּן תַּחַת מַצַּב רַגְלֵי הַכֹּהֲנִים נֹשְׂאֵי אֲרוֹן הַבְּרִית וַיִּהְיוּ שָׁם עַד הַיּוֹם

י הַזֶּה: וְהַכֹּהֲנִים נֹשְׂאֵי הָאָרוֹן עֹמְדִים בְּתוֹךְ הַיַּרְדֵּן עַד תֹּם כָּל־הַדָּבָר

אֲשֶׁר־צִוָּה יהוה אֶת־יְהוֹשֻׁעַ לְדַבֵּר אֶל־הָעָם כְּכֹל אֲשֶׁר־צִוָּה מֹשֶׁה

יא אֶת־יְהוֹשֻׁעַ וַיְמַהֲרוּ הָעָם וַיַּעֲבֹרוּ: וַיְהִי כַּאֲשֶׁר־תַּם כָּל־הָעָם לַעֲבוֹר

יב וַיַּעֲבֹר אֲרוֹן־יהוה וְהַכֹּהֲנִים לִפְנֵי הָעָם: וַיַּעַבְרוּ בְּנֵי־רְאוּבֵן וּבְנֵי־גָד

וַחֲצִי שֵׁבֶט הַמְנַשֶּׁה חֲמֻשִׁים לִפְנֵי בְּנֵי יִשְׂרָאֵל כַּאֲשֶׁר דִּבֶּר אֲלֵיהֶם

יג מֹשֶׁה: כְּאַרְבָּעִים אֶלֶף חֲלוּצֵי הַצָּבָא עָבְרוּ לִפְנֵי יהוה לַמִּלְחָמָה

יד אֶל עַרְבוֹת יְרִיחוֹ: בַּיּוֹם הַהוּא גִּדַּל יהוה אֶת־

יְהוֹשֻׁעַ בְּעֵינֵי כָּל־יִשְׂרָאֵל וַיִּרְאוּ אֹתוֹ כַּאֲשֶׁר יָרְאוּ אֶת־מֹשֶׁה כָּל־יְמֵי

טו־טז חַיָּיו: וַיֹּאמֶר יהוה אֶל־יְהוֹשֻׁעַ לֵאמֹר: צַוֵּה אֶת־

הַכֹּהֲנִים נֹשְׂאֵי אֲרוֹן הָעֵדוּת וְיַעֲלוּ מִן־הַיַּרְדֵּן: וַיְצַו יְהוֹשֻׁעַ אֶת־הַכֹּהֲנִים

יח לֵאמֹר עֲלוּ מִן־הַיַּרְדֵּן: וַיְהִי *בַעֲלוֹת [כַּעֲלוֹת ק] הַכֹּהֲנִים נֹשְׂאֵי אֲרוֹן

בְּרִית־יהוה מִתּוֹךְ הַיַּרְדֵּן נִתְּקוּ כַּפּוֹת רַגְלֵי הַכֹּהֲנִים אֶל הֶחָרָבָה

וַיָּשֻׁבוּ מֵי־הַיַּרְדֵּן לִמְקוֹמָם וַיֵּלְכוּ כִתְמוֹל־שִׁלְשׁוֹם עַל־כָּל־גְּדוֹתָיו: וְהָעָם

יט עָלוּ מִן־הַיַּרְדֵּן בֶּעָשׂוֹר לַחֹדֶשׁ הָרִאשׁוֹן וַיַּחֲנוּ בַּגִּלְגָּל בִּקְצֵה מִזְרַח

כ יְרִיחוֹ: וְאֵת שְׁתֵּים עֶשְׂרֵה הָאֲבָנִים הָאֵלֶּה אֲשֶׁר לָקְחוּ מִן־הַיַּרְדֵּן

כא הֵקִים יְהוֹשֻׁעַ בַּגִּלְגָּל: וַיֹּאמֶר אֶל־בְּנֵי יִשְׂרָאֵל לֵאמֹר אֲשֶׁר יִשְׁאָלוּן

כב בְּנֵיכֶם מָחָר אֶת־אֲבוֹתָם לֵאמֹר מָה הָאֲבָנִים הָאֵלֶּה: וְהוֹדַעְתֶּם אֶת־

4:7. These stones would testify that the Torah, in the form of the Tablets, had protected the nation from the over- flowing Jordan, and this would signify that their existence in the future depended on their allegiance to the Torah.

4

¹ It happened when the entire nation had finished crossing the Jordan: HASHEM spoke to Joshua, saying, ² "Take for yourselves twelve men from the people, one man from each tribe; ³ and command them, saying, 'Carry for yourselves from here, from the middle of the Jordan, from the station of the feet of the Kohanim, making ready twelve stones and bring them across with you and set them in the lodging place where you will spend the night.' "

A permanent memorial of the miracle

⁴ Joshua summoned the twelve men whom he had prepared from the Children of Israel, one man from each tribe, ⁵ and Joshua said to them, "Pass before the Ark of HASHEM, your God, into the middle of the Jordan, and each of you lift for yourselves one stone upon his shoulder, [corresponding] to the number of tribes of the Children of Israel. ⁶ So that this will be a sign in your midst, when your children ask tomorrow, saying, '[Of] what [significance] are these stones to you?' ⁷ You shall tell them, '[They signify] that the waters of the Jordan were cut off before the Ark of the Covenant of HASHEM — when it crossed the Jordan the waters of the Jordan were cut off' — and these stones shall remain a remembrance for the Children of Israel forever."*

A stone for each tribe

⁸ The Children of Israel did so, as Joshua commanded. They carried twelve stones from the Jordan, as HASHEM had told Joshua, [corresponding] to the number of the tribes of the Children of Israel, and brought them across with them to the lodging place and set them there. ⁹ Joshua erected twelve [other] stones in the middle of the Jordan, under the station of the feet of the Kohanim, the bearers of the Ark of the Covenant; and they remained there to this day. ¹⁰ The Kohanim, the bearers of the Ark, were standing in the middle of the Jordan until the completion of the entire procedure that HASHEM had commanded Joshua to tell the people, according to all that Moses commanded Joshua. * The people hastened and crossed.

The crossing is completed

¹¹ It happened when the entire people had completed crossing that the Ark of HASHEM and the Kohanim passed in front of the people. ¹² The children of Reuben, the children of Gad, and half the tribe of Manasseh crossed, armed, before the Children of Israel, as Moses had spoken to them. * ¹³ About forty thousand armed men of the legion passed before HASHEM for the battle, to the plains of Jericho. ¹⁴ On that day HASHEM exalted Joshua in the eyes of all Israel, and they revered him as they had revered Moses all the days of his life.

Joshua is exalted

¹⁵ HASHEM spoke to Joshua, saying, ¹⁶ "Command the Kohanim, bearers of the Ark of Testimony, that they should ascend from the Jordan." ¹⁷ So Joshua commanded the Kohanim, saying, "Ascend from the Jordan." ¹⁸ It happened when the Kohanim, the bearers of the Ark of the Covenant of HASHEM, ascended from the middle of the Jordan and the soles of the Kohanim's feet were removed to the dry ground: The waters of the Jordan returned to their place and flowed — as [they had] yesterday and before yesterday — upon all its banks.

The crossing ends and the waters descend

¹⁹ The people ascended from the Jordan on the tenth of the first month, and encamped at Gilgal at the eastern end of Jericho. ²⁰ And these twelve stones that they had taken from the Jordan, Joshua erected at Gilgal. ²¹ He spoke to the Children of Israel, saying, "When your children ask their fathers tomorrow, saying, 'What are these stones?' ²² you should inform your

The memorial is erected

4:10. The entire procedure mentioned above was completed, in addition to the instructions that Moses had

given Joshua in *Deuteronomy* 27:2.
4:12. See *Numbers* 32.

כג בְּנֵיכֶ֣ם לֵאמֹ֑ר בַּיַּבָּשָׁה֙ עָבַ֣ר יִשְׂרָאֵ֔ל אֶת־הַיַּרְדֵּ֖ן הַזֶּֽה: אֲשֶׁר־הוֹבִ֣ישׁ יהוה
אֱלֹֽהֵיכֶ֜ם אֶת־מֵ֧י הַיַּרְדֵּ֛ן מִפְּנֵיכֶ֖ם עַד־עׇבְרְכֶ֑ם כַּאֲשֶׁ֣ר עָשָׂ֩ה יהוה
כד אֱלֹהֵיכֶ֨ם לְיַם־ס֜וּף אֲשֶׁר־הוֹבִ֥ישׁ מִפָּנֵ֖ינוּ עַד־עׇבְרֵֽנוּ: לְ֠מַ֠עַן דַּ֜עַת כׇּל־
עַמֵּ֤י הָאָ֙רֶץ֙ אֶת־יַ֣ד יהוה כִּ֥י חֲזָקָ֖ה הִ֑יא לְמַ֧עַן יְרָאתֶ֛ם אֶת־יהוה
א אֱלֹהֵיכֶ֖ם כׇּל־הַיָּמִֽים: וַיְהִ֣י כִשְׁמֹ֣עַ כׇּל־מַלְכֵ֣י הָאֱמֹרִ֡י אֲשֶׁר֩
בְּעֵ֨בֶר הַיַּרְדֵּ֜ן יָ֗מָּה וְכׇל־מַלְכֵ֤י הַֽכְּנַעֲנִי֙ אֲשֶׁ֣ר עַל־הַיָּ֔ם אֵ֣ת אֲשֶׁר־הוֹבִ֣ישׁ
יהוה אֶת־מֵ֧י הַיַּרְדֵּ֛ן מִפְּנֵ֥י בְנֵֽי־יִשְׂרָאֵ֖ל עַד־°עברנו [°עׇבְרָ֑ם ק] וַיִּמַּ֣ס
ב לְבָבָ֗ם וְלֹא־הָ֨יָה בָ֥ם עוֹד֙ ר֔וּחַ מִפְּנֵ֖י בְּנֵֽי־יִשְׂרָאֵֽל: ◂ בָּעֵ֣ת
הַהִ֗יא אָמַ֤ר יהוה אֶל־יְהוֹשֻׁ֔עַ עֲשֵׂ֥ה לְךָ֖ חַֽרְב֣וֹת צֻרִ֑ים וְשׁ֛וּב מֹ֥ל אֶת־בְּנֵֽי־
ג יִשְׂרָאֵ֖ל שֵׁנִֽית: וַיַּֽעַשׂ־ל֥וֹ יְהוֹשֻׁ֖עַ חַֽרְב֣וֹת צֻרִ֑ים וַיָּ֙מׇל֙ אֶת־בְּנֵ֣י יִשְׂרָאֵ֔ל
ד אֶל־גִּבְעַ֖ת הָעֲרָלֽוֹת: וְזֶ֥ה הַדָּבָ֖ר אֲשֶׁר־מָ֣ל יְהוֹשֻׁ֑עַ כׇּל־הָעָ֣ם הַיֹּצֵ֣א
מִמִּצְרַ֡יִם הַזְּכָרִ֡ים כֹּ֣ל ׀ אַנְשֵׁ֣י הַמִּלְחָמָ֡ה מֵ֣תוּ בַמִּדְבָּר֙ בַּדֶּ֔רֶךְ בְּצֵאתָ֖ם
ה מִמִּצְרָֽיִם: כִּֽי־מֻלִ֣ים הָי֔וּ כׇּל־הָעָ֖ם הַיֹּצְאִ֑ים וְכׇל־הָ֠עָ֠ם הַיִּלֹּדִ֨ים בַּמִּדְבָּ֧ר
ו בַּדֶּ֛רֶךְ בְּצֵאתָ֥ם מִמִּצְרַ֖יִם לֹא־מָֽלוּ: כִּ֣י ׀ אַרְבָּעִ֣ים שָׁנָ֗ה הָלְכ֣וּ בְנֵֽי־יִשְׂרָאֵל֮
בַּמִּדְבָּר֒ עַד־תֹּ֨ם כׇּל־הַגּ֜וֹי אַנְשֵׁ֤י הַמִּלְחָמָה֙ הַיֹּצְאִ֣ים מִמִּצְרַ֔יִם אֲשֶׁ֥ר
לֹא־שָׁמְע֖וּ בְּק֣וֹל יהוה אֲשֶׁ֨ר נִשְׁבַּ֤ע יהוה לָהֶם֙ לְבִלְתִּ֣י הַרְאוֹתָ֔ם אֶת־
ז הָאָ֗רֶץ אֲשֶׁר֩ נִשְׁבַּ֨ע יהוה לַאֲבוֹתָ֜ם לָ֣תֶת לָ֗נוּ אֶ֛רֶץ זָבַ֥ת חָלָ֖ב וּדְבָֽשׁ: וְאֶת־
בְּנֵיהֶם֙ הֵקִ֣ים תַּחְתָּ֔ם אֹתָ֖ם מָ֣ל יְהוֹשֻׁ֑עַ כִּֽי־עֲרֵלִ֣ים הָי֔וּ כִּ֛י לֹא־מָ֥לוּ אוֹתָ֖ם
ח בַּדָּֽרֶךְ: וַיְהִ֛י כַּאֲשֶׁר־תַּ֥מּוּ כׇל־הַגּ֖וֹי לְהִמּ֑וֹל וַיֵּשְׁב֥וּ תַחְתָּ֛ם בַּמַּחֲנֶ֖ה עַ֥ד
ט חֲיוֹתָֽם: וַיֹּ֤אמֶר יהוה אֶל־יְהוֹשֻׁ֔עַ הַיּ֗וֹם גַּלּ֛וֹתִי אֶת־
חֶרְפַּ֥ת מִצְרַ֖יִם מֵעֲלֵיכֶ֑ם וַיִּקְרָ֞א שֵׁ֣ם הַמָּק֤וֹם הַהוּא֙ גִּלְגָּ֔ל עַ֖ד הַיּ֥וֹם הַזֶּֽה:
י וַיַּחֲנ֥וּ בְנֵֽי־יִשְׂרָאֵ֖ל בַּגִּלְגָּ֑ל וַיַּעֲשׂ֣וּ אֶת־הַפֶּ֗סַח בְּאַרְבָּעָ֠ה עָשָׂ֨ר י֥וֹם לַחֹ֛דֶשׁ
יא בָּעֶ֖רֶב בְּעַֽרְב֣וֹת יְרִיחֽוֹ: וַיֹּ֨אכְל֜וּ מֵעֲב֥וּר הָאָ֛רֶץ מִמׇּחֳרַ֥ת הַפֶּ֖סַח מַצּ֣וֹת
יב וְקָל֑וּי בְּעֶ֖צֶם הַיּ֥וֹם הַזֶּֽה: וַיִּשְׁבֹּ֨ת הַמָּ֜ן מִמׇּחֳרָ֗ת בְּאׇכְלָם֙ מֵעֲב֣וּר הָאָ֔רֶץ
וְלֹא־הָ֨יָה ע֤וֹד לִבְנֵ֤י יִשְׂרָאֵל֙ מָ֔ן וַיֹּאכְל֗וּ מִתְּבוּאַת֙ אֶ֣רֶץ כְּנַ֔עַן בַּשָּׁנָ֖ה
יג הַהִֽיא: וַיְהִ֗י בִּֽהְי֣וֹת יְהוֹשֻׁ֘עַ֮ בִּירִיחוֹ֒ וַיִּשָּׂ֤א עֵינָיו֙ וַיַּ֔רְא
וְהִנֵּה־אִישׁ֙ עֹמֵ֣ד לְנֶגְדּ֔וֹ וְחַרְבּ֥וֹ שְׁלוּפָ֖ה בְּיָד֑וֹ וַיֵּ֨לֶךְ יְהוֹשֻׁ֤עַ אֵלָיו֙
יד וַיֹּ֣אמֶר ל֔וֹ הֲלָ֥נוּ אַתָּ֖ה אִם־לְצָרֵֽינוּ: וַיֹּ֣אמֶר ׀ לֹ֗א כִּ֛י אֲנִ֥י שַׂר־צְבָֽא־יהוה
עַתָּ֣ה בָ֑אתִי וַיִּפֹּל֩ יְהוֹשֻׁ֨עַ אֶל־פָּנָ֤יו אַ֙רְצָה֙ וַיִּשְׁתָּ֔חוּ וַיֹּ֣אמֶר ל֔וֹ מָ֥ה אֲדֹנִ֖י
טו מְדַבֵּ֥ר אֶל־עַבְדּֽוֹ: וַיֹּ֩אמֶר֩ שַׂר־צְבָ֨א יהוה אֶל־יְהוֹשֻׁ֗עַ שַׁל־נַֽעַלְךָ֙ מֵעַ֣ל
רַגְלֶ֔ךָ כִּ֣י הַמָּק֗וֹם אֲשֶׁ֥ר אַתָּ֛ה עֹמֵ֥ד עָלָ֖יו קֹ֣דֶשׁ ה֑וּא וַיַּ֥עַשׂ יְהוֹשֻׁ֖עַ כֵּֽן:

Haftarah for first day Pesach continues here: 5:2-6:1; 6:27

5:2. When God promised Moses that He would deliver the Israelites from Egypt, He concluded, "And I will bring you to the land" (*Exodus* 6:8). *Sifre* explains that the Jews merited being freed from Egypt because they performed the rite of circumcision and brought the *pesach*-offering. There had been a mass circumcision in Egypt just before

the Exodus (see *Exodus* 12:44,48). In the Wilderness, it was unhealthy to perform circumcision, so the great majority of the people did not do so. Now that they had entered the land, God commanded Joshua to arrange a nationwide circumcision for a second time.

5:14. The "man" reassured Joshua that he was not an

children, saying, 'Israel crossed this Jordan on dry land.' ^{23} For HASHEM, your God, dried up the waters of the Jordan before you until you crossed, as HASHEM, your God, did to the Sea of Reeds, which He dried up before us until we crossed. ^{24} So that all the peoples of the earth would know the hand of HASHEM, that it is mighty, so that you would fear HASHEM, your God, all the days."

5

The terror of the native kings

^{1} It happened that when all the Amorite kings who were on the western side of the Jordan and all the Canaanite kings who were by the sea heard that HASHEM had dried up the Jordan's waters for the sake of the Children of Israel until they had crossed, their hearts melted, and there was no longer [any] spirit within them because of the Children of Israel.

The national circumcision

. . .

^{2} At that time HASHEM said to Joshua, "Make sharp knives for yourself and circumcise the Children of Israel again, a second time."* ^{3} So Joshua made sharp knives for himself and circumcised the Children of Israel at Gibeath-haaraloth [the Hill of the Foreskins].

^{4} This is the reason why Joshua circumcised [them]: The entire people that had gone forth from Egypt — the males, all the men of war — had died in the Wilderness on the way, after they went forth from Egypt. ^{5} All the people that went forth were circumcised, but all the people that were born in the Wilderness on the way, after they went forth from Egypt, were not circumcised, ^{6} because for forty years the Children of Israel journeyed in the Wilderness until the demise of the entire nation — the men of war — who went forth from Egypt and had not heeded the voice of HASHEM, about whom HASHEM had sworn not to show them the land that HASHEM had sworn to their forefathers to give us, a land flowing with milk and honey. ^{7} But He raised their children in their stead — them Joshua circumcised, for they were uncircumcised since they did not circumcise them on the way. ^{8} When all the nation had finished being circumcised, they remained in their place in the camp until they had recuperated.

. . . removes the national disgrace

^{9} HASHEM said to Joshua, "Today I have rolled away the disgrace of Egypt from upon you." He named that place Gilgal [Rolling], to this day. ^{10} The Children of Israel encamped at Gilgal and performed the pesach-offering on the

The Pesach-offering

fourteenth day of the month in the evening, in the plains of Jericho. ^{11} They ate from the grain of the land on the day after the pesach-offering, matzos and roasted grain, on this very day. ^{12} The manna was depleted the following day, when they ate from the grain of the land; there was no longer any manna for the Children of Israel. They ate from the grain of the Land of Canaan that year.

The appearance of the angel

^{13} It happened when Joshua was in Jericho that he raised his eyes and saw, and behold! — a man was standing opposite him with his sword drawn in his hand. Joshua went toward him and said to him, "Are you with us or with our enemies?"

^{14} He said, "No, for I am the commander of HASHEM's legion; now I have come."* Joshua fell before him to the ground and prostrated himself, and said to him, "What does my master say to his servant?"

^{15} The commander of HASHEM's legion said to Joshua, "Remove your shoe from upon your foot, for the place upon which you stand is holy." And Joshua did so.

---

enemy, but an angel who had come to guarantee success in the battle of Jericho (*Rashi*). According to the Sages, the drawn sword signified that the angel was angry with

Joshua, for in the press of entering the land and performing the circumcisions and so on, Joshua had allowed the people to neglect their Torah study (*Radak*).

ו א־ב וְירִיחוֹ סֹגֶרֶת וּמְסֻגֶּרֶת מִפְּנֵי בְּנֵי יִשְׂרָאֵל אֵין יוֹצֵא וְאֵין בָּא: ◄ וַיֹּאמֶר
יְהוָה אֶל־יְהוֹשֻׁעַ רְאֵה נָתַתִּי בְיָדְךָ֙ אֶת־יְרִיחוֹ וְאֶת־מַלְכָּהּ גִּבּוֹרֵי הֶחָיִל:

Haftarah
continues
on p. 530

ג וְסַבֹּתֶם אֶת־הָעִיר כֹּל אַנְשֵׁי הַמִּלְחָמָה הַקֵּיף אֶת־הָעִיר פַּעַם אֶחָת כֹּה
ד תַעֲשֶׂה שֵׁשֶׁת יָמִים: וְשִׁבְעָה כֹהֲנִים יִשְׂאוּ שִׁבְעָה שׁוֹפְרוֹת הַיּוֹבְלִים לִפְנֵי
הָאָרוֹן וּבַיּוֹם הַשְּׁבִיעִי תָּסֹבּוּ אֶת־הָעִיר שֶׁבַע פְּעָמִים וְהַכֹּהֲנִים יִתְקְעוּ
ה בַּשּׁוֹפָרוֹת: וְהָיָה בִּמְשֹׁךְ ׀ בְּקֶרֶן הַיּוֹבֵל °בְּשָׁמְעֲכֶם [כְּשָׁמְעֲכֶם ק] אֶת־
קוֹל הַשּׁוֹפָר יָרִיעוּ כָל־הָעָם תְּרוּעָה גְדוֹלָה וְנָפְלָה חוֹמַת הָעִיר תַּחְתֶּיהָ
ו וְעָלוּ הָעָם אִישׁ נֶגְדּוֹ: וַיִּקְרָא יְהוֹשֻׁעַ בִּן־נוּן אֶל־הַכֹּהֲנִים וַיֹּאמֶר אֲלֵהֶם
שְׂאוּ אֶת־אֲרוֹן הַבְּרִית וְשִׁבְעָה כֹהֲנִים יִשְׂאוּ שִׁבְעָה שׁוֹפְרוֹת יוֹבְלִים
ז לִפְנֵי אֲרוֹן יְהוָה: °וַיֹּאמְרוּ [וַיֹּאמֶר ק] אֶל־הָעָם עִבְרוּ וְסֹבּוּ אֶת־הָעִיר
ח וְהֶחָלוּץ יַעֲבֹר לִפְנֵי אֲרוֹן יְהוָה: וַיְהִי כֶּאֱמֹר יְהוֹשֻׁעַ אֶל־הָעָם וְשִׁבְעָה
הַכֹּהֲנִים נֹשְׂאִים שִׁבְעָה שׁוֹפְרוֹת הַיּוֹבְלִים לִפְנֵי יְהוָה עָבְרוּ וְתָקְעוּ
ט בַּשּׁוֹפָרוֹת וַאֲרוֹן בְּרִית יְהוָה הֹלֵךְ אַחֲרֵיהֶם: וְהֶחָלוּץ הֹלֵךְ לִפְנֵי הַכֹּהֲנִים
°תֹּקְעֵי [תָּקְעוּ ק] הַשּׁוֹפָרוֹת וְהַמְאַסֵּף הֹלֵךְ אַחֲרֵי הָאָרוֹן הָלוֹךְ וְתָקוֹעַ
י בַּשּׁוֹפָרוֹת: וְאֶת־הָעָם צִוָּה יְהוֹשֻׁעַ לֵאמֹר לֹא תָרִיעוּ וְלֹא־תַשְׁמִיעוּ אֶת־
קוֹלְכֶם וְלֹא־יֵצֵא מִפִּיכֶם דָּבָר עַד יוֹם אָמְרִי אֲלֵיכֶם הָרִיעוּ וַהֲרִיעֹתֶם:
יא וַיַּסֵּב אֲרוֹן־יְהוָה אֶת־הָעִיר הַקֵּף פַּעַם אֶחָת וַיָּבֹאוּ הַמַּחֲנֶה וַיָּלִינוּ
יב בַּמַּחֲנֶה: וַיַּשְׁכֵּם יְהוֹשֻׁעַ בַּבֹּקֶר וַיִּשְׂאוּ הַכֹּהֲנִים אֶת־אֲרוֹן
יג יְהוָה: וְשִׁבְעָה הַכֹּהֲנִים נֹשְׂאִים שִׁבְעָה שׁוֹפְרוֹת הַיֹּבְלִים לִפְנֵי אֲרוֹן יְהוָה
הֹלְכִים הָלוֹךְ וְתָקְעוּ בַּשּׁוֹפָרוֹת וְהֶחָלוּץ הֹלֵךְ לִפְנֵיהֶם וְהַמְאַסֵּף הֹלֵךְ
יד אַחֲרֵי אֲרוֹן יְהוָה °הוֹלֵךְ [הָלוֹךְ ק] וְתָקוֹעַ בַּשּׁוֹפָרוֹת: וַיָּסֹבּוּ אֶת־הָעִיר
בַּיּוֹם הַשֵּׁנִי פַּעַם אַחַת וַיָּשֻׁבוּ הַמַּחֲנֶה כֹּה עָשׂוּ שֵׁשֶׁת יָמִים: וַיְהִי ׀ בַּיּוֹם
טו הַשְּׁבִיעִי וַיַּשְׁכִּמוּ כַּעֲלוֹת הַשַּׁחַר וַיָּסֹבּוּ אֶת־הָעִיר כַּמִּשְׁפָּט הַזֶּה שֶׁבַע
טז פְּעָמִים רַק בַּיּוֹם הַהוּא סָבְבוּ אֶת־הָעִיר שֶׁבַע פְּעָמִים: וַיְהִי בַּפַּעַם
הַשְּׁבִיעִית תָּקְעוּ הַכֹּהֲנִים בַּשּׁוֹפָרוֹת וַיֹּאמֶר יְהוֹשֻׁעַ אֶל־הָעָם הָרִיעוּ כִּי־
יז נָתַן יְהוָה לָכֶם אֶת־הָעִיר: וְהָיְתָה הָעִיר חֵרֶם הִיא וְכָל־אֲשֶׁר־בָּהּ לַיהוָה
רַק רָחָב הַזּוֹנָה תִּחְיֶה הִיא וְכָל־אֲשֶׁר אִתָּהּ בַּבַּיִת כִּי הֶחְבְּאַתָה אֶת־
יח הַמַּלְאָכִים אֲשֶׁר שָׁלָחְנוּ: וְרַק־אַתֶּם שִׁמְרוּ מִן־הַחֵרֶם פֶּן־תַּחֲרִימוּ
וּלְקַחְתֶּם מִן־הַחֵרֶם וְשַׂמְתֶּם אֶת־מַחֲנֵה יִשְׂרָאֵל לְחֵרֶם וַעֲכַרְתֶּם אוֹתוֹ:
יט וְכֹל ׀ כֶּסֶף וְזָהָב וּכְלֵי נְחֹשֶׁת וּבַרְזֶל קֹדֶשׁ הוּא לַיהוָה אוֹצַר יְהוָה
כ יָבוֹא: וַיָּרַע הָעָם וַיִּתְקְעוּ בַּשֹּׁפָרוֹת וַיְהִי כִשְׁמֹעַ הָעָם אֶת־קוֹל הַשּׁוֹפָר
וַיָּרִיעוּ הָעָם תְּרוּעָה גְדוֹלָה וַתִּפֹּל הַחוֹמָה תַּחְתֶּיהָ וַיַּעַל הָעָם הָעִירָה

6:5. As the first campaign in the conquest of the land, the miracle of Jericho demonstrated conclusively that success would come with God's help. There was nothing military about the operation; it was spiritual in every way, from the leadership of the Kohanim, to the blowing of the shofar, to the emphasis on cycles of seven, the number that symbolizes spiritual completion, as in the case of the Sabbath and the Sabbatical year.

6

THE
CONQUEST
OF JERICHO
6:1-27
(See Appendix D,
map 3)

Joshua
instructs the
Kohanim
and the
people

They
encircle
the city

The
seventh day

Jericho's
walls come
down

¹ Jericho was completely sealed before the Children of Israel; no one left and no one entered. ² HASHEM said to Joshua, "See, I have delivered into your hand Jericho and its king, the mighty warriors. ³ You shall go around the city, all the men of war, encircling the city one time; thus shall you do for a period of six days. ⁴ And seven Kohanim shall carry seven ram-shofars before the Ark; on the seventh day you shall go around the city seven times, and the Kohanim shall blow with the shofars. ⁵ It shall be that upon an extended blast with the ram's horn — when you hear the sound of the shofar — all the people shall cry out with a great cry, and the wall of the city will drop down in its place, and the people shall advance, each man straight ahead."*

⁶ Joshua son of Nun summoned the Kohanim and said to them, "Carry the Ark of the Covenant, and seven Kohanim shall carry seven ram-shofars before the Ark of HASHEM."

⁷ He said to the people, "Advance and go around the city; let the armed troop pass before the Ark of HASHEM."

⁸ It happened that as soon as Joshua spoke to the people, the seven Kohanim carrying seven ram-shofars before the [Ark of] HASHEM advanced and blew with the shofars, and the Ark of the Covenant of HASHEM went after them. ⁹ The armed troop went before the Kohanim who blew the shofars, and the rear guard went after the Ark — walking and blowing with the shofars. ¹⁰ Joshua commanded the people, saying, "You shall not cry out, and you shall not let your voice be heard, nor shall any word issue from your mouth, until the day I tell you to cry out — then you shall cry out." ¹¹ He had the Ark of HASHEM go around the city, encircling one time; then they came [back] to the camp and lodged in the camp.

¹² Joshua arose early the [next] morning. The Kohanim carried the Ark of HASHEM, ¹³ and the seven Kohanim carrying the seven ram-shofars before the Ark of HASHEM walked onward and blew with the shofars — and the armed troop went before them and the rear guard went after the Ark of HASHEM walking and blowing with the shofars. ¹⁴ They went around the city one time on the second day and they returned to the camp; they did thus for a period of six days.

¹⁵ It happened on the seventh day: They arose early at daybreak, and they went around the city in this same manner seven times; only on that day they went around the city seven times. ¹⁶ It happened on the seventh time: The Kohanim were blowing with the shofars, and Joshua said to the people, "Cry out, for HASHEM has given you the city! ¹⁷ The city — it and all that is in it — shall be consecrated property for HASHEM. Only Rahab the innkeeper shall live — she and all who are with her in the house — because she hid the emissaries whom we sent. ¹⁸ Only you — beware of the consecrated property, lest you cause destruction if you take from the consecrated property and you bring destruction upon the camp of Israel and cause it trouble. ¹⁹ All the silver and gold and vessels of copper and iron are holy to HASHEM; they shall go to the treasury of HASHEM."

²⁰ The people cried out, and [the Kohanim] blew with the shofars. It happened when the people heard the sound of the shofar that the people cried out with a great shout: The wall fell in its place and the people went up to the city —

כא אִישׁ נֶגְדּוֹ וַיִּלְכְּדוּ אֶת־הָעִיר: וַיַּחֲרִימוּ אֶת־כָּל־אֲשֶׁר בָּעִיר מֵאִישׁ וְעַד־

כב אִשָּׁה מִנַּעַר וְעַד־זָקֵן וְעַד שׁוֹר וָשֶׂה וַחֲמוֹר לְפִי־חָרֶב: וְלִשְׁנַיִם הָאֲנָשִׁים הַמְרַגְּלִים אֶת־הָאָרֶץ אָמַר יְהוֹשֻׁעַ בֹּאוּ בֵּית־הָאִשָּׁה הַזּוֹנָה וְהוֹצִיאוּ

כג מִשָּׁם אֶת־הָאִשָּׁה וְאֶת־כָּל־אֲשֶׁר־לָהּ כַּאֲשֶׁר נִשְׁבַּעְתֶּם לָהּ: וַיָּבֹאוּ הַנְּעָרִים הַמְרַגְּלִים וַיֹּצִיאוּ אֶת־רָחָב וְאֶת־אָבִיהָ וְאֶת־אִמָּהּ וְאֶת־אַחֶיהָ וְאֶת־כָּל־אֲשֶׁר־לָהּ וְאֵת כָּל־מִשְׁפְּחוֹתֶיהָ הוֹצִיאוּ וַיַּנִּיחוּם מִחוּץ לְמַחֲנֵה

כד יִשְׂרָאֵל: וְהָעִיר שָׂרְפוּ בָאֵשׁ וְכָל־אֲשֶׁר־בָּהּ רַק ׀ הַכֶּסֶף וְהַזָּהָב וּכְלֵי

כה הַנְּחֹשֶׁת וְהַבַּרְזֶל נָתְנוּ אוֹצַר בֵּית־יְהוָֹה: וְאֶת־רָחָב הַזּוֹנָה וְאֶת־בֵּית אָבִיהָ וְאֶת־כָּל־אֲשֶׁר־לָהּ הֶחֱיָה יְהוֹשֻׁעַ וַתֵּשֶׁב בְּקֶרֶב יִשְׂרָאֵל עַד הַיּוֹם הַזֶּה כִּי הֶחְבִּיאָה אֶת־הַמַּלְאָכִים אֲשֶׁר שָׁלַח יְהוֹשֻׁעַ לְרַגֵּל אֶת־

כו יְרִיחוֹ:   וַיַּשְׁבַּע יְהוֹשֻׁעַ בָּעֵת הַהִיא לֵאמֹר אָרוּר הָאִישׁ לִפְנֵי יְהוָֹה אֲשֶׁר יָקוּם וּבָנָה אֶת־הָעִיר הַזֹּאת אֶת־יְרִיחוֹ בִּבְכֹרוֹ יְיַסְּדֶנָּה

כז וּבִצְעִירוֹ יַצִּיב דְּלָתֶיהָ: ◀וַיְהִי יְהוָֹה אֶת־יְהוֹשֻׁעַ וַיְהִי

Haftarah for first day Pesach concludes here: 6:27

ז שָׁמְעוֹ בְּכָל־הָאָרֶץ: ◀וַיִּמְעֲלוּ בְנֵי־יִשְׂרָאֵל מַעַל בַּחֵרֶם וַיִּקַּח עָכָן בֶּן־

א כַּרְמִי בֶן־זַבְדִּי בֶן־זֶרַח לְמַטֵּה יְהוּדָה מִן־הַחֵרֶם וַיִּחַר־אַף יְהוָֹה בִּבְנֵי

ב יִשְׂרָאֵל: וַיִּשְׁלַח יְהוֹשֻׁעַ אֲנָשִׁים מִירִיחוֹ הָעַי אֲשֶׁר עִם־בֵּית אָוֶן מִקֶּדֶם לְבֵית־אֵל וַיֹּאמֶר אֲלֵיהֶם לֵאמֹר עֲלוּ וְרַגְּלוּ אֶת־הָאָרֶץ

ג וַיַּעֲלוּ הָאֲנָשִׁים וַיְרַגְּלוּ אֶת־הָעָי: וַיָּשֻׁבוּ אֶל־יְהוֹשֻׁעַ וַיֹּאמְרוּ אֵלָיו אַל־יַעַל כָּל־הָעָם כְּאַלְפַּיִם אִישׁ אוֹ כִּשְׁלֹשֶׁת אֲלָפִים אִישׁ יַעֲלוּ וְיַכּוּ אֶת־הָעָי אַל־

ד תְּיַגַּע־שָׁמָּה אֶת־כָּל־הָעָם כִּי מְעַט הֵמָּה: וַיַּעֲלוּ מִן־הָעָם שָׁמָּה כִּשְׁלֹשֶׁת

ה אֲלָפִים אִישׁ וַיָּנֻסוּ לִפְנֵי אַנְשֵׁי הָעָי: וַיַּכּוּ מֵהֶם אַנְשֵׁי הָעַי כִּשְׁלֹשִׁים וְשִׁשָּׁה אִישׁ וַיִּרְדְּפוּם לִפְנֵי הַשַּׁעַר עַד־הַשְּׁבָרִים וַיַּכּוּם בַּמּוֹרָד וַיִּמַּס לְבַב־הָעָם

ו וַיְהִי לְמָיִם: וַיִּקְרַע יְהוֹשֻׁעַ שִׂמְלֹתָיו וַיִּפֹּל עַל־פָּנָיו אַרְצָה לִפְנֵי אֲרוֹן

ז יְהוָֹה עַד־הָעֶרֶב הוּא וְזִקְנֵי יִשְׂרָאֵל וַיַּעֲלוּ עָפָר עַל־רֹאשָׁם: וַיֹּאמֶר יְהוֹשֻׁעַ אֲהָהּ ׀ אֲדֹנָי יֱהֹוִה לָמָה הֵעֲבַרְתָּ הַעֲבִיר אֶת־הָעָם הַזֶּה אֶת־הַיַּרְדֵּן לָתֵת

ח אֹתָנוּ בְּיַד הָאֱמֹרִי לְהַאֲבִידֵנוּ וְלוּ הוֹאַלְנוּ וַנֵּשֶׁב בְּעֵבֶר הַיַּרְדֵּן: בִּי אֲדֹנָי מָה

ט אֹמַר אַחֲרֵי אֲשֶׁר הָפַךְ יִשְׂרָאֵל עֹרֶף לִפְנֵי אֹיְבָיו: וְיִשְׁמְעוּ הַכְּנַעֲנִי וְכֹל יֹשְׁבֵי הָאָרֶץ וְנָסַבּוּ עָלֵינוּ וְהִכְרִיתוּ אֶת־שְׁמֵנוּ מִן־הָאָרֶץ וּמַה־תַּעֲשֵׂה

י לְשִׁמְךָ הַגָּדוֹל: וַיֹּאמֶר יְהוָֹה אֶל־יְהוֹשֻׁעַ קֻם לָךְ לָמָּה

יא זֶּה אַתָּה נֹפֵל עַל־פָּנֶיךָ: חָטָא יִשְׂרָאֵל וְגַם עָבְרוּ אֶת־בְּרִיתִי אֲשֶׁר צִוִּיתִי אוֹתָם וְגַם לָקְחוּ מִן־הַחֵרֶם וְגַם גָּנְבוּ וְגַם כִּחֲשׁוּ וְגַם שָׂמוּ בִכְלֵיהֶם:

6:26. The children of the builder will die one by one in the course of the construction, starting when he lays the foundation and ending when he puts up its gates. Some five centuries later, Joshua's ban was defied by Hiel of Beth-el, and the curse was fulfilled (*I Kings* 16:34).

7:1. Collective responsibility is a cardinal precept in Jewish life. The extent to which the community at large is held responsible for the actions of an individual is the theme of this chapter.

7:7. See *Genesis* 15:2.

7:9. How can You permit this desecration of Your Great Name?

each man straight ahead — and they conquered the city. ²¹ They destroyed everything that was in the city — man and woman, youth and elder, ox and sheep and ass — by the edge of the sword.

²² To the two men who had spied out the country, Joshua said, "Go to the house of the woman, the innkeeper, and bring forth from there the woman and all that is hers, as you swore to her."

²³ So they entered — the youthful ones, the spies — and they brought out Rahab, and her father, mother, brothers and all that was hers; they brought out all her families and placed them outside the camp of Israel.

Jericho is destroyed

Rahab and her family are spared

²⁴ They burned [down] the city in fire, and everything that was in it; only the silver and the gold, and the vessels of copper and iron they gave to the treasury of the House of HASHEM. ²⁵ But Rahab the innkeeper, and her father's household and all that was hers, Joshua allowed to live. She dwelled in the midst of Israel until this day, because she hid the messengers that Joshua had sent to spy out Jericho.

Joshua's curse

²⁶ Joshua adjured [the people] at that time saying, "Cursed before HASHEM be the man who rises up and rebuilds this city, Jericho; with his oldest [child] he will lay its foundation and with his youngest he will set up its gates."*

²⁷ HASHEM was with Joshua, and his renown was [spread] through the entire land.

7

THE
CONQUEST
OF AI
7:1-8:35

¹ The Children of Israel trespassed against the consecrated property: Achan son of Carmi, son of Zabdi, son of Zerah, of the tribe of Judah, took of the consecrated property, and the wrath of HASHEM flared against the Children of Israel.*

A small force to attack Ai

² Joshua sent men from Jericho to Ai, which is near Beth-aven, east of Beth-el, and spoke to them, saying, "Go up and spy out the land." The men went up and spied out Ai. ³ They returned to Joshua and said to him, "The entire people need not go up; about two thousand men or three thousand men should go up and smite Ai. Do not weary the entire nation there, because they are few."

The Israelite force is defeated

⁴ About three thousand men of the people went up there; but they fled before the men of Ai. ⁵ The men of Ai struck down about thirty-six of them; they pursued them from the front of the gate until Shebarim and smote them on the downward slope. The people's heart melted and became like water. ⁶ Joshua tore his garments and fell on his face to the ground before the Ark of HASHEM until evening, he and the elders of Israel; and they placed dirt upon their heads.

Joshua's prayer

⁷ Joshua said, "Alas, my Lord, HASHEM/ELOHIM.* Why did you bring this people across the Jordan to deliver us into the hand of the Amorites, to make us perish? If only we had been content to dwell on the other side of the Jordan! ⁸ If you please, my Lord, what shall I say now that Israel has turned [the back of its] neck before its enemies? ⁹ The Canaanite and all the inhabitants of the land will hear and will surround us and cut off our name from the earth. What will You do for Your Great Name?"*

God's answer

¹⁰ HASHEM said to Joshua, "Raise yourself up! Why do you fall on your face? ¹¹ Israel has sinned; they have also violated My Covenant that I commanded them; they have also taken from the consecrated property; they have also stolen; they have also denied; they have also placed [it] in their vessels.

יב וְלֹא יֻכְלוּ בְּנֵי יִשְׂרָאֵל לָקוּם לִפְנֵי אֹיְבֵיהֶם עֹרֶף יִפְנוּ לִפְנֵי אֹיְבֵיהֶם
כִּי הָיוּ לְחֵרֶם לֹא אוֹסִיף לִהְיוֹת עִמָּכֶם אִם־לֹא תַשְׁמִידוּ הַחֵרֶם
יג מִקִּרְבְּכֶם: קֻם קַדֵּשׁ אֶת־הָעָם וְאָמַרְתָּ הִתְקַדְּשׁוּ לְמָחָר כִּי כֹה אָמַר
יְהוָֹה אֱלֹהֵי יִשְׂרָאֵל חֵרֶם בְּקִרְבְּךָ יִשְׂרָאֵל לֹא תוּכַל לָקוּם לִפְנֵי אֹיְבֶיךָ
יד עַד־הֲסִירְכֶם הַחֵרֶם מִקִּרְבְּכֶם: וְנִקְרַבְתֶּם בַּבֹּקֶר לְשִׁבְטֵיכֶם וְהָיָה הַשֵּׁבֶט
אֲשֶׁר־יִלְכְּדֶנּוּ יְהוָֹה יִקְרַב לַמִּשְׁפָּחוֹת וְהַמִּשְׁפָּחָה אֲשֶׁר־יִלְכְּדֶנָּה יְהוָֹה
טו תִּקְרַב לַבָּתִּים וְהַבַּיִת אֲשֶׁר יִלְכְּדֶנּוּ יְהוָֹה יִקְרַב לַגְּבָרִים: וְהָיָה הַנִּלְכָּד
בַּחֵרֶם יִשָּׂרֵף בָּאֵשׁ אֹתוֹ וְאֶת־כָּל־אֲשֶׁר־לוֹ כִּי עָבַר אֶת־בְּרִית יְהוָֹה
טז וְכִי־עָשָׂה נְבָלָה בְּיִשְׂרָאֵל: וַיַּשְׁכֵּם יְהוֹשֻׁעַ בַּבֹּקֶר וַיַּקְרֵב אֶת־יִשְׂרָאֵל
יז לִשְׁבָטָיו וַיִּלָּכֵד שֵׁבֶט יְהוּדָה: וַיַּקְרֵב אֶת־מִשְׁפַּחַת יְהוּדָה וַיִּלְכֹּד אֵת
מִשְׁפַּחַת הַזַּרְחִי וַיַּקְרֵב אֶת־מִשְׁפַּחַת הַזַּרְחִי לַגְּבָרִים וַיִּלָּכֵד זַבְדִּי:
יח וַיַּקְרֵב אֶת־בֵּיתוֹ לַגְּבָרִים וַיִּלָּכֵד עָכָן בֶּן־כַּרְמִי בֶן־זַבְדִּי בֶּן־זֶרַח לְמַטֵּה
יט יְהוּדָה: וַיֹּאמֶר יְהוֹשֻׁעַ אֶל־עָכָן בְּנִי שִׂים־נָא כָבוֹד לַיהוָֹה אֱלֹהֵי יִשְׂרָאֵל
וְתֶן־לוֹ תוֹדָה וְהַגֶּד־נָא לִי מֶה עָשִׂיתָ אַל־תְּכַחֵד מִמֶּנִּי: וַיַּעַן עָכָן
כ אֶת־יְהוֹשֻׁעַ וַיֹּאמַר אָמְנָה אָנֹכִי חָטָאתִי לַיהוָֹה אֱלֹהֵי יִשְׂרָאֵל וְכָזֹאת
כא וְכָזֹאת עָשִׂיתִי: °וָאֶרְאֶה [°וָאֵרֶא ק] בַּשָּׁלָל אַדֶּרֶת שִׁנְעָר אַחַת טוֹבָה
וּמָאתַיִם שְׁקָלִים כֶּסֶף וּלְשׁוֹן זָהָב אֶחָד חֲמִשִּׁים שְׁקָלִים מִשְׁקָלוֹ
וָאֶחְמְדֵם וָאֶקָּחֵם וְהִנָּם טְמוּנִים בָּאָרֶץ בְּתוֹךְ הָאָהֳלִי וְהַכֶּסֶף תַּחְתֶּיהָ:
כב וַיִּשְׁלַח יְהוֹשֻׁעַ מַלְאָכִים וַיָּרֻצוּ הָאֹהֱלָה וְהִנֵּה טְמוּנָה בְּאָהֳלוֹ וְהַכֶּסֶף
כג תַּחְתֶּיהָ: וַיִּקָּחוּם מִתּוֹךְ הָאֹהֶל וַיְבִאוּם אֶל־יְהוֹשֻׁעַ וְאֶל כָּל־בְּנֵי
כד יִשְׂרָאֵל וַיַּצִּקֻם לִפְנֵי יְהוָֹה: וַיִּקַּח יְהוֹשֻׁעַ אֶת־עָכָן בֶּן־זֶרַח וְאֶת־
הַכֶּסֶף וְאֶת־הָאַדֶּרֶת וְאֶת־לְשׁוֹן הַזָּהָב וְאֶת־בָּנָיו וְאֶת־בְּנֹתָיו וְאֶת־
שׁוֹרוֹ וְאֶת־חֲמֹרוֹ וְאֶת־צֹאנוֹ וְאֶת־אָהֳלוֹ וְאֶת־כָּל־אֲשֶׁר־לוֹ וְכָל־
כה יִשְׂרָאֵל עִמּוֹ וַיַּעֲלוּ אֹתָם עֵמֶק עָכוֹר: וַיֹּאמֶר יְהוֹשֻׁעַ מֶה עֲכַרְתָּנוּ יַעְכָּרְךָ
יְהוָֹה בַּיּוֹם הַזֶּה וַיִּרְגְּמוּ אֹתוֹ כָל־יִשְׂרָאֵל אֶבֶן וַיִּשְׂרְפוּ אֹתָם בָּאֵשׁ
כו וַיִּסְקְלוּ אֹתָם בָּאֲבָנִים: וַיָּקִימוּ עָלָיו גַּל־אֲבָנִים גָּדוֹל עַד הַיּוֹם הַזֶּה
וַיָּשָׁב יְהוָֹה מֵחֲרוֹן אַפּוֹ עַל־כֵּן קָרָא שֵׁם הַמָּקוֹם הַהוּא עֵמֶק עָכוֹר עַד
הַיּוֹם הַזֶּה:

7:12. Although only Achan sinned, it was regarded as a national violation of the covenant with God, because those who knew did not protest. When something is universally condemned as an unthinkable sin, even individuals would not take it lightly. Thus, Achan's sin was indicative of a general failure to treat God's word, spoken by His prophet, with the necessary gravity.

7:14. The transgressor would be identified by means of the *Choshen*, the breastplate of the Kohen Gadol, upon which were inscribed the names of all the tribes. When the responsible party passed in front of the *Choshen*, the stone containing that tribe's name would grow dim. The leaders of the tribes, representing their brethren, would approach. Then would come the leaders of the indicated families, and, finally, each individual. Since Achan was from the tribe of Judah, the stone of that tribe grew dim each time Achan's representative passed by, and finally, it singled him out as the sinner.

7:21. שִׁנְעָר, *Shinar*, is Babylon (*Genesis* 11:1-9).

7:24. Achan's family was not liable to the death penalty,

¹² *The Children of Israel will not be able to stand before their enemies; they will turn the [back of their] necks to their enemies because they have become worthy of destruction.* * *I will not continue to be with you if you do not destroy the transgressor from your midst.*

¹³ *"Arise, prepare the people and say, 'Prepare yourselves for tomorrow, for thus said* HASHEM, *God of Israel: There is a transgressor in your midst, Israel. You will not be able to stand before your enemies until you remove the transgressor from your midst.* ¹⁴ *You shall approach in the morning according to your tribes. It will be that the tribe that* HASHEM *singles out shall approach by families; and the family that* HASHEM *singles out shall approach by households; and the household that* HASHEM *singles out shall approach by [individual] men.* * ¹⁵ *It will be that the one singled out with consecrated property shall be burned, he and all that is his, because he has violated the covenant of* HASHEM, *and because he has committed an abomination in Israel.' "*

¹⁶ *Joshua arose early in the morning and had Israel approach according to its tribes; the tribe of Judah was singled out.* ¹⁷ *Then he had each family of Judah approach, and he singled out the Zerahite family; he had the Zerahite family approach by [individual] men, and Zabdi was singled out.* ¹⁸ *He had his*

The lottery household approach man by man, and Achan, son of Carmi, son of Zabdi, son
identifies the of Zerah of the tribe of Judah was singled out.
sinner

¹⁹ *Then Joshua said to Achan, "My son, please give honor to* HASHEM, *God of Israel, and confess to Him. Tell me, please, what you have done; do not withhold from me."*

Achan ²⁰ *Achan answered Joshua and said, "Indeed, I have sinned against* HASHEM,
confesses *God of Israel; thus and thus have I done.* ²¹ *I saw among the spoils a lovely*
. . . *Babylonian garment* * *and two hundred shekels of silver and one bar of gold — fifty shekels its weight. I desired them and took them, and behold, they are hidden in the ground within my tent, with the silver beneath it."*

²² *Joshua sent messengers. They ran to the tent, and behold, it was hidden in his tent, and the silver was beneath it.* ²³ *They took them from inside the tent and brought them to Joshua and to all the Children of Israel; and they spread them out before* HASHEM.

²⁴ *And Joshua took Achan son of Zerah and the silver and the garment and the bar of gold and his sons and his daughters* * *and his ox and his ass and his flock and his tent and all that was his, and all of Israel was with him. They brought them up to the Valley of Achor.*

²⁵ *Joshua said, "How greatly have you caused us trouble!* HASHEM *will cause*
. . . *and is* *you trouble this day." Then all of Israel pelted him with stones, burned them*
executed *with fire, and stoned* * *them with stones.* ²⁶ *They piled a great heap of stones over him [which is there] until this day, and* HASHEM *relented from His flaring wrath. Therefore, he called the name of that place the Valley of Achor [Troubling] until this day.*

---

since only he had sinned. The members of his family, like the rest of Israel, were taken to witness the punishment as a deterrent against such conduct in the future. Achan was liable to the death penalty in accordance with 1:18.
7:25. They pelted him, burned his belongings and

stoned his animals (*Rashi*).

It should be noted that the conduct of the people at this time would set precedents, since they had a new leader and were in a new land. Therefore, deviations could not be tolerated.

ח א וַיֹּ֨אמֶר יְהוָ֜ה אֶל־יְהוֹשֻׁ֗עַ אַל־תִּירָא֙ וְאַל־תֵּחָ֔ת קַ֣ח עִמְּךָ֗ אֵ֚ת כָּל־עַ֣ם הַמִּלְחָמָ֔ה וְק֖וּם עֲלֵ֣ה הָעָ֑י רְאֵ֣ה ׀ נָתַ֣תִּי בְיָדְךָ֗ אֶת־מֶ֤לֶךְ הָעַי֙ וְאֶת־עַמּ֔וֹ וְאֶת־עִיר֖וֹ וְאֶת־אַרְצֽוֹ: ב וְעָשִׂ֨יתָ לָעַ֜י וּלְמַלְכָּ֗הּ כַּאֲשֶׁ֨ר עָשִׂ֤יתָ לִֽירִיחוֹ֙ וּלְמַלְכָּ֔הּ רַק־שְׁלָלָ֥הּ וּבְהֶמְתָּ֖הּ תָּבֹ֣זּוּ לָכֶ֑ם שִֽׂים־לְךָ֥ אֹרֵ֖ב לָעִ֥יר מֵאַחֲרֶֽיהָ: ג וַיָּ֧קָם יְהוֹשֻׁ֛עַ וְכָל־עַ֥ם הַמִּלְחָמָ֖ה לַעֲל֣וֹת הָעָ֑י וַיִּבְחַ֣ר יְ֠הוֹשֻׁעַ שְׁלֹשִׁ֨ים אֶ֤לֶף אִישׁ֙ גִּבּוֹרֵ֣י הַחַ֔יִל וַיִּשְׁלָחֵ֖ם לָֽיְלָה: ד וַיְצַ֨ו אֹתָ֜ם לֵאמֹ֗ר רְ֠אוּ אַתֶּ֞ם אֹרְבִ֤ים לָעִיר֙ מֵאַחֲרֵ֣י הָעִ֔יר אַל־תַּרְחִ֥יקוּ מִן־הָעִ֖יר מְאֹ֑ד וִהְיִיתֶ֥ם כֻּלְּכֶ֖ם נְכֹנִֽים: ה וַאֲנִ֗י וְכָל־הָעָם֙ אֲשֶׁ֣ר אִתִּ֔י נִקְרַ֖ב אֶל־הָעִ֑יר וְהָיָ֗ה כִּֽי־יֵצְא֤וּ לִקְרָאתֵ֙נוּ֙ כַּאֲשֶׁ֣ר בָּרִֽאשֹׁנָ֔ה וְנַ֖סְנוּ לִפְנֵיהֶֽם: ו וְיָצְא֣וּ אַחֲרֵ֗ינוּ עַ֣ד הַתִּיקֵ֤נוּ אוֹתָם֙ מִן־הָעִ֔יר כִּ֣י יֹֽאמְר֔וּ נָסִ֣ים לְפָנֵ֔ינוּ כַּאֲשֶׁ֖ר בָּרִֽאשֹׁנָ֑ה וְנַ֖סְנוּ לִפְנֵיהֶֽם: ז וְאַתֶּ֗ם תָּקֻ֙מוּ֙ מֵהָ֣אוֹרֵ֔ב וְהוֹרַשְׁתֶּ֖ם אֶת־הָעִ֑יר וּנְתָנָ֛הּ יְהוָ֥ה אֱלֹֽהֵיכֶ֖ם בְּיֶדְכֶֽם: ח וְהָיָ֞ה כְּתָפְשְׂכֶ֣ם אֶת־הָעִ֗יר תַּצִּ֤יתוּ אֶת־הָעִיר֙ בָּאֵ֔שׁ כִּדְבַ֥ר יְהוָ֖ה תַּעֲשׂ֑וּ רְא֖וּ צִוִּ֥יתִי אֶתְכֶֽם: ט וַיִּשְׁלָחֵ֣ם יְהוֹשֻׁ֗עַ וַיֵּֽלְכוּ֙ אֶל־הַמַּאְרָ֔ב וַיֵּשְׁב֗וּ בֵּ֧ין בֵּֽית־אֵ֛ל וּבֵ֥ין הָעַ֖י מִיָּ֣ם לָעָ֑י וַיָּ֧לֶן יְהוֹשֻׁ֛עַ בַּלַּ֥יְלָה הַה֖וּא בְּת֥וֹךְ הָעָֽם: י וַיַּשְׁכֵּ֤ם יְהוֹשֻׁ֙עַ֙ בַּבֹּ֔קֶר וַיִּפְקֹ֖ד אֶת־הָעָ֑ם וַיַּ֨עַל ה֜וּא וְזִקְנֵ֧י יִשְׂרָאֵ֛ל לִפְנֵ֥י הָעָ֖ם הָעָֽי: יא וְכָל־הָעָ֨ם הַמִּלְחָמָ֜ה אֲשֶׁ֣ר אִתּ֗וֹ עָלוּ֙ וַֽיִּגְּשׁ֔וּ וַיָּבֹ֖אוּ נֶ֣גֶד הָעִ֑יר וַֽיַּחֲנוּ֙ מִצְּפ֣וֹן לָעַ֔י וְהַגַּ֖י °בֵּינ֥וֹ ק °בֵינָ֥יו ק וּבֵֽין־הָעָֽי: יב וַיִּקַּ֕ח כַּחֲמֵ֥שֶׁת אֲלָפִ֖ים אִ֑ישׁ וַיָּ֨שֶׂם אוֹתָ֜ם אֹרֵ֗ב בֵּ֧ין בֵּֽית־אֵ֛ל וּבֵ֥ין הָעַ֖י מִיָּ֥ם °לָעִ֥יר ק °לָעָֽי ק: יג וַיָּשִׂ֨ימוּ הָעָ֜ם אֶת־כָּל־הַֽמַּחֲנֶ֗ה אֲשֶׁר֙ מִצְּפ֣וֹן לָעִ֔יר וְאֶת־עֲקֵב֖וֹ מִיָּ֣ם לָעִ֑יר וַיֵּ֧לֶךְ יְהוֹשֻׁ֛עַ בַּלַּ֥יְלָה הַה֖וּא בְּת֥וֹךְ הָעֵֽמֶק: יד וַיְהִ֞י כִּרְא֣וֹת מֶֽלֶךְ־הָעַ֗י וַֽיְמַהֲר֡וּ וַיַּשְׁכִּ֡ימוּ וַיֵּצְא֣וּ אַנְשֵֽׁי־הָעִיר֩ לִקְרַֽאת־יִשְׂרָאֵ֨ל לַֽמִּלְחָמָ֜ה ה֧וּא וְכָל־עַמּ֛וֹ לַמּוֹעֵ֖ד לִפְנֵ֣י הָֽעֲרָבָ֑ה וְהוּא֙ לֹ֣א יָדַ֔ע כִּי־אֹרֵ֥ב ל֖וֹ מֵאַחֲרֵ֥י הָעִֽיר: טו וַיִּנָּֽגְע֛וּ יְהוֹשֻׁ֥עַ וְכָל־יִשְׂרָאֵ֖ל לִפְנֵיהֶ֑ם וַיָּנֻ֖סוּ דֶּ֥רֶךְ הַמִּדְבָּֽר: טז וַיִּזָּֽעֲק֗וּ כָּל־הָעָם֙ אֲשֶׁ֣ר °בָּעִ֥יר ק °בָּעַ֥י ק לִרְדֹּ֖ף אַחֲרֵיהֶ֑ם וַֽיִּרְדְּפ֗וּ אַחֲרֵי֙ יְהוֹשֻׁ֔עַ וַיִּנָּתְק֖וּ מִן־הָעִֽיר: יז וְלֹֽא־נִשְׁאַ֣ר אִ֗ישׁ בָּעַי֙ וּבֵ֣ית אֵ֔ל אֲשֶׁ֥ר לֹֽא־יָצְא֖וּ אַחֲרֵ֣י יִשְׂרָאֵ֑ל וַיַּעַזְב֤וּ אֶת־הָעִיר֙ פְּתוּחָ֔ה וַֽיִּרְדְּפ֖וּ אַחֲרֵ֥י יִשְׂרָאֵֽל: יח וַיֹּ֨אמֶר יְהוָ֜ה אֶל־יְהוֹשֻׁ֗עַ נְטֵ֞ה בַּכִּיד֤וֹן אֲשֶׁר־בְּיָֽדְךָ֙ אֶל־הָעַ֔י כִּ֥י בְיָֽדְךָ֖ אֶתְּנֶ֑נָּה וַיֵּ֧ט יְהוֹשֻׁ֛עַ בַּכִּיד֥וֹן אֲשֶׁר־בְּיָד֖וֹ אֶל־הָעִֽיר: יט וְהָאוֹרֵ֡ב קָם֩ מְהֵרָ֨ה מִמְּקוֹמ֜וֹ וַיָּר֙וּצוּ֙ כִּנְט֣וֹת יָד֔וֹ וַיָּבֹ֥אוּ הָעִ֖יר וַֽיִּלְכְּד֑וּהָ וַֽיְמַהֲר֔וּ וַיַּצִּ֥יתוּ אֶת־הָעִ֖יר בָּאֵֽשׁ: כ וַיִּפְנ֣וּ אַנְשֵׁי֩ הָעַ֨י אַחֲרֵיהֶ֜ם וַיִּרְא֗וּ וְהִנֵּ֨ה עָלָ֜ה עֲשַׁ֤ן הָעִיר֙ הַשָּׁמַ֔יְמָה וְלֹא־הָיָ֨ה בָהֶ֥ם יָדַ֛יִם לָנ֖וּס הֵ֣נָּה וָהֵ֑נָּה וְהָעָם֙ הַנָּ֣ס הַמִּדְבָּ֔ר נֶהְפַּ֖ךְ אֶל־הָרוֹדֵֽף: כא וִיהוֹשֻׁ֨עַ וְכָל־יִשְׂרָאֵ֜ל רָא֗וּ כִּֽי־לָכַ֤ד הָֽאֹרֵב֙ אֶת־הָעִ֔יר וְכִ֥י עָלָ֖ה עֲשַׁ֣ן הָעִ֑יר וַיָּשֻׁ֙בוּ֙ וַיַּכּ֖וּ אֶת־אַנְשֵׁ֥י הָעָֽי: כב וְאֵ֨לֶּה יָצְא֤וּ מִן־הָעִיר֙

8:14. The king had set a specific time for his army to attack (*Radak*).

8:18. The outstretched spear was the signal for the ambush party to occupy the city (*Rashi*).

8

The second attempt to conquer Ai
(See Appendix D, map 3)

¹ HASHEM said to Joshua, "Do not fear and do not lose resolve. Take all the people of war with you; arise and go up to Ai. See, I have given into your hand the king of Ai, and his people, and his city, and his land. ² You shall do to Ai and its king as you did to Jericho and its king, except that you may plunder its spoils and its animals for yourselves. Set yourself an ambush for the city from its rear."

The strategy

³ So Joshua arose along with all the people of war to go up to Ai. Joshua chose thirty thousand mighty warriors and dispatched them at night. ⁴ He commanded them saying, "See, you shall ambush the city from the city's rear. Do not be too far from the city, and all of you should be ready. ⁵ I and all the people who are with me will approach the city, and it will be that when they go out to oppose us, like the first time, we will flee before them. ⁶ They will come out after us until we have drawn them from the city, for they will say, 'They are fleeing before us, like the first time!' And we will flee before them. ⁷ Then you shall rise up from the ambush and drive out [the remaining people of] the city, and HASHEM, your God, will deliver it into your hand. ⁸ It will be that when you seize the city, you shall set the city on fire; you shall act according to the word of HASHEM. See, I have commanded you!"

⁹ Joshua dispatched them, and they went to the place of ambush and situated themselves between Beth-el and Ai, to the west of Ai. Joshua lodged among the people that night. ¹⁰ Joshua arose early in the morning and inspected the people; then he ascended with the elders of Israel before the people to Ai. ¹¹ All the people of war who were with him ascended, approached, and arrived before the city. They encamped to the north of Ai, and the valley was between them and Ai. ¹² He took about five thousand men and set them to lie in ambush between Beth-el and Ai, to the west of Ai. ¹³ The people readied the entire camp, which was to the north of the city, and the ambush party to the west. That night Joshua went into the midst of the valley.

The ruse succeeds

¹⁴ And it was [as soon] as the king of Ai saw this, the men of the city hastened, rose early, and went out to oppose Israel in battle — he and all his people — at the appointed time, * before the plain. He did not know that an ambush awaited him behind the city. ¹⁵ Joshua and all Israel "were beaten" before them, and they "fled" toward the wilderness. ¹⁶ All the people [remaining] in Ai were mustered to pursue them. They pursued Joshua and were drawn from the city. ¹⁷ Not a man remained in Ai and Beth-el who did not go forth after Israel; they left the city exposed and pursued Israel.

Joshua leads the Israelites to victory

¹⁸ HASHEM said to Joshua, "Stretch forth with the spear that is in your hand toward Ai, * for in your hand will I give it"; and Joshua stretched forth with the spear that was in his hand toward the city. ¹⁹ The ambush party rose quickly from its place and ran when he stretched forth his hand; they entered the city and conquered it; then they hastened and set the city afire. ²⁰ The men of Ai turned behind them and saw and behold, smoke of the city was ascending to the sky! They did not have the strength to flee this way or that way. Then the people who had "fled" to the wilderness turned upon the pursuer.

²¹ When Joshua and all Israel saw that the ambush party had conquered the city and that smoke of the city was ascending, they turned back and struck the men of Ai. ²² [The ambush party] went toward them from the city,

לִקְרָאתָ֑ם וַיִּהְי֣וּ לְיִשְׂרָאֵ֗ל בַּתָּ֙וֶךְ֙ אֵ֤לֶּה מִזֶּה֙ וְאֵ֣לֶּה מִזֶּ֔ה וַיַּכּ֣וּ אוֹתָ֗ם עַד־

כג בִּלְתִּ֥י הִשְׁאִֽיר־ל֖וֹ שָׂרִ֣יד וּפָלִֽיט: וְאֶת־מֶ֥לֶךְ הָעַ֖י תָּ֣פְשׂוּ חָ֑י וַיַּקְרִ֥בוּ אֹת֖וֹ

כד אֶל־יְהוֹשֻֽׁעַ: וַיְהִ֣י כְּכַלּ֣וֹת יִשְׂרָאֵ֗ל לַהֲרֹ֛ג אֶת־כָּל־יֹשְׁבֵ֥י הָעַ֖י בַּשָּׂדֶ֣ה בַּמִּדְבָּ֔ר

אֲשֶׁ֥ר רְדָפ֖וּם בּ֑וֹ וַיִּפְּל֥וּ כֻלָּ֛ם לְפִי־חֶ֖רֶב עַד־תֻּמָּ֑ם וַיָּשֻׁ֣בוּ

כה כָל־יִשְׂרָאֵל֙ הָעַ֔י וַיַּכּ֥וּ אֹתָ֖הּ לְפִי־חָֽרֶב: וַיְהִי֩ כָל־הַנֹּ֨פְלִ֜ים בַּיּ֣וֹם הַה֗וּא

כו מֵאִ֤ישׁ וְעַד־אִשָּׁה֙ שְׁנֵ֣ים עָשָׂ֣ר אָ֑לֶף כֹּ֖ל אַנְשֵׁ֥י הָעָֽי: וִיהוֹשֻׁ֙עַ֙ לֹא־הֵשִׁ֣יב יָד֔וֹ

אֲשֶׁ֥ר נָטָ֖ה בַּכִּיד֑וֹן עַ֚ד אֲשֶׁ֣ר הֶחֱרִ֔ים אֵ֖ת כָּל־יֹשְׁבֵ֥י הָעָֽי: רַ֣ק הַבְּהֵמָ֗ה וּשְׁלַ֤ל

כז הָעִ֤יר הַהִיא֙ בָּזְז֣וּ לָהֶ֔ם יִשְׂרָאֵ֑ל כִּדְבַ֣ר יְהוָֹ֔ה אֲשֶׁ֥ר צִוָּ֖ה אֶת־יְהוֹשֻֽׁעַ: וַיִּשְׂרֹ֥ף

כח יְהוֹשֻׁ֖עַ אֶת־הָעָ֑י וַיְשִׂימֶ֛הָ תֵּל־עוֹלָ֥ם שְׁמָמָ֖ה עַ֥ד הַיּ֥וֹם הַזֶּֽה: וְאֶת־מֶ֣לֶךְ הָעַ֗י

כט תָּלָ֣ה עַל־הָעֵ֔ץ עַד־עֵ֖ת הָעָ֑רֶב וּכְב֣וֹא הַשֶּׁ֗מֶשׁ צִוָּ֤ה יְהוֹשֻׁ֙עַ֙ וַיֹּרִ֤ידוּ אֶת־

נִבְלָתוֹ֙ מִן־הָעֵ֔ץ וַיַּשְׁלִ֜יכוּ אוֹתָ֗הּ אֶל־פֶּ֙תַח֙ שַׁ֣עַר הָעִ֔יר וַיָּקִ֤ימוּ עָלָיו֙ גַּל־

אֲבָנִ֣ים גָּד֔וֹל עַ֖ד הַיּ֥וֹם הַזֶּֽה:

ל-לא אָ֣ז יִבְנֶ֤ה יְהוֹשֻׁ֙עַ֙ מִזְבֵּ֔חַ לַֽיהוָֹ֖ה אֱלֹהֵ֣י יִשְׂרָאֵ֑ל בְּהַ֖ר עֵיבָֽל: כַּאֲשֶׁ֣ר צִוָּ֩ה

מֹשֶׁ֨ה עֶֽבֶד־יְהוָֹ֜ה אֶת־בְּנֵ֣י יִשְׂרָאֵ֗ל כַּכָּתוּב֙ בְּסֵ֙פֶר֙ תּוֹרַ֣ת מֹשֶׁ֔ה מִזְבַּ֣ח

אֲבָנִ֣ים שְׁלֵמ֔וֹת אֲשֶׁ֛ר לֹֽא־הֵנִ֥יף עֲלֵיהֶ֖ן בַּרְזֶ֑ל וַיַּעֲל֤וּ עָלָיו֙ עֹלוֹת֙ לַֽיהוָֹ֔ה

לב וַֽיִּזְבְּח֖וּ שְׁלָמִֽים: וַיִּכְתָּב־שָׁ֖ם עַל־הָאֲבָנִ֑ים אֵ֗ת מִשְׁנֵה֙ תּוֹרַ֣ת מֹשֶׁ֔ה אֲשֶׁ֣ר

לג כָּתַ֔ב לִפְנֵ֖י בְּנֵ֥י יִשְׂרָאֵֽל: וְכָל־יִשְׂרָאֵ֡ל וּזְקֵנָ֣יו וְשֹׁטְרִ֣ים | וְשֹׁפְטָ֡יו עֹמְדִ֣ים

מִזֶּ֣ה | וּמִזֶּ֣ה | לָאָר֡וֹן נֶ֩גֶד֩ הַכֹּהֲנִ֨ים הַלְוִיִּ֜ם נֹשְׂאֵ֣י | אֲר֣וֹן בְּרִית־יְהוָֹ֗ה כַּגֵּר֙

כָּֽאֶזְרָ֔ח חֶצְיוֹ֙ אֶל־מ֣וּל הַר־גְּרִזִ֔ים וְהַֽחֶצְי֖וֹ אֶל־מ֣וּל הַר־עֵיבָ֑ל כַּאֲשֶׁ֣ר צִוָּ֩ה

לד מֹשֶׁ֙ה עֶֽבֶד־יְהוָֹ֜ה לְבָרֵ֛ךְ אֶת־הָעָ֥ם יִשְׂרָאֵ֖ל בָּרִֽאשֹׁנָֽה: וְאַֽחֲרֵי־כֵ֗ן קָרָא֙

אֶת־כָּל־דִּבְרֵ֣י הַתּוֹרָ֔ה הַבְּרָכָ֖ה וְהַקְּלָלָ֑ה כְּכָל־הַכָּת֖וּב בְּסֵ֥פֶר הַתּוֹרָֽה:

לה לֹֽא־הָיָ֣ה דָבָ֗ר מִכֹּ֛ל אֲשֶׁר־צִוָּ֥ה מֹשֶׁ֖ה אֲשֶׁ֣ר לֹֽא־קָרָ֣א יְהוֹשֻׁ֗עַ נֶ֣גֶד כָּל־קְהַ֣ל

א יִשְׂרָאֵל֙ וְהַנָּשִׁ֣ים וְהַטַּ֔ף וְהַגֵּ֖ר הַהֹלֵ֣ךְ בְּקִרְבָּֽם: וַיְהִ֣י כִשְׁמֹ֣עַ

ט

כָּל־הַמְּלָכִ֡ים אֲשֶׁר֩ בְּעֵ֨בֶר הַיַּרְדֵּ֜ן בָּהָ֣ר וּבַשְּׁפֵלָ֗ה וּבְכֹל֙ ח֣וֹף הַיָּ֣ם הַגָּד֔וֹל

ב אֶל־מ֖וּל הַלְּבָנ֑וֹן הַחִתִּ֨י וְהָאֱמֹרִ֜י הַֽכְּנַעֲנִ֣י הַפְּרִזִּ֗י הַחִוִּ֛י וְהַיְבוּסִ֖י וַיִּֽתְקַבְּצ֣וּ

ג יַחְדָּ֔ו לְהִלָּחֵ֥ם עִם־יְהוֹשֻׁ֖עַ וְעִם־יִשְׂרָאֵ֑ל פֶּ֖ה אֶחָֽד: וְיֹשְׁבֵ֙י

ד גִבְעוֹן֙ שָֽׁמְע֔וּ אֵ֧ת אֲשֶׁ֛ר עָשָׂ֥ה יְהוֹשֻׁ֖עַ לִֽירִיח֣וֹ וְלָעָ֑י וַיַּעֲשׂ֤וּ גַם־

הֵ֙מָּה֙ בְּעָרְמָ֔ה וַיֵּלְכ֖וּ וַיִּצְטַיָּ֑רוּ וַיִּקְח֞וּ שַׂקִּ֤ים בָּלִים֙ לַחֲמ֣וֹרֵיהֶ֔ם וְנֹאד֥וֹת

ה יַ֙יִן֙ בָּלִ֔ים וּמְבֻקָּעִ֖ים וּמְצֹרָרִֽים: וּנְעָל֤וֹת בָּלוֹת֙ וּמְטֻלָּא֔וֹת בְּרַגְלֵיהֶ֑ם

ו וּשְׂלָמ֥וֹת בָּל֖וֹת עֲלֵיהֶ֑ם וְכֹל֙ לֶ֣חֶם צֵידָ֔ם יָבֵ֖שׁ הָיָ֥ה נִקֻּדִֽים: וַיֵּלְכ֧וּ

אֶל־יְהוֹשֻׁ֛עַ אֶל־הַמַּחֲנֶ֖ה הַגִּלְגָּ֑ל וַיֹּאמְר֤וּ אֵלָיו֙ וְאֶל־אִ֣ישׁ יִשְׂרָאֵ֔ל

8:22. Once the ambush party secured the city, they set upon the army of Ai from the rear, so that the army of Ai was under attack on two fronts.

8:29. See *Deuteronomy* 21:23.

8:30. See *Deuteronomy* 27:1-8.

8:33. The blessings were pronounced first, followed by the curses, as prescribed in *Deuteronomy* Ch. 27. Then Joshua read to them all the words of the Torah, i.e., the admonition of *Deuteronomy* Ch. 28. According to *Radak*, he also read to them all the positive and negative comso it was that they were in the midst of the Israelite [forces], some on this [side] and some on that. * They struck them down until they did not leave them a remnant or survivor. ²³ They captured the king of Ai alive and brought him to Joshua. ²⁴ And it was when Israel finished slaying all the inhabitants of Ai in the field — in the wilderness where they had chased them — and they had all fallen by the edge of the sword until their annihilation that all the Israelites returned to Ai and smote it by the edge of the sword.

The city is destroyed ²⁵ All who fell on that day, both men and women, were twelve thousand, all the people of Ai. ²⁶ Joshua did not withdraw his hand that he had stretched out with the spear until he had destroyed all the inhabitants of Ai. ²⁷ Only the animals and booty of that city Israel took as spoils for themselves, according to the word of HASHEM, which He had commanded Joshua. ²⁸ Joshua burned Ai and made it a mound forever, a wasteland, until this day. ²⁹ He hanged the king of Ai on the gallows until the time of evening. When the sun went down, Joshua commanded, and they lowered his corpse from the gallows. * They threw it [down] at the entrance to the city gates and piled a great heap of stones on him, until this day.

The altar on Mount Ebal ³⁰ Then Joshua built an altar to HASHEM, God of Israel, on Mount Ebal, * ³¹ as Moses, the servant of HASHEM, had commanded the Children of Israel, as it is written in the Book of the Torah of Moses — an altar of whole stones upon which no one had lifted up iron, and they brought elevation-offerings to HASHEM upon it, and they slaughtered peace-offerings. ³² He inscribed there, on the stones, a repetition of the Torah of Moses, which he wrote before the Children of Israel.

The blessings and the curses ³³ And all Israel and its elders and officers and its judges stood on this [side] and that of the Ark opposite the Kohanim, the Levites, bearers of the Ark of the Covenant of HASHEM, proselyte and native alike, half of them on the slope of Mount Gerizim and half of them on the slope of Mount Ebal, as Moses the servant of HASHEM had commanded, to first bless the people of Israel. * ³⁴ After that, he read all the words of the Torah, the blessing and the curse, according to all that is written in the Book of the Torah. ³⁵ There was not a word of all that Moses commanded that Joshua did not read to the entire congregation of Israel, the women and the children and the converts that walked among them.

9

THE GIBEONITES
9:1-27

¹ When all the kings that were on the [western] side of the Jordan — in the mountain and in the lowland and on the entire shore of the Great [Mediterranean] Sea opposite the Lebanon, the Hittite and the Amorite, the Canaanite, the Perizzite, the Hivvite, and the Jebusite — heard, ² they gathered together to wage war with Joshua and with Israel, with a single accord.

The Gibeonites' ruse ³ The inhabitants of Gibeon heard* what Joshua had done to Jericho and to Ai. ⁴ They also acted — [but] with guile — and went and disguised themselves as ambassadors. They took well-worn sacks for their donkeys; well-worn, cracked, and split wineskins; ⁵ well-worn and patched shoes on their feet; and well-worn garments on themselves. All the bread of their provisions was dry, toasted. ⁶ They went to Joshua at the camp at Gilgal and said to him and to the men of Israel,

---

mandments.
9:3. Like the people of Jericho and Ai before them, the Gibeonites chose to resist the Israelite conquest, but in a different manner. Jericho chose defense; Ai chose offense; the Gibeonites chose deception (*Radak*). According to the Sages, they also acted with guile, meaning the Gibeonites imitated the tactics of Jacob's sons against Shechem; see *Genesis* 34:13.

ז מֵאֶרֶץ רְחוֹקָה בָּאנוּ וְעַתָּה כִּרְתוּ־לָנוּ בְרִית: ⁰וַיֹּאמְרוּ [°וַיֹּאמֶר ק] אִישׁ־
יִשְׂרָאֵל אֶל־הַחִוִּי אוּלַי בְּקִרְבִּי אַתָּה יוֹשֵׁב וְאֵיךְ ⁰אכרות [°אֶכְרָת־ ק]

ח לְךָ בְרִית: וַיֹּאמְרוּ אֶל־יְהוֹשֻׁעַ עֲבָדֶיךָ אֲנָחְנוּ וַיֹּאמֶר אֲלֵהֶם יְהוֹשֻׁעַ מִי

ט אַתֶּם וּמֵאַיִן תָּבֹאוּ: וַיֹּאמְרוּ אֵלָיו מֵאֶרֶץ רְחוֹקָה מְאֹד בָּאוּ עֲבָדֶיךָ
לְשֵׁם יְהוָה אֱלֹהֶיךָ כִּי־שָׁמַעְנוּ שָׁמְעוֹ וְאֵת כָּל־אֲשֶׁר עָשָׂה בְּמִצְרָיִם:

י וְאֵת ׀ כָּל־אֲשֶׁר עָשָׂה לִשְׁנֵי מַלְכֵי הָאֱמֹרִי אֲשֶׁר בְּעֵבֶר הַיַּרְדֵּן לְסִיחוֹן

יא מֶלֶךְ חֶשְׁבּוֹן וּלְעוֹג מֶלֶךְ־הַבָּשָׁן אֲשֶׁר בְּעַשְׁתָּרוֹת: וַיֹּאמְרוּ אֵלֵינוּ זְקֵינֵינוּ
וְכָל־יֹשְׁבֵי אַרְצֵנוּ לֵאמֹר קְחוּ בְיֶדְכֶם צֵידָה לַדֶּרֶךְ וּלְכוּ לִקְרָאתָם

יב וַאֲמַרְתֶּם אֲלֵיהֶם עַבְדֵיכֶם אֲנַחְנוּ וְעַתָּה כִּרְתוּ־לָנוּ בְרִית: זֶה ׀ לַחְמֵנוּ
חָם הִצְטַיַּדְנוּ אֹתוֹ מִבָּתֵּינוּ בְּיוֹם צֵאתֵנוּ לָלֶכֶת אֲלֵיכֶם וְעַתָּה הִנֵּה

יג יָבֵשׁ וְהָיָה נִקֻּדִים: וְאֵלֶּה נֹאדוֹת הַיַּיִן אֲשֶׁר מִלֵּאנוּ חֲדָשִׁים וְהִנֵּה
הִתְבַּקָּעוּ וְאֵלֶּה שַׂלְמוֹתֵינוּ וּנְעָלֵינוּ בָּלוּ מֵרֹב הַדֶּרֶךְ מְאֹד: וַיִּקְחוּ

יד הָאֲנָשִׁים מִצֵּידָם וְאֶת־פִּי יְהוָה לֹא שָׁאָלוּ: וַיַּעַשׂ לָהֶם יְהוֹשֻׁעַ שָׁלוֹם

טו וַיִּכְרֹת לָהֶם בְּרִית לְחַיּוֹתָם וַיִּשָּׁבְעוּ לָהֶם נְשִׂיאֵי הָעֵדָה: וַיְהִי מִקְצֵה

טז שְׁלֹשֶׁת יָמִים אַחֲרֵי אֲשֶׁר־כָּרְתוּ לָהֶם בְּרִית וַיִּשְׁמְעוּ כִּי־קְרֹבִים הֵם
אֵלָיו וּבְקִרְבּוֹ הֵם יֹשְׁבִים: וַיִּסְעוּ בְנֵי־יִשְׂרָאֵל וַיָּבֹאוּ אֶל־עָרֵיהֶם בַּיּוֹם

יז הַשְּׁלִישִׁי וְעָרֵיהֶם גִּבְעוֹן וְהַכְּפִירָה וּבְאֵרוֹת וְקִרְיַת יְעָרִים: וְלֹא הִכּוּם

יח בְּנֵי יִשְׂרָאֵל כִּי־נִשְׁבְּעוּ לָהֶם נְשִׂיאֵי הָעֵדָה בַּיהוָה אֱלֹהֵי יִשְׂרָאֵל וַיִּלֹּנוּ
כָל־הָעֵדָה עַל־הַנְּשִׂיאִים: וַיֹּאמְרוּ כָל־הַנְּשִׂיאִים אֶל־כָּל־הָעֵדָה אֲנַחְנוּ

יט נִשְׁבַּעְנוּ לָהֶם בַּיהוָה אֱלֹהֵי יִשְׂרָאֵל וְעַתָּה לֹא נוּכַל לִנְגֹּעַ בָּהֶם: זֹאת

כ נַעֲשֶׂה לָהֶם וְהַחֲיֵה אוֹתָם וְלֹא־יִהְיֶה עָלֵינוּ קֶצֶף עַל־הַשְּׁבוּעָה אֲשֶׁר־

כא נִשְׁבַּעְנוּ לָהֶם: וַיֹּאמְרוּ אֲלֵיהֶם הַנְּשִׂיאִים יִחְיוּ וַיִּהְיוּ חֹטְבֵי עֵצִים וְשֹׁאֲבֵי־
מַיִם לְכָל־הָעֵדָה כַּאֲשֶׁר דִּבְּרוּ לָהֶם הַנְּשִׂיאִים: וַיִּקְרָא לָהֶם יְהוֹשֻׁעַ

כב וַיְדַבֵּר אֲלֵיהֶם לֵאמֹר לָמָּה רִמִּיתֶם אֹתָנוּ לֵאמֹר רְחוֹקִים אֲנַחְנוּ מִכֶּם

כג מְאֹד וְאַתֶּם בְּקִרְבֵּנוּ יֹשְׁבִים: וְעַתָּה אֲרוּרִים אַתֶּם וְלֹא־יִכָּרֵת מִכֶּם
עֶבֶד וְחֹטְבֵי עֵצִים וְשֹׁאֲבֵי מַיִם לְבֵית אֱלֹהָי: וַיַּעֲנוּ אֶת־יְהוֹשֻׁעַ וַיֹּאמְרוּ כִּי

כד הֻגֵּד הֻגַּד לַעֲבָדֶיךָ אֵת אֲשֶׁר צִוָּה יְהוָה אֱלֹהֶיךָ אֶת־מֹשֶׁה עַבְדּוֹ
לָתֵת לָכֶם אֶת־כָּל־הָאָרֶץ וּלְהַשְׁמִיד אֶת־כָּל־יֹשְׁבֵי הָאָרֶץ מִפְּנֵיכֶם

כה וַנִּירָא מְאֹד לְנַפְשֹׁתֵינוּ מִפְּנֵיכֶם וַנַּעֲשֶׂה אֶת־הַדָּבָר הַזֶּה: וְעַתָּה הִנְנוּ

כו בְיָדֶךָ כַּטּוֹב וְכַיָּשָׁר בְּעֵינֶיךָ לַעֲשׂוֹת לָנוּ עֲשֵׂה: וַיַּעַשׂ לָהֶם כֵּן וַיַּצֵּל אוֹתָם

כז מִיַּד בְּנֵי־יִשְׂרָאֵל וְלֹא הֲרָגוּם: וַיִּתְּנֵם יְהוֹשֻׁעַ בַּיּוֹם הַהוּא חֹטְבֵי עֵצִים

9:7. The Israelites suspected that the Gibeonites were not foreigners at all, but inhabitants of the land, i.e., in my midst. As members of the seven Canaanite nations, they could not be accepted as full-fledged members of a covenant unless they accepted a vassal status and agreed to

keep the Seven Noachide Laws (*Radak*). Seeing that the Israelites were not receptive, the Gibeonites turned to Joshua alone (v. 8) and pleaded with him (*Abarbanel*).
9:19. Since the oath was obtained through deception, it was not valid, but Joshua and the elders maintained that

"We have come from a distant land; now seal a covenant with us."

⁷ *The men of Israel said to the Hivvite, "Perhaps you dwell in my midst. How can I seal a covenant with you?"**

⁸ *They said to Joshua, "We are your servants." Joshua said to them, "Who are you and from where do you come?"* ⁹ *They said to him, "Your servants have come from a very distant land for the sake of HASHEM, your God. We have heard of His fame and all that He did in Egypt,* ¹⁰ *and all that He did to the two Amorite kings that were on the [other] side of the Jordan, to Sihon, king of Heshbon, and to Og, king of Bashan, who was in Ashtaroth.* ¹¹ *Our elders and all the inhabitants of our country spoke to us, saying, 'Take in your hands provisions for the journey and go meet them and say to them: We are your servants. Now seal a covenant with us.'* ¹² *This is our bread: It was hot when we packed it for our provisions from our houses, on the day we went forth to go to you; now behold, it is dry and has become toasted.* ¹³ *These wineskins were new when we filled them; [now] behold, they are cracked! These are our clothes and our shoes; they are well-worn from the very long journey."*

¹⁴ *The men accepted their deception, but they did not ask for the word of HASHEM.* ¹⁵ *Joshua made peace with them and sealed a covenant with them to let them live; the leaders of the assembly swore to them.*

A covenant is mistakenly made

¹⁶ *It happened at the end of three days after they had sealed a covenant with them that they heard that they were neighbors of theirs and that they dwelled in their midst.* ¹⁷ *The Children of Israel traveled and came to their cities on the third day; their cities were Gibeon, Chephirah, Beroth, and Kiriath-jearim.* ¹⁸ *The Children of Israel did not smite them, because the leaders of the assembly had sworn to them by HASHEM, God of Israel; but the entire assembly complained against the leaders.* ¹⁹ *All the leaders said to the entire assembly, "We have sworn to them by HASHEM, God of Israel; now we may not touch them.* * ²⁰ *This we will do to them — let them live; there will be no wrath upon us because of the oath that we have sworn to them . . ."* ²¹ *So the leaders said to them, "Let them live." They became woodchoppers and water drawers for the entire assembly, as the leaders had told them.*

The Gibeonites' deception is uncovered

The Gibeonites are spared and relegated to lowly positions

²² *Then Joshua summoned [the Gibeonites] and spoke to them, saying, "Why have you deceived us, saying, 'We are very distant from you,' when you dwell in our midst?* ²³ *Now you are cursed; slaves shall never cease from among you — woodchoppers and water drawers — for the House of my God."**

The Gibeonites explain themselves and accept their status

²⁴ *They answered Joshua and said, "Because it was told to your servants that HASHEM, your God, had commanded Moses His servant to give you the entire land and to exterminate all the inhabitants of the land from before you, we were most fearful for our lives because of you, so we did this thing.* ²⁵ *And now, we are in your hand; whatever seems good and right in your eyes to do with us — do."*

²⁶ *He did this to them: He rescued them from the hand of the Children of Israel, and they did not kill them.* ²⁷ *That day Joshua made them woodchoppers*

---

it would have been a desecration of God's Name for Jews to nullify an oath made to non-Jews.

9:23. The leaders had made them servants to the entire assembly (v. 21), and now Joshua modified that decree.

As long as all the people lived together, the Gibeonites were general servants; after the land was divided among the tribes, the servitude would be limited to serving in the Temple (*Radak*).

וְשׁאֲבֵי מַיִם לָעֵדָה וּלְמִזְבַּח יהוה עַד־הַיּוֹם הַזֶּה אֶל־הַמָּקוֹם אֲשֶׁר
יִבְחָר:　　　א　וַיְהִי כִשְׁמֹעַ אֲדֹנִי־צֶדֶק מֶלֶךְ יְרוּשָׁלַ͏ִם כִּי־לָכַד
יְהוֹשֻׁעַ אֶת־הָעַי וַיַּחֲרִימָהּ כַּאֲשֶׁר עָשָׂה לִירִיחוֹ וּלְמַלְכָּהּ כֵּן־עָשָׂה לָעַי
ב וּלְמַלְכָּהּ וְכִי הִשְׁלִימוּ יֹשְׁבֵי גִבְעוֹן אֶת־יִשְׂרָאֵל וַיִּהְיוּ בְּקִרְבָּם: וַיִּירְאוּ
מְאֹד כִּי עִיר גְּדוֹלָה גִּבְעוֹן כְּאַחַת עָרֵי הַמַּמְלָכָה וְכִי הִיא גְדוֹלָה מִן־הָעַי
ג וְכָל־אֲנָשֶׁיהָ גִּבֹּרִים: וַיִּשְׁלַח אֲדֹנִי־צֶדֶק מֶלֶךְ יְרוּשָׁלַ͏ִם אֶל־הוֹהָם מֶלֶךְ־
חֶבְרוֹן וְאֶל־פִּרְאָם מֶלֶךְ־יַרְמוּת וְאֶל־יָפִיעַ מֶלֶךְ־לָכִישׁ וְאֶל־דְּבִיר
ד מֶלֶךְ־עֶגְלוֹן לֵאמֹר: עֲלוּ־אֵלַי וְעִזְרֻנִי וְנַכֶּה אֶת־גִּבְעוֹן כִּי־הִשְׁלִימָה אֶת־
ה יְהוֹשֻׁעַ וְאֶת־בְּנֵי יִשְׂרָאֵל: וַיֵּאָסְפוּ וַיַּעֲלוּ חֲמֵשֶׁת ׀ מַלְכֵי הָאֱמֹרִי מֶלֶךְ
יְרוּשָׁלַ͏ִם מֶלֶךְ־חֶבְרוֹן מֶלֶךְ־יַרְמוּת מֶלֶךְ־לָכִישׁ מֶלֶךְ־עֶגְלוֹן הֵם וְכָל־
ו מַחֲנֵיהֶם וַיַּחֲנוּ עַל־גִּבְעוֹן וַיִּלָּחֲמוּ עָלֶיהָ: וַיִּשְׁלְחוּ אַנְשֵׁי גִבְעוֹן אֶל־
יְהוֹשֻׁעַ אֶל־הַמַּחֲנֶה הַגִּלְגָּלָה לֵאמֹר אַל־תֶּרֶף יָדֶיךָ מֵעֲבָדֶיךָ עֲלֵה אֵלֵינוּ
מְהֵרָה וְהוֹשִׁיעָה לָּנוּ וְעָזְרֵנוּ כִּי נִקְבְּצוּ אֵלֵינוּ כָּל־מַלְכֵי הָאֱמֹרִי יֹשְׁבֵי
ז הָהָר: וַיַּעַל יְהוֹשֻׁעַ מִן־הַגִּלְגָּל הוּא וְכָל־עַם הַמִּלְחָמָה עִמּוֹ וְכֹל גִּבּוֹרֵי
ח הֶחָיִל:　　　　　　　　וַיֹּאמֶר יהוה אֶל־יְהוֹשֻׁעַ אַל־תִּירָא מֵהֶם כִּי בְיָדְךָ
ט נְתַתִּים לֹא־יַעֲמֹד אִישׁ מֵהֶם בְּפָנֶיךָ: וַיָּבֹא אֲלֵיהֶם יְהוֹשֻׁעַ פִּתְאֹם כָּל־
י הַלַּיְלָה עָלָה מִן־הַגִּלְגָּל: וַיְהֻמֵּם יהוה לִפְנֵי יִשְׂרָאֵל וַיַּכֵּם מַכָּה־גְדוֹלָה
בְּגִבְעוֹן וַיִּרְדְּפֵם דֶּרֶךְ מַעֲלֵה בֵית־חוֹרֹן וַיַּכֵּם עַד־עֲזֵקָה וְעַד־מַקֵּדָה:
יא וַיְהִי בְּנֻסָם ׀ מִפְּנֵי יִשְׂרָאֵל הֵם בְּמוֹרַד בֵּית־חוֹרֹן וַיהוה הִשְׁלִיךְ עֲלֵיהֶם
אֲבָנִים גְּדֹלוֹת מִן־הַשָּׁמַיִם עַד־עֲזֵקָה וַיָּמֻתוּ רַבִּים אֲשֶׁר־מֵתוּ בְּאַבְנֵי
הַבָּרָד מֵאֲשֶׁר הָרְגוּ בְּנֵי יִשְׂרָאֵל בֶּחָרֶב:　　　　אָז יְדַבֵּר יְהוֹשֻׁעַ
יב לַיהוה בְּיוֹם תֵּת יהוה אֶת־הָאֱמֹרִי לִפְנֵי בְּנֵי יִשְׂרָאֵל וַיֹּאמֶר ׀ לְעֵינֵי
יִשְׂרָאֵל שֶׁמֶשׁ בְּגִבְעוֹן דּוֹם וְיָרֵחַ בְּעֵמֶק אַיָּלוֹן: וַיִּדֹּם הַשֶּׁמֶשׁ וְיָרֵחַ עָמָד
יג עַד־יִקֹּם גּוֹי אֹיְבָיו הֲלֹא־הִיא כְתוּבָה עַל־סֵפֶר הַיָּשָׁר וַיַּעֲמֹד הַשֶּׁמֶשׁ
בַּחֲצִי הַשָּׁמַיִם וְלֹא־אָץ לָבוֹא כְּיוֹם תָּמִים: וְלֹא הָיָה כַּיּוֹם הַהוּא לְפָנָיו
יד וְאַחֲרָיו לִשְׁמֹעַ יהוה בְּקוֹל אִישׁ כִּי יהוה נִלְחָם לְיִשְׂרָאֵל:　　　וַיָּשָׁב
טו יְהוֹשֻׁעַ וְכָל־יִשְׂרָאֵל עִמּוֹ אֶל־הַמַּחֲנֶה הַגִּלְגָּלָה: וַיָּנֻסוּ חֲמֵשֶׁת הַמְּלָכִים
טז הָאֵלֶּה וַיֵּחָבְאוּ בַמְּעָרָה בְּמַקֵּדָה: וַיֻּגַּד לִיהוֹשֻׁעַ לֵאמֹר נִמְצְאוּ חֲמֵשֶׁת
יז הַמְּלָכִים נֶחְבְּאִים בַּמְּעָרָה בְּמַקֵּדָה: וַיֹּאמֶר יְהוֹשֻׁעַ גֹּלּוּ אֲבָנִים גְּדֹלוֹת
יח אֶל־פִּי הַמְּעָרָה וְהַפְקִידוּ עָלֶיהָ אֲנָשִׁים לְשָׁמְרָם: וְאַתֶּם אַל־תַּעֲמֹדוּ
יט רִדְפוּ אַחֲרֵי אֹיְבֵיכֶם וְזִנַּבְתֶּם אוֹתָם אַל־תִּתְּנוּם לָבוֹא אֶל־עָרֵיהֶם כִּי

10:1. This chapter relates details of Joshua's conquest of the southern part of Canaan. Divine Providence assisted the Israelites by causing the Canaanites of the South to unite and attack Gibeon. As a result, the Jews were able to defeat the confederacy of five kings in a single battle.

10:12. Alternatively: . . . and he said, "Before the eyes of Israel, O Sun, stand still . . . " (*Radak*).

10:13. The Book of the Upright is the Torah, in which God told Moses (*Exodus* 34:10) that He would act in an unprecedented manner for the benefit of Israel (*Radak*).

and water drawers for the assembly and for the Altar of HASHEM until this day, in the place that He would choose.

10

THE
CONQUEST
OF THE
SOUTH
10:1-43

Five Amorite
kings unite
against
Gibeon

(See Appendix D,
map 3)

¹ It happened when Adoni-zedek king of Jerusalem* heard that Joshua had conquered Ai and had destroyed it, as he had done to Jericho and its king so had he done to Ai and its king, and that the inhabitants of Gibeon had made peace with Israel and were in their midst: ² They feared greatly, because Gibeon was a great city, like one of the royal cities, and because it was greater than Ai and all its men were mighty. ³ So Adoni-zedek king of Jerusalem sent to Hoham king of Hebron, and to Piram king of Jarmuth, and to Japhia king of Lachish, and to Debir king of Eglon, saying, ⁴ "Come up to me and help me, and let us smite Gibeon, for it has made peace with Joshua and with the Children of Israel."

⁵ The five Amorite kings joined together and ascended — the king of Jerusalem, the king of Hebron, the king of Jarmuth, the king of Lachish, the king of Eglon — they and all their camps. They encamped at Gibeon and waged war against it.

⁶ The men of Gibeon sent to Joshua, to the camp, to Gilgal, saying, "Do not loosen your hands from your servants; come up to us quickly, save us and help us, for all the Amorite kings who dwell in the mountains have gathered against us."

Joshua
saves
Gibeon

⁷ Joshua ascended from Gilgal, he and all the people of war with him, and all the mighty warriors. ⁸ HASHEM said to Joshua, "Do not fear them, for I have delivered them into your hand; not a man of them shall stand against you."

⁹ Joshua came upon them suddenly; he had ascended from Gilgal all night. ¹⁰ HASHEM confounded them before Israel and smote them with a mighty blow at Gibeon. They pursued them by way of the ascent to Beth-horon and struck them until Azekah and until Makkedah. ¹¹ It happened when they fled before Israel; they were on the descent of Beth-horon when HASHEM cast

Hailstones
pummel
Israel's
enemies

upon them large stones from heaven until [they reached] Azekah and they died; more died through the hailstones than the Children of Israel killed with the sword.

¹² Then Joshua spoke to HASHEM on the day HASHEM delivered the Amorites before the Children of Israel, and he said before the eyes of Israel,* "Sun, stand

Joshua
orders the
sun to stand
still

still at Gibeon, and moon, in the Valley of Aijalon."

¹³ Then the sun stood still, and the moon stopped, until the people took retribution against their enemies. Is this not written in the Book of the Upright* So the sun stood in the middle of the sky and did not hasten to set for a whole day. ¹⁴ There was no day like that before it or after it, that HASHEM heeded the voice of a man, for HASHEM did battle for Israel.

¹⁵ Joshua and all Israel with him returned to the camp, to Gilgal. ¹⁶ These five kings had fled and were concealed in the cave at Makkedah. ¹⁷ It was told to Joshua, saying, "The five kings have been found concealed in the cave at Makkedah."

¹⁸ Joshua said, "Roll large stones up against the mouth of the cave and appoint men to guard them by it. ¹⁹ But you, do not stand still; pursue your enemies and attack their stragglers. Do not let them enter their cities, because

כ נְתָנָם יְהוָה אֱלֹהֵיכֶם בְּיֶדְכֶם: וַיְהִי כְּכַלּוֹת יְהוֹשֻׁעַ וּבְנֵי יִשְׂרָאֵל לְהַכּוֹתָם
מַכָּה גְדוֹלָה־מְאֹד עַד־תֻּמָּם וְהַשְּׂרִידִים שָׂרְדוּ מֵהֶם וַיָּבֹאוּ אֶל־עָרֵי
כא הַמִּבְצָר: וַיָּשֻׁבוּ כָל־הָעָם אֶל־הַמַּחֲנֶה אֶל־יְהוֹשֻׁעַ מַקֵּדָה בְּשָׁלוֹם לֹא־
כב חָרַץ לִבְנֵי יִשְׂרָאֵל לְאִישׁ אֶת־לְשֹׁנוֹ: וַיֹּאמֶר יְהוֹשֻׁעַ פִּתְחוּ אֶת־פִּי
הַמְּעָרָה וְהוֹצִיאוּ אֵלַי אֶת־חֲמֵשֶׁת הַמְּלָכִים הָאֵלֶּה מִן־הַמְּעָרָה: וַיַּעֲשׂוּ
כג כֵן וַיֹּצִיאוּ אֵלָיו אֶת־חֲמֵשֶׁת הַמְּלָכִים הָאֵלֶּה מִן־הַמְּעָרָה אֵת ׀ מֶלֶךְ
יְרוּשָׁלַ͏ִם אֶת־מֶלֶךְ חֶבְרוֹן אֶת־מֶלֶךְ יַרְמוּת אֶת־מֶלֶךְ לָכִישׁ אֶת־מֶלֶךְ
כד עֶגְלוֹן: וַיְהִי כְּהוֹצִיאָם אֶת־הַמְּלָכִים הָאֵלֶּה אֶל־יְהוֹשֻׁעַ וַיִּקְרָא יְהוֹשֻׁעַ
אֶל־כָּל־אִישׁ יִשְׂרָאֵל וַיֹּאמֶר אֶל־קְצִינֵי אַנְשֵׁי הַמִּלְחָמָה הֶהָלְכוּא אִתּוֹ
קִרְבוּ שִׂימוּ אֶת־רַגְלֵיכֶם עַל־צַוְּארֵי הַמְּלָכִים הָאֵלֶּה וַיִּקְרְבוּ וַיָּשִׂימוּ אֶת־
כה רַגְלֵיהֶם עַל־צַוְּארֵיהֶם: וַיֹּאמֶר אֲלֵיהֶם יְהוֹשֻׁעַ אַל־תִּירְאוּ וְאַל־תֵּחָתּוּ
חִזְקוּ וְאִמְצוּ כִּי כָכָה יַעֲשֶׂה יְהוָה לְכָל־אֹיְבֵיכֶם אֲשֶׁר אַתֶּם נִלְחָמִים
כו אוֹתָם: וַיַּכֵּם יְהוֹשֻׁעַ אַחֲרֵי־כֵן וַיְמִיתֵם וַיִּתְלֵם עַל חֲמִשָּׁה עֵצִים וַיִּהְיוּ
כז תְּלוּיִם עַל־הָעֵצִים עַד־הָעָרֶב: וַיְהִי לְעֵת ׀ בּוֹא הַשֶּׁמֶשׁ צִוָּה יְהוֹשֻׁעַ
וַיֹּרִידוּם מֵעַל הָעֵצִים וַיַּשְׁלִכֻם אֶל־הַמְּעָרָה אֲשֶׁר נֶחְבְּאוּ־שָׁם וַיָּשִׂמוּ
כח אֲבָנִים גְּדֹלוֹת עַל־פִּי הַמְּעָרָה עַד־עֶצֶם הַיּוֹם הַזֶּה: וְאֶת־
מַקֵּדָה לָכַד יְהוֹשֻׁעַ בַּיּוֹם הַהוּא וַיַּכֶּהָ לְפִי־חֶרֶב וְאֶת־מַלְכָּהּ הֶחֱרִם אוֹתָם
וְאֶת־כָּל־הַנֶּפֶשׁ אֲשֶׁר־בָּהּ לֹא הִשְׁאִיר שָׂרִיד וַיַּעַשׂ לְמֶלֶךְ מַקֵּדָה כַּאֲשֶׁר
כט עָשָׂה לְמֶלֶךְ יְרִיחוֹ:   וַיַּעֲבֹר יְהוֹשֻׁעַ וְכָל־יִשְׂרָאֵל עִמּוֹ מִמַּקֵּדָה
לִבְנָה וַיִּלָּחֶם עִם־לִבְנָה: וַיִּתֵּן יְהוָה גַּם־אוֹתָהּ בְּיַד יִשְׂרָאֵל וְאֶת־מַלְכָּהּ
ל וַיַּכֶּהָ לְפִי־חֶרֶב וְאֶת־כָּל־הַנֶּפֶשׁ אֲשֶׁר־בָּהּ לֹא־הִשְׁאִיר בָּהּ שָׂרִיד וַיַּעַשׂ
לא לְמַלְכָּהּ כַּאֲשֶׁר עָשָׂה לְמֶלֶךְ יְרִיחוֹ:   וַיַּעֲבֹר יְהוֹשֻׁעַ וְכָל־יִשְׂרָאֵל
עִמּוֹ מִלִּבְנָה לָכִישָׁה וַיִּחַן עָלֶיהָ וַיִּלָּחֶם בָּהּ: וַיִּתֵּן יְהוָה אֶת־לָכִישׁ בְּיַד
לב יִשְׂרָאֵל וַיִּלְכְּדָהּ בַּיּוֹם הַשֵּׁנִי וַיַּכֶּהָ לְפִי־חֶרֶב וְאֶת־כָּל־הַנֶּפֶשׁ אֲשֶׁר־בָּהּ
לג כְּכֹל אֲשֶׁר־עָשָׂה לְלִבְנָה: אָז עָלָה הֹרָם מֶלֶךְ גֶּזֶר לַעְזֹר אֶת־
לד לָכִישׁ וַיַּכֵּהוּ יְהוֹשֻׁעַ וְאֶת־עַמּוֹ עַד־בִּלְתִּי הִשְׁאִיר־לוֹ שָׂרִיד: וַיַּעֲבֹר
יְהוֹשֻׁעַ וְכָל־יִשְׂרָאֵל עִמּוֹ מִלָּכִישׁ עֶגְלֹנָה וַיַּחֲנוּ עָלֶיהָ וַיִּלָּחֲמוּ עָלֶיהָ:
לה וַיִּלְכְּדוּהָ בַּיּוֹם הַהוּא וַיַּכּוּהָ לְפִי־חֶרֶב וְאֵת כָּל־הַנֶּפֶשׁ אֲשֶׁר־בָּהּ בַּיּוֹם
לו הַהוּא הֶחֱרִים כְּכֹל אֲשֶׁר־עָשָׂה לְלָכִישׁ:   וַיַּעַל יְהוֹשֻׁעַ וְכָל־
יִשְׂרָאֵל עִמּוֹ מֵעֶגְלוֹנָה חֶבְרוֹנָה וַיִּלָּחֲמוּ עָלֶיהָ: וַיִּלְכְּדוּהָ וַיַּכּוּהָ לְפִי־
חֶרֶב וְאֶת־מַלְכָּהּ וְאֶת־כָּל־עָרֶיהָ וְאֶת־כָּל־הַנֶּפֶשׁ אֲשֶׁר־בָּהּ לֹא־
הִשְׁאִיר שָׂרִיד כְּכֹל אֲשֶׁר־עָשָׂה לְעֶגְלוֹן וַיַּחֲרֵם אוֹתָהּ וְאֶת־כָּל־הַנֶּפֶשׁ
לח אֲשֶׁר־בָּהּ:   וַיָּשָׁב יְהוֹשֻׁעַ וְכָל־יִשְׂרָאֵל עִמּוֹ דְּבִרָה וַיִּלָּחֶם

HASHEM, your God, has delivered them into your hand."

²⁰ It happened when Joshua and the Children of Israel finished striking them an exceedingly great blow until their annihilation* that the remnant that remained of them entered the fortified cities. ²¹ Then the entire nation [of Israel] returned to the camp, to Joshua, to Makkedah, in peace. No one [even] whetted his tongue against any man of the Children of Israel. ²² Joshua said, "Open the mouth of the cave and bring out to me those five kings from the cave."²³ So they did; they brought out to him those five kings from the cave — the king of Jerusalem, the king of Hebron, the king of Jarmuth, the king of Lachish, the king of Eglon. ²⁴ It happened when they brought out those kings to Joshua that Joshua summoned all the men of Israel and said to the officers of the men of war who had gone with him, "Approach, place your feet on the necks of these kings." They approached and placed their feet on their necks. * ²⁵ Joshua said to them, "Do not fear, and do not lose resolve; be strong and courageous, for thus shall HASHEM do to all your enemies with whom you battle." ²⁶ Joshua struck them after that and killed them, and hanged them on five gallows, and they remained hanging on the gallows until evening. ²⁷ It happened at the time the sun set that Joshua ordered and they lowered them from the gallows and they threw them into the cave in which they had concealed themselves. They placed large stones at the mouth of the cave — [which are there] to this very day.

Joshua kills the five kings

²⁸ Joshua captured Makkedah on that day, and smote it by the edge of the sword and its king he destroyed; [he killed] them and every soul that was in it; he did not leave a remnant. He did to the king of Makkedah as he had done to the king of Jericho.

City by city conquest: Makkedah (See Appendix D, map 3)

²⁹ Joshua and all Israel with him passed over from Makkedah to Libnah, and he waged war against Libnah. ³⁰ HASHEM also delivered it and its king into the hand of Israel; they smote it by the edge of the sword and every soul that was in it; he did not leave a remnant in it. He did to its king as he had done to the king of Jericho.

Libnah

³¹ Joshua and all Israel with him passed over from Libnah to Lachish; he encamped by it and waged war against it. ³² HASHEM delivered Lachish into the hand of Israel, and they conquered it on the second day. He smote it by the edge of the sword and every soul that was in it, like all that he had done to Libnah.

Lachish

³³ Then Horam, king of Gezer, went up to help Lachish. Joshua struck him and his people until he did not leave him a remnant.

Gezer

³⁴ Joshua and all Israel with him passed over from Lachish to Eglon; they encamped by it and waged war against it. ³⁵ On that day they conquered it and they struck it by the edge of the sword and destroyed every soul that was in it that day, like all that he had done to Lachish.

Eglon

³⁶ Joshua and all Israel with him went up from Eglon to Hebron and waged war against it. ³⁷ They conquered it and struck it by the edge of the sword — its king and all its villages and every soul that was in it; he did not leave a remnant, like all that he had done to Eglon. He destroyed it and every soul that was in it.

Hebron

³⁸ Joshua and all Israel with him returned to Debir and waged war against

Debir

10:20. Even though there were still some survivors, they were so few that, for all practical purposes, the entire army had been annihilated (*Metzudos*).

10:24. This was to symbolize that the Jews had nothing to fear from any of the Canaanite kings.

לט עָלֶ֔יהָ וַֽיִּלְכְּדָ֜הּ וְאֶת־מַלְכָּ֣הּ וְאֶת־כָּל־עָרֶ֗יהָ וַיַּכּ֣וּם לְפִי־חֶ֙רֶב֙ וַיַּחֲרִ֙ימוּ֙ אֶת־כָּל־נֶ֙פֶשׁ֙ אֲשֶׁר־בָּ֔הּ לֹ֥א הִשְׁאִ֖יר שָׂרִ֑יד כַּאֲשֶׁ֙ר עָשָׂ֜ה לְחֶבְר֗וֹן כֵּן־

מ עָשָׂ֤ה לִדְבִרָה֙ וּלְמַלְכָּ֔הּ וְכַאֲשֶׁ֥ר עָשָׂ֖ה לְלִבְנָ֥ה וּלְמַלְכָּֽהּ: וַיַּכֶּ֣ה יְהוֹשֻׁ֣עַ אֶת־כָּל־הָאָ֡רֶץ הָהָר֩ וְהַנֶּ֙גֶב וְהַשְּׁפֵלָ֜ה וְהָאֲשֵׁד֗וֹת וְאֵ֖ת כָּל־מַלְכֵיהֶ֑ם לֹ֤א הִשְׁאִ֙יר שָׂרִ֔יד וְאֵ֤ת כָּל־הַנְּשָׁמָה֙ הֶחֱרִ֔ים כַּאֲשֶׁ֣ר צִוָּ֔ה יְהוָ֖ה אֱלֹהֵ֥י

מא יִשְׂרָאֵֽל: וַיַּכֵּ֧ם יְהוֹשֻׁ֛עַ מִקָּדֵ֥שׁ בַּרְנֵ֖עַ וְעַד־עַזָּ֑ה וְאֵ֛ת כָּל־אֶ֥רֶץ גֹּ֖שֶׁן וְעַד־

מב גִּבְעֽוֹן: וְאֵ֣ת כָּל־הַמְּלָכִ֤ים הָאֵ֙לֶּה֙ וְאֶת־אַרְצָ֔ם לָכַ֥ד יְהוֹשֻׁ֖עַ פַּ֣עַם אֶחָ֑ת

מג כִּ֚י יְהוָ֣ה אֱלֹהֵ֣י יִשְׂרָאֵ֔ל נִלְחָ֖ם לְיִשְׂרָאֵֽל: וַיָּ֤שָׁב יְהוֹשֻׁ֙עַ֙ וְכָל־יִשְׂרָאֵ֣ל עִמּ֔וֹ אֶל־הַֽמַּחֲנֶ֖ה הַגִּלְגָּֽלָה: יא   א וַיְהִ֕י כִּשְׁמֹ֖עַ יָבִ֣ין מֶֽלֶךְ־

חָצ֑וֹר וַיִּשְׁלַ֗ח אֶל־יוֹבָב֙ מֶ֣לֶךְ מָד֔וֹן וְאֶל־מֶ֥לֶךְ שִׁמְר֖וֹן וְאֶל־מֶ֥לֶךְ אַכְשָֽׁף:

ב וְֽאֶל־הַמְּלָכִ֞ים אֲשֶׁ֣ר מִצְּפ֗וֹן בָּהָ֧ר וּבָעֲרָבָ֛ה נֶ֥גֶב כִּנְר֖וֹת וּבַשְּׁפֵלָ֑ה

ג וּבְנָפ֥וֹת דּ֖וֹר מִיָּֽם: הַֽכְּנַעֲנִי֙ מִמִּזְרָ֣ח וּמִיָּ֔ם וְהָאֱמֹרִ֙י וְהַחִתִּ֤י וְהַפְּרִזִּי֙ וְהַיְבוּסִ֔י

ד בָּהָ֑ר וְהַֽחִוִּי֙ תַּ֣חַת חֶרְמ֔וֹן בְּאֶ֖רֶץ הַמִּצְפָּֽה: וַיֵּצְא֣וּ הֵ֗ם וְכָל־מַחֲנֵיהֶם֙ עִמָּ֔ם

ה עַם־רָ֕ב כַּח֛וֹל אֲשֶׁ֥ר עַל־שְׂפַת־הַיָּ֖ם לָרֹ֑ב וְס֥וּס וָרֶ֖כֶב רַב־מְאֹֽד: וַיִּוָּ֣עֲד֔וּ כֹּ֖ל הַמְּלָכִ֣ים הָאֵ֑לֶּה וַיָּבֹ֜אוּ וַיַּחֲנ֤וּ יַחְדָּו֙ אֶל־מֵ֣י מֵר֔וֹם לְהִלָּחֵ֖ם עִם־

ו יִשְׂרָאֵֽל: וַיֹּ֙אמֶר יְהוָ֤ה אֶל־יְהוֹשֻׁ֙עַ֙ אַל־תִּירָ֣א מִפְּנֵיהֶ֔ם כִּֽי־מָחָ֞ר כָּעֵ֤ת הַזֹּאת֙ אָנֹכִ֗י נֹתֵ֧ן אֶת־כֻּלָּ֛ם חֲלָלִ֖ים לִפְנֵ֣י יִשְׂרָאֵ֑ל

ז אֶת־סוּסֵיהֶ֣ם תְּעַקֵּ֔ר וְאֶת־מַרְכְּבֹתֵיהֶ֖ם תִּשְׂרֹ֥ף בָּאֵֽשׁ: וַיָּבֹ֣א יְהוֹשֻׁ֡עַ וְכָל־עַם֩ הַמִּלְחָמָ֙ה עִמּ֜וֹ עֲלֵיהֶ֛ם עַל־מֵ֥י מֵר֖וֹם פִּתְאֹ֑ם וַֽיִּפְּל֖וּ בָּהֶֽם:

ח וַיִּתְּנֵ֙ם יְהוָ֣ה בְּיַֽד־יִשְׂרָאֵל֮ וַיַּכּוּם֒ וַֽיִּרְדְּפ֞וּם עַד־צִיד֣וֹן רַבָּ֗ה וְעַד֙ מִשְׂרְפ֣וֹת מַ֔יִם וְעַד־בִּקְעַ֥ת מִצְפֶּ֖ה מִזְרָ֑חָה וַיַּכֻּ֕ם עַד־בִּלְתִּ֥י הִשְׁאִֽיר־לָהֶ֖ם שָׂרִֽיד:

ט וַיַּ֧עַשׂ לָהֶ֛ם יְהוֹשֻׁ֖עַ כַּאֲשֶׁ֣ר אָֽמַר־ל֣וֹ יְהוָ֑ה אֶת־סוּסֵיהֶ֣ם עִקֵּ֔ר וְאֶת־

י מַרְכְּבֹתֵיהֶ֖ם שָׂרַ֥ף בָּאֵֽשׁ: וַיָּ֙שָׁב יְהוֹשֻׁ֜עַ בָּעֵ֤ת הַהִיא֙ וַיִּלְכֹּ֣ד אֶת־חָצ֔וֹר וְאֶת־מַלְכָּ֖הּ הִכָּ֣ה בֶחָ֑רֶב כִּֽי־חָצ֣וֹר לְפָנִ֔ים הִ֥יא

יא רֹ֖אשׁ כָּל־הַמַּמְלָכ֥וֹת הָאֵֽלֶּה: וַ֠יַּכּוּ אֶת־כָּל־הַנֶּ֙פֶשׁ אֲשֶׁר־בָּ֤הּ לְפִי־חֶ֙רֶב֙ הַֽחֲרֵ֔ם לֹ֥א נוֹתַ֖ר כָּל־נְשָׁמָ֑ה וְאֶת־חָצ֖וֹר שָׂרַ֥ף בָּאֵֽשׁ: וְֽאֶת־כָּל־עָרֵ֙י

יב הַמְּלָכִֽים־הָאֵ֜לֶּה וְֽאֶת־כָּל־מַלְכֵיהֶ֗ם לָכַ֧ד יְהוֹשֻׁ֛עַ וַיַּכֵּ֥ם לְפִי־חֶ֖רֶב הֶחֱרִ֣ים אוֹתָ֑ם כַּאֲשֶׁ֣ר צִוָּ֔ה מֹשֶׁ֖ה עֶ֥בֶד יְהוָֽה: רַ֣ק כָּל־הֶֽעָרִים֙ הָעֹמְד֣וֹת

יג עַל־תִּלָּ֔ם לֹ֥א שְׂרָפָ֖ם יִשְׂרָאֵ֑ל זוּלָתִ֛י אֶת־חָצ֥וֹר לְבַדָּ֖הּ שָׂרַ֥ף יְהוֹשֻֽׁעַ:

יד וְ֠כֹל שְׁלַ֙ל הֶעָרִ֤ים הָאֵ֙לֶּה֙ וְהַבְּהֵמָ֔ה בָּזְז֥וּ לָהֶ֖ם בְּנֵ֣י יִשְׂרָאֵ֑ל רַ֣ק אֶֽת־כָּל־הָאָדָ֞ם הִכּ֣וּ לְפִי־חֶ֗רֶב עַד־הִשְׁמִדָם֙ אוֹתָ֔ם לֹ֥א הִשְׁאִ֖ירוּ כָּל־

טו נְשָׁמָֽה: כַּאֲשֶׁ֙ר צִוָּ֤ה יְהוָה֙ אֶת־מֹשֶׁ֣ה עַבְדּ֔וֹ כֵּן־צִוָּ֥ה מֹשֶׁ֖ה אֶת־יְהוֹשֻׁ֑עַ וְכֵ֤ן עָשָׂה֙ יְהוֹשֻׁ֔עַ לֹֽא־הֵסִ֣יר דָּבָ֔ר מִכֹּ֛ל אֲשֶׁר־צִוָּ֥ה יְהוָ֖ה אֶת־מֹשֶֽׁה:

11:1. After the Israelites' success in their campaign against the Canaanites in the South, they turned to the final stage of their conquest — the northern Canaanite kingdoms. Again, Divine Providence assisted them, as it. [39] He conquered it and its king and all its villages, and he struck them with the edge of the sword and destroyed every soul that was in it; he did not leave a remnant. As he had done to Hebron, so he did to Debir and to its king, and as *The* he had done to Libnah and to its king. [40] Joshua smote the entire land — the *conclusion* mountain, the South, the lowland, the [land of the] waterfalls and all their *of the* kings. He did not leave a remnant. He destroyed every soul as HASHEM, God of *southern* Israel, had commanded. [41] Joshua smote them from Kadesh-barnea to Gaza *conquest* and the entire land of Goshen to Gibeon. [42] All those kings and their land Joshua conquered at the same time, because HASHEM, God of Israel, was waging war for Israel. [43] Joshua and all Israel with him returned to the camp, to Gilgal.

11   [1] It happened when Jabin king of Hazor heard: * He sent to Jobab king of Madon, to the king of Shimron, and to the king of Achshaph, [2] and to the
THE   kings who were from the north, in the mountain, and in the plain south of
CONQUEST   Kinnereth, and in the lowland and in the districts of Dor to the west; [3] the
OF THE   Canaanite on the east and on the west; and the Amorite and the Hittite and the
NORTH   Perizzite and the Jebusite in the mountain; and the Hivvite at the foothills of
11:1-15   Hermon in the land of Mizpah. [4] They went out — they and all their camps with
(See Appendix D, them — many people, [as numerous] as the sand on the seashore, and very
map 3)   many horses and chariots. [5] All these kings gathered [together]; they came and
             encamped together at the waters of Merom to wage war with Israel.

[6] HASHEM said to Joshua, "Do not fear them, for tomorrow at this time I will deliver them all as corpses before Israel. You shall hamstring their horses and burn their chariots in fire."

Joshua's   [7] Joshua and all the people of war with him attacked them suddenly at the
preemptive waters of Merom and fell upon them. [8] HASHEM delivered them into the hand
strike   of Israel, and they struck them and pursued them all the way to the Great
             Sidon and Misrephoth-maim and to the Valley of Mizpeh eastward. They struck
             them until they had not left them a remnant. [9] Joshua dealt with them as
             HASHEM had told him; he hamstrung their horses and burned their chariots in
             fire.

[10] Joshua turned back at that time and conquered Hazor and struck its king with the sword, because Hazor had formerly been the leader of all those kingdoms. [11] They smote every soul that was in it, destroying them by the edge of the sword; not a soul was left. He burned Hazor in fire. [12] Joshua conquered all the cities of these kings and all their kings; he struck them with the edge of the sword, destroying them, as Moses the servant of HASHEM had commanded. [13] However, all the cities [whose walls] remained steadfast, Israel did not burn. Only Hazor alone did Joshua burn. * [14] All the spoils of these cities and the livestock, the Children of Israel took for themselves as booty; but they struck every man by the edge of the sword until they exterminated them. They did not leave any soul. [15] As HASHEM had commanded Moses His servant, so Moses commanded Joshua; and so Joshua did. He did not omit a thing of all that HASHEM had commanded Moses.

---

the king of Hazor formed a confederacy of the most powerful northern kingdoms to attack the Israelites, thus enabling Joshua to strike the unsuspecting confederacy

while it was organizing its attack against the Israelites. **11:13.** Joshua did not burn the cities whose walls remained intact. The only city he razed was Hazor (*Rashi*).

טז וַיִּקַּח יְהוֹשֻׁעַ אֶת־כָּל־הָאָרֶץ הַזֹּאת הָהָר וְאֶת־כָּל־הַנֶּגֶב וְאֵת כָּל־אֶרֶץ
הַגֹּשֶׁן וְאֶת־הַשְּׁפֵלָה וְאֶת־הָעֲרָבָה וְאֶת־הַר יִשְׂרָאֵל וּשְׁפֵלָתֹה: מִן־הָהָר
יז הֶחָלָק הָעוֹלֶה שֵׂעִיר וְעַד־בַּעַל־גָּד בְּבִקְעַת הַלְּבָנוֹן תַּחַת הַר־חֶרְמוֹן
יח וְאֵת כָּל־מַלְכֵיהֶם לָכַד וַיַּכֵּם וַיְמִיתֵם: יָמִים רַבִּים עָשָׂה יְהוֹשֻׁעַ אֶת־
יט כָּל־הַמְּלָכִים הָאֵלֶּה מִלְחָמָה: לֹא־הָיְתָה עִיר אֲשֶׁר הִשְׁלִימָה אֶל־בְּנֵי
כ יִשְׂרָאֵל בִּלְתִּי הַחִוִּי יֹשְׁבֵי גִבְעוֹן אֶת־הַכֹּל לָקְחוּ בַמִּלְחָמָה: כִּי־מֵאֵת
יְהֹוָה ׀ הָיְתָה לְחַזֵּק אֶת־לִבָּם לִקְרַאת הַמִּלְחָמָה אֶת־יִשְׂרָאֵל לְמַעַן
הַחֲרִימָם לְבִלְתִּי הֱיוֹת־לָהֶם תְּחִנָּה כִּי לְמַעַן הַשְׁמִידָם כַּאֲשֶׁר צִוָּה יְהֹוָה
כא אֶת־מֹשֶׁה: וַיָּבֹא יְהוֹשֻׁעַ בָּעֵת הַהִיא וַיַּכְרֵת אֶת־הָעֲנָקִים
מִן־הָהָר מִן־חֶבְרוֹן מִן־דְּבִר מִן־עֲנָב וּמִכֹּל הַר יְהוּדָה וּמִכֹּל הַר יִשְׂרָאֵל
כב עִם־עָרֵיהֶם הֶחֱרִימָם יְהוֹשֻׁעַ: לֹא־נוֹתַר עֲנָקִים בְּאֶרֶץ בְּנֵי יִשְׂרָאֵל רַק
כג בְּעַזָּה בְּגַת וּבְאַשְׁדּוֹד נִשְׁאָרוּ: וַיִּקַּח יְהוֹשֻׁעַ אֶת־כָּל־הָאָרֶץ כְּכֹל אֲשֶׁר
דִּבֶּר יְהֹוָה אֶל־מֹשֶׁה וַיִּתְּנָהּ יְהוֹשֻׁעַ לְנַחֲלָה לְיִשְׂרָאֵל כְּמַחְלְקֹתָם
לְשִׁבְטֵיהֶם וְהָאָרֶץ שָׁקְטָה מִמִּלְחָמָה:

יב א וְאֵלֶּה ׀ מַלְכֵי
הָאָרֶץ אֲשֶׁר הִכּוּ בְנֵי־יִשְׂרָאֵל וַיִּרְשׁוּ אֶת־אַרְצָם בְּעֵבֶר הַיַּרְדֵּן מִזְרְחָה
ב הַשֶּׁמֶשׁ מִנַּחַל אַרְנוֹן עַד־הַר חֶרְמוֹן וְכָל־הָעֲרָבָה מִזְרָחָה: סִיחוֹן מֶלֶךְ
הָאֱמֹרִי הַיּוֹשֵׁב בְּחֶשְׁבּוֹן מֹשֵׁל מֵעֲרוֹעֵר אֲשֶׁר עַל־שְׂפַת־נַחַל אַרְנוֹן וְתוֹךְ
ג הַנַּחַל וַחֲצִי הַגִּלְעָד וְעַד יַבֹּק הַנַּחַל גְּבוּל בְּנֵי עַמּוֹן: וְהָעֲרָבָה עַד־יָם
כִּנְרוֹת מִזְרָחָה וְעַד יָם הָעֲרָבָה יָם־הַמֶּלַח מִזְרָחָה דֶּרֶךְ בֵּית הַיְשִׁמוֹת
ד וּמִתֵּימָן תַּחַת אַשְׁדּוֹת הַפִּסְגָּה: וּגְבוּל עוֹג מֶלֶךְ הַבָּשָׁן מִיֶּתֶר הָרְפָאִים
ה הַיּוֹשֵׁב בְּעַשְׁתָּרוֹת וּבְאֶדְרֶעִי: וּמֹשֵׁל בְּהַר חֶרְמוֹן וּבְסַלְכָה וּבְכָל־הַבָּשָׁן
עַד־גְּבוּל הַגְּשׁוּרִי וְהַמַּעֲכָתִי וַחֲצִי הַגִּלְעָד גְּבוּל סִיחוֹן מֶלֶךְ־חֶשְׁבּוֹן:
ו מֹשֶׁה עֶבֶד־יְהֹוָה וּבְנֵי יִשְׂרָאֵל הִכּוּם וַיִּתְּנָהּ מֹשֶׁה עֶבֶד־יְהֹוָה יְרֻשָּׁה
ז לָרֻאוּבֵנִי וְלַגָּדִי וְלַחֲצִי שֵׁבֶט הַמְנַשֶּׁה: וְאֵלֶּה מַלְכֵי
הָאָרֶץ אֲשֶׁר הִכָּה יְהוֹשֻׁעַ וּבְנֵי יִשְׂרָאֵל בְּעֵבֶר הַיַּרְדֵּן יָמָּה מִבַּעַל גָּד
בְּבִקְעַת הַלְּבָנוֹן וְעַד־הָהָר הֶחָלָק הָעֹלֶה שֵׂעִירָה וַיִּתְּנָהּ יְהוֹשֻׁעַ לְשִׁבְטֵי
ח יִשְׂרָאֵל יְרֻשָּׁה כְּמַחְלְקֹתָם: בָּהָר וּבַשְּׁפֵלָה וּבָעֲרָבָה וּבָאֲשֵׁדוֹת וּבַמִּדְבָּר
וּבַנֶּגֶב הַחִתִּי הָאֱמֹרִי וְהַכְּנַעֲנִי הַפְּרִזִּי הַחִוִּי וְהַיְבוּסִי:

ט מֶלֶךְ יְרִיחוֹ אֶחָד
מֶלֶךְ הָעַי אֲשֶׁר־מִצַּד בֵּית־אֵל אֶחָד:
י מֶלֶךְ יְרוּשָׁלַ͏ִם אֶחָד
מֶלֶךְ חֶבְרוֹן אֶחָד:

11:16. The mountain was named for Jacob (Israel), who had lived there.

11:21. The Anakim were a family of giants that lived in the Hebron area and terrified all their opponents.

11:22. These were Philistine cities. Goliath, the giant slain by David, was from Gath (*I Samuel* 17:23).

11:23. When the Canaanites ceased their futile attempts at battle the Jews stopped the war, although much of the

SUMMARY
OF THE
CONQUESTS
11:16-12:24

¹⁶ And Joshua took this entire land: the mountain and the entire South and the entire land of Goshen and the lowland and the Arabah and Mount Israel* and its lowland. ¹⁷ From the split mountain that ascends to Seir, to the plain of Gad in the valley of the Lebanon at the foot of Mount Hermon; he conquered all their kings, struck them, and killed them.

¹⁸ Joshua waged war with all these kings for a long time. ¹⁹ There was not a city that made peace with the Children of Israel except for the Hivvite inhabitants of Gibeon; they took everything in battle. ²⁰ For it was from HASHEM, to harden their hearts toward battle against Israel, in order to destroy them — that they not find favor — so that they would be exterminated, as HASHEM had commanded Moses.

²¹ At that time Joshua came and cut down the Anakim* from the mountain, from Hebron, from Debir, from Anab and from all the Mountains of Judah, and from all of Mount Israel; Joshua destroyed them with their cities. ²² No Anakim were left in the land of the Children of Israel; however, in Gaza, Gath, and Ashdod* they remained. ²³ Thus, Joshua took the entire land, according to all that HASHEM had spoken to Moses. Joshua gave it to Israel as a heritage, according to their divisions, to their tribes. The land then rested from war.*

12

Moses'
conquest:
Sihon's
territory
(See Appendix D,
map 1)

Og's territory

¹ **T**hese are the kings of the land whom the Children of Israel smote* and whose land they inherited on the other side of the Jordan, towards the rising sun, from the River Arnon to Mount Hermon and the entire plain to the east: ² Sihon, king of the Amorite, who dwelled in Heshbon and who ruled from Aroer, that is on the edge of the River Arnon, and the middle of the river, and half of the Gilead, until the River Jabbok, the border of the Children of Ammon; ³ and the plain until the Kinnereth Sea to the east and until the sea of the plain, the Salt [Dead] Sea, to the east, the way to Beth-jeshimoth; and from the south under the falls of Pisgah. ⁴ And the boundary of Og, king of Bashan, who was a remnant of the giants, who lived in Ashtaroth and in Edrei, ⁵ and who reigned in Mount Hermon and Salcah, and in all of Bashan up to the border of the Geshurite and the Maacathite and half of the Gilead, [up to] the border of Sihon, king of Heshbon. ⁶ Moses, servant of HASHEM, and the Children of Israel defeated them; and Moses, servant of HASHEM, gave it as an inheritance to the Reubenite and to the Gadite and to half the tribe of Manasseh.

Joshua's
conquest
(See Appendix D,
map 3)

⁷ These are the kings of the land whom Joshua and the Children of Israel smote on the western side of the Jordan, from the plain of Gad in the Lebanon valley to the split mountain that ascends to Seir; Joshua gave it as an inheritance to the tribes of Israel according to their divisions, ⁸ in the mountain and in the lowland, in the plain and in [the land of] the waterfalls, and in the wilderness and in the South — the Hittite, the Amorite and the Canaanite, the Perizzite, the Hivvite and the Jebusite:

The
thirty-one
Canaanite
kings

⁹ The king of Jericho,   one;
the king of Ai, which was near Beth-el,   one;
¹⁰ the king of Jerusalem,   one;
the king of Hebron,   one;

---

land was yet to be conquered. However, before his death, Joshua exhorted them to complete their occupation of the land or face disastrous consequences (Ch. 23).

12:1. The previous chapter ends with the conclusion of

Joshua's battles, the close of the seven years of conquest and the beginning of the seven years of division. This chapter records all the territories that the Israelites had conquered until this time, under both Moses and Joshua.

מֶ֣לֶךְ יַרְמוּת֙	יא	אֶחָ֔ד
מֶ֥לֶךְ לָכִ֖ישׁ		אֶחָ֑ד׃
מֶ֤לֶךְ עֶגְלוֹן֙	יב	אֶחָ֔ד
מֶ֥לֶךְ גֶּ֖זֶר		אֶחָ֑ד׃
מֶ֣לֶךְ דְּבִ֔ר	יג	אֶחָ֔ד
מֶ֥לֶךְ גֶּ֖דֶר		אֶחָ֑ד׃
מֶ֤לֶךְ חָרְמָה֙	יד	אֶחָ֔ד
מֶ֥לֶךְ עֲרָ֖ד		אֶחָ֑ד׃
מֶ֣לֶךְ לִבְנָ֔ה	טו	אֶחָ֔ד
מֶ֥לֶךְ עֲדֻלָּ֖ם		אֶחָ֑ד׃
מֶ֤לֶךְ מַקֵּדָה֙	טז	אֶחָ֔ד
מֶ֥לֶךְ בֵּֽית־אֵ֖ל		אֶחָ֑ד׃
מֶ֤לֶךְ תַּפּ֙וּחַ֙	יז	אֶחָ֔ד
מֶ֥לֶךְ חֵ֖פֶר		אֶחָ֑ד׃
מֶ֤לֶךְ אֲפֵק֙	יח	אֶחָ֔ד
מֶ֥לֶךְ לַשָּׁר֖וֹן		אֶחָ֑ד׃
מֶ֤לֶךְ מָדוֹן֙	יט	אֶחָ֔ד
מֶ֥לֶךְ חָצ֖וֹר		אֶחָ֑ד׃
מֶ֤לֶךְ שִׁמְרוֹן֙ מְראֹ֔ון	כ	אֶחָ֔ד
מֶ֥לֶךְ אַכְשָׁ֖ף		אֶחָ֑ד׃
מֶ֤לֶךְ תַּעְנַךְ֙	כא	אֶחָ֔ד
מֶ֥לֶךְ מְגִדּ֖וֹ		אֶחָ֑ד׃
מֶ֤לֶךְ קֶ֙דֶשׁ֙	כב	אֶחָ֔ד
מֶ֥לֶךְ יׇקְנְעָ֖ם לַכַּרְמֶֽל		אֶחָ֑ד׃
מֶ֤לֶךְ דּוֹר֙ לְנָפַ֣ת דּ֔וֹר	כג	אֶחָ֔ד
מֶֽלֶךְ־גּוֹיִ֖ם לְגִלְגָּֽל		אֶחָ֑ד׃
מֶ֥לֶךְ תִּרְצָ֖ה	כד	אֶחָ֑ד

כׇּל־מְלָכִ֖ים שְׁלֹשִׁ֥ים וְאֶחָֽד׃

יג א וִיהוֹשֻׁ֣עַ זָקֵ֔ן בָּ֖א בַּיָּמִ֑ים וַיֹּ֨אמֶר יְהֹוָ֜ה אֵלָ֗יו אַתָּ֤ה זָקַ֙נְתָּה֙ בָּ֣אתָ בַיָּמִ֔ים וְהָאָ֛רֶץ
ב נִשְׁאֲרָ֥ה הַרְבֵּֽה־מְאֹ֖ד לְרִשְׁתָּֽהּ׃ זֹ֥את הָאָ֖רֶץ הַנִּשְׁאָ֑רֶת כׇּל־גְּלִילֹ֣ות
ג הַפְּלִשְׁתִּ֔ים וְכׇל־הַגְּשׁוּרִֽי׃ מִן־הַשִּׁיח֗וֹר אֲשֶׁ֣ר ׀ עַל־פְּנֵ֣י מִצְרַ֔יִם וְעַ֨ד גְּב֤וּל
עֶקְרוֹן֙ צָפ֔וֹנָה לַֽכְּנַעֲנִ֖י תֵּחָשֵׁ֑ב חֲמֵ֣שֶׁת ׀ סַרְנֵ֣י פְלִשְׁתִּ֗ים הָעַזָּתִ֤י וְהָאַשְׁדּוֹדִי֙
ד הָאֶשְׁקְלוֹנִ֣י הַגִּתִּ֔י וְהָעֶקְרוֹנִ֖י וְהָעַוִּֽים׃ מִתֵּימָ֞ן כׇּל־אֶ֣רֶץ הַֽכְּנַעֲנִ֗י וּמְעָרָה֙ אֲשֶׁ֣ר
ה לַצִּ֣ידֹנִ֔ים עַד־אֲפֵ֖קָה עַ֣ד גְּב֣וּל הָאֱמֹרִֽי׃ וְהָאָ֣רֶץ הַגִּבְלִ֗י וְכׇל־הַלְּבָנוֹן֙ מִזְרַ֣ח
ו הַשֶּׁ֔מֶשׁ מִבַּ֣עַל גָּ֔ד תַּ֖חַת הַר־חֶרְמ֑וֹן עַ֖ד לְב֣וֹא חֲמָ֑ת כׇּל־יֹשְׁבֵ֣י הָהָ֡ר

¹¹ *the king of Jarmuth,*   *one;*
the king of Lachish,   *one;*
¹² *the king of Eglon,*   *one;*
the king of Gezer,   *one;*
¹³ *the king of Debir,*   *one;*
the king of Geder,   *one;*
¹⁴ *the king of Hormah,*   *one;*
the king of Arad,   *one;*
¹⁵ *the king of Libnah,*   *one;*
the king of Adullam,   *one;*
¹⁶ *the king of Makkedah,*   *one;*
the king of Beth-el,   *one;*
¹⁷ *the king of Tappuah,*   *one;*
the king of Hepher,   *one;*
¹⁸ *the king of Aphek,*   *one;*
the king of the Sharon,   *one;*
¹⁹ *the king of Madon,*   *one;*
the king of Hazor,   *one;*
²⁰ *the king of Shimron Meron,*   *one;*
the king of Achshaph,   *one;*
²¹ *the king of Taanach,*   *one;*
the king of Megiddo,   *one;*
²² *the king of Kedesh,*   *one;*
the king of Jokneam in the Carmel,   *one;*
²³ *the king of Dor, of the district of Dor,*   *one;*
the king of Goiim in Gilgal,   *one;*
²⁴ *the king of Tirzah,*   *one;*
all the kings, thirty-one.

13

**DIVISION OF
THE LAND
13:1-21:40**
(See Appendix D,
map 4)

¹ Joshua *was old, well on in years, and* Hashem *said to him, "You have grown old, you are well on in years, and very much land still remains to be possessed.* ² *This is the land that remains: all the districts of the Philistines and all the Geshurite [territory];* ³ *from the Shihor that is before Egypt to the border of Ekron northward is considered to be the Canaanite's [territory]; the five governors of the Philistines, [who are] the Gazite and the Ashdodite and the Ashkelonite, the Gittite and the Ekronite; and the Avvites.* ⁴ *From the south: all the land of the Canaanite; Mearah that belongs to the Sidonians to Aphekah, until the border of the Amorite;* ⁵ *and the land of the Giblite, and all the Lebanon toward the rising sun — from the plain of Gad at the foot of Mount Hermon until the approach to Hamath;* ⁶ *all the inhabitants of the mountains,*

מִן־הַלְּבָנוֹן עַד־מִשְׂרְפֹת מַיִם כָּל־צִידֹנִים אָנֹכִי אוֹרִישֵׁם מִפְּנֵי בְּנֵי
ז יִשְׂרָאֵל רַק הַפִּלֶהָ לְיִשְׂרָאֵל בְּנַחֲלָה כַּאֲשֶׁר צִוִּיתִיךָ: וְעַתָּה חַלֵּק אֶת־
ח הָאָרֶץ הַזֹּאת בְּנַחֲלָה לְתִשְׁעַת הַשְּׁבָטִים וַחֲצִי הַשֵּׁבֶט הַמְנַשֶּׁה: עִמּוֹ
הָרְאוּבֵנִי וְהַגָּדִי לָקְחוּ נַחֲלָתָם אֲשֶׁר נָתַן לָהֶם מֹשֶׁה בְּעֵבֶר הַיַּרְדֵּן מִזְרָחָה
ט כַּאֲשֶׁר נָתַן לָהֶם מֹשֶׁה עֶבֶד יְהוָה: מֵעֲרוֹעֵר אֲשֶׁר עַל־שְׂפַת־נַחַל אַרְנוֹן
י וְהָעִיר אֲשֶׁר בְּתוֹךְ־הַנַּחַל וְכָל־הַמִּישֹׁר מֵידְבָא עַד־דִּיבוֹן: וְכֹל עָרֵי
יא סִיחוֹן מֶלֶךְ הָאֱמֹרִי אֲשֶׁר מָלַךְ בְּחֶשְׁבּוֹן עַד־גְּבוּל בְּנֵי עַמּוֹן: וְהַגִּלְעָד
יב וּגְבוּל הַגְּשׁוּרִי וְהַמַּעֲכָתִי וְכֹל הַר חֶרְמוֹן וְכָל־הַבָּשָׁן עַד־סַלְכָה: כָּל־
מַמְלְכוּת עוֹג בַּבָּשָׁן אֲשֶׁר מָלַךְ בְּעַשְׁתָּרוֹת וּבְאֶדְרֶעִי הוּא נִשְׁאַר מִיֶּתֶר
יג הָרְפָאִים וַיַּכֵּם מֹשֶׁה וַיֹּרִשֵׁם: וְלֹא הוֹרִישׁוּ בְּנֵי יִשְׂרָאֵל אֶת־הַגְּשׁוּרִי וְאֶת־
הַמַּעֲכָתִי וַיֵּשֶׁב גְּשׁוּר וּמַעֲכָת בְּקֶרֶב יִשְׂרָאֵל עַד הַיּוֹם הַזֶּה: רַק לְשֵׁבֶט
יד הַלֵּוִי לֹא נָתַן נַחֲלָה אִשֵּׁי יְהוָה אֱלֹהֵי יִשְׂרָאֵל הוּא נַחֲלָתוֹ כַּאֲשֶׁר דִּבֶּר־
טו-טז לוֹ: וַיִּתֵּן מֹשֶׁה לְמַטֵּה בְנֵי־רְאוּבֵן לְמִשְׁפְּחֹתָם: וַיְהִי לָהֶם הַגְּבוּל
מֵעֲרוֹעֵר אֲשֶׁר עַל־שְׂפַת־נַחַל אַרְנוֹן וְהָעִיר אֲשֶׁר בְּתוֹךְ־הַנַּחַל וְכָל־
יז הַמִּישֹׁר עַל־מֵידְבָא: חֶשְׁבּוֹן וְכָל־עָרֶיהָ אֲשֶׁר בַּמִּישֹׁר דִּיבוֹן וּבָמוֹת בַּעַל
יח-יט וּבֵית בַּעַל מְעוֹן: וְיַהְצָה וּקְדֵמֹת וּמֵפָעַת: וְקִרְיָתַיִם וְשִׂבְמָה וְצֶרֶת הַשַּׁחַר
כ-כא בְּהַר הָעֵמֶק: וּבֵית פְּעוֹר וְאַשְׁדּוֹת הַפִּסְגָּה וּבֵית הַיְשִׁמוֹת: וְכֹל עָרֵי
הַמִּישֹׁר וְכָל־מַמְלְכוּת סִיחוֹן מֶלֶךְ הָאֱמֹרִי אֲשֶׁר מָלַךְ בְּחֶשְׁבּוֹן אֲשֶׁר
הִכָּה מֹשֶׁה אֹתוֹ וְאֶת־נְשִׂיאֵי מִדְיָן אֶת־אֱוִי וְאֶת־רֶקֶם וְאֶת־צוּר וְאֶת־
כב חוּר וְאֶת־רֶבַע נְסִיכֵי סִיחוֹן יֹשְׁבֵי הָאָרֶץ: וְאֶת־בִּלְעָם בֶּן־בְּעוֹר הַקּוֹסֵם
כג הָרְגוּ בְנֵי־יִשְׂרָאֵל בַּחֶרֶב אֶל־חַלְלֵיהֶם: וַיְהִי גְּבוּל בְּנֵי רְאוּבֵן הַיַּרְדֵּן וּגְבוּל
כד וְזֹאת נַחֲלַת בְּנֵי־רְאוּבֵן לְמִשְׁפְּחֹתָם הֶעָרִים וְחַצְרֵיהֶן: וַיִּתֵּן
כה מֹשֶׁה לְמַטֵּה גָד לִבְנֵי גָד לְמִשְׁפְּחֹתָם: וַיְהִי לָהֶם הַגְּבוּל יַעְזֵר וְכָל־עָרֵי
כו הַגִּלְעָד וַחֲצִי אֶרֶץ בְּנֵי עַמּוֹן עַד־עֲרוֹעֵר אֲשֶׁר עַל־פְּנֵי רַבָּה: וּמֵחֶשְׁבּוֹן
כז עַד־רָמַת הַמִּצְפֶּה וּבְטֹנִים וּמִמַּחֲנַיִם עַד־גְּבוּל לִדְבִר: וּבָעֵמֶק בֵּית הָרָם
וּבֵית נִמְרָה וְסֻכּוֹת וְצָפוֹן יֶתֶר מַמְלְכוּת סִיחוֹן מֶלֶךְ חֶשְׁבּוֹן הַיַּרְדֵּן וּגְבֻל
כח עַד־קְצֵה יָם־כִּנֶּרֶת עֵבֶר הַיַּרְדֵּן מִזְרָחָה: זֹאת נַחֲלַת בְּנֵי־גָד לְמִשְׁפְּחֹתָם
כט הֶעָרִים וְחַצְרֵיהֶם: וַיִּתֵּן מֹשֶׁה לַחֲצִי שֵׁבֶט מְנַשֶּׁה וַיְהִי לַחֲצִי
ל מַטֵּה בְנֵי־מְנַשֶּׁה לְמִשְׁפְּחוֹתָם: וַיְהִי גְבוּלָם מִמַּחֲנַיִם כָּל־הַבָּשָׁן כָּל־
לא מַמְלְכוּת עוֹג מֶלֶךְ־הַבָּשָׁן וְכָל־חַוֹּת יָאִיר אֲשֶׁר בַּבָּשָׁן שִׁשִּׁים עִיר: וַחֲצִי
הַגִּלְעָד וְעַשְׁתָּרוֹת וְאֶדְרֶעִי עָרֵי מַמְלְכוּת עוֹג בַּבָּשָׁן לִבְנֵי מָכִיר בֶּן־
לב מְנַשֶּׁה לַחֲצִי בְּנֵי־מָכִיר לְמִשְׁפְּחוֹתָם: אֵלֶּה אֲשֶׁר־נִחַל מֹשֶׁה בְּעַרְבוֹת

13:8. I.e., with the other half of Manasseh, which took its allotment east of the Jordan.

13:14. See *Numbers* 18:20.

13:23. That is, the Jordan and the towns along its banks (*Radak*).

from the Lebanon to Misrephoth-maim — all the Sidonians — I will drive them out on behalf of the Children of Israel. You have only to allot it to Israel as a heritage, as I have commanded you. [7] *So now, divide this land as a heritage for the nine tribes and half the tribe of Manasseh."*

[8] *With it, * the Reubenite and the Gadite took their heritage that Moses had given them on the eastern side of the Jordan, according to that which Moses,*

The boundaries of trans-Jordan (See Appendix D, map 1)

servant of HASHEM, had given them. [9] *From Aroer that is on the edge of the River Arnon and the city that is in the middle of the river — the entire plain from Medeba to Dibon;* [10] *and all the cities of Sihon, the king of the Amorite, who ruled in Heshbon to the border of the Children of Ammon;* [11] *and Gilead, and the border of the Geshurite and the Maacathite, all of Mount Hermon, and all of Bashan to Salcah;* [12] *the entire kingdom of Og in Bashan who ruled in Ashtaroth and in Edrei; it is he who remained from the remnant of the giants — Moses defeated them and drove them out.* [13] *But the Children of Israel did not drive out the Geshurite and the Maacathite, rather the Geshurite and Maacathite dwell in the midst of Israel until this day.* [14] *To the tribe of Levi, however, he did not give a heritage; the fire-offerings of HASHEM, the God of Israel, are his heritage, as He had spoken to him. **

Reuben's territory

[15] *Moses gave to the tribe of the children of Reuben according to their families.* [16] *Their border was from Aroer that is on the edge of the River Arnon and the city that is in the middle of the river and all the plain to Medeba;* [17] *Heshbon and all its cities that are in the plain — Dibon and Bamoth-baal and Beth-baal-meon;* [18] *and Jahaz and Kedemoth and Mephaath;* [19] *and Kiriathaim and Sibmah and Zeres-hashahar on the mount of the valley;* [20] *and Beth-peor and the falls of Pisgah and Beth-jeshimoth;* [21] *and all the cities of the plain; and all the kingdom of Sihon, king of the Amorite, who ruled in Heshbon, whom Moses had smitten: him and the princes of Midian — Evi and Rekem and Zur and Hur and Reba — dukes of Sihon, the inhabitants of the land.* [22] *The Children of Israel slayed Balaam son of Beor, the sorcerer, with the sword, along with their [other] slain.* [23] *The border of the children of Reuben was the Jordan and its border. * This was the inheritance of the children of Reuben, according to their families — the cities and their villages.*

Gad's territory

[24] *Moses also gave to the tribe of Gad, to the children of Gad, according to their families.* [25] *Their border was Jazer, and all the cities of Gilead, and half the land of the Children of Ammon, to Aroer, which is before Rabbah;* [26] *and from Heshbon to Ramath-hamizpeh and Betonim; and from Mahanaim to the border toward Debir.* [27] *And in the valley: Beth-haram and Beth-nimrah and Succoth and Zaphon — the rest of the kingdom of Sihon, king of Heshbon — the Jordan and its border, to the shore of the Kinnereth Sea on the eastern side of the Jordan.* [28] *This is the heritage of the children of Gad according to their families — the cities and their villages.*

Manasseh's territory

[29] *Moses also gave to half the tribe of Manasseh; and it was for half of the tribe of the children of Manasseh according to their families.* [30] *Their boundary was from Mahanaim, all the Bashan, all the kingdom of Og, king of Bashan, and all of Havvoth-jair in Bashan — sixty cities;* [31] *and half of the Gilead, and Ashtaroth and Edrei — the royal cities of Og in Bashan — were given to the children of Machir son of Manasseh, to half the children of Machir, according to their families.* [32] *These are the ones to whom Moses distributed inheritances in the plains*

לג מוֹאָ֗ב מֵעֵ֛בֶר לְיַרְדֵּ֥ן יְרֵח֖וֹ מִזְרָֽחָה: וּלְשֵׁ֙בֶט֙ הַלֵּוִ֔י לֹא־נָתַ֥ן מֹשֶׁ֖ה נַחֲלָֽה:

יד א יְהֹוָ֞ה אֱלֹהֵ֤י יִשְׂרָאֵל֙ ה֣וּא נַחֲלָתָ֔ם כַּאֲשֶׁ֖ר דִּבֶּ֥ר לָהֶֽם: וְאֵ֗לֶּה אֲשֶׁר־נָֽחֲל֛וּ בְּנֵֽי־יִשְׂרָאֵ֖ל בְּאֶ֣רֶץ כְּנָ֑עַן אֲשֶׁ֙ר נִֽחֲל֜וּ אוֹתָ֗ם אֶלְעָזָ֤ר הַכֹּהֵן֙ וִיהוֹשֻׁ֣עַ בִּן־נ֔וּן

ב וְרָאשֵׁ֛י אֲב֥וֹת הַמַּטּ֖וֹת לִבְנֵ֣י יִשְׂרָאֵֽל: בְּגוֹרַ֖ל נַחֲלָתָ֑ם כַּאֲשֶׁ֨ר צִוָּ֤ה יְהֹוָה֙ בְּיַד־מֹשֶׁ֔ה לְתִשְׁעַ֥ת הַמַּטּ֖וֹת וַחֲצִ֥י הַמַּטֶּֽה:

ג כִּֽי־נָתַ֨ן מֹשֶׁ֜ה נַחֲלַ֣ת שְׁנֵ֣י הַמַּטּ֗וֹת וַחֲצִ֤י הַמַּטֶּה֙ מֵעֵ֣בֶר לַיַּרְדֵּ֔ן וְלַ֨לְוִיִּ֔ם לֹֽא־נָתַ֥ן נַחֲלָ֖ה בְּתוֹכָֽם:

ד כִּֽי־הָי֤וּ בְנֵֽי־יוֹסֵף֙ שְׁנֵ֣י מַטּ֔וֹת מְנַשֶּׁ֖ה וְאֶפְרָ֑יִם וְלֹֽא־נָתְנ֨וּ חֵ֤לֶק לַלְוִיִּם֙ בָּאָ֔רֶץ כִּ֚י אִם־עָרִ֣ים לָשֶׁ֔בֶת וּמִ֨גְרְשֵׁיהֶ֔ם לְמִקְנֵיהֶ֖ם וּלְקִנְיָנָֽם:

ה כַּאֲשֶׁ֙ר צִוָּ֤ה יְהֹוָה֙ אֶת־מֹשֶׁ֔ה כֵּ֥ן עָשׂ֖וּ בְּנֵ֣י יִשְׂרָאֵ֑ל וַֽיַּחְלְק֖וּ אֶת־הָאָֽרֶץ:

ו וַיִּגְּשׁ֙וּ בְנֵֽי־יְהוּדָ֤ה אֶל־יְהוֹשֻׁ֙עַ֙ בַּגִּלְגָּ֔ל וַיֹּ֣אמֶר אֵלָ֔יו כָּלֵ֥ב בֶּן־יְפֻנֶּ֖ה הַקְּנִזִּ֑י אַתָּ֣ה יָדַ֗עְתָּ אֶֽת־הַדָּבָ֞ר אֲשֶׁר־דִּבֶּ֤ר יְהֹוָה֙ אֶל־מֹשֶׁ֣ה אִישׁ־הָאֱלֹהִ֔ים עַ֥ל אֹדוֹתַ֖י וְעַ֣ל אֹדוֹתֶ֑יךָ בְּקָדֵ֖שׁ בַּרְנֵֽעַ:

ז בֶּן־אַרְבָּעִ֥ים שָׁנָ֛ה אָנֹכִ֖י בִּשְׁלֹ֣חַ מֹשֶׁ֣ה עֶֽבֶד־יְהֹוָ֜ה אֹתִ֗י מִקָּדֵ֥שׁ בַּרְנֵ֖עַ לְרַגֵּ֣ל אֶת־הָאָ֑רֶץ וָאָשֵׁ֤ב אֹתוֹ֙ דָּבָ֔ר כַּאֲשֶׁ֖ר עִם־לְבָבִֽי:

ח וְאַחַי֙ אֲשֶׁ֣ר עָל֣וּ עִמִּ֔י הִמְסִ֖יו אֶת־לֵ֣ב הָעָ֑ם וְאָנֹכִ֣י מִלֵּ֔אתִי אַחֲרֵ֖י יְהֹוָ֥ה אֱלֹהָֽי:

ט וַיִּשָּׁבַ֣ע מֹשֶׁ֗ה בַּיּ֣וֹם הַהוּא֮ לֵאמֹר֒ אִם־לֹ֗א הָאָ֙רֶץ֙ אֲשֶׁ֨ר דָּֽרְכָ֤ה רַגְלְךָ֙ בָּ֔הּ לְךָ֙ תִֽהְיֶ֣ה לְנַחֲלָ֔ה וּלְבָנֶ֖יךָ עַד־עוֹלָ֑ם כִּ֣י מִלֵּ֔אתָ אַחֲרֵ֖י יְהֹוָ֥ה אֱלֹהָֽי:

י וְעַתָּ֗ה הִנֵּה֩ הֶחֱיָ֙ה יְהֹוָ֤ה ׀ אוֹתִי֙ כַּאֲשֶׁ֣ר דִּבֵּ֔ר זֶ֣ה אַרְבָּעִ֤ים וְחָמֵשׁ֙ שָׁנָ֔ה מֵ֠אָ֠ז דִּבֶּ֨ר יְהֹוָ֜ה אֶת־הַדָּבָ֤ר הַזֶּה֙ אֶל־מֹשֶׁ֔ה אֲשֶׁר־הָלַ֥ךְ יִשְׂרָאֵ֖ל בַּמִּדְבָּ֑ר וְעַתָּ֗ה

יא הִנֵּ֙ה אָנֹכִ֤י הַיּוֹם֙ בֶּן־חָמֵ֥שׁ וּשְׁמוֹנִ֖ים שָׁנָֽה: עוֹדֶ֙נִּי֙ הַיּ֔וֹם חָזָ֕ק כַּאֲשֶׁ֖ר בְּי֣וֹם שְׁלֹ֥חַ אוֹתִ֖י מֹשֶׁ֑ה כְּכֹ֥חִי אָ֙ז֙ וּכְכֹ֣חִי עָ֔תָּה לַמִּלְחָמָ֖ה וְלָצֵ֥את וְלָבֽוֹא:

יב וְעַתָּ֗ה תְּנָה־לִּי֙ אֶת־הָהָ֣ר הַזֶּ֔ה אֲשֶׁר־דִּבֶּ֥ר יְהֹוָ֖ה בַּיּ֣וֹם הַה֑וּא כִּ֣י אַתָּֽה־שָׁמַ֣עְתָּ בַיּוֹם־הַ֠ה֠וּא כִּֽי־עֲנָקִ֥ים שָׁם֙ וְעָרִ֣ים גְּדֹל֣וֹת בְּצֻר֔וֹת אוּלַ֙י יְהֹוָ֤ה אוֹתִי֙ וְהֽוֹרַשְׁתִּ֔ים כַּאֲשֶׁ֖ר דִּבֶּ֥ר יְהֹוָֽה:

יג וַֽיְבָרְכֵ֖הוּ יְהוֹשֻׁ֑עַ וַיִּתֵּ֧ן אֶת־חֶבְר֛וֹן לְכָלֵ֥ב בֶּן־יְפֻנֶּ֖ה לְנַחֲלָֽה:

יד עַל־כֵּ֣ן הָיְתָה־חֶ֠בְר֠וֹן לְכָלֵ֙ב בֶּן־יְפֻנֶּ֤ה הַקְּנִזִּי֙ לְֽנַחֲלָ֔ה עַ֖ד הַיּ֣וֹם הַזֶּ֑ה יַ֚עַן אֲשֶׁ֣ר מִלֵּ֔א אַחֲרֵ֕י יְהֹוָ֖ה אֱלֹהֵ֥י יִשְׂרָאֵֽל:

טו וְשֵׁ֨ם חֶבְר֤וֹן לְפָנִים֙ קִרְיַ֣ת אַרְבַּ֔ע הָאָדָ֧ם הַגָּד֛וֹל בָּעֲנָקִ֖ים ה֑וּא וְהָאָ֥רֶץ שָׁקְטָ֖ה מִמִּלְחָמָֽה:

טו א וַיְהִ֣י הַגּוֹרָ֗ל לְמַטֵּ֛ה בְּנֵ֥י יְהוּדָ֖ה לְמִשְׁפְּחֹתָ֑ם אֶל־

ב גְּב֣וּל אֱד֑וֹם מִדְבַּר־צִ֛ן נֶ֖גְבָּה מִקְצֵ֥ה תֵימָֽן: וַיְהִ֤י לָהֶם֙ גְּב֣וּל נֶ֔גֶב מִקְצֵ֖ה יָ֣ם הַמֶּ֑לַח מִן־הַלָּשֹׁ֖ן הַפֹּנֶ֥ה נֶֽגְבָּה:

ג וְ֠יָצָ֠א אֶל־מִנֶּ֙גֶב֙ לְמַעֲלֵ֣ה עַקְרַבִּ֔ים וְעָ֥בַר צִ֙נָה֙ וְעָלָ֣ה מִנֶּ֣גֶב לְקָדֵ֣שׁ בַּרְנֵ֗עַ וְעָבַ֤ר חֶצְרוֹן֙ וְעָלָ֣ה אַדָּ֔רָה וְנָסַ֖ב הַקַּרְקָֽעָה:

14:4. Although Levi was excluded from the division of the land, the grand total of tribal territories was twelve, because Joseph's two sons were treated as tribes.

14:6. Before any of the territories in Eretz Yisrael had been allocated to the tribes, Caleb, one of the twelve spies sent by Moses (see *Numbers* Ch. 13), asked Joshua for the city of Hebron, which Moses had promised him. The leaders of Judah accompanied Caleb in a show of support for his claim. (See also *Numbers* 14:24, 30.)

14:11. That is, to lead the people out to battle and to lead them back home safely.

14:15. Literally, "City of Arba," i.e., the city was named for Arba, the tallest of the Anakim.

of Moab, on the eastern side of the Jordan, across from Jericho.
³³ *But to the tribe of Levi, Moses gave no heritage; HASHEM, the God of Israel, is their heritage, as He had spoken to them.*

14

The division
of Canaan
(See Appendix D,
map 5)

¹ These are [the areas] that the Children of Israel inherited in the land of Canaan, which were distributed to them as heritages — by Elazar the Kohen and Joshua son of Nun and the heads of the ancestral [families] of the tribes of the Children of Israel — ² by the lottery of their inheritance, as HASHEM had commanded through Moses, for the nine tribes and the half tribe. ³ For Moses had given the heritage of the two tribes and the half tribe across the Jordan, but to the Levites he had given no heritage among them. ⁴ The children of Joseph, however, were two tribes, * Manasseh and Ephraim. They gave no share to the Levites in the land, only cities for dwelling and their open land around them for their cattle and their flocks. ⁵ As HASHEM had commanded Moses, so the Children of Israel did, and they divided the land.

Caleb's
request

⁶ The Children of Judah approached Joshua in Gilgal, and Caleb son of Jephunneh the Kenizzite said to him, "You are aware of the matter that HASHEM told Moses, the man of God, concerning me and concerning you in Kadesh-barnea. * ⁷ I was forty years old when Moses, the servant of HASHEM, sent me from Kadesh-barnea to spy out the land, and I brought him back a report as was in my heart. ⁸ My brethren who went up with me melted the heart of the people, but I fulfilled [the will of] HASHEM, my God. ⁹ Moses swore on that day, saying, 'Surely the land on which your foot trod will be to you as a heritage, and to your children forever, because you fulfilled [the will of] HASHEM, my God.' ¹⁰ And now, behold — HASHEM has kept me alive as He had spoken, these forty-five years, from the time HASHEM spoke this word to Moses when Israel went in the Wilderness; and now, behold, I am eighty-five years old today. ¹¹ I am still as strong today as I was on the day that Moses sent me. As my strength was then, so my strength is now for war — to go out and to come in. * ¹² So now, give me this mountain of which HASHEM spoke on that day, because you heard on that day that the Anakim were there and that the cities were large and fortified. Perhaps HASHEM will be with me, and I will drive them out, as HASHEM had spoken."

Joshua
gives Hebron
to Caleb

¹³ Joshua blessed him and gave Hebron to Caleb son of Jephunneh as a heritage. ¹⁴ Therefore, Hebron became the heritage of Caleb son of Jephunneh the Kenizzite to this day, because he fulfilled the will of HASHEM, God of Israel. ¹⁵ The name of Hebron was formerly Kiriath-arba, * who was the biggest man among the Anakim. Then the land had rest from war.

15

JUDAH'S
TERRITORY
15:1-63
Judah's
southern
border

¹ The lot for the tribe of the children of Judah according to their families was: * up to the border of Edom, the Wilderness of Zin southward, at the southernmost edge. ² Their southern border was from the edge of the Dead Sea from the tip that faces south. ³ It went out to the south of Maaleh-akrabbim, passed to Zin, ascended to the south of Kadesh-barnea, passed Hezron, ascended toward Addar, and circled Karka.

15:1. This chapter gives the borders and cities of Judah in minute detail, a thoroughness that characterizes approximately one-third of the *Book of Joshua*. The Talmud states that had the Israelites not sinned, only six books would have been included in Scripture — the *Five Books*

of Moses and the *Book of Joshua* (*Nedarim* 22b). Joshua would have been included because it details the inheritance of each tribe (*Rashi*), and thus the exact borders of the Land of Israel, which must be known precisely since certain *mitzvos* can be performed only in the land.

ד וְעָבַר עַצְמוֹנָה וְיָצָא נַחַל מִצְרַיִם °והיה °וְהָיָ֣ה ק] תְּצְאוֹת הַגְּבוּל יָמָּה

ה זֶה־יִהְיֶ֣ה לָכֶ֥ם גְּב֖וּל נֶֽגֶב: וּגְב֣וּל קֵ֗דְמָה יָ֤ם הַמֶּ֨לַח֙ עַד־קְצֵ֣ה הַיַּרְדֵּ֑ן וּגְב֞וּל

ו לִפְאַ֤ת צָפ֨וֹנָה֙ מִלְּשׁ֣וֹן הַיָּ֔ם מִקְצֵ֖ה הַיַּרְדֵּֽן: וְעָלָ֤ה הַגְּבוּל֙ בֵּ֣ית חָגְלָ֔ה וְעָבַ֕ר

ז מִצְּפ֖וֹן לְבֵ֣ית הָעֲרָבָ֑ה וְעָלָ֣ה הַגְּב֔וּל אֶ֥בֶן בֹּ֖הַן בֶּן־רְאוּבֵֽן: וְעָלָ֣ה הַגְּב֣וּל ׀

דְּבִ֨רָה֙ מֵעֵ֣מֶק עָכ֔וֹר וְצָפ֜וֹנָה פֹּנֶ֣ה אֶל־הַגִּלְגָּ֗ל אֲשֶׁר־נֹ֨כַח֙ לְמַעֲלֵ֣ה אֲדֻמִּ֔ים

אֲשֶׁ֥ר מִנֶּ֖גֶב לַנָּ֑חַל וְעָבַ֤ר הַגְּבוּל֙ אֶל־מֵי־עֵ֣ין שֶׁ֔מֶשׁ וְהָי֥וּ תֹצְאֹתָ֖יו אֶל־עֵ֥ין

ח רֹגֵֽל: וְעָלָ֣ה הַגְּבוּל֩ גֵּ֨י בֶן־הִנֹּ֜ם אֶל־כֶּ֤תֶף הַיְבוּסִי֙ מִנֶּ֔גֶב הִ֖יא יְרוּשָׁלָ֑͏ִם וְעָלָ֣ה

הַגְּב֣וּל אֶל־רֹ֣אשׁ הָהָ֡ר אֲשֶׁר֩ עַל־פְּנֵ֨י גֵֽי־הִנֹּ֜ם יָ֗מָּה אֲשֶׁ֛ר בִּקְצֵ֥ה עֵֽמֶק־

ט רְפָאִ֖ים צָפֹֽנָה: וְתָאַ֨ר הַגְּב֜וּל מֵרֹ֣אשׁ הָהָ֗ר אֶל־מַעְיַן֙ מֵ֣י נֶפְתּ֔וֹחַ וְיָצָ֖א אֶל־

י עָרֵ֣י הַר־עֶפְר֑וֹן וְתָאַ֤ר הַגְּבוּל֙ בַּֽעֲלָ֔ה הִ֖יא קִרְיַ֥ת יְעָרִֽים: וְנָסַב֩ הַגְּב֨וּל

מִבַּעֲלָ֥ה יָ֨מָּה֙ אֶל־הַ֣ר שֵׂעִ֔יר וְעָבַ֕ר אֶל־כֶּ֧תֶף הַר־יְעָרִ֛ים מִצָּפ֖וֹנָה הִ֣יא

יא כְסָל֑וֹן וְיָרַ֤ד בֵּֽית־שֶׁ֨מֶשׁ֙ וְעָבַ֣ר תִּמְנָֽה: וְיָצָ֤א הַגְּבוּל֙ אֶל־כֶּ֣תֶף עֶקְר֖וֹן צָפ֑וֹנָה

וְתָאַ֤ר הַגְּבוּל֙ שִׁכְּר֔וֹנָה וְעָבַ֥ר הַר־הַֽבַּעֲלָ֖ה וְיָצָ֣א יַבְנְאֵ֑ל וְהָי֛וּ תֹּצְא֥וֹת

יב הַגְּב֖וּל יָֽמָּה: וּגְב֣וּל יָ֔ם הַיָּ֥מָּה הַגָּד֖וֹל וּגְב֑וּל זֶ֠ה גְּב֧וּל בְּנֵֽי־יְהוּדָ֛ה סָבִ֖יב

יג לְמִשְׁפְּחֹתָֽם: וּלְכָלֵ֣ב בֶּן־יְפֻנֶּ֗ה נָ֤תַן חֵ֨לֶק֙ בְּת֣וֹךְ בְּנֵֽי־יְהוּדָ֔ה אֶל־פִּ֖י יְהוָ֑ה

ליהוֹשֻׁ֑עַ אֶת־קִרְיַ֥ת אַרְבַּ֛ע אֲבִ֥י הָעֲנָ֖ק הִ֣יא חֶבְר֑וֹן: וַיֹּ֤רֶשׁ מִשָּׁם֙ כָּלֵ֔ב אֶת־

יד שְׁלוֹשָׁ֖ה בְּנֵ֣י הָעֲנָ֑ק אֶת־שֵׁשַׁ֤י וְאֶת־אֲחִימַן֙ וְאֶת־תַּלְמַ֔י יְלִידֵ֖י הָֽעֲנָֽק: וַיַּ֣עַל מִשָּׁ֔ם אֶל־

טו יֹשְׁבֵ֖י דְּבִ֑ר וְשֵׁם־דְּבִ֥ר לְפָנִ֖ים קִרְיַת־סֵֽפֶר: וַיֹּ֣אמֶר כָּלֵ֔ב אֲשֶׁר־

טז יַכֶּ֥ה אֶת־קִרְיַת־סֵ֖פֶר וּלְכָדָ֑הּ וְנָתַ֥תִּי ל֛וֹ אֶת־עַכְסָ֥ה בִתִּ֖י לְאִשָּֽׁה: וַֽיִּלְכְּדָ֛הּ

יז עָתְנִיאֵ֥ל בֶּן־קְנַ֖ז אֲחִ֣י כָלֵ֑ב וַיִּתֶּן־ל֛וֹ אֶת־עַכְסָ֥ה בִתּ֖וֹ לְאִשָּֽׁה: וַיְהִ֣י בְּבוֹאָ֗הּ

יח וַתְּסִיתֵ֨הוּ֙ לִשְׁא֤וֹל מֵֽאֵת־אָבִ֨יהָ֙ שָׂדֶ֔ה וַתִּצְנַ֖ח מֵעַ֣ל הַחֲמ֑וֹר וַיֹּֽאמֶר־לָ֥הּ

כָּלֵ֖ב מַה־לָּֽךְ: וַתֹּ֜אמֶר תְּנָה־לִּ֣י בְרָכָ֗ה כִּ֣י אֶ֤רֶץ הַנֶּ֨גֶב֙ נְתַתָּ֔נִי וְנָתַתָּ֥ה לִּ֖י גֻּלֹּ֣ת

יט מָ֑יִם וַיִּתֶּן־לָ֗הּ אֵ֚ת גֻּלֹּ֣ת עִלִּיּ֔וֹת וְאֵ֖ת גֻּלֹּ֥ת תַּחְתִּיּֽוֹת: זֹ֗את

כ נַחֲלַ֛ת מַטֵּ֥ה בְנֵֽי־יְהוּדָ֖ה לְמִשְׁפְּחֹתָֽם: וַיִּֽהְי֣וּ הֶעָרִ֗ים מִקְצֵה֙ לְמַטֵּ֣ה בְנֵֽי־

כא יְהוּדָ֔ה אֶל־גְּב֥וּל אֱד֖וֹם בַּנֶּ֑גְבָּה קַבְצְאֵ֥ל וְעֵ֖דֶר וְיָגֽוּר: וְקִינָ֥ה וְדִֽימוֹנָ֖ה

כב־כג וְעַדְעָדָֽה: וְקֶ֥דֶשׁ וְחָצ֖וֹר וְיִתְנָֽן: זִ֥יף וָטֶ֖לֶם וּבְעָל֑וֹת: וְחָצ֤וֹר ׀ חֲדַתָּה֙ וּקְרִיּ֔וֹת

כד־כו חֶצְר֖וֹן הִ֥יא חָצֽוֹר: אֲמָ֥ם וּשְׁמַ֖ע וּמוֹלָדָֽה: וַחֲצַ֥ר גַּדָּ֛ה וְחֶשְׁמ֖וֹן וּבֵ֥ית פָּֽלֶט:

כז־כח וַחֲצַ֥ר שׁוּעָ֛ל וּבְאֵ֥ר שֶׁ֖בַע וּבִזְיוֹתְיָֽה: בַּֽעֲלָ֥ה וְעִיִּ֖ים וָעָֽצֶם: וְאֶלְתּוֹלַ֥ד וּכְסִ֖יל

ל־לב וְחָרְמָֽה: וְצִֽקְלַ֥ג וּמַדְמַנָּ֖ה וְסַנְסַנָּֽה: וּלְבָא֥וֹת וְשִׁלְחִ֖ים וְעַ֣יִן וְרִמּ֑וֹן כָּל־עָרִ֛ים

לג עֶשְׂרִ֥ים וָתֵ֖שַׁע וְחַצְרֵיהֶֽן: בַּשְּׁפֵלָ֑ה אֶשְׁתָּא֥וֹל וְצָרְעָ֖ה וְאַשְׁנָֽה:

לד־לה וְזָנ֨וֹחַ֙ וְעֵ֣ין גַּנִּ֔ים תַּפּ֖וּחַ וְהָעֵינָֽם: יַרְמוּת֙ וַעֲדֻלָּ֔ם שׂוֹכֹ֖ה וַעֲזֵקָֽה: צְנָ֥ן

לו וַעֲדִיתַ֖יִם וְהַגְּדֵרָ֣ה וּגְדֵרֹתָ֑יִם עָרִ֥ים אַרְבַּֽע־עֶשְׂרֵ֖ה וְחַצְרֵיהֶֽן:

15:12. According to the Talmud, "and its border" is meant to include the islands off the coast of the land.

15:13. See 14:15.

15:17. Caleb and Othniel were half brothers through their mother. Kenaz was the father of Othniel and the stepfather of Caleb (*Radak*).

15:18. To prostrate herself before Caleb.

15:32. Nine of the thirty-eight cities listed here —

⁴ *It passed to Azmon and went out to the Brook of Egypt; the border's outlets*
_{The eastern} *were to the Sea. This shall be your southern border.* ⁵ *The eastern border was*
_{border} *from the Salt Sea to the end of the Jordan. The border on the northern side*
_{(See Appendix D,} *stretched from the tip of the Sea at the end of the Jordan River;* ⁶ *the border*
_{map 2)} *ascended to Beth-haglah and passed to the north of Beth-haarabah; the border*
ascended to the Stone of Bohan son of Reuben. ⁷ *The border ascended toward*
Debir from the Valley of Achor and northward facing Gilgal which is opposite
Maaleh-adummim, which is south of the valley. The border passed to the waters
of En-shemesh and its outlets were into En-rogel. ⁸ *The border ascended by the*
Valley of the Son of Hinnom to the southern shoulder of the Jebusite, which is
Jerusalem. The border ascended to the top of the mountain that faces the Valley
of Hinnom on the west, which is at the northern edge of the Valley of Rephaim.
⁹ *The border curved from the top of the mountain to the spring of the Waters of*
Nephtoah and went out to the cities of Mount Ephron. The border curved toward
_{The northern} *Baalah, which is Kiriath-jearim.* ¹⁰ *The border went around from Baalah to the*
_{border} *west to Mount Seir and passed to the flank of Mount Jearim from the north,*
which is Chesalon. It descended to Beth-shemesh and passed Timnah. ¹¹ *The*
border went out to the flank of Ekron to the north; the border curved toward
Shicron, passed Mount Baalah, and went out to Jabneel; the border's outlets
_{The western} *were to the Sea.* ¹² *The western border was the Great Sea and its border.* * *This*
_{border} *is the border of the children of Judah all around, according to their families.*

¹³ *To Caleb son of Jephunneh he gave a portion among the Children of Judah*
_{Caleb's} *in accordance with* HASHEM's *word to Joshua — Kiriath-arba,* * *the father of the*
_{inheritance} *Anakim, which is Hebron.* ¹⁴ *Caleb drove out the three sons of the Anak from*
there — Sheshai and Ahiman, and Talmai, the offspring of the Anak. ¹⁵ *He*
ascended from there to the inhabitants of Debir; the former name of Debir was
Kiriath-sefer. ¹⁶ *Caleb said, "Whoever smites Kiriath-sefer and conquers it, I shall*
give him my daughter Achsah as a wife."

¹⁷ *Othniel son of Kenaz, brother* * *of Caleb, conquered it; so he gave him his*
daughter Achsah as a wife. ¹⁸ *When she came [to him], she urged him to let her*
ask her father for a field. Then she slid off the donkey, * *and Caleb said to her,*
"What do you wish?" ¹⁹ *She said, "Give me a [source of] blessing, for you have*
given me an arid land; give me springs of water." So he gave her the upper
springs and the lower springs.

²⁰ *This is the heritage of the tribe of the children of Judah according to their*
_{Judah's} *families.* ²¹ *The cities at the extremity of [the territory of] the tribe of the children*
_{southern} *of Judah at the border of Edom in the south were: Kabzeal, Eder, Jagur,*
_{cities} ²² *Kinah, Dimonah, Ad'adah,* ²³ *Kedesh, Hazor, Ithnan,* ²⁴ *Ziph, Telem, Bealoth,*
²⁵ *Hazor, Hadattah, Kerioth, Hezron which is Hazor,* ²⁶ *Amam, Shema,*
Moladah, ²⁷ *Hazar-gaddah, Heshmon, Beth-pelet,* ²⁸ *Hazar-shual, Beer-sheba,*
Biziothiah, ²⁹ *Baalah, Iim, Ezem,* ³⁰ *Eltolad, Chesil, Hormah,* ³¹ *Ziklag, Madman-*
nah, Sansannah, ³² *Lebaoth, Shilhim, Ain, Rimmon — all the cities twenty-*
nine, * *and their villages.*

_{The lowland} ³³ *In the lowland: Eshtaol, Zorah, Ashnah,* ³⁴ *Zanoah, En-gannim, Tapuah,*
Enam, ³⁵ *Jarmuth, Adullam, Socoh, Azekah;* ³⁶ *Shaaraim, Adithaim, Haged-*
erah [which is] Gederothaim — fourteen cities and their villages.

Beer-sheba, Moladah, Hazar-shual, Ezem, Eltolad, Hor-   Simeon (see 19:2-7). Thus, Judah retained twenty-nine of
mah, Ziklag, Ain, Rimmon — were eventually given to   these cities (*Rashi*).

לח-מ וַחֲדָשָׁה וּמִגְדַּל־גָּד: וְדִלְעָן וְהַמִּצְפֶּה וְיׇקְתְאֵל: לָכִישׁ וּבׇצְקַת וְעֶגְלוֹן: וְכַבּוֹן

מא וְלַחְמָס וְכִתְלִישׁ: וּגְדֵרוֹת בֵּית־דָּגוֹן וְנַעֲמָה וּמַקֵּדָה עָרִים שֵׁשׁ־עֶשְׂרֵה

מב-מד וְחַצְרֵיהֶן: לִבְנָה וָעֶתֶר וְעָשָׁן: וְיִפְתָּח וְאַשְׁנָה וּנְצִיב: וּקְעִילָה

מה וְאַכְזִיב וּמָרֵאשָׁה עָרִים תֵּשַׁע וְחַצְרֵיהֶן: עֶקְרוֹן וּבְנֹתֶיהָ וַחֲצֵרֶיהָ:

מו-מז מֵעֶקְרוֹן וָיָמָּה כֹּל אֲשֶׁר־עַל־יַד אַשְׁדּוֹד וְחַצְרֵיהֶן: אַשְׁדּוֹד

בְּנוֹתֶיהָ וַחֲצֵרֶיהָ עַזָּה בְּנוֹתֶיהָ וַחֲצֵרֶיהָ עַד־נַחַל מִצְרָיִם וְהַיָּם הַגְּבוֹל °הַגָּדוֹל ק:

מח-מט וּגְבֽוּל: וּבָהָר שָׁמִיר וְיַתִּיר וְשׂוֹכֹה: וְדַנָּה וְקִרְיַת־סַנָּה הִיא

נ-נא דְבִר: וַעֲנָב וְאֶשְׁתְּמֹה וְעָנִים: וְגֹשֶׁן וְחֹלֹן וְגִלֹה עָרִים אַחַת־עֶשְׂרֵה

נב-נג וְחַצְרֵיהֶן: אֲרַב °וְרוּמָה [נ"א °וְדוּמָה] וְאֶשְׁעָן: °יָנִים [°יָנוּם ק]

נד וּבֵית־תַּפּוּחַ וַאֲפֵקָה: וְחֻמְטָה וְקִרְיַת־אַרְבַּע הִיא חֶבְרוֹן וְצִיעֹר עָרִים

נה-נו תֵּשַׁע וְחַצְרֵיהֶן: מָעוֹן ׀ כַּרְמֶל וָזִיף וְיוּטָּה: וְיִזְרְעֶאל וְיׇקְדְעָם וְזָנוֹחַ:

נז-נח הַקַּיִן גִּבְעָה וְתִמְנָה עָרִים עֶשֶׂר וְחַצְרֵיהֶן: חַלְחוּל בֵּית־צוּר

נט-ס וּגְדוֹר: וּמַעֲרָת וּבֵית־עֲנוֹת וְאֶלְתְּקֹן עָרִים שֵׁשׁ וְחַצְרֵיהֶן: קִרְיַת־

סא בַּעַל הִיא קִרְיַת יְעָרִים וְהָרַבָּה עָרִים שְׁתַּיִם וְחַצְרֵיהֶן: בַּמִּדְבָּר

סב בֵּית הָעֲרָבָה מִדִּין וּסְכָכָה: וְהַנִּבְשָׁן וְעִיר־הַמֶּלַח וְעֵין גֶּדִי עָרִים שֵׁשׁ

סג וְחַצְרֵיהֶן: וְאֶת־הַיְבוּסִי יוֹשְׁבֵי יְרוּשָׁלַ͏ִם לֹא־°יוּכְלוּ [°יָכְלוּ ק]

בְנֵי־יְהוּדָה לְהוֹרִישָׁם וַיֵּשֶׁב הַיְבוּסִי אֶת־בְּנֵי יְהוּדָה בִּירוּשָׁלַ͏ִם עַד הַיּוֹם

הַזֶּה:

טז א וַיֵּצֵא הַגּוֹרָל לִבְנֵי יוֹסֵף מִיַּרְדֵּן יְרִיחוֹ לְמֵי יְרִיחוֹ מִזְרָחָה

ב הַמִּדְבָּר עֹלֶה מִירִיחוֹ בָּהָר בֵּית־אֵל: וְיָצָא מִבֵּית־אֵל לוּזָה וְעָבַר אֶל־

ג גְּבוּל הָאַרְכִּי עֲטָרוֹת: וְיָרַד־יָמָּה אֶל־גְּבוּל הַיַּפְלֵטִי עַד גְּבוּל בֵּית־חוֹרֹן

ד תַּחְתּוֹן וְעַד־גָּזֶר וְהָיוּ °תֹצְאֹתָו [°תֹצְאֹתָיו ק] יָמָּה: וַיִּנְחֲלוּ בְנֵי־יוֹסֵף

ה מְנַשֶּׁה וְאֶפְרָיִם: וַיְהִי גְּבוּל בְּנֵי־אֶפְרַיִם לְמִשְׁפְּחֹתָם וַיְהִי גְּבוּל נַחֲלָתָם

ו מִזְרָחָה עַטְרוֹת אַדָּר עַד־בֵּית חוֹרֹן עֶלְיוֹן: וְיָצָא הַגְּבוּל הַיָּמָּה הַמִּכְמְתָת

ז מִצָּפוֹן וְנָסַב הַגְּבוּל מִזְרָחָה תַּאֲנַת שִׁלֹה וְעָבַר אוֹתוֹ מִמִּזְרַח יָנוֹחָה: וְיָרַד

ח מִיָּנוֹחָה עֲטָרוֹת וְנַעֲרָתָה וּפָגַע בִּירִיחוֹ וְיָצָא הַיַּרְדֵּן: מִתַּפּוּחַ יֵלֵךְ הַגְּבוּל

יָמָּה נַחַל קָנָה וְהָיוּ תֹצְאֹתָיו הַיָּמָּה זֹאת נַחֲלַת מַטֵּה בְנֵי־אֶפְרַיִם

ט לְמִשְׁפְּחֹתָם: וְהֶעָרִים הַמִּבְדָּלוֹת לִבְנֵי אֶפְרַיִם בְּתוֹךְ נַחֲלַת בְּנֵי־מְנַשֶּׁה

י כׇּל־הֶעָרִים וְחַצְרֵיהֶן: וְלֹא הוֹרִישׁוּ אֶת־הַכְּנַעֲנִי הַיּוֹשֵׁב בְּגָזֶר וַיֵּשֶׁב

יז א הַכְּנַעֲנִי בְּקֶרֶב אֶפְרַיִם עַד־הַיּוֹם הַזֶּה וַיְהִי לְמַס־עֹבֵד: וַיְהִי

הַגּוֹרָל לְמַטֵּה מְנַשֶּׁה כִּי־הוּא בְּכוֹר יוֹסֵף לְמָכִיר בְּכוֹר מְנַשֶּׁה אֲבִי

ב הַגִּלְעָד כִּי הוּא הָיָה אִישׁ מִלְחָמָה וַיְהִי־לוֹ הַגִּלְעָד וְהַבָּשָׁן: וַיְהִי לִבְנֵי

מְנַשֶּׁה הַנּוֹתָרִים לְמִשְׁפְּחֹתָם לִבְנֵי אֲבִיעֶזֶר וְלִבְנֵי־חֵלֶק וְלִבְנֵי אַשְׂרִיאֵל

17:1. Ephraim's lottery (Ch. 16) had preceded Manasseh's, even though Manasseh was Joseph's firstborn. The reason for this was that Jacob had given preference to Ephraim when he blessed the two (see *Genesis* 48:20). Within Manasseh, Machir received his portion first, partly because he was the firstborn and partly because he was an able fighter and thus could readily conquer his territory.

37 Zenan, Hadashah, Migdal-gad, 38 Dilan, Mizpeh, Joktheel, 39 Lachish, Bozkath, Eglon, 40 Cabbon, Lahmas, Chithlish, 41 Gederoth, Beth-dagon, Naamah, Makkedah — sixteen cities and their villages.

42 Libnah, Ether, Ashan, 43 Iphtah, Ashnah, Nezib, 44 Keilah, Achzib, Mareshah — nine cities and their villages.

45 Ekron and its towns and villages; 46 from Ekron to the Sea, all that lay near Ashdod and their villages: 47 Ashdod, its towns and villages; Gaza, its towns and villages to the Brook of Egypt and the Great [Mediterranean] Sea, and its *The* border. 48 And in the mountain: Shamir, Jattir, Socoh, 49 Dannah, Kiriath-san- *mountain* nah which is Debir, 50 Anab, Eshtemoh, Anim, 51 Goshen, Holon, Giloh — *region* eleven cities and their villages.

52 Arab, Rumah, Eshan, 53 Janum, Beth-tappuah, Aphekah, 54 Humtah, Kiriath-arba which is Hebron, and Zior — nine cities and their villages.

55 Maon, Carmel, Ziph, Juttah, 56 Jezreel, Jokdeam, Zanoah, 57 Kain, Gibeah, and Timnah — ten cities and their villages.

58 Halhul, Beth-zur, Gedor; 59 Maarath, Beth-anoth, Eltekon — six cities and their villages.

60 Kiriath-baal which is Kiriath-jearim, and Harabbah — two cities and their villages.

The 61 In the wilderness: Beth-haarabah, Middin, Secacah, 62 and Nibshan, the *Wilderness* City of Salt and En-gedi — six cities and their villages. *of Judah* 63 But the Jebusite, the inhabitants of Jerusalem, the children of Judah were not able to drive out; and the Jebusite dwelled among the children of Judah, in Jerusalem, until this day.

16

JOSEPH'S
TERRITORIES
16:1-18:1

Ephraim's
territory
(See Appendix D,
map 2)

Ephraim's
isolated
cities

1 The lot for the children of Joseph went out from the Jordan opposite Jericho to the Waters of Jericho to the east; the wilderness that ascends from Jericho to the mountain to Beth-el. 2 It went out from Beth-el to Luz and passed to the border of the Archite, to Ataroth. 3 It descended westward to the border of the Japhletite until the border of Lower Beth-horon and until Gezer; its outlets were to the Sea. 4 The children of Joseph — Manasseh and Ephraim — received their heritages. 5 The border of the children of Ephraim, according to their families, was: The border of their inheritance to the east was from Atroth Addar to Upper Beth-horon. 6 The border went out westward north of Mich-methath, and the border circled to the east of Taanath-shiloh, passing it on the east of Janoah. 7 It descended from Janoah to Ataroth and Naarath and reached Jericho, and went out to the Jordan. 8 From Tappuah the border went westward to the Brook of Kanah and its outlets were to the Sea. This is the heritage of the children of Ephraim according to their families. 9 There were isolated cities belonging to the children of Ephraim that were within the heritage of the children of Manasseh, all these cities and their villages. 10 They did not drive out the Canaanite that dwelled in Gezer; rather the Canaanite dwelled in the midst of Ephraim until this day, and they were indentured laborers.

17

Manasseh's
family

1 Then was the lot for the tribe of Manasseh, though he was Joseph's first-born. * For Machir the firstborn of Manasseh, the father of Gilead — be-cause he was a man of war — unto him was Gilead and the Bashan. 2 There was [also a portion] for the remaining sons of Manasseh according to their families: for the children of Abiezer, for the children of Helek, for the children of Asriel,

וְלִבְנֵי־שֶׁכֶם וְלִבְנֵי־חֵפֶר וְלִבְנֵי שְׁמִידָע אֵלֶּה בְּנֵי מְנַשֶּׁה בֶן־יוֹסֵף הַזְּכָרִים
לְמִשְׁפְּחֹתָם: וְלִצְלָפְחָד בֶּן־חֵפֶר בֶּן־גִּלְעָד בֶּן־מָכִיר בֶּן־מְנַשֶּׁה לֹא־הָיוּ
לוֹ בָּנִים כִּי אִם־בָּנוֹת וְאֵלֶּה שְׁמוֹת בְּנֹתָיו מַחְלָה וְנֹעָה חָגְלָה מִלְכָּה
וְתִרְצָה: וַתִּקְרַבְנָה לִפְנֵי אֶלְעָזָר הַכֹּהֵן וְלִפְנֵי | יְהוֹשֻׁעַ בִּן־נוּן וְלִפְנֵי
הַנְּשִׂיאִים לֵאמֹר יְהוָה צִוָּה אֶת־מֹשֶׁה לָתֶת־לָנוּ נַחֲלָה בְּתוֹךְ אַחֵינוּ וַיִּתֵּן
לָהֶם אֶל־פִּי יְהוָה נַחֲלָה בְּתוֹךְ אֲחֵי אֲבִיהֶן: וַיִּפְּלוּ חַבְלֵי־מְנַשֶּׁה עֲשָׂרָה
לְבַד מֵאֶרֶץ הַגִּלְעָד וְהַבָּשָׁן אֲשֶׁר מֵעֵבֶר לַיַּרְדֵּן: כִּי בְּנוֹת מְנַשֶּׁה נָחֲלוּ
נַחֲלָה בְּתוֹךְ בָּנָיו וְאֶרֶץ הַגִּלְעָד הָיְתָה לִבְנֵי־מְנַשֶּׁה הַנּוֹתָרִים: וַיְהִי גְבוּל־
מְנַשֶּׁה מֵאָשֵׁר הַמִּכְמְתָת אֲשֶׁר עַל־פְּנֵי שְׁכֶם וְהָלַךְ הַגְּבוּל אֶל־הַיָּמִין אֶל־
יֹשְׁבֵי עֵין תַּפּוּחַ: לִמְנַשֶּׁה הָיְתָה אֶרֶץ תַּפּוּחַ וְתַפּוּחַ אֶל־גְּבוּל מְנַשֶּׁה לִבְנֵי
אֶפְרָיִם: וְיָרַד הַגְּבוּל נַחַל קָנָה נֶגְבָּה לַנַּחַל עָרִים הָאֵלֶּה לְאֶפְרַיִם בְּתוֹךְ
עָרֵי מְנַשֶּׁה וּגְבוּל מְנַשֶּׁה מִצְּפוֹן לַנַּחַל וַיְהִי תֹצְאֹתָיו הַיָּמָּה: נֶגְבָּה לְאֶפְרַיִם
וְצָפוֹנָה לִמְנַשֶּׁה וַיְהִי הַיָּם גְּבוּלוֹ וּבְאָשֵׁר יִפְגְּעוּן מִצָּפוֹן וּבְיִשָּׂשכָר מִמִּזְרָח:
וַיְהִי לִמְנַשֶּׁה בְּיִשָּׂשכָר וּבְאָשֵׁר בֵּית־שְׁאָן וּבְנוֹתֶיהָ וְיִבְלְעָם וּבְנוֹתֶיהָ וְאֶת־
יֹשְׁבֵי דֹאר וּבְנוֹתֶיהָ וְיֹשְׁבֵי עֵין־דֹּר וּבְנֹתֶיהָ וְיֹשְׁבֵי תַעְנַךְ וּבְנֹתֶיהָ וְיֹשְׁבֵי
מְגִדּוֹ וּבְנוֹתֶיהָ שְׁלֹשֶׁת הַנָּפֶת: וְלֹא יָכְלוּ בְּנֵי מְנַשֶּׁה לְהוֹרִישׁ אֶת־הֶעָרִים
הָאֵלֶּה וַיּוֹאֶל הַכְּנַעֲנִי לָשֶׁבֶת בָּאָרֶץ הַזֹּאת: וַיְהִי כִּי חָזְקוּ בְּנֵי יִשְׂרָאֵל וַיִּתְּנוּ
אֶת־הַכְּנַעֲנִי לָמַס וְהוֹרֵשׁ לֹא הוֹרִישׁוֹ: וַיְדַבְּרוּ בְּנֵי יוֹסֵף
אֶת־יְהוֹשֻׁעַ לֵאמֹר מַדּוּעַ נָתַתָּה לִּי נַחֲלָה גּוֹרָל אֶחָד וְחֶבֶל אֶחָד וַאֲנִי
עַם־רָב עַד אֲשֶׁר־עַד־כֹּה בֵּרְכַנִי יְהוָה: וַיֹּאמֶר אֲלֵיהֶם יְהוֹשֻׁעַ אִם־עַם־
רַב אַתָּה עֲלֵה לְךָ הַיַּעְרָה וּבֵרֵאתָ לְךָ שָׁם בְּאֶרֶץ הַפְּרִזִּי וְהָרְפָאִים כִּי־אָץ
לְךָ הַר־אֶפְרָיִם: וַיֹּאמְרוּ בְּנֵי יוֹסֵף לֹא־יִמָּצֵא לָנוּ הָהָר וְרֶכֶב בַּרְזֶל בְּכָל־
הַכְּנַעֲנִי הַיֹּשֵׁב בְּאֶרֶץ הָעֵמֶק לַאֲשֶׁר בְּבֵית־שְׁאָן וּבְנוֹתֶיהָ וְלַאֲשֶׁר בְּעֵמֶק
יִזְרְעֶאל: וַיֹּאמֶר יְהוֹשֻׁעַ אֶל־בֵּית יוֹסֵף לְאֶפְרַיִם וְלִמְנַשֶּׁה לֵאמֹר עַם־רָב
אַתָּה וְכֹחַ גָּדוֹל לָךְ לֹא־יִהְיֶה לְךָ גּוֹרָל אֶחָד: כִּי הַר יִהְיֶה־לָּךְ כִּי־יַעַר הוּא
וּבֵרֵאתוֹ וְהָיָה לְךָ תֹּצְאֹתָיו כִּי־תוֹרִישׁ אֶת־הַכְּנַעֲנִי כִּי רֶכֶב בַּרְזֶל לוֹ כִּי
חָזָק הוּא:
                            וַיִּקָּהֲלוּ כָּל־עֲדַת בְּנֵי־יִשְׂרָאֵל שִׁלֹה וַיַּשְׁכִּינוּ   **יח**
שָׁם אֶת־אֹהֶל מוֹעֵד וְהָאָרֶץ נִכְבְּשָׁה לִפְנֵיהֶם: וַיִּוָּתְרוּ בִּבְנֵי יִשְׂרָאֵל אֲשֶׁר
לֹא־חָלְקוּ אֶת־נַחֲלָתָם שִׁבְעָה שְׁבָטִים: וַיֹּאמֶר יְהוֹשֻׁעַ אֶל־בְּנֵי יִשְׂרָאֵל

17:3. See *Numbers* 27:1; 36:11.
17:8. The city of Tappuah belonged to Ephraim, but the countryside around it belonged to Manasseh.
17:16. They complained that Joshua's solution was untenable because the Canaanites were too well armed to be displaced.
17:18. Joshua countered that the large population of Manasseh would enable them both to clear a large forest and to defeat the Canaanites.

18:1. After seven years of conquest and seven years of allocation, the Tabernacle, which had been located in Gilgal, was moved to the city of Shiloh, in Ephraim's territory, where it would remain for 369 years as the focal point of the national service to God (see *Tosefta, Zevachim* 13:6). Whereas the portable Tabernacle in the Wilderness had been made of collapsible wooden walls and a roof of draperies, the Tabernacle at Shiloh was made of stone walls and a roof of draperies.

for the children of Shechem, for the children of Hepher, and for the children of Shemida. These were the male children of Manasseh son of Joseph according to their families.

³ *But Zelophehad, son of Hepher, son of Gilead, son of Machir, son of Manasseh, had no sons, only daughters; and these are the names of his daughters: Mahlah, Noah, Hoglah, Milcah, and Tirzah.* * ⁴ *They approached before Elazar the Kohen, before Joshua son of Nun, and before the leaders, saying, "*HASHEM *commanded Moses to give us a heritage among our brethren"; and he gave them, according to the word of* HASHEM, *a heritage among their father's brothers.* ⁵ *Ten portions fell to Manasseh — besides the land of Gilead and the Bashan which are on the other side of the Jordan —* ⁶ *because the women of Manasseh received a heritage among his sons. The land of Gilead went to Manasseh's remaining sons.*

⁷ *The border of Manasseh was from Asher to Michmethath which faces Shechem, and the border went to the south to the inhabitants of En-tappuah.* ⁸ *The land of Tappuah belonged to Manasseh, but Tappuah on the border of Manasseh belonged to the children of Ephraim.* * ⁹ *The border descended to the Brook of Kanah — south of the brook. These cities were Ephraim's, in the midst of the cities of Manasseh. The border of Manasseh was on the north of the brook, and its outlets were to the Sea.* ¹⁰ *The southern part [of Joseph's portion] was Ephraim's and the northern part was Manasseh's. The Sea was their [western] border; they met with Asher on the north and Issachar on the east.* ¹¹ *There was unto Manasseh, within [the territory of] Issachar and within [the territory of] Asher: Beth-shean and its towns, Ibleam and its towns, the inhabitants of Dor and its towns, the inhabitants of En-dor and its towns, the inhabitants of Taanach and its towns, and the inhabitants of Megiddo and its towns — three provinces.* ¹² *But the children of Manasseh were not able to drive out [the inhabitants of] these cities, and the Canaanite wished to dwell in this land.* ¹³ *It happened when the Children of Israel became strong that they imposed tribute on the Canaanite, but they did not drive them out.*

¹⁴ *The children of Joseph spoke to Joshua, saying, "Why have you given me an inheritance of [only] a single lot and a single portion, seeing that I am a numerous people, for* HASHEM *has blessed me to such an extent?"*

¹⁵ *Joshua said to them, "If you are such a numerous people, ascend to the forest and clear an area for yourselves there — in the land of the Perizzite and the Rephaim — since the mountain range of Ephraim is too confined for you."*

¹⁶ *The children of Joseph said, "The mountain is insufficient for us, and all the Canaanite that dwell in the land of the valley — those in Beth-shean and its villages and those in the Valley of Jezreel — have iron chariots."* *

¹⁷ *Joshua spoke to the House of Joseph, to Ephraim and to Manasseh, saying, "You are a numerous people and you have great strength. You should not have [only] one lot.* ¹⁸ *That mountain shall be yours because it is a forest; you can cut it down and its outskirts will be yours, for you shall drive out the Canaanite even though they have iron chariots and are strong."* *

18   ¹ *The entire assembly of the Children of Israel gathered at Shiloh and erected the Tent of Meeting there,* * *and the land had been conquered before them,* ² *but there was left among the Children of Israel seven tribes that had not yet received their heritage.* ³ *Joshua said to the Children of Israel,*

Zelophehad's daughters

Manasseh's territory

Ephraim's separated cities

Manasseh's separated cities

Joseph's demand . . .

. . . and Joshua's response

THE REMAINING TRIBES' TERRITORIES
18:2-19:51

עַד־אָ֗נָה אַתֶּם֙ מִתְרַפִּ֔ים לָבוֹא֙ לָרֶ֣שֶׁת אֶת־הָאָ֔רֶץ אֲשֶׁר֙ נָתַ֣ן לָכֶ֔ם יְהוָ֖ה

ד אֱלֹהֵ֥י אֲבֽוֹתֵיכֶֽם: הָב֨וּ לָכֶ֤ם שְׁלֹשָׁה֙ אֲנָשִׁ֣ים לַשָּׁ֔בֶט וְאֶשְׁלָחֵ֕ם וְיָקֻ֜מוּ

ה וְיִֽתְהַלְּכ֣וּ בָאָ֗רֶץ וְיִכְתְּב֨וּ אוֹתָ֜הּ לְפִ֤י נַֽחֲלָתָם֙ וְיָבֹ֣אוּ אֵלָֽי: וְהִֽתְחַלְּק֥וּ אֹתָ֖הּ לְשִׁבְעָ֣ה חֲלָקִ֑ים יְהוּדָ֞ה יַֽעֲמֹ֤ד עַל־גְּבוּלוֹ֙ מִנֶּ֔גֶב וּבֵ֥ית יוֹסֵ֛ף יַֽעַמְד֥וּ עַל־

ו גְּבוּלָ֖ם מִצָּפֽוֹן: וְאַתֶּ֞ם תִּכְתְּב֤וּ אֶת־הָאָ֙רֶץ֙ שִׁבְעָ֣ה חֲלָקִ֔ים וַֽהֲבֵאתֶ֥ם אֵלַ֖י

ז הֵ֑נָּה וְיָרִ֧יתִי לָכֶ֛ם גּוֹרָ֖ל פֹּ֑ה לִפְנֵ֥י יְהוָ֖ה אֱלֹהֵֽינוּ: כִּ֠י אֵֽין־חֵ֤לֶק לַֽלְוִיִּם֙ בְּקִרְבְּכֶ֔ם כִּֽי־כְהֻנַּ֥ת יְהוָ֖ה נַֽחֲלָת֑וֹ וְגָ֡ד וּרְאוּבֵ֡ן וַֽחֲצִ֣י שֵֽׁבֶט הַֽמְנַשֶּׁה֩ לָֽקְח֨וּ

ח נַֽחֲלָתָ֜ם מֵעֵ֤בֶר לַיַּרְדֵּן֙ מִזְרָ֔חָה אֲשֶׁ֣ר נָתַ֣ן לָהֶ֔ם מֹשֶׁ֖ה עֶ֣בֶד יְהוָֽה: וַיָּקֻ֥מוּ הָֽאֲנָשִׁ֖ים וַיֵּלֵ֑כוּ וַיְצַ֣ו יְהוֹשֻׁ֡עַ אֶת־הַהֹֽלְכִים֩ לִכְתֹּ֨ב אֶת־הָאָ֜רֶץ לֵאמֹ֗ר לְכ֨וּ וְהִתְהַלְּכ֤וּ בָאָ֙רֶץ֙ וְכִתְב֣וּ אוֹתָ֔הּ וְשׁ֥וּבוּ אֵלַ֖י וּפֹ֗ה אַשְׁלִ֥יךְ לָכֶ֛ם גּוֹרָ֖ל לִפְנֵ֥י

ט יְהוָ֖ה בְּשִׁלֹֽה: וַיֵּֽלְכ֤וּ הָֽאֲנָשִׁים֙ וַיַּֽעַבְר֣וּ בָאָ֔רֶץ וַיִּכְתְּב֧וּהָ לֶֽעָרִ֛ים לְשִׁבְעָ֥ה

י חֲלָקִ֖ים עַל־סֵ֑פֶר וַיָּבֹ֧אוּ אֶל־יְהוֹשֻׁ֛עַ אֶל־הַֽמַּֽחֲנֶ֖ה שִׁלֹֽה: וַיַּשְׁלֵךְ֩ לָהֶ֨ם יְהוֹשֻׁ֧עַ גּוֹרָ֛ל בְּשִׁלֹ֖ה לִפְנֵ֣י יְהוָ֑ה וַיְחַלֶּק־שָׁ֨ם יְהוֹשֻׁ֧עַ אֶת־הָאָ֛רֶץ לִבְנֵ֥י

יא יִשְׂרָאֵ֖ל כְּמַחְלְקֹתָֽם: וַיַּ֗עַל גּוֹרַ֛ל מַטֵּ֥ה בְנֵֽי־בִנְיָמִ֖ן לְמִשְׁפְּחֹתָ֑ם

יב וַיֵּצֵא֙ גְּב֣וּל גּֽוֹרָלָ֔ם בֵּ֚ין בְּנֵ֣י יְהוּדָ֔ה וּבֵ֖ין בְּנֵ֣י יוֹסֵ֑ף וַיְהִ֨י לָהֶ֤ם הַגְּבוּל֙ לִפְאַ֣ת צָפ֔וֹנָה מִן־הַיַּרְדֵּ֑ן וְעָלָ֣ה הַגְּבוּל֩ אֶל־כֶּ֨תֶף יְרִיח֤וֹ מִצָּפוֹן֙ וְעָלָ֤ה בָהָר֙ יָ֔מָּה

יג °והיה [וְהָיוּ֙ ק] תֹּֽצְאֹתָ֔יו מִדְבַּ֖רָה בֵּ֣ית אָ֑וֶן: וְעָבַ֨ר מִשָּׁ֥ם הַגְּב֛וּל ל֥וּזָה אֶל־כֶּ֖תֶף ל֣וּזָה נֶ֑גְבָּה הִ֣יא בֵּֽית־אֵ֑ל וְיָרַ֤ד הַגְּבוּל֙ עַטְר֣וֹת אַדָּ֔ר עַל־הָהָ֕ר

יד אֲשֶׁ֕ר מִנֶּ֥גֶב לְבֵית־חֹר֖וֹן תַּחְתּֽוֹן: וְתָאַ֣ר הַגְּב֗וּל וְנָסַ֞ב לִפְאַת־יָ֤ם נֶ֙גְבָּה֙ מִן־הָהָ֔ר אֲשֶׁ֛ר עַל־פְּנֵ֥י בֵית־חֹר֖וֹן נֶ֑גְבָּה °והיה [וְהָי֣וּ ק] תֹֽצְאֹתָ֗יו אֶל־

טו קִרְיַת־בַּ֙עַל֙ הִ֚יא קִרְיַ֣ת יְעָרִ֔ים עִ֖יר בְּנֵ֣י יְהוּדָ֑ה זֹ֖את פְּאַת־יָֽם: וּפְאַת־נֶ֗גְבָּה מִקְצֵה֙ קִרְיַ֣ת יְעָרִ֔ים וְיָצָ֤א הַגְּבוּל֙ יָ֔מָּה וְיָצָ֕א אֶל־מַעְיַ֖ן מֵ֥י נֶפְתּֽוֹחַ: וְיָרַ֨ד

טז הַגְּב֜וּל אֶל־קְצֵ֣ה הָהָ֗ר אֲשֶׁר֙ עַל־פְּנֵ֙י גֵּ֣י בֶן־הִנֹּ֔ם אֲשֶׁ֛ר בְּעֵ֥מֶק רְפָאִ֖ים צָפ֑וֹנָה וְיָרַד֩ גֵּ֨י הִנֹּ֜ם אֶל־כֶּ֤תֶף הַיְבוּסִי֙ נֶ֔גְבָּה וְיָרַ֖ד עֵ֥ין רֹגֵֽל: וְתָאַ֣ר מִצָּפ֗וֹן

יז וְיָצָא֙ עֵ֣ין שֶׁ֔מֶשׁ וְיָצָא֙ אֶל־גְּלִיל֔וֹת אֲשֶׁר־נֹ֖כַח מַֽעֲלֵ֣ה אֲדֻמִּ֑ים וְיָרַ֖ד אֶ֥בֶן

יח בֹּ֖הַן בֶּן־רְאוּבֵֽן: וְעָבַ֛ר אֶל־כֶּ֥תֶף מֽוּל־הָֽעֲרָבָ֖ה צָפ֑וֹנָה וְיָרַ֖ד הָֽעֲרָבָֽתָה:

יט וְעָבַ֨ר הַגְּב֜וּל אֶל־כֶּ֣תֶף בֵּית־חָגְלָה֮ צָפוֹנָה֒ °והיה [וְהָי֣וּ ׀ ק] תֹֽצְאוֹתָ֣יו [תֹצְא֣וֹת ק] הַגְּב֗וּל אֶל־לְשׁ֤וֹן יָֽם־הַמֶּ֙לַח֙ צָפ֔וֹנָה אֶל־קְצֵ֥ה הַיַּרְדֵּ֖ן נֶ֑גְבָּה

כ זֶ֖ה גְּב֥וּל נֶֽגֶב: וְהַיַּרְדֵּ֥ן יִגְבֹּל־אֹת֖וֹ לִפְאַת־קֵ֑דְמָה זֹ֡את נַֽחֲלַת֩ בְּנֵ֨י בִנְיָמִ֧ן

כא לִגְבֽוּלֹתֶ֛יהָ סָבִ֖יב לְמִשְׁפְּחֹתָֽם: וְהָי֣וּ הֶֽעָרִ֗ים לְמַטֵּ֛ה בְּנֵ֥י בִנְיָמִ֖ן

כב לְמִשְׁפְּחֽוֹתֵיהֶ֑ם יְרִיח֥וֹ וּבֵית־חָגְלָ֖ה וְעֵ֥מֶק קְצִֽיץ: וּבֵ֤ית הָֽעֲרָבָה֙ וּצְמָרַ֙יִם֙

18:3. God had said long before this (13:1,7) that lots should be drawn to divide the land, and He would assist in the conquest, but the tribes had been lax in doing so (*Malbim*). They were afraid that if each tribe knew where it was to live, the united army would disperse, and the individual tribes would not be strong enough to conquer their assigned lands. The stronger tribes, such as Judah and Joseph, however, had no such fears and had occupied their portions (*Abarbanel*).

18:5. The emissaries would map the land into seven

"How long will you be lax in coming to possess the Land that HASHEM, the God of your fathers, has given you?* ⁴ Appoint for yourselves three men for each tribe. I will dispatch them, and they will arise and traverse the land and describe it in writing according to their heritage; then they will come back to me. ⁵ They will divide it into seven portions; Judah will remain at his border to the south and the House of Joseph will remain at their border to the north. * ⁶ You shall describe in writing seven portions of the land and bring it to me here. I will then draw lots for you here before HASHEM, our God. ⁷ For there is no share for the Levites in your midst, since the service of HASHEM is their heritage. Gad, Reuben, and half the tribe of Manasseh have taken their heritage across the Jordan to the east, which Moses the servant of HASHEM gave them."

⁸ The men arose and went. Joshua commanded those who went to write about the land, saying, "Go walk through the land, describe it in writing, and return to me. I will cast a lottery for you here before HASHEM in Shiloh."

⁹ The men went and passed through the land; they described it in writing, according to the cities, in seven portions, in a book; then they came to Joshua, to the encampment at Shiloh. ¹⁰ Joshua cast a lottery for them in Shiloh before HASHEM; there Joshua apportioned the land for the Children of Israel according to their portions.

Benjamin's territory (See Appendix D, map 2)

¹¹ The lottery for the tribe of the children of Benjamin came up, according to their families; the boundary of their lot went out between the children of Judah and the children of Joseph. ¹² Their northern border was from the Jordan, and it ascended to the flank of Jericho on the north and ascended the mountain to the west; its outlets were to the wilderness of Beth-aven. ¹³ From there the border passed toward Luz, to the southern flank of Luz which is Beth-el; and the border descended to Atroth-addar, to the mountain that is south of Lower Beth-horon. ¹⁴ The border curved and circled around the western side, going southward from the mountain that faces Beth-horon on the south. Its outlets were toward Kiriath-baal which is Kiriath-jearim, a city of the children of Judah. This was the western side. ¹⁵ The southern side [was] from the edge of Kiriath-jearim; and the border went out from the west and went out to the spring of the Waters of Nephtoah. ¹⁶ The border descended to the edge of the mountain that faces the Valley of the Son of Hinnom, which is north of the Valley of Rephaim, and descended to the Valley of Hinnom to the southern flank of the Jebusite, and descended to En-rogel. ¹⁷ It curved from the north and went out to En-shemesh; it went out to Geliloth which was across from Maaleh-adummim. It then descended toward the Stone of Bohan son of Reuben. ¹⁸ It passed to the northern flank opposite the plain, and it descended to the plain. ¹⁹ The border passed the northern flank of Beth-hoglah; the border's outlets were to the northern tip of the Salt Sea, to the southern end of the Jordan. This was the southern border. ²⁰ The Jordan bordered it on the eastern side. This is the heritage of the children of Benjamin according to its borders all around, according to their families.

²¹ These are the cities of the tribe of the children of Benjamin according to their families: Jericho, Beth-hoglah, and Emek Keziz, ²² Beth-haarabah, Zemaraim,

portions and the Divinely guided lottery would match the portions with the appropriate tribes. Judah's position to the south and Joseph's to the north guaranteed the security of those borders, permitting the seven tribes in the central part of the land to concentrate on the conquest.

כג-כד וּבֵ֣ית אֵ֔ל: וְהָעַוִּ֥ים וְהַפָּרָ֖ה וְעָפְרָ֑ה: וּכְפַ֧ר °הָעַמֹּנִי [°הָעַמֹּנָ֛ה ק] וְהָעָפְנִ֥י

כה-כו וָגָ֑בַע עָרִ֥ים שְׁתֵּים־עֶשְׂרֵ֖ה וְחַצְרֵיהֶֽן: גִּבְע֥וֹן וְהָֽרָמָ֖ה וּבְאֵרֽוֹת: וְהַמִּצְפֶּ֥ה

כז-כח וְהַכְּפִירָ֖ה וְהַמֹּצָ֑ה: וְרֶ֥קֶם וְיִרְפְּאֵ֖ל וְתַרְאֲלָֽה: וְצֵ֥לַע הָאֶ֛לֶף וְהַיְבוּסִ֥י הִ֖יא יְרֽוּשָׁלִַ֑ם גִּבְעַ֣ת קִרְיַ֗ת עָרִ֤ים אַרְבַּֽע־עֶשְׂרֵ֖ה וְחַצְרֵיהֶ֑ן זֹ֗את נַחֲלַ֛ת בְּנֵֽי־

יט א בִנְיָמִ֖ן לְמִשְׁפְּחֹתָֽם: וַיֵּצֵ֞א הַגּוֹרָ֤ל הַשֵּׁנִי֙ לְשִׁמְע֔וֹן לְמַטֵּ֥ה בְנֵֽי־

ב שִׁמְע֖וֹן לְמִשְׁפְּחוֹתָ֑ם וַֽיְהִי֙ נַֽחֲלָתָ֔ם בְּת֖וֹךְ נַֽחֲלַ֥ת בְּנֵֽי־יְהוּדָֽה: וַֽיְהִ֣י לָהֶ֔ם

ג-ד בְּנַֽחֲלָתָ֑ם בְּאֵֽר־שֶׁ֥בַע וְשֶׁ֖בַע וּמוֹלָדָֽה: וַֽחֲצַ֥ר שׁוּעָ֛ל וּבָלָ֖ה וָעָֽצֶם: וְאֶלְתּוֹלַ֥ד

ה וּבְת֖וּל וְחָרְמָֽה: וְצִֽקְלַ֥ג וּבֵֽית־הַמַּרְכָּב֖וֹת וַֽחֲצַ֥ר סוּסָֽה: וּבֵ֥ית

ו לְבָא֛וֹת וְשָׁרֽוּחֶ֖ן עָרִ֥ים שְׁלֹֽשׁ־עֶשְׂרֵ֖ה וְחַצְרֵיהֶֽן: עַ֥יִן רִמּ֛וֹן וָעֶ֥תֶר וְעָשָׁ֖ן עָרִ֥ים אַרְבַּ֖ע

ז-ח וְחַצְרֵיהֶֽן: וְכָל־הַֽחֲצֵרִ֗ים אֲשֶׁ֤ר סְבִיבוֹת֙ הֶֽעָרִ֣ים הָאֵ֔לֶּה עַד־בַּֽעֲלַ֖ת בְּאֵ֑ר

ט רָ֥אמַת נֶ֖גֶב זֹ֗את נַֽחֲלַ֛ת מַטֵּ֥ה בְנֵֽי־שִׁמְע֖וֹן לְמִשְׁפְּחֹתָֽם: מֵחֶ֨בֶל֙ בְּנֵ֣י יְהוּדָ֔ה נַֽחֲלַ֖ת בְּנֵ֣י שִׁמְע֑וֹן כִּֽי־הָיָ֞ה חֵ֤לֶק בְּנֵֽי־יְהוּדָה֙ רַ֣ב מֵהֶ֔ם וַיִּנְחֲל֥וּ בְנֵֽי־שִׁמְע֖וֹן

י בְּת֥וֹךְ נַֽחֲלָתָֽם: וַיַּ֙עַל֙ הַגּוֹרָ֣ל הַשְּׁלִישִׁ֔י לִבְנֵ֥י זְבוּלֻ֖ן

יא לְמִשְׁפְּחֹתָ֑ם וַיְהִ֛י גְּב֥וּל נַֽחֲלָתָ֖ם עַד־שָׂרִֽיד: וְעָלָ֨ה גְבוּלָ֧ם ׀ לַיָּ֣מָּה וּמַרְעֲלָ֗ה

יב וּפָגַ֣ע בְּדַבָּ֔שֶׁת וּפָגַע֙ אֶל־הַנַּ֔חַל אֲשֶׁ֖ר עַל־פְּנֵ֣י יָקְנְעָ֑ם וְשָׁ֤ב מִשָּׂרִיד֙ קֵ֔דְמָה

יג מִזְרַ֣ח הַשֶּׁ֗מֶשׁ עַל־גְּב֛וּל כִּסְלֹ֥ת תָּבֹ֖ר וְיָצָ֣א אֶל־הַדָּֽבְרַ֔ת וְעָלָ֖ה יָפִֽיעַ: וּמִשָּׁ֤ם עָבַר֙ קֵ֣דְמָה מִזְרָ֔חָה גִּתָּ֥ה חֵ֖פֶר עִתָּ֣ה קָצִ֑ין וְיָצָ֛א רִמּ֥וֹן הַמְּתֹאָ֖ר הַנֵּעָֽה:

יד-טו וְנָסַ֤ב אֹתוֹ֙ הַגְּב֔וּל מִצְּפ֥וֹן חַנָּתֹ֑ן וְהָיוּ֙ תֹּֽצְאֹתָ֔יו גֵּ֖י יִפְתַּח־אֵֽל: וְקַטָּ֤ת וְנַֽהֲלָ֙ל וְשִׁמְר֥וֹן וְיִדְאֲלָ֖ה וּבֵ֣ית לָ֑חֶם עָרִ֥ים שְׁתֵּים־עֶשְׂרֵ֖ה וְחַצְרֵיהֶֽן: זֹ֚את נַֽחֲלַ֣ת

טז בְּנֵֽי־זְבוּלֻ֔ן לְמִשְׁפְּחוֹתָ֑ם הֶֽעָרִ֥ים הָאֵ֖לֶּה וְחַצְרֵיהֶֽן: וּלְיִשָּׂשכָ֕ר

יז יָצָ֖א הַגּוֹרָ֣ל הָֽרְבִיעִ֑י לִבְנֵ֥י יִשָּׂשכָ֖ר לְמִשְׁפְּחוֹתָֽם: וַיְהִ֖י גְּבוּלָ֑ם יִזְרְעֶ֥אלָה

יח-יט וְהַכְּסוּלֹ֖ת וְשׁוּנֵֽם: וַֽחֲפָרַ֥יִם וְשִׁיאֹ֖ן וַֽאֲנָֽחֲרַֽת: וְהָֽרַבִּ֥ית וְקִשְׁי֖וֹן וָאָֽבֶץ:

כ-כב וְרֶ֧מֶת וְעֵֽין־גַּנִּ֛ים וְעֵ֥ין חַדָּ֖ה וּבֵ֥ית פַּצֵּֽץ: וּפָגַע֩ הַגְּב֨וּל בְּתָב֜וֹר °וְשַׁחֲצוֹמָה [°וְשַׁ חֲצִ֧ימָה ק] וּבֵ֣ית שֶׁ֗מֶשׁ וְהָי֛וּ תֹּֽצְא֥וֹת גְּבוּלָ֖ם הַיַּרְדֵּ֑ן עָרִ֥ים שֵׁשׁ־

כג עֶשְׂרֵ֖ה וְחַצְרֵיהֶֽן: זֹ֗את נַֽחֲלַ֛ת מַטֵּ֥ה בְנֵֽי־יִשָּׂשכָ֖ר לְמִשְׁפְּחֹתָ֑ם הֶֽעָרִ֖ים

כד וְחַצְרֵיהֶֽן: וַיֵּצֵא֙ הַגּוֹרָ֣ל הַֽחֲמִישִׁ֔י לְמַטֵּ֥ה בְנֵֽי־אָשֵׁ֖ר לְמִשְׁפְּחוֹתָֽם:

כה-כו וַיְהִ֖י גְּבוּלָ֑ם חֶלְקַ֥ת וַֽחֲלִ֖י וָבֶ֥טֶן וְאַכְשָֽׁף: וְאַֽלַמֶּ֥לֶךְ וְעַמְעָ֖ד וּמִשְׁאָ֑ל וּפָגַ֤ע בְּכַרְמֶל֙ הַיָּ֔מָּה וּבְשִׁיח֖וֹר לִבְנָֽת: וְשָׁ֨ב מִזְרַ֣ח הַשֶּׁ֗מֶשׁ בֵּ֚ית דָּגֹ֔ן וּפָגַ֣ע בִּזְבֻל֗וּן

כז-כט וּבְגֵ֤י יִפְתַּח־אֵל֙ צָפ֔וֹנָה בֵּ֥ית הָעֵ֖מֶק וּנְעִיאֵ֑ל וְיָצָ֥א אֶל־כָּב֖וּל מִשְּׂמֹֽאל: וְעֶבְרֹ֥ן וּרְחֹ֖ב וְחַמּ֣וֹן וְקָנָ֑ה עַ֖ד צִיד֥וֹן רַבָּֽה: וְשָׁ֤ב הַגְּבוּל֙ הָֽרָמָ֔ה וְעַד־עִ֖יר מִבְצַר־צֹ֑ר וְשָׁ֤ב הַגְּבוּל֙ חֹסָ֔ה °וַיְהִ֥יוּ [°וְהָי֛וּ ק] תֹֽצְאֹתָ֥יו הַיָּ֖מָּה מֵחֶ֥בֶל

19:8. Whereas all the tribes received separate territories within the land, Simeon was not allocated any territory, but only scattered patches of land within the territory of Judah. *Ramban* explains that this was in fulfillment of Jacob's words, "I will divide them [i.e., Simeon and Levi] in Jacob and scatter them in Israel" (*Genesis* 49:7), implying that the tribes of Simeon and Levi would be given a series of cities, but not complete provinces.

Beth-el, ²³ Avvim, Parah, Ophrah, ²⁴ Cephar-ammonah, Ophni, Geba — twelve cities and their villages; ²⁵ Gibeon, Ramah, Beeroth, ²⁶ Mizpeh, Chephirah, Mozah; ²⁷ Rekem, Irpeel, Taralah, ²⁸ Zela, Eleph, the Jebusite [city] which is Jerusalem, Gibeath, [and] Kiriath — fourteen cities and their villages. This is the heritage of the children of Benjamin according to their families.

19

Simeon's
territory
(See Appendix D,
map 2)

¹ The second lottery came out for Simeon, for the tribe of the children of Simeon according to their families. Their heritage was situated in the midst of the heritage of the children of Judah. ² They received for their heritage: Beer-sheba [which is] Sheba, Moladah, ³ Hazar-shual, Balah, Ezem, ⁴ Eltolad, Bethul, Hormah, ⁵ Ziklag, Beth-marcaboth, Hazar-susah, ⁶ Beth-lebaoth, and Sharuhen — thirteen cities and their villages. ⁷ Ain, Rimmon, Ether, and Ashan — four cities and their villages — ⁸ and all the villages that surrounded these cities until Baalath-beer and Ramah of the south; this is the heritage of the tribe of the children of Simeon according to their families. * ⁹ The heritage of the children of Simeon was from the portion of the children of Judah, because the lot of the children of Judah was too large for them. Therefore, the children of Simeon received their heritage within [Judah's] heritage. *

Zebulun's
territory

¹⁰ The third lottery came up for the children of Zebulun according to their families; the border of their heritage extended to Sarid. ¹¹ Their border ascended to the west and Maralah and reached to Dabbesheth; it reached the river that is alongside Jokneam. ¹² It returned from Sarid eastward, toward the rising sun on the border of Chisloth-tabor, and it went out to Dobrath and ascended to Japhia. ¹³ From there it passed to the east, to Gath-hepher and to Ittah-kazin, and it went out to Rimmon, curving to Neah. ¹⁴ The border circled it, at the north of Hannathon, and its outlets were the Valley of Iphtah-el, ¹⁵ with Kattath, Nahalal, Shimron, Idalah, and Beth-lehem — twelve cities* and their villages. ¹⁶ This is the heritage of the children of Zebulun according to their families, these cities and their villages.

Issachar's
territory

¹⁷ The fourth lottery came out for Issachar, for the children of Issachar according to their families. ¹⁸ Their border was: Jezreel, Chesuloth, Shunem, ¹⁹ Hapharaim, Shion, Anaharath, ²⁰ Rabbith, Kishion, Ebez, ²¹ Remeth, En-gannim, En-chaddah, and Beth-pazzez. ²² The border reached Tabor, Sha-hazim, Beth-shemesh; their border's outlets were to the Jordan — sixteen cities and their villages. ²³ This is the heritage of the tribe of the children of Issachar according to their families, the cities and their villages.

Asher's
territory

²⁴ The fifth lottery came out for the tribe of the children of Asher according to their families. ²⁵ Their border was: Helkath, Hali, Beten, Achshaph, ²⁶ and Alammelech, Amad, Mishal; and it reached Carmel at the sea and at Shihor-libnath. ²⁷ It turned toward the rising sun, to Beth-dagon, and it reached Zebulun and the north of the Valley of Iphtah-el and Beth-haemek and Neiel. It then went out to the north of Cabul, ²⁸ and to Ebron, Rehob, Hammon, and Kanah, until Great Sidon. ²⁹ The border turned to Ramah and to the fortified city of Tyre; * the border turned to Hosah, and its outlets were to the Sea from the portion of

---

19:9. Judah conquered more than it required. Since Simeon was allied with the army of Judah (see *Judges* 1:3), Judah's excess cities were allocated to Simeon.

19:15. Some of the cities listed along the borders

belonged to Zebulun; others were just across the border and belonged to the neighboring tribe.

19:29. Tyre belonged to Naphtali and is listed here only as a border landmark.

ל-לא אַכְזִיבָה: וְעֻמָה וַאֲפֵק וּרְחֹב עָרִים עֶשְׂרִים וּשְׁתַּיִם וְחַצְרֵיהֶן: זֹאת נַחֲלַת

לב מַטֵּה בְנֵי־אָשֵׁר לְמִשְׁפְּחֹתָם הֶעָרִים הָאֵלֶּה וְחַצְרֵיהֶן: לִבְנֵי

לג נַפְתָּלִי יָצָא הַגּוֹרָל הַשִּׁשִּׁי לִבְנֵי נַפְתָּלִי לְמִשְׁפְּחֹתָם: וַיְהִי גְבוּלָם

מֵחֵלֶף מֵאֵלוֹן בְּצַעֲנַנִּים וַאֲדָמִי הַנֶּקֶב וְיַבְנְאֵל עַד־לַקּוּם וַיְהִי תֹצְאֹתָיו

לד הַיַּרְדֵּן: וְשָׁב הַגְּבוּל יָמָּה אַזְנוֹת תָּבוֹר וְיָצָא מִשָּׁם חוּקֹקָה וּפָגַע בִּזְבֻלוּן

לה מִנֶּגֶב וּבְאָשֵׁר פָּגַע מִיָּם וּבִיהוּדָה הַיַּרְדֵּן מִזְרַח הַשָּׁמֶשׁ: וְעָרֵי מִבְצָר

לו-לז הַצִּדִּים צֵר וְחַמַּת רַקַּת וְכִנָּרֶת: וַאֲדָמָה וְהָרָמָה וְחָצוֹר: וְקֶדֶשׁ וְאֶדְרֶעִי

לח וְעֵין חָצוֹר: וְיִרְאוֹן וּמִגְדַּל־אֵל חֳרֵם וּבֵית־עֲנָת וּבֵית שָׁמֶשׁ עָרִים תֵּשַׁע־

לט עֶשְׂרֵה וְחַצְרֵיהֶן: זֹאת נַחֲלַת מַטֵּה בְנֵי־נַפְתָּלִי לְמִשְׁפְּחֹתָם הֶעָרִים

מ-מא וְחַצְרֵיהֶן: לְמַטֵּה בְנֵי־דָן לְמִשְׁפְּחֹתָם יָצָא הַגּוֹרָל הַשְּׁבִיעִי: וַיְהִי

מב גְּבוּל נַחֲלָתָם צָרְעָה וְאֶשְׁתָּאוֹל וְעִיר שָׁמֶשׁ: וְשַׁעֲלַבִּין וְאַיָּלוֹן וְיִתְלָה:

מג-מה וְאֵילוֹן וְתִמְנָתָה וְעֶקְרוֹן: וְאֶלְתְּקֵה וְגִבְּתוֹן וּבַעֲלָת: וִיהֻד וּבְנֵי־בְרַק וְגַת־

מו-מז רִמּוֹן: וּמֵי הַיַּרְקוֹן וְהָרַקּוֹן עִם־הַגְּבוּל מוּל יָפוֹ: וַיֵּצֵא גְבוּל־בְּנֵי־דָן מֵהֶם

וַיַּעֲלוּ בְנֵי־דָן וַיִּלָּחֲמוּ עִם־לֶשֶׁם וַיִּלְכְּדוּ אוֹתָהּ | וַיַּכּוּ אוֹתָהּ לְפִי־חֶרֶב

מח וַיִּרְשׁוּ אוֹתָהּ וַיֵּשְׁבוּ בָהּ וַיִּקְרְאוּ לְלֶשֶׁם דָּן כְּשֵׁם דָּן אֲבִיהֶם: זֹאת נַחֲלַת

מט מַטֵּה בְנֵי־דָן לְמִשְׁפְּחֹתָם הֶעָרִים הָאֵלֶּה וְחַצְרֵיהֶן: וַיְכַלּוּ לִנְחֹל־

אֶת־הָאָרֶץ לִגְבוּלֹתֶיהָ וַיִּתְּנוּ בְנֵי־יִשְׂרָאֵל נַחֲלָה לִיהוֹשֻׁעַ בִּן־נוּן בְּתוֹכָם:

נ עַל־פִּי יהוה נָתְנוּ לוֹ אֶת־הָעִיר אֲשֶׁר שָׁאָל אֶת־תִּמְנַת־סֶרַח בְּהַר אֶפְרָיִם

נא וַיִּבְנֶה אֶת־הָעִיר וַיֵּשֶׁב בָּהּ: אֵלֶּה הַנְּחָלֹת אֲשֶׁר נִחֲלוּ אֶלְעָזָר

הַכֹּהֵן | וִיהוֹשֻׁעַ בִּן־נוּן וְרָאשֵׁי הָאָבוֹת לְמַטּוֹת בְּנֵי־יִשְׂרָאֵל | בְּגוֹרָל |

בְּשִׁלֹה לִפְנֵי יהוה פֶּתַח אֹהֶל מוֹעֵד וַיְכַלּוּ מֵחַלֵּק אֶת־הָאָרֶץ:

כ

א-ב וַיְדַבֵּר יהוה אֶל־יְהוֹשֻׁעַ לֵאמֹר: דַּבֵּר אֶל־בְּנֵי יִשְׂרָאֵל לֵאמֹר תְּנוּ

ג לָכֶם אֶת־עָרֵי הַמִּקְלָט אֲשֶׁר־דִּבַּרְתִּי אֲלֵיכֶם בְּיַד־מֹשֶׁה: לָנוּס שָׁמָּה

ד רוֹצֵחַ מַכֵּה־נֶפֶשׁ בִּשְׁגָגָה בִּבְלִי־דָעַת וְהָיוּ לָכֶם לְמִקְלָט מִגֹּאֵל הַדָּם: וְנָס

אֶל־אַחַת | מֵהֶעָרִים הָאֵלֶּה וְעָמַד פֶּתַח שַׁעַר הָעִיר וְדִבֶּר בְּאָזְנֵי זִקְנֵי

הָעִיר־הַהִיא אֶת־דְּבָרָיו וְאָסְפוּ אֹתוֹ הָעִירָה אֲלֵיהֶם וְנָתְנוּ־לוֹ מָקוֹם

ה וְיָשַׁב עִמָּם: וְכִי יִרְדֹּף גֹּאֵל הַדָּם אַחֲרָיו וְלֹא־יַסְגִּרוּ אֶת־הָרֹצֵחַ בְּיָדוֹ

כִּי בִבְלִי־דַעַת הִכָּה אֶת־רֵעֵהוּ וְלֹא־שֹׂנֵא הוּא לוֹ מִתְּמוֹל שִׁלְשׁוֹם:

ו וְיָשַׁב | בָּעִיר הַהִיא עַד־עָמְדוֹ לִפְנֵי הָעֵדָה לַמִּשְׁפָּט עַד־מוֹת הַכֹּהֵן

הַגָּדוֹל אֲשֶׁר יִהְיֶה בַּיָּמִים הָהֵם אָז | יָשׁוּב הָרוֹצֵחַ וּבָא אֶל־עִירוֹ וְאֶל־

ז בֵּיתוֹ אֶל־הָעִיר אֲשֶׁר־נָס מִשָּׁם: וַיַּקְדִּשׁוּ אֶת־קֶדֶשׁ בַּגָּלִיל בְּהַר נַפְתָּלִי

19:38. Some of the border cities listed above belonged to neighboring tribes.

20:2. See *Numbers* 35:9-34 for the background of the laws in this chapter.

20:6. If the killer is found to have exercised all reasonable care, he is acquitted and does not go into exile. If he is found guilty of carelessness, he is exiled to a city of refuge where he must remain until the death of the Kohen Gadol.

Achzib; ³⁰ with Ummah and Aphek and Rehob — twenty-two cities and their villages. ³¹ This is the heritage of the tribe of the children of Asher according to their families, these cities and their villages.

Naphtali's territory
(See Appendix D, map 2)

³² The sixth lottery came out for the children of Naphtali, for the children of Naphtali according to their families. ³³ Their border was: from Heleph, from Elon-bezaanannim, Adami, Nekeb, and Jabneel until Lakkum, and its outlets were the Jordan. ³⁴ The border turned westward to Aznoth-tabor and went out from there to Hukok; it reached Zebulun in the south, and reached Asher in the west, and Judah at the Jordan toward the rising sun. ³⁵ The fortified cities were: Ziddim, Zer, Hammath, Rakkath, Kinnereth, ³⁶ Adamah, Haramath, Hazor, ³⁷ Kedesh, Edrei, En-hazor, ³⁸ Iron, Migdal-el, Horem, Beth-anath, and Beth-shemesh — nineteen cities* and their villages. ³⁹ This is the heritage of the tribe of the children of Naphtali according to their families, the cities and their villages.

Dan's territory

⁴⁰ For the tribe of the children of Dan according to their families, the seventh lottery went out. ⁴¹ The border of their heritage was: Zorah, Eshtaol, Ir-shemesh, ⁴² Shaalabbin, Aijalon, Ithlah, ⁴³ Elon, Timnah, Ekron, ⁴⁴ Eltekeh, Gibbethon, Baalath, ⁴⁵ Jehud, Bene-berak, Gath-rimmon, ⁴⁶ Mei-jarkon, and Rakkon, with the border opposite Jaffa. ⁴⁷ The boundary of the children of Dan was not sufficient for them, so the children of Dan ascended and battled with Leshem, and conquered it, smiting it by the edge of the sword. They took possession of it and dwelled there, and changed the name of Leshem to Dan, after the name of Dan their ancestor. ⁴⁸ This is the heritage of the tribe of the children of Dan according to their families, these cities and their villages.

⁴⁹ Thus they finished apportioning the land according to its borders. The Children of Israel gave a heritage to Joshua son of Nun within their midst. ⁵⁰ By the word of HASHEM they gave him the city that he requested, Timnath-serah in Mount Ephraim; and he built the city and dwelled there.

⁵¹ These are the heritages that Elazar the Kohen, and Joshua son of Nun, and the heads of the ancestral [families] of the tribes of the Children of Israel apportioned by lottery, in Shiloh, before HASHEM, at the entrance of the Tent of Meeting. Thus they finished dividing the land.

20

THE CITIES OF REFUGE
20:1-9
(See Appendix D, map 5)

¹ HASHEM spoke to Joshua, saying, ² "Speak to the Children of Israel, saying, 'Prepare for yourselves the cities of refuge, about which I spoke to you through Moses,* ³ where a killer may flee — one who kills a person through carelessness, unintentionally. They will be a refuge for you from the avenger of the blood. ⁴ He shall flee to one of these cities, stand at the entrance to the city gate, and speak his words into the ears of the elders of that city; they shall bring him into the city, to them, and provide him a place, and he shall dwell among them. ⁵ If the avenger of the blood chases after him, they shall not deliver the killer into his hand, for he struck his fellow unintentionally; he did not hate him from yesterday and before yesterday. ⁶ He shall dwell in that city until he stands before the tribunal for judgment, until the death of the Kohen Gadol who will be in those days. Then the killer may return and go to his city and to his house, to the city from which he fled.' "*

⁷ They designated Kedesh in the Galilee in the mountains of Naphtali,

ח וְאֶת־שְׁכֶם בְּהַר אֶפְרַיִם וְאֶת־קִרְיַת אַרְבַּע הִיא חֶבְרוֹן בְּהַר יְהוּדָה: וּמֵעֵבֶר
לְיַרְדֵּן יְרִיחוֹ מִזְרָחָה נָתְנוּ אֶת־בֶּצֶר בַּמִּדְבָּר בַּמִּישֹׁר מִמַּטֵּה רְאוּבֵן וְאֶת־
רָאמֹת בַּגִּלְעָד מִמַּטֵּה־גָד וְאֶת־°גָּלוֹן [°גּוֹלָן ק] בַּבָּשָׁן מִמַּטֵּה מְנַשֶּׁה: אֵלֶּה
ט הָיוּ עָרֵי הַמּוּעָדָה לְכֹל | בְּנֵי יִשְׂרָאֵל וְלַגֵּר הַגָּר בְּתוֹכָם לָנוּס
שָׁמָּה כָּל־מַכֵּה־נֶפֶשׁ בִּשְׁגָגָה וְלֹא יָמוּת בְּיַד גֹּאֵל הַדָּם עַד־עָמְדוֹ לִפְנֵי
א הָעֵדָה: וַיִּגְּשׁוּ רָאשֵׁי אֲבוֹת הַלְוִיִּם אֶל־אֶלְעָזָר הַכֹּהֵן וְאֶל־ כא
ב יְהוֹשֻׁעַ בִּן־נוּן וְאֶל־רָאשֵׁי אֲבוֹת הַמַּטּוֹת לִבְנֵי יִשְׂרָאֵל: וַיְדַבְּרוּ אֲלֵיהֶם
בְּשִׁלֹה בְּאֶרֶץ כְּנַעַן לֵאמֹר יְהוָה צִוָּה בְיַד־מֹשֶׁה לָתֶת־לָנוּ עָרִים לָשָׁבֶת
ג וּמִגְרְשֵׁיהֶן לִבְהֶמְתֵּנוּ: וַיִּתְּנוּ בְנֵי־יִשְׂרָאֵל לַלְוִיִּם מִנַּחֲלָתָם אֶל־פִּי יְהוָה
ד אֶת־הֶעָרִים הָאֵלֶּה וְאֶת־מִגְרְשֵׁיהֶן: וַיֵּצֵא הַגּוֹרָל לְמִשְׁפְּחֹת
הַקְּהָתִי וַיְהִי לִבְנֵי אַהֲרֹן הַכֹּהֵן מִן־הַלְוִיִּם מִמַּטֵּה יְהוּדָה וּמִמַּטֵּה הַשִּׁמְעֹנִי
ה וּמִמַּטֵּה בִנְיָמִן בַּגּוֹרָל עָרִים שְׁלֹשׁ עֶשְׂרֵה: וְלִבְנֵי קְהָת
הַנּוֹתָרִים מִמִּשְׁפְּחֹת מַטֵּה־אֶפְרַיִם וּמִמַּטֵּה־דָן וּמֵחֲצִי מַטֵּה מְנַשֶּׁה
ו בַּגּוֹרָל עָרִים עָשֶׂר: וְלִבְנֵי גֵרְשׁוֹן מִמִּשְׁפְּחוֹת מַטֵּה־יִשָּׂשכָר
וּמִמַּטֵּה־אָשֵׁר וּמִמַּטֵּה נַפְתָּלִי וּמֵחֲצִי מַטֵּה מְנַשֶּׁה בַבָּשָׁן בַּגּוֹרָל עָרִים
ז שְׁלֹשׁ עֶשְׂרֵה: לִבְנֵי מְרָרִי לְמִשְׁפְּחֹתָם מִמַּטֵּה רְאוּבֵן וּמִמַּטֵּה־
ח גָד וּמִמַּטֵּה זְבוּלֻן עָרִים שְׁתֵּים עֶשְׂרֵה: וַיִּתְּנוּ בְנֵי־יִשְׂרָאֵל
לַלְוִיִּם אֶת־הֶעָרִים הָאֵלֶּה וְאֶת־מִגְרְשֵׁיהֶן כַּאֲשֶׁר צִוָּה יְהוָה בְּיַד־מֹשֶׁה
ט בַּגּוֹרָל: וַיִּתְּנוּ מִמַּטֵּה בְּנֵי יְהוּדָה וּמִמַּטֵּה בְּנֵי שִׁמְעוֹן אֵת הֶעָרִים
י הָאֵלֶּה אֲשֶׁר־יִקְרָא אֶתְהֶן בְּשֵׁם: וַיְהִי לִבְנֵי אַהֲרֹן מִמִּשְׁפְּחוֹת הַקְּהָתִי
יא מִבְּנֵי לֵוִי כִּי לָהֶם הָיָה הַגּוֹרָל רִאשֹׁנָה: וַיִּתְּנוּ לָהֶם אֶת־קִרְיַת אַרְבַּע אֲבִי
יב הָעֲנוֹק הִיא חֶבְרוֹן בְּהַר יְהוּדָה וְאֶת־מִגְרָשֶׁהָ סְבִיבֹתֶיהָ: וְאֶת־שְׂדֵה הָעִיר
יג וְאֶת־חֲצֵרֶיהָ נָתְנוּ לְכָלֵב בֶּן־יְפֻנֶּה בַּאֲחֻזָּתוֹ: וְלִבְנֵי | אַהֲרֹן
הַכֹּהֵן נָתְנוּ אֶת־עִיר מִקְלַט הָרֹצֵחַ אֶת־חֶבְרוֹן וְאֶת־מִגְרָשֶׁהָ וְאֶת־לִבְנָה
יד-טו וְאֶת־מִגְרָשֶׁהָ: וְאֶת־יַתִּר וְאֶת־מִגְרָשֶׁהָ וְאֶת־אֶשְׁתְּמֹעַ וְאֶת־מִגְרָשֶׁהָ: וְאֶת־
טז חֹלֹן וְאֶת־מִגְרָשֶׁהָ וְאֶת־דְּבִיר וְאֶת־מִגְרָשֶׁהָ: וְאֶת־עַיִן וְאֶת־מִגְרָשֶׁהָ וְאֶת־
יֻטָּה וְאֶת־מִגְרָשֶׁהָ אֶת־בֵּית־שֶׁמֶשׁ וְאֶת־מִגְרָשֶׁהָ עָרִים תֵּשַׁע מֵאֵת שְׁנֵי
יז הַשְּׁבָטִים הָאֵלֶּה: וּמִמַּטֵּה בִנְיָמִן אֶת־גִּבְעוֹן וְאֶת־מִגְרָשֶׁהָ
יח אֶת־גֶּבַע וְאֶת־מִגְרָשֶׁהָ: אֶת־עֲנָתוֹת וְאֶת־מִגְרָשֶׁהָ וְאֶת־עַלְמוֹן וְאֶת־
יט מִגְרָשֶׁהָ עָרִים אַרְבַּע: כָּל־עָרֵי בְנֵי־אַהֲרֹן הַכֹּהֲנִים שְׁלֹשׁ־עֶשְׂרֵה
כ עָרִים וּמִגְרְשֵׁיהֶן: וּלְמִשְׁפְּחוֹת בְּנֵי־קְהָת הַלְוִיִּם הַנּוֹתָרִים

20:8. Although Moses designated the three cities to the east of the Jordan before his death (*Deuteronomy* 4:41-43), they did not assume their official status until Joshua designated the remaining three (*Talmud*).

21:2. The Levite cities were spread throughout the land in fulfillment of Jacob's utterance, "I will scatter them in Israel" (*Genesis* 49:7). The Torah granted the Levites cities, but not a tribal province in the land (*Numbers* 18:20), so that they would devote themselves to Divine service in the Holy Temple and teach the Torah to the other tribes

The six cities

and Shechem in the mountains of Ephraim, and Kiriath-arba which is Hebron in the mountains of Judah. ⁸ On the other side of the Jordan, by Jericho, to the east, they designated Bezer in the wilderness in the plain from the tribe of Reuben, and Ramoth in Gilead from the tribe of Gad, and Golan in the Bashan from the tribe of Manasseh. * ⁹ These were the cities appointed for all the Children of Israel and for the resident who dwells among them — to which any person who kills through carelessness may flee, and not die by the hand of the avenger of the blood before he stands before the tribunal.

21

THE CITIES OF THE LEVITES AND KOHANIM

21:1-40

(See Appendix D, map 5)

¹ **T**he heads of the ancestral [families] of the Levites approached Elazar the Kohen, Joshua son of Nun, and the heads of the fathers' [household] of the tribes of the Children of Israel. ² They spoke to them in Shiloh, in the land of Canaan, saying, "HASHEM commanded through Moses to give us cities in which to dwell and their open [surrounding] spaces for our animals."* ³ So the Children of Israel gave to the Levites from their heritages, according to the word of HASHEM, these cities and their open spaces.

⁴ The lottery came out for the families of the Kohathite: for the sons of Aaron the Kohen, [who were] of the Levites, [there were] from the tribe of Judah, from the tribe of the Simeonite, and from the tribe of Benjamin, by lottery, thirteen cities.

⁵ For the remaining sons of Kohath: from the families of the tribe of Ephraim, from the tribe of Dan, and from half the tribe of Manasseh, by lottery, ten cities.

⁶ To the sons of Gershon: from the families of the tribe of Issachar, from the tribe of Asher, from the tribe of Naphtali, and from half the tribe of Manasseh in the Bashan, by lottery, thirteen cities.

⁷ For the sons of Merari according to their families: from the tribe of Reuben, from the tribe of Gad, and from the tribe of Zebulun, twelve cities.

⁸ The Children of Israel gave these cities and their open spaces to the Levites, as HASHEM had commanded through Moses, by lottery.

The cities of the Kohanim — from Judah, Simeon, and Benjamin

⁹ They gave — from the tribe of the children of Judah and from the tribe of the children of Simeon — these cities which will be mentioned by name, ¹⁰ and they belonged to the sons of Aaron from the Kohathite family of the children of Levi, for theirs was the first lottery. ¹¹ They gave them Kiriath-arba, * father of the giants, which is Hebron in Mount Judah, and its open spaces around it; ¹² but the fields of the city and its villages they gave to Caleb son of Jephunneh as his possession.

¹³ To the sons of Aaron the Kohen they gave the city of refuge for killers, Hebron and its open spaces, Libnah and its open spaces, ¹⁴ Jattir and its open spaces, Eshtemoa and its open spaces, ¹⁵ Holon and its open spaces, Debir and its open spaces, ¹⁶ Ain and its open spaces, Juttah and its open spaces, and Beth-shemesh and its open spaces — nine cities from these two tribes.

¹⁷ From the tribe of Benjamin: Gibeon and its open spaces, Geba and its open spaces, ¹⁸ Anathoth and its open spaces, and Almon and its open spaces — four cities. ¹⁹ All the cities of the sons of Aaron, the Kohanim, were thirteen cities and their open spaces.

²⁰ As for the families of the sons of Kohath, the Levites — those that were left

---

(Rambam). They were supported by the tithes given them by their brethren, a process that was facilitated by their

dispersion throughout the land. See Numbers 35:1-8. **21:11.** See 14:15.

כא מִבְּנֵי קְהָת וַיְהִי עָרֵי גוֹרָלָם מִמַּטֵּה אֶפְרָיִם: וַיִּתְּנוּ לָהֶם אֶת־עִיר מִקְלַט הָרֹצֵחַ אֶת־שְׁכֶם וְאֶת־מִגְרָשֶׁהָ בְּהַר אֶפְרָיִם וְאֶת־גֶּזֶר וְאֶת־

כב מִגְרָשֶׁהָ: וְאֶת־קִבְצַיִם וְאֶת־מִגְרָשֶׁהָ וְאֶת־בֵּית חוֹרֹן וְאֶת־מִגְרָשֶׁהָ עָרִים

כג אַרְבַּע: וּמִמַּטֵּה־דָן אֶת־אֶלְתְּקֵא וְאֶת־מִגְרָשֶׁהָ אֶת־גִּבְּתוֹן

כד וְאֶת־מִגְרָשֶׁהָ: אֶת־אַיָּלוֹן וְאֶת־מִגְרָשֶׁהָ אֶת־גַּת־רִמּוֹן וְאֶת־מִגְרָשֶׁהָ

כה עָרִים אַרְבַּע: וּמִמַּחֲצִית מַטֵּה מְנַשֶּׁה אֶת־תַּעְנַךְ וְאֶת־

כו מִגְרָשֶׁהָ וְאֶת־גַּת־רִמּוֹן וְאֶת־מִגְרָשֶׁהָ עָרִים שְׁתָּיִם: כָּל־עָרִים עֶשֶׂר וּמִגְרָשֵׁיהֶן לְמִשְׁפְּחוֹת בְּנֵי־קְהָת הַנּוֹתָרִים: וְלִבְנֵי גֵרְשׁוֹן

כז מִמִּשְׁפְּחֹת הַלְוִיִּם מֵחֲצִי מַטֵּה מְנַשֶּׁה אֶת־עִיר מִקְלַט הָרֹצֵחַ אֶת־ °גלון [°גּוֹלָן ק] בַּבָּשָׁן וְאֶת־מִגְרָשֶׁהָ וְאֶת־בְּעֶשְׁתְּרָה וְאֶת־מִגְרָשֶׁהָ עָרִים

כח שְׁתָּיִם: וּמִמַּטֵּה יִשָּׂשכָר אֶת־קִשְׁיוֹן וְאֶת־מִגְרָשֶׁהָ אֶת־

כט דָּבְרַת וְאֶת־מִגְרָשֶׁהָ: אֶת־יַרְמוּת וְאֶת־מִגְרָשֶׁהָ אֶת־עֵין גַּנִּים וְאֶת־

ל מִגְרָשֶׁהָ עָרִים אַרְבַּע: וּמִמַּטֵּה אָשֵׁר אֶת־מִשְׁאָל וְאֶת־

לא מִגְרָשֶׁהָ אֶת־עַבְדּוֹן וְאֶת־מִגְרָשֶׁהָ: אֶת־חֶלְקָת וְאֶת־מִגְרָשֶׁהָ וְאֶת־רְחֹב

לב וְאֶת־מִגְרָשֶׁהָ עָרִים אַרְבַּע: וּמִמַּטֵּה נַפְתָּלִי אֶת־עִיר ׀ מִקְלַט הָרֹצֵחַ אֶת־קֶדֶשׁ בַּגָּלִיל וְאֶת־מִגְרָשֶׁהָ וְאֶת־חַמֹּת דֹּאר וְאֶת־

לג מִגְרָשֶׁהָ וְאֶת־קַרְתָּן וְאֶת־מִגְרָשֶׁהָ עָרִים שָׁלֹשׁ: כָּל־עָרֵי הַגֵּרְשֻׁנִּי

לד לְמִשְׁפְּחֹתָם שְׁלֹשׁ־עֶשְׂרֵה עִיר וּמִגְרָשֵׁיהֶן: וּלְמִשְׁפְּחוֹת בְּנֵי־מְרָרִי הַלְוִיִּם הַנּוֹתָרִים מֵאֵת מַטֵּה זְבוּלֻן אֶת־יָקְנְעָם וְאֶת־מִגְרָשֶׁהָ

לה אֶת־קַרְתָּה וְאֶת־מִגְרָשֶׁהָ: אֶת־דִּמְנָה וְאֶת־מִגְרָשֶׁהָ אֶת־נַהֲלָל וְאֶת־

לו מִגְרָשֶׁהָ עָרִים אַרְבַּע: °° וּמִמַּטֵּה־גָד אֶת־עִיר מִקְלַט הָרֹצֵחַ

לז אֶת־רָמֹת בַּגִּלְעָד וְאֶת־מִגְרָשֶׁהָ וְאֶת־מַחֲנַיִם וְאֶת־מִגְרָשֶׁהָ: אֶת־חֶשְׁבּוֹן

לח וְאֶת־מִגְרָשֶׁהָ אֶת־יַעְזֵר וְאֶת־מִגְרָשֶׁהָ כָּל־עָרִים אַרְבַּע: כָּל־ הֶעָרִים לִבְנֵי מְרָרִי לְמִשְׁפְּחֹתָם הַנּוֹתָרִים מִמִּשְׁפְּחוֹת הַלְוִיִּם וַיְהִי

לט גוֹרָלָם עָרִים שְׁתֵּים עֶשְׂרֵה: כֹּל עָרֵי הַלְוִיִּם בְּתוֹךְ אֲחֻזַּת בְּנֵי־יִשְׂרָאֵל

מ עָרִים אַרְבָּעִים וּשְׁמֹנֶה וּמִגְרְשֵׁיהֶן: תִּהְיֶינָה הֶעָרִים הָאֵלֶּה עִיר עִיר

מא וּמִגְרָשֶׁיהָ סְבִיבֹתֶיהָ כֵּן לְכָל־הֶעָרִים הָאֵלֶּה: וַיִּתֵּן יְהוָה לְיִשְׂרָאֵל אֶת־כָּל־הָאָרֶץ אֲשֶׁר נִשְׁבַּע לָתֵת לַאֲבוֹתָם וַיִּרָשׁוּהָ וַיֵּשְׁבוּ

מב בָהּ: וַיָּנַח יְהוָה לָהֶם מִסָּבִיב כְּכֹל אֲשֶׁר־נִשְׁבַּע לַאֲבוֹתָם וְלֹא־עָמַד

מג אִישׁ בִּפְנֵיהֶם מִכָּל־אֹיְבֵיהֶם אֵת כָּל־אֹיְבֵיהֶם נָתַן יְהוָה בְּיָדָם: לֹא־ נָפַל דָּבָר מִכֹּל הַדָּבָר הַטּוֹב אֲשֶׁר־דִּבֶּר יְהוָה אֶל־בֵּית יִשְׂרָאֵל הַכֹּל

°° בְּקְצָת סְפָרִים אַחַר פָּסוּק לה:

וּמִמַּטֵּה רְאוּבֵן אֶת־בֶּצֶר וְאֶת־מִגְרָשֶׁהָ וְאֶת־יַהְצָה וְאֶת־מִגְרָשֶׁהָ: אֶת־קְדֵמוֹת וְאֶת־מִגְרָשֶׁהָ וְאֶת־מֵיפַעַת וְאֶת־מִגְרָשֶׁהָ עָרִים אַרְבַּע:

The cities of Kohath — from Ephraim, Dan, and half of Manasseh

from the sons of Kohath — the cities of their lottery were from the tribe of Ephraim. ²¹ They gave them the city of refuge for killers, Shechem and its open spaces in Mount Ephraim, Gezer and its open spaces, ²² Kivzaim and its open spaces, and Beth-horon and its open spaces — four cities.

²³ From the tribe of Dan — Elteke and its open spaces, Gibbethon and its open spaces, ²⁴ Aijalon and its open spaces, and Gath-rimmon and its open spaces — four cities.

²⁵ From half the tribe of Manasseh: Taanach and its open spaces and Gath-rimmon and its open spaces — two cities. ²⁶ In all there were ten cities and their open spaces for the remaining families of the sons of Kohath.

The cities of Gershon — from half of Manasseh, Issachar, Asher, and Naphtali

²⁷ For the sons of Gershon of the families of the Levites: from half the tribe of Manasseh, the city of refuge for the killer, Golan in the Bashan and its open spaces, and Beeshterah and its open spaces — two cities.

²⁸ From the tribe of Issachar: Kishion and its open spaces, Dobrath and its open spaces, ²⁹ Jarmuth and its open spaces, and En-gannim and its open spaces — four cities.

³⁰ From the tribe of Asher: Mishal and its open spaces, Abdon and its open spaces, ³¹ Helkath and its open spaces, and Rehob and its open spaces — four cities.

³² From the tribe of Naphtali: the city of refuge for the killers, Kedesh in the Galilee and its open spaces, Hammoth-dor and its open spaces, and Kartan and its open spaces — three cities. ³³ All the Gershonite cities according to their families were thirteen cities and their open spaces.

The cities of Merari — from Zebulun, Reuben, and Gad

³⁴ For the families of the sons of Merari, the remaining Levites: from the tribe of Zebulun, Jokneam and its open spaces, Kartah and its open spaces, ³⁵ Dimnah and its open spaces, and Nahalal and its open spaces — four cities. *

³⁶ From the tribe of Gad: the city of refuge for the killers, Ramoth, in the Gilead, and its open spaces, Mahanaim and its open spaces, ³⁷ Heshbon and its open spaces, and Jazer and its open spaces — all the cities four.

³⁸ All the cities for the sons of Merari according to their families, the remaining families of the Levites — their lot was twelve cities.

³⁹ All the cities of the Levites within the possession of the Children of Israel were forty-eight, and their open spaces. ⁴⁰ Every single city of these cities shall be [given] with its open spaces all around it; so shall it be for all these cities.

DIVISION OF TERRITORIES CONCLUDED
21:41-22:34

God's promises fulfilled

⁴¹ Thus HASHEM gave to Israel the entire land that He swore to their forefathers to give; they inherited it and dwelled in it. ⁴² HASHEM granted them rest from all around, according to all that He had sworn to their forefathers; no man from among all their enemies stood before them; HASHEM delivered all their enemies into their hands. ⁴³ Nothing of all the good things of which HASHEM had spoken to the House of Israel was lacking; everything came to pass.

21:35. Some editions contain the following two verses after verse 35: *From the tribe of Reuben: Bezer and its open spaces, Jahaz and its open spaces, Kedemoth and its open spaces, Mephaath and its open spaces — four cities.*

However, most Masoretic authorities maintain that although the information contained in these verses is recorded in *I Chronicles* 6:63-64, it is nevertheless not part of the original Masoretic text of *Joshua (Radak).*

כב

א בָּא: אָז יִקְרָא יְהוֹשֻׁעַ לָרֽאוּבֵנִי וְלַגָּדִי וְלַחֲצִי מַטֵּה מְנַשֶּׁה:

ב וַיֹּאמֶר אֲלֵיהֶם אַתֶּם שְׁמַרְתֶּם אֵת כָּל־אֲשֶׁר צִוָּה אֶתְכֶם מֹשֶׁה עֶבֶד יְהוָה

ג וַתִּשְׁמְעוּ בְקוֹלִי לְכֹל אֲשֶׁר־צִוִּיתִי אֶתְכֶם: לֹא־עֲזַבְתֶּם אֶת־אֲחֵיכֶם זֶה יָמִים רַבִּים עַד הַיּוֹם הַזֶּה וּשְׁמַרְתֶּם אֶת־מִשְׁמֶרֶת מִצְוַת יְהוָה אֱלֹהֵיכֶם:

ד וְעַתָּה הֵנִיחַ יְהוָה אֱלֹהֵיכֶם לַאֲחֵיכֶם כַּאֲשֶׁר דִּבֶּר לָהֶם וְעַתָּה פְּנוּ וּלְכוּ לָכֶם לְאָהֳלֵיכֶם אֶל־אֶרֶץ אֲחֻזַּתְכֶם אֲשֶׁר ׀ נָתַן לָכֶם מֹשֶׁה עֶבֶד יְהוָה

ה בְּעֵבֶר הַיַּרְדֵּן: רַק ׀ שִׁמְרוּ מְאֹד לַעֲשׂוֹת אֶת־הַמִּצְוָה וְאֶת־הַתּוֹרָה אֲשֶׁר צִוָּה אֶתְכֶם מֹשֶׁה עֶבֶד־יְהוָה לְאַהֲבָה אֶת־יְהוָה אֱלֹהֵיכֶם וְלָלֶכֶת בְּכָל־ דְּרָכָיו וְלִשְׁמֹר מִצְוֹתָיו וּלְדָבְקָה־בוֹ וּלְעָבְדוֹ בְּכָל־לְבַבְכֶם וּבְכָל־נַפְשְׁכֶם:

ו וַיְבָרֲכֵם יְהוֹשֻׁעַ וַיְשַׁלְּחֵם וַיֵּלְכוּ אֶל־אָהֳלֵיהֶם: וְלַחֲצִי ׀ שֵׁבֶט הַמְנַשֶּׁה נָתַן מֹשֶׁה בַּבָּשָׁן וּלְחֶצְיוֹ נָתַן יְהוֹשֻׁעַ עִם־אֲחֵיהֶם °מֵעֵבֶר

ז [בְּעֵבֶר ק'] הַיַּרְדֵּן יָמָּה וְגַם כִּי שִׁלְּחָם יְהוֹשֻׁעַ אֶל־אָהֳלֵיהֶם וַיְבָרֲכֵם:

ח וַיֹּאמֶר אֲלֵיהֶם לֵאמֹר בִּנְכָסִים רַבִּים שׁוּבוּ אֶל־אָהֳלֵיכֶם וּבְמִקְנֶה רַב־ מְאֹד בְּכֶסֶף וּבְזָהָב וּבִנְחֹשֶׁת וּבְבַרְזֶל וּבִשְׂלָמוֹת הַרְבֵּה מְאֹד חִלְקוּ שְׁלַל־ אֹיְבֵיכֶם עִם־אֲחֵיכֶם:

ט וַיָּשֻׁבוּ וַיֵּלְכוּ בְּנֵי־רְאוּבֵן וּבְנֵי־גָד וַחֲצִי ׀ שֵׁבֶט הַמְנַשֶּׁה מֵאֵת בְּנֵי יִשְׂרָאֵל מִשִּׁלֹה אֲשֶׁר בְּאֶרֶץ־כְּנַעַן לָלֶכֶת אֶל־אֶרֶץ הַגִּלְעָד אֶל־אֶרֶץ אֲחֻזָּתָם אֲשֶׁר נֹאחֲזוּ־בָהּ עַל־פִּי יְהוָה בְּיַד־מֹשֶׁה:

י וַיָּבֹאוּ אֶל־גְּלִילוֹת הַיַּרְדֵּן אֲשֶׁר בְּאֶרֶץ כְּנַעַן וַיִּבְנוּ בְנֵי־רְאוּבֵן וּבְנֵי־ גָד וַחֲצִי שֵׁבֶט הַמְנַשֶּׁה שָׁם מִזְבֵּחַ עַל־הַיַּרְדֵּן מִזְבֵּחַ גָּדוֹל לְמַרְאֶה:

יא וַיִּשְׁמְעוּ בְנֵי־יִשְׂרָאֵל לֵאמֹר הִנֵּה בָנוּ בְנֵי־רְאוּבֵן וּבְנֵי־גָד וַחֲצִי שֵׁבֶט הַמְנַשֶּׁה אֶת־הַמִּזְבֵּחַ אֶל־מוּל אֶרֶץ כְּנַעַן אֶל־גְּלִילוֹת הַיַּרְדֵּן אֶל־עֵבֶר בְּנֵי יִשְׂרָאֵל:

יב וַיִּשְׁמְעוּ בְּנֵי יִשְׂרָאֵל וַיִּקָּהֲלוּ כָּל־עֲדַת בְּנֵי־יִשְׂרָאֵל שִׁלֹה לַעֲלוֹת עֲלֵיהֶם לַצָּבָא:

יג וַיִּשְׁלְחוּ בְנֵי־יִשְׂרָאֵל אֶל־בְּנֵי־ רְאוּבֵן וְאֶל־בְּנֵי־גָד וְאֶל־חֲצִי שֵׁבֶט־מְנַשֶּׁה אֶל־אֶרֶץ הַגִּלְעָד אֶת־פִּינְחָס בֶּן־אֶלְעָזָר הַכֹּהֵן:

יד וַעֲשָׂרָה נְשִׂאִים עִמּוֹ נָשִׂיא אֶחָד נָשִׂיא אֶחָד לְבֵית אָב לְכֹל מַטּוֹת יִשְׂרָאֵל וְאִישׁ רֹאשׁ בֵּית־אֲבוֹתָם הֵמָּה לְאַלְפֵי יִשְׂרָאֵל: וַיָּבֹאוּ

טו אֶל־בְּנֵי־רְאוּבֵן וְאֶל־בְּנֵי־גָד וְאֶל־חֲצִי שֵׁבֶט־מְנַשֶּׁה אֶל־אֶרֶץ הַגִּלְעָד וַיְדַבְּרוּ אִתָּם לֵאמֹר:

טז כֹּה אָמְרוּ כֹּל ׀ עֲדַת יְהוָה מָה־הַמַּעַל הַזֶּה אֲשֶׁר מְעַלְתֶּם בֵּאלֹהֵי יִשְׂרָאֵל לָשׁוּב הַיּוֹם מֵאַחֲרֵי יְהוָה בִּבְנוֹתְכֶם לָכֶם מִזְבֵּחַ

יז לִמְרָדְכֶם הַיּוֹם בַּיהוָה: הַמְעַט־לָנוּ אֶת־עֲוֹן פְּעוֹר אֲשֶׁר לֹא־הִטַּהַרְנוּ מִמֶּנּוּ עַד הַיּוֹם הַזֶּה וַיְהִי הַנֶּגֶף בַּעֲדַת יְהוָה:

יח וְאַתֶּם תָּשֻׁבוּ הַיּוֹם מֵאַחֲרֵי יְהוָה וְהָיָה אַתֶּם תִּמְרְדוּ הַיּוֹם בַּיהוָה וּמָחָר אֶל־כָּל־עֲדַת יִשְׂרָאֵל יִקְצֹף:

22:1. The two-and-a-half tribes east of the Jordan were in a uniquely precarious position. Their separation from the bulk of their brethren created the danger that they would view themselves as a separate nation. This chapter deals with this fear and the entire nation's efforts to prevent it from happening.

22:7. This parenthetical verse explains why Joshua

22

Farewell to Reuben, Gad, and Manasseh

[1] Then Joshua summoned the Reubenite, and the Gadite and half of the tribe of Manasseh. * [2] He said to them, "You have observed all that Moses, the servant of HASHEM, has commanded you, and you have obeyed my voice, in all that I have commanded you. [3] You have not forsaken your brethren these many days — until this day; you have kept the charge of the commandment of HASHEM, your God. [4] And now HASHEM, your God, has granted rest to your brethren as He had told them; so now turn and go to your tents, to the land of your possession, which Moses, the servant of HASHEM, gave you across the Jordan. [5] Only be very careful to fulfill the commandment and the Torah that Moses, the servant of HASHEM, commanded you: to love HASHEM, your God, and to walk in all His ways and to observe His commandments and to cling to Him and to serve Him with all your heart and with all your soul." [6] Then Joshua blessed them and sent them forth, and they went to their tents.

[7] To half the tribe of Manasseh, Moses had given [territory] in the Bashan, and to half of it, Joshua had given [territory] among their brothers on the western side of the Jordan. When Joshua sent them away to their dwellings he blessed them, as well. * [8] And he said to them saying, "With much wealth return to your tents, and with very much cattle, with silver, gold, copper, and iron, and garments, very much. Divide the spoils of your enemies with your brothers." *

[9] They returned and went — the children of Reuben, the children of Gad, and half the tribe of Manasseh — from the Children of Israel, from Shiloh that is in the land of Canaan, to go to the land of Gilead, to the land of their possession, of which they took possession in accordance with the word of HASHEM through the hand of Moses.

The suspected rebellion

[10] They came to the regions of the Jordan that are in the land of Canaan. The children of Reuben, the children of Gad, and half the tribe of Manasseh built an altar there, near the Jordan — a large altar as a showpiece. [11] The Children of Israel heard, saying, "Behold, the children of Reuben, the children of Gad, and half the tribe of Manasseh have built the altar opposite the land of Canaan in the regions of the Jordan, across from the side of the Children of Israel." [12] When the Children of Israel heard, the entire assembly of the Children of Israel congregated at Shiloh to advance upon them with an army.

[13] To the children of Reuben, the children of Gad, and half the tribe of Manasseh, the Children of Israel sent Phinehas the son of Elazar the Kohen to the land of Gilead. [14] Ten leaders were with him, one head of an ancestral family for each tribe of Israel; each man was the head of his ancestral family of the thousands of Israel. [15] They came to the children of Reuben, the children of Gad, and half the tribe of Manasseh, to the land of Gilead, and they spoke with them, saying, [16] "Thus said the entire assembly of HASHEM: 'What is this treachery that you have committed against the God of Israel — to turn away from HASHEM this day, by building for yourselves an altar for your rebellion this day against HASHEM? [17] Is the sin of Peor not enough for us — from which we have not become cleansed until this day, and which resulted in the plague in the assembly of HASHEM? * [18] Yet today you would turn away from HASHEM? If you rebel against HASHEM today, tomorrow He will be angry with the entire assembly of Israel.

---

blessed half of Manasseh along with Gad and Reuben, the other eastern tribes (*Radak*).

22:8. Joshua applied the principle that the warriors

should share the spoils with those who had remained behind to guard the women, children, and property (*Rashi*).

22:17. See *Numbers* 25:1-9.

יט וְאַךְ אִם־טְמֵאָה אֶרֶץ אֲחֻזַּתְכֶם עִבְרוּ לָכֶם אֶל־אֶרֶץ אֲחֻזַּת יְהוָה אֲשֶׁר
שָׁכַן־שָׁם מִשְׁכַּן יְהוָה וְהֵאָחֲזוּ בְּתוֹכֵנוּ וּבַיהוָה אַל־תִּמְרֹדוּ וְאֹתָנוּ אַל־
כ תִּמְרֹדוּ בִּבְנֹתְכֶם לָכֶם מִזְבֵּחַ מִבַּלְעֲדֵי מִזְבַּח יְהוָה אֱלֹהֵינוּ: הֲלוֹא ׀ עָכָן
בֶּן־זֶרַח מָעַל מַעַל בַּחֵרֶם וְעַל־כָּל־עֲדַת יִשְׂרָאֵל הָיָה קָצֶף וְהוּא אִישׁ
כא אֶחָד לֹא גָוַע בַּעֲוֹנוֹ: וַיַּעֲנוּ בְּנֵי־רְאוּבֵן וּבְנֵי־גָד וַחֲצִי שֵׁבֶט
כב הַמְנַשֶּׁה וַיְדַבְּרוּ אֶת־רָאשֵׁי אַלְפֵי יִשְׂרָאֵל: אֵל ׀ אֱלֹהִים ׀ יְהוָה אֵל ׀ יְהוָה אֵל ׀
אֱלֹהִים ׀ יְהוָה הוּא יֹדֵעַ וְיִשְׂרָאֵל הוּא יֵדָע אִם־בְּמֶרֶד וְאִם־בְּמַעַל
כג בַּיהוָה אַל־תּוֹשִׁיעֵנוּ הַיּוֹם הַזֶּה: לִבְנוֹת לָנוּ מִזְבֵּחַ לָשׁוּב מֵאַחֲרֵי יְהוָה
וְאִם־לְהַעֲלוֹת עָלָיו עוֹלָה וּמִנְחָה וְאִם־לַעֲשׂוֹת עָלָיו זִבְחֵי שְׁלָמִים יְהוָה
כד הוּא יְבַקֵּשׁ: וְאִם־לֹא מִדְּאָגָה מִדָּבָר עָשִׂינוּ אֶת־זֹאת לֵאמֹר מָחָר יֹאמְרוּ
בְנֵיכֶם לְבָנֵינוּ לֵאמֹר מַה־לָכֶם וְלַיהוָה אֱלֹהֵי יִשְׂרָאֵל: וּגְבוּל נָתַן־יְהוָה
כה בֵּינֵנוּ וּבֵינֵיכֶם בְּנֵי־רְאוּבֵן וּבְנֵי־גָד אֶת־הַיַּרְדֵּן אֵין־לָכֶם חֵלֶק בַּיהוָה
כו וְהִשְׁבִּיתוּ בְנֵיכֶם אֶת־בָּנֵינוּ לְבִלְתִּי יְרֹא אֶת־יְהוָה: וַנֹּאמֶר נַעֲשֶׂה־נָּא לָנוּ
כז לִבְנוֹת אֶת־הַמִּזְבֵּחַ לֹא לְעוֹלָה וְלֹא לְזָבַח: כִּי עֵד הוּא בֵּינֵינוּ וּבֵינֵיכֶם
וּבֵין דֹּרוֹתֵינוּ אַחֲרֵינוּ לַעֲבֹד אֶת־עֲבֹדַת יְהוָה לְפָנָיו בְּעֹלוֹתֵינוּ וּבִזְבָחֵינוּ
וּבִשְׁלָמֵינוּ וְלֹא־יֹאמְרוּ בְנֵיכֶם מָחָר לְבָנֵינוּ אֵין־לָכֶם חֵלֶק בַּיהוָה:
כח וַנֹּאמֶר וְהָיָה כִּי־יֹאמְרוּ אֵלֵינוּ וְאֶל־דֹּרֹתֵינוּ מָחָר וְאָמַרְנוּ רְאוּ אֶת־
תַּבְנִית מִזְבַּח יְהוָה אֲשֶׁר־עָשׂוּ אֲבוֹתֵינוּ לֹא לְעוֹלָה וְלֹא לְזֶבַח כִּי־עֵד
כט הוּא בֵּינֵינוּ וּבֵינֵיכֶם: חָלִילָה לָּנוּ מִמֶּנּוּ לִמְרֹד בַּיהוָה וְלָשׁוּב הַיּוֹם
מֵאַחֲרֵי יְהוָה לִבְנוֹת מִזְבֵּחַ לְעֹלָה לְמִנְחָה וּלְזָבַח מִלְּבַד מִזְבַּח יְהוָה
ל אֱלֹהֵינוּ אֲשֶׁר לִפְנֵי מִשְׁכָּנוֹ: וַיִּשְׁמַע פִּינְחָס הַכֹּהֵן וּנְשִׂיאֵי
הָעֵדָה וְרָאשֵׁי אַלְפֵי יִשְׂרָאֵל אֲשֶׁר אִתּוֹ אֶת־הַדְּבָרִים אֲשֶׁר דִּבְּרוּ בְּנֵי־
לא רְאוּבֵן וּבְנֵי־גָד וּבְנֵי מְנַשֶּׁה וַיִּיטַב בְּעֵינֵיהֶם: וַיֹּאמֶר פִּינְחָס בֶּן־אֶלְעָזָר
הַכֹּהֵן אֶל־בְּנֵי־רְאוּבֵן וְאֶל־בְּנֵי־גָד וְאֶל־בְּנֵי מְנַשֶּׁה הַיּוֹם ׀ יָדַעְנוּ כִּי־
בְתוֹכֵנוּ יְהוָה אֲשֶׁר לֹא־מְעַלְתֶּם בַּיהוָה הַמַּעַל הַזֶּה אָז הִצַּלְתֶּם אֶת־בְּנֵי
לב יִשְׂרָאֵל מִיַּד יְהוָה: וַיָּשָׁב פִּינְחָס בֶּן־אֶלְעָזָר הַכֹּהֵן ׀ וְהַנְּשִׂיאִים מֵאֵת בְּנֵי־
רְאוּבֵן וּמֵאֵת בְּנֵי־גָד מֵאֶרֶץ הַגִּלְעָד אֶל־אֶרֶץ כְּנַעַן אֶל־בְּנֵי יִשְׂרָאֵל
לג וַיָּשִׁבוּ אוֹתָם דָּבָר: וַיִּיטַב הַדָּבָר בְּעֵינֵי בְּנֵי יִשְׂרָאֵל וַיְבָרֲכוּ אֱלֹהִים בְּנֵי
יִשְׂרָאֵל וְלֹא אָמְרוּ לַעֲלוֹת עֲלֵיהֶם לַצָּבָא לְשַׁחֵת אֶת־הָאָרֶץ אֲשֶׁר בְּנֵי־
לד רְאוּבֵן וּבְנֵי־גָד יֹשְׁבִים בָּהּ: וַיִּקְרְאוּ בְּנֵי־רְאוּבֵן וּבְנֵי־גָד לַמִּזְבֵּחַ כִּי־עֵד
הוּא בֵּינֹתֵינוּ כִּי יְהוָה הָאֱלֹהִים:

22:19. If you consider the east bank of the Jordan to lack the sanctity of Eretz Yisrael because the Tabernacle is not there (*Radak*), then join your brethren in the west and we will redistribute the land to give you portions among us.

22:20. Achan's sin is recorded in Chapter 7.

22:22. They were addressing God, as it were, saying that if they were not sincere, He should not save them (*Rashi*).

22:31. Your explanation has prevented the calamity of future generations sinning in the manner you described (*Metzudos*), or an attack against innocent people.

¹⁹ But if the land of your possession is contaminated, * cross over to the land of HASHEM's possession where the Sanctuary of HASHEM is, and take your possession among us; but do not rebel against HASHEM and do not rebel against us by building for yourselves an altar other than the Altar of HASHEM, our God. ²⁰ Did not Achan son of Zerah commit treachery* regarding the consecrated property, and wrath fell upon the entire assembly of Israel? That man was not the only one to perish for his sin!' "

The explanation

²¹ The children of Reuben, the children of Gad, and half the tribe of Manasseh responded and spoke to the heads of the thousands of Israel, ²² "Almighty, God, HASHEM; Almighty, God, HASHEM: He knows and Israel shall know. If it is in rebellion or in treachery against HASHEM, save us not this day. * ²³ [If we meant] to build an altar for ourselves to turn away from following HASHEM, or to offer an elevation-offering or meal-offering upon it, or to offer peace-offerings upon it, let HASHEM Himself exact [retribution], ²⁴ if we did not do this out of fear, saying [to ourselves]: In the future your children might say to our children, 'What have you to do with HASHEM the God of Israel? ²⁵ HASHEM has established a border between us and you, O children of Reuben and children of Gad — the Jordan! You have no share in HASHEM!' So your children will cause our children to stop fearing HASHEM. ²⁶ Therefore, we said, 'Let us do this for ourselves — to build the altar, not for elevation-offering and not for sacrifice, ²⁷ but so that it will be a witness between us and you and our generations after us, to per-form the service of HASHEM before Him with our elevation-offerings, and with our offerings and with our peace-offerings.' Then your children will not say to our children in the future, 'You have no share in HASHEM.' ²⁸ So we said, 'When they say this to us or to our generations tomorrow, we will say, "See the structure of the altar of HASHEM that our fathers made — not for elevation-offering and not for offering, but as a testimony between us and you." ' ²⁹ It would be sacrilegious for us to rebel against HASHEM and to turn away this day from following HASHEM, to build an altar for burnt-offering, meal-offering, and sacrifice — other than the Altar of HASHEM, our God, which is before His Sanctuary!"

The rest of the tribes approve

³⁰ When Phinehas the Kohen and the leaders of the assembly and the heads of the thousands of Israel that were with him heard the words that the children of Reuben, the children of Gad and the children of Manasseh spoke, it was good in their eyes. ³¹ And Phinehas son of Elazar the Kohen said to the children of Reuben, the children of Gad, and the children of Manasseh, "Today we know that HASHEM is in our midst, since you did not commit this treachery against HASHEM. Now you have saved the Children of Israel from the hand of HASHEM."*

³² Then Phinehas son of Elazar the Kohen and the leaders returned from the children of Reuben and the children of Gad, from the land of Gilead, to the land of Canaan, to the Children of Israel, and they gave them a report. ³³ The matter was good in the eyes of the Children of Israel; and the Children of Israel blessed God and no longer spoke of advancing upon them with an army, to destroy the land in which the children of Reuben and the children of Gad dwelled. ³⁴ The children of Reuben and the children of Gad named the altar ["Witness"], for "it is a witness between us that HASHEM is God."

כג א וַיְהִי מִיָּמִים רַבִּים אַחֲרֵי אֲשֶׁר־הֵנִיחַ יהוה לְיִשְׂרָאֵל מִכָּל־אֹיְבֵיהֶם
ב מִסָּבִיב וִיהוֹשֻׁעַ זָקֵן בָּא בַּיָּמִים: וַיִּקְרָא יְהוֹשֻׁעַ לְכָל־יִשְׂרָאֵל לִזְקֵנָיו
וּלְרָאשָׁיו וּלְשֹׁפְטָיו וּלְשֹׁטְרָיו וַיֹּאמֶר אֲלֵהֶם אֲנִי זָקַנְתִּי בָּאתִי בַּיָּמִים:
ג וְאַתֶּם רְאִיתֶם אֵת כָּל־אֲשֶׁר עָשָׂה יהוה אֱלֹהֵיכֶם לְכָל־הַגּוֹיִם הָאֵלֶּה
ד מִפְּנֵיכֶם כִּי יהוה אֱלֹהֵיכֶם הוּא הַנִּלְחָם לָכֶם: רְאוּ הִפַּלְתִּי לָכֶם אֶת־
הַגּוֹיִם הַנִּשְׁאָרִים הָאֵלֶּה בְּנַחֲלָה לְשִׁבְטֵיכֶם מִן־הַיַּרְדֵּן וְכָל־הַגּוֹיִם
ה אֲשֶׁר הִכְרַתִּי וְהַיָּם הַגָּדוֹל מְבוֹא הַשָּׁמֶשׁ: וַיהוה אֱלֹהֵיכֶם הוּא יֶהְדֳּפֵם
מִפְּנֵיכֶם וְהוֹרִישׁ אֹתָם מִלִּפְנֵיכֶם וִירִשְׁתֶּם אֶת־אַרְצָם כַּאֲשֶׁר דִּבֶּר
ו יהוה אֱלֹהֵיכֶם לָכֶם: וַחֲזַקְתֶּם מְאֹד לִשְׁמֹר וְלַעֲשׂוֹת אֵת כָּל־הַכָּתוּב
ז בְּסֵפֶר תּוֹרַת מֹשֶׁה לְבִלְתִּי סוּר־מִמֶּנּוּ יָמִין וּשְׂמֹאול: לְבִלְתִּי־בוֹא בַּגּוֹיִם
הָאֵלֶּה הַנִּשְׁאָרִים הָאֵלֶּה אִתְּכֶם וּבְשֵׁם אֱלֹהֵיהֶם לֹא־תַזְכִּירוּ וְלֹא
ח תַשְׁבִּיעוּ וְלֹא תַעַבְדוּם וְלֹא תִשְׁתַּחֲווּ לָהֶם: כִּי אִם־בַּיהוה אֱלֹהֵיכֶם
ט תִּדְבָּקוּ כַּאֲשֶׁר עֲשִׂיתֶם עַד הַיּוֹם הַזֶּה: וַיּוֹרֶשׁ יהוה מִפְּנֵיכֶם גּוֹיִם גְּדֹלִים
י וַעֲצוּמִים וְאַתֶּם לֹא־עָמַד אִישׁ בִּפְנֵיכֶם עַד הַיּוֹם הַזֶּה: אִישׁ־אֶחָד מִכֶּם
יִרְדָּף־אָלֶף כִּי ׀ יהוה אֱלֹהֵיכֶם הוּא הַנִּלְחָם לָכֶם כַּאֲשֶׁר דִּבֶּר לָכֶם:
יא־יב וְנִשְׁמַרְתֶּם מְאֹד לְנַפְשֹׁתֵיכֶם לְאַהֲבָה אֶת־יהוה אֱלֹהֵיכֶם: כִּי ׀ אִם־
שׁוֹב תָּשׁוּבוּ וּדְבַקְתֶּם בְּיֶתֶר הַגּוֹיִם הָאֵלֶּה הַנִּשְׁאָרִים הָאֵלֶּה אִתְּכֶם
יג וְהִתְחַתַּנְתֶּם בָּהֶם וּבָאתֶם בָּהֶם וְהֵם בָּכֶם: יָדוֹעַ תֵּדְעוּ כִּי לֹא יוֹסִיף
יהוה אֱלֹהֵיכֶם לְהוֹרִישׁ אֶת־הַגּוֹיִם הָאֵלֶּה מִלִּפְנֵיכֶם וְהָיוּ לָכֶם לְפַח
וּלְמוֹקֵשׁ וּלְשֹׁטֵט בְּצִדֵּיכֶם וְלִצְנִנִים בְּעֵינֵיכֶם עַד־אֲבָדְכֶם מֵעַל הָאֲדָמָה
יד הַטּוֹבָה הַזֹּאת אֲשֶׁר נָתַן לָכֶם יהוה אֱלֹהֵיכֶם: וְהִנֵּה אָנֹכִי הוֹלֵךְ הַיּוֹם
בְּדֶרֶךְ כָּל־הָאָרֶץ וִידַעְתֶּם בְּכָל־לְבַבְכֶם וּבְכָל־נַפְשְׁכֶם כִּי לֹא־נָפַל
דָּבָר אֶחָד מִכֹּל ׀ הַדְּבָרִים הַטּוֹבִים אֲשֶׁר דִּבֶּר יהוה אֱלֹהֵיכֶם עֲלֵיכֶם
טו הַכֹּל בָּאוּ לָכֶם לֹא־נָפַל מִמֶּנּוּ דָּבָר אֶחָד: וְהָיָה כַּאֲשֶׁר־בָּא עֲלֵיכֶם
כָּל־הַדָּבָר הַטּוֹב אֲשֶׁר דִּבֶּר יהוה אֱלֹהֵיכֶם אֲלֵיכֶם כֵּן יָבִיא יהוה עֲלֵיכֶם
אֵת כָּל־הַדָּבָר הָרָע עַד־הַשְׁמִידוֹ אוֹתְכֶם מֵעַל הָאֲדָמָה הַטּוֹבָה
טז הַזֹּאת אֲשֶׁר נָתַן לָכֶם יהוה אֱלֹהֵיכֶם: בְּעָבְרְכֶם אֶת־בְּרִית יהוה
אֱלֹהֵיכֶם אֲשֶׁר צִוָּה אֶתְכֶם וַהֲלַכְתֶּם וַעֲבַדְתֶּם אֱלֹהִים אֲחֵרִים
וְהִשְׁתַּחֲוִיתֶם לָהֶם וְחָרָה אַף־יהוה בָּכֶם וַאֲבַדְתֶּם מְהֵרָה מֵעַל הָאָרֶץ
כד א הַטּוֹבָה אֲשֶׁר נָתַן לָכֶם: וַיֶּאֱסֹף יְהוֹשֻׁעַ אֶת־כָּל־שִׁבְטֵי
יִשְׂרָאֵל שְׁכֶמָה וַיִּקְרָא לְזִקְנֵי יִשְׂרָאֵל וּלְרָאשָׁיו וּלְשֹׁפְטָיו וּלְשֹׁטְרָיו
ב וַיִּתְיַצְּבוּ לִפְנֵי הָאֱלֹהִים: וַיֹּאמֶר יְהוֹשֻׁעַ אֶל־כָּל־הָעָם כֹּה־אָמַר יהוה

23:2. At the end of his life, Joshua was acutely aware that many Canaanites still remained in the land. He knew that these idolaters were a threat to the existence of the Israelites, and that without his leadership, the Israelites might lose confidence in their worthiness of the Divine protection that had assured their previous

23

¹ It happened many days after HASHEM had given rest to Israel from all their surrounding enemies, and Joshua was old, well on in years; ² Joshua summoned all of Israel* — their elders, their heads, their judges, and their marshals — and said to them, "I have aged and am well on in years. ³ You have seen all that HASHEM, your God, has done to all these nations before you; that HASHEM, your God, has fought for you. ⁴ See, I have allotted to you [the territories of] these remaining nations as a heritage for your tribes, from the Jordan, including all the nations that I have destroyed, up to the Great Sea toward the setting of the sun. ⁵ HASHEM, your God, will push them out from your presence and drive them out from before you, and you will inherit their land, as HASHEM, your God, has spoken to you. ⁶ Strengthen yourselves very much to observe and to do all that is written in the book of the Torah of Moses, not to deviate from it to the right or to the left, ⁷ not to come into these nations, those who still remain with you; you shall not mention the name of their gods and you shall not cause others to swear by them, you shall not serve them and you shall not bow down to them. ⁸ Only cling to HASHEM, your God, as you have done up to this day. ⁹ HASHEM has driven out great and powerful nations from before you, and not a man has stood against you, to this day. ¹⁰ One of you chased a thousand, because HASHEM, your God, it is He Who fought for you, as He spoke to you.

¹¹ "You shall beware greatly for your souls, to love HASHEM, your God. ¹² For if you should turn away and cling to the rest of these nations, these which remain with you, by intermarrying with them and coming into them and they into you, ¹³ you should know with certainty that HASHEM, your God, will not continue to drive these nations out from before you; they will be a snare and an obstacle to you, a lash in your sides and thorns in your eyes, until you are banished from this goodly land that HASHEM, your God, has given to you. ¹⁴ Behold, this day I am going the way of all the world. You know with all your heart and with all your soul that not one of all the good things that HASHEM your God has promised you has fallen short; all have come about for you, not one word of it has fallen short.

¹⁵ "But it shall be that just as every good thing that HASHEM, your God, has told you has come to you, so will HASHEM bring upon you every bad thing until He will have eliminated you from upon this goodly land that HASHEM, your God, has given you. ¹⁶ If you transgress the covenant of HASHEM, your God, that He has commanded you, and you go and serve gods of others and bow down to them, the wrath of HASHEM will burn against you, and you will perish swiftly from the goodly land that He has given you."

24

¹ Joshua assembled all the tribes of Israel at Shechem; he summoned the elders of Israel, their heads, their judges, and their officers, and they stood before God. * ² Joshua said to the entire nation, "Thus said HASHEM,

---

victories. He summoned the entire nation and explained to them that their success was dependent not on his presence, but rather upon their faithfulness to the Torah. If they would be scrupulous in their observance, then God would continue to make them victorious. If, however, they would fail in their observance, then the Canaanites would remain and be a thorn in their sides (v. 13).

24:1. Joshua convoked a second assembly of the Israelites before his death. He reviewed the panorama of Jewish history and recounted God's manifold kindness to the Jewish people. Then he urged them to remain loyal to God, and to destroy any gold and silver objects used for idol worship that were in their possession. Finally, just as Moses had done before his death, Joshua urged them to reaffirm their adherence to the Torah.

אֱלֹהֵי יִשְׂרָאֵל בְּעֵבֶר הַנָּהָר יָשְׁבוּ אֲבוֹתֵיכֶם מֵעוֹלָם תֶּרַח אֲבִי אַבְרָהָם

ג וַאֲבִי נָחוֹר וַיַּעַבְדוּ אֱלֹהִים אֲחֵרִים: וָאֶקַּח אֶת־אֲבִיכֶם אֶת־אַבְרָהָם מֵעֵבֶר הַנָּהָר וָאוֹלֵךְ אוֹתוֹ בְּכָל־אֶרֶץ כְּנָעַן [ואֹרֶב ק°] וָאַרְבֶּה אֶת־זַרְעוֹ

ד וָאֶתֶּן־לוֹ אֶת־יִצְחָק: וָאֶתֵּן לְיִצְחָק אֶת־יַעֲקֹב וְאֶת־עֵשָׂו וָאֶתֵּן לְעֵשָׂו אֶת־הַר שֵׂעִיר לָרֶשֶׁת אוֹתוֹ וְיַעֲקֹב וּבָנָיו יָרְדוּ מִצְרָיִם: וָאֶשְׁלַח אֶת־מֹשֶׁה

ה וְאֶת־אַהֲרֹן וָאֶגֹּף אֶת־מִצְרַיִם כַּאֲשֶׁר עָשִׂיתִי בְּקִרְבּוֹ וְאַחַר הוֹצֵאתִי

ו אֶתְכֶם: וָאוֹצִיא אֶת־אֲבוֹתֵיכֶם מִמִּצְרַיִם וַתָּבֹאוּ הַיָּמָּה וַיִּרְדְּפוּ מִצְרַיִם

ז אַחֲרֵי אֲבוֹתֵיכֶם בְּרֶכֶב וּבְפָרָשִׁים יַם־סוּף: וַיִּצְעֲקוּ אֶל־יהוה וַיָּשֶׂם מַאֲפֵל בֵּינֵיכֶם וּבֵין הַמִּצְרִים וַיָּבֵא עָלָיו אֶת־הַיָּם וַיְכַסֵּהוּ וַתִּרְאֶינָה עֵינֵיכֶם אֵת

ח אֲשֶׁר־עָשִׂיתִי בְּמִצְרָיִם וַתֵּשְׁבוּ בַמִּדְבָּר יָמִים רַבִּים: [וָאבֹאה° וָאָבִיא ק°] אֶתְכֶם אֶל־אֶרֶץ הָאֱמֹרִי הַיּוֹשֵׁב בְּעֵבֶר הַיַּרְדֵּן וַיִּלָּחֲמוּ אִתְּכֶם וָאֶתֵּן אוֹתָם

ט בְּיֶדְכֶם וַתִּירְשׁוּ אֶת־אַרְצָם וָאַשְׁמִידֵם מִפְּנֵיכֶם: וַיָּקָם בָּלָק בֶּן־צִפּוֹר מֶלֶךְ מוֹאָב וַיִּלָּחֶם בְּיִשְׂרָאֵל וַיִּשְׁלַח וַיִּקְרָא לְבִלְעָם בֶּן־בְּעוֹר לְקַלֵּל אֶתְכֶם:

י וְלֹא אָבִיתִי לִשְׁמֹעַ לְבִלְעָם וַיְבָרֶךְ בָּרוֹךְ אֶתְכֶם וָאַצִּל אֶתְכֶם מִיָּדוֹ:

יא וַתַּעַבְרוּ אֶת־הַיַּרְדֵּן וַתָּבֹאוּ אֶל־יְרִיחוֹ וַיִּלָּחֲמוּ בָכֶם בַּעֲלֵי־יְרִיחוֹ הָאֱמֹרִי וְהַפְּרִזִּי וְהַכְּנַעֲנִי וְהַחִתִּי וְהַגִּרְגָּשִׁי הַחִוִּי וְהַיְבוּסִי וָאֶתֵּן אוֹתָם בְּיֶדְכֶם:

יב וָאֶשְׁלַח לִפְנֵיכֶם אֶת־הַצִּרְעָה וַתְּגָרֶשׁ אוֹתָם מִפְּנֵיכֶם שְׁנֵי מַלְכֵי הָאֱמֹרִי

יג לֹא בְחַרְבְּךָ וְלֹא בְקַשְׁתֶּךָ: וָאֶתֵּן לָכֶם אֶרֶץ ׀ אֲשֶׁר לֹא־יָגַעְתָּ בָּהּ וְעָרִים אֲשֶׁר לֹא־בְנִיתֶם וַתֵּשְׁבוּ בָּהֶם כְּרָמִים וְזֵיתִים אֲשֶׁר לֹא־נְטַעְתֶּם אַתֶּם

יד אֹכְלִים: וְעַתָּה יְראוּ אֶת־יהוה וְעִבְדוּ אֹתוֹ בְּתָמִים וּבֶאֱמֶת וְהָסִירוּ אֶת־אֱלֹהִים אֲשֶׁר עָבְדוּ אֲבוֹתֵיכֶם בְּעֵבֶר הַנָּהָר וּבְמִצְרַיִם וְעִבְדוּ אֶת־יהוה:

טו וְאִם רַע בְּעֵינֵיכֶם לַעֲבֹד אֶת־יהוה בַּחֲרוּ לָכֶם הַיּוֹם אֶת־מִי תַעֲבֹדוּן אִם אֶת־אֱלֹהִים אֲשֶׁר־עָבְדוּ אֲבוֹתֵיכֶם אֲשֶׁר [בעבר° מֵעֵבֶר ק°] הַנָּהָר וְאִם אֶת־אֱלֹהֵי הָאֱמֹרִי אֲשֶׁר אַתֶּם יֹשְׁבִים בְּאַרְצָם וְאָנֹכִי וּבֵיתִי נַעֲבֹד אֶת־

טז יהוה: וַיַּעַן הָעָם וַיֹּאמֶר חָלִילָה לָּנוּ מֵעֲזֹב אֶת־יהוה לַעֲבֹד

יז אֱלֹהִים אֲחֵרִים: כִּי יהוה אֱלֹהֵינוּ הוּא הַמַּעֲלֶה אֹתָנוּ וְאֶת־אֲבוֹתֵינוּ מֵאֶרֶץ מִצְרַיִם מִבֵּית עֲבָדִים וַאֲשֶׁר עָשָׂה לְעֵינֵינוּ אֶת־הָאֹתוֹת הַגְּדֹלוֹת הָאֵלֶּה וַיִּשְׁמְרֵנוּ בְּכָל־הַדֶּרֶךְ אֲשֶׁר הָלַכְנוּ בָהּ וּבְכֹל הָעַמִּים אֲשֶׁר עָבַרְנוּ

יח בְּקִרְבָּם: וַיְגָרֶשׁ יהוה אֶת־כָּל־הָעַמִּים וְאֶת־הָאֱמֹרִי יֹשֵׁב הָאָרֶץ מִפָּנֵינוּ

יט גַּם־אֲנַחְנוּ נַעֲבֹד אֶת־יהוה כִּי־הוּא אֱלֹהֵינוּ:   וַיֹּאמֶר יְהוֹשֻׁעַ אֶל־הָעָם לֹא תוּכְלוּ לַעֲבֹד אֶת־יהוה כִּי־אֱלֹהִים קְדֹשִׁים הוּא

כ אֵל־קַנּוֹא הוּא לֹא־יִשָּׂא לְפִשְׁעֲכֶם וּלְחַטֹּאותֵיכֶם: כִּי תַעַזְבוּ אֶת־יהוה וַעֲבַדְתֶּם אֱלֹהֵי נֵכָר וְשָׁב וְהֵרַע לָכֶם וְכִלָּה אֶתְכֶם אַחֲרֵי אֲשֶׁר־הֵיטִיב

כא־כב לָכֶם: וַיֹּאמֶר הָעָם אֶל־יְהוֹשֻׁעַ לֹא כִּי אֶת־יהוה נַעֲבֹד: וַיֹּאמֶר יְהוֹשֻׁעַ

the God of Israel: 'Your forefathers — Terah, the father of Abraham and the father of Nahor — always dwelt beyond the [Euphrates] River and they served gods of others. ³ But I took your forefather Abraham from beyond the River and led him throughout all the land of Canaan; I multiplied his seed and I gave him Isaac. ⁴ To Isaac I gave Jacob and Esau. To Esau I gave Mount Seir to inherit, and Jacob and his sons went down to Egypt.

⁵ " 'I sent Moses and Aaron, and I plagued Egypt with all that I did in their midst, and afterwards I brought you out. ⁶ I brought your forefathers out of Egypt and you arrived at the sea. The Egyptians pursued your forefathers with chariot and horsemen to the Sea of Reeds. ⁷ They cried out to HASHEM, and He placed darkness between you and the Egyptians and brought the sea upon them and covered them — your own eyes saw what I did with the Egyptians — and then you dwelled in the Wilderness for many years. ⁸ I brought you to the land of the Amorite, who dwelled across the Jordan, and they battled with you, but I delivered them into your hand and you inherited their land; I destroyed them from before you. ⁹ Then Balak the son of Zippor, king of Moab, arose and battled against Israel. He sent and summoned Balaam son of Beor to curse you, ¹⁰ but I refused to listen to Balaam, and he pronounced a blessing upon you; thus I rescued you from his power.

¹¹ " 'Then you crossed the Jordan and came to Jericho. The inhabitants of Jericho battled against you — the Amorite and the Perizzite and the Canaanite and the Hittite and the Girgashite, the Hivvite and the Jebusite — and I delivered them into your hand. ¹² I sent the hornet-swarm ahead of you, and it drove them out before you — the two kings of the Amorite — not by your sword and not by your bow. ¹³ I gave you a land for which you did not labor and cities that you did not build, yet you occupied them; vineyards and olive groves that you did not plant, yet you are eating from them.'

Joshua's ¹⁴ "And now, fear HASHEM and serve Him with wholeheartedness and truth;
discourse remove the gods that your forefathers served on the other side of the River and in Egypt, and serve HASHEM. ¹⁵ If it is evil in your eyes to serve HASHEM, choose today whom you will serve: the gods your forefathers served across the River, or the gods of the Amorite in whose land you dwell. But as for me and my house, we will serve HASHEM!"

¹⁶ The nation responded and said, "It would be sacrilegious for us to forsake HASHEM, to serve gods of others. ¹⁷ For it is HASHEM our God Who brought us and our fathers up from the land of Egypt, from the house of bondage, Who performed these great wondrous signs before our eyes; He safeguarded us on all the paths upon which we walked and among all the peoples in whose midst we passed. ¹⁸ HASHEM drove out all the peoples and the Amorite who inhabited the land from before us. We, too, will serve HASHEM, for He is our God!"

¹⁹ But Joshua said to the people, "You will not be able to serve HASHEM, for He is a holy God; He is a jealous God; He will not forgive your rebellious sins or your transgressions. ²⁰ If you forsake HASHEM and serve gods of the foreigner, He will turn and act harshly toward you and destroy you after having done good with you."

²¹ The people said to Joshua, "No, we will serve only HASHEM!" ²² Joshua said

אֶל־הָעָם עֵדִים אַתֶּם בָּכֶ֫ם כִּי־אַתֶּם בְּחַרְתֶּם לָכֶם אֶת־יהוה לַעֲבֹד אוֹתוֹ

כג וַיֹּאמְרוּ עֵדִים: וְעַתָּ֫ה הָסִירוּ אֶת־אֱלֹהֵי הַנֵּכָר אֲשֶׁר בְּקִרְבְּכֶם וְהַטּוּ אֶת־

כד לְבַבְכֶ֫ם אֶל־יהוה אֱלֹהֵי יִשְׂרָאֵל: וַיֹּאמְרוּ הָעָם אֶל־יְהוֹשֻׁעַ אֶת־יהוה

כה אֱלֹהֵ֫ינוּ נַעֲבֹד וּבְקוֹלוֹ נִשְׁמָע: וַיִּכְרֹת יְהוֹשֻׁעַ בְּרִית לָעָם בַּיּוֹם הַהוּא

כו וַיָּ֫שֶׂם לוֹ חֹק וּמִשְׁפָּט בִּשְׁכֶם: וַיִּכְתֹּב יְהוֹשֻׁעַ אֶת־הַדְּבָרִים הָאֵלֶּה בְּסֵפֶר

תּוֹרַת אֱלֹהִים וַיִּקַּח אֶבֶן גְּדוֹלָה וַיְקִימֶהָ שָּׁם תַּחַת הָאַלָּה אֲשֶׁר בְּמִקְדַּשׁ

כז יהוה: וַיֹּאמֶר יְהוֹשֻׁעַ אֶל־כָּל־הָעָם הִנֵּה הָאֶבֶן הַזֹּאת

תִּהְיֶה־בָּנוּ לְעֵדָה כִּי־הִיא שָׁמְעָ֫ה אֵת כָּל־אִמְרֵי יהוה אֲשֶׁר דִּבֶּר עִמָּ֫נוּ

כח וְהָיְתָה בָכֶם לְעֵדָה פֶּן־תְּכַחֲשׁוּן בֵּאלֹהֵיכֶם: וַיְשַׁלַּח יְהוֹשֻׁעַ אֶת־הָעָם

כט אִישׁ לְנַחֲלָתוֹ:   וַיְהִי אַחֲרֵי הַדְּבָרִים הָאֵלֶּה וַיָּמָת יְהוֹשֻׁעַ

ל בִּן־נוּן עֶבֶד יהוה בֶּן־מֵאָה וָעֶשֶׂר שָׁנִים: וַיִּקְבְּרוּ אֹתוֹ בִּגְבוּל נַחֲלָתוֹ

לא בְּתִמְנַת־סֶרַח אֲשֶׁר בְּהַר־אֶפְרָיִם מִצְּפוֹן לְהַר־גָּעַשׁ: וַיַּעֲבֹד יִשְׂרָאֵל

אֶת־יהוה כֹּל יְמֵי יְהוֹשֻׁעַ וְכֹל | יְמֵי הַזְּקֵנִים אֲשֶׁר הֶאֱרִיכוּ יָמִים אַחֲרֵי

לב יְהוֹשֻׁעַ וַאֲשֶׁר יָדְעוּ אֵת כָּל־מַעֲשֵׂה יהוה אֲשֶׁר עָשָׂה לְיִשְׂרָאֵל: וְאֶת־

עַצְמוֹת יוֹסֵף אֲשֶׁר־הֶעֱלוּ בְנֵי־יִשְׂרָאֵל | מִמִּצְרַ֫יִם קָבְרוּ בִשְׁכֶם בְּחֶלְקַת

הַשָּׂדֶה אֲשֶׁר קָנָה יַעֲקֹב מֵאֵת בְּנֵי־חֲמוֹר אֲבִי־שְׁכֶם בְּמֵאָה קְשִׂיטָה וַיִּהְיוּ

לג לִבְנֵי־יוֹסֵף לְנַחֲלָה: וְאֶלְעָזָר בֶּן־אַהֲרֹן מֵת וַיִּקְבְּרוּ אֹתוֹ בְּגִבְעַת פִּינְחָס

בְּנוֹ אֲשֶׁר נִתַּן־לוֹ בְּהַר אֶפְרָיִם:

סכום הפסוקים של ספר יהושע שש מאות וחמשים וששה. **ותרן** לשון אלם סימן.

24:25. He reviewed the laws of the Torah (*Rashi*).
24:26. Joshua wrote the words he had just proclaimed, and placed the parchment together with the Torah scroll

(*Targum*). At that time the Holy Ark, which the verse refers to as the Sanctuary, was in Shechem (*Radak*).
24:32. See *Genesis* 33:19.

to the people, "You bear witness upon yourselves that you have chosen HASHEM, to serve Him"; and they said, "We are witnesses."

²³ "So now, remove the gods of the foreigner that are among you and direct your hearts to HASHEM, the God of Israel." ²⁴ The people replied to Joshua, "We shall serve HASHEM, our God, and we shall heed His voice."

The covenant and conclusion

²⁵ Joshua made a covenant with the people that day and he set down decrees and laws for them in Shechem. * ²⁶ Joshua wrote these words [and placed them] with the Book of God's Torah. * He took a large stone and stood it there beneath the doorpost that was in the Sanctuary of HASHEM, ²⁷ and Joshua declared to all the people, "Behold, this stone will be a witness for us, for it has heard all the words of HASHEM that He has spoken to us; it will be a witness against you if you ever deny your God." ²⁸ Then Joshua sent the people forth, each man to his heritage.

Joshua's death and burial
(See Appendix A, timeline 3)

²⁹ It was after these events that Joshua son of Nun, the servant of HASHEM, died at the age of one hundred and ten years. ³⁰ They buried him in the border of his heritage in Timnath-serah, which is in Mount Ephraim, north of Mount Gaash.

³¹ Israel served HASHEM all the days of Joshua and all the days of the Elders whose days were lengthened after Joshua, and who had known all the deeds of HASHEM, which He had done for Israel.

Joseph's burial

³² Joseph's bones, which the Children of Israel had brought up from Egypt, they buried in Shechem, in the portion of the field that Jacob acquired from the children of Hamor, the father of Shechem, for a hundred kesitahs; * and it became a heritage for the children of Joseph.

Elazar's death and burial

³³ Elazar son of Aaron died, and they buried him in the Hill of Phinehas his son, which was given to him on Mount Ephraim.

Judges שופטים

With the death of Joshua, the Jewish nation entered a new era. No longer was there a single national leader, a virtual king of the nation, as Moses and Joshua had been. True, there were courts in every town and city, as commanded by the Torah, so that there would be a system of justice, but there was no formally constituted national leader. There should have been a general acknowledgment that, as Samuel had insisted centuries later, "HASHEM your God is your king," and all questions of law and policy should have been decided by the national or tribal Sanhedrins. Instead, the tribes became involved in settling their respective provinces, setting up homes and farms and — because of their reluctance to eradicate all Canaanite influence from the land — often tended to adopt the corrupt practices of their neighbors.

As the Book of Judges notes all too sadly, "In those days there was no king in Israel; every man did what was proper in his own eyes" (17:6, 21:25). There were episodes of extreme sinfulness that caused God to remove His protective providence from Israel, and foreign oppressors would exercise predatory control over parts of the country. Nevertheless, the masses of the people never lost their faith in God and their basic allegiance to the Torah. God would choose a leader, known as a judge, who would rally the people to repent and thus deserve God's help once again. Then, generally, the judge would conquer and expel the oppressor and the nation would enjoy a long period of tranquility — until it slid downward again.

Sometimes the judge would be someone of great renown, such as Deborah or Othniel, who was one of Joshua's greatest contemporaries. Sometimes he would be a young man of enormous but unknown potential, such as Gideon. There was a time when the nation did not merit a leader as great as these historic figures, so Jephthah became their judge; or a time when they did not deserve to conquer their enemies, so God gave them Samson, whose individual exploits kept the brutal Philistines at bay.

In reading the Book of Judges, it is essential to note that the combined years of peace and righteousness far outnumbered the years of failure and persecution. Always, the judge was chosen by God, and whenever he or she called upon the people to repent, they responded. The nation had shortcomings, but it was essentially righteous and true to the Torah and its Giver.

א

א וַיְהִי אַחֲרֵי מוֹת יְהוֹשֻׁעַ וַיִּשְׁאֲלוּ בְּנֵי יִשְׂרָאֵל בַּיהוָה לֵאמֹר מִי־יַעֲלֶה־
ב לָּנוּ אֶל־הַכְּנַעֲנִי בַּתְּחִלָּה לְהִלָּחֶם בּוֹ: וַיֹּאמֶר יְהוָה יְהוּדָה יַעֲלֶה הִנֵּה
ג נָתַתִּי אֶת־הָאָרֶץ בְּיָדוֹ: וַיֹּאמֶר יְהוּדָה לְשִׁמְעוֹן אָחִיו עֲלֵה אִתִּי בְגוֹרָלִי
ד וְנִלָּחֲמָה בַּכְּנַעֲנִי וְהָלַכְתִּי גַם־אֲנִי אִתְּךָ בְּגוֹרָלֶךָ וַיֵּלֶךְ אִתּוֹ שִׁמְעוֹן: וַיַּעַל
יְהוּדָה וַיִּתֵּן יְהוָה אֶת־הַכְּנַעֲנִי וְהַפְּרִזִּי בְּיָדָם וַיַּכּוּם בְּבֶזֶק עֲשֶׂרֶת אֲלָפִים
ה אִישׁ: וַיִּמְצְאוּ אֶת־אֲדֹנִי בֶזֶק בְּבֶזֶק וַיִּלָּחֲמוּ בּוֹ וַיַּכּוּ אֶת־הַכְּנַעֲנִי וְאֶת־
ו הַפְּרִזִּי: וַיָּנָס אֲדֹנִי בֶזֶק וַיִּרְדְּפוּ אַחֲרָיו וַיֹּאחֲזוּ אֹתוֹ וַיְקַצְּצוּ אֶת־בְּהֹנוֹת יָדָיו
ז וְרַגְלָיו: וַיֹּאמֶר אֲדֹנִי־בֶזֶק שִׁבְעִים מְלָכִים בְּהֹנוֹת יְדֵיהֶם וְרַגְלֵיהֶם
מְקֻצָּצִים הָיוּ מְלַקְּטִים תַּחַת שֻׁלְחָנִי כַּאֲשֶׁר עָשִׂיתִי כֵּן שִׁלַּם־לִי אֱלֹהִים
וַיְבִיאֻהוּ יְרוּשָׁלִַם וַיָּמָת שָׁם:
ח וַיִּלָּחֲמוּ בְנֵי־יְהוּדָה בִּירוּשָׁלִַם וַיִּלְכְּדוּ אוֹתָהּ וַיַּכּוּהָ לְפִי־חָרֶב וְאֶת־הָעִיר
ט שִׁלְּחוּ בָאֵשׁ: וְאַחַר יָרְדוּ בְּנֵי יְהוּדָה לְהִלָּחֵם בַּכְּנַעֲנִי יוֹשֵׁב הָהָר וְהַנֶּגֶב
י וְהַשְּׁפֵלָה: וַיֵּלֶךְ יְהוּדָה אֶל־הַכְּנַעֲנִי הַיּוֹשֵׁב בְּחֶבְרוֹן וְשֵׁם־חֶבְרוֹן לְפָנִים
יא קִרְיַת אַרְבַּע וַיַּכּוּ אֶת־שֵׁשַׁי וְאֶת־אֲחִימַן וְאֶת־תַּלְמָי: וַיֵּלֶךְ מִשָּׁם אֶל־
יב יוֹשְׁבֵי דְּבִיר וְשֵׁם־דְּבִיר לְפָנִים קִרְיַת־סֵפֶר: וַיֹּאמֶר כָּלֵב אֲשֶׁר־יַכֶּה אֶת־
יג קִרְיַת־סֵפֶר וּלְכָדָהּ וְנָתַתִּי לוֹ אֶת־עַכְסָה בִתִּי לְאִשָּׁה: וַיִּלְכְּדָהּ עָתְנִיאֵל
יד בֶּן־קְנַז אֲחִי כָלֵב הַקָּטֹן מִמֶּנּוּ וַיִּתֶּן־לוֹ אֶת־עַכְסָה בִתּוֹ לְאִשָּׁה: וַיְהִי בְּבוֹאָהּ
וַתְּסִיתֵהוּ לִשְׁאוֹל מֵאֵת־אָבִיהָ הַשָּׂדֶה וַתִּצְנַח מֵעַל הַחֲמוֹר וַיֹּאמֶר־לָהּ
טו כָּלֵב מַה־לָּךְ: וַתֹּאמֶר לוֹ הָבָה־לִּי בְרָכָה כִּי אֶרֶץ הַנֶּגֶב נְתַתָּנִי וְנָתַתָּה לִי
טז גֻּלֹּת מָיִם וַיִּתֶּן־לָהּ כָּלֵב אֵת גֻּלֹּת עִלִּית וְאֵת גֻּלֹּת תַּחְתִּית: וּבְנֵי
קֵינִי חֹתֵן מֹשֶׁה עָלוּ מֵעִיר הַתְּמָרִים אֶת־בְּנֵי יְהוּדָה מִדְבַּר יְהוּדָה אֲשֶׁר
יז בְּנֶגֶב עֲרָד וַיֵּלֶךְ וַיֵּשֶׁב אֶת־הָעָם: וַיֵּלֶךְ יְהוּדָה אֶת־שִׁמְעוֹן אָחִיו וַיַּכּוּ
אֶת־הַכְּנַעֲנִי יוֹשֵׁב צְפַת וַיַּחֲרִימוּ אוֹתָהּ וַיִּקְרָא אֶת־שֵׁם־הָעִיר חָרְמָה:
יח וַיִּלְכֹּד יְהוּדָה אֶת־עַזָּה וְאֶת־גְּבוּלָהּ וְאֶת־אַשְׁקְלוֹן וְאֶת־גְּבוּלָהּ וְאֶת־
יט עֶקְרוֹן וְאֶת־גְּבוּלָהּ: וַיְהִי יְהוָה אֶת־יְהוּדָה וַיֹּרֶשׁ אֶת־הָהָר כִּי לֹא לְהוֹרִישׁ
כ אֶת־יֹשְׁבֵי הָעֵמֶק כִּי־רֶכֶב בַּרְזֶל לָהֶם: וַיִּתְּנוּ לְכָלֵב אֶת־חֶבְרוֹן כַּאֲשֶׁר
כא דִּבֶּר מֹשֶׁה וַיּוֹרֶשׁ מִשָּׁם אֶת־שְׁלֹשָׁה בְּנֵי הָעֲנָק: וְאֶת־הַיְבוּסִי יֹשֵׁב
יְרוּשָׁלִַם לֹא הוֹרִישׁוּ בְּנֵי בִנְיָמִן וַיֵּשֶׁב הַיְבוּסִי אֶת־בְּנֵי בִנְיָמִן בִּירוּשָׁלִַם

1:1. Seeing that Joshua had died, the Canaanites would be emboldened, convinced that without its leader, Israel would be vulnerable. But if the very first battle were to end in a decisive Jewish victory, the Canaanites would become disheartened. Therefore, the nation inquired of the *Urim VeTumim* (see *Exodus* 28:30) which tribe should initiate the crucial first battle (*Ralbag*).

1:3. The tribe of Simeon received scattered cities within the boundaries of Judah, but had no separate, contiguous territory of its own (see *Joshua* 19:1).

1:6. Nowhere else do we find Jews mutilating their

opponents, as they did to Adoni-bezek. God prompted them to do this in order to frighten the remaining Canaanite rulers and to punish Adoni-bezek measure for measure for the atrocities he had inflicted on his victims (*Ralbag*).

1:8. Scripture reviews the important areas taken in Judah's earlier wars under the leadership of Joshua, the conquests of Caleb and Othniel, and the request of Caleb's daughter Achsah. See *Joshua* 15:13-20,63.

1:16. Like their ancestor Jethro, the Kenites were loyal friends and allies of Israel, and the Jews reciprocated this friendship by evacuating the Kenite families whenever

1

CONQUEST
OF CANAAN
1:1-36

Simeon
assists
Judah

Judah's
conquests
(See Appendix D,
map 3)

Othniel
marries
Caleb's
daughter

The Kenites

Jerusalem

¹ It happened after the death of Joshua that the Children of Israel inquired of HASHEM, saying, "Who should go up for us first against the Canaanite, to wage war against him?"*

² HASHEM said, "Judah should go up. Behold, I have delivered the land into his hand."

³ Judah said to Simeon his brother, "Go up [in battle] with me for my portion * and let us wage war against the Canaanite; then I, too, will go with you for your portion." So Simeon went with him. ⁴ Judah attacked and HASHEM delivered the Canaanite and the Perizzite into their hand; they struck them down at Bezek — ten thousand men.

⁵ They found Adoni-bezek in Bezek, and battled against him, and they struck down the Canaanite and the Perizzite. ⁶ Adoni-bezek fled and they chased after him. They seized him and cut off his thumbs and his big toes. * ⁷ Adoni-bezek said, "Seventy kings with their thumbs and big toes cut off used to glean under my table; as I did, so God requited me." They brought him to Jerusalem and he died there.

⁸ The children of Judah then waged war against Jerusalem. * They conquered it and struck it down by the edge of the sword, and they set the city on fire. ⁹ Afterward, the children of Judah descended to wage war against the Canaanite who inhabited the mountain, the South, and the lowland.

¹⁰ Judah had gone forth against the Canaanite who dwelled in Hebron — the name of Hebron in early times had been Kiriath-arba — and they struck down Sheshai, Ahiman, and Talmai. ¹¹ From there he went [to fight] against the inhabitants of Debir, and the name of Debir in early times had been Kiriath-sefer. ¹² Caleb said, "Whoever smites Kiriath-sefer and conquers it — I shall give him my daughter Achsah as a wife." ¹³ Othniel son of Kenaz, Caleb's younger brother, conquered it; so he gave him his daughter Achsah as a wife.

¹⁴ When she came [to Othniel], she urged him to let her ask her father for a field. Then she slid off the donkey, and Caleb said to her, "What do you wish?" ¹⁵ She said to him, "Give me a [source of] blessing — for you have given me an arid land; give me springs of water." So Caleb gave her the upper springs and the lower springs.

¹⁶ The children of the Kenite, * Moses' father-in-law, ascended from the City of Date Palms with the children of Judah to the Wilderness of Judah that is south of Arad; they went and settled with the people. ¹⁷ Judah went with his brother Simeon and they struck down the Canaanite who dwelled in Zephath and destroyed it. He named the city Hormah [Destruction]. ¹⁸ Judah conquered Gaza and its territory, Ashkelon and its territory, and Ekron and its territory. ¹⁹ HASHEM was with Judah and he drove out the [inhabitants of the] mountains, but the inhabitants of the valley could not be driven out, because they had iron chariots. ²⁰ They granted Hebron to Caleb, as Moses had spoken, and he drove the three sons of the giant from there.

²¹ But the children of Benjamin did not drive out the Jebusite, inhabitant of Jerusalem, * so the Jebusite dwelt with the children of Benjamin, in Jerusalem,

---

they might be caught in the crossfire of war. The Kenites had settled in Jericho (the City of Date Palms), and when the battle for the city took place, they left it and settled with the tribe of Judah (*Radak*).

1:21. Although Judah had captured and razed Jerusalem

(v. 8), the Jebusite inhabitants took refuge in the city's citadel, from which Judah was unable to dislodge them (*Abarbanel*). Part of Jerusalem was in the province of Benjamin, and that part remained in the possession of the Jebusites.

כב   וַיַּעֲלוּ בֵית־יוֹסֵף גַּם־הֵם בֵּית־אֵל וַיהוָה עִמָּם: עַד הַיּוֹם הַזֶּה:

כג־כד   וַיָּתִירוּ בֵית־יוֹסֵף בְּבֵית־אֵל וְשֵׁם־הָעִיר לְפָנִים לוּז: וַיִּרְאוּ הַשֹּׁמְרִים אִישׁ יוֹצֵא מִן־הָעִיר וַיֹּאמְרוּ לוֹ הַרְאֵנוּ נָא אֶת־מְבוֹא הָעִיר וְעָשִׂינוּ עִמְּךָ

כה   חָסֶד: וַיַּרְאֵם אֶת־מְבוֹא הָעִיר וַיַּכּוּ אֶת־הָעִיר לְפִי־חָרֶב וְאֶת־הָאִישׁ וְאֶת־

כו   כָּל־מִשְׁפַּחְתּוֹ שִׁלֵּחוּ: וַיֵּלֶךְ הָאִישׁ אֶרֶץ הַחִתִּים וַיִּבֶן עִיר וַיִּקְרָא שְׁמָהּ לוּז הוּא שְׁמָהּ עַד הַיּוֹם הַזֶּה:

כז   וְלֹא־הוֹרִישׁ מְנַשֶּׁה אֶת־בֵּית־ שְׁאָן וְאֶת־בְּנוֹתֶיהָ וְאֶת־תַּעְנַךְ וְאֶת־בְּנֹתֶיהָ וְאֶת־°יֹשֵׁב [יוֹשְׁבֵי ק] דוֹר וְאֶת־בְּנוֹתֶיהָ וְאֶת־יוֹשְׁבֵי יִבְלְעָם וְאֶת־בְּנֹתֶיהָ וְאֶת־יוֹשְׁבֵי מְגִדּוֹ וְאֶת־

כח   בְּנוֹתֶיהָ וַיּוֹאֶל הַכְּנַעֲנִי לָשֶׁבֶת בָּאָרֶץ הַזֹּאת: וַיְהִי כִּי־חָזַק יִשְׂרָאֵל וַיָּשֶׂם

כט   אֶת־הַכְּנַעֲנִי לָמַס וְהוֹרֵישׁ לֹא הוֹרִישׁוֹ: וְאֶפְרַיִם לֹא הוֹרִישׁ אֶת־הַכְּנַעֲנִי הַיּוֹשֵׁב בְּגָזֶר וַיֵּשֶׁב הַכְּנַעֲנִי בְּקִרְבּוֹ בְּגָזֶר:

ל   זְבוּלֻן לֹא הוֹרִישׁ אֶת־יוֹשְׁבֵי קִטְרוֹן וְאֶת־יוֹשְׁבֵי נַהֲלֹל וַיֵּשֶׁב הַכְּנַעֲנִי בְּקִרְבּוֹ

לא   וַיִּהְיוּ לָמַס: אָשֵׁר לֹא הוֹרִישׁ אֶת־יֹשְׁבֵי עַכּוֹ וְאֶת־יוֹשְׁבֵי צִידוֹן

לב   וְאֶת־אַחְלָב וְאֶת־אַכְזִיב וְאֶת־חֶלְבָּה וְאֶת־אֲפִיק וְאֶת־רְחֹב: וַיֵּשֶׁב הָאָשֵׁרִי בְּקֶרֶב הַכְּנַעֲנִי יֹשְׁבֵי הָאָרֶץ כִּי לֹא הוֹרִישׁוֹ:   נַפְתָּלִי

לג   לֹא־הוֹרִישׁ אֶת־יֹשְׁבֵי בֵית־שֶׁמֶשׁ וְאֶת־יֹשְׁבֵי בֵית־עֲנָת וַיֵּשֶׁב בְּקֶרֶב הַכְּנַעֲנִי יֹשְׁבֵי הָאָרֶץ וְיֹשְׁבֵי בֵית־שֶׁמֶשׁ וּבֵית עֲנָת הָיוּ לָהֶם לָמַס: וַיִּלְחֲצוּ

לד   הָאֱמֹרִי אֶת־בְּנֵי־דָן הָהָרָה כִּי־לֹא נְתָנוֹ לָרֶדֶת לָעֵמֶק: וַיּוֹאֶל הָאֱמֹרִי

לה   לָשֶׁבֶת בְּהַר־חֶרֶס בְּאַיָּלוֹן וּבְשַׁעַלְבִים וַתִּכְבַּד יַד בֵּית־יוֹסֵף וַיִּהְיוּ לָמַס:

לו־א   וּגְבוּל הָאֱמֹרִי מִמַּעֲלֵה עַקְרַבִּים מֵהַסֶּלַע וָמָעְלָה: וַיַּעַל

ב   מַלְאַךְ־יְהוָה מִן־הַגִּלְגָּל אֶל־הַבֹּכִים   וַיֹּאמֶר אַעֲלֶה אֶתְכֶם מִמִּצְרַיִם וָאָבִיא אֶתְכֶם אֶל־הָאָרֶץ אֲשֶׁר נִשְׁבַּעְתִּי לַאֲבֹתֵיכֶם וָאֹמַר

ב   לֹא־אָפֵר בְּרִיתִי אִתְּכֶם לְעוֹלָם: וְאַתֶּם לֹא־תִכְרְתוּ בְרִית לְיוֹשְׁבֵי הָאָרֶץ הַזֹּאת מִזְבְּחוֹתֵיהֶם תִּתֹּצוּן וְלֹא־שְׁמַעְתֶּם בְּקֹלִי מַה־זֹּאת עֲשִׂיתֶם: וְגַם

ג   אָמַרְתִּי לֹא־אֲגָרֵשׁ אוֹתָם מִפְּנֵיכֶם וְהָיוּ לָכֶם לְצִדִּים וֵאלֹהֵיהֶם יִהְיוּ לָכֶם

ד   לְמוֹקֵשׁ: וַיְהִי כְּדַבֵּר מַלְאַךְ יְהוָה אֶת־הַדְּבָרִים הָאֵלֶּה אֶל־כָּל־בְּנֵי

ה   יִשְׂרָאֵל וַיִּשְׂאוּ הָעָם אֶת־קוֹלָם וַיִּבְכּוּ: וַיִּקְרְאוּ שֵׁם־הַמָּקוֹם הַהוּא בֹּכִים וַיִּזְבְּחוּ־שָׁם לַיהוָה: וַיְשַׁלַּח יְהוֹשֻׁעַ אֶת־הָעָם וַיֵּלְכוּ

ו   בְנֵי־יִשְׂרָאֵל אִישׁ לְנַחֲלָתוֹ לָרֶשֶׁת אֶת־הָאָרֶץ: וַיַּעַבְדוּ הָעָם אֶת־

ז   יְהוָה כֹּל יְמֵי יְהוֹשֻׁעַ וְכֹל יְמֵי הַזְּקֵנִים אֲשֶׁר הֶאֱרִיכוּ יָמִים אַחֲרֵי יְהוֹשֻׁעַ אֲשֶׁר רָאוּ אֵת כָּל־מַעֲשֵׂה יְהוָה הַגָּדוֹל אֲשֶׁר עָשָׂה לְיִשְׂרָאֵל:

1:27-36. Nearly all the tribes were derelict in not persevering to rid the land of its inhabitants. Indeed, had this pernicious seed of idol worship not been permitted to take root in the land, the spiritual degeneration that led to the destruction of the Temple more than eight hundred years later would not have occurred.

2:1. The word מַלְאַךְ means "emissary" and is used to describe both an angel and a prophet, as each is an emissary who carries out God's mission. Since the emissary speaks in God's name, he uses the first person.

2:3. See *Numbers* 33:55. Measure for measure, if Israel would choose to establish ties to the Canaanite nations, it *until this day.*

The tribes of   ²² *The House of Joseph went up, as well, to Beth-el, and HASHEM was with*
Joseph . . .   *them.* ²³ *The House of Joseph spied out Beth-el — the name of the city in early*
times had been Luz. ²⁴ *The lookouts saw a man leaving the city and they said*
to him, "Show us the approach to the city and we shall deal kindly with you."
²⁵ *He showed them the approach to the city and they struck down the city by the*
edge of the sword, but they released the man and his entire family. ²⁶ *The man*
went to the land of the Hittites. He built a city and called it Luz; that is its name
until this day.

. . . Manasseh   ²⁷ *Manasseh did not drive out [the inhabitants of] Beth-shean and its towns,*
. . .   *Taanach and its towns, the inhabitants of Dor and its towns, the inhabitants of*
Ibleam and its towns, and the inhabitants of Megiddo and its towns. The
Canaanite were determined to dwell in this land. * ²⁸ *So it was that when Israel*
was strong, they imposed tribute upon the Canaanite, but did not drive him out.

. . . and   ²⁹ *Ephraim did not drive out the Canaanite that was dwelling in Gezer, so the*
Ephraim   *Canaanite dwelt in their midst in Gezer.*

Zebulun   ³⁰ *Zebulun did not drive out the inhabitants of Kitron and the inhabitants of*
Nahalol, so the Canaanite dwelt in their midst, and became tributary.

Asher   ³¹ *Asher did not drive out the inhabitants of Acco nor the inhabitants of Sidon,*
[nor of] Ahlab, Achzib, Helbah, Aphik, and Rehob. ³² *So the Asherite dwelt*
amid the Canaanite, the inhabitants of the land, for they did not drive them out.

Naphtali   ³³ *Naphtali did not drive out the inhabitants of Beth-shemesh and the inhabi-*
tants of Beth-anath, so they dwelt among the Canaanite, the inhabitants of the
land. The inhabitants of Beth-shemesh and Beth-anath became tributary to
them.

Dan   ³⁴ *The Amorite forced the children of Dan up the mountain, for they did not let*
them descend to the valley. ³⁵ *The Amorite was determined to dwell in Har-*
heres, Aijalon, and Shaalbim, but the hand of the House of Joseph prevailed, so
[the Amorite] became tributary. ³⁶ *The border of the Amorite was from Maaleh-*
akrabbim, from the rock upward.

2   ¹ *An emissary* * *of HASHEM went up from Gilgal to Bochim. He said, "I*
THE PERIOD   *brought you up from Egypt and I brought you to the land that I swore to*
OF THE   *your forefathers. And I said, 'I shall never annul My covenant with you,* ² *but*
JUDGES: *you shall not seal a covenant with the inhabitants of this land; you shall break*
CYCLES OF
IDOLATRY,   *apart their altars.' But you did not hearken to My voice! What is this that you*
CHASTENING   *have done?* ³ *So I also said, 'I shall not chase them out before you, and they will*
AND   *be unto you [as thorns in your] sides,* * *and their gods will be a trap for you.' "*
DELIVER-
ANCE   ⁴ *It happened that when the emissary of HASHEM spoke these words to all the*
2:1-3:6   *Children of Israel, the people raised their voices and wept.* ⁵ *They named that*
place Bochim [Crying], and they brought offerings there to HASHEM.

⁶ *Joshua had sent the people away* * *and the Children of Israel had gone,*
every man to his heritage, to possess the land. ⁷ *The people served HASHEM*
all the days of Joshua and all the days of the elders who outlived Joshua,
who had seen all the great work of HASHEM, which He had done for Israel. *

---

would be saddled with them, as permanent challenges.
2:6. The rest of this chapter provides the background for
the events of the entire period of the Judges, which
began with Joshua's death.

2:7. Although the people erred in not continuing the
wars of conquest, they did not turn to sin as long as they
remembered the great leaders and the miracles they had
witnessed (*Radak*).

ח־ט וַיָּמָת יְהוֹשֻׁעַ בִּן־נוּן עֶבֶד יהוה בֶּן־מֵאָה וָעֶשֶׂר שָׁנִים: וַיִּקְבְּרוּ אוֹתוֹ
י בִּגְבוּל נַחֲלָתוֹ בְּתִמְנַת־חֶרֶס בְּהַר אֶפְרָיִם מִצְּפוֹן לְהַר־גָּעַשׁ: וְגַם כָּל־
הַדּוֹר הַהוּא נֶאֶסְפוּ אֶל־אֲבוֹתָיו וַיָּקָם דּוֹר אַחֵר אַחֲרֵיהֶם אֲשֶׁר לֹא־יָדְעוּ
יא אֶת־יהוה וְגַם אֶת־הַמַּעֲשֶׂה אֲשֶׁר עָשָׂה לְיִשְׂרָאֵל: וַיַּעֲשׂוּ
יב בְנֵי־יִשְׂרָאֵל אֶת־הָרַע בְּעֵינֵי יהוה וַיַּעַבְדוּ אֶת־הַבְּעָלִים: וַיַּעַזְבוּ אֶת־
יהוה ׀ אֱלֹהֵי אֲבוֹתָם הַמּוֹצִיא אוֹתָם מֵאֶרֶץ מִצְרַיִם וַיֵּלְכוּ אַחֲרֵי ׀ אֱלֹהִים
אֲחֵרִים מֵאֱלֹהֵי הָעַמִּים אֲשֶׁר סְבִיבוֹתֵיהֶם וַיִּשְׁתַּחֲווּ לָהֶם וַיַּכְעִסוּ אֶת־
יג־יד יהוה: וַיַּעַזְבוּ אֶת־יהוה וַיַּעַבְדוּ לַבַּעַל וְלָעַשְׁתָּרוֹת: וַיִּחַר־אַף יהוה
בְּיִשְׂרָאֵל וַיִּתְּנֵם בְּיַד־שֹׁסִים וַיָּשֹׁסּוּ אוֹתָם וַיִּמְכְּרֵם בְּיַד אוֹיְבֵיהֶם מִסָּבִיב
טו וְלֹא־יָכְלוּ עוֹד לַעֲמֹד לִפְנֵי אוֹיְבֵיהֶם: בְּכֹל ׀ אֲשֶׁר יָצְאוּ יַד־יהוה הָיְתָה־
בָּם לְרָעָה כַּאֲשֶׁר דִּבֶּר יהוה וְכַאֲשֶׁר נִשְׁבַּע יהוה לָהֶם וַיֵּצֶר לָהֶם מְאֹד:
טז־יז וַיָּקֶם יהוה שֹׁפְטִים וַיּוֹשִׁיעוּם מִיַּד שֹׁסֵיהֶם: וְגַם אֶל־שֹׁפְטֵיהֶם לֹא שָׁמֵעוּ
כִּי זָנוּ אַחֲרֵי אֱלֹהִים אֲחֵרִים וַיִּשְׁתַּחֲווּ לָהֶם סָרוּ מַהֵר מִן־הַדֶּרֶךְ אֲשֶׁר
יח הָלְכוּ אֲבוֹתָם לִשְׁמֹעַ מִצְוֹת־יהוה לֹא־עָשׂוּ כֵן: וְכִי־הֵקִים יהוה ׀ לָהֶם
שֹׁפְטִים וְהָיָה יהוה עִם־הַשֹּׁפֵט וְהוֹשִׁיעָם מִיַּד אֹיְבֵיהֶם כֹּל יְמֵי הַשּׁוֹפֵט
יט כִּי־יִנָּחֵם יהוה מִנַּאֲקָתָם מִפְּנֵי לֹחֲצֵיהֶם וְדֹחֲקֵיהֶם: וְהָיָה ׀ בְּמוֹת הַשּׁוֹפֵט
יָשֻׁבוּ וְהִשְׁחִיתוּ מֵאֲבוֹתָם לָלֶכֶת אַחֲרֵי אֱלֹהִים אֲחֵרִים לְעָבְדָם
כ וּלְהִשְׁתַּחֲוֹת לָהֶם לֹא הִפִּילוּ מִמַּעַלְלֵיהֶם וּמִדַּרְכָּם הַקָּשָׁה: וַיִּחַר־אַף
יהוה בְּיִשְׂרָאֵל וַיֹּאמֶר יַעַן אֲשֶׁר עָבְרוּ הַגּוֹי הַזֶּה אֶת־בְּרִיתִי אֲשֶׁר צִוִּיתִי
כא אֶת־אֲבוֹתָם וְלֹא שָׁמְעוּ לְקוֹלִי: גַּם־אֲנִי לֹא אוֹסִיף לְהוֹרִישׁ אִישׁ
כב מִפְּנֵיהֶם מִן־הַגּוֹיִם אֲשֶׁר־עָזַב יְהוֹשֻׁעַ וַיָּמֹת: לְמַעַן נַסּוֹת בָּם אֶת־יִשְׂרָאֵל
הֲשֹׁמְרִים הֵם אֶת־דֶּרֶךְ יהוה לָלֶכֶת בָּם כַּאֲשֶׁר שָׁמְרוּ אֲבוֹתָם אִם־לֹא:
כג וַיַּנַּח יהוה אֶת־הַגּוֹיִם הָאֵלֶּה לְבִלְתִּי הוֹרִישָׁם מַהֵר וְלֹא נְתָנָם בְּיַד
ג א יְהוֹשֻׁעַ:   וְאֵלֶּה הַגּוֹיִם אֲשֶׁר הִנִּיחַ יהוה לְנַסּוֹת בָּם
ב אֶת־יִשְׂרָאֵל אֵת כָּל־אֲשֶׁר לֹא־יָדְעוּ אֵת כָּל־מִלְחֲמוֹת כְּנָעַן: רַק לְמַעַן
דַּעַת דֹּרוֹת בְּנֵי־יִשְׂרָאֵל לְלַמְּדָם מִלְחָמָה רַק אֲשֶׁר־לְפָנִים לֹא יְדָעוּם:
ג חֲמֵשֶׁת ׀ סַרְנֵי פְלִשְׁתִּים וְכָל־הַכְּנַעֲנִי וְהַצִּידֹנִי וְהַחִוִּי יֹשֵׁב הַר הַלְּבָנוֹן
ד מֵהַר בַּעַל חֶרְמוֹן עַד לְבוֹא חֲמָת: וַיִּהְיוּ לְנַסּוֹת בָּם אֶת־יִשְׂרָאֵל וּבְנֵי־
ה לָדַעַת הֲיִשְׁמְעוּ אֶת־מִצְוֹת יהוה אֲשֶׁר־צִוָּה אֶת־אֲבוֹתָם בְּיַד־מֹשֶׁה: וּבְנֵי

2:11. As chronicled in the Book of Judges, Scripture outlines the pattern of events that continued repeatedly throughout the centuries. Thus, the translation *they would do* instead of the simple past "they did."

Baal is a generic term for idols; the word means *master*. Ashtaroth (v. 13) was a statue of a female sheep or goat [see *Deuteronomy* 7:13] (*Radak*), worshiped by the Canaanites as the goddess of fertility.

2:17. The root of their continual sinfulness was their

failure to heed their leaders; this shortcoming served as an impediment to repentance (*Alshich*).

2:22. It was as if they had willed that their spiritual enemies should live among them, and if so their test was to prove that they would not be influenced by them.

3:2. Because they did not exert themselves to drive out the Canaanites, the next generation would not see the miraculous victories that their fathers saw. Rather, they would have to learn the art of warfare (*Radak*).

⁸ *Joshua son of Nun, the servant of* HASHEM, *died at the age of a hundred and ten years.* ⁹ *They buried him within the borders of his heritage, in Timnath-heres in Mount Ephraim, north of Mount Gaash.* ¹⁰ *That entire generation, as well, was gathered in to its forefathers. A new generation arose after them that did not know* HASHEM, *nor the deeds that He had performed for Israel.*

Idolatry ¹¹ *The Children of Israel would do what was evil in the eyes of* HASHEM, *and would worship the Baalim.* * ¹² *They would forsake* HASHEM, *the God of their forefathers, Who took them out of the land of Egypt, and follow the gods of others, from among the gods of the peoples that were around them; they would prostrate themselves to them and anger* HASHEM. ¹³ *They would forsake* HASHEM *and worship the Baal and the Ashtaroth.*

Chastening ¹⁴ *Then the wrath of* HASHEM *would flare against Israel and He would deliver them into the hands of plunderers and they would plunder them, and He would deliver them into the hands of their enemies all around, so that they could no longer stand before their enemies.* ¹⁵ *Wherever they would go out [in battle], the hand of* HASHEM *would be upon them for evil — as* HASHEM *had spoken and as* HASHEM *had sworn to them — and they would be very distressed.*

¹⁶ *Then* HASHEM *would set up judges who would save them from the hand of their plunderers.* ¹⁷ *But they would not hearken to their judges either, for they would stray after the gods of others and prostrate themselves to them. They would turn away quickly from the path that their forefathers had traveled, to hearken to the commandments of* HASHEM; *they did not do so.* *

Deliverance ¹⁸ *When* HASHEM *would set up judges for them,* HASHEM *would be with the judge and he would save them from the hand of their enemies all the days of the judge, for* HASHEM *would have relented because of their outcry before those who oppressed them and who crushed them.*

¹⁹ *But then it would happen that upon the death of the judge they would turn back and be even more corrupt than their forefathers, to follow the gods of others, to worship them, and to prostrate themselves before them. They would not omit any of their misdeeds or their stubborn way.* ²⁰ *So the wrath of* HASHEM *would flare against Israel and He would say, "Because this nation has violated My covenant that I commanded their forefathers and they did not hearken to My voice,* ²¹ *I, too, shall no longer drive away any man from before them, from among the nations that Joshua left when he died,* ²² *in order to test Israel through them: Are they observing the way of* HASHEM, *to follow them as their forefathers observed, or not?"**

²³ *So* HASHEM *let those nations remain, without driving them out quickly, and He did not deliver them into Joshua's hand.*

3

The remaining nations

(See Appendix D, map 4)

¹ T*hese are the nations that* HASHEM *let remain, to test Israel through them, all those who did not know all the Canaanite wars —* ² *[they remained] only so that the generations of the Children of Israel would know, to teach them warfare; but those who preceded [them] did not [need to] know:** ³ *the five governors of the Philistines, all the Canaanite, the Sidonite, and the Hivvite that dwell on Mount Lebanon, from the mountain of the plain of Hermon until the approach to Hamath.* ⁴ *They were [for God] to test Israel through them, to know whether they would hearken to the commandments of* HASHEM, *which He commanded their forefathers through the hand of Moses.* ⁵ *So the Children of*

ו יִשְׂרָאֵל יָשְׁבוּ בְּקֶרֶב הַכְּנַעֲנִי הַחִתִּי וְהָאֱמֹרִי וְהַפְּרִזִּי וְהַחִוִּי וְהַיְבוּסִי: וַיִּקְחוּ
אֶת־בְּנוֹתֵיהֶם לָהֶם לְנָשִׁים וְאֶת־בְּנוֹתֵיהֶם נָתְנוּ לִבְנֵיהֶם וַיַּעַבְדוּ אֶת־
ז אֱלֹהֵיהֶם: וַיַּעֲשׂוּ בְנֵי־יִשְׂרָאֵל אֶת־הָרַע בְּעֵינֵי יהוה
ח וַיִּשְׁכְּחוּ אֶת־יהוה אֱלֹהֵיהֶם וַיַּעַבְדוּ אֶת־הַבְּעָלִים וְאֶת־הָאֲשֵׁרוֹת: וַיִּחַר־
אַף יהוה בְּיִשְׂרָאֵל וַיִּמְכְּרֵם בְּיַד כּוּשַׁן רִשְׁעָתַיִם מֶלֶךְ אֲרַם נַהֲרָיִם וַיַּעַבְדוּ
ט בְנֵי־יִשְׂרָאֵל אֶת־כּוּשַׁן רִשְׁעָתַיִם שְׁמֹנֶה שָׁנִים: וַיִּזְעֲקוּ בְנֵי־יִשְׂרָאֵל אֶל־
יהוה וַיָּקֶם יהוה מוֹשִׁיעַ לִבְנֵי יִשְׂרָאֵל וַיּוֹשִׁיעֵם אֵת עָתְנִיאֵל בֶּן־קְנַז אֲחִי
י כָלֵב הַקָּטֹן מִמֶּנּוּ: וַתְּהִי עָלָיו רוּחַ־יהוה וַיִּשְׁפֹּט אֶת־יִשְׂרָאֵל וַיֵּצֵא
לַמִּלְחָמָה וַיִּתֵּן יהוה בְּיָדוֹ אֶת־כּוּשַׁן רִשְׁעָתַיִם מֶלֶךְ אֲרָם וַתָּעָז יָדוֹ
יא עַל כּוּשַׁן רִשְׁעָתָיִם: וַתִּשְׁקֹט הָאָרֶץ אַרְבָּעִים שָׁנָה וַיָּמָת עָתְנִיאֵל בֶּן־
יב קְנַז: וַיֹּסִפוּ בְּנֵי יִשְׂרָאֵל לַעֲשׂוֹת הָרַע בְּעֵינֵי יהוה
וַיְחַזֵּק יהוה אֶת־עֶגְלוֹן מֶלֶךְ־מוֹאָב עַל־יִשְׂרָאֵל עַל כִּי־עָשׂוּ אֶת־הָרַע
יג בְּעֵינֵי יהוה: וַיֶּאֱסֹף אֵלָיו אֶת־בְּנֵי עַמּוֹן וַעֲמָלֵק וַיֵּלֶךְ וַיַּךְ אֶת־יִשְׂרָאֵל
יד וַיִּירְשׁוּ אֶת־עִיר הַתְּמָרִים: וַיַּעַבְדוּ בְנֵי־יִשְׂרָאֵל אֶת־עֶגְלוֹן מֶלֶךְ־מוֹאָב
טו שְׁמוֹנֶה עֶשְׂרֵה שָׁנָה: וַיִּזְעֲקוּ בְנֵי־יִשְׂרָאֵל אֶל־יהוה וַיָּקֶם יהוה לָהֶם
מוֹשִׁיעַ אֶת־אֵהוּד בֶּן־גֵּרָא בֶּן־הַיְמִינִי אִישׁ אִטֵּר יַד־יְמִינוֹ וַיִּשְׁלְחוּ בְנֵי־
טז יִשְׂרָאֵל בְּיָדוֹ מִנְחָה לְעֶגְלוֹן מֶלֶךְ מוֹאָב: וַיַּעַשׂ לוֹ אֵהוּד חֶרֶב וְלָהּ שְׁנֵי
יז פֵיוֹת גֹּמֶד אָרְכָּהּ וַיַּחְגֹּר אוֹתָהּ מִתַּחַת לְמַדָּיו עַל יֶרֶךְ יְמִינוֹ: וַיַּקְרֵב אֶת־
יח הַמִּנְחָה לְעֶגְלוֹן מֶלֶךְ מוֹאָב וְעֶגְלוֹן אִישׁ בָּרִיא מְאֹד: וַיְהִי כַּאֲשֶׁר כִּלָּה
יט לְהַקְרִיב אֶת־הַמִּנְחָה וַיְשַׁלַּח אֶת־הָעָם נֹשְׂאֵי הַמִּנְחָה: וְהוּא שָׁב מִן־
הַפְּסִילִים אֲשֶׁר אֶת־הַגִּלְגָּל וַיֹּאמֶר דְּבַר־סֵתֶר לִי אֵלֶיךָ הַמֶּלֶךְ וַיֹּאמֶר
כ הָס וַיֵּצְאוּ מֵעָלָיו כָּל־הָעֹמְדִים עָלָיו: וְאֵהוּד בָּא אֵלָיו וְהוּא־יֹשֵׁב
בַּעֲלִיַּת הַמְּקֵרָה אֲשֶׁר־לוֹ לְבַדּוֹ וַיֹּאמֶר אֵהוּד דְּבַר־אֱלֹהִים לִי אֵלֶיךָ
כא וַיָּקָם מֵעַל הַכִּסֵּא: וַיִּשְׁלַח אֵהוּד אֶת־יַד שְׂמֹאלוֹ וַיִּקַּח אֶת־הַחֶרֶב מֵעַל
כב יֶרֶךְ יְמִינוֹ וַיִּתְקָעֶהָ בְּבִטְנוֹ: וַיָּבֹא גַם־הַנִּצָּב אַחַר הַלַּהַב וַיִּסְגֹּר הַחֵלֶב
כג בְּעַד הַלַּהַב כִּי לֹא שָׁלַף הַחֶרֶב מִבִּטְנוֹ וַיֵּצֵא הַפַּרְשְׁדֹנָה: וַיֵּצֵא אֵהוּד
כד הַמִּסְדְּרוֹנָה וַיִּסְגֹּר דַּלְתוֹת הָעֲלִיָּה בַּעֲדוֹ וְנָעָל: וְהוּא יָצָא וַעֲבָדָיו בָּאוּ
וַיִּרְאוּ וְהִנֵּה דַּלְתוֹת הָעֲלִיָּה נְעֻלוֹת וַיֹּאמְרוּ אַךְ מֵסִיךְ הוּא אֶת־רַגְלָיו
כה בַּחֲדַר הַמְּקֵרָה: וַיָּחִילוּ עַד־בּוֹשׁ וְהִנֵּה אֵינֶנּוּ פֹּתֵחַ דַּלְתוֹת הָעֲלִיָּה
כו וַיִּקְחוּ אֶת־הַמַּפְתֵּחַ וַיִּפְתָּחוּ וְהִנֵּה אֲדֹנֵיהֶם נֹפֵל אַרְצָה מֵת: וְאֵהוּד
נִמְלַט עַד הִתְמַהְמְהָם וְהוּא עָבַר אֶת־הַפְּסִילִים וַיִּמָּלֵט הַשְּׂעִירָתָה:

3:9. The generation that had never seen God's miracles may not have realized that their fate was inextricably tied to their degree of virtue and sin. Only when the persecution became unbearable did they pray for help.

3:11. This pattern would be repeated many times in the Book: National sinfulness would bring about foreign domination, until Israel would cry out to God and He would designate a judge to save them.

Though the Book's accounts of sin and war are lengthy, it records not a single event during the forty-year period

Israel dwelt among the Canaanite, the Hittite, the Amorite, the Perizzite, the Hivvite, and the Jebusite. [6] *[The Israelites] took [the nations'] daughters for themselves as wives and gave their daughters to their sons, and they served their gods.*

THE FIRST JUDGE: OTHNIEL SON OF KENAZ
3:7-11

Aramean oppression
(See Appendix A, timeline 3)

[7] *The Children of Israel did what was evil in the eyes of HASHEM and they forgot HASHEM, their God, and worshiped the Baalim and the Asherah-trees.* [8] *The wrath of HASHEM flared against Israel and He delivered them into the hand of Cushan-rishathaim, king of Aram-naharaim, and the Children of Israel served Cushan-rishathaim for eight years.* [9] *The Children of Israel cried out to HASHEM,* * *and HASHEM set up a savior for the Children of Israel and he saved them: Othniel son of Kenaz, Caleb's younger brother.* [10] *The spirit of HASHEM was upon him and he judged Israel. He went out to war and HASHEM delivered Cushan-rishathaim, king of Aram, into his hand; and his hand dominated Cushan-rishathaim.* [11] *The land was tranquil for forty years;* * *and Othniel son of Kenaz died.*

EHUD SON OF GERA
3:12-30

Moabite oppression

[12] *The Children of Israel continued to do that which was evil in the eyes of HASHEM, and HASHEM strengthened Eglon, king of Moab, over Israel, because they had done that which was evil in the eyes of HASHEM.* [13] *He gathered to himself the Children of Ammon and Amalek, then he went and struck Israel and took possession of the City of Date Palms [Jericho].* [14] *The Children of Israel served Eglon, king of Moab, for eighteen years.*

[15] *The Children of Israel cried out to HASHEM, and HASHEM set up a savior for them: Ehud son of Gera, a Benjaminite, a man with a withered right hand. The Children of Israel sent a tribute with him to Eglon, king of Moab.* [16] *Ehud made himself a sword with two sharp edges, a cubit its length, and he girded it under his garments on his right thigh.*

Ehud confronts Eglon, king of Moab . . .

[17] *He brought the tribute to Eglon, king of Moab. (Now Eglon was a very obese man.)* [18] *It happened that when he finished offering the tribute, he led away the people, the bearers of the tribute,* [19] *and then he returned from the quarries near Gilgal and said, "I have a secret matter for you, O king."*

[The King] said, "Silence!" — and all who stood before him went out.

[20] *Then Ehud came to him as he was sitting alone in his cool upper chamber. Ehud said, "I have a word of God for you," so he stood up* * *from the chair.*

. . . and dispatches him

[21] *Ehud then stretched out his left hand and took the sword from upon his right thigh and thrust it into [Eglon's] belly.* [22] *Even the hilt went in after the blade and the fat closed around the blade, for he did not pull the sword out of his belly; the excrement poured out.*

[23] *Ehud went out to the porch, closed the doors of the upper chamber behind him, and locked [them].* [24] *When he had left, [Eglon's] servants came and saw that — behold! the doors of the upper chamber were locked, they said, "He is but relieving himself in the cool chamber."* [25] *They waited for a long time, but behold, he was not opening the doors of the upper chamber. They took the key and opened them and — behold! their master was fallen on the ground, dead!* [26] *Ehud had escaped while they were waiting, and he passed the quarries and escaped to Seirah.*

---

of tranquility. In the context of the narrative it is clear that it was a time when the nation maintained the high standard of righteousness that the Torah demands. In fact, of the nearly four hundred years spanned by the period of the Judges, the people were sinful during only one hundred and ten (*Rashi* to *Ezekiel* 4:5).

3:20. Eglon's respect for God was rewarded: Ruth, ancestress of the Davidic dynasty, descended from him (*Rashi*).

כז וַיְהִי בְּבוֹאוֹ וַיִּתְקַע בַּשּׁוֹפָר בְּהַר אֶפְרָיִם וַיֵּרְדוּ עִמּוֹ בְנֵי־יִשְׂרָאֵל מִן־הָהָר

כח וְהוּא לִפְנֵיהֶם: וַיֹּאמֶר אֲלֵהֶם רִדְפוּ אַחֲרַי כִּי־נָתַן יהוה אֶת־אֹיְבֵיכֶם אֶת־ מוֹאָב בְּיֶדְכֶם וַיֵּרְדוּ אַחֲרָיו וַיִּלְכְּדוּ אֶת־מַעְבְּרוֹת הַיַּרְדֵּן לְמוֹאָב וְלֹא־

כט נָתְנוּ אִישׁ לַעֲבֹר: וַיַּכּוּ אֶת־מוֹאָב בָּעֵת הַהִיא כַּעֲשֶׂרֶת אֲלָפִים אִישׁ כָּל־

ל שָׁמֵן וְכָל־אִישׁ חָיִל וְלֹא נִמְלַט אִישׁ: וַתִּכָּנַע מוֹאָב בַּיּוֹם הַהוּא תַּחַת יַד יִשְׂרָאֵל וַתִּשְׁקֹט הָאָרֶץ שְׁמוֹנִים שָׁנָה:

לא וְאַחֲרָיו הָיָה שַׁמְגַּר בֶּן־עֲנָת וַיַּךְ אֶת־פְּלִשְׁתִּים שֵׁשׁ־מֵאוֹת אִישׁ בְּמַלְמַד הַבָּקָר וַיֹּשַׁע גַּם־הוּא אֶת־יִשְׂרָאֵל:

ד א וַיֹּסִפוּ בְּנֵי יִשְׂרָאֵל לַעֲשׂוֹת הָרַע

ב בְּעֵינֵי יהוה וְאֵהוּד מֵת: וַיִּמְכְּרֵם יהוה בְּיַד־יָבִין מֶלֶךְ־כְּנַעַן אֲשֶׁר מָלַךְ

ג בְּחָצוֹר וְשַׂר־צְבָאוֹ סִיסְרָא וְהוּא יוֹשֵׁב בַּחֲרֹשֶׁת הַגּוֹיִם: וַיִּצְעֲקוּ בְנֵי־ יִשְׂרָאֵל אֶל־יהוה כִּי תְּשַׁע מֵאוֹת רֶכֶב־בַּרְזֶל לוֹ וְהוּא לָחַץ אֶת־בְּנֵי יִשְׂרָאֵל בְּחָזְקָה עֶשְׂרִים שָׁנָה:

▶ ד וּדְבוֹרָה אִשָּׁה נְבִיאָה אֵשֶׁת לַפִּידוֹת הִיא שֹׁפְטָה אֶת־יִשְׂרָאֵל בָּעֵת

ה הַהִיא: וְהִיא יוֹשֶׁבֶת תַּחַת־תֹּמֶר דְּבוֹרָה בֵּין הָרָמָה וּבֵין בֵּית־אֵל בְּהַר

ו אֶפְרָיִם וַיַּעֲלוּ אֵלֶיהָ בְּנֵי יִשְׂרָאֵל לַמִּשְׁפָּט: וַתִּשְׁלַח וַתִּקְרָא לְבָרָק בֶּן־ אֲבִינֹעַם מִקֶּדֶשׁ נַפְתָּלִי וַתֹּאמֶר אֵלָיו הֲלֹא צִוָּה ׀ יהוה אֱלֹהֵי־יִשְׂרָאֵל לֵךְ וּמָשַׁכְתָּ בְּהַר תָּבוֹר וְלָקַחְתָּ עִמְּךָ עֲשֶׂרֶת אֲלָפִים אִישׁ מִבְּנֵי נַפְתָּלִי וּמִבְּנֵי

ז זְבֻלוּן: וּמָשַׁכְתִּי אֵלֶיךָ אֶל־נַחַל קִישׁוֹן אֶת־סִיסְרָא שַׂר־צְבָא יָבִין וְאֶת־

ח רִכְבּוֹ וְאֶת־הֲמוֹנוֹ וּנְתַתִּיהוּ בְּיָדֶךָ: וַיֹּאמֶר אֵלֶיהָ בָּרָק אִם־תֵּלְכִי עִמִּי

ט וְהָלָכְתִּי וְאִם־לֹא תֵלְכִי עִמִּי לֹא אֵלֵךְ: וַתֹּאמֶר הָלֹךְ אֵלֵךְ עִמָּךְ אֶפֶס כִּי לֹא תִהְיֶה תִּפְאַרְתְּךָ עַל־הַדֶּרֶךְ אֲשֶׁר אַתָּה הוֹלֵךְ כִּי בְיַד־אִשָּׁה יִמְכֹּר

י יהוה אֶת־סִיסְרָא וַתָּקָם דְּבוֹרָה וַתֵּלֶךְ עִם־בָּרָק קֶדְשָׁה: וַיַּזְעֵק בָּרָק אֶת־ זְבוּלֻן וְאֶת־נַפְתָּלִי קֶדְשָׁה וַיַּעַל בְּרַגְלָיו עֲשֶׂרֶת אַלְפֵי אִישׁ וַתַּעַל עִמּוֹ

יא דְּבוֹרָה: וְחֶבֶר הַקֵּינִי נִפְרָד מִקַּיִן מִבְּנֵי חֹבָב חֹתֵן מֹשֶׁה וַיֵּט אָהֳלוֹ עַד־

יב אֵלוֹן °בצענים [°בְּצַעֲנַנִּים ק] אֲשֶׁר אֶת־קֶדֶשׁ: וַיַּגִּדוּ לְסִיסְרָא כִּי עָלָה

יג בָּרָק בֶּן־אֲבִינֹעַם הַר־תָּבוֹר: וַיַּזְעֵק סִיסְרָא אֶת־כָּל־רִכְבּוֹ תְּשַׁע מֵאוֹת רֶכֶב בַּרְזֶל וְאֶת־כָּל־הָעָם אֲשֶׁר אִתּוֹ מֵחֲרֹשֶׁת הַגּוֹיִם אֶל־נַחַל קִישׁוֹן:

יד וַתֹּאמֶר דְּבֹרָה אֶל־בָּרָק קוּם כִּי זֶה הַיּוֹם אֲשֶׁר נָתַן יהוה אֶת־סִיסְרָא בְּיָדֶךָ הֲלֹא יהוה יָצָא לְפָנֶיךָ וַיֵּרֶד בָּרָק מֵהַר תָּבוֹר וַעֲשֶׂרֶת אֲלָפִים אִישׁ

טו אַחֲרָיו: וַיָּהָם יהוה אֶת־סִיסְרָא וְאֶת־כָּל־הָרֶכֶב וְאֶת־כָּל־הַמַּחֲנֶה לְפִי־

**HAFTARAS
BESHALACH**
Ashkenazim:
4:4-5:31

3:31. Shamgar, a Levite, was a judge for a period of only several months. His brief reign is included in the eighty years of tranquility mentioned in verse 30 (*Seder Olam*).

4:2. The people again lapsed into sinful conduct and were punished by the ascendancy of Canaan, in fulfillment of the prophecy (2:3) that God would cause the Canaanites to be a source of pain and irritation (*Malbim*).

4:4. Deborah was the first judge to be described as a prophet and as a decider of questions of law for the nation. Literally, לַפִּידוֹת means *torches*. The phrase אֵשֶׁת לַפִּידוֹת then indicates that Deborah was either "a woman who made wicks" for the Tabernacle Menorah (*Rashi*), or "a fiery, energetic woman" (*Ralbag*). Alternatively, *Lappidoth* (Torches) was another name for *Barak* (v. 6), a name

²⁷ It happened when he arrived that he sounded the shofar at Mount Ephraim. The Children of Israel descended with him from the mountain, and he was before them. ²⁸ He said to them, "Give chase behind me, for HASHEM has delivered your enemies, Moab, into your hand!" They descended after him. They conquered the Jordan's crossings into Moab and did not let anyone cross. ²⁹ They struck Moab at that time, about ten thousand men, every fearsome man and every mighty hero, not a man escaped.

SHAMGAR
SON OF
ANATH
3:31
(See Appendix A,
timeline 3)

³⁰ On that day Moab was subjugated under the hand of Israel, and the land was tranquil for eighty years.

³¹ After him was Shamgar son of Anath.* He struck the Philistines, six hundred men, with a cattle goad; and he, too, saved Israel.

4

¹ The Children of Israel continued to do what was evil in the eyes of HASHEM, once Ehud died. ² HASHEM delivered them into the hand of Jabin, king of Canaan, * who reigned in Hazor. The general of his army was Sisera, who dwelt in Harosheth-goiim. ³ The Children of Israel cried out to HASHEM, for [Sisera] had nine hundred iron chariots, and he oppressed the Children of Israel forcefully for twenty years.

DEBORAH
THE
PROPHETESS
AND BARAK
4:1-5:31

Canaannite
oppression:
Jabin and
Sisera

⁴ Deborah was a prophetess,* the wife of Lappidoth;* she judged Israel at that time. ⁵ She would sit under the date palm of Deborah,* between Ramah and Beth-el on Mount Ephraim, and the Children of Israel would go up to her for judgment. ⁶ She sent and summoned Barak son of Abinoam of Kedesh-naphtali and said to him, "Behold, HASHEM, the God of Israel, has commanded, 'Go and convince [the people to go] toward Mount Tabor, and take with you ten thousand men from the children of Naphtali and from the children of Zebulun! ⁷ I will draw toward you — to Kishon Brook — Sisera, the general of Jabin's army, with his chariot and his multitude; and I shall deliver him into your hand.' "

⁸ Barak said to her, "If you go with me, I will go; but if you do not go with me, I will not go."*

⁹ She said, "Indeed, I will go with you — but the path on which you have chosen to go will not be for your glory, for HASHEM will have delivered Sisera into the hand of a woman." Then Deborah got up and went with Barak to Kedesh.

Zebulun and
Naphtali
mustered

¹⁰ Barak mustered Zebulun and Naphtali to Kedesh, and ten thousand men ascended in his footsteps; and Deborah went up with him.

¹¹ (Heber the Kenite had become separated from the Kenites, from the children of Hobab, father-in-law of Moses, and pitched his tents as far as the Plain of Zaanannim, which is near Kedesh.)*

¹² They told Sisera that Barak son of Abinoam had gone up to Mount Tabor. ¹³ Sisera mustered all his chariots — nine hundred iron chariots — and all the people who were with him, from Harosheth-goiim to Kishon Brook. ¹⁴ Deborah said to Barak, "Arise! For this is the day when HASHEM has delivered Sisera into your hand — behold, HASHEM has gone forth before you!" So Barak descended from Mount Tabor with the ten thousand men behind him.

Sisera's flight

¹⁵ HASHEM panicked Sisera and all the chariots and the entire camp by the edge

---

that means flash (Radak).
4:5. Named for an earlier Deborah who was buried in that area (see Genesis 35:8; Abarbanel).
4:8. Considering himself unworthy of such a momentous

miracle, Barak felt that he needed the merit of the judge and prophetess to insure the success of his mission.
4:11. This sets the stage for the later heroics of Heber's wife (v. 17ff).

טו חֶרֶב לִפְנֵי בָרָק וַיֵּרֶד סִיסְרָא מֵעַל הַמֶּרְכָּבָה וַיָּנָס בְּרַגְלָיו: וּבָרָק רָדַף
אַחֲרֵי הָרֶכֶב וְאַחֲרֵי הַמַּחֲנֶה עַד חֲרֹשֶׁת הַגּוֹיִם וַיִּפֹּל כָּל־מַחֲנֵה סִיסְרָא

טז לְפִי־חֶרֶב לֹא נִשְׁאַר עַד־אֶחָד: וְסִיסְרָא נָס בְּרַגְלָיו אֶל־אֹהֶל יָעֵל אֵשֶׁת

יז חֶבֶר הַקֵּינִי כִּי שָׁלוֹם בֵּין יָבִין מֶלֶךְ־חָצוֹר וּבֵין בֵּית חֶבֶר הַקֵּינִי: וַתֵּצֵא
יָעֵל לִקְרַאת סִיסְרָא וַתֹּאמֶר אֵלָיו סוּרָה אֲדֹנִי סוּרָה אֵלַי אַל־תִּירָא

יח וַיָּסַר אֵלֶיהָ הָאֹהֱלָה וַתְּכַסֵּהוּ בַּשְּׂמִיכָה: וַיֹּאמֶר אֵלֶיהָ הַשְׁקִינִי־נָא מְעַט־

יט מַיִם כִּי צָמֵאתִי וַתִּפְתַּח אֶת־נֹאוד הֶחָלָב וַתַּשְׁקֵהוּ וַתְּכַסֵּהוּ: וַיֹּאמֶר
אֵלֶיהָ עֲמֹד פֶּתַח הָאֹהֶל וְהָיָה אִם־אִישׁ יָבֹא וּשְׁאֵלֵךְ וְאָמַר הֲיֵשׁ־פֹּה

כ אִישׁ וְאָמַרְתְּ אָיִן: וַתִּקַּח יָעֵל אֵשֶׁת־חֶבֶר אֶת־יְתַד הָאֹהֶל וַתָּשֶׂם אֶת־
הַמַּקֶּבֶת בְּיָדָהּ וַתָּבוֹא אֵלָיו בַּלָּאט וַתִּתְקַע אֶת־הַיָּתֵד בְּרַקָּתוֹ וַתִּצְנַח

כא בָּאָרֶץ וְהוּא־נִרְדָּם וַיָּעַף וַיָּמֹת: וְהִנֵּה בָרָק רֹדֵף אֶת־סִיסְרָא וַתֵּצֵא יָעֵל
לִקְרָאתוֹ וַתֹּאמֶר לוֹ לֵךְ וְאַרְאֶךָּ אֶת־הָאִישׁ אֲשֶׁר־אַתָּה מְבַקֵּשׁ וַיָּבֹא

כב אֵלֶיהָ וְהִנֵּה סִיסְרָא נֹפֵל מֵת וְהַיָּתֵד בְּרַקָּתוֹ: וַיַּכְנַע אֱלֹהִים בַּיּוֹם הַהוּא

כג אֵת יָבִין מֶלֶךְ־כְּנָעַן לִפְנֵי בְּנֵי יִשְׂרָאֵל: וַתֵּלֶךְ יַד בְּנֵי־יִשְׂרָאֵל הָלוֹךְ וְקָשָׁה

כד עַל יָבִין מֶלֶךְ־כְּנָעַן עַד אֲשֶׁר הִכְרִיתוּ אֵת יָבִין מֶלֶךְ־כְּנָעַן:

ה

HAFTARAS BESHALACH Sephardim: 5:1-31

א וַתָּשַׁר דְּבוֹרָה וּבָרָק בֶּן־אֲבִינֹעַם בַּיּוֹם הַהוּא

ב לֵאמֹר: בִּפְרֹעַ פְּרָעוֹת בְּיִשְׂרָאֵל בְּהִתְנַדֵּב

ג עָם בָּרֲכוּ יְהוָה: שִׁמְעוּ מְלָכִים הַאֲזִינוּ
רֹזְנִים אָנֹכִי לַיהֹוָה אָנֹכִי אָשִׁירָה אֲזַמֵּר

ד לַיהוָה אֱלֹהֵי יִשְׂרָאֵל: יְהוָה בְּצֵאתְךָ
מִשֵּׂעִיר בְּצַעְדְּךָ מִשְּׂדֵה אֱדוֹם אֶרֶץ
רָעָשָׁה גַּם־שָׁמַיִם נָטָפוּ גַּם־עָבִים נָטְפוּ

ה מָיִם: הָרִים נָזְלוּ מִפְּנֵי יְהוָה זֶה
סִינַי מִפְּנֵי יְהוָה אֱלֹהֵי יִשְׂרָאֵל: בִּימֵי שַׁמְגַּר בֶּן־

ו עֲנָת בִּימֵי יָעֵל חָדְלוּ אֳרָחוֹת וְהֹלְכֵי
נְתִיבוֹת יֵלְכוּ אֳרָחוֹת עֲקַלְקַלּוֹת: חָדְלוּ פְרָזוֹן בְּיִשְׂרָאֵל

ז חָדֵלּוּ עַד שַׁקַּמְתִּי דְּבוֹרָה שַׁקַּמְתִּי
אֵם בְּיִשְׂרָאֵל: יִבְחַר אֱלֹהִים

ח חֲדָשִׁים אָז לָחֶם שְׁעָרִים מָגֵן
אִם־יֵרָאֶה וָרֹמַח בְּאַרְבָּעִים אֶלֶף

ט בְּיִשְׂרָאֵל: לִבִּי לְחוֹקְקֵי יִשְׂרָאֵל הַמִּתְנַדְּבִים

י בָּעָם בָּרֲכוּ יְהוָה: רֹכְבֵי אֲתֹנוֹת
צְחֹרוֹת יֹשְׁבֵי עַל־מִדִּין וְהֹלְכֵי

of the sword before Barak; Sisera dismounted from his chariot and fled on his feet. [16] *Barak chased after the chariots and after the camp until Harosheth-goiim; and the entire camp of Sisera fell by the edge of the sword; not even one was left.*

Jael lures Sisera . . .   [17] *Sisera fled on his feet to the tent of Jael, the wife of Heber the Kenite, for there was peace between Jabin, king of Hazor, and the House of Heber the Kenite.* [18] *Jael went out toward Sisera and said to him, "Turn aside, my lord, turn aside to me, do not fear." So he turned aside to her to the tent, and she covered him with a blanket.*

[19] *He said to her, "Give me now a bit of water to drink, because I am thirsty." She opened a skin of milk, gave him to drink, and covered him.* [20] *He said to her, "Stand at the entrance of the tent, and it shall be that if any man will come and ask you and say, 'Is anyone here?' you shall say, 'No!' "*

. . . and dispatches him   [21] *Jael, wife of Heber, took a tent peg, placed a hammer in her hand, came to him stealthily, and drove the peg into his temple and it went through into the ground — [while] he was sleeping deeply and exhausted — and he died.* [22] *Behold — Barak was pursuing Sisera, and Jael went out toward him and told him, "Come and I will show you the man whom you seek!" He came to her and behold — Sisera was fallen, dead, with the peg in his temple.*

[23] *On that day God subjugated Jabin, king of Canaan, before the Children of Israel.* [24] *The hand of the Children of Israel became progressively harsh over Jabin, king of Canaan, until they destroyed Jabin, king of Canaan.*

5

The Song of Deborah   [1] **D**eborah sang — as well as Barak son of Abinoam — on that day, saying:

[2] *When vengeances are inflicted upon Israel and the people dedicates itself [to God] — bless* HASHEM.

[3] *Hear, O kings; give ear, O princes! I, to* HASHEM *shall I sing; I shall sing praise to* HASHEM*, God of Israel!*

[4] HASHEM*, as You left Seir, * as You strode from the fields of Edom, the earth quaked and even the heavens trickled; even the clouds dripped water.*

[5] *Mountains melted before* HASHEM *— as did Sinai — before* HASHEM*, the God of Israel.*

[6] *In the days of Shamgar son of Anath, in the days of Jael, highway travel ceased, and those who traveled on paths went by circuitous roads.*

[7] *They stopped living in unwalled towns in Israel, they stopped; until I, Deborah, arose; I arose as a mother in Israel.*

[8] *When it chose new gods, war came to its gates; was even a shield or a spear seen among forty thousand in Israel?*

The new situation after the war   [9] *My heart is with the lawgivers of Israel who are devoted to the people, [saying,] "Bless* HASHEM*."**

[10] *O riders of white donkeys, [you] who sit in judgment, and you who walk*

5:1. A Scriptural "song" is an unusual spiritual phenomenon. Just as music consists of a combination of notes and instruments so harmonious that every part is indispensable, similarly the spiritual experience that erupts into Scriptural song consists of a perception that all events — even those previously incomprehensible — are part of God's plan and were for the benefit of its players. As Deborah sets forth rapturously, even the forces of nature joined Israel in battle.

5:4. Poetically, Deborah depicts the Giving of the Torah at Mount Sinai (see *Deuteronomy* 33:2).

5:9. Deborah expresses her heartfelt gratitude to the devoted *lawgivers*, who circulated among the people tirelessly in their time of degradation, teaching them to bless HASHEM (Rashi).

יא עַל־דֶּרֶךְ שִׂיחוּ:   מִקּוֹל מְחַצְצִים בֵּין

מַשְׁאַבִּים   שָׁם יְתַנּוּ צִדְקוֹת יהוה   צִדְקֹת

פִּרְזוֹנוֹ בְּיִשְׂרָאֵל   אָז יָרְדוּ לַשְּׁעָרִים עַם־

יב יהוָה: עוּרִי עוּרִי דְּבוֹרָה   עוּרִי

עוּרִי דַּבְּרִי־שִׁיר   קוּם בָּרָק וּשֲׁבֵה שֶׁבְיְךָ בֶּן־

יג אֲבִינֹעַם: אָז יְרַד שָׂרִיד לְאַדִּירִים עָם   יהוָה

יד יְרַד־לִי בַּגִּבּוֹרִים: מִנִּי אֶפְרַיִם שָׁרְשָׁם

בַּעֲמָלֵק   אַחֲרֶיךָ בִנְיָמִין בַּעֲמָמֶיךָ   מִנִּי

מָכִיר יָרְדוּ מְחֹקְקִים   וּמִזְּבוּלֻן מֹשְׁכִים בְּשֵׁבֶט

טו סֹפֵר: וְשָׂרַי בְּיִשָּׂשכָר עִם־דְּבֹרָה   וְיִשָּׂשכָר

כֵּן בָּרָק   בָּעֵמֶק שֻׁלַּח

בְּרַגְלָיו   בִּפְלַגּוֹת רְאוּבֵן   גְּדֹלִים

טז לָמָּה יָשַׁבְתָּ בֵּין   חִקְקֵי־לֵב:

הַמִּשְׁפְּתַיִם   לִשְׁמֹעַ שְׁרִקוֹת עֲדָרִים   לִפְלַגּוֹת

יז רְאוּבֵן גְּדוֹלִים חִקְרֵי־לֵב: גִּלְעָד בְּעֵבֶר הַיַּרְדֵּן

שָׁכֵן   וְדָן לָמָּה יָגוּר אֳנִיּוֹת   אָשֵׁר

יָשַׁב לְחוֹף יַמִּים   וְעַל מִפְרָצָיו

יח יִשְׁכּוֹן: זְבֻלוּן עַם חֵרֵף נַפְשׁוֹ לָמוּת   וְנַפְתָּלִי

יט עַל מְרוֹמֵי שָׂדֶה: בָּאוּ מְלָכִים

נִלְחָמוּ   אָז נִלְחֲמוּ מַלְכֵי כְנַעַן   בְּתַעְנַךְ

עַל־מֵי מְגִדּוֹ   בֶּצַע כֶּסֶף לֹא

כ לָקָחוּ:   מִן־שָׁמַיִם נִלְחָמוּ   הַכּוֹכָבִים

כא מִמְּסִלּוֹתָם נִלְחֲמוּ עִם־סִיסְרָא: נַחַל קִישׁוֹן

גְּרָפָם   נַחַל קְדוּמִים נַחַל קִישׁוֹן   תִּדְרְכִי

כב נַפְשִׁי עֹז: אָז הָלְמוּ עִקְּבֵי־

כג סוּס   מִדַּהֲרוֹת דַּהֲרוֹת אַבִּירָיו: אוֹרוּ

מֵרוֹז אָמַר מַלְאַךְ יהוה   אֹרוּ אָרוֹר

יֹשְׁבֶיהָ   כִּי לֹא־בָאוּ לְעֶזְרַת יהוה   לְעֶזְרַת

כד יהוה בַּגִּבּוֹרִים: תְּבֹרַךְ מִנָּשִׁים

יָעֵל   אֵשֶׁת חֶבֶר הַקֵּינִי   מִנָּשִׁים

כה בָּאֹהֶל תְּבֹרָךְ:   מַיִם שָׁאַל חָלָב

נָתָנָה   בְּסֵפֶל אַדִּירִים הִקְרִיבָה חֶמְאָה: כו

יָדָהּ לַיָּתֵד תִּשְׁלַחְנָה   וִימִינָהּ לְהַלְמוּת

עֲמֵלִים   וְהָלְמָה סִיסְרָא מָחֲקָה רֹאשׁוֹ   וּמָחֲצָה

the roads, speak up!

¹¹ *Rather than the sound of arrows [aimed] at the water-drawers, there they will recount the righteous deeds of HASHEM, the righteous deeds for His open cities in Israel. Then the people of HASHEM descended [again] to the [open] cities.* *

¹² *Give praise, give praise, O Deborah! Give praise, give praise, utter a song! Arise, O Barak, and capture your prisoners, O son of Abinoam!*

¹³ *Now the survivor dominates the mightiest of the people; HASHEM has given me dominion over the strong ones.*

The response of her fellow Jews

¹⁴ *From Ephraim,* * whose root [fought] against Amalek;* * after you came Benjamin with your peoples. From Machir descended lawgivers; and from Zebulun, those who ply the scribal quill.*

¹⁵ *The leaders of Issachar were with Deborah, and so was [the rest of] Issachar with Barak; into the valley he was sent on his feet. But in the indecision of Reuben there was great deceit.*

¹⁶ *Why did you remain sitting at the borders to hear the bleatings of the flocks? The indecision of Reuben demands great investigation.* *

¹⁷ *Gilead dwelled across the Jordan; and Dan — why did he gather [his valuables] onto ships? But Asher lived by the shores of seas and remained [to protect] his open [borders].*

¹⁸ *Zebulun is a people that risked its life to the death, and so did Naphtali, on the heights of the battlefield.*

The miraculous rout of Sisera's army

¹⁹ *Kings came and fought* * — then the kings of Canaan fought, from Taanach to the waters of Megiddo, without accepting monetary reward.*

²⁰ *From heaven they fought, the very stars from their orbits did battle with Sisera.* *

²¹ *Kishon Brook swept them away — the ancient brook, Kishon Brook — but I myself trod it vigorously.* *

²² *Then the horses' heels were pounded by the gallopings, the gallopings of their mighty riders.*

²³ *"Curse Meroz,"* * said the angel of HASHEM, "Curse! Cursed are its inhabitants, for they failed to come to aid [the nation of] HASHEM, to aid [the nation of] HASHEM against the mighty."*

Jael: Blessed for her valor

²⁴ *Blessed by women is Jael, wife of Heber the Kenite; by women in the tent will she blessed.*

²⁵ *He asked for water, she gave him milk; in a stately saucer she presented cream.*

²⁶ *She stretched her hand to the peg and her right hand to the laborers' hammer. She hammered Sisera, severed his head, smashed and pierced his temple.*

5:11. No longer need Jews fear ambushes at their wells. No longer need they flee their unwalled cities.

5:14. Deborah speaks of the varying Jewish responses to Barak's summons. Although Barak summoned only Zebulun and Naphtali (4:10), who were nearest to the battlefield, some but not all of the other tribes also responded nobly.

Ephraim's descendant, Joshua, fought Amalek (*Exodus* 17:9-10,13); Machir represents the tribe of his father Manasseh.

5:16. Incomprehensibly, the Reubenites remained on the sidelines, with their flocks (*Radak*).

5:19. Israel's foes came unselfishly to join Sisera, only to be vanquished by miraculous intervention.

5:20. The rout was so decisive that it was as if the very heavens fought Sisera (*Radak*).

5:21. The Canaanite army rode into Kishon, either to flee or to maneuver for an attack, and the shallow, lazy brook suddenly became a raging torrent. But when the Jews waded into the water, they were able to walk firmly and confidently (*Radak; Ralbag*).

5:23. *Meroz* was the name of a prominent person (*Rashi*) or a city (*Radak*) located near the battlefield, that did not join Barak's cause.

כז בֵּין רַגְלֶיהָ כָּרַע נָפַל   וְחָלְפָה רַקָּתוֹ:

בֵּין רַגְלֶיהָ כָּרַע נָפַל בַּאֲשֶׁר   שָׁכֵב

כח כָּרַע שָׁם נָפַל שָׁדוּד: בְּעַד הַחַלּוֹן נִשְׁקְפָה

אֵם סִיסְרָא בְּעַד הָאֶשְׁנָב וַתְּיַבֵּב   מַדּוּעַ

בֹּשֵׁשׁ רִכְבּוֹ לָבוֹא   מַדּוּעַ אֶחֱרוּ פַּעֲמֵי

כט מַרְכְּבוֹתָיו: חַכְמוֹת שָׂרוֹתֶיהָ תַּעֲנֶינָה   אַף

ל הִיא תָּשִׁיב אֲמָרֶיהָ לָהּ:   הֲלֹא יִמְצְאוּ יְחַלְּקוּ

רַחַם רַחֲמָתַיִם לְרֹאשׁ גֶּבֶר   שָׁלָל

צְבָעִים לְסִיסְרָא שְׁלַל   שְׁלַל צְבָעִים

לא רִקְמָה צֶבַע רִקְמָתַיִם לְצַוְּארֵי שָׁלָל: כֵּן

יֹאבְדוּ כָל אוֹיְבֶיךָ יְהוָה   וְאֹהֲבָיו כְּצֵאת הַשֶּׁמֶשׁ

בִּגְבֻרָתוֹ וַתִּשְׁקֹט הָאָרֶץ   אַרְבָּעִים שָׁנָה: ▸

ו א וַיַּעֲשׂוּ בְנֵי־יִשְׂרָאֵל הָרַע בְּעֵינֵי יְהוָה וַיִּתְּנֵם יְהוָה בְּיַד־מִדְיָן שֶׁבַע שָׁנִים:

ב וַתָּעָז יַד־מִדְיָן עַל־יִשְׂרָאֵל מִפְּנֵי מִדְיָן עָשׂוּ לָהֶם ׀ בְּנֵי יִשְׂרָאֵל אֶת־הַמִּנְהָרוֹת אֲשֶׁר בֶּהָרִים וְאֶת־הַמְּעָרוֹת וְאֶת־הַמְּצָדוֹת:

ג וְהָיָה אִם־זָרַע יִשְׂרָאֵל וְעָלָה מִדְיָן וַעֲמָלֵק וּבְנֵי־קֶדֶם וְעָלוּ עָלָיו: ד וַיַּחֲנוּ עֲלֵיהֶם וַיַּשְׁחִיתוּ אֶת־יְבוּל הָאָרֶץ עַד־בּוֹאֲךָ עַזָּה וְלֹא־יַשְׁאִירוּ מִחְיָה בְּיִשְׂרָאֵל וְשֶׂה וָשׁוֹר וַחֲמוֹר: ה כִּי הֵם וּמִקְנֵיהֶם יַעֲלוּ וְאָהֳלֵיהֶם °יבאו [וּבָאוּ ק] כְּדֵי־אַרְבֶּה לָרֹב וְלָהֶם וְלִגְמַלֵּיהֶם אֵין מִסְפָּר וַיָּבֹאוּ בָאָרֶץ לְשַׁחֲתָהּ: ו וַיִּדַּל יִשְׂרָאֵל מְאֹד מִפְּנֵי מִדְיָן וַיִּזְעֲקוּ בְנֵי־יִשְׂרָאֵל אֶל־יְהוָה: ז וַיְהִי כִּי־זָעֲקוּ בְנֵי־יִשְׂרָאֵל אֶל־יְהוָה עַל אֹדוֹת מִדְיָן: ח וַיִּשְׁלַח יְהוָה אִישׁ נָבִיא אֶל־בְּנֵי יִשְׂרָאֵל וַיֹּאמֶר לָהֶם כֹּה־אָמַר יְהוָה ׀ אֱלֹהֵי יִשְׂרָאֵל אָנֹכִי הֶעֱלֵיתִי אֶתְכֶם מִמִּצְרַיִם וָאֹצִיא אֶתְכֶם מִבֵּית עֲבָדִים: ט וָאַצִּל אֶתְכֶם מִיַּד מִצְרַיִם וּמִיַּד כָּל־לֹחֲצֵיכֶם וָאֲגָרֵשׁ אוֹתָם מִפְּנֵיכֶם וָאֶתְּנָה לָכֶם אֶת־אַרְצָם: י וָאֹמְרָה לָכֶם אֲנִי יְהוָה אֱלֹהֵיכֶם לֹא תִירְאוּ אֶת־אֱלֹהֵי הָאֱמֹרִי אֲשֶׁר אַתֶּם יוֹשְׁבִים בְּאַרְצָם וְלֹא שְׁמַעְתֶּם בְּקוֹלִי: יא וַיָּבֹא מַלְאַךְ יְהוָה וַיֵּשֶׁב תַּחַת הָאֵלָה אֲשֶׁר בְּעָפְרָה אֲשֶׁר לְיוֹאָשׁ אֲבִי הָעֶזְרִי וְגִדְעוֹן בְּנוֹ חֹבֵט חִטִּים בַּגַּת לְהָנִיס מִפְּנֵי מִדְיָן: יב וַיֵּרָא אֵלָיו מַלְאַךְ יְהוָה וַיֹּאמֶר אֵלָיו יְהוָה עִמְּךָ גִּבּוֹר הֶחָיִל: יג וַיֹּאמֶר אֵלָיו גִּדְעוֹן בִּי אֲדֹנִי וְיֵשׁ יְהוָה עִמָּנוּ וְלָמָּה מְצָאַתְנוּ כָּל־זֹאת וְאַיֵּה כָל־נִפְלְאֹתָיו אֲשֶׁר סִפְּרוּ־לָנוּ אֲבוֹתֵינוּ לֵאמֹר הֲלֹא מִמִּצְרַיִם הֶעֱלָנוּ יְהוָה וְעַתָּה נְטָשָׁנוּ יְהוָה וַיִּתְּנֵנוּ בְּכַף־מִדְיָן: יד וַיִּפֶן אֵלָיו יְהוָה וַיֹּאמֶר לֵךְ בְּכֹחֲךָ זֶה וְהוֹשַׁעְתָּ אֶת־יִשְׂרָאֵל מִכַּף מִדְיָן הֲלֹא שְׁלַחְתִּיךָ: טו וַיֹּאמֶר אֵלָיו בִּי אֲדֹנָי בַּמָּה אוֹשִׁיעַ אֶת־יִשְׂרָאֵל הִנֵּה אַלְפִּי הַדַּל בִּמְנַשֶּׁה וְאָנֹכִי הַצָּעִיר בְּבֵית אָבִי:

²⁷ *At her feet he knelt, he fell, he lay. At her feet he knelt, he fell; where he knelt, there he fell, vanquished.*

²⁸ *Through the window she gazed; Sisera's mother peered through the window. "Why is his chariot delayed in coming? Why are the hoofbeats of his carriages so late?"*

Sisera's mother yearns

²⁹ *The wisest of her ladies answer her, and she, too, offers herself responses.*

³⁰ *"Are they not finding [and] dividing loot? A comely [captive], two comely [captives], for every man; booty of colored garments for Sisera, booty of colored embroidery, colored, doubly embroidered garments for the necks of the looters."*

³¹ *So may all Your enemies be destroyed, O HASHEM! And let those who love Him be like the powerfully rising sun.*

And the land was tranquil for forty years.

6

GIDEON [JERUBAAL] 6:1-8:35 (See Appendix A, timeline 3)

¹ *T*he Children of Israel did what was evil in the eyes of HASHEM, so HASHEM delivered them into the hand of Midian [for] seven years. ² The hand of Midian grew powerful over Israel. In the face of Midian, the Children of Israel made themselves the dugouts that are in the mountains, and the caves and strongholds. ³ It happened that whenever Israel would sow, Midian would ascend — as well as Amalek and the people of the east — and they would overrun it. ⁴ They would encamp against them and destroy the produce of the land, until the approach to Gaza. They would leave no sustenance in Israel, [nor] sheep, [nor] ox, [nor] donkey. ⁵ For they and their livestock would ascend with their tents, and they would come as abundantly as a locust-swarm; they and their camels were countless, and they came into the land to destroy it.*

Midianite oppression

⁶ *Israel became very impoverished because of Midian, and the Children of Israel cried out to HASHEM. ⁷ So it happened that when the Children of Israel cried out to HASHEM concerning Midian, ⁸ that HASHEM sent a man, a prophet, to the Children of Israel, and he said to them, "Thus said HASHEM, God of Israel, 'I brought you up from Egypt and I took you out of the house of slavery. ⁹ I rescued you from the hand of Egypt and from the hand of all your oppressors and I drove them away before you and gave you their land. ¹⁰ I said to you: I am HASHEM, your God, you shall not fear the gods of the Amorite, in whose land you dwell — but you did not heed My voice!'"*

Gideon is chosen

¹¹ *An angel of HASHEM came and sat under the elm tree in Ophrah, that belonged to Joash, the Abi-ezrite. His son Gideon was threshing wheat at the winepress, to hide it from Midian. ¹² The angel of HASHEM appeared to him, and said to him, "HASHEM is with you, O mighty hero!"*

¹³ *Gideon said to him, "I beg you, my lord, if HASHEM is with us, why has all this happened to us? And where are all His wonders of which our forefathers told us, saying, 'Behold, HASHEM brought us up from Egypt'? For now HASHEM has deserted us, and He has delivered us into the grip of Midian."*

¹⁴ *Then HASHEM turned to him and said, "Go with this strength of yours and you shall save Israel from the grip of Midian. Behold I have sent you!"*

The angel's sign

¹⁵ *He said, "I beg of You, my Lord, with what shall I save Israel? Behold, my thousand* is the most impoverished of Manasseh, and I am the youngest of my father's house."*

6:15. Gideon was referring to the administrative division of each of the twelve tribes into groups of one   thousand men (see *Exodus* 18:17-26).

טז-יז וַיֹּ֤אמֶר אֵלָיו֙ יְהֹוָ֔ה כִּ֥י אֶֽהְיֶ֖ה עִמָּ֑ךְ וְהִכִּיתָ֥ אֶת־מִדְיָ֖ן כְּאִ֥ישׁ אֶחָֽד: וַיֹּ֣אמֶר
אֵלָ֗יו אִם־נָ֞א מָצָ֤אתִי חֵן֙ בְּעֵינֶ֔יךָ וְעָשִׂ֥יתָ לִּ֛י א֖וֹת שָׁאַתָּ֥ה מְדַבֵּ֖ר עִמִּֽי:
יח אַל־נָ֞א תָּ֤מֻשׁ מִזֶּה֙ עַד־בֹּאִ֣י אֵלֶ֔יךָ וְהֹֽצֵאתִי֙ אֶת־מִנְחָתִ֔י וְהִנַּחְתִּ֖י לְפָנֶ֑יךָ
יט וַיֹּ֕אמַר אָנֹכִ֥י אֵשֵׁ֖ב עַד־שׁוּבֶֽךָ: וְגִדְע֣וֹן בָּ֗א וַיַּ֤עַשׂ גְּדִֽי־עִזִּים֙ וְאֵיפַת־קֶ֣מַח
מַצּ֔וֹת הַבָּשָׂר֙ שָׂ֣ם בַּסַּ֔ל וְהַמָּרַ֖ק שָׂ֣ם בַּפָּר֑וּר וַיּוֹצֵ֥א אֵלָ֛יו אֶל־תַּ֥חַת הָֽאֵלָ֖ה
כ וַיַּגַּֽשׁ:   וַיֹּ֨אמֶר אֵלָ֜יו מַלְאַ֣ךְ הָֽאֱלֹהִ֗ים קַ֣ח אֶת־הַבָּשָׂ֞ר
כא וְאֶת־הַמַּצּ֗וֹת וְהַנַּח֙ אֶל־הַסֶּ֣לַע הַלָּ֔ז וְאֶת־הַמָּרַ֖ק שְׁפ֑וֹךְ וַיַּ֖עַשׂ כֵּֽן: וַיִּשְׁלַ֞ח
מַלְאַ֣ךְ יְהֹוָ֗ה אֶת־קְצֵ֤ה הַמִּשְׁעֶ֙נֶת֙ אֲשֶׁ֣ר בְּיָד֔וֹ וַיִּגַּ֥ע בַּבָּשָׂ֖ר וּבַמַּצּ֑וֹת וַתַּ֣עַל
הָאֵ֗שׁ מִן־הַצּ֤וּר וַתֹּ֙אכַל֙ אֶת־הַבָּשָׂ֣ר וְאֶת־הַמַּצּ֔וֹת וּמַלְאַ֣ךְ יְהֹוָ֔ה הָלַ֖ךְ
כב מֵֽעֵינָֽיו: וַיַּ֣רְא גִּדְע֔וֹן כִּֽי־מַלְאַ֥ךְ יְהֹוָ֖ה ה֑וּא וַיֹּ֣אמֶר גִּדְע֗וֹן אֲהָהּ֙ אֲדֹנָ֣י יֱהֹוִ֔ה
כג כִּֽי־עַל־כֵּ֤ן רָאִ֙יתִי֙ מַלְאַ֣ךְ יְהֹוָ֔ה פָּנִ֖ים אֶל־פָּנִֽים: וַיֹּ֨אמֶר ל֧וֹ יְהֹוָ֛ה שָׁל֥וֹם לְךָ֖
כד אַל־תִּירָ֖א לֹ֥א תָמֽוּת: וַיִּ֧בֶן שָׁ֛ם גִּדְע֥וֹן מִזְבֵּ֖חַ לַֽיהֹוָ֑ה וַיִּקְרָא־ל֣וֹ יְהֹוָ֣ה
כה שָׁל֔וֹם עַ֚ד הַיּ֣וֹם הַזֶּ֔ה עוֹדֶ֕נּוּ בְּעָפְרָ֖ת אֲבִ֥י הָֽעֶזְרִֽי: וַֽיְהִי֙
בַּלַּ֣יְלָה הַה֔וּא וַיֹּ֧אמֶר ל֣וֹ יְהֹוָ֗ה קַ֤ח אֶת־פַּר־הַשּׁוֹר֙ אֲשֶׁ֣ר לְאָבִ֔יךָ וּפַ֥ר הַשֵּׁנִ֖י
שֶׁ֣בַע שָׁנִ֑ים וְהָרַסְתָּ֗ אֶת־מִזְבַּ֤ח הַבַּ֙עַל֙ אֲשֶׁ֣ר לְאָבִ֔יךָ וְאֶת־הָֽאֲשֵׁרָ֥ה אֲשֶׁר־
כו עָלָ֖יו תִּכְרֹֽת: וּבָנִ֨יתָ מִזְבֵּ֜חַ לַיהֹוָ֣ה אֱלֹהֶ֗יךָ עַ֣ל רֹ֤אשׁ הַמָּע֤וֹז הַזֶּה֙ בַּמַּֽעֲרָכָ֔ה
וְלָֽקַחְתָּ֙ אֶת־הַפָּ֣ר הַשֵּׁנִ֔י וְהַֽעֲלִ֣יתָ עוֹלָ֔ה בַּעֲצֵ֥י הָֽאֲשֵׁרָ֖ה אֲשֶׁ֥ר תִּכְרֹֽת:
כז וַיִּקַּ֨ח גִּדְע֜וֹן עֲשָׂרָ֤ה אֲנָשִׁים֙ מֵֽעֲבָדָ֔יו וַיַּ֕עַשׂ כַּֽאֲשֶׁ֛ר דִּבֶּ֥ר אֵלָ֖יו יְהֹוָ֑ה וַיְהִ֡י
כַּֽאֲשֶׁ֣ר יָרֵא֩ אֶת־בֵּ֨ית אָבִ֜יו וְאֶת־אַנְשֵׁ֤י הָעִיר֙ מֵֽעֲשׂ֣וֹת יוֹמָ֔ם וַיַּ֖עַשׂ לָֽיְלָה:
כח וַיַּשְׁכִּ֜ימוּ אַנְשֵׁ֤י הָעִיר֙ בַּבֹּ֔קֶר וְהִנֵּ֤ה נֻתַּץ֙ מִזְבַּ֣ח הַבַּ֔עַל וְהָֽאֲשֵׁרָ֥ה אֲשֶׁר־
כט עָלָ֖יו כֹּרָ֑תָה וְאֵת֙ הַפָּ֣ר הַשֵּׁנִ֔י הֹֽעֲלָ֖ה עַל־הַמִּזְבֵּ֥חַ הַבָּנֽוּי: וַיֹּֽאמְרוּ֙ אִ֣ישׁ
אֶל־רֵעֵ֔הוּ מִ֥י עָשָׂ֖ה הַדָּבָ֣ר הַזֶּ֑ה וַֽיִּדְרְשׁוּ֙ וַיְבַקְשׁ֔וּ וַיֹּ֣אמְר֔וּ גִּדְע֥וֹן בֶּן־יוֹאָ֖שׁ
ל עָשָׂ֥ה הַדָּבָ֥ר הַזֶּֽה: וַיֹּ֨אמְר֜וּ אַנְשֵׁ֤י הָעִיר֙ אֶל־יוֹאָ֔שׁ הוֹצֵ֥א אֶת־בִּנְךָ֖ וְיָמֹ֑ת
לא כִּ֤י נָתַץ֙ אֶת־מִזְבַּ֣ח הַבַּ֔עַל וְכִ֥י כָרַ֖ת הָֽאֲשֵׁרָ֥ה אֲשֶׁר־עָלָֽיו: וַיֹּ֣אמֶר יוֹאָ֡שׁ
לְכֹל֩ אֲשֶׁר־עָמְד֨וּ עָלָ֜יו הַֽאַתֶּ֣ם ׀ תְּרִיב֣וּן לַבַּ֗עַל אִם־אַתֶּם֙ תּֽוֹשִׁיע֣וּן אוֹת֔וֹ
אֲשֶׁ֨ר יָרִ֥יב ל֛וֹ יוּמַ֖ת עַד־הַבֹּ֑קֶר אִם־אֱלֹהִ֥ים הוּא֙ יָ֣רֶב ל֔וֹ כִּ֥י נָתַ֖ץ אֶת־
לב מִזְבְּחֽוֹ: וַיִּקְרָא־ל֥וֹ בַיּֽוֹם־הַה֖וּא יְרֻבַּ֣עַל לֵאמֹ֑ר יָ֤רֶב בּוֹ֙ הַבַּ֔עַל כִּ֥י נָתַ֖ץ אֶת־
לג מִזְבְּחֽוֹ:   וְכָל־מִדְיָ֧ן וַֽעֲמָלֵ֛ק וּבְנֵי־קֶ֖דֶם נֶֽאֶסְפ֣וּ יַחְדָּ֑ו
לד וַיַּֽעַבְר֥וּ וַֽיַּחֲנ֖וּ בְּעֵ֥מֶק יִזְרְעֶֽאל: וְר֣וּחַ יְהֹוָ֔ה לָֽבְשָׁ֖ה אֶת־גִּדְע֑וֹן וַיִּתְקַע֙
לה בַּשּׁוֹפָ֔ר וַיִּזָּעֵ֥ק אֲבִיעֶ֖זֶר אַחֲרָֽיו: וּמַלְאָכִ֣ים שָׁלַ֗ח בְּכָל־מְנַשֶּׁה֙ וַיִּזָּעֵ֥ק גַּם־
ה֖וּא אַֽחֲרָ֑יו וּמַלְאָכִ֣ים שָׁלַ֗ח בְּאָשֵׁ֤ר וּבִזְבֻלוּן֙ וּבְנַפְתָּלִ֔י וַֽיַּעֲל֖וּ לִקְרָאתָֽם:

6:19. Gideon prepared matzos. This indicates that this
event took place during Pesach (*Rashi*; see 7:13).

6:24. He did not build this altar for sacrificial use, since
it was forbidden to bring offerings at personal altars
[therefore God commanded explicitly to build another
altar upon which he was to bring an offering (v. 26)].

Rather he built it to commemorate his gratitude for
having been shown a degree of revelation (see *Genesis*
12:7, 35:7).

6:32. As a result of his father's successful argument,
Gideon received the nickname Jerubaal, a contraction of
יָרֶב בַּעַל, *let Baal take up the grievance*.

¹⁶ HASHEM said to him, "For I shall be with you, and you shall strike down Midian as if it were a single man."

¹⁷ He said to Him, "If I have now found favor in Your eyes, then perform a sign for me that it is You Who speaks with me. ¹⁸ Please do not depart from here until I return to You; I will bring forth my tribute and place it before You." He said, "I shall remain until your return."

¹⁹ So Gideon went inside and prepared a young goat, and matzos* from an ephah of flour. He put the meat in a basket and put the broth in a pot. He brought it out to Him beneath the elm, and presented it. ²⁰ The angel of God said to him, "Take the meat and the matzos and place them on that rock, and pour out the broth," and he did so.

²¹ The angel of HASHEM stretched out the edge of the staff that was in his hand and touched the meat and the matzos. A flame went up from the rock and consumed the meat and the matzos. Then the angel of HASHEM left [from before] his eyes. ²² Gideon realized that it had been an angel of HASHEM! Gideon said, "Alas, my Lord, HASHEM/ELOHIM, inasmuch as I have seen an angel of HASHEM, face to face . . .!"

²³ HASHEM said to him, "Peace to you. Do not be afraid; you will not die!"

²⁴ Gideon built an altar* there to HASHEM, and called it, "HASHEM [is the source of our] Peace." Until this day it is at Ophrah of the Abi-ezrite.

Gideon destroys his own people's idol ²⁵ It happened that night that HASHEM said to him, "Take the young bull that belongs to your father and the second bull, which is seven years old, and break apart the altar of the Baal that belongs to your father, and cut down the Asherah-tree that is near it. ²⁶ Then build an altar for HASHEM, your God, atop the strong rock, on a level place. Take the second bull and offer it up as an elevation-offering, using the wood of the Asherah-tree that you will cut down."

²⁷ Gideon took ten men from among his servants and did as HASHEM spoke to him — but since he was afraid to do it by day, because of his father's household and the people of his city, he did it at night.

²⁸ The people of the city arose early in the morning and behold — the altar of the Baal had been broken and the Asherah-tree that was near it had been cut down, and the second bull had been offered up on the newly built altar! ²⁹ Each man said to his fellow, "Who did this thing?" They searched and sought, and they said, "Gideon son of Joash did this thing!" ³⁰ The men of the city then said to Joash, "Bring out your son and he shall die, because he has broken the altar of the Baal and because he has cut down the Asherah-tree that was near it."

³¹ Joash said to all who were standing near him, "Will you take up the Baal's grievance? Will you save him? Whoever aggrieved him should die by morning; if [Baal] is a god, it will take up its grievance against him, for breaking its altar."

³² On that day [Joash] named him Jerubaal,* saying, "Let the Baal take up the grievance against him, for breaking its altar."

Midian and Amalek invade Israel ³³ All of Midian, Amalek, and the people of the East gathered together. They crossed [the Jordan] and encamped in the Valley of Jezreel. ³⁴ The spirit of HASHEM clothed Gideon. He blew the shofar, and [the family of] Abiezer was mustered after him. ³⁵ He sent messengers throughout Manasseh, and it, too, was mustered after him. He sent messengers to Asher, Zebulun, and Naphtali, and they ascended to confront them.

לו וַיֹּ֥אמֶר גִּדְע֖וֹן אֶל־הָאֱלֹהִ֑ים אִם־יֶשְׁךָ֞ מוֹשִׁ֧יעַ בְּיָדִ֛י אֶת־יִשְׂרָאֵ֖ל כַּאֲשֶׁ֥ר

לז דִּבַּֽרְתָּ׃ הִנֵּ֣ה אָנֹכִ֗י מַצִּ֛יג אֶת־גִּזַּ֥ת הַצֶּ֖מֶר בַּגֹּ֑רֶן אִם֩ טַ֨ל יִהְיֶ֤ה עַל־הַגִּזָּה֙ לְבַדָּ֔הּ וְעַל־כָּל־הָאָ֖רֶץ חֹ֑רֶב וְיָדַעְתִּ֗י כִּי־תוֹשִׁ֧יעַ בְּיָדִ֛י אֶת־יִשְׂרָאֵ֖ל כַּאֲשֶׁ֥ר

לח דִּבַּֽרְתָּ׃ וַיְהִי־כֵ֔ן וַיַּשְׁכֵּם֙ מִֽמׇּחֳרָ֔ת וַיָּ֖זַר אֶת־הַגִּזָּ֑ה וַיִּ֤מֶץ טַל֙ מִן־הַגִּזָּ֔ה מְל֖וֹא

לט הַסֵּ֥פֶל מָֽיִם׃ וַיֹּ֤אמֶר גִּדְעוֹן֙ אֶל־הָ֣אֱלֹהִ֔ים אַל־יִ֤חַר אַפְּךָ֙ בִּ֔י וַאֲדַבְּרָ֖ה אַ֣ךְ הַפָּ֑עַם אֲנַסֶּ֤ה נָּא־רַק־הַפַּ֙עַם֙ בַּגִּזָּ֔ה יְהִי־נָ֨א חֹ֤רֶב אֶל־הַגִּזָּה֙ לְבַדָּ֔הּ וְעַל־

מ כָּל־הָאָ֖רֶץ יִֽהְיֶה־טָּֽל׃ וַיַּ֧עַשׂ אֱלֹהִ֛ים כֵּ֖ן בַּלַּ֣יְלָה הַה֑וּא וַיְהִי־חֹ֤רֶב אֶל־

ז א הַגִּזָּה֙ לְבַדָּ֔הּ וְעַל־כָּל־הָאָ֖רֶץ הָ֥יָה טָֽל׃ וַיַּשְׁכֵּ֨ם יְרֻבַּ֜עַל ה֣וּא גִדְע֗וֹן וְכָל־הָעָם֙ אֲשֶׁ֣ר אִתּ֔וֹ וַֽיַּחֲנ֖וּ עַל־עֵ֣ין חֲרֹ֑ד וּמַחֲנֵ֤ה מִדְיָן֙ הָיָה־ל֣וֹ מִצָּפ֔וֹן מִגִּבְעַ֥ת

ב הַמּוֹרֶ֖ה בָּעֵֽמֶק׃ וַיֹּ֤אמֶר יְהֹוָה֙ אֶל־גִּדְע֔וֹן רַ֤ב הָעָם֙ אֲשֶׁ֣ר אִתָּ֔ךְ מִתִּתִּ֥י אֶת־מִדְיָ֖ן בְּיָדָ֑ם פֶּן־יִתְפָּאֵ֤ר עָלַי֙ יִשְׂרָאֵ֣ל לֵאמֹ֔ר יָדִ֖י

ג הוֹשִׁ֥יעָה לִּֽי׃ וְעַתָּ֗ה קְרָ֨א נָ֜א בְּאׇזְנֵ֤י הָעָם֙ לֵאמֹ֔ר מִֽי־יָרֵ֣א וְחָרֵ֔ד יָשֹׁ֥ב וְיִצְפֹּ֖ר מֵהַ֣ר הַגִּלְעָ֑ד וַיָּ֣שׇׁב מִן־הָעָ֗ם עֶשְׂרִ֤ים וּשְׁנַ֙יִם֙ אֶ֔לֶף וַעֲשֶׂ֥רֶת אֲלָפִ֖ים

ד נִשְׁאָֽרוּ׃ וַיֹּ֨אמֶר יְהֹוָ֜ה אֶל־גִּדְע֗וֹן עוֹד֮ הָעָ֣ם רָב֒ הוֹרֵ֤ד אוֹתָם֙ אֶל־הַמַּ֔יִם וְאֶצְרְפֶ֥נּוּ לְךָ֖ שָׁ֑ם וְהָיָ֡ה אֲשֶׁר֩ אֹמַ֨ר אֵלֶ֜יךָ זֶ֣ה ׀ יֵלֵ֣ךְ אִתָּ֗ךְ ה֚וּא יֵלֵ֣ךְ אִתָּ֔ךְ וְכֹ֨ל אֲשֶׁר־אֹמַ֜ר אֵלֶ֗יךָ זֶ֚ה לֹא־יֵלֵ֣ךְ עִמָּ֔ךְ ה֖וּא לֹ֥א יֵלֵֽךְ׃

ה וַיּ֥וֹרֶד אֶת־הָעָ֖ם אֶל־הַמָּ֑יִם וַיֹּ֨אמֶר יְהֹוָ֜ה אֶל־גִּדְע֗וֹן כֹּ֣ל אֲשֶׁר־יָלֹק֩ בִּלְשׁוֹנ֨וֹ מִן־הַמַּ֜יִם כַּאֲשֶׁ֧ר יָלֹ֣ק הַכֶּ֗לֶב תַּצִּ֤יג אוֹתוֹ֙ לְבָ֔ד וְכֹ֛ל אֲשֶׁר־יִכְרַ֥ע

ו עַל־בִּרְכָּ֖יו לִשְׁתּֽוֹת׃ וַיְהִ֗י מִסְפַּ֞ר הַֽמְלַקְקִ֤ים בְּיָדָם֙ אֶל־פִּיהֶ֔ם שְׁלֹ֥שׁ מֵא֖וֹת אִ֑ישׁ וְכֹל֙ יֶ֣תֶר הָעָ֔ם כָּרְע֥וּ עַל־בִּרְכֵיהֶ֖ם לִשְׁתּ֥וֹת מָֽיִם׃ וַיֹּ֣אמֶר

ז יְהֹוָה֙ אֶל־גִּדְע֔וֹן בִּשְׁלֹ֣שׁ מֵא֨וֹת הָאִ֤ישׁ הַֽמְלַקְקִים֙ אוֹשִׁ֣יעַ אֶתְכֶ֔ם וְנָתַתִּ֥י אֶת־מִדְיָ֖ן בְּיָדֶ֑ךָ וְכָל־הָעָ֔ם יֵלְכ֖וּ אִ֥ישׁ לִמְקֹמֽוֹ׃ וַיִּקְח֣וּ אֶת־צֵדָ֣ה

ח הָעָם֩ בְּיָדָ֨ם וְאֵ֜ת שׁוֹפְרֹֽתֵיהֶ֗ם וְאֵ֨ת כָּל־אִ֤ישׁ יִשְׂרָאֵל֙ שִׁלַּח֙ אִ֣ישׁ לְאֹהָלָ֔יו וּבִשְׁלֹשׁ־מֵא֥וֹת הָאִ֖ישׁ הֶחֱזִ֑יק וּמַחֲנֵ֣ה מִדְיָ֔ן הָ֥יָה ל֖וֹ מִתַּ֥חַת

ט בָּעֵֽמֶק׃ וַֽיְהִי֙ בַּלַּ֣יְלָה הַה֔וּא וַיֹּ֤אמֶר אֵלָיו֙ יְהֹוָ֔ה ק֖וּם רֵ֣ד

י בַּֽמַּחֲנֶ֑ה כִּ֥י נְתַתִּ֖יו בְּיָדֶֽךָ׃ וְאִם־יָרֵ֥א אַתָּ֖ה לָרֶ֑דֶת רֵ֥ד אַתָּ֛ה וּפֻרָ֥ה נַעַרְךָ֖

יא אֶל־הַֽמַּחֲנֶֽה׃ וְשָֽׁמַעְתָּ֙ מַה־יְדַבֵּ֔רוּ וְאַחַר֙ תֶּחֱזַ֣קְנָה יָדֶ֔יךָ וְיָרַדְתָּ֖ בַּֽמַּחֲנֶ֑ה

יב וַיֵּ֤רֶד הוּא֙ וּפֻרָ֣ה נַעֲר֔וֹ אֶל־קְצֵ֥ה הַחֲמֻשִׁ֖ים אֲשֶׁ֥ר בַּֽמַּחֲנֶֽה׃ וּמִדְיָ֨ן וַעֲמָלֵ֤ק וְכָל־בְּנֵי־קֶ֙דֶם֙ נֹפְלִ֣ים בָּעֵ֔מֶק כָּאַרְבֶּ֖ה לָרֹ֑ב וְלִגְמַלֵּיהֶם֙ אֵ֣ין מִסְפָּ֔ר כַּח֛וֹל

יג שֶׁעַל־שְׂפַ֥ת הַיָּ֖ם לָרֹֽב׃ וַיָּבֹ֣א גִדְע֔וֹן וְהִנֵּה־אִ֗ישׁ מְסַפֵּ֥ר לְרֵעֵ֖הוּ חֲל֑וֹם

6:36-37. Gideon asked God to perform two specific miracles for him, as proof that he was worthy of the miracles he would need to defeat Midian (*Radak*). Moreover, Gideon wanted proofs that he could present to his fellow Jews, in case they doubted him (*Emek HaNetziv*).

7:2. God wanted the conquest to be recognized without question as a miracle. Even though the initial Jewish

force of thirty-two thousand would have been an underdog against the Midianite army of one hundred and thirty-five thousand (see 8:10), its size was such that a victory was conceivable, though unlikely.

7:3. The fearful men were to withdraw before the others awoke, so that they would not be embarrassed by a retreat visible to all their comrades (*Abarbanel*).

Gideon
requests
assurance
from God

³⁶ Gideon said to God, "If You wish to save Israel through my hand, as You spoke, ³⁷ behold, I am spreading out a fleece of wool on the threshing floor. If there will be dew only on the fleece, and the entire ground will be dry, then I will know that You will help Israel through my hand,* as You have spoken." ³⁸ And so it was. He arose the next morning and squeezed the fleece. He pressed dew from the fleece, a full bowl of water.

³⁹ Then Gideon said to God, "Let Your wrath not flare against me and I will speak only this time. I will test but this time through the fleece: Let there be dryness only on the fleece, and let there be dew on the entire ground." ⁴⁰ God did so that night, and there was dryness only on the fleece, and there was dew on the entire ground.

7

¹ Jerubaal, who is Gideon, arose early with all the people who were with him and they encamped near En-harod; the camp of Midian was to his north, from the Hill of Moreh, in the valley.

God
chooses
those who
will fight
Midian

² HASHEM said to Gideon, "The people that are with you are too numerous for Me to deliver Midian into their hand, lest Israel aggrandize itself over Me, saying, 'My own strength has saved me!'* ³ So now call out in the ears of the people, saying, 'Whoever fears and trembles, let him turn back and depart at dawn from Mount Gilead.' "* Twenty-two thousand of the people withdrew, and ten thousand remained. ⁴ Then HASHEM said to Gideon, "The people are still too numerous; bring them down to the water and I shall purge them for you there. And it shall be, that of whomever I say to you, 'This one shall go with you,' he shall go with you, and of whomever I say to you, 'This one shall not go with you,' he shall not go."

⁵ He brought the people down to the water, and HASHEM said to Gideon, "Everyone who laps from the water with his tongue as a dog laps, stand him apart, and [so, too], everyone who kneels on his knees to drink."*

⁶ It happened that the number of those who lapped with their hands to their mouth were three hundred men, and all the rest of the people knelt on their knees to drink water. ⁷ HASHEM said to Gideon, "Through the three hundred men who lap shall I save you and I shall deliver Midian into your hand — and let all the [other] people leave, each to his place." ⁸ And they took the provisions of the [other] people in their hands, as well as their shofars. And as for all the men of Israel, he sent them each to his home, and he kept the three hundred men. The camp of Midian was below him, in the valley.

Omen of
the roasted
barley bread

⁹ It happened that night that HASHEM said to him, "Arise and descend into the camp, for I have delivered it into your hand. ¹⁰ But if you are afraid to descend, go down to the camp, you and Purah your attendant. ¹¹ Listen to what they will speak; then your hands will be strengthened, and you will descend into the camp." So he descended with Purah his attendant to the edge of the armed troops in the camp. ¹² Midian, Amalek, and all the people of the East were encamping in the valley, as numerous as a locust-swarm; and their camels were countless, as numerous as the sand at the seashore.

¹³ Gideon arrived, and behold, a man was relating a dream to his fellow,

---

7:5. In order to thoroughly discredit the idea that idols had any power, God commanded Gideon to test his volunteers in a manner that would exclude anyone with even a tendency toward idolatry. Less than one percent of the original army was deemed worthy. Whether they lay prostrate on the ground to lap like dogs, or knelt to reach the water, their actions indicated that they were in the habit of making obeisance to idols (*Rashi*).

וַיֹּ֣אמֶר הִנֵּ֣ה חֲלֹ֣ום חָלַ֔מְתִּי וְהִנֵּ֨ה °צְלוּל [°צְלִיל ק] לֶ֤חֶם שְׂעֹרִים֙ מִתְהַפֵּ֔ךְ בְּמַחֲנֵ֣ה מִדְיָ֔ן וַיָּבֹ֣א עַד־הָאֹ֜הֶל וַיַּכֵּ֤הוּ וַיִּפֹּ֙ל וַיַּֽהַפְכֵ֣הוּ לְמַ֔עְלָה וְנָפַ֥ל הָאֹֽהֶל:

יד וַיַּ֣עַן רֵעֵ֗הוּ וַיֹּ֙אמֶר֙ אֵ֣ין זֹ֔את בִּלְתִּ֗י אִם־חֶ֛רֶב גִּדְעֹ֥ון בֶּן־יֹואָ֖שׁ אִ֣ישׁ יִשְׂרָאֵ֑ל

טו נָתַ֤ן הָֽאֱלֹהִים֙ בְּיָדֹ֔ו אֶת־מִדְיָ֖ן וְאֶת־כָּל־הַֽמַּחֲנֶֽה: וַיְהִ֤י כִשְׁמֹ֙עַ֙ גִּדְעֹ֔ון אֶת־מִסְפַּ֥ר הַֽחֲלֹ֖ום וְאֶת־שִׁבְרֹ֑ו וַיִּשְׁתָּ֔חוּ וַיָּ֙שָׁב֙ אֶל־מַחֲנֵ֣ה יִשְׂרָאֵ֔ל

טז וַיֹּ֙אמֶר֙ ק֣וּמוּ כִּֽי־נָתַ֧ן יְהוָ֛ה בְּיֶדְכֶ֖ם אֶת־מַֽחֲנֵ֥ה מִדְיָֽן: וַיַּ֜חַץ אֶת־שְׁלֹשׁ־מֵאֹ֣ות הָאִ֗ישׁ שְׁלֹשָׁ֣ה רָאשִׁ֑ים וַיִּתֵּ֨ן שֹׁופָרֹ֤ות בְּיַד־כֻּלָּם֙ וְכַדִּ֣ים רֵקִ֔ים

יז וְלַפִּדִ֖ים בְּתֹ֣וךְ הַכַּדִּֽים: וַיֹּ֣אמֶר אֲלֵיהֶ֔ם מִמֶּ֥נִּי תִרְא֖וּ וְכֵ֣ן תַּעֲשׂ֑וּ וְהִנֵּ֨ה אָנֹכִ֥י

יח בָ֣א בִּקְצֵ֣ה הַֽמַּחֲנֶ֗ה וְהָיָ֛ה כַאֲשֶׁר־אֶעֱשֶׂ֖ה כֵּ֥ן תַּעֲשֽׂוּן: וְתָקַעְתִּי֙ בַּשֹּׁופָ֔ר אָֽנֹכִ֖י וְכָל־אֲשֶׁ֣ר אִתִּ֑י וּתְקַעְתֶּ֨ם בַּשֹּׁופָרֹ֜ות גַּם־אַתֶּ֗ם סְבִיבֹות֙ כָּל־הַֽמַּחֲנֶ֔ה

יט וַֽאֲמַרְתֶּ֖ם לַֽיהוָ֥ה וּלְגִדְעֹֽון: וַיָּבֹ֣א גִ֠דְעֹ֠ון וּמֵאָה־אִ֨ישׁ אֲשֶׁר־אִתֹּ֜ו בִּקְצֵ֣ה הַֽמַּחֲנֶ֗ה רֹ֚אשׁ הָאַשְׁמֹ֣רֶת הַתִּֽיכֹונָ֔ה אַ֖ךְ הָקֵ֣ם הֵקִ֑ימוּ אֶת־הַשֹּֽׁמְרִ֑ים

כ וַֽיִּתְקְעוּ֙ בַּשֹּׁ֣ופָרֹ֔ות וְנָפֹ֥וץ הַכַּדִּ֖ים אֲשֶׁ֣ר בְּיָדָ֑ם: וַֽיִּתְקְ֡עוּ שְׁלֹ֣שֶׁת הָֽרָאשִׁים֩ בַּשֹּׁ֨ופָרֹ֜ות וַיִּשְׁבְּר֣וּ הַכַּדִּ֗ים וַיַּֽחֲזִ֤יקוּ בְיַד־שְׂמֹאולָם֙ בַּלַּפִּדִ֔ים וּבְיַד־יְמִינָ֔ם

כא הַשֹּֽׁופָרֹ֖ות לִתְקֹ֑ועַ וַֽיִּקְרְא֗וּ חֶ֚רֶב לַֽיהוָ֣ה וּלְגִדְעֹ֔ון: וַיַּֽעַמְדוּ֙ אִ֣ישׁ תַּחְתָּ֔יו סָבִ֖יב לַֽמַּחֲנֶ֑ה וַיָּ֧רָץ כָּל־הַֽמַּחֲנֶ֛ה וַיָּרִ֖יעוּ °וַיָּרִ֑יעוּ [°וַיָּנֻ֑סוּ ק]:

כב וַֽיִּתְקְעוּ֮ שְׁלֹשׁ־מֵאֹ֣ות הַשֹּׁופָרֹות֒ וַיָּ֣שֶׂם יְהוָ֗ה אֵ֣ת חֶ֥רֶב אִ֛ישׁ בְּרֵעֵ֖הוּ וּבְכָל־הַֽמַּחֲנֶ֑ה וַיָּ֨נָס הַֽמַּחֲנֶ֜ה עַד־בֵּ֤ית הַשִּׁטָּה֙ צְרֵ֣רָתָה עַ֚ד שְׂפַת־אָבֵ֣ל מְחֹולָ֔ה עַל־טַבָּֽת:

כג וַיִּצָּעֵ֧ק אִֽישׁ־יִשְׂרָאֵ֛ל מִנַּפְתָּלִ֖י וּמִן־אָשֵׁ֑ר וּמִן־כָּל־מְנַשֶּׁ֔ה וַֽיִּרְדְּפ֖וּ אַחֲרֵ֥י

כד מִדְיָֽן: וּמַלְאָכִ֡ים שָׁלַ֣ח גִּדְעֹון֩ בְּכָל־הַ֨ר אֶפְרַ֜יִם לֵאמֹ֗ר רְד֞וּ לִקְרַ֣את מִדְיָ֗ן וְלִכְד֤וּ לָהֶם֙ אֶת־הַמַּ֔יִם עַ֚ד בֵּ֣ית בָּרָ֔ה וְאֶת־הַיַּרְדֵּ֑ן וַיִּצָּעֵ֞ק כָּל־אִ֤ישׁ אֶפְרַ֨יִם֙

כה וַיִּלְכְּד֤וּ אֶת־הַמַּ֙יִם֙ עַד־בֵּ֣ית בָּרָ֔ה וְאֶת־הַיַּרְדֵּ֑ן וַֽיִּלְכְּד֗וּ שְׁנֵֽי־שָׂרֵ֤י מִדְיָן֙ אֶת־עֹרֵ֣ב וְאֶת־זְאֵ֔ב וַיַּהַרְג֤וּ אֶת־עֹורֵב֙ בְּצוּר־עֹורֵ֔ב וְאֶת־זְאֵ֥ב הָרְג֖וּ בְיֶ֣קֶב־זְאֵ֑ב וַֽיִּרְדְּפ֣וּ אֶל־מִדְיָ֔ן וְרֹֽאשׁ־עֹרֵ֣ב וּזְאֵ֔ב הֵבִ֙יאוּ֙ אֶל־גִּדְעֹ֔ון מֵעֵ֖בֶר לַיַּרְדֵּֽן:

ח א וַיֹּֽאמְר֨וּ אֵלָ֜יו אִ֣ישׁ אֶפְרַ֗יִם מָֽה־הַדָּבָ֤ר הַזֶּה֙ עָשִׂ֣יתָ לָּ֔נוּ לְבִלְתִּי֙ קְרֹ֣אות לָ֔נוּ

ב כִּ֥י הָלַ֖כְתָּ לְהִלָּחֵ֣ם בְּמִדְיָ֑ן וַיְרִיב֥וּן אִתֹּ֖ו בְּחָזְקָֽה: וַיֹּ֣אמֶר אֲלֵיהֶ֔ם מֶה־עָשִׂ֥יתִי

ג עַתָּ֖ה כָּכֶ֑ם הֲלֹ֗וא טֹ֛וב עֹֽלְלֹ֥ות אֶפְרַ֖יִם מִבְצִ֣יר אֲבִיעֶ֑זֶר: בְּיֶדְכֶם֩ נָתַ֨ן אֱלֹהִ֜ים אֶת־שָׂרֵ֤י מִדְיָן֙ אֶת־עֹרֵ֣ב וְאֶת־זְאֵ֔ב וּמַה־יָּכֹ֖לְתִּי עֲשֹׂ֣ות כָּכֶ֑ם אָ֗ז רָפְתָ֤ה רוּחָם֙

ד מֵֽעָלָ֔יו בְּדַבְּרֹ֖ו הַדָּבָ֥ר הַזֶּֽה: וַיָּבֹ֥א גִדְעֹ֖ון הַיַּרְדֵּ֑נָה עֹבֵ֣ר ה֗וּא וּשְׁלֹשׁ־מֵאֹ֤ות

ה הָאִישׁ֙ אֲשֶׁ֣ר אִתֹּ֔ו עֲיֵפִ֖ים וְרֹדְפִֽים: וַיֹּ֙אמֶר֙ לְאַנְשֵׁ֣י סֻכֹּ֔ות תְּנוּ־נָא֙ כִּכְּרֹ֣ות לֶ֔חֶם לָעָ֖ם אֲשֶׁ֣ר בְּרַגְלָ֑י כִּֽי־עֲיֵפִ֣ים הֵ֔ם וְאָ֣נֹכִ֔י רֹדֵ֗ף אַֽחֲרֵ֛י זֶ֥בַח וְצַלְמֻנָּ֖ע

7:13. The omen of salvation was a *barley bread*, because this event took place on the second day of Pesach (see 6:19), the day on which the once-a-year *omer*-offering of barley is brought in the Tabernacle. In the merit of this offering, God was about to save Israel (*Rashi*).

7:23. Now that the battle was won with only three hundred men, thus proving that the salvation was a miracle, Gideon called upon thousands of others to come and complete the rout.

8:1. Gideon's original call to arms did not include Eph-

and said, "Behold, I dreamt a dream. Behold, a roasted barley bread* was rolling in the Midianite camp. It came to the tent and struck it and it fell; it turned it upside down and the tent fell."

¹⁴ His fellow answered and said, "This is none other than the sword of Gideon son of Joash, the man of Israel; God has delivered Midian and the entire camp into his hand!"

¹⁵ It happened that when Gideon heard the recounting of the dream and its interpretation, he prostrated himself. He returned to the camp of Israel and said, "Rise up, for HASHEM has delivered the camp of Midian into your hand!"

Gideon attacks. . . ¹⁶ He divided the three hundred men into three companies. Into the hand of them all he gave shofars and empty jugs, with torches inside the jugs. ¹⁷ He said to them, "See my example and do the same. Behold, when I arrive at the edge of the camp, then as I do, so shall you do. ¹⁸ I will sound the shofar — I and all who are with me — then you, too, shall sound shofars all around the entire camp, and you shall say, 'For HASHEM and for Gideon!' "

¹⁹ Gideon and the hundred men with him arrived at the edge of the camp at the beginning of the middle watch, when they had just barely set up the guards. They sounded the shofars and broke the jugs that were in their hand. ²⁰ The three companies sounded the shofars and broke the jugs; in their left hand they grasped the torches and in their right hand the shofars to sound, and they called out, "The sword for HASHEM and for Gideon!" ²¹ Each of them stood in his place, all around the camp — and the entire camp ran, they shouted and fled. ²² They sounded the three hundred shofars and HASHEM set each man's sword against his fellow, and throughout the entire camp. The camp fled as far as Beth-shittah, toward Zererah, as far as the border of Abel-meholah, near Tabbath.

. . . and pursues Midian ²³ The men of Israel were mustered from Naphtali and from Asher and from all of Manasseh, * and they pursued Midian. ²⁴ Gideon sent messengers throughout Mount Ephraim, saying, "Come down toward Midian and secure the waterway to block them, until Beth-barah, and the Jordan." All the men of Ephraim were mustered and they occupied the water until Beth-barah, and the Jordan. ²⁵ They captured two leaders of Midian, Oreb and Zeeb; they killed Oreb at the Rock of Oreb and they killed Zeeb at the Winepress of Zeeb, and they pursued Midian. They brought the heads of Oreb and Zeeb to Gideon across the Jordan.

8

Gideon mollifies Ephraim ¹ The men of Ephraim* said to [Gideon], "What is this thing that you have done to us, not summoning us when you went to fight with Midian?" and they contended with him vehemently. ² He said to them, "What have I now done compared to you? Are not the gleanings of Ephraim better than the vintage of Abiezer? ³ Into your hand did God give the leaders of Midian, Oreb and Zeeb, and what could I do compared to you?" Then their indignation against him abated, when he made this statement.

Insolence of the people of Succoth and Penuel ⁴ Gideon then arrived at the Jordan. He and the three hundred men who were with him were crossing, exhausted, yet pursuing. ⁵ He said to the people of Succoth, "Give now loaves of bread to the people that follow at my feet, for they are exhausted, and I am pursuing Zebah and Zalmunna,

---

raim, apparently because the Midianites were blocking their way. The tribe of Ephraim, however, was insulted that Gideon ignored them until the war was all but won, as if he considered them to be inferior warriors (see 12:1).

מַלְכֵי מִדְיָן: וַיֹּאמֶר שָׂרֵי סֻכּוֹת הֲכַף זֶבַח וְצַלְמֻנָּע עַתָּה בְּיָדֶךָ כִּי־נִתֵּן ו

לִצְבָאֲךָ לָחֶם: וַיֹּאמֶר גִּדְעוֹן לָכֵן בְּתֵת יהוה אֶת־זֶבַח וְאֶת־צַלְמֻנָּע בְּיָדִי ז

וְדַשְׁתִּי אֶת־בְּשַׂרְכֶם אֶת־קוֹצֵי הַמִּדְבָּר וְאֶת־הַבַּרְקֳנִים: וַיַּעַל מִשָּׁם ח

פְּנוּאֵל וַיְדַבֵּר אֲלֵיהֶם כָּזֹאת וַיַּעֲנוּ אוֹתוֹ אַנְשֵׁי פְנוּאֵל כַּאֲשֶׁר עָנוּ אַנְשֵׁי

סֻכּוֹת: וַיֹּאמֶר גַּם־לְאַנְשֵׁי פְנוּאֵל לֵאמֹר בְּשׁוּבִי בְשָׁלוֹם אֶתֹּץ אֶת־ ט

הַמִּגְדָּל הַזֶּה: וְזֶבַח וְצַלְמֻנָּע בַּקַּרְקֹר וּמַחֲנֵיהֶם עִמָּם י

כַּחֲמֵשֶׁת עָשָׂר אֶלֶף כֹּל הַנּוֹתָרִים מִכֹּל מַחֲנֵה בְנֵי־קֶדֶם וְהַנֹּפְלִים מֵאָה

וְעֶשְׂרִים אֶלֶף אִישׁ שֹׁלֵף חָרֶב: וַיַּעַל גִּדְעוֹן דֶּרֶךְ הַשְּׁכוּנֵי בָאֳהָלִים יא

מִקֶּדֶם לְנֹבַח וְיָגְבְּהָה וַיַּךְ אֶת־הַמַּחֲנֶה וְהַמַּחֲנֶה הָיָה בֶטַח: וַיָּנוּסוּ זֶבַח יב

וְצַלְמֻנָּע וַיִּרְדֹּף אַחֲרֵיהֶם וַיִּלְכֹּד אֶת־שְׁנֵי ׀ מַלְכֵי מִדְיָן אֶת־זֶבַח וְאֶת־

צַלְמֻנָּע וְכָל־הַמַּחֲנֶה הֶחֱרִיד: וַיָּשָׁב גִּדְעוֹן בֶּן־יוֹאָשׁ מִן־הַמִּלְחָמָה יג

מִלְמַעֲלֵה הֶחָרֶס: וַיִּלְכָּד־נַעַר מֵאַנְשֵׁי סֻכּוֹת וַיִּשְׁאָלֵהוּ וַיִּכְתֹּב אֵלָיו אֶת־ יד

שָׂרֵי סֻכּוֹת וְאֶת־זְקֵנֶיהָ שִׁבְעִים וְשִׁבְעָה אִישׁ: וַיָּבֹא אֶל־אַנְשֵׁי סֻכּוֹת טו

וַיֹּאמֶר הִנֵּה זֶבַח וְצַלְמֻנָּע אֲשֶׁר חֵרַפְתֶּם אוֹתִי לֵאמֹר הֲכַף זֶבַח וְצַלְמֻנָּע

עַתָּה בְּיָדֶךָ כִּי נִתֵּן לַאֲנָשֶׁיךָ הַיְּעֵפִים לָחֶם: וַיִּקַּח אֶת־זִקְנֵי הָעִיר וְאֶת־ טז

קוֹצֵי הַמִּדְבָּר וְאֶת־הַבַּרְקֳנִים וַיֹּדַע בָּהֶם אֵת אַנְשֵׁי סֻכּוֹת: וְאֶת־מִגְדַּל יז

פְּנוּאֵל נָתָץ וַיַּהֲרֹג אֶת־אַנְשֵׁי הָעִיר: וַיֹּאמֶר אֶל־זֶבַח וְאֶל־צַלְמֻנָּע אֵיפֹה יח

הָאֲנָשִׁים אֲשֶׁר הֲרַגְתֶּם בְּתָבוֹר וַיֹּאמְרוּ כָּמוֹךָ כְמוֹהֶם אֶחָד כְּתֹאַר בְּנֵי

הַמֶּלֶךְ: וַיֹּאמַר אַחַי בְּנֵי־אִמִּי הֵם חַי־יהוה לוּ הַחֲיִתֶם אוֹתָם לֹא הָרַגְתִּי יט

אֶתְכֶם: וַיֹּאמֶר לְיֶתֶר בְּכוֹרוֹ קוּם הֲרֹג אוֹתָם וְלֹא־שָׁלַף הַנַּעַר חַרְבּוֹ כִּי כ

יָרֵא כִּי עוֹדֶנּוּ נָעַר: וַיֹּאמֶר זֶבַח וְצַלְמֻנָּע קוּם אַתָּה וּפְגַע־בָּנוּ כִּי כָאִישׁ כא

גְּבוּרָתוֹ וַיָּקָם גִּדְעוֹן וַיַּהֲרֹג אֶת־זֶבַח וְאֶת־צַלְמֻנָּע וַיִּקַּח אֶת־הַשַּׂהֲרֹנִים

אֲשֶׁר בְּצַוְּארֵי גְמַלֵּיהֶם: וַיֹּאמְרוּ אִישׁ־יִשְׂרָאֵל אֶל־גִּדְעוֹן כב

מְשָׁל־בָּנוּ גַּם־אַתָּה גַּם־בִּנְךָ גַּם בֶּן־בְּנֶךָ כִּי הוֹשַׁעְתָּנוּ מִיַּד מִדְיָן: וַיֹּאמֶר כג

אֲלֵהֶם גִּדְעוֹן לֹא־אֶמְשֹׁל אֲנִי בָּכֶם וְלֹא־יִמְשֹׁל בְּנִי בָּכֶם יהוה יִמְשֹׁל

בָּכֶם: וַיֹּאמֶר אֲלֵהֶם גִּדְעוֹן אֶשְׁאֲלָה מִכֶּם שְׁאֵלָה וּתְנוּ־לִי אִישׁ נֶזֶם שְׁלָלוֹ כד

כִּי־נִזְמֵי זָהָב לָהֶם כִּי יִשְׁמְעֵאלִים הֵם: וַיֹּאמְרוּ נָתוֹן נִתֵּן וַיִּפְרְשׂוּ אֶת־ כה

הַשִּׂמְלָה וַיַּשְׁלִיכוּ שָׁמָּה אִישׁ נֶזֶם שְׁלָלוֹ: וַיְהִי מִשְׁקַל נִזְמֵי הַזָּהָב אֲשֶׁר כו

שָׁאַל אֶלֶף וּשְׁבַע־מֵאוֹת זָהָב לְבַד מִן־הַשַּׂהֲרֹנִים וְהַנְּטִפוֹת וּבִגְדֵי

הָאַרְגָּמָן שֶׁעַל מַלְכֵי מִדְיָן וּלְבַד מִן־הָעֲנָקוֹת אֲשֶׁר בְּצַוְּארֵי גְמַלֵּיהֶם:

8:7. The disheartening lack of gratitude and simple compassion shown by the residents of Succoth and Penuel was a traitorous act that Gideon had to punish.

8:14. Aware that the entire community was not responsible for the attitude of some leaders, Gideon seized one of the citizens to ascertain the identity of the guilty parties.

8:17. He killed only those who attacked him when he began to raze the tower (*Radak*).

8:21. They said, "Your son is not strong enough to kill us quickly. If he would smite us we would linger in a painful, drawn-out death. You can kill us with one blow."

8:24. Since Ishmael and Midian were brothers (see *Genesis* 16:16 and 25:1-2), Scripture sometimes identifies the Midianites as Ishmaelites (cf. *Genesis* 37:28).

the kings of Midian."

⁶ But the leaders of Succoth said, "Is the palm of Zebah and Zalmunna already in your hand, that we should give bread to your legion?"

⁷ So Gideon said, "Therefore, when God delivers Zebah and Zalmunna into my hand, I shall thrash your flesh with desert thorns and briers!"*

⁸ He ascended from there to Penuel, and spoke similarly to them. The men of Penuel answered him as the men of Succoth had answered. ⁹ So he said also to the men of Penuel, saying, "When I return in peace, I shall break down this tower!"

Gideon captures the two Midianite kings . . .   ¹⁰ Zebah and Zalmunna were in Karkor and their camps were with them, about fifteen thousand, all the survivors from the entire camp of the people of the East, for the fallen ones were a hundred and twenty thousand swordsmen. ¹¹ Gideon ascended by way of the tent dwellers, east of Nobah and Jogbehah; he struck the camp while the camp was complacent. ¹² Zebah and Zalmunna fled, and he chased after them. He captured the two kings of Midian, Zebah and Zalmunna, and terrified the entire camp.

. . . punishes Succoth and Penuel . . .   ¹³ Gideon son of Joash returned from the battle while the sun was high. ¹⁴ He seized a youth from among the men of Succoth and questioned him.* He wrote for him the [names of the] leaders of Succoth and her elders, seventy-seven men. ¹⁵ He came to the men of Succoth and said, "Here are Zebah and Zalmunna about whom you scorned me, saying, 'Is the palm of Zebah and Zalmunna already in your hand, that we should give bread to your exhausted people?' " ¹⁶ He took the elders of the city and some desert thorns and briers, and with them he thrashed the men of Succoth. ¹⁷ Then he broke down the tower of Penuel and killed the men of the city.*

. . .then kills the two kings   ¹⁸ He said to Zebah and Zalmunna, "What sort of men did you kill in Tabor?" They said, "Your appearance is like theirs, identical, like the form of the king's sons."

¹⁹ He said, "They were my brothers, the sons of my mother. As HASHEM lives, had you let them live, I would not kill you!" ²⁰ He said to Jether his firstborn, "Arise and kill them!" But the youth did not draw his sword, for he was afraid, since he was still a youth.

²¹ Zebah and Zalmunna said, "You arise and slay us, for as a man is, so is his strength."* So Gideon arose and killed Zebah and Zalmunna, and took the crescents that were on the necks of their camels.

Gideon declines rulership   ²² The men of Israel said to Gideon, "Rule over us — you, your son, and your grandson, for you have saved us from the hand of Midian!"

²³ But Gideon said to them, "I shall not rule over you, nor shall my son rule over you; HASHEM shall rule over you!"

²⁴ Then Gideon said to them, "I shall make a request of you. Let each of you give me a nose ring from his booty" (for they had golden nose rings, since they were Ishmaelites*).

²⁵ They said, "We shall surely give." They spread out a garment and every man threw into it a nose ring from his booty. ²⁶ The weight of the nose rings that he requested was one thousand seven hundred gold [dinars], aside from the crescents and the pendants, and the purple wool garments worn by the kings of Midian, and aside from the chains on the necks of their camels.

כז וַיַּ֣עַשׂ אוֹתוֹ֩ גִדְע֨וֹן לְאֵפ֜וֹד וַיַּצֵּ֣ג אוֹת֣וֹ בְעִיר֗וֹ בְּעׇפְרָה֙ וַיִּזְנ֤וּ כׇל־יִשְׂרָאֵל֙

כח אַחֲרָ֣יו שָׁ֔ם וַיְהִ֛י לְגִדְע֥וֹן וּלְבֵית֖וֹ לְמוֹקֵֽשׁ: וַיִּכָּנַ֣ע מִדְיָ֗ן לִפְנֵי֙ בְּנֵ֣י

יִשְׂרָאֵ֔ל וְלֹ֥א יָסְפ֖וּ לָשֵׂ֣את רֹאשָׁ֑ם וַתִּשְׁקֹ֥ט הָאָ֛רֶץ אַרְבָּעִ֥ים שָׁנָ֖ה בִּימֵ֥י

כט-ל גִדְעֽוֹן: וַיֵּ֛לֶךְ יְרֻבַּ֥עַל בֶּן־יוֹאָ֖שׁ וַיֵּ֥שֶׁב בְּבֵיתֽוֹ: וּלְגִדְע֗וֹן הָי֛וּ שִׁבְעִ֥ים

לא בָּנִ֖ים יֹצְאֵ֣י יְרֵכ֑וֹ כִּֽי־נָשִׁ֥ים רַבּ֖וֹת הָ֥יוּ לֽוֹ: וּפִ֨ילַגְשׁ֜וֹ אֲשֶׁ֣ר בִּשְׁכֶ֗ם יָֽלְדָה־לּ֥וֹ

לב גַם־הִ֖יא בֵּ֑ן וַיָּ֥שֶׂם אֶת־שְׁמ֖וֹ אֲבִימֶֽלֶךְ: וַיָּ֛מׇת גִּדְע֥וֹן בֶּן־יוֹאָ֖שׁ בְּשֵׂיבָ֣ה טוֹבָ֑ה

לג וַיִּקָּבֵ֗ר בְּקֶ֨בֶר֙ יוֹאָ֣שׁ אָבִ֔יו בְּעׇפְרָ֖ה אֲבִ֥י הָעֶזְרִֽי: וַֽיְהִ֗י כַּֽאֲשֶׁר֙

מֵ֣ת גִּדְע֔וֹן וַיָּשׁ֙וּבוּ֙ בְּנֵ֣י יִשְׂרָאֵ֔ל וַיִּזְנ֖וּ אַחֲרֵ֣י הַבְּעָלִ֑ים וַיָּשִׂ֧ימוּ לָהֶ֛ם בַּ֥עַל

לד בְּרִ֖ית לֵֽאלֹהִֽים: וְלֹ֤א זָֽכְרוּ֙ בְּנֵ֣י יִשְׂרָאֵ֔ל אֶת־יהו֖ה אֱלֹֽהֵיהֶ֑ם הַמַּצִּ֥יל אוֹתָ֛ם

לה מִיַּ֥ד כׇּל־אֹֽיְבֵיהֶ֖ם מִסָּבִֽיב: וְלֹֽא־עָשׂ֣וּ חֶ֔סֶד עִם־בֵּ֥ית יְרֻבַּ֖עַל גִּדְע֑וֹן כְּכׇל־

א הַטּוֹבָ֔ה אֲשֶׁ֥ר עָשָׂ֖ה עִם־יִשְׂרָאֵֽל: וַיֵּ֨לֶךְ אֲבִימֶ֤לֶךְ בֶּן־יְרֻבַּ֙עַל֙

שְׁכֶ֔מָה אֶל־אֲחֵ֖י אִמּ֑וֹ וַיְדַבֵּ֣ר אֲלֵיהֶ֔ם וְאֶל־כׇּל־מִשְׁפַּ֖חַת בֵּֽית־אֲבִ֥י אִמּ֖וֹ

ב לֵאמֹֽר: דַּבְּרוּ־נָ֞א בְּאׇזְנֵ֨י כׇל־בַּעֲלֵ֣י שְׁכֶם֮ מַה־טּ֣וֹב לָכֶם֒ הַמְשֹׁ֨ל בָּכֶ֜ם

שִׁבְעִ֣ים אִ֗ישׁ כֹּ֚ל בְּנֵ֣י יְרֻבַּ֔עַל אִם־מְשֹׁ֥ל בָּכֶ֖ם אִ֣ישׁ אֶחָ֑ד וּזְכַרְתֶּ֕ם כִּֽי־

ג עַצְמְכֶ֥ם וּבְשַׂרְכֶ֖ם אָֽנִי: וַיְדַבְּר֨וּ אֲחֵֽי־אִמּ֜וֹ עָלָ֗יו בְּאׇזְנֵי֙ כׇּל־בַּעֲלֵ֣י שְׁכֶ֔ם אֵ֥ת

כׇּל־הַדְּבָרִ֖ים הָאֵ֑לֶּה וַיֵּ֤ט לִבָּם֙ אַחֲרֵ֣י אֲבִימֶ֔לֶךְ כִּ֥י אָמְר֖וּ אָחִ֥ינוּ הֽוּא: וַיִּתְּנוּ־

ד ל֗וֹ שִׁבְעִ֥ים כֶּ֙סֶף֙ מִבֵּ֣ית בַּ֣עַל בְּרִ֔ית וַיִּשְׂכֹּ֤ר בָּהֶם֙ אֲבִימֶ֔לֶךְ אֲנָשִׁ֥ים רֵיקִ֖ים

ה וּפֹחֲזִ֑ים וַיֵּלְכ֖וּ אַחֲרָֽיו: וַיָּבֹ֤א בֵית־אָבִיו֙ עׇפְרָ֔תָה וַֽיַּהֲרֹ֞ג אֶת־אֶחָ֧יו בְּנֵֽי־

יְרֻבַּ֛עַל שִׁבְעִ֥ים אִ֖ישׁ עַל־אֶ֣בֶן אֶחָ֑ת וַיִּוָּתֵ֞ר יוֹתָ֧ם בֶּן־יְרֻבַּ֛עַל הַקָּטֹ֖ן

ו כִּ֥י נֶחְבָּֽא: וַיֵּאָֽסְפ֞וּ כׇּל־בַּעֲלֵ֣י שְׁכֶם֮ וְכׇל־בֵּ֣ית מִלּוֹא֒ וַיֵּ֣לְכ֔וּ

ז וַיַּמְלִ֥יכוּ אֶת־אֲבִימֶ֖לֶךְ לְמֶ֑לֶךְ עִם־אֵל֥וֹן מֻצָּ֖ב אֲשֶׁ֥ר בִּשְׁכֶֽם: וַיַּגִּ֣דוּ לְיוֹתָ֔ם

וַיֵּ֙לֶךְ֙ וַֽיַּעֲמֹ֔ד בְּרֹ֖אשׁ הַר־גְּרִזִ֑ים וַיִּשָּׂ֤א קוֹלוֹ֙ וַיִּקְרָ֔א וַיֹּ֣אמֶר לָהֶ֔ם שִׁמְע֤וּ

ח אֵלַי֙ בַּעֲלֵ֣י שְׁכֶ֔ם וְיִשְׁמַ֥ע אֲלֵיכֶ֖ם אֱלֹהִֽים: הָל֤וֹךְ הָֽלְכוּ֙ הָֽעֵצִ֔ים לִמְשֹׁ֥חַ

ט עֲלֵיהֶ֖ם מֶ֑לֶךְ וַיֹּאמְר֥וּ לַזַּ֖יִת מׇלְכ֣ה [°מלוכה ק] עָלֵֽינוּ: וַיֹּ֤אמֶר לָהֶם֙ הַזַּ֔יִת

הֶחֳדַ֙לְתִּי֙ אֶת־דִּשְׁנִ֔י אֲשֶׁר־בִּ֛י יְכַבְּד֥וּ אֱלֹהִ֖ים וַאֲנָשִׁ֑ים וְהָ֣לַכְתִּ֔י לָנ֖וּעַ עַל־

י הָעֵצִֽים: וַיֹּאמְר֥וּ הָעֵצִ֖ים לַתְּאֵנָ֑ה לְכִי־אַ֖תְּ מׇלְכִ֥י עָלֵֽינוּ: וַתֹּ֤אמֶר לָהֶם֙

יא הַתְּאֵנָ֔ה הֶחֳדַ֙לְתִּי֙ אֶת־מׇתְקִ֔י וְאֶת־תְּנוּבָתִ֖י הַטּוֹבָ֑ה וְהָ֣לַכְתִּ֔י לָנ֖וּעַ עַל־

יב הָעֵצִֽים: וַיֹּאמְר֥וּ הָעֵצִ֖ים לַגָּ֑פֶן לְכִי־אַ֖תְּ °מלוכי [°מׇלְכִ֥י ק] עָלֵֽינוּ: וַתֹּ֤אמֶר

יג לָהֶם֙ הַגֶּ֔פֶן הֶחֳדַ֙לְתִּי֙ אֶת־תִּ֣ירוֹשִׁ֔י הַֽמְשַׂמֵּ֥חַ אֱלֹהִ֖ים וַאֲנָשִׁ֑ים וְהָ֣לַכְתִּ֔י

לָנ֖וּעַ עַל־הָעֵצִֽים: וַיֹּאמְר֥וּ כׇל־הָעֵצִ֖ים אֶל־הָאָטָ֑ד לֵ֥ךְ אַתָּ֖ה מְלׇךְ־עָלֵֽינוּ:

טו וַיֹּ֣אמֶר הָאָטָד֮ אֶל־הָעֵצִים֒ אִ֡ם בֶּאֱמֶ֣ת אַתֶּם֩ מֹשְׁחִ֨ים אֹתִ֤י לְמֶ֙לֶךְ֙ עֲלֵיכֶ֔ם

בֹּ֖אוּ חֲס֣וּ בְצִלִּ֑י וְאִם־אַ֗יִן תֵּ֤צֵא אֵשׁ֙ מִן־הָ֣אָטָ֔ד וְתֹאכַ֖ל אֶת־אַרְזֵ֥י הַלְּבָנֽוֹן:

ט

8:27. He intended it to commemorate the miracle of deliverance, but later generations deified it.

9:7. Jotham, Gideon's orphan, pronounced a parable and a curse. The moral of his parable: Three great judges —

Othniel, Deborah, and Gideon — could have claimed sovereignty but did not. Instead, the people of Shechem chose Abimelech, a person as inferior as a thorn, and they would pay a heavy price for their decision (*Rashi*).

²⁷ *Gideon made it into an ephod* and hung it in his city, in Ophrah. [Eventually] all Israel strayed after it there, and it became a snare for Gideon and his household.*

Gideon's final years

²⁸ *Thus Midian was subdued before the Children of Israel, and they did not continue to raise their head; and the land was tranquil for forty years in the days of Gideon.*

²⁹ *Jerubaal son of Joash went and settled in his home.* ³⁰ *Gideon had seventy sons emerging from his loins, for he had many wives.* ³¹ *His concubine, who was in Shechem, also bore him a son and he called his name Abimelech.* ³² *Gideon son of Joash died at a good old age, and he was buried by the grave of Joash, his father, in Ophrah, of the Abi-ezrites.*

Idolatry recurs

³³ *It happened when Gideon died that the Children of Israel once again went astray after the Baalim, and they set Baal-berith as a god for themselves.* ³⁴ *The Children of Israel did not remember* HASHEM, *their God, Who rescued them from the hand of all their surrounding enemies.* ³⁵ *Also, they did not perform kindness with the household of Jerubaal, [who is] Gideon, commensurate with all the goodness that he had done with Israel.*

9

ABIMELECH SON OF GIDEON: KING IN SHECHEM

9:1-57

(See Appendix A, timeline 3)

¹ A*bimelech son of Jerubaal went to Shechem, to his mother's brothers, and spoke to them and to the entire family of his mother's father's household, saying,* ² *"Speak now in the ears of all the inhabitants of Shechem: 'What is better for you — that seventy men rule over you, all the sons of Jerubaal, or that one man rule over you? And remember that I am your bone and flesh!' "* ³ *So his mother's brothers spoke all these words about him in the ears of all the inhabitants of Shechem. Their heart inclined after Abimelech, for they said, "He is our kinsman."* ⁴ *They gave him seventy pieces of silver from the temple of Baal-berith, and with them Abimelech hired boorish, impetuous men, and they followed him.* ⁵ *He came to his father's house, to Ophrah, and murdered his brothers, the sons of Jerubaal, seventy men, at one rock, but Jotham, Jerubaal's youngest son, was left, for he had hidden.*

⁶ *All the inhabitants of Shechem and all of Beth-millo gathered together, and they went and crowned Abimelech as king, by the Plain of the Monument, which was in Shechem.*

Jotham's parable and curse

⁷ *They told Jotham, so he went and stood atop Mount Gerizzim and raised his voice and cried out; he said to them, "Listen to me,* O inhabitants of Shechem, so that God may listen to you!* ⁸ *The trees went to anoint a king over themselves. They said to the olive tree, 'Reign over us!'* ⁹ *But the olive tree said to them, 'Shall I cause my richness to cease, whereby God and men honor themselves through me, and go to wave over the trees?'* ¹⁰ *Then the trees said to the fig tree, 'You go and reign over us!'* ¹¹ *But the fig tree said to them, 'Shall I cause my sweetness and my goodly produce to cease, and go to wave over the trees?'* ¹² *Then the trees said to the grapevine, 'You go and reign over us!'* ¹³ *But the grapevine said to them, 'Shall I give up my vintage that gladdens God and men, and go to wave over the trees?'* ¹⁴ *Then all the trees went to the thorn and said, 'You go and reign over us!'* ¹⁵ *The thorn said to the trees, 'If with honesty do you anoint me as king over you, then come and take shelter in my shade; but if not, then may a flame come forth from the thorn and consume the cedars of Lebanon!'*

טז וְעַתָּ֞ה אִם־בֶּאֱמֶ֤ת וּבְתָמִים֙ עֲשִׂיתֶ֔ם וַתַּמְלִ֖יכוּ אֶת־אֲבִימֶ֑לֶךְ וְאִם־טוֹבָ֣ה

יז עֲשִׂיתֶ֗ם עִם־יְרֻבַּ֙עַל֙ וְעִם־בֵּית֔וֹ וְאִם־כִּגְמ֥וּל יָדָ֖יו עֲשִׂ֥יתֶם לֽוֹ: אֲשֶׁר־

יח נִלְחַ֥ם אָבִ֛י עֲלֵיכֶ֖ם וַיַּשְׁלֵ֣ךְ אֶת־נַפְשׁ֣וֹ מִנֶּ֑גֶד וַיַּצֵּ֥ל אֶתְכֶ֖ם מִיַּ֣ד מִדְיָ֑ן וְאַתֶּ֞ם קַמְתֶּ֤ם עַל־בֵּית֙ אָבִי֙ הַיּ֔וֹם וַתַּהַרְג֧וּ אֶת־בָּנָ֛יו שִׁבְעִ֥ים אִ֖ישׁ עַל־אֶ֣בֶן אֶחָ֑ת וַתַּמְלִ֜יכוּ אֶת־אֲבִימֶ֤לֶךְ בֶּן־אֲמָתוֹ֙ עַל־בַּעֲלֵ֣י שְׁכֶ֔ם כִּ֥י אֲחִיכֶ֖ם

יט הֽוּא: וְאִם־בֶּאֱמֶ֨ת וּבְתָמִ֧ים עֲשִׂיתֶ֛ם עִם־יְרֻבַּ֥עַל וְעִם־בֵּית֖וֹ הַיּ֣וֹם הַזֶּ֑ה

כ שִׂמְחוּ֙ בַּאֲבִימֶ֔לֶךְ וְיִשְׂמַ֥ח גַּם־ה֖וּא בָּכֶֽם: וְאִם־אַ֕יִן תֵּ֤צֵא אֵשׁ֙ מֵאֲבִימֶ֔לֶךְ וְתֹאכַ֛ל אֶת־בַּעֲלֵ֥י שְׁכֶ֖ם וְאֶת־בֵּ֣ית מִלּ֑וֹא וְתֵצֵ֣א אֵ֗שׁ מִבַּעֲלֵ֤י שְׁכֶם֙

כא וּמִבֵּ֣ית מִלּ֔וֹא וְתֹאכַ֖ל אֶת־אֲבִימֶֽלֶךְ: וַיָּ֣נָס יוֹתָ֔ם וַיִּבְרַ֖ח וַיֵּ֣לֶךְ בְּאֵ֑רָה וַיֵּ֣שֶׁב שָׁ֔ם מִפְּנֵ֖י אֲבִימֶ֥לֶךְ אָחִֽיו:

כב וַיָּ֧שַׂר אֲבִימֶ֛לֶךְ

כג עַל־יִשְׂרָאֵ֖ל שָׁלֹ֥שׁ שָׁנִֽים: וַיִּשְׁלַ֤ח אֱלֹהִים֙ ר֣וּחַ רָעָ֔ה בֵּ֚ין אֲבִימֶ֔לֶךְ

כד וּבֵ֖ין בַּעֲלֵ֣י שְׁכֶ֑ם וַיִּבְגְּד֥וּ בַעֲלֵי־שְׁכֶ֖ם בַּאֲבִימֶֽלֶךְ: לָבֹ֕וא חֲמַ֖ס שִׁבְעִ֣ים בְּנֵֽי־יְרֻבָּ֑עַל וְדָמָ֗ם לָשׂ֞וּם עַל־אֲבִימֶ֤לֶךְ אֲחִיהֶם֙ אֲשֶׁ֣ר הָרַ֣ג אוֹתָ֔ם וְעַל֙

כה בַּעֲלֵ֣י שְׁכֶ֔ם אֲשֶׁר־חִזְּק֥וּ אֶת־יָדָ֖יו לַהֲרֹ֥ג אֶת־אֶחָֽיו: וַיָּשִׂ֣ימוּ לוֹ֩ בַעֲלֵ֨י שְׁכֶ֜ם מְאָרְבִ֗ים עַ֚ל רָאשֵׁ֣י הֶהָרִ֔ים וַיִּגְזְל֗וּ אֵ֛ת כָּל־אֲשֶׁר־יַעֲבֹ֥ר עֲלֵיהֶ֖ם

כו בַּדָּ֑רֶךְ וַיֻּגַּ֖ד לַאֲבִימֶֽלֶךְ: וַיָּבֹ֞א גַּ֤עַל בֶּן־עֶ֙בֶד֙

כז וְאֶחָ֔יו וַיַּעַבְר֖וּ בִּשְׁכֶ֑ם וַיִּבְטְחוּ־ב֖וֹ בַּעֲלֵ֥י שְׁכֶֽם: וַיֵּצְא֨וּ הַשָּׂדֶ֜ה וַיִּבְצְר֤וּ אֶת־כַּרְמֵיהֶם֙ וַֽיִּדְרְכ֔וּ וַֽיַּעֲשׂ֖וּ הִלּוּלִ֑ים וַיָּבֹ֙אוּ֙ בֵּ֣ית אֱלֹֽהֵיהֶ֔ם וַיֹּֽאכְלוּ֙

כח וַיִּשְׁתּ֔וּ וַֽיְקַלְל֖וּ אֶת־אֲבִימֶֽלֶךְ: וַיֹּ֣אמֶר ׀ גַּ֣עַל בֶּן־עֶ֗בֶד מִֽי־אֲבִימֶ֤לֶךְ וּמִֽי־שְׁכֶם֙ כִּ֣י נַעַבְדֶ֔נּוּ הֲלֹ֥א בֶן־יְרֻבַּ֖עַל וּזְבֻ֣ל פְּקִיד֑וֹ עִבְד֗וּ אֶת־אַנְשֵׁ֤י חֲמוֹר֙

כט אֲבִ֣י שְׁכֶ֔ם וּמַדּ֖וּעַ נַעַבְדֶ֥נּֽוּ אֲנָֽחְנוּ: וּמִ֨י יִתֵּ֜ן אֶת־הָעָ֤ם הַזֶּה֙ בְּיָדִ֔י וְאָסִ֖ירָה אֶת־אֲבִימֶ֑לֶךְ וַיֹּ֙אמֶר֙ לַאֲבִימֶ֔לֶךְ רַבֶּ֥ה צְבָאֲךָ֖ וָצֵֽאָה: וַיִּשְׁמַ֗ע זְבֻל֙

ל שַׂר־הָעִ֔יר אֶת־דִּבְרֵ֖י גַּ֣עַל בֶּן־עָ֑בֶד וַיִּ֖חַר אַפּֽוֹ: וַיִּשְׁלַ֧ח מַלְאָכִ֛ים אֶל־

לא אֲבִימֶ֖לֶךְ בְּתָרְמָ֣ה לֵאמֹ֑ר הִנֵּה֩ גַ֨עַל בֶּן־עֶ֤בֶד וְאֶחָיו֙ בָּאִ֣ים שְׁכֶ֔מָה

לב וְהִנָּ֛ם צָרִ֥ים אֶת־הָעִ֖יר עָלֶֽיךָ: וְעַתָּה֙ ק֣וּם לַ֔יְלָה אַתָּ֖ה וְהָעָ֣ם אֲשֶׁר־אִתָּ֑ךְ

לג וֶאֱרֹ֖ב בַּשָּׂדֶֽה: וְהָיָ֤ה בַבֹּ֙קֶר֙ כִּזְרֹ֣חַ הַשֶּׁ֔מֶשׁ תַּשְׁכִּ֖ים וּפָשַׁטְתָּ֣ עַל־הָעִ֑יר וְהִנֵּה־ה֨וּא וְהָעָ֤ם אֲשֶׁר־אִתּוֹ֙ יֹצְאִ֣ים אֵלֶ֔יךָ וְעָשִׂ֣יתָ לּ֔וֹ כַּאֲשֶׁ֖ר תִּמְצָ֥א יָדֶֽךָ:

לד וַיָּ֧קָם אֲבִימֶ֛לֶךְ וְכָל־הָעָ֥ם אֲשֶׁר־עִמּ֖וֹ לָ֑יְלָה וַיֶּאֶרְב֣וּ עַל־שְׁכֶ֔ם אַרְבָּעָ֖ה

לה רָאשִֽׁים: וַיֵּצֵא֙ גַּ֣עַל בֶּן־עֶ֔בֶד וַיַּעֲמֹ֕ד פֶּ֖תַח שַׁ֣עַר הָעִ֑יר וַיָּ֣קָם אֲבִימֶ֗לֶךְ

לו וְהָעָ֛ם אֲשֶׁר־אִתּ֖וֹ מִן־הַמַּאְרָֽב: וַיַּרְא־גַּעַל֮ אֶת־הָעָם֒ וַיֹּ֣אמֶר אֶל־זְבֻ֔ל הִנֵּֽה־עָ֣ם יוֹרֵ֔ד מֵרָאשֵׁ֖י הֶהָרִ֑ים וַיֹּ֤אמֶר אֵלָיו֙ זְבֻ֔ל אֵ֣ת צֵ֧ל הֶהָרִ֛ים אַתָּ֥ה

לז רֹאֶ֖ה כָּאֲנָשִֽׁים: וַיֹּ֨סֶף ע֣וֹד גַּעַל֮ לְדַבֵּר֒ וַיֹּ֕אמֶר הִנֵּה־עָ֗ם יֽוֹרְדִים֙ מֵעִ֣ם

9:26. Gaal was a heathen (*Rashi*).

9:28. Gaal railed against Abimelech, saying that, as a son of Jerubaal, he was an Abiezrite, not a Shechemite, and

his officer Zebul was unworthy of their respect. He urged them to choose a descendant of Hamor, Shechem's original ruler (see *Genesis* Ch. 34) in Jacob's days (*Rashi*).

¹⁶ "So now, if you have acted with honesty and sincerity and crowned Abimelech, and if you have done good with Jerubaal and his household, and if you have acted toward him corresponding to the kindness of his hands — ¹⁷ as my father went to war for you; as he cast his life aside and rescued you from the hand of Midian, ¹⁸ yet you rose up against my father's house today and murdered his sons, seventy souls, on one rock, and you crowned Abimelech son of his maidservant over the inhabitants of Shechem, because he is your kinsman — ¹⁹ so if you have acted with honesty and sincerity toward Jerubaal and toward his household this day, then rejoice with Abimelech and let him also rejoice with you. ²⁰ But if not, may a fire go forth from Abimelech and consume the inhabitants of Shechem and Beth-millo, and may a fire go forth from the inhabitants of Shechem and Beth-millo and consume Abimelech!"

²¹ Then Jotham ran away. He fled and went to Beer and settled there because of Abimelech, his brother.

Discord between Abimelech and Shechem

²² Abimelech was master over Israel for three years. ²³ Then God sent a spirit of ill will between Abimelech and the inhabitants of Shechem, and the inhabitants of Shechem betrayed Abimelech, ²⁴ so that the violence against the seventy sons of Jerubaal would come [back] upon — and their blood would be placed upon — Abimelech their brother, who murdered them, and upon the inhabitants of Shechem, who strengthened his hands to murder his brothers.

²⁵ The inhabitants of Shechem set up ambushes against him on the mountaintops and they robbed anyone who would pass them on the road. And this was told to Abimelech.

Gaal's challenge to Abimelech

²⁶ Gaal son of Ebed* came with his kinsmen and they passed into Shechem; the inhabitants of Shechem had confidence in him. ²⁷ They went out to the field, harvested their vineyards and trod [their grapes], and made celebrations. They came to the temple of their god, and they ate and drank, and cursed Abimelech. ²⁸ Gaal son of Ebed said, "Who is Abimelech and who is Shechem that we should serve him? Is he not the son of Jerubaal, and is Zebul not his officer? Go, serve the people of Hamor* the father of Shechem! Why should we serve him? ²⁹ If only someone would give this people into my hand, then I would depose Abimelech!" He said to Abimelech, "Reinforce your army and come out!"

³⁰ Zebul, the leader of the city, heard the words of Gaal son of Ebed and his wrath flared. ³¹ He sent messengers to Abimelech stealthily, saying, "Behold, Gaal son of Ebed and his kinsmen are arriving in Shechem, and behold, they are fortifying the city against you. ³² So now, rise up at night, you and the people who are with you, and set an ambush in the field. ³³ It shall be, in the morning, when the sun shines, you will arise early and spread out by the city. Then behold, just as he and the people with him are going out toward you, you will do to them whatever your strength permits."

Gaal's defeat

³⁴ So Abimelech and all the people with him rose up at night and set an ambush against Shechem, of four companies. ³⁵ Gaal son of Ebed went out and stood at the entrance of the city gate. Then Abimelech and the people with him rose up from the ambush.

³⁶ Gaal saw the people and said to Zebul, "Behold! People are descending from the mountaintops!"

Zebul said to him, "You see the shadow of the mountains as people."

³⁷ Gaal continued to speak and said, "Behold! People are descending from the

לח טַבּ֣וּר הָאָ֔רֶץ וְרֹאשׁ־אֶחָ֣ד בָּ֔א מִדֶּ֖רֶךְ אֵל֥וֹן מְעֽוֹנְנִֽים: וַיֹּ֨אמֶר אֵלָ֜יו זְבֻ֗ל אַיֵּ֨ה אֵפ֤וֹא פִ֙יךָ֙ אֲשֶׁ֣ר תֹּאמַ֔ר מִ֥י אֲבִימֶ֖לֶךְ כִּ֣י נַֽעַבְדֶ֑נּוּ הֲלֹ֨א זֶ֤ה הָעָם֙

לט אֲשֶׁ֣ר מָאַ֣סְתָּה בּ֔וֹ צֵא־נָ֥א עַתָּ֖ה וְהִלָּ֥חֶם בּֽוֹ: וַיֵּ֣צֵא גַ֔עַל לִפְנֵ֖י בַּֽעֲלֵ֥י שְׁכֶֽם

מ וַיִּלָּ֖חֶם בַּֽאֲבִימֶֽלֶךְ: וַיִּרְדְּפֵ֣הוּ אֲבִימֶ֔לֶךְ וַיָּ֖נָס מִפָּנָ֑יו וַיִּפְּל֛וּ חֲלָלִ֥ים רַבִּ֖ים

מא עַד־פֶּ֥תַח הַשָּֽׁעַר: וַיֵּ֥שֶׁב אֲבִימֶ֖לֶךְ בָּֽארוּמָ֑ה וַיְגָ֧רֶשׁ זְבֻ֛ל אֶת־גַּ֖עַל וְאֶת־

מב אֶחָ֑יו מִשֶּׁ֖בֶת בִּשְׁכֶֽם: וַֽיְהִי֙ מִֽמָּֽחֳרָ֔ת וַיֵּצֵ֥א הָעָ֖ם הַשָּׂדֶ֑ה

מג וַיַּגִּ֖דוּ לַֽאֲבִימֶֽלֶךְ: וַיִּקַּ֣ח אֶת־הָעָ֗ם וַֽיֶּֽחֱצֵם֙ לִשְׁלֹשָׁ֣ה רָאשִׁ֔ים וַיֶּֽאֱרֹ֖ב בַּשָּׂדֶ֑ה

מד וַיַּ֗רְא וְהִנֵּ֤ה הָעָם֙ יֹצֵ֣א מִן־הָעִ֔יר וַיָּ֥קָם עֲלֵיהֶ֖ם וַיַּכֵּֽם: וַֽאֲבִימֶ֗לֶךְ וְהָֽרָאשִׁים֙ אֲשֶׁ֣ר עִמּ֔וֹ פָּֽשְׁט֕וּ וַיַּֽעַמְד֖וּ פֶּ֣תַח שַׁ֣עַר הָעִ֑יר וּשְׁנֵ֣י הָֽרָאשִׁ֗ים פָּֽשְׁט֛וּ

מה עַֽל־כָּל־אֲשֶׁ֥ר בַּשָּׂדֶ֖ה וַיַּכּֽוּם: וַֽאֲבִימֶ֜לֶךְ נִלְחָ֣ם בָּעִ֗יר כֹּ֚ל הַיּ֣וֹם הַה֔וּא וַיִּלְכֹּד֙ אֶת־הָעִ֔יר וְאֶת־הָעָ֥ם אֲשֶׁר־בָּ֖הּ הָרָ֑ג וַיִּתֹּץ֙ אֶת־הָעִ֔יר וַיִּזְרָעֶ֖הָ

מו מֶֽלַח: וַֽיִּשְׁמְע֔וּ כָּל־בַּֽעֲלֵ֖י מִגְדַּל־שְׁכֶ֑ם וַיָּבֹ֖אוּ אֶל־צְרִ֥יחַ

מז-מח בֵּ֥ית אֵ֖ל בְּרִֽית: וַיֻּגַּ֖ד לַֽאֲבִימֶ֑לֶךְ כִּ֣י הִֽתְקַבְּצ֔וּ כָּל־בַּֽעֲלֵ֖י מִגְדַּל־שְׁכֶֽם: וַיַּ֣עַל אֲבִימֶ֡לֶךְ הַר־צַלְמ֨וֹן הוּא֩ וְכָל־הָעָ֨ם אֲשֶׁר־אִתּ֜וֹ וַיִּקַּ֧ח אֲבִימֶ֣לֶךְ אֶת־הַקַּרְדֻּמּוֹת֙ בְּיָד֔וֹ וַיִּכְרֹת֙ שׂוֹכַ֣ת עֵצִ֔ים וַיִּ֨שָּׂאֶ֔הָ וַיָּ֖שֶׂם עַל־שִׁכְמ֑וֹ וַיֹּ֜אמֶר

מט אֶל־הָעָ֣ם אֲשֶׁר־עִמּ֗וֹ מָ֤ה רְאִיתֶם֙ עָשִׂ֔יתִי מַֽהֲר֖וּ עֲשׂ֥וּ כָמֽוֹנִי: וַיִּכְרְת֨וּ גַם־ כָּל־הָעָ֜ם אִ֣ישׁ שׂוֹכֹ֗ה וַיֵּ֤לְכוּ אַֽחֲרֵי֙ אֲבִימֶ֔לֶךְ וַיָּשִׂ֣ימוּ עַל־הַצְּרִ֔יחַ וַיַּצִּ֧יתוּ עֲלֵיהֶ֛ם אֶת־הַצְּרִ֖יחַ בָּאֵ֑שׁ וַיָּמֻ֜תוּ גַּ֗ם כָּל־אַנְשֵׁ֤י מִגְדַּל־שְׁכֶם֙ כְּאֶ֣לֶף אִ֔ישׁ

נ וְאִשָּֽׁה: וַיֵּ֥לֶךְ אֲבִימֶ֖לֶךְ אֶל־תֵּבֵ֑ץ וַיִּ֥חַן בְּתֵבֵ֖ץ וַֽיִּלְכְּדָֽהּ:

נא וּמִגְדַּל־עֹ֞ז הָיָ֣ה בְתֽוֹךְ־הָעִ֗יר וַיָּנֻ֨סוּ שָׁ֜מָּה כָּל־הָֽאֲנָשִׁ֤ים וְהַנָּשִׁים֙ וְכֹל֙ בַּֽעֲלֵ֣י

נב הָעִ֔יר וַֽיִּסְגְּר֖וּ בַּֽעֲדָ֑ם וַיַּֽעֲל֖וּ עַל־גַּ֣ג הַמִּגְדָּֽל: וַיָּבֹ֤א אֲבִימֶ֙לֶךְ֙ עַד־הַמִּגְדָּ֔ל וַיִּלָּ֖חֶם בּ֑וֹ וַיִּגַּ֛שׁ עַד־פֶּ֥תַח הַמִּגְדָּ֖ל לְשָׂרְפ֥וֹ בָאֵֽשׁ: וַתַּשְׁלֵ֞ךְ אִשָּׁ֥ה אַחַ֛ת

נג-נד פֶּ֥לַח רֶ֖כֶב עַל־רֹ֣אשׁ אֲבִימֶ֑לֶךְ וַתָּ֖רִץ אֶת־גֻּלְגָּלְתּֽוֹ: וַיִּקְרָ֣א מְהֵרָ֡ה אֶל־ הַנַּ֣עַר ׀ נֹשֵׂ֣א כֵלָיו֩ וַיֹּ֨אמֶר ל֜וֹ שְׁלֹ֤ף חַרְבְּךָ֙ וּמ֣וֹתְתֵ֔נִי פֶּן־יֹ֥אמְרוּ לִ֖י אִשָּׁ֣ה

נה הֲרָגָ֑תְהוּ וַיִּדְקְרֵ֥הוּ נַֽעֲר֖וֹ וַיָּמֹֽת: וַיִּרְא֥וּ אִֽישׁ־יִשְׂרָאֵ֖ל כִּ֣י מֵ֣ת אֲבִימֶ֑לֶךְ

נו וַיֵּֽלְכ֖וּ אִ֥ישׁ לִמְקֹמֽוֹ: וַיָּ֣שֶׁב אֱלֹהִ֔ים אֵ֖ת רָעַ֣ת אֲבִימֶ֑לֶךְ אֲשֶׁ֤ר עָשָׂה֙ לְאָבִ֔יו

נז לַֽהֲרֹ֖ג אֶת־שִׁבְעִ֥ים אֶחָֽיו: וְאֵ֗ת כָּל־רָעַת֙ אַנְשֵׁ֣י שְׁכֶ֔ם הֵשִׁ֥יב אֱלֹהִ֖ים

י א בְּרֹאשָׁ֑ם וַתָּבֹ֣א אֲלֵיהֶ֔ם קִֽלֲלַ֖ת יוֹתָ֥ם בֶּן־יְרֻבָּֽעַל: וַיָּ֨קָם֙ אַֽחֲרֵ֣י אֲבִימֶ֔לֶךְ לְהוֹשִׁ֖יעַ אֶת־יִשְׂרָאֵ֑ל תּוֹלָ֧ע בֶּן־פּוּאָ֛ה בֶּן־דּוֹד֖וֹ אִ֣ישׁ יִשָּׂשכָ֑ר

ב וְהֽוּא־יֹשֵׁ֥ב בְּשָׁמִ֖יר בְּהַ֥ר אֶפְרָֽיִם: וַיִּשְׁפֹּט֙ אֶת־יִשְׂרָאֵ֔ל עֶשְׂרִ֥ים וְשָׁלֹ֖שׁ

ג שָׁנָ֑ה וַיָּ֖מָת וַיִּקָּבֵ֥ר בְּשָׁמִֽיר: וַיָּ֣קָם אַֽחֲרָ֔יו יָאִ֖יר הַגִּלְעָדִ֑י

ד וַיִּשְׁפֹּ֥ט אֶת־יִשְׂרָאֵ֖ל עֶשְׂרִ֥ים וּשְׁתַּ֥יִם שָׁנָֽה: וַֽיְהִי־ל֞וֹ שְׁלֹשִׁ֣ים בָּנִ֗ים רֹֽכְבִים֙ עַל־שְׁלֹשִׁ֣ים עֲיָרִ֔ים וּשְׁלֹשִׁ֥ים עֲיָרִ֖ים לָהֶ֑ם לָהֶ֞ם יִקְרְא֣וּ ׀ חַוֺּ֣ת יָאִ֗יר עַ֚ד

ה הַיּ֣וֹם הַזֶּ֔ה אֲשֶׁ֖ר בְּאֶ֣רֶץ הַגִּלְעָ֑ד: וַיָּ֣מָת יָאִ֔יר וַיִּקָּבֵ֖ר בְּקָמֽוֹן:

navel of the land, and one company is coming by way of the Plain of Me-onenim!'"

³⁸ Zebul said to him, "Where then is your mouth that would say, 'Who is Abimelech that we should serve him?' Is this not the people you scorned? Go out now, if you please, and battle it!"

³⁹ Gaal went out before the inhabitants of Shechem and battled Abimelech. ⁴⁰ Abimelech pursued him, and he fled before him. Many corpses fell up to the entrance of the gate. ⁴¹ Abimelech settled in Arumah, and Zebul drove out Gaal and his kinsmen from living in Shechem.

⁴² It happened the next day that the people went out to the field, and they told [this] to Abimelech. ⁴³ He took [his] people and divided them into three companies and he set an ambush in the field. He watched, and behold, as the people were leaving the city, he rose up against them and struck them. ⁴⁴ Abimelech and the companies that were with him spread out and stood at the entrance of the city gate, and the [other] two companies spread out against all who were in the field and struck them. ⁴⁵ Abimelech fought against the city all that day, and he occupied the city and killed the people who were in it. He tore down the city and sowed it with salt.

Abimelech destroys Shechem

⁴⁶ When all the inhabitants of the Tower of Shechem heard, they came to the citadel of Beth-el-berith. ⁴⁷ Abimelech was told that all the inhabitants of the Tower of Shechem had gathered, ⁴⁸ so Abimelech went up to Mount Zalmon, he and all the people that were with him. Abimelech took the axes in his hand and cut down a branch of the trees, lifted it and placed it on his shoulder, and said to the people that were with him, "What you have seen me do, hurry and do as I did!" ⁴⁹ Each of the people also cut down a branch and they followed Abimelech. They placed them by the citadel and with them set the citadel on fire. All the people of the Tower of Shechem died, about a thousand men and women.

Abimelech burns Thebez but is killed

⁵⁰ Then Abimelech went to Thebez, and encamped in Thebez and occupied it. ⁵¹ There was a strong tower in the midst of the city, and all the men and women and the inhabitants of the city fled and locked themselves in, and they climbed to the roof of the tower. ⁵² Abimelech reached the tower and fought against it. He approached the tower's entrance to burn it in fire.

⁵³ A certain woman threw down part of an upper millstone on Abimelech's head, and crushed his skull. ⁵⁴ He called quickly to the attendant who was his armor-bearer and said to him, "Draw your sword and kill me, lest they say of me, 'A woman killed him.'" His attendant stabbed him and he died. ⁵⁵ The men of Israel saw that Abimelech had died, and each man went back to his place.

⁵⁶ [Thus] God repaid the evil of Abimelech that he had done to his father [by] murdering his seventy brothers; ⁵⁷ and all the evil of the men of Shechem, God brought back upon their heads, and the curse of Jotham son of Jerubaal came upon them.

10

TOLA SON OF PUAH
10:1-2

¹ After Abimelech there arose to save Israel, Tola son of Puah son of Dodo, a man of Issachar; he dwelt in Shamir, in Mount Ephraim. ² He judged Israel for twenty-three years; he died and was buried in Shamir.

JAIR THE GILEADITE
10:3-5
(See Appendix A, timeline 3)

³ After him there arose Jair the Gileadite, and he judged Israel for twenty-two years. ⁴ He had thirty sons riding thirty colts, and they owned thirty towns — they would call them the villages of Jair until this day — which were in the land of Gilead. ⁵ Jair died and was buried in Kamon.

וַיֹּסִפוּ ׀ בְּנֵי יִשְׂרָאֵל לַעֲשׂוֹת הָרַע בְּעֵינֵי יהוה וַיַּעַבְדוּ אֶת־הַבְּעָלִים וְאֶת־ ו
הָעַשְׁתָּרוֹת וְאֶת־אֱלֹהֵי אֲרָם וְאֶת־אֱלֹהֵי צִידוֹן וְאֵת ׀ אֱלֹהֵי מוֹאָב וְאֵת
אֱלֹהֵי בְנֵי־עַמּוֹן וְאֵת אֱלֹהֵי פְלִשְׁתִּים וַיַּעַזְבוּ אֶת־יהוה וְלֹא עֲבָדֽוּהוּ:
וַיִּחַר־אַף יהוה בְּיִשְׂרָאֵל וַיִּמְכְּרֵם בְּיַד־פְּלִשְׁתִּים וּבְיַד בְּנֵי עַמּוֹן: וַיִּרְעֲצוּ ז-ח
וַיְרֹצְצוּ אֶת־בְּנֵי יִשְׂרָאֵל בַּשָּׁנָה הַהִיא שְׁמֹנֶה עֶשְׂרֵה שָׁנָה אֶת־כָּל־בְּנֵי
יִשְׂרָאֵל אֲשֶׁר בְּעֵבֶר הַיַּרְדֵּן בְּאֶרֶץ הָאֱמֹרִי אֲשֶׁר בַּגִּלְעָד: וַיַּעַבְרוּ בְנֵי־ ט
עַמּוֹן אֶת־הַיַּרְדֵּן לְהִלָּחֵם גַּם־בִּיהוּדָה וּבְבִנְיָמִין וּבְבֵית אֶפְרָיִם וַתֵּצֶר
לְיִשְׂרָאֵל מְאֹד: וַיִּזְעֲקוּ בְּנֵי יִשְׂרָאֵל אֶל־יהוה לֵאמֹר חָטָאנוּ לָךְ וְכִי עָזַבְנוּ י
אֶת־אֱלֹהֵינוּ וַנַּעֲבֹד אֶת־הַבְּעָלִים: וַיֹּאמֶר יהוה אֶל־בְּנֵי יא
יִשְׂרָאֵל הֲלֹא מִמִּצְרַיִם וּמִן־הָאֱמֹרִי וּמִן־בְּנֵי עַמּוֹן וּמִן־פְּלִשְׁתִּים: וְצִידוֹנִים יב
וַעֲמָלֵק וּמָעוֹן לָחֲצוּ אֶתְכֶם וַתִּצְעֲקוּ אֵלַי וָאוֹשִׁיעָה אֶתְכֶם מִיָּדָם: וְאַתֶּם יג
עֲזַבְתֶּם אוֹתִי וַתַּעַבְדוּ אֱלֹהִים אֲחֵרִים לָכֵן לֹא־אוֹסִיף לְהוֹשִׁיעַ אֶתְכֶם:
לְכוּ וְזַעֲקוּ אֶל־הָאֱלֹהִים אֲשֶׁר בְּחַרְתֶּם בָּם הֵמָּה יוֹשִׁיעוּ לָכֶם בְּעֵת יד
צָרַתְכֶם: וַיֹּאמְרוּ בְנֵי־יִשְׂרָאֵל אֶל־יהוה חָטָאנוּ עֲשֵׂה־אַתָּה לָנוּ כְּכָל־ טו
הַטּוֹב בְּעֵינֶיךָ אַךְ הַצִּילֵנוּ נָא הַיּוֹם הַזֶּה: וַיָּסִירוּ אֶת־אֱלֹהֵי הַנֵּכָר מִקִּרְבָּם טז
וַיַּעַבְדוּ אֶת־יהוה וַתִּקְצַר נַפְשׁוֹ בַּעֲמַל יִשְׂרָאֵל:
וַיִּצָּעֲקוּ
בְנֵי עַמּוֹן וַיַּחֲנוּ בַּגִּלְעָד וַיֵּאָסְפוּ בְּנֵי יִשְׂרָאֵל וַיַּחֲנוּ בַּמִּצְפָּה: וַיֹּאמְרוּ הָעָם יז
שָׂרֵי גִלְעָד אִישׁ אֶל־רֵעֵהוּ מִי הָאִישׁ אֲשֶׁר יָחֵל לְהִלָּחֵם בִּבְנֵי עַמּוֹן יִהְיֶה יח

יא
HAFTARAS
CHUKAS
11:1-33

לְרֹאשׁ לְכֹל יֹשְׁבֵי גִלְעָד: ◄ וְיִפְתָּח הַגִּלְעָדִי הָיָה גִּבּוֹר חַיִל א
וְהוּא בֶּן־אִשָּׁה זוֹנָה וַיּוֹלֶד גִּלְעָד אֶת־יִפְתָּח: וַתֵּלֶד אֵשֶׁת־גִּלְעָד לוֹ בָּנִים ב
וַיִּגְדְּלוּ בְנֵי־הָאִשָּׁה וַיְגָרְשׁוּ אֶת־יִפְתָּח וַיֹּאמְרוּ לוֹ לֹא־תִנְחַל בְּבֵית־אָבִינוּ
כִּי בֶּן־אִשָּׁה אַחֶרֶת אָתָּה: וַיִּבְרַח יִפְתָּח מִפְּנֵי אֶחָיו וַיֵּשֶׁב בְּאֶרֶץ טוֹב ג
וַיִּתְלַקְּטוּ אֶל־יִפְתָּח אֲנָשִׁים רֵיקִים וַיֵּצְאוּ עִמּוֹ: וַיְהִי מִיָּמִים ד
וַיִּלָּחֲמוּ בְנֵי־עַמּוֹן עִם־יִשְׂרָאֵל: וַיְהִי כַּאֲשֶׁר־נִלְחֲמוּ בְנֵי־עַמּוֹן עִם־ ה
יִשְׂרָאֵל וַיֵּלְכוּ זִקְנֵי גִלְעָד לָקַחַת אֶת־יִפְתָּח מֵאֶרֶץ טוֹב: וַיֹּאמְרוּ לְיִפְתָּח ו
לְכָה וְהָיִיתָה לָּנוּ לְקָצִין וְנִלָּחֲמָה בִּבְנֵי עַמּוֹן: וַיֹּאמֶר יִפְתָּח לְזִקְנֵי גִלְעָד ז
הֲלֹא אַתֶּם שְׂנֵאתֶם אוֹתִי וַתְּגָרְשׁוּנִי מִבֵּית אָבִי וּמַדּוּעַ בָּאתֶם אֵלַי עַתָּה
כַּאֲשֶׁר צַר לָכֶם: וַיֹּאמְרוּ זִקְנֵי גִלְעָד אֶל־יִפְתָּח לָכֵן עַתָּה שַׁבְנוּ אֵלֶיךָ ח

10:6. During seven periods, the nation successively worshiped seven different idols. Each period of disloyalty to God was followed by a period of suffering, remorse and eventual salvation. Nevertheless, Israel was again disloyal to God (*Talmud, Beitzah* 25b).

10:8. The year of Jair's death (*Rashi*).

10:14. God answered, through His prophet, that this time a mere declaration of remorse would not suffice. Thoroughly chastened by God's rebuke, the people made a new plea and backed it with action, whereupon God commenced His salvation.

10:16. This incident shows that one may never despair even if a sharp sword is on his neck. Though God had said that the people had lost their chance to regain His favor, they continued to repent and to plead — and prevailed.

11:1. From this point until the rise of Samuel, God did not provide great leaders to bring Israel triumph and tranquility. There were leaders of lesser stature, victories of lesser magnitude, and even civil war and factiousness among Israel. Now, as they sought a warrior to defeat Ammon, the people were forced to call upon Jephthah, who did not measure up to their usual standards.

A NEW CYCLE
BEGINS
10:6-18

Idolatry

Chastening
(See Appendix A,
timeline 3)

⁶ *The Children of Israel continued to do that which was evil in the eyes of HASHEM and they worshiped the Baalim, the Ashtaroth, the gods of Aram, the gods of Sidon, the gods of Moab, the gods of the Children of Ammon, and the gods of the Philistines; they forsook HASHEM and did not serve Him.* * ⁷ *The wrath of HASHEM flared against Israel and He delivered them into the hand of the Philistines and into the hand of the Children of Ammon.* ⁸ *They broke and crushed the Children of Israel [starting] that year,* * *for eighteen years — all the Children of Israel who were of the other side of the Jordan, in the land of the Amorite, which is in Gilead.* ⁹ *The Children of Ammon crossed the Jordan to make war even against Judah and Benjamin and the house of Ephraim. Israel was greatly distressed.*

¹⁰ *The Children of Israel cried out to HASHEM, saying, "We have sinned to You, for we have forsaken our God and we have worshiped the Baalim!"*

*Divine
reprimand*

¹¹ *Then HASHEM said to the Children of Israel, "Did [I] not [save you] from Egypt and from the Amorite and from the Children of Ammon and from the Philistines?* ¹² *The Sidonians and Amalek and Maon oppressed you; and you cried out to Me, and I saved you from their hand.* ¹³ *But you forsook Me and worshiped the gods of others. Therefore I shall not continue to help you.* ¹⁴ *Go and cry out to the gods that you have chosen — let them save you in your time of distress!"* *

¹⁵ *The Children of Israel then said to HASHEM, "We have sinned! May You do with us whatever is good in Your eyes, but rescue us now, this day!"* ¹⁶ *They removed the foreign gods from their midst and they served HASHEM — then His spirit could not tolerate the travail of Israel.* *

¹⁷ *The Children of Ammon were mustered and they encamped in Gilead. The Children of Israel were gathered and they encamped in Mizpah.* ¹⁸ *The people — the princes of Gilead — said, each to his fellow, "Whichever man will begin to do battle against the Children of Ammon will become the leader of all the inhabitants of Gilead."*

11

JEPHTHAH
THE
GILEADITE
11:1-12:7
(See Appendix A,
timeline 3)

*Jephthah's
expulsion . . .*

*. . . and
recall*

¹ **J**ephthah the Gileadite was a mighty man of valor and he was the son of a concubine; * Gilead begat Jephthah. ² Gilead's wife bore him sons, and when the wife's sons grew up they drove Jephthah away and said to him, "You will not inherit in the household of our father, for you are the son of another woman."

³ Jephthah fled because of his brothers and settled in the land of Tob. Boorish men collected around Jephthah, and ventured forth with him.

⁴ It happened after a period of time that the Children of Ammon made war with Israel. ⁵ And it happened when the Children of Ammon waged war against Israel that the elders of Gilead went to bring Jephthah [back] from the land of Tob. ⁶ They said to Jephthah, "Come and be our chief, and we will do battle with the Children of Ammon."

⁷ But Jephthah said to the elders of Gilead, "Was it not you who hated me and drove me away from my father's house? Why have you come to me now when you are in distress?"

⁸ The elders of Gilead said to Jephthah, "For this have we now returned to you

During this period, it was still considered unseemly for an heiress to marry out of her father's tribe (see *Numbers* 36:5-9). Having broken this tradition, Jephthah's mother was called a זונה, literally, *harlot*, even though she remained faithful to her husband Gilead

(*Radak; Ralbag*). Though Jephthah's mother was called a harlot, the verse testifies that Gilead was his father to show that his brothers mistreated him (see below), because, as a son, he was fully entitled to share in Gilead's estate.

וְהָלַכְתִּ֤י עִמָּ֙נוּ֙ וְנִלְחַמְתָּ֙ בִּבְנֵ֣י עַמּ֔וֹן וְהָיִ֤יתָ לָ֙נוּ֙ לְרֹ֔אשׁ לְכֹ֖ל יֹשְׁבֵ֥י גִלְעָֽד:

ט וַיֹּ֨אמֶר יִפְתָּ֜ח אֶל־זִקְנֵ֣י גִלְעָ֗ד אִם־מְשִׁיבִ֨ים אַתֶּ֤ם אוֹתִי֙ לְהִלָּחֵם֙ בִּבְנֵ֣י

י עַמּ֔וֹן וְנָתַ֧ן יְהֹוָ֛ה אוֹתָ֖ם לְפָנָ֑י אָנֹכִ֕י אֶהְיֶ֥ה לָכֶ֖ם לְרֹֽאשׁ: וַיֹּֽאמְר֥וּ זִקְנֵֽי־גִלְעָ֖ד

יא אֶל־יִפְתָּ֑ח יְהֹוָ֗ה יִהְיֶ֤ה שֹׁמֵ֙עַ֙ בֵּֽינוֹתֵ֔ינוּ אִם־לֹ֥א כִדְבָרְךָ֖ כֵּ֥ן נַעֲשֶֽׂה: וַיֵּ֤לֶךְ

יִפְתָּח֙ עִם־זִקְנֵ֣י גִלְעָ֔ד וַיָּשִׂ֨ימוּ הָעָ֥ם אוֹת֛וֹ עֲלֵיהֶ֖ם לְרֹ֣אשׁ וּלְקָצִ֑ין וַיְדַבֵּ֨ר

יב יִפְתָּ֧ח אֶת־כָּל־דְּבָרָ֛יו לִפְנֵ֥י יְהֹוָ֖ה בַּמִּצְפָּֽה: וַיִּשְׁלַ֤ח

יִפְתָּח֙ מַלְאָכִ֔ים אֶל־מֶ֥לֶךְ בְּנֵֽי־עַמּ֖וֹן לֵאמֹ֑ר מַה־לִּ֣י וָלָ֔ךְ כִּֽי־בָ֥אתָ אֵלַ֖י

יג לְהִלָּחֵ֥ם בְּאַרְצִֽי: וַיֹּ֩אמֶר֩ מֶ֨לֶךְ בְּנֵי־עַמּ֜וֹן אֶל־מַלְאֲכֵ֣י יִפְתָּ֗ח כִּֽי־לָקַ֣ח

יִשְׂרָאֵ֤ל אֶת־אַרְצִי֙ בַּעֲלוֹת֣וֹ מִמִּצְרַ֔יִם מֵאַרְנ֥וֹן וְעַד־הַיַּבֹּ֖ק וְעַד־הַיַּרְדֵּ֑ן

יד וְעַתָּ֕ה הָשִׁ֥יבָה אֶתְהֶ֖ן בְּשָׁלֽוֹם: וַיּ֥וֹסֶף ע֖וֹד יִפְתָּ֑ח וַיִּשְׁלַח֙ מַלְאָכִ֔ים אֶל־

טו מֶ֖לֶךְ בְּנֵ֥י עַמּֽוֹן: וַיֹּ֣אמֶר ל֔וֹ כֹּ֖ה אָמַ֣ר יִפְתָּ֑ח לֹֽא־לָקַ֤ח יִשְׂרָאֵל֙ אֶת־אֶ֣רֶץ

טז מוֹאָ֔ב וְאֶת־אֶ֖רֶץ בְּנֵ֥י עַמּֽוֹן: כִּ֖י בַּעֲלוֹתָ֣ם מִמִּצְרָ֑יִם וַיֵּ֨לֶךְ יִשְׂרָאֵ֤ל בַּמִּדְבָּר֙

יז עַד־יַם־ס֔וּף וַיָּבֹ֖א קָדֵֽשָׁה: וַיִּשְׁלַ֣ח יִשְׂרָאֵ֣ל מַלְאָכִ֣ים ׀ אֶל־מֶ֩לֶךְ֩ אֱד֨וֹם

לֵאמֹ֜ר אֶעְבְּרָה־נָּ֣א בְאַרְצֶ֗ךָ וְלֹ֤א שָׁמַע֙ מֶ֣לֶךְ אֱד֔וֹם וְגַ֛ם אֶל־מֶ֥לֶךְ מוֹאָ֖ב

יח שָׁלַ֣ח וְלֹ֣א אָבָ֑ה וַיֵּ֣שֶׁב יִשְׂרָאֵ֖ל בְּקָדֵֽשׁ: וַיֵּ֣לֶךְ בַּמִּדְבָּ֗ר וַיָּ֜סָב אֶת־אֶ֤רֶץ

אֱדוֹם֙ וְאֶת־אֶ֣רֶץ מוֹאָ֔ב וַיָּבֹ֤א מִמִּזְרַח־שֶׁ֙מֶשׁ֙ לְאֶ֣רֶץ מוֹאָ֔ב וַיַּחֲנ֖וּן בְּעֵ֣בֶר

יט אַרְנ֑וֹן וְלֹא־בָ֙אוּ֙ בִּגְב֣וּל מוֹאָ֔ב כִּ֥י אַרְנ֖וֹן גְּב֥וּל מוֹאָֽב: וַיִּשְׁלַ֤ח יִשְׂרָאֵל֙

מַלְאָכִ֔ים אֶל־סִיח֥וֹן מֶֽלֶךְ־הָאֱמֹרִ֖י מֶ֣לֶךְ חֶשְׁבּ֑וֹן וַיֹּ֤אמֶר לוֹ֙ יִשְׂרָאֵ֔ל

כ נַעְבְּרָה־נָּ֥א בְאַרְצְךָ֖ עַד־מְקוֹמִֽי: וְלֹֽא־הֶאֱמִ֙ין סִיח֤וֹן אֶת־יִשְׂרָאֵל֙ עֲבֹ֣ר

בִּגְבֻל֔וֹ וַיֶּאֱסֹ֤ף סִיחוֹן֙ אֶת־כָּל־עַמּ֔וֹ וַֽיַּחֲנ֖וּ בְּיָ֑הְצָה וַיִּלָּ֖חֶם עִם־יִשְׂרָאֵֽל:

כא וַ֠יִּתֵּ֠ן יְהֹוָ֨ה אֱלֹהֵֽי־יִשְׂרָאֵ֜ל אֶת־סִיח֧וֹן וְאֶת־כָּל־עַמּ֛וֹ בְּיַ֥ד יִשְׂרָאֵ֖ל וַיַּכּ֑וּם

כב וַיִּירַשׁ֙ יִשְׂרָאֵ֔ל אֵ֚ת כָּל־אֶ֣רֶץ הָאֱמֹרִ֔י יוֹשֵׁ֖ב הָאָ֣רֶץ הַהִ֑יא: וַיִּ֣ירְשׁ֔וּ אֵ֖ת כָּל־

כג גְּב֣וּל הָאֱמֹרִ֑י מֵֽאַרְנוֹן֙ וְעַד־הַיַּבֹּ֔ק וּמִן־הַמִּדְבָּ֖ר וְעַד־הַיַּרְדֵּֽן: וְעַתָּ֞ה יְהֹוָ֣ה ׀

אֱלֹהֵ֣י יִשְׂרָאֵ֗ל הוֹרִישׁ֙ אֶת־הָ֣אֱמֹרִ֔י מִפְּנֵ֖י עַמּ֣וֹ יִשְׂרָאֵ֑ל וְאַתָּ֖ה תִּירָשֶֽׁנּוּ:

כד הֲלֹ֞א אֵ֣ת אֲשֶׁ֧ר יֽוֹרִישְׁךָ֛ כְּמ֥וֹשׁ אֱלֹהֶ֖יךָ אוֹת֣וֹ תִירָ֑שׁ וְאֵת֩ כָּל־אֲשֶׁ֨ר הוֹרִ֜ישׁ

כה יְהֹוָ֧ה אֱלֹהֵ֛ינוּ מִפָּנֵ֖ינוּ אוֹת֥וֹ נִירָֽשׁ: וְעַתָּ֗ה הֲט֥וֹב טוֹב֙ אַתָּ֔ה מִבָּלָ֖ק בֶּן־צִפּ֑וֹר

כו מֶ֖לֶךְ מוֹאָ֑ב הֲר֥וֹב רָב֙ עִם־יִשְׂרָאֵ֔ל אִם־נִלְחֹ֥ם נִלְחַ֖ם בָּֽם: בְּשֶׁ֣בֶת יִ֠שְׂרָאֵ֠ל

בְּחֶשְׁבּ֨וֹן וּבִבְנוֹתֶ֜יהָ וּבְעַרְע֣וֹר וּבִבְנוֹתֶ֗יהָ וּבְכָל־הֶֽעָרִים֙ אֲשֶׁר֙ עַל־יְדֵ֣י

כז אַרְנ֔וֹן שְׁלֹ֥שׁ מֵא֖וֹת שָׁנָ֑ה וּמַדּ֥וּעַ לֹֽא־הִצַּלְתֶּ֖ם בָּעֵ֥ת הַהִֽיא: וְאָֽנֹכִי֙ לֹֽא־

חָטָ֣אתִי לָ֔ךְ וְאַתָּ֞ה עֹשֶׂ֥ה אִתִּ֛י רָעָ֖ה לְהִלָּ֣חֶם בִּ֑י יִשְׁפֹּ֙ט יְהֹוָ֤ה הַשֹּׁפֵט֙ הַיּ֔וֹם

כח בֵּ֚ין בְּנֵ֣י יִשְׂרָאֵ֔ל וּבֵ֖ין בְּנֵ֣י עַמּ֑וֹן: וְלֹ֣א שָׁמַ֔ע מֶ֖לֶךְ בְּנֵ֣י עַמּ֑וֹן אֶל־דִּבְרֵ֣י יִפְתָּ֔ח

כט אֲשֶׁ֖ר שָׁלַ֥ח אֵלָֽיו: וַתְּהִ֤י עַל־יִפְתָּח֙ ר֣וּחַ יְהֹוָ֔ה וַיַּעֲבֹ֖ר אֶת־הַגִּלְעָ֑ד

11:11. Where large numbers of Jews gather, the *Shechinah* (Immanent Presence of God) is manifest, and Jephthah used the occasion to have God bear witness, so to speak, to the nation's acceptance of the elders' promise to bestow leadership upon him (*Rashi*).

— that you go with us and do battle with the Children of Ammon, and that you become a leader over us, over all the inhabitants of Gilead!"

⁹ Jephthah said to the elders of Gilead, "If you bring me back to do battle with the Children of Ammon and HASHEM delivers them before me, I will become your leader."

¹⁰ Then the elders of Gilead said to Jephthah, "May HASHEM bear witness between us, if we do not do according to your word." ¹¹ So Jephthah went with the elders of Gilead, and the people set him as a leader and a chief over them. Jephthah spoke all his words before HASHEM* in Mizpah.

Jephthah confronts the king of Ammon

¹² Jephthah sent emissaries to the king of the Children of Ammon, saying, "What is there between you and me that you have come to me to make war in my land?"

¹³ The king of the Children of Ammon said to Jephthah's emissaries, "Because Israel took away my land when it ascended from Egypt, from Arnon to the Jabbok to the Jordan! So now return them in peace."

¹⁴ Jephthah once again sent emissaries to the king of the Children of Ammon, ¹⁵ and said to him, "So said Jephthah: Israel did not take away the land of Moab and the land of the Children of Ammon. ¹⁶ For when they ascended from Egypt, Israel went in the Wilderness until the Sea of Reeds, and then they arrived at Kadesh. ¹⁷ Israel sent emissaries to the king of Edom, saying, 'Let me now pass through your land,' but the king of Edom did not take heed. It sent also to the king of Moab, but he was not willing, so Israel dwelt in Kadesh. ¹⁸ It went through the Wilderness and went around the land of Edom and the land of Moab, and came to the land of Moab from the east, where they encamped across the Arnon; but they did not enter the border of Moab, for the Arnon is the border of Moab. ¹⁹ Then Israel sent emissaries to Sihon, king of the Amorite, the king of Heshbon, and Israel said to him, 'Let us now pass through your land until my place.' ²⁰ But Sihon did not trust Israel to pass through his border. Rather, Sihon assembled his entire people and they encamped at Jahaz, and he made war against Israel. ²¹ Then HASHEM, God of Israel, delivered Sihon and his entire people into the hand of Israel and they struck them down. Israel took possession of the entire land of the Amorite, the inhabitants of that land. ²² They took possession of the entire territory of the Amorite, from Arnon to the Jabbok, and from the Wilderness to the Jordan.

²³ "And now HASHEM, the God of Israel, has driven out the Amorite because of His people Israel — yet you would possess it? ²⁴ Surely, whatever your god Chemosh lets you possess, that you shall possess; and whichever [people] God drives away before us, that [land] we shall possess. ²⁵ And now, are you any better than Balak son of Zippor, king of Moab? Did he pursue any grievance against Israel, or did he make any war against them? ²⁶ While Israel dwelt in Heshbon and its suburbs, in Aroer and its suburbs, and in all the cities that are near Arnon for three hundred years — why did you not recover [them] during that time? ²⁷ I have not sinned against you; but you do me wrong to make war against me! Let HASHEM, the Judge, decide today between the Children of Israel and the Children of Ammon!"

²⁸ But the king of the Children of Ammon did not heed the words of Jephthah, which he sent to him.

²⁹ A spirit of HASHEM was upon Jephthah, and he passed through the Gilead

ל וְאֶת־מְנַשֶּׁה וַיַּעֲבֹר אֶת־מִצְפֵּה גִלְעָד וּמִמִּצְפֵּה גִלְעָד עָבַר בְּנֵי עַמּוֹן: וַיִּדַּר

לא יִפְתָּח נֶדֶר לַיהוָה וַיֹּאמַר אִם־נָתוֹן תִּתֵּן אֶת־בְּנֵי עַמּוֹן בְּיָדִי: וְהָיָה הַיּוֹצֵא אֲשֶׁר יֵצֵא מִדַּלְתֵי בֵיתִי לִקְרָאתִי בְּשׁוּבִי בְשָׁלוֹם מִבְּנֵי עַמּוֹן וְהָיָה לַיהוָה וְהַעֲלִיתִיהוּ עוֹלָה:

לב-לג וַיַּעֲבֹר יִפְתָּח אֶל־בְּנֵי עַמּוֹן לְהִלָּחֶם בָּם וַיִּתְּנֵם יהוה בְּיָדוֹ: וַיַּכֵּם מֵעֲרוֹעֵר וְעַד־בּוֹאֲךָ מִנִּית עֶשְׂרִים עִיר וְעַד אָבֵל כְּרָמִים מַכָּה גְּדוֹלָה מְאֹד וַיִּכָּנְעוּ בְּנֵי עַמּוֹן מִפְּנֵי בְּנֵי יִשְׂרָאֵל: ◄

לד וַיָּבֹא יִפְתָּח הַמִּצְפָּה אֶל־בֵּיתוֹ וְהִנֵּה בִתּוֹ יֹצֵאת לִקְרָאתוֹ בְּתֻפִּים וּבִמְחֹלוֹת וְרַק הִיא יְחִידָה אֵין־לוֹ

לה מִמֶּנּוּ בֵּן אוֹ־בַת: וַיְהִי כִרְאוֹתוֹ אוֹתָהּ וַיִּקְרַע אֶת־בְּגָדָיו וַיֹּאמֶר אֲהָהּ בִּתִּי הַכְרֵעַ הִכְרַעְתִּנִי וְאַתְּ הָיִית בְּעֹכְרָי וְאָנֹכִי פָּצִיתִי פִי אֶל־יהוה וְלֹא אוּכַל

לו לָשׁוּב: וַתֹּאמֶר אֵלָיו אָבִי פָּצִיתָה אֶת־פִּיךָ אֶל־יהוה עֲשֵׂה לִי כַּאֲשֶׁר יָצָא

לז מִפִּיךָ אַחֲרֵי אֲשֶׁר עָשָׂה לְךָ יהוה נְקָמוֹת מֵאֹיְבֶיךָ מִבְּנֵי עַמּוֹן: וַתֹּאמֶר אֶל־אָבִיהָ יֵעָשֶׂה לִּי הַדָּבָר הַזֶּה הַרְפֵּה מִמֶּנִּי שְׁנַיִם חֳדָשִׁים וְאֵלְכָה וְיָרַדְתִּי עַל־הֶהָרִים וְאֶבְכֶּה עַל־בְּתוּלַי אָנֹכִי °וְרֵעיתִי [°וְרֵעוֹתָי ק]:

לח וַיֹּאמֶר לֵכִי וַיִּשְׁלַח אוֹתָהּ שְׁנֵי חֳדָשִׁים וַתֵּלֶךְ הִיא וְרֵעוֹתֶיהָ וַתֵּבְךְּ עַל־

לט בְּתוּלֶיהָ עַל־הֶהָרִים: וַיְהִי מִקֵּץ | שְׁנַיִם חֳדָשִׁים וַתָּשָׁב אֶל־אָבִיהָ וַיַּעַשׂ לָהּ

מ אֶת־נִדְרוֹ אֲשֶׁר נָדָר וְהִיא לֹא־יָדְעָה אִישׁ וַתְּהִי־חֹק בְּיִשְׂרָאֵל: מִיָּמִים | יָמִימָה תֵּלַכְנָה בְּנוֹת יִשְׂרָאֵל לְתַנּוֹת לְבַת־יִפְתָּח הַגִּלְעָדִי אַרְבַּעַת יָמִים בַּשָּׁנָה:

יב א וַיִּצָּעֵק אִישׁ אֶפְרַיִם וַיַּעֲבֹר צָפוֹנָה וַיֹּאמְרוּ לְיִפְתָּח מַדּוּעַ | עָבַרְתָּ | לְהִלָּחֵם בִּבְנֵי־עַמּוֹן וְלָנוּ לֹא קָרָאתָ לָלֶכֶת עִמָּךְ בֵּיתְךָ נִשְׂרֹף

ב עָלֶיךָ בָּאֵשׁ: וַיֹּאמֶר יִפְתָּח אֲלֵיהֶם אִישׁ רִיב הָיִיתִי אֲנִי וְעַמִּי וּבְנֵי־עַמּוֹן

ג מְאֹד וָאֶזְעַק אֶתְכֶם וְלֹא־הוֹשַׁעְתֶּם אוֹתִי מִיָּדָם: וָאֶרְאֶה כִּי־אֵינְךָ מוֹשִׁיעַ וָאָשִׂימָה נַפְשִׁי בְכַפִּי וָאֶעְבְּרָה אֶל־בְּנֵי עַמּוֹן וַיִּתְּנֵם יהוה בְּיָדִי וְלָמָה

ד עֲלִיתֶם אֵלַי הַיּוֹם הַזֶּה לְהִלָּחֶם בִּי: וַיִּקְבֹּץ יִפְתָּח אֶת־כָּל־אַנְשֵׁי גִלְעָד וַיִּלָּחֶם אֶת־אֶפְרָיִם וַיַּכּוּ אַנְשֵׁי גִלְעָד אֶת־אֶפְרַיִם כִּי אָמְרוּ פְּלִיטֵי אֶפְרַיִם

ה אַתֶּם גִּלְעָד בְּתוֹךְ אֶפְרַיִם בְּתוֹךְ מְנַשֶּׁה: וַיִּלְכֹּד גִּלְעָד אֶת־מַעְבְּרוֹת הַיַּרְדֵּן לְאֶפְרָיִם וְהָיָה כִּי יֹאמְרוּ פְּלִיטֵי אֶפְרַיִם אֶעֱבֹרָה וַיֹּאמְרוּ לוֹ אַנְשֵׁי־גִלְעָד

11:31. Jephthah acted improperly by vowing that he would make an altar offering of the first thing to emerge from his house — for how could he be certain that it would be an animal? (*Talmud, Taanis* 4a).

11:35. Under no circumstances was Jephthah permitted to sacrifice his daughter, nor could he obligate her to a course of behavior. Jephthah should have gone to Phinehas to have his vow annulled, but he felt that since he was the leader of the nation, Phinehas should come to him. Phinehas, however, felt that since he was a prophet and Kohen, Jephthah should come to him. Thus, the two never met, and the daughter's tragedy was sealed. God punished both of them. Phinehas lost his exalted posi-

tion, and Jephthah contracted a disease that caused his limbs to atrophy (see 12:7).

11:36. Jephthah's daughter volunteered to submit and Jephthah carried out his vow figuratively, by having her live in seclusion, and devote herself to prayer.

11:37. Before the vow was carried out, she wanted to grieve with her friends, because she would remain a virgin, never to marry and bring children into the world.

12:1. A tragic civil war illustrates the lowered spiritual state of the nation. Jephthah had rallied his own kinsmen to defeat Ammon, and now the tribe of Ephraim came *en masse* to protest that he had slighted them. They felt that and Manasseh, and he passed through Mizpeh of Gilead, and from Mizpeh of Gilead he passed through [to] the Children of Ammon.

Jephthah's vow

³⁰ Jephthah declared a vow to Hashem, and said, "If You will indeed deliver the Children of Ammon into my hand, ³¹ then it shall be that whatever emerges — what will emerge from the doors of my house — toward me when I return in peace from the Children of Ammon, it shall belong to Hashem and I shall offer it up as an elevation-offering."*

Jephthah defeats Ammon

³² Then Jephthah crossed to the Children of Ammon to do battle against them, and Hashem delivered them into his hand. ³³ He struck them from Aroer until your approach to Minnith, twenty cities, and until the plain of Cheramim — a very great blow — and the Children of Ammon were subdued before the Children of Israel.

His daughter's fate

³⁴ Jephthah arrived at Mizpah, to his home, and behold! his daughter was coming out toward him with drums and dances — and she was an only child; he did not have [another] son or daughter of his own. ³⁵ When he saw her, he tore his clothes and said, "Alas, my daughter! You have brought me to my knees, and you have joined those who trouble me. I have opened my mouth to Hashem and I cannot recant!"*

³⁶ She said to him, "My father, you have opened your mouth to Hashem — do to me according to what has gone out of your mouth,* since Hashem has wreaked vengeance for you against your enemies, against the Children of Ammon!" ³⁷ But she said to her father, "Let this thing be done for me: Let me be for two months, and I shall go and wail upon the mountains and weep over my virginity, I and my friends."*

³⁸ He said, "Go!" and he sent her off for two months. She went with her friends and wept over her virginity upon the mountains. ³⁹ At the end of two months she returned to her father. He carried out with her the vow that he had vowed, and she never knew a man. This became a practice in Israel: ⁴⁰ From year to year the daughters of Israel would go to lament with the daughter of Jephthah the Gileadite, four days of the year.

12

Ephraim challenges Jephthah

¹ The men of Ephraim were mustered and crossed to the north. They said to Jephthah, "Why did you cross over to make war against the Children of Ammon, and did not call on us to go with you? We shall burn down your house in fire upon you!"*

² Jephthah said to them, "A man of great strife was I — I and my people — against the Children of Ammon; I summoned you, but you did not save me from their hand. ³ I saw that you were not helping, so I placed my life in my hand and I crossed over to the Children of Ammon — and Hashem delivered them into my hand. Now why have you come up to me this day to make war with me?"

Civil war

⁴ Jephthah assembled all the men of Gilead and warred against Ephraim, and the men of Gilead struck Ephraim, for [even] the rabble of Ephraim had said, "[Of what worth are] you Gilead? [You who dwell] in the midst of Ephraim, in the midst of Manasseh!"

⁵ Gilead occupied the crossings of the Jordan against Ephraim, so it was that when the "rabble of Ephraim" would say, "Let me cross," the men of Gilead

---

by ignoring them, Jephthah had usurped the primacy that was legitimately theirs. They had done likewise to Gideon (8:1-3), but he, with modesty and tact, had molli-

fied them (*Malbim; Daas Soferim*). Jephthah, however, would not, or could not, appease them; instead, he responded with violence (*Ralbag*).

ו הָאֶפְרָתִי אַתָּה וַיֹּאמֶר ׀ לֹא: וַיֹּאמְרוּ לוֹ אֱמָר־נָא שִׁבֹּלֶת וַיֹּאמֶר סִבֹּלֶת
וְלֹא יָכִין לְדַבֵּר כֵּן וַיֹּאחֲזוּ אוֹתוֹ וַיִּשְׁחָטוּהוּ אֶל־מַעְבְּרוֹת הַיַּרְדֵּן וַיִּפֹּל
בָּעֵת הַהִיא מֵאֶפְרַיִם אַרְבָּעִים וּשְׁנַיִם אָלֶף: וַיִּשְׁפֹּט יִפְתָּח אֶת־יִשְׂרָאֵל
ז שֵׁשׁ שָׁנִים וַיָּמָת יִפְתָּח הַגִּלְעָדִי וַיִּקָּבֵר בְּעָרֵי גִלְעָד: וַיִּשְׁפֹּט
ח אַחֲרָיו אֶת־יִשְׂרָאֵל אִבְצָן מִבֵּית לָחֶם: וַיְהִי־לוֹ שְׁלֹשִׁים בָּנִים וּשְׁלֹשִׁים
בָּנוֹת שִׁלַּח הַחוּצָה וּשְׁלֹשִׁים בָּנוֹת הֵבִיא לְבָנָיו מִן־הַחוּץ וַיִּשְׁפֹּט אֶת־
י יִשְׂרָאֵל שֶׁבַע שָׁנִים: וַיָּמָת אִבְצָן וַיִּקָּבֵר בְּבֵית לָחֶם:
יא אַחֲרָיו אֶת־יִשְׂרָאֵל אֵילוֹן הַזְּבוּלֹנִי וַיִּשְׁפֹּט אֶת־יִשְׂרָאֵל עֶשֶׂר שָׁנִים: וַיָּמָת
יב אֵילוֹן הַזְּבוּלֹנִי וַיִּקָּבֵר בְּאַיָּלוֹן בְּאֶרֶץ זְבוּלֻן: וַיִּשְׁפֹּט אַחֲרָיו
יג אֶת־יִשְׂרָאֵל עַבְדּוֹן בֶּן־הִלֵּל הַפִּרְעָתוֹנִי: וַיְהִי־לוֹ אַרְבָּעִים בָּנִים וּשְׁלֹשִׁים
יד בְּנֵי בָנִים רֹכְבִים עַל־שִׁבְעִים עֲיָרִם וַיִּשְׁפֹּט אֶת־יִשְׂרָאֵל שְׁמֹנֶה שָׁנִים:
טו וַיָּמָת עַבְדּוֹן בֶּן־הִלֵּל הַפִּרְעָתוֹנִי וַיִּקָּבֵר בְּפִרְעָתוֹן בְּאֶרֶץ אֶפְרַיִם בְּהַר

א הָעֲמָלֵקִי: וַיֹּסִפוּ בְּנֵי יִשְׂרָאֵל לַעֲשׂוֹת הָרַע בְּעֵינֵי יהוה וַיִּתְּנֵם   **יג**
ב יהוה בְּיַד־פְּלִשְׁתִּים אַרְבָּעִים שָׁנָה: ◄ וַיְהִי אִישׁ אֶחָד מִצָּרְעָה   HAFTARAS
NASSO
13:2-25
ג מִמִּשְׁפַּחַת הַדָּנִי וּשְׁמוֹ מָנוֹחַ וְאִשְׁתּוֹ עֲקָרָה וְלֹא יָלָדָה: וַיֵּרָא מַלְאַךְ־יהוה
אֶל־הָאִשָּׁה וַיֹּאמֶר אֵלֶיהָ הִנֵּה־נָא אַתְּ־עֲקָרָה וְלֹא יָלַדְתְּ וְהָרִית וְיָלַדְתְּ
ד-ה בֵּן: וְעַתָּה הִשָּׁמְרִי נָא וְאַל־תִּשְׁתִּי יַיִן וְשֵׁכָר וְאַל־תֹּאכְלִי כָּל־טָמֵא: כִּי הִנָּךְ
הָרָה וְיֹלַדְתְּ בֵּן וּמוֹרָה לֹא־יַעֲלֶה עַל־רֹאשׁוֹ כִּי־נְזִיר אֱלֹהִים יִהְיֶה הַנַּעַר
ו מִן־הַבָּטֶן וְהוּא יָחֵל לְהוֹשִׁיעַ אֶת־יִשְׂרָאֵל מִיַּד פְּלִשְׁתִּים: וַתָּבֹא הָאִשָּׁה
וַתֹּאמֶר לְאִישָׁהּ לֵאמֹר אִישׁ הָאֱלֹהִים בָּא אֵלַי וּמַרְאֵהוּ כְּמַרְאֵה מַלְאַךְ
הָאֱלֹהִים נוֹרָא מְאֹד וְלֹא שְׁאִלְתִּיהוּ אֵי־מִזֶּה הוּא וְאֶת־שְׁמוֹ לֹא־הִגִּיד
ז לִי: וַיֹּאמֶר לִי הִנָּךְ הָרָה וְיֹלַדְתְּ בֵּן וְעַתָּה אַל־תִּשְׁתִּי ׀ יַיִן וְשֵׁכָר וְאַל־תֹּאכְלִי
כָּל־טֻמְאָה כִּי־נְזִיר אֱלֹהִים יִהְיֶה הַנַּעַר מִן־הַבֶּטֶן עַד־יוֹם מוֹתוֹ:
ח וַיֶּעְתַּר מָנוֹחַ אֶל־יהוה וַיֹּאמַר בִּי אֲדוֹנָי אִישׁ הָאֱלֹהִים אֲשֶׁר שָׁלַחְתָּ
ט יָבוֹא־נָא עוֹד אֵלֵינוּ וְיוֹרֵנוּ מַה־נַּעֲשֶׂה לַנַּעַר הַיּוּלָּד: וַיִּשְׁמַע הָאֱלֹהִים
בְּקוֹל מָנוֹחַ וַיָּבֹא מַלְאַךְ הָאֱלֹהִים עוֹד אֶל־הָאִשָּׁה וְהִיא יוֹשֶׁבֶת
י בַּשָּׂדֶה וּמָנוֹחַ אִישָׁהּ אֵין עִמָּהּ: וַתְּמַהֵר הָאִשָּׁה וַתָּרָץ וַתַּגֵּד לְאִישָׁהּ
יא וַתֹּאמֶר אֵלָיו הִנֵּה נִרְאָה אֵלַי הָאִישׁ אֲשֶׁר־בָּא בַיּוֹם אֵלָי: וַיָּקָם וַיֵּלֶךְ
מָנוֹחַ אַחֲרֵי אִשְׁתּוֹ וַיָּבֹא אֶל־הָאִישׁ וַיֹּאמֶר לוֹ הַאַתָּה הָאִישׁ אֲשֶׁר־דִּבַּרְתָּ
יב אֶל־הָאִשָּׁה וַיֹּאמֶר אָנִי: וַיֹּאמֶר מָנוֹחַ עַתָּה יָבֹא דְבָרֶיךָ מַה־יִּהְיֶה

12:6. The people of Gilead took advantage of an Ephraimite speech defect to identify who was from that tribe. The people of Ephraim could not pronounce a "sh" sound, and that was their undoing.

12:7. Jephthah "was buried in *cities* of Gilead" implies that he received more than one burial. According to the *Midrash* (see 11:3), his limbs atrophied and fell off one by

one; each was buried in the city he was in at the time.

12:9. Scripture implies that Ibzan was a very virtuous man, for he became judge of his nation and merited to see all his sixty children happily married (*Radak*).

13:5. The people once more fell into sinfulness and God permitted the Philistines to take control of the country. Israel was not worthy of the complete salvation brought would say to him, "Are you an Ephrathite?" and he would answer, "No." ⁶ Then they would say to him, "Now say, 'Shibboleth,'" but he said, "Sibboleth" — for he could not enunciate properly. Then they would seize him and slaughter him by the crossings of the Jordan. During that time, forty-two thousand fell from Ephraim. *

⁷ Jephthah judged Israel for six years. Jephthah the Gileadite died and was buried in cities of Gilead. *

IBZAN
12:8-10
(See Appendix A, timeline 3)

⁸ After him, Ibzan of Beth-lehem judged Israel. ⁹ He had thirty sons and he sent out thirty daughters; he brought thirty daughters for his sons from without. * He judged Israel for seven years. ¹⁰ Ibzan died and was buried in Beth-lehem.

ELON THE
ZEBULUNITE
12:11-12

¹¹ After him, Elon the Zebulunite judged Israel; he judged Israel for ten years. ¹² Elon the Zebulunite died and was buried in Aijalon, in the land of Zebulun.

ABDON SON
OF HILLEL
12:13-15

¹³ After him, Abdon son of Hillel the Pirathonite judged Israel. ¹⁴ He had forty sons and thirty grandsons, riding on seventy colts. He judged Israel for eight years. ¹⁵ Abdon son of Hillel the Pirathonite died and was buried in Pirathon, in the land of Ephraim, on the Amalekite mountain.

13

SAMSON
13:1—16:31

An angelic
visitation

¹ The Children of Israel continued to do what was evil in the eyes of Hashem, and Hashem delivered them into the hand of the Philistines for forty years. ² There was a certain man of Zorah, of the family of the Danite, whose name was Manoah; his wife was barren and had not given birth. ³ An angel of God appeared to the woman and said to her, "Behold now — you are barren and have not given birth, but you shall conceive and give birth to a son. ⁴ And now, be careful not to drink wine or aged wine, and not to eat anything contaminated. ⁵ For you shall conceive and give birth to a son; a razor shall not come upon his head, for the lad shall be a nazirite of God from the womb, * and he will begin to save Israel from the hand of the Philistines."

⁶ The woman came and told her husband, saying, "A man of God came to me, and his appearance was like the appearance of an angel of God — very awesome! I did not ask him where he was from and he did not tell me his name. ⁷ He said to me, 'Behold, you shall conceive and give birth to a son. And now, do not drink wine or aged wine, and do not eat anything contaminated, for the lad shall be a nazirite unto God from the womb until the day of his death.'"

Manoah's
prayer

⁸ Manoah prayed to Hashem and said, "Please, my Lord, may the man of God whom you sent come now again to us and teach us what we should do with the lad who is to be born."

The angel's
reappearance

⁹ God heeded the call of Manoah and the angel of God came again to the woman when she was sitting in the field, but Manoah her husband was not with her. ¹⁰ The woman hastened; she ran and told her husband; she said to him, "Behold, the man who came to me that day has appeared to me."

¹¹ Manoah arose and went after his wife. He came to the man and said to him, "Are you the man who spoke to the woman?"

He said, "I am."

¹² Manoah said, "Now, may your words come true! What should be the

---

about in earlier times by such great judges as Deborah and Gideon, but God did not wish to let the Philistines go completely unpunished. So He sent Samson, whom He endowed with superhuman strength, to carry out sporadic attacks against the Philistines. Moreover, he was to

do so as a lone "vigilante," so to speak, not as the leader of the people. As a symbol of his holiness, and the source of his strength, he was to be a nazirite from the womb, and even his very birth from a barren, infertile mother would be miraculous.

יג מִשְׁפַּט־הַנַּעַר וּמַעֲשֵׂהוּ: וַיֹּאמֶר מַלְאַךְ יהוה אֶל־מָנוֹחַ מִכֹּל אֲשֶׁר־אָמַרְתִּי
אֶל־הָאִשָּׁה תִּשָּׁמֵר: מִכֹּל אֲשֶׁר־יֵצֵא מִגֶּפֶן הַיַּיִן לֹא תֹאכַל וְיַיִן וְשֵׁכָר אַל־ יד
תֵּשְׁתְּ וְכָל־טֻמְאָה אַל־תֹּאכַל כֹּל אֲשֶׁר־צִוִּיתִיהָ תִּשְׁמֹר: וַיֹּאמֶר מָנוֹחַ טו
אֶל־מַלְאַךְ יהוה נַעְצְרָה־נָּא אוֹתָךְ וְנַעֲשֶׂה לְפָנֶיךָ גְּדִי עִזִּים: וַיֹּאמֶר טז
מַלְאַךְ יהוה אֶל־מָנוֹחַ אִם־תַּעְצְרֵנִי לֹא־אֹכַל בְּלַחְמֶךָ וְאִם־תַּעֲשֶׂה עֹלָה
לַיהוה תַּעֲלֶנָּה כִּי לֹא־יָדַע מָנוֹחַ כִּי־מַלְאַךְ יהוה הוּא: וַיֹּאמֶר מָנוֹחַ אֶל־ יז
מַלְאַךְ יהוה מִי שְׁמֶךָ כִּי־יָבֹא °דְבָרֶיךָ [°דְבָרְךָ ק] וְכִבַּדְנוּךָ: וַיֹּאמֶר לוֹ יח
מַלְאַךְ יהוה לָמָּה זֶּה תִּשְׁאַל לִשְׁמִי וְהוּא־פֶלִאי: וַיִּקַּח מָנוֹחַ אֶת־גְּדִי־ יט
הָעִזִּים וְאֶת־הַמִּנְחָה וַיַּעַל עַל־הַצּוּר לַיהוה וּמַפְלִא לַעֲשׂוֹת וּמָנוֹחַ
וְאִשְׁתּוֹ רֹאִים: וַיְהִי בַעֲלוֹת הַלַּהַב מֵעַל הַמִּזְבֵּחַ הַשָּׁמַיְמָה וַיַּעַל מַלְאַךְ־ כ
יהוה בְּלַהַב הַמִּזְבֵּחַ וּמָנוֹחַ וְאִשְׁתּוֹ רֹאִים וַיִּפְּלוּ עַל־פְּנֵיהֶם אָרְצָה: וְלֹא־ כא
יָסַף עוֹד מַלְאַךְ יהוה לְהֵרָאֹה אֶל־מָנוֹחַ וְאֶל־אִשְׁתּוֹ אָז יָדַע מָנוֹחַ כִּי־
מַלְאַךְ יהוה הוּא: וַיֹּאמֶר מָנוֹחַ אֶל־אִשְׁתּוֹ מוֹת נָמוּת כִּי אֱלֹהִים רָאִינוּ: כב
וַתֹּאמֶר לוֹ אִשְׁתּוֹ לוּ חָפֵץ יהוה לַהֲמִיתֵנוּ לֹא־לָקַח מִיָּדֵנוּ עֹלָה וּמִנְחָה כג
וְלֹא הֶרְאָנוּ אֶת־כָּל־אֵלֶּה וְכָעֵת לֹא הִשְׁמִיעָנוּ כָּזֹאת: וַתֵּלֶד הָאִשָּׁה בֵּן כד
וַתִּקְרָא אֶת־שְׁמוֹ שִׁמְשׁוֹן וַיִּגְדַּל הַנַּעַר וַיְבָרְכֵהוּ יהוה: וַתָּחֶל רוּחַ יהוה כה
לְפַעֲמוֹ בְּמַחֲנֵה־דָן בֵּין צָרְעָה וּבֵין אֶשְׁתָּאֹל: ◄   וַיֵּרֶד שִׁמְשׁוֹן   **יד** א
תִּמְנָתָה וַיַּרְא אִשָּׁה בְּתִמְנָתָה מִבְּנוֹת פְּלִשְׁתִּים: וַיַּעַל וַיַּגֵּד לְאָבִיו וּלְאִמּוֹ ב
וַיֹּאמֶר אִשָּׁה רָאִיתִי בְתִמְנָתָה מִבְּנוֹת פְּלִשְׁתִּים וְעַתָּה קְחוּ־אוֹתָהּ לִי
לְאִשָּׁה: וַיֹּאמֶר לוֹ אָבִיו וְאִמּוֹ הַאֵין בִּבְנוֹת אַחֶיךָ וּבְכָל־עַמִּי אִשָּׁה כִּי־ ג
אַתָּה הוֹלֵךְ לָקַחַת אִשָּׁה מִפְּלִשְׁתִּים הָעֲרֵלִים וַיֹּאמֶר שִׁמְשׁוֹן אֶל־אָבִיו
אוֹתָהּ קַח־לִי כִּי־הִיא יָשְׁרָה בְעֵינָי: וְאָבִיו וְאִמּוֹ לֹא יָדְעוּ כִּי מֵיהוה הִיא ד
כִּי־תֹאֲנָה הוּא־מְבַקֵּשׁ מִפְּלִשְׁתִּים וּבָעֵת הַהִיא פְּלִשְׁתִּים מֹשְׁלִים
בְּיִשְׂרָאֵל: וַיֵּרֶד שִׁמְשׁוֹן וְאָבִיו וְאִמּוֹ תִּמְנָתָה וַיָּבֹאוּ עַד־כַּרְמֵי תִמְנָתָה ה
וְהִנֵּה כְּפִיר אֲרָיוֹת שֹׁאֵג לִקְרָאתוֹ: וַתִּצְלַח עָלָיו רוּחַ יהוה וַיְשַׁסְּעֵהוּ ו
כְּשַׁסַּע הַגְּדִי וּמְאוּמָה אֵין בְּיָדוֹ וְלֹא הִגִּיד לְאָבִיו וּלְאִמּוֹ אֵת אֲשֶׁר עָשָׂה:
וַיֵּרֶד וַיְדַבֵּר לָאִשָּׁה וַתִּישַׁר בְּעֵינֵי שִׁמְשׁוֹן: וַיָּשָׁב מִיָּמִים לְקַחְתָּהּ וַיָּסַר ז-ח
לִרְאוֹת אֵת מַפֶּלֶת הָאַרְיֵה וְהִנֵּה עֲדַת דְּבוֹרִים בִּגְוִיַּת הָאַרְיֵה וּדְבָשׁ:
וַיִּרְדֵּהוּ אֶל־כַּפָּיו וַיֵּלֶךְ הָלוֹךְ וְאָכֹל וַיֵּלֶךְ אֶל־אָבִיו וְאֶל־אִמּוֹ וַיִּתֵּן לָהֶם ט

14:1. Samson's mode of operation was to find pretexts for the oppressors to wrong him, thus giving him plausible excuses to lash out against them.

In the beginning of his career as a savior, he entered into marriages with Philistine women purely for the sake of Heaven, so that he could manufacture justifications for his battles against the Philistines, and all his Philistine wives converted to Judaism before they were married. As time went on, however, his righteousness diminished, and

he began to be attracted by physical beauty, which ultimately led to his downfall (*Radak; Talmud, Sotah* 10a).

14:4. Only he knew of this mission; he did not even tell his parents.

14:6. As a nazirite who is forbidden wine, Samson would not even walk through a vineyard (see *Talmud, Pesachim* 40b). Thus, he was separated from his parents at this time (*Vilna Gaon*).

conduct of the lad and his behavior?"

¹³ The angel of God said to Manoah, "Of everything that I spoke to the woman, she should beware. ¹⁴ Of anything that comes from the grapevine, she shall not eat; wine or aged wine, she shall not drink; anything contaminated, she shall not eat. Everything that I commanded her, she shall observe."

Manoah's ¹⁵ Manoah said to the angel of HASHEM, "Please let us detain you, and we **offering** shall prepare a goat kid for you."

¹⁶ The angel of HASHEM said to Manoah, "If you detain me, I shall not eat of your food. If you wish to prepare an elevation-offering, offer it up to HASHEM" — for Manoah did not know that he was an angel of HASHEM.

¹⁷ Manoah said to the angel of HASHEM, "What is your name, so that when your word comes about, we may honor you?"

¹⁸ The angel of HASHEM said to him, "Why is it that you ask for my name ? It is hidden!"

¹⁹ Manoah took the goat kid and the meal-offering and brought [them] up on the rock to HASHEM — and [the angel] performed a miracle, as Manoah and his wife watched. ²⁰ It happened that as the flame rose up from atop the altar to the heavens, the angel of HASHEM went up in the flame of the altar. Manoah and his wife were watching and they fell upon their faces to the ground.

²¹ The angel of HASHEM no longer appeared to Manoah and his wife; then Manoah realized that he was an angel of HASHEM. ²² Manoah said to his wife, "We shall surely die, for we have seen a Godly angel!"

²³ His wife said to him, "Had HASHEM wanted to put us to death, He would not have accepted from our hand an elevation-offering and a meal-offering, nor would He have shown us all this, nor would He let us hear such [tidings] at this time."

Blessing ²⁴ The woman gave birth to a son, and she called his name Samson; the lad **fulfilled** grew and HASHEM blessed him. ²⁵ The spirit of HASHEM began to resound in him in the camp of Dan, between Zorah and Eshtaol.

14   ¹ Samson went down to Timnath, and in Timnath he saw a woman of the **The woman** daughters of the Philistines. * ² He went up and told his father and mother, **of Timnath** and said, "I have seen a woman in Timnath, of the daughters of the Philistines. Now, take her for me as a wife." ³ His father and mother said to him, "Is there no woman among the daughters of your brothers and in all my people that you go to take a wife from the uncircumcised Philistines?" But Samson said to his father, "Take her for me, for she is fitting in my eyes." ⁴ His father and mother did not know that it was from HASHEM, for he was seeking a pretext against the Philistines; * at that time the Philistines were ruling in Israel.

The lion ⁵ So Samson and his father and mother descended to Timnath. They reached **and the bees** the vineyards of Timnath, and behold — a young lion was roaring toward him! ⁶ The spirit of HASHEM came over him and he tore it apart as one tears apart a kid, though he had nothing in his hand. He did not tell his father and mother what he had done. *

⁷ He went down and spoke with the woman, and she was fitting in the eyes of Samson. ⁸ He returned after some time to marry her, but he turned aside to see the fallen carcass of the lion, and behold, a swarm of bees was in the body of the lion, with honey. ⁹ He scraped it into his hands and went, walking and eating; he went to his father and mother and gave them, and

י וַיֹּאכֵל וְלֹא־הִגִּיד לָהֶם כִּי מִגְוִיַּת הָאַרְיֵה רָדָה הַדְּבָשׁ: וַיֵּרֶד אָבִיהוּ

יא אֶל־הָאִשָּׁה וַיַּעַשׂ שָׁם שִׁמְשׁוֹן מִשְׁתֶּה כִּי כֵּן יַעֲשׂוּ הַבַּחוּרִים: וַיְהִי

יב כִּרְאוֹתָם אוֹתוֹ וַיִּקְחוּ שְׁלֹשִׁים מֵרֵעִים וַיִּהְיוּ אִתּוֹ: וַיֹּאמֶר לָהֶם שִׁמְשׁוֹן אָחוּדָה־נָּא לָכֶם חִידָה אִם־הַגֵּד תַּגִּידוּ אוֹתָהּ לִי שִׁבְעַת יְמֵי הַמִּשְׁתֶּה

יג וּמְצָאתֶם וְנָתַתִּי לָכֶם שְׁלֹשִׁים סְדִינִים וּשְׁלֹשִׁים חֲלִפֹת בְּגָדִים: וְאִם־לֹא תוּכְלוּ לְהַגִּיד לִי וּנְתַתֶּם אַתֶּם לִי שְׁלֹשִׁים סְדִינִים וּשְׁלֹשִׁים

יד חֲלִיפוֹת בְּגָדִים וַיֹּאמְרוּ לוֹ חוּדָה חִידָתְךָ וְנִשְׁמָעֶנָּה: וַיֹּאמֶר לָהֶם מֵהָאֹכֵל יָצָא מַאֲכָל וּמֵעַז יָצָא מָתוֹק וְלֹא יָכְלוּ לְהַגִּיד הַחִידָה שְׁלֹשֶׁת

טו יָמִים: וַיְהִי | בַּיּוֹם הַשְּׁבִיעִי וַיֹּאמְרוּ לְאֵשֶׁת־שִׁמְשׁוֹן פַּתִּי אֶת־אִישֵׁךְ וְיַגֶּד־לָנוּ אֶת־הַחִידָה פֶּן־נִשְׂרֹף אוֹתָךְ וְאֶת־בֵּית אָבִיךְ בָּאֵשׁ הַלְיָרְשֵׁנוּ

טז קְרָאתֶם לָנוּ הֲלֹא: וַתֵּבְךְּ אֵשֶׁת שִׁמְשׁוֹן עָלָיו וַתֹּאמֶר רַק־שְׂנֵאתַנִי וְלֹא אֲהַבְתָּנִי הַחִידָה חַדְתָּ לִבְנֵי עַמִּי וְלִי לֹא הִגַּדְתָּה וַיֹּאמֶר לָהּ הִנֵּה

יז לְאָבִי וּלְאִמִּי לֹא הִגַּדְתִּי וְלָךְ אַגִּיד: וַתֵּבְךְּ עָלָיו שִׁבְעַת הַיָּמִים אֲשֶׁר־הָיָה לָהֶם הַמִּשְׁתֶּה וַיְהִי | בַּיּוֹם הַשְּׁבִיעִי וַיַּגֶּד־לָהּ כִּי הֱצִיקַתְהוּ וַתַּגֵּד

יח הַחִידָה לִבְנֵי עַמָּהּ: וַיֹּאמְרוּ לוֹ אַנְשֵׁי הָעִיר בַּיּוֹם הַשְּׁבִיעִי בְּטֶרֶם יָבֹא הַחַרְסָה מַה־מָּתוֹק מִדְּבַשׁ וּמֶה עַז מֵאֲרִי וַיֹּאמֶר לָהֶם לוּלֵא חֲרַשְׁתֶּם

יט בְּעֶגְלָתִי לֹא מְצָאתֶם חִידָתִי: וַתִּצְלַח עָלָיו רוּחַ יְהוָה וַיֵּרֶד אַשְׁקְלוֹן וַיַּךְ מֵהֶם | שְׁלֹשִׁים אִישׁ וַיִּקַּח אֶת־חֲלִיצוֹתָם וַיִּתֵּן הַחֲלִיפוֹת לְמַגִּידֵי

כ הַחִידָה וַיִּחַר אַפּוֹ וַיַּעַל בֵּית אָבִיהוּ: וַתְּהִי אֵשֶׁת שִׁמְשׁוֹן לְמֵרֵעֵהוּ אֲשֶׁר רֵעָה לוֹ:

טו א וַיְהִי מִיָּמִים בִּימֵי קְצִיר־חִטִּים וַיִּפְקֹד שִׁמְשׁוֹן אֶת־אִשְׁתּוֹ בִּגְדִי עִזִּים וַיֹּאמֶר אָבֹאָה אֶל־אִשְׁתִּי הֶחָדְרָה

ב וְלֹא־נְתָנוֹ אָבִיהָ לָבוֹא: וַיֹּאמֶר אָבִיהָ אָמֹר אָמַרְתִּי כִּי־שָׂנֹא שְׂנֵאתָהּ וָאֶתְּנֶנָּה לְמֵרֵעֶךָ הֲלֹא אֲחֹתָהּ הַקְּטַנָּה טוֹבָה מִמֶּנָּה תְּהִי־נָא לְךָ

ג תַּחְתֶּיהָ: וַיֹּאמֶר לָהֶם שִׁמְשׁוֹן נִקֵּיתִי הַפַּעַם מִפְּלִשְׁתִּים כִּי־עֹשֶׂה אֲנִי

ד עִמָּם רָעָה: וַיֵּלֶךְ שִׁמְשׁוֹן וַיִּלְכֹּד שְׁלֹשׁ־מֵאוֹת שׁוּעָלִים וַיִּקַּח לַפִּדִים וַיֶּפֶן

ה זָנָב אֶל־זָנָב וַיָּשֶׂם לַפִּיד אֶחָד בֵּין־שְׁנֵי הַזְּנָבוֹת בַּתָּוֶךְ: וַיַּבְעֶר־אֵשׁ בַּלַּפִּידִים וַיְשַׁלַּח בְּקָמוֹת פְּלִשְׁתִּים וַיַּבְעֵר מִגָּדִישׁ וְעַד־קָמָה וְעַד־כֶּרֶם

ו זָיִת: וַיֹּאמְרוּ פְלִשְׁתִּים מִי עָשָׂה זֹאת וַיֹּאמְרוּ שִׁמְשׁוֹן חֲתַן הַתִּמְנִי כִּי לָקַח אֶת־אִשְׁתּוֹ וַיִּתְּנָהּ לְמֵרֵעֵהוּ וַיַּעֲלוּ פְלִשְׁתִּים וַיִּשְׂרְפוּ אוֹתָהּ

ז וְאֶת־אָבִיהָ בָּאֵשׁ: וַיֹּאמֶר לָהֶם שִׁמְשׁוֹן אִם־תַּעֲשׂוּן כָּזֹאת כִּי אִם־נִקַּמְתִּי

14:20. His wife's betrayal gave Samson an excuse to avenge himself. Then, the woman's father unwittingly set the stage for the next exploit by giving Samson's wife in marriage to another man.

15:3. His wife's marriage to one of his erstwhile "friends"

provided him with a perfect pretext for vengeance.

15:7. Had you intervened against her family's treachery when it happened, I would have respected you, but you did nothing until I avenged myself — therefore I shall not rest until I exact more punishment from you (*Radak*).

they ate, but he did not tell them that he had scraped it from the body of the lion.

Samson's first marriage ¹⁰ *His father went down to the woman and Samson made a feast there, for that was what the young men would do.* ¹¹ *It happened when [the woman and her father] saw him that they took thirty companions to be with him.* ¹² *Samson said to them, "Let me now pose you a riddle. If you tell me [its solution] during the seven days of feasting and you solve it, I will give you thirty sheets and thirty changes of clothing.* ¹³ *But if you cannot tell it to me, then you will give me thirty sheets and thirty changes of clothing."*

They said to him, "Pose your riddle and let us hear it."

¹⁴ *He said to them, "From the eater came forth food; and from the strong came forth sweetness." They could not tell [the solution of] the riddle for three days.*

¹⁵ *It was on the Sabbath day that they said to Samson's wife, "Entice your husband to tell [you] the riddle for us — lest we will burn you and your father's house with fire! Did you invite us here to impoverish us?"*

Samson's wife's treachery ¹⁶ *So Samson's wife wept near him and said, "You only hate me and do not love me! You posed the riddle to the sons of my people, but you did not tell me [the solution]."*

He said to her, "Behold, I did not even tell my father and mother; shall I tell you?"

¹⁷ *She wept near him for the [remainder of the] seven days that they had the feast. It happened on the seventh day that he told her, for she had distressed him. Then she told [the solution to the] riddle to the sons of her people.*

¹⁸ *So the men of the city said to [Samson] on the seventh day, before the sun had set, "What is sweeter than honey, and what is stronger than a lion?" He replied to them, "Had you not 'plowed with my calf,' you would not have solved my riddle!"*

¹⁹ *Then a spirit of HASHEM came over him, and he went down to Ashkelon and struck down thirty men of them; he took their garments and gave the changes [of clothing] to those who had told [the solution] of his riddle. His wrath flared, and he went up to his father's house.* ²⁰ *Meanwhile, Samson's wife was [given in marriage] to his companion,* * *whom he had befriended.*

15

Samson's pretext ¹ *It happened some time later, in the days of the wheat harvest, that Samson remembered his wife with a goat kid. He said, "I wish to come to my wife, to the chamber," but her father would not permit him to enter.*

² *Her father said, "I thought that you surely hate her, so I gave her over to your companion. Behold, her younger sister is better than she; let her be yours, instead of her."*

³ *Samson said to them, "This time I will be blameless from the Philistines,* * *when I do evil to them."*

Foxtails and torches ⁴ *Samson went and caught three hundred foxes; he took torches and turned [the foxes] tail to tail, and put one torch between each pair of tails, in the middle.* ⁵ *He set fire to the torches, and sent [the foxes] off to the grain fields of the Philistines; thus he burnt down [everything] from grain stacks to standing grain to olive groves.*

⁶ *The Philistines said, "Who did this?"*

And [others] answered, "Samson, the son-in-law of the Timnite, because he took his wife and gave her to his companion." The Philistines then went and burned her and her father in fire.

⁷ *Samson said to them, "If only you had done so [before]!* * *Now I will avenge*

ח בָּכֶם וְאַחַר אֶחְדָּל: וַיַּ֤ךְ אוֹתָם֙ שׁ֣וֹק עַל־יָרֵ֔ךְ מַכָּ֖ה גְדוֹלָ֑ה וַיֵּ֣רֶד וַיֵּ֔שֶׁב

ט בִּסְעִ֖יף סֶ֥לַע עֵיטָֽם: וַיַּעֲל֣וּ פְלִשְׁתִּ֔ים וַיַּחֲנ֖וּ בִּֽיהוּדָ֑ה

י וַיִּנָּטְשׁ֖וּ בַּלֶּֽחִי: וַיֹּֽאמְרוּ֙ אִ֣ישׁ יְהוּדָ֔ה לָמָ֖ה עֲלִיתֶ֣ם עָלֵ֑ינוּ וַיֹּֽאמְר֗וּ לֶאֱס֤וֹר

יא אֶת־שִׁמְשׁוֹן֙ עָלִ֔ינוּ לַעֲשׂ֣וֹת ל֔וֹ כַּאֲשֶׁ֖ר עָ֣שָׂה לָ֑נוּ וַיֵּרְד֡וּ שְׁלֹ֣שֶׁת אֲלָפִ֣ים

אִישׁ֩ מִֽיהוּדָ֨ה אֶל־סְעִ֜יף סֶ֣לַע עֵיטָ֗ם וַיֹּאמְר֣וּ לְשִׁמְשׁ֗וֹן הֲלֹ֤א יָדַ֙עְתָּ֙ כִּֽי־

מֹשְׁלִ֥ים בָּ֙נוּ֙ פְּלִשְׁתִּ֔ים וּמַה־זֹּ֖את עָשִׂ֣יתָ לָּ֑נוּ וַיֹּ֣אמֶר לָהֶ֗ם כַּאֲשֶׁר֙ עָ֣שׂוּ לִ֔י כֵּ֖ן

יב עָשִׂ֥יתִי לָהֶֽם: וַיֹּ֤אמְרוּ לוֹ֙ לֶֽאֱסָרְךָ֣ יָרַ֔דְנוּ לְתִתְּךָ֖ בְּיַד־פְּלִשְׁתִּ֑ים וַיֹּ֤אמֶר לָהֶם֙

יג שִׁמְשׁ֔וֹן הִשָּֽׁבְע֣וּ לִ֔י פֶּֽן־תִּפְגְּע֥וּן בִּ֖י אַתֶּֽם: וַיֹּ֨אמְרוּ ל֤וֹ לֵאמֹר֙ לֹ֔א כִּֽי־אָסֹ֤ר

נֶֽאֱסָרְךָ֙ וּנְתַנּ֣וּךָ בְיָדָ֔ם וְהָמֵ֖ת לֹ֣א נְמִיתֶ֑ךָ וַיַּאַסְרֻ֗הוּ בִּשְׁנַ֙יִם֙ עֲבֹתִ֣ים חֲדָשִׁ֔ים

יד וַיַּעֲל֖וּהוּ מִן־הַסָּֽלַע: הוּא־בָ֣א עַד־לֶ֔חִי וּפְלִשְׁתִּ֖ים הֵרִ֣יעוּ לִקְרָאת֑וֹ וַתִּצְלַ֨ח

עָלָ֜יו ר֣וּחַ יְהֹוָ֗ה וַתִּהְיֶ֤֙ינָה הָעֲבֹתִים֙ אֲשֶׁ֣ר עַל־זְרֽוֹעוֹתָ֔יו כַּפִּשְׁתִּ֖ים אֲשֶׁ֤ר

טו בָּעֲר֣וּ בָאֵ֔שׁ וַיִּמַּ֥סּוּ אֱסוּרָ֖יו מֵעַ֥ל יָדָֽיו: וַיִּמְצָ֥א לְחִֽי־חֲמ֖וֹר טְרִיָּ֑ה וַיִּשְׁלַ֤ח יָדוֹ֙

טז וַיִּקָּחֶ֔הָ וַיַּךְ־בָּ֖הּ אֶ֥לֶף אִֽישׁ: וַיֹּ֣אמֶר שִׁמְשׁ֔וֹן בִּלְחִ֣י הַחֲמ֔וֹר חֲמ֖וֹר חֲמֹרָתָ֑יִם

יז בִּלְחִ֣י הַחֲמ֔וֹר הִכֵּ֖יתִי אֶ֥לֶף אִֽישׁ: וַֽיְהִי֙ כְּכַלֹּת֣וֹ לְדַבֵּ֔ר וַיַּשְׁלֵ֥ךְ הַלְּחִ֖י מִיָּד֑וֹ

יח וַיִּקְרָ֛א לַמָּק֥וֹם הַה֖וּא רָ֥מַת לֶֽחִי: וַיִּצְמָ֣א מְאֹ֔ד וַיִּקְרָ֤א אֶל־יְהֹוָה֙ וַיֹּאמַ֔ר

אַתָּה֙ נָתַ֣תָּ בְיַֽד־עַבְדְּךָ֔ אֶת־הַתְּשׁוּעָ֥ה הַגְּדֹלָ֖ה הַזֹּ֑את וְעַתָּ֗ה אָמ֛וּת בַּצָּמָ֖א

יט וְנָפַלְתִּ֖י בְּיַ֥ד הָעֲרֵלִֽים: וַיִּבְקַ֨ע אֱלֹהִ֜ים אֶת־הַמַּכְתֵּ֣שׁ אֲשֶׁר־בַּלֶּ֗חִי וַיֵּצְא֤וּ

מִמֶּ֙נּוּ֙ מַ֔יִם וַיֵּ֖שְׁתְּ וַתָּ֣שׇׁב רוּח֖וֹ וַיֶּ֑חִי עַל־כֵּ֣ן ׀ קָרָ֣א שְׁמָ֗הּ עֵ֤ין הַקּוֹרֵא֙

כ אֲשֶׁ֣ר בַּלֶּ֔חִי עַ֖ד הַיּ֥וֹם הַזֶּֽה: וַיִּשְׁפֹּ֧ט אֶת־יִשְׂרָאֵ֛ל בִּימֵ֥י פְלִשְׁתִּ֖ים עֶשְׂרִ֥ים

טז א שָׁנָֽה: וַיֵּ֥לֶךְ שִׁמְשׁ֖וֹן עַזָּ֑תָה וַיַּרְא־שָׁם֙ אִשָּׁ֣ה זוֹנָ֔ה וַיָּבֹ֖א

ב אֵלֶֽיהָ: לַֽעַזָּתִ֣ים ׀ לֵאמֹ֗ר בָּ֤א שִׁמְשׁוֹן֙ הֵ֔נָּה וַיָּסֹ֛בּוּ וַיֶּאֶרְבוּ־ל֥וֹ כׇל־הַלַּ֖יְלָה

בְּשַׁ֣עַר הָעִ֑יר וַיִּֽתְחָרְשׁ֣וּ כׇל־הַלַּ֗יְלָה לֵאמֹ֛ר עַד־א֥וֹר הַבֹּ֖קֶר וַהֲרַגְנֻֽהוּ:

ג וַיִּשְׁכַּ֣ב שִׁמְשׁוֹן֮ עַד־חֲצִ֣י הַלַּ֒יְלָה֒ וַיָּ֣קׇם ׀ בַּחֲצִ֣י הַלַּ֗יְלָה וַיֶּאֱחֹ֞ז בְּדַלְת֣וֹת

שַֽׁעַר־הָ֠עִ֠יר וּבִשְׁתֵּ֨י הַמְּזוּז֜וֹת וַיִּסָּעֵ֣ם עִֽם־הַבְּרִ֗יחַ וַיָּ֤שֶׂם עַל־כְּתֵפָ֔יו

ד וַֽיַּעֲלֵם֙ אֶל־רֹ֣אשׁ הָהָ֔ר אֲשֶׁ֖ר עַל־פְּנֵ֥י חֶבְרֽוֹן: וַֽיְהִי֙

ה אַחֲרֵי־כֵ֔ן וַיֶּאֱהַ֣ב אִשָּׁ֔ה בְּנַ֖חַל שֹׂרֵ֑ק וּשְׁמָ֖הּ דְּלִילָֽה: וַיַּעֲל֨וּ אֵלֶ֜יהָ סַרְנֵ֣י

פְלִשְׁתִּ֗ים וַיֹּ֨אמְרוּ לָ֜הּ פַּתִּ֣י אוֹת֗וֹ וּרְאִי֙ בַּמֶּה֙ כֹּח֣וֹ גָד֔וֹל וּבַמֶּה֙ נ֣וּכַל ל֔וֹ

ו וַאֲסַרְנֻ֖הוּ לְעַנֹּת֑וֹ וַאֲנַ֗חְנוּ נִתַּן־לְךָ֗ אִ֛ישׁ אֶ֥לֶף וּמֵאָ֖ה כָּֽסֶף: וַתֹּ֤אמֶר דְּלִילָה֙

אֶל־שִׁמְשׁ֔וֹן הַגִּֽידָה־נָּ֣א לִ֔י בַּמֶּ֖ה כֹּחֲךָ֣ גָד֑וֹל וּבַמֶּ֥ה תֵאָסֵ֖ר לְעַנּוֹתֶֽךָ:

15:9. The place was given this name after the event described below.

15:11. By telling Samson that the Philistines were their rulers, they justified their decision to hand him over to the enemy. They implied that Samson had endangered the entire population by inciting the Philistines to take reprisals against helpless, innocent people.

15:16. I.e., heaps of slain Philistines. This is a play on words; חֲמוֹר is used for both "donkey" and "heap."

15:17. Alternatively, "Casting of the Jawbone."

15:19. The hollows from which the teeth grow (Rashi). Alternatively, the depression in a large rock in the place named Lehi (Radak).

15:20. Despite Samson's scattered victories over them, the Philistines maintained their control over the land.

16:1. To continue his provocations against the Philistines, Samson went to a public house in Gaza where his presence would quickly become known.

myself against you and afterwards I will stop." [8] *Then Samson struck them calf upon thigh a great blow. Then he descended and dwelt in the cleft of the Rock of Etam.*

[9] *The Philistines went up [for war], and they encamped in Judah, spreading out at Lehi [Jawbone].* * [10] *The men of Judah said, "Why have you come up against us?"*

They responded, "We have come up to arrest Samson, to do to him as he did to us!"

[11] *Three thousand men of Judah then went down to the cleft of the Rock of Etam, and they said to Samson, "Do you not know that the Philistines rule over us?* * *What is this [that] you have done to us?"*

But he answered them, "As they did to me, so I did to them!"

Judah arrests Samson [12] *They said to him, "We have come to arrest you, to hand you over into the hand of the Philistines."*

Samson said to them, "Swear to me that you yourselves will not harm me."

[13] *They said to him, "No, rather we will only arrest you and give you over into their hand; but we will surely not put you to death." So they bound him with two new ropes and brought him up from the rock.*

A donkey's jawbone; a thousand Philistines ... [14] *He came to Lehi and the Philistines shouted at him. A spirit of HASHEM came over him and the ropes that were on his arms became like flax that had been singed with fire; his bonds melted from upon his hands.* [15] *He found a fresh jawbone of a donkey, and stretched out his hand and took it. He struck down a thousand people with it.* [16] *Samson then said, "With the jawbone of a donkey, heap upon heaps;* * *with the jawbone of a donkey I have struck down a thousand men!"* [17] *When he finished speaking he cast the jawbone from his hand. That place was called Ramath-lehi [Jawbone Hill].* *

... and fresh water [18] *He became very thirsty. He called out to HASHEM and said, "You have granted this great salvation through the hand of Your servant, and now, shall I die of thirst and fall into the hand of the uncircumcised?"* [19] *So God split open the hollow that was in the jawbone,* * *and water came from it and he drank; his spirit returned to him and he was revived. Therefore that place is called En-hakkorei [Spring of the Caller], which is in Lehi — until this day.*

[20] *[Samson] judged Israel in the days of the Philistines* * *for twenty years.*

16 [1] **S**amson went to Gaza. He saw there a harlot and consorted with her. * [2] It was said to the Gazites, "Samson has come here!" So they went around and lay in wait for him all night at the city gate. They remained silent all night, thinking, "By the dawn light, we will kill him." [3] Samson slept until midnight. He arose at midnight and grasped the doors of the city gate and the two doorposts and tore them out, with the crossbar, and placed them on his shoulders. He brought them to the top of the mountain that faces Hebron.

The gates of Gaza

Delilah's first treachery [4] It happened after this that he loved a woman from the Sorek Brook; her name was Delilah. [5] The governors of the Philistines went up to her and said to her, "Entice him and find out by what [means] his strength is so great, and by what [means] we may overpower him, so that we may bind him, to afflict him. Each one of us will give you eleven hundred [pieces of] silver."

[6] So Delilah said to Samson, "Please tell me what makes your strength so great, and how you could be bound, to afflict you."

ז וַיֹּ֣אמֶר אֵלֶ֣יהָ שִׁמְשׁ֗וֹן אִם־יַאַסְרֻ֜נִי בְּשִׁבְעָ֨ה יְתָרִ֤ים לַחִים֙ אֲשֶׁ֣ר לֹא־חֹרָ֔בוּ

ח וְחָלִ֥יתִי וְהָיִ֖יתִי כְּאַחַ֥ד הָאָדָֽם: וַיַּעֲלוּ־לָ֞הּ סַרְנֵ֣י פְלִשְׁתִּ֗ים שִׁבְעָ֛ה יְתָרִ֥ים

ט לַחִ֖ים אֲשֶׁ֣ר לֹא־חֹרָ֑בוּ וַתַּאַסְרֵ֖הוּ בָּהֶֽם: וְהָאֹרֵ֗ב יֹשֵׁ֥ב לָהּ֙ בַּחֶ֔דֶר וַתֹּ֣אמֶר
   אֵלָ֔יו פְּלִשְׁתִּ֥ים עָלֶ֖יךָ שִׁמְשׁ֑וֹן וַיְנַתֵּק֙ אֶת־הַיְתָרִ֔ים כַּאֲשֶׁ֨ר יִנָּתֵ֤ק פְּתִֽיל־

י הַנְּעֹ֨רֶת֙ בַּהֲרִ֣יחוֹ אֵ֔שׁ וְלֹ֥א נוֹדַ֖ע כֹּחֽוֹ: וַתֹּ֤אמֶר דְּלִילָה֙ אֶל־שִׁמְשׁ֔וֹן הִנֵּה֙

יא הֵתַ֣לְתָּ בִּ֔י וַתְּדַבֵּ֥ר אֵלַ֖י כְּזָבִ֑ים עַתָּה֙ הַגִּֽידָה־נָּ֣א לִ֔י בַּמֶּ֖ה תֵּאָסֵֽר: וַיֹּ֣אמֶר
   אֵלֶ֔יהָ אִם־אָס֤וֹר יַאַסְר֨וּנִי֙ בַּעֲבֹתִ֣ים חֲדָשִׁ֔ים אֲשֶׁ֥ר לֹֽא־נַעֲשָׂ֖ה בָהֶ֖ם

יב מְלָאכָ֑ה וְחָלִ֥יתִי וְהָיִ֖יתִי כְּאַחַ֥ד הָאָדָֽם: וַתִּקַּ֣ח דְּלִילָ֡ה עֲבֹתִים֩ חֲדָשִׁ֨ים
   וַתַּאַסְרֵ֜הוּ בָהֶ֗ם וַתֹּ֤אמֶר אֵלָיו֙ פְּלִשְׁתִּ֤ים עָלֶ֨יךָ֙ שִׁמְשׁ֔וֹן וְהָאֹרֵ֖ב יֹשֵׁ֣ב בֶּחָ֑דֶר

יג וַֽיְנַתְּקֵ֛ם מֵעַ֥ל זְרֹעֹתָ֖יו כַּחֽוּט: וַתֹּ֨אמֶר דְּלִילָ֜ה אֶל־שִׁמְשׁ֗וֹן עַד־הֵ֜נָּה הֵתַ֤לְתָּ
   בִּי֙ וַתְּדַבֵּ֤ר אֵלַי֙ כְּזָבִ֔ים הַגִּ֣ידָה לִּ֔י בַּמֶּ֖ה תֵּאָסֵ֑ר וַיֹּ֣אמֶר אֵלֶ֔יהָ אִם־תַּאַרְגִ֗י
   אֶת־שֶׁ֨בַע מַחְלְפ֥וֹת רֹאשִׁ֖י עִם־הַמַּסָּֽכֶת: וַתִּתְקַ֣ע בַּיָּתֵ֔ד וַתֹּ֣אמֶר אֵלָ֔יו

יד פְּלִשְׁתִּ֥ים עָלֶ֖יךָ שִׁמְשׁ֑וֹן וַיִּיקַץ֙ מִשְּׁנָת֔וֹ וַיִּסַּ֛ע אֶת־הַיְתַ֥ד הָאֶ֖רֶג וְאֶת־

טו הַמַּסָּֽכֶת: וַתֹּ֣אמֶר אֵלָ֗יו אֵ֚יךְ תֹּאמַ֣ר אֲהַבְתִּ֔יךְ וְלִבְּךָ֖ אֵ֣ין אִתִּ֑י זֶ֣ה שָׁלֹ֤שׁ
   פְּעָמִים֙ הֵתַ֣לְתָּ בִּ֔י וְלֹא־הִגַּ֣דְתָּ לִּ֔י בַּמֶּ֖ה כֹּחֲךָ֥ גָדֽוֹל: ‏°וַיְהִ֡י כִּֽי־הֵצִ֣יקָה לּ֩וֹ

טז בִדְבָרֶ֨יהָ כָּל־הַיָּמִ֤ים וַתְּאַֽלֲצֵ֔הוּ וַתִּקְצַ֥ר נַפְשׁ֖וֹ לָמֽוּת: וַיַּגֶּד־לָ֣הּ אֶת־כָּל־

יז לִבּ֗וֹ וַיֹּ֤אמֶר לָהּ֙ מוֹרָה֙ לֹא־עָלָ֣ה עַל־רֹאשִׁ֔י כִּֽי־נְזִ֧יר אֱלֹהִ֛ים אֲנִ֖י מִבֶּ֣טֶן
   אִמִּ֑י אִם־גֻּלַּ֨חְתִּי֙ וְסָ֣ר מִמֶּ֣נִּי כֹחִ֔י וְחָלִ֥יתִי וְהָיִ֖יתִי כְּכָל־הָאָדָֽם: וַתֵּ֣רֶא

יח דְלִילָ֗ה כִּֽי־הִגִּ֣יד לָהּ֮ אֶת־כָּל־לִבּוֹ֒ וַתִּשְׁלַ֡ח וַתִּקְרָא֩ לְסַרְנֵ֨י פְלִשְׁתִּ֜ים
   לֵאמֹ֗ר עֲל֣וּ הַפַּ֘עַם֮ כִּֽי־הִגִּ֣יד °לָ֣הּ [לִ֣י ק] אֶת־כָּל־לִבּ֑וֹ וְעָל֤וּ אֵלֶ֨יהָ֙ סַרְנֵ֣י

יט פְלִשְׁתִּ֔ים וַיַּעֲל֥וּ הַכֶּ֖סֶף בְּיָדָֽם: וַתְּיַשְּׁנֵ֨הוּ֙ עַל־בִּרְכֶּ֔יהָ וַתִּקְרָ֣א לָאִ֔ישׁ וַתְּגַלַּ֕ח
   אֶת־שֶׁ֖בַע מַחְלְפ֣וֹת רֹאשׁ֑וֹ וַתָּ֣חֶל לְעַנּוֹת֔וֹ וַיָּ֥סַר כֹּח֖וֹ מֵעָלָֽיו: וַתֹּ֕אמֶר

כ פְּלִשְׁתִּ֥ים עָלֶ֖יךָ שִׁמְשׁ֑וֹן וַיִּקַ֣ץ מִשְּׁנָת֗וֹ וַיֹּ֨אמֶר֙ אֵצֵ֞א כְּפַ֤עַם בְּפַ֨עַם֙ וְאִנָּעֵ֔ר
   וְה֣וּא לֹ֣א יָדַ֔ע כִּ֥י יְהוָ֖ה סָ֥ר מֵעָלָֽיו: וַיֹּאחֲז֣וּהוּ פְלִשְׁתִּ֗ים וַֽיְנַקְּרוּ֙ אֶת־עֵינָ֔יו

כא וַיּוֹרִ֨ידוּ אוֹת֜וֹ עַזָּ֗תָה וַיַּאַסְר֨וּהוּ֙ בַּֽנְחֻשְׁתַּ֔יִם וַיְהִ֥י טוֹחֵ֖ן בְּבֵ֥ית °הָאֲסִירִֽים
   [הָאֲסוּרִֽים ק]: וַיָּ֤חֶל שְׂעַר־רֹאשׁוֹ֙ לְצַמֵּ֔חַ כַּאֲשֶׁ֖ר גֻּלָּֽח:

כב-כג וְסַרְנֵ֣י
   פְלִשְׁתִּ֗ים נֶֽאֶסְפוּ֙ לִזְבֹּ֧חַ זֶֽבַח־גָּד֛וֹל לְדָג֥וֹן אֱלֹהֵיהֶ֖ם וּלְשִׂמְחָ֑ה וַיֹּ֣אמְר֔וּ נָתַ֤ן

כד אֱלֹהֵ֨ינוּ֙ בְּיָדֵ֔נוּ אֵ֖ת שִׁמְשׁ֥וֹן אוֹיְבֵֽנוּ: וַיִּרְא֤וּ אֹתוֹ֙ הָעָ֔ם וַֽיְהַלְל֖וּ אֶת־אֱלֹהֵיהֶ֑ם
   כִּ֣י אָמְר֗וּ נָתַ֨ן אֱלֹהֵ֤ינוּ בְיָדֵ֨נוּ֙ אֶת־אֽוֹיְבֵ֔נוּ וְאֵת֙ מַחֲרִ֣יב אַרְצֵ֔נוּ וַאֲשֶׁ֥ר

כה הִרְבָּ֖ה אֶת־חֲלָלֵֽינוּ: וַֽיְהִי֙ °כִּ֣י טֹ֣וב [כְּט֣וֹב ק] לִבָּ֔ם וַיֹּ֣אמְר֔וּ קִרְא֥וּ
   לְשִׁמְשׁ֖וֹן וִֽישַֽׂחֶק־לָ֑נוּ וַיִּקְרְא֨וּ לְשִׁמְשׁ֜וֹן מִבֵּ֣ית °הָאֲסִירִ֗ים [הָאֲסוּרִ֗ים ק]

16:19. It was not simply hair that gave Samson his great strength. Rather, it was his obedience to the command that he be a nazirite. When he permitted that status to be desecrated by revealing his secret to please his wife — who had his hair shorn — he lost his strength. Later, when he repented [and resumed his nazirite observance (*Kli Yakar*)], his strength returned (*Abarbanel*).

16:21. Because Samson allowed his eyes to entice him (14:3), he suffered the loss of his eyes (*Talmud, Sotah* 10a).

⁷ Samson told her, "If they bind me with seven wet twines that have never been dried, I would become weak and be like any other man."

⁸ The governors of the Philistines then brought her seven wet twines that had never been dried, and she bound him with them; ⁹ and there was an ambush party sitting for her in the room. She said to him, "Philistines are upon you, Samson!" and he snapped the twines as flax straw snaps when it smells fire; and his [full] strength was not even apparent.

Delilah's second treachery
¹⁰ Delilah said to Samson, "Behold, you have mocked me and told me lies! Now tell me how you can be bound."

¹¹ He said to her, 'If they bind me up with new ropes with which work was never done, then I would become weak and be like any other man."

¹² So Delilah took new ropes and bound him with them and said to him, "Philistines are upon you, Samson!" and the ambush party was sitting in the room. [Samson] snapped them off his arms like a thread.

Delilah's third treachery
¹³ Then Delilah said to Samson, "Up to now you have mocked me and told me lies! Tell me how you can be bound!"

He told her, "If you weave the seven locks of my head onto a weaving rod." ¹⁴ She fastened [it] with the peg of the loom.

She said to him, "Philistines are upon you, Samson!" He awoke from his sleep and tore out the peg of the loom and the weaving rod.

¹⁵ She said to him, "How can you say, 'I love you,' when your heart is not with me? This makes three times that you have mocked me and not told me what makes your strength so great!"

Delilah finally succeeds
¹⁶ It happened that after she tormented him with her words every day and pressed him, he became exasperated to death. ¹⁷ So he told her all [that was in] his heart and said to her, "A razor has never gone up upon my head, for I am a nazirite unto God from my mother's womb. If I would be shaven, my strength would leave me; I would become weak and be like any [other] man."

¹⁸ Delilah saw that he had told her all [that was in] his heart, so she sent and summoned all the governors of the Philistines, saying, "Come up this time, for he has told me all [that was in] his heart." So the governors of the Philistines came up and brought up the money in their hands. ¹⁹ She lulled him to sleep on

Samson's downfall
her knees, and she called over the man and had him shave off the seven locks of his head, thus beginning to afflict him, and his strength departed from him. *

²⁰ She said, "Philistines are upon you, Samson!"

He awoke from his sleep and said [to himself], "I will go out [to fight] like every other time, and arouse myself!" But he did not know that HASHEM had departed from him.

²¹ The Philistines seized him and gouged out his eyes. * They brought him down to Gaza and bound him in copper fetters; he was made to grind [grain] in prison. ²² The hair of his head began to sprout after he had been shaven.

The Philistines celebrate . . .
²³ The governors of the Philistines gathered to make a great sacrifice unto their god Dagon, and for a celebration. They said, "Our god has delivered Samson our enemy into our hand!" ²⁴ The people saw him and praised their god, for they said, "Our god has delivered into our hand our enemy and the destroyer of our land, the one who increased the numbers of our slain."

²⁵ It happened when their heart became merry that they said, "Summon Samson and let him entertain us!" They summoned Samson from the prison

כו וַיִּצְחַק לִפְנֵיהֶם וַיַּעֲמִידוּ אוֹתוֹ בֵּין הָעַמּוּדִים: וַיֹּאמֶר שִׁמְשׁוֹן אֶל־הַנַּעַר
הַמַּחֲזִיק בְּיָדוֹ הַנִּיחָה אוֹתִי °והימשני [°וַהֲמִישֵׁנִי ק] אֶת־הָעַמֻּדִים אֲשֶׁר
כז הַבַּיִת נָכוֹן עֲלֵיהֶם וְאֶשָּׁעֵן עֲלֵיהֶם: וְהַבַּיִת מָלֵא הָאֲנָשִׁים וְהַנָּשִׁים וְשָׁמָּה
כֹּל סַרְנֵי פְלִשְׁתִּים וְעַל־הַגָּג כִּשְׁלֹשֶׁת אֲלָפִים אִישׁ וְאִשָּׁה הָרֹאִים בִּשְׂחוֹק
כח שִׁמְשׁוֹן: וַיִּקְרָא שִׁמְשׁוֹן אֶל־יְהֹוָה וַיֹּאמַר אֲדֹנָי יֱהֹוִה זָכְרֵנִי נָא וְחַזְּקֵנִי נָא
אַךְ הַפַּעַם הַזֶּה הָאֱלֹהִים וְאִנָּקְמָה נְקַם־אַחַת מִשְּׁתֵי עֵינַי מִפְּלִשְׁתִּים:
כט וַיִּלְפֹּת שִׁמְשׁוֹן אֶת־שְׁנֵי ׀ עַמּוּדֵי הַתָּוֶךְ אֲשֶׁר הַבַּיִת נָכוֹן עֲלֵיהֶם וַיִּסָּמֵךְ
ל עֲלֵיהֶם אֶחָד בִּימִינוֹ וְאֶחָד בִּשְׂמֹאלוֹ: וַיֹּאמֶר שִׁמְשׁוֹן תָּמוֹת נַפְשִׁי עִם־
פְּלִשְׁתִּים וַיֵּט בְּכֹחַ וַיִּפֹּל הַבַּיִת עַל־הַסְּרָנִים וְעַל־כָּל־הָעָם אֲשֶׁר־בּוֹ וַיִּהְיוּ
לא הַמֵּתִים אֲשֶׁר הֵמִית בְּמוֹתוֹ רַבִּים מֵאֲשֶׁר הֵמִית בְּחַיָּיו: וַיֵּרְדוּ אֶחָיו וְכָל־
בֵּית אָבִיהוּ וַיִּשְׂאוּ אֹתוֹ וַיַּעֲלוּ ׀ וַיִּקְבְּרוּ אוֹתוֹ בֵּין צָרְעָה וּבֵין אֶשְׁתָּאֹל
בְּקֶבֶר מָנוֹחַ אָבִיו וְהוּא שָׁפַט אֶת־יִשְׂרָאֵל עֶשְׂרִים שָׁנָה: וַיְהִי־

יז א

ב אִישׁ מֵהַר־אֶפְרָיִם וּשְׁמוֹ מִיכָיְהוּ: וַיֹּאמֶר לְאִמּוֹ אֶלֶף וּמֵאָה הַכֶּסֶף אֲשֶׁר
לֻקַּח־לָךְ °ואתי [°וְאַתְּ ק] אָלִית וְגַם אָמַרְתְּ בְּאָזְנַי הִנֵּה־הַכֶּסֶף אִתִּי אֲנִי
ג לְקַחְתִּיו וַתֹּאמֶר אִמּוֹ בָּרוּךְ בְּנִי לַיהֹוָה: וַיָּשֶׁב אֶת־אֶלֶף־וּמֵאָה הַכֶּסֶף
לְאִמּוֹ וַתֹּאמֶר אִמּוֹ הַקְדֵּשׁ הִקְדַּשְׁתִּי אֶת־הַכֶּסֶף לַיהֹוָה מִיָּדִי לִבְנִי לַעֲשׂוֹת
ד פֶּסֶל וּמַסֵּכָה וְעַתָּה אֲשִׁיבֶנּוּ לָךְ: וַיָּשֶׁב אֶת־הַכֶּסֶף לְאִמּוֹ וַתִּקַּח אִמּוֹ
מָאתַיִם כֶּסֶף וַתִּתְּנֵהוּ לַצּוֹרֵף וַיַּעֲשֵׂהוּ פֶּסֶל וּמַסֵּכָה וַיְהִי בְּבֵית מִיכָיְהוּ:
ה וְהָאִישׁ מִיכָה לוֹ בֵּית אֱלֹהִים וַיַּעַשׂ אֵפוֹד וּתְרָפִים וַיְמַלֵּא אֶת־יַד אַחַד
ו מִבָּנָיו וַיְהִי־לוֹ לְכֹהֵן: בַּיָּמִים הָהֵם אֵין מֶלֶךְ בְּיִשְׂרָאֵל אִישׁ הַיָּשָׁר בְּעֵינָיו
ז יַעֲשֶׂה: וַיְהִי־נַעַר מִבֵּית לֶחֶם יְהוּדָה מִמִּשְׁפַּחַת יְהוּדָה
ח וְהוּא לֵוִי וְהוּא גָר־שָׁם: וַיֵּלֶךְ הָאִישׁ מֵהָעִיר מִבֵּית לֶחֶם יְהוּדָה
לָגוּר בַּאֲשֶׁר יִמְצָא וַיָּבֹא הַר־אֶפְרַיִם עַד־בֵּית מִיכָה לַעֲשׂוֹת דַּרְכּוֹ:
ט וַיֹּאמֶר־לוֹ מִיכָה מֵאַיִן תָּבוֹא וַיֹּאמֶר אֵלָיו לֵוִי אָנֹכִי מִבֵּית לֶחֶם יְהוּדָה
י וְאָנֹכִי הֹלֵךְ לָגוּר בַּאֲשֶׁר אֶמְצָא: וַיֹּאמֶר לוֹ מִיכָה שְׁבָה עִמָּדִי
וֶהְיֵה־לִי לְאָב וּלְכֹהֵן וְאָנֹכִי אֶתֶּן־לְךָ עֲשֶׂרֶת כֶּסֶף לַיָּמִים וְעֵרֶךְ בְּגָדִים
יא וּמִחְיָתֶךָ וַיֵּלֶךְ הַלֵּוִי: וַיּוֹאֶל הַלֵּוִי לָשֶׁבֶת אֶת־הָאִישׁ וַיְהִי הַנַּעַר לוֹ כְּאַחַד
יב מִבָּנָיו: וַיְמַלֵּא מִיכָה אֶת־יַד הַלֵּוִי וַיְהִי־לוֹ הַנַּעַר לְכֹהֵן וַיְהִי בְּבֵית מִיכָה:
יג וַיֹּאמֶר מִיכָה עַתָּה יָדַעְתִּי כִּי־יֵיטִיב יְהֹוָה לִי כִּי הָיָה־לִי הַלֵּוִי לְכֹהֵן:

17:1. From here to the end of *Judges*, the events described are not in their chronological place, for they occurred at the very beginning of the period of the Judges, soon after Joshua's death (*Rashi*, from *Seder Olam*).

17:3. Her original intention was to makes images that would serve either as intermediaries between her and God or as mediums with which to foretell the future (*Ralbag*).

17:4. Micajehu did not wish to make the images, so his

mother paid two hundred silver pieces to the smith, and had the remaining silver melted down and fashioned into the images (*Radak*).

17:5. Micajehu and Micah are the same person.

17:6. The lack of a king, an authority to prevent such a sacrilege, was at the root of this tragedy. Because the same was true of the shocking incidents recorded in the succeeding chapters, this verse is repeated several times.

17:7. The lad was a Levite who lived in Beth-lehem, in

and he sported before them. They stood him between the pillars.

²⁶ Samson said to the boy who was holding his hand, "Let go of me and let me touch the pillars that the building rests upon, so that I may lean on them." ²⁷ Now the building was full of men and women, and all the governors of the Philistines were there; and on the roof [there were] about three thousand men and women watching Samson's sport.

. . . and pay a heavy price

²⁸ Samson called out to HASHEM and said, "My Lord, HASHEM/ELOHIM! Remember me and strengthen me just this one time, O God, and I will exact vengeance from the Philistines for one of my two eyes." ²⁹ Samson grasped the two central pillars upon which the building rested, and he leaned on them; one with his right hand and one with his left hand. ³⁰ Samson said, "Let my soul die with the Philistines!" He leaned with force, and the building collapsed on the governors and on all the people inside it. The dead whom he killed at his own death were more than he had killed in his lifetime.

³¹ His brothers and all his father's household came and carried him away; they brought him up and buried him between Zoreah and Eshtaol, in the burial plot of Manoah, his father. He had judged Israel for twenty years.

17

MICAH'S [MICAJEHU'S] MOLTEN IMAGE 17:1-18:31

¹ There was a man from Mount Ephraim whose name was Micajehu. * ² He said to his mother, "The eleven hundred [pieces of] silver that were taken from you, and you cursed [whoever stole it] and even said [the curse] in my ears — behold, the money is with me! I took it!"

His mother said, "Blessed be my son to HASHEM!" ³ He returned the eleven hundred [pieces of] silver to his mother, but his mother said, "I had resolved to consecrate the money for HASHEM from my hand to my son to make a carved image and a molten image, * so now I will give it back to you."

⁴ He [again] returned the money to his mother, so his mother took two hundred [pieces of] silver and gave it to the silversmith, and he made it into a carved image and a molten image, * and it remained in Micajehu's house. ⁵ The man Micah* had a house of idolatry; he made an ephod and icons, and he installed one of his sons to be his priest. ⁶ (In those days there was no king in Israel; a man would do whatever seemed proper in his eyes. *)

Micah's Levite priest

⁷ There was a lad from Beth-lehem of Judah, of the family of Judah; he was a Levite, but he lived there. * ⁸ The man went from the city, from Beth-lehem of Judah, to sojourn where he would find [it suitable]. He came to Mount Ephraim, up to the house of Micah, to make his way.

⁹ Micah said to him, "From where do you come?"

He said to him, "I am a Levite from Beth-lehem of Judah, and I am traveling to sojourn where I will find [it suitable]."

¹⁰ Micah said to him, "Stay with me, and be a father and a priest for me. I will give you ten [pieces of] silver a year, a set of clothes and your livelihood." So the Levite went [in]. ¹¹ The Levite desired to settle with the man, and the lad became to him like one of his own sons. ¹² Micah installed the Levite, and the lad became his priest, and remained in Micah's house. ¹³ Micah thought, "Now I know that HASHEM will be good to me, for this Levite has become my priest."*

---

the territory of Judah (*Radak*).

17:13. Micah knew it had not been proper for his son,

who was not a Levite, to be a priest. Now that he had a "qualified" priest, he felt assured of success.

יח א בַּיָּמִים הָהֵם אֵין מֶלֶךְ בְּיִשְׂרָאֵל וּבַיָּמִים הָהֵם שֵׁבֶט הַדָּנִי מְבַקֶּשׁ־לוֹ
נַחֲלָה לָשֶׁבֶת כִּי לֹא־נָפְלָה לּוֹ עַד־הַיּוֹם הַהוּא בְּתוֹךְ שִׁבְטֵי־יִשְׂרָאֵל
ב בְּנַחֲלָה: וַיִּשְׁלְחוּ בְנֵי־דָן מִמִּשְׁפַּחְתָּם חֲמִשָּׁה
אֲנָשִׁים מִקְצוֹתָם אֲנָשִׁים בְּנֵי־חַיִל מִצָּרְעָה וּמֵאֶשְׁתָּאֹל לְרַגֵּל אֶת־הָאָרֶץ
וּלְחָקְרָהּ וַיֹּאמְרוּ אֲלֵהֶם לְכוּ חִקְרוּ אֶת־הָאָרֶץ וַיָּבֹאוּ הַר־אֶפְרַיִם עַד־
ג בֵּית מִיכָה וַיָּלִינוּ שָׁם: הֵמָּה עִם־בֵּית מִיכָה וְהֵמָּה הִכִּירוּ אֶת־קוֹל הַנַּעַר
הַלֵּוִי וַיָּסוּרוּ שָׁם וַיֹּאמְרוּ לוֹ מִי־הֱבִיאֲךָ הֲלֹם וּמָה־אַתָּה עֹשֶׂה בָּזֶה וּמַה־
ד לְּךָ פֹה: וַיֹּאמֶר אֲלֵהֶם כָּזֹה וְכָזֶה עָשָׂה לִי מִיכָה וַיִּשְׂכְּרֵנִי וָאֱהִי־לוֹ לְכֹהֵן:
ה וַיֹּאמְרוּ לוֹ שְׁאַל־נָא בֵאלֹהִים וְנֵדְעָה הֲתַצְלִיחַ דַּרְכֵּנוּ אֲשֶׁר אֲנַחְנוּ
ו הֹלְכִים עָלֶיהָ: וַיֹּאמֶר לָהֶם הַכֹּהֵן לְכוּ לְשָׁלוֹם נֹכַח יְהוָה דַּרְכְּכֶם אֲשֶׁר
ז תֵּלְכוּ־בָהּ:   וַיֵּלְכוּ חֲמֵשֶׁת הָאֲנָשִׁים וַיָּבֹאוּ לַיְשָׁה
וַיִּרְאוּ אֶת־הָעָם אֲשֶׁר־בְּקִרְבָּהּ יוֹשֶׁבֶת־לָבֶטַח כְּמִשְׁפַּט צִדֹנִים שֹׁקֵט ׀
וּבֹטֵחַ וְאֵין־מַכְלִים דָּבָר בָּאָרֶץ יוֹרֵשׁ עֶצֶר וּרְחֹקִים הֵמָּה מִצִּדֹנִים
ח וְדָבָר אֵין־לָהֶם עִם־אָדָם: וַיָּבֹאוּ אֶל־אֲחֵיהֶם צָרְעָה וְאֶשְׁתָּאֹל וַיֹּאמְרוּ
ט לָהֶם אֲחֵיהֶם מָה אַתֶּם: וַיֹּאמְרוּ קוּמָה וְנַעֲלֶה עֲלֵיהֶם כִּי רָאִינוּ אֶת־
הָאָרֶץ וְהִנֵּה טוֹבָה מְאֹד וְאַתֶּם מַחְשִׁים אַל־תֵּעָצְלוּ לָלֶכֶת לָבֹא לָרֶשֶׁת
י אֶת־הָאָרֶץ: כְּבֹאֲכֶם תָּבֹאוּ ׀ אֶל־עַם בֹּטֵחַ וְהָאָרֶץ רַחֲבַת יָדַיִם כִּי־נְתָנָהּ
אֱלֹהִים בְּיֶדְכֶם מָקוֹם אֲשֶׁר אֵין־שָׁם מַחְסוֹר כָּל־דָּבָר אֲשֶׁר בָּאָרֶץ:
יא וַיִּסְעוּ מִשָּׁם מִמִּשְׁפַּחַת הַדָּנִי מִצָּרְעָה וּמֵאֶשְׁתָּאֹל שֵׁשׁ־מֵאוֹת אִישׁ
יב חָגוּר כְּלֵי מִלְחָמָה: וַיַּעֲלוּ וַיַּחֲנוּ בְּקִרְיַת יְעָרִים בִּיהוּדָה עַל־כֵּן קָרְאוּ
לַמָּקוֹם הַהוּא מַחֲנֵה־דָן עַד הַיּוֹם הַזֶּה הִנֵּה אַחֲרֵי קִרְיַת יְעָרִים: וַיַּעַבְרוּ
יג מִשָּׁם הַר־אֶפְרָיִם וַיָּבֹאוּ עַד־בֵּית מִיכָה: וַיַּעֲנוּ חֲמֵשֶׁת הָאֲנָשִׁים הַהֹלְכִים
יד לְרַגֵּל אֶת־הָאָרֶץ לַיִשׁ וַיֹּאמְרוּ אֶל־אֲחֵיהֶם הַיְדַעְתֶּם כִּי יֵשׁ בַּבָּתִּים
טו הָאֵלֶּה אֵפוֹד וּתְרָפִים וּפֶסֶל וּמַסֵּכָה וְעַתָּה דְּעוּ מַה־תַּעֲשׂוּ: וַיָּסוּרוּ
טז שָׁמָּה וַיָּבֹאוּ אֶל־בֵּית־הַנַּעַר הַלֵּוִי בֵּית מִיכָה וַיִּשְׁאֲלוּ־לוֹ לְשָׁלוֹם: וְשֵׁשׁ־
מֵאוֹת אִישׁ חֲגוּרִים כְּלֵי מִלְחַמְתָּם נִצָּבִים פֶּתַח הַשָּׁעַר אֲשֶׁר מִבְּנֵי־
יז דָן: וַיַּעֲלוּ חֲמֵשֶׁת הָאֲנָשִׁים הַהֹלְכִים לְרַגֵּל אֶת־הָאָרֶץ בָּאוּ שָׁמָּה
לָקְחוּ אֶת־הַפֶּסֶל וְאֶת־הָאֵפוֹד וְאֶת־הַתְּרָפִים וְאֶת־הַמַּסֵּכָה וְהַכֹּהֵן
יח נִצָּב פֶּתַח הַשַּׁעַר וְשֵׁשׁ־מֵאוֹת הָאִישׁ הֶחָגוּר כְּלֵי הַמִּלְחָמָה: וְאֵלֶּה
בָּאוּ בֵּית מִיכָה וַיִּקְחוּ אֶת־פֶּסֶל הָאֵפוֹד וְאֶת־הַתְּרָפִים וְאֶת־הַמַּסֵּכָה
יט וַיֹּאמֶר אֲלֵיהֶם הַכֹּהֵן מָה אַתֶּם עֹשִׂים: וַיֹּאמְרוּ לוֹ הַחֲרֵשׁ שִׂים־יָדְךָ
עַל־פִּיךָ וְלֵךְ עִמָּנוּ וֶהְיֵה־לָנוּ לְאָב וּלְכֹהֵן הֲטוֹב ׀ הֱיוֹתְךָ כֹהֵן לְבֵית

18:1. See Joshua 19:47.
18:7. The people of Laish had no enemies, no conflicts and no dynasty to fight to retake the city if it fell.

Furthermore, they were too isolated to summon help and had no allies to defend them. Consequently they were ripe for conquest.

18

The Danite spies

¹ In those days there was no king in Israel. In those days the tribe of the Danite was seeking a heritage in which to dwell * for an [adequate] heritage had not yet fallen to them up to that day among the tribes of Israel. ² The children of Dan sent five men from their families — from among their leaders — men of valor from Zorah and from Eshtaol, to spy out the land and to investigate it. They said to them, "Go, investigate the land."

They arrived at Mount Ephraim, to the house of Micah, and spent the night there. ³ When they were in Micah's house they recognized the voice of the Levite lad. They turned there and said to him, "Who brought you here? What are you doing here? What do you have here?"

⁴ He answered them, "Micah did such and such for me; he hired me and I became a priest for him."

⁵ They said to him, "Inquire please of God, so that we may know if our journey upon which we go will be successful."

⁶ The priest said to them, "Go in peace; the journey on which you go is in accord with Hashem."

⁷ So the five men went, and they arrived at Laish. They saw that the people who were in it were living securely, after the manner of the Sidonians, complacent and secure. No issue in the land could cause them embarrassment and there was no heir to the dynasty; they were far from the Sidonians and they had no alliance with any person. *

The spies' report

⁸ [The Danites] went back to their brothers in Zorah and Eshtaol, and their brothers said to them, "What do you [say]?"

⁹ They said, "Arise, let us advance against them, for we have seen the land, and it is very good — yet you remain still! Do not be too lazy to go, to arrive and inherit the land! ¹⁰ When you arrive, you will come upon a trusting people, and the land is expansive, for God has delivered it into your hand. It is a place where there is no shortage of anything that is in the land!"

¹¹ So they journeyed forth from there — from the family of the Danite, from Zorah and Eshtaol — six hundred men girded with weapons of war. ¹² They ascended and encamped in Kiriath-jearim in Judah. (For this reason they called that place "the Camp of Dan," to this day — behold, it is west of Kiriath-jearim.) ¹³ They passed on from there to Mount Ephraim, and arrived near Micah's house. ¹⁴ The five men who had gone to spy out the land of Laish spoke up and said to their brothers, "Did you know that in these buildings there are an ephod and icons, a carved image and molten image? Now, you know what you should do!"

¹⁵ So they turned there and came to the house of the Levite lad, at the house of Micah, and they greeted him. ¹⁶ The six hundred men girded with their weapons of war were standing at the entrance of the gate; [they were] of the tribe

Dan seizes Micah's image and priest . . .

of Dan. ¹⁷ The five men who had gone to spy out the land arrived there. They took the carved image, the ephod, the icons and the molten image. The priest was standing at the opening of the gate, as were the six hundred men girded with weapons of war.

¹⁸ And as these [men] entered Micah's house and took the carved image of the ephod, the icons and the molten image, the priest said to them, "What are you doing?"

¹⁹ They said to him, "Be quiet! Put your hand over your mouth and go with us, and be a father and a priest for us. Is it better for you to be a priest in the house

כ אִישׁ אֶחָד אוֹ הֱיוֹתְךָ כֹהֵן לְשֵׁבֶט וּלְמִשְׁפָּחָה בְּיִשְׂרָאֵל: וַיִּיטַב לֵב הַכֹּהֵן

כא וַיִּקַּח אֶת־הָאֵפוֹד וְאֶת־הַתְּרָפִים וְאֶת־הַפָּסֶל וַיָּבֹא בְּקֶרֶב הָעָם: וַיִּפְנוּ

כב וַיֵּלֵכוּ וַיָּשִׂימוּ אֶת־הַטַּף וְאֶת־הַמִּקְנֶה וְאֶת־הַכְּבוּדָּה לִפְנֵיהֶם: הֵמָּה

הִרְחִיקוּ מִבֵּית מִיכָה וְהָאֲנָשִׁים אֲשֶׁר בַּבָּתִּים אֲשֶׁר עִם־בֵּית מִיכָה נִזְעֲקוּ

כג וַיַּדְבִּיקוּ אֶת־בְּנֵי־דָן: וַיִּקְרְאוּ אֶל־בְּנֵי־דָן וַיַּסֵּבּוּ פְּנֵיהֶם וַיֹּאמְרוּ לְמִיכָה

כד מַה־לְּךָ כִּי נִזְעָקְתָּ: וַיֹּאמֶר אֶת־אֱלֹהַי אֲשֶׁר־עָשִׂיתִי לְקַחְתֶּם וְאֶת־הַכֹּהֵן

כה וַתֵּלְכוּ וּמַה־לִּי עוֹד וּמַה־זֶּה תֹּאמְרוּ אֵלַי מַה־לָּךְ: וַיֹּאמְרוּ אֵלָיו בְּנֵי־דָן

אַל־תַּשְׁמַע קוֹלְךָ עִמָּנוּ פֶּן־יִפְגְּעוּ בָכֶם אֲנָשִׁים מָרֵי נֶפֶשׁ וְאָסַפְתָּה נַפְשְׁךָ

כו וְנֶפֶשׁ בֵּיתֶךָ: וַיֵּלְכוּ בְנֵי־דָן לְדַרְכָּם וַיַּרְא מִיכָה כִּי־חֲזָקִים הֵמָּה מִמֶּנּוּ וַיִּפֶן

כז וַיָּשָׁב אֶל־בֵּיתוֹ: וְהֵמָּה לָקְחוּ אֵת אֲשֶׁר־עָשָׂה מִיכָה וְאֶת־הַכֹּהֵן אֲשֶׁר

הָיָה־לוֹ וַיָּבֹאוּ עַל־לַיִשׁ עַל־עַם שֹׁקֵט וּבֹטֵחַ וַיַּכּוּ אוֹתָם לְפִי־חָרֶב וְאֶת־

כח הָעִיר שָׂרְפוּ בָאֵשׁ: וְאֵין מַצִּיל כִּי רְחוֹקָה־הִיא מִצִּידוֹן וְדָבָר אֵין־לָהֶם

עִם־אָדָם וְהִיא בָּעֵמֶק אֲשֶׁר לְבֵית־רְחוֹב וַיִּבְנוּ אֶת־הָעִיר וַיֵּשְׁבוּ בָהּ:

כט וַיִּקְרְאוּ שֵׁם־הָעִיר דָּן בְּשֵׁם דָּן אֲבִיהֶם אֲשֶׁר יוּלַּד לְיִשְׂרָאֵל וְאוּלָם לַיִשׁ

ל שֵׁם־הָעִיר לָרִאשֹׁנָה: וַיָּקִימוּ לָהֶם בְּנֵי־דָן אֶת־הַפָּסֶל וִיהוֹנָתָן בֶּן־גֵּרְשֹׁם

בֶּן־מְ^נשֶׁה הוּא וּבָנָיו הָיוּ כֹהֲנִים לְשֵׁבֶט הַדָּנִי עַד־יוֹם גְּלוֹת הָאָרֶץ: °נ**ּון תלויה**

לא וַיָּשִׂימוּ לָהֶם אֶת־פֶּסֶל מִיכָה אֲשֶׁר עָשָׂה כָּל־יְמֵי הֱיוֹת בֵּית־הָאֱלֹהִים

א בְּשִׁלֹה: וַיְהִי בַּיָּמִים הָהֵם וּמֶלֶךְ אֵין בְּיִשְׂרָאֵל וַיְהִי ׀ אִישׁ לֵוִי   **יט**

ב גָּר בְּיַרְכְּתֵי הַר־אֶפְרַיִם וַיִּקַּח־לוֹ אִשָּׁה פִילֶגֶשׁ מִבֵּית לֶחֶם יְהוּדָה: וַתִּזְנֶה

עָלָיו פִּילַגְשׁוֹ וַתֵּלֶךְ מֵאִתּוֹ אֶל־בֵּית אָבִיהָ אֶל־בֵּית לֶחֶם יְהוּדָה וַתְּהִי־

ג שָׁם יָמִים אַרְבָּעָה חֳדָשִׁים: וַיָּקָם אִישָׁהּ וַיֵּלֶךְ אַחֲרֶיהָ לְדַבֵּר עַל־לִבָּהּ

לַהֲשִׁיבו [°לַהֲשִׁיבָהּ ק] וְנַעֲרוֹ עִמּוֹ וְצֶמֶד חֲמֹרִים וַתְּבִיאֵהוּ בֵּית אָבִיהָ

ד וַיִּרְאֵהוּ אֲבִי הַנַּעֲרָה וַיִּשְׂמַח לִקְרָאתוֹ: וַיֶּחֱזַק־בּוֹ חֹתְנוֹ אֲבִי הַנַּעֲרָה וַיֵּשֶׁב

ה אִתּוֹ שְׁלֹשֶׁת יָמִים וַיֹּאכְלוּ וַיִּשְׁתּוּ וַיָּלִינוּ שָׁם: וַיְהִי בַּיּוֹם הָרְבִיעִי וַיַּשְׁכִּימוּ

בַבֹּקֶר וַיָּקָם לָלֶכֶת וַיֹּאמֶר אֲבִי הַנַּעֲרָה אֶל־חֲתָנוֹ סְעָד לִבְּךָ פַּת־לֶחֶם

ו וְאַחַר תֵּלֵכוּ: וַיֵּשְׁבוּ וַיֹּאכְלוּ שְׁנֵיהֶם יַחְדָּו וַיִּשְׁתּוּ וַיֹּאמֶר אֲבִי הַנַּעֲרָה אֶל־

ז הָאִישׁ הוֹאֶל־נָא וְלִין וְיִטַב לִבֶּךָ: וַיָּקָם הָאִישׁ לָלֶכֶת וַיִּפְצַר־בּוֹ חֹתְנוֹ

18:21. Expecting to be pursued from the rear by local people resisting their theft, they placed the children and livestock in front of them, out of harm's way.

18:27. They set the fire during the attack to terrify potential defenders, and the fire went out of control. Alternatively, they burned the city because it was filled with idols. Although the people of Dan had brought the Levite with his idols, they wrongly considered those to be a means of serving God (*Radak*; see 17:13).

18:30. In the Masoretic text, the letter נ of מנשה, *Manasseh*, is suspended above the line. This implies that the remaining letters are to be read as an independent word, משה, *Moshe*/"Moses." The Talmud therefore identifies

the Jonathan of our verse as the son of Gershom son of Moses (see *Exodus* 2:21,22), but out of respect for Moses a letter was added to mask his name.

19:1. This episode, like the preceding one, is not written in its chronological place. It occurred in the very beginning of the era of the Judges, shortly after the death of Joshua (*Rashi*).

Ramban (*Genesis* 19:8) explains at length how the incident in Gibeah, horrifying and inexcusable though it was, is not comparable to the seemingly identical conduct of Sodom (see *Genesis* Ch. 19). In Gibeah, a lawless band of thugs terrorized the decent majority, but in Sodom, as Scripture states explicitly, all elements of the city particiof one man or to be a priest for an [entire] tribe and a family in Israel?" [20] The priest was pleased, and he took the ephod, the icons and the carved image, and went along amid the people. [21] They turned away and left; they placed the children and the livestock and the possessions before them. *

[22] They had gone a distance from Micah's house, when the men who were in the houses near Micah's house were mustered, and they overtook the children of Dan. [23] They called out to the children of Dan, who turned to face them. They said to Micah, "What concerns you that you have been mustered?"

[24] He said, "You took my god that I made and the priest, and have gone away! What more do I possess? So how can you say to me, 'What concerns you?' "

[25] But the children of Dan said to him, "Let your voice not be heard among us, lest embittered men strike out at you, and you bring about the death of yourself and your household!"

. . . destroys a city . . .

[26] Then the children of Dan went on their way. Micah saw that they were stronger than he, so he turned and went back to his house. [27] Thus they took what Micah had made and the priest who had been his. They came upon Laish, upon a complacent and secure people, and they struck them down by the sword and burnt the city down. * [28] There was no one to save [them], for it was distant from Sidon, and they had no alliance with any person. It was situated in the valley which is near Beth-rehob. Then they built up the city and settled in it.

. . . and builds an idolatrous sanctuary

[29] They named the city Dan, after the name of Dan their ancestor, who was born to Israel; but Laish was the name of the city at first. [30] The children of Dan set up for themselves the carved image, and Jonathan son of Gershom son of Manasseh * — he and his children — were priests for the tribe of the Danite, up until the day the land was exiled. [31] They accepted upon themselves Micah's carved image that he had made, all the days that the House of God was in Shiloh.

19

THE CONCUBINE AT GIBEAH
19:1-21:25

[1] **A**nd it was that in those days there was no king in Israel. * It happened that there was a Levite man who dwelled in the foothills of Mount Ephraim. He married a concubine wife from Beth-lehem of Judah. [2] His concubine deserted him and left him for her father's house in Beth-lehem of Judah, and she remained there for a period of four months. [3] Then her husband rose up and went after her, to cajole her, * to bring her back. His attendant was with him, as well as a pair of donkeys. She brought him into her father's house; the father of the girl saw him and greeted him gladly.

[4] His father-in-law, the father of the girl, detained him, and he stayed with him for three days. They ate and drank and lodged there. [5] It happened on the fourth day that they arose early in the morning and he rose up to leave, but the father of the girl said to his son-in-law, "Sustain yourself with some bread and go afterwards." [6] So they both sat and ate together and drank. The father of the girl then said to the man, "Please agree to stay overnight, so that your heart will be at ease." [7] The man rose up to leave, but his father-in-law pressed him,

---

pated in the crime. The Sodomites had a concerted campaign to frighten all potential immigrants away, but in Gibeah there was no institutionalized cruelty, only a small, lustful mob that came to satisfy its appetite. Despite their viciousness, the sinners of Gibeah did not intend to commit murder; they released the concubine, apparently unaware that they had mortally injured her. Finally, in the aftermath of this atrocity, the entire nation

rose up in organized, forceful protest, while no one made an effort to curb the constant brutality of Sodom.

19:3. Lit., he went "to speak upon her heart." Apparently, the man felt that his own conduct had provoked her to desert him, so he took the initiative of trying to win her back (Ralbag). Trying to cement the newly positive relationship, the woman's father went out of his way to be warm and gracious.

ח וַיֵּשֶׁב וַיֵּלֶן שָׁם: וַיַּשְׁכֵּם בַּבֹּקֶר בַּיּוֹם הַחֲמִישִׁי לָלֶכֶת וַיֹּאמֶר ׀ אֲבִי הַנַּעֲרָה

ט סְעָד־נָא לְבָבְךָ וְהִתְמַהְמְהוּ עַד־נְטוֹת הַיּוֹם וַיֹּאכְלוּ שְׁנֵיהֶם: וַיָּקָם הָאִישׁ לָלֶכֶת הוּא וּפִילַגְשׁוֹ וְנַעֲרוֹ וַיֹּאמֶר לוֹ חֹתְנוֹ אֲבִי הַנַּעֲרָה הִנֵּה נָא רָפָה הַיּוֹם לַעֲרוֹב לִינוּ־נָא הִנֵּה חֲנוֹת הַיּוֹם לִין פֹּה וְיִיטַב לְבָבֶךָ וְהִשְׁכַּמְתֶּם

י מָחָר לְדַרְכְּכֶם וְהָלַכְתָּ לְאֹהָלֶךָ: וְלֹא־אָבָה הָאִישׁ לָלוּן וַיָּקָם וַיֵּלֶךְ וַיָּבֹא עַד־נֹכַח יְבוּס הִיא יְרוּשָׁלִָם וְעִמּוֹ צֶמֶד חֲמוֹרִים חֲבוּשִׁים וּפִילַגְשׁוֹ עִמּוֹ:

יא הֵם עִם־יְבוּס וְהַיּוֹם רַד מְאֹד וַיֹּאמֶר הַנַּעַר אֶל־אֲדֹנָיו לְכָה־נָּא וְנָסוּרָה אֶל־עִיר־הַיְבוּסִי הַזֹּאת וְנָלִין בָּהּ:

יב וַיֹּאמֶר אֵלָיו אֲדֹנָיו לֹא נָסוּר אֶל־עִיר נָכְרִי אֲשֶׁר לֹא־מִבְּנֵי יִשְׂרָאֵל הֵנָּה וְעָבַרְנוּ עַד־גִּבְעָה: וַיֹּאמֶר לְנַעֲרוֹ לְךָ

יג וְנִקְרְבָה בְּאַחַד הַמְּקֹמוֹת וְלַנּוּ בַגִּבְעָה אוֹ בָרָמָה: וַיַּעַבְרוּ וַיֵּלֵכוּ וַתָּבֹא

יד לָהֶם הַשֶּׁמֶשׁ אֵצֶל הַגִּבְעָה אֲשֶׁר לְבִנְיָמִן: וַיָּסֻרוּ שָׁם לָבוֹא לָלוּן בַּגִּבְעָה

טו וַיָּבֹא וַיֵּשֶׁב בִּרְחוֹב הָעִיר וְאֵין אִישׁ מְאַסֵּף־אוֹתָם הַבַּיְתָה לָלוּן: וְהִנֵּה ׀

טז אִישׁ זָקֵן בָּא מִן־מַעֲשֵׂהוּ מִן־הַשָּׂדֶה בָּעֶרֶב וְהָאִישׁ מֵהַר אֶפְרַיִם וְהוּא־גָר בַּגִּבְעָה וְאַנְשֵׁי הַמָּקוֹם בְּנֵי יְמִינִי: וַיִּשָּׂא עֵינָיו וַיַּרְא אֶת־הָאִישׁ הָאֹרֵחַ

יז בִּרְחוֹב הָעִיר וַיֹּאמֶר הָאִישׁ הַזָּקֵן אָנָה תֵלֵךְ וּמֵאַיִן תָּבוֹא: וַיֹּאמֶר אֵלָיו

יח עֹבְרִים אֲנַחְנוּ מִבֵּית־לֶחֶם יְהוּדָה עַד־יַרְכְּתֵי הַר־אֶפְרַיִם מִשָּׁם אָנֹכִי וָאֵלֵךְ עַד־בֵּית לֶחֶם יְהוּדָה וְאֶת־בֵּית יְהוָה אֲנִי הֹלֵךְ וְאֵין אִישׁ מְאַסֵּף

יט אוֹתִי הַבָּיְתָה: וְגַם־תֶּבֶן גַּם־מִסְפּוֹא יֵשׁ לַחֲמוֹרֵינוּ וְגַם לֶחֶם וָיַיִן יֶשׁ־לִי וְלַאֲמָתֶךָ וְלַנַּעַר עִם־עֲבָדֶיךָ אֵין מַחְסוֹר כָּל־דָּבָר: וַיֹּאמֶר הָאִישׁ הַזָּקֵן

כ שָׁלוֹם לָךְ רַק כָּל־מַחְסוֹרְךָ עָלָי רַק בָּרְחוֹב אַל־תָּלַן: וַיְבִיאֵהוּ לְבֵיתוֹ

כא וַיָּבוֹל [°וַיָּבָל קֹ] לַחֲמוֹרִים וַיִּרְחֲצוּ רַגְלֵיהֶם וַיֹּאכְלוּ וַיִּשְׁתּוּ: הֵמָּה

כב מֵיטִיבִים אֶת־לִבָּם וְהִנֵּה אַנְשֵׁי הָעִיר אַנְשֵׁי בְנֵי־בְלִיַּעַל נָסַבּוּ אֶת־הַבַּיִת מִתְדַּפְּקִים עַל־הַדָּלֶת וַיֹּאמְרוּ אֶל־הָאִישׁ בַּעַל הַבַּיִת הַזָּקֵן לֵאמֹר הוֹצֵא

כג אֶת־הָאִישׁ אֲשֶׁר־בָּא אֶל־בֵּיתְךָ וְנֵדָעֶנּוּ: וַיֵּצֵא אֲלֵיהֶם הָאִישׁ בַּעַל הַבַּיִת וַיֹּאמֶר אֲלֵהֶם אַל־אַחַי אַל־תָּרֵעוּ נָא אַחֲרֵי אֲשֶׁר־בָּא הָאִישׁ הַזֶּה אֶל־

כד בֵּיתִי אַל־תַּעֲשׂוּ אֶת־הַנְּבָלָה הַזֹּאת: הִנֵּה בִתִּי הַבְּתוּלָה וּפִילַגְשֵׁהוּ אוֹצִיאָה־נָּא אוֹתָם וְעַנּוּ אוֹתָם וַעֲשׂוּ לָהֶם הַטּוֹב בְּעֵינֵיכֶם וְלָאִישׁ

כה הַזֶּה לֹא תַעֲשׂוּ דְּבַר הַנְּבָלָה הַזֹּאת: וְלֹא־אָבוּ הָאֲנָשִׁים לִשְׁמֹעַ לוֹ וַיַּחֲזֵק הָאִישׁ בְּפִילַגְשׁוֹ וַיֹּצֵא אֲלֵיהֶם הַחוּץ וַיֵּדְעוּ אוֹתָהּ וַיִּתְעַלְּלוּ־בָהּ כָּל־הַלַּיְלָה עַד־הַבֹּקֶר וַיְשַׁלְּחוּהָ °בעלות [°כַּעֲלוֹת קֹ] הַשָּׁחַר:

19:18. The sanctuary at Shiloh was in the foothills of Ephraim. The man planned to stop there to pray on his way home; or perhaps he lived in Shiloh.

19:24. The lawless mob wanted to sodomize the guest. Knowing that the mob would overpower them, the host tried to protect his guest by making a revolting offer: to give them his daughter and the concubine. [They rational-ized that since the concubine was not legally married there was no death penalty in her case; thus, they thought, it would be preferable to turn her over, rather than let the mob sodomize the man, which is a capital sin (*Ramban*). Nevertheless, they were wrong, for it was forbidden to turn over one person to save another.] The rabble satisfied their lust with the concubine, and she died from the abuse.

and he spent the night there once again. [8] He arose early in the morning on the fifth day to go, but the father of the girl said, "Sustain yourself now and wait until afternoon," so the two of them ate. [9] When the man rose up to go — he and his concubine and his attendant — his father-in-law, the father of the girl, said to him, "See, now, the sun is waning and is about to set; please stay overnight. Behold, it is the time of day to set up camp; spend the night here so that your heart will be at ease, and tomorrow you can arise early for your journey and go to your tent."

The journey home

[10] But the man would not consent to stay overnight, and he rose up and left. He arrived as far as opposite Jebus, which is Jerusalem; with him were a pair of laden donkeys, and his concubine was with him. [11] They were near Jebus when the sun was very low, so the attendant said to his master, "Come, let us turn into this Jebusite city and spend the night in it."

[12] But his master said to him, "Let us not turn into a city of a foreign [people] who are not of the Children of Israel. Let us pass on to Gibeah." [13] So he said to his attendant, "Come, let us approach one of the [Jewish] places, and we will spend the night in Gibeah or in Ramah." [14] So they passed [Jebus] and went on, and the sun set upon them near Gibeah of Benjamin. [15] They turned there to come and spend the night in Gibeah. He entered and sat in the town square, but no one brought them into a home to spend the night.

Hospitality of the Ephraimite

[16] Just then an old man came from his work, from the field, in the evening. The man was from Mount Ephraim, but he was living in Gibeah; the local people were Benjamites. [17] When he raised his eyes and saw the traveler in the town square, the old man said, "Where are you headed? From where have you come?"

[18] He answered him, "We are passing from Beth-lehem of Judah to the foothills of Mount Ephraim; I am from there. I went to Beth-lehem of Judah, and I am headed for the House of HASHEM. * And no man is bringing me into his home. [19] We even have straw and fodder for our donkeys, and there is even bread and wine for me and your maidservant and the boy who is with your servants; not a thing is lacking."

[20] The old man said, "Peace be with you! However, all your provisions shall be upon me. Just don't spend the night in the [town] square!"

[21] He brought them to his house and prepared food for the donkeys; they washed their feet and ate and drank. [22] As they were feeling merry, behold — people of the city, lawless people, surrounded the house, banging on the door, and saying to the old man, the owner of the house, "Send out the man who came to your house, so that we may know him."

[23] The man who was the owner of the house went out to them. He said to them, "No, my brothers! Please do not be wicked! Since this man has come to my house, do not do this disgusting thing! [24] Here are my virgin daughter and his concubine! I will bring them out and you may molest them and do to them whatever you please. But do not do this disgusting thing to this man!"*

The concubine is violated

[25] But the men were not willing to listen to him. The man grabbed his concubine and thrust [her] outside to them. They knew her and they molested her all night long until the morning; they sent her away as the dawn began to break.

כו וַתָּבֹא הָאִשָּׁה לִפְנוֹת הַבֹּקֶר וַתִּפֹּל פֶּתַח בֵּית־הָאִישׁ אֲשֶׁר־אֲדוֹנֶיהָ שָּׁם

כז עַד־הָאוֹר: וַיָּקָם אֲדֹנֶיהָ בַּבֹּקֶר וַיִּפְתַּח דַּלְתוֹת הַבַּיִת וַיֵּצֵא לָלֶכֶת לְדַרְכּוֹ

כח וְהִנֵּה הָאִשָּׁה פִילַגְשׁוֹ נֹפֶלֶת פֶּתַח הַבַּיִת וְיָדֶיהָ עַל־הַסַּף: וַיֹּאמֶר אֵלֶיהָ

כט קוּמִי וְנֵלֵכָה וְאֵין עֹנֶה וַיִּקָּחֶהָ עַל־הַחֲמוֹר וַיָּקָם הָאִישׁ וַיֵּלֶךְ לִמְקֹמוֹ: וַיָּבֹא אֶל־בֵּיתוֹ וַיִּקַּח אֶת־הַמַּאֲכֶלֶת וַיַּחֲזֵק בְּפִילַגְשׁוֹ וַיְנַתְּחֶהָ לַעֲצָמֶיהָ לִשְׁנֵים

ל עָשָׂר נְתָחִים וַיְשַׁלְּחֶהָ בְּכֹל גְּבוּל יִשְׂרָאֵל: וְהָיָה כָל־הָרֹאֶה וְאָמַר לֹא־נִהְיְתָה וְלֹא־נִרְאֲתָה כָּזֹאת לְמִיּוֹם עֲלוֹת בְּנֵי־יִשְׂרָאֵל מֵאֶרֶץ מִצְרַיִם עַד

א הַיּוֹם הַזֶּה שִׂימוּ־לָכֶם עָלֶיהָ עֻצוּ וְדַבֵּרוּ:   וַיֵּצְאוּ כָּל־בְּנֵי   **כ**

יִשְׂרָאֵל וַתִּקָּהֵל הָעֵדָה כְּאִישׁ אֶחָד לְמִדָּן וְעַד־בְּאֵר שֶׁבַע וְאֶרֶץ הַגִּלְעָד

ב אֶל־יְהוָה הַמִּצְפָּה: וַיִּתְיַצְּבוּ פִּנּוֹת כָּל־הָעָם כֹּל שִׁבְטֵי יִשְׂרָאֵל בִּקְהַל עַם

ג הָאֱלֹהִים אַרְבַּע מֵאוֹת אֶלֶף אִישׁ רַגְלִי שֹׁלֵף חָרֶב: וַיִּשְׁמְעוּ בְּנֵי בִנְיָמִן כִּי־עָלוּ בְנֵי־יִשְׂרָאֵל הַמִּצְפָּה וַיֹּאמְרוּ בְּנֵי יִשְׂרָאֵל דַּבְּרוּ אֵיכָה

ד נִהְיְתָה הָרָעָה הַזֹּאת: וַיַּעַן הָאִישׁ הַלֵּוִי אִישׁ הָאִשָּׁה הַנִּרְצָחָה וַיֹּאמֶר

ה הַגִּבְעָתָה אֲשֶׁר לְבִנְיָמִן בָּאתִי אֲנִי וּפִילַגְשִׁי לָלוּן: וַיָּקֻמוּ עָלַי בַּעֲלֵי הַגִּבְעָה וַיָּסֹבּוּ עָלַי אֶת־הַבַּיִת לָיְלָה אוֹתִי דִּמּוּ לַהֲרֹג וְאֶת־פִּילַגְשִׁי עִנּוּ

ו וַתָּמֹת: וָאֹחֵז בְּפִילַגְשִׁי וָאֲנַתְּחֶהָ וָאֲשַׁלְּחֶהָ בְּכָל־שְׂדֵה נַחֲלַת יִשְׂרָאֵל

ז כִּי עָשׂוּ זִמָּה וּנְבָלָה בְּיִשְׂרָאֵל: הִנֵּה כֻלְּכֶם בְּנֵי יִשְׂרָאֵל הָבוּ לָכֶם דָּבָר

ח וְעֵצָה הֲלֹם: וַיָּקָם כָּל־הָעָם כְּאִישׁ אֶחָד לֵאמֹר לֹא נֵלֵךְ אִישׁ לְאָהֳלוֹ וְלֹא

ט נָסוּר אִישׁ לְבֵיתוֹ: וְעַתָּה זֶה הַדָּבָר אֲשֶׁר נַעֲשֶׂה לַגִּבְעָה עָלֶיהָ בְּגוֹרָל:

י וְלָקַחְנוּ עֲשָׂרָה אֲנָשִׁים לַמֵּאָה לְכֹל ׀ שִׁבְטֵי יִשְׂרָאֵל וּמֵאָה לָאֶלֶף וְאֶלֶף לָרְבָבָה לָקַחַת צֵדָה לָעָם לַעֲשׂוֹת לְבוֹאָם לְגֶבַע בִּנְיָמִן כְּכָל־הַנְּבָלָה

יא אֲשֶׁר עָשָׂה בְּיִשְׂרָאֵל: וַיֵּאָסֵף כָּל־אִישׁ יִשְׂרָאֵל אֶל־הָעִיר כְּאִישׁ אֶחָד

יב חֲבֵרִים: וַיִּשְׁלְחוּ שִׁבְטֵי יִשְׂרָאֵל אֲנָשִׁים בְּכָל־שִׁבְטֵי בִנְיָמִן לֵאמֹר

יג מָה הָרָעָה הַזֹּאת אֲשֶׁר נִהְיְתָה בָּכֶם: וְעַתָּה תְּנוּ אֶת־הָאֲנָשִׁים בְּנֵי־ בְלִיַּעַל אֲשֶׁר בַּגִּבְעָה וּנְמִיתֵם וּנְבַעֲרָה רָעָה מִיִּשְׂרָאֵל וְלֹא אָבוּ [בְּנֵי ק׳ ולא

יד כ׳] בִּנְיָמִן לִשְׁמֹעַ בְּקוֹל אֲחֵיהֶם בְּנֵי־יִשְׂרָאֵל: וַיֵּאָסְפוּ בְנֵי־בִנְיָמִן מִן־

טו הֶעָרִים הַגִּבְעָתָה לָצֵאת לַמִּלְחָמָה עִם־בְּנֵי יִשְׂרָאֵל: וַיִּתְפָּקְדוּ בְנֵי בִנְיָמִן בַּיּוֹם הַהוּא מֵהֶעָרִים עֶשְׂרִים וְשִׁשָּׁה אֶלֶף אִישׁ שֹׁלֵף חָרֶב לְבַד מִיֹּשְׁבֵי

טז הַגִּבְעָה הִתְפָּקְדוּ שְׁבַע מֵאוֹת אִישׁ בָּחוּר: מִכֹּל ׀ הָעָם הַזֶּה שְׁבַע מֵאוֹת

19:29. Again, the man did not act in accordance with Torah law, since the desecration of a body is forbidden. He took it upon himself to thus rouse the entire population to act against the perpetrators of the atrocity and to ensure that such an episode would never happen again.

20:1. Although no capital offense had been committed at Gibeah (since the concubine was not a married woman and her death was unintended), the nation was appalled at the unprecedented atrocity. They wished to exercise the right to act extralegally in an emergency situation. The Benjamites refused to cooperate, for several reasons: (a) The crime committed, heinous though it was, was not a capital offense; (b) the other tribes were acting high-handedly, without consulting Benjamin; and (c) the responsibility to take action lay exclusively in the hands of the high court of the tribe of Benjamin. All parties acted wrongly, and God allowed them to suffer heavy casualties as a result: The tribes should not have gone to war before

²⁶ The woman arrived towards morning and collapsed at the door of the man's house, where her master was staying until it was light. ²⁷ Her master got up in the morning, opened the doors of the house, and left to go on his way, and behold — his concubine wife was fallen at the entrance of the house, with her hands on the threshold! ²⁸ He said to her, "Get up, let us go!" but there was no answer. He took her upon the donkey, and then the man got up and went to his place.

The Levite's reaction   ²⁹ When he arrived in his house, he took a knife and took hold of his concubine. He sliced her body limb by limb, into twelve pieces, and sent her [parts] throughout all the borders of Israel. * ³⁰ It happened that whoever saw it said, "Such a thing has never happened nor been seen since the day the Children of Israel went up from the Land of Egypt to this day! You must contemplate this, take counsel and speak up!"

20   ¹ **A**ll the Children of Israel went out* and the assembly gathered together as a single man, from Dan to Beer-sheba and the land of Gilead, to HASHEM, *Israel gathers at Mizpah*   at Mizpah. ² The chiefs of all the people, of all the tribes of Israel, stood in the congregation of the people of God, four hundred thousand sword-wielding foot soldiers.

³ The children of Benjamin heard that the Children of Israel had gone up to Mizpah. The Children of Israel said, "Tell us; how did this outrage happen?"

⁴ The Levite man, the husband of the murdered woman, answered and said, "I arrived with my concubine at Gibeah of Benjamin, to spend the night. ⁵ The inhabitants of Gibeah rose up against me and surrounded the house against me at night. They proposed to kill me, and they tormented my concubine so that she died. ⁶ I took hold of my concubine and cut her apart and sent her [body] throughout all the territory of the heritage of Israel, for they had done an indecent and disgusting thing in Israel. ⁷ Here you all are, O Children of Israel, produce a decision and counsel right here!"

All Israel respond as one   ⁸ All the people arose as one man, saying, "No man will go to his tent and no man will turn away to his house! ⁹ Now, this is the thing that we should do to Gibeah: [We will advance] against it by lot; ¹⁰ we will choose ten men out of every hundred of all the tribes of Israel — and a hundred out of every thousand and a thousand out of every ten thousand — to obtain provisions for the people, so that they may act, when they go to Geba of Benjamin, in accordance with the disgusting act that was committed in Israel." ¹¹ Then all the people of Israel gathered together at the city, as one man, as comrades.

Israel's demand   ¹² The tribes of Israel then sent men through all the clans of Benjamin, saying, "What is this outrage that occurred among you? ¹³ Now turn over the lawless men who are in Gibeah, and we will put them to death and eliminate the evil from Israel."

Benjamin's refusal   But the children of Benjamin refused to heed the voice of their brothers, the Children of Israel. ¹⁴ The children of Benjamin were gathered together from the cities to Gibeah, to go out to war with the Children of Israel. ¹⁵ The children of Benjamin from the cities were numbered that day at twenty-six thousand sword-wielding men, besides the inhabitants of Gibeah, who were numbered at seven hundred choice men. ¹⁶ Among all these people there were seven hundred

consulting Benjamin, and Benjamin should not have turned a blind eye to the atrocity (*Ramban*).

אִישׁ בָּחוּר אִטֵּר יַד־יְמִינֵוֹ כָּל־זֶה קֹלֵעַ בָּאֶבֶן אֶל־הַשַּׂעֲרָה וְלֹא
יַחֲטִא: וְאִישׁ יִשְׂרָאֵל הִתְפָּקְדוּ לְבַד מִבִּנְיָמִן אַרְבַּע
מֵאוֹת אֶלֶף אִישׁ שֹׁלֵף חָרֶב כָּל־זֶה אִישׁ מִלְחָמָה: וַיָּקֻמוּ וַיַּעֲלוּ בֵית־אֵל
וַיִּשְׁאֲלוּ בֵאלֹהִים וַיֹּאמְרוּ בְּנֵי יִשְׂרָאֵל מִי יַעֲלֶה־לָּנוּ בַתְּחִלָּה לַמִּלְחָמָה
עִם־בְּנֵי בִנְיָמִן וַיֹּאמֶר יְהוָה יְהוּדָה בַתְּחִלָּה: וַיָּקוּמוּ בְנֵי־יִשְׂרָאֵל בַּבֹּקֶר
וַיַּחֲנוּ עַל־הַגִּבְעָה: וַיֵּצֵא אִישׁ יִשְׂרָאֵל לַמִּלְחָמָה עִם־בִּנְיָמִן וַיַּעַרְכוּ אִתָּם
אִישׁ־יִשְׂרָאֵל מִלְחָמָה אֶל־הַגִּבְעָה: וַיֵּצְאוּ בְנֵי־בִנְיָמִן מִן־הַגִּבְעָה
וַיַּשְׁחִיתוּ בְיִשְׂרָאֵל בַּיּוֹם הַהוּא שְׁנַיִם וְעֶשְׂרִים אֶלֶף אִישׁ אָרְצָה: וַיִּתְחַזֵּק
הָעָם אִישׁ יִשְׂרָאֵל וַיֹּסִפוּ לַעֲרֹךְ מִלְחָמָה בַּמָּקוֹם אֲשֶׁר־עָרְכוּ שָׁם בַּיּוֹם
הָרִאשׁוֹן: וַיַּעֲלוּ בְנֵי־יִשְׂרָאֵל וַיִּבְכּוּ לִפְנֵי־יְהוָה עַד־הָעֶרֶב וַיִּשְׁאֲלוּ בַיהוָה
לֵאמֹר הַאוֹסִיף לָגֶשֶׁת לַמִּלְחָמָה עִם־בְּנֵי בִנְיָמִן אָחִי וַיֹּאמֶר יְהוָה עֲלוּ
אֵלָיו: וַיִּקְרְבוּ בְנֵי־יִשְׂרָאֵל אֶל־בְּנֵי בִנְיָמִן בַּיּוֹם הַשֵּׁנִי: וַיֵּצֵא
בִנְיָמִן לִקְרָאתָם מִן־הַגִּבְעָה בַּיּוֹם הַשֵּׁנִי וַיַּשְׁחִיתוּ בִבְנֵי יִשְׂרָאֵל עוֹד
שְׁמֹנַת עָשָׂר אֶלֶף אִישׁ אָרְצָה כָּל־אֵלֶּה שֹׁלְפֵי חָרֶב: וַיַּעֲלוּ כָל־בְּנֵי
יִשְׂרָאֵל וְכָל־הָעָם וַיָּבֹאוּ בֵית־אֵל וַיִּבְכּוּ וַיֵּשְׁבוּ שָׁם לִפְנֵי יְהוָה וַיָּצוּמוּ
בַיּוֹם־הַהוּא עַד־הָעָרֶב וַיַּעֲלוּ עֹלוֹת וּשְׁלָמִים לִפְנֵי יְהוָה: וַיִּשְׁאֲלוּ בְנֵי־
יִשְׂרָאֵל בַּיהוָה וְשָׁם אֲרוֹן בְּרִית הָאֱלֹהִים בַּיָּמִים הָהֵם: וּפִינְחָס בֶּן־
אֶלְעָזָר בֶּן־אַהֲרֹן עֹמֵד לְפָנָיו בַּיָּמִים הָהֵם לֵאמֹר הַאוֹסִף עוֹד לָצֵאת
לַמִּלְחָמָה עִם־בְּנֵי־בִנְיָמִן אָחִי אִם־אֶחְדָּל וַיֹּאמֶר יְהוָה עֲלוּ כִּי מָחָר
אֶתְּנֶנּוּ בְיָדֶךָ: וַיָּשֶׂם יִשְׂרָאֵל אֹרְבִים אֶל־הַגִּבְעָה סָבִיב: וַיַּעֲלוּ
בְנֵי־יִשְׂרָאֵל אֶל־בְּנֵי בִנְיָמִן בַּיּוֹם הַשְּׁלִישִׁי וַיַּעַרְכוּ אֶל־הַגִּבְעָה כְּפַעַם
בְּפָעַם: וַיֵּצְאוּ בְנֵי־בִנְיָמִן לִקְרַאת הָעָם הָנְתְּקוּ מִן־הָעִיר וַיָּחֵלּוּ לְהַכּוֹת
מֵהָעָם חֲלָלִים כְּפַעַם ׀ בְּפַעַם בַּמְסִלּוֹת אֲשֶׁר אַחַת עֹלָה בֵית־אֵל
וְאַחַת גִּבְעָתָה בַּשָּׂדֶה כִּשְׁלֹשִׁים אִישׁ בְּיִשְׂרָאֵל: וַיֹּאמְרוּ בְּנֵי בִנְיָמִן
נִגָּפִים הֵם לְפָנֵינוּ כְּבָרִאשֹׁנָה וּבְנֵי יִשְׂרָאֵל אָמְרוּ נָנוּסָה וּנְתַקְנֻהוּ מִן־
הָעִיר אֶל־הַמְסִלּוֹת: וְכֹל ׀ אִישׁ יִשְׂרָאֵל קָמוּ מִמְּקוֹמוֹ וַיַּעַרְכוּ בְּבַעַל תָּמָר
וְאֹרֵב יִשְׂרָאֵל מֵגִיחַ מִמְּקֹמוֹ מִמַּעֲרֵה־גָבַע: וַיָּבֹאוּ מִנֶּגֶד לַגִּבְעָה עֲשֶׂרֶת
אֲלָפִים אִישׁ בָּחוּר מִכָּל־יִשְׂרָאֵל וְהַמִּלְחָמָה כָּבֵדָה וְהֵם לֹא יָדְעוּ
כִּי־נֹגַעַת עֲלֵיהֶם הָרָעָה: וַיִּגֹּף יְהוָה ׀ אֶת־בִּנְיָמִן
לִפְנֵי יִשְׂרָאֵל וַיַּשְׁחִיתוּ בְנֵי יִשְׂרָאֵל בְּבִנְיָמִן בַּיּוֹם הַהוּא עֶשְׂרִים
וַחֲמִשָּׁה אֶלֶף וּמֵאָה אִישׁ כָּל־אֵלֶּה שֹׁלֵף חָרֶב: וַיִּרְאוּ בְנֵי־בִנְיָמִן כִּי

20:16. Lit., "impaired in their right hands."

20:18. The people erred. They should have asked, "Should we go to war?" to which the answer would have been that they should seek an accommodation with Benjamin. Instead, they made their own decision to fight; their only question was who should lead them. They paid a heavy price for their pride (Ramban).

20:23. This time they asked God for permission to fight; but they lost again because they arrogantly trusted in their own superior numbers. The Benjamites, on the choice left-handed* men, all of whom could sling a stone at a hair and not miss. [17] Besides Benjamin, the men of Israel were numbered at four hundred thousand sword-wielding men, all these were warriors.

Divine guidance sought [18] They got up and went to Beth-el and inquired of God. The Children of Israel said, "Who among us should advance first to [wage] war against the children of Benjamin?"*

HASHEM answered, "Judah should be first."

First encounter: Benjamin victorious [19] The Children of Israel rose up in the morning and encamped against Gibeah. [20] The men of Israel went out to war against Benjamin, and the men of Israel arrayed themselves for war against Gibeah. [21] The children of Benjamin came out of Gibeah and on that day they destroyed twenty-two thousand men of Israel to the ground. [22] The people, the men of Israel, strengthened themselves and continued to array themselves for war in the place where they had arrayed themselves on the first day. [23] The Children of Israel went up and cried before HASHEM until evening. They inquired of HASHEM, saying, "Should I once again approach for war against the children of Benjamin, my brother?"

HASHEM said, "Go up against him."*

Second encounter: Benjamin victorious [24] So the Children of Israel advanced against the children of Benjamin on the second day. [25] Benjamin went out towards them from Gibeah on the second day, and they destroyed another eighteen thousand men of the Children of Israel to the ground, sword wielders all of them.

[26] All the Children of Israel and all the people went up and came to Beth-el; they cried and remained there before HASHEM, and they fasted on that day until evening; they brought up elevation-offerings and peace-offerings before HASHEM. [27] The Children of Israel then inquired of HASHEM (the Ark of the Covenant of God was there in those days, [28] and Phinehas son of Elazar son of Aaron ministered before it in those days), saying, "Should I go out again to [make] war against the children of Benjamin my brother, or should I withdraw?"

HASHEM said, "Go up, for tomorrow I shall deliver them into your hand."*

Third encounter: Israel prevails [29] Israel then set up ambushes all around Gibeah. [30] The Children of Israel went up to war against the children of Benjamin on the third day, and they arrayed themselves against Gibeah, like the other times. [31] The children of Benjamin came out towards the people; they were drawn away from the city. They began to strike down casualties from the people as in the other times, on the roads in the field, of which one led up to Beth-el and the other to Gibeah, around thirty men of Israel. [32] So the children of Benjamin said, "They are being beaten before us, as before," but the Children of Israel said, "Let us retreat and cut them off from the city, into the roads." [33] So they arose, each man of Israel from his place, and they arrayed themselves in Baal-tamar. Meanwhile the Israelite ambush was withdrawing from its place, from the Plain of Gibeah. [34] They arrived opposite Gibeah, ten thousand choice men of all Israel, and the battle was intense. [The Benjamites] did not realize that evil was befalling them.

[35] HASHEM then struck Benjamin before Israel, and the Children of Israel destroyed twenty-five thousand and one hundred men from Benjamin on that day, sword wielders all of them. [36] The children of Benjamin saw that they were

---

other hand, acted improperly in pursuing the carnage so zealously, rather than merely defending themselves.

20:28. After the second defeat, the Israelites repented and prayed sincerely, and they prevailed on the third day.

נִגְּפוּ וַיִּתְּנוּ אִישׁ־יִשְׂרָאֵל מָקוֹם לְבִנְיָמִן כִּי בָטְחוּ אֶל־הָאֹרֵב אֲשֶׁר שָׂמוּ

לז אֶל־הַגִּבְעָה: וְהָאֹרֵב הֵחִישׁוּ וַיִּפְשְׁטוּ אֶל־הַגִּבְעָה וַיִּמְשֹׁךְ הָאֹרֵב וַיַּךְ

לח אֶת־כָּל־הָעִיר לְפִי־חָרֶב: וְהַמּוֹעֵד הָיָה לְאִישׁ יִשְׂרָאֵל עִם־הָאֹרֵב הֶרֶב

לט לְהַעֲלוֹתָם מַשְׂאַת הֶעָשָׁן מִן־הָעִיר: וַיַּהֲפֹךְ אִישׁ־יִשְׂרָאֵל בַּמִּלְחָמָה

וּבִנְיָמִן הֵחֵל לְהַכּוֹת חֲלָלִים בְּאִישׁ־יִשְׂרָאֵל כִּשְׁלֹשִׁים אִישׁ כִּי אָמְרוּ אַךְ

מ נָגוֹף נִגָּף הוּא לְפָנֵינוּ כַּמִּלְחָמָה הָרִאשֹׁנָה: וְהַמַּשְׂאֵת הֵחֵלָּה לַעֲלוֹת מִן־

הָעִיר עַמּוּד עָשָׁן וַיִּפֶן בִּנְיָמִן אַחֲרָיו וְהִנֵּה עָלָה כְלִיל־הָעִיר הַשָּׁמָיְמָה:

מא וְאִישׁ יִשְׂרָאֵל הָפַךְ וַיִּבָּהֵל אִישׁ בִּנְיָמִן כִּי רָאָה כִּי־נָגְעָה עָלָיו הָרָעָה:

מב וַיִּפְנוּ לִפְנֵי אִישׁ יִשְׂרָאֵל אֶל־דֶּרֶךְ הַמִּדְבָּר וְהַמִּלְחָמָה הִדְבִּיקָתְהוּ וַאֲשֶׁר

מג מֵהֶעָרִים מַשְׁחִיתִים אוֹתוֹ בְּתוֹכוֹ: כִּתְּרוּ אֶת־בִּנְיָמִן הִרְדִיפֻהוּ מְנוּחָה

מד הִדְרִיכֻהוּ עַד נֹכַח הַגִּבְעָה מִמִּזְרַח־שָׁמֶשׁ: וַיִּפְּלוּ מִבִּנְיָמִן שְׁמֹנָה־עָשָׂר

מה אֶלֶף אִישׁ אֶת־כָּל־אֵלֶּה אַנְשֵׁי־חָיִל: וַיִּפְנוּ וַיָּנֻסוּ הַמִּדְבָּרָה אֶל־סֶלַע

הָרִמּוֹן וַיְעֹלְלֻהוּ בַּמְסִלּוֹת חֲמֵשֶׁת אֲלָפִים אִישׁ וַיַּדְבִּיקוּ אַחֲרָיו עַד־

מו גִּדְעֹם וַיַּכּוּ מִמֶּנּוּ אַלְפַּיִם אִישׁ: וַיְהִי כָל־הַנֹּפְלִים מִבִּנְיָמִן עֶשְׂרִים וַחֲמִשָּׁה

מז אֶלֶף אִישׁ שֹׁלֵף חֶרֶב בַּיּוֹם הַהוּא אֶת־כָּל־אֵלֶּה אַנְשֵׁי־חָיִל: וַיִּפְנוּ

וַיָּנֻסוּ הַמִּדְבָּרָה אֶל־סֶלַע הָרִמּוֹן שֵׁשׁ מֵאוֹת אִישׁ וַיֵּשְׁבוּ בְּסֶלַע רִמּוֹן

מח אַרְבָּעָה חֳדָשִׁים: וְאִישׁ יִשְׂרָאֵל שָׁבוּ אֶל־בְּנֵי בִנְיָמִן וַיַּכּוּם לְפִי־חֶרֶב

מֵעִיר מְתֹם עַד־בְּהֵמָה עַד כָּל־הַנִּמְצָא גַּם כָּל־הֶעָרִים הַנִּמְצָאוֹת שִׁלְּחוּ

כא א בָאֵשׁ: וְאִישׁ יִשְׂרָאֵל נִשְׁבַּע בַּמִּצְפָּה לֵאמֹר אִישׁ

ב מִמֶּנּוּ לֹא־יִתֵּן בִּתּוֹ לְבִנְיָמִן לְאִשָּׁה: וַיָּבֹא הָעָם בֵּית־אֵל וַיֵּשְׁבוּ שָׁם

ג עַד־הָעֶרֶב לִפְנֵי הָאֱלֹהִים וַיִּשְׂאוּ קוֹלָם וַיִּבְכּוּ בְּכִי גָדוֹל: וַיֹּאמְרוּ לָמָה

יהוה אֱלֹהֵי יִשְׂרָאֵל הָיְתָה זֹּאת בְּיִשְׂרָאֵל לְהִפָּקֵד הַיּוֹם מִיִּשְׂרָאֵל שֵׁבֶט

ד אֶחָד: וַיְהִי מִמָּחֳרָת וַיַּשְׁכִּימוּ הָעָם וַיִּבְנוּ־שָׁם מִזְבֵּחַ וַיַּעֲלוּ עֹלוֹת

ה וּשְׁלָמִים: וַיֹּאמְרוּ בְּנֵי יִשְׂרָאֵל מִי אֲשֶׁר לֹא־עָלָה

בַקָּהָל מִכָּל־שִׁבְטֵי יִשְׂרָאֵל אֶל־יהוה כִּי הַשְּׁבוּעָה הַגְּדוֹלָה הָיְתָה

ו לַאֲשֶׁר לֹא־עָלָה אֶל־יהוה הַמִּצְפָּה לֵאמֹר מוֹת יוּמָת: וַיִּנָּחֲמוּ בְּנֵי

יִשְׂרָאֵל אֶל־בִּנְיָמִן אָחִיו וַיֹּאמְרוּ נִגְדַּע הַיּוֹם שֵׁבֶט אֶחָד מִיִּשְׂרָאֵל:

ז מַה־נַּעֲשֶׂה לָהֶם לַנּוֹתָרִים לְנָשִׁים וַאֲנַחְנוּ נִשְׁבַּעְנוּ בַיהוה לְבִלְתִּי תֵּת־

ח לָהֶם מִבְּנוֹתֵינוּ לְנָשִׁים: וַיֹּאמְרוּ מִי אֶחָד מִשִּׁבְטֵי יִשְׂרָאֵל אֲשֶׁר לֹא־

עָלָה אֶל־יהוה הַמִּצְפָּה וְהִנֵּה לֹא בָא־אִישׁ אֶל־הַמַּחֲנֶה מִיָּבֵישׁ גִּלְעָד

ט אֶל־הַקָּהָל: וַיִּתְפָּקֵד הָעָם וְהִנֵּה אֵין־שָׁם אִישׁ מִיּוֹשְׁבֵי יָבֵשׁ גִּלְעָד:

21:2. Beth-el here refers to Shiloh, the site of the Tabernacle (see 20:26). Although the national Altar was there, the Jews built another altar to express their sense of the tragedy and to pray for God's help (Radak; Ralbag).

21:8. The people felt sure that one cause of the catastrophe that took the lives of so many of their number was that some segments of the nation had flouted the national oath that all communities must gather to deal with the atrocity in Gibeah (v. 5). Then, they used that defection as a means to rebuild the tribe of Benjamin (Malbim).

being beaten, and the men of Israel made way for Benjamin [to retreat], for they were relying on the ambush they had laid against Gibeah. ³⁷ *The ambushers hastened and spread out against Gibeah; the ambushers sounded [the shofar] and struck down the entire city by the edge of the sword.*

Details of
the battle

³⁸ *The signal between the men of Israel and the ambushers was that they would send up a thick column of smoke from the city.* ³⁹ *The men of Israel had retreated in the battle, and Benjamin had begun to strike down casualties among the men of Israel, about thirty men, for they said [to themselves], "They are certainly being beaten before us, as in the first battle."* ⁴⁰ *But as the column began to rise from the city, a pillar of smoke, [the army of] Benjamin looked behind itself and behold — the city in its entirety was going up to the sky!* ⁴¹ *Then the men of Israel turned around, and the men of Benjamin became terrified, because they realized that the evil had befallen them.* ⁴² *They turned before the men of Israel, [to flee] towards the desert, but [the army of] the battle[field] overtook them; and [the ambushers] of the cities destroyed them within it.* ⁴³ *They surrounded [the army of] Benjamin and pursued it; they trampled it [where it sought] rest, until opposite Gibeah toward the east.*

Benjamin
in flight

⁴⁴ *Eighteen thousand men of Benjamin fell, all of them men of valor.* ⁴⁵ *[Others] turned and fled to the desert, to the Rock of Rimmon. [The Children of Israel killed] the stragglers on the roads, five thousand men, and they overtook them until Gidom, where they struck down of them two thousand men.* ⁴⁶ *All those who fell from Benjamin on that day were twenty-five thousand sword-wielding men, all of them men of valor.*

⁴⁷ *Six hundred men turned and fled to the desert, to the Rock of Rimmon, and they stayed at the Rock of Rimmon for four months.* ⁴⁸ *The men of Israel went back to the children of Benjamin and struck them down by the edge of the sword, from the populated cities to animals to everything else that was found. Also all the cities that they discovered, they set on fire.*

21

The oath
at Mizpah

¹ *The men of Israel had taken an oath at Mizpah, saying, "None of us will give his daughter as a wife to Benjamin."* ² *The people came to Beth-el* and remained there until evening before God. They raised their voices and wept in a loud lament.* ³ *They said, "Why, O HASHEM, God of Israel, has this happened in Israel, that one tribe of Israel should be missing in Israel today?"* ⁴ *It happened on the following day that the people arose early and built an altar there, and they offered elevation-offerings and peace-offerings.*

Remorse
over
Benjamin's
fate

⁵ *The Children of Israel then said, "From among all the tribes of Israel, who did not come up to the assembly to HASHEM?" For there had been a great oath against anyone who would not come up to HASHEM, to Mizpah, saying, "He shall surely be put to death."* ⁶ *For the Children of Israel had relented towards their brother Benjamin, and they said, "Today one tribe will be eliminated from Israel!* ⁷ *What can we do [to provide] wives for the survivors? For we have sworn by HASHEM not to give them our daughters for wives!"* ⁸ *So they said, "Who is there of the tribes of Israel who did not come up to HASHEM at Mizpah?" And behold, no one had come to the camp, to the assembly, from Jabesh-gilead.** ⁹ *The people took an account and behold, there was no man there from the inhabitants of Jabesh-gilead.*

י וַיִּשְׁלְחוּ־שָׁם הָעֵדָה שְׁנֵים־עָשָׂר אֶלֶף אִישׁ מִבְּנֵי הֶחָיִל וַיְצַוּוּ אוֹתָם

יא לֵאמֹר לְכוּ וְהִכִּיתֶם אֶת־יוֹשְׁבֵי יָבֵשׁ גִּלְעָד לְפִי־חֶרֶב וְהַנָּשִׁים וְהַטָּף: וְזֶה
הַדָּבָר אֲשֶׁר תַּעֲשׂוּ כָּל־זָכָר וְכָל־אִשָּׁה יֹדַעַת מִשְׁכַּב־זָכָר תַּחֲרִימוּ:

יב וַיִּמְצְאוּ מִיּוֹשְׁבֵי | יָבֵישׁ גִּלְעָד אַרְבַּע מֵאוֹת נַעֲרָה בְתוּלָה אֲשֶׁר לֹא־
יָדְעָה אִישׁ לְמִשְׁכַּב זָכָר וַיָּבִיאוּ אוֹתָם אֶל־הַמַּחֲנֶה שִׁלֹה אֲשֶׁר בְּאֶרֶץ
כְּנָעַן: יג וַיִּשְׁלְחוּ כָּל־הָעֵדָה וַיְדַבְּרוּ אֶל־בְּנֵי בִנְיָמִן אֲשֶׁר

בְּסֶלַע רִמּוֹן וַיִּקְרְאוּ לָהֶם שָׁלוֹם: יד וַיָּשָׁב בִּנְיָמִן בָּעֵת הַהִיא וַיִּתְּנוּ לָהֶם
הַנָּשִׁים אֲשֶׁר חִיּוּ מִנְּשֵׁי יָבֵשׁ גִּלְעָד וְלֹא־מָצְאוּ לָהֶם כֵּן: טו וְהָעָם נִחָם

טז לְבִנְיָמִן כִּי־עָשָׂה יְהֹוָה פֶּרֶץ בְּשִׁבְטֵי יִשְׂרָאֵל: וַיֹּאמְרוּ זִקְנֵי הָעֵדָה מַה־
נַּעֲשֶׂה לַנּוֹתָרִים לְנָשִׁים כִּי־נִשְׁמְדָה מִבִּנְיָמִן אִשָּׁה: יז וַיֹּאמְרוּ יְרֻשַּׁת פְּלֵיטָה

יח לְבִנְיָמִן וְלֹא־יִמָּחֶה שֵׁבֶט מִיִּשְׂרָאֵל: וַאֲנַחְנוּ לֹא־נוּכַל לָתֵת לָהֶם נָשִׁים
מִבְּנוֹתֵינוּ כִּי־נִשְׁבְּעוּ בְנֵי־יִשְׂרָאֵל לֵאמֹר אָרוּר נֹתֵן אִשָּׁה לְבִנְיָמִן:

יט וַיֹּאמְרוּ הִנֵּה חַג־יְהֹוָה בְּשִׁלוֹ מִיָּמִים | יָמִימָה אֲשֶׁר מִצְּפוֹנָה לְבֵית־אֵל
מִזְרְחָה הַשֶּׁמֶשׁ לִמְסִלָּה הָעֹלָה מִבֵּית־אֵל שְׁכֶמָה וּמִנֶּגֶב לִלְבוֹנָה:

כ-כא °וַיְצַו [וַיְצַוּוּ ק] אֶת־בְּנֵי בִנְיָמִן לֵאמֹר לְכוּ וַאֲרַבְתֶּם בַּכְּרָמִים: וּרְאִיתֶם
וְהִנֵּה אִם־יֵצְאוּ בְנוֹת־שִׁילוֹ לָחוּל בַּמְּחֹלוֹת וִיצָאתֶם מִן־הַכְּרָמִים

כב וַחֲטַפְתֶּם לָכֶם אִישׁ אִשְׁתּוֹ מִבְּנוֹת שִׁילוֹ וַהֲלַכְתֶּם אֶרֶץ בִּנְיָמִן: וְהָיָה כִּי־
יָבֹאוּ אֲבוֹתָם אוֹ אֲחֵיהֶם °לָרוֹב [לָרִיב ק] | אֵלֵינוּ וְאָמַרְנוּ אֲלֵיהֶם
חָנּוּנוּ אוֹתָם כִּי לֹא לָקַחְנוּ אִישׁ אִשְׁתּוֹ בַּמִּלְחָמָה כִּי לֹא אַתֶּם נְתַתֶּם

כג לָהֶם כָּעֵת תֶּאְשָׁמוּ: וַיַּעֲשׂוּ־כֵן בְּנֵי בִנְיָמִן וַיִּשְׂאוּ נָשִׁים לְמִסְפָּרָם מִן־
הַמְּחֹלְלוֹת אֲשֶׁר גָּזָלוּ וַיֵּלְכוּ וַיָּשׁוּבוּ אֶל־נַחֲלָתָם וַיִּבְנוּ אֶת־הֶעָרִים

כד וַיֵּשְׁבוּ בָּהֶם: וַיִּתְהַלְּכוּ מִשָּׁם בְּנֵי־יִשְׂרָאֵל בָּעֵת הַהִיא אִישׁ לְשִׁבְטוֹ
כה וּלְמִשְׁפַּחְתּוֹ וַיֵּצְאוּ מִשָּׁם אִישׁ לְנַחֲלָתוֹ: בַּיָּמִים הָהֵם אֵין מֶלֶךְ בְּיִשְׂרָאֵל
אִישׁ הַיָּשָׁר בְּעֵינָיו יַעֲשֶׂה:

סכום הפסוקים של ספר שופטים שש מאות ושמנה עשר. **אברתיה** בירקרק חרוץ סימן.

21:12. Jabesh-gilead was across the Jordan.
21:14. There were six hundred Benjamite men and only
four hundred girls.

21:22. You are not guilty of violating the oath not to
"give" your daughters to the Benjamites, because the
brides were "taken," without your permission.

Jabesh-
gilead's
recompense

¹⁰ *The congregation sent twelve thousand men of valor there, and they commanded them, saying, "Go and strike down the inhabitants of Jabesh-gilead by the edge of the sword, including women and children.* ¹¹ *This is the thing that you shall do: Destroy all males, and all females who have had relations with males."* ¹² *They found among the inhabitants of Jabesh-gilead four hundred virgin girls who had never had relations with a man, and they brought them to the camp at Shiloh, which is in the land of Canaan.* *

Peace
overtures

¹³ *The entire congregation sent [messengers] and spoke to the children of Benjamin who were at the Rock of Rimmon, and they called to them in peace.* ¹⁴ *So Benjamin returned at that time. They gave them the women whom they had spared of the women of Jabesh-gilead; but they were not sufficient for them.* *

¹⁵ *The people had relented toward Benjamin, for HASHEM had made a breach in the tribes of Israel.* ¹⁶ *The elders of the congregation said, "What can we do [to provide] wives for the survivors? For the women of Benjamin have been destroyed."* ¹⁷ *They said, "The inheritance of the remnant of Benjamin [must survive], and let a tribe not be eliminated from Israel!* ¹⁸ *But we cannot give them wives from our daughters, for the Children of Israel have sworn, saying, 'Cursed be whoever gives a woman to Benjamin.' "*

Brides
from Shiloh

¹⁹ *They said, "Behold, there is a yearly holiday unto HASHEM at Shiloh, which is north of Beth-el, east of the road going up from Beth-el to Shechem, and south of Lebonah."* ²⁰ *So they directed the sons of Benjamin, saying, "Go and lie in wait in the vineyards.* ²¹ *And see; and behold, if the daughters of Shiloh go out to perform the dances, you shall emerge from the vineyards, and each of you grab his wife from the daughters of Shiloh, and go to the land of Benjamin.* ²² *It shall be that if their fathers or brothers come to protest to us, we will say to them, 'Be compassionate toward [the Benjamites], for we did not capture a wife for each man in the war [with Jabesh-gilead], and because you did not give the [wives] to them, so that you should incur guilt now.' "* *

²³ *The children of Benjamin did so. They took wives according to their number from the dancers whom they abducted, and they went and returned to their heritage; they rebuilt the cities and settled in them.*

²⁴ *At that time the Children of Israel went off from there, everyone to his tribe and his family; they left there, each man to his own heritage.*

²⁵ *In those days there was no king in Israel; a man would do whatever seemed proper in his eyes.*

Samuel שמואל

T he Book of Samuel begins with the longing of a barren woman, who became one of history's models of prayer. In response to Hannah's entreaty from the heart, God made her the mother of Samuel, the greatest of all the judges, and a prophet who was of the stature of Moses and Aaron. Samuel became the nation's leader during one of its most dismal periods to date, and he raised it back to its earlier eminence. From his home in Ramah, he traveled the length and breadth of the land, teaching, adjudicating, and inspiring.

During his tenure, the people insisted that they needed a king, and Samuel inaugurated the era of Jewish monarchy, anointing both Saul and David. Although Saul towered head and shoulders over his peers, he failed as a leader. His tragedy cost him the throne, and he was succeeded by David, who became the epitome of royal greatness.

Most of this Book is the story of David: man of faith, unselfish leader, great warrior, loyal friend, compassionate in victory, humble in defeat, and model of repentance. Only by studying his life in the light of the Talmudic and Rabbinic commentaries can one begin to imagine his stature. Even a superficial reading of the episode of Bath-sheba shows David's humility and powerful conscience. When the prophet Nathan criticized him harshly, David did not defend himself — even though, as the Talmud explains, he was technically in the right. His remorse was so great that it became the textbook for repentance.

David consolidated the twelve often competing tribes into a single nation. He defeated external enemies and left his successor with a united, secure, prosperous kingdom. To the rest of us in all generations, he bequeathed legacies of pure faith, the seeds of the Messiah, and the Book of Psalms.

The Book of Samuel marks a historic transition in Jewish history in more ways than one, because the change from judges to kings also led to a change in the role of the prophets. Since the judges had been chosen by God because of their righteousness, there was no danger that they would defy Him or falsify His message. The monarchy, however, was hereditary, and — as seen in the sad history of the Books of Kings and Chronicles — many of the kings sinned grievously and ultimately brought the nation down. The kings could not be the moral leaders of the nation, as the judges had been. That role had to be assumed by prophets. Thus, after the Book of Samuel, we find the prophets assuming a new kind of authority and prominence, as the succeeding Books will show.

א

א וַיְהִי֩ אִ֨ישׁ אֶחָ֜ד מִן־הָרָמָתַ֛יִם צוֹפִ֖ים מֵהַ֣ר אֶפְרָ֑יִם וּשְׁמ֡וֹ אֶ֠לְקָנָה בֶּן־יְרֹחָ֨ם

ב בֶּן־אֱלִיה֤וּא בֶּן־תֹּ֙חוּ֙ בֶן־צ֔וּף אֶפְרָתִֽי׃ וְלוֹ֙ שְׁתֵּ֣י נָשִׁ֔ים שֵׁ֤ם אַחַת֙ חַנָּ֔ה וְשֵׁ֥ם

ג הַשֵּׁנִ֖ית פְּנִנָּ֑ה וַיְהִ֤י לִפְנִנָּה֙ יְלָדִ֔ים וּלְחַנָּ֖ה אֵ֥ין יְלָדִֽים׃ וְעָלָה֩ הָאִ֨ישׁ הַה֤וּא

מֵעִירוֹ֙ מִיָּמִ֣ים ׀ יָמִ֔ימָה לְהִֽשְׁתַּחֲוֺ֧ת וְלִזְבֹּ֛חַ לַֽיהוָ֥ה צְבָא֖וֹת בְּשִׁלֹ֑ה וְשָׁ֗ם שְׁנֵ֤י

ד בְנֵֽי־עֵלִי֙ חָפְנִ֣י וּפִֽנְחָ֔ס כֹּהֲנִ֖ים לַֽיהוָֽה׃ וַיְהִ֣י הַיּ֔וֹם וַיִּזְבַּ֖ח אֶלְקָנָ֑ה וְנָתַ֞ן לִפְנִנָּ֣ה

ה אִשְׁתּ֗וֹ וּֽלְכָל־בָּנֶ֛יהָ וּבְנוֹתֶ֖יהָ מָנֽוֹת׃ וּלְחַנָּ֕ה יִתֵּ֛ן מָנָ֥ה אַחַ֖ת אַפָּ֑יִם כִּ֤י אֶת־

ו חַנָּה֙ אָהֵ֔ב וַֽיהוָ֖ה סָגַ֥ר רַחְמָֽהּ׃ וְכִֽעֲסַ֤תָּה צָֽרָתָהּ֙ גַּם־כַּ֔עַס בַּעֲב֖וּר הַרְּעִמָ֑הּ

ז כִּֽי־סָגַ֥ר יְהוָ֖ה בְּעַ֣ד רַחְמָֽהּ׃ וְכֵ֨ן יַעֲשֶׂ֜ה שָׁנָ֣ה בְשָׁנָ֗ה מִדֵּ֤י עֲלֹתָהּ֙ בְּבֵ֣ית יְהוָ֔ה

ח כֵּ֖ן תַּכְעִסֶ֑נָּה וַתִּבְכֶּ֖ה וְלֹ֥א תֹאכַֽל׃ וַיֹּ֨אמֶר לָ֜הּ אֶלְקָנָ֣ה אִישָׁ֗הּ חַנָּה֙ לָ֣מֶה

תִבְכִּ֗י וְלָ֙מֶה֙ לֹ֣א תֹֽאכְלִ֔י וְלָ֖מֶה יֵרַ֣ע לְבָבֵ֑ךְ הֲל֤וֹא אָֽנֹכִי֙ ט֣וֹב לָ֔ךְ מֵעֲשָׂרָ֖ה

ט בָּנִֽים׃ וַתָּ֣קָם חַנָּ֔ה אַחֲרֵ֛י אָכְלָ֥ה בְשִׁלֹ֖ה וְאַחֲרֵ֣י שָׁתֹ֑ה וְעֵלִ֣י הַכֹּהֵ֗ן יֹשֵׁב֙ עַל־

י הַכִּסֵּ֔א עַל־מְזוּזַ֖ת הֵיכַ֥ל יְהוָֽה׃ וְהִ֖יא מָ֣רַת נָ֑פֶשׁ וַתִּתְפַּלֵּ֥ל עַל־יְהוָ֖ה וּבָכֹ֥ה

יא תִבְכֶּֽה׃ וַתִּדֹּ֨ר נֶ֜דֶר וַתֹּאמַ֗ר יְהוָ֨ה צְבָא֜וֹת אִם־רָאֹ֥ה תִרְאֶ֣ה ׀ בָּֽעֳנִ֣י אֲמָתֶ֗ךָ

וּזְכַרְתַּ֙נִי֙ וְלֹֽא־תִשְׁכַּ֣ח אֶת־אֲמָתֶ֔ךָ וְנָתַתָּ֥ה לַאֲמָתְךָ֖ זֶ֣רַע אֲנָשִׁ֑ים וּנְתַתִּ֤יו

יב לַֽיהוָה֙ כָּל־יְמֵ֣י חַיָּ֔יו וּמוֹרָ֖ה לֹא־יַעֲלֶ֥ה עַל־רֹאשֽׁוֹ׃ וְהָיָה֙ כִּ֣י הִרְבְּתָ֔ה

יג לְהִתְפַּלֵּ֖ל לִפְנֵ֣י יְהוָ֑ה וְעֵלִ֖י שֹׁמֵ֥ר אֶת־פִּֽיהָ׃ וְחַנָּ֗ה הִ֚יא מְדַבֶּ֣רֶת עַל־לִבָּ֔הּ

יד רַ֚ק שְׂפָתֶ֣יהָ נָּע֔וֹת וְקוֹלָ֖הּ לֹ֣א יִשָּׁמֵ֑עַ וַיַּחְשְׁבֶ֥הָ עֵלִ֖י לְשִׁכֹּרָֽה׃ וַיֹּ֤אמֶר אֵלֶ֙יהָ֙

טו עֵלִ֔י עַד־מָתַ֖י תִּשְׁתַּכָּרִ֑ין הָסִ֥ירִי אֶת־יֵינֵ֖ךְ מֵעָלָֽיִךְ׃ וַתַּ֨עַן חַנָּ֤ה וַתֹּ֨אמֶר֙ לֹ֣א

אֲדֹנִ֔י אִשָּׁ֤ה קְשַׁת־ר֙וּחַ֙ אָנֹ֔כִי וְיַ֥יִן וְשֵׁכָ֖ר לֹ֣א שָׁתִ֑יתִי וָאֶשְׁפֹּ֥ךְ אֶת־נַפְשִׁ֖י

טז לִפְנֵ֥י יְהוָֽה׃ אַל־תִּתֵּן֙ אֶת־אֲמָ֣תְךָ֔ לִפְנֵ֖י בַּת־בְּלִיָּ֑עַל כִּֽי־מֵרֹ֥ב שִׂיחִ֛י וְכַעְסִ֖י

יז דִּבַּ֥רְתִּי עַד־הֵֽנָּה׃ וַיַּ֧עַן עֵלִ֛י וַיֹּ֖אמֶר לְכִ֣י לְשָׁל֑וֹם וֵֽאלֹהֵ֣י יִשְׂרָאֵ֗ל יִתֵּן֙ אֶת־

יח שֵׁ֣לָתֵ֔ךְ אֲשֶׁ֥ר שָׁאַ֖לְתְּ מֵעִמּֽוֹ׃ וַתֹּ֗אמֶר תִּמְצָ֧א שִׁפְחָתְךָ֛ חֵ֖ן בְּעֵינֶ֑יךָ וַתֵּ֨לֶךְ

יט הָאִשָּׁ֤ה לְדַרְכָּהּ֙ וַתֹּאכַ֔ל וּפָנֶ֥יהָ לֹא־הָ֥יוּ לָ֖הּ עֽוֹד׃ וַיַּשְׁכִּ֣מוּ בַבֹּ֗קֶר וַיִּֽשְׁתַּחֲווּ֙

לִפְנֵ֣י יְהוָ֔ה וַיָּשֻׁ֛בוּ וַיָּבֹ֥אוּ אֶל־בֵּיתָ֖ם הָרָמָ֑תָה וַיֵּ֤דַע אֶלְקָנָה֙ אֶת־חַנָּ֣ה

כ אִשְׁתּ֔וֹ וַיִּזְכְּרֶ֖הָ יְהוָֽה׃ וַיְהִי֙ לִתְקֻפ֣וֹת הַיָּמִ֔ים וַתַּ֥הַר חַנָּ֖ה וַתֵּ֣לֶד בֵּ֑ן וַתִּקְרָ֤א

כא אֶת־שְׁמוֹ֙ שְׁמוּאֵ֔ל כִּ֥י מֵֽיהוָ֖ה שְׁאִלְתִּֽיו׃ וַיַּ֛עַל הָאִ֥ישׁ אֶלְקָנָ֖ה וְכָל־בֵּית֑וֹ

כב לִזְבֹּ֧חַ לַֽיהוָ֛ה אֶת־זֶ֥בַח הַיָּמִ֖ים וְאֶת־נִדְרֽוֹ׃ וְחַנָּ֖ה לֹ֣א עָלָ֑תָה כִּֽי־אָמְרָ֣ה

לְאִישָׁ֗הּ עַ֣ד יִגָּמֵ֤ל הַנַּ֙עַר֙ וַהֲבִאֹתִ֔יו וְנִרְאָה֙ אֶת־פְּנֵ֣י יְהוָ֔ה וְיָ֥שַׁב שָׁ֖ם עַד־

כג עוֹלָֽם׃ וַיֹּ֣אמֶר לָהּ֩ אֶלְקָנָ֨ה אִישָׁ֜הּ עֲשִׂ֧י הַטּ֣וֹב בְּעֵינַ֗יִךְ שְׁבִי֙ עַד־גָּמְלֵ֣ךְ אֹת֔וֹ

אַ֛ךְ יָקֵ֥ם יְהוָ֖ה אֶת־דְּבָר֑וֹ וַתֵּ֤שֶׁב הָֽאִשָּׁה֙ וַתֵּ֣ינֶק אֶת־בְּנָ֔הּ עַד־גָּמְלָ֖הּ אֹתֽוֹ׃

1:1. Elkanah, a Levite, lived in the territory of Ephraim.
His complete lineage is recorded in *I Chronicles* 6:18-23.

1:6. Peninnah taunted her by saying such things as,
"Have you bought something new for your baby?" She
meant to provoke Hannah to pray, but was punished for
doing so in a cruel manner.

1:11. He would be a nazirite, who is forbidden to cut his
hair. See *Numbers* 6:5.

1:18. To pray for the fulfillment of your blessing.

1:20. The name combines the words שָׁאוּל מֵאֵל, *requested of God (Radak)*.

1:21. He had vowed an offering in gratitude for Samuel's

1

BIRTH OF
SAMUEL
1:1-28

Elkanah and
his family

¹ There was a certain man from Ramathaim-zophim, from Mount Ephraim, whose name was Elkanah, son of Jeroham, son of Elihu, son of Tohu, son of Zuph, from the land of Ephraim. * ² He had two wives; one's name was Hannah and the second's name was Peninnah. Peninnah had children, but Hannah had no children. ³ This man would ascend from his city from year to year to prostrate himself and to bring offerings to HASHEM, Master of Legions, in Shiloh, where the two sons of Eli — Hophni and Phinehas — were Kohanim to HASHEM.

Hannah's
suffering

⁴ It happened on the day that Elkanah brought offerings that he gave portions to Peninnah, his wife, and to all her sons and daughters. ⁵ But to Hannah he gave a double portion, for he loved Hannah and HASHEM had closed her womb. ⁶ Her rival [Peninnah] provoked her again and again in order to irritate her, for HASHEM had closed her womb. * ⁷ This is what he would do year after year, and whenever [Peninnah] would go up to the house of HASHEM, she would provoke her; she would cry and not eat. ⁸ Elkanah, her husband, said to her, "Hannah, why do you cry and why do you not eat? Why is your heart broken? Am I not better to you than ten children?"

(See Appendix A,
timeline 3)

Hannah's
prayer

⁹ Hannah arose after eating in Shiloh and after drinking; and Eli the Kohen was sitting on the chair, near the doorpost of the Sanctuary of HASHEM. ¹⁰ She was feeling bitter, and she prayed to HASHEM, weeping continuously. ¹¹ She made a vow and said, "HASHEM, Master of Legions, if You take note of the suffering of Your maidservant, and You remember me, and do not forget Your maidservant, and give Your maidservant male offspring, then I shall give him to HASHEM all the days of his life, and a razor shall not come upon his head."*

Eli's
misjudgment
and blessing

¹² It happened as she continued to pray before HASHEM that Eli observed her mouth. ¹³ Hannah was speaking to her heart — only her lips moved, but her voice was not heard — so Eli thought she was drunk. ¹⁴ Eli said to her, "How long will you be drunk? Remove your wine from yourself!" ¹⁵ Hannah answered and said, "No, my lord, I am a woman of aggrieved spirit. I have drunk neither wine nor strong drink, and I have poured out my soul before HASHEM. ¹⁶ Do not deem your maidservant to be a base woman — for it is out of much grievance and anger that I have spoken until now." ¹⁷ Eli then answered and said, "Go in peace. The God of Israel will grant the request you have made of Him." ¹⁸ She said, "May your maidservant find favor in your eyes."* Then the woman went on her way and she ate, and no longer had the same look on her face.

Samuel's
birth

¹⁹ They arose early in the morning and prostrated themselves before HASHEM; then they returned and came to their home, to Ramah. Elkanah knew Hannah his wife and HASHEM remembered her. ²⁰ And it happened with the passage of the period of days that Hannah had conceived, and she gave birth to a son. She named him Samuel, for [she said,] "I requested him from HASHEM."*

²¹ The man Elkanah ascended with his entire household to bring to HASHEM the annual offering and his vow. * ²² But Hannah did not ascend, as she told her husband, "When the child is weaned, then I will bring him, and he shall appear before HASHEM and shall settle there forever." ²³ Elkanah her husband said to her, "Do what is good in your eyes; remain until you wean him — but may HASHEM fulfill His word."* So the woman remained and nursed her son until she weaned him.

---

birth (Radak).
1:23. Hannah had been told prophetically that Samuel

would be the leader of Israel. Elkanah now prayed that the promise be fulfilled (Malbim).

כד וַתַּעֲלֵהוּ עִמָּהּ כַּאֲשֶׁר גְּמָלַתּוּ בְּפָרִים שְׁלֹשָׁה וְאֵיפָה אַחַת קֶמַח וְנֵבֶל
כה יַיִן וַתְּבִאֵהוּ בֵית־יהוָה שִׁלוֹ וְהַנַּעַר נָעַר: וַיִּשְׁחֲטוּ אֶת־הַפָּר וַיָּבִיאוּ
כו אֶת־הַנַּעַר אֶל־עֵלִי: וַתֹּאמֶר בִּי אֲדֹנִי חֵי נַפְשְׁךָ אֲדֹנִי אֲנִי הָאִשָּׁה
כז הַנִּצֶּבֶת עִמְּכָה בָּזֶה לְהִתְפַּלֵּל אֶל־יהוָה: אֶל־הַנַּעַר הַזֶּה הִתְפַּלָּלְתִּי
כח וַיִּתֵּן יהוָה לִי אֶת־שְׁאֵלָתִי אֲשֶׁר שָׁאַלְתִּי מֵעִמּוֹ: וְגַם אָנֹכִי הִשְׁאִלְתִּהוּ
לַיהוָה כָּל־הַיָּמִים אֲשֶׁר הָיָה הוּא שָׁאוּל לַיהוָה וַיִּשְׁתַּחוּ שָׁם

ב א לַיהוָה: וַתִּתְפַּלֵּל חַנָּה וַתֹּאמַר עָלַץ לִבִּי בַּיהוָה
ב רָמָה קַרְנִי בַּיהוָה רָחַב פִּי עַל־אוֹיְבַי כִּי שָׂמַחְתִּי בִּישׁוּעָתֶךָ: אֵין־קָדוֹשׁ
ג כַּיהוָה כִּי־אֵין בִּלְתֶּךָ וְאֵין צוּר כֵּאלֹהֵינוּ: אַל־תַּרְבּוּ תְדַבְּרוּ גְּבֹהָה
גְבֹהָה יֵצֵא עָתָק מִפִּיכֶם כִּי אֵל דֵּעוֹת יהוָה °וְלֹא [°וְלוֹ ק] נִתְכְּנוּ עֲלִלוֹת:
ד-ה קֶשֶׁת גִּבֹּרִים חַתִּים וְנִכְשָׁלִים אָזְרוּ חָיִל: שְׂבֵעִים בַּלֶּחֶם נִשְׂכָּרוּ וּרְעֵבִים
ו חָדֵלּוּ עַד־עֲקָרָה יָלְדָה שִׁבְעָה וְרַבַּת בָּנִים אֻמְלָלָה: יהוָה מֵמִית
ז וּמְחַיֶּה מוֹרִיד שְׁאוֹל וַיָּעַל: יהוָה מוֹרִישׁ וּמַעֲשִׁיר מַשְׁפִּיל אַף־מְרוֹמֵם:
ח מֵקִים מֵעָפָר דָּל מֵאַשְׁפֹּת יָרִים אֶבְיוֹן לְהוֹשִׁיב עִם־נְדִיבִים וְכִסֵּא
ט כָבוֹד יַנְחִלֵם כִּי לַיהוָה מְצֻקֵי אֶרֶץ וַיָּשֶׁת עֲלֵיהֶם תֵּבֵל: רַגְלֵי °חֲסִידוֹ
י [°חֲסִידָיו ק] יִשְׁמֹר וּרְשָׁעִים בַּחֹשֶׁךְ יִדָּמּוּ כִּי־לֹא בְכֹחַ יִגְבַּר־אִישׁ: יהוָה
יֵחַתּוּ °מְרִיבוֹ [°מְרִיבָיו ק] °עֲלוֹ [°עָלָיו ק] בַּשָּׁמַיִם יַרְעֵם יהוָה יָדִין
אַפְסֵי־אָרֶץ וְיִתֶּן־עֹז לְמַלְכּוֹ וְיָרֵם קֶרֶן מְשִׁיחוֹ: ◀

יא וַיֵּלֶךְ אֶלְקָנָה הָרָמָתָה עַל־בֵּיתוֹ וְהַנַּעַר הָיָה מְשָׁרֵת אֶת־יהוָה אֶת־פְּנֵי
יב-יג עֵלִי הַכֹּהֵן: וּבְנֵי עֵלִי בְּנֵי בְלִיָּעַל לֹא יָדְעוּ אֶת־יהוָה: וּמִשְׁפַּט הַכֹּהֲנִים
אֶת־הָעָם כָּל־אִישׁ זֹבֵחַ זֶבַח וּבָא נַעַר הַכֹּהֵן כְּבַשֵּׁל הַבָּשָׂר וְהַמַּזְלֵג
יד שְׁלֹשׁ־הַשִּׁנַּיִם בְּיָדוֹ: וְהִכָּה בַכִּיּוֹר אוֹ בַדּוּד אוֹ בַקַּלַּחַת אוֹ בַפָּרוּר
כֹּל אֲשֶׁר יַעֲלֶה הַמַּזְלֵג יִקַּח הַכֹּהֵן בּוֹ כָּכָה יַעֲשׂוּ לְכָל־יִשְׂרָאֵל הַבָּאִים
טו שָׁם בְּשִׁלֹה: גַּם בְּטֶרֶם יַקְטִרוּן אֶת־הַחֵלֶב וּבָא נַעַר הַכֹּהֵן וְאָמַר לָאִישׁ
הַזֹּבֵחַ תְּנָה בָשָׂר לִצְלוֹת לַכֹּהֵן וְלֹא־יִקַּח מִמְּךָ בָּשָׂר מְבֻשָּׁל כִּי אִם־חָי:
טז וַיֹּאמֶר אֵלָיו הָאִישׁ קַטֵּר יַקְטִירוּן כַּיּוֹם הַחֵלֶב וְקַח־לְךָ כַּאֲשֶׁר תְּאַוֶּה
נַפְשֶׁךָ וְאָמַר | °לוֹ [°לֹא ק] כִּי עַתָּה תִתֵּן וְאִם־לֹא לָקַחְתִּי בְחָזְקָה:

1:28. Either Elkanah or Samuel prostrated himself in assent to Hannah's decision.

2:1-10. Hannah's lyrical expression of gratitude is regarded by the Sages as one of history's great prophetic songs. Its theme is the acknowledgment that triumph and defeat, wealth and poverty, grandeur and degradation are not permanent conditions. God apportions them according to what people deserve or need; therefore, good deeds and prayer can cause changes in the human condition.

2:5. Hannah alluded to Peninah's arrogant taunts (1:6).

The end was that Hannah would bear many children, while most of Peninah's would die.

2:10. Her prayer was prophetic: May God crush Samuel's Philistine enemies, and bless Saul and David, the two kings he would anoint.

2:11. Samuel served Eli, yet the verse states that he "served HASHEM"; this teaches that serving righteous scholars is tantamount to serving God Himself (*Rashi*).

2:12-16. These lawless priests intimidated the people into giving them larger portions than those apportioned to them by the Torah.

Samuel's dedication as a servant of God

²⁴ She brought him up with her when she weaned him, with three bulls, one ephah of flour, and a flask of wine; she brought him to the house of HASHEM in Shiloh, though the child was still tender. ²⁵ They slaughtered the bull, and brought the child to Eli. ²⁶ She said, "Please, my lord! By your life, my lord, I am the woman who was standing by you here praying to HASHEM. ²⁷ This is the child that I prayed for; HASHEM granted me my request that I asked of Him. ²⁸ Furthermore, I have dedicated him to HASHEM — all the days that he lives he is dedicated to HASHEM." He* then prostrated himself to HASHEM.

2

HANNAH'S SONG OF PRAYER
2:1-10

¹ Then Hannah prayed and said: *

My heart exults in HASHEM, my pride has been raised through HASHEM;
my mouth is opened wide against my antagonists,
for I rejoice in Your salvation.
² There is none as holy as HASHEM, for there is none besides You,
and there is no Rock like our God.
³ Do not abound in speaking with arrogance upon arrogance,
let not haughtiness come from your mouth;
for HASHEM is the God of thoughts, and [men's] deeds are accounted by Him.

Man's shifting fortunes

⁴ The bow of the mighty is broken,
while the foundering are girded with strength.
⁵ The sated ones are hired out for bread,
while the hungry ones cease to be so;
while the barren woman bears seven,
the one with many children becomes bereft. *
⁶ HASHEM brings death and gives life, He lowers to the grave and raises up.
⁷ HASHEM impoverishes and makes rich, He humbles and He elevates.
⁸ He raises the needy from the dirt, from the trash heaps He lifts the destitute,
to seat [them] with nobles and to endow them with a seat of honor —
for HASHEM's are the pillars of the earth, and upon them He set the world.
⁹ He guards the steps of His devout ones, but the wicked are stilled in darkness; for not through strength does man prevail.

A prayer for Samuel

¹⁰ HASHEM — may those that contend with Him be shattered,
let the heavens thunder against them.
May HASHEM judge to the ends of the earth;
may He give power to His king and raise the pride of His anointed one. *

SAMUEL'S YOUTH
2:11-3:21

¹¹ Elkanah then went to Ramah, to his house, while the boy served HASHEM before Eli the Kohen. * ¹² The sons of Eli were lawless men; they did not recognize HASHEM.

Shortcomings of Eli's sons

¹³ This was the practice of the Kohanim with the people: When any person would slaughter a sacrifice the Kohen's attendant would come while the meat was cooking, with a three-pronged fork in his hand. ¹⁴ He would thrust it into the pot or the cauldron or the pan or the kettle, and everything the fork would bring up the Kohen would take with it. This is what they would do with all the Israelites who would come there, to Shiloh. ¹⁵ Even before they would burn the fat [upon the Altar] the Kohen's attendant would come and say to the man who was bringing the offering, "Give some meat for roasting for the Kohen; he will not take cooked meat from you, but only raw [meat]." ¹⁶ The man would say, "Let them first burn the fat [upon the altar] and then take for yourself whatever your soul desires." But [the attendant] would say, "No; give it now, or else I will take it by force."*

יז וַתְּהִ֣י חַטַּ֧את הַנְּעָרִ֛ים גְּדוֹלָ֥ה מְאֹ֖ד אֶת־פְּנֵ֣י יְהֹוָ֑ה כִּ֤י נִֽאֲצוּ֙ הָֽאֲנָשִׁ֔ים אֵ֖ת

יח־יט מִנְחַ֥ת יְהֹוָֽה: וּשְׁמוּאֵ֕ל מְשָׁרֵ֖ת אֶת־פְּנֵ֣י יְהֹוָ֑ה נַ֕עַר חָג֖וּר אֵפ֥וֹד בָּֽד: וּמְעִ֤יל

קָטֹן֙ תַּֽעֲשֶׂה־לּ֣וֹ אִמּ֔וֹ וְהַֽעַלְתָ֥ה ל֖וֹ מִיָּמִ֣ים ׀ יָמִ֑ימָה בַּֽעֲלוֹתָהּ֙ אֶת־אִישָׁ֔הּ

כ לִזְבֹּ֖חַ אֶת־זֶ֥בַח הַיָּמִֽים: וּבֵרַ֨ךְ עֵלִ֜י אֶת־אֶלְקָנָ֣ה וְאֶת־אִשְׁתּ֗וֹ וְאָמַר֙ יָשֵׂם֩

יְהֹוָ֨ה לְךָ֥ זֶ֨רַע֙ מִן־הָֽאִשָּׁ֣ה הַזֹּ֔את תַּ֚חַת הַשְּׁאֵלָ֔ה אֲשֶׁ֥ר שָׁאַ֖ל לַֽיהֹוָ֑ה וְהָֽלְכ֖וּ

כא לִמְקֹמֽוֹ: כִּֽי־פָקַ֤ד יְהֹוָה֙ אֶת־חַנָּ֔ה וַתַּ֛הַר וַתֵּ֥לֶד שְׁלֹשָֽׁה־בָנִ֖ים וּשְׁתֵּ֣י בָנ֑וֹת

כב וַיִּגְדַּ֛ל הַנַּ֥עַר שְׁמוּאֵ֖ל עִם־יְהֹוָֽה: וְעֵלִ֖י זָקֵ֣ן מְאֹ֑ד וְשָׁמַ֗ע

אֵת֩ כָּל־אֲשֶׁ֨ר יַֽעֲשׂ֤וּן בָּנָיו֙ לְכָל־יִשְׂרָאֵ֔ל וְאֵ֤ת אֲשֶֽׁר־יִשְׁכְּבוּן֙ אֶת־הַנָּשִׁ֔ים

כג הַצֹּֽבְא֔וֹת פֶּ֖תַח אֹ֥הֶל מוֹעֵֽד: וַיֹּ֣אמֶר לָהֶ֔ם לָ֥מָּה תַֽעֲשׂ֖וּן כַּדְּבָרִ֣ים הָאֵ֑לֶּה

כד אֲשֶׁ֨ר אָֽנֹכִ֤י שֹׁמֵ֨עַ֙ אֶת־דִּבְרֵיכֶ֣ם רָעִ֔ים מֵאֵ֖ת כָּל־הָעָ֥ם אֵֽלֶּה: אַ֖ל בָּנָ֑י כִּ֠י

כה לֽוֹא־טוֹבָ֤ה הַשְּׁמֻעָה֙ אֲשֶׁ֣ר אָֽנֹכִ֣י שֹׁמֵ֔עַ מַֽעֲבִרִ֖ים עַם־יְהֹוָֽה: אִם־יֶֽחֱטָ֨א

אִ֤ישׁ לְאִישׁ֙ וּפִֽלְל֣וֹ אֱלֹהִ֔ים וְאִ֤ם לַֽיהֹוָה֙ יֶֽחֱטָא־אִ֔ישׁ מִ֖י יִתְפַּלֶּל־ל֑וֹ וְלֹ֤א

כו יִשְׁמְעוּ֙ לְק֣וֹל אֲבִיהֶ֔ם כִּֽי־חָפֵ֥ץ יְהֹוָ֖ה לַֽהֲמִיתָֽם: וְהַנַּ֣עַר שְׁמוּאֵ֔ל הֹלֵ֥ךְ וְגָדֵ֖ל

כז וָט֑וֹב גַּ֚ם עִם־יְהֹוָ֔ה וְגַ֖ם עִם־אֲנָשִֽׁים: וַיָּבֹ֥א אִישׁ־אֱלֹהִ֖ים אֶל־עֵלִ֑י וַיֹּ֣אמֶר אֵלָ֗יו כֹּ֚ה אָמַ֣ר יְהֹוָ֔ה הֲנִגְלֹ֤ה נִגְלֵ֨יתִי֙

כח אֶל־בֵּ֣ית אָבִ֔יךָ בִּֽהְיוֹתָ֥ם בְּמִצְרַ֖יִם לְבֵ֣ית פַּרְעֹֽה: וּבָחֹ֣ר אֹ֠ת֠וֹ מִכָּל־שִׁבְטֵ֨י

יִשְׂרָאֵ֥ל לִי֙ לְכֹהֵ֔ן לַֽעֲל֣וֹת עַל־מִזְבְּחִ֗י לְהַקְטִ֥יר קְטֹ֨רֶת֙ לָשֵׂ֣את אֵפ֔וֹד לְפָנָ֑י

כט וָֽאֶתְּנָה֙ לְבֵ֣ית אָבִ֔יךָ אֶת־כָּל־אִשֵּׁ֖י בְּנֵ֣י יִשְׂרָאֵֽל: לָ֣מָּה תִבְעֲט֗וּ בְּזִבְחִי֙

וּבְמִנְחָתִ֔י אֲשֶׁ֥ר צִוִּ֖יתִי מָע֑וֹן וַתְּכַבֵּ֤ד אֶת־בָּנֶ֨יךָ֙ מִמֶּ֔נִּי לְהַבְרִֽיאֲכֶ֗ם מֵֽרֵאשִׁ֛ית

ל כָּל־מִנְחַ֥ת יִשְׂרָאֵ֖ל לְעַמִּֽי: לָכֵ֗ן נְאֻם־יְהֹוָה֮ אֱלֹהֵ֣י יִשְׂרָאֵל֒ אָמ֣וֹר אָמַ֔רְתִּי

בֵּֽיתְךָ֙ וּבֵ֣ית אָבִ֔יךָ יִתְהַלְּכ֥וּ לְפָנַ֖י עַד־עוֹלָ֑ם וְעַתָּ֤ה נְאֻם־יְהֹוָה֙ חָלִ֣ילָה לִּ֔י

לא כִּי־מְכַבְּדַ֥י אֲכַבֵּ֖ד וּבֹזַ֥י יֵקָֽלּוּ: הִנֵּה֙ יָמִ֣ים בָּאִ֔ים וְגָֽדַעְתִּי֙ אֶת־זְרֹ֣עֲךָ֔ וְאֶת־זְרֹ֖עַ

לב בֵּ֣ית אָבִ֑יךָ מִֽהְי֥וֹת זָקֵ֖ן בְּבֵיתֶֽךָ: וְהִבַּטְתָּ֞ צַ֣ר מָע֗וֹן בְּכֹ֛ל אֲשֶׁר־יֵיטִ֥יב אֶת־

לג יִשְׂרָאֵ֑ל וְלֹֽא־יִהְיֶ֥ה זָקֵ֛ן בְּבֵֽיתְךָ֖ כָּל־הַיָּמִֽים: וְאִ֗ישׁ לֹֽא־אַכְרִ֤ית לְךָ֙ מֵעִ֣ם

מִזְבְּחִ֔י לְכַלּ֥וֹת אֶת־עֵינֶ֖יךָ וְלַֽאֲדִ֣יב אֶת־נַפְשֶׁ֑ךָ וְכָל־מַרְבִּ֥ית בֵּֽיתְךָ֖ יָמ֥וּתוּ

לד אֲנָשִֽׁים: וְזֶה־לְּךָ֣ הָא֗וֹת אֲשֶׁ֤ר יָבֹא֙ אֶל־שְׁנֵ֣י בָנֶ֔יךָ אֶל־חָפְנִ֖י וּפִ֣ינְחָ֑ס בְּי֥וֹם

לה אֶחָ֖ד יָמ֥וּתוּ שְׁנֵיהֶֽם: וַהֲקִֽימֹתִ֥י לִ֨י כֹּהֵ֜ן נֶֽאֱמָ֗ן כַּֽאֲשֶׁ֧ר בִּלְבָבִ֛י וּבְנַפְשִׁ֖י יַֽעֲשֶׂ֑ה

לו וּבָנִ֤יתִי לוֹ֙ בַּ֣יִת נֶֽאֱמָ֔ן וְהִתְהַלֵּ֥ךְ לִפְנֵֽי־מְשִׁיחִ֖י כָּל־הַיָּמִֽים: וְהָיָ֗ה כָּל־הַנּוֹתָר֙

בְּבֵ֣יתְךָ֔ יָבוֹא֙ לְהִשְׁתַּֽחֲו֣‍ֹת ל֔וֹ לַֽאֲג֥וֹרַת כֶּ֖סֶף וְכִכַּר־לָ֑חֶם וְאָמַ֕ר סְפָחֵ֥נִי נָ֛א

ג א אֶל־אַחַ֥ת הַכְּהֻנּ֖וֹת לֶֽאֱכֹ֥ל פַּת־לָֽחֶם: וְהַנַּ֧עַר שְׁמוּאֵ֛ל מְשָׁרֵ֥ת אֶת־

ב יְהֹוָ֖ה לִפְנֵ֣י עֵלִ֑י וּדְבַר־יְהֹוָ֗ה הָיָ֤ה יָקָר֙ בַּיָּמִ֣ים הָהֵ֔ם אֵ֥ין חָז֖וֹן נִפְרָֽץ: וַיְהִי֙ בַּיּ֣וֹם

2:20. Elkanah had asked Eli to bless him with more children from his wife Hannah.

2:22. According to the Midrash this phrase has a figurative meaning: They callously delayed bringing the women's bird-offerings (see *Leviticus* 12:8 and 15:29), so that the women could not return home to their husbands, but had to remain in Shiloh overnight. Scripture considers this breach of modesty as a form of adultery.

¹⁷ *The sin of the attendants was very great before* HASHEM, *for the men had disgraced* HASHEM'S *offering.*

¹⁸ *Samuel was serving before* HASHEM — *a lad girded with a linen robe.* ¹⁹ *His mother would make him a small robe and bring it up to him from year to year, when she came up with her husband to slaughter the annual offering.* ²⁰ *Then Eli would bless Elkanah and his wife and say, "May* HASHEM *grant you offspring from this woman,"* *because of the request that he had made of* HASHEM,* *and they would return to [Elkanah's] place.* ²¹ *For* HASHEM *had remembered Hannah, and she conceived and gave birth to three sons and two daughters. And the boy Samuel grew up with* HASHEM.

²² *Eli became very old. He heard about all that his sons were doing to all of Israel, and that they would lie with the women** *who congregated at the entrance of the Tent of Meeting,* ²³ *so he said to them, "Why do you do such things? For I hear of your evil deeds from all these people.* ²⁴ *No, my sons! — for the report that I hear* HASHEM'S *people passing on is not good.* ²⁵ *If man sins against man, a judge tries him; but if he sins against* HASHEM, *who can speak in his defense?" But they would not listen to their father's voice, for* HASHEM *desired to kill them.** ²⁶ *But the boy Samuel kept growing and improving, both with* HASHEM *and with people.*

²⁷ *A man of God came to Eli and said to him: Thus said* HASHEM, *"Did I not appear to your ancestor's family when they were in Egypt [enslaved] to the house of Pharaoh,* ²⁸ *and choose him from among all the tribes of Israel to be a Kohen to Me, to ascend My altar, to burn incense, to wear an Ephod** *before me; and [didn't] I give your ancestor's family all the fire-offerings of the Children of Israel?* ²⁹ *Why do you scorn My sacrifice and My meal-offering which I have commanded [to be brought in My] dwelling place, and you honor your sons more than Me,** *to fatten yourselves from the choicest parts of all the offerings of Israel, before My people?"* ³⁰ *Therefore, [this is] the word of* HASHEM, *God of Israel: "I had indeed said that your family and your father's family would walk before Me forever — but now," — the word of* HASHEM — *"far be it from Me [to do so]; for I honor those who honor Me, and those that scorn Me will be accursed.* ³¹ *Behold, days are coming when I shall cut off your arm and the arm of your father's family, from there being any old person in your family.* ³² *And you will see a rival [Kohen in My] dwelling place throughout all the good [times] that He will bring upon Israel, but there will be no old people in your family for all time.* ³³ *But I will not [completely] cut off any of your men from upon My altar, to make your eyes pine and your soul sad; and all those raised in your house will die as [young] men.* ³⁴ *This [will be] the sign for you: that which will befall your two sons, Hophni and Phinehas — they will both die on the same day.* ³⁵ *And I will appoint for Myself a faithful Kohen, who will do as is in My heart and in My desire, and I will build for him a faithful house, and he will walk before My anointed one all the days.* ³⁶ *And it shall be that anyone left over of your family will come to bow down to him for a small coin or a loaf of bread, and will say, 'Please attach me to one of the priestly divisions to eat a morsel of bread.'"*

Eli blesses
Hannah

Eli's sons
disobey him

Prophetic
judgment
against Eli

3 (See Appendix
A, timeline 3)

¹ **T**he lad Samuel was serving HASHEM before Eli. The word of HASHEM was scarce in those days; vision was not widespread.* ² It happened one day

---

2:25. Since they deserved to die, God influenced them to be stubborn and not repent.

2:28. One of Aaron's priestly garments. See *Exodus* 28:4.

2:29. Eli shared his sons' guilt because he did not

chastise them sufficiently.

3:1. Since prophecy was not common then, Samuel did not realize that the voice he heard (vv. 5-8) was that of God.

הַהוּא וְעֵלִי שֹׁכֵב בִּמְקֹמוֹ °וְעֵינוֹ [°וְעֵינָיו ק] הֵחֵלּוּ כֵהוֹת לֹא יוּכַל

לִרְאוֹת: וְנֵר אֱלֹהִים טֶרֶם יִכְבֶּה וּשְׁמוּאֵל שֹׁכֵב בְּהֵיכַל יהוה אֲשֶׁר־שָׁם ג

ד־ה אֲרוֹן אֱלֹהִים: וַיִּקְרָא יהוה אֶל־שְׁמוּאֵל וַיֹּאמֶר הִנֵּנִי: וַיָּרָץ אֶל־

עֵלִי וַיֹּאמֶר הִנְנִי כִּי־קָרָאתָ לִּי וַיֹּאמֶר לֹא־קָרָאתִי שׁוּב שְׁכָב וַיֵּלֶךְ וַיִּשְׁכָּב:

ו וַיֹּסֶף יהוה קְרֹא עוֹד שְׁמוּאֵל וַיָּקָם שְׁמוּאֵל וַיֵּלֶךְ אֶל־עֵלִי וַיֹּאמֶר הִנְנִי

כִּי קָרָאתָ לִּי וַיֹּאמֶר לֹא־קָרָאתִי בְנִי שׁוּב שְׁכָב: וּשְׁמוּאֵל טֶרֶם יָדַע אֶת־ ז

יהוה וְטֶרֶם יִגָּלֶה אֵלָיו דְּבַר־יהוה: וַיֹּסֶף יהוה קְרֹא־שְׁמוּאֵל בַּשְּׁלִשִׁית ח

וַיָּקָם וַיֵּלֶךְ אֶל־עֵלִי וַיֹּאמֶר הִנְנִי כִּי קָרָאתָ לִי וַיָּבֶן עֵלִי כִּי יהוה קֹרֵא

ט לַנָּעַר: וַיֹּאמֶר עֵלִי לִשְׁמוּאֵל לֵךְ שְׁכָב וְהָיָה אִם־יִקְרָא אֵלֶיךָ וְאָמַרְתָּ דַּבֵּר

י יהוה כִּי שֹׁמֵעַ עַבְדֶּךָ וַיֵּלֶךְ שְׁמוּאֵל וַיִּשְׁכַּב בִּמְקוֹמוֹ: וַיָּבֹא יהוה וַיִּתְיַצַּב

וַיִּקְרָא כְפַעַם־בְּפַעַם שְׁמוּאֵל | שְׁמוּאֵל וַיֹּאמֶר שְׁמוּאֵל דַּבֵּר כִּי שֹׁמֵעַ

יא עַבְדֶּךָ: וַיֹּאמֶר יהוה אֶל־שְׁמוּאֵל הִנֵּה אָנֹכִי עֹשֶׂה דָבָר בְּיִשְׂרָאֵל

יב אֲשֶׁר כָּל־שֹׁמְעוֹ תְּצִלֶּינָה שְׁתֵּי אָזְנָיו: בַּיּוֹם הַהוּא אָקִים אֶל־עֵלִי אֵת כָּל־

יג אֲשֶׁר דִּבַּרְתִּי אֶל־בֵּיתוֹ הָחֵל וְכַלֵּה: וְהִגַּדְתִּי לוֹ כִּי־שֹׁפֵט אֲנִי אֶת־בֵּיתוֹ

עַד־עוֹלָם בַּעֲוֹן אֲשֶׁר־יָדַע כִּי־מְקַלְלִים לָהֶם בָּנָיו וְלֹא כִהָה בָּם: וְלָכֵן יד

נִשְׁבַּעְתִּי לְבֵית עֵלִי אִם־יִתְכַּפֵּר עֲוֹן בֵּית־עֵלִי בְּזֶבַח וּבְמִנְחָה עַד־עוֹלָם:

טו וַיִּשְׁכַּב שְׁמוּאֵל עַד־הַבֹּקֶר וַיִּפְתַּח אֶת־דַּלְתוֹת בֵּית־יהוה וּשְׁמוּאֵל יָרֵא

טז מֵהַגִּיד אֶת־הַמַּרְאָה אֶל־עֵלִי: וַיִּקְרָא עֵלִי אֶת־שְׁמוּאֵל וַיֹּאמֶר שְׁמוּאֵל

יז בְּנִי וַיֹּאמֶר הִנֵּנִי: וַיֹּאמֶר מָה הַדָּבָר אֲשֶׁר דִּבֶּר אֵלֶיךָ אַל־נָא תְכַחֵד מִמֶּנִּי

כֹּה יַעֲשֶׂה־לְּךָ אֱלֹהִים וְכֹה יוֹסִיף אִם־תְּכַחֵד מִמֶּנִּי דָּבָר מִכָּל־הַדָּבָר

יח אֲשֶׁר־דִּבֶּר אֵלֶיךָ: וַיַּגֶּד־לוֹ שְׁמוּאֵל אֶת־כָּל־הַדְּבָרִים וְלֹא כִחֵד מִמֶּנּוּ

וַיֹּאמַר יהוה הוּא הַטּוֹב °בְּעֵינוֹ [°בְּעֵינָיו ק] יַעֲשֶׂה: וַיִּגְדַּל שְׁמוּאֵל וַיהוה יט

כ הָיָה עִמּוֹ וְלֹא־הִפִּיל מִכָּל־דְּבָרָיו אָרְצָה: וַיֵּדַע כָּל־יִשְׂרָאֵל מִדָּן וְעַד־

כא בְּאֵר שָׁבַע כִּי נֶאֱמָן שְׁמוּאֵל לְנָבִיא לַיהוה: וַיֹּסֶף יהוה לְהֵרָאֹה

ד א בְשִׁלֹה כִּי־נִגְלָה יהוה אֶל־שְׁמוּאֵל בְּשִׁלוֹ בִּדְבַר יהוה: וַיְהִי

דְבַר־שְׁמוּאֵל לְכָל־יִשְׂרָאֵל וַיֵּצֵא יִשְׂרָאֵל לִקְרַאת פְּלִשְׁתִּים

ב לַמִּלְחָמָה וַיַּחֲנוּ עַל־הָאֶבֶן הָעֵזֶר וּפְלִשְׁתִּים חָנוּ בַאֲפֵק: וַיַּעַרְכוּ

פְלִשְׁתִּים לִקְרַאת יִשְׂרָאֵל וַתִּטֹּשׁ הַמִּלְחָמָה וַיִּנָּגֶף יִשְׂרָאֵל לִפְנֵי פְלִשְׁתִּים

ג וַיַּכּוּ בַמַּעֲרָכָה בַּשָּׂדֶה כְּאַרְבַּעַת אֲלָפִים אִישׁ: וַיָּבֹא הָעָם אֶל־הַמַּחֲנֶה

וַיֹּאמְרוּ זִקְנֵי יִשְׂרָאֵל לָמָּה נְגָפָנוּ יהוה הַיּוֹם לִפְנֵי פְלִשְׁתִּים נִקְחָה

אֵלֵינוּ מִשִּׁלֹה אֶת־אֲרוֹן בְּרִית יהוה וְיָבֹא בְקִרְבֵּנוּ וְיֹשִׁעֵנוּ מִכַּף אֹיְבֵינוּ:

3:13. This is a euphemism; the intent of the verse is "his sons were blaspheming *Me*," i.e., God.

3:17. "May unspoken punishments befall you if you do not tell me." According to the Midrash, "If you do not tell

me, may whatever was said about me happen to you."

3:18. With these words, Eli accepted God's judgment.

3:19. God did not reject anything Samuel said; rather, He caused it all to come true.

Samuel's call
to prophecy

that Eli was lying in his place; his eyes had begun to become dim, he could not see. ³ The lamp of HASHEM had not yet gone out — and Samuel was lying — in the Temple of HASHEM where the Ark of God was.

Samuel's
bewilderment

⁴ HASHEM called to Samuel, and he said, "Here I am." ⁵ He ran to Eli and said, "Here I am, for you called me." But he said, "I did not call; go back and lie down," so he went and lay down. ⁶ HASHEM continued to call again, "Samuel!" so Samuel arose and went to Eli and said, "Here I am, for you called me." But he said, "I did not call, my son; go back and lie down." ⁷ Samuel had not yet known HASHEM, and the word of HASHEM had not yet been revealed to him. ⁸ HASHEM continued to call, "Samuel!" a third time, and he arose and went to Eli and said, "Here I am, for you called me." Then Eli realized that HASHEM was calling the lad.

⁹ Eli said to Samuel, "Go and lie down; and if He calls you, you should say, 'Speak, HASHEM, for Your servant is listening.' " Samuel went and lay down in his place. ¹⁰ HASHEM came and appeared, and called as the other times, "Samuel, Samuel!" and Samuel said, "Speak, for Your servant is listening."

The downfall
of the house
of Eli

¹¹ HASHEM said to Samuel, "Behold, I am going to do [such] a thing in Israel that when anyone hears about it, both of his ears will ring. ¹² On that day, I will fulfill for Eli all that I have spoken concerning his house, beginning to destroy. ¹³ I have told him that I am executing judgment against his house forever for the sin [he committed] that he was aware that his sons were blaspheming themselves * and he did not censure them. ¹⁴ Therefore I have sworn concerning the house of Eli that the sin of the house of Eli would never be atoned for by sacrifice or meal-offering."

Eli accepts
the bitter
decree

¹⁵ Samuel lay until the morning, when he opened the doors of the House of HASHEM; and Samuel was fearful of relating the vision to Eli. ¹⁶ Eli called Samuel and said, "Samuel, my son!" and he said, "Here I am." ¹⁷ He said, "What is the word that He spoke to you? Please do not withhold from me! Such shall God do to you and such shall He do further, * if you withhold from me anything from the word that He spoke to you!" ¹⁸ Samuel told him all the words and did not withhold from him. [Eli] said, "He is HASHEM; He will do what is good in His eyes."*

¹⁹ Samuel grew up, and HASHEM was with him; He did not cast any of his words to the ground. * ²⁰ All of Israel, from Dan to Beer-sheba, knew that Samuel was faithful as a prophet to HASHEM.

²¹ [Thus] HASHEM once again appeared in Shiloh, for HASHEM appeared to Samuel in Shiloh, with the word of HASHEM.

4

THE ARK'S
CAPTURE
4:1-5:12

¹ The word of Samuel* befell all of Israel.

Israel went out to war against the Philistines. They encamped at Eben-ezer, while the Philistines encamped at Aphek. ² The Philistines arrayed themselves opposite Israel and the battle spread. Israel was smitten before the Philistines; they slew about four thousand men in the battlefield.

The
Philistines
defeat Israel

³ The people came to the camp, and the elders of Israel said, "Why did HASHEM smite us today before the Philistines? Let us take with us from Shiloh the Ark of the Covenant of HASHEM that He may come in our midst and save us from the hands of our enemies!"

4:1. The fearsome prophecy of 3:11-14.

ד וַיִּשְׁלַ֣ח הָעָם֮ שִׁלֹה֒ וַיִּשְׂא֣וּ מִשָּׁ֗ם אֵ֚ת אֲרוֹן֙ בְּרִית־יְהֹוָ֣ה צְבָא֔וֹת יֹשֵׁ֖ב

ה הַכְּרֻבִ֑ים וְשָׁ֞ם שְׁנֵ֣י בְנֵֽי־עֵלִ֗י עִם־אֲרוֹן֙ בְּרִ֣ית הָאֱלֹהִ֔ים חׇפְנִ֖י וּפִֽינְחָ֑ס: וַיְהִ֗י

כְּב֨וֹא אֲר֤וֹן בְּרִית־יְהֹוָה֙ אֶל־הַֽמַּחֲנֶ֔ה וַיָּרִ֥עוּ כׇל־יִשְׂרָאֵ֖ל תְּרוּעָ֣ה גְדוֹלָ֑ה

ו וַתֵּהֹ֖ם הָאָֽרֶץ: וַיִּשְׁמְע֤וּ פְלִשְׁתִּים֙ אֶת־ק֣וֹל הַתְּרוּעָ֔ה וַיֹּ֣אמְר֔וּ מֶ֠ה ק֣וֹל

הַתְּרוּעָ֧ה הַגְּדוֹלָ֛ה הַזֹּ֖את בְּמַחֲנֵ֣ה הָֽעִבְרִ֑ים וַיֵּ֣דְע֔וּ כִּ֚י אֲר֣וֹן יְהֹוָ֔ה בָּ֖א אֶל־

ז הַֽמַּחֲנֶֽה: וַיִּֽרְאוּ֙ הַפְּלִשְׁתִּ֔ים כִּ֣י אָמְר֔וּ בָּ֥א אֱלֹהִ֖ים אֶל־הַֽמַּחֲנֶ֑ה וַיֹּֽאמְרוּ֙ א֣וֹי

ח לָ֔נוּ כִּ֣י לֹ֤א הָֽיְתָה֙ כָּזֹ֔את אֶתְמ֖וֹל שִׁלְשֹֽׁם: א֣וֹי לָ֔נוּ מִ֣י יַצִּילֵ֔נוּ מִיַּ֛ד הָאֱלֹהִ֥ים

הָאַדִּירִ֖ים הָאֵ֑לֶּה אֵ֣לֶּה הֵ֗ם הָאֱלֹהִ֞ים הַמַּכִּ֧ים אֶת־מִצְרַ֛יִם בְּכׇל־מַכָּ֖ה

ט בַּמִּדְבָּֽר: הִֽתְחַזְּק֞וּ וִֽהְי֣וּ לַֽאֲנָשִׁ֗ים פְּלִשְׁתִּים֙ פֶּ֚ן תַּֽעַבְד֣וּ לָֽעִבְרִ֔ים כַּֽאֲשֶׁ֥ר

י עָֽבְד֖וּ לָכֶ֑ם וִֽהְיִיתֶ֥ם לַֽאֲנָשִׁ֖ים וְנִלְחַמְתֶּֽם: וַיִּלָּֽחֲמ֣וּ פְלִשְׁתִּ֗ים וַיִּנָּ֤גֶף יִשְׂרָאֵל֙

וַיָּנֻ֨סוּ֙ אִ֣ישׁ לְאֹֽהָלָ֔יו וַתְּהִ֥י הַמַּכָּ֖ה גְּדוֹלָ֣ה מְאֹ֑ד וַיִּפֹּל֙ מִיִּשְׂרָאֵ֔ל שְׁלֹשִׁ֥ים

יא אֶ֖לֶף רַגְלִֽי: וַֽאֲר֥וֹן אֱלֹהִ֖ים נִלְקָ֑ח וּשְׁנֵ֤י בְנֵֽי־עֵלִי֙ מֵ֔תוּ חׇפְנִ֖י וּפִֽינְחָֽס: וַיָּ֣רׇץ

יב אִֽישׁ־בִּנְיָמִן֮ מֵהַֽמַּֽעֲרָכָה֒ וַיָּבֹ֥א שִׁלֹ֖ה בַּיּ֣וֹם הַה֑וּא וּמַדָּ֣יו קְרֻעִ֔ים וַֽאֲדָמָ֖ה עַל־

יג רֹאשֽׁוֹ: וַיָּב֗וֹא וְהִנֵּ֣ה עֵלִ֡י יֹשֵׁב֩ עַל־הַכִּסֵּ֨א [יָ֜ד ק׳] °יׇ֣יׇ דֶּ֗רֶךְ מְצַפֶּה֙ כִּֽי־הָיָ֤ה

לִבּוֹ֙ חָרֵ֔ד עַ֖ל אֲר֣וֹן הָֽאֱלֹהִ֑ים וְהָאִ֗ישׁ בָּ֚א לְהַגִּ֣יד בָּעִ֔יר וַתִּזְעַ֖ק כׇּל־הָעִֽיר:

יד וַיִּשְׁמַ֤ע עֵלִי֙ אֶת־ק֣וֹל הַצְּעָקָ֔ה וַיֹּ֕אמֶר מֶ֛ה ק֥וֹל הֶהָמ֖וֹן הַזֶּ֑ה וְהָאִ֣ישׁ מִהַ֔ר

טו וַיָּבֹ֖א וַיַּגֵּ֥ד לְעֵלִֽי: וְעֵלִ֕י בֶּן־תִּשְׁעִ֥ים וּשְׁמֹנֶ֖ה שָׁנָ֑ה וְעֵינָ֣יו קָ֔מָה וְלֹ֥א יָכ֖וֹל

טז לִרְאֽוֹת: וַיֹּ֨אמֶר הָאִ֜ישׁ אֶל־עֵלִ֗י אָֽנֹכִי֙ הַבָּ֣א מִן־הַֽמַּֽעֲרָכָ֔ה וַֽאֲנִ֕י מִן־

הַֽמַּֽעֲרָכָ֖ה נַ֣סְתִּי הַיּ֑וֹם וַיֹּ֛אמֶר מֶה־הָיָ֥ה הַדָּבָ֖ר בְּנִֽי: וַיַּ֣עַן הַֽמְבַשֵּׂ֣ר וַיֹּ֗אמֶר נָ֤ס

יז יִשְׂרָאֵל֙ לִפְנֵ֣י פְלִשְׁתִּ֔ים וְגַ֛ם מַגֵּפָ֥ה גְדוֹלָ֖ה הָֽיְתָ֣ה בָעָ֑ם וְגַם־שְׁנֵ֨י בָנֶ֜יךָ מֵ֗תוּ

יח חׇפְנִי֙ וּפִ֣ינְחָ֔ס וַֽאֲר֥וֹן הָֽאֱלֹהִ֖ים נִלְקָֽחָה: וַיְהִ֞י כְּהַזְכִּיר֣וֹ ׀ אֶת־אֲר֣וֹן הָֽאֱלֹהִ֗ים

וַיִּפֹּ֣ל מֵֽעַל־הַ֠כִּסֵּ֠א אֲחֹֽרַנִּ֞ית בְּעַ֣ד ׀ יַ֣ד הַשַּׁ֗עַר וַתִּשָּׁבֵ֤ר מַפְרַקְתּוֹ֙ וַיָּמֹ֔ת כִּֽי־

יט זָקֵ֥ן הָאִ֖ישׁ וְכָבֵ֑ד וְה֛וּא שָׁפַ֥ט אֶת־יִשְׂרָאֵ֖ל אַרְבָּעִ֥ים שָׁנָֽה: וְכַלָּת֣וֹ אֵֽשֶׁת־

פִּֽינְחָס֮ הָרָ֣ה לָלַת֒ וַתִּשְׁמַ֣ע אֶת־הַשְּׁמוּעָ֔ה אֶל־הִלָּקַח֙ אֲר֣וֹן הָֽאֱלֹהִ֔ים וּמֵ֥ת

כ חָמִ֖יהָ וְאִישָׁ֑הּ וַתִּכְרַ֣ע וַתֵּ֔לֶד כִּֽי־נֶהֶפְכ֥וּ עָלֶ֖יהָ צִרֶ֑יהָ: וּכְעֵ֣ת מוּתָ֗הּ

וַתְּדַבֵּ֨רְנָה֙ הַנִּצָּב֣וֹת עָלֶ֔יהָ אַל־תִּֽירְאִ֖י כִּ֣י בֵ֣ן יָלָ֑דְתְּ וְלֹ֥א עָֽנְתָ֖ה וְלֹא־שָׁ֥תָה

כא לִבָּֽהּ: וַתִּקְרָ֣א לַנַּ֗עַר אִֽי־כָבוֹד֙ לֵאמֹ֔ר גָּלָ֥ה כָב֖וֹד מִיִּשְׂרָאֵ֑ל אֶל־הִלָּקַ֤ח אֲרוֹן֙

כב הָֽאֱלֹהִ֔ים וְאֶל־חָמִ֖יהָ וְאִישָֽׁהּ: וַתֹּ֨אמֶר֙ גָּלָ֣ה כָב֖וֹד מִיִּשְׂרָאֵ֑ל כִּ֥י נִלְקַ֖ח אֲר֥וֹן

הָֽאֱלֹהִֽים:

ה א־ב וּפְלִשְׁתִּים֙ לָ֣קְח֔וּ אֵ֖ת אֲר֣וֹן הָֽאֱלֹהִ֑ים וַיְבִאֻ֛הוּ מֵאֶ֥בֶן הָעֵ֖זֶר אַשְׁדּֽוֹדָה: וַיִּקְח֤וּ

פְלִשְׁתִּים֙ אֶת־אֲר֣וֹן הָֽאֱלֹהִ֔ים וַיָּבִ֥יאוּ אֹת֖וֹ בֵּ֣ית דָּג֑וֹן וַיַּצִּ֥יגוּ אֹת֖וֹ אֵ֥צֶל דָּגֽוֹן:

ג וַיַּשְׁכִּ֤מוּ אַשְׁדּוֹדִים֙ מִֽמׇּחֳרָ֔ת וְהִנֵּ֣ה דָג֗וֹן נֹפֵ֤ל לְפָנָיו֙ אַ֔רְצָה לִפְנֵ֖י אֲר֣וֹן יְהֹוָ֑ה

4:16. Knowing how shocking the story would be to Eli, the man revealed it gradually.

4:21. The Hebrew term אִי כָבוֹד means *there is no glory.*

The Ark is brought to the front

⁴ So the people sent to Shiloh and carried from there the Ark of the Covenant of HASHEM, Master of Legions, Who dwells atop the Cherubim, and the two sons of Eli — Hophni and Phinehas — were there along with the Ark of the Covenant of God. ⁵ When the Ark of the Covenant of HASHEM arrived at the camp, all of Israel sounded a great shofar blast and the ground shook.

The Philistines are frightened

⁶ The Philistines heard the sound of the blast and they said, "What is the sound of this great blast in the camp of the Hebrews?" And they became aware that the Ark of HASHEM had come to the camp. ⁷ The Philistines were afraid, as they said, "God has come to the camp!" And they said, "Woe to us, for such a thing had not happened yesterday or the day before! ⁸ Woe to us! Who will save us from the hand of this mighty God? This is the God Who struck the Egyptians with all kinds of plagues in the wilderness! ⁹ Be strong; be men, O Philistines, lest you become enslaved to the Hebrews as they have been enslaved to you! Be men and fight!"

Israel is defeated and the Ark is captured

¹⁰ So the Philistines fought. Israel was smitten and they ran, every man to his tents. The blow was very great: Thirty thousand foot soldiers fell from Israel; ¹¹ the Ark of God was taken; and the two sons of Eli — Hophni and Phinehas — died.

¹² A Benjamite man ran from the battlefront and came to Shiloh that day, his clothing ripped and dirt upon his head. ¹³ When he came Eli was seated in a chair next to the road, looking out, for his heart was fearful about the Ark of God. The man arrived to inform the city, and the entire city cried out. ¹⁴ Eli heard the sound of the outcry and said, "What is the commotion of this multitude?" And the man hastened — he came and told Eli. ¹⁵ Now Eli was ninety-eight years old; his eyes had become motionless and he could not see.

Eli hears the tragic news and dies

¹⁶ The man said to Eli, "I am the one who came from the battlefront. And I ran from the battlefront today."* [Eli] said, "What is the report, my son?" ¹⁷ The bearer of the tidings answered him saying, "Israel ran from before the Philistines; and there was a great blow among the people; also, your two sons — Hophni and Phinehas — died; and the Ark of God was taken!" ¹⁸ As soon as he mentioned the Ark of God, [Eli] fell backwards off his chair, opposite the site of the city gate, breaking his neck, and he died, for the man was old and heavy. He had judged Israel for forty years.

The wife of Phinehas gives birth

¹⁹ His daughter-in-law, the wife of Phinehas, was soon to give birth, and when she heard the news about the capture of the Ark of God and [that] her father-in-law died, and her husband, she crouched down and gave birth, for her labor pains came upon her. ²⁰ As she was about to die, those standing around her spoke to her, "Fear not, for you have borne a son!" But she did not answer, and she did not take it to her heart. ²¹ She called the boy Ichabod* saying, "Glory has been exiled from Israel," because of the capture of the Ark of God and because of [the deaths of] her father-in-law and her husband. ²² And she said, "Glory has been exiled from Israel, for the Ark of God has been captured."*

5

The Ark wreaks havoc in Ashdod

¹ The Philistines had taken the Ark of God and brought it from Eben-ezer to Ashdod. ² The Philistines took the Ark of God and brought it to the House of Dagon, placing it next to Dagon. * ³ The Ashdodites arose early the next day and behold, Dagon had fallen upon its face to the ground, before the Ark of HASHEM.

4:22. Despite their personal grief, both she and Eli (v. 18) were most affected by the capture of the Ark.

5:2. A Philistine idol with the body of a fish (דָּג) and the head and hands of a human.

ה וַיִּקְחוּ אֶת־דָּגוֹן וַיָּשִׁבוּ אֹתוֹ לִמְקוֹמוֹ: וַיַּשְׁכִּמוּ בַבֹּקֶר מִמָּחֳרָת וְהִנֵּה דָגוֹן
נֹפֵל לְפָנָיו אַרְצָה לִפְנֵי אֲרוֹן יהוה וְרֹאשׁ דָּגוֹן וּשְׁתֵּי ׀ כַּפּוֹת יָדָיו כְּרֻתוֹת

ה אֶל־הַמִּפְתָּן רַק דָּגוֹן נִשְׁאַר עָלָיו: עַל־כֵּן לֹא־יִדְרְכוּ כֹהֲנֵי דָגוֹן וְכָל־
ו הַבָּאִים בֵּית־דָּגוֹן עַל־מִפְתַּן דָּגוֹן בְּאַשְׁדּוֹד עַד הַיּוֹם הַזֶּה: וַתִּכְבַּד
יַד־יהוה אֶל־הָאַשְׁדּוֹדִים וַיְשִׁמֵּם וַיַּךְ אֹתָם °בֶּעְפֹלִים [°בַּטְּחֹרִים ק] אֶת־
ז אַשְׁדּוֹד וְאֶת־גְּבוּלֶיהָ: וַיִּרְאוּ אַנְשֵׁי־אַשְׁדּוֹד כִּי־כֵן וְאָמְרוּ לֹא־יֵשֵׁב אֲרוֹן
ח אֱלֹהֵי יִשְׂרָאֵל עִמָּנוּ כִּי־קָשְׁתָה יָדוֹ עָלֵינוּ וְעַל דָּגוֹן אֱלֹהֵינוּ: וַיִּשְׁלְחוּ
וַיַּאַסְפוּ אֶת־כָּל־סַרְנֵי פְלִשְׁתִּים אֲלֵיהֶם וַיֹּאמְרוּ מַה־נַּעֲשֶׂה לַאֲרוֹן אֱלֹהֵי
יִשְׂרָאֵל וַיֹּאמְרוּ גַּת יִסֹּב אֲרוֹן אֱלֹהֵי יִשְׂרָאֵל וַיַּסֵּבּוּ אֶת־אֲרוֹן אֱלֹהֵי
ט יִשְׂרָאֵל: וַיְהִי אַחֲרֵי ׀ הֵסַבּוּ אֹתוֹ וַתְּהִי יַד־יהוה ׀ בָּעִיר מְהוּמָה גְּדוֹלָה
מְאֹד וַיַּךְ אֶת־אַנְשֵׁי הָעִיר מִקָּטֹן וְעַד־גָּדוֹל וַיִּשָּׂתְרוּ לָהֶם °עֳפֹלִים
י [°טְחֹרִים ק]: וַיְשַׁלְּחוּ אֶת־אֲרוֹן הָאֱלֹהִים עֶקְרוֹן וַיְהִי כְּבוֹא אֲרוֹן
הָאֱלֹהִים עֶקְרוֹן וַיִּזְעֲקוּ הָעֶקְרֹנִים לֵאמֹר הֵסַבּוּ אֵלַי אֶת־אֲרוֹן אֱלֹהֵי
יא יִשְׂרָאֵל לַהֲמִיתֵנִי וְאֶת־עַמִּי: וַיִּשְׁלְחוּ וַיַּאַסְפוּ אֶת־כָּל־סַרְנֵי פְלִשְׁתִּים
וַיֹּאמְרוּ שַׁלְּחוּ אֶת־אֲרוֹן אֱלֹהֵי יִשְׂרָאֵל וְיָשֹׁב לִמְקֹמוֹ וְלֹא־יָמִית אֹתִי
וְאֶת־עַמִּי כִּי־הָיְתָה מְהוּמַת־מָוֶת בְּכָל־הָעִיר כָּבְדָה מְאֹד יַד הָאֱלֹהִים
יב שָׁם: וְהָאֲנָשִׁים אֲשֶׁר לֹא־מֵתוּ הֻכּוּ °בֶּעְפֹלִים [°בַּטְּחֹרִים ק] וַתַּעַל שַׁוְעַת
הָעִיר הַשָּׁמָיִם:

ו א וַיְהִי אֲרוֹן־יהוה בִּשְׂדֵה פְלִשְׁתִּים שִׁבְעָה
ב חֳדָשִׁים: וַיִּקְרְאוּ פְלִשְׁתִּים לַכֹּהֲנִים וְלַקֹּסְמִים לֵאמֹר מַה־נַּעֲשֶׂה לַאֲרוֹן
ג יהוה הוֹדִעֻנוּ בַּמֶּה נְשַׁלְּחֶנּוּ לִמְקוֹמוֹ: וַיֹּאמְרוּ אִם־מְשַׁלְּחִים אֶת־אֲרוֹן
אֱלֹהֵי יִשְׂרָאֵל אַל־תְּשַׁלְּחוּ אֹתוֹ רֵיקָם כִּי־הָשֵׁב תָּשִׁיבוּ לוֹ אָשָׁם אָז
ד תֵּרָפְאוּ וְנוֹדַע לָכֶם לָמָּה לֹא־תָסוּר יָדוֹ מִכֶּם: וַיֹּאמְרוּ מָה הָאָשָׁם אֲשֶׁר
נָשִׁיב לוֹ וַיֹּאמְרוּ מִסְפַּר סַרְנֵי פְלִשְׁתִּים חֲמִשָּׁה °עָפֹלֵי [°טְחֹרֵי ק] זָהָב
ה וַחֲמִשָּׁה עַכְבְּרֵי זָהָב כִּי־מַגֵּפָה אַחַת לְכֻלָּם וּלְסַרְנֵיכֶם: וַעֲשִׂיתֶם צַלְמֵי
°עָפֹלֵיכֶם [°טְחֹרֵיכֶם ק] וְצַלְמֵי עַכְבְּרֵיכֶם הַמַּשְׁחִיתִם אֶת־הָאָרֶץ
וּנְתַתֶּם לֵאלֹהֵי יִשְׂרָאֵל כָּבוֹד אוּלַי יָקֵל אֶת־יָדוֹ מֵעֲלֵיכֶם וּמֵעַל
ו אֱלֹהֵיכֶם וּמֵעַל אַרְצְכֶם: וְלָמָּה תְכַבְּדוּ אֶת־לְבַבְכֶם כַּאֲשֶׁר כִּבְּדוּ
מִצְרַיִם וּפַרְעֹה אֶת־לִבָּם הֲלוֹא כַּאֲשֶׁר הִתְעַלֵּל בָּהֶם וַיְשַׁלְּחוּם
ז וַיֵּלֵכוּ: וְעַתָּה קְחוּ וַעֲשׂוּ עֲגָלָה חֲדָשָׁה אֶחָת וּשְׁתֵּי פָרוֹת עָלוֹת אֲשֶׁר
לֹא־עָלָה עֲלֵיהֶם עֹל וַאֲסַרְתֶּם אֶת־הַפָּרוֹת בָּעֲגָלָה וַהֲשֵׁיבֹתֶם בְּנֵיהֶם
ח מֵאַחֲרֵיהֶם הַבָּיְתָה: וּלְקַחְתֶּם אֶת־אֲרוֹן יהוה וּנְתַתֶּם אֹתוֹ אֶל־הָעֲגָלָה

5:4. The head and hand were severed; but the fish part — *Dagon* — was still intact.

They consulted on how to do so in a way that would show their remorse, and thus assuage God's anger.

6:1. The foregoing series of transfers and tribulations convinced the Philistines that the Ark must be returned.

6:4. Because when the people would relieve themselves, mice would attack the bleeding hemorrhoids (*Radak*).

So they took Dagon and returned it to its place. ⁴ They arose early the next morning and [again] Dagon had fallen upon its face to the ground before the Ark of HASHEM, and Dagon's head and the two palms of its hands were severed, [lying] upon the threshold; only Dagon's body remained intact. * ⁵ (This is why the priests of Dagon and all those who come to the House of Dagon do not tread upon the threshold of Dagon in Ashdod to this day.)

⁶ The hand of HASHEM then became heavy against the Ashdodites, and He devastated them; He struck them — Ashdod and its surrounding areas — with hemorrhoids.

⁷ The men of Ashdod saw that it was so, and they said, "Let the Ark of the God of Israel not stay with us, for its hand has been hard against us and against Dagon, our god." ⁸ They summoned and gathered all the governors of the Philistines to them, and they said, "What shall we do about the Ark of the God of Israel?" They replied, "Let the Ark of the God of Israel be transferred to Gath." So they transferred the Ark of the God of Israel.

Gath is afflicted

⁹ It was after they transferred it that the hand of HASHEM was [set] against the city [causing] a great commotion; He struck the people of the city, from small to great, and He afflicted them internally with hemorrhoids. ¹⁰ They then sent the Ark of HASHEM to Ekron. It happened when the Ark of God arrived in Ekron that the people of Ekron cried out saying, "They have transferred to me the Ark of the God of Israel, to kill me and my people!"

Ekron is punished in turn

¹¹ So they summoned and gathered all the governors of the Philistines and said [to them], "Send away the Ark of the God of Israel. Let it return to its place and not kill me and my people!" For there was a panic of death in the whole city; the hand of God was very heavy there. ¹² The people who did not die were stricken with hemorrhoids, and the cry of the city ascended to heaven.

6

THE ARK'S
RETURN
6:1-7:1

¹ The Ark of HASHEM had been in the land of the Philistines for seven months. *
² The Philistines called upon the priests and the sorcerers, saying, "What shall we do about the Ark of HASHEM? Inform us how we should send it [back] to its place!"

The Philistines plan for the Ark's return

³ They replied, "If [you] are sending [back] the Ark of the God of Israel, you must not send it [back] empty-handed, but you must certainly send back a guilt-offering to Him. Then you will be healed, and you will realize why His hand would not turn away from against you."

A guilt-offering to accompany the Ark

⁴ So they said, "What is the guilt-offering that we should send back to Him?" They answered, "According to the number of Philistine governors — five golden [images of] hemorrhoids and five golden mice; * for the same plague is upon all [of you] and upon your governors. ⁵ Make your images of hemorrhoids and your images of mice, which are demolishing the country, and give them as homage to the God of Israel; perhaps He will alleviate His hand from upon you and your gods and your land. ⁶ Why should you harden your hearts as Egypt and Pharaoh hardened their hearts? * Did it not happen that when He mocked them they had to send [the Israelites] forth, and they left? ⁷ So now, take [materials] and make one new wagon, and [take] two nursing cows upon whom a yoke was never placed, and tie the cows to the wagon, and send their calves back home from behind them. * ⁸ Then take the Ark of HASHEM and place it onto the wagon,

---

6:6. See *Exodus* 7-10.
6:7. If the nursing cows would ignore their calves and

follow the Ark, it would prove that God wanted the Ark brought back.

וְאֵ֣ת ׀ כְּלֵ֣י הַזָּהָ֗ב אֲשֶׁ֨ר הֲשֵׁבֹתֶ֥ם לוֹ֙ אָשָׁם֙ תָּשִׂ֣ימוּ בָאַרְגַּ֔ז מִצִּדּ֖וֹ וְשִׁלַּחְתֶּ֥ם

ט אֹת֖וֹ וְהָלָֽךְ: וּרְאִיתֶ֗ם אִם־דֶּ֨רֶךְ גְּבוּל֤וֹ יַעֲלֶה֙ בֵּ֣ית שֶׁ֔מֶשׁ ה֚וּא עָ֣שָׂה לָ֔נוּ אֶת־
הָרָעָ֥ה הַגְּדוֹלָ֖ה הַזֹּ֑את וְאִם־לֹ֗א וְיָדַ֙עְנוּ֙ כִּ֣י לֹ֤א יָדוֹ֙ נָ֣גְעָה בָּ֔נוּ מִקְרֶ֥ה ה֖וּא

י הָ֥יָה לָֽנוּ: וַיַּעֲשׂ֤וּ הָֽאֲנָשִׁים֙ כֵּ֔ן וַיִּקְח֗וּ שְׁתֵּ֤י פָרוֹת֙ עָל֔וֹת וַיַּאַסְר֖וּם בָּעֲגָלָ֑ה

יא וְאֶת־בְּנֵיהֶ֖ם כָּל֥וּ בַבָּֽיִת: וַיָּשִׂ֛מוּ אֶת־אֲר֥וֹן יְהוָ֖ה אֶל־הָעֲגָלָ֑ה וְאֵ֣ת הָאַרְגַּ֗ז

יב וְאֵ֚ת עַכְבְּרֵ֣י הַזָּהָ֔ב וְאֵ֖ת צַלְמֵ֥י טְחֹרֵיהֶֽם: וַיִשַּׁ֣רְנָה הַפָּר֣וֹת בַּדֶּ֗רֶךְ עַל־דֶּ֙רֶךְ֙
בֵּ֣ית שֶׁ֔מֶשׁ בִּמְסִלָּ֣ה אַחַ֗ת הָלְכ֤וּ הָלֹךְ֙ וְגָע֔וֹ וְלֹא־סָ֖רוּ יָמִ֣ין וּשְׂמֹ֑אול וְסַרְנֵ֣י

יג פְלִשְׁתִּ֗ים הֹלְכִ֤ים אַחֲרֵיהֶם֙ עַד־גְּב֖וּל בֵּ֣ית שָֽׁמֶשׁ: וּבֵ֣ית שֶׁ֡מֶשׁ קֹצְרִ֣ים
קְצִיר־חִטִּים֮ בָּעֵמֶק֒ וַיִּשְׂא֣וּ אֶת־עֵינֵיהֶ֗ם וַֽיִּרְאוּ֙ אֶת־הָ֣אָר֔וֹן וַֽיִּשְׂמְח֖וּ

יד לִרְאֽוֹת: וְהָעֲגָלָ֡ה בָּ֠אָה אֶל־שְׂדֵ֞ה יְהוֹשֻׁ֤עַ בֵּֽית־הַשִּׁמְשִׁי֙ וַתַּעֲמֹ֣ד שָׁ֔ם
וְשָׁ֖ם אֶ֣בֶן גְּדוֹלָ֑ה וַֽיְבַקְּעוּ֙ אֶת־עֲצֵ֣י הָעֲגָלָ֔ה וְאֶת־הַ֨פָּר֔וֹת הֶעֱל֥וּ עֹלָ֖ה

טו לַֽיהוָֽה: וְהַלְוִיִּ֞ם הוֹרִ֣ידוּ ׀ אֶת־אֲר֣וֹן יְהוָ֗ה וְאֶת־הָֽאַרְגַּ֤ז אֲשֶׁר־אִתּוֹ֙
אֲשֶׁר־בּ֣וֹ כְלֵי־זָהָ֔ב וַיָּשִׂ֖מוּ אֶל־הָאֶ֣בֶן הַגְּדוֹלָ֑ה וְאַנְשֵׁ֣י בֵֽית־שֶׁ֗מֶשׁ הֶעֱל֥וּ עֹל֛וֹת

טז וַֽיִּזְבְּח֧וּ זְבָחִ֛ים בַּיּ֥וֹם הַה֖וּא לַֽיהוָֽה: וַחֲמִשָּׁ֥ה סַרְנֵֽי־פְלִשְׁתִּ֖ים רָא֑וּ וַיָּשֻׁ֥בוּ

יז עֶקְר֖וֹן בַּיּ֥וֹם הַהֽוּא: וְאֵ֙לֶּה֙ טְחֹרֵ֣י הַזָּהָ֔ב אֲשֶׁ֨ר הֵשִׁ֧יבוּ פְלִשְׁתִּ֛ים
אָשָׁ֖ם לַֽיהוָ֑ה לְאַשְׁדּ֨וֹד אֶחָ֜ד לְעַזָּ֤ה אֶחָד֙ לְאַשְׁקְל֣וֹן אֶחָ֔ד לְגַ֥ת אֶחָ֖ד

יח לְעֶקְר֥וֹן אֶחָֽד: וְעַכְבְּרֵ֣י הַזָּהָ֗ב מִסְפַּ֞ר כָּל־עָרֵ֤י פְלִשְׁתִּים֙ לַחֲמֵ֣שֶׁת
הַסְּרָנִ֔ים מֵעִ֥יר מִבְצָ֖ר וְעַ֣ד כֹּ֣פֶר הַפְּרָזִ֑י וְעַ֣ד ׀ אָבֵ֣ל הַגְּדוֹלָ֗ה אֲשֶׁ֨ר הִנִּ֤יחוּ

יט עָלֶ֙יהָ֙ אֵ֚ת אֲר֣וֹן יְהוָ֔ה עַ֖ד הַיּ֣וֹם הַזֶּ֑ה בִּשְׂדֵ֖ה יְהוֹשֻׁ֣עַ בֵּֽית־הַשִּׁמְשִֽׁי: וַיַּ֞ךְ
בְּאַנְשֵׁ֣י בֵֽית־שֶׁ֗מֶשׁ כִּ֤י רָאוּ֙ בַּאֲר֣וֹן יְהוָ֔ה וַיַּ֤ךְ בָּעָם֙ שִׁבְעִ֣ים אִ֔ישׁ חֲמִשִּׁ֥ים

כ אֶ֖לֶף אִ֑ישׁ וַיִּֽתְאַבְּל֣וּ הָעָ֔ם כִּֽי־הִכָּ֧ה יְהוָ֛ה בָּעָ֖ם מַכָּ֣ה גְדוֹלָֽה: וַיֹּֽאמְרוּ֙ אַנְשֵׁ֣י
בֵֽית־שֶׁ֔מֶשׁ מִ֚י יוּכַ֣ל לַעֲמֹ֔ד לִפְנֵ֨י יְהוָ֧ה הָאֱלֹהִ֛ים הַקָּד֖וֹשׁ הַזֶּ֑ה וְאֶל־מִ֖י יַעֲלֶ֥ה

כא מֵעָלֵֽינוּ: וַֽיִּשְׁלְח֣וּ מַלְאָכִ֗ים אֶל־יוֹשְׁבֵ֨י קִרְיַת־יְעָרִ֜ים לֵאמֹ֗ר הֵשִׁ֤בוּ פְלִשְׁתִּים֙

ז א אֶת־אֲר֣וֹן יְהוָ֔ה רְד֕וּ הַעֲל֥וּ אֹת֖וֹ אֲלֵיכֶֽם: וַיָּבֹ֜אוּ אַנְשֵׁ֣י ׀ קִרְיַ֣ת יְעָרִ֗ים וַֽיַּעֲלוּ֙
אֶת־אֲר֣וֹן יְהוָ֔ה וַיָּבִ֤אוּ אֹתוֹ֙ אֶל־בֵּ֣ית אֲבִֽינָדָ֔ב בַּגִּבְעָ֑ה וְאֶת־אֶלְעָזָ֤ר בְּנוֹ֙

ב קִדְּשׁ֔וּ לִשְׁמֹ֖ר אֶת־אֲר֥וֹן יְהוָֽה: וַיְהִ֗י מִיּ֞וֹם שֶׁ֤בֶת הָֽאָרוֹן֙ בְּקִרְיַ֣ת
יְעָרִ֔ים וַיִּרְבּוּ֙ הַיָּמִ֔ים וַיִּֽהְי֖וּ עֶשְׂרִ֣ים שָׁנָ֑ה וַיִּנָּה֛וּ כָּל־בֵּ֥ית יִשְׂרָאֵ֖ל אַחֲרֵ֥י

ג יְהוָֽה: וַיֹּ֣אמֶר שְׁמוּאֵ֗ל אֶל־כָּל־בֵּ֣ית יִשְׂרָאֵל֮ לֵאמֹר֒ אִם־בְּכָל־
לְבַבְכֶ֗ם אַתֶּ֤ם שָׁבִים֙ אֶל־יְהוָ֔ה הָסִ֜ירוּ אֶת־אֱלֹהֵ֧י הַנֵּכָ֛ר מִתּוֹכְכֶ֖ם
וְהָעַשְׁתָּר֑וֹת וְהָכִ֨ינוּ לְבַבְכֶ֤ם אֶל־יְהוָה֙ וְעִבְדֻ֣הוּ לְבַדּ֔וֹ וְיַצֵּ֥ל אֶתְכֶ֖ם מִיַּ֥ד

ד פְּלִשְׁתִּֽים: וַיָּסִ֙ירוּ֙ בְּנֵ֣י יִשְׂרָאֵ֔ל אֶת־הַבְּעָלִ֖ים וְאֶת־הָעַשְׁתָּרֹ֑ת וַיַּעַבְד֖וּ

6:9. See *Joshua* 15:10.

6:18. This was the rock mentioned in verse 14. It was named "Mourning" after the event of the next verse.

6:19. Seventy elders and 50,000 of the common people

(*Targum*). Or seventy men, each as worthy as 50,000; or 50,000, each worthy of being one of the seventy elders (*Rashi*).

6:21. See *Joshua* 15:9.

Proof that the Ark's return is God's will and put the golden objects that you are sending back to Him as a guilt-offering in a box at its side. Send it forth and it will go. [9] Then you will see: If it ascends by the road to its boundary, towards Beth-shemesh, * then it was He Who brought upon us all this great evil; but if not, we will know that His hand did not afflict us, but it was all by chance that this befell us."

[10] The men did so — they took two nursing cows and tied them to the wagon, and secured their calves at home. [11] They placed the Ark of HASHEM onto the wagon, along with the box and the golden mice and their images of hemorrhoids. [12] The cows set out on the direct road — on the road to Beth-shemesh — on a single road did they go, lowing as they went, and they did not veer right or left. The governors of the Philistines went behind them until the border of Beth-shemesh.

The Ark arrives at Beth-shemesh [13] [The people of] Beth-shemesh were reaping the wheat harvest in the valley, when they raised their eyes and saw the Ark, and they rejoiced to see [it]. [14] The wagon came to the field of Joshua, a Beth-shemeshite, and stopped there, where there was a large rock. They chopped the boards of the wagon, and offered up the cows as an elevation-offering to HASHEM.

[15] The Levites had unloaded the Ark of HASHEM and the box that was with it, in which were the golden objects, and placed them upon the large rock. The people of Beth-shemesh offered up elevation-offerings and slaughtered feast-offerings on that day to HASHEM. [16] The five Philistine governors saw all this and returned to Ekron on that day.

[17] These are the golden hemorrhoids that the Philistines sent as a guilt-offering to HASHEM: for Ashdod one; for Gaza one; for Ashkelon one; for Gath one; for Ekron one; [18] and golden mice corresponding to the number of all Philistine cities of the five governors, [who ruled] from fortified city until the open village, until the Great Mourning [Stone], * upon which they placed the Ark of HASHEM, which to this day is in the field of Joshua the Beth-shemeshite.

The people are disrespectful [19] And He smote some of the men of Beth-shemesh because they peered [disrespectfully] into the Ark of HASHEM. He struck among them seventy men, fifty thousand men. * The people mourned because HASHEM had smitten the people with a great blow. [20] And the people of Beth-shemesh said, "Who can [possibly] stand before HASHEM, this Holy God? To whom among us can [the Ark] ascend?" [21] They then sent emissaries to the inhabitants of Kiriath-jearim, * saying, "The Philistines have returned the Ark of HASHEM. Come down and bring it up unto yourselves."

7

The Ark is transferred to Kiriath-jearim [1] So the men of Kiriath-jearim came and brought up the Ark of HASHEM, and they brought it to the house of Abinadab on the hill, and they designated Elazar his son to guard the Ark of HASHEM. *

SAMUEL THE JUDGE 7:2-8:3 [2] From the time the Ark was stationed at Kiriath-jearim there ensued many days, they were twenty years, during which the entire House of Israel was drawn after HASHEM. [3] Samuel said to the entire House of Israel, saying, "If you are returning unto HASHEM with all your hearts, then remove the foreign gods and the Ashtaroth from your midst, and direct your hearts to HASHEM, serving Him alone; then He will rescue you from the hand of the Philistines." [4] So the Children of Israel removed the Baalim and the Ashtaroth, and served

---

7:1. Others were afraid to harbor the Ark, but to the people of Kiriath-jearim the honor of being host to the Tablets of the Law — the Torah of Israel — drove away all apprehension, and they harbored the Ark for twenty years.

ה אֶת־יהוה לְבַדּֽוֹ:   וַיֹּ֣אמֶר שְׁמוּאֵ֔ל קִבְצ֥וּ אֶת־כָּל־יִשְׂרָאֵ֖ל
ו הַמִּצְפָּ֑תָה וְאֶתְפַּלֵּ֥ל בַּעַדְכֶ֖ם אֶל־יהוֽה: וַיִּקָּבְצ֣וּ הַמִּצְפָּ֩תָה֩ וַיִּֽשְׁאֲבוּ־מַ֜יִם
   וַיִּשְׁפְּכ֣וּ ׀ לִפְנֵ֣י יהוה וַיָּצ֣וּמוּ בַּיּ֣וֹם הַה֔וּא וַיֹּ֣אמְרוּ שָׁ֔ם חָטָ֖אנוּ לַיהוֹ֑ה וַיִּשְׁפֹּ֧ט
ז שְׁמוּאֵ֛ל אֶת־בְּנֵ֥י יִשְׂרָאֵ֖ל בַּמִּצְפָּֽה: וַיִּשְׁמְע֣וּ פְלִשְׁתִּ֗ים כִּֽי־הִתְקַבְּצ֤וּ בְנֵֽי־
   יִשְׂרָאֵל֙ הַמִּצְפָּ֔תָה וַיַּעֲל֥וּ סַרְנֵֽי־פְלִשְׁתִּ֖ים אֶל־יִשְׂרָאֵ֑ל וַיִּשְׁמְעוּ֙ בְּנֵ֣י יִשְׂרָאֵ֔ל
ח וַיִּֽרְא֖וּ מִפְּנֵ֥י פְלִשְׁתִּֽים: וַיֹּֽאמְר֤וּ בְנֵֽי־יִשְׂרָאֵל֙ אֶל־שְׁמוּאֵ֔ל אַל־תַּחֲרֵ֥שׁ מִמֶּ֖נּוּ
ט מִזְּעֹ֣ק אֶל־יהוה אֱלֹהֵ֑ינוּ וְיֹשִׁעֵ֖נוּ מִיַּ֥ד פְּלִשְׁתִּֽים: וַיִּקַּ֣ח שְׁמוּאֵ֗ל טְלֵ֤ה חָלָב֙
   אֶחָ֔ד °וַיַּעֲלֵהוּ ק°[וַֽיַעֲלֶ֥ה] עוֹלָ֛ה כָּלִ֖יל לַֽיהוֹ֑ה וַיִּזְעַ֨ק שְׁמוּאֵ֤ל אֶל־יהוֹה
י בְּעַ֣ד יִשְׂרָאֵ֔ל וַיַּעֲנֵ֖הוּ יהוֹֽה: וַיְהִ֣י שְׁמוּאֵ֗ל מַעֲלֶ֣ה הָֽעוֹלָ֔ה וּפְלִשְׁתִּ֥ים נִגְּשׁ֖וּ
   לַמִּלְחָמָ֣ה בְּיִשְׂרָאֵ֑ל וַיַּרְעֵ֣ם יהוֹ֣ה ׀ בְּקוֹל־גָּד֠וֹל בַּיּ֨וֹם הַה֤וּא עַל־פְּלִשְׁתִּים֙
יא וַיְהֻמֵּ֔ם וַיִּנָּגְפ֖וּ לִפְנֵ֥י יִשְׂרָאֵֽל: וַיֵּ֨צְא֜וּ אַנְשֵׁ֤י יִשְׂרָאֵל֙ מִן־הַמִּצְפָּ֔ה וַיִּרְדְּפ֖וּ
יב אֶת־פְּלִשְׁתִּ֑ים וַיַּכּ֕וּם עַד־מִתַּ֖חַת לְבֵ֥ית כָּֽר: וַיִּקַּ֨ח שְׁמוּאֵ֜ל אֶ֣בֶן אַחַ֗ת וַיָּ֤שֶׂם
   בֵּֽין־הַמִּצְפָּה֙ וּבֵ֣ין הַשֵּׁ֔ן וַיִּקְרָ֥א אֶת־שְׁמָ֖הּ אֶ֣בֶן הָעָ֑זֶר וַיֹּאמַ֕ר עַד־הֵ֖נָּה עֲזָרָ֥נוּ
יג יהוֹֽה: וַיִּכָּֽנְעוּ֙ הַפְּלִשְׁתִּ֔ים וְלֹא־יָסְפ֣וּ ע֔וֹד לָב֖וֹא בִּגְב֣וּל יִשְׂרָאֵ֑ל וַתְּהִ֤י יַד־
יד יהוה בַּֽפְּלִשְׁתִּ֔ים כֹּ֖ל יְמֵ֥י שְׁמוּאֵֽל: וַתָּשֹׁ֣בְנָה הֶעָרִ֡ים אֲשֶׁ֣ר לָֽקְחוּ־פְלִשְׁתִּ֣ים
   מֵאֵ֣ת יִשְׂרָאֵ֣ל ׀ לְיִשְׂרָאֵ֡ל מֵעֶקְר֤וֹן וְעַד־גַּת֙ וְאֶת־גְּבוּלָ֔ן הִצִּ֥יל יִשְׂרָאֵ֖ל מִיַּ֣ד
טו פְּלִשְׁתִּ֑ים וַיְהִ֣י שָׁל֔וֹם בֵּ֥ין יִשְׂרָאֵ֖ל וּבֵ֥ין הָאֱמֹרִֽי: וַיִּשְׁפֹּ֤ט שְׁמוּאֵל֙ אֶת־
טז יִשְׂרָאֵ֔ל כֹּ֖ל יְמֵ֥י חַיָּֽיו: וְהָלַ֗ךְ מִדֵּ֤י שָׁנָה֙ בְּשָׁנָ֔ה וְסָבַב֙ בֵּֽית־אֵ֔ל וְהַגִּלְגָּ֖ל
יז וְהַמִּצְפָּ֑ה וְשָׁפַט֙ אֶת־יִשְׂרָאֵ֔ל אֵ֥ת כָּל־הַמְּקוֹמ֖וֹת הָאֵֽלֶּה: וּתְשֻׁבָת֤וֹ הָרָמָ֨תָה֙
   כִּֽי־שָׁ֣ם בֵּית֔וֹ וְשָׁ֥ם שָׁפַ֖ט אֶת־יִשְׂרָאֵ֑ל וַיִּֽבֶן־שָׁ֥ם מִזְבֵּ֖חַ לַיהוֹֽה:

ח א־ב וַיְהִ֕י כַּאֲשֶׁ֥ר זָקֵ֖ן שְׁמוּאֵ֑ל וַיָּ֧שֶׂם אֶת־בָּנָ֛יו שֹׁפְטִ֖ים לְיִשְׂרָאֵֽל: וַיְהִ֛י שֶׁם־
ג בְּנ֤וֹ הַבְּכוֹר֙ יוֹאֵ֔ל וְשֵׁ֥ם מִשְׁנֵ֖הוּ אֲבִיָּ֑ה שֹׁפְטִ֖ים בִּבְאֵ֥ר שָֽׁבַע: וְלֹֽא־
   הָלְכ֤וּ בָנָיו֙ °בדרכו °[בִּדְרָכָ֔יו ק] וַיִּטּ֖וּ אַֽחֲרֵ֣י הַבָּ֑צַע וַיִּקְחוּ־שֹׁ֔חַד וַיַּטּ֖וּ
ד מִשְׁפָּֽט: וַיִּֽתְקַבְּצ֔וּ כֹּ֖ל זִקְנֵ֣י יִשְׂרָאֵ֑ל וַיָּבֹ֥אוּ אֶל־שְׁמוּאֵ֖ל
ה הָרָמָֽתָה: וַיֹּאמְר֣וּ אֵלָ֗יו הִנֵּה֙ אַתָּ֣ה זָקַ֔נְתָּ וּבָנֶ֕יךָ לֹ֥א הָלְכ֖וּ בִּדְרָכֶ֑יךָ
ו עַתָּ֗ה שִֽׂימָה־לָּ֥נוּ מֶ֛לֶךְ לְשָׁפְטֵ֖נוּ כְּכָל־הַגּוֹיִֽם: וַיֵּ֤רַע הַדָּבָר֙ בְּעֵינֵ֣י
   שְׁמוּאֵ֔ל כַּאֲשֶׁ֣ר אָמְר֔וּ תְּנָה־לָּ֥נוּ מֶ֖לֶךְ לְשָׁפְטֵ֑נוּ וַיִּתְפַּלֵּ֥ל שְׁמוּאֵ֖ל אֶל־
ז יהוֹֽה: וַיֹּ֤אמֶר יהוה אֶל־שְׁמוּאֵ֔ל שְׁמַע֙ בְּק֣וֹל הָעָ֔ם לְכֹ֥ל
   אֲשֶׁר־יֹאמְר֖וּ אֵלֶ֑יךָ כִּ֣י לֹ֤א אֹֽתְךָ֙ מָאָ֔סוּ כִּֽי־אֹתִ֥י מָאֲס֖וּ מִמְּלֹ֥ךְ עֲלֵיהֶֽם:
ח כְּכָֽל־הַֽמַּעֲשִׂ֣ים אֲשֶׁר־עָשׂ֗וּ מִיּוֹם֩ הַעֲלֹתִ֨י אֹתָ֜ם מִמִּצְרַ֗יִם וְעַד־הַיּ֣וֹם
ט הַזֶּ֔ה וַיַּ֣עַזְבֻ֔נִי וַיַּעַבְד֖וּ אֱלֹהִ֣ים אֲחֵרִ֑ים כֵּ֛ן הֵ֥מָּה עֹשִׂ֖ים גַּם־לָֽךְ: וְעַתָּ֖ה
   שְׁמַ֣ע בְּקוֹלָ֑ם אַ֗ךְ כִּֽי־הָעֵ֤ד תָּעִיד֙ בָּהֶ֔ם וְהִגַּדְתָּ֣ לָהֶ֔ם מִשְׁפַּ֣ט הַמֶּ֔לֶךְ אֲשֶׁ֥ר

7:6. In a symbolic gesture of pouring out their hearts in submission to God.

Samuel adjudicated disputes (*Rashi*), because God does not help those who mistreat others. Alternatively, Samuel punished sinners according to their misdeeds (*Radak*).

HASHEM alone.

The people repent ⁵ Then Samuel said, "Gather all of Israel to Mizpah, and I will pray to HASHEM for you." ⁶ So they gathered at Mizpah. They drew water and poured it out before HASHEM * and fasted on that day; they said there, "We have sinned to HASHEM!" And Samuel judged the Children of Israel at Mizpah. *

⁷ The Philistines heard that the Children of Israel had gathered together at Mizpah, and the governors of the Philistines came up against Israel. The Children of Israel heard and were afraid of the Philistines. ⁸ The Children of Israel said to Samuel, "Do not be silent from crying out on our behalf to HASHEM, our God, that He save us from the hands of the Philistines."

Salvation from the Philistines ⁹ Samuel took a suckling lamb and offered it up entirely as an elevation-offering to HASHEM; Samuel cried out to HASHEM on behalf of Israel and HASHEM answered him. ¹⁰ Samuel was offering up the elevation-offering when the Philistines approached for the battle with Israel. HASHEM then thundered with a great noise on that day against the Philistines and confounded them, so that they were defeated by Israel. ¹¹ The men of Israel went out of Mizpah and pursued the Philistines, striking them down until beneath Beth-car. ¹² Samuel then took one rock and placed it between Mizpah and the cliff and called it Eben-ezer (the Rock of Help), saying, "HASHEM helped us until here."

Israel's cities are liberated ¹³ The Philistines were humbled and no longer continued to enter the borders of Israel; and the hand of HASHEM was against the Philistines all the days of Samuel. ¹⁴ The cities that the Philistines had taken from Israel reverted to Israel from Ekron to Gath; and Israel rescued their surrounding areas from the hand of the Philistines. Furthermore, there was peace between Israel and the Amorite.

¹⁵ Samuel judged Israel all the days of his life. ¹⁶ He would travel year after year, **Samuel's route** circling to Beth-el, Gilgal, and Mizpah, and judging Israel in all these places. ¹⁷ Then he would return to Ramah, for his home was there, and there he would judge Israel. And there he built an altar to HASHEM.

8

¹ **W**hen Samuel became old, he appointed his sons judges over Israel. ² The **Samuel's sons prove disappointing** name of his firstborn son was Joel and the name of his second was Abijah; they were judges in Beer-sheba. ³ But his sons did not follow his ways. They were swayed by profit; they took bribes and they perverted justice. *

EVENTS LEADING TO THE MONARCHY 8:4-8:22 ⁴ All the elders of Israel then gathered together and came to Samuel, to Ramah. ⁵ They said to him, "Behold! You are old, and your sons did not follow your ways. So now appoint for us a king to judge us, like all the nations."

⁶ It was wrong in Samuel's eyes that they said, "Give us a king to judge us," * and Samuel prayed to HASHEM.

Rejecting God by demanding a king ⁷ HASHEM said to Samuel, "Listen to the voice of the people in all that they say to you, for it is not you whom they have rejected, but it is Me whom they have rejected from reigning over them. ⁸ Like all their deeds that they have done from the day I brought them up from Egypt until this day — they forsook Me and worshiped the gods of others. So are they doing to you, as well. ⁹ And now, heed their voice, but be sure to warn them and tell them about the protocol of the king who

---

8:3. The Sages explain that these charges are figurative. Instead of traveling to all Jewish communities as Samuel had done, his sons remained in Ramah, so that their officials and scribes could earn fees from litigants. When great people make important decisions based on such financial considerations, it is tantamount to bribery.

8:6. For they wanted to be "like all the nations" (Rashi).

י וַיֹּאמֶר שְׁמוּאֵל אֵת כָּל־דִּבְרֵי יהוה אֶל־הָעָם   יִמְלֹךְ עֲלֵיהֶם:

יא הַשֹּׁאֲלִים מֵאִתּוֹ מֶלֶךְ:   וַיֹּאמֶר זֶה יִהְיֶה מִשְׁפַּט הַמֶּלֶךְ אֲשֶׁר יִמְלֹךְ עֲלֵיכֶם אֶת־בְּנֵיכֶם יִקָּח וְשָׂם לוֹ בְּמֶרְכַּבְתּוֹ וּבְפָרָשָׁיו וְרָצוּ לִפְנֵי

יב מֶרְכַּבְתּוֹ: וְלָשׂוּם לוֹ שָׂרֵי אֲלָפִים וְשָׂרֵי חֲמִשִּׁים וְלַחֲרֹשׁ חֲרִישׁוֹ וְלִקְצֹר

יג קְצִירוֹ וְלַעֲשׂוֹת כְּלֵי־מִלְחַמְתּוֹ וּכְלֵי רִכְבּוֹ: וְאֶת־בְּנוֹתֵיכֶם יִקָּח לְרַקָּחוֹת

יד וּלְטַבָּחוֹת וּלְאֹפוֹת: וְאֶת־שְׂדוֹתֵיכֶם וְאֶת־כַּרְמֵיכֶם וְזֵיתֵיכֶם הַטּוֹבִים יִקָּח

טו-טז וְנָתַן לַעֲבָדָיו: וְזַרְעֵיכֶם וְכַרְמֵיכֶם יַעְשֹׂר וְנָתַן לְסָרִיסָיו וְלַעֲבָדָיו: וְאֶת־עַבְדֵיכֶם וְאֶת־שִׁפְחוֹתֵיכֶם וְאֶת־בַּחוּרֵיכֶם הַטּוֹבִים וְאֶת־חֲמוֹרֵיכֶם יִקָּח

יז-יח וְעָשָׂה לִמְלַאכְתּוֹ: צֹאנְכֶם יַעְשֹׂר וְאַתֶּם תִּהְיוּ־לוֹ לַעֲבָדִים: וּזְעַקְתֶּם בַּיּוֹם הַהוּא מִלִּפְנֵי מַלְכְּכֶם אֲשֶׁר בְּחַרְתֶּם לָכֶם וְלֹא־יַעֲנֶה יהוה אֶתְכֶם בַּיּוֹם

יט הַהוּא: וַיְמָאֲנוּ הָעָם לִשְׁמֹעַ בְּקוֹל שְׁמוּאֵל וַיֹּאמְרוּ לֹּא כִּי אִם־מֶלֶךְ יִהְיֶה

כ עָלֵינוּ: וְהָיִינוּ גַם־אֲנַחְנוּ כְּכָל־הַגּוֹיִם וּשְׁפָטָנוּ מַלְכֵּנוּ וְיָצָא לְפָנֵינוּ

כא וְנִלְחַם אֶת־מִלְחֲמֹתֵנוּ: וַיִּשְׁמַע שְׁמוּאֵל אֵת כָּל־דִּבְרֵי הָעָם וַיְדַבְּרֵם בְּאָזְנֵי

כב יהוה: וַיֹּאמֶר יהוה אֶל־שְׁמוּאֵל שְׁמַע בְּקוֹלָם וְהִמְלַכְתָּ לָהֶם מֶלֶךְ

ט א וַיֹּאמֶר שְׁמוּאֵל אֶל־אַנְשֵׁי יִשְׂרָאֵל לְכוּ אִישׁ לְעִירוֹ: וַיְהִי־אִישׁ מבן ימין [°מִבִּנְיָמִין ק] וּשְׁמוֹ קִישׁ בֶּן־אֲבִיאֵל בֶּן־צְרוֹר בֶּן־בְּכוֹרַת בֶּן־

ב אֲפִיחַ בֶּן־אִישׁ יְמִינִי גִּבּוֹר חָיִל: וְלוֹ־הָיָה בֵן וּשְׁמוֹ שָׁאוּל בָּחוּר וָטוֹב וְאֵין

ג אִישׁ מִבְּנֵי יִשְׂרָאֵל טוֹב מִמֶּנּוּ מִשִּׁכְמוֹ וָמַעְלָה גָּבֹהַּ מִכָּל־הָעָם: וַתֹּאבַדְנָה הָאֲתֹנוֹת לְקִישׁ אֲבִי שָׁאוּל וַיֹּאמֶר קִישׁ אֶל־שָׁאוּל בְּנוֹ קַח־נָא אִתְּךָ אֶת־

ד אַחַד מֵהַנְּעָרִים וְקוּם לֵךְ בַּקֵּשׁ אֶת־הָאֲתֹנֹת: וַיַּעֲבֹר בְּהַר־אֶפְרַיִם וַיַּעֲבֹר בְּאֶרֶץ־שָׁלִשָׁה וְלֹא מָצָאוּ וַיַּעַבְרוּ בְאֶרֶץ־שַׁעֲלִים וָאַיִן וַיַּעֲבֹר בְּאֶרֶץ־

ה יְמִינִי וְלֹא מָצָאוּ: הֵמָּה בָּאוּ בְּאֶרֶץ צוּף וְשָׁאוּל אָמַר לְנַעֲרוֹ אֲשֶׁר־עִמּוֹ

ו לְכָה וְנָשׁוּבָה פֶּן־יֶחְדַּל אָבִי מִן־הָאֲתֹנוֹת וְדָאַג לָנוּ: וַיֹּאמֶר לוֹ הִנֵּה־נָא אִישׁ־אֱלֹהִים בָּעִיר הַזֹּאת וְהָאִישׁ נִכְבָּד כֹּל אֲשֶׁר־יְדַבֵּר בּוֹא יָבוֹא עַתָּה

ז נֵלְכָה שָּׁם אוּלַי יַגִּיד לָנוּ אֶת־דַּרְכֵּנוּ אֲשֶׁר־הָלַכְנוּ עָלֶיהָ: וַיֹּאמֶר שָׁאוּל לְנַעֲרוֹ וְהִנֵּה נֵלֵךְ וּמַה־נָּבִיא לָאִישׁ כִּי הַלֶּחֶם אָזַל מִכֵּלֵינוּ וּתְשׁוּרָה

ח אֵין־לְהָבִיא לְאִישׁ הָאֱלֹהִים מָה אִתָּנוּ: וַיֹּסֶף הַנַּעַר לַעֲנוֹת אֶת־שָׁאוּל וַיֹּאמֶר הִנֵּה נִמְצָא בְיָדִי רֶבַע שֶׁקֶל כָּסֶף וְנָתַתִּי לְאִישׁ הָאֱלֹהִים וְהִגִּיד

ט לָנוּ אֶת־דַּרְכֵּנוּ: בְּיִשְׂרָאֵל כֹּה־אָמַר הָאִישׁ בְּלֶכְתּוֹ לִדְרוֹשׁ אֱלֹהִים לְכוּ וְנֵלְכָה עַד־הָרֹאֶה כִּי לַנָּבִיא הַיּוֹם יִקָּרֵא לְפָנִים הָרֹאֶה:

8:18. Some Sages understand that a king is entitled to do all of the above. Others maintain that Samuel meant to frighten the people by citing possible abuses of power.

8:20. Typically, those swept up by enthusiasm choose to see only advantages and close their eyes to danger.

9:2. That is, he was of attractive appearance (*Targum*).

9:7. Unfamiliar with Samuel, Saul and his servant thought he would not help them unless they brought him a gift.

9:9. The Hebrew word for prophet, נָבִיא, literally means "speaker." A prophet conveys the word of God; a seer *will reign over them."*

¹⁰ *Samuel told all the words of* HASHEM *to the people who had requested a king of him.* ¹¹ *He said, "This is the protocol of the king who will reign over you: He will* *Royal* *take away your sons and place them in his chariots and cavalry, and they will run* *prerogatives* *before his chariot;* ¹² *he will appoint for himself captains of thousands and captains of fifty, to plow his furrow and to reap his harvest, and to produce his implements of battle and the furnishings of his chariot.* ¹³ *He will take your daughters to be perfumers, cooks, and bakers.* ¹⁴ *He will confiscate your best fields, vineyards, and olive trees, and present them to his servants.* ¹⁵ *He will take a tenth of your grain and vines, and present them to his officers and servants.* ¹⁶ *He will take your servants and maidservants and your best young men and your donkeys and press them into his service.* ¹⁷ *He will take a tenth of your sheep, and you will be his slaves.* ¹⁸ *On that day you will cry out because of your king whom you have chosen for yourselves — but* HASHEM *will not answer you on that day."** ¹⁹ *But the people refused to listen to the voice of Samuel. They said, "No! There shall be a king over us,* ²⁰ *and we will be like all the other nations; our king will judge us, and go forth before us, and fight our wars!"** ²¹ *Samuel heard all the words of the people and repeated them to* HASHEM.

God concurs ²² HASHEM *told Samuel, "Listen to their voice, and crown a king for them." Samuel told the men of Israel, "Go, each man to his city."*

9

APPOINTMENT,
ANOINTMENT
AND
ACCEPTANCE
OF SAUL
9:1-10:27

¹ **T**here *was a man of Benjamin whose name was Kish son of Abiel, son of Zeror, son of Becorath, son of Aphiah, son of a distinguished Benjamite — a mighty man of valor.* ² *He had a son named Saul who was exceptional and goodly;* no one in Israel was handsomer than he. From his shoulders up, he was taller than any of the people.*

³ *[One day] the donkeys of Kish, Saul's father, were lost, and Kish said to Saul his son, "Please take one of the attendants with you, arise and go; search for the donkeys."*

Saul seeks ⁴ *He passed through Mount Ephraim and he passed through the land of* *the lost* *Shalishah, but they did not find [them]; they passed through the land of Shaalim,* *donkeys* *but they were not there; and he passed through the land of the Benjamite but they did not find them.* ⁵ *They came to the land of Zuph and Saul said to his attendant who was with him, "Come, let us return, lest my father stop thinking about the donkeys and worry about us!"* ⁶ *But [the attendant] said to him, "Behold now, there is a man of God in this city, and the man is esteemed; everything he says is certain to occur. Let us go there now; perhaps he will tell us [which is] our road upon which we should travel."*

A tribute for ⁷ *Saul replied to his attendant, "Behold, if we go, what shall we bring to the man,* *the "seer"* *for the bread is gone from our vessels and we have no gift to bring to the man of God. What do we have with us?"** ⁸ *The servant spoke up once more to Saul, and said, "Behold! I have a quarter of a silver shekel with me. I will give it to the man of God and he will tell us about our way."*

⁹ *(Formerly in Israel, this is what someone said when he went to inquire of God: "Let us go to the seer"; for "the prophet" of today was formerly called "the seer."*)*

---

foresees the future or directs people to lost or hidden property. The primary prophetic function of teaching and   chastising had not yet begun in those days (*R' Yaakov Kamenetsky*).

י וַיֹּאמֶר שָׁאוּל לְנַעֲרוֹ טוֹב דְּבָרְךָ לְכָה | נֵלֵכָה וַיֵּלְכוּ אֶל־הָעִיר אֲשֶׁר־שָׁם
יא אִישׁ הָאֱלֹהִים: הֵמָּה עֹלִים בְּמַעֲלֵה הָעִיר וְהֵמָּה מָצְאוּ נְעָרוֹת יֹצְאוֹת
לִשְׁאֹב מָיִם וַיֹּאמְרוּ לָהֶן הֲיֵשׁ בָּזֶה הָרֹאֶה: וַתַּעֲנֶינָה אוֹתָם וַתֹּאמַרְנָה יֵשׁ
יב הִנֵּה לְפָנֶיךָ מַהֵר | עַתָּה כִּי הַיּוֹם בָּא לָעִיר כִּי זֶבַח הַיּוֹם לָעָם בַּבָּמָה:
יג כְּבֹאֲכֶם הָעִיר כֵּן תִּמְצְאוּן אֹתוֹ בְּטֶרֶם יַעֲלֶה הַבָּמָתָה לֶאֱכֹל כִּי לֹא־יֹאכַל
הָעָם עַד־בֹּאוֹ כִּי־הוּא יְבָרֵךְ הַזֶּבַח אַחֲרֵי־כֵן יֹאכְלוּ הַקְּרֻאִים וְעַתָּה עֲלוּ
יד כִּי־אֹתוֹ כְהַיּוֹם תִּמְצְאוּן אֹתוֹ: וַיַּעֲלוּ הָעִיר הֵמָּה בָּאִים בְּתוֹךְ הָעִיר וְהִנֵּה
טו שְׁמוּאֵל יֹצֵא לִקְרָאתָם לַעֲלוֹת הַבָּמָה: וַיהֹוָה גָּלָה אֶת־אֹזֶן
טז שְׁמוּאֵל יוֹם אֶחָד לִפְנֵי בוֹא־שָׁאוּל לֵאמֹר: כָּעֵת | מָחָר אֶשְׁלַח אֵלֶיךָ אִישׁ
מֵאֶרֶץ בִּנְיָמִן וּמְשַׁחְתּוֹ לְנָגִיד עַל־עַמִּי יִשְׂרָאֵל וְהוֹשִׁיעַ אֶת־עַמִּי מִיַּד
יז פְּלִשְׁתִּים כִּי רָאִיתִי אֶת־עַמִּי כִּי בָּאָה צַעֲקָתוֹ אֵלָי: וּשְׁמוּאֵל רָאָה אֶת־
יח שָׁאוּל וַיהֹוָה עָנָהוּ הִנֵּה הָאִישׁ אֲשֶׁר אָמַרְתִּי אֵלֶיךָ זֶה יַעְצֹר בְּעַמִּי: וַיִּגַּשׁ
שָׁאוּל אֶת־שְׁמוּאֵל בְּתוֹךְ הַשָּׁעַר וַיֹּאמֶר הַגִּידָה־נָּא לִי אֵי־זֶה בֵּית הָרֹאֶה:
יט וַיַּעַן שְׁמוּאֵל אֶת־שָׁאוּל וַיֹּאמֶר אָנֹכִי הָרֹאֶה עֲלֵה לְפָנַי הַבָּמָה וַאֲכַלְתֶּם
כ עִמִּי הַיּוֹם וְשִׁלַּחְתִּיךָ בַבֹּקֶר וְכֹל אֲשֶׁר בִּלְבָבְךָ אַגִּיד לָךְ: וְלָאֲתֹנוֹת
הָאֹבְדוֹת לְךָ הַיּוֹם שְׁלֹשֶׁת הַיָּמִים אַל־תָּשֶׂם אֶת־לִבְּךָ לָהֶם כִּי נִמְצָאוּ
כא וּלְמִי כָּל־חֶמְדַּת יִשְׂרָאֵל הֲלוֹא לְךָ וּלְכֹל בֵּית אָבִיךָ:   וַיַּעַן
שָׁאוּל וַיֹּאמֶר הֲלוֹא בֶן־יְמִינִי אָנֹכִי מִקַּטַנֵּי שִׁבְטֵי יִשְׂרָאֵל וּמִשְׁפַּחְתִּי
הַצְּעִרָה מִכָּל־מִשְׁפְּחוֹת שִׁבְטֵי בִנְיָמִן וְלָמָּה דִּבַּרְתָּ אֵלַי כַּדָּבָר
כב הַזֶּה: וַיִּקַּח שְׁמוּאֵל אֶת־שָׁאוּל וְאֶת־נַעֲרוֹ וַיְבִיאֵם לִשְׁכָּתָה
כג וַיִּתֵּן לָהֶם מָקוֹם בְּרֹאשׁ הַקְּרוּאִים וְהֵמָּה כִּשְׁלֹשִׁים אִישׁ: וַיֹּאמֶר שְׁמוּאֵל
לַטַּבָּח תְּנָה אֶת־הַמָּנָה אֲשֶׁר נָתַתִּי לָךְ אֲשֶׁר אָמַרְתִּי אֵלֶיךָ שִׂים אֹתָהּ
כד עִמָּךְ: וַיָּרֶם הַטַּבָּח אֶת־הַשּׁוֹק וְהֶעָלֶיהָ וַיָּשֶׂם | לִפְנֵי שָׁאוּל וַיֹּאמֶר הִנֵּה
הַנִּשְׁאָר שִׂים־לְפָנֶיךָ אֱכֹל כִּי לַמּוֹעֵד שָׁמוּר־לְךָ לֵאמֹר הָעָם קָרָאתִי
כה וַיֹּאכַל שָׁאוּל עִם־שְׁמוּאֵל בַּיּוֹם הַהוּא: וַיֵּרְדוּ מֵהַבָּמָה הָעִיר וַיְדַבֵּר עִם־
כו שָׁאוּל עַל־הַגָּג: וַיַּשְׁכִּמוּ וַיְהִי כַּעֲלוֹת הַשַּׁחַר וַיִּקְרָא שְׁמוּאֵל אֶל־שָׁאוּל
הַגָּג [הַגָּגָה ק] לֵאמֹר קוּמָה וַאֲשַׁלְּחֶךָּ וַיָּקָם שָׁאוּל וַיֵּצְאוּ שְׁנֵיהֶם הוּא
כז וּשְׁמוּאֵל הַחוּצָה: הֵמָּה יוֹרְדִים בִּקְצֵה הָעִיר וּשְׁמוּאֵל אָמַר אֶל־שָׁאוּל
אֱמֹר לַנַּעַר וְיַעֲבֹר לְפָנֵינוּ וַיַּעֲבֹר וְאַתָּה עֲמֹד כַּיּוֹם וְאַשְׁמִיעֲךָ אֶת־דְּבַר
י א אֱלֹהִים: וַיִּקַּח שְׁמוּאֵל אֶת־פַּךְ הַשֶּׁמֶן וַיִּצֹק עַל־רֹאשׁוֹ וַיִּשָּׁקֵהוּ
ב וַיֹּאמֶר הֲלוֹא כִּי־מְשָׁחֲךָ יְהֹוָה עַל־נַחֲלָתוֹ לְנָגִיד: בְּלֶכְתְּךָ הַיּוֹם מֵעִמָּדִי
וּמָצָאתָ שְׁנֵי אֲנָשִׁים עִם־קְבֻרַת רָחֵל בִּגְבוּל בִּנְיָמִן בְּצֶלְצַח וְאָמְרוּ אֵלֶיךָ

9:20. Samuel hinted to him that he would be king, as if to say: Why should the master of all the nation's wealth be concerned with mere donkeys?

9:21. Saul understood Samuel's hint.

Saul receives directions

¹⁰ Saul said to his attendant, "You have spoken well; come, let us go." So they went to the city where the man of God was. ¹¹ As they were climbing the ascent to the city they encountered some maidens going out to draw water, and they said to them, "Is this where the seer is?" ¹² They answered them saying, "It is. Behold, he is just ahead of you. Hurry now, for he came to the city today, for the people are bringing a feast-offering today at the High Place. ¹³ As you enter the city you will find him before he ascends to the High Place to eat, for the people will not eat before he comes, since he blesses the offering; only afterwards do the invited guests eat. Now go up, for you will find him as surely as it is day." ¹⁴ So they ascended to the city. As they were entering the city, behold, Samuel was coming out towards them, to go up to the High Place.

God prepares Samuel

¹⁵ Now HASHEM had revealed in Samuel's ear, one day before Saul had come, saying, ¹⁶ "At this time tomorrow I will send a man to you from the land of Benjamin; you shall anoint him to be ruler over My people Israel, and he will save My people from the hand of the Philistines — for I have seen [the distress] of My people, since its cry has come before Me."

Samuel honors Saul

¹⁷ When Samuel saw Saul, HASHEM spoke up to him, "This is the man of whom I said to you, 'This one will rule over My people.' " ¹⁸ Saul approached Samuel inside the [city] gate and said, "Tell me, please, which is the house of the seer?" ¹⁹ Samuel answered Saul, saying, "I am the seer! Go up before me to the High Place and you shall eat with me today. I will send you away in the morning, and I will tell you whatever is in your heart. ²⁰ As for your donkeys which have been lost to you now for three days — do not concern yourself over them, for they have been found. Besides, to whom does all the desirable property in Israel belong, if not to you and to all your father's family?"*

²¹ Saul answered, saying, "But I am only a Benjamite, and am from the smallest of the tribes of Israel, and furthermore my family is the youngest of all the families of the tribe of Benjamin; why, then, have you spoken to me in this way?"*

²² Samuel then took Saul and his attendant and brought them into the chamber. He gave them a place at the head of the invited guests, who were some thirty men. ²³ Samuel said to the cook, "Bring the portion that I gave you, about which I told you, 'Keep it with yourself.' " ²⁴ So the cook lifted up the thigh piece with what was attached to it, and placed it before Saul. [Samuel] then said, "This is the set-aside [portion]. Put it before yourself — eat; for it was reserved for you for the [feast] time when I told [the cook about] the people I had invited." So Saul ate with Samuel on that day.

Samuel and Saul meet in the morning

²⁵ When they descended from the High Place to the city, he spoke with Saul on the rooftop. ²⁶ They arose early [the next morning], and at daybreak Samuel called Saul to the roof, saying, "Arise, I will send you off." So Saul arose and the two of them — he and Samuel — went outside. ²⁷ As they were going down at the edge of town, Samuel said to Saul, "Tell the attendant to go on

Saul is anointed and given prophetic proof
(See Appendix A, timeline 4)

ahead of us"; so he passed ahead. "You stand here now and I will let you hear the word of God."

10 ¹ Then Samuel took a flask of oil and poured some onto [Saul's] head, and he kissed him. He said, "Indeed, HASHEM has anointed you as ruler over His heritage. ² When you leave me today you will encounter two men near Rachel's Tomb, at the border of Benjamin, in Zelzah. They will tell you

ג נִמְצְא֣וּ הָאֲתֹנ֔וֹת אֲשֶׁ֥ר הָלַ֖כְתָּ לְבַקֵּ֑שׁ וְהִנֵּ֨ה נָטַ֤שׁ אָבִ֙יךָ֙ אֶת־דִּבְרֵ֣י
הָאֲתֹנ֔וֹת וְדָאַ֥ג לָכֶ֖ם לֵאמֹ֑ר מָ֥ה אֶעֱשֶׂ֖ה לִבְנִֽי: וְחָלַפְתָּ֨ מִשָּׁ֜ם וָהָ֗לְאָה וּבָ֙אתָ֙
עַד־אֵל֣וֹן תָּב֔וֹר וּמְצָא֣וּךָ שָּׁ֗ם שְׁלֹשָׁ֤ה אֲנָשִׁים֙ עֹלִ֣ים אֶל־הָֽאֱלֹהִ֖ים בֵּֽית־
אֵ֑ל אֶחָ֞ד נֹשֵׂ֣א ׀ שְׁלֹשָׁ֣ה גְדָיִ֗ים וְאֶחָד֙ נֹשֵׂ֗א שְׁלֹ֣שֶׁת כִּכְּר֣וֹת לֶ֔חֶם וְאֶחָ֖ד
ד נֹשֵׂ֥א נֵֽבֶל־יָֽיִן: וְשָׁאֲל֥וּ לְךָ֖ לְשָׁל֑וֹם וְנָתְנ֤וּ לְךָ֙ שְׁתֵּי־לֶ֔חֶם וְלָקַחְתָּ֖ מִיָּדָֽם:
ה אַחַ֣ר כֵּ֗ן תָּבוֹא֙ גִּבְעַ֣ת הָאֱלֹהִ֔ים אֲשֶׁר־שָׁ֖ם נְצִבֵ֣י פְלִשְׁתִּ֑ים וִיהִי֩ כְבֹאֲךָ֨ שָׁ֜ם
הָעִ֗יר וּפָגַעְתָּ֞ חֶ֤בֶל נְבִיאִים֙ יֹרְדִ֣ים מֵֽהַבָּמָ֔ה וְלִפְנֵיהֶ֞ם נֵ֤בֶל וְתֹף֙ וְחָלִ֣יל
ו וְכִנּ֔וֹר וְהֵ֖מָּה מִֽתְנַבְּאִֽים: וְצָלְחָ֤ה עָלֶ֙יךָ֙ ר֣וּחַ יְהֹוָ֔ה וְהִתְנַבִּ֖יתָ עִמָּ֑ם וְנֶהְפַּכְתָּ֖
ז לְאִ֥ישׁ אַחֵֽר: וְהָיָ֞ה כִּ֥י °תבאנה [°תָבֹ֙אנָה ק] הָאֹת֥וֹת הָאֵ֖לֶּה לָ֑ךְ עֲשֵׂ֤ה לְךָ֙
ח אֲשֶׁ֣ר תִּמְצָ֣א יָדֶ֔ךָ כִּ֥י הָאֱלֹהִ֖ים עִמָּֽךְ: וְיָרַדְתָּ֣ לְפָנַי֮ הַגִּלְגָּל֒ וְהִנֵּ֤ה אָֽנֹכִי֙ יֹרֵ֣ד
אֵלֶ֔יךָ לְהַעֲל֣וֹת עֹל֔וֹת לִזְבֹּ֖חַ זִבְחֵ֣י שְׁלָמִ֑ים שִׁבְעַ֣ת יָמִ֣ים תּוֹחֵ֔ל עַד־בּוֹאִ֣י
ט אֵלֶ֔יךָ וְהוֹדַעְתִּ֣י לְךָ֔ אֵ֖ת אֲשֶׁ֥ר תַּעֲשֶֽׂה: וְהָיָ֗ה כְּהַפְנֹת֤וֹ שִׁכְמוֹ֙ לָלֶ֙כֶת֙ מֵעִ֣ם
שְׁמוּאֵ֔ל וַיַּהֲפָךְ־ל֥וֹ אֱלֹהִ֖ים לֵ֣ב אַחֵ֑ר וַיָּבֹ֛אוּ כָּל־הָאֹת֥וֹת הָאֵ֖לֶּה בַּיּ֥וֹם
י הַהֽוּא: וַיָּבֹ֤אוּ שָׁם֙ הַגִּבְעָ֔תָה וְהִנֵּ֥ה חֶֽבֶל־נְבִאִ֖ים לִקְרָאת֑וֹ וַתִּצְלַ֤ח
יא עָלָיו֙ ר֣וּחַ אֱלֹהִ֔ים וַיִּתְנַבֵּ֖א בְּתוֹכָֽם: וַיְהִ֗י כָּֽל־יֽוֹדְעוֹ֙ מֵֽאִתְּמ֣וֹל שִׁלְשֹׁ֔ם
וַיִּרְא֕וּ וְהִנֵּ֥ה עִם־נְבִאִ֖ים נִבָּ֑א   וַיֹּ֤אמֶר הָעָם֙ אִ֣ישׁ אֶל־רֵעֵ֔הוּ מַה־
יב זֶּ֤ה הָיָה֙ לְבֶן־קִ֔ישׁ הֲגַ֥ם שָׁא֖וּל בַּנְּבִיאִֽים: וַיַּ֨עַן אִ֤ישׁ מִשָּׁם֙ וַיֹּ֔אמֶר וּמִ֖י
יג אֲבִיהֶ֑ם עַל־כֵּן֙ הָיְתָ֣ה לְמָשָׁ֔ל הֲגַ֥ם שָׁא֖וּל בַּנְּבִאִֽים: וַיְכַל֙ מֵֽהִתְנַבֵּ֔וֹת וַיָּבֹ֖א
יד הַבָּמָֽה: וַיֹּ֩אמֶר֩ דּ֨וֹד שָׁא֤וּל אֵלָיו֙ וְאֶֽל־נַעֲר֔וֹ אָ֖ן הֲלַכְתֶּ֑ם וַיֹּ֕אמֶר לְבַקֵּ֥שׁ
טו אֶת־הָ֣אֲתֹנ֔וֹת וַנִּרְאֶ֣ה כִי־אַ֔יִן וַנָּב֖וֹא אֶל־שְׁמוּאֵֽל: וַיֹּ֖אמֶר דּ֣וֹד שָׁא֑וּל
טז הַגִּֽידָה־נָּ֣א לִ֔י מָֽה־אָמַ֥ר לָכֶ֖ם שְׁמוּאֵֽל: וַיֹּ֤אמֶר שָׁאוּל֙ אֶל־דּוֹד֔וֹ הַגֵּ֤ד הִגִּיד֙
לָ֔נוּ כִּ֥י נִמְצְא֖וּ הָאֲתֹנ֑וֹת וְאֶת־דְּבַ֤ר הַמְּלוּכָה֙ לֹֽא־הִגִּ֣יד ל֔וֹ אֲשֶׁ֥ר אָמַ֖ר
יז שְׁמוּאֵֽל: וַיַּצְעֵ֤ק שְׁמוּאֵל֙ אֶת־הָעָ֔ם אֶל־יְהֹוָ֖ה הַמִּצְפָּֽה: וַיֹּ֣אמֶר ׀
יח אֶל־בְּנֵ֣י יִשְׂרָאֵ֗ל כֹּֽה־אָמַ֣ר יְהֹוָה֮ אֱלֹהֵ֣י יִשְׂרָאֵל֒ אָנֹכִ֞י הֶעֱלֵ֤יתִי אֶת־יִשְׂרָאֵל֙
מִמִּצְרָ֔יִם וָאַצִּ֤יל אֶתְכֶם֙ מִיַּ֣ד מִצְרַ֔יִם וּמִיַּד֙ כָּל־הַמַּמְלָכ֔וֹת הַלֹּחֲצִ֖ים
יט אֶתְכֶֽם: וְאַתֶּ֨ם הַיּ֜וֹם מְאַסְתֶּ֣ם אֶת־אֱלֹֽהֵיכֶ֗ם אֲשֶׁר־ה֞וּא מוֹשִׁ֤יעַ לָכֶם֙ מִכָּל־
רָעֽוֹתֵיכֶ֣ם וְצָרֹֽתֵיכֶ֔ם וַתֹּ֣אמְרוּ ל֔וֹ כִּי־מֶ֖לֶךְ תָּשִׂ֣ים עָלֵ֑ינוּ וְעַתָּ֗ה הִֽתְיַצְּבוּ֙
כ לִפְנֵ֣י יְהֹוָ֔ה לְשִׁבְטֵיכֶ֖ם וּלְאַלְפֵיכֶֽם: וַיַּקְרֵ֣ב שְׁמוּאֵ֔ל אֵ֖ת כָּל־שִׁבְטֵ֣י יִשְׂרָאֵ֑ל
כא וַיִּלָּכֵ֖ד שֵׁ֥בֶט בִּנְיָמִֽן: וַיַּקְרֵ֞ב אֶת־שֵׁ֤בֶט בִּנְיָמִן֙ °למשפחתו [°לְמִשְׁפְּחֹתָ֔יו
ק] וַתִּלָּכֵ֖ד מִשְׁפַּ֣חַת הַמַּטְרִ֑י וַיִּלָּכֵד֙ שָׁא֣וּל בֶּן־קִ֔ישׁ וַיְבַקְשֻׁ֖הוּ וְלֹ֥א נִמְצָֽא:
כב וַיִּשְׁאֲלוּ־עוֹד֙ בַּֽיהֹוָ֔ה הֲבָ֥א ע֖וֹד הֲלֹ֣ם אִ֑ישׁ   וַיֹּ֣אמֶר יְהֹוָ֔ה הִנֵּה־
כג ה֥וּא נֶחְבָּ֖א אֶל־הַכֵּלִֽים: וַיָּרֻ֙צוּ֙ וַיִּקָּחֻ֣הוּ מִשָּׁ֔ם וַיִּתְיַצֵּ֖ב בְּת֣וֹךְ הָעָ֑ם וַיִּגְבַּהּ֙

10:5. Kiriath-jearim, where the Ark was located at the time (see 6:21-7:2; *Targum*).

10:12. It should not be surprising that Saul, who did not come from a family of prophets, joined in with the band, for — "Who is their father?" — the other prophets are also of undistinguished parentage. Prophecy does not that the donkeys that you went to seek were found, and that your father has abandoned the matter of the donkeys and has begun to worry about you, saying, 'What shall I do about my son?' ³ Then you will travel beyond there and come to the Plain of Tabor, where you will be encountered by three men on their way to [worship before] God at Beth-el — one carrying three kids, one carrying three loaves of bread, and one carrying a container of wine. ⁴ They will greet you and give you two breads, which you should take from them. ⁵ After that you will arrive at the Hill of God,* where the Philistine commissioners are stationed. It shall be that when you arrive at the city you will encounter a band of prophets descending from the High Place, and before them [players of] lyre, drum, flute, and harp and they will be prophesying. ⁶ The spirit of HASHEM will then pass over you, and you will prophesy with them, and you will be transformed into another person. ⁷ After these signs come upon you, do for yourself [to prepare for kingship] as best as you can, for God is with you. ⁸ Then you shall go down to Gilgal ahead of me; behold! I will go down to you, to offer burnt-offerings, to slaughter peace-offerings. You shall wait for seven days until I come to you and I will inform you what you are to do."

Samuel arranges a meeting

⁹ As soon as [Saul] turned away to depart from Samuel, God transformed him with a new heart and all these signs came about on that day.

Saul among the prophets

¹⁰ They arrived there at the Hill and behold! a band of prophets was opposite him. The spirit of God passed over him, and he prophesied among them. ¹¹ All those who had known him from yesterday and before then saw that behold! he was prophesying along with the prophets, and they said one to another, "What is this that has happened to the son of Kish? Is Saul also among the prophets?" ¹² A man spoke up from there and said, "And who is their father?"* It thus became an aphorism: "Is Saul also among the prophets?" ¹³ Then he stopped prophesying and arrived at the High Place.

Saul conceals his royal status

¹⁴ Saul's uncle said to him and his attendant, "Where did you go?" He replied, "To look for the donkeys, but when we saw that they were gone we went to Samuel." ¹⁵ Saul's uncle said, "Tell me now what Samuel said to you." ¹⁶ Saul answered his uncle, "He told us that the donkeys had been found," but he did not tell him about the matter of the kingship of which Samuel had spoken.

Samuel summons the nation

¹⁷ Samuel gathered the people to HASHEM at Mizpah. ¹⁸ He said to the Children of Israel, "Thus said HASHEM, the God of Israel: 'I brought Israel up from Egypt. I rescued you from the hand of Egypt and from the hand of all the kingdoms that oppressed you. ¹⁹ Today you have rejected your God, Who saves you from all your calamities and troubles, and you said to Him, "Only place a king over us!" Now stand before HASHEM, according to your tribes and your thousands.'"

Saul is singled out

²⁰ Samuel then brought all the tribes of Israel near, and the tribe of Benjamin was singled out.* ²¹ Then he brought the tribe of Benjamin near according to its families, and the Matrite family was singled out; [eventually] Saul son of Kish was singled out. They searched for him but he was not found. ²² They then asked HASHEM further, "Has the man arrived here as yet?"

And HASHEM replied, "He is hidden among the baggage."* ²³ They ran and took him from there, and he stood in the midst of the people. He was taller than

---

run in families (*Rashi*); God's spirit rests upon those who deserve it.

10:20. By lottery (*Rashi*), or by the *Urim VeTumim* (see

14:3; *Radak*).

10:22. In his modesty, Saul did not seek the honor, so he hid from the people.

כד מִכָּל־הָעָם מִשְׁכְּמוֹ וָמָעְלָה: וַיֹּאמֶר שְׁמוּאֵל אֶל־כָּל־הָעָם הַרְאִיתֶם אֲשֶׁר בָּחַר־בּוֹ יהוה כִּי אֵין כָּמֹהוּ בְּכָל־הָעָם וַיָּרִעוּ כָל־הָעָם וַיֹּאמְרוּ יְחִי

כה הַמֶּלֶךְ: וַיְדַבֵּר שְׁמוּאֵל אֶל־הָעָם אֵת מִשְׁפַּט הַמְּלֻכָה וַיִּכְתֹּב

כו בַּסֵּפֶר וַיַּנַּח לִפְנֵי יהוה וַיְשַׁלַּח שְׁמוּאֵל אֶת־כָּל־הָעָם אִישׁ לְבֵיתוֹ: וְגַם־ שָׁאוּל הָלַךְ לְבֵיתוֹ גִּבְעָתָה וַיֵּלְכוּ עִמּוֹ הַחַיִל אֲשֶׁר־נָגַע אֱלֹהִים בְּלִבָּם:

כז וּבְנֵי בְלִיַּעַל אָמְרוּ מַה־יֹּשִׁעֵנוּ זֶה וַיִּבְזֻהוּ וְלֹא־הֵבִיאוּ לוֹ מִנְחָה וַיְהִי

יא כְּמַחֲרִישׁ:   א וַיַּעַל נָחָשׁ הָעַמּוֹנִי וַיִּחַן עַל־יָבֵישׁ גִּלְעָד וַיֹּאמְרוּ

ב כָּל־אַנְשֵׁי יָבֵישׁ אֶל־נָחָשׁ כְּרָת־לָנוּ בְרִית וְנַעַבְדֶךָּ: וַיֹּאמֶר אֲלֵיהֶם נָחָשׁ הָעַמּוֹנִי בְּזֹאת אֶכְרֹת לָכֶם בִּנְקוֹר לָכֶם כָּל־עֵין יָמִין וְשַׂמְתִּיהָ חֶרְפָּה עַל־

ג כָּל־יִשְׂרָאֵל: וַיֹּאמְרוּ אֵלָיו זִקְנֵי יָבֵישׁ הֶרֶף לָנוּ שִׁבְעַת יָמִים וְנִשְׁלְחָה מַלְאָכִים בְּכֹל גְּבוּל יִשְׂרָאֵל וְאִם־אֵין מוֹשִׁיעַ אֹתָנוּ וְיָצָאנוּ אֵלֶיךָ: וַיָּבֹאוּ

ד הַמַּלְאָכִים גִּבְעַת שָׁאוּל וַיְדַבְּרוּ הַדְּבָרִים בְּאָזְנֵי הָעָם וַיִּשְׂאוּ כָל־הָעָם

ה אֶת־קוֹלָם וַיִּבְכּוּ: וְהִנֵּה שָׁאוּל בָּא אַחֲרֵי הַבָּקָר מִן־הַשָּׂדֶה וַיֹּאמֶר שָׁאוּל מַה־לָּעָם כִּי יִבְכּוּ וַיְסַפְּרוּ־לוֹ אֶת־דִּבְרֵי אַנְשֵׁי יָבֵישׁ: וַתִּצְלַח רוּחַ־אֱלֹהִים

ו עַל־שָׁאוּל °בשמעו [כְּשָׁמְעוֹ ק] אֶת־הַדְּבָרִים הָאֵלֶּה וַיִּחַר אַפּוֹ מְאֹד:

ז וַיִּקַּח צֶמֶד בָּקָר וַיְנַתְּחֵהוּ וַיְשַׁלַּח בְּכָל־גְּבוּל יִשְׂרָאֵל בְּיַד הַמַּלְאָכִים לֵאמֹר אֲשֶׁר אֵינֶנּוּ יֹצֵא אַחֲרֵי שָׁאוּל וְאַחַר שְׁמוּאֵל כֹּה יֵעָשֶׂה לִבְקָרוֹ

ח וַיִּפֹּל פַּחַד־יהוה עַל־הָעָם וַיֵּצְאוּ כְּאִישׁ אֶחָד: וַיִּפְקְדֵם בְּבָזֶק וַיִּהְיוּ בְנֵי־

ט יִשְׂרָאֵל שְׁלֹשׁ מֵאוֹת אֶלֶף וְאִישׁ יְהוּדָה שְׁלֹשִׁים אָלֶף: וַיֹּאמְרוּ לַמַּלְאָכִים הַבָּאִים כֹּה תֹאמְרוּן לְאִישׁ יָבֵישׁ גִּלְעָד מָחָר תִּהְיֶה־לָכֶם תְּשׁוּעָה °בחם [כְּחֹם ק] הַשָּׁמֶשׁ וַיָּבֹאוּ הַמַּלְאָכִים וַיַּגִּידוּ לְאַנְשֵׁי יָבֵישׁ

י וַיִּשְׂמָחוּ: וַיֹּאמְרוּ אַנְשֵׁי יָבֵישׁ מָחָר נֵצֵא אֲלֵיכֶם וַעֲשִׂיתֶם לָנוּ כְּכָל־הַטּוֹב

יא בְּעֵינֵיכֶם: וַיְהִי מִמָּחֳרָת וַיָּשֶׂם שָׁאוּל אֶת־הָעָם שְׁלֹשָׁה רָאשִׁים וַיָּבֹאוּ בְתוֹךְ־הַמַּחֲנֶה בְּאַשְׁמֹרֶת הַבֹּקֶר וַיַּכּוּ אֶת־עַמּוֹן עַד־חֹם הַיּוֹם וַיְהִי

יב הַנִּשְׁאָרִים וַיָּפֻצוּ וְלֹא נִשְׁאֲרוּ־בָם שְׁנַיִם יָחַד: וַיֹּאמֶר הָעָם אֶל־שְׁמוּאֵל

יג מִי הָאֹמֵר שָׁאוּל יִמְלֹךְ עָלֵינוּ תְּנוּ הָאֲנָשִׁים וּנְמִיתֵם: וַיֹּאמֶר שָׁאוּל לֹא־

יד יוּמַת אִישׁ בַּיּוֹם הַזֶּה כִּי הַיּוֹם עָשָׂה־יהוה תְּשׁוּעָה בְּיִשְׂרָאֵל: וַיֹּאמֶר

טו שְׁמוּאֵל אֶל־הָעָם לְכוּ וְנֵלְכָה הַגִּלְגָּל וּנְחַדֵּשׁ שָׁם הַמְּלוּכָה: וַיֵּלְכוּ כָל־הָעָם הַגִּלְגָּל וַיַּמְלִכוּ שָׁם אֶת־שָׁאוּל לִפְנֵי יהוה בַּגִּלְגָּל וַיִּזְבְּחוּ־ שָׁם זְבָחִים שְׁלָמִים לִפְנֵי יהוה וַיִּשְׂמַח שָׁם שָׁאוּל וְכָל־אַנְשֵׁי יִשְׂרָאֵל

HAFTARAS KORACH 11:14-12:22

10:27. Saul, still modest, ignored the slights of his detractors. This is a virtue in an ordinary person but a king must be a strong leader and demand the allegiance of his people. Early in his reign, Saul's humility proved to be his undoing (see 15:17).

11:2. Homiletically, the Midrash comments that Judaism's "right eye" is the Torah. Nahash wanted to burn a Torah scroll publicly (*Rashi*).

11:3. Nahash wanted the mutilation to testify to the helplessness of the nation. If so, the people of Jabesh argued, give us time to appeal for help. A failure to respond to us will indeed be the "sign of shame" you desire.

11:5. In his humility, Saul had not yet begun to function as official monarch, and had returned to his civilian *any of the people from his shoulder upward.* ²⁴ *Samuel said to all the people,* "Have you seen [the one] whom HASHEM has chosen, that there is none like him among all the people?" And all the people shouted, saying, "May the king live!" ²⁵ *Samuel then told the people the protocol of the kingship. He wrote it in a book and placed it before HASHEM. Then Samuel sent away all the people, everyone to his home.* ²⁶ *Saul, too, went to his home, to Gibeah, and with him went all the army of those whose heart was inspired by [fear of] God.* ²⁷ *But base men said, "How can this person save us!" They ridiculed him and did not bring him a tribute, but he remained mute.* *

Skeptics ridicule Saul

11

SAUL PROVES HIMSELF
11:1-15

The Ammonite invasion

¹ **T**hen *Nahash the Ammonite went up and besieged Jabesh-gilead, and all the people of Jabesh said to Nahash, "Seal a covenant with us, and we will serve you."* ² *But Nahash the Ammonite replied to them, "On this [condition] I will seal [a covenant] with you: when each right eye of yours is put out.* * *It will be a sign of shame for all of Israel.* ³ *The elders of Jabesh replied to him, "Hold off from [attacking] us for seven days while we send messengers throughout all the Land of Israel.* * *If there is no one to save us, then we will go out to you [and submit]."*

⁴ *When the messengers arrived at Gibeath-shaul and reported these words to the people, all the people raised their voices and wept.* ⁵ *Just then Saul came in from the field, behind his oxen,* * *and Saul said, "Why are the people crying?" They told him the words of the men from Jabesh.* ⁶ *The spirit of God passed over Saul when he heard these things, and he became very angry.* ⁷ *He took a pair of oxen and cut them into pieces, which he sent with the messengers throughout the Land of Israel, saying, "Whoever does not go out after Saul and Samuel [to battle], so shall be done to his oxen." A dread of HASHEM fell upon the people and they went forth as one man.*

Saul demands national mobilization

The nation responds

⁸ *He counted them at Bezek, and the Children of Israel were three hundred thousand, and the men of Judah, thirty thousand.* ⁹ *They said to the messengers who had come, "So shall you tell the people of Jabesh-gilead: 'Tomorrow there will be a salvation for you by the time the sun gets hot.'" The messengers came and told the people of Jabesh, and they rejoiced.* ¹⁰ *So the people of Jabesh said [to Nahash], "Tomorrow we will go forth to you, and you may do to us whatever seems good in your eyes."*

¹¹ *It was on the next day that Saul set the people into three companies, and they entered the camp [of the Ammonites] at the approach of dawn, and they struck down Ammon by the time the day became hot. There were survivors but they scattered; there did not remain of them two [men] together.* ¹² *The people then said to Samuel, "Who is it that said, 'Will Saul reign over us?'* * *Give the men over and we will put them to death!"*

Saul establishes his authority

Samuel rallies the people

¹³ *But Saul said to them, "Let no man be put to death this day, for today HASHEM has wrought salvation in Israel."* ¹⁴ *Then Samuel said to the people, "Come and let us go to Gilgal,* * *and let us renew the kingdom there."* ¹⁵ *So all the people went to Gilgal: there they made Saul king before HASHEM in Gilgal, and there they slaughtered feast peace-offerings before HASHEM; and there Saul, as well as all the men of Israel,*

---

occupation, perhaps because of the opposition of the "base men" (10:27) and their followers (*Radak*).
11:12. The "base men" who refused to accept Saul.

11:14. Gilgal had been regarded as a sacred place from the time the Ark and Tabernacle were there, when Joshua entered the land (*Joshua 4:19*).

יב   א   וַיֹּאמֶר שְׁמוּאֵל אֶל־כָּל־יִשְׂרָאֵל הִנֵּה שָׁמַעְתִּי עַד־מְאָד:

ב בְּקֹלְכֶם לְכֹל אֲשֶׁר־אֲמַרְתֶּם לִי וָאַמְלִיךְ עֲלֵיכֶם מֶלֶךְ: וְעַתָּה הִנֵּה הַמֶּלֶךְ | מִתְהַלֵּךְ לִפְנֵיכֶם וַאֲנִי זָקַנְתִּי וָשַׂבְתִּי וּבָנַי הִנָּם אִתְּכֶם וַאֲנִי

ג הִתְהַלַּכְתִּי לִפְנֵיכֶם מִנְּעֻרַי עַד־הַיּוֹם הַזֶּה: הִנְנִי עֲנוּ בִי נֶגֶד יהוה וְנֶגֶד מְשִׁיחוֹ אֶת־שׁוֹר | מִי לָקַחְתִּי וַחֲמוֹר מִי לָקַחְתִּי וְאֶת־מִי עָשַׁקְתִּי אֶת־מִי

ד רַצּוֹתִי וּמִיַּד־מִי לָקַחְתִּי כֹפֶר וְאַעְלִים עֵינַי בּוֹ וְאָשִׁיב לָכֶם: וַיֹּאמְרוּ לֹא

ה עֲשַׁקְתָּנוּ וְלֹא רַצּוֹתָנוּ וְלֹא־לָקַחְתָּ מִיַּד־אִישׁ מְאוּמָה: וַיֹּאמֶר אֲלֵיהֶם עֵד יהוה בָּכֶם וְעֵד מְשִׁיחוֹ הַיּוֹם הַזֶּה כִּי לֹא מְצָאתֶם בְּיָדִי מְאוּמָה וַיֹּאמֶר

ו עֵד: וַיֹּאמֶר שְׁמוּאֵל אֶל־הָעָם יהוה אֲשֶׁר עָשָׂה אֶת־מֹשֶׁה

ז וְאֶת־אַהֲרֹן וַאֲשֶׁר הֶעֱלָה אֶת־אֲבֹתֵיכֶם מֵאֶרֶץ מִצְרָיִם: וְעַתָּה הִתְיַצְּבוּ וְאִשָּׁפְטָה אִתְּכֶם לִפְנֵי יהוה אֵת כָּל־צִדְקוֹת יהוה אֲשֶׁר־עָשָׂה אִתְּכֶם

ח וְאֶת־אֲבוֹתֵיכֶם: כַּאֲשֶׁר־בָּא יַעֲקֹב מִצְרָיִם וַיִּזְעֲקוּ אֲבוֹתֵיכֶם אֶל־יהוה וַיִּשְׁלַח יהוה אֶת־מֹשֶׁה וְאֶת־אַהֲרֹן וַיּוֹצִיאוּ אֶת־אֲבֹתֵיכֶם מִמִּצְרַיִם

ט וַיֹּשִׁבוּם בַּמָּקוֹם הַזֶּה: וַיִּשְׁכְּחוּ אֶת־יהוה אֱלֹהֵיהֶם וַיִּמְכֹּר אֹתָם בְּיַד סִיסְרָא שַׂר־צְבָא חָצוֹר וּבְיַד־פְּלִשְׁתִּים וּבְיַד מֶלֶךְ מוֹאָב וַיִּלָּחֲמוּ בָּם:

י וַיִּזְעֲקוּ אֶל־יהוה °וַיֹּאמֶר [וַיֹּאמְרוּ ק] חָטָאנוּ כִּי עָזַבְנוּ אֶת־יהוה וַנַּעֲבֹד אֶת־הַבְּעָלִים וְאֶת־הָעַשְׁתָּרוֹת וְעַתָּה הַצִּילֵנוּ מִיַּד אֹיְבֵינוּ וְנַעַבְדֶךָּ: וַיִּשְׁלַח

יא יהוה אֶת־יְרֻבַּעַל וְאֶת־בְּדָן וְאֶת־יִפְתָּח וְאֶת־שְׁמוּאֵל וַיַּצֵּל אֶתְכֶם מִיַּד

יב אֹיְבֵיכֶם מִסָּבִיב וַתֵּשְׁבוּ בֶּטַח: וַתִּרְאוּ כִּי־נָחָשׁ מֶלֶךְ בְּנֵי־עַמּוֹן בָּא עֲלֵיכֶם

יג וַתֹּאמְרוּ לִי לֹא כִּי־מֶלֶךְ יִמְלֹךְ עָלֵינוּ וַיהוה אֱלֹהֵיכֶם מַלְכְּכֶם: וְעַתָּה הִנֵּה

יד הַמֶּלֶךְ אֲשֶׁר בְּחַרְתֶּם אֲשֶׁר שְׁאֶלְתֶּם וְהִנֵּה נָתַן יהוה עֲלֵיכֶם מֶלֶךְ: אִם־תִּירְאוּ אֶת־יהוה וַעֲבַדְתֶּם אֹתוֹ וּשְׁמַעְתֶּם בְּקֹלוֹ וְלֹא תַמְרוּ אֶת־פִּי יהוה וִהְיִתֶם גַּם־אַתֶּם וְגַם־הַמֶּלֶךְ אֲשֶׁר מָלַךְ עֲלֵיכֶם אַחַר יהוה אֱלֹהֵיכֶם:

טו וְאִם־לֹא תִשְׁמְעוּ בְּקוֹל יהוה וּמְרִיתֶם אֶת־פִּי יהוה וְהָיְתָה יַד־יהוה

טז בָּכֶם וּבַאֲבֹתֵיכֶם: גַּם־עַתָּה הִתְיַצְּבוּ וּרְאוּ אֶת־הַדָּבָר הַגָּדוֹל הַזֶּה אֲשֶׁר

יז יהוה עֹשֶׂה לְעֵינֵיכֶם: הֲלוֹא קְצִיר־חִטִּים הַיּוֹם אֶקְרָא אֶל־יהוה וְיִתֵּן קֹלוֹת וּמָטָר וּדְעוּ וּרְאוּ כִּי־רָעַתְכֶם רַבָּה אֲשֶׁר עֲשִׂיתֶם בְּעֵינֵי יהוה לִשְׁאוֹל

יח לָכֶם מֶלֶךְ: וַיִּקְרָא שְׁמוּאֵל אֶל־יהוה וַיִּתֵּן יהוה קֹלֹת וּמָטָר

12:1. The Israelites' request for a king constituted an ungrateful rejection both of Samuel and of God Himself (cf. 8:7). Here Samuel chastises the people. First, he points out that he has derived no personal benefit from his lifelong, dedicated service to them — on the contrary, his hard service made him old before his time (he was only fifty). Then he criticizes them for having rejected God's mastery over them (*Abarbanel, Malbim*). Furthermore, by asserting his own moral authority and then chastising the people, he meant to stiffen the national resolve to remain loyal to God and Torah.

12:5. The singular verb וַיֹּאמֶר implies that they spoke in unison (*Radak*). Alternatively: A Heavenly voice testified that everything Samuel said was true (*Rashi*).

12:11. Jerubaal is Gideon (*Judges* 6-9); Bedan is the equivalent of *ben dan*, son of Dan, and refers to Samson (*Targum*) who was a Danite (*Judges* 13-16); for Jephthah, see *Judges* 11:1-12:7.

12:15. Their graves will be desecrated (*Rashi*). Alternatively: The kings, as heads of the nation, are referred to figuratively as their fathers (*Radak*).

rejoiced exceedingly.

12
SAMUEL'S ADMONITION
12:1-25

¹ Then Samuel said to all of Israel, * "Behold! I have hearkened to your voice, to everything that you have said to me, and I have crowned a king over you. ² And now, behold! — the king goes before you, but I have become old and gray. As for my sons — here they are with you. And as for me, I have walked before you from my youth until this day. ³ Here I am; testify about me in the presence of HASHEM and in the presence of His anointed: Whose ox have I taken? Whose donkey have I taken? Whom have I robbed? Whom have I coerced? From whose hand have I taken redemption-money that I should avert my eyes from him? And I shall make restitution to you."

The people assert their faith in Samuel

⁴ And they said, "You have not robbed us; you have not coerced us; and you have not taken anything from any person's hand."

⁵ So he said to them, "HASHEM is your witness, and His anointed one is a witness this day, that you have not found anything in my hand." And they said as one, * "A witness!"

Samuel reviews God's historic kindness

⁶ Samuel then said to the people, "[It is] HASHEM Who produced Moses and Aaron, and Who brought your forefathers up from the land of Egypt. ⁷ And now, stand erect, and I shall enter into judgment with you before HASHEM, concerning all the righteous deeds of HASHEM that He has done with you and with your forefathers. ⁸ When Jacob came to Egypt and your forefathers cried out to HASHEM, HASHEM sent Moses and Aaron, and they brought your forefathers out of Egypt, and settled them in this place. ⁹ But they forgot HASHEM, their God, so He delivered them into the hand of Sisera, general of the army of Hazor, and into the hand of the Philistines, and into the hand of the king of Moab; and they battled them. ¹⁰ Then they cried out to HASHEM, and said, 'We have sinned! For we have forsaken HASHEM, and we have worshiped the Baalim and the Ashtaroth; but now, rescue us from the hand of our enemies, and we will worship You.'

Unjustified fear

¹¹ So HASHEM sent Jerubaal and Bedan* and Jephthah and Samuel, and He rescued you from the hand of your enemies from all around, and you dwelt in security. ¹² But when you saw that Nahash, king of the Children of Ammon, came upon you, you said to me, 'No, but a king shall reign over us!' But HASHEM, your God, is your King!

¹³ "And now, here is the king whom you have chosen, whom you have requested; and behold, HASHEM has set a king over you. ¹⁴ If you will fear HASHEM and worship Him and hearken to His voice and not rebel against the word of HASHEM, then you and the king who reigns over you will remain [following] after HASHEM, your God. ¹⁵ But if you do not hearken to the voice of HASHEM, and you rebel against the word of HASHEM, then the hand of HASHEM shall be against you and against your fathers. *

A Divine warning

¹⁶ "Even now, stand erect and see this great thing that HASHEM will do before your eyes. ¹⁷ Is today not the wheat harvest season? I shall call to HASHEM and He will set forth thunder and rain;* then you will recognize and see that your wickedness is great, that which you have perpetrated before the eyes of HASHEM, in requesting a king for yourselves."

¹⁸ Then Samuel called to HASHEM, and HASHEM set forth thunder and rain

---

12:17. The wheat harvest season is in the summertime, when no rain normally falls in Israel. Rainfall then is harmful, as it prevents the harvested wheat from drying and can even ruin the crop. Samuel was proving to the people that God was displeased with their actions (*Kara*).

יט בַּיּ֤וֹם הַהוּא֙ וַיִּֽירְא֣וּ כָל־הָעָ֧ם מְאֹ֛ד אֶת־יְהוָ֖ה וְאֶת־שְׁמוּאֵ֑ל וַיֹּאמְר֣וּ כָל־הָעָ֗ם אֶל־שְׁמוּאֵ֜ל הִתְפַּלֵּ֧ל בְּעַד־עֲבָדֶ֛יךָ אֶל־יְהוָ֥ה אֱלֹהֶ֖יךָ וְאַל־נָמ֑וּת כִּֽי־

כ יָסַ֤פְנוּ עַל־כָּל־חַטֹּאתֵ֙ינוּ֙ רָעָ֔ה לִשְׁאֹ֥ל לָ֖נוּ מֶֽלֶךְ: וַיֹּ֨אמֶר שְׁמוּאֵ֤ל אֶל־הָעָם֙ אַל־תִּירָ֔אוּ אַתֶּ֣ם עֲשִׂיתֶ֔ם אֵ֥ת כָּל־הָרָעָ֖ה הַזֹּ֑את אַ֗ךְ

כא אַל־תָּס֙וּרוּ֙ מֵאַחֲרֵ֣י יְהוָ֔ה וַעֲבַדְתֶּ֥ם אֶת־יְהוָ֖ה בְּכָל־לְבַבְכֶֽם: וְלֹ֖א תָּס֑וּרוּ

כב כִּ֣י ׀ אַחֲרֵ֣י הַתֹּ֗הוּ אֲשֶׁ֧ר לֹֽא־יוֹעִ֛ילוּ וְלֹ֥א יַצִּ֖ילוּ כִּי־תֹ֥הוּ הֵֽמָּה: כִּ֠י לֹֽא־יִטֹּ֤שׁ יְהוָה֙ אֶת־עַמּ֔וֹ בַּעֲב֖וּר שְׁמ֣וֹ הַגָּד֑וֹל כִּ֚י הוֹאִ֣יל יְהוָ֔ה לַעֲשׂ֥וֹת אֶתְכֶ֛ם ל֖וֹ

כג לְעָֽם: גַּ֣ם אָנֹכִ֗י חָלִ֤ילָה לִּי֙ מֵחֲטֹ֣א לַֽיהוָ֔ה מֵחֲדֹ֖ל לְהִתְפַּלֵּ֣ל בַּעַדְכֶ֑ם וְהֽוֹרֵיתִ֣י אֶתְכֶ֔ם בְּדֶ֥רֶךְ הַטּוֹבָ֖ה וְהַיְשָׁרָֽה: אַ֣ךְ ׀ יְר֣אוּ אֶת־יְהוָ֗ה וַעֲבַדְתֶּ֥ם

כד אֹת֛וֹ בֶּאֱמֶ֖ת בְּכָל־לְבַבְכֶ֑ם כִּ֣י רְא֔וּ אֵ֥ת אֲשֶׁר־הִגְדִּ֖ל עִמָּכֶֽם: וְאִם־הָרֵ֣עַ

כה תָּרֵ֑עוּ גַּם־אַתֶּ֥ם גַּם־מַלְכְּכֶ֖ם תִּסָּפֽוּ:

יג א בֶּן־שָׁנָ֖ה שָׁא֣וּל בְּמָלְכ֑וֹ וּשְׁתֵּ֣י שָׁנִ֔ים מָלַ֖ךְ עַל־יִשְׂרָאֵֽל: וַיִּבְחַר־ל֨וֹ שָׁא֜וּל

ב שְׁלֹ֣שֶׁת אֲלָפִ֣ים מִיִּשְׂרָאֵ֗ל וַיִּֽהְי֤וּ עִם־שָׁאוּל֙ אַלְפַּ֙יִם֙ בְּמִכְמָ֣שׂ וּבְהַ֣ר בֵּֽית־אֵ֔ל וְאֶ֗לֶף הָיוּ֙ עִם־יֽוֹנָתָ֔ן בְּגִבְעַ֖ת בִּנְיָמִ֑ין וְיֶ֣תֶר הָעָ֔ם שִׁלַּ֖ח אִ֥ישׁ לְאֹהָלָֽיו:

ג וַיַּ֣ךְ יוֹנָתָ֗ן אֵ֚ת נְצִ֣יב פְּלִשְׁתִּ֔ים אֲשֶׁ֖ר בְּגָ֑בַע וַיִּשְׁמְע֖וּ פְּלִשְׁתִּ֑ים וְשָׁאוּל֩ תָּקַ֨ע

ד בַּשּׁוֹפָר֙ בְּכָל־הָאָ֣רֶץ לֵאמֹ֔ר יִשְׁמְע֖וּ הָעִבְרִֽים: וְכָל־יִשְׂרָאֵ֞ל שָׁמְע֣וּ לֵאמֹ֗ר הִכָּ֤ה שָׁאוּל֙ אֶת־נְצִ֣יב פְּלִשְׁתִּ֔ים וְגַם־נִבְאַ֥שׁ יִשְׂרָאֵ֖ל בַּפְּלִשְׁתִּ֑ים וַיִּצָּעֲק֥וּ

ה הָעָ֛ם אַחֲרֵ֥י שָׁא֖וּל הַגִּלְגָּֽל: וּפְלִשְׁתִּ֞ים נֶאֶסְפ֣וּ ׀ לְהִלָּחֵ֣ם עִם־יִשְׂרָאֵ֗ל שְׁלֹשִׁ֨ים אֶ֜לֶף רֶ֗כֶב וְשֵׁ֤שֶׁת אֲלָפִים֙ פָּרָשִׁ֔ים וְעָ֕ם כַּח֛וֹל אֲשֶׁ֥ר עַל־שְׂפַ֖ת־

ו הַיָּ֣ם לָרֹ֑ב וַיַּעֲל֗וּ וַיַּחֲנ֤וּ בְמִכְמָשׂ֙ קִדְמַ֖ת בֵּ֣ית אָֽוֶן: וְאִ֨ישׁ יִשְׂרָאֵ֤ל רָאוּ֙ כִּ֣י צַר־ל֔וֹ כִּ֥י נִגַּ֖שׂ הָעָ֑ם וַיִּֽתְחַבְּא֣וּ הָעָ֗ם בַּמְּעָר֤וֹת וּבַֽחֲוָחִים֙ וּבַסְּלָעִ֔ים וּבַצְּרִחִ֖ים

ז וּבַבֹּרֽוֹת: וְעִבְרִ֗ים עָֽבְרוּ֙ אֶת־הַיַּרְדֵּ֔ן אֶ֥רֶץ גָּ֖ד וְגִלְעָ֑ד וְשָׁאוּל֙ עוֹדֶ֣נּוּ בַגִּלְגָּ֔ל

ח וְכָל־הָעָ֖ם חָרְד֣וּ אַחֲרָֽיו: °וַיֵּיחֶל [פ] °וַיּ֣וֹחֶל ק | שִׁבְעַ֤ת יָמִים֙ לַמּוֹעֵד֙ אֲשֶׁ֣ר שְׁמוּאֵ֔ל וְלֹא־בָ֥א שְׁמוּאֵ֖ל הַגִּלְגָּ֑ל וַיָּ֥פֶץ הָעָ֖ם מֵעָלָֽיו: וַיֹּ֣אמֶר שָׁא֔וּל הַגִּ֤שׁוּ

ט י אֵלַי֙ הָעֹלָ֣ה וְהַשְּׁלָמִ֔ים וַיַּ֖עַל הָעֹלָֽה: וַיְהִ֗י כְּכַלֹּתוֹ֙ לְהַעֲל֣וֹת הָעֹלָ֔ה וְהִנֵּ֥ה

יא שְׁמוּאֵ֖ל בָּ֑א וַיֵּצֵ֥א שָׁא֛וּל לִקְרָאת֖וֹ לְבָרֲכֽוֹ: וַיֹּ֣אמֶר שְׁמוּאֵ֔ל מֶ֖ה עָשִׂ֑יתָ וַיֹּ֣אמֶר שָׁא֗וּל כִּֽי־רָאִ֙יתִי֙ כִֽי־נָפַ֤ץ הָעָם֙ מֵֽעָלַ֔י וְאַתָּה֙ לֹֽא־בָ֙אתָ֙ לְמוֹעֵ֣ד

יב הַיָּמִ֔ים וּפְלִשְׁתִּ֖ים נֶאֱסָפִ֣ים מִכְמָֽשׂ: וָאֹמַ֗ר עַ֠תָּה יֵרְד֨וּ פְלִשְׁתִּ֤ים אֵלַי֙ הַגִּלְגָּ֔ל וּפְנֵ֥י יְהוָ֖ה לֹ֣א חִלִּ֑יתִי וָֽאֶתְאַפַּ֔ק וָאַעֲלֶ֖ה הָעֹלָֽה: וַיֹּ֤אמֶר

יג שְׁמוּאֵל֙ אֶל־שָׁא֔וּל נִסְכָּ֑לְתָּ לֹ֣א שָׁמַ֗רְתָּ אֶת־מִצְוַ֞ת יְהוָ֤ה אֱלֹהֶ֙יךָ֙ אֲשֶׁ֣ר צִוָּ֔ךְ כִּ֣י עַתָּ֗ה הֵכִ֧ין יְהוָ֛ה אֶת־מַמְלַכְתְּךָ֥ אֶל־יִשְׂרָאֵ֖ל עַד־עוֹלָֽם: וְעַתָּ֖ה

יד

12:24. If you act properly, I will overlook the slights to me (8:8) and God will forgive your sin of demanding a king in an improper, sinful manner (*Abarbanel*).

13:1. Literally, *a year-old Saul in his reign,* i.e., the narrative of this chapter occurred during the first year of his two-year reign. As soon as his authority was accepted at Gilgal, he selected three thousand soldiers with whom he and Jonathan would repel the Philistines, who had occupied part of the country since the time of Eli (Ch. 4). Alternatively: When Saul became king, he was as free of on that day; and all the people greatly feared HASHEM and Samuel. ¹⁹ All the people then said to Samuel, "Pray on behalf of your servants to HASHEM, your God, that we not die; for we have added evil upon all of our sins, to request a king for ourselves."

Samuel
reassures
the people ²⁰ Samuel said to the people, "Fear not. You have done all this evil — but do not turn away from following HASHEM, rather serve HASHEM with all your heart. ²¹ Do not turn away for [that would be to] pursue futilities that cannot avail and cannot rescue, for they are futile. ²² For HASHEM shall not forsake His people for the sake of His great Name; for HASHEM has sworn to make you for a people unto Him. ²³ And I, also — far be it from me to sin against HASHEM and refrain from praying on your behalf; rather I shall instruct you in the good and proper path. ²⁴ Only fear HASHEM and serve Him faithfully, with all your hearts, for look at how much He has done for you. * ²⁵ But if you act wickedly, both you and your king will perish."

13

WAR WITH
THE
PHILISTINES
13:1-14:52 ¹ It was in the first year of Saul's reign* (he reigned over Israel for two years) ² that Saul chose three thousand [troops] from Israel — two thousand were with Saul at Michmas and at Mount Beth-el, and one thousand were with Jonathan at Gibeath-benjamin — and the rest of the people he sent off, each man to his tent.

³ Jonathan slew the Philistine commissioner in Geba, and the Philistines heard [about it]. Saul had the shofar blown throughout the land, announcing, "Let the Hebrews hear."* ⁴ All Israel heard [the announcement], saying, "Saul has slain the Philistine commissioner, and Israel has become despicable in the eyes of the Philistines," and the people were summoned to Saul at Gilgal. ⁵ The Philistines gathered to wage war against Israel, with thirty thousand chariots, six thousand cavalry, and foot-soldiers as numerous as the sand of the seashore. They went up and encamped at Michmas, east of Beth-aven. ⁶ The Israel is
terror-
stricken
and fails to
heed Samuel men of Israel saw that they were in trouble, for the people were hard pressed; and the people hid in caves and in fortresses and in rocks and in towers and in pits. ⁷ Some Hebrews even crossed the Jordan to the land of Gad and Gilead. Saul was still in Gilgal, and all the people [who remained] hurried after him. ⁸ He waited seven days, for the time set by Samuel;* but Samuel did not arrive at Gilgal, so the people began to disband from him. ⁹ So Saul said, "Bring me the elevation-offering and the peace-offering!" and he offered up the burnt-offering. ¹⁰ It was just as he finished offering up the burnt-offering when behold! Samuel arrived, and Saul went forth to greet him.

¹¹ Samuel said, "What have you done?"

Saul said, "Because I saw that the people were disbanding from me and you had not arrived by the arranged day, and that the Philistines were gathering at Michmas, ¹² and I thought, 'Now the Philistines will descend upon me to Gilgal and I have not supplicated before HASHEM,' so I fortified myself and offered up the burnt-offering."

Samuel
admonishes
Saul
severely ¹³ Samuel said to Saul, "You have acted foolishly! You did not keep the commandment of HASHEM, your God, that He commanded you. [Until] now HASHEM would have established your kingdom over Israel forever, ¹⁴ but now

---

sin as a one-year-old (*Rashi*).   **13:8.** See 10:8.
13:3. And prepare themselves for Philistine retaliation.

מַמְלַכְתְּךָ֛ לֹא־תָק֑וּם בִּקֵּשׁ֩ יְהֹוָ֨ה ל֜וֹ אִ֣ישׁ כִּלְבָב֗וֹ וַיְצַוֵּ֤הוּ יְהֹוָה֙ לְנָגִיד֙ עַל־

טו עַמּ֔וֹ כִּ֚י לֹ֣א שָׁמַ֔רְתָּ אֵ֥ת אֲשֶׁר־צִוְּךָ֖ יְהֹוָֽה: וַיָּ֣קׇם שְׁמוּאֵ֗ל וַיַּ֛עַל מִן־הַגִּלְגָּ֖ל גִּבְעַ֣ת בִּנְיָמִ֑ן וַיִּפְקֹ֣ד שָׁא֗וּל אֶת־הָעָם֙ הַנִּמְצְאִ֣ים עִמּ֔וֹ כְּשֵׁ֥שׁ

טז מֵא֖וֹת אִֽישׁ: וְשָׁא֞וּל וְיוֹנָתָ֣ן בְּנ֗וֹ וְהָעָם֙ הַנִּמְצָ֣א עִמָּ֔ם יֹשְׁבִ֖ים בְּגֶ֣בַע בִּנְיָמִ֑ן

יז וּפְלִשְׁתִּ֖ים חָנ֣וּ בְמִכְמָ֑שׂ וַיֵּצֵ֧א הַמַּשְׁחִ֛ית מִמַּחֲנֵ֥ה פְלִשְׁתִּ֖ים שְׁלֹשָׁ֣ה רָאשִׁ֑ים הָרֹ֨אשׁ אֶחָ֥ד יִפְנֶ֛ה אֶל־דֶּ֥רֶךְ עׇפְרָ֖ה אֶל־אֶ֥רֶץ שׁוּעָֽל: וְהָרֹ֨אשׁ

יח אֶחָ֤ד יִפְנֶה֙ דֶּ֣רֶךְ בֵּ֣ית חֹר֔וֹן וְהָרֹ֨אשׁ אֶחָ֤ד יִפְנֶה֙ דֶּ֣רֶךְ הַגְּב֔וּל הַנִּשְׁקָ֛ף עַל־גֵּ֥י

יט הַצְּבֹעִ֖ים הַמִּדְבָּֽרָה: וְחָרָשׁ֙ לֹ֣א יִמָּצֵ֔א בְּכֹ֖ל אֶ֣רֶץ יִשְׂרָאֵ֑ל כִּֽי־

כ אׇמַ֣ר [°אָמְר֣וּ ק] פְלִשְׁתִּ֔ים פֶּ֚ן יַעֲשׂ֣וּ הָעִבְרִ֔ים חֶ֖רֶב א֣וֹ חֲנִֽית: וַיֵּרְד֣וּ כׇֽל־יִשְׂרָאֵ֜ל הַפְּלִשְׁתִּ֗ים לִלְטֹ֞ושׁ אִ֣ישׁ אֶת־מַחֲרַשְׁתּ֤וֹ וְאֶת־אֵתוֹ֙ וְאֶת־קַרְדֻּמּ֔וֹ

כא וְאֵ֖ת מַחֲרֵשָׁתֽוֹ: וְהָיְתָ֞ה הַפְּצִירָ֣ה פִ֗ים לַמַּֽחֲרֵשֹׁת֙ וְלָ֣אֵתִ֔ים וְלִשְׁלֹ֥שׁ קִלְּשׁ֖וֹן

כב וּלְהַקַּרְדֻּמִּ֑ים וּלְהַצִּ֖יב הַדׇּרְבָֽן: וְהָיָה֙ בְּי֣וֹם מִלְחֶ֔מֶת וְלֹ֣א נִמְצָ֗א חֶ֚רֶב וַחֲנִ֔ית בְּיַ֣ד כׇּל־הָעָ֔ם אֲשֶׁ֥ר אֶת־שָׁא֖וּל וְאֶת־יוֹנָתָ֑ן וַתִּמָּצֵ֣א לְשָׁא֔וּל וּלְיוֹנָתָ֖ן בְּנֽוֹ:

כג וַיֵּצֵא֙ מַצַּ֣ב פְּלִשְׁתִּ֔ים אֶֽל־מַעֲבַ֖ר מִכְמָֽשׂ:   וַֽיְהִ֣י הַיּ֗וֹם וַיֹּ֡אמֶר

יד יוֹנָתָ֣ן בֶּן־שָׁאוּל֩ אֶל־הַנַּ֨עַר נֹשֵׂ֤א כֵלָיו֙ לְכָ֣ה וְנַעְבְּרָ֗ה אֶל־מַצַּ֤ב פְּלִשְׁתִּים֙

ב אֲשֶׁ֣ר מֵעֵ֣בֶר הַלָּ֑ז וּלְאָבִ֖יו לֹ֥א הִגִּֽיד: וְשָׁא֗וּל יוֹשֵׁב֙ בִּקְצֵ֣ה הַגִּבְעָ֔ה תַּ֥חַת

ג הָרִמּ֖וֹן אֲשֶׁ֣ר בְּמִגְר֑וֹן וְהָעָ֛ם אֲשֶׁ֥ר עִמּ֖וֹ כְּשֵׁ֥שׁ מֵא֥וֹת אִֽישׁ: וַאֲחִיָּ֣ה בֶן־אֲחִט֡וּב אֲחִ֣י אִיכָב֠וֹד ׀ בֶּן־פִּ֨ינְחָ֜ס בֶּן־עֵלִ֗י כֹּהֵ֧ן ׀ יְהֹוָ֛ה בְּשִׁל֖וֹ נֹשֵׂ֣א אֵפ֑וֹד

ד וְהָעָם֙ לֹ֣א יָדַ֔ע כִּ֥י הָלַ֖ךְ יוֹנָתָֽן: וּבֵ֣ין הַֽמַּעְבְּר֗וֹת אֲשֶׁ֨ר בִּקֵּ֤שׁ יֽוֹנָתָן֙ לַֽעֲבֹר֙ עַל־מַצַּ֣ב פְּלִשְׁתִּ֔ים שֵׁן־הַסֶּ֤לַע מֵהָעֵ֙בֶר֙ מִזֶּ֔ה וְשֵׁן־הַסֶּ֥לַע מֵהָעֵ֖בֶר מִזֶּ֑ה וְשֵׁ֧ם

ה הָאֶחָ֣ד בּוֹצֵ֗ץ וְשֵׁ֤ם הָאֶחָד֙ סֶ֔נֶּה: הַשֵּׁ֧ן הָאֶחָ֛ד מָצ֥וּק מִצָּפ֖וֹן מ֣וּל מִכְמָ֑שׂ

ו וְהָאֶחָ֥ד מִנֶּ֖גֶב מ֥וּל גָּֽבַע: וַיֹּ֨אמֶר יְהוֹנָתָ֜ן אֶל־הַנַּ֣עַר ׀ נֹשֵׂ֣א כֵלָ֗יו לְכָה֙ וְנַעְבְּרָ֗ה אֶל־מַצַּב֙ הָעֲרֵלִ֣ים הָאֵ֔לֶּה אוּלַ֛י יַעֲשֶׂ֥ה יְהֹוָ֖ה לָ֑נוּ כִּ֣י אֵ֤ין

ז לַֽיהֹוָה֙ מַעְצ֔וֹר לְהוֹשִׁ֥יעַ בְּרַ֖ב א֥וֹ בִמְעָֽט: וַיֹּ֤אמֶר לוֹ֙ נֹשֵׂ֣א כֵלָ֔יו עֲשֵׂ֖ה כׇּל־

ח אֲשֶׁ֣ר בִּלְבָבֶ֑ךָ נְטֵ֣ה לָ֔ךְ הִנְנִ֥י עִמְּךָ֖ כִּלְבָבֶֽךָ:   וַיֹּ֙אמֶר֙ יְה֣וֹנָתָ֔ן הִנֵּ֛ה

ט אֲנַ֛חְנוּ עֹבְרִ֥ים אֶל־הָאֲנָשִׁ֖ים וְנִגְלִ֣ינוּ אֲלֵיהֶֽם: אִם־כֹּ֤ה יֹֽאמְרוּ֙ אֵלֵ֔ינוּ דֹּ֕מּוּ

י עַד־הַגִּיעֵ֖נוּ אֲלֵיכֶ֑ם וְעָמַ֣דְנוּ תַחְתֵּ֔ינוּ וְלֹ֥א נַעֲלֶ֖ה אֲלֵיהֶֽם: וְאִם־כֹּ֨ה יֹאמְר֜וּ

יא עֲל֤וּ עָלֵ֙ינוּ֙ וְעָלִ֔ינוּ כִּֽי־נְתָנָ֥ם יְהֹוָ֖ה בְּיָדֵ֑נוּ וְזֶה־לָּ֖נוּ הָאֽוֹת: וַיִּגָּל֣וּ שְׁנֵיהֶ֔ם אֶל־מַצַּ֖ב פְּלִשְׁתִּ֑ים וַיֹּאמְר֣וּ פְלִשְׁתִּ֔ים הִנֵּ֤ה עִבְרִים֙ יֹֽצְאִ֔ים מִן־הַחֹרִ֖ים

יב אֲשֶׁ֥ר הִתְחַבְּאוּ־שָֽׁם: וַיַּעֲנוּ֩ אַנְשֵׁ֨י הַמַּצָּבָ֜ה אֶת־יוֹנָתָ֣ן ׀ וְאֶת־נֹשֵׂ֣א כֵלָ֗יו

13:14. Saul's justification was logical, but not adequate for a king. A Jewish ruler must be strong enough to resist public opinion and, most of all, he must obey the word of God, as conveyed by His prophet, to the letter.

  Samuel knew that God had chosen Saul's successor, but he did not know as yet who the next king would be (*Radak*).

13:21. The Jews used a file when they could not go to Philistine territory for this service.

14:3. The *Ephod* was one of the eight vestments of the High Priest. The *Urim VeTumim* affixed to it revealed the will of God in response to the Kohen Gadol's queries (see *Exodus* 28:30).

14:10. It will be an omen that we will "come up" and

*your kingdom shall not endure. * HASHEM has sought a man after His own heart and appointed him as ruler over His people, * because you have not observed that which HASHEM has commanded you."* ¹⁵ Then Samuel arose and went up from Gilgal to Gibeath-benjamin.*

Saul mobilizes his out-numbered, poorly armed soldiers

Saul counted the people who were [still] found with him: about six hundred men. ¹⁶ Saul and his son Jonathan and the people who were found with them were staying in Geba-benjamin, while the Philistines were encamped at Michmas. ¹⁷ A raiding party went forth from the Philistine camp in three companies — one company turned toward the road to Ophrah, to the land of Shual; ¹⁸ one company turned toward the road to Beth-horon; and one company turned toward the road of the border, which overlooks the Valley of the Zeboim, toward the desert.

¹⁹ Now there was no smith to be found anywhere in the entire Land of Israel, for the Philistines said, "Lest the Hebrews produce a sword or spear." ²⁰ (So all the Israelites would have to go down to the Philistines, each man to sharpen his plow and his spade, his axe and his hoe. ²¹ There was a multi-grooved file that they used* to [sharpen] hoes, spades, three-pronged pitchforks, and axes, and for setting the peg of an ox-goad.) ²² Thus it was on the day of war that there was not to be found sword or spear in the possession of any of the people who were with Saul and Jonathan; but they could be found with Saul and his son Jonathan. ²³ A Philistine garrison went forth towards the Michmas Pass.

14

Jonathan's secret foray

¹ It happened one day that Jonathan son of Saul said to the attendant who bore his armor, "Come, let us cross over to the Philistine garrison that is on the other side," but he did not tell his father.

² Saul was staying at the outskirts of Gibeah, under the pomegranate tree that is in Migron, along with the people who were with him, about six hundred men, ³ and Ahijah, son of Ichabod's brother Ahitub, son of Phinehas, son of Eli the Kohen of HASHEM at Shiloh, who wore the Ephod. * The people did not know that Jonathan had gone.

⁴ Between the passes that Jonathan wanted to cross to the Philistine garrison there was a rocky precipice on one side and a rocky precipice on the other side; one was named Bozez and the other was named Seneh. ⁵ One precipice jutted out on the north, facing Michmas, and the other was on the south, facing Geba.

⁶ Jonathan said to the attendant, his armor-bearer, "Come, let us cross over to the garrison of these uncircumcised ones. Perhaps HASHEM will act on our behalf, for nothing prevents HASHEM from saving, whether through many or through few." ⁷ His armor-bearer said to him, "Do whatever is in your heart.

Jonathan formulates an omen

Choose your direction; I am with you as you desire." ⁸ Jonathan said, "Behold! — we are crossing over to the men, and we will show ourselves to them. ⁹ If they say this to us, 'Halt until we reach you!' we will stay where we are and not go up to them. ¹⁰ But if they say this: 'Come up to us!' then we will go up, for HASHEM will have delivered them into our hand, and that will be our sign!"*

The signal to advance

¹¹ So the two of them showed themselves to the Philistine garrison, and the Philistines said, "Look! The Hebrews are emerging from the holes where they were hiding!" ¹² The men of the garrison called out to Jonathan and his armor-bearer,

---

they will fall down. The omen will thus give Jonathan and his armor-bearer encouragement and strength.

וַיֹּאמְרוּ עֲלוּ אֵלֵינוּ וְנוֹדִיעָה אֶתְכֶם דָּבָר   וַיֹּאמֶר יוֹנָתָן אֶל־

יג נֹשֵׂא כֵלָיו עֲלֵה אַחֲרַי כִּי־נְתָנָם יהוה בְּיַד יִשְׂרָאֵל: וַיַּעַל יוֹנָתָן עַל־יָדָיו
וְעַל־רַגְלָיו וְנֹשֵׂא כֵלָיו אַחֲרָיו וַיִּפְּלוּ לִפְנֵי יוֹנָתָן וְנֹשֵׂא כֵלָיו מְמוֹתֵת

יד אַחֲרָיו: וַתְּהִי הַמַּכָּה הָרִאשֹׁנָה אֲשֶׁר הִכָּה יוֹנָתָן וְנֹשֵׂא כֵלָיו כְּעֶשְׂרִים
אִישׁ כְּבַחֲצִי מַעֲנָה צֶמֶד שָׂדֶה: וַתְּהִי חֲרָדָה בַמַּחֲנֶה בַשָּׂדֶה וּבְכָל־

טו הָעָם הַמַּצָּב וְהַמַּשְׁחִית חָרְדוּ גַם־הֵמָּה וַתִּרְגַּז הָאָרֶץ וַתְּהִי לְחֶרְדַּת
אֱלֹהִים: וַיִּרְאוּ הַצֹּפִים לְשָׁאוּל בְּגִבְעַת בִּנְיָמִן וְהִנֵּה הֶהָמוֹן נָמוֹג וַיֵּלֶךְ

טז וַהֲלֹם: וַיֹּאמֶר שָׁאוּל לָעָם אֲשֶׁר אִתּוֹ פִּקְדוּ־נָא וּרְאוּ מִי הָלַךְ
מֵעִמָּנוּ וַיִּפְקְדוּ וְהִנֵּה אֵין יוֹנָתָן וְנֹשֵׂא כֵלָיו: וַיֹּאמֶר שָׁאוּל לַאֲחִיָּה הַגִּישָׁה

יח אֲרוֹן הָאֱלֹהִים כִּי־הָיָה אֲרוֹן הָאֱלֹהִים בַּיּוֹם הַהוּא וּבְנֵי יִשְׂרָאֵל: וַיְהִי עַד
דִּבֶּר שָׁאוּל אֶל־הַכֹּהֵן וְהֶהָמוֹן אֲשֶׁר בְּמַחֲנֵה פְלִשְׁתִּים וַיֵּלֶךְ הָלוֹךְ

כ וָרָב   וַיֹּאמֶר שָׁאוּל אֶל־הַכֹּהֵן אֱסֹף יָדֶךָ: וַיִּזָּעֵק שָׁאוּל וְכָל־
הָעָם אֲשֶׁר אִתּוֹ וַיָּבֹאוּ עַד־הַמִּלְחָמָה וְהִנֵּה הָיְתָה חֶרֶב אִישׁ בְּרֵעֵהוּ

כא מְהוּמָה גְדוֹלָה מְאֹד: וְהָעִבְרִים הָיוּ לַפְּלִשְׁתִּים כְּאֶתְמוֹל שִׁלְשׁוֹם אֲשֶׁר
עָלוּ עִמָּם בַּמַּחֲנֶה סָבִיב וְגַם־הֵמָּה לִהְיוֹת עִם־יִשְׂרָאֵל אֲשֶׁר עִם־שָׁאוּל

כב וְיוֹנָתָן: וְכֹל אִישׁ יִשְׂרָאֵל הַמִּתְחַבְּאִים בְּהַר־אֶפְרַיִם שָׁמְעוּ כִּי־נָסוּ
פְלִשְׁתִּים וַיַּדְבְּקוּ גַם־הֵמָּה אַחֲרֵיהֶם בַּמִּלְחָמָה: וַיּוֹשַׁע יהוה בַּיּוֹם הַהוּא

כד אֶת־יִשְׂרָאֵל וְהַמִּלְחָמָה עָבְרָה אֶת־בֵּית אָוֶן: וְאִישׁ־יִשְׂרָאֵל נִגַּשׂ בַּיּוֹם
הַהוּא וַיֹּאֶל שָׁאוּל אֶת־הָעָם לֵאמֹר אָרוּר הָאִישׁ אֲשֶׁר־יֹאכַל לֶחֶם עַד־

כה הָעֶרֶב וְנִקַּמְתִּי מֵאֹיְבַי וְלֹא־טָעַם כָּל־הָעָם לָחֶם: וְכָל־הָאָרֶץ בָּאוּ בַיַּעַר
כו וַיְהִי דְבַשׁ עַל־פְּנֵי הַשָּׂדֶה: וַיָּבֹא הָעָם אֶל־הַיַּעַר וְהִנֵּה הֵלֶךְ דְּבָשׁ וְאֵין
כז מַשִּׂיג יָדוֹ אֶל־פִּיו כִּי־יָרֵא הָעָם אֶת־הַשְּׁבֻעָה: וְיוֹנָתָן לֹא־שָׁמַע בְּהַשְׁבִּיעַ
אָבִיו אֶת־הָעָם וַיִּשְׁלַח אֶת־קְצֵה הַמַּטֶּה אֲשֶׁר בְּיָדוֹ וַיִּטְבֹּל אוֹתָהּ בְּיַעְרַת
כח הַדְּבָשׁ וַיָּשֶׁב יָדוֹ אֶל־פִּיו °וַתֹּארְנָה [°וַתָּאֹרְנָה ק] עֵינָיו: וַיַּעַן אִישׁ מֵהָעָם
וַיֹּאמֶר הַשְׁבֵּעַ הִשְׁבִּיעַ אָבִיךָ אֶת־הָעָם לֵאמֹר אָרוּר הָאִישׁ אֲשֶׁר־יֹאכַל
כט לֶחֶם הַיּוֹם וַיָּעַף הָעָם: וַיֹּאמֶר יוֹנָתָן עָכַר אָבִי אֶת־הָאָרֶץ רְאוּ־נָא
ל כִּי־אֹרוּ עֵינַי כִּי טָעַמְתִּי מְעַט דְּבַשׁ הַזֶּה: אַף כִּי לוּא אָכֹל אָכַל הַיּוֹם
הָעָם מִשְּׁלַל אֹיְבָיו אֲשֶׁר מָצָא כִּי־עַתָּה לֹא־רָבְתָה מַכָּה בַּפְּלִשְׁתִּים:
לא-לב וַיַּכּוּ בַּיּוֹם הַהוּא בַּפְּלִשְׁתִּים מִמִּכְמָשׂ אַיָּלֹנָה וַיָּעַף הָעָם מְאֹד: °וַיַּעַשׂ
[°וַיַּעַט ק] הָעָם אֶל־°שָׁלָל [°הַשָּׁלָל ק] וַיִּקְחוּ צֹאן וּבָקָר וּבְנֵי בָקָר
לג וַיִּשְׁחֲטוּ־אָרְצָה וַיֹּאכַל הָעָם עַל־הַדָּם: וַיַּגִּידוּ לְשָׁאוּל לֵאמֹר הִנֵּה

14:14. Although the Philistines were crowded together and should have been able to overpower him, Jonathan still managed to kill them all (Rashi).

14:18. Saul wanted Ahijah, the Kohen Gadol, to come with the Urim VeTumim, to seek Heavenly counsel in the presence of the Ark (Rashi). Then, seeing that there was no time for delay, Saul said it was not necessary (v. 19).

14:21. There were Jews who had sided with the Philistines out of fear (Rashi). Alternatively: They lived in Philistia and were forced to join its army (Radak).

saying, "Come up to us! We have something to tell you!" Jonathan then said to his armor-bearer, "Come up after me, for HASHEM has delivered them into the hand of Israel!" [13] Jonathan then climbed up on his hands and feet, with his armor-bearer behind him, and [the Philistines] fell before Jonathan, while his armor-bearer slew people behind him. [14] The first blow that Jonathan and his armor-bearer dealt [killed] about twenty men within about [the area of] half a furrow

The
Philistines
are routed

of a pair [of oxen plowing] in the field. * [15] Then a great terror took hold in the camp, on the field, and among all the people; the raiding party and the garrison, too, were terrified. The very ground trembled and a God-inspired terror took hold.

[16] Saul's sentries at Gibeath-benjamin saw that, behold! the multitude [of Philistines] was scattering and approaching them. [17] Saul said to the people who were with him, "Check and see who has gone forth from us." They checked and behold! — Jonathan and his armor-bearer were not [there]. [18] Saul then said to Ahijah, "Bring near the Ark of God,"* for the Ark of God [was there] with the Children of Israel on that day. [19] But as Saul was speaking to the Kohen, the tumult in the Philistine camp grew greater and greater, so Saul told the Kohen, "Stay your hand!"

All Israelites
join the
chase

[20] Saul and the entire people with him mustered and came into the battle. And behold! every [Philistine] man's sword was turned against his colleague — a very great panic! [21] And the Hebrews who had sided with the Philistines* from yesterday and earlier, who had come up with them in the camp all around, they, too, [joined] with the Israelites who were with Saul and Jonathan. [22] All the men of Israel who were hiding in Mount Ephraim heard that the Philistines were running away, and they too gave chase after them in the battle.

[23] So HASHEM saved Israel on that day and the battle passed by Beth-aven.

Saul decrees
a fast

[24] The people of Israel were hard pressed on that day, and Saul adjured the people, saying, "Cursed be the man who shall eat food until the evening, when I shall be avenged of my enemies."* So the entire people did not taste food. [25] Then all [the people of] the land came into the forest, where there was nectar on the surface of the field. [26] The people came to the forest and behold! there was an oozing of nectar, but no one put his hand to his mouth, for the people feared the oath.

Jonathan
unwittingly
transgresses
the oath

[27] But Jonathan had not heard when his father adjured the people, so he stretched out the edge of the staff that was in his hand, and dipped it into the nectar of the cane; he then brought his hand to his mouth and his eyes lit up. [28] Then one of the people called out and said, "Your father has adjured the people saying, 'Cursed be the man who eats food today,' and the people have become weary."

[29] Jonathan said, "My father has distressed the land. See now how my eyes lit up when I tasted just a bit of this nectar; [30] surely if the people had eaten today of the spoils of their enemy that they have acquired, would there not now have been an even greater blow against the Philistines?"

[31] The people smote the Philistines on that day, from Michmas to Aijalon, and the people were very weary. [32] The people swooped down upon the spoils, and took sheep, cattle, and young cattle. They slaughtered them on the ground; and the people ate with the blood.* [33] They told Saul, saying, "Behold! —

14:24. The people pursued the Philistines so ardently that Saul adjured them not to eat lest they be distracted from the rout (Rashi).

14:32. The people had consecrated the animals to be sacrificed, but were so famished that they did not wait

until the required sprinkling of the blood before eating the meat (Talmud). Alternatively, since the people slaughtered the animals "on the ground" they could not properly drain the blood from the meat, transgressing the prohibition of eating blood (Radak).

הָעָם חַטָּאִים לַיהוָה לֶאֱכֹל עַל־הַדָּם וַיֹּאמֶר בְּגַדְתֶּם גֹּלּוּ־אֵלַי הַיּוֹם

לד אֶבֶן גְּדוֹלָה: וַיֹּאמֶר שָׁאוּל פֻּצוּ בָעָם וַאֲמַרְתֶּם לָהֶם הַגִּישׁוּ אֵלַי אִישׁ
שׁוֹרוֹ וְאִישׁ שְׂיֵהוּ וּשְׁחַטְתֶּם בָּזֶה וַאֲכַלְתֶּם וְלֹא־תֶחֶטְאוּ לַיהוָה לֶאֱכֹל

לה אֶל־הַדָּם וַיַּגִּשׁוּ כָל־הָעָם אִישׁ שׁוֹרוֹ בְיָדוֹ הַלַּיְלָה וַיִּשְׁחֲטוּ־שָׁם: וַיִּבֶן
שָׁאוּל מִזְבֵּחַ לַיהוָה אֹתוֹ הֵחֵל לִבְנוֹת מִזְבֵּחַ לַיהוָה: וַיֹּאמֶר

לו שָׁאוּל נֵרְדָה אַחֲרֵי פְלִשְׁתִּים לַיְלָה וְנָבֹזָה בָהֶם ׀ עַד־אוֹר הַבֹּקֶר וְלֹא־
נַשְׁאֵר בָּהֶם אִישׁ וַיֹּאמְרוּ כָּל־הַטּוֹב בְּעֵינֶיךָ עֲשֵׂה   וַיֹּאמֶר

לז הַכֹּהֵן נִקְרְבָה הֲלֹם אֶל־הָאֱלֹהִים: וַיִּשְׁאַל שָׁאוּל בֵּאלֹהִים הַאֵרֵד אַחֲרֵי
לח פְלִשְׁתִּים הֲתִתְּנֵם בְּיַד יִשְׂרָאֵל וְלֹא עָנָהוּ בַּיּוֹם הַהוּא: וַיֹּאמֶר שָׁאוּל
גֹּשׁוּ הֲלֹם כֹּל פִּנּוֹת הָעָם וּדְעוּ וּרְאוּ בַּמָּה הָיְתָה הַחַטָּאת הַזֹּאת הַיּוֹם:

לט כִּי חַי־יְהֹוָה הַמּוֹשִׁיעַ אֶת־יִשְׂרָאֵל כִּי אִם־יֶשְׁנוֹ בְּיוֹנָתָן בְּנִי כִּי מוֹת
יָמוּת וְאֵין עֹנֵהוּ מִכָּל־הָעָם: וַיֹּאמֶר אֶל־כָּל־יִשְׂרָאֵל אַתֶּם תִּהְיוּ
לְעֵבֶר אֶחָד וַאֲנִי וְיוֹנָתָן בְּנִי נִהְיֶה לְעֵבֶר אֶחָד וַיֹּאמְרוּ הָעָם אֶל־

מא שָׁאוּל הַטּוֹב בְּעֵינֶיךָ עֲשֵׂה: וַיֹּאמֶר שָׁאוּל אֶל־יְהֹוָה אֱלֹהֵי
מב יִשְׂרָאֵל הָבָה תָמִים וַיִּלָּכֵד יוֹנָתָן וְשָׁאוּל וְהָעָם יָצָאוּ: וַיֹּאמֶר שָׁאוּל
הַפִּילוּ בֵּינִי וּבֵין יוֹנָתָן בְּנִי וַיִּלָּכֵד יוֹנָתָן: וַיֹּאמֶר שָׁאוּל אֶל־יוֹנָתָן הַגִּידָה

מג לִּי מֶה עָשִׂיתָה וַיַּגֶּד־לוֹ יוֹנָתָן וַיֹּאמֶר טָעֹם טָעַמְתִּי בִּקְצֵה הַמַּטֶּה
מד אֲשֶׁר־בְּיָדִי מְעַט דְּבַשׁ הִנְנִי אָמוּת: וַיֹּאמֶר שָׁאוּל כֹּה־יַעֲשֶׂה אֱלֹהִים
מה וְכֹה יוֹסִף כִּי־מוֹת תָּמוּת יוֹנָתָן: וַיֹּאמֶר הָעָם אֶל־שָׁאוּל הֲיוֹנָתָן ׀ יָמוּת
אֲשֶׁר עָשָׂה הַיְשׁוּעָה הַגְּדוֹלָה הַזֹּאת בְּיִשְׂרָאֵל חָלִילָה חַי־יְהֹוָה
אִם־יִפֹּל מִשַּׂעֲרַת רֹאשׁוֹ אַרְצָה כִּי־עִם־אֱלֹהִים עָשָׂה הַיּוֹם הַזֶּה

מו וַיִּפְדּוּ הָעָם אֶת־יוֹנָתָן וְלֹא־מֵת: וַיַּעַל שָׁאוּל מֵאַחֲרֵי
מז פְלִשְׁתִּים וּפְלִשְׁתִּים הָלְכוּ לִמְקוֹמָם: וְשָׁאוּל לָכַד הַמְּלוּכָה עַל־
יִשְׂרָאֵל וַיִּלָּחֶם סָבִיב ׀ בְּכָל־אֹיְבָיו בְּמוֹאָב ׀ וּבִבְנֵי־עַמּוֹן וּבֶאֱדוֹם
מח וּבְמַלְכֵי צוֹבָה וּבַפְּלִשְׁתִּים וּבְכֹל אֲשֶׁר־יִפְנֶה יַרְשִׁיעַ: וַיַּעַשׂ חַיִל וַיַּךְ
מט אֶת־עֲמָלֵק וַיַּצֵּל אֶת־יִשְׂרָאֵל מִיַּד שֹׁסֵהוּ:   וַיִּהְיוּ בְּנֵי
שָׁאוּל יוֹנָתָן וְיִשְׁוִי וּמַלְכִּי־שׁוּעַ וְשֵׁם שְׁתֵּי בְנֹתָיו שֵׁם הַבְּכִירָה מֵרַב
נ וְשֵׁם הַקְּטַנָּה מִיכַל: וְשֵׁם אֵשֶׁת שָׁאוּל אֲחִינֹעַם בַּת־אֲחִימָעַץ וְשֵׁם שַׂר־
נא צְבָאוֹ אֲבִינֵר בֶּן־נֵר דּוֹד שָׁאוּל: וְקִישׁ אֲבִי־שָׁאוּל וְנֵר אֲבִי־אַבְנֵר בֶּן־
נב אֲבִיאֵל: וַתְּהִי הַמִּלְחָמָה חֲזָקָה עַל־פְּלִשְׁתִּים כֹּל יְמֵי שָׁאוּל:

14:33. This boulder was to serve either as a makeshift altar to facilitate the sprinkling of the blood, or as a convenient place for slaughter with adequate drainage.

14:36. Let us consult Him through the *Urim VeTumim* (*Targum*).

14:38-42. It was clear to Saul that God's refusal to respond implied that sin had soiled the nation. By means of the *Urim VeTumim*, it was determined that the guilt lay with Jonathan.

14:46. He did not continue the chase, since he had not received God's approval (*Radak*).

the people are sinning to HASHEM by eating with the blood!"

He said, "You have transgressed. Roll over to me a large boulder today."*

Saul forestalls a sin ³⁴ Saul said, "Spread out among the people and say to them, 'Let each man bring to me his ox and each man his sheep, and you shall slaughter [them] here and eat them, so that you not sin unto HASHEM by eating with the blood.' " So each man of the people brought his ox with him that night, and they slaughtered them there. ³⁵ Saul built an altar to HASHEM; this was the first of the altars that he built to HASHEM.

³⁶ Saul said, "Let us go down after the Philistines at night and plunder them until the morning's light; let us not let any man of them remain."

And [the people] answered, "Whatever is good in your eyes, do!"

God does not respond The Kohen then said, "Let us approach God at this point."* ³⁷ So Saul asked of God: "Shall I go down after the Philistines? Will You deliver them into the hand of Israel?" But He did not answer him on that day.

³⁸ Saul said, "Draw near to here, all you captains of the people, and find out and see through whom this sin occurred today.* ³⁹ For as HASHEM, the Savior of Israel, lives, even if the sin is found to be with my son Jonathan, he shall surely die!" But no one of all the people answered him. ⁴⁰ He then said to all Israel, "You will be on one side and I and my son Jonathan will be on the other side [and let the lot be conducted]."

The people said to Saul, "Do what is proper in your eyes."

Jonathan's error is revealed and the people save him ⁴¹ Saul said to HASHEM, "God of Israel, produce a flawless [verdict]!" [The side of] Jonathan and Saul was singled out, and the people were absolved. ⁴² Then Saul said, "Cast [a lot] between me and my son Jonathan," and Jonathan was singled out. ⁴³ Saul said to Jonathan, "Tell me, what have you done?" And Jonathan told him, and he said, "I did indeed taste a bit of nectar from the tip of the staff that was in my hand; I am prepared to die."

⁴⁴ So Saul said, "So shall HASHEM do and so shall He do further [if I do not carry out my oath], for you must surely die, Jonathan."

⁴⁵ But the people said to Saul, "Shall Jonathan die, he who has achieved this great salvation for Israel? A sacrilege! — as HASHEM lives, not a hair of his head shall fall to the ground, for he has acted for God's sake this day!" So the people redeemed Jonathan and he did not die.

Saul consolidates his rule ⁴⁶ Saul then went back up from [chasing] after the Philistines,* and the Philistines went to their place.

⁴⁷ Saul consolidated the kingdom over Israel. He waged war against all his enemies all around — with Moab and with the Children of Ammon and with Edom and with the kings of Zobah and with the Philistines; wherever he turned he inspired terror. ⁴⁸ He assembled an army and struck Amalek, and he rescued Israel from the hand of its oppressor.

⁴⁹ And the sons of Saul were Jonathan, Ishvi, and Malchi-shua; and the names of his two daughters — the name of the older one [was] Merab, and the name of the younger one [was] Michal; ⁵⁰ the name of Saul's wife [was] Ahinoam daughter of Ahimaaz; the name of the leader of his army [was] Abner, son of Saul's uncle Ner; ⁵¹ and Saul's father Kish and Abner's father Ner were sons of Abiel.

⁵² The war against the Philistines was intense all the days of Saul. Whenever

טו

HAFTARAS
PARASHAS
ZACHOR
Ashkenazim:
15:2-34
Sephardim:
15:1-34

א וְרָאָה שָׁאוּל כָּל־אִישׁ גִּבּוֹר וְכָל־בֶּן־חַיִל וַיַּאַסְפֵהוּ אֵלָיו: ◄ וַיֹּאמֶר
שְׁמוּאֵל אֶל־שָׁאוּל אֹתִי שָׁלַח יהוה לִמְשָׁחֲךָ לְמֶלֶךְ עַל־עַמּוֹ עַל־
יִשְׂרָאֵל וְעַתָּה שְׁמַע לְקוֹל דִּבְרֵי יהוה: ◄ ב כֹּה אָמַר יהוה צְבָאוֹת
פָּקַדְתִּי אֵת אֲשֶׁר־עָשָׂה עֲמָלֵק לְיִשְׂרָאֵל אֲשֶׁר־שָׂם לוֹ בַּדֶּרֶךְ בַּעֲלֹתוֹ
ג מִמִּצְרָיִם: עַתָּה לֵךְ וְהִכִּיתָה אֶת־עֲמָלֵק וְהַחֲרַמְתֶּם אֶת־כָּל־אֲשֶׁר־לוֹ
וְלֹא תַחְמֹל עָלָיו וְהֵמַתָּה מֵאִישׁ עַד־אִשָּׁה מֵעֹלֵל וְעַד־יוֹנֵק מִשּׁוֹר וְעַד־
ד שֶׂה מִגָּמָל וְעַד־חֲמוֹר: וַיְשַׁמַּע שָׁאוּל אֶת־הָעָם וַיִּפְקְדֵם
ה בַּטְּלָאִים מָאתַיִם אֶלֶף רַגְלִי וַעֲשֶׂרֶת אֲלָפִים אֶת־אִישׁ יְהוּדָה: וַיָּבֹא
שָׁאוּל עַד־עִיר עֲמָלֵק וַיָּרֶב בַּנָּחַל: ו וַיֹּאמֶר שָׁאוּל אֶל־הַקֵּינִי לְכוּ סֻּרוּ רְדוּ
מִתּוֹךְ עֲמָלֵקִי פֶּן־אֹסִפְךָ עִמּוֹ וְאַתָּה עָשִׂיתָה חֶסֶד עִם־כָּל־בְּנֵי יִשְׂרָאֵל
ז בַּעֲלוֹתָם מִמִּצְרָיִם וַיָּסַר קֵינִי מִתּוֹךְ עֲמָלֵק: וַיַּךְ שָׁאוּל אֶת־עֲמָלֵק מֵחֲוִילָה
ח בּוֹאֲךָ שׁוּר אֲשֶׁר עַל־פְּנֵי מִצְרָיִם: וַיִּתְפֹּשׂ אֶת־אֲגַג מֶלֶךְ־עֲמָלֵק חָי וְאֶת־
ט כָּל־הָעָם הֶחֱרִים לְפִי־חָרֶב: וַיַּחְמֹל שָׁאוּל וְהָעָם עַל־אֲגָג וְעַל־מֵיטַב
הַצֹּאן וְהַבָּקָר וְהַמִּשְׁנִים וְעַל־הַכָּרִים וְעַל־כָּל־הַטּוֹב וְלֹא אָבוּ הַחֲרִימָם
י וְכָל־הַמְּלָאכָה נְמִבְזָה וְנָמֵס אֹתָהּ הֶחֱרִימוּ: וַיְהִי דְּבַר־
יא יהוה אֶל־שְׁמוּאֵל לֵאמֹר: נִחַמְתִּי כִּי־הִמְלַכְתִּי אֶת־שָׁאוּל לְמֶלֶךְ כִּי־
שָׁב מֵאַחֲרַי וְאֶת־דְּבָרַי לֹא הֵקִים וַיִּחַר לִשְׁמוּאֵל וַיִּזְעַק אֶל־יהוה
יב כָּל־הַלָּיְלָה: וַיַּשְׁכֵּם שְׁמוּאֵל לִקְרַאת שָׁאוּל בַּבֹּקֶר וַיֻּגַּד לִשְׁמוּאֵל
לֵאמֹר בָּא־שָׁאוּל הַכַּרְמֶלָה וְהִנֵּה מַצִּיב לוֹ יָד וַיִּסֹּב וַיַּעֲבֹר וַיֵּרֶד
יג הַגִּלְגָּל: וַיָּבֹא שְׁמוּאֵל אֶל־שָׁאוּל וַיֹּאמֶר לוֹ שָׁאוּל בָּרוּךְ אַתָּה לַיהוה
יד הֲקִימֹתִי אֶת־דְּבַר יהוה: וַיֹּאמֶר שְׁמוּאֵל וּמֶה קוֹל־הַצֹּאן הַזֶּה בְּאָזְנָי
טו וְקוֹל הַבָּקָר אֲשֶׁר אָנֹכִי שֹׁמֵעַ: וַיֹּאמֶר שָׁאוּל מֵעֲמָלֵקִי הֱבִיאוּם אֲשֶׁר חָמַל
הָעָם עַל־מֵיטַב הַצֹּאן וְהַבָּקָר לְמַעַן זְבֹחַ לַיהוה אֱלֹהֶיךָ וְאֶת־הַיּוֹתֵר
טז הֶחֱרַמְנוּ: וַיֹּאמֶר שְׁמוּאֵל אֶל־שָׁאוּל הֶרֶף וְאַגִּידָה לְּךָ אֵת אֲשֶׁר
יז דִּבֶּר יהוה אֵלַי הַלָּיְלָה °וַיֹּאמְרוּ °וַיֹּאמֶר ק] לוֹ דַּבֵּר: וַיֹּאמֶר
שְׁמוּאֵל הֲלוֹא אִם־קָטֹן אַתָּה בְּעֵינֶיךָ רֹאשׁ שִׁבְטֵי יִשְׂרָאֵל אָתָּה
יח וַיִּמְשָׁחֲךָ יהוה לְמֶלֶךְ עַל־יִשְׂרָאֵל: וַיִּשְׁלָחֲךָ יהוה בְּדָרֶךְ וַיֹּאמֶר לֵךְ
וְהַחֲרַמְתָּה אֶת־הַחַטָּאִים אֶת־עֲמָלֵק וְנִלְחַמְתָּ בוֹ עַד־כַּלּוֹתָם אֹתָם:
יט וְלָמָּה לֹא־שָׁמַעְתָּ בְּקוֹל יהוה וַתַּעַט אֶל־הַשָּׁלָל וַתַּעַשׂ הָרַע בְּעֵינֵי
כ יהוה: וַיֹּאמֶר שָׁאוּל אֶל־שְׁמוּאֵל אֲשֶׁר שָׁמַעְתִּי בְּקוֹל יהוה וָאֵלֵךְ

15:1. The Torah commanded Israel to do three things after completing the conquest of the land: to appoint a king, to eradicate Amalek, and to build the Temple (*Talmud*). Hence, Samuel introduced this commandment to battle Amalek by telling Saul that since he had been anointed as king (*Radak*), Amalek, as the leading force of evil in the world, was to be wiped out entirely. See verse 3.

15:4. In order to avoid counting Israel directly, each one took a lamb from Saul's flocks. These lambs were then counted to determine the census (*Rashi*).

15:6. The Kenites descended from Jethro, father-in-law of Moses, who was a valuable adviser in the Wilderness.

15:11. This chapter states that Saul lost his throne only because of his failure against Amalek, but his downfall

*Saul saw any mighty warrior or military strategist, he would take him to himself
[into his army].*

15

**SAUL'S
ILL-FATED
VICTORY
OVER
AMALEK**
15:1-35
*A command
to destroy
Amalek*

¹ **S**amuel said to Saul: *"HASHEM sent me to anoint you as king over His
people, over Israel, so now hear the sound of HASHEM's words.* * ² *So said
HASHEM, Master of Legions: 'I have remembered what Amalek did to Israel —
[the ambush] he emplaced against him on the way, as he went up from Egypt.
³ Now go and strike down Amalek and destroy everything he has. Have no pity
on him — kill man and woman alike, infant and suckling alike, ox and sheep
alike, camel and donkey alike.' "*

⁴ *Saul had all the people summoned, and he counted them through lambs:* *
*two hundred thousand infantrymen, and the men of Judah were ten thousand.
⁵ Saul came to the city of Amalek, and he fought [them] in the valley. ⁶ Saul said
to the Kenite,* * *"Go, withdraw, descend from among the Amalekite, lest I
destroy you with them; for you acted kindly to all the Children of Israel when
they went up from Egypt." So the Kenite withdrew from among Amalek.*

*Amalek is
conquered;
King Agag
is captured*

⁷ *Saul struck down Amalek, from Havilah to the approach to Shur, which is
alongside Egypt. ⁸ He captured Agag, king of Amalek, alive, and the entire
people he destroyed by the edge of the sword. ⁹ Saul, as well as the people, took
pity on Agag, on the best of the sheep, the cattle, the fatted bulls, the fatted
sheep, and on all that was good; and they were not willing to destroy them; but
the inferior and wretched livestock, that they did destroy.*

*Saul's
weakness
and God's
wrath*

¹⁰ *The word of HASHEM then came to Samuel, saying, ¹¹ "I have reconsidered
My having made Saul king, for he has turned away from Me and has not fulfilled
My word!"* * *Samuel was aggrieved [by this] and he cried out to HASHEM the entire
night.*

¹² *Samuel arose early in the morning to meet Saul. (It had been told to Samuel,
saying, "Saul came to the Carmel and set up for himself a place [for an altar].
He turned and descended to Gilgal.") ¹³ When Samuel came to Saul, Saul said
to him, "Blessed are you to HASHEM! I have fulfilled the word of HASHEM."*

¹⁴ *Samuel said, "And what is this sound of the sheep in my ears and the sound
of the cattle that I hear?"*

¹⁵ *Saul said, "I have brought them from the Amalekite, for the people took pity
on the best of the sheep and cattle in order to bring them as offerings to HASHEM,
your God, but we have destroyed the remainder."*

*Samuel
condemns
Saul*

¹⁶ *Samuel said to Saul, "Desist, and I shall tell you what HASHEM spoke to me
last night."*

He said to him, "Speak."

¹⁷ *Samuel said, "Is this not so? — Though you may be small in your own eyes,
you are the head of the tribes of Israel; and HASHEM has anointed you to be king
over Israel.* * ¹⁸ *HASHEM sent you on the way, and He said, 'Go, destroy the
sinners, Amalek, and wage war with him until you have exterminated him.'
¹⁹ Why did you not obey the voice of HASHEM? You rushed after the spoils,* * *and
you did what was evil in the eyes of HASHEM."*

²⁰ *Saul said to Samuel, "But I did heed the voice of HASHEM, and I did walk*

---

had already been decreed above (13:13-14). Possibly
he had repented and was forgiven. Alternatively, the
earlier decree was that his son would not become king;
the new failure caused his own reign to be terminated
(*Radak*).

15:17. A leader must do the right thing, even if he must
override popular opinion; humility is not a virtue if it
interferes with duty.

15:19. Though Saul did not take loot for himself, he, as
king, was responsible.

בַּדֶּרֶךְ אֲשֶׁר־שְׁלָחַנִי יהוה וָאָבִיא אֶת־אֲגַג מֶלֶךְ עֲמָלֵק וְאֶת־עֲמָלֵק

כא הֶחֱרַמְתִּי: וַיִּקַּח הָעָם מֵהַשָּׁלָל צֹאן וּבָקָר רֵאשִׁית הַחֵרֶם לִזְבֹּחַ לַיהוה

כב אֱלֹהֶיךָ בַּגִּלְגָּל: וַיֹּאמֶר שְׁמוּאֵל הַחֵפֶץ לַיהוה בְּעֹלוֹת וּזְבָחִים

כג כִּשְׁמֹעַ בְּקוֹל יהוה הִנֵּה שְׁמֹעַ מִזֶּבַח טוֹב לְהַקְשִׁיב מֵחֵלֶב אֵילִים: כִּי

חַטַּאת־קֶסֶם מֶרִי וְאָוֶן וּתְרָפִים הַפְצַר יַעַן מָאַסְתָּ אֶת־דְּבַר יהוה וַיִּמְאָסְךָ

כד מִמֶּלֶךְ: וַיֹּאמֶר שָׁאוּל אֶל־שְׁמוּאֵל חָטָאתִי כִּי־עָבַרְתִּי אֶת־פִּי־

כה יהוה וְאֶת־דְּבָרֶיךָ כִּי יָרֵאתִי אֶת־הָעָם וָאֶשְׁמַע בְּקוֹלָם: וְעַתָּה שָׂא נָא

כו אֶת־חַטָּאתִי וְשׁוּב עִמִּי וְאֶשְׁתַּחֲוֶה לַיהוה: וַיֹּאמֶר שְׁמוּאֵל אֶל־שָׁאוּל לֹא

אָשׁוּב עִמָּךְ כִּי מָאַסְתָּה אֶת־דְּבַר יהוה וַיִּמְאָסְךָ יהוה מִהְיוֹת מֶלֶךְ עַל־

כז-כח יִשְׂרָאֵל: וַיִּסֹּב שְׁמוּאֵל לָלֶכֶת וַיַּחֲזֵק בִּכְנַף־מְעִילוֹ וַיִּקָּרַע: וַיֹּאמֶר אֵלָיו

שְׁמוּאֵל קָרַע יהוה אֶת־מַמְלְכוּת יִשְׂרָאֵל מֵעָלֶיךָ הַיּוֹם וּנְתָנָהּ לְרֵעֲךָ

כט הַטּוֹב מִמֶּךָּ: וְגַם נֵצַח יִשְׂרָאֵל לֹא יְשַׁקֵּר וְלֹא יִנָּחֵם כִּי לֹא אָדָם הוּא

ל לְהִנָּחֵם: וַיֹּאמֶר חָטָאתִי עַתָּה כַּבְּדֵנִי נָא נֶגֶד־זִקְנֵי עַמִּי וְנֶגֶד יִשְׂרָאֵל וְשׁוּב

לא עִמִּי וְהִשְׁתַּחֲוֵיתִי לַיהוה אֱלֹהֶיךָ: וַיָּשָׁב שְׁמוּאֵל אַחֲרֵי שָׁאוּל וַיִּשְׁתַּחוּ

לב שָׁאוּל לַיהוה: וַיֹּאמֶר שְׁמוּאֵל הַגִּישׁוּ אֵלַי אֶת־אֲגַג מֶלֶךְ עֲמָלֵק

לג וַיֵּלֶךְ אֵלָיו אֲגַג מַעֲדַנֹּת וַיֹּאמֶר אֲגַג אָכֵן סָר מַר־הַמָּוֶת: וַיֹּאמֶר שְׁמוּאֵל

כַּאֲשֶׁר שִׁכְּלָה נָשִׁים חַרְבֶּךָ כֵּן־תִּשְׁכַּל מִנָּשִׁים אִמֶּךָ וַיְשַׁסֵּף שְׁמוּאֵל אֶת־

לד אֲגַג לִפְנֵי יהוה בַּגִּלְגָּל: וַיֵּלֶךְ שְׁמוּאֵל הָרָמָתָה וְשָׁאוּל עָלָה

לה אֶל־בֵּיתוֹ גִּבְעַת שָׁאוּל: וְלֹא־יָסַף שְׁמוּאֵל לִרְאוֹת אֶת־שָׁאוּל עַד־

יוֹם מוֹתוֹ כִּי־הִתְאַבֵּל שְׁמוּאֵל אֶל־שָׁאוּל וַיהוה נִחָם כִּי־הִמְלִיךְ אֶת־

טז א שָׁאוּל עַל־יִשְׂרָאֵל: וַיֹּאמֶר יהוה אֶל־שְׁמוּאֵל עַד־מָתַי אַתָּה

מִתְאַבֵּל אֶל־שָׁאוּל וַאֲנִי מְאַסְתִּיו מִמְּלֹךְ עַל־יִשְׂרָאֵל מַלֵּא קַרְנְךָ שֶׁמֶן

ב וְלֵךְ אֶשְׁלָחֲךָ אֶל־יִשַׁי בֵּית־הַלַּחְמִי כִּי־רָאִיתִי בְּבָנָיו לִי מֶלֶךְ: וַיֹּאמֶר

שְׁמוּאֵל אֵיךְ אֵלֵךְ וְשָׁמַע שָׁאוּל וַהֲרָגָנִי וַיֹּאמֶר יהוה עֶגְלַת

ג בָּקָר תִּקַּח בְּיָדֶךָ וְאָמַרְתָּ לִזְבֹּחַ לַיהוה בָּאתִי: וְקָרָאתָ לְיִשַׁי בַּזָּבַח וְאָנֹכִי

ד אוֹדִיעֲךָ אֵת אֲשֶׁר־תַּעֲשֶׂה וּמָשַׁחְתָּ לִי אֵת אֲשֶׁר־אֹמַר אֵלֶיךָ: וַיַּעַשׂ

שְׁמוּאֵל אֵת אֲשֶׁר דִּבֶּר יהוה וַיָּבֹא בֵּית לָחֶם וַיֶּחֶרְדוּ זִקְנֵי הָעִיר לִקְרָאתוֹ

ה וַיֹּאמֶר שָׁלֹם בּוֹאֶךָ: וַיֹּאמֶר ׀ שָׁלוֹם לִזְבֹּחַ לַיהוה בָּאתִי הִתְקַדְּשׁוּ וּבָאתֶם

ו אִתִּי בַּזָּבַח וַיְקַדֵּשׁ אֶת־יִשַׁי וְאֶת־בָּנָיו וַיִּקְרָא לָהֶם לַזָּבַח: וַיְהִי בְּבוֹאָם

ז וַיַּרְא אֶת־אֱלִיאָב וַיֹּאמֶר אַךְ נֶגֶד יהוה מְשִׁיחוֹ:

וַיֹּאמֶר

15:22-23. Samuel made three points: (a) Offerings and contributions are no substitute for obedience to God; (b) reliance on sorcery and omens is equivalent to rebellion against God; and (c) verbose rationalizations are as empty as the extravagant rituals of idol worship.

15:28. Prophets commonly use a physical act to symbolize the reality of a prophecy.

15:29. The decree is final; repentance will not rescind it.

16:2. For Samuel to anoint a new king could be considered a subversive act, which the reigning king may punish by death.

16:4. They feared that Samuel's unexpected arrival was prompted by a grievous sin.

the path on which HASHEM sent me! I brought Agag, king of Amalek, and I destroyed Amalek! ²¹ The people took sheep and cattle from the spoils — the best of that which was to be destroyed — in order to bring offerings to HASHEM, your God, in Gilgal."

²² Samuel said, * "Does HASHEM delight in elevation-offerings and feast-offerings as in obedience to the voice of HASHEM? Behold! — to obey is better than a choice offering, to be attentive than the fat of rams. ²³ For rebelliousness is like the sin of sorcery, and verbosity is like the iniquity of idolatry. Because you have rejected the word of God, He has rejected you as king!"

²⁴ Saul said to Samuel, "I have sinned, for I have transgressed the word of HASHEM and your word, for I feared the people and I hearkened to their voice. ²⁵ But now, please forgive my sin and return with me, and I will prostrate myself to HASHEM."

²⁶ Samuel said to Saul, "I will not return with you, for you have rejected the word of HASHEM and HASHEM has rejected you from being king over Israel!" ²⁷ Samuel then turned away to leave, but [Saul] grabbed the hem of his tunic,
and it tore. ²⁸ Samuel said to him, "HASHEM has torn the kingship of Israel from upon you this day, and has given it to your fellow who is better than you. * ²⁹ Moreover, the Eternal One of Israel does not lie and does not relent, for He is not a human that He should relent."*

³⁰ He said, "I have sinned. Now, please honor me in the presence of the elders of my people and in the presence of Israel; return with me, and I shall prostrate myself to HASHEM, your God." ³¹ So Samuel returned after Saul, and Saul prostrated himself before HASHEM.

³² Samuel then said, "Bring me Agag, king of Amalek."

Agag went to him in chains, and Agag said, "Alas, the bitterness of death approaches."

³³ Samuel said, "Just as your sword made women childless, so shall your mother be childless among women!" And Samuel severed Agag before HASHEM in Gilgal.

³⁴ Samuel went to Ramah, and Saul went up to his home at Gibeath-shaul. ³⁵ Samuel never again saw Saul until the day of his death, for Samuel mourned over Saul, but HASHEM had reconsidered His making Saul king over Israel.

16

THE RISE
OF DAVID
16:1-23
God sends
Samuel to
anoint Saul's
successor ¹ HASHEM said to Samuel, "How long will you mourn over Saul, when I have rejected him from reigning over Israel? Fill your horn with oil and go forth — I shall send you to Jesse the Bethlehemite, for I have seen a king for Myself among his sons." ² But Samuel asked, "How can I go? If Saul finds out he will kill me."*

So HASHEM said, "Take along a heifer, and say, 'I have come to bring an offering to HASHEM.' ³ Invite Jesse to the feast; I will then tell you what to do, and you shall anoint for Me the one whom I shall tell you."

⁴ So Samuel did as HASHEM had spoken, and he arrived in Bethlehem. The elders of the city hurried nervously toward him, and one of them said, "Do you come in peace?"* ⁵ And he answered, " Peace. To bring an offering to HASHEM have I come. Prepare yourselves and join me at the feast." And he invited Jesse and his sons, calling them to the feast.

⁶ And it was upon their arrival that Samuel saw Eliab; he said, "Surely, before HASHEM is His anointed one."

יְהוָה אֶל־שְׁמוּאֵל אַל־תַּבֵּט אֶל־מַרְאֵהוּ וְאֶל־גְּבֹהַּ קוֹמָתוֹ כִּי מְאַסְתִּיהוּ
כִּי ׀ לֹא אֲשֶׁר יִרְאֶה הָאָדָם כִּי הָאָדָם יִרְאֶה לַעֵינַיִם וַיהוָה יִרְאֶה לַלֵּבָב:

ח וַיִּקְרָא יִשַׁי אֶל־אֲבִינָדָב וַיַּעֲבִרֵהוּ לִפְנֵי שְׁמוּאֵל וַיֹּאמֶר גַּם־בָּזֶה לֹא־בָחַר
ט-י יְהוָה: וַיַּעֲבֵר יִשַׁי שַׁמָּה וַיֹּאמֶר גַּם־בָּזֶה לֹא־בָחַר יְהוָה: וַיַּעֲבֵר יִשַׁי שִׁבְעַת
בָּנָיו לִפְנֵי שְׁמוּאֵל וַיֹּאמֶר שְׁמוּאֵל אֶל־יִשַׁי לֹא־בָחַר יְהוָה בָּאֵלֶּה: וַיֹּאמֶר
יא שְׁמוּאֵל אֶל־יִשַׁי הֲתַמּוּ הַנְּעָרִים וַיֹּאמֶר עוֹד שָׁאַר הַקָּטָן וְהִנֵּה רֹעֶה בַּצֹּאן
יב וַיֹּאמֶר שְׁמוּאֵל אֶל־יִשַׁי שִׁלְחָה וְקָחֶנּוּ כִּי לֹא־נָסֹב עַד־בֹּאוֹ פֹה: וַיִּשְׁלַח
וַיְבִיאֵהוּ וְהוּא אַדְמוֹנִי עִם־יְפֵה עֵינַיִם וְטוֹב רֹאִי
יג קוּם מְשָׁחֵהוּ כִּי־זֶה הוּא: וַיִּקַּח שְׁמוּאֵל אֶת־קֶרֶן הַשֶּׁמֶן וַיִּמְשַׁח אֹתוֹ בְּקֶרֶב
אֶחָיו וַתִּצְלַח רוּחַ־יְהוָה אֶל־דָּוִד מֵהַיּוֹם הַהוּא וָמָעְלָה וַיָּקָם שְׁמוּאֵל וַיֵּלֶךְ
יד הָרָמָתָה: וְרוּחַ יְהוָה סָרָה מֵעִם שָׁאוּל וּבִעֲתַתּוּ רוּחַ־רָעָה מֵאֵת יְהוָה:
טו-טז וַיֹּאמְרוּ עַבְדֵי־שָׁאוּל אֵלָיו הִנֵּה־נָא רוּחַ־אֱלֹהִים רָעָה מְבַעִתֶּךָ: יֹאמַר־נָא
אֲדֹנֵנוּ עֲבָדֶיךָ לְפָנֶיךָ יְבַקְשׁוּ אִישׁ יֹדֵעַ מְנַגֵּן בַּכִּנּוֹר וְהָיָה בִּהְיוֹת עָלֶיךָ
רוּחַ־אֱלֹהִים רָעָה וְנִגֵּן בְּיָדוֹ וְטוֹב לָךְ: וַיֹּאמֶר שָׁאוּל אֶל־עֲבָדָיו רְאוּ־נָא
יז-יח לִי אִישׁ מֵיטִיב לְנַגֵּן וַהֲבִיאוֹתֶם אֵלָי: וַיַּעַן אֶחָד מֵהַנְּעָרִים וַיֹּאמֶר הִנֵּה
רָאִיתִי בֵּן לְיִשַׁי בֵּית הַלַּחְמִי יֹדֵעַ נַגֵּן וְגִבּוֹר חַיִל וְאִישׁ מִלְחָמָה וּנְבוֹן דָּבָר
יט וְאִישׁ תֹּאַר וַיהוָה עִמּוֹ: וַיִּשְׁלַח שָׁאוּל מַלְאָכִים אֶל־יִשַׁי וַיֹּאמֶר שִׁלְחָה
כ אֵלַי אֶת־דָּוִד בִּנְךָ אֲשֶׁר בַּצֹּאן: וַיִּקַּח יִשַׁי חֲמוֹר לֶחֶם וְנֹאד יַיִן וּגְדִי עִזִּים
כא אֶחָד וַיִּשְׁלַח בְּיַד־דָּוִד בְּנוֹ אֶל־שָׁאוּל: וַיָּבֹא דָוִד אֶל־שָׁאוּל וַיַּעֲמֹד לְפָנָיו
כב וַיֶּאֱהָבֵהוּ מְאֹד וַיְהִי־לוֹ נֹשֵׂא כֵלִים: וַיִּשְׁלַח שָׁאוּל אֶל־יִשַׁי לֵאמֹר יַעֲמָד־
כג נָא דָוִד לְפָנַי כִּי־מָצָא חֵן בְּעֵינָי: וְהָיָה בִּהְיוֹת רוּחַ־אֱלֹהִים אֶל־שָׁאוּל
וְלָקַח דָּוִד אֶת־הַכִּנּוֹר וְנִגֵּן בְּיָדוֹ וְרָוַח לְשָׁאוּל וְטוֹב לוֹ וְסָרָה מֵעָלָיו רוּחַ
א הָרָעָה: וַיַּאַסְפוּ פְלִשְׁתִּים אֶת־מַחֲנֵיהֶם לַמִּלְחָמָה וַיֵּאָסְפוּ שֹׂכֹה   יז

ב אֲשֶׁר לִיהוּדָה וַיַּחֲנוּ בֵּין־שׂוֹכֹה וּבֵין־עֲזֵקָה בְּאֶפֶס דַּמִּים: וְשָׁאוּל וְאִישׁ־
יִשְׂרָאֵל נֶאֶסְפוּ וַיַּחֲנוּ בְּעֵמֶק הָאֵלָה וַיַּעַרְכוּ מִלְחָמָה לִקְרַאת פְּלִשְׁתִּים:
ג וּפְלִשְׁתִּים עֹמְדִים אֶל־הָהָר מִזֶּה וְיִשְׂרָאֵל עֹמְדִים אֶל־הָהָר מִזֶּה וְהַגַּיְא
ד בֵּינֵיהֶם: וַיֵּצֵא אִישׁ־הַבֵּנַיִם מִמַּחֲנוֹת פְּלִשְׁתִּים גָּלְיָת שְׁמוֹ מִגַּת גָּבְהוֹ שֵׁשׁ
ה אַמּוֹת וָזָרֶת: וְכוֹבַע נְחֹשֶׁת עַל־רֹאשׁוֹ וְשִׁרְיוֹן קַשְׂקַשִּׂים הוּא לָבוּשׁ וּמִשְׁקַל
ו הַשִּׁרְיוֹן חֲמֵשֶׁת־אֲלָפִים שְׁקָלִים נְחֹשֶׁת: וּמִצְחַת נְחֹשֶׁת עַל־רַגְלָיו וְכִידוֹן
ז נְחֹשֶׁת בֵּין כְּתֵפָיו: °וַחֵץ [°וְעֵץ ק] חֲנִיתוֹ כִּמְנוֹר אֹרְגִים וְלַהֶבֶת חֲנִיתוֹ
ח שֵׁשׁ־מֵאוֹת שְׁקָלִים בַּרְזֶל וְנֹשֵׂא הַצִּנָּה הֹלֵךְ לְפָנָיו: וַיַּעֲמֹד וַיִּקְרָא אֶל־
מַעַרְכֹת יִשְׂרָאֵל וַיֹּאמֶר לָהֶם לָמָּה תֵצְאוּ לַעֲרֹךְ מִלְחָמָה הֲלוֹא אָנֹכִי

17:4. Lit., "the man of the middle," i.e., a mighty
warrior who would leave his camp and stand alone
between the warring armies, challenging the opposing

force (Rashi).
He was 12-13 feet tall. A cubit is just under two feet,
and a span is half a cubit.

Samuel
seeks to
identify
God's
anointed

⁷ But HASHEM said to Samuel, "Do not look at his appearance or at his tall stature, for I have rejected him. For it is not as man sees — man sees what his eyes behold, but HASHEM sees into the heart." ⁸ Jesse then called Abinadab and brought him before Samuel, but he said, "HASHEM has not chosen this one either." ⁹ Then Jesse brought Shammah, but [Samuel] said, "HASHEM has not chosen this one either." ¹⁰ Jesse presented his seven sons before Samuel, but Samuel said to Jesse, "HASHEM has not chosen these." ¹¹ Samuel said, "Are these all the boys?" And he said, "The youngest one is still left; he is tending the sheep now." So Samuel said to Jesse, "Send and bring him, for we will not sit [to dine] until he arrives here."

¹² He sent and brought him. He was ruddy, with fair eyes and a pleasing appearance. HASHEM then said, "Arise and anoint him, for this is he!" ¹³ Samuel took the horn of oil and anointed him in the midst of his brothers, and the spirit of HASHEM passed over David from that day on. Then Samuel arose and went to Ramah.

Saul suffers
melancholia

¹⁴ The spirit of HASHEM departed from Saul, and he was tormented by a spirit of melancholy from HASHEM. ¹⁵ Saul's servants said him, "Behold now! a spirit of melancholy from God torments you. ¹⁶ Let our lord tell your servants [who are] before you [that] they should seek a man who knows how to play the harp, so that when the spirit of melancholy from God is upon you, he will play [the harp] with his hand and it will be well with you." ¹⁷ So Saul said to his servants, "Seek now for me someone who plays well and bring him to me." ¹⁸ One of the young servants spoke up and said, "Behold! I have seen a son of Jesse the Beth-lehemite, who knows how to play, is a mighty man of valor and a man of war, who understands a matter, and is a handsome man; and HASHEM is with him."

David
comes to
soothe Saul

¹⁹ Saul sent messengers to Jesse, and said, "Send me David your son who is with the sheep." ²⁰ Jesse took a donkey [laden with] bread, a jug of wine, and one kid, and sent it with his son David, for Saul. ²¹ David came to Saul and stood before him. He loved him very much, and he became his armor-bearer. ²² Saul sent to Jesse, saying, "Let David stand before me, for he has found favor in my eyes." ²³ And it happened that whenever the spirit [of melancholy] from God was upon Saul, David would take the harp and play [it] with his hand, and Saul would feel relieved and it would be well with him, and the spirit of melancholy would depart from him.

17

DAVID
FACES
GOLIATH
17:1-54

The
Philistines
invade again

¹ The Philistines assembled their camps for war, and assembled themselves at Socoh that is to Judah; they encamped between Socoh and Azekah, in Ephes-dammim. ² So Saul and the people of Israel assembled themselves, they encamped in the Terebinth Valley, and they arranged for war against the Philis-tines. ³ The Philistines were standing on the mountain on one side and Israel was standing on the mountain on the other side, and the valley was between them. ⁴ A champion* went forth from the Philistine camps, whose name was Goliath of Gath; his height six cubits and one span. * ⁵ [He had] a copper helmet on his head, and was wearing armor of mail; the weight of the armor [was] five thousand copper shekels. ⁶ [He had] a copper shield on his legs and a copper neck-guard between his shoulders. ⁷ The shaft of his spear was like a weavers' beam and the blade of his spear [weighed] six hundred iron shekels. The shield-bearer walked before him. ⁸ He stood and called out to the battalions of Israel and said to them, "Why are you going forth to wage war? Am I not

ט　הַפְּלִשְׁתִּי וְאַתֶּם עֲבָדִים לְשָׁאוּל בְּרוּ־לָכֶם אִישׁ וְיֵרֵד אֵלָי: אִם־יוּכַל

להִלָּחֵם אִתִּי וְהִכָּנִי וְהָיִינוּ לָכֶם לַעֲבָדִים וְאִם־אֲנִי אוּכַל־לוֹ וְהִכֵּיתִיו

י　וִהְיִיתֶם לָנוּ לַעֲבָדִים וַעֲבַדְתֶּם אֹתָנוּ: וַיֹּאמֶר הַפְּלִשְׁתִּי אֲנִי חֵרַפְתִּי אֶת־

יא　מַעַרְכוֹת יִשְׂרָאֵל הַיּוֹם הַזֶּה תְּנוּ־לִי אִישׁ וְנִלָּחֲמָה יָחַד: וַיִּשְׁמַע שָׁאוּל

יב　וְכָל־יִשְׂרָאֵל אֶת־דִּבְרֵי הַפְּלִשְׁתִּי הָאֵלֶּה וַיֵּחַתּוּ וַיִּרְאוּ מְאֹד: וְדָוִד

בֶּן־אִישׁ אֶפְרָתִי הַזֶּה מִבֵּית לֶחֶם יְהוּדָה וּשְׁמוֹ יִשַׁי וְלוֹ שְׁמֹנָה בָנִים וְהָאִישׁ

יג　בִּימֵי שָׁאוּל זָקֵן בָּא בַאֲנָשִׁים: וַיֵּלְכוּ שְׁלֹשֶׁת בְּנֵי־יִשַׁי הַגְּדֹלִים הָלְכוּ אַחֲרֵי־

שָׁאוּל לַמִּלְחָמָה וְשֵׁם ׀ שְׁלֹשֶׁת בָּנָיו אֲשֶׁר הָלְכוּ בַּמִּלְחָמָה אֱלִיאָב הַבְּכוֹר

יד　וּמִשְׁנֵהוּ אֲבִינָדָב וְהַשְּׁלִשִׁי שַׁמָּה: וְדָוִד הוּא הַקָּטָן וּשְׁלֹשָׁה הַגְּדֹלִים הָלְכוּ

טו　אַחֲרֵי שָׁאוּל: וְדָוִד הֹלֵךְ וָשָׁב מֵעַל שָׁאוּל לִרְעוֹת אֶת־צֹאן אָבִיו בֵּית־

טז-יז　לָחֶם: וַיִּגַּשׁ הַפְּלִשְׁתִּי הַשְׁכֵּם וְהַעֲרֵב וַיִּתְיַצֵּב אַרְבָּעִים יוֹם: וַיֹּאמֶר

יִשַׁי לְדָוִד בְּנוֹ קַח־נָא לְאַחֶיךָ אֵיפַת הַקָּלִיא הַזֶּה וַעֲשָׂרָה לֶחֶם הַזֶּה וְהָרֵץ

יח　הַמַּחֲנֶה לְאַחֶיךָ: וְאֵת עֲשֶׂרֶת חֲרִצֵי הֶחָלָב הָאֵלֶּה תָּבִיא לְשַׂר־הָאָלֶף

יט　וְאֶת־אַחֶיךָ תִּפְקֹד לְשָׁלוֹם וְאֶת־עֲרֻבָּתָם תִּקָּח: וְשָׁאוּל וְהֵמָּה וְכָל־אִישׁ

כ　יִשְׂרָאֵל בְּעֵמֶק הָאֵלָה נִלְחָמִים עִם־פְּלִשְׁתִּים: וַיַּשְׁכֵּם דָּוִד

בַּבֹּקֶר וַיִּטֹּשׁ אֶת־הַצֹּאן עַל־שֹׁמֵר וַיִּשָּׂא וַיֵּלֶךְ כַּאֲשֶׁר צִוָּהוּ יִשָׁי וַיָּבֹא

כא　הַמַּעְגָּלָה וְהַחַיִל הַיֹּצֵא אֶל־הַמַּעֲרָכָה וְהֵרֵעוּ בַּמִּלְחָמָה: וַתַּעֲרֹךְ יִשְׂרָאֵל

כב　וּפְלִשְׁתִּים מַעֲרָכָה לִקְרַאת מַעֲרָכָה: וַיִּטֹּשׁ דָּוִד אֶת־הַכֵּלִים מֵעָלָיו עַל־יַד

כג　שׁוֹמֵר הַכֵּלִים וַיָּרָץ הַמַּעֲרָכָה וַיָּבֹא וַיִּשְׁאַל לְאֶחָיו לְשָׁלוֹם: וְהוּא ׀ מְדַבֵּר

עִמָּם וְהִנֵּה אִישׁ הַבֵּנַיִם עוֹלֶה גָּלְיָת הַפְּלִשְׁתִּי שְׁמוֹ מִגַּת °מִמַּעְרוֹת

כד　[°מִמַּעַרְכוֹת ק] פְּלִשְׁתִּים וַיְדַבֵּר כַּדְּבָרִים הָאֵלֶּה וַיִּשְׁמַע דָּוִד: וְכֹל ׀ אִישׁ

יִשְׂרָאֵל בִּרְאוֹתָם אֶת־הָאִישׁ וַיָּנֻסוּ מִפָּנָיו וַיִּרְאוּ מְאֹד: וַיֹּאמֶר ׀ אִישׁ

כה　יִשְׂרָאֵל הַרְאִיתֶם הָאִישׁ הָעֹלֶה הַזֶּה כִּי לְחָרֵף אֶת־יִשְׂרָאֵל עֹלֶה וְהָיָה

הָאִישׁ אֲשֶׁר־יַכֶּנּוּ יַעְשְׁרֶנּוּ הַמֶּלֶךְ ׀ עֹשֶׁר גָּדוֹל וְאֶת־בִּתּוֹ יִתֶּן־לוֹ וְאֵת בֵּית

כו　אָבִיו יַעֲשֶׂה חָפְשִׁי בְּיִשְׂרָאֵל: וַיֹּאמֶר דָּוִד אֶל־הָאֲנָשִׁים הָעֹמְדִים

עִמּוֹ לֵאמֹר מַה־יֵּעָשֶׂה לָאִישׁ אֲשֶׁר יַכֶּה אֶת־הַפְּלִשְׁתִּי הַלָּז וְהֵסִיר חֶרְפָּה

מֵעַל יִשְׂרָאֵל כִּי מִי הַפְּלִשְׁתִּי הֶעָרֵל הַזֶּה כִּי חֵרֵף מַעַרְכוֹת אֱלֹהִים חַיִּים:

כז-כח　וַיֹּאמֶר לוֹ הָעָם כַּדָּבָר הַזֶּה לֵאמֹר כֹּה יֵעָשֶׂה לָאִישׁ אֲשֶׁר יַכֶּנּוּ: וַיִּשְׁמַע

אֱלִיאָב אָחִיו הַגָּדוֹל בְּדַבְּרוֹ אֶל־הָאֲנָשִׁים וַיִּחַר־אַף אֱלִיאָב בְּדָוִד וַיֹּאמֶר ׀

לָמָּה־זֶּה יָרַדְתָּ וְעַל־מִי נָטַשְׁתָּ מְעַט הַצֹּאן הָהֵנָּה בַּמִּדְבָּר אֲנִי יָדַעְתִּי

17:8. Why fight a full-scale war? I challenge you to represent your king in a one-on-one duel (*Kara*). Alternatively: "I am an ordinary Philistine soldier, yet I have distinguished myself in battle; what has your king Saul done for you? Let him come and fight me!" (*Rashi*).

17:10. Seeing that no one was willing to duel him,

Goliath taunted them as cowards.

17:12. Bethlehem, in the province of Judah, was in an area known as Ephrath. Scripture recapitulates Jesse's background because David is about to become the savior of the nation.

17:15. David would shuttle back and forth from

Goliath
humiliates
Israel with a
challenge the Philistine, while you are the servants of Saul?* Choose yourselves a man and let him come down to me! ⁹ If he can fight me and kill me, we will be slaves to you; and if I defeat him and kill him, you will be slaves to us and serve us."
¹⁰ Then the Philistine said, "I have disgraced the battalions of Israel this day, [saying,] 'Give me a man and we will fight together.' "* ¹¹ Saul and all Israel heard these words of the Philistine, and they were terrified and greatly afraid.

¹² David was the son of a certain Ephrathite* man from Bethlehem [in] Judah; his name was Jesse and he had eight sons. In the days of Saul, the man was old, and would come among the elders. ¹³ Jesse's three oldest sons left home and followed Saul to war. The names of his three sons who went to war were Eliab, the firstborn; the second to him, Abinadab; and the third, Shammah. ¹⁴ But David was the youngest; just the three oldest followed Saul. ¹⁵ David would travel back and forth from Saul's presence to tend his father's flocks in Bethlehem.*

¹⁶ The Philistine would approach [the Israelite camp] early morning and evening; he presented himself for forty days.

David brings
provisions
for his
brothers ¹⁷ Jesse said to his son David, "Please take this ephah of toasted grain and these ten loaves of bread for your brothers and hurry to the camp to your brothers, ¹⁸ and bring these ten cheeses to the captain of the thousand. Inquire after the welfare of your brothers, and obtain a report of their welfare."*

¹⁹ Saul, they, and all the men of Israel were in the Terebinth Valley, fighting with the Philistines. ²⁰ David arose early in the morning, left the sheep with a watchman, and set out as Jesse had commanded him. He came to the encirclement, and the army was going forth to the battle line, shouting battle cries. ²¹ Israel and the Philistines deployed, battalions facing battalion. ²² David left the baggage that was upon him with the keeper of the baggage and ran to the line. When he arrived he inquired after the welfare of his brothers.

David sees
Israel's fear
of Goliath ²³ As he was speaking to them, behold — the champion went forth from the Philistine battalions, Goliath the Philistine of Gath was his name, and spoke the [above] words, and David heard. ²⁴ All the men of Israel, when they saw the man, fled from him, and they were very frightened. ²⁵ The men of Israel were saying, "Have you seen this man who goes forth? He goes forth to disgrace Israel! The king will enrich whoever kills him with great wealth and give his daughter to him [in marriage], and he will free his father's family [from royal service] in Israel."

He implies
his readiness
to fight ²⁶ David spoke to the men standing with him, saying, "What will be done for the man who slays this Philistine and removes disgrace from Israel? For who is this uncircumcised Philistine, that he disgraces the battalions of the Living God?" ²⁷ So the people told him regarding this matter, saying, "Such and such shall be done for the man who kills him."

²⁸ Eliab, [his] older brother, heard as he was talking to the men, and Eliab became angry with David,* and said, "Why did you come down [here]? And with whom did you leave those few sheep in the wilderness? I am aware of

---

Jesse's sheep to his duties as Saul's minstrel. At the time of Goliath's insolent challenge, David was at Bethlehem.

17:18. Following *Targum.* According to *Kara* and *Radak*, the meaning is, "redeem their pledges," for soldiers often

are short of money and have to pawn items as security in order to buy provisions; Jesse gave David money to redeem these pledges.

17:28. Eliab lashed out because he sensed that David was thinking "unrealistically" of fighting the Philistine.

כט אֶת־זְדֹנְךָ וְאֵת רֹעַ לְבָבֶךָ כִּי לְמַעַן רְאוֹת הַמִּלְחָמָה יָרָדְתָּ: וַיֹּאמֶר דָּוִד מֶה

ל עָשִׂיתִי עָתָּה הֲלוֹא דָבָר הוּא: וַיִּסֹּב מֵאֶצְלוֹ אֶל־מוּל אַחֵר וַיֹּאמֶר כַּדָּבָר

לא הַזֶּה וַיְשִׁבֻהוּ הָעָם דָּבָר כַּדָּבָר הָרִאשׁוֹן: וַיִּשָּׁמְעוּ הַדְּבָרִים אֲשֶׁר דִּבֶּר דָּוִד

לב וַיַּגִּדוּ לִפְנֵי־שָׁאוּל וַיִּקָּחֵהוּ: וַיֹּאמֶר דָּוִד אֶל־שָׁאוּל אַל־יִפֹּל לֵב־אָדָם עָלָיו

לג עַבְדְּךָ יֵלֵךְ וְנִלְחַם עִם־הַפְּלִשְׁתִּי הַזֶּה: וַיֹּאמֶר שָׁאוּל אֶל־דָּוִד לֹא תוּכַל

לָלֶכֶת אֶל־הַפְּלִשְׁתִּי הַזֶּה לְהִלָּחֵם עִמּוֹ כִּי־נַעַר אַתָּה וְהוּא אִישׁ מִלְחָמָה

לד מִנְּעֻרָיו: וַיֹּאמֶר דָּוִד אֶל־שָׁאוּל רֹעֶה הָיָה עַבְדְּךָ לְאָבִיו בַּצֹּאן

לה וּבָא הָאֲרִי וְאֶת־הַדּוֹב וְנָשָׂא שֶׂה מֵהָעֵדֶר: וְיָצָאתִי אַחֲרָיו וְהִכִּתִיו   °נ״א זֶה

לו וְהִצַּלְתִּי מִפִּיו וַיָּקָם עָלַי וְהֶחֱזַקְתִּי בִּזְקָנוֹ וְהִכִּתִיו וַהֲמִיתִּיו: גַּם אֶת־הָאֲרִי

גַּם־הַדּוֹב הִכָּה עַבְדֶּךָ וְהָיָה הַפְּלִשְׁתִּי הֶעָרֵל הַזֶּה כְּאַחַד מֵהֶם כִּי חֵרֵף

לז מַעַרְכֹת אֱלֹהִים חַיִּים: וַיֹּאמֶר דָּוִד יהוה אֲשֶׁר הִצִּלַנִי מִיַּד הָאֲרִי

וּמִיַּד הַדֹּב הוּא יַצִּילֵנִי מִיַּד הַפְּלִשְׁתִּי הַזֶּה   וַיֹּאמֶר שָׁאוּל אֶל־דָּוִד

לח לֵךְ וַיהוה יִהְיֶה עִמָּךְ: וַיַּלְבֵּשׁ שָׁאוּל אֶת־דָּוִד מַדָּיו וְנָתַן קוֹבַע נְחֹשֶׁת עַל־

לט רֹאשׁוֹ וַיַּלְבֵּשׁ אֹתוֹ שִׁרְיוֹן: וַיַּחְגֹּר דָּוִד אֶת־חַרְבּוֹ מֵעַל לְמַדָּיו וַיֹּאֶל לָלֶכֶת

כִּי לֹא־נִסָּה וַיֹּאמֶר דָּוִד אֶל־שָׁאוּל לֹא־אוּכַל לָלֶכֶת בָּאֵלֶּה כִּי לֹא נִסִּיתִי

מ וַיְסִרֵם דָּוִד מֵעָלָיו: וַיִּקַּח מַקְלוֹ בְּיָדוֹ וַיִּבְחַר־לוֹ חֲמִשָּׁה חַלֻּקֵי־אֲבָנִים ׀ מִן־

הַנַּחַל וַיָּשֶׂם אֹתָם בִּכְלִי הָרֹעִים אֲשֶׁר־לוֹ וּבַיַּלְקוּט וְקַלְעוֹ בְיָדוֹ וַיִּגַּשׁ אֶל־

מא הַפְּלִשְׁתִּי: וַיֵּלֶךְ הַפְּלִשְׁתִּי הֹלֵךְ וְקָרֵב אֶל־דָּוִד וְהָאִישׁ נֹשֵׂא הַצִּנָּה לְפָנָיו:

מב וַיַּבֵּט הַפְּלִשְׁתִּי וַיִּרְאֶה אֶת־דָּוִד וַיִּבְזֵהוּ כִּי־הָיָה נַעַר וְאַדְמֹנִי עִם־יְפֵה

מג מַרְאֶה: וַיֹּאמֶר הַפְּלִשְׁתִּי אֶל־דָּוִד הֲכֶלֶב אָנֹכִי כִּי־אַתָּה בָא־אֵלַי בַּמַּקְלוֹת

מד וַיְקַלֵּל הַפְּלִשְׁתִּי אֶת־דָּוִד בֵּאלֹהָיו: וַיֹּאמֶר הַפְּלִשְׁתִּי אֶל־דָּוִד לְכָה אֵלַי

מה וְאֶתְּנָה אֶת־בְּשָׂרְךָ לְעוֹף הַשָּׁמַיִם וּלְבֶהֱמַת הַשָּׂדֶה: וַיֹּאמֶר דָּוִד

אֶל־הַפְּלִשְׁתִּי אַתָּה בָּא אֵלַי בְּחֶרֶב וּבַחֲנִית וּבְכִידוֹן וְאָנֹכִי בָא־אֵלֶיךָ

מו בְּשֵׁם יהוה צְבָאוֹת אֱלֹהֵי מַעַרְכוֹת יִשְׂרָאֵל אֲשֶׁר חֵרַפְתָּ: הַיּוֹם הַזֶּה

יְסַגֶּרְךָ יהוה בְּיָדִי וְהִכִּיתִךָ וַהֲסִרֹתִי אֶת־רֹאשְׁךָ מֵעָלֶיךָ וְנָתַתִּי פֶּגֶר מַחֲנֵה

פְלִשְׁתִּים הַיּוֹם הַזֶּה לְעוֹף הַשָּׁמַיִם וּלְחַיַּת הָאָרֶץ וְיֵדְעוּ כָּל־הָאָרֶץ כִּי יֵשׁ

מז אֱלֹהִים לְיִשְׂרָאֵל: וְיֵדְעוּ כָּל־הַקָּהָל הַזֶּה כִּי־לֹא בְּחֶרֶב וּבַחֲנִית יְהוֹשִׁיעַ

יהוה כִּי לַיהוה הַמִּלְחָמָה וְנָתַן אֶתְכֶם בְּיָדֵנוּ: וְהָיָה כִּי־קָם הַפְּלִשְׁתִּי וַיֵּלֶךְ

מט וַיִּקְרַב לִקְרַאת דָּוִד וַיְמַהֵר דָּוִד וַיָּרָץ הַמַּעֲרָכָה לִקְרַאת הַפְּלִשְׁתִּי: וַיִּשְׁלַח

דָּוִד אֶת־יָדוֹ אֶל־הַכֶּלִי וַיִּקַּח מִשָּׁם אֶבֶן וַיְקַלַּע וַיַּךְ אֶת־הַפְּלִשְׁתִּי אֶל־מִצְחוֹ

נ וַתִּטְבַּע הָאֶבֶן בְּמִצְחוֹ וַיִּפֹּל עַל־פָּנָיו אָרְצָה: וַיֶּחֱזַק דָּוִד מִן־הַפְּלִשְׁתִּי

נא בַּקֶּלַע וּבָאֶבֶן וַיַּךְ אֶת־הַפְּלִשְׁתִּי וַיְמִיתֵהוּ וְחֶרֶב אֵין בְּיַד־דָּוִד: וַיָּרָץ דָּוִד

וַיַּעֲמֹד אֶל־הַפְּלִשְׁתִּי וַיִּקַּח אֶת־חַרְבּוֹ וַיִּשְׁלְפָהּ מִתַּעְרָהּ וַיְמֹתְתֵהוּ וַיִּכְרָת־

17:39. Having never worn armor, he felt too constricted to fight Goliath.

your willfulness and your evil thoughts, that you have come down here in order to watch the fighting!" [29] David replied, *"What have I done now? Was it not mere talk?"* [30] He then turned away from him toward someone else, and said the same thing to him; and the people answered him as before.

David volunteers to Saul, expressing faith in God

[31] The words David was saying became heard; people related [them] to Saul, and he summoned [David]. [32] David said to Saul, *"Let no man lose heart because of him. Your servant will go forth and fight this Philistine!"* [33] But Saul said to David, *"You cannot go forth to this Philistine to fight with him, for you are a lad, while he is a warrior from his youth."*

[34] David said to Saul, *"Your servant was a shepherd for his father among the flocks; the lion or the bear would come and carry off a sheep from the flock,* [35] *and I would go after it, strike it down, and rescue [the sheep] from its mouth. If it would attack me I would grab onto its beard and strike it and kill it.* [36] *Your servant has slain even lion and bear; and this uncircumcised Philistine shall be like one of them, for he has disgraced the battalions of the Living God!"* [37] Then David said, *"HASHEM Who rescued me from the hand of the lion and from the hand of the bear, He will rescue me from this Philistine!"*

David refuses armor

So Saul said to David, *"Go, and may HASHEM be with you!"* [38] Saul dressed David with his own battle garments; he put a copper helmet on his head and dressed him in armor. [39] David then girded his sword over his battle garments. But he was unwilling to go forth [that way], for he was not accustomed [to it], * so David said to Saul, *"I cannot walk with these, for I am not accustomed [to them],"* and David removed them from on himself. [40] He took his staff in his hand and picked out five smooth stones from the brook and put them in his shepherd's bag and in the knapsack, and his slingshot was in his hand. Then he approached the Philistine.

With his faith, David confronts Goliath

[41] The Philistine walked, going closer and closer to David, and the man bearing his shield was before him. [42] The Philistine peered and saw David, and he derided him, for he was a youth, ruddy and handsome. [43] The Philistine said to David, *"Am I a dog that you come after me with sticks?"* and the Philistine cursed David by his gods. [44] Then the Philistine said to David, *"Come to me, so that I may offer your flesh to the fowl of the heavens and to the beast of the field!"*

[45] David said to the Philistine, *"You come to me with a sword, a spear, and a javelin — but I come to you with the Name of HASHEM, Master of Legions, the God of the battalions of Israel that you have ridiculed.* [46] *On this day HASHEM will deliver you into my hand. I shall smite you and I will remove your head from upon you; and I shall offer the carcass of the Philistine camp this day to the fowl of the heavens and to the beast of earth! Then the whole earth will know that there is a God in Israel,* [47] *and all this assembly will know that not through sword and spear does HASHEM grant salvation; for unto HASHEM is the battle, and He shall deliver you into our hands!"*

David fells the giant and the Philistines flee

[48] It happened that when the Philistine arose and moved closer towards David that David hurried and ran to the line, towards the Philistine. [49] David stretched his hand into the sack. He took a stone from there and slung it, and struck the Philistine in the forehead. The stone penetrated his forehead, and he fell upon his face, upon the ground. [50] Thus David overpowered the Philistine with the slingshot and stone, he smote the Philistine and killed him; there was no sword in David's hand. [51] David ran and stood by the Philistine; he took [Goliath's] sword and drew it from its sheath, having already killed him, and he cut off

נב בָּהּ אֶת־רֹאשׁוֹ וַיִּרְאוּ הַפְּלִשְׁתִּים כִּי־מֵת גִּבּוֹרָם וַיָּנֻסוּ: וַיָּקֻמוּ אַנְשֵׁי יִשְׂרָאֵל
וִיהוּדָה וַיָּרִעוּ וַיִּרְדְּפוּ אֶת־הַפְּלִשְׁתִּים עַד־בּוֹאֲךָ גַיְא וְעַד שַׁעֲרֵי עֶקְרוֹן
נג וַיִּפְּלוּ חַלְלֵי פְלִשְׁתִּים בְּדֶרֶךְ שַׁעֲרַיִם וְעַד־גַּת וְעַד־עֶקְרוֹן: וַיָּשֻׁבוּ בְּנֵי
נד יִשְׂרָאֵל מִדְּלֹק אַחֲרֵי פְלִשְׁתִּים וַיָּשֹׁסּוּ אֶת־מַחֲנֵיהֶם: וַיִּקַּח דָּוִד אֶת־רֹאשׁ
הַפְּלִשְׁתִּי וַיְבִאֵהוּ יְרוּשָׁלָ͏ִם וְאֶת־כֵּלָיו שָׂם בְּאָהֳלוֹ:   וְכִרְאוֹת שָׁאוּל
נה אֶת־דָּוִד יֹצֵא לִקְרַאת הַפְּלִשְׁתִּי אָמַר אֶל־אַבְנֵר שַׂר הַצָּבָא בֶּן־מִי־זֶה
הַנַּעַר אַבְנֵר וַיֹּאמֶר אַבְנֵר חֵי־נַפְשְׁךָ הַמֶּלֶךְ אִם־יָדָעְתִּי: וַיֹּאמֶר הַמֶּלֶךְ
נו שְׁאַל אַתָּה בֶּן־מִי־זֶה הָעָלֶם: וּכְשׁוּב דָּוִד מֵהַכּוֹת אֶת־הַפְּלִשְׁתִּי
נז וַיִּקַּח אֹתוֹ אַבְנֵר וַיְבִאֵהוּ לִפְנֵי שָׁאוּל וְרֹאשׁ הַפְּלִשְׁתִּי בְּיָדוֹ: וַיֹּאמֶר אֵלָיו

יח
א שָׁאוּל בֶּן־מִי אַתָּה הַנָּעַר וַיֹּאמֶר דָּוִד בֶּן־עַבְדְּךָ יִשַׁי בֵּית הַלַּחְמִי: וַיְהִי
כְּכַלֹּתוֹ לְדַבֵּר אֶל־שָׁאוּל וְנֶפֶשׁ יְהוֹנָתָן נִקְשְׁרָה בְּנֶפֶשׁ דָּוִד °וַיֶּאֱהָבוֹ
ב [°וַיֶּאֱהָבֵהוּ ק] יְהוֹנָתָן כְּנַפְשׁוֹ: וַיִּקָּחֵהוּ שָׁאוּל בַּיּוֹם הַהוּא וְלֹא נְתָנוֹ לָשׁוּב
ג בֵּית אָבִיו: וַיִּכְרֹת יְהוֹנָתָן וְדָוִד בְּרִית בְּאַהֲבָתוֹ אֹתוֹ כְּנַפְשׁוֹ: וַיִּתְפַּשֵּׁט
יְהוֹנָתָן אֶת־הַמְּעִיל אֲשֶׁר עָלָיו וַיִּתְּנֵהוּ לְדָוִד וּמַדָּיו וְעַד־חַרְבּוֹ וְעַד־
ה קַשְׁתּוֹ וְעַד־חֲגֹרוֹ: וַיֵּצֵא דָוִד בְּכֹל אֲשֶׁר יִשְׁלָחֶנּוּ שָׁאוּל יַשְׂכִּיל וַיְשִׂמֵהוּ
שָׁאוּל עַל אַנְשֵׁי הַמִּלְחָמָה וַיִּיטַב בְּעֵינֵי כָל־הָעָם וְגַם בְּעֵינֵי עַבְדֵי
ו שָׁאוּל: וַיְהִי בְּבוֹאָם בְּשׁוּב דָּוִד מֵהַכּוֹת אֶת־הַפְּלִשְׁתִּי וַתֵּצֶאנָה
הַנָּשִׁים מִכָּל־עָרֵי יִשְׂרָאֵל °לָשׁוֹר [°לָשִׁיר ק] וְהַמְּחֹלוֹת לִקְרַאת שָׁאוּל
ז הַמֶּלֶךְ בְּתֻפִּים בְּשִׂמְחָה וּבְשָׁלִשִׁים: וַתַּעֲנֶינָה הַנָּשִׁים הַמְשַׂחֲקוֹת וַתֹּאמַרְןָ
ח הִכָּה שָׁאוּל °בַּאֲלָפוֹ [°בַּאֲלָפָיו ק] וְדָוִד בְּרִבְבֹתָיו: וַיִּחַר לְשָׁאוּל מְאֹד
וַיֵּרַע בְּעֵינָיו הַדָּבָר הַזֶּה וַיֹּאמֶר נָתְנוּ לְדָוִד רְבָבוֹת וְלִי נָתְנוּ הָאֲלָפִים
ט וְעוֹד לוֹ אַךְ הַמְּלוּכָה: וַיְהִי שָׁאוּל °עוֹיֵן [°עוֹיֵן ק] אֶת־דָּוִד מֵהַיּוֹם הַהוּא
י וָהָלְאָה: וַיְהִי מִמָּחֳרָת וַתִּצְלַח רוּחַ אֱלֹהִים ׀ רָעָה ׀ אֶל־שָׁאוּל
יא וַיִּתְנַבֵּא בְתוֹךְ־הַבַּיִת וְדָוִד מְנַגֵּן בְּיָדוֹ כְּיוֹם ׀ בְּיוֹם וְהַחֲנִית בְּיַד־שָׁאוּל: וַיָּטֶל
שָׁאוּל אֶת־הַחֲנִית וַיֹּאמֶר אַכֶּה בְדָוִד וּבַקִּיר וַיִּסֹּב דָּוִד מִפָּנָיו פַּעֲמָיִם: וַיִּרָא
יב שָׁאוּל מִלִּפְנֵי דָוִד כִּי־הָיָה יְהוָה עִמּוֹ וּמֵעִם שָׁאוּל סָר: וַיְסִרֵהוּ שָׁאוּל מֵעִמּוֹ
יג וַיְשִׂמֵהוּ לוֹ שַׂר־אָלֶף וַיֵּצֵא וַיָּבֹא לִפְנֵי הָעָם: וַיְהִי דָוִד לְכָל־דְּרָכָו
יד מַשְׂכִּיל וַיהוָה עִמּוֹ: וַיַּרְא שָׁאוּל אֲשֶׁר־הוּא מַשְׂכִּיל מְאֹד וַיָּגָר מִפָּנָיו: וְכָל־
טו־טז יִשְׂרָאֵל וִיהוּדָה אֹהֵב אֶת־דָּוִד כִּי־הוּא יוֹצֵא וָבָא לִפְנֵיהֶם: וַיֹּאמֶר
יז שָׁאוּל אֶל־דָּוִד הִנֵּה בִתִּי הַגְּדוֹלָה מֵרַב אֹתָהּ אֶתֶּן־לְךָ לְאִשָּׁה אַךְ הֱיֵה־לִּי
לְבֶן־חַיִל וְהִלָּחֵם מִלְחֲמוֹת יְהוָה וְשָׁאוּל אָמַר אַל־תְּהִי יָדִי בּוֹ וּתְהִי־בוֹ

17:54. He brought Goliath's weapons home to Bethlehem (*Radak*) as mementos of his triumph. Goliath's sword, however, was stored in the sanctuary at Nob, as related in 21:10.

17:55. By this time Saul knew David quite well (see 16:21); his question was if David came from a brave, heroic lineage (*Radak*). According to the *Midrash*, Saul wanted to know if David descended from the Peretz his head with it. The Philistines saw that their hero was dead, and they ran away. ⁵² The men of Israel and Judah rose up, and shouted exultantly, and pursued the Philistines up to the approach to the valley and to the gates of Ekron. Philistine corpses were strewn along the Shaaraim Road, until Gath and Ekron. ⁵³ Then the Children of Israel returned from pursuing Philistines and plundered their camp. ⁵⁴ David took the head of the Philistine, and [eventually] brought it to Jerusalem, and his weapons he put in his tent. *

SAUL, DAVID'S JEALOUS FATHER-IN-LAW
17:55-19:24

Saul inquires about David

⁵⁵ When Saul had seen David going forth towards the Philistine, he said to Abner, the minister of the army, "Abner, whose son is this lad?"* And Abner replied, "By your life, O king, I do not know." ⁵⁶ So the king instructed him, "You ask whose son this youth is." ⁵⁷ So when David returned from smiting the Philistine, Abner took him and brought him before Saul, while the head of the Philistine was [still] in his hand. ⁵⁸ Saul said to him, "Whose son are you, young man?" David replied, "The son of your servant Jesse, the Bethlehemite."

18

David and Jonathan become friends

¹ It was after [David] finished speaking to Saul that Jonathan's soul became attached to David's soul, and Jonathan loved him as himself. ² Saul conscripted him that day and did not permit him to return to his father's home. ³ Jonathan and David sealed a covenant, since each loved the other like himself. ⁴ And Jonathan took off the robe he was wearing and gave it to David; also his battle garments, down to his sword, his bow, and his belt. ⁵ David went forth, and in whatever Saul would send him to do he would be successful. Saul appointed him over the warriors, and it was good in the eyes of all the people and also in the eyes of Saul's servants.

⁶ It happened that when [the troops] came [back] — when David returned from slaying the Philistine — that the women from all the towns of Israel came out to sing with timbrels to greet King Saul, with drums, with gladness, and with cymbals.

Saul becomes morbidly jealous

⁷ The rejoicing women called out, and said, "Saul has slain his thousands, and David his tens of thousands." ⁸ Saul grew very angry, and this matter was disturbing in his eyes. He said, "They have attributed to David ten thousands, while to me they have attributed thousands! He is lacking only the kingship." ⁹ And Saul eyed David with suspicion from that day on.

¹⁰ It happened the next day that a spirit of melancholy from God came upon Saul and he raved incoherently in the house. David was playing [the harp] with his hand as [he did] every day, and the spear was in Saul's hand. ¹¹ Then Saul hurled the spear, saying [to himself], "I will thrust it through David into the wall." But David eluded him twice.

¹² Saul feared David, for HASHEM was with him, but He had turned away from Saul. ¹³ So Saul removed him from his presence and made him captain of a thousand, and he came and went before the people. ¹⁴ David was successful in all his ways, and HASHEM was with him. ¹⁵ Saul saw that he was very successful, and he was intimidated by him. ¹⁶ All of Israel and Judah loved David, for he came and went before them.

Saul plots against David

¹⁷ Saul said to David, "Here is my older daughter, Merab; I shall give her to you for a wife, but you must be a warrior for me and fight the wars of HASHEM." Saul said [to himself], "Let my hand not be against him; let the

---

branch of Judah, for if so he was a potential rival for the throne (*Rashi*).

יח וַיֹּאמֶר דָּוִד אֶל־שָׁאוּל מִי אָנֹכִי וּמִי חַיַּי מִשְׁפַּחַת יַד־פְּלִשְׁתִּים:

יט אָבִי בְּיִשְׂרָאֵל כִּי־אֶהְיֶה חָתָן לַמֶּלֶךְ: וַיְהִי בְּעֵת תֵּת אֶת־מֵרַב בַּת־שָׁאוּל לְדָוִד וְהִיא נִתְּנָה לְעַדְרִיאֵל הַמְּחֹלָתִי לְאִשָּׁה: וַתֶּאֱהַב מִיכַל בַּת־שָׁאוּל

כ אֶת־דָּוִד וַיַּגִּדוּ לְשָׁאוּל וַיִּשַׁר הַדָּבָר בְּעֵינָיו: וַיֹּאמֶר שָׁאוּל אֶתְּנֶנָּה לּוֹ

כא וּתְהִי־לוֹ לְמוֹקֵשׁ וּתְהִי־בוֹ יַד־פְּלִשְׁתִּים וַיֹּאמֶר שָׁאוּל אֶל־דָּוִד בִּשְׁתַּיִם

כב תִּתְחַתֵּן בִּי הַיּוֹם: וַיְצַו שָׁאוּל אֶת־עֲבָדָו דַּבְּרוּ אֶל־דָּוִד בַּלָּט לֵאמֹר הִנֵּה

כג חָפֵץ בְּךָ הַמֶּלֶךְ וְכָל־עֲבָדָיו אֲהֵבוּךָ וְעַתָּה הִתְחַתֵּן בַּמֶּלֶךְ: וַיְדַבְּרוּ עַבְדֵי שָׁאוּל בְּאָזְנֵי דָוִד אֶת־הַדְּבָרִים הָאֵלֶּה וַיֹּאמֶר דָּוִד הַנְקַלָּה בְעֵינֵיכֶם

כד הִתְחַתֵּן בַּמֶּלֶךְ וְאָנֹכִי אִישׁ־רָשׁ וְנִקְלֶה: וַיַּגִּדוּ עַבְדֵי שָׁאוּל לוֹ לֵאמֹר

כה כַּדְּבָרִים הָאֵלֶּה דִּבֶּר דָּוִד: וַיֹּאמֶר שָׁאוּל כֹּה־תֹאמְרוּ לְדָוִד אֵין־חֵפֶץ לַמֶּלֶךְ בְּמֹהַר כִּי בְּמֵאָה עָרְלוֹת פְּלִשְׁתִּים לְהִנָּקֵם בְּאֹיְבֵי הַמֶּלֶךְ

כו וְשָׁאוּל חָשַׁב לְהַפִּיל אֶת־דָּוִד בְּיַד־פְּלִשְׁתִּים: וַיַּגִּדוּ עֲבָדָיו לְדָוִד אֶת־הַדְּבָרִים הָאֵלֶּה וַיִּשַׁר הַדָּבָר בְּעֵינֵי דָוִד לְהִתְחַתֵּן בַּמֶּלֶךְ וְלֹא מָלְאוּ

כז הַיָּמִים: וַיָּקָם דָּוִד וַיֵּלֶךְ הוּא וַאֲנָשָׁיו וַיַּךְ בַּפְּלִשְׁתִּים מָאתַיִם אִישׁ וַיָּבֵא דָוִד אֶת־עָרְלֹתֵיהֶם וַיְמַלְאוּם לַמֶּלֶךְ לְהִתְחַתֵּן בַּמֶּלֶךְ וַיִּתֶּן־לוֹ שָׁאוּל אֶת־

כח מִיכַל בִּתּוֹ לְאִשָּׁה: וַיַּרְא שָׁאוּל וַיֵּדַע כִּי יהוה עִם־דָּוִד וּמִיכַל בַּת־שָׁאוּל

כט אֲהֵבַתְהוּ: וַיֹּאסֶף שָׁאוּל לֵרֹא מִפְּנֵי דָוִד עוֹד וַיְהִי שָׁאוּל אֹיֵב אֶת־דָּוִד כָּל־

ל הַיָּמִים: וַיֵּצְאוּ שָׂרֵי פְלִשְׁתִּים וַיְהִי מִדֵּי צֵאתָם שָׂכַל דָּוִד מִכֹּל עַבְדֵי שָׁאוּל וַיִּיקַר שְׁמוֹ מְאֹד:

יט א וַיְדַבֵּר שָׁאוּל אֶל־יוֹנָתָן בְּנוֹ וְאֶל־כָּל־עֲבָדָיו לְהָמִית אֶת־דָּוִד וִיהוֹנָתָן בֶּן־שָׁאוּל חָפֵץ בְּדָוִד

ב מְאֹד: וַיַּגֵּד יְהוֹנָתָן לְדָוִד לֵאמֹר מְבַקֵּשׁ שָׁאוּל אָבִי לַהֲמִיתֶךָ וְעַתָּה

ג הִשָּׁמֶר־נָא בַבֹּקֶר וְיָשַׁבְתָּ בַסֵּתֶר וְנַחְבֵּאתָ: וַאֲנִי אֵצֵא וְעָמַדְתִּי לְיַד־אָבִי בַּשָּׂדֶה אֲשֶׁר אַתָּה שָׁם וַאֲנִי אֲדַבֵּר בְּךָ אֶל־אָבִי וְרָאִיתִי מָה וְהִגַּדְתִּי

ד לָךְ: וַיְדַבֵּר יְהוֹנָתָן בְּדָוִד טוֹב אֶל־שָׁאוּל אָבִיו וַיֹּאמֶר אֵלָיו אַל־יֶחֱטָא הַמֶּלֶךְ בְּעַבְדּוֹ בְדָוִד כִּי לוֹא חָטָא לָךְ וְכִי מַעֲשָׂיו טוֹב־לְךָ מְאֹד:

ה וַיָּשֶׂם אֶת־נַפְשׁוֹ בְכַפּוֹ וַיַּךְ אֶת־הַפְּלִשְׁתִּי וַיַּעַשׂ יהוה תְּשׁוּעָה גְדוֹלָה לְכָל־יִשְׂרָאֵל רָאִיתָ וַתִּשְׂמָח וְלָמָּה תֶחֱטָא בְּדָם נָקִי לְהָמִית אֶת־דָּוִד חִנָּם:

ו וַיִּשְׁמַע שָׁאוּל בְּקוֹל יְהוֹנָתָן וַיִּשָּׁבַע שָׁאוּל חַי־יהוה אִם־יוּמָת: וַיִּקְרָא

ז יְהוֹנָתָן לְדָוִד וַיַּגֶּד־לוֹ יְהוֹנָתָן אֵת כָּל־הַדְּבָרִים הָאֵלֶּה וַיָּבֵא יְהוֹנָתָן אֶת־דָּוִד אֶל־שָׁאוּל וַיְהִי לְפָנָיו כְּאֶתְמוֹל שִׁלְשׁוֹם: וַתּוֹסֶף הַמִּלְחָמָה

ח לִהְיוֹת וַיֵּצֵא דָוִד וַיִּלָּחֶם בַּפְּלִשְׁתִּים וַיַּךְ בָּהֶם מַכָּה גְדוֹלָה וַיָּנֻסוּ מִפָּנָיו:

18:21. Saul was confident that Michal would remain loyal to him and encourage David to endanger himself in battle with the Philistines.

18:22. Apparently, David had lost interest after the first marriage proposal was so callously broken, and needed

to be persuaded anew (*Radak*).

18:26. Saul had requested the foreskins by a specific time.

18:28. Now Saul had two reasons to fear David — God was always with him, and Michal, who Saul had hoped hand of the Philistines be against him." ¹⁸ David said to Saul, "Who am I and what is my life, [or] my father's family in Israel that I should become a son-in-law to the king?" ¹⁹ But it happened that when the time came to give Merab daughter of Saul to David, she was given [instead] to Adriel the Meholathite as a wife.

²⁰ But Michal daughter of Saul loved David. They told [this] to Saul and it was proper in his eyes. ²¹ Saul thought, "I will give her to him and she will be a snare to him, * and the hand of the Philistines will act against him." So Saul said to David, "Through [one of] my two [daughters] you will become my son-in-law today." ²² Saul then commanded his servants, "Speak to David in secret, saying, 'Behold, the king desires you, and all his servants like you, so become now the king's son-in-law.' "* ²³ So Saul's servants spoke these words in David's ears. And David said, "Is it a trivial matter in your eyes to become a son-in-law to the king? I am a poor and simple person!"

²⁴ Saul's servants told him saying, "David spoke these words." ²⁵ Saul said, "So shall you say to David: 'The King desires no dowry, only one hundred Philistine foreskins to avenge the enemies of the King.' " Saul intended to have David fall at the hands of the Philistines.

David marries Michal ²⁶ His servants told these words to David, and the proposal was proper in David's eyes, to become the King's son-in-law. The days had not yet expired, * ²⁷ when David arose and went — he and his men — and slew two hundred Philistine men. David brought their foreskins and sent them all to the King in order to become the King's son-in-law. Then Saul gave him his daughter Michal for a wife. ²⁸ Saul saw and understood that HASHEM was with David, and that Michal, Saul's daughter, loved him. * ²⁹ So Saul continued to fear David even more; and Saul harbored enmity towards David all the days.

³⁰ The officers of the Philistines would venture forth * — and whenever they ventured forth, David was more successful than all the other servants of Saul, and his reputation became very outstanding.

19

Jonathan makes peace between Saul and David

¹ Saul spoke to Jonathan his son and to all his servants about killing David, but Jonathan son of Saul liked David very much. ² So Jonathan told David, saying, "My father Saul is trying to kill you, so now be cautious tomorrow morning and stay in the secret place, and hide yourself. ³ I will go out and stand near my father in the field where you will be, and I will speak to my father about you. I will see what happens and tell you."

⁴ So Jonathan spoke favorably of David to his father Saul, saying to him, "Let the king not sin against his servant David, for he has not sinned against you, and because his deeds are very good for you. ⁵ He put his life in his hand and slew the Philistine and HASHEM granted a great salvation to all of Israel; you saw [it] and rejoiced — so why should you sin with innocent blood, to kill David for no reason?"

⁶ Saul listened to Jonathan's voice, and Saul swore, "As HASHEM lives, he shall not die." ⁷ So Jonathan called David, and Jonathan told David all these things. Jonathan brought David to Saul and he was before him as he had been yesterday and before.

⁸ And there was war again, and David went forth and fought against the Philistines. He smote them a great blow, and they ran from him.

---

would help him do away with David (v. 21), truly loved   **18:30.** On occasional forays into Israelite territory.
him (*Radak*).

ט וַתְּהִי רוּחַ יְהוָה ׀ רָעָה אֶל־שָׁאוּל וְהוּא בְּבֵיתוֹ יוֹשֵׁב וַחֲנִיתוֹ בְּיָדוֹ וְדָוִד

י מְנַגֵּן בְּיָד: וַיְבַקֵּשׁ שָׁאוּל לְהַכּוֹת בַּחֲנִית בְּדָוִד וּבַקִּיר וַיִּפְטַר מִפְּנֵי שָׁאוּל

יא וַיַּךְ אֶת־הַחֲנִית בַּקִּיר וְדָוִד נָס וַיִּמָּלֵט בַּלַּיְלָה הוּא: וַיִּשְׁלַח

שָׁאוּל מַלְאָכִים אֶל־בֵּית דָּוִד לְשָׁמְרוֹ וְלַהֲמִיתוֹ בַּבֹּקֶר וַתַּגֵּד לְדָוִד מִיכַל

אִשְׁתּוֹ לֵאמֹר אִם־אֵינְךָ מְמַלֵּט אֶת־נַפְשְׁךָ הַלַּיְלָה מָחָר אַתָּה מוּמָת:

יב-יג וַתֹּרֶד מִיכַל אֶת־דָּוִד בְּעַד הַחַלּוֹן וַיֵּלֶךְ וַיִּבְרַח וַיִּמָּלֵט: וַתִּקַּח מִיכַל אֶת־

הַתְּרָפִים וַתָּשֶׂם אֶל־הַמִּטָּה וְאֵת כְּבִיר הָעִזִּים שָׂמָה מְרַאֲשֹׁתָיו וַתְּכַס

יד בַּבָּגֶד: וַיִּשְׁלַח שָׁאוּל מַלְאָכִים לָקַחַת אֶת־דָּוִד וַתֹּאמֶר חֹלֶה

טו הוּא: וַיִּשְׁלַח שָׁאוּל אֶת־הַמַּלְאָכִים לִרְאוֹת אֶת־דָּוִד לֵאמֹר

טז הַעֲלוּ אֹתוֹ בַמִּטָּה אֵלַי לַהֲמִתוֹ: וַיָּבֹאוּ הַמַּלְאָכִים וְהִנֵּה הַתְּרָפִים אֶל־

יז הַמִּטָּה וּכְבִיר הָעִזִּים מְרַאֲשֹׁתָיו: וַיֹּאמֶר שָׁאוּל אֶל־מִיכַל

לָמָּה כָּכָה רִמִּיתִנִי וַתְּשַׁלְּחִי אֶת־אֹיְבִי וַיִּמָּלֵט וַתֹּאמֶר מִיכַל אֶל־שָׁאוּל

יח הוּא־אָמַר אֵלַי שַׁלְּחִנִי לָמָּה אֲמִיתֵךְ: וְדָוִד בָּרַח וַיִּמָּלֵט וַיָּבֹא אֶל־

שְׁמוּאֵל הָרָמָתָה וַיַּגֶּד־לוֹ אֵת כָּל־אֲשֶׁר עָשָׂה־לוֹ שָׁאוּל וַיֵּלֶךְ הוּא

יט וּשְׁמוּאֵל וַיֵּשְׁבוּ °בְּנָיוֹת [°בְּנָיוֹת ק]: וַיֻּגַּד לְשָׁאוּל לֵאמֹר הִנֵּה דָוִד °בְּנָיוֹת

כ [°בְּנָיוֹת ק] בָּרָמָה: וַיִּשְׁלַח שָׁאוּל מַלְאָכִים לָקַחַת אֶת־דָּוִד וַיַּרְא אֶת־

לַהֲקַת הַנְּבִיאִים נִבְּאִים וּשְׁמוּאֵל עֹמֵד נִצָּב עֲלֵיהֶם וַתְּהִי עַל־מַלְאֲכֵי

כא שָׁאוּל רוּחַ אֱלֹהִים וַיִּתְנַבְּאוּ גַּם־הֵמָּה: וַיַּגִּדוּ לְשָׁאוּל וַיִּשְׁלַח מַלְאָכִים

אֲחֵרִים וַיִּתְנַבְּאוּ גַם־הֵמָּה וַיֹּסֶף שָׁאוּל וַיִּשְׁלַח מַלְאָכִים שְׁלִשִׁים

כב וַיִּתְנַבְּאוּ גַם־הֵמָּה: וַיֵּלֶךְ גַּם־הוּא הָרָמָתָה וַיָּבֹא עַד־בּוֹר הַגָּדוֹל אֲשֶׁר

בַּשֶּׂכוּ וַיִּשְׁאַל וַיֹּאמֶר אֵיפֹה שְׁמוּאֵל וְדָוִד וַיֹּאמֶר הִנֵּה °בְּנָיוֹת [°בְּנָיוֹת ק]

כג בָּרָמָה: וַיֵּלֶךְ שָׁם אֶל־°נָוִית [°נָיוֹת ק] בָּרָמָה וַתְּהִי עָלָיו גַּם־הוּא רוּחַ

כד אֱלֹהִים וַיֵּלֶךְ הָלוֹךְ וַיִּתְנַבֵּא עַד־בֹּאוֹ °בְּנָוִית [°בְּנָיוֹת ק] בָּרָמָה: וַיִּפְשַׁט

גַּם־הוּא בְּגָדָיו וַיִּתְנַבֵּא גַם־הוּא לִפְנֵי שְׁמוּאֵל וַיִּפֹּל עָרֹם כָּל־הַיּוֹם הַהוּא

א וְכָל־הַלַּיְלָה עַל־כֵּן יֹאמְרוּ הֲגַם שָׁאוּל בַּנְּבִיאִם: וַיִּבְרַח דָּוִד

°מִנָּווֹת [°מִנָּיוֹת ק] בָּרָמָה וַיָּבֹא וַיֹּאמֶר ׀ לִפְנֵי יְהוֹנָתָן מֶה עָשִׂיתִי מֶה

ב עֲוֹנִי וּמֶה־חַטָּאתִי לִפְנֵי אָבִיךָ כִּי מְבַקֵּשׁ אֶת־נַפְשִׁי: וַיֹּאמֶר לוֹ חָלִילָה

לֹא תָמוּת הִנֵּה °לֹו־עשה [°לֹא־יַעֲשֶׂה ק] אָבִי דָּבָר גָּדוֹל אוֹ דָבָר קָטֹן

וְלֹא יִגְלֶה אֶת־אָזְנִי וּמַדּוּעַ יַסְתִּיר אָבִי מִמֶּנִּי אֶת־הַדָּבָר הַזֶּה אֵין זֹאת:

ג וַיִּשָּׁבַע עוֹד דָּוִד וַיֹּאמֶר יָדֹעַ יָדַע אָבִיךָ כִּי־מָצָאתִי חֵן בְּעֵינֶיךָ וַיֹּאמֶר

אַל־יֵדַע־זֹאת יְהוֹנָתָן פֶּן־יֵעָצֵב וְאוּלָם חַי־יְהוָה וְחֵי נַפְשֶׁךָ כִּי כְפֶשַׂע

ד בֵּינִי וּבֵין הַמָּוֶת: וַיֹּאמֶר יְהוֹנָתָן אֶל־דָּוִד מַה־תֹּאמַר נַפְשְׁךָ וְאֶעֱשֶׂה־

19:10. Two events occurred: David fled from Saul, and during the night Michal arranged an escape that saved his life a second time (*Radak*).

19:11. Not wanting David to be killed in the presence of Michal, Saul wanted David to be kept from fleeing during the night so that he could be taken into custody the next

⁹ Then HASHEM'S spirit of melancholy befell Saul, while he was sitting in his house with his spear in his hand and David was playing [the harp] with his hand. ¹⁰ Saul tried to thrust the spear through David and the wall, but he slipped away from Saul and the spear hit the wall.

David ran away and escaped that night. *

Saul sets an ambush but Michal saves David

¹¹ Saul sent messengers to David's house to keep watch over him and kill him in the morning. * His wife Michal told David, saying, "If you do not [act to] escape with your life tonight, you will be killed tomorrow." ¹² So Michal lowered David through the window, and he left; he fled and escaped. ¹³ Michal then took mannequins and placed them in the bed, and she put a goat-skin at its head and covered it with a cloth.

¹⁴ Saul sent agents to take David, but she said, "He is ill."

¹⁵ Then Saul sent the agents again to inquire after David, * telling them, "Bring him up to me in the bed, to have him killed." ¹⁶ The agents came and behold! — the mannequins were in the bed and a goat-skin at its head!

¹⁷ Saul asked Michal, "Why did you deceive me this way? You sent away my enemy so that he escaped." And Michal replied, "He said to me, 'Let me go or I will kill you.' "*

David flees to Samuel and God protects him

¹⁸ David fled and escaped, and came to Samuel at Ramah. He told him all that Saul had done to him, so he and Samuel went and stayed at Naioth. ¹⁹ It was told to Saul, saying, "Behold! David is in Naioth, in Ramah." ²⁰ Saul sent messengers to arrest David. [When they arrived] they saw a group of prophets prophesying * with Samuel standing erect, overseeing them, and a spirit of God came upon Saul's messengers and they, too, prophesied. ²¹ People told Saul and he sent other messengers, but they, too, prophesied. Saul persisted and sent a third group of messengers, but they, too, prophesied. ²² So he went to Ramah himself, arriving at the cistern in Secu. He inquired and said, "Where are Samuel and David?" Someone said, "They are in Naioth, in Ramah." ²³ He went there, to Naioth in Ramah, and the spirit of God came upon him, as well; and he kept on prophesying until he arrived at Naioth in Ramah. ²⁴ He too removed his [royal] raiment and he, too, prophesied before Samuel; he fell unclothed that entire day and night. Therefore there people say, "Is Saul also among the prophets?"

20
JONATHAN'S ALLEGIANCE TO DAVID
20:1-42

David pleads his case with Jonathan

¹ Then David fled from Naioth in Ramah. He came and said before Jonathan, "What have I done? What is my iniquity and my sin before your father, that he seeks my life?" ² He said to him, "It would be a sacrilege; you shall not die! Behold, my father does not do a major thing or a minor thing without revealing it to me, so why should my father conceal this matter from me?* It is not so!" ³ But David swore to him again, and said, "Your father knows very well I have found favor in your eyes, so he said [to himself], 'Jonathan should not know about this, lest he be saddened.' However, as HASHEM lives, and by your life, there is but a footstep between me and death."

⁴ Jonathan said to David, "Whatever your soul shall say I shall do for you."

---

morning (*Radak*).

19:15. They were to tell Michal that they had come to inquire after her sick husband, so that she should not resist them.

19:17. Lit., why should I [have to] kill you? Michal lied in

self-defense.

19:20. See note to 10:5.

20:2. Although Saul had informed Jonathan of his intention to have David killed (19:1), Jonathan wholeheartedly believed his father's oath recanting it (19:6).

ה לֵךְ: וַיֹּאמֶר דָּוִד אֶל־יְהוֹנָתָן הִנֵּה־חֹדֶשׁ מָחָר וְאָנֹכִי יָשֹׁב־אֵשֵׁב

ו עִם־הַמֶּלֶךְ לֶאֱכוֹל וְשִׁלַּחְתַּנִי וְנִסְתַּרְתִּי בַשָּׂדֶה עַד הָעֶרֶב הַשְּׁלִשִׁית: אִם־
פָּקֹד יִפְקְדֵנִי אָבִיךָ וְאָמַרְתָּ נִשְׁאֹל נִשְׁאַל מִמֶּנִּי דָוִד לָרוּץ בֵּית־לֶחֶם עִירוֹ

ז כִּי זֶבַח הַיָּמִים שָׁם לְכָל־הַמִּשְׁפָּחָה: אִם־כֹּה יֹאמַר טוֹב שָׁלוֹם לְעַבְדֶּךָ

ח וְאִם־חָרֹה יֶחֱרֶה לוֹ דַּע כִּי־כָלְתָה הָרָעָה מֵעִמּוֹ: וְעָשִׂיתָ חֶסֶד עַל־עַבְדֶּךָ
כִּי בִּבְרִית יְהוָה הֵבֵאתָ אֶת־עַבְדְּךָ עִמָּךְ וְאִם־יֶשׁ־בִּי עָוֹן הֲמִיתֵנִי אַתָּה

ט וְעַד־אָבִיךָ לָמָּה־זֶּה תְבִיאֵנִי: וַיֹּאמֶר יְהוֹנָתָן חָלִילָה לָּךְ
כִּי ׀ אִם־יָדֹעַ אֵדַע כִּי־כָלְתָה הָרָעָה מֵעִם אָבִי לָבוֹא עָלֶיךָ וְלֹא אֹתָהּ

י אַגִּיד לָךְ: וַיֹּאמֶר דָּוִד אֶל־יְהוֹנָתָן מִי יַגִּיד לִי אוֹ מַה־יַּעַנְךָ

יא אָבִיךָ קָשָׁה: וַיֹּאמֶר יְהוֹנָתָן אֶל־דָּוִד לְכָה וְנֵצֵא הַשָּׂדֶה וַיֵּצְאוּ שְׁנֵיהֶם

יב הַשָּׂדֶה: וַיֹּאמֶר יְהוֹנָתָן אֶל־דָּוִד יְהוָה אֱלֹהֵי יִשְׂרָאֵל כִּי־אֶחְקֹר
אֶת־אָבִי כָּעֵת ׀ מָחָר הַשְּׁלִשִׁית וְהִנֵּה־טוֹב אֶל־דָּוִד וְלֹא־אָז אֶשְׁלַח

יג אֵלֶיךָ וְגָלִיתִי אֶת־אָזְנֶךָ: כֹּה־יַעֲשֶׂה יְהוָה לִיהוֹנָתָן וְכֹה יֹסִיף כִּי־יֵיטִב אֶל־
אָבִי אֶת־הָרָעָה עָלֶיךָ וְגָלִיתִי אֶת־אָזְנֶךָ וְשִׁלַּחְתִּיךָ וְהָלַכְתָּ לְשָׁלוֹם וִיהִי

יד יְהוָה עִמָּךְ כַּאֲשֶׁר הָיָה עִם־אָבִי: וְלֹא אִם־עוֹדֶנִּי חָי וְלֹא־תַעֲשֶׂה עִמָּדִי

טו חֶסֶד יְהוָה וְלֹא אָמוּת: וְלֹא־תַכְרִת אֶת־חַסְדְּךָ מֵעִם בֵּיתִי עַד־עוֹלָם: וְלֹא

טז בְּהַכְרִת יְהוָה אֶת־אֹיְבֵי דָוִד אִישׁ מֵעַל פְּנֵי הָאֲדָמָה: וַיִּכְרֹת יְהוֹנָתָן

יז עִם־בֵּית דָּוִד וּבִקֵּשׁ יְהוָה מִיַּד אֹיְבֵי דָוִד: וַיּוֹסֶף יְהוֹנָתָן לְהַשְׁבִּיעַ אֶת־דָּוִד
בְּאַהֲבָתוֹ אֹתוֹ כִּי־אַהֲבַת נַפְשׁוֹ אֲהֵבוֹ: ◀ וַיֹּאמֶר־לוֹ יְהוֹנָתָן מָחָר

יח חֹדֶשׁ וְנִפְקַדְתָּ כִּי יִפָּקֵד מוֹשָׁבֶךָ: וְשִׁלַּשְׁתָּ תֵּרֵד מְאֹד וּבָאתָ אֶל־הַמָּקוֹם

HAFTARAS
EREV ROSH
CHODESH
20:18-42

כ אֲשֶׁר־נִסְתַּרְתָּ שָּׁם בְּיוֹם הַמַּעֲשֶׂה וְיָשַׁבְתָּ אֵצֶל הָאֶבֶן הָאָזֶל: וַאֲנִי שְׁלֹשֶׁת

כא הַחִצִּים צִדָּה אוֹרֶה לְשַׁלַּח־לִי לְמַטָּרָה: וְהִנֵּה אֶשְׁלַח אֶת־הַנַּעַר לֵךְ מְצָא
אֶת־הַחִצִּים אִם־אָמֹר אֹמַר לַנַּעַר הִנֵּה הַחִצִּים ׀ מִמְּךָ וָהֵנָּה קָחֶנּוּ ׀ וָבֹאָה

כב כִּי־שָׁלוֹם לְךָ וְאֵין דָּבָר חַי־יְהוָה: וְאִם־כֹּה אֹמַר לָעֶלֶם הִנֵּה הַחִצִּים מִמְּךָ

כג וָהָלְאָה לֵךְ כִּי שִׁלַּחֲךָ יְהוָה: וְהַדָּבָר אֲשֶׁר דִּבַּרְנוּ אֲנִי וָאָתָּה הִנֵּה יְהוָה

כד בֵּינִי וּבֵינְךָ עַד־עוֹלָם: וַיִּסָּתֵר דָּוִד בַּשָּׂדֶה וַיְהִי הַחֹדֶשׁ וַיֵּשֶׁב

כה הַמֶּלֶךְ °עַל [אֶל־ ק] הַלֶּחֶם לֶאֱכוֹל: וַיֵּשֶׁב הַמֶּלֶךְ עַל־מוֹשָׁבוֹ כְּפַעַם ׀
בְּפַעַם אֶל־מוֹשַׁב הַקִּיר וַיָּקָם יְהוֹנָתָן וַיֵּשֶׁב אַבְנֵר מִצַּד שָׁאוּל וַיִּפָּקֵד מְקוֹם

כו דָּוִד: וְלֹא־דִבֶּר שָׁאוּל מְאוּמָה בַּיּוֹם הַהוּא כִּי אָמַר מִקְרֶה הוּא בִּלְתִּי

כז טָהוֹר הוּא כִּי־לֹא טָהוֹר: וַיְהִי מִמָּחֳרַת הַחֹדֶשׁ הַשֵּׁנִי

20:8. See 18:3.

20:9. You have no right to suspect me of withholding such information from you!

20:11. Where we can speak in private.

20:14-15. I know that when you become king, you will surely deal kindly with me. But if I die before then, I implore you to deal kindly with my descendants.

20:16. Jonathan promised that as long as Saul reigned, he would protect David's family from the king.

20:17. He asked David to repeat the oath of brotherhood because Jonathan cherished it as an expression of love.

20:19. Described above in 19:1-3.

A plan to
test Saul's
intention

⁵ David said to Jonathan, "Behold, tomorrow is the New Moon, when I would usually sit with the king to eat. Grant me leave and I will hide in the field until the third evening [of the month]. ⁶ If your father notices my absence, you shall say to him, 'David asked me to let him run to his hometown Bethlehem, for there is an annual feast-offering there for the entire family.' ⁷ If he says thus, 'Good!' then it is well for your servant. But if he gets very angry, then know that the evil [decree] has become final with him. ⁸ Do this favor for your servant, for you have brought your servant into a covenant of HASHEM with you. * If I am guilty of an iniquity, kill me yourself; why bring me to your father?"

⁹ Jonathan said, "Far be it from you!* For if I knew that the evil [decree] has become final with my father, would I not tell it to you?"

¹⁰ David then said to Jonathan, "Who will tell me [if your father answers favorably] or if your father answers you harshly?"

Jonathan's
pledge and
plea

¹¹ So Jonathan said to David, "Come, let us go out to the field,"* and they both went out to the field. ¹² Jonathan said to David, "[I swear by] HASHEM the God of Israel that I will probe my father at this time on the third day from now, and behold, if it is good for David will I not then send for you and reveal it to you? ¹³ Such shall HASHEM do to Jonathan and such shall He do further — if it pleases my father to harm you I will reveal it to you, and I will send you away that you may go to peace; and may HASHEM be with you as He was with my father. ¹⁴ I need not [ask anything of you] if I will still be alive [when you become king], for would you not do with me the kindness of HASHEM, so that I will not die? ¹⁵ But do not cut off your kindness from my descendants forever, not even when HASHEM cuts each of David's enemies from the face of the earth."* ¹⁶ Jonathan also sealed [a covenant] regarding David's household,* and added, "May HASHEM exact punishment from the enemies of David." ¹⁷ Jonathan again adjured David because of his love for him, * for he loved him as he loved himself.

The signal

¹⁸ Jonathan said to him, "Tomorrow is the New Moon, and you will be missed because your seat will be empty. ¹⁹ For three days you are to remain far down and come to the place where you hid on the day of the incident, * and stay near the marker stone. ²⁰ I will shoot three arrows in that direction as if I were shooting at a target. ²¹ Behold, I will then send the lad [saying], 'Go find the arrows.' If I say to the lad, 'Behold, the arrows are on this side of you!' then you yourself may take the arrows and return, for it is well with you and there is no concern, as HASHEM lives. ²² But if I say this to the boy: 'Behold, the arrows are beyond you!' then go, for [this is a signal that] HASHEM has sent you away. ²³ But this matter of which we have spoken, I and you — behold, HASHEM remains [witness] between me and you forever."*

An
uneventful
day

²⁴ David concealed himself in the field. It was the New Moon and the king sat at the meal to eat. ²⁵ The king sat at his seat as at other times, at the seat by the wall; Jonathan stood up and Abner sat at Saul's side, * and David's seat was empty. ²⁶ Saul said nothing on that day, for he thought, "It is a coincidence; he must be impure, for he has not been cleansed."

²⁷ It was the day after the New Moon, the second [day of the month], and

---

20:23. Even if you are forced to flee, God is witness that our covenant of friendship remains eternal.

20:25. David usually sat between Jonathan and Saul. Since David was absent, Jonathan had been sitting next

to his father, but then gave that place to Abner, as it was not considered respectful for a son to recline right next to his father (Rashi), or because he was apprehensive that Saul might become enraged (Radak).

וַיִּפְקֹד מְקוֹם דָּוִד וַיֹּאמֶר שָׁאוּל אֶל־יְהוֹנָתָן בְּנוֹ מַדּוּעַ לֹא־בָא בֶן־יִשַׁי גַּם־ כח
תְּמוֹל גַּם־הַיּוֹם אֶל־הַלָּחֶם: וַיַּעַן יְהוֹנָתָן אֶת־שָׁאוּל נִשְׁאֹל נִשְׁאַל דָּוִד כט
מֵעִמָּדִי עַד־בֵּית לָחֶם: וַיֹּאמֶר שַׁלְּחֵנִי נָא כִּי זֶבַח מִשְׁפָּחָה לָנוּ בָּעִיר וְהוּא
צִוָּה־לִי אָחִי וְעַתָּה אִם־מָצָאתִי חֵן בְּעֵינֶיךָ אִמָּלְטָה נָּא וְאֶרְאֶה אֶת־אֶחָי
עַל־כֵּן לֹא־בָא אֶל־שֻׁלְחַן הַמֶּלֶךְ: וַיִּחַר־אַף שָׁאוּל בִּיהוֹנָתָן ל
וַיֹּאמֶר לוֹ בֶּן־נַעֲוַת הַמַּרְדּוּת הֲלוֹא יָדַעְתִּי כִּי־בֹחֵר אַתָּה לְבֶן־יִשַׁי לְבָשְׁתְּךָ
וּלְבֹשֶׁת עֶרְוַת אִמֶּךָ: כִּי כָל־הַיָּמִים אֲשֶׁר בֶּן־יִשַׁי חַי עַל־הָאֲדָמָה לֹא תִכּוֹן לא
אַתָּה וּמַלְכוּתֶךָ וְעַתָּה שְׁלַח וְקַח אֹתוֹ אֵלַי כִּי בֶן־מָוֶת הוּא: וַיַּעַן לב
יְהוֹנָתָן אֶת־שָׁאוּל אָבִיו וַיֹּאמֶר אֵלָיו לָמָּה יוּמַת מֶה עָשָׂה: וַיָּטֶל שָׁאוּל לג
אֶת־הַחֲנִית עָלָיו לְהַכֹּתוֹ וַיֵּדַע יְהוֹנָתָן כִּי־כָלָה הִיא מֵעִם אָבִיו לְהָמִית
אֶת־דָּוִד: וַיָּקָם יְהוֹנָתָן מֵעִם הַשֻּׁלְחָן בָּחֳרִי־אָף וְלֹא־אָכַל בְּיוֹם־ לד
הַחֹדֶשׁ הַשֵּׁנִי לֶחֶם כִּי נֶעְצַב אֶל־דָּוִד כִּי הִכְלִמוֹ אָבִיו: וַיְהִי לה
בַבֹּקֶר וַיֵּצֵא יְהוֹנָתָן הַשָּׂדֶה לְמוֹעֵד דָּוִד וְנַעַר קָטֹן עִמּוֹ: וַיֹּאמֶר לְנַעֲרוֹ רֻץ לו
מְצָא נָא אֶת־הַחִצִּים אֲשֶׁר אָנֹכִי מוֹרֶה הַנַּעַר רָץ וְהוּא־יָרָה הַחֵצִי
לְהַעֲבִרוֹ: וַיָּבֹא הַנַּעַר עַד־מְקוֹם הַחֵצִי אֲשֶׁר יָרָה יְהוֹנָתָן וַיִּקְרָא יְהוֹנָתָן לז
אַחֲרֵי הַנַּעַר וַיֹּאמֶר הֲלוֹא הַחֵצִי מִמְּךָ וָהָלְאָה: וַיִּקְרָא יְהוֹנָתָן אַחֲרֵי הַנַּעַר לח
מְהֵרָה חוּשָׁה אַל־תַּעֲמֹד וַיְלַקֵּט נַעַר יְהוֹנָתָן אֶת־°הַחִצִּי [°הַחִצִּים ק]
וַיָּבֹא אֶל־אֲדֹנָיו: וְהַנַּעַר לֹא־יָדַע מְאוּמָה אַךְ יְהוֹנָתָן וְדָוִד יָדְעוּ אֶת־הַדָּבָר: לט
וַיִּתֵּן יְהוֹנָתָן אֶת־כֵּלָיו אֶל־הַנַּעַר אֲשֶׁר־לוֹ וַיֹּאמֶר לוֹ לֵךְ הָבֵיא הָעִיר: מ
הַנַּעַר בָּא וְדָוִד קָם מֵאֵצֶל הַנֶּגֶב וַיִּפֹּל לְאַפָּיו אַרְצָה וַיִּשְׁתַּחוּ שָׁלֹשׁ פְּעָמִים מא
וַיִּשְּׁקוּ אִישׁ אֶת־רֵעֵהוּ וַיִּבְכּוּ אִישׁ אֶת־רֵעֵהוּ עַד־דָּוִד הִגְדִּיל: וַיֹּאמֶר מב
יְהוֹנָתָן לְדָוִד לֵךְ לְשָׁלוֹם אֲשֶׁר נִשְׁבַּעְנוּ שְׁנֵינוּ אֲנַחְנוּ בְּשֵׁם יהוה לֵאמֹר
יהוה יִהְיֶה בֵּינִי וּבֵינֶךָ וּבֵין זַרְעִי וּבֵין זַרְעֲךָ עַד־עוֹלָם: ◄ וַיָּקָם א כא
וַיֵּלֶךְ וִיהוֹנָתָן בָּא הָעִיר: וַיָּבֹא דָוִד נֹבֶה אֶל־אֲחִימֶלֶךְ הַכֹּהֵן וַיֶּחֱרַד ב
אֲחִימֶלֶךְ לִקְרַאת דָּוִד וַיֹּאמֶר לוֹ מַדּוּעַ אַתָּה לְבַדֶּךָ וְאִישׁ אֵין אִתָּךְ:
וַיֹּאמֶר דָּוִד לַאֲחִימֶלֶךְ הַכֹּהֵן הַמֶּלֶךְ צִוַּנִי דָבָר וַיֹּאמֶר אֵלַי אִישׁ אַל־יֵדַע ג
מְאוּמָה אֶת־הַדָּבָר אֲשֶׁר־אָנֹכִי שֹׁלֵחֲךָ וַאֲשֶׁר צִוִּיתִךָ וְאֶת־הַנְּעָרִים
יוֹדַעְתִּי אֶל־מְקוֹם פְּלֹנִי אַלְמוֹנִי: וְעַתָּה מַה־יֵּשׁ תַּחַת־יָדְךָ חֲמִשָּׁה־לֶחֶם ד
תְּנָה בְיָדִי אוֹ הַנִּמְצָא: וַיַּעַן הַכֹּהֵן אֶת־דָּוִד וַיֹּאמֶר אֵין־לֶחֶם חֹל אֶל־תַּחַת ה
יָדִי כִּי־אִם־לֶחֶם קֹדֶשׁ יֵשׁ אִם־נִשְׁמְרוּ הַנְּעָרִים אַךְ מֵאִשָּׁה: וַיַּעַן ו

20:30. People seeing you support my enemy will assume that you were born of an adulterous relationship (*Radak*).

20:42. Above, v. 23.

21:2. After the Philistines destroyed the Tabernacle at Shiloh, a new national altar was erected at Nob, and the communal sacrificial service was performed there.

21:4. David implied that five attendants awaited him in the secret place (*Malbim*).

21:5-7. The only bread Ahimelech had available was the show-bread (see *Leviticus* 24:5-9), which only Kohanim were allowed to eat and which must be kept in a state of the highest ritual purity. Since David's need for food was a life-or-death matter, the Kohen ruled that he could give

David's place was empty. So Saul said to Jonathan, his son, "Why did the son of Jesse not come to the meal either yesterday or today?"

²⁸ *Jonathan answered Saul, "David asked me for permission to go to Bethlehem.* ²⁹ *He said, 'Please grant me leave, for we have a family feast-offering in the city, and he — my brother — summoned me; so now, if I have found favor in your eyes, please let me be excused that I may see my brothers.' That is why he did not come to the king's table."*

Saul reveals
his hatred ³⁰ *Saul's anger flared up at Jonathan, and he said to him, "Son of a pervertedly rebellious woman! Do I not know that you choose the son of Jesse, to your own shame and the shame of your mother's nakedness?* * ³¹ *For all the days that the son of Jesse is alive on the earth, you and your kingdom will not be established! And now send and bring him to me, for he is deserving of death!"*

³² *But Jonathan spoke up to his father Saul, and said to him, "Why should he die? What has he done?"*

³³ *Saul hurled the spear at him to strike him. Jonathan then realized that his father had decided to kill David.* ³⁴ *Jonathan arose from the table enraged; he did not partake of food on that second day of the month, for he was saddened over David, and because his father had humiliated him.*

The dear
friends'
emotional
parting ³⁵ *It happened the next morning that Jonathan went out to the field for the meeting with David, and a young attendant was with him.* ³⁶ *He said to his attendant, "Please run and find the arrows that I shoot." The attendant ran, and he shot the arrow to go beyond him.* ³⁷ *The attendant arrived at the place of the arrow that Jonathan had shot, and Jonathan called out after the attendant and said, "Is not the arrow beyond you?"* ³⁸ *Jonathan then called out after the attendant, "Quickly, hurry, do not stand still!" Jonathan's attendant gathered the arrows and came to his master.* ³⁹ *The attendant knew nothing; only Jonathan and David understood the matter.* ⁴⁰ *Jonathan gave his equipment to his attendant and said to him, "Go, bring it to the city."*

⁴¹ *The attendant went and David stood up from near the south [side of the stone], and he fell on his face to the ground and prostrated himself three times. Each man kissed the other and they wept with one another, until David [wept] greatly.* ⁴² *Jonathan said to David, "Go to peace. What the two of us have sworn* * in the Name of HASHEM — saying, 'HASHEM shall be [a witness] between me and you, and between my offspring and your offspring' — shall be forever!"*

21
SAUL'S WAR
AGAINST
DAVID
21:1-24:23 ¹ [**D**avid] *arose and left, and Jonathan came back to the city.* ² *David came to Nob,* * to Ahimelech the Kohen. Ahimelech hurried to greet David, and said to him, "Why are you alone, with no one accompanying you?"*

³ *David said to Ahimelech the Kohen, "The king ordered me on a mission, and told me, 'No man may know anything about the matter for which I have sent you and commanded you.' Thus, I informed my attendants to be at a certain secret place.* A hungry
David
requests
food ⁴ *And now, what do you have available? Five loaves of bread? Give them* * — or whatever there is — into my hand."*

⁵ *The Kohen answered David, saying, "I have no ordinary bread available; there is only sacred bread,* * provided that your attendants have kept themselves from women."* *

---

the breads to David, but they had to be kept ritually pure (*Rashi*). In response, David assured him that this would be done, and that he and his men would be even more careful now that they would have the sacred bread. **21:5.** Had they been intimate, they would have become impure (see *Leviticus* 15:18).

דָּוִד אֶת־הַכֹּהֵן וַיֹּאמֶר לוֹ כִּי אִם־אִשָּׁה עֲצֻרָה־לָנוּ כִּתְמוֹל שִׁלְשֹׁם בְּצֵאתִי

ז וַיִּהְיוּ כְלֵי־הַנְּעָרִים קֹדֶשׁ וְהוּא דֶרֶךְ חֹל וְאַף כִּי הַיּוֹם יִקְדַּשׁ בַּכֶּלִי: וַיִּתֶּן־לוֹ הַכֹּהֵן קֹדֶשׁ כִּי לֹא־הָיָה שָׁם לֶחֶם כִּי־אִם־לֶחֶם הַפָּנִים הַמּוּסָרִים מִלִּפְנֵי

ח יהוה לָשׂוּם לֶחֶם חֹם בְּיוֹם הִלָּקְחוֹ: וְשָׁם אִישׁ מֵעַבְדֵי שָׁאוּל בַּיּוֹם הַהוּא נֶעְצָר לִפְנֵי יהוה וּשְׁמוֹ דֹּאֵג הָאֲדֹמִי אַבִּיר הָרֹעִים אֲשֶׁר לְשָׁאוּל: וַיֹּאמֶר

ט דָּוִד לַאֲחִימֶלֶךְ וְאִין יֶשׁ־פֹּה תַחַת־יָדְךָ חֲנִית אוֹ־חָרֶב כִּי גַם־חַרְבִּי וְגַם־ כֵּלַי לֹא־לָקַחְתִּי בְיָדִי כִּי־הָיָה דְבַר־הַמֶּלֶךְ נָחוּץ: וַיֹּאמֶר

י הַכֹּהֵן חֶרֶב גָּלְיָת הַפְּלִשְׁתִּי אֲשֶׁר־הִכִּיתָ | בְּעֵמֶק הָאֵלָה הִנֵּה־הִיא לוּטָה בַשִּׂמְלָה אַחֲרֵי הָאֵפוֹד אִם־אֹתָהּ תִּקַּח־לְךָ קָח כִּי אֵין אַחֶרֶת זוּלָתָהּ

יא בָּזֶה וַיֹּאמֶר דָּוִד אֵין כָּמוֹהָ תְּנֶנָּה לִּי: וַיָּקָם דָּוִד וַיִּבְרַח בַּיּוֹם־ הַהוּא מִפְּנֵי שָׁאוּל וַיָּבֹא אֶל־אָכִישׁ מֶלֶךְ גַּת: וַיֹּאמְרוּ עַבְדֵי אָכִישׁ אֵלָיו

יב הֲלוֹא־זֶה דָוִד מֶלֶךְ הָאָרֶץ הֲלוֹא לָזֶה יַעֲנוּ בַמְּחֹלֹת לֵאמֹר הִכָּה שָׁאוּל בְּ[אֲלָפָו כ] [בַּאֲלָפָיו ק] וְדָוִד בְּ[רִבְבֹתוֹ כ] [בְּרִבְבֹתָיו ק]: וַיָּשֶׂם דָּוִד אֶת־

יג הַדְּבָרִים הָאֵלֶּה בִּלְבָבוֹ וַיִּרָא מְאֹד מִפְּנֵי אָכִישׁ מֶלֶךְ־גַּת: וַיְשַׁנּוֹ אֶת־טַעְמוֹ בְּעֵינֵיהֶם וַיִּתְהֹלֵל בְּיָדָם וַ[יְתָו כ] [וַיְתָיו ק] עַל־דַּלְתוֹת הַשַּׁעַר וַיּוֹרֶד רִירוֹ

יד אֶל־זְקָנוֹ: וַיֹּאמֶר אָכִישׁ אֶל־עֲבָדָיו הִנֵּה תִרְאוּ אִישׁ מִשְׁתַּגֵּעַ לָמָּה

טו תָּבִיאוּ אֹתוֹ אֵלָי: חֲסַר מְשֻׁגָּעִים אָנִי כִּי־הֲבֵאתֶם אֶת־זֶה לְהִשְׁתַּגֵּעַ עָלָי

טז הֲזֶה יָבוֹא אֶל־בֵּיתִי:

כב

א וַיֵּלֶךְ דָּוִד מִשָּׁם וַיִּמָּלֵט אֶל־מְעָרַת עֲדֻלָּם וַיִּשְׁמְעוּ אֶחָיו וְכָל־בֵּית אָבִיו וַיֵּרְדוּ אֵלָיו שָׁמָּה: וַיִּתְקַבְּצוּ אֵלָיו כָל־אִישׁ

ב מָצוֹק וְכָל־אִישׁ אֲשֶׁר־לוֹ נֹשֶׁא וְכָל־אִישׁ מַר־נֶפֶשׁ וַיְהִי עֲלֵיהֶם לְשָׂר וַיִּהְיוּ עִמּוֹ כְּאַרְבַּע מֵאוֹת אִישׁ: וַיֵּלֶךְ דָּוִד מִשָּׁם מִצְפֵּה מוֹאָב וַיֹּאמֶר אֶל־

ג מֶלֶךְ מוֹאָב יֵצֵא־נָא אָבִי וְאִמִּי אִתְּכֶם עַד אֲשֶׁר אֵדַע מַה־יַּעֲשֶׂה־לִּי

ד אֱלֹהִים: וַיַּנְחֵם אֶת־פְּנֵי מֶלֶךְ מוֹאָב וַיֵּשְׁבוּ עִמּוֹ כָּל־יְמֵי הֱיוֹת־דָּוִד

ה בַּמְּצוּדָה: וַיֹּאמֶר גָּד הַנָּבִיא אֶל־דָּוִד לֹא תֵשֵׁב בַּמְּצוּדָה לֵךְ

ו וּבָאתָ־לְּךָ אֶרֶץ יְהוּדָה וַיֵּלֶךְ דָּוִד וַיָּבֹא יַעַר חָרֶת: וַיִּשְׁמַע שָׁאוּל כִּי נוֹדַע דָּוִד וַאֲנָשִׁים אֲשֶׁר אִתּוֹ וְשָׁאוּל יוֹשֵׁב בַּגִּבְעָה תַּחַת־ הָאֶשֶׁל בָּרָמָה וַחֲנִיתוֹ בְיָדוֹ וְכָל־עֲבָדָיו נִצָּבִים עָלָיו: וַיֹּאמֶר שָׁאוּל

ז לַעֲבָדָיו הַנִּצָּבִים עָלָיו שִׁמְעוּ־נָא בְּנֵי יְמִינִי גַּם־לְכֻלְּכֶם יִתֵּן בֶּן־יִשַׁי

ח שָׂדוֹת וּכְרָמִים לְכֻלְּכֶם יָשִׂים שָׂרֵי אֲלָפִים וְשָׂרֵי מֵאוֹת: כִּי קְשַׁרְתֶּם כֻּלְּכֶם עָלַי וְאֵין־גֹּלֶה אֶת־אָזְנִי בִּכְרָת־בְּנִי עִם־בֶּן־יִשַׁי וְאֵין־חֹלֶה מִכֶּם עָלַי וְגֹלֶה אֶת־אָזְנִי כִּי הֵקִים בְּנִי אֶת־עַבְדִּי עָלַי לְאֹרֵב

ט כַּיּוֹם הַזֶּה: וַיַּעַן דֹּאֵג הָאֲדֹמִי וְהוּא נִצָּב עַל־עַבְדֵי־שָׁאוּל

21:8. Doeg, who resided in Edomite territory, had come to the Tabernacle to bring offerings or to worship. According to the Sages, he was *chief of the shepherds* who lead the nation's spiritual life, i.e. a chief judge.

21:16. David's ruse succeeded. Achish felt that this madman could not be the famed David (*Metzudos*).

⁶ David answered the Kohen, and said to him, "Women have been withheld from us yesterday and the day before; [moreover], when I left, the garments of the attendants were pure, even though this is a mundane mission — surely today it will remain sacred in a [proper] vessel." ⁷ So the Kohen gave him sacred food, for there was no other bread there except for the show-bread that was being removed from before HASHEM, in order to place hot bread on the day it is taken off.

The Kohen gives David both sacred bread and Goliath's sword

⁸ Now there on that day was one of Saul's servants, who lingered before HASHEM. His name was Doeg the Edomite; he was the chief of Saul's shepherds. *

⁹ David then said to Ahimelech, "Perhaps you have here under your hand a spear or a sword, for I did not take my sword and my weapons with me, since the king's mission was urgent."

¹⁰ The Kohen said, "The sword of Goliath, whom you slew in the Terebinth Valley, is wrapped up in a cloth behind the Ephod; if you want to take it, take it, for there is none other here except for it."

And David said, "There is none like it; give it to me."

¹¹ David arose and fled from Saul on that day, and he came to Achish, king of Gath. ¹² The servants of Achish said to him, "Is this not David, the king of the land? Is it not of him that they sing with the timbrels, saying, 'Saul has slain his thousands, and David his tens of thousands'?"

¹³ David took this matter to heart and was greatly afraid of Achish, king of Gath. ¹⁴ So he changed his demeanor in their eyes and feigned madness while in their presence; he scribbled on the doors of the gateway and let his saliva drip into his beard. ¹⁵ Achish said to his servants, "Behold — you see the man is mad; why do you bring him to me? ¹⁶ Do I lack madmen that you have brought this one to carry on madly before me? Should this person enter my house?"*

22

David's flight

¹ **D**avid went from there and escaped to the cave of Adullam. His brothers and all his father's house heard about this, and went down to him there. ² They gathered to him — every man in distress, every man with a creditor, and every man embittered of spirit — and he became their leader. With him were about four hundred men.

The beleaguered gather around David

³ David went from there to Mizpeh of Moab, and he said to the king of Moab, "Let my father and mother come out here and be with you until I know what God will do with me." ⁴ So he escorted them to the king of Moab and they stayed with him all the days that David was in the fortress. ⁵ Gad the Prophet said to David, "Do not stay in the fortress; go and get yourself to the land of Judah." So David went and arrived at the forest of Hereth.

Saul appeals for loyalty

⁶ Saul heard that David and the men with him had been discovered. Saul was sitting in Gibeah under the tamarisk tree in Ramah with his spear in his hand, with all his servants standing about him. ⁷ Saul said to his servants who were standing about him, "Listen now, [fellow] Benjamites. Is the son of Jesse going to give you all fields and vineyards, is he going to make you all captains of thousands and captains of hundreds, ⁸ that you have all organized against me and no one revealed to me that my son covenanted with the son of Jesse; and that none among you is distressed for me or reveals to me that my son has incited my servant to rise up and ambush me, [as clearly] as this day?"

Doeg's treachery

⁹ Then Doeg the Edomite, who was appointed over Saul's servants, spoke up

י וַיֹּאמֶר רָאִיתִי אֶת־בֶּן־יִשַׁי בָּא נֹבֶה אֶל־אֲחִימֶלֶךְ בֶּן־אֲחִטוּב: וַיִּשְׁאַל־לוֹ

יא בַּיהוָה וְצֵידָה נָתַן לוֹ וְאֵת חֶרֶב גָּלְיָת הַפְּלִשְׁתִּי נָתַן לוֹ: וַיִּשְׁלַח הַמֶּלֶךְ
לִקְרֹא אֶת־אֲחִימֶלֶךְ בֶּן־אֲחִיטוּב הַכֹּהֵן וְאֵת כָּל־בֵּית אָבִיו הַכֹּהֲנִים אֲשֶׁר

יב בְּנֹב וַיָּבֹאוּ כֻלָּם אֶל־הַמֶּלֶךְ:   וַיֹּאמֶר שָׁאוּל שְׁמַע־נָא בֶּן־

יג אֲחִיטוּב וַיֹּאמֶר הִנְנִי אֲדֹנִי: וַיֹּאמֶר °אֵלוֹ [°אֵלָיו ק] שָׁאוּל לָמָּה קְשַׁרְתֶּם
עָלַי אַתָּה וּבֶן־יִשַׁי בְּתִתְּךָ לוֹ לֶחֶם וְחֶרֶב וְשָׁאוֹל לוֹ בֵּאלֹהִים לָקוּם אֵלַי

יד לָאֹרֵב כַּיּוֹם הַזֶּה: וַיַּעַן אֲחִימֶלֶךְ אֶת־הַמֶּלֶךְ וַיֹּאמֶר וּמִי בְכָל־

טו עֲבָדֶיךָ כְּדָוִד נֶאֱמָן וַחֲתַן הַמֶּלֶךְ וְסָר אֶל־מִשְׁמַעְתֶּךָ וְנִכְבָּד בְּבֵיתֶךָ: הַיּוֹם
הַחִלֹּתִי °לִשְׁאָול [°לִשְׁאָל ק] לוֹ בֵאלֹהִים חָלִילָה לִּי אַל־יָשֵׂם הַמֶּלֶךְ
בְּעַבְדּוֹ דָבָר בְּכָל־בֵּית אָבִי כִּי לֹא־יָדַע עַבְדְּךָ בְּכָל־זֹאת דָּבָר קָטֹן אוֹ

טז־יז גָדוֹל: וַיֹּאמֶר הַמֶּלֶךְ מוֹת תָּמוּת אֲחִימֶלֶךְ אַתָּה וְכָל־בֵּית אָבִיךָ: וַיֹּאמֶר
הַמֶּלֶךְ לָרָצִים הַנִּצָּבִים עָלָיו סֹבּוּ וְהָמִיתוּ ׀ כֹּהֲנֵי יהוה כִּי גַם־יָדָם עִם־דָּוִד
וְכִי יָדְעוּ כִּי־בֹרֵחַ הוּא וְלֹא גָלוּ אֶת־°אֹזנוֹ [°אָזְנִי ק] וְלֹא־אָבוּ עַבְדֵי

יח הַמֶּלֶךְ לִשְׁלֹחַ אֶת־יָדָם לִפְגֹעַ בְּכֹהֲנֵי יהוה: וַיֹּאמֶר הַמֶּלֶךְ
°לְדֹויֵג [°לְדוֹאֵג ק] סֹב אַתָּה וּפְגַע בַּכֹּהֲנִים וַיִּסֹּב °דֹויֵג [°דּוֹאֵג ק] הָאֲדֹמִי
וַיִּפְגַּע־הוּא בַּכֹּהֲנִים וַיָּמֶת ׀ בַּיּוֹם הַהוּא שְׁמֹנִים וַחֲמִשָּׁה אִישׁ נֹשֵׂא אֵפוֹד

יט בָּד: וְאֵת נֹב עִיר־הַכֹּהֲנִים הִכָּה לְפִי־חֶרֶב מֵאִישׁ וְעַד־אִשָּׁה מֵעוֹלֵל

כ וְעַד־יוֹנֵק וְשׁוֹר וַחֲמוֹר וָשֶׂה לְפִי־חָרֶב: וַיִּמָּלֵט בֶּן־אֶחָד לַאֲחִימֶלֶךְ בֶּן־

כא אֲחִטוּב וּשְׁמוֹ אֶבְיָתָר וַיִּבְרַח אַחֲרֵי דָוִד: וַיַּגֵּד אֶבְיָתָר לְדָוִד כִּי הָרַג שָׁאוּל

כב אֵת כֹּהֲנֵי יהוה: וַיֹּאמֶר דָּוִד לְאֶבְיָתָר יָדַעְתִּי בַּיּוֹם הַהוּא כִּי־שָׁם °דֹויֵג
[°דּוֹאֵג ק] הָאֲדֹמִי כִּי־הַגֵּד יַגִּיד לְשָׁאוּל אָנֹכִי סַבֹּתִי בְּכָל־נֶפֶשׁ בֵּית

כג אָבִיךָ: שְׁבָה אִתִּי אַל־תִּירָא כִּי אֲשֶׁר־יְבַקֵּשׁ אֶת־נַפְשִׁי יְבַקֵּשׁ אֶת־נַפְשֶׁךָ

כג א כִּי־מִשְׁמֶרֶת אַתָּה עִמָּדִי: וַיַּגִּדוּ לְדָוִד לֵאמֹר הִנֵּה פְלִשְׁתִּים נִלְחָמִים

ב בִּקְעִילָה וְהֵמָּה שֹׁסִים אֶת־הַגֳּרָנוֹת: וַיִּשְׁאַל דָּוִד בַּיהוָה לֵאמֹר הַאֵלֵךְ
וְהִכֵּיתִי בַּפְּלִשְׁתִּים הָאֵלֶּה   וַיֹּאמֶר יהוה אֶל־דָּוִד לֵךְ וְהִכִּיתָ בַפְּלִשְׁתִּים

ג וְהוֹשַׁעְתָּ אֶת־קְעִילָה: וַיֹּאמְרוּ אַנְשֵׁי דָוִד אֵלָיו הִנֵּה אֲנַחְנוּ פֹה בִיהוּדָה

ד יְרֵאִים וְאַף כִּי־נֵלֵךְ קְעִלָה אֶל־מַעַרְכוֹת פְּלִשְׁתִּים: וַיּוֹסֶף עוֹד
דָּוִד לִשְׁאֹל בַּיהוָה   וַיַּעֲנֵהוּ יהוה וַיֹּאמֶר קוּם רֵד קְעִילָה כִּי־

ה אֲנִי נֹתֵן אֶת־פְּלִשְׁתִּים בְּיָדֶךָ: וַיֵּלֶךְ דָּוִד °ואנשו [°וַאֲנָשָׁיו ק] קְעִילָה וַיִּלָּחֶם
בַּפְּלִשְׁתִּים וַיִּנְהַג אֶת־מִקְנֵיהֶם וַיַּךְ בָּהֶם מַכָּה גְדוֹלָה וַיֹּשַׁע דָּוִד אֵת יֹשְׁבֵי

ו קְעִילָה: וַיְהִי בִּבְרֹחַ אֶבְיָתָר בֶּן־אֲחִימֶלֶךְ אֶל־דָּוִד קְעִילָה אֵפוֹד

ז יָרַד בְּיָדוֹ: וַיֻּגַּד לְשָׁאוּל כִּי־בָא דָוִד קְעִילָה וַיֹּאמֶר שָׁאוּל נִכַּר אֹתוֹ אֱלֹהִים

22:15. Ahimelech was shocked at the accusation. He said
that he had often inquired of God for David, since David
was known to be a leading member of Saul's court, and he

had no knowledge of the friction between Saul and David.
22:16. A king has the right to supersede the judicial
process to put down a rebellion. Thus, since he was

and said, "I saw the son of Jesse come to Nob, to Ahimelech son of Ahitub.
¹⁰ He inquired of HASHEM for him and gave him provisions, and he gave him the
sword of Goliath the Philistine."

Saul accuses
Ahimelech
¹¹ So the king sent for Ahimelech son of Ahitub the Kohen and all his father's
house, the Kohanim of Nob, and they all came to the king. ¹² Saul said, "Listen
now, son of Ahitub!" And he said, "Here I am, my lord." ¹³ Saul said to him,
"Why did you organize against me — you and the son of Jesse — by giving him
food and a sword, and inquiring of God for him, so that he could arise and
ambush me, [as clearly] as this day?"

¹⁴ Ahimelech answered the king, and said, "Who among all your servants is
as trustworthy as David? He is the king's son-in-law, obeys your bidding, and
is honored in your household. ¹⁵ Did I begin today to inquire for him of God? It
would be sacrilegious for me [to betray the king]! Let the king not accuse his
servant or my father's entire household of anything, for your servant did not
know anything small or great about all of this."*

The
annihilation
of Nob's
Kohanim
¹⁶ But the king said, "You must die, Ahimelech, you and all your father's
house!"*

¹⁷ The king then said to the footmen who stood about him, "Surround and kill
the Kohanim of HASHEM, because their hand is also with David, and because
they knew that he was fleeing and did not inform me." But the servants of the
king were not willing to send forth their hand to slay the Kohanim of HASHEM.
¹⁸ So the king said to Doeg, "You circle around and slay the Kohanim!" Doeg the
Edomite circled around and he killed the Kohanim; on that day he killed
eighty-five men, wearers of linen robes. ¹⁹ And Nob, the city of Kohanim, he
killed by the blade of the sword: man and woman alike; child and suckling alike;
ox, donkey and sheep.

David
shelters the
lone survivor
²⁰ One son of Ahimelech son of Ahitub — his name was Abiathar — escaped,
and he fled to David. ²¹ Abiathar told David that Saul had massacred the
Kohanim of HASHEM. ²² David said to Abiathar, "I knew on that day that Doeg
the Edomite was there and that he would certainly inform Saul. I am responsible
for every life of your father's house! ²³ Stay with me and fear not, for the man
who seeks my life seeks your life, as well. You are safe with me."

23

David
saves Keilah
¹ They told David, saying, "Behold, the Philistines are battling against Keilah
and they are pillaging the granaries." ² David then inquired of HASHEM, *
saying, "Shall I go and strike down these Philistines?" And HASHEM replied to
David, "Go, strike the Philistines and save Keilah." ³ But David's men said to
him, "Behold, we are afraid [even] here in Judah; how much more so if we go
to Keilah to the Philistine lines!" ⁴ So David inquired again of HASHEM, and
HASHEM answered him, "Arise, go down to Keilah, for I am delivering the
Philistines into your hand." ⁵ David and his men went to Keilah and battled the
Philistines; he led away their livestock and struck them a great blow. Thus David
saved the residents of Keilah.

⁶ When Abiathar son of Ahimelech fled to David to Keilah, he brought the
Ephod with him.

⁷ Saul was told that David had come to Keilah, and Saul said, "God has

---

convinced that the Kohanim were out to depose or kill
him, Saul could impose the death penalty.

23:2. Abiathar had brought the *Urim VeTumim* (see v. 6)
through which the Kohen could make inquiries of God.

ח בְּיָדִי כִּי נִסְגַּר לָבוֹא בְּעִיר בִּדְלָתַיִם וּבְרִיחַ: וַיְשַׁמַּע שָׁאוּל אֶת־כָּל־

ט הָעָם לַמִּלְחָמָה לָרֶדֶת קְעִילָה לָצוּר אֶל־דָּוִד וְאֶל־אֲנָשָׁיו: וַיֵּדַע

דָּוִד כִּי עָלָיו שָׁאוּל מַחֲרִישׁ הָרָעָה וַיֹּאמֶר אֶל־אֶבְיָתָר הַכֹּהֵן הַגִּישָׁה

י הָאֵפוֹד: וַיֹּאמֶר דָּוִד יְהוָה אֱלֹהֵי יִשְׂרָאֵל שָׁמֹעַ שָׁמַע עַבְדְּךָ

יא כִּי־מְבַקֵּשׁ שָׁאוּל לָבוֹא אֶל־קְעִילָה לְשַׁחֵת לָעִיר בַּעֲבוּרִי: הֲיַסְגִּרֻנִי בַעֲלֵי

קְעִילָה בְיָדוֹ הֲיֵרֵד שָׁאוּל כַּאֲשֶׁר שָׁמַע עַבְדֶּךָ יְהוָה אֱלֹהֵי יִשְׂרָאֵל הַגֶּד־

יב נָא לְעַבְדֶּךָ: וַיֹּאמֶר יְהוָה יֵרֵד: וַיֹּאמֶר דָּוִד הֲיַסְגִּרוּ בַעֲלֵי

יג קְעִילָה אֹתִי וְאֶת־אֲנָשַׁי בְּיַד־שָׁאוּל וַיֹּאמֶר יְהוָה יַסְגִּירוּ: וַיָּקָם

דָּוִד וַאֲנָשָׁיו כְּשֵׁשׁ־מֵאוֹת אִישׁ וַיֵּצְאוּ מִקְּעִלָה וַיִּתְהַלְּכוּ בַּאֲשֶׁר יִתְהַלָּכוּ

יד וּלְשָׁאוּל הֻגַּד כִּי־נִמְלַט דָּוִד מִקְּעִילָה וַיֶּחְדַּל לָצֵאת: וַיֵּשֶׁב דָּוִד בַּמִּדְבָּר

בַּמְּצָדוֹת וַיֵּשֶׁב בָּהָר בְּמִדְבַּר־זִיף וַיְבַקְשֵׁהוּ שָׁאוּל כָּל־הַיָּמִים וְלֹא־נְתָנוֹ

טו אֱלֹהִים בְּיָדוֹ: וַיַּרְא דָוִד כִּי־יָצָא שָׁאוּל לְבַקֵּשׁ אֶת־נַפְשׁוֹ וְדָוִד בְּמִדְבַּר־

טז זִיף בַּחֹרְשָׁה: וַיָּקָם יְהוֹנָתָן בֶּן־שָׁאוּל וַיֵּלֶךְ אֶל־דָּוִד חֹרְשָׁה:

יז וַיְחַזֵּק אֶת־יָדוֹ בֵּאלֹהִים: וַיֹּאמֶר אֵלָיו אַל־תִּירָא כִּי לֹא תִמְצָאֲךָ יַד־

שָׁאוּל אָבִי וְאַתָּה תִּמְלֹךְ עַל־יִשְׂרָאֵל וְאָנֹכִי אֶהְיֶה־לְּךָ לְמִשְׁנֶה וְגַם־

יח שָׁאוּל אָבִי יֹדֵעַ כֵּן: וַיִּכְרְתוּ שְׁנֵיהֶם בְּרִית לִפְנֵי יְהוָה וַיֵּשֶׁב דָּוִד בַּחֹרְשָׁה

יט וִיהוֹנָתָן הָלַךְ לְבֵיתוֹ: וַיַּעֲלוּ זִפִים אֶל־שָׁאוּל הַגִּבְעָתָה

לֵאמֹר הֲלוֹא דָוִד מִסְתַּתֵּר עִמָּנוּ בַמְּצָדוֹת בַּחֹרְשָׁה בְּגִבְעַת הַחֲכִילָה

כ אֲשֶׁר מִימִין הַיְשִׁימוֹן: וְעַתָּה לְכָל־אַוַּת נַפְשְׁךָ הַמֶּלֶךְ לָרֶדֶת רֵד וְלָנוּ

כא הַסְגִּירוֹ בְּיַד הַמֶּלֶךְ: וַיֹּאמֶר שָׁאוּל בְּרוּכִים אַתֶּם לַיהוָה כִּי חֲמַלְתֶּם עָלָי:

כב לְכוּ־נָא הָכִינוּ עוֹד וּדְעוּ וּרְאוּ אֶת־מְקוֹמוֹ אֲשֶׁר תִּהְיֶה רַגְלוֹ מִי רָאָהוּ שָׁם

כג כִּי אָמַר אֵלַי עָרוֹם יַעְרִם הוּא: וּרְאוּ וּדְעוּ מִכֹּל הַמַּחֲבֹאִים אֲשֶׁר יִתְחַבֵּא

שָׁם וְשַׁבְתֶּם אֵלַי אֶל־נָכוֹן וְהָלַכְתִּי אִתְּכֶם וְהָיָה אִם־יֶשְׁנוֹ בָאָרֶץ וְחִפַּשְׂתִּי

כד אֹתוֹ בְּכֹל אַלְפֵי יְהוּדָה: וַיָּקוּמוּ וַיֵּלְכוּ זִיפָה לִפְנֵי שָׁאוּל וְדָוִד וַאֲנָשָׁיו

בְּמִדְבַּר מָעוֹן בָּעֲרָבָה אֶל יְמִין הַיְשִׁימוֹן: כה וַיֵּלֶךְ שָׁאוּל וַאֲנָשָׁיו לְבַקֵּשׁ וַיַּגִּדוּ

לְדָוִד וַיֵּרֶד הַסֶּלַע וַיֵּשֶׁב בְּמִדְבַּר מָעוֹן וַיִּשְׁמַע שָׁאוּל וַיִּרְדֹּף אַחֲרֵי־דָוִד

כו מִדְבַּר מָעוֹן: וַיֵּלֶךְ שָׁאוּל מִצַּד הָהָר מִזֶּה וְדָוִד וַאֲנָשָׁיו מִצַּד הָהָר מִזֶּה וַיְהִי

דָוִד נֶחְפָּז לָלֶכֶת מִפְּנֵי שָׁאוּל וְשָׁאוּל וַאֲנָשָׁיו עֹטְרִים אֶל־דָּוִד וְאֶל־אֲנָשָׁיו

כז לְתָפְשָׂם: וּמַלְאָךְ בָּא אֶל־שָׁאוּל לֵאמֹר מַהֲרָה וְלֵכָה כִּי־פָשְׁטוּ פְלִשְׁתִּים

כח עַל־הָאָרֶץ: וַיָּשָׁב שָׁאוּל מִרְדֹף אַחֲרֵי דָוִד וַיֵּלֶךְ לִקְרַאת פְּלִשְׁתִּים עַל־כֵּן

א קָרְאוּ לַמָּקוֹם הַהוּא סֶלַע הַמַּחְלְקוֹת: וַיַּעַל דָּוִד מִשָּׁם וַיֵּשֶׁב בִּמְצָדוֹת עֵין

כד

ב גֶּדִי: וַיְהִי כַּאֲשֶׁר שָׁב שָׁאוּל מֵאַחֲרֵי פְּלִשְׁתִּים וַיַּגִּדוּ לוֹ לֵאמֹר

23:7. If the gates of a walled city are guarded, there is no
escape from it.

23:17. Jonathan reiterated Samuel's prophecy (Ch. 16)

that David would one day reign over Israel (*Radak*).

23:22. Do not rely on hearsay evidence. Obtain eyewitness reports (*Abarbanel*).

delivered him into my hand, for he has been trapped by coming into a city of

Saul pursues David gates and bar."* ⁸ So Saul summoned all the people for war, to go down to Keilah to besiege David and his men. ⁹ David learned that Saul was planning evil against him, and he said to Abiathar the Kohen, "Bring forth the Ephod." ¹⁰ David said, "HASHEM, God of Israel, Your servant has heard that Saul seeks to come to Keilah to destroy the city on my account. ¹¹ Will the inhabitants of Keilah give me over into his hand? Will Saul come down here, as Your servant has heard? HASHEM, God of Israel, please tell Your servant!" And HASHEM said, "He will come down." ¹² David then said, "Will the inhabitants of Keilah give me and my men over into the hand of Saul?" And HASHEM replied, "They will give

David eludes Saul [you] over." ¹³ So David and his men — about six hundred men — arose and left Keilah and went wherever they could go. When Saul was told that David had escaped from Keilah, he stopped advancing.

¹⁴ David then dwelled in the wilderness in strongholds, or he dwelt in the mountain, in the Wilderness of Ziph. Saul searched for him all the days, but God did not deliver him into his hand. ¹⁵ David saw that Saul had gone forth to seek

Jonathan's secret rendezvous his life, and David was in the Wilderness of Ziph, in the forest. ¹⁶ Jonathan son of Saul arose and went to see David in the forest, and he encouraged him with the word of God. ¹⁷ He said to him, "Fear not, for the hand of my father Saul will not find you; you will reign over Israel and I will be second to you, and even my father Saul knows it."* ¹⁸ The two of them sealed a covenant before HASHEM. David stayed on in the forest, and Jonathan went to his home.

The Ziphites betray David ¹⁹ Some Ziphites went up to Saul in Gibeah, saying, "David is hiding among us in the strongholds in the forest in Hachilah Hill, south of Jeshimon. ²⁰ So now, however your soul desires to come down, O king, come down — and we undertake to give him over into the hand of the king." ²¹ Saul said, "Blessed are you unto HASHEM, for you have shown me compassion! ²² Go now and prepare further, ascertain and observe his location, where he dwells, and who has seen him there, * for someone has told me he acts with great cunning. ²³ Observe and ascertain all the hiding places where he conceals himself and come back to me with a precise report, and then I shall go with you. And it will be [that] if he is in the land, I will search him out from among all the thousands of Judah."

²⁴ So they arose and went back to Ziph ahead of Saul. David and his men were in the Wilderness of Maon in the Arabah, south of Jeshimon. ²⁵ Saul and his men went to search, and people told David, so he descended to the Rock and stayed in the Wilderness of Maon. Saul heard and pursued David to the Wilderness of Maon. ²⁶ Saul went on this side of the mountain while David and his men were on that side of the mountain; David hastened to go away from Saul, but Saul

An unexpected rescue and his men were surrounding David and his men, to capture them. ²⁷ Then a messenger came to Saul saying, "Hurry and go — for the Philistines have spread out over the land!" ²⁸ So Saul returned from chasing after David, and went toward the Philistines. This is why that place is called "the Rock of Divisions."*

24

¹ David ascended from there and dwelt in the strongholds of En-gedi. ² When Saul returned from [chasing] after the Philistines, people told him, saying,

---

23:28. Because the two camps separated from each other (*Kara*). Alternatively: Saul's mind was "divided,"   i.e., indecisive, about whether to continue pursuing David or to turn back and confront the Philistines (*Targum*).

ג הִנֵּה דָוִד בְּמִדְבַּר עֵין גֶּדִי: וַיִּקַּח שָׁאוּל שְׁלֹשֶׁת אֲלָפִים אִישׁ בָּחוּר מִכָּל־יִשְׂרָאֵל וַיֵּלֶךְ לְבַקֵּשׁ אֶת־דָּוִד וַאֲנָשָׁיו עַל־פְּנֵי צוּרֵי הַיְּעֵלִים:

ד וַיָּבֹא אֶל־גִּדְרוֹת הַצֹּאן עַל־הַדֶּרֶךְ וְשָׁם מְעָרָה וַיָּבֹא שָׁאוּל לְהָסֵךְ אֶת־רַגְלָיו וְדָוִד וַאֲנָשָׁיו בְּיַרְכְּתֵי הַמְּעָרָה יֹשְׁבִים:

ה וַיֹּאמְרוּ אַנְשֵׁי דָוִד אֵלָיו הִנֵּה הַיּוֹם אֲשֶׁר־אָמַר יהוה אֵלֶיךָ הִנֵּה אָנֹכִי נֹתֵן אֶת־[אֹיִבְךָ ק] °אֹיְבֶיךָ בְּיָדֶךָ וְעָשִׂיתָ לּוֹ כַּאֲשֶׁר יִטַב בְּעֵינֶיךָ וַיָּקָם דָּוִד וַיִּכְרֹת אֶת־כְּנַף־הַמְּעִיל אֲשֶׁר־

ו לְשָׁאוּל בַּלָּט: וַיְהִי אַחֲרֵי־כֵן וַיַּךְ לֵב־דָּוִד אֹתוֹ עַל אֲשֶׁר כָּרַת אֶת־כְּנָף אֲשֶׁר לְשָׁאוּל:

ז וַיֹּאמֶר לַאֲנָשָׁיו חָלִילָה לִּי מֵיהוה אִם־אֶעֱשֶׂה אֶת־הַדָּבָר הַזֶּה לַאדֹנִי לִמְשִׁיחַ יהוה לִשְׁלֹחַ יָדִי בּוֹ כִּי־מְשִׁיחַ יהוה הוּא: וַיְשַׁסַּע דָּוִד

ח אֶת־אֲנָשָׁיו בַּדְּבָרִים וְלֹא נְתָנָם לָקוּם אֶל־שָׁאוּל וְשָׁאוּל קָם מֵהַמְּעָרָה וַיֵּלֶךְ בַּדָּרֶךְ:

ט וַיָּקָם דָּוִד אַחֲרֵי־כֵן וַיֵּצֵא °מִן־הַמְּעָרָה [מֵהַמְּעָרָה ק] וַיִּקְרָא אַחֲרֵי־שָׁאוּל לֵאמֹר אֲדֹנִי הַמֶּלֶךְ וַיַּבֵּט שָׁאוּל אַחֲרָיו וַיִּקֹּד דָּוִד אַפַּיִם אַרְצָה וַיִּשְׁתָּחוּ:

י וַיֹּאמֶר דָּוִד לְשָׁאוּל לָמָּה תִשְׁמַע אֶת־דִּבְרֵי אָדָם לֵאמֹר הִנֵּה דָוִד מְבַקֵּשׁ רָעָתֶךָ:

יא הִנֵּה הַיּוֹם הַזֶּה רָאוּ עֵינֶיךָ אֵת אֲשֶׁר־נְתָנְךָ יהוה ׀ הַיּוֹם בְּיָדִי בַּמְּעָרָה וְאָמַר לַהֲרָגְךָ וַתָּחָס עָלֶיךָ וָאֹמַר לֹא־אֶשְׁלַח יָדִי בַּאדֹנִי כִּי־מְשִׁיחַ יהוה הוּא:

יב וְאָבִי רְאֵה גַם רְאֵה אֶת־כְּנַף מְעִילְךָ בְּיָדִי כִּי בְּכָרְתִי אֶת־כְּנַף מְעִילְךָ וְלֹא הֲרַגְתִּיךָ דַּע וּרְאֵה כִּי אֵין בְּיָדִי רָעָה וָפֶשַׁע וְלֹא־חָטָאתִי לָךְ וְאַתָּה צֹדֶה אֶת־נַפְשִׁי לְקַחְתָּהּ:

יג יִשְׁפֹּט יהוה בֵּינִי וּבֵינֶךָ וּנְקָמַנִי יהוה מִמֶּךָּ וְיָדִי לֹא תִהְיֶה־בָּךְ: כַּאֲשֶׁר יֹאמַר מְשַׁל הַקַּדְמֹנִי

יד מֵרְשָׁעִים יֵצֵא רֶשַׁע וְיָדִי לֹא תִהְיֶה־בָּךְ: אַחֲרֵי מִי יָצָא מֶלֶךְ יִשְׂרָאֵל אַחֲרֵי

טו מִי אַתָּה רֹדֵף אַחֲרֵי כֶּלֶב מֵת אַחֲרֵי פַּרְעֹשׁ אֶחָד: וְהָיָה יהוה לְדַיָּן וְשָׁפַט

טז בֵּינִי וּבֵינֶךָ וְיֵרֶא וְיָרֵב אֶת־רִיבִי וְיִשְׁפְּטֵנִי מִיָּדֶךָ: וַיְהִי ׀ כְּכַלּוֹת

יז דָּוִד לְדַבֵּר אֶת־הַדְּבָרִים הָאֵלֶּה אֶל־שָׁאוּל וַיֹּאמֶר שָׁאוּל הֲקֹלְךָ זֶה בְּנִי דָוִד וַיִּשָּׂא שָׁאוּל קֹלוֹ וַיֵּבְךְּ:

יח וַיֹּאמֶר אֶל־דָּוִד צַדִּיק אַתָּה מִמֶּנִּי כִּי אַתָּה גְּמַלְתַּנִי הַטּוֹבָה וַאֲנִי גְּמַלְתִּיךָ הָרָעָה: °וְאַת [וְאַתָּה ק] הִגַּדְתָּ הַיּוֹם

יט אֵת אֲשֶׁר־עָשִׂיתָה אִתִּי טוֹבָה אֵת אֲשֶׁר סִגְּרַנִי יהוה בְּיָדְךָ וְלֹא הֲרַגְתָּנִי:

כ וְכִי־יִמְצָא אִישׁ אֶת־אֹיְבוֹ וְשִׁלְּחוֹ בְּדֶרֶךְ טוֹבָה וַיהוה יְשַׁלֶּמְךָ טוֹבָה תַּחַת הַיּוֹם הַזֶּה אֲשֶׁר עָשִׂיתָה לִי:

כא וְעַתָּה הִנֵּה יָדַעְתִּי כִּי מָלֹךְ תִּמְלוֹךְ וְקָמָה בְּיָדְךָ מַמְלֶכֶת יִשְׂרָאֵל:

כב וְעַתָּה הִשָּׁבְעָה לִּי בַּיהוה אִם־תַּכְרִית אֶת־זַרְעִי אַחֲרָי וְאִם־תַּשְׁמִיד אֶת־שְׁמִי מִבֵּית אָבִי: וַיִּשָּׁבַע דָּוִד לְשָׁאוּל

כג וַיֵּלֶךְ שָׁאוּל אֶל־בֵּיתוֹ וְדָוִד וַאֲנָשָׁיו עָלוּ עַל־הַמְּצוּדָה:

כה א וַיָּמָת שְׁמוּאֵל וַיִּקָּבְצוּ כָל־יִשְׂרָאֵל וַיִּסְפְּדוּ־לוֹ וַיִּקְבְּרֻהוּ בְּבֵיתוֹ בָּרָמָה

24:6. David felt that it was disrespectful for him to have damaged a garment of the king, so surely David rejected his men's contention that he should slay Saul.

24:8. They had been unanimous in their insistence that Saul be attacked, but David broke their ranks with his vehement verbal onslaught.

24:13. If God brings retribution upon you, it will not be through me.

Saul resumes his pursuit "Behold, David is in the Wilderness of En-gedi." ³ So Saul took three thousand chosen men, from all of Israel, and went to seek David and his men over the rocks of the wild goats. ⁴ He came to sheep enclosures along the road, and there was a cave there, which Saul entered to relieve himself. David and his men were sitting at the far end of the cave.

David spares Saul's life ⁵ David's men said to him, "Behold, this is the day of which HASHEM said to you, 'Behold, I am delivering your enemy into your hand, and you may do to him as you please'!" So David arose and stealthily cut off a corner of Saul's robe. ⁶ Afterwards, however, David's conscience troubled him for having cut off the corner of Saul's [garment]. * ⁷ He said to his men, "It would be sacrilegious before HASHEM for me to do this thing to my lord, the anointed of HASHEM, to send forth my hand against him, for he is the anointed of HASHEM!" ⁸ And David sundered his men with rhetoric, * and did not permit them to rise up against Saul. Then Saul rose up from the cave and continued on the way.

A passionate declamation ⁹ After that David arose and stepped out of the cave, calling after Saul, saying, "My lord, the king!" Saul looked behind him, and David bowed down on his face to the ground, and he prostrated himself. ¹⁰ David said to Saul, "Why do you listen to the words of someone who says, 'Behold, David seeks to harm you'? ¹¹ Behold! This day your eyes have seen that HASHEM delivered you into my hand in the cave today, and [although] someone said to kill you, [my soul] took pity on you, and I said, 'I shall not send forth my hand against my lord, for he is the anointed of HASHEM!' ¹² See now, my father, indeed, see the corner of your coat that is in my hand, for since I have cut off the corner of your coat and have not killed you, you should know and see that there is no evil or rebellion in my hand, and that I have not sinned against you — yet you hunt my soul to take it! ¹³ May HASHEM judge between me and you, and may HASHEM avenge me from you — but my hand will not act against you. * ¹⁴ As the ancient proverb says, 'Wickedness issues from the wicked'; but my hand will not act against you. ¹⁵ After whom has the king of Israel gone out? Whom are you pursuing? After [someone as insignificant as] a dead dog, after a single flea! ¹⁶ May HASHEM be an arbiter, and judge between me and you; may He see and take up my grievance, and vindicate me from your hand."

Saul's remorse ¹⁷ And it was when David finished speaking these words to Saul, Saul said, "Is that your voice, my son David?" — and Saul raised his voice and wept. ¹⁸ He said to David, "You are more righteous than I, for you have repaid me with goodness while I have repaid you with wickedness. ¹⁹ You have proven today that you have done [only] good with me, for HASHEM delivered me into your hand but you did not kill me. ²⁰ Does a man find his enemy and then send him off on a good way? May HASHEM repay you with beneficence for what you have done to me this day. ²¹ Now behold! I know that you will certainly reign, and the kingship over Israel shall be established in your hand. ²² So now, swear to me by HASHEM that you will not annihilate my descendants after me and that you will not destroy my name from my father's house."

²³ David swore to Saul. Saul went to his house and David and his men ascended to the stronghold.

25 *Samuel dies* ¹ **S**amuel died, and all of Israel gathered and eulogized him, and they buried him at his home in Ramah.

ב וַיָּ֣קָם דָּוִ֔ד וַיֵּ֖רֶד אֶל־מִדְבַּ֣ר פָּארָ֑ן: וְאִ֨ישׁ בְּמָע֜וֹן וּמַעֲשֵׂ֣הוּ בַכַּרְמֶ֗ל
וְהָאִישׁ֙ גָּד֣וֹל מְאֹ֔ד וְל֣וֹ צֹ֗אן שְׁלֹֽשֶׁת־אֲלָפִ֛ים וְאֶ֥לֶף עִזִּ֖ים וַיְהִ֛י בִּגְזֹ֥ז אֶת־
ג צֹאנ֖וֹ בַּכַּרְמֶֽל: וְשֵׁ֤ם הָאִישׁ֙ נָבָ֔ל וְשֵׁ֥ם אִשְׁתּ֖וֹ אֲבִגָ֑יִל וְהָאִשָּׁ֤ה טֽוֹבַת־שֶׂ֙כֶל֙
ד וִ֣יפַת תֹּ֔אַר וְהָאִ֥ישׁ קָשֶׁ֛ה וְרַ֥ע מַעֲלָלִ֖ים וְה֥וּא °כלבו [°כָלִבִּ֖י ק]: וַיִּשְׁמַ֥ע
ה דָוִ֖ד בַּמִּדְבָּ֑ר כִּֽי־גֹזֵ֥ז נָבָ֖ל אֶת־צֹאנֽוֹ: וַיִּשְׁלַ֥ח דָּוִ֖ד עֲשָׂרָ֣ה נְעָרִ֑ים וַיֹּ֨אמֶר דָּוִ֜ד
לַנְּעָרִ֗ים עֲל֤וּ כַרְמֶ֙לָה֙ וּבָאתֶ֣ם אֶל־נָבָ֔ל וּשְׁאֶלְתֶּם־ל֥וֹ בִשְׁמִ֖י לְשָׁלֽוֹם:
ו וַאֲמַרְתֶּ֣ם כֹּ֣ה לֶחָ֑י וְאַתָּ֤ה שָׁלוֹם֙ וּבֵֽיתְךָ֣ שָׁל֔וֹם וְכֹ֥ל אֲשֶׁר־לְךָ֖ שָׁלֽוֹם: וְעַתָּ֗ה
ז שָׁמַ֙עְתִּי֙ כִּ֣י גֹזְזִ֣ים לָ֔ךְ עַתָּ֣ה הָרֹעִ֤ים אֲשֶׁר־לְךָ֙ הָי֣וּ עִמָּ֔נוּ לֹ֣א הֶכְלַמְנ֔וּם וְלֹֽא־
ח נִפְקַ֤ד לָהֶם֙ מְא֔וּמָה כָּל־יְמֵ֖י הֱיוֹתָ֣ם בַּכַּרְמֶֽל: שְׁאַ֨ל אֶת־נְעָרֶ֜יךָ וְיַגִּ֣ידוּ לָ֗ךְ
וְיִמְצְא֨וּ הַנְּעָרִ֥ים חֵן֙ בְּעֵינֶ֔יךָ כִּֽי־עַל־י֥וֹם ט֖וֹב °בנו [°בָּ֑אנוּ ק] תְּנָה־נָּ֗א אֵת֩
ט אֲשֶׁ֨ר תִּמְצָ֤א יָֽדְךָ֙ לַעֲבָדֶ֔יךָ וּלְבִנְךָ֖ לְדָוִֽד: וַיָּבֹ֙אוּ֙ נַעֲרֵ֣י דָוִ֔ד וַיְדַבְּר֧וּ אֶל־נָבָ֛ל
י כְּכָל־הַדְּבָרִ֥ים הָאֵ֖לֶּה בְּשֵׁ֣ם דָּוִ֑ד וַיָּנֽוּחוּ: וַיַּ֨עַן נָבָ֜ל אֶת־עַבְדֵ֤י דָוִד֙ וַיֹּ֔אמֶר מִ֣י
יא דָוִ֔ד וּמִ֖י בֶן־יִשָׁ֑י הַיּוֹם֙ רַבּ֣וּ עֲבָדִ֔ים הַמִּתְפָּ֣רְצִ֔ים אִ֖ישׁ מִפְּנֵ֥י אֲדֹנָֽיו: וְלָקַחְתִּ֞י
אֶת־לַחְמִ֣י וְאֶת־מֵימַ֗י וְאֵת֙ טִבְחָתִ֔י אֲשֶׁ֥ר טָבַ֖חְתִּי לְגֹֽזְזָ֑י וְנָֽתַתִּי֙ לַאֲנָשִׁ֔ים
יב אֲשֶׁר֙ לֹ֣א יָדַ֔עְתִּי אֵ֥י מִזֶּ֖ה הֵֽמָּה: וַיַּהַפְכ֥וּ נַעֲרֵֽי־דָוִ֖ד לְדַרְכָּ֑ם וַיָּשֻׁ֙בוּ֙ וַיָּבֹ֔אוּ
יג וַיַּגִּ֣דוּ ל֔וֹ כְּכֹ֖ל הַדְּבָרִ֥ים הָאֵֽלֶּה: וַיֹּ֩אמֶר֩ דָּוִ֨ד לַאֲנָשָׁ֜יו חִגְר֣וּ ׀ אִ֣ישׁ אֶת־חַרְבּ֗וֹ
וַֽיַּחְגְּר֙וּ֙ אִ֣ישׁ אֶת־חַרְבּ֔וֹ וַיַּחְגֹּ֥ר גַּם־דָּוִ֖ד אֶת־חַרְבּ֑וֹ וַֽיַּעֲל֣וּ ׀ אַחֲרֵ֣י דָוִ֗ד
יד כְּאַרְבַּ֤ע מֵאוֹת֙ אִ֔ישׁ וּמָאתַ֖יִם יָשְׁב֥וּ עַל־הַכֵּלִֽים: וְלַאֲבִיגַ֙יִל֙ אֵ֣שֶׁת נָבָ֔ל
הִגִּ֣יד נַֽעַר־אֶחָ֣ד מֵהַנְּעָרִ֣ים לֵאמֹ֑ר הִנֵּ֣ה שָׁלַח֩ דָּוִ֨ד ׀ מַלְאָכִ֤ים ׀ מֵֽהַמִּדְבָּר֙
טו לְבָרֵ֣ךְ אֶת־אֲדֹנֵ֔ינוּ וַיָּ֖עַט בָּהֶֽם: וְהָ֣אֲנָשִׁ֔ים טֹבִ֥ים לָ֖נוּ מְאֹ֑ד וְלֹ֤א הָכְלַ֙מְנוּ֙
טז וְלֹֽא־פָקַ֣דְנוּ מְא֔וּמָה כָּל־יְמֵי֙ הִתְהַלַּ֣כְנוּ אִתָּ֔ם בִּֽהְיוֹתֵ֖נוּ בַּשָּׂדֶֽה: חוֹמָה֙ הָי֣וּ
יז עָלֵ֔ינוּ גַּם־לַ֖יְלָה גַּם־יוֹמָ֑ם כָּל־יְמֵ֛י הֱיוֹתֵ֥נוּ עִמָּ֖ם רֹעִ֥ים הַצֹּֽאן: וְעַתָּ֗ה דְּעִ֤י
וּרְאִי֙ מַֽה־תַּעֲשִׂ֔י כִּֽי־כָלְתָ֧ה הָרָעָ֛ה אֶל־אֲדֹנֵ֖ינוּ וְעַ֣ל כָּל־בֵּית֑וֹ וְהוּא֙ בֶּן־
יח בְּלִיַּ֔עַל מִדַּבֵּ֖ר אֵלָֽיו: וַתְּמַהֵ֣ר °אבוגיל [°אֲבִיגַ֗יִל ק] וַתִּקַּח֩ מָאתַ֨יִם לֶ֜חֶם
וּשְׁנַ֣יִם נִבְלֵי־יַ֗יִן וְחָמֵ֤שׁ צֹאן֙ °עשוות [°עֲשׂוּיֹת֙ ק] וְחָמֵ֤שׁ סְאִים֙ קָלִ֔י וּמֵאָ֤ה
יט צִמֻּקִים֙ וּמָאתַ֣יִם דְּבֵלִ֔ים וַתָּ֖שֶׂם עַל־הַחֲמֹרִֽים: וַתֹּ֤אמֶר לִנְעָרֶ֙יהָ֙ עִבְר֣וּ לְפָנַ֔י
הִנְנִ֖י אַחֲרֵיכֶ֣ם בָּאָ֑ה וּלְאִישָׁ֥הּ נָבָ֖ל לֹ֥א הִגִּֽידָה: וְהָיָ֡ה הִ֣יא ׀ רֹכֶ֣בֶת עַל־
כ הַחֲמ֡וֹר וְיֹרֶ֜דֶת בְּסֵ֣תֶר הָהָ֗ר וְהִנֵּ֤ה דָוִד֙ וַאֲנָשָׁ֔יו יֹרְדִ֖ים לִקְרָאתָ֑הּ וַתִּפְגֹּ֖שׁ
כא אֹתָֽם: וְדָוִ֣ד אָמַ֗ר אַךְ֩ לַשֶּׁ֨קֶר שָׁמַ֜רְתִּי אֶת־כָּל־אֲשֶׁ֤ר לָזֶה֙ בַּמִּדְבָּ֔ר וְלֹֽא־נִפְקַ֥ד
כב מִכָּל־אֲשֶׁר־ל֖וֹ מְא֑וּמָה וַיָּֽשֶׁב־לִ֥י רָעָ֖ה תַּ֥חַת טוֹבָֽה: כֹּֽה־יַעֲשֶׂ֧ה אֱלֹהִ֛ים
לְאֹיְבֵ֥י דָוִ֖ד וְכֹ֣ה יֹסִ֑יף אִם־אַשְׁאִ֧יר מִכָּל־אֲשֶׁר־ל֛וֹ עַד־הַבֹּ֖קֶר מַשְׁתִּ֥ין בְּקִֽיר:

25:6. May the prosperity of this sheep-shearing be repeated as long as you live! (*Rashi*).
25:7. We fulfilled their every request and did not shame them with rejection (*Rashi*).
25:9. Though exhausted from the trip, they did not rest until they had delivered the message to Nabal.

25:22. "David's enemies" is a euphemism for David himself. He took an oath to punish Nabal's cruelty. Since it was known that David had been anointed as the future king, Nabal's insolence was tantamount to rebellion and punishable by death (*Ralbag*).
The term מַשְׁתִּין בְּקִיר, literally, *one that urinates against*

NABAL AND
ABIGAIL
25:1-44

David arose and descended to the Wilderness of Paran.
² *There was a man in Maon whose business was in Carmel. The man was very wealthy; he owned three thousand sheep and a thousand goats. [The following once] happened at the shearing of his sheep in Carmel:* ³ *(The man's name was Nabal and his wife's name was Abigail; the woman was intelligent and beautiful, but the man was difficult and an evildoer; he was a descendant*

David asks
for food

of Caleb.) ⁴ *David heard in the wilderness that Nabal was shearing his sheep,* ⁵ *so David sent ten attendants, and David said to the attendants, "Go up to Carmel and approach Nabal, inquiring after his welfare, in my name.* ⁶ *And say: 'Such [success] for life!* *Peace be upon you, peace be upon your household, and peace be upon all that is yours!* ⁷ *And now, I have heard that they are shearing for you. Now, your shepherds stayed with us, we did not shame them* *and they did not lack anything all the days they were in Carmel —* ⁸ *ask your attendants and they will tell you [so]. [Therefore] let my attendants find favor in your eyes, for we have come because of [your] celebration — please give whatever you can to your servants and to your son, to David.' "*

Nabal's
insolent
selfishness

⁹ *David's attendants came and spoke in accordance with all these words to Nabal in David's name, and then rested.* * ¹⁰ *Nabal replied to David's servants, and said, "Who is David and who is the son of Jesse? These days the rebellious servants have increased, each against his master!* ¹¹ *Should I take from my bread and my water and my meat that I have slaughtered for my shearers and give them to men about whose origin I do not know?"*

¹² *David's attendants turned around to their way, and they went back, arrived and reported to him in accordance with all these words.* ¹³ *David said to his men, "Each man gird his sword!" Each man girded his sword, and David, too, girded his sword. About four hundred men went after David, and two hundred others stayed with the belongings.*

¹⁴ *One young man from the attendants told Abigail, Nabal's wife, saying, "Behold! David sent messengers from the wilderness to greet our master and he drove them off.* ¹⁵ *These men were very good to us; we were not shamed, nor were we lacking anything all the days that we traveled with them, when we were in the field.* ¹⁶ *They were a [protective] wall over us, both by night and by day, all the days we were with them tending the sheep.* ¹⁷ *And now be aware and determine what to do, for the evil [decree] has been made final against our master and against his entire household, and he himself is too base a person even to talk to."*

Abigail's
wisdom and
courage
saves her
undeserving
husband

¹⁸ *So Abigail hurried and took two hundred breads, two containers of wine, five cooked sheep, five se'ahs of toasted grain, a hundred raisin-clusters, and two hundred cakes of pressed figs, and she put them on the donkeys.* ¹⁹ *She said to her attendants, "Go on ahead of me; behold, I am coming behind you." But she did not tell Nabal her husband.* ²⁰ *Then it happened, as she was riding on the donkey, clandestinely descending the mountain, behold — David and his men were descending [the other mountain] toward her, and she met them.*

²¹ *Now David had said, "It was for naught that I guarded all of this man's possessions in the desert and there was not missing anything from all that belonged to him; yet he has repaid my kindness with evil.* ²² *Such shall God do to David's enemies* *and such shall He do further, if I leave over until morning of all that belongs to him so much as a dog!"* *

כג וַתֵּ֤רֶא אֲבִיגַ֙יִל֙ אֶת־דָּוִ֔ד וַתְּמַהֵ֕ר וַתֵּ֖רֶד מֵעַ֣ל הַחֲמ֑וֹר וַתִּפֹּ֞ל לְאַפֵּ֤י דָוִד֙ עַל־

כד פָּנֶ֔יהָ וַתִּשְׁתַּ֖חוּ אָֽרֶץ: וַתִּפֹּל֙ עַל־רַגְלָ֔יו וַתֹּ֕אמֶר בִּי־אֲנִ֥י אֲדֹנִ֖י הֶֽעָוֺ֑ן וּתְדַבֶּר־

כה נָ֤א אֲמָֽתְךָ֙ בְּאָזְנֶ֔יךָ וּשְׁמַ֕ע אֵ֖ת דִּבְרֵ֥י אֲמָתֶֽךָ: אַל־נָ֣א יָשִׂ֣ים אֲדֹנִ֣י ׀ אֶת־לִבּ֡וֹ

אֶל־אִישׁ֩ הַבְּלִיַּ֨עַל הַזֶּ֜ה עַל־נָבָ֗ל כִּ֤י כִשְׁמוֹ֙ כֶּן־ה֔וּא נָבָ֣ל שְׁמ֔וֹ וּנְבָלָ֖ה עִמּ֑וֹ

כו וַאֲנִי֙ אֲמָ֣תְךָ֔ לֹ֤א רָאִ֙יתִי֙ אֶת־נַעֲרֵ֣י אֲדֹנִ֔י אֲשֶׁ֖ר שָׁלָֽחְתָּ: °וְעַתָּ֣ה אֲדֹנִ֣י חַי־ °נ״א וְאַתָּה

יְהוָ֣ה וְחֵי־נַפְשְׁךָ֗ אֲשֶׁ֨ר מְנָעֲךָ֤ יְהוָה֙ מִבּ֣וֹא בְדָמִ֔ים וְהוֹשֵׁ֥עַ יָדְךָ֖ לָ֑ךְ וְעַתָּ֗ה

כז יִֽהְי֤וּ כְנָבָל֙ אֹֽיְבֶ֔יךָ וְהַֽמְבַקְשִׁ֥ים אֶל־אֲדֹנִ֖י רָעָ֑ה וְעַתָּה֙ הַבְּרָכָ֣ה הַזֹּ֔את אֲשֶׁר־

כח הֵבִ֤יא שִׁפְחָֽתְךָ֙ לַֽאדֹנִ֔י וְנִתְּנָה֙ לַנְּעָרִ֔ים הַמִּֽתְהַלְּכִ֖ים בְּרַגְלֵ֥י אֲדֹנִֽי: שָׂ֣א נָ֗א

לְפֶ֣שַׁע אֲמָתֶ֔ךָ כִּ֣י עָשֹֽׂה־יַעֲשֶׂ֩ה יְהוָ֨ה לַֽאדֹנִ֜י בַּ֣יִת נֶאֱמָ֗ן כִּֽי־מִלְחֲמ֤וֹת יְהוָה֙

כט אֲדֹנִ֣י נִלְחָ֔ם וְרָעָ֛ה לֹא־תִמָּצֵ֥א בְךָ֖ מִיָּמֶֽיךָ: וַיָּ֤קָם אָדָם֙ לִרְדָפְךָ֔ וּלְבַקֵּ֖שׁ אֶת־

נַפְשֶׁ֑ךָ וְֽהָיְתָה֩ נֶ֨פֶשׁ אֲדֹנִ֜י צְרוּרָ֣ה ׀ בִּצְר֣וֹר הַחַיִּ֗ים אֵ֚ת יְהוָ֣ה אֱלֹהֶ֔יךָ וְאֵ֨ת

ל נֶ֤פֶשׁ אֹֽיְבֶ֙יךָ֙ יְקַלְּעֶ֔נָּה בְּת֖וֹךְ כַּ֥ף הַקָּֽלַע: וְהָיָ֗ה כִּֽי־יַעֲשֶׂ֤ה יְהוָה֙ לַֽאדֹנִ֔י כְּכֹ֛ל

לא אֲשֶׁר־דִּבֶּ֥ר אֶת־הַטּוֹבָ֖ה עָלֶ֑יךָ וְצִוְּךָ֥ לְנָגִ֖יד עַל־יִשְׂרָאֵֽל: וְלֹ֣א תִֽהְיֶ֣ה זֹ֣את ׀

לְךָ֡ לְפוּקָה֩ וּלְמִכְשׁ֨וֹל לֵ֜ב לַֽאדֹנִ֗י וְלִשְׁפָּךְ־דָּם֙ חִנָּ֔ם וּלְהוֹשִׁ֥יעַ אֲדֹנִ֖י ל֑וֹ וְהֵיטִ֤ב

לב יְהוָה֙ לַֽאדֹנִ֔י וְזָכַרְתָּ֖ אֶת־אֲמָתֶֽךָ: וַיֹּ֥אמֶר דָּוִ֖ד לַאֲבִיגַ֑יִל בָּר֤וּךְ יְהוָה֙

לג אֱלֹהֵ֣י יִשְׂרָאֵ֔ל אֲשֶׁ֧ר שְׁלָחֵ֛ךְ הַיּ֥וֹם הַזֶּ֖ה לִקְרָאתִֽי: וּבָר֣וּךְ טַעְמֵ֔ךְ וּבְרוּכָ֖ה אָ֑תְּ

לד אֲשֶׁ֨ר כְּלִתִ֜נִי הַיּ֤וֹם הַזֶּה֙ מִבּ֣וֹא בְדָמִ֔ים וְהֹשֵׁ֥עַ יָדִ֖י לִֽי: וְאוּלָ֗ם חַי־יְהוָה֙ אֱלֹהֵ֣י

יִשְׂרָאֵ֔ל אֲשֶׁ֣ר מְנָעַ֔נִי מֵהָרַ֖ע אֹתָ֑ךְ כִּ֣י ׀ לוּלֵ֣י מִהַ֗רְתְּ °וַתָּבֹ֙אתִ֙ °וַתָּבֹ֣את ק׳

[

לה לִקְרָאתִ֔י כִּ֣י אִם־נוֹתַ֤ר לְנָבָל֙ עַד־א֣וֹר הַבֹּ֔קֶר מַשְׁתִּ֖ין בְּקִֽיר: וַיִּקַּ֤ח דָּוִד֙ מִיָּדָ֔הּ

אֵ֥ת אֲשֶׁר־הֵבִ֖יאָה ל֑וֹ וְלָ֣הּ אָמַ֗ר עֲלִ֤י לְשָׁלוֹם֙ לְבֵיתֵ֔ךְ רְאִי֙ שָׁמַ֣עְתִּי בְקוֹלֵ֔ךְ

לו וָאֶשָּׂ֖א פָּנָֽיִךְ: וַתָּבֹ֣א אֲבִיגַ֣יִל ׀ אֶל־נָבָ֗ל וְהִנֵּה־לוֹ֨ מִשְׁתֶּ֤ה בְּבֵיתוֹ֙ כְּמִשְׁתֵּ֣ה

הַמֶּ֔לֶךְ וְלֵ֤ב נָבָל֙ ט֣וֹב עָלָ֔יו וְה֥וּא שִׁכֹּ֖ר עַד־מְאֹ֑ד וְלֹֽא־הִגִּ֤ידָה לּוֹ֙ דָּבָ֣ר קָטֹ֣ן

לז וְגָד֔וֹל עַד־א֖וֹר הַבֹּֽקֶר: וַיְהִ֣י בַבֹּ֗קֶר בְּצֵ֤את הַיַּ֙יִן֙ מִנָּבָ֔ל וַתַּגֶּד־ל֣וֹ אִשְׁתּ֔וֹ אֶת־

לח הַדְּבָרִ֣ים הָאֵ֑לֶּה וַיָּ֤מָת לִבּוֹ֙ בְּקִרְבּ֔וֹ וְה֖וּא הָיָ֥ה לְאָֽבֶן: וַֽיְהִ֖י כַּעֲשֶׂ֣רֶת הַיָּמִ֑ים

לט וַיִּגֹּ֧ף יְהוָ֛ה אֶת־נָבָ֖ל וַיָּמֹֽת: וַיִּשְׁמַ֣ע דָּוִד֮ כִּ֣י מֵ֣ת נָבָל֒ וַיֹּ֡אמֶר בָּר֣וּךְ יְהוָ֡ה אֲשֶׁ֣ר

רָב֩ אֶת־רִ֨יב חֶרְפָּתִ֜י מִיַּ֣ד נָבָ֗ל וְאֶת־עַבְדּוֹ֙ חָשַׂ֣ךְ מֵֽרָעָ֔ה וְאֵ֗ת רָעַ֤ת נָבָל֙

הֵשִׁ֤יב יְהוָה֙ בְּרֹאשׁ֑וֹ וַיִּשְׁלַ֤ח דָּוִד֙ וַיְדַבֵּ֣ר בַּאֲבִיגַ֔יִל לְקַחְתָּ֥הּ ל֖וֹ לְאִשָּֽׁה:

מ וַיָּבֹ֜אוּ עַבְדֵ֥י דָוִ֛ד אֶל־אֲבִיגַ֖יִל הַכַּרְמֶ֑לָה וַיְדַבְּר֤וּ אֵלֶ֙יהָ֙ לֵאמֹ֔ר דָּוִד֙ שְׁלָחָ֣נוּ

מא אֵלַ֔יִךְ לְקַחְתֵּ֥ךְ ל֖וֹ לְאִשָּֽׁה: וַתָּ֕קָם וַתִּשְׁתַּ֖חוּ אַפַּ֣יִם אָ֑רְצָה וַתֹּ֗אמֶר הִנֵּ֤ה אֲמָֽתְךָ֙

מב לְשִׁפְחָ֔ה לִרְחֹ֕ץ רַגְלֵ֖י עַבְדֵ֥י אֲדֹנִֽי: וַתְּמַהֵ֞ר וַתָּ֣קָם אֲבִיגַ֗יִל וַתִּרְכַּב֙ עַֽל־

הַחֲמ֔וֹר וְחָמֵשׁ֙ נַעֲרֹתֶ֔יהָ הַהֹלְכ֖וֹת לְרַגְלָ֑הּ וַתֵּ֗לֶךְ אַֽחֲרֵי֙ מַלְאֲכֵ֣י דָוִ֔ד וַתְּהִי־

---

the wall, refers to males, and can be applied to either human beings or dogs. Thus, David warns that no male offspring of Nabal's will remain (*Metzudos*); or, not even a dog of Nabal's will remain (*Radak*).

25:25. A play on words: The Hebrew name נָבָל, *Nabal*, is

related to נְבָלָה, *revulsion*.

25:26. Though wealthy (v. 2), he is unimportant and powerless. May all your enemies be as weak and insignificant!

25:37. Nabal was distressed by her extravagant gift to David.

²³ When Abigail saw David she hurried and dismounted from the donkey, and fell on her face before David and prostrated herself to the ground. ²⁴ She fell at his feet and said, "With me myself, my lord, lies the sin. Let your maidservant please speak in your ears, and hear out the words of your maidservant. ²⁵ Let my lord not set his heart against this base man — against Nabal — for he is as his name implies — Nabal is his name and revulsion is his trait; * and I, your maidservant, did not see my lord's attendants whom you sent. ²⁶ Now, my lord, as HASHEM lives — and by your life — as HASHEM has prevented you from coming to bloodshed and from your own hand avenging you, may all your enemies and all those who wish evil upon my lord be like Nabal!* ²⁷ And now, this homage that your maidservant has brought to my lord — let it be given to the attendants who are traveling with my lord. ²⁸ Please forgive the sin of your maidservant, for HASHEM shall certainly make for my lord an enduring house, for my lord fights the wars of HASHEM; and no blame has been found in you in your days. ²⁹ A man has risen up to pursue you and to seek your life! May my lord's soul be bound up in the bond of life, with HASHEM, your God, and may He hurl away the soul of your enemies as one shoots a stone from a slingshot. ³⁰ And may it be that when HASHEM performs for my lord all the beneficence of which He has spoken regarding you, and appoints you as leader over Israel, ³¹ that this not be for you a stumbling block and a moral hindrance for my lord, to have shed innocent blood for my lord to have avenged himself! And may HASHEM act beneficently towards my lord, and may you [then] remember your maidservant."

David relents and expresses admiration for Abigail ³² David then said to Abigail, "Blessed is HASHEM, God of Israel, Who sent you this day to meet me. ³³ And blessed is your advice and blessed are you, who have restrained me from coming to bloodshed and avenging myself by my own hand. ³⁴ Truly, as HASHEM, God of Israel, lives — Who has prevented me from harming you — had you not hurried and come to meet me, by morning's light there would not have remained to Nabal as much as a dog." ³⁵ David then accepted from her what she had brought to him. He said to her, "Go up in peace to your house. See, I have heeded your advice, and I shall show you grace."

³⁶ Abigail then came to Nabal and behold, he was having a feast in his house — a feast fit for the king. Nabal's heart was pleased about himself, and he was very drunk, so she did not tell him anything minor or major until the morning's light. ³⁷ And it was in the morning, when Nabal had become sober, his wife told him of these matters, his heart [seemed to have] died within him, and he was stunned. *

Nabal dies and David marries Abigail ³⁸ It happened after ten days that HASHEM struck Nabal and he died. ³⁹ When David heard that Nabal had died, he said, "Blessed is HASHEM, Who has taken up the cause of my disgrace from the hand of Nabal, and has prevented His servant from wrongdoing; and HASHEM has returned Nabal's evil upon his head." Then David sent [agents] and spoke regarding Abigail to take her to himself as a wife.

⁴⁰ David's servants came to Abigail to Carmel and spoke to her saying, "David has sent us to you, to take you for himself as a wife." ⁴¹ She arose and prostrated herself to the ground and said, "Your maidservant is merely a handmaid to wash the feet of the servants of my lord."

⁴² Abigail then hurried, arose and mounted the donkey, with her five maids traveling with her, and she followed David's messengers and became

מג לוֹ לְאִשָּׁה: וְאֶת־אֲחִינֹעַם לָקַח דָּוִד מִיִּזְרְעֶאל וַתִּהְיֶיןָ גַּם־שְׁתֵּיהֶן לוֹ

מד לְנָשִׁים: וְשָׁאוּל נָתַן אֶת־מִיכַל בִּתּוֹ אֵשֶׁת דָּוִד לְפַלְטִי בֶן־לַיִשׁ

כו א אֲשֶׁר מִגַּלִּים: וַיָּבֹאוּ הַזִּפִים אֶל־שָׁאוּל הַגִּבְעָתָה לֵאמֹר הֲלוֹא דָוִד

ב מִסְתַּתֵּר בְּגִבְעַת הַחֲכִילָה עַל פְּנֵי הַיְשִׁימֹן: וַיָּקָם שָׁאוּל וַיֵּרֶד אֶל־מִדְבַּר־

זִיף וְאִתּוֹ שְׁלֹשֶׁת־אֲלָפִים אִישׁ בְּחוּרֵי יִשְׂרָאֵל לְבַקֵּשׁ אֶת־דָּוִד בְּמִדְבַּר־

ג זִיף: וַיִּחַן שָׁאוּל בְּגִבְעַת הַחֲכִילָה אֲשֶׁר עַל־פְּנֵי הַיְשִׁימֹן עַל־הַדָּרֶךְ וְדָוִד

ד יֹשֵׁב בַּמִּדְבָּר וַיַּרְא כִּי בָא שָׁאוּל אַחֲרָיו הַמִּדְבָּרָה: וַיִּשְׁלַח דָּוִד מְרַגְּלִים

ה וַיֵּדַע כִּי־בָא שָׁאוּל אֶל־נָכוֹן: וַיָּקָם דָּוִד וַיָּבֹא אֶל־הַמָּקוֹם אֲשֶׁר חָנָה־שָׁם

שָׁאוּל וַיַּרְא דָּוִד אֶת־הַמָּקוֹם אֲשֶׁר שָׁכַב־שָׁם שָׁאוּל וְאַבְנֵר בֶּן־נֵר שַׂר־

ו צְבָאוֹ וְשָׁאוּל שֹׁכֵב בַּמַּעְגָּל וְהָעָם חֹנִים °סביבתו [°סְבִיבֹתָיו ק]: וַיַּעַן

דָּוִד וַיֹּאמֶר | אֶל־אֲחִימֶלֶךְ הַחִתִּי וְאֶל־אֲבִישַׁי בֶּן־צְרוּיָה אֲחִי יוֹאָב לֵאמֹר

ז מִי־יֵרֵד אִתִּי אֶל־שָׁאוּל אֶל־הַמַּחֲנֶה וַיֹּאמֶר אֲבִישַׁי אֲנִי אֵרֵד עִמָּךְ: וַיָּבֹא

דָוִד וַאֲבִישַׁי | אֶל־הָעָם לַיְלָה וְהִנֵּה שָׁאוּל שֹׁכֵב יָשֵׁן בַּמַּעְגָּל וַחֲנִיתוֹ

מְעוּכָה־בָאָרֶץ [°מראשתו °מְרַאֲשֹׁתָיו ק] וְאַבְנֵר וְהָעָם שֹׁכְבִים °סביבתו

ח [°סְבִיבֹתָיו ק]: וַיֹּאמֶר אֲבִישַׁי אֶל־דָּוִד סִגַּר אֱלֹהִים הַיּוֹם

אֶת־אוֹיִבְךָ בְּיָדֶךָ וְעַתָּה אַכֶּנּוּ נָא בַּחֲנִית וּבָאָרֶץ פַּעַם אַחַת וְלֹא אֶשְׁנֶה

ט לוֹ: וַיֹּאמֶר דָּוִד אֶל־אֲבִישַׁי אַל־תַּשְׁחִיתֵהוּ כִּי מִי שָׁלַח יָדוֹ בִּמְשִׁיחַ

י יְהֹוָה וְנִקָּה: וַיֹּאמֶר דָּוִד חַי־יְהֹוָה כִּי אִם־יְהֹוָה יִגָּפֶנּוּ אוֹ־יוֹמוֹ יָבוֹא וָמֵת

יא אוֹ בַמִּלְחָמָה יֵרֵד וְנִסְפָּה: חָלִילָה לִּי מֵיהֹוָה מִשְּׁלֹחַ יָדִי בִּמְשִׁיחַ יְהֹוָה

וְעַתָּה קַח־נָא אֶת־הַחֲנִית אֲשֶׁר [°מראשתו °מְרַאֲשֹׁתָיו ק] וְאֶת־צַפַּחַת

יב הַמַּיִם וְנֵלֵכָה לָּנוּ: וַיִּקַּח דָּוִד אֶת־הַחֲנִית וְאֶת־צַפַּחַת הַמַּיִם מֵרַאֲשֹׁתֵי

שָׁאוּל וַיֵּלְכוּ לָהֶם וְאֵין רֹאֶה וְאֵין יוֹדֵעַ וְאֵין מֵקִיץ כִּי כֻלָּם יְשֵׁנִים כִּי

יג תַּרְדֵּמַת יְהֹוָה נָפְלָה עֲלֵיהֶם: וַיַּעֲבֹר דָּוִד הָעֵבֶר וַיַּעֲמֹד עַל־רֹאשׁ־הָהָר

יד מֵרָחֹק רַב־הַמָּקוֹם בֵּינֵיהֶם: וַיִּקְרָא דָוִד אֶל־הָעָם וְאֶל־אַבְנֵר בֶּן־נֵר לֵאמֹר

הֲלוֹא תַעֲנֶה אַבְנֵר וַיַּעַן אַבְנֵר וַיֹּאמֶר מִי אַתָּה קָרָאתָ אֶל־הַמֶּלֶךְ: וַיֹּאמֶר

טו דָּוִד אֶל־אַבְנֵר הֲלוֹא־אִישׁ אַתָּה וּמִי כָמוֹךָ בְּיִשְׂרָאֵל וְלָמָּה לֹא שָׁמַרְתָּ

אֶל־אֲדֹנֶיךָ הַמֶּלֶךְ כִּי־בָא אַחַד הָעָם לְהַשְׁחִית אֶת־הַמֶּלֶךְ אֲדֹנֶיךָ: לֹא־

טז טוֹב הַדָּבָר הַזֶּה אֲשֶׁר עָשִׂיתָ חַי־יְהֹוָה כִּי בְנֵי־מָוֶת אַתֶּם אֲשֶׁר לֹא־

שְׁמַרְתֶּם עַל־אֲדֹנֵיכֶם עַל־מְשִׁיחַ יְהֹוָה וְעַתָּה | רְאֵה אֵי־חֲנִית הַמֶּלֶךְ

וְאֶת־צַפַּחַת הַמַּיִם אֲשֶׁר [°מראשתו °מְרַאֲשֹׁתָיו ק]: וַיַּכֵּר שָׁאוּל אֶת־

יז קוֹל דָּוִד וַיֹּאמֶר הֲקוֹלְךָ זֶה בְּנִי דָוִד וַיֹּאמֶר דָּוִד קוֹלִי אֲדֹנִי הַמֶּלֶךְ: וַיֹּאמֶר

יח לָמָּה זֶּה אֲדֹנִי רֹדֵף אַחֲרֵי עַבְדּוֹ כִּי מֶה עָשִׂיתִי וּמַה־בְּיָדִי רָעָה: וְעַתָּה

יט יִשְׁמַע־נָא אֲדֹנִי הַמֶּלֶךְ אֵת דִּבְרֵי עַבְדּוֹ אִם־יְהֹוָה הֱסִיתְךָ בִי יָרַח

25:44. Saul contended that David's betrothal of Michal was invalid, so he gave her to Palti. Palti, however, was righteous and did not cohabit with her (*Sanhedrin* 19b).

26:14-16. Abner berated David for disturbing Saul's

his wife. ⁴³ David also married Ahinoam of Jezreel, and both of them were his wives. ⁴⁴ Saul had given his daughter Michal, David's [intended] wife, to Palti son of Laish of Gallim. *

26

DAVID SPARES SAUL AGAIN
26:1-25

The Ziphites reveal David's whereabouts

David and Abishai come upon the defenseless Saul

David saves Saul again

David proves his loyalty to Saul

¹ The Ziphites came to Saul at Gibeah, saying, "Is David not hiding himself in Hachilah Hill, which faces Jeshimon?" ² So Saul arose and went down to the Wilderness of Ziph, with three thousand choice men of Israel, to search for David in the Wilderness of Ziph. ³ Saul encamped at Hachilah Hill, which faces Jeshimon, beside the road. David was staying in the wilderness, and he saw that Saul was coming after him, towards the wilderness. ⁴ David sent out scouts and ascertained that Saul was definitely coming.

⁵ David then arose and came to the place where Saul was encamped. David saw the place where Saul and Abner, the commander of his army, lay; Saul lay within the circle, with the people encamped all around him. ⁶ David spoke up and said to Ahimelech the Hittite and Abishai son of Zeruiah, Joab's brother, saying, "Who will go down with me to Saul, to the camp?" And Abishai said, "I will go down with you." ⁷ So David and Abishai came to [Saul's] people at night, and behold — Saul lay asleep in the circle, his spear plunged into the ground by his head, and Abner and the people lay all around him!

⁸ Abishai said to David, "God has delivered your enemy into your hand this day! Now let me strike him with the spear, [driving it] into the ground with a single thrust — I will not need [to strike] a second time!" ⁹ But David said to Abishai, "Do not destroy him, for who can send forth his hand against the anointed one of HASHEM and be absolved?" ¹⁰ David said, "As HASHEM lives, HASHEM will strike him with illness, or his day will come and he will die, or he will go forth into battle and perish. ¹¹ It would be sacrilegious before HASHEM for me to send forth my hand against HASHEM's anointed one. Now, please take the spear that is near Saul's head and the flask of water, and let us go."

¹² So David took the spear and the flask of water from near Saul's head and they left. No one saw, no one knew, and no one awoke, for they were all asleep, for a deep sleep from HASHEM had fallen upon them.

¹³ David then crossed the ford and stood on a mountaintop from afar; there was considerable distance between them. ¹⁴ And David called out to the people and to Abner son of Ner, saying, "Won't you answer, Abner?" So Abner answered and said, "Who are you that you shout at the king!"*

¹⁵ David said to Abner, "Are you not a great man? Who is your equal in Israel? So why did you not guard your lord, the king? For someone from among the people came to assassinate the king, your master! ¹⁶ This thing that you have done is not proper! As HASHEM lives, you all deserve to die for you have not watched over your master, over the anointed one of HASHEM. Now, look — where are the king's spear and the flask of water that were near his head?"

¹⁷ Saul recognized David's voice and said, "Is that your voice, my son David?" David replied, "It is my voice, my lord, the king." ¹⁸ And he said [further], "Why is this, my lord pursuing his servant? For what have I done and what evil is in my hand? ¹⁹ And now, let my lord the king listen to the words of his servant: If it is HASHEM Who has incited you against me, then He will be appeased

---

sleep by shouting, whereupon David accused Abner of neglecting his duty to guard Saul. By showing that he had

had the opportunity to assassinate Saul, David wanted to prove yet again that he was not the King's enemy.

מִנְחָה וְאִם ׀ בְּנֵי הָאָדָם אֲרוּרִים הֵם לִפְנֵי יהוה כִּי־גֵרְשׁוּנִי הַיּוֹם

כ מֵהִסְתַּפֵּחַ בְּנַחֲלַת יהוה לֵאמֹר לֵךְ עֲבֹד אֱלֹהִים אֲחֵרִים: וְעַתָּה אַל־יִפֹּל דָּמִי אַרְצָה מִנֶּגֶד פְּנֵי יהוה כִּי־יָצָא מֶלֶךְ יִשְׂרָאֵל לְבַקֵּשׁ אֶת־פַּרְעֹשׁ אֶחָד

כא כַּאֲשֶׁר יִרְדֹּף הַקֹּרֵא בֶּהָרִים: וַיֹּאמֶר שָׁאוּל חָטָאתִי שׁוּב בְּנִי־דָוִד כִּי לֹא־אָרַע לְךָ עוֹד תַּחַת אֲשֶׁר יָקְרָה נַפְשִׁי בְּעֵינֶיךָ הַיּוֹם הַזֶּה הִנֵּה הִסְכַּלְתִּי

כב וָאֶשְׁגֶּה הַרְבֵּה מְאֹד: וַיַּעַן דָּוִד וַיֹּאמֶר הִנֵּה הַחֲנִית [הַחֲנִית ק] הַמֶּלֶךְ

כג וְיַעֲבֹר אֶחָד מֵהַנְּעָרִים וְיִקָּחֶהָ: וַיהוה יָשִׁיב לָאִישׁ אֶת־צִדְקָתוֹ וְאֶת־אֱמֻנָתוֹ אֲשֶׁר נְתָנְךָ יהוה ׀ הַיּוֹם בְּיָד וְלֹא אָבִיתִי לִשְׁלֹחַ יָדִי בִּמְשִׁיחַ

כד יהוה: וְהִנֵּה כַּאֲשֶׁר גָּדְלָה נַפְשְׁךָ הַיּוֹם הַזֶּה בְּעֵינָי כֵּן תִּגְדַּל נַפְשִׁי

כה בְּעֵינֵי יהוה וְיַצִּלֵנִי מִכָּל־צָרָה: וַיֹּאמֶר שָׁאוּל אֶל־דָּוִד בָּרוּךְ אַתָּה בְּנִי דָוִד גַּם עָשֹׂה תַעֲשֶׂה וְגַם יָכֹל תּוּכָל וַיֵּלֶךְ דָּוִד לְדַרְכּוֹ וְשָׁאוּל שָׁב לִמְקוֹמוֹ:

כז א וַיֹּאמֶר דָּוִד אֶל־לִבּוֹ עַתָּה אֶסָּפֶה יוֹם־אֶחָד בְּיַד־שָׁאוּל אֵין־לִי טוֹב כִּי הִמָּלֵט אִמָּלֵט ׀ אֶל־אֶרֶץ פְּלִשְׁתִּים וְנוֹאַשׁ מִמֶּנִּי שָׁאוּל

ב לְבַקְשֵׁנִי עוֹד בְּכָל־גְּבוּל יִשְׂרָאֵל וְנִמְלַטְתִּי מִיָּדוֹ: וַיָּקָם דָּוִד וַיַּעֲבֹר הוּא

ג וְשֵׁשׁ־מֵאוֹת אִישׁ אֲשֶׁר עִמּוֹ אֶל־אָכִישׁ בֶּן־מָעוֹךְ מֶלֶךְ גַּת: וַיֵּשֶׁב דָּוִד עִם־אָכִישׁ בְּגַת הוּא וַאֲנָשָׁיו אִישׁ וּבֵיתוֹ דָּוִד וּשְׁתֵּי נָשָׁיו אֲחִינֹעַם

ד הַיִּזְרְעֵאלִית וַאֲבִיגַיִל אֵשֶׁת־נָבָל הַכַּרְמְלִית: וַיֻּגַּד לְשָׁאוּל כִּי־בָרַח דָּוִד

ה גַּת וְלֹא־יוֹסִף [יָסַף ק] עוֹד לְבַקְשׁוֹ: וַיֹּאמֶר דָּוִד אֶל־אָכִישׁ אִם־נָא מָצָאתִי חֵן בְּעֵינֶיךָ יִתְּנוּ־לִי מָקוֹם בְּאַחַת עָרֵי הַשָּׂדֶה וְאֵשְׁבָה שָּׁם

ו וְלָמָּה יֵשֵׁב עַבְדְּךָ בְּעִיר הַמַּמְלָכָה עִמָּךְ: וַיִּתֶּן־לוֹ אָכִישׁ בַּיּוֹם הַהוּא אֶת־

ז צִקְלָג לָכֵן הָיְתָה צִקְלַג לְמַלְכֵי יְהוּדָה עַד הַיּוֹם הַזֶּה: וַיְהִי מִסְפַּר

ח הַיָּמִים אֲשֶׁר־יָשַׁב דָּוִד בִּשְׂדֵה פְלִשְׁתִּים יָמִים וְאַרְבָּעָה חֳדָשִׁים: וַיַּעַל דָּוִד וַאֲנָשָׁיו וַיִּפְשְׁטוּ אֶל־הַגְּשׁוּרִי וְהַגִּרְזִי [וְהַגִּזְרִי ק] וְהָעֲמָלֵקִי כִּי הֵנָּה

ט יֹשְׁבוֹת הָאָרֶץ אֲשֶׁר מֵעוֹלָם בּוֹאֲךָ שׁוּרָה וְעַד־אֶרֶץ מִצְרָיִם: וְהִכָּה דָוִד אֶת־הָאָרֶץ וְלֹא יְחַיֶּה אִישׁ וְאִשָּׁה וְלָקַח צֹאן וּבָקָר וַחֲמֹרִים וּגְמַלִּים

י וּבְגָדִים וַיָּשָׁב וַיָּבֹא אֶל־אָכִישׁ: וַיֹּאמֶר אָכִישׁ אַל־פְּשַׁטְתֶּם הַיּוֹם וַיֹּאמֶר

יא דָּוִד עַל־נֶגֶב יְהוּדָה וְעַל־נֶגֶב הַיְּרַחְמְאֵלִי וְאֶל־נֶגֶב הַקֵּינִי: וְאִישׁ וְאִשָּׁה לֹא־יְחַיֶּה דָוִד לְהָבִיא גַת לֵאמֹר פֶּן־יַגִּדוּ עָלֵינוּ לֵאמֹר כֹּה־עָשָׂה דָוִד

יב וְכֹה מִשְׁפָּטוֹ כָּל־הַיָּמִים אֲשֶׁר יָשַׁב בִּשְׂדֵה פְלִשְׁתִּים: וַיַּאֲמֵן אָכִישׁ בְּדָוִד

כח א לֵאמֹר הַבְאֵשׁ הִבְאִישׁ בְּעַמּוֹ בְיִשְׂרָאֵל וְהָיָה לִי לְעֶבֶד עוֹלָם: וַיְהִי

26:19. If your anger is God's punishment for me, then I can appease Him through repentance and an offering.

David was angered that people might have conspired to drive him from *Eretz Yisrael,* God's "heritage," for to leave the holiness of the Land of Israel and live among non-Jews is comparable to worshiping false gods (see *Kesubos* 110b).

26:20. May the constant threat to my life not go

unnoticed by God. You are chasing me — an insignificant flea — as if I were an elusive, tempting partridge.

27:1. David did not accept Saul's assurance that he could return and feel secure. It was not the first time Saul had had short-lived regrets.

27:2. David had fled from Achish once before (see 21:11 ff.), but this time he apparently made a prior agreement with Achish noting, as implied by verse 12, that he had with an offering* — but if it is men, may they be cursed before HASHEM, for they have driven me away this day from attaching myself to the heritage of HASHEM, [as if] to say, 'Go worship the gods of others!'* ²⁰ And now, let my blood not be cast to the ground, away from HASHEM's attention, for the king of Israel has gone to seek out a single flea as one hunts the partridge in the mountains."*

Saul pleads for reconciliation ²¹ Saul then said, "I have sinned! Come back, my son David, for I will no longer cause you harm, because my life has been precious in your eyes this day. Behold, I have been foolish and have very greatly erred." ²² David then spoke up and said, "Here is the spear of the King; let one of the attendants cross over and take it. ²³ May HASHEM repay every man his righteousness and his faithfulness; for HASHEM delivered you into [my] hand today, but I had no desire to send forth my hand against the anointed one of HASHEM. ²⁴ Behold, just as your life was important to me this day, so may my life be important in the eyes of HASHEM, and may He save me from all misfortune."

²⁵ Saul then said to David, "Blessed are you, my son David. May you accomplish much and may you be very successful." Then David went on his way and Saul returned to his place.

27

DAVID IN THE "SERVICE" OF KING ACHISH
27:1-28:2

In desperation, David goes to Philistia

David convinces Achish that he hates the Israelites . . .

. . . but David carries out raids on the Israelites' enemies

¹ **D**avid said to himself, "Now I may well perish one day at the hand of Saul. * There is nothing better for me than to escape to the land of the Philistines; then Saul will despair of searching for me again anywhere in the borders of Israel, and I will have escaped from his hand." ² So David arose and crossed over, with the six hundred men who were with him, to Achish son of Maoch, * king of Gath. ³ David dwelt with Achish in Gath, he and his men, each man with his household; David with his two wives, Ahinoam of Jezreel and Abigail, the [former] wife of Nabal, the Carmelite. ⁴ It was told to Saul that David had fled to Gath, so he no longer searched for him.

⁵ David said to Achish, "If I have found favor in your eyes, let them give me a place in one of the towns of the countryside that I may settle there. Why should your servant dwell in the royal city with you?" ⁶ So Achish gave him Ziklag on that day; this is why Ziklag belongs to the kings of Judah to this day. ⁷ The number of days that David dwelled in the Philistine countryside was four months and two days. ⁸ David and his men went up and spread out against the Geshurite and the Gizrite and the Amalekite, for they were the original inhabitants of the land, from where you approach Shur until the land of Egypt. * ⁹ David would smite the land, and would not leave a man or woman alive; he would take sheep and cattle and donkeys and camels and clothing, and would return and come to Achish. ¹⁰ Achish would ask, "Where did you raid today?" And David would say, "Against the south of Judah," or "against the south of the Jerahmeelite,"* or "against the south of the Kenite." ¹¹ And David would not leave alive any man or woman to bring back [captive] to Gath, saying [to himself], "Lest they inform about us, saying, 'This is what David did and this has been his practice all the days that he has been dwelling in the Philistine countryside.' " ¹² And Achish believed David, thinking, "He has really come to abhor his people Israel, and he will be my servant always."

---

run afoul of Saul (Radak).

27:8. Thus they were subject to the command given to Israel (Deuteronomy 20:16-18) that they should be driven from the Land of Israel (Malbim) and, in fact, there had

been a state of war between them and the people of Israel.

27:10. One of the families of Judah. David gained the confidence of Achish by convincing him that he was attacking his fellow Jews. (See 15:6 regarding the Kenite.)

בַּיָּמִים הָהֵם וַיִּקְבְּצ֥וּ פְלִשְׁתִּ֛ים אֶת־מַחֲנֵיהֶ֖ם לַצָּבָ֖א לְהִלָּחֵ֣ם בְּיִשְׂרָאֵ֑ל
וַיֹּ֣אמֶר אָכִ֗ישׁ אֶל־דָּוִ֔ד יָדֹ֣עַ תֵּדַ֗ע כִּ֤י אִתִּי֙ תֵּצֵ֣א בַמַּחֲנֶ֔ה אַתָּ֖ה וַאֲנָשֶֽׁיךָ:
ב וַיֹּ֤אמֶר דָּוִד֙ אֶל־אָכִ֔ישׁ לָכֵן֙ אַתָּ֣ה תֵדַ֔ע אֵ֥ת אֲשֶׁר־יַעֲשֶׂ֖ה עַבְדֶּ֑ךָ וַיֹּ֤אמֶר
אָכִישׁ֙ אֶל־דָּוִ֔ד לָכֵ֗ן שֹׁמֵ֧ר לְרֹאשִׁ֛י אֲשִֽׂימְךָ֖ כָּל־הַיָּמִֽים:
ג וּשְׁמוּאֵ֣ל מֵ֗ת וַיִּסְפְּדוּ־לוֹ֙ כָּל־יִשְׂרָאֵ֔ל וַיִּקְבְּרֻ֥הוּ בָרָמָ֖ה וּבְעִירֹ֑ו וְשָׁא֗וּל
הֵסִ֤יר הָאֹבוֹת֙ וְאֶת־הַיִּדְּעֹנִ֔ים מֵהָאָֽרֶץ: ד וַיִּקָּבְצ֣וּ פְלִשְׁתִּ֔ים וַיָּבֹ֖אוּ וַיַּחֲנ֣וּ
בְשׁוּנֵ֑ם וַיִּקְבֹּ֤ץ שָׁאוּל֙ אֶת־כָּל־יִשְׂרָאֵ֔ל וַֽיַּחֲנ֖וּ בַּגִּלְבֹּֽעַ: ה וַיַּ֥רְא שָׁא֖וּל אֶת־
מַחֲנֵ֣ה פְלִשְׁתִּ֑ים וַיִּרָ֕א וַיֶּחֱרַ֥ד לִבֹּ֖ו מְאֹֽד: ו וַיִּשְׁאַ֤ל שָׁאוּל֙ בַּֽיהוָ֔ה וְלֹ֥א עָנָ֖הוּ
יְהוָ֑ה גַּ֧ם בַּחֲלֹמֹ֛ות גַּ֥ם בָּאוּרִ֖ים גַּ֥ם בַּנְּבִיאִֽם: ז וַיֹּ֨אמֶר שָׁא֜וּל לַעֲבָדָ֗יו בַּקְּשׁוּ־
לִ֞י אֵ֣שֶׁת בַּעֲלַת־אֹ֗וב וְאֵלְכָ֤ה אֵלֶ֙יהָ֙ וְאֶדְרְשָׁה־בָּ֔הּ וַיֹּאמְר֤וּ עֲבָדָיו֙ אֵלָ֔יו
ח הִנֵּ֛ה אֵ֥שֶׁת בַּֽעֲלַת־אֹ֖וב בְּעֵ֥ין דֹּֽור: וַיִּתְחַפֵּ֣שׂ שָׁא֗וּל וַיִּלְבַּשׁ֙ בְּגָדִ֣ים אֲחֵרִ֔ים
וַיֵּ֣לֶךְ ה֗וּא וּשְׁנֵ֤י אֲנָשִׁים֙ עִמֹּ֔ו וַיָּבֹ֥אוּ אֶל־הָאִשָּׁ֖ה לָ֑יְלָה וַיֹּ֗אמֶר °קָסֳמִי־
ט [קָֽסֳמִי־ ק] נָ֥א לִי֙ בָּאֹ֔וב וְהַ֣עֲלִי לִ֔י אֵ֥ת אֲשֶׁר־אֹמַ֖ר אֵלָֽיִךְ: וַתֹּ֨אמֶר הָאִשָּׁ֜ה
אֵלָ֗יו הִנֵּ֨ה אַתָּ֤ה יָדַ֙עְתָּ֙ אֵ֣ת אֲשֶׁר־עָשָׂ֣ה שָׁא֔וּל אֲשֶׁ֥ר הִכְרִ֛ית אֶת־הָאֹב֥וֹת
וְאֶת־הַיִּדְּעֹנִ֖י מִן־הָאָ֑רֶץ וְלָמָ֥ה אַתָּ֛ה מִתְנַקֵּ֥שׁ בְּנַפְשִׁ֖י לַהֲמִיתֵֽנִי: י וַיִּשָּׁ֨בַֽע לָ֤הּ
שָׁאוּל֙ בַּֽיהוָ֣ה לֵאמֹ֔ר חַי־יְהוָ֖ה אִֽם־יִקְּרֵ֥ךְ עָוֹ֖ן בַּדָּבָ֥ר הַזֶּֽה: יא וַתֹּ֙אמֶר֙ הָֽאִשָּׁ֔ה
אֶת־מִ֖י אַֽעֲלֶה־לָּ֑ךְ וַיֹּ֕אמֶר אֶת־שְׁמוּאֵ֖ל הַֽעֲלִי־לִֽי: יב וַתֵּ֤רֶא הָֽאִשָּׁה֙ אֶת־
שְׁמוּאֵ֔ל וַתִּזְעַ֖ק בְּק֣וֹל גָּד֑וֹל וַתֹּאמֶר֩ הָאִשָּׁ֨ה אֶל־שָׁא֤וּל לֵאמֹר֙ לָ֣מָּה רִמִּיתָ֔נִי
וְאַתָּ֖ה שָׁאֽוּל: יג וַיֹּ֨אמֶר לָ֥הּ הַמֶּ֛לֶךְ אַל־תִּֽירְאִ֖י כִּ֣י מָ֣ה רָאִ֑ית וַתֹּ֤אמֶר הָֽאִשָּׁה֙
אֶל־שָׁא֔וּל אֱלֹהִ֥ים רָאִ֖יתִי עֹלִ֥ים מִן־הָאָֽרֶץ: יד וַיֹּ֤אמֶר לָהּ֙ מַֽה־תָּאֳר֔וֹ וַתֹּ֗אמֶר
אִ֤ישׁ זָקֵן֙ עֹלֶ֔ה וְה֖וּא עֹטֶ֣ה מְעִ֑יל וַיֵּ֤דַע שָׁאוּל֙ כִּֽי־שְׁמוּאֵ֣ל ה֔וּא וַיִּקֹּ֨ד אַפַּ֥יִם
טו אַ֖רְצָה וַיִּשְׁתָּֽחוּ: וַיֹּ֤אמֶר שְׁמוּאֵל֙ אֶל־שָׁא֔וּל לָ֥מָּה הִרְגַּזְתַּ֖נִי לְהַעֲל֣וֹת
אֹתִ֑י וַיֹּ֣אמֶר שָׁ֠אוּל צַר־לִ֨י מְאֹ֜ד וּפְלִשְׁתִּ֣ים ׀ נִלְחָמִ֣ים בִּ֗י וֵֽאלֹהִ֞ים סָ֤ר מֵֽעָלַי֙
וְלֹֽא־עָנָ֣נִי ע֗וֹד גַּ֤ם בְּיַֽד־הַנְּבִיאִם֙ גַּם־בַּ֣חֲלֹמ֔וֹת וָאֶקְרָאֶ֣ה לְךָ֔ לְהוֹדִיעֵ֖נִי מָ֥ה
טז-יז אֶעֱשֶֽׂה: וַיֹּ֣אמֶר שְׁמוּאֵ֔ל וְלָ֖מָּה תִּשְׁאָלֵ֑נִי וַֽיהוָ֛ה סָ֥ר מֵעָלֶ֖יךָ וַיְהִ֥י עָרֶֽךָ: וַיַּ֧עַשׂ
יְהוָ֣ה ל֔וֹ כַּֽאֲשֶׁ֖ר דִּבֶּ֣ר בְּיָדִ֑י וַיִּקְרַ֨ע יְהוָ֤ה אֶת־הַמַּמְלָכָה֙ מִיָּדֶ֔ךָ וַֽיִּתְּנָ֖הּ לְרֵֽעֲךָ֥
יח לְדָוִֽד: כַּאֲשֶׁ֤ר לֹֽא־שָׁמַ֙עְתָּ֙ בְּק֣וֹל יְהוָ֔ה וְלֹֽא־עָשִׂ֥יתָ חֲרֹֽון־אַפֹּ֖ו בַּֽעֲמָלֵ֑ק
יט עַל־כֵּן֙ הַדָּבָ֣ר הַזֶּ֔ה עָשָֽׂה־לְךָ֥ יְהוָ֖ה הַיֹּ֣ום הַזֶּֽה: וְיִתֵּ֣ן יְ֠הוָה גַּ֣ם אֶת־יִשְׂרָאֵ֤ל
עִמְּךָ֙ בְּיַד־פְּלִשְׁתִּ֔ים וּמָחָ֕ר אַתָּ֥ה וּבָנֶ֖יךָ עִמִּ֑י גַּ֚ם אֶת־מַחֲנֵ֣ה יִשְׂרָאֵ֔ל יִתֵּ֥ן
כ יְהוָ֖ה בְּיַד־פְּלִשְׁתִּֽים: וַיְמַהֵ֣ר שָׁא֗וּל וַיִּפֹּ֤ל מְלֹֽא־קֽוֹמָתוֹ֙ אַ֔רְצָה וַיִּרָ֥א מְאֹ֖ד

28:2. David was deliberately vague in his reply; he certainly had no intention of fighting against his people. However, his answer was good enough to make Achish think, wishfully, that David was loyal enough to be his personal bodyguard.

28:3. Thus, Saul could not inquire of Samuel. Nor could he inquire of those who divined through the dead (see

Leviticus 19:31; *Deuteronomy* 18:11) because he had banished them. This sets the stage for the ensuing narrative.
28:6. See *Exodus* 28:30.

28:11. Just as God gave great powers to the forces of holiness, as is plain from the exploits of patriarchs and prophets, so He gave great powers to the forces of profanity. This was in order to create tests of faith, so that

28

Achish drafts David

[1] It happened in those days that the Philistines mobilized their camps to the army, to fight against Israel, and Achish said to David, "Know that you will go forth with me to the camp — you and your men." [2] David replied to Achish, "Therefore you shall see what your servant will do!" Achish then said to David, "Therefore I will appoint you as my permanent bodyguard."*

SAUL SEEKS A NECRO-MANCER
28:3-25

[3] Samuel had died and all Israel eulogized him and buried him in Ramah, in his home town. Saul had banished the necromancers and the Yidoni-diviners* from the Land.

[4] The Philistines mobilized, they came and encamped at Shunem, and Saul mobilized all Israel and they encamped at Gilboa. [5] When Saul saw the Philistine camp he was afraid and his heart trembled greatly. [6] Saul inquired of HASHEM, but HASHEM did not answer him; neither in a dream, nor through the Urim [VeTumim], * nor through the prophets. [7] So Saul said to his servants, "Seek out a woman who practices necromancy, and I will go to her and inquire through her." His servants said to him, "Behold, there is a woman who practices necromancy in En-dor."

[8] So Saul disguised himself; he donned different clothing, and he went [taking] two men with him. They came to the woman at night, and he said to her, "Please divine for me through necromancy, and raise up whomever I shall tell you." [9] But the woman said to him, "Behold, you surely know what Saul has done — that he has eliminated the necromancers and Yidoni-diviner from the land — so why do you seek to entrap me, to have me killed?" [10] Saul then swore to her by HASHEM, saying, "As HASHEM lives, this thing will not be held against you as an iniquity."

She raises up the soul of Samuel

[11] The woman asked, "Whom shall I raise up for you?" And he said, "Raise up Samuel for me."* [12] The woman then saw Samuel, and she screamed in a loud voice. The woman said to Saul, "Why did you deceive me? You are Saul!" [13] The king then said to her, "Fear not. What did you see?" The woman said to Saul, "I saw a great man ascending from the earth." [14] He then said to her, "What does he look like?" She said, "An elderly man is ascending, and he is garbed in a cloak." Saul realized that it was Samuel, and he bowed down upon his face to the ground and prostrated himself.

[15] Samuel said to Saul, "Why did you disturb me, to raise me up?" Saul replied, "I am in great distress, and the Philistines are at war against me; God has turned away from me and does not answer me anymore, neither through the hand of the prophets nor in dreams — so I called upon you to inform me what I should do."

Samuel delivers a dire prediction

[16] Samuel then said, "But why do you ask me, since HASHEM has turned away from you and has become your adversary, [17] and HASHEM has done for Himself that which He spoke through me, * for HASHEM has torn the kingship from your hand and given it to your fellow, to David? [18] Because you did not obey the word of HASHEM and did not carry out His wrath against Amalek, therefore HASHEM has done this thing to you this day. [19] And HASHEM will deliver Israel with you into the hand of the Philistines; tomorrow you and your sons will be with me, and also the Israelite camp will HASHEM deliver into the hand of the Philistines."

Saul is devastated by the news

[20] Saul quickly fell his full height to the ground and he was exceedingly fright-

---

people could choose between good and evil. Now, in his desperation for counsel, Saul resorted to this forbidden device to call upon the spirit of Samuel.
28:17. See 13:14; 15:23-29.

מִדִּבְרֵי שְׁמוּאֵל גַּם־כֹּחַ לֹא־הָיָה בוֹ כִּי לֹא אָכַל לֶחֶם כָּל־הַיּוֹם וְכָל־
הַלָּיְלָה: וַתָּבוֹא הָאִשָּׁה אֶל־שָׁאוּל וַתֵּרֶא כִּי־נִבְהַל מְאֹד וַתֹּאמֶר אֵלָיו כא
הִנֵּה שָׁמְעָה שִׁפְחָתְךָ בְּקוֹלֶךָ וָאָשִׂים נַפְשִׁי בְּכַפִּי וָאֶשְׁמַע אֶת־דְּבָרֶיךָ
אֲשֶׁר דִּבַּרְתָּ אֵלָי: וְעַתָּה שְׁמַע־נָא גַם־אַתָּה בְּקוֹל שִׁפְחָתֶךָ וְאָשִׂמָה כב
לְפָנֶיךָ פַּת־לֶחֶם וֶאֱכוֹל וִיהִי בְךָ כֹּחַ כִּי תֵלֵךְ בַּדָּרֶךְ: וַיְמָאֵן וַיֹּאמֶר לֹא אֹכַל כג
וַיִּפְרְצוּ־בוֹ עֲבָדָיו וְגַם־הָאִשָּׁה וַיִּשְׁמַע לְקֹלָם וַיָּקָם מֵהָאָרֶץ וַיֵּשֶׁב אֶל־
הַמִּטָּה: וְלָאִשָּׁה עֵגֶל־מַרְבֵּק בַּבַּיִת וַתְּמַהֵר וַתִּזְבָּחֵהוּ וַתִּקַּח־קֶמַח וַתָּלָשׁ כד
וַתֹּפֵהוּ מַצּוֹת: וַתַּגֵּשׁ לִפְנֵי־שָׁאוּל וְלִפְנֵי עֲבָדָיו וַיֹּאכֵלוּ וַיָּקֻמוּ וַיֵּלְכוּ בַּלַּיְלָה כה
הַהוּא:

וַיִּקְבְּצוּ פְלִשְׁתִּים אֶת־כָּל־מַחֲנֵיהֶם אֲפֵקָה וְיִשְׂרָאֵל כט א
חֹנִים בַּעַיִן אֲשֶׁר בְּיִזְרְעֶאל: וְסַרְנֵי פְלִשְׁתִּים עֹבְרִים לְמֵאוֹת וְלַאֲלָפִים ב
וְדָוִד וַאֲנָשָׁיו עֹבְרִים בָּאַחֲרֹנָה עִם־אָכִישׁ: וַיֹּאמְרוּ שָׂרֵי פְלִשְׁתִּים מָה ג
הָעִבְרִים הָאֵלֶּה וַיֹּאמֶר אָכִישׁ אֶל־שָׂרֵי פְלִשְׁתִּים הֲלוֹא־זֶה דָוִד עֶבֶד |
שָׁאוּל מֶלֶךְ־יִשְׂרָאֵל אֲשֶׁר הָיָה אִתִּי זֶה יָמִים אוֹ־זֶה שָׁנִים וְלֹא־מָצָאתִי בוֹ
מְאוּמָה מִיּוֹם נָפְלוֹ עַד־הַיּוֹם הַזֶּה: וַיִּקְצְפוּ עָלָיו שָׂרֵי ד
פְלִשְׁתִּים וַיֹּאמְרוּ לוֹ שָׂרֵי פְלִשְׁתִּים הָשֵׁב אֶת־הָאִישׁ וְיָשֹׁב אֶל־מְקוֹמוֹ
אֲשֶׁר הִפְקַדְתּוֹ שָׁם וְלֹא־יֵרֵד עִמָּנוּ בַּמִּלְחָמָה וְלֹא־יִהְיֶה־לָּנוּ לְשָׂטָן
בַּמִּלְחָמָה וּבַמֶּה יִתְרַצֶּה זֶה אֶל־אֲדֹנָיו הֲלוֹא בְּרָאשֵׁי הָאֲנָשִׁים הָהֵם:
הֲלוֹא־זֶה דָוִד אֲשֶׁר יַעֲנוּ־לוֹ בַּמְּחֹלוֹת לֵאמֹר הִכָּה שָׁאוּל בַּאֲלָפָיו וְדָוִד ה
בְּרִבְבֹתָו [°בְּרִבְבֹתָיו ק]: וַיִּקְרָא אָכִישׁ אֶל־דָּוִד וַיֹּאמֶר ו
אֵלָיו חַי־יהֹוָה כִּי־יָשָׁר אַתָּה וְטוֹב בְּעֵינַי צֵאתְךָ וּבֹאֲךָ אִתִּי בַּמַּחֲנֶה כִּי
לֹא־מָצָאתִי בְךָ רָעָה מִיּוֹם בֹּאֲךָ אֵלַי עַד־הַיּוֹם הַזֶּה וּבְעֵינֵי הַסְּרָנִים
לֹא־טוֹב אָתָּה: וְעַתָּה שׁוּב וְלֵךְ בְּשָׁלוֹם וְלֹא־תַעֲשֶׂה רָע בְּעֵינֵי סַרְנֵי ז
פְלִשְׁתִּים: וַיֹּאמֶר דָּוִד אֶל־אָכִישׁ כִּי מֶה עָשִׂיתִי וּמַה־ ח
מָּצָאתָ בְעַבְדְּךָ מִיּוֹם אֲשֶׁר הָיִיתִי לְפָנֶיךָ עַד הַיּוֹם הַזֶּה כִּי לֹא אָבוֹא
וְנִלְחַמְתִּי בְּאֹיְבֵי אֲדֹנִי הַמֶּלֶךְ: וַיַּעַן אָכִישׁ וַיֹּאמֶר אֶל־דָּוִד יָדַעְתִּי כִּי טוֹב ט
אַתָּה בְּעֵינַי כְּמַלְאַךְ אֱלֹהִים אַךְ שָׂרֵי פְלִשְׁתִּים אָמְרוּ לֹא־יַעֲלֶה עִמָּנוּ
בַּמִּלְחָמָה: וְעַתָּה הַשְׁכֵּם בַּבֹּקֶר וְעַבְדֵי אֲדֹנֶיךָ אֲשֶׁר־בָּאוּ אִתָּךְ וְהִשְׁכַּמְתֶּם י
בַּבֹּקֶר וְאוֹר לָכֶם וָלֵכוּ: וַיַּשְׁכֵּם דָּוִד הוּא וַאֲנָשָׁיו לָלֶכֶת בַּבֹּקֶר לָשׁוּב אֶל־ יא
אֶרֶץ פְּלִשְׁתִּים וּפְלִשְׁתִּים עָלוּ יִזְרְעֶאל: וַיְהִי בְּבֹא דָוִד ל א
וַאֲנָשָׁיו צִקְלַג בַּיּוֹם הַשְּׁלִישִׁי וַעֲמָלֵקִי פָשְׁטוּ אֶל־נֶגֶב וְאֶל־צִקְלַג וַיַּכּוּ אֶת־
צִקְלַג וַיִּשְׂרְפוּ אֹתָהּ בָּאֵשׁ: וַיִּשְׁבּוּ אֶת־הַנָּשִׁים אֲשֶׁר־בָּהּ מִקָּטֹן וְעַד־גָּדוֹל ב
לֹא הֵמִיתוּ אִישׁ וַיִּנְהֲגוּ וַיֵּלְכוּ לְדַרְכָּם: וַיָּבֹא דָוִד וַאֲנָשָׁיו אֶל־הָעִיר וְהִנֵּה ג

29:3. Achish meant to say that although David had been there for only a bit over four months (27:7), he felt as if he had known David for years (*Radak*).

30:2. The men were with David at the front, so the Amalekites could take the women and children without resistance or fatalities (*Radak*).

ened by Samuel's words; also he had no strength for he had not eaten any food all the day and all the night. ²¹ *The woman came over to Saul and saw that he was greatly terrified, and she said to him, "Behold, your maidservant heeded your voice and I put my life in my hand, and I listened to your words that you spoke to me.* ²² *Now you, too, listen to the voice of your maidservant. I will place before you a piece of bread so that you may eat, so that you may have strength when you go on your way."* ²³ *But he refused, and said, "I shall not eat." His servants, and also the woman, urged him strongly, and he listened to their voice. He arose from the ground and sat on the bed.* ²⁴ *The woman had a fattened calf in her house, she hurried and slaughtered it; and she took flour and kneaded it and baked it into matzos.* ²⁵ *She set it before Saul and before his servants and they ate; and they arose and left that night.*

29

THE
PHILISTINES
DISMISS
DAVID
29:1-11

¹ The Philistines mobilized their entire army to Aphek, and Israel was encamped by the spring that is in Jezreel. ² *The governors of the Philistines were passing by with hundreds and thousands, and David and his men were passing at the rear with Achish.* ³ *The Philistine officers said, "What are these Hebrews [doing here]?" And Achish replied to the Philistine officers, "Is this not David, the servant of Saul, king of Israel, who has been with me for these days or these years, * and I have found no fault with him from the day he encamped [with me] until this very day."* ⁴ *But the Philistine officers were angry with him, and the Philistine officers said to him, "Send this man back, and let him return to the place that you assigned to him. Let him not go down to battle with us, so that he not be an antagonist to us in the battle. With what can this person ingratiate himself to his lord? Is it not with the heads of these [our] men?* ⁵ *Is this not David, of whom they sing with the timbrels, saying, 'Saul has slain his thousands and David his tens of thousands'?"*

⁶ *So Achish called David and said to him, "As HASHEM lives, you are an upright person, and your going forth and coming in with me in the camp would have been fine with me, for I have found nothing wrong with you from the day of your coming to me until this very day; but in the eyes of the governors you are not good.* ⁷ *So now, return, and go in peace, and do not do what is wrong in the eyes of the Philistine governors."*

*"Reluctantly"
and
protesting his
innocence,
David leaves
the front*

⁸ *David then said to Achish, "But what have I done, and what [fault] have you found with your servant from the day I have been before you to this very day, that I should not come and fight against the enemies of my lord the king?"*

⁹ *So Achish answered, and said to David, "I know — for in my eyes you are as good as an angel of God — but the Philistine officers have said, 'He shall not go up with us into battle.'* ¹⁰ *So now, arise early in the morning along with the servants of your lord who came with you; all of you arise early in the morning, and, when it becomes light enough for you, go."* ¹¹ *So David and his men arose early, to leave in the morning to return to the land of the Philistines, while the Philistines ascended to Jezreel.*

30

DAVID
AVENGES
ZIKLAG
30:1-31

¹ It happened that when David and his men arrived in Ziklag on the third day, *that the Amalekite had spread out to the south and to Ziklag. They had attacked Ziklag and burned it with fire.* ² *They had captured the women in it, * from small to great, they did not kill a person but led them off and went their way.* ³ *When David and his men arrived at the city — and, behold, it was*

ד שְׂרוּפָ֣ה בָאֵ֔שׁ וּנְשֵׁיהֶ֧ם וּבְנֵיהֶ֛ם וּבְנֹתֵיהֶ֖ם נִשְׁבּ֑וּ וַיִּשָּׂ֨א דָוִ֤ד וְהָעָם֙ אֲשֶׁר־

ה אִתּ֖וֹ אֶת־קוֹלָ֑ם וַיִּבְכּ֔וּ עַ֣ד אֲשֶׁ֧ר אֵין־בָּהֶ֛ם כֹּ֖חַ לִבְכּֽוֹת׃ וּשְׁתֵּ֥י נְשֵׁי־דָוִ֖ד

ו נִשְׁבּ֑וּ אֲחִינֹ֙עַם֙ הַיִּזְרְעֵלִ֔ית וַאֲבִיגַ֕יִל אֵ֖שֶׁת נָבָ֣ל הַכַּרְמְלִֽי׃ וַתֵּ֨צֶר לְדָוִ֜ד מְאֹ֗ד
   כִּֽי־אָמְר֤וּ הָעָם֙ לְסָקְל֔וֹ כִּֽי־מָ֙רָה֙ נֶ֣פֶשׁ כָּל־הָעָ֔ם אִ֖ישׁ עַל־בנו [°בָּנָ֑יו ק׳]

ז וְעַל־בְּנֹתָ֑יו וַיִּתְחַזֵּ֣ק דָּוִ֔ד בַּיהוָ֖ה אֱלֹהָֽיו׃   וַיֹּ֣אמֶר דָּוִ֗ד אֶל־אֶבְיָתָ֤ר
   הַכֹּהֵן֙ בֶּן־אֲחִימֶ֔לֶךְ הַגִּֽישָׁה־נָּ֥א לִ֖י הָאֵפֹ֑ד וַיַּגֵּ֧שׁ אֶבְיָתָ֛ר אֶת־הָאֵפֹ֖ד אֶל־

ח דָּוִֽד׃ וַיִּשְׁאַ֨ל דָּוִ֤ד בַּֽיהוָה֙ לֵאמֹ֔ר אֶרְדֹּ֛ף אַחֲרֵ֥י הַגְּדוּד־הַזֶּ֖ה הַֽאַשִּׂגֶ֑נּוּ וַיֹּ֤אמֶר

ט לוֹ֙ רְדֹ֔ף כִּֽי־הַשֵּׂ֥ג תַּשִּׂ֖יג וְהַצֵּ֥ל תַּצִּֽיל׃ וַיֵּ֣לֶךְ דָּוִ֗ד ה֚וּא וְשֵׁשׁ־מֵא֣וֹת אִ֔ישׁ

י אֲשֶׁ֣ר אִתּ֑וֹ וַיָּבֹ֖אוּ עַד־נַ֣חַל הַבְּשׂ֑וֹר וְהַנּֽוֹתָרִ֖ים עָמָֽדוּ׃ וַיִּרְדֹּ֣ף דָּוִ֔ד ה֖וּא
   וְאַרְבַּע־מֵא֣וֹת אִ֑ישׁ וַיַּֽעַמְדוּ֙ מָאתַ֣יִם אִ֔ישׁ אֲשֶׁ֣ר פִּגְּר֔וּ מֵֽעֲבֹ֖ר אֶת־נַ֥חַל

יא הַבְּשֽׂוֹר׃ וַיִּמְצְא֤וּ אִישׁ־מִצְרִי֙ בַּשָּׂדֶ֔ה וַיִּקְח֥וּ אֹת֖וֹ אֶל־דָּוִ֑ד וַיִּתְּנוּ־ל֥וֹ לֶ֙חֶם֙

יב וַיֹּ֣אכַל וַיַּשְׁקֻ֖הוּ מָֽיִם׃ וַיִּתְּנוּ־ל֩וֹ פֶ֨לַח דְּבֵלָ֜ה וּשְׁנֵ֣י צִמֻּקִ֗ים וַיֹּ֙אכַל֙ וַתָּ֣שָׁב
   רוּח֣וֹ אֵלָ֔יו כִּ֠י לֹֽא־אָ֤כַל לֶ֙חֶם֙ וְלֹא־שָׁ֣תָה מַ֔יִם שְׁלֹשָׁ֥ה יָמִ֖ים וּשְׁלֹשָׁ֥ה

יג לֵילֽוֹת׃   וַיֹּ֙אמֶר ל֤וֹ דָוִד֙ לְמִֽי־אַ֔תָּה וְאֵ֥י מִזֶּ֖ה אָ֑תָּה וַיֹּ֗אמֶר נַ֤עַר
   מִצְרִי֙ אָנֹ֔כִי עֶ֖בֶד לְאִ֣ישׁ עֲמָלֵקִ֑י וַיַּעַזְבֵ֣נִי אֲדֹנִ֔י כִּ֥י חָלִ֖יתִי הַיּ֥וֹם שְׁלֹשָֽׁה׃

יד אֲנַ֡חְנוּ פָּשַׁ֜טְנוּ נֶ֧גֶב הַכְּרֵתִ֛י וְעַל־אֲשֶׁ֥ר לִֽיהוּדָ֖ה וְעַל־נֶ֣גֶב כָּלֵ֑ב וְאֶת־צִקְלַ֖ג

טו שָׂרַ֥פְנוּ בָאֵֽשׁ׃ וַיֹּ֤אמֶר אֵלָיו֙ דָּוִ֔ד הֲתֽוֹרִדֵ֖נִי אֶל־הַגְּד֣וּד הַזֶּ֑ה וַיֹּ֡אמֶר הִשָּׁבְעָה֩
   לִּ֨י בֵֽאלֹהִ֜ים אִם־תְּמִיתֵ֗נִי וְאִם־תַּסְגִּרֵ֙נִי֙ בְּיַד־אֲדֹנִ֔י וְאֽוֹרִֽדְךָ֖ אֶל־הַגְּד֥וּד הַזֶּֽה׃

טז וַיֹּ֣רִדֵ֔הוּ וְהִנֵּ֥ה נְטֻשִׁ֖ים עַל־פְּנֵ֣י כָל־הָאָ֑רֶץ אֹכְלִ֤ים וְשֹׁתִים֙ וְחֹ֣גְגִ֔ים בְּכֹל֙
   הַשָּׁלָ֣ל הַגָּד֔וֹל אֲשֶׁ֥ר לָקְח֖וּ מֵאֶ֣רֶץ פְּלִשְׁתִּ֑ים וּמֵאֶ֖רֶץ יְהוּדָֽה׃ וַיַּכֵּ֥ם דָּוִ֛ד

יז מֵהַנֶּ֥שֶׁף וְעַד־הָעֶ֖רֶב לְמָֽחֳרָתָ֑ם וְלֹֽא־נִמְלַ֤ט מֵהֶם֙ אִ֔ישׁ כִּ֣י אִם־אַרְבַּ֣ע מֵא֗וֹת

יח אִֽישׁ־נַ֙עַר֙ אֲשֶׁ֣ר רָכְב֣וּ עַל־הַגְּמַלִּ֔ים וַיָּנֻֽסוּ׃ וַיַּצֵּ֣ל דָּוִ֔ד אֵ֥ת כָּל־אֲשֶׁ֥ר לָקְח֖וּ

יט עֲמָלֵ֑ק וְאֶת־שְׁתֵּ֥י נָשָׁ֖יו הִצִּ֥יל דָּוִֽד׃ וְלֹ֣א נֶעְדַּר־לָ֠הֶם מִן־הַקָּטֹ֨ן וְעַד־הַגָּד֜וֹל
   וְעַד־בָּנִ֤ים וּבָנוֹת֙ וּמִשָּׁלָ֔ל וְעַ֛ד כָּל־אֲשֶׁ֥ר לָקְח֖וּ לָהֶ֑ם הַכֹּ֖ל הֵשִׁ֥יב דָּוִֽד׃ וַיִּקַּ֣ח

כ דָּוִ֔ד אֶת־כָּל־הַצֹּ֖אן וְהַבָּקָ֑ר נָהֲג֗וּ לִפְנֵי֙ הַמִּקְנֶ֣ה הַה֔וּא וַיֹּ֣אמְר֔וּ זֶ֖ה שְׁלַ֥ל דָּוִֽד׃

כא וַיָּבֹ֣א דָוִ֗ד אֶל־מָאתַ֣יִם הָאֲנָשִׁ֡ים אֲשֶֽׁר־פִּגְּר֣וּ ׀ מִלֶּ֣כֶת ׀ אַחֲרֵ֣י דָוִ֗ד וַיּֽשִׁיבֻם֙
   בְּנַ֣חַל הַבְּשׂ֔וֹר וַיֵּֽצְאוּ֙ לִקְרַ֣את דָּוִ֔ד וְלִקְרַ֖את הָעָ֣ם אֲשֶׁר־אִתּ֑וֹ וַיִּגַּ֤שׁ דָּוִד֙

כב אֶת־הָעָ֔ם וַיִּשְׁאַ֥ל לָהֶ֖ם לְשָׁלֽוֹם׃   וַיַּ֜עַן כָּל־אִֽישׁ־רָ֣ע וּבְלִיַּ֗עַל
   מֵֽהָאֲנָשִׁים֮ אֲשֶׁ֣ר הָלְכ֣וּ עִם־דָּוִד֒ וַיֹּאמְר֗וּ יַ֚עַן אֲשֶׁ֣ר לֹֽא־הָלְכ֣וּ עִמִּ֔י לֹֽא־
   נִתֵּ֣ן לָהֶ֔ם מֵהַשָּׁלָ֖ל אֲשֶׁ֣ר הִצַּ֑לְנוּ כִּֽי־אִם־אִ֤ישׁ אֶת־אִשְׁתּוֹ֙ וְאֶת־בָּנָ֔יו וְיִנְהֲג֖וּ

כג וְיֵלֵֽכוּ׃   וַיֹּ֣אמֶר דָּוִ֔ד לֹֽא־תַעֲשׂ֥וּ כֵ֖ן אֶחָ֑י אֵ֠ת אֲשֶׁר־נָתַ֨ן יהוָ֥ה לָ֙נוּ֙

כד וַיִּשְׁמֹ֣ר אֹתָ֔נוּ וַיִּתֵּ֗ן אֶֽת־הַגְּד֛וּד הַבָּ֥א עָלֵ֖ינוּ בְּיָדֵֽנוּ׃ וּמִי֙ יִשְׁמַ֣ע לָכֶ֔ם לַדָּבָ֖ר

30:6. David did not despair, but trusted that God would enable him to recover the captives and the booty (*Radak*).

30:20. David returned the flocks and herds of Ziklag and Judah, but kept the Amalekite livestock as spoils of war.

The burned in fire, and their wives and sons and daughters had been captured! —
Amalekites ⁴ David and the people who were with him raised their voices and wept, until
abduct the
women and they had no strength to weep. ⁵ Both of David's wives had been captured —
children Ahinoam of Jezreel and Abigail, the [former] wife of Nabal the Carmelite.
⁶ David was very distressed, for the people were ready to stone him, for the soul
of all the people was embittered, each over his sons and his daughters; but David
drew strength from HASHEM, his God. *

David ⁷ David said to Ebiathar the Kohen, the son of Ahimelech, "Bring the
seeks Ephod to me now," so Ebiathar brought the Ephod to David. ⁸ David inquired
Divine
sanction of HASHEM, saying, "Shall I pursue this band? Will I overtake them?" And He said
to him, "Pursue, for you will surely overtake them and you will surely rescue."
⁹ So David went, he and the six hundred men who were with him, and they
came to the Besor Brook, where some men remained behind. ¹⁰ David pursued,
he together with four hundred men, while two hundred men remained, who were
too exhausted to cross the Besor Brook. ¹¹ They found an Egyptian man in the
A fugitive field and took him to David; they gave him bread and he ate, and they gave him
leads David
to the water to drink. ¹² They gave him a cake of pressed figs and two raisin-clusters
marauders and he ate, and his spirit returned to him, for he had not eaten bread nor drunk
water for three days and three nights. ¹³ David said to him, "To whom do you
belong? And where are you from?" He replied, "I am an Egyptian youth, the
slave of an Amalekite man. My master abandoned me because I became ill,
three days ago. ¹⁴ We raided the south of the Cherethite and the territory of
Judah and the south of Caleb, and we burned down Ziklag with fire." ¹⁵ So David
asked him, "Will you lead me to that band?" And he replied, "Swear to me by
God that you will not kill me nor hand me over to my master, and I will lead you
to that band."

The chase ¹⁶ So he led him and there they were! — spread out across the face of the entire
succeeds land, eating and drinking and celebrating with all the great spoils they had taken
from the land of the Philistines and the land of Judah. ¹⁷ And David smote them
from twilight until the evening of the next day; not a man of them survived,
except four hundred youths who were riding camels, who fled. ¹⁸ So David
rescued everything that Amalek had taken, and David rescued his two wives.
¹⁹ No one among them was missing, from small to great, sons and daughters,
as well as the spoils, including everything they had taken for themselves; David
returned everything. ²⁰ David took all the [Amalekite] sheep and cattle; they
led them before all that livestock and said, "This is the booty of David."*

²¹ David then came to the two hundred men who were too exhausted to
go follow after David, whom he had stationed at the Besor Brook, and they
went to meet David and to meet the people who were with him. David
approached the people and inquired after their welfare. ²² Every mean-spirited
and base person of the men who had gone with David spoke up and said,
"Since they did not go with me, we will not give them of the spoils that
we rescued, except to each man his wife and his children; let them take them
and go." ²³ But David said, "Do not act so, my brothers, with that which HASHEM
has given us, for He has watched over us and delivered into our hands the
band that had come upon us. ²⁴ Who could hearken to you to such a thing!

His men led these spoils ahead of the other livestock and announced that they were intended for David.

הַזֶּה כִּי כְּחֵלֶק | הַיֹּרֵד בַּמִּלְחָמָה וּכְחֵלֶק הַיֹּשֵׁב עַל־הַכֵּלִים יַחְדָּו
כה יַחֲלֹקוּ: וַיְהִי מֵהַיּוֹם הַהוּא וָמָעְלָה וַיְשִׂמֶהָ לְחֹק וּלְמִשְׁפָּט
כו לְיִשְׂרָאֵל עַד הַיּוֹם הַזֶּה: וַיָּבֹא דָוִד אֶל־צִקְלַג וַיְשַׁלַּח
מֵהַשָּׁלָל לְזִקְנֵי יְהוּדָה לְרֵעֵהוּ לֵאמֹר הִנֵּה לָכֶם בְּרָכָה מִשְּׁלַל אֹיְבֵי יְהוָה:
כז־כח לַאֲשֶׁר בְּבֵית־אֵל וְלַאֲשֶׁר בְּרָמוֹת־נֶגֶב וְלַאֲשֶׁר בְּיַתִּר: וְלַאֲשֶׁר בַּעֲרֹעֵר
כט וְלַאֲשֶׁר בְּשִׂפְמוֹת וְלַאֲשֶׁר בְּאֶשְׁתְּמֹעַ: וְלַאֲשֶׁר בְּרָכָל וְלַאֲשֶׁר בְּעָרֵי
ל הַיְּרַחְמְאֵלִי וְלַאֲשֶׁר בְּעָרֵי הַקֵּינִי: וְלַאֲשֶׁר בְּחָרְמָה וְלַאֲשֶׁר °בְּבוֹר־עָשָׁן   °נ"א בְּכוֹר
לא וְלַאֲשֶׁר בַּעֲתָךְ: וְלַאֲשֶׁר בְּחֶבְרוֹן וּלְכָל־הַמְּקֹמוֹת אֲשֶׁר־הִתְהַלֶּךְ־שָׁם דָּוִד
הוּא וַאֲנָשָׁיו:

לא   א וּפְלִשְׁתִּים נִלְחָמִים בְּיִשְׂרָאֵל וַיָּנֻסוּ אַנְשֵׁי יִשְׂרָאֵל מִפְּנֵי פְלִשְׁתִּים וַיִּפְּלוּ
ב חֲלָלִים בְּהַר הַגִּלְבֹּעַ: וַיַּדְבְּקוּ פְלִשְׁתִּים אֶת־שָׁאוּל וְאֶת־בָּנָיו וַיַּכּוּ
ג פְלִשְׁתִּים אֶת־יְהוֹנָתָן וְאֶת־אֲבִינָדָב וְאֶת־מַלְכִּי־שׁוּעַ בְּנֵי שָׁאוּל: וַתִּכְבַּד
הַמִּלְחָמָה אֶל־שָׁאוּל וַיִּמְצָאֻהוּ הַמּוֹרִים אֲנָשִׁים בַּקָּשֶׁת וַיָּחֶל מְאֹד
ד מֵהַמּוֹרִים: וַיֹּאמֶר שָׁאוּל לְנֹשֵׂא כֵלָיו שְׁלֹף חַרְבְּךָ | וְדָקְרֵנִי בָהּ פֶּן־יָבוֹאוּ
הָעֲרֵלִים הָאֵלֶּה וּדְקָרֻנִי וְהִתְעַלְּלוּ־בִי וְלֹא אָבָה נֹשֵׂא כֵלָיו כִּי יָרֵא מְאֹד
ה וַיִּקַּח שָׁאוּל אֶת־הַחֶרֶב וַיִּפֹּל עָלֶיהָ: וַיַּרְא נֹשֵׂא כֵלָיו כִּי־מֵת שָׁאוּל וַיִּפֹּל
ו גַּם־הוּא עַל־חַרְבּוֹ וַיָּמָת עִמּוֹ: וַיָּמָת שָׁאוּל וּשְׁלֹשֶׁת בָּנָיו וְנֹשֵׂא כֵלָיו גַּם
ז כָּל־אֲנָשָׁיו בַּיּוֹם הַהוּא יַחְדָּו: וַיִּרְאוּ אַנְשֵׁי־יִשְׂרָאֵל אֲשֶׁר־בְּעֵבֶר הָעֵמֶק
וַאֲשֶׁר | בְּעֵבֶר הַיַּרְדֵּן כִּי־נָסוּ אַנְשֵׁי יִשְׂרָאֵל וְכִי־מֵתוּ שָׁאוּל וּבָנָיו
ח וַיַּעַזְבוּ אֶת־הֶעָרִים וַיָּנֻסוּ וַיָּבֹאוּ פְלִשְׁתִּים וַיֵּשְׁבוּ בָּהֶן: וַיְהִי
מִמָּחֳרָת וַיָּבֹאוּ פְלִשְׁתִּים לְפַשֵּׁט אֶת־הַחֲלָלִים וַיִּמְצְאוּ אֶת־שָׁאוּל וְאֶת־
ט שְׁלֹשֶׁת בָּנָיו נֹפְלִים בְּהַר הַגִּלְבֹּעַ: וַיִּכְרְתוּ אֶת־רֹאשׁוֹ וַיַּפְשִׁיטוּ אֶת־כֵּלָיו
י וַיְשַׁלְּחוּ בְאֶרֶץ־פְּלִשְׁתִּים סָבִיב לְבַשֵּׂר בֵּית עֲצַבֵּיהֶם וְאֶת־הָעָם: וַיָּשִׂמוּ
יא אֶת־כֵּלָיו בֵּית עַשְׁתָּרוֹת וְאֶת־גְּוִיָּתוֹ תָּקְעוּ בְּחוֹמַת בֵּית שָׁן: וַיִּשְׁמְעוּ אֵלָיו
יב יֹשְׁבֵי יָבֵישׁ גִּלְעָד אֵת אֲשֶׁר־עָשׂוּ פְלִשְׁתִּים לְשָׁאוּל: וַיָּקוּמוּ כָּל־אִישׁ חַיִל
וַיֵּלְכוּ כָל־הַלַּיְלָה וַיִּקְחוּ אֶת־גְּוִיַּת שָׁאוּל וְאֵת גְּוִיֹּת בָּנָיו מֵחוֹמַת בֵּית שָׁן
יג וַיָּבֹאוּ יָבֵשָׁה וַיִּשְׂרְפוּ אֹתָם שָׁם: וַיִּקְחוּ אֶת־עַצְמֹתֵיהֶם וַיִּקְבְּרוּ תַחַת־

שמואל ב   א הָאֶשֶׁל בְּיָבֵשָׁה וַיָּצֻמוּ שִׁבְעַת יָמִים: וַיְהִי אַחֲרֵי מוֹת שָׁאוּל
א   ב וְדָוִד שָׁב מֵהַכּוֹת אֶת־הָעֲמָלֵק וַיֵּשֶׁב דָּוִד בְּצִקְלָג יָמִים שְׁנָיִם: וַיְהִי |

31:4. Although suicide is normally a grave transgression of Jewish law, the Sages explain that Saul's case was an exception. *Radak* suggests that this is because he knew that he would surely die anyway, as Samuel had prophesied, and reasoned that it was better to die by his own hand than to be killed in a mocking, disgraceful way by the Philistines.

31:5. Details of the narrative of Saul's death are in *II Samuel* 1:5-10.

31:12. According to most commentators, they burned Saul's belongings, in accord with the dictum that no one may use a king's possessions. *Radak* suggests that the bodies had become decomposed and infested, so the people burned the flesh, leaving the bones for burial.

The new decree: an equal division of spoils

Rather, like the portion of the one who went into battle, so is the portion of the one who remained with the baggage; they shall divide [it] equally." ²⁵ And it was from that day on, that [David] made this a decree and a law in Israel, until this day.

²⁶ When David arrived at Ziklag, he sent some of the spoils to the elders of Judah, to his allies, saying, "Here is a gift for you, from the spoils of the enemies of HASHEM!" ²⁷ [He sent] to those in Beth-el, to those in Ramot of the South, and to those in Jattir; ²⁸ and to those in Aroer and to those in Siphmoth and to those in Eshtemoa; ²⁹ and to those in Rachal and to those in the Jerahmeelite cities and to those in the Kenite cities; ³⁰ and to those in Hormah and to those in Cor Ashan and to those in Athach, ³¹ and to those in Hebron; and to those in all the places where David had traveled — he and his men.

31

THE DEATH OF SAUL

31:1 — II-1:27

(See Appendix A, timeline 4)

¹ The Philistines were battling with Israel, and the men of Israel ran off from before the Philistines and fell slain upon Mount Gilboa. ² The Philistines overtook Saul and his sons, and the Philistines slew Jonathan, Abinadab, and Malchi-shua, the son's of Saul. ³ The battle then concentrated against Saul. The archers — the men with bows — found him, and Saul was terrified of the archers. ⁴ Saul said to his armor-bearer, "Draw your sword and stab me with it, lest these uncircumcised people come and stab me and make sport of me." But his armor-bearer did not consent, for he was very frightened, so Saul took the sword himself and fell upon it. * ⁵ When the armor-bearer saw that Saul was dying* he also fell upon his sword to die with him. ⁶ So Saul and his three sons and his armor-bearer, as well as all of his men, died together on that day.

Jewish demoralization and Philistine plunder

⁷ When the men of Israel, who were on the other side of the valley and on the other side of the Jordan, saw that the men of Israel had fled and that Saul and his sons had died, they abandoned their cities and fled, and the Philistines came and settled in them. ⁸ It happened the next day, when the Philistines came to plunder the corpses, that they found Saul and his three sons, fallen on Mount Gilboa. ⁹ They severed his head and stripped off his gear, and sent heralds all about the land of the Philistines to inform [those in] the temple of their idols and the people. ¹⁰ They placed his gear in the temple of Ashtaroth, and they hung up his remains upon the wall of Beth-shan.

A daring rescue of Saul's remains

¹¹ The inhabitants of Jabesh-gilead heard about him — about what the Philistines had done to Saul — ¹² and all the daring men arose and went throughout the night, and took the remains of Saul and the remains of his sons from the wall of Beth-shan, and came back to Jabesh. They burned them there. * ¹³ They then took their bones and buried them under the tamarisk tree in Jabesh, and they fasted seven days.

II SAMUEL

1

¹ It happened after the death of Saul, when David had returned from striking Amalek, and David had been living in Ziklag for two days — ² it was on

---

⤳§ II Samuel

According to the masoretic tradition, the "books" of *I Samuel* and *II Samuel* are actually *one* long book; their designation as two separate books is of non-Jewish origin. Thus, in the total of the twenty-four books of

Tanach, all of *Samuel* is counted as a single book. The same applies to the "books" of *Kings* and *Chronicles*. However, for the convenience of the reader, we refer to chapters and verses in the familiar way, e.g. *II Samuel* 3:10.

בַּיּוֹם הַשְּׁלִישִׁי וְהִנֵּה אִישׁ בָּא מִן־הַמַּחֲנֶה מֵעִם שָׁאוּל וּבְגָדָיו קְרֻעִים

ג וַאֲדָמָה עַל־רֹאשׁוֹ וַיְהִי בְּבֹאוֹ אֶל־דָּוִד וַיִּפֹּל אַרְצָה וַיִּשְׁתָּחוּ: וַיֹּאמֶר

ד לוֹ דָוִד אֵי מִזֶּה תָּבוֹא וַיֹּאמֶר אֵלָיו מִמַּחֲנֵה יִשְׂרָאֵל נִמְלָטְתִּי: וַיֹּאמֶר

אֵלָיו דָּוִד מֶה־הָיָה הַדָּבָר הַגֶּד־נָא לִי וַיֹּאמֶר אֲשֶׁר־נָס הָעָם מִן־

הַמִּלְחָמָה וְגַם־הַרְבֵּה נָפַל מִן־הָעָם וַיָּמֻתוּ וְגַם שָׁאוּל וִיהוֹנָתָן בְּנוֹ

ה מֵתוּ: וַיֹּאמֶר דָּוִד אֶל־הַנַּעַר הַמַּגִּיד לוֹ אֵיךְ יָדַעְתָּ כִּי־מֵת שָׁאוּל וִיהוֹנָתָן

ו בְּנוֹ: וַיֹּאמֶר הַנַּעַר | הַמַּגִּיד לוֹ נִקְרֹא נִקְרֵיתִי בְּהַר הַגִּלְבֹּעַ וְהִנֵּה שָׁאוּל

ז נִשְׁעָן עַל־חֲנִיתוֹ וְהִנֵּה הָרֶכֶב וּבַעֲלֵי הַפָּרָשִׁים הִדְבִּקֻהוּ: וַיִּפֶן אַחֲרָיו

ח וַיִּרְאֵנִי וַיִּקְרָא אֵלָי וָאֹמַר הִנֵּנִי: וַיֹּאמֶר לִי מִי־אָתָּה °וָיֹּאמֶר [°וָאֹמַר ק]

ט אֵלָיו עֲמָלֵקִי אָנֹכִי: וַיֹּאמֶר אֵלַי עֲמָד־נָא עָלַי וּמֹתְתֵנִי כִּי אֲחָזַנִי הַשָּׁבָץ

י כִּי־כָל־עוֹד נַפְשִׁי בִּי: וָאֶעֱמֹד עָלָיו וַאֲמֹתְתֵהוּ כִּי יָדַעְתִּי כִּי לֹא

יִחְיֶה אַחֲרֵי נִפְלוֹ וָאֶקַּח הַנֵּזֶר | אֲשֶׁר עַל־רֹאשׁוֹ וְאֶצְעָדָה אֲשֶׁר עַל־זְרֹעוֹ

יא וָאֲבִיאֵם אֶל־אֲדֹנִי הֵנָּה: וַיַּחֲזֵק דָּוִד °בבגדו [°בִּבְגָדָיו ק] וַיִּקְרָעֵם וְגַם

יב כָּל־הָאֲנָשִׁים אֲשֶׁר אִתּוֹ: וַיִּסְפְּדוּ וַיִּבְכּוּ וַיָּצֻמוּ עַד־הָעָרֶב עַל־

שָׁאוּל וְעַל־יְהוֹנָתָן בְּנוֹ וְעַל־עַם יְהוָה וְעַל־בֵּית יִשְׂרָאֵל כִּי נָפְלוּ

יג בֶּחָרֶב: וַיֹּאמֶר דָּוִד אֶל־הַנַּעַר הַמַּגִּיד לוֹ אֵי מִזֶּה

יד אָתָּה וַיֹּאמֶר בֶּן־אִישׁ גֵּר עֲמָלֵקִי אָנֹכִי: וַיֹּאמֶר אֵלָיו דָּוִד אֵיךְ אֵיךְ לֹא

טו יָרֵאתָ לִשְׁלֹחַ יָדְךָ לְשַׁחֵת אֶת־מְשִׁיחַ יְהוָה: וַיִּקְרָא דָוִד לְאַחַד

טז מֵהַנְּעָרִים וַיֹּאמֶר גַּשׁ פְּגַע־בּוֹ וַיַּכֵּהוּ וַיָּמֹת: וַיֹּאמֶר אֵלָיו דָּוִד °דמיך

[°דָּמְךָ ק] עַל־רֹאשֶׁךָ כִּי פִיךָ עָנָה בְךָ לֵאמֹר אָנֹכִי מֹתַתִּי אֶת־

יז מְשִׁיחַ יְהוָה: וַיְקֹנֵן דָּוִד אֶת־הַקִּינָה הַזֹּאת עַל־

יח שָׁאוּל וְעַל־יְהוֹנָתָן בְּנוֹ: וַיֹּאמֶר לְלַמֵּד בְּנֵי־יְהוּדָה קָשֶׁת הִנֵּה כְתוּבָה

יט עַל־סֵפֶר הַיָּשָׁר: הַצְּבִי יִשְׂרָאֵל עַל־בָּמוֹתֶיךָ חָלָל אֵיךְ נָפְלוּ גִבּוֹרִים:

כ אַל־תַּגִּידוּ בְגַת אַל־תְּבַשְּׂרוּ בְּחוּצֹת אַשְׁקְלוֹן פֶּן־תִּשְׂמַחְנָה בְּנוֹת

כא פְּלִשְׁתִּים פֶּן־תַּעֲלֹזְנָה בְּנוֹת הָעֲרֵלִים: הָרֵי בַגִּלְבֹּעַ אַל־טַל וְאַל־מָטָר

עֲלֵיכֶם וּשְׂדֵי תְרוּמֹת כִּי שָׁם נִגְעַל מָגֵן גִּבּוֹרִים מָגֵן שָׁאוּל בְּלִי

כב מָשִׁיחַ בַּשָּׁמֶן: מִדַּם חֲלָלִים מֵחֵלֶב גִּבּוֹרִים קֶשֶׁת יְהוֹנָתָן לֹא נָשׂוֹג

כג אָחוֹר וְחֶרֶב שָׁאוּל לֹא תָשׁוּב רֵיקָם: שָׁאוּל וִיהוֹנָתָן הַנֶּאֱהָבִים

וְהַנְּעִימִם בְּחַיֵּיהֶם וּבְמוֹתָם לֹא נִפְרָדוּ מִנְּשָׁרִים קַלּוּ מֵאֲרָיוֹת גָּבֵרוּ:

1:9. Saul wanted to die before the Philistines could taunt and disgrace him (see *I Samuel* 31:4).

1:16. Although there were no witnesses and no legal process, David ordered the execution as an emergency measure [הוֹרָאַת שָׁעָה], lest anarchy displace respect for the throne. Halachically, the Amalekite had no right to kill Saul, despite his request.

1:18. The Torah, which alludes to Judah's prowess in archery (*Genesis* 49:8).

1:19. This refers to Saul (*Kara*); or the Land of Israel (*Radak*; see *Daniel* 11:16). Alternatively: צְּבִי means "station, standing" and refers to Israel's stature that has fallen with Saul's death (*Rashi*).

1:21. Lit., fields of *terumah*, i.e., beautiful fields that yield abundant tithes.

Leather shields would be oiled so that arrows or spears would slide harmlessly off them.

the third day that, behold! a man came from the camp, from Saul, with his garments torn and with earth upon his head. When he reached David he fell to the ground and prostrated himself. ³ David said to him, "Where are you coming from?" He said to him, "I escaped from the Israelite camp." ⁴ David then said to him, "What happened? Tell me now!" And he said, "The people fled from the battle, and also many of the people fell and died. And even Saul and Jonathan his son died."

The report of Saul's death

⁵ David then said to the young man who was telling him, "How do you know that Saul and Jonathan his son died?" ⁶ The young man who was telling him said, "I happened to be at Mount Gilboa, and Saul was leaning on his spear. And behold! the chariots and cavalry were overtaking him. ⁷ He turned around and saw me. He called out to me and I answered, 'Here I am.' ⁸ He asked me, 'Who are you?' and I told him, 'I am an Amalekite.' ⁹ Then he said, 'Stand up over me and put an end to my life, for the throes of death have gripped me, while my soul is still within me.' * ¹⁰ So I stood over him and ended his life, for I knew that he would not survive after he had fallen [on his sword]. I then took the crown that was on his head and a bracelet that was on his arm and brought them here to my lord."

David and his people mourn

¹¹ David took hold of his garments and tore them, as did all the people who were with him. ¹² They lamented and wept and fasted until evening, over Saul, over Jonathan his son, over the nation of HASHEM, and over the House of Israel, for they had fallen by the sword.

¹³ David then asked the young man who was telling him, "Where are you from?" And he replied, "I am the son of an Amalekite convert." ¹⁴ David then said to him, "How could you not be afraid to send forth your hand to destroy the anointed one of HASHEM?"

¹⁵ David then called one of the attendants and said, "Approach and strike him down!" So he struck him and he died. ¹⁶ David said to him, "Your blood is on your own head, for your own mouth testified against you, saying, 'I put to death the anointed one of HASHEM!' "*

David's mournful dirge

¹⁷ David lamented this dirge over Saul and Jonathan his son. ¹⁸ He said:
   [We must] teach the Children of Judah the archer's bow,
   Behold, this is written in the Book of Uprightness. *
¹⁹ O precious One of Israel* — upon your heights lie the slain!
   How have the mighty fallen!
²⁰ Do not tell [it] in Gath; do not spread the tidings
     in the streets of Ashkelon —
   Lest the Philistine girls rejoice,
     lest the daughters of the uncircumcised jubilate.
²¹ O mountains of Gilboa — let neither dew nor rain be upon you,
     nor fields of bounty, *
   For rejected there was the shield of the mighty ones, the shield of Saul,
     as if unanointed with oil. *
²² From the blood of the slain, from the fat of the mighty,
     the bow of Jonathan would not recoil,
     the sword of Saul would not return empty.
²³ Saul and Jonathan, beloved and pleasant in their lives,
     and in their death not parted.
   They were swifter than eagles, stronger than lions.

כד בְּנוֹת֙ יִשְׂרָאֵ֔ל אֶל־שָׁא֖וּל בְּכֶ֑ינָה הַמַּלְבִּֽשְׁכֶ֤ם שָׁנִי֙ עִם־עֲדָנִ֔ים הַמַּעֲלֶ֥ה

כה עֲדִ֣י זָהָ֔ב עַ֖ל לְבוּשְׁכֶֽן׃ אֵ֚יךְ נָפְל֣וּ גִבֹּרִ֔ים בְּת֖וֹךְ הַמִּלְחָמָ֑ה יְה֣וֹנָתָ֔ן

כו עַל־בָּמוֹתֶ֖יךָ חָלָֽל׃ צַר־לִ֣י עָלֶ֗יךָ אָחִי֙ יְה֣וֹנָתָ֔ן נָעַ֥מְתָּ לִּ֖י מְאֹ֑ד

כז נִפְלְאַ֤תָה אַהֲבָֽתְךָ֙ לִ֔י מֵאַהֲבַ֖ת נָשִֽׁים׃ אֵ֚יךְ נָפְל֣וּ גִבּוֹרִ֔ים וַיֹּאבְד֖וּ כְּלֵ֥י

ב מִלְחָמָֽה׃   א וַיְהִ֣י אַֽחֲרֵי־כֵ֗ן וַיִּשְׁאַל֩ דָּוִ֨ד בַּֽיהֹוָ֜ה ׀ לֵאמֹ֗ר הַאֶֽעֱלֶה֙

בְּאַחַת֙ עָרֵ֣י יְהוּדָ֔ה וַיֹּ֧אמֶר יְהֹוָ֛ה אֵלָ֖יו עֲלֵ֑ה וַיֹּ֧אמֶר דָּוִ֛ד אָ֥נָה אֶעֱלֶ֖ה

ב וַיֹּ֥אמֶר חֶבְרֹֽנָה׃ וַיַּ֣עַל שָׁ֣ם דָּוִ֗ד וְגַ֚ם שְׁתֵּ֣י נָשָׁ֔יו אֲחִינֹ֙עַם֙ הַיִּזְרְעֵלִ֔ית

ג וַאֲבִיגַ֕יִל אֵ֖שֶׁת נָבָ֣ל הַֽכַּרְמְלִֽי׃ וַאֲנָשָׁ֧יו אֲשֶׁר־עִמּ֛וֹ הֶעֱלָ֥ה דָוִ֖ד אִ֣ישׁ וּבֵית֑וֹ

ד וַיֵּשְׁב֖וּ בְּעָרֵ֣י חֶבְרֽוֹן׃ וַיָּבֹ֙אוּ֙ אַנְשֵׁ֣י יְהוּדָ֔ה וַיִּמְשְׁחוּ־שָׁ֥ם אֶת־דָּוִ֖ד לְמֶ֑לֶךְ

עַל־בֵּ֣ית יְהוּדָ֑ה וַיַּגִּ֤דוּ לְדָוִד֙ לֵאמֹ֔ר אַנְשֵׁי֙ יָבֵ֣ישׁ גִּלְעָ֔ד אֲשֶׁ֥ר קָֽבְר֖וּ אֶת־

ה שָׁאֽוּל׃   וַיִּשְׁלַ֤ח דָּוִד֙ מַלְאָכִ֔ים אֶל־אַנְשֵׁ֖י יָבֵ֣ישׁ גִּלְעָ֑ד וַיֹּ֣אמֶר

אֲלֵיהֶ֗ם בְּרֻכִ֚ים אַתֶּם֙ לַֽיהֹוָ֔ה אֲשֶׁ֨ר עֲשִׂיתֶ֜ם הַחֶ֣סֶד הַזֶּ֗ה עִם־אֲדֹֽנֵיכֶם֙ עִם־

ו שָׁא֔וּל וַֽתִּקְבְּר֖וּ אֹתֽוֹ׃ וְעַתָּ֕ה יַֽעַשׂ־יְהֹוָ֥ה עִמָּכֶ֖ם חֶ֣סֶד וֶאֱמֶ֑ת וְגַ֣ם אָנֹכִ֗י

ז אֶעֱשֶׂ֤ה אִתְּכֶם֙ הַטּוֹבָ֣ה הַזֹּ֔את אֲשֶׁ֥ר עֲשִׂיתֶ֖ם הַדָּבָ֣ר הַזֶּֽה׃ וְעַתָּ֣ה ׀ תֶּחֱזַ֣קְנָה

יְדֵיכֶ֗ם וִֽהְיוּ֙ לִבְנֵי־חַ֔יִל כִּי־מֵ֖ת אֲדֹֽנֵיכֶ֣ם שָׁא֑וּל וְגַם־אֹתִ֗י מָֽשְׁח֧וּ בֵית־

ח יְהוּדָ֛ה לְמֶ֖לֶךְ עֲלֵיהֶֽם׃   וְאַבְנֵ֣ר בֶּן־נֵ֔ר שַׂר־צָבָ֖א אֲשֶׁ֣ר לְשָׁא֑וּל

ט לָקַ֗ח אֶת־אִ֥ישׁ בֹּ֙שֶׁת֙ בֶּן־שָׁא֔וּל וַיַּֽעֲבִרֵ֖הוּ מַֽחֲנָֽיִם׃ וַיַּמְלִכֵ֙הוּ֙ אֶל־הַגִּלְעָ֔ד

וְאֶל־הָאֲשׁוּרִ֖י וְאֶל־יִזְרְעֶ֑אל וְעַל־אֶפְרַ֙יִם֙ וְעַל־בִּנְיָמִ֔ן וְעַל־יִשְׂרָאֵ֖ל

י כֻּלֹּֽה׃ בֶּן־אַרְבָּעִ֣ים שָׁנָ֗ה אִֽישׁ־בֹּ֙שֶׁת֙ בֶּן־שָׁא֔וּל בְּמָלְכ֖וֹ עַל־

יא יִשְׂרָאֵ֔ל וּשְׁתַּ֥יִם שָׁנִ֖ים מָלָ֑ךְ אַ֚ךְ בֵּ֣ית יְהוּדָ֔ה הָי֖וּ אַחֲרֵ֥י דָוִֽד׃ וַיְהִי֙ מִסְפַּ֣ר

הַיָּמִ֗ים אֲשֶׁר֩ הָיָ֨ה דָוִ֥ד מֶ֙לֶךְ֙ בְּחֶבְר֔וֹן עַל־בֵּ֣ית יְהוּדָ֑ה שֶׁ֥בַע שָׁנִ֖ים וְשִׁשָּׁ֥ה

יב חֳדָשִֽׁים׃   וַיֵּצֵא֙ אַבְנֵ֣ר בֶּן־נֵ֔ר וְעַבְדֵ֖י אִֽישׁ־בֹּ֣שֶׁת בֶּן־שָׁא֑וּל

יג מִֽמַּחֲנַ֖יִם גִּבְעֽוֹנָה׃ וְיוֹאָ֣ב בֶּן־צְרוּיָ֗ה וְעַבְדֵ֤י דָוִד֙ יָֽצְא֔וּ וַֽיִּפְגְּשׁ֛וּם עַל־בְּרֵכַ֥ת

יד גִּבְע֖וֹן יַחְדָּ֑ו וַיֵּ֨שְׁב֜וּ אֵ֤לֶּה עַל־הַבְּרֵכָה֙ מִזֶּ֔ה וְאֵ֥לֶּה עַל־הַבְּרֵכָ֖ה מִזֶּֽה׃ וַיֹּ֤אמֶר

אַבְנֵר֙ אֶל־יוֹאָ֔ב יָק֚וּמוּ נָא֙ הַנְּעָרִ֔ים וִישַֽׂחֲק֖וּ לְפָנֵ֑ינוּ וַיֹּ֥אמֶר יוֹאָ֖ב יָקֻֽמוּ׃

טו וַיָּקֻ֖מוּ וַיַּֽעַבְר֣וּ בְמִסְפָּ֑ר שְׁנֵ֧ים עָשָׂ֣ר לְבִנְיָמִ֗ן וּלְאִ֥ישׁ בֹּ֙שֶׁת֙ בֶּן־שָׁא֔וּל וּשְׁנֵ֥ים

טז עָשָׂ֖ר מֵֽעַבְדֵ֥י דָוִֽד׃ וַֽיַּחֲזִ֜קוּ אִ֣ישׁ ׀ בְּרֹ֣אשׁ רֵעֵ֗הוּ וְחַרְבּוֹ֙ בְּצַ֣ד רֵעֵ֔הוּ וַיִּפְּל֖וּ

יז יַחְדָּ֑ו וַיִּקְרָ֙א לַמָּק֤וֹם הַהוּא֙ חֶלְקַ֣ת הַצֻּרִ֔ים אֲשֶׁ֖ר בְּגִבְעֽוֹן׃ וַתְּהִ֧י הַמִּלְחָמָ֛ה

קָשָׁ֥ה עַד־מְאֹ֖ד בַּיּ֣וֹם הַה֑וּא וַיִּנָּ֤גֶף אַבְנֵר֙ וְאַנְשֵׁ֣י יִשְׂרָאֵ֔ל לִפְנֵ֖י עַבְדֵ֥י דָוִֽד׃

יח וַיִּֽהְיוּ־שָׁ֗ם שְׁלֹשָׁה֙ בְּנֵ֣י צְרוּיָ֔ה יוֹאָ֥ב וַאֲבִישַׁ֖י וַֽעֲשָׂהאֵ֑ל וַֽעֲשָׂהאֵל֙ קַ֣ל

יט בְּרַגְלָ֔יו כְּאַחַ֥ד הַצְּבָיִ֖ם אֲשֶׁ֣ר בַּשָּׂדֶֽה׃ וַיִּרְדֹּ֣ף עֲשָׂהאֵ֔ל אַחֲרֵ֖י אַבְנֵ֑ר וְלֹֽא־

1:27. Saul and Jonathan were the weapons of Israel.

2:1. David would reign only with explicit Divine sanction.

2:10. Ish-bosheth reigned only two years during David's term in Hebron. Thus, Israel was without a king for about five-and-a-half years (*Radak*).

2:14. Gibeon, in the land of Benjamin, was only a few miles from Judean territory. Abner suggested a friendly duel, but the fighting got out of hand and ended in tragedy (*Metzudos*).

2:18. Zeruiah was David's sister (*I Chronicles* 2:15-16).

²⁴ O daughters of Israel, weep over Saul,
> who would clothe you in scarlet with finery,
> who would place golden jewelry upon your clothing.
²⁵ How have [the] mighty fallen in the midst of the battle —
> Jonathan, slain upon your heights?
²⁶ I am distressed over you, my brother Jonathan;
> you were so pleasant to me!
> Your love was more wondrous to me than the love of women!
²⁷ How have [the] mighty fallen and the weapons of war* gone to waste?

2

DAVID AND
ISH-
BOSHETH
2:1-4:12
(See Appendix A,
timeline 4)

David reigns
in Hebron

¹ It happened after this that David inquired of HASHEM, saying, "Shall I go up to one of the cities of Judah?"* And HASHEM answered him, "Go up!" David then asked, "To where shall I go up?" And He responded, "To Hebron." ² So David went up there with his two wives — Ahinoam of Jezreel and Abigail, the [former] wife of Nabal the Carmelite. ³ David also brought up his men who were with him, each man with his household, and they settled in the towns around Hebron. ⁴ The men of Judah came and there they anointed David as king of the House of Judah.

David
blesses
those who
buried Saul

It was told to David, saying, "[It was] the men of Jabesh-gilead who buried Saul." ⁵ So David sent messengers to the men of Jabesh-gilead, and said to them, "Blessed are you to HASHEM for you have performed this act of kindness for your lord, Saul, for you have buried him. ⁶ So now, may HASHEM perform acts of kindness and truth for you. I, too, shall repay you for this benevolence, because you have done this deed. ⁷ And now, may your hands be strong and may you be courageous, for your lord Saul has died; moreover the House of Judah has anointed me as king over them."

Ish-bosheth
assumes
Saul's
kingship

⁸ Now Abner son of Ner, the commander of Saul's army, had taken Ish-bosheth son of Saul and brought him across to Mahanaim, ⁹ and made him king over Gilead, over the Asherite, over Jezreel, over Ephraim, over Benjamin and over all of Israel.

¹⁰ Ish-bosheth son of Saul was forty years old when he reigned over Israel, and he reigned for two years.* (However, the House of Judah was loyal to David; ¹¹ the number of days that David was king over the House of Judah in Hebron was seven years and six months.)

A bloody
duel

¹² Abner son of Ner went forth with the servants of Ish-bosheth son of Saul, from Mahanaim to Gibeon. ¹³ Joab son of Zeruiah and David's servants went forth, and they met together at the Pool of Gibeon; these were sitting at one end of the pool and these were sitting at the other end of the pool. ¹⁴ Abner then said to Joab, "Let the young soldiers arise and duel before us!"* And Joab answered, "Let them arise!" ¹⁵ So they arose and crossed [the pool] according to a set number — twelve for Benjamin and Ish-bosheth son of Saul, and twelve of David's servants. ¹⁶ Each man grabbed his opponent's head, and then thrust his sword into his opponent's side, and they fell together. They called that place Helkat-hazzurim (Field of the Swords), which is in Gibeon.

¹⁷ A very intense battle ensued on that day, and Abner was defeated along with the men of Israel, by the servants of David. ¹⁸ The three sons of Zeruiah* were there — Joab, Abishai and Asahel. Asahel was as swift on his feet as one of the deer that are in the field. ¹⁹ Asahel pursued Abner; he did not

כ נָטָה לָלֶכֶת עַל־הַיָּמִין וְעַל־הַשְּׂמֹאל מֵאַחֲרֵי אַבְנֵר: וַיִּפֶן אַבְנֵר אַחֲרָיו

כא וַיֹּאמֶר הַאַתָּה זֶה עֲשָׂהאֵל וַיֹּאמֶר אָנֹכִי: וַיֹּאמֶר לוֹ אַבְנֵר נְטֵה לְךָ עַל־

יְמִינְךָ אוֹ עַל־שְׂמֹאלֶךָ וֶאֱחֹז לְךָ אֶחָד מֵהַנְּעָרִים וְקַח־לְךָ אֶת־חֲלִצָתוֹ

כב וְלֹא־אָבָה עֲשָׂהאֵל לָסוּר מֵאַחֲרָיו: וַיֹּסֶף עוֹד אַבְנֵר לֵאמֹר אֶל־עֲשָׂהאֵל

סוּר לְךָ מֵאַחֲרָי לָמָּה אַכֶּכָּה אַרְצָה וְאֵיךְ אֶשָּׂא פָנַי אֶל־יוֹאָב אָחִיךָ:

כג וַיְמָאֵן לָסוּר וַיַּכֵּהוּ אַבְנֵר בְּאַחֲרֵי הַחֲנִית אֶל־הַחֹמֶשׁ וַתֵּצֵא הַחֲנִית

מֵאַחֲרָיו וַיִּפָּל־שָׁם וַיָּמָת °תחתו [תַּחְתָּיו ק] וַיְהִי כָּל־הַבָּא אֶל־הַמָּקוֹם

כד אֲשֶׁר־נָפַל שָׁם עֲשָׂהאֵל וַיָּמֹת וַיַּעֲמֹדוּ: וַיִּרְדְּפוּ יוֹאָב וַאֲבִישַׁי אַחֲרֵי אַבְנֵר

וְהַשֶּׁמֶשׁ בָּאָה וְהֵמָּה בָּאוּ עַד־גִּבְעַת אַמָּה אֲשֶׁר עַל־פְּנֵי־גִיחַ דֶּרֶךְ מִדְבַּר

כה גִּבְעוֹן: וַיִּתְקַבְּצוּ בְנֵי־בִנְיָמִן אַחֲרֵי אַבְנֵר וַיִּהְיוּ לַאֲגֻדָּה אֶחָת וַיַּעַמְדוּ עַל

כו רֹאשׁ־גִּבְעָה אֶחָת: וַיִּקְרָא אַבְנֵר אֶל־יוֹאָב וַיֹּאמֶר הֲלָנֶצַח תֹּאכַל חֶרֶב הֲלוֹא יָדַעְתָּה כִּי־מָרָה תִהְיֶה בָּאַחֲרוֹנָה וְעַד־מָתַי לֹא־תֹאמַר לָעָם לָשׁוּב

כז מֵאַחֲרֵי אֲחֵיהֶם: וַיֹּאמֶר יוֹאָב חַי הָאֱלֹהִים כִּי לוּלֵא דִּבַּרְתָּ כִּי אָז מֵהַבֹּקֶר

כח נַעֲלָה הָעָם אִישׁ מֵאַחֲרֵי אָחִיו: וַיִּתְקַע יוֹאָב בַּשּׁוֹפָר וַיַּעַמְדוּ כָּל־הָעָם

כט וְלֹא־יִרְדְּפוּ עוֹד אַחֲרֵי יִשְׂרָאֵל וְלֹא־יָסְפוּ עוֹד לְהִלָּחֵם: וְאַבְנֵר וַאֲנָשָׁיו

הָלְכוּ בָּעֲרָבָה כֹּל הַלַּיְלָה הַהוּא וַיַּעַבְרוּ אֶת־הַיַּרְדֵּן וַיֵּלְכוּ כָּל־הַבִּתְרוֹן

ל וַיָּבֹאוּ מַחֲנָיִם: וְיוֹאָב שָׁב מֵאַחֲרֵי אַבְנֵר וַיִּקְבֹּץ אֶת־כָּל־הָעָם וַיִּפָּקְדוּ

לא מֵעַבְדֵי דָוִד תִּשְׁעָה־עָשָׂר אִישׁ וַעֲשָׂהאֵל: וְעַבְדֵי דָוִד הִכּוּ מִבִּנְיָמִן

לב וּבְאַנְשֵׁי אַבְנֵר שְׁלֹשׁ־מֵאוֹת וְשִׁשִּׁים אִישׁ מֵתוּ: וַיִּשְׂאוּ אֶת־עֲשָׂהאֵל

וַיִּקְבְּרֻהוּ בְּקֶבֶר אָבִיו אֲשֶׁר בֵּית לָחֶם וַיֵּלְכוּ כָל־הַלַּיְלָה יוֹאָב וַאֲנָשָׁיו

ג וַיֵּאֹר לָהֶם בְּחֶבְרוֹן: וַתְּהִי הַמִּלְחָמָה אֲרֻכָּה בֵּין בֵּית שָׁאוּל וּבֵין בֵּית דָּוִד

ב וְדָוִד הֹלֵךְ וְחָזֵק וּבֵית שָׁאוּל הֹלְכִים וְדַלִּים: °ילדו [וַיִּוָּלְדוּ ק]

ג לְדָוִד בָּנִים בְּחֶבְרוֹן וַיְהִי בְכוֹרוֹ אַמְנוֹן לַאֲחִינֹעַם הַיִּזְרְעֵאלִת: וּמִשְׁנֵהוּ

כִלְאָב °לאביגל [לַאֲבִיגַיִל ק] אֵשֶׁת נָבָל הַכַּרְמְלִי וְהַשְּׁלִשִׁי אַבְשָׁלוֹם

ד בֶּן־מַעֲכָה בַּת־תַּלְמַי מֶלֶךְ גְּשׁוּר: וְהָרְבִיעִי אֲדֹנִיָּה בֶן־חַגִּית וְהַחֲמִישִׁי

ה שְׁפַטְיָה בֶן־אֲבִיטָל: וְהַשִּׁשִּׁי יִתְרְעָם לְעֶגְלָה אֵשֶׁת דָּוִד אֵלֶּה יֻלְּדוּ לְדָוִד

ו בְּחֶבְרוֹן: וַיְהִי בִּהְיוֹת הַמִּלְחָמָה בֵּין בֵּית שָׁאוּל וּבֵין בֵּית

ז דָּוִד וְאַבְנֵר הָיָה מִתְחַזֵּק בְּבֵית שָׁאוּל: וּלְשָׁאוּל פִּלֶגֶשׁ וּשְׁמָהּ רִצְפָּה

ח בַת־אַיָּה וַיֹּאמֶר אֶל־אַבְנֵר מַדּוּעַ בָּאתָה אֶל־פִּילֶגֶשׁ אָבִי: וַיִּחַר לְאַבְנֵר

מְאֹד עַל־דִּבְרֵי אִישׁ־בֹּשֶׁת וַיֹּאמֶר הֲרֹאשׁ כֶּלֶב אָנֹכִי אֲשֶׁר לִיהוּדָה

הַיּוֹם אֶעֱשֶׂה־חֶסֶד עִם־בֵּית | שָׁאוּל אָבִיךָ אֶל־אֶחָיו וְאֶל־מֵרֵעֵהוּ וְלֹא

2:21. Not wanting to harm Asahel, Abner urged him to settle for stripping a minor soldier of his armaments.

2:27. If you had not issued your challenge for a duel, this whole tragic episode would never have happened!

3:3. The Sages tell us that Maacah was a war captive (see

I Samuel 27:8) whom David married according to the law described in *Deuteronomy* 21:10-14 (*Radak*).

3:5. This was another name of Michal, daughter of Saul, David's first and most beloved wife (*Rashi*).

3:7. Both morally and halachically it is forbidden for a turn away — going to the right or to the left — from behind Abner. ²⁰ Abner turned around and said, "Is that you, Asahel?" And he replied, "It is I." ²¹ Abner then said to him, "Turn yourself away to your right or to your left and capture one of the young soldiers and his weapon for yourself." But Asahel would not agree to turn aside from after him. * ²² So Abner once again said to Asahel, "Turn aside from behind me! Why should I strike you to the ground? How will I be able to show my face to your brother Joab?" ²³ But he refused to turn aside, and Abner struck him with the back of his spear, into his fifth rib; and the spear came out of his back, and he fell there and died in his place. It happened that whoever came to the place where Asahel had fallen and died, stood still [in shock]. ²⁴ Joab and Abishai chased after Abner. The sun was setting as they reached Ammah Hill which is alongside Giah, on the way to the Wilderness of Gibeon. ²⁵ The children of Benjamin assembled themselves behind Abner and became a single group, and they stood atop a hill. ²⁶ Abner then called out to Joab and said, "Must the sword consume forever? Do you not know that there will be a bitter ending to this? How long will you not tell the people to turn back from after their brethren?"

²⁷ Joab then said, "As God lives, had you not spoken [first], already in the morning every one of the people would have gone back from going after his brother."* ²⁸ So Joab blew the shofar, and all the people halted, no longer chasing after [their fellow] Israelites, and they did not continue to fight. ²⁹ Abner and his men traveled through the Arabah that entire night; they crossed the Jordan and went through the entire Bithron, and came to Mahanaim. ³⁰ Joab thus withdrew from pursuing Abner and gathered together all the people. There were missing from David's subjects nineteen men and Asahel. ³¹ But David's subjects had slain [many] of Benjamin and of Abner's men; three hundred and sixty men died. ³² They carried Asahel and buried him in his father's burial plot in Bethlehem. Joab and his men walked all night, and light broke upon them at Hebron.

3

¹ The war was long between the House of Saul and the House of David; David grew continuously stronger, while the House of Saul grew continuously weaker.

² Sons were born to David in Hebron: his firstborn was Amnon, [born] to Ahinoam of Jezreel; ³ his second [son] was Chileab, [born] to Abigail, the [former] wife of Nabal the Carmelite; the third was Absalom, the son of Maacah, daughter of Talmai, king of Geshur;* ⁴ the fourth was Adonijah, the son of Hagith; the fifth was Shephatiah, the son of Abital; ⁵ the sixth was Ithream, [born] to Eglah, David's [main] wife.* These were born to David in Hebron.

⁶ And it happened while there was war between the House of Saul and the House of David, that Abner exerted himself on behalf of the House of Saul. ⁷ Now Saul had had a concubine, her name was Rizpah daughter of Aiah. [Ish-bosheth] said to Abner, "Why were you intimate with my father's concubine?"* ⁸ Abner was infuriated over the words of Ish-bosheth, and he said, "Am I the chief dog warden of Judah? Shall I perform acts of kindness today for the house of your father Saul, for his brothers and for his friends, when I have not

Marginal notes:

Abner kills Asahel in self-defense

Abner convinces Joab to avoid civil war

The combatants withdraw and bury their dead

David's sons

Ish-bosheth alienates Abner

---

commoner to live with a king's widow, so Ish-bosheth felt obligated to defend the honor of his late father. Abner, however, was furious. He felt that, as the defender of Saul and his family, he was entitled to gratitude and deference. So insulted was he, that he deserted Ish-bosheth and defected to David.

ט הַמְצִיאֹתֶךָ בְּיַד־דָּוִד וַתִּפְקֹד עָלַי עֲוֹן הָאִשָּׁה הַיּוֹם: כֹּה־יַעֲשֶׂה אֱלֹהִים
לְאַבְנֵר וְכֹה יֹסִיף לוֹ כִּי כַּאֲשֶׁר נִשְׁבַּע יהוה לְדָוִד כִּי־כֵן אֶעֱשֶׂה־לּוֹ:
י לְהַעֲבִיר הַמַּמְלָכָה מִבֵּית שָׁאוּל וּלְהָקִים אֶת־כִּסֵּא דָוִד עַל־יִשְׂרָאֵל וְעַל־
יא יְהוּדָה מִדָּן וְעַד־בְּאֵר שָׁבַע: וְלֹא־יָכֹל עוֹד לְהָשִׁיב אֶת־אַבְנֵר דָּבָר
יב מִיִּרְאָתוֹ אֹתוֹ: וַיִּשְׁלַח אַבְנֵר מַלְאָכִים ׀ אֶל־דָּוִד תַּחְתָּו
[תַּחְתָּיו ק] לֵאמֹר לְמִי־אָרֶץ לֵאמֹר כָּרְתָה בְרִיתְךָ אִתִּי וְהִנֵּה יָדִי עִמָּךְ
יג לְהָסֵב אֵלֶיךָ אֶת־כָּל־יִשְׂרָאֵל: וַיֹּאמֶר טוֹב אֲנִי אֶכְרֹת אִתְּךָ בְּרִית אַךְ דָּבָר
אֶחָד אָנֹכִי שֹׁאֵל מֵאִתְּךָ לֵאמֹר לֹא־תִרְאֶה אֶת־פָּנַי כִּי ׀ אִם־לִפְנֵי הֱבִיאֲךָ
יד אֵת מִיכַל בַּת־שָׁאוּל בְּבֹאֲךָ לִרְאוֹת אֶת־פָּנָי: וַיִּשְׁלַח
דָּוִד מַלְאָכִים אֶל־אִישׁ־בֹּשֶׁת בֶּן־שָׁאוּל לֵאמֹר תְּנָה אֶת־אִשְׁתִּי אֶת־
טו מִיכַל אֲשֶׁר אֵרַשְׂתִּי לִי בְּמֵאָה עָרְלוֹת פְּלִשְׁתִּים: וַיִּשְׁלַח אִישׁ בֹּשֶׁת
טז וַיִּקָּחֶהָ מֵעִם אִישׁ מֵעִם פַּלְטִיאֵל בֶּן־לוּשׁ [לָיִשׁ ק]: וַיֵּלֶךְ אִתָּהּ אִישָׁהּ
הָלוֹךְ וּבָכֹה אַחֲרֶיהָ עַד־בַּחֻרִים וַיֹּאמֶר אֵלָיו אַבְנֵר לֵךְ שׁוּב וַיָּשֹׁב: וּדְבַר־
יז אַבְנֵר הָיָה עִם־זִקְנֵי יִשְׂרָאֵל לֵאמֹר גַּם־תְּמוֹל גַּם־שִׁלְשֹׁם הֱיִיתֶם
יח מְבַקְשִׁים אֶת־דָּוִד לְמֶלֶךְ עֲלֵיכֶם: וְעַתָּה עֲשׂוּ כִּי יהוה אָמַר אֶל־דָּוִד
לֵאמֹר בְּיַד ׀ דָּוִד עַבְדִּי הוֹשִׁיעַ אֶת־עַמִּי יִשְׂרָאֵל מִיַּד פְּלִשְׁתִּים וּמִיַּד כָּל־
יט אֹיְבֵיהֶם: וַיְדַבֵּר גַּם־אַבְנֵר בְּאָזְנֵי בִנְיָמִין וַיֵּלֶךְ גַּם־אַבְנֵר לְדַבֵּר בְּאָזְנֵי דָוִד
כ בְּחֶבְרוֹן אֵת כָּל־אֲשֶׁר־טוֹב בְּעֵינֵי יִשְׂרָאֵל וּבְעֵינֵי כָּל־בֵּית בִּנְיָמִן: וַיָּבֹא
אַבְנֵר אֶל־דָּוִד חֶבְרוֹן וְאִתּוֹ עֶשְׂרִים אֲנָשִׁים וַיַּעַשׂ דָּוִד לְאַבְנֵר וְלָאֲנָשִׁים
כא אֲשֶׁר־אִתּוֹ מִשְׁתֶּה: וַיֹּאמֶר אַבְנֵר אֶל־דָּוִד אָקוּמָה ׀ וְאֵלֵכָה וְאֶקְבְּצָה אֶל־
אֲדֹנִי הַמֶּלֶךְ אֶת־כָּל־יִשְׂרָאֵל וְיִכְרְתוּ אִתְּךָ בְּרִית וּמָלַכְתָּ בְּכֹל אֲשֶׁר־
כב תְּאַוֶּה נַפְשֶׁךָ וַיְשַׁלַּח דָּוִד אֶת־אַבְנֵר וַיֵּלֶךְ בְּשָׁלוֹם: וְהִנֵּה עַבְדֵי דָוִד וְיוֹאָב
בָּא מֵהַגְּדוּד וְשָׁלָל רָב עִמָּם הֵבִיאוּ וְאַבְנֵר אֵינֶנּוּ עִם־דָּוִד בְּחֶבְרוֹן כִּי
כג שִׁלְּחוֹ וַיֵּלֶךְ בְּשָׁלוֹם: וְיוֹאָב וְכָל־הַצָּבָא אֲשֶׁר־אִתּוֹ בָּאוּ וַיַּגִּדוּ לְיוֹאָב
כד לֵאמֹר בָּא־אַבְנֵר בֶּן־נֵר אֶל־הַמֶּלֶךְ וַיְשַׁלְּחֵהוּ וַיֵּלֶךְ בְּשָׁלוֹם: וַיָּבֹא יוֹאָב
אֶל־הַמֶּלֶךְ וַיֹּאמֶר מֶה עָשִׂיתָה הִנֵּה־בָא אַבְנֵר אֵלֶיךָ לָמָּה־זֶּה שִׁלַּחְתּוֹ
כה וַיֵּלֶךְ הָלוֹךְ: יָדַעְתָּ אֶת־אַבְנֵר בֶּן־נֵר כִּי לְפַתֹּתְךָ בָּא וְלָדַעַת אֶת־מוֹצָאֲךָ
כו וְאֶת־מוֹבָאֶךָ [מוֹבָאֲךָ ק] וְלָדַעַת אֵת כָּל־אֲשֶׁר אַתָּה עֹשֶׂה: וַיֵּצֵא יוֹאָב
מֵעִם דָּוִד וַיִּשְׁלַח מַלְאָכִים אַחֲרֵי אַבְנֵר וַיָּשִׁבוּ אֹתוֹ מִבּוֹר הַסִּרָה וְדָוִד לֹא
כז יָדָע: וַיָּשָׁב אַבְנֵר חֶבְרוֹן וַיַּטֵּהוּ יוֹאָב אֶל־תּוֹךְ הַשַּׁעַר לְדַבֵּר אִתּוֹ בַּשֶּׁלִי
כח וַיַּכֵּהוּ שָׁם הַחֹמֶשׁ וַיָּמָת בְּדַם עֲשָׂה־אֵל אָחִיו: וַיִּשְׁמַע דָּוִד מֵאַחֲרֵי כֵן
כט וַיֹּאמֶר נָקִי אָנֹכִי וּמַמְלַכְתִּי מֵעִם יהוה עַד־עוֹלָם מִדְּמֵי אַבְנֵר בֶּן־נֵר: יָחֻלוּ

3:14. See *I Samuel* 18:25-27. David did not want it to appear as if Abner was abducting Michal without the consent of Ish-bosheth (*Radak*).

3:15. Paltiel (referred to in *I Samuel* 25:44 as Palti) had never cohabited with Michal; otherwise, she would have been forbidden to return to David (*Talmud*).

handed you over into the hand of David, yet today you accuse me of sinning with this woman? [9] So may God do to Abner and so may He do further to him [if he does not keep this oath] . . .; for just as HASHEM has sworn to David, so shall I do for him: [10] to remove the kingship from the House of Saul and to establish the throne of David upon Israel and upon Judah, from Dan to Beer-sheba!" [11] [Ish-bosheth] was no longer able to respond to Abner a word, because of his fear of him.

Abner defects and brings Michal back to David

[12] Abner sent messengers to David from his place, saying, "Whose is the land [if not yours]?" and saying, "Seal your covenant with me and behold — my hand will be with you, to turn all of Israel to you."

[13] [David] said, "Good. I shall seal a covenant with you — but I request one thing of you, that is, 'You shall not see my face, unless you bring Michal daughter of Saul when you enter to see my face.' "

[14] David then sent messengers to Ish-bosheth son of Saul, saying, "Give me my wife, Michal, whom I married to myself with one hundred Philistine fore-skins."* [15] So Ish-bosheth sent and took her away from her husband, from Paltiel son of Laish. * [16] Her husband accompanied her, constantly weeping for her, until Bahurim. Then Abner told him, "Go. Turn back," and he turned back.

Abner rallies Israel to David

[17] Abner's message had been sent to all the elders of Israel, saying, "From yesterday and before yesterday you wanted David as king over you; [18] so now do it! For HASHEM has said of David, 'By the hand of My servant David I shall save My people Israel from the hand of the Philistines and from the hand of all their enemies.' "

[19] Abner also spoke in the ears of Benjamin. Then Abner set out to speak in the ears of David in Hebron that it was all good in the eyes of Israel and in the eyes of the entire House of Benjamin. [20] Abner came to David in Hebron, and with him twenty men, and David made a feast for Abner and the men who were with him.

[21] Abner said to David, "I shall arise and go to rally all of Israel behind my lord the king, so that they will seal a covenant with you so that you may reign over all that your soul desires." David sent Abner away, and he went in peace.

[22] Just then behold — the servants of David and Joab were returning from a raid, and brought many spoils with them. Abner was no longer with David in Hebron, for he had already sent him away and he had left in peace. [23] When Joab and all the army that was with him arrived, they told Joab, saying, "Abner son of Ner came to the king, and he sent him away and he left in peace!" [24] So Joab came to the king and said, "What have you done? Behold — Abner came to you — why did you send him away and allow him to leave? [25] You know Abner son of Ner — that he has come to entice you and to learn of your comings and goings and to learn all that you do!"

Joab assassinates Abner

[26] Joab then left David's presence and sent messengers after Abner. * They brought him back from Bor-hassirah, but David did not know. [27] When Abner returned to Hebron, Joab led him aside to the middle of the gateway [as if] to talk to him casually. He struck him there in the fifth rib, and he died [as revenge] for the blood of his brother Asahel.

[28] When David heard afterwards, he declared, "I and my kingdom are guiltless before HASHEM forever, for the blood of Abner son of Ner! [29] [The guilt] shall rest

---

3:26. To inform Abner falsely that the king wanted to speak to him (*Metzudos*).

עַל־רֹאשׁ יוֹאָב וְאֶל כָּל־בֵּית אָבִיו וְאַל־יִכָּרֵת מִבֵּית יוֹאָב זָב וּמְצֹרָע
ל וּמַחֲזִיק בַּפֶּלֶךְ וְנֹפֵל בַּחֶרֶב וַחֲסַר־לָחֶם: וְיוֹאָב וַאֲבִישַׁי אָחִיו הָרְגוּ לְאַבְנֵר
לא עַל אֲשֶׁר הֵמִית אֶת־עֲשָׂה־אֵל אֲחִיהֶם בְּגִבְעוֹן בַּמִּלְחָמָה: וַיֹּאמֶר
דָּוִד אֶל־יוֹאָב וְאֶל־כָּל־הָעָם אֲשֶׁר־אִתּוֹ קִרְעוּ בִגְדֵיכֶם וְחִגְרוּ שַׂקִּים
וְסִפְדוּ לִפְנֵי אַבְנֵר וְהַמֶּלֶךְ דָּוִד הֹלֵךְ אַחֲרֵי הַמִּטָּה: וַיִּקְבְּרוּ אֶת־
אַבְנֵר בְּחֶבְרוֹן וַיִּשָּׂא הַמֶּלֶךְ אֶת־קוֹלוֹ וַיֵּבְךְּ אֶל־קֶבֶר אַבְנֵר וַיִּבְכּוּ כָּל־
לג הָעָם: וַיְקֹנֵן הַמֶּלֶךְ אֶל־אַבְנֵר וַיֹּאמַר הַכְּמוֹת נָבָל יָמוּת אַבְנֵר:
לד יָדֶךָ לֹא־אֲסֻרוֹת וְרַגְלֶיךָ לֹא־לִנְחֻשְׁתַּיִם הֻגָּשׁוּ כִּנְפוֹל לִפְנֵי בְנֵי־עַוְלָה
לה נָפָלְתָּ וַיֹּסִפוּ כָל־הָעָם לִבְכּוֹת עָלָיו: וַיָּבֹא כָל־הָעָם לְהַבְרוֹת אֶת־דָּוִד
לֶחֶם בְּעוֹד הַיּוֹם וַיִּשָּׁבַע דָּוִד לֵאמֹר כֹּה יַעֲשֶׂה־לִּי אֱלֹהִים וְכֹה יֹסִיף כִּי
לו אִם־לִפְנֵי בוֹא־הַשֶּׁמֶשׁ אֶטְעַם־לֶחֶם אוֹ כָל־מְאוּמָה: וְכָל־הָעָם הִכִּירוּ
לז וַיִּיטַב בְּעֵינֵיהֶם כְּכֹל אֲשֶׁר עָשָׂה הַמֶּלֶךְ בְּעֵינֵי כָל־הָעָם טוֹב: וַיֵּדְעוּ כָל־
הָעָם וְכָל־יִשְׂרָאֵל בַּיּוֹם הַהוּא כִּי לֹא הָיְתָה מֵהַמֶּלֶךְ לְהָמִית אֶת־אַבְנֵר
לח בֶּן־נֵר: וַיֹּאמֶר הַמֶּלֶךְ אֶל־עֲבָדָיו הֲלוֹא תֵדְעוּ כִּי־שַׂר וְגָדוֹל נָפַל
לט הַיּוֹם הַזֶּה בְּיִשְׂרָאֵל: וְאָנֹכִי הַיּוֹם רַךְ וּמָשׁוּחַ מֶלֶךְ וְהָאֲנָשִׁים הָאֵלֶּה בְּנֵי
צְרוּיָה קָשִׁים מִמֶּנִּי יְשַׁלֵּם יְהוָה לְעֹשֵׂה הָרָעָה כְּרָעָתוֹ:   ד   וַיִּשְׁמַע
א בֶּן־שָׁאוּל כִּי מֵת אַבְנֵר בְּחֶבְרוֹן וַיִּרְפּוּ יָדָיו וְכָל־יִשְׂרָאֵל נִבְהָלוּ: וּשְׁנֵי
ב אֲנָשִׁים שָׂרֵי־גְדוּדִים הָיוּ בֶן־שָׁאוּל שֵׁם הָאֶחָד בַּעֲנָה וְשֵׁם הַשֵּׁנִי רֵכָב בְּנֵי
ג רִמּוֹן הַבְּאֵרֹתִי מִבְּנֵי בִנְיָמִן כִּי גַם־בְּאֵרוֹת תֵּחָשֵׁב עַל־בִּנְיָמִן: וַיִּבְרְחוּ
ד הַבְּאֵרֹתִים גִּתָּיְמָה וַיִּהְיוּ־שָׁם גָּרִים עַד הַיּוֹם הַזֶּה: וְלִיהוֹנָתָן
בֶּן־שָׁאוּל בֵּן נְכֵה רַגְלָיִם בֶּן־חָמֵשׁ שָׁנִים הָיָה בְּבֹא שְׁמֻעַת שָׁאוּל
וִיהוֹנָתָן מִיִּזְרְעֶאל וַתִּשָּׂאֵהוּ אֹמַנְתּוֹ וַתָּנֹס וַיְהִי בְּחָפְזָהּ לָנוּס וַיִּפֹּל וַיִּפָּסֵחַ
ה וּשְׁמוֹ מְפִיבֹשֶׁת: וַיֵּלְכוּ בְּנֵי־רִמּוֹן הַבְּאֵרֹתִי רֵכָב וּבַעֲנָה וַיָּבֹאוּ כְּחֹם
הַיּוֹם אֶל־בֵּית אִישׁ בֹּשֶׁת וְהוּא שֹׁכֵב אֵת מִשְׁכַּב הַצָּהֳרָיִם: וְהֵנָּה בָּאוּ
ו עַד־תּוֹךְ הַבַּיִת לֹקְחֵי חִטִּים וַיַּכֻּהוּ אֶל־הַחֹמֶשׁ וְרֵכָב וּבַעֲנָה אָחִיו
ז נִמְלָטוּ: וַיָּבֹאוּ הַבַּיִת וְהוּא־שֹׁכֵב עַל־מִטָּתוֹ בַּחֲדַר מִשְׁכָּבוֹ וַיַּכֻּהוּ וַיְמִתֻהוּ
וַיָּסִירוּ אֶת־רֹאשׁוֹ וַיִּקְחוּ אֶת־רֹאשׁוֹ וַיֵּלְכוּ דֶּרֶךְ הָעֲרָבָה כָּל־הַלָּיְלָה:
ח וַיָּבִאוּ אֶת־רֹאשׁ אִישׁ־בֹּשֶׁת אֶל־דָּוִד חֶבְרוֹן וַיֹּאמְרוּ אֶל־הַמֶּלֶךְ הִנֵּה
רֹאשׁ אִישׁ־בֹּשֶׁת בֶּן־שָׁאוּל אֹיִבְךָ אֲשֶׁר בִּקֵּשׁ אֶת־נַפְשֶׁךָ וַיִּתֵּן יְהוָה

3:29-30. Knowing that Joab had conspired with his
relatives, David cursed Joab and all his accomplices, but
not the innocent, for their treachery. Abner had killed
Asahel in self-defense, but Joab had committed un-
provoked murder (*Radak*).
3:34. Normally the only way to overpower such a mighty
warrior as yourself would be to capture him and render
him defenseless before killing him. You, however, were
not even granted this "dignity"; you were slain through a

despicable act of trickery and deception (*Kara*).
3:38. A court could not act against Joab because he had
not been given a formal warning and there were no
witnesses; but as king, David had the authority to take
extralegal action. Now he explained that he was not yet
strong enough to act against the powerful Joab.
4:3. This parenthetical insertion informs us that these
two captains were actually from Benjamin, Saul's tribe,
although they lived in a "non-Jewish" city.

David
condemns
Joab

upon the head of Joab and upon all his father's house, * and may there never cease from Joab's house contaminated men, lepers, those who lean on crutches, who fall by the sword, and who lack food." [30] Joab and his brother Abishai had killed Abner because he had killed their brother Asahel in Gibeon, in the battle.

David
leads the
mourning for
Abner . . .

[31] David said to Joab and to all the people who were with him, "Tear your clothes and don sackcloth, and lament over Abner." King David himself walked behind the bier. [32] And they buried Abner in Hebron. The king raised his voice and wept at Abner's grave, and all the people wept. [33] The king lamented a dirge for Abner, and said,

"Should Abner have died the death of a knave?
[34] Your hands were not bound and your feet were not placed in chains;
as one who falls before villains have you fallen!" *
And all the people wept even more over him.

[35] All the people came to [comfort] David by bringing him a meal on that same day, but David swore, saying, "So shall God do to me and so shall He do further if I taste any bread or anything else before the sun sets!" [36] All the people recognized [David's sincerity] and it was well in their eyes; whatever the king did was well in the eyes of all the people. [37] And all the people and all of Israel realized on that day that it was not [ordered] by the king to kill Abner son of Ner.

[38] The king said to his servants, "Surely you realize that an officer and a great man has fallen in Israel this day, [39] but today I am still weak and newly anointed as king, and these sons of Zeruiah are harder than I. * But may HASHEM repay the evildoer according to his evil!"

. . . but feels
too weak to
punish Joab

4

[1] Saul's son heard that Abner had died in Hebron and he despaired, and all Israel was shocked.

[2] Two men, heads of legions, were with Saul's son; the name of the one was Baanah and the name of the second was Rechab, sons of Rimmon the Beerothite of the tribe of Benjamin, since Beeroth was also considered part of Benjamin. [3] The original Beerothites had fled to Gittaim, where they became sojourners, to this day. *

[4] (Jonathan son of Saul had a son who was lame. He had been five years old when word came from Jezreel about [the deaths of] Saul and Jonathan; his nursemaid had picked him up and fled, and in her hurry to flee she dropped him and he became lame. His name was Mephibosheth.)

[5] The sons of Rimmon the Beerothite — Rechab and Baanah — went forth, and arrived in the heat of the day at the house of Ish-bosheth, while he was

Traitors
assassinate
Ish-bosheth

having his afternoon rest. [6] Behold — they entered into the house [posing] as wheat merchants and struck him in the fifth rib; then Rechab and his brother Baanah escaped. *

[7] After they had entered the house while he was asleep in his bed in his bedroom, and struck him, and killed him, they had severed his head. They then took

They try to
ingratiate
themselves
to David . . .

his head and traveled through the Arabah all night. [8] They brought the head of Ish-bosheth to David in Hebron, and said to the king, "Here is the head of Ish-bosheth, son of Saul your enemy, who sought [to take] your life! HASHEM has

---

4:6. Since, as Scripture had informed us, the only heir to Saul's throne, other than Ish-bosheth, was not fit to reign   because of his lameness, this assassination was the deathblow to the House of Saul (*Radak*).

ט לַאדֹנִי הַמֶּלֶךְ נְקָמוֹת הַיּוֹם הַזֶּה מִשָּׁאוּל וּמִזַּרְעוֹ: וַיַּעַן דָּוִד אֶת־רֵכָב ׀ וְאֶת־
בַּעֲנָה אָחִיו בְּנֵי רִמּוֹן הַבְּאֵרֹתִי וַיֹּאמֶר לָהֶם חַי־יְהֹוָה אֲשֶׁר־פָּדָה אֶת־
י נַפְשִׁי מִכָּל־צָרָה: כִּי הַמַּגִּיד לִי לֵאמֹר הִנֵּה־מֵת שָׁאוּל וְהוּא־הָיָה כִמְבַשֵּׂר
יא בְּעֵינָיו וָאֹחֲזָה בוֹ וָאֶהְרְגֵהוּ בְּצִקְלָג אֲשֶׁר לְתִתִּי־לוֹ בְּשֹׂרָה: אַף כִּי־אֲנָשִׁים
רְשָׁעִים הָרְגוּ אֶת־אִישׁ־צַדִּיק בְּבֵיתוֹ עַל־מִשְׁכָּבוֹ וְעַתָּה הֲלוֹא אֲבַקֵּשׁ אֶת־
יב דָּמוֹ מִיֶּדְכֶם וּבִעַרְתִּי אֶתְכֶם מִן־הָאָרֶץ: וַיְצַו דָּוִד אֶת־הַנְּעָרִים וַיַּהַרְגוּם
וַיְקַצְּצוּ אֶת־יְדֵיהֶם וְאֶת־רַגְלֵיהֶם וַיִּתְלוּ עַל־הַבְּרֵכָה בְּחֶבְרוֹן וְאֵת רֹאשׁ
ה א אִישׁ־בֹּשֶׁת לָקָחוּ וַיִּקְבְּרוּ בְקֶבֶר־אַבְנֵר בְּחֶבְרוֹן: וַיָּבֹאוּ כָּל־שִׁבְטֵי
ב יִשְׂרָאֵל אֶל־דָּוִד חֶבְרוֹנָה וַיֹּאמְרוּ לֵאמֹר הִנְנוּ עַצְמְךָ וּבְשָׂרְךָ אֲנָחְנוּ: גַּם־
אֶתְמוֹל גַּם־שִׁלְשׁוֹם בִּהְיוֹת שָׁאוּל מֶלֶךְ עָלֵינוּ אַתָּה °הייתה [°הָיִיתָ ק]
°מוֹצִיא [°הַמּוֹצִיא ק] °והמבי [°וְהַמֵּבִיא ק] אֶת־יִשְׂרָאֵל וַיֹּאמֶר
יְהֹוָה לְךָ אַתָּה תִרְעֶה אֶת־עַמִּי אֶת־יִשְׂרָאֵל וְאַתָּה תִּהְיֶה לְנָגִיד עַל־
ג יִשְׂרָאֵל: וַיָּבֹאוּ כָּל־זִקְנֵי יִשְׂרָאֵל אֶל־הַמֶּלֶךְ חֶבְרוֹנָה וַיִּכְרֹת לָהֶם
הַמֶּלֶךְ דָּוִד בְּרִית בְּחֶבְרוֹן לִפְנֵי יְהֹוָה וַיִּמְשְׁחוּ אֶת־דָּוִד לְמֶלֶךְ עַל־
ד יִשְׂרָאֵל: בֶּן־שְׁלֹשִׁים שָׁנָה דָּוִד בְּמָלְכוֹ אַרְבָּעִים שָׁנָה מָלָךְ:
ה בְּחֶבְרוֹן מָלַךְ עַל־יְהוּדָה שֶׁבַע שָׁנִים וְשִׁשָּׁה חֳדָשִׁים וּבִירוּשָׁלַ͏ִם מָלַךְ
ו שְׁלֹשִׁים וְשָׁלֹשׁ שָׁנָה עַל כָּל־יִשְׂרָאֵל וִיהוּדָה: וַיֵּלֶךְ הַמֶּלֶךְ וַאֲנָשָׁיו
יְרוּשָׁלַ͏ִם אֶל־הַיְבֻסִי יוֹשֵׁב הָאָרֶץ וַיֹּאמֶר לְדָוִד לֵאמֹר לֹא־תָבוֹא הֵנָּה כִּי
ז אִם־הֱסִירְךָ הַעִוְרִים וְהַפִּסְחִים לֵאמֹר לֹא־יָבוֹא דָוִד הֵנָּה: וַיִּלְכֹּד דָּוִד אֵת
ח מְצֻדַת צִיּוֹן הִיא עִיר דָּוִד: וַיֹּאמֶר דָּוִד בַּיּוֹם הַהוּא כָּל־מַכֵּה יְבֻסִי וְיִגַּע
בַּצִּנּוֹר וְאֶת־הַפִּסְחִים וְאֶת־הָעִוְרִים °שנאו [°שְׂנֻאֵי ק] נֶפֶשׁ דָּוִד עַל־
ט כֵּן יֹאמְרוּ עִוֵּר וּפִסֵּחַ לֹא יָבוֹא אֶל־הַבָּיִת: וַיֵּשֶׁב דָּוִד בַּמְּצֻדָה וַיִּקְרָא־
י לָהּ עִיר דָּוִד וַיִּבֶן דָּוִד סָבִיב מִן־הַמִּלּוֹא וָבָיְתָה: וַיֵּלֶךְ דָּוִד הָלוֹךְ וְגָדוֹל
יא וַיהֹוָה אֱלֹהֵי צְבָאוֹת עִמּוֹ:   וַיִּשְׁלַח חִירָם מֶלֶךְ־צֹר מַלְאָכִים
יב אֶל־דָּוִד וַעֲצֵי אֲרָזִים וְחָרָשֵׁי עֵץ וְחָרָשֵׁי אֶבֶן קִיר וַיִּבְנוּ־בַיִת לְדָוִד: וַיֵּדַע
דָּוִד כִּי־הֱכִינוֹ יְהֹוָה לְמֶלֶךְ עַל־יִשְׂרָאֵל וְכִי נִשֵּׂא מַמְלַכְתּוֹ בַּעֲבוּר עַמּוֹ
יג יִשְׂרָאֵל: וַיִּקַּח דָּוִד עוֹד פִּלַגְשִׁים וְנָשִׁים מִירוּשָׁלַ͏ִם אַחֲרֵי בֹּאוֹ
יד מֵחֶבְרוֹן וַיִּוָּלְדוּ עוֹד לְדָוִד בָּנִים וּבָנוֹת: וְאֵלֶּה שְׁמוֹת הַיִּלֹּדִים לוֹ בִּירוּשָׁלָ͏ִם
טו-טז שַׁמּוּעַ וְשׁוֹבָב וְנָתָן וּשְׁלֹמֹה: וְיִבְחָר וֶאֱלִישׁוּעַ וְנֶפֶג וְיָפִיעַ: וֶאֱלִישָׁמָע
יז וְאֶלְיָדָע וֶאֱלִיפָלֶט: וַיִּשְׁמְעוּ פְלִשְׁתִּים כִּי־מָשְׁחוּ אֶת־דָּוִד לְמֶלֶךְ

4:10. He had expected to be rewarded for bringing the "good news" of his crime, but instead David treated him as a murderer.

4:12. David took this drastic step in order to convince everyone that he had no part in, nor was he pleased with, the destruction of the House of Saul.

5:6. "This city is so well fortified that you could not conquer it even if it were guarded only by the blind and lame" (*Abarbanel*). According to the *Midrash*, the Jebusites alluded to the Patriarchs. Abraham had made a treaty of peace with Abimelech, a Jebusite ancestor (*Genesis* 21:23). To commemorate the binding nature of the treaty, the Jebusites set up statues of a blind man, alluding to the blind Isaac (see *Genesis* 27:1), and a *granted my lord the king revenge from Saul and his offspring this day!"*

... but
David has
them exe-
cuted

⁹ *David answered Rechab and his brother Baanah, the sons of Rimmon the Beerothite, and said to them, "As HASHEM lives, Who has redeemed my soul from all adversity,* ¹⁰ *if the one who informed me, saying, 'Behold! Saul is dead,' saw himself as a bearer of good tidings, yet I seized him and killed him in Ziklag, instead of giving him [reward for his] tidings,* * ¹¹ *surely [this should be done] to wicked people who have killed an innocent man in his house upon his bed! Shall I not avenge his blood from your hand and eradicate you from the earth?"* ¹² *David then commanded the soldiers and they killed them. They cut off their hands and feet, and hung them over the pool in Hebron.* * *Then they took the head of Ish-bosheth and buried [it] in Abner's tomb, in Hebron.*

5

JERUSALEM,
CITY OF
DAVID
5:1-7:29

The entire
nation
accepts
David

¹ **A**ll the tribes of Israel came to David in Hebron and spoke, saying, "Behold, we are your bone and your flesh. ² Even yesterday and before yesterday, when Saul was king over us, you were the one who brought Israel out and brought them in; and HASHEM had said of you, 'You shall shepherd My people Israel and you shall be ruler over Israel.' " ³ All the elders of Israel came to the king at Hebron, and King David sealed a covenant with them in Hebron before HASHEM, and they anointed David as king over Israel.

⁴ David was thirty years old when he began to reign; he ruled for forty years — ⁵ in Hebron he ruled over Judah for seven years and six months, and in Jerusalem he ruled for thirty-three years over all of Israel and Judah.

⁶ The king and his men went to Jerusalem, to the Jebusite inhabitants of the land, and [one of them] spoke to David, saying, "You shall not enter here unless you remove the blind and the lame,"* as if to say, "David will not enter here."

David
occupies
Jerusalem
as his capital

⁷ David then captured Zion Fortress, which is [called] the City of David. ⁸ David declared on that day, "Whoever smites the Jebusite and reaches the stronghold, and the blind and the lame, that David detests . . .!* Therefore [people] say, "The blind and the lame [are here]; he shall not enter the house!" ⁹ David settled in the fortress and called it "The City of David." David built around [the city], from the Millo* and inward. ¹⁰David kept becoming greater, and HASHEM, the God of Legions, was with him.

Hiram
befriends
David

¹¹ Hiram, king of Tyre, sent a delegation to David, with cedar wood,* and carpenters, and masons of wall-stones, and they built a palace for David. ¹² David realized that HASHEM had established him as king over Israel and that He had exalted his kingdom for the sake of His people Israel. *

David's
family
grows

¹³ David took additional concubines and wives from Jerusalem after his coming from Hebron, and more sons and daughters were born to David. ¹⁴ These are the names of those born to him in Jerusalem: Shammua, Shobab, Nathan, Solomon, ¹⁵ Ibhar, Elishua, Nepheg, Japhia, ¹⁶ Elishama, Eliada, and Eliphelet. ¹⁷ The Philistines heard that [all the tribes] had anointed David as king

---

cripple, alluding to Jacob (see *Genesis* 32:26), and placed the words of the treaty in the statues' mouths.

5:8. The phrase is left unfinished [common practice for exclamations, curses and oaths in the Bible], but is quoted in full in *I Chronicles* 11:6: "Whoever strikes the Jebusites first will become a chief and an officer." David was no longer bound by Abraham's oath because more than 700 years had passed, ("my son and my grandson") and the term of the oath had expired.

5:9. The Millo was a landfill (*Rashi*), an open plaza for large gatherings (*Radak*), or a moat (*Abarbanel*).

5:11. Tyre is in Lebanon, famed for its cedar trees.

5:12. His great success and the homage of the powerful king of Tyre made David realize that he was indeed ordained to rule Israel, but he accepted it with the humility that typified his greatness: God had given him greatness only for the sake of Israel.

עַל־יִשְׂרָאֵל וַיַּעֲלוּ כָל־פְּלִשְׁתִּים לְבַקֵּשׁ אֶת־דָּוִד וַיִּשְׁמַע דָּוִד וַיֵּרֶד אֶל־
יח־יט הַמְּצוּדָה: וּפְלִשְׁתִּים בָּאוּ וַיִּנָּטְשׁוּ בְּעֵמֶק רְפָאִים: וַיִּשְׁאַל דָּוִד בַּיהוה
לֵאמֹר הַאֶעֱלֶה אֶל־פְּלִשְׁתִּים הֲתִתְּנֵם בְּיָדִי   וַיֹּאמֶר יהוה אֶל־
כ דָּוִד עֲלֵה כִּי־נָתֹן אֶתֵּן אֶת־הַפְּלִשְׁתִּים בְּיָדֶךָ: וַיָּבֹא דָוִד בְּבַעַל־פְּרָצִים
וַיַּכֵּם שָׁם דָּוִד וַיֹּאמֶר פָּרַץ יהוה אֶת־אֹיְבַי לְפָנַי כְּפֶרֶץ מָיִם עַל־כֵּן קָרָא
כא שֵׁם־הַמָּקוֹם הַהוּא בַּעַל פְּרָצִים: וַיַּעַזְבוּ־שָׁם אֶת־עֲצַבֵּיהֶם וַיִּשָּׂאֵם דָּוִד
כב וַאֲנָשָׁיו: וַיֹּסִפוּ עוֹד פְּלִשְׁתִּים לַעֲלוֹת וַיִּנָּטְשׁוּ בְּעֵמֶק רְפָאִים:
כג וַיִּשְׁאַל דָּוִד בַּיהוה וַיֹּאמֶר לֹא תַעֲלֶה הָסֵב אֶל־אַחֲרֵיהֶם וּבָאתָ לָהֶם
כד מִמּוּל בְּכָאִים: וִיהִי °בשמעך [קְכְּשָׁמְעֲךָ] אֶת־קוֹל צְעָדָה בְּרָאשֵׁי
הַבְּכָאִים אָז תֶּחֱרָץ כִּי אָז יָצָא יהוה לְפָנֶיךָ לְהַכּוֹת בְּמַחֲנֵה פְלִשְׁתִּים:
כה וַיַּעַשׂ דָּוִד כֵּן כַּאֲשֶׁר צִוָּהוּ יהוה וַיַּךְ אֶת־פְּלִשְׁתִּים מִגֶּבַע עַד־בֹּאֲךָ
א ו גָזֶר: ◀ וַיֹּסֶף עוֹד דָּוִד אֶת־כָּל־בָּחוּר בְּיִשְׂרָאֵל שְׁלֹשִׁים אָלֶף:

HAFTARAS
SHEMINI
Ashkenazim:
6:1-7:17
Sephardim:
6:1-19

ב וַיָּקָם ׀ וַיֵּלֶךְ דָּוִד וְכָל־הָעָם אֲשֶׁר אִתּוֹ מִבַּעֲלֵי יְהוּדָה לְהַעֲלוֹת מִשָּׁם אֵת
אֲרוֹן הָאֱלֹהִים אֲשֶׁר־נִקְרָא שֵׁם שֵׁם יהוה צְבָאוֹת יֹשֵׁב הַכְּרֻבִים עָלָיו:
ג וַיַּרְכִּבוּ אֶת־אֲרוֹן הָאֱלֹהִים אֶל־עֲגָלָה חֲדָשָׁה וַיִּשָּׂאֻהוּ מִבֵּית אֲבִינָדָב
אֲשֶׁר בַּגִּבְעָה וְעֻזָּא וְאַחְיוֹ בְּנֵי אֲבִינָדָב נֹהֲגִים אֶת־הָעֲגָלָה חֲדָשָׁה:
ד וַיִּשָּׂאֻהוּ מִבֵּית אֲבִינָדָב אֲשֶׁר בַּגִּבְעָה עִם אֲרוֹן הָאֱלֹהִים וְאַחְיוֹ הֹלֵךְ לִפְנֵי
ה הָאָרוֹן: וְדָוִד ׀ וְכָל־בֵּית יִשְׂרָאֵל מְשַׂחֲקִים לִפְנֵי יהוה בְּכֹל עֲצֵי בְרוֹשִׁים
ו וּבְכִנֹּרוֹת וּבִנְבָלִים וּבְתֻפִּים וּבִמְנַעַנְעִים וּבְצֶלְצֶלִים: וַיָּבֹאוּ עַד־גֹּרֶן נָכוֹן
ז וַיִּשְׁלַח עֻזָּה אֶל־אֲרוֹן הָאֱלֹהִים וַיֹּאחֶז בּוֹ כִּי שָׁמְטוּ הַבָּקָר: וַיִּחַר־אַף יהוה
ח בְּעֻזָּה וַיַּכֵּהוּ שָׁם הָאֱלֹהִים עַל־הַשַּׁל וַיָּמָת שָׁם עִם אֲרוֹן הָאֱלֹהִים: וַיִּחַר
לְדָוִד עַל אֲשֶׁר פָּרַץ יהוה פֶּרֶץ בְּעֻזָּה וַיִּקְרָא לַמָּקוֹם הַהוּא פֶּרֶץ עֻזָּה עַד
ט הַיּוֹם הַזֶּה: וַיִּרָא דָוִד אֶת־יהוה בַּיּוֹם הַהוּא וַיֹּאמֶר אֵיךְ יָבוֹא אֵלַי אֲרוֹן
י יהוה: וְלֹא־אָבָה דָוִד לְהָסִיר אֵלָיו אֶת־אֲרוֹן יהוה עַל־עִיר דָּוִד וַיַּטֵּהוּ דָוִד
יא בֵּית עֹבֵד־אֱדֹם הַגִּתִּי: וַיֵּשֶׁב אֲרוֹן יהוה בֵּית עֹבֵד אֱדֹם הַגִּתִּי שְׁלֹשָׁה
יב חֳדָשִׁים וַיְבָרֶךְ יהוה אֶת־עֹבֵד אֱדֹם וְאֶת־כָּל־בֵּיתוֹ: וַיֻּגַּד לַמֶּלֶךְ דָּוִד
לֵאמֹר בֵּרַךְ יהוה אֶת־בֵּית עֹבֵד אֱדֹם וְאֶת־כָּל־אֲשֶׁר־לוֹ בַּעֲבוּר אֲרוֹן
הָאֱלֹהִים וַיֵּלֶךְ דָּוִד וַיַּעַל אֶת־אֲרוֹן הָאֱלֹהִים מִבֵּית עֹבֵד אֱדֹם עִיר דָּוִד
יג בְּשִׂמְחָה: וַיְהִי כִּי צָעֲדוּ נֹשְׂאֵי אֲרוֹן־יהוה שִׁשָּׁה צְעָדִים וַיִּזְבַּח שׁוֹר וּמְרִיא:
יד־טו וְדָוִד מְכַרְכֵּר בְּכָל־עֹז לִפְנֵי יהוה וְדָוִד חָגוּר אֵפוֹד בָּד: וְדָוִד וְכָל־בֵּית

5:17. Hearing that all twelve tribes had accepted David as their king, the Philistines perceived him as a threat.

5:24. The rustling of the tree leaves would sound like a marching army, signifying that Hashem's angels had come to fight for Israel (*Rashi*). By telling David to wait for this sign — and ignore the entreaties of his own men who were anxious to attack the Philistines — God was

testing David to see if he would display the sort of impetuosity that had caused Saul to lose his throne (see *I Samuel* 10:8; 13:8-14).

6:2. Literally, *Plain of Judah;* another name for Kiriath-jearim (see *Joshua* 15:9), where the Ark had been located since its return by the Philistines (*I Samuel* 7:1-2).

6:7. The Sages explain that Uzzah committed a gross

over Israel, * so all the Philistines came up to seek out David. David heard and went down to the fortress. [18] The Philistines had come and spread out in the Rephaim Valley. [19] David inquired of HASHEM, saying, "Shall I go up against the Philistines? Will You deliver them into my hand?" And HASHEM answered David,* **David defeats the attacking Philistines** *"Go up, for I shall indeed deliver the Philistines into your hand." [20] David came to the Plain of Perazim, and David struck them there. He said, "HASHEM breached my enemies as water breaches [a barrier]"; therefore he named that place the Plain of Perazim [Breaches]. [21] [The Philistines] had left their idols there, and David and his men burned them.*

[22] *The Philistines came up once again and spread out in the Rephaim Valley.* [23] *So David inquired of HASHEM, and He said, "Do not go [directly] up; circle around to their rear, and approach them from opposite the mulberry trees. [24] It shall be that when you hear a sound like marching at the tops of the mulberry trees you shall shout [your battle cry], for then HASHEM will have gone out before you to strike at the Philistine camp."* * [25] *David did so, as HASHEM had commanded him, and he struck the Philistines from Geba until the approach to Gezer.*

6

David and his people retrieve the Ark

[1] **D**avid again gathered all the chosen men of Israel, thirty thousand. [2] *David and all the people that were with him arose and went forth from Baale-judah* * *to bring up from there the Ark of God, which is called by [its] name: "The Name of HASHEM, Master of Legions, Who is enthroned upon the Cherubim, is upon it." [3] They placed the Ark of God upon a new wagon and carried it from the house of Abinadab which was in Gibeah. Uzzah and Ahio, the sons of Abinadab, guided the new wagon. [4] They carried it from Abinadab's house which was in Gibeah, with the Ark of God, and Ahio walked in front of the Ark. [5] David and the entire House of Israel were rejoicing before HASHEM with all kinds of cypress-wood instruments — with harps, lyres, drums, timbrels and cymbals.*

Uzzah dies and the Ark is diverted

[6] *They came to the threshing-floor of Nacon, and Uzzah reached out to the Ark of God and grasped it, for the oxen had dislodged it. [7] HASHEM became angry at Uzzah and God struck him there for the blunder; and Uzzah died there by the Ark of God.* *

[8] *David was upset [with himself] because HASHEM had inflicted a breach against Uzzah; he named that place Perez-uzzah [Breach of Uzzah], [which is its name] to this day. [9] David feared HASHEM on that day, and he said, "How can the Ark of HASHEM come to me?" [10] So David refused to move the Ark of HASHEM to himself to the City of David, and David diverted it to the house of Obed-edom the Gittite.* * [11] *The Ark remained in the house of Obed-edom the Gittite for three months, and HASHEM blessed Obed-edom and his entire household.*

[12] *King David was told, "HASHEM has blessed the house of Obed-edom* **David leads the celebration for the Ark** *and everything he has because of the Ark of God." David then went and brought up the Ark of God from the house of Obed-edom to the City of David with joy. [13] Whenever the bearers of the Ark walked six paces, he slaughtered an ox and a fatted ox. [14] David danced with all [his] strength before HASHEM; David was girded in a linen tunic. [15] David and the entire House of*

---

error. The Ark was so holy that its customary bearers, the Levites, never felt its great weight; *they* were borne by *it.* How, then, could Uzzah think it was in danger of falling to the ground? (*Rashi*). David, on the other hand, was upset

with himself for having failed to take the necessary precautions to avoid such a mishap (*Malbim*).

6:10. He was a Levite (*I Chronicles* 15:18) who had lived in Gath (*Radak*).

טו יִשְׂרָאֵל מַעֲלִים אֶת־אֲרוֹן יהוה בִּתְרוּעָה וּבְקוֹל שׁוֹפָר: וְהָיָה אֲרוֹן יהוה
בָּא עִיר דָּוִד וּמִיכַל בַּת־שָׁאוּל נִשְׁקְפָה ׀ בְּעַד הַחַלּוֹן וַתֵּרֶא אֶת־הַמֶּלֶךְ
יז דָּוִד מְפַזֵּז וּמְכַרְכֵּר לִפְנֵי יהוה וַתִּבֶז לוֹ בְּלִבָּהּ: וַיָּבִאוּ אֶת־אֲרוֹן יהוה
וַיַּצִּגוּ אֹתוֹ בִּמְקוֹמוֹ בְּתוֹךְ הָאֹהֶל אֲשֶׁר נָטָה־לוֹ דָּוִד וַיַּעַל דָּוִד עֹלוֹת לִפְנֵי
יח יהוה וּשְׁלָמִים: וַיְכַל דָּוִד מֵהַעֲלוֹת הָעוֹלָה וְהַשְּׁלָמִים וַיְבָרֶךְ אֶת־הָעָם
יט בְּשֵׁם יהוה צְבָאוֹת: וַיְחַלֵּק לְכָל־הָעָם לְכָל־הֲמוֹן יִשְׂרָאֵל לְמֵאִישׁ וְעַד־
אִשָּׁה לְאִישׁ חַלַּת לֶחֶם אַחַת וְאֶשְׁפָּר אֶחָד וַאֲשִׁישָׁה אֶחָת וַיֵּלֶךְ כָּל־
כ הָעָם אִישׁ לְבֵיתוֹ: ◄ וַיָּשָׁב דָּוִד לְבָרֵךְ אֶת־בֵּיתוֹ וַתֵּצֵא מִיכַל בַּת־שָׁאוּל
לִקְרַאת דָּוִד וַתֹּאמֶר מַה־נִּכְבַּד הַיּוֹם מֶלֶךְ יִשְׂרָאֵל אֲשֶׁר נִגְלָה הַיּוֹם
כא לְעֵינֵי אַמְהוֹת עֲבָדָיו כְּהִגָּלוֹת נִגְלוֹת אַחַד הָרֵקִים: וַיֹּאמֶר דָּוִד אֶל־
מִיכַל לִפְנֵי יהוה אֲשֶׁר בָּחַר־בִּי מֵאָבִיךְ וּמִכָּל־בֵּיתוֹ לְצַוֹּת אֹתִי נָגִיד
כב עַל־עַם יהוה עַל־יִשְׂרָאֵל וְשִׂחַקְתִּי לִפְנֵי יהוה: וּנְקַלֹּתִי עוֹד מִזֹּאת
כג וְהָיִיתִי שָׁפָל בְּעֵינָי וְעִם־הָאֲמָהוֹת אֲשֶׁר אָמַרְתְּ עִמָּם אִכָּבֵדָה: וּלְמִיכַל
ז א בַּת־שָׁאוּל לֹא־הָיָה לָהּ יָלֶד עַד יוֹם מוֹתָהּ:　　　　　　וַיְהִי כִּי־
ב יָשַׁב הַמֶּלֶךְ בְּבֵיתוֹ וַיהוה הֵנִיחַ־לוֹ מִסָּבִיב מִכָּל־אֹיְבָיו: וַיֹּאמֶר הַמֶּלֶךְ
אֶל־נָתָן הַנָּבִיא רְאֵה נָא אָנֹכִי יוֹשֵׁב בְּבֵית אֲרָזִים וַאֲרוֹן הָאֱלֹהִים יֹשֵׁב
ג בְּתוֹךְ הַיְרִיעָה: וַיֹּאמֶר נָתָן אֶל־הַמֶּלֶךְ כֹּל אֲשֶׁר בִּלְבָבְךָ לֵךְ עֲשֵׂה
ד כִּי יהוה עִמָּךְ:　　　　　　וַיְהִי בַּלַּיְלָה הַהוּא וַיְהִי
ה דְבַר־יהוה אֶל־נָתָן לֵאמֹר: לֵךְ וְאָמַרְתָּ אֶל־עַבְדִּי אֶל־דָּוִד כֹּה אָמַר
ו יהוה הַאַתָּה תִּבְנֶה־לִּי בַיִת לְשִׁבְתִּי: כִּי לֹא יָשַׁבְתִּי בְּבַיִת לְמִיּוֹם הַעֲלֹתִי
אֶת־בְּנֵי יִשְׂרָאֵל מִמִּצְרַיִם וְעַד הַיּוֹם הַזֶּה וָאֶהְיֶה מִתְהַלֵּךְ בְּאֹהֶל
ז וּבְמִשְׁכָּן: בְּכֹל אֲשֶׁר־הִתְהַלַּכְתִּי בְּכָל־בְּנֵי יִשְׂרָאֵל הֲדָבָר דִּבַּרְתִּי אֶת־
אַחַד שִׁבְטֵי יִשְׂרָאֵל אֲשֶׁר צִוִּיתִי לִרְעוֹת אֶת־עַמִּי אֶת־יִשְׂרָאֵל לֵאמֹר
ח לָמָּה לֹא־בְנִיתֶם לִי בֵּית אֲרָזִים: וְעַתָּה כֹּה־תֹאמַר לְעַבְדִּי לְדָוִד כֹּה
אָמַר יהוה צְבָאוֹת אֲנִי לְקַחְתִּיךָ מִן־הַנָּוֶה מֵאַחַר הַצֹּאן לִהְיוֹת נָגִיד
ט עַל־עַמִּי עַל־יִשְׂרָאֵל: וָאֶהְיֶה עִמְּךָ בְּכֹל אֲשֶׁר הָלַכְתָּ וָאַכְרִתָה אֶת־
כָּל־אֹיְבֶיךָ מִפָּנֶיךָ וְעָשִׂתִי לְךָ שֵׁם גָּדוֹל כְּשֵׁם הַגְּדֹלִים אֲשֶׁר בָּאָרֶץ:
י וְשַׂמְתִּי מָקוֹם לְעַמִּי לְיִשְׂרָאֵל וּנְטַעְתִּיו וְשָׁכַן תַּחְתָּיו וְלֹא יִרְגַּז עוֹד וְלֹא־
יא יֹסִיפוּ בְנֵי־עַוְלָה לְעַנּוֹתוֹ כַּאֲשֶׁר בָּרִאשׁוֹנָה: וּלְמִן־הַיּוֹם אֲשֶׁר צִוִּיתִי
שֹׁפְטִים עַל־עַמִּי יִשְׂרָאֵל וַהֲנִיחֹתִי לְךָ מִכָּל־אֹיְבֶיךָ וְהִגִּיד לְךָ יהוה כִּי־

6:22. Unlike you, the maidservants of whom you have spoken so contemptuously will honor me for my humbleness before HASHEM.

6:23. As a punishment for her haughtiness, she bore no children *after* this incident, but she had given birth previously (see 3:5). The Sages interpret "no child until the day of her death" to mean that she died in childbirth (*Rashi*).

7:3. Nathan had assumed that David should build the Holy Temple, but God overruled him. For about 450 years since the Exodus, there had been no Temple, only a tent or a Tabernacle — nor had God requested one. The time was not yet ripe. Although God had given David unprecedented blessing and renown, the era of complete serenity would not be at hand until the reign of his son.

Israel brought up the Ark of HASHEM with loud, joyous sound, and the sound of the shofar.

¹⁶ And it happened as the Ark of HASHEM arrived at the City of David, that Michal daughter of Saul peered out the window and saw King David leaping and dancing before HASHEM, and she became contemptuous of him in her heart.

¹⁷ They brought the Ark of HASHEM and set it up in its place, within the tent that David had pitched for it; and David brought up elevation-offerings before HASHEM, and peace-offerings. ¹⁸ When David had finished bringing up the elevation-offering and the peace-offerings, he blessed the people with the Name of HASHEM, Master of Legions. ¹⁹ He distributed to all the people — to the entire multitude of Israel, man and woman alike — to each person: one loaf of bread, one portion of beef, and one container of wine. Then all the people left, everyone to his home.

Michal's contempt and David's rebuke ²⁰ David returned to bless his household. Michal daughter of Saul went out to meet David and said, "How honored was the king of Israel today, who was exposed today in the presence of his servants' maidservants, as one of the boors would be exposed!"

²¹ David answered Michal, "In the presence of HASHEM, Who chose me over your father and over his entire house to appoint me as ruler over the people of HASHEM, over Israel — before HASHEM I shall rejoice! ²² And I shall behave even more humbly than this, and I shall be lowly in my eyes; and among the maidservants of whom you spoke — among them will I be honored!"*

²³ Michal daughter of Saul had no child until the day of her death. *

7

David longs to build the Holy Temple ¹ It happened after the king was settled into his home and HASHEM had given him respite from his enemies all around, ² that the king said to Nathan the prophet, "See now, I am living in a house of cedar while the Ark of God dwells within the curtain!"

³ Nathan said to the king, "Whatever is in your heart go and do, for HASHEM is with you."*

God does not request a Temple ⁴ It happened that night that the word of HASHEM came to Nathan, saying, ⁵ "Go and say to My servant, to David: 'Thus said HASHEM: Will you build Me a house for My dwelling? ⁶ For I have not dwelt in a house from the day I brought the Children of Israel up from Egypt to this day; I have moved about in a tent and a Tabernacle. ⁷ Wherever I moved about among all the Children of Israel, did I say a word to one of the leaders of Israel, whom I have appointed to shepherd My people Israel, saying, 'Why have you not built Me a house of cedar?' ⁸ And now, so shall you say to My servant, to David: 'Thus said HASHEM, Master of Legions: I have taken you from the sheepfold, from following the flocks, to become ruler over My people, over Israel. ⁹ I was with you wherever you went — I cut down all your enemies before you and I gave you great renown, like the renown of the great men of the world. ¹⁰ I shall yet establish a place for My people, for Israel; I shall plant it there and it shall dwell in its place so that it shall be disturbed no more; iniquitous people will no longer afflict it as in early times, ¹¹ and also from the day that I appointed judges over My people Israel — and I shall give you respite from all your enemies. And HASHEM informs you that

---

God assured David that he would found a dynasty and that his son Solomon would build the Temple. God would be a loving Father to Solomon, even when it would be necessary to chastise him.

יב בַּיִת יַעֲשֶׂה־לְּךָ יהוה: כִּי ׀ יִמְלְאוּ יָמֶיךָ וְשָׁכַבְתָּ אֶת־אֲבֹתֶיךָ וַהֲקִימֹתִי אֶת־
יג זַרְעֲךָ אַחֲרֶיךָ אֲשֶׁר יֵצֵא מִמֵּעֶיךָ וַהֲכִינֹתִי אֶת־מַמְלַכְתּוֹ: הוּא יִבְנֶה־בַּיִת
יד לִשְׁמִי וְכֹנַנְתִּי אֶת־כִּסֵּא מַמְלַכְתּוֹ עַד־עוֹלָם: אֲנִי אֶהְיֶה־לּוֹ לְאָב וְהוּא
יִהְיֶה־לִּי לְבֵן אֲשֶׁר בְּהַעֲוֺתוֹ וְהֹכַחְתִּיו בְּשֵׁבֶט אֲנָשִׁים וּבְנִגְעֵי בְּנֵי אָדָם:
טו וְחַסְדִּי לֹא־יָסוּר מִמֶּנּוּ כַּאֲשֶׁר הֲסִרֹתִי מֵעִם שָׁאוּל אֲשֶׁר הֲסִרֹתִי מִלְּפָנֶיךָ:
טז וְנֶאְמַן בֵּיתְךָ וּמַמְלַכְתְּךָ עַד־עוֹלָם לְפָנֶיךָ כִּסְאֲךָ יִהְיֶה נָכוֹן עַד־עוֹלָם:
יז כְּכֹל הַדְּבָרִים הָאֵלֶּה וּכְכֹל הַחִזָּיוֹן הַזֶּה כֵּן דִּבֶּר נָתָן אֶל־דָּוִד:
יח וַיָּבֹא הַמֶּלֶךְ דָּוִד וַיֵּשֶׁב לִפְנֵי יהוה וַיֹּאמֶר מִי אָנֹכִי אֲדֹנָי יֱהוִה וּמִי בֵיתִי
יט כִּי הֲבִיאֹתַנִי עַד־הֲלֹם: וַתִּקְטַן עוֹד זֹאת בְּעֵינֶיךָ אֲדֹנָי יֱהוִה וַתְּדַבֵּר
כ גַּם אֶל־בֵּית־עַבְדְּךָ לְמֵרָחוֹק וְזֹאת תּוֹרַת הָאָדָם אֲדֹנָי יֱהוִה: וּמַה־
כא יּוֹסִיף דָּוִד עוֹד לְדַבֵּר אֵלֶיךָ וְאַתָּה יָדַעְתָּ אֶת־עַבְדְּךָ אֲדֹנָי יֱהוִה: בַּעֲבוּר
כב דְּבָרְךָ וּכְלִבְּךָ עָשִׂיתָ אֵת כָּל־הַגְּדוּלָּה הַזֹּאת לְהוֹדִיעַ אֶת־עַבְדֶּךָ: עַל־
כֵּן גָּדַלְתָּ אֲדֹנָי יֱהוִה כִּי־אֵין כָּמוֹךָ וְאֵין אֱלֹהִים זוּלָתֶךָ בְּכֹל אֲשֶׁר־
כג שָׁמַעְנוּ בְּאָזְנֵינוּ: וּמִי כְעַמְּךָ כְּיִשְׂרָאֵל גּוֹי אֶחָד בָּאָרֶץ אֲשֶׁר הָלְכוּ־
אֱלֹהִים לִפְדּוֹת־לוֹ לְעָם וְלָשׂוּם לוֹ שֵׁם וְלַעֲשׂוֹת לָכֶם הַגְּדוּלָּה וְנֹרָאוֹת
כד לְאַרְצֶךָ מִפְּנֵי עַמְּךָ אֲשֶׁר פָּדִיתָ לְּךָ מִמִּצְרַיִם גּוֹיִם וֵאלֹהָיו: וַתְּכוֹנֵן לְךָ
אֶת־עַמְּךָ יִשְׂרָאֵל ׀ לְךָ לְעָם עַד־עוֹלָם וְאַתָּה יהוה הָיִיתָ לָהֶם לֵאלֹהִים:
כה וְעַתָּה יהוה אֱלֹהִים הַדָּבָר אֲשֶׁר דִּבַּרְתָּ עַל־עַבְדְּךָ וְעַל־בֵּיתוֹ הָקֵם עַד־
כו עוֹלָם וַעֲשֵׂה כַּאֲשֶׁר דִּבַּרְתָּ: וְיִגְדַּל שִׁמְךָ עַד־עוֹלָם לֵאמֹר יהוה צְבָאוֹת
כז אֱלֹהִים עַל־יִשְׂרָאֵל וּבֵית עַבְדְּךָ דָוִד יִהְיֶה נָכוֹן לְפָנֶיךָ: כִּי־אַתָּה יהוה
צְבָאוֹת אֱלֹהֵי יִשְׂרָאֵל גָּלִיתָה אֶת־אֹזֶן עַבְדְּךָ לֵאמֹר בַּיִת אֶבְנֶה־לָּךְ
עַל־כֵּן מָצָא עַבְדְּךָ אֶת־לִבּוֹ לְהִתְפַּלֵּל אֵלֶיךָ אֶת־הַתְּפִלָּה הַזֹּאת:
כח וְעַתָּה ׀ אֲדֹנָי יֱהוִה אַתָּה־הוּא הָאֱלֹהִים וּדְבָרֶיךָ יִהְיוּ אֱמֶת וַתְּדַבֵּר
כט אֶל־עַבְדְּךָ אֶת־הַטּוֹבָה הַזֹּאת: וְעַתָּה הוֹאֵל וּבָרֵךְ אֶת־בֵּית עַבְדְּךָ
לִהְיוֹת לְעוֹלָם לְפָנֶיךָ כִּי־אַתָּה אֲדֹנָי יֱהוִה דִּבַּרְתָּ וּמִבִּרְכָתְךָ יְבֹרַךְ בֵּית־
ח א עַבְדְּךָ לְעוֹלָם: וַיְהִי אַחֲרֵי־כֵן וַיַּךְ דָּוִד אֶת־
ב פְּלִשְׁתִּים וַיַּכְנִיעֵם וַיִּקַּח דָּוִד אֶת־מֶתֶג הָאַמָּה מִיַּד פְּלִשְׁתִּים: וַיַּךְ
אֶת־מוֹאָב וַיְמַדְּדֵם בַּחֶבֶל הַשְׁכֵּב אוֹתָם אַרְצָה וַיְמַדֵּד שְׁנֵי־חֲבָלִים
לְהָמִית וּמְלֹא הַחֶבֶל לְהַחֲיוֹת וַתְּהִי מוֹאָב לְדָוִד לַעֲבָדִים נֹשְׂאֵי מִנְחָה:

7:14. I will chastise him as a father would a son, but not too severely, never abandoning My affection for him and never abrogating My promise concerning the permanence of your dynasty.

7:19. Only a great man — not I — is deserving of such honor (*Radak*).

7:20. I need not praise You, for You know the deepest thoughts of my heart (*Radak*). Or, "What else could I request; You have granted all I could want" (*Targum, Rashi*).

7:23. Since You are the One and Only great God, how fortunate are Your people Israel that You have chosen (*Metzudos*).

7:27. Only because You have told me that You desire to create a dynasty from me have I dared to approach You with the request that my offspring rule forever (*Kara*).

8:1. Lit., "Harness of the Arm." The city was also known as Gath (*I Chronicles* 18:1), and was the capital of the Philistine confederation and the seat of the monarchy (*Rashi*).

God will establish David's dynasty, and his son will build the Temple HASHEM will establish a dynasty for you. ¹² When your days are complete and you lie with your forefathers, I shall raise up after you your offspring who will issue from your loins, and I shall make his kingdom firm. ¹³ He shall build a Temple for My sake, and I shall make firm the throne of his kingdom forever. ¹⁴ I shall be a Father unto him and he shall be a son unto Me, so that when he sins I will chastise him with the rod of men and with afflictions of human beings. *

¹⁵ But My kindness will not be removed from him as I removed [it] from Saul, whom I removed from before you. ¹⁶ Your dynasty and your kingdom will remain steadfast before you for all time; your throne will remain firm forever.' "

¹⁷ In accordance with all these words and this entire vision, so did Nathan speak to David.

David thanks God . . . ¹⁸ King David then came and sat down before HASHEM, and said, "Who am I, O my Lord, HASHEM/ELOHIM, and who is my household, that You should have brought me this far? ¹⁹ And yet this was still insufficient in Your eyes, my Lord HASHEM/ELOHIM, so You have spoken even of Your servant's household in the distant future — and that would be fitting for [great] men * — O my Lord, HASHEM/ELOHIM. ²⁰ What more can David say to You; You know Your servant, my Lord, HASHEM/ELOHIM. * ²¹ It is because of Your word and Your desire that You have bestowed all this greatness [upon me], and informed Your servant of it; ²² because You are great, HASHEM, God, for there is none like You and there *. . . and prays for Israel and his dynasty* is no god besides You, according to all that we have heard with our ears. ²³ And who is like Your people, like Israel, a unique nation on earth, whom God went forth to redeem unto Himself for a people * — thus gaining Himself renown — and to perform great works for you [Israel] and wonders for Your Land, [driving out] nations and their gods from before Your people, whom You have redeemed for Yourself from Egypt. ²⁴ You have established for Yourself Your people Israel as a people unto You forever, and You, HASHEM, have been a God for them. ²⁵ And now, HASHEM, God, may You forever uphold the matter that You have spoken concerning Your servant and his house and do as You have spoken. ²⁶ And may Your Name thereby be glorified forever, saying, 'HASHEM, Master of Legions, is God over Israel!' And may the house of Your servant David remain firm before You; ²⁷ for You, HASHEM, Master of Legions, God of Israel, have revealed to the ear of Your servant, saying, 'I shall create a dynasty for you'; therefore Your servant has found it proper in his heart to pray this prayer to You. * ²⁸ And now, O my Lord, HASHEM/ELOHIM, You are God and Your words will come true, and You have spoken to Your servant of this benevolence. ²⁹ And now, may You desire to bless the house of Your servant, that it may remain forever before You, for You, my Lord, HASHEM/ELOHIM, have spoken; and from Your blessing may the House of Your servant be blessed forever."

8

DAVID SUBDUES FOREIGN ENEMIES
8:1-18

¹ It happened after this that David struck the Philistines and subdued them. David took Metheg-ammah* from the hands of the Philistines.

² He [also] struck Moab. He measured [his captives] with a rope, laying them down on the ground and measuring two ropes' length to be put to death and one rope's length to be kept alive. * The Moabites became subjects to David, bearers of tribute.

8:2. According to the *Midrash,* David punished the Moabites because they had murdered his parents and brothers after he had brought them to Moab for safekeeping (see *I Samuel* 22:3-5).

ג וַיַּ֤ךְ דָּוִד֙ אֶת־הֲדַדְעֶ֣זֶר בֶּן־רְחֹ֔ב מֶ֣לֶךְ צוֹבָ֑ה בְּלֶכְתּ֕וֹ לְהָשִׁ֥יב יָד֖וֹ בִּנְהַר־
ד [פְּרָת ק' ולא כ':] וַיִּלְכֹּ֨ד דָּוִ֜ד מִמֶּ֗נּוּ אֶ֤לֶף וּשְׁבַע־מֵאוֹת֙ פָּ֣רָשִׁ֔ים וְעֶשְׂרִ֥ים אֶ֖לֶף
ה אִ֣ישׁ רַגְלִ֑י וַיְעַקֵּ֤ר דָּוִד֙ אֶת־כָּל־הָרֶ֔כֶב וַיּוֹתֵ֥ר מִמֶּ֖נּוּ מֵ֥אָה רָֽכֶב: וַתָּבֹא֙ אֲרַ֣ם
דַּמֶּ֔שֶׂק לַעְזֹ֕ר לַהֲדַדְעֶ֖זֶר מֶ֣לֶךְ צוֹבָ֑ה וַיַּ֤ךְ דָּוִד֙ בַּֽאֲרָ֔ם עֶשְׂרִֽים־וּשְׁנַ֥יִם אֶ֖לֶף
ו אִֽישׁ: וַיָּ֨שֶׂם דָּוִ֤ד נְצִבִים֙ בַּאֲרַ֣ם דַּמֶּ֔שֶׂק וַתְּהִ֤י אֲרָם֙ לְדָוִ֔ד לַעֲבָדִ֖ים נוֹשְׂאֵ֣י
מִנְחָ֑ה וַיֹּ֤שַׁע יהוה֙ אֶת־דָּוִ֔ד בְּכֹ֖ל אֲשֶׁ֥ר הָלָֽךְ: ז וַיִּקַּ֣ח דָּוִ֗ד אֵ֚ת שִׁלְטֵ֣י הַזָּהָ֔ב
אֲשֶׁ֣ר הָי֔וּ אֶ֖ל עַבְדֵ֣י הֲדַדְעָ֑זֶר וַיְבִיאֵ֖ם יְרוּשָׁלָֽ͏ִם: ח וּמִבֶּ֥טַח וּמִבֵּרֹתַ֖י עָרֵ֣י
הֲדַדְעָ֑זֶר לָקַ֞ח הַמֶּ֧לֶךְ דָּוִ֛ד נְחֹ֖שֶׁת הַרְבֵּ֥ה מְאֹֽד: ט וַיִּשְׁמַ֕ע תֹּ֖עִי
מֶ֣לֶךְ חֲמָ֑ת כִּ֚י הִכָּ֣ה דָוִ֔ד אֵ֖ת כָּל־חֵ֥יל הֲדַדְעָֽזֶר: י וַיִּשְׁלַ֣ח תֹּ֣עִי אֶת־יֽוֹרָם־בְּנ֣וֹ
אֶל־הַמֶּֽלֶךְ־דָּ֠וִד לִשְׁאָל־ל֨וֹ לְשָׁל֜וֹם וּֽלְבָרֲכ֗וֹ עַל֩ אֲשֶׁ֨ר נִלְחַ֤ם בַּהֲדַדְעֶ֙זֶר֙
וַיַּכֵּ֔הוּ כִּי־אִ֛ישׁ מִלְחֲמ֥וֹת תֹּ֖עִי הָיָ֣ה הֲדַדְעָ֑זֶר וּבְיָד֗וֹ הָי֛וּ כְּלֵי־כֶ֥סֶף וּכְלֵי־זָהָ֖ב
יא וּכְלֵ֥י נְחֹֽשֶׁת: גַּם־אֹתָ֗ם הִקְדִּ֞ישׁ הַמֶּ֤לֶךְ דָּוִד֙ לַֽיהוה֔ עִם־הַכֶּ֖סֶף וְהַזָּהָ֑ב אֲשֶׁ֣ר
הִקְדִּ֗ישׁ מִכָּל־הַגּוֹיִ֖ם אֲשֶׁ֥ר כִּבֵּֽשׁ: יב מֵאֲרָ֣ם וּמִמּוֹאָ֗ב וּמִבְּנֵ֤י עַמּוֹן֙ וּמִפְּלִשְׁתִּ֔ים
וּמֵֽעֲמָלֵ֑ק וּמִשְּׁלַ֛ל הֲדַדְעֶ֥זֶר בֶּן־רְחֹ֖ב מֶ֥לֶךְ צוֹבָֽה: יג וַיַּ֤עַשׂ דָּוִד֙ שֵׁ֔ם בְּשֻׁב֕וֹ
מֵהַכּוֹת֥וֹ אֶת־אֲרָ֖ם בְּגֵיא־מֶ֑לַח שְׁמוֹנָ֥ה עָשָׂ֖ר אָֽלֶף: יד וַיָּ֨שֶׂם בֶּאֱד֜וֹם נְצִבִ֗ים
בְּכָל־אֱדוֹם֙ שָׂ֣ם נְצִבִ֔ים וַיְהִ֥י כָל־אֱד֖וֹם עֲבָדִ֣ים לְדָוִ֑ד וַיּ֤וֹשַׁע יהוה֙ אֶת־דָּוִ֔ד
בְּכֹ֖ל אֲשֶׁ֥ר הָלָֽךְ: טו וַיִּמְלֹ֥ךְ דָּוִ֖ד עַל־כָּל־יִשְׂרָאֵ֑ל וַיְהִ֣י דָוִ֗ד עֹשֶׂ֛ה מִשְׁפָּ֥ט
וּצְדָקָ֖ה לְכָל־עַמּֽוֹ: טז וְיוֹאָ֥ב בֶּן־צְרוּיָ֖ה עַל־הַצָּבָ֑א וִיהוֹשָׁפָ֥ט בֶּן־אֲחִיל֖וּד
מַזְכִּֽיר: יז וְצָד֧וֹק בֶּן־אֲחִיט֛וּב וַאֲחִימֶ֥לֶךְ בֶּן־אֶבְיָתָ֖ר כֹּהֲנִ֑ים וּשְׂרָיָ֖ה סוֹפֵֽר:
יח וּבְנָיָ֙הוּ֙ בֶּן־יְה֣וֹיָדָ֔ע וְהַכְּרֵתִ֖י וְהַפְּלֵתִ֑י וּבְנֵ֥י דָוִ֖ד כֹּהֲנִ֥ים הָיֽוּ: ט:א וַיֹּ֣אמֶר
דָּוִ֔ד הֲכִ֣י יֶשׁ־ע֔וֹד אֲשֶׁ֥ר נוֹתַ֖ר לְבֵ֣ית שָׁא֑וּל וְאֶעֱשֶׂ֤ה עִמּוֹ֙ חֶ֔סֶד בַּעֲב֖וּר
יְהוֹנָתָֽן: ב וּלְבֵ֨ית שָׁא֥וּל עֶ֙בֶד֙ וּשְׁמ֣וֹ צִיבָ֔א וַיִּקְרְאוּ־ל֖וֹ אֶל־דָּוִ֑ד וַיֹּ֨אמֶר הַמֶּ֤לֶךְ
אֵלָיו֙ הַאַתָּ֣ה צִיבָ֔א וַיֹּ֖אמֶר עַבְדֶּֽךָ: ג וַיֹּ֣אמֶר הַמֶּ֗לֶךְ הַאֶ֨פֶס ע֥וֹד אִישׁ֙ לְבֵ֣ית
שָׁא֔וּל וְאֶעֱשֶׂ֥ה עִמּ֖וֹ חֶ֣סֶד אֱלֹהִ֑ים וַיֹּ֤אמֶר צִיבָא֙ אֶל־הַמֶּ֔לֶךְ ע֥וֹד בֵּ֛ן
לִיהוֹנָתָ֖ן נְכֵ֥ה רַגְלָֽיִם: ד וַיֹּֽאמֶר־ל֥וֹ הַמֶּ֖לֶךְ אֵיפֹ֣ה ה֑וּא וַיֹּ֤אמֶר צִיבָא֙ אֶל־
הַמֶּ֔לֶךְ הִנֵּה־ה֗וּא בֵּ֛ית מָכִ֥יר בֶּן־עַמִּיאֵ֖ל בְּל֥וֹ דְבָֽר: ה וַיִּשְׁלַ֖ח הַמֶּ֣לֶךְ דָּוִ֑ד
וַיִּקָּחֵ֗הוּ מִבֵּ֛ית מָכִ֥יר בֶּן־עַמִּיאֵ֖ל מִלּ֥וֹ דְבָֽר: ו וַ֠יָּבֹא מְפִיבֹ֣שֶׁת בֶּן־יְהוֹנָתָ֤ן
בֶּן־שָׁאוּל֙ אֶל־דָּוִ֔ד וַיִּפֹּ֥ל עַל־פָּנָ֖יו וַיִּשְׁתָּ֑חוּ וַיֹּ֤אמֶר דָּוִד֙ מְפִיבֹ֔שֶׁת וַיֹּ֖אמֶר
הִנֵּ֥ה עַבְדֶּֽךָ: ז וַיֹּאמֶר֩ ל֨וֹ דָוִ֜ד אַל־תִּירָ֗א כִּ֣י עָשֹׂ֩ה אֶעֱשֶׂ֨ה עִמְּךָ֤ חֶ֙סֶד֙
בַּֽעֲבוּר֙ יְהוֹנָתָ֣ן אָבִ֔יךָ וַהֲשִׁבֹתִ֣י לְךָ֔ אֶת־כָּל־שְׂדֵ֖ה שָׁא֣וּל אָבִ֑יךָ וְאַתָּ֗ה

8:3. In the process of controlling the Euphrates, Hadadezer would have to overrun part of *Eretz Yisrael* (*Radak*).

8:11. For use in the construction of the Temple (see *I Chronicles* 18:8; *I Kings* 7:51).

8:13. Because he fought valiantly there (*Kara*). The Sages attribute his renown to his virtuous conduct in war: He had the slain enemy soldiers properly buried.

The Valley of Salt is located in Edom (see *II Kings* 14:7). As may be seen from *Psalms* 60:2 and as suggested here by the following verse, there was a war against *Edom*, which was apparently fought immediately after, or simultaneously with, the war with Aram. See also *I Chronicles* 18:12 (*Radak*).

³ *David [also] struck Hadadezer son of Rehob, king of Zobah, as he was on the way to extend his control over the Euphrates River.* * ⁴ *David captured from him one thousand seven hundred horsemen, and twenty thousand foot soldiers; David hamstrung all the chariot [horses], while he left over of them one hundred chariot [horses].* ⁵ *Aram of Damascus came to assist Hadadezer, king of Zobah, and David struck down twenty-two thousand men of Aram.* ⁶ *David appointed authorities in Aram of Damascus, and Aram became servants of David, bearers of tribute. HASHEM caused salvation for David wherever he went.* ⁷ *David took the golden shields of Hadadezer's servants and brought them to Jerusalem.* ⁸ *And from Betah and Berothai — cities of Hadadezer — King David took a great deal of copper.*

King Toi pays tribute ⁹ *Toi, king of Hamath, heard that David had struck down the entire army of Hadadezer.* ¹⁰ *So Toi sent his son Joram to King David to greet him and to wish him well for having fought and defeated Hadadezer, for Hadadezer was a battle foe of Toi; in his hand were silver vessels, gold vessels and copper vessels.* ¹¹ *King David consecrated them also unto HASHEM,* * *along with the silver and gold of all the nations he had conquered, which he had already consecrated —* ¹² *from Aram, from Moab, from the Children of Ammon, from the Philistines, from Amalek, and from the spoils of Hadadezer son of Rehob, king of Zobah.*

David consolidates his reign ¹³ *David gained renown* * *upon returning from striking down Aram at the Valley of Salt:* * *eighteen thousand [men].* ¹⁴ *He appointed authorities in Edom — throughout Edom he appointed authorities — and all of Edom became subjects of David. HASHEM caused salvation for David wherever he went.*

¹⁵ *David reigned over all of Israel; David administered justice and kindness to his entire people.* ¹⁶ *Joab son of Zeruiah was in command of the army; Jehoshaphat son of Ahilud was the chronicler;* ¹⁷ *Zadok son of Ahitub and Ahimelech son of Ebiathar were Kohanim; Seraiah was the scribe;* ¹⁸ *Benaiahu son of Jehoiada was in charge of the archers and slingers,* * *and David's sons were senior ministers.*

9

DAVID AND MEPHI- BOSHETH 9:1-13

David learns of Jonathan's young surviving son . . .

¹ **D**avid inquired, "Is there anyone else who has survived of the House of Saul, so that I may deal kindly with him for the sake of Jonathan?" ² *The House of Saul had a servant named Ziba, and they summoned him to David. The king said to him, "Are you Ziba?" and he answered, "[I am] your servant."* ³ *The king said, "Is there any man at all left of the House of Saul, so that I may perform Godly kindness with him?" Ziba said to the king, "There remains a son of Jonathan, whose legs are crippled."* ⁴ *The king said, "Where is he?" and Ziba said to the king, "Behold, he is in the house of Machir son of Ammiel, in Lo-debar."* ⁵ *King David sent and had him brought from the house of Machir son of Ammiel, from Lo-debar.* ⁶ *Mephibosheth son of Jonathan son of Saul came before David and fell upon his face and prostrated himself. David said, "[Are you] Mephibosheth?" and he said, "Behold! [I am] your servant."* ⁷ *David told him, "Fear not, for I shall surely deal kindly with you for the sake of your father Jonathan; I shall return to you the entire estate of your father Saul,* * *and you*

8:18. The translation of וְהַכְּרֵתִי וְהַפְּלֵתִי follows *Targum*. *Radak* suggests the Cherethite and the Pelethite, two families loyal to David. The Talmud says that the two terms refer to the *Urim VeTumim* (see *Exodus* 28:30) or the Sanhedrin.

9:7. That is, your *grandfather* Saul. It is common in the Bible for grandsons to be referred to as "sons," as here, and as in vv. 9 and 10.

ח תֹּאכַל לֶ֫חֶם עַל־שֻׁלְחָנִ֖י תָּמִ֑יד וַיִּשְׁתַּ֣חוּ וַיֹּ֔אמֶר מֶ֖ה עַבְדֶּ֑ךָ כִּ֣י פָנִ֔יתָ אֶל־

ט הַכֶּ֥לֶב הַמֵּ֖ת אֲשֶׁ֥ר כָּמֽוֹנִי׃ וַיִּקְרָ֣א הַמֶּ֗לֶךְ אֶל־צִיבָ֛א נַ֥עַר שָׁא֖וּל וַיֹּ֣אמֶר אֵלָ֑יו

י כֹּל֩ אֲשֶׁ֨ר הָיָ֤ה לְשָׁאוּל֙ וּלְכָל־בֵּית֔וֹ נָתַ֖תִּי לְבֶן־אֲדֹנֶֽיךָ׃ וְעָבַ֣דְתָּ לּ֣וֹ אֶת־
הָאֲדָמָ֡ה אַתָּה֩ וּבָנֶ֨יךָ וַעֲבָדֶ֜יךָ וְהֵבֵ֗אתָ וְהָיָ֤ה לְבֶן־אֲדֹנֶ֙יךָ֙ לֶ֔חֶם וַאֲכָל֔וֹ
וּמְפִיבֹ֙שֶׁת֙ בֶּן־אֲדֹנֶ֔יךָ יֹאכַ֥ל תָּמִ֖יד לֶ֣חֶם עַל־שֻׁלְחָנִ֑י וּלְצִיבָ֗א חֲמִשָּׁ֥ה עָשָׂ֛ר

יא בָּנִ֖ים וְעֶשְׂרִ֥ים עֲבָדִֽים׃ וַיֹּ֤אמֶר צִיבָא֙ אֶל־הַמֶּ֔לֶךְ כְּכֹל֩ אֲשֶׁ֨ר יְצַוֶּ֜ה אֲדֹנִ֤י
הַמֶּ֙לֶךְ֙ אֶת־עַבְדּ֔וֹ כֵּ֖ן יַעֲשֶׂ֣ה עַבְדֶּ֑ךָ וּמְפִיבֹ֗שֶׁת אֹכֵל֙ עַל־שֻׁלְחָנִ֔י כְּאַחַ֖ד

יב מִבְּנֵ֥י הַמֶּֽלֶךְ׃ וְלִמְפִיבֹ֥שֶׁת בֵּן־קָטָ֖ן וּשְׁמ֣וֹ מִיכָ֑א וְכֹל֙ מוֹשַׁ֣ב בֵּית־צִיבָ֔א

יג עֲבָדִ֖ים לִמְפִיבֹֽשֶׁת׃ וּמְפִיבֹ֗שֶׁת יֹשֵׁב֙ בִּיר֣וּשָׁלַ֔͏ִם כִּ֣י עַל־שֻׁלְחַ֥ן הַמֶּ֛לֶךְ תָּמִ֖יד
ה֥וּא אֹכֵ֖ל וְה֥וּא פִּסֵּ֖חַ שְׁתֵּ֥י רַגְלָֽיו׃

י א וַיְהִי֙ אַֽחֲרֵי־כֵ֔ן וַיָּ֕מָת מֶ֖לֶךְ

ב בְּנֵ֣י עַמּ֑וֹן וַיִּמְלֹ֛ךְ חָנ֥וּן בְּנ֖וֹ תַּחְתָּֽיו׃ וַיֹּ֨אמֶר דָּוִ֜ד אֶעֱשֶׂה־חֶ֣סֶד ׀ עִם־חָנ֣וּן בֶּן־
נָחָ֗שׁ כַּאֲשֶׁר֩ עָשָׂ֨ה אָבִ֤יו עִמָּדִי֙ חֶ֔סֶד וַיִּשְׁלַ֨ח דָּוִ֧ד לְנַחֲמ֛וֹ בְּיַד־עֲבָדָ֖יו אֶל־

ג אָבִ֑יו וַיָּבֹ֙אוּ֙ עַבְדֵ֣י דָוִ֔ד אֶ֖רֶץ בְּנֵ֥י עַמּֽוֹן׃ וַיֹּאמְרוּ֩ שָׂרֵ֨י בְנֵֽי־עַמּ֜וֹן אֶל־חָנ֣וּן
אֲדֹֽנֵיהֶ֗ם הַֽמְכַבֵּ֨ד דָּוִ֤ד אֶת־אָבִ֙יךָ֙ בְּעֵינֶ֔יךָ כִּֽי־שָׁלַ֥ח לְךָ֖ מְנַֽחֲמִ֑ים הֲ֠לוֹא
בַּעֲב֞וּר חֲק֤וֹר אֶת־הָעִיר֙ וּלְרַגְּלָ֣הּ וּלְהָפְכָ֔הּ שָׁלַ֥ח דָּוִ֛ד אֶת־עֲבָדָ֖יו אֵלֶֽיךָ׃

ד וַיִּקַּ֨ח חָנ֜וּן אֶת־עַבְדֵ֣י דָוִ֗ד וַיְגַלַּח֙ אֶת־חֲצִ֣י זְקָנָ֔ם וַיִּכְרֹ֧ת אֶת־מַדְוֵיהֶ֛ם בַּחֵ֖צִי

ה עַ֣ד שְׁתֽוֹתֵיהֶ֑ם וַֽיְשַׁלְּחֵֽם׃ וַיַּגִּ֣דוּ לְדָוִד֮ וַיִּשְׁלַ֣ח לִקְרָאתָם֒ כִּֽי־הָי֥וּ הָאֲנָשִׁ֖ים
נִכְלָמִ֣ים מְאֹ֑ד וַיֹּ֤אמֶר הַמֶּ֙לֶךְ֙ שְׁב֣וּ בִירֵח֔וֹ עַד־יְצַמַּ֥ח זְקַנְכֶ֖ם וְשַׁבְתֶּֽם׃ וַיִּרְא֨וּ

ו בְּנֵ֣י עַמּ֗וֹן כִּ֤י נִבְאֲשׁוּ֙ בְּדָוִ֔ד וַיִּשְׁלְח֣וּ בְנֵֽי־עַמּ֡וֹן וַיִּשְׂכְּרוּ֩ אֶת־אֲרַ֨ם בֵּית־רְח֜וֹב
וְאֶת־אֲרַ֣ם צוֹבָ֗א עֶשְׂרִ֥ים אֶ֙לֶף֙ רַגְלִ֔י וְאֶת־מֶ֤לֶךְ מַֽעֲכָה֙ אֶ֣לֶף אִ֔ישׁ וְאִ֣ישׁ

ז ט֔וֹב שְׁנֵים־עָשָׂ֥ר אֶ֖לֶף אִֽישׁ׃ וַיִּשְׁמַ֖ע דָּוִ֑ד וַיִּשְׁלַח֙ אֶת־יוֹאָ֔ב וְאֵ֥ת כָּל־הַצָּבָ֖א

ח הַגִּבֹּרִֽים׃ וַיֵּֽצְאוּ֙ בְּנֵ֣י עַמּ֔וֹן וַיַּֽעַרְכ֖וּ מִלְחָמָ֑ה פֶּ֖תַח הַשָּׁ֑עַר וַאֲרַ֣ם צוֹבָ֣א

ט וּרְח֗וֹב וְאִֽישׁ־ט֥וֹב וּמַֽעֲכָ֖ה לְבַדָּ֥ם בַּשָּׂדֶֽה׃ וַיַּ֣רְא יוֹאָ֗ב כִּֽי־הָיְתָ֤ה אֵלָיו֙ פְּנֵ֣י
הַמִּלְחָמָ֔ה מִפָּנִ֖ים וּמֵֽאָח֑וֹר וַיִּבְחַ֗ר מִכֹּל֙ בְּחוּרֵ֣י בְיִשְׂרָאֵ֔ל °בְישראל [יִשְׂרָאֵ֖ל ק]

י וַֽיַּעֲרֹ֖ךְ לִקְרַ֥את אֲרָֽם׃ וְאֵת֙ יֶ֣תֶר הָעָ֔ם נָתַ֕ן בְּיַ֖ד אַבְשַׁ֣י אָחִ֑יו וַֽיַּעֲרֹ֔ךְ לִקְרַ֖את

יא בְּנֵ֥י עַמּֽוֹן׃ וַיֹּ֗אמֶר אִם־תֶּחֱזַ֤ק אֲרָם֙ מִמֶּ֔נִּי וְהָיִ֥תָה לִּ֖י לִֽישׁוּעָ֑ה וְאִם־

יב בְּנֵ֤י עַמּוֹן֙ יֶֽחֶזְק֣וּ מִמְּךָ֔ וְהָלַכְתִּ֖י לְהוֹשִׁ֥יעַֽ לָֽךְ׃ חֲזַ֤ק וְנִתְחַזַּק֙ בְּעַד־עַמֵּ֔נוּ

יג וּבְעַ֖ד עָרֵ֣י אֱלֹהֵ֑ינוּ וַֽיהֹוָ֔ה יַעֲשֶׂ֥ה הַטּ֖וֹב בְּעֵינָֽיו׃ וַיִּגַּ֣שׁ יוֹאָ֗ב וְהָעָם֙ אֲשֶׁ֣ר

יד עִמּ֔וֹ לַמִּלְחָמָ֖ה בַּֽאֲרָ֑ם וַיָּנֻ֖סוּ מִפָּנָֽיו׃ וּבְנֵ֣י עַמּ֗וֹן רָאוּ֙ כִּי־נָ֣ס אֲרָ֔ם וַיָּנֻ֙סוּ֙
מִפְּנֵ֣י אֲבִישַׁ֔י וַיָּבֹ֖אוּ הָעִ֑יר וַיָּ֣שָׁב יוֹאָ֗ב מֵעַל֙ בְּנֵ֣י עַמּ֔וֹן וַיָּבֹ֖א יְרוּשָׁלָֽ͏ִם׃

9:10. Although Ziba's large retinue was more than adequate to provide for Mephibosheth, David wanted him as his personal guest, in honor of Jonathan's memory.

9:13. Being lame and unable to travel easily, he dwelled in Jerusalem proper in order to partake of the king's meals (*Malbim*).

10:2. According to the *Midrash,* Hanun's father Nahash had protected David's brother after the king of Moab wiped out the rest of his family (see note to 8:2).

10:5. They could not shave off the rest of their beards, because Jews did not cut their beards in those days (*Radak*).

10:8. Presumably at the Ammonite capital.

10:12. If we do not prevail, our people will be taken captive and our cities conquered by heathens (*Radak*).

shall eat bread at my table continually." [8] *[Mephibosheth] prostrated himself and said, "What is your servant, that you should pay attention to a dead dog such as myself?"*

[9] *The king then called Ziba, Saul's attendant, and said to him, "I have given all that belonged to Saul and all of his family to your master's son.* [10] *You shall work the land for him — you and your sons and your servants — and bring in [its produce] to be bread for [Mica] the son of your master [Mephibosheth] to eat; but Mephibosheth son of your master [Jonathan] shall always eat at my table." (Ziba had fifteen sons and twenty servants.)** [11] *And Ziba said to the king, "According to all that my lord the king commands his servant, so shall your servant do." [David repeated,] "Mephibosheth will be eating at my table, like one of the king's sons."*

... and orders that he be provided and cared for

[12] *Mephibosheth had a young son whose name was Mica, and all of Ziba's household were servants to Mephibosheth.* [13] *Mephibosheth dwelled in Jerusalem, for he would always eat at the table of the king, and he was lame in both his legs.**

10

DAVID DEFEATS AMMON
10:1-11:1

[1] *It happened after this that the king of the Children of Ammon died, and his son Hanun reigned after him.* [2] *David thought, "I shall do an act of kindness for Hanun son of Nahash, just as his father acted with kindness for me."** *So David sent [a message] to him by the hand of his servants to console him over his father; David's servants arrived in the land of the Children of Ammon.* [3] *The ministers of the Children of Ammon said to their master Hanun, "Do you think that David has sent consolers to you to honor your father in your eyes? Is it not in order to explore the city, to spy it out and to overthrow it that David has sent*

Ammon's gratuitous cruelty

his servants to you?" [4] *So Hanun took David's servants and shaved off half of their beards and cut their garments in half until their buttocks, and sent them away.* [5] *They sent word to David, and he sent [messengers] to them, for the men were deeply humiliated. The king said, "Stay in Jericho until your beards grow back and then return."**

Ammon hires Aramean mercenaries

[6] *The Children of Ammon realized that they had become repugnant to David, so the Children of Ammon sent and hired [from] Aram of Beth-rehob and Aram of Zoba, twenty thousand footmen; and [from] the king of Maacah, a thousand men; and [from] Ish-tob, twelve thousand men.* [7] *David heard and he dispatched Joab and all the mighty men of the army.*

The allies surround Joab's force

[8] *The Children of Ammon came out and waged war at the opening of the gateway,** *while Aram of Zoba and Rehob, and Ish-tob, and Maacah were in the field by themselves.* [9] *Joab saw that the battlefield faced him from the front and from the rear, so he selected from among all the chosen ones of Israel, and deployed against Aram.* [10] *He placed the rest of the people in the hand of his brother Abishai, and he deployed against the Children of Ammon.* [11] *He said, "If Aram will overpower me, then you will be my salvation; and if the Children of Ammon will overpower you, I will go to save you.* [12] *Be strong and let us both be strong, for the sake of our people and for the sake of the cities of our God;** *and HASHEM will do what is good in His eyes."*

Joab's successful strategy

The enemies are subdued and make peace

[13] *Then Joab, as well as the people who were with him, approached to do battle against Aram, and they fled from him.* [14] *When the Children of Ammon saw that Aram had fled, they also fled from Abishai, and entered the city. Joab then turned back from the Children of Ammon and came to Jerusalem.*

טו-טז	וַיַּ֣רְא אֲרָ֗ם כִּ֣י נִגַּף֮ לִפְנֵ֣י יִשְׂרָאֵל֒ וַיֵּאָסְפ֖וּ יָֽחַד׃ וַיִּשְׁלַ֣ח הֲדַדְעֶ֗זֶר וַיֹּצֵ֣א אֶת־אֲרָם֮ אֲשֶׁ֣ר מֵעֵ֣בֶר הַנָּהָר֒ וַיָּבֹ֖אוּ חֵילָ֑ם וְשׁוֹבַ֛ךְ שַׂר־צְבָ֥א הֲדַדְעֶ֖זֶר לִפְנֵיהֶֽם׃
יז	וַיֻּגַּ֣ד לְדָוִ֗ד וַיֶּאֱסֹ֤ף אֶת־כָּל־יִשְׂרָאֵל֙ וַיַּעֲבֹ֣ר אֶת־הַיַּרְדֵּ֔ן וַיָּבֹ֖א חֵלָ֑אמָה וַיַּעַרְכ֣וּ אֲרָ֗ם לִקְרַ֤את דָּוִד֙ וַיִּלָּ֣חֲמ֔וּ עִמּֽוֹ׃ וַיָּ֣נָס אֲרָם֮ מִפְּנֵ֣י יִשְׂרָאֵל֒
יח	וַיַּהֲרֹ֨ג דָּוִ֜ד מֵאֲרָ֗ם שְׁבַ֤ע מֵאוֹת֙ רֶ֔כֶב וְאַרְבָּעִ֥ים אֶ֖לֶף פָּרָשִׁ֑ים וְאֵ֨ת שׁוֹבַ֤ךְ שַׂר־צְבָאוֹ֙ הִכָּ֔ה וַיָּ֖מָת שָֽׁם׃
יט	וַיִּרְא֨וּ כָֽל־הַמְּלָכִ֜ים עַבְדֵ֣י הֲדַדְעֶ֗זֶר כִּ֤י נִגְּפוּ֙ לִפְנֵ֣י יִשְׂרָאֵ֔ל וַיַּשְׁלִ֥מוּ אֶת־יִשְׂרָאֵ֖ל וַיַּֽעַבְד֑וּם וַיִּרְא֣וּ אֲרָ֔ם לְהוֹשִׁ֥יעַ ע֖וֹד אֶת־בְּנֵ֥י עַמּֽוֹן׃

יא	
א	וַיְהִי֩ לִתְשׁוּבַ֨ת הַשָּׁנָ֜ה לְעֵ֣ת ׀ צֵ֣את הַמַּלְאכִ֗ים וַיִּשְׁלַ֣ח דָּוִ֡ד אֶת־יוֹאָב֩ וְאֶת־עֲבָדָ֨יו עִמּ֜וֹ וְאֶת־כָּל־יִשְׂרָאֵ֗ל וַיַּשְׁחִ֙תוּ֙ אֶת־בְּנֵ֣י עַמּ֔וֹן וַיָּצֻ֖רוּ עַל־רַבָּ֑ה וְדָוִ֖ד יוֹשֵׁ֥ב בִּירֽוּשָׁלָֽםִ׃
ב	וַיְהִ֣י ׀ לְעֵ֣ת הָעֶ֗רֶב וַיָּ֜קָם דָּוִ֤ד מֵעַ֣ל מִשְׁכָּב֗וֹ וַיִּתְהַלֵּךְ֙ עַל־גַּ֣ג בֵּית־הַמֶּ֔לֶךְ וַיַּ֥רְא אִשָּׁ֛ה רֹחֶ֖צֶת מֵעַ֣ל הַגָּ֑ג וְהָ֣אִשָּׁ֔ה טוֹבַ֥ת מַרְאֶ֖ה מְאֹֽד׃
ג	וַיִּשְׁלַ֣ח דָּוִ֔ד וַיִּדְרֹ֖שׁ לָֽאִשָּׁ֑ה וַיֹּ֗אמֶר הֲלוֹא־זֹאת֙ בַּת־שֶׁ֣בַע בַּת־אֱלִיעָ֔ם אֵ֖שֶׁת אֽוּרִיָּ֥ה הַחִתִּֽי׃
ד	וַיִּשְׁלַח֩ דָּוִ֨ד מַלְאָכִ֜ים וַיִּקָּחֶ֗הָ וַתָּב֤וֹא אֵלָיו֙ וַיִּשְׁכַּ֣ב עִמָּ֔הּ וְהִ֥יא מִתְקַדֶּ֖שֶׁת מִטֻּמְאָתָ֑הּ וַתָּ֖שָׁב אֶל־בֵּיתָֽהּ׃
ה	וַתַּ֖הַר הָאִשָּׁ֑ה וַתִּשְׁלַ֗ח וַתַּגֵּ֤ד לְדָוִד֙ וַתֹּ֔אמֶר הָרָ֖ה אָנֹֽכִי׃
ו	וַיִּשְׁלַ֤ח דָּוִד֙ אֶל־יוֹאָ֔ב שְׁלַ֣ח אֵלַ֔י אֶת־אֽוּרִיָּ֖ה הַחִתִּ֑י וַיִּשְׁלַ֥ח יוֹאָ֛ב אֶת־אֽוּרִיָּ֖ה אֶל־דָּוִֽד׃
ז	וַיָּבֹ֥א אֽוּרִיָּ֖ה אֵלָ֑יו וַיִּשְׁאַ֣ל דָּוִ֗ד לִשְׁל֤וֹם יוֹאָב֙ וְלִשְׁל֣וֹם הָעָ֔ם וְלִשְׁל֖וֹם הַמִּלְחָמָֽה׃
ח	וַיֹּ֤אמֶר דָּוִד֙ לְא֣וּרִיָּ֔ה רֵ֥ד לְבֵיתְךָ֖ וּרְחַ֣ץ רַגְלֶ֑יךָ וַיֵּצֵ֤א אֽוּרִיָּה֙ מִבֵּ֣ית הַמֶּ֔לֶךְ וַתֵּצֵ֥א אַחֲרָ֖יו מַשְׂאַ֥ת הַמֶּֽלֶךְ׃
ט	וַיִּשְׁכַּ֣ב אֽוּרִיָּ֗ה פֶּ֚תַח בֵּ֣ית הַמֶּ֔לֶךְ אֵ֖ת כָּל־עַבְדֵ֣י אֲדֹנָ֑יו וְלֹ֥א יָרַ֖ד אֶל־בֵּיתֽוֹ׃
י	וַיַּגִּ֤דוּ לְדָוִד֙ לֵאמֹ֔ר לֹֽא־יָרַ֥ד אֽוּרִיָּ֖ה אֶל־בֵּית֑וֹ וַיֹּ֨אמֶר דָּוִ֜ד אֶל־אֽוּרִיָּ֗ה הֲל֤וֹא מִדֶּ֙רֶךְ֙ אַתָּ֣ה בָ֔א מַדּ֖וּעַ לֹֽא־יָרַ֥דְתָּ אֶל־בֵּיתֶֽךָ׃
יא	וַיֹּ֨אמֶר אֽוּרִיָּ֜ה אֶל־דָּוִ֗ד הָ֠אָר֠וֹן וְיִשְׂרָאֵ֨ל וִֽיהוּדָ֜ה יֹשְׁבִ֣ים בַּסֻּכּ֗וֹת וַֽאדֹנִ֨י יוֹאָ֜ב וְעַבְדֵ֤י אֲדֹנִי֙ עַל־פְּנֵ֤י הַשָּׂדֶה֙ חֹנִ֔ים וַאֲנִ֞י אָב֧וֹא אֶל־בֵּיתִ֛י לֶאֱכֹ֥ל וְלִשְׁתּ֖וֹת וְלִשְׁכַּ֣ב עִם־אִשְׁתִּ֑י חַיֶּ֙ךָ֙ וְחֵ֣י נַפְשֶׁ֔ךָ אִֽם־אֶעֱשֶׂ֖ה אֶת־הַדָּבָ֥ר הַזֶּֽה׃
יב	וַיֹּ֨אמֶר דָּוִ֜ד אֶל־אֽוּרִיָּ֗ה שֵׁ֥ב בָּזֶ֛ה גַּם־הַיּ֖וֹם וּמָחָ֣ר אֲשַׁלְּחֶ֑ךָּ וַיֵּ֨שֶׁב אֽוּרִיָּ֧ה בִירוּשָׁלַ֛םִ בַּיּ֥וֹם הַה֖וּא וּמִֽמָּחֳרָֽת׃
יג	וַיִּקְרָא־ל֣וֹ דָוִ֗ד וַיֹּ֧אכַל לְפָנָ֛יו וַיֵּ֖שְׁתְּ וַֽיְשַׁכְּרֵ֑הוּ וַיֵּצֵ֣א בָעֶ֗רֶב לִשְׁכַּ֤ב בְּמִשְׁכָּבוֹ֙ עִם־עַבְדֵ֣י אֲדֹנָ֔יו וְאֶל־בֵּית֖וֹ לֹ֥א יָרָֽד׃
יד	וַיְהִ֣י בַבֹּ֔קֶר וַיִּכְתֹּ֥ב דָּוִ֛ד סֵ֖פֶר אֶל־יוֹאָ֑ב וַיִּשְׁלַ֖ח בְּיַ֥ד אֽוּרִיָּֽה׃
טו	וַיִּכְתֹּ֥ב בַּסֵּ֖פֶר לֵאמֹ֑ר הָב֣וּ אֶת־אֽוּרִיָּ֗ה אֶל־מוּל֙ פְּנֵ֤י הַמִּלְחָמָה֙ הַֽחֲזָקָ֔ה וְשַׁבְתֶּ֥ם מֵאַחֲרָ֖יו וְנִכָּ֥ה וָמֵֽת׃
טז	וַיְהִ֕י

11:1. I.e., summertime, when the abundance of food in the fields and orchards is conducive to the undertaking of expeditions (*Rashi*). *Radak* translates, "exactly a year after the aforementioned battle."

11:3. He was either a proselyte of Hittite descent or an Israelite who had dwelt in a Hittite area (*Radak*).

11:4. Technically, Bath-sheba could be considered an unmarried woman, for, as the Talmud (*Shabbos* 56b) states, David's troops always gave their wives conditional divorces, lest a soldier be missing in action leaving his wife unable to remarry. [Furthermore, the Talmud (*Sanhedrin* 107b) notes that David recognized that Bath-sheba was his Divinely intended mate.] Nevertheless, the Sages teach that he repented for many years. See *Psalms* 51:5.

¹⁵ *Aram saw that they were beaten by Israel and they banded together.* ¹⁶ *Hadarezer sent and brought over Aram from the other side of the [Euphrates] River, and they came with their armies, and Shobach, the commander of Hadarezer's army, leading them.* ¹⁷ *This was told to David, and he gathered together all of Israel and crossed the Jordan, and came to Helam. Aram deployed against David and fought him.* ¹⁸ *Aram fled before Israel, and David slew of Aram seven hundred charioteers and forty thousand horsemen; he struck Shobach, commander of the army, and he died there.* ¹⁹ *When all the kings, the subjects of Hadarezer, saw that they were defeated by Israel, they made peace with Israel and became subservient to them. Aram became afraid to help the Children of Ammon any longer.*

11

DAVID AND
BATH-SHEBA
11:2-12:25

¹ *It happened at the turn of the year,* * *at the time when kings go forth, that David had sent Joab along with his servants and all of Israel, and they destroyed the Children of Ammon and besieged Rabbah; and David was staying in Jerusalem.* ² *It happened towards evening that David arose from his bed and strolled on the roof of the king's house. From atop the roof he saw a woman bathing, and the woman was very beautiful.* ³ *David sent to inquire about the woman, and someone said, "Is this not Bath-sheba daughter of Eliam, the wife of Uriah the Hittite?"** ⁴ *David sent messengers and took her. She came to him and he lay with her;* * *she had been cleansing herself from her impurity.* * *She then returned to her house.* ⁵ *The woman conceived. She sent [a message in which] she told David; "I have conceived."*

⁶ *David sent [a message] to Joab: "Send me Uriah the Hittite," so Joab sent Uriah to David.* ⁷ *Uriah came to him, and David inquired after the welfare of Joab and the welfare of the people and the welfare of the warriors.* ⁸ *David then said to Uriah, "Go down to your house and wash your feet." So Uriah left the*

Uriah
disobeys
David . . .

house of the king, and a royal feast was sent after him. ⁹ *But Uriah lay down at the entrance to the king's house along with all of his lord's servants, and did not go down to his house.*

¹⁰ *They told David, saying, "Uriah did not go down to his house"; so David said to Uriah, "Are you not coming from a journey? Why did you not go down*

. . . and
explains
why

to your house?" ¹¹ *Uriah said to David, "The Ark and Israel and Judah are staying in huts, and my lord Joab and the servants of my lord are camping out in the field — shall I then come to my house to eat and to drink and to lie with my wife? By your life and the life of your soul,* * *I will not do such a thing!"*

¹² *David then said to Uriah, "Stay here today also, and tomorrow I will send you off." So Uriah stayed in Jerusalem that day and the next.* ¹³ *Then David summoned him, and he ate and drank before him; and he made him drunk. He went out in the evening to lie down in his place among his lord's servants, but did not go down to his house.* ¹⁴ *And it was in the morning that David wrote a letter to Joab and sent it by Uriah's hand.* ¹⁵ *He wrote in the note, saying, "Place Uriah directly in front of the fierce fighting; then withdraw from behind him so that he shall be struck and die."*

When David spied Bath-sheba, she was cleansing herself from her menstrual impurity; thus David did not transgress the prohibition of having relations with a menstruant woman (*Radak*). Moreover, Scripture means to show that she was not pregnant at that time. Thus, the concep-

tion of verse 5 must have issued from David (*Kara*).

11:11. By your life in this world and by your soul's life in the World to Come. Thus, Uriah swore that he would not obey David's command, making him liable to the death penalty for his insubordination and disrespect of the King.

בִּשְׁמֹ֣ור יֹואָ֔ב אֶל־הָעִ֑יר וַיִּתֵּ֣ן אֶת־אֽוּרִיָּ֗ה אֶל־הַמָּקֹום֙ אֲשֶׁ֣ר יָדַ֔ע כִּ֥י אַנְשֵׁי־

יז חַ֖יִל שָׁ֑ם: וַיֵּ֨צְא֜וּ אַנְשֵׁ֤י הָעִיר֙ וַיִּלָּחֲמ֣וּ אֶת־יֹואָ֔ב וַיִּפֹּ֥ל מִן־הָעָ֖ם מֵעַבְדֵ֣י דָוִ֑ד

יח וַיָּ֕מָת גַּ֖ם אֽוּרִיָּ֥ה הַחִתִּֽי: וַיִּשְׁלַ֣ח יֹואָ֔ב וַיַּגֵּ֣ד לְדָוִ֔ד אֶת־כָּל־דִּבְרֵ֥י הַמִּלְחָמָֽה:

יט וַיְצַ֥ו אֶת־הַמַּלְאָ֖ךְ לֵאמֹ֑ר כְּכַלֹּֽותְךָ֗ אֵ֛ת כָּל־דִּבְרֵ֥י הַמִּלְחָמָ֖ה לְדַבֵּ֥ר אֶל־

כ הַמֶּֽלֶךְ: וְהָיָ֗ה אִֽם־תַּעֲלֶה֙ חֲמַ֣ת הַמֶּ֔לֶךְ וְאָמַ֣ר לְךָ֔ מַדּ֛וּעַ נִגַּשְׁתֶּ֥ם אֶל־הָעִ֖יר

כא לְהִלָּחֵ֑ם הֲלֹ֤וא יְדַעְתֶּם֙ אֵ֣ת אֲשֶׁר־יֹר֣וּ מֵעַ֣ל הַחֹומָֽה: מִֽי־הִכָּ֞ה אֶת־אֲבִימֶ֣לֶךְ בֶּן־יְרֻבֶּ֗שֶׁת הֲלֹֽוא־אִשָּׁ֡ה הִשְׁלִ֣יכָה עָלָיו֩ פֶּ֨לַח רֶ֜כֶב מֵעַ֤ל הַֽחֹומָה֙ וַיָּ֣מָת בְּתֵבֵ֔ץ לָ֥מָּה נִגַּשְׁתֶּ֖ם אֶל־הַֽחֹומָ֑ה וְאָ֣מַרְתָּ֔ גַּ֗ם עַבְדְּךָ֛ אֽוּרִיָּ֥ה הַחִתִּ֖י

כב מֵֽת: וַיֵּ֖לֶךְ הַמַּלְאָ֑ךְ וַיָּבֹא֙ וַיַּגֵּ֣ד לְדָוִ֔ד אֵ֛ת כָּל־אֲשֶׁ֥ר שְׁלָחֹ֖ו יֹואָֽב: וַיֹּ֤אמֶר

כג-כד הַמַּלְאָךְ֙ אֶל־דָּוִ֔ד כִּֽי־גָבְר֤וּ עָלֵ֨ינוּ֙ הָֽאֲנָשִׁ֔ים וַיֵּצְא֥וּ אֵלֵ֖ינוּ הַשָּׂדֶ֑ה וַנִּהְיֶ֥ה עֲלֵיהֶ֖ם עַד־פֶּ֥תַח הַשָּֽׁעַר: °וַיֹּר֨וּ הַמֹּורְאִ֤ים [°וַיֹּר֨וּ הַמֹּורִים֙ ק] אֶל־עֲבָדֶ֨יךָ֙ מֵעַ֣ל הַחֹומָ֔ה וַיָּמ֖וּתוּ מֵעַבְדֵ֣י הַמֶּ֑לֶךְ וְגַ֗ם עַבְדְּךָ֛ אֽוּרִיָּ֥ה הַחִתִּ֖י

כה מֵֽת: וַיֹּ֨אמֶר דָּוִ֜ד אֶל־הַמַּלְאָ֗ךְ כֹּֽה־תֹאמַ֤ר אֶל־יֹואָב֙ אַל־יֵרַ֤ע בְּעֵינֶ֨יךָ֙ אֶת־הַדָּבָ֣ר הַזֶּ֔ה כִּֽי־כָזֹ֥ה וְכָזֶ֖ה תֹּאכַ֣ל הֶחָ֑רֶב הַחֲזֵ֨ק מִלְחַמְתְּךָ֧ אֶל־

כו הָעִ֛יר וְהָרְסָ֖הּ וְחַזְּקֵֽהוּ: וַתִּשְׁמַע֙ אֵ֣שֶׁת אֽוּרִיָּ֔ה כִּי־מֵ֖ת אֽוּרִיָּ֣ה אִישָׁ֑הּ וַתִּסְפֹּ֖ד

כז עַל־בַּעְלָֽהּ: וַיַּעֲבֹ֣ר הָאֵ֗בֶל וַיִּשְׁלַ֨ח דָּוִ֜ד וַיַּֽאַסְפָ֣הּ אֶל־בֵּיתֹ֗ו וַתְּהִי־לֹ֤ו לְאִשָּׁה֙ וַתֵּ֣לֶד לֹ֣ו בֵּ֔ן וַיֵּ֧רַע הַדָּבָ֛ר אֲשֶׁר־עָשָׂ֥ה דָוִ֖ד בְּעֵינֵ֥י יְהוָֽה: וַיִּשְׁלַ֧ח

יב א יְהוָ֛ה אֶת־נָתָ֖ן אֶל־דָּוִ֑ד וַיָּבֹ֣א אֵלָ֗יו וַיֹּ֤אמֶר לֹו֙ שְׁנֵ֣י אֲנָשִׁ֗ים הָיוּ֙ בְּעִ֣יר אֶחָ֔ת

ב-ג אֶחָ֥ד עָשִׁ֖יר וְאֶחָ֥ד רָֽאשׁ: לְעָשִׁ֗יר הָיָ֛ה צֹ֥אן וּבָקָ֖ר הַרְבֵּ֥ה מְאֹֽד: וְלָרָ֣שׁ אֵֽין־ כֹּ֗ל כִּ֩י אִם־כִּבְשָׂ֨ה אַחַ֤ת קְטַנָּה֙ אֲשֶׁ֣ר קָנָ֔ה וַֽיְחַיֶּ֔הָ וַתִּגְדַּ֥ל עִמֹּ֛ו וְעִם־בָּנָ֖יו

ד יַחְדָּ֑ו מִפִּתֹּ֤ו תֹאכַל֙ וּמִכֹּסֹ֣ו תִשְׁתֶּ֔ה וּבְחֵיקֹ֣ו תִשְׁכָּ֔ב וַתְּהִי־לֹ֖ו כְּבַֽת: וַיָּ֣בֹא הֵלֶךְ֮ לְאִ֣ישׁ הֶֽעָשִׁיר֒ וַיַּחְמֹ֗ל לָקַ֤חַת מִצֹּאנֹו֙ וּמִבְּקָרֹ֔ו לַעֲשֹׂ֕ות לָאֹרֵ֖חַ הַבָּא־

ה לֹ֑ו וַיִּקַּ֗ח אֶת־כִּבְשַׂת֙ הָאִ֣ישׁ הָרָ֔אשׁ וַֽיַּעֲשֶׂ֔הָ לָאִ֖ישׁ הַבָּ֥א אֵלָֽיו: וַיִּֽחַר־אַ֥ף דָּוִ֛ד בָּאִ֖ישׁ מְאֹ֑ד וַיֹּ֨אמֶר֙ אֶל־נָתָ֔ן חַי־יְהוָ֕ה כִּ֣י בֶן־מָ֔וֶת הָאִ֖ישׁ הָעֹשֶׂ֥ה זֹֽאת:

ו וְאֶת־הַכִּבְשָׂ֖ה יְשַׁלֵּ֣ם אַרְבַּעְתָּ֑יִם עֵ֗קֶב אֲשֶׁ֤ר עָשָׂה֙ אֶת־הַדָּבָ֣ר הַזֶּ֔ה וְעַ֖ל

ז אֲשֶׁ֥ר לֹֽא־חָמָֽל: וַיֹּ֧אמֶר נָתָ֛ן אֶל־דָּוִ֖ד אַתָּ֣ה הָאִ֑ישׁ כֹּה־אָמַ֨ר יְהוָ֜ה אֱלֹהֵ֣י יִשְׂרָאֵ֗ל אָנֹכִ֞י מְשַׁחְתִּ֤יךָֽ לְמֶ֨לֶךְ֙ עַל־יִשְׂרָאֵ֔ל וְאָנֹכִ֥י הִצַּלְתִּ֖יךָ

ח מִיַּ֥ד שָׁאֽוּל: וָאֶתְּנָ֨ה לְךָ֜ אֶת־בֵּ֣ית אֲדֹנֶ֗יךָ וְאֶת־נְשֵׁ֤י אֲדֹנֶ֨יךָ֙ בְּחֵיקֶ֔ךָ וָאֶתְּנָ֣ה לְךָ֗ אֶת־בֵּ֤ית יִשְׂרָאֵל֙ וִֽיהוּדָ֔ה וְאִ֨ם־מְעָ֔ט וְאֹסִ֥פָה לְּךָ֖ כָּהֵ֣נָּה וְכָהֵֽנָּה: מַדּ֜וּעַ

ט בָּזִ֣יתָ ׀ אֶת־דְּבַ֣ר יְהוָ֗ה לַעֲשֹׂ֣ות הָרַע֮ °בְּעֵינֹו [°בְּעֵינַ֔י ק] אֵ֣ת אֽוּרִיָּ֣ה הַחִתִּי֮ הִכִּ֣יתָ בַחֶ֒רֶב֒ וְאֶ֨ת־אִשְׁתֹּ֜ו לָקַ֤חְתָּ לְּךָ֙ לְאִשָּׁ֔ה וְאֹתֹ֣ו הָרַ֔גְתָּ בְּחֶ֖רֶב בְּנֵ֥י עַמֹּֽון:

11:21. Jerubbesheth is another name of Gideon. The story of Abimelech is in *Judges* 9:50-55.

11:27. Though this verse states clearly that David acted improperly, and Chapter 12 says so even more forcefully, the Sages explain that, while David was morally wrong,

he did not commit adultery in the literal sense.

12:6. The payment of four sheep for the one he stole is in accordance with *Exodus* 21:37. There is no death penalty for theft, however; David's "death sentence" was a figurative condemnation of the rich man's depravity.

Uriah is sent to the front, and is killed ¹⁶ So it was that when Joab was besieging the city, he stationed Uriah in a place where he knew that the powerful warriors were. ¹⁷ The men of the city came out and fought against Joab, and some people from among David's servants fell; and Uriah the Hittite also died.

¹⁸ Joab sent and told David all the matters concerning the war. ¹⁹ He instructed the messenger, saying, "When you finish telling the king all the matters concerning the war, ²⁰ if the king's ire flares up and he says to you, 'Why did you draw close to the city to fight? Did you not know that they shoot from atop the wall? ²¹ Who killed Abimelech son of Jerubbesheth* — was it not a woman who threw a millstone over the wall so that he died in Thebez? Why, then, did you draw close to the wall?' Then you should say, 'Also your servant Uriah the Hittite died.' "

David hears the news and encourages Joab ²² The messenger went and came and told David all that Joab had sent him [to say]. ²³ The messenger told David, "When the men overpowered us and they came out to us in the field, we repulsed them up to the opening of the gate. ²⁴ The archers shot at your servants from atop the wall, and some of the king's servants died; and your servant Uriah the Hittite also died."

²⁵ David then told the messenger, "Say thus to Joab: 'Do not let this matter be deemed evil in your eyes, for the sword consumes one way or another. Strengthen your offense against the city and destroy it!' Then encourage him."

David marries Bath-sheba, but God is displeased ²⁶ Uriah's wife heard that her husband Uriah had died, and she mourned over her husband. ²⁷ The mourning passed, and David sent [for her] and brought her into his house, and she became his wife and bore him a son.

The deed that David had done was deemed evil in the eyes of HASHEM. *

12

Nathan's rebuke: A parable of selfish cruelty ¹ HASHEM sent Nathan to David. He came to him and told him: "There were two men in one city; one rich and one poor. ² The rich man had very many sheep and cattle, ³ but the poor man had nothing except one small ewe that he had acquired. He raised it and it grew up together with him and his children. It ate from his bread and drank from his cup and lay in his bosom; it became like a daughter to him. ⁴ A wayfarer came to the rich man. He was reluctant to take from his own sheep or cattle to prepare for the visitor who had come to him, so he took the poor man's ewe and prepared it for the man who had come to him."

⁵ David was very indignant about this man, and he said to Nathan, "As HASHEM lives, any man who does this deserves to die! ⁶ And he must pay fourfold for the ewe, * because he did this deed and because he had no pity!"

Nathan accuses David . . . ⁷ Nathan then said to David, "You are that man!* Thus said HASHEM, God of Israel: 'I anointed you as king over Israel and I saved you from Saul's hand. ⁸ I gave you the house of your lord, and the women of your lord into your bosom, * and I gave over to you the house of Israel and Judah; and if this were not enough I would have increased for you this much and this much again. ⁹ Why have you scorned the word of HASHEM, doing that which is evil in My eyes? You have struck Uriah the Hittite with the sword; his wife you have taken to yourself for a wife, while him you have killed by the sword of the Children of Ammon!

12:7. David is the rich man, Uriah is the poor man, and Bath-sheba is the ewe. The hungry wayfarer represents David's passion, which he could have satisfied through one of his wives (*Radak*).

12:8. God said that He had given Michal, Saul's daughter, to David as his wife (*Rashi*).

וְעַתָּ֗ה לֹא־תָס֥וּר חֶ֛רֶב מִבֵּיתְךָ֖ עַד־עוֹלָ֑ם עֵ֚קֶב כִּ֣י בְזִתָ֔נִי וַתִּקַּ֗ח אֶת־אֵ֙שֶׁת֙ י
אֽוּרִיָּ֣ה הַֽחִתִּ֔י לִהְי֥וֹת לְךָ֖ לְאִשָּֽׁה: כֹּ֣ה ׀ אָמַ֣ר יהוה הִנְנִי֩ מֵקִ֨ים יא
עָלֶ֤יךָ רָעָה֙ מִבֵּיתֶ֔ךָ וְלָקַחְתִּ֤י אֶת־נָשֶׁ֙יךָ֙ לְעֵינֶ֔יךָ וְנָתַתִּ֖י לְרֵעֶ֑יךָ וְשָׁכַ֣ב עִם־
נָשֶׁ֔יךָ לְעֵינֵ֖י הַשֶּׁ֥מֶשׁ הַזֹּֽאת: כִּ֥י אַתָּ֖ה עָשִׂ֣יתָ בַסָּ֑תֶר וַֽאֲנִ֗י אֶֽעֱשֶׂה֙ אֶת־הַדָּבָ֣ר יב
הַזֶּ֔ה נֶ֥גֶד כָּל־יִשְׂרָאֵ֖ל וְנֶ֥גֶד הַשָּֽׁמֶשׁ: וַיֹּ֧אמֶר דָּוִ֛ד אֶל־נָתָ֖ן חָטָ֣אתִי יג
לַֽיהוה וַיֹּ֨אמֶר נָתָ֜ן אֶל־דָּוִ֗ד גַּם־יהוה הֶֽעֱבִ֥יר חַטָּֽאתְךָ֖ לֹ֥א
תָמֽוּת: אֶ֗פֶס כִּֽי־נִאֵ֤ץ נִאַ֙צְתָּ֙ אֶת־אֹֽיְבֵ֣י יהוה בַּדָּבָ֣ר הַזֶּ֑ה גַּ֗ם הַבֵּ֛ן הַיִּלּ֥וֹד יד
לְךָ֖ מ֥וֹת יָמֽוּת: וַיֵּ֥לֶךְ נָתָ֖ן אֶל־בֵּית֑וֹ וַיִּגֹּ֣ף יהוה אֶת־הַיֶּ֗לֶד אֲשֶׁ֨ר יָֽלְדָ֧ה טו
אֵֽשֶׁת־אֽוּרִיָּ֛ה לְדָוִ֖ד וַיֵּֽאָנַֽשׁ: וַיְבַקֵּ֥שׁ דָּוִ֛ד אֶת־הָֽאֱלֹהִ֖ים בְּעַ֣ד הַנָּ֑עַר וַיָּ֤צָם טז
דָּוִד֙ צ֔וֹם וּבָ֛א וְלָ֖ן וְשָׁכַ֥ב אָֽרְצָה: וַיָּקֻ֜מוּ זִקְנֵ֤י בֵיתוֹ֙ עָלָ֔יו לַֽהֲקִימ֖וֹ מִן־הָאָ֑רֶץ יז
וְלֹ֣א אָבָ֔ה וְלֹֽא־בָרָ֥א אִתָּ֖ם לָֽחֶם: וַֽיְהִ֛י בַּיּ֥וֹם הַשְּׁבִיעִ֖י וַיָּ֣מָת הַיָּ֑לֶד וַיִּֽרְא֩וּ יח
עַבְדֵ֨י דָוִ֜ד לְהַגִּ֥יד ל֣וֹ ׀ כִּי־מֵ֣ת הַיֶּ֗לֶד כִּ֤י אָֽמְרוּ֙ הִנֵּה֩ בִֽהְי֨וֹת הַיֶּ֤לֶד חַי֙ דִּבַּ֣רְנוּ
אֵלָ֗יו וְלֹֽא־שָׁמַע֙ בְּקוֹלֵ֔נוּ וְאֵ֛יךְ נֹאמַ֥ר אֵלָ֖יו מֵ֣ת הַיֶּ֑לֶד וְעָשָׂ֖ה רָעָֽה: וַיַּ֣רְא יט
דָּוִ֗ד כִּ֤י עֲבָדָיו֙ מִתְלַֽחֲשִׁ֔ים וַיָּ֥בֶן דָּוִ֖ד כִּ֣י מֵ֣ת הַיָּ֑לֶד וַיֹּ֧אמֶר דָּוִ֛ד אֶל־עֲבָדָ֖יו
הֲמֵ֣ת הַיֶּ֑לֶד וַיֹּֽאמְר֖וּ מֵֽת: וַיָּ֣קָם דָּוִ֣ד מֵֽהָאָ֡רֶץ וַיִּרְחַ֣ץ וַיָּ֗סֶךְ וַיְחַלֵּף֙ °שִׂמְלֹתוֹ כ
[°שִׂמְלֹתָ֔יו ק] וַיָּבֹ֥א בֵית־יהוה וַיִּשְׁתָּ֑חוּ וַיָּבֹא֙ אֶל־בֵּית֔וֹ וַיִּשְׁאַ֕ל וַיָּשִׂ֥ימוּ ל֛וֹ
לֶ֖חֶם וַיֹּאכַֽל: וַיֹּֽאמְר֤וּ עֲבָדָיו֙ אֵלָ֔יו מָֽה־הַדָּבָ֥ר הַזֶּ֖ה אֲשֶׁ֣ר עָשִׂ֑יתָה בַּֽעֲב֤וּר כא
הַיֶּ֙לֶד֙ חַ֣י צַ֔מְתָּ וַתֵּ֑בְךְּ וְכַֽאֲשֶׁר֙ מֵ֣ת הַיֶּ֔לֶד קַ֖מְתָּ וַתֹּ֥אכַל לָֽחֶם: וַיֹּ֕אמֶר בְּעוֹד֙ כב
הַיֶּ֣לֶד חַ֔י צַ֖מְתִּי וָֽאֶבְכֶּ֑ה כִּ֤י אָמַ֙רְתִּי֙ מִ֣י יוֹדֵ֔עַ °יְחָנַּ֥נִי [°וְחַנַּ֖נִי ק] יהוה וְחַ֥י
הַיָּֽלֶד: וְעַתָּ֣ה ׀ מֵ֗ת לָ֤מָּה זֶּה֙ אֲנִ֣י צָ֔ם הַֽאוּכַ֥ל לַֽהֲשִׁיב֖וֹ ע֑וֹד אֲנִי֙ הֹלֵ֣ךְ אֵלָ֔יו כג
וְה֖וּא לֹֽא־יָשׁ֥וּב אֵלָֽי: וַיְנַחֵ֣ם דָּוִ֗ד אֵ֚ת בַּת־שֶׁ֣בַע אִשְׁתּ֔וֹ וַיָּבֹ֥א אֵלֶ֖יהָ וַיִּשְׁכַּ֣ב כד
עִמָּ֑הּ וַתֵּ֣לֶד בֵּ֗ן °וַיִּקְרָ֤א [°וַתִּקְרָ֤א ק] אֶת־שְׁמ֙וֹ שְׁלֹמֹ֔ה וַֽיהוה אֲהֵבֽוֹ: וַיִּשְׁלַ֗ח
בְּיַד֙ נָתָ֣ן הַנָּבִ֔יא וַיִּקְרָ֥א אֶת־שְׁמ֖וֹ יְדִ֣ידְיָ֑הּ בַּֽעֲב֖וּר יהוה: כה
יוֹאָ֔ב בְּרַבַּ֖ת בְּנֵ֣י עַמּ֑וֹן וַיִּלְכֹּ֖ד אֶת־עִ֥יר הַמְּלוּכָֽה: וַיִּשְׁלַ֤ח יוֹאָב֙ מַלְאָכִ֔ים כו כז
אֶל־דָּוִ֑ד וַיֹּ֕אמֶר נִלְחַ֣מְתִּי בְרַבָּ֔ה גַּם־לָכַ֖דְתִּי אֶת־עִ֥יר הַמָּֽיִם: וְעַתָּ֗ה כח
אֱסֹף֙ אֶת־יֶ֣תֶר הָעָ֔ם וַֽחֲנֵ֥ה עַל־הָעִ֖יר וְלָכְדָ֑הּ פֶּן־אֶלְכֹּ֤ד אֲנִי֙ אֶת־הָעִ֔יר
וְנִקְרָ֥א שְׁמִ֖י עָלֶֽיהָ: וַיֶּֽאֱסֹ֥ף דָּוִ֛ד אֶת־כָּל־הָעָ֖ם וַיֵּ֣לֶךְ רַבָּ֑תָה וַיִּלָּ֥חֶם בָּ֖הּ כט
וַֽיִּלְכְּדָֽהּ: וַיִּקַּ֣ח אֶת־עֲטֶֽרֶת־מַלְכָּ֣ם מֵעַ֣ל רֹאשׁ֗וֹ וּמִשְׁקָלָ֞הּ כִּכַּ֤ר זָהָב֙ ל
וְאֶ֣בֶן יְקָרָ֔ה וַתְּהִ֖י עַל־רֹ֣אשׁ דָּוִ֑ד וּשְׁלַ֥ל הָעִ֛יר הוֹצִ֖יא הַרְבֵּ֥ה מְאֹֽד:

12:13. In response to your immediate admission of guilt (cf. Saul's reaction to Samuel's accusations in I Samuel 13:11 and 15:20 — *Malbim*), God has mitigated the severity of the punishment you really deserve. Sincere confession is the first step of repentance.

12:14. A euphemism for having blasphemed God Himself.

12:20. David had avoided these pleasures during his days of fasting and prayer. Although these pleasures are for-

bidden to a mourner, David was not obligated to mourn ["sit *shivah*" for] the baby, for halachic mourning is not required for a baby who died before it was thirty days old.

12:25. That is, "because of HASHEM's love for Solomon." The name Jedidiah, which means "Beloved of God," signified God's love. Indeed, God designated Solomon as David's successor.

12:27. Joab conquered the royal quarter of Rabbah, which was also known as the "City of Water." In verse 28,

¹⁰ *And now, the sword shall not cease from your house forever, because you have scorned Me and have taken the wife of Uriah the Hittite to be a wife unto you.*

... and prophesies David's punishment

¹¹ *"So says* HASHEM: *'Behold! — I shall raise evil against you from your own household, I shall take your wives away in front of your eyes and give them to your fellowman, who will lie with them in the sight of this sun.* ¹² *Though you have acted in secrecy, I shall perform this deed in the presence of all Israel and before the sun!' "*

David confesses and repents

¹³ *David said to Nathan, "I have sinned to* HASHEM!"

Nathan responded to David, "So, too, HASHEM *has commuted your sin;* * *you will not die.* ¹⁴ *However, because you have thoroughly blasphemed the enemies of* HASHEM * *in this matter, the son that has been born to you shall surely die."*

Bath-sheba's baby is stricken; David prays and fasts

¹⁵ *Nathan then went to his house; and* HASHEM *struck the child that Uriah's wife had borne to David, and he became gravely ill.* ¹⁶ *David pleaded with God on behalf of the boy; David undertook a fast, and when he came in for the night, he lay on the floor.* ¹⁷ *The elders of his house stood over him to raise him from the ground, but he would not consent; and he did not eat food with them.*

¹⁸ *It happened on the seventh day that the child died. David's servants were afraid to tell him that the baby had died, for they said, "Behold! — if when the baby was alive we spoke to him but he would not listen to us, how can we tell him the baby has died — he will do something terrible!"* ¹⁹ *David saw that his servants were whispering to themselves and David understood that the child had died. David said to his servants, "Is the child dead?" And they answered, "He is dead."*

David ends his fast

²⁰ *David got up from the floor and bathed and anointed himself and changed his clothes,* * *and he came to the House of* HASHEM *and prostrated himself. He then came to his house and, at his request, they served him food and he ate.* ²¹ *His servants said to him, "What is this thing that you are doing? For the living baby you fasted and wept — and when the baby died you got up and ate a meal?"* ²² *He said, "While the baby was still alive I fasted and cried, for I thought, 'Who knows? Perhaps* HASHEM *will show me favor and the baby will live.'* ²³ *But now that he is dead why should I fast? Can I bring him back again? I will be going to him, but he will not return to me."*

Bath-sheba gives birth to Solomon

²⁴ *David comforted his wife Bath-sheba, and he came to her and lay with her; she gave birth to a boy and called his name Solomon.* HASHEM *loved him;* ²⁵ *He sent word through Nathan the prophet and called his name Jedidiah, because of* HASHEM. *

DAVID CONQUERS AMMON
12:26-31

²⁶ *Joab fought against Rabbah of the Children of Ammon, and he captured the royal city.* ²⁷ *Joab sent messengers to David, saying, "I fought against Rabbah and have even captured the City of Water.* * ²⁸ *And now, you gather the rest of the people together and encamp against the city and capture it, lest I capture the city myself and my name will be attached to it."*

²⁹ *So David gathered together all the people and he went to Rabbah; he battled it and captured it.* ³⁰ *He removed their king's crown from his head — it weighed a talent of gold and had a precious stone — and it remained over David's head.* * *He also took out a great deal of booty from the city.*

---

he urged David to lead the conquest of the rest of the city. **12:30.** The crown was much too heavy (about 64 pounds) to be on the king's head; it was apparently suspended symbolically over the throne (*Radak*).

לא וְאֶת־הָעָם אֲשֶׁר־בָּהּ הוֹצִיא וַיָּשֶׂם בַּמְּגֵרָה וּבַחֲרִצֵי הַבַּרְזֶל וּבְמַגְזְרֹת
הַבַּרְזֶל וְהֶעֱבִיר אוֹתָם ׳בַּמַּלְכֵּן [°בַּמַּלְבֵּן] ׆ וְכֵן יַעֲשֶׂה לְכֹל עָרֵי בְנֵי־

יג א עַמּוֹן וַיָּשָׁב דָּוִד וְכָל־הָעָם יְרוּשָׁלָםִ: ס וַיְהִי אַחֲרֵי־כֵן וּלְאַבְשָׁלוֹם
ב בֶּן־דָּוִד אָחוֹת יָפָה וּשְׁמָהּ תָּמָר וַיֶּאֱהָבֶהָ אַמְנוֹן בֶּן־דָּוִד: וַיֵּצֶר לְאַמְנוֹן
לְהִתְחַלּוֹת בַּעֲבוּר תָּמָר אֲחֹתוֹ כִּי בְתוּלָה הִיא וַיִּפָּלֵא בְּעֵינֵי אַמְנוֹן
ג לַעֲשׂוֹת לָהּ מְאוּמָה: וּלְאַמְנוֹן רֵעַ וּשְׁמוֹ יוֹנָדָב בֶּן־שִׁמְעָה אֲחִי דָוִד וְיוֹנָדָב
ד אִישׁ חָכָם מְאֹד: וַיֹּאמֶר לוֹ מַדּוּעַ אַתָּה כָּכָה דַּל בֶּן־הַמֶּלֶךְ בַּבֹּקֶר בַּבֹּקֶר
הֲלוֹא תַּגִּיד לִי וַיֹּאמֶר לוֹ אַמְנוֹן אֶת־תָּמָר אֲחוֹת אַבְשָׁלֹם אָחִי אֲנִי אֹהֵב:
ה וַיֹּאמֶר לוֹ יְהוֹנָדָב שְׁכַב עַל־מִשְׁכָּבְךָ וְהִתְחָל וּבָא אָבִיךָ לִרְאוֹתֶךָ וְאָמַרְתָּ
אֵלָיו תָּבֹא נָא תָמָר אֲחוֹתִי וְתַבְרֵנִי לֶחֶם וְעָשְׂתָה לְעֵינַי אֶת־הַבִּרְיָה
ו לְמַעַן אֲשֶׁר אֶרְאֶה וְאָכַלְתִּי מִיָּדָהּ: וַיִּשְׁכַּב אַמְנוֹן וַיִּתְחָל וַיָּבֹא הַמֶּלֶךְ
לִרְאֹתוֹ וַיֹּאמֶר אַמְנוֹן אֶל־הַמֶּלֶךְ תָּבוֹא־נָא תָּמָר אֲחֹתִי וּתְלַבֵּב לְעֵינַי
ז שְׁתֵּי לְבִבוֹת וְאֶבְרֶה מִיָּדָהּ: וַיִּשְׁלַח דָּוִד אֶל־תָּמָר הַבַּיְתָה לֵאמֹר לְכִי נָא
ח בֵּית אַמְנוֹן אָחִיךְ וַעֲשִׂי־לוֹ הַבִּרְיָה: וַתֵּלֶךְ תָּמָר בֵּית אַמְנוֹן אָחִיהָ וְהוּא
שֹׁכֵב וַתִּקַּח אֶת־הַבָּצֵק ׳וַתָּלוֹשׁ [°וַתָּלָשׁ] ׆ וַתְּלַבֵּב לְעֵינָיו וַתְּבַשֵּׁל אֶת־
ט הַלְּבִבוֹת: וַתִּקַּח אֶת־הַמַּשְׂרֵת וַתִּצֹק לְפָנָיו וַיְמָאֵן לֶאֱכוֹל וַיֹּאמֶר אַמְנוֹן
י הוֹצִיאוּ כָל־אִישׁ מֵעָלַי וַיֵּצְאוּ כָל־אִישׁ מֵעָלָיו: וַיֹּאמֶר אַמְנוֹן אֶל־תָּמָר
הָבִיאִי הַבִּרְיָה הַחֶדֶר וְאֶבְרֶה מִיָּדֵךְ וַתִּקַּח תָּמָר אֶת־הַלְּבִבוֹת אֲשֶׁר
יא עָשָׂתָה וַתָּבֵא לְאַמְנוֹן אָחִיהָ הֶחָדְרָה: וַתַּגֵּשׁ אֵלָיו לֶאֱכֹל וַיַּחֲזֶק־בָּהּ
יב וַיֹּאמֶר לָהּ בּוֹאִי שִׁכְבִי עִמִּי אֲחוֹתִי: וַתֹּאמֶר לוֹ אַל־אָחִי אַל־תְּעַנֵּנִי כִּי
יג לֹא־יֵעָשֶׂה כֵן בְּיִשְׂרָאֵל אַל־תַּעֲשֵׂה אֶת־הַנְּבָלָה הַזֹּאת: וַאֲנִי אָנָה אוֹלִיךְ
אֶת־חֶרְפָּתִי וְאַתָּה תִּהְיֶה כְּאַחַד הַנְּבָלִים בְּיִשְׂרָאֵל וְעַתָּה דַּבֶּר־נָא אֶל־
יד הַמֶּלֶךְ כִּי לֹא יִמְנָעֵנִי מִמֶּךָּ: וְלֹא אָבָה לִשְׁמֹעַ בְּקוֹלָהּ וַיֶּחֱזַק מִמֶּנָּה וַיְעַנֶּהָ
טו וַיִּשְׁכַּב אֹתָהּ: וַיִּשְׂנָאֶהָ אַמְנוֹן שִׂנְאָה גְּדוֹלָה מְאֹד כִּי גְדוֹלָה הַשִּׂנְאָה אֲשֶׁר
טז שְׂנֵאָהּ מֵאַהֲבָה אֲשֶׁר אֲהֵבָהּ וַיֹּאמֶר־לָהּ אַמְנוֹן קוּמִי לֵכִי: וַתֹּאמֶר לוֹ אַל־
אוֹדֹת הָרָעָה הַגְּדוֹלָה הַזֹּאת מֵאַחֶרֶת אֲשֶׁר־עָשִׂיתָ עִמִּי לְשַׁלְּחֵנִי וְלֹא
יז אָבָה לִשְׁמֹעַ לָהּ: וַיִּקְרָא אֶת־נַעֲרוֹ מְשָׁרְתוֹ וַיֹּאמֶר שִׁלְחוּ־נָא אֶת־זֹאת
יח מֵעָלַי הַחוּצָה וּנְעֹל הַדֶּלֶת אַחֲרֶיהָ: וְעָלֶיהָ כְּתֹנֶת פַּסִּים כִּי כֵן תִּלְבַּשְׁןָ
בְנוֹת־הַמֶּלֶךְ הַבְּתוּלֹת מְעִילִים וַיֹּצֵא אוֹתָהּ מְשָׁרְתוֹ הַחוּץ וְנָעַל הַדֶּלֶת
יט אַחֲרֶיהָ: וַתִּקַּח תָּמָר אֵפֶר עַל־רֹאשָׁהּ וּכְתֹנֶת הַפַּסִּים אֲשֶׁר עָלֶיהָ קָרָעָה
כ וַתָּשֶׂם יָדָהּ עַל־רֹאשָׁהּ וַתֵּלֶךְ הָלוֹךְ וְזָעָקָה: וַיֹּאמֶר אֵלֶיהָ אַבְשָׁלוֹם אָחִיהָ

12:31. David felt that the gratuitous cruelty of the Ammonites — of which their treachery in 10:1-4 was a small example — had to be punished in a public manner that would be a deterrent to others.

13:1. Absalom and Tamar were children of David's wife

Maacah (above 3:3) who, as noted there, was a captive of war. The Sages teach that Tamar was conceived before her mother converted. Therefore, Tamar was born as a convert and, halachically, was not a sister of her blood siblings. Consequently, Amnon's abhorrent deed did not fall

³¹ He took out the people of the city and punished them with saws, with iron threshing boards and with iron axes, and he had them dragged through muddy streets; and this is what he would do to all the cities of the Children of Ammon. * David and all the people then returned to Jerusalem.

13

¹ This is what happened afterwards: Absalom son of David had a beautiful sister whose name was Tamar, * and Amnon son of David loved her. ² Amnon lusted to the point of illness for his sister Tamar, for she was a virgin, but it seemed impossible for Amnon to do anything to her.

AMNON LUSTS FOR TAMAR
13:1-13:22

³ Amnon had a friend named Jonadab, the son of David's brother Shimeah, and Jonadab was a very cunning man. ⁴ He said to him, "Why are you so downtrodden, O son of the king, morning after morning? Will you not tell me?" So Amnon said to him, "I love Tamar, my brother Absalom's sister." ⁵ Jonadab said to him, "Lie on your bed and feign illness. When your father comes to visit you, say to him, 'Please, let my sister Tamar come and serve me some food. Let her prepare a light meal in my sight so that I may see and eat from her hand.' "

Amnon's plot

⁶ So Amnon lay down and feigned illness, and the king came to visit him. Amnon said to the king, "Please let my sister Tamar come and prepare two dumplings in my sight, so that I may eat from her hand." ⁷ David sent to Tamar, at the house, saying, "Go now to your brother Amnon's house and prepare a light meal for him."

⁸ Tamar went to her brother Amnon's house, where he was lying down. She took some dough and kneaded it and prepared it in his sight, and she cooked the dumplings. ⁹ She then took the pan and poured it before him, but he refused to eat. Amnon then said, "Remove everyone from before me"; and everyone went away from before him. ¹⁰ Amnon then said to Tamar, "Bring the light meal into the room, so that I may eat from your hand"; so Tamar took the [dish of] dumplings that she had made and brought it to her brother Amnon, into the room. ¹¹ She was serving [them] to him, when he grabbed her and said to her, "Come lie with me, my sister!" ¹² But she said to him, "No, my brother; do not violate me, for such things are not done in Israel. Do not commit this despicable act! ¹³ Where could I go with my shame? And you — you would be considered in Israel as one of the despicable men! So now, speak to the king, for he would not withhold me from you [in marriage]."* ¹⁴ But he refused to heed her voice. He overpowered her and violated her and lay with her.

Tamar serves the "sick" Amnon

He violates her. . .

¹⁵ Afterwards Amnon despised her with a great hatred; his hatred was even greater than his love that he had felt for her. So Amnon said to her, "Get up and go away!" ¹⁶ But she said to him, "Do not do this greater evil than that which you have already done to me — to send me away!"* But he refused to listen to her. ¹⁷ He called in his attendant who ministered to him, and said, "Send this [person] out from me now, and lock the door behind her!" ¹⁸ (She was wearing a colorful tunic, for such robes were worn by the maidens among the king's daughters.) His minister took her out and locked the door behind her. ¹⁹ Tamar put dirt upon her head and tore the colorful tunic that was on her; she put her hand to her head and left, crying out as she went. ²⁰ Her brother Absalom said to her,

. . . and expels her in disgrace

---

under the halachic definition of incest (see v. 13).
13:13. Since, as noted above, she and Amnon were not considered siblings, they could have married.

13:16. Tamar begged Amnon not to humiliate her publicly by throwing her out (*Radak*). Alternatively, she wanted him to marry her (*Malbim*).

הֶאֱמִינֻון אָחִיךְ הָיָה עִמָּךְ וְעַתָּה אֲחוֹתִי אֲחוֹתִי הַחֲרִישִׁי אָחִיךְ הוּא אַל־תָּשִׁיתִי

כא אֶת־לִבֵּךְ לַדָּבָר הַזֶּה וַתֵּשֶׁב תָּמָר וְשֹׁמֵמָה בֵּית אַבְשָׁלוֹם אָחִיהָ: וְהַמֶּלֶךְ

כב דָּוִד שָׁמַע אֵת כָּל־הַדְּבָרִים הָאֵלֶּה וַיִּחַר לוֹ מְאֹד: וְלֹא־דִבֶּר אַבְשָׁלוֹם

עִם־אַמְנוֹן לְמֵרָע וְעַד־טוֹב כִּי־שָׂנֵא אַבְשָׁלוֹם אֶת־אַמְנוֹן עַל־דְּבַר

כג אֲשֶׁר עִנָּה אֵת תָּמָר אֲחֹתוֹ: וַיְהִי לִשְׁנָתַיִם יָמִים וַיִּהְיוּ גֹזְזִים

לְאַבְשָׁלוֹם בְּבַעַל חָצוֹר אֲשֶׁר עִם־אֶפְרָיִם וַיִּקְרָא אַבְשָׁלוֹם לְכָל־בְּנֵי

כד הַמֶּלֶךְ: וַיָּבֹא אַבְשָׁלוֹם אֶל־הַמֶּלֶךְ וַיֹּאמֶר הִנֵּה־נָא גֹזְזִים לְעַבְדֶּךָ יֵלֶךְ־נָא

כה הַמֶּלֶךְ וַעֲבָדָיו עִם־עַבְדֶּךָ: וַיֹּאמֶר הַמֶּלֶךְ אֶל־אַבְשָׁלוֹם אַל־בְּנִי אַל־נָא

נֵלֵךְ כֻּלָּנוּ וְלֹא נִכְבַּד עָלֶיךָ וַיִּפְרָץ־בּוֹ וְלֹא־אָבָה לָלֶכֶת וַיְבָרֲכֵהוּ:

כו וַיֹּאמֶר אַבְשָׁלוֹם וָלֹא יֵלֶךְ־נָא אִתָּנוּ אַמְנוֹן אָחִי וַיֹּאמֶר לוֹ הַמֶּלֶךְ לָמָּה

כז יֵלֵךְ עִמָּךְ: וַיִּפְרָץ־בּוֹ אַבְשָׁלוֹם וַיִּשְׁלַח אִתּוֹ אֶת־אַמְנוֹן וְאֵת כָּל־בְּנֵי

כח הַמֶּלֶךְ: וַיְצַו אַבְשָׁלוֹם אֶת־נְעָרָיו לֵאמֹר רְאוּ נָא כְּטוֹב לֵב־

אַמְנוֹן בַּיַּיִן וְאָמַרְתִּי אֲלֵיכֶם הַכּוּ אֶת־אַמְנוֹן וַהֲמִתֶּם אֹתוֹ אַל־תִּירָאוּ

כט הֲלוֹא כִּי אָנֹכִי צִוִּיתִי אֶתְכֶם חִזְקוּ וִהְיוּ לִבְנֵי־חָיִל: וַיַּעֲשׂוּ נַעֲרֵי אַבְשָׁלוֹם

לְאַמְנוֹן כַּאֲשֶׁר צִוָּה אַבְשָׁלוֹם וַיָּקֻמוּ ׀ כָּל־בְּנֵי הַמֶּלֶךְ וַיִּרְכְּבוּ אִישׁ עַל־

ל פִּרְדּוֹ וַיָּנֻסוּ: וַיְהִי הֵמָּה בַדֶּרֶךְ וְהַשְּׁמֻעָה בָאָה אֶל־דָּוִד לֵאמֹר הִכָּה

אַבְשָׁלוֹם אֶת־כָּל־בְּנֵי הַמֶּלֶךְ וְלֹא־נוֹתַר מֵהֶם אֶחָד: וַיָּקָם

לא הַמֶּלֶךְ וַיִּקְרַע אֶת־בְּגָדָיו וַיִּשְׁכַּב אָרְצָה וְכָל־עֲבָדָיו נִצָּבִים קְרֻעֵי

לב בְגָדִים: וַיַּעַן יוֹנָדָב ׀ בֶּן־שִׁמְעָה אֲחִי־דָוִד וַיֹּאמֶר אַל־יֹאמַר

אֲדֹנִי אֵת כָּל־הַנְּעָרִים בְּנֵי־הַמֶּלֶךְ הֵמִיתוּ כִּי־אַמְנוֹן לְבַדּוֹ מֵת כִּי־עַל־פִּי

לג אַבְשָׁלוֹם הָיְתָה שִׂימָה °שׂוּמָה ק מִיּוֹם עַנֹּתוֹ אֵת תָּמָר אֲחֹתוֹ: וְעַתָּה

אַל־יָשֵׂם אֲדֹנִי הַמֶּלֶךְ אֶל־לִבּוֹ דָּבָר לֵאמֹר כָּל־בְּנֵי הַמֶּלֶךְ מֵתוּ כִּי־

לד אִם ב ולא ק אַמְנוֹן לְבַדּוֹ מֵת: וַיִּבְרַח אַבְשָׁלוֹם וַיִּשָּׂא

הַנַּעַר הַצֹּפֶה אֶת־°עֵינֹו °עֵינָיו ק וַיַּרְא וְהִנֵּה עַם־רַב הֹלְכִים מִדֶּרֶךְ

לה אַחֲרָיו מִצַּד הָהָר: וַיֹּאמֶר יוֹנָדָב אֶל־הַמֶּלֶךְ הִנֵּה בְנֵי־הַמֶּלֶךְ בָּאוּ

לו כִּדְבַר עַבְדְּךָ כֵּן הָיָה: וַיְהִי ׀ כְּכַלֹּתוֹ לְדַבֵּר וְהִנֵּה בְנֵי־הַמֶּלֶךְ בָּאוּ

וַיִּשְׂאוּ קוֹלָם וַיִּבְכּוּ וְגַם־הַמֶּלֶךְ וְכָל־עֲבָדָיו בָּכוּ בְּכִי גָּדוֹל מְאֹד:

לז וְאַבְשָׁלוֹם בָּרַח וַיֵּלֶךְ אֶל־תַּלְמַי בֶּן־°עַמִּיחוּר °עַמִּיהוּד ק מֶלֶךְ גְּשׁוּר

וַיִּתְאַבֵּל עַל־בְּנוֹ כָּל־הַיָּמִים: וְאַבְשָׁלוֹם בָּרַח וַיֵּלֶךְ גְּשׁוּר וַיְהִי־שָׁם שָׁלֹשׁ

לט שָׁנִים: וַתְּכַל דָּוִד הַמֶּלֶךְ לָצֵאת אֶל־אַבְשָׁלוֹם כִּי־נִחַם עַל־אַמְנוֹן כִּי־

יד א מֵת: וַיֵּדַע יוֹאָב בֶּן־צְרֻיָה כִּי־לֵב הַמֶּלֶךְ עַל־אַבְשָׁלוֹם:

ב וַיִּשְׁלַח יוֹאָב תְּקוֹעָה וַיִּקַּח מִשָּׁם אִשָּׁה חֲכָמָה וַיֹּאמֶר אֵלֶיהָ הִתְאַבְּלִי־

נָא וְלִבְשִׁי־נָא בִגְדֵי־אֵבֶל וְאַל־תָּסוּכִי שֶׁמֶן וְהָיִית כְּאִשָּׁה זֶה יָמִים

ג רַבִּים מִתְאַבֶּלֶת עַל־מֵת: וּבָאת אֶל־הַמֶּלֶךְ וְדִבַּרְתְּ אֵלָיו כַּדָּבָר הַזֶּה

"Has your brother Aminon been with you? Be silent for now, my sister. He is your brother; do not concern your heart over this matter." * *So Tamar dwelled, devastated, in the house of her brother Absalom.*

²¹ *King David heard about all these events, and he was very angry.* ²² *Absalom would not speak with Amnon — neither bad nor good — for Absalom hated Amnon because he had violated his sister Tamar.*

²³ *It happened two years later that they were shearing Absalom's [sheep] in the Plain of Hazor, which is in Ephraim; and Absalom invited all the king's sons.* ²⁴ *Absalom came to the king and said, "Behold, they are shearing for your servant; let the king and his servants accompany your servant."* ²⁵ *The king said to Absalom, "No, my son, let us not all go, so that we do not overburden you." He importuned but he would not consent to go, but he blessed him.* ²⁶ *Absalom said, "If not, then let my brother Amnon go with us." But David said, "Why should he go with you?"* ²⁷ *Absalom importuned him, so he sent Amnon and all the king's sons along with him.*

²⁸ *Absalom instructed his servants, saying, "Take note when Amnon's heart is giddy with wine. Then, I will tell you, 'Strike down Amnon.' Kill him and fear not! Have I not commanded you? Be strong, and be brave men!"*

²⁹ *Absalom's servants did to Amnon as Absalom had commanded them. Then all the king's sons arose; each man mounted his mule and ran away.* ³⁰ *While they were on the way a rumor reached David, saying, "Absalom has struck down all the king's sons; not one of them survived!"* ³¹ *The king arose and tore his garments and lay on the ground, and all his servants stood with torn clothing.* ³² *Jonadab, the son of David's brother Shimeah, spoke up and said, "Let my lord not think that they killed all the young men, the king's sons, for Amnon alone is dead; for Absalom had issued that order since the day [Amnon] violated his sister Tamar.* ³³ *And now, let my lord the king not take the matter to his heart, saying, 'All the king's sons have died'; for only Amnon is dead."*

³⁴ *Absalom fled. The lookout soldier raised his eyes and saw that — behold! — a large group of people was traveling on the road behind him, from the direction of the mountain.* ³⁵ *Jonadab then said to the king, "Behold — the king's sons have arrived! Like your servant's word, so it was!"* ³⁶ *Just as he finished speaking, the king's sons came; they raised up their voices and wept; also the king and all his servants wept a very great weeping.*

³⁷ *Absalom had fled; he went to Talmai son of Ammihud, the king of Geshur.* * *And [David] mourned for his son [Amnon] many years.* ³⁸ *Absalom had fled; he went to Geshur, and he remained there for three years.* ³⁹ *Then [the soul of] King David pined for Absalom, for he had become consoled over Amnon, who had died.*

14

¹ J*oab son of Zeruiah perceived that David's heart was set on Absalom.* * ² *So Joab sent to Tekoa and brought a wise woman from there. He said to her, "If you please, pretend to be a mourner. Wear garments of mourning and do not anoint yourself with oil; be like this for many days as a woman mourning over a dead person.* ³ *Then come before the king and speak these words to him . . ."*

13:20. Absalom tried to comfort Tamar by saying that the outrage would have been even more humiliating had it been committed by an outsider. Furthermore, he urged her to try and forget the traumatic incident and get on with her life (*Malbim*). In his heart, however, Absalom was plotting revenge.

13:37. Talmai was Absalom's maternal grandfather (above 3:3).
14:1. Joab realized that David longed for a reconciliation with Absalom, but that he refrained from taking the initiative, lest he seem to condone Absalom's fratricide.

ד וַיָּ֣שֶׂם יוֹאָ֗ב אֶת־הַדְּבָרִ֖ים בְּפִֽיהָ: וַתֹּ֡אמֶר הָאִשָּׁה֩ הַתְּקֹעִית֙ אֶל־הַמֶּ֔לֶךְ

ה וַתִּפֹּ֧ל עַל־אַפֶּ֛יהָ אַ֖רְצָה וַתִּשְׁתָּ֑חוּ וַתֹּ֖אמֶר הוֹשִׁ֣עָה הַמֶּֽלֶךְ:   וַיֹּֽאמֶר־

ו לָ֧הּ הַמֶּ֛לֶךְ מַה־לָּ֖ךְ וַתֹּ֑אמֶר אֲבָ֣ל אִשָּֽׁה־אַלְמָנָ֤ה אָ֙נִי֙ וַיָּ֣מׇת אִישִֽׁי: וּלְשִׁפְחָֽתְךָ֙
שְׁנֵ֣י בָנִ֔ים וַיִּנָּצ֤וּ שְׁנֵיהֶם֙ בַּשָּׂדֶ֔ה וְאֵ֥ין מַצִּ֖יל בֵּֽינֵיהֶ֑ם וַיַּכּ֧וֹ הָאֶחָ֛ד אֶת־הָאֶחָ֖ד

ז וַיָּ֣מֶת אֹתֽוֹ: וְהִנֵּה֩ קָ֨מָה כׇל־הַמִּשְׁפָּחָ֜ה עַל־שִׁפְחָתֶ֗ךָ וַיֹּֽאמְרוּ֙ תְּנִ֣י ׀ אֶת־
מַכֵּ֣ה אָחִ֗יו וּנְמִתֵ֙הוּ֙ בְּנֶ֣פֶשׁ אָחִ֔יו אֲשֶׁ֣ר הָרָ֔ג וְנַשְׁמִ֖ידָה גַּ֣ם אֶת־הַיּוֹרֵ֑שׁ וְכִבּ֗וּ
אֶת־גַּֽחַלְתִּי֙ אֲשֶׁ֣ר נִשְׁאָ֔רָה לְבִלְתִּ֧י °שׂ֥וּם [°שִֽׂים ק] לְאִישִׁ֛י שֵׁ֥ם

ח וּשְׁאֵרִ֖ית עַל־פְּנֵ֥י הָאֲדָמָֽה: וַיֹּ֧אמֶר הַמֶּ֛לֶךְ אֶל־הָאִשָּׁ֖ה לְכִ֣י לְבֵיתֵ֑ךְ וַאֲנִ֖י

ט אֲצַוֶּ֥ה עָלָֽיִךְ: וַתֹּ֜אמֶר הָאִשָּׁ֤ה הַתְּקוֹעִית֙ אֶל־הַמֶּ֔לֶךְ עָלַ֛י אֲדֹנִ֥י הַמֶּ֖לֶךְ הֶעָוֺ֑ן

י וְעַל־בֵּ֣ית אָבִ֔י וְהַמֶּ֥לֶךְ וְכִסְא֖וֹ נָקִֽי: וַיֹּ֣אמֶר הַמֶּ֔לֶךְ הַֽמְדַבֵּ֥ר אֵלַ֖יִךְ

יא וַֽהֲבֵאתֹ֣ו אֵלַ֔י וְלֹֽא־יֹסִ֥יף ע֖וֹד לָגַ֥עַת בָּֽךְ: וַתֹּ֩אמֶר֩ יִזְכׇּר־נָ֨א הַמֶּ֜לֶךְ אֶת־יְהֹוָ֣ה
אֱלֹהֶ֗יךָ °מֵהַרְבִּ֞ית [°מֵהַרְבַּ֞ת ק] גֹּאֵ֤ל הַדָּם֙ לְשַׁחֵ֔ת וְלֹ֥א יַשְׁמִ֖ידוּ אֶת־בְּנִ֑י

יב וַיֹּ֙אמֶר֙ חַי־יְהֹוָ֔ה אִם־יִפֹּ֛ל מִשַּׂעֲרַ֥ת בְּנֵ֖ךְ אָֽרְצָה: וַתֹּ֙אמֶר֙ הָֽאִשָּׁ֔ה תְּדַבֶּר־

יג נָ֧א שִׁפְחָֽתְךָ֛ אֶל־אֲדֹנִ֥י הַמֶּ֖לֶךְ דָּבָ֑ר וַיֹּ֖אמֶר דַּבֵּֽרִי: וַתֹּ֙אמֶר֙
הָֽאִשָּׁ֔ה וְלָ֧מָּה חָשַׁ֛בְתָּה כָּזֹ֖את עַל־עַ֣ם אֱלֹהִ֑ים וּמִדַּבֵּ֤ר הַמֶּ֙לֶךְ֙ הַדָּבָ֤ר הַזֶּה֙

יד כְּאָשֵׁ֔ם לְבִלְתִּ֛י הָשִׁ֥יב הַמֶּ֖לֶךְ אֶת־נִדְּחֽוֹ: כִּי־מ֣וֹת נָמ֔וּת וְכַמַּ֙יִם֙ הַנִּגָּרִ֣ים
אַ֔רְצָה אֲשֶׁ֖ר לֹ֣א יֵאָסֵ֑פוּ וְלֹֽא־יִשָּׂ֤א אֱלֹהִים֙ נֶ֔פֶשׁ וְחָשַׁ֣ב מַֽחֲשָׁב֔וֹת לְבִלְתִּ֛י

טו יִדַּ֥ח מִמֶּ֖נּוּ נִדָּֽח: וְ֠עַתָּ֠ה אֲשֶׁר־בָּ֜אתִי לְדַבֵּ֨ר אֶל־הַמֶּ֤לֶךְ אֲדֹנִי֙ אֶת־הַדָּבָ֣ר
הַזֶּ֔ה כִּ֥י יֵֽרְאֻ֖נִי הָעָ֑ם וַתֹּ֤אמֶר שִׁפְחָֽתְךָ֙ אֲדַבְּרָה־נָּ֣א אֶל־הַמֶּ֔לֶךְ אוּלַ֛י יַעֲשֶׂ֥ה

טז הַמֶּ֖לֶךְ אֶת־דְּבַ֥ר אֲמָתֽוֹ: כִּ֣י יִשְׁמַ֣ע הַמֶּ֗לֶךְ לְהַצִּ֤יל אֶת־אֲמָתוֹ֙ מִכַּ֣ף הָאִ֔ישׁ

יז לְהַשְׁמִ֞יד אֹתִ֤י וְאֶת־בְּנִ֛י יַ֖חַד מִֽנַּחֲלַ֥ת אֱלֹהִֽים: וַתֹּ֙אמֶר֙ שִׁפְחָֽתְךָ֔ יִֽהְיֶה־נָּ֛א
דְּבַר־אֲדֹנִ֥י הַמֶּ֖לֶךְ לִמְנֻחָ֑ה כִּ֣י ׀ כְּמַלְאַ֣ךְ הָאֱלֹהִ֗ים כֵּ֣ן אֲדֹנִ֤י הַמֶּ֙לֶךְ֙ לִשְׁמֹ֙עַ֙

יח הַטּ֣וֹב וְהָרָ֔ע וַֽיהֹוָ֥ה אֱלֹהֶ֖יךָ יְהִ֥י עִמָּֽךְ:   וַיַּ֙עַן֙ הַמֶּ֙לֶךְ֙ וַיֹּ֙אמֶר֙
אֶל־הָ֣אִשָּׁ֔ה אַל־נָ֨א תְכַחֲדִ֤י מִמֶּ֙נִּי֙ דָּבָ֔ר אֲשֶׁ֥ר אָנֹכִ֖י שֹׁאֵ֣ל אֹתָ֑ךְ וַתֹּ֙אמֶר֙

יט הָ֣אִשָּׁ֔ה יְדַבֶּר־נָ֖א אֲדֹנִ֥י הַמֶּֽלֶךְ: וַיֹּ֣אמֶר הַמֶּ֗לֶךְ הֲיַ֥ד יוֹאָ֛ב אִתָּ֖ךְ בְּכׇל־זֹ֑את
וַתַּ֣עַן הָאִשָּׁ֞ה וַתֹּ֗אמֶר חֵֽי־נַפְשְׁךָ֙ אֲדֹנִ֣י הַמֶּ֔לֶךְ אִם־אִ֣שׁ ׀ לְהֵמִ֣ין וּלְהַשְׂמִ֗יל
מִכֹּ֤ל אֲשֶׁר־דִּבֶּר֙ אֲדֹנִ֣י הַמֶּ֔לֶךְ כִּֽי־עַבְדְּךָ֤ יוֹאָב֙ ה֣וּא צִוָּ֔נִי וְה֗וּא שָׂ֚ם אֵ֣ת כׇּל־

כ הַדְּבָרִ֣ים הָאֵ֔לֶּה בְּפִ֖י שִׁפְחָתֶֽךָ: לְבַעֲב֤וּר סַבֵּב֙ אֶת־פְּנֵ֣י הַדָּבָ֔ר עָשָׂ֖ה
עַבְדְּךָ֣ יוֹאָ֑ב אֶת־הַדָּבָ֣ר הַזֶּ֔ה וַֽאדֹנִ֣י חָכָ֗ם כְּחׇכְמַת֙ מַלְאַ֣ךְ הָֽאֱלֹהִ֔ים לָדַ֖עַת

כא אֶֽת־כׇּל־אֲשֶׁ֥ר בָּאָֽרֶץ: וַיֹּ֤אמֶר הַמֶּ֙לֶךְ֙ אֶל־יוֹאָ֔ב הִנֵּה־נָ֥א עָשִׂ֖יתִי   °עָשִׂ֖יתָ נ"א

כב אֶת־הַדָּבָ֣ר הַזֶּ֑ה וְלֵ֛ךְ הָשֵׁ֥ב אֶת־הַנַּ֖עַר אֶת־אַבְשָׁלֽוֹם: וַיִּפֹּל֩ יוֹאָ֨ב אֶל־פָּנָ֜יו

14:7. The family argued that it was immoral for the murderer, who was the slain brother's heir, to benefit from his crime.

14:9. Euphemistically interchanging herself and the king, she intimated that if something did happen to her

son after David had guaranteed his safety, it would be the king's fault (*Rashi*).

14:13. Surely you realize that my story never happened, for God's people would never act so cruelly! My story was really a parable for Absalom and Amnon. Your own

And Joab put the words into her mouth.

The wise woman's predicament

⁴ The woman from Tekoa spoke to the king as she fell on her face to the ground and prostrated herself. She said, "Save [me], O king!" ⁵ The king said to her, "What [problem] do you have?" She said, "In truth, I am a widowed woman, my husband has died. ⁶ Your maidservant had two sons. They quarreled in the field, and there was no rescuer between them. One struck the other and killed him. ⁷ Now behold! the entire family rose up against your maidservant and said, 'Hand over the one who struck down his brother and we shall put him to death for the life of his brother whom he murdered; we shall also destroy [this] heir!'* They would thus extinguish my last remaining coal, not leaving for my husband a name and a remnant on the face of the earth!"

David promises to help her

⁸ The king said to the woman, "Go home, and I will issue a command concerning you."

⁹ The woman of Tekoa said to the king, "The sin will be upon me and upon my father's family, my lord the king; the king and his throne are innocent!"* ¹⁰ The king replied, "Whoever speaks [ill] to you, bring him to me, and he will no longer harm you." ¹¹ She said, "May the king remember HASHEM, your God, [to protect me] from the many destructive blood-avengers, so that they not destroy my son!" And he said, "As HASHEM lives, not one hair of your son shall fall to the ground!" ¹² The woman then said, "May your maidservant speak a word to my lord the king?" And he said, "Speak."

The woman turns the tables

¹³ The woman said, "Why do you think such a thing about God's people? And let the king not say now about this matter that he was mistaken, in order for the king not to return his own banished one.* ¹⁴ For we shall all die, like water flowing along the ground that cannot be collected, God spares no one. [Let the king, therefore,] ponder thoughts so that no one be banished from him. ¹⁵ And now, the reason I have come to speak to the king, my lord, in this manner is because the people frightened me;* so your maidservant thought, 'I shall speak to the king and perhaps the king will carry out the word of his maidservant.' ¹⁶ For the king would listen, to save his maidservant from the clutches of "that man" [who wishes] to obliterate me and my son alike from the heritage of God.' ¹⁷ So your maidservant said, 'Let the word of my lord the king bring about tranquility [for his own son].' For like an angel of God, so is my lord, the king, listening to the good and the bad. May HASHEM your God be with you!"

David deduces Joab's involvement . . .

¹⁸ The king then spoke up and said to the woman, "Do not conceal from me anything of that which I ask of you"; and the woman said, "Let my lord, the king, speak." ¹⁹ The king asked, "Is Joab's hand [involved] with you in all this?" The woman spoke up and said, "As your soul lives, my lord, the king, one cannot veer right or left from all that my lord, the king, has spoken; for your servant Joab was the one who instructed me, and he put all these words into the mouth of your maidservant; ²⁰ your servant Joab did this thing to lead up to the matter [of Absalom] in a roundabout way. My lord is wise like the wisdom of an angel of God, knowing everything in the land!"

. . . and sends Joab to bring Absalom back

²¹ The king then said to Joab, "Behold now! — I have done this thing, so go and bring back the lad, Absalom." ²² Joab then fell upon his face

---

judgment requires that you reconcile with Absalom. Please do not retract your response to my parable in   order to keep Absalom in exile.
14:15. I was warned not to broach the subject directly.

אַ֥רְצָה וַיִּשְׁתַּ֖חוּ וַיְבָ֣רֶךְ אֶת־הַמֶּ֑לֶךְ וַיֹּ֣אמֶר יוֹאָ֗ב הַיּ֩וֹם֩ יָדַ֨ע עַבְדְּךָ֜
כִּי־מָצָ֤אתִי חֵן֙ בְּעֵינֶ֙יךָ֙ אֲדֹנִ֣י הַמֶּ֔לֶךְ אֲשֶׁר־עָשָׂ֥ה הַמֶּ֖לֶךְ אֶת־דְּבַ֥ר
כג עַבְדֶּךָ ‬[עַבְדּ֑וֹ]: וַיָּ֣קָם יוֹאָ֗ב וַיֵּ֛לֶךְ גְּשׁ֖וּרָה וַיָּבֵ֥א אֶת־אַבְשָׁל֖וֹם
כד יְרוּשָׁלָֽ͏ִם: וַיֹּ֣אמֶר הַמֶּ֗לֶךְ יִסֹּ֤ב אֶל־בֵּיתוֹ֙ וּפָנַ֣י לֹ֣א יִרְאֶ֔ה וַיִּסֹּ֤ב

14:26. Being a nazirite, Absalom was permitted to cut his hair only annually, when it became uncomfortably heavy.

14:29. Joab refused because he felt that he would not be able to effect a full reconciliation between David and

Absalom (*Malbim*).

14:30. Through this criminal act, Absalom was in effect telling Joab that it was a grave injustice to have brought him back to Jerusalem only to subject him to humiliating confinement (*Malbim*).

to the ground, and he prostrated himself and blessed the king. Joab said, "Today your servant realizes that I have found favor in your eyes, my lord, the king, for the king has carried out the request of your servant."

²³ Joab then got up and went to Geshur, and brought Absalom to Jerusalem. ²⁴ The king said, "Let him go around to his house, but let him not see my face!" So Absalom went around to his house and did not see the king's face.

Absalom's physical beauty ²⁵ There was no one in all of Israel as praiseworthy for his beauty as Absalom; from the bottom of his foot to the top of his head there was no blemish in him. ²⁶ When he would have his head barbered — at the end of every year he would have his hair barbered, because it became heavy upon him* and he had it barbered — he weighed the hair of his head at two hundred shekels by the king's weight. ²⁷ To Absalom were born three sons and one daughter, named Tamar, who was a beautiful woman.

Absalom forces a reunion with David ²⁸ Absalom lived in Jerusalem for two full years and did not see the king's face. ²⁹ Absalom then sent for Joab, in order to send him to the king, but he refused to come to him. He sent again, but he refused to come. * ³⁰ He then said to his servants, "Take note of Joab's field that is next to mine, where he has barley, and go and set it on fire."* So Absalom's servants set the field on fire. ³¹ Joab then arose and went to Absalom, into the house, and said to him, "Why did your servants set my field on fire?" ³² Absalom answered Joab, "Behold! — I sent for you, saying, 'Come here that I may send you to the king to say, "Why have I come from Geshur? It would be better for me if I were still there!" And now, let me see the king's face, and if I am guilty of a sin, let him put me to death!' "

³³ So Joab came to the king and told him. He summoned Absalom and he came to the king, prostrating himself upon his face to the ground before the king, and the king kissed Absalom.

15

ABSALOM'S REBELLION
15:1-19:9

Absalom connives to gain a following

¹ It happened after this that Absalom prepared for himself chariot and horses and fifty men to run before him. * ² Absalom would arise early and stand by the way toward the gate; and it happened when any man who would have a dispute to bring to the king for judgment, Absalom called to him and said, "Which city are you from?" And he said, "Your servant is from such and such tribe of Israel." ³ Then Absalom said to him, "Look, your words are good and proper, but there is no one before the king to understand you." ⁴ Then Absalom said, "If only someone would appoint me judge in the land, and any man who had a dispute or a judgment could come to me — I would judge him fairly!" ⁵ And it was that whenever anyone came near him to prostrate himself before him, he would stretch out his hand and take hold of him and kiss him. * ⁶ Absalom did this sort of thing to all of Israel who would come for judgment to the king; and Absalom stole the hearts of the men of Israel.

⁷ It happened at the end of forty years* that Absalom said to the king, "I would like to go now and pay my vow that I made to Hashem, in Hebron. ⁸ For your servant took a vow, when I lived in Geshur in Aram, saying,

---

15:1. Absalom started to lay the groundwork for a rebellion against David. He began by projecting himself as the only committed friend of the common people.

15:5. By showing them lavish affection, agreeing with

their grievances, and not letting them bow to him, Absalom slyly gained the trust and love of the masses.

15:7. That is, forty years since the institution of Saul's monarchy in Israel (*Talmud*), this being the thirty-seventh year of David's reign (*Radak*).

ט אִם־יָשִׁיב [יָשׁוֹב ק׳] יְשִׁבֵנִי יהוה יְרוּשָׁלַ͏ִם וְעָבַדְתִּי אֶת־יהוה: וַיֹּאמֶר־
י לוֹ הַמֶּלֶךְ לֵךְ בְּשָׁלוֹם וַיָּקָם וַיֵּלֶךְ חֶבְרוֹנָה: וַיִּשְׁלַח אַבְשָׁלוֹם
מְרַגְּלִים בְּכָל־שִׁבְטֵי יִשְׂרָאֵל לֵאמֹר כְּשָׁמְעֲכֶם אֶת־קוֹל הַשֹּׁפָר וַאֲמַרְתֶּם
יא מָלַךְ אַבְשָׁלוֹם בְּחֶבְרוֹן: וְאֶת־אַבְשָׁלוֹם הָלְכוּ מָאתַיִם אִישׁ מִירוּשָׁלַ͏ִם
קְרֻאִים וְהֹלְכִים לְתֻמָּם וְלֹא יָדְעוּ כָּל־דָּבָר: וַיִּשְׁלַח אַבְשָׁלוֹם אֶת־
יב אֲחִיתֹפֶל הַגִּילֹנִי יוֹעֵץ דָּוִד מֵעִירוֹ מִגִּלֹה בְּזָבְחוֹ אֶת־הַזְּבָחִים וַיְהִי הַקֶּשֶׁר
אַמִּץ וְהָעָם הוֹלֵךְ וָרָב אֶת־אַבְשָׁלוֹם: וַיָּבֹא הַמַּגִּיד אֶל־דָּוִד לֵאמֹר הָיָה
יג לֶב־אִישׁ יִשְׂרָאֵל אַחֲרֵי אַבְשָׁלוֹם: וַיֹּאמֶר דָּוִד לְכָל־עֲבָדָיו אֲשֶׁר־אִתּוֹ
יד בִירוּשָׁלַ͏ִם קוּמוּ וְנִבְרָחָה כִּי לֹא־תִהְיֶה־לָּנוּ פְלֵיטָה מִפְּנֵי אַבְשָׁלוֹם מַהֲרוּ
לָלֶכֶת פֶּן־יְמַהֵר וְהִשִּׂגָנוּ וְהִדִּיחַ עָלֵינוּ אֶת־הָרָעָה וְהִכָּה הָעִיר לְפִי־חָרֶב:
טו וַיֹּאמְרוּ עַבְדֵי־הַמֶּלֶךְ אֶל־הַמֶּלֶךְ כְּכֹל אֲשֶׁר־יִבְחַר אֲדֹנִי הַמֶּלֶךְ הִנֵּה
טז עֲבָדֶיךָ: וַיֵּצֵא הַמֶּלֶךְ וְכָל־בֵּיתוֹ בְּרַגְלָיו וַיַּעֲזֹב הַמֶּלֶךְ אֵת עֶשֶׂר נָשִׁים
יז פִּלַגְשִׁים לִשְׁמֹר הַבָּיִת: וַיֵּצֵא הַמֶּלֶךְ וְכָל־הָעָם בְּרַגְלָיו וַיַּעַמְדוּ בֵּית
יח הַמֶּרְחָק: וְכָל־עֲבָדָיו עֹבְרִים עַל־יָדוֹ וְכָל־הַכְּרֵתִי וְכָל־הַפְּלֵתִי וְכָל־
הַגִּתִּים שֵׁשׁ־מֵאוֹת אִישׁ אֲשֶׁר־בָּאוּ בְרַגְלוֹ מִגַּת עֹבְרִים עַל־פְּנֵי
יט הַמֶּלֶךְ: וַיֹּאמֶר הַמֶּלֶךְ אֶל־אִתַּי הַגִּתִּי לָמָּה תֵלֵךְ גַּם־אַתָּה
כ אִתָּנוּ שׁוּב וְשֵׁב עִם־הַמֶּלֶךְ כִּי־נָכְרִי אַתָּה וְגַם־גֹּלֶה אַתָּה לִמְקוֹמֶךָ: תְּמוֹל
בּוֹאֶךָ וְהַיּוֹם אֲנוֹעֲךָ [אֲנִיעֲךָ ק׳] עִמָּנוּ לָלֶכֶת וַאֲנִי הוֹלֵךְ עַל אֲשֶׁר־אֲנִי
כא הוֹלֵךְ שׁוּב וְהָשֵׁב אֶת־אַחֶיךָ עִמָּךְ חֶסֶד וֶאֱמֶת: וַיַּעַן אִתַּי אֶת־הַמֶּלֶךְ
וַיֹּאמַר חַי־יהוה וְחֵי אֲדֹנִי הַמֶּלֶךְ כִּי [אִם כ׳ ולא ק׳] בִּמְקוֹם אֲשֶׁר יִהְיֶה־שָּׁם ׀
כב אֲדֹנִי הַמֶּלֶךְ אִם־לְמָוֶת אִם־לְחַיִּים כִּי־שָׁם יִהְיֶה עַבְדֶּךָ: וַיֹּאמֶר דָּוִד אֶל־
כג אִתַּי לֵךְ וַעֲבֹר וַיַּעֲבֹר אִתַּי הַגִּתִּי וְכָל־אֲנָשָׁיו וְכָל־הַטַּף אֲשֶׁר אִתּוֹ: וְכָל־
הָאָרֶץ בּוֹכִים קוֹל גָּדוֹל וְכָל־הָעָם עֹבְרִים וְהַמֶּלֶךְ עֹבֵר בְּנַחַל קִדְרוֹן
כד וְכָל־הָעָם עֹבְרִים עַל־פְּנֵי־דֶרֶךְ אֶת־הַמִּדְבָּר: וְהִנֵּה גַם־צָדוֹק וְכָל־הַלְוִיִּם
אִתּוֹ נֹשְׂאִים אֶת־אֲרוֹן בְּרִית הָאֱלֹהִים וַיַּצִּקוּ אֶת־אֲרוֹן הָאֱלֹהִים וַיַּעַל
כה אֶבְיָתָר עַד־תֹּם כָּל־הָעָם לַעֲבוֹר מִן־הָעִיר: וַיֹּאמֶר הַמֶּלֶךְ
לְצָדוֹק הָשֵׁב אֶת־אֲרוֹן הָאֱלֹהִים הָעִיר אִם־אֶמְצָא חֵן בְּעֵינֵי יהוה
כו וֶהֱשִׁבַנִי וְהִרְאַנִי אֹתוֹ וְאֶת־נָוֵהוּ: וְאִם כֹּה יֹאמַר לֹא חָפַצְתִּי בָּךְ הִנְנִי
כז יַעֲשֶׂה־לִּי כַּאֲשֶׁר טוֹב בְּעֵינָיו: וַיֹּאמֶר הַמֶּלֶךְ אֶל־צָדוֹק הַכֹּהֵן
הֲרוֹאֶה אַתָּה שֻׁבָה הָעִיר בְּשָׁלוֹם וַאֲחִימַעַץ בִּנְךָ וִיהוֹנָתָן בֶּן־אֶבְיָתָר שְׁנֵי
כח בְנֵיכֶם אִתְּכֶם: רְאוּ אָנֹכִי מִתְמַהְמֵהַּ בְּעַבְרֹות [בְּעַרְבוֹת ק׳] הַמִּדְבָּר עַד

15:11. David had given Absalom the right to take dignitaries with him (*Yalkut*), and he took advantage of this offer to make it seem as if he enjoyed the widespread support of national leaders.
15:18. See note to 8:18.

15:19. "You have only recently settled in Jerusalem; how could I now dislocate you again by having you wander about with me? Return to your [new-found] place [in Jerusalem]" (*Radak*). *Targum* translates, "And even if you prefer exile [to serving Absalom], [go back] to your

'If HASHEM shall return me to Jerusalem, I shall worship unto HASHEM.' " ⁹ *The king said to him, "Go in peace," and he arose and went to Hebron.*

Absalom declares his rebellion

¹⁰ *Absalom then sent spies throughout all the tribes of Israel saying, "When you hear the sound of the shofar, announce, 'Absalom has become king in Hebron.' "* ¹¹ *With Absalom went two hundred men from Jerusalem, who were invited and went along innocently; they did not know anything [of Absalom's intention].* * ¹² *And Absalom sent for Ahithophel the Gilonite, David's adviser, from his city, from Giloh, when he slaughtered the sacrifices. The conspiracy was powerful, and the people with Absalom continually increased.*

David goes into exile

¹³ *The bearer of news came to David saying, "The heart of [every] man of Israel has turned to Absalom."* ¹⁴ *David then said to all his servants who were with him in Jerusalem, "Arise, let us flee; for there will be no escape for us from before Absalom! Hurry to leave, lest he hurry and catch up to us and thrust evil upon us, and smite the city by the blade of the sword."*

His servants prove their loyalty

¹⁵ *The king's servants said to the king, "Whatever my lord the king decides, your servants are ready!"*

¹⁶ *The king left, and all his household [went] with him, but the king left ten concubine wives to keep the house.* ¹⁷ *The king left, and all the people [went] with him. They stopped at a faraway house.* ¹⁸ *All his servants passed near him, along with all the archers and slingers;* * *and the Gittites — six hundred men who had come with him from Gath — passed before the king.*

¹⁹ *The king said to Ittai the Gittite, "Why should you also go with us? Go back and remain with the [new] king, for you are a foreigner and also an exile; [return] to your place.* * ²⁰ *You arrived just yesterday; shall I displace you today to take flight with us, while I go wherever I go? Return, and take your brethren back with you — [your offer is] kindness and truth."* ²¹ *But Ittai answered the king and said, "As HASHEM lives, and by the life of my lord the king, [I swear] that in whatever place my lord the king will be — whether for death or for life — there your servant will be."*

²² *David then said to Ittai, "Go, then, pass ahead." So Ittai the Gittite passed ahead with all his men and all the children who were with him.* ²³ *The entire land was crying in a loud voice, and all the people were passing by. The king was passing through the Kidron Valley and all the people were passing along the road, toward the wilderness.* ²⁴ *Behold, Zadok and all the Levites with him were carrying the Ark of the Covenant of God.* * *They set down the Ark of God — and Abiathar came up [as well] — until all the people of the city finished passing from the city.*

The Ark is returned to Jerusalem

²⁵ *The king said to Zadok, "Return the Ark of God to the city. If I find favor in HASHEM's eyes He will bring me back and let me behold Him and His Abode.* ²⁶ *And if He says thus, 'I desire you not,' then I am prepared; let Him do with me as He sees fit."*

²⁷ *The king then said to Zadok the Kohen, "Do you agree?* * *Return to the city in peace, your son Ahimaaz and Jonathan son of Abiathar — your two sons going with you.* ²⁸ *See, I am remaining in the Plains of the Wilderness, until*

[original] place [in Gath]."

15:24. The Kohanim and Levites had thought to accompany David with the Ark so that it might afford him protection during his wanderings, but David believed that it would be disrespectful to carry the Ark about from

place to place (*Abarbanel*).

15:27. Having already instructed Zadok to return the Ark to Jerusalem, David now proposes that Zadok himself should also remain there, in order to act as a spy and informant on behalf of David.

כט בּוֹא דָבָר מֵעִמָּכֶם לְהַגִּיד לִי: וַיָּשֶׁב צָדוֹק וְאֶבְיָתָר אֶת־אֲרוֹן הָאֱלֹהִים
ל יְרוּשָׁלֵַם וַיֵּשְׁבוּ שָׁם: וְדָוִד עֹלֶה בְמַעֲלֵה הַזֵּיתִים עֹלֶה ׀ וּבוֹכֶה וְרֹאשׁ לוֹ
חָפוּי וְהוּא הֹלֵךְ יָחֵף וְכָל־הָעָם אֲשֶׁר־אִתּוֹ חָפוּ אִישׁ רֹאשׁוֹ וְעָלוּ עָלֹה
לא וּבָכֹה: וְדָוִד הִגִּיד לֵאמֹר אֲחִיתֹפֶל בַּקֹּשְׁרִים עִם־אַבְשָׁלוֹם וַיֹּאמֶר דָּוִד
לב סַכֶּל־נָא אֶת־עֲצַת אֲחִיתֹפֶל יְהוָה: וַיְהִי דָוִד בָּא עַד־הָרֹאשׁ אֲשֶׁר־
יִשְׁתַּחֲוֶה שָׁם לֵאלֹהִים וְהִנֵּה לִקְרָאתוֹ חוּשַׁי הָאַרְכִּי קָרוּעַ כֻּתָּנְתּוֹ וַאֲדָמָה
לג־לד עַל־רֹאשׁוֹ: וַיֹּאמֶר לוֹ דָּוִד אִם עָבַרְתָּ אִתִּי וְהָיָתָ עָלַי לְמַשָּׂא: וְאִם־הָעִיר
תָּשׁוּב וְאָמַרְתָּ לְאַבְשָׁלוֹם עַבְדְּךָ אֲנִי הַמֶּלֶךְ אֶהְיֶה עֶבֶד אָבִיךָ וַאֲנִי מֵאָז
לה וְעַתָּה וַאֲנִי עַבְדֶּךָ וְהֵפַרְתָּה לִי אֵת עֲצַת אֲחִיתֹפֶל: וַהֲלוֹא עִמְּךָ שָׁם צָדוֹק
וְאֶבְיָתָר הַכֹּהֲנִים וְהָיָה כָּל־הַדָּבָר אֲשֶׁר תִּשְׁמַע מִבֵּית הַמֶּלֶךְ תַּגִּיד
לו לְצָדוֹק וּלְאֶבְיָתָר הַכֹּהֲנִים: הִנֵּה־שָׁם עִמָּם שְׁנֵי בְנֵיהֶם אֲחִימַעַץ לְצָדוֹק
לז וְלִיהוֹנָתָן לְאֶבְיָתָר וּשְׁלַחְתֶּם בְּיָדָם אֵלַי כָּל־דָּבָר אֲשֶׁר תִּשְׁמָעוּ: וַיָּבֹא
חוּשַׁי רֵעֶה דָוִד הָעִיר וְאַבְשָׁלֹם יָבֹא יְרוּשָׁלָ͏ִם:

טז

א וְדָוִד עָבַר
מְעַט מֵהָרֹאשׁ וְהִנֵּה צִיבָא נַעַר מְפִי־בֹשֶׁת לִקְרָאתוֹ וְצֶמֶד חֲמֹרִים חֲבֻשִׁים
ב וַעֲלֵיהֶם מָאתַיִם לֶחֶם וּמֵאָה צִמּוּקִים וּמֵאָה קַיִץ וְנֵבֶל יָיִן: וַיֹּאמֶר הַמֶּלֶךְ
אֶל־צִיבָא מָה־אֵלֶּה לָּךְ וַיֹּאמֶר צִיבָא הַחֲמוֹרִים לְבֵית־הַמֶּלֶךְ לִרְכֹּב
וְלַהלהם [°וְהַלֶּחֶם ק׳] וְהַקַּיִץ לֶאֱכוֹל הַנְּעָרִים וְהַיַּיִן לִשְׁתּוֹת הַיָּעֵף
ג בַּמִּדְבָּר: וַיֹּאמֶר הַמֶּלֶךְ וְאַיֵּה בֶּן־אֲדֹנֶיךָ וַיֹּאמֶר צִיבָא אֶל־הַמֶּלֶךְ הִנֵּה
יוֹשֵׁב בִּירוּשָׁלַ͏ִם כִּי אָמַר הַיּוֹם יָשִׁיבוּ לִי בֵּית יִשְׂרָאֵל אֵת מַמְלְכוּת אָבִי:
ד וַיֹּאמֶר הַמֶּלֶךְ לְצִבָא הִנֵּה לְךָ כֹּל אֲשֶׁר לִמְפִי־בֹשֶׁת וַיֹּאמֶר צִיבָא
ה הִשְׁתַּחֲוֵיתִי אֶמְצָא־חֵן בְּעֵינֶיךָ אֲדֹנִי הַמֶּלֶךְ: וּבָא הַמֶּלֶךְ דָּוִד עַד־בַּחוּרִים
וְהִנֵּה מִשָּׁם אִישׁ יוֹצֵא מִמִּשְׁפַּחַת בֵּית־שָׁאוּל וּשְׁמוֹ שִׁמְעִי בֶן־גֵּרָא יֹצֵא יָצוֹא
ו וּמְקַלֵּל: וַיְסַקֵּל בָּאֲבָנִים אֶת־דָּוִד וְאֶת־כָּל־עַבְדֵי הַמֶּלֶךְ דָּוִד וְכָל־
ז הָעָם וְכָל־הַגִּבֹּרִים מִימִינוֹ וּמִשְּׂמֹאלוֹ: וְכֹה־אָמַר שִׁמְעִי בְּקַלְלוֹ צֵא צֵא אִישׁ
ח הַדָּמִים וְאִישׁ הַבְּלִיָּעַל: הֵשִׁיב עָלֶיךָ יְהוָה כֹּל ׀ דְּמֵי בֵית־שָׁאוּל
אֲשֶׁר מָלַכְתָּ תחתו [°תַּחְתָּיו ק׳] וַיִּתֵּן יְהוָה אֶת־הַמְּלוּכָה בְּיַד אַבְשָׁלוֹם
ט בְּנֶךָ וְהִנְּךָ בְּרָעָתֶךָ כִּי אִישׁ דָּמִים אָתָּה: וַיֹּאמֶר אֲבִישַׁי בֶּן־צְרוּיָה אֶל־
הַמֶּלֶךְ לָמָּה יְקַלֵּל הַכֶּלֶב הַמֵּת הַזֶּה אֶת־אֲדֹנִי הַמֶּלֶךְ אֶעְבְּרָה־נָּא
י וְאָסִירָה אֶת־רֹאשׁוֹ: וַיֹּאמֶר הַמֶּלֶךְ מַה־לִּי וְלָכֶם בְּנֵי צְרֻיָה
כי [°כֹּה ק׳] יְקַלֵּל וכי [°וְכִי ק׳] יְהוָה אָמַר לוֹ קַלֵּל אֶת־דָּוִד וּמִי יֹאמַר
יא מַדּוּעַ עָשִׂיתָה כֵּן: וַיֹּאמֶר דָּוִד אֶל־אֲבִישַׁי וְאֶל־כָּל־עֲבָדָיו

15:30. Going barefoot and wrapping one's head with a scarf are traditional symbols of mourning (*Rashi*).

15:31. The shrewd counsel of Ahithophel was one of Absalom's greatest assets. David now prayed that his advice would lead to Absalom's undoing.

15:32. The summit of the Mount of Olives overlooked the Tent of the Ark in Jerusalem. Whenever he approached Jerusalem, David would prostrate himself as soon as the Tent came into view (*Rashi*).

15:33. Hushai was elderly and unsuited to the rigors of

word comes from you to inform me." [29] So Zadok and Abiathar returned the Ark of God to Jerusalem, and they stayed there.

[30] David was going up on the ascent of [the Mount of] Olives, crying as he ascended, with his head covered, going barefoot. * And all the people with him wrapped their heads and went up, crying as they ascended. [31] It was told to David, saying, "Ahithophel is among the conspirators with Absalom." And David said, "Please confound the advice of Ahithophel, O HASHEM!" *

Ahithophel's treachery

[32] David was approaching the summit where he would prostrate himself to God, * and there before him was Hushai the Archite, with his tunic torn and dirt upon his head. [33] David said to him, "If you pass over with me you will be a burden to me, * [34] but if you return to the city and say to Absalom, 'I shall be your servant, O king; I have always been your father's servant and now I am your servant,' you will be able to nullify Ahithophel's counsel for me. [35] Are not Zadok and Abiathar the Kohanim there with you? And it will be that anything you hear from the king's house, you will tell to Zadok and Abiathar the Kohanim. [36] Behold, their two sons are there with them — Zadok's Ahimaaz and Abiathar's Jonathan; send me by their hand any word you may hear." [37] So Hushai, David's friend, came to the city, as Absalom was about to enter Jerusalem.

Hushai becomes David's secret agent

16

[1] **D**avid had just passed beyond the summit, and, behold, Ziba, Mephibosheth's servant, was in front of him, with a pair of donkeys laden with two hundred breads, a hundred [clusters of] raisins, a hundred [portions of] dried figs and a container of wine. [2] The king asked Ziba, "Why do you have these things?" And Ziba answered, "The donkeys are for the king's household to ride upon, the bread and the dried figs are for the youths to eat, and the wine is for the exhausted one in the desert to drink." [3] The king then said, "And where is your master's son [Mephibosheth]?" Ziba said to the king, "Behold, he is staying in Jerusalem, for he said, 'Today the House of Israel will restore my father's * kingdom to me.' " [4] The king then said to Ziba, "Behold — everything that Mephibosheth owns is now yours!" And Ziba said, "I prostrate myself; may I find favor in the eyes of my lord the king!"

Ziba condemns Mephibosheth

[5] King David came until Bahurim, and behold — a man of Saul's family was coming out from there, named Shimei son of Gera, and he was cursing as he was coming out. [6] He pelted David and all of King David's servants with stones, as well as all the people and the soldiers, to his right and to his left. [7] And this is what Shimei said as he cursed, "Go out, go out, you man of bloodshed, you base man! [8] HASHEM is repaying you for all the blood of the House of Saul, * in whose stead you have reigned, and has given over the kingdom into the hand of Absalom your son. Behold — you are now afflicted because you are a man of bloodshed!" [9] Abishai son of Zeruiah said to the king, "Why should this dead dog curse my lord the king? I will go on ahead and take off his head!"

Shimei reviles David . . .

[10] But the king said, "What does it matter to me or to you, O sons of Zeruiah? He is cursing because HASHEM has said to him, 'Curse David.' * Who can then say, 'Why have you done this?' " [11] David then said to Abishai and all his servants,

. . . but David shields him

---

flight in rugged territory.

16:3. Mephibosheth referred to Saul, who was actually his grandfather (see 9:7 and the note there).

16:8. Shimei was accusing David of complicity in the assassinations of Ish-bosheth and Abner (*Radak*).

16:10. God, Who has ordained that I suffer this degrading exile as punishment for my sins, has invoked this man as His agent to augment my suffering (*Radak*). Alternatively, Shimei is the head of a sanhedrin, and such a personage would not have cursed me without Divine sanction (*Rashi*).

הִנֵּה בְנִי אֲשֶׁר־יָצָא מִמֵּעַי מְבַקֵּשׁ אֶת־נַפְשִׁי וְאַף כִּי־עַתָּה בֶן־הַיְמִינִי

יב הַנִּחוּ לוֹ וִיקַלֵּל כִּי־אָמַר לוֹ יְהֹוָה: אוּלַי יִרְאֶה יְהֹוָה °בְּעֵנִי [°בְּעֵנִי ק]

יג וְהֵשִׁיב יְהֹוָה לִי טוֹבָה תַּחַת קִלְלָתוֹ הַיּוֹם הַזֶּה: וַיֵּלֶךְ דָּוִד וַאֲנָשָׁיו

בַּדָּרֶךְ וְשִׁמְעִי הֹלֵךְ בְּצֵלַע הָהָר לְעֻמָּתוֹ הָלוֹךְ וַיְקַלֵּל וַיְסַקֵּל

יד בָּאֲבָנִים לְעֻמָּתוֹ וְעִפַּר בֶּעָפָר: וַיָּבֹא הַמֶּלֶךְ וְכָל־הָעָם אֲשֶׁר־

טו אִתּוֹ עֲיֵפִים וַיִּנָּפֵשׁ שָׁם: וְאַבְשָׁלוֹם וְכָל־הָעָם אִישׁ יִשְׂרָאֵל בָּאוּ יְרוּשָׁלָ͏ִם

טז וַאֲחִיתֹפֶל אִתּוֹ: וַיְהִי כַּאֲשֶׁר־בָּא חוּשַׁי הָאַרְכִּי רֵעֶה דָוִד אֶל־אַבְשָׁלוֹם

יז וַיֹּאמֶר חוּשַׁי אֶל־אַבְשָׁלֹם יְחִי הַמֶּלֶךְ יְחִי הַמֶּלֶךְ: וַיֹּאמֶר אַבְשָׁלוֹם אֶל־

יח חוּשַׁי זֶה חַסְדְּךָ אֶת־רֵעֶךָ לָמָּה לֹא־הָלַכְתָּ אֶת־רֵעֶךָ: וַיֹּאמֶר חוּשַׁי אֶל־

אַבְשָׁלֹם לֹא כִּי אֲשֶׁר בָּחַר יְהֹוָה וְהָעָם הַזֶּה וְכָל־אִישׁ יִשְׂרָאֵל °לֹא

יט [°לוֹ ק] אֶהְיֶה וְאִתּוֹ אֵשֵׁב: וְהַשֵּׁנִית לְמִי אֲנִי אֶעֱבֹד הֲלוֹא לִפְנֵי בְנוֹ כַּאֲשֶׁר

כ עָבַדְתִּי לִפְנֵי אָבִיךָ כֵּן אֶהְיֶה לְפָנֶיךָ: וַיֹּאמֶר אַבְשָׁלוֹם אֶל־

כא אֲחִיתֹפֶל הָבוּ לָכֶם עֵצָה מַה־נַּעֲשֶׂה: וַיֹּאמֶר אֲחִיתֹפֶל אֶל־אַבְשָׁלֹם בּוֹא

אֶל־פִּלַגְשֵׁי אָבִיךָ אֲשֶׁר הִנִּיחַ לִשְׁמוֹר הַבָּיִת וְשָׁמַע כָּל־יִשְׂרָאֵל כִּי־

כב נִבְאַשְׁתָּ אֶת־אָבִיךָ וְחָזְקוּ יְדֵי כָּל־אֲשֶׁר אִתָּךְ: וַיַּטּוּ לְאַבְשָׁלוֹם הָאֹהֶל עַל־

כג הַגָּג וַיָּבֹא אַבְשָׁלוֹם אֶל־פִּלַגְשֵׁי אָבִיו לְעֵינֵי כָּל־יִשְׂרָאֵל: וַעֲצַת אֲחִיתֹפֶל

אֲשֶׁר יָעַץ בַּיָּמִים הָהֵם כַּאֲשֶׁר יִשְׁאַל־[אִישׁ ק ולא כ] בִּדְבַר הָאֱלֹהִים

יז א כֵּן כָּל־עֲצַת אֲחִיתֹפֶל גַּם־לְדָוִד גַּם־לְאַבְשָׁלֹם: וַיֹּאמֶר

אֲחִיתֹפֶל אֶל־אַבְשָׁלֹם אֶבְחֲרָה נָּא שְׁנֵים־עָשָׂר אֶלֶף אִישׁ וְאָקוּמָה

ב וְאֶרְדְּפָה אַחֲרֵי־דָוִד הַלָּיְלָה: וְאָבוֹא עָלָיו וְהוּא יָגֵעַ וּרְפֵה יָדַיִם וְהַחֲרַדְתִּי

ג אֹתוֹ וְנָס כָּל־הָעָם אֲשֶׁר־אִתּוֹ וְהִכֵּיתִי אֶת־הַמֶּלֶךְ לְבַדּוֹ: וְאָשִׁיבָה כָל־

הָעָם אֵלֶיךָ כְּשׁוּב הַכֹּל הָאִישׁ אֲשֶׁר אַתָּה מְבַקֵּשׁ כָּל־הָעָם יִהְיֶה שָׁלוֹם:

ד־ה וַיִּישַׁר הַדָּבָר בְּעֵינֵי אַבְשָׁלֹם וּבְעֵינֵי כָּל־זִקְנֵי יִשְׂרָאֵל: וַיֹּאמֶר

אַבְשָׁלוֹם קְרָא נָא גַם לְחוּשַׁי הָאַרְכִּי וְנִשְׁמְעָה מַה־בְּפִיו גַּם־הוּא: וַיָּבֹא

ו חוּשַׁי אֶל־אַבְשָׁלוֹם וַיֹּאמֶר אַבְשָׁלוֹם אֵלָיו לֵאמֹר כַּדָּבָר הַזֶּה דִּבֶּר

ז אֲחִיתֹפֶל הֲנַעֲשֶׂה אֶת־דְּבָרוֹ אִם־אַיִן אַתָּה דַבֵּר: וַיֹּאמֶר

חוּשַׁי אֶל־אַבְשָׁלוֹם לֹא־טוֹבָה הָעֵצָה אֲשֶׁר־יָעַץ אֲחִיתֹפֶל בַּפַּעַם

ח הַזֹּאת: וַיֹּאמֶר חוּשַׁי אַתָּה יָדַעְתָּ אֶת־אָבִיךָ וְאֶת־אֲנָשָׁיו כִּי גִבֹּרִים

הֵמָּה וּמָרֵי נֶפֶשׁ הֵמָּה כְּדֹב שַׁכּוּל בַּשָּׂדֶה וְאָבִיךָ אִישׁ מִלְחָמָה וְלֹא יָלִין

ט אֶת־הָעָם: הִנֵּה עַתָּה הוּא־נֶחְבָּא בְּאַחַת הַפְּחָתִים אוֹ בְּאַחַד הַמְּקֹמֹת

וְהָיָה כִּנְפֹל בָּהֶם בַּתְּחִלָּה וְשָׁמַע הַשֹּׁמֵעַ וְאָמַר הָיְתָה מַגֵּפָה בָּעָם

י אֲשֶׁר אַחֲרֵי אַבְשָׁלֹם: וְהוּא גַם־בֶּן־חַיִל אֲשֶׁר לִבּוֹ כְּלֵב הָאַרְיֵה הִמֵּס

יא יִמָּס כִּי־יֹדֵעַ כָּל־יִשְׂרָאֵל כִּי־גִבּוֹר אָבִיךָ וּבְנֵי־חַיִל אֲשֶׁר אִתּוֹ: כִּי יָעַצְתִּי

16:21. Until you do something to irrevocably break your ties to David, your followers might not support you whole-   heartedly, fearing that you might become reconciled with your father and leave them branded as traitors (*Rashi*).

"Here my own son, who has issued from my innards, seeks my life, so what now of this Benjamite? Let him be; let him curse, for HASHEM has told him to. ¹² *Perhaps HASHEM will see [the tears in] my eye and HASHEM will repay me with goodness instead of his curse this day."* ¹³ *David and his men continued on the way, with Shimei walking along the side of the mountain opposite him; going, he cursed and flung stones in his direction, and threw dirt.*

¹⁴ *The king and all the people who were with him arrived [in Bahurim] exhausted, and they rested there.*

¹⁵ *Absalom and all the people, [every] man of Israel, came to Jerusalem, and Ahithophel with him.* ¹⁶ *When Hushai the Archite, David's friend, came to*

Hushai wins Absalom's trust

Absalom, he said, "May the king live! May the king live!" ¹⁷ *Absalom then said to Hushai, "Is this your kindness to your friend? Why did you not go with your friend?"* ¹⁸ *Hushai said to Absalom, "No! Rather, he whom HASHEM — as well as this people and every man of Israel — has chosen, his shall I be and with him shall I stay!* ¹⁹ *Secondly, whom shall I be serving — is it not [my friend's] son? Just as I served before your father so shall I be before you!"*

²⁰ *Absalom said to Ahithophel, "Give counsel; what should we do?"*

Ahithophel's immoral counsel

²¹ *Ahithophel advised Absalom, "Consort with your father's concubines, whom he left to keep the house. All of Israel will hear that you have totally repudiated your father, and all who are with you will strengthen their resolve."* * ²² *So they pitched a tent on the roof for Absalom, and Absalom consorted with his father's concubines in front of all of Israel.*

²³ *Now the counsel of Ahithophel that he advised in those days was as if someone would inquire of the word of God; such was all the counsel of Ahithophel both to David and to Absalom.*

17

Ahithophel proposes a surprise attack on David . . .

¹ **A**hithophel told Absalom, *"Let me please choose twelve thousand men, and I will arise and chase after David tonight!* ² *I will come upon him while he is exhausted and weak-handed; I will frighten him so that all the people who are with him will flee, and I will strike down only the king.* ³ *Then I will return all the people to you. When everyone will have returned, the man whom you are seeking [will be dead] and all the people will be at peace."* * ⁴ *This proposal was proper in the eyes of Absalom and in the eyes of all the elders of Israel.*

⁵ *Absalom then said, "Call now Hushai the Archite also; let us also hear what he says."* ⁶ *So Hushai came to Absalom. Absalom said to him, saying, "In this manner has Ahithophel spoken; shall we follow his word? If not, then you speak*

. . . but Hushai disputes him

up." ⁷ *Hushai said to Absalom, "This time the advice that Ahithophel suggested is not good."* ⁸ *Hushai said, "You know your father and his men, that they are mighty men and that they are as embittered as a bereaved bear in the field. Your father is a skilled warrior; he will not sleep with the people.* ⁹ *Behold, he is now hiding in one of the pits or in one of the [other hiding] places; when the first soldiers fall, whoever hears will say, 'There has been a calamity among the people who are with Absalom'* — ¹⁰ *even if someone is a valiant man whose heart is like a lion's heart, it will certainly melt — for all of Israel knows that your father is a mighty man, as are the soldiers who are with him.* * ¹¹ *I would suggest*

17:3. Radak suggests that the reason Ahithophel turned so bitterly against David is because he was incensed at his conduct with Bath-sheba, Ahithophel's granddaughter (see 11:3 and 23:34).

17:10. Since David's military prowess is well known, the cries of the first victims will be attributed — rightly or wrongly — to casualties in Absalom's army, terrifying even your most courageous soldiers (Kara, Radak).

הֵאָסֹף יֵאָסֵף עָלֶ֫יךָ כָל־יִשְׂרָאֵל מִדָּן וְעַד־בְּאֵר שֶׁ֫בַע כַּח֫וֹל אֲשֶׁר־עַל־הַיָּם
לָרֹב וּפָנֶ֫יךָ הֹלְכִ֫ים בַּקְּרָב: וּבָ֫אנוּ אֵלָיו °בְּאַחַת ק׳] הַמְּקוֹמֹת אֲשֶׁר יב
נִמְצָא שָׁם וְנַ֫חְנוּ עָלָיו כַּאֲשֶׁר יִפֹּל הַטַּל עַל־הָאֲדָמָה וְלֹא־נ֫וֹתַר בּ֫וֹ וּבְכָל־
הָאֲנָשִׁים אֲשֶׁר־אִתּ֫וֹ גַּם־אֶחָד: וְאִם־אֶל־עִיר יֵאָסֵף וְהִשִּׂ֫יאוּ כָל־יִשְׂרָאֵל יג
אֶל־הָעִיר הַהִ֫יא חֲבָלִ֫ים וְסָחַבְנוּ אֹת֫וֹ עַד־הַנַּ֫חַל עַד אֲשֶׁר־לֹא־נִמְצָא שָׁם
גַּם־צְרֽוֹר: וַיֹּ֫אמֶר אַבְשָׁלוֹם וְכָל־אִישׁ יִשְׂרָאֵל ט֫וֹבָה עֲצַת חוּשַׁ֫י יד
הָאַרְכִּ֫י מֵעֲצַ֫ת אֲחִיתֹ֫פֶל   וַיהֹוָה צִוָּה לְהָפֵ֫ר אֶת־עֲצַ֫ת אֲחִיתֹ֫פֶל
הַטּוֹבָ֫ה לְבַעֲב֫וּר הָבִ֫יא יְהֹוָ֫ה אֶל־אַבְשָׁל֫וֹם אֶת־הָרָעָֽה: וַיֹּ֫אמֶר טו
חוּשַׁי אֶל־צָד֫וֹק וְאֶל־אֶבְיָתָ֫ר הַכֹּהֲנִ֫ים כָּזֹ֫את וְכָזֹ֫את יָעַ֫ץ אֲחִיתֹ֫פֶל אֶת־
אַבְשָׁלֹ֫ם וְאֵת זִקְנֵ֫י יִשְׂרָאֵל וְכָזֹ֫את וְכָזֹ֫את יָעַ֫צְתִּי אָֽנִי: וְעַתָּ֫ה שִׁלְח֫וּ מְהֵרָה֫ טז
וְהַגִּ֫ידוּ לְדָוִד֫ לֵאמֹר אַל־תָּ֫לֶן הַלַּ֫יְלָה °בְּעַרְבוֹת ק׳] הַמִּדְבָּ֫ר וְגַם֫
עָב֫וֹר תַּעֲב֫וֹר פֶּ֫ן יְבֻלַּ֫ע לַמֶּ֫לֶךְ וּלְכָל־הָעָ֫ם אֲשֶׁר אִתּֽוֹ: וִיהוֹנָתָ֫ן וַאֲחִימַ֫עַץ יז
עֹמְדִ֫ים בְּעֵֽין־רֹגֵ֫ל וְהָלְכָ֫ה הַשִּׁפְחָה֫ וְהִגִּ֫ידָה לָהֶ֫ם וְהֵ֫ם יֵלְכ֫וּ וְהִגִּ֫ידוּ לַמֶּ֫לֶךְ
דָּוִ֫ד כִּ֫י לֹ֫א יֽוּכְל֫וּ לְהֵרָא֫וֹת לָב֫וֹא הָעִֽירָה: וַיַּ֫רְא אֹתָ֫ם נַ֫עַר וַיַּגֵּ֫ד לְאַבְשָׁלֹ֫ם יח
וַיֵּלְכ֫וּ שְׁנֵיהֶ֫ם מְהֵרָה֫ וַיָּבֹ֫אוּ ׀ אֶל־בֵּית־אִ֫ישׁ בְּבַחוּרִ֫ים וְל֫וֹ בְאֵ֫ר בַּחֲצֵר֫וֹ
וַיֵּ֫רְדוּ שָֽׁם: וַתִּקַּ֫ח הָאִשָּׁה֫ וַתִּפְרֹ֫שׂ אֶת־הַמָּסָךְ֫ עַל־פְּנֵ֫י הַבְּאֵ֫ר וַתִּשְׁטַ֫ח עָלָ֫יו יט
הָרִפ֫וֹת וְלֹ֫א נוֹדַ֫ע דָּבָֽר: וַיָּבֹ֫אוּ עַבְדֵ֫י אַבְשָׁל֫וֹם אֶל־הָאִשָּׁה֫ הַבַּ֫יְתָה וַיֹּ֫אמְרוּ כ
אַיֵּ֫ה אֲחִימַ֫עַץ וִיהֽוֹנָתָ֫ן וַתֹּ֫אמֶר לָהֶ֫ם הָאִשָּׁה֫ עָבְר֫וּ מִיכַ֫ל הַמָּ֫יִם וַיְבַקְשׁ֫וּ
וְלֹ֫א מָצָ֫אוּ וַיָּשֻׁ֫בוּ יְרוּשָׁלָֽ͏ִם: וַיְהִ֫י ׀ אַֽחֲרֵ֫י ׀ לֶכְתָּ֫ם וַיַּעֲל֫וּ כא
מֵֽהַבְּאֵ֫ר וַיֵּלְכ֫וּ וַיַּגִּ֫דוּ לַמֶּ֫לֶךְ דָּוִ֫ד וַיֹּאמְר֫וּ אֶל־דָּוִ֫ד ק֫וּמוּ וְעִבְר֫וּ מְהֵרָה֫ אֶת־
הַמַּ֫יִם כִּי־כָ֫כָה יָעַ֫ץ עֲלֵיכֶ֫ם אֲחִיתֹֽפֶל: וַיָּ֫קָם דָּוִ֫ד וְכָל־הָעָ֫ם אֲשֶׁ֫ר אִתּ֫וֹ כב
וַיַּעַבְר֫וּ אֶת־הַיַּרְדֵּ֫ן עַד־א֫וֹר הַבֹּ֫קֶר עַד־אַחַ֫ד לֹ֫א נֶעְדָּ֫ר אֲשֶׁ֫ר לֹֽא־עָ֫בַר
אֶת־הַיַּרְדֵּֽן: וַאֲחִיתֹ֫פֶל רָאָ֫ה כִּ֫י לֹ֫א נֶֽעֶשְׂתָה֫ עֲצָת֫וֹ וַֽיַּחֲבֹ֫שׁ אֶת־הַחֲמ֫וֹר כג
וַיָּ֫קָם וַיֵּ֫לֶךְ אֶל־בֵּית֫וֹ אֶל־עִיר֫וֹ וַיְצַ֫ו אֶל־בֵּית֫וֹ וַיֵּחָנַ֫ק וַיָּ֫מָת וַיִּקָּבֵ֫ר בְּקֶ֫בֶר
אָבִֽיו: וְדָוִ֫ד בָּ֫א מַחֲנָ֫יְמָה וְאַבְשָׁל֫וֹם עָבַ֫ר אֶת־הַיַּרְדֵּ֫ן כד
ה֫וּא וְכָל־אִ֫ישׁ יִשְׂרָאֵ֫ל עִמּֽוֹ: וְאֶת־עֲמָשָׂ֫א שָׂ֫ם אַבְשָׁלֹ֫ם תַּ֫חַת יוֹאָ֫ב כה
עַל־הַצָּבָ֫א וַעֲמָשָׂ֫א בֶן־אִ֫ישׁ וּשְׁמ֫וֹ יִתְרָ֫א הַיִּשְׂרְאֵלִ֫י אֲשֶׁר־בָּ֫א אֶל־אֲבִיגַ֫ל
בַּת־נָחָ֫שׁ אֲח֫וֹת צְרוּיָ֫ה אֵ֫ם יוֹאָֽב: וַיִּ֫חַן יִשְׂרָאֵ֫ל וְאַבְשָׁלֹ֫ם אֶ֫רֶץ כו
הַגִּלְעָֽד: וַיְהִ֫י כְּב֫וֹא דָוִד֫ מַחֲנָ֫יְמָה וְשֹׁבִ֫י בֶן־נָחָ֫שׁ מֵרַבַּ֫ת כז
בְּנֵֽי־עַמּ֫וֹן וּמָכִ֫יר בֶּן־עַמִּיאֵ֫ל מִלֹּ֫א דְבָ֫ר וּבַרְזִלַּ֫י הַגִּלְעָדִ֫י מֵרֹגְלִֽים: מִשְׁכָּ֫ב כח

17:14. Unless God had decreed it, it would have been sheer folly to reject Ahithophel's plan of a surprise attack in favor of Hushai's unwieldy suggestion.

17:16. Hushai was afraid that Absalom would follow Ahithophel's plan after all, and destroy David and his army.

17:17. It would have appeared suspicious if the two

young Kohanim had come into the city to meet with their fathers, and then dashed off in the direction of David's camp.

17:18-19. Knowing that they had been observed, Jonathan and Ahimaaz hurried into hiding. The woman covered their hiding place with groats, which are normally spread out to dry in the sun, to give the impression that all of Israel should be gathered unto you, from Dan to Beer-sheba, numerous as the sand upon the sea, and that you should personally lead the battle. [12] Then we will come upon him in one of the places where he is [hiding], and descend upon him as the dew falls upon the earth, and there will not be even one person left of him of all the men who are with him. [13] And if he will be brought into a city, all of Israel will muster battalions to that city, and we will drag [its wall] to the ravine, until not even a pebble will be found there!"

Absalom sides with Hushai [14] Absalom and all the men of Israel said, "Hushai the Archite's suggestion is better than Ahithophel's suggestion." For HASHEM had ordained to nullify the good advice of Ahithophel, in order for HASHEM to bring a calamity upon Absalom. *

Hushai sends informers to David [15] Hushai then told Zadok and Abiathar the Kohanim, "Such and such has Ahithophel advised Absalom and the elders of Israel, and such and such I myself advised. [16] So now, send quickly and tell David saying, 'Do not spend the night in the Plains of the Wilderness, but you must cross over [the Jordan], lest the king — along with all the people who are with him — be swallowed up.'* [17] Jonathan and Ahimaaz are staying in En-rogel; let the maidservant go and tell them so that they may go and tell King David, for they will not be observed entering the city."*

The informers elude capture and warn David [18] But a youth saw them and he told Absalom; so they both left quickly and came to the house of a man in Bahurim. He had a well in his courtyard, into which they descended. [19] His wife took a curtain and spread it over the opening of the well and she scattered some crushed groats upon it, so that nothing could have been suspected. * [20] When Absalom's servants came to the woman, into the house, and said, "Where are Ahimaaz and Jonathan?" the woman said to them, "They crossed the body of water." They searched but could not find them, so they returned to Jerusalem. [21] It happened that after their departure that they ascended from the well and they went and told King David. They said to David, "Arise and quickly cross the water, for such has Ahithophel advised concerning you." [22] So David arose — along with all the people who were with him — and they crossed the Jordan; by morning's light not one person was missing who had not crossed the Jordan.

Ahithophel's suicide [23] When Ahithophel saw that his advice was not carried out, he saddled the donkey and arose and went to his house, to his city. He instructed his family and strangled himself;* he died and was buried in his father's grave.

Absalom and David face off [24] David arrived at Mahanaim. Absalom crossed the Jordan, he and every man of Israel with him. [25] Absalom appointed Amasa over the army in place of Joab; Amasa was the son of a man named Ithra the Israelite, who consorted with Abigal daughter of Nahash, * the sister of Joab's mother Zeruiah. [26] Israel and Absalom encamped in the land of Gilead.

David's loyalists bring provisions [27] It happened that when David came to Mahanaim, Shobi son of Nahash from Rabbah the [capital] of the Children of Ammon and Machir son of Ammiel from Lo-debar and Barzillai of Gilead from Roglim [28] [took] bedding,

---

that the curtain had been there for some time.

17:23. Certain that Hushai's plan would fail and that David would eventually regain power, Ahithophel knew he would be executed for treason. He therefore chose to die by his own hand (Radak).

17:25. As a Jew who lived in the land of the Ishmaelites (I Chronicles 2:17), Ithra was given the appellation "the

Israelite" (Radak).

Since it does not say "who married Abigal," Radak conjectures that Amasa was conceived out of wedlock. At any rate, Amasa and Joab were first cousins, and nephews of David. Zeruiah and Abigal were sisters of David (I Chronicles 2:16), so "Nahash" must be another name for "Jesse" (Talmud).

כט וְסַפּוֹת וּכְלִי יוֹצֵר וְחִטִּים וּשְׂעֹרִים וְקֶמַח וְקָלִי וּפוֹל וַעֲדָשִׁים וְקָלִי: וּדְבַשׁ
וְחֶמְאָה וְצֹאן וּשְׁפוֹת בָּקָר הִגִּישׁוּ לְדָוִד וְלָעָם אֲשֶׁר־אִתּוֹ לֶאֱכוֹל כִּי

יח א אָמְרוּ הָעָם רָעֵב וְעָיֵף וְצָמֵא בַּמִּדְבָּר: וַיִּפְקֹד דָּוִד אֶת־הָעָם אֲשֶׁר אִתּוֹ
ב וַיָּשֶׂם עֲלֵיהֶם שָׂרֵי אֲלָפִים וְשָׂרֵי מֵאוֹת: וַיְשַׁלַּח דָּוִד אֶת־הָעָם הַשְּׁלִשִׁית
בְּיַד־יוֹאָב וְהַשְּׁלִשִׁית בְּיַד אֲבִישַׁי בֶּן־צְרוּיָה אֲחִי יוֹאָב וְהַשְּׁלִשִׁת בְּיַד
אִתַּי הַגִּתִּי   וַיֹּאמֶר הַמֶּלֶךְ אֶל־הָעָם יָצֹא אֵצֵא גַּם־אָנִי
ג עִמָּכֶם: וַיֹּאמֶר הָעָם לֹא תֵצֵא כִּי אִם־נֹס נָנוּס לֹא־יָשִׂימוּ אֵלֵינוּ לֵב
וְאִם־יָמֻתוּ חֶצְיֵנוּ לֹא־יָשִׂימוּ אֵלֵינוּ לֵב כִּי־עַתָּה כָמֹנוּ עֲשָׂרָה אֲלָפִים
ד וְעַתָּה טוֹב כִּי־תִהְיֶה־לָּנוּ מֵעִיר °לעזר [°לַעְזוֹר ק]: וַיֹּאמֶר
אֲלֵיהֶם הַמֶּלֶךְ אֲשֶׁר־יִיטַב בְּעֵינֵיכֶם אֶעֱשֶׂה וַיַּעֲמֹד הַמֶּלֶךְ אֶל־יַד הַשַּׁעַר
ה וְכָל־הָעָם יָצְאוּ לְמֵאוֹת וְלַאֲלָפִים: וַיְצַו הַמֶּלֶךְ אֶת־יוֹאָב וְאֶת־אֲבִישַׁי
וְאֶת־אִתַּי לֵאמֹר לְאַט־לִי לַנַּעַר לְאַבְשָׁלוֹם וְכָל־הָעָם שָׁמְעוּ בְּצַוֺּת
ו הַמֶּלֶךְ אֶת־כָּל־הַשָּׂרִים עַל־דְּבַר אַבְשָׁלוֹם: וַיֵּצֵא הָעָם הַשָּׂדֶה לִקְרַאת
ז יִשְׂרָאֵל וַתְּהִי הַמִּלְחָמָה בְּיַעַר אֶפְרָיִם: וַיִּנָּגְפוּ שָׁם עַם יִשְׂרָאֵל לִפְנֵי
ח עַבְדֵי דָוִד וַתְּהִי־שָׁם הַמַּגֵּפָה גְדוֹלָה בַּיּוֹם הַהוּא עֶשְׂרִים אָלֶף: וַתְּהִי־שָׁם
הַמִּלְחָמָה °נפצית [°נָפֹצֶת ק] עַל־פְּנֵי כָל־הָאָרֶץ וַיֶּרֶב הַיַּעַר לֶאֱכֹל
ט בָּעָם מֵאֲשֶׁר אָכְלָה הַחֶרֶב בַּיּוֹם הַהוּא: וַיִּקָּרֵא אַבְשָׁלוֹם לִפְנֵי עַבְדֵי דָוִד
וְאַבְשָׁלוֹם רֹכֵב עַל־הַפֶּרֶד וַיָּבֹא הַפֶּרֶד תַּחַת שׂוֹבֶךְ הָאֵלָה הַגְּדוֹלָה
וַיֶּחֱזַק רֹאשׁוֹ בָאֵלָה וַיֻּתַּן בֵּין הַשָּׁמַיִם וּבֵין הָאָרֶץ וְהַפֶּרֶד אֲשֶׁר־תַּחְתָּיו
י עָבָר: וַיַּרְא אִישׁ אֶחָד וַיַּגֵּד לְיוֹאָב וַיֹּאמֶר הִנֵּה רָאִיתִי אֶת־אַבְשָׁלֹם תָּלוּי
יא בָּאֵלָה: וַיֹּאמֶר יוֹאָב לָאִישׁ הַמַּגִּיד לוֹ וְהִנֵּה רָאִיתָ וּמַדּוּעַ לֹא־הִכִּיתוֹ שָׁם
יב אָרְצָה וְעָלַי לָתֶת לְךָ עֲשָׂרָה כֶסֶף וַחֲגֹרָה אֶחָת: וַיֹּאמֶר הָאִישׁ אֶל־יוֹאָב
°ולא [°וְלוּא ק] אָנֹכִי שֹׁקֵל עַל־כַּפִּי אֶלֶף כֶּסֶף לֹא־אֶשְׁלַח יָדִי אֶל־בֶּן־
הַמֶּלֶךְ כִּי בְאָזְנֵינוּ צִוָּה הַמֶּלֶךְ אֹתְךָ וְאֶת־אֲבִישַׁי וְאֶת־אִתַּי לֵאמֹר
יג שִׁמְרוּ־מִי בַּנַּעַר בְּאַבְשָׁלוֹם: אוֹ־עָשִׂיתִי °בנפשו [°בְנַפְשִׁי ק] שֶׁקֶר וְכָל־
יד דָּבָר לֹא־יִכָּחֵד מִן־הַמֶּלֶךְ וְאַתָּה תִּתְיַצֵּב מִנֶּגֶד: וַיֹּאמֶר יוֹאָב לֹא־כֵן
אֹחִילָה לְפָנֶיךָ וַיִּקַּח שְׁלֹשָׁה שְׁבָטִים בְּכַפּוֹ וַיִּתְקָעֵם בְּלֵב אַבְשָׁלוֹם עוֹדֶנּוּ
טו חַי בְּלֵב הָאֵלָה: וַיָּסֹבּוּ עֲשָׂרָה נְעָרִים נֹשְׂאֵי כְּלֵי יוֹאָב וַיַּכּוּ אֶת־אַבְשָׁלוֹם
טז וַיְמִיתֻהוּ: וַיִּתְקַע יוֹאָב בַּשֹּׁפָר וַיָּשָׁב הָעָם מִרְדֹף אַחֲרֵי יִשְׂרָאֵל כִּי־חָשַׂךְ
יז יוֹאָב אֶת־הָעָם: וַיִּקְחוּ אֶת־אַבְשָׁלוֹם וַיַּשְׁלִיכוּ אֹתוֹ בַיַּעַר אֶל־הַפַּחַת
הַגָּדוֹל וַיַּצִּבוּ עָלָיו גַּל־אֲבָנִים גָּדוֹל מְאֹד וְכָל־יִשְׂרָאֵל נָסוּ אִישׁ °לאהלו
יח [°לְאֹהָלָיו ק]: וְאַבְשָׁלֹם לָקַח וַיַּצֶּב־לוֹ °בחיו [בְחַיָּיו ק] אֶת־מַצֶּבֶת

18:3. Since it is only you that they seek, they will not fight as enthusiastically once they see that you are not with us, and will not bother to pursue us if we are forced to retreat or if our forces become severely weakened. It is thus to our advantage if you stay behind (*Abarbanel*). By remaining in the city, you can help us with your military advice bowls, pottery, wheat, barley, flour, toasted grain, beans, lentils, toasted legumes, [29] honey, butter, sheep, and cows' [milk] cheeses [and] they brought [them] to David and to the people with him to eat, for they said, "The people are hungry and exhausted and thirsty in the desert."

18

David plans his strategy . . .

[1] **D**avid counted the people who were with him and appointed over them officers of thousands and officers of hundreds. [2] David then sent the people away — a third under the hand of Joab, a third under the hand of Abishai son of Zeruiah, Joab's brother, and a third under the hand of Ittai the Gittite. The king then said to the people, "I shall also go forth with you." [3] But the people said, "You should not go forth! For if we will have to flee they will not care about us. If half of us die they will not care about us, even if we would be ten thousand times as many as we are. Therefore it is better that you help us from the city."* [4] The king replied to them, "Whatever is best in your eyes I shall do." So the king stayed near the gate, while all the people went forth by their hundreds and thousands. [5] The king commanded Joab and Abishai and Ittai, saying, "For my sake, be gentle with the boy Absalom"; and the people all heard as the king commanded all the officers concerning Absalom.

. . . and his army defeats Absalom's

[6] The people went out to the field, towards [the army of] Israel; the battle took place in the forest of Ephraim. [7] The people of Israel were defeated by David's servants; the casualties were heavy on that day — twenty thousand. [8] The battle spread out from there all across the land; the forest consumed more people than the sword* consumed on that day.

Absalom is spared at David's orders . . .

[9] Absalom chanced upon David's servants. Absalom was riding upon a mule, and the mule came under the thick branches of a large elm tree; his head became entangled in the elm,* and he was suspended between the heavens and the earth, while the mule that was under him moved on. [10] One man saw and told Joab; he said, "Behold I saw Absalom hanging from an elm!" [11] Joab then said to the man who had told him, "And if you saw this, why did you not strike him there down to the ground? I would have been obligated to reward you with ten silver pieces and one belt!" [12] The man said to Joab, "Even if I were holding a thousand silver pieces in my hands, I would not send forth my hand against the king's son, for in our own earshot the king commanded you and Abishai and Ittai saying, 'Whichever one of you [finds him], take care of the boy, of Absalom.' [13] Even if I had acted deceitfully on my own, nothing remains hidden from the king — and you would stand aside."*

. . . but then Joab kills him

[14] Joab then said, "I will not beg you any more!" He then took three staves in his hand and thrust them into Absalom's heart — yet he was still alive in the midst of the elm. [15] Ten soldiers, the armor-bearers of Joab, circled around and beat Absalom, and killed him. [16] Joab then blew the shofar, and the people refrained from chasing after Israel, for Joab restrained the people. [17] They took Absalom's [body] and threw it in the forest, into the great pit, and they erected a very large mound of stones. Meanwhile all of Israel fled, each man to his tent. [18] (Absalom had undertaken in his lifetime and erected for himself the pillar

---

(Radak), or with your prayers (Targum).

18:8. The soldiers constantly became entangled in the thick branches of the trees (Radak), or they were attacked by the wild animals of the forest (Targum).

18:9. Absalom was a nazirite (see 14:26) and his long hair

now became caught in the branches of the tree (Talmud).

18:13. Even if I had betrayed the king and killed Absalom, the king would learn what I did. When he would order me punished for the killing, you would not come to my aid.

אֲשֶׁר בְּעֵמֶק־הַמֶּלֶךְ כִּי אָמַר אֵין־לִי בֵן בַּעֲבוּר הַזְכִּיר שְׁמִי וַיִּקְרָא לַמַּצֶּבֶת
עַל־שְׁמוֹ וַיִּקָּרֵא לָהּ יַד אַבְשָׁלֹם עַד הַיּוֹם הַזֶּה: יט וַאֲחִימַעַץ בֶּן־
צָדוֹק אָמַר אָרוּצָה נָּא וַאֲבַשְּׂרָה אֶת־הַמֶּלֶךְ כִּי־שְׁפָטוֹ יְהֹוָה מִיַּד אֹיְבָיו:
כ וַיֹּאמֶר לוֹ יוֹאָב לֹא אִישׁ בְּשֹׂרָה אַתָּה הַיּוֹם הַזֶּה וּבִשַּׂרְתָּ בְּיוֹם אַחֵר וְהַיּוֹם
כא הַזֶּה לֹא תְבַשֵּׂר כִּי־עַל [כֵּן ק ולא כ] בֶּן־הַמֶּלֶךְ מֵת: וַיֹּאמֶר יוֹאָב לַכּוּשִׁי
כב לֵךְ הַגֵּד לַמֶּלֶךְ אֲשֶׁר רָאִיתָה וַיִּשְׁתַּחוּ כוּשִׁי לְיוֹאָב וַיָּרֹץ: וַיֹּסֶף עוֹד
אֲחִימַעַץ בֶּן־צָדוֹק וַיֹּאמֶר אֶל־יוֹאָב וִיהִי מָה אָרֻצָה־נָּא גַם־אָנִי אַחֲרֵי
הַכּוּשִׁי וַיֹּאמֶר יוֹאָב לָמָּה־זֶּה אַתָּה רָץ בְּנִי וּלְכָה אֵין־בְּשׂוֹרָה מֹצֵאת:
כג וִיהִי־מָה אָרוּץ וַיֹּאמֶר לוֹ רוּץ וַיָּרָץ אֲחִימַעַץ דֶּרֶךְ הַכִּכָּר וַיַּעֲבֹר אֶת־
כד הַכּוּשִׁי: וְדָוִד יוֹשֵׁב בֵּין־שְׁנֵי הַשְּׁעָרִים וַיֵּלֶךְ הַצֹּפֶה אֶל־גַּג הַשַּׁעַר אֶל־
כה הַחוֹמָה וַיִּשָּׂא אֶת־עֵינָיו וַיַּרְא וְהִנֵּה־אִישׁ רָץ לְבַדּוֹ: וַיִּקְרָא הַצֹּפֶה וַיַּגֵּד
כו לַמֶּלֶךְ וַיֹּאמֶר הַמֶּלֶךְ אִם־לְבַדּוֹ בְּשׂוֹרָה בְּפִיו וַיֵּלֶךְ הָלוֹךְ וְקָרֵב: וַיַּרְא
הַצֹּפֶה אִישׁ־אַחֵר רָץ וַיִּקְרָא הַצֹּפֶה אֶל־הַשֹּׁעֵר וַיֹּאמֶר הִנֵּה־אִישׁ רָץ
כז לְבַדּוֹ וַיֹּאמֶר הַמֶּלֶךְ גַּם־זֶה מְבַשֵּׂר: וַיֹּאמֶר הַצֹּפֶה אֲנִי רֹאֶה אֶת־מְרוּצַת
הָרִאשׁוֹן כִּמְרֻצַת אֲחִימַעַץ בֶּן־צָדוֹק וַיֹּאמֶר הַמֶּלֶךְ אִישׁ־טוֹב זֶה וְאֶל־
כח בְּשׂוֹרָה טוֹבָה יָבוֹא: וַיִּקְרָא אֲחִימַעַץ וַיֹּאמֶר אֶל־הַמֶּלֶךְ שָׁלוֹם וַיִּשְׁתַּחוּ
לַמֶּלֶךְ לְאַפָּיו אָרְצָה וַיֹּאמֶר בָּרוּךְ יְהֹוָה אֱלֹהֶיךָ אֲשֶׁר סִגַּר אֶת־הָאֲנָשִׁים
כט אֲשֶׁר־נָשְׂאוּ אֶת־יָדָם בַּאדֹנִי הַמֶּלֶךְ: וַיֹּאמֶר הַמֶּלֶךְ שָׁלוֹם לַנַּעַר
לְאַבְשָׁלוֹם וַיֹּאמֶר אֲחִימַעַץ רָאִיתִי הֶהָמוֹן הַגָּדוֹל לִשְׁלֹחַ אֶת־עֶבֶד
ל הַמֶּלֶךְ יוֹאָב וְאֶת־עַבְדֶּךָ וְלֹא יָדַעְתִּי מָה: וַיֹּאמֶר הַמֶּלֶךְ סֹב הִתְיַצֵּב כֹּה
לא וַיִּסֹּב וַיַּעֲמֹד: וְהִנֵּה הַכּוּשִׁי בָּא וַיֹּאמֶר הַכּוּשִׁי יִתְבַּשֵּׂר אֲדֹנִי הַמֶּלֶךְ כִּי־
לב שְׁפָטְךָ יְהֹוָה הַיּוֹם מִיַּד כָּל־הַקָּמִים עָלֶיךָ: וַיֹּאמֶר הַמֶּלֶךְ אֶל־
הַכּוּשִׁי הֲשָׁלוֹם לַנַּעַר לְאַבְשָׁלוֹם וַיֹּאמֶר הַכּוּשִׁי יִהְיוּ כַנַּעַר אֹיְבֵי אֲדֹנִי
יט א הַמֶּלֶךְ וְכֹל אֲשֶׁר־קָמוּ עָלֶיךָ לְרָעָה: וַיִּרְגַּז הַמֶּלֶךְ וַיַּעַל עַל־
עֲלִיַּת הַשַּׁעַר וַיֵּבְךְּ וְכֹה ׀ אָמַר בְּלֶכְתּוֹ בְּנִי אַבְשָׁלוֹם בְּנִי בְנִי אַבְשָׁלוֹם מִי־
ב יִתֵּן מוּתִי אֲנִי תַחְתֶּיךָ אַבְשָׁלוֹם בְּנִי בְנִי: וַיֻּגַּד לְיוֹאָב הִנֵּה הַמֶּלֶךְ בֹּכֶה
ג וַיִּתְאַבֵּל עַל־אַבְשָׁלֹם: וַתְּהִי הַתְּשֻׁעָה בַּיּוֹם הַהוּא לְאֵבֶל לְכָל־הָעָם כִּי־
ד שָׁמַע הָעָם בַּיּוֹם הַהוּא לֵאמֹר נֶעֱצַב הַמֶּלֶךְ עַל־בְּנוֹ: וַיִּתְגַּנֵּב הָעָם בַּיּוֹם
הַהוּא לָבוֹא הָעִיר כַּאֲשֶׁר יִתְגַּנֵּב הָעָם הַנִּכְלָמִים בְּנוּסָם בַּמִּלְחָמָה:
ה וְהַמֶּלֶךְ לָאַט אֶת־פָּנָיו וַיִּזְעַק הַמֶּלֶךְ קוֹל גָּדוֹל בְּנִי אַבְשָׁלוֹם אַבְשָׁלוֹם בְּנִי
ו בְנִי: וַיָּבֹא יוֹאָב אֶל־הַמֶּלֶךְ הַבָּיִת וַיֹּאמֶר הֹבַשְׁתָּ הַיּוֹם אֶת־

18:18. Noting that Absalom had three sons (14:27), the Talmud offers two possible solutions: Either they had died, or Absalom meant that none of them was worthy of taking his place.

This parenthetical verse notes the ironic contradiction between Absalom's delusions of grandeur during his lifetime and his humiliating disgrace at death (*Abarbanel*).

18:21. The Cushite was either a proselyte from the land of Cush, or an Israelite who was as dark as a Cushite (*Radak*). Alternatively: The man's name was "Cushi" (*Targum*).

Absalom's monument that is in the Valley of the King; for he said, "I have no son; * [this is] in order that my name should be remembered." He called the pillar by his name, and it is called "Absalom's Monument" until this day.)*

Runners hurry to tell David ¹⁹ Ahimaaz son of Zadok said, "I shall run and tell the king the news — that HASHEM has granted him justice from his enemies!" ²⁰ But Joab told him, "You should not be the bearer of news today. You can bring news another day; but do not bring news today, for the king's son is dead." ²¹ Joab then said to the Cushite, * "Go tell the king what you have seen"; and the Cushite prostrated himself to Joab and ran off. ²² Ahimaaz son of Zadok continued to persist, and said to Joab, "Whatever happens — please let me also run after the Cushite." But Joab said, "Why should you run, my son? This news will not provide any [benefit] for you." ²³ "Whatever happens — let me run!" So he said to him, "Run." Ahimaaz ran by the route of the plain and overtook the Cushite.

²⁴ David was sitting between the two gates [of the city]. The lookout went up to the roof of the gate, to the wall; he raised his eyes and looked — and behold, a man running alone! ²⁵ The lookout called out and told the king. The king said, "If he is alone, there is news in his mouth," and he kept drawing closer. ²⁶ Then the lookout saw another man running; the lookout called out to the gatekeeper and said, "Behold, [another] man is running alone!" The king said, "This man is also a herald!" ²⁷ The lookout said, "I recognize the first one's stride as the stride of Ahimaaz son of Zadok." And the king said, "He is a good man; he is coming

David hears the good news first . . . with good news." ²⁸ Ahimaaz called out and said to the king, "Peace!" and he prostrated himself to the king with his face to the ground. Then he said [further], "Blessed is HASHEM, your God, Who has delivered [into our hands] the men who lifted up their hand against my lord the king!" ²⁹ The king then asked, "Is it well with the boy Absalom?" Ahimaaz replied, "I saw the great commotion when Joab sent the [Cushite] servant of the king and [myself,] your servant, and I do not know what happened."* ³⁰ The king then said, "Move aside and stand here," so he moved aside and stood. ³¹ Then behold — at that point the Cushite arrived. The Cushite said, "Let my lord the king be informed that HASHEM has granted you justice today from all those who rose up against you!" ³² Then the

. . . and then hears of the fate of Absalom king asked the Cushite, "Is it well with the boy Absalom?" The Cushite replied, "May the enemies of my lord the king be like the boy, as well as all others who rise up against you to do you harm!"

19 ¹ The king trembled. He ascended to the upper chamber of the gateway and wept; and thus he said as he went: "My son, Absalom! My son, my son, Absalom! If only I could have died in your place! Absalom, my son, my son!" ² It was told to Joab, "Behold, the king is crying and lamenting over Absalom!"

The people join David's grief ³ The salvation of that day was transformed to mourning for all the people, for the people heard it said on that day, "The king is saddened over his son." ⁴ The people stole themselves into the city on that day, as those people who are ashamed would steal away when they run from the battle. ⁵ The king wrapped his face, * and the king cried out in a loud voice, "My son, Absalom! Absalom, my son, my son!"

⁶ Joab then came to the king, into the chamber, and said, "Today you have

---

18:29. Ahimaaz understood how concerned the king was with Absalom's welfare; therefore, he did not break the news of Absalom's death at once. Rather he first hinted to   it by speaking of the commotion.
19:5. A traditional gesture of mourning (see 15:30, and footnote there).

פְּנֵי כָל־עֲבָדֶיךָ הַמְמַלְּטִים אֶת־נַפְשְׁךָ הַיּוֹם וְאֵת נֶפֶשׁ בָּנֶיךָ וּבְנֹתֶיךָ וְנֶפֶשׁ

ז נָשֶׁיךָ וְנֶפֶשׁ פִּלַגְשֶׁיךָ: לְאַהֲבָה אֶת־שֹׂנְאֶיךָ וְלִשְׂנֹא אֶת־אֹהֲבֶיךָ כִּי ׀ הִגַּדְתָּ הַיּוֹם כִּי אֵין לְךָ שָׂרִים וַעֲבָדִים כִּי ׀ יָדַעְתִּי הַיּוֹם כִּי °לֹא

ח [°לוּ ק] אַבְשָׁלוֹם חַי וְכֻלָּנוּ הַיּוֹם מֵתִים כִּי־אָז יָשָׁר בְּעֵינֶיךָ: וְעַתָּה קוּם צֵא וְדַבֵּר עַל־לֵב עֲבָדֶיךָ כִּי בַיהוָה נִשְׁבַּעְתִּי כִּי־אֵינְךָ יוֹצֵא אִם־יָלִין אִישׁ אִתְּךָ הַלַּיְלָה וְרָעָה לְךָ זֹאת מִכָּל־הָרָעָה אֲשֶׁר־בָּאָה עָלֶיךָ מִנְּעֻרֶיךָ

ט עַד־עָתָּה: וַיָּקָם הַמֶּלֶךְ וַיֵּשֶׁב בַּשָּׁעַר וּלְכָל־הָעָם הִגִּידוּ לֵאמֹר הִנֵּה הַמֶּלֶךְ יוֹשֵׁב בַּשַּׁעַר וַיָּבֹא כָל־הָעָם לִפְנֵי הַמֶּלֶךְ וְיִשְׂרָאֵל נָס

י אִישׁ לְאֹהָלָיו: וַיְהִי כָל־הָעָם נָדוֹן בְּכָל־שִׁבְטֵי יִשְׂרָאֵל לֵאמֹר הַמֶּלֶךְ הִצִּילָנוּ ׀ מִכַּף אֹיְבֵינוּ וְהוּא מִלְּטָנוּ מִכַּף פְּלִשְׁתִּים וְעַתָּה בָּרַח מִן־

יא הָאָרֶץ מֵעַל אַבְשָׁלוֹם: וְאַבְשָׁלוֹם אֲשֶׁר מָשַׁחְנוּ עָלֵינוּ מֵת בַּמִּלְחָמָה וְעַתָּה לָמָה אַתֶּם מַחֲרִשִׁים לְהָשִׁיב אֶת־הַמֶּלֶךְ: וְהַמֶּלֶךְ

יב דָּוִד שָׁלַח אֶל־צָדוֹק וְאֶל־אֶבְיָתָר הַכֹּהֲנִים לֵאמֹר דַּבְּרוּ אֶל־זִקְנֵי יְהוּדָה לֵאמֹר לָמָּה תִהְיוּ אַחֲרֹנִים לְהָשִׁיב אֶת־הַמֶּלֶךְ אֶל־בֵּיתוֹ וּדְבַר כָּל־

יג יִשְׂרָאֵל בָּא אֶל־הַמֶּלֶךְ אֶל־בֵּיתוֹ: אַחַי אַתֶּם עַצְמִי וּבְשָׂרִי אַתֶּם וְלָמָּה תִהְיוּ אַחֲרֹנִים לְהָשִׁיב אֶת־הַמֶּלֶךְ: וְלַעֲמָשָׂא תֹּמְרוּ הֲלוֹא עַצְמִי וּבְשָׂרִי

יד אָתָּה כֹּה יַעֲשֶׂה־לִּי אֱלֹהִים וְכֹה יוֹסִיף אִם־לֹא שַׂר־צָבָא תִּהְיֶה לְפָנַי כָּל־הַיָּמִים תַּחַת יוֹאָב: וַיַּט אֶת־לְבַב כָּל־אִישׁ־יְהוּדָה כְּאִישׁ אֶחָד

טו וַיִּשְׁלְחוּ אֶל־הַמֶּלֶךְ שׁוּב אַתָּה וְכָל־עֲבָדֶיךָ: וַיָּשָׁב הַמֶּלֶךְ וַיָּבֹא עַד־

טז הַיַּרְדֵּן וִיהוּדָה בָּא הַגִּלְגָּלָה לָלֶכֶת לִקְרַאת הַמֶּלֶךְ לְהַעֲבִיר אֶת־הַמֶּלֶךְ אֶת־הַיַּרְדֵּן: וַיְמַהֵר שִׁמְעִי בֶן־גֵּרָא בֶּן־הַיְמִינִי אֲשֶׁר מִבַּחוּרִים וַיֵּרֶד

יז עִם־אִישׁ יְהוּדָה לִקְרַאת הַמֶּלֶךְ דָּוִד: וְאֶלֶף אִישׁ עִמּוֹ מִבִּנְיָמִן וְצִיבָא נַעַר בֵּית שָׁאוּל וַחֲמֵשֶׁת עָשָׂר בָּנָיו וְעֶשְׂרִים עֲבָדָיו אִתּוֹ וְצָלְחוּ

יח הַיַּרְדֵּן לִפְנֵי הַמֶּלֶךְ: וְעָבְרָה הָעֲבָרָה לַעֲבִיר אֶת־בֵּית הַמֶּלֶךְ וְלַעֲשׂוֹת הַטּוֹב °בעינו [°בְּעֵינָיו ק] וְשִׁמְעִי בֶן־גֵּרָא נָפַל לִפְנֵי הַמֶּלֶךְ בְּעָבְרוֹ

יט בַּיַּרְדֵּן: וַיֹּאמֶר אֶל־הַמֶּלֶךְ אַל־יַחֲשָׁב־לִי אֲדֹנִי עָוֹן וְאַל־תִּזְכֹּר אֵת אֲשֶׁר הֶעֱוָה עַבְדְּךָ בַּיּוֹם אֲשֶׁר־*יָצָא אֲדֹנִי־הַמֶּלֶךְ מִירוּשָׁלָ͏ִם לָשׂוּם

כ הַמֶּלֶךְ אֶל־לִבּוֹ: כִּי יָדַע עַבְדְּךָ כִּי אֲנִי חָטָאתִי וְהִנֵּה־בָאתִי הַיּוֹם רִאשׁוֹן לְכָל־בֵּית יוֹסֵף לָרֶדֶת לִקְרַאת אֲדֹנִי הַמֶּלֶךְ: וַיַּעַן

כא אֲבִישַׁי בֶּן־צְרוּיָה וַיֹּאמֶר הֲתַחַת זֹאת לֹא יוּמַת שִׁמְעִי כִּי קִלֵּל אֶת־

כב מְשִׁיחַ יְהוָה: וַיֹּאמֶר דָּוִד מַה־לִּי וְלָכֶם בְּנֵי צְרוּיָה כִּי־תִהְיוּ־

כג

*נקוד על יצא

19:10. In this verse and in most of the remainder of the chapter, as in many other books of the Bible, "Israel" comprises ten tribes, the excluded tribes being Judah and Benjamin.

19:14. David dismissed Joab from his post for having

killed Absalom (Radak). David appointed Amasa, who had led the mutinous army in its attack against David, as a sign that David sought reconciliation rather than retribution from the former insurgents (Ralbag).

19:21. The "House of Joseph" includes all of Rachel's

humiliated the faces of all your servants who saved your soul and the soul of your sons and daughters and the soul of your wives and the soul of your concubines, ⁷ by expressing love for those who hate you and hatred for those who love you; for you have declared today that you do not have officers or servants, for today I know that were Absalom alive and all of us dead today, it would be preferable in your eyes! ⁸ So now, arise, and go out; speak to the heart of your servants, for I swear by HASHEM that if you do not go out, no man will stay to spend the night with you; and this will be worse for you than any harm

David accepts Joab's protest that has ever come upon you from your youth until this day!" ⁹ So the king arose and sat at the [city] gate. They told all the people, saying, "Behold, the king is sitting at the gate"; and all the people came before the king. Meanwhile [the army of] Israel had run away, each man to his tents.

DAVID'S RETURN TO JERUSALEM 19:10-44

The people return to David . . . ¹⁰ Then it happened that all the people, among all the tribes of Israel, * were reproachful [toward each other], saying, "The king rescued us from the hand of our enemies, and he delivered us from the hand of the Philistines. Now he has fled from the land, from before Absalom, ¹¹ and Absalom, whom we had anointed over us, has died in the battle; and now, why are you silent regarding bringing back the king?"

. . . and he regains Judah's loyalty ¹² King David then sent [a message] to Zadok and Abiathar, the Kohanim, saying, "Speak to the elders of Judah, saying, 'Why should you be last to return the king to his house? The word of all of Israel has come to the king, [to return him] to his house. ¹³ You are my brothers, you are my bone and my flesh — so why should you be last to return the king?' ¹⁴ And to Amasa say, 'Are you not my bone and my flesh? Such may God do to me and such may He do further, if I do not make you commander of the army before me always, in place of Joab.' " * ¹⁵ [King David] thus turned the hearts of all the men of Judah as one man; and they sent [a message] to the king, "Return, you and all your servants."

¹⁶ So the king returned, and he reached the Jordan, and [the people of] Judah came to Gilgal, to go and greet the king, to escort him across the Jordan.

Shimei comes to beg for mercy ¹⁷ Shimei son of Gera, the Benjamite who was from Bahurim, hastened and went down with the men of Judah to greet King David. ¹⁸ With him were a thousand men from Benjamin, and Ziba, the attendant of the House of Saul, with his fifteen sons and twenty servants, and they forded the Jordan [to go] before the king. ¹⁹ When the ferry crossed over to bring across the household of the king and to do whatever was proper in his eyes, Shimei son of Gera fell before the king, as he was crossing in the Jordan.

²⁰ He said to the king, "Let my lord not consider it an iniquity for me, and do not remember that which your servant sinned on the day when my master the king left Jerusalem, that the king should take it to his heart. ²¹ For your servant knows that I have sinned, and here I have come today, first among all the House of Joseph, * to come down and greet my master the king." ²² Abishai son of Zeruiah then spoke up and said, "Shall Shimei not be put to death, despite this [apology]? For he has cursed the anointed one of HASHEM!" ²³ David then said, "What does it matter to me or to you, O sons of Zeruiah, that you should be

---

descendants, namely the tribes of Manasseh, Ephraim and Benjamin. Alternatively, it is a collective term for all of Israel (*Radak*).

Shimei was insinuating that, as the first non-Judean to

greet the king, he would be considered a "test case" by all of Israel, and if he were not shown clemency, the other people, out of fear that they would all be dealt with harshly, would continue their insurrection (*Rashi*).

לִי הַיּוֹם לְשָׂטָן הַיּוֹם יוּמַת אִישׁ בְּיִשְׂרָאֵל כִּי הֲלוֹא יָדַעְתִּי כִּי הַיּוֹם

כד אֲנִי־מֶלֶךְ עַל־יִשְׂרָאֵל: וַיֹּאמֶר הַמֶּלֶךְ אֶל־שִׁמְעִי לֹא תָמוּת וַיִּשָּׁבַע לוֹ

כה הַמֶּלֶךְ: וּמְפִבֹשֶׁת בֶּן־שָׁאוּל יָרַד לִקְרַאת הַמֶּלֶךְ וְלֹא־

עָשָׂה רַגְלָיו וְלֹא־עָשָׂה שְׂפָמוֹ וְאֶת־בְּגָדָיו לֹא כִבֵּס לְמִן־הַיּוֹם לֶכֶת

כו הַמֶּלֶךְ עַד־הַיּוֹם אֲשֶׁר־בָּא בְשָׁלוֹם: וַיְהִי כִּי־בָא יְרוּשָׁלַ͏ִם לִקְרַאת הַמֶּלֶךְ

כז וַיֹּאמֶר לוֹ הַמֶּלֶךְ לָמָּה לֹא־הָלַכְתָּ עִמִּי מְפִיבֹשֶׁת: וַיֹּאמַר אֲדֹנִי הַמֶּלֶךְ

עַבְדִּי רִמָּנִי כִּי־אָמַר עַבְדְּךָ אֶחְבְּשָׁה־לִּי הַחֲמוֹר וְאֶרְכַּב עָלֶיהָ וְאֵלֵךְ

כח אֶת־הַמֶּלֶךְ כִּי פִסֵּחַ עַבְדֶּךָ: וַיְרַגֵּל בְּעַבְדְּךָ אֶל־אֲדֹנִי הַמֶּלֶךְ וַאדֹנִי הַמֶּלֶךְ

כט כְּמַלְאַךְ הָאֱלֹהִים וַעֲשֵׂה הַטּוֹב בְּעֵינֶיךָ: כִּי לֹא הָיָה כָּל־בֵּית אָבִי כִּי אִם־

אַנְשֵׁי־מָוֶת לַאדֹנִי הַמֶּלֶךְ וַתָּשֶׁת אֶת־עַבְדְּךָ בְּאֹכְלֵי שֻׁלְחָנֶךָ וּמַה־יֶּשׁ־לִי

ל עוֹד צְדָקָה וְלִזְעֹק עוֹד אֶל־הַמֶּלֶךְ:   וַיֹּאמֶר לוֹ הַמֶּלֶךְ

לָמָּה תְּדַבֵּר עוֹד דְּבָרֶיךָ אָמַרְתִּי אַתָּה וְצִיבָא תַּחְלְקוּ אֶת־הַשָּׂדֶה:

לא וַיֹּאמֶר מְפִיבֹשֶׁת אֶל־הַמֶּלֶךְ גַּם אֶת־הַכֹּל יִקָּח אַחֲרֵי אֲשֶׁר־בָּא אֲדֹנִי

לב הַמֶּלֶךְ בְּשָׁלוֹם אֶל־בֵּיתוֹ:   וּבַרְזִלַּי הַגִּלְעָדִי יָרַד מֵרֹגְלִים

לג וַיַּעֲבֹר אֶת־הַמֶּלֶךְ הַיַּרְדֵּן לְשַׁלְּחוֹ אֶת־°בַּיַּרְדֵּן [הַיַּרְדֵּן ק]: וּבַרְזִלַּי זָקֵן

מְאֹד בֶּן־שְׁמֹנִים שָׁנָה וְהוּא־כִלְכַּל אֶת־הַמֶּלֶךְ בְשִׁיבָתוֹ בְמַחֲנַיִם כִּי־

לד אִישׁ גָּדוֹל הוּא מְאֹד: וַיֹּאמֶר הַמֶּלֶךְ אֶל־בַּרְזִלָּי אַתָּה עֲבֹר אִתִּי וְכִלְכַּלְתִּי

לה אֹתְךָ עִמָּדִי בִּירוּשָׁלָ͏ִם: וַיֹּאמֶר בַּרְזִלַּי אֶל־הַמֶּלֶךְ כַּמָּה יְמֵי שְׁנֵי חַיַּי כִּי

לו אֶעֱלֶה אֶת־הַמֶּלֶךְ יְרוּשָׁלָ͏ִם: בֶּן־שְׁמֹנִים שָׁנָה אָנֹכִי הַיּוֹם הַאֵדַע בֵּין־

טוֹב לְרָע אִם־יִטְעַם עַבְדְּךָ אֶת־אֲשֶׁר אֹכַל וְאֶת־אֲשֶׁר אֶשְׁתֶּה אִם־

אֶשְׁמַע עוֹד בְּקוֹל שָׁרִים וְשָׁרוֹת וְלָמָּה יִהְיֶה עַבְדְּךָ עוֹד לְמַשָּׂא אֶל־אֲדֹנִי

לז הַמֶּלֶךְ: כִּמְעַט יַעֲבֹר עַבְדְּךָ אֶת־הַיַּרְדֵּן אֶת־הַמֶּלֶךְ וְלָמָּה יִגְמְלֵנִי הַמֶּלֶךְ

לח הַגְּמוּלָה הַזֹּאת: יָשָׁב־נָא עַבְדְּךָ וְאָמֻת בְּעִירִי עִם קֶבֶר אָבִי וְאִמִּי

וְהִנֵּה ׀ עַבְדְּךָ כִמְהָם יַעֲבֹר עִם־אֲדֹנִי הַמֶּלֶךְ וַעֲשֵׂה־לּוֹ אֵת אֲשֶׁר־טוֹב

לט בְּעֵינֶיךָ:   וַיֹּאמֶר הַמֶּלֶךְ אִתִּי יַעֲבֹר כִּמְהָם וַאֲנִי אֶעֱשֶׂה־

מ לּוֹ אֶת־הַטּוֹב בְּעֵינֶיךָ וְכֹל אֲשֶׁר־תִּבְחַר עָלַי אֶעֱשֶׂה־לָּךְ: וַיַּעֲבֹר כָּל־

הָעָם אֶת־הַיַּרְדֵּן וְהַמֶּלֶךְ עָבָר וַיִּשַּׁק הַמֶּלֶךְ לְבַרְזִלַּי וַיְבָרֲכֵהוּ וַיָּשָׁב

מא לִמְקֹמוֹ:   וַיַּעֲבֹר הַמֶּלֶךְ הַגִּלְגָּלָה וְכִמְהָן עָבַר עִמּוֹ וְכָל־עַם

מב יְהוּדָה °וַיְעִבְרוּ [הֶעֱבִירוּ ק] אֶת־הַמֶּלֶךְ וְגַם חֲצִי עַם יִשְׂרָאֵל וְהִנֵּה כָּל־

אִישׁ יִשְׂרָאֵל בָּאִים אֶל־הַמֶּלֶךְ וַיֹּאמְרוּ אֶל־הַמֶּלֶךְ מַדּוּעַ גְּנָבוּךָ אַחֵינוּ

אִישׁ יְהוּדָה וַיַּעֲבִרוּ אֶת־הַמֶּלֶךְ וְאֶת־בֵּיתוֹ אֶת־הַיַּרְדֵּן וְכָל־אַנְשֵׁי דָוִד

19:23. David said, "It is not appropriate for a king to sentence someone to death on the day of his ascension — or, in my case, reascencion — to the throne" (*Malbim*).

19:25. This passage is not in chronological order, since it took place in Jerusalem (v. 26), while the previous and following passages (vv. 32-45) took place at the Jordan. This passage is interpolated here because the lame Mephibosheth had been accused by his servant Ziba of disloyalty to David (16:3) and the obsequious Ziba had been among the first to greet the victorious David (v. 18).

David
spares
Shimei

an adversary unto me today? Shall a man of Israel be put to death today? For do I not know that today I am king over Israel?"* ²⁴ So the king said to Shimei, "You shall not die"; and the king swore to him.

Mephi-
bosheth
refutes
Ziba's
slander

²⁵ Mephibosheth son of Saul came down to greet the king. He had not bathed his feet and had not trimmed his mustache, he had not laundered his clothing from the day the king left until the day that he returned in peace. * ²⁶ And it happened that when he came to Jerusalem to greet the king, that the king said to him, "Why didn't you go with me, Mephibosheth?" ²⁷ He replied, "My lord the king, my servant [Ziba] tricked me; for your servant said, 'I shall saddle up the donkey and ride upon it and go with the king,' for your servant is crippled. ²⁸ He then slandered your servant to my lord the king. My lord the king is like an angel of God; do what is proper in your eyes. ²⁹ For my entire father's family was nothing but condemned men before my lord the king, and yet you placed your servant among those who eat at your table. So what further justification have I to cry out further to the king?" ³⁰ The king then said to him, "Why do you still speak your words? I hereby declare that you and Ziba should divide the property."* ³¹ Mephibosheth replied to the king, "Let him take it all, since my lord the king has arrived safely to his house."

David
rewards
Barzillai

³² Barzillai of Gilead came down from Roglim, and he crossed the Jordan with the king, to see him off at the Jordan. ³³ Barzillai was very old — eighty years of age. He had sustained the king when he dwelt in Mahanaim, for he was a very wealthy man. ³⁴ The king said to Barzillai, "You cross over with me and I shall sustain you with me in Jerusalem." ³⁵ But Barzillai said to the king, "How many are the days [remaining] of the years of my life that I should go up with the king to Jerusalem? ³⁶ I am eighty years old today; can I distinguish good from bad;* does your servant taste what I eat or what I drink? Can I still hear the sound of male or female singers? Why then should your servant be a burden any longer on my lord the king? ³⁷ I will accompany the king across the Jordan for a bit, but why should the king reward me with this benefit? ³⁸ Let your servant return and I will die in my own city, near the grave of my father and my mother. Behold, your servant Chimham* will cross with my lord the king; do with him what is proper in your eyes." ³⁹ The king said, "Chimham will cross with me, and I shall do for him what is proper in your eyes; anything you choose for me I shall do for you."

⁴⁰ All the people then crossed the Jordan, and the king crossed. The king kissed Barzillai and blessed him, and he returned to his place. ⁴¹ The king crossed over to Gilgal, and Chimham crossed over with him; all the people of Judah brought the king across, and also half of the people of Israel.

⁴² Then behold! — all the men of Israel came to the king, and said to the king, "Why have our brethren, the men of Judah, abducted you? They have brought the king and his household across the Jordan, and all of David's men

---

Now we are told how Mephibosheth defended himself — and indeed, that he was telling the truth. The verse testifies to his grief over David's overthrow since abstention from bathing, haircutting, and laundering of clothes are symbols of mourning.

19:30. David was not sure whether to believe Mephibosheth or Ziba, so he silenced Mephibosheth and decreed a compromise. According to the Talmud, David

was punished for believing Ziba's slanderous tale by having his own kingdom split in two during the days of his grandson Rehoboam (Radak).

19:36. I cannot even tell the difference between good food and bad (Rashi). Abarbanel interprets, "If you want me to live in Jerusalem in order to be your adviser, it will be of no use, for I do not know a good idea from a bad one."

19:38. Barzillai's son (Rashi).

מג וַיַּ֨עַן כָּל־אִ֣ישׁ יְהוּדָ֗ה עַל־אִ֣ישׁ יִשְׂרָאֵל֮ כִּֽי־קָר֣וֹב הַמֶּ֣לֶךְ עֵלַ֒י֒ וְלָ֤מָּה זֶּה֙ חָ֣רָה לְךָ֔ עַל־הַדָּבָ֖ר הַזֶּ֑ה הֶאָכ֤וֹל אָכַ֨לְנוּ֙ מִן־הַמֶּ֔לֶךְ אִם־נִשֵּׂ֖את נִשָּׂ֥א לָֽנוּ: מד וַיַּ֣עַן אִֽישׁ־יִשְׂרָאֵל֩ אֶת־אִ֨ישׁ יְהוּדָ֜ה וַיֹּ֗אמֶר עֶֽשֶׂר־יָד֨וֹת לִ֣י בַמֶּ֘לֶךְ֘ וְגַם־בְּדָוִד֮ אֲנִ֣י מִמְּךָ֒ וּמַדּ֨וּעַ֙ הֱקִלֹּתַ֔נִי וְלֹא־הָ֨יָה דְבָרִ֥י רִֽאשׁ֛וֹן לִ֖י לְהָשִׁ֣יב אֶת־מַלְכִּ֑י וַיִּ֨קֶשׁ֙ דְּבַר־אִ֣ישׁ יְהוּדָ֔ה מִדְּבַ֖ר אִ֥ישׁ

כ
א יִשְׂרָאֵֽל: וְשָׁ֨ם נִקְרָ֜א אִ֣ישׁ בְּלִיַּ֗עַל וּשְׁמוֹ֙ שֶׁ֤בַע בֶּן־בִּכְרִי֙ אִ֣ישׁ יְמִינִ֔י וַיִּתְקַ֖ע בַּשֹּׁפָ֑ר וַיֹּ֡אמֶר אֵֽין־לָנוּ֩ חֵ֨לֶק בְּדָוִ֜ד וְלֹ֤א נַֽחֲלָה־לָ֨נוּ֙ בְּבֶן־יִשַׁ֔י אִ֥ישׁ לְאֹֽהָלָ֖יו ב יִשְׂרָאֵֽל: וַיַּ֜עַל כָּל־אִ֤ישׁ יִשְׂרָאֵל֙ מֵאַֽחֲרֵ֣י דָוִ֔ד מֵאַֽחֲרֵ֖י שֶׁ֣בַע בֶּן־בִּכְרִ֑י וְאִ֤ישׁ ג יְהוּדָה֙ דָּֽבְק֣וּ בְמַלְכָּ֔ם מִן־הַיַּרְדֵּ֖ן וְעַד־יְרֽוּשָׁלָֽ͏ִם: וַיָּבֹ֨א דָוִ֣ד אֶל־בֵּית֥וֹ יְרֽוּשָׁלַ֒ם֒ וַיִּקַּ֣ח הַמֶּ֡לֶךְ אֵ֣ת עֶֽשֶׂר־נָשִׁ֣ים | פִּֽלַגְשִׁ֗ים אֲשֶׁ֤ר הִנִּ֨יחַ֙ לִשְׁמֹ֣ר הַבַּ֔יִת וַֽיִּתְּנֵ֞ם בֵּֽית־מִשְׁמֶ֨רֶת֙ וַֽיְכַלְכְּלֵ֔ם וַֽאֲלֵיהֶ֖ם לֹא־בָ֑א וַתִּֽהְיֶ֨ינָה֙ צְרֻר֣וֹת עַד־י֣וֹם ד מֻתָ֔ן אַלְמְנ֖וּת חַיּֽוּת: וַיֹּ֤אמֶר הַמֶּ֨לֶךְ֙ אֶל־עֲמָשָׂ֔א הַזְעֶק־לִ֥י אֶת־אִֽישׁ־יְהוּדָ֖ה שְׁלֹ֣שֶׁת יָמִ֑ים וְאַתָּ֖ה פֹּ֥ה עֲמֹֽד: ה וַיֵּ֥לֶךְ עֲמָשָׂ֖א לְהַזְעִ֣יק אֶת־ ו יְהוּדָ֑ה °וַיֹּ֔יחֶר [ק׳ וַיִּיחֶ֔ר] מִן־הַמּוֹעֵ֖ד אֲשֶׁ֥ר יְעָדֽוֹ: וַיֹּ֣אמֶר דָּוִ֣ד אֶל־אֲבִישַׁ֗י עַתָּ֞ה יֵ֤רַ֤ע לָ֨נוּ֙ שֶׁ֤בַע בֶּן־בִּכְרִי֙ מִן־אַבְשָׁל֑וֹם אַתָּ֡ה קַ֣ח אֶת־עַבְדֵ֤י אֲדֹנֶ֨יךָ֙ וּרְדֹ֣ף אַֽחֲרָ֔יו פֶּן־מָ֥צָא ל֛וֹ עָרִ֥ים בְּצֻר֖וֹת וְהִצִּ֥יל עֵינֵֽנוּ: ז וַיֵּֽצְא֤וּ אַֽחֲרָיו֙ אַנְשֵׁ֣י יוֹאָ֔ב וְהַכְּרֵתִ֥י וְהַפְּלֵתִ֖י וְכָל־הַגִּבֹּרִ֑ים וַיֵּֽצְאוּ֙ מִיר֣וּשָׁלַ֔͏ִם ח לִרְדֹּ֕ף אַֽחֲרֵ֖י שֶׁ֥בַע בֶּן־בִּכְרִֽי: הֵ֣ם עִם־הָאֶ֣בֶן הַגְּדוֹלָה֮ אֲשֶׁ֣ר בְּגִבְעוֹן֒ וַֽעֲמָשָׂ֗א בָּ֚א לִפְנֵיהֶ֔ם וְיוֹאָ֞ב חָג֣וּר | מִדּ֣וֹ לְבֻשׁ֗וּ °וְעָלֹה [ק׳ וְעָלָ֜יו] חֲג֣וֹר ט חֶ֗רֶב מְצֻמֶּ֤דֶת עַל־מָתְנָיו֙ בְּתַעְרָ֔הּ וְה֥וּא יָצָ֖א וַתִּפֹּֽל: וַיֹּ֤אמֶר יוֹאָב֙ לַֽעֲמָשָׂ֔א הֲשָׁל֥וֹם אַתָּ֖ה אָחִ֑י וַתֹּ֜חֶז יַד־יְמִ֥ין יוֹאָ֛ב בִּזְקַ֥ן עֲמָשָׂ֖א י לִנְשָׁק־לֽוֹ: וַֽעֲמָשָׂ֨א לֹֽא־נִשְׁמַ֜ר בַּחֶ֣רֶב | אֲשֶׁ֣ר בְּיַד־יוֹאָ֗ב וַיַּכֵּ֩הוּ֩ בָ֨הּ אֶל־הַחֹ֜מֶשׁ וַיִּשְׁפֹּ֤ךְ מֵעָיו֙ אַ֔רְצָה וְלֹא־שָׁ֥נָה ל֖וֹ וַיָּמֹ֑ת וְיוֹאָב֙ יא וַֽאֲבִישַׁ֣י אָחִ֔יו רָדַ֕ף אַֽחֲרֵ֖י שֶׁ֥בַע בֶּן־בִּכְרִֽי: וְאִ֗ישׁ עָמַ֤ד עָלָיו֙ מִנַּֽעֲרֵ֣י יוֹאָ֔ב יב וַיֹּ֗אמֶר מִ֣י אֲשֶׁ֤ר חָפֵץ֙ בְּיוֹאָ֔ב וּמִ֥י אֲשֶׁר־לְדָוִ֖ד אַֽחֲרֵ֥י יוֹאָֽב: וַֽעֲמָשָׂ֨א מִתְגֹּלֵ֥ל בַּדָּ֖ם בְּת֣וֹךְ הַֽמְסִלָּ֑ה וַיַּ֣רְא הָאִ֗ישׁ כִּֽי־עָמַ֣ד כָּל־הָעָם֒ וַיַּסֵּב֩ אֶת־עֲמָשָׂ֨א מִן־הַֽמְסִלָּ֤ה הַשָּׂדֶה֙ וַיַּשְׁלֵ֤ךְ עָלָיו֙ בֶּ֔גֶד כַּֽאֲשֶׁ֣ר רָאָ֔ה כָּל־הַבָּ֥א יג עָלָ֖יו וְעָמָֽד: כַּֽאֲשֶׁ֤ר הֹגָה֙ מִן־הַֽמְסִלָּ֔ה עָבַ֧ר כָּל־אִ֛ישׁ אַֽחֲרֵ֥י יוֹאָ֖ב לִרְדֹּ֑ף יד אַֽחֲרֵ֖י שֶׁ֥בַע בֶּן־בִּכְרִֽי: וַֽיַּֽעֲבֹ֞ר בְּכָל־שִׁבְטֵ֣י יִשְׂרָאֵ֗ל אָבֵ֛לָה וּבֵ֥ית מַֽעֲכָ֖ה

19:42. You should have notified us of the king's arrival so that we could take part in the welcoming celebrations.

19:44. Even though this king is David, who is from your tribe, we are still the majority of the nation.

20:3. Having been violated by Absalom (see 16:21), they were no longer appropriate for the king; having been intimate with the king, they were forbidden to commoners. Thus, David could neither live with them, nor divorce them so that they could marry others.

20:7. For the explanation of these terms, see note to 8:18.

20:8. Joab was seized with jealous hatred for having been replaced by Amasa, and planned this opportunity to settle the score. He wore his scabbard horizontally so that the sword would slide out unnoticed when he leaned over. Thus, he would not alert Amasa to the danger by actually drawing his sword.

20:11. There were undoubtedly many men — especially from Amasa's force — who felt revulsion at Joab's treach-

with him."* ⁴³ And all the men of Judah [as one] answered the men of Israel, "Because the king is related to me. Why, then, are you angry over this matter? Have we partaken of the king's [food]? Has he granted us special portions?"

Israel protests that Judah slights them

⁴⁴ But the men of Israel [as one] answered the men of Judah and said, "I have ten times as much share in the king — though he be David* — I [have more] than you [do], so why do you slight me? Was it not my initiative to bring back my king?" But the words of the men of Judah were harsher than the words of the men of Israel.

20

SHEBA SON OF BICHRI'S REBELLION
20:1-26

¹ There happened to be there a certain base man by the name of Sheba son of Bichri, a Benjamite; he sounded the shofar and said, "We have no part in David and we have no heritage in the son of Jesse! Every man [back] to his tents, O Israel!" ² So all the men of Israel went up from behind David, and followed Sheba son of Bichri. But the men of Judah clung to their king, from the Jordan to Jerusalem.

David returns home

³ David arrived at his house in Jerusalem. The king took the ten concubine wives whom he had left behind to keep the house, and put them up in a guarded house and sustained them, but he no longer lived with them; they were bound up in living widowhood until the day they died. *

David sends a force to subdue Sheba

⁴ The king then said to Amasa, "Muster for me the men of Judah within the next three days, and you [also] stand here [then]." ⁵ So Amasa went to muster [the men of] Judah; but he was late for the appointed time which [the king] had set for him. ⁶ David then said to Abishai, "Now Sheba son of Bichri will do us more harm than Absalom! So you take your lord's servants yourself and chase after him, lest he find himself some fortified cities and [secure his] rescue [before] our eyes."⁷ Joab's men went after him, as well as the archers and the slingers* and all the mighty men; they left Jerusalem to chase after Sheba son of Bichri.

⁸ When they were at the Great Stone that is in Gibeon, Amasa was coming towards them. Joab was girded with his battle garments, and had a sword girded upon himself, which was fastened upon his loins in its scabbard; and as he moved forward, it fell out. * ⁹ Joab then said to Amasa, "Is all well with you, my brother?" And Joab's right hand grabbed hold of Amasa's beard, to kiss him. ¹⁰ Amasa was not vigilant of the sword in Joab's [left] hand, and he struck him with it, into his fifth rib, and spilled his innards out onto the ground; he did not [need to] repeat [the blow], and he died. Joab and his brother Abishai then took up the chase after Sheba son of Bichri.

Joab kills Amasa and assumes command

¹¹ A man, one of Joab's attendants, stood over [Amasa] and said, "Whoever approves of Joab and whoever is for David, follow Joab."* ¹² But Amasa was wallowing in blood in the middle of the road, and the man saw that all the people stood still; so he moved Amasa from the road into the field, and threw a garment over him, when he saw that everyone who came to it stood still . ¹³ Once he was removed from the road, all the men passed and followed Joab, to chase after Sheba son of Bichri.

¹⁴ He* passed through all the tribes of Israel, to Abel and to Beth-maacah

---

erous behavior. This soldier of Joab announced that there was no time for quibbling now, and that all soldiers present, whether they were followers of Joab or simply loyal to King David, had to disregard what had happened and follow Joab into the battle against Sheba's insurrection.

20:14. *Rashi* understands "he" as a reference to Sheba who enlisted the citizens of all these towns in his rebellion. *Radak* understands "he" as a reference to Joab who passed through all the towns of Israel soliciting and gaining support for David.

וְכָל־הָעָ֗ם °וַיִּקָּלֵ֑הוּ [°וַיַּקְהִ֖לוּ ק] וַיָּבֹ֨אוּ אַף־אַחֲרָ֑יו וַיָּבֹ֜אוּ וַיָּצֻ֤רוּ עָלָיו֙ טו
בְּאָבֵ֙לָה֙ בֵּ֣ית הַֽמַּעֲכָ֔ה וַיִּשְׁפְּכ֤וּ סֹֽלְלָה֙ אֶל־הָעִ֔יר וַֽתַּעֲמֹ֖ד בַּחֵ֑ל וְכָל־הָעָם֙
אֲשֶׁ֣ר אֶת־יוֹאָ֔ב מַשְׁחִיתִ֖ם לְהַפִּ֥יל הַחוֹמָֽה: וַתִּקְרָ֣א אִשָּׁ֧ה חֲכָמָ֛ה מִן־הָעִ֖יר טז
שִׁמְע֣וּ שִׁמְע֗וּ אִמְרוּ־נָ֤א אֶל־יוֹאָב֙ קְרַ֣ב עַד־הֵ֔נָּה וַאֲדַבְּרָ֖ה אֵלֶ֑יךָ: וַיִּקְרַ֣ב יז
אֵלֶ֗יהָ וַתֹּ֤אמֶר הָֽאִשָּׁה֙ הַאַתָּ֣ה יוֹאָ֔ב וַיֹּ֖אמֶר אָ֑נִי וַתֹּ֣אמֶר ל֔וֹ שְׁמַ֕ע דִּבְרֵ֖י
אֲמָתֶ֑ךָ וַיֹּ֖אמֶר שֹׁמֵ֥עַ אָנֹֽכִי: וַתֹּ֣אמֶר לֵאמֹ֔ר דַּבֵּ֥ר יְדַבְּר֛וּ בָרִֽאשֹׁנָ֖ה לֵאמֹ֑ר יח
שָׁאֹ֧ל יְשָׁאֲל֛וּ בְּאָבֵ֖ל וְכֵ֥ן הֵתַֽמּוּ: אָ֠נֹכִֽי שְׁלֻמֵ֞י אֱמוּנֵ֣י יִשְׂרָאֵ֗ל אַתָּ֣ה מְבַקֵּ֗שׁ יט
לְהָמִ֤ית עִיר֙ וְאֵ֣ם בְּיִשְׂרָאֵ֔ל לָ֥מָּה תְבַלַּ֖ע נַחֲלַ֥ת יְהוָֽה: וַיַּ֣עַן יוֹאָ֔ב כ
וַיֹּאמַ֑ר חָלִ֤ילָה חָלִ֙ילָה֙ לִ֔י אִם־אֲבַלַּ֖ע וְאִם־אַשְׁחִֽית: לֹא־כֵ֣ן הַדָּבָ֗ר כִּ֡י כא
אִ֣ישׁ מֵהַ֣ר אֶפְרַ֡יִם שֶׁ֣בַע בֶּן־בִּכְרִ֨י שְׁמ֜וֹ נָשָׂ֤א יָד֙וֹ בַּמֶּ֣לֶךְ בְּדָוִ֔ד תְּנוּ־אֹת֣וֹ
לְבַדּ֔וֹ וְאֵלְכָ֖ה מֵעַ֣ל הָעִ֑יר וַתֹּ֤אמֶר הָֽאִשָּׁה֙ אֶל־יוֹאָ֔ב הִנֵּ֥ה רֹאשׁ֛וֹ מֻשְׁלָ֥ךְ
אֵלֶ֖יךָ בְּעַ֥ד הַֽחוֹמָֽה: וַתָּבוֹא֩ הָאִשָּׁ֨ה אֶל־כָּל־הָעָ֜ם בְּחָכְמָתָ֗הּ וַֽיִּכְרְת֞וּ אֶת־ כב
רֹ֨אשׁ שֶׁ֤בַע בֶּן־בִּכְרִי֙ וַיַּשְׁלִ֣כוּ אֶל־יוֹאָ֔ב וַיִּתְקַע֙ בַּשּׁוֹפָ֔ר וַיָּפֻ֥צוּ מֵֽעַל־הָעִ֖יר
אִ֣ישׁ לְאֹֽהָלָ֑יו וְיוֹאָ֣ב שָׁ֔ב יְרוּשָׁלַ֖͏ִם אֶל־הַמֶּֽלֶךְ:   וְיוֹאָ֗ב אֶ֚ל כָּל־ כג
הַצָּבָ֖א יִשְׂרָאֵ֑ל וּבְנָיָ֙ה֙ בֶּן־יְה֣וֹיָדָ֔ע עַל־°הכרי [°הַכְּרֵתִ֖י ק] וְעַל־הַפְּלֵתִֽי:
וַאֲדֹרָ֖ם עַל־הַמַּ֑ס וִיהוֹשָׁפָ֥ט בֶּן־אֲחִיל֖וּד הַמַּזְכִּֽיר: °וְשִׁיָ֖א [°וּשְׁוָ֖א ק] סֹפֵ֑ר כד-כה

כא וְצָד֥וֹק וְאֶבְיָתָ֖ר כֹּהֲנִֽים: וְגַ֣ם עִירָ֣א הַיָּאִרִ֔י הָיָ֥ה כֹהֵ֖ן לְדָוִֽד: וַיְהִ֣י א
רָעָב֩ בִּימֵ֨י דָוִ֜ד שָׁלֹ֣שׁ שָׁנִ֗ים שָׁנָה֙ אַחֲרֵ֣י שָׁנָ֔ה וַיְבַקֵּ֥שׁ דָּוִ֖ד אֶת־פְּנֵ֣י
יְהוָ֑ה   וַיֹּ֣אמֶר יְהוָ֗ה אֶל־שָׁאוּל֙ וְאֶל־בֵּ֣ית הַדָּמִ֔ים עַל־אֲשֶׁר־
הֵמִ֖ית אֶת־הַגִּבְעֹנִֽים: וַיִּקְרָ֥א הַמֶּ֛לֶךְ לַגִּבְעֹנִ֖ים וַיֹּ֣אמֶר אֲלֵיהֶ֑ם וְהַגִּבְעֹנִ֗ים ב
לֹ֤א מִבְּנֵ֣י יִשְׂרָאֵל֙ הֵ֔מָּה כִּ֛י אִם־מִיֶּ֥תֶר הָאֱמֹרִ֖י וּבְנֵ֣י יִשְׂרָאֵ֗ל נִשְׁבְּע֣וּ לָהֶ֔ם
וַיְבַקֵּ֤שׁ שָׁאוּל֙ לְהַכֹּתָ֔ם בְּקַנֹּאת֥וֹ לִבְנֵֽי־יִשְׂרָאֵ֖ל וִיהוּדָֽה: וַיֹּ֤אמֶר דָּוִד֙ אֶל־ ג
הַגִּבְעֹנִ֔ים מָ֥ה אֶעֱשֶׂ֖ה לָכֶ֑ם וּבַמָּ֣ה אֲכַפֵּ֔ר וּבָרְכ֖וּ אֶת־נַחֲלַ֥ת יְהוָֽה: וַיֹּ֧אמְרוּ ד
ל֣וֹ הַגִּבְעֹנִ֗ים אֵֽין־°לִי [°לָ֜נוּ ק] כֶּ֤סֶף וְזָהָב֙ עִם־שָׁא֣וּל וְעִם־בֵּית֔וֹ וְאֵֽין־לָ֥נוּ
אִ֖ישׁ לְהָמִ֣ית בְּיִשְׂרָאֵ֑ל וַיֹּ֖אמֶר מָֽה־אַתֶּ֥ם אֹמְרִ֖ים אֶעֱשֶׂ֥ה לָכֶֽם: וַיֹּֽאמְרוּ֙ ה
אֶל־הַמֶּ֔לֶךְ הָאִישׁ֙ אֲשֶׁ֣ר כִּלָּ֔נוּ וַאֲשֶׁ֖ר דִּמָּה־לָ֑נוּ נִשְׁמַ֕דְנוּ מֵֽהִתְיַצֵּ֖ב בְּכָל־
גְּבֻ֥ל יִשְׂרָאֵֽל: °יֻנְתַן [°יֻתַּן־ ק] לָ֜נוּ שִׁבְעָ֤ה אֲנָשִׁים֙ מִבָּנָ֔יו וְהֽוֹקַעֲנ֤וּם ו
לַֽיהוָ֔ה בְּגִבְעַ֥ת שָׁא֖וּל בְּחִ֣יר יְהוָ֑ה   וַיֹּ֥אמֶר הַמֶּ֖לֶךְ

20:15. The siege of a fortified city was carried out by pouring a huge mound, or ramp, of earth next to the wall until the besieging troops could ascend to the top of the wall and enter the city.

20:23. When he saw Joab's immense popularity after the victory (*Malbim*) and his spectacular handling of the Sheba affair (*Radak*), David felt he had no choice but to reinstate Joab as commander. Eventually, however, he saw to it that Joab would be punished for his barbaric and treacherous acts (*I Kings* 2:5-6).

20:26. Others translate, "a senior officer" (*Targum*).

Chapters 21-24. Each of the events described from here to the end of the Book is related in some way to the events recorded before and after it. However, they are not given in chronological order (see *Rashi* 21:18; *Kara* 21:15).

21:1. Saul's family is described as the "House of Blood" because they took part in his campaign against the Gibeonites. Exactly what Saul did is not stated explicitly in Scripture. The Sages teach that Gibeonites were wood-choppers and water drawers for the priestly city of Nob, and to all the Berites; they gathered together, and they too followed him. [15] They came and besieged him at Abel of Beth-maacah; they poured a ramp against the city until it stood even with the outer wall, * and all the people who were with Joab began demolishing, to topple the main wall.

A wise woman saves her city . . .

[16] A wise woman called out from the city, "Listen! Listen! Please say to Joab, 'Come close to here, so that I may speak to you.' " [17] So he drew close to her, and the woman said, "Are you Joab?" He replied, "I am." She said, "Hear the words of your maidservant!" and he said, "I am listening." [18] She spoke [on], saying, "[Your men] should have spoken at the start, saying, 'Let them inquire in Abel [about surrender],' for they would have made peace. [19] I [represent] the loyal, faithful people of Israel. You are seeking to annihilate a metropolis in Israel! Why will you swallow up the heritage of HASHEM?" [20] Joab answered and said, "Far be it, far be it from me, that I should swallow up or destroy! [21] The matter is not so. Rather a man from Mount Ephraim, his name is Sheba son of Bichri, has raised up his hand against the king, against David. Turn over him alone, and I will go away from the city." The woman then said to Joab, "Behold, his head will be thrown to you over the wall!"

. . . by executing Sheba

[22] In her wisdom, the woman then went to all the people and they cut off the head of Sheba son of Bichri and threw it to Joab. He sounded the shofar and they all disbanded from the city, every man to his tents. And Joab then returned to Jerusalem, to the king.

The leaders of David's court

[23] Joab was [commander] of the entire army of Israel; * with Benaiah son of Jehoiada over the archers and the slingers; [24] Adoram over the tax; Jehoshaphat son of Ahilud the secretary; [25] Sheva the scribe; Zadok and Abiathar the Kohanim; [26] and also Ira the Jairite was a Kohen * unto David.

21

THE THREE-YEAR FAMINE 21:1-14

[1] In the days of David there was [once] a famine for three years, year after year. David inquired of HASHEM, and HASHEM said, "It is for Saul and for the House of Blood, for his having killed the Gibeonites." *

[2] So the king called the Gibeonites and spoke to them. (The Gibeonites were not of the Children of Israel, but from the remnant of the Amorite; the Children of Israel had sworn [not to harm] them, * but Saul had tried to strike them down in his zeal for the Children of Israel and Judah.) [3] David said to the Gibeonites, "What can I do for you, and how can I atone [for this sin], so that you will bless the heritage of HASHEM?" * [4] The Gibeonites replied to him, "We have no [claim of] silver or gold against Saul nor against his house, and we have no [innocent] man in Israel to put to death." He then said [to them], "Whatever you say I will do for you."

The Gibeonites' cruel demand

[5] They said to the king, "The man who annihilated us and who schemed against us that we be eliminated from remaining within the entire border of Israel — [6] let seven men of his sons be given to us and we will hang them for the sake of HASHEM in the Gibeah of Saul (the chosen one of HASHEM)." The king then

---

and when Saul ordered the massacre of Nob (see *I Samuel* 22:17-19), seven Gibeonites were killed and the rest were left without a livelihood (*Rashi*). *Kara* and *Radak* suggest that Saul drove them from the country, killing many in the process, because the Gibeonites were members of the Hivvite nation, and as such were not entitled to remain in *Eretz Yisrael*. Saul held that Joshua's promise to them was invalid because the Gibeonites had acquired it through

deception (see *Joshua* Ch. 9). Whatever Saul did, it was not justified, and his family incurred God's wrath because he, and they, had desecrated God's Name.

21:2. See *Joshua* Ch. 9.

21:3. David tried to appease the Gibeonites so that they would forgive Israel and pray that God end the drought (*Rashi*).

ז אֲנִי אֶתֵּן: וַיַּחְמֹל הַמֶּלֶךְ עַל־מְפִיבֹשֶׁת בֶּן־יְהוֹנָתָן בֶּן־שָׁאוּל עַל־שְׁבֻעַת
ח יהוה אֲשֶׁר בֵּינֹתָם בֵּין דָּוִד וּבֵין יְהוֹנָתָן בֶּן־שָׁאוּל: וַיִּקַּח הַמֶּלֶךְ אֶת־שְׁנֵי
בְּנֵי רִצְפָּה בַת־אַיָּה אֲשֶׁר יָלְדָה לְשָׁאוּל אֶת־אַרְמֹנִי וְאֶת־מְפִבֹשֶׁת
וְאֶת־חֲמֵשֶׁת בְּנֵי מִיכַל בַּת־שָׁאוּל אֲשֶׁר יָלְדָה לְעַדְרִיאֵל בֶּן־בַּרְזִלַּי
ט הַמְּחֹלָתִי: וַיִּתְּנֵם בְּיַד הַגִּבְעֹנִים וַיֹּקִיעֻם בָּהָר לִפְנֵי יהוה וַיִּפְּלוּ °שבעתים
[°שְׁבַעְתָּם ק] יָחַד °והם [°וְהֵמָּה ק] הֻמְתוּ בִּימֵי קָצִיר בָּרִאשֹׁנִים
י °תחלת [°בִּתְחִלַּת ק] קְצִיר שְׂעֹרִים: וַתִּקַּח רִצְפָּה בַת־אַיָּה אֶת־
הַשַּׂק וַתַּטֵּהוּ לָהּ אֶל־הַצּוּר מִתְּחִלַּת קָצִיר עַד נִתַּךְ־מַיִם עֲלֵיהֶם
מִן־הַשָּׁמָיִם וְלֹא־נָתְנָה עוֹף הַשָּׁמַיִם לָנוּחַ עֲלֵיהֶם יוֹמָם וְאֶת־חַיַּת
יא הַשָּׂדֶה לָיְלָה: וַיֻּגַּד לְדָוִד אֵת אֲשֶׁר־עָשְׂתָה רִצְפָּה בַת־אַיָּה פִּלֶגֶשׁ
יב שָׁאוּל: וַיֵּלֶךְ דָּוִד וַיִּקַּח אֶת־עַצְמוֹת שָׁאוּל וְאֶת־עַצְמוֹת יְהוֹנָתָן בְּנוֹ
מֵאֵת בַּעֲלֵי יָבֵישׁ גִּלְעָד אֲשֶׁר גָּנְבוּ אֹתָם מֵרְחֹב בֵּית־שַׁן אֲשֶׁר °תלום
°שם הפלשתים [°תְּלָאוּם שָׁמָּה פְלִשְׁתִּים ק] בְּיוֹם הַכּוֹת פְּלִשְׁתִּים
יג אֶת־שָׁאוּל בַּגִּלְבֹּעַ: וַיַּעַל מִשָּׁם אֶת־עַצְמוֹת שָׁאוּל וְאֶת־עַצְמוֹת יְהוֹנָתָן
יד בְּנוֹ וַיַּאַסְפוּ אֶת־עַצְמוֹת הַמּוּקָעִים: וַיִּקְבְּרוּ אֶת־עַצְמוֹת־שָׁאוּל
וִיהוֹנָתָן־בְּנוֹ בְּאֶרֶץ בִּנְיָמִן בְּצֵלָע בְּקֶבֶר קִישׁ אָבִיו וַיַּעֲשׂוּ כֹּל אֲשֶׁר־צִוָּה
טו הַמֶּלֶךְ וַיֵּעָתֵר אֱלֹהִים לָאָרֶץ אַחֲרֵי־כֵן: וַתְּהִי־עוֹד
מִלְחָמָה לַפְּלִשְׁתִּים אֶת־יִשְׂרָאֵל וַיֵּרֶד דָּוִד וַעֲבָדָיו עִמּוֹ וַיִּלָּחֲמוּ אֶת־
טז פְּלִשְׁתִּים וַיָּעַף דָּוִד: °וישבו [°וְיִשְׁבִּי ק] בְּנֹב אֲשֶׁר | בִּילִידֵי הָרָפָה
וּמִשְׁקַל קֵינוֹ שְׁלֹשׁ מֵאוֹת מִשְׁקַל נְחֹשֶׁת וְהוּא חָגוּר חֲדָשָׁה וַיֹּאמֶר
יז לְהַכּוֹת אֶת־דָּוִד: וַיַּעֲזָר־לוֹ אֲבִישַׁי בֶּן־צְרוּיָה וַיַּךְ אֶת־הַפְּלִשְׁתִּי וַיְמִיתֵהוּ
אָז נִשְׁבְּעוּ אַנְשֵׁי־דָוִד לוֹ לֵאמֹר לֹא־תֵצֵא עוֹד אִתָּנוּ לַמִּלְחָמָה
יח וְלֹא תְכַבֶּה אֶת־נֵר יִשְׂרָאֵל: וַיְהִי אַחֲרֵי־כֵן וַתְּהִי־עוֹד
הַמִּלְחָמָה בְּגוֹב עִם־פְּלִשְׁתִּים אָז הִכָּה סִבְּכַי הַחֻשָׁתִי אֶת־סַף אֲשֶׁר
יט בִּילִידֵי הָרָפָה: וַתְּהִי־עוֹד הַמִּלְחָמָה בְּגוֹב עִם־פְּלִשְׁתִּים וַיַּךְ
אֶלְחָנָן בֶּן־יַעְרֵי אֹרְגִים בֵּית הַלַּחְמִי אֵת גָּלְיָת הַגִּתִּי וְעֵץ חֲנִיתוֹ כִּמְנוֹר
כ אֹרְגִים: וַתְּהִי־עוֹד מִלְחָמָה בְּגַת וַיְהִי | אִישׁ °מדין [°מָדוֹן ק]

21:6. The hanging would show the justice of HASHEM, for He had punished the entire land for three years because of their cruelty to the Gibeonites (*Radak*). Scripture — not the Gibeonites — gave Saul the accolade, "the chosen one of HASHEM" (*Talmud*).

How could these seven people be executed for the sin of Saul? A court would not have the right to do so, but this was a Heavenly imposed penalty, since the seven were chosen by the *Urim VeTumim*; in God's judgment all of a person's deeds are considered. R' Yochanan declared that in order to end a desecration of the Name, which had been caused by Saul's treatment of the Gibeonites, a commandment of the Torah was set aside, so that the

seven men were chosen to atone for Saul's sin (*Radak*). According to R' Saadyah Gaon, they participated in Saul's deed.

21:7. He prayed to HASHEM that Mephibosheth should not be among the men chosen by God to meet this fate (*Rashi*). R' Saadyah Gaon translates, "David rejoiced over Mephibosheth," meaning that David was relieved that Mephibosheth was not involved in the persecution of the Gibeonites and would not have to be handed over.

21:8. Actually Michal did not have so many children (6:23). Furthermore, her sister Merab was the one married to Adriel (*I Samuel* 18:19). The Talmud explains that Merab gave birth to these five children, but they were said, "I will give [them to you]."*

David designates seven victims   [7] The king had mercy on Mephibosheth son of Jonathan son of Saul,* because of the oath of HASHEM that was between them — between David and Jonathan son of Saul. [8] So the king took the two sons of Rizpah daughter of Aiah, whom she bore to Saul — Armoni and Mephibosheth — and the five sons of Michal* daughter of Saul, whom she bore to Adriel son of Barzillai the Meholathite. [9] He delivered them into the hand of the Gibeonites, and they hanged them on the mountain before HASHEM; all seven of them fell together. They were put to death during the first days of the harvest, at the beginning of the barley harvest.

Rizpah's vigil   [10] Rizpah daughter of Aiah took a sackcloth and spread it for herself over a rock, from the beginning of the harvest until water fell down on [the corpses] from heaven;* she did not allow the birds of the heaven to descend upon them during the day, nor the beasts of the field during the night. [11] David was told what Rizpah daughter of Aiah, Saul's concubine, had done; [12] and David went* and took the bones of Saul and the bones of his son Jonathan from the inhabitants of Jabesh-gilead, who had stolen them from the square of Beth-shan, where the Philistines had hanged them on the day that the Philistines defeated Saul at Gilboa. [13] He brought up from there the bones of Saul and the bones of his son Jonathan. They gathered together the bones of those who were hanged; [14] and they buried the bones of Saul and his son Jonathan in the land of Benjamin, in Zela, in the grave of [Saul's] father, Kish. They did all that the king commanded, and God answered the prayers of the land after that.

THE GIANT'S CHILDREN 21:15-22   [15] The Philistines again made war with Israel. David and his servants went down and fought with the Philistines, and David became faint. [16] Ishbi-benob — who was one of the children of the giant, and whose spear weighed three hundred copper weights and who was girded with a new [sword] — declared that he would strike down David.* [17] Abishai son of Zeruiah came to his aid and he struck the Philistine, killing him. Then David's men swore to him, saying, "You shall not go out to war with us anymore, so that you not extinguish the lamp of Israel!"

[18] It happened after this that there was another war with the Philistines in Gob. It was then that Sibbecai the Hushathite struck down Saph, who was one of the children of the giant.

[19] There was another war with the Philistines in Gob, and Elhanan son of Jaare-oregim the Bethlehemite struck down [the brother of] Goliath of Gath,* who had a spear with a shaft like a weaver's beam.

[20] There was another war, in Gath. There was a man of huge dimensions,

---

adopted and raised by Michal, so she was considered their mother.

21:10. Rizpah, mother of two of the victims, put up a sackcloth shelter for herself and protected the bodies, from the springtime harvest until the fall rainy season.

Although the Torah prohibits leaving a corpse unburied even for one night (Deut. 21:23), God decreed that the bodies should be left there for a lengthy time so that all would see that He condemns those who take advantage of the poor and powerless. Such a powerful impression did this sanctification of the Name make that 150,000 people converted to Judaism (Radak, quoting the Talmud).

21:12. The rainfall proved that Israel's sin had been atoned for. Having learned that the bodies had been preserved through Rizpah's devoted efforts, David now arranged that these remains together with those of Saul and Jonathan [see I Samuel 31:10-12] would receive a proper burial (Di Trani).

21:16. It was customary for a warrior to kill someone on his first day in battle, in order to become fully "initiated" into the army. Ishbi-benob chose the exhausted David as his victim (Rashi).

21:19. The reference is to Goliath's brother, Lahmi, as stated in I Chronicles 20:5 (Kara, Radak).

וְאֶצְבְּעֹת יָדָיו וְאֶצְבְּעֹת רַגְלָיו שֵׁשׁ וָשֵׁשׁ עֶשְׂרִים וְאַרְבַּע מִסְפָּר וְגַם־הוּא

כא יֻלַּד לְהָרָפָה: וַיְחָרֵף אֶת־יִשְׂרָאֵל וַיַּכֵּהוּ יְהוֹנָתָן בֶּן־°שִׁמְעִי [שִׁמְעָה קּ]

כב אֲחִי דָוִד: אֶת־אַרְבַּעַת אֵלֶּה יֻלְּדוּ לְהָרָפָה בְּגַת וַיִּפְּלוּ בְיַד־דָּוִד וּבְיַד עֲבָדָיו:

כב

HAFTARAS HAAZINU (when it is read after Yom Kippur)

HAFTARAH SEVENTH DAY OF PESACH 22:1-51

א ◀ וַיְדַבֵּר דָּוִד לַיהוָה אֶת־דִּבְרֵי הַשִּׁירָה הַזֹּאת בְּיוֹם הִצִּיל יְהוָה אֹתוֹ מִכַּף כָּל־אֹיְבָיו וּמִכַּף שָׁאוּל:

ב-ג וַיֹּאמַר יְהוָה סַלְעִי וּמְצֻדָתִי וּמְפַלְטִי־לִי: אֱלֹהֵי צוּרִי אֶחֱסֶה־בּוֹ מָגִנִּי וְקֶרֶן יִשְׁעִי מִשְׂגַּבִּי

ד וּמְנוּסִי מְשִׁעִי מֵחָמָס תֹּשִׁעֵנִי: מְהֻלָּל

ה אֶקְרָא יְהוָה וּמֵאֹיְבַי אִוָּשֵׁעַ: כִּי אֲפָפֻנִי מִשְׁבְּרֵי

ו מָוֶת נַחֲלֵי בְלִיַּעַל יְבַעֲתֻנִי: חֶבְלֵי שְׁאוֹל סַבֻּנִי קִדְּמֻנִי מֹקְשֵׁי

ז מָוֶת: בַּצַּר־לִי אֶקְרָא יְהוָה וְאֶל־ אֱלֹהַי אֶקְרָא וַיִּשְׁמַע מֵהֵיכָלוֹ

ח קוֹלִי וְשַׁוְעָתִי בְּאָזְנָיו: °וַיִּתְגָּעַשׁ [וַתִּגְעַשׁ קּ] וַתִּרְעַשׁ הָאָרֶץ מוֹסְדוֹת הַשָּׁמַיִם

ט יִרְגָּזוּ וַיִּתְגָּעֲשׁוּ כִּי־חָרָה לוֹ: עָלָה עָשָׁן בְּאַפּוֹ וְאֵשׁ מִפִּיו

י תֹּאכֵל גֶּחָלִים בָּעֲרוּ מִמֶּנּוּ: וַיֵּט שָׁמַיִם וַיֵּרַד וַעֲרָפֶל תַּחַת

יא רַגְלָיו: וַיִּרְכַּב עַל־כְּרוּב וַיָּעֹף וַיֵּרָא

יב עַל־כַּנְפֵי־רוּחַ: וַיָּשֶׁת חֹשֶׁךְ סְבִיבֹתָיו סֻכּוֹת

יג חַשְׁרַת־מַיִם עָבֵי שְׁחָקִים: מִנֹּגַהּ נֶגְדּוֹ בָּעֲרוּ גַּחֲלֵי־אֵשׁ: יַרְעֵם מִן־שָׁמַיִם

יד יְהוָה וְעֶלְיוֹן יִתֵּן קוֹלוֹ: וַיִּשְׁלַח

טו חִצִּים וַיְפִיצֵם בָּרָק °וַיהמם [וַיָּהֹם קּ]: יָם

טז בְּגַעֲרַת יָגֻלּוּ מֹסְדוֹת תֵּבֵל

יז יְהוָה מִנִּשְׁמַת רוּחַ אַפּוֹ: יִשְׁלַח מִמָּרוֹם

יח יַקָּחֵנִי יַמְשֵׁנִי מִמַּיִם רַבִּים: יַצִּילֵנִי מֵאֹיְבִי עָז מִשֹּׂנְאַי כִּי אָמְצוּ

יט מִמֶּנִּי: יְקַדְּמֻנִי בְּיוֹם אֵידִי וַיְהִי

כ יְהוָה מִשְׁעָן לִי: וַיֹּצֵא לַמֶּרְחָב

כא אֹתִי יְחַלְּצֵנִי כִּי־חָפֵץ בִּי: יִגְמְלֵנִי

whose fingers and toes were six each, twenty-four in number; he, too, was born to the giant. ²¹ He ridiculed Israel, and Jonathan, the son of David's brother Shimea, struck him down.

²² These four were born to the giant in Gath, and they fell by the hand of David and by the hand of his servants.

22

SONG OF
GRATITUDE
22:1-51

¹ **D**avid spoke to HASHEM the words of this song* on the day that HASHEM delivered him from the hand of all his enemies and from the hand of Saul. ² He said:

HASHEM is my Rock,* my Fortress, and my Rescuer.
³ God, my Rock* in Whom I take shelter, my Shield,
   and the Horn* of my Salvation, my Stronghold and my Refuge.
   My Savior, You save me from violence.
⁴ With praises I call unto HASHEM, and I am saved from my enemies.
⁵ When the pains of death encircled me
   and torrents of godless men would frighten me,
⁶ the pains of the grave surrounded me, the snares of death confronted me —

David
prays . . .

⁷ in my distress I would call upon HASHEM, and to my God I would call;
   from His abode He heard my voice, and my cry was in His ears.

. . . and God
answers him

⁸ Then the earth quaked and roared, the foundations of the heavens shook;
   they quaked when His wrath flared.
⁹ Smoke rose up in His nostrils, a devouring fire from His mouth,*
   flaming coals blazed forth from Him.
¹⁰ He bent down the heavens and descended,*
   with thick darkness beneath His feet.
¹¹ He mounted a cherub and flew, He appeared on the wings of the wind.
¹² He made darkness into shelters all around Him —
   the darkness of water, the clouds of heaven.*
¹³ From out of the brilliance that is before Him burned fiery coals.
¹⁴ HASHEM thundered from the heavens, the Most High gave forth His voice.
¹⁵ He sent forth His arrows and scattered them; lightning, and He terrified them.
¹⁶ The depths of the sea became visible,
   the foundations of the earth were laid bare,*
   by the rebuke of HASHEM, by the blowing of the breath of His nostrils.

Support
against his
enemies . . .

¹⁷ He sent from on high and took me, He drew me out of deep waters.
¹⁸ He saved me from my mighty foe,
   and from my enemies, when they overpowered me.
¹⁹ They confronted me on the day of my misfortune,
   but HASHEM was a support unto me.
²⁰ He brought me out into a broad space; He released me, for He desired me.

22:1. This song also appears, with minor differences, as the eighteenth psalm. See commentary there.

22:2. Heb., קֶלַע — that is, fortress (*Rashi*).

22:3. Heb., צוּר — that is, refuge, as a mountainside cave shelters one from the elements (*Rashi*).

   "Horn" is a metaphor for strength, just as the horn of an animal is its "weapon" (*Radak*).

22:9. The word of God itself consumes the wicked, like

a fire (*Rashi*).

22:10. God intervened in human affairs (*Ralbag*), and cast His enemies into despair.

22:12. Even when He intervenes, He conceals Himself in natural phenomena (*Ibn Ezra*).

22:16. A reference to the Splitting of the Sea after the Exodus (*Rashi*).

יהוה כְּצִדְקָתִי   כְּבֹר יָדַי יָשִׁיב

כב לִי: כִּי שָׁמַרְתִּי דַּרְכֵי יהוה   וְלֹא

כג רָשַׁעְתִּי מֵאֱלֹהָי   כִּי כָל־°מִשְׁפָּטוֹ [מִשְׁפָּטָיו ק]

כד וְחֻקֹּתָיו לֹא־אָסוּר מִמֶּנָּה   לְנֶגְדִּי וָאֶהְיֶה

כה תָמִים לוֹ וָאֶשְׁתַּמְּרָה מֵעֲוֺנִי: וַיָּשֶׁב יהוה לִי

כו כְצִדְקָתִי כְּבֹרִי לְנֶגֶד עֵינָיו: עִם־

חָסִיד תִּתְחַסָּד   עִם־גִּבּוֹר תָּמִים

כז עִם־נָבָר תִּתָּבָר: תִּתַּמָּם וְעִם־

כח עִקֵּשׁ תִּתַּפָּל: וְאֶת־עַם עָנִי

כט וְעֵינֶיךָ עַל־רָמִים תַּשְׁפִּיל: תּוֹשִׁיעַ כִּי־

אַתָּה נֵרִי יהוה   וַיהוה יַגִּיהַּ

ל חָשְׁכִּי: כִּי בְכָה אָרוּץ גְּדוּד בֵּאלֹהַי

לא אֲדַלֶּג־שׁוּר: הָאֵל תָּמִים

דַּרְכּוֹ   אִמְרַת יהוה צְרוּפָה מָגֵן

לב הוּא לְכֹל הַחֹסִים בּוֹ:   כִּי מִי־אֵל מִבַּלְעֲדֵי

לג יהוה   וּמִי צוּר מִבַּלְעֲדֵי אֱלֹהֵינוּ: הָאֵל

מָעוּזִּי חָיִל   וַיַּתֵּר תָּמִים

לד °דרכו [דַּרְכִּי ק]:   מְשַׁוֶּה °רגליו [רַגְלַי ק] כָּאַיָּלוֹת וְעַל־

לה בָּמֹתַי יַעֲמִדֵנִי: מְלַמֵּד יָדַי

לו לַמִּלְחָמָה   וְנִחַת קֶשֶׁת־נְחוּשָׁה זְרֹעֹתָי: וַתִּתֶּן־

לז לִי מָגֵן יִשְׁעֶךָ וַעֲנֹתְךָ תַּרְבֵּנִי: תַּרְחִיב צַעֲדִי

לח תַחְתֵּנִי   וְלֹא מָעֲדוּ קַרְסֻלָּי: אֶרְדְּפָה

אֹיְבַי וָאַשְׁמִידֵם   וְלֹא אָשׁוּב עַד־

לט כַּלּוֹתָם: וָאֲכַלֵּם וָאֶמְחָצֵם וְלֹא יְקוּמוּן וַיִּפְּלוּ

מ תַּחַת רַגְלָי: וַתַּזְרֵנִי חַיִל

לַמִּלְחָמָה   וְאֹיְבַי

מא תַּכְרִיעַ קָמַי תַּחְתֵּנִי: מְשַׂנְאַי וָאַצְמִיתֵם: יִשְׁעוּ וְאֵין

מב מֹשִׁיעַ   אֶל־יהוה וְלֹא עָנָם: וָאֶשְׁחָקֵם

כְּעֲפַר־אָרֶץ   כְּטִיט־חוּצוֹת אֲדִקֵּם

מג אֶרְקָעֵם: וַתְּפַלְּטֵנִי מֵרִיבֵי עַמִּי תִּשְׁמְרֵנִי

מד לְרֹאשׁ גּוֹיִם   עַם לֹא־יָדַעְתִּי

מה יַעַבְדֻנִי: בְּנֵי נֵכָר יִתְכַּחֲשׁוּ־לִי לִשְׁמוֹעַ

מו אֹזֶן יִשָּׁמְעוּ לִי: בְּנֵי נֵכָר יִבֹּלוּ וְיַחְגְּרוּ

מז חַי־יהוה וּבָרוּךְ צוּרִי   מִמִּסְגְּרוֹתָם: וְיָרֻם

. . . in return
for righteous-
ness

²¹ HASHEM recompensed me according to my righteousness;
    He repaid me befitting the cleanliness of my hands.
²² For I have kept the ways of HASHEM,
    and I have not departed wickedly from my God.
²³ For all His judgments are before me; I do not remove myself from His decrees.
²⁴ I have been perfectly innocent with Him, and I was vigilant against my sin.
²⁵ HASHEM repaid me in accordance with my righteousness,
    according to my purity before His eyes.
²⁶ With the devout You deal devoutly.
    with the one who is strong in his wholeheartedness You act wholeheartedly.
²⁷ With the pure You act purely, with the corrupt You act perversely.
²⁸ You save the humble people,
    while Your eyes are upon the haughty to lower them.
²⁹ For You are my lamp, HASHEM; HASHEM illuminates my darkness.
³⁰ For with You I smash a troop, with my God I leap over a wall. *
³¹ The God! His way is perfect; the promise of HASHEM is flawless.

Only in God
is there
safety

    He is a shield for all who take refuge in Him.
³² For who is God besides HASHEM, and who is a Rock besides our God? ³³ God!
My Fortress of strength; He cleared my way, with perfection.
³⁴ Who straightened my feet like the hinds, and stood me upon my heights.
³⁵ Who trained my hands for battle,
    so that a copper bow could be bent by my arms.

David
defeats his
enemies . . .

³⁶ You have given me the shield of Your salvation,
    and Your humility made me great. *
³⁷ You widened my stride beneath me; and my ankles have not faltered.
³⁸ I pursued my foes and eradicated them,
    and returned not until they were destroyed.
³⁹ I destroyed them and struck them down so that they did not rise,
    and they fell beneath my feet.
⁴⁰ You girded me with strength for battle;
    You brought my adversaries to their knees beneath me.
⁴¹ And my enemies — you gave to me in retreat;
    my antagonists, and I cut them down.
⁴² They cried out, but there was no savior;
    [they turned] to HASHEM, but He answered them not.
⁴³ I pulverized them like dust of the earth;
    like the mud in the streets I crushed them and trampled them.

. . . and wins
allegiance
from friend
and foe

⁴⁴ You rescued me from the strife of my people; *
You preserved me to be the head of nations; a people I did not know serves me.
⁴⁵ Foreigners dissemble to me;
    at the ear's hearing, they become obedient to me. *

Gratitude
to HASHEM

⁴⁶ Foreigners are withered and terrified from within their fortified enclosures.
⁴⁷ HASHEM lives! Blessed is my Rock!

22:30. With God by my side I have the strength to engage and conquer my enemies.

22:36. God's "humility," by which He deigns to bestow goodness upon human beings, was illustrated many times for me, through His miraculous acts of salvation.

22:44. You have delivered me from my foes in the Israelite camp — Saul, Doeg, Absalom, Sheba, etc.

22:45. Out of apprehension for me, they conceal the truth when they fear it will displease me, but the mere report that I have issued an order is enough to make them cower with obeisance.

מח הָאֵל הַנֹּתֵן נְקָמֹת   אֱלֹהֵי צוּר יִשְׁעִי:

מט וּמוֹרִיד עַמִּים תַּחְתֵּנִי: לִי   וּמוֹצִיאִי

מֵאִיְבָי וּמִקָּמַי תְּרוֹמְמֵנִי   מֵאִישׁ חֲמָסִים

נ תַּצִּילֵנִי: עַל־כֵּן אוֹדְךָ יְהוָה בַּגּוֹיִם   וּלְשִׁמְךָ

נא אֲזַמֵּר: °מַגְדִּיל [°מִגְדּוֹל ק]   יְשׁוּעוֹת

מַלְכּוֹ   וְעֹשֶׂה־חֶסֶד   לִמְשִׁיחוֹ

לְדָוִד וּלְזַרְעוֹ   עַד־עוֹלָם: ◀

כג א וְאֵלֶּה דִּבְרֵי דָוִד הָאַחֲרֹנִים נְאֻם דָּוִד בֶּן־יִשַׁי וּנְאֻם הַגֶּבֶר הֻקַם עָל מְשִׁיחַ

ב אֱלֹהֵי יַעֲקֹב וּנְעִים זְמִרוֹת יִשְׂרָאֵל: רוּחַ יְהוָה דִּבֶּר־בִּי וּמִלָּתוֹ עַל־לְשׁוֹנִי:

ג אָמַר אֱלֹהֵי יִשְׂרָאֵל לִי דִבֶּר צוּר יִשְׂרָאֵל מוֹשֵׁל בָּאָדָם צַדִּיק מוֹשֵׁל יִרְאַת

ד אֱלֹהִים: וּכְאוֹר בֹּקֶר יִזְרַח־שָׁמֶשׁ בֹּקֶר לֹא עָבוֹת מִנֹּגַהּ מִמָּטָר דֶּשֶׁא

ה מֵאָרֶץ: כִּי־לֹא־כֵן בֵּיתִי עִם־אֵל כִּי בְרִית עוֹלָם שָׂם לִי עֲרוּכָה בַכֹּל

ו וּשְׁמֻרָה כִּי־כָל־יִשְׁעִי וְכָל־חֵפֶץ כִּי־לֹא יַצְמִיחַ: וּבְלִיַּעַל כְּקוֹץ מֻנָד כֻּלָּהַם

ז כִּי־לֹא בְיָד יִקָּחוּ: וְאִישׁ יִגַּע בָּהֶם יִמָּלֵא בַרְזֶל וְעֵץ חֲנִית וּבָאֵשׁ שָׂרוֹף

יִשָּׂרְפוּ בַּשָּׁבֶת:

ח אֵלֶּה שְׁמוֹת הַגִּבֹּרִים אֲשֶׁר לְדָוִד יֹשֵׁב בַּשֶּׁבֶת תַּחְכְּמֹנִי ׀ רֹאשׁ הַשָּׁלִשִׁי

הוּא עֲדִינוֹ [°הָעֶצְנוֹ ק] °הָעֶצְנִי [ק] עַל־שְׁמֹנֶה מֵאוֹת חָלָל בְּפַעַם °אֶחָד

ט [°אֶחָת ק]: °ואחרו [°וְאַחֲרָיו ק] אֶלְעָזָר בֶּן־°דֹדִי [°דֹּדוֹ ק] בֶּן־אֲחֹחִי

בִּשְׁלֹשָׁה °גברים [°הַגִּבֹּרִים ק] עִם־דָּוִד בְּחָרְפָם בַּפְּלִשְׁתִּים נֶאֶסְפוּ־שָׁם

י לַמִּלְחָמָה וַיַּעֲלוּ אִישׁ יִשְׂרָאֵל: הוּא קָם וַיַּךְ בַּפְּלִשְׁתִּים עַד ׀ כִּי־יָגְעָה יָדוֹ

וַתִּדְבַּק יָדוֹ אֶל־הַחֶרֶב וַיַּעַשׂ יְהוָה תְּשׁוּעָה גְדוֹלָה בַּיּוֹם הַהוּא וְהָעָם יָשֻׁבוּ

יא אַחֲרָיו אַךְ־לְפַשֵּׁט: וְאַחֲרָיו שַׁמָּא בֶן־אָגֵא הָרָרִי וַיֵּאָסְפוּ

פְלִשְׁתִּים לַחַיָּה וַתְּהִי־שָׁם חֶלְקַת הַשָּׂדֶה מְלֵאָה עֲדָשִׁים וְהָעָם נָס

יב מִפְּנֵי פְלִשְׁתִּים: וַיִּתְיַצֵּב בְּתוֹךְ־הַחֶלְקָה וַיַּצִּילֶהָ וַיַּךְ אֶת־פְּלִשְׁתִּים וַיַּעַשׂ

יג יְהוָה תְּשׁוּעָה גְדוֹלָה: וַיֵּרְדוּ °שְׁלשִׁים [°שְׁלֹשָׁה ק] מֵהַשְּׁלֹשִׁים

רֹאשׁ וַיָּבֹאוּ אֶל־קָצִיר אֶל־דָּוִד אֶל־מְעָרַת עֲדֻלָּם וְחַיַּת פְּלִשְׁתִּים

23:1. These are the last words David uttered through Divine inspiration (*Targum*).

David was "established on high" when he was "taken from the sheepfold, from following the flocks, to become ruler over God's people, over Israel" (7:8).

23:4. Grass needs both rain and sunshine to grow. David likens his reign to a sunny morning after a night's rain, a time for optimism, growth and prosperity (*Di Trani*).

23:5. The glory of the kingdom of the house of David was not meant to be "clouded over" by constant subversion or lack of endurance, as other royal houses of Israel (the house of Saul, the houses of future kings, the Hasmonean dynasty, etc.).

23:7. Just as thistles and thorns must be removed with implements or burned in their place, lest they prick the one who gathers them, so too the wicked must be obliterated, either through mercenaries or by directly destroying them in the places where they lurk (*Radak*).

23:8. Adino once slew eight hundred men in one battle.

23:9. The three mighty men were Adino, Elazar and Shammah (*Radak*).

23:10. Elazar defeated the Philistine army singlehandedly; the people had nothing to do except to come afterwards to plunder the fallen soldiers.

23:11. Lit., "into a beast"; i.e., they formed into a raiding party that, like the wild beasts, would pillage the produce

Exalted is God, Rock of my salvation,

⁴⁸ The God Who grants me vengeance and subdues nations beneath me,

⁴⁹ and extricates me from my enemies!

You raised me above my adversaries; from the man of violence You rescued me.

⁵⁰ Therefore, I shall give thanks to You, HASHEM, among the nations,
and to Your Name I will sing.

⁵¹ He is a tower of His king's salvations,
and does kindness to His anointed one, to David and his offspring, forever!

23

**DAVID'S
LAST
PROPHETIC
WORDS**
23:1-7

*The
command
that he
reign . . .*

*. . . and his
enemies will
be swept
aside*

¹ **T**hese are the last words* of David: The words of David son of Jesse,
and the words of the man who was established on high, *
the anointed one of the God of Jacob,
and the pleasing [composer] of the songs of Israel:

² The spirit of HASHEM spoke through me; His word is upon my tongue.

³ The God of Israel has said — the Rock of Israel has spoken to me —
"[Become a] ruler over men; a righteous one,
who rules through the fear of God,

⁴ like the morning light when the sun shines — a morning without clouds,
from the shine out of the rain, grass [sprouts forth] from the earth."*

⁵ For was my house not [set up] thus with God;*
for He has granted me an everlasting covenant,
established for all [time] and secure;
for my entire salvation and desire [have been fulfilled],
for He will not [allow other kingdoms to] sprout.

⁶ But godless men are all like a wind-blown thistle,
which they cannot take by hand.

⁷ [For] a man to touch them, he must equip himself with iron [tools]
and the shaft of a spear,
and they must be thoroughly burnt where they are. *

**DAVID'S
MIGHTY
WARRIORS**
23:8-39

⁸ These are the names of David's warriors: One who sat in the assembly, a
sagacious man, head of the captains — he is Adino the Eznite, [who stood] over
eight hundred corpses at one time. *

⁹ After him was Elazar son of Dodo an Ahohite; [he was] among the three
mighty men* who were with David when they fought defiantly against the
Philistines who had gathered there for war, and the men of Israel ran off. ¹⁰ He
rose up and struck the Philistines until his hand tired and his hand stuck to the
sword; and HASHEM performed a great salvation on that day. The people returned
after him only to strip [the corpses]. *

¹¹ After him was Shammah son of Age, from the mountain. The Philistines had
gathered into a raiding party* where there was a portion of the field full of lentils,
and the people fled from the Philistines. ¹² So he stood in the middle of the portion
and rescued it, and slayed the Philistines; and HASHEM performed a great
salvation.

¹³ Once three men, who were officers over the thirty men, went down and
came to David at harvest, to the cave of Adullam, * and a Philistine raiding party

---

of the fields (Rashi, Ralbag).
23:13. The three heroes mentioned above (Di Trani), or
perhaps "the three" referred to in v. 18 (Ralbag), had

under their command the thirty men mentioned below.
They were with David at the stronghold of Adullam, where
he was hiding from Saul (I Samuel 22:1).

יד חֹנָה בְּעֵמֶק רְפָאִים: וְדָוִד אָז בַּמְּצוּדָה וּמַצַּב פְּלִשְׁתִּים אָז בֵּית

טו לָחֶם: וַיִּתְאַוֶּה דָוִד וַיֹּאמַר מִי יַשְׁקֵנִי מַיִם מִבֹּאר בֵּית־לֶחֶם אֲשֶׁר

טז בַּשָּׁעַר: וַיִּבְקְעוּ שְׁלֹשֶׁת הַגִּבֹּרִים בְּמַחֲנֵה פְלִשְׁתִּים וַיִּשְׁאֲבוּ־מַיִם מִבֹּאר בֵּית־לֶחֶם אֲשֶׁר בַּשַּׁעַר וַיִּשְׂאוּ וַיָּבִאוּ אֶל־דָּוִד וְלֹא אָבָה

יז לִשְׁתּוֹתָם וַיַּסֵּךְ אֹתָם לַיהֹוָה: וַיֹּאמֶר חָלִילָה לִּי יהֹוָה מֵעֲשֹׂתִי זֹאת הֲדַם הָאֲנָשִׁים הַהֹלְכִים בְּנַפְשׁוֹתָם וְלֹא אָבָה לִשְׁתּוֹתָם אֵלֶּה עָשׂוּ שְׁלֹשֶׁת

יח הַגִּבֹּרִים: וַאֲבִישַׁי אֲחִי ׀ יוֹאָב בֶּן־צְרוּיָה הוּא רֹאשׁ °הַשְּׁלֹשִׁי [°הַשְּׁלֹשָׁה ק] וְהוּא עוֹרֵר אֶת־חֲנִיתוֹ עַל־שְׁלֹשׁ מֵאוֹת חָלָל

יט וְלוֹ־שֵׁם בַּשְּׁלֹשָׁה: מִן־הַשְּׁלֹשָׁה הֲכִי נִכְבָּד וַיְהִי לָהֶם לְשָׂר וְעַד־הַשְּׁלֹשָׁה

כ לֹא־בָא: וּבְנָיָהוּ בֶן־יְהוֹיָדָע בֶּן־אִישׁ־°חַי [°חַיִל ק] רַב־פְּעָלִים מִקַּבְצְאֵל הוּא הִכָּה אֵת שְׁנֵי אֲרִאֵל מוֹאָב וְהוּא יָרַד וְהִכָּה

כא אֶת־°הָאֲרִיה [°הָאֲרִי ק] בְּתוֹךְ הַבֹּאר בְּיוֹם הַשָּׁלֶג: וְהוּא־הִכָּה אֶת־אִישׁ מִצְרִי °אֲשֶׁר [°אִישׁ ק] מַרְאֶה וּבְיַד הַמִּצְרִי חֲנִית וַיֵּרֶד אֵלָיו בַּשָּׁבֶט וַיִּגְזֹל

כב אֶת־הַחֲנִית מִיַּד הַמִּצְרִי וַיַּהַרְגֵהוּ בַּחֲנִיתוֹ: אֵלֶּה עָשָׂה בְּנָיָהוּ בֶּן־יְהוֹיָדָע

כג וְלוֹ־שֵׁם בִּשְׁלֹשָׁה הַגִּבֹּרִים: מִן־הַשְּׁלֹשִׁים נִכְבָּד וְאֶל־הַשְּׁלֹשָׁה לֹא־בָא

כד וַיְשִׂמֵהוּ דָוִד אֶל־מִשְׁמַעְתּוֹ: עֲשָׂה־אֵל אֲחִי־יוֹאָב בַּשְּׁלֹשִׁים אֶלְחָנָן בֶּן־דֹּדוֹ בֵּית לָחֶם: שַׁמָּה הַחֲרֹדִי אֱלִיקָא הַחֲרֹדִי

כה־כו חֶלֶץ הַפַּלְטִי עִירָא בֶן־עִקֵּשׁ הַתְּקוֹעִי: אֲבִיעֶזֶר הָעַנְּתֹתִי מְבֻנַּי

כז הַחֻשָׁתִי: צַלְמוֹן הָאֲחֹחִי מַהְרַי הַנְּטֹפָתִי: חֵלֶב בֶּן־בַּעֲנָה

כח־כט הַנְּטֹפָתִי אִתַּי בֶּן־רִיבַי מִגִּבְעַת בְּנֵי בִנְיָמִן: בְּנָיָהוּ פִּרְעָתֹנִי הִדַּי

ל מִנַּחֲלֵי גָעַשׁ: אֲבִי־עַלְבוֹן הָעַרְבָתִי עַזְמָוֶת הַבַּרְחֻמִי: אֶלְיַחְבָּא

לא־לב הַשַּׁעַלְבֹנִי בְּנֵי יָשֵׁן יְהוֹנָתָן: שַׁמָּה הַהֲרָרִי אֲחִיאָם בֶּן־שָׁרָר

לג הָאֲרָרִי: אֱלִיפֶלֶט בֶּן־אֲחַסְבַּי בֶּן־הַמַּעֲכָתִי אֱלִיעָם בֶּן־אֲחִיתֹפֶל

לד הַגִּלֹנִי: חֶצְרוֹ °הַכַּרְמְלִי [°חֶצְרַי ק] פַּעֲרַי הָאַרְבִּי: יִגְאָל

לה־לו בֶּן־נָתָן מִצֹּבָה בָּנִי הַגָּדִי: צֶלֶק הָעַמֹּנִי נַחְרַי הַבְּאֵרֹתִי

לז °נֹשְׂאֵי [°נֹשֵׂא ק] כְּלֵי יוֹאָב בֶּן־צְרוּיָה: עִירָא הַיִּתְרִי גָּרֵב

לח־לט הַיִּתְרִי: אוּרִיָּה הַחִתִּי כֹּל שְׁלֹשִׁים וְשִׁבְעָה: וַיֹּסֶף אַף־יהֹוָה

כד לַחֲרוֹת בְּיִשְׂרָאֵל וַיָּסֶת אֶת־דָּוִד בָּהֶם לֵאמֹר לֵךְ מְנֵה אֶת־יִשְׂרָאֵל וְאֶת־

ב יְהוּדָה: וַיֹּאמֶר הַמֶּלֶךְ אֶל־יוֹאָב ׀ שַׂר־הַחַיִל אֲשֶׁר־אִתּוֹ שׁוּט־נָא בְּכָל־

23:16. According to one Talmudic opinion, this event took place on Succos, the only time of the year when water libations are offered, so that David must have had an altar at Adullam. *Radak* suggests that the intent is figurative: David spilled out the water in a gesture of devotion to God.

23:18. These three are not the same as the three mighty men described above.

23:20. Unlike the previously described heroes, for whom only one daring deed is reported for each man, Benaiahu was a man of *many* deeds, as the verses go on to detail (*Kara*). The Sages interpret the account of his exploits as a metaphor for spiritual and scholarly successes.

23:22. I.e., the three who risked their lives to bring water for David.

23:39. There are many versions of how to arrive at the number of thirty-seven mighty men.

24:1. This episode continues the misfortunes listed in the *was encamped in the Valley of Rephaim.* ¹⁴ *David was then in the stronghold, and there was a Philistine garrison in Bethlehem.* ¹⁵ *David had a craving and said, "If only someone could give me water to drink from the well of Bethlehem, which is in the city gate!"* ¹⁶ *So the three mighty men broke into the camp of the Philistines and drew water from the well of Bethlehem, which is at the gate, and they carried it and brought it to David. But he refused to drink it, and he poured it out unto HASHEM.* * ¹⁷ *He said, "Far be it from me, HASHEM, that I should do this! Is this not [tantamount to] the blood of the men who risked their lives to go?" And he refused to drink it. These are what the three mighty men did.*

Abishai ¹⁸ *Abishai, the brother of Joab son of Zeruiah — he was the head of the three;* * *he wielded his sword over three hundred corpses; he was the best known of the three.* ¹⁹ *Of the three, he was the most honored, and he became their leader, but he did not compare to the first three.*

Benaiah ²⁰ *Benaiah son of Jehoiada was a valiant man of many achievements,* * *from Kabzeel; he struck down the two commanders of Moab, and he [also] went down and slew a lion in the middle of a well on a snowy day.* ²¹ *He also struck down an Egyptian man, a man of imposing appearance; in the hand of the Egyptian was a spear, and he came down upon him with a stick, and stole the spear from the hand of the Egyptian, and killed him with his own spear.* ²² *These [things] Benaiah son of Jehoiada did; he was well known among the three mighty men.* * ²³ *He was more honored than the thirty, but he did not compare to the [first] three; and David set him as his confidant.*

The rest of his heroic warriors ²⁴ *Asahel, the brother of Joab, was among the thirty, [who were]: Elhanan son of Dodo of Bethlehem,* ²⁵ *Shammah the Harodite, Elika the Harodite,* ²⁶ *Helez the Paltite, Ira son of Ikkesh the Tekoite,* ²⁷ *Abiezer the Anathothite, Mebunnai the Hushathite,* ²⁸ *Zalmon the Ahohite, Maharai the Netophathite,* ²⁹ *Heleb son of Baanah the Netophathite, Ittai son of Ribai from Gibeah of the Children of Benjamin,* ³⁰ *Benaiah a Pirathonite, Hiddai from Nahale-gaash,* ³¹ *Abi-albon the Arbathite, Azmaveth the Barhumite,* ³² *Eliahba the Shaalbonite; of the sons of Jashen, Jonathan;* ³³ *Shammah from the mountain, Ahiam son of Sharar the Ararite,* ³⁴ *Eliphelet son of Ahasbai son of the Maacathite, Eliam son of Ahithophel the Gilonite,* ³⁵ *Hezrai the Carmelite, Paarai the Arbite,* ³⁶ *Igal son of Nathan from Zobah, Bani the Gadite,* ³⁷ *Zelek the Ammonite, Nahrai the Beerothite — who was Joab son of Zeruiah's armor-bearer —* ³⁸ *Ira the Ithrite, Gareb the Ithrite,* ³⁹ *Uriah the Hittite. Altogether there were thirty-seven [mighty men].* *

24

DAVID'S WRONGFUL CENSUS

24:1-25

¹ *The anger of HASHEM again flared against Israel, and He enticed David because of them, to say, "Go count the people of Israel and Judah."* * ² *So the king said to Joab, the commander of his army, "Travel around among all the*

---

previous chapters. Although Scripture does not specify which sin had precipitated God's anger against Israel, the *Midrash* asserts that the people sinned by not seeking a more active role in the building of the Temple, although David himself had made such an effort and was rebuffed (Ch. 7). [It is interesting to note that in fact the entire episode ends when an altar is built upon the threshing floor of Araunah, the future site of the Temple.]

Radak explains that all such calamities are the result of national sinfulness, but God brings about the punishments by means of natural and common phenomena such as political discord or droughts. In this case, David

was enticed to conduct a national census. The verse does not necessarily mean that God commanded or caused David to do so. The parallel verse in *I Chronicles* (21:1) reads "A *satan*, i.e., an evil impulse (*Radak*), enticed David to count Israel."

Counting the population is improper, even sinful, because it is likely to be motivated by a vain desire to know the exact strategic potency of the nation, which in turn leads the people to believe that their salvation is in strength of numbers and not in God's desire for their well-being. Consequently, such a counting of the population is likely to bode ill for the people involved, which is

שִׁבְטֵי יִשְׂרָאֵל מִדָּן וְעַד־בְּאֵר שֶׁבַע וּפִקְדוּ אֶת־הָעָם וְיָדַעְתִּי אֵת מִסְפַּר

הָעָם: ג   וַיֹּאמֶר יוֹאָב אֶל־הַמֶּלֶךְ וְיוֹסֵף יהוה אֱלֹהֶיךָ אֶל־הָעָם

כָּהֵם ׀ וְכָהֵם מֵאָה פְעָמִים וְעֵינֵי אֲדֹנִי־הַמֶּלֶךְ רֹאוֹת וַאדֹנִי הַמֶּלֶךְ לָמָּה

חָפֵץ בַּדָּבָר הַזֶּה: ד   וַיֶּחֱזַק דְּבַר־הַמֶּלֶךְ אֶל־יוֹאָב וְעַל שָׂרֵי הֶחָיִל וַיֵּצֵא יוֹאָב

וְשָׂרֵי הַחַיִל לִפְנֵי הַמֶּלֶךְ לִפְקֹד אֶת־הָעָם אֶת־יִשְׂרָאֵל: ה   וַיַּעַבְרוּ אֶת־

הַיַּרְדֵּן וַיַּחֲנוּ בַעֲרוֹעֵר יְמִין הָעִיר אֲשֶׁר בְּתוֹךְ־הַנַּחַל הַגָּד וְאֶל־יַעְזֵר:

וַיָּבֹאוּ הַגִּלְעָדָה וְאֶל־אֶרֶץ תַּחְתִּים חָדְשִׁי וַיָּבֹאוּ דָּנָה יַּעַן וְסָבִיב אֶל־   ו

צִידוֹן: ז   וַיָּבֹאוּ מִבְצַר־צֹר וְכָל־עָרֵי הַחִוִּי וְהַכְּנַעֲנִי וַיֵּצְאוּ אֶל־נֶגֶב יְהוּדָה

בְּאֵר שָׁבַע: ח   וַיָּשֻׁטוּ בְּכָל־הָאָרֶץ וַיָּבֹאוּ מִקְצֵה תִשְׁעָה חֳדָשִׁים וְעֶשְׂרִים יוֹם

יְרוּשָׁלָ͏ִם: ט   וַיִּתֵּן יוֹאָב אֶת־מִסְפַּר מִפְקַד־הָעָם אֶל־הַמֶּלֶךְ וַתְּהִי יִשְׂרָאֵל

שְׁמֹנֶה מֵאוֹת אֶלֶף אִישׁ־חַיִל שֹׁלֵף חֶרֶב וְאִישׁ יְהוּדָה חֲמֵשׁ־מֵאוֹת אֶלֶף

אִישׁ:   י   וַיַּךְ לֵב־דָּוִד אֹתוֹ אַחֲרֵי־כֵן סָפַר אֶת־הָעָם   וַיֹּאמֶר

דָּוִד אֶל־יהוה חָטָאתִי מְאֹד אֲשֶׁר עָשִׂיתִי וְעַתָּה יהוה הַעֲבֶר־נָא אֶת־עֲוֹן

עַבְדְּךָ כִּי נִסְכַּלְתִּי מְאֹד: וַיָּקָם דָּוִד בַּבֹּקֶר   וּדְבַר־יהוה הָיָה אֶל־   יא

גָּד הַנָּבִיא חֹזֵה דָוִד לֵאמֹר: יב   הָלוֹךְ וְדִבַּרְתָּ אֶל־דָּוִד כֹּה אָמַר יהוה שָׁלֹשׁ

אָנֹכִי נוֹטֵל עָלֶיךָ בְּחַר־לְךָ אַחַת־מֵהֶם וְאֶעֱשֶׂה־לָּךְ:   יג   וַיָּבֹא־גָד אֶל־דָּוִד

וַיַּגֶּד־לוֹ וַיֹּאמֶר לוֹ הֲתָבוֹא לְךָ שֶׁבַע־שָׁנִים ׀ רָעָב ׀ בְּאַרְצֶךָ וְאִם־שְׁלֹשָׁה

חֳדָשִׁים נֻסְךָ לִפְנֵי־צָרֶיךָ וְהוּא רֹדְפֶךָ וְאִם־הֱיוֹת שְׁלֹשֶׁת יָמִים דֶּבֶר

בְּאַרְצֶךָ עַתָּה דַּע וּרְאֵה מָה־אָשִׁיב שֹׁלְחִי דָּבָר: וַיֹּאמֶר דָּוִד   יד

אֶל־גָּד צַר־לִי מְאֹד נִפְּלָה־נָּא בְיַד־יהוה כִּי־רַבִּים °רַחֲמָיו ק׳ רחמו]

וּבְיַד־אָדָם אַל־אֶפֹּלָה: טו   וַיִּתֵּן יהוה דֶּבֶר בְּיִשְׂרָאֵל מֵהַבֹּקֶר וְעַד־עֵת מוֹעֵד

וַיָּמָת מִן־הָעָם מִדָּן וְעַד־בְּאֵר שֶׁבַע שִׁבְעִים אֶלֶף אִישׁ:   טז   וַיִּשְׁלַח יָדוֹ

הַמַּלְאָךְ ׀ יְרוּשָׁלַ͏ִם לְשַׁחֲתָהּ וַיִּנָּחֶם יהוה אֶל־הָרָעָה וַיֹּאמֶר לַמַּלְאָךְ

הַמַּשְׁחִית בָּעָם רַב עַתָּה הֶרֶף יָדֶךָ וּמַלְאַךְ יהוה הָיָה עִם־גֹּרֶן °הָאֲוַרְנָה

°הָאֲרַוְנָה ק׳] הַיְבֻסִי: וַיֹּאמֶר דָּוִד אֶל־יהוה בִּרְאֹתוֹ ׀ אֶת־   יז

הַמַּלְאָךְ ׀ הַמַּכֶּה בָעָם וַיֹּאמֶר הִנֵּה אָנֹכִי חָטָאתִי וְאָנֹכִי הֶעֱוֵיתִי וְאֵלֶּה

הַצֹּאן מֶה עָשׂוּ תְּהִי נָא יָדְךָ בִּי וּבְבֵית אָבִי: יח   וַיָּבֹא־גָד אֶל־דָּוִד

בַּיּוֹם הַהוּא וַיֹּאמֶר לוֹ עֲלֵה הָקֵם לַיהוה מִזְבֵּחַ בְּגֹרֶן °ארניה °אֲרַוְנָה ק׳]

הַיְבֻסִי: יט   וַיַּעַל דָּוִד כִּדְבַר־גָּד כַּאֲשֶׁר צִוָּה יהוה: וַיַּשְׁקֵף אֲרַוְנָה וַיַּרְא אֶת־

הַמֶּלֶךְ וְאֶת־עֲבָדָיו עֹבְרִים עָלָיו וַיֵּצֵא אֲרַוְנָה וַיִּשְׁתַּחוּ לַמֶּלֶךְ אַפָּיו אָרְצָה:

---

why Joab tried to convince David not to do it (v. 3). To dispel the notion that salvation is in numbers, the Torah (*Exodus* 30:12-16) commands that a census always be done in such a way that there is another reason for it, e.g., the raising of funds. See *Ralbag*.

24:14. If there were seven years of famine, the people would be dependent on the mercies of the countries where they would wander in search of food. If there were a three-month military defeat, they would be at the mercy of the conquerors. But if there were a plague, God in His mercy would decide whom and how to punish. Also, in the case of war or famine, David himself would be perceived by his people as having an advantage, due to his military powers or wealth.

tribes of Israel, from Dan to Beer-sheba, and count the people, so that I may know the number of the people." ³ *But Joab said to the king, "May HASHEM your God increase the number of the people over and over a hundred times, while the eyes of my lord the king [live to] see [it]; but why should my lord the king desire such a thing?"* ⁴ *But the king's word prevailed over Joab and the officers of the army; so Joab and the officers of the army who were before the king went to count the people, Israel.*

A lengthy
expedition

⁵ *They crossed the Jordan and encamped in Aroer, south of the city that was in the middle of the Valley of Gad, and [then] to Jazer.* ⁶ *They came to Gilead and to the land of Tahtim-hodshi, and they came to Dan-jaan, and went around to Sidon.* ⁷ *They came to the fortress of Tyre and to all the Hivvite and Canaanite cities, and they went to the south of Judah, to Beer-sheba.* ⁸ *They traveled around the entire land, coming back to Jerusalem at the end of nine months and twenty days.* ⁹ *Joab gave the sum of the number of people over to the king: [In] Israel were eight hundred thousand men of war — drawers of the sword — and the men of Judah, five hundred thousand men.*

David
chooses his
punishment

¹⁰ *David's heart smote him after having counted the people, and David said to HASHEM, "I have sinned greatly in what I have done. Now, HASHEM, please re- move the sin of Your servant, for I have acted very foolishly."* ¹¹ *David arose the next morning; and the word of HASHEM had come to the prophet Gad, David's seer, saying,* ¹² *"Go and say to David, 'Thus says HASHEM: I am holding three [things] upon you; choose for yourself one of them and I shall do it to you.'"* ¹³ *So Gad came to David and told him; he said to him, "[Would you rather have] seven years of famine come to your land, or three months of fleeing from your enemy while he pursues you, or three days' pestilence in your land? Now deter- mine and consider what answer I should return to the One Who has sent me."* ¹⁴ *David said to Gad, "I am exceedingly distressed. Let us fall into the hand of HASHEM, for His mercies are abundant; but let me not fall into human hands."* *

Early end to
the pestilence

¹⁵ *So HASHEM sent a pestilence in Israel, from the morning until the set time;* * *there died from the people, from Dan to Beer-sheba, seventy thousand men.* ¹⁶ *When the angel stretched out his hand against Jerusalem to destroy it, HASHEM relented of the evil and told the angel who was destroying among the people, "Enough! Now stay your hand!" The angel of HASHEM was at the threshing floor of Araunah the Jebusite.* *

Araunah's
threshing
floor

¹⁷ *David said to HASHEM when he saw the angel who was striking down the people, "Behold, I have sinned and I have transgressed; but these sheep — what have they done? Let Your hand be against me and my father's family."*

¹⁸ *Gad came to David on that day and said to him, "Go up, erect an altar to HASHEM on the threshing floor of Araunah the Jebusite."* ¹⁹ *So David went up as Gad had said, as HASHEM had commanded.* ²⁰ *Araunah looked out and saw the king and his servants coming across to him, and Araunah went out and prostrated himself to the king, with his face to the ground.*

He wanted to be no better off than his people (*Radak*, et al.).

24:15. *Targum* interprets this to be the time of the burning of the daily offering on the Altar, in mid-morn- ing. *Radak* cites an opinion that it was noontime. Either

way, the three-day time span mentioned by Gad (v. 13) was drastically reduced.

24:16. Araunah's property was on Mount Moriah (*II Chronicles* 3:1), the site of Abraham's intended sacrifice of Isaac (*Genesis* 22:2).

כא וַיֹּ֣אמֶר אֲרַ֔וְנָה מַדּ֥וּעַ בָּ֛א אֲדֹנִֽי־הַמֶּ֖לֶךְ אֶל־עַבְדּ֑וֹ וַיֹּ֨אמֶר דָּוִ֜ד לִקְנ֧וֹת מֵעִמְּךָ֣ אֶת־הַגֹּ֗רֶן לִבְנ֤וֹת מִזְבֵּ֙חַ֙ לַֽיהוָ֔ה וְתֵעָצַ֥ר הַמַּגֵּפָ֖ה מֵעַ֥ל הָעָֽם:
כב וַיֹּ֤אמֶר אֲרַ֙וְנָה֙ אֶל־דָּוִ֔ד יִקַּ֥ח וְיַ֛עַל אֲדֹנִ֥י הַמֶּ֖לֶךְ הַטּ֣וֹב °בעינו [°בְּעֵינָ֑יו ק] רְאֵה֙ הַבָּקָ֣ר לָעֹלָ֔ה וְהַמֹּרִגִּ֛ים וּכְלֵ֥י הַבָּקָ֖ר לָעֵצִֽים:
כג הַכֹּ֗ל נָתַ֛ן אֲרַ֥וְנָה הַמֶּ֖לֶךְ לַמֶּ֑לֶךְ וַיֹּ֤אמֶר אֲרַ֙וְנָה֙ אֶל־הַמֶּ֔לֶךְ יְהוָ֥ה אֱלֹהֶ֖יךָ יִרְצֶֽךָ:
כד וַיֹּ֨אמֶר הַמֶּ֜לֶךְ אֶל־אֲרַ֗וְנָה לֹ֚א כִּֽי־קָנ֤וֹ אֶקְנֶה֙ מֵאֽוֹתְךָ֙ בִּמְחִ֔יר וְלֹ֥א אַֽעֲלֶ֛ה לַיהוָ֥ה אֱלֹהַ֖י עֹל֣וֹת חִנָּ֑ם וַיִּ֩קֶן דָּוִ֨ד אֶת־הַגֹּ֤רֶן וְאֶת־הַבָּקָר֙ בְּכֶ֣סֶף שְׁקָלִ֔ים חֲמִשִּֽׁים:
כה וַיִּ֩בֶן שָׁ֨ם דָּוִ֤ד מִזְבֵּ֙חַ֙ לַֽיהוָ֔ה וַיַּ֥עַל עֹל֖וֹת וּשְׁלָמִ֑ים וַיֵּעָתֵ֤ר יְהוָה֙ לָאָ֔רֶץ וַתֵּעָצַ֥ר הַמַּגֵּפָ֖ה מֵעַ֥ל יִשְׂרָאֵֽל:

24:23. Araunah was the chieftain of the remaining Jebusites of Jerusalem (*Rashi*).
24:24. This was the site of the future Temple.

The parallel verse in *I Chronicles* (21:25) has "six hundred gold shekels." The Talmud explains that David assessed each tribe fifty shekels.

²¹ Araunah asked, "Why has my lord the king come to his servant?" And David replied, "To buy the threshing floor from you in order to build an altar to HASHEM, so that the pestilence may cease from the people." ²² But Araunah said to David, "Let my lord the king take [it] and offer whatever is proper in his eyes. See, the cattle are [available] for elevation-offerings, and the threshing tools and the implements of the cattle are [available] for firewood." ²³ Araunah the king* gave all of it to the king, and Araunah said to the king, "May HASHEM your God accept your [offerings]."

David buys it and builds an altar   ²⁴ But the king told Araunah, "No; I shall purchase it from you for a price, * and I shall not offer up to HASHEM my God free elevation-offerings!" So David bought the threshing floor and the cattle for money — fifty shekels. * ²⁵ David built an altar there to HASHEM, and he offered elevation-offerings and peace-offerings. HASHEM then answered the prayers of the land, and the pestilence ceased from Israel.

Kings מלכים

*T*he first part of the Book of Kings begins in glory and ends in
disgrace; the second begins in turmoil and ends in disaster.
Twelve-year-old Solomon assumes the throne and makes only one
request of God: that he be granted the wisdom to judge the people
of Israel in accordance with the Divine will. Because Solomon asked
for wisdom instead of power, security and wealth, God granted him
wisdom — beyond precedent and imagination — as well as great
wealth and respect. He built the Holy Temple and created a prosperous,
righteous realm. But after his death, the kingdom split. Only Judah and
Benjamin remained loyal to the Davidic dynasty, while the other ten
tribes broke away, under King Jeroboam.

Jeroboam's wickedness became the Book's standard for measuring
his sorry line of successors. Most imitated his evil ways; some even
surpassed it. Although the Kingdom of Judah remained relatively loyal
to God and the Torah — though with frequent lapses — the Kingdom of
the Ten Tribes fell into a downward spiritual spiral.

Over the course of the Book's second part, both competing Jewish
kingdoms decline. Wicked King Ahab of Israel is dead, Moab rebels
against his successors, and King Ahaziah is badly hurt in an accidental
fall — but instead of turning to the prophet Elijah, he asks the god
of Ekron whether he will recover! This was typical of the disgraceful
conduct that brought destruction and exile without a trace.

Judah had brighter moments. There were such kings as Hezekiah and
Josiah, whose righteousness was comparable to that of their ancestors
David and Solomon. But increasingly, there was deterioration, as some
kings tried to institutionalize idolatry. Even the great Hezekiah, of whom
the Sages say that he was worthy to have been the ultimate Messiah,
was succeeded by his son Manasseh, whose wickedness rivaled that of
the worst Samarian kings. Many of the historic events that took place
during the era of Kings are detailed in Jeremiah and Chronicles. Indeed,
the prophecies of such monumental figures as Isaiah, Hosea, Jeremiah,
and Ezekiel, who were active during the period, fill over a hundred
and fifty chapters in the Books of the Later Prophets. Thus, the events of
this Book can be understood best in the context of the prophets whose
messages dominated its spiritual life.

א‑ב וְהַמֶּלֶךְ דָּוִד זָקֵן בָּא בַּיָּמִים וַיְכַסֻּהוּ בַּבְּגָדִים וְלֹא יִחַם לוֹ: וַיֹּאמְרוּ לוֹ עֲבָדָיו יְבַקְשׁוּ לַאדֹנִי הַמֶּלֶךְ נַעֲרָה בְתוּלָה וְעָמְדָה לִפְנֵי הַמֶּלֶךְ וּתְהִי־לוֹ

ג סֹכֶנֶת וְשָׁכְבָה בְחֵיקֶךָ וְחַם לַאדֹנִי הַמֶּלֶךְ: וַיְבַקְשׁוּ נַעֲרָה יָפָה בְּכֹל גְּבוּל

ד יִשְׂרָאֵל וַיִּמְצְאוּ אֶת־אֲבִישַׁג הַשּׁוּנַמִּית וַיָּבִאוּ אֹתָהּ לַמֶּלֶךְ: וְהַנַּעֲרָה יָפָה

ה עַד־מְאֹד וַתְּהִי לַמֶּלֶךְ סֹכֶנֶת וַתְּשָׁרְתֵהוּ וְהַמֶּלֶךְ לֹא יְדָעָהּ: וַאֲדֹנִיָּה בֶן־ חַגִּית מִתְנַשֵּׂא לֵאמֹר אֲנִי אֶמְלֹךְ וַיַּעַשׂ לוֹ רֶכֶב וּפָרָשִׁים וַחֲמִשִּׁים אִישׁ

ו רָצִים לְפָנָיו: וְלֹא־עֲצָבוֹ אָבִיו מִיָּמָיו לֵאמֹר מַדּוּעַ כָּכָה עָשִׂיתָ וְגַם־הוּא

ז טוֹב־תֹּאַר מְאֹד וְאֹתוֹ יָלְדָה אַחֲרֵי אַבְשָׁלוֹם: וַיִּהְיוּ דְבָרָיו עִם יוֹאָב בֶּן־

ח צְרוּיָה וְעִם אֶבְיָתָר הַכֹּהֵן וַיַּעְזְרוּ אַחֲרֵי אֲדֹנִיָּה: וְצָדוֹק הַכֹּהֵן וּבְנָיָהוּ בֶן־ יְהוֹיָדָע וְנָתָן הַנָּבִיא וְשִׁמְעִי וְרֵעִי וְהַגִּבּוֹרִים אֲשֶׁר לְדָוִד לֹא הָיוּ עִם־

ט אֲדֹנִיָּהוּ: וַיִּזְבַּח אֲדֹנִיָּהוּ צֹאן וּבָקָר וּמְרִיא עִם אֶבֶן הַזֹּחֶלֶת אֲשֶׁר־אֵצֶל עֵין רֹגֵל וַיִּקְרָא אֶת־כָּל־אֶחָיו בְּנֵי הַמֶּלֶךְ וּלְכָל־אַנְשֵׁי יְהוּדָה עַבְדֵי

י הַמֶּלֶךְ: וְאֶת־נָתָן הַנָּבִיא וּבְנָיָהוּ וְאֶת־הַגִּבּוֹרִים וְאֶת־שְׁלֹמֹה אָחִיו לֹא

יא קָרָא: וַיֹּאמֶר נָתָן אֶל־בַּת־שֶׁבַע אֵם־שְׁלֹמֹה לֵאמֹר הֲלוֹא שָׁמַעַתְּ כִּי מָלַךְ

יב אֲדֹנִיָּהוּ בֶן־חַגִּית וַאֲדֹנֵינוּ דָוִד לֹא יָדָע: וְעַתָּה לְכִי אִיעָצֵךְ נָא עֵצָה

יג וּמַלְּטִי אֶת־נַפְשֵׁךְ וְאֶת־נֶפֶשׁ בְּנֵךְ שְׁלֹמֹה: לְכִי וּבֹאִי אֶל־הַמֶּלֶךְ דָּוִד וְאָמַרְתְּ אֵלָיו הֲלֹא־אַתָּה אֲדֹנִי הַמֶּלֶךְ נִשְׁבַּעְתָּ לַאֲמָתְךָ לֵאמֹר כִּי־

יד שְׁלֹמֹה בְנֵךְ יִמְלֹךְ אַחֲרַי וְהוּא יֵשֵׁב עַל־כִּסְאִי וּמַדּוּעַ מָלַךְ אֲדֹנִיָּהוּ: הִנֵּה עוֹדָךְ מְדַבֶּרֶת שָׁם עִם־הַמֶּלֶךְ וַאֲנִי אָבוֹא אַחֲרַיִךְ וּמִלֵּאתִי אֶת־דְּבָרָיִךְ:

טו וַתָּבֹא בַת־שֶׁבַע אֶל־הַמֶּלֶךְ הַחַדְרָה וְהַמֶּלֶךְ זָקֵן מְאֹד וַאֲבִישַׁג הַשּׁוּנַמִּית

טז מְשָׁרַת אֶת־הַמֶּלֶךְ: וַתִּקֹּד בַּת־שֶׁבַע וַתִּשְׁתַּחוּ לַמֶּלֶךְ וַיֹּאמֶר הַמֶּלֶךְ מַה־

יז לָךְ: וַתֹּאמֶר לוֹ אֲדֹנִי אַתָּה נִשְׁבַּעְתָּ בַּיהוָה אֱלֹהֶיךָ לַאֲמָתֶךָ כִּי־שְׁלֹמֹה

יח בְנֵךְ יִמְלֹךְ אַחֲרָי וְהוּא יֵשֵׁב עַל־כִּסְאִי: וְעַתָּה הִנֵּה אֲדֹנִיָּה מָלָךְ וְעַתָּה

יט אֲדֹנִי הַמֶּלֶךְ לֹא יָדָעְתָּ: וַיִּזְבַּח שׁוֹר וּמְרִיא־וְצֹאן לָרֹב וַיִּקְרָא לְכָל־בְּנֵי הַמֶּלֶךְ וּלְאֶבְיָתָר הַכֹּהֵן וּלְיֹאָב שַׂר הַצָּבָא וְלִשְׁלֹמֹה עַבְדְּךָ לֹא קָרָא:

כ וְאַתָּה אֲדֹנִי הַמֶּלֶךְ עֵינֵי כָל־יִשְׂרָאֵל עָלֶיךָ לְהַגִּיד לָהֶם מִי יֵשֵׁב עַל־

כא כִּסֵּא אֲדֹנִי־הַמֶּלֶךְ אַחֲרָיו: וְהָיָה כִּשְׁכַב אֲדֹנִי־הַמֶּלֶךְ עִם־אֲבֹתָיו

כב וְהָיִיתִי אֲנִי וּבְנִי שְׁלֹמֹה חַטָּאִים: וְהִנֵּה עוֹדֶנָּה מְדַבֶּרֶת עִם־הַמֶּלֶךְ

כג וְנָתָן הַנָּבִיא בָּא: וַיַּגִּידוּ לַמֶּלֶךְ לֵאמֹר הִנֵּה נָתָן הַנָּבִיא וַיָּבֹא לִפְנֵי

כד הַמֶּלֶךְ וַיִּשְׁתַּחוּ לַמֶּלֶךְ עַל־אַפָּיו אָרְצָה: וַיֹּאמֶר נָתָן אֲדֹנִי הַמֶּלֶךְ

כה אַתָּה אָמַרְתָּ אֲדֹנִיָּהוּ יִמְלֹךְ אַחֲרָי וְהוּא יֵשֵׁב עַל־כִּסְאִי: כִּי וְיָרַד הַיּוֹם

1:5. Adonijah was David's fourth son; Haggith was his mother (*II Samuel* 3:4).

1:6. That is, he was the oldest surviving son of David after his older brothers [Amnon (*II Samuel* 13:32), Chileab (apparently), and Absalom (*II Samuel* 18:15)]

had died. This, together with his attractive appearance, led him to believe that he would be David's successor.

1:7. Joab knew that David would charge his successor to have him executed for his unsanctioned assassinations

1

DAVID'S
LAST DAYS
1:1-2:11

An attendant
for the aged
king

¹ **K**ing David was old, advanced in years. They covered him with garments, but he did not become warm. ² His servants said to him, "Let there be sought for my lord the king a young virgin, who will stand before the king and be his attendant; she will lie in your bosom and it will be warm for my lord the king." ³ They sought a beautiful girl throughout the boundary of Israel, and they found Abishag the Shunammite and brought her to the king. ⁴ The girl was exceedingly beautiful, and she became the king's attendant and she served him, but the king was not intimate with her.

Adonijah
proclaims
himself
crown
prince. . .

⁵ Adonijah son of Haggith * exalted himself, saying, "I shall reign!" He provided himself with chariot and riders, and fifty men to run before him. ⁶ All his days his father had never saddened him [by] saying, "Why have you done this?" Moreover, he was very handsome and [his mother] bore him after Absalom. * ⁷ He discussed his intentions with Joab son of Zeruiah * and Abiathar the Kohen, and they assisted, [following] after Adonijah. ⁸ But Zadok the Kohen, Benaiah son of Jehoiada, Nathan the prophet, Shimei, Rei and David's mighty men were not with Adonijah. ⁹ Adonijah slaughtered sheep, cattle, and fatted bull at the Zoheleth Stone which is near En-rogel, and he invited all his brothers, the sons of the king, and all the men of Judah, the king's servants. ¹⁰ But Nathan the prophet, Benaiah, the mighty men and his brother Solomon he did not invite.

. . . but
excludes
Solomon's
supporters

Nathan's
plan

¹¹ Nathan spoke to Bath-sheba, Solomon's mother, saying, "Have you not heard that Adonijah son of Haggith has become king? But our lord David does not know. ¹² So now go, I will give you counsel now, so that you may save your soul and the soul of your son Solomon. * ¹³ Go and come to King David and say to him, 'Have you not, my lord the king, sworn to your maidservant saying: Your son Solomon will reign after me and he will sit on my throne? Why has Adonijah become king?' ¹⁴ While you are still speaking there with the king, I will come in after you and supplement your words."

¹⁵ So Bath-sheba came to the king, into the chamber; the king was very old, and Abishag the Shunammite was serving the king. ¹⁶ Bath-sheba bowed and prostrated herself to the king, and the king said, "What concerns you?"

Bath-sheba
pleads with
David

¹⁷ She said to him, "My lord, you swore to your maidservant by HASHEM, your God, 'Only Solomon, your son, will reign after me, and he will sit on my throne.' ¹⁸ But now, behold, Adonijah has become king and now, my lord the king, you did not know! ¹⁹ He has slaughtered ox, fatted bull, and sheep in abundance, and has invited all the king's sons, as well as Abiathar the Kohen and Joab, the commander of the army; but he has not invited your servant Solomon. ²⁰ And you, my lord the king, the eyes of all Israel are upon you, to tell them who will sit on the throne of my lord the king after him. ²¹ For it will happen that when my lord the king lies with his forefathers, I and my son Solomon will be [deemed] sinners."

²² Behold she was still speaking with the king, when Nathan the prophet arrived. ²³ They told the king, saying, "Nathan the prophet is here."

Nathan
supports
Bath-sheba's
claim

He came before the king and prostrated himself to the king with his face to the ground. ²⁴ Nathan said, "My lord the king, have you said, 'Adonijah will reign after me and he will sit on my throne'? ²⁵ For he has gone down today

---

(see 2:5-6) and hoped to thwart this plan by putting his own man on the throne (*Rashi*).
1:12. For Adonijah might eliminate Solomon and his

mother to prevent a challenge to his authority. At the very least, they would suffer the humiliation of becoming subjects to Adonijah (*Radak*).

וַיִּזְבַּ֞ח שׁ֣וֹר וּמְרִיא־וְצֹאן֮ לָרֹב֒ וַיִּקְרָא֙ לְכָל־בְּנֵ֣י הַמֶּ֔לֶךְ וּלְשָׂרֵ֖י הַצָּבָ֑א
וּלְאֶבְיָתָ֖ר הַכֹּהֵ֑ן וְהִנָּ֣ם אֹכְלִ֗ים וְשֹׁתִ֛ים לְפָנָ֖יו וַיֹּ֣אמְר֔וּ יְחִ֖י הַמֶּ֥לֶךְ אֲדֹנִיָּֽהוּ:

כו וְלִ֣י אֲנִֽי־עַ֠בְדֶּ֠ךָ וּלְצָדֹ֨ק הַכֹּהֵ֜ן וְלִבְנָיָ֣הוּ בֶן־יְהוֹיָדָ֗ע וְלִשְׁלֹמֹ֛ה עַבְדְּךָ֖ לֹ֥א
כז קָרָ֑א: אִ֗ם מֵאֵת֙ אֲדֹנִ֣י הַמֶּ֔לֶךְ נִֽהְיָ֖ה הַדָּבָ֣ר הַזֶּ֑ה וְלֹ֤א הוֹדַ֙עְתָּ֙ אֶֽת־°עבדיך
[°עַבְדְּךָ֔ ק] מִ֚י יֵשֵׁ֔ב עַל־כִּסֵּ֥א אֲדֹֽנִי־הַמֶּ֖לֶךְ אַחֲרָֽיו: {פ}

כח וַיַּ֨עַן הַמֶּ֤לֶךְ דָּוִד֙
וַיֹּ֔אמֶר קִרְאוּ־לִ֖י לְבַת־שָׁ֑בַע וַתָּבֹא֙ לִפְנֵ֣י הַמֶּ֔לֶךְ וַֽתַּעֲמֹ֖ד לִפְנֵ֥י הַמֶּֽלֶךְ:
כט-ל וַיִּשָּׁבַ֥ע הַמֶּ֖לֶךְ וַיֹּאמַ֑ר חַי־יְהֹוָ֕ה אֲשֶׁר־פָּדָ֥ה אֶת־נַפְשִׁ֖י מִכָּל־צָרָֽה: כִּ֡י
כַּאֲשֶׁר֩ נִשְׁבַּ֨עְתִּי לָ֜ךְ בַּיהֹוָ֣ה אֱלֹהֵ֣י יִשְׂרָאֵ֮ל לֵאמֹר֒ כִּֽי־שְׁלֹמֹ֤ה בְנֵךְ֙
לא יִמְלֹ֣ךְ אַחֲרַ֔י וְה֛וּא יֵשֵׁ֥ב עַל־כִּסְאִ֖י תַּחְתָּ֑י כִּ֛י כֵּ֥ן אֶעֱשֶׂ֖ה הַיּ֥וֹם הַזֶּֽה: וַתִּקֹּ֨ד
בַּת־שֶׁ֤בַע אַפַּ֙יִם֙ אֶ֔רֶץ וַתִּשְׁתַּ֖חוּ לַמֶּ֑לֶךְ וַתֹּ֕אמֶר יְחִ֛י אֲדֹנִ֥י הַמֶּ֥לֶךְ דָּוִ֖ד
לב לְעֹלָֽם: ◀   וַיֹּ֣אמֶר | הַמֶּ֣לֶךְ דָּוִ֗ד קִרְאוּ־לִ֤י לְצָד֙וֹק֙ הַכֹּהֵ֔ן

לג וּלְנָתָן֙ הַנָּבִ֔יא וְלִבְנָיָ֖הוּ בֶּן־יְהֽוֹיָדָ֑ע וַיָּבֹ֖אוּ לִפְנֵ֣י הַמֶּֽלֶךְ: וַיֹּ֨אמֶר הַמֶּ֜לֶךְ לָהֶ֗ם
קְח֤וּ עִמָּכֶם֙ אֶת־עַבְדֵ֣י אֲדֹֽנֵיכֶ֔ם וְהִרְכַּבְתֶּ֣ם אֶת־שְׁלֹמֹ֣ה בְנִ֔י עַל־הַפִּרְדָּ֖ה
לד אֲשֶׁר־לִ֑י וְהֽוֹרַדְתֶּ֥ם אֹת֖וֹ °אֶל־[°עַל־ ק] גִּחֽוֹן: וּמָשַׁ֣ח אֹת֣וֹ שָׁ֠ם צָד֨וֹק
הַכֹּהֵ֜ן וְנָתָ֤ן הַנָּבִיא֙ לְמֶ֣לֶךְ עַל־יִשְׂרָאֵ֔ל וּתְקַעְתֶּם֙ בַּשּׁוֹפָ֔ר וַאֲמַרְתֶּ֕ם יְחִ֖י
לה הַמֶּ֥לֶךְ שְׁלֹמֹֽה: וַעֲלִיתֶ֣ם אַחֲרָ֗יו וּבָא֙ וְיָשַׁ֣ב עַל־כִּסְאִ֔י וְה֥וּא יִמְלֹ֖ךְ תַּחְתָּ֑י
לו וְאֹת֤וֹ צִוִּ֙יתִי֙ לִֽהְי֣וֹת נָגִ֔יד עַל־יִשְׂרָאֵ֖ל וְעַל־יְהוּדָֽה: וַיַּ֨עַן בְּנָיָ֧הוּ בֶן־יְהֽוֹיָדָ֛ע
אֶת־הַמֶּ֖לֶךְ וַיֹּ֣אמֶר | אָמֵ֑ן כֵּ֚ן יֹאמַ֣ר יְהֹוָ֔ה אֱלֹהֵ֖י אֲדֹנִ֥י הַמֶּֽלֶךְ: כַּאֲשֶׁ֨ר הָיָ֤ה
לז יְהֹוָה֙ עִם־אֲדֹנִ֣י הַמֶּ֔לֶךְ כֵּ֖ן °יהי [°יִֽהְיֶ֣ה ק] עִם־שְׁלֹמֹ֑ה [°וִיהִ֣יֶ֥ה ק] וִֽיגַדֵּל֙ אֶת־כִּסְא֔וֹ
לח מִ֨כִּסֵּ֔א אֲדֹנִ֥י הַמֶּ֖לֶךְ דָּוִֽד: וַיֵּ֣רֶד צָד֣וֹק הַ֠כֹּהֵ֠ן וְנָתָ֨ן הַנָּבִ֜יא וּבְנָיָ֣הוּ בֶן־
יְהֽוֹיָדָ֗ע וְהַכְּרֵתִי֙ וְהַפְּלֵתִ֔י וַיַּרְכִּ֙בוּ֙ אֶת־שְׁלֹמֹ֔ה עַל־פִּרְדַּ֖ת הַמֶּ֣לֶךְ דָּוִ֑ד
לט וַיֹּלִ֥כוּ אֹת֖וֹ עַל־גִּחֽוֹן: וַיִּקַּח֩ צָד֨וֹק הַכֹּהֵ֜ן אֶת־קֶ֤רֶן הַשֶּׁ֙מֶן֙ מִן־הָאֹ֔הֶל
וַיִּמְשַׁ֖ח אֶת־שְׁלֹמֹ֑ה וַֽיִּתְקְעוּ֙ בַּשּׁוֹפָ֔ר וַיֹּֽאמְרוּ֙ כָּל־הָעָ֔ם יְחִ֖י הַמֶּ֥לֶךְ
מ שְׁלֹמֹֽה: וַיַּעֲל֤וּ כָל־הָעָם֙ אַחֲרָ֔יו וְהָעָם֙ מְחַלְּלִ֣ים בַּחֲלִלִ֔ים וּשְׂמֵחִ֖ים
מא שִׂמְחָ֣ה גְדוֹלָ֑ה וַתִּבָּקַ֥ע הָאָ֖רֶץ בְּקוֹלָֽם: וַיִּשְׁמַ֣ע אֲדֹנִיָּ֗הוּ וְכָל־הַקְּרֻאִים֙
אֲשֶׁ֣ר אִתּ֔וֹ וְהֵ֖ם כִּלּ֣וּ לֶאֱכֹ֑ל וַיִּשְׁמַ֤ע יוֹאָב֙ אֶת־ק֣וֹל הַשּׁוֹפָ֔ר וַיֹּ֕אמֶר מַדּ֥וּעַ
מב קֽוֹל־הַקִּרְיָ֖ה הוֹמָֽה: עוֹדֶ֣נּוּ מְדַבֵּ֔ר וְהִנֵּ֛ה יוֹנָתָ֥ן בֶּן־אֶבְיָתָ֥ר הַכֹּהֵ֖ן בָּ֑א וַיֹּ֤אמֶר
מג אֲדֹנִיָּ֙הוּ֙ בֹּ֔א כִּ֣י אִ֥ישׁ חַ֛יִל אַ֖תָּה וְט֥וֹב תְּבַשֵּֽׂר: וַיַּ֙עַן֙ יֽוֹנָתָ֔ן וַיֹּ֖אמֶר לַאֲדֹנִיָּ֑הוּ
מד אֲבָ֕ל אֲדֹנֵ֥ינוּ הַמֶּֽלֶךְ־דָּוִ֖ד הִמְלִ֥יךְ אֶת־שְׁלֹמֹֽה: וַיִּשְׁלַ֣ח אִתּֽוֹ־הַ֠מֶּ֠לֶךְ אֶת־
צָד֨וֹק הַכֹּהֵ֜ן וְאֶת־נָתָ֣ן הַנָּבִ֗יא וּבְנָיָ֙הוּ֙ בֶּן־יְה֣וֹיָדָ֔ע וְהַכְּרֵתִ֖י וְהַפְּלֵתִ֑י וַיַּרְכִּ֣בוּ
מה אֹת֔וֹ עַ֖ל פִּרְדַּ֥ת הַמֶּֽלֶךְ: וַיִּמְשְׁח֣וּ אֹת֡וֹ צָד֣וֹק הַכֹּהֵ֣ן וְנָתָן֩ הַנָּבִ֨יא לְמֶ֜לֶךְ
מו בְּגִח֗וֹן וַיַּעֲל֤וּ מִשָּׁם֙ שְׂמֵחִ֔ים וַתֵּהֹ֖ם הַקִּרְיָ֑ה ה֚וּא הַקּ֣וֹל אֲשֶׁ֣ר שְׁמַעְתֶּ֑ם: וְגַ֛ם

1:28. Apparently Bath-sheba had stepped away when the prophet came to speak with the King (*Radak*).
1:37. This wish is an illustration of the dictum that a father is not jealous if his son surpasses him. To wish that Solomon become greater than David was not disrespectful; it was an expression of David's own hope (*Ralbag*).

and slaughtered ox, fatted bull, and sheep in abundance, and he has invited all the king's sons, the generals of the army and Abiathar the Kohen; and behold, they are eating and drinking before him, and they have said, 'Long live King Adonijah!' [26] But me — I, your servant — Zadok the Kohen, Benaiah son of Jehoiada, and your servant Solomon he did not invite. [27] Can it be that this matter has come from my lord the king, and you have not informed your servant who will sit on the throne of my lord the king after him?"

David affirms his pledge . . . [28] Then King David answered and said, "Summon Bath-sheba to me."* She came before the king and stood before the king. [29] The king swore and said, "As HASHEM lives, Who has redeemed my life from every trouble, [30] [I swear] that as I have sworn to you by HASHEM, the God of Israel, saying, 'Solomon your son will reign after me and he will sit on my throne in my place,' so shall I fulfill it this very day."

[31] Bath-sheba bowed down to the ground and prostrated herself to the king, and she said, "May my lord King David live forever!"

. . . and commands that it be executed [32] King David then said, "Summon Zadok the Kohen, Nathan the prophet, and Benaiah son of Jehoiada to me"; and they came before the king. [33] The king said to them, "Take with you your master's servants and mount my son Solomon upon my mule and take him down to Gihon. [34] There Zadok the Kohen and Nathan the prophet shall anoint him as king over Israel; sound the shofar and proclaim, '[Long] live King Solomon!' [35] Then come back up after him, and let him come and sit upon my throne, and he shall reign in my place, for it is he whom I have commanded to become ruler over Israel and Judah."

[36] Benaiah son of Jehoiada then answered the king, saying, "Amen! And so may HASHEM, God of my lord the king, say! [37] Just as HASHEM was with my lord the king, so may He be with Solomon, and may He make his throne even greater than the throne of my lord King David!"*

Solomon is proclaimed the next king (See Appendix A, timeline 4) [38] So Zadok the Kohen and Nathan the prophet and Benaiah son of Jehoiada and the archers and slingers* went down and mounted Solomon upon King David's mule, and led him to Gihon. [39] Zadok the Kohen had taken the horn of oil from the Tent,* and he anointed Solomon; they sounded the shofar, and all the people proclaimed, "[Long] live King Solomon!" [40] All the people then ascended after him, and the people were playing flutes and rejoicing with great joy; the ground [virtually] burst from their noise.

Adonijah hears the news . . . [41] Adonijah and all the guests who were with him heard this just when they had finished eating. Joab heard the sound of the shofar, and said, "Why is the sound of the city [so] turbulent?" [42] He was still speaking, when Jonathan son of Abiathar the Kohen came.

Adonijah said, "Come, for you are a man of accomplishment and you will bring good tidings!"

[43] Jonathan answered and said to Adonijah, "To the contrary, our lord King David has made Solomon king! [44] The king sent with him Zadok the Kohen, Nathan the prophet, Benaiah son of Jehoiada, and the archers and slingers, and they mounted him upon the king's mule. [45] Zadok the Kohen and Nathan the prophet anointed him as king at Gihon. They ascended from there rejoicing, and the city became turbulent; that is the noise that you heard. [46] Furthermore,

---

1:38. See note to *II Samuel* 8:18.
1:39. This refers either to the Tent that David had set up

to house the Ark [*II Samuel* 6:17] (*Rashi*), or to the national Tabernacle in Gibeon (*Radak*).

מז יָשַׁב שְׁלֹמֹה עַל כִּסֵּא הַמְּלוּכָה: וְגַם־בָּאוּ עַבְדֵי הַמֶּלֶךְ לְבָרֵךְ אֶת־אֲדֹנֵינוּ הַמֶּלֶךְ דָּוִד לֵאמֹר יֵיטֵב °אֱלֹהֶיךָ [°אֱלֹהִים ק] אֶת־שֵׁם שְׁלֹמֹה מִשְּׁמֶךָ

מח וִיגַדֵּל אֶת־כִּסְאוֹ מִכִּסְאֶךָ וַיִּשְׁתַּחוּ הַמֶּלֶךְ עַל־הַמִּשְׁכָּב: וְגַם־כָּכָה אָמַר הַמֶּלֶךְ בָּרוּךְ יְהוָה אֱלֹהֵי יִשְׂרָאֵל אֲשֶׁר נָתַן הַיּוֹם יֹשֵׁב עַל־כִּסְאִי וְעֵינַי רֹאוֹת:

מט וַיֶּחֶרְדוּ וַיָּקֻמוּ כָּל־הַקְּרֻאִים אֲשֶׁר לַאֲדֹנִיָּהוּ וַיֵּלְכוּ אִישׁ לְדַרְכּוֹ:

נ-נא וַאֲדֹנִיָּהוּ יָרֵא מִפְּנֵי שְׁלֹמֹה וַיָּקָם וַיֵּלֶךְ וַיַּחֲזֵק בְּקַרְנוֹת הַמִּזְבֵּחַ: וַיֻּגַּד לִשְׁלֹמֹה לֵאמֹר הִנֵּה אֲדֹנִיָּהוּ יָרֵא אֶת־הַמֶּלֶךְ שְׁלֹמֹה וְהִנֵּה אָחַז בְּקַרְנוֹת הַמִּזְבֵּחַ לֵאמֹר יִשָּׁבַע־לִי כַיּוֹם הַמֶּלֶךְ שְׁלֹמֹה אִם־יָמִית אֶת־עַבְדּוֹ בֶּחָרֶב:

נב וַיֹּאמֶר שְׁלֹמֹה אִם יִהְיֶה לְבֶן־חַיִל לֹא־יִפֹּל מִשַּׂעֲרָתוֹ אָרְצָה וְאִם־רָעָה

נג תִמָּצֵא־בוֹ וָמֵת: וַיִּשְׁלַח הַמֶּלֶךְ שְׁלֹמֹה וַיֹּרִדֻהוּ מֵעַל הַמִּזְבֵּחַ וַיָּבֹא וַיִּשְׁתַּחוּ

ב

א לַמֶּלֶךְ שְׁלֹמֹה וַיֹּאמֶר־לוֹ שְׁלֹמֹה לֵךְ לְבֵיתֶךָ: ◀וַיִּקְרְבוּ יְמֵי־

HAFTARAS VAYECHI 2:1-12

ב דָוִד לָמוּת וַיְצַו אֶת־שְׁלֹמֹה בְנוֹ לֵאמֹר: אָנֹכִי הֹלֵךְ בְּדֶרֶךְ כָּל־הָאָרֶץ

ג וְחָזַקְתָּ וְהָיִיתָ לְאִישׁ: וְשָׁמַרְתָּ אֶת־מִשְׁמֶרֶת ׀ יְהוָה אֱלֹהֶיךָ לָלֶכֶת בִּדְרָכָיו לִשְׁמֹר חֻקֹּתָיו מִצְוֹתָיו וּמִשְׁפָּטָיו וְעֵדְוֹתָיו כַּכָּתוּב בְּתוֹרַת מֹשֶׁה לְמַעַן

ד תַּשְׂכִּיל אֵת כָּל־אֲשֶׁר תַּעֲשֶׂה וְאֵת כָּל־אֲשֶׁר תִּפְנֶה שָׁם: לְמַעַן יָקִים יְהוָה אֶת־דְּבָרוֹ אֲשֶׁר דִּבֶּר עָלַי לֵאמֹר אִם־יִשְׁמְרוּ בָנֶיךָ אֶת־דַּרְכָּם לָלֶכֶת לְפָנַי בֶּאֱמֶת בְּכָל־לְבָבָם וּבְכָל־נַפְשָׁם לֵאמֹר לֹא־יִכָּרֵת לְךָ אִישׁ מֵעַל כִּסֵּא

ה יִשְׂרָאֵל: וְגַם אַתָּה יָדַעְתָּ אֵת אֲשֶׁר־עָשָׂה לִי יוֹאָב בֶּן־צְרוּיָה אֲשֶׁר עָשָׂה לִשְׁנֵי־שָׂרֵי צִבְאוֹת יִשְׂרָאֵל לְאַבְנֵר בֶּן־נֵר וְלַעֲמָשָׂא בֶן־יֶתֶר וַיַּהַרְגֵם וַיָּשֶׂם דְּמֵי־מִלְחָמָה בְּשָׁלֹם וַיִּתֵּן דְּמֵי מִלְחָמָה בַּחֲגֹרָתוֹ אֲשֶׁר בְּמָתְנָיו

ו וּבְנַעֲלוֹ אֲשֶׁר בְּרַגְלָיו: וְעָשִׂיתָ כְּחָכְמָתֶךָ וְלֹא־תוֹרֵד שֵׂיבָתוֹ בְּשָׁלֹם

ז שְׁאֹל: וְלִבְנֵי בַרְזִלַּי הַגִּלְעָדִי תַּעֲשֶׂה־חֶסֶד וְהָיוּ בְּאֹכְלֵי

ח שֻׁלְחָנֶךָ כִּי־כֵן קָרְבוּ אֵלַי בְּבָרְחִי מִפְּנֵי אַבְשָׁלוֹם אָחִיךָ: וְהִנֵּה עִמְּךָ שִׁמְעִי בֶן־גֵּרָא בֶן־הַיְמִינִי מִבַּחֻרִים וְהוּא קִלְלַנִי קְלָלָה נִמְרֶצֶת בְּיוֹם לֶכְתִּי מַחֲנָיִם וְהוּא־יָרַד לִקְרָאתִי הַיַּרְדֵּן וָאֶשָּׁבַע לוֹ בַיהוָה לֵאמֹר אִם־אֲמִיתְךָ

ט בֶּחָרֶב: וְעַתָּה אַל־תְּנַקֵּהוּ כִּי אִישׁ חָכָם אָתָּה וְיָדַעְתָּ אֵת אֲשֶׁר תַּעֲשֶׂה־

י לּוֹ וְהוֹרַדְתָּ אֶת־שֵׂיבָתוֹ בְּדָם שְׁאוֹל: וַיִּשְׁכַּב דָּוִד עִם־אֲבֹתָיו וַיִּקָּבֵר בְּעִיר

יא דָּוִד: וְהַיָּמִים אֲשֶׁר מָלַךְ דָּוִד עַל־יִשְׂרָאֵל אַרְבָּעִים שָׁנָה בְּחֶבְרוֹן מָלַךְ שֶׁבַע שָׁנִים וּבִירוּשָׁלַם מָלַךְ שְׁלֹשִׁים וְשָׁלֹשׁ שָׁנִים:

1:49. The word of David was all that was needed. Having heard that David had arranged for Solomon to be anointed, Adonijah's supporters deserted him; and he thought only of saving himself, lest Solomon judge him to be a rebel.

1:50. This may have been that national Altar at Gibeon (*Rashi*) or a private altar in Jerusalem (*Radak*). Adonijah grasped the square protrusions, called "horns" (*Exodus* 27:2) at the Altar's four corners, for he was confident

that Solomon would not do violence at the site of the Altar.

2:5. Joab killed them while feigning peaceful friendliness with them (see *II Samuel* 3:27 and 20:9-10). He killed Amasa by fastening his sword onto his belt in an unusual manner (see *II Samuel* 20:8), and Amasa fell dead at Joab's feet (*Abarbanel*), so Joab is described as having placed blood on his belt and his shoes. David was too dependent on Joab's support to punish him for his

Solomon has sat upon the royal throne, [47] and the kings's servants have come to bless our lord King David, saying, 'May God grant Solomon a reputation even better than your own reputation, and may He make his throne even greater than your throne,' and the king prostrated himself on his bed. [48] Furthermore, the king said thus, 'Blessed is HASHEM, God of Israel, Who has granted today someone who sits upon my throne and my eyes can see it.' "

. . . his supporters disperse and he pleads for his life [49] All of Adonijah's guests were alarmed and arose; each man went on his way. * [50] Adonijah was afraid of Solomon, so he arose and went and took hold of the horns of the Altar. * [51] Solomon was told, saying, "Behold, Adonijah is afraid of King Solomon, and behold, he has taken hold of the horns of the Altar, saying, 'Let King Solomon swear to me this very day that he will not execute his servant by the sword!' "

[52] Solomon said, "If he will be a loyal man, not a single hair of his will fall to the ground, but if any evil will be found in him, he shall die." [53] King Solomon sent messengers and they took him down from the Altar. He came and prostrated himself before King Solomon, and Solomon said to him, "You may go to your home."

2

[1] $\mathbf{D}$avid's days drew near to die, and he instructed his son Solomon, saying; *David's charge to Solomon: Be loyal to the Torah* [2] "I am going the way of all the earth; be strong and become a man. [3] Safeguard the charge of HASHEM, your God, to walk in His ways, to observe His decrees, commandments, ordinances and testimonies, as written in the Torah of Moses, so that you will succeed in all that you do and wherever you turn; [4] so that HASHEM will uphold His word that He spoke regarding me, saying, 'If your children will safeguard their way, to walk before Me sincerely, with all their heart and with all their soul,' saying, 'no man of yours will ever be cut off from upon the throne of Israel.'

Pass judgment on Joab [5] "Furthermore, you know what Joab son of Zeruiah did to me, what he did to two commanders of the armies of Israel — to Abner son of Ner and to Amasa son of Jether — whom he killed, shedding blood of war in peacetime, and placing the blood of war in the girdle that is on his loins and on his shoes that are on his feet. * [6] You shall act according to your wisdom, and do not allow his white hair to go down to the grave in peace.

Gratitude to Barzillai [7] "Towards the children of Barzillai the Gileadite act with kindness, and they shall be among those who eat at your table, for in this way * they befriended me when I fled from Absalom your brother.

Shimei's guilt [8] "Behold, with you is Shimei son of Gera, * the Benjamite from Bahurim. He cursed me with a powerful curse on the day I went to Mahanaim; but he came down to meet me at the Jordan, and I swore to him by HASHEM, saying, 'I will not put you to death by the sword.' [9] But now, you shall not hold him guiltless, for you are a wise man, and you will know what you are to do to him; and you *David's death* shall bring his white hair to the grave in blood." [10] David lay with his forefathers and was buried in the City of David.

(See Appendix A, timeline 4) [11] The days that David reigned over Israel were forty years; in Hebron he reigned for seven years and in Jerusalem he reigned for thirty-three years.

---

crimes, but he urged Solomon to take appropriate measures against him.

2:7. Barzillai's family gave me food and provisions (see *II*

Samuel 17:27-29; 19:33); you should do likewise for them.

2:8. (See *II Samuel* 16:5-13.)

יב-יג ◀ וּשְׁלֹמֹה יָשַׁב עַל־כִּסֵּא דָּוִד אָבִיו וַתִּכֹּן מַלְכֻתוֹ מְאֹד: וַיָּבֹא

אֲדֹנִיָּהוּ בֶן־חַגִּית אֶל־בַּת־שֶׁבַע אֵם־שְׁלֹמֹה וַתֹּאמֶר הֲשָׁלוֹם בֹּאֶךָ וַיֹּאמֶר

יד-טו שָׁלוֹם: וַיֹּאמֶר דָּבָר לִי אֵלָיִךְ וַתֹּאמֶר דַּבֵּר: וַיֹּאמֶר אַתְּ יָדַעַתְּ כִּי־לִי הָיְתָה

הַמְּלוּכָה וְעָלַי שָׂמוּ כָל־יִשְׂרָאֵל פְּנֵיהֶם לִמְלֹךְ וַתִּסֹּב הַמְּלוּכָה וַתְּהִי

טז לְאָחִי כִּי מֵיהוָה הָיְתָה לּוֹ:   וְעַתָּה שְׁאֵלָה אַחַת אָנֹכִי שֹׁאֵל מֵאִתָּךְ אַל־

יז תָּשִׁבִי אֶת־פָּנָי וַתֹּאמֶר אֵלָיו דַּבֵּר: וַיֹּאמֶר אִמְרִי־נָא לִשְׁלֹמֹה הַמֶּלֶךְ כִּי

יח לֹא־יָשִׁיב אֶת־פָּנָיִךְ וְיִתֶּן־לִי אֶת־אֲבִישַׁג הַשּׁוּנַמִּית לְאִשָּׁה: וַתֹּאמֶר בַּת־

יט שֶׁבַע טוֹב אָנֹכִי אֲדַבֵּר עָלֶיךָ אֶל־הַמֶּלֶךְ:   וַתָּבֹא בַת־שֶׁבַע אֶל־הַמֶּלֶךְ

שְׁלֹמֹה לְדַבֶּר־לוֹ עַל־אֲדֹנִיָּהוּ וַיָּקָם הַמֶּלֶךְ לִקְרָאתָהּ וַיִּשְׁתַּחוּ לָהּ וַיֵּשֶׁב

כ עַל־כִּסְאוֹ וַיָּשֶׂם כִּסֵּא לְאֵם הַמֶּלֶךְ וַתֵּשֶׁב לִימִינוֹ:   וַתֹּאמֶר שְׁאֵלָה אַחַת

קְטַנָּה אָנֹכִי שֹׁאֶלֶת מֵאִתָּךְ אַל־תָּשֶׁב אֶת־פָּנָי וַיֹּאמֶר־לָהּ הַמֶּלֶךְ שַׁאֲלִי

כא אִמִּי כִּי לֹא־אָשִׁיב אֶת־פָּנָיִךְ:   וַתֹּאמֶר יֻתַּן אֶת־אֲבִישַׁג הַשֻּׁנַמִּית לַאֲדֹנִיָּהוּ

כב אָחִיךָ לְאִשָּׁה: וַיַּעַן הַמֶּלֶךְ שְׁלֹמֹה וַיֹּאמֶר לְאִמּוֹ וְלָמָה אַתְּ שֹׁאֶלֶת אֶת־

אֲבִישַׁג הַשֻּׁנַמִּית לַאֲדֹנִיָּהוּ וְשַׁאֲלִי־לוֹ אֶת־הַמְּלוּכָה כִּי הוּא אָחִי הַגָּדוֹל

כג מִמֶּנִּי וְלוֹ וּלְאֶבְיָתָר הַכֹּהֵן וּלְיוֹאָב בֶּן־צְרוּיָה: וַיִּשָּׁבַע

הַמֶּלֶךְ שְׁלֹמֹה בַּיהוָה לֵאמֹר כֹּה יַעֲשֶׂה־לִּי אֱלֹהִים וְכֹה יוֹסִיף כִּי בְנַפְשׁוֹ

כד דִּבֶּר אֲדֹנִיָּהוּ אֶת־הַדָּבָר הַזֶּה: וְעַתָּה חַי־יְהוָה אֲשֶׁר הֱכִינַנִי °וַיּוֹשִׁיבִינִי

[וַיּוֹשִׁיבַנִי ק] עַל־כִּסֵּא דָּוִד אָבִי וַאֲשֶׁר עָשָׂה־לִי בַּיִת כַּאֲשֶׁר דִּבֵּר כִּי

כה הַיּוֹם יוּמַת אֲדֹנִיָּהוּ:   וַיִּשְׁלַח הַמֶּלֶךְ שְׁלֹמֹה בְּיַד בְּנָיָהוּ בֶן־יְהוֹיָדָע וַיִּפְגַּע־

כו בּוֹ וַיָּמֹת: וּלְאֶבְיָתָר הַכֹּהֵן אָמַר הַמֶּלֶךְ עֲנָתֹת לֵךְ עַל־שָׂדֶיךָ

כִּי אִישׁ מָוֶת אָתָּה וּבַיּוֹם הַזֶּה לֹא אֲמִיתֶךָ כִּי־נָשָׂאתָ אֶת־אֲרוֹן אֲדֹנָי יְהוִֹה

כז לִפְנֵי דָּוִד אָבִי וְכִי הִתְעַנִּיתָ בְּכֹל אֲשֶׁר־הִתְעַנָּה אָבִי: וַיְגָרֶשׁ שְׁלֹמֹה אֶת־

אֶבְיָתָר מִהְיוֹת כֹּהֵן לַיהוָה לְמַלֵּא אֶת־דְּבַר יהוה אֲשֶׁר דִּבֶּר עַל־בֵּית עֵלִי

כח בְּשִׁלֹה: וְהַשְּׁמֻעָה בָּאָה עַד־יוֹאָב כִּי יוֹאָב נָטָה אַחֲרֵי אֲדֹנִיָּה

וְאַחֲרֵי אַבְשָׁלוֹם לֹא נָטָה וַיָּנָס יוֹאָב אֶל־אֹהֶל יהוה וַיַּחֲזֵק בְּקַרְנוֹת

כט הַמִּזְבֵּחַ:   וַיֻּגַּד לַמֶּלֶךְ שְׁלֹמֹה כִּי נָס יוֹאָב אֶל־אֹהֶל יהוה וְהִנֵּה אֵצֶל

ל הַמִּזְבֵּחַ וַיִּשְׁלַח שְׁלֹמֹה אֶת־בְּנָיָהוּ בֶן־יְהוֹיָדָע לֵאמֹר לֵךְ פְּגַע־בּוֹ:   וַיָּבֹא

בְנָיָהוּ אֶל־אֹהֶל יהוה וַיֹּאמֶר אֵלָיו כֹּה־אָמַר הַמֶּלֶךְ צֵא וַיֹּאמֶר לֹא כִי

פֹה אָמוּת וַיָּשֶׁב בְּנָיָהוּ אֶת־הַמֶּלֶךְ דָּבָר לֵאמֹר כֹּה־דִבֶּר יוֹאָב וְכֹה עָנָנִי:

2:22. Solomon understood that Adonijah, with the help of Abiathar and Joab, was still conspiring to seize the throne. His marrying Abishag, who had been David's companion, would lay the groundwork for another attempt (*Rashi*). Therefore, Solomon exercised the royal prerogative to execute those who rebel against the crown.

2:23. ". . . If I do not carry out the following oath." This is a common expression in the Bible.

2:26. Abiathar was guilty of treason, for having supported Adonijah against David's will, but because of his priestly service and his loyalty to David when he was hiding from Saul (*I Samuel* Ch. 23), Solomon limited his punishment to banishment from Jerusalem and demotion from the High Priesthood (see v. 35 and 4:4).

2:27. "You will see a rival Kohen in My dwelling place, etc." (*I Samuel* 2:31-36).

2:28. The fact that Joab had not joined Absalom's well-organized rebellion made his support of the upstart

SOLOMON'S
REIGN
2:12-11:43

THE EARLY
YEARS
2:13-5:14

Adonijah's
request
of Bath-
sheba . . .

. . . which
Solomon
recognizes as
insurrection

Solomon
dismisses
Abiathar

Joab
flees for
his life . . .

¹² Solomon sat on the throne of his father David, and his kingship was firmly established.

¹³ Adonijah son of Haggith came to Bath-sheba, Solomon's mother. She asked, "Do you come in peace?"

He replied, "[I come in] peace." ¹⁴ He said, "I have something to say to you." She said, "Speak."

¹⁵ He said, "You know that the kingship was mine, and that all of Israel looked to me to reign, but the kingship was diverted [from me] and became my brother's, for it was his from HASHEM. ¹⁶ Now, I have one request to make of you; do not turn me away."

She said to him, "Speak."

¹⁷ He said, "Please speak to King Solomon — for he will not turn you away — that he give me Abishag the Shunammite as a wife."

¹⁸ Bath-sheba said, "Very well. I shall speak to the king on your behalf."

¹⁹ Bath-sheba came to King Solomon to speak to him concerning Adonijah. The king rose to greet her and prostrated himself to her. He then sat upon his throne and placed a chair for the king's mother, and she sat to his right. ²⁰ She said, "I have one small request that I ask of you; do not turn me away."

The king said to her, "Ask, my mother, for I shall not turn you away."

²¹ She said, "Let Abishag the Shunnamite be given to your brother Adonijah for a wife."

²² King Solomon answered, saying to his mother, "Why do you request Abishag the Shunnamite for Adonijah? Request for him rather the kingship, for he is my older brother, for him, for Abiathar the Kohen and for Joab son of Zeruiah!"* ²³ King Solomon then swore by HASHEM, saying, "So should HASHEM do to me and so should He do further . . .* For Adonijah has spoken of this matter at the cost of his life. ²⁴ And now, as HASHEM lives — Who has established me and has set me upon the throne of my father David, and Who has made a dynasty for me as He had spoken — [I swear] that today Adonijah shall be put to death." ²⁵ So King Solomon dispatched Benaiah son of Jehoiada and he struck him, killing him.

²⁶ To Abiathar the Kohen the king said, "Go to Anathoth, to your fields. For you are deserving of death; but I shall not put you to death this day, because you have carried the Ark of my Lord HASHEM/ELOHIM, before my father David, and because you suffered in all that my father suffered."* ²⁷ Solomon then dismissed Abiathar from being a Kohen to HASHEM, to fulfill the word of HASHEM that He had spoken concerning the house of Eli in Shiloh. *

²⁸ The news reached Joab [and he was frightened,] for Joab had sided with Adonijah (although he had not sided with Absalom). * Joab fled to the Tent of HASHEM and took hold of the horns of the Altar. * ²⁹ It was told to King Solomon that Joab had fled to the Tent of HASHEM and that he was there next to the Altar; so Solomon sent Benaiah son of Jehoiada, saying, "Go, strike him down."

³⁰ Benaiah then came to the Tent of HASHEM and said to [Joab], "Thus said the king: 'Go out!' "

But he replied, "No; for I shall die here."

Benaiah sent back word to the king, saying, "Thus spoke Joab, and thus did he answer me."

Adonijah even more poignant and insulting to Solomon (Abarbanel). Regarding the Tent and the Altar, see 1:39 and 1:50.

לא וַיֹּאמֶר לוֹ הַמֶּלֶךְ עֲשֵׂה כַּאֲשֶׁר דִּבֶּר וּפְגַע־בּוֹ וּקְבַרְתּוֹ וַהֲסִירֹתָ ׀ דְּמֵי חִנָּם

לב אֲשֶׁר שָׁפַךְ יוֹאָב מֵעָלַי וּמֵעַל בֵּית אָבִי: וְהֵשִׁיב יהוה אֶת־דָּמוֹ עַל־רֹאשׁוֹ

אֲשֶׁר פָּגַע בִּשְׁנֵי־אֲנָשִׁים צַדִּקִים וְטֹבִים מִמֶּנּוּ וַיַּהַרְגֵם בַּחֶרֶב וְאָבִי דָוִד

לֹא יָדָע אֶת־אַבְנֵר בֶּן־נֵר שַׂר־צְבָא יִשְׂרָאֵל וְאֶת־עֲמָשָׂא בֶן־יֶתֶר שַׂר־

לג צְבָא יְהוּדָה: וְשָׁבוּ דְמֵיהֶם בְּרֹאשׁ יוֹאָב וּבְרֹאשׁ זַרְעוֹ לְעֹלָם וּלְדָוִד וּלְזַרְעוֹ

לד וּלְבֵיתוֹ וּלְכִסְאוֹ יִהְיֶה שָׁלוֹם עַד־עוֹלָם מֵעִם יהוה: וַיַּעַל בְּנָיָהוּ בֶּן־יְהוֹיָדָע

לה וַיִּפְגַּע־בּוֹ וַיְמִתֵהוּ וַיִּקָּבֵר בְּבֵיתוֹ בַּמִּדְבָּר: וַיִּתֵּן הַמֶּלֶךְ אֶת־בְּנָיָהוּ בֶן־יְהוֹיָדָע

לו תַּחְתָּיו עַל־הַצָּבָא וְאֶת־צָדוֹק הַכֹּהֵן נָתַן הַמֶּלֶךְ תַּחַת אֶבְיָתָר: וַיִּשְׁלַח

הַמֶּלֶךְ וַיִּקְרָא לְשִׁמְעִי וַיֹּאמֶר לוֹ בְּנֵה־לְךָ בַיִת בִּירוּשָׁלַם וְיָשַׁבְתָּ שָׁם וְלֹא־

לז תֵצֵא מִשָּׁם אָנֶה וָאָנָה: וְהָיָה ׀ בְּיוֹם צֵאתְךָ וְעָבַרְתָּ אֶת־נַחַל קִדְרוֹן יָדֹעַ

לח תֵּדַע כִּי מוֹת תָּמוּת דָּמְךָ יִהְיֶה בְרֹאשֶׁךָ: וַיֹּאמֶר שִׁמְעִי לַמֶּלֶךְ טוֹב הַדָּבָר

כַּאֲשֶׁר דִּבֶּר אֲדֹנִי הַמֶּלֶךְ כֵּן יַעֲשֶׂה עַבְדֶּךָ וַיֵּשֶׁב שִׁמְעִי בִּירוּשָׁלַם יָמִים

לט רַבִּים: וַיְהִי מִקֵּץ שָׁלֹשׁ שָׁנִים וַיִּבְרְחוּ שְׁנֵי־עֲבָדִים לְשִׁמְעִי

אֶל־אָכִישׁ בֶּן־מַעֲכָה מֶלֶךְ גַּת וַיַּגִּידוּ לְשִׁמְעִי לֵאמֹר הִנֵּה עֲבָדֶיךָ בְּגַת:

מ וַיָּקָם שִׁמְעִי וַיַּחֲבֹשׁ אֶת־חֲמֹרוֹ וַיֵּלֶךְ גַּתָה אֶל־אָכִישׁ לְבַקֵּשׁ אֶת־עֲבָדָיו

מא וַיֵּלֶךְ שִׁמְעִי וַיָּבֵא אֶת־עֲבָדָיו מִגַּת: וַיֻּגַּד לִשְׁלֹמֹה כִּי־הָלַךְ

מב שִׁמְעִי מִירוּשָׁלַם גַּת וַיָּשֹׁב: וַיִּשְׁלַח הַמֶּלֶךְ וַיִּקְרָא לְשִׁמְעִי וַיֹּאמֶר אֵלָיו

הֲלוֹא הִשְׁבַּעְתִּיךָ בַיהוה וָאָעִד בְּךָ לֵאמֹר בְּיוֹם צֵאתְךָ וְהָלַכְתָּ אָנֶה וָאָנָה

מג יָדֹעַ תֵּדַע כִּי מוֹת תָּמוּת וַתֹּאמֶר אֵלַי טוֹב הַדָּבָר שָׁמָעְתִּי: וּמַדּוּעַ לֹא

מד שָׁמַרְתָּ אֵת שְׁבֻעַת יהוה וְאֶת־הַמִּצְוָה אֲשֶׁר־צִוִּיתִי עָלֶיךָ: וַיֹּאמֶר הַמֶּלֶךְ

אֶל־שִׁמְעִי אַתָּה יָדַעְתָּ אֵת כָּל־הָרָעָה אֲשֶׁר יָדַע לְבָבְךָ אֲשֶׁר עָשִׂיתָ לְדָוִד

מה אָבִי וְהֵשִׁיב יהוה אֶת־רָעָתְךָ בְּרֹאשֶׁךָ: וְהַמֶּלֶךְ שְׁלֹמֹה בָּרוּךְ וְכִסֵּא דָוִד

מו יִהְיֶה נָכוֹן לִפְנֵי יהוה עַד־עוֹלָם: וַיְצַו הַמֶּלֶךְ אֶת־בְּנָיָהוּ בֶּן־יְהוֹיָדָע וַיֵּצֵא

ג א וַיִּפְגַּע־בּוֹ וַיָּמֹת וְהַמַּמְלָכָה נָכוֹנָה בְּיַד־שְׁלֹמֹה: וַיִּתְחַתֵּן

שְׁלֹמֹה אֶת־פַּרְעֹה מֶלֶךְ מִצְרָיִם וַיִּקַּח אֶת־בַּת־פַּרְעֹה וַיְבִיאֶהָ אֶל־עִיר

דָּוִד עַד כַּלֹּתוֹ לִבְנוֹת אֶת־בֵּיתוֹ וְאֶת־בֵּית יהוה וְאֶת־חוֹמַת יְרוּשָׁלַם

ב סָבִיב: רַק הָעָם מְזַבְּחִים בַּבָּמוֹת כִּי לֹא־נִבְנָה בַיִת לְשֵׁם יהוה עַד הַיָּמִים

ג הָהֵם: וַיֶּאֱהַב שְׁלֹמֹה אֶת־יהוה לָלֶכֶת בְּחֻקּוֹת דָּוִד אָבִיו רַק

2:31. As long as I have not avenged the deaths of Abner and Amasa it is as if their blood is on my head and my father's.

2:44. What you did publicly was bad enough, but you know that there was more hatred in your heart than you expressed verbally (*Radak*).

2:45. Your curses were to no avail.

3:1. To further consolidate his reign, Solomon married a princess from the neighboring superpower (*Malbim*). During a period of general tranquility and well-being in

Israel, the Sanhedrin (national *beth din*) does not accept converts to Judaism, for the court suspects that insincere persons might petition to convert for less than noble motives, such as a share in the nation's prosperity. Such was the case during the reigns of David and Solomon. Nevertheless, lesser *beth dins* or individual rabbinic authorities did accept converts whom they deemed sincere, and the Sanhedrin did not reject them out of hand. Rather, they waited to see how loyal the newcomers would remain over a period of time.

Solomon, as a Torah scholar, converted Pharaoh's

³¹ The king then said to him, "Do as he said — strike him down [there], and bury him; eliminate thereby the innocent blood which Joab spilled, from me and from my father's house. * ³² HASHEM will thus return his blood upon his head because he struck two men who were more righteous and good than he, and he killed them by the sword, yet my father David did not know — Abner son of Ner, commander of the army of Israel, and Amasa son of Jether, commander of the army of Judah. ³³ Let their blood return upon the head of Joab and the head of his offspring forever, while for David and his offspring and his house and his throne there shall be peace forever from HASHEM."

. . . but Benaiah carries out the sentence ³⁴ So Benaiah son of Jehoiada went up and struck him and killed him, and he was buried at his house in the desert. ³⁵ The king appointed Benaiah son of Jehoiada in his place over the army, and the king appointed Zadok the Kohen in place of Abiathar.

Solomon puts Shimei on notice . . . ³⁶ The king then sent a message summoning Shimei, and said to him, "Build yourself a house in Jerusalem and live there; you may not leave it [to go] anywhere. ³⁷ It shall be that on the day that you leave it and cross over the Kidron Valley you should know well that you will certainly die; your blood will be upon your own head."

³⁸ Shimei said to the king, "The word that my lord the king has spoken is good; so shall your servant do." So Shimei lived in Jerusalem for many days.

. . . but he causes his own undoing ³⁹ It happened after three years that two of Shimei's servants fled to Achish son of Maacah, king of Gath. They told Shimei, saying, "Behold, your servants are in Gath!" ⁴⁰ So Shimei got up and saddled his donkey and left for Gath, to Achish, to seek his servants. Shimei went and brought his servants from Gath. ⁴¹ It was told to Solomon that Shimei had gone from Jerusalem to Gath and returned. ⁴² The king sent a message summoning Shimei, and said to him, "Did I not adjure you by HASHEM and warn you, saying, 'On the day that you leave to go here or there, you should know well that you shall certainly die'? And you answered me, 'The word is good; I have heard.' ⁴³ So why have you not kept the oath of HASHEM and the commandment that I commanded you?" ⁴⁴ The king then said to Shimei, "You know of all the evil that your heart knows * that you did to my father David; HASHEM has now brought your evil upon your head. ⁴⁵ For King Solomon is blessed, and the throne of David shall be established before HASHEM forever."* ⁴⁶ The king then commanded Benaiah son of Jehoiada, and he went out and struck him and he died.

The kingdom was thus established in the hand of Solomon.

3

Solomon marries an Egyptian princess ¹ Solomon made a marriage alliance with Pharaoh, king of Egypt; he took Pharaoh's daughter in marriage* and brought her to the City of David until he finished building his house and the House of HASHEM and the wall of Jerusalem all around. ² However, the people brought offerings upon high places, for a House for the Name of HASHEM had not yet been built in those days. * ³ Solomon loved HASHEM, acting in accordance with the decrees of his father David, only

---

daughter (as well as each of his subsequent foreign wives) before he married her. However, since these foreign-born wives were not converted with the prior consent of the Sanhedrin, Scripture censures Solomon for marrying them. Moreover, in the end, the Sanhedrin's fears proved valid (see 11:1-10), as these wives never fully abandoned

their idol worship (*Rambam*).

3:2. Despite Solomon's efforts to consolidate his rule, the nation suffered due to the lack of a central Temple (*Malbim*). Although there was a national Altar at Gibeon, it was permissible to bring offerings on *high places* (private altars).

ד בַּבָּמוֹת הוּא מְזַבֵּחַ וּמַקְטִיר: וַיֵּלֶךְ הַמֶּלֶךְ גִּבְעֹנָה לִזְבֹּחַ שָׁם כִּי הִיא הַבָּמָה

ה הַגְּדוֹלָה אֶלֶף עֹלוֹת יַעֲלֶה שְׁלֹמֹה עַל הַמִּזְבֵּחַ הַהוּא: בְּגִבְעוֹן

נִרְאָה יהוה אֶל שְׁלֹמֹה בַּחֲלוֹם הַלָּיְלָה וַיֹּאמֶר אֱלֹהִים שְׁאַל מָה אֶתֶּן

ו לָךְ: וַיֹּאמֶר שְׁלֹמֹה אַתָּה עָשִׂיתָ עִם עַבְדְּךָ דָוִד אָבִי חֶסֶד גָּדוֹל כַּאֲשֶׁר

הָלַךְ לְפָנֶיךָ בֶּאֱמֶת וּבִצְדָקָה וּבְיִשְׁרַת לֵבָב עִמָּךְ וַתִּשְׁמָר לוֹ אֶת הַחֶסֶד

ז הַגָּדוֹל הַזֶּה וַתִּתֶּן לוֹ בֵן יֹשֵׁב עַל כִּסְאוֹ כַּיּוֹם הַזֶּה: וְעַתָּה יהוה אֱלֹהָי

אַתָּה הִמְלַכְתָּ אֶת עַבְדְּךָ תַּחַת דָּוִד אָבִי וְאָנֹכִי נַעַר קָטֹן לֹא אֵדַע צֵאת

ח וָבֹא: וְעַבְדְּךָ בְּתוֹךְ עַמְּךָ אֲשֶׁר בָּחָרְתָּ עַם רָב אֲשֶׁר לֹא יִמָּנֶה וְלֹא יִסָּפֵר

ט מֵרֹב: וְנָתַתָּ לְעַבְדְּךָ לֵב שֹׁמֵעַ לִשְׁפֹּט אֶת עַמְּךָ לְהָבִין בֵּין טוֹב לְרָע כִּי מִי

י יוּכַל לִשְׁפֹּט אֶת עַמְּךָ הַכָּבֵד הַזֶּה: וַיִּיטַב הַדָּבָר בְּעֵינֵי אֲדֹנָי כִּי שָׁאַל

יא שְׁלֹמֹה אֶת הַדָּבָר הַזֶּה: וַיֹּאמֶר אֱלֹהִים אֵלָיו יַעַן אֲשֶׁר שָׁאַלְתָּ אֶת הַדָּבָר

הַזֶּה וְלֹא שָׁאַלְתָּ לְּךָ יָמִים רַבִּים וְלֹא שָׁאַלְתָּ לְּךָ עֹשֶׁר וְלֹא שָׁאַלְתָּ נֶפֶשׁ

יב אֹיְבֶיךָ וְשָׁאַלְתָּ לְּךָ הָבִין לִשְׁמֹעַ מִשְׁפָּט: הִנֵּה עָשִׂיתִי כִּדְבָרֶיךָ הִנֵּה נָתַתִּי

לְךָ לֵב חָכָם וְנָבוֹן אֲשֶׁר כָּמוֹךָ לֹא הָיָה לְפָנֶיךָ וְאַחֲרֶיךָ לֹא יָקוּם כָּמוֹךָ:

יג וְגַם אֲשֶׁר לֹא שָׁאַלְתָּ נָתַתִּי לָךְ גַּם עֹשֶׁר גַּם כָּבוֹד אֲשֶׁר לֹא הָיָה כָמוֹךָ

יד אִישׁ בַּמְּלָכִים כָּל יָמֶיךָ: וְאִם תֵּלֵךְ בִּדְרָכַי לִשְׁמֹר חֻקַּי וּמִצְוֹתַי כַּאֲשֶׁר

הָלַךְ דָּוִיד אָבִיךָ וְהַאֲרַכְתִּי אֶת יָמֶיךָ:

טו וַיִּקַץ שְׁלֹמֹה וְהִנֵּה חֲלוֹם   ◄ HAFTARAS MIKEITZ 3:15-4:1

וַיָּבוֹא יְרוּשָׁלַםִ וַיַּעֲמֹד לִפְנֵי אֲרוֹן בְּרִית אֲדֹנָי וַיַּעַל עֹלוֹת וַיַּעַשׂ שְׁלָמִים

וַיַּעַשׂ מִשְׁתֶּה לְכָל עֲבָדָיו: אָז תָּבֹאנָה שְׁתַּיִם נָשִׁים זֹנוֹת אֶל

טז הַמֶּלֶךְ וַתַּעֲמֹדְנָה לְפָנָיו: וַתֹּאמֶר הָאִשָּׁה הָאַחַת בִּי אֲדֹנִי אֲנִי וְהָאִשָּׁה

יז הַזֹּאת יֹשְׁבֹת בְּבַיִת אֶחָד וָאֵלֵד עִמָּהּ בַּבָּיִת: וַיְהִי בַּיּוֹם הַשְּׁלִישִׁי לְלִדְתִּי

וַתֵּלֶד גַּם הָאִשָּׁה הַזֹּאת וַאֲנַחְנוּ יַחְדָּו אֵין זָר אִתָּנוּ בַּבַּיִת זוּלָתִי שְׁתַּיִם

יח-כ אֲנַחְנוּ בַּבָּיִת: וַיָּמָת בֶּן הָאִשָּׁה הַזֹּאת לָיְלָה אֲשֶׁר שָׁכְבָה עָלָיו: וַתָּקָם בְּתוֹךְ

הַלַּיְלָה וַתִּקַּח אֶת בְּנִי מֵאֶצְלִי וַאֲמָתְךָ יְשֵׁנָה וַתַּשְׁכִּיבֵהוּ בְּחֵיקָהּ וְאֶת

כא בְּנָהּ הַמֵּת הִשְׁכִּיבָה בְחֵיקִי: וָאָקֻם בַּבֹּקֶר לְהֵינִיק אֶת בְּנִי וְהִנֵּה מֵת

כב וָאֶתְבּוֹנֵן אֵלָיו בַּבֹּקֶר וְהִנֵּה לֹא הָיָה בְנִי אֲשֶׁר יָלָדְתִּי: וַתֹּאמֶר הָאִשָּׁה

הָאַחֶרֶת לֹא כִי בְּנִי הַחַי וּבְנֵךְ הַמֵּת וְזֹאת אֹמֶרֶת לֹא כִי בְּנֵךְ הַמֵּת וּבְנִי

כג הֶחָי וַתְּדַבֵּרְנָה לִפְנֵי הַמֶּלֶךְ: וַיֹּאמֶר הַמֶּלֶךְ זֹאת אֹמֶרֶת זֶה בְּנִי הַחַי וּבְנֵךְ

כד הַמֵּת וְזֹאת אֹמֶרֶת לֹא כִי בְּנֵךְ הַמֵּת וּבְנִי הֶחָי: וַיֹּאמֶר הַמֶּלֶךְ קְחוּ

כה לִי חָרֶב וַיָּבִאוּ הַחֶרֶב לִפְנֵי הַמֶּלֶךְ: וַיֹּאמֶר הַמֶּלֶךְ גִּזְרוּ אֶת הַיֶּלֶד הַחַי

3:3. Although sacrificing at *high places* was permissible before the building of the Temple, David always tried to bring his offerings at the Great High Place at Gibeon or to the Tent of the Ark in Jerusalem, which were the preferable places of worship. In this respect Solomon did not follow the ways of his father (*Radak*).

3:4. This is the Altar built by Bezalel (*Exodus* 27:1-8) under the supervision of Moses (*Rashi*).

3:7. A metaphor for leadership; the king must be able to lead the people out in battle and back home in peace. See *Numbers* 27:17.

3:16. See *Joshua* 2:1.

upon high places he slaughtered and burned offerings. * ⁴ The king went to Gibeon to sacrifice there, for that was the Great High Place. * Solomon offered up a thousand elevation-offerings on that Altar.

⁵ In Gibeon HASHEM appeared to Solomon in a dream of the night. God said to him, "Request what I should give to you."

Solomon prays for wisdom . . .

⁶ Solomon said, "You have done a great kindness with Your servant, David my father, because he walked before You with truth and justice and with uprightness of heart with You; and You have preserved for him this great kindness and have granted him a son who sits on his throne this very day. ⁷ And now, HASHEM, my God, You have crowned Your servant in place of David my father, but I am a young lad; I do not know how to go out and come in. * ⁸ Your servant is in the midst of Your people whom You have chosen, a large nation that can neither be counted nor numbered because of its abundance. ⁹ May You grant Your servant an understanding heart, to judge Your people, to distinguish between good and evil; for who can judge this formidable people of Yours?"

. . . and God grants him much more

¹⁰ It was good in the eyes of the Lord that Solomon had requested this thing. ¹¹ God said to him, "Because you have requested this thing, and you have not requested length of days and have not requested riches and have not requested the life of your enemies, but you have requested understanding, to comprehend justice — ¹² behold, I have acted in accordance with your words; behold, I have given you a wise and understanding heart, such that there has never been anyone like you before, nor will anyone like you ever arise. ¹³ Furthermore, even that which you did not request I have granted you — even riches and honor — all your days, such that there has never been any man among the kings like you. ¹⁴ If you walk in My ways, observing My decrees and commandments, as your father David walked, I shall prolong your days."

¹⁵ Solomon awoke, and behold, it had been a dream. When he came to Jerusalem, he stood before the Ark of the Covenant of the Lord and brought up elevation-offerings and offered peace-offerings; and he made a feast for all of his servants.

Two women claim the one living baby

¹⁶ Then two women, innkeepers, * came to the king and stood before him. ¹⁷ One woman said, "Please, my lord: I and this woman dwell in one house, and I gave birth while with her in the house. ¹⁸ On the third day after I gave birth, this woman gave birth as well. We [were] together; there was no outsider with us in the house; only the two of us were in the house. ¹⁹ The son of this woman died at night, because she lay upon him. ²⁰ She arose during the night and took my son from my side while your maidservant was asleep, and laid him in her bosom, and her dead son she laid in my bosom. ²¹ When I arose in the morning to nurse my son, behold, he was dead! When I studied him in the morning, behold it was not my son to whom I had given birth."

²² But the other woman said, "It is not so! My son is the live one, and your son is the dead one!"

But this one said, "It is not so! Your son is the dead one, and my son is the live one!" And they went on speaking before the king.

²³ The king said, "This one claims, 'This is my son, who is alive, and your son is the dead one,' and this one claims, 'It is not so! Your son is the dead one, and my son is the live one.' " ²⁴ So the king said, "Fetch me a sword!" and they brought a sword before the king. ²⁵ The king said, "Cut the living child

כו לִשְׁנַ֔יִם וּתְנ֤וּ אֶת־הַחֲצִי֙ לְאַחַ֔ת וְאֶת־הַחֲצִ֖י לְאֶחָ֑ת וַתֹּ֣אמֶר הָאִשָּׁ֣ה אֲשֶׁר־
בְּנָ֣הּ הַחַ֣י אֶל־הַמֶּ֗לֶךְ כִּֽי־נִכְמְרוּ֮ רַחֲמֶ֣יהָ עַל־בְּנָהּ֒ וַתֹּ֣אמֶר ׀ בִּ֣י אֲדֹנִ֗י תְּנוּ־
לָהּ֙ אֶת־הַיָּל֣וּד הַחַ֔י וְהָמֵ֖ת אַל־תְּמִיתֻ֑הוּ וְזֹ֣את אֹמֶ֗רֶת גַּם־לִ֥י גַם־לָ֛ךְ לֹ֥א
כז יִֽהְיֶ֖ה גְּזֹֽרוּ: וַיַּ֨עַן הַמֶּ֜לֶךְ וַיֹּ֗אמֶר תְּנוּ־לָהּ֙ אֶת־הַיָּל֣וּד הַחַ֔י וְהָמֵ֖ת לֹ֣א תְמִיתֻ֑הוּ
כח הִ֖יא אִמּֽוֹ: וַיִּשְׁמְע֣וּ כָל־יִשְׂרָאֵ֗ל אֶת־הַמִּשְׁפָּט֙ אֲשֶׁ֣ר שָׁפַ֣ט הַמֶּ֔לֶךְ וַיִּֽרְא֖וּ
א מִפְּנֵ֣י הַמֶּ֑לֶךְ כִּ֣י רָא֔וּ כִּֽי־חָכְמַ֧ת אֱלֹהִ֛ים בְּקִרְבּ֖וֹ לַעֲשׂ֥וֹת מִשְׁפָּֽט: וַיְהִי֙
ד ב הַמֶּ֣לֶךְ שְׁלֹמֹ֔ה מֶ֖לֶךְ עַל־כָּל־יִשְׂרָאֵֽל: ◄ וְאֵ֥לֶּה הַשָּׂרִ֖ים אֲשֶׁר־לֽוֹ
ג עֲזַרְיָ֥הוּ בֶן־צָד֖וֹק הַכֹּהֵֽן: אֱלִיחֹ֧רֶף וַאֲחִיָּ֛ה בְּנֵ֥י שִׁישָׁ֖א סֹפְרִ֑ים יְהוֹשָׁפָ֥ט בֶּן־
ד אֲחִיל֖וּד הַמַּזְכִּֽיר: וּבְנָיָ֥הוּ בֶן־יְהוֹיָדָ֖ע עַל־הַצָּבָ֑א וְצָד֥וֹק וְאֶבְיָתָ֖ר כֹּהֲנִֽים:
ה־ה וַעֲזַרְיָ֥הוּ בֶן־נָתָ֖ן עַל־הַנִּצָּבִ֑ים וְזָב֧וּד בֶּן־נָתָ֛ן כֹּהֵ֖ן רֵעֶ֥ה הַמֶּֽלֶךְ: וַאֲחִישָׁ֖ר
ז עַל־הַבָּ֑יִת וַאֲדֹנִירָ֥ם בֶּן־עַבְדָּ֖א עַל־הַמַּֽס: וְלִשְׁלֹמֹ֞ה שְׁנֵים־
עָשָׂ֤ר נִצָּבִים֙ עַל־כָּל־יִשְׂרָאֵ֔ל וְכִלְכְּל֥וּ אֶת־הַמֶּ֖לֶךְ וְאֶת־בֵּית֑וֹ חֹ֧דֶשׁ בַּשָּׁנָ֛ה
ח יִהְיֶ֥ה עַל־אֶחָ֖ד [°הָאֶחָ֖ד ק] לְכַלְכֵּֽל: וְאֵ֣לֶּה שְׁמוֹתָ֔ם בֶּן־ח֖וּר בְּהַ֥ר
ט־ט אֶפְרָֽיִם: בֶּן־דֶּ֣קֶר בְּמָקַ֔ץ וּבְשַֽׁעַלְבִ֖ים וּבֵ֣ית שָׁ֑מֶשׁ וְאֵיל֥וֹן בֵּ֥ית חָנָ֖ן: בֶּן־חֶ֑סֶד
יא בָּאֲרֻבּ֑וֹת ל֣וֹ שֹׂכֹ֔ה וְכָל־אֶ֖רֶץ חֵֽפֶר: בֶּן־אֲבִינָדָ֗ב כָּל־נָ֥פַת דֹּ֖אר טָפַ֣ת בַּת־
יב שְׁלֹמֹ֖ה הָ֥יְתָה לּ֖וֹ לְאִשָּֽׁה: בַּֽעֲנָא֙ בֶּן־אֲחִיל֔וּד תַּעְנַ֖ךְ וּמְגִדּ֑וֹ
וְכָל־בֵּ֣ית שְׁאָ֡ן אֲשֶׁר֩ אֵ֨צֶל צָֽרְתַ֜נָה מִתַּ֣חַת לְיִזְרְעֶ֗אל מִבֵּ֣ית שְׁאָ֜ן עַ֣ד
יג אָבֵ֤ל מְחוֹלָה֙ עַ֚ד מֵעֵ֣בֶר לְיָקְמֳעָֽם: בֶּן־גֶּ֖בֶר בְּרָמֹ֣ת גִּלְעָ֑ד
ל֣וֹ חַוֺּ֞ת יָאִ֤יר בֶּן־מְנַשֶּׁה֙ אֲשֶׁ֣ר בַּגִּלְעָ֔ד ל֚וֹ חֶ֣בֶל אַרְגֹּ֗ב אֲשֶׁ֣ר בַּבָּשָׁ֔ן שִׁשִּׁים֙
יד עָרִ֣ים גְּדֹל֔וֹת חוֹמָ֖ה וּבְרִ֥יחַ נְחֹֽשֶׁת: אֲחִֽינָדָ֖ב בֶּן־עִדֹּ֑א
טו מַֽחֲנָֽיְמָה: אֲחִימַ֖עַץ בְּנַפְתָּלִ֑י גַּם־ה֗וּא לָקַ֛ח אֶת־בָּשְׂמַ֥ת בַּת־
טז־יז שְׁלֹמֹ֖ה לְאִשָּֽׁה: בַּֽעֲנָא֙ בֶּן־חוּשָׁ֔י בְּאָשֵׁ֖ר וּבְעָל֑וֹת: יְהוֹשָׁפָ֥ט
יח־יט בֶּן־פָּר֖וּחַ בְּיִשָׂשכָֽר: שִׁמְעִ֥י בֶן־אֵלָ֖א בְּבִנְיָמִֽן: גֶּ֖בֶר בֶּן־
אֻרִ֖י בְּאֶ֣רֶץ גִּלְעָ֑ד אֶ֜רֶץ סִיח֣וֹן ׀ מֶ֣לֶךְ הָאֱמֹרִ֗י וְעֹג֙ מֶ֣לֶךְ הַבָּשָׁ֔ן וּנְצִ֥יב
כ אֶחָ֖ד אֲשֶׁ֥ר בָּאָֽרֶץ: יְהוּדָ֤ה וְיִשְׂרָאֵל֙ רַבִּ֔ים כַּח֛וֹל אֲשֶׁר־עַל־הַיָּ֖ם לָרֹ֑ב
א אֹכְלִ֥ים וְשֹׁתִ֖ים וּשְׂמֵחִֽים: וּשְׁלֹמֹ֗ה הָיָ֤ה מוֹשֵׁל֙ בְּכָל־הַמַּמְלָכ֔וֹת מִן־
ה הַנָּהָר֙ אֶ֣רֶץ פְּלִשְׁתִּ֔ים וְעַ֖ד גְּב֣וּל מִצְרָ֑יִם מַגִּשִׁ֥ים מִנְחָ֛ה וְעֹבְדִ֥ים אֶת־
ב שְׁלֹמֹ֖ה כָּל־יְמֵ֥י חַיָּֽיו: וַיְהִ֥י לֶֽחֶם־שְׁלֹמֹ֖ה לְי֣וֹם אֶחָ֑ד שְׁלֹשִׁ֥ים
ג כֹּ֣ר סֹ֗לֶת וְשִׁשִּׁ֥ים כֹּ֖ר קָֽמַח: עֲשָׂרָ֨ה בָקָ֤ר בְּרִאִים֙ וְעֶשְׂרִ֣ים בָּקָ֔ר רְעִ֖י וּמֵאָ֣ה
ד צֹ֑אן לְ֠בַד מֵֽאַיָּ֤ל וּצְבִי֙ וְיַחְמ֔וּר וּבַרְבֻּרִ֖ים אֲבוּסִֽים: כִּי־ה֞וּא רֹדֶ֣ה ׀ בְּכָל־
עֵ֣בֶר הַנָּהָ֗ר מִתִּפְסַח֙ וְעַד־עַזָּ֔ה בְּכָל־מַלְכֵ֖י עֵ֣בֶר הַנָּהָ֑ר וְשָׁל֗וֹם הָ֥יָה ל֖וֹ

4:1. Awed at Solomon's insight and wisdom, the people unanimously accepted his reign. *Radak* contrasts this with David's reign, which was contested at its outset, and was continuously beset by insurrection and revolt.

4:3. See *II Samuel* 8:16.

4:4. Although Solomon had dismissed Abiathar from being the Kohen Gadol (2:26), he apparently retained some status as a major Kohen (*Ralbag*).

4:5. Those mentioned below, in vv. 8-19.

4:7. They collected the necessary funds from their re-

Solomon's decision . . . in two and give half to one and half to the other."

²⁶ The woman whose son was the live one spoke to the king — because her compassion was aroused for her son — and she said, "Please, my lord, give her the living newborn, and do not put it to death!"

But the other one said, "Neither mine nor yours shall he be. Cut!"

. . . proves his God-given wisdom ²⁷ The king spoke up and said, "Give her [the first one] the living newborn and do not put it to death; she is his mother!"

²⁸ All Israel heard the judgment that the king rendered and they were in awe of the king, for they saw that the wisdom of God was within him, to do justice.

4

¹ So King Solomon was king over all Israel. *

Solomon's chief ministers ² These were his ministers: Azariah son of Zadok the Kohen; ³ Elihoreph and Ahijah, sons of Shisha, scribes; Jehoshaphat son of Ahilud, the secretary; * ⁴ Benaiah son of Jehoiada, over the army; Zadok and Abiathar, * Kohanim; ⁵ Azariah son of Nathan, over the commissioners; * Zabud son of Nathan, a senior minister, a friend of the king; ⁶ Ahishar, the chamberlain; and Adoniram son of Abda, over the taxes.

Twelve regional commissioners ⁷ Solomon had twelve commissioners over all of Israel, who sustained the king and his household; * each one sustained [him] one month out of the year. ⁸ These were their names: The son of Hur at Mount Ephraim; ⁹ the son of Deker at Makaz, Shaalbim, Beth-shemesh, and Elon-beth-hanan; ¹⁰ the son of Hesed at Arubboth, he was in charge of Socoh and the entire land of Hepher; ¹¹ the son of Abinadab [was in charge of] the entire Dor district, Taphath daughter of Solomon became his wife; ¹² Baana son of Ahilud [at] Taanach and Megiddo and all of Beth-shean which is near Zarethan, below Jezreel, from Beth-shean until the Plain of Meholah, until beyond Jokmeam; ¹³ the son of Geber at Ramoth-gilead, he was in charge of the villages of Jair son of Manasseh in the Gilead, and he was in charge of the Argob region, which is in the Bashan, sixty great cities, with walls and copper bars; ¹⁴ Ahinadab son of Iddo at Mahanaim; ¹⁵ Ahimaaz in Naphtali, he also married Basemath daughter of Solomon; ¹⁶ Baana son of Hushai in Asher and in Be'aloth; ¹⁷ Jehoshaphat son of Paruah in Issachar; ¹⁸ Shimei son of Ela in Benjamin; ¹⁹ Geber son of Uri in the land of Gilead — the land of Sihon, king of the Amorite, and of Og, king of Bashan; and *National joy and prosperity* one [main] commissioner who was over the [entire] land. *

²⁰ Judah and Israel were numerous, like the sand that is by the sea for multitude, eating, drinking and rejoicing. *

5

Extent of his kingdom ¹ Solomon ruled over all the kingdoms, from the [Euphrates] River [to] the land of the Philistines, until the border of Egypt; they brought tributes and served Solomon all the days of his life.

² Solomon's provision for one day was: thirty kor of fine flour, sixty kor* of flour; ³ ten fattened oxen, twenty oxen from the pasture, and a hundred sheep and goats, besides gazelle, deer, yachmur, and fattened fowl. ⁴ For he ruled over the entire area beyond the [Euphrates] River, from Tiphsah to Gaza, * over all the kings of the area beyond the [Euphrates] River; and he was at peace [with

---

spective districts to keep the royal treasuries viable.

4:19. See v. 5.

4:20. This was a period of unprecedented peace and prosperity for the Israelites, and the tax that they paid to the royal treasury was not a burden for them (*Malbim*).

5:2. Opinions regarding the capacity of a *kor* range from 67.5 to 120 gallons. Thus, ninety *kor* of flour was enough to feed thousands of people.

5:4. From Tiphsah on the Euphrates in the northeast to Gaza on the Mediterranean in the southwest.

ה מִכָּל־עֲבָרָיו מִסָּבִיב: וַיֵּשֶׁב יְהוּדָה וְיִשְׂרָאֵל לָבֶטַח אִישׁ תַּחַת גַּפְנוֹ וְתַחַת

ו תְּאֵנָתוֹ מִדָּן וְעַד־בְּאֵר שָׁבַע כֹּל יְמֵי שְׁלֹמֹה: וַיְהִי לִשְׁלֹמֹה

ז אַרְבָּעִים אֶלֶף אֻרְוֹת סוּסִים לְמֶרְכָּבוֹ וּשְׁנֵים־עָשָׂר אֶלֶף פָּרָשִׁים: וְכִלְכְּלוּ

הַנִּצָּבִים הָאֵלֶּה אֶת־הַמֶּלֶךְ שְׁלֹמֹה וְאֵת כָּל־הַקָּרֵב אֶל־שֻׁלְחַן הַמֶּלֶךְ־

ח שְׁלֹמֹה אִישׁ חָדְשׁוֹ לֹא יְעַדְּרוּ דָּבָר: וְהַשְּׂעֹרִים וְהַתֶּבֶן לַסּוּסִים וְלָרֶכֶשׁ

ט יָבִאוּ אֶל־הַמָּקוֹם אֲשֶׁר יִהְיֶה־שָּׁם אִישׁ כְּמִשְׁפָּטוֹ: וַיִּתֵּן

אֱלֹהִים חָכְמָה לִשְׁלֹמֹה וּתְבוּנָה הַרְבֵּה מְאֹד וְרֹחַב לֵב כַּחוֹל אֲשֶׁר עַל־

י שְׂפַת הַיָּם: וַתֵּרֶב חָכְמַת שְׁלֹמֹה מֵחָכְמַת כָּל־בְּנֵי־קֶדֶם וּמִכֹּל חָכְמַת

יא מִצְרָיִם: וַיֶּחְכַּם מִכָּל־הָאָדָם מֵאֵיתָן הָאֶזְרָחִי וְהֵימָן וְכַלְכֹּל וְדַרְדַּע בְּנֵי

יב מָחוֹל וַיְהִי־שְׁמוֹ בְכָל־הַגּוֹיִם סָבִיב: וַיְדַבֵּר שְׁלֹשֶׁת אֲלָפִים מָשָׁל וַיְהִי

יג שִׁירוֹ חֲמִשָּׁה וָאָלֶף: וַיְדַבֵּר עַל־הָעֵצִים מִן־הָאֶרֶז אֲשֶׁר בַּלְּבָנוֹן וְעַד

הָאֵזוֹב אֲשֶׁר יֹצֵא בַּקִּיר וַיְדַבֵּר עַל־הַבְּהֵמָה וְעַל־הָעוֹף וְעַל־הָרֶמֶשׂ וְעַל־

יד הַדָּגִים: וַיָּבֹאוּ מִכָּל־הָעַמִּים לִשְׁמֹעַ אֵת חָכְמַת שְׁלֹמֹה מֵאֵת כָּל־מַלְכֵי

טו הָאָרֶץ אֲשֶׁר שָׁמְעוּ אֶת־חָכְמָתוֹ: וַיִּשְׁלַח חִירָם מֶלֶךְ־צוֹר

אֶת־עֲבָדָיו אֶל־שְׁלֹמֹה כִּי שָׁמַע כִּי אֹתוֹ מָשְׁחוּ לְמֶלֶךְ תַּחַת אָבִיהוּ כִּי

טז אֹהֵב הָיָה חִירָם לְדָוִד כָּל־הַיָּמִים: וַיִּשְׁלַח שְׁלֹמֹה אֶל־חִירָם

יז לֵאמֹר: אַתָּה יָדַעְתָּ אֶת־דָּוִד אָבִי כִּי לֹא יָכֹל לִבְנוֹת בַּיִת לְשֵׁם יְהוָה

אֱלֹהָיו מִפְּנֵי הַמִּלְחָמָה אֲשֶׁר סְבָבֻהוּ עַד תֵּת־יְהוָה אֹתָם תַּחַת כַּפּוֹת

יח רַגְלַי [רַגְלָי ק׳]: וְעַתָּה הֵנִיחַ יְהוָה אֱלֹהַי לִי מִסָּבִיב אֵין שָׂטָן וְאֵין פֶּגַע

יט רָע: וְהִנְנִי אֹמֵר לִבְנוֹת בַּיִת לְשֵׁם יְהוָה אֱלֹהָי כַּאֲשֶׁר | דִּבֶּר יְהוָה אֶל־דָּוִד

אָבִי לֵאמֹר בִּנְךָ אֲשֶׁר אֶתֵּן תַּחְתֶּיךָ עַל־כִּסְאֶךָ הוּא־יִבְנֶה הַבַּיִת לִשְׁמִי:

כ וְעַתָּה צַוֵּה וְיִכְרְתוּ־לִי אֲרָזִים מִן־הַלְּבָנוֹן וַעֲבָדַי יִהְיוּ עִם־עֲבָדֶיךָ וּשְׂכַר

עֲבָדֶיךָ אֶתֵּן לְךָ כְּכֹל אֲשֶׁר תֹּאמֵר כִּי | אַתָּה יָדַעְתָּ כִּי אֵין בָּנוּ אִישׁ יֹדֵעַ

כא לִכְרָת־עֵצִים כַּצִּדֹנִים: וַיְהִי כִשְׁמֹעַ חִירָם אֶת־דִּבְרֵי שְׁלֹמֹה

וַיִּשְׂמַח מְאֹד וַיֹּאמֶר בָּרוּךְ יְהוָה הַיּוֹם אֲשֶׁר נָתַן לְדָוִד בֵּן חָכָם עַל־הָעָם

כב הָרָב הַזֶּה: וַיִּשְׁלַח חִירָם אֶל־שְׁלֹמֹה לֵאמֹר שָׁמַעְתִּי אֵת אֲשֶׁר־שָׁלַחְתָּ

כג אֵלָי אֲנִי אֶעֱשֶׂה אֶת־כָּל־חֶפְצְךָ בַּעֲצֵי אֲרָזִים וּבַעֲצֵי בְרוֹשִׁים: עֲבָדַי

יֹרִדוּ מִן־הַלְּבָנוֹן יָמָּה וַאֲנִי אֲשִׂימֵם דֹּבְרוֹת בַּיָּם עַד־הַמָּקוֹם אֲשֶׁר־

תִּשְׁלַח אֵלַי וְנִפַּצְתִּים שָׁם וְאַתָּה תִשָּׂא וְאַתָּה תַּעֲשֶׂה אֶת־חֶפְצִי לָתֵת

כד לֶחֶם בֵּיתִי: וַיְהִי חִירוֹם נֹתֵן לִשְׁלֹמֹה עֲצֵי אֲרָזִים וַעֲצֵי בְרוֹשִׁים כָּל־

כה חֶפְצוֹ: וּשְׁלֹמֹה נָתַן לְחִירָם עֶשְׂרִים אֶלֶף כֹּר חִטִּים מַכֹּלֶת לְבֵיתוֹ

וְעֶשְׂרִים כֹּר שֶׁמֶן כָּתִית כֹּה־יִתֵּן שְׁלֹמֹה לְחִירָם שָׁנָה בְשָׁנָה:

5:7. Enumerated above, 4:7-19.

5:11. The identity of these people is not certain.

5:12. The vast majority of Solomon's proverbs and songs are not found in Scripture; apparently they were not pre-

served (*Radak*).

5:13. He instructed people about the scientific and medicinal properties of each species of flora and fauna (*Rashi*).

5:15. Hiram's good will towards David is described in

the lands] on all sides, roundabout. ⁵ Judah and Israel dwelt in security, each man under his grapevine and under his fig tree, from Dan to Beer-sheba, all the days of Solomon.

Rotating providers ⁶ Solomon had forty thousand stalls of horses for his chariots, and twelve thousand horsemen. ⁷ These commissioners* sustained King Solomon, and all who came to King Solomon's table, each in his assigned month; they did not leave anything lacking. ⁸ The barley and straw for the horses and the speedy mounts, they would bring to whatever place they were [quartered]; each one [providing it] according to his responsibility.

Solomon's vast wisdom ⁹ God gave wisdom and considerable understanding to Solomon, and breadth of heart as [immense as] the sand which is upon the seashore. ¹⁰ Solomon's wisdom surpassed the wisdom of all the people of the East and all the wisdom of Egypt. ¹¹ He was wiser than all men — than Ethan the Ezrahite and Heman and Calcol and Darda, the sons of Mahol;* his fame spread to all the nations around him. ¹² He spoke three thousand proverbs, and his songs were one thousand and five. * ¹³ He spoke of the trees, * from the cedar which is in Lebanon down to the hyssop which grows out of the wall; he spoke of animal, of fowl, of crawling creature, and of fish. ¹⁴ They came from all the nations to hear the wisdom of Solomon, [emissaries] from all the kings of the land who had heard of his wisdom.

SOLOMON ERECTS THE BEIS HAMIKDASH (HOLY TEMPLE) 5:15-7:51 ¹⁵ Hiram, king of Tyre, sent his servants to Solomon, for he had heard that he had been anointed king in place of his father, for Hiram had always been a friend of David. * ¹⁶ Solomon sent [back] to Hiram, saying, ¹⁷ "You knew that my father David was not able to build a house for the Name of HASHEM his God because of the war that surrounded him, until HASHEM would subdue [our enemies] under the soles of my feet. * ¹⁸ And now HASHEM my God has granted me rest on all sides — there is no adversary and no misfortune. ¹⁹ Therefore I

Solomon's proposal to Hiram have decided to build a house for the Name of HASHEM my God, as HASHEM spoke to my father David, saying, 'Your son, whom I shall place upon your throne in your stead — he will build a house for My Name.' ²⁰ And now, command [your servants] that they cut down cedars for me from Lebanon; my servants will be with your servants, and I will provide you with the wages of your servants according to whatever you say, for you know that we have no one who knows how to hew down trees like the Sidonians."

Hiram's acceptance ²¹ And it was when Hiram heard the words of Solomon he was very glad and said, "Blessed is HASHEM this day, Who has granted David a wise son [to rule] over this numerous people."

²² Hiram sent [a message] to Solomon saying, "I received what you sent me; I shall do all that you desire, with cedar wood and cypress wood. ²³ My servants will bring [the logs] down from the Lebanon to the sea; I will make them into rafts on the sea, [to go] to the place that you shall appoint for me; I will dismantle them there, and you will carry them away. And you do what I desire, providing food [for] my household." ²⁴ Hiram would give Solomon cedar wood and cypress wood, as much as he desired; ²⁵ and Solomon would give Hiram twenty thousand kor* of wheat as sustenance for his household, and twenty kor of squeezed oil — this is what Solomon would give Hiram year by year.

II Samuel 5:11. Now he pledges the same friendship and support to Solomon.

5:17. See II Samuel 7:3.
5:25. See 5:2.

HAFTARAS
TERUMAH
5:26-6:13

כו ◀ וַיהוָה נָתַן חָכְמָה לִשְׁלֹמֹה כַּאֲשֶׁר דִּבֶּר־לוֹ וַיְהִי שָׁלֹם בֵּין חִירָם וּבֵין

כז שְׁלֹמֹה וַיִּכְרְתוּ בְרִית שְׁנֵיהֶם: וַיַּעַל הַמֶּלֶךְ שְׁלֹמֹה מַס מִכָּל־יִשְׂרָאֵל

כח וַיְהִי הַמַּס שְׁלֹשִׁים אֶלֶף אִישׁ: וַיִּשְׁלָחֵם לְבָנוֹנָה עֲשֶׂרֶת אֲלָפִים בַּחֹדֶשׁ

חֲלִיפוֹת חֹדֶשׁ יִהְיוּ בַלְּבָנוֹן שְׁנַיִם חֳדָשִׁים בְּבֵיתוֹ וַאֲדֹנִירָם עַל־

כט הַמַּס: וַיְהִי לִשְׁלֹמֹה שִׁבְעִים אֶלֶף נֹשֵׂא סַבָּל וּשְׁמֹנִים

ל אֶלֶף חֹצֵב בָּהָר: לְבַד מִשָּׂרֵי הַנִּצָּבִים לִשְׁלֹמֹה אֲשֶׁר עַל־הַמְּלָאכָה

לא שְׁלֹשֶׁת אֲלָפִים וּשְׁלֹשׁ מֵאוֹת הָרֹדִים בָּעָם הָעֹשִׂים בַּמְּלָאכָה: וַיְצַו

הַמֶּלֶךְ וַיַּסִּעוּ אֲבָנִים גְּדֹלוֹת אֲבָנִים יְקָרוֹת לְיַסֵּד הַבָּיִת אַבְנֵי גָזִית: וַיִּפְסְלוּ

לב בֹּנֵי שְׁלֹמֹה וּבֹנֵי חִירוֹם וְהַגִּבְלִים וַיָּכִינוּ הָעֵצִים וְהָאֲבָנִים לִבְנוֹת

ו א הַבָּיִת: וַיְהִי בִשְׁמוֹנִים שָׁנָה וְאַרְבַּע מֵאוֹת שָׁנָה לְצֵאת

בְּנֵי־יִשְׂרָאֵל מֵאֶרֶץ־מִצְרַיִם בַּשָּׁנָה הָרְבִיעִית בְּחֹדֶשׁ זִו הוּא הַחֹדֶשׁ הַשֵּׁנִי

ב לִמְלֹךְ שְׁלֹמֹה עַל־יִשְׂרָאֵל וַיִּבֶן הַבַּיִת לַיהוָה: וְהַבַּיִת אֲשֶׁר בָּנָה הַמֶּלֶךְ

שְׁלֹמֹה לַיהוָה שִׁשִּׁים־אַמָּה אָרְכּוֹ וְעֶשְׂרִים רָחְבּוֹ וּשְׁלֹשִׁים אַמָּה קוֹמָתוֹ:

ג וְהָאוּלָם עַל־פְּנֵי הֵיכַל הַבַּיִת עֶשְׂרִים אַמָּה אָרְכּוֹ עַל־פְּנֵי רֹחַב הַבָּיִת

ד עֶשֶׂר בָּאַמָּה רָחְבּוֹ עַל־פְּנֵי הַבָּיִת: וַיַּעַשׂ לַבָּיִת חַלּוֹנֵי שְׁקֻפִים אֲטֻמִים:

ה וַיִּבֶן עַל־קִיר הַבַּיִת °יצוע [יָצִיעַ ק] סָבִיב אֶת־קִירוֹת הַבַּיִת סָבִיב

לַהֵיכָל וְלַדְּבִיר וַיַּעַשׂ צְלָעוֹת סָבִיב: °היצוע [הַיָּצִיעַ ק] הַתַּחְתֹּנָה חָמֵשׁ

ו בָּאַמָּה רָחְבָּהּ וְהַתִּיכֹנָה שֵׁשׁ בָּאַמָּה רָחְבָּהּ וְהַשְּׁלִישִׁית שֶׁבַע בָּאַמָּה

רָחְבָּהּ כִּי מִגְרָעוֹת נָתַן לַבַּיִת סָבִיב חוּצָה לְבִלְתִּי אֲחֹז בְּקִירוֹת הַבָּיִת:

ז וְהַבַּיִת בְּהִבָּנֹתוֹ אֶבֶן־שְׁלֵמָה מַסָּע נִבְנָה וּמַקָּבוֹת וְהַגַּרְזֶן כָּל־כְּלִי בַרְזֶל

ח לֹא־נִשְׁמַע בַּבַּיִת בְּהִבָּנֹתוֹ: פֶּתַח הַצֵּלָע הַתִּיכֹנָה אֶל־כֶּתֶף הַבַּיִת הַיְמָנִית

וּבְלוּלִּים יַעֲלוּ עַל־הַתִּיכֹנָה וּמִן־הַתִּיכֹנָה אֶל־הַשְּׁלִשִׁים: וַיִּבֶן אֶת־הַבַּיִת

ט י וַיְכַלֵּהוּ וַיִּסְפֹּן אֶת־הַבַּיִת גֵּבִים וּשְׂדֵרֹת בָּאֲרָזִים: וַיִּבֶן אֶת־°היצוע

[הַיָּצִיעַ ק] עַל־כָּל־הַבַּיִת חָמֵשׁ אַמּוֹת קוֹמָתוֹ וַיֶּאֱחֹז אֶת־הַבַּיִת בַּעֲצֵי

יא־יב אֲרָזִים: וַיְהִי דְּבַר־יְהוָה אֶל־שְׁלֹמֹה לֵאמֹר: הַבַּיִת הַזֶּה אֲשֶׁר־

אַתָּה בֹנֶה אִם־תֵּלֵךְ בְּחֻקֹּתַי וְאֶת־מִשְׁפָּטַי תַּעֲשֶׂה וְשָׁמַרְתָּ אֶת־כָּל־

מִצְוֹתַי לָלֶכֶת בָּהֶם וַהֲקִמֹתִי אֶת־דְּבָרִי אִתָּךְ אֲשֶׁר דִּבַּרְתִּי אֶל־דָּוִד אָבִיךָ:

יג־יד וְשָׁכַנְתִּי בְּתוֹךְ בְּנֵי יִשְׂרָאֵל וְלֹא אֶעֱזֹב אֶת־עַמִּי יִשְׂרָאֵל: ◀ וַיִּבֶן

5:32. The people of Gebal, a city in northern Lebanon, were known for their masonry skills (*Rashi*).

6:1. The spring month of Iyar.

6:2. These sixty cubits of length were divided into two chambers: the Hall (Sanctuary) which was forty cubits long, and the Inner Sanctum (Holy of Holies), which was twenty. The plans for the Temple had been drawn by David, who received his instructions and inspiration from God, through a prophet (*I Chronicles* 28:19). The Temple's basic format was basically similar to the Tabernacle

of Moses (*Exodus* Chs. 25-27), but with various deviations.

6:4. The Talmud explains that, contrary to ordinary window frames, which are wider on the inside of the building in order to maximize the amount of light that is diffused in the room, the windows of the Temple became narrower on the inside, in order to show that the House of God did not require any light from the outside. According to the *Midrash*, it was to show that the *outside* world benefited from the "light" of the Temple.

Armies of workers build the Temple

²⁶ HASHEM gave wisdom to Solomon, as He had spoken to him; there was peace between Hiram and Solomon, and the two of them sealed a covenant. ²⁷ King Solomon imposed a levy from all of Israel; the levy consisted of thirty thousand men. ²⁸ He sent them to Lebanon in shifts of ten thousand each month; for one month they would be in Lebanon and for two months each [would be] at home. Adoniram was in charge of the levy.

²⁹ Solomon had seventy thousand who carried burdens and eighty thousand who hewed in the mountain, ³⁰ in addition to Solomon's three thousand three hundred chief officers who were [appointed] over the work, who directed the people performing the work. ³¹ The king commanded and they quarried great stones, heavy stones, to lay the foundation of the Temple with hewn stones. ³² The builders of Solomon, the builders of Hiram and the Gebalites* carved the stones, and they prepared the wood and the stones to build the Temple.

6

Solomon commences building the Temple

Chambers and materials

¹ In the four hundred and eightieth year after the Children of Israel's exodus from the land of Egypt — in the fourth year of Solomon's reign over Israel, in the month of Ziv,* which is the second month — he built the Temple for HASHEM. ² The Temple that King Solomon built for HASHEM: sixty cubits was its length,* twenty cubits was its width, and thirty cubits was its height. ³ The Hall in front of the Sanctuary of the Temple: twenty cubits [was] its length across the width of the Temple; and ten cubits its width, in front of the Temple. ⁴ He made narrowing windows* for the Temple.

⁵ Against the wall of the Temple he built an annex all around, [built into] the walls of the Temple all around the Sanctuary and the Inner Sanctum, and he made side-chambers* all around. ⁶ The lowest [story] of the annex, its width [was] five cubits; the middle [story], six cubits its width, and the third [story], seven cubits its width; for he had provided recesses around the outside of the wall of the Temple, in order not to penetrate the walls of the Temple.*

⁷ When the Temple was being built, it was built of complete quarried stone; but the hammers, the chisel, any iron utensil, was not heard in the Temple when it was being built.*

⁸ The entrance to the central [ground level] side-chamber was at the south side of the Temple, and they would ascend on winding stairs to the middle [story], and from the middle [story] to the third.

⁹ He built the Temple and completed it; he made the Temple ceiling of decorative [wooden] panels [under] cedar planks. ¹⁰ He built the annex along the entire Temple, five cubits was its height, and he covered the house with cedar wood.*

God's promise

¹¹ The word of HASHEM then came to Solomon, saying, ¹² "This Temple that you build — if you follow My decrees, perform My statutes, and observe all My commandments, to follow them, I shall uphold My word with you that I spoke to David your father. ¹³ I shall dwell among the Children of Israel, and I shall not forsake My people Israel."

6:5. To be used for storage and other needs of the Temple.

6:6. Rather than making large holes in the Temple wall for the beams that would support the annex's upper stories, Solomon indented the wall's thickness by one cubit at different levels, to form ledges upon which to place the beams.

6:7. Solomon did not use iron tools because "The Temple

was constructed in order to prolong men's lives, and iron implements are used to shorten men's lives; it is not fitting that the thing that shortens should be given power over the thing that prolongs" (Mechilta).

6:10. He roofed the annex with cedar wood, which rested upon the highest ledge in the outer wall, as described above (6:6).

טו שְׁלֹמֹה אֶת־הַבַּיִת וַיְכַלֵּהוּ וַיִּבֶן אֶת־קִירוֹת הַבַּיִת מִבַּיְתָה בְּצַלְעוֹת
אֲרָזִים מִקַּרְקַע הַבַּיִת עַד־קִירוֹת הַסִּפֻּן צִפָּה עֵץ מִבָּיִת וַיְצַף אֶת־קַרְקַע
טז הַבַּיִת בְּצַלְעוֹת בְּרוֹשִׁים: וַיִּבֶן אֶת־עֶשְׂרִים אַמָּה °מירכותי [מִיַּרְכְּתֵי
ק] הַבַּיִת בְּצַלְעוֹת אֲרָזִים מִן־הַקַּרְקַע עַד־הַקִּירוֹת וַיִּבֶן לוֹ מִבַּיִת לִדְבִיר
יז-יח לְקֹדֶשׁ הַקֳּדָשִׁים: וְאַרְבָּעִים בָּאַמָּה הָיָה הַבָּיִת הוּא הַהֵיכָל לִפְנָי: וְאֶרֶז
אֶל־הַבַּיִת פְּנִימָה מִקְלַעַת פְּקָעִים וּפְטוּרֵי צִצִּים הַכֹּל אֶרֶז אֵין אֶבֶן
יט נִרְאָה: וּדְבִיר בְּתוֹךְ־הַבַּיִת מִפְּנִימָה הֵכִין לְתִתֵּן שָׁם אֶת־אֲרוֹן בְּרִית
כ יְהוָה: וְלִפְנֵי הַדְּבִיר עֶשְׂרִים אַמָּה אֹרֶךְ וְעֶשְׂרִים אַמָּה רֹחַב וְעֶשְׂרִים
כא אַמָּה קוֹמָתוֹ וַיְצַפֵּהוּ זָהָב סָגוּר וַיְצַף מִזְבֵּחַ אָרֶז: וַיְצַף שְׁלֹמֹה אֶת־
הַבַּיִת מִפְּנִימָה זָהָב סָגוּר וַיְעַבֵּר °ברתיקות [בְּרַתּוּקוֹת ק] זָהָב לִפְנֵי
כב הַדְּבִיר וַיְצַפֵּהוּ זָהָב: וְאֶת־כָּל־הַבַּיִת צִפָּה זָהָב עַד־תֹּם כָּל־הַבָּיִת וְכָל־
כג הַמִּזְבֵּחַ אֲשֶׁר־לַדְּבִיר צִפָּה זָהָב: וַיַּעַשׂ בַּדְּבִיר שְׁנֵי כְרוּבִים עֲצֵי־
כד שָׁמֶן עֶשֶׂר אַמּוֹת קוֹמָתוֹ: וְחָמֵשׁ אַמּוֹת כְּנַף הַכְּרוּב הָאֶחָת וְחָמֵשׁ
אַמּוֹת כְּנַף הַכְּרוּב הַשֵּׁנִית עֶשֶׂר אַמּוֹת מִקְצוֹת כְּנָפָיו וְעַד־קְצוֹת
כה כְּנָפָיו: וְעֶשֶׂר בָּאַמָּה הַכְּרוּב הַשֵּׁנִי מִדָּה אַחַת וְקֶצֶב אֶחָד לִשְׁנֵי הַכְּרֻבִים:
כו-כז קוֹמַת הַכְּרוּב הָאֶחָד עֶשֶׂר בָּאַמָּה וְכֵן הַכְּרוּב הַשֵּׁנִי: וַיִּתֵּן אֶת־הַכְּרוּבִים
בְּתוֹךְ | הַבַּיִת הַפְּנִימִי וַיִּפְרְשׂוּ אֶת־כַּנְפֵי הַכְּרֻבִים וַתִּגַּע כְּנַף הָאֶחָד
בַּקִּיר וּכְנַף הַכְּרוּב הַשֵּׁנִי נֹגַעַת בַּקִּיר הַשֵּׁנִי וְכַנְפֵיהֶם אֶל־תּוֹךְ הַבַּיִת
כח-כט נֹגְעֹת כָּנָף אֶל־כָּנָף: וַיְצַף אֶת־הַכְּרוּבִים זָהָב: וְאֵת כָּל־קִירוֹת הַבַּיִת
מֵסַב | קָלַע פִּתּוּחֵי מִקְלְעוֹת כְּרוּבִים וְתִמֹרֹת וּפְטוּרֵי צִצִּים מִלִּפְנִים
ל-לא וְלַחִיצוֹן: וְאֶת־קַרְקַע הַבַּיִת צִפָּה זָהָב לִפְנִימָה וְלַחִיצוֹן: וְאֵת פֶּתַח
לב הַדְּבִיר עָשָׂה דַּלְתוֹת עֲצֵי־שָׁמֶן הָאַיִל מְזוּזוֹת חֲמִשִׁית: וּשְׁתֵּי דַּלְתוֹת
עֲצֵי־שֶׁמֶן וְקָלַע עֲלֵיהֶם מִקְלְעוֹת כְּרוּבִים וְתִמֹרוֹת וּפְטוּרֵי צִצִּים וְצִפָּה
לג זָהָב וַיָּרֶד עַל־הַכְּרוּבִים וְעַל־הַתִּמֹרוֹת אֶת־הַזָּהָב: וְכֵן עָשָׂה לְפֶתַח
לד הַהֵיכָל מְזוּזוֹת עֲצֵי־שָׁמֶן מֵאֵת רְבִעִית: וּשְׁתֵּי דַלְתוֹת עֲצֵי בְרוֹשִׁים
שְׁנֵי צְלָעִים הַדֶּלֶת הָאַחַת גְּלִילִים וּשְׁנֵי קְלָעִים הַדֶּלֶת הַשֵּׁנִית גְּלִילִים:
לה וְקָלַע כְּרוּבִים וְתִמֹרוֹת וּפְטוּרֵי צִצִּים וְצִפָּה זָהָב מְיֻשָּׁר עַל־הַמְחֻקֶּה:

6:15. Since he wanted the interior of the Temple to be overlaid with gold (vv. 19-22), he had to first cover the walls with wood, as it is impossible to attach gold sheets to stone (*Rashi*).

6:16. The word דְּבִיר refers either to the entire Holy of Holies, or to the Inner Sanctum (as in v. 5), (as in this verse), or to the Partition separating the forty-cubit Sanctuary from the twenty-cubit Inner Sanctum.

6:20. The ceiling above the Inner Sanctum was apparently ten cubits lower than that of the rest of the Temple, whose height was given before as thirty cubits (v. 2) (*Rashi*); the Talmud, however, explains that the height of

the Inner Sanctum was twenty cubits *above* the Cherubim, which were ten cubits tall (see v. 23).

The Altar mentioned here is the Incense Altar (see *Exodus* 30:6) that was in front of the Partition (*Radak*). Since the sixty-by-twenty-cubit Temple was twice the width and twice the length of the thirty-by-ten-cubit Tabernacle, Solomon enlarged the Incense Altar proportionately by adding cedar panels covered with gold (*Vilna Gaon*).

6:26. Unlike those made in the time of Moses (*Exodus* 25:18), these Cherubim stood on the floor.

6:27. The Cherubim stood alongside one another,

Walls and floor ¹⁴ Solomon had built the Temple and finished it. ¹⁵ He built the walls of the Temple on the inside with cedar boards; from the Temple floor to the ceiling beams he overlaid it with wood on the inside. * He also overlaid the Temple floor with cypress boards. ¹⁶ He built [an overlay for] the twenty cubits at the rear of the Temple of cedar boards, from the floor to the beams; and he prepared this area inside the Partition * to be the Holy of Holies. ¹⁷ The Temple was forty cubits long — that is, the Sanctuary at the front. ¹⁸ The cedar upon the Temple on the inside was [decorated with] a network of designs of knobs and blossoming flowers. Everything was [covered with] cedar wood; stone was not visible.

The Inner Sanctum ¹⁹ He prepared an Inner Sanctum in the Temple towards the inside, there to place the Ark of the Covenant of HASHEM. ²⁰ Behind the Partition [was an area] twenty cubits in length and twenty cubits in width and twenty cubits its height. * He overlaid [the Partition] with fine gold; he also overlaid an altar with cedar wood. * ²¹ Solomon then overlaid the inner section of the Temple with fine gold; and he drew golden chains in front of the Partition, and he overlaid it with gold. ²² He then overlaid the whole Temple with gold, until the entire Temple was completely [overlaid]; the whole altar [that stood opposite the entrance] of the Inner Sanctum he overlaid with gold.

The Cherubim ²³ In the Inner Sanctum he made two Cherubim out of olive wood, [each one,] its height ten cubits; ²⁴ and five cubits the one wing of the Cherub, and five cubits the second wing of the Cherub, ten cubits from the edge of its [one] wing to the edge of its [other] wing. ²⁵ The other Cherub was [also] ten cubits; one size and one form for the two Cherubim. ²⁶ The height of one Cherub [was] ten cubits, * and so the second Cherub. ²⁷ He put the Cherubim inside the inner chamber, and they spread out the Cherubim's wings; the wing of one touched the wall and the wing of the other touched the second wall, and their [other] wings, which were in the center of the chamber, were touching wing to wing. *

Walls and floor ²⁸ He overlaid the Cherubim with gold. ²⁹ All the walls of the Temple were surrounded by designs, an engraved network of figures of cherubim and palm trees and blossoming flowers, in the inside [chamber] and in the outside [chamber]. ³⁰ He overlaid the floor of the house with gold also, in the inner [chamber] and in the outer [chamber].

Entrance doors ³¹ For the entrance of the Inner Sanctum he made doors of olive wood — the door frame was five-sided* — ³² and two doors of olive wood upon which he engraved designs of cherubim, palms and blossoming flowers, and he overlaid [them] with gold; he pressed the gold over the cherubim and the palms. ³³ He also made door-posts of olive wood for the entrance of the Sanctuary, which were four-sided, ³⁴ and two doors of cypress wood, with two rounded hinges for the one door and two rounded hinges for the second door. ³⁵ He [then] engraved [on the doors] designs of cherubim and palms and blossoming flowers, and he overlaid [them] with gold, which was flattened over the engraved designs.

---

facing the Partition, with their wing spans spread out north to south. Thus the combined ten-foot wing spans covered the twenty-foot width of the Inner Sanctum, touching the northern and southern walls.

6:31. The doorposts were not square, but pentagonal in cross-section (*Rashi*). Alternatively, each doorpost was made of five boards, presumably for decoration (*Rashi*).

לו-לז וַיִּבֶן אֶת־הֶחָצֵר הַפְּנִימִית שְׁלֹשָׁה טוּרֵי גָזִית וְטוּר כְּרֻתֹת אֲרָזִים: בַּשָּׁנָה
לח הָרְבִיעִית יֻסַּד בֵּית יהוה בְּיֶרַח זִו: וּבַשָּׁנָה הָאַחַת עֶשְׂרֵה בְּיֶרַח בּוּל הוּא
הַחֹדֶשׁ הַשְּׁמִינִי כָּלָה הַבַּיִת לְכָל־דְּבָרָיו וּלְכָל־ °מִשְׁפָּטוֹ [מִשְׁפָּטָיו ק]

ז א וַיִּבְנֵהוּ שֶׁבַע שָׁנִים: וְאֶת־בֵּיתוֹ בָּנָה שְׁלֹמֹה שְׁלֹשׁ עֶשְׂרֵה שָׁנָה וַיְכַל אֶת־
ב כָּל־בֵּיתוֹ: וַיִּבֶן אֶת־בֵּית ׀ יַעַר הַלְּבָנוֹן מֵאָה אַמָּה אָרְכּוֹ וַחֲמִשִּׁים אַמָּה
רָחְבּוֹ וּשְׁלֹשִׁים אַמָּה קוֹמָתוֹ עַל אַרְבָּעָה טוּרֵי עַמּוּדֵי אֲרָזִים וּכְרֻתוֹת
ג אֲרָזִים עַל־הָעַמּוּדִים: וְסָפֻן בָּאֶרֶז מִמַּעַל עַל־הַצְּלָעֹת אֲשֶׁר עַל־
ד הָעַמּוּדִים אַרְבָּעִים וַחֲמִשָּׁה חֲמִשָּׁה עָשָׂר הַטּוּר: וּשְׁקֻפִים שְׁלֹשָׁה טוּרִים
ה וּמֶחֱזָה אֶל־מֶחֱזָה שָׁלֹשׁ פְּעָמִים: וְכָל־הַפְּתָחִים וְהַמְּזוּזוֹת רְבֻעִים שָׁקֶף
ו וּמוּל מֶחֱזָה אֶל־מֶחֱזָה שָׁלֹשׁ פְּעָמִים: וְאֵת אוּלָם הָעַמּוּדִים עָשָׂה
חֲמִשִּׁים אַמָּה אָרְכּוֹ וּשְׁלֹשִׁים אַמָּה רָחְבּוֹ וְאוּלָם עַל־פְּנֵיהֶם וְעַמֻּדִים
ז וְעָב עַל־פְּנֵיהֶם: וְאוּלָם הַכִּסֵּא אֲשֶׁר יִשְׁפָּט־שָׁם אֻלָם הַמִּשְׁפָּט עָשָׂה
ח וְסָפוּן בָּאֶרֶז מֵהַקַּרְקַע עַד־הַקַּרְקָע: וּבֵיתוֹ אֲשֶׁר־יֵשֵׁב שָׁם חָצֵר הָאַחֶרֶת
מִבֵּית לָאוּלָם כַּמַּעֲשֶׂה הַזֶּה הָיָה וּבַיִת יַעֲשֶׂה לְבַת־פַּרְעֹה אֲשֶׁר לָקַח
ט שְׁלֹמֹה כָּאוּלָם הַזֶּה: כָּל־אֵלֶּה אֲבָנִים יְקָרֹת כְּמִדֹּת גָּזִית מְגֹרָרוֹת בַּמְּגֵרָה
י מִבַּיִת וּמִחוּץ וּמִמַּסָּד עַד־הַטְּפָחוֹת וּמִחוּץ עַד־הֶחָצֵר הַגְּדוֹלָה: וּמְיֻסָּד
אֲבָנִים יְקָרוֹת אֲבָנִים גְּדֹלוֹת אַבְנֵי עֶשֶׂר אַמּוֹת וְאַבְנֵי שְׁמֹנֶה אַמּוֹת:
יא-יב וּמִלְמַעְלָה אֲבָנִים יְקָרוֹת כְּמִדּוֹת גָּזִית וָאָרֶז: וְחָצֵר הַגְּדוֹלָה סָבִיב
שְׁלֹשָׁה טוּרִים גָּזִית וְטוּר כְּרֻתֹת אֲרָזִים וְלַחֲצַר בֵּית־יהוה הַפְּנִימִית
יג וּלְאֻלָם הַבָּיִת: ◄ וַיִּשְׁלַח הַמֶּלֶךְ שְׁלֹמֹה וַיִּקַּח אֶת־חִירָם

HAFTARAS
VAYAKHEL
Sephardim:
7:13-26

יד מִצֹּר: בֶּן־אִשָּׁה אַלְמָנָה הוּא מִמַּטֵּה נַפְתָּלִי וְאָבִיו אִישׁ־צֹרִי חֹרֵשׁ נְחֹשֶׁת
וַיִּמָּלֵא אֶת־הַחָכְמָה וְאֶת־הַתְּבוּנָה וְאֶת־הַדַּעַת לַעֲשׂוֹת כָּל־מְלָאכָה
טו בַּנְּחֹשֶׁת וַיָּבוֹא אֶל־הַמֶּלֶךְ שְׁלֹמֹה וַיַּעַשׂ אֶת־כָּל־מְלַאכְתּוֹ: וַיָּצַר אֶת־
שְׁנֵי הָעַמּוּדִים נְחֹשֶׁת שְׁמֹנֶה עֶשְׂרֵה אַמָּה קוֹמַת הָעַמּוּד הָאֶחָד וְחוּט
טז שְׁתֵּים־עֶשְׂרֵה אַמָּה יָסֹב אֶת־הָעַמּוּד הַשֵּׁנִי: וּשְׁתֵּי כֹתָרֹת עָשָׂה
לָתֵת עַל־רָאשֵׁי הָעַמּוּדִים מֻצַק נְחֹשֶׁת חָמֵשׁ אַמּוֹת קוֹמַת הַכֹּתֶרֶת
יז הָאֶחָת וְחָמֵשׁ אַמּוֹת קוֹמַת הַכֹּתֶרֶת הַשֵּׁנִית: שְׂבָכִים מַעֲשֵׂה שְׂבָכָה
גְּדִלִים מַעֲשֵׂה שַׁרְשְׁרוֹת לַכֹּתָרֹת אֲשֶׁר עַל־רֹאשׁ הָעַמּוּדִים שִׁבְעָה

6:36. This was a continuous pattern used for the entire height of the wall — three layers of stone followed by one of cedar.

6:37-38. *Ziv* is the month of Iyar; *Bul* is the month of Cheshvan.

7:1. After stating that Solomon worked with alacrity for seven years to build the Temple, Scripture contrasts it with the slow pace with which he worked on his own palace (*Rashi*).

7:2. A summer house (*Targum*), with many doors and windows to allow an ample flow of air. It was called "House of the Forest of Lebanon" because the numerous pillars (which were made of cedars imported from Lebanon) made it look like a forest (*Rashi* to v. 5). Alternatively, this royal summer home was built in the cool shade of the forest called Lebanon (*Radak*).

7:3. The four rows of pillars supported three rows of roofing planks.

7:4. (*Radak*). Alternatively, this refers not to windows, but to additional smaller roofing planks, because forty-

Courtyard wall | [36] He then built [a wall around] the inner courtyard, three rows of hewn stone and a row of cedar beams. *

Seven-year construction | [37] In [Solomon's] fourth year the foundation of the House of HASHEM was laid, in the month of Ziv. * [38] And in the eleventh year, in the month of Bul, * which is the eighth month, the House was completed according to all its particulars and all its specifications; he built it over seven years.

7

Solomon builds his palace | [1] **H**is own house Solomon built over thirteen years, and he finished his entire palace. * [2] He built the "House of the Forest of Lebanon,"* one hundred cubits it length, fifty cubits its width, and thirty cubits its height; over four rows of cedar pillars, with cedar beams over the pillars. [3] It was roofed with cedar overhead, upon the boards that were atop the pillars; there were forty-five [boards], fifteen per row. * [4] There were also three rows of windows, * opening opposite opening, three times. [5] All the doorways and doorposts had four-sided frames; they were aligned, opening opposite opening, three times. [6] He made a portico of pillars for [this building], fifty cubits its length, and thirty cubits its width. * The portico was situated in front of [the doors of the building]; it had [its own] pillars with a thick beam upon them.

Hall of Justice | [7] He made a hall for the throne where he would judge, a hall of judgment; it was covered with cedarwood from one end of the floor to the other.

[8] His house where he dwelt, which was in another courtyard, beyond the hall, was of the same construction. He [also] made a house like this hall for the daughter of Pharaoh, whom Solomon had taken [as a wife].

Precious materials | [9] All these were [built of] valuable stones, the size of hewn stones, filed smooth with a file, on the inside and on the outside and from the foundation to the ceiling — and outdoors until the great courtyard. [10] It was founded upon valuable stones, large stones — stones of ten cubits and stones of eight cubits. [11] But above ground, there were valuable stones the size of hewn stones, and cedar. * [12] The great courtyard all around [the king's buildings], its [walls] were made of three rows of hewn stone and a row of cedar boards, as was done for the Inner Courtyard of the Temple of HASHEM * and for the Hall of the Temple.

An imported coppersmith | [13] King Solomon sent and took Hiram from Tyre. * [14] He was the son of a widowed woman, from the tribe of Naphtali; his father had been a Tyrian coppersmith. He was full of wisdom, insight and knowledge to do all sorts of work with copper; so he came to King Solomon and performed all his work.

Ornamental pillars; Jachin and Boaz | [15] He designed the two pillars of copper; eighteen cubits the height of the one pillar, and a twelve-cubit string could go around [its circumference] — [and likewise for the] second pillar. [16] He made two capitals to place upon the tops of the pillars, of molten copper; five cubits the height of the one capital, and five cubits the height of the second capital. * [17] There were nettings of meshwork and ropes of chainwork on the capitals that were upon the pillars; seven [designs]

---

five planks could not cover the larger area of the house (*Rashi*).

7:6. The length of the portico ran along the fifty-cubit width of the building (*Rashi*).

7:11. Above ground level, the stones used for the walls were of the standard hewn-stone size, as mentioned just previously, and cedarwood was used for the

ceiling (*Abarbanel*).

7:12. As described above, 6:36.

7:13. This Hiram was not the king of Tyre. In *II Chronicles* 2:12, he is called Huram.

7:16. The lower two cubits of the capitals were hollow and fit over the pillars; the upper three cubits were decorated as described below (*Rashi*; see *II Kings* 25:17).

יח לְכֹתֶרֶת הָאֶחָת וְשִׁבְעָה לַכֹּתֶרֶת הַשֵּׁנִית: וַיַּעַשׂ אֶת־הָעַמּוּדִים וּשְׁנֵי
טוּרִים סָבִיב עַל־הַשְּׂבָכָה הָאֶחָת לְכַסּוֹת אֶת־הַכֹּתָרֹת אֲשֶׁר עַל־רֹאשׁ

יט הָרִמֹּנִים וְכֵן עָשָׂה לַכֹּתֶרֶת הַשֵּׁנִית: וְכֹתָרֹת אֲשֶׁר עַל־רֹאשׁ הָעַמּוּדִים

כ מַעֲשֵׂה שׁוּשָׁן בָּאוּלָם אַרְבַּע אַמּוֹת: וְכֹתָרֹת עַל־שְׁנֵי הָעַמּוּדִים גַּם־
מִמַּעַל מִלְּעֻמַּת הַבֶּטֶן אֲשֶׁר לְעֵבֶר °שבכה [הַשְּׂבָכָה קּ] וְהָרִמּוֹנִים

כא מָאתַיִם טֻרִים סָבִיב עַל הַכֹּתֶרֶת הַשֵּׁנִית: וַיָּקֶם אֶת־הָעַמֻּדִים לְאֻלָם
הַהֵיכָל וַיָּקֶם אֶת־הָעַמּוּד הַיְמָנִי וַיִּקְרָא אֶת־שְׁמוֹ יָכִין וַיָּקֶם אֶת־הָעַמּוּד

כב הַשְּׂמָאלִי וַיִּקְרָא אֶת־שְׁמוֹ בֹּעַז: וְעַל רֹאשׁ הָעַמּוּדִים מַעֲשֵׂה שׁוֹשָׁן וַתִּתֹּם

כג מְלֶאכֶת הָעַמּוּדִים: וַיַּעַשׂ אֶת־הַיָּם מוּצָק עֶשֶׂר בָּאַמָּה
מִשְּׂפָתוֹ עַד־שְׂפָתוֹ עָגֹל | סָבִיב וְחָמֵשׁ בָּאַמָּה קוֹמָתוֹ °וקוה [וְקָו קּ]

כד שְׁלֹשִׁים בָּאַמָּה יָסֹב אֹתוֹ סָבִיב: וּפְקָעִים מִתַּחַת לִשְׂפָתוֹ | סָבִיב סְבָבִים
אֹתוֹ עֶשֶׂר בָּאַמָּה מַקִּפִים אֶת־הַיָּם סָבִיב שְׁנֵי טוּרִים הַפְּקָעִים יְצֻקִים

כה בִּיצֻקָתוֹ: עֹמֵד עַל־שְׁנֵי עָשָׂר בָּקָר שְׁלֹשָׁה פֹנִים | צָפוֹנָה וּשְׁלֹשָׁה פֹנִים |
יָמָּה וּשְׁלֹשָׁה | פֹּנִים נֶגְבָּה וּשְׁלֹשָׁה פֹּנִים מִזְרָחָה וְהַיָּם עֲלֵיהֶם מִלְמָעְלָה

כו וְכָל־אֲחֹרֵיהֶם בָּיְתָה: וְעָבְיוֹ טֶפַח וּשְׂפָתוֹ כְּמַעֲשֵׂה שְׂפַת־כּוֹס פֶּרַח שׁוֹשָׁן
אַלְפַּיִם בַּת יָכִיל: ▸ וַיַּעַשׂ אֶת־הַמְּכֹנוֹת עֶשֶׂר נְחֹשֶׁת אַרְבַּע

כז בָּאַמָּה אֹרֶךְ הַמְּכוֹנָה הָאֶחָת וְאַרְבַּע בָּאַמָּה רָחְבָּהּ וְשָׁלֹשׁ בָּאַמָּה

כח קוֹמָתָהּ: וְזֶה מַעֲשֵׂה הַמְּכוֹנָה מִסְגְּרֹת לָהֶם וּמִסְגְּרֹת בֵּין הַשְׁלַבִּים: וְעַל־
הַמִּסְגְּרוֹת אֲשֶׁר | בֵּין הַשְׁלַבִּים אֲרָיוֹת | בָּקָר וּכְרוּבִים וְעַל־הַשְׁלַבִּים כֵּן

ל מִמָּעַל וּמִתַּחַת לַאֲרָיוֹת וְלַבָּקָר לֹיוֹת מַעֲשֵׂה מוֹרָד: וְאַרְבָּעָה אוֹפַנֵּי
נְחֹשֶׁת לַמְּכוֹנָה הָאֶחָת וְסַרְנֵי נְחֹשֶׁת וְאַרְבָּעָה פַעֲמֹתָיו כְּתֵפֹת לָהֶם

לא מִתַּחַת לַכִּיֹּר הַכְּתֵפֹת יְצֻקוֹת מֵעֵבֶר אִישׁ לֹיוֹת: וּפִיהוּ מִבֵּית לַכֹּתֶרֶת
וָמַעְלָה בָּאַמָּה וּפִיהָ עָגֹל מַעֲשֵׂה־כֵן אַמָּה וַחֲצִי הָאַמָּה וְגַם־עַל־פִּיהָ

לב מִקְלָעוֹת וּמִסְגְּרֹתֵיהֶם מְרֻבָּעוֹת לֹא עֲגֻלּוֹת: וְאַרְבַּעַת הָאוֹפַנִּים לְמִתַּחַת
לַמִּסְגְּרוֹת וִידוֹת הָאוֹפַנִּים בַּמְּכוֹנָה וְקוֹמַת הָאוֹפַן הָאֶחָד אַמָּה וַחֲצִי

לג הָאַמָּה: וּמַעֲשֵׂה הָאוֹפַנִּים כְּמַעֲשֵׂה אוֹפַן הַמֶּרְכָּבָה יְדוֹתָם וְגַבֵּיהֶם
וְחִשֻּׁקֵיהֶם וְחִשֻּׁרֵיהֶם הַכֹּל מוּצָק: וְאַרְבַּע כְּתֵפוֹת אֶל אַרְבַּע פִּנּוֹת

לה הַמְּכֹנָה הָאֶחָת מִן־הַמְּכֹנָה כְּתֵפֶיהָ: וּבְרֹאשׁ הַמְּכוֹנָה חֲצִי הָאַמָּה קוֹמָה
עָגֹל | סָבִיב וְעַל רֹאשׁ הַמְּכֹנָה יְדֹתֶיהָ וּמִסְגְּרֹתֶיהָ מִמֶּנָּה: וַיְפַתַּח עַל־

לו הַלֻּחֹת יְדֹתֶיהָ וְעַל °ומסגרתיה [מִסְגְּרֹתֶיהָ קּ] כְּרוּבִים אֲרָיוֹת וְתִמֹרֹת

7:18. Hundreds of brass pomegranates were attached to the capital, on top of the netting design. Two "rows" (of chains or lines) were strung around the capital, on which two rows of pomegranates were hung (*Abarbanel*).

7:19. The pillars were placed at the entrance to the Temple's hall, as mentioned below (*Abarbanel*).

7:20. The capitals consisted of two sections: an upper

one, which was shaped like a bowl turned over, had the network and chain designs, and a lower one, which was shaped like a bowl, was unornamented. The seam where the lips of the two bowls were joined is referred to here as the *bulge*, since it was spherical.

7:21. Solomon gave them these names to symbolize his prayer that the Temple be firmly established and be for the one capital and seven for the second capital. ¹⁸ He made the pillars; [he placed] two rows going all around upon the one netting, to cover the capitals that were on top, with the pomegranates, * and he did likewise for the second capital. ¹⁹ [Over] the capitals, which were atop the pillars, was a molded flower — in the hall* — four cubits high. ²⁰ [These molded flowers over] the capitals on the two pillars also extended over opposite the bulge which was at the edge of the netting. * There were two hundred pomegranate figures, [arranged in] rows all around; [and likewise] for the second capital. ²¹ He erected the pillars by the hall of the Sanctuary; he erected the right pillar and called its name "Jachin" [Establish], and he erected the left pillar and called its name "Boaz" [Strength Is in It]. * ²² Upon the top of the pillars [was placed] a flowered figure, and the work of the pillars was complete.

The "sea" ²³ He made the "sea" of cast [metal] * ten cubits from its one lip to its [other] lip, circular all around, five cubits its height; a thirty-cubit line could encircle it all around. * ²⁴ Knobs under its lip surrounded it ten cubits [in length], girdling the sea all around, * two rows of the knobs, which were cast with the casting [of the sea]. ²⁵ It stood upon twelve oxen, three facing north, three facing west, three facing south and three facing east; the sea was on top of them, and their haunches were toward the center [of the sea]. ²⁶ Its thickness was one hand-breadth; its lip was like the lip of a cup, with a rose-blossom design; its capacity was two thousand bath-measures. *

Ten stands ²⁷ He then made ten copper stands, four cubits each stand, four cubits its for width and three cubits its height. * ²⁸ This is the workmanship of the stands: ten lavers They had frames, and [more] frames between the rods; ²⁹ and on the frames which were between the rods [were engraved] lions, oxen and cherubim. There was a base upon the rods, above them. Under the lions and the oxen there were braces of hammered metal. ³⁰ There were four copper wheels to each stand, and copper bars that had shafts at their four corners; the shafts were cast under the basin, opposite each brace. ³¹ The opening [of the stand] extended from inside the capital [of the stand] one cubit upward; its opening was round, like the workmanship of the stand, one and a half cubits [in diameter]. There were designs upon the rim also. The frames were square, not circular. ³² As for the four wheels that were under the frames — the axles of the wheels were [built] into the stand, and the height of each wheel was one and a half cubits. ³³ The workmanship of the wheels was like the workmanship of the chariot's wheel; their axles, their hubs, their rims and their spokes were all made of cast [copper]. ³⁴ [There were] four shafts at the four corners of each stand; from the stand its shafts came. ³⁵ At the top of the stand there was a round [frame] half a cubit high surrounding [the opening], and on the top of the stand its rods and its frames were all from it. ³⁶ And he engraved upon the tablets, upon its rods and upon its frames, cherubim, lions and palms,

---

blessed with the strength of God forever (Radak).

7:23. The "sea" was a copper tank that was filled with water and used by the Kohanim for ritual immersion (II Chronicles 4:6).

Either the given numbers are approximations, or the ten-cubit diameter is measured outer lip to outer lip, while the thirty-cubit circumference is measured on the inner surface (Ralbag).

7:24. The Talmud explains that the upper two cubits of the sea were round, while the lower three cubits were in the form of a ten-cubit square. The knobs decorated the lower three cubits, ten cubits on each side (Rashi).

7:26. Opinions regarding the modern equivalent of a bath range between 6.75 and 12 gallon. Thus, the sea held 13,500-24,000 gallons.

7:27. The stands supported the lavers described in v. 38.

לז כְּמַעַר־אִישׁ וְלֹיֹות סָבִיב: כָּזֹאת עָשָׂה אֵת עֶשֶׂר הַמְּכֹנוֹת מוּצָק אֶחָד

לח מִדָּה אַחַת קֶצֶב אֶחָד לְכֻלָּהְנָה: וַיַּעַשׂ עֲשָׂרָה כִּיֹרוֹת נְחֹשֶׁת אַרְבָּעִים בַּת יָכִיל | הַכִּיּוֹר הָאֶחָד אַרְבַּע בָּאַמָּה הַכִּיּוֹר הָאֶחָד כִּיּוֹר אֶחָד

לט עַל־הַמְּכוֹנָה הָאַחַת לְעֶשֶׂר הַמְּכֹנוֹת: וַיִּתֵּן אֶת־הַמְּכֹנוֹת חָמֵשׁ עַל־כֶּתֶף הַבַּיִת מִיָּמִין וְחָמֵשׁ עַל־כֶּתֶף הַבַּיִת מִשְּׂמֹאלוֹ וְאֶת־הַיָּם נָתַן מִכֶּתֶף הַבַּיִת

מ הַיְמָנִית קֵדְמָה מִמּוּל נֶגֶב: ◀ וַיַּעַשׂ חִירוֹם אֶת־הַכִּיֹּרוֹת וְאֶת־הַיָּעִים וְאֶת־הַמִּזְרָקוֹת וַיְכַל חִירָם לַעֲשׂוֹת אֶת־כָּל־הַמְּלָאכָה אֲשֶׁר

מא עָשָׂה לַמֶּלֶךְ שְׁלֹמֹה בֵּית יְהֹוָה: עַמֻּדִים שְׁנַיִם וְגֻלֹּת הַכֹּתָרֹת אֲשֶׁר־עַל־רֹאשׁ הָעַמּוּדִים שְׁתָּיִם וְהַשְּׂבָכוֹת שְׁתַּיִם לְכַסּוֹת אֶת־שְׁתֵּי גֻּלֹּת הַכֹּתָרֹת

מב אֲשֶׁר עַל־רֹאשׁ הָעַמּוּדִים: וְאֶת־הָרִמֹּנִים אַרְבַּע מֵאוֹת לִשְׁתֵּי הַשְּׂבָכוֹת שְׁנֵי־טוּרִים רִמֹּנִים לַשְּׂבָכָה הָאֶחָת לְכַסּוֹת אֶת־שְׁתֵּי גֻּלֹּת הַכֹּתָרֹת

מג אֲשֶׁר עַל־פְּנֵי הָעַמּוּדִים: וְאֶת־הַמְּכֹנוֹת עָשֶׂר וְאֶת־הַכִּיֹּרֹת עֲשָׂרָה עַל־הַמְּכֹנוֹת:

מד-מה וְאֶת־הַיָּם הָאֶחָד וְאֶת־הַבָּקָר שְׁנֵים־עָשָׂר תַּחַת הַיָּם: וְאֶת־הַסִּירוֹת וְאֶת־הַיָּעִים וְאֶת־הַמִּזְרָקוֹת וְאֵת כָּל־הַכֵּלִים הָאֵהֶל °הָאֵלֶּה ק]

מו אֲשֶׁר עָשָׂה חִירָם לַמֶּלֶךְ שְׁלֹמֹה בֵּית יְהֹוָה נְחֹשֶׁת מְמֹרָט: בְּכִכַּר הַיַּרְדֵּן יְצָקָם הַמֶּלֶךְ בְּמַעֲבֵה הָאֲדָמָה בֵּין סֻכּוֹת וּבֵין צָרְתָן: וַיַּנַּח שְׁלֹמֹה אֶת־

מז כָּל־הַכֵּלִים מֵרֹב מְאֹד מְאֹד לֹא נֶחְקַר מִשְׁקַל הַנְּחֹשֶׁת: וַיַּעַשׂ שְׁלֹמֹה אֵת

מח כָּל־הַכֵּלִים אֲשֶׁר בֵּית יְהֹוָה אֵת מִזְבַּח הַזָּהָב וְאֶת־הַשֻּׁלְחָן אֲשֶׁר עָלָיו

מט לֶחֶם הַפָּנִים זָהָב: וְאֶת־הַמְּנֹרוֹת חָמֵשׁ מִיָּמִין וְחָמֵשׁ מִשְּׂמֹאול לִפְנֵי

נ הַדְּבִיר זָהָב סָגוּר וְהַפֶּרַח וְהַנֵּרֹת וְהַמֶּלְקָחַיִם זָהָב: וְהַסִּפּוֹת וְהַמְזַמְּרוֹת וְהַמִּזְרָקוֹת וְהַכַּפּוֹת וְהַמַּחְתּוֹת זָהָב סָגוּר וְהַפֹּתוֹת לְדַלְתוֹת הַבַּיִת

נא הַפְּנִימִי לְקֹדֶשׁ הַקֳּדָשִׁים לְדַלְתֵי הַבַּיִת לַהֵיכָל זָהָב: ◀ וַתִּשְׁלַם כָּל־הַמְּלָאכָה אֲשֶׁר עָשָׂה הַמֶּלֶךְ שְׁלֹמֹה בֵּית יְהֹוָה וַיָּבֵא שְׁלֹמֹה אֶת־קָדְשֵׁי | דָּוִד אָבִיו אֶת־הַכֶּסֶף וְאֶת־הַזָּהָב וְאֶת־הַכֵּלִים נָתַן בְּאֹצְרוֹת בֵּית

א יְהֹוָה: **ח** אָז יַקְהֵל שְׁלֹמֹה אֶת־זִקְנֵי יִשְׂרָאֵל אֶת־כָּל־רָאשֵׁי הַמַּטּוֹת נְשִׂיאֵי הָאָבוֹת לִבְנֵי יִשְׂרָאֵל אֶל־הַמֶּלֶךְ שְׁלֹמֹה יְרוּשָׁלָ͏ִם

ב לְהַעֲלוֹת אֶת־אֲרוֹן בְּרִית־יְהֹוָה מֵעִיר דָּוִד הִיא צִיּוֹן: ◀ וַיִּקָּהֲלוּ אֶל־הַמֶּלֶךְ שְׁלֹמֹה כָּל־אִישׁ יִשְׂרָאֵל בְּיֶרַח הָאֵתָנִים בֶּחָג הוּא הַחֹדֶשׁ הַשְּׁבִיעִי:

ג-ד וַיָּבֹאוּ כֹּל זִקְנֵי יִשְׂרָאֵל וַיִּשְׂאוּ הַכֹּהֲנִים אֶת־הָאָרוֹן: וַיַּעֲלוּ אֶת־אֲרוֹן יְהֹוָה וְאֶת־אֹהֶל מוֹעֵד וְאֶת־כָּל־כְּלֵי הַקֹּדֶשׁ אֲשֶׁר בָּאֹהֶל וַיַּעֲלוּ אֹתָם

ה הַכֹּהֲנִים וְהַלְוִיִּם: וְהַמֶּלֶךְ שְׁלֹמֹה וְכָל־עֲדַת יִשְׂרָאֵל הַנּוֹעָדִים עָלָיו אִתּוֹ לִפְנֵי הָאָרוֹן מְזַבְּחִים צֹאן וּבָקָר אֲשֶׁר לֹא־יִסָּפְרוּ וְלֹא יִמָּנוּ מֵרֹב:

HAFTARAS VAYAKHEL *Ashkenazim;* HAFTARAS PEKUDEI *Sephardim;* HAFTARAH SECOND SABBATH OF CHANUKAH 7:40-50

HAFTARAS PEKUDEI *Ashkenazim* 7:51-8:21

HAFTARAH SECOND DAY OF SUCCOS 8:2-21

7:38. The Kohanim used the lavers to wash their hands and feet (see *Exodus* 30:18-19), and to rinse the parts of the sacrificial animals offered upon the Altar (*II Chronicles* 4:6).

7:39. "Opposite the south" means "in the north."
7:40. The pans and shovels were used in removing the accumulated ash from the surface of the Altar (*Rashi*).

all braced firmly roundabout. [37] Thus he did for the ten stands — one casting, one measure, one form for all of them.

[38] He then made ten copper lavers. * Each laver had a capacity of forty bath-measures; each laver was four cubits [high]. There was one laver for each of the ten stands. [39] He placed the stands, five at the side of the Temple to the right and five at the side of the Temple to its left; and he placed the Sea at the right side of the Temple, eastward, opposite the south. *

The handiwork of Hiram the coppersmith

[40] Hiram made the lavers, the shovels, * and the bowls; and Hiram finished doing all the work that he did for King Solomon for the Temple of HASHEM: [41] two pillars; the two basins of the capitals that were on top of the pillars; the two nettings to cover the two basins of the capitals that were on top of the pillars; [42] the pomegranates, four hundred for the two nettings, two rows of pomegranates for each netting to cover the two basins of the capitals that were on top of the pillars; [43] the ten stands and the ten lavers upon the stands; [44] the one sea and the twelve bulls under the sea; [45] the pots, the shovels, the bowls, and all these vessels that Hiram had made for King Solomon for the Temple of HASHEM — [all made from] pure copper. [46] The king cast them in the Plain of the Jordan, in firm clay, between Succoth and Zarethan. [47] Solomon set aside all the vessels because there were so very, very many; the weight of the copper could not be determined.

Solomon's gold furnishings

[48] And Solomon made all the furnishings for the Temple of HASHEM: the golden Altar; the Table upon which was the showbread, of gold; [49] the candelabra, five on the right and five on the left, placed in front of the Inner Sanctum, of fine gold; with their flowers, lamps, and tongs of gold; [50] the jugs, musical instruments, bowls, spoons and pans were of fine gold; and the hinge-sockets of the doors of the inner House, the Holy of Holies, and those of the doors of the Temple, that is, the Hall, of gold.

David's sanctities

[51] When all the work that King Solomon had done for the Temple of HASHEM was completed, Solomon brought that which his father David had sanctified, the silver, the gold and the articles — and placed them in the treasuries of the Temple of HASHEM. *

8

SOLOMON AND THE NATION DEDICATE THE TEMPLE 8:1-9:9

[1] Then Solomon gathered together the elders of Israel and all the heads of the tribes, the leaders of the ancestral families of the Children of Israel, to King Solomon in Jerusalem, to bring up the Ark of the Covenant of HASHEM from the City of David, which is Zion. [2] They gathered before King Solomon — every man of Israel — for the festival [of Succos], * in the month of Ethanim, which is the seventh month. [3] All the elders of Israel came, and the Kohanim bore the Ark. [4] They brought up the Ark of HASHEM, and the Tent of Meeting, * and all the sacred vessels that were in that Tent; the Kohanim and the Levites brought them up. [5] King Solomon and the entire assembly of Israel that had assembled with him were with him before the Ark, offering sheep and cattle, too abundant to be numbered or counted.

7:51. David had prepared vast amounts of silver, gold, building materials, etc., that had been used in the construction of the Temple (I Chronicles 22:2-19), and Solomon now stored the leftover materials for future use.

8:2. Actually the celebration began a week before the festival; see v. 65. Ethanim is the month of Tishrei.

8:4. After building the new Temple, Solomon stored the Tent of Meeting [the Tabernacle built by Moses] within the Temple precincts (Rashi).

וַיָּבִאוּ הַכֹּהֲנִים אֶת־אֲרוֹן בְּרִית־יְהֹוָה אֶל־מְקוֹמוֹ אֶל־דְּבִיר הַבַּיִת אֶל־ ו
קֹדֶשׁ הַקֳּדָשִׁים אֶל־תַּחַת כַּנְפֵי הַכְּרוּבִים: כִּי הַכְּרוּבִים פְּרְשִׂים כְּנָפַיִם ז
אֶל־מְקוֹם הָאָרוֹן וַיָּסֹכּוּ הַכְּרֻבִים עַל־הָאָרוֹן וְעַל־בַּדָּיו מִלְמָעְלָה:
וַיַּאֲרִכוּ הַבַּדִּים וַיֵּרָאוּ רָאשֵׁי הַבַּדִּים מִן־הַקֹּדֶשׁ עַל־פְּנֵי הַדְּבִיר וְלֹא יֵרָאוּ ח
הַחוּצָה וַיִּהְיוּ שָׁם עַד הַיּוֹם הַזֶּה: אֵין בָּאָרוֹן רַק שְׁנֵי לֻחוֹת הָאֲבָנִים אֲשֶׁר ט
הִנִּחַ שָׁם מֹשֶׁה בְּחֹרֵב אֲשֶׁר כָּרַת יְהֹוָה עִם־בְּנֵי יִשְׂרָאֵל בְּצֵאתָם מֵאֶרֶץ
מִצְרָיִם: וַיְהִי בְּצֵאת הַכֹּהֲנִים מִן־הַקֹּדֶשׁ וְהֶעָנָן מָלֵא אֶת־בֵּית יְהֹוָה: י
וְלֹא־יָכְלוּ הַכֹּהֲנִים לַעֲמֹד לְשָׁרֵת מִפְּנֵי הֶעָנָן כִּי־מָלֵא כְבוֹד־יְהֹוָה אֶת־ יא
בֵּית יְהֹוָה:
אָז אָמַר שְׁלֹמֹה יְהֹוָה אָמַר לִשְׁכֹּן בָּעֲרָפֶל: בָּנֹה יב־יג
בָנִיתִי בֵּית זְבֻל לָךְ מָכוֹן לְשִׁבְתְּךָ עוֹלָמִים: וַיַּסֵּב הַמֶּלֶךְ אֶת־פָּנָיו וַיְבָרֶךְ יד
אֵת כָּל־קְהַל יִשְׂרָאֵל וְכָל־קְהַל יִשְׂרָאֵל עֹמֵד: וַיֹּאמֶר בָּרוּךְ יְהֹוָה אֱלֹהֵי טו
יִשְׂרָאֵל אֲשֶׁר דִּבֶּר בְּפִיו אֵת דָּוִד אָבִי וּבְיָדוֹ מִלֵּא לֵאמֹר: מִן־הַיּוֹם אֲשֶׁר טז
הוֹצֵאתִי אֶת־עַמִּי אֶת־יִשְׂרָאֵל מִמִּצְרַיִם לֹא־בָחַרְתִּי בְעִיר מִכֹּל שִׁבְטֵי
יִשְׂרָאֵל לִבְנוֹת בַּיִת לִהְיוֹת שְׁמִי שָׁם וָאֶבְחַר בְּדָוִד לִהְיוֹת עַל־עַמִּי
יִשְׂרָאֵל: וַיְהִי עִם־לְבַב דָּוִד אָבִי לִבְנוֹת בַּיִת לְשֵׁם יְהֹוָה אֱלֹהֵי יִשְׂרָאֵל: יז
וַיֹּאמֶר יְהֹוָה אֶל־דָּוִד אָבִי יַעַן אֲשֶׁר הָיָה עִם־לְבָבְךָ לִבְנוֹת בַּיִת לִשְׁמִי יח
הֱטִיבֹתָ כִּי הָיָה עִם־לְבָבֶךָ: רַק אַתָּה לֹא תִבְנֶה הַבָּיִת כִּי אִם־בִּנְךָ הַיֹּצֵא יט
מֵחֲלָצֶיךָ הוּא־יִבְנֶה הַבַּיִת לִשְׁמִי: וַיָּקֶם יְהֹוָה אֶת־דְּבָרוֹ אֲשֶׁר דִּבֵּר וָאָקֻם כ
תַּחַת דָּוִד אָבִי וָאֵשֵׁב עַל־כִּסֵּא יִשְׂרָאֵל כַּאֲשֶׁר דִּבֶּר יְהֹוָה וָאֶבְנֶה הַבַּיִת
לְשֵׁם יְהֹוָה אֱלֹהֵי יִשְׂרָאֵל: וָאָשִׂם שָׁם מָקוֹם לָאָרוֹן אֲשֶׁר־שָׁם בְּרִית יְהֹוָה כא
אֲשֶׁר כָּרַת עִם־אֲבֹתֵינוּ בְּהוֹצִיאוֹ אֹתָם מֵאֶרֶץ מִצְרָיִם: ◄ וַיַּעֲמֹד כב
שְׁלֹמֹה לִפְנֵי מִזְבַּח יְהֹוָה נֶגֶד כָּל־קְהַל יִשְׂרָאֵל וַיִּפְרֹשׂ כַּפָּיו הַשָּׁמָיִם:
וַיֹּאמַר יְהֹוָה אֱלֹהֵי יִשְׂרָאֵל אֵין־כָּמוֹךָ אֱלֹהִים בַּשָּׁמַיִם מִמַּעַל וְעַל־ כג
הָאָרֶץ מִתָּחַת שֹׁמֵר הַבְּרִית וְהַחֶסֶד לַעֲבָדֶיךָ הַהֹלְכִים לְפָנֶיךָ בְּכָל־לִבָּם:
אֲשֶׁר שָׁמַרְתָּ לְעַבְדְּךָ דָּוִד אָבִי אֵת אֲשֶׁר־דִּבַּרְתָּ לּוֹ וַתְּדַבֵּר בְּפִיךָ וּבְיָדְךָ כד
מִלֵּאתָ כַּיּוֹם הַזֶּה: וְעַתָּה יְהֹוָה ׀ אֱלֹהֵי יִשְׂרָאֵל שְׁמֹר לְעַבְדְּךָ דָוִד אָבִי כה
אֵת אֲשֶׁר דִּבַּרְתָּ לּוֹ לֵאמֹר לֹא־יִכָּרֵת לְךָ אִישׁ מִלְּפָנַי יֹשֵׁב עַל־כִּסֵּא
יִשְׂרָאֵל רַק אִם־יִשְׁמְרוּ בָנֶיךָ אֶת־דַּרְכָּם לָלֶכֶת לְפָנַי כַּאֲשֶׁר הָלַכְתָּ
לְפָנָי: וְעַתָּה אֱלֹהֵי יִשְׂרָאֵל יֵאָמֶן נָא °דבריך [דְּבָרְךָ ק] אֲשֶׁר דִּבַּרְתָּ כו
לְעַבְדְּךָ דָּוִד אָבִי: כִּי הַאֻמְנָם יֵשֵׁב אֱלֹהִים עַל־הָאָרֶץ הִנֵּה הַשָּׁמַיִם וּשְׁמֵי כז

8:7. See *Exodus* 25:13-15.

8:8. The doors of the Partition wall remained permanently open, and a curtain was hung in the doorway. The staves of the Ark pushed against this curtain, but did not go through it. As viewed from the Sanctuary, the tips of the staves appeared as two bumps in the curtain.

8:9. I.e., Sinai, where God gave Moses the Tablets,

signifying His covenant with Israel.

8:10. The Divine Presence (שְׁכִינָה), as represented by the cloud, rested in the Temple as soon as the Ark was placed there.

8:18. See *II Samuel*, Ch.7.

8:22. Solomon stood before the Altar and then knelt while offering his inaugural prayer (see v. 54).

The Ark is emplaced

⁶ *The Kohanim brought the Ark of the Covenant of* HASHEM *to its place, to the Inner Sanctum of the Temple, to the Holy of Holies, to beneath the wings of the Cherubim.* ⁷ *For the Cherubim spread their wings over the place of the Ark; the Cherubim covered over the Ark and its staves* from above.* ⁸ *They extended the staves so that the tips of the staves were noticeable upon the Partition from the Sanctuary, but could not be seen on the outside;* and they remained there to this very day.* ⁹ *Nothing was in the Ark but the two stone Tablets that Moses placed there in Horeb,* by which* HASHEM *covenanted with the Children of Israel when they left the land of Egypt.* ¹⁰ *And it was as the Kohanim left the Sanctuary, that the cloud filled the Temple of* HASHEM.* ¹¹ *The Kohanim could not stand and minister because of the cloud, for the glory of* HASHEM *filled the Temple of* HASHEM.

Solomon's declaration

¹² *Then Solomon said, "*HASHEM *said that He would dwell in the thick cloud.* ¹³ *I have surely built a house of habitation for You, the foundation for Your dwelling forever."*

¹⁴ *Then the king turned his face and blessed the entire congregation of Israel, while the entire congregation of Israel was standing.* ¹⁵ *He then said, "Blessed is* HASHEM, *God of Israel, Who spoke with His word to my father David — and fulfilled with His power, saying,* ¹⁶ *'From the day when I took My people Israel out of Egypt, I did not choose a city from among all the tribes of Israel in which to build a Temple where My Name would be; but I chose David to rule over My people Israel.'*

David's desire fulfilled

¹⁷ *"It was in the heart of my father David to build a Temple for the sake of the Name of* HASHEM, *God of Israel.* ¹⁸ *But* HASHEM *said to my father David,* 'Inasmuch as it has been in your heart to build a Temple for My Name, you have done well by having this in your heart.* ¹⁹ *You, however, shall not build the Temple. Rather, your son, who will emerge from your loins — he will build the Temple for My Name.'* ²⁰ *Now* HASHEM *has fulfilled His word that He spoke, for I have risen in place of my father David, and I sit on the throne of Israel as* HASHEM *spoke, and I have built the Temple for the Name of* HASHEM, *God of Israel.* ²¹ *And I have set there a place for the Ark wherein is the covenant of* HASHEM, *which He made with our forefathers when He took them out of the land of Egypt."*

A plea for the Davidic dynasty . . .

²² *Solomon stood* before the Altar of* HASHEM, *in front of the entire congregation of Israel, and spread out his hands toward Heaven,* ²³ *and he said, "*HASHEM, *God of Israel, there is none like You, O God, in the heavens above nor on the earth below, Who preserves the covenant and kindness for Your servants who walk before You with all their heart;* ²⁴ *for You have preserved for Your servant, my father David, all that You have spoken to him. You spoke with Your mouth and with Your power fulfilled this very day.* ²⁵ *And now, O* HASHEM, *God of Israel, preserve [Your promise] to Your servant, my father David, that You spoke to him, saying, 'There shall not cease from you a man to sit before Me upon the throne of Israel — provided that your children preserve their way, to go before Me, as you have gone before Me.'* ²⁶ *So now, O God of Israel, cause Your word that You spoke to Your servant my father David to come true.*

²⁷ *"Would God truly dwell on earth? Behold, the heavens and the highest*

כח הַשָּׁמַ֨יִם לֹ֣א יְכַלְכְּל֔וּךָ אַ֕ף כִּֽי־הַבַּ֥יִת הַזֶּ֖ה אֲשֶׁ֥ר בָּנִֽיתִי: וּפָנִ֜יתָ אֶל־תְּפִלַּ֤ת
עַבְדְּךָ֙ וְאֶל־תְּחִנָּת֔וֹ יְהֹוָ֖ה אֱלֹהָ֑י לִשְׁמֹ֤עַ אֶל־הָֽרִנָּה֙ וְאֶל־הַתְּפִלָּ֔ה אֲשֶׁ֧ר
כט עַבְדְּךָ֛ מִתְפַּלֵּ֥ל לְפָנֶ֖יךָ הַיּֽוֹם: לִהְי֨וֹת עֵינֶ֤ךָ פְתֻחוֹת֙ אֶל־הַבַּ֣יִת הַזֶּ֔ה לַ֣יְלָה
וָי֔וֹם אֶל־הַ֨מָּק֔וֹם אֲשֶׁ֣ר אָמַ֔רְתָּ יִהְיֶ֥ה שְׁמִ֖י שָׁ֑ם לִשְׁמֹ֙עַ֙ אֶל־הַתְּפִלָּ֔ה אֲשֶׁ֥ר
ל יִתְפַּלֵּ֥ל עַבְדְּךָ֖ אֶל־הַמָּק֥וֹם הַזֶּֽה: וְשָׁ֨מַעְתָּ֜ אֶל־תְּחִנַּ֤ת עַבְדְּךָ֙ וְעַמְּךָ֣ יִשְׂרָאֵ֔ל
אֲשֶׁ֥ר יִֽתְפַּֽלְל֖וּ אֶל־הַמָּק֣וֹם הַזֶּ֑ה וְ֠אַתָּ֠ה תִּשְׁמַ֞ע אֶל־מְק֤וֹם שִׁבְתְּךָ֙ אֶל־
לא הַשָּׁמַ֔יִם וְשָׁמַעְתָּ֖ וְסָלָֽחְתָּ: אֵת֩ אֲשֶׁ֨ר יֶחֱטָ֥א אִישׁ֙ לְרֵעֵ֔הוּ וְנָֽשָׁא־ב֖וֹ אָלָ֑ה   ^{נ״א וְנָשָׁא}
לב לְהַֽאֲלֹת֑וֹ וּבָ֗א אָלָ֛ה לִפְנֵ֥י מִֽזְבַּחֲךָ֖ בַּבַּ֣יִת הַזֶּֽה: וְאַתָּ֣ה ׀ תִּשְׁמַ֣ע הַשָּׁמַ֗יִם
וְעָשִׂ֨יתָ֙ וְשָׁפַטְתָּ֣ אֶת־עֲבָדֶ֔יךָ לְהַרְשִׁ֣יעַ רָשָׁ֔ע לָתֵ֥ת דַּרְכּ֖וֹ בְּרֹאשׁ֑וֹ וּלְהַצְדִּ֣יק
לג צַדִּ֔יק לָ֥תֶת ל֖וֹ כְּצִדְקָתֽוֹ: בְּהִנָּגֵ֨ף עַמְּךָ֧ יִשְׂרָאֵ֛ל לִפְנֵ֥י אוֹיֵ֖ב אֲשֶׁ֣ר
יֶֽחֶטְאוּ־לָ֑ךְ וְשָׁ֤בוּ אֵלֶ֙יךָ֙ וְהוֹד֣וּ אֶת־שְׁמֶ֔ךָ וְהִֽתְפַּֽלְל֧וּ וְהִֽתְחַֽנְּנ֛וּ אֵלֶ֖יךָ בַּבַּ֥יִת
לד הַזֶּֽה: וְאַתָּה֙ תִּשְׁמַ֣ע הַשָּׁמַ֔יִם וְסָ֣לַחְתָּ֔ לְחַטַּ֖את עַמְּךָ֣ יִשְׂרָאֵ֑ל וַהֲשֵֽׁבֹתָם֙
לה אֶל־הָ֣אֲדָמָ֔ה אֲשֶׁ֥ר נָתַ֖תָּ לַאֲבוֹתָֽם: בְּהֵעָצֵ֥ר שָׁמַ֛יִם וְלֹא־יִהְיֶ֥ה מָטָ֖ר
כִּ֣י יֶחֶטְאוּ־לָ֑ךְ וְהִֽתְפַּֽלְל֞וּ אֶל־הַמָּק֤וֹם הַזֶּה֙ וְהוֹד֣וּ אֶת־שְׁמֶ֔ךָ
לו וּמֵחַטָּאתָ֖ם יְשׁוּב֑וּן כִּ֥י תַעֲנֵֽם: וְאַתָּ֣ה ׀ תִּשְׁמַ֣ע הַשָּׁמַ֗יִם וְסָ֨לַחְתָּ֜ לְחַטַּ֤את
עֲבָדֶ֙יךָ֙ וְעַמְּךָ֣ יִשְׂרָאֵ֔ל כִּ֥י תוֹרֵ֛ם אֶת־הַדֶּ֥רֶךְ הַטּוֹבָ֖ה אֲשֶׁ֣ר יֵֽלְכוּ־בָ֑הּ וְנָתַתָּ֤ה
לז מָטָר֙ עַל־אַרְצְךָ֔ אֲשֶׁר־נָתַ֥תָּה לְעַמְּךָ֖ לְנַחֲלָֽה: רָעָ֞ב כִּֽי־יִהְיֶ֣ה
בָאָ֗רֶץ דֶּ֣בֶר כִּֽי־יִ֠הְיֶ֠ה שִׁדָּפ֨וֹן יֵרָק֜וֹן אַרְבֶּ֤ה חָסִיל֙ כִּ֣י יִהְיֶ֔ה כִּ֧י יָֽצַר־ל֣וֹ אֹיְב֗וֹ
לח בְּאֶ֣רֶץ שְׁעָרָ֑יו כָּל־נֶ֖גַע כָּל־מַֽחֲלָֽה: כָּל־תְּפִלָּ֣ה כָל־תְּחִנָּ֗ה אֲשֶׁ֤ר תִּֽהְיֶה֙
לְכָל־הָ֣אָדָ֔ם לְכֹ֖ל עַמְּךָ֣ יִשְׂרָאֵ֑ל אֲשֶׁ֣ר יֵֽדְע֗וּן אִ֚ישׁ נֶ֣גַע לְבָב֔וֹ וּפָרַ֥שׂ
לט כַּפָּ֖יו אֶל־הַבַּ֥יִת הַזֶּֽה: וְ֠אַתָּ֠ה תִּשְׁמַ֨ע הַשָּׁמַ֜יִם מְכ֤וֹן שִׁבְתֶּ֙ךָ֙ וְסָלַחְתָּ֣
וְעָשִׂ֔יתָ וְנָתַתָּ֤ לָאִישׁ֙ כְּכָל־דְּרָכָ֔יו אֲשֶׁ֥ר תֵּדַ֖ע אֶת־לְבָב֑וֹ כִּֽי־אַתָּ֤ה יָדַ֙עְתָּ֙
מ לְבַדְּךָ֔ אֶת־לְבַ֖ב כָּל־בְּנֵ֥י הָֽאָדָֽם: לְמַ֙עַן֙ יִֽרָא֔וּךָ כָּל־הַ֨יָּמִ֔ים אֲשֶׁר־הֵ֣ם
מא חַיִּ֔ים עַל־פְּנֵ֣י הָ֣אֲדָמָ֔ה אֲשֶׁ֥ר נָתַ֖תָּה לַֽאֲבֹתֵֽינוּ: וְגַ֣ם אֶל־
הַנָּכְרִ֗י אֲשֶׁ֧ר לֹא־מֵעַמְּךָ֛ יִשְׂרָאֵ֖ל ה֑וּא וּבָ֛א מֵאֶ֥רֶץ רְחוֹקָ֖ה לְמַ֥עַן שְׁמֶֽךָ:
מב כִּ֤י יִשְׁמְעוּן֙ אֶת־שִׁמְךָ֣ הַגָּד֔וֹל וְאֶת־יָֽדְךָ֙ הַ֣חֲזָקָ֔ה וּֽזְרֹעֲךָ֖ הַנְּטוּיָ֑ה וּבָ֥א
מג וְהִתְפַּלֵּ֖ל אֶל־הַבַּ֥יִת הַזֶּֽה: אַתָּ֞ה תִּשְׁמַ֤ע הַשָּׁמַ֙יִם֙ מְכ֣וֹן שִׁבְתֶּ֔ךָ וְעָשִׂ֕יתָ
כְּכֹ֛ל אֲשֶׁר־יִקְרָ֥א אֵלֶ֖יךָ הַנָּכְרִ֑י לְמַ֣עַן יֵֽדְע֞וּן כָּל־עַמֵּ֤י הָאָ֙רֶץ֙ אֶת־שְׁמֶ֔ךָ
לְיִרְאָ֣ה אֹֽתְךָ֗ כְּעַמְּךָ֣ יִשְׂרָאֵ֔ל וְלָדַ֕עַת כִּֽי־שִׁמְךָ֣ נִקְרָ֔א עַל־הַבַּ֥יִת הַזֶּ֖ה אֲשֶׁ֥ר
מד בָּנִֽיתִי: כִּֽי־יֵצֵ֨א עַמְּךָ֤ לַמִּלְחָמָה֙ עַל־אֹ֣יְב֔וֹ בַּדֶּ֖רֶךְ אֲשֶׁ֣ר תִּשְׁלָחֵ֑ם
וְהִתְפַּֽלְל֣וּ אֶל־יְהֹוָ֗ה דֶּ֚רֶךְ הָעִיר֙ אֲשֶׁ֣ר בָּחַ֣רְתָּ בָּ֔הּ וְהַבַּ֖יִת אֲשֶׁר־בָּנִ֥תִי
מה לִשְׁמֶֽךָ: וְשָׁמַעְתָּ֙ הַשָּׁמַ֔יִם אֶת־תְּפִלָּתָ֖ם וְאֶת־תְּחִנָּתָ֑ם וְעָשִׂ֖יתָ מִשְׁפָּטָֽם:

8:27. The purpose of this Temple was not to serve as a "residence" for God; that would be absurd. Rather, the Temple would be a conduit to God for the prayers of Israel — and of all mankind.

8:31-32. Solomon referred to sins involving property, and prayed that God treat monetary oaths — especially those sworn in the Temple precincts — with gravity, and that the reward and punishment of the parties

heavens cannot contain You, and surely not this Temple that I have built! * [28] But,
. . . and that   may You turn to the prayer of Your servant and to his supplication, O HASHEM
God heed   my God, to hear the cry and the prayer that Your servant prays before You today:
Israel's   [29] that Your eyes be open toward this Temple night and day, to the place of which
prayers . . .   You said, 'My Name shall be there,' to hear the prayer that Your servant shall
pray toward this place. [30] And may You hear the supplication of Your servant
and of Your people Israel, which they shall pray toward this place; may You hear
from the place of Your habitation in Heaven — may You hear and forgive.

[31] "If a man should wrong his fellow, who imposes an oath upon him and
adjures him, and the oath comes before Your Altar in this Temple, [32] may You
. . . vindicate   hear from Heaven, may You act and judge Your servants, condemning the
the   wicked party, to place the [consequences of] his way upon his head, and
righteous . . .   vindicating the righteous party, to give him according to his righteousness. *

. . . reverse   [33] "If Your people are defeated by an enemy, because they sinned against You,
their   and then they return to You and praise Your Name, and pray and supplicate to
defeats . . .   You in this Temple, [34] may You hear from Heaven and forgive the sin of Your
people Israel, and return them to the land* that You gave their forefathers.

. . . send   [35] "If the heavens are restrained and there be no rain, for they have sinned
rain . . .   against You, and they pray toward this place and praise Your Name, and they
repent from their sin so that You will respond to them, [36] may You hear from
Heaven and forgive the sin of Your servants and Your people Israel, when You
teach them the proper path in which they should walk, and may You give rain
upon Your land, * which You gave to Your people as a heritage.

[37] "If there be a famine in the land, if there be a pestilence, if there be windblast
or withering or locust or grasshopper, if [Israel's] enemy oppresses it in the land
. . . and   of their cities — any plague, any disease — [38] for any prayer and any supplica-
respond to   tion that any person of Your entire people Israel may have — each man knowing
their pleas   the affliction of his heart — when he spreads out his hands [in prayer] toward
this Temple, [39] may You hear from Heaven, the foundation of Your abode, and
forgive and act, and recompense that man according to his ways as You know
his heart, for You alone know the hearts of all people; [40] so that they may fear
You all the days that they live upon the land that You gave to our forefathers.

May He hear   [41] "Also a gentile who is not of Your people Israel, but will come from a distant
the gentile's   land, for Your Name's sake [42] — for they will hear of Your great Name and Your
prayer   strong hand and Your outstretched arm — and will come and pray toward this
Temple — [43] may You hear from Heaven, the foundation of Your abode, and act
according to all that the gentile calls out to You, so that all the peoples of the
world may know Your Name, to fear You as [does] Your people Israel, and to
know that Your Name is proclaimed upon this Temple that I have built.

Help Jews   [44] "When Your people goes to war against its enemy, along the course on
in war . . .   which You shall send them, and they direct their prayers to HASHEM by way of
the city that You have chosen and the Temple that I have built for Your Name,
[45] from Heaven may You hear their prayer and their supplication, and carry out
their judgment [against their enemies].

---

should be swift and noticeable, so that people would   exile and their brethren come to the Temple to pray . . .
recognize the unique level of sanctity present in the   (*Radak*).
Temple (*Radak*).   **8:36.** Let them know which sin caused You to withhold
8:34. If the defeated Jews were forced into captivity or   the rain, so that they can repent (*Radak*).

מו כִּי יֶחֶטְאוּ־לָךְ כִּי אֵין אָדָם אֲשֶׁר לֹא־יֶחֱטָא וְאָנַפְתָּ בָם וּנְתַתָּם לִפְנֵי אוֹיֵב

מז וְשָׁבוּם שְׁבֵיהֶם אֶל־אֶרֶץ הָאוֹיֵב רְחוֹקָה אוֹ קְרוֹבָה: וְהֵשִׁיבוּ אֶל־לִבָּם בָּאָרֶץ אֲשֶׁר נִשְׁבּוּ־שָׁם וְשָׁבוּ | וְהִתְחַנְּנוּ אֵלֶיךָ בְּאֶרֶץ שֹׁבֵיהֶם לֵאמֹר

מח חָטָאנוּ וְהֶעֱוִינוּ רָשָׁעְנוּ: וְשָׁבוּ אֵלֶיךָ בְּכָל־לְבָבָם וּבְכָל־נַפְשָׁם בְּאֶרֶץ אֹיְבֵיהֶם אֲשֶׁר־שָׁבוּ אֹתָם וְהִתְפַּלְלוּ אֵלֶיךָ דֶּרֶךְ אַרְצָם אֲשֶׁר נָתַתָּה לַאֲבוֹתָם הָעִיר אֲשֶׁר בָּחַרְתָּ וְהַבַּיִת אֲשֶׁר־בנית [°בָּנִיתִי ק] לִשְׁמֶךָ:

מט וְשָׁמַעְתָּ הַשָּׁמַיִם מְכוֹן שִׁבְתְּךָ אֶת־תְּפִלָּתָם וְאֶת־תְּחִנָּתָם וְעָשִׂיתָ מִשְׁפָּטָם: וְסָלַחְתָּ לְעַמְּךָ אֲשֶׁר חָטְאוּ־לָךְ וּלְכָל־פִּשְׁעֵיהֶם אֲשֶׁר פָּשְׁעוּ־

נ בָךְ וּנְתַתָּם לְרַחֲמִים לִפְנֵי שֹׁבֵיהֶם וְרִחֲמוּם: כִּי־עַמְּךָ וְנַחֲלָתְךָ הֵם אֲשֶׁר

נב הוֹצֵאתָ מִמִּצְרַיִם מִתּוֹךְ כּוּר הַבַּרְזֶל: לִהְיוֹת עֵינֶיךָ פְתֻחוֹת אֶל־תְּחִנַּת עַבְדְּךָ וְאֶל־תְּחִנַּת עַמְּךָ יִשְׂרָאֵל לִשְׁמֹעַ אֲלֵיהֶם בְּכֹל קָרְאָם אֵלֶיךָ: כִּי־

נג אַתָּה הִבְדַּלְתָּם לְךָ לְנַחֲלָה מִכֹּל עַמֵּי הָאָרֶץ כַּאֲשֶׁר דִּבַּרְתָּ בְּיַד | מֹשֶׁה עַבְדֶּךָ בְּהוֹצִיאֲךָ אֶת־אֲבֹתֵינוּ מִמִּצְרַיִם אֲדֹנָי יֱהוִֹה:

נד **וַיְהִי |** כְּכַלּוֹת שְׁלֹמֹה לְהִתְפַּלֵּל אֶל־יְהוָה אֵת כָּל־הַתְּפִלָּה וְהַתְּחִנָּה הַזֹּאת קָם מִלִּפְנֵי מִזְבַּח יְהוָה מִכְּרֹעַ עַל־בִּרְכָּיו וְכַפָּיו פְּרֻשׂוֹת הַשָּׁמָיִם: וַיַּעֲמֹד

נה וַיְבָרֶךְ אֵת כָּל־קְהַל יִשְׂרָאֵל קוֹל גָּדוֹל לֵאמֹר: בָּרוּךְ יְהוָה אֲשֶׁר נָתַן מְנוּחָה לְעַמּוֹ יִשְׂרָאֵל כְּכֹל אֲשֶׁר דִּבֵּר לֹא־נָפַל דָּבָר אֶחָד מִכֹּל דְּבָרוֹ

נז הַטּוֹב אֲשֶׁר דִּבֶּר בְּיַד מֹשֶׁה עַבְדּוֹ: יְהִי יְהוָה אֱלֹהֵינוּ עִמָּנוּ כַּאֲשֶׁר הָיָה עִם־אֲבֹתֵינוּ אַל־יַעַזְבֵנוּ וְאַל־יִטְּשֵׁנוּ: לְהַטּוֹת לְבָבֵנוּ אֵלָיו לָלֶכֶת בְּכָל־

נט דְּרָכָיו וְלִשְׁמֹר מִצְוֹתָיו וְחֻקָּיו וּמִשְׁפָּטָיו אֲשֶׁר צִוָּה אֶת־אֲבֹתֵינוּ: וְיִהְיוּ דְבָרַי אֵלֶּה אֲשֶׁר הִתְחַנַּנְתִּי לִפְנֵי יְהוָה קְרֹבִים אֶל־יְהוָה אֱלֹהֵינוּ יוֹמָם

ס וָלָיְלָה לַעֲשׂוֹת | מִשְׁפַּט עַבְדּוֹ וּמִשְׁפַּט עַמּוֹ יִשְׂרָאֵל דְּבַר־יוֹם בְּיוֹמוֹ: לְמַעַן

סא דַּעַת כָּל־עַמֵּי הָאָרֶץ כִּי יְהוָה הוּא הָאֱלֹהִים אֵין עוֹד: וְהָיָה לְבַבְכֶם שָׁלֵם עִם יְהוָה אֱלֹהֵינוּ לָלֶכֶת בְּחֻקָּיו וְלִשְׁמֹר מִצְוֹתָיו כַּיּוֹם הַזֶּה: וְהַמֶּלֶךְ וְכָל־

סג יִשְׂרָאֵל עִמּוֹ זֹבְחִים זֶבַח לִפְנֵי יְהוָה: וַיִּזְבַּח שְׁלֹמֹה אֵת זֶבַח הַשְּׁלָמִים אֲשֶׁר זָבַח לַיהוָה בָּקָר עֶשְׂרִים וּשְׁנַיִם אֶלֶף וְצֹאן מֵאָה וְעֶשְׂרִים אָלֶף

סד וַיַּחְנְכוּ אֶת־בֵּית יְהוָה הַמֶּלֶךְ וְכָל־בְּנֵי יִשְׂרָאֵל: בַּיּוֹם הַהוּא קִדַּשׁ הַמֶּלֶךְ אֶת־תּוֹךְ הֶחָצֵר אֲשֶׁר לִפְנֵי בֵית־יְהוָה כִּי־עָשָׂה שָׁם אֶת־הָעֹלָה וְאֶת־הַמִּנְחָה וְאֵת חֶלְבֵי הַשְּׁלָמִים כִּי־מִזְבַּח הַנְּחֹשֶׁת אֲשֶׁר לִפְנֵי יְהוָה

סה קָטֹן מֵהָכִיל אֶת־הָעֹלָה וְאֶת־הַמִּנְחָה וְאֵת חֶלְבֵי הַשְּׁלָמִים: וַיַּעַשׂ שְׁלֹמֹה בָעֵת־הַהִיא | אֶת־הֶחָג וְכָל־יִשְׂרָאֵל עִמּוֹ קָהָל גָּדוֹל מִלְּבוֹא חֲמָת | עַד־נַחַל מִצְרַיִם לִפְנֵי יְהוָה אֱלֹהֵינוּ שִׁבְעַת יָמִים וְשִׁבְעַת יָמִים

HAFTARAS SHEMINI ATZERES (outside Israel) *Ashkenazim:* 8:54-9:1 *Sephardim:* 8:54-66

8:51. The oppression the Israelites suffered in Egypt is likened to a furnace in which metal is purified.

8:56. A reference to the promise in *Deuteronomy* 12:10 that the nation will dwell securely in the Holy Land (*Rashi*).

⁴⁶ *"When they sin against You — for there is no man who never sins — and You become angry with them, and You deliver them to an enemy, and their captors take them captive to the enemy's land, faraway or nearby,* ⁴⁷ *and they take it to heart in the land where they were taken captive and they repent and supplicate to You in the land of their captors, saying, 'We have sinned; we have been iniquitous; we have been wicked,'* ⁴⁸ *and they return to You with all their heart and with all their soul in the land of their enemies who had captured them, and pray to You by way of their land that You gave to their forefathers, and [by way of] the city that You have chosen and [through] the Temple that I built for Your Name —* ⁴⁹ *may You hear their prayer and their supplication from Heaven, the foundation of Your abode, and carry out their judgment,* ⁵⁰ *and forgive Your people who sinned against You, and all their transgressions that they transgressed against You, and let them inspire mercy before their captors, so that they will treat them mercifully.*

. . . and accept their repentance . . .

⁵¹ *"For they are Your people and Your heritage, whom You have taken out of Egypt, from the midst of the iron furnace;** ⁵² *may Your eyes thus be open to the supplication of Your servant and the supplication of Your people Israel, to listen to them whenever they call out to You.* ⁵³ *For You have separated them for Yourself as a heritage from all the peoples of the earth, as You spoke through Your servant Moses, when You took our forefathers out of Egypt, O my Lord, HASHEM/ELOHIM."*

. . . because You made them Yours

⁵⁴ *And it was when Solomon had finished praying to HASHEM this entire prayer and supplication, he stood up from having knelt on his knees before the Altar of HASHEM with his hands spread out heavenward.* ⁵⁵ *He stood and blessed the entire congregation of Israel in a loud voice, saying,* ⁵⁶ *"Blessed is HASHEM Who has granted rest to His people Israel, according to all that He has spoken;* not one word has gone unfulfilled from the entire gracious promise that He pronounced through the hand of His servant Moses.* ⁵⁷ *May HASHEM, our God, be with us as He was with our forefathers, may He not forsake us nor cast us off,* ⁵⁸ *to turn our hearts to Him, to walk in all His ways and to observe His commandments, decrees and statutes that He commanded our forefathers.* ⁵⁹ *And may these words of mine that I have supplicated before HASHEM be near to HASHEM, our God, day and night, that He may grant the just due of His servant and the just due of His people Israel, each day's need in its day,* ⁶⁰ *so that all the peoples of the earth shall know that HASHEM is God — there is no other.* ⁶¹ *May your hearts remain perfect with HASHEM our God, to follow His decrees and to observe His commandments as on this very day."*

Solomon blesses the people

⁶² *The king and all Israel with him were bringing an offering before HASHEM.* ⁶³ *Solomon brought the peace-offering that he offered to HASHEM: cattle, twenty-two thousand, and of the flock, one hundred and twenty thousand; and they dedicated the Temple of HASHEM — the king and all the Children of Israel.*

Solomon's offerings

⁶⁴ *On that day the king sanctified the interior of the Courtyard that was before the Temple of HASHEM, for there he performed the service of the elevation-offering, the meal-offering and the fats of the peace-offering; for the Copper Altar that was before HASHEM was too small to contain the elevation-offering, the meal-offering and the fats of the peace-offering.*

⁶⁵ *At that time Solomon instituted the celebration — and all Israel was with him, a huge congregation, from the Approach of Hamath until the Brook of Egypt — before HASHEM our God, for seven days and seven [more] days,*

סו אַרְבָּעָה עָשָׂר יוֹם: בַּיּוֹם הַשְּׁמִינִי שִׁלַּח אֶת־הָעָם וַיְבָרְכוּ אֶת־הַמֶּלֶךְ
וַיֵּלְכוּ לְאָהֳלֵיהֶם שְׂמֵחִים וְטוֹבֵי לֵב עַל כָּל־הַטּוֹבָה אֲשֶׁר עָשָׂה יהוה לְדָוִד

ט

א עַבְדּוֹ וּלְיִשְׂרָאֵל עַמּוֹ: ◀ וַיְהִי כְּכַלּוֹת שְׁלֹמֹה לִבְנוֹת אֶת־בֵּית־יהוה
ב וְאֶת־בֵּית הַמֶּלֶךְ וְאֵת כָּל־חֵשֶׁק שְׁלֹמֹה אֲשֶׁר חָפֵץ לַעֲשׂוֹת: ◀ וַיֵּרָא
ג יהוה אֶל־שְׁלֹמֹה שֵׁנִית כַּאֲשֶׁר נִרְאָה אֵלָיו בְּגִבְעוֹן: וַיֹּאמֶר יהוה אֵלָיו
שָׁמַ֫עְתִּי אֶת־תְּפִלָּתְךָ וְאֶת־תְּחִנָּתְךָ אֲשֶׁר הִתְחַנַּ֫נְתָּה לְפָנַי הִקְדַּ֫שְׁתִּי אֶת־
הַבַּיִת הַזֶּה אֲשֶׁר בָּנִ֫תָה לָשׂוּם־שְׁמִי שָׁם עַד־עוֹלָם וְהָיוּ עֵינַי וְלִבִּי שָׁם כָּל־
ד הַיָּמִים: וְאַתָּה אִם־תֵּלֵךְ לְפָנַי כַּאֲשֶׁר הָלַךְ דָּוִד אָבִיךָ בְּתָם־לֵבָב וּבְיֹשֶׁר
ה לַעֲשׂוֹת כְּכֹל אֲשֶׁר צִוִּיתִיךָ חֻקַּי וּמִשְׁפָּטַי תִּשְׁמֹר: וַהֲקִמֹתִי אֶת־כִּסֵּא
מַמְלַכְתְּךָ עַל־יִשְׂרָאֵל לְעֹלָם כַּאֲשֶׁר דִּבַּ֫רְתִּי עַל־דָּוִד אָבִיךָ לֵאמֹר לֹא־
ו יִכָּרֵת לְךָ אִישׁ מֵעַל כִּסֵּא יִשְׂרָאֵל: אִם־שׁוֹב תְּשֻׁבוּן אַתֶּם וּבְנֵיכֶם מֵאַחֲרַי
וְלֹא תִשְׁמְרוּ מִצְוֺתַי חֻקֹּתַי אֲשֶׁר נָתַ֫תִּי לִפְנֵיכֶם וַהֲלַכְתֶּם וַעֲבַדְתֶּם אֱלֹהִים
ז אֲחֵרִים וְהִשְׁתַּחֲוִיתֶם לָהֶם: וְהִכְרַתִּי אֶת־יִשְׂרָאֵל מֵעַל פְּנֵי הָאֲדָמָה אֲשֶׁר
נָתַ֫תִּי לָהֶם וְאֶת־הַבַּיִת אֲשֶׁר הִקְדַּ֫שְׁתִּי לִשְׁמִי אֲשַׁלַּח מֵעַל פָּנָי וְהָיָה
ח יִשְׂרָאֵל לְמָשָׁל וְלִשְׁנִינָה בְּכָל־הָעַמִּים: וְהַבַּיִת הַזֶּה יִהְיֶה עֶלְיוֹן כָּל־עֹבֵר
עָלָיו יִשֹּׁם וְשָׁרָק וְאָמְרוּ עַל־מֶה עָשָׂה יהוה כָּ֫כָה לָאָרֶץ הַזֹּאת וְלַבַּיִת
ט הַזֶּה: וְאָמְרוּ עַל אֲשֶׁר עָזְבוּ אֶת־יהוה אֱלֹהֵיהֶם אֲשֶׁר הוֹצִיא אֶת־אֲבֹתָם
מֵאֶ֫רֶץ מִצְרַיִם וַיַּחֲזִקוּ בֵּאלֹהִים אֲחֵרִים °וַיִּשְׁתַּחוּ [°וַיִּשְׁתַּחֲווּ ק] לָהֶם
וַיַּעַבְדֻם עַל־כֵּן הֵבִיא יהוה עֲלֵיהֶם אֵת כָּל־הָרָעָה הַזֹּאת: וַיְהִי
י מִקְצֵה עֶשְׂרִים שָׁנָה אֲשֶׁר־בָּנָה שְׁלֹמֹה אֶת־שְׁנֵי הַבָּתִּים אֶת־בֵּית יהוה
יא וְאֶת־בֵּית הַמֶּלֶךְ: חִירָם מֶלֶךְ־צֹר נִשָּׂא אֶת־שְׁלֹמֹה בַּעֲצֵי אֲרָזִים וּבַעֲצֵי
בְרוֹשִׁים וּבַזָּהָב לְכָל־חֶפְצוֹ אָז יִתֵּן הַמֶּלֶךְ שְׁלֹמֹה לְחִירָם עֶשְׂרִים עִיר
יב בְּאֶ֫רֶץ הַגָּלִיל: וַיֵּצֵא חִירָם מִצֹּר לִרְאוֹת אֶת־הֶעָרִים אֲשֶׁר נָתַן־לוֹ שְׁלֹמֹה
יג וְלֹא יָשְׁרוּ בְּעֵינָיו: וַיֹּאמֶר מָה הֶעָרִים הָאֵלֶּה אֲשֶׁר־נָתַ֫תָּה לִּי אָחִי וַיִּקְרָא
יד לָהֶם אֶ֫רֶץ כָּבוּל עַד הַיּוֹם הַזֶּה: וַיִּשְׁלַח חִירָם לַמֶּלֶךְ מֵאָה
טו וְעֶשְׂרִים כִּכַּר זָהָב: וְזֶה דְבַר־הַמַּס אֲשֶׁר־הֶעֱלָה ׀ הַמֶּלֶךְ שְׁלֹמֹה לִבְנוֹת
אֶת־בֵּית יהוה וְאֶת־בֵּיתוֹ וְאֶת־הַמִּלּוֹא וְאֵת חוֹמַת יְרוּשָׁלָ֫͏ִם וְאֶת־
טז חָצֹר וְאֶת־מְגִדּוֹ וְאֶת־גָּ֫זֶר: פַּרְעֹה מֶלֶךְ־מִצְרַיִם עָלָה וַיִּלְכֹּד אֶת־גֶּ֫זֶר
וַיִּשְׂרְפָהּ בָּאֵשׁ וְאֶת־הַכְּנַעֲנִי הַיֹּשֵׁב בָּעִיר הָרָג וַיִּתְּנָהּ שִׁלֻּחִים לְבִתּוֹ
יז־יח אֵ֫שֶׁת שְׁלֹמֹה: וַיִּבֶן שְׁלֹמֹה אֶת־גָּ֫זֶר וְאֶת־בֵּית חֹרֹן תַּחְתּוֹן: וְאֶת־בַּעֲלָת
יט וְאֶת־°תָּמֹר [°תַּדְמֹר ק] בַּמִּדְבָּר בָּאָ֫רֶץ: וְאֵת כָּל־עָרֵי הַמִּסְכְּנוֹת
אֲשֶׁר הָיוּ לִשְׁלֹמֹה וְאֵת עָרֵי הָרֶ֫כֶב וְאֵת עָרֵי הַפָּרָשִׁים וְאֵת ׀ חֵשֶׁק

8:65. *II Chronicles* 7:9 indicates that they held a seven-day inaugural celebration, followed by the seven-day festival of Succos, for a total of fourteen days of joy.

8:66. Solomon bade them farewell, but the people remained in Jerusalem one more day to observe the festival of Shemini Atzeres (*Chronicles* ibid.).

9:6. The Hebrew word for "you" here is in the plural [אַתֶּם]; thus the warning applies to all the people of Israel.

A
fourteen-day
celebration
fourteen days. * ⁶⁶ On the eighth day, he sent the people off, * and they blessed the king. They then went to their homes, joyous and good-hearted over all the goodness that HASHEM had shown to His servant David and to His people Israel.

9   ¹ It happened when Solomon had finished building the Temple of HASHEM and the king's palace, and every luxury of Solomon that he had wished to
God
repeats His
pledge to
Solomon . . .
make: ² HASHEM appeared to Solomon a second time, as He had appeared to him at Gibeon. ³ HASHEM said to him, "I have heard your prayer and supplication that you supplicated before Me. I have sanctified this Temple that you have built, to place My Name there forever, and My eyes and My heart shall be there all the days. ⁴ And as for you — if you walk before Me as your father David walked, with wholeheartedness and with uprightness, to do in accordance with all that I have commanded you, and you will observe My decrees and My statutes; ⁵ then I shall uphold the throne of your kingdom over Israel forever, as I spoke about your father David, saying, 'No man of yours will be cut off from
. . . but on
the condition
that he and
Israel obey
the Torah
upon the throne of Israel.' ⁶ But if you * and your children turn away from Me and will not observe My commandments, My decrees that I have placed before you, and you go and worship the gods of others and prostrate yourselves to them, ⁷ then I shall cut off Israel from upon the face of the land that I gave them, and the Temple that I have sanctified for My Name I shall dismiss from My presence, and Israel shall become a parable and a conversation piece among all the nations. ⁸ And this Temple, which will be so exalted — all who pass by it will be appalled and will whistle, and they will say, 'Why did HASHEM do such a thing to this land and to this Temple?' ⁹ And they will say, 'Because they forsook HASHEM, their God, Who brought their forefathers out of the land of Egypt, and they grasped the gods of others, and prostrated themselves to them and worshiped them; therefore HASHEM brought all this evil upon them.' "

SOLOMON'S
LATER
YEARS
9:10-11:43
¹⁰ It happened at the end of the twenty years during which Solomon built the two buildings, the Temple of HASHEM and the king's palace: ¹¹ Hiram, king of Tyre, had supplied Solomon with cedar trees and cypress trees and gold according to his desire; then King Solomon gave Hiram twenty cities in the Land of Galilee. * ¹² Hiram left Tyre to see the cities that Solomon had given him, and
Solomon
repays Hiram
they were not acceptable in his eyes. ¹³ He said, "What are these cities you have given me, my brother?" And he called them "the Land of Cabul," * [which is its name] to this day. ¹⁴ Hiram sent the king a hundred and twenty talents of gold.
Solomon's
tax and
administra-
tors
¹⁵ This is a description of the levy * that King Solomon imposed to build the Temple of HASHEM; his own palace; the Millo * and the wall of Jerusalem; Hazor and Megiddo; Gezer ¹⁶ (Pharaoh, king of Egypt, had come up and conquered Gezer and burnt it in fire, and killed the Canaanite who lived in the city; he gave it as a wedding present to his daughter, Solomon's wife, ¹⁷ and Solomon then built up Gezer) and Lower Beth-horon; ¹⁸ Baalath and Tadmor in the desert, near the [populated] land; ¹⁹ and all the storage cities that Solomon had, and the chariot cities and the cavalry cities; and every luxury of

---

9:11. This was in addition to the handsome payments Solomon had been making to Hiram during the course of the twenty years (5:25). II Chronicles (8:2) implies that these twenty cities were *exchanged* for other cities from Hiram's territory (*Radak*), for it is unthinkable that Solomon would diminish the size of *Eretz Yisrael* (*Ralbag*).

9:13. Lit., *Shackles*. It was a marshland, where it was as

difficult to walk as it is for a man in shackles (*Rashi*).

9:15. The levy is described in verses 20-23.

The *Millo* from מלא, *to fill*, has been variously explained as a landfill (*Rashi*), an open plaza for large gatherings (*Radak*) or a moat (*Abarbanel*). Following the *Millo* is a list of cities that Solomon built at various strategic locations throughout Israel.

כ שְׁלֹמֹה אֲשֶׁר חָשַׁק לִבְנוֹת בִּירוּשָׁלַ͏ִם וּבַלְּבָנוֹן וּבְכֹל אֶרֶץ מֶמְשַׁלְתּוֹ: כָּל־
הָעָם הַנּוֹתָר מִן־הָאֱמֹרִי הַחִתִּי הַפְּרִזִּי הַחִוִּי וְהַיְבוּסִי אֲשֶׁר לֹא־מִבְּנֵי
כא יִשְׂרָאֵל הֵמָּה: בְּנֵיהֶם אֲשֶׁר נֹתְרוּ אַחֲרֵיהֶם בָּאָרֶץ אֲשֶׁר לֹא־יָכְלוּ בְּנֵי
כב יִשְׂרָאֵל לְהַחֲרִימָם וַיַּעֲלֵם שְׁלֹמֹה לְמַס־עֹבֵד עַד הַיּוֹם הַזֶּה: וּמִבְּנֵי יִשְׂרָאֵל
לֹא־נָתַן שְׁלֹמֹה עָבֶד כִּי־הֵם אַנְשֵׁי הַמִּלְחָמָה וַעֲבָדָיו וְשָׂרָיו וְשָׁלִשָׁיו
כג וְשָׂרֵי רִכְבּוֹ וּפָרָשָׁיו: אֵלֶּה ׀ שָׂרֵי הַנִּצָּבִים אֲשֶׁר עַל־הַמְּלָאכָה
כד לִשְׁלֹמֹה חֲמִשִּׁים וַחֲמֵשׁ מֵאוֹת הָרֹדִים בָּעָם הָעֹשִׂים בַּמְּלָאכָה: אַךְ בַּת־
פַּרְעֹה עָלְתָה מֵעִיר דָּוִד אֶל־בֵּיתָהּ אֲשֶׁר בָּנָה־לָהּ אָז בָּנָה אֶת־הַמִּלּוֹא:
כה וְהֶעֱלָה שְׁלֹמֹה שָׁלֹשׁ פְּעָמִים בַּשָּׁנָה עֹלוֹת וּשְׁלָמִים עַל־הַמִּזְבֵּחַ אֲשֶׁר
בָּנָה לַיהוָה וְהַקְטֵיר אִתּוֹ אֲשֶׁר לִפְנֵי יְהוָה וְשִׁלַּם אֶת־הַבָּיִת: וָאֳנִי עָשָׂה
כו הַמֶּלֶךְ שְׁלֹמֹה בְּעֶצְיוֹן־גֶּבֶר אֲשֶׁר אֶת־אֵלוֹת עַל־שְׂפַת יַם־סוּף בְּאֶרֶץ
כז אֱדוֹם: וַיִּשְׁלַח חִירָם בָּאֳנִי אֶת־עֲבָדָיו אַנְשֵׁי אֳנִיּוֹת יֹדְעֵי הַיָּם עִם עַבְדֵי
כח שְׁלֹמֹה: וַיָּבֹאוּ אוֹפִירָה וַיִּקְחוּ מִשָּׁם זָהָב אַרְבַּע־מֵאוֹת וְעֶשְׂרִים כִּכָּר

י

א וַיָּבִאוּ אֶל־הַמֶּלֶךְ שְׁלֹמֹה: וּמַלְכַּת־שְׁבָא שֹׁמַעַת אֶת־שֵׁמַע
שְׁלֹמֹה לְשֵׁם יְהוָה וַתָּבֹא לְנַסֹּתוֹ בְּחִידוֹת: וַתָּבֹא יְרוּשָׁלְַמָה בְּחַיִל כָּבֵד
ב מְאֹד גְּמַלִּים נֹשְׂאִים בְּשָׂמִים וְזָהָב רַב־מְאֹד וְאֶבֶן יְקָרָה וַתָּבֹא אֶל־שְׁלֹמֹה
ג וַתְּדַבֵּר אֵלָיו אֵת כָּל־אֲשֶׁר הָיָה עִם־לְבָבָהּ: וַיַּגֶּד־לָהּ שְׁלֹמֹה אֶת־כָּל־
ד דְּבָרֶיהָ לֹא־הָיָה דָבָר נֶעְלָם מִן־הַמֶּלֶךְ אֲשֶׁר לֹא הִגִּיד לָהּ: וַתֵּרֶא מַלְכַּת־
ה שְׁבָא אֵת כָּל־חָכְמַת שְׁלֹמֹה וְהַבַּיִת אֲשֶׁר בָּנָה: וּמַאֲכַל שֻׁלְחָנוֹ וּמוֹשַׁב
עֲבָדָיו וּמַעֲמַד °מְשָׁרְתָו [°מְשָׁרְתָיו ק] וּמַלְבֻּשֵׁיהֶם וּמַשְׁקָיו וְעֹלָתוֹ אֲשֶׁר
ו יַעֲלֶה בֵּית יְהוָה וְלֹא־הָיָה בָהּ עוֹד רוּחַ: וַתֹּאמֶר אֶל־הַמֶּלֶךְ אֱמֶת הָיָה
ז הַדָּבָר אֲשֶׁר שָׁמַעְתִּי בְּאַרְצִי עַל־דְּבָרֶיךָ וְעַל־חָכְמָתֶךָ: וְלֹא־הֶאֱמַנְתִּי
לַדְּבָרִים עַד אֲשֶׁר־בָּאתִי וַתִּרְאֶינָה עֵינַי וְהִנֵּה לֹא־הֻגַּד־לִי הַחֵצִי הוֹסַפְתָּ
ח חָכְמָה וָטוֹב אֶל־הַשְּׁמוּעָה אֲשֶׁר שָׁמָעְתִּי: אַשְׁרֵי אֲנָשֶׁיךָ אַשְׁרֵי עֲבָדֶיךָ
ט אֵלֶּה הָעֹמְדִים לְפָנֶיךָ תָּמִיד הַשֹּׁמְעִים אֶת־חָכְמָתֶךָ: יְהִי יְהוָה אֱלֹהֶיךָ בָּרוּךְ
אֲשֶׁר חָפֵץ בְּךָ לְתִתְּךָ עַל־כִּסֵּא יִשְׂרָאֵל בְּאַהֲבַת יְהוָה אֶת־יִשְׂרָאֵל לְעֹלָם
י וַיְשִׂימְךָ לְמֶלֶךְ לַעֲשׂוֹת מִשְׁפָּט וּצְדָקָה: וַתִּתֵּן לַמֶּלֶךְ מֵאָה וְעֶשְׂרִים ׀ כִּכַּר
זָהָב וּבְשָׂמִים הַרְבֵּה מְאֹד וְאֶבֶן יְקָרָה לֹא־בָא כַבֹּשֶׂם הַהוּא עוֹד לָרֹב
יא אֲשֶׁר־נָתְנָה מַלְכַּת־שְׁבָא לַמֶּלֶךְ שְׁלֹמֹה: וְגַם אֳנִי חִירָם אֲשֶׁר־נָשָׂא זָהָב
יב מֵאוֹפִיר הֵבִיא מֵאֹפִיר עֲצֵי אַלְמֻגִּים הַרְבֵּה מְאֹד וְאֶבֶן יְקָרָה: וַיַּעַשׂ הַמֶּלֶךְ

9:24. Although Solomon's grandiose construction plans included a great royal palace, he did not have his queen live there, because [Solomon] thought, *"I should not have a wife stay in the City of David, king of Israel, for it is a holy place, being that the Ark of HASHEM was brought there" (II Chronicles 8:11).*

9:25. Having built the Temple, Solomon undertook to

assure a supply of offerings and incense. Though our verse singles out those of the three pilgrimage festivals, Solomon also supplied the daily, Sabbath, and New Moon offerings as well *(II Chronicles 8:13).* He also *completed [the arrangements]* by setting up systems of rotations for the Kohanim and Levites *(II Chronicles 8:14).*

9:26. Also called Elath *(Deut. 2:8)*, or Eilat.

Solomon that he wished to build in Jerusalem and in the Lebanon and in all the land of his dominion. ²⁰ All the people who were left of the Amorite, the Hittite, the Perizzite, the Hivite and Jebusite, who were not of the Children of Israel — ²¹ their descendants who were left after them in the land, whom the Children of Israel were not able to eradicate — Solomon conscripted them as indentured laborers, until this day. ²² But Solomon did not enslave anyone of the Children of Israel, for they were the men of war, and they were his servants, commanders and officers, and the commanders of his chariots and his riders. ²³ And these were the commanders of his commissioners who were in charge of the work for Solomon: five hundred and fifty [men] who directed the people doing the work.

The queen's palace ²⁴ However* Pharaoh's daughter went up from the City of David to her house that [Solomon] had built for her; then he built [up] the Millo.

His Temple offerings ²⁵ Three times a year Solomon had elevation-offerings and peace-offerings brought upon the Altar that he had built for HASHEM, and had incense burned [on the other Altar that was] with it before HASHEM, and he completed [the arrangements of] the Temple. *

His fleet ²⁶ King Solomon made a fleet in Ezion-geber, which is near Eloth, * on the coast of the Sea of Reeds, in the land of Edom. ²⁷ Hiram sent in the fleet his servants, shipmen who knew the sea, together with Solomon's servants; ²⁸ they came to Ophir and took gold from there, four hundred and twenty talents, * and brought them to King Solomon.

10

The queen of Sheba arrives . . . ¹ The queen of Sheba heard of Solomon's fame, that it was for the Name of HASHEM, * and she came to test him with riddles. ² She arrived in Jerusalem with a very large entourage, with camels bearing very large amounts of spices and gold, and precious stones. She came before Solomon, and she spoke to him about all that was in her heart. ³ Solomon told her [the solutions to] all her questions; there was not a thing hidden from the king that he could not tell her. ⁴ The queen of Sheba saw all the wisdom of Solomon: the palace that he had erected; ⁵ the food

. . . and is overwhelmed [served] at his table and the seating of his servants; the station of his attendants and their uniforms; his drinks; and his passageway by which he ascended to the Temple of HASHEM * — and she was overwhelmed.

⁶ She said to the king, "True was the word that I had heard in my country about your words and your wisdom! ⁷ I had not believed the words until I came and my own eyes saw; and behold — even the half of it was not told to me! You have surpassed [in] wisdom and goodness the report that I had heard. ⁸ Fortunate are your men — fortunate are these servants of yours — who stand before you constantly, who hear your wisdom! ⁹ May HASHEM, your God, be blessed, Who has chosen you, to place you upon the throne of Israel; in HASHEM's everlasting love for Israel He has established you as king, to do justice and righteousness."

¹⁰ She then gave the king a hundred and twenty talents of gold, very many spices and precious stones; there has never again come such a large quantity of spice as that which the queen of Sheba gave to King Solomon.

More magnificence ¹¹ (In addition, Hiram's fleet, which had carried gold from Ophir, also brought a large amount of almog-trees, * and precious stones from Ophir. ¹² The king made

---

9:28. A talent is approximately 64 pounds.
10:1. His wisdom was a gift of God and he used it to do God's will (*Ralbag*).

10:5. Solomon had built himself a ramp or stairway from his palace to the Temple (see *II Chronicles* 9:4).
10:11. Branching, tree-like coral (*Rashi; Radak*).

אֶת־עֲצֵי הָאַלְמֻגִּים מִסְעָד לְבֵית־יְהוָה וּלְבֵית הַמֶּלֶךְ וְכִנֹּרוֹת וּנְבָלִים

יג לַשָּׁרִים לֹא בָא־כֵן עֲצֵי אַלְמֻגִּים וְלֹא נִרְאָה עַד הַיּוֹם הַזֶּה: וְהַמֶּלֶךְ
שְׁלֹמֹה נָתַן לְמַלְכַּת־שְׁבָא אֶת־כָּל־חֶפְצָהּ אֲשֶׁר שָׁאָלָה מִלְּבַד אֲשֶׁר

יד נָתַן־לָהּ כְּיַד הַמֶּלֶךְ שְׁלֹמֹה וַתֵּפֶן וַתֵּלֶךְ לְאַרְצָהּ הִיא וַעֲבָדֶיהָ: וַיְהִי
מִשְׁקַל הַזָּהָב אֲשֶׁר־בָּא לִשְׁלֹמֹה בְּשָׁנָה אֶחָת שֵׁשׁ מֵאוֹת שִׁשִּׁים וָשֵׁשׁ

טו כִּכַּר זָהָב: לְבַד מֵאַנְשֵׁי הַתָּרִים וּמִסְחַר הָרֹכְלִים וְכָל־מַלְכֵי הָעֶרֶב וּפַחוֹת

טז הָאָרֶץ: וַיַּעַשׂ הַמֶּלֶךְ שְׁלֹמֹה מָאתַיִם צִנָּה זָהָב שָׁחוּט שֵׁשׁ־מֵאוֹת זָהָב

יז יַעֲלֶה עַל־הַצִּנָּה הָאֶחָת: וּשְׁלֹשׁ־מֵאוֹת מָגִנִּים זָהָב שָׁחוּט שְׁלֹשֶׁת מָנִים
זָהָב יַעֲלֶה עַל־הַמָּגֵן הָאֶחָת וַיִּתְּנֵם הַמֶּלֶךְ בֵּית יַעַר הַלְּבָנוֹן: וַיַּעַשׂ

יח הַמֶּלֶךְ כִּסֵּא־שֵׁן גָּדוֹל וַיְצַפֵּהוּ זָהָב מוּפָז: שֵׁשׁ מַעֲלוֹת לַכִּסֵּה וְרֹאשׁ־עָגֹל

יט לַכִּסֵּה מֵאַחֲרָיו וְיָדֹת מִזֶּה וּמִזֶּה אֶל־מְקוֹם הַשָּׁבֶת וּשְׁנַיִם אֲרָיוֹת עֹמְדִים

כ אֵצֶל הַיָּדוֹת: וּשְׁנֵים עָשָׂר אֲרָיִים עֹמְדִים שָׁם עַל־שֵׁשׁ הַמַּעֲלוֹת מִזֶּה וּמִזֶּה
לֹא־נַעֲשָׂה כֵן לְכָל־מַמְלָכוֹת: וְכֹל כְּלֵי מַשְׁקֵה הַמֶּלֶךְ שְׁלֹמֹה זָהָב וְכֹל

כא כְּלֵי בֵּית־יַעַר הַלְּבָנוֹן זָהָב סָגוּר אֵין כֶּסֶף לֹא נֶחְשָׁב בִּימֵי שְׁלֹמֹה

כב לִמְאוּמָה: כִּי אֳנִי תַרְשִׁישׁ לַמֶּלֶךְ בַּיָּם עִם אֳנִי חִירָם אַחַת לְשָׁלֹשׁ שָׁנִים

כג תָּבוֹא ׀ אֳנִי תַרְשִׁישׁ נֹשְׂאֵת זָהָב וָכֶסֶף שֶׁנְהַבִּים וְקֹפִים וְתֻכִּיִּים: וַיִּגְדַּל
הַמֶּלֶךְ שְׁלֹמֹה מִכֹּל מַלְכֵי הָאָרֶץ לְעֹשֶׁר וּלְחָכְמָה: וְכָל־הָאָרֶץ מְבַקְשִׁים

כד אֶת־פְּנֵי שְׁלֹמֹה לִשְׁמֹעַ אֶת־חָכְמָתוֹ אֲשֶׁר־נָתַן אֱלֹהִים בְּלִבּוֹ: וְהֵמָּה

כה מְבִאִים אִישׁ מִנְחָתוֹ כְּלֵי כֶסֶף וּכְלֵי זָהָב וּשְׂלָמוֹת וְנֵשֶׁק וּבְשָׂמִים סוּסִים
וּפְרָדִים דְּבַר־שָׁנָה בְּשָׁנָה: וַיֶּאֱסֹף שְׁלֹמֹה רֶכֶב וּפָרָשִׁים וַיְהִי־לוֹ

כו אֶלֶף וְאַרְבַּע־מֵאוֹת רֶכֶב וּשְׁנֵים־עָשָׂר אֶלֶף פָּרָשִׁים וַיַּנְחֵם בְּעָרֵי הָרֶכֶב

כז וְעִם־הַמֶּלֶךְ בִּירוּשָׁלָ‍ִם: וַיִּתֵּן הַמֶּלֶךְ אֶת־הַכֶּסֶף בִּירוּשָׁלַ‍ִם כָּאֲבָנִים וְאֵת

כח הָאֲרָזִים נָתַן כַּשִּׁקְמִים אֲשֶׁר־בַּשְּׁפֵלָה לָרֹב: וּמוֹצָא הַסּוּסִים אֲשֶׁר לִשְׁלֹמֹה

כט מִמִּצְרָיִם וּמִקְוֵה סֹחֲרֵי הַמֶּלֶךְ יִקְחוּ מִקְוֵה בִּמְחִיר: וַתַּעֲלֶה וַתֵּצֵא מֶרְכָּבָה
מִמִּצְרַיִם בְּשֵׁשׁ מֵאוֹת כֶּסֶף וְסוּס בַּחֲמִשִּׁים וּמֵאָה וְכֵן לְכָל־מַלְכֵי הַחִתִּים

יא א וּלְמַלְכֵי אֲרָם בְּיָדָם יֹצִאוּ:   וְהַמֶּלֶךְ שְׁלֹמֹה אָהַב נָשִׁים נָכְרִיּוֹת

ב רַבּוֹת וְאֶת־בַּת־פַּרְעֹה מוֹאֲבִיּוֹת עַמֳּנִיּוֹת אֲדֹמִיֹּת צֵדְנִיֹּת חִתִּיֹּת: מִן־
הַגּוֹיִם אֲשֶׁר אָמַר־יְהוָה אֶל־בְּנֵי יִשְׂרָאֵל לֹא־תָבֹאוּ בָהֶם וְהֵם לֹא־יָבֹאוּ
בָכֶם אָכֵן יַטּוּ אֶת־לְבַבְכֶם אַחֲרֵי אֱלֹהֵיהֶם בָּהֶם דָּבַק שְׁלֹמֹה לְאַהֲבָה:

ג וַיְהִי־לוֹ נָשִׁים שָׂרוֹת שְׁבַע מֵאוֹת וּפִלַגְשִׁים שְׁלֹשׁ מֵאוֹת וַיַּטּוּ נָשָׁיו אֶת־

ד לִבּוֹ: וַיְהִי לְעֵת זִקְנַת שְׁלֹמֹה נָשָׁיו הִטּוּ אֶת־לְבָבוֹ אַחֲרֵי אֱלֹהִים אֲחֵרִים

10:22. The term "Tarshish ship" refers to a large sturdy seafaring vessel. (Tarshish has been variously identified as a place in Turkey, Spain or North Africa.)

10:28. As Pharaoh's son-in-law, Solomon was able to obtain horses from Egypt without paying any duties or fees, but the horses that were brought from Keveh were much more expensive (*Abarbanel*).

10:29. Solomon's favorable arrangement with Egypt enabled him to develop a profitable international trading system (*Abarbanel*).

the almog-trees into a walkway for the Temple of HASHEM and the palace of the king, and into harps and lyres for the singers; there had never come such almog-trees before, nor was there seen [afterwards] to this day.)

The queen returns home

¹³ King Solomon gave the queen of Sheba whatever desire she requested, besides that which he gave according to the generosity of King Solomon, and she turned and went to her land, she and her servants.

Annual receipts of gold

¹⁴ The amount of gold that came to Solomon in one year was six hundred sixty-six talents of gold, ¹⁵ besides [tax income] from merchants and the commerce of the spice-peddlers, and from all the vassal kings and the governors of the land. ¹⁶ King Solomon made two hundred shields of beaten gold, he would put six hundred [measures] of gold into each shield; ¹⁷ and three hundred bucklers of beaten gold, he would put three maneh of gold into each buckler; and the king placed them in the "House of the Forest of Lebanon."

Solomon's magnificent throne

¹⁸ The king made a great throne of ivory, and overlaid it with sparkling gold. ¹⁹ The throne had six steps; a rounded top to the throne at its back; arms on either side at the place of the seat, with two [figures of] lions standing next to the arms; ²⁰ and twelve [figures of] lions standing there, on the six steps on either side. Nothing like it had ever been made for any of the kingdoms.

His unparalleled wealth

²¹ All of King Solomon's drinking vessels were gold, and all the fixtures of the "House of the Forest of Lebanon" were pure gold; there was no silver, [for silver] was not considered of any worth in the days of Solomon. ²² For the king had a Tarshish fleet* in the sea with Hiram's fleet; once in three years the Tarshish fleet would arrive, carrying gold, silver, ivory, and monkeys and peacocks.

²³ King Solomon became greater than all the kings of the land in wealth and in wisdom. ²⁴ And the whole world wanted to see Solomon to hear his wisdom, which God had put in his heart. ²⁵ And each one of them would bring his gift — silver articles, golden articles, clothing, weapons, spices, horses, and mules — each year's due in its year.

His horses and chariots

²⁶ Solomon assembled chariots and horsemen — he had one thousand four hundred chariots and twelve thousand riders; he kept them in the chariot cities, and [left some] with the king in Jerusalem. ²⁷ King Solomon made silver in Jerusalem [as common] as stones, and he made cedars as abundant as sycamores in the lowland. ²⁸ Solomon's horses were imported from Egypt. An association of the King's traders would purchase as an association at a set price.* ²⁹ A chariot could be brought out of Egypt for six hundred [pieces of] silver and horses for a hundred and fifty; [Solomon's traders] would also export for all the kings of the Hittites and the kings of Aram.*

11

Solomon's many wives lead him astray

*¹ **K**ing Solomon loved many foreign women,* in addition to the daughter of Pharaoh* — Moabites, Ammonites, Edomites, Sidonians and Hittites — ² from the nations of which HASHEM had said to the Children of Israel, "Do not come into [marriage with] them, and they shall not come into [marriage with] you; for they will surely sway your hearts after their gods." Solomon clung to them for love. ³ He had seven hundred wives who were noblewomen and three hundred concubines, and his wives swayed his heart. ⁴ So it was that when Solomon grew old his wives swayed his heart after the gods of others,*

11:1. Although every one of Solomon's spouses converted (*Rambam*; see 3:1), he committed two offenses: A king should not marry many wives (*Deut.* 17:17); and, as

mentioned in the following verse, even a commoner is not permitted to marry an idolater.

ה וְלֹא־הָיָה לְבָבוֹ שָׁלֵם עִם־יהוה אֱלֹהָיו כִּלְבַב דָּוִיד אָבִיו: וַיֵּלֶךְ שְׁלֹמֹה

ו אַחֲרֵי עַשְׁתֹּרֶת אֱלֹהֵי צִדֹנִים וְאַחֲרֵי מִלְכֹּם שִׁקֻּץ עַמֹּנִים: וַיַּעַשׂ שְׁלֹמֹה

ז הָרַע בְּעֵינֵי יהוה וְלֹא מִלֵּא אַחֲרֵי יהוה כְּדָוִד אָבִיו: אָז יִבְנֶה
שְׁלֹמֹה בָּמָה לִכְמוֹשׁ שִׁקֻּץ מוֹאָב בָּהָר אֲשֶׁר עַל־פְּנֵי יְרוּשָׁלָ͏ִם וּלְמֹלֶךְ

ח שִׁקֻּץ בְּנֵי עַמּוֹן: וְכֵן עָשָׂה לְכָל־נָשָׁיו הַנָּכְרִיּוֹת מַקְטִירוֹת וּמְזַבְּחוֹת

ט לֵאלֹהֵיהֶן: וַיִּתְאַנַּף יהוה בִּשְׁלֹמֹה כִּי־נָטָה לְבָבוֹ מֵעִם יהוה אֱלֹהֵי יִשְׂרָאֵל

י הַנִּרְאָה אֵלָיו פַּעֲמָיִם: וְצִוָּה אֵלָיו עַל־הַדָּבָר הַזֶּה לְבִלְתִּי־לֶכֶת אַחֲרֵי
אֱלֹהִים אֲחֵרִים וְלֹא שָׁמַר אֵת אֲשֶׁר־צִוָּה יהוה: וַיֹּאמֶר יהוה

יא לִשְׁלֹמֹה יַעַן אֲשֶׁר הָיְתָה־זֹּאת עִמָּךְ וְלֹא שָׁמַרְתָּ בְּרִיתִי וְחֻקֹּתַי אֲשֶׁר

יב צִוִּיתִי עָלֶיךָ קָרֹעַ אֶקְרַע אֶת־הַמַּמְלָכָה מֵעָלֶיךָ וּנְתַתִּיהָ לְעַבְדֶּךָ: אַךְ־
בְּיָמֶיךָ לֹא אֶעֱשֶׂנָּה לְמַעַן דָּוִד אָבִיךָ מִיַּד בִּנְךָ אֶקְרָעֶנָּה: רַק אֶת־כָּל־

יג הַמַּמְלָכָה לֹא אֶקְרָע שֵׁבֶט אֶחָד אֶתֵּן לִבְנֶךָ לְמַעַן דָּוִד עַבְדִּי וּלְמַעַן

יד יְרוּשָׁלַ͏ִם אֲשֶׁר בָּחָרְתִּי: וַיָּקֶם יהוה שָׂטָן לִשְׁלֹמֹה אֵת הֲדַד

טו הָאֲדֹמִי מִזֶּרַע הַמֶּלֶךְ הוּא בֶּאֱדוֹם: וַיְהִי בִּהְיוֹת דָּוִד אֶת־אֱדוֹם בַּעֲלוֹת

טז יוֹאָב שַׂר הַצָּבָא לְקַבֵּר אֶת־הַחֲלָלִים וַיַּךְ כָּל־זָכָר בֶּאֱדוֹם: כִּי שֵׁשֶׁת
חֳדָשִׁים יָשַׁב־שָׁם יוֹאָב וְכָל־יִשְׂרָאֵל עַד־הִכְרִית כָּל־זָכָר בֶּאֱדוֹם: וַיִּבְרַח

יז אֲדַד הוּא וַאֲנָשִׁים אֲדֹמִיִּים מֵעַבְדֵי אָבִיו אִתּוֹ לָבוֹא מִצְרָיִם וַהֲדַד נַעַר

יח קָטָן: וַיָּקֻמוּ מִמִּדְיָן וַיָּבֹאוּ פָּארָן וַיִּקְחוּ אֲנָשִׁים עִמָּם מִפָּארָן וַיָּבֹאוּ מִצְרַיִם
אֶל־פַּרְעֹה מֶלֶךְ־מִצְרַיִם וַיִּתֶּן־לוֹ בַיִת וְלֶחֶם אָמַר לוֹ וְאֶרֶץ נָתַן לוֹ: וַיִּמְצָא

יט הֲדַד חֵן בְּעֵינֵי פַרְעֹה מְאֹד וַיִּתֶּן־לוֹ אִשָּׁה אֶת־אֲחוֹת אִשְׁתּוֹ אֲחוֹת

כ תַּחְפְּנֵיס הַגְּבִירָה: וַתֵּלֶד לוֹ אֲחוֹת תַּחְפְּנֵיס אֵת גְּנֻבַת בְּנוֹ וַתִּגְמְלֵהוּ

כא תַחְפְּנֵס בְּתוֹךְ בֵּית פַּרְעֹה וַיְהִי גְנֻבַת בֵּית פַּרְעֹה בְּתוֹךְ בְּנֵי פַרְעֹה: וַהֲדַד
שָׁמַע בְּמִצְרַיִם כִּי־שָׁכַב דָּוִד עִם־אֲבֹתָיו וְכִי־מֵת יוֹאָב שַׂר־הַצָּבָא וַיֹּאמֶר

כב הֲדַד אֶל־פַּרְעֹה שַׁלְּחֵנִי וְאֵלֵךְ אֶל־אַרְצִי: וַיֹּאמֶר לוֹ פַרְעֹה כִּי מָה־אַתָּה
חָסֵר עִמִּי וְהִנְּךָ מְבַקֵּשׁ לָלֶכֶת אֶל־אַרְצֶךָ וַיֹּאמֶר ׀ לֹא כִּי שַׁלֵּחַ תְּשַׁלְּחֵנִי:

כג וַיָּקֶם אֱלֹהִים לוֹ שָׂטָן אֶת־רְזוֹן בֶּן־אֶלְיָדָע אֲשֶׁר בָּרַח מֵאֵת הֲדַדְעֶזֶר

כד מֶלֶךְ־צוֹבָה אֲדֹנָיו: וַיִּקְבֹּץ עָלָיו אֲנָשִׁים וַיְהִי שַׂר־גְּדוּד בַּהֲרֹג דָּוִד אֹתָם

כה וַיֵּלְכוּ דַמֶּשֶׂק וַיֵּשְׁבוּ בָהּ וַיִּמְלְכוּ בְּדַמָּשֶׂק: וַיְהִי שָׂטָן לְיִשְׂרָאֵל כָּל־

11:4. Since Solomon is criticized not as a sinner, but only as being less virtuous than David, the Sages of the Talmud infer that he was not *personally* involved in idolatry or in building altars to strange gods. Rather, he was responsible because he did not prevent his wives from carrying on their idolatrous practices freely, even though he himself did not participate in such worship. This imputation of guilt to Solomon follows two principles: A Jew is responsible for the behavior of those subject to his influence; and great people, such as Solomon, are held to more exacting standards than others. What may be tolerated in others is considered a grievous sin for them.

11:10. The Sages comment that Solomon was led astray by his unprecedented wisdom. The Torah forbade a king to have many wives lest they sway his heart, and to have too many horses, lest he establish too close a relationship with Egypt, the source of the finest horses (*Deut.* 17:16-17). Solomon was confident that his wisdom would enable him to avoid both snares. He was wrong; no human being may substitute his wisdom for God's word.

and his heart was not as perfect with HASHEM his God as [had been] the heart of his father David. * [5] Solomon went after Ashtoreth, the god of the Sidonians, and after Milcom, the abomination of the Ammonites. [6] And Solomon did what was sinful in the eyes of HASHEM, and did not wholeheartedly follow HASHEM as his father David had done.

. . . as if he were an idolater

[7] Then Solomon built a high place for Chemosh, the abomination of Moab, on the Mount [of Olives] facing Jerusalem; and for Molech, the abomination of the Children of Ammon; [8] and he did likewise for all his foreign wives, they burned incense and sacrificed to their gods. [9] So HASHEM became angry with Solomon, for his heart had strayed from HASHEM, the God of Israel, Who had appeared to him twice, [10] and commanded him about this matter, not to go after the gods of others; but he did not heed that which HASHEM had commanded him. *

The kingdom will be split

[11] So HASHEM said to Solomon, "Since this has happened to you, and you have not kept My covenant and My decrees that I have commanded you, I shall surely tear away the kingship from you and give it to your servant. [12] In your days, however, I will not do it, because of your father David; from the hand of your son will I tear it away. [13] Only I shall not tear away the entire kingdom from him; one tribe shall I give to your son, for the sake of David My servant and for the sake of Jerusalem, which I have chosen."

Hadad becomes Solomon's antagonist . . .

[14] HASHEM then stirred up an antagonist against Solomon, Hadad the Edomite; he was a member of the royal family of Edom. [15] It had happened when David was in Edom, when Joab, the commander of the army, went up to bury the slain* (for he had killed all the males of Edom; [16] Joab and all of Israel stayed there for six months until he had destroyed all the males in Edom), [17] that Hadad, along with some other Edomite men of his father's servants, had fled to Egypt, while Hadad was a young boy. [18] They arose from Midian and came to Paran; they took men with them from Paran and came to Egypt, to Pharaoh, king of Egypt, and he gave him a house, arranged food for him and gave him land. * [19] Hadad found grace in Pharaoh's eyes, and [Pharaoh] gave him his wife's sister — the sister of Tahpenes the queen — for a wife. [20] The sister of Tahpenes bore him his son Genubath; Tahpenes weaned him in Pharaoh's house, and Genubath lived in Pharaoh's house, among Pharaoh's children. * [21] When Hadad heard in Egypt that David lay with his forefathers and that Joab, the commander of the army, had died, Hadad said to Pharaoh, "Grant me leave, and I shall go to my homeland."

[22] Pharaoh said to him, "What do you lack with me, that you desire to go to your homeland?"

But he replied, "Nevertheless, grant me leave."

. . . and Rezon joins him

[23] And God stirred up [another] antagonist against [Solomon] — Rezon son of Eliada, who had escaped from his master, Hadadezer, king of Zobah. [24] He gathered men to himself and became a captain of a force after David had decimated them; they went to Damascus and lived there, and they reigned in Damascus. [25] He was an antagonist against Israel all the [remaining]

11:15. See note to *II Samuel* 8:13.

11:18. After Hadad fled to Midian, he went to Paran and from there to Egypt, where the king made him governor of a province (*Radak*).

11:20. Scripture provides so much personal data about

Hadad to show that his desire for revenge was so great that he gave up all his success in Egypt and sought to retaliate against Israel. Nevertheless, it was only because Solomon sinned that God allowed Hadad to become Israel's main adversary.

כו יְמֵי שְׁלֹמֹה וְאֵת־הָרָעָה אֲשֶׁר הֲדָד וַיָּקָץ בְּיִשְׂרָאֵל וַיִּמְלֹךְ עַל־
אֲרָם: וְיָרָבְעָם בֶּן־נְבָט אֶפְרָתִי מִן־הַצְּרֵדָה וְשֵׁם אִמּוֹ

כז צְרוּעָה אִשָּׁה אַלְמָנָה עֶבֶד לִשְׁלֹמֹה וַיָּרֶם יָד בַּמֶּלֶךְ: וְזֶה הַדָּבָר אֲשֶׁר־
הֵרִים יָד בַּמֶּלֶךְ שְׁלֹמֹה בָּנָה אֶת־הַמִּלּוֹא סָגַר אֶת־פֶּרֶץ עִיר דָּוִד

כח אָבִיו: וְהָאִישׁ יָרָבְעָם גִּבּוֹר חָיִל וַיַּרְא שְׁלֹמֹה אֶת־הַנַּעַר כִּי־עֹשֵׂה
כט מְלָאכָה הוּא וַיַּפְקֵד אֹתוֹ לְכָל־סֵבֶל בֵּית יוֹסֵף: וַיְהִי
בָּעֵת הַהִיא וְיָרָבְעָם יָצָא מִירוּשָׁלִַם וַיִּמְצָא אֹתוֹ אֲחִיָּה הַשִּׁילֹנִי הַנָּבִיא

ל בַּדֶּרֶךְ וְהוּא מִתְכַּסֶּה בְּשַׂלְמָה חֲדָשָׁה וּשְׁנֵיהֶם לְבַדָּם בַּשָּׂדֶה: וַיִּתְפֹּשׂ
לא אֲחִיָּה בַּשַּׂלְמָה הַחֲדָשָׁה אֲשֶׁר עָלָיו וַיִּקְרָעֶהָ שְׁנֵים עָשָׂר קְרָעִים: וַיֹּאמֶר
לְיָרָבְעָם קַח־לְךָ עֲשָׂרָה קְרָעִים כִּי כֹה אָמַר יְהוָֹה אֱלֹהֵי יִשְׂרָאֵל הִנְנִי

לב קֹרֵעַ אֶת־הַמַּמְלָכָה מִיַּד שְׁלֹמֹה וְנָתַתִּי לְךָ אֵת עֲשָׂרָה הַשְּׁבָטִים: וְהַשֵּׁבֶט
הָאֶחָד יִהְיֶה־לּוֹ לְמַעַן עַבְדִּי דָוִד וּלְמַעַן יְרוּשָׁלִַם הָעִיר אֲשֶׁר בָּחַרְתִּי

לג בָהּ מִכֹּל שִׁבְטֵי יִשְׂרָאֵל: יַעַן אֲשֶׁר עֲזָבוּנִי וַיִּשְׁתַּחֲווּ לְעַשְׁתֹּרֶת אֱלֹהֵי
צִדֹנִין לִכְמוֹשׁ אֱלֹהֵי מוֹאָב וּלְמִלְכֹּם אֱלֹהֵי בְנֵי־עַמּוֹן וְלֹא־הָלְכוּ בִדְרָכַי

לד לַעֲשׂוֹת הַיָּשָׁר בְּעֵינַי וְחֻקֹּתַי וּמִשְׁפָּטַי כְּדָוִד אָבִיו: וְלֹא־אֶקַּח אֶת־כָּל־
הַמַּמְלָכָה מִיָּדוֹ כִּי נָשִׂיא אֲשִׁתֶנּוּ כֹּל יְמֵי חַיָּיו לְמַעַן דָּוִד עַבְדִּי אֲשֶׁר

לה בָּחַרְתִּי אֹתוֹ אֲשֶׁר שָׁמַר מִצְוֹתַי וְחֻקֹּתָי: וְלָקַחְתִּי הַמְּלוּכָה מִיַּד בְּנוֹ
לו וּנְתַתִּיהָ לְּךָ אֵת עֲשֶׂרֶת הַשְּׁבָטִים: וְלִבְנוֹ אֶתֵּן שֵׁבֶט־אֶחָד לְמַעַן הֱיוֹת־
נִיר לְדָוִיד־עַבְדִּי כָּל־הַיָּמִים לְפָנַי בִּירוּשָׁלִַם הָעִיר אֲשֶׁר בָּחַרְתִּי

לז לִי לָשׂוּם שְׁמִי שָׁם: וְאֹתְךָ אֶקַּח וּמָלַכְתָּ בְּכֹל אֲשֶׁר־תְּאַוֶּה נַפְשֶׁךָ וְהָיִיתָ
לח מֶּלֶךְ עַל־יִשְׂרָאֵל: וְהָיָה אִם־תִּשְׁמַע אֶת־כָּל־אֲשֶׁר אֲצַוֶּךָ וְהָלַכְתָּ בִדְרָכַי
וְעָשִׂיתָ הַיָּשָׁר בְּעֵינַי לִשְׁמוֹר חֻקּוֹתַי וּמִצְוֹתַי כַּאֲשֶׁר עָשָׂה דָּוִד עַבְדִּי
וְהָיִיתִי עִמָּךְ וּבָנִיתִי לְךָ בַיִת־נֶאֱמָן כַּאֲשֶׁר בָּנִיתִי לְדָוִד וְנָתַתִּי לְךָ אֶת־

לט יִשְׂרָאֵל: וַאֲעַנֶּה אֶת־זֶרַע דָּוִד לְמַעַן זֹאת אַךְ לֹא כָל־הַיָּמִים: וַיְבַקֵּשׁ
מ שְׁלֹמֹה לְהָמִית אֶת־יָרָבְעָם וַיָּקָם יָרָבְעָם וַיִּבְרַח מִצְרַיִם אֶל־שִׁישַׁק

מֶלֶךְ־מִצְרַיִם וַיְהִי בְמִצְרַיִם עַד־מוֹת שְׁלֹמֹה: וְיֶתֶר דִּבְרֵי שְׁלֹמֹה וְכָל־
מא אֲשֶׁר עָשָׂה וְחָכְמָתוֹ הֲלוֹא־הֵם כְּתֻבִים עַל־סֵפֶר דִּבְרֵי שְׁלֹמֹה:
מב וְהַיָּמִים אֲשֶׁר מָלַךְ שְׁלֹמֹה בִירוּשָׁלִַם עַל־כָּל־יִשְׂרָאֵל אַרְבָּעִים שָׁנָה:
מג וַיִּשְׁכַּב שְׁלֹמֹה עִם־אֲבֹתָיו וַיִּקָּבֵר בְּעִיר דָּוִד אָבִיו וַיִּמְלֹךְ רְחַבְעָם בְּנוֹ

11:27. Jeroboam publicly criticized Solomon for blocking the Millo in order to build a palace for Pharaoh's daughter (9:24). Until then it had been an open area providing public access to the Temple. The next passage explains that Jeroboam was encouraged in this flagrant breach of protocol by his prior success and reputation, and by the prophecy of Ahijah.

11:32. Judah would remain with Solomon's family, and Benjamin, the twelfth tribe, was considered a part of

Judah in this instance (see 12:21), because Jerusalem straddled the territory of both Judah and Benjamin [*Joshua* 15:8; 18:16] (*Radak*).

11:33. I.e. the House of Solomon.

11:39. God would afflict the Davidic dynasty by not allowing it to reign over the entire nation (*Radak*), but this punishment would not be permanent. The Messiah, scion of the House of David, will once again reign over a united Israel (*Rashi*).

days of Solomon, together with the evil Hadad; he despised Israel, and ruled over Aram.

Jeroboam
protests

²⁶ *Also Jeroboam son of Nebat, an Ephraimite from Zeredah — his mother's name was Zeruah, a widow — who was a servant to Solomon, raised his hand against the king.* ²⁷ *This is the matter [about] which he raised his hand against the king: Solomon had built [up] the Millo and closed up the breach left by his father David!* *

God ordains
that Israel
will split into
two nations

²⁸ *This man Jeroboam was a mighty man of valor. Solomon had seen in the young man that he was one who did his work [well], and he appointed him over all the taxation of the House of Joseph.*

²⁹ *It happened at that time, while Jeroboam was leaving Jerusalem, the prophet Ahijah the Shilonite found him on the way; he was clothed in a new garment, and the two of them were alone in the field.* ³⁰ *Ahijah grabbed hold of the new garment that was upon him, and he tore it into twelve pieces.* ³¹ *He said to Jeroboam, "Take for yourself ten pieces, for so said HASHEM, God of Israel,'I am tearing the kingdom away from the hand of Solomon and I shall give the ten tribes to you.* ³² *But the one tribe shall remain for him,* * *for the sake of My servant David and for the sake of Jerusalem, the city which I have chosen of all the tribes of Israel.* ³³ *[This is] because they* * *have forsaken Me and bowed down to Ashtoreth, the god of the Sidonians, to Chemosh, the god of Moab, and to Milcom, the god of the Children of Ammon, and they did not walk in My ways, to do what is proper in My eyes, My decrees and My statutes, as [did] David his father.* ³⁴ *But I shall not take away any of the kingdom from his own hand, for I shall set him as ruler all the days of his life, for the sake of My servant David whom I chose, who observed My commandments and My decrees.* ³⁵ *Rather I shall take away the kingdom from the hand of his son and I shall give it to you — the ten tribes;* ³⁶ *and to his son I shall give one tribe, so that there may remain a dominion for the House of David for all the days before Me in Jerusalem, the city that I have chosen for Myself to place My Name there.* ³⁷ *But you I shall take, and you shall reign over all that you desire, and you will be king over Israel.* ³⁸ *And it shall be that if you obey all that I will command you and walk in My ways, and you do that which is upright in My eyes, to observe My decrees and My commandments as David My servant did, then I shall be with you and I shall build an enduring dynasty for you, just as I built for David, and I shall give Israel to you.* ³⁹ *And I shall afflict the descendants of David for this — but not for all time.' "* *

⁴⁰ *Solomon sought to put Jeroboam to death,* * *so Jeroboam arose and ran away to Egypt, to Shishak, king of Egypt; and he stayed in Egypt until Solomon's death.*

Solomon
dies
(See Appendix A,
timeline 4)

⁴¹ *As for all the rest of the deeds of Solomon and all that he did and his wisdom — behold, they are written in the Book of the Words of Solomon.* * ⁴² *The duration of Solomon's reign in Jerusalem over all Israel was forty years.* ⁴³ *Solomon lay with his forefathers, and was buried in the City of David his father. His son Rehoboam reigned in his place.*

11:40. After recording the meeting of Jeroboam and the prophet Ahijah, the narrative returns to Solomon's reac-

tion to Jeroboam's public criticism (see vv. 26-28). **11:41.** This book is no longer extant (*Abarbanel*).

יב

א תַּחְתָּיו: וַיֵּלֶךְ רְחַבְעָם שְׁכֶם כִּי שְׁכֶם בָּא כָל־יִשְׂרָאֵל

ב לְהַמְלִיךְ אֹתוֹ: וַיְהִי כִּשְׁמֹעַ ׀ יָרָבְעָם בֶּן־נְבָט וְהוּא עוֹדֶנּוּ בְמִצְרַיִם אֲשֶׁר

ג בָּרַח מִפְּנֵי הַמֶּלֶךְ שְׁלֹמֹה וַיֵּשֶׁב יָרָבְעָם בְּמִצְרָיִם: וַיִּשְׁלְחוּ וַיִּקְרְאוּ־לֹו °וַיָּבֹא [וַיָּבֹאוּ ק] יָרָבְעָם וְכָל־קְהַל יִשְׂרָאֵל וַיְדַבְּרוּ אֶל־רְחַבְעָם לֵאמֹר:

ד אָבִיךָ הִקְשָׁה אֶת־עֻלֵּנוּ וְאַתָּה עַתָּה הָקֵל מֵעֲבֹדַת אָבִיךָ הַקָּשָׁה וּמֵעֻלּוֹ

ה הַכָּבֵד אֲשֶׁר־נָתַן עָלֵינוּ וְנַעַבְדֶךָּ: וַיֹּאמֶר אֲלֵיהֶם לְכוּ עֹד שְׁלֹשָׁה יָמִים

ו וְשׁוּבוּ אֵלָי וַיֵּלְכוּ הָעָם: וַיִּוָּעַץ הַמֶּלֶךְ רְחַבְעָם אֶת־הַזְּקֵנִים אֲשֶׁר־הָיוּ עֹמְדִים אֶת־פְּנֵי שְׁלֹמֹה אָבִיו בִּהְיֹתוֹ חַי לֵאמֹר אֵיךְ אַתֶּם נוֹעָצִים

ז לְהָשִׁיב אֶת־הָעָם־הַזֶּה דָבָר: °וַיְדַבֵּר [וַיְדַבְּרוּ ק] אֵלָיו לֵאמֹר אִם־הַיּוֹם תִּהְיֶה־עֶבֶד לָעָם הַזֶּה וַעֲבַדְתָּם וַעֲנִיתָם וְדִבַּרְתָּ אֲלֵיהֶם דְּבָרִים טוֹבִים

ח וְהָיוּ לְךָ עֲבָדִים כָּל־הַיָּמִים: וַיַּעֲזֹב אֶת־עֲצַת הַזְּקֵנִים אֲשֶׁר יְעָצֻהוּ וַיִּוָּעַץ

ט אֶת־הַיְלָדִים אֲשֶׁר גָּדְלוּ אִתּוֹ אֲשֶׁר הָעֹמְדִים לְפָנָיו: וַיֹּאמֶר אֲלֵיהֶם מָה אַתֶּם נוֹעָצִים וְנָשִׁיב דָּבָר אֶת־הָעָם הַזֶּה אֲשֶׁר דִּבְּרוּ אֵלַי לֵאמֹר הָקֵל

י מִן־הָעֹל אֲשֶׁר־נָתַן אָבִיךָ עָלֵינוּ: וַיְדַבְּרוּ אֵלָיו הַיְלָדִים אֲשֶׁר גָּדְלוּ אִתּוֹ לֵאמֹר כֹּה־תֹאמַר לָעָם הַזֶּה אֲשֶׁר דִּבְּרוּ אֵלֶיךָ לֵאמֹר אָבִיךָ הִכְבִּיד אֶת־עֻלֵּנוּ וְאַתָּה הָקֵל מֵעָלֵינוּ כֹּה תְּדַבֵּר אֲלֵיהֶם קָטָנִּי עָבָה מִמָּתְנֵי אָבִי:

יא וְעַתָּה אָבִי הֶעְמִיס עֲלֵיכֶם עֹל כָּבֵד וַאֲנִי אוֹסִיף עַל־עֻלְּכֶם אָבִי יִסַּר אֶתְכֶם בַּשּׁוֹטִים וַאֲנִי אֲיַסֵּר אֶתְכֶם בָּעַקְרַבִּים: °וַיָּבֹו [וַיָּבוֹא ק] יָרָבְעָם

יב וְכָל־הָעָם אֶל־רְחַבְעָם בַּיּוֹם הַשְּׁלִישִׁי כַּאֲשֶׁר דִּבֶּר הַמֶּלֶךְ לֵאמֹר שׁוּבוּ

יג אֵלַי בַּיּוֹם הַשְּׁלִישִׁי: וַיַּעַן הַמֶּלֶךְ אֶת־הָעָם קָשָׁה וַיַּעֲזֹב אֶת־עֲצַת הַזְּקֵנִים

יד אֲשֶׁר יְעָצֻהוּ: וַיְדַבֵּר אֲלֵיהֶם כַּעֲצַת הַיְלָדִים לֵאמֹר אָבִי הִכְבִּיד אֶת־עֻלְּכֶם וַאֲנִי אֹסִיף עַל־עֻלְּכֶם אָבִי יִסַּר אֶתְכֶם בַּשּׁוֹטִים וַאֲנִי אֲיַסֵּר אֶתְכֶם

טו בָּעַקְרַבִּים: וְלֹא־שָׁמַע הַמֶּלֶךְ אֶל־הָעָם כִּי־הָיְתָה סִבָּה מֵעִם יְהֹוָה לְמַעַן הָקִים אֶת־דְּבָרוֹ אֲשֶׁר דִּבֶּר יְהֹוָה בְּיַד אֲחִיָּה הַשִּׁילֹנִי אֶל־יָרָבְעָם בֶּן־נְבָט:

טז וַיַּרְא כָּל־יִשְׂרָאֵל כִּי לֹא־שָׁמַע הַמֶּלֶךְ אֲלֵיהֶם וַיָּשִׁבוּ הָעָם אֶת־הַמֶּלֶךְ דָּבָר ׀ לֵאמֹר מַה־לָּנוּ חֵלֶק בְּדָוִד וְלֹא־נַחֲלָה בְּבֶן־יִשַׁי לְאֹהָלֶיךָ יִשְׂרָאֵל

יז עַתָּה רְאֵה בֵיתְךָ דָּוִד וַיֵּלֶךְ יִשְׂרָאֵל לְאֹהָלָיו: וּבְנֵי יִשְׂרָאֵל הַיֹּשְׁבִים בְּעָרֵי יְהוּדָה וַיִּמְלֹךְ עֲלֵיהֶם רְחַבְעָם:

יח וַיִּשְׁלַח הַמֶּלֶךְ רְחַבְעָם אֶת־אֲדֹרָם אֲשֶׁר עַל־הַמַּס וַיִּרְגְּמוּ כָל־יִשְׂרָאֵל בּוֹ אֶבֶן וַיָּמֹת וְהַמֶּלֶךְ רְחַבְעָם הִתְאַמֵּץ לַעֲלוֹת בַּמֶּרְכָּבָה לָנוּס יְרוּשָׁלָ‍ִם:

יט-כ וַיִּפְשְׁעוּ יִשְׂרָאֵל בְּבֵית דָּוִד עַד הַיּוֹם הַזֶּה: וַיְהִי

12:8. Rehoboam was forty-one years old (14-21); his peers were hardly youngsters. Scripture calls them "youths" as a comment on their immaturity.

12:15. See 11:31.

12:16. Rule over your own tribe, not over us! (*Targum*).

Alternatively: The Temple that your father built is yours alone (*Rashi*).

12:18. Adoram and Adoniram were the same person (see 4:6, 5:28 and *II Samuel* 20:24; *Rashi*).

12

THE TWO
KINGDOMS:
REHOBOAM,
KING OF
JUDAH;
JEROBOAM,
KING OF
ISRAEL
12:1-14:31
(See Appendix A,
timeline 4)

¹ Rehoboam went to Shechem, for all of Israel had come to Shechem to make him king. ² When Jeroboam son of Nebat heard this while he was still in Egypt (where he had fled from before King Solomon, and Jeroboam had settled in Egypt), ³ for [the people] sent for him and summoned him, Jeroboam came, along with all of the Congregation of Israel, and they spoke to Rehoboam, saying, ⁴ "Your father made our yoke [of taxation] difficult; now, you alleviate your father's difficult workload and his heavy yoke that he placed upon us, and we will serve you."

⁵ He said to them, "Go away for three more days and then come back to me." So the people left.

⁶ King Rehoboam took counsel with the elders, who had stood before his father Solomon while he was alive, saying, "How do you advise; what word to respond to this people?"

⁷ They spoke to him, saying, "If today you become a servant to this people and serve them, and respond [favorably] to them and speak kind words to them, they will be your servants all the days."

Rehoboam ignores the sage advice of his elders . . .
⁸ But he ignored the advice of the elders who had counseled him, and he took counsel with the youths * who had grown up with him, who ministered before him. ⁹ He said to them, "What do you advise; what word shall we respond to this people who have spoken to me, saying, 'Alleviate the yoke that your father placed upon us'?"

. . . and accepts the impetuous counsel of his friends
¹⁰ The young men who had grown up with him spoke to him, saying, "This is what you should say to this people who have spoken to you, saying, 'Your father made our yoke heavy; you alleviate it for us' — this is what you should say to them: 'My little finger is thicker than my father's loins! ¹¹ So now, my father saddled you with a heavy yoke; I shall add to your yoke! My father chastised you with sticks; I shall chastise you with scorpions!' "

¹² Jeroboam and all the people came to Rehoboam on the third day, as the king had spoken, saying, "Return to me on the third day." ¹³ The king responded harshly to the people; he ignored the advice of the elders who had counseled him. ¹⁴ He spoke to them according to the counsel of the youths, saying, "My father made your yoke heavy, and I shall add to your yoke! My father chastised you with sticks; I shall chastise you with scorpions!"

He antagonizes the populace and they rebel
¹⁵ The king did not listen to the people, for it was a design from HASHEM, in order to fulfill His word that HASHEM had spoken through the hand of Ahijah the Shilonite to Jeroboam son of Nebat. * ¹⁶ All of Israel saw that the king did not listen to them, and the people gave their response to the king, saying, "What share have we in [the House of] David? [We have] no heritage in the son of Jesse! Back to your homes, O Israel! Now see to your own house, O [kingdom of] David!"* And [the men of] Israel left for home. ¹⁷ As for the Children of Israel who lived in the cities of Judah — Rehoboam ruled over them.

¹⁸ King Rehoboam dispatched Adoram, who was in charge of the tax* — and all of Israel pelted him with stones, and he died. King Rehoboam then hastened to mount his chariot to flee to Jerusalem. ¹⁹ Thus Israel rebelled against the House of David, to this day.

כִּשְׁמֹעַ כָּל־יִשְׂרָאֵל כִּי־שָׁב יָרָבְעָם וַיִּשְׁלְחוּ וַיִּקְרְאוּ אֹתוֹ אֶל־הָעֵדָה
וַיַּמְלִיכוּ אֹתוֹ עַל־כָּל־יִשְׂרָאֵל לֹא הָיָה אַחֲרֵי בֵית־דָּוִד זוּלָתִי שֵׁבֶט־יְהוּדָה
כא לְבַדּוֹ: ⁰וַיָּבֹא [°וַיָּבֹא ק] רְחַבְעָם יְרוּשָׁלַם וַיַּקְהֵל אֶת־כָּל־בֵּית יְהוּדָה
וְאֶת־שֵׁבֶט בִּנְיָמִן מֵאָה וּשְׁמֹנִים אֶלֶף בָּחוּר עֹשֵׂה מִלְחָמָה לְהִלָּחֵם עִם־
כב בֵּית יִשְׂרָאֵל לְהָשִׁיב אֶת־הַמְּלוּכָה לִרְחַבְעָם בֶּן־שְׁלֹמֹה: וַיְהִי
כג דְּבַר הָאֱלֹהִים אֶל־שְׁמַעְיָה אִישׁ־הָאֱלֹהִים לֵאמֹר: אֱמֹר אֶל־רְחַבְעָם בֶּן־
כד שְׁלֹמֹה מֶלֶךְ יְהוּדָה וְאֶל־כָּל־בֵּית יְהוּדָה וּבִנְיָמִין וְיֶתֶר הָעָם לֵאמֹר: כֹּה
אָמַר יְהוָה לֹא־תַעֲלוּ וְלֹא־תִלָּחֲמוּן עִם־אֲחֵיכֶם בְּנֵי־יִשְׂרָאֵל שׁוּבוּ אִישׁ
לְבֵיתוֹ כִּי מֵאִתִּי נִהְיָה הַדָּבָר הַזֶּה וַיִּשְׁמְעוּ אֶת־דְּבַר יְהוָה וַיָּשֻׁבוּ לָלֶכֶת
כה כִּדְבַר יְהוָה: וַיִּבֶן יָרָבְעָם אֶת־שְׁכֶם בְּהַר אֶפְרַיִם וַיֵּשֶׁב בָּהּ וַיֵּצֵא
כו מִשָּׁם וַיִּבֶן אֶת־פְּנוּאֵל: וַיֹּאמֶר יָרָבְעָם בְּלִבּוֹ עַתָּה תָּשׁוּב הַמַּמְלָכָה לְבֵית
כז דָּוִד: אִם־יַעֲלֶה | הָעָם הַזֶּה לַעֲשׂוֹת זְבָחִים בְּבֵית־יְהוָה בִּירוּשָׁלַם וְשָׁב לֵב
הָעָם הַזֶּה אֶל־אֲדֹנֵיהֶם אֶל־רְחַבְעָם מֶלֶךְ יְהוּדָה וַהֲרָגֻנִי וְשָׁבוּ אֶל־
כח רְחַבְעָם מֶלֶךְ־יְהוּדָה: וַיִּוָּעַץ הַמֶּלֶךְ וַיַּעַשׂ שְׁנֵי עֶגְלֵי זָהָב וַיֹּאמֶר אֲלֵהֶם
רַב־לָכֶם מֵעֲלוֹת יְרוּשָׁלַם הִנֵּה אֱלֹהֶיךָ יִשְׂרָאֵל אֲשֶׁר הֶעֱלוּךָ מֵאֶרֶץ
כט־ל מִצְרָיִם: וַיָּשֶׂם אֶת־הָאֶחָד בְּבֵית־אֵל וְאֶת־הָאֶחָד נָתַן בְּדָן: וַיְהִי הַדָּבָר
לא הַזֶּה לְחַטָּאת וַיֵּלְכוּ הָעָם לִפְנֵי הָאֶחָד עַד־דָּן: וַיַּעַשׂ אֶת־בֵּית בָּמוֹת וַיַּעַשׂ
לב כֹּהֲנִים מִקְצוֹת הָעָם אֲשֶׁר לֹא־הָיוּ מִבְּנֵי לֵוִי: וַיַּעַשׂ יָרָבְעָם | חָג בַּחֹדֶשׁ
הַשְּׁמִינִי בַּחֲמִשָּׁה־עָשָׂר יוֹם | לַחֹדֶשׁ כֶּחָג | אֲשֶׁר בִּיהוּדָה וַיַּעַל עַל־
הַמִּזְבֵּחַ כֵּן עָשָׂה בְּבֵית־אֵל לְזַבֵּחַ לָעֲגָלִים אֲשֶׁר־עָשָׂה וְהֶעֱמִיד בְּבֵית אֵל
לג אֶת־כֹּהֲנֵי הַבָּמוֹת אֲשֶׁר עָשָׂה: וַיַּעַל עַל־הַמִּזְבֵּחַ | אֲשֶׁר־עָשָׂה בְּבֵית־אֵל
בַּחֲמִשָּׁה עָשָׂר יוֹם בַּחֹדֶשׁ הַשְּׁמִינִי בַּחֹדֶשׁ אֲשֶׁר־בָּדָא °מִלְבַּד [°מִלִּבּוֹ ק]
יג א וַיַּעַשׂ חָג לִבְנֵי יִשְׂרָאֵל וַיַּעַל עַל־הַמִּזְבֵּחַ לְהַקְטִיר: וְהִנֵּה |
אִישׁ אֱלֹהִים בָּא מִיהוּדָה בִּדְבַר יְהוָה אֶל־בֵּית־אֵל וְיָרָבְעָם עֹמֵד עַל־
ב הַמִּזְבֵּחַ לְהַקְטִיר: וַיִּקְרָא עַל־הַמִּזְבֵּחַ בִּדְבַר יְהוָה וַיֹּאמֶר מִזְבֵּחַ מִזְבֵּחַ
כֹּה אָמַר יְהוָה הִנֵּה־בֵן נוֹלָד לְבֵית־דָּוִד יֹאשִׁיָּהוּ שְׁמוֹ וְזָבַח עָלֶיךָ אֶת־
ג כֹּהֲנֵי הַבָּמוֹת הַמַּקְטִרִים עָלֶיךָ וְעַצְמוֹת אָדָם יִשְׂרְפוּ עָלֶיךָ: וְנָתַן בַּיּוֹם
הַהוּא מוֹפֵת לֵאמֹר זֶה הַמּוֹפֵת אֲשֶׁר דִּבֶּר יְהוָה הִנֵּה הַמִּזְבֵּחַ נִקְרָע
ד וְנִשְׁפַּךְ הַדֶּשֶׁן אֲשֶׁר־עָלָיו: וַיְהִי כִשְׁמֹעַ הַמֶּלֶךְ אֶת־דְּבַר אִישׁ־הָאֱלֹהִים
אֲשֶׁר קָרָא עַל־הַמִּזְבֵּחַ בְּבֵית־אֵל וַיִּשְׁלַח יָרָבְעָם אֶת־יָדוֹ מֵעַל הַמִּזְבֵּחַ
לֵאמֹר | תִּפְשֻׂהוּ וַתִּיבַשׁ יָדוֹ אֲשֶׁר שָׁלַח עָלָיו וְלֹא יָכֹל לַהֲשִׁיבָהּ אֵלָיו:

12:23. Those residents of Jerusalem who were from
other tribes and some members of Simeon, who lived in
scattered enclaves within the territory of Judah (see
Joshua 19:1,9; Ralbag).

12:31. None of the Levites would cooperate with his

villainous scheme (*Radak*), so Jeroboam expelled them
from his kingdom (*II Chronicles 11:14*).

12:32. Jeroboam's eighth-month (*Cheshvan*) festival
was to replace the seventh-month (*Tishrei*) festival of
Succos.

Rehoboam
mobilizes to
fight . . .
(See Appendix A,
timeline 4)
²⁰ It happened when all of Israel heard that Jeroboam had returned, that they sent and summoned him to the assembly, and they made him king over all of Israel; no one followed the house of David except the tribe of Judah alone. ²¹ Rehoboam came to Jerusalem, and gathered together the entire House of Judah and the tribe of Benjamin, one hundred eighty thousand choice warriors, to fight against the House of Israel, to return the kingship to Rehoboam son of Solomon.

*. . . but
obeys God's
command to
desist*

²² The word of God then came to Shemaiah, the man of God, saying, ²³ "Speak to Rehoboam son of Solomon, king of Judah, and to all the House of Judah and Benjamin and to the rest of the people, * saying, ²⁴ 'Thus said HASHEM: Do not go up and fight with your brethren, the Children of Israel; let each man return to his home, for this matter was brought about by Me.' " They obeyed the word of HASHEM and turned back from going [to war], in accordance with the word of HASHEM.

*Jeroboam
establishes
idol worship
for political
reasons*

²⁵ Jeroboam built [up] Shechem in the Mountain of Ephraim and dwelled in it; then he left there and built [up] Penuel. ²⁶ Jeroboam then thought, "Now the kingship may revert to the house of David. ²⁷ If this people will go up to bring offerings in the Temple of HASHEM in Jerusalem, the heart of this people will revert to their lord, to Rehoboam, king of Judah, and they will kill me and return to Rehoboam, king of Judah."

²⁸ The king took counsel, and he made two golden calves; and he said to [the people], "It is too far for you to go up to Jerusalem. These are your gods, O Israel, who brought you up from the land of Egypt!" ²⁹ He placed the one in Beth-el and the [other] one in Dan. ³⁰ This matter became a sin, and the people traveled [all the way] to Dan [to worship] before one [of them]. ³¹ He also made a temple of high places, and he appointed priests from the commoners of the people, who were not of the children of Levi. * ³² Jeroboam also innovated a holiday in the eighth month, on the fifteenth day of the month, in imitation of the holiday in Judah, * and brought offerings on the altar. He did the same in Beth-el, sacrificing to the calves that he had made; and in Beth-el he set up the priests of the high places that he had made. ³³ He ascended the altar that he had made in Beth-el on the fifteenth day of the eighth month, in the month that he had fabricated with his imagination; he made a holiday for the Children of Israel — he ascended the altar to burn incense.

13

*A prophet
denounces
Jeroboam's
idolatry*

¹ Just then a man of God came to Beth-el from Judah by the word of HASHEM, while Jeroboam was standing atop the altar to burn incense. ² He called out to the altar, by the word of HASHEM, and said, "Altar, altar! Thus said HASHEM: Behold a son will be born to the house of David, — Josiah [will be] his name — and he will slaughter upon you the priests of the high places, who burn sacrifices upon you; human bones will be burnt upon you." ³ And he provided a proof on that day, saying, "This is the proof of which HASHEM spoke: Behold, the altar is split and the ashes upon it are spilled."

*Jeroboam is
punished and
the prophet
leaves him*

⁴ It happened when the king heard the words of the man of God who had called out to the altar in Beth-el, that Jeroboam stretched out his hand from upon the altar, saying, "Seize him!" and his hand that he had stretched out towards him became paralyzed; he was not able to bring it back to himself.

ה וְהַמִּזְבֵּחַ נִקְרָע וַיִּשָּׁפֵךְ הַדֶּשֶׁן מִן־הַמִּזְבֵּחַ כַּמּוֹפֵת אֲשֶׁר נָתַן אִישׁ
הָאֱלֹהִים בִּדְבַר יהוָה: ו וַיַּעַן הַמֶּלֶךְ וַיֹּאמֶר ׀ אֶל־אִישׁ הָאֱלֹהִים חַל־נָא
אֶת־פְּנֵי יהוָה אֱלֹהֶיךָ וְהִתְפַּלֵּל בַּעֲדִי וְתָשֹׁב יָדִי אֵלָי וַיְחַל אִישׁ־הָאֱלֹהִים
אֶת־פְּנֵי יהוָה וַתָּשָׁב יַד־הַמֶּלֶךְ אֵלָיו וַתְּהִי כְּבָרִאשֹׁנָה: ז וַיְדַבֵּר הַמֶּלֶךְ אֶל־
ח אִישׁ הָאֱלֹהִים בֹּאָה־אִתִּי הַבַּיְתָה וּסְעָדָה וְאֶתְּנָה לְךָ מַתָּת: וַיֹּאמֶר אִישׁ־
הָאֱלֹהִים אֶל־הַמֶּלֶךְ אִם־תִּתֶּן־לִי אֶת־חֲצִי בֵיתֶךָ לֹא אָבֹא עִמָּךְ וְלֹא־
ט אֹכַל לֶחֶם וְלֹא אֶשְׁתֶּה־מַּיִם בַּמָּקוֹם הַזֶּה: כִּי־כֵן ׀ צִוָּה אֹתִי בִדְבַר יהוָה
לֵאמֹר לֹא־תֹאכַל לֶחֶם וְלֹא תִשְׁתֶּה־מָּיִם וְלֹא תָשׁוּב בַּדֶּרֶךְ אֲשֶׁר הָלָכְתָּ:
יא וַיֵּלֶךְ בְּדֶרֶךְ אַחֵר וְלֹא־שָׁב בַּדֶּרֶךְ אֲשֶׁר בָּא בָהּ אֶל־בֵּית־אֵל: וְנָבִיא
אֶחָד זָקֵן יֹשֵׁב בְּבֵית־אֵל וַיָּבוֹא בְנוֹ וַיְסַפֶּר־לוֹ אֶת־כָּל־הַמַּעֲשֶׂה אֲשֶׁר־
עָשָׂה אִישׁ־הָאֱלֹהִים ׀ הַיּוֹם בְּבֵית־אֵל אֶת־הַדְּבָרִים אֲשֶׁר דִּבֶּר אֶל־
יב הַמֶּלֶךְ וַיְסַפְּרוּם לַאֲבִיהֶם: וַיְדַבֵּר אֲלֵהֶם אֲבִיהֶם אֵי־זֶה הַדֶּרֶךְ הָלָךְ וַיִּרְאוּ
יג בָנָיו אֶת־הַדֶּרֶךְ אֲשֶׁר הָלַךְ אִישׁ הָאֱלֹהִים אֲשֶׁר־בָּא מִיהוּדָה: וַיֹּאמֶר
יד אֶל־בָּנָיו חִבְשׁוּ־לִי הַחֲמוֹר וַיַּחְבְּשׁוּ־לוֹ הַחֲמוֹר וַיִּרְכַּב עָלָיו: וַיֵּלֶךְ אַחֲרֵי
אִישׁ הָאֱלֹהִים וַיִּמְצָאֵהוּ יֹשֵׁב תַּחַת הָאֵלָה וַיֹּאמֶר אֵלָיו הַאַתָּה אִישׁ־
טו הָאֱלֹהִים אֲשֶׁר־בָּאתָ מִיהוּדָה וַיֹּאמֶר אָנִי: וַיֹּאמֶר אֵלָיו לֵךְ אִתִּי הַבָּיְתָה
טז וֶאֱכֹל לָחֶם: וַיֹּאמֶר לֹא אוּכַל לָשׁוּב לָלֶכֶת אִתָּךְ וְלָבוֹא אִתָּךְ וְלֹא־אֹכַל לֶחֶם
יז וְלֹא־אֶשְׁתֶּה אִתְּךָ מַיִם בַּמָּקוֹם הַזֶּה: כִּי־דָבָר אֵלַי בִּדְבַר יהוָה לֹא־
תֹאכַל לֶחֶם וְלֹא־תִשְׁתֶּה שָׁם מָיִם לֹא־תָשׁוּב לָלֶכֶת בַּדֶּרֶךְ אֲשֶׁר הָלַכְתָּ
יח בָהּ: וַיֹּאמֶר לוֹ גַּם־אֲנִי נָבִיא כָּמוֹךָ וּמַלְאָךְ דִּבֶּר אֵלַי בִּדְבַר יהוָה לֵאמֹר
יט הֲשִׁבֵהוּ אִתְּךָ אֶל־בֵּיתֶךָ וְיֹאכַל לֶחֶם וְיֵשְׁתְּ מָיִם כִּחֵשׁ לוֹ: וַיָּשָׁב אִתּוֹ
כ וַיֹּאכַל לֶחֶם בְּבֵיתוֹ וַיֵּשְׁתְּ מָיִם: וַיְהִי הֵם יֹשְׁבִים אֶל־הַשֻּׁלְחָן וַיְהִי
כא דְּבַר־יהוָה אֶל־הַנָּבִיא אֲשֶׁר הֱשִׁיבוֹ: וַיִּקְרָא אֶל־אִישׁ הָאֱלֹהִים אֲשֶׁר־בָּא
מִיהוּדָה לֵאמֹר כֹּה אָמַר יהוָה יַעַן כִּי מָרִיתָ פִּי יהוָה וְלֹא שָׁמַרְתָּ אֶת־
כב הַמִּצְוָה אֲשֶׁר צִוְּךָ יהוָה אֱלֹהֶיךָ: וַתָּשָׁב וַתֹּאכַל לֶחֶם וַתֵּשְׁתְּ מַיִם בַּמָּקוֹם
אֲשֶׁר דִּבֶּר אֵלֶיךָ אַל־תֹּאכַל לֶחֶם וְאַל־תֵּשְׁתְּ מָיִם לֹא־תָבוֹא נִבְלָתְךָ
כג אֶל־קֶבֶר אֲבֹתֶיךָ: וַיְהִי אַחֲרֵי אָכְלוֹ לֶחֶם וְאַחֲרֵי שְׁתוֹתוֹ וַיַּחֲבָשׁ־לוֹ
כד הַחֲמוֹר לַנָּבִיא אֲשֶׁר הֱשִׁיבוֹ: וַיֵּלֶךְ וַיִּמְצָאֵהוּ אַרְיֵה בַּדֶּרֶךְ וַיְמִיתֵהוּ וַתְּהִי
נִבְלָתוֹ מֻשְׁלֶכֶת בַּדֶּרֶךְ וְהַחֲמוֹר עֹמֵד אֶצְלָהּ וְהָאַרְיֵה עֹמֵד אֵצֶל הַנְּבֵלָה:
כה וְהִנֵּה אֲנָשִׁים עֹבְרִים וַיִּרְאוּ אֶת־הַנְּבֵלָה מֻשְׁלֶכֶת בַּדֶּרֶךְ וְאֶת־הָאַרְיֵה
עֹמֵד אֵצֶל הַנְּבֵלָה וַיָּבֹאוּ וַיְדַבְּרוּ בָעִיר אֲשֶׁר הַנָּבִיא הַזָּקֵן יֹשֵׁב בָּהּ:

13:11. He was a false prophet (*Targum*) who was originally from Samaria; see *II Kings* 23:18.

13:20. Had HASHEM's message not been transmitted to
the false prophet beforehand, the people might not have
taken the true prophet's admonitions seriously, be-

cause they would have thought that his unnatural death
proved him to be a charlatan (*Malbim*).

13:22. The man of God should have ascertained if the
false prophet was speaking in the Name of God (*Radak*).
13:23. This is the man of God.

[5] *The altar then split and the ashes spilled from the altar, in accordance with the proof that the man of God had given by the word of H*ASHEM. [6] *The king then spoke up and said to the man of God, "Please entreat the presence of H*ASHEM *your God and pray for me, so that my hand may return to me!" So the man of God entreated the presence of H*ASHEM; *[the use of] the king's hand returned to him, and it became as it had been before.* [7] *The king then spoke to the man of God, "Come home with me and dine, and I shall give you a gift."*

[8] *But the man of God said to the king, "Even if you give me half your house, I shall not come with you, I shall not eat bread, I shall not drink water in this place.* [9] *For thus has it been commanded to me by the word of H*ASHEM, *saying, 'Do not eat a meal and do not drink water, and do not return on the road by which you went.'"* [10] *So he went on a different road, and did not return on the road by which he had come to Beth-el.*

A false prophet pursues the man of God . . .

[11] *There was a certain old prophet who was living in Beth-el.* * *His son came and told him all about the deed that the man of God had done that day in Beth-el, and the words he had spoken to the king. [His other sons] also told their father.* [12] *Their father said to them, "By which road did he go?" His sons showed him the road by which the man of God, who had come from Judah, had gone.* [13] *He then said to his sons, "Saddle up the donkey for me!" They saddled up the donkey, and he mounted it.*

. . . and deceives him

[14] *He went after the man of God and found him sitting under an elm tree. He said to him, "Are you the man of God who came from Judah?"*

And he said, "I am."

[15] *He said to him, "Come home with me and eat a meal."*

[16] *He replied, "I cannot return with you and come with you, and I shall not eat a meal nor drink water in this place!* [17] *For a decree [has come] to me by the word of H*ASHEM, *'You shall not eat a meal nor drink water there, and you shall not return on the road by which you went.'"*

[18] *But he said to him, "I am also a prophet like you, and an angel spoke to me by the word of H*ASHEM, *saying, 'Bring him back with you to your house, so that he may eat a meal and drink water.'" (He lied to him.)* [19] *So he returned with him and ate a meal in his house and drank water.*

A dire prophecy . . .

[20] *As they were sitting at the table, the word of H*ASHEM *came to the prophet* * *who had brought back [the man of God].* [21] *He called out to the man of God who had come from Judah, saying, "Thus said H*ASHEM: *Because you have rebelled against the word of H*ASHEM, *and did not keep the commandment that H*ASHEM *your God commanded you,* [22] *and you returned and ate a meal and drank water in the place where He told you, 'Do not eat a meal and do not drink water,' your corpse shall not reach your fathers' grave."* *

. . . and the true prophet is mauled to death

[23] *It happened after he had eaten a meal and after he had drunk [that] he saddled the donkey for the prophet* * *whom he had brought back.* [24] *He went and a lion encountered him on the way and killed him, and his corpse was cast down on the road, and the donkey stood next to it, and the lion [also] stood next to the corpse.* * [25] *Then behold — some people were passing, and they saw the corpse cast down on the road and the lion standing next to the corpse, and they came and related it in the city where the old prophet lived.*

13:24. That the lion did not devour the corpse nor kill the donkey was a clear indication that the man's death   had been a supernatural occurrence.

כו וַיִּשְׁמַע הַנָּבִיא אֲשֶׁר הֱשִׁיבוֹ מִן־הַדֶּרֶךְ וַיֹּאמֶר אִישׁ הָאֱלֹהִים הוּא אֲשֶׁר מָרָה אֶת־פִּי יהוה וַיִּתְּנֵהוּ יהוה לָאַרְיֵה וַיִּשְׁבְּרֵהוּ וַיְמִתֵהוּ כִּדְבַר יהוה

כז אֲשֶׁר דִּבֶּר־לוֹ: וַיְדַבֵּר אֶל־בָּנָיו לֵאמֹר חִבְשׁוּ־לִי אֶת־הַחֲמוֹר וַיַּחֲבֹשׁוּ:

כח וַיֵּלֶךְ וַיִּמְצָא אֶת־נִבְלָתוֹ מֻשְׁלֶכֶת בַּדֶּרֶךְ וַחֲמוֹר וְהָאַרְיֵה עֹמְדִים אֵצֶל הַנְּבֵלָה לֹא־אָכַל הָאַרְיֵה אֶת־הַנְּבֵלָה וְלֹא שָׁבַר אֶת־הַחֲמוֹר:

כט וַיִּשָּׂא הַנָּבִיא אֶת־נִבְלַת אִישׁ־הָאֱלֹהִים וַיַּנִּחֵהוּ אֶל־הַחֲמוֹר וַיְשִׁיבֵהוּ וַיָּבֹא אֶל־עִיר הַנָּבִיא הַזָּקֵן לִסְפֹּד וּלְקָבְרוֹ:

ל וַיַּנַּח אֶת־נִבְלָתוֹ בְּקִבְרוֹ וַיִּסְפְּדוּ עָלָיו הוֹי אָחִי:

לא וַיְהִי אַחֲרֵי קָבְרוֹ אֹתוֹ וַיֹּאמֶר אֶל־בָּנָיו לֵאמֹר בְּמוֹתִי וּקְבַרְתֶּם אֹתִי בַּקֶּבֶר אֲשֶׁר אִישׁ הָאֱלֹהִים קָבוּר בּוֹ אֵצֶל עַצְמֹתָיו הַנִּיחוּ אֶת־עַצְמֹתָי:

לב כִּי הָיֹה יִהְיֶה הַדָּבָר אֲשֶׁר קָרָא בִּדְבַר יהוה עַל־הַמִּזְבֵּחַ אֲשֶׁר בְּבֵית־אֵל וְעַל כָּל־בָּתֵּי הַבָּמוֹת אֲשֶׁר בְּעָרֵי שֹׁמְרוֹן:

לג אַחַר הַדָּבָר הַזֶּה לֹא־שָׁב יָרָבְעָם מִדַּרְכּוֹ הָרָעָה וַיָּשָׁב וַיַּעַשׂ מִקְצוֹת הָעָם כֹּהֲנֵי בָמוֹת הֶחָפֵץ יְמַלֵּא אֶת־יָדוֹ וִיהִי כֹּהֲנֵי בָמוֹת:

לד וַיְהִי בַּדָּבָר הַזֶּה לְחַטַּאת בֵּית יָרָבְעָם וּלְהַכְחִיד וּלְהַשְׁמִיד מֵעַל פְּנֵי הָאֲדָמָה:

יד

א בָּעֵת הַהִיא חָלָה אֲבִיָּה בֶן־יָרָבְעָם:

ב וַיֹּאמֶר יָרָבְעָם לְאִשְׁתּוֹ קוּמִי נָא וְהִשְׁתַּנִּית וְלֹא יֵדְעוּ כִּי־°אַתְּ [ק° אַתְּ] אֵשֶׁת יָרָבְעָם וְהָלַכְתְּ שִׁלֹה הִנֵּה־שָׁם אֲחִיָּה הַנָּבִיא הוּא־

ג דִּבֶּר עָלַי לְמֶלֶךְ עַל־הָעָם הַזֶּה: וְלָקַחַתְּ בְּיָדֵךְ עֲשָׂרָה לֶחֶם וְנִקֻּדִים וּבַקְבֻּק

ד דְּבַשׁ וּבָאת אֵלָיו הוּא יַגִּיד לָךְ מַה־יִּהְיֶה לַנָּעַר: וַתַּעַשׂ כֵּן אֵשֶׁת יָרָבְעָם וַתָּקָם וַתֵּלֶךְ שִׁלֹה וַתָּבֹא בֵּית אֲחִיָּה וַאֲחִיָּהוּ לֹא־יָכֹל לִרְאוֹת כִּי קָמוּ

ה עֵינָיו מִשֵּׂיבוֹ: וַיהוֹה אָמַר אֶל־אֲחִיָּהוּ הִנֵּה אֵשֶׁת יָרָבְעָם בָּאָה לִדְרֹשׁ דָּבָר מֵעִמָּךְ אֶל־בְּנָהּ כִּי־חֹלֶה הוּא כָּזֹה וְכָזֶה תְּדַבֵּר אֵלֶיהָ וִיהִי

ו כְבֹאָהּ וְהִיא מִתְנַכֵּרָה: וַיְהִי כִשְׁמֹעַ אֲחִיָּהוּ אֶת־קוֹל רַגְלֶיהָ בָּאָה בַפֶּתַח וַיֹּאמֶר בֹּאִי אֵשֶׁת יָרָבְעָם לָמָּה זֶּה אַתְּ מִתְנַכֵּרָה וְאָנֹכִי שָׁלוּחַ אֵלַיִךְ קָשָׁה:

ז לְכִי אִמְרִי לְיָרָבְעָם כֹּה־אָמַר יהוה אֱלֹהֵי יִשְׂרָאֵל יַעַן אֲשֶׁר הֲרִימֹתִיךָ מִתּוֹךְ הָעָם וָאֶתֶּנְךָ נָגִיד עַל עַמִּי יִשְׂרָאֵל:

ח וָאֶקְרַע אֶת־הַמַּמְלָכָה מִבֵּית דָּוִד וָאֶתְּנֶהָ לָךְ וְלֹא־הָיִיתָ כְּעַבְדִּי דָוִד אֲשֶׁר שָׁמַר מִצְוֹתַי וַאֲשֶׁר־הָלַךְ

ט אַחֲרַי בְּכָל־לְבָבוֹ לַעֲשׂוֹת רַק הַיָּשָׁר בְּעֵינָי: וַתָּרַע לַעֲשׂוֹת מִכֹּל אֲשֶׁר־הָיוּ לְפָנֶיךָ וַתֵּלֶךְ וַתַּעֲשֶׂה־לְּךָ אֱלֹהִים אֲחֵרִים וּמַסֵּכוֹת לְהַכְעִיסֵנִי וְאֹתִי

י הִשְׁלַכְתָּ אַחֲרֵי גַוֶּךָ: לָכֵן הִנְנִי מֵבִיא רָעָה אֶל־בֵּית יָרָבְעָם וְהִכְרַתִּי לְיָרָבְעָם מַשְׁתִּין בְּקִיר עָצוּר וְעָזוּב בְּיִשְׂרָאֵל וּבִעַרְתִּי אַחֲרֵי בֵית־יָרָבְעָם

יא כַּאֲשֶׁר יְבַעֵר הַגָּלָל עַד־תֻּמּוֹ: הַמֵּת לְיָרָבְעָם בָּעִיר יֹאכְלוּ הַכְּלָבִים וְהַמֵּת

13:32. The prophecy that human bones would be burned on Jeroboam's altar (v. 2) would surely come about. To ensure that his remains would not be among them, the false prophet wanted his bones mingled with those of the true prophet. See *II Kings* 23:15-20, and especially v. 18.

14:10. Literally, *one who urinates against the wall.* See *I Samuel* 25:22.

²⁶ The prophet who had brought back [the man of God] from the road heard, and he said, "It is the man of God, who rebelled against the word of HASHEM; HASHEM gave him over to the lion, and it mauled him and killed him, like the word of HASHEM that He had spoken to him."

The false prophet confirms the truth

²⁷ He spoke to his sons, saying, "Saddle up the donkey for me," and they saddled it. ²⁸ He went and found his corpse cast down on the road, and the donkey and the lion standing next to the corpse; the lion had not eaten the corpse, nor had it mauled the donkey. ²⁹ The prophet then lifted up the corpse of the man of God, and placed it upon the donkey and brought it back; he came to the city of the old prophet to eulogize and to bury him. ³⁰ He laid his corpse in his [own] grave, and they lamented over him, "Alas, my brother." ³¹ It happened after he buried him that he spoke to his sons, saying, "When I die, bury me in the grave in which the man of God is buried; next to his bones place my bones. ³² For the words that he proclaimed by the word of HASHEM to the altar in Beth-el shall certainly come about, * and [it will also come] upon all the houses of the high places that are in the cities of Samaria."

Jeroboam's evil persists

³³ After this incident, Jeroboam did not repent from his evil way, and he again appointed commoners of the people as priests for the high places; whomever he desired he would appoint, and they would be priests for the high places. ³⁴ This matter became a [source of] punishment for the house of Jeroboam, to eradicate it and destroy it from the face of the earth.

14

Jeroboam's queen goes to Ahijah

¹ At that time Jeroboam's son Abijah became ill. ² Jeroboam said to his wife, "Get up now and disguise yourself so that people will not know that you are Jeroboam's wife, and go to Shiloh. Ahijah the prophet is there, the one who spoke of me as becoming king over this people. ³ Take with you ten breads, wafers, and a bottle of honey, and come to him; he will tell you what will happen to the boy."

⁴ Jeroboam's wife did so; she arose and went to Shiloh, and arrived at Ahijah's house. Now Ahijah could not see, for his eyes had stopped [functioning] because of his old age. ⁵ But HASHEM had told Ahijah, "Behold, Jeroboam's wife is coming to seek a pronouncement from you about her son, for he is sick. Such and such shall you say to her. When she comes she will be disguised."

Ahijah prophesies Jeroboam's horrible end . . .

⁶ It happened that when Ahijah heard the sound of her feet coming in the door, he said, "Enter, wife of Jeroboam! Why do you disguise yourself? I have a harsh message for you. ⁷ Go tell Jeroboam, 'Thus said HASHEM, God of Israel: Inasmuch as I elevated you from the midst of the people and emplaced you as ruler over My people Israel, ⁸ and I tore away the kingship from the house of David and gave it to you, but you were not like My servant David, who kept My commandments and who went after Me with all his heart, to do only what is proper in My eyes. ⁹ But you have acted more wickedly than any who were before you, and you went and made for yourself the gods of others and molten images to anger Me, and you have cast Me behind your back. ¹⁰ Therefore, behold — I am bringing evil upon the house of Jeroboam, and I shall eliminate [every] male offspring* from Jeroboam and all property, whether hidden or public in Israel, and I shall destructively pursue the House of Jeroboam, as one completely consumes food until it is waste. ¹¹ Anyone [of the House] of Jeroboam who dies in the city, the dogs will eat; and whoever dies

יב בַּשָּׂדֶ֖ה יֹאכְל֣וּ ע֣וֹף הַשָּׁמָ֑יִם כִּ֥י יְהֹוָ֖ה דִּבֵּֽר: וְאַ֣תְּ ק֚וּמִי לְכִ֣י לְבֵיתֵ֔ךְ בְּבֹאָ֥ה

יג רַגְלַ֖יִךְ הָעִ֑ירָה וּמֵ֣ת הַיָּֽלֶד: וְסָֽפְדוּ־ל֣וֹ כָל־יִשְׂרָאֵל֮ וְקָֽבְר֣וּ אֹתוֹ֒ כִּי־זֶ֣ה לְבַדּ֗וֹ יָבֹ֤א לְיָֽרָבְעָם֙ אֶל־קָ֔בֶר יַ֗עַן נִמְצָא־ב֞וֹ דָּבָ֣ר ט֗וֹב אֶל־יְהֹוָ֛ה אֱלֹהֵ֥י

יד יִשְׂרָאֵ֖ל בְּבֵ֥ית יָֽרָבְעָֽם: וְהֵקִים֩ יְהֹוָ֨ה ל֥וֹ מֶ֙לֶךְ֙ עַל־יִשְׂרָאֵ֔ל אֲשֶׁ֥ר יַכְרִ֛ית אֶת־בֵּ֥ית יָֽרָבְעָ֖ם זֶ֣ה הַיּ֑וֹם וּמֶ֖ה גַּם־עָֽתָּה: וְהִכָּ֨ה יְהֹוָ֜ה אֶת־יִשְׂרָאֵ֗ל כַּֽאֲשֶׁ֨ר

טו יָנ֣וּד הַקָּנֶה֮ בַּמַּיִם֒ וְנָתַ֣שׁ אֶת־יִשְׂרָאֵ֗ל מֵעַ֨ל הָֽאֲדָמָ֤ה הַטּוֹבָה֙ הַזֹּ֔את אֲשֶׁ֥ר נָתַ֖ן לַֽאֲבֽוֹתֵיהֶ֑ם וְזֵֽרָ֖ם מֵעֵ֣בֶר לַנָּהָ֑ר יַ֗עַן אֲשֶׁ֤ר עָשׂוּ֙ אֶת־אֲשֵׁ֣רֵיהֶ֔ם

טז מַכְעִיסִ֖ים אֶת־יְהֹוָֽה: וְיִתֵּ֖ן אֶת־יִשְׂרָאֵ֑ל בִּגְלַ֞ל חַטֹּ֤אות יָֽרָבְעָם֙ אֲשֶׁ֣ר חָטָ֔א

יז וַֽאֲשֶׁ֥ר הֶֽחֱטִ֖יא אֶת־יִשְׂרָאֵֽל: וַתָּ֙קָם֙ אֵ֣שֶׁת יָֽרָבְעָ֔ם וַתֵּ֖לֶךְ וַתָּבֹ֣א תִרְצָ֑תָה

יח הִ֚יא בָּאָ֣ה בְסַף־הַבַּ֔יִת וְהַנַּ֖עַר מֵֽת: וַיִּקְבְּר֣וּ אֹת֗וֹ וַיִּסְפְּדוּ־לוֹ֙ כָּל־יִשְׂרָאֵ֔ל

יט כִּדְבַ֤ר יְהֹוָה֙ אֲשֶׁ֣ר דִּבֶּ֔ר בְּיַד־עַבְדּ֖וֹ אֲחִיָּ֥הוּ הַנָּבִֽיא: וְיֶ֙תֶר֙ דִּבְרֵ֣י יָֽרָבְעָ֔ם אֲשֶׁ֥ר נִלְחַ֖ם וַֽאֲשֶׁ֣ר מָלָ֑ךְ הִנָּ֣ם כְּתוּבִ֗ים עַל־סֵ֛פֶר דִּבְרֵ֥י הַיָּמִ֖ים לְמַלְכֵ֥י

כ יִשְׂרָאֵֽל: וְהַיָּמִים֙ אֲשֶׁ֣ר מָלַ֣ךְ יָֽרָבְעָ֔ם עֶשְׂרִ֥ים וּשְׁתַּ֖יִם שָׁנָ֑ה וַיִּשְׁכַּב֙ עִם־אֲבֹתָ֔יו וַיִּמְלֹ֛ךְ נָדָ֥ב בְּנ֖וֹ תַּחְתָּֽיו: וּרְחַבְעָ֣ם בֶּן־שְׁלֹמֹ֗ה

כא מָלַ֣ךְ בִּֽיהוּדָ֑ה בֶּן־אַרְבָּעִ֣ים וְאַחַ֣ת שָׁנָ֡ה רְחַבְעָ֣ם בְּמָלְכ֡וֹ וּשֲׁבַ֣ע עֶשְׂרֵ֣ה שָׁנָ֣ה ׀ מָלַ֣ךְ בִּירֽוּשָׁלַ֗͏ִם הָ֠עִ֠יר אֲשֶׁר־בָּחַ֨ר יְהֹוָ֜ה לָשׂ֨וּם אֶת־שְׁמ֥וֹ שָׁם֙ מִכֹּל֙

כב שִׁבְטֵ֣י יִשְׂרָאֵ֔ל וְשֵׁ֣ם אִמּ֔וֹ נַֽעֲמָ֖ה הָֽעַמֹּנִֽית: וַיַּ֧עַשׂ יְהוּדָ֛ה הָרַ֖ע בְּעֵינֵ֣י יְהֹוָ֑ה וַיְקַנְא֣וּ אֹת֗וֹ מִכֹּל֙ אֲשֶׁ֣ר עָשׂ֣וּ אֲבֹתָ֔ם בְּחַטֹּאתָ֖ם אֲשֶׁ֥ר חָטָֽאוּ: וַיִּבְנ֨וּ גַם־

כג הֵ֧מָּה לָהֶ֛ם בָּמ֥וֹת וּמַצֵּב֖וֹת וַֽאֲשֵׁרִ֑ים עַ֚ל כָּל־גִּבְעָ֣ה גְבֹהָ֔ה וְתַ֖חַת כָּל־עֵ֥ץ

כד רַֽעֲנָֽן: וְגַם־קָדֵ֖שׁ הָיָ֣ה בָאָ֑רֶץ עָשׂ֕וּ כְּכֹל֙ הַתּֽוֹעֲבֹ֣ת הַגּוֹיִ֔ם אֲשֶׁר֙ הוֹרִ֣ישׁ יְהֹוָ֔ה מִפְּנֵ֖י בְּנֵ֥י יִשְׂרָאֵֽל: וַֽיְהִ֞י בַּשָּׁנָ֤ה הַֽחֲמִישִׁית֙ לַמֶּ֣לֶךְ

כה רְחַבְעָ֑ם עָלָ֛ה שׁוּשַׁ֖ק °שׁוּשַׁק [שִׁישַׁ֥ק ק] מֶֽלֶךְ־מִצְרַ֖יִם עַל־יְרֽוּשָׁלָֽ͏ִם: וַיִּקַּ֣ח אֶת־

כו אֹֽצְר֣וֹת בֵּית־יְהֹוָ֗ה וְאֶת־אֽוֹצְרוֹת֙ בֵּ֣ית הַמֶּ֔לֶךְ וְאֶת־הַכֹּ֖ל לָקָ֑ח וַיִּקַּח֙ אֶת־

כז כָּל־מָֽגִנֵּ֣י הַזָּהָ֔ב אֲשֶׁ֥ר עָשָׂ֖ה שְׁלֹמֹֽה: וַיַּ֨עַשׂ הַמֶּ֤לֶךְ רְחַבְעָם֙ תַּחְתָּ֔ם מָֽגִנֵּ֖י

כח נְחֹ֑שֶׁת וְהִפְקִ֗יד עַל־יַד֙ שָׂרֵ֣י הָֽרָצִ֔ים הַשֹּׁ֣מְרִ֔ים פֶּ֖תַח בֵּ֥ית הַמֶּֽלֶךְ: וַֽיְהִ֛י מִדֵּֽי־בֹ֥א הַמֶּ֖לֶךְ בֵּ֣ית יְהֹוָ֑ה יִשָּׂא֣וּם הָֽרָצִ֔ים וֶהֱשִׁיב֖וּם אֶל־תָּ֥א הָֽרָצִֽים:

כט וְיֶ֙תֶר֙ דִּבְרֵ֣י רְחַבְעָ֔ם וְכָל־אֲשֶׁ֖ר עָשָׂ֑ה הֲלֹא־הֵ֣מָּה כְתוּבִ֗ים עַל־סֵ֛פֶר דִּבְרֵ֥י

ל הַיָּמִ֖ים לְמַלְכֵ֥י יְהוּדָֽה: וּמִלְחָמָ֨ה הָֽיְתָ֧ה בֵֽין־רְחַבְעָ֛ם וּבֵ֥ין יָֽרָבְעָ֖ם כָּל־

לא הַיָּמִֽים: וַיִּשְׁכַּ֨ב רְחַבְעָ֜ם עִם־אֲבֹתָ֗יו וַיִּקָּבֵ֤ר עִם־אֲבֹתָיו֙ בְּעִ֣יר דָּוִ֔ד וְשֵׁ֣ם

טו א אִמּ֔וֹ נַֽעֲמָ֖ה הָֽעַמֹּנִ֑ית וַיִּמְלֹ֛ךְ אֲבִיָּ֥ם בְּנ֖וֹ תַּחְתָּֽיו: וּבִשְׁנַת֙

14:13. Jeroboam had set up guards along the roads to prevent his people from making the festival pilgrimages to Jerusalem, but Abijah dismissed them (*Talmud*).

14:14. The tragedies of the House of Jeroboam will pale in comparison with the calamities that will befall the people of Israel, for HASHEM will smite . . . (*Radak*).

14:17. Apparently the royal capital, originally in She-

chem and then in Penuel (12:25), had been moved to Tirzah (see 15:21; 16:15). When she returned to Tirzah, her son's condition worsened; when she arrived at her door, he died (*Radak*).

14:19. No longer extant. This book was the official Court history of the Kingdom of Israel, including its wars and internal affairs.

in the field, the birds of the heaven will eat — for HASHEM has spoken!' 12 And
. . . and the death of the child
you — arise and go to your house; as your feet enter the city, the child shall die!
13 All of Israel will lament for him and bury him, for this one alone of Jeroboam's
[House] will be brought to a grave, because something good for HASHEM, God
of Israel, has been found in him of [all] the house of Jeroboam. 14 Then, HASHEM*
will appoint for Himself a king over Israel who will eliminate the house of
Israel, too, will suffer
Jeroboam on that day. But of what does this matter now! 15 For HASHEM will*
smite Israel as a reed lurches about in the water, and He will uproot Israel from
upon this bountiful land that He gave to their forefathers, and He will scatter
them beyond the [Euphrates] River — because they have made their Asherah-
trees, angering HASHEM. 16 And He will give Israel over [to this curse], because
of the sins of Jeroboam that he committed himself and which he caused Israel
to commit."

The boy dies
17 Jeroboam's wife arose and left, and she came to Tirzah. As she entered*
the threshold of the house, the boy died. 18 All of Israel buried him and lamented
him, like the word of HASHEM which He spoke through the hand of His servant
Ahijah the prophet.

Jeroboam dies (See Appendix A, timeline 4)
19 The rest of the deeds of Jeroboam — how he fought wars and how he
reigned — behold, they are recorded in the Book of the Chronicles of the Kings
of Israel. 20 The duration of Jeroboam's reign was twenty-two years; then he*
lay with his forefathers and Nadab his son reigned in his place.

Rehoboam's kingdom declines
21 Rehoboam son of Solomon reigned in Judah. Rehoboam was forty-one
years old when he became king and he reigned for seventeen years in Jerusa-
lem, the city that HASHEM chose of all the tribes of Israel to place His Name there.
[Rehoboam's] mother's name was Naamah the Ammonite. 22 [The people of]*
Judah did evil in the eyes of HASHEM, angering Him more than their ancestors
had done with the sins they committed. 23 They, too, built for themselves high
places and pillars and Asherah-trees on every lofty hill and under every leafy
tree. 24 There was also prostitution in the land; they did all the abominations of
the nations that HASHEM had driven out from before the Children of Israel.

Egypt loots the kingdom
25 It was in King Rehoboam's fifth year that Shishak, king of Egypt, ascended
against Jerusalem. 26 He took away the treasures of the Temple of HASHEM and
the treasures of the king's palace — he took everything. He also took all the
*golden shields that Solomon had made.**

27 King Rehoboam made copper shields in their place, and he placed them in
the charge of the captains of the runners, who guarded the entrance to the king's
palace; 28 and it would be that whenever the king would come to the Temple of
HASHEM, the runners would bear them and then return them to the chamber of
the runners.

Rehoboam dies
29 The rest of the deeds of Rehoboam and all that he did — behold, they are
*recorded in the Book of the Chronicles of the Kings of Judah.**

30 There was warfare between Rehoboam and Jeroboam, all the days.

31 Rehoboam lay with his forefathers and was buried with his forefathers in the
City of David. His mother's name was Naamah the Ammonite. Abijam his son
reigned in his place.

14:21. Her non-Jewish origin may explain why Rehoboam was drawn after idolatry (*Radak*).

14:26. Described above in 10:16-17.

14:29. See *II Chronicles* 9:31-12:16.

ב שְׁמֹנֶה עֶשְׂרֵה לַמֶּלֶךְ יָרׇבְעָם בֶּן־נְבָט מָלַךְ אֲבִיָּם עַל־יְהוּדָה: שָׁלֹשׁ שָׁנִים

ג מָלַךְ בִּירוּשָׁלׇ͏ִם וְשֵׁם אִמּוֹ מַעֲכָה בַּת־אֲבִישָׁלוֹם: וַיֵּלֶךְ בְּכׇל־חַטֹּאות אָבִיו

אֲשֶׁר־עָשָׂה לְפָנָיו וְלֹא־הָיָה לְבָבוֹ שָׁלֵם עִם־יהוה אֱלֹהָיו כִּלְבַב דָּוִד

ד אָבִיו: כִּי לְמַעַן דָּוִד נָתַן יהוה אֱלֹהָיו לוֹ נִיר בִּירוּשָׁלׇ͏ִם לְהָקִים אֶת־בְּנוֹ

ה אַחֲרָיו וּלְהַעֲמִיד אֶת־יְרוּשָׁלׇ͏ִם: אֲשֶׁר עָשָׂה דָוִד אֶת־הַיָּשָׁר בְּעֵינֵי יהוה

ו וְלֹא־סָר מִכֹּל אֲשֶׁר־צִוָּהוּ כֹּל יְמֵי חַיָּיו רַק בִּדְבַר אוּרִיָּה הַחִתִּי: וּמִלְחָמָה

ז הָיְתָה בֵין־רְחַבְעָם וּבֵין יָרׇבְעָם כׇּל־יְמֵי חַיָּיו: וְיֶתֶר דִּבְרֵי אֲבִיָּם וְכׇל־אֲשֶׁר

עָשָׂה הֲלוֹא־הֵם כְּתוּבִים עַל־סֵפֶר דִּבְרֵי הַיָּמִים לְמַלְכֵי יְהוּדָה וּמִלְחָמָה

ח הָיְתָה בֵּין אֲבִיָּם וּבֵין יָרׇבְעָם: וַיִּשְׁכַּב אֲבִיָּם עִם־אֲבֹתָיו וַיִּקְבְּרוּ אֹתוֹ בְּעִיר

ט דָּוִד וַיִּמְלֹךְ אָסָא בְנוֹ תַּחְתָּיו: וּבִשְׁנַת עֶשְׂרִים לְיָרׇבְעָם מֶלֶךְ

י יִשְׂרָאֵל מָלַךְ אָסָא °עַל־יְהוּדָה: וְאַרְבָּעִים וְאַחַת שָׁנָה מָלַךְ בִּירוּשָׁלׇ͏ִם °נ״א מֶלֶךְ

יא וְשֵׁם אִמּוֹ מַעֲכָה בַּת־אֲבִישָׁלוֹם: וַיַּעַשׂ אָסָא הַיָּשָׁר בְּעֵינֵי יהוה כְּדָוִד אָבִיו:

יב וַיַּעֲבֵר הַקְּדֵשִׁים מִן־הָאָרֶץ וַיָּסַר אֶת־כׇּל־הַגִּלֻּלִים אֲשֶׁר עָשׂוּ אֲבֹתָיו: וְגַם ׀

יג אֶת־מַעֲכָה אִמּוֹ וַיְסִרֶהָ מִגְּבִירָה אֲשֶׁר־עָשְׂתָה מִפְלֶצֶת לָאֲשֵׁרָה וַיִּכְרֹת

יד אָסָא אֶת־מִפְלַצְתָּהּ וַיִּשְׂרֹף בְּנַחַל קִדְרוֹן: וְהַבָּמוֹת לֹא־סָרוּ רַק לְבַב־

טו אָסָא הָיָה שָׁלֵם עִם־יהוה כׇּל־יָמָיו: וַיָּבֵא אֶת־קׇדְשֵׁי אָבִיו °וְקׇדְשׁוֹ °[וְקׇדְשֵׁי ק׳]

טז בֵּית יהוה כֶּסֶף וְזָהָב וְכֵלִים: וּמִלְחָמָה הָיְתָה בֵּין אָסָא וּבֵין

יז בַּעְשָׁא מֶלֶךְ־יִשְׂרָאֵל כׇּל־יְמֵיהֶם: וַיַּעַל בַּעְשָׁא מֶלֶךְ־יִשְׂרָאֵל עַל־יְהוּדָה

יח וַיִּבֶן אֶת־הָרָמָה לְבִלְתִּי תֵּת יֹצֵא וָבָא לְאָסָא מֶלֶךְ יְהוּדָה: וַיִּקַּח אָסָא אֶת־

כׇּל־הַכֶּסֶף וְהַזָּהָב הַנּוֹתָרִים ׀ בְּאוֹצְרוֹת בֵּית־יהוה וְאֶת־אוֹצְרוֹת בֵּית °מֶלֶךְ °[הַמֶּלֶךְ ק׳]

וַיִּתְּנֵם בְּיַד־עֲבָדָיו וַיִּשְׁלָחֵם הַמֶּלֶךְ אָסָא אֶל־בֶּן־הֲדַד בֶּן־

יט טַבְרִמֹּן בֶּן־חֶזְיוֹן מֶלֶךְ אֲרָם הַיֹּשֵׁב בְּדַמֶּשֶׂק לֵאמֹר: בְּרִית בֵּינִי וּבֵינֶךָ בֵּין

אָבִי וּבֵין אָבִיךָ הִנֵּה שָׁלַחְתִּי לְךָ שֹׁחַד כֶּסֶף וְזָהָב לֵךְ הָפֵרָה אֶת־בְּרִיתְךָ

כ אֶת־בַּעְשָׁא מֶלֶךְ־יִשְׂרָאֵל וְיַעֲלֶה מֵעָלָי: וַיִּשְׁמַע בֶּן־הֲדַד אֶל־הַמֶּלֶךְ אָסָא

וַיִּשְׁלַח אֶת־שָׂרֵי הַחֲיָלִים אֲשֶׁר־לוֹ עַל־עָרֵי יִשְׂרָאֵל וַיַּךְ אֶת־עִיּוֹן וְאֶת־

כא דָּן וְאֵת אָבֵל בֵּית־מַעֲכָה וְאֵת כׇּל־כִּנְּרוֹת עַל כׇּל־אֶרֶץ נַפְתָּלִי: וַיְהִי

כב כִּשְׁמֹעַ בַּעְשָׁא וַיֶּחְדַּל מִבְּנוֹת אֶת־הָרָמָה וַיֵּשֶׁב בְּתִרְצָה: וְהַמֶּלֶךְ אָסָא

הִשְׁמִיעַ אֶת־כׇּל־יְהוּדָה אֵין נָקִי וַיִּשְׂאוּ אֶת־אַבְנֵי הָרָמָה וְאֶת־עֵצֶיהָ אֲשֶׁר

כג בָּנָה בַּעְשָׁא וַיִּבֶן בָּם הַמֶּלֶךְ אָסָא אֶת־גֶּבַע בִּנְיָמִן וְאֶת־הַמִּצְפָּה: וְיֶתֶר כׇּל־

דִּבְרֵי־אָסָא וְכׇל־גְּבוּרָתוֹ וְכׇל־אֲשֶׁר עָשָׂה וְהֶעָרִים אֲשֶׁר בָּנָה הֲלֹא־הֵמָּה

כְתוּבִים עַל־סֵפֶר דִּבְרֵי הַיָּמִים לְמַלְכֵי יְהוּדָה רַק לְעֵת זִקְנָתוֹ חָלָה אֶת־

כד רַגְלָיו: וַיִּשְׁכַּב אָסָא עִם־אֲבֹתָיו וַיִּקָּבֵר עִם־אֲבֹתָיו בְּעִיר דָּוִד אָבִיו

15:5. See *II Samuel*, Ch. 11.

15:6. Although Rehoboam initially heeded the word of the prophet (12:22-24) not to do battle with Jeroboam, he later sent his son Abijam to do so (*Ralbag; Abarbanel*).

15:7. See *II Chronicles* 12:16-13:23.

15:15. See *II Chronicles* 15:18.

15

ABIJAM, KING OF JUDAH
15:1-8
(See Appendix A, timeline 4)
A short, flawed, battle-scarred reign

¹ *In the eighteenth year of King Jeroboam son of Nebat, Abijam became king over Judah.* ² *For three years he reigned in Jerusalem; his mother's name was Maacah daughter of Abishalom.* ³ *He went in [the way of] all the sins of his father that he had done before him; and his heart was not whole with* HASHEM, *his God, as the heart of his forefather David [had been].* ⁴ *It was [only] for David's sake that* HASHEM *his God had given him dominion in Jerusalem, to raise up his son after him and to establish Jerusalem,* ⁵ *because David had done what is proper in the eyes of* HASHEM, *and did not veer from all that He had commanded him all the days of his life (except for the matter of Uriah the Hittite).* *

⁶ *There was warfare between Rehoboam and Jeroboam all the days of [Abijam's] life.* * ⁷ *The rest of the deeds of Abijam and all that he did — behold, they are recorded in the Book of the Chronicles of the Kings of Judah.* * *There was warfare between Abijam and Jeroboam.* ⁸ *Abijam lay with his forefathers, and they buried him in the City of David; Asa his son reigned in his place.*

ASA, KING OF JUDAH
15:9-24
A righteous king

⁹ *In the twentieth year of Jeroboam king of Israel, Asa became king over Judah.* ¹⁰ *He reigned in Jerusalem for forty-one years, and his [grand]mother's name was Maacah daughter of Abishalom.* ¹¹ *Asa did what was proper in the eyes of* HASHEM, *like his forefather David.* ¹² *He removed the prostitutes from the land, and removed all the idols that his forefathers had made.* ¹³ *And even his [grand]mother Maacah he deposed from being a queen for she had made an abomination unto an Asherah-tree; Asa chopped up the abomination and burned it in the Kidron Valley.* ¹⁴ *But they did not take away the high places; nevertheless, Asa's heart was whole with* HASHEM *all his days.* ¹⁵ *He brought in the consecrated goods of his father and his own consecrated goods* * *to the Temple of* HASHEM — *silver and gold and articles.*

BAASA, KING OF ISRAEL
15:16-22;
15:27-16:7
Asa seeks a foreign ally

¹⁶ *There was warfare between Asa and Baasa, the king of Israel, all their days.* ¹⁷ *Baasa, king of Israel, attacked Judah and built up Ramah, in order to prevent Asa, king of Judah, from leaving or entering.* * ¹⁸ *Asa then took all the silver and gold remaining in the treasuries of the Temple of* HASHEM *and the treasuries of the king's palace and placed it in the hands of his servants. King Asa sent them to Ben-hadad son of Tabrimmon son of Hezion, the king of Aram, who dwelled in Damascus, saying,* ¹⁹ *"[There is] a treaty between me and you, between my father and your father. Behold, I have sent you an inducement of silver and gold; go, annul your treaty with Baasa king of Israel, so that he will depart from me."* ²⁰ *Ben-hadad heeded King Asa, and he sent the officers of his soldiers against cities of Israel. He struck at Ijon, Dan and Abel-beth-maacah, and the whole Chinneroth area, together with the entire land of Naphtali.* ²¹ *When Baasa heard this he ceased his building of Ramah, and he settled in Tirzah.* *

²² *And King Asa called together all of Judah — no one was exempt — and they carried away the stones of Ramah and its wood, with which Baasa had built, and with them King Asa built up Geba of Benjamin and Mizpah.* ²³ *All the rest of the deeds of Asa and all his heroic acts and all that he did and the cities that he built — behold, they are recorded in the Book of the Chronicles of the Kings of Judah.* * *Only in his old age, his legs ailed.* ²⁴ *Asa lay with his forefathers and was buried with his forefathers, in the city of David his forefather;*

15:17. The city of Jerusalem.
15:21. The capital city of the Israelite kingdom (see 14:17).
15:23. See *II Chronicles* 13:23-16:14.

כה וַיִּמְלֹךְ יְהוֹשָׁפָט בְּנוֹ תַּחְתָּיו: וְנָדָב בֶּן־יָרָבְעָם מָלַךְ עַל־יִשְׂרָאֵל בִּשְׁנַת שְׁתַּיִם לְאָסָא מֶלֶךְ יְהוּדָה וַיִּמְלֹךְ עַל־יִשְׂרָאֵל שְׁנָתָיִם: כו וַיַּעַשׂ הָרַע בְּעֵינֵי יְהוָה וַיֵּלֶךְ בְּדֶרֶךְ אָבִיו וּבְחַטָּאתוֹ אֲשֶׁר הֶחֱטִיא אֶת־יִשְׂרָאֵל: כז וַיִּקְשֹׁר עָלָיו בַּעְשָׁא בֶן־אֲחִיָּה לְבֵית יִשָּׂשכָר וַיַּכֵּהוּ בַעְשָׁא בְגִבְּתוֹן אֲשֶׁר לַפְּלִשְׁתִּים וְנָדָב וְכָל־יִשְׂרָאֵל צָרִים עַל־גִּבְּתוֹן: כח וַיְמִתֵהוּ בַעְשָׁא בִּשְׁנַת שָׁלֹשׁ לְאָסָא מֶלֶךְ יְהוּדָה וַיִּמְלֹךְ תַּחְתָּיו: כט וַיְהִי כְמָלְכוֹ הִכָּה אֶת־כָּל־בֵּית יָרָבְעָם לֹא־הִשְׁאִיר כָּל־נְשָׁמָה לְיָרָבְעָם עַד־הִשְׁמִדוֹ כִּדְבַר יְהוָה אֲשֶׁר דִּבֶּר בְּיַד־עַבְדּוֹ אֲחִיָּה הַשִּׁילֹנִי: עַל־חַטֹּאות יָרָבְעָם אֲשֶׁר ל חָטָא וַאֲשֶׁר הֶחֱטִיא אֶת־יִשְׂרָאֵל בְּכַעְסוֹ אֲשֶׁר הִכְעִיס אֶת־יְהוָה אֱלֹהֵי לא יִשְׂרָאֵל: וְיֶתֶר דִּבְרֵי נָדָב וְכָל־אֲשֶׁר עָשָׂה הֲלֹא־הֵם כְּתוּבִים עַל־סֵפֶר לב דִּבְרֵי הַיָּמִים לְמַלְכֵי יִשְׂרָאֵל: וּמִלְחָמָה הָיְתָה בֵּין אָסָא וּבֵין בַּעְשָׁא מֶלֶךְ־ לג יִשְׂרָאֵל כָּל־יְמֵיהֶם: בִּשְׁנַת שָׁלֹשׁ לְאָסָא מֶלֶךְ יְהוּדָה מָלַךְ בַּעְשָׁא בֶן־אֲחִיָּה עַל־כָּל־יִשְׂרָאֵל בְּתִרְצָה עֶשְׂרִים וְאַרְבַּע שָׁנָה: לד וַיַּעַשׂ הָרַע בְּעֵינֵי יְהוָה וַיֵּלֶךְ בְּדֶרֶךְ יָרָבְעָם וּבְחַטָּאתוֹ אֲשֶׁר הֶחֱטִיא אֶת־ טז א יִשְׂרָאֵל: וַיְהִי דְבַר־יְהוָה אֶל־יֵהוּא בֶן־חֲנָנִי עַל־בַּעְשָׁא ב לֵאמֹר: יַעַן אֲשֶׁר הֲרִימֹתִיךָ מִן־הֶעָפָר וָאֶתֶּנְךָ נָגִיד עַל עַמִּי יִשְׂרָאֵל וַתֵּלֶךְ בְּדֶרֶךְ יָרָבְעָם וַתַּחֲטִא אֶת־עַמִּי יִשְׂרָאֵל לְהַכְעִיסֵנִי בְּחַטֹּאתָם: ג הִנְנִי מַבְעִיר אַחֲרֵי בַעְשָׁא וְאַחֲרֵי בֵיתוֹ וְנָתַתִּי אֶת־בֵּיתְךָ כְּבֵית יָרָבְעָם ד בֶּן־נְבָט: הַמֵּת לְבַעְשָׁא בָּעִיר יֹאכְלוּ הַכְּלָבִים וְהַמֵּת לוֹ בַּשָּׂדֶה יֹאכְלוּ ה עוֹף הַשָּׁמָיִם: וְיֶתֶר דִּבְרֵי בַעְשָׁא וַאֲשֶׁר עָשָׂה וּגְבוּרָתוֹ הֲלֹא־הֵם כְּתוּבִים ו עַל־סֵפֶר דִּבְרֵי הַיָּמִים לְמַלְכֵי יִשְׂרָאֵל: וַיִּשְׁכַּב בַּעְשָׁא עִם־אֲבֹתָיו וַיִּקָּבֵר ז בְּתִרְצָה וַיִּמְלֹךְ אֵלָה בְנוֹ תַּחְתָּיו: וְגַם בְּיַד־יֵהוּא בֶן־חֲנָנִי הַנָּבִיא דְּבַר־ יְהוָה הָיָה אֶל־בַּעְשָׁא וְאֶל־בֵּיתוֹ וְעַל כָּל־הָרָעָה אֲשֶׁר־עָשָׂה בְּעֵינֵי יְהוָה לְהַכְעִיסוֹ בְּמַעֲשֵׂה יָדָיו לִהְיוֹת כְּבֵית יָרָבְעָם וְעַל אֲשֶׁר־הִכָּה ח אֹתוֹ: בִּשְׁנַת עֶשְׂרִים וָשֵׁשׁ שָׁנָה לְאָסָא מֶלֶךְ יְהוּדָה ט מָלַךְ אֵלָה בֶן־בַּעְשָׁא עַל־יִשְׂרָאֵל בְּתִרְצָה שְׁנָתָיִם: וַיִּקְשֹׁר עָלָיו עַבְדּוֹ זִמְרִי שַׂר מַחֲצִית הָרָכֶב וְהוּא בְתִרְצָה שֹׁתֶה שִׁכּוֹר בֵּית אַרְצָא אֲשֶׁר י עַל־הַבַּיִת בְּתִרְצָה: וַיָּבֹא זִמְרִי וַיַּכֵּהוּ וַיְמִיתֵהוּ בִּשְׁנַת עֶשְׂרִים וָשֶׁבַע יא לְאָסָא מֶלֶךְ יְהוּדָה וַיִּמְלֹךְ תַּחְתָּיו: וַיְהִי בְמָלְכוֹ כְּשִׁבְתּוֹ עַל־כִּסְאוֹ הִכָּה אֶת־כָּל־בֵּית בַּעְשָׁא לֹא־הִשְׁאִיר לוֹ מַשְׁתִּין בְּקִיר וְגֹאֲלָיו וְרֵעֵהוּ: וַיַּשְׁמֵד יב זִמְרִי אֵת כָּל־בֵּית בַּעְשָׁא כִּדְבַר יְהוָה אֲשֶׁר דִּבֶּר אֶל־בַּעְשָׁא בְּיַד יֵהוּא יג הַנָּבִיא: אֶל כָּל־חַטֹּאות בַּעְשָׁא וְחַטֹּאות אֵלָה בְנוֹ אֲשֶׁר חָטְאוּ וַאֲשֶׁר הֶחֱטִיאוּ אֶת־יִשְׂרָאֵל לְהַכְעִיס אֶת־יְהוָה אֱלֹהֵי יִשְׂרָאֵל בְּהַבְלֵיהֶם:

15:31. See note to 14:19.　　**16:5.** See note to 14:19.　　**16:11.** See note to 14:10.

his son Jehoshaphat reigned in his place.

NADAB, KING OF ISRAEL
15:25-27
(See Appendix A, timeline 4)

²⁵ *Nadab son of Jeroboam became king over Israel in the second year of Asa, king of Judah, and he reigned over Israel for two years.* ²⁶ *He did evil in the eyes of HASHEM, he went in the path of his father and his sins, by which he caused Israel to sin.* ²⁷ *Baasa son of Ahijah of the house of Issachar conspired against him, and Baasa struck him down at Gibbethon of the Philistines, while Nadab and all of Israel were besieging Gibbethon.* ²⁸ *Baasa killed him in the third year of Asa, king of Judah, and reigned in his place.* ²⁹ *It happened that when he became king he struck down the entire house of Jeroboam; he did not leave a soul in [the house of] Jeroboam, until he annihilated it, according to the word of HASHEM, which He had spoken through the hand of His servant Ahijah the Shilonite,* ³⁰ *for the sins of Jeroboam that he had committed and caused Israel to commit, with his provocations by which he angered HASHEM, God of Israel.* ³¹ *The rest of the deeds of Nadab and all that he did — behold, they are recorded in the Book of the Chronicles of the Kings of Israel. **

BAASA, KING OF ISRAEL
15:28-16:7

Baasa annihilates the House of Jeroboam . . .

. . . but proves to be a wicked king

³² *There was warfare between Asa and Baasa king of Israel all their days.* ³³ *In the third year of Asa, king of Judah, Baasa son of Ahijah became king over all of Israel at Tirzah, [and reigned] for twenty-four years.* ³⁴ *He did what was evil in the eyes of HASHEM, he went in the way of Jeroboam and his sins that he caused Israel to sin.*

16

Baasa's ignominious end

¹ *The word of HASHEM came to Jehu son of Hanani concerning Baasa, saying,* ² *"Inasmuch as I have elevated you from the dirt, and emplaced you as ruler over My people Israel, yet you have gone in the path of Jeroboam, and have caused My people Israel to sin, to anger Me with their sins,* ³ *therefore I shall destructively pursue Baasa and his house with annihilation, and I shall make your house like the house of Jeroboam son of Nebat.* ⁴ *Anyone [of the house] of Baasa who dies in the city, the dogs will eat; and whoever of his dies in the field, the birds of the heavens will eat."*

⁵ *The rest of the deeds of Baasa and that which he did and his might — behold, they are recorded in the Book of the Chronicles of the Kings of Israel. ** ⁶ *Baasa lay with his forefathers and was buried in Tirzah, and his son Elah reigned in his place.* ⁷ *And also through the hand of Jehu son of Hanani the prophet was the word of HASHEM concerning Baasa and his house, because of all the evil that he had done in the eyes of HASHEM, angering Him by his own handiwork, by being like the house of Jeroboam, and because he struck [Jeroboam] down.*

ELAH, KING OF ISRAEL
16:8-14

ZIMRI, KING OF ISRAEL
16:10-20

⁸ *In the twenty-sixth year of Asa, king of Judah, Elah son of Baasa became king over Israel in Tirzah, [ruling] for two years.* ⁹ *His servant Zimri, commander of half the chariots, conspired against him. [Elah] was in Tirzah, drinking himself drunk, in the house of Arza, who was in charge of the palace in Tirzah.* ¹⁰ *Zimri came, struck [Elah] down and killed him, in the twenty-seventh year of Asa, king of Judah, and he reigned in his place.* ¹¹ *It happened that when he became king, when he sat upon the throne, he struck down the entire house of Baasa — he did not leave over any male offspring* — *and all his relatives and friends.* ¹² *Zimri annihilated the entire house of Baasa, in accordance with the word of HASHEM, which He had spoken concerning Baasa through the hand of the prophet Jehu,* ¹³ *because of all the sins of Baasa and the sins of his son Elah, who sinned and caused Israel to sin, angering HASHEM, God of Israel, with their vanities.*

Zimri assassinates the House of Baasa

יד וְיֶ֙תֶר֙ דִּבְרֵ֣י אֵלָ֔ה וְכָל־אֲשֶׁ֖ר עָשָׂ֑ה הֲלוֹא־הֵ֣ם כְּתוּבִ֗ים עַל־סֵ֛פֶר דִּבְרֵ֥י הַיָּמִ֖ים לְמַלְכֵ֥י יִשְׂרָאֵֽל:

טו בִּשְׁנַת֩ עֶשְׂרִ֨ים וָשֶׁ֤בַע שָׁנָה֙ לְאָסָ֣א מֶ֣לֶךְ יְהוּדָ֔ה מָלַ֥ךְ זִמְרִ֛י שִׁבְעַ֥ת יָמִ֖ים בְּתִרְצָ֑ה וְהָעָ֣ם חֹנִ֔ים עַל־גִּבְּת֖וֹן אֲשֶׁ֥ר לַפְּלִשְׁתִּֽים:

טז וַיִּשְׁמַ֤ע הָעָם֙ הַחֹנִ֣ים לֵאמֹ֔ר קָשַׁ֣ר זִמְרִ֔י וְגַ֖ם הִכָּ֣ה אֶת־הַמֶּ֑לֶךְ וַיַּמְלִ֣כוּ כָֽל־יִ֠שְׂרָאֵ֠ל אֶת־עָמְרִ֨י שַׂר־צָבָ֧א עַל־יִשְׂרָאֵ֛ל בַּיּ֥וֹם הַה֖וּא בַּֽמַּחֲנֶֽה: יז וַיַּעֲלֶ֤ה עָמְרִי֙ וְכָל־יִשְׂרָאֵ֣ל עִמּ֔וֹ מִגִּבְּת֑וֹן וַיָּצֻ֖רוּ עַל־תִּרְצָֽה: יח וַיְהִ֞י כִּרְא֤וֹת זִמְרִי֙ כִּֽי־נִלְכְּדָ֣ה הָעִ֔יר וַיָּבֹ֖א אֶל־אַרְמ֣וֹן בֵּית־הַמֶּ֑לֶךְ וַיִּשְׂרֹ֨ף עָלָ֧יו אֶת־בֵּֽית־מֶ֛לֶךְ בָּאֵ֖שׁ וַיָּמֹֽת: יט עַל־°חטאתו [°חַטֹּאתָ֜יו ק] אֲשֶׁ֣ר חָטָ֗א לַעֲשׂ֥וֹת הָרַ֖ע בְּעֵינֵ֣י יְהֹוָ֑ה לָלֶ֙כֶת֙ בְּדֶ֣רֶךְ יָרָבְעָ֔ם וּבְחַטָּאת֔וֹ אֲשֶׁ֥ר עָשָׂ֖ה לְהַחֲטִ֥יא אֶת־יִשְׂרָאֵֽל:

כ וְיֶ֙תֶר֙ דִּבְרֵ֣י זִמְרִ֔י וְקִשְׁר֖וֹ אֲשֶׁ֣ר קָשָׁ֑ר הֲלֹֽא־הֵ֣ם כְּתוּבִ֗ים עַל־סֵ֛פֶר דִּבְרֵ֥י הַיָּמִ֖ים לְמַלְכֵ֥י יִשְׂרָאֵֽל:

כא אָ֤ז יֵֽחָלֵק֙ הָעָ֣ם יִשְׂרָאֵ֔ל לַחֵ֖צִי חֲצִ֣י הָעָ֗ם הָיָ֞ה אַחֲרֵ֤י תִבְנִי֙ בֶן־גִּינַ֣ת לְהַמְלִיכ֔וֹ וְהַחֲצִ֖י אַחֲרֵ֥י עָמְרִֽי: כב וַיֶּחֱזַ֤ק הָעָם֙ אֲשֶׁ֣ר אַחֲרֵ֣י עָמְרִ֔י אֶת־הָעָ֔ם אֲשֶׁ֣ר אַחֲרֵ֖י תִּבְנִ֣י בֶן־גִּינַ֑ת וַיָּ֣מָת תִּבְנִ֔י וַיִּמְלֹ֖ךְ עָמְרִֽי:

כג בִּשְׁנַת֩ שְׁלֹשִׁ֨ים וְאַחַ֜ת שָׁנָ֗ה לְאָסָא֙ מֶ֣לֶךְ יְהוּדָ֔ה מָלַ֤ךְ עָמְרִי֙ עַל־יִשְׂרָאֵ֔ל שְׁתֵּ֥ים עֶשְׂרֵ֖ה שָׁנָ֑ה בְּתִרְצָ֖ה מָלַ֥ךְ שֵׁשׁ־שָׁנִֽים: כד וַיִּ֜קֶן אֶת־הָהָ֥ר שֹׁמְר֛וֹן מֵאֶ֥ת שֶׁ֖מֶר בְּכִכְּרַ֣יִם כָּ֑סֶף וַיִּ֙בֶן֙ אֶת־הָהָ֔ר וַיִּקְרָ֗א אֶת־שֵׁ֤ם הָעִיר֙ אֲשֶׁ֣ר בָּנָ֔ה עַ֣ל שֶׁם־שֶׁ֔מֶר אֲדֹנֵ֖י הָהָ֥ר שֹׁמְרֽוֹן: כה וַיַּעֲשֶׂ֥ה עָמְרִ֛י הָרַ֖ע בְּעֵינֵ֣י יְהֹוָ֑ה וַיָּ֕רַע מִכֹּ֖ל אֲשֶׁ֥ר לְפָנָֽיו: כו וַיֵּ֗לֶךְ בְּכָל־דֶּ֙רֶךְ֙ יָרָבְעָ֣ם בֶּן־נְבָ֔ט וּבְחַטֹּאת֔יו [°וּבְחַטָּאת֔וֹ ק] אֲשֶׁ֣ר הֶחֱטִ֣יא אֶת־יִשְׂרָאֵ֔ל לְהַכְעִ֗יס אֶת־יְהֹוָ֛ה אֱלֹהֵ֥י יִשְׂרָאֵ֖ל בְּהַבְלֵיהֶֽם:

כז וְיֶ֙תֶר֙ דִּבְרֵ֤י עָמְרִי֙ אֲשֶׁ֣ר עָשָׂ֔ה וּגְבֽוּרָת֖וֹ אֲשֶׁ֣ר עָשָׂ֑ה הֲלֹא־הֵ֣ם כְּתוּבִ֗ים עַל־סֵ֛פֶר דִּבְרֵ֥י הַיָּמִ֖ים לְמַלְכֵ֥י יִשְׂרָאֵֽל: כח וַיִּשְׁכַּ֤ב עָמְרִי֙ עִם־אֲבֹתָ֔יו וַיִּקָּבֵ֖ר בְּשֹׁמְר֑וֹן וַיִּמְלֹ֛ךְ אַחְאָ֥ב בְּנ֖וֹ תַּחְתָּֽיו:

כט וְאַחְאָ֣ב בֶּן־עָמְרִ֗י מָלַךְ֙ עַל־יִשְׂרָאֵ֔ל בִּשְׁנַת֙ שְׁלֹשִׁ֣ים וּשְׁמֹנֶ֣ה שָׁנָ֔ה לְאָסָ֖א מֶ֣לֶךְ יְהוּדָ֑ה וַ֠יִּמְלֹ֠ךְ אַחְאָ֨ב בֶּן־עָמְרִ֤י עַל־יִשְׂרָאֵל֙ בְּשֹׁמְר֔וֹן עֶשְׂרִ֥ים וּשְׁתַּ֖יִם שָׁנָֽה: ל וַיַּ֙עַשׂ֙ אַחְאָ֣ב בֶּן־עָמְרִ֔י הָרַ֖ע בְּעֵינֵ֣י יְהֹוָ֑ה מִכֹּ֖ל אֲשֶׁ֥ר לְפָנָֽיו: לא וַיְהִי֙ הֲנָקֵ֣ל לֶכְתּ֔וֹ בְּחַטֹּ֖אות יָרָבְעָ֣ם בֶּן־נְבָ֑ט וַיִּקַּ֨ח אִשָּׁ֜ה אֶת־אִיזֶ֗בֶל בַּת־אֶתְבַּ֨עַל֙ מֶ֣לֶךְ צִידֹנִ֔ים וַיֵּ֙לֶךְ֙ וַֽיַּעֲבֹ֣ד אֶת־הַבַּ֔עַל וַיִּשְׁתַּ֖חוּ לֽוֹ: לב וַיָּ֥קֶם מִזְבֵּ֖חַ לַבָּ֑עַל בֵּ֣ית הַבַּ֔עַל אֲשֶׁ֥ר בָּנָ֖ה בְּשֹׁמְרֽוֹן: לג וַיַּ֥עַשׂ אַחְאָ֖ב אֶת־הָאֲשֵׁרָ֑ה וַיּ֨וֹסֶף אַחְאָ֜ב לַעֲשׂ֗וֹת לְהַכְעִיס֙ אֶת־יְהֹוָה֙ אֱלֹהֵ֣י יִשְׂרָאֵ֔ל מִכֹּ֕ל מַלְכֵ֣י יִשְׂרָאֵ֔ל אֲשֶׁ֥ר הָי֖וּ לְפָנָֽיו: לד בְּיָמָ֞יו בָּנָ֥ה חִיאֵ֛ל בֵּ֥ית הָאֱלִ֖י אֶת־יְרִיחֹ֑ה בַּאֲבִירָ֣ם בְּכֹר֗וֹ יִסְּדָ֞הּ וּבִשְׂג֤וּב [°וּבִשְׂגֻ֥יב ק] צְעִיר֙וֹ הִצִּ֣יב דְּלָתֶ֔יהָ כִּדְבַ֣ר יְהֹוָ֔ה אֲשֶׁ֣ר דִּבֶּ֔ר בְּיַ֖ד יְהוֹשֻׁ֥עַ בִּן־נֽוּן:

יז א וַיֹּאמֶר֩ אֵלִיָּ֨הוּ הַתִּשְׁבִּ֜י מִתֹּשָׁבֵ֣י גִלְעָ֗ד אֶל־אַחְאָב֙ חַי־יְהֹוָ֞ה אֱלֹהֵ֤י יִשְׂרָאֵל֙ אֲשֶׁ֣ר עָמַ֣דְתִּי לְפָנָ֔יו אִם־יִהְיֶ֛ה הַשָּׁנִ֥ים הָאֵ֖לֶּה טַ֣ל וּמָטָ֑ר כִּ֖י אִם־לְפִ֥י

¹⁴ *The rest of the deeds of Elah and all that he did — behold, they are recorded in the Book of the Chronicles of the Kings of Israel.* *

(See Appendix A, timeline 4)

OMRI, KING OF ISRAEL
16:16-28

¹⁵ *In the twenty-seventh year of Asa, king of Judah, Zimri reigned for seven days in Tirzah, while the people were encamped against Gibbethon of the Philistines.* ¹⁶ *The encamped people heard [the news], saying, "Zimri has conspired and has even struck down the king!" So all of Israel made Omri, the commander of the army, king over Israel on that day, in the camp.* ¹⁷ *Omri, and all of Israel with him, went up from Gibbethon and besieged Tirzah.* ¹⁸ *When Zimri saw that the city was being captured, he entered the hall of the king's palace, and he burned down the king's palace upon him in fire, and he died,* ¹⁹ *because of his sins that he committed, doing what is evil in the eyes of HASHEM, going in the way of Jeroboam and his sins that he committed, causing Israel to sin.* ²⁰ *The rest of the deeds of Zimri, and his conspiracy that he organized — behold, they are recorded in the Book of the Chronicles of the Kings of Israel.* *

Tibni's rebellion

²¹ *At that time the people of Israel became split into halves: half the people followed Tibni son of Ginath, to make him king, and the other half followed after Omri.* ²² *The half that followed after Omri prevailed over the half that followed Tibni son of Ginath; Tibni died, and Omri became king.*

Omri consolidates his sinful reign

²³ *In the thirty-first year of Asa,* * *king of Judah, Omri became king over Israel for twelve years. In Tirzah he reigned for six years;* ²⁴ *then he bought the Mountain of Samaria from Shemer for two talents of silver, and he built up the mountain, and he called the name of the city that he built after Shemer, the lord of the Mountain of Samaria.* ²⁵ *Omri did what was evil in the eyes of HASHEM; he was more wicked than all those who had preceded him.* ²⁶ *He went in the entire path of Jeroboam son of Nebat and his sins that he caused Israel to commit, angering HASHEM, God of Israel, with their vanities.* ²⁷ *The rest of the deeds of Omri that he did, and his acts of might that he performed — behold, they are recorded in the Book of the Chronicles of the Kings of Israel.* * ²⁸ *Omri lay with his forefathers and was buried in Samaria, and his son Ahab reigned in his place.*

AHAB, KING OF ISRAEL
16:28-22:40

²⁹ *Ahab son of Omri became king over Israel in the thirty-eighth year of Asa, king of Judah. Ahab son of Omri ruled over Israel in Samaria for twenty-two years.* ³⁰ *Ahab son of Omri did what was evil in the eyes of HASHEM, more than all who had preceded him.* ³¹ *The least [of his evils] was his going in [the way of] the sins of Jeroboam son of Nebat. He took a wife, Jezebel daughter of Ethbaal, king of the Sidonians; and he went and worshiped the Baal and prostrated himself to it.* ³² *He erected an altar for the Baal, in the Temple of the Baal that he built in Samaria.* ³³ *Ahab made an Asherah-tree; and Ahab did more to anger HASHEM, God of Israel, than all the kings of Israel who had preceded him.*

Ahab and Jezebel become rulers

The curse of Jericho

³⁴ *In his days, Hiel the Beth-elite built [up] Jericho; with [the death of] Abiram, his firstborn, he laid its foundations; and with [the death of] Segub, his youngest, he installed its doors; like the word of HASHEM that He had spoken through the hand of Joshua son of Nun.* *

17
ELIJAH THE PROPHET
17:1-II 2:14

¹ **E**lijah the Tishbite, a resident of Gilead, said to Ahab, "As HASHEM, God of Israel, lives — before Whom I stand — [I swear that] there will not be dew nor rain during these years, except by my word."

16:14,20. See note to 14:19.

16:23. The civil war with Tibni lasted four years, until Asa's thirty-first year, so it was not until then that Omri's

reign was secure.

16:27. See note to 14:19.

16:34. See *Joshua* 6:26.

ב-ג דְּבָרָי: וַיְהִי דְבַר־יהוה אֵלָיו לֵאמֹר: לֵךְ מִזֶּה וּפָנִיתָ לְּךָ קֵדְמָה

ד וְנִסְתַּרְתָּ בְּנַחַל כְּרִית אֲשֶׁר עַל־פְּנֵי הַיַּרְדֵּן: וְהָיָה מֵהַנַּחַל תִּשְׁתֶּה וְאֶת־

ה הָעֹרְבִים צִוִּיתִי לְכַלְכֶּלְךָ שָׁם: וַיֵּלֶךְ וַיַּעַשׂ כִּדְבַר יהוה וַיֵּלֶךְ וַיֵּשֶׁב בְּנַחַל

ו כְּרִית אֲשֶׁר עַל־פְּנֵי הַיַּרְדֵּן: וְהָעֹרְבִים מְבִיאִים לוֹ לֶחֶם וּבָשָׂר בַּבֹּקֶר וְלֶחֶם

ז וּבָשָׂר בָּעָרֶב וּמִן־הַנַּחַל יִשְׁתֶּה: וַיְהִי מִקֵּץ יָמִים וַיִּיבַשׁ הַנָּחַל כִּי לֹא־הָיָה

ח-ט גֶשֶׁם בָּאָרֶץ: וַיְהִי דְבַר־יהוה אֵלָיו לֵאמֹר: קוּם לֵךְ צָרְפַתָה אֲשֶׁר

י לְצִידוֹן וְיָשַׁבְתָּ שָׁם הִנֵּה צִוִּיתִי שָׁם אִשָּׁה אַלְמָנָה לְכַלְכְּלֶךָ: וַיָּקָם ׀ וַיֵּלֶךְ

צָרְפַתָה וַיָּבֹא אֶל־פֶּתַח הָעִיר וְהִנֵּה־שָׁם אִשָּׁה אַלְמָנָה מְקֹשֶׁשֶׁת עֵצִים

יא וַיִּקְרָא אֵלֶיהָ וַיֹּאמַר קְחִי־נָא לִי מְעַט־מַיִם בַּכְּלִי וְאֶשְׁתֶּה: וַתֵּלֶךְ לָקַחַת

יב וַיִּקְרָא אֵלֶיהָ וַיֹּאמַר לִקְחִי־נָא לִי פַּת־לֶחֶם בְּיָדֵךְ: וַתֹּאמֶר חַי־יהוה

אֱלֹהֶיךָ אִם־יֶשׁ־לִי מָעוֹג כִּי אִם־מְלֹא כַף־קֶמַח בַּכַּד וּמְעַט־שֶׁמֶן בַּצַּפָּחַת

וְהִנְנִי מְקֹשֶׁשֶׁת שְׁנַיִם עֵצִים וּבָאתִי וַעֲשִׂיתִיהוּ לִי וְלִבְנִי וַאֲכַלְנֻהוּ וָמָתְנוּ:

יג וַיֹּאמֶר אֵלֶיהָ אֵלִיָּהוּ אַל־תִּירְאִי בֹּאִי עֲשִׂי כִדְבָרֵךְ אַךְ עֲשִׂי־לִי מִשָּׁם עֻגָה

יד קְטַנָּה בָרִאשֹׁנָה וְהוֹצֵאת לִי וְלָךְ וְלִבְנֵךְ תַּעֲשִׂי בָּאַחֲרֹנָה: כִּי

כֹה אָמַר יהוה אֱלֹהֵי יִשְׂרָאֵל כַּד הַקֶּמַח לֹא תִכְלָה וְצַפַּחַת הַשֶּׁמֶן לֹא

תֶחְסָר עַד יוֹם °תתן [°תֵּת ק] יהוה גֶּשֶׁם עַל־פְּנֵי הָאֲדָמָה: וַתֵּלֶךְ

טו וַתַּעֲשֶׂה כִּדְבַר אֵלִיָּהוּ וַתֹּאכַל °הוא וָאֵכַל [°הִיא־וָהוּא ק] וּבֵיתָהּ יָמִים:

טז כַּד הַקֶּמַח לֹא כָלָתָה וְצַפַּחַת הַשֶּׁמֶן לֹא חָסֵר כִּדְבַר יהוה אֲשֶׁר דִּבֶּר בְּיַד

יז אֵלִיָּהוּ: וַיְהִי אַחַר הַדְּבָרִים הָאֵלֶּה חָלָה בֶּן־הָאִשָּׁה בַּעֲלַת

יח הַבָּיִת וַיְהִי חָלְיוֹ חָזָק מְאֹד עַד אֲשֶׁר לֹא־נוֹתְרָה־בּוֹ נְשָׁמָה: וַתֹּאמֶר אֶל־

אֵלִיָּהוּ מַה־לִּי וָלָךְ אִישׁ הָאֱלֹהִים בָּאתָ אֵלַי לְהַזְכִּיר אֶת־עֲוֹנִי וּלְהָמִית

יט אֶת־בְּנִי: וַיֹּאמֶר אֵלֶיהָ תְּנִי־לִי אֶת־בְּנֵךְ וַיִּקָּחֵהוּ מֵחֵיקָהּ וַיַּעֲלֵהוּ אֶל־

כ הָעֲלִיָּה אֲשֶׁר־הוּא יֹשֵׁב שָׁם וַיַּשְׁכִּבֵהוּ עַל־מִטָּתוֹ: וַיִּקְרָא אֶל־יהוה וַיֹּאמַר

יהוה אֱלֹהָי הֲגַם עַל־הָאַלְמָנָה אֲשֶׁר־אֲנִי מִתְגּוֹרֵר עִמָּהּ הֲרֵעוֹתָ לְהָמִית

כא אֶת־בְּנָהּ: וַיִּתְמֹדֵד עַל־הַיֶּלֶד שָׁלֹשׁ פְּעָמִים וַיִּקְרָא אֶל־יהוה וַיֹּאמַר יהוה

כב אֱלֹהָי תָּשָׁב־נָא נֶפֶשׁ־הַיֶּלֶד הַזֶּה עַל־קִרְבּוֹ: וַיִּשְׁמַע יהוה בְּקוֹל אֵלִיָּהוּ

כג וַתָּשָׁב נֶפֶשׁ־הַיֶּלֶד עַל־קִרְבּוֹ וַיֶּחִי: וַיִּקַּח אֵלִיָּהוּ אֶת־הַיֶּלֶד וַיֹּרִדֵהוּ מִן־

כד הָעֲלִיָּה הַבַּיְתָה וַיִּתְּנֵהוּ לְאִמּוֹ וַיֹּאמֶר אֵלִיָּהוּ רְאִי חַי בְּנֵךְ: וַתֹּאמֶר הָאִשָּׁה

אֶל־אֵלִיָּהוּ עַתָּה זֶה יָדַעְתִּי כִּי אִישׁ אֱלֹהִים אָתָּה וּדְבַר־יהוה בְּפִיךָ

א אֱמֶת: ◀וַיְהִי יָמִים רַבִּים וּדְבַר־יהוה הָיָה אֶל־אֵלִיָּהוּ בַּשָּׁנָה

יח

הַשְּׁלִישִׁית לֵאמֹר לֵךְ הֵרָאֵה אֶל־אַחְאָב וְאֶתְּנָה מָטָר עַל־פְּנֵי הָאֲדָמָה:

17:7. God dried up Elijah's source of water so that he would feel the suffering of his thirsty fellow men (*Rashi*).

17:10. Elijah tested the woman's kindness to determine if she was the widow of whom God had spoken. In doing so, Elijah followed the precedent of Eliezer in *Genesis*

24:12-15 (*Rashi*).

17:18. Your very presence in my house, with your impeccable standards of piety and Godliness, has caused God to take note of my sins and has brought this tragedy upon me (*Ralbag*).

Drought ^{2} The word of HASHEM came to him, saying, ^{3} "Go from here and turn eastward. You shall hide in the Cherith Brook, which faces the Jordan. ^{4} It shall be that you will drink from the brook; and I have commanded the ravens to supply you with food there." ^{5} So he went and acted according to the word of *The ravens* HASHEM; he went and settled in the Cherith Brook, which faces the Jordan. ^{6} The *bring food* ravens would bring him bread and meat in the morning and bread and meat in *to Elijah* the evening, and he would drink from the brook. ^{7} It happened at the end of a year that the brook dried up, * for there was no rain in the land.

^{8} The word of HASHEM then came to him, saying, ^{9} "Arise, go to Zarephath, of [the territory of] Sidon, and settle there. Behold, I have commanded a widow to sustain you there."

A widow ^{10} So he arose and went to Zarephath and arrived at the entrance to the city. *sustains him* Behold, a widow was gathering wood there; he called to her and said, "Please *and is* fetch me some water in a vessel, that I may drink."* ^{11} She went to get it, and *rewarded* he called to her, saying, "Please fetch me [also] a piece of bread in your hand."

^{12} She said, "As HASHEM, your God, lives, [I swear that] I have not so much as a cookie, but only a handful of flour in a jug, and a bit of oil in a cruse. Behold, I am gathering two pieces of wood; then I will go and prepare it for myself and my son. We will eat it and then we will die." ^{13} But Elijah said to her, "Fear not! Go do as you have said; but first prepare a small cake from it for me, and bring it out to me. And prepare for yourself and your son, afterward. ^{14} For thus said HASHEM, God of Israel: The jug of flour shall not run out and the flask of oil shall not lack, until the day that HASHEM provides rain upon the face of the earth."

^{15} She went and did according to the word of Elijah; and she ate — she and he and her household — for a year. ^{16} The jug of flour did not run out and the cruse of oil did not lack, in accordance with the word of HASHEM, which He had spoken through Elijah.

^{17} And it happened after these events: The son of the woman, the landlady, became ill. His illness became very serious, until there was no more breath left in him. ^{18} She said to Elijah, "What is there between me and you, O man of God, that you have come to me to call attention to my sins * and to cause my son to die!"

^{19} He said to her, "Give me your son." He took him from her bosom and brought him up to the upper story where he was dwelling, and laid him on his [own] bed. ^{20} He called out to HASHEM and said, "HASHEM, my God, have You brought harm even upon the widow with whom I dwell, to cause her son to die?" ^{21} He stretched himself out over the boy three times, and he called out to HASHEM and said, "O HASHEM, my God, please let this boy's soul come back within him!" *He restores* ^{22} HASHEM hearkened to the voice of Elijah, and the soul of the boy came back *her son to* within him, and he came to life. ^{23} Elijah took the boy and brought him down *life* from the upper story to the house, and delivered him to his mother. Elijah said, "See, your son is alive!"

^{24} The woman said to Elijah, "Now I know [through] this that you are a man of God, and that the word of HASHEM in your mouth is true!"

18 ^{1} It happened [after] many days: The word of HASHEM came to Elijah in the third year, * saying, "Go, appear to Ahab; and I shall send rain upon the face of the land."

18:1. In the third year of the drought, God sent Elijah to persuade the people to repent.

ב־ג וַיֵּ֥לֶךְ אֵלִיָּ֖הוּ לְהֵרָא֣וֹת אֶל־אַחְאָ֑ב וְהָרָעָ֖ב חָזָ֥ק בְּשֹׁמְרֽוֹן: וַיִּקְרָ֣א אַחְאָ֔ב
ד אֶל־עֹבַדְיָ֖הוּ אֲשֶׁ֣ר עַל־הַבָּ֑יִת וְעֹבַדְיָ֕הוּ הָיָ֥ה יָרֵ֛א אֶת־יְהֹוָ֖ה מְאֹֽד: וַיְהִי֙
בְּהַכְרִ֣ית אִיזֶ֔בֶל אֵ֖ת נְבִיאֵ֣י יְהֹוָ֑ה וַיִּקַּ֨ח עֹבַדְיָ֜הוּ מֵאָ֣ה נְבִאִ֗ים וַֽיַּחְבִּיאֵ֞ם
ה חֲמִשִּׁ֥ים אִישׁ֙ בַּמְּעָרָ֔ה וְכִלְכְּלָ֖ם לֶ֣חֶם וָמָֽיִם: וַיֹּ֤אמֶר אַחְאָב֙ אֶל־עֹ֣בַדְיָ֔הוּ
לֵ֣ךְ בָּאָ֗רֶץ אֶל־כָּל־מַעְיְנֵ֤י הַמַּ֙יִם֙ וְאֶ֣ל כָּל־הַנְּחָלִ֔ים אוּלַ֣י ׀ נִמְצָ֣א חָצִ֗יר
ו וּנְחַיֶּ֥ה ס֙וּס֙ וָפֶ֔רֶד וְל֥וֹא נַכְרִ֖ית מֵהַבְּהֵמָֽה: וַיְחַלְּק֥וּ לָהֶ֛ם אֶת־הָאָ֖רֶץ לַֽעֲבָר־
ז בָּ֑הּ אַחְאָ֞ב הָלַ֨ךְ בְּדֶ֤רֶךְ אֶחָד֙ לְבַדּ֔וֹ וְעֹבַדְיָ֛הוּ הָלַ֥ךְ בְּדֶֽרֶךְ־אֶחָ֖ד לְבַדּֽוֹ: וַיְהִ֤י
עֹבַדְיָ֙הוּ֙ בַּדֶּ֔רֶךְ וְהִנֵּ֥ה אֵלִיָּ֖הוּ לִקְרָאת֑וֹ וַיַּכִּרֵ֙הוּ֙ וַיִּפֹּ֣ל עַל־פָּנָ֔יו וַיֹּ֕אמֶר הַאַתָּ֥ה
ח־ט זֶ֛ה אֲדֹנִ֖י אֵלִיָּֽהוּ: וַיֹּ֥אמֶר ל֖וֹ אֲנִ֑י לֵ֛ךְ אֱמֹ֥ר לַֽאדֹנֶ֖יךָ הִנֵּ֥ה אֵלִיָּֽהוּ: וַיֹּ֣אמֶר מֶ֣ה
י חָטָ֔אתִי כִּֽי־אַתָּ֞ה נֹתֵ֧ן אֶֽת־עַבְדְּךָ֛ בְּיַד־אַחְאָ֖ב לַֽהֲמִיתֵֽנִי: חַ֣י ׀ יְהֹוָ֣ה אֱלֹהֶ֗יךָ
אִם־יֶשׁ־גּ֤וֹי וּמַמְלָכָה֙ אֲשֶׁ֨ר לֹֽא־שָׁלַ֜ח אֲדֹנִ֥י שָׁם֙ לְבַקֶּשְׁךָ֔ וְאָמְר֖וּ אָ֑יִן
יא וְהִשְׁבִּ֤יעַ אֶת־הַמַּמְלָכָה֙ וְאֶת־הַגּ֔וֹי כִּ֖י לֹ֣א יִמְצָאֶֽכָּה: וְעַתָּ֖ה אַתָּ֣ה אֹמֵ֑ר לֵ֛ךְ
יב אֱמֹ֥ר לַֽאדֹנֶ֖יךָ הִנֵּ֥ה אֵלִיָּֽהוּ: וְהָיָ֞ה אֲנִ֣י ׀ אֵלֵ֣ךְ מֵֽאִתָּ֗ךְ וְר֨וּחַ יְהֹוָ֤ה ׀ יִֽשָּׂאֲךָ֙ עַל־
אֲשֶׁ֣ר לֹֽא־אֵדָ֔ע וּבָ֨אתִי לְהַגִּ֤יד לְאַחְאָב֙ וְלֹ֣א יִמְצָֽאֲךָ֔ וַֽהֲרָגָ֑נִי וְעַבְדְּךָ֛
יג יָרֵ֥א אֶת־יְהֹוָ֖ה מִנְּעֻרָֽי: הֲלֹֽא־הֻגַּ֣ד לַֽאדֹנִ֔י אֵ֥ת אֲשֶׁר־עָשִׂ֖יתִי בַּהֲרֹ֣ג אִיזֶ֔בֶל
אֵ֖ת נְבִיאֵ֣י יְהֹוָ֑ה וָֽאַחְבִּא֩ מִנְּבִיאֵ֨י יְהֹוָ֜ה מֵאָ֣ה אִ֗ישׁ חֲמִשִּׁ֨ים חֲמִשִּׁ֥ים אִישׁ֙
יד בַּמְּעָרָ֔ה וָֽאֲכַלְכְּלֵ֖ם לֶ֣חֶם וָמָֽיִם: וְעַתָּ֗ה אַתָּ֤ה אֹמֵר֙ לֵ֚ךְ אֱמֹ֣ר לַֽאדֹנֶ֔יךָ
הִנֵּ֥ה אֵלִיָּ֖הוּ וַֽהֲרָגָֽנִי: וַיֹּ֙אמֶר֙ אֵ֣לִיָּ֔הוּ חַ֚י יְהֹוָ֣ה צְבָא֔וֹת אֲשֶׁ֥ר עָמַ֖דְתִּי
טו לְפָנָ֑יו כִּ֥י הַיּ֖וֹם אֵרָאֶ֥ה אֵלָֽיו: וַיֵּ֧לֶךְ עֹבַדְיָ֛הוּ לִקְרַ֥את אַחְאָ֖ב וַיַּגֶּד־ל֑וֹ וַיֵּ֣לֶךְ
טז אַחְאָ֔ב לִקְרַ֖את אֵלִיָּֽהוּ: וַיְהִ֛י כִּרְא֥וֹת אַחְאָ֖ב אֶת־אֵלִיָּ֑הוּ וַיֹּ֤אמֶר אַחְאָב֙
יז אֵלָ֔יו הַֽאַתָּ֥ה זֶ֖ה עֹכֵ֥ר יִשְׂרָאֵֽל: וַיֹּ֗אמֶר לֹ֤א עָכַ֙רְתִּי֙ אֶת־יִשְׂרָאֵ֔ל כִּ֖י אִם־
יח אַתָּ֣ה וּבֵית־אָבִ֑יךָ בַּֽעֲזָבְכֶם֙ אֶת־מִצְוֺ֣ת יְהֹוָ֔ה וַתֵּ֖לֶךְ אַֽחֲרֵ֥י הַבְּעָלִֽים: וְעַתָּ֗ה
יט שְׁלַ֨ח קְבֹ֥ץ אֵלַ֛י אֶת־כָּל־יִשְׂרָאֵ֖ל אֶל־הַ֣ר הַכַּרְמֶ֑ל וְאֶת־נְבִיאֵ֣י הַבַּ֡עַל
אַרְבַּ֣ע מֵא֣וֹת וַֽחֲמִשִּׁ֗ים וּנְבִיאֵ֤י הָֽאֲשֵׁרָה֙ אַרְבַּ֣ע מֵא֔וֹת אֹכְלֵ֖י שֻׁלְחַ֥ן אִיזָֽבֶל:
כ וַיִּשְׁלַ֥ח אַחְאָ֖ב בְּכָל־בְּנֵ֣י יִשְׂרָאֵ֑ל וַיִּקְבֹּ֥ץ אֶת־הַנְּבִיאִ֖ים אֶל־הַ֥ר הַכַּרְמֶֽל:

HAFTARAS
KI SISA
Sephardim:
18:20-39

כא וַיִּגַּ֨שׁ אֵלִיָּ֜הוּ אֶל־כָּל־הָעָ֗ם וַיֹּ֙אמֶר֙ עַד־מָתַ֞י אַתֶּ֣ם פֹּֽסְחִים֮ עַל־שְׁתֵּ֣י
הַסְּעִפִּים֒ אִם־יְהֹוָ֤ה הָֽאֱלֹהִים֙ לְכ֣וּ אַֽחֲרָ֔יו וְאִם־הַבַּ֖עַל לְכ֣וּ אַֽחֲרָ֑יו וְלֹֽא־
כב עָנ֥וּ הָעָ֛ם אֹת֖וֹ דָּבָֽר: וַיֹּ֤אמֶר אֵֽלִיָּ֙הוּ֙ אֶל־הָעָ֔ם אֲנִ֞י נוֹתַ֧רְתִּי נָבִ֛יא לַֽיהֹוָ֖ה
כג לְבַדִּ֑י וּנְבִיאֵ֣י הַבַּ֔עַל אַרְבַּע־מֵא֥וֹת וַֽחֲמִשִּׁ֖ים אִֽישׁ: וְיִתְּנוּ־לָ֜נוּ שְׁנַ֣יִם
פָּרִ֗ים וְיִבְחֲר֣וּ לָהֶם֩ הַפָּ֨ר הָֽאֶחָ֜ד וִינַתְּחֻ֗הוּ וְיָשִׂ֙ימוּ֙ עַל־הָ֣עֵצִ֔ים וְאֵ֖שׁ לֹ֣א
יָשִׂ֑ימוּ וַֽאֲנִ֞י אֶֽעֱשֶׂ֣ה ׀ אֶת־הַפָּ֣ר הָֽאֶחָ֗ד וְנָֽתַתִּי֙ עַל־הָ֣עֵצִ֔ים וְאֵ֖שׁ לֹ֥א
כד אָשִֽׂים: וּקְרָאתֶ֞ם בְּשֵׁ֣ם אֱלֹֽהֵיכֶ֗ם וַֽאֲנִי֙ אֶקְרָ֣א בְשֵׁם־יְהֹוָ֔ה וְהָיָ֧ה הָֽאֱלֹהִ֛ים
אֲשֶׁר־יַֽעֲנֶ֥ה בָאֵ֖שׁ ה֣וּא הָֽאֱלֹהִ֑ים וַיַּ֧עַן כָּל־הָעָ֛ם וַיֹּֽאמְר֖וּ ט֥וֹב הַדָּבָֽר:

18:21. Apparently, they saw nothing wrong with combining the contradictory beliefs of Baalism and monotheism.

² So Elijah went to appear to Ahab, and the famine was severe in Samaria. ³ Ahab summoned Obadiah, who was in charge of the household. (Obadiah feared God greatly. ⁴ And it was when Jezebel had decimated the prophets of HASHEM, Obadiah took a hundred prophets and hid them, fifty men to a cave, and sustained them with food and water.) ⁵ Ahab said to Obadiah, "Go through the land, to every spring of water and to all the streams; perhaps we may find grass and keep horses and mules alive, so that we should not be deprived of animals."

⁶ They divided the land between them to traverse it; Ahab went alone on one road and Obadiah went alone on another road. ⁷ Obadiah was on the road, and
behold! — Elijah was in front of him! He recognized him and fell on his face and said, "Is that you, my lord Elijah?"

⁸ He said to him, "It is I. Go tell your lord: Elijah is here!"

⁹ [Obadiah] said, "What is my sin, that you deliver your servant into Ahab's hand to put me to death? ¹⁰ As HASHEM, your God, lives, [I swear that] there is not a nation or kingdom where my lord has not sent to seek you, and they have responded, '[He is] not [here]!' He had the kingdom and the nation swear that they could not find you. ¹¹ And now you say, 'Go tell your lord: Elijah is here!' ¹² As soon as I go from you, a spirit of HASHEM will carry you to where I will not know. I will have come to tell Ahab, and he will not find you — and he will kill me! But your servant has feared HASHEM since my youth! ¹³ Has it not been told to my lord what I did when Jezebel killed the prophets of HASHEM — that I hid a hundred men of the prophets of HASHEM, fifty men to each cave, and sustained them with food and water. ¹⁴ And now you say to me, 'Go tell your lord: Elijah is here'! He will kill me!"

¹⁵ Elijah said, "As HASHEM, Master of Legions, before Whom I have stood, lives, [I swear] that today I will appear to him!"

¹⁶ Obadiah went toward Ahab and told him, so Ahab went toward Elijah. ¹⁷ And it was when Ahab saw Elijah, Ahab said to him, "Is that you, the troubler of Israel?"

¹⁸ He said [to him], "Not I have troubled Israel, rather you and your father's house [have], by your forsaking the commandments of HASHEM; and you have gone after the Baalim! ¹⁹ And now, send and gather all of Israel to me at Mount Carmel, and also the four hundred and fifty prophets of the Baal and the four hundred prophets of the Asherah-tree, who eat at Jezebel's table."

²⁰ Ahab sent among all the Children of Israel and he gathered the prophets to Mount Carmel. ²¹ Elijah approached all the people and said, "How long will you dance between two opinions? If HASHEM is the God, go after Him! And if the Baal, go after it!"

But the people did not answer him at all. *

²² Elijah then said to the people, "I alone have remained as a prophet of HASHEM, and the prophets of the Baal are four hundred and fifty men. ²³ Let us be given two bulls. Let them choose the one bull for themselves, cut it, and put it on the wood, but not apply fire; and I too will prepare the other bull and place it on the wood, and I will not apply fire. ²⁴ You shall call out in the name of your gods and I shall call out in the Name of HASHEM, and whichever God responds with fire, He is the [true] God!"

All the people responded, "The proposal is good!"

כה וַיֹּ֨אמֶר אֵלִיָּ֜הוּ לִנְבִיאֵ֣י הַבַּ֗עַל בַּחֲר֣וּ לָכֶ֞ם הַפָּ֤ר הָֽאֶחָד֙ וַעֲשׂ֣וּ רִֽאשֹׁנָ֔ה כִּ֥י
כו אַתֶּ֖ם הָֽרַבִּ֑ים וְקִרְאוּ֙ בְּשֵׁ֣ם אֱלֹֽהֵיכֶ֔ם וְאֵ֖שׁ לֹ֥א תָשִֽׂימוּ: וַ֠יִּקְחוּ אֶת־הַפָּ֨ר
אֲשֶׁר־נָתַ֣ן לָהֶם֮ וַֽיַּעֲשׂוּ֒ וַיִּקְרְא֣וּ בְשֵׁם־הַ֠בַּעַל מֵהַבֹּ֨קֶר וְעַד־הַֽצָּהֳרַ֤יִם
לֵאמֹר֙ הַבַּ֣עַל עֲנֵ֔נוּ וְאֵ֥ין ק֖וֹל וְאֵ֣ין עֹנֶ֑ה וַֽיְפַסְּח֔וּ עַל־הַמִּזְבֵּ֖חַ אֲשֶׁ֥ר עָשָֽׂה:
כז וַיְהִ֨י בַֽצָּהֳרַ֜יִם וַיְהַתֵּ֧ל בָּהֶ֣ם אֵלִיָּ֗הוּ וַיֹּ֙אמֶר֙ קִרְא֤וּ בְקוֹל־גָּדוֹל֙ כִּֽי־אֱלֹהִ֣ים
כח ה֔וּא כִּ֣י שִׂ֧יחַ וְכִי־שִׂ֛יג ל֖וֹ וְכִי־דֶ֣רֶךְ ל֑וֹ אוּלַ֛י יָשֵׁ֥ן ה֖וּא וְיִקָֽץ: וַֽיִּקְרְאוּ֙ בְּק֣וֹל
גָּד֔וֹל וַיִּתְגֹּֽדְד֗וּ כְּמִשְׁפָּטָ֛ם בַּחֲרָב֖וֹת וּבָֽרְמָחִ֑ים עַד־שְׁפָךְ־דָּ֖ם עֲלֵיהֶֽם: וַיְהִ֤י
כט כַֽעֲבֹ֣ר הַֽצָּהֳרַ֔יִם וַיִּֽתְנַבְּא֔וּ עַ֖ד לַעֲל֣וֹת הַמִּנְחָ֑ה וְאֵֽין־ק֥וֹל וְאֵֽין־עֹנֶ֖ה וְאֵ֥ין
ל קָֽשֶׁב: וַיֹּ֨אמֶר אֵלִיָּ֜הוּ לְכָל־הָעָ֗ם גְּשׁ֤וּ אֵלַי֙ וַיִּגְּשׁ֤וּ כָל־הָעָם֙ אֵלָ֔יו וַיְרַפֵּ֕א
לא אֶת־מִזְבַּ֥ח יְהֹוָ֖ה הֶֽהָרֽוּס: וַיִּקַּ֣ח אֵלִיָּ֗הוּ שְׁתֵּ֤ים עֶשְׂרֵה֙ אֲבָנִ֔ים כְּמִסְפַּ֖ר
שִׁבְטֵ֣י בְנֵֽי־יַעֲקֹ֑ב אֲשֶׁר֩ הָיָ֨ה דְבַר־יְהֹוָ֤ה אֵלָיו֙ לֵאמֹ֔ר יִשְׂרָאֵ֖ל יִהְיֶ֥ה שְׁמֶֽךָ:
לב וַיִּבְנֶ֧ה אֶת־הָאֲבָנִ֛ים מִזְבֵּ֖חַ בְּשֵׁ֣ם יְהֹוָ֑ה וַיַּ֣עַשׂ תְּעָלָ֗ה כְּבֵית֙ סָאתַ֣יִם זֶ֔רַע
לג סָבִ֖יב לַמִּזְבֵּֽחַ: וַֽיַּעֲרֹ֖ךְ אֶת־הָֽעֵצִ֑ים וַיְנַתַּח֙ אֶת־הַפָּ֔ר וַיָּ֖שֶׂם עַל־הָֽעֵצִֽים:
לד וַיֹּ֗אמֶר מִלְא֨וּ אַרְבָּעָ֤ה כַדִּים֙ מַ֔יִם וְיִֽצְק֥וּ עַל־הָֽעֹלָ֖ה וְעַל־הָֽעֵצִ֑ים וַיֹּ֤אמֶר
שְׁנוּ֙ וַיִּשְׁנ֔וּ וַיֹּ֥אמֶר שַׁלֵּ֖שׁוּ וַיְשַׁלֵּֽשׁוּ: וַיֵּֽלְכ֣וּ הַמַּ֔יִם סָבִ֖יב לַמִּזְבֵּ֑חַ וְגַ֥ם אֶת־
לה הַתְּעָלָ֖ה מִלֵּא־מָֽיִם: וַיְהִ֣י ׀ בַּֽעֲל֣וֹת הַמִּנְחָ֗ה וַיִּגַּ֞שׁ אֵלִיָּ֤הוּ הַנָּבִיא֙ וַיֹּאמַ֔ר
לו יְהֹוָ֗ה אֱלֹהֵי֙ אַבְרָהָם֙ יִצְחָ֣ק וְיִשְׂרָאֵ֔ל הַיּ֣וֹם יִוָּדַ֗ע כִּֽי־אַתָּ֧ה אֱלֹהִ֛ים בְּיִשְׂרָאֵ֖ל
וַֽאֲנִ֣י עַבְדֶּ֑ךָ °וּבִדְבָרֶ֔יךָ [°וּבִדְבָֽרְךָ ק] עָשִׂ֕יתִי אֵ֥ת כָּל־הַדְּבָרִ֖ים הָאֵֽלֶּה:
לז עֲנֵ֤נִי יְהֹוָה֙ עֲנֵ֔נִי וְיֵֽדְעוּ֙ הָעָ֣ם הַזֶּ֔ה כִּֽי־אַתָּ֥ה יְהֹוָ֖ה הָאֱלֹהִ֑ים וְאַתָּ֛ה הֲסִבֹּ֥תָ
לח אֶת־לִבָּ֖ם אֲחֹֽרַנִּֽית: וַתִּפֹּ֣ל אֵשׁ־יְהֹוָ֗ה וַתֹּ֤אכַל אֶת־הָֽעֹלָה֙ וְאֶת־הָ֣עֵצִ֔ים
וְאֶת־הָֽאֲבָנִ֖ים וְאֶת־הֶֽעָפָ֑ר וְאֶת־הַמַּ֥יִם אֲשֶׁר־בַּתְּעָלָ֖ה לִחֵֽכָה: וַיַּרְא֙ כָּל־
לט הָעָ֔ם וַֽיִּפְּל֖וּ עַל־פְּנֵיהֶ֑ם וַיֹּ֣אמְר֔וּ יְהֹוָה֙ ה֣וּא הָֽאֱלֹהִ֔ים יְהֹוָ֖ה ה֥וּא הָֽאֱלֹהִֽים: ◄
מ וַיֹּ֩אמֶר֩ אֵלִיָּ֨הוּ לָהֶ֜ם תִּפְשׂ֣וּ ׀ אֶת־נְבִיאֵ֣י הַבַּ֗עַל אִ֛ישׁ אַל־יִמָּלֵ֥ט מֵהֶ֖ם
מא וַֽיִּתְפְּשׂ֑וּם וַיּֽוֹרִדֵ֤ם אֵלִיָּ֙הוּ֙ אֶל־נַ֣חַל קִישׁ֔וֹן וַיִּשְׁחָטֵ֖ם שָֽׁם: וַיֹּ֤אמֶר אֵלִיָּ֙הוּ֙
מב לְאַחְאָ֔ב עֲלֵ֖ה אֱכֹ֣ל וּשְׁתֵ֑ה כִּי־ק֖וֹל הֲמ֥וֹן הַגָּֽשֶׁם: וַיַּעֲלֶ֥ה אַחְאָ֖ב לֶאֱכֹ֣ל וְלִשְׁתּ֑וֹת
וְאֵ֨לִיָּ֜הוּ עָלָ֨ה אֶל־רֹ֤אשׁ הַכַּרְמֶל֙ וַיִּגְהַ֣ר אַ֔רְצָה וַיָּ֥שֶׂם פָּנָ֖יו
מג בֵּ֣ין °בִּרְכּו [°בִּרְכָּֽיו ק]: וַיֹּ֣אמֶר אֶֽל־נַעֲר֗וֹ עֲלֵה־נָא֙ הַבֵּ֣ט דֶּֽרֶךְ־יָ֔ם וַיַּ֙עַל֙
מד וַיַּבֵּ֣ט וַיֹּ֖אמֶר אֵ֣ין מְא֑וּמָה וַיֹּ֙אמֶר֙ שֻׁ֣ב שֶׁ֣בַע פְּעָמִֽים: וַיְהִי֙ בַּשְּׁבִעִ֔ית וַיֹּ֕אמֶר
הִנֵּה־עָ֛ב קְטַנָּ֥ה כְּכַף־אִ֖ישׁ עֹלָ֣ה מִיָּ֑ם וַיֹּ֗אמֶר עֲלֵ֞ה אֱמֹ֤ר אֶל־אַחְאָ֙ב
מה אֱסֹ֣ר וָרֵ֔ד וְלֹ֥א יַֽעֲצָרְכָ֖ה הַגָּֽשֶׁם: וַיְהִ֣י ׀ עַד־כֹּ֣ה וְעַד־כֹּ֗ה וְהַשָּׁמַ֙יִם֙ הִֽתְקַדְּרוּ֙

18:29. Prescribed in *Exodus* 29:38-41 and *Numbers* 28:1-8.

18:31. Elijah's twelve stones symbolized that all twelve tribes actually comprise one unit. He mentioned Jacob's name of Israel because it was in Beth-el that God had appeared to Jacob and changed his name to Israel, promising him that his descendants would become a great nation (*Genesis* 35:9-15). Now Elijah reprimanded the people for having chosen that very location as the site of their idolatrous temple (*Radak*).

18:32. Opinions regarding modern-day equivalents range from 12,400 to 18,000 square feet.

18:42. Elijah prayed in this position (*Rashi*).

²⁵ Elijah said to the prophets of the Baal, "Choose for yourselves the one bull and prepare it first, for you are the many, and call out in the name of your god, but do not apply fire." ²⁶ They took the bull that he gave them and prepared it, and called out in the name of the Baal from morning until noon, saying, "O Baal, answer us!" But there was neither sound nor response; and they danced by the altar that he had made.

²⁷ And it was at noontime, Elijah ridiculed them, and said, "Cry out in a loud voice, for he is a god! Perhaps he is conversing, or pursuing [enemies], or relieving himself; perhaps he is asleep and he will awaken!"

²⁸ They called out with a loud voice and cut themselves with swords and spears, according to their custom, until blood spurted on them. ²⁹ When the noon hour passed they prophesied until the [time of] the afternoon-offering * — but there was neither sound, nor response, nor listener.

³⁰ Elijah then said to all the people, "Draw near to me," and all the people drew near to him. He repaired the ruined altar of HASHEM. ³¹ Elijah took twelve stones, corresponding to the number of the tribes of the children of Jacob (to whom the word of HASHEM came, saying, "Your name shall be Israel"). * ³² He built the stones into an altar for the Name of HASHEM, and he made a trench large enough to plant two se'ahs of seed* around the altar. ³³ He arranged the wood, he cut up the bull, and put it on the wood. ³⁴ Then he said, "Fill four jugs with water and pour them over the elevation-offering and over the wood." He said, "Do it a second time!" and they did it a second time. He said, "Do it a third time!" and they did it a third time. ³⁵ The water went all around the altar and he also filled the trench with water.

³⁶ And it was at the time of the afternoon-offering, Elijah the prophet approached and said, "HASHEM, God of Abraham, Isaac and Israel, today it will become known that You are God in Israel and I am Your servant, and that it is by Your word that I have done all these things. ³⁷ Answer me, HASHEM, answer me! And let this people know that You, HASHEM, are the God; thus You will turn their hearts back."

³⁸ A fire of HASHEM descended and consumed the elevation-offering and the wood, and the stones, and the earth; and it licked up the water in the trench. ³⁹ The entire people saw and fell on their faces and exclaimed, "HASHEM — He is the God! HASHEM — He is the God!"

⁴⁰ Elijah said to them, "Seize the prophets of Baal! Let none of them escape!" So they seized them. Elijah took them down to the Kishon Brook and slaughtered them there.

⁴¹ Elijah said to Ahab, "Go up and eat and drink, for a rumbling sound of rain [is coming]." ⁴² So Ahab went up to eat and drink; but Elijah went up to the summit of the Carmel, bent down to the ground, * and put his face between his knees. ⁴³ He said to his attendant, "Go up now and gaze westward."

He went up and gazed, and he said, "There is nothing at all."

[Elijah] said seven times, "Go back!"

⁴⁴ It was at the seventh time, and he said, "Behold, a cloud, as small as a man's hand is coming up from the west."

[Elijah] said, "Go up and tell Ahab, 'Harness [your chariot] and go down, so that the rain does not hold you back.' "

⁴⁵ It happened that in the meantime the heavens had become darkened with

HAFTARAS
PINCHAS
18:46-19:21

מו עָבִים וְרוּחַ וַיְהִי גֶּשֶׁם גָּדוֹל וַיִּרְכַּב אַחְאָב וַיֵּלֶךְ יִזְרְעֶאלָה: וְיַד־
יהוה הָיְתָה אֶל־אֵלִיָּהוּ וַיְשַׁנֵּס מָתְנָיו וַיָּרָץ לִפְנֵי אַחְאָב עַד־בֹּאֲכָה
א יִזְרְעֶאלָה: וַיַּגֵּד אַחְאָב לְאִיזֶבֶל אֵת כָּל־אֲשֶׁר עָשָׂה אֵלִיָּהוּ וְאֵת כָּל־
ב אֲשֶׁר הָרַג אֶת־כָּל־הַנְּבִיאִים בֶּחָרֶב: וַתִּשְׁלַח אִיזֶבֶל מַלְאָךְ אֶל־אֵלִיָּהוּ
לֵאמֹר כֹּה־יַעֲשׂוּן אֱלֹהִים וְכֹה יוֹסִפוּן כִּי־כָעֵת מָחָר אָשִׂים אֶת־נַפְשְׁךָ
ג כְּנֶפֶשׁ אַחַד מֵהֶם: וַיַּרְא וַיָּקָם וַיֵּלֶךְ אֶל־נַפְשׁוֹ וַיָּבֹא בְּאֵר שֶׁבַע אֲשֶׁר
ד לִיהוּדָה וַיַּנַּח אֶת־נַעֲרוֹ שָׁם: וְהוּא־הָלַךְ בַּמִּדְבָּר דֶּרֶךְ יוֹם וַיָּבֹא וַיֵּשֶׁב
תַּחַת רֹתֶם °אֶחָת ק] אֶחָד וַיִּשְׁאַל אֶת־נַפְשׁוֹ לָמוּת וַיֹּאמֶר ׀ רַב עַתָּה
ה יהוה קַח נַפְשִׁי כִּי לֹא־טוֹב אָנֹכִי מֵאֲבֹתָי: וַיִּשְׁכַּב וַיִּישַׁן תַּחַת רֹתֶם אֶחָד
ו וְהִנֵּה־זֶה מַלְאָךְ נֹגֵעַ בּוֹ וַיֹּאמֶר לוֹ קוּם אֱכֹל: וַיַּבֵּט וְהִנֵּה מְרַאֲשֹׁתָיו עֻגַת
ז רְצָפִים וְצַפַּחַת מָיִם וַיֹּאכַל וַיֵּשְׁתְּ וַיָּשָׁב וַיִּשְׁכָּב: וַיָּשָׁב מַלְאַךְ יהוה ׀ שֵׁנִית
ח וַיִּגַּע־בּוֹ וַיֹּאמֶר קוּם אֱכֹל כִּי רַב מִמְּךָ הַדָּרֶךְ: וַיָּקָם וַיֹּאכַל וַיִּשְׁתֶּה וַיֵּלֶךְ
בְּכֹחַ ׀ הָאֲכִילָה הַהִיא אַרְבָּעִים יוֹם וְאַרְבָּעִים לַיְלָה עַד הַר הָאֱלֹהִים
ט חֹרֵב: וַיָּבֹא־שָׁם אֶל־הַמְּעָרָה וַיָּלֶן שָׁם וְהִנֵּה דְבַר־יהוה אֵלָיו וַיֹּאמֶר לוֹ
י מַה־לְּךָ פֹה אֵלִיָּהוּ: וַיֹּאמֶר קַנֹּא קִנֵּאתִי לַיהוה ׀ אֱלֹהֵי צְבָאוֹת כִּי־עָזְבוּ
בְרִיתְךָ בְּנֵי יִשְׂרָאֵל אֶת־מִזְבְּחֹתֶיךָ הָרָסוּ וְאֶת־נְבִיאֶיךָ הָרְגוּ בֶחָרֶב
יא וָאִוָּתֵר אֲנִי לְבַדִּי וַיְבַקְשׁוּ אֶת־נַפְשִׁי לְקַחְתָּהּ: וַיֹּאמֶר צֵא וְעָמַדְתָּ בָהָר
לִפְנֵי יהוה וְהִנֵּה יהוה עֹבֵר וְרוּחַ גְּדוֹלָה וְחָזָק מְפָרֵק הָרִים וּמְשַׁבֵּר
סְלָעִים לִפְנֵי יהוה לֹא בָרוּחַ יהוה וְאַחַר הָרוּחַ רַעַשׁ לֹא בָרַעַשׁ יהוה:
יב-יג וְאַחַר הָרַעַשׁ אֵשׁ לֹא בָאֵשׁ יהוה וְאַחַר הָאֵשׁ קוֹל דְּמָמָה דַקָּה ׀ וַיְהִי ׀
כִּשְׁמֹעַ אֵלִיָּהוּ וַיָּלֶט פָּנָיו בְּאַדַּרְתּוֹ וַיֵּצֵא וַיַּעֲמֹד פֶּתַח הַמְּעָרָה וְהִנֵּה אֵלָיו
יד קוֹל וַיֹּאמֶר מַה־לְּךָ פֹה אֵלִיָּהוּ: וַיֹּאמֶר קַנֹּא קִנֵּאתִי לַיהוה ׀ אֱלֹהֵי צְבָאוֹת
כִּי־עָזְבוּ בְרִיתְךָ בְּנֵי יִשְׂרָאֵל אֶת־מִזְבְּחֹתֶיךָ הָרָסוּ וְאֶת־נְבִיאֶיךָ הָרְגוּ
טו בֶחָרֶב וָאִוָּתֵר אֲנִי לְבַדִּי וַיְבַקְשׁוּ אֶת־נַפְשִׁי לְקַחְתָּהּ: וַיֹּאמֶר
יהוה אֵלָיו לֵךְ שׁוּב לְדַרְכְּךָ מִדְבַּרָה דַמָּשֶׂק וּבָאתָ וּמָשַׁחְתָּ אֶת־חֲזָאֵל
טז לְמֶלֶךְ עַל־אֲרָם: וְאֵת יֵהוּא בֶן־נִמְשִׁי תִּמְשַׁח לְמֶלֶךְ עַל־יִשְׂרָאֵל וְאֶת־
יז אֱלִישָׁע בֶּן־שָׁפָט מֵאָבֵל מְחוֹלָה תִּמְשַׁח לְנָבִיא תַּחְתֶּיךָ: וְהָיָה הַנִּמְלָט
יח מֵחֶרֶב חֲזָאֵל יָמִית יֵהוּא וְהַנִּמְלָט מֵחֶרֶב יֵהוּא יָמִית אֱלִישָׁע: וְהִשְׁאַרְתִּי

19:2. ". . . if I do not fulfill my word." This is a common expression of oath in the Bible.

19:4. After wandering for a day without food, water, or shelter, Elijah despaired and exclaimed that he had suffered enough. He was not more worthy than his forebears; why should he live longer than they? (*Radak*).

19:8. Horeb is another name for Mount Sinai (see *Deut.* 5:2ff).

19:10. Elijah intimated that God should take vengeance against the Israelites (*Ralbag*).

19:12. God taught Elijah that He does not administer indiscriminate, harsh justice to sinners. Rather, with silent restraint and patience, He awaits their repentance.

19:16. See *II Kings*, Chs. 9-10.

19:17. After showing him that he was wrong in his harsh attitude toward Israel, God commanded Elijah to set in motion the forces that would bring retribution to the sinners: Kings Hazael and Jehu who would implement the death penalty, and Elisha who would admonish the Jewish sinners so that those who ignored him would deserve punishment.

Additionally, the command to anoint Elisha as his

clouds and [filled with] wind, and there was a great rain. Ahab rode off and went towards Jezreel. ⁴⁶ The hand of HASHEM was upon Elijah, and he girded his loins and ran before Ahab until the approach to Jezreel.

19

Elijah flees from Jezebel's death threat

¹ Then Ahab told Jezebel everything that Elijah had done and everything about how he had slain all the [false] prophets by the sword. ² So Jezebel sent a messenger to Elijah, saying, "Such may the gods do [to me] and such may they do further . . . * for at this time tomorrow I shall make your soul like the soul of one of them."

³ When he saw [the danger], he arose and fled for his life; he came to Beer-sheba which is in Judah, and left his attendant there. ⁴ He then went a day's journey into the wilderness; he went and sat under a solitary *retem* tree, and requested for his soul to die. He said, "It is enough! Now, HASHEM, take my soul, for I am no better than my forefathers."*

God sends food to Elijah

⁵ He lay down and slept under a solitary *retem* tree; and behold! — an angel was touching him and said to him, "Get up and eat!" ⁶ He looked up and behold, near his head [were] a coal-baked cake and a cruse of water; he ate and drank, then went back and lay down.

⁷ The angel of HASHEM returned to him a second time, and he touched him and said, "Get up and eat [more], for there is a long way ahead for you." ⁸ So he arose, and ate and drank; he walked on the strength of that meal for forty days and forty nights, until the Mountain of God, Horeb. * ⁹ He arrived there at the cave and spent the night in it; then behold, the word of HASHEM came to him and said to him, "Why are you here, Elijah?"

¹⁰ He said, "I have acted with great zeal for HASHEM, God of Legions, for the Children of Israel have forsaken Your covenant; they have razed Your altars and have killed Your prophets by the sword, so [that] I alone have remained, and they now seek to take my life."*

Elijah's vision; the still, thin sound

¹¹ [The word of God] then said, "Go out [of the cave] and stand on the mountain before HASHEM." And behold, HASHEM was passing, and a great, powerful wind, smashing mountains and breaking rocks, went before HASHEM. "HASHEM is not in the wind!" [Elijah was told]. After the wind came an earthquake. "HASHEM is not in the earthquake." ¹² After the earthquake came a fire. "HASHEM is not in the fire." After the fire came a still, thin sound. *

¹³ It happened that when Elijah heard [this], he wrapped his face in his mantle, and he went out and stood by the cave's entrance; and behold, a voice [spoke] unto him, and said, "Why are you here, Elijah?"

¹⁴ He said, "I have acted with great zeal for HASHEM, God of Legions, for the Children of Israel have forsaken Your covenant; they have razed Your altars and have killed Your prophets by the sword, so [that] I alone have remained, and they now seek to take my life."

God sends Elijah to anoint kings and a prophet

¹⁵ Then HASHEM said to him, "Go, return on your way, and go to the Wilderness of Damascus. When you arrive, you shall anoint Hazael as king over Aram. ¹⁶ And you shall anoint Jehu son of Nimshi as king over Israel, * and anoint Elisha son of Shaphat from Abel-meholah as a prophet in your stead. ¹⁷ And it shall happen that whoever escapes the sword of Hazael, Jehu will kill; and whoever escapes the sword of Jehu, Elisha will kill. * ¹⁸ But I will leave over

---

successor was an implied rebuke to Elijah for his demand that Israel be punished (*Rashi*).

בְיִשְׂרָאֵל שִׁבְעַת אֲלָפִים כָּל־הַבִּרְכַּ֫יִם אֲשֶׁר לֹא־כָרְעוּ לַבַּעַל וְכָל־הַפֶּ֫ה
^{יט} אֲשֶׁר לֹא־נָשַׁק לֽוֹ: וַיֵּ֫לֶךְ מִשָּׁם וַיִּמְצָא אֶת־אֱלִישָׁע בֶּן־שָׁפָט וְה֣וּא חֹרֵ֫שׁ
שְׁנֵים־עָשָׂר צְמָדִים לְפָנָיו וְה֖וּא בִּשְׁנֵים הֶעָשָׂר וַיַּעֲבֹר אֵלִיָּ֫הוּ אֵלָיו וַיַּשְׁלֵ֥ךְ
^כ אַדַּרְתּ֖וֹ אֵלָיו: וַיַּעֲזֹב אֶת־הַבָּקָר וַיָּ֫רָץ אַחֲרֵי אֵלִיָּ֫הוּ וַיֹּ֫אמֶר אֶשְּׁקָה־נָּ֫א
^{כא} לְאָבִי וּלְאִמִּ֫י וְאֵלְכָ֣ה אַחֲרֶ֫יךָ וַיֹּ֫אמֶר ל֖וֹ לֵ֣ךְ שׁ֔וּב כִּ֥י מֶה־עָשִׂ֥יתִי לָֽךְ: וַיָּ֫שָׁב
מֵאַחֲרָיו וַיִּקַּ֫ח אֶת־צֶ֫מֶד הַבָּקָר וַיִּזְבָּחֵ֫הוּ וּבִכְלִ֣י הַבָּקָר בִּשְּׁלָ֣ם הַבָּשָׂר וַיִּתֵּ֥ן
^כ   לָעָם וַיֹּאכֵ֫לוּ וַיָּ֫קָם וַיֵּ֫לֶךְ אַחֲרֵ֥י אֵלִיָּ֖הוּ וַיְשָׁרְתֵֽהוּ:   ▸   וּבֶן־

^א הֲדַ֣ד מֶֽלֶךְ־אֲרָ֗ם קָבַץ֙ אֶת־כָּל־חֵיל֔וֹ וּשְׁלֹשִׁ֤ים וּשְׁנַ֨יִם֙ מֶ֣לֶךְ אִתּ֔וֹ וְס֖וּס
^ב וָרָ֑כֶב וַיַּ֨עַל֙ וַיָּ֣צַר עַל־שֹׁמְר֔וֹן וַיִּלָּ֖חֶם בָּֽהּ: וַיִּשְׁלַ֧ח מַלְאָכִ֛ים אֶל־אַחְאָ֖ב
^ג מֶֽלֶךְ־יִשְׂרָאֵ֖ל הָעִֽירָה: וַיֹּ֣אמֶר ל֗וֹ כֹּ֚ה אָמַ֣ר בֶּן־הֲדַ֔ד כַּסְפְּךָ֥ וּֽזְהָבְךָ֖ לִי־ה֑וּא
^ד וְנָשֶׁ֧יךָ וּבָנֶ֛יךָ הַטּוֹבִ֖ים לִי־הֵֽם: וַיַּ֨עַן֙ מֶ֣לֶךְ־יִשְׂרָאֵ֔ל וַיֹּ֖אמֶר כִּדְבָֽרְךָ֣ אֲדֹנִ֣י
^ה הַמֶּ֑לֶךְ לְךָ֥ אֲנִ֖י וְכָל־אֲשֶׁר־לִֽי: וַיָּשֻׁ֨בוּ֙ הַמַּלְאָכִ֔ים וַיֹּ֣אמְר֔וּ כֹּה־אָמַ֥ר בֶּן־
הֲדַ֖ד לֵאמֹ֑ר כִּֽי־שָׁלַ֤חְתִּי אֵלֶ֨יךָ֙ לֵאמֹ֔ר כַּסְפְּךָ֧ וּֽזְהָבְךָ֛ וְנָשֶׁ֥יךָ וּבָנֶ֖יךָ לִ֥י תִתֵּֽן:
^ו כִּ֣י ׀ אִם־כָּעֵ֣ת מָחָ֗ר אֶשְׁלַ֤ח אֶת־עֲבָדַי֙ אֵלֶ֔יךָ וְחִפְּשׂוּ֙ אֶת־בֵּ֣יתְךָ֔ וְאֵ֖ת בָּתֵּ֣י
^ז עֲבָדֶ֑יךָ וְהָיָה֩ כָּל־מַחְמַ֨ד עֵינֶ֜יךָ יָשִׂ֤ימוּ בְיָדָם֙ וְלָקָֽחוּ: וַיִּקְרָ֤א מֶֽלֶךְ־יִשְׂרָאֵל֙
לְכָל־זִקְנֵ֣י הָאָ֔רֶץ וַיֹּ֨אמֶר֙ דְּעֽוּ־נָ֣א וּרְא֔וּ כִּ֥י רָעָ֖ה זֶ֣ה מְבַקֵּ֑שׁ כִּֽי־שָׁלַ֨ח אֵלַ֜י
^ח לְנָשַׁ֤י וּלְבָנַי֙ וּלְכַסְפִּ֣י וְלִזְהָבִ֔י וְלֹ֥א מָנַ֖עְתִּי מִמֶּֽנּוּ: וַיֹּאמְר֥וּ אֵלָ֛יו כָּל־הַזְּקֵנִ֖ים
^ט וְכָל־הָעָ֑ם אַל־תִּשְׁמַ֖ע וְל֥וֹא תֹאבֶֽה: וַיֹּ֜אמֶר לְמַלְאֲכֵ֣י בֶן־הֲדַ֗ד אִמְר֞וּ
לַֽאדֹנִ֤י הַמֶּ֨לֶךְ֙ כֹּל֩ אֲשֶׁר־שָׁלַ֨חְתָּ אֶל־עַבְדְּךָ֤ בָרִֽאשֹׁנָה֙ אֶעֱשֶׂ֔ה וְהַדָּבָ֣ר
^י הַזֶּ֔ה לֹ֥א אוּכַ֖ל לַעֲשׂ֑וֹת וַיֵּֽלְכוּ֙ הַמַּלְאָכִ֔ים וַיְשִׁבֻ֖הוּ דָּבָֽר: וַיִּשְׁלַ֨ח אֵלָ֜יו בֶּן־
הֲדַ֗ד וַיֹּ֨אמֶר֙ כֹּֽה־יַעֲשׂ֥וּן לִ֛י אֱלֹהִ֖ים וְכֹ֣ה יוֹסִ֑פוּ אִם־יִשְׂפֹּק֙ עֲפַ֣ר שֹׁמְר֔וֹן
^{יא} לִשְׁעָלִ֕ים לְכָל־הָעָ֖ם אֲשֶׁ֥ר בְּרַגְלָֽי: וַיַּ֨עַן֙ מֶ֣לֶךְ־יִשְׂרָאֵ֔ל וַיֹּ֖אמֶר דַּבְּר֑וּ אַל־
^{יב} יִתְהַלֵּ֥ל חֹגֵ֖ר כִּמְפַתֵּֽחַ: וַיְהִ֗י כִּשְׁמֹ֨עַ֙ אֶת־הַדָּבָ֣ר הַזֶּ֔ה וְה֥וּא שֹׁתֶ֖ה ה֣וּא
וְהַמְּלָכִ֖ים בַּסֻּכּ֑וֹת וַיֹּ֤אמֶר אֶל־עֲבָדָיו֙ שִׂ֔ימוּ וַיָּשִׂ֖ימוּ עַל־הָעִֽיר: וְהִנֵּ֣ה ׀ נָבִ֣יא
^{יג} אֶחָ֗ד נִגַּשׁ֙ אֶל־אַחְאָ֣ב מֶֽלֶךְ־יִשְׂרָאֵ֔ל וַיֹּ֗אמֶר כֹּ֚ה אָמַ֣ר יְהֹוָ֔ה הֲרָאִ֕יתָ
אֵ֛ת כָּל־הֶהָמ֥וֹן הַגָּד֖וֹל הַזֶּ֑ה הִנְנִ֨י נֹתְנ֤וֹ בְיָֽדְךָ֙ הַיּ֔וֹם וְיָדַעְתָּ֖ כִּֽי־אֲנִ֥י יְהֹוָֽה:

19:20. Elijah thus tested Elisha's resolve (*Radak*).

20:5. Ahab had thought that Ben-hadad would demand tribute in the form of taxes and labor, to which Ahab meekly complied. Now Ben-hadad made it clear that he would actually carry women and children off to servitude in Aram (*Radak*).

20:6. Since Ahab had already agreed to relinquish his money, women, and children, what were these "precious" things that Ben-Hadad now demanded? The Sages (*Sanhedrin* 102b) explain that Ben-hadad now added that he would search for and confiscate the people's "precious" Torah scrolls. To this Ahab responded by summoning the elders (v. 7), for he felt that these treasures belonged to the nation, and he could not

give them away without consulting the elders (*Rashi; Radak*).

20:8. Ben-hadad's newly clarified demand for the Torah scrolls was too outrageous. According to the Sages, the elders, though they were idolaters, would not surrender the Torah itself, which symbolizes the very essence of Israel.

20:11. A warrior may boast of his prowess when he removes his sword belt after a victorious battle, but not when he is just beginning to arm himself to go out to the battlefield!

20:13. According to the Sages, Micaiah son of Imlah (see Ch. 22) is meant each time our chapter mentions a prophet.

in Israel seven thousand [people], all the knees that did not kneel to the Baal and every mouth that did not kiss it."

Elisha
follows
Elijah
 ¹⁹ So he went forth from there and he came upon Elisha son of Shaphat while he was plowing, twelve pairs [of oxen] going before him, he being with the twelfth, so Elijah went over to him and cast his mantle upon him. ²⁰ He left the oxen and ran after Elijah, and said, "Please let me kiss my father and mother, and then I shall go after you."

But he said to him, "Go, return, for what have I done to you?"*

²¹ [Elisha] turned back from following him; he took a pair of oxen and slaughtered them. He cooked the meat with the oxen's implements and gave [it] to the people, and they ate. He then arose and went after Elijah and ministered unto him.

20

Ahab
cravenly
submits to
Ben-hadad
¹ Ben-hadad king of Aram gathered together his whole army, and with him thirty-two kings, and horse and chariot; he went up and besieged Samaria and waged war against it. ² He sent messengers to Ahab king of Israel, into the city, ³ and said to him, "Thus said Ben-hadad: 'Your silver and your gold are mine, and your best women and children are mine.'"

⁴ The king of Israel replied, saying, "Just as you say, my lord the king; I and all I own are yours."

Ben-hadad
oversteps
⁵ The messengers returned [to Ahab] and said, "Thus spoke Ben-hadad, saying: I sent [word] to you, saying, 'Your silver and your gold and your women and your sons you shall give to me,'* ⁶ because at this time tomorrow, I shall send my servants to you, and they will search your house and the houses of your servants; and it shall be that everything precious in your eyes, * they will place in their hands and take [away].''

⁷ The king of Israel summoned all the elders of the land, and said, "Understand now and realize that this [man] is seeking evil, for he sent to me for my women and my children and my silver and my gold, and I did not withhold anything from him."

⁸ All the elders and all the people said to him, "Do not listen and do not consent!"*

⁹ So he said to Ben-hadad's messengers, "Tell my lord the king: Everything concerning which you sent word to your servant the first time I shall do, but this [second] thing I cannot do." The messengers left, and they brought back a reply.

Boast and
defiance
¹⁰ Ben-hadad sent word to [Ahab], saying, "Such may the gods do to me and such may they do further, if the dust of Samaria will be sufficient to [cover] the soles of all the people who accompany me!"

¹¹ The king of Israel replied, saying, "Tell [Hadad]: Let one who girds [his sword] not boast like one who unfastens [it]!"*

¹² It happened when [Ben-hadad] heard this reply, he was drinking — he and the [other] kings — in huts; he said to his servants, "Set up!" And they set up [for the attack] against the city.

God
promises
victory
¹³ Then behold, a certain prophet* approached Ahab, king of Israel, and said, "Thus said HASHEM: Have you seen all this great multitude [of people]? Behold, I shall deliver them into your hand today, and you will know that I am HASHEM."

יד וַיֹּאמֶר אַחְאָב בְּמִי וַיֹּאמֶר כֹּה־אָמַר יהוה בְּנַעֲרֵי שָׂרֵי הַמְּדִינוֹת וַיֹּאמֶר

טו מִי־יֶאְסֹר הַמִּלְחָמָה וַיֹּאמֶר אָתָּה: וַיִּפְקֹד אֶת־נַעֲרֵי שָׂרֵי הַמְּדִינוֹת וַיִּהְיוּ מָאתַיִם שְׁנַיִם וּשְׁלֹשִׁים וְאַחֲרֵיהֶם פָּקַד אֶת־כָּל־הָעָם כָּל־בְּנֵי יִשְׂרָאֵל

טז שִׁבְעַת אֲלָפִים: וַיֵּצְאוּ בַּצָּהֳרָיִם וּבֶן־הֲדַד שֹׁתֶה שִׁכּוֹר בַּסֻּכּוֹת הוּא

יז וְהַמְּלָכִים שְׁלֹשִׁים־וּשְׁנַיִם מֶלֶךְ עֹזֵר אֹתוֹ: וַיֵּצְאוּ נַעֲרֵי שָׂרֵי הַמְּדִינוֹת בָּרִאשֹׁנָה וַיִּשְׁלַח בֶּן־הֲדַד וַיַּגִּידוּ לוֹ לֵאמֹר אֲנָשִׁים יָצְאוּ מִשֹּׁמְרוֹן:

יח וַיֹּאמֶר אִם־לְשָׁלוֹם יָצָאוּ תִּפְשׂוּם חַיִּים וְאִם לְמִלְחָמָה יָצָאוּ חַיִּים

יט תִּפְשׂוּם: וְאֵלֶּה יָצְאוּ מִן־הָעִיר נַעֲרֵי שָׂרֵי הַמְּדִינוֹת וְהַחַיִל אֲשֶׁר

כ אַחֲרֵיהֶם: וַיַּכּוּ אִישׁ אִישׁוֹ וַיָּנֻסוּ אֲרָם וַיִּרְדְּפֵם יִשְׂרָאֵל וַיִּמָּלֵט בֶּן־הֲדַד

כא מֶלֶךְ אֲרָם עַל־סוּס וּפָרָשִׁים: וַיֵּצֵא מֶלֶךְ יִשְׂרָאֵל וַיַּךְ אֶת־הַסּוּס וְאֶת־

כב הָרָכֶב וְהִכָּה בַאֲרָם מַכָּה גְדוֹלָה: וַיִּגַּשׁ הַנָּבִיא אֶל־מֶלֶךְ יִשְׂרָאֵל וַיֹּאמֶר לוֹ לֵךְ הִתְחַזַּק וְדַע וּרְאֵה אֵת אֲשֶׁר־תַּעֲשֶׂה כִּי לִתְשׁוּבַת הַשָּׁנָה מֶלֶךְ אֲרָם עֹלֶה עָלֶיךָ:

כג וְעַבְדֵי מֶלֶךְ־אֲרָם אָמְרוּ אֵלָיו אֱלֹהֵי הָרִים אֱלֹהֵיהֶם עַל־כֵּן חָזְקוּ

כד מִמֶּנּוּ וְאוּלָם נִלָּחֵם אִתָּם בַּמִּישׁוֹר אִם־לֹא נֶחֱזַק מֵהֶם: וְאֶת־הַדָּבָר הַזֶּה עֲשֵׂה הָסֵר הַמְּלָכִים אִישׁ מִמְּקֹמוֹ וְשִׂים פַּחוֹת תַּחְתֵּיהֶם:

כה וְאַתָּה תִמְנֶה־לְךָ | חַיִל כַּחַיִל הַנֹּפֵל מֵאוֹתָךְ וְסוּס כַּסּוּס | וְרֶכֶב כָּרֶכֶב וְנִלָּחֲמָה אוֹתָם בַּמִּישׁוֹר אִם־לֹא נֶחֱזַק מֵהֶם וַיִּשְׁמַע לְקֹלָם וַיַּעַשׂ

כו כֵּן: וַיְהִי לִתְשׁוּבַת הַשָּׁנָה וַיִּפְקֹד בֶּן־הֲדַד אֶת־אֲרָם וַיַּעַל

כז אֲפֵקָה לַמִּלְחָמָה עִם־יִשְׂרָאֵל: וּבְנֵי יִשְׂרָאֵל הָתְפָּקְדוּ וְכָלְכְּלוּ וַיֵּלְכוּ לִקְרָאתָם וַיַּחֲנוּ בְנֵי־יִשְׂרָאֵל נֶגְדָּם כִּשְׁנֵי חֲשִׂפֵי עִזִּים וַאֲרָם מִלְאוּ אֶת־

כח הָאָרֶץ: וַיִּגַּשׁ אִישׁ הָאֱלֹהִים וַיֹּאמֶר אֶל־מֶלֶךְ יִשְׂרָאֵל וַיֹּאמֶר כֹּה־אָמַר יהוה יַעַן אֲשֶׁר אָמְרוּ אֲרָם אֱלֹהֵי הָרִים יהוה וְלֹא־אֱלֹהֵי עֲמָקִים הוּא וְנָתַתִּי אֶת־כָּל־הֶהָמוֹן הַגָּדוֹל הַזֶּה בְּיָדֶךָ וִידַעְתֶּם כִּי־אֲנִי יהוה:

כט וַיַּחֲנוּ אֵלֶּה נֹכַח אֵלֶּה שִׁבְעַת יָמִים וַיְהִי | בַּיּוֹם הַשְּׁבִיעִי וַתִּקְרַב הַמִּלְחָמָה וַיַּכּוּ בְנֵי־יִשְׂרָאֵל אֶת־אֲרָם מֵאָה־אֶלֶף רַגְלִי בְּיוֹם אֶחָד:

ל וַיָּנֻסוּ הַנּוֹתָרִים | אֲפֵקָה אֶל־הָעִיר וַתִּפֹּל הַחוֹמָה עַל־עֶשְׂרִים וְשִׁבְעָה אֶלֶף אִישׁ הַנּוֹתָרִים וּבֶן־הֲדַד נָס וַיָּבֹא אֶל־הָעִיר חֶדֶר בְּחָדֶר:

20:14. These youths had been sent to be educated and trained in the capital city.

20:15. *Rashi* explains that these were the people whose "knees did not kneel to the Baal" (see 19:18).

20:20. The scouts who had gone out to capture the youths were caught off guard by their daring, and were utterly routed.

20:22. Do not let your victory lead to complacency!

Act righteously so that you will merit God's miraculous intervention the next time Ben-hadad attacks (*Radak*).

20:24. Soldiers from the lower ranks will fight harder in order to make a name for themselves (*Rashi*).

20:27. The verse compares the two armies. The Aramean force was immense while the Israelites consisted of two paltry groups: the two hundred thirty-

¹⁴ *Ahab asked, "Through whom?"*

And he answered, "Thus said HASHEM: *Through the young [sons] of the officers of the provinces."* *

[Ahab] then asked, "Who will lead the battle?"

And he answered, "You!"

Ahab's great triumph   ¹⁵ *[Ahab] counted the young [sons] of the officers of the provinces, and they were two hundred and thirty-two. Afterwards he counted all the people — all the Children of Israel — [and they were] seven thousand.* *

¹⁶ *They went forth [from the city] at noontime, while Ben-hadad was drinking himself drunk — he and the thirty-two kings who helped him — in [their] huts.* ¹⁷ *The young [sons] of the officers of the provinces went out first. Ben-hadad had sent out [scouts], who now told him, saying, "Some men have left Samaria!"*

¹⁸ *He said, "If they have come forth in peace, capture them alive; and if they have come forth for war, capture them alive."*

¹⁹ *But these — the young [sons] of the officers of the provinces — went forth from the city, with the army that was behind them;* ²⁰ *and each man struck down his opponent.* * *Aram fled, and Israel chased after them; Ben-hadad, king of Aram, escaped on a horse, with horsemen.* ²¹ *The king of Israel then came out and struck down the horse and the chariot, and struck a severe blow in Aram.*

²² *The prophet approached the king of Israel and said to him, "Go and strengthen yourself; understand and realize what you should do,* * *for at the turn of the year the king of Aram will come up against you [again]."*

Aram prepares a new attack   ²³ *The servants of the king of Aram told him, "Their God is a God of mountains, and therefore they were stronger than us; but, let us fight them on the plain, [see] if we will not be stronger than them!* ²⁴ *This thing shall you do: Remove the kings, each one from his post, and replace them with captains.* * ²⁵ *And count out for yourselves an army like the army that fell from you, and horse like horse, and chariot like chariot; we will fight them on the plain, and [see] if we do not overpower them!" He hearkened to their voice and did so.*

²⁶ *It happened at the turn of the year that Ben-hadad counted Aram, and he went up to Aphek to wage war against Israel.* ²⁷ *The Children of Israel were counted and outfitted, and they went towards them. The Children of Israel encamped opposite them like two groups of goats, while Aram filled the land.* *

A prophet assures Ahab   ²⁸ *The man of God approached and spoke to the king of Israel and said, "Thus said* HASHEM: *Because Aram said, '*HASHEM *is a God of mountains and not a God of lowlands,' I shall deliver all this great multitude into your hand, and you will know that I am* HASHEM."

Aram is routed   ²⁹ *They were encamped one opposite the other for a seven-day period. It happened on the seventh day that the battle was joined, and the Children of Israel struck down Aram — a hundred thousand foot soldiers in one day.* ³⁰ *The remainder fled to Aphek,* * *into the city, and the [city] wall fell over upon the twenty-seven thousand surviving men. Ben-hadad fled, and entered into the city, [hiding] in a room within a room.*

---

two youths, and the seven thousand soldiers (*Me-tzudos*).   **20:30.** Aphek was in the territory of the Kingdom of Judah, which had a peace treaty with Aram (see 15:18-20).

לא וַיֹּאמְר֣וּ אֵלָ֡יו עֲבָדָיו֩ הִנֵּה־נָ֨א שָׁמַ֜עְנוּ כִּ֗י מַלְכֵי֙ בֵּ֣ית יִשְׂרָאֵ֔ל כִּֽי־מַלְכֵ֥י חֶ֖סֶד הֵ֑ם נָשִׂ֣ימָה נָּא֩ שַׂקִּ֨ים בְּמָתְנֵ֜ינוּ וַחֲבָלִ֣ים בְּרֹאשֵׁ֗נוּ וְנֵצֵא֙ אֶל־מֶ֣לֶךְ

לב יִשְׂרָאֵ֔ל אוּלַ֖י יְחַיֶּ֥ה אֶת־נַפְשֶֽׁךָ: וַיַּחְגְּר֣וּ שַׂקִּ֣ים בְּמָתְנֵיהֶ֗ם וַחֲבָלִים֮ בְּרֹאשֵׁיהֶם֒ וַיָּבֹ֙אוּ֙ אֶל־מֶ֣לֶךְ יִשְׂרָאֵ֔ל וַיֹּ֣אמְר֔וּ עַבְדְּךָ֧ בֶן־הֲדַ֛ד אָמַ֖ר תְּחִֽי־

לג נָ֣א נַפְשִׁ֑י וַיֹּ֙אמֶר֙ הַעוֹדֶ֣נּוּ חַ֔י אָחִ֖י הֽוּא: וְהָאֲנָשִׁ֞ים יְנַחֲשׁ֙וּ֙ וַֽיְמַהֲר֔וּ וַיַּחְלְט֣וּ הֲמִמֶּ֗נּוּ וַיֹּֽאמְרוּ֙ אָחִ֣יךָ בֶן־הֲדַ֔ד וַיֹּ֖אמֶר בֹּ֣אוּ קָחֻ֑הוּ וַיֵּצֵ֤א אֵלָיו֙ בֶּן־הֲדַ֔ד

לד וַֽיַּעֲלֵ֖הוּ עַל־הַמֶּרְכָּבָֽה: וַיֹּ֣אמֶר אֵלָ֡יו הֶעָרִ֣ים אֲשֶׁר־לָֽקַח־אָבִי֩ מֵאֵ֨ת אָבִ֜יךָ אָשִׁ֗יב וְֽחוּצ֞וֹת תָּשִׂ֤ים לְךָ֙ בְדַמֶּ֔שֶׂק כַּאֲשֶׁר־שָׂ֥ם אָבִ֖י בְּשֹׁמְר֑וֹן וַאֲנִ֤י

לה בַבְּרִית֙ אֲשַׁלְּחֶ֔ךָ וַיִּכְרָת־ל֥וֹ בְרִ֖ית וַֽיְשַׁלְּחֵֽהוּ: וְאִ֜ישׁ אֶחָ֣ד מִבְּנֵ֣י הַנְּבִיאִ֗ים אָמַ֤ר אֶל־רֵעֵ֙הוּ֙ בִּדְבַ֣ר יְהוָ֔ה הַכֵּ֖ינִי נָ֑א וַיְמָאֵ֥ן

לו הָאִ֖ישׁ לְהַכֹּתֽוֹ: וַיֹּ֣אמֶר ל֗וֹ יַ֚עַן אֲשֶׁ֤ר לֹֽא־שָׁמַ֙עְתָּ֙ בְּק֣וֹל יְהוָ֔ה הִנְּךָ֤ הוֹלֵךְ֙ מֵֽאִתִּ֔י וְהִכְּךָ֖ הָאַרְיֵ֑ה וַיֵּ֙לֶךְ֙ מֵֽאֶצְל֔וֹ וַיִּמְצָאֵ֥הוּ הָאַרְיֵ֖ה וַיַּכֵּֽהוּ: וַיִּמְצָא֩

לז אִ֨ישׁ אַחֵ֜ר וַיֹּ֣אמֶר הַכֵּ֣ינִי נָ֑א וַיַּכֵּ֥הוּ הָאִ֖ישׁ הַכֵּ֥ה וּפָצֹֽעַ: וַיֵּ֙לֶךְ֙ הַנָּבִ֔יא וַיַּעֲמֹ֥ד

לח לַמֶּ֖לֶךְ עַל־הַדָּ֑רֶךְ וַיִּתְחַפֵּ֥שׂ בָּאֲפֵ֖ר עַל־עֵינָֽיו: וַיְהִ֤י הַמֶּ֙לֶךְ֙ עֹבֵ֔ר וְה֖וּא

לט צָעַ֣ק אֶל־הַמֶּ֑לֶךְ וַיֹּ֡אמֶר עַבְדְּךָ֣ ׀ יָצָ֣א בְקֶֽרֶב־הַמִּלְחָמָ֗ה וְהִנֵּֽה־אִ֣ישׁ סָ֡ר וַיָּבֵא֩ אֵלַ֨י אִ֜ישׁ וַיֹּ֗אמֶר שְׁמֹר֙ אֶת־הָאִ֣ישׁ הַזֶּ֔ה אִם־הִפָּקֵד֙ יִפָּקֵ֔ד וְהָיְתָ֤ה

מ נַפְשְׁךָ֙ תַּ֣חַת נַפְשׁ֔וֹ א֥וֹ כִכַּר־כֶּ֖סֶף תִּשְׁקֽוֹל: וַיְהִ֣י עַבְדְּךָ֗ עֹשֵׂ֥ה הֵ֙נָּה֙ וָהֵ֔נָּה

מא וְה֖וּא אֵינֶ֑נּוּ וַיֹּ֤אמֶר אֵלָיו֙ מֶ֣לֶךְ־יִשְׂרָאֵ֔ל כֵּ֥ן מִשְׁפָּטֶ֖ךָ אַתָּ֥ה חָרָֽצְתָּ: וַיְמַהֵ֕ר וַיָּ֙סַר֙ אֶת־הָ֣אֲפֵ֔ר מֵעַ֖ל [מֵעֲלֵ֖י ק] עֵינָ֑יו וַיַּכֵּ֤ר אֹתוֹ֙ מֶ֣לֶךְ יִשְׂרָאֵ֔ל כִּ֥י

מב מֵֽהַנְּבִאִ֖ים הֽוּא: וַיֹּ֣אמֶר אֵלָ֗יו כֹּ֚ה אָמַ֣ר יְהוָ֔ה יַ֛עַן שִׁלַּ֥חְתָּ אֶת־

מג אִישׁ־חֶרְמִ֖י מִיָּ֑ד וְהָיְתָ֤ה נַפְשְׁךָ֙ תַּ֣חַת נַפְשׁ֔וֹ וְעַמְּךָ֖ תַּ֥חַת עַמּֽוֹ: וַיֵּ֧לֶךְ

א מֶֽלֶךְ־יִשְׂרָאֵ֛ל עַל־בֵּית֖וֹ סַ֣ר וְזָעֵ֑ף וַיָּבֹ֖א שֹׁמְרֽוֹנָה: וַיְהִ֗י

כא

אַחַר֙ הַדְּבָרִ֣ים הָאֵ֔לֶּה כֶּ֧רֶם הָיָ֛ה לְנָב֥וֹת הַיִּזְרְעֵאלִ֖י אֲשֶׁ֣ר בְּיִזְרְעֶ֑אל

ב אֵ֚צֶל הֵיכַ֣ל אַחְאָ֔ב מֶ֖לֶךְ שֹׁמְרֽוֹן: וַיְדַבֵּ֣ר אַחְאָ֣ב אֶל־נָב֣וֹת ׀ לֵאמֹר֩ תְּנָה־לִּ֨י אֶֽת־כַּרְמְךָ֜ וִיהִי־לִ֣י לְגַן־יָרָ֗ק כִּ֣י ה֤וּא קָרוֹב֙ אֵ֣צֶל בֵּיתִ֔י וְאֶתְּנָ֤ה לְךָ֙ תַּחְתָּ֔יו כֶּ֖רֶם ט֣וֹב מִמֶּ֑נּוּ אִ֣ם ט֣וֹב בְּעֵינֶ֗יךָ אֶתְּנָה־לְךָ֥ כֶ֖סֶף

ג מְחִ֥יר זֶֽה: וַיֹּ֥אמֶר נָב֖וֹת אֶל־אַחְאָ֑ב חָלִ֤ילָה לִּי֙ מֵֽיהוָ֔ה מִתִּתִּ֥י אֶת־

ד נַחֲלַ֥ת אֲבֹתַ֖י לָֽךְ: וַיָּבֹא֩ אַחְאָ֨ב אֶל־בֵּית֜וֹ סַ֣ר וְזָעֵ֗ף עַל־הַדָּבָר֙ אֲשֶׁר־ דִּבֶּ֣ר אֵלָ֗יו נָבוֹת֙ הַיִּזְרְעֵאלִ֔י וַיֹּ֕אמֶר לֹֽא־אֶתֵּ֣ן לְךָ֔ אֶת־נַחֲלַ֖ת אֲבוֹתָ֑י

20:35. The same prophet who had brought God's word to Ahab several times in this chapter. Now he was to convey a new prophecy to the king: Ahab had been commanded prophetically to destroy the Arameans, yet he had chosen to be gracious and treat Ben-hadad like a brother. But mercy to the evil is in itself a manifestation of cruelty, for the surviving evildoer will cause others to suffer (*Radak*).

20:36. Since he was a known prophet, his command in God's Name (v. 35) had the force of a Divine command. Just as this man was punished for putting his own sense of propriety and leniency before the express command of God, so would Ahab meet a similar fate (*Rashi*).

Ahab's
mercy to
Ben-hadad
— an
alliance . . .

³¹ *His servants said to him, "Behold, we have heard that the kings of the House of Israel are merciful kings; let us put sackcloth on our loins and ropes upon our heads and go forth to the king of Israel — perhaps he will let you live."* ³² *So they girded their loins with sackcloth and [put] ropes upon their heads, and they came to the king of Israel and said, "Your servant Ben-hadad said, 'Please let me live!' "*

[Ahab] said, "Is he still alive? He is my brother!"

³³ *The men interpreted this as a [good] omen and seized upon the expression from him, and said, "Your brother Ben-hadad."*

And [Ahab] said, "Go and bring him."

So Ben-hadad came out to him, and [Ahab] helped him onto the chariot. ³⁴ *[Ben-hadad] said to him, "The cities that my father took from your father, I shall return; and you may control markets in Damascus, just as my father did in Samaria."*

[Ahab agreed,] "And with this covenant I shall send you off." So he sealed a covenant with him and sent him off.

The penalty
for misplaced
mercy

³⁵ *One man, of the disciples of the prophets,* * *said to his fellow, "By the word of* HASHEM, *please hit me!" But the man refused to hit him.* ³⁶ *He then said to him, "Because you did not listen to the voice of* HASHEM, *behold, when you go away from me a lion will strike you down!"* * *He went away from him, and a lion came upon him and struck him down.*

³⁷ *He then found another man and said, "Please hit me!" The man struck him, hitting [him] and wounding [him].* ³⁸ *The prophet then went and stood [awaiting] the king on the road, and disguised himself with a scarf over his eyes.* ³⁹ *As the king passed by he cried out to the king; he said, "Your servant had gone out to the thick of the battle, when behold, one man turned aside, and brought to me a man, saying, 'Guard this man; if he will be missing, your soul will be instead of his soul, or you will weigh out [as a fine] a talent of silver.'* ⁴⁰ *Your servant was busy going here and there, and [now] he is gone!"*

So the king of Israel said to him, "The judgment against you is fair; you have decided it!"

⁴¹ *Quickly he removed the scarf from his eyes, and the king of Israel recognized him, that he was one of the prophets.* ⁴² *[The prophet] said to him, "Thus said* HASHEM: *Because you sent forth from [your] hand the man whom I had condemned to destruction, your life shall be in place of his life, and your people instead of his people!"* ⁴³ *The king of Israel went to his house angry and upset, and he came to Samaria.*

21

¹ *It happened after these events: There was a vineyard [belonging] to Naboth the Jezreelite in Jezreel that was adjacent to the palace of Ahab, king of Samaria.* ² *Ahab spoke to Naboth, saying, "Give me your vineyard, so that I may have it as an herb garden, for it is close by my house; in its place I will give you a better vineyard, or, if you prefer, I will give you its price in money."*

Naboth
rebuffs
Ahab

³ *But Naboth said to Ahab, "Far be it from me before* HASHEM *that I should give you my ancestors' heritage!"*

⁴ *Ahab came home sullen and angry over the matter that Naboth the Jezreelite had spoken to him, [when] he said, "I will not give you my ancestors' herit-*

ה וַיִּשְׁכַּב֙ עַל־מִטָּת֔וֹ וַיַּסֵּ֖ב אֶת־פָּנָ֑יו וְלֹֽא־אָ֖כַל לָֽחֶם׃ וַתָּבֹ֤א אֵלָיו֙ אִיזֶ֣בֶל

ו אִשְׁתּ֔וֹ וַתְּדַבֵּ֣ר אֵלָ֔יו מַה־זֶּה֙ רֽוּחֲךָ֣ סָרָ֔ה וְאֵינְךָ֖ אֹכֵ֥ל לָֽחֶם׃ וַיְדַבֵּ֣ר אֵלֶ֗יהָ

כִּֽי־אֲדַבֵּ֣ר אֶל־נָבוֹת֩ הַיִּזְרְעֵאלִ֨י וָאֹ֜מַר ל֗וֹ תְּנָה־לִּ֤י אֶֽת־כַּרְמְךָ֙ בְּכֶ֔סֶף א֚וֹ

אִם־חָפֵ֣ץ אַתָּ֔ה אֶתְּנָה־לְךָ֥ כֶ֖רֶם תַּחְתָּ֑יו וַיֹּ֕אמֶר לֹֽא־אֶתֵּ֥ן לְךָ֖ אֶת־

ז כַּרְמִֽי׃ וַתֹּ֤אמֶר אֵלָיו֙ אִיזֶ֣בֶל אִשְׁתּ֔וֹ אַתָּ֕ה עַתָּ֛ה תַּעֲשֶׂ֥ה מְלוּכָ֖ה עַל־

יִשְׂרָאֵ֑ל ק֤וּם אֱכָל־לֶ֙חֶם֙ וְיִטַ֣ב לִבֶּ֔ךָ אֲנִ֣י אֶתֵּ֣ן לְךָ֔ אֶת־כֶּ֖רֶם נָב֥וֹת

ח הַיִּזְרְעֵאלִֽי׃ וַתִּכְתֹּ֤ב סְפָרִים֙ בְּשֵׁ֣ם אַחְאָ֔ב וַתַּחְתֹּ֖ם בְּחֹתָמ֑וֹ וַתִּשְׁלַ֣ח

°הַסְּפָרִים [°סְפָרִ֗ים ק] אֶל־הַזְּקֵנִ֤ים וְאֶל־הַֽחֹרִים֙ אֲשֶׁ֣ר בְּעִיר֔וֹ הַיֹּשְׁבִ֖ים

ט אֶת־נָבֽוֹת׃ וַתִּכְתֹּ֥ב בַּסְּפָרִ֖ים לֵאמֹ֑ר קִרְאוּ־צ֔וֹם וְהוֹשִׁ֥יבוּ אֶת־נָב֖וֹת

י בְּרֹ֥אשׁ הָעָֽם׃ וְ֠הוֹשִׁ֠יבוּ שְׁנַ֨יִם אֲנָשִׁ֥ים בְּנֵֽי־בְלִיַּ֖עַל נֶגְדּ֑וֹ וִיעִדֻ֣הוּ לֵאמֹ֔ר

יא בֵּרַ֥כְתָּ אֱלֹהִ֖ים וָמֶ֑לֶךְ וְהוֹצִיאֻ֥הוּ וְסִקְלֻ֖הוּ וְיָמֹֽת׃ וַיַּעֲשׂ֣וּ אַנְשֵׁ֣י עִיר֡וֹ הַזְּקֵנִ֣ים

וְהַֽחֹרִ֡ים אֲשֶׁ֣ר הַיֹּשְׁבִים֩ בְּעִיר֨וֹ כַּאֲשֶׁ֜ר שָׁלְחָ֤ה אֲלֵיהֶם֙ אִיזָ֔בֶל כַּֽאֲשֶׁ֤ר

יב כָּתוּב֙ בַּסְּפָרִ֔ים אֲשֶׁ֥ר שָׁלְחָ֖ה אֲלֵיהֶ֑ם קָרְא֥וּ צוֹם֙ וְהֹשִׁ֥יבוּ אֶת־נָב֖וֹת

יג בְּרֹ֥אשׁ הָעָֽם׃ וַ֠יָּבֹ֠אוּ שְׁנֵ֨י הָאֲנָשִׁ֥ים בְּנֵֽי־בְלִיַּעַל֮ וַיֵּשְׁב֣וּ נֶגְדּוֹ֒ וַ֠יְעִדֻ֠הוּ אַנְשֵׁ֣י

הַבְּלִיַּ֜עַל אֶת־נָב֗וֹת נֶ֤גֶד הָעָם֙ לֵאמֹ֔ר בֵּרַ֥ךְ נָב֛וֹת אֱלֹהִ֖ים וָמֶ֑לֶךְ וַיֹּצִאֻ֙הוּ֙

יד מִח֣וּץ לָעִ֔יר וַיִּסְקְלֻ֥הוּ בָאֲבָנִ֖ים וַיָּמֹֽת׃ וַֽיִּשְׁלְח֖וּ אֶל־אִיזֶ֣בֶל לֵאמֹ֑ר סֻקַּ֥ל

טו נָב֖וֹת וַיָּמֹֽת׃ וַיְהִ֞י כִּשְׁמֹ֤עַ אִיזֶ֙בֶל֙ כִּֽי־סֻקַּ֥ל נָב֖וֹת וַיָּמֹ֑ת וַתֹּ֤אמֶר אִיזֶ֙בֶל֙ אֶל־

אַחְאָ֗ב ק֣וּם רֵ֞שׁ אֶת־כֶּ֣רֶם ׀ נָב֣וֹת הַיִּזְרְעֵאלִ֗י אֲשֶׁ֤ר מֵאֵן֙ לָתֶת־לְךָ֣ בְכֶ֔סֶף

טז כִּ֣י אֵ֥ין נָב֖וֹת חַ֣י כִּי־מֵֽת׃ וַיְהִ֗י כִּשְׁמֹ֤עַ אַחְאָב֙ כִּ֣י מֵ֣ת נָב֔וֹת וַיָּ֣קָם אַחְאָ֗ב

לָרֶ֛דֶת אֶל־כֶּ֛רֶם נָב֥וֹת הַיִּזְרְעֵאלִ֖י לְרִשְׁתּֽוֹ׃   וַיְהִ֤י דְבַר־

יז יְהֹוָ֔ה אֶל־אֵלִיָּ֥הוּ הַתִּשְׁבִּ֖י לֵאמֹֽר׃ ק֣וּם רֵ֗ד לִקְרַ֛את אַחְאָ֥ב מֶ֥לֶךְ־

יח יִשְׂרָאֵ֖ל אֲשֶׁ֣ר בְּשֹׁמְר֑וֹן הִנֵּה֙ בְּכֶ֣רֶם נָב֔וֹת אֲשֶׁר־יָ֥רַד שָׁ֖ם לְרִשְׁתּֽוֹ׃ וְדִבַּרְתָּ֨

יט אֵלָ֜יו לֵאמֹ֗ר כֹּ֚ה אָמַ֣ר יְהֹוָ֔ה הֲרָצַ֖חְתָּ וְגַם־יָרָ֑שְׁתָּ וְדִבַּרְתָּ֨ אֵלָ֜יו לֵאמֹ֗ר

כֹּ֚ה אָמַ֣ר יְהֹוָ֔ה בִּמְק֗וֹם אֲשֶׁ֨ר לָקְק֤וּ הַכְּלָבִים֙ אֶת־דַּ֣ם נָב֔וֹת יָלֹ֧קּוּ

כ הַכְּלָבִ֛ים אֶת־דָּמְךָ֖ גַּם־אָֽתָּה׃ וַיֹּ֤אמֶר אַחְאָב֙ אֶל־אֵ֣לִיָּ֔הוּ הַֽמְצָאתַ֖נִי אֹיְבִ֑י

כא וַיֹּ֣אמֶר מָצָ֔אתִי יַ֚עַן הִתְמַכֶּרְךָ֔ לַעֲשׂ֥וֹת הָרַ֖ע בְּעֵינֵ֣י יְהֹוָֽה׃ הִנְנִ֨י °מֵבִ֤י

[°מֵבִ֤יא ק] אֵלֶ֙יךָ֙ רָעָ֔ה וּבִעַרְתִּ֖י אַחֲרֶ֑יךָ וְהִכְרַתִּ֤י לְאַחְאָב֙ מַשְׁתִּ֣ין בְּקִ֔יר

כב וְעָצ֥וּר וְעָז֖וּב בְּיִשְׂרָאֵֽל׃ וְנָתַתִּ֣י אֶת־בֵּֽיתְךָ֗ כְּבֵית֙ יָרׇבְעָ֣ם בֶּן־נְבָ֔ט

וּכְבֵ֖ית בַּעְשָׁ֣א בֶן־אֲחִיָּ֑ה אֶל־הַכַּ֙עַס֙ אֲשֶׁ֣ר הִכְעַ֔סְתָּ וַֽתַּחֲטִ֖א אֶת־יִשְׂרָאֵֽל׃

21:8. Although the people could not or would not control Ahab and Jezebel's idolatry, they would not tolerate royal injustice. Thus, Jezebel resorted to the only "legal" avenue available: to conspire with corrupt officials to convict Naboth of a capital offense, thus allowing the king to confiscate his property (*Radak*; see v. 15).

21:9. Fast days were proclaimed in order to assemble the

people for collective prayer and to determine what sins had to be remedied (*Rashi*).

21:10. This is a euphemism for blasphemy and cursing. Both the one who blasphemes and the one who curses the king are liable to death.

21:15. The Talmud gives two opinions for Ahab's "right" to the property: (a) Naboth was put to death for *age." He lay on his bed, turned his face [to the wall] and would not eat any food.*

Jezebel to the rescue ⁵ His wife Jezebel came to him and spoke to him, "Why is it that your mood is so sullen and you do not eat any food?"

⁶ He said to her, "Because I spoke to Naboth the Jezreelite, and said to him, 'Give me your vineyard for money, or, if you prefer, I will give you a[nother] vineyard in its place.' But he said, 'I will not give you my vineyard.' "

⁷ His wife Jezebel said to him, "Are you now exercising your sovereignty over Israel? Arise. Eat some food, and let your heart be. I shall present you with the vineyard of Naboth the Jezreelite!"

Jezebel's plan . . . ⁸ She then wrote scrolls in Ahab's name, sealing them with his signet, and she sent scrolls to the elders and the officials who were in his city, who dwelt with Naboth.* ⁹ She wrote in the scrolls, saying, "Declare a fast,* and seat Naboth at the head of the people. ¹⁰ Then seat two unscrupulous people opposite him, who will testify against him, saying, 'You blessed* God and the king!' Then take him out and stone him, so he will die."

. . . to kill an innocent man ¹¹ The men of his city — the elders and the officials who dwelt in his city — did as Jezebel had sent [word] to them, as was written in the scrolls that she had sent them. ¹² They declared a fast and seated Naboth at the head of the people. ¹³ Two unscrupulous men came and sat opposite him, and the unscrupulous men testified against Naboth in the presence of the people, saying, "Naboth has 'blessed' God and the king." Then they took him outside of the city and stoned him with stones, and he died.

¹⁴ They then sent word to Jezebel, saying, "Naboth has been stoned and has died."

Ahab occupies the vineyard ¹⁵ When Jezebel heard that Naboth had been stoned and had died, Jezebel said to Ahab, "Arise and inherit* the vineyard of Naboth the Jezreelite, which he had refused to give you for money; for Naboth is not alive, for he is dead." ¹⁶ When Ahab heard that Naboth had died, Ahab arose to go down to the vineyard of Naboth the Jezreelite, to inherit it.

Elijah rebukes him . . . ¹⁷ The word of HASHEM then came to Elijah the Tishbite, saying, ¹⁸ "Arise and go down to meet Ahab, king of Israel, who [lives] in Samaria; behold he is at the vineyard of Naboth, which he has gone down to inherit. ¹⁹ You shall speak to him, saying, 'Thus said HASHEM: Will you murder and also inherit?' Then you shall speak to him [further], saying, 'Thus said HASHEM: In the place where the dogs licked up the blood of Naboth, the dogs will lick up your blood as well.' "

²⁰ Ahab said to Elijah, "Have you found me [guilty], my adversary?"

. . . with a fearsome curse He said, "I have found [you guilty], because you have sold yourself to do what is evil in the eyes of HASHEM. ²¹ Behold! [says HASHEM] I am bringing evil upon you, and I shall annihilate after you, and I shall eliminate [every] male offspring* from Ahab and all property, whether hidden or public, in Israel. ²² And I shall set your house like the house of Jeroboam son of Nebat and like the house of Baasa son of Ahijah, because of the provocation with which you have provoked [Me], and because you caused Israel to sin.*

---

sedition against the king and such a person forfeits his property to the royal estate; or (b) Ahab was Naboth's next of kin, and thus his legal heir.
21:21. See 14:10.

כג וְגַם־לְאִיזֶבֶל דִּבֶּר יהוה לֵאמֹר הַכְּלָבִים יֹאכְלוּ אֶת־אִיזֶבֶל בְּחֵל
כד יִזְרְעֶאל: הַמֵּת לְאַחְאָב בָּעִיר יֹאכְלוּ הַכְּלָבִים וְהַמֵּת בַּשָּׂדֶה יֹאכְלוּ עוֹף
כה הַשָּׁמָיִם: רַק לֹא־הָיָה כְאַחְאָב אֲשֶׁר הִתְמַכֵּר לַעֲשׂוֹת הָרַע בְּעֵינֵי יהוה
כו אֲשֶׁר־הֵסַתָּה אֹתוֹ אִיזֶבֶל אִשְׁתּוֹ: וַיַּתְעֵב מְאֹד לָלֶכֶת אַחֲרֵי הַגִּלֻּלִים
כז כְּכֹל אֲשֶׁר עָשׂוּ הָאֱמֹרִי אֲשֶׁר הוֹרִישׁ יהוה מִפְּנֵי בְּנֵי יִשְׂרָאֵל: וַיְהִי
כִשְׁמֹעַ אַחְאָב אֶת־הַדְּבָרִים הָאֵלֶּה וַיִּקְרַע בְּגָדָיו וַיָּשֶׂם־שַׂק עַל־
כח בְּשָׂרוֹ וַיָּצוֹם וַיִּשְׁכַּב בַּשָּׂק וַיְהַלֵּךְ אַט: וַיְהִי דְּבַר־
כט יהוה אֶל־אֵלִיָּהוּ הַתִּשְׁבִּי לֵאמֹר: הֲרָאִיתָ כִּי־נִכְנַע אַחְאָב מִלְּפָנָי
יַעַן כִּי־נִכְנַע מִפָּנַי לֹא־[°אָבִי אָבִיא ק] הָרָעָה בְּיָמָיו בִּימֵי בְנוֹ אָבִיא

כב א הָרָעָה עַל־בֵּיתוֹ: וַיֵּשְׁבוּ שָׁלֹשׁ שָׁנִים אֵין מִלְחָמָה בֵּין אֲרָם וּבֵין
יִשְׂרָאֵל:
ב וַיְהִי בַּשָּׁנָה הַשְּׁלִישִׁית וַיֵּרֶד יְהוֹשָׁפָט מֶלֶךְ־יְהוּדָה אֶל־מֶלֶךְ יִשְׂרָאֵל:
ג וַיֹּאמֶר מֶלֶךְ־יִשְׂרָאֵל אֶל־עֲבָדָיו הַיְדַעְתֶּם כִּי־לָנוּ רָמֹת גִּלְעָד וַאֲנַחְנוּ
ד מַחְשִׁים מִקַּחַת אֹתָהּ מִיַּד מֶלֶךְ אֲרָם: וַיֹּאמֶר אֶל־יְהוֹשָׁפָט הֲתֵלֵךְ
אִתִּי לַמִּלְחָמָה רָמֹת גִּלְעָד וַיֹּאמֶר יְהוֹשָׁפָט אֶל־מֶלֶךְ יִשְׂרָאֵל כָּמוֹנִי
ה כָמוֹךָ כְּעַמִּי כְעַמֶּךָ כְּסוּסַי כְּסוּסֶיךָ: וַיֹּאמֶר יְהוֹשָׁפָט אֶל־מֶלֶךְ יִשְׂרָאֵל
ו דְּרָשׁ־נָא כַיּוֹם אֶת־דְּבַר יהוה: וַיִּקְבֹּץ מֶלֶךְ־יִשְׂרָאֵל אֶת־הַנְּבִיאִים
כְּאַרְבַּע מֵאוֹת אִישׁ וַיֹּאמֶר אֲלֵהֶם הַאֵלֵךְ עַל־רָמֹת גִּלְעָד לַמִּלְחָמָה
ז אִם־אֶחְדָּל וַיֹּאמְרוּ עֲלֵה וְיִתֵּן אֲדֹנָי בְּיַד הַמֶּלֶךְ: וַיֹּאמֶר יְהוֹשָׁפָט הַאֵין
ח פֹּה נָבִיא לַיהוה עוֹד וְנִדְרְשָׁה מֵאֹתוֹ: וַיֹּאמֶר מֶלֶךְ־יִשְׂרָאֵל ׀ אֶל־
יְהוֹשָׁפָט עוֹד אִישׁ־אֶחָד לִדְרֹשׁ אֶת־יהוה מֵאֹתוֹ וַאֲנִי שְׂנֵאתִיו כִּי לֹא־
יִתְנַבֵּא עָלַי טוֹב כִּי אִם־רָע מִיכָיְהוּ בֶן־יִמְלָה וַיֹּאמֶר יְהוֹשָׁפָט אַל־יֹאמַר
ט הַמֶּלֶךְ כֵּן: וַיִּקְרָא מֶלֶךְ יִשְׂרָאֵל אֶל־סָרִיס אֶחָד וַיֹּאמֶר מַהֲרָה מִיכָיְהוּ
י בֶן־יִמְלָה: וּמֶלֶךְ יִשְׂרָאֵל וִיהוֹשָׁפָט מֶלֶךְ־יְהוּדָה יֹשְׁבִים אִישׁ עַל־כִּסְאוֹ
מְלֻבָּשִׁים בְּגָדִים בְּגֹרֶן פֶּתַח שַׁעַר שֹׁמְרוֹן וְכָל־הַנְּבִיאִים מִתְנַבְּאִים
יא לִפְנֵיהֶם: וַיַּעַשׂ לוֹ צִדְקִיָּה בֶן־כְּנַעֲנָה קַרְנֵי בַרְזֶל וַיֹּאמֶר כֹּה־אָמַר יהוה
יב בְּאֵלֶּה תְּנַגַּח אֶת־אֲרָם עַד־כַּלֹּתָם: וְכָל־הַנְּבִאִים נִבְּאִים כֵּן לֵאמֹר
יג עֲלֵה רָמֹת גִּלְעָד וְהַצְלַח וְנָתַן יהוה בְּיַד הַמֶּלֶךְ: וְהַמַּלְאָךְ אֲשֶׁר־הָלַךְ ׀
לִקְרֹא מִיכָיְהוּ דִּבֶּר אֵלָיו לֵאמֹר הִנֵּה־נָא דִּבְרֵי הַנְּבִיאִים פֶּה־אֶחָד טוֹב
אֶל־הַמֶּלֶךְ יְהִי־נָא [°דְבָרֶיךָ דְבָרְךָ ק] כִּדְבַר אַחַד מֵהֶם וְדִבַּרְתָּ טּוֹב:

22:2. After Ben-hadad was released (see 20:29-43).
22:3. The king of Aram had promised to return all the cities of Israel captured by his father (20:34), but apparently had retained his hold on Ramoth-gilead.

22:7. The Talmud explains that Jehoshaphat recognized these prophets as charlatans because they all proclaimed the same "prophecy" word for word; with true prophets, "no two prophets ever prophesy with the same words."

²³ HASHEM has spoken also concerning Jezebel, saying, 'The dogs shall eat Jezebel in the Valley of Jezreel.' ²⁴ Anyone [of the house] of Ahab who dies in the city, the dogs will eat; and whoever dies in the field, the birds of the heavens will eat."

²⁵ (There had never been anyone like Ahab, who sold himself to do what was evil in the eyes of HASHEM, because Jezebel his wife had incited him. ²⁶ He became very depraved, going after idols, according to all that was done by the Amorite, whom HASHEM had driven out from before the Children of Israel.)

Ahab humbles himself

²⁷ It happened that when Ahab heard these words, he tore his clothes and placed sackcloth upon his skin and fasted; he slept with the sackcloth, and he walked about slowly.

²⁸ The word of HASHEM came to Elijah the Tishbite, saying, ²⁹ "Have you seen that Ahab has humbled himself before Me? Since he has humbled himself before Me, I will not bring the evil during his days; I will rather bring the evil upon his house in the days of his son."

22

JEHOSHA-PHAT, KING OF JUDAH
22:2-51
(See Appendix A, timeline 4)

Jehoshaphat travels to Samaria

¹ They lived for three years [during which] there was not any war between Aram and Israel. ² But it happened in the third year* [that] Jehoshaphat, king of Judah, came down to [visit] the king of Israel. ³ The king of Israel said to his servants, "Did you know that Ramoth-gilead belongs to us? Yet we have been lax in taking it [back] from the king of Aram."* ⁴ He then said to Jehoshaphat, "Will you go with me to do battle [for] Ramoth-gilead?"

Jehoshaphat answered the king of Israel, "I shall be like you, my people shall be like your people, my horses shall be like your horses." ⁵ Jehoshaphat then said to the king of Israel, "Inquire, please, today, of the word of HASHEM."

⁶ The king of Israel gathered the prophets, some four hundred men, and said to them, "Shall I go to war for Ramoth-gilead, or shall I refrain?"

They answered, "Go up, for my Lord will deliver it into the hand of the king."

⁷ Jehoshaphat said, "Is there no longer here a prophet of HASHEM of whom we may inquire?"*

⁸ The king of Israel answered Jehoshaphat, "There is one more man through whom to inquire of HASHEM; but I hate him, for he never prophesies good for me, only bad — Micaiahu son of Imlah."

Jehoshaphat said, "Let the king not speak this way!"

⁹ So the king of Israel summoned one officer and said, "Rush Micaiahu son of Imlah [here]."

¹⁰ The king of Israel and Jehoshaphat king of Judah were sitting, each man on his throne, dressed in [royal] garb, at the threshing floor at the gateway of Samaria, and all the prophets were prophesying before them. ¹¹ Zedekiah son of Chenaanah made himself iron horns and said, "Thus said HASHEM: With these you shall gore Aram, until they are obliterated!"

¹² All the prophets were prophesying similarly, saying, "Go up to Ramoth-gilead and triumph, for HASHEM will deliver it into the hand of the king."

¹³ The messenger who had gone to summon Micaiahu spoke to him, saying, "Behold, the words of the prophets are unanimously favorable towards the king; please let your words be like the word of one of them, and speak favorably!"

יד-טו וַיֹּאמֶר מִיכָיְהוּ חַי־יהוֹה כִּי אֶת־אֲשֶׁר יֹאמַר יהוֹה אֵלַי אֹתוֹ אֲדַבֵּר: וַיָּבוֹא
אֶל־הַמֶּלֶךְ וַיֹּאמֶר הַמֶּלֶךְ אֵלָיו מִיכָיְהוּ הֲנֵלֵךְ אֶל־רָמֹת גִּלְעָד לַמִּלְחָמָה

טז אִם־נֶחְדָּל וַיֹּאמֶר אֵלָיו עֲלֵה וְהַצְלַח וְנָתַן יהוֹה בְּיַד הַמֶּלֶךְ: וַיֹּאמֶר אֵלָיו
הַמֶּלֶךְ עַד־כַּמֶּה פְעָמִים אֲנִי מַשְׁבִּעֶךָ אֲשֶׁר לֹא־תְדַבֵּר אֵלַי רַק־אֱמֶת

יז בְּשֵׁם יהוֹה: וַיֹּאמֶר רָאִיתִי אֶת־כָּל־יִשְׂרָאֵל נְפֹצִים אֶל־הֶהָרִים כַּצֹּאן
אֲשֶׁר אֵין־לָהֶם רֹעֶה וַיֹּאמֶר יהוֹה לֹא־אֲדֹנִים לָאֵלֶּה יָשׁוּבוּ אִישׁ־לְבֵיתוֹ

יח בְּשָׁלוֹם: וַיֹּאמֶר מֶלֶךְ־יִשְׂרָאֵל אֶל־יְהוֹשָׁפָט הֲלוֹא אָמַרְתִּי אֵלֶיךָ לוֹא־
יט יִתְנַבֵּא עָלַי טוֹב כִּי אִם־רָע: וַיֹּאמֶר לָכֵן שְׁמַע דְּבַר־יהוֹה רָאִיתִי אֶת־
יהוֹה יֹשֵׁב עַל־כִּסְאוֹ וְכָל־צְבָא הַשָּׁמַיִם עֹמֵד עָלָיו מִימִינוֹ וּמִשְּׂמֹאלוֹ:

כ וַיֹּאמֶר יהוֹה מִי יְפַתֶּה אֶת־אַחְאָב וְיַעַל וְיִפֹּל בְּרָמֹת גִּלְעָד וַיֹּאמֶר זֶה בְּכֹה
כא וְזֶה אֹמֵר בְּכֹה: וַיֵּצֵא הָרוּחַ וַיַּעֲמֹד לִפְנֵי יהוֹה וַיֹּאמֶר אֲנִי אֲפַתֶּנּוּ וַיֹּאמֶר
כב יהוֹה אֵלָיו בַּמָּה: וַיֹּאמֶר אֵצֵא וְהָיִיתִי רוּחַ שֶׁקֶר בְּפִי כָּל־נְבִיאָיו וַיֹּאמֶר
כג תְּפַתֶּה וְגַם־תּוּכָל צֵא וַעֲשֵׂה־כֵן: וְעַתָּה הִנֵּה נָתַן יהוֹה רוּחַ שֶׁקֶר בְּפִי כָּל־
כד נְבִיאֶיךָ אֵלֶּה וַיהוֹה דִּבֶּר עָלֶיךָ רָעָה: וַיִּגַּשׁ צִדְקִיָּהוּ בֶן־כְּנַעֲנָה וַיַּכֶּה אֶת־
מִיכָיְהוּ עַל־הַלֶּחִי וַיֹּאמֶר אֵי־זֶה עָבַר רוּחַ־יהוֹה מֵאִתִּי לְדַבֵּר אוֹתָךְ:

כה וַיֹּאמֶר מִיכָיְהוּ הִנְּךָ רֹאֶה בַּיּוֹם הַהוּא אֲשֶׁר תָּבֹא חֶדֶר בְּחֶדֶר לְהֵחָבֵה:
כו וַיֹּאמֶר מֶלֶךְ יִשְׂרָאֵל קַח אֶת־מִיכָיְהוּ וַהֲשִׁיבֵהוּ אֶל־אָמֹן שַׂר־הָעִיר וְאֶל־
כז יוֹאָשׁ בֶּן־הַמֶּלֶךְ: וְאָמַרְתָּ כֹּה אָמַר הַמֶּלֶךְ שִׂימוּ אֶת־זֶה בֵּית הַכֶּלֶא
כח וְהַאֲכִילֻהוּ לֶחֶם לַחַץ וּמַיִם לַחַץ עַד בֹּאִי בְשָׁלוֹם: וַיֹּאמֶר מִיכָיְהוּ אִם־
שׁוֹב תָּשׁוּב בְּשָׁלוֹם לֹא־דִבֶּר יהוֹה בִּי וַיֹּאמֶר שִׁמְעוּ עַמִּים כֻּלָּם: וַיַּעַל

כט-ל מֶלֶךְ־יִשְׂרָאֵל וִיהוֹשָׁפָט מֶלֶךְ־יְהוּדָה רָמֹת גִּלְעָד: וַיֹּאמֶר מֶלֶךְ יִשְׂרָאֵל
אֶל־יְהוֹשָׁפָט הִתְחַפֵּשׂ וָבֹא בַמִּלְחָמָה וְאַתָּה לְבַשׁ בְּגָדֶיךָ וַיִּתְחַפֵּשׂ

לא מֶלֶךְ יִשְׂרָאֵל וַיָּבוֹא בַּמִּלְחָמָה: וּמֶלֶךְ אֲרָם צִוָּה אֶת־שָׂרֵי הָרֶכֶב אֲשֶׁר־לוֹ
שְׁלֹשִׁים וּשְׁנַיִם לֵאמֹר לֹא תִּלָּחֲמוּ אֶת־קָטֹן וְאֶת־גָּדוֹל כִּי אִם־

לב אֶת־מֶלֶךְ יִשְׂרָאֵל לְבַדּוֹ: וַיְהִי כִּרְאוֹת שָׂרֵי הָרֶכֶב אֶת־יְהוֹשָׁפָט וְהֵמָּה
אָמְרוּ אַךְ מֶלֶךְ־יִשְׂרָאֵל הוּא וַיָּסֻרוּ עָלָיו לְהִלָּחֵם וַיִּזְעַק יְהוֹשָׁפָט:

לג וַיְהִי כִּרְאוֹת שָׂרֵי הָרֶכֶב כִּי־לֹא־מֶלֶךְ יִשְׂרָאֵל הוּא וַיָּשׁוּבוּ מֵאַחֲרָיו:

22:15. This was not said in God's Name, but in cynical mimicry of the false prophets. Thus, Ahab insisted that he speak the truth.

22:17. Ahab would die in battle, but Israel would scatter and escape unharmed.

22:21. It was the "spirit" of Naboth, the victim of Ahab and Jezebel (Ch. 21; *Rashi*). All this was part of the prophetic vision (*Radak*).

22:25. Zedekiah would desperately hide from the returning vanquished army, which would seek to vent its anger at him for having encouraged the fiasco (*Abarbanel*).

22:28. That is, all the tribes of Israel (*Metzudos*).

22:30. Ahab knew that the Arameans would kill him immediately if they recognized him, but that Jehoshaphat was in no such danger.

22:31. He was not primarily concerned with the lives of the Israelite soldiers, only fearful that Ahab might escape if the fighting became fierce. He wanted to postpone the decimation of the Israelite army until after Ahab was apprehended (*Radak*).

22:33. Seeing that only the soldiers of Judah came to Jehoshaphat's rescue, they understood that this was not Ahab (*Metzudos*).

¹⁴ But Micaiahu said, "As HASHEM lives, [I swear] that whatever HASHEM says to me, that shall I speak!"

¹⁵ He came to the king, and the king said to him, "Micaiahu, shall we go to war for Ramoth-gilead or shall we refrain?"

He said to him, "Go up and triumph, for HASHEM will deliver it into the king's hand."*

¹⁶ The king then said to him, "I adjure you many times over that you speak to me nothing but the truth, in the name of HASHEM!"

¹⁷ [Micaiahu] then said, "I have seen all of Israel scattering to the mountains, like sheep that have no shepherd; and HASHEM saying, 'These have no masters; let each man go to his house in peace!' "*

¹⁸ The king of Israel said to Jehoshaphat,· "Did I not I tell you that he never prophesies good for me, but only bad?"

¹⁹ [Micaiahu] said [further], "Therefore listen to the word of HASHEM! I have seen HASHEM sitting upon His throne, with all the host of Heaven standing by Him, on His right and on His left. ²⁰ And HASHEM said, 'Who will lure Ahab to go up [to war] that he may fall in Ramoth-gilead?' This one said, 'Like this!' and this one said, 'Like this!' ²¹ Then the spirit* came forward and stood before HASHEM and said, 'I shall lure him!' And HASHEM said, 'How?' ²² [The spirit] replied, 'I will go out and be a spirit of falsehood in the mouths of all his prophets.' And [HASHEM] said, 'You will lure him and you will succeed! Go forth and do so!' ²³ And now, behold! HASHEM has put a spirit of falsehood in the mouths of all these prophets of yours, for HASHEM has decreed evil upon you."

²⁴ Zedekiah son of Chenaanah then approached and struck Micaiahu on the cheek and said, "How is it that the spirit of HASHEM passed from me to speak to you?"

²⁵ Micaiahu said, "Behold, you will see for yourself on that day, when you go inside a room within a room to be hidden!"*

²⁶ The king of Israel said, "Take Micaiahu and turn him over to Amon, the minister of the city, and to Joash, the king's son, ²⁷ and say, 'Thus said the king: Put this one in the prison and feed him a minimum of food and a minimum of water, until I return in peace.' "

²⁸ Micaiahu said, "If you indeed return in peace, then HASHEM did not speak through me!" and he said [further], "Hear this, all the peoples!"*

²⁹ The king of Israel and Jehoshaphat the king of Judah then went up [to wage war] at Ramoth-gilead. ³⁰ The king of Israel said to Jehoshaphat, "[I] will disguise [myself] when [I] come to the battle, but you wear your royal garments,"* so the king of Israel disguised himself and went out to battle. ³¹ The king of Aram commanded his thirty-two chariot commanders, saying, "Do not wage war with anyone weak or strong, but only with the king of Israel himself."* ³² It happened that when the chariot commanders saw Jehoshaphat, they said, "This must be the king of Israel!" — and they went towards him to fight him. Jehoshaphat cried out. ³³ When the chariot commanders realized that he was not the king of Israel,* they turned away from him.

Micaiahu is consulted

Micaiahu prophesies disaster for Ahab

The false prophet challenges him

The kings go to war, and Ahab is killed

לד וְאִישׁ מָשַׁךְ בַּקֶּשֶׁת לְתֻמּוֹ וַיַּכֶּה אֶת־מֶלֶךְ יִשְׂרָאֵל בֵּין הַדְּבָקִים וּבֵין

לה הַשִּׁרְיָן וַיֹּאמֶר לְרַכָּבוֹ הֲפֹךְ יָדְךָ וְהוֹצִיאֵנִי מִן־הַמַּחֲנֶה כִּי הָחֳלֵיתִי: וַתַּעֲלֶה הַמִּלְחָמָה בַּיּוֹם הַהוּא וְהַמֶּלֶךְ הָיָה מׇעֳמָד בַּמֶּרְכָּבָה נֹכַח אֲרָם וַיָּמׇת בָּעֶרֶב

לו וַיִּצֶק דַּם־הַמַּכָּה אֶל־חֵיק הָרָכֶב: וַיַּעֲבֹר הָרִנָּה בַּמַּחֲנֶה כְּבֹא

לז הַשֶּׁמֶשׁ לֵאמֹר אִישׁ אֶל־עִירוֹ וְאִישׁ אֶל־אַרְצוֹ: וַיָּמׇת הַמֶּלֶךְ וַיָּבוֹא שֹׁמְרוֹן

לח וַיִּקְבְּרוּ אֶת־הַמֶּלֶךְ בְּשֹׁמְרוֹן: וַיִּשְׁטֹף אֶת־הָרֶכֶב עַל ׀ בְּרֵכַת שֹׁמְרוֹן וַיָּלֹקּוּ

לט הַכְּלָבִים אֶת־דָּמוֹ וְהַזֹּנוֹת רָחָצוּ כִּדְבַר יְהֹוָה אֲשֶׁר דִּבֵּר: וְיֶתֶר דִּבְרֵי אַחְאָב וְכׇל־אֲשֶׁר עָשָׂה וּבֵית הַשֵּׁן אֲשֶׁר בָּנָה וְכׇל־הֶעָרִים אֲשֶׁר בָּנָה

מ הֲלוֹא־הֵם כְּתוּבִים עַל־סֵפֶר דִּבְרֵי הַיָּמִים לְמַלְכֵי יִשְׂרָאֵל: וַיִּשְׁכַּב אַחְאָב עִם־אֲבֹתָיו וַיִּמְלֹךְ אֲחַזְיָהוּ בְנוֹ תַּחְתָּיו: וִיהוֹשָׁפָט

מא בֶּן־אָסָא מָלַךְ עַל־יְהוּדָה בִּשְׁנַת אַרְבַּע לְאַחְאָב מֶלֶךְ יִשְׂרָאֵל: יְהוֹשָׁפָט

מב בֶּן־שְׁלֹשִׁים וְחָמֵשׁ שָׁנָה בְּמׇלְכוֹ וְעֶשְׂרִים וְחָמֵשׁ שָׁנָה מָלַךְ בִּירוּשָׁלָ͏ִם וְשֵׁם אִמּוֹ עֲזוּבָה בַּת־שִׁלְחִי: וַיֵּלֶךְ בְּכׇל־דֶּרֶךְ אָסָא אָבִיו לֹא־סָר מִמֶּנּוּ

מד לַעֲשׂוֹת הַיָּשָׁר בְּעֵינֵי יְהֹוָה: אַךְ הַבָּמוֹת לֹא־סָרוּ עוֹד הָעָם מְזַבְּחִים

מה–מו וּמְקַטְּרִים בַּבָּמוֹת: וַיַּשְׁלֵם יְהוֹשָׁפָט עִם־מֶלֶךְ יִשְׂרָאֵל: וְיֶתֶר דִּבְרֵי יְהוֹשָׁפָט וּגְבוּרָתוֹ אֲשֶׁר־עָשָׂה וַאֲשֶׁר נִלְחָם הֲלֹא־הֵם כְּתוּבִים עַל־

מז סֵפֶר דִּבְרֵי הַיָּמִים לְמַלְכֵי יְהוּדָה: וְיֶתֶר הַקָּדֵשׁ אֲשֶׁר נִשְׁאַר בִּימֵי אָסָא

מח–מט אָבִיו בִּעֵר מִן־הָאָרֶץ: וּמֶלֶךְ אֵין בֶּאֱדוֹם נִצָּב מֶלֶךְ: יְהוֹשָׁפָט °עשר [°עָשָׂה ק] אֳנִיּוֹת תַּרְשִׁישׁ לָלֶכֶת אוֹפִירָה לַזָּהָב וְלֹא הָלָךְ כִּי־°נשברה [°נִשְׁבְּרוּ ק] אֳנִיּוֹת בְּעֶצְיוֹן גָּבֶר: אָז אָמַר אֲחַזְיָהוּ בֶן־אַחְאָב אֶל־

נא יְהוֹשָׁפָט יֵלְכוּ עֲבָדַי עִם־עֲבָדֶיךָ בָּאֳנִיּוֹת וְלֹא אָבָה יְהוֹשָׁפָט: וַיִּשְׁכַּב יְהוֹשָׁפָט עִם־אֲבֹתָיו וַיִּקָּבֵר עִם־אֲבֹתָיו בְּעִיר דָּוִד אָבִיו וַיִּמְלֹךְ יְהוֹרָם בְּנוֹ

נב תַּחְתָּיו: אֲחַזְיָהוּ בֶן־אַחְאָב מָלַךְ עַל־יִשְׂרָאֵל בְּשֹׁמְרוֹן בִּשְׁנַת שְׁבַע עֶשְׂרֵה לִיהוֹשָׁפָט מֶלֶךְ יְהוּדָה וַיִּמְלֹךְ עַל־יִשְׂרָאֵל שְׁנָתָיִם:

נג וַיַּעַשׂ הָרַע בְּעֵינֵי יְהֹוָה וַיֵּלֶךְ בְּדֶרֶךְ אָבִיו וּבְדֶרֶךְ אִמּוֹ וּבְדֶרֶךְ יָרׇבְעָם

נד בֶּן־נְבָט אֲשֶׁר הֶחֱטִיא אֶת־יִשְׂרָאֵל: וַיַּעֲבֹד אֶת־הַבַּעַל וַיִּשְׁתַּחֲוֶה לוֹ וַיַּכְעֵס אֶת־יְהֹוָה אֱלֹהֵי יִשְׂרָאֵל כְּכֹל אֲשֶׁר־עָשָׂה אָבִיו: **מלכים ב**

א וַיִּפְשַׁע מוֹאָב

ב בְּיִשְׂרָאֵל אַחֲרֵי מוֹת אַחְאָב: וַיִּפֹּל אֲחַזְיָה בְּעַד הַשְּׂבָכָה בַּעֲלִיָּתוֹ אֲשֶׁר בְּשֹׁמְרוֹן וַיָּחַל וַיִּשְׁלַח מַלְאָכִים וַיֹּאמֶר אֲלֵהֶם לְכוּ דִרְשׁוּ בְּבַעַל זְבוּב

22:34. See *II Kings 5:1*.

22:35. Ahab had himself propped up so that his soldiers would not be demoralized and flee.

22:38. See *21:19*.

22:39. See note to *14:19*.

22:46. See *II Chronicles 17:1-21:1*.

22:48. See *II Samuel 8:14*. This fact is emphasized here

because, under Jehoshaphat's son Jehoram, Edom rebelled and appointed their own king (see *II Kings 8:20*; *Rashi*).

22:49. See *10:22*.

22:50. In punishment for allying himself with the wicked Ahaziah, Jehoshaphat's ships broke down (*II Chronicles 20:37*). For this reason Jehoshaphat refused Ahaziah's offer to join forces again.

³⁴ *A man [of Aram]* * *drew his bow aimlessly, yet hit the king of Israel between the joints of his armor. [The king] said to his driver, "Reverse your hand and take me out of the camp, for I am wounded."* ³⁵ *The war intensified on that day, and the king was propped up in his chariot in the presence of Aram.* * *He died in the evening, the blood of the wound spilling into the bosom of the chariot.*

³⁶ *The call went out in the camp as the sun was setting, saying, "Every man back to his city and his land!"*

His ignominious end

³⁷ *The king had died and was brought to Samaria, and they buried the king in Samaria.* ³⁸ *[The driver] rinsed out the chariot at the pool of Samaria; the dogs licked up [the king's] blood, and the harlots bathed [in it] — like the word of* HASHEM *that He had spoken.* *

³⁹ *The rest of the deeds of Ahab and all that he did, and the ivory house that he built, and all the cities which he built — behold, they are recorded in the Book of the Chronicles of the Kings of Israel.* * ⁴⁰ *Ahab lay with his forefathers, and Ahaziah his son reigned in his place.*

AHAZIAH, KING OF ISRAEL
22:40—II 1:18
(See Appendix A, timeline 4)

Jehoshaphat's righteous reign

⁴¹ *Jehoshaphat son of Asa had become king over Judah in the fourth year of Ahab, king of Israel.* ⁴² *Jehoshaphat was thirty-five years old when he became king, and he reigned for twenty-five years in Jerusalem. His mother's name was Azubah daughter of Shilhi.* ⁴³ *He followed completely the way of his father Asa; he did not deviate from it, doing what was proper in the eyes of* HASHEM. ⁴⁴ *But they did not remove the high places; the people still slaughtered and burnt sacrifices at the high places.* ⁴⁵ *And Jehoshaphat made peace with the king of Israel.*

⁴⁶ *The rest of the deeds of Jehoshaphat and the acts of might that he did, and how he waged wars — behold, they are recorded in the Book of the Chronicles of the Kings of Judah.* * ⁴⁷ *Whatever prostitution was left from the days of his father Asa, he eradicated from the land.* ⁴⁸ *There was [still] no king in Edom; a commissioner [from Judah] ruled.* * ⁴⁹ *Jehoshaphat built Tarshish ships* * *to travel to Ophir for gold, but he did not go, because the ships broke down at Etzion-geber.* ⁵⁰ *Then Ahaziah son of Ahab said to Jehoshaphat, "Let my servants travel together with your servants in ships," but Jehoshaphat did not consent.* *

⁵¹ *Jehoshaphat lay with his forefathers and was buried with his forefathers in the city of David his forefather; his son Jehoram reigned in his place.*

Ahaziah emulates Ahab

⁵² *Ahaziah son of Ahab became king over Israel in Samaria in the seventeenth year of Jehoshaphat king of Judah, and he reigned over Israel for two years.* ⁵³ *He did what was evil in the eyes of* HASHEM, *and he went in the way of his father and in the way of his mother, and in the way of Jeroboam son of Nebat, who caused Israel to sin.* ⁵⁴ *He worshiped the Baal and prostrated himself to it, and he angered* HASHEM, *God of Israel, like all that his father had done.*

II KINGS
1

ELIJAH THE PROPHET
1:1—2:11

¹ Moab *rebelled against Israel after Ahab's death.* * ² *Ahaziah fell through the balustrade of his upper-chamber in Samaria, and took ill. He sent messengers, saying to them, "Go inquire of Baal-zebub*

◆§ II Kings

According to the masoretic tradition, the "books" of *I Kings* and *II Kings* are actually *one* long book; their designation as two separate books is of non-Jewish origin. Thus, in the total of the twenty-four books of *Tanach*, all of *Kings* is counted as a single book. The same applies to the "books" of *Samuel* and *Chronicles*. However, for the convenience of the reader, we refer to chapters and verses in the familiar way, e.g. *II Kings* 3:10.

1:1. This provides the background for a punishment to be meted out to Ahaziah. It is discussed more fully in Chapter 3.

ג אֱלֹהֵי עֶקְרוֹן אִם־אֶחְיֶה מֵחֳלִי זֶה: וּמַלְאַךְ
יְהוָה דִּבֶּר אֶל־אֵלִיָּה הַתִּשְׁבִּי קוּם עֲלֵה לִקְרַאת מַלְאֲכֵי מֶלֶךְ־שֹׁמְרוֹן
וְדַבֵּר אֲלֵהֶם הַמִבְּלִי אֵין־אֱלֹהִים בְּיִשְׂרָאֵל אַתֶּם הֹלְכִים לִדְרֹשׁ בְּבַעַל
ד זְבוּב אֱלֹהֵי עֶקְרוֹן: וְלָכֵן כֹּה־אָמַר יְהוָה הַמִּטָּה אֲשֶׁר־עָלִיתָ שָּׁם לֹא־
ה תֵרֵד מִמֶּנָּה כִּי מוֹת תָּמוּת וַיֵּלֶךְ אֵלִיָּה: וַיָּשׁוּבוּ הַמַּלְאָכִים אֵלָיו וַיֹּאמֶר
ו אֲלֵהֶם מַה־זֶּה שַׁבְתֶּם: וַיֹּאמְרוּ אֵלָיו אִישׁ ׀ עָלָה לִקְרָאתֵנוּ וַיֹּאמֶר אֵלֵינוּ
לְכוּ שׁוּבוּ אֶל־הַמֶּלֶךְ אֲשֶׁר־שָׁלַח אֶתְכֶם וְדִבַּרְתֶּם אֵלָיו כֹּה אָמַר יְהוָה
הַמִבְּלִי אֵין־אֱלֹהִים בְּיִשְׂרָאֵל אַתָּה שֹׁלֵחַ לִדְרֹשׁ בְּבַעַל זְבוּב אֱלֹהֵי
עֶקְרוֹן לָכֵן הַמִּטָּה אֲשֶׁר־עָלִיתָ שָּׁם לֹא־תֵרֵד מִמֶּנָּה כִּי־מוֹת תָּמוּת:
ז וַיְדַבֵּר אֲלֵהֶם מֶה מִשְׁפַּט הָאִישׁ אֲשֶׁר עָלָה לִקְרַאתְכֶם וַיְדַבֵּר אֲלֵיכֶם
ח אֶת־הַדְּבָרִים הָאֵלֶּה: וַיֹּאמְרוּ אֵלָיו אִישׁ בַּעַל שֵׂעָר וְאֵזוֹר עוֹר אָזוּר
ט בְּמָתְנָיו וַיֹּאמַר אֵלִיָּה הַתִּשְׁבִּי הוּא: וַיִּשְׁלַח אֵלָיו שַׂר־חֲמִשִּׁים וַחֲמִשָּׁיו
וַיַּעַל אֵלָיו וְהִנֵּה יֹשֵׁב עַל־רֹאשׁ הָהָר וַיְדַבֵּר אֵלָיו אִישׁ הָאֱלֹהִים הַמֶּלֶךְ
י דִּבֶּר רֵדָה: וַיַּעֲנֶה אֵלִיָּהוּ וַיְדַבֵּר אֶל־שַׂר הַחֲמִשִּׁים וְאִם־אִישׁ אֱלֹהִים אָנִי
תֵּרֶד אֵשׁ מִן־הַשָּׁמַיִם וְתֹאכַל אֹתְךָ וְאֶת־חֲמִשֶּׁיךָ וַתֵּרֶד אֵשׁ מִן־הַשָּׁמַיִם
יא וַתֹּאכַל אֹתוֹ וְאֶת־חֲמִשָּׁיו: וַיָּשָׁב וַיִּשְׁלַח אֵלָיו שַׂר־חֲמִשִּׁים אַחֵר וַחֲמִשָּׁיו
יב וַיַּעַן וַיְדַבֵּר אֵלָיו אִישׁ הָאֱלֹהִים כֹּה־אָמַר הַמֶּלֶךְ מְהֵרָה רֵדָה: וַיַּעַן אֵלִיָּה
וַיְדַבֵּר אֲלֵיהֶם אִם־אִישׁ הָאֱלֹהִים אָנִי תֵּרֶד אֵשׁ מִן־הַשָּׁמַיִם וְתֹאכַל אֹתְךָ
וְאֶת־חֲמִשֶּׁיךָ וַתֵּרֶד אֵשׁ־אֱלֹהִים מִן־הַשָּׁמַיִם וַתֹּאכַל אֹתוֹ וְאֶת־חֲמִשָּׁיו:
יג וַיָּשָׁב וַיִּשְׁלַח שַׂר־חֲמִשִּׁים שְׁלִשִׁים וַחֲמִשָּׁיו וַיַּעַל וַיָּבֹא שַׂר־הַחֲמִשִּׁים
הַשְּׁלִישִׁי וַיִּכְרַע עַל־בִּרְכָּיו ׀ לְנֶגֶד אֵלִיָּהוּ וַיִּתְחַנֵּן אֵלָיו וַיְדַבֵּר אֵלָיו אִישׁ
יד הָאֱלֹהִים תִּיקַר־נָא נַפְשִׁי וְנֶפֶשׁ עֲבָדֶיךָ אֵלֶּה חֲמִשִּׁים בְּעֵינֶיךָ: הִנֵּה יָרְדָה
אֵשׁ מִן־הַשָּׁמַיִם וַתֹּאכַל אֶת־שְׁנֵי שָׂרֵי הַחֲמִשִּׁים הָרִאשֹׁנִים וְאֶת־
טו חֲמִשֵּׁיהֶם וְעַתָּה תִּיקַר נַפְשִׁי בְּעֵינֶיךָ: וַיְדַבֵּר מַלְאַךְ יְהוָה
אֶל־אֵלִיָּהוּ רֵד אוֹתוֹ אַל־תִּירָא מִפָּנָיו וַיָּקָם וַיֵּרֶד אוֹתוֹ אֶל־הַמֶּלֶךְ:
טז וַיְדַבֵּר אֵלָיו כֹּה־אָמַר יְהוָה יַעַן אֲשֶׁר־שָׁלַחְתָּ מַלְאָכִים לִדְרֹשׁ בְּבַעַל
זְבוּב אֱלֹהֵי עֶקְרוֹן הַמִבְּלִי אֵין־אֱלֹהִים בְּיִשְׂרָאֵל לִדְרֹשׁ בִּדְבָרוֹ לָכֵן
יז הַמִּטָּה אֲשֶׁר־עָלִיתָ שָּׁם לֹא־תֵרֵד מִמֶּנָּה כִּי־מוֹת תָּמוּת: וַיָּמָת כִּדְבַר
יְהוָה ׀ אֲשֶׁר־דִּבֶּר אֵלִיָּהוּ וַיִּמְלֹךְ יְהוֹרָם תַּחְתָּיו בִּשְׁנַת
שְׁתַּיִם לִיהוֹרָם בֶּן־יְהוֹשָׁפָט מֶלֶךְ יְהוּדָה כִּי לֹא־הָיָה לוֹ בֵּן: וְיֶתֶר דִּבְרֵי יח
אֲחַזְיָהוּ אֲשֶׁר עָשָׂה הֲלוֹא־הֵמָּה כְתוּבִים עַל־סֵפֶר דִּבְרֵי הַיָּמִים לְמַלְכֵי

1:10. Though the captain addressed Elijah as Man of God, he spoke peremptorily and impudently, suggesting that his first loyalty was to the idol (see below). By calling for Heavenly assistance, Elijah left it to God to judge whether or not the men deserved to die.

1:15. Since the angel appeared for the first time at this juncture, it is clear that the first two troops intended to harm Elijah, thus explaining why they deserved to die.

1:18. See note to *I Kings* 14:19.

the god of Ekron, whether I will recover from this illness."

Elijah intercepts Ahaziah's messenger

³ An angel of HASHEM then said to Elijah the Tishbite, "Arise and go up towards the messengers of the king of Samaria and speak to them, 'Is there no God in Israel that you go to inquire of Baal-zebub, the god of Ekron? ⁴ Therefore, thus said HASHEM [of Ahaziah]: The bed onto which you have climbed — you shall never go down from it, for you shall surely die.' " Elijah then set off.

⁵ The messengers returned to [Ahaziah], and he asked them, "Why have you returned?"

⁶ They answered him, "A man came up toward us and said to us, 'Go and return to the king who sent you, and speak to him: Thus said HASHEM: Is there no God in Israel that you send to inquire of Baal-zebub, the god of Ekron? Therefore, the bed onto which you have climbed — you shall never go down from it, for you shall surely die.' "

Ahaziah identifies him

⁷ He asked them, "What is the appearance of the man who came up towards you, and spoke these words to you?"

⁸ They said to him, "He was a hairy man, with a leather belt girded on his waist." [Ahaziah] said, "He is Elijah the Tishbite!"

⁹ So [Ahaziah] dispatched to him a captain of fifty, along with his fifty [men]. He came up to [Elijah], and he was sitting at the top of a mountain; he said to him, "Man of God, the king has spoken: Come down!"

Elijah is saved from the pursuers

¹⁰ Elijah responded and spoke to the captain of the fifty, "If I am a 'Man of God' let a fire descend from Heaven and consume you and your fifty [men]!"* A fire then descended from Heaven and consumed him and his fifty [men]. ¹¹ [Ahaziah] repeated and sent another captain of fifty, along with his fifty [men], to him. He spoke up and said to [Elijah], "Man of God, thus said the king: Come down quickly!"

¹² Elijah responded and spoke to them, "If I am a 'Man of God,' let a fire descend from Heaven and consume you and your fifty [men]!" The fire of God then descended from Heaven and consumed him and his fifty [men]. ¹³ [Ahaziah] repeated and sent a third captain of fifty [men], along with his fifty men. This third captain of fifty went up, arrived, and fell on his knees in front of Elijah and entreated him and spoke to him, "Man of God, please let my soul and the souls of these fifty servants of yours be worthy in your eyes! ¹⁴ Behold, a fire has descended from Heaven and consumed the [first] two captains of fifty, along with their [groups of] fifty; but now, may my soul be worthy in your eyes!"

Elijah faces Ahaziah

¹⁵ An angel of HASHEM then said to Elijah, "Go down with him; do not fear him."* So he arose and went down with him to the king.

¹⁶ [Elijah] said to [Ahaziah], "Thus said HASHEM: Because you sent messengers to inquire of Baal-zebub, the god of Ekron — is there no God in Israel of Whose word to inquire? Therefore, the bed onto which you have climbed — you shall never go down from it, for you shall surely die."

(See Appendix A, timeline 4)

¹⁷ [Ahaziah] died, in accordance with the word of HASHEM that Elijah had spoken. [His brother] Jehoram reigned in his place, in the second year of Jehoram son of Jehoshaphat, king of Judah, for [Ahaziah] had no son.

¹⁸ The rest of Ahaziah's deeds that he did — behold, they are recorded in the Book of the Chronicles of the Kings of Israel. *

ב   א יִשְׂרָאֵל: וַיְהִי בְּהַעֲלוֹת יהוה אֶת־אֵלִיָּהוּ בַּסְעָרָה הַשָּׁמָיִם

ב וַיֵּלֶךְ אֵלִיָּהוּ וֶאֱלִישָׁע מִן־הַגִּלְגָּל: וַיֹּאמֶר אֵלִיָּהוּ אֶל־אֱלִישָׁע שֵׁב־נָא

פֹה כִּי יהוה שְׁלָחַנִי עַד־בֵּית־אֵל וַיֹּאמֶר אֱלִישָׁע חַי־יהוה וְחֵי־

ג נַפְשְׁךָ אִם־אֶעֶזְבֶךָּ וַיֵּרְדוּ בֵּית־אֵל: וַיֵּצְאוּ בְנֵי־הַנְּבִיאִים אֲשֶׁר־בֵּית־

אֵל אֶל־אֱלִישָׁע וַיֹּאמְרוּ אֵלָיו הֲיָדַעְתָּ כִּי הַיּוֹם יהוה לֹקֵחַ אֶת־אֲדֹנֶיךָ

ד מֵעַל רֹאשֶׁךָ וַיֹּאמֶר גַּם־אֲנִי יָדַעְתִּי הֶחֱשׁוּ: וַיֹּאמֶר לוֹ אֵלִיָּהוּ אֱלִישָׁע ׀

שֵׁב־נָא פֹה כִּי יהוה שְׁלָחַנִי יְרִיחוֹ וַיֹּאמֶר חַי־יהוה וְחֵי־נַפְשְׁךָ אִם־

ה אֶעֶזְבֶךָּ וַיָּבֹאוּ יְרִיחוֹ: וַיִּגְּשׁוּ בְנֵי־הַנְּבִיאִים אֲשֶׁר־בִּירִיחוֹ אֶל־אֱלִישָׁע

וַיֹּאמְרוּ אֵלָיו הֲיָדַעְתָּ כִּי הַיּוֹם יהוה לֹקֵחַ אֶת־אֲדֹנֶיךָ מֵעַל רֹאשֶׁךָ

ו וַיֹּאמֶר גַּם־אֲנִי יָדַעְתִּי הֶחֱשׁוּ: וַיֹּאמֶר לוֹ אֵלִיָּהוּ שֵׁב־נָא פֹה כִּי יהוה

שְׁלָחַנִי הַיַּרְדֵּנָה וַיֹּאמֶר חַי־יהוה וְחֵי־נַפְשְׁךָ אִם־אֶעֶזְבֶךָּ וַיֵּלְכוּ שְׁנֵיהֶם:

ז וַחֲמִשִּׁים אִישׁ מִבְּנֵי הַנְּבִיאִים הָלְכוּ וַיַּעַמְדוּ מִנֶּגֶד מֵרָחוֹק וּשְׁנֵיהֶם

ח עָמְדוּ עַל־הַיַּרְדֵּן: וַיִּקַּח אֵלִיָּהוּ אֶת־אַדַּרְתּוֹ וַיִּגְלֹם וַיַּכֶּה אֶת־הַמַּיִם

ט וַיֵּחָצוּ הֵנָּה וָהֵנָּה וַיַּעַבְרוּ שְׁנֵיהֶם בֶּחָרָבָה: וַיְהִי כְעָבְרָם וְאֵלִיָּהוּ

אָמַר אֶל־אֱלִישָׁע שְׁאַל מָה אֶעֱשֶׂה־לָּךְ בְּטֶרֶם אֶלָּקַח מֵעִמָּךְ וַיֹּאמֶר

י אֱלִישָׁע וִיהִי־נָא פִּי־שְׁנַיִם בְּרוּחֲךָ אֵלָי: וַיֹּאמֶר הִקְשִׁיתָ לִשְׁאוֹל אִם־

יא תִּרְאֶה אֹתִי לֻקָּח מֵאִתָּךְ יְהִי־לְךָ כֵן וְאִם־אַיִן לֹא יִהְיֶה: וַיְהִי הֵמָּה

הֹלְכִים הָלוֹךְ וְדַבֵּר וְהִנֵּה רֶכֶב־אֵשׁ וְסוּסֵי אֵשׁ וַיַּפְרִדוּ בֵּין שְׁנֵיהֶם

יב וַיַּעַל אֵלִיָּהוּ בַּסְעָרָה הַשָּׁמָיִם: וֶאֱלִישָׁע רֹאֶה וְהוּא מְצַעֵק אָבִי ׀ אָבִי

רֶכֶב יִשְׂרָאֵל וּפָרָשָׁיו וְלֹא רָאָהוּ עוֹד וַיַּחֲזֵק בִּבְגָדָיו וַיִּקְרָעֵם לִשְׁנַיִם

יג קְרָעִים: וַיָּרֶם אֶת־אַדֶּרֶת אֵלִיָּהוּ אֲשֶׁר נָפְלָה מֵעָלָיו וַיָּשָׁב וַיַּעֲמֹד

יד עַל־שְׂפַת הַיַּרְדֵּן: וַיִּקַּח אֶת־אַדֶּרֶת אֵלִיָּהוּ אֲשֶׁר־נָפְלָה מֵעָלָיו וַיַּכֶּה

אֶת־הַמַּיִם וַיֹּאמַר אַיֵּה יהוה אֱלֹהֵי אֵלִיָּהוּ אַף־הוּא ׀ וַיַּכֶּה אֶת־הַמַּיִם

טו וַיֵּחָצוּ הֵנָּה וָהֵנָּה וַיַּעֲבֹר אֱלִישָׁע: וַיִּרְאֻהוּ בְנֵי־הַנְּבִיאִים אֲשֶׁר־בִּירִיחוֹ

מִנֶּגֶד וַיֹּאמְרוּ נָחָה רוּחַ אֵלִיָּהוּ עַל־אֱלִישָׁע וַיָּבֹאוּ לִקְרָאתוֹ וַיִּשְׁתַּחֲווּ־

טז לוֹ אָרְצָה: וַיֹּאמְרוּ אֵלָיו הִנֵּה־נָא יֵשׁ־אֶת־עֲבָדֶיךָ חֲמִשִּׁים אֲנָשִׁים בְּנֵי־

חַיִל יֵלְכוּ נָא וִיבַקְשׁוּ אֶת־אֲדֹנֶיךָ פֶּן־נְשָׂאוֹ רוּחַ יהוה וַיַּשְׁלִכֵהוּ

בְּאַחַד הֶהָרִים אוֹ בְּאַחַת °הַגֵּיאוֹת [°הַגֵּאָיוֹת ק] וַיֹּאמֶר לֹא תִשְׁלָחוּ:

יז וַיִּפְצְרוּ־בוֹ עַד־בֹּשׁ וַיֹּאמֶר שְׁלָחוּ וַיִּשְׁלְחוּ חֲמִשִּׁים אִישׁ וַיְבַקְשׁוּ

2:2. Out of modesty, Elijah did not want anyone present when he was to ascend to Heaven.

2:10. If Elisha was spiritually elevated enough to see Elijah's miraculous ascent to Heaven, it would be an indication that his request would be granted.

2:14. Elisha meant, "Is He with me as He was with my master?" In reply, the river split for him, as it had for Elijah.

2:16. Although the disciples knew that Elijah was to be "taken away" on that day (vv. 3,5), they thought that he might merely have been transported to some other place (cf. *I Kings* 18:12), where he might yet be found (*Radak*).

2

Elijah's ascent to heaven

¹ It happened when HASHEM took Elijah up to Heaven in a whirlwind: Elijah went with Elisha from Gilgal, ² Elijah said to Elisha, "Please stay here, for HASHEM has sent me to Beth-el."*

But Elisha said, "[I swear] as HASHEM lives and by your life that I shall not leave you!" So they went down to Beth-el.

³ The prophets' disciples who had been in Beth-el came out to Elisha and said to him, "Did you know that today HASHEM is taking your master from upon your head?"

He said, "I know also. Be silent!"

⁴ Elijah then said to him, "Elisha, please stay here, for HASHEM has sent me to Jericho."

But he said, "[I swear] as HASHEM lives and by your life that I shall not leave you!" So they came to Jericho.

⁵ The prophets' disciples who had been in Jericho approached Elisha and said to him, "Did you know that today HASHEM is taking your master from upon your head?"

He said, "I know also. Be silent!"

⁶ Elijah then said to him, "Please stay here, for HASHEM has sent me to the Jordan."

Elijah and Elisha at the Jordan

He said, "[I swear] as HASHEM lives and by your life that I shall not leave you!" So they both went. ⁷ Fifty men of the prophets' disciples went, standing opposite them at a distance, and the two of them stood at the Jordan.

⁸ Elijah took his mantle and folded it over, and struck the water, which split apart this way and that, and they both crossed over on dry land. ⁹ As they were crossing, Elijah said to Elisha, "Request what I should do for you before I am taken away from you."

Elisha's request

Elisha said, "May twice as much as your spirit be mine."

¹⁰ [Elijah] said, "You have made a difficult request. If you see me taken from you, it shall be so for you; but if you do not, then it will not happen."*

Elijah ascends to Heaven

¹¹ As they were walking and conversing, behold! — a chariot of fire and horses of fire [appeared] and separated between the two of them, and Elijah ascended to Heaven in the whirlwind. ¹² Elisha was watching and shouting, "Father! Father! Israel's chariot and horsemen!" And then he saw him no more. He took hold of his garments and rent them into two pieces.

ELISHA THE PROPHET
2:12-13:21

¹³ He picked up Elijah's mantle, which had fallen from him, and he returned and stood at the bank of the Jordan. ¹⁴ He took Elijah's mantle, which had fallen from him, and struck the water, and said, "Where is HASHEM, the God of Elijah?"* He too struck the water and it split apart this way and that, and Elisha crossed over.

The spirit rests upon Elisha

¹⁵ The prophets' disciples who were from Jericho saw him from a distance and said, "The spirit of Elijah has rested upon Elisha!" They came towards him and prostrated themselves to the ground before him. ¹⁶ They said to him, "Behold, among your servants there are fifty able-bodied men. Let them go and search for your master; perhaps a spirit of HASHEM has carried him off and hurled him onto one of the mountains or one of the valleys."*

A futile search

But [Elisha] said, "Don't send them." ¹⁷ They badgered him until it was embarrassing [to refuse] so he said, "Send [them]"; they sent fifty men, who searched

שְׁלֹשָׁה יָמִים וְלֹא מְצָאֻהוּ: וַיָּשֻׁבוּ אֵלָיו וְהוּא יֹשֵׁב בִּירִיחוֹ וַיֹּאמֶר אֲלֵהֶם יח

הֲלוֹא־אָמַרְתִּי אֲלֵיכֶם אַל־תֵּלֵכוּ: וַיֹּאמְרוּ אַנְשֵׁי הָעִיר אֶל־אֱלִישָׁע יט

הִנֵּה־נָא מוֹשַׁב הָעִיר טוֹב כַּאֲשֶׁר אֲדֹנִי רֹאֶה וְהַמַּיִם רָעִים וְהָאָרֶץ

מְשַׁכָּלֶת: וַיֹּאמֶר קְחוּ־לִי צְלֹחִית חֲדָשָׁה וְשִׂימוּ שָׁם מֶלַח וַיִּקְחוּ אֵלָיו: כ

וַיֵּצֵא אֶל־מוֹצָא הַמַּיִם וַיַּשְׁלֶךְ־שָׁם מֶלַח וַיֹּאמֶר כֹּה־אָמַר יְהוָה רִפִּאתִי כא

לַמַּיִם הָאֵלֶּה לֹא־יִהְיֶה מִשָּׁם עוֹד מָוֶת וּמְשַׁכָּלֶת: וַיֵּרָפוּ הַמַּיִם עַד הַיּוֹם כב

הַזֶּה כִּדְבַר אֱלִישָׁע אֲשֶׁר דִּבֵּר: וַיַּעַל מִשָּׁם בֵּית־אֵל וְהוּא ׀ כג

עֹלֶה בַדֶּרֶךְ וּנְעָרִים קְטַנִּים יָצְאוּ מִן־הָעִיר וַיִּתְקַלְּסוּ־בוֹ וַיֹּאמְרוּ לוֹ עֲלֵה

קֵרֵחַ עֲלֵה קֵרֵחַ: וַיִּפֶן אַחֲרָיו וַיִּרְאֵם וַיְקַלְלֵם בְּשֵׁם יְהוָה וַתֵּצֶאנָה שְׁתַּיִם כד

דֻּבִּים מִן־הַיַּעַר וַתְּבַקַּעְנָה מֵהֶם אַרְבָּעִים וּשְׁנֵי יְלָדִים: וַיֵּלֶךְ מִשָּׁם אֶל־ כה

הַר הַכַּרְמֶל וּמִשָּׁם שָׁב שֹׁמְרוֹן: וִיהוֹרָם בֶּן־אַחְאָב מָלַךְ עַל־ א   **ג**

יִשְׂרָאֵל בְּשֹׁמְרוֹן בִּשְׁנַת שְׁמֹנֶה עֶשְׂרֵה לִיהוֹשָׁפָט מֶלֶךְ יְהוּדָה וַיִּמְלֹךְ

שְׁתֵּים־עֶשְׂרֵה שָׁנָה: וַיַּעֲשֶׂה הָרַע בְּעֵינֵי יְהוָה רַק לֹא כְאָבִיו וּכְאִמּוֹ וַיָּסַר ב

אֶת־מַצְּבַת הַבַּעַל אֲשֶׁר עָשָׂה אָבִיו: רַק בְּחַטֹּאות יָרָבְעָם בֶּן־נְבָט ג

אֲשֶׁר־הֶחֱטִיא אֶת־יִשְׂרָאֵל דָּבֵק לֹא־סָר מִמֶּנָּה: וּמֵישַׁע ד

מֶלֶךְ־מוֹאָב הָיָה נֹקֵד וְהֵשִׁיב לְמֶלֶךְ־יִשְׂרָאֵל מֵאָה־אֶלֶף כָּרִים וּמֵאָה

אֶלֶף אֵילִים צָמֶר: וַיְהִי כְּמוֹת אַחְאָב וַיִּפְשַׁע מֶלֶךְ־מוֹאָב בְּמֶלֶךְ יִשְׂרָאֵל: ה

וַיֵּצֵא הַמֶּלֶךְ יְהוֹרָם בַּיּוֹם הַהוּא מִשֹּׁמְרוֹן וַיִּפְקֹד אֶת־כָּל־יִשְׂרָאֵל: וַיֵּלֶךְ ו-ז

וַיִּשְׁלַח אֶל־יְהוֹשָׁפָט מֶלֶךְ־יְהוּדָה לֵאמֹר מֶלֶךְ מוֹאָב פָּשַׁע בִּי הֲתֵלֵךְ

אִתִּי אֶל־מוֹאָב לַמִּלְחָמָה וַיֹּאמֶר אֶעֱלֶה כָּמוֹנִי כָמוֹךָ כְּעַמִּי כְעַמֶּךָ

כְּסוּסַי כְּסוּסֶיךָ: וַיֹּאמֶר אֵי־זֶה הַדֶּרֶךְ נַעֲלֶה וַיֹּאמֶר דֶּרֶךְ מִדְבַּר אֱדוֹם: ח

וַיֵּלֶךְ מֶלֶךְ יִשְׂרָאֵל וּמֶלֶךְ־יְהוּדָה וּמֶלֶךְ אֱדוֹם וַיָּסֹבּוּ דֶּרֶךְ שִׁבְעַת יָמִים ט

וְלֹא־הָיָה מַיִם לַמַּחֲנֶה וְלַבְּהֵמָה אֲשֶׁר בְּרַגְלֵיהֶם: וַיֹּאמֶר מֶלֶךְ יִשְׂרָאֵל י

אֲהָהּ כִּי־קָרָא יְהוָה לִשְׁלֹשֶׁת הַמְּלָכִים הָאֵלֶּה לָתֵת אוֹתָם בְּיַד־מוֹאָב:

וַיֹּאמֶר יְהוֹשָׁפָט הַאֵין פֹּה נָבִיא לַיהוָה וְנִדְרְשָׁה אֶת־יְהוָה מֵאוֹתוֹ יא

וַיַּעַן אֶחָד מֵעַבְדֵי מֶלֶךְ־יִשְׂרָאֵל וַיֹּאמֶר פֹּה אֱלִישָׁע בֶּן־שָׁפָט אֲשֶׁר־

יָצַק מַיִם עַל־יְדֵי אֵלִיָּהוּ: וַיֹּאמֶר יְהוֹשָׁפָט יֵשׁ אוֹתוֹ דְּבַר־יְהוָה וַיֵּרְדוּ יב

אֵלָיו מֶלֶךְ יִשְׂרָאֵל וִיהוֹשָׁפָט וּמֶלֶךְ אֱדוֹם: וַיֹּאמֶר אֱלִישָׁע אֶל־מֶלֶךְ יג

יִשְׂרָאֵל מַה־לִּי וָלָךְ לֵךְ אֶל־נְבִיאֵי אָבִיךָ וְאֶל־נְבִיאֵי אִמֶּךָ וַיֹּאמֶר

לוֹ מֶלֶךְ יִשְׂרָאֵל אַל כִּי־קָרָא יְהוָה לִשְׁלֹשֶׁת הַמְּלָכִים הָאֵלֶּה לָתֵת

אוֹתָם בְּיַד מוֹאָב: וַיֹּאמֶר אֱלִישָׁע חַי־יְהוָה צְבָאוֹת אֲשֶׁר עָמַדְתִּי לְפָנָיו יד

2:24. The Talmud (*Sotah* 46b) explains that Elisha cursed them because he "saw" that they were degenerate and depraved, and he foresaw that no good would ever come out of them. Nevertheless, Elisha was later punished for treating them so harshly.

3:3. Jehoram maintained the worship of Jeroboam's golden calves, for fear that if he acknowledged the validity of the Temple in Jerusalem, his kingdom would disintegrate (*Rashi*).

3:5. The rebellion had begun earlier (1:1).

for three days but could not find him. ¹⁸ They returned to him — he was staying in Jericho — and he said to them, "Did I not say to you, 'Do not go!'?"

Supernatural powers ¹⁹ The people of the city told Elisha, "Behold, living in this city is pleasant, as my master can see, but the water is bad, making the land deadly." ²⁰ He said, "Get me a new jar and put salt in it," and they brought it to him. ²¹ He went out to the source of the water and threw salt there, and he said, "Thus said HASHEM: I have cured this water; there shall no longer be from it death and bereavement." ²² So the water became cured, until this day, like the word of Elisha that he had spoken.

²³ He went up from there to Beth-el. As he was going up on the road, some young lads came out from the city and mocked him, saying to him, "Go on up, Baldhead! Go on up, Baldhead!" ²⁴ He turned around and saw them* and cursed them in the name of HASHEM. Two bears then came out of the forest and tore apart forty-two of the lads.

²⁵ He went from there to Mount Carmel; and from there he returned to Samaria.

3

JEHORAM, KING OF ISRAEL
3:1-9:24
(See Appendix A, timeline 4)

¹ Jehoram son of Ahab had become king over Israel in Samaria in the eighteenth year of Jehoshaphat, king of Judah, and he reigned for twelve years. ² He did what was evil in the eyes of HASHEM, albeit not like his father and mother; he removed the pillar of the Baal that his father had erected. ³ However, he clung to the sins of Jeroboam son of Nebat, * who caused Israel to sin; he did not deviate from them.

His alliance with Judah

⁴ Mesha, king of Moab, was a herdsman; he paid the king of Israel a hundred thousand fatted sheep and a hundred thousand woolly rams. ⁵ It happened that when Ahab died, the king of Moab had rebelled against the king of Israel. * ⁶ King Jehoram went out of Samaria that day* and mobilized all of Israel. ⁷ He went and sent to Jehoshaphat, king of Judah, saying, "The king of Moab has rebelled against me; will you go to war with me against Moab?" He said, "I will go up; I [will be] like you; my people [shall be] like your people, my horses [shall be] like your horses."

⁸ He then asked, "By which route shall we go up?"
He replied, "By way of the Wilderness of Edom."

⁹ The king of Israel, the king of Judah, and the king of Edom then went and traveled round about for seven days; but there was no more water for the camp and for the animals that were with them. ¹⁰ The king of Israel then said, "Alas, HASHEM has summoned these three kings in order to deliver them into the hands of Moab!"

¹¹ Jehoshaphat said, "Is there no prophet of HASHEM here, that we may inquire of HASHEM through him?"
One of the servants of the king of Israel spoke up and said, "Elisha son of Shaphat is here, who poured water over the hands of Elijah!"

Jehoshaphat consults Elisha . . .

¹² Jehoshaphat said, "The word of HASHEM is [indeed] with him." So they went down to him — the king of Israel, Jehoshaphat, and the king of Edom.

¹³ Elisha said to the king of Israel, "What have we to do with one another? Go to your father's prophets or your mother's prophets!"
The king of Israel said to him, "Do not [speak thus]! For HASHEM has summoned these three kings to deliver them into the hand of Moab!"

¹⁴ Elisha said, "As HASHEM, Master of Legions, lives, before Whom I stand,

---

3:6. On the day Elisha arrived in Samaria (see 2:25; Metzudos).

כִּי לוּלֵי פְּנֵי יְהוֹשָׁפָט מֶלֶךְ־יְהוּדָה אֲנִי נֹשֵׂא אִם־אַבִּיט אֵלֶיךָ וְאִם־

טו-טז אֶרְאֶךָּ: וְעַתָּה קְחוּ־לִי מְנַגֵּן וְהָיָה כְּנַגֵּן הַמְנַגֵּן וַתְּהִי עָלָיו יַד־יְהוָה: וַיֹּאמֶר

יז כֹּה אָמַר יְהוָה עָשֹׂה הַנַּחַל הַזֶּה גֵּבִים ׀ גֵּבִים: כִּי־כֹה ׀ אָמַר יְהוֹה לֹא־

תִרְאוּ רוּחַ וְלֹא־תִרְאוּ גֶשֶׁם וְהַנַּחַל הַהוּא יִמָּלֵא מָיִם וּשְׁתִיתֶם אַתֶּם

יח וּמִקְנֵיכֶם וּבְהֶמְתְּכֶם: וְנָקַל זֹאת בְּעֵינֵי יְהוָה וְנָתַן אֶת־מוֹאָב בְּיֶדְכֶם:

יט וְהִכִּיתֶם כָּל־עִיר מִבְצָר וְכָל־עִיר מִבְחוֹר וְכָל־עֵץ טוֹב תַּפִּילוּ וְכָל־

כ מַעְיְנֵי־מַיִם תִּסְתֹּמוּ וְכֹל הַחֶלְקָה הַטּוֹבָה תַּכְאִבוּ בָּאֲבָנִים: וַיְהִי בַבֹּקֶר

כַּעֲלוֹת הַמִּנְחָה וְהִנֵּה־מַיִם בָּאִים מִדֶּרֶךְ אֱדוֹם וַתִּמָּלֵא הָאָרֶץ אֶת־

כא הַמָּיִם: וְכָל־מוֹאָב שָׁמְעוּ כִּי־עָלוּ הַמְּלָכִים לְהִלָּחֶם בָּם וַיִּצָּעֲקוּ מִכֹּל

כב חֹגֵר חֲגֹרָה וָמַעְלָה וַיַּעַמְדוּ עַל־הַגְּבוּל: וַיַּשְׁכִּימוּ בַבֹּקֶר וְהַשֶּׁמֶשׁ זָרְחָה

כג עַל־הַמָּיִם וַיִּרְאוּ מוֹאָב מִנֶּגֶד אֶת־הַמַּיִם אֲדֻמִּים כַּדָּם: וַיֹּאמְרוּ דָּם זֶה

הֶחֳרֵב נֶחֶרְבוּ הַמְּלָכִים וַיַּכּוּ אִישׁ אֶת־רֵעֵהוּ וְעַתָּה לַשָּׁלָל מוֹאָב: וַיָּבֹאוּ

כד אֶל־מַחֲנֵה יִשְׂרָאֵל וַיָּקֻמוּ יִשְׂרָאֵל וַיַּכּוּ אֶת־מוֹאָב וַיָּנֻסוּ מִפְּנֵיהֶם °וַיָּבוֹ־

כה [וַיַּכּוּ ק׳] בָהּ וְהַכּוֹת אֶת־מוֹאָב: וְהֶעָרִים יַהֲרֹסוּ וְכָל־חֶלְקָה טוֹבָה

יַשְׁלִיכוּ אִישׁ־אַבְנוֹ וּמִלְאוּהָ וְכָל־מַעְיַן־מַיִם יִסְתֹּמוּ וְכָל־עֵץ־טוֹב יַפִּילוּ

עַד־הִשְׁאִיר אֲבָנֶיהָ בַּקִּיר חֲרָשֶׂת וַיָּסֹבּוּ הַקַּלָּעִים וַיַּכּוּהָ: וַיַּרְא מֶלֶךְ מוֹאָב

כו כִּי־חָזַק מִמֶּנּוּ הַמִּלְחָמָה וַיִּקַּח אוֹתוֹ שְׁבַע־מֵאוֹת אִישׁ שֹׁלֵף חֶרֶב

כז לְהַבְקִיעַ אֶל־מֶלֶךְ אֱדוֹם וְלֹא יָכֹלוּ: וַיִּקַּח אֶת־בְּנוֹ הַבְּכוֹר אֲשֶׁר־יִמְלֹךְ

תַּחְתָּיו וַיַּעֲלֵהוּ עֹלָה עַל־הַחֹמָה וַיְהִי קֶצֶף־גָּדוֹל עַל־יִשְׂרָאֵל וַיִּסְעוּ

א מֵעָלָיו וַיָּשֻׁבוּ לָאָרֶץ: וְאִשָּׁה אַחַת מִנְּשֵׁי בְנֵי־הַנְּבִיאִים

ד

HAFTARAS VAYEIRA
Ashkenazim:
4:1-37
Sephardim:
4:1-23

צָעֲקָה אֶל־אֱלִישָׁע לֵאמֹר עַבְדְּךָ אִישִׁי מֵת וְאַתָּה יָדַעְתָּ כִּי עַבְדְּךָ

ב הָיָה יָרֵא אֶת־יְהוָה וְהַנֹּשֶׁה בָּא לָקַחַת אֶת־שְׁנֵי יְלָדַי לוֹ לַעֲבָדִים: וַיֹּאמֶר

אֵלֶיהָ אֱלִישָׁע מָה אֶעֱשֶׂה־לָּךְ הַגִּידִי לִי מַה־יֶּשׁ־°לְכִי [לָךְ ק׳] בַּבָּיִת

ג וַתֹּאמֶר אֵין לְשִׁפְחָתְךָ כֹל בַּבַּיִת כִּי אִם־אָסוּךְ שָׁמֶן: וַיֹּאמֶר לְכִי שַׁאֲלִי־

לָךְ כֵּלִים מִן־הַחוּץ מֵאֵת כָּל־°שְׁכֵנָכִי [שְׁכֵנָיִךְ ק׳] כֵּלִים רֵקִים אַל־

ד תַּמְעִיטִי: וּבָאת וְסָגַרְתְּ הַדֶּלֶת בַּעֲדֵךְ וּבְעַד־בָּנַיִךְ וְיָצַקְתְּ עַל כָּל־הַכֵּלִים

ה הָאֵלֶּה וְהַמָּלֵא תַּסִּיעִי: וַתֵּלֶךְ מֵאִתּוֹ וַתִּסְגֹּר הַדֶּלֶת בַּעֲדָהּ וּבְעַד בָּנֶיהָ הֵם

ו מַגִּשִׁים אֵלֶיהָ וְהִיא °מיצקת [מוֹצָקֶת ק׳]: וַיְהִי ׀ כִּמְלֹאת הַכֵּלִים וַתֹּאמֶר

אֶל־בְּנָהּ הַגִּישָׁה אֵלַי עוֹד כֶּלִי וַיֹּאמֶר אֵלֶיהָ אֵין עוֹד כֶּלִי וַיַּעֲמֹד הַשָּׁמֶן:

3:15. Because Elisha had become agitated over Jehoram's hypocrisy, the prophetic spirit departed from him. The musician improved his mood, so that he could receive the Divine presence again (*Rashi*).

3:21. From the simplest soldier to the most skilled warriors.

3:22. Since that area had always been an arid ravine, it never dawned on the Moabites that they were looking at a reflection from water (*Rashi*).

3:25. They took so many stones from the walls to clutter up the land that the only part of the wall that was left was the mortar that had held its stones together. Then, the "shooters," who fling rocks by means of catapults, slingshots, etc., destroyed whatever was left of the wall (*Rashi*).

3:27. Mesha slew the firstborn of the Edomite king

[I swear] that were it not for the presence of Jehoshaphat, king of Judah, whom I respect, I would not look at you nor see you! ¹⁵ And now, bring me a musician."* It happened that as the musician played, the hand of HASHEM came upon him. ¹⁶ He said, "Thus said HASHEM: This valley shall be made into many pools. ¹⁷ For thus said HASHEM: You will not see wind and you will not see rain, but that valley will be filled with water, and you, your cattle, and your animals will drink.

... who
prophesies
victory

¹⁸ But this is yet trivial in the eyes of HASHEM; for He will [also] deliver Moab into your hands. ¹⁹ You will smite every fortified city and every major city; you will fell every goodly tree and stop up all springs of water, and you will clutter up every goodly piece of land with stones." ²⁰ It happened in the morning, when the meal-offering is brought up, that water began to come from the direction of Edom, and the land was filled with the water.

²¹ All of Moab heard that the kings had come up to wage war against them, and they were mustered — from everyone who girds a [sword-]belt and upward* — and they stood at the border. ²² When they arose early in the morning, as the sun shone upon the water, from afar the Moabites saw the water as red as blood.* ²³ They exclaimed, "This is blood! The kings must have drawn swords and smitten one another! So now — Moab, to the spoils!" ²⁴ So they entered the

Moab is
routed

camp of Israel; the Israelites rose up and smote Moab, and they fled from them, they struck at them, repeatedly smiting Moab. ²⁵ They destroyed the cities; into every goodly piece of land, each man threw his stone and filled it; every spring of water they stopped up, and every goodly tree they felled; the only "stones" they left in the wall was the mortar. The shooters then went around and destroyed it.* ²⁶ When the king of Moab saw that the war was too difficult for him, he took seven hundred swordsmen with him to break through to [attack] the king of Edom, but they could not do so. ²⁷ He then took his firstborn son, who was to reign after him, and sacrificed him as a burnt-offering upon the wall, and a great wrath took effect against Israel;* so they turned away from [Mesha] and returned to the land.

4

A widow's
plight

¹ **O**ne woman from among the wives of the prophets' disciples cried out to Elisha, saying, "Your servant, my husband, has died, and you know that your servant feared God. But now the creditor has come to take my two sons to be his slaves."

² Elisha said to her, "What can I do for you? Tell me, what have you in the house?"

An unending
flow of oil

She said, "Your maidservant has nothing in the house except for a jar of oil." ³ He said, "Go, borrow vessels for yourself from the outside, from all your neighbors — empty vessels; do not be sparing. ⁴ Then go in and shut the door behind you and behind your sons. Pour [oil] into all these vessels, and carry away the full ones."

⁵ She went from him and shut the door behind her and behind her children. They brought [vessels] to her and she poured. ⁶ When all the containers were full she said to her son, "Bring me another vessel."

He said to her, "There is not another vessel," and the oil stopped.

(whom he had apparently captured and for whose sake the Edomites joined Israel against Moab) and the Edomites were furious with their erstwhile Israelite allies for not having prevented this barbaric murder (*Radak*). Then the tide of war suddenly turned against the Israelite army and they abandoned the siege of Moab.

וַתָּבֹא וַתַּגֵּד לְאִישׁ הָאֱלֹהִים וַיֹּאמֶר לְכִי מִכְרִי אֶת־הַשֶּׁמֶן וְשַׁלְּמִי אֶת־ ז
°נִשְׁיֵכִי [°נִשְׁיֵךְ ק׳] וְאַתְּ °בְּנֵיכִי [°וּבָנַיִךְ ק׳] תִּחְיִי בַּנּוֹתָר: וַיְהִי ח
הַיּוֹם וַיַּעֲבֹר אֱלִישָׁע אֶל־שׁוּנֵם וְשָׁם אִשָּׁה גְדוֹלָה וַתַּחֲזֶק־בּוֹ לֶאֱכָל־
לָחֶם וַיְהִי מִדֵּי עָבְרוֹ יָסֻר שָׁמָּה לֶאֱכָל־לָחֶם: וַתֹּאמֶר אֶל־אִישָׁהּ הִנֵּה־ ט
נָא יָדַעְתִּי כִּי אִישׁ אֱלֹהִים קָדוֹשׁ הוּא עֹבֵר עָלֵינוּ תָּמִיד: נַעֲשֶׂה־נָּא י
עֲלִיַּת־קִיר קְטַנָּה וְנָשִׂים לוֹ שָׁם מִטָּה וְשֻׁלְחָן וְכִסֵּא וּמְנוֹרָה וְהָיָה בְּבֹאוֹ
אֵלֵינוּ יָסוּר שָׁמָּה: וַיְהִי הַיּוֹם וַיָּבֹא שָׁמָּה וַיָּסַר אֶל־הָעֲלִיָּה וַיִּשְׁכַּב־שָׁמָּה: יא
וַיֹּאמֶר אֶל־גֵּיחֲזִי נַעֲרוֹ קְרָא לַשּׁוּנַמִּית הַזֹּאת וַיִּקְרָא־לָהּ וַתַּעֲמֹד לְפָנָיו: יב
וַיֹּאמֶר לוֹ אֱמָר־נָא אֵלֶיהָ הִנֵּה חָרַדְתְּ ׀ אֵלֵינוּ אֶת־כָּל־הַחֲרָדָה הַזֹּאת יג
מֶה לַעֲשׂוֹת לָךְ הֲיֵשׁ לְדַבֶּר־לָךְ אֶל־הַמֶּלֶךְ אוֹ אֶל־שַׂר הַצָּבָא וַתֹּאמֶר
בְּתוֹךְ עַמִּי אָנֹכִי יֹשָׁבֶת: וַיֹּאמֶר וּמֶה לַעֲשׂוֹת לָהּ וַיֹּאמֶר גֵּיחֲזִי אֲבָל בֵּן יד
אֵין־לָהּ וְאִישָׁהּ זָקֵן: וַיֹּאמֶר קְרָא־לָהּ וַיִּקְרָא־לָהּ וַתַּעֲמֹד בַּפָּתַח: וַיֹּאמֶר טו-טז
לַמּוֹעֵד הַזֶּה כָּעֵת חַיָּה °אֹתִי [°אַתְּ ק׳] חֹבֶקֶת בֵּן וַתֹּאמֶר אַל־אֲדֹנִי אִישׁ
הָאֱלֹהִים אַל־תְּכַזֵּב בְּשִׁפְחָתֶךָ: וַתַּהַר הָאִשָּׁה וַתֵּלֶד בֵּן לַמּוֹעֵד הַזֶּה יז
כָּעֵת חַיָּה אֲשֶׁר־דִּבֶּר אֵלֶיהָ אֱלִישָׁע: וַיִּגְדַּל הַיָּלֶד וַיְהִי הַיּוֹם וַיֵּצֵא אֶל־ יח
אָבִיו אֶל־הַקֹּצְרִים: וַיֹּאמֶר אֶל־אָבִיו רֹאשִׁי ׀ רֹאשִׁי וַיֹּאמֶר אֶל־הַנַּעַר יט
שָׂאֵהוּ אֶל־אִמּוֹ: וַיִּשָּׂאֵהוּ וַיְבִיאֵהוּ אֶל־אִמּוֹ וַיֵּשֶׁב עַל־בִּרְכֶּיהָ עַד־ כ
הַצָּהֳרַיִם וַיָּמֹת: וַתַּעַל וַתַּשְׁכִּבֵהוּ עַל־מִטַּת אִישׁ הָאֱלֹהִים וַתִּסְגֹּר בַּעֲדוֹ כא
וַתֵּצֵא: וַתִּקְרָא אֶל־אִישָׁהּ וַתֹּאמֶר שִׁלְחָה נָא לִי אֶחָד מִן־הַנְּעָרִים כב
וְאַחַת הָאֲתֹנוֹת וְאָרוּצָה עַד־אִישׁ הָאֱלֹהִים וְאָשׁוּבָה: וַיֹּאמֶר מַדּוּעַ כג
°אתי הלכתי [°אַתְּ הֹלֶכֶת ק׳] אֵלָיו הַיּוֹם לֹא־חֹדֶשׁ וְלֹא שַׁבָּת וַתֹּאמֶר
שָׁלוֹם: ▶ וַתַּחֲבֹשׁ הָאָתוֹן וַתֹּאמֶר אֶל־נַעֲרָהּ נְהַג וָלֵךְ אַל־תַּעֲצָר־לִי כד
לִרְכֹּב כִּי אִם־אָמַרְתִּי לָךְ: וַתֵּלֶךְ וַתָּבֹא אֶל־אִישׁ הָאֱלֹהִים אֶל־הַר כה
הַכַּרְמֶל וַיְהִי כִּרְאוֹת אִישׁ־הָאֱלֹהִים אֹתָהּ מִנֶּגֶד וַיֹּאמֶר אֶל־גֵּיחֲזִי נַעֲרוֹ
הִנֵּה הַשּׁוּנַמִּית הַלָּז: עַתָּה רוּץ־נָא לִקְרָאתָהּ וֶאֱמָר־לָהּ הֲשָׁלוֹם לָךְ כו
הֲשָׁלוֹם לְאִישֵׁךְ הֲשָׁלוֹם לַיָּלֶד וַתֹּאמֶר שָׁלוֹם: וַתָּבֹא אֶל־אִישׁ הָאֱלֹהִים כז
אֶל־הָהָר וַתַּחֲזֵק בְּרַגְלָיו וַיִּגַּשׁ גֵּיחֲזִי לְהָדְפָהּ וַיֹּאמֶר אִישׁ הָאֱלֹהִים
הַרְפֵּה־לָהּ כִּי־נַפְשָׁהּ מָרָה־לָהּ וַיהוֹה הֶעְלִים מִמֶּנִּי וְלֹא הִגִּיד לִי:
וַתֹּאמֶר הֲשָׁאַלְתִּי בֵן מֵאֵת אֲדֹנִי הֲלֹא אָמַרְתִּי לֹא תַשְׁלֶה אֹתִי: וַיֹּאמֶר כח-כט
לְגֵיחֲזִי חֲגֹר מָתְנֶיךָ וְקַח מִשְׁעַנְתִּי בְיָדְךָ וָלֵךְ כִּי תִמְצָא אִישׁ לֹא
תְבָרְכֶנּוּ וְכִי־יְבָרֶכְךָ אִישׁ לֹא תַעֲנֶנּוּ וְשַׂמְתָּ מִשְׁעַנְתִּי עַל־פְּנֵי הַנָּעַר:

4:13. Elisha called her to express thanks for her hospitality (v. 12); after she left, he instructed Gehazi to put this question to her (*Abarbanel*). She said, "I have no trouble with anyone that requires intervention with the authorities" (*Rashi*).

4:23. It was customary to visit great men on such days, for inspiration and instruction (*Ralbag*).

⁷ She came and told the man of God, and he said, "Go sell the oil and pay your creditor, and you and your sons will live on the remainder."

⁸ It happened one day that Elisha traveled to Shunem. There was a prominent woman there and she importuned him to eat a meal; and so it was, whenever he passed by, he would turn in there to eat a meal. ⁹ She [once] said to her husband, "Behold, I now know that he is a holy man of God who passes by us regularly.

The Shunammite woman's hospitality

¹⁰ Let us now make a small, walled attic and place there for him a bed, a table, a chair, and a lamp, so that whenever he comes to us, he can turn in there."

¹¹ It happened one day that he arrived there, and he turned in to the attic and lay down there. ¹² He said to Gehazi his attendant, "Summon that Shunammite woman." He summoned her and she stood before him. ¹³ He then said to [Gehazi], "Please say to her, 'Behold, you have undertaken all this exertion on our behalf — what [favor] can be done for you? Can something be said on your behalf to the king or the army commander?' "

She replied, "I dwell among my people."*

¹⁴ So he said [to Gehazi], "What can be done for her?"

Gehazi said, "Actually, she has no child, and her husband is old."

Elisha's blessing of a son . . .

¹⁵ He said, "Summon her"; so he summoned her and she stood in the doorway. ¹⁶ [Elisha] said, "At this season next year you will be embracing a son."

She said, "Do not, my master, O man of God, do not disappoint your maidservant!"

¹⁷ The woman conceived and bore a son at that season the next year, as Elisha had told her.

¹⁸ The boy grew up. It happened one day, he went out to his father, to the reapers [in the field]. ¹⁹ He said to his father, "My head! My head!"

[His father] said to the attendant, "Carry him to his mother."

. . . who suddenly dies

²⁰ He carried him and brought him to his mother; he sat in her lap until noon, and then he died. ²¹ She went up and laid him on the bed of the man of God, shut [the door] upon him and left.

²² She then called her husband and said, "Please send me one of the attendants and one of the donkeys, so that I can hurry to the man of God and return."

²³ He said, "Why are you going to him today? It is not a New Moon or a Sabbath!"*

She replied, "It is well."

She goes to Elisha

²⁴ She saddled the donkey and said to her attendant, "Lead and go, and do not impede me from riding unless I tell you." ²⁵ She set out and came to the man of God at Mount Carmel.

When the man of God saw her from afar, he said to Gehazi, his attendant, "Behold — it is that Shunammite woman! ²⁶ Now, please run toward her and say to her, 'Is it well with you? Is it well with your husband? Is it well with the boy?' "

She replied [to Gehazi], "It is well."

The prophet's compassion

²⁷ She came before the man of God at the mountain and grasped his legs. Gehazi approached to push her away, but the man of God said, "Leave her, for her soul is bitter within her, HASHEM has hidden it from me and not told me."

²⁸ She said, "Did I request a son of my master? Did I not say, 'Do not mislead me!'?"

²⁹ He said to Gehazi, "Gird your loins; take my staff in your hand and go. If you meet a man, do not greet him, and if a man greets you, do not respond to him. Place my staff upon the lad's face."

ל וַתֹּאמֶר אֵם הַנַּעַר חַי־יְהוָה וְחֵי־נַפְשְׁךָ אִם־אֶעֶזְבֶךָּ וַיָּקָם וַיֵּלֶךְ אַחֲרֶיהָ:

לא וְגֵחֲזִי עָבַר לִפְנֵיהֶם וַיָּשֶׂם אֶת־הַמִּשְׁעֶנֶת עַל־פְּנֵי הַנַּעַר וְאֵין קוֹל וְאֵין קָשֶׁב וַיָּשָׁב לִקְרָאתוֹ וַיַּגֶּד־לוֹ לֵאמֹר לֹא הֵקִיץ הַנָּעַר: וַיָּבֹא

לב אֱלִישָׁע הַבָּיְתָה וְהִנֵּה הַנַּעַר מֵת מֻשְׁכָּב עַל־מִטָּתוֹ: וַיָּבֹא וַיִּסְגֹּר הַדֶּלֶת

לג בְּעַד שְׁנֵיהֶם וַיִּתְפַּלֵּל אֶל־יְהוָה: וַיַּעַל וַיִּשְׁכַּב עַל־הַיֶּלֶד וַיָּשֶׂם פִּיו

לד עַל־פִּיו וְעֵינָיו עַל־עֵינָיו וְכַפָּיו עַל־°כפו [°כַּפָּיו ק] וַיִּגְהַר עָלָיו וַיָּחָם

לה בְּשַׂר הַיָּלֶד: וַיָּשָׁב וַיֵּלֶךְ בַּבַּיִת אַחַת הֵנָּה וְאַחַת הֵנָּה וַיַּעַל וַיִּגְהַר עָלָיו

לו וַיְזוֹרֵר הַנַּעַר עַד־שֶׁבַע פְּעָמִים וַיִּפְקַח הַנַּעַר אֶת־עֵינָיו: וַיִּקְרָא אֶל־גֵּיחֲזִי וַיֹּאמֶר קְרָא אֶל־הַשֻּׁנַמִּית הַזֹּאת וַיִּקְרָאֶהָ וַתָּבֹא אֵלָיו וַיֹּאמֶר שְׂאִי

לז בְנֵךְ: וַתָּבֹא וַתִּפֹּל עַל־רַגְלָיו וַתִּשְׁתַּחוּ אָרְצָה וַתִּשָּׂא אֶת־בְּנָהּ

לח וַתֵּצֵא: ◄ וֶאֱלִישָׁע שָׁב הַגִּלְגָּלָה וְהָרָעָב בָּאָרֶץ וּבְנֵי הַנְּבִיאִים יֹשְׁבִים לְפָנָיו וַיֹּאמֶר לְנַעֲרוֹ שְׁפֹת הַסִּיר הַגְּדוֹלָה וּבַשֵּׁל נָזִיד

לט לִבְנֵי הַנְּבִיאִים: וַיֵּצֵא אֶחָד אֶל־הַשָּׂדֶה לְלַקֵּט אֹרֹת וַיִּמְצָא גֶּפֶן שָׂדֶה וַיְלַקֵּט מִמֶּנּוּ פַּקֻּעֹת שָׂדֶה מְלֹא בִגְדוֹ וַיָּבֹא וַיְפַלַּח אֶל־סִיר הַנָּזִיד

מ כִּי־לֹא יָדָעוּ: וַיִּצְקוּ לַאֲנָשִׁים לֶאֱכוֹל וַיְהִי כְּאָכְלָם מֵהַנָּזִיד וְהֵמָּה צָעָקוּ וַיֹּאמְרוּ מָוֶת בַּסִּיר אִישׁ הָאֱלֹהִים וְלֹא יָכְלוּ לֶאֱכֹל: וַיֹּאמֶר וּקְחוּ־

מא קֶמַח וַיַּשְׁלֵךְ אֶל־הַסִּיר וַיֹּאמֶר צַק לָעָם וְיֹאכֵלוּ וְלֹא הָיָה דָּבָר רָע בַּסִּיר:

מב וְאִישׁ בָּא מִבַּעַל שָׁלִשָׁה וַיָּבֵא לְאִישׁ הָאֱלֹהִים לֶחֶם בִּכּוּרִים עֶשְׂרִים־לֶחֶם שְׂעֹרִים וְכַרְמֶל בְּצִקְלֹנוֹ וַיֹּאמֶר

מג תֵּן לָעָם וְיֹאכֵלוּ: וַיֹּאמֶר מְשָׁרְתוֹ מָה אֶתֵּן זֶה לִפְנֵי מֵאָה אִישׁ וַיֹּאמֶר

מד תֵּן לָעָם וְיֹאכֵלוּ כִּי כֹה אָמַר יְהוָה אָכוֹל וְהוֹתֵר: וַיִּתֵּן לִפְנֵיהֶם וַיֹּאכְלוּ וַיּוֹתִרוּ כִּדְבַר יְהוָה:

ה

א וְנַעֲמָן שַׂר־צְבָא מֶלֶךְ־אֲרָם הָיָה אִישׁ גָּדוֹל לִפְנֵי אֲדֹנָיו וּנְשֻׂא פָנִים כִּי־בוֹ נָתַן־יְהוָה תְּשׁוּעָה

ב לַאֲרָם וְהָאִישׁ הָיָה גִּבּוֹר חַיִל מְצֹרָע: וַאֲרָם יָצְאוּ גְדוּדִים וַיִּשְׁבּוּ

ג מֵאֶרֶץ יִשְׂרָאֵל נַעֲרָה קְטַנָּה וַתְּהִי לִפְנֵי אֵשֶׁת נַעֲמָן: וַתֹּאמֶר אֶל־גְּבִרְתָּהּ אַחֲלֵי אֲדֹנִי לִפְנֵי הַנָּבִיא אֲשֶׁר בְּשֹׁמְרוֹן אָז יֶאֱסֹף אֹתוֹ מִצָּרַעְתּוֹ:

ד וַיָּבֹא וַיַּגֵּד לַאדֹנָיו לֵאמֹר כָּזֹאת וְכָזֹאת דִּבְּרָה הַנַּעֲרָה אֲשֶׁר מֵאֶרֶץ

ה יִשְׂרָאֵל: וַיֹּאמֶר מֶלֶךְ־אֲרָם לֶךְ־בֹּא וְאֶשְׁלְחָה סֵפֶר אֶל־מֶלֶךְ יִשְׂרָאֵל וַיֵּלֶךְ וַיִּקַּח בְּיָדוֹ עֶשֶׂר כִּכְּרֵי־כֶסֶף וְשֵׁשֶׁת אֲלָפִים זָהָב וְעֶשֶׂר חֲלִיפוֹת

ו בְּגָדִים: וַיָּבֵא הַסֵּפֶר אֶל־מֶלֶךְ יִשְׂרָאֵל לֵאמֹר וְעַתָּה כְּבוֹא הַסֵּפֶר הַזֶּה אֵלֶיךָ הִנֵּה שָׁלַחְתִּי אֵלֶיךָ אֶת־נַעֲמָן עַבְדִּי וַאֲסַפְתּוֹ מִצָּרַעְתּוֹ:

4:39. They did not realize that the mushrooms were poisonous.

5:1. He was the unnamed archer who slew Ahab (see I Kings 22:34; Rashi).

Regarding the affliction of the מְצֹרָע (here rendered leper), see Leviticus, Ch. 13.

³⁰ The lad's mother said. "[I swear] as HASHEM lives and [I swear] as you live, I will not leave you!" So he arose and went after her.

³¹ Gehazi went ahead of them and placed the staff on the lad's face, but there was no sound and nothing was heard. He returned toward [Elisha] and told him, saying, "The lad has not awakened."

³² Elisha came into the house and behold — the lad was dead, laid out on his bed. ³³ He entered and shut the door behind them both, and prayed to HASHEM.

Elisha returns the child to life ³⁴ Then he went up and lay upon the boy, placing his mouth upon his mouth, his eyes upon his eyes, and his palms upon his palms. He stretched himself out over him, and warmed the flesh of the boy. ³⁵ He withdrew and walked through the house, once this way and once that way, then he went up and stretched himself over him. The lad sneezed seven times, and the lad opened his eyes.

³⁶ [Elisha] called Gehazi and said, "Summon this Shunammite woman." He summoned her and she came to him; he said, "Pick up your son!" ³⁷ She came and fell at his feet and bowed down to the ground; she then picked up her son and left.

Food for the starving prophets ³⁸ Elisha then returned to Gilgal, and there was a famine in the land. The prophets' disciples were sitting before him. He said to his attendant, "Put up the large pot and cook a stew for the prophets' disciples."

³⁹ One of them went out to the field to gather herbs; he came across a vine in the field and picked [enough] from it [and from the] wild mushrooms [around it] to fill up his garment. He came and cut [them] into the pot of stew, for they did not recognize [these fruits]. * ⁴⁰ They poured it out for the men to eat, and it happened as they ate the soup, they shouted; they said, "There is death in the pot, O man of God!" and they could not eat.

⁴¹ Elisha said, "Get some flour!" and he threw it into the pot; and he said, "Pour for the people and let them eat"; and there was no longer anything harmful in the pot.

⁴² A man came from Baal-shalishah, and he brought to the man of God food from the first reaping: twenty loaves of barley bread — and some fresh kernels in their husks. [Elisha] said, "Give it to the people that they may eat."

⁴³ His servant said, "How can I place this before a hundred people?"

But he said, "Give it to the people and let them eat, for thus said HASHEM: Eat and leave over!" ⁴⁴ He placed it before them, and they ate and left over, as the word of HASHEM.

5

Naaman the leper seeks a cure in the Land of Israel ¹ **N**aaman, the commander of the army of the king of Aram, was an eminent man before his master and well honored, for through him HASHEM had granted victory to Aram. The man was a great warrior — a leper. * ² Aram had gone out in raiding parties, and had captured a young girl from the Land of Israel, and she was [serving] before Naaman's wife. ³ She said to her mistress, "My master's prayers [should be brought] before the prophet who is in Samaria; for then he will heal him from his leprosy."

⁴ So [Naaman] went and told his master, saying, "Such and such spoke the girl who is from the Land of Israel."

⁵ The king of Aram said, "Go and approach [him], and I will send a letter to the king of Israel." He went and took in his hand ten talents of silver, six thousand [pieces of] gold and ten changes of clothes.

⁶ He brought to the king of Israel the letter which said, ". . . and now, when this letter reaches you, behold I have sent my servant Naaman to you, that you should heal him from his leprosy."

ז וַיְהִי כִּקְרֹא מֶלֶךְ־יִשְׂרָאֵל אֶת־הַסֵּפֶר וַיִּקְרַע בְּגָדָיו וַיֹּאמֶר הַאֱלֹהִים אָנִי
לְהָמִית וּלְהַחֲיוֹת כִּי־זֶה שֹׁלֵחַ אֵלַי לֶאֱסֹף אִישׁ מִצָּרַעְתּוֹ כִּי אַךְ־דְּעוּ־נָא
ח וּרְאוּ כִּי־מִתְאַנֶּה הוּא לִי: וַיְהִי כִּשְׁמֹעַ ׀ אֱלִישָׁע אִישׁ־הָאֱלֹהִים כִּי־קָרַע
מֶלֶךְ־יִשְׂרָאֵל אֶת־בְּגָדָיו וַיִּשְׁלַח אֶל־הַמֶּלֶךְ לֵאמֹר לָמָּה קָרַעְתָּ בְּגָדֶיךָ
ט יָבֹא־נָא אֵלַי וְיֵדַע כִּי יֵשׁ נָבִיא בְּיִשְׂרָאֵל: וַיָּבֹא נַעֲמָן [°בְּסוּסָו] בּסוסיו
י ק'] וּבְרִכְבּוֹ וַיַּעֲמֹד פֶּתַח־הַבַּיִת לֶאֱלִישָׁע: וַיִּשְׁלַח אֵלָיו אֱלִישָׁע מַלְאָךְ
יא לֵאמֹר הָלוֹךְ וְרָחַצְתָּ שֶׁבַע־פְּעָמִים בַּיַּרְדֵּן וְיָשֹׁב בְּשָׂרְךָ לְךָ וּטְהָר: וַיִּקְצֹף
נַעֲמָן וַיֵּלַךְ וַיֹּאמֶר הִנֵּה אָמַרְתִּי אֵלַי ׀ יֵצֵא יָצוֹא וְעָמַד וְקָרָא בְּשֵׁם־
יב יהוה אֱלֹהָיו וְהֵנִיף יָדוֹ אֶל־הַמָּקוֹם וְאָסַף הַמְּצֹרָע: הֲלֹא טוֹב [°אֲבָנָה
°אֲמָנָה ק'] וּפַרְפַּר נַהֲרוֹת דַּמֶּשֶׂק מִכֹּל מֵימֵי יִשְׂרָאֵל הֲלֹא־אֶרְחַץ בָּהֶם
יג וְטָהָרְתִּי וַיִּפֶן וַיֵּלֶךְ בְּחֵמָה: וַיִּגְּשׁוּ עֲבָדָיו וַיְדַבְּרוּ אֵלָיו וַיֹּאמְרוּ אָבִי דָּבָר
יד גָּדוֹל הַנָּבִיא דִּבֶּר אֵלֶיךָ הֲלוֹא תַעֲשֶׂה וְאַף כִּי־אָמַר אֵלֶיךָ רְחַץ וּטְהָר:
וַיֵּרֶד וַיִּטְבֹּל בַּיַּרְדֵּן שֶׁבַע פְּעָמִים כִּדְבַר אִישׁ הָאֱלֹהִים וַיָּשָׁב בְּשָׂרוֹ
טו כִּבְשַׂר נַעַר קָטֹן וַיִּטְהָר: וַיָּשָׁב אֶל־אִישׁ הָאֱלֹהִים הוּא וְכָל־מַחֲנֵהוּ וַיָּבֹא
וַיַּעֲמֹד לְפָנָיו וַיֹּאמֶר הִנֵּה־נָא יָדַעְתִּי כִּי אֵין אֱלֹהִים בְּכָל־הָאָרֶץ כִּי אִם־
טז בְּיִשְׂרָאֵל וְעַתָּה קַח־נָא בְרָכָה מֵאֵת עַבְדֶּךָ: וַיֹּאמֶר חַי־יהוה אֲשֶׁר־
יז עָמַדְתִּי לְפָנָיו אִם־אֶקָּח וַיִּפְצַר־בּוֹ לָקַחַת וַיְמָאֵן: וַיֹּאמֶר נַעֲמָן וָלֹא יֻתַּן־
נָא לְעַבְדְּךָ מַשָּׂא צֶמֶד־פְּרָדִים אֲדָמָה כִּי לוֹא־יַעֲשֶׂה עוֹד עַבְדְּךָ עֹלָה
יח וָזֶבַח לֵאלֹהִים אֲחֵרִים כִּי אִם־לַיהוה: לַדָּבָר הַזֶּה יִסְלַח יהוה לְעַבְדֶּךָ
בְּבוֹא אֲדֹנִי בֵית־רִמּוֹן לְהִשְׁתַּחֲוֹת שָׁמָּה וְהוּא ׀ נִשְׁעָן עַל־יָדִי
וְהִשְׁתַּחֲוֵיתִי בֵּית רִמֹּן בְּהִשְׁתַּחֲוָיָתִי בֵּית רִמֹּן יִסְלַח־[°נָא כ' וְלֹא ק'] יהוה
יט לְעַבְדְּךָ בַּדָּבָר הַזֶּה: וַיֹּאמֶר לוֹ לֵךְ לְשָׁלוֹם וַיֵּלֶךְ מֵאִתּוֹ כִּבְרַת
כ אָרֶץ: ▶   וַיֹּאמֶר גֵּיחֲזִי נַעַר אֱלִישָׁע אִישׁ־הָאֱלֹהִים הִנֵּה ׀ חָשַׂךְ
אֲדֹנִי אֶת נַעֲמָן הָאֲרַמִּי הַזֶּה מִקַּחַת מִיָּדוֹ אֵת אֲשֶׁר־הֵבִיא חַי־יהוה כִּי־
כא אִם־רַצְתִּי אַחֲרָיו וְלָקַחְתִּי מֵאִתּוֹ מְאוּמָה: וַיִּרְדֹּף גֵּיחֲזִי אַחֲרֵי נַעֲמָן
וַיִּרְאֶה נַעֲמָן רָץ אַחֲרָיו וַיִּפֹּל מֵעַל הַמֶּרְכָּבָה לִקְרָאתוֹ וַיֹּאמֶר הֲשָׁלוֹם:
כב וַיֹּאמֶר ׀ שָׁלוֹם אֲדֹנִי שְׁלָחַנִי לֵאמֹר הִנֵּה עַתָּה זֶה בָּאוּ אֵלַי שְׁנֵי־נְעָרִים
מֵהַר אֶפְרַיִם מִבְּנֵי הַנְּבִיאִים תְּנָה־נָּא לָהֶם כִּכַּר־כֶּסֶף וּשְׁתֵּי חֲלִפוֹת
כג בְּגָדִים: וַיֹּאמֶר נַעֲמָן הוֹאֵל קַח כִּכָּרָיִם וַיִּפְרָץ־בּוֹ וַיָּצַר כִּכְּרַיִם כֶּסֶף
בִּשְׁנֵי חֲרִטִים וּשְׁתֵּי חֲלִפוֹת בְּגָדִים וַיִּתֵּן אֶל־שְׁנֵי נְעָרָיו וַיִּשְׂאוּ לְפָנָיו:
כד וַיָּבֹא אֶל־הָעֹפֶל וַיִּקַּח מִיָּדָם וַיִּפְקֹד בַּבָּיִת וַיְשַׁלַּח אֶת־הָאֲנָשִׁים וַיֵּלֵכוּ:

5:17. Naaman requested permission to take a large amount of earth from Elisha's property (*Ralbag*) in order to build an altar to Elisha's God in his own town.

The Jewish king's fear | [7] When the king of Israel read the letter, he rent his garments and said, "Am I God that I can take and give life, that this person sends me [instructions] to heal a man of his leprosy? Understand and realize that he seeks a pretext against me!"

Elisha sends for Naaman | [8] When Elisha, the man of God, heard that the king of Israel had rent his garments, he sent word to the king, saying, "Why did you rend your garments? Let him come to me now, and he will realize that there is a prophet in Israel!"

[9] Naaman came with his horses and chariot and stood at the entrance of Elisha's house. [10] Elisha sent him a messenger, saying, "Go and bathe seven times in the Jordan; your flesh will become normal again and you will be cleansed."

Arrogant Naaman . . . | [11] Naaman was enraged and left. He said, "Behold, I said [to myself] that he would surely come out to me, and stand and call in the Name of HASHEM, his God, and wave his hand over the [diseased] area — and the leper would be healed! [12] Are not Amanah and Pharpar, the rivers of Damascus, better than all the waters of Israel? Do I not always bathe in them? Have I become cleansed?" Then he turned and went in a fury.

. . . accedes and is cured | [13] But his servants approached and spoke to him, and said, "My father, had the prophet told you to do a difficult thing, would you not have done it? How much more so [now] that he has told you 'bathe and become cleansed.' " [14] So he went down and immersed himself seven times in the Jordan, in accordance with the word of the man of God, and his flesh became like the flesh of a young boy, and he became cleansed.

Naaman's respect for Elisha | [15] He returned to the man of God, he and his entire retinue. He arrived and stood before him and said, "Behold, now I know that there is no God in the whole world except in Israel! And now, please accept a tribute from your servant."

[16] But [Elisha] answered, "As HASHEM before Whom I stood lives, [I swear that] I will not accept." He urged him to accept, but he refused.

[17] Naaman said, "At least, let there be given to your servant a mule-team's load of earth, * for your servant will never again offer a burnt-offering or any sacrifice to other gods, but only to HASHEM. [18] May HASHEM forgive your servant for this [one] thing, however: When my master comes to the temple of Rimmon to bow down there, he leans on my arm, so I must bow in the temple of Rimmon; when I bow down in the temple of Rimmon, may HASHEM forgive your servant for this [one] thing."

[19] He said to him, "Go to peace." And [Naaman] traveled a short distance from him.

Gehazi's greed . . . | [20] Gehazi, the attendant of Elisha, the man of God, said to himself, "Behold, my master has spared this Aramean Naaman by not accepting from his hand what he had brought. As HASHEM lives, [I swear] that I shall run after him and take something from him."

[21] So Gehazi chased after Naaman. Naaman saw him running after him, and he alighted from the chariot to greet him, and said, "Is [all] well?"

[22] He said, "[All is] well. My master sent me saying, 'Just now two young men of the prophets' disciples have arrived to me from Mount Ephraim. Please give them a talent of silver and two changes of clothing.' "

[23] Naaman said, "Please! Take two talents!" He prevailed upon him, and he wrapped up two talents of silver in two pouches, and [took] two changes of clothing, and gave [it] to his two attendants, who carried it before [Gehazi]. [24] When they came to a secluded place he took [it] from their hands and hid [it] in his house. He then sent off the men, and they went.

כה וְהוּא־בָא אֶל־אֲדֹנָיו וַיַּעֲמֹד וַיֹּאמֶר אֵלָיו אֱלִישָׁע °מֵאָן [°מֵאַיִן ק] גֵּחֲזִי

כו וַיֹּאמֶר לֹא־הָלַךְ עַבְדְּךָ אָנֶה וָאָנָה וַיֹּאמֶר אֵלָיו לֹא־לִבִּי הָלַךְ כַּאֲשֶׁר הָפַךְ־
אִישׁ מֵעַל מֶרְכַּבְתּוֹ לִקְרָאתֶךָ הַעֵת לָקַחַת אֶת־הַכֶּסֶף וְלָקַחַת בְּגָדִים

כז וְזֵיתִים וּכְרָמִים וְצֹאן וּבָקָר וַעֲבָדִים וּשְׁפָחוֹת: וְצָרַעַת נַעֲמָן תִּדְבַּק־בְּךָ
וּבְזַרְעֲךָ לְעוֹלָם וַיֵּצֵא מִלְּפָנָיו מְצֹרָע כַּשָּׁלֶג:

ו א וַיֹּאמְרוּ בְנֵי־הַנְּבִיאִים
אֶל־אֱלִישָׁע הִנֵּה־נָא הַמָּקוֹם אֲשֶׁר אֲנַחְנוּ יֹשְׁבִים שָׁם לְפָנֶיךָ צַר מִמֶּנּוּ:

ב נֵלְכָה־נָּא עַד־הַיַּרְדֵּן וְנִקְחָה מִשָּׁם אִישׁ קוֹרָה אֶחָת וְנַעֲשֶׂה־לָּנוּ שָׁם מָקוֹם
לָשֶׁבֶת שָׁם וַיֹּאמֶר לֵכוּ:

ג וַיֹּאמֶר הָאֶחָד הוֹאֶל נָא וְלֵךְ אֶת־עֲבָדֶיךָ וַיֹּאמֶר
אֲנִי אֵלֵךְ:

ד-ה וַיֵּלֶךְ אִתָּם וַיָּבֹאוּ הַיַּרְדֵּנָה וַיִּגְזְרוּ הָעֵצִים: וַיְהִי הָאֶחָד מַפִּיל
הַקּוֹרָה וְאֶת־הַבַּרְזֶל נָפַל אֶל־הַמָּיִם וַיִּצְעַק וַיֹּאמֶר אֲהָהּ אֲדֹנִי וְהוּא שָׁאוּל:

ו וַיֹּאמֶר אִישׁ־הָאֱלֹהִים אָנָה נָפָל וַיַּרְאֵהוּ אֶת־הַמָּקוֹם וַיִּקְצָב־עֵץ וַיַּשְׁלֶךְ־
שָׁמָּה וַיָּצֶף הַבַּרְזֶל:

ז וַיֹּאמֶר הָרֶם לָךְ וַיִּשְׁלַח יָדוֹ וַיִּקָּחֵהוּ:

ח וּמֶלֶךְ
אֲרָם הָיָה נִלְחָם בְּיִשְׂרָאֵל וַיִּוָּעַץ אֶל־עֲבָדָיו לֵאמֹר אֶל־מְקוֹם פְּלֹנִי אַלְמֹנִי
תַּחֲנֹתִי:

ט וַיִּשְׁלַח אִישׁ הָאֱלֹהִים אֶל־מֶלֶךְ יִשְׂרָאֵל לֵאמֹר הִשָּׁמֶר מֵעֲבֹר
הַמָּקוֹם הַזֶּה כִּי־שָׁם אֲרָם נְחִתִּים:

י וַיִּשְׁלַח מֶלֶךְ יִשְׂרָאֵל אֶל־הַמָּקוֹם אֲשֶׁר
אָמַר־לוֹ אִישׁ הָאֱלֹהִים °וְהִזְהִירָה [°וְהִזְהִירוֹ ק] וְנִשְׁמַר שָׁם לֹא אַחַת
וְלֹא שְׁתָּיִם:

יא וַיִּסָּעֵר לֵב מֶלֶךְ־אֲרָם עַל־הַדָּבָר הַזֶּה וַיִּקְרָא אֶל־עֲבָדָיו וַיֹּאמֶר
אֲלֵיהֶם הֲלוֹא תַּגִּידוּ לִי מִי מִשֶּׁלָּנוּ אֶל־מֶלֶךְ יִשְׂרָאֵל:

יב וַיֹּאמֶר אַחַד מֵעֲבָדָיו
לוֹא אֲדֹנִי הַמֶּלֶךְ כִּי־אֱלִישָׁע הַנָּבִיא אֲשֶׁר בְּיִשְׂרָאֵל יַגִּיד לְמֶלֶךְ יִשְׂרָאֵל
אֶת־הַדְּבָרִים אֲשֶׁר תְּדַבֵּר בַּחֲדַר מִשְׁכָּבֶךָ:

יג וַיֹּאמֶר לְכוּ וּרְאוּ אֵיכֹה הוּא
וְאֶשְׁלַח וְאֶקָּחֵהוּ וַיֻּגַּד־לוֹ לֵאמֹר הִנֵּה בְדֹתָן:

יד וַיִּשְׁלַח־שָׁמָּה סוּסִים וְרֶכֶב
וְחַיִל כָּבֵד וַיָּבֹאוּ לַיְלָה וַיַּקִּפוּ עַל־הָעִיר: וַיַּשְׁכֵּם מְשָׁרֵת אִישׁ הָאֱלֹהִים

טו לָקוּם וַיֵּצֵא וְהִנֵּה־חַיִל סוֹבֵב אֶת־הָעִיר וְסוּס וָרָכֶב וַיֹּאמֶר נַעֲרוֹ אֵלָיו אֲהָהּ
אֲדֹנִי אֵיכָה נַעֲשֶׂה:

טז וַיֹּאמֶר אַל־תִּירָא כִּי רַבִּים אֲשֶׁר אִתָּנוּ מֵאֲשֶׁר אוֹתָם:

יז וַיִּתְפַּלֵּל אֱלִישָׁע וַיֹּאמַר יְהוָה פְּקַח־נָא אֶת־עֵינָיו וְיִרְאֶה וַיִּפְקַח
יְהוָה אֶת־עֵינֵי הַנַּעַר וַיַּרְא וְהִנֵּה הָהָר מָלֵא סוּסִים וְרֶכֶב אֵשׁ סְבִיבֹת
אֱלִישָׁע:

יח וַיֵּרְדוּ אֵלָיו וַיִּתְפַּלֵּל אֱלִישָׁע אֶל־יְהוָה וַיֹּאמַר הַךְ־נָא אֶת־
הַגּוֹי־הַזֶּה בַּסַּנְוֵרִים וַיַּכֵּם בַּסַּנְוֵרִים כִּדְבַר אֱלִישָׁע:

יט וַיֹּאמֶר אֲלֵהֶם אֱלִישָׁע
לֹא זֶה הַדֶּרֶךְ וְלֹא זֹה הָעִיר לְכוּ אַחֲרַי וְאוֹלִיכָה אֶתְכֶם אֶל־הָאִישׁ אֲשֶׁר
תְּבַקֵּשׁוּן וַיֹּלֶךְ אוֹתָם שֹׁמְרוֹנָה:

כ וַיְהִי כְּבֹאָם שֹׁמְרוֹן וַיֹּאמֶר אֱלִישָׁע יְהוָה
פְּקַח אֶת־עֵינֵי־אֵלֶּה וְיִרְאוּ וַיִּפְקַח יְהוָה אֶת־עֵינֵיהֶם וַיִּרְאוּ וְהִנֵּה בְּתוֹךְ

5:26. Through prophetic vision, my heart exactly knew what happened (*Targum*). Gehazi's greed had detracted from the sanctification of God's Name that had resulted from Elisha's unselfish aid to the ailing stranger.

5:27. Gehazi's children were apparently guilty of com-

plicity in his deeds (*Radak*).

6:5. And I cannot afford to pay for it.

6:10. After the king's scouts verified Elisha's intelligence reports (*Rashi*), the Israelites eluded the ambush several times.

²⁵ He then came and stood before his master. Elisha said to him, "Where are you coming from, Gehazi?"

He said, "Your servant did not go here or there."

. . . causes his expulsion ²⁶ [Elisha] then said to him, "Did my heart not go along, * when a man turned aside from upon his chariot to greet you! Is this a [proper] time to accept money [with which] to buy clothing, olive trees, vineyards, sheep, cattle, slaves and maid-servants? ²⁷ Naaman's leprosy shall therefore cleave to you and to your children * forever!" When [Gehazi] left his presence, he was [white] as snow with leprosy.

6 ¹ The prophets' disciples [once] said to Elisha, "Behold, the place where we are dwelling before you is too crowded for us. ² Let us go to the Jordan and each one of us will take one beam, and there we will make ourselves a place to dwell."

[Elisha] replied, "Go."

³ One of them said, "Please agree to go with your servants." [Elisha] replied, "I will go."

The floating axehead ⁴ So he went with them, and they arrived at the Jordan and cut down the trees. ⁵ It happened as one of them was felling a beam that the iron [axehead] fell into the water. He cried out and said, "Woe is me, my master, it is borrowed!" *

⁶ The man of God asked him, "Where did it fall?" and he showed him the place. [Elisha] then cut a piece of wood and threw it there, and the blade floated up. ⁷ He said, "Pick it up for yourself!" and he stretched out his hand and took it.

Elisha warns against Aram's ambush ⁸ The king of Aram was fighting against Israel. He took counsel with his serv-ants, saying, "My encampments will be in such and such a place." ⁹ The man of God sent [word] to the king of Israel, saying, "Beware of passing by this place, for that is where Aram is lurking." ¹⁰ The king of Israel sent [scouts] to the place about which the man of God had spoken to him and had warned him, and he took care [to avoid] that place. [This happened] not [just] once and not [just] twice. *

¹¹ The heart of the king of Aram became perturbed over this matter. He summoned his servants and said to them, "Won't you tell me which of our people is [reporting] to the king of Israel?"

¹² One of his servants said, "It is not so, my master the king! Rather, Elisha, the prophet who is in Israel, tells the king of Israel [even] the things that you discuss in your bedroom."

Aram seeks to capture him ¹³ He said, "Go and see where he is, and I will send [men] and capture him." It was told to him, saying, "He is in Dothan." ¹⁴ He sent horses and chariot and a large army there; they came at night and surrounded the city.

¹⁵ The attendant of the man of God was early to arise and he set out, when behold — an army was surrounding the city, with horse and chariot. His attendant said to him, "Alas, my master, what shall we do?"

The disciple sees the heavenly army ¹⁶ [Elisha] said, "Fear not, for we have more [forces] with us than they have with them!" ¹⁷ Elisha then prayed and said, "HASHEM, please open up his eyes that he may see!" HASHEM then opened up the attendant's eyes and he saw that, behold, the mountain was full of horses and a chariot of fire, all around Elisha.

Elisha leads Aram to defeat ¹⁸ [The Arameans] then descended upon him; Elisha prayed to HASHEM, and said, "Please strike this nation with blindness!" And He struck them with blind-ness, according to the word of Elisha. ¹⁹ Elisha then said to them, "This is not the [right] way, and this is not the [right] city! Follow me and I will lead you to the man whom you seek," and he led them to Samaria. ²⁰ It happened when they arrived at Samaria that Elisha said, "HASHEM, open the eyes of these [people] that they may see!" HASHEM opened up their eyes and they realized that there they were in

כא שִׁמְרוֹן: וַיֹּאמֶר מֶלֶךְ־יִשְׂרָאֵל אֶל־אֱלִישָׁע כִּרְאֹתוֹ אוֹתָם הַאַכֶּה אַכֶּה
כב אָבִי: וַיֹּאמֶר לֹא תַכֶּה הַאֲשֶׁר שָׁבִיתָ בְּחַרְבְּךָ וּבְקַשְׁתְּךָ אַתָּה מַכֶּה שִׂים
לֶחֶם וָמַיִם לִפְנֵיהֶם וְיֹאכְלוּ וְיִשְׁתּוּ וְיֵלְכוּ אֶל־אֲדֹנֵיהֶם: וַיִּכְרֶה לָהֶם כֵּרָה
כג גְדוֹלָה וַיֹּאכְלוּ וַיִּשְׁתּוּ וַיְשַׁלְּחֵם וַיֵּלְכוּ אֶל־אֲדֹנֵיהֶם וְלֹא־יָסְפוּ עוֹד גְּדוּדֵי
כד אֲרָם לָבוֹא בְּאֶרֶץ יִשְׂרָאֵל: וַיְהִי אַחֲרֵי־כֵן וַיִּקְבֹּץ בֶּן־הֲדַד מֶלֶךְ־
כה אֲרָם אֶת־כָּל־מַחֲנֵהוּ וַיַּעַל וַיָּצַר עַל־שֹׁמְרוֹן: וַיְהִי רָעָב גָּדוֹל בְּשֹׁמְרוֹן וְהִנֵּה
צָרִים עָלֶיהָ עַד הֱיוֹת רֹאשׁ־חֲמוֹר בִּשְׁמֹנִים כֶּסֶף וְרֹבַע הַקַּב °חריונים
כו [דִּבְיוֹנִים ק׳] בַּחֲמִשָּׁה־כָסֶף: וַיְהִי מֶלֶךְ יִשְׂרָאֵל עֹבֵר עַל־הַחֹמָה וְאִשָּׁה
כז צָעֲקָה אֵלָיו לֵאמֹר הוֹשִׁיעָה אֲדֹנִי הַמֶּלֶךְ: וַיֹּאמֶר אַל־יוֹשִׁעֵךְ יְהוָה מֵאַיִן
כח אוֹשִׁיעֵךְ הֲמִן־הַגֹּרֶן אוֹ מִן־הַיָּקֶב: וַיֹּאמֶר־לָהּ הַמֶּלֶךְ מַה־לָּךְ וַתֹּאמֶר הָאִשָּׁה
הַזֹּאת אָמְרָה אֵלַי תְּנִי אֶת־בְּנֵךְ וְנֹאכְלֶנּוּ הַיּוֹם וְאֶת־בְּנִי נֹאכַל מָחָר:
כט וַנְּבַשֵּׁל אֶת־בְּנִי וַנֹּאכְלֵהוּ וָאֹמַר אֵלֶיהָ בַּיּוֹם הָאַחֵר תְּנִי אֶת־בְּנֵךְ וְנֹאכְלֶנּוּ
ל וַתַּחְבִּא אֶת־בְּנָהּ: וַיְהִי כִשְׁמֹעַ הַמֶּלֶךְ אֶת־דִּבְרֵי הָאִשָּׁה וַיִּקְרַע אֶת־בְּגָדָיו
לא וְהוּא עֹבֵר עַל־הַחֹמָה וַיַּרְא הָעָם וְהִנֵּה הַשַּׂק עַל־בְּשָׂרוֹ מִבָּיִת: וַיֹּאמֶר כֹּה־
יַעֲשֶׂה־לִּי אֱלֹהִים וְכֹה יוֹסִף אִם־יַעֲמֹד רֹאשׁ אֱלִישָׁע בֶּן־שָׁפָט עָלָיו הַיּוֹם:
לב וֶאֱלִישָׁע יֹשֵׁב בְּבֵיתוֹ וְהַזְּקֵנִים יֹשְׁבִים אִתּוֹ וַיִּשְׁלַח אִישׁ מִלְּפָנָיו בְּטֶרֶם יָבֹא
הַמַּלְאָךְ אֵלָיו וְהוּא אָמַר אֶל־הַזְּקֵנִים הַרְּאִיתֶם כִּי־שָׁלַח בֶּן־הַמְרַצֵּחַ
הַזֶּה לְהָסִיר אֶת־רֹאשִׁי רְאוּ כְּבֹא הַמַּלְאָךְ סִגְרוּ הַדֶּלֶת וּלְחַצְתֶּם
לג אֹתוֹ בַּדֶּלֶת הֲלוֹא קוֹל רַגְלֵי אֲדֹנָיו אַחֲרָיו: עוֹדֶנּוּ מְדַבֵּר עִמָּם וְהִנֵּה
הַמַּלְאָךְ יֹרֵד אֵלָיו וַיֹּאמֶר הִנֵּה־זֹאת הָרָעָה מֵאֵת יְהוָה מָה־אוֹחִיל לַיהוָה
ז א עוֹד: וַיֹּאמֶר אֱלִישָׁע שִׁמְעוּ דְּבַר־יְהוָה כֹּה אָמַר יְהוָה כָּעֵת
ב מָחָר סְאָה־סֹלֶת בְּשֶׁקֶל וְסָאתַיִם שְׂעֹרִים בְּשֶׁקֶל בְּשַׁעַר שֹׁמְרוֹן: וַיַּעַן
הַשָּׁלִישׁ אֲשֶׁר־לַמֶּלֶךְ נִשְׁעָן עַל־יָדוֹ אֶת־אִישׁ הָאֱלֹהִים וַיֹּאמַר הִנֵּה יְהוָה
עֹשֶׂה אֲרֻבּוֹת בַּשָּׁמַיִם הֲיִהְיֶה הַדָּבָר הַזֶּה וַיֹּאמֶר הִנְּכָה רֹאֶה בְּעֵינֶיךָ וּמִשָּׁם
ג לֹא תֹאכֵל: וְאַרְבָּעָה אֲנָשִׁים הָיוּ מְצֹרָעִים פֶּתַח הַשָּׁעַר וַיֹּאמְרוּ
ד אִישׁ אֶל־רֵעֵהוּ מָה אֲנַחְנוּ יֹשְׁבִים פֹּה עַד־מָתְנוּ: אִם־אָמַרְנוּ נָבוֹא הָעִיר

HAFTARAS
METZORA
7:3-20

ז

6:22. It is unscrupulous to kill unarmed prisoners of war (*Rashi*).

6:23. The Arameans abandoned their ambushes and terrorist forays. As the next verse attests, however, they later turned to conventional warfare (*Ralbag*).

6:25. A natural famine (see 4:38 and 8:1) was further aggravated by the siege (*Abarbanel*).

6:27. At first, he thought the woman was appealing to him for nonexistent food (*Rashi*).

6:30. The king was wearing sackcloth in a gesture of repentance and contrition, but the royal protocol required that this not be displayed in public. Then, when he tore his outer garment in grief upon hearing the woman's shocking story, the sackcloth was revealed.

6:31. Elisha could have ended the famine by praying to God, as Elijah had once done (I *Kings*, Ch. 18); the king felt that he deserved to die for ignoring the people's suffering (*Rashi*). Alternatively, the king blamed Elisha for not having allowed him to end the Arameans' threat by killing them when he had had the chance (v. 21).

6:32. Seeing prophetically that King Jehoram was stealthily following his messenger in order to hear what the prophet would say, Elisha instructed the elders to hold the door shut until the king arrived. Elisha wanted to address Jehoram directly (*Abarbanel*).

6:33. Despite his rage at Elisha (v. 31), Jehoram had an underlying faith in God; in verse 30, he was praying. Now he exclaimed that the tragedy, including the cannibalism, the midst of Samaria.

²¹ The king of Israel said to Elisha when he saw them, "Shall I strike [them] down? Shall I strike [them] down, my father?"

²² But he said, "Do not strike [them] down! Would you strike down people whom you have captured with your sword and your bow?* Rather, place food and water before them. Let them eat and drink and then return to their masters."

²³ So he prepared a large meal for them, and they ate and drank; and he sent them away and they went to their masters. And the bands of Arameans no longer came into the Land of Israel. *

Siege, famine . . . ²⁴ It happened after that that Ben-hadad, the king of Aram, gathered together his entire camp, and he went up and laid siege to Samaria. ²⁵ There was a great famine in Samaria, and — behold! — they were besieging it, until a donkey's head cost eighty silver pieces and a quarter of a kav of pigeon's dung cost five silver pieces. *

²⁶ The king of Israel was [once] passing on the [city] wall, and a woman called out to him, "Help, my lord the king!"

²⁷ He replied, "If HASHEM does not help you, how shall I help you? From the threshing floor or from the winepress?!"* ²⁸ The king then said to her, "What troubles you?"

and shocking cannibalism She said, "This woman said to me, 'Give over your son and we will eat him today, and we will eat my son tomorrow.' ²⁹ So we cooked my son and ate him, and I said to her on the next day, 'Give over your son and let us eat him' — but she has hidden her son!"

The king blames Elisha ³⁰ It happened when the king heard the woman's words that he rent his garments while he was passing on the wall, and the people saw that there was sackcloth upon his flesh underneath. * ³¹ He said, "Such may HASHEM do to me and such may He do further, if the head of Elisha son of Shaphat remains on him today!"*

³² Elisha was sitting in his house, and the elders were sitting with him, [when the king] sent a man ahead of him. Before the messenger had come to him, [Elisha] said to the elders, "Have you seen that this son of a murderer has sent to remove my head? See to it that when the messenger comes you close the door and push him out with the door; for surely the sound of his master's feet is behind him."*

³³ As he was speaking with them behold, the messenger was coming down to him. Then [the king] said, "Behold, this misfortune is from HASHEM; what hope can I have from HASHEM?"*

7

Elisha guarantees a surfeit of food ¹ Elisha then said, "Hear the word of HASHEM! Thus said HASHEM: At this time tomorrow, a se'ah* of fine flour [will be bought] for one shekel and two se'ahs of barley for one shekel at the gateway of Samaria!"

² The king's captain, upon whose arm he was leaning, answered the man of God and said, "Even if HASHEM were to make windows in the heavens, can this thing happen?"

[Elisha] replied, "You will see it with your own eyes, but you will not eat from it!"

³ There were four men who were lepers* at the city gate. They said one to the other, "Why should we sit here until we die? ⁴ If we propose to enter the city,

---

was the result of his and his people's wickedness (see *Deuteronomy* 28:53). If so, he despaired, what hope could he have for salvation?

7:1. Six *kav.* Opinions of the modern equivalent of a *kav*

range between 1.5 and 2.65 quarts.

7:3. For a discussion of this disease, see the introduction to *Leviticus,* Ch. 13. People thus afflicted may not enter any walled city in Israel (*Leviticus* 13:46).

וְהָרָעָב בָּעִיר וָמַתְנוּ שָׁם וְאִם־יָשַׁבְנוּ פֹה וָמָתְנוּ וְעַתָּה לְכוּ וְנִפְּלָה אֶל־
ה מַחֲנֵה אֲרָם אִם־יְחַיֻּנוּ נִחְיֶה וְאִם־יְמִיתֻנוּ וָמָתְנוּ: וַיָּקֻמוּ בַנֶּשֶׁף לָבוֹא אֶל־
ו מַחֲנֵה אֲרָם וַיָּבֹאוּ עַד־קְצֵה מַחֲנֵה אֲרָם וְהִנֵּה אֵין־שָׁם אִישׁ: וַאדֹנָי
הִשְׁמִיעַ ׀ אֶת־מַחֲנֵה אֲרָם קוֹל רֶכֶב קוֹל סוּס קוֹל חַיִל גָּדוֹל וַיֹּאמְרוּ אִישׁ
אֶל־אָחִיו הִנֵּה שָׂכַר־עָלֵינוּ מֶלֶךְ יִשְׂרָאֵל אֶת־מַלְכֵי הַחִתִּים וְאֶת־מַלְכֵי
ז מִצְרַיִם לָבוֹא עָלֵינוּ: וַיָּקוּמוּ וַיָּנוּסוּ בַנֶּשֶׁף וַיַּעַזְבוּ אֶת־אָהֳלֵיהֶם וְאֶת־
ח סוּסֵיהֶם וְאֶת־חֲמֹרֵיהֶם הַמַּחֲנֶה כַּאֲשֶׁר־הִיא וַיָּנֻסוּ אֶל־נַפְשָׁם: וַיָּבֹאוּ
הַמְצֹרָעִים הָאֵלֶּה עַד־קְצֵה הַמַּחֲנֶה וַיָּבֹאוּ אֶל־אֹהֶל אֶחָד וַיֹּאכְלוּ וַיִּשְׁתּוּ
וַיִּשְׂאוּ מִשָּׁם כֶּסֶף וְזָהָב וּבְגָדִים וַיֵּלְכוּ וַיַּטְמִנוּ וַיָּשֻׁבוּ וַיָּבֹאוּ אֶל־אֹהֶל אַחֵר
ט וַיִּשְׂאוּ מִשָּׁם וַיֵּלְכוּ וַיַּטְמִנוּ: וַיֹּאמְרוּ אִישׁ אֶל־רֵעֵהוּ לֹא־כֵן ׀ אֲנַחְנוּ עֹשִׂים
הַיּוֹם הַזֶּה יוֹם־בְּשֹׂרָה הוּא וַאֲנַחְנוּ מַחְשִׁים וְחִכִּינוּ עַד־אוֹר הַבֹּקֶר וּמְצָאָנוּ
י עָווֹן וְעַתָּה לְכוּ וְנָבֹאָה וְנַגִּידָה בֵּית הַמֶּלֶךְ: וַיָּבֹאוּ וַיִּקְרְאוּ אֶל־שֹׁעֵר הָעִיר
וַיַּגִּידוּ לָהֶם לֵאמֹר בָּאנוּ אֶל־מַחֲנֵה אֲרָם וְהִנֵּה אֵין־שָׁם אִישׁ וְקוֹל אָדָם כִּי
יא אִם־הַסּוּס אָסוּר וְהַחֲמוֹר אָסוּר וְאֹהָלִים כַּאֲשֶׁר־הֵמָּה: וַיִּקְרָא הַשֹּׁעֲרִים
יב וַיַּגִּידוּ בֵּית הַמֶּלֶךְ פְּנִימָה: וַיָּקָם הַמֶּלֶךְ לַיְלָה וַיֹּאמֶר אֶל־עֲבָדָיו אַגִּידָה־נָּא
לָכֶם אֵת אֲשֶׁר־עָשׂוּ לָנוּ אֲרָם יָדְעוּ כִּי־רְעֵבִים אֲנַחְנוּ וַיֵּצְאוּ מִן־הַמַּחֲנֶה
לְהֵחָבֵה °בהשדה [°בַשָּׂדֶה ק] לֵאמֹר כִּי־יֵצְאוּ מִן־הָעִיר וְנִתְפְּשֵׂם חַיִּים
יג וְאֶל־הָעִיר נָבֹא: וַיַּעַן אֶחָד מֵעֲבָדָיו וַיֹּאמֶר וְיִקְחוּ־נָא חֲמִשָּׁה מִן־הַסּוּסִים
הַנִּשְׁאָרִים אֲשֶׁר נִשְׁאֲרוּ־בָהּ הִנָּם כְּכָל־°ההמון [°הֲמוֹן ק] יִשְׂרָאֵל אֲשֶׁר
יד נִשְׁאֲרוּ־בָהּ הִנָּם כְּכָל־הֲמוֹן יִשְׂרָאֵל אֲשֶׁר־תָּמּוּ וְנִשְׁלְחָה וְנִרְאֶה: וַיִּקְחוּ
טו שְׁנֵי רֶכֶב סוּסִים וַיִּשְׁלַח הַמֶּלֶךְ אַחֲרֵי מַחֲנֵה־אֲרָם לֵאמֹר לְכוּ וּרְאוּ: וַיֵּלְכוּ
אַחֲרֵיהֶם עַד־הַיַּרְדֵּן וְהִנֵּה כָל־הַדֶּרֶךְ מְלֵאָה בְגָדִים וְכֵלִים אֲשֶׁר־הִשְׁלִיכוּ
טז אֲרָם °בהחפזם [°בְּחָפְזָם ק] וַיָּשֻׁבוּ הַמַּלְאָכִים וַיַּגִּדוּ לַמֶּלֶךְ: וַיֵּצֵא הָעָם
וַיָּבֹזּוּ אֵת מַחֲנֵה אֲרָם וַיְהִי סְאָה־סֹלֶת בְּשֶׁקֶל וְסָאתַיִם שְׂעֹרִים בְּשֶׁקֶל
יז כִּדְבַר יְהֹוָה: וְהַמֶּלֶךְ הִפְקִיד אֶת־הַשָּׁלִישׁ אֲשֶׁר־נִשְׁעָן עַל־יָדוֹ עַל־הַשַּׁעַר
וַיִּרְמְסֻהוּ הָעָם בַּשַּׁעַר וַיָּמֹת כַּאֲשֶׁר דִּבֶּר אִישׁ הָאֱלֹהִים אֲשֶׁר דִּבֶּר בְּרֶדֶת
יח הַמֶּלֶךְ אֵלָיו: וַיְהִי כְּדַבֵּר אִישׁ הָאֱלֹהִים אֶל־הַמֶּלֶךְ לֵאמֹר סָאתַיִם שְׂעֹרִים
יט בְּשֶׁקֶל וּסְאָה־סֹלֶת בְּשֶׁקֶל יִהְיֶה כָּעֵת מָחָר בְּשַׁעַר שֹׁמְרוֹן: וַיַּעַן הַשָּׁלִישׁ
אֶת־אִישׁ הָאֱלֹהִים וַיֹּאמַר וְהִנֵּה יְהֹוָה עֹשֶׂה אֲרֻבּוֹת בַּשָּׁמַיִם הֲיִהְיֶה כַּדָּבָר
כ הַזֶּה וַיֹּאמֶר הִנְּךָ רֹאֶה בְּעֵינֶיךָ וּמִשָּׁם לֹא תֹאכֵל: וַיְהִי־לוֹ כֵּן וַיִּרְמְסוּ אֹתוֹ
הָעָם בַּשַּׁעַר וַיָּמֹת: ◄

ח א וֶאֱלִישָׁע דִּבֶּר אֶל־הָאִשָּׁה אֲשֶׁר־הֶחֱיָה
אֶת־בְּנָהּ לֵאמֹר קוּמִי וּלְכִי °אתי [°אַתְּ ק] °את [°אַתְּ ק] וּבֵיתֵךְ וְגוּרִי בַּאֲשֶׁר תָּגוּרִי

7:13. The horsemen we send out will be in no greater danger from the Arameans than if they remain with the starving, dying multitudes in the city (*Rashi*). The king agreed to risk only two men.

8:1. See 4:8-37.

there is a famine in the city and we will die there; and if we remain here we will
die. So let us now go and throw ourselves upon the camp of Aram; if they let us
live we will live, and if they put us to death we will die."

 ⁵ So they arose at twilight to go to the Aramean camp and they arrived at the
edge of the Aramean camp, and behold — not a man was there! ⁶ HASHEM had
caused the Aramean camp to hear the sound of chariot, the sound of horse, the
sound of a great army; and they said to one another, "Behold, the king of Israel
has hired against us the Hittite kings and the Egyptian kings to come upon us!"
⁷ So they arose and fled in the twilight; they abandoned their tents, their horses
and their donkeys, [leaving] the camp just as it was, and they fled for their lives.

⁸ These lepers arrived at the edge of the camp. They came to one tent and ate
and drank. They carried from there silver, gold and clothing, which they went and
hid. Then they returned and went to another tent, and carried [loot] away from
there, which they went and hid.

⁹ Then they said, one to the other, "We are not acting properly — today is a day
of [good] tidings, yet we remain silent! If we wait until the light of dawn we will
be considered sinful. So now come, let us go and report to the king's palace!"

¹⁰ They came and called out to the gate patrol of the city and told them, saying,
"We came to the Aramean camp and behold — not a man or a human sound is
there; only each horse is tethered and each donkey is tethered, and the tents are
[abandoned] as they were!" ¹¹ The gatekeepers announced it, and it was related
inside the king's palace.

¹² The king arose in the night and said to his servants, "Let me tell you what
Aram has done to us. They knew that we are famished, so they left the camp to
conceal themselves in the field, saying, 'When they leave the city we will capture
them alive, and then we will enter the city.'"

¹³ One of his servants spoke up and said, "Let them take five of the remaining
horses that are still in [the city] — behold, they are like the entire multitude of Israel
that still survives within; behold, they are like the entire multitude of Israel that has
perished. * Let us send [them] and we will see."

¹⁴ They chose two horsemen, and the king sent them after the Aramean camp,
saying, "Go and see." ¹⁵ They followed their [tracks] until the Jordan and behold,
the whole way was filled with clothing and gear that Aram had thrown away in
their haste. The messengers returned and told the king. ¹⁶ The people went out and
plundered the Aramean camp; a se'ah of fine flour cost a shekel and two se'ahs
of barley cost a shekel, like the word of HASHEM.

¹⁷ The king had appointed the captain on whose arm he had leaned to be in
charge of the gate, and the people trampled him to death in the gateway, just as
the man of God had spoken — as he had spoken when the king had come down
to him. ¹⁸ It had happened that when the man of God had spoken to the king,
saying, "Two se'ahs of barley [will be bought] for a shekel and a se'ah of fine flour
[will be bought] for a shekel at this time tomorrow in the gate of Samaria," ¹⁹ that
captain had answered the man of God and said, "Even if HASHEM were to make
windows in the heavens, could this thing happen?" And [Elisha] had replied, "You
will see it with your own eyes, but you will not eat from it!" ²⁰ And so it happened
to him, for the people trampled him in the gate, and he died.

8

¹ E lisha had spoken to the woman whose son he had revived, * saying, "Arise
and go forth, you and your household, and sojourn where you would sojourn,

Margin notes:

Jewish
lepers find an
abandoned
camp . . .

. . . and
report to
their brethren

The king
suspects
a trick

Abundant
food

The doubter
is trampled

ב כִּי־קָרָא יהוה לָרָעָב וְגַם־בָּא אֶל־הָאָרֶץ שֶׁבַע שָׁנִים: וַתָּקָם הָאִשָּׁה וַתַּעַשׂ
כִּדְבַר אִישׁ הָאֱלֹהִים וַתֵּלֶךְ הִיא וּבֵיתָהּ וַתָּגָר בְּאֶרֶץ־פְּלִשְׁתִּים שֶׁבַע

ג שָׁנִים: וַיְהִי מִקְצֵה שֶׁבַע שָׁנִים וַתָּשָׁב הָאִשָּׁה מֵאֶרֶץ פְּלִשְׁתִּים וַתֵּצֵא

ד לִצְעֹק אֶל־הַמֶּלֶךְ אֶל־בֵּיתָהּ וְאֶל־שָׂדָהּ: וְהַמֶּלֶךְ מְדַבֵּר אֶל־גֵּחֲזִי נַעַר אִישׁ־

ה הָאֱלֹהִים לֵאמֹר סַפְּרָה־נָּא לִי אֵת כָּל־הַגְּדֹלוֹת אֲשֶׁר־עָשָׂה אֱלִישָׁע: וַיְהִי
הוּא מְסַפֵּר לַמֶּלֶךְ אֵת אֲשֶׁר־הֶחֱיָה אֶת־הַמֵּת וְהִנֵּה הָאִשָּׁה אֲשֶׁר־הֶחֱיָה
אֶת־בְּנָהּ צֹעֶקֶת אֶל־הַמֶּלֶךְ עַל־בֵּיתָהּ וְעַל־שָׂדָהּ וַיֹּאמֶר גֵּחֲזִי אֲדֹנִי

ו הַמֶּלֶךְ זֹאת הָאִשָּׁה וְזֶה־בְּנָהּ אֲשֶׁר־הֶחֱיָה אֱלִישָׁע: וַיִּשְׁאַל הַמֶּלֶךְ לָאִשָּׁה
וַתְּסַפֶּר־לוֹ וַיִּתֶּן־לָהּ הַמֶּלֶךְ סָרִיס אֶחָד לֵאמֹר הָשֵׁיב אֶת־כָּל־אֲשֶׁר־לָהּ
וְאֵת כָּל־תְּבוּאֹת הַשָּׂדֶה מִיּוֹם עָזְבָה אֶת־הָאָרֶץ וְעַד־עָתָּה:

ז וַיָּבֹא אֱלִישָׁע דַּמֶּשֶׂק וּבֶן־הֲדַד מֶלֶךְ־אֲרָם חֹלֶה וַיֻּגַּד־לוֹ לֵאמֹר בָּא אִישׁ

ח הָאֱלֹהִים עַד־הֵנָּה: וַיֹּאמֶר הַמֶּלֶךְ אֶל־חֲזָהאֵל קַח בְּיָדְךָ מִנְחָה וְלֵךְ
לִקְרַאת אִישׁ הָאֱלֹהִים וְדָרַשְׁתָּ אֶת־יהוה מֵאוֹתוֹ לֵאמֹר הַאֶחְיֶה מֵחֳלִי זֶה:

ט וַיֵּלֶךְ חֲזָאֵל לִקְרָאתוֹ וַיִּקַּח מִנְחָה בְיָדוֹ וְכָל־טוּב דַּמֶּשֶׂק מַשָּׂא אַרְבָּעִים
גָּמָל וַיָּבֹא וַיַּעֲמֹד לְפָנָיו וַיֹּאמֶר בִּנְךָ בֶן־הֲדַד מֶלֶךְ־אֲרָם שְׁלָחַנִי אֵלֶיךָ

י לֵאמֹר הַאֶחְיֶה מֵחֳלִי זֶה: וַיֹּאמֶר אֵלָיו אֱלִישָׁע לֵךְ אֱמָר־°לא אָמַר־לוֹ

יא [לוֹ ק] חָיֹה תִחְיֶה וְהִרְאַנִי יהוה כִּי־מוֹת יָמוּת: וַיַּעֲמֵד אֶת־פָּנָיו וַיָּשֶׂם

יב עַד־בֹּשׁ וַיֵּבְךְּ אִישׁ הָאֱלֹהִים: וַיֹּאמֶר חֲזָאֵל מַדּוּעַ אֲדֹנִי בֹכֶה וַיֹּאמֶר כִּי־
יָדַעְתִּי אֵת אֲשֶׁר־תַּעֲשֶׂה לִבְנֵי יִשְׂרָאֵל רָעָה מִבְצְרֵיהֶם תְּשַׁלַּח בָּאֵשׁ

יג וּבַחֻרֵיהֶם בַּחֶרֶב תַּהֲרֹג וְעֹלְלֵיהֶם תְּרַטֵּשׁ וְהָרֹתֵיהֶם תְּבַקֵּעַ: וַיֹּאמֶר חֲזָהאֵל
כִּי מָה עַבְדְּךָ הַכֶּלֶב כִּי יַעֲשֶׂה הַדָּבָר הַגָּדוֹל הַזֶּה וַיֹּאמֶר אֱלִישָׁע הִרְאַנִי

יד יהוה אֹתְךָ מֶלֶךְ עַל־אֲרָם: וַיֵּלֶךְ ׀ מֵאֵת אֱלִישָׁע וַיָּבֹא אֶל־אֲדֹנָיו וַיֹּאמֶר לוֹ

טו מַה־אָמַר לְךָ אֱלִישָׁע וַיֹּאמֶר אָמַר לִי חָיֹה תִחְיֶה: וַיְהִי מִמָּחֳרָת וַיִּקַּח
הַמַּכְבֵּר וַיִּטְבֹּל בַּמַּיִם וַיִּפְרֹשׂ עַל־פָּנָיו וַיָּמֹת וַיִּמְלֹךְ חֲזָהאֵל

טז תַּחְתָּיו: וּבִשְׁנַת חָמֵשׁ לְיוֹרָם בֶּן־אַחְאָב מֶלֶךְ יִשְׂרָאֵל
וִיהוֹשָׁפָט מֶלֶךְ יְהוּדָה מָלַךְ יְהוֹרָם בֶּן־יְהוֹשָׁפָט מֶלֶךְ יְהוּדָה: בֶּן־שְׁלֹשִׁים

יז וּשְׁתַּיִם שָׁנָה הָיָה בְמָלְכוֹ וּשְׁמֹנֶה °שנה [שָׁנִים ק] מָלַךְ בִּירוּשָׁלָ‍ִם: וַיֵּלֶךְ

יח בְּדֶרֶךְ ׀ מַלְכֵי יִשְׂרָאֵל כַּאֲשֶׁר עָשׂוּ בֵּית אַחְאָב כִּי בַּת־אַחְאָב הָיְתָה־

יט לוֹ לְאִשָּׁה וַיַּעַשׂ הָרַע בְּעֵינֵי יהוה: וְלֹא־אָבָה יהוה לְהַשְׁחִית אֶת־
יְהוּדָה לְמַעַן דָּוִד עַבְדּוֹ כַּאֲשֶׁר אָמַר־לוֹ לָתֵת לוֹ נִיר לְבָנָיו כָּל־הַיָּמִים:

8:3. Her property had apparently been usurped in her absence.

8:7. To carry out HASHEM's charge to Elijah which is found in *I Kings* 19:15 (*Radak*).

8:10. Elisha meant that under normal circumstances Ben-hadad would recover from this illness. However, he will die of other causes before he recovers.

8:11. Knowing what he was about to say, Elisha tried to hide his tears from Hazael.

8:15. Hazael told Ben-hadad that the wet blanket would lower his fever. But Hazael's true purpose was to assassinate the king (*Radak*).

8:16. In the fifth year of the close alliance between Jehoram son of Ahab and Jehoshaphat, (see 3:7), for HASHEM has called for a famine, and it is coming to the land for seven years. ² So the woman arose and did as the man of God had told her, and she went with her household, and sojourned in the land of the Philistines [for] seven years. ³ It *The* happened at the end of seven years, the woman returned from the land of the *Shunammite* Philistines, and she went to appeal to the king about her house and her field. *

woman's
property is ⁴ The king had been speaking with Gehazi, the attendant of the man of God,
stolen . . . saying, "Please tell me about all the great deeds that Elisha has performed." ⁵ Just when [Gehazi] was telling him about how [Elisha] had revived the dead [boy], behold — the woman whose son he had revived was appealing to the king about her house and her field!

Gehazi exclaimed, "My lord, the king! This is the woman, and this is her son whom Elisha had revived!"

. . . and the ⁶ The king asked the woman, and she told him [that it was true]. The king then
king orders it designated a certain servant for her, saying [to him], "Return everything that is hers,
returned as well as all the produce of the land from the day she left the land to the present."

Ben-hadad's ⁷ Elisha went to Damascus, * where Ben-hadad, king of Aram, was ill. It was
illness told to [the king], saying, "The man of God has come here."

⁸ The king said to Hazael, "Take a tribute with you and go to meet the man of God. Inquire of HASHEM through him, asking, 'Will I recover from this illness?' "

⁹ So Hazael went to meet [Elisha], taking as a tribute all the bounty of Damascus with him, forty camel-loads. He came and stood before him and said, "Your son Ben-hadad, the king of Aram, has sent me to you saying, 'Will I recover from this illness?' "

¹⁰ Elisha said to him, "Go say to him, 'You should indeed recover'; but in fact HASHEM has shown me that he will indeed die* [from another cause]."

¹¹ [Elisha] turned his face aside for some time, and then the man of God cried. ¹² Hazael asked him, "Why is my lord crying?"

Prophecy of And he replied, "Because I know what evil you will do to the Children of Israel:
Hazael's Their strongholds you will set on fire; their young men you will kill by the sword,
cruelty to their babies you will tear apart, and their pregnant women you will split open."
Israel
¹³ Hazael said, "But what is your servant, a dog, that he could do such a terrible deed?"

Elisha answered him, "HASHEM has shown me you as king of Aram."

¹⁴ He went from Elisha and came to his master, who said to him, "What did Elisha say to you?"

He said, "He said to me, 'You should indeed recover.' " ¹⁵ The next day [Hazael] took a cover, dipped it in water, and spread it over [Ben-hadad's] face, * and he died. Hazael became king in his place.

JEHORAM, ¹⁶ In the fifth year of Jehoram son of Ahab king of Israel, and Jehoshaphat king
KING OF of Judah* — Jehoram, son of Jehoshaphat king of Judah, became king. ¹⁷ He
JUDAH was thirty-two years old when he reigned, and he reigned for eight years in
8:16-24 Jerusalem. ¹⁸ He went in the way of the kings of Israel, just as the house of Ahab
(See Appendix A, had done, for Ahab's daughter had become his wife; he did what was evil in the
timeline 4) eyes of HASHEM. ¹⁹ But HASHEM did not wish to destroy Judah, for the sake of His servant David; in accordance with what He had said to him — that he would give dominion to his descendants all the days.

Jehoshaphat died. His son Jehoram succeeded as king of Judah (*Ralbag*).

בְּיָמָיו פָּשַׁע אֱדֹום מִתַּחַת יַד־יְהוּדָה וַיַּמְלִכוּ עֲלֵיהֶם מֶלֶךְ: וַיַּעֲבֹר יֹורָם   כ־כא

צָעִירָה וְכָל־הָרֶכֶב עִמֹּו וַיְהִי־הוּא קָם לַיְלָה וַיַּכֶּה אֶת־אֱדֹום הַסֹּבֵיב

אֵלָיו וְאֵת שָׂרֵי הָרֶכֶב וַיָּנָס הָעָם לְאֹהָלָיו: וַיִּפְשַׁע אֱדֹום מִתַּחַת יַד־   כב

יְהוּדָה עַד הַיֹּום הַזֶּה אָז תִּפְשַׁע לִבְנָה בָּעֵת הַהִיא: וְיֶתֶר דִּבְרֵי יֹורָם   כג

וְכָל־אֲשֶׁר עָשָׂה הֲלֹוא־הֵם כְּתוּבִים עַל־סֵפֶר דִּבְרֵי הַיָּמִים לְמַלְכֵי

יְהוּדָה: וַיִּשְׁכַּב יֹורָם עִם־אֲבֹתָיו וַיִּקָּבֵר עִם־אֲבֹתָיו בְּעִיר דָּוִד וַיִּמְלֹךְ   כד

אֲחַזְיָהוּ בְנֹו תַּחְתָּיו: בִּשְׁנַת שְׁתֵּים־עֶשְׂרֵה שָׁנָה לְיֹורָם   כה

בֶּן־אַחְאָב מֶלֶךְ יִשְׂרָאֵל מָלַךְ אֲחַזְיָהוּ בֶן־יְהֹורָם מֶלֶךְ יְהוּדָה: בֶּן־

עֶשְׂרִים וּשְׁתַּיִם שָׁנָה אֲחַזְיָהוּ בְמָלְכֹו וְשָׁנָה אַחַת מָלַךְ בִּירוּשָׁלִָם וְשֵׁם   כו

אִמֹּו עֲתַלְיָהוּ בַּת־עָמְרִי מֶלֶךְ יִשְׂרָאֵל: וַיֵּלֶךְ בְּדֶרֶךְ בֵּית אַחְאָב וַיַּעַשׂ   כז

הָרַע בְּעֵינֵי יְהוָה כְּבֵית אַחְאָב כִּי חֲתַן בֵּית־אַחְאָב הוּא: וַיֵּלֶךְ אֶת־   כח

יֹורָם בֶּן־אַחְאָב לַמִּלְחָמָה עִם־חֲזָהאֵל מֶלֶךְ־אֲרָם בְּרָמֹת גִּלְעָד וַיַּכּוּ

אֲרַמִּים אֶת־יֹורָם: וַיָּשָׁב יֹורָם הַמֶּלֶךְ לְהִתְרַפֵּא בְיִזְרְעֶאל מִן־הַמַּכִּים   כט

אֲשֶׁר יַכֻּהוּ אֲרַמִּים בָּרָמָה בְּהִלָּחֲמֹו אֶת־חֲזָהאֵל מֶלֶךְ אֲרָם וַאֲחַזְיָהוּ

בֶן־יְהֹורָם מֶלֶךְ יְהוּדָה יָרַד לִרְאֹות אֶת־יֹורָם בֶּן־אַחְאָב בְּיִזְרְעֶאל

כִּי־חֹלֶה הוּא: וֶאֱלִישָׁע הַנָּבִיא קָרָא לְאַחַד מִבְּנֵי   א   ט

הַנְּבִיאִים וַיֹּאמֶר לֹו חֲגֹר מָתְנֶיךָ וְקַח פַּךְ הַשֶּׁמֶן הַזֶּה בְּיָדֶךָ וְלֵךְ רָמֹת

גִּלְעָד: וּבָאתָ שָׁמָּה וּרְאֵה־שָׁם יֵהוּא בֶן־יְהֹושָׁפָט בֶּן־נִמְשִׁי וּבָאתָ   ב

וַהֲקֵמֹתֹו מִתֹּוךְ אֶחָיו וְהֵבֵיאתָ אֹתֹו חֶדֶר בְּחָדֶר: וְלָקַחְתָּ פַךְ־הַשֶּׁמֶן   ג

וְיָצַקְתָּ עַל־רֹאשֹׁו וְאָמַרְתָּ כֹּה־אָמַר יְהוָה מְשַׁחְתִּיךָ לְמֶלֶךְ אֶל־יִשְׂרָאֵל

וּפָתַחְתָּ הַדֶּלֶת וְנַסְתָּה וְלֹא תְחַכֶּה: וַיֵּלֶךְ הַנַּעַר הַנַּעַר הַנָּבִיא רָמֹת   ד

גִּלְעָד: וַיָּבֹא וְהִנֵּה שָׂרֵי הַחַיִל יֹשְׁבִים וַיֹּאמֶר דָּבָר לִי אֵלֶיךָ הַשָּׂר וַיֹּאמֶר   ה

יֵהוּא אֶל־מִי מִכֻּלָּנוּ וַיֹּאמֶר אֵלֶיךָ הַשָּׂר: וַיָּקָם וַיָּבֹא הַבַּיְתָה וַיִּצֹק הַשֶּׁמֶן   ו

אֶל־רֹאשֹׁו וַיֹּאמֶר לֹו כֹּה־אָמַר יְהוָה אֱלֹהֵי יִשְׂרָאֵל מְשַׁחְתִּיךָ לְמֶלֶךְ אֶל־

עַם יְהוָה אֶל־יִשְׂרָאֵל: וְהִכִּיתָה אֶת־בֵּית אַחְאָב אֲדֹנֶיךָ וְנִקַּמְתִּי דְּמֵי ׀   ז

עֲבָדַי הַנְּבִיאִים וּדְמֵי כָּל־עַבְדֵי יְהוָה מִיַּד אִיזָבֶל: וְאָבַד כָּל־בֵּית אַחְאָב   ח

וְהִכְרַתִּי לְאַחְאָב מַשְׁתִּין בְּקִיר וְעָצוּר וְעָזוּב בְּיִשְׂרָאֵל: וְנָתַתִּי אֶת־בֵּית   ט

אַחְאָב כְּבֵית יָרָבְעָם בֶּן־נְבָט וּכְבֵית בַּעְשָׁא בֶן־אֲחִיָּה: וְאֶת־אִיזֶבֶל   י

יֹאכְלוּ הַכְּלָבִים בְּחֵלֶק יִזְרְעֶאל וְאֵין קֹבֵר וַיִּפְתַּח הַדֶּלֶת וַיָּנֹס: וְיֵהוּא יָצָא   יא

אֶל־עַבְדֵי אֲדֹנָיו וַיֹּאמֶר לֹו הֲשָׁלֹום מַדּוּעַ בָּא־הַמְשֻׁגָּע הַזֶּה אֵלֶיךָ וַיֹּאמֶר

אֲלֵיהֶם אַתֶּם יְדַעְתֶּם אֶת־הָאִישׁ וְאֶת־שִׂיחֹו: וַיֹּאמְרוּ שֶׁקֶר הַגֶּד־נָא לָנוּ   יב

8:20. Since the time of David, Edom had been ruled by a governor subservient to the kingdom of Judah (see II Samuel 8:14 and I Kings 22:48).

8:23. See II Chronicles, Ch. 21.

9:8. See I Samuel 25:22.

²⁰ In his days Edom rebelled against the rule of Judah, and they appointed a king over themselves. * ²¹ So Jehoram went to Zair, and [took] all his chariots with him; he rose in the night and smote Edom which had surrounded him and *Edom* the chariot captains; then the people fled back to their tents. ²² But Edom rebelled *declares* against [being] under the hand of Judah to this day. Then Libnah rebelled at that *independence* time. ²³ The rest of the deeds of Jehoram and all that he did — behold, they are recorded in the Book of the Chronicles of the Kings of Judah. * ²⁴ Jehoram lay with his forefathers and was buried with his forefathers in the City of David; and his son Ahaziah reigned in his place.

AHAZIAH, 　²⁵ In the twelfth year of Jehoram son of Ahab, king of Israel — Ahaziah, the
KING OF son of Jehoram king of Judah, became king. ²⁶ Ahaziah was twenty-two years
JUDAH old when he became king, and he reigned for one year in Jerusalem. His
8:25-9:29 mother's name was Athaliah, the [grand]daughter of Omri king of Israel. ²⁷ He
(See Appendix A, followed the way of the house of Ahab, and did what was evil in the eyes of
timeline 4) HASHEM, like the house of Ahab, for he was [the son of] a [grand]son-in-law of
the house of Ahab.

Jehoram is 　²⁸ [Ahaziah] went with Jehoram son of Ahab to war against Hazael king of
wounded in Aram at Ramoth-gilead, and the Arameans wounded Jehoram. ²⁹ King Jehoram
battle returned to convalesce in Jezreel from the wounds that the Arameans had
inflicted upon him at Ramah as he battled against Hazael king of Aram. Ahaziah
son of Jehoram, king of Judah, went down to visit Jehoram son of Ahab in
Jezreel, for he was ill.

9　　　　　　¹ [At that time] Elisha the prophet called one of the prophets' disciples and
Elisha sends 　　said to him, "Gird your loins; take this jar of oil in your hand and go to
a disciple to Ramoth-gilead. ² When you arrive there, find Jehu son of Jehoshaphat son of
crown Jehu Nimshi; tell him to arise from among his colleagues and bring him into an inner
chamber. ³ Then take the jar of oil and pour it on his head and say, 'Thus said
HASHEM: I have anointed you king over Israel!' Then open the door and flee; do
not delay."

JEHU, KING 　⁴ So the young man, the youthful prophet, went to Ramoth-gilead. ⁵ He ar-
OF ISRAEL rived, and behold, the commanders of the army were sitting, and he said, "I have
9:4-10:36 a message for you, O commander."

　　Jehu said, "For which of all of us?"

　　And he replied, "For you, O commander." ⁶ So he arose and went inside; [the
prophet] poured the oil upon his head and said to him, "Thus said HASHEM, God
of Israel: I have anointed you king over the people of HASHEM, over Israel. ⁷ You
The disciple shall strike down your masters, the house of Ahab; then I shall be avenged of the
foretells the blood of My servants the prophets and the blood of all the servants of HASHEM,
bloody end from the hand of Jezebel. ⁸ The entire house of Ahab shall perish; I shall obliter-
of Ahab's ate male offspring* from Ahab, and anyone who survives or remains anywhere
house in Israel. ⁹ And I shall make the house of Ahab like the house of Jeroboam son of
Nebat and like the house of Baasha son of Ahijah. ¹⁰ And Jezebel shall be eaten
by the dogs in the portion of Jezreel, and no one will bury [her]." He then opened
the door and fled.

　¹¹ Jehu went out to his master's servants, and one of them said to him, "Is all
well? Why did this lunatic come to you?"

　　And he said to them, "You know that man and his prattle."

　¹² But they said, "It's a lie! Tell us now!"

וַיֹּאמֶר כָּזֹאת וְכָזֹאת אָמַר אֵלַי לֵאמֹר כֹּה אָמַר יְהוָה מְשַׁחְתִּיךָ
לְמֶלֶךְ אֶל־יִשְׂרָאֵל: וַיְמַהֲרוּ וַיִּקְחוּ אִישׁ בִּגְדוֹ וַיָּשִׂימוּ תַחְתָּיו אֶל־ יג
גֶּרֶם הַמַּעֲלוֹת וַיִּתְקְעוּ בַּשּׁוֹפָר וַיֹּאמְרוּ מָלַךְ יֵהוּא: וַיִּתְקַשֵּׁר יֵהוּא יד
בֶּן־יְהוֹשָׁפָט בֶּן־נִמְשִׁי אֶל־יוֹרָם וְיוֹרָם הָיָה שֹׁמֵר בְּרָמֹת גִּלְעָד הוּא
וְכָל־יִשְׂרָאֵל מִפְּנֵי חֲזָאֵל מֶלֶךְ אֲרָם: וַיָּשָׁב יְהוֹרָם הַמֶּלֶךְ לְהִתְרַפֵּא טו
בְיִזְרְעֶאל מִן־הַמַּכִּים אֲשֶׁר יַכֻּהוּ אֲרַמִּים בְּהִלָּחֲמוֹ אֶת־חֲזָאֵל מֶלֶךְ
אֲרָם וַיֹּאמֶר יֵהוּא אִם־יֵשׁ נַפְשְׁכֶם אַל־יֵצֵא פָלִיט מִן־הָעִיר לָלֶכֶת
°לַגִּיד [לְהַגִּיד ק׳] בְּיִזְרְעֶאל: וַיִּרְכַּב יֵהוּא וַיֵּלֶךְ יִזְרְעֶאלָה כִּי יוֹרָם שֹׁכֵב טז
שָׁמָּה וַאֲחַזְיָה מֶלֶךְ יְהוּדָה יָרַד לִרְאוֹת אֶת־יוֹרָם: וְהַצֹּפֶה עֹמֵד עַל־ יז
הַמִּגְדָּל בְּיִזְרְעֶאל וַיַּרְא אֶת־שִׁפְעַת יֵהוּא בְּבֹאוֹ וַיֹּאמֶר שִׁפְעַת אֲנִי
רֹאֶה וַיֹּאמֶר יְהוֹרָם קַח רַכָּב וּשְׁלַח לִקְרָאתָם וְיֹאמַר הֲשָׁלוֹם: וַיֵּלֶךְ יח
רֹכֵב הַסּוּס לִקְרָאתוֹ וַיֹּאמֶר כֹּה־אָמַר הַמֶּלֶךְ הֲשָׁלוֹם וַיֹּאמֶר יֵהוּא
מַה־לְּךָ וּלְשָׁלוֹם סֹב אֶל־אַחֲרָי וַיַּגֵּד הַצֹּפֶה לֵאמֹר בָּא־הַמַּלְאָךְ עַד־הֶם
וְלֹא־שָׁב: וַיִּשְׁלַח רֹכֵב סוּס שֵׁנִי וַיָּבֹא אֲלֵהֶם וַיֹּאמֶר כֹּה־אָמַר הַמֶּלֶךְ יט
שָׁלוֹם וַיֹּאמֶר יֵהוּא מַה־לְּךָ וּלְשָׁלוֹם סֹב אֶל־אַחֲרָי: וַיַּגֵּד הַצֹּפֶה לֵאמֹר כ
בָּא עַד־אֲלֵיהֶם וְלֹא־שָׁב וְהַמִּנְהָג כְּמִנְהַג יֵהוּא בֶן־נִמְשִׁי כִּי בְשִׁגָּעוֹן
יִנְהָג: וַיֹּאמֶר יְהוֹרָם אֱסֹר וַיֶּאְסֹר רִכְבּוֹ וַיֵּצֵא יְהוֹרָם מֶלֶךְ־יִשְׂרָאֵל כא
וַאֲחַזְיָהוּ מֶלֶךְ־יְהוּדָה אִישׁ בְּרִכְבּוֹ וַיֵּצְאוּ לִקְרַאת יֵהוּא וַיִּמְצָאֻהוּ
בְּחֶלְקַת נָבוֹת הַיִּזְרְעֵאלִי: וַיְהִי כִּרְאוֹת יְהוֹרָם אֶת־יֵהוּא וַיֹּאמֶר הֲשָׁלוֹם כב
יֵהוּא וַיֹּאמֶר מָה הַשָּׁלוֹם עַד־זְנוּנֵי אִיזֶבֶל אִמְּךָ וּכְשָׁפֶיהָ הָרַבִּים:
וַיַּהֲפֹךְ יְהוֹרָם יָדָיו וַיָּנֹס וַיֹּאמֶר אֶל־אֲחַזְיָהוּ מִרְמָה אֲחַזְיָה: וְיֵהוּא כג-כד
מִלֵּא יָדוֹ בַקֶּשֶׁת וַיַּךְ אֶת־יְהוֹרָם בֵּין זְרֹעָיו וַיֵּצֵא הַחֵצִי מִלִּבּוֹ וַיִּכְרַע
בְּרִכְבּוֹ: וַיֹּאמֶר אֶל־בִּדְקַר °שָׁלִשֹׁה [שָׁלִשׁוֹ ק׳] שָׂא הַשְׁלִכֵהוּ בְּחֶלְקַת כה
שְׂדֵה נָבוֹת הַיִּזְרְעֵאלִי כִּי־זְכֹר אֲנִי וָאַתָּה אֵת רֹכְבִים צְמָדִים אַחֲרֵי
אַחְאָב אָבִיו וַיהוָה נָשָׂא עָלָיו אֶת־הַמַּשָּׂא הַזֶּה: אִם־לֹא אֶת־דְּמֵי כו
נָבוֹת וְאֶת־דְּמֵי בָנָיו רָאִיתִי אֶמֶשׁ נְאֻם־יְהוָה וְשִׁלַּמְתִּי לְךָ בַּחֶלְקָה
הַזֹּאת נְאֻם־יְהוָה וְעַתָּה שָׂא הַשְׁלִכֵהוּ בַּחֶלְקָה כִּדְבַר יְהוָה: וַאֲחַזְיָה כז
מֶלֶךְ־יְהוּדָה רָאָה וַיָּנָס דֶּרֶךְ בֵּית הַגָּן וַיִּרְדֹּף אַחֲרָיו יֵהוּא וַיֹּאמֶר
גַּם־אֹתוֹ הַכֻּהוּ אֶל־הַמֶּרְכָּבָה בְּמַעֲלֵה־גוּר אֲשֶׁר אֶת־יִבְלְעָם וַיָּנָס
מְגִדּוֹ וַיָּמָת שָׁם: וַיַּרְכִּבוּ אֹתוֹ עֲבָדָיו יְרוּשָׁלְמָה וַיִּקְבְּרוּ אֹתוֹ בִקְבֻרָתוֹ כח

9:13. The garments formed a makeshift throne (*Metzudos*). **9:21.** See *I Kings* 21:1-22.

He replied, "Such and such did he say to me, saying, 'Thus said HASHEM: I have anointed you king over Israel.' " [13] Hurriedly, each of them took his garment and put it underneath him, on the top of the steps; * they sounded the shofar and said, "Jehu has become king!"

Jehu embarks on his mission

[14] Jehu son of Jehoshaphat son of Nimshi then organized against Jehoram. (Jehoram had been protecting Ramoth-gilead, he and all of Israel, against Hazael king of Aram; [15] and then King Jehoram returned to convalesce in Jezreel from the wounds that the Arameans had inflicted upon him when he was fighting Hazael king of Aram.) Jehu said, "If this is truly your will, let no refugee leave the city to go and tell [the news] in the Jezreelite."

[16] Jehu rode and went to Jezreel, for Jehoram was lying there, and Ahaziah king of Judah had come down to visit Jehoram. [17] The watchman was standing on the tower in Jezreel, and he saw the company of Jehu as he approached, and he said, "I see a company."

Jehoram said, "Select a rider and send him to meet them and ask, '[Do you come] in peace?' "

[18] So the horseman went toward him and said, "Thus said the king, '[Do you come] in peace?' "

Jehu said [to him], "What is it to you whether [it is] in for peace? Come around to my rear."

Jehoram's messengers defect

The watchman reported, saying, "The messenger reached them, but he did not return."

[19] So he sent a second horseman, who came to them and said, "Thus said the king, '[Do you come in] peace?' "

Jehu said to him, "What is it to you whether [it is] for peace? Come around to my rear."

[20] The watchman reported, saying, "He has reached them, but has not returned. The driving is like the driving of Jehu [grand]son of Nimshi, for he is driving [his chariot] recklessly."

[21] Jehoram then said, "Harness [my chariot]!" and he harnessed his chariot. Jehoram king of Israel and Ahaziah king of Judah then set out, each man in his chariot, going out towards Jehu, and they encountered him at the portion [of land] belonging to Naboth the Jezreelite. *

[22] When Jehoram saw Jehu he said, "[Do you come] in peace, Jehu?"

And he replied, "What is the peace that it should extend to the harlotries of your mother Jezebel and to her abundant witchcraft!" [23] Jehoram then turned [the reins in] his hands and fled, and said to Ahaziah, "It is a trick, Ahaziah!"

Jehu kills Jehoram . . .

[24] Jehu drew his bow fully and hit Jehoram between his shoulder blades; the arrow protruded from his heart, and he collapsed in his chariot. [25] [Jehu] then said to Bidkar his captain, "Pick [him] up and throw him into the portion of the field belonging to Naboth the Jezreelite, for remember that I and you were riding together behind his father Ahab when [the prophet of] HASHEM proclaimed this prophecy about him: [26] 'Did I not see the blood of Naboth and the blood of his descendants last night? — the word of HASHEM. I shall therefore bring retribution upon you in this very portion — the word of HASHEM.' So now pick [him] up and throw him into the portion, according to the word of HASHEM."

. . . and throws his body into Naboth's field

Jehu kills Ahaziah . . .

[27] Ahaziah king of Judah saw and he fled by way of the garden house; Jehu chased after him and said, "Strike him down also in the chariot." [They wounded him] in the ascent of Gur which is by Ibleam; he fled to Megiddo and died there. [28] His servants brought him by chariot to Jerusalem and buried him in his grave,

כט עִם־אֲבֹתָיו בְּעִיר דָּוִד: וּבִשְׁנַת֩ אַחַ֨ת עֶשְׂרֵ֤ה שָׁנָה֙ לְיוֹרָם

ל בֶּן־אַחְאָ֔ב מָלַ֥ךְ אֲחַזְיָ֖ה עַל־יְהוּדָֽה: וַיָּב֥וֹא יֵה֖וּא יִזְרְעֶ֑אלָה וְאִיזֶ֣בֶל
שָׁמְעָ֔ה וַתָּ֨שֶׂם בַּפּ֤וּךְ עֵינֶ֙יהָ֙ וַתֵּ֣יטֶב אֶת־רֹאשָׁ֔הּ וַתַּשְׁקֵ֖ף בְּעַ֥ד הַחַלּֽוֹן:

לא-לב וְיֵה֖וּא בָּ֣א בַשָּׁ֑עַר וַתֹּ֕אמֶר הֲשָׁל֖וֹם זִמְרִ֥י הֹרֵ֥ג אֲדֹנָֽיו: וַיִּשָּׂ֤א פָנָיו֙ אֶל־הַֽחַלּ֔וֹן
וַיֹּ֕אמֶר מִ֥י אִתִּ֖י מִ֑י וַיַּשְׁקִ֣יפוּ אֵלָ֔יו שְׁנַ֥יִם שְׁלֹשָׁ֖ה סָרִיסִֽים: וַיֹּ֖אמֶר °שִׁמְטֻ֑הוּ

לג [°שִׁמְט֖וּהָ ק] וַיִּשְׁמְט֔וּהָ וַיִּ֧ז מִדָּמָ֛הּ אֶל־הַקִּ֖יר וְאֶל־הַסּוּסִ֑ים וַֽיִּרְמְסֶֽנָּה: וַיָּבֹ֖א
לד וַיֹּ֣אכַל וַיֵּ֑שְׁתְּ וַיֹּ֗אמֶר פִּקְדוּ־נָ֞א אֶת־הָאֲרוּרָ֤ה הַזֹּאת֙ וְקִבְר֔וּהָ כִּ֥י בַת־מֶ֖לֶךְ

לה הִֽיא: וַיֵּלְכ֖וּ לְקָבְרָ֑הּ וְלֹֽא־מָ֣צְאוּ בָ֗הּ כִּ֧י אִם־הַגֻּלְגֹּ֛לֶת וְהָרַגְלַ֖יִם וְכַפּ֥וֹת
לו הַיָּדָֽיִם: וַיָּשֻׁ֘בוּ֮ וַיַּגִּ֣ידוּ לוֹ֒ וַיֹּ֗אמֶר דְּבַר־יְהוָ֣ה ה֔וּא אֲשֶׁ֣ר דִּבֶּ֗ר בְּיַד־עַבְדּ֣וֹ
אֵלִיָּ֖הוּ הַתִּשְׁבִּ֣י לֵאמֹ֑ר בְּחֵ֣לֶק יִזְרְעֶ֔אל יֹאכְל֥וּ הַכְּלָבִ֖ים אֶת־בְּשַׂ֥ר אִיזָֽבֶל:

לז °וְהָֽיְתָ֞ה [°וְהָיָ֞ת ק] נִבְלַ֣ת אִיזֶ֗בֶל כְּדֹ֛מֶן עַל־פְּנֵ֥י הַשָּׂדֶ֖ה בְּחֵ֣לֶק יִזְרְעֶ֑אל
א אֲשֶׁ֥ר לֹֽא־יֹאמְר֖וּ זֹ֥את אִיזָֽבֶל: וּלְאַחְאָ֛ב שִׁבְעִ֥ים בָּנִ֖ים **י**
בְּשֹׁמְר֑וֹן וַיִּכְתֹּב֩ יֵה֨וּא סְפָרִ֜ים וַיִּשְׁלַ֣ח שֹׁמְר֗וֹן אֶל־שָׂרֵ֤י יִזְרְעֶאל֙ הַזְּקֵנִ֔ים
ב וְאֶל־הָאֹמְנִ֖ים אַחְאָ֣ב לֵאמֹֽר: וְעַתָּ֗ה כְּבֹ֨א הַסֵּ֤פֶר הַזֶּה֙ אֲלֵיכֶ֔ם וְאִתְּכֶ֖ם בְּנֵ֣י
ג אֲדֹנֵיכֶ֑ם וְאִתְּכֶ֛ם הָרֶ֥כֶב וְהַסּוּסִ֖ים וְעִ֣יר מִבְצָ֑ר וְהַנָּֽשֶׁק: וּרְאִיתֶ֞ם הַטּ֣וֹב
וְהַיָּשָׁ֗ר מִבְּנֵ֤י אֲדֹֽנֵיכֶם֙ וְשַׂמְתֶּ֣ם עַל־כִּסֵּ֣א אָבִ֔יו וְהִֽלָּחֲמ֖וּ עַל־בֵּ֥ית אֲדֹנֵיכֶֽם:
ד וַיִּֽרְא֙וּ֙ מְאֹ֣ד מְאֹ֔ד וַיֹּ֣אמְר֔וּ הִנֵּ֞ה שְׁנֵ֤י הַמְּלָכִים֙ לֹ֣א עָ֣מְד֣וּ לְפָנָ֔יו וְאֵ֖יךְ נַעֲמֹ֥ד
ה אֲנָֽחְנוּ: וַיִּשְׁלַ֣ח אֲשֶׁר־עַל־הַבַּ֣יִת וַאֲשֶׁ֣ר עַל־הָעִ֗יר וְהַזְּקֵנִים֙ וְהָאֹ֣מְנִ֔ים אֶל־
יֵה֣וּא ׀ לֵאמֹ֗ר עֲבָדֶ֣יךָ אֲנַ֔חְנוּ וְכֹ֛ל אֲשֶׁר־תֹּאמַ֥ר אֵלֵ֖ינוּ נַעֲשֶׂ֑ה לֹֽא־נַמְלִ֣יךְ
ו אִ֔ישׁ הַטּ֥וֹב בְּעֵינֶ֖יךָ עֲשֵֽׂה: וַיִּכְתֹּ֣ב אֲלֵיהֶ֣ם סֵ֣פֶר ׀ שֵׁנִית֘ לֵאמֹר֒ אִם־לִ֨י אַתֶּ֜ם
וּלְקֹלִ֣י ׀ אַתֶּ֣ם שֹׁמְעִ֗ים קְח֤וּ אֶת־רָאשֵׁי֙ אַנְשֵׁ֣י בְנֵֽי־אֲדֹֽנֵיכֶ֔ם וּבֹ֧אוּ אֵלַ֛י כָּעֵ֥ת
מָחָ֖ר יִזְרְעֶ֑אלָה וּבְנֵ֤י הַמֶּ֙לֶךְ֙ שִׁבְעִ֣ים אִ֔ישׁ אֶת־גְּדֹלֵ֥י הָעִ֖יר מְגַדְּלִ֥ים אוֹתָֽם:
ז וַיְהִ֗י כְּבֹ֤א הַסֵּ֙פֶר֙ אֲלֵיהֶ֔ם וַיִּקְח֖וּ אֶת־בְּנֵ֣י הַמֶּ֑לֶךְ וַֽיִּשְׁחֲט֖וּ שִׁבְעִ֣ים אִ֑ישׁ
ח וַיָּשִׂ֤ימוּ אֶת־רָֽאשֵׁיהֶם֙ בַּדּוּדִ֔ים וַיִּשְׁלְח֥וּ אֵלָ֖יו יִזְרְעֶֽאלָה: וַיָּבֹ֤א הַמַּלְאָךְ֙
וַיַּגֶּד־ל֣וֹ לֵאמֹ֔ר הֵבִ֖יאוּ רָאשֵׁ֣י בְנֵי־הַמֶּ֑לֶךְ וַיֹּ֕אמֶר שִׂ֣ימוּ אֹתָ֞ם שְׁנֵ֧י צִבֻּרִ֛ים
ט פֶּ֥תַח הַשַּׁ֖עַר עַד־הַבֹּֽקֶר: וַיְהִ֤י בַבֹּ֙קֶר֙ וַיֵּצֵ֣א וַֽיַּעֲמֹ֔ד וַיֹּ֙אמֶר֙ אֶל־כָּל־הָעָ֔ם
צַדִּקִ֖ים אַתֶּ֑ם הִנֵּ֨ה אֲנִ֜י קָשַׁ֤רְתִּי עַל־אֲדֹנִי֙ וָאֶהְרְגֵ֔הוּ וּמִ֥י הִכָּ֖ה אֶת־
י כָּל־אֵֽלֶּה: דְּע֣וּ אֵפ֗וֹא כִּ֣י לֹ֤א יִפֹּ֤ל מִדְּבַ֤ר יְהוָה֙ אַ֔רְצָה אֲשֶׁר־דִּבֶּ֖ר יְהוָ֑ה

9:29. But 8:25 states that Ahaziah became king in the twelfth year of Jehoram. Actually, Ahaziah ruled for one year in the lifetime of his father, who was too ill to rule (see *II Chronicles* 21:18; *Rashi*).

9:30. Either Jezebel hoped to find favor or even seduce Jehu in a desperate attempt to save her life (*Rashi; Radak*), or she wanted to show scornful defiance of the murderous usurper (*Ralbag*).

9:31. A reference to Zimri (*I Kings* 16:9ff), who murdered his master, King Elah, and usurped the throne. Either she

was trying to gain Jehu's favor by implying that what she had done had precedent and was acceptable, or she was being sarcastic and insolent.

9:34. He occupied the palace to symbolize that he was the new ruler.

9:36. See *I Kings* 21:23.

10:3. Jehu was challenging Ahab's followers to appoint a successor from Ahab's dynasty and defend it from the insurrection.

with his forefathers in the City of David.

²⁹ *And in the eleventh year of Jehoram son of Ahab, Ahaziah reigned over Judah.* *

³⁰ *Jehu then came to Jezreel. Jezebel heard and she put mascara on her eyes and adorned her head,* * *and she looked out of the window.* ³¹ *Jehu was coming through the gate and she said, "Is all well, Zimri, murderer of his master?"* *

... and then kills Jezebel and leaves her body for the dogs

³² *He raised his face towards the window and said, "Who is with me? Who?"; and two or three officials looked out to him.* ³³ *He said, "Push her out [of the window]!" They pushed her out, and some of her blood flowed to the wall and to the horses, and [Jehu] trampled her body.* ³⁴ *He then came in and ate and drank.* * *Then he said, "Attend to this cursed woman and bury her, for she is the daughter of a king."*

³⁵ *So they went to bury her, but they did not find anything left of her except the skull, the feet, and the palms of the hands.* ³⁶ *They returned and told him; and he said, "It is the word of HASHEM that he spoke through the hand of his servant Elijah the Tishbite,* * *saying, 'In the portion of Jezreel, the dogs will devour the flesh of Jezebel.* ³⁷ *And Jezebel's carcass shall be like fertilizer spread over the face of the earth in the portion of Jezreel, so that they will not be able to say, This is Jezebel.'"*

10

Jehu intimidates Ahab's loyalists ...

¹ A*hab had seventy sons in Samaria. Jehu wrote scrolls and sent them to Samaria, to the elder officials of Jezreel, and to those who were rearing [the children of] Ahab saying,* ² *". . . and now, when this letter reaches you, since your master's children are with you, and with you the chariot force and the horses, fortified city and weapons —* ³ *see [who is] the best and most virtuous of your master's sons and place him upon his father's throne, and fight for the sake of your master's house."* *

⁴ *They were exceedingly frightened, for they said, "If even those two kings* * *could not stand against him, how can we stand?"*

⁵ *So the one in charge of the household, and the one in charge of the city, and the elders, and those who were rearing [the children] sent to Jehu, saying, "We are your servants, and everything you tell us, we will do. We will not appoint anyone as king; do whatever is good in your eyes."*

⁶ *[Jehu] wrote them a second scroll, saying, "If you are with me and you wish to listen to my voice, take the heads of the male offspring of your master and come to me at this time tomorrow, to Jezreel. Now the sons of the king number seventy men, and the great men of the city are raising them."*

... and they annihilate Ahab's sons

⁷ *And so it happened; when the scroll reached them they took the king's sons and slaughtered the seventy men; they put their heads in kettles and sent them to [Jehu], to Jezreel.*

⁸ *A messenger came and told him, saying, "They have brought the heads of the king's sons!"*

And he said, "Place them in two piles at the gateway until the morning." ⁹ *It happened in the morning that he went out and stood, and said to all the people, "You are righteous!* * *Behold, I organized a rebellion against my master and killed him, but who has struck down all of these [men]?* ¹⁰ *Know, therefore, that there shall not fall [unfulfilled] to the earth any word of HASHEM; for HASHEM spoke*

10:4. Jehoram of Israel and Ahaziah of Judah (see 9:24,27).

10:9. Jehu was being sarcastic. The populace considered itself righteous and disdained Jehu's regicide as repre-

hensible. Now he showed them the heads and said, "The great men of Samaria terminated Ahab's dynasty; this is a clear indication that I have not sinned in killing Jehoram."

יא עַל־בֵּית אַחְאָב וַיהוָה עָשָׂה אֵת אֲשֶׁר דִּבֶּר בְּיַד עֲבָדָו אֵלִיָּהוּ: וַיַּךְ יֵהוּא
אֵת כָּל־הַנִּשְׁאָרִים לְבֵית־אַחְאָב בְּיִזְרְעֶאל וְכָל־גְּדֹלָיו וּמְיֻדָּעָיו וְכֹהֲנָיו
עַד־בִּלְתִּי הִשְׁאִיר־לוֹ שָׂרִיד: וַיָּקָם וַיָּבֹא וַיֵּלֶךְ שֹׁמְרוֹן הוּא בֵּית־עֵקֶד

יב הָרֹעִים בַּדָּרֶךְ: וְיֵהוּא מָצָא אֶת־אֲחֵי אֲחַזְיָהוּ מֶלֶךְ־יְהוּדָה וַיֹּאמֶר מִי

יג אַתֶּם וַיֹּאמְרוּ אֲחֵי אֲחַזְיָהוּ אֲנַחְנוּ וַנֵּרֶד לִשְׁלוֹם בְּנֵי־הַמֶּלֶךְ וּבְנֵי
הַגְּבִירָה: וַיֹּאמֶר תִּפְשׂוּם חַיִּים וַיִּתְפְּשׂוּם חַיִּים וַיִּשְׁחָטוּם אֶל־בּוֹר בֵּית־

יד עֵקֶד אַרְבָּעִים וּשְׁנַיִם אִישׁ וְלֹא־הִשְׁאִיר אִישׁ מֵהֶם: וַיֵּלֶךְ

טו מִשָּׁם וַיִּמְצָא אֶת־יְהוֹנָדָב בֶּן־רֵכָב לִקְרָאתוֹ וַיְבָרְכֵהוּ וַיֹּאמֶר אֵלָיו
הֲיֵשׁ אֶת־לְבָבְךָ יָשָׁר כַּאֲשֶׁר לְבָבִי עִם־לְבָבֶךָ וַיֹּאמֶר יְהוֹנָדָב יֵשׁ וָיֵשׁ

טז תְּנָה אֶת־יָדֶךָ וַיִּתֵּן יָדוֹ וַיַּעֲלֵהוּ אֵלָיו אֶל־הַמֶּרְכָּבָה: וַיֹּאמֶר לְכָה אִתִּי

יז וּרְאֵה בְּקִנְאָתִי לַיהוָה וַיַּרְכִּבוּ אֹתוֹ בְּרִכְבּוֹ: וַיָּבֹא שֹׁמְרוֹן וַיַּךְ אֶת־כָּל־
הַנִּשְׁאָרִים לְאַחְאָב בְּשֹׁמְרוֹן עַד־הִשְׁמִידוֹ כִּדְבַר יְהוָה אֲשֶׁר דִּבֶּר אֶל־

יח אֵלִיָּהוּ: וַיִּקְבֹּץ יֵהוּא אֶת־כָּל־הָעָם וַיֹּאמֶר אֲלֵהֶם אַחְאָב

יט עָבַד אֶת־הַבַּעַל מְעָט יֵהוּא יַעַבְדֶנּוּ הַרְבֵּה: וְעַתָּה כָל־נְבִיאֵי הַבַּעַל
כָּל־עֹבְדָיו וְכָל־כֹּהֲנָיו קִרְאוּ אֵלַי אִישׁ אַל־יִפָּקֵד כִּי זֶבַח גָּדוֹל לִי
לַבַּעַל כֹּל אֲשֶׁר־יִפָּקֵד לֹא יִחְיֶה וְיֵהוּא עָשָׂה בְעָקְבָּה לְמַעַן הַאֲבִיד אֶת־

כ-כא עֹבְדֵי הַבָּעַל: וַיֹּאמֶר יֵהוּא קַדְּשׁוּ עֲצָרָה לַבַּעַל וַיִּקְרָאוּ: וַיִּשְׁלַח יֵהוּא
בְּכָל־יִשְׂרָאֵל וַיָּבֹאוּ כָּל־עֹבְדֵי הַבַּעַל וְלֹא־נִשְׁאַר אִישׁ אֲשֶׁר לֹא־בָא

כב וַיָּבֹאוּ בֵּית הַבַּעַל וַיִּמָּלֵא בֵית־הַבַּעַל פֶּה לָפֶה: וַיֹּאמֶר לַאֲשֶׁר עַל־
הַמֶּלְתָּחָה הוֹצֵא לְבוּשׁ לְכֹל עֹבְדֵי הַבָּעַל וַיֹּצֵא לָהֶם הַמַּלְבּוּשׁ: וַיָּבֹא

כג יֵהוּא וִיהוֹנָדָב בֶּן־רֵכָב בֵּית הַבָּעַל וַיֹּאמֶר לְעֹבְדֵי הַבַּעַל חַפְּשׂוּ וּרְאוּ

כד פֶּן־יֶשׁ־פֹּה עִמָּכֶם מֵעַבְדֵי יְהוָה כִּי אִם־עֹבְדֵי הַבַּעַל לְבַדָּם: וַיָּבֹאוּ
לַעֲשׂוֹת זְבָחִים וְעֹלוֹת וְיֵהוּא שָׂם־לוֹ בַחוּץ שְׁמֹנִים אִישׁ וַיֹּאמֶר הָאִישׁ
אֲשֶׁר־יִמָּלֵט מִן־הָאֲנָשִׁים אֲשֶׁר אֲנִי מֵבִיא עַל־יְדֵיכֶם נַפְשׁוֹ תַּחַת נַפְשׁוֹ:

כה וַיְהִי כְּכַלֹּתוֹ ׀ לַעֲשׂוֹת הָעֹלָה וַיֹּאמֶר יֵהוּא לָרָצִים וְלַשָּׁלִשִׁים בֹּאוּ הַכּוּם
אִישׁ אַל־יֵצֵא וַיַּכּוּם לְפִי־חָרֶב וַיַּשְׁלִכוּ הָרָצִים וְהַשָּׁלִשִׁים וַיֵּלְכוּ

כו-כז עַד־עִיר בֵּית־הַבָּעַל: וַיֹּצִאוּ אֶת־מַצְּבוֹת בֵּית־הַבַּעַל וַיִּשְׂרְפוּהָ: וַיִּתְּצוּ
אֵת מַצְּבַת הַבָּעַל וַיִּתְּצוּ אֶת־בֵּית הַבַּעַל וַיְשִׂמֻהוּ °לְמַחֲרָאוֹת

כח-כט [°לְמוֹצָאוֹת ק] עַד־הַיּוֹם: וַיַּשְׁמֵד יֵהוּא אֶת־הַבַּעַל מִיִּשְׂרָאֵל: רַק חַטָּאֵי
יָרָבְעָם בֶּן־נְבָט אֲשֶׁר הֶחֱטִיא אֶת־יִשְׂרָאֵל לֹא־סָר יֵהוּא מֵאַחֲרֵיהֶם

ל עֶגְלֵי הַזָּהָב אֲשֶׁר בֵּית־אֵל וַאֲשֶׁר בְּדָן: וַיֹּאמֶר

10:13. They did not realize that they were speaking to the murderer of the entire family. Jehu ordered that they be arrested and executed (*Radak*).

10:15. Jehonadab was a widely respected man, who is mentioned along with his descendants in *Jeremiah* (Ch. 35) as a paragon of righteousness and piety. Jehu asked Jehonadab if he wholeheartedly supported his zealous revolution against the House of Ahab and the cult of the Baal, just as Jehu wholeheartedly respected Jehonadab's sincerity and devoutness.

concerning the house of Ahab, and HASHEM has carried out all that He had spoken through the hand of His servant Elijah." ¹¹ Jehu then struck down all those who remained of the house of Ahab in Jezreel, and all of his notables, acquaintances and priests, until he left him not a survivor.

¹² He arose and came [home], then set out for Samaria. He was at a gathering-house for shepherds along the way, ¹³ and Jehu encountered some relatives of Ahaziah king of Judah, and he said, "Who are you?"

They replied, "We are relatives of Ahaziah and have come for the welfare of the sons of the king and the sons of the queen."*

He slaughters Ahaziah's brethren . . .

¹⁴ [Jehu] then said, "Capture them alive," and they captured them alive. He then slaughtered forty-two men into the pit of the gathering-house; he did not leave any of them alive.

¹⁵ [Jehu] went on from there and encountered Jehonadab son of Rechab* coming towards him; he greeted him, and said to him, "Is your heart sincere as my heart is with your heart?"

And Jehonadab said, "It is! It is! Give [me] your hand!"

[Jehu] gave him his hand and pulled him up to him into the chariot, ¹⁶ and he said, "Come with me and see my zealous vengeance for HASHEM!" And they drove [Jehonadab] in [Jehu's] chariot.

. . . and the remnant of Ahab's family

¹⁷ [Jehu] arrived at Samaria and struck down all those that remained of Ahab in Samaria, until he annihilated him; in accordance with the word of HASHEM, which He had spoken to Elijah.

Jehu feigns loyalty to the Baal . . .

¹⁸ Jehu then gathered together all the people and said to them, "Ahab worshiped the Baal just a bit; Jehu will worship it a great deal! ¹⁹ So now, all the prophets of the Baal and all its servants and all its priests, gather them unto me — let no man be absent — for I have a great sacrifice for the Baal, and anyone who is absent shall not live!" (Jehu was acting with cunning, in order to eliminate the worshipers of the Baal.) ²⁰ Jehu said, "Convoke an assembly unto the Baal," and they declared it. ²¹ Jehu sent [messages] throughout all of Israel, and all the worshipers of the Baal came; there was no man left who did not come. They arrived at the Temple of the Baal, and the Temple of the Baal became filled from end to end.

²² [Jehu] then said to the one in charge of the wardrobe, "Bring out a vestment for each of the worshipers of the Baal," and he brought out the vestments for them. ²³ Jehu and Jehonadab son of Rechab arrived at the Temple of the Baal, and he said to the worshipers of the Baal, "Search and ascertain, lest there be among you worshipers of HASHEM, for only worshipers of the Baal alone [may attend]." ²⁴ They came to offer peace-offerings and burnt-offerings; Jehu posted eighty men outside and said, "If any one of these men whom I am putting under your charge escapes, your soul shall be in place of his soul!"

. . . and destroys its worshipers and idols

²⁵ It happened when he finished performing the burnt-offering, that Jehu said to the runners and to the captains, "Come and strike them down! Let no man get away!" They struck them down by the sword. The runners and the captains threw themselves onward, as they advanced going to the city of the Temple of the Baal. ²⁶ They removed the monuments of the Temple of the Baal and burned them. ²⁷ They smashed the pillar of the Baal, and they demolished the Temple of the Baal and designated it for latrines, until today.

²⁸ Thus Jehu eliminated the Baal from Israel, ²⁹ but regarding the sins of Jeroboam son of Nebat, who caused Israel to sin — the golden calves that were [in] Beth-el and in Dan — Jehu did not turn away from them.

יְהֹוָה אֶל־יֵהוּא יַעַן אֲשֶׁר־הֱטִיבֹתָ לַעֲשׂוֹת הַיָּשָׁר בְּעֵינַי כְּכֹל אֲשֶׁר בִּלְבָבִי

לא עָשִׂיתָ לְבֵית אַחְאָב בְּנֵי רְבִעִים יֵשְׁבוּ לְךָ עַל־כִּסֵּא יִשְׂרָאֵל: וְיֵהוּא לֹא שָׁמַר לָלֶכֶת בְּתוֹרַת־יְהֹוָה אֱלֹהֵי־יִשְׂרָאֵל בְּכָל־לְבָבוֹ לֹא סָר מֵעַל

לב חַטֹּאות יָרָבְעָם אֲשֶׁר הֶחֱטִיא אֶת־יִשְׂרָאֵל: בַּיָּמִים הָהֵם הֵחֵל יְהֹוָה

לג לְקַצּוֹת בְּיִשְׂרָאֵל וַיַּכֵּם חֲזָאֵל בְּכָל־גְּבוּל יִשְׂרָאֵל: מִן־הַיַּרְדֵּן מִזְרַח הַשֶּׁמֶשׁ אֵת כָּל־אֶרֶץ הַגִּלְעָד הַגָּדִי וְהָרֵאוּבֵנִי וְהַמְנַשִּׁי מֵעֲרֹעֵר אֲשֶׁר־

לד עַל־נַחַל אַרְנֹן וְהַגִּלְעָד וְהַבָּשָׁן: וְיֶתֶר דִּבְרֵי יֵהוּא וְכָל־אֲשֶׁר עָשָׂה וְכָל־ גְּבוּרָתוֹ הֲלוֹא־הֵם כְּתוּבִים עַל־סֵפֶר דִּבְרֵי הַיָּמִים לְמַלְכֵי יִשְׂרָאֵל:

לה וַיִּשְׁכַּב יֵהוּא עִם־אֲבֹתָיו וַיִּקְבְּרוּ אֹתוֹ בְּשֹׁמְרוֹן וַיִּמְלֹךְ יְהוֹאָחָז בְּנוֹ

לו תַּחְתָּיו: וְהַיָּמִים אֲשֶׁר מָלַךְ יֵהוּא עַל־יִשְׂרָאֵל עֶשְׂרִים וּשְׁמֹנֶה־שָׁנָה

א בְּשֹׁמְרוֹן: וַעֲתַלְיָה אֵם אֲחַזְיָהוּ °וראתה [רָאֲתָה ק] כִּי מֵת

יא

ב בְּנָהּ וַתָּקָם וַתְּאַבֵּד אֵת כָּל־זֶרַע הַמַּמְלָכָה: וַתִּקַּח יְהוֹשֶׁבַע בַּת־הַמֶּלֶךְ־ יוֹרָם אֲחוֹת אֲחַזְיָהוּ אֶת־יוֹאָשׁ בֶּן־אֲחַזְיָה וַתִּגְנֹב אֹתוֹ מִתּוֹךְ בְּנֵי־הַמֶּלֶךְ °הממותתים [הַמּוּמָתִים ק] אֹתוֹ וְאֶת־מֵינִקְתּוֹ בַּחֲדַר הַמִּטּוֹת וַיַּסְתִּרוּ

ג אֹתוֹ מִפְּנֵי עֲתַלְיָהוּ וְלֹא הוּמָת: וַיְהִי אִתָּהּ בֵּית יְהֹוָה מִתְחַבֵּא שֵׁשׁ שָׁנִים

ד וַעֲתַלְיָה מֹלֶכֶת עַל־הָאָרֶץ: וּבַשָּׁנָה הַשְּׁבִיעִית שָׁלַח יְהוֹיָדָע וַיִּקַּח | אֶת־שָׂרֵי °המיאית [הַמֵּאוֹת ק] לַכָּרִי וְלָרָצִים וַיָּבֵא אֹתָם אֵלָיו בֵּית יְהֹוָה וַיִּכְרֹת לָהֶם בְּרִית וַיַּשְׁבַּע אֹתָם בְּבֵית יְהֹוָה וַיַּרְא אֹתָם אֶת־בֶּן־

ה הַמֶּלֶךְ: וַיְצַוֵּם לֵאמֹר זֶה הַדָּבָר אֲשֶׁר תַּעֲשׂוּן הַשְּׁלִשִׁית מִכֶּם בָּאֵי הַשַּׁבָּת

ו וְשֹׁמְרֵי מִשְׁמֶרֶת בֵּית הַמֶּלֶךְ: וְהַשְּׁלִשִׁית בְּשַׁעַר סוּר וְהַשְּׁלִשִׁית בַּשַּׁעַר

ז אַחַר הָרָצִים וּשְׁמַרְתֶּם אֶת־מִשְׁמֶרֶת הַבַּיִת מַסָּח: וּשְׁתֵּי הַיָּדוֹת בָּכֶם כֹּל

ח יֹצְאֵי הַשַּׁבָּת וְשָׁמְרוּ אֶת־מִשְׁמֶרֶת בֵּית־יְהֹוָה אֶל־הַמֶּלֶךְ: וְהִקַּפְתֶּם עַל־ הַמֶּלֶךְ סָבִיב אִישׁ וְכֵלָיו בְּיָדוֹ וְהַבָּא אֶל־הַשְּׂדֵרוֹת יוּמָת וִהְיוּ אֶת־הַמֶּלֶךְ

ט בְּצֵאתוֹ וּבְבֹאוֹ: וַיַּעֲשׂוּ שָׂרֵי °המיאית [הַמֵּאוֹת ק] כְּכֹל אֲשֶׁר־צִוָּה יְהוֹיָדָע הַכֹּהֵן וַיִּקְחוּ אִישׁ אֶת־אֲנָשָׁיו בָּאֵי הַשַּׁבָּת עִם יֹצְאֵי הַשַּׁבָּת וַיָּבֹאוּ

י אֶל־יְהוֹיָדָע הַכֹּהֵן: וַיִּתֵּן הַכֹּהֵן לְשָׂרֵי °המיאית [הַמֵּאוֹת ק] אֶת־הַחֲנִית

יא וְאֶת־הַשְּׁלָטִים אֲשֶׁר לַמֶּלֶךְ דָּוִד אֲשֶׁר בְּבֵית יְהֹוָה: וַיַּעַמְדוּ הָרָצִים אִישׁ | וְכֵלָיו בְּיָדוֹ מִכֶּתֶף הַבַּיִת הַיְמָנִית עַד־כֶּתֶף הַבַּיִת הַשְּׂמָאלִית לַמִּזְבֵּחַ

יב וְלַבָּיִת עַל־הַמֶּלֶךְ סָבִיב: וַיּוֹצִא אֶת־בֶּן־הַמֶּלֶךְ וַיִּתֵּן עָלָיו אֶת־הַנֵּזֶר וְאֶת־

10:34. See *I Kings* 14:19.

11:2. This was an upper chamber located above the Holy of Holies of the Temple in Jerusalem (*Rashi*). As the wife of Jehoiada the Kohen Gadol (*II Chronicles* 22:11), Jehosheba had access to the Temple. They bided their time until they felt it was opportune to overthrow Athaliah and place Joash on the throne.

11:5. In order to enlist the Kohanim and Levites, who

could be trusted, Jehoiada now addressed their captains. The Kohanim and Levites were divided into twenty-four shifts, called watches, (see *I Chronicles* Chs. 24-25), which changed places on the Sabbath. Since both the incoming and outgoing shifts would be present, the additional numbers of loyalists made the Sabbath the best day to overcome Athaliah's supporters. Now Jehoiada gave them their assignments.

³⁰ HASHEM said to Jehu, "Because you have done well, doing that which is proper in My eyes, for you have done to the house of Ahab according to all that was in My heart, four generations of your descendants will sit upon the throne of Israel for your sake."

His reign is partially righteous ³¹ But Jehu did not watch to follow the Torah of HASHEM, God of Israel, with all his heart; he did not turn away from the sins of Jeroboam that he caused Israel to sin.

³² In those days HASHEM began to cut away at Israel: Hazael struck at them along the entire border of Israel: ³³ from the Jordan toward the rising sun, all the land of Gilead of the Gadite, the Reubenite, and the Manassite — from Aroer which is on the Arnon Brook to Gilead and Bashan.

Jehu is succeeded by Jehoahaz (See Appendix A, timeline 4) ³⁴ The rest of the deeds of Jehu and all that he did, and all of his might — behold, they are recorded in the Book of the Chronicles of the Kings of Israel. * ³⁵ Jehu lay with his forefathers and they buried him in Samaria. His son Jehoahaz reigned in his place. ³⁶ The days that Jehu ruled over Israel were twenty-eight years, in Samaria.

11

ATHALIAH, QUEEN REG- NANT OF JUDAH 11:1-20

The child Joash is hidden

Jehoiada enlists allies . . .

¹ **W**hen Athaliah, Ahaziah's mother, saw that her son had died, she arose and exterminated all the offspring of the royal family. ² But Jehosheba, King Jehoram's daughter, Ahaziah's sister, took Joash son of Ahaziah and smuggled him from the midst of the king's sons who were being killed, [and put] him and his nursemaid in the bed chamber; * they hid him from Athaliah, so he was not put to death. ³ He remained with her in the Temple of HASHEM, hidden for six years, while Athaliah reigned over the land.

⁴ In the seventh year Jehoiada sent for and took the captains of hundreds, who were over the mighty men and the foot soldiers, and he brought them to [meet with] him in the Temple of HASHEM. He made a covenant with them and adjured them in the Temple of HASHEM, and he showed them the king's son. ⁵ He commanded them, saying, "This is what you are to do: A third of those of you who are arriving on the Sabbath* will be in charge of the watch of the king's palace, ⁶ a third will be stationed at the Sur Gate, and a third will be stationed at the gate behind which is the Gate of the Infantry. Be careful to keep the watch of the palace diligently. ⁷ The other two groups among you will be joined by all those who are leaving on the Sabbath; they shall keep the guard of the Temple of HASHEM, for the king. ⁸ You will thus encircle the king all around, each man with his weapons in his hand; any [outsider] who breaks into [your] ranks should be put to death. You must remain with the king when he goes out and when he comes in."

⁹ So the captains of hundreds did according to all that Jehoiada the Kohen had commanded them; each [captain] took his men, those who were arriving on the Sabbath and those who were leaving on the Sabbath, and came to Jehoiada the Kohen. ¹⁰ The Kohen gave to the captains of hundreds the spear arsenal and the shields of King David, * which were in the Temple of HASHEM. ¹¹ The infantry stood, each man with his weapons in his hand, from the right flank of the Temple to the left flank of the Temple, near the Altar and the Sanctuary, surrounding the king. ¹² Then [Jehoiada] brought out the king's son and placed the crown and the

---

11:10. See *II Samuel* 8:7 and *I Kings* 10:16-17.

יג הָעֵד֗וּת וַיַּמְלִ֤כוּ אֹתוֹ֙ וַיִּמְשָׁחֻ֔הוּ וַיַּכּוּ־כָ֔ף וַיֹּאמְר֖וּ יְחִ֣י הַמֶּֽלֶךְ: וַתִּשְׁמַ֣ע

יד עֲתַלְיָ֗ה אֶת־ק֤וֹל הָֽרָצִין֙ הָעָ֔ם וַתָּבֹ֥א אֶל־הָעָ֖ם בֵּ֥ית יְהוָֽה: וַתֵּ֡רֶא וְהִנֵּ֣ה
הַמֶּ֩לֶךְ֩ עֹמֵ֨ד עַֽל־הָעַמּ֜וּד כַּמִּשְׁפָּ֗ט וְהַשָּׂרִ֤ים וְהַחֲצֹֽצְרוֹת֙ אֶל־הַמֶּ֔לֶךְ וְכָל־
עַ֤ם הָאָ֨רֶץ֙ שָׂמֵ֔חַ וְתֹקֵ֖עַ בַּֽחֲצֹֽצְר֑וֹת וַתִּקְרַ֤ע עֲתַלְיָה֙ אֶת־בְּגָדֶ֔יהָ וַתִּקְרָ֖א

טו קֶ֥שֶׁר קָֽשֶׁר: וַיְצַ֣ו יְהוֹיָדָ֣ע הַכֹּהֵ֡ן אֶת־שָׂרֵ֣י °הַמֵּאיוֹת [°הַמֵּא֗וֹת ק] ׀ פְּקֻדֵ֣י
הַחַ֜יִל וַיֹּ֤אמֶר אֲלֵיהֶם֙ הֽוֹצִ֤יאוּ אֹתָהּ֙ אֶל־מִבֵּ֣ית לַשְּׂדֵרֹ֔ת וְהַבָּ֥א אַֽחֲרֶ֖יהָ

טז הָמֵ֣ת בֶּחָ֑רֶב כִּ֚י אָמַ֣ר הַכֹּהֵ֔ן אַל־תּוּמַ֖ת בֵּ֣ית יְהוָֽה: וַיָּשִׂ֤מוּ לָהּ֙ יָדַ֔יִם וַתָּב֗וֹא

יז דֶּֽרֶךְ־מְב֥וֹא הַסּוּסִ֖ים בֵּ֣ית הַמֶּ֑לֶךְ וַתּוּמַ֖ת שָֽׁם: ◄ וַיִּכְרֹ֣ת יְהוֹיָדָ֡ע

HAFTARAS
PARASHAS
SHEKALIM
Sephardim:
11:17-
12:17

אֶת־הַבְּרִ֗ית בֵּ֤ין יְהוָה֙ וּבֵ֤ין הַמֶּ֨לֶךְ֙ וּבֵ֣ין הָעָ֔ם לִֽהְי֥וֹת לְעָ֖ם לַֽיהוָ֑ה וּבֵ֥ין
יח הַמֶּ֖לֶךְ וּבֵ֥ין הָעָֽם: וַיָּבֹ֣אוּ כָל־עַם֩ הָאָ֨רֶץ בֵּֽית־הַבַּ֜עַל וַֽיִּתְּצֻ֗הוּ אֶת־
°מִזְבְּחֹתָו [°מִזְבְּחֹתָ֞יו ק] וְֽאֶת־צְלָמָיו֙ שִׁבְּר֣וּ הֵיטֵ֔ב וְאֵ֗ת מַתָּן֙ כֹּהֵ֣ן הַבַּ֔עַל

יט הָֽרְג֖וּ לִפְנֵ֣י הַֽמִּזְבְּח֑וֹת וַיָּ֧שֶׂם הַכֹּהֵ֛ן פְּקֻדּ֖וֹת עַל־בֵּ֣ית יְהוָֽה: וַיִּקַּ֣ח אֶת־שָׂרֵ֣י
הַמֵּא֡וֹת וְאֶת־הַכָּרִי֩ וְאֶת־הָֽרָצִ֨ים וְאֵ֣ת ׀ כָּל־עַ֣ם הָאָ֗רֶץ וַיֹּרִ֤ידוּ אֶת־
הַמֶּ֨לֶךְ֙ מִבֵּ֣ית יְהוָ֔ה וַיָּב֤וֹאוּ דֶּֽרֶךְ־שַׁ֥עַר הָֽרָצִ֖ים בֵּ֣ית הַמֶּ֑לֶךְ וַיֵּ֖שֶׁב עַל־כִּסֵּ֥א

כ הַמְּלָכִֽים: וַיִּשְׂמַ֣ח כָּל־עַם־הָאָ֔רֶץ וְהָעִ֖יר שָׁקָ֑טָה וְאֶת־עֲתַלְיָ֛הוּ הֵמִ֥יתוּ

יב בַחֶ֖רֶב בֵּ֥ית °מלך [°הַמֶּֽלֶךְ ק]: ◄ בֶּן־שֶׁ֤בַע שָׁנִים֙ יְהוֹאָ֖שׁ בְּמָלְכֽוֹ:

HAFTARAS
PARASHAS
SHEKALIM
Ashkenazim:
12:1-17

א בִּשְׁנַת־שֶׁ֤בַע לְיֵהוּא֙ מָלַ֣ךְ יְהוֹאָ֔שׁ וְאַרְבָּעִ֣ים שָׁנָ֔ה מָלַ֖ךְ בִּירֽוּשָׁלָ֑ם וְשֵׁ֣ם

ב אִמּ֔וֹ צִבְיָ֖ה מִבְּאֵ֥ר שָֽׁבַע: וַיַּ֨עַשׂ יְהוֹאָ֜שׁ הַיָּשָׁ֤ר בְּעֵינֵ֣י יְהוָ֔ה כָּל־יָמָ֑יו אֲשֶׁ֣ר

ג הוֹרָ֖הוּ יְהוֹיָדָ֥ע הַכֹּהֵֽן: רַ֥ק הַבָּמ֖וֹת לֹא־סָ֑רוּ ע֥וֹד הָעָ֛ם מְזַבְּחִ֥ים וּֽמְקַטְּרִ֖ים

ד בַּבָּמֽוֹת: וַיֹּ֨אמֶר יְהוֹאָ֜שׁ אֶל־הַכֹּֽהֲנִ֗ים כֹּל֩ כֶּ֨סֶף הַקֳּדָשִׁ֜ים אֲשֶׁר־יוּבָ֣א

ה בֵֽית־יְהוָה֮ כֶּ֣סֶף עוֹבֵר֒ אִ֕ישׁ כֶּ֥סֶף נַפְשׁ֖וֹת עֶרְכּ֑וֹ כָּל־כֶּ֗סֶף אֲשֶׁ֤ר יַֽעֲלֶה֙ עַל־
לֶב־אִ֔ישׁ לְהָבִ֖יא בֵּ֥ית יְהוָֽה: יִקְח֤וּ לָהֶם֙ הַכֹּ֣הֲנִ֔ים אִ֖ישׁ מֵאֵ֣ת מַכָּר֑וֹ וְהֵ֣ם

ו יְחַזְּק֗וּ אֶת־בֶּ֣דֶק הַבַּ֔יִת לְכֹ֛ל אֲשֶׁר־יִמָּצֵ֥א שָׁ֖ם בָּֽדֶק: וַיְהִ֗י

ז בִּשְׁנַ֨ת עֶשְׂרִ֤ים וְשָׁלֹשׁ֙ שָׁנָ֔ה לַמֶּ֖לֶךְ יְהוֹאָ֑שׁ לֹֽא־חִזְּק֥וּ הַכֹּֽהֲנִ֖ים אֶת־

ח בֶּ֥דֶק הַבָּֽיִת: וַיִּקְרָא֩ הַמֶּ֨לֶךְ יְהוֹאָ֜שׁ לִיהוֹיָדָ֤ע הַכֹּהֵן֙ וְלַכֹּ֣הֲנִ֔ים וַיֹּ֣אמֶר
אֲלֵהֶ֔ם מַדּ֛וּעַ אֵֽינְכֶ֥ם מְחַזְּקִ֖ים אֶת־בֶּ֣דֶק הַבָּ֑יִת וְעַתָּ֗ה אַל־תִּקְחוּ־כֶ֨סֶף֙

ט מֵאֵ֣ת מַכָּֽרֵיכֶ֔ם כִּֽי־לְבֶ֥דֶק הַבַּ֖יִת תִּתְּנֻֽהוּ: וַיֵּאֹ֖תוּ הַכֹּֽהֲנִ֑ים לְבִלְתִּ֤י קְחַת־

י כֶּ֨סֶף֙ מֵאֵ֣ת הָעָ֔ם וּלְבִלְתִּ֥י חַזֵּ֖ק אֶת־בֶּ֥דֶק הַבָּֽיִת: וַיִּקַּ֣ח יְהוֹיָדָ֣ע הַכֹּהֵ֡ן
אֲרוֹן֩ אֶחָ֨ד וַיִּקֹּ֥ב חֹר֙ בְּדַלְתּ֔וֹ וַיִּתֵּ֣ן אֹת֗וֹ אֵ֚צֶל הַמִּזְבֵּ֔חַ °בימין [°מִיָּמִ֗ין ק]

11:12. I.e., Jehoiada gave Joash a Torah scroll, which a
king must have with him at all times, in accordance with
Deuteronomy 17:18-19 (*Rashi*).

11:17. The covenant obligated the king and the people
to be faithful to HASHEM, and uproot the cult of the Baal
which had infiltrated Judah through the reign of Athaliah
and her predecessors; and in addition it obligated the
people to be loyal to Joash.

11:18. Jehoiada reinstituted the routine of the Temple

service, which had apparently fallen into a degree of
disarray under Athaliah's reign (*Rashi*).

12:5. The annual half-*shekel* contribution is described as
"money of those who pass through" (*Exodus* 30:13) and,
according to *Leviticus* 27:1-8, a person may undertake to
dedicate the fixed value of himself or another person to
the Temple.

12:9. Up to then, each Kohen was authorized to accept
funds and use them, at his own discretion, for repairs.

. . . and crowns Joash

Divine testimony* upon him; they declared him king and anointed him, and they clapped [their] hands and said, "Long live the king!"

¹³ Athaliah heard the sound of the people who were rushing, and she came to the people in the Temple of HASHEM. ¹⁴ She looked, and there was the king standing at the position, in the royal manner, with the officers and the trumpets next to the king, and all the people of the land rejoicing and blowing trumpets. Athaliah tore her garments and shouted, "A rebellion! A rebellion!"

¹⁵ Jehoiada the Kohen commanded the captains of hundreds, the officers of the force, and said to them, "Take her away, but keep her within the ranks [of the guards], and anyone who comes after her slay with the sword!" For the Kohen said, "Let her not be put to death in the Temple of HASHEM." ¹⁶ They made place

Athaliah is executed

for her and she came by the way of the horses' entrance to the palace of the king, and there she was put to death.

¹⁷ Jehoiada then sealed the covenant between HASHEM and the king and the people, to be a people of HASHEM; and between the king and the people. * ¹⁸ All the people of the land came to the Temple of Baal and tore it down; they smashed its altars and images; and Mattan, priest of the Baal, they slew in front of the altars. [Jehoiada] the Kohen then established administrators over the Temple of

Joash assumes the throne

HASHEM. * ¹⁹ He took the captains of hundreds, the mighty men, the infantry and all the people of the land, and they escorted the king down from the Temple of HASHEM; they proceeded by way of the Gate of the Infantry to the royal palace, and he sat on the royal throne.

²⁰ The entire people of the land rejoiced and the city was tranquil, for they had put Athaliah to death by the sword in the king's palace.

12

JEHOASH,
KING OF
JUDAH
12:1-22
(See Appendix A,
timeline 4)

¹ Jehoash was seven years old when he became king. ² In the seventh year of Jehu, Jehoash became king, and he reigned for forty years in Jerusalem; his mother's name was Zibiah of Beer-sheba. ³ Jehoash did what was proper in the eyes of HASHEM all his days that Jehoiada the Kohen taught him. ⁴ However, the high places did not cease; the people continued to sacrifice and burn incense at the high places.

The child-king's devotion to the Temple

⁵ Jehoash said to the Kohanim, "All the money for holy purposes that is brought to the Temple of HASHEM — whether the money of 'those who pass through' or any man's money for his personal valuation* or any money that a man's heart may move him to bring to the Temple of HASHEM — ⁶ let the Kohanim take it, each man from his acquaintance, and let them repair the deterioration of the Temple, wherever deterioration will be found."

Jehoash imposes a new system of Temple maintenance

⁷ It was in the twenty-third year of King Jehoash: The Kohanim did not repair the deterioration of the Temple. ⁸ King Jehoash summoned Jehoiada the Kohen and the other Kohanim and said to them, "Why are you not repairing the deterioration of the Temple? [From] now [on], do not take money from your acquaintances; rather give it over [directly] for the deterioration [repair fund] of the Temple."

⁹ The Kohanim agreed not to accept money from the people and not to [personally] repair the deterioration of the Temple;* ¹⁰ Jehoiada the Kohen took one chest, * bored a hole in its lid, and placed it near the Altar, on the right side

---

Over the years, however, the system did not work, either because some Kohanim kept the money or because the system was inefficient. Now they agreed to forward the money directly to the repair fund, as Joash had ordained. **12:10.** This was one of the thirteen collection chests mentioned in the Mishnah (*Shekalim*, Ch. 6; *Malbim*).

בְּבוֹא־אִ֗ישׁ בֵּ֣ית יהוה וְנָתְנוּ־שָׁ֜מָּה הַכֹּהֲנִים֙ שֹׁמְרֵ֣י הַסַּ֔ף אֵֽת־כׇּל־הַכֶּ֖סֶף

יא   הַמּוּבָ֣א בֵית־יהוה: וַיְהִ֗י כִּרְאוֹתָם֙ אֶת־רַ֣ב הַכֶּ֔סֶף בָּאָר֔וֹן וַיַּ֗עַל סֹפֵ֤ר הַמֶּ֙לֶךְ֙

יב   וְהַכֹּהֵ֣ן הַגָּד֔וֹל וַיָּצֻ֙רוּ֙ וַיִּמְנ֔וּ אֶת־הַכֶּ֖סֶף הַנִּמְצָ֣א בֵית־יהוה: וְנָתְנוּ֙ אֶת־הַכֶּ֙סֶף֙ הַֽמְתֻכָּ֔ן עַל־ [יְדֵ֣י ק] [יַ֣ד כ] עֹשֵׂ֣י הַמְּלָאכָ֗ה הַפְּקֻדִ֖ים [הַֽמֻּפְקָדִ֖ים ק]

יג   בֵּ֣ית יהוה וַיּוֹצִיאֻ֜הוּ לְחָרָשֵׁ֤י הָעֵץ֙ וְלַבֹּנִ֔ים הָעֹשִׂ֖ים בֵּ֥ית יהוה: וְלַגֹּֽדְרִ֙ים֙

וּלְחֹצְבֵ֣י הָאֶ֔בֶן וְלִקְנ֤וֹת עֵצִים֙ וְאַבְנֵ֣י מַחְצֵ֔ב לְחַזֵּ֖ק אֶת־בֶּ֣דֶק בֵּית־יהוה

יד   וּלְכֹ֛ל אֲשֶׁר־יֵצֵ֥א עַל־הַבַּ֖יִת לְחׇזְקָֽה: אַ֣ךְ לֹ֣א יֵעָשֶׂה֩ בֵּ֨ית יהוה סִפּ֜וֹת כֶּ֗סֶף

מְזַמְּר֤וֹת מִזְרָקוֹת֙ חֲצֹ֣צְר֔וֹת כׇּל־כְּלִ֥י זָהָ֖ב וּכְלִי־כָ֑סֶף מִן־הַכֶּ֖סֶף הַמּוּבָ֥א

טו–טז   בֵית־יהוה: כִּֽי־לְעֹשֵׂ֥י הַמְּלָאכָ֖ה יִתְּנֻ֑הוּ וְחִזְּקוּ־ב֖וֹ אֶת־בֵּ֥ית יהוה: וְלֹ֧א

יְחַשְּׁב֣וּ אֶת־הָאֲנָשִׁ֗ים אֲשֶׁ֨ר יִתְּנ֤וּ אֶת־הַכֶּ֙סֶף֙ עַל־יָדָ֔ם לָתֵ֖ת לְעֹשֵׂ֣י

יז   הַמְּלָאכָ֑ה כִּ֥י בֶאֱמֻנָ֖ה הֵ֥ם עֹשִֽׂים: כֶּ֤סֶף אָשָׁם֙ וְכֶ֣סֶף חַטָּא֔וֹת לֹ֥א יוּבָ֖א בֵּ֣ית

יח   יהוה לַכֹּהֲנִ֖ים יִֽהְיֽוּ: ▸ אָ֣ז יַעֲלֶ֗ה חֲזָאֵל֙ מֶ֣לֶךְ אֲרָ֔ם וַיִּלָּ֖חֶם עַל־

יט   גַּ֑ת וַֽיִּלְכְּדָ֑הּ וַיָּ֤שֶׂם חֲזָאֵל֙ פָּנָ֔יו לַעֲל֖וֹת עַל־יְרוּשָׁלָֽ͏ִם: וַיִּקַּ֞ח יְהוֹאָ֣שׁ מֶֽלֶךְ־

יְהוּדָ֗ה אֵ֣ת כׇּל־הַקֳּדָשִׁ֡ים אֲשֶׁר־הִקְדִּ֣ישׁוּ יְהוֹשָׁפָ֣ט וִיהוֹרָם֩ וַאֲחַזְיָ֨הוּ אֲבֹתָ֜יו

מַלְכֵ֤י יְהוּדָה֙ וְאֶת־קֳדָשָׁ֔יו וְאֵ֣ת כׇּל־הַזָּהָ֗ב הַנִּמְצָ֛א בְּאֹצְר֥וֹת בֵּית־יהוה

כ   וּבֵ֣ית הַמֶּ֑לֶךְ וַיִּשְׁלַ֕ח לַחֲזָאֵ֖ל מֶ֣לֶךְ אֲרָ֑ם וַיַּ֖עַל מֵעַ֥ל יְרוּשָׁלָֽ͏ִם: וְיֶ֙תֶר֙ דִּבְרֵ֣י

יוֹאָ֔שׁ וְכׇל־אֲשֶׁ֖ר עָשָׂ֑ה הֲלֽוֹא־הֵ֣ם כְּתוּבִ֗ים עַל־סֵ֛פֶר דִּבְרֵ֥י הַיָּמִ֖ים לְמַלְכֵ֥י

כא   יְהוּדָֽה: וַיָּקֻ֥מוּ עֲבָדָ֖יו וַיִּקְשְׁרוּ־קָ֑שֶׁר וַיַּכּוּ֙ אֶת־יוֹאָ֔שׁ בֵּ֥ית מִלֹּ֖א הַיּוֹרֵ֥ד סִלָּֽא:

כב   וְיוֹזָבָ֣ד בֶּן־שִׁמְעָ֡ת וִיהוֹזָבָ֣ד בֶּן־שֹׁמֵ֣ר ׀ עֲבָדָ֣יו הִכֻּ֥הוּ וַיָּמֹ֛ת וַיִּקְבְּר֥וּ אֹת֖וֹ עִם־

יג   א   אֲבֹתָ֖יו בְּעִ֣יר דָּוִ֑ד וַיִּמְלֹ֛ךְ אֲמַצְיָ֥ה בְנ֖וֹ תַּחְתָּֽיו: בִּשְׁנַ֨ת עֶשְׂרִ֤ים

וְשָׁלֹשׁ֙ שָׁנָ֔ה לְיוֹאָ֥שׁ בֶּן־אֲחַזְיָ֖הוּ מֶ֣לֶךְ יְהוּדָ֑ה מָ֠לַ֠ךְ יְהוֹאָחָ֨ז בֶּן־יֵה֤וּא עַל־

ב   יִשְׂרָאֵל֙ בְּשֹׁ֣מְר֔וֹן שְׁבַ֥ע עֶשְׂרֵ֖ה שָׁנָֽה: וַיַּ֥עַשׂ הָרַ֖ע בְּעֵינֵ֣י יהוה וַיֵּ֗לֶךְ אַחַ֞ר

ג   חַטֹּ֞את יָרׇבְעָ֧ם בֶּן־נְבָ֛ט אֲשֶׁר־הֶחֱטִ֥יא אֶת־יִשְׂרָאֵ֖ל לֹא־סָ֥ר מִמֶּֽנָּה: וַיִּֽחַר־

אַ֥ף יהוה בְּיִשְׂרָאֵ֑ל וַֽיִּתְּנֵ֞ם בְּיַ֣ד ׀ חֲזָאֵ֣ל מֶֽלֶךְ־אֲרָ֗ם וּבְיַ֛ד בֶּן־הֲדַ֥ד בֶּן־חֲזָאֵ֖ל

ד   כׇּל־הַיָּמִֽים: וַיְחַ֥ל יְהוֹאָחָ֖ז אֶת־פְּנֵ֣י יהוה וַיִּשְׁמַ֤ע אֵלָיו֙ יהוה כִּ֤י רָאָה֙ אֶת־

ה   לַ֣חַץ יִשְׂרָאֵ֔ל כִּֽי־לָחַ֥ץ אֹתָ֖ם מֶ֣לֶךְ אֲרָֽם: וַיִּתֵּ֨ן יהוה לְיִשְׂרָאֵ֜ל מוֹשִׁ֗יעַ וַיֵּ֙צְאוּ֙

מִתַּ֣חַת יַ֣ד־אֲרָ֔ם וַיֵּשְׁב֧וּ בְנֵֽי־יִשְׂרָאֵ֛ל בְּאׇהֳלֵיהֶ֖ם כִּתְמ֣וֹל שִׁלְשֽׁוֹם: אַ֣ךְ לֹֽא־

ו   סָ֜רוּ מֵחַטֹּ֧אות בֵּית־יָרׇבְעָ֛ם אֲשֶׁ֥ר־ [הֶחֱטִ֥יא ק] [הֶחֱטִ֥י כ] אֶת־יִשְׂרָאֵ֖ל בָּ֣הּ

ז   הָלָ֑ךְ וְגַם֙ הָאֲשֵׁרָ֔ה עָמְדָ֖ה בְּשֹׁמְרֽוֹן: כִּ֣י לֹא֩ הִשְׁאִ֨יר לִיהוֹאָחָ֜ז עָ֗ם כִּ֣י אִם־

חֲמִשִּׁ֣ים פָּֽרָשִׁ֗ים וַעֲשָׂרָה֙ רֶ֔כֶב וַעֲשֶׂ֣רֶת אֲלָפִ֖ים רַגְלִ֑י כִּ֤י אִבְּדָם֙ מֶ֣לֶךְ אֲרָ֔ם

12:17. If money had been set aside for a guilt-offering or a sin-offering, and some was left over after the animal was purchased, this money was to be used for something that could bring personal benefit for the Kohanim. The Talmud explains that it was used to buy public elevation-offerings, the hides of which became the personal property of the Kohanim.

12:20. See *II Chronicles* Ch. 24.

13:5. That is, Jehoahaz' evil son Jehoash saved them from Aram (vv. 22-25). Jehoahaz was able to witness this salvation because Jehoash's reign began two years before his father's death (see v. 10).

13:7. After the parenthetical allusion to Jehoahaz' son Jehoash, the narrative returns to where it left off in as one enters the Temple of HASHEM, and the Kohanim who were the overseers of the threshold put into it all the money that was brought to the Temple of HASHEM. ¹¹ Whenever they saw that there was much money in the chest, the king's scribe and the Kohen Gadol would come up and they bagged and counted the money that was found in the Temple of HASHEM. ¹² They gave the counted money into the hands of the workmen, who were appointed [as overseers in] the Temple of HASHEM; and they paid it out to the carpenters and the builders who were working in the Temple of HASHEM, ¹³ and to the masons and the hewers of stone, and to purchase lumber and quarried stones to repair the deterioration of the Temple of HASHEM, and for any other expense that was spent for the Temple to repair it. ¹⁴ But there would not be made for the Temple of HASHEM silver musical instruments, basins, trumpets, or any implements of gold or silver from the money that was brought to the Temple of HASHEM, ¹⁵ for they gave it all to the workmen, and with it they repaired the Temple of HASHEM. ¹⁶ They did not make an accounting with the men into whose hand they gave the money to pay out to the workmen, for they acted with integrity.

¹⁷ The [leftover] money of guilt-offerings and the [leftover] money of sin-offerings was not brought to the Temple of HASHEM; they were for the Kohanim. *

¹⁸ Then Hazael king of Aram went up and did battle with Gath and conquered

Jehoash bribes an invader

it; Hazael then set his face to come upon Jerusalem. ¹⁹ Jehoash king of Judah took all the sacred objects that Jehoshaphat and Jehoram and Ahaziah his forefathers, the kings of Judah, had consecrated, and his own consecrated objects, along with all the gold that was found in the treasuries of the Temple of HASHEM and the king's palace, and he sent them to Hazael king of Aram; and he arose and left Jerusalem.

²⁰ The rest of the deeds of Jehoash and all that he did — behold, they are

Jehoash is assassinated

recorded in the Book of the Chronicles of the Kings of Judah. * ²¹ His servants rose up and instigated a rebellion, and they killed Jehoash at Beth-millo, which is on the descent to Silla. ²² Jozacar son of Shimeath and Jehozabad son of Shomer, his servants, struck him and he died. They buried him with his forefathers in the City of David. His son Amaziah reigned in his place.

13

JEHOAHAZ,
KING OF
ISRAEL
13:1-9
(See Appendix A,
timeline 4)

¹ In the twenty-third year of Jehoash son of Ahaziah, king of Judah, Jehoahaz son of Jehu became king over Israel in Samaria, [and reigned] for seventeen years. ² He did what was evil in the eyes of HASHEM; he went after the sins of Jeroboam son of Nebat, that he caused Israel to sin; he did not turn aside from them. ³ So HASHEM became angry with Israel, and He delivered them into the hand of Hazael king of Aram, and into the hand of Hazael's son Ben-hadad, all the days [of Jehoahaz]. ⁴ Jehoahaz pleaded before HASHEM, and HASHEM hearkened to him, for He had seen the oppression of Israel, for

A partial salvation from Aram

the king of Aram had oppressed them. ⁵ So HASHEM supplied Israel with a savior, * and they escaped from under the rule of Aram; the Children of Israel dwelt securely in their homes as they had in the past. ⁶ Nevertheless, they did not turn away from the sins of the house of Jeroboam, that he caused Israel to sin, he went in that [path]; also, an Asherah-tree stood in Samaria. ⁷ For* [Aram] left no [armed] people to Jehoahaz, except for fifty horsemen, ten chariots, and ten thousand foot soldiers, for the king of Aram had destroyed [the rest],

---

verse 4: Aram had oppressed them, by leaving no [armed] people to Jehoahaz . . . (*Radak*).

ח וַיִּשְׂמֵם כֶּעָפָר לָדֻשׁ: וְיֶתֶר דִּבְרֵי יְהוֹאָחָז וְכָל־אֲשֶׁר עָשָׂה וּגְבוּרָתוֹ הֲלוֹא־
ט הֵם כְּתוּבִים עַל־סֵפֶר דִּבְרֵי הַיָּמִים לְמַלְכֵי יִשְׂרָאֵל: וַיִּשְׁכַּב יְהוֹאָחָז עִם־
אֲבֹתָיו וַיִּקְבְּרֻהוּ בְּשֹׁמְרוֹן וַיִּמְלֹךְ יוֹאָשׁ בְּנוֹ תַּחְתָּיו:
י בִּשְׁנַת שְׁלֹשִׁים וָשֶׁבַע שָׁנָה לְיוֹאָשׁ מֶלֶךְ יְהוּדָה מָלַךְ יְהוֹאָשׁ בֶּן־יְהוֹאָחָז
יא עַל־יִשְׂרָאֵל בְּשֹׁמְרוֹן שֵׁשׁ עֶשְׂרֵה שָׁנָה: וַיַּעֲשֶׂה הָרַע בְּעֵינֵי יְהוָה לֹא סָר
יב מִכָּל־חַטֹּאות יָרָבְעָם בֶּן־נְבָט אֲשֶׁר־הֶחֱטִיא אֶת־יִשְׂרָאֵל בָּהּ הָלָךְ: וְיֶתֶר
דִּבְרֵי יוֹאָשׁ וְכָל־אֲשֶׁר עָשָׂה וּגְבוּרָתוֹ אֲשֶׁר נִלְחַם עִם אֲמַצְיָה מֶלֶךְ־
יג יְהוּדָה הֲלוֹא־הֵם כְּתוּבִים עַל־סֵפֶר דִּבְרֵי הַיָּמִים לְמַלְכֵי יִשְׂרָאֵל: וַיִּשְׁכַּב
יוֹאָשׁ עִם־אֲבֹתָיו וְיָרָבְעָם יָשַׁב עַל־כִּסְאוֹ וַיִּקָּבֵר יוֹאָשׁ בְּשֹׁמְרוֹן עִם מַלְכֵי
יד יִשְׂרָאֵל: וֶאֱלִישָׁע חָלָה אֶת־חָלְיוֹ אֲשֶׁר יָמוּת בּוֹ וַיֵּרֶד אֵלָיו
יוֹאָשׁ מֶלֶךְ־יִשְׂרָאֵל וַיֵּבְךְּ עַל־פָּנָיו וַיֹּאמַר אָבִי אָבִי רֶכֶב יִשְׂרָאֵל וּפָרָשָׁיו:
טו-טז וַיֹּאמֶר לוֹ אֱלִישָׁע קַח קֶשֶׁת וְחִצִּים וַיִּקַּח אֵלָיו קֶשֶׁת וְחִצִּים: וַיֹּאמֶר ו
לְמֶלֶךְ יִשְׂרָאֵל הַרְכֵּב יָדְךָ עַל־הַקֶּשֶׁת וַיַּרְכֵּב יָדוֹ וַיָּשֶׂם אֱלִישָׁע יָדָיו עַל־
יז יְדֵי הַמֶּלֶךְ: וַיֹּאמֶר פְּתַח הַחַלּוֹן קֵדְמָה וַיִּפְתָּח וַיֹּאמֶר אֱלִישָׁע יְרֵה וַיּוֹר
וַיֹּאמֶר חֵץ־תְּשׁוּעָה לַיהוָה וְחֵץ תְּשׁוּעָה בַאֲרָם וְהִכִּיתָ אֶת־אֲרָם בַּאֲפֵק
יח עַד־כַּלֵּה: וַיֹּאמֶר קַח הַחִצִּים וַיִּקָּח וַיֹּאמֶר לְמֶלֶךְ יִשְׂרָאֵל הַךְ אַרְצָה וַיַּךְ
יט שָׁלֹשׁ־פְּעָמִים וַיַּעֲמֹד: וַיִּקְצֹף עָלָיו אִישׁ הָאֱלֹהִים וַיֹּאמֶר לְהַכּוֹת חָמֵשׁ
אוֹ־שֵׁשׁ פְּעָמִים אָז הִכִּיתָ אֶת־אֲרָם עַד־כַּלֵּה וְעַתָּה שָׁלֹשׁ פְּעָמִים תַּכֶּה
כ אֶת־אֲרָם: וַיָּמָת אֱלִישָׁע וַיִּקְבְּרֻהוּ וּגְדוּדֵי מוֹאָב יָבֹאוּ בָאָרֶץ
כא בָּא שָׁנָה: וַיְהִי הֵם ו קֹבְרִים אִישׁ וְהִנֵּה רָאוּ אֶת־הַגְּדוּד וַיַּשְׁלִיכוּ אֶת־
הָאִישׁ בְּקֶבֶר אֱלִישָׁע וַיֵּלֶךְ וַיִּגַּע הָאִישׁ בְּעַצְמוֹת אֱלִישָׁע וַיְחִי וַיָּקָם עַל־
כב-כג רַגְלָיו: וַחֲזָאֵל מֶלֶךְ אֲרָם לָחַץ אֶת־יִשְׂרָאֵל כֹּל יְמֵי יְהוֹאָחָז: וַיָּחָן יְהוָה
אֹתָם וַיְרַחֲמֵם וַיִּפֶן אֲלֵיהֶם לְמַעַן בְּרִיתוֹ אֶת־אַבְרָהָם יִצְחָק וְיַעֲקֹב וְלֹא
כד אָבָה הַשְׁחִיתָם וְלֹא־הִשְׁלִיכָם מֵעַל־פָּנָיו עַד־עָתָּה: וַיָּמָת חֲזָאֵל מֶלֶךְ־
כה אֲרָם וַיִּמְלֹךְ בֶּן־הֲדַד בְּנוֹ תַּחְתָּיו: וַיָּשָׁב יְהוֹאָשׁ בֶּן־יְהוֹאָחָז וַיִּקַּח אֶת־
הֶעָרִים מִיַּד בֶּן־הֲדַד בֶּן־חֲזָאֵל אֲשֶׁר לָקַח מִיַּד יְהוֹאָחָז אָבִיו בַּמִּלְחָמָה
שָׁלֹשׁ פְּעָמִים הִכָּהוּ יוֹאָשׁ וַיָּשֶׁב אֶת־עָרֵי יִשְׂרָאֵל: בִּשְׁנַת שְׁתַּיִם
יד א לְיוֹאָשׁ בֶּן־יוֹאָחָז מֶלֶךְ יִשְׂרָאֵל מָלַךְ אֲמַצְיָהוּ בֶן־יוֹאָשׁ מֶלֶךְ יְהוּדָה: בֶּן־
ב עֶשְׂרִים וְחָמֵשׁ שָׁנָה הָיָה בְמָלְכוֹ וְעֶשְׂרִים וָתֵשַׁע שָׁנָה מָלַךְ בִּירוּשָׁלָ͏ם
ג וְשֵׁם אִמּוֹ °יְהוֹעַדִּין [°יְהוֹעַדָּן ק] מִן־יְרוּשָׁלָ͏ם: וַיַּעַשׂ הַיָּשָׁר בְּעֵינֵי

13:8. See note to I Kings 14:19.

13:10. According to verse 1 of this chapter, Jehoahaz reigned from the middle of the twenty-third to the middle of the thirty-*ninth* year of Jehoash of Judah. Thus, the reign of Jehoash of Israel must have begun two years before his father's death (*Rashi*).

13:14. The same words with which Elisha lamented over Elijah (2:12).

13:19. In prophecy a simple physical sign is often used to symbolize a future event. Elisha wanted Jehoash to cast all his remaining arrows into the ground, which would symbolize the complete rout of Aram. By diminishing the scope of Elisha's intended sign, Jehoash diminished the future event it symbolized.

and made them like dirt to be trampled upon.

⁸ *The rest of the deeds of Jehoahaz and all that he did, and his might — behold, they are recorded in the Book of the Chronicles of the Kings of Israel.* * ⁹ *Jehoahaz lay with his forefathers, and they buried him in Samaria; his son Jehoash reigned in his place.*

JEHOASH KING OF ISRAEL 13:10-14:16

¹⁰ *In the thirty-seventh year of Jehoash king of Judah, Jehoash son of Jehoahaz began to reign* * over Israel in Samaria, [and reigned] for sixteen years.* ¹¹ *He did what was evil in the eyes of HASHEM; he did not turn away from all the sins of Jeroboam son of Nebat that he caused Israel to sin, he went in that [path].*

Jehoash, another evil king (See Appendix A, timeline 4)

¹² *The rest of the deeds of Jehoash and all that he did and his might — how he fought against Amaziah king of Judah — behold, they are recorded in the Book of the Chronicles of the Kings of Israel.* ¹³ *Jehoash lay with his forefathers, and [his son] Jeroboam sat on his throne. Jehoash was buried in Samaria with the kings of Israel.*

¹⁴ *Elisha became ill with the disease from which he was to die. Jehoash, king of Israel, went down to [visit] him, and he cried before him and said, "Father! Father! Israel's chariot and horsemen!"* *

Elisha's last miracle

¹⁵ *Elisha said to him, "Get a bow and arrows," so he took for himself a bow and arrows.* ¹⁶ *He then said to the king of Israel, "Position your hand upon the bow," and he positioned his hand. Elisha placed his hand upon the hands of the king.* ¹⁷ *He then said, "Open the window towards the east," and he opened [it]; Elisha said, "Shoot!" and he shot; [Elisha] said, "[It is] an arrow of salvation unto HASHEM, and an arrow of salvation against Aram; you shall strike Aram at Aphek to utter destruction!"* ¹⁸ *Then he said, "Take the arrows," and he took [them]; he said to the king of Israel, "Strike [them] to the ground!" and he struck three times and stopped.* ¹⁹ *The man of God became angry with him and said, "[Were you] to strike five or six times, you would have smitten Aram to utter destruction!* * But now you will strike at Aram [only] three times."*

²⁰ *Then Elisha died and they buried him.*

[It happened that] troops from Moab would come into the land at the start of the year. * ²¹ *Some people were burying a man, and just then they saw the troop coming, so they threw the man into Elisha's grave. The man's body rolled over and touched the bones of Elisha, and [the man] came back to life and rose up on his feet.*

²² *Hazael king of Aram oppressed Israel all the days of Jehoahaz.* ²³ *But HASHEM showed them grace and had mercy on them, and He was attentive to them, because of His covenant with Abraham, Isaac and Jacob, and He did not wish to destroy them, so He did not cast them away from His presence up to now.* ²⁴ *Hazael king of Aram died, and his son Ben-hadad reigned in his place.*

Jehoash's victory over Aram

²⁵ *Jehoash son of Jehoahaz returned and took back from Ben-hadad son of Hazael the cities that [Ben-hadad] had taken in battle from his father Jehoahaz. Jehoash struck him three times, and retrieved the cities of Israel.*

14

AMAZIAH, KING OF JUDAH 14:1-22

¹ *In the second year of Jehoash son of Jehoahaz, king of Israel, Amaziah, son of Jehoash king of Judah, became king.* ² *He was twenty-five years old when he became king, and he reigned for twenty-nine years in Jerusalem. His mother's name was Jehoaddan of Jerusalem.* ³ *He did what was proper in the eyes of*

13:20. The Moabites would raid at the beginning of the year, when there was plenty of vegetation on the ground for their animals (*Rashi*).

Alternatively, "Troops from Moab came into the land that very year [when Elisha, the protector of Israel, died]" (*Radak*).

ד יְהֹוָה רַק לֹא כְדָוִד אָבִיו כְּכֹל אֲשֶׁר־עָשָׂה יוֹאָשׁ אָבִיו עָשָׂה: רַק הַבָּמוֹת
ה לֹא־סָרוּ עוֹד הָעָם מְזַבְּחִים וּמְקַטְּרִים בַּבָּמוֹת: וַיְהִי כַּאֲשֶׁר חָזְקָה
ו הַמַּמְלָכָה בְּיָדוֹ וַיַּךְ אֶת־עֲבָדָיו הַמַּכִּים אֶת־הַמֶּלֶךְ אָבִיו: וְאֶת־בְּנֵי
הַמַּכִּים לֹא הֵמִית כַּכָּתוּב בְּסֵפֶר־תּוֹרַת־מֹשֶׁה אֲשֶׁר־צִוָּה יְהֹוָה לֵאמֹר
לֹא־יוּמְתוּ אָבוֹת עַל־בָּנִים וּבָנִים לֹא־יוּמְתוּ עַל־אָבוֹת כִּי אִם־אִישׁ
ז בְּחֶטְאוֹ °יָמוּת [°יוּמָת ק]: הוּא־הִכָּה אֶת־אֱדוֹם בְּגֵיא־°הַמֶּלַח [°מֶלַח ק]
עֲשֶׂרֶת אֲלָפִים וְתָפַשׂ אֶת־הַסֶּלַע בַּמִּלְחָמָה וַיִּקְרָא אֶת־שְׁמָהּ יָקְתְאֵל
ח עַד הַיּוֹם הַזֶּה: אָז שָׁלַח אֲמַצְיָה מַלְאָכִים אֶל־יְהוֹאָשׁ בֶּן־
ט יְהוֹאָחָז בֶּן־יֵהוּא מֶלֶךְ יִשְׂרָאֵל לֵאמֹר לְכָה נִתְרָאֶה פָנִים: וַיִּשְׁלַח יְהוֹאָשׁ
מֶלֶךְ־יִשְׂרָאֵל אֶל־אֲמַצְיָהוּ מֶלֶךְ־יְהוּדָה לֵאמֹר הַחוֹחַ אֲשֶׁר בַּלְּבָנוֹן
שָׁלַח אֶל־הָאֶרֶז אֲשֶׁר בַּלְּבָנוֹן לֵאמֹר תְּנָה אֶת־בִּתְּךָ לִבְנִי לְאִשָּׁה
י וַתַּעֲבֹר חַיַּת הַשָּׂדֶה אֲשֶׁר בַּלְּבָנוֹן וַתִּרְמֹס אֶת־הַחוֹחַ: הַכֵּה הִכִּיתָ אֶת־
אֱדוֹם וּנְשָׂאֲךָ לִבֶּךָ הִכָּבֵד וְשֵׁב בְּבֵיתֶךָ וְלָמָּה תִתְגָּרֶה בְּרָעָה וְנָפַלְתָּה
יא אַתָּה וִיהוּדָה עִמָּךְ: וְלֹא־שָׁמַע אֲמַצְיָהוּ וַיַּעַל יְהוֹאָשׁ מֶלֶךְ־יִשְׂרָאֵל
וַיִּתְרָאוּ פָנִים הוּא וַאֲמַצְיָהוּ מֶלֶךְ־יְהוּדָה בְּבֵית שֶׁמֶשׁ אֲשֶׁר לִיהוּדָה:
יב-יג וַיִּנָּגֶף יְהוּדָה לִפְנֵי יִשְׂרָאֵל וַיָּנֻסוּ אִישׁ °לְאֹהֱלוֹ [°לְאֹהָלָיו ק]: וְאֵת
אֲמַצְיָהוּ מֶלֶךְ־יְהוּדָה בֶּן־יְהוֹאָשׁ בֶּן־אֲחַזְיָהוּ תָּפַשׂ יְהוֹאָשׁ מֶלֶךְ־יִשְׂרָאֵל
בְּבֵית שָׁמֶשׁ °וַיָּבֹאוּ [°וַיָּבֹא ק] יְרוּשָׁלַ͏ִם וַיִּפְרֹץ בְּחוֹמַת יְרוּשָׁלַ͏ִם בְּשַׁעַר
יד אֶפְרַיִם עַד־שַׁעַר הַפִּנָּה אַרְבַּע מֵאוֹת אַמָּה: וְלָקַח אֶת־כָּל־הַזָּהָב
וְהַכֶּסֶף וְאֵת כָּל־הַכֵּלִים הַנִּמְצְאִים בֵּית־יְהֹוָה וּבְאֹצְרוֹת בֵּית הַמֶּלֶךְ וְאֵת
טו בְּנֵי הַתַּעֲרֻבוֹת וַיָּשָׁב שֹׁמְרוֹנָה: וְיֶתֶר דִּבְרֵי יְהוֹאָשׁ אֲשֶׁר עָשָׂה וּגְבוּרָתוֹ
וַאֲשֶׁר נִלְחַם עִם אֲמַצְיָהוּ מֶלֶךְ־יְהוּדָה הֲלֹא־הֵם כְּתוּבִים עַל־סֵפֶר דִּבְרֵי
טז הַיָּמִים לְמַלְכֵי יִשְׂרָאֵל: וַיִּשְׁכַּב יְהוֹאָשׁ עִם־אֲבֹתָיו וַיִּקָּבֵר בְּשֹׁמְרוֹן עִם
מַלְכֵי יִשְׂרָאֵל וַיִּמְלֹךְ יָרָבְעָם בְּנוֹ תַּחְתָּיו: וַיְחִי אֲמַצְיָהוּ בֶן־
יז יוֹאָשׁ מֶלֶךְ יְהוּדָה אַחֲרֵי מוֹת יְהוֹאָשׁ בֶּן־יְהוֹאָחָז מֶלֶךְ יִשְׂרָאֵל חֲמֵשׁ
יח עֶשְׂרֵה שָׁנָה: וְיֶתֶר דִּבְרֵי אֲמַצְיָהוּ הֲלֹא־הֵם כְּתוּבִים עַל־סֵפֶר דִּבְרֵי
יט הַיָּמִים לְמַלְכֵי יְהוּדָה: וַיִּקְשְׁרוּ עָלָיו קֶשֶׁר בִּירוּשָׁלַ͏ִם וַיָּנָס לָכִישָׁה וַיִּשְׁלְחוּ
כ אַחֲרָיו לָכִישָׁה וַיְמִתֻהוּ שָׁם: וַיִּשְׂאוּ אֹתוֹ עַל־הַסּוּסִים וַיִּקָּבֵר בִּירוּשָׁלַ͏ִם
כא עִם־אֲבֹתָיו בְּעִיר דָּוִד: וַיִּקְחוּ כָּל־עַם יְהוּדָה אֶת־עֲזַרְיָה וְהוּא בֶּן־שֵׁשׁ
כב עֶשְׂרֵה שָׁנָה וַיַּמְלִכוּ אֹתוֹ תַּחַת אָבִיו אֲמַצְיָהוּ: הוּא בָּנָה אֶת־אֵילַת
כג וַיְשִׁבֶהָ לִיהוּדָה אַחֲרֵי שְׁכַב־הַמֶּלֶךְ עִם־אֲבֹתָיו: בִּשְׁנַת

14:6. *Deuteronomy* 24:16. The final clause is a paraphrase.

14:7. *Targum* renders כְּרַךְ, *large city, metropolis.* Presumably, it alludes to Petra (Greek for "rock"), a well-known site in present-day Jordan.

14:8. Amaziah wanted to go to war against Jehoash because Israelite mercenaries had gone on a rampage and attacked several Judean cities (*II Chronicles* Ch. 25).

14:14. It was common for kings to have children of senior officers stay at their courts in a sort of "hostage"

Righteous to HASHEM, but not like his forefather David; he did everything as his father Jehoash
a point had done. ⁴ However, the high places did not cease; the people continued to
sacrifice and burn incense at the high places. ⁵ It happened when the kingship
was firmly in his power that he struck down his servants who had assassinated
the king, his father, ⁶ but he did not put to death the sons of the assassins, as it
is written in the Book of the Torah of Moses, which HASHEM had commanded,
saying, "Fathers shall not be put to death because of sons, and sons shall not be
put to death because of fathers; rather a man should be put to death for his own
sin."*

⁷ He struck Edom at the Valley of Salt — ten thousand [men]; and captured
the Rock* in battle. He called its name "Joktheel" [which is its name] to this
day.

⁸ Thereupon, Amaziah sent messengers to Jehoash son of Jehoahaz son of
Jehu, king of Israel, saying, "Let us confront one another [in battle]."*

⁹ Jehoash king of Israel sent [word back] to Amaziah king of Judah,
saying, "The thornbush in Lebanon [once] sent [word] to the cedar of Lebanon,
saying, 'Give your daughter to my son for a wife'; the wild beast of Lebanon
then came by and trampled the thornbush. ¹⁰ You have routed Edom, so
your heart became arrogant. Maintain your honor and stay at your home; why
should you provoke evil against yourself and be defeated, you and Judah with
you?"

¹¹ But Amaziah did not listen, so Jehoash, king of Israel, went up and they
confronted one another — he and Amaziah king of Judah — in Beth-shemesh,
which is in Judah. ¹² Judah was defeated before Israel and they fled, each man
Amaziah to his home. ¹³ Jehoash king of Israel captured Amaziah king of Judah, the son
is routed of Jehoash son of Ahaziah, in Beth-shemesh; he then came to Jerusalem and he
by King made a breach in the wall of Jerusalem, from the Ephraim Gate to the Corner
Jehoash Gate, [a distance of] four hundred cubits. ¹⁴ And he took all the gold and silver
of Israel and all the articles that were found in the Temple of HASHEM and in the treasuries
of the king's palace, along with the "hostage children"* and he returned to
Samaria.

¹⁵ The rest of the deeds of Jehoash that he did and his might, and how he went
to war against Amaziah king of Judah — behold, they are recorded in the Book
Jehoash is of the Chronicles of the Kings of Israel.* ¹⁶ Jehoash lay with his forefathers and
succeeded was buried in Samaria with the kings of Israel. His son Jeroboam reigned in his
by Jeroboam place.

¹⁷ Amaziah son of Jehoash, king of Judah, lived for fifteen years after the
death of Jehoash son of Jehoahaz, king of Israel. ¹⁸ The rest of the deeds of
Amaziah — behold, they are recorded in the Book of the Chronicles of the Kings
of Judah.* ¹⁹ They organized a revolt against him in Jerusalem, so he fled to
Amaziah is Lachish; but they sent after him to Lachish and killed him there. ²⁰ They carried
assassinated him with horses, and he was buried in Jerusalem, with his forefathers, in the City
in a camp of David. ²¹ All the people of Judah then took Azariah, who was sixteen years
old, and crowned him in place of his father Amaziah. ²² He built up Elath, after
having retrieved it for Judah after the king lay with his forefathers.

---

arrangement, to ensure the loyalty of their influential   Samaria and Amaziah escaped back to Jerusalem.
fathers. Jehoash brought them to Samaria. According to   **14:15.** See note to *I Kings* 14:19.
Seder Olam, Jehoash died shortly after returning to   **14:18.** See *II Chronicles* Ch. 25.

חֲמֵשׁ־עֶשְׂרֵה שָׁנָה לַאֲמַצְיָהוּ בֶן־יוֹאָשׁ מֶלֶךְ יְהוּדָה מָלַךְ יָרָבְעָם בֶּן־

כד יוֹאָשׁ מֶלֶךְ־יִשְׂרָאֵל בְּשֹׁמְרוֹן אַרְבָּעִים וְאַחַת שָׁנָה: וַיַּעַשׂ הָרַע בְּעֵינֵי
יְהוֹוָה לֹא סָר מִכָּל־חַטֹּאות יָרָבְעָם בֶּן־נְבָט אֲשֶׁר הֶחֱטִיא אֶת־יִשְׂרָאֵל:

כה הוּא הֵשִׁיב אֶת־גְּבוּל יִשְׂרָאֵל מִלְּבוֹא חֲמָת עַד־יָם הָעֲרָבָה כִּדְבַר יְהֹוָה
אֱלֹהֵי יִשְׂרָאֵל אֲשֶׁר דִּבֶּר בְּיַד־עַבְדּוֹ יוֹנָה בֶן־אֲמִתַּי הַנָּבִיא אֲשֶׁר מִגַּת

כו הַחֵפֶר: כִּי־רָאָה יְהֹוָה אֶת־עֳנִי יִשְׂרָאֵל מֹרֶה מְאֹד וְאֶפֶס עָצוּר וְאֶפֶס

כז עָזוּב וְאֵין עֹזֵר לְיִשְׂרָאֵל: וְלֹא־דִבֶּר יְהֹוָה לִמְחוֹת אֶת־שֵׁם יִשְׂרָאֵל
מִתַּחַת הַשָּׁמָיִם וַיּוֹשִׁיעֵם בְּיַד יָרָבְעָם בֶּן־יוֹאָשׁ: וְיֶתֶר דִּבְרֵי יָרָבְעָם

כח וְכָל־אֲשֶׁר עָשָׂה וּגְבוּרָתוֹ אֲשֶׁר־נִלְחָם וַאֲשֶׁר הֵשִׁיב אֶת־דַּמֶּשֶׂק
וְאֶת־חֲמָת לִיהוּדָה בְּיִשְׂרָאֵל הֲלֹא־הֵם כְּתוּבִים עַל־סֵפֶר דִּבְרֵי הַיָּמִים

כט לְמַלְכֵי יִשְׂרָאֵל: וַיִּשְׁכַּב יָרָבְעָם עִם־אֲבֹתָיו עִם מַלְכֵי יִשְׂרָאֵל וַיִּמְלֹךְ

טו   א זְכַרְיָה בְנוֹ תַּחְתָּיו: בִּשְׁנַת עֶשְׂרִים וָשֶׁבַע שָׁנָה לְיָרָבְעָם

ב מֶלֶךְ יִשְׂרָאֵל מָלַךְ עֲזַרְיָה בֶן־אֲמַצְיָה מֶלֶךְ יְהוּדָה: בֶּן־שֵׁשׁ עֶשְׂרֵה שָׁנָה
הָיָה בְמָלְכוֹ וַחֲמִשִּׁים וּשְׁתַּיִם שָׁנָה מָלַךְ בִּירוּשָׁלָ͏ִם וְשֵׁם אִמּוֹ יְכָלְיָהוּ

ג מִירוּשָׁלָ͏ִם: וַיַּעַשׂ הַיָּשָׁר בְּעֵינֵי יְהֹוָה כְּכֹל אֲשֶׁר־עָשָׂה אֲמַצְיָהוּ אָבִיו:

ד-ה רַק הַבָּמוֹת לֹא־סָרוּ עוֹד הָעָם מְזַבְּחִים וּמְקַטְּרִים בַּבָּמוֹת: וַיְנַגַּע יְהֹוָה
אֶת־הַמֶּלֶךְ וַיְהִי מְצֹרָע עַד־יוֹם מֹתוֹ וַיֵּשֶׁב בְּבֵית הַחׇפְשִׁית וְיוֹתָם בֶּן־

ו הַמֶּלֶךְ עַל־הַבַּיִת שֹׁפֵט אֶת־עַם הָאָרֶץ: וְיֶתֶר דִּבְרֵי עֲזַרְיָהוּ וְכָל־אֲשֶׁר

ז עָשָׂה הֲלֹא־הֵם כְּתוּבִים עַל־סֵפֶר דִּבְרֵי הַיָּמִים לְמַלְכֵי יְהוּדָה: וַיִּשְׁכַּב
עֲזַרְיָה עִם־אֲבֹתָיו וַיִּקְבְּרוּ אֹתוֹ עִם־אֲבֹתָיו בְּעִיר דָּוִד וַיִּמְלֹךְ יוֹתָם בְּנוֹ

ח תַּחְתָּיו: בִּשְׁנַת שְׁלֹשִׁים וּשְׁמֹנֶה שָׁנָה לַעֲזַרְיָהוּ מֶלֶךְ יְהוּדָה מָלַךְ

ט זְכַרְיָהוּ בֶן־יָרָבְעָם עַל־יִשְׂרָאֵל בְּשֹׁמְרוֹן שִׁשָּׁה חֳדָשִׁים: וַיַּעַשׂ הָרַע
בְּעֵינֵי יְהֹוָה כַּאֲשֶׁר עָשׂוּ אֲבֹתָיו לֹא סָר מֵחַטֹּאות יָרָבְעָם בֶּן־נְבָט אֲשֶׁר

י הֶחֱטִיא אֶת־יִשְׂרָאֵל: וַיִּקְשֹׁר עָלָיו שַׁלֻּם בֶּן־יָבֵשׁ וַיַּכֵּהוּ קׇבׇל־עָם וַיְמִיתֵהוּ

יא וַיִּמְלֹךְ תַּחְתָּיו: וְיֶתֶר דִּבְרֵי זְכַרְיָה הִנָּם כְּתוּבִים עַל־סֵפֶר דִּבְרֵי הַיָּמִים

יב לְמַלְכֵי יִשְׂרָאֵל: הוּא דְבַר־יְהֹוָה אֲשֶׁר דִּבֶּר אֶל־יֵהוּא לֵאמֹר בְּנֵי רְבִיעִים

יג יֵשְׁבוּ לְךָ עַל־כִּסֵּא יִשְׂרָאֵל וַיְהִי־כֵן: שַׁלּוּם בֶּן־יָבֵישׁ מָלַךְ בִּשְׁנַת
שְׁלֹשִׁים וָתֵשַׁע שָׁנָה לְעֻזִּיָּה מֶלֶךְ יְהוּדָה וַיִּמְלֹךְ יֶרַח־יָמִים בְּשֹׁמְרוֹן:

יד וַיַּעַל מְנַחֵם בֶּן־גָּדִי מִתִּרְצָה וַיָּבֹא שֹׁמְרוֹן וַיַּךְ אֶת־שַׁלּוּם בֶּן־יָבֵישׁ

טו בְּשֹׁמְרוֹן וַיְמִיתֵהוּ וַיִּמְלֹךְ תַּחְתָּיו: וְיֶתֶר דִּבְרֵי שַׁלּוּם וְקִשְׁרוֹ אֲשֶׁר קָשָׁר

14:25. He is the prophet for whom the Book of *Jonah* is named. The prophecy referred to here is not recorded in Scripture (*Radak*).

14:28. Aram, including Damascus and Hamath, had originally been captured and administered by David (*II Samuel* Chs. 8,10), but subsequently freed itself. Jeroboam's army recaptured it and returned it to

Judah (*Abarbanel*).

15:5. Lit., "house of freedom." As a leper he was forced to live in isolation, outside the city wall, and was not able to attend to his royal duties; he was thus "freed," or relieved, of his responsibilities. The reason he was punished this way is given in *II Chronicles* 26:16-20.

JEROBOAM, KING OF ISRAEL
14:23-29
(See Appendix A, timeline 4)

²³ In the fifteenth year of [the reign of] Amaziah son of Jehoash king of Judah, Jeroboam son of Jehoash king of Israel became king, in Samaria, [and reigned] for forty-one years. ²⁴ He did what was evil in the eyes of HASHEM; he did not turn away from all the sins of Jeroboam son of Nebat, that he caused Israel to sin. ²⁵ He restored the boundary of Israel from the Approach of Hamath until the Sea of the Arabah, like the word of HASHEM, God of Israel, which He had spoken by the hand of His servant Jonah son of Amittai* the prophet, who was from Gath-hepher. ²⁶ For HASHEM had seen that Israel's suffering was very severe, with none surviving and none remaining, and there was no helper for Israel. ²⁷ But HASHEM did not say to erase the name of Israel from under the heavens, so He saved them through the hand of Jeroboam son of Jehoash.

²⁸ The rest of the deeds of Jeroboam and all that he did, and his might that he performed in battle, and how he restored Damascus and Hamath to Judah with [the army of] Israel* — behold, they are recorded in the Book of Chronicles of the Kings of Israel. ²⁹ Jeroboam lay with his forefathers, the kings of Israel; and his son Zechariah reigned in his place.

15

AZARIAH, KING OF JUDAH
15:1-7
A long, righteous, and uneventful reign

¹ In the twenty-seventh year of Jeroboam king of Israel — Azariah, son of Amaziah king of Judah, became king. ² He was sixteen years old when he became king, and he reigned for fifty-two years in Jerusalem. His mother's name was Jecoliah of Jerusalem. ³ He did what was proper in the eyes of HASHEM, entirely as his father Amaziah had done. ⁴ However, the high places did not cease; the people continued to sacrifice and burn incense at the high places. ⁵ HASHEM inflicted disease upon the king; he was a leper until the day of his death, and he dwelt in a place of asylum.* Jotham, the king's son, was appointed over the palace, judging the people of the land.

⁶ The rest of the deeds of Azariah and all that he did — behold, they are recorded in the Book of the Chronicles of the Kings of Judah.* ⁷ Azariah lay with his forefathers and they buried him with his forefathers in the City of David; his son Jotham reigned in his place.

ZECHARIAH, KING OF ISRAEL
15:8-12

⁸ In the thirty-eighth year of Azariah king of Judah, Zechariah son of Jeroboam became king over Israel, [and reigned] in Samaria for six months. ⁹ He did what was evil in the eyes of HASHEM, as his forefathers had done; he did not turn away from the sins of Jeroboam son of Nebat, that he caused Israel to sin. ¹⁰ Shallum

SHALLUM, KING OF ISRAEL
15:10-15

son of Jabesh conspired against him, and he struck him in front of the people, killing him; and he reigned in his place. ¹¹ The rest of the deeds of Zechariah — behold, they are recorded in the Book of the Chronicles of the Kings of Israel. ¹² This was [the fulfillment of] the word of HASHEM that He had spoken to Jehu, saying, "Four generations [of your descendants] will sit upon the throne of Israel for your sake," and so it was.*

¹³ Shallum son of Jabesh became king in the thirty-ninth year of Uzziah king of Judah, and reigned for one month in Samaria. ¹⁴ Menahem son of Gadi went up from Tirzah and came to Samaria, and he struck down Shallum son of Jabesh in Samaria, killed him, and he reigned in his place.

MENAHEM, KING OF ISRAEL
15:14-22

¹⁵ The rest of the deeds of Shallum, and his conspiracy that he organized —

15:6. See *II Chronicles* 26:16-21, where Azariah is called Uzziah, as in v. 13 below.

15:12. See 10:30. The assumption of the throne by Zechariah fulfilled that prophecy.

טז הֲנֵה כְתֻבִים עַל־סֵפֶר דִּבְרֵי הַיָּמִים לְמַלְכֵי יִשְׂרָאֵל: אָז יַכֶּה־מְנַחֵם אֶת־
תִּפְסַח וְאֶת־כָּל־אֲשֶׁר־בָּהּ וְאֶת־גְּבוּלֶיהָ מִתִּרְצָה כִּי לֹא פָתַח וַיַּךְ אֵת
כָּל־הֶהָרוֹתֶיהָ בִּקֵּעַ:

יז בִּשְׁנַת שְׁלֹשִׁים וָתֵשַׁע שָׁנָה לַעֲזַרְיָה
מֶלֶךְ יְהוּדָה מָלַךְ מְנַחֵם בֶּן־גָּדִי עַל־יִשְׂרָאֵל עֶשֶׂר שָׁנִים בְּשֹׁמְרוֹן: וַיַּעַשׂ
יח הָרַע בְּעֵינֵי יהוה לֹא סָר מֵעַל חַטֹּאות יָרָבְעָם בֶּן־נְבָט אֲשֶׁר־הֶחֱטִיא
יט אֶת־יִשְׂרָאֵל כָּל־יָמָיו: בָּא פוּל מֶלֶךְ־אַשּׁוּר עַל־הָאָרֶץ וַיִּתֵּן מְנַחֵם
כ לְפוּל אֶלֶף כִּכַּר־כָּסֶף לִהְיוֹת יָדָיו אִתּוֹ לְהַחֲזִיק הַמַּמְלָכָה בְּיָדוֹ: וַיֹּצֵא
מְנַחֵם אֶת־הַכֶּסֶף עַל־יִשְׂרָאֵל עַל כָּל־גִּבּוֹרֵי הַחַיִל לָתֵת לְמֶלֶךְ אַשּׁוּר
חֲמִשִּׁים שְׁקָלִים כֶּסֶף לְאִישׁ אֶחָד וַיָּשָׁב מֶלֶךְ אַשּׁוּר וְלֹא־עָמַד שָׁם בָּאָרֶץ:
כא וְיֶתֶר דִּבְרֵי מְנַחֵם וְכָל־אֲשֶׁר עָשָׂה הֲלוֹא־הֵם כְּתוּבִים עַל־סֵפֶר דִּבְרֵי
כב הַיָּמִים לְמַלְכֵי יִשְׂרָאֵל: וַיִּשְׁכַּב מְנַחֵם עִם־אֲבֹתָיו וַיִּמְלֹךְ פְּקַחְיָה בְנוֹ
כג תַּחְתָּיו:

בִּשְׁנַת חֲמִשִּׁים שָׁנָה לַעֲזַרְיָה מֶלֶךְ יְהוּדָה מָלַךְ
פְקַחְיָה בֶן־מְנַחֵם עַל־יִשְׂרָאֵל בְּשֹׁמְרוֹן שְׁנָתָיִם: וַיַּעַשׂ הָרַע בְּעֵינֵי יהוה
כד לֹא סָר מֵחַטֹּאות יָרָבְעָם בֶּן־נְבָט אֲשֶׁר הֶחֱטִיא אֶת־יִשְׂרָאֵל: וַיִּקְשֹׁר עָלָיו
כה פֶּקַח בֶּן־רְמַלְיָהוּ שָׁלִישׁוֹ וַיַּכֵּהוּ בְשֹׁמְרוֹן בְּאַרְמוֹן בֵּית־°מלך ק° [הַמֶּלֶךְ]
אֶת־אַרְגֹּב וְאֶת־הָאַרְיֵה וְעִמּוֹ חֲמִשִּׁים אִישׁ מִבְּנֵי גִלְעָדִים וַיְמִיתֵהוּ וַיִּמְלֹךְ
כו תַּחְתָּיו: וְיֶתֶר דִּבְרֵי פְקַחְיָה וְכָל־אֲשֶׁר עָשָׂה הִנָּם כְּתוּבִים עַל־סֵפֶר דִּבְרֵי
כז הַיָּמִים לְמַלְכֵי יִשְׂרָאֵל:

בִּשְׁנַת חֲמִשִּׁים וּשְׁתַּיִם שָׁנָה לַעֲזַרְיָה
מֶלֶךְ יְהוּדָה מָלַךְ פֶּקַח בֶּן־רְמַלְיָהוּ עַל־יִשְׂרָאֵל בְּשֹׁמְרוֹן עֶשְׂרִים שָׁנָה:
כח וַיַּעַשׂ הָרַע בְּעֵינֵי יהוה לֹא סָר מִן־חַטֹּאות יָרָבְעָם בֶּן־נְבָט אֲשֶׁר הֶחֱטִיא
כט אֶת־יִשְׂרָאֵל: בִּימֵי פֶּקַח מֶלֶךְ־יִשְׂרָאֵל בָּא תִּגְלַת פִּלְאֶסֶר מֶלֶךְ אַשּׁוּר
וַיִּקַּח אֶת־עִיּוֹן וְאֶת־אָבֵל בֵּית־מַעֲכָה וְאֶת־יָנוֹחַ וְאֶת־קֶדֶשׁ וְאֶת־חָצוֹר
ל וְאֶת־הַגִּלְעָד וְאֶת־הַגָּלִילָה כֹּל אֶרֶץ נַפְתָּלִי וַיַּגְלֵם אַשּׁוּרָה: וַיִּקְשָׁר־קֶשֶׁר
הוֹשֵׁעַ בֶּן־אֵלָה עַל־פֶּקַח בֶּן־רְמַלְיָהוּ וַיַּכֵּהוּ וַיְמִיתֵהוּ וַיִּמְלֹךְ תַּחְתָּיו בִּשְׁנַת
לא עֶשְׂרִים לְיוֹתָם בֶּן־עֻזִּיָּה: וְיֶתֶר דִּבְרֵי־פֶקַח וְכָל־אֲשֶׁר עָשָׂה הִנָּם כְּתוּבִים
לב עַל־סֵפֶר דִּבְרֵי הַיָּמִים לְמַלְכֵי יִשְׂרָאֵל:

בִּשְׁנַת שְׁתַּיִם לְפֶקַח בֶּן־
לג רְמַלְיָהוּ מֶלֶךְ יִשְׂרָאֵל מָלַךְ יוֹתָם בֶּן־עֻזִּיָּהוּ מֶלֶךְ יְהוּדָה: בֶּן־עֶשְׂרִים וְחָמֵשׁ
שָׁנָה הָיָה בְמָלְכוֹ וְשֵׁשׁ־עֶשְׂרֵה שָׁנָה מָלַךְ בִּירוּשָׁלָ͏ִם וְשֵׁם אִמּוֹ יְרוּשָׁא
לד בַת־צָדוֹק: וַיַּעַשׂ הַיָּשָׁר בְּעֵינֵי יהוה כְּכֹל אֲשֶׁר־עָשָׂה עֻזִּיָּהוּ אָבִיו עָשָׂה:
לה רַק הַבָּמוֹת לֹא סָרוּ עוֹד הָעָם מְזַבְּחִים וּמְקַטְּרִים בַּבָּמוֹת הוּא בָּנָה אֶת־
לו שַׁעַר בֵּית־יהוה הָעֶלְיוֹן: וְיֶתֶר דִּבְרֵי יוֹתָם הֲלֹא־הֵם כְּתוּבִים

°נ״א וְכָל־אֲשֶׁר

15:16. Tiphsah was an Aramite city that resisted Menahem's forces. He attacked it and committed atrocities
against its women.

15:20. He did not honor his commitment to protect
Menahem and Israel (*Radak*). Alternatively, he took the

money and left in peace, not carrying out his original
hostile and destructive plans (*Targum*).

15:25. Apparently there was a well-known sculpture of a
lion near the mansion where the assassination took place
(*Rashi*).

behold, they are recorded in the Book of the Chronicles of the Kings of Israel.

¹⁶ *At that time Menahem launched an attack from Tirzah, against Tiphsah — all that was in it and its outlying areas — because it would not capitulate, so he struck it down. He split open all its pregnant women.* *

¹⁷ *In the thirty-ninth year of Azariah king of Judah, Menahem son of Gadi became king over Israel, [and reigned] ten years in Samaria.* ¹⁸ *He did what was evil in the eyes of HASHEM; he did not turn away from the sins of Jeroboam son of Nebat, that he caused Israel to sin, all his days.*

¹⁹ *Pul, king of Assyria, came upon the land, and Menahem gave Pul a thousand talents of silver that his hands should be with him, to secure the kingship in his hand.* ²⁰ *Menahem exacted the money [with a tax] upon Israel, upon all the powerful men of the army, to give fifty shekels of silver per person for the king of Assyria. The king of Assyria then went back; he did not remain there in the land.* *

PEKAHIAH,
KING OF
ISRAEL
15:22-26
(See Appendix A,
timeline 4)

²¹ *The rest of the deeds of Menahem and all that he did — behold, they are recorded in the Book of the Chronicles of the Kings of Israel.* ²² *Menahem lay with his forefathers, and his son Pekahiah reigned in his place.*

²³ *In the fiftieth year of Azariah king of Judah, Pekahiah son of Menahem became king over Israel, [and reigned] in Samaria for two years.* ²⁴ *He did what was evil in the eyes of HASHEM; he did not turn away from the sins of Jeroboam son of Nebat, that he caused Israel to sin.* ²⁵ *His captain Pekah son of Remaliah conspired against him, striking him in Samaria in the hall of the king's palace, by the mansion and the lion* — with him were fifty men of the Gileadites — he killed him and reigned in his place.*

²⁶ *The rest of the deeds of Pekahiah and all that he did — behold, they are recorded in the Book of the Chronicles of the Kings of Israel.*

²⁷ *In the fifty-second year of Azariah king of Judah, Pekah son of Remaliah became king over Israel, [and reigned] in Samaria for twenty years.* ²⁸ *He did that which was evil in the eyes of HASHEM; he did not turn away from the sins of Jeroboam son of Nebat, that he caused Israel to sin.*

²⁹ *In the days of Pekah king of Israel, Tiglath-pileser king of Assyria came and took Ijon, Abel-beth-maacah, Janoah, Kedesh, Hazor, Gilead, and the Galilee — all of the land of Naphtali — and he exiled them to Assyria.* ³⁰ *Hoshea son of Elah conspired against Pekah son of Remaliah, and he struck him, and killed him; and he reigned in his place, in the twentieth year of Jotham* son of Uzziah.*

³¹ *The rest of the deeds of Pekah and all that he did — behold, they are recorded in the Book of the Chronicles of the Kings of Israel.*

³² *In the second year of Pekah son of Remaliah king of Israel, Jotham, son of Uzziah king of Judah, became king.* ³³ *He was twenty-five years old when he became king, and he reigned for sixteen years in Jerusalem. His mother's name was Jerusha daughter of Zadok.* ³⁴ *He did what was proper in the eyes of HASHEM, just as his father Uzziah had done, he did.* ³⁵ *However, the high places did not cease; the people continued to sacrifice and burn incense at the high places. He built the upper gate of the Temple of HASHEM.*

³⁶ *The rest of the deeds of Jotham that he did — behold, they are recorded*

15:30. Although Jotham died after only sixteen years on the throne (v. 33), Scripture prefers to record dates according to the reign of the righteous Jotham, even after his death, rather than according to the reign of his wicked successor (*Seder Olam*).

לז עַל־סֵפֶר דִּבְרֵי הַיָּמִים לְמַלְכֵי יְהוּדָה: בַּיָּמִים הָהֵם הֵחֵל יהוה לְהַשְׁלִיחַ

לח בִּיהוּדָה רְצִין מֶלֶךְ אֲרָם וְאֵת פֶּקַח בֶּן־רְמַלְיָהוּ: וַיִּשְׁכַּב יוֹתָם עִם־אֲבֹתָיו

טז א וַיִּקָּבֵר עִם־אֲבֹתָיו בְּעִיר דָּוִד אָבִיו וַיִּמְלֹךְ אָחָז בְּנוֹ תַּחְתָּיו: בִּשְׁנַת

שְׁבַע־עֶשְׂרֵה שָׁנָה לְפֶקַח בֶּן־רְמַלְיָהוּ מָלַךְ אָחָז בֶּן־יוֹתָם מֶלֶךְ יְהוּדָה: בֶּן־

ב עֶשְׂרִים שָׁנָה אָחָז בְּמָלְכוֹ וְשֵׁשׁ־עֶשְׂרֵה שָׁנָה מָלַךְ בִּירוּשָׁלִָם וְלֹא־עָשָׂה

ג הַיָּשָׁר בְּעֵינֵי יהוה אֱלֹהָיו כְּדָוִד אָבִיו: וַיֵּלֶךְ בְּדֶרֶךְ מַלְכֵי יִשְׂרָאֵל וְגַם אֶת־

בְּנוֹ הֶעֱבִיר בָּאֵשׁ כְּתֹעֲבוֹת הַגּוֹיִם אֲשֶׁר הוֹרִישׁ יהוה אֹתָם מִפְּנֵי בְּנֵי

ד-ה יִשְׂרָאֵל: וַיְזַבֵּחַ וַיְקַטֵּר בַּבָּמוֹת וְעַל־הַגְּבָעוֹת וְתַחַת כָּל־עֵץ רַעֲנָן: אָז יַעֲלֶה

רְצִין מֶלֶךְ־אֲרָם וּפֶקַח בֶּן־רְמַלְיָהוּ מֶלֶךְ־יִשְׂרָאֵל יְרוּשָׁלִַם לַמִּלְחָמָה

ו וַיָּצֻרוּ עַל־אָחָז וְלֹא יָכְלוּ לְהִלָּחֵם: בָּעֵת הַהִיא הֵשִׁיב רְצִין מֶלֶךְ־אֲרָם

אֶת־אֵילַת לַאֲרָם וַיְנַשֵּׁל אֶת־הַיְהוּדִים מֵאֵילוֹת °וארמים [°וַאֲדוֹמִים ק]

ז בָּאוּ אֵילַת וַיֵּשְׁבוּ שָׁם עַד הַיּוֹם הַזֶּה: וַיִּשְׁלַח אָחָז מַלְאָכִים אֶל־תִּגְלַת

פְּלֶסֶר מֶלֶךְ־אַשּׁוּר לֵאמֹר עַבְדְּךָ וּבִנְךָ אָנִי עֲלֵה וְהוֹשִׁעֵנִי מִכַּף מֶלֶךְ־אֲרָם

ח וּמִכַּף מֶלֶךְ יִשְׂרָאֵל הַקּוֹמִים עָלָי: וַיִּקַּח אָחָז אֶת־הַכֶּסֶף וְאֶת־הַזָּהָב

הַנִּמְצָא בֵּית יהוה וּבְאֹצְרוֹת בֵּית הַמֶּלֶךְ וַיִּשְׁלַח לְמֶלֶךְ־אַשּׁוּר שֹׁחַד:

ט וַיִּשְׁמַע אֵלָיו מֶלֶךְ אַשּׁוּר וַיַּעַל מֶלֶךְ אַשּׁוּר אֶל־דַּמֶּשֶׂק וַיִּתְפְּשֶׂהָ וַיַּגְלֶהָ

י קִירָה וְאֶת־רְצִין הֵמִית: וַיֵּלֶךְ הַמֶּלֶךְ אָחָז לִקְרַאת תִּגְלַת פִּלְאֶסֶר מֶלֶךְ־

אַשּׁוּר דּוּמֶּשֶׂק וַיַּרְא אֶת־הַמִּזְבֵּחַ אֲשֶׁר בְּדַמָּשֶׂק וַיִּשְׁלַח הַמֶּלֶךְ אָחָז אֶל־

יא אוּרִיָּה הַכֹּהֵן אֶת־דְּמוּת הַמִּזְבֵּחַ וְאֶת־תַּבְנִיתוֹ לְכָל־מַעֲשֵׂהוּ: וַיִּבֶן אוּרִיָּה

הַכֹּהֵן אֶת־הַמִּזְבֵּחַ כְּכֹל אֲשֶׁר־שָׁלַח הַמֶּלֶךְ אָחָז מִדַּמֶּשֶׂק כֵּן עָשָׂה אוּרִיָּה

יב הַכֹּהֵן עַד־בּוֹא הַמֶּלֶךְ־אָחָז מִדַּמָּשֶׂק: וַיָּבֹא הַמֶּלֶךְ מִדַּמֶּשֶׂק וַיַּרְא הַמֶּלֶךְ

יג אֶת־הַמִּזְבֵּחַ וַיִּקְרַב הַמֶּלֶךְ עַל־הַמִּזְבֵּחַ וַיַּעַל עָלָיו: וַיַּקְטֵר אֶת־עֹלָתוֹ וְאֶת־

יד מִנְחָתוֹ וַיַּסֵּךְ אֶת־נִסְכּוֹ וַיִּזְרֹק אֶת־דַּם־הַשְּׁלָמִים אֲשֶׁר־לוֹ עַל־הַמִּזְבֵּחַ: וְאֵת

הַמִּזְבַּח הַנְּחֹשֶׁת אֲשֶׁר לִפְנֵי יהוה וַיַּקְרֵב מֵאֵת פְּנֵי הַבַּיִת מִבֵּין הַמִּזְבֵּחַ

טו וּמִבֵּין בֵּית יהוה וַיִּתֵּן אֹתוֹ עַל־יֶרֶךְ הַמִּזְבֵּחַ צָפוֹנָה: °ויצוהו [°וַיְצַוֶּה ק]

הַמֶּלֶךְ־אָחָז אֶת־אוּרִיָּה הַכֹּהֵן לֵאמֹר עַל הַמִּזְבֵּחַ הַגָּדוֹל הַקְטֵר אֶת־

עֹלַת־הַבֹּקֶר וְאֶת־מִנְחַת הָעֶרֶב וְאֶת־עֹלַת הַמֶּלֶךְ וְאֶת־מִנְחָתוֹ וְאֵת עֹלַת

כָּל־עַם הָאָרֶץ וּמִנְחָתָם וְנִסְכֵּיהֶם וְכָל־דַּם עֹלָה וְכָל־דַּם־זֶבַח עָלָיו תִּזְרֹק

טז וּמִזְבַּח הַנְּחֹשֶׁת יִהְיֶה־לִּי לְבַקֵּר: וַיַּעַשׂ אוּרִיָּה הַכֹּהֵן כְּכֹל אֲשֶׁר־צִוָּה

יז הַמֶּלֶךְ אָחָז: וַיְקַצֵּץ הַמֶּלֶךְ אָחָז אֶת־הַמִּסְגְּרוֹת הַמְּכֹנוֹת וַיָּסַר מֵעֲלֵיהֶם

°ואת־ [°וְאֶת ק] הַכִּיֹּר וְאֶת־הַיָּם הוֹרִד מֵעַל הַבָּקָר הַנְּחֹשֶׁת אֲשֶׁר תַּחְתֶּיהָ

יח וַיִּתֵּן אֹתוֹ עַל מַרְצֶפֶת אֲבָנִים: וְאֶת־°מיסך [°מוּסַךְ ק] הַשַּׁבָּת אֲשֶׁר־בָּנוּ

15:36. See *II Chronicles* Ch. 27.

16:3. See *Deuteronomy* 18:9-10.

16:6. Another name for Elath.

16:10. *II Chronicles* 28:23 explains why Ahaz reproduced the altar of Damascus: "Because the gods of the kings of Aram help them; I will sacrifice to them that in the Book of Chronicles of the Kings of Judah. * ³⁷ In those days HASHEM began to incite Rezin, king of Aram, and Pekah son of Remaliah against Judah.

³⁸ Jotham lay with his forefathers and was buried with his forefathers, in the City of David his forefather. His son Ahaz reigned in his place.

16

AHAZ, KING OF JUDAH
15:38-16:20
(See Appendix A, timeline 4)

¹ In the seventeenth year of Pekah son of Remaliah, Ahaz son of Jotham king of Judah, became king. ² Ahaz was twenty years old when he became king, and he reigned for sixteen years in Jerusalem. He did not do what is proper in the eyes of HASHEM, his God, as David his forefather [had done]. ³ He went the way of the kings of Israel; he even passed his son through the fire, like the abominations of the nations whom HASHEM had driven out before the Children of Israel. * ⁴ He [also] sacrificed and burned incense at the high places and upon the hilltops and under every leafy tree.

Rezin of Aram, a new regional power

⁵ After this Rezin king of Aram and Pekah son of Remaliah king of Israel went up to do battle against Jerusalem; they besieged Ahaz, but could not defeat [him]. ⁶ At that time Rezin king of Aram restored Elath to Aram and he evicted the Jews from Eloth; * Edomites then came to Elath and dwelled there, to this day.

Ahaz bribes Assyria for help . . .

⁷ Ahaz sent messengers to Tiglath-pileser king of Assyria, saying, "Your servant and your son am I. Come up and save me from the clutches of the king of Aram and from the clutches of the king of Israel, who are rising up against me." ⁸ Ahaz took whatever silver and gold was found in the Temple of HASHEM and in the treasuries of the king's palace, and he sent a bribe to the king of Assyria. ⁹ The king of Assyria heeded him. The king of Assyria went up to Damascus and seized it, exiling its [inhabitants] to Kir, and killed Rezin.

¹⁰ King Ahaz went to greet Tiglath-pileser in Damascus; he saw the altar that was in Damascus, and King Ahaz sent a model of the altar and its plans, according to all its workings, to Urijah the Kohen. * ¹¹ Urijah the Kohen then built the altar; according to everything that King Ahaz had sent from Damascus, so Urijah the Kohen did, before King Ahaz arrived from Damascus. ¹² When the king arrived from Damascus, the king saw the altar; the king approached the altar and offered upon it. ¹³ He burned his elevation-offering and his meal-offering, poured out his libations, and sprinkled the blood of his peace-offerings upon the altar. ¹⁴ And as for the Copper Altar * that was before HASHEM — he drew [the new altar] closer to the entrance of the Sanctuary, between the [true] Altar and the Temple of HASHEM and placed it upon the northern side of the Altar.

. . . and becomes an unctuous worshiper of the Assyrian idol

¹⁵ King Ahaz commanded Urijah the Kohen, saying, "Upon the great altar you shall burn the elevation-offering of the morning and the meal-offering of the evening, the elevation-offering of the king and his meal-offering, the elevation-offering of the general populace and their meal-offerings and libations, and the blood of all elevation-offerings and the blood of any sacrifice you shall sprinkle upon it; the Copper Altar will be for me to visit." ¹⁶ Urijah the Kohen did according to all that King Ahaz had commanded.

Ahaz violates the Temple

¹⁷ King Ahaz cut off the stands of the lavers * and removed the laver from them; he also took down the sea from upon the copper oxen that were under it and placed it upon a stone floor. ¹⁸ He removed the Sabbath awning that they had built

---

they may help me."   **16:17.** See I Kings 7:23-27.
16:14. The Temple's sacred Altar.

בַּבַּ֗יִת וְאֶת־מְב֤וֹא הַמֶּ֙לֶךְ֙ הַֽחִיצ֔וֹנָה הֵסֵ֛ב בֵּ֥ית יהֹוָ֖ה מִפְּנֵ֥י מֶ֥לֶךְ אַשּֽׁוּר׃

יט וְיֶ֛תֶר דִּבְרֵ֥י אָחָ֖ז אֲשֶׁ֣ר עָשָׂ֑ה הֲלֹא־הֵ֣ם כְּתוּבִ֗ים עַל־סֵ֛פֶר דִּבְרֵ֥י הַיָּמִ֖ים

כ לְמַלְכֵ֥י יְהוּדָֽה׃ וַיִּשְׁכַּ֤ב אָחָז֙ עִם־אֲבֹתָ֔יו וַיִּקָּבֵ֥ר עִם־אֲבֹתָ֖יו בְּעִ֣יר דָּוִ֑ד

א וַיִּמְלֹ֛ךְ חִזְקִיָּ֥הוּ בְנ֖וֹ תַּחְתָּֽיו׃   בִּשְׁנַת֙ שְׁתֵּ֣ים עֶשְׂרֵ֔ה לְאָחָ֖ז מֶ֣לֶךְ   **יז**

ב יְהוּדָ֑ה מָ֠לַ֠ךְ הוֹשֵׁ֨עַ בֶּן־אֵלָ֧ה בְשֹׁמְר֛וֹן עַל־יִשְׂרָאֵ֖ל תֵּ֥שַׁע שָׁנִֽים׃ וַיַּ֥עַשׂ הָרַ֖ע

ג בְּעֵינֵ֣י יהֹוָ֑ה רַ֗ק לֹ֚א כְּמַלְכֵ֣י יִשְׂרָאֵ֔ל אֲשֶׁ֥ר הָי֖וּ לְפָנָֽיו׃ עָלָ֣יו עָלָ֔ה שַׁלְמַנְאֶ֖סֶר

ד מֶ֣לֶךְ אַשּׁ֑וּר וַֽיְהִי־ל֤וֹ הוֹשֵׁ֙עַ֙ עֶ֔בֶד וַיָּ֥שֶׁב ל֖וֹ מִנְחָֽה׃ וַיִּמְצָא֩ מֶֽלֶךְ־אַשּׁ֨וּר

בְּהוֹשֵׁ֜עַ קֶ֗שֶׁר אֲשֶׁ֨ר שָׁלַ֤ח מַלְאָכִים֙ אֶל־ס֣וֹא מֶֽלֶךְ־מִצְרַ֔יִם וְלֹא־הֶעֱלָ֥ה

מִנְחָ֛ה לְמֶ֥לֶךְ אַשּׁ֖וּר כְּשָׁנָ֣ה בְשָׁנָ֑ה וַיַּעַצְרֵ֙הוּ֙ מֶ֣לֶךְ אַשּׁ֔וּר וַיַּאַסְרֵ֖הוּ בֵּ֥ית

ה כֶּֽלֶא׃ וַיַּ֥עַל מֶֽלֶךְ־אַשּׁ֖וּר בְּכׇל־הָאָ֑רֶץ וַיַּ֙עַל֙ שֹׁ֣מְר֔וֹן וַיָּ֥צַר עָלֶ֖יהָ שָׁלֹ֥שׁ שָׁנִֽים׃

ו בִּשְׁנַ֣ת הַ֠תְּשִׁיעִ֠ית לְהוֹשֵׁ֗עַ לָכַ֤ד מֶֽלֶךְ־אַשּׁוּר֙ אֶת־שֹׁ֣מְר֔וֹן וַיֶּ֥גֶל אֶת־יִשְׂרָאֵ֖ל   וַיְהִ֣י

אַשּׁ֑וּרָה וַיֹּ֨שֶׁב אֹתָ֤ם בַּחְלַח֙ וּבְחָב֔וֹר נְהַ֖ר גּוֹזָ֑ן וְעָרֵ֥י מָדָֽי׃

ז כִּ֣י חָטְא֣וּ בְנֵֽי־יִשְׂרָאֵ֗ל לַיהֹוָ֤ה אֱלֹֽהֵיהֶם֙ הַמַּעֲלֶ֤ה אֹתָם֙ מֵאֶ֣רֶץ מִצְרַ֔יִם

ח מִתַּ֕חַת יַ֖ד פַּרְעֹ֣ה מֶֽלֶךְ־מִצְרָ֑יִם וַיִּ֣ירְא֔וּ אֱלֹהִ֖ים אֲחֵרִֽים׃ וַיֵּלְכוּ֙ בְּחֻקּ֣וֹת

הַגּוֹיִ֔ם אֲשֶׁ֨ר הוֹרִ֤ישׁ יהֹוָה֙ מִפְּנֵ֣י בְּנֵ֣י יִשְׂרָאֵ֑ל וּמַלְכֵ֥י יִשְׂרָאֵ֖ל אֲשֶׁ֥ר עָשֽׂוּ׃

ט וַיְחַפְּא֣וּ בְנֵי־יִשְׂרָאֵ֗ל דְּבָרִים֙ אֲשֶׁ֣ר לֹא־כֵ֔ן עַל־יהֹוָ֖ה אֱלֹהֵיהֶ֑ם וַיִּבְנ֨וּ

י לָהֶ֤ם בָּמוֹת֙ בְּכׇל־עָ֣רֵיהֶ֔ם מִמִּגְדַּ֥ל נֽוֹצְרִ֖ים עַד־עִ֥יר מִבְצָֽר׃ וַיַּצִּ֧בוּ לָהֶ֛ם

יא מַצֵּב֖וֹת וַאֲשֵׁרִ֑ים עַ֚ל כׇּל־גִּבְעָ֣ה גְבֹהָ֔ה וְתַ֖חַת כׇּל־עֵ֥ץ רַעֲנָֽן׃ וַיְקַטְּרוּ־שָׁם֙

בְּכׇל־בָּמ֔וֹת כַּגּוֹיִ֕ם אֲשֶׁר־הֶגְלָ֥ה יהֹוָ֖ה מִפְּנֵיהֶ֑ם וַיַּֽעֲשׂוּ֙ דְּבָרִ֣ים רָעִ֔ים

יב לְהַכְעִ֖יס אֶת־יהֹוָֽה׃ וַיַּ֙עַבְד֖וּ הַגִּלֻּלִ֑ים אֲשֶׁ֨ר אָמַ֤ר יהֹוָה֙ לָהֶ֔ם לֹ֥א תַעֲשׂ֖וּ

יג אֶת־הַדָּבָ֥ר הַזֶּֽה׃ וַיָּ֣עַד יהֹוָ֡ה בְּיִשְׂרָאֵ֣ל וּבִיהוּדָ֡ה בְּיַד֩ כׇּל־נְבִיא֨וֹ

[נְבִיאֵ֜י ק] כׇל־חֹזֶ֗ה לֵאמֹ֞ר °שֻׁ֤בוּ מִדַּרְכֵיכֶ֤ם הָֽרָעִים֙ וְשִׁמְרוּ֙ מִצְוֺתַ֣י חֻקּוֹתַ֔י   * הקורא יטעים
האולא גרש
קורם התליּשא

כְּכׇל־הַ֨תּוֹרָ֔ה אֲשֶׁ֥ר צִוִּ֖יתִי אֶת־אֲבֹֽתֵיכֶ֑ם וַֽאֲשֶׁר֙ שָׁלַ֣חְתִּי אֲלֵיכֶ֔ם בְּיַ֖ד עֲבָדַ֥י

יד הַנְּבִיאִֽים׃ וְלֹ֖א שָׁמֵ֑עוּ וַיַּקְשׁ֤וּ אֶת־עׇרְפָּם֙ כְּעֹ֣רֶף אֲבוֹתָ֔ם אֲשֶׁר֙ לֹ֣א הֶאֱמִ֔ינוּ

טו בַּיהֹוָ֖ה אֱלֹהֵיהֶֽם׃ וַיִּמְאֲס֣וּ אֶת־חֻקָּ֗יו וְאֶת־בְּרִיתוֹ֙ אֲשֶׁ֣ר כָּרַ֣ת אֶת־אֲבוֹתָ֔ם

וְאֵת֙ עֵדְוֺתָ֔יו אֲשֶׁ֥ר הֵעִ֖יד בָּ֑ם וַיֵּ֨לְכ֜וּ אַחֲרֵ֤י הַהֶ֙בֶל֙ וַיֶּהְבָּ֔לוּ וְאַֽחֲרֵי֙ הַגּוֹיִ֔ם

טז אֲשֶׁ֣ר סְבִֽיבֹתָ֔ם אֲשֶׁ֨ר צִוָּ֤ה יהֹוָה֙ אֹתָ֔ם לְבִלְתִּ֖י עֲשׂ֥וֹת כָּהֶֽם׃ וַיַּעַזְב֗וּ

אֶת־כׇּל־מִצְוֺת֙ יהֹוָ֣ה אֱלֹֽהֵיהֶ֔ם וַיַּעֲשׂ֥וּ לָהֶ֛ם מַסֵּכָ֖ה °שְׁנַ֣יִם [°שְׁנֵ֣י ק]

עֲגָלִ֑ים וַיַּעֲשׂ֣וּ אֲשֵׁרָ֗ה וַיִּֽשְׁתַּחֲווּ֙ לְכׇל־צְבָ֣א הַשָּׁמַ֔יִם וַיַּעַבְד֖וּ אֶת־הַבָּֽעַל׃

16:18. This awning had been installed for the comfort of the outgoing shift of Kohanim (see 11:5-7), whose duties ended on Sabbath morning, but who could not travel to their homes until after the Sabbath. All of the deeds of Ahaz described here, as well as others described in *II Chronicles* (28:23-25), were intended to disrupt the Temple service and display his scorn and disdain for the religion of Israel.

     Ahaz rerouted the royal entrance to the Temple out of

concern for his personal security. Until then, he had used a public thoroughfare; now he made a passageway directly from the palace to the Temple.

16:19. See *II Chronicles*, Ch. 28.

17:1. Hoshea actually reigned in the *fourth* year of Ahaz (see 15:30), but the commentators explain that Hoshea was initially a vassal king under Assyria, and only in the twelfth year of Ahaz did he rebel and declare his independence (*Ralbag*).

in the Temple. * He routed the king's outer entrance to go directly to the Temple of HASHEM, out of fear of the king of Assyria. *

¹⁹ The rest of the deeds of Ahaz that he did — behold, they are recorded in the Book of Chronicles of the Kings of Judah. * ²⁰ Ahaz lay with his forefathers and was buried with his forefathers in the City of David; his son Hezekiah reigned in his place.

Ahaz is succeeded by Hezekiah

17

HOSHEA, LAST KING OF ISRAEL
17:1-18:12

¹ In the twelfth year of Ahaz* king of Judah, Hoshea son of Elah became king over Israel in Samaria, [and reigned] for nine years. ² He did what was evil in the eyes of HASHEM, albeit not like the kings of Israel who were before him. * ³ Shalmaneser king of Assyria went up against him; and Hoshea became his vassal and sent him a tribute.

⁴ Then the king of Assyria discovered that Hoshea, had betrayed him, for he had sent messengers to So, the king of Egypt, and he did not send up his tribute to the king of Assyria as he had year by year; therefore the king of Assyria arrested him and incarcerated him in prison. ⁵ The king of Assyria then invaded the entire country; he went up to Samaria and besieged it for three years.

Assyria conquers the Ten Tribes and exiles the people

⁶ In the ninth year of [the reign of] Hoshea, the king of Assyria captured Samaria and exiled Israel to Assyria. He settled them in Halah, in Habor, by the Gozan River, and in the cities of Media.

Summary of the sad history of the Ten Tribes . . .

⁷ And so it was that the Children of Israel sinned to HASHEM their God, Who had taken them up out of the land of Egypt from under the oppression of Pharaoh king of Egypt, and they feared the gods of others. ⁸ They walked in the decrees of the nations whom HASHEM had driven out from before the Children of Israel, and [in the decrees] that the kings of Israel had enacted. ⁹ The Children of Israel imputed things that were not so to HASHEM their God and built themselves high places in all their cities, from the [solitary] watchtower to the fortified city. ¹⁰ They erected for themselves pillars and Asherah-trees upon every tall hill and under every leafy tree. ¹¹ They burned incense there at all their high places, like the nations whom HASHEM had exiled before them; and they did wicked things, to anger HASHEM. ¹² They worshiped the execrable idols, concerning which HASHEM had told them, "Do not do this thing."* ¹³ HASHEM had issued warning in Israel and in Judah through the hand of all prophets of any vision, saying, "Repent from your evil ways, and observe My commandments and My decrees in accordance with the entire Torah that I commanded your forefathers, and that I have sent you through My servants the prophets." ¹⁴ But they did not listen, and they stiffened their neck like the neck of their forefathers, who did not believe in HASHEM their God. ¹⁵ They rejected His decrees and His covenant that He had sealed with their forefathers, and His warnings that He had warned about them; and they went after the worthless, and became worthless; and after [the ways of] the nations that surrounded them, concerning whom HASHEM had commanded them not to do like them. ¹⁶ They forsook all the commandments of HASHEM, their God, and made a molten image for themselves — two calves; and they made Asherah-trees and prostrated themselves to all the hosts of the heavens and worshiped the Baal.

. . . their refusal to heed prophetic warnings . . .

. . . worsening rebellion . . .

17:2. Hoshea was the only king of the Ten Tribes to let his people go to the Temple in Jerusalem for the three pilgrimage festivals (*Seder Olam*).

17:12. This is not a direct quote, but a paraphrase of various verses that forbid idolatry (e.g., *Leviticus* 18:3; 26:1).

יז וַיַּעֲבִ֨ירוּ אֶת־בְּנֵיהֶ֤ם וְאֶת־בְּנֽוֹתֵיהֶם֙ בָּאֵ֔שׁ וַיִּקְסְמ֥וּ קְסָמִ֖ים וַיְנַחֵ֑שׁוּ
יח וַיִּֽתְמַכְּר֗וּ לַעֲשׂ֥וֹת הָרַ֛ע בְּעֵינֵ֥י יהו֖ה לְהַכְעִיסֽוֹ: וַיִּתְאַנַּ֨ף יהו֤ה מְאֹד֙
בְּיִשְׂרָאֵ֔ל וַיְסִרֵ֖ם מֵעַ֣ל פָּנָ֑יו לֹ֣א נִשְׁאַ֗ר רַ֚ק שֵׁ֣בֶט יְהוּדָ֖ה לְבַדּֽוֹ: יט גַּם־יְהוּדָ֕ה
לֹ֣א שָׁמַ֔ר אֶת־מִצְוֺ֖ת יהו֣ה אֱלֹהֵיהֶ֑ם וַיֵּ֣לְכ֔וּ בְּחֻקּ֥וֹת יִשְׂרָאֵ֖ל אֲשֶׁ֥ר עָשֽׂוּ:
כ וַיִּמְאַ֣ס יהו֗ה בְּכָל־זֶ֨רַע֙ יִשְׂרָאֵ֔ל וַיְעַנֵּ֕ם וַֽיִּתְּנֵ֖ם בְּיַד־שֹׁסִ֑ים עַ֛ד אֲשֶׁ֥ר
הִשְׁלִיכָ֖ם מִפָּנָֽיו: כא כִּֽי־קָרַ֣ע יִשְׂרָאֵ֗ל מֵעַל֙ בֵּ֣ית דָּוִ֔ד וַיַּמְלִ֖יכוּ אֶת־יָרׇבְעָ֣ם
בֶּן־נְבָ֑ט [°וַיַּדַּ֨ח ק] °ויד֤א יָֽרׇבְעָם֙ אֶת־יִשְׂרָאֵ֔ל מֵאַחֲרֵ֣י יהו֔ה וְהֶחֱטִיאָ֖ם
חֲטָאָ֥ה גְדוֹלָֽה: כב וַיֵּֽלְכוּ֙ בְּנֵ֣י יִשְׂרָאֵ֔ל בְּכָל־חַטֹּ֥אות יָֽרׇבְעָ֖ם אֲשֶׁ֣ר עָשָׂ֑ה לֹא־
סָ֖רוּ מִמֶּֽנָּה: כג עַ֠ד אֲשֶׁר־הֵסִ֨יר יהו֤ה אֶת־יִשְׂרָאֵל֙ מֵעַ֣ל פָּנָ֔יו כַּאֲשֶׁ֣ר דִּבֶּ֔ר
בְּיַ֖ד כָּל־עֲבָדָ֣יו הַנְּבִיאִ֑ים וַיִּ֤גֶל יִשְׂרָאֵל֙ מֵעַ֣ל אַדְמָת֔וֹ אַשּׁ֖וּרָה עַ֥ד הַיּ֥וֹם
הַזֶּֽה: כד וַיָּבֵ֣א מֶֽלֶךְ־אַשּׁ֡וּר מִבָּבֶ֡ל וּ֠מִכּ֠וּתָה וּמֵֽעַוָּ֤א וּמֵֽחֲמָת֙
°וּסְפַרְוַ֔יִם [°וּמִסְּפַרְוַ֔יִם ק] וַיֹּ֙שֶׁב֙ בְּעָרֵ֣י שֹֽׁמְר֔וֹן תַּ֖חַת בְּנֵ֣י יִשְׂרָאֵ֑ל וַיִּֽרְשׁוּ֙
אֶת־שֹׁ֣מְר֔וֹן וַיֵּֽשְׁב֖וּ בְּעָרֶֽיהָ: כה וַיְהִ֗י בִּתְחִלַּת֙ שִׁבְתָּ֣ם שָׁ֔ם לֹ֥א יָֽרְא֖וּ אֶת־יהו֑ה
וַיְשַׁלַּ֨ח יהו֤ה בָּהֶם֙ אֶת־הָ֣אֲרָי֔וֹת וַיִּֽהְי֥וּ הֹרְגִ֖ים בָּהֶֽם: כו וַיֹּאמְר֣וּ לְמֶ֣לֶךְ
אַשּׁ֢וּר לֵאמֹ֡ר הַגּוֹיִ֡ם אֲשֶׁ֣ר הִגְלִ֩יתָ֩ וַתּ֨וֹשֶׁב בְּעָרֵ֜י שֹׁמְר֗וֹן לֹ֤א יָֽדְעוּ֙ אֶת־
מִשְׁפַּט֙ אֱלֹהֵ֣י הָאָ֔רֶץ וַיְשַׁלַּח־בָּ֣ם אֶת־הָֽאֲרָי֔וֹת וְהִנָּם֙ מְמִיתִ֣ים אוֹתָ֔ם
כז כַּֽאֲשֶׁר֙ אֵינָ֣ם יֹֽדְעִ֔ים אֶת־מִשְׁפַּ֖ט אֱלֹהֵ֣י הָאָ֑רֶץ וַיְצַ֨ו מֶֽלֶךְ־אַשּׁ֜וּר לֵאמֹ֗ר
הֹלִ֤יכוּ שָׁ֙מָּה֙ אֶחָ֣ד מֵהַכֹּ֣הֲנִ֔ים אֲשֶׁ֥ר הִגְלִיתֶ֖ם מִשָּׁ֑ם וְיֵלְכ֖וּ וְיֵ֣שְׁבוּ שָׁ֑ם
וְיֹרֵ֕ם אֶת־מִשְׁפַּ֖ט אֱלֹהֵ֥י הָאָֽרֶץ: כח וַיָּבֹ֞א אֶחָ֣ד מֵהַכֹּֽהֲנִ֗ים אֲשֶׁ֤ר הִגְל֙וּ
מִשֹּׁ֣מְר֔וֹן וַיֵּ֖שֶׁב בְּבֵֽית־אֵ֑ל וַֽיְהִי֙ מוֹרֶ֣ה אֹתָ֔ם אֵ֖יךְ יִֽירְא֥וּ אֶת־יהוֽה: כט וַיִּֽהְי֣וּ
עֹשִׂ֔ים גּ֥וֹי גּ֖וֹי אֱלֹהָ֑יו וַיַּנִּ֣יחוּ ׀ בְּבֵ֣ית הַבָּמ֗וֹת אֲשֶׁ֤ר עָשׂוּ֙ הַשֹּׁ֣מְרֹנִ֔ים גּ֖וֹי
גּ֣וֹי בְּעָֽרֵיהֶ֔ם אֲשֶׁ֛ר הֵ֥ם יֹֽשְׁבִ֖ים שָֽׁם: ל וְאַנְשֵׁ֣י בָבֶ֗ל עָשׂוּ֙ אֶת־סֻכּ֣וֹת בְּנ֔וֹת
לא וְאַנְשֵׁי־כ֗וּת עָשׂוּ֙ אֶת־נֵ֣רְגַּ֔ל וְאַנְשֵׁ֥י חֲמָ֖ת עָשׂ֣וּ אֶת־אֲשִׁימָ֑א וְהָעַוִּ֛ים
עָשׂ֥וּ נִבְחַ֖ז וְאֶת־תַּרְתָּ֑ק וְהַסְפַרְוִ֗ים שֹׂרְפִ֤ים אֶת־בְּנֵיהֶם֙ בָּאֵ֔שׁ לְאַדְרַמֶּ֥לֶךְ
לב וַעֲנַמֶּ֖לֶךְ °אֱלֹהֵ֣י ספרים [°אֱלֹהֵ֣י סְפַרְוָֽיִם ק]: וַיִּֽהְי֥וּ יְרֵאִ֖ים אֶת־יהו֑ה
וַיַּֽעֲשׂ֣וּ לָהֶ֗ם מִקְצוֹתָם֙ כֹּהֲנֵ֣י בָמ֔וֹת וַיִּֽהְי֤וּ עֹשִׂ֤ים לָהֶם֙ בְּבֵ֣ית הַבָּמֽוֹת:
לג אֶת־יהו֖ה הָי֣וּ יְרֵאִ֑ים וְאֶת־אֱלֹֽהֵיהֶם֙ הָי֣וּ עֹֽבְדִ֔ים כְּמִשְׁפַּ֖ט הַגּוֹיִ֔ם
אֲשֶׁר־הִגְל֥וּ אֹתָ֖ם מִשָּֽׁם: לד עַ֣ד הַיּ֤וֹם הַזֶּה֙ הֵ֣ם עֹשִׂ֔ים כַּמִּשְׁפָּטִ֖ים
הָרִֽאשֹׁנִ֑ים אֵינָ֤ם יְרֵאִים֙ אֶת־יהו֔ה וְאֵינָ֣ם עֹשִׂ֗ים כְּחֻקֹּתָם֙ וּכְמִשְׁפָּטָ֔ם
וְכַתּוֹרָ֣ה וְכַמִּצְוָ֔ה אֲשֶׁ֥ר צִוָּ֖ה יהו֣ה אֶת־בְּנֵ֣י יַעֲקֹ֑ב אֲשֶׁר־שָׂ֥ם שְׁמ֖וֹ יִשְׂרָאֵֽל:

°יד רבתי

17:18. That is, He exiled them from the Land of Israel (*Targum*).

17:28. Realizing that he could not uproot centuries of idolatry from these people, the Kohen allowed them to continue serving their idols, not as deities, but rather as intermediaries. Thus, he instructed them to direct their thoughts to God, even while performing the rituals of their old beliefs (*Radak*).

17:34. God changed Jacob's name to Israel only after he ordered his entourage to discard all their alien gods (*Genesis 35:2-4,10*), because a person cannot earn God's blessing unless his loyalty is complete and unequivocal

¹⁷ They passed their sons and their daughters through fire and practiced divinations and sorcery; and they dedicated themselves to do that which was evil in the
eyes of HASHEM, to anger Him.

... and total
downfall

¹⁸ Then HASHEM became very angry with Israel and removed them from His
Presence;* none remained except the tribe of Judah alone. ¹⁹ (And even Judah
did not observe the commandments of HASHEM their God, and they walked in the
decrees of Israel, which they had enacted.) ²⁰ So HASHEM rejected the entire
offspring of Israel, and oppressed them; He delivered them into the hands of
plunderers, until He had cast them away from His Presence. ²¹ For Israel had torn
[itself] away from the house of David, crowning Jeroboam son of Nebat [over
themselves], and Jeroboam pushed Israel away from following HASHEM and
caused them to commit a grave sin. ²² The Children of Israel went in [the way of]
all the sins of Jeroboam, which he committed, they did not turn away from them,
²³ until HASHEM removed Israel from His Presence, as He had spoken through the
hand of all His servants the prophets. So Israel went into exile from their land to
Assyria, to this day.

Assyria
settles
foreigners
in Samaria

²⁴ The king of Assyria brought [people] from Babylonia and Cuthah and Avva
and Hamath and Sepharvaim, and settled [them] in the cities of Samaria in place
of the Children of Israel; they took possession of Samaria and dwelled in its cities.
²⁵ It happened that at the beginning [of the period] of their dwelling there they did
not fear HASHEM, and HASHEM incited lions against them, and they were killing

The
newcomers
are
frightened
into serving
Hashem ...

among them. ²⁶ They spoke to the king of Assyria, saying, "The nations that you
have exiled and settled in the cities of Samaria do not know the law of the God of
the land. He has incited lions against them, and they are now killing them
because they do not know the law of the God of the land."

²⁷ The king of Assyria issued a command, saying, "Bring to there one of the
Kohanim whom you exiled from there and let them go and settle there and teach
them the law of the God of the land."

²⁸ One of the Kohanim whom they had exiled from Samaria came and settled
in Beth-el, and he would teach them how to fear HASHEM. ²⁹ They would make —
each nation — its own god,* and they set up [their idols] in the high place
temples that the [Israelite] Samaritans had built — each nation in their cities,
where they dwelled. ³⁰ The people of Babylonia made Succoth-benoth; the people of Cuthah made Nergal; the people of Hamath made Ashima, ³¹ the Avvites
made Nivhaz and Tartak; and the Sepharvites burned their children in fire unto
Adrammelech and Anammelech, the gods of Sepharvaim. ³² They feared
HASHEM, and they appointed some from among themselves as priests for the
high places, and they would perform [the rituals] for them in the high place
temples.

... but they
continue
their idolatry

³³ They feared HASHEM, but they worshiped their own gods [as well], according
to the practice of the nations from which they had been exiled. ³⁴ Until this day
they act according to the original practice; they do not fear HASHEM sincerely;
they do not act according to their customs and practices, or according to the
Torah and the commandments that HASHEM had commanded the Children of
Jacob, whose name He had changed to Israel.*

(*Radak*). But the Samaritans could not bring themselves
to do so. They adopted Jewish practices out of fear of the
lions, but they retained their idols as well.

לה וַיִּכְרֹת יְהֹוָה אִתָּם בְּרִית וַיְצַוֵּם לֵאמֹר לֹא תִּירְאוּ אֱלֹהִים אֲחֵרִים וְלֹא־
תִשְׁתַּחֲווּ לָהֶם וְלֹא תַעַבְדוּם וְלֹא תִזְבְּחוּ לָהֶם: כִּי אִם־אֶת־יְהֹוָה אֲשֶׁר
לו הֶעֱלָה אֶתְכֶם מֵאֶרֶץ מִצְרַיִם בְּכֹחַ גָּדוֹל וּבִזְרוֹעַ נְטוּיָה אֹתוֹ תִירָאוּ וְלוֹ
תִשְׁתַּחֲווּ וְלוֹ תִזְבָּחוּ: וְאֶת־הַחֻקִּים וְאֶת־הַמִּשְׁפָּטִים וְהַתּוֹרָה וְהַמִּצְוָה
לז אֲשֶׁר כָּתַב לָכֶם תִּשְׁמְרוּן לַעֲשׂוֹת כָּל־הַיָּמִים וְלֹא תִירְאוּ אֱלֹהִים
לח אֲחֵרִים: וְהַבְּרִית אֲשֶׁר־כָּרַתִּי אִתְּכֶם לֹא תִשְׁכָּחוּ וְלֹא תִירְאוּ אֱלֹהִים
לט אֲחֵרִים: כִּי אִם־אֶת־יְהֹוָה אֱלֹהֵיכֶם תִּירָאוּ וְהוּא יַצִּיל אֶתְכֶם מִיַּד כָּל־
מ-מא אֹיְבֵיכֶם: וְלֹא שָׁמֵעוּ כִּי אִם־כְּמִשְׁפָּטָם הָרִאשׁוֹן הֵם עֹשִׂים: וַיִּהְיוּ | הַגּוֹיִם
הָאֵלֶּה יְרֵאִים אֶת־יְהֹוָה וְאֶת־פְּסִילֵיהֶם הָיוּ עֹבְדִים גַּם־בְּנֵיהֶם | וּבְנֵי
יח א בְנֵיהֶם כַּאֲשֶׁר עָשׂוּ אֲבֹתָם הֵם עֹשִׂים עַד הַיּוֹם הַזֶּה: וַיְהִי
בִּשְׁנַת שָׁלֹשׁ לְהוֹשֵׁעַ בֶּן־אֵלָה מֶלֶךְ יִשְׂרָאֵל מָלַךְ חִזְקִיָּה בֶן־אָחָז מֶלֶךְ
ב יְהוּדָה: בֶּן־עֶשְׂרִים וְחָמֵשׁ שָׁנָה הָיָה בְמָלְכוֹ וְעֶשְׂרִים וָתֵשַׁע שָׁנָה מָלַךְ
ג בִּירוּשָׁלָ͏ִם וְשֵׁם אִמּוֹ אֲבִי בַּת־זְכַרְיָה: וַיַּעַשׂ הַיָּשָׁר בְּעֵינֵי יְהֹוָה כְּכֹל
ד אֲשֶׁר־עָשָׂה דָּוִד אָבִיו: הוּא | הֵסִיר אֶת־הַבָּמוֹת וְשִׁבַּר אֶת־הַמַּצֵּבֹת
וְכָרַת אֶת־הָאֲשֵׁרָה וְכִתַּת נְחַשׁ הַנְּחֹשֶׁת אֲשֶׁר־עָשָׂה מֹשֶׁה כִּי עַד־
ה הַיָּמִים הָהֵמָּה הָיוּ בְנֵי־יִשְׂרָאֵל מְקַטְּרִים לוֹ וַיִּקְרָא־לוֹ נְחֻשְׁתָּן: בַּיהֹוָה
אֱלֹהֵי־יִשְׂרָאֵל בָּטָח וְאַחֲרָיו לֹא־הָיָה כָמֹהוּ בְּכֹל מַלְכֵי יְהוּדָה וַאֲשֶׁר
ו הָיוּ לְפָנָיו: וַיִּדְבַּק בַּיהֹוָה לֹא־סָר מֵאַחֲרָיו וַיִּשְׁמֹר מִצְוֹתָיו אֲשֶׁר־צִוָּה
ז יְהֹוָה אֶת־מֹשֶׁה: וְהָיָה יְהֹוָה עִמּוֹ בְּכֹל אֲשֶׁר־יֵצֵא יַשְׂכִּיל וַיִּמְרֹד בְּמֶלֶךְ־
ח אַשּׁוּר וְלֹא עֲבָדוֹ: הוּא־הִכָּה אֶת־פְּלִשְׁתִּים עַד־עַזָּה וְאֶת־גְּבוּלֶיהָ
ט מִמִּגְדַּל נוֹצְרִים עַד־עִיר מִבְצָר: וַיְהִי בַּשָּׁנָה הָרְבִיעִית
לַמֶּלֶךְ חִזְקִיָּהוּ הִיא הַשָּׁנָה הַשְּׁבִיעִית לְהוֹשֵׁעַ בֶּן־אֵלָה מֶלֶךְ יִשְׂרָאֵל
י עָלָה שַׁלְמַנְאֶסֶר מֶלֶךְ־אַשּׁוּר עַל־שֹׁמְרוֹן וַיָּצַר עָלֶיהָ: וַיִּלְכְּדֻהָ מִקְצֵה
שָׁלֹשׁ שָׁנִים בִּשְׁנַת־שֵׁשׁ לְחִזְקִיָּה הִיא שְׁנַת־תֵּשַׁע לְהוֹשֵׁעַ מֶלֶךְ יִשְׂרָאֵל
יא נִלְכְּדָה שֹׁמְרוֹן: וַיֶּגֶל מֶלֶךְ־אַשּׁוּר אֶת־יִשְׂרָאֵל אַשּׁוּרָה וַיַּנְחֵם בַּחְלַח
יב וּבְחָבוֹר נְהַר גּוֹזָן וְעָרֵי מָדָי: עַל | אֲשֶׁר לֹא־שָׁמְעוּ בְּקוֹל יְהֹוָה אֱלֹהֵיהֶם
וַיַּעַבְרוּ אֶת־בְּרִיתוֹ אֵת כָּל־אֲשֶׁר צִוָּה מֹשֶׁה עֶבֶד יְהֹוָה וְלֹא שָׁמְעוּ
וְלֹא עָשׂוּ:
יג וּבְאַרְבַּע עֶשְׂרֵה שָׁנָה לַמֶּלֶךְ חִזְקִיָּה עָלָה סַנְחֵרִיב מֶלֶךְ־אַשּׁוּר עַל כָּל־
יד עָרֵי יְהוּדָה הַבְּצֻרוֹת וַיִּתְפְּשֵׂם: וַיִּשְׁלַח חִזְקִיָּה מֶלֶךְ־יְהוּדָה אֶל־מֶלֶךְ־
אַשּׁוּר | לָכִישָׁה | לֵאמֹר | חָטָאתִי שׁוּב מֵעָלַי אֵת אֲשֶׁר־תִּתֵּן עָלַי
אֶשָּׂא וַיָּשֶׂם מֶלֶךְ־אַשּׁוּר עַל־חִזְקִיָּה מֶלֶךְ־יְהוּדָה שְׁלֹשׁ מֵאוֹת כִּכַּר־

18:4. "A thing of copper," a pejorative term. Regarding the copper serpent, see *Numbers* 21:4-9. Although Moses made it for a noble purpose, in later centuries it began to

be looked upon by some as a deity. Therefore, Hezekiah destroyed it.

18:13. This passage, until 20:19, appears with minor

³⁵ *(For* HASHEM *had made a covenant with [Israel], and had commanded them, saying, "You shall not fear the gods of others; and you shall not bow down to them, and you shall not worship them, and you shall not slaughter to them.* ³⁶ *Rather, only* HASHEM *Who brought you up from the land of Egypt, with great force and with an outstretched arm — Him shall you fear, and to Him shall you bow down, and to Him shall you slaughter.* ³⁷ *And the decrees and the laws, and the Torah and the commandment that He wrote for you, you shall observe to do all the days, and you shall not fear the gods of others.* ³⁸ *And the covenant that I sealed with you, you shall not forget; and you shall not fear the gods of others.* ³⁹ *Rather, you shall fear* HASHEM *your God, and He will save you from the hand of your enemies.")*

⁴⁰ *But they did not obey, rather they act according to their original practice.* ⁴¹ *So these nations feared* HASHEM, *yet worshiped their graven images. Also their children and children's children, as their forefathers had done, so do they do, to this day.*

18

HEZEKIAH, KING OF JUDAH
18:1-20:21
(See Appendix A, timeline 4)

Hezekiah's historic righteousness

¹ **I**t *was in the third year of Hoshea son of Elah king of Israel: Hezekiah, * son of Ahaz king of Judah, became king.* ² *He was twenty-five years old when he became king, and he reigned for twenty-nine years in Jerusalem. His mother's name was Abi daughter of Zechariah.* ³ *He did what was proper in the eyes of* HASHEM, *just as his forefather David had done.* ⁴ *He removed the high places, shattered the pillars, and cut down the Asherah-trees; he [also] ground up the copper serpent that Moses had made — for until those days the Children of Israel used to burn incense before it; he called it Nehushtan. ** ⁵ *He trusted in* HASHEM, *the God of Israel; after him there was not anyone like him among all the kings of Judah, nor among those who preceded him.* ⁶ *He clung to* HASHEM *and did not turn aside from [following] after Him; he observed His commandments, which* HASHEM *had commanded Moses.* ⁷ HASHEM *was with him; wherever he ventured he was successful. He rebelled against the king of Assyria and did not serve him.* ⁸ *He struck the Philistines until Gaza and its environs, from the [solitary] watchtower to the fortified city.*

Assyria, which had destroyed Samaria . . .

⁹ *It was in the fourth year of King Hezekiah, * it was the seventh year of Hoshea son of Elah king of Israel: Shalmaneser king of Assyria invaded Samaria and besieged it.* ¹⁰ *They captured it after three years — in the sixth year of Hezekiah, it was the ninth year of Hoshea king of Israel — Samaria was captured.* ¹¹ *The king of Assyria exiled Israel to Assyria, placing them in Halah, in Habor, by the Gozan River, and in the cities of Media.* ¹² *[This was] because they did not heed the voice of* HASHEM *their God, and they transgressed His covenant — all that Moses, the servant of* HASHEM, *had commanded, they did not heed and they did not fulfill.*

. . . turns on Judah, and Hezekiah pays tribute

¹³ *In the fourteenth year of King Hezekiah, Sennacherib king of Assyria attacked all the fortified cities of Judah, and captured them.* ¹⁴ *Hezekiah king of Judah sent [word] to the king of Assyria, to Lachish, * saying, "I have sinned. Withdraw from me, and whatever you impose upon me I will bear." So the king of Assyria imposed upon Hezekiah king of Judah a levy of three hundred talents*

---

differences in *Isaiah* 36:1-38:8, 39:1-8.
18:14. Lachish was one of the main fortified cities of

Judah, which Assyrian King Shalmaneser had apparently captured and made his base.

טו כֶּסֶף וּשְׁלֹשִׁים כִּכַּר זָהָב: וַיִּתֵּן חִזְקִיָּה אֶת־כָּל־הַכֶּסֶף הַנִּמְצָא בֵית־

טז יהוה וּבְאֹצְרוֹת בֵּית הַמֶּלֶךְ: בָּעֵת הַהִיא קִצַּץ חִזְקִיָּה אֶת־דַּלְתוֹת הֵיכַל יהוה וְאֶת־הָאֹמְנוֹת אֲשֶׁר צִפָּה חִזְקִיָּה מֶלֶךְ יְהוּדָה וַיִּתְּנֵם לְמֶלֶךְ

יז אַשּׁוּר: וַיִּשְׁלַח מֶלֶךְ־אַשּׁוּר אֶת־תַּרְתָּן וְאֶת־רַב־סָרִיס ׀ וְאֶת־ רַב־שָׁקֵה מִן־לָכִישׁ אֶל־הַמֶּלֶךְ חִזְקִיָּהוּ בְּחֵיל כָּבֵד יְרוּשָׁלָ͏ִם וַיַּעֲלוּ וַיָּבֹאוּ יְרוּשָׁלַ͏ִם וַיַּעֲלוּ וַיָּבֹאוּ וַיַּעַמְדוּ בִּתְעָלַת הַבְּרֵכָה הָעֶלְיוֹנָה אֲשֶׁר בִּמְסִלַּת

יח שְׂדֵה כוֹבֵס: וַיִּקְרְאוּ אֶל־הַמֶּלֶךְ וַיֵּצֵא אֲלֵהֶם אֶלְיָקִים בֶּן־חִלְקִיָּהוּ אֲשֶׁר

יט עַל־הַבָּיִת וְשֶׁבְנָה הַסֹּפֵר וְיוֹאָח בֶּן־אָסָף הַמַּזְכִּיר: וַיֹּאמֶר אֲלֵהֶם רַב־שָׁקֵה אִמְרוּ־נָא אֶל־חִזְקִיָּהוּ כֹּה־אָמַר הַמֶּלֶךְ הַגָּדוֹל מֶלֶךְ אַשּׁוּר מָה הַבִּטָּחוֹן

כ הַזֶּה אֲשֶׁר בָּטָחְתָּ: אָמַרְתָּ אַךְ־דְּבַר־שְׂפָתַיִם עֵצָה וּגְבוּרָה לַמִּלְחָמָה עַתָּה

כא עַל־מִי בָטַחְתָּ כִּי מָרַדְתָּ בִּי: עַתָּה הִנֵּה בָטַחְתָּ לְּךָ עַל־מִשְׁעֶנֶת הַקָּנֶה הָרָצוּץ הַזֶּה עַל־מִצְרַיִם אֲשֶׁר יִסָּמֵךְ אִישׁ עָלָיו וּבָא בְכַפּוֹ וּנְקָבָהּ כֵּן פַּרְעֹה

כב מֶלֶךְ־מִצְרַיִם לְכָל־הַבֹּטְחִים עָלָיו: וְכִי־תֹאמְרוּן אֵלַי אֶל־יהוה אֱלֹהֵינוּ בָּטָחְנוּ הֲלוֹא־הוּא אֲשֶׁר הֵסִיר חִזְקִיָּהוּ אֶת־בָּמֹתָיו וְאֶת־מִזְבְּחֹתָיו וַיֹּאמֶר לִיהוּדָה וְלִירוּשָׁלַ͏ִם לִפְנֵי הַמִּזְבֵּחַ הַזֶּה תִּשְׁתַּחֲווּ בִּירוּשָׁלָ͏ִם: וְעַתָּה הִתְעָרֶב

כג נָא אֶת־אֲדֹנִי אֶת־מֶלֶךְ אַשּׁוּר וְאֶתְּנָה לְךָ אַלְפַּיִם סוּסִים אִם־תּוּכַל לָתֶת

כד לְךָ רֹכְבִים עֲלֵיהֶם: וְאֵיךְ תָּשִׁיב אֵת פְּנֵי פַחַת אַחַד עַבְדֵי אֲדֹנִי הַקְּטַנִּים וַתִּבְטַח לְךָ עַל־מִצְרַיִם לְרֶכֶב וּלְפָרָשִׁים: עַתָּה הֲמִבַּלְעֲדֵי יהוה עָלִיתִי

כה עַל־הַמָּקוֹם הַזֶּה לְהַשְׁחִתוֹ יהוה אָמַר אֵלַי עֲלֵה עַל־הָאָרֶץ הַזֹּאת

כו וְהַשְׁחִיתָהּ: וַיֹּאמֶר אֶלְיָקִים בֶּן־חִלְקִיָּהוּ וְשֶׁבְנָה וְיוֹאָח אֶל־רַב־שָׁקֵה דַּבֶּר־ נָא אֶל־עֲבָדֶיךָ אֲרָמִית כִּי שֹׁמְעִים אֲנָחְנוּ וְאַל־תְּדַבֵּר עִמָּנוּ יְהוּדִית

כז בְּאָזְנֵי הָעָם אֲשֶׁר עַל־הַחֹמָה: וַיֹּאמֶר אֲלֵיהֶם רַב־שָׁקֵה הַעַל אֲדֹנֶיךָ וְאֵלֶיךָ שְׁלָחַנִי אֲדֹנִי לְדַבֵּר אֶת־הַדְּבָרִים הָאֵלֶּה הֲלֹא עַל־ הָאֲנָשִׁים הַיֹּשְׁבִים עַל־הַחֹמָה לֶאֱכֹל אֶת־°חרֵיהֶם [°צוֹאָתָם ק] וְלִשְׁתּוֹת

כח אֶת־°שינֵיהֶם [°מֵימֵי רַגְלֵיהֶם ק] עִמָּכֶם: וַיַּעֲמֹד רַב־שָׁקֵה וַיִּקְרָא בְקוֹל־גָּדוֹל יְהוּדִית וַיְדַבֵּר וַיֹּאמֶר שִׁמְעוּ דְּבַר־הַמֶּלֶךְ הַגָּדוֹל מֶלֶךְ

כט אַשּׁוּר: כֹּה אָמַר הַמֶּלֶךְ אַל־יַשִּׁא לָכֶם חִזְקִיָּהוּ כִּי־לֹא יוּכַל לְהַצִּיל

ל אֶתְכֶם מִיָּדוֹ: וְאַל־יַבְטַח אֶתְכֶם חִזְקִיָּהוּ אֶל־יהוה לֵאמֹר הַצֵּל יַצִּילֵנוּ

לא יהוה וְלֹא תִנָּתֵן אֶת־הָעִיר הַזֹּאת בְּיַד מֶלֶךְ אַשּׁוּר: אַל־תִּשְׁמְעוּ אֶל־ חִזְקִיָּהוּ כִּי כֹה אָמַר מֶלֶךְ אַשּׁוּר עֲשׂוּ־אִתִּי בְרָכָה וּצְאוּ אֵלַי וְאִכְלוּ אִישׁ־

לב גַּפְנוֹ וְאִישׁ תְּאֵנָתוֹ וּשְׁתוּ אִישׁ מֵי־בוֹרוֹ: עַד־בֹּאִי וְלָקַחְתִּי אֶתְכֶם אֶל־אֶרֶץ כְּאַרְצְכֶם אֶרֶץ דָּגָן וְתִירוֹשׁ אֶרֶץ לֶחֶם וּכְרָמִים אֶרֶץ זֵית יִצְהָר וּדְבַשׁ

18:20. You fooled your people with false promises, assuring them that you had the military capabilities to back up your rebellion against Assyria.

18:23. Rabshakeh offered to call off the siege for a price. If Hezekiah would provide a bond to guarantee his loyalty — which would be forfeited if he rebelled again — then As-

of silver and thirty talents of gold. [15] *Hezekiah gave all the money that was found in the Temple of HASHEM and in the treasuries of the king's palace.* [16] *At that time Hezekiah stripped the [golden overlay of] the doors of the Sanctuary of HASHEM and the thresholds, which Hezekiah king of Judah had overlaid, and he gave them to the king of Assyria.*

But Assyria wants conquest
[17] *The king of Assyria sent Tartan and Rabsaris and Rabshakeh from Lachish with a great army to King Hezekiah, to Jerusalem. They came up and arrived at Jerusalem; they came up and arrived and stood at the channel of the upper pool, which is in the road of the launderer's field.* [18] *They called out for the king, and Eliakim son of Hilkiah, who was in charge of the palace, went out to them, with Shebnah the scribe, and Joah son of Asaph the recorder.*

Assyria's spokesman's ultimatum . . .
[19] *Rabshakeh said to them, "Say now to Hezekiah: Thus said the great king, the king of Assyria: What is this confidence of which you are so confident?* [20] *You have spoken but [idle] word of the lips [claiming that you had] strategy and power for battle!* * *Now — upon whom have you placed your trust, that you have rebelled against me?* [21] *Now, behold! You have relied upon the support of this splintered cane, upon Egypt, which, if a man leans on it, it will enter his palm and puncture it; so is Pharaoh king of Egypt to all who rely on him.* [22] *And if you will tell me, 'We trust in HASHEM our God' — is He not the One Whose high places and altars Hezekiah has removed; and he said to Judah and Jerusalem, '[Only] before this Altar may you prostrate yourselves, in Jerusalem'?* [23] *So now, provide a security guarantee to my master the king of Assyria, and I will give you two thousand horses — if you can put riders on them!* * [24] *How dare you turn away even a single minor captain from among the servants of my master, and depend on Egypt for chariot and horsemen!* [25] *Now, is it without [the consent of] HASHEM that I have come up to this place to destroy it? HASHEM told me, 'Go up against this land and destroy it!' "*

[26] *Eliakim son of Hilkiah, as well as Shebnah and Joah, then said to Rabshakeh, "Please speak to your servants in Aramaic, for we understand it, and do not speak Hebrew with us within earshot of the people on the wall."*

. . . is intended to terrorize the people
[27] *But Rabshakeh said to them, "Is it to your master and to you that my master has sent me to speak these words? Is it not to the people sitting on the wall, who will eat their own excrement and drink their own urine with you!"* *

[28] *Rabshakeh then stood up and called out in a loud voice in Hebrew; he spoke and said, "Hear the word of the great king, the king of Assyria!* [29] *Thus said the king: Let not Hezekiah delude you, for he cannot save you from [Assyria's] hand!* [30] *And let not Hezekiah reassure you with HASHEM, saying, 'HASHEM will surely save us, and this city shall not be delivered into the hand of the king of Assyria!'* [31] *Do not listen to Hezekiah, for thus said the king of Assyria: Make peace with me and come out to me, and each man will be able to eat [the fruits of] his grapevine and each man [the fruits of] his fig tree, and each man will drink the water of his well,* [32] *until I come and I bring you to a land like your land* * — *a land of grain and wine, a land of bread and vineyards, a land of oil-laden olives and date-honey —*

---

syria would provide two thousand horses for Hezekiah's government. Rabshakeh added a sarcastic comment implying that Hezekiah would not even have enough riders for the horses, much less to mount a rebellion (*Ralbag*).
18:27. So severe will be the prolonged siege that will ensue if you do not capitulate to us.

18:32. The Assyrian practice was to deport all conquered populations to faraway lands in order to thwart any future attempts at regaining independence (see 17:6,24). The only alternative, Rabshakeh threatened, would be certain death, either during the prolonged siege or after the disastrous defeat that was sure to follow.

וְחָיוּ וְלֹא תָמֻתוּ וְאַל־תִּשְׁמְעוּ אֶל־חִזְקִיָּהוּ כִּי־יַסִּית אֶתְכֶם לֵאמֹר יְהֹוָה
לג־לד יַצִּילֵנוּ: הַהַצֵּל הִצִּילוּ אֱלֹהֵי הַגּוֹיִם אִישׁ אֶת־אַרְצוֹ מִיַּד מֶלֶךְ אַשּׁוּר: אַיֵּה
אֱלֹהֵי חֲמָת וְאַרְפָּד אַיֵּה אֱלֹהֵי סְפַרְוַיִם הֵנַע וְעִוָּה כִּי־הִצִּילוּ אֶת־שֹׁמְרוֹן
לה מִיָּדִי: מִי בְּכָל־אֱלֹהֵי הָאֲרָצוֹת אֲשֶׁר־הִצִּילוּ אֶת־אַרְצָם מִיָּדִי כִּי־יַצִּיל
לו יְהֹוָה אֶת־יְרוּשָׁלַ͏ִם מִיָּדִי: וְהֶחֱרִישׁוּ הָעָם וְלֹא־עָנוּ אֹתוֹ דָּבָר כִּי־מִצְוַת
לז הַמֶּלֶךְ הִיא לֵאמֹר לֹא תַעֲנֻהוּ: וַיָּבֹא אֶלְיָקִים בֶּן־חִלְקִיָּה אֲשֶׁר־עַל־הַבַּיִת
וְשֶׁבְנָא הַסֹּפֵר וְיוֹאָח בֶּן־אָסָף הַמַּזְכִּיר אֶל־חִזְקִיָּהוּ קְרוּעֵי בְגָדִים וַיַּגִּדוּ לוֹ

יט   א דִּבְרֵי רַב־שָׁקֵה: וַיְהִי כִּשְׁמֹעַ הַמֶּלֶךְ חִזְקִיָּהוּ וַיִּקְרַע אֶת־בְּגָדָיו וַיִּתְכַּס
ב בַּשָּׂק וַיָּבֹא בֵּית יְהֹוָה: וַיִּשְׁלַח אֶת־אֶלְיָקִים אֲשֶׁר־עַל־הַבַּיִת וְשֶׁבְנָא
הַסֹּפֵר וְאֵת זִקְנֵי הַכֹּהֲנִים מִתְכַּסִּים בַּשַּׂקִּים אֶל־יְשַׁעְיָהוּ הַנָּבִיא בֶן־אָמוֹץ:
ג וַיֹּאמְרוּ אֵלָיו כֹּה אָמַר חִזְקִיָּהוּ יוֹם־צָרָה וְתוֹכֵחָה וּנְאָצָה הַיּוֹם הַזֶּה כִּי
ד בָאוּ בָנִים עַד־מַשְׁבֵּר וְכֹחַ אַיִן לְלֵדָה: אוּלַי יִשְׁמַע יְהֹוָה אֱלֹהֶיךָ אֵת ׀ כָּל־
דִּבְרֵי רַב־שָׁקֵה אֲשֶׁר שְׁלָחוֹ מֶלֶךְ־אַשּׁוּר ׀ אֲדֹנָיו לְחָרֵף אֱלֹהִים חַי
וְהוֹכִיחַ בַּדְּבָרִים אֲשֶׁר שָׁמַע יְהֹוָה אֱלֹהֶיךָ וְנָשָׂאתָ תְפִלָּה בְּעַד הַשְּׁאֵרִית
ה־ו הַנִּמְצָאָה: וַיָּבֹאוּ עַבְדֵי הַמֶּלֶךְ חִזְקִיָּהוּ אֶל־יְשַׁעְיָהוּ: וַיֹּאמֶר לָהֶם יְשַׁעְיָהוּ
כֹּה תֹאמְרוּן אֶל־אֲדֹנֵיכֶם כֹּה ׀ אָמַר יְהֹוָה אַל־תִּירָא מִפְּנֵי הַדְּבָרִים אֲשֶׁר
ז שָׁמַעְתָּ אֲשֶׁר גִּדְּפוּ נַעֲרֵי מֶלֶךְ־אַשּׁוּר אֹתִי: הִנְנִי נֹתֵן בּוֹ רוּחַ וְשָׁמַע
שְׁמוּעָה וְשָׁב לְאַרְצוֹ וְהִפַּלְתִּיו בַּחֶרֶב בְּאַרְצוֹ: וַיָּשָׁב רַב־שָׁקֵה וַיִּמְצָא
ח
ט אֶת־מֶלֶךְ אַשּׁוּר נִלְחָם עַל־לִבְנָה כִּי שָׁמַע כִּי נָסַע מִלָּכִישׁ: וַיִּשְׁמַע אֶל־
תִּרְהָקָה מֶלֶךְ־כּוּשׁ לֵאמֹר הִנֵּה יָצָא לְהִלָּחֵם אִתָּךְ וַיָּשָׁב וַיִּשְׁלַח מַלְאָכִים
י אֶל־חִזְקִיָּהוּ לֵאמֹר: כֹּה תֹאמְרוּן אֶל־חִזְקִיָּהוּ מֶלֶךְ־יְהוּדָה לֵאמֹר אַל־
יַשִּׁאֲךָ אֱלֹהֶיךָ אֲשֶׁר אַתָּה בֹּטֵחַ בּוֹ לֵאמֹר לֹא תִנָּתֵן יְרוּשָׁלַ͏ִם בְּיַד מֶלֶךְ
יא אַשּׁוּר: הִנֵּה ׀ אַתָּה שָׁמַעְתָּ אֵת אֲשֶׁר עָשׂוּ מַלְכֵי אַשּׁוּר לְכָל־הָאֲרָצוֹת
יב לְהַחֲרִימָם וְאַתָּה תִּנָּצֵל: הַהִצִּילוּ אֹתָם אֱלֹהֵי הַגּוֹיִם אֲשֶׁר שִׁחֲתוּ אֲבוֹתַי
יג אֶת־גּוֹזָן וְאֶת־חָרָן וְרֶצֶף וּבְנֵי־עֶדֶן אֲשֶׁר בִּתְלַאשָּׂר: אַיּוֹ מֶלֶךְ־חֲמָת וּמֶלֶךְ
יד אַרְפָּד וּמֶלֶךְ לָעִיר סְפַרְוָיִם הֵנַע וְעִוָּה: וַיִּקַּח חִזְקִיָּהוּ אֶת־הַסְּפָרִים מִיַּד
הַמַּלְאָכִים וַיִּקְרָאֵם וַיַּעַל בֵּית יְהֹוָה וַיִּפְרְשֵׂהוּ חִזְקִיָּהוּ לִפְנֵי יְהֹוָה:
טו וַיִּתְפַּלֵּל חִזְקִיָּהוּ לִפְנֵי יְהֹוָה וַיֹּאמַר יְהֹוָה אֱלֹהֵי יִשְׂרָאֵל יֹשֵׁב הַכְּרֻבִים
אַתָּה־הוּא הָאֱלֹהִים לְבַדְּךָ לְכֹל מַמְלְכוֹת הָאָרֶץ אַתָּה עָשִׂיתָ אֶת־הַשָּׁמַיִם
טז וְאֶת־הָאָרֶץ: הַטֵּה יְהֹוָה ׀ אָזְנְךָ וּשֲׁמָע פְּקַח יְהֹוָה עֵינֶיךָ וּרְאֵה וּשְׁמַע אֵת
יז דִּבְרֵי סַנְחֵרִיב אֲשֶׁר שְׁלָחוֹ לְחָרֵף אֱלֹהִים חָי: אָמְנָם יְהֹוָה הֶחֱרִיבוּ מַלְכֵי

18:37. They were in grief and consternation over the seemingly hopeless situation and over the shocking blasphemy uttered by Rabshakeh.

19:3. The battle for Jerusalem is about to begin, but we are powerless.

19:8. This began the fulfillment of Isaiah's prophecy. Sennacherib had broken camp to advance against Jerusalem, and then (v. 9) went back to Assyria to repel an attack by Tirhakah.

19:9. Cush is usually identified as Ethiopia.

and you will live and not die. Do not listen to Hezekiah when he tries to entice you, saying, 'HASHEM will save us!' ³³ Did the gods of the nations save any person in his land from the hand of the king of Assyria? ³⁴ Where are the gods of Hamath and Arpad? Where are the gods of Sepharvaim, Hena and Ivvah; did they save Samaria from my hand? ³⁵ Which among all the gods of the lands saved their land from my hand, that HASHEM should save Jerusalem from my hand?"

Grief-stricken report to Hezekiah

³⁶ The people remained silent and did not answer him a word, for there was a command from the king, saying, "Do not answer him." ³⁷ Eliakim son of Hilkiah, who was in charge of the palace, came, as well as Shebna the scribe and Joah son of Asaph the recorder, to Hezekiah with rent garments, * and told him the words of Rabshakeh.

19

The distressed Hezekiah asks Isaiah to pray

¹ It happened when King Hezekiah heard this: He rent his garments; he donned sackcloth and went to the Temple of HASHEM. ² He sent Eliakim, who was in charge of the palace, and Shebna the scribe and the elders of the Kohanim, all dressed in sackcloth, to Isaiah the prophet, the son of Amoz. ³ They said to him, "Thus said Hezekiah: Today is a day of distress, rebuke, and sacrilege. [We are like] babies who have entered the birth canal, but [the mother] has no strength to give birth. * ⁴ If only HASHEM, your God, will hear all the words of Rabshakeh, whom the king of Assyria, his master, sent to insult the living God, and He will punish him for those words that HASHEM your God heard. And may you offer a prayer for the remnant [of the people] that is still here!"

Isaiah promises victory

⁵ King Hezekiah's servants came to Isaiah, ⁶ and Isaiah said to them, "Thus shall you say to your master: Thus said HASHEM: Do not be frightened by the words that you have heard, by which the attendants of the king of Assyria have blasphemed Me. ⁷ Behold, I am instilling a desire within him. He will hear a report and return to his land, and I will strike him down by the sword in his own land."

Sennacherib withdraws to fight a war . . .

⁸ Rabshakeh went back and found the king of Assyria fighting against Libnah, because [Rabshakeh] had heard that he had journeyed from Lachish. * ⁹ Then [Sennacherib] heard a report about Tirhakah, the king of Cush*, saying, "He has gone out to do battle against you."

. . . but sends an abusive threat to Hezekiah

But he once again sent messengers to Hezekiah, saying, * ¹⁰ "Thus shall you speak unto Hezekiah king of Judah, saying: Do not let your God, in Whom you trust, persuade you, saying, 'Jerusalem will not be delivered into the hand of the king of Assyria.' ¹¹ Behold, you have heard what the kings of Assyria have done to all the lands, laying them waste; will you be spared? ¹² Did the gods of the nations rescue those whom my fathers destroyed — Gozan, Haran, Rezeph, and people of Eden who are in Telassar? ¹³ Where is the king of Hamath or the king of Arpad or the king of the city of Sepharvaim, or [of] Hena, or [of] Ivvah?"

Hezekiah beseeches God

¹⁴ Hezekiah took the letters from the hand of the messengers and read them, and he went up to the Temple of HASHEM and Hezekiah spread out each [of them] before HASHEM. ¹⁵ Hezekiah then prayed before HASHEM, and said, "HASHEM, God of Israel, Who dwells atop the Cherubim:* You alone are God of all the kingdoms of the world; You made heaven and earth. ¹⁶ Incline Your ear, HASHEM, and hear; open Your eyes, HASHEM, and see! Hear the words of Sennacherib that he has sent to insult the living God! ¹⁷ Indeed, HASHEM, the kings of Assyria have destroyed

---

Before leaving to repel advances by the Cushites, Sennacherib sent another intimidating message to   Hezekiah.
19:15. See *Exodus* 25:22.

יח אַשּׁוּר אֶת־הַגּוֹיִם וְאֶת־אַרְצָם: וְנָתְנוּ אֶת־אֱלֹהֵיהֶם בָּאֵשׁ כִּי לֹא אֱלֹהִים
יט הֵמָּה כִּי אִם־מַעֲשֵׂה יְדֵי־אָדָם עֵץ וָאֶבֶן וַיְאַבְּדוּם: וְעַתָּה יהוה אֱלֹהֵינוּ
הוֹשִׁיעֵנוּ נָא מִיָּדוֹ וְיֵדְעוּ כָּל־מַמְלְכוֹת הָאָרֶץ כִּי אַתָּה יהוה אֱלֹהִים
כ לְבַדֶּךָ: וַיִּשְׁלַח יְשַׁעְיָהוּ בֶן־אָמוֹץ אֶל־חִזְקִיָּהוּ לֵאמֹר כֹּה־אָמַר
יהוה אֱלֹהֵי יִשְׂרָאֵל אֲשֶׁר הִתְפַּלַּלְתָּ אֵלַי אֶל־סַנְחֵרִב מֶלֶךְ־אַשּׁוּר
כא שָׁמָעְתִּי: זֶה הַדָּבָר אֲשֶׁר־דִּבֶּר יהוה עָלָיו בָּזָה לְךָ לָעֲגָה לְךָ בְּתוּלַת בַּת־
כב צִיּוֹן אַחֲרֶיךָ רֹאשׁ הֵנִיעָה בַּת יְרוּשָׁלָ͏ִם: אֶת־מִי חֵרַפְתָּ וְגִדַּפְתָּ וְעַל־מִי
כג הֲרִימוֹתָ קּוֹל וַתִּשָּׂא מָרוֹם עֵינֶיךָ עַל־קְדוֹשׁ יִשְׂרָאֵל: בְּיַד מַלְאָכֶיךָ חֵרַפְתָּ ׀
אֲדֹנָי וַתֹּאמֶר °ברכב [בְּרֹב ק] רִכְבִּי אֲנִי עָלִיתִי מְרוֹם הָרִים יַרְכְּתֵי
לְבָנוֹן וְאֶכְרֹת קוֹמַת אֲרָזָיו מִבְחוֹר בְּרֹשָׁיו וְאָבוֹאָה מְלוֹן קִצֹּה יַעַר
כד כַּרְמִלּוֹ: אֲנִי קַרְתִּי וְשָׁתִיתִי מַיִם זָרִים וְאַחֲרִב בְּכַף־פְּעָמַי כֹּל יְאֹרֵי מָצוֹר:
כה הֲלֹא־שָׁמַעְתָּ לְמֵרָחוֹק אֹתָהּ עָשִׂיתִי לְמִימֵי קֶדֶם וִיצַרְתִּיהָ עַתָּה
כו הֲבֵיאתִיהָ וּתְהִי לַהְשׁוֹת גַּלִּים נִצִּים עָרִים בְּצֻרוֹת: וְיֹשְׁבֵיהֶן קִצְרֵי־יָד
חַתּוּ וַיֵּבֹשׁוּ הָיוּ עֵשֶׂב שָׂדֶה וִירַק דֶּשֶׁא חֲצִיר גַּגּוֹת וּשְׁדֵפָה לִפְנֵי קָמָה:
כז-כח וְשִׁבְתְּךָ וְצֵאתְךָ וּבֹאֲךָ יָדָעְתִּי וְאֵת הִתְרַגֶּזְךָ אֵלָי: יַעַן הִתְרַגֶּזְךָ אֵלַי
וְשַׁאֲנַנְךָ עָלָה בְאָזְנָי וְשַׂמְתִּי חַחִי בְּאַפֶּךָ וּמִתְגִּי בִּשְׂפָתֶיךָ וַהֲשִׁבֹתִיךָ
כט בַּדֶּרֶךְ אֲשֶׁר־בָּאתָ בָּהּ: וְזֶה־לְּךָ הָאוֹת אָכוֹל הַשָּׁנָה סָפִיחַ וּבַשָּׁנָה הַשֵּׁנִית
ל סָחִישׁ וּבַשָּׁנָה הַשְּׁלִישִׁית זִרְעוּ וְקִצְרוּ וְנִטְעוּ כְרָמִים וְאִכְלוּ פִרְיָם: וְיָסְפָה
לא פְּלֵיטַת בֵּית־יְהוּדָה הַנִּשְׁאָרָה שֹׁרֶשׁ לְמָטָּה וְעָשָׂה פְרִי לְמָעְלָה: כִּי
מִירוּשָׁלַ͏ִם תֵּצֵא שְׁאֵרִית וּפְלֵיטָה מֵהַר צִיּוֹן קִנְאַת יהוה [צְבָאוֹת ק יא ב]
לב תַּעֲשֶׂה־זֹּאת: לָכֵן כֹּה־אָמַר יהוה אֶל־מֶלֶךְ אַשּׁוּר לֹא
יָבֹא אֶל־הָעִיר הַזֹּאת וְלֹא־יוֹרֶה שָׁם חֵץ וְלֹא־יְקַדְּמֶנָּה מָגֵן וְלֹא־
לג יִשְׁפֹּךְ עָלֶיהָ סֹלְלָה: בַּדֶּרֶךְ אֲשֶׁר־יָבֹא בָּהּ יָשׁוּב וְאֶל־הָעִיר הַזֹּאת לֹא
לד יָבֹא נְאֻם־יהוה: וְגַנּוֹתִי אֶל־הָעִיר הַזֹּאת לְהוֹשִׁיעָהּ לְמַעֲנִי וּלְמַעַן דָּוִד
לה עַבְדִּי: וַיְהִי בַּלַּיְלָה הַהוּא וַיֵּצֵא ׀ מַלְאַךְ יהוה וַיַּךְ בְּמַחֲנֵה אַשּׁוּר
מֵאָה שְׁמוֹנִים וַחֲמִשָּׁה אָלֶף וַיַּשְׁכִּימוּ בַבֹּקֶר וְהִנֵּה כֻלָּם פְּגָרִים מֵתִים:

19:23. In his prophecy, Isaiah poetically likened the Land of Israel, Jerusalem, and the Temple to majestic forests and stately trees.

19:24. So vast were my armies of foot soldiers, that they had their pack animals drink up all the known water sources of the countries they have invaded, so I was forced to dig deep for unknown sources of water.

19:25-26. God rebukes the arrogant Sennacherib, saying: Your remarkable military victories are not your own doing. All your acts of destruction were foreordained by Me as punishment for the wickedness of your victims; you were merely the messenger who delivered the preordained blow. Your hubris and contemptuousness are totally unjustified.

19:28. Isaiah prophesied that God would bring Sennacherib back to Jerusalem, where his army would be destroyed.

19:29. Isaiah now prophesied to Hezekiah that unimagined prosperity would come in the wake of Assyria's downfall. There would be an abundance of wild grain, and fruit would grow from the stumps of the trees that Sennacherib had chopped down. This would symbolize the recovery of the decimated remainder of Judah into a strong, vibrant nation (*Rashi*).

19:35. Although Scripture does not say so explicitly, it is clear that Sennacherib had now resumed his siege of Jerusalem.

the nations and their land, [18] and have placed their gods into the fire — for they are not gods, but the work of man's hands, wood and stone — so they destroyed them. [19] So now, HASHEM, our God, save us please from his hand, then all the kingdoms of the world shall know that You alone are HASHEM, God."

[20] Isaiah son of Amoz sent [word] to Hezekiah, saying: Thus said HASHEM, God of Israel: Regarding what you prayed to Me concerning Sennacherib king of Assyria. [21] This is the word that HASHEM has spoken about him:

She scorns you, she mocks you, [she] the maiden daughter of Zion;
    she shakes her head at you, [she] the daughter of Jerusalem.
[22] Whom have you insulted and blasphemed;
    against Whom have you raised a voice, and lifted your eyes on high?
    Against the Holy One of Israel!
[23] By the hand of your messengers you have insulted my Lord, and said,
    'With my multitude of chariots I climbed the highest mountains,
    [to] the ends of the Lebanon [forest];
    I shall cut down its tallest cedars, its choicest cypresses,
    and I shall enter His ultimate abode, the forest of His fruitful field. *
[24] I dug and drank unknown waters,
    for the soles of my feet dried up all the rivers of the besieged area.'*
[25] Have you not heard from the distant [past that] I have done it?
    From earliest days [that] I have formed it?
    Now I have brought it about,
    to raze [into] desolate heaps [your] fortified cities. *
[26] Their inhabitants were short of power, crushed and ashamed;
    they were [like] herbage of the field and grassy vegetation,
    like grass on rooftops, like stalks wind-blasted, before standing [full].
[27] Your sitting [in counsel], your going forth, and your coming in —
    I know [them]; and [also] your provocation against Me.
[28] Because you provoked Me, and your arrogance has risen unto My ears,
    I shall place My hook into your nose and My bridle into your lips,
    and I shall make you return by the route on which you came. *

[29] And this shall be the sign for you:* You will eat this year of the aftercrop; the second year, fruits from tree stumps; and in the third year —

sow and harvest, and plant vineyards and eat their fruits. [30] And the survivors that remained of the House of Judah shall take root below and produce fruit above. [31] For from Jerusalem shall emerge a remnant, and survivors from Mount Zion. The zeal of HASHEM, Master of Legions, shall do this!

[32] Therefore, thus says HASHEM about the king of Assyria: He will not enter this city, and will not shoot there an arrow; he will not approach it with a shield, and will not pour a ramp against it. [33] On the route by which he came he will retreat, but he will not enter this city — the word of HASHEM. [34] And I shall protect this city, to save it, for My sake and for the sake of My servant David.

[35] And it was that [very] night:* An angel of HASHEM went out and struck down one hundred eighty-five thousand [people] of the Assyrian camp. The rest arose [early] in the morning and behold — they were all dead corpses!

לו-לז וַיִּסַּ֣ע וַיֵּ֔לֶךְ וַיָּ֖שָׁב סַנְחֵרִ֣יב מֶֽלֶךְ־אַשּׁ֑וּר וַיֵּ֖שֶׁב בְּנִֽינְוֵֽה: וַיְהִי֩ ה֨וּא מִֽשְׁתַּחֲוֶ֜ה
בֵּ֣ית ׀ נִסְרֹ֣ךְ אֱלֹהָ֗יו וְֽאַדְרַמֶּ֨לֶךְ וְשַׂרְאֶ֜צֶר [בָּנָ֗יו ק״ וּלא כ״] הִכֻּ֣הוּ בַחֶ֗רֶב וְהֵ֤מָּה
ב נִמְלְטוּ֙ אֶ֣רֶץ אֲרָרָ֔ט וַיִּמְלֹ֛ךְ אֵֽסַר־חַדֹּ֥ן בְּנ֖וֹ תַּחְתָּֽיו: בַּיָּמִ֣ים הָהֵ֔ם

א חָלָ֥ה חִזְקִיָּ֖הוּ לָמ֑וּת וַיָּבֹ֣א אֵלָ֡יו יְשַֽׁעְיָ֣הוּ בֶן־אָמוֹץ֩ הַנָּבִ֨יא וַיֹּ֤אמֶר אֵלָיו֙
ב כֹּֽה־אָמַ֣ר יהו֗ה צַ֤ו לְבֵֽיתְךָ֙ כִּ֣י מֵ֤ת אַתָּה֙ וְלֹ֣א תִֽחְיֶ֔ה: וַיַּסֵּ֥ב אֶת־פָּנָ֖יו אֶל־
ג הַקִּ֑יר וַיִּתְפַּלֵּ֖ל אֶל־יהו֥ה לֵאמֹֽר: אָנָּ֣ה יהו֗ה זְכָר־נָ֞א אֵ֣ת אֲשֶׁ֧ר הִתְהַלַּ֣כְתִּי
לְפָנֶ֗יךָ בֶּֽאֱמֶת֙ וּבְלֵבָ֣ב שָׁלֵ֔ם וְהַטּ֥וֹב בְּעֵינֶ֖יךָ עָשִׂ֑יתִי וַיֵּ֥בְךְּ חִזְקִיָּ֖הוּ בְּכִ֥י
ד גָדֽוֹל: וַֽיְהִ֣י יְשַֽׁעְיָ֔הוּ לֹ֣א יָצָ֔א °הֶעִ֑יר [°חָצֵ֖ר ק״] הַתִּֽיכֹנָ֑ה וּדְבַר־
ה יהו֖ה הָיָ֣ה אֵלָ֣יו לֵאמֹֽר: שׁ֣וּב וְאָֽמַרְתָּ֞ אֶל־חִזְקִיָּ֣הוּ נְגִיד־עַמִּ֗י כֹּֽה־אָמַ֤ר
יהוה֙ אֱלֹהֵי֙ דָּוִ֣ד אָבִ֔יךָ שָׁמַ֨עְתִּי֙ אֶת־תְּפִלָּתֶ֔ךָ רָאִ֖יתִי אֶת־דִּמְעָתֶ֑ךָ הִנְנִי֙
ו רֹ֣פֶא לָ֔ךְ בַּיּוֹם֙ הַשְּׁלִישִׁ֔י תַּֽעֲלֶ֖ה בֵּ֥ית יהוֽה: וְהֹֽסַפְתִּ֣י עַל־יָמֶ֗יךָ חֲמֵ֤שׁ עֶשְׂרֵה֙
שָׁנָ֔ה וּמִכַּ֤ף מֶֽלֶךְ־אַשּׁוּר֙ אַצִּ֣ילְךָ֔ וְאֵ֖ת הָעִ֣יר הַזֹּ֑את וְגַנּוֹתִ֖י עַל־הָעִ֥יר הַזֹּ֛את
ז לְמַֽעֲנִ֖י וּלְמַ֥עַן דָּוִ֣ד עַבְדִּֽי: וַיֹּ֣אמֶר יְשַֽׁעְיָ֔הוּ קְח֖וּ דְּבֶ֣לֶת תְּאֵנִ֑ים וַיִּקְח֛וּ וַיָּשִׂ֥ימוּ
ח עַל־הַשְּׁחִ֖ין וַיֶּֽחִי: וַיֹּ֤אמֶר חִזְקִיָּ֨הוּ֙ אֶל־יְשַֽׁעְיָ֔הוּ מָ֣ה א֔וֹת כִּֽי־יִרְפָּ֥א יהו֖ה
ט לִ֑י וְעָלִ֛יתִי בַּיּ֥וֹם הַשְּׁלִישִׁ֖י בֵּ֥ית יהוֽה: וַיֹּ֣אמֶר יְשַֽׁעְיָ֗הוּ זֶה־לְּךָ֤ הָאוֹת֙ מֵאֵ֣ת
יהו֔ה כִּ֚י יַֽעֲשֶׂ֣ה יהו֔ה אֶת־הַדָּבָ֖ר אֲשֶׁ֣ר דִּבֵּ֑ר הָלַ֤ךְ הַצֵּל֙ עֶ֣שֶׂר מַֽעֲל֔וֹת
י אִם־יָשׁ֖וּב עֶ֥שֶׂר מַֽעֲלֽוֹת: וַיֹּ֨אמֶר֙ יְחִזְקִיָּ֔הוּ נָקֵ֕ל לַצֵּ֖ל לִנְט֣וֹת עֶ֣שֶׂר מַֽעֲל֑וֹת
יא לֹ֣א כִ֔י יָשׁ֥וּב הַצֵּ֛ל אֲחֹֽרַנִּ֖ית עֶ֣שֶׂר מַֽעֲל֑וֹת: וַיִּקְרָ֞א יְשַֽׁעְיָ֤הוּ הַנָּבִיא֙ אֶל־יהו֔ה
וַיָּ֣שֶׁב אֶת־הַצֵּ֗ל בַּֽמַּֽעֲלוֹת֩ אֲשֶׁ֨ר יָֽרְדָ֜ה בְּמַֽעֲל֥וֹת אָחָ֛ז אֲחֹֽרַנִּ֖ית עֶ֥שֶׂר
יב מַֽעֲלֽוֹת: בָּעֵ֣ת הַהִ֗יא שָׁלַ֡ח בְּרֹֽאדַךְ בַּֽלְאֲדָ֛ן בֶּֽן־בַּלְאֲדָ֖ן מֶֽלֶךְ־
יג בָּבֶ֛ל סְפָרִ֥ים וּמִנְחָ֖ה אֶל־חִזְקִיָּ֑הוּ כִּ֣י שָׁמַ֔ע כִּ֥י חָלָ֖ה חִזְקִיָּֽהוּ: וַיִּשְׁמַ֣ע
עֲלֵיהֶם֮ חִזְקִיָּהוּ֒ וַיַּרְאֵ֣ם אֶת־כָּל־בֵּ֣ית נְכֹתֹ֡ה אֶת־הַכֶּ֣סֶף וְאֶת־הַזָּהָב֩
וְאֶת־הַבְּשָׂמִ֨ים וְאֵ֣ת ׀ שֶׁ֣מֶן הַטּ֗וֹב וְאֵת֙ בֵּ֣ית כֵּלָ֔יו וְאֵ֛ת כָּל־אֲשֶׁ֥ר נִמְצָ֖א
בְּאֽוֹצְרֹתָ֑יו לֹֽא־הָיָ֣ה דָבָ֗ר אֲשֶׁ֧ר לֹא־הֶרְאָ֛ם חִזְקִיָּ֖הוּ בְּבֵית֥וֹ וּבְכָל־
יד מֶמְשַׁלְתּֽוֹ: וַיָּבֹא֙ יְשַֽׁעְיָ֣הוּ הַנָּבִ֔יא אֶל־הַמֶּ֖לֶךְ חִזְקִיָּ֑הוּ וַיֹּ֨אמֶר אֵלָ֜יו מָ֥ה
אָֽמְר֣וּ ׀ הָֽאֲנָשִׁ֣ים הָאֵ֗לֶּה וּמֵאַ֨יִן֙ יָבֹ֣אוּ אֵלֶ֔יךָ וַיֹּ֨אמֶר֙ חִזְקִיָּ֔הוּ מֵאֶ֧רֶץ
טו רְחוֹקָ֛ה בָּ֖אוּ מִבָּבֶֽל: וַיֹּ֕אמֶר מָ֥ה רָא֖וּ בְּבֵיתֶ֑ךָ וַיֹּ֣אמֶר חִזְקִיָּ֗הוּ אֵ֣ת כָּל־
טז אֲשֶׁ֤ר בְּבֵיתִי֙ רָא֔וּ לֹֽא־הָיָ֥ה דָבָ֛ר אֲשֶׁ֥ר לֹֽא־הִרְאִיתִ֖ם בְּאֽוֹצְרֹתָֽי: וַיֹּ֥אמֶר
יז יְשַֽׁעְיָ֖הוּ אֶל־חִזְקִיָּ֑הוּ שְׁמַ֖ע דְּבַר־יהוֽה: הִנֵּה֮ יָמִ֣ים בָּאִים֒ וְנִשָּׂ֣א ׀ כָּל־
אֲשֶׁ֣ר בְּבֵיתֶ֗ךָ וַֽאֲשֶׁ֨ר אָֽצְר֤וּ אֲבֹתֶ֨יךָ֙ עַד־הַיּ֣וֹם הַזֶּ֔ה בָּבֶ֑לָה לֹֽא־יִוָּתֵ֖ר דָּבָ֑ר

20:1. As implied by verse 6, these events happened just
before the abortive Assyrian invasion of the previous
chapter. According to the Talmud, they took place three
days before.

20:8. Hezekiah suspected that Isaiah was not relating the
true word of God, but was only trying to console him after
seeing how upset he was by the prophecy that he would

die (*Radak*).

20:9. Ahaz had built a sun-clock (v. 11), which consisted
of a tall pillar with a number of indentations etched out
on it at regular intervals, with the time indicated by the
location of the shadow cast by the rising and setting sun.
Isaiah gave Hezekiah a choice of two miraculous signs —
the shade would suddenly move by ten notches, either

³⁶ So Sennacherib king of Assyria journeyed forth, went and returned; and he settled in Nineveh. ³⁷ It happened that he was worshiping in the temple of his god Nisroch: His sons Adrammelech and Sarezer struck him down by the sword; they then fled to the land of Ararat, and Esar-haddon his son reigned in his place.

20

Hezekiah's illness

¹ In those days Hezekiah became deathly ill. * Isaiah son of Amoz, the prophet, came to him and said to him, "Thus said HASHEM: Instruct your household, for you shall die; and you shall not live."

² [Hezekiah] then turned his face to the wall and prayed to HASHEM, saying, ³ "Please, HASHEM, remember now that I have walked before You faithfully and wholeheartedly, and I have done what is good in Your eyes." And Hezekiah wept an intense weeping.

Isaiah prophesies recovery . . .

⁴ And it was when Isaiah had not yet left the middle courtyard: The word of HASHEM came to him, saying, ⁵ "Go back and tell Hezekiah, the ruler of My people, 'Thus said HASHEM, the God of your forefather David: I have heard your prayer; I have seen your tears. Behold, I am healing you; on the third day you will go up to the Temple of HASHEM. ⁶ I will add fifteen years to your life and I will rescue you and this city from the grip of the king of Assyria. I will protect this city for My sake and for the sake of My servant David.' "

⁷ Then Isaiah said, "Take a cake of figs." They took it and placed it on [Hezekiah's] boil, and it was healed.

⁸ Hezekiah said to Isaiah, "What sign [can you show me] that HASHEM will heal me, and that I will go up on the third day to the Temple of HASHEM?" *

. . . and proves it with a sign

⁹ Isaiah said, "This is the sign for you from HASHEM that HASHEM will do the deed of which He spoke: Shall the shade move ten degrees ahead [on the clock], or shall it go back ten degrees?" *

¹⁰ Hezekiah said, "It is easier for the shade to be extended by ten degrees. No — rather let the shade turn backwards ten degrees."

¹¹ Isaiah the prophet called out unto HASHEM, and He turned the shade backward by ten degrees from the levels where it had descended [on the sun-clock] of Ahaz.

Hezekiah flatters the king of Babylonia . . .

¹² At that time Berodach-baladan son of Baladan, the king of Babylonia, sent letters and a gift to Hezekiah, for he had heard that Hezekiah was ill. ¹³ Hezekiah hearkened to them and showed them his whole treasure house — the silver, the gold, the spices, the fine oil, his warehouse, and everything that was found in his treasuries; there was nothing that Hezekiah did not show them in his palace and in all his realm. *

¹⁴ Isaiah the prophet came to King Hezekiah and said to him, "What did these men say, and from where did they come to you?"

Hezekiah said, "They came from a faraway land, from Babylonia."

¹⁵ He said, "And what did they see in your house?"

Hezekiah said, "They saw everything in my house; there was nothing that I did not show them in my treasuries."

. . . and God rebukes him

¹⁶ Isaiah then said to Hezekiah, "Hear the word of HASHEM: * ¹⁷ 'Behold, the days are coming when everything in your house, and that which your forefathers have accumulated until this day, will be carried off to Babylonia. Not a thing will be left,'

---

forward or backwards.

20:13. The parallel verse in *Isaiah* (39:2) reads, "He rejoiced over them . . ."

20:16. The reason for God's anger at Hezekiah is ex-

plained in *II Chronicles* (32:31): The king of Babylonia had sent this delegation because he had heard of the miraculous sign that God had performed for Hezekiah. Hezekiah should not have distracted them from the glory of God to impress them with his own wealth and grandeur.

יח אָמַ֣ר יְהֹוָ֑ה וּמִבָּנֶ֜יךָ אֲשֶׁ֤ר יֵצְא֣וּ מִמְּךָ֙ אֲשֶׁ֣ר תּוֹלִ֔יד °יִקָּח [°יֻקָּ֔חוּ ק] וְהָיוּ֙

יט סָֽרִיסִ֔ים בְּהֵיכַ֖ל מֶ֣לֶךְ בָּבֶֽל: וַיֹּ֤אמֶר חִזְקִיָּ֙הוּ֙ אֶל־יְשַֽׁעְיָ֔הוּ ט֥וֹב דְּבַר־יְהֹוָ֖ה

כ אֲשֶׁ֣ר דִּבַּ֑רְתָּ וַיֹּ֕אמֶר הֲל֥וֹא אִם־שָׁל֛וֹם וֶאֱמֶ֥ת יִהְיֶ֖ה בְיָמָֽי: וְיֶ֩תֶר֩ דִּבְרֵ֨י

חִזְקִיָּ֜הוּ וְכׇל־גְּבֽוּרָת֗וֹ וַֽאֲשֶׁ֣ר עָשָׂ֣ה אֶת־הַבְּרֵכָ֣ה וְאֶת־הַ֠תְּעָלָ֠ה וַיָּבֵ֤א אֶת־

הַמַּ֙יִם֙ הָעִ֔ירָה הֲלֹא־הֵ֣ם כְּתוּבִ֗ים עַל־סֵ֛פֶר דִּבְרֵ֥י הַיָּמִ֖ים לְמַלְכֵ֥י יְהוּדָֽה:

כא כא-א וַיִּשְׁכַּ֤ב חִזְקִיָּ֙הוּ֙ עִם־אֲבֹתָ֔יו וַיִּמְלֹ֛ךְ מְנַשֶּׁ֥ה בְנ֖וֹ תַּחְתָּֽיו: בֶּן־שְׁתֵּ֣ים

עֶשְׂרֵ֨ה שָׁנָ֤ה מְנַשֶּׁה֙ בְּמׇלְכ֔וֹ וַחֲמִשִּׁ֤ים וְחָמֵשׁ֙ שָׁנָ֔ה מָלַ֖ךְ בִּירֽוּשָׁלָ֑͏ִם וְשֵׁ֥ם

ב אִמּ֖וֹ חֶפְצִי־בָֽהּ: וַיַּ֥עַשׂ הָרַ֖ע בְּעֵינֵ֣י יְהֹוָ֑ה כְּתֽוֹעֲבֹת֙ הַגּוֹיִ֔ם אֲשֶׁר֙ הוֹרִ֣ישׁ

ג יְהֹוָ֔ה מִפְּנֵ֖י בְּנֵ֥י יִשְׂרָאֵֽל: וַיָּ֗שׇׁב וַיִּ֙בֶן֙ אֶת־הַבָּמ֔וֹת אֲשֶׁ֥ר אִבַּ֖ד חִזְקִיָּ֣הוּ אָבִ֑יו

וַיָּ֨קֶם מִזְבְּחֹ֜ת לַבַּ֗עַל וַיַּ֤עַשׂ אֲשֵׁרָה֙ כַּאֲשֶׁ֣ר עָשָׂ֗ה אַחְאָב֙ מֶ֣לֶךְ יִשְׂרָאֵ֔ל

ד וַיִּשְׁתַּ֙חוּ֙ לְכׇל־צְבָ֣א הַשָּׁמַ֔יִם וַֽיַּעֲבֹ֖ד אֹתָֽם: וּבָנָ֥ה מִזְבְּחֹ֖ת בְּבֵ֣ית יְהֹוָ֑ה

ה אֲשֶׁר֙ אָמַ֣ר יְהֹוָ֔ה בִּירֽוּשָׁלַ֖͏ִם אָשִׂ֥ים אֶת־שְׁמִֽי: וַיִּ֥בֶן מִזְבְּח֖וֹת לְכׇל־צְבָ֣א

ו הַשָּׁמָ֑יִם בִּשְׁתֵּ֖י חַצְר֥וֹת בֵּית־יְהֹוָֽה: וְהֶעֱבִ֤יר אֶת־בְּנוֹ֙ בָּאֵ֔שׁ וְעוֹנֵ֣ן וְנִחֵ֔שׁ

ז וְעָ֥שָׂה א֖וֹב וְיִדְּעֹנִ֑ים הִרְבָּ֗ה לַעֲשׂ֥וֹת הָרַ֛ע בְּעֵינֵ֥י יְהֹוָ֖ה לְהַכְעִֽיס: וַיָּ֕שֶׂם

אֶת־פֶּ֥סֶל הָאֲשֵׁרָ֖ה אֲשֶׁ֣ר עָשָׂ֑ה בַּבַּ֗יִת אֲשֶׁ֨ר אָמַ֤ר יְהֹוָה֙ אֶל־דָּוִ֔ד וְאֶל־

שְׁלֹמֹ֣ה בְנ֔וֹ בַּבַּ֤יִת הַזֶּה֙ וּבִיר֣וּשָׁלַ֔͏ִם אֲשֶׁ֤ר בָּחַ֙רְתִּי֙ מִכֹּל֙ שִׁבְטֵ֣י יִשְׂרָאֵ֔ל

ח אָשִׂ֥ים אֶת־שְׁמִ֖י לְעוֹלָֽם: וְלֹ֣א אֹסִ֗יף לְהָנִיד֙ רֶ֣גֶל יִשְׂרָאֵ֔ל מִן־הָ֣אֲדָמָ֔ה

אֲשֶׁ֥ר נָתַ֖תִּי לַֽאֲבוֹתָ֑ם רַ֣ק ׀ אִם־יִשְׁמְר֣וּ לַעֲשׂ֗וֹת כְּכֹל֙ אֲשֶׁ֣ר צִוִּיתִ֔ים וּלְכׇל־

ט הַתּוֹרָ֔ה אֲשֶׁר־צִוָּ֥ה אֹתָ֖ם עַבְדִּ֣י מֹשֶׁ֑ה וְלֹ֖א שָׁמֵ֑עוּ וַיַּתְעֵ֤ם מְנַשֶּׁה֙ לַעֲשׂ֣וֹת

י אֶת־הָרָ֔ע מִן־הַ֨גּוֹיִ֔ם אֲשֶׁר֙ הִשְׁמִ֣יד יְהֹוָ֔ה מִפְּנֵ֖י בְּנֵ֣י יִשְׂרָאֵֽל: וַיְדַבֵּ֧ר יְהֹוָ֛ה

יא בְּיַד־עֲבָדָ֥יו הַנְּבִיאִ֖ים לֵאמֹֽר: יַ֩עַן֩ אֲשֶׁ֨ר עָשָׂ֜ה מְנַשֶּׁ֤ה מֶֽלֶךְ־יְהוּדָה֙

הַתֹּעֵב֣וֹת הָאֵ֔לֶּה הֵרַ֕ע מִכֹּ֛ל אֲשֶׁר־עָשׂ֥וּ הָאֱמֹרִ֖י אֲשֶׁ֣ר לְפָנָ֑יו וַיַּחֲטִ֥א גַם־

יב אֶת־יְהוּדָ֖ה בְּגִלּוּלָֽיו: לָכֵ֗ן כֹּֽה־אָמַ֤ר יְהֹוָה֙ אֱלֹהֵ֣י יִשְׂרָאֵ֔ל

הִנְנִ֥י מֵבִ֛יא רָעָ֖ה עַל־יְרֽוּשָׁלַ֣͏ִם וִיהוּדָ֑ה אֲשֶׁר֙ כׇּל־°שמעיו [°שֹֽׁמְעָ֔הּ ק]

יג תִּצַּ֖לְנָה שְׁתֵּ֥י אׇזְנָֽיו: וְנָטִ֣יתִי עַל־יְרֽוּשָׁלַ֗͏ִם אֵ֚ת קָ֣ו שֹֽׁמְר֔וֹן וְאֶת־מִשְׁקֹ֖לֶת

בֵּ֣ית אַחְאָ֑ב וּמָחִ֙יתִי֙ אֶת־יְר֣וּשָׁלַ֔͏ִם כַּֽאֲשֶׁר־יִמְחֶ֥ה אֶת־הַצַּלַּ֖חַת מָחָ֥ה

יד וְהָפַ֖ךְ עַל־פָּנֶֽיהָ: וְנָטַשְׁתִּ֗י אֵ֚ת שְׁאֵרִ֣ית נַחֲלָתִ֔י וּנְתַתִּ֖ים בְּיַ֣ד אֹֽיְבֵיהֶ֑ם

טו וְהָי֥וּ לְבַ֛ז וְלִמְשִׁסָּ֖ה לְכׇל־אֹֽיְבֵיהֶֽם: יַ֗עַן אֲשֶׁ֤ר עָשׂוּ֙ אֶת־הָרַ֣ע בְּעֵינַ֔י

וַיִּֽהְי֥וּ מַכְעִסִ֖ים אֹתִ֑י מִן־הַיּ֗וֹם אֲשֶׁ֨ר יָצְא֤וּ אֲבוֹתָם֙ מִמִּצְרַ֔יִם וְעַ֖ד הַיּ֥וֹם

טז הַזֶּֽה: וְגַם֩ דָּ֨ם נָקִ֜י שָׁפַ֤ךְ מְנַשֶּׁה֙ הַרְבֵּ֣ה מְאֹ֔ד עַ֛ד אֲשֶׁר־מִלֵּ֥א אֶת־יְרֽוּשָׁלַ֖͏ִם

20:18. This prophecy found fulfillment in the appoint-ment of Daniel, Hananiah, Mishael, and Azariah, descen-dants of Hezekiah, to the court of Nebuchadnezzar (see *Daniel* 1:1-6; *Rashi*; *Radak*).

20:19. Humbly, Hezekiah accepted Isaiah's rebuke. Then he turned to the "bright side" of Isaiah's prophecy — that the punishment would not be meted out until some time

in the future, after his death.

20:20. See *II Chronicles* 29:1-32:33.

21:13. The destruction of Jerusalem will be just as thorough and meticulous as the destruction of Samaria and the family of Ahab. Jerusalem will be "wiped clean" of its inhabitants and then "turned over," i.e., destroyed (*Radak*), so that it will no longer be habitable.

said HASHEM. [18] 'And they will also take some of your children who will issue from you, whom you will beget, and they shall become officers in the palace of the king of Babylonia.' "*

[19] Hezekiah said to Isaiah, "The word of HASHEM that you have spoken is good"; and he said [to himself], "Is it not true that there will be peace and truth in my days?"*

[20] The rest of the deeds of Hezekiah and all his might, and how he made the pool and the channel, bringing the water source into the city — behold, they are recorded in the Book of the Chronicles of the Kings of Judah.*
[21] Hezekiah lay with his forefathers, and his son Manasseh reigned in his place.

21

MANASSEH, KING OF JUDAH
20:21-21:18

Manasseh reigns and is appallingly evil

[1] **M**anasseh was twelve years old when he became king, and he reigned for fifty-five years in Jerusalem. His mother's name was Hephzi-bah. [2] He did what was evil in the eyes of HASHEM, like the abominations of the nations that HASHEM had driven out before the Children of Israel. [3] He rebuilt the high places that his father Hezekiah had destroyed. He erected altars to Baal. He made an Asherah [idol] as Ahab king of Israel had done; he bowed down to the entire host of the heaven and worshiped them. [4] He built altars in the Temple of HASHEM — about which HASHEM had said, "I shall place My Name in Jerusalem" — [5] he built altars to the entire host of the heaven in the two courtyards of the Temple of HASHEM. [6] He passed his son through the fire, practiced astrology and read omens, and performed necromancy and conjured up spirits; he was profuse in doing what was evil in the eyes of HASHEM, to anger [Him]. [7] The Asherah idol that he had made he placed in the Temple, concerning which HASHEM said to David and his son Solomon, "In this Temple and in Jerusalem, which I have chosen from among all the tribes of Israel, I shall place My Name forever. [8] And I shall no longer cause the feet of Israel to wander from the land that I have given to their fore-fathers — provided they are careful to act according to all that I have commanded them, and to the entire Torah that My servant Moses com-manded them." [9] But they did not listen; Manasseh led them astray to do more evil than the nations that HASHEM had destroyed from before the Children of Israel.

Manasseh is the cause of destruction

[10] HASHEM spoke through His servants the prophets, saying, [11] "Because Manasseh king of Judah has committed these abominations, he did worse than all that the Amorite who was before him had done, and he caused even Judah to sin with his idols — [12] therefore, thus said HASHEM, God of Israel: Behold, I am bringing such evil upon Jerusalem and Judah, that both ears of anyone who hears of it will ring! [13] I will stretch out upon Jerusalem the level of Samaria and the plumbline of the house of Ahab; I will wipe out Jerusalem, as one would wipe a plate thoroughly, and then turn it upside down.* [14] I shall abandon the remnant of My heritage and deliver them into the hands of their enemies, where they will be plundered and trampled by all their enemies, [15] because they did what is evil in My eyes, and angered Me, from the day that their forefathers left Egypt and to this day."

[16] Manasseh also shed very much innocent blood, until he filled Jerusalem

פֶּה לָפֶה לְבַד מֵחַטָּאתוֹ אֲשֶׁר הֶחֱטִיא אֶת־יְהוּדָה לַעֲשׂוֹת הָרַע בְּעֵינֵי

יז יְהוָה: וְיֶתֶר דִּבְרֵי מְנַשֶּׁה וְכָל־אֲשֶׁר עָשָׂה וְחַטָּאתוֹ אֲשֶׁר חָטָא הֲלֹא־הֵם

יח כְּתוּבִים עַל־סֵפֶר דִּבְרֵי הַיָּמִים לְמַלְכֵי יְהוּדָה: וַיִּשְׁכַּב מְנַשֶּׁה עִם־אֲבֹתָיו

יט וַיִּקָּבֵר בְּגַן־בֵּיתוֹ בְּגַן־עֻזָּא וַיִּמְלֹךְ אָמוֹן בְּנוֹ תַּחְתָּיו: בֶּן־עֶשְׂרִים

וּשְׁתַּיִם שָׁנָה אָמוֹן בְּמָלְכוֹ וּשְׁתַּיִם שָׁנִים מָלַךְ בִּירוּשָׁלָ͏ִם וְשֵׁם אִמּוֹ

כ מְשֻׁלֶּמֶת בַּת־חָרוּץ מִן־יָטְבָה: וַיַּעַשׂ הָרַע בְּעֵינֵי יְהוָה כַּאֲשֶׁר עָשָׂה מְנַשֶּׁה

כא אָבִיו: וַיֵּלֶךְ בְּכָל־הַדֶּרֶךְ אֲשֶׁר־הָלַךְ אָבִיו וַיַּעֲבֹד אֶת־הַגִּלֻּלִים אֲשֶׁר עָבַד

כב אָבִיו וַיִּשְׁתַּחוּ לָהֶם: וַיַּעֲזֹב אֶת־יְהוָה אֱלֹהֵי אֲבֹתָיו וְלֹא הָלַךְ בְּדֶרֶךְ יְהוָה:

כג-כד וַיִּקְשְׁרוּ עַבְדֵי־אָמוֹן עָלָיו וַיָּמִיתוּ אֶת־הַמֶּלֶךְ בְּבֵיתוֹ: וַיַּךְ עַם־הָאָרֶץ אֵת

כָּל־הַקֹּשְׁרִים עַל־הַמֶּלֶךְ אָמוֹן וַיַּמְלִיכוּ עַם־הָאָרֶץ אֶת־יֹאשִׁיָּהוּ בְנוֹ

כה תַּחְתָּיו: וְיֶתֶר דִּבְרֵי אָמוֹן אֲשֶׁר עָשָׂה הֲלֹא־הֵם כְּתוּבִים עַל־סֵפֶר דִּבְרֵי

כו הַיָּמִים לְמַלְכֵי יְהוּדָה: וַיִּקְבֹּר אֹתוֹ בִּקְבֻרָתוֹ בְּגַן־עֻזָּא וַיִּמְלֹךְ יֹאשִׁיָּהוּ בְנוֹ

כב א תַּחְתָּיו: בֶּן־שְׁמֹנֶה שָׁנָה יֹאשִׁיָּהוּ בְמָלְכוֹ וּשְׁלֹשִׁים וְאַחַת

ב שָׁנָה מָלַךְ בִּירוּשָׁלָ͏ִם וְשֵׁם אִמּוֹ יְדִידָה בַת־עֲדָיָה מִבָּצְקַת: וַיַּעַשׂ הַיָּשָׁר

ג בְּעֵינֵי יְהוָה וַיֵּלֶךְ בְּכָל־דֶּרֶךְ דָּוִד אָבִיו וְלֹא־סָר יָמִין וּשְׂמֹאול: וַיְהִי

בִּשְׁמֹנֶה עֶשְׂרֵה שָׁנָה לַמֶּלֶךְ יֹאשִׁיָּהוּ שָׁלַח הַמֶּלֶךְ אֶת־שָׁפָן בֶּן־אֲצַלְיָהוּ

ד בֶן־מְשֻׁלָּם הַסֹּפֵר בֵּית יְהוָה לֵאמֹר: עֲלֵה אֶל־חִלְקִיָּהוּ הַכֹּהֵן הַגָּדוֹל וְיַתֵּם

ה אֶת־הַכֶּסֶף הַמּוּבָא בֵּית יְהוָה אֲשֶׁר אָסְפוּ שֹׁמְרֵי הַסַּף מֵאֵת הָעָם: °וְיִתְּנֻה

[וְיִתְּנֹהוּ ק] עַל־יַד עֹשֵׂי הַמְּלָאכָה הַמֻּפְקָדִים °בבית [בֵּית ק] יְהוָה וְיִתְּנוּ

ו אֹתוֹ לְעֹשֵׂי הַמְּלָאכָה אֲשֶׁר בְּבֵית יְהוָה לְחַזֵּק אֶת־בֶּדֶק הַבָּיִת: לֶחָרָשִׁים

ז וְלַבֹּנִים וְלַגֹּדְרִים וְלִקְנוֹת עֵצִים וְאַבְנֵי מַחְצֵב לְחַזֵּק אֶת־הַבָּיִת: אַךְ לֹא־

ח יֵחָשֵׁב אִתָּם הַכֶּסֶף הַנִּתָּן עַל־יָדָם כִּי בֶאֱמוּנָה הֵם עֹשִׂים: וַיֹּאמֶר חִלְקִיָּהוּ

הַכֹּהֵן הַגָּדוֹל עַל־שָׁפָן הַסֹּפֵר סֵפֶר הַתּוֹרָה מָצָאתִי בְּבֵית יְהוָה וַיִּתֵּן

ט חִלְקִיָּה אֶת־הַסֵּפֶר אֶל־שָׁפָן וַיִּקְרָאֵהוּ: וַיָּבֹא שָׁפָן הַסֹּפֵר אֶל־הַמֶּלֶךְ וַיָּשֶׁב

אֶת־הַמֶּלֶךְ דָּבָר וַיֹּאמֶר הִתִּיכוּ עֲבָדֶיךָ אֶת־הַכֶּסֶף הַנִּמְצָא בַבַּיִת וַיִּתְּנֻהוּ

י עַל־יַד עֹשֵׂי הַמְּלָאכָה הַמֻּפְקָדִים בֵּית יְהוָה: וַיַּגֵּד שָׁפָן הַסֹּפֵר לַמֶּלֶךְ

יא לֵאמֹר סֵפֶר נָתַן לִי חִלְקִיָּה הַכֹּהֵן וַיִּקְרָאֵהוּ שָׁפָן לִפְנֵי הַמֶּלֶךְ: וַיְהִי

יב כִּשְׁמֹעַ הַמֶּלֶךְ אֶת־דִּבְרֵי סֵפֶר הַתּוֹרָה וַיִּקְרַע אֶת־בְּגָדָיו: וַיְצַו הַמֶּלֶךְ אֶת־

חִלְקִיָּה הַכֹּהֵן וְאֶת־אֲחִיקָם בֶּן־שָׁפָן וְאֶת־עַכְבּוֹר בֶּן־מִיכָיָה וְאֵת ׀ שָׁפָן

יג הַסֹּפֵר וְאֵת עֲשָׂיָה עֶבֶד־הַמֶּלֶךְ לֵאמֹר: לְכוּ דִרְשׁוּ אֶת־יְהוָה בַּעֲדִי וּבְעַד־

הָעָם וּבְעַד כָּל־יְהוּדָה עַל־דִּבְרֵי הַסֵּפֶר הַנִּמְצָא הַזֶּה כִּי־גְדוֹלָה חֲמַת

21:17. See *II Chronicles 33:1-20*.

22:5. The last extensive repairs had been carried out in the days of Joash more than two centuries earlier (Ch. 12).

22:8. Manasseh had systematically destroyed all the Torah Scrolls and alienated the nation so thoroughly from

the Torah that the people were completely unfamiliar with its contents. Sixty-seven years had elapsed since the beginning of Manasseh's reign, so that this discovery was a surprising revelation to everyone (*Radak*).

22:11. Josiah was deeply distressed at what he heard.

[from] end to end [with it]; aside from his sin of causing Judah to sin, to do what was evil in the eyes of HASHEM.

¹⁷ *The rest of the deeds of Manasseh and all that he did and his sins that he committed — behold, they are recorded in the Book of the Chronicles of the Kings of Judah.* * ¹⁸ *Manasseh lay with his forefathers and was buried in the garden of his palace, in the garden of Uzza. His son Amon reigned in his place.*

¹⁹ *Amon was twenty-two years old when he became king, and he reigned for two years in Jerusalem. His mother's name was Meshullemeth daughter of Haruz, from Jotbah.* ²⁰ *He did what was evil in the eyes of HASHEM, as Manasseh his father had done.* ²¹ *He went the same way as his father had gone; he worshiped the idols that his father had worshiped and he prostrated himself to them.* ²² *He forsook HASHEM, the God of his forefathers, and he did not follow the way of HASHEM.* ²³ *Amon's servants conspired against him, and they killed the king in his palace,* ²⁴ *but the people of the land struck down all the conspirators against King Amon; the people of the land crowned Josiah his son in his place.*

²⁵ *The rest of the deeds of Amon that he did — behold, they are recorded in the Book of the Chronicles of the Kings of Judah.* ²⁶ *They buried him in his grave in the garden of Uzza, and his son Josiah reigned in his place.*

22 ¹ *Josiah was eight years old when he became king, and he reigned for thirty-one years in Jerusalem. His mother's name was Jedidah daughter of Adaiah, of Bozkath.* ² *He did what was proper in the eyes of HASHEM, following the ways of his forefather David; he did not veer right or left.*

³ *It happened in the eighteenth year of King Josiah that the king sent Shaphan son of Azaliah son of Meshullam, the scribe, to the Temple of HASHEM, saying,* ⁴ *"Go up to Hilkiah the Kohen Gadol, and [tell him] that he should collect all the money that is brought to the Temple of HASHEM, which the gatekeepers have collected from the people,* ⁵ *and they should give it over to the workmen-in-charge in the Temple of HASHEM, and they should give it to the workmen in the Temple of HASHEM, to repair the deterioration of the Temple,* * ⁶ *for the carpenters, the builders, and the stonemasons, and for buying wood and quarried stones to repair the Temple.* ⁷ *However, no accounting shall be made with them for the money given over into their hand, for they act with integrity."*

⁸ *Hilkiah, the Kohen Gadol, said to Shaphan the scribe, "I have found a Scroll of the Torah in the Temple of HASHEM."* * *Hilkiah gave the Scroll to Shaphan, and he read it.* ⁹ *Shaphan the scribe came to the king and brought a report to the king, and he said, "Your servants have counted the money that was found in the Temple, and have given it into the hand of the workmen-in-charge in the Temple of HASHEM."* ¹⁰ *Shaphan the scribe then told the king, saying, "Hilkiah the Kohen has given me a Scroll." Shaphan then read it before the king.* ¹¹ *It happened that when the king heard the words of the Scroll of the Torah, he rent his garments.* * ¹² *The king commanded Hilkiah the Kohen, Ahikam son of Shaphan, Achbor son of Micaiah, Shaphan the scribe, and Asaiah, the king's servant, saying,* ¹³ *"Go and inquire of HASHEM on my behalf, and on behalf of the people and on behalf of all of Judah, concerning the words of this Scroll that was found; for great is the wrath*

AMON, KING OF JUDAH
21:18-26
(See Appendix A, timeline 4)

Amon walks in Manasseh's footsteps . . .

JOSIAH, KING OF JUDAH
21:24-23:30
. . . and is assassinated

The righteous King Josiah

Josiah and the Temple maintenance

The "Book" is discovered

According to the Talmud, the selection was from the Admonition of *Deuteronomy*, Chapter 28; verse 36 of that

chapter especially affected the king.

יְהֹוָה אֲשֶׁר־הִיא נִצְּתָה בָנוּ עַל אֲשֶׁר לֹא־שָׁמְעוּ אֲבֹתֵ֫ינוּ עַל־דִּבְרֵי

יד הַסֵּ֫פֶר הַזֶּה לַעֲשׂוֹת כְּכָל־הַכָּת֫וּב עָלֵ֫ינוּ: וַיֵּ֫לֶךְ חִלְקִיָּ֫הוּ הַכֹּהֵן וַאֲחִיקָם

וְעַכְבּוֹר וְשָׁפָן וַעֲשָׂיָ֫ה אֶל־חֻלְדָּה הַנְּבִיאָה אֵ֫שֶׁת ׀ שַׁלֻּם בֶּן־תִּקְוָ֫ה בֶּן־

חַרְחַ֫ס שֹׁמֵ֫ר הַבְּגָדִים וְהִיא יֹשֶׁ֫בֶת בִּירוּשָׁלַ֫͏ִם בַּמִּשְׁנֶ֫ה וַיְדַבְּר֫וּ אֵלֶ֫יהָ:

טו וַתֹּ֫אמֶר אֲלֵיהֶם כֹּה־אָמַר יְהֹוָה אֱלֹהֵי יִשְׂרָאֵל אִמְר֫וּ לָאִ֫ישׁ אֲשֶׁר־שָׁלַ֫ח

טז אֶתְכֶם אֵלָ֫י: כֹּה אָמַר יְהֹוָה הִנְנִי מֵבִ֫יא רָעָ֫ה אֶל־הַמָּקוֹם הַזֶּה וְעַל־יֹשְׁבָ֫יו

אֵת כָּל־דִּבְרֵי הַסֵּ֫פֶר אֲשֶׁר קָרָ֫א מֶ֫לֶךְ יְהוּדָה: תַּ֫חַת ׀ אֲשֶׁר עֲזָב֫וּנִי וַיְקַטְּר֫וּ

יז לֵאלֹהִים אֲחֵרִים לְמַ֫עַן הַכְעִיסֵ֫נִי בְּכֹל מַעֲשֵׂ֫ה יְדֵיהֶם וְנִצְּתָ֫ה חֲמָתִ֫י

יח בַּמָּקוֹם הַזֶּ֫ה וְלֹא תִכְבֶּ֫ה: וְאֶל־מֶ֫לֶךְ יְהוּדָ֫ה הַשֹּׁלֵ֫חַ אֶתְכֶם לִדְרֹשׁ אֶת־

יְהֹוָה כֹּה תֹאמְר֫וּ אֵלָ֫יו כֹּה־אָמַר יְהֹוָה אֱלֹהֵי יִשְׂרָאֵל הַדְּבָרִים אֲשֶׁ֫ר

יט שָׁמָֽעְתָּ֫: יַ֫עַן רַךְ־לְבָבְךָ֫ וַתִּכָּנַ֫ע ׀ מִפְּנֵ֫י יְהֹוָה בְּשָׁמְעֲךָ֫ אֲשֶׁר דִּבַּ֫רְתִּי עַל־

הַמָּקוֹם הַזֶּה וְעַל־יֹשְׁבָ֫יו לִהְי֫וֹת לְשַׁמָּה֫ וְלִקְלָלָ֫ה וַתִּקְרַ֫ע אֶת־בְּגָדֶ֫יךָ

כ וַתִּבְכֶּ֫ה לְפָנָ֫י וְגַם אָנֹכִ֫י שָׁמַ֫עְתִּי נְאֻם־יְהֹוָ֫ה: לָכֵן הִנְנִ֫י אֹסִפְךָ֫ עַל־אֲבֹתֶ֫יךָ

וְנֶאֱסַפְתָּ֫ אֶל־קִבְרֹתֶ֫יךָ בְּשָׁל֫וֹם וְלֹא־תִרְאֶ֫ינָה עֵינֶ֫יךָ בְּכֹ֫ל הָרָעָ֫ה אֲשֶׁר־

אֲנִ֫י מֵבִ֫יא עַל־הַמָּקוֹם הַזֶּ֫ה וַיָּשִׁ֫יבוּ אֶת־הַמֶּ֫לֶךְ דָּבָ֫ר: **וַיִּשְׁלַ֫ח הַמֶּ֫לֶךְ**

כג

HAFTARAH
SECOND
DAY OF
PESACH
23:1-9,
21-25

א **וַיַּֽאַסְפ֫וּ אֵלָ֫יו כָּל־זִקְנֵ֫י יְהוּדָ֫ה וִירוּשָׁלָֽ͏ִם:** וַיַּ֫עַל הַמֶּ֫לֶךְ בֵּית־יְהֹוָ֫ה וְכָל־אִ֫ישׁ

יְהוּדָ֫ה וְכָל־יֹֽשְׁבֵ֫י יְרוּשָׁלַ֫͏ִם אִתּ֫וֹ וְהַכֹּֽהֲנִ֫ים וְהַנְּבִיאִ֫ים וְכָל־הָעָ֫ם לְמִקָּטֹ֫ן

וְעַד־גָּד֫וֹל וַיִּקְרָ֫א בְאָזְנֵיהֶ֫ם אֶת־כָּל־דִּבְרֵ֫י סֵ֫פֶר הַבְּרִ֫ית הַנִּמְצָ֫א בְּבֵ֫ית

ג יְהֹוָֽה: וַיַּעֲמֹ֫ד הַמֶּ֫לֶךְ עַל־הָעַמּ֫וּד וַיִּכְרֹ֫ת אֶת־הַבְּרִ֫ית ׀ לִפְנֵ֫י יְהֹוָ֫ה לָלֶ֫כֶת

אַחַ֫ר יְהֹוָ֫ה וְלִשְׁמֹ֫ר מִצְוֹתָ֫יו וְאֶת־עֵדְוֹתָ֫יו וְאֶת־חֻקֹּתָ֫יו בְּכָל־לֵ֫ב וּבְכָל־

נֶ֫פֶשׁ לְהָקִ֫ים אֶת־דִּבְרֵ֫י הַבְּרִ֫ית הַזֹּ֫את הַכְּתֻבִ֫ים עַל־הַסֵּ֫פֶר הַזֶּ֫ה וַיַּעֲמֹ֫ד

ד כָּל־הָעָ֫ם בַּבְּרִֽית: וַיְצַ֫ו הַמֶּ֫לֶךְ אֶת־חִלְקִיָּ֫הוּ הַכֹּהֵ֫ן הַגָּדוֹל וְאֶת־כֹּֽהֲנֵ֫י

הַמִּשְׁנֶה֫ וְאֶת־שֹׁמְרֵ֫י הַסַּ֫ף לְהוֹצִ֫יא מֵהֵיכַ֫ל יְהֹוָ֫ה אֵ֫ת כָּל־הַכֵּלִ֫ים הָעֲשׂוּ֫ים

לַבַּ֫עַל וְלָֽאֲשֵׁרָ֫ה וּלְכֹ֫ל צְבָ֫א הַשָּׁמָ֫יִם וַיִּשְׂרְפֵ֫ם מִח֫וּץ לִירוּשָׁלַ֫͏ִם בְּשַׁדְמ֫וֹת

ה קִדְר֫וֹן וְנָשָׂ֫א אֶת־עֲפָרָ֫ם בֵּֽית־אֵֽל: וְהִשְׁבִּ֫ית אֶת־הַכְּמָרִ֫ים אֲשֶׁ֫ר נָֽתְנ֫וּ

מַלְכֵ֫י יְהוּדָ֫ה וַיְקַטֵּ֫ר בַּבָּמוֹת֫ בְּעָרֵ֫י יְהוּדָ֫ה וּמְסִבֵּ֫י יְרוּשָׁלָ֫͏ִם וְאֶת־הַֽמְקַטְּרִ֫ים

ו לַבַּ֫עַל לַשֶּׁ֫מֶשׁ וְלַיָּרֵ֫חַ וְלַמַּזָּל֫וֹת וּלְכֹ֫ל צְבָ֫א הַשָּׁמָֽיִם: וַיֹּצֵ֫א אֶת־הָֽאֲשֵׁרָ֫ה

מִבֵּ֫ית יְהֹוָ֫ה מִח֫וּץ לִירוּשָׁלַ֫͏ִם אֶל־נַ֫חַל קִדְר֫וֹן וַיִּשְׂרֹ֫ף אֹתָ֫הּ בְּנַ֫חַל קִדְר֫וֹן

ז וַיָּ֫דֶק לְעָפָ֫ר וַיַּשְׁלֵ֫ךְ אֶת־עֲפָרָ֫הּ עַל־קֶ֫בֶר בְּנֵ֫י הָעָֽם: וַיִּתֹּץ֫ אֶת־בָּתֵּ֫י

הַקְּדֵשִׁ֫ים אֲשֶׁ֫ר בְּבֵ֫ית יְהֹוָ֫ה אֲשֶׁ֫ר הַנָּשִׁ֫ים אֹֽרְג֫וֹת שָׁ֫ם בָּתִּ֫ים לָֽאֲשֵׁרָֽה: וַיָּבֵ֫א

ח אֶת־כָּל־הַכֹּֽהֲנִ֫ים מֵעָרֵ֫י יְהוּדָ֫ה וַיְטַמֵּ֫א אֶת־הַבָּמ֫וֹת אֲשֶׁ֫ר קִטְּרוּ־שָׁ֫מָּה

הַכֹּֽהֲנִ֫ים מִגֶּ֫בַע עַד־בְּאֵ֫ר שָׁ֫בַע וְנָתַ֫ץ אֶת־בָּמ֫וֹת הַשְּׁעָרִ֫ים אֲשֶׁר־פֶּ֫תַח

23:4. Josiah had the ashes scattered on the site of Jeroboam's temple, which he would soon defile (v. 15). He wanted even the ashes that remained of these idolatrous objects to be disposed of in an unclean place. **23:8.** These were true Kohanim who had sinned by serving as priests to the idols.

of HASHEM that has been incited against us, because our fathers have not listened to the words of this Scroll, to fulfill all that was written for us."

¹⁴ So Hilkiah the Kohen, Ahikam, Achbor, Shaphan and Asaiah went to Huldah the prophetess, the wife of Shallum son of Tikvah son of Harhas, the keeper of the [royal] garments, who dwelled in Jerusalem, in the study house, and they spoke to her.

Hulda's ominous prophecy

¹⁵ She said to them, "Thus said HASHEM, God of Israel: Say to the man who sent you to me, ¹⁶ 'Thus said HASHEM: Behold, I am bringing evil upon this place and upon its inhabitants — [namely] all the words of the Scroll that the king of Judah read — ¹⁷ because they have forsaken Me and burned offerings to the gods of others, in order to anger Me with all their handiwork; My wrath has been incited against this place, and it will not be extinguished.' ¹⁸ And concerning the king of Judah who sent you to inquire of HASHEM, thus should you say to him: 'Thus said HASHEM, God of Israel: [Regarding] the words that you have just heard — ¹⁹ because your heart is soft and you humbled yourself before HASHEM when you heard that which I have spoken about this place and its inhabitants, that they would become a desolation and a curse; and you rent your garments and cried before Me, and I, too, have heard — the word of HASHEM. ²⁰ Therefore, behold, I will gather you in to your forefathers — you will be gathered to your grave in peace — and your eyes will not see all the evil that I am bringing upon this place.' "

They brought this report back to the king.

23

Josiah seals a covenant . . .

¹ The king sent out and gathered to himself all the elders of Judah and Jerusalem. ² The king went up to the Temple of HASHEM, and all the men of Judah and all the inhabitants of Jerusalem with him, as well as the Kohanim and the prophets and all the people, from small to great, and he read in their ears all the words of the Book of the Covenant that had been found in the Temple of HASHEM.

³ The king then stood at his place and sealed a covenant before HASHEM, to follow HASHEM and to observe His commandments and His testimonies and His decrees with all [his] heart and all [his] soul, to uphold the words of this covenant written in this book; and the entire people accepted the covenant.

. . . cleanses the land of idolatry . . .

⁴ The king then instructed Hilkiah the Kohen Gadol, the Kohanim of the second rank, and the gatekeepers to remove from the Temple of HASHEM all the articles that had been made for the Baal, for the Asherah, and for all the hosts of the heavens. He had them burned outside Jerusalem, in the plains of Kidron, and their ashes carried away to Beth-el. * ⁵ He also dismissed the priests whom the kings of Judah had appointed to burn offerings at the high places in the cities of Judah and in the surrounding areas of Jerusalem, as well as those who burned offerings to the Baal, to the sun and to the moon and to the constellations and to all the heavenly hosts. ⁶ He removed the Asherah from the Temple of HASHEM to the Kidron Valley outside Jerusalem; he burned it in the Kidron Valley and ground it to dust, and then scattered its dust over the graves of the [idolatrous] common people. ⁷ He demolished the rooms of the idolaters that were in the Temple of HASHEM, where the women would weave curtains for the Asherah.

. . . and destroys the idols

⁸ He brought all the priests* from the cities of Judah, and he defiled the high places where these priests used to burn offerings from Geba to Beer-sheba; he smashed the high places at the gates and the one that was at the entrance of

ט שַׁעַר יְהוֹשֻׁעַ שַׂר־הָעִיר אֲשֶׁר־עַל־שְׂמֹאול אִישׁ בְּשַׁעַר הָעִיר: אַךְ לֹא
יַעֲלוּ כֹּהֲנֵי הַבָּמוֹת אֶל־מִזְבַּח יהוה בִּירוּשָׁלָ͏ִם כִּי אִם־אָכְלוּ מַצּוֹת בְּתוֹךְ
אֲחֵיהֶם: ◀ וְטִמֵּא אֶת־הַתֹּפֶת אֲשֶׁר בְּגֵי °בְנֵי [°בֶן קּ] הִנֹּם לְבִלְתִּי

Haftarah continues below, v. 21

יא לְהַעֲבִיר אִישׁ אֶת־בְּנוֹ וְאֶת־בִּתּוֹ בָּאֵשׁ לַמֹּלֶךְ: וַיַּשְׁבֵּת אֶת־הַסּוּסִים אֲשֶׁר
נָתְנוּ מַלְכֵי יְהוּדָה לַשֶּׁמֶשׁ מִבֹּא בֵית־יהוה אֶל־לִשְׁכַּת נְתַן־מֶלֶךְ הַסָּרִיס
יב אֲשֶׁר בַּפַּרְוָרִים וְאֶת־מַרְכְּבוֹת הַשֶּׁמֶשׁ שָׂרַף בָּאֵשׁ: וְאֶת־הַמִּזְבְּחוֹת אֲשֶׁר
עַל־הַגָּג עֲלִיַּת אָחָז אֲשֶׁר־עָשׂוּ ׀ מַלְכֵי יְהוּדָה וְאֶת־הַמִּזְבְּחוֹת אֲשֶׁר־
עָשָׂה מְנַשֶּׁה בִּשְׁתֵּי חַצְרוֹת בֵּית־יהוה נָתַץ הַמֶּלֶךְ וַיָּרָץ מִשָּׁם וְהִשְׁלִיךְ
יג אֶת־עֲפָרָם אֶל־נַחַל קִדְרוֹן: וְאֶת־הַבָּמוֹת אֲשֶׁר ׀ עַל־פְּנֵי יְרוּשָׁלַ͏ִם אֲשֶׁר
מִימִין לְהַר־הַמַּשְׁחִית אֲשֶׁר בָּנָה שְׁלֹמֹה מֶלֶךְ־יִשְׂרָאֵל לְעַשְׁתֹּרֶת ׀ שִׁקֻּץ
צִידֹנִים וְלִכְמוֹשׁ שִׁקֻּץ מוֹאָב וּלְמִלְכֹּם תּוֹעֲבַת בְּנֵי־עַמּוֹן טִמֵּא הַמֶּלֶךְ:
יד וְשִׁבַּר אֶת־הַמַּצֵּבוֹת וַיִּכְרֹת אֶת־הָאֲשֵׁרִים וַיְמַלֵּא אֶת־מְקוֹמָם עַצְמוֹת
טו אָדָם: וְגַם אֶת־הַמִּזְבֵּחַ אֲשֶׁר בְּבֵית־אֵל הַבָּמָה אֲשֶׁר עָשָׂה יָרָבְעָם בֶּן־
נְבָט אֲשֶׁר הֶחֱטִיא אֶת־יִשְׂרָאֵל גַּם אֶת־הַמִּזְבֵּחַ הַהוּא וְאֶת־הַבָּמָה נָתָץ
טז וַיִּשְׂרֹף אֶת־הַבָּמָה הֵדַק לְעָפָר וְשָׂרַף אֲשֵׁרָה: וַיִּפֶן יֹאשִׁיָּהוּ וַיַּרְא אֶת־
הַקְּבָרִים אֲשֶׁר־שָׁם בָּהָר וַיִּשְׁלַח וַיִּקַּח אֶת־הָעֲצָמוֹת מִן־הַקְּבָרִים וַיִּשְׂרֹף
עַל־הַמִּזְבֵּחַ וַיְטַמְּאֵהוּ כִּדְבַר יהוה אֲשֶׁר קָרָא אִישׁ הָאֱלֹהִים אֲשֶׁר קָרָא
יז אֶת־הַדְּבָרִים הָאֵלֶּה: וַיֹּאמֶר מָה הַצִּיּוּן הַלָּז אֲשֶׁר אֲנִי רֹאֶה וַיֹּאמְרוּ אֵלָיו
אַנְשֵׁי הָעִיר הַקֶּבֶר אִישׁ־הָאֱלֹהִים אֲשֶׁר־בָּא מִיהוּדָה וַיִּקְרָא אֶת־
יח הַדְּבָרִים הָאֵלֶּה אֲשֶׁר עָשִׂיתָ עַל הַמִּזְבֵּחַ בֵּית־אֵל: וַיֹּאמֶר הַנִּיחוּ לוֹ אִישׁ
אַל־יָנַע עַצְמֹתָיו וַיְמַלְּטוּ עַצְמֹתָיו אֵת עַצְמוֹת הַנָּבִיא אֲשֶׁר־בָּא
יט מִשֹּׁמְרוֹן: וְגַם אֶת־כָּל־בָּתֵּי הַבָּמוֹת אֲשֶׁר ׀ בְּעָרֵי שֹׁמְרוֹן אֲשֶׁר עָשׂוּ מַלְכֵי
יִשְׂרָאֵל לְהַכְעִיס הֵסִיר יֹאשִׁיָּהוּ וַיַּעַשׂ לָהֶם כְּכָל־הַמַּעֲשִׂים אֲשֶׁר עָשָׂה
כ בְּבֵית־אֵל: וַיִּזְבַּח אֶת־כָּל־כֹּהֲנֵי הַבָּמוֹת אֲשֶׁר־שָׁם עַל־הַמִּזְבְּחוֹת

Haftarah of second day Pesach continues here: 23:21-25

כא וַיִּשְׂרֹף אֶת־עַצְמוֹת אָדָם עֲלֵיהֶם וַיָּשָׁב יְרוּשָׁלָ͏ִם: ◀ וַיְצַו הַמֶּלֶךְ אֶת־כָּל־
הָעָם לֵאמֹר עֲשׂוּ פֶסַח לַיהוה אֱלֹהֵיכֶם כַּכָּתוּב עַל סֵפֶר הַבְּרִית הַזֶּה:
כב כִּי לֹא נַעֲשָׂה כַּפֶּסַח הַזֶּה מִימֵי הַשֹּׁפְטִים אֲשֶׁר שָׁפְטוּ אֶת־יִשְׂרָאֵל וְכֹל
כג יְמֵי מַלְכֵי יִשְׂרָאֵל וּמַלְכֵי יְהוּדָה: כִּי אִם־בִּשְׁמֹנֶה עֶשְׂרֵה שָׁנָה לַמֶּלֶךְ
כד יֹאשִׁיָּהוּ נַעֲשָׂה הַפֶּסַח הַזֶּה לַיהוה בִּירוּשָׁלָ͏ִם: וְגַם אֶת־הָאֹבוֹת וְאֶת־
הַיִּדְּעֹנִים וְאֶת־הַתְּרָפִים וְאֶת־הַגִּלֻּלִים וְאֵת כָּל־הַשִּׁקֻּצִים אֲשֶׁר נִרְאוּ
בְּאֶרֶץ יְהוּדָה וּבִירוּשָׁלַ͏ִם בִּעֵר יֹאשִׁיָּהוּ לְמַעַן הָקִים אֶת־דִּבְרֵי הַתּוֹרָה

23:9. These Kohanim who had served as priests were not permitted to participate in the actual Temple service, but they were allowed to partake of the sacrificial foods that were distributed among their fellow Kohanim. All meal-offerings were prepared in an unleavened state, as matzos (*Lev.* 2:10-11).

23:11. The worship of the sun consisted in racing out towards the east at daybreak, in horse-drawn chariots, to "greet" the rising sun.
23:14. As a graphic illustration of his disdain for the idols, he exhumed their worshipers and scattered their bones over the ruins of the idols.

the gate of Joshua the governor of the city, which was situated at one's left [when entering] the city gate. ⁹ But, the priests of the high places were not permitted to ascend the Altar of HASHEM in Jerusalem; rather they would only eat unleavened bread among their brethren. *

¹⁰ He also defiled the Topheth, which was in the Valley of Ben Hinnom, so that no man could pass his son or daughter through the fire for the Molech. ¹¹ He also abolished the horses that the kings of Judah had designated for [worship of] the sun, * [which would race] from the entrance to the Temple of HASHEM to the office of Nethan-melech, the officer in the outlying area of the city. He burned the chariots of the sun in fire. ¹² And the altars that were on the roof of the upper story built by Ahaz, which the kings of Judah had set up, and the altars that Manasseh had set up in the two courtyards of the Temple of HASHEM, the king smashed; he eliminated [them] from there and threw their dust into the Kidron Valley. ¹³ And the high places facing Jerusalem, south of the Mount of Olives, which Solomon king of Israel had built for Ashtoreth the abomination of the Sidonians, for Chemosh the abomination of Moab, and for Milcom the abomination of the Children of Ammon, the king defiled. ¹⁴ He shattered the pillars and cut down the Asherah-trees, and he filled up their places with human bones. *

¹⁵ Also the altar that was in Beth-el — the high place that Jeroboam son of Nebat built, with which he caused Israel to sin — also that altar and its high place he demolished; he burned the high place and ground it into dust, and burned the Asherah-tree. ¹⁶ Josiah then turned and saw the graves that were there on the mountain and he sent [men] to take the bones out of the graves, and he burned them upon the altar and defiled it; in accordance with the word of HASHEM, which the man of God who had prophesied about these events, * had proclaimed.

¹⁷ [Josiah] then said, "What is this tombstone that I see?"

The people of the city said to him, "It is the grave of the man of God who came from Judah and prophesied about these deeds that you have done upon the altar of Beth-el." ¹⁸ He said, "Leave it alone. Let no man move those bones." His bones saved the bones of the prophet who came from Samaria. *

¹⁹ Furthermore, all the temples of the high places in the cities of Samaria, which the kings of Israel had built to anger [HASHEM], Josiah removed and he did to them like all the deeds that he had done at Beth-el. ²⁰ He slaughtered all the priests of the high places who were there upon the altars, and burned human bones upon them, and he returned to Jerusalem.

Unprecedented Pesach ²¹ The king then commanded the people, saying, "Perform the pesach-offering unto HASHEM your God, as written in this Book of the Covenant." ²² For such a pesach-offering had not been celebrated since the days of the Judges who judged Israel, and all the days of the kings of Israel and the kings of Judah; * ²³ but in the eighteenth year of King Josiah this Passover was celebrated unto HASHEM in Jerusalem.

²⁴ Furthermore, the necromancers and conjurers of spirits, the teraphim, the execrable-idols and all the abominations that had been seen in the land of Judah and Jerusalem, Josiah removed in order to uphold the words of the Torah that

---

ipation by the people, partly because it was the first time in centuries that the Israelites of the northern tribes participated in the observance of Passover at Jerusalem.

כה הַכְּתֻבִים עַל־הַסֵּפֶר אֲשֶׁר מָצָא חִלְקִיָּהוּ הַכֹּהֵן בֵּית יְהֹוָה: וְכָמֹהוּ לֹא־הָיָה לְפָנָיו מֶלֶךְ אֲשֶׁר־שָׁב אֶל־יְהֹוָה בְּכָל־לְבָבוֹ וּבְכָל־נַפְשׁוֹ וּבְכָל־

כו מְאֹדוֹ כְּכֹל תּוֹרַת מֹשֶׁה וְאַחֲרָיו לֹא־קָם כָּמֹהוּ: ◀ אַךְ | לֹא־שָׁב יְהֹוָה מֵחֲרוֹן אַפּוֹ הַגָּדוֹל אֲשֶׁר־חָרָה אַפּוֹ בִּיהוּדָה עַל כָּל־הַכְּעָסִים אֲשֶׁר

כז הִכְעִיסוֹ מְנַשֶּׁה: וַיֹּאמֶר יְהֹוָה גַּם אֶת־יְהוּדָה אָסִיר מֵעַל פָּנַי כַּאֲשֶׁר הֲסִרֹתִי אֶת־יִשְׂרָאֵל וּמָאַסְתִּי אֶת־הָעִיר הַזֹּאת אֲשֶׁר־בָּחַרְתִּי אֶת־

כח יְרוּשָׁלַם וְאֶת־הַבַּיִת אֲשֶׁר אָמַרְתִּי יִהְיֶה שְׁמִי שָׁם: וְיֶתֶר דִּבְרֵי יֹאשִׁיָּהוּ וְכָל־אֲשֶׁר עָשָׂה הֲלֹא־הֵם כְּתוּבִים עַל־סֵפֶר דִּבְרֵי הַיָּמִים לְמַלְכֵי

כט יְהוּדָה: בְּיָמָיו עָלָה פַרְעֹה נְכֹה מֶלֶךְ־מִצְרַיִם עַל־מֶלֶךְ אַשּׁוּר עַל־נְהַר־פְּרָת וַיֵּלֶךְ הַמֶּלֶךְ יֹאשִׁיָּהוּ לִקְרָאתוֹ וַיְמִיתֵהוּ בִּמְגִדּוֹ כִּרְאֹתוֹ אֹתוֹ:

ל וַיַּרְכִּבֻהוּ עֲבָדָיו מֵת מִמְּגִדּוֹ וַיְבִאֻהוּ יְרוּשָׁלַם וַיִּקְבְּרֻהוּ בִּקְבֻרָתוֹ וַיִּקַּח עַם־הָאָרֶץ אֶת־יְהוֹאָחָז בֶּן־יֹאשִׁיָּהוּ וַיִּמְשְׁחוּ אֹתוֹ וַיַּמְלִיכוּ אֹתוֹ תַּחַת

לא אָבִיו: בֶּן־עֶשְׂרִים וְשָׁלֹשׁ שָׁנָה יְהוֹאָחָז בְּמָלְכוֹ וּשְׁלֹשָׁה חֳדָשִׁים מָלַךְ בִּירוּשָׁלַם וְשֵׁם אִמּוֹ חֲמוּטַל בַּת־יִרְמְיָהוּ מִלִּבְנָה: וַיַּעַשׂ

לב הָרַע בְּעֵינֵי יְהֹוָה כְּכֹל אֲשֶׁר־עָשׂוּ אֲבֹתָיו: וַיַּאַסְרֵהוּ פַרְעֹה נְכֹה בְרִבְלָה

לג בְּאֶרֶץ חֲמָת °במלך [°מִמְּלֹךְ ק] בִּירוּשָׁלָם וַיִּתֶּן־עֹנֶשׁ עַל־הָאָרֶץ מֵאָה

לד כִכַּר־כֶּסֶף וְכִכַּר זָהָב: וַיַּמְלֵךְ פַּרְעֹה נְכֹה אֶת־אֶלְיָקִים בֶּן־יֹאשִׁיָּהוּ תַּחַת יֹאשִׁיָּהוּ אָבִיו וַיַּסֵּב אֶת־שְׁמוֹ יְהוֹיָקִים וְאֶת־יְהוֹאָחָז לָקָח וַיָּבֹא מִצְרַיִם

לה וַיָּמָת שָׁם: וְהַכֶּסֶף וְהַזָּהָב נָתַן יְהוֹיָקִים לְפַרְעֹה אַךְ הֶעֱרִיךְ אֶת־הָאָרֶץ לָתֵת אֶת־הַכֶּסֶף עַל־פִּי פַרְעֹה אִישׁ כְּעֶרְכּוֹ נָגַשׂ אֶת־הַכֶּסֶף וְאֶת־

לו הַזָּהָב אֶת־עַם הָאָרֶץ לָתֵת לְפַרְעֹה נְכֹה: בֶּן־עֶשְׂרִים וְחָמֵשׁ שָׁנָה יְהוֹיָקִים בְּמָלְכוֹ וְאַחַת עֶשְׂרֵה שָׁנָה מָלַךְ בִּירוּשָׁלָם וְשֵׁם

לז אִמּוֹ °זבידה [°זְבוּדָּה ק] בַת־פְּדָיָה מִן־רוּמָה: וַיַּעַשׂ הָרַע בְּעֵינֵי יְהֹוָה

כד א כְּכֹל אֲשֶׁר־עָשׂוּ אֲבֹתָיו: בְּיָמָיו עָלָה נְבֻכַדְנֶאצַּר מֶלֶךְ בָּבֶל וַיְהִי־לוֹ

ב יְהוֹיָקִים עֶבֶד שָׁלֹשׁ שָׁנִים וַיָּשָׁב וַיִּמְרָד־בּוֹ: וַיְשַׁלַּח יְהֹוָה | בּוֹ אֶת־גְּדוּדֵי כַשְׂדִּים וְאֶת־גְּדוּדֵי אֲרָם וְאֵת | גְּדוּדֵי מוֹאָב וְאֵת גְּדוּדֵי בְנֵי־עַמּוֹן וַיְשַׁלְּחֵם בִּיהוּדָה לְהַאֲבִידוֹ כִּדְבַר יְהֹוָה אֲשֶׁר דִּבֶּר בְּיַד עֲבָדָיו הַנְּבִיאִים:

ג אַךְ | עַל־פִּי יְהֹוָה הָיְתָה בִּיהוּדָה לְהָסִיר מֵעַל פָּנָיו בְּחַטֹּאת מְנַשֶּׁה

ד כְּכֹל אֲשֶׁר עָשָׂה: וְגַם דַּם־הַנָּקִי אֲשֶׁר שָׁפָךְ וַיְמַלֵּא אֶת־יְרוּשָׁלַם דָּם נָקִי וְלֹא־אָבָה יְהֹוָה לִסְלֹחַ: וְיֶתֶר דִּבְרֵי יְהוֹיָקִים וְכָל־אֲשֶׁר עָשָׂה הֲלֹא־

ה הֵם כְּתוּבִים עַל־סֵפֶר דִּבְרֵי הַיָּמִים לְמַלְכֵי יְהוּדָה: וַיִּשְׁכַּב יְהוֹיָקִים

ו

23:28. See *II Chronicles 34:1-35:27.*
23:29. Although Pharaoh Neco informed Josiah that he was using the Land of Israel only for passage to Assyria, and had no belligerent intentions towards him, Josiah went to prevent him from crossing through

the land (*II Chronicles 35:20-24*). When Pharaoh saw that Josiah insisted on a confrontation, he killed him (*Radak*).

23:34. The change of name, like the peremptory appointment of a new king, was to demonstrate that

were written in the Scroll that Hilkiah the Kohen found in the Temple of HASHEM.
Unprecedented king *25 Before him there had never been a king like him who returned to HASHEM with all his heart, with all his soul, and with all his resources, in accordance with the entire Torah of Moses, and after him no one arose like him.* **But God's decree stands** *26 Nevertheless, HASHEM did not relent from His great flaring anger, for His anger had flared up against Judah because of all the provocations with which Manasseh had angered Him. 27 So HASHEM said, "Judah, as well, will I remove from My presence, as I removed Israel; and I will reject this city which I have chosen, Jerusalem, and the Temple of which I had said, 'My Name would remain there.'"*

28 The rest of the deeds of Josiah and all that he did — behold, they are recorded in the Book of Chronicles of the Kings of Judah. * 29 In his days Pharaoh Neco **Josiah dies in battle** *the king of Egypt, went up to wage war against the king of Assyria by the Euphrates River; King Josiah went to confront him, and [Pharaoh] killed him in* **JEHOAHAZ, KING OF JUDAH 23:30-34** *Megiddo when he saw him. * 30 His servants drove him, dead from Megiddo in a chariot, brought him to Jerusalem and buried him in his grave. The common people took Jehoahaz son of Josiah, anointed him, and crowned him king in place of his father.*

(See Appendix A, timeline 4)

King Jehoahaz is evil *31 Jehoahaz was twenty-three years old when he became king, and he reigned for three months in Jerusalem. His mother's name was Hamutal daughter of Jeremiah of Libnah. 32 He did what was evil in the eyes of HASHEM, like everything* **Pharaoh Neco replaces him and despoils Israel** *that his forefathers had done. 33 Pharaoh Neco imprisoned him at Riblah in the land of Hamath, [to prevent him] from reigning in Jerusalem, and he levied a fine upon the land — a hundred talents of silver and a talent of gold. 34 Pharaoh Neco then crowned Eliakim son of Josiah in place of his father Josiah, and changed his name to Jehoiakim. * [Pharaoh] took Jehoahaz and returned to Egypt; and* **JEHOIAKIM, KING OF JUDAH 23:34-24:6** *[Jehoahaz] died there. 35 Jehoiakim delivered the silver and the gold to Pharaoh; but he assessed upon the populace to pay the money that Phararoh had demanded; he imposed upon the populace, each man according to his means, the silver and gold [that he had] to give to Pharaoh Neco.*

36 Jehoiakim was twenty-five years old when he became king, and he reigned for eleven years in Jerusalem. His mother's name was Zebudah daughter of Pedaiah of Rumah. 37 He did what was evil in the eyes of HASHEM, like everything that his forefathers had done.

24

Nebuchadnezzar becomes God's agent of punishment

(See Appendix A, timeline 5)

1 In his days Nebuchadnezzar, king of Babylonia, invaded; Jehoiakim became a vassal to him for three years, but then he reneged and rebelled against him. 2 HASHEM incited against him troops of Chaldeans, troops of Aram, troops of Moab and troops of the Children of Ammon, and sent them against Judah* to annihilate it, in accordance with the word of HASHEM that He had spoken through His servants the prophets. 3 Indeed, the [decree] was issued against Judah by the word of HASHEM, to remove them from His presence, for the sins of Manasseh, for everything that he had done, 4 and also [for] the innocent blood that he had shed; he had filled Jerusalem with innocent blood, and HASHEM did not want to forgive.

5 The rest of the deeds of Jehoiakim and all that he did — behold, they are recorded in the Book of Chronicles of the Kings of Judah. * 6 Jehoiakim lay

---

Pharaoh was master of the country.
24:2. These troops were mercenaries, sent by Nebuchadnezzar to punish the Judeans for their disloyalty (*Radak*).

When this tactic proved inadequate, the Babylonians mounted a full-scale invasion (v. 10).
24:5. See *II Chronicles 36:5-8.*

עִם־אֲבֹתָיו וַיִּמְלֹךְ יְהוֹיָכִין בְּנוֹ תַּחְתָּיו: וְלֹא־הֹסִיף עוֹד מֶלֶךְ מִצְרַיִם ז
לָצֵאת מֵאַרְצוֹ כִּי־לָקַח מֶלֶךְ בָּבֶל מִנַּחַל מִצְרַיִם עַד־נְהַר־פְּרָת כֹּל אֲשֶׁר
הָיְתָה לְמֶלֶךְ מִצְרָיִם: בֶּן־שְׁמֹנֶה עֶשְׂרֵה שָׁנָה יְהוֹיָכִין ח
בְּמָלְכוֹ וּשְׁלֹשָׁה חֳדָשִׁים מָלַךְ בִּירוּשָׁלָ͏ִם וְשֵׁם אִמּוֹ נְחֻשְׁתָּא בַת־אֶלְנָתָן
מִירוּשָׁלָ͏ִם: וַיַּעַשׂ הָרַע בְּעֵינֵי יְהוָה כְּכֹל אֲשֶׁר־עָשָׂה אָבִיו: בָּעֵת הַהִיא ט
°עלה [עָלוּ ק] עַבְדֵי נְבֻכַדְנֶאצַּר מֶלֶךְ־בָּבֶל יְרוּשָׁלָ͏ִם וַתָּבֹא הָעִיר
בַּמָּצוֹר: וַיָּבֹא נְבוּכַדְנֶאצַּר מֶלֶךְ־בָּבֶל עַל־הָעִיר וַעֲבָדָיו צָרִים עָלֶיהָ: וַיֵּצֵא יא-יב
יְהוֹיָכִין מֶלֶךְ־יְהוּדָה עַל־מֶלֶךְ בָּבֶל הוּא וְאִמּוֹ וַעֲבָדָיו וְשָׂרָיו וְסָרִיסָיו
וַיִּקַּח אֹתוֹ מֶלֶךְ בָּבֶל בִּשְׁנַת שְׁמֹנֶה לְמָלְכוֹ: וַיּוֹצֵא מִשָּׁם אֶת־כָּל־אוֹצְרוֹת יג
בֵּית יְהוָה וְאוֹצְרוֹת בֵּית הַמֶּלֶךְ וַיְקַצֵּץ אֶת־כָּל־כְּלֵי הַזָּהָב אֲשֶׁר עָשָׂה
שְׁלֹמֹה מֶלֶךְ־יִשְׂרָאֵל בְּהֵיכַל יְהוָה כַּאֲשֶׁר דִּבֶּר יְהוָה: וְהִגְלָה אֶת־כָּל־ יד
יְרוּשָׁלַ͏ִם וְאֶת־כָּל־הַשָּׂרִים וְאֵת ׀ כָּל־גִּבּוֹרֵי הַחַיִל °עשרה [עֲשֶׂרֶת ק]
אֲלָפִים גּוֹלֶה וְכָל־הֶחָרָשׁ וְהַמַּסְגֵּר לֹא נִשְׁאַר זוּלַת דַּלַּת עַם־הָאָרֶץ:
וַיֶּגֶל אֶת־יְהוֹיָכִין בָּבֶלָה וְאֶת־אֵם־הַמֶּלֶךְ וְאֶת־נְשֵׁי הַמֶּלֶךְ וְאֶת־סָרִיסָיו טו
°ואת [וְאֵת ק] °אולי [אֵילֵי ק] הָאָרֶץ הוֹלִיךְ גּוֹלָה מִירוּשָׁלַ͏ִם בָּבֶלָה: וְאֵת כָּל־ טז
אַנְשֵׁי הַחַיִל שִׁבְעַת אֲלָפִים וְהֶחָרָשׁ וְהַמַּסְגֵּר אֶלֶף הַכֹּל גִּבּוֹרִים עֹשֵׂי
מִלְחָמָה וַיְבִיאֵם מֶלֶךְ־בָּבֶל גּוֹלָה בָּבֶלָה: וַיַּמְלֵךְ מֶלֶךְ־בָּבֶל אֶת־מַתַּנְיָה יז
דֹדוֹ תַּחְתָּיו וַיַּסֵּב אֶת־שְׁמוֹ צִדְקִיָּהוּ:   בֶּן־עֶשְׂרִים וְאַחַת שָׁנָה יח
צִדְקִיָּהוּ בְמָלְכוֹ וְאַחַת עֶשְׂרֵה שָׁנָה מָלַךְ בִּירוּשָׁלָ͏ִם וְשֵׁם אִמּוֹ °חמיטל
[חֲמוּטַל ק] בַּת־יִרְמְיָהוּ מִלִּבְנָה: וַיַּעַשׂ הָרַע בְּעֵינֵי יְהוָה כְּכֹל אֲשֶׁר־ יט
עָשָׂה יְהוֹיָקִים: כִּי ׀ עַל־אַף יְהוָה הָיְתָה בִירוּשָׁלַ͏ִם וּבִיהוּדָה עַד־הִשְׁלִכוֹ כ
אֹתָם מֵעַל פָּנָיו וַיִּמְרֹד צִדְקִיָּהוּ בְּמֶלֶךְ בָּבֶל: וַיְהִי בִשְׁנַת כה א
הַתְּשִׁיעִית לְמָלְכוֹ בַּחֹדֶשׁ הָעֲשִׂירִי בֶּעָשׂוֹר לַחֹדֶשׁ בָּא נְבֻכַדְנֶאצַּר מֶלֶךְ־
בָּבֶל הוּא וְכָל־חֵילוֹ עַל־יְרוּשָׁלַ͏ִם וַיִּחַן עָלֶיהָ וַיִּבְנוּ עָלֶיהָ דָּיֵק סָבִיב: וַתָּבֹא ב
הָעִיר בַּמָּצוֹר עַד עַשְׁתֵּי עֶשְׂרֵה שָׁנָה לַמֶּלֶךְ צִדְקִיָּהוּ: בְּתִשְׁעָה לַחֹדֶשׁ ג
וַיֶּחֱזַק הָרָעָב בָּעִיר וְלֹא־הָיָה לֶחֶם לְעַם הָאָרֶץ: וַתִּבָּקַע הָעִיר וְכָל־אַנְשֵׁי ד
הַמִּלְחָמָה ׀ הַלַּיְלָה דֶּרֶךְ שַׁעַר בֵּין הַחֹמֹתַיִם אֲשֶׁר עַל־גַּן הַמֶּלֶךְ וְכַשְׂדִּים
עַל־הָעִיר סָבִיב וַיֵּלֶךְ דֶּרֶךְ הָעֲרָבָה: וַיִּרְדְּפוּ חֵיל־כַּשְׂדִּים אַחַר הַמֶּלֶךְ ה
וַיַּשִּׂגוּ אֹתוֹ בְּעַרְבוֹת יְרֵחוֹ וְכָל־חֵילוֹ נָפֹצוּ מֵעָלָיו: וַיִּתְפְּשׂוּ אֶת־הַמֶּלֶךְ ו
וַיַּעֲלוּ אֹתוֹ אֶל־מֶלֶךְ בָּבֶל רִבְלָתָה וַיְדַבְּרוּ אִתּוֹ מִשְׁפָּט: וְאֶת־בְּנֵי צִדְקִיָּהוּ ז
שָׁחֲטוּ לְעֵינָיו וְאֶת־עֵינֵי צִדְקִיָּהוּ עִוֵּר וַיַּאַסְרֵהוּ בַנְחֻשְׁתַּיִם וַיְבִאֵהוּ

24:14. The Talmud explains "the artisans and the gate-keepers" as a metaphoric allusion to the Torah scholars and leaders.

24:17. Mattaniah was the brother of the former kings Jehoahaz and Jehoiakim; they were all sons of Josiah.

24:18-25:21. Aside from a few minor differences, this passage is identical to *Jeremiah 52:1-27*.

24:20. In his great wrath against the people, God incited Zedekiah to rebel against Nebuchadnezzar, in order that He might thereby bring an end to the with his forefathers, and his son Jehoiachin reigned in his place. [7] The king of Egypt no longer left his country, for the king of Babylonia had occupied from the Brook of Egypt to the Euphrates River, all [the land] that had belonged to the king of Egypt.

JEHOIACHIN, KING OF JUDAH
24:8-16
(See Appendix A, timeline 4)

[8] Jehoiachin was eighteen years old when he became king, and he reigned for three months in Jerusalem. His mother's name was Nehushta daughter of Elnathan of Jerusalem. [9] He did what was evil in the eyes of HASHEM, like everything that his father had done.

Nebuchadnezzar besieges and pillages Jerusalem

[10] At that time, the servants of Nebuchadnezzar king of Babylonia came up to wage war against Jerusalem, and the city came under siege. [11] Nebuchadnezzar king of Babylonia came upon the city while his servants were besieging it. [12] Jehoiachin, king of Judah, went out to the king of Babylonia — he, his mother, his servants, his ministers, and his officers — and the king of Babylonia took him [captive], in the eighth year of his reign. [13] He also removed from there all the treasures of the Temple of HASHEM and the treasures of the king's palace, and he dismantled all the golden articles that Solomon king of Israel had made in the

He exiles the king and the distinguished people

Sanctuary of HASHEM, as HASHEM had said. [14] He exiled all of Jerusalem — all the officers and all the men of war, ten thousand exiles, as well as all the artisans and the gatekeepers* — there was no one left except for the poorest of the common people. [15] He exiled Jehoiachin to Babylonia; and the king's mother, the king's wives, his officers, and the noblemen of the land he brought into exile from Jerusalem to Babylonia. [16] All of the men of war, seven thousand; and the artisans and the gatekeepers; one thousand, all of them mighty men, warriors — the king

ZEDEKIAH, KING OF JUDAH
24:17-25:7

of Babylonia brought them to exile, to Babylonia. [17] The king of Babylonia then crowned Mattaniah, [Jehoiachin's] uncle, * in his place, and changed his name to Zedekiah.

[18] Zedekiah* was twenty-one years old when he became king, and he reigned for eleven years in Jerusalem. His mother's name was Hamutal daughter of Jeremiah of Libnah. [19] He did what was evil in the eyes of HASHEM, like everything that Jehoiakim had done. [20] It was because the wrath of HASHEM was upon Jerusalem and Judah until He would cast them away from His presence that Zedekiah rebelled against the king of Babylonia. *

25
(See Appendix A, timeline 5)
The last battle

[1] It happened in the ninth year of [Zedekiah's] reign, in the tenth month, on the tenth of the month, * that Nebuchadnezzar king of Babylonia, he and his entire army, came [to wage war] against Jerusalem and encamped near it, and built a siege tower around it. [2] The city came under siege until the eleventh year of King Zedekiah. [3] On the ninth [day] of the [fourth] month the famine in the city became

Jerusalem is conquered, amid slaughter

critical; there was no food for the people of the land. [4] The city was breached, and all the men of war [fled] during the night, by way of the gate between the walls, which was near the king's garden, although the Chaldeans were upon the city all around; and [the king] went [into flight] by way of the Arabah. [5] The Chaldean army pursued the king and overtook him at the plains of Jericho, and his entire army dispersed from him. [6] They seized the king and brought him up to the king of Babylonia at Riblah, and they spoke [words of] judgment to him. [7] They slaughtered Zedekiah's sons before his eyes; [Nebuchadnezzar] blinded Zedekiah's eyes, then he bound him in leg-irons and brought him to Babylonia.

Jewish presence in the land.   **25:1.** The tenth of Teves. See *Zechariah* 8:19.

ח בָּבֶֽל: וּבַחֹ֤דֶשׁ הַֽחֲמִישִׁי֙ בְּשִׁבְעָ֣ה לַחֹ֔דֶשׁ הִ֚יא שְׁנַת֙ תְּשַֽׁע־עֶשְׂרֵ֣ה
שָׁנָ֔ה לַמֶּ֖לֶךְ נְבֻכַדְנֶאצַּ֣ר מֶֽלֶךְ־בָּבֶ֑ל בָּ֞א נְבוּזַרְאֲדָ֧ן רַב־טַבָּחִ֛ים עֶ֥בֶד מֶֽלֶךְ־
ט בָּבֶ֖ל יְרוּשָׁלָֽ͏ִם: וַיִּשְׂרֹ֥ף אֶת־בֵּֽית־יְהֹוָ֖ה וְאֶת־בֵּ֣ית הַמֶּ֑לֶךְ וְאֵ֨ת כָּל־בָּתֵּ֧י
י יְרֽוּשָׁלַ֛͏ִם וְאֶת־כָּל־בֵּ֥ית גָּד֖וֹל שָׂרַ֥ף בָּאֵֽשׁ: וְאֶת־חוֹמֹ֥ת יְרֽוּשָׁלַ֖͏ִם סָבִ֑יב נָ͏ֽתְצוּ֙
יא כָּל־חֵ֣יל כַּשְׂדִּ֔ים אֲשֶׁ֖ר רַב־טַבָּחִֽים: וְאֵת֩ יֶ֨תֶר הָעָ֜ם הַנִּשְׁאָרִ֣ים בָּעִ֗יר וְאֶת־
הַנֹּֽפְלִים֙ אֲשֶׁ֤ר נָֽפְלוּ֙ עַל־הַמֶּ֣לֶךְ בָּבֶ֔ל וְאֵ֖ת יֶ֣תֶר הֶֽהָמ֑וֹן הֶגְלָ֕ה נְבֽוּזַרְאֲדָ֖ן
יב־יג רַב־טַבָּחִֽים: וּמִדַּלַּ֣ת הָאָ֔רֶץ הִשְׁאִ֖יר רַב־טַבָּחִ֑ים לְכֹֽרְמִ֖ים וּלְיֹֽגְבִֽים: וְאֶת־
עַמּוּדֵ֨י הַנְּחֹ֜שֶׁת אֲשֶׁ֣ר בֵּֽית־יְהֹוָ֗ה וְֽאֶת־הַמְּכֹנ֞וֹת וְאֶת־יָ֧ם הַנְּחֹ֛שֶׁת אֲשֶׁ֥ר
יד בְּבֵֽית־יְהֹוָ֖ה שִׁבְּר֣וּ כַשְׂדִּ֑ים וַיִּשְׂא֥וּ אֶת־נְחֻשְׁתָּ֖ם בָּבֶֽלָה: וְאֶת־הַסִּירֹ֨ת
וְאֶת־הַיָּעִ֜ים וְאֶת־הַֽמְזַמְּר֣וֹת וְאֶת־הַכַּפּ֗וֹת וְאֵ֨ת כָּל־כְּלֵ֧י הַנְּחֹ֛שֶׁת אֲשֶׁ֥ר
טו יְשָֽׁרְתוּ־בָ֖ם לָקָֽחוּ: וְאֶת־הַמַּחְתּ֗וֹת וְאֶת־הַמִּזְרָקוֹת֙ אֲשֶׁ֤ר זָהָב֙ זָהָ֔ב וַֽאֲשֶׁר־
טז כֶּ֥סֶף כֶּ֖סֶף לָקַ֥ח רַב־טַבָּחִֽים: הָעַמּוּדִ֣ים ׀ שְׁנַ֗יִם הַיָּ֤ם הָֽאֶחָד֙ וְהַמְּכֹנ֔וֹת
אֲשֶׁר־עָשָׂ֥ה שְׁלֹמֹ֖ה לְבֵ֣ית יְהֹוָ֑ה לֹֽא־הָיָ֣ה מִשְׁקָ֔ל לִנְחֹ֖שֶׁת כָּל־הַכֵּלִ֥ים
יז הָאֵֽלֶּה: שְׁמֹנֶ֨ה עֶשְׂרֵ֜ה אַמָּ֗ה קוֹמַת֮ ׀ הָֽעַמּ֣וּד הָֽאֶחָד֒ וְכֹתֶ֨רֶת עָלָ֥יו ׀ נְחֹ֘שֶׁת֮
וְקוֹמַ֣ת הַכֹּתֶ֣רֶת שָׁלֹ֣שׁ °אַמָּה֒ [°אַמּ֒וֹת ק] וּשְׂבָכָ֨ה וְרִמֹּנִ֧ים עַל־הַכֹּתֶ֛רֶת
יח סָבִ֖יב הַכֹּ֣ל נְחֹ֑שֶׁת וְכָאֵ֛לֶּה לַֽעַמּ֥וּד הַשֵּׁנִ֖י עַל־הַשְּׂבָכָֽה: וַיִּקַּ֣ח רַב־טַבָּחִ֗ים
אֶת־שְׂרָיָה֙ כֹּהֵ֣ן הָרֹ֔אשׁ וְאֶת־צְפַנְיָ֖הוּ כֹּהֵ֣ן מִשְׁנֶ֑ה וְאֶת־שְׁלֹ֖שֶׁת שֹׁמְרֵ֥י
יט הַסַּֽף: וּמִן־הָעִ֡יר לָקַח֩ סָרִ֨יס אֶחָ֜ד אֲ‍ֽשֶׁר־ה֥וּא פָקִ֣יד ׀ עַל־אַנְשֵׁ֣י הַמִּלְחָמָ֗ה
וַֽחֲמִשָּׁ֨ה אֲנָשִׁ֜ים מֵֽרֹאֵ֤י פְנֵֽי־הַמֶּ֨לֶךְ֙ אֲשֶׁ֣ר נִמְצְא֣וּ בָעִ֔יר וְ֠אֵ֠ת הַסֹּפֵ֞ר שַׂ֤ר
הַצָּבָא֙ הַמַּצְבִּ֣א אֶת־עַ֣ם הָאָ֔רֶץ וְשִׁשִּׁ֥ים אִישׁ֙ מֵעַ֣ם הָאָ֔רֶץ הַֽנִּמְצְאִ֖ים
כ בָּעִֽיר: וַיִּקַּ֣ח אֹתָ֔ם נְבֽוּזַרְאֲדָ֖ן רַב־טַבָּחִ֑ים וַיֹּ֧לֶךְ אֹתָ֛ם עַל־מֶ֥לֶךְ בָּבֶ֖ל
כא רִבְלָֽתָה: וַיַּ֣ךְ אֹתָם֩ מֶ֨לֶךְ בָּבֶ֧ל וַיְמִיתֵ֛ם בְּרִבְלָ֖ה בְּאֶ֣רֶץ חֲמָ֑ת וַיִּ֥גֶל יְהוּדָ֖ה
כב מֵעַ֥ל אַדְמָתֽוֹ: וְהָעָ֗ם הַנִּשְׁאָר֙ בְּאֶ֣רֶץ יְהוּדָ֔ה אֲשֶׁ֣ר הִשְׁאִ֔יר נְבֽוּכַדְנֶאצַּ֖ר
כג מֶ֣לֶךְ בָּבֶ֑ל וַיַּפְקֵ֣ד עֲלֵיהֶ֔ם אֶת־גְּדַלְיָ֖הוּ בֶּן־אֲחִיקָ֥ם בֶּן־שָׁפָֽן: וַיִּשְׁמְע֣וּ כָל־
שָׂרֵ֣י הַֽחֲיָלִ֡ים הֵ֣מָּה וְהָֽאֲנָשִׁים֩ כִּֽי־הִפְקִ֨יד מֶֽלֶךְ־בָּבֶ֜ל אֶת־גְּדַלְיָ֗הוּ וַיָּבֹ֣אוּ
אֶל־גְּדַלְיָה֮ הַמִּצְפָּה֒ וְיִשְׁמָעֵ֣אל בֶּן־נְתַנְיָ֗ה וְיֽוֹחָנָ֤ן בֶּן־קָרֵ֨חַ֙ וּשְׂרָיָ֣ה בֶן־
כד תַּנְחֻ֜מֶת הַנְּטֹֽפָתִ֗י וְיַֽאֲזַנְיָ֨הוּ֙ בֶּן־הַמַּ֣עֲכָתִ֔י הֵ֖מָּה וְאַנְשֵׁיהֶֽם: וַיִּשָּׁבַ֨ע לָהֶ֤ם
גְּדַלְיָ֨הוּ֙ וּלְאַנְשֵׁיהֶ֔ם וַיֹּ֣אמֶר לָהֶ֗ם אַל־תִּֽירְא֖וּ מֵֽעַבְדֵ֣י הַכַּשְׂדִּ֑ים שְׁב֣וּ בָאָ֗רֶץ
כה וְעִבְד֛וּ אֶת־מֶ֥לֶךְ בָּבֶ֖ל וְיִטַ֥ב לָכֶֽם: וַיְהִ֣י ׀ בַּחֹ֣דֶשׁ הַשְּׁבִיעִ֗י בָּ֣א
יִשְׁמָעֵ֣אל בֶּן־נְ֠תַנְיָ֠ה בֶּן־אֱלִ֨ישָׁמָ֜ע מִזֶּ֣רַע הַמְּלוּכָ֗ה וַֽעֲשָׂרָ֤ה אֲנָשִׁים֙ אִתּ֔וֹ וַיַּכּ֣וּ
אֶת־גְּדַלְיָ֖הוּ וַיָּמֹ֑ת וְאֶת־הַיְּהוּדִים֙ וְאֶת־הַכַּשְׂדִּ֔ים אֲשֶׁ֥ר הָי֛וּ אִתּ֖וֹ בַּמִּצְפָּֽה:
כו וַיָּקֻ֨מוּ כָל־הָעָ֜ם מִקָּטֹ֤ן וְעַד־גָּדוֹל֙ וְשָׂרֵ֣י הַֽחֲיָלִ֔ים וַיָּבֹ֖אוּ מִצְרָ֑יִם כִּ֥י יָ͏ֽרְא֖וּ

25:8. Nebuzaradan arrived on the seventh of Av (the fifth month), and set the Temple afire on the ninth of the month, Tishah B'Av (cf. *Jeremiah* 52:12).

25:13-17. These parts of the Temple are described in

I Kings, Ch. 7. A more detailed description of the pillars appears in *Jeremiah* 52:21-23.

25:22. Gedaliah was to be the governor of the remnant of Judah, completely subservient to the Babylonian con-

The Temple is burned and the people exiled

8 In the fifth month, on the seventh of the month, * which was the nineteenth year of Nebuchadnezzar king of Babylonia, Nebuzaradan, the chief executioner, servant of the king of Babylonia, came to Jerusalem. 9 He burned the Temple of HASHEM, the king's palace and all the buildings of Jerusalem; and every great house he burned in fire. 10 And the walls of Jerusalem all around, the entire Chaldean army that was with the chief executioner smashed. 11 The remainder of the people who were left in the city and the defectors who had surrendered to the king of Babylonia, and the rest of the masses, Nebuzaradan the chief executioner sent into exile. 12 But some of the poor people of the land the chief executioner left to be workers in vineyards and in fields.

The remnant destroyed

13 The copper pillars of the Temple of HASHEM, and the laver-stands and the copper sea* that were in the Temple of HASHEM, the Chaldeans shattered and carried off their copper to Babylonia. 14 The pots, the shovels, the musical instruments, the spoons and all the copper utensils with which [the Kohanim] served, they took away. 15 The pans and the bowls, whether of gold or of silver, the chief executioner took away. 16 The two pillars, the one sea, and the laver-stands that Solomon had made for the Temple of HASHEM — there was no weight [with which to measure] the copper of all these items; 17 eighteen cubits the height of the one pillar; [there was] a copper capital upon it, the height of the capital [extended] three cubits [above the pillar]; and [there were] a netting and pomegranate figures upon the capital all around, all of copper; the second pillar had the same [ornaments] upon the netting.

Arrest, execution, exile

18 The chief executioner took Seraiah the chief Kohen and Zephaniah the deputy Kohen and the three gatekeepers. 19 From the city he took one officer who was in charge of the men of war; five men from those [advisors] who see the king's face, who were found in the city; the secretary of the general of the army, who would marshal the common people for war; and sixty men of the common people who were found in the city. 20 Nebuzaradan, the chief executioner, took them and brought them to the king of Babylonia at Riblah, 21 and the king of Babylonia struck them down and killed them at Riblah, in the land of Hamath. And Judah was exiled from its land.

Gedaliah, governor of Judah

22 As for the people who remained in the land of Judah, whom Nebuchadnezzar king of Babylonia allowed to remain — he appointed over them Gedaliah son of Ahikam son of Shaphan. * 23 All the officers of the army [who were in hiding], they and their men, heard that the king of Babylonia had appointed Gedaliah, and they came to Gedaliah at Mizpah, along with Ishmael son of Nethaniah, Johanan son of Kareah, Seraiah son of Tanhumeth of Netophah and Jaazaniah son of the Maacathite, they and their men. 24 Gedaliah swore to them and to their men and said to them, "Do not fear the servants of the Chaldeans; settle in the land and serve the king of Babylonia and all will be well for you."

Gedaliah, the last hope, assassinated

25 And it was in the seventh month: There came Ishmael son of Nethaniah son of Elishama, [who was] of the royal family, and with him ten men; they struck down Gedaliah, and he died, as well as the Jews and the Chaldeans who were with him at Mizpah. 26 All the people, from small to great, as well as the army officers, arose and came to Egypt, for they feared the Chaldeans. *

---

querors. A fuller account of this episode is found in *Jeremiah*, Chs. 40-43.
25:26. The Jewish remnant fled the land out of fear that they would be punished for the slaughter carried out by

Ishmael. The day of the assassination was designated as a national fast day, the Fast of Gedaliah. Ishmael's crime was the final step of the Destruction, since it caused the land to be denuded of its remaining children.

מִפְּנֵי כַשְׂדִּים: כז וַיְהִי בִשְׁלֹשִׁים וָשֶׁבַע שָׁנָה לְגָלוּת יְהוֹיָכִין מֶלֶךְ־יְהוּדָה בִּשְׁנֵים עָשָׂר חֹדֶשׁ בְּעֶשְׂרִים וְשִׁבְעָה לַחֹדֶשׁ נָשָׂא אֱוִיל מְרֹדַךְ מֶלֶךְ בָּבֶל בִּשְׁנַת מָלְכוֹ אֶת־רֹאשׁ יְהוֹיָכִין מֶלֶךְ־יְהוּדָה מִבֵּית כֶּלֶא: כח וַיְדַבֵּר אִתּוֹ טֹבוֹת וַיִּתֵּן אֶת־כִּסְאוֹ מֵעַל כִּסֵּא הַמְּלָכִים אֲשֶׁר אִתּוֹ בְּבָבֶל: כט וְשִׁנָּא אֵת בִּגְדֵי כִלְאוֹ וְאָכַל לֶחֶם תָּמִיד לְפָנָיו כָּל־יְמֵי חַיָּיו: ל וַאֲרֻחָתוֹ אֲרֻחַת תָּמִיד נִתְּנָה־לּוֹ מֵאֵת הַמֶּלֶךְ דְּבַר־יוֹם בְּיוֹמוֹ כֹּל יְמֵי חַיָּו:

25:27-30. Aside from a few minor differences, this passage is identical to *Jeremiah* 52:31-34.

25:27. Evil-merodach was Nebuchadnezzar's son and successor. He released Jehoiachin, who had been king before Zedekiah, and whom Nebuchadnezzar had imprisoned when he conquered Jerusalem (24:12-16).

Scant comfort for the deposed King Jehoiachin

²⁷ * *It happened in the thirty-seventh year of the exile of Jehoiachin king of Judah, in the twelfth month, on the twenty-seventh of the month: Evil-merodach, the king of Babylonia, in the year of his coronation, elevated Jehoiachin* king of Judah [and released him] from prison.* ²⁸ *He spoke kindly with him, and set his seat above the seats of the [other] kings who were with him in Babylonia.* ²⁹ *He changed [from] his prison clothing, and he ate [his] meal before him regularly, all the days of his life.* ³⁰ *His allowance was a regular allowance given to him from the king, each day's portion on its day, all the days of his life.*

Seat
comfort-
for the
deposed
king
Jehoiachin

Isaiah ישעיה

*I*saiah was a member of the Judean aristocracy and his long career
as a prophet spanned eighty-six years (619-533 B.C.E.), a period
during which he uttered some of the most stirring and lyrical
prophecies in all of Scripture. Far more Haftaros are taken from
the Book of Isaiah than from any other Book. Isaiah lashes out at the
wicked among his people and warns them of dire destruction, but he
also consoles and comforts. Interestingly, this Book is the source both
of the chilling "Vision of Isaiah" that is read on the Sabbath before the
Ninth of Av and of the seven prophecies of consolation that follow it.
He foretold the exile that took place during his lifetime, as the powerful
Assyrian army under Sennacherib conquered the Northern Kingdom
and scattered its people around the Assyrian kingdom, so that they
would lose their Jewish identity. Then the seemingly invincible
Assyrian ruler moved against Judah, but Isaiah prophesied that this
time the army would be wiped out.

Isaiah's contemporary, Hosea, prophesied to the Northern Kingdom
at the time Isaiah prophesied to the Kingdom of Judah. Like the other
prophets of that era, he railed against idolatry — indeed, as soon as the
notorious idolater, King Manasseh, assumed the throne, he had Isaiah
murdered. The prophet stressed the holiness of the people and the
sanctity of the Temple service. He condemned hypocrisy and the attitude
that habitually performed commandments were satisfactory, and taught
that a Judaism empty of sincerity and striving is not Judaism. Could
anyone think that lip service without content would satisfy God? It
is ironic that the secular scholars praise Isaiah for his cadences and
lyricism. People speak of Isaiah as a "poet" — he, the prophet who so
condemned empty talk and insincere service! He also offered hope and
encouragement to the downtrodden, the forlorn, and the childless.

His prophecies have yet to be fulfilled; they clearly await the final
Redemption, when the earth will be filled with the purity and holiness
he demanded. This could have happened in his day. It could have
happened when the Second Temple was built. It could have happened
at any time, had people heeded his message and been worthy of its
realization. But it did not, because they did not. Not yet. But because we
know, as he said in his final stirring declaration, that no word of God
goes back unless it has accomplished what He desired, we can read
Isaiah's words as harbingers of a future better than anyone has ever
known. And this has always been Israel's consolation, no matter how
dreadful the circumstances.

HAFTARAS
DEVARIM
1:1-27

א א חֲזוֹן יְשַׁעְיָהוּ בֶן־אָמוֹץ אֲשֶׁר חָזָה עַל־יְהוּדָה וִירוּשָׁלֶָם בִּימֵי עֻזִּיָּהוּ
ב יוֹתָם אָחָז יְחִזְקִיָּהוּ מַלְכֵי יְהוּדָה: שִׁמְעוּ שָׁמַיִם וְהַאֲזִינִי אֶרֶץ כִּי יְהוָה
ג דִּבֵּר בָּנִים גִּדַּלְתִּי וְרוֹמַמְתִּי וְהֵם פָּשְׁעוּ בִי: יָדַע שׁוֹר קֹנֵהוּ וַחֲמוֹר אֵבוּס
ד בְּעָלָיו יִשְׂרָאֵל לֹא יָדַע עַמִּי לֹא הִתְבּוֹנָן: הוֹי ׀ גּוֹי חֹטֵא עַם כֶּבֶד
עָוֹן זֶרַע מְרֵעִים בָּנִים מַשְׁחִיתִים עָזְבוּ אֶת־יְהוָה נִאֲצוּ אֶת־קְדוֹשׁ
ה יִשְׂרָאֵל נָזֹרוּ אָחוֹר: עַל מֶה תֻכּוּ עוֹד תּוֹסִיפוּ סָרָה כָּל־רֹאשׁ לָחֳלִי
ו וְכָל־לֵבָב דַּוָּי: מִכַּף־רֶגֶל וְעַד־רֹאשׁ אֵין־בּוֹ מְתֹם פֶּצַע וְחַבּוּרָה וּמַכָּה
ז טְרִיָּה לֹא־זֹרוּ וְלֹא חֻבָּשׁוּ וְלֹא רֻכְּכָה בַּשָּׁמֶן: אַרְצְכֶם שְׁמָמָה עָרֵיכֶם
שְׂרֻפוֹת אֵשׁ אַדְמַתְכֶם לְנֶגְדְּכֶם זָרִים אֹכְלִים אֹתָהּ וּשְׁמָמָה כְּמַהְפֵּכַת
ח זָרִים: וְנוֹתְרָה בַת־צִיּוֹן כְּסֻכָּה בְכָרֶם כִּמְלוּנָה בְמִקְשָׁה כְּעִיר נְצוּרָה:
ט לוּלֵי יְהוָה צְבָאוֹת הוֹתִיר לָנוּ שָׂרִיד כִּמְעָט כִּסְדֹם הָיִינוּ לַעֲמֹרָה
י דָּמִינוּ: שִׁמְעוּ דְבַר־יְהוָה קְצִינֵי סְדֹם הַאֲזִינוּ תּוֹרַת
יא אֱלֹהֵינוּ עַם עֲמֹרָה: לָמָּה־לִּי רֹב־זִבְחֵיכֶם יֹאמַר יְהוָה שָׂבַעְתִּי עֹלוֹת
אֵילִים וְחֵלֶב מְרִיאִים וְדַם פָּרִים וּכְבָשִׂים וְעַתּוּדִים לֹא חָפָצְתִּי:
יב־יג כִּי תָבֹאוּ לֵרָאוֹת פָּנָי מִי־בִקֵּשׁ זֹאת מִיֶּדְכֶם רְמֹס חֲצֵרָי: לֹא תוֹסִיפוּ
הָבִיא מִנְחַת־שָׁוְא קְטֹרֶת תּוֹעֵבָה הִיא לִי חֹדֶשׁ וְשַׁבָּת קְרֹא מִקְרָא
יד לֹא־אוּכַל אָוֶן וַעֲצָרָה: חָדְשֵׁיכֶם וּמוֹעֲדֵיכֶם שָׂנְאָה נַפְשִׁי הָיוּ עָלַי
טו לָטֹרַח נִלְאֵיתִי נְשֹׂא: וּבְפָרִשְׂכֶם כַּפֵּיכֶם אַעְלִים עֵינַי מִכֶּם גַּם כִּי־תַרְבּוּ
טז תְפִלָּה אֵינֶנִּי שֹׁמֵעַ יְדֵיכֶם דָּמִים מָלֵאוּ: רַחֲצוּ הִזַּכּוּ הָסִירוּ רֹעַ מַעַלְלֵיכֶם
יז מִנֶּגֶד עֵינָי חִדְלוּ הָרֵעַ: לִמְדוּ הֵיטֵב דִּרְשׁוּ מִשְׁפָּט אַשְּׁרוּ חָמוֹץ שִׁפְטוּ
יח יָתוֹם רִיבוּ אַלְמָנָה: לְכוּ־נָא וְנִוָּכְחָה יֹאמַר יְהוָה
אִם־יִהְיוּ חֲטָאֵיכֶם כַּשָּׁנִים כַּשֶּׁלֶג יַלְבִּינוּ אִם־יַאְדִּימוּ כַתּוֹלָע כַּצֶּמֶר
יט־כ יִהְיוּ: אִם־תֹּאבוּ וּשְׁמַעְתֶּם טוּב הָאָרֶץ תֹּאכֵלוּ: וְאִם־תְּמָאֲנוּ וּמְרִיתֶם
כא חֶרֶב תְּאֻכְּלוּ כִּי פִּי יְהוָה דִּבֵּר: אֵיכָה הָיְתָה
לְזוֹנָה קִרְיָה נֶאֱמָנָה מְלֵאֲתִי מִשְׁפָּט צֶדֶק יָלִין בָּהּ וְעַתָּה מְרַצְּחִים:
כב־כג כַּסְפֵּךְ הָיָה לְסִיגִים סָבְאֵךְ מָהוּל בַּמָּיִם: שָׂרַיִךְ סוֹרְרִים וְחַבְרֵי גַּנָּבִים כֻּלּוֹ
אֹהֵב שֹׁחַד וְרֹדֵף שַׁלְמֹנִים יָתוֹם לֹא יִשְׁפֹּטוּ וְרִיב אַלְמָנָה לֹא־יָבוֹא
כד אֲלֵיהֶם: לָכֵן נְאֻם הָאָדוֹן יְהוָה צְבָאוֹת אֲבִיר יִשְׂרָאֵל הוֹי
כה אֶנָּחֵם מִצָּרַי וְאִנָּקְמָה מֵאוֹיְבָי: וְאָשִׁיבָה יָדִי עָלַיִךְ וְאֶצְרֹף כַּבֹּר סִיגָיִךְ

1:1. Uzziah (also called Azariah) reigned fifty-two years, Jotham and Ahaz each reigned sixteen years, and Hezekiah reigned twenty-nine years. Their histories are recorded in *II Kings* Chs. 15,16,18 and *II Chronicles* Chs. 26-32.

1:5. These harsh punishments should have made you realize that you should cease your evildoing! (*Rashi*).

1:8. Those appointed to guard the crop until it is gathered abandon their temporary shelters in the field as soon as the growing season is over. Similarly, the tents of the attacking army are deserted when the siege is lifted.

1:18. Let us honestly discuss and decide who wronged whom, and you will admit that you were at fault. That will lead to repentance, and I will forgive your sins ... (*Radak*).

1

(See Appendix A, timeline 4)

A rebellious people . . .

. . . and their chastisement

¹ The vision of Isaiah son of Amoz, which he saw concerning Judah and Jerusalem, in the days of Uzziah, Jotham, Ahaz, and Hezekiah, kings of Judah: * ² Hear, O heavens, and give ear, O earth, for HASHEM has spoken: "Children have I raised and exalted, but they have rebelled against Me. ³ An ox knows his owner, and a donkey his master's trough; but Israel does not know, My people does not comprehend."

⁴ Woe! [They are] a sinful nation, a people weighed down by iniquity, evil offspring, destructive children! They have forsaken HASHEM; they have angered the Holy One of Israel, and have turned their back [to Him]. ⁵ For what have you been smitten, since you continue to act perversely? Each head [is smitten] with sickness; each heart [with] infirmity. * ⁶ From the sole of the foot to the head, nothing in him is whole; [only] injury, bruise, and festering wound: They have not been treated and they have not been bandaged, and [the wound] has not been softened with oil. ⁷ Your country is desolate; your cities are burned with fire; as for your land — strangers consume its [yield] in your presence; it is desolate as if overturned by foreigners. ⁸ The daughter of Zion is left like a booth in a vineyard, like a shed in a field of gourds, like a city besieged. * ⁹ Had not HASHEM, Master of Legions, left us a trace of a remnant, we would have been like Sodom; we would have resembled Gomorrah!

¹⁰ Hear the word of HASHEM, O chiefs of Sodom; give ear to the teaching of our God, O people of Gomorrah:

Worthless offerings

¹¹ Why do I need your numerous sacrifices? says HASHEM. I am sated with elevation-offerings of rams and the fat of fatlings; the blood of bulls, sheep and goats I do not desire. ¹² When you come to appear before Me, who sought this from your hand, to trample My courtyards? ¹³ Bring your worthless meal-offering no longer, it is incense of abomination to Me. [As for] the New Moon and Sabbath, and your calling of convocations, I cannot abide mendacity with solemn assembly. ¹⁴ My soul detests your New Moons and your appointed times; they have become a burden upon Me; I am weary of bearing [them]. ¹⁵ When you spread your hands [in prayer], I will hide My eyes from you; even if you were to intensify your prayer, I will not listen; your hands are replete with blood. ¹⁶ Wash yourselves, purify yourselves, remove the evil of your deeds from before My eyes; cease doing evil. ¹⁷ Learn to do good, seek justice, vindicate the victim, render justice to the orphan, take up the grievance of the widow.

Repent!

¹⁸ Come, now, let us reason together, says HASHEM. * If your sins are like scarlet they will become white as snow; if they have become red as crimson, they will become [white] as wool. ¹⁹ If you are willing and obey, you will eat the goodness of the land. ²⁰ But if you refuse and rebel, you will be devoured by the sword — for the mouth of HASHEM has spoken.

²¹ How the faithful city has become a harlot! — she had been full of justice, righteousness lodged in her, but now murderers! ²² Your silver has become dross, your heady wine diluted with water. ²³ Your princes are rebellious and associates of thieves; each of them loves bribery and pursues payments. They do not render justice to the orphan; the grievance of the widow does not come to them.

Divine punishment . . .

²⁴ Therefore — the word of the Lord, HASHEM, Master of Legions, Mighty One of Israel:

Oh, I shall be relieved of My adversaries, and I shall avenge Myself of My enemies! ²⁵ I will turn My hand against you, until I refine your dross as with lye

כו וְאָשִׁיבָה כָּל־בְּדִילָיִךְ: וְאָשִׁיבָה שֹׁפְטַיִךְ כְּבָרִאשֹׁנָה וְיֹעֲצַיִךְ כְּבַתְּחִלָּה

כז אַחֲרֵי־כֵן יִקָּרֵא לָךְ עִיר הַצֶּדֶק קִרְיָה נֶאֱמָנָה: צִיּוֹן בְּמִשְׁפָּט תִּפָּדֶה וְשָׁבֶיהָ

כח-כט בִּצְדָקָה: ◄ וְשֶׁבֶר פֹּשְׁעִים וְחַטָּאִים יַחְדָּו וְעֹזְבֵי יְהוָה יִכְלוּ: כִּי יֵבֹשׁוּ

ל מֵאֵילִים אֲשֶׁר חֲמַדְתֶּם וְתַחְפְּרוּ מֵהַגַּנּוֹת אֲשֶׁר בְּחַרְתֶּם: כִּי תִהְיוּ כְּאֵלָה

לא נֹבֶלֶת עָלֶהָ וּכְגַנָּה אֲשֶׁר־מַיִם אֵין לָהּ: וְהָיָה הֶחָסֹן לִנְעֹרֶת וּפֹעֲלוֹ לְנִיצוֹץ

א וּבָעֲרוּ שְׁנֵיהֶם יַחְדָּו וְאֵין מְכַבֶּה: הַדָּבָר אֲשֶׁר חָזָה יְשַׁעְיָהוּ

ב ‖

ב בֶּן־אָמוֹץ עַל־יְהוּדָה וִירוּשָׁלָםִ: וְהָיָה | בְּאַחֲרִית הַיָּמִים נָכוֹן יִהְיֶה

הַר בֵּית־יְהוָה בְּרֹאשׁ הֶהָרִים וְנִשָּׂא מִגְּבָעוֹת וְנָהֲרוּ אֵלָיו כָּל־הַגּוֹיִם:

ג וְהָלְכוּ עַמִּים רַבִּים וְאָמְרוּ לְכוּ | וְנַעֲלֶה אֶל־הַר־יְהוָה אֶל־בֵּית אֱלֹהֵי

יַעֲקֹב וְיֹרֵנוּ מִדְּרָכָיו וְנֵלְכָה בְּאֹרְחֹתָיו כִּי מִצִּיּוֹן תֵּצֵא תוֹרָה וּדְבַר־

ד יְהוָה מִירוּשָׁלָםִ: וְשָׁפַט בֵּין הַגּוֹיִם וְהוֹכִיחַ לְעַמִּים רַבִּים וְכִתְּתוּ חַרְבוֹתָם

לְאִתִּים וַחֲנִיתוֹתֵיהֶם לְמַזְמֵרוֹת לֹא־יִשָּׂא גוֹי אֶל־גּוֹי חֶרֶב וְלֹא־

ה-ו יִלְמְדוּ עוֹד מִלְחָמָה: בֵּית יַעֲקֹב לְכוּ וְנֵלְכָה בְּאוֹר יְהוָה: כִּי

נָטַשְׁתָּה עַמְּךָ בֵּית יַעֲקֹב כִּי מָלְאוּ מִקֶּדֶם וְעֹנְנִים כַּפְּלִשְׁתִּים וּבְיַלְדֵי

ז נָכְרִים יַשְׂפִּיקוּ: וַתִּמָּלֵא אַרְצוֹ כֶּסֶף וְזָהָב וְאֵין קֵצֶה לְאֹצְרֹתָיו וַתִּמָּלֵא

ח אַרְצוֹ סוּסִים וְאֵין קֵצֶה לְמַרְכְּבֹתָיו: וַתִּמָּלֵא אַרְצוֹ אֱלִילִים לְמַעֲשֵׂה

ט יָדָיו יִשְׁתַּחֲווּ לַאֲשֶׁר עָשׂוּ אֶצְבְּעֹתָיו: וַיִּשַּׁח אָדָם וַיִּשְׁפַּל־אִישׁ

י וְאַל־תִּשָּׂא לָהֶם: בּוֹא בַצּוּר וְהִטָּמֵן בֶּעָפָר מִפְּנֵי פַּחַד יְהוָה וּמֵהֲדַר

יא גְּאֹנוֹ: עֵינֵי גַּבְהוּת אָדָם שָׁפֵל וְשַׁח רוּם אֲנָשִׁים וְנִשְׂגַּב יְהוָה לְבַדּוֹ בַּיּוֹם

יב הַהוּא: כִּי יוֹם לַיהוָה צְבָאוֹת עַל כָּל־גֵּאֶה וָרָם וְעַל כָּל־נִשָּׂא

יג וְשָׁפֵל: וְעַל כָּל־אַרְזֵי הַלְּבָנוֹן הָרָמִים וְהַנִּשָּׂאִים וְעַל כָּל־אַלּוֹנֵי הַבָּשָׁן:

יד-טו וְעַל כָּל־הֶהָרִים הָרָמִים וְעַל כָּל־הַגְּבָעוֹת הַנִּשָּׂאוֹת: וְעַל כָּל־מִגְדָּל גָּבֹהַּ

טז וְעַל כָּל־חוֹמָה בְצוּרָה: וְעַל כָּל־אֳנִיּוֹת תַּרְשִׁישׁ וְעַל כָּל־שְׂכִיּוֹת

יז הַחֶמְדָּה: וְשַׁח גַּבְהוּת הָאָדָם וְשָׁפֵל רוּם אֲנָשִׁים וְנִשְׂגַּב יְהוָה לְבַדּוֹ בַּיּוֹם

יח-יט הַהוּא: וְהָאֱלִילִים כָּלִיל יַחֲלֹף: וּבָאוּ בִּמְעָרוֹת צֻרִים וּבִמְחִלּוֹת עָפָר

כ מִפְּנֵי פַּחַד יְהוָה וּמֵהֲדַר גְּאוֹנוֹ בְּקוּמוֹ לַעֲרֹץ הָאָרֶץ: בַּיּוֹם הַהוּא יַשְׁלִיךְ

הָאָדָם אֵת אֱלִילֵי כַסְפּוֹ וְאֵת אֱלִילֵי זְהָבוֹ אֲשֶׁר עָשׂוּ־לוֹ לְהִשְׁתַּחֲוֹת

1:31. Flax is highly combustible, but its fire burns out very quickly. The idols and those who erect them will perish in an instant at the time of judgment.

2:4. "He" refers to the King Messiah, who will judge disputes between nations; they will accept his decisions, and no longer resort to war for settling disputes (*Radak*).

2:5. Either the prophet is interjecting his own message to Israel (*Radak*) or this verse is a continuation of the words of the "many peoples" of verse 3 (*Rashi*).

2:6-8. The prophet addresses God, saying that He forsook Israel because, after becoming wealthy, the people absorbed the sorcery of other nations, and traded the

ancient wisdom of the Torah for modern, fashionable notions, i.e., the children of foreign philosophies. This theme echoes *Deuteronomy* 32:14-18; see also *Hosea* 2:10 (*Radak*). Alternatively: "they content themselves with the children of foreigners" refers to the children of sinful intermarriage with non-Jewish women (*Rashi*).

2:9. When the nations will attempt to battle the King Messiah, they will eventually capitulate and realize the folly of their ways. Nevertheless, You will exact retribution from them for all the physical and spiritual havoc they wreaked upon Israel (*Radak*).

2:10-21. Isaiah warns the arrogant sinners, whom he

. . . and redemption

and I remove all your base metal. ²⁶ Then I will restore your judges as at first, and your counselors as at the beginning; after that you will be called 'City of Righteousness,' 'Faithful City.' ²⁷ Zion will be redeemed through justice, and those who return to her through righteousness; ²⁸ but calamity [awaits] rebels and sinners together, and those who forsake HASHEM will perish; ²⁹ for they will become ashamed of the idolatrous elms that you desired, and you will be embarrassed over the gardens that you chose. ³⁰ For you will be like an elm tree with withered leaves, and like a garden without water. ³¹ The mighty will be like flax and its maker like a spark; * and the two of them will burn together, with no one to extinguish it.

2

In Messianic times

¹ The prophecy that Isaiah son of Amoz saw, concerning Judah and Jerusalem: ² It will happen in the end of days: The mountain of the Temple of HASHEM will be firmly established as the head of the mountains, and it will be exalted above the hills, and all the nations will stream to it. ³ Many peoples will go and say, 'Come, let us go up to the Mountain of HASHEM, to the Temple of the God of Jacob, and He will teach us of His ways and we will walk in His paths.' For from Zion will the Torah come forth, and the word of HASHEM from Jerusalem. ⁴ He* will judge among the nations, and will settle the arguments of many peoples. They shall beat their swords into plowshares and their spears into pruning hooks; nation will not lift sword against nation and they will no longer study warfare;

⁵ O House of Jacob: * Come, let us walk by the light of HASHEM!

⁶ For You* have abandoned Your people, the House of Jacob, because they were filled with [sorceries] of the East and divinations, like the Philistines; and they content themselves with the children of foreigners. ⁷ Its land became full of silver and gold, with no end to its treasures; its land became full of horses, with no end to its chariots. ⁸ Then its land became full of false gods; each one of them bows to his own handiwork, to what his fingers have made.

⁹ Humankind will have bowed and man will have humbled himself; yet You will not forgive them. *

The Day of Judgment

¹⁰ Enter the rock* and be hidden in the ground, because of the fear of HASHEM, and from the glory of His greatness. ¹¹ Humankind's haughty eyes will be brought low and men's arrogance will be humbled; and HASHEM alone will be exalted on that day. ¹² For HASHEM, Master of Legions, has a day [for retribution] against every proud and arrogant person and against every exalted person — and he will be brought low; ¹³ and against all the lofty and exalted cedars of Lebanon and against all the oaks of the Bashan; ¹⁴ and against all the lofty mountains, and against all the exalted hills; ¹⁵ and against every tall tower and against every fortified wall; ¹⁶ and against all the ships of Tarshish and against all the splendid palaces. ¹⁷ Humankind's haughtiness will be humbled and men's arrogance will be brought down; and HASHEM alone will be exalted on that day. ¹⁸ And the false gods will perish completely, ¹⁹ and [idolaters] will enter caves in the rocks and tunnels in the ground, because of the fear of HASHEM and from the glory of His greatness, when He arises to break the land. ²⁰ On that day * man will throw away his false gods of silver and his false gods of gold, which they made for him to prostrate himself,

---

likens to trees and hills, that their presumed power and wealth brought from foreign lands will not avail them against God's judgment.

2:20. Isaiah uses the expression בַּיּוֹם הַהוּא, *on that day*, as a reference to the Day of Judgment that will take place in Messianic times (*Radak*).

כא לַחְפֹּר פֵּרוֹת וְלָעֲטַלֵּפִים: לָבוֹא בְּנִקְרוֹת הַצֻּרִים וּבִסְעִפֵי הַסְּלָעִים מִפְּנֵי
כב פַּחַד יהוה וּמֵהֲדַר גְּאוֹנוֹ בְּקוּמוֹ לַעֲרֹץ הָאָרֶץ: חִדְלוּ לָכֶם מִן־הָאָדָם

ג א אֲשֶׁר נְשָׁמָה בְּאַפּוֹ כִּי־בַמֶּה נֶחְשָׁב הוּא: כִּי הִנֵּה הָאָדוֹן יהוה
צְבָאוֹת מֵסִיר מִירוּשָׁלַםִ וּמִיהוּדָה מַשְׁעֵן וּמַשְׁעֵנָה כֹּל מִשְׁעַן־לֶחֶם וְכֹל
ב־ג מִשְׁעַן־מָיִם: גִּבּוֹר וְאִישׁ מִלְחָמָה שׁוֹפֵט וְנָבִיא וְקֹסֵם וְזָקֵן: שַׂר־חֲמִשִּׁים
ד וּנְשׂוּא פָנִים וְיוֹעֵץ וַחֲכַם חֲרָשִׁים וּנְבוֹן לָחַשׁ: וְנָתַתִּי נְעָרִים שָׂרֵיהֶם
ה וְתַעֲלוּלִים יִמְשְׁלוּ־בָם: וְנִגַּשׂ הָעָם אִישׁ בְּאִישׁ וְאִישׁ בְּרֵעֵהוּ יִרְהֲבוּ
ו הַנַּעַר בַּזָּקֵן וְהַנִּקְלֶה בַּנִּכְבָּד: כִּי־יִתְפֹּשׂ אִישׁ בְּאָחִיו בֵּית אָבִיו שִׂמְלָה
ז לְכָה קָצִין תִּהְיֶה־לָּנוּ וְהַמַּכְשֵׁלָה הַזֹּאת תַּחַת יָדֶךָ: יִשָּׂא בַיּוֹם הַהוּא |
לֵאמֹר לֹא־אֶהְיֶה חֹבֵשׁ וּבְבֵיתִי אֵין לֶחֶם וְאֵין שִׂמְלָה לֹא תְשִׂימֻנִי
ח קְצִין עָם: כִּי כָשְׁלָה יְרוּשָׁלַםִ וִיהוּדָה נָפָל כִּי־לְשׁוֹנָם וּמַעַלְלֵיהֶם אֶל־
ט יהוה לַמְרוֹת עֵנֵי כְבוֹדוֹ: הַכָּרַת פְּנֵיהֶם עָנְתָה בָּם וְחַטָּאתָם כִּסְדֹם
י הִגִּידוּ לֹא כִחֵדוּ אוֹי לְנַפְשָׁם כִּי־גָמְלוּ לָהֶם רָעָה: אִמְרוּ צַדִּיק כִּי־
יא טוֹב כִּי־פְרִי מַעַלְלֵיהֶם יֹאכֵלוּ: אוֹי לְרָשָׁע רָע כִּי־גְמוּל יָדָיו יֵעָשֶׂה לּוֹ:
יב עַמִּי נֹגְשָׂיו מְעוֹלֵל וְנָשִׁים מָשְׁלוּ בוֹ עַמִּי מְאַשְּׁרֶיךָ מַתְעִים וְדֶרֶךְ
יג־יד אֹרְחֹתֶיךָ בִּלֵּעוּ:   נִצָּב לָרִיב יהוה וְעֹמֵד לָדִין עַמִּים: יהוה
בְּמִשְׁפָּט יָבוֹא עִם־זִקְנֵי עַמּוֹ וְשָׂרָיו וְאַתֶּם בִּעַרְתֶּם הַכֶּרֶם גְּזֵלַת הֶעָנִי
טו בְּבָתֵּיכֶם: °מַלְכֶם [°מַה־לָּכֶם ק] תְּדַכְּאוּ עַמִּי וּפְנֵי עֲנִיִּים תִּטְחָנוּ נְאֻם־
טז אֲדֹנָי יהוה צְבָאוֹת: וַיֹּאמֶר יהוה יַעַן כִּי גָבְהוּ בְּנוֹת צִיּוֹן
וַתֵּלַכְנָה °נטוות [°נְטוּיוֹת ק] גָּרוֹן וּמְשַׂקְּרוֹת עֵינָיִם הָלוֹךְ וְטָפֹף תֵּלַכְנָה
יז וּבְרַגְלֵיהֶם תְּעַכַּסְנָה: וְשִׂפַּח אֲדֹנָי קָדְקֹד בְּנוֹת צִיּוֹן וַיהוה פָּתְהֵן
יח יְעָרֶה: בַּיּוֹם הַהוּא יָסִיר אֲדֹנָי אֵת תִּפְאֶרֶת הָעֲכָסִים וְהַשְּׁבִיסִים
יט־כ וְהַשַּׂהֲרֹנִים: הַנְּטִיפוֹת וְהַשֵּׁירוֹת וְהָרְעָלוֹת: הַפְּאֵרִים וְהַצְּעָדוֹת
כא־כב וְהַקִּשֻּׁרִים וּבָתֵּי הַנֶּפֶשׁ וְהַלְּחָשִׁים: הַטַּבָּעוֹת וְנִזְמֵי הָאָף: הַמַּחֲלָצוֹת
כג וְהַמַּעֲטָפוֹת וְהַמִּטְפָּחוֹת וְהָחֲרִיטִים: וְהַגִּלְיֹנִים וְהַסְּדִינִים וְהַצְּנִיפוֹת
כד וְהָרְדִידִים: וְהָיָה תַחַת בֹּשֶׂם מַק יִהְיֶה וְתַחַת חֲגוֹרָה נִקְפָּה וְתַחַת מַעֲשֶׂה
כה מִקְשֶׁה קָרְחָה וְתַחַת פְּתִיגִיל מַחֲגֹרֶת שָׂק כִּי־תַחַת יֹפִי: מְתַיִךְ בַּחֶרֶב
כו יִפֹּלוּ וּגְבוּרָתֵךְ בַּמִּלְחָמָה: וְאָנוּ וְאָבְלוּ פְּתָחֶיהָ וְנִקָּתָה לָאָרֶץ תֵּשֵׁב:

3:1. This explains why Israel should distance themselves from evil, arrogant people (2:22): because God will depose men of power and influence, by depriving them of food and water (*Ibn Ezra*).

3:6-7. The poverty will be so overwhelming that even family members will be unable to help their less fortunate relatives when requested to do so (*Kara*).

3:10. Tell him that his deeds are good (*Metzudos*); or, that a goodly reward awaits him (*Kara*). Alternatively: Tell the world about the rewards enjoyed by the righteous

in the World to Come (*Radak*).

3:12. The people have become so driven to satisfy their lusts, that they do anything to please their immoral women (*Radak*).

3:18. See 2:20.

3:25. The prophet is still addressing "the daughters of Zion" (*Ibn Ezra*; *Radak*).

3:26. This verse alludes to the razing of Jerusalem's buildings (*Radak*).

to moles and to bats, 21 to enter clefts of the rocks and the cracks of the crags, because of the fear of HASHEM and from the glory of His greatness, when He arises to break the land.

22 Withdraw from man who has breath in his nostrils, for with what is he deemed worthy?

3

Dire prophecy of the siege of Jerusalem

1 For behold, the Lord, HASHEM, Master of Legions, is removing from Jerusalem and from Judah support of men and support of women, every support of bread and every support of water; * 2 hero and man of war, judge, prophet, diviner and elder; 3 captain of fifty, respected person, adviser, teacher of the wise and comprehender of mysteries. 4 I shall make youngsters their leaders, and mockers will rule them. 5 The people will be oppressed, man by man and man by his fellow; they will domineer, the youngster over the elder and the base over the respectable. 6 When a man will grasp his relative, a member of his father's house, [saying,] 'You have a garment! Become a benefactor for us; and let this obstacle [of poverty] be under [the control of] your hand!'* — 7 he will swear on that day, saying, 'I cannot become a patron, for in my house there is neither bread nor garment. Do not make me a benefactor of the people!' 8 [All this has come about] because Jerusalem has stumbled and Judah has fallen; for their speech and their actions are against HASHEM, rebelling before the eyes of His glory. 9 Their brazen countenance testifies against them; their sins, like Sodom's, speak out and do not withhold [anything]. Woe to their souls, for they have brought evil upon themselves! 10 Tell [each] righteous man that it is good; * for they shall eat the fruit of their deeds. 11 But woe to the wicked person who does evil, for the recompense of his hands will be dealt to him. 12 My people — their oppressors are mockers and women dominate them. * O My people, your leaders mislead you, and they have corrupted the direction of your ways.

13 HASHEM stands erect to contend, and stands to judge peoples. 14 HASHEM will enter into judgment with the elders and officers of His people, [saying,] 'You have consumed the vineyard; what you have robbed from the poor man is in your houses. 15 What has become of you that you crush My people and grind the faces of the poor?' — the word of My Lord, HASHEM/ELOHIM, Master of Legions.

16 HASHEM said:

Fate of the immoral women

Because the daughters of Zion are haughty, walking with outstretched necks and winking eyes; walking with dainty steps, jingling with their feet, 17 [therefore] the Lord will afflict the heads of the daughters of Zion with lesions, and HASHEM will bare their private parts. 18 On that day * the Lord will remove the splendor of the shoe-bells, the head scarves, the moon-shaped ornaments, 19 the necklaces, the bracelets, the veils, 20 the bonnets, the leg bands, the hair-ties, the brooches, the earrings, 21 the rings, the nose rings, 22 the robes, the shawls, the kerchiefs, the pouches, 23 the mirrors, the linens, the turbans and the clasps. 24 And it shall be that in the place of fragrance there will be rot; and in the place of the belt, abrasion; and in the place of coiffure, baldness; and in the place of the ornamental belt, a belt of sackcloth; a burn in the place of beauty. 25 Your men * will fall by the sword and your might in war. 26 Her doorways will mourn and lament; she will be wiped out; she will sit on the ground. *

ד א וְהֶחֱזִיקוּ שֶׁבַע נָשִׁים בְּאִישׁ אֶחָד בַּיּוֹם הַהוּא לֵאמֹר לַחְמֵנוּ נֹאכֵל
ב וְשִׂמְלָתֵנוּ נִלְבָּשׁ רַק יִקָּרֵא שִׁמְךָ עָלֵינוּ אֱסֹף חֶרְפָּתֵנוּ: בַּיּוֹם
הַהוּא יִהְיֶה צֶמַח יהוה לִצְבִי וּלְכָבוֹד וּפְרִי הָאָרֶץ לְגָאוֹן וּלְתִפְאֶרֶת
ג לִפְלֵיטַת יִשְׂרָאֵל: וְהָיָה | הַנִּשְׁאָר בְּצִיּוֹן וְהַנּוֹתָר בִּירוּשָׁלַ͏ִם קָדוֹשׁ יֵאָמֶר
ד לוֹ כָּל־הַכָּתוּב לַחַיִּים בִּירוּשָׁלָ͏ִם: אִם | רָחַץ אֲדֹנָי אֵת צֹאַת בְּנוֹת־צִיּוֹן
ה וְאֶת־דְּמֵי יְרוּשָׁלַ͏ִם יָדִיחַ מִקִּרְבָּהּ בְּרוּחַ מִשְׁפָּט וּבְרוּחַ בָּעֵר: וּבָרָא יהוה
עַל כָּל־מְכוֹן הַר־צִיּוֹן וְעַל־מִקְרָאֶהָ עָנָן | יוֹמָם וְעָשָׁן וְנֹגַהּ אֵשׁ לֶהָבָה
ו לָיְלָה כִּי עַל־כָּל־כָּבוֹד חֻפָּה: וְסֻכָּה תִּהְיֶה לְצֵל־יוֹמָם מֵחֹרֶב וּלְמַחְסֶה
ה א וּלְמִסְתּוֹר מִזֶּרֶם וּמִמָּטָר: אָשִׁירָה נָּא לִידִידִי שִׁירַת דּוֹדִי
ב לְכַרְמוֹ כֶּרֶם הָיָה לִידִידִי בְּקֶרֶן בֶּן־שָׁמֶן: וַיְעַזְּקֵהוּ וַיְסַקְּלֵהוּ וַיִּטָּעֵהוּ שֹׂרֵק
וַיִּבֶן מִגְדָּל בְּתוֹכוֹ וְגַם־יֶקֶב חָצֵב בּוֹ וַיְקַו לַעֲשׂוֹת עֲנָבִים וַיַּעַשׂ בְּאֻשִׁים:
ג–ד וְעַתָּה יוֹשֵׁב יְרוּשָׁלַ͏ִם וְאִישׁ יְהוּדָה שִׁפְטוּ־נָא בֵּינִי וּבֵין כַּרְמִי: מַה־
לַעֲשׂוֹת עוֹד לְכַרְמִי וְלֹא עָשִׂיתִי בּוֹ מַדּוּעַ קִוֵּיתִי לַעֲשׂוֹת עֲנָבִים וַיַּעַשׂ
ה בְּאֻשִׁים: וְעַתָּה אוֹדִיעָה־נָּא אֶתְכֶם אֵת אֲשֶׁר־אֲנִי עֹשֶׂה לְכַרְמִי הָסֵר
ו מְשׂוּכָּתוֹ וְהָיָה לְבָעֵר פָּרֹץ גְּדֵרוֹ וְהָיָה לְמִרְמָס: וַאֲשִׁיתֵהוּ בָתָה לֹא יִזָּמֵר
ז וְלֹא יֵעָדֵר וְעָלָה שָׁמִיר וָשָׁיִת וְעַל הֶעָבִים אֲצַוֶּה מֵהַמְטִיר עָלָיו מָטָר: כִּי
כֶרֶם יהוה צְבָאוֹת בֵּית יִשְׂרָאֵל וְאִישׁ יְהוּדָה נְטַע שַׁעֲשׁוּעָיו וַיְקַו
ח לְמִשְׁפָּט וְהִנֵּה מִשְׂפָּח לִצְדָקָה וְהִנֵּה צְעָקָה: הוֹי מַגִּיעֵי בַיִת
בְּבַיִת שָׂדֶה בְשָׂדֶה יַקְרִיבוּ עַד אֶפֶס מָקוֹם וְהוּשַׁבְתֶּם לְבַדְּכֶם בְּקֶרֶב
ט הָאָרֶץ: בְּאָזְנָי יהוה צְבָאוֹת אִם־לֹא בָּתִּים רַבִּים לְשַׁמָּה יִהְיוּ גְּדֹלִים
י וְטוֹבִים מֵאֵין יוֹשֵׁב: כִּי עֲשֶׂרֶת צִמְדֵּי־כֶרֶם יַעֲשׂוּ בַּת אֶחָת וְזֶרַע חֹמֶר
יא יַעֲשֶׂה אֵיפָה: הוֹי מַשְׁכִּימֵי בַבֹּקֶר שֵׁכָר יִרְדֹּפוּ מְאַחֲרֵי בַנֶּשֶׁף
יב יַיִן יַדְלִיקֵם: וְהָיָה כִנּוֹר וָנֶבֶל תֹּף וְחָלִיל וָיַיִן מִשְׁתֵּיהֶם וְאֵת פֹּעַל יהוה
יג לֹא יַבִּיטוּ וּמַעֲשֵׂה יָדָיו לֹא רָאוּ: לָכֵן גָּלָה עַמִּי מִבְּלִי־דָעַת וּכְבוֹדוֹ מְתֵי
יד רָעָב וַהֲמוֹנוֹ צִחֵה צָמָא: לָכֵן הִרְחִיבָה שְּׁאוֹל נַפְשָׁהּ וּפָעֲרָה פִיהָ לִבְלִי־
טו חֹק וְיָרַד הֲדָרָהּ וַהֲמוֹנָהּ וּשְׁאוֹנָהּ וְעָלֵז בָּהּ: וַיִּשַּׁח אָדָם וַיִּשְׁפַּל־אִישׁ

4:1. In a graphic illustration of the downfall described in the previous chapter, Isaiah says that there will be so many widows that women will far outnumber men, and they will offer themselves in marriage without any promise of support.

4:2. Once the above punishments have been carried out, providing atonement for Israel's sins, the Messianic era will begin. The Messiah is referred to as a sprout and fruit of the land (Radak).

4:3. Only holy and righteous people will survive and be inscribed for life.

4:6. That is, there will be Divine protection afforded to those who remain in Jerusalem, to protect them from the destruction that will "rain down" upon the wicked.

5:2. A winepress (Rashi); a watchtower (Ibn Ezra; Radak).

5:5. A vineyard had two fences around it: a stone wall to keep out animals, and a hedge of sharp thorns outside or on top of the stone wall to prevent people from climbing over it. The removal of the hedge would allow people to come in and eat its produce; the removal of the wall would let animals in to trample it (Kara; Radak).

5:7. Instead of producing justice and righteousness, God's "vineyard" produced the affliction and outcry of persecuted and victimized people.

5:8. If a rich man wanted to enlarge his house or field, he would simply encroach on the adjacent property of a poor, defenseless owner.

5:10. The volumes of the liquid measure bath and the dry

4

¹ *And seven women will grasp one man on that day,* * *saying, 'We will eat our own food and wear our own clothes; just let us be called by your name, and end our disgrace!'*

² *On that day* HASHEM's *sprout* * *will come forth for splendor and honor; and the fruit of the land will be for pride and glory for the survivors of Israel.* ³ *Of every remnant that will be in Zion and every remaining one in Jerusalem,*

Zion
cleansed

'Holy' will be said of him, * *everyone who is inscribed for life in Jerusalem.* ⁴ *When my Lord will have washed the filth of the daughters of Zion and rinsed the blood of Jerusalem from her midst, with a spirit of judgment and a spirit of purging.* ⁵ *And* HASHEM *will create over every structure of Mount Zion and over those who assemble in it a cloud by day, and smoke and a glow of flaming fire by night, for this will be a canopy over all the honor.* ⁶ *And there will be a tabernacle as a shade from heat in the daytime, as a protection and refuge from storm and from rain.* *

5

¹ I *will now sing on behalf of my Beloved, my Beloved's song concerning His vineyard:*

Song
of the
vineyard

My Beloved had a vineyard in a fertile corner. ² *He fenced it around and cleared it of stones; He planted it with choice shoots and built a tower* * *inside it; He even hewed a wine vat in it. He hoped to produce [fine] grapes, but it produced only inferior grapes.*

³ *[So my Beloved said,] 'Now, O inhabitant of Jerusalem and people of Judah, judge between Me and My vineyard.* ⁴ *What more could have been done for my vineyard that I did not do for it? Why — though I had hoped to produce [fine] grapes — did it produce only inferior grapes?* ⁵ *So now, I will tell you what I am doing to my vineyard: I will remove its hedge and it will be consumed; I will breach its fence and it will trampled.* * ⁶ *I will make it a wasteland; it will not be pruned, and it will not be hoed; thorns and weeds will grow. And I will command the clouds not to pour rain upon it.*

⁷ *Now, the vineyard of* HASHEM, *Master of Legions, is the House of Israel, and the people of Judah are the shoot of His delight; He had hoped for justice, but behold, affliction! For righteousness, but behold, an outcry!* *

Fate of the
selfish . . .

⁸ *Woe to you who caused house to encroach against house,* * *and make field approach field, until there is no more place; are you the only ones to be settled in the midst of the land?* ⁹ *'[It has entered] into My ears,' [said]* HASHEM, *Master of Legions, 'I swear that many houses, great and splendid ones, will be laid ruin, without inhabitant.* ¹⁰ *For ten portions of vineyard will produce only one bath, and a homer of seeds will produce only one ephah.'* *

. . . the
drunk . . .

¹¹ *Woe to those who arise early in the morning to pursue liquor, who stay up late at night while wine inflames them.* ¹² *There are harp and lyre and drum and flute, and wine at their drinking parties; but they would not contemplate the deed of* HASHEM, *and would not look at the work of His hands.* ¹³ *There-*

. . . the
ignorant . . .

fore, my people is being exiled because of ignorance; its honored ones dying of starvation, and its multitude parched from thirst. ¹⁴ *Therefore, the nether-world has enlarged its appetite and opened its mouth wide without limit; and [into it] will descend her* * *glory and her multitude and her horde, and who-*

. . . and the
haughty

soever revels within her. ¹⁵ *Man will be humbled and people will be brought*

---

measure *ephah* are the same, one-tenth of a *homer*. Not only would the yield be less than usual, each field would   produce only a tenth of the seed with which it was sown. **5:14.** "Her" refers to Jerusalem.

טז וְעֵינֵי גְבֹהִים תִּשְׁפַּלְנָה: וַיִּגְבַּה יהוה צְבָאוֹת בַּמִּשְׁפָּט וְהָאֵל הַקָּדוֹשׁ נִקְדָּשׁ

יז-יח בִּצְדָקָה: וְרָעוּ כְבָשִׂים כְּדָבְרָם וְחָרְבוֹת מֵחִים גָּרִים יֹאכֵלוּ:   הוֹי

יט מֹשְׁכֵי הֶעָוֺן בְּחַבְלֵי הַשָּׁוְא וְכַעֲבוֹת הָעֲגָלָה חַטָּאָה: הָאֹמְרִים יְמַהֵר ׀

יָחִישָׁה מַעֲשֵׂהוּ לְמַעַן נִרְאֶה וְתִקְרַב וְתָבוֹאָה עֲצַת קְדוֹשׁ יִשְׂרָאֵל

כ וְנֵדָעָה: הוֹי הָאֹמְרִים לָרַע טוֹב וְלַטּוֹב רָע שָׂמִים חֹשֶׁךְ לְאוֹר

כא וְאוֹר לְחֹשֶׁךְ שָׂמִים מַר לְמָתוֹק וּמָתוֹק לְמָר: הוֹי חֲכָמִים

כב בְּעֵינֵיהֶם וְנֶגֶד פְּנֵיהֶם נְבֹנִים: הוֹי גִּבּוֹרִים לִשְׁתּוֹת יָיִן וְאַנְשֵׁי־

כג חַיִל לִמְסֹךְ שֵׁכָר: מַצְדִּיקֵי רָשָׁע עֵקֶב שֹׁחַד וְצִדְקַת צַדִּיקִים יָסִירוּ

כד מִמֶּנּוּ: לָכֵן כֶּאֱכֹל קַשׁ לְשׁוֹן אֵשׁ וַחֲשַׁשׁ לֶהָבָה יִרְפֶּה שָׁרְשָׁם

כַּמָּק יִהְיֶה וּפִרְחָם כָּאָבָק יַעֲלֶה כִּי מָאֲסוּ אֵת תּוֹרַת יהוה צְבָאוֹת וְאֵת

כה אִמְרַת קְדוֹשׁ־יִשְׂרָאֵל נִאֵצוּ: עַל־כֵּן חָרָה אַף־יהוה בְּעַמּוֹ וַיֵּט יָדוֹ עָלָיו

וַיַּכֵּהוּ וַיִּרְגְּזוּ הֶהָרִים וַתְּהִי נִבְלָתָם כַּסּוּחָה בְּקֶרֶב חוּצוֹת בְּכָל־זֹאת לֹא־

כו שָׁב אַפּוֹ וְעוֹד יָדוֹ נְטוּיָה: וְנָשָׂא־נֵס לַגּוֹיִם מֵרָחוֹק וְשָׁרַק לוֹ מִקְצֵה הָאָרֶץ

כז וְהִנֵּה מְהֵרָה קַל יָבוֹא: אֵין־עָיֵף וְאֵין־כּוֹשֵׁל בּוֹ לֹא יָנוּם וְלֹא יִישָׁן וְלֹא

כח נִפְתַּח אֵזוֹר חֲלָצָיו וְלֹא נִתַּק שְׂרוֹךְ נְעָלָיו: אֲשֶׁר חִצָּיו שְׁנוּנִים וְכָל־

כט קַשְּׁתֹתָיו דְּרֻכוֹת פַּרְסוֹת סוּסָיו כַּצַּר נֶחְשָׁבוּ וְגַלְגִּלָּיו כַּסּוּפָה: שְׁאָגָה לוֹ

כַּלָּבִיא °וְשָׁאַג [יִשְׁאַג ק] כַּכְּפִירִים וְיִנְהֹם וְיֹאחֵז טֶרֶף וְיַפְלִיט וְאֵין מַצִּיל:

ל וְיִנְהֹם עָלָיו בַּיּוֹם הַהוּא כְּנַהֲמַת־יָם וְנִבַּט לָאָרֶץ וְהִנֵּה־חֹשֶׁךְ צַר וָאוֹר

חָשַׁךְ בַּעֲרִיפֶיהָ:   ▸ בִּשְׁנַת־מוֹת הַמֶּלֶךְ עֻזִּיָּהוּ וָאֶרְאֶה אֶת־אֲדֹנָי

א

ב יֹשֵׁב עַל־כִּסֵּא רָם וְנִשָּׂא וְשׁוּלָיו מְלֵאִים אֶת־הַהֵיכָל: שְׂרָפִים עֹמְדִים ׀

מִמַּעַל לוֹ שֵׁשׁ כְּנָפַיִם שֵׁשׁ כְּנָפַיִם לְאֶחָד בִּשְׁתַּיִם ׀ יְכַסֶּה פָנָיו וּבִשְׁתַּיִם

ג יְכַסֶּה רַגְלָיו וּבִשְׁתַּיִם יְעוֹפֵף: וְקָרָא זֶה אֶל־זֶה וְאָמַר קָדוֹשׁ ׀ קָדוֹשׁ קָדוֹשׁ

ד יהוה צְבָאוֹת מְלֹא כָל־הָאָרֶץ כְּבוֹדוֹ: וַיָּנֻעוּ אַמּוֹת הַסִּפִּים מִקּוֹל הַקּוֹרֵא

ה וְהַבַּיִת יִמָּלֵא עָשָׁן: וָאֹמַר אוֹי־לִי כִי־נִדְמֵיתִי כִּי אִישׁ טְמֵא־שְׂפָתַיִם אָנֹכִי

וּבְתוֹךְ עַם־טְמֵא שְׂפָתַיִם אָנֹכִי יוֹשֵׁב כִּי אֶת־הַמֶּלֶךְ יהוה צְבָאוֹת רָאוּ

ו עֵינָי: וַיָּעָף אֵלַי אֶחָד מִן־הַשְּׂרָפִים וּבְיָדוֹ רִצְפָּה בְּמֶלְקַחַיִם לָקַח מֵעַל

ז הַמִּזְבֵּחַ: וַיַּגַּע עַל־פִּי וַיֹּאמֶר הִנֵּה נָגַע זֶה עַל־שְׂפָתֶיךָ וְסָר עֲוֺנֶךָ וְחַטָּאתְךָ

ח תְּכֻפָּר: וָאֶשְׁמַע אֶת־קוֹל אֲדֹנָי אֹמֵר אֶת־מִי אֶשְׁלַח וּמִי יֵלֶךְ־לָנוּ

5:16. When God punishes the wicked He becomes exalted and feared.

5:17. The sheep and sojourners are the righteous and downtrodden, who will live peacefully after God punishes the wicked. The fattened animals are the greedy wicked, whose destroyed property will revert to their victims.

5:25-6. Because the people did not take their punishments to heart (*Rashi*), God will signal foreign nations to come and attack.

5:30. The translation follows *Radak*. According to *Rashi,*

the end of the verse reads "*. . . but there will be darkness; the distressed one (Israel) and the [would-be] light (its allies) become darkened by the thick clouds [of doom].*"

6:1. According to a tradition of the *Midrash*, "death" here refers to the leprous disease contracted by Uzziah (see *II Chronicles* 26:16-19) sometime after he consolidated his kingdom (*Targum*; *Rashi*). Others understand "death" literally (*Ibn Ezra*; *Radak*).

6:5. Isaiah was sure he would die, because no human can see [God's] face and live (*Exodus* 33:20).

HAFTARAS
YISRO
Ashkenazim:
6:1-7:6,
9:5-6
Sephardim:
6:1-13

lower, and the eyes of the haughty will be brought low. ¹⁶ HASHEM, Master of Legions, will become exalted through judgment, and the Holy God will be sanctified through justice. * ¹⁷ Then the sheep will graze in their usual way, and sojourners will eat of the ruins of the fattened animals. *

Woe to the deceitful

¹⁸ Woe to those who pull iniquity upon themselves with cords of false-hood, and sin like the ropes of a wagon. ¹⁹ Those who say, 'Let Him hurry, let Him hasten His action, so that we may see it; let the plan of the Holy One of Israel approach and take place, so that we may know it.'

²⁰ Woe to those who speak of evil as good and of good as evil; who make darkness into light and light into darkness; they make bitter into sweet and sweet into bitter!

²¹ Woe to those who are wise in their own eyes, and in their own view, understanding. ²² Woe to those who are mighty in drinking wine and are men of accomplishment in pouring liquor. ²³ They acquit the wicked one because of a bribe, and strip the righteous one of his innocence.

God's wrath

²⁴ Therefore, just as a tongue of fire consumes straw, and a flame destroys stubble, so will their root become rot and their flower will be blown away like dust; for they have abhorred the Torah of HASHEM, Master of Legions, and they have scorned the word of the Holy One of Israel. ²⁵ Therefore, HASHEM's wrath has flared up against His people and He has stretched forth His hand against them and stricken them; the mountains have quaked, and their corpses are like refuse in the middle of the streets. Yet still His wrath has not ceased and His hand is still stretched out. ²⁶ He will raise a banner for far-off nations* and He will whistle for [the enemy to come] from the ends of the earth; and then, behold, he will come with quickness, with alacrity. ²⁷ None among him is tired or stumbles; he neither sleeps nor slumbers; the belt around his waist will not be opened, and the laces of his shoes will not be untied. ²⁸ His arrows are sharpened and all his bows are drawn; his horses' hooves are considered like flint, and his [chariots'] wheels like a storm. ²⁹ His roar is like a lion's; he will roar like young lions, growl, seize prey and pull it away, and none can save it. ³⁰ He will growl at [Israel] on that day like the rumble of the sea; [Israel] will peer across the land, but there will be only the darkness of the enemy; the light [of day] has darkened in the sky. *

6

Isaiah's vision of the Heavenly Court

¹ In the year of King Uzziah's death, * I saw the Lord sitting upon a high and lofty throne, and its legs filled the Temple. ² Seraphim were standing above, at His service. Each one had six wings: with two it would cover its face, with two it would cover its legs, and with two it would fly. ³ And one would call to another and say, "Holy, holy, holy is HASHEM, Master of Legions; the whole world is filled with His glory." ⁴ The doorposts moved many cubits at the sound of the calling, and the Temple became filled with smoke.

⁵ Then I said, "Woe is me, for I am doomed:* for I am a man of impure lips and I dwell among a people with impure lips, for my eyes have seen the King, HASHEM, Master of Legions."

⁶ One of the Seraphim flew to me and in his hand was a coal; he had taken it with tongs from atop the altar. ⁷ He touched it to my mouth and said, "Behold, this has touched your lips; your iniquity has gone away and your sin shall be atoned for."

⁸ I heard the voice of the Lord, saying, "Whom shall I send, and who shall go for us?"

ט וָאֹמֶר הִנְנִי שְׁלָחֵנִי: וַיֹּאמֶר לֵךְ וְאָמַרְתָּ לָעָם הַזֶּה שִׁמְעוּ שָׁמוֹעַ וְאַל־תָּבִינוּ

י וּרְאוּ רָאוֹ וְאַל־תֵּדָעוּ: הַשְׁמֵן לֵב־הָעָם הַזֶּה וְאָזְנָיו הַכְבֵּד וְעֵינָיו הָשַׁע פֶּן־

יא יִרְאֶה בְעֵינָיו וּבְאָזְנָיו יִשְׁמָע וּלְבָבוֹ יָבִין וָשָׁב וְרָפָא לוֹ: וָאֹמַר עַד־מָתַי אֲדֹנָי וַיֹּאמֶר עַד אֲשֶׁר אִם־שָׁאוּ עָרִים מֵאֵין יוֹשֵׁב וּבָתִּים מֵאֵין אָדָם

יב וְהָאֲדָמָה תִּשָּׁאֶה שְׁמָמָה: וְרִחַק יְהוָה אֶת־הָאָדָם וְרַבָּה הָעֲזוּבָה בְּקֶרֶב

יג הָאָרֶץ: וְעוֹד בָּהּ עֲשִׂרִיָּה וְשָׁבָה וְהָיְתָה לְבָעֵר כָּאֵלָה וְכָאַלּוֹן אֲשֶׁר

ז א בְּשַׁלֶּכֶת מַצֶּבֶת בָּם זֶרַע קֹדֶשׁ מַצַּבְתָּהּ: ◄ וַיְהִי בִּימֵי אָחָז בֶּן־יוֹתָם בֶּן־עֻזִּיָּהוּ מֶלֶךְ יְהוּדָה עָלָה רְצִין מֶלֶךְ־אֲרָם וּפֶקַח בֶּן־רְמַלְיָהוּ

ב מֶלֶךְ־יִשְׂרָאֵל יְרוּשָׁלַם לַמִּלְחָמָה עָלֶיהָ וְלֹא יָכֹל לְהִלָּחֵם עָלֶיהָ: וַיֻּגַּד לְבֵית דָּוִד לֵאמֹר נָחָה אֲרָם עַל־אֶפְרָיִם וַיָּנַע לְבָבוֹ וּלְבַב עַמּוֹ כְּנוֹעַ עֲצֵי־

ג יַעַר מִפְּנֵי־רוּחַ: וַיֹּאמֶר יְהוָה אֶל־יְשַׁעְיָהוּ צֵא־נָא לִקְרַאת אָחָז אַתָּה וּשְׁאָר יָשׁוּב בְּנֶךָ אֶל־קְצֵה תְּעָלַת הַבְּרֵכָה הָעֶלְיוֹנָה אֶל־מְסִלַּת

ד שְׂדֵה כוֹבֵס: וְאָמַרְתָּ אֵלָיו הִשָּׁמֵר וְהַשְׁקֵט אַל־תִּירָא וּלְבָבְךָ אַל־יֵרַךְ מִשְּׁנֵי זַנְבוֹת הָאוּדִים הָעֲשֵׁנִים הָאֵלֶּה בָּחֳרִי־אַף רְצִין וַאֲרָם וּבֶן־רְמַלְיָהוּ:

ה־ו יַעַן כִּי־יָעַץ עָלֶיךָ אֲרָם רָעָה אֶפְרַיִם וּבֶן־רְמַלְיָהוּ לֵאמֹר: נַעֲלֶה בִיהוּדָה וּנְקִיצֶנָּה וְנַבְקִעֶנָּה אֵלֵינוּ וְנַמְלִיךְ מֶלֶךְ בְּתוֹכָהּ אֵת בֶּן־טָבְאַל: ◄ כֹּה

ז אָמַר אֲדֹנָי יְהוִה לֹא תָקוּם וְלֹא תִהְיֶה: כִּי רֹאשׁ אֲרָם דַּמֶּשֶׂק וְרֹאשׁ

ח דַּמֶּשֶׂק רְצִין וּבְעוֹד שִׁשִּׁים וְחָמֵשׁ שָׁנָה יֵחַת אֶפְרַיִם מֵעָם: וְרֹאשׁ

ט אֶפְרַיִם שֹׁמְרוֹן וְרֹאשׁ שֹׁמְרוֹן בֶּן־רְמַלְיָהוּ אִם לֹא תַאֲמִינוּ כִּי לֹא תֵאָמֵנוּ:

י־יא וַיּוֹסֶף יְהוָה דַּבֵּר אֶל־אָחָז לֵאמֹר: שְׁאַל־לְךָ אוֹת מֵעִם

יב יְהוָה אֱלֹהֶיךָ הַעֲמֵק שְׁאָלָה אוֹ הַגְבֵּהַּ לְמָעְלָה: וַיֹּאמֶר אָחָז לֹא־אֶשְׁאַל

יג וְלֹא־אֲנַסֶּה אֶת־יְהוָה: וַיֹּאמֶר שִׁמְעוּ־נָא בֵּית דָּוִד הַמְעַט מִכֶּם הַלְאוֹת

יד אֲנָשִׁים כִּי תַלְאוּ גַּם אֶת־אֱלֹהָי: לָכֵן יִתֵּן אֲדֹנָי הוּא לָכֶם אוֹת הִנֵּה הָעַלְמָה הָרָה וְיֹלֶדֶת בֵּן וְקָרָאת שְׁמוֹ עִמָּנוּ אֵל:

טו חֶמְאָה וּדְבַשׁ יֹאכֵל לְדַעְתּוֹ מָאוֹס בָּרָע וּבָחוֹר בַּטּוֹב: כִּי בְּטֶרֶם יֵדַע הַנַּעַר מָאֹס בָּרָע וּבָחֹר

טז־יז בַּטּוֹב תֵּעָזֵב הָאֲדָמָה אֲשֶׁר אַתָּה קָץ מִפְּנֵי שְׁנֵי מְלָכֶיהָ: יָבִיא יְהוָה עָלֶיךָ וְעַל־עַמְּךָ וְעַל־בֵּית אָבִיךָ יָמִים אֲשֶׁר לֹא־בָאוּ לְמִיּוֹם סוּר־אֶפְרַיִם

Haftaras Yisro for Ashkenazim continues on p. 968

6:10. They adamantly refuse to heed the prophets' words, as if to prevent an improvement in their situation.

6:12. The area of abandonment will be vast (*Rashi*) and its duration (*Radak*) will be lengthy.

6:13. From the time of Uzziah, when Isaiah received this prophecy and when the Ten Tribes were exiled, there would be ten more kings of Judah, and then it, too, would be exiled and the Temple destroyed (*Radak*). Alternatively: "A tenth will still be in it," i.e., when the wicked ones among them have been killed, only one-tenth of the people will remain (*Targum; Rashi*).

When a tree loses its leaves it gives the appearance of being completely dead, but the truth is that in the spring its leaves sprout once again. So too the Land of Israel, although it appears to have been completely emptied of its inhabitants, will once again be populated by the "holy seed" — the righteous of Israel.

7:1. Lit., "could not wage war against it." The phrase in singular refers to Pekah (*Ibn Ezra*). Jerusalem was militarily weak and Ahaz was a wicked king, but God protected the city in the merit of Ahaz' righteous predecessors (*Rashi; Radak*).

7:6. Our siege will cause Jerusalem so much distress that it will surrender (*Radak*); then we will annex it (*Rashi*).

7:8-9. Rezin has no business in Jerusalem, and Ephraim belongs in its capital of Samaria. The exile of the Ten

Call to prophecy
And I said, "Here I am! Send me!"

⁹ He said, "Go and say to this people, 'Surely you hear, but you do not comprehend; and surely you see, but you fail to know.' ¹⁰ This people is fattening its heart, hardening its ears, and sealing its eyes, lest it see with its eyes, hear with its ears and understand with its heart, so that it will repent and be healed."*

¹¹ I then asked, "How long, my Lord?"

And He said, "Until the cities become desolate without inhabitant, the houses without a person, and the land becomes desolate, wasted; ¹² and HASHEM will drive the people far away, and abandonment will be great* amid the land. ¹³ There will be ten more [kings] in it,* then it shall regress and become barren — like an elm and an oak which, when shedding [their leaves], still have vitality in them, so will the holy seed be the vitality of [the land]."*

7

Aram and Israel attack Jerusalem
(See Appendix A, timeline 4)

¹ It happened in the days of Ahaz son of Jotham son of Uzziah, king of Judah: Rezin, king of Aram, and Pekah son of Remaliah, king of Israel, went up to wage war against Jerusalem, but he could not triumph over it. * ² It was told to the House of David, saying, "Aram has joined with Ephraim"; and his heart shuddered, and the heart of his people, like the shuddering of the trees of the forest in the wind.

³ HASHEM said to Isaiah, "Go out and meet Ahaz, you and your son Shear-jashub [A Remainder Will Return], at the edge of the channel of the Upper Pool, at the road of the Launderer's Field, ⁴ and say to him, 'Be calm and still; fear not.

They will not succeed
Let your heart not grow faint before these two smoldering spent firebrands: before the burning wrath of Rezin and Aram, and [before] the son of Remaliah. ⁵ Because Aram, along with Ephraim and the son of Remaliah, has counseled evil against you, saying, ⁶ "Let us attack Judah and vex it and annex it to ourselves, * and crown the son of Tabeel as king within it" — ⁷ thus said my Lord HASHEM/ELOHIM: It shall not endure and it shall not be! ⁸ For the capital of Aram is Damascus and the head of Damascus is Rezin; in sixty-five more years, Ephraim will cease to be a people. * ⁹ And the capital of Ephraim is Samaria and the head of Samaria is the son of Remaliah. If you do not believe this, it is because you lack faith.' "

¹⁰ HASHEM spoke further to Ahaz, saying, ¹¹ "Request a sign for yourself from HASHEM your God; request it in the depths, or high, above."

¹² But Ahaz said, "I will not request; I will not test HASHEM."*

¹³ [Isaiah] responded, "Hear now, O House of David: Is it not enough for you that you scorn human [prophets], that you scorn even my God? ¹⁴ Therefore, my Lord

A sign, a son
Himself will give you a sign: Behold, the maiden will become pregnant and bear a son, and you will name him Immanuel. * ¹⁵ He will eat cream and honey as soon as he knows to abhor evil and choose good. * ¹⁶ For before the child will know to abhor evil and choose good, the land of the two kings whom you fear will be abandoned. ¹⁷ [Later] HASHEM will bring upon you and upon your people and upon your father's family* days such as have not come since the day Ephraim turned

---

Tribes, led by Ephraim (as prophesied in Amos 7:11 and 17), will take place in sixty-five years.

7:11-12. Isaiah told Ahaz to ask for a sign [from the depths, i.e., to revive a dead person, or from the heavens (Rashi)] to prove the veracity of the prophecy, but Ahaz answered contemptuously, as if to say, "I do not believe that HASHEM can supply any sign" (Ibn Ezra).

7:14. Either Isaiah's (Rashi) or Ahaz' (Radak) young wife will bear a son and, through prophetic inspiration, will give him the name Immanuel, which means "God is With

Us," thus in effect prophesying that Judah will be saved from the threat of Rezin and Pekah.

7:15. Although the land was now impoverished, there will be such prosperity that from an early age the child will be pampered with the richest delicacies. This prophecy is explained in verses 16 and 22.

7:17. The reference is to Ahaz's son, the righteous King Hezekiah. In his time, God will signal to the armies of Egypt and Assyria, which will swarm like flies and bees, to swoop down upon the Land of Israel.

יח מֵעַל יְהוּדָה אֵת מֶלֶךְ אַשּׁוּר: וְהָיָה ׀ בַּיּוֹם הַהוּא יִשְׁרֹק יְהוָה

יט לַזְּבוּב אֲשֶׁר בִּקְצֵה יְאֹרֵי מִצְרָיִם וְלַדְּבוֹרָה אֲשֶׁר בְּאֶרֶץ אַשּׁוּר: וּבָאוּ וְנָחוּ

כֻלָּם בְּנַחֲלֵי הַבַּתּוֹת וּבִנְקִיקֵי הַסְּלָעִים וּבְכֹל הַנַּעֲצוּצִים וּבְכֹל הַנַּהֲלֹלִים:

כ בַּיּוֹם הַהוּא יְגַלַּח אֲדֹנָי בְּתַעַר הַשְּׂכִירָה בְּעֶבְרֵי נָהָר בְּמֶלֶךְ אַשּׁוּר אֶת-

הָרֹאשׁ וְשַׂעַר הָרַגְלָיִם וְגַם אֶת-הַזָּקָן תִּסְפֶּה: וְהָיָה בַּיּוֹם

כא הַהוּא יְחַיֶּה-אִישׁ עֶגְלַת בָּקָר וּשְׁתֵּי-צֹאן: וְהָיָה מֵרֹב עֲשׂוֹת חָלָב יֹאכַל

כב חֶמְאָה כִּי-חֶמְאָה וּדְבַשׁ יֹאכֵל כָּל-הַנּוֹתָר בְּקֶרֶב הָאָרֶץ: וְהָיָה בַּיּוֹם

כג הַהוּא יִהְיֶה כָל-מָקוֹם אֲשֶׁר יִהְיֶה-שָּׁם אֶלֶף גֶּפֶן בְּאֶלֶף כָּסֶף לַשָּׁמִיר

כד וְלַשַּׁיִת יִהְיֶה: בַּחִצִּים וּבַקֶּשֶׁת יָבוֹא שָׁמָּה כִּי-שָׁמִיר וָשַׁיִת תִּהְיֶה כָל-

כה הָאָרֶץ: וְכֹל הֶהָרִים אֲשֶׁר בַּמַּעְדֵּר יֵעָדֵרוּן לֹא-תָבוֹא שָׁמָּה יִרְאַת שָׁמִיר

וָשָׁיִת וְהָיָה לְמִשְׁלַח שׁוֹר וּלְמִרְמַס שֶׂה: וַיֹּאמֶר יְהוָה

ח

א אֵלַי קַח-לְךָ גִּלָּיוֹן גָּדוֹל וּכְתֹב עָלָיו בְּחֶרֶט אֱנוֹשׁ לְמַהֵר שָׁלָל חָשׁ בַּז:

ב וְאָעִידָה לִּי עֵדִים נֶאֱמָנִים אֵת אוּרִיָּה הַכֹּהֵן וְאֶת-זְכַרְיָהוּ בֶּן יְבֶרֶכְיָהוּ:

ג וָאֶקְרַב אֶל-הַנְּבִיאָה וַתַּהַר וַתֵּלֶד בֵּן וַיֹּאמֶר יְהוָה אֵלַי קְרָא שְׁמוֹ מַהֵר

ד שָׁלָל חָשׁ בַּז: כִּי בְּטֶרֶם יֵדַע הַנַּעַר קְרֹא אָבִי וְאִמִּי יִשָּׂא ׀ אֶת-חֵיל דַּמֶּשֶׂק

ה וְאֵת שְׁלַל שֹׁמְרוֹן לִפְנֵי מֶלֶךְ אַשּׁוּר: וַיֹּסֶף יְהוָה דַּבֵּר

ו אֵלַי עוֹד לֵאמֹר: יַעַן כִּי מָאַס הָעָם הַזֶּה אֵת מֵי הַשִּׁלֹחַ הַהֹלְכִים לְאַט

ז וּמְשׂוֹשׂ אֶת-רְצִין וּבֶן-רְמַלְיָהוּ: וְלָכֵן הִנֵּה אֲדֹנָי מַעֲלֶה עֲלֵיהֶם אֶת-מֵי

הַנָּהָר הָעֲצוּמִים וְהָרַבִּים אֶת-מֶלֶךְ אַשּׁוּר וְאֶת-כָּל-כְּבוֹדוֹ וְעָלָה עַל-

ח כָּל-אֲפִיקָיו וְהָלַךְ עַל-כָּל-גְּדוֹתָיו: וְחָלַף בִּיהוּדָה שָׁטַף וְעָבַר עַד-צַוָּאר

ט יַגִּיעַ וְהָיָה מֻטּוֹת כְּנָפָיו מְלֹא רֹחַב-אַרְצְךָ עִמָּנוּ אֵל: רֹעוּ

עַמִּים וָחֹתּוּ וְהַאֲזִינוּ כֹּל מֶרְחַקֵּי-אָרֶץ הִתְאַזְּרוּ וָחֹתּוּ הִתְאַזְּרוּ וָחֹתּוּ:

י עֻצוּ עֵצָה וְתֻפָר דַּבְּרוּ דָבָר וְלֹא יָקוּם כִּי עִמָּנוּ אֵל: כִּי כֹה

יא אָמַר יְהוָה אֵלַי כְּחֶזְקַת הַיָּד וְיִסְּרֵנִי מִלֶּכֶת בְּדֶרֶךְ הָעָם-הַזֶּה לֵאמֹר:

יב לֹא-תֹאמְרוּן קֶשֶׁר לְכֹל אֲשֶׁר-יֹאמַר הָעָם הַזֶּה קָשֶׁר וְאֶת-מוֹרָאוֹ לֹא-

יג תִירְאוּ וְלֹא תַעֲרִיצוּ: אֶת-יְהוָה צְבָאוֹת אֹתוֹ תַקְדִּישׁוּ וְהוּא מוֹרַאֲכֶם

יד וְהוּא מַעֲרִצְכֶם: וְהָיָה לְמִקְדָּשׁ וּלְאֶבֶן נֶגֶף וּלְצוּר מִכְשׁוֹל לִשְׁנֵי בָתֵּי

טו יִשְׂרָאֵל לְפַח וּלְמוֹקֵשׁ לְיוֹשֵׁב יְרוּשָׁלָ͏ִם: וְכָשְׁלוּ בָם רַבִּים וְנָפְלוּ

7:20. The hair of the head represents the king; of the legs, his soldiers; and of the beard, his officials. All will be shorn, i.e., perish (*Targum*).

7:21-25. After the defeat of the Assyrian invaders, there will be miraculous prosperity in the desolate land. A minimum of animals will produce abundant dairy products. People will forsake wine because they will be on a lofty spiritual level; the neglected wine region will become filled with wild animals and too treacherous for an unarmed man to traverse (*Rashi*). The remaining land will be so fertile that people will let animals use much of

it for grazing (*Radak*).

8:1. To strengthen the message of his prophecy, Isaiah was commanded to inscribe it in an easily and universally understandable manner (*Rashi*). He was to inform the people that Sennacherib's plunder of the Ten Tribes was at hand, and that Nebuchadnezzar's spoil of Jerusalem, though years away, was already approaching.

8:3. Isaiah speaks of his wife as the prophetess.

8:6. The humble and unassuming House of David (*Targum*) is likened to the Shiloah, Jerusalem's water sup-

away from Judah: the king of Assyria's invasion.

Assyria's attack and defeat

¹⁸ "It shall be on that day that HASHEM will whistle to the fly that is at the far end of Egypt's rivers and to the bee that is in the land of Assyria. ¹⁹ They will come and all will encamp in the desolate valleys, in the crags of the rocks and upon all the brushes and all the bushes. ²⁰ On that day the Lord will shave with a large razor those who crossed the [Euphrates] River with the king of Assyria; the head, the hair of the legs, and the beard, as well, will be destroyed. *

²¹ "It shall be on that day that each man will raise a heifer and two sheep, ²² but it shall be that from the abundant production of milk he will eat cream, and whoever is left in the midst of the land will eat cream and honey. ²³ It will happen on that day: Where there had been a thousand vines, worth a thousand silver pieces, it will become thorns and weeds. ²⁴ One will be able to enter there [only] with arrows and a bow, for all the land will be thorns and weeds. ²⁵ But all the mountains that are hoed with a hoe — the fear of thorns and weeds will not come there, but they will be for the grazing of oxen and the roaming of sheep." *

8

¹ HASHEM said to me, "Take a large scroll and write on it in clear script: 'Plunder hastens; spoil quickens.'"* ² I appointed trustworthy witnesses for myself: Uriah the Kohen and Zechariah son of Jeberechiah. ³ I approached the prophetess, * and she conceived and bore a son; and HASHEM said to me: "Name

Maher-shalal-hash-baz

him Maher-shalal-hash-baz [Plunder Hastens; Spoil Quickens]. ⁴ For before the child knows how to say 'My father' and 'My mother,' the wealth of Damascus and the spoils of Samaria will be carried off before the king of Assyria."

⁵ HASHEM spoke further to me, saying:

The Shiloah and the Euphrates

⁶ Because this people has rejected the gently flowing water of the Shiloah, * and has rejoiced with Rezin and the son of Remaliah, ⁷ therefore, behold, the Lord is bringing upon them the mighty and abundant waters of the [Euphrates] River, the king of Assyria and all his glory, and it will rise above all its channels and overflow all its banks. ⁸ It will pass through Judah, flooding as it passes, and reaching to the neck; and its wingspread will be the full breadth of your land, O Immanuel.

⁹ Destroy, O you peoples, and then be devastated yourselves; hear this, all you faraway parts of the world: Gird yourselves, and then be shattered! Gird yourselves, and then be shattered! ¹⁰ Plan a conspiracy and it shall be annulled; speak your piece and it shall not stand, for God is with us!

¹¹ For thus said HASHEM to me with a strong hand; He admonished me not to follow the way of this people, [but] to say:

Castigation of the defectors

¹² Do not speak of a cabal, for everything this people speaks of is a cabal; * do not fear what they fear and do not be overwhelmed by it. ¹³ HASHEM, Master of Legions, Him shall you sanctify; He is Your reverence and He is your strength. ¹⁴ He shall be a sanctuary, but also a striking stone and a stumbling rock, for the two houses of Israel; * a trap and a snare for the inhabitants of Jerusalem. ¹⁵ And many people will stumble over them; they will fall down

---

ply. There were people in Judah who preferred the rule of Aram and the Ten Tribes to that of the Davidic dynasty. This chapter refers to them as "the people."

8:12. The majority wanted to conspire against Ahaz (*Radak*) or Hezekiah (*Rashi*), and surrender to the

enemy. Isaiah warned the loyalists not to think that such a cabal had any legitimacy.

8:14. God will be a fortress of protection for the loyalists in Jerusalem, and a stumbling rock for the rebels (*Radak*).

טז וְנִשְׁבָּרוּ וְנוֹקְשׁוּ וְנִלְכָּדוּ: צוֹר תְּעוּדָה חֲתוֹם תּוֹרָה בְּלִמֻּדָי:

יז–יח וְחִכִּיתִי לַיהוָה הַמַּסְתִּיר פָּנָיו מִבֵּית יַעֲקֹב וְקִוֵּיתִי־לוֹ: הִנֵּה אָנֹכִי וְהַיְלָדִים אֲשֶׁר נָתַן־לִי יְהוָה לְאֹתוֹת וּלְמוֹפְתִים בְּיִשְׂרָאֵל מֵעִם יְהוָה צְבָאוֹת הַשֹּׁכֵן בְּהַר צִיּוֹן:

יט וְכִי־יֹאמְרוּ אֲלֵיכֶם דִּרְשׁוּ אֶל־הָאֹבוֹת וְאֶל־הַיִּדְּעֹנִים הַמְצַפְצְפִים וְהַמַּהְגִּים הֲלוֹא־עַם אֶל־אֱלֹהָיו יִדְרֹשׁ בְּעַד

כ הַחַיִּים אֶל־הַמֵּתִים: לְתוֹרָה וְלִתְעוּדָה אִם־לֹא יֹאמְרוּ כַּדָּבָר הַזֶּה אֲשֶׁר

כא אֵין־לוֹ שָׁחַר: וְעָבַר בָּהּ נִקְשֶׁה וְרָעֵב וְהָיָה כִי־יִרְעַב וְהִתְקַצַּף וְקִלֵּל בְּמַלְכּוֹ

כב וּבֵאלֹהָיו וּפָנָה לְמָעְלָה: וְאֶל־אֶרֶץ יַבִּיט וְהִנֵּה צָרָה וַחֲשֵׁכָה מְעוּף צוּקָה

כג וַאֲפֵלָה מְנֻדָּח: כִּי לֹא מוּעָף לַאֲשֶׁר מוּצָק לָהּ כָּעֵת הָרִאשׁוֹן הֵקַל אַרְצָה זְבֻלוּן וְאַרְצָה נַפְתָּלִי וְהָאַחֲרוֹן הִכְבִּיד דֶּרֶךְ הַיָּם עֵבֶר הַיַּרְדֵּן גְּלִיל הַגּוֹיִם:

א הָעָם הַהֹלְכִים בַּחֹשֶׁךְ רָאוּ אוֹר גָּדוֹל יֹשְׁבֵי בְּאֶרֶץ צַלְמָוֶת אוֹר נָגַהּ

ב עֲלֵיהֶם: הִרְבִּיתָ הַגּוֹי °לֹא [לוֹ ק] הִגְדַּלְתָּ הַשִּׂמְחָה שָׂמְחוּ לְפָנֶיךָ

ג כְּשִׂמְחַת בַּקָּצִיר כַּאֲשֶׁר יָגִילוּ בְּחַלְּקָם שָׁלָל: כִּי ׀ אֶת־עֹל סֻבֳּלוֹ וְאֵת מַטֵּה

ד שִׁכְמוֹ שֵׁבֶט הַנֹּגֵשׂ בּוֹ הַחִתֹּתָ כְּיוֹם מִדְיָן: כִּי כָל־סְאוֹן סֹאֵן בְּרַעַשׁ וְשִׂמְלָה

ה מְגוֹלָלָה בְדָמִים וְהָיְתָה לִשְׂרֵפָה מַאֲכֹלֶת אֵשׁ: כִּי־יֶלֶד יֻלַּד־לָנוּ בֵּן נִתַּן־ לָנוּ וַתְּהִי הַמִּשְׂרָה עַל־שִׁכְמוֹ וַיִּקְרָא שְׁמוֹ פֶּלֶא יוֹעֵץ אֵל גִּבּוֹר אֲבִי־עַד

ו שַׂר־שָׁלוֹם: °לְמַרְבֵּה [לְמַרְבֵּה ק] הַמִּשְׂרָה וּלְשָׁלוֹם אֵין־קֵץ עַל־כִּסֵּא דָוִד וְעַל־מַמְלַכְתּוֹ לְהָכִין אֹתָהּ וּלְסַעֲדָהּ בְּמִשְׁפָּט וּבִצְדָקָה מֵעַתָּה וְעַד־

ז עוֹלָם קִנְאַת יְהוָה צְבָאוֹת תַּעֲשֶׂה־זֹּאת: ◄ דָּבָר שָׁלַח אֲדֹנָי

ח בְּיַעֲקֹב וְנָפַל בְּיִשְׂרָאֵל: וְיָדְעוּ הָעָם כֻּלּוֹ אֶפְרַיִם וְיוֹשֵׁב שֹׁמְרוֹן בְּגַאֲוָה

ט וּבְגֹדֶל לֵבָב לֵאמֹר: לְבֵנִים נָפָלוּ וְגָזִית נִבְנֶה שִׁקְמִים גֻּדָּעוּ וַאֲרָזִים נַחֲלִיף:

י–יא וַיְשַׂגֵּב יְהוָה אֶת־צָרֵי רְצִין עָלָיו וְאֶת־אֹיְבָיו יְסַכְסֵךְ: אֲרָם מִקֶּדֶם וּפְלִשְׁתִּים מֵאָחוֹר וַיֹּאכְלוּ אֶת־יִשְׂרָאֵל בְּכָל־פֶּה בְּכָל־זֹאת לֹא־שָׁב

יב אַפּוֹ וְעוֹד יָדוֹ נְטוּיָה: וְהָעָם לֹא־שָׁב עַד־הַמַּכֵּהוּ וְאֶת־יְהוָה צְבָאוֹת לֹא

יג דָרָשׁוּ: וַיַּכְרֵת יְהוָה מִיִּשְׂרָאֵל רֹאשׁ וְזָנָב כִּפָּה וְאַגְמוֹן

יד יוֹם אֶחָד: זָקֵן וּנְשׂוּא־פָנִים הוּא הָרֹאשׁ וְנָבִיא מוֹרֶה־שֶּׁקֶר הוּא הַזָּנָב:

Haftaras
Yisro for
Ashkenazim
continues
here:
9:5-6

ט

8:17-18. Isaiah interrupts his prophecy to declare which of the two groups he will join.

8:18. My actions, such as the writing on the scroll (v. 1), and the names of my children — Maher-shalal-hash-baz, Shear-jashub, Immanuel — are Divinely ordained signs for events that will befall the people of Israel.

8:20. I am telling you for certain that the people will indeed try to entice you [v. 19] with arguments that have no substance (Radak).

8:21. Realizing that his king and gods cannot save him, he will look to Heaven and pray to the true God.

8:23. The Assyrians exiled the Ten Tribes in three stages (see II Kings Chs. 15, 17). The first time the people were not so severely shocked and alarmed, but when Senna-

cherib would return and uproot the remaining population of the Northern Kingdom, the distress would be felt much more intensely. The land is called region of the nations, because so many peoples desired it.

9:1-6. Isaiah again interrupts his prophecy to address God. The salvation to which he refers is the miraculous end of Sennacherib's siege of Jerusalem [see Chs. 36-37] (Rashi).

9:3. The rout of the Assyrian army will be reminiscent of the miracle granted Gideon and his small force against Midian (Judges Chs. 7-8).

9:5. This wondrous salvation took place in the days of the child of Ahaz, the righteous King Hezekiah, whom God — the Wondrous Adviser, Mighty God, Eternal and be broken, trapped and ensnared. ¹⁶ Fasten this warning and seal the teaching onto [the hearts of] My students.

God will
conceal
Himself

¹⁷ I shall await HASHEM, * Who has concealed His face from the House of Jacob, and I will hope to Him. ¹⁸ Behold, I and the children whom HASHEM has given me are signs and symbols for Israel, * from HASHEM, Master of Legions, Who dwells in Mount Zion.

¹⁹ If people say to you, 'Enquire of the necromancers and the diviners who chirp and snort,' [respond:] 'Should not a people inquire of their own God? [Should we inquire] of the dead for the living?!' ²⁰ [I swear] by the Torah and the teaching that they will make this statement to you, which has no light of dawn. * ²¹ Through [the land] will pass the troubled and hungry. When he will be hungry he will be angry and curse his king and his gods, and direct his

Tripartite
exile

face on high. * ²² He will gaze throughout the land; but behold — misfortune and darkness, the weariness of distress! He will be buffeted to darkness. ²³ For he was not wearied the first time [the land] was distressed, when [Assyria] exiled the land of Zebulun and the land of Naphtali, * but the last time [Assyria] will be severe, by the way of the sea, beyond the Jordan, the region of the nations.

9

Isaiah
praises
God's
salvation

¹ The people* that walked in darkness have seen a great light; those who dwelled in the land of the shadow of death, light has shone upon them. ² You exalted the nation; You increased its joy. They rejoiced before You like the joy of harvest time, as they would exult when they divide spoils. ³ For the yoke of its burden and the staff on its shoulder, the rod that oppressed them, You smashed like the day of Midian. * ⁴ For all tumultuous battles are fought with an uproar, and the garments wallow in blood, but [Sennacherib] became a blaze and was consumed by fire. ⁵ For a child* has been born to us, a son has been given to us, and the dominion will rest on his shoulder; the Wondrous Adviser, Mighty God, Eternal Father, called his name Sar-shalom [Prince of Peace]; ⁶ upon the one with the greatness in dominion and the boundless peace that will prevail on the throne of David and on his kingdom, to establish it and sustain it through justice and righteousness, from now to eternity. The zealousness of HASHEM, Master of Legions, will accomplish this!

His anger
has not
subsided
from
Ephraim . . .

⁷ The word [that] the Lord has sent for Jacob will befall Israel. * ⁸ Then the entire people will realize, Ephraim and the inhabitants of Samaria, who had said with pride and with arrogant heart, ⁹ "Bricks have fallen, we will rebuild with hewn stone; sycamores have been cut down, we will replace them with cedars." ¹⁰ HASHEM set Rezin's enemies over him, and roused his adversaries; ¹¹ Aram from the east and the Philistines from the west, they have consumed Israel with every mouth. Yet despite all this, His anger has not subsided and His hand is still outstretched.

. . . from
those who
mislead . . .

¹² But the people has not returned to the One Who smites it; they do not seek HASHEM, Master of Legions. ¹³ HASHEM will cut off from Israel the head and the tail, * the canopied tree and the reed, in one day. ¹⁴ The elder and the distinguished man, he is the head; and the prophet who teaches falsehood, he is the tail.

Father — called "Prince of Peace."

9:7. After praising God for the miraculous future salvation of Jerusalem, Isaiah turns to the people and warns them of the disaster awaiting the arrogant and over-confident Northern Kingdom. Assyria will defeat Aram.

Then, Aram and Philistia will viciously attack Israel from east and west, but the people will still refuse to acknowledge their dependence on God.

9:13. I.e., all the greater and lesser leaders of the people, and the major and minor members of society.

וַיִּהְיוּ מְאַשְּׁרֵי הָעָם־הַזֶּה מַתְעִים וּמְאֻשָּׁרָיו מְבֻלָּעִים: עַל־כֵּן עַל־ טו־טז
בַּחוּרָיו לֹא־יִשְׂמַח | אֲדֹנָי וְאֶת־יְתֹמָיו וְאֶת־אַלְמְנֹתָיו לֹא יְרַחֵם כִּי
כֻלּוֹ חָנֵף וּמֵרַע וְכָל־פֶּה דֹּבֵר נְבָלָה בְּכָל־זֹאת לֹא־שָׁב אַפּוֹ וְעוֹד יָדוֹ
נְטוּיָה: כִּי־בָעֲרָה כָאֵשׁ רִשְׁעָה שָׁמִיר וָשַׁיִת תֹּאכֵל וַתִּצַּת בְּסִבְכֵי הַיַּעַר יז
וַיִּתְאַבְּכוּ גֵּאוּת עָשָׁן: בְּעֶבְרַת יהוה צְבָאוֹת נֶעְתַּם אָרֶץ וַיְהִי הָעָם יח
כְּמַאֲכֹלֶת אֵשׁ אִישׁ אֶל־אָחִיו לֹא יַחְמֹלוּ: וַיִּגְזֹר עַל־יָמִין וְרָעֵב וַיֹּאכַל יט
עַל־שְׂמֹאול וְלֹא שָׂבֵעוּ אִישׁ בְּשַׂר־זְרֹעוֹ יֹאכֵלוּ: מְנַשֶּׁה אֶת־אֶפְרַיִם כ
וְאֶפְרַיִם אֶת־מְנַשֶּׁה יַחְדָּו הֵמָּה עַל־יְהוּדָה בְּכָל־זֹאת לֹא־שָׁב אַפּוֹ וְעוֹד
יָדוֹ נְטוּיָה: הוֹי הַחֹקְקִים חִקְקֵי־אָוֶן וּמְכַתְּבִים עָמָל כִּתֵּבוּ: א **י**
לְהַטּוֹת מִדִּין דַּלִּים וְלִגְזֹל מִשְׁפַּט עֲנִיֵּי עַמִּי לִהְיוֹת אַלְמָנוֹת שְׁלָלָם וְאֶת־ ב
יְתוֹמִים יָבֹזּוּ: וּמַה־תַּעֲשׂוּ לְיוֹם פְּקֻדָּה וּלְשׁוֹאָה מִמֶּרְחָק תָּבוֹא עַל־מִי ג
תָּנוּסוּ לְעֶזְרָה וְאָנָה תַעַזְבוּ כְּבוֹדְכֶם: בִּלְתִּי כָרַע תַּחַת אַסִּיר וְתַחַת ד
הֲרוּגִים יִפֹּלוּ בְּכָל־זֹאת לֹא־שָׁב אַפּוֹ וְעוֹד יָדוֹ נְטוּיָה: הוֹי ה
אַשּׁוּר שֵׁבֶט אַפִּי וּמַטֶּה־הוּא בְיָדָם זַעְמִי: בְּגוֹי חָנֵף אֲשַׁלְּחֶנּוּ וְעַל־עַם ו
עֶבְרָתִי אֲצַוֶּנּוּ לִשְׁלֹל שָׁלָל וְלָבֹז בַּז °וּלְשִׂימוֹ [°וּלְשׂוּמוֹ ק] מִרְמָס
כְּחֹמֶר חוּצוֹת: וְהוּא לֹא־כֵן יְדַמֶּה וּלְבָבוֹ לֹא־כֵן יַחְשֹׁב כִּי לְהַשְׁמִיד ז
בִּלְבָבוֹ וּלְהַכְרִית גּוֹיִם לֹא מְעָט: כִּי יֹאמַר הֲלֹא שָׂרַי יַחְדָּו מְלָכִים: ח
הֲלֹא כְּכַרְכְּמִישׁ כַּלְנוֹ אִם־לֹא כְאַרְפַּד חֲמָת אִם־לֹא כְדַמֶּשֶׂק ט
שֹׁמְרוֹן: כַּאֲשֶׁר מָצְאָה יָדִי לְמַמְלְכֹת הָאֱלִיל וּפְסִילֵיהֶם מִירוּשָׁלַ͏ִם י
וּמִשֹּׁמְרוֹן: הֲלֹא כַּאֲשֶׁר עָשִׂיתִי לְשֹׁמְרוֹן וְלֶאֱלִילֶיהָ כֵּן אֶעֱשֶׂה לִירוּשָׁלַ͏ִם יא
וְלַעֲצַבֶּיהָ:   וְהָיָה כִּי־יְבַצַּע אֲדֹנָי אֶת־כָּל־מַעֲשֵׂהוּ בְּהַר צִיּוֹן יב
וּבִירוּשָׁלָ͏ִם אֶפְקֹד עַל־פְּרִי־גֹדֶל לְבַב מֶלֶךְ־אַשּׁוּר וְעַל־תִּפְאֶרֶת רוּם
עֵינָיו: כִּי אָמַר בְּכֹחַ יָדִי עָשִׂיתִי וּבְחָכְמָתִי כִּי נְבֻנוֹתִי וְאָסִיר | גְּבוּלֹת יג
עַמִּים °וַעֲתִידֹתֵיהֶם °[וַעֲתוּדֹתֵיהֶם ק] שׁוֹשֵׂתִי וְאוֹרִיד כַּאבִּיר יוֹשְׁבִים:
וַתִּמְצָא כַקֵּן | יָדִי לְחֵיל הָעַמִּים וְכֶאֱסֹף בֵּיצִים עֲזֻבוֹת כָּל־הָאָרֶץ אֲנִי יד
אָסָפְתִּי וְלֹא הָיָה נֹדֵד כָּנָף וּפֹצֶה פֶה וּמְצַפְצֵף: הֲיִתְפָּאֵר הַגַּרְזֶן עַל הַחֹצֵב טו
בּוֹ אִם־יִתְגַּדֵּל הַמַּשּׂוֹר עַל־מְנִיפוֹ כְּהָנִיף שֵׁבֶט אֶת־מְרִימָיו כְּהָרִים מַטֶּה
לֹא־עֵץ: לָכֵן יְשַׁלַּח הָאָדוֹן יהוה צְבָאוֹת בְּמִשְׁמַנָּיו טז
רָזוֹן וְתַחַת כְּבֹדוֹ יֵקַד יְקֹד כִּיקוֹד אֵשׁ: וְהָיָה אוֹר־יִשְׂרָאֵל לְאֵשׁ וּקְדוֹשׁוֹ יז

9:16. Despite the disaster, Israel did not repent, so God's anger persisted.

9:18-19. Just as one burning log ignites the next, so too the people, out of panic and starvation, will act cruelly toward one another (*Radak*). They will steal provisions, but will not find enough to satisfy their hunger (*Rashi*).

10:1. Isaiah addresses dishonest judges and others who use the judicial process to enrich themselves unlawfully.

10:4. The slaughter and exile will be so complete that even the wealthiest people will be doomed. The only hope will be to pretend to be one of the prisoners or to feign death among the corpses (*Kara*). But even then, the people will not repent, so God will not relent.

10:6-7. God sent Assyria to punish hypocritical Israel, which had angered Him, but the Assyrian king thinks his conquests are due to his own strength.

10:12-14. After using the Assyrians as His "rod of anger," God will punish them for their arrogance.

¹⁵ The guides of this people mislead, and the guided ones are devoured. ¹⁶ Therefore, my Lord shall not rejoice over their young men, and He shall not pity their orphans and widows, for they are all hypocritical and evil, and every mouth utters degeneracy. Yet despite all this, * His anger has not subsided and His hand is still outstretched.

... from the cruel ...   ¹⁷ For [their] wickedness will burn [within them] like the fire; it will consume thorns and weeds, and will kindle the branches of the forest; they will be overcome by the intensity of the smoke. ¹⁸ By the wrath of HASHEM, Master of Legions, the land is charred. The people has become like fuel for a fire; * they have no mercy one for another. ¹⁹ He snatched from his right and remains hungry; he consumed on his left, but they are not sated; everyone will eat the flesh of his own arm. ²⁰ Manasseh is against Ephraim, Ephraim is against Manasseh, [but] they are both together against Judah. Yet despite all this, His anger has not subsided and His hand is still outstretched.

10   ¹ Woe to those * who inscribe inscriptions of falsehood and who write fraud-
... and from the unjust   ulent documents, ² to deprive the destitute of justice and to rob the justice of the poor of My people, so that widows be their spoil; and they plunder orphans. ³ What will you do about the day of retribution, about catastrophe that comes from afar? To whom will you run for help? Where will you leave your wealth? ⁴ [You will not survive] unless you kneel in the prisoner's place or fall down in the place of the slain. Yet despite all this, His anger has not subsided, and His hand is still outstretched. *

Assyria's conceit   ⁵ Woe to Assyria, the rod of My anger; My wrath is a staff in their hand. ⁶ Against a hypocritical people * shall I send them, and against a people that angers Me shall I charge them, to take spoils and to plunder booty, and to make them trampled like the mire of the streets. ⁷ But he does not imagine this, and his heart does not think this way; for his heart is set to destroy, and to cut off nations, without leaving even a bit. ⁸ For he says, 'Are not all my officers [like] kings? ⁹ Is not Calno like Carchemish; is not Hamath like Arpad; is not Samaria like Damascus? ¹⁰ Just as my hand has overpowered the kingdoms of the false god — and their graven images are from Jerusalem and Samaria — ¹¹ surely, just as I have done to Samaria and its false gods, so shall I do to Jerusalem and its idols!'

¹² But it will be that after the Lord completes all His work, at Mount Zion and Jerusalem, I will deal with the fruits of the Assyrian king's conceit, and with the glory of his arrogant eyes. * ¹³ For he said, 'With the strength of my hand have I accomplished, and with my wisdom, for I am understanding; I have removed the boundaries of peoples and have plundered their treasures; I have brought down dwellers in strongholds. ¹⁴ My hand has found the wealth of the peoples like a nest; as one gathers abandoned eggs, so have I gathered the whole world, and no one shook a wing or opened a mouth and chirped [in protest].'

¹⁵ Can a hatchet glory over the one who chops with it? Can a saw be greater than the one who wields it? It is as if a rod could shake those who lift it; as if a stick could lift one who is not wood!

Parable of the forest fire   ¹⁶ Therefore, the Lord, HASHEM, Master of Legions, will send a leanness among his fatted ones, and instead of his glory a burning will burn like a blaze of fire. ¹⁷ And the Light of Israel will be like fire and his Holy One will be like

יח לְלַהֲבָה וּבָעֲרָה וְאָכְלָה שִׁיתוֹ וּשְׁמִירוֹ בְּיוֹם אֶחָד: וּכְבוֹד יַעְרוֹ וְכַרְמִלּוֹ
יט מִנֶּפֶשׁ וְעַד-בָּשָׂר יְכַלֶּה וְהָיָה כִּמְסֹס נֹסֵס: וּשְׁאָר עֵץ יַעְרוֹ מִסְפָּר יִהְיוּ
כ וְנַעַר יִכְתְּבֵם: וְהָיָה ׀ בַּיּוֹם הַהוּא לֹא-יוֹסִיף עוֹד שְׁאָר יִשְׂרָאֵל
וּפְלֵיטַת בֵּית-יַעֲקֹב לְהִשָּׁעֵן עַל-מַכֵּהוּ וְנִשְׁעַן עַל-יְהוָה קְדוֹשׁ יִשְׂרָאֵל
כא-כב בֶּאֱמֶת: שְׁאָר יָשׁוּב שְׁאָר יַעֲקֹב אֶל-אֵל גִּבּוֹר: כִּי אִם-יִהְיֶה עַמְּךָ יִשְׂרָאֵל
כג כְּחוֹל הַיָּם שְׁאָר יָשׁוּב בּוֹ כִּלָּיוֹן חָרוּץ שׁוֹטֵף צְדָקָה: כִּי כָלָה וְנֶחֱרָצָה
כד אֲדֹנָי יְהוִה צְבָאוֹת עֹשֶׂה בְּקֶרֶב כָּל-הָאָרֶץ: לָכֵן כֹּה-אָמַר
אֲדֹנָי יְהוִה צְבָאוֹת אַל-תִּירָא עַמִּי יֹשֵׁב צִיּוֹן מֵאַשּׁוּר בַּשֵּׁבֶט יַכֶּכָּה וּמַטֵּהוּ
כה יִשָּׂא-עָלֶיךָ בְּדֶרֶךְ מִצְרָיִם: כִּי-עוֹד מְעַט מִזְעָר וְכָלָה זַעַם וְאַפִּי עַל-
כו תַּבְלִיתָם: וְעוֹרֵר עָלָיו יְהוָה צְבָאוֹת שׁוֹט כְּמַכַּת מִדְיָן בְּצוּר עוֹרֵב וּמַטֵּהוּ
כז עַל-הַיָּם וּנְשָׂאוֹ בְּדֶרֶךְ מִצְרָיִם: וְהָיָה ׀ בַּיּוֹם הַהוּא יָסוּר סֻבֳּלוֹ מֵעַל שִׁכְמֶךָ
כח וְעֻלּוֹ מֵעַל צַוָּארֶךָ וְחֻבַּל עֹל מִפְּנֵי-שָׁמֶן: בָּא עַל-עַיַּת עָבַר בְּמִגְרוֹן
כט לְמִכְמָשׂ יַפְקִיד כֵּלָיו: עָבְרוּ מַעְבָּרָה גֶּבַע מָלוֹן לָנוּ חָרְדָה הָרָמָה גִּבְעַת
ל-לא שָׁאוּל נָסָה: צַהֲלִי קוֹלֵךְ בַּת-גַּלִּים הַקְשִׁיבִי לַיְשָׁה עֲנִיָּה עֲנָתוֹת: נָדְדָה
לב מַדְמֵנָה יֹשְׁבֵי הַגֵּבִים הֵעִיזוּ ◄ עוֹד הַיּוֹם בְּנֹב לַעֲמֹד יְנֹפֵף יָדוֹ הַר °בֵּית-
לג [°בַּת- ק] צִיּוֹן גִּבְעַת יְרוּשָׁלָ͏ִם: הִנֵּה הָאָדוֹן יְהוָה
צְבָאוֹת מְסָעֵף פֻּארָה בְּמַעֲרָצָה וְרָמֵי הַקּוֹמָה גְּדֻעִים וְהַגְּבֹהִים יִשְׁפָּלוּ:
יא לד-א וְנִקַּף סִבְכֵי הַיַּעַר בַּבַּרְזֶל וְהַלְּבָנוֹן בְּאַדִּיר יִפּוֹל: וְיָצָא
ב חֹטֶר מִגֵּזַע יִשָׁי וְנֵצֶר מִשָּׁרָשָׁיו יִפְרֶה: וְנָחָה עָלָיו רוּחַ יְהוָה רוּחַ חָכְמָה
ג וּבִינָה רוּחַ עֵצָה וּגְבוּרָה רוּחַ דַּעַת וְיִרְאַת יְהוָה: וַהֲרִיחוֹ בְּיִרְאַת יְהוָה
ד וְלֹא-לְמַרְאֵה עֵינָיו יִשְׁפּוֹט וְלֹא-לְמִשְׁמַע אָזְנָיו יוֹכִיחַ: וְשָׁפַט בְּצֶדֶק
דַּלִּים וְהוֹכִיחַ בְּמִישׁוֹר לְעַנְוֵי-אָרֶץ וְהִכָּה-אֶרֶץ בְּשֵׁבֶט פִּיו וּבְרוּחַ
ה-ו שְׂפָתָיו יָמִית רָשָׁע: וְהָיָה צֶדֶק אֵזוֹר מָתְנָיו וְהָאֱמוּנָה אֵזוֹר חֲלָצָיו: וְגָר
זְאֵב עִם-כֶּבֶשׂ וְנָמֵר עִם-גְּדִי יִרְבָּץ וְעֵגֶל וּכְפִיר וּמְרִיא יַחְדָּו וְנַעַר קָטֹן
ז נֹהֵג בָּם: וּפָרָה וָדֹב תִּרְעֶינָה יַחְדָּו יִרְבְּצוּ יַלְדֵיהֶן וְאַרְיֵה כַּבָּקָר יֹאכַל-
ח-ט תֶּבֶן: וְשִׁעֲשַׁע יוֹנֵק עַל-חֻר פָּתֶן וְעַל מְאוּרַת צִפְעוֹנִי גָּמוּל יָדוֹ הָדָה: לֹא-
יָרֵעוּ וְלֹא-יַשְׁחִיתוּ בְּכָל-הַר קָדְשִׁי כִּי-מָלְאָה הָאָרֶץ דֵּעָה אֶת-יְהוָה

HAFTARAH
EIGHTH
DAY OF
PESACH
10:32-12:6

10:17-18. Sennacherib's captains and officers are likened to plants and fields.

10:22. The prophecy addresses Hezekiah. Since the Ten Tribes will have been exiled, even the large populace under Hezekiah will be reckoned as a remnant of the total (Radak).

10:24. Do not fear that Assyria will exterminate you. There will be persecution as in ancient Egypt, but the nation will survive (Radak).

10:26. See Judges Ch. 7. God will defeat Sennacherib as He did Midian, and as He wiped away Egypt at the sea, by means of Moses' staff.

10:27. An ox's neck is usually oiled to keep the yoke from tearing its skin (Kara). The Sages comment that Hezekiah earned the miracle of the destruction of the Assyrian forces because of the copious amounts of oil that he used to keep lamps burning in the study halls so that the people could learn Torah late into the night.

10:34. I.e., the angel mentioned in 37:36.

11:1. The Ten Tribes, which were exiled by the Assyrians, will also be redeemed by the future Messiah, who will descend from the son of Jesse i.e., David (Rashi).

11:6. A metaphor for the abundant peace of Messianic times (Rambam; Ibn Ezra). Radak cites a view that the a flame; it will burn and consume his thorns and weeds in a single day; [18] and his glorious forest and his fertile field, * it will annihilate from soul to flesh, and they will be like a termite's chewings. [19] The tree-remnant of his forest will be few; a child will record them.

Israel's remnant will return . . .

[20] It will be on that day that the remnant of Israel and the survivors of the House of Jacob will no longer rely on its attacker, but will rely on HASHEM, the Holy One of Israel, in truth. [21] The remnant will return, the remnant of Jacob, to the mighty God. [22] For even if your* people Israel will be like the sand of the sea, only a remnant of it will return; [for] an intense destruction will surge forth, with justification. [23] For an intense devastation does the Lord HASHEM/ELOHIM, Master of Legions, carry out in the midst of the land.

[24] Therefore, thus said My Lord HASHEM/ELOHIM, Master of Legions: Do not be afraid of Assyria, O My people who dwell in Zion, though he will strike you with a staff and raise his rod over you in the manner of Egypt. * [25] For in a very short while, My fury and My anger will destroy [them] for their sacrilege. [26] HASHEM, Master of Legions, will arouse a rod upon him like the defeat of Midian at the rock of Oreb, and His staff [as] at the Sea [of Reeds], and carry him away, in the manner of Egypt. * [27] It will be on that day that He will lift [Assyria's] affliction from your shoulders, and his yoke from upon your neck, and the yoke will be broken because of the oil. *

[28] [Sennacherib] has come to Ayyath and passed through Migron; he deposits his belongings at Michmas. [29] They passed by the river crossing, they lodged at Geba; Ramah trembled, Gibeath-shaul fled. [30] Let out your voice, Bath-gallim! Hear, O Laish! Anathoth is wretched. [31] Madmenah has moved away; the inhabitants of Gebim have mustered themselves. [32] Yet today he will stand in Nob; he will wave his hand [contemptuously] at the mountain of the daughter of Zion, at the hill of Jerusalem. [33] Behold, the Lord, HASHEM, Master of Legions, will chop off branches with an ax; those of lofty stature will be severed, and the haughty ones brought low. [34] Forest thickets will be hewn by iron, and the Lebanon will fall by a mighty one. *

. . . and Assyria's forest will be cut down

11

The Davidic Messiah

[1] A staff will emerge from the stump of Jesse* and a shoot will sprout from his roots. [2] The spirit of HASHEM will rest upon him — a spirit of wisdom and understanding, a spirit of counsel and strength, a spirit of knowledge and fear of HASHEM. [3] He will be imbued with a spirit of fear for HASHEM; and will not need to judge by what his eyes see nor decide by what his ears hear. [4] He will judge the destitute with righteousness, and decide with fairness for the humble of the earth. He will strike [the wicked of] the world with the rod of his mouth, and with the breath of his lips he will slay the wicked. [5] Righteousness will be the girdle round his loins, and faith will be the girdle round his waist.

[6] The wolf will live with the sheep* and the leopard will lie down with the kid; and a calf, a lion whelp and a fatling [will walk] together, and a young child will lead them. [7] A cow and bear will graze and their young will lie down together; and a lion, like cattle, will eat hay. [8] A suckling will play by a viper's hole; and a newly weaned child will stretch his hand toward an adder's lair. [9] They will neither injure nor destroy in all of My sacred mountain; for the earth will be as filled with knowledge of HASHEM

---

prophecy means literally that even animals will coexist in harmony. *Radak's* own view is that the prophecy applies

to *Eretz Yisrael*, where the righteous people will be protected from the violence of nature (see v. 9).

וְהָיָה בַּיּוֹם הַהוּא שֹׁרֶשׁ יִשַׁי אֲשֶׁר עֹמֵד ‏ כְּנֵס לַיָּם מְכַסִּים: י

וְהָיָה | לְנֵס עַמִּים אֵלָיו גּוֹיִם יִדְרֹשׁוּ וְהָיְתָה מְנֻחָתוֹ כָּבוֹד: יא

בַּיּוֹם הַהוּא יוֹסִיף אֲדֹנָי | שֵׁנִית יָדוֹ לִקְנוֹת אֶת־שְׁאָר עַמּוֹ אֲשֶׁר יִשָּׁאֵר

מֵאַשּׁוּר וּמִמִּצְרַיִם וּמִפַּתְרוֹס וּמִכּוּשׁ וּמֵעֵילָם וּמִשִּׁנְעָר וּמֵחֲמָת וּמֵאִיֵּי

הַיָּם: וְנָשָׂא נֵס לַגּוֹיִם וְאָסַף נִדְחֵי יִשְׂרָאֵל וּנְפֻצוֹת יְהוּדָה יְקַבֵּץ מֵאַרְבַּע יב

כַּנְפוֹת הָאָרֶץ: וְסָרָה קִנְאַת אֶפְרַיִם וְצֹרְרֵי יְהוּדָה יִכָּרֵתוּ אֶפְרַיִם לֹא־ יג

יְקַנֵּא אֶת־יְהוּדָה וִיהוּדָה לֹא־יָצֹר אֶת־אֶפְרָיִם: וְעָפוּ בְכָתֵף פְּלִשְׁתִּים יד

יָמָּה יַחְדָּו יָבֹזּוּ אֶת־בְּנֵי־קֶדֶם אֱדוֹם וּמוֹאָב מִשְׁלוֹחַ יָדָם וּבְנֵי עַמּוֹן

מִשְׁמַעְתָּם: וְהֶחֱרִים יהוה אֵת לְשׁוֹן יָם־מִצְרַיִם וְהֵנִיף יָדוֹ עַל־הַנָּהָר טו

בַּעְיָם רוּחוֹ וְהִכָּהוּ לְשִׁבְעָה נְחָלִים וְהִדְרִיךְ בַּנְּעָלִים: וְהָיְתָה מְסִלָּה טז

לִשְׁאָר עַמּוֹ אֲשֶׁר יִשָּׁאֵר מֵאַשּׁוּר כַּאֲשֶׁר הָיְתָה לְיִשְׂרָאֵל בְּיוֹם עֲלֹתוֹ

מֵאֶרֶץ מִצְרָיִם: וְאָמַרְתָּ בַּיּוֹם הַהוּא אוֹדְךָ יהוה כִּי אָנַפְתָּ בִּי יָשֹׁב ‏ יב ‏ א

אַפְּךָ וּתְנַחֲמֵנִי: הִנֵּה אֵל יְשׁוּעָתִי אֶבְטַח וְלֹא אֶפְחָד כִּי־עָזִּי וְזִמְרָת יָהּ ב

יהוה וַיְהִי־לִי לִישׁוּעָה: וּשְׁאַבְתֶּם־מַיִם בְּשָׂשׂוֹן מִמַּעַיְנֵי הַיְשׁוּעָה: ג

וַאֲמַרְתֶּם בַּיּוֹם הַהוּא הוֹדוּ לַיהוה קִרְאוּ בִשְׁמוֹ הוֹדִיעוּ בָעַמִּים עֲלִילֹתָיו ד

הַזְכִּירוּ כִּי נִשְׂגָּב שְׁמוֹ: זַמְּרוּ יהוה כִּי גֵאוּת עָשָׂה °מִידַעַת [°מוּדַעַת ק] ה

זֹאת בְּכָל־הָאָרֶץ: צַהֲלִי וָרֹנִּי יוֹשֶׁבֶת צִיּוֹן כִּי־גָדוֹל בְּקִרְבֵּךְ קְדוֹשׁ ו

יִשְׂרָאֵל: ‏ ◀ ‏ מַשָּׂא בָּבֶל אֲשֶׁר חָזָה יְשַׁעְיָהוּ בֶּן־ ‏ יג ‏ א

אָמוֹץ: עַל הַר־נִשְׁפֶּה שְׂאוּ־נֵס הָרִימוּ קוֹל לָהֶם הָנִיפוּ יָד וְיָבֹאוּ ב

פִּתְחֵי נְדִיבִים: אֲנִי צִוֵּיתִי לִמְקֻדָּשָׁי גַּם קָרָאתִי גִבּוֹרַי לְאַפִּי עַלִּיזֵי ג

גַּאֲוָתִי: קוֹל הָמוֹן בֶּהָרִים דְּמוּת עַם־רָב קוֹל שְׁאוֹן מַמְלְכוֹת גּוֹיִם ד

נֶאֱסָפִים יהוה צְבָאוֹת מְפַקֵּד צְבָא מִלְחָמָה: בָּאִים מֵאֶרֶץ מֶרְחָק ה

מִקְצֵה הַשָּׁמָיִם יהוה וּכְלֵי זַעְמוֹ לְחַבֵּל כָּל־הָאָרֶץ: הֵילִילוּ כִּי קָרוֹב ו

יוֹם יהוה כְּשֹׁד מִשַּׁדַּי יָבוֹא: עַל־כֵּן כָּל־יָדַיִם תִּרְפֶּינָה וְכָל־לְבַב אֱנוֹשׁ ז

יִמָּס: וְנִבְהָלוּ | צִירִים וַחֲבָלִים יֹאחֵזוּן כַּיּוֹלֵדָה יְחִילוּן אִישׁ אֶל־רֵעֵהוּ ח

יִתְמָהוּ פְּנֵי לְהָבִים פְּנֵיהֶם: הִנֵּה יוֹם־יהוה בָּא אַכְזָרִי וְעֶבְרָה וַחֲרוֹן ט

אָף לָשׂוּם הָאָרֶץ לְשַׁמָּה וְחַטָּאֶיהָ יַשְׁמִיד מִמֶּנָּה: כִּי־כוֹכְבֵי הַשָּׁמַיִם י

וּכְסִילֵיהֶם לֹא יָהֵלּוּ אוֹרָם חָשַׁךְ הַשֶּׁמֶשׁ בְּצֵאתוֹ וְיָרֵחַ לֹא־יַגִּיהַּ

אוֹרוֹ: וּפָקַדְתִּי עַל־תֵּבֵל רָעָה וְעַל־רְשָׁעִים עֲוֺנָם וְהִשְׁבַּתִּי גְּאוֹן זֵדִים יא

12:1. The punishment of exile afforded me atonement for my sin so that complete forgiveness is now possible (*Rashi*).

12:3. Salvation will be as inexhaustible as water from a spring.

12:6. That is, He has wrought many great miracles for you.

13:2. These are all ways to summon multitudes of people, in this case for war against Babylonia.

13:3. God made the Persians and Medes His agents to overthrow the wicked Babylonians.

13:10. These are metaphors for the dismal and gloomy conditions that will prevail when Babylonia is invaded.

as water covering the sea bed.

¹⁰ It shall be on that day that the descendant of Jesse who stands as a banner for the peoples, nations will seek him, and his resting place will be glorious.

Ingathering
of the exiles

¹¹ It shall be on that day that the Lord will once again show His hand, to acquire the remnant of His people, who will have remained, from Assyria and from Egypt and from Pathros and from Cush and from Elam and from Shinar and from Hamath and from the islands of the sea. ¹² He will raise a banner for the nations and assemble the castaways of Israel; and He will gather in the dispersed ones of Judah from the four corners of the earth. ¹³ The jealousy of Ephraim shall stop and the oppressors of Judah shall be cut off; Ephraim will not be jealous of Judah and Judah will not harass Ephraim. ¹⁴ They will fly in unison against the Philistine to the west, and together they will plunder the people of the East; their hand will extend over Edom and Moab, and their discipline over the Children of Ammon. ¹⁵ HASHEM will dry up the gulf of the Sea of Egypt and He will wave His hand over the [Euphrates] River with the power of His breath; He will break it into seven streams and lead [the people] across in [dry] shoes. ¹⁶ There will be a road for the remnant of His people that will remain from Assyria, as there was for Israel on the day it went up from the land of Egypt.

12

¹ **Y**ou will say on that day, 'I thank You, HASHEM, for You were angry with me, * and now Your wrath has subsided and You have comforted me. ² Behold, God is my salvation; I shall trust and not fear. For God is my might and my praise — HASHEM! — and He is a salvation for me.'

Thanksgiving

³ You can draw water with joy from the springs of salvation. * ⁴ And you will say on that day, 'Give thanks to HASHEM, declare His Name, make His acts known among the peoples; declare that His Name is exalted.' ⁵ Make music for HASHEM, for He has acted with grandeur; make this known throughout the world. ⁶ Exult and shout for joy, O inhabitant of Zion, for the Holy One of Israel is great in your midst! *

13

PROPHECIES
REGARDING
THE
NATIONS
13:1-23:18

*Downfall
of Babylonia*

¹ **A** prophecy concerning Babylonia, which Isaiah son of Amoz envisioned: ² Upon the high mountain hoist a banner; raise a voice to them; wave a hand, * and let them come to the doors of the nobles. ³ I have commanded My dedicated ones; I have also summoned My warriors to [execute] My wrath, * to be exuberant over My grandeur. ⁴ The sound of commotion is in the mountains, like that of an enormous people, the crescendo of the king-doms of gathering nations; HASHEM, Master of the Legions, is assigning officers for the legion of war. ⁵ They come from a faraway land, from the end of the heavens — HASHEM and His weapons of anger, to devastate the entire land. ⁶ Wail, for the day of HASHEM is near; it will come like a sudden attack from the Almighty. ⁷ Therefore, all hands will grow weak and every human heart will melt. ⁸ They will be terrorized; aches and pains will seize them; they will be in travail like a woman in childbirth. Each man will be astonished at his friend; their faces are faces of flame. ⁹ Behold, the day of HASHEM is coming: [a day] of cruelty, rage and burning anger, to make the land desolate; and He will annihilate its sinners from it. ¹⁰ For the stars of the heavens and their constellations will not radiate their light; the sun will be dark when it rises, and the moon will not shine forth its light. * ¹¹ I will visit evil upon the earth and upon the wicked their iniquity; and I will end the pride of the wanton

יב-יג וְגַאֲוַת עָרִיצִים אַשְׁפִּיל: אוֹקִיר אֱנוֹשׁ מִפָּז וְאָדָם מִכֶּתֶם אוֹפִיר: עַל־כֵּן
שָׁמַיִם אַרְגִּיז וְתִרְעַשׁ הָאָרֶץ מִמְּקוֹמָהּ בְּעֶבְרַת יהוה צְבָאוֹת וּבְיוֹם חֲרוֹן

יד אַפּוֹ: וְהָיָה כִּצְבִי מֻדָּח וּכְצֹאן וְאֵין מְקַבֵּץ אִישׁ אֶל־עַמּוֹ יִפְנוּ וְאִישׁ אֶל־

טו-טז אַרְצוֹ יָנוּסוּ: כָּל־הַנִּמְצָא יִדָּקֵר וְכָל־הַנִּסְפֶּה יִפּוֹל בֶּחָרֶב: וְעֹלְלֵיהֶם
יְרֻטְּשׁוּ לְעֵינֵיהֶם יִשַּׁסּוּ בָּתֵּיהֶם וּנְשֵׁיהֶם °תִּשָּׁגַלְנָה [°תִּשָּׁכַבְנָה ק]: הִנְנִי
מֵעִיר עֲלֵיהֶם אֶת־מָדַי אֲשֶׁר־כֶּסֶף לֹא יַחְשֹׁבוּ וְזָהָב לֹא יַחְפְּצוּ־בוֹ:

יח וְקַשָּׁתוֹת נְעָרִים תְּרַטַּשְׁנָה וּפְרִי־בֶטֶן לֹא יְרַחֵמוּ עַל־בָּנִים לֹא־תָחוּס

יט עֵינָם: וְהָיְתָה בָבֶל צְבִי מַמְלָכוֹת תִּפְאֶרֶת גְּאוֹן כַּשְׂדִּים כְּמַהְפֵּכַת

כ אֱלֹהִים אֶת־סְדֹם וְאֶת־עֲמֹרָה: לֹא־תֵשֵׁב לָנֶצַח וְלֹא תִשְׁכֹּן עַד־דּוֹר

כא וָדוֹר וְלֹא־יַהֵל שָׁם עֲרָבִי וְרֹעִים לֹא־יַרְבִּצוּ שָׁם: וְרָבְצוּ־שָׁם צִיִּים

כב וּמָלְאוּ בָתֵּיהֶם אֹחִים וְשָׁכְנוּ שָׁם בְּנוֹת יַעֲנָה וּשְׂעִירִים יְרַקְּדוּ־שָׁם: וְעָנָה
אִיִּים בְּאַלְמְנוֹתָיו וְתַנִּים בְּהֵיכְלֵי עֹנֶג וְקָרוֹב לָבוֹא עִתָּהּ וְיָמֶיהָ לֹא

יד א יִמָּשֵׁכוּ: כִּי יְרַחֵם יהוה אֶת־יַעֲקֹב וּבָחַר עוֹד בְּיִשְׂרָאֵל וְהִנִּיחָם עַל־

ב אַדְמָתָם וְנִלְוָה הַגֵּר עֲלֵיהֶם וְנִסְפְּחוּ עַל־בֵּית יַעֲקֹב: וּלְקָחוּם עַמִּים
וֶהֱבִיאוּם אֶל־מְקוֹמָם וְהִתְנַחֲלוּם בֵּית־יִשְׂרָאֵל עַל אַדְמַת יהוה לַעֲבָדִים

ג וְלִשְׁפָחוֹת וְהָיוּ שֹׁבִים לְשֹׁבֵיהֶם וְרָדוּ בְּנֹגְשֵׂיהֶם: וְהָיָה
בְּיוֹם הָנִיחַ יהוה לְךָ מֵעָצְבְּךָ וּמֵרָגְזֶךָ וּמִן־הָעֲבֹדָה הַקָּשָׁה אֲשֶׁר עֻבַּד־

ד בָּךְ: וְנָשָׂאתָ הַמָּשָׁל הַזֶּה עַל־מֶלֶךְ בָּבֶל וְאָמָרְתָּ אֵיךְ שָׁבַת נֹגֵשׂ שָׁבְתָה

ה-ו מַדְהֵבָה: שָׁבַר יהוה מַטֵּה רְשָׁעִים שֵׁבֶט מֹשְׁלִים: מַכֶּה עַמִּים בְּעֶבְרָה

ז מַכַּת בִּלְתִּי סָרָה רֹדֶה בָאַף גּוֹיִם מֻרְדָּף בְּלִי חָשָׂךְ: נָחָה שָׁקְטָה

ח כָּל־הָאָרֶץ פָּצְחוּ רִנָּה: גַּם־בְּרוֹשִׁים שָׂמְחוּ לְךָ אַרְזֵי לְבָנוֹן מֵאָז שָׁכַבְתָּ

ט לֹא־יַעֲלֶה הַכֹּרֵת עָלֵינוּ: שְׁאוֹל מִתַּחַת רָגְזָה לְךָ לִקְרַאת בּוֹאֶךָ עוֹרֵר
י לְךָ רְפָאִים כָּל־עַתּוּדֵי אָרֶץ הֵקִים מִכִּסְאוֹתָם כֹּל מַלְכֵי גוֹיִם: כֻּלָּם

יא יַעֲנוּ וְיֹאמְרוּ אֵלֶיךָ גַּם־אַתָּה חֻלֵּיתָ כָמוֹנוּ אֵלֵינוּ נִמְשָׁלְתָּ: הוּרַד שְׁאוֹל
גְּאוֹנֶךָ הֶמְיַת נְבָלֶיךָ תַּחְתֶּיךָ יֻצַּע רִמָּה וּמְכַסֶּיךָ תּוֹלֵעָה: אֵיךְ נָפַלְתָּ

יב מִשָּׁמַיִם הֵילֵל בֶּן־שָׁחַר נִגְדַּעְתָּ לָאָרֶץ חוֹלֵשׁ עַל־גּוֹיִם: וְאַתָּה אָמָרְתָּ

יג בִלְבָבְךָ הַשָּׁמַיִם אֶעֱלֶה מִמַּעַל לְכוֹכְבֵי־אֵל אָרִים כִּסְאִי וְאֵשֵׁב

יד-טו בְּהַר־מוֹעֵד בְּיַרְכְּתֵי צָפוֹן: אֶעֱלֶה עַל־בָּמֳתֵי עָב אֶדַּמֶּה לְעֶלְיוֹן: אַךְ

טז אֶל־שְׁאוֹל תּוּרָד אֶל־יַרְכְּתֵי־בוֹר: רֹאֶיךָ אֵלֶיךָ יַשְׁגִּיחוּ אֵלֶיךָ יִתְבּוֹנָנוּ

13:12. The Persians and Medes will not accept ransom to spare their Babylonian captives (*Radak*).

13:13. I.e., because the evil of Babylonia caused Me to decree its destruction.

14:1-2. The first part of this verse refers to the great kindness that God will cause Cyrus the Persian, the conqueror of Babylonia, to show the Jews. The prophet then goes on to speak of the Messianic era (*Rashi*; *Radak*).

14:2. Non-Jews will volunteer to become servants in the Land of Israel (*Ibn Ezra*).

14:11. Instead of the fine bed linens you were pampered with in your lifetime (*Radak*).

14:13. The Mountain of Meeting refers to the Temple Mount. The northern side was the holiest area of the Temple Courtyard (*Rashi*). Alternatively: The Temple was on the north side of Jerusalem (*Radak*).

and bring low the haughtiness of the mighty. [12] I will make man more valuable than rare gold, * and people more than the precious gold of Ophir. [13] Therefore * I will make the heavens tremble and the earth will rumble from its place at the fury of HASHEM, Master of Legions, on the day of His burning wrath. [14] They will be like a chased-away deer and like sheep with no one to gather [them]; each person will turn to his people and each person will flee to his land. [15] Anyone found will be pierced, and anyone who is gathered in will fall by the sword. [16] Their babies will be sundered before their eyes; their houses will be pillaged and their women ravished. [17] Behold, I shall arouse Medea against them, who will not value silver and will not desire gold. [18] Their bows will sunder young men; they will show no mercy for the fruit of the womb, and their eyes will not have pity on children. [19] And Babylonia, the choicest of the kingdoms, the splendor of the glory of the Chaldeans, will be like God's overturning of Sodom and Gomorrah. [20] It will not be inhabited forever and it will not be settled from generation to generation; no Arab will pitch tent there, and shepherds will not make their flocks lie there. [21] Martens will lie there and their houses will be full of ferrets; owls will live there and demons will dance there; [22] cats will howl in their mansions, and jackals in their palaces of delight. Her time is soon to come; her days will not long endure!

14

Israel will return from Babylonia

[1] For HASHEM will show mercy to Jacob. * He will choose Israel again and grant them rest upon their land. The proselyte will join them and be attached to the House of Jacob. [2] The nations will take them and bring them to their place, and the House of Israel will possess them as slaves and maidservants upon the land of HASHEM; * they will be captors over their captors and they will rule over their oppressors.

[3] It shall be on the day when HASHEM grants you relief from your distress and your anxiety and from the hard labor with which you were worked: [4] You will recite this parable about the king of Babylonia:

The parable about the king of Babylonia

How has the oppressor come to an end, the arrogance been ended? [5] HASHEM has broken the staff of the wicked, the rod of rulers [6] who would strike peoples with fury, with unrelenting blows, who would oppress nations with wrath, [the nations] were pursued [by them] without respite. [7] 'The entire land is at rest and tranquil,' they broke out in glad song. [8] Even the cypresses rejoice over you, the cedars of Lebanon, [saying,] 'From the time that you were laid low, the woodcutter would not come up against us.' [9] The nether-world from below trembles for you to greet your arrival; it has awakened the giants for you, all the leaders of the world, it has roused all the kings of the land out of their thrones. [10] They will all proclaim and say to you, 'You also have been stricken as we were; you are compared to us. [11] Brought down to the nether-world were your pride and the tumult of your stringed instruments; maggots are spread out under you, and worms are your covers. * [12] How have you fallen from the heavens, O glowing morning star; been cut down to the ground, O conqueror of nations? [13] You had said in your heart, "I will ascend to the heavens; higher than the stars of God I shall raise my throne; I will sit at the Mountain of Meeting, on the northern side; * [14] I will ascend over the tops of the clouds; I will liken myself to the Most High!" [15] But to the nether-world have you been lowered, to the bottom of the pit!' [16] Those who see you will take note, they will contemplate you carefully;

יז הֲזֶה הָאִישׁ מַרְגִּיז הָאָרֶץ מַרְעִישׁ מַמְלָכוֹת: שָׂם תֵּבֵל כַּמִּדְבָּר וְעָרָיו הָרָס

יח אֲסִירָיו לֹא־פָתַח בָּיְתָה: כָּל־מַלְכֵי גוֹיִם כֻּלָּם שָׁכְבוּ בְכָבוֹד אִישׁ בְּבֵיתוֹ:

יט וְאַתָּה הָשְׁלַכְתָּ מִקִּבְרְךָ כְּנֵצֶר נִתְעָב לְבֻשׁ הֲרֻגִים מְטֹעֲנֵי חָרֶב יוֹרְדֵי

כ אֶל־אַבְנֵי־בוֹר כְּפֶגֶר מוּבָס: לֹא־תֵחַד אִתָּם בִּקְבוּרָה כִּי־אַרְצְךָ שִׁחַתָּ

כא עַמְּךָ הָרָגְתָּ לֹא־יִקָּרֵא לְעוֹלָם זֶרַע מְרֵעִים: הָכִינוּ לְבָנָיו מַטְבֵּחַ בַּעֲוֹן

כב אֲבוֹתָם בַּל־יָקֻמוּ וְיָרְשׁוּ אָרֶץ וּמָלְאוּ פְנֵי־תֵבֵל עָרִים: וְקַמְתִּי עֲלֵיהֶם נְאֻם

כג יְהוָה צְבָאוֹת וְהִכְרַתִּי לְבָבֶל שֵׁם וּשְׁאָר וְנִין וָנֶכֶד נְאֻם־יְהוָה: וְשַׂמְתִּיהָ

כד לְמוֹרַשׁ קִפֹּד וְאַגְמֵי־מָיִם וְטֵאטֵאתִיהָ בְּמַטְאֲטֵא הַשְׁמֵד נְאֻם יְהוָה
צְבָאוֹת: נִשְׁבַּע יְהוָה צְבָאוֹת לֵאמֹר אִם־לֹא כַּאֲשֶׁר דִּמִּיתִי כֵּן

כה הָיָתָה וְכַאֲשֶׁר יָעַצְתִּי הִיא תָקוּם: לִשְׁבֹּר אַשּׁוּר בְּאַרְצִי וְעַל־הָרַי אֲבוּסֶנּוּ

כו וְסָר מֵעֲלֵיהֶם עֻלּוֹ וְסֻבֳּלוֹ מֵעַל שִׁכְמוֹ יָסוּר: זֹאת הָעֵצָה הַיְּעוּצָה עַל־כָּל־

כז הָאָרֶץ וְזֹאת הַיָּד הַנְּטוּיָה עַל־כָּל־הַגּוֹיִם: כִּי־יְהוָה צְבָאוֹת יָעָץ וּמִי יָפֵר

כח וְיָדוֹ הַנְּטוּיָה וּמִי יְשִׁיבֶנָּה: בִּשְׁנַת־מוֹת הַמֶּלֶךְ אָחָז הָיָה

כט הַמַּשָּׂא הַזֶּה: אַל־תִּשְׂמְחִי פְלֶשֶׁת כֻּלֵּךְ כִּי נִשְׁבַּר שֵׁבֶט מַכֵּךְ כִּי־מִשֹּׁרֶשׁ

ל נָחָשׁ יֵצֵא צֶפַע וּפִרְיוֹ שָׂרָף מְעוֹפֵף: וְרָעוּ בְּכוֹרֵי דַלִּים וְאֶבְיוֹנִים לָבֶטַח

לא יִרְבָּצוּ וְהֵמַתִּי בָרָעָב שָׁרְשֵׁךְ וּשְׁאֵרִיתֵךְ יַהֲרֹג: הֵילִילִי שַׁעַר זַעֲקִי־עִיר

לב נָמוֹג פְּלֶשֶׁת כֻּלֵּךְ כִּי מִצָּפוֹן עָשָׁן בָּא וְאֵין בּוֹדֵד בְּמוֹעָדָיו: וּמַה־יַּעֲנֶה

א מַלְאֲכֵי־גוֹי כִּי יְהוָה יִסַּד צִיּוֹן וּבָהּ יֶחֱסוּ עֲנִיֵּי עַמּוֹ:   מַשָּׂא מוֹאָב
טו

ב כִּי בְּלֵיל שֻׁדַּד עָר מוֹאָב נִדְמָה כִּי בְּלֵיל שֻׁדַּד קִיר־מוֹאָב נִדְמָה: עָלָה

הַבַּיִת וְדִיבֹן הַבָּמוֹת לְבֶכִי עַל־נְבוֹ וְעַל מֵידְבָא מוֹאָב יְיֵלִיל בְּכָל־רֹאשָׁיו

ג קָרְחָה כָּל־זָקָן גְּרוּעָה: בְּחוּצֹתָיו חָגְרוּ שָׂק עַל גַּגּוֹתֶיהָ וּבִרְחֹבֹתֶיהָ כֻּלֹּה

ד יְיֵלִיל יֹרֵד בַּבֶּכִי: וַתִּזְעַק חֶשְׁבּוֹן וְאֶלְעָלֵה עַד־יַהַץ נִשְׁמַע קוֹלָם עַל־כֵּן

ה חֲלֻצֵי מוֹאָב יָרִיעוּ נַפְשׁוֹ יָרְעָה לּוֹ: לִבִּי לְמוֹאָב יִזְעָק בְּרִיחֶהָ עַד־צֹעַר

עֶגְלַת שְׁלִשִׁיָּה כִּי מַעֲלֵה הַלּוּחִית בִּבְכִי יַעֲלֶה־בּוֹ כִּי דֶּרֶךְ חוֹרֹנַיִם

ו זַעֲקַת־שֶׁבֶר יְעֹעֵרוּ: כִּי־מֵי נִמְרִים מְשַׁמּוֹת יִהְיוּ כִּי־יָבֵשׁ חָצִיר כָּלָה דֶשֶׁא

ז יֶרֶק לֹא הָיָה: עַל־כֵּן יִתְרָה עָשָׂה וּפְקֻדָּתָם עַל נַחַל הָעֲרָבִים יִשָּׂאוּם:

14:18-20. Lit., in his home; i.e., Nebuchadnezzar will not rest in peace like other dead kings who lie peacefully in their graves (*Rashi*), for his body will be exhumed and desecrated by his own people (*Seder Olam*). Moreover, his dynasty will end with his grandson.

14:24-27. This prophecy concerns Assyria. *Rashi* connects it to the previous prophecy against Babylonia: "When you, Nebuchadnezzar, see God's word come true against Assyria, you will realize that His prophecy concerning you will come about, as well."

14:29. The Philistines should not rejoice over a death in the Davidic dynasty, which always triumphed over them, for from David and Uzziah, who defeated them (*II Samuel* 8:1; *II Chronicles* 26:6), will emerge Hezekiah,

who will deal them a severe blow (*II Kings* 18:8).

14:31. Hezekiah will swoop down from the north upon the Philistine capital, Gaza, every one of his troops in full formation.

15:2. Pulling out the hair of the head and of the beard are signs of intense grief and consternation.

15:5. The prophets of Israel feel compassion even for their enemies (*Rashi*).

"Third-born calf" was a common expression used to denote prime quality and value, since the third calf born to a cow is considered the strongest and healthiest of her offspring (see *Jeremiah* 48:34).

15:7. This refers to Babylonia (see *Psalms* 137:1-2; *Rashi*).

'Is this the man who made the land tremble, who made kingdoms quake; [17] who made the world like a wilderness and tore down its cities; who never released his captives to go home?' [18] All the kings of the nations, all of them, lie in honor, each in his place, * [19] but you have been flung from your grave like a detested tree shoot; like the garment of corpses pierced by the sword, which are lowered into the stones of the pit, like a trampled carcass. [20] You will not join them in burial, for you have destroyed your land and killed your people; your evil offspring will not be called [by your name] for long. [21] Prepare a slaughter for his sons for their father's iniquity; let them not arise and inherit the land, lest the world become full of enemies.

[22] I will rise up against them — the word of HASHEM, Master of Legions — and I will cut off for Babylonia name and remnant, child and grandchild — the word of HASHEM. [23] And I will make it an inheritance for the hedgehog and marshes of water, and I will sweep it clean with the broom of destruction — the word of HASHEM, Master of Legions.

God's plan for Assyria is fulfilled

[24] HASHEM, Master of Legions, has sworn, saying: * 'Surely as I have conceived, so shall come about; and as I have devised, so shall be established: [25] To break Assyria in My land; I will trample him on My mountains; his yoke will be removed from upon [Israel] and his burden will be removed from upon [Israel's] shoulder. [26] This is the plan that is devised against all the land, and this is the hand that is outstretched against all the nations.' [27] For HASHEM, Master of Legions, has devised, and who can annul? His hand is outstretched, and who can turn it back?

[28] In the year of King Ahaz' death, this prophecy came:

Warning to Philistia

[29] Do not rejoice, O Philistia, all of you, because the staff that beat you has been broken; for from the root of the snake will emerge a viper, and his progeny will be a flying fiery serpent. * [30] The foremost of the poor will then graze, and the destitute will lie down in security; and I will kill your root with famine, and he will slay your remnant. [31] Wail, O gate! Cry out, O city! Melt [in fear], O Philistia, all of you! For smoke comes from the North, and no one is isolated among his appointed troops. * [32] What will the messengers of the nation say? That HASHEM has established Zion and in it the poor of His people take shelter.

15 [1] **A** prophecy concerning Moab:

Downfall of Moab

On the night Ar of Moab was pillaged, it was silenced; on the night that Kir of Moab was pillaged, it was silenced. [2] [Its populace] went up to the temple, and Dibon went up to the high places to weep; Moab wails for Nebo and for Medeba. On all of its heads there is baldness; every beard is diminished. * [3] In their streets they have donned sackcloth; upon their rooftops and in their plazas every one wails and laments with weeping. [4] Heshbon cries out, and Elealeh, their voice is heard until Jahaz. Therefore, the armed soldiers of Moab shout; its soul shouts for it. [5] My heart cries out for Moab! * Her refugees flee until Zoar, the third-born calf; * for they ascend the Luhith ascent with weeping, for on the road of Horonaim they howl with the cry of catastrophe. [6] For the waters of Nimrim will be laid waste; for the grass is withered, the herbage is finished; the greenery is gone. [7] For the wealth they had accrued and their possessions will be carried off to the Willow Brook. *

ח כִּי־הִקִּיפָה הַזְּעָקָה אֶת־גְּבוּל מוֹאָב עַד־אֶגְלַיִם יִלְלָתָהּ וּבְאֵר אֵילִים
ט יִלְלָתָהּ: כִּי מֵי דִימוֹן מָלְאוּ דָם כִּי־אָשִׁית עַל־דִּימוֹן נוֹסָפוֹת לִפְלֵיטַת

טז א מוֹאָב אַרְיֵה וְלִשְׁאֵרִית אֲדָמָה: שִׁלְחוּ־כַר מֹשֵׁל־אֶרֶץ מִסֶּלַע מִדְבָּרָה
ב אֶל־הַר בַּת־צִיּוֹן: וְהָיָה כְעוֹף־נוֹדֵד קֵן מְשֻׁלָּח תִּהְיֶינָה בְּנוֹת מוֹאָב
ג מַעְבָּרֹת לְאַרְנוֹן: °הביאו [°הָבִיאִי ק] עֵצָה [°עשי °עשׂי [°עֲשׂוּ ק] פְלִילָה
ד שִׁיתִי כַלַּיִל צִלֵּךְ בְּתוֹךְ צָהֳרַיִם סַתְּרִי נִדָּחִים נֹדֵד אַל־תְּגַלִּי: יָגוּרוּ בָךְ
נִדָּחַי מוֹאָב הֱוִי־סֵתֶר לָמוֹ מִפְּנֵי שׁוֹדֵד כִּי־אָפֵס הַמֵּץ כָּלָה שֹׁד תַּמּוּ רֹמֵס
ה מִן־הָאָרֶץ: וְהוּכַן בַּחֶסֶד כִּסֵּא וְיָשַׁב עָלָיו בֶּאֱמֶת בְּאֹהֶל דָּוִד
שֹׁפֵט וְדֹרֵשׁ מִשְׁפָּט וּמְהִר צֶדֶק: שָׁמַעְנוּ גְאוֹן־מוֹאָב גֵּא מְאֹד גַּאֲוָתוֹ
ו וּגְאוֹנוֹ וְעֶבְרָתוֹ לֹא־כֵן בַּדָּיו: לָכֵן יְיֵלִיל מוֹאָב לְמוֹאָב כֻּלֹּה יְיֵלִיל
ז לַאֲשִׁישֵׁי קִיר־חֲרֶשֶׂת תֶּהְגּוּ אַךְ־נְכָאִים: כִּי שַׁדְמוֹת חֶשְׁבּוֹן אֻמְלָל גֶּפֶן
ח שִׂבְמָה בַּעֲלֵי גוֹיִם הָלְמוּ שְׂרוּקֶיהָ עַד־יַעְזֵר נָגָעוּ תָּעוּ מִדְבָּר שְׁלֻחוֹתֶיהָ
נִטְּשׁוּ עָבְרוּ יָם: עַל־כֵּן אֶבְכֶּה בִּבְכִי יַעְזֵר גֶּפֶן שִׂבְמָה אֲרַיָּוֶךְ דִּמְעָתִי
ט חֶשְׁבּוֹן וְאֶלְעָלֵה כִּי עַל־קֵיצֵךְ וְעַל־קְצִירֵךְ הֵידָד נָפָל: וְנֶאֱסַף שִׂמְחָה
י וָגִיל מִן־הַכַּרְמֶל וּבַכְּרָמִים לֹא־יְרֻנָּן לֹא יְרֹעָע יַיִן בַּיְקָבִים לֹא־יִדְרֹךְ
הַדֹּרֵךְ הֵידָד הִשְׁבַּתִּי: עַל־כֵּן מֵעַי לְמוֹאָב כַּכִּנּוֹר יֶהֱמוּ וְקִרְבִּי לְקִיר חָרֶשׂ:
יא וְהָיָה כִי־נִרְאָה כִּי־נִלְאָה מוֹאָב עַל־הַבָּמָה וּבָא אֶל־מִקְדָּשׁוֹ לְהִתְפַּלֵּל
יב וְלֹא יוּכָל: זֶה הַדָּבָר אֲשֶׁר דִּבֶּר יהוה אֶל־מוֹאָב מֵאָז: וְעַתָּה
יג–יד דִּבֶּר יהוה לֵאמֹר בְּשָׁלֹשׁ שָׁנִים כִּשְׁנֵי שָׂכִיר וְנִקְלָה כְּבוֹד מוֹאָב בְּכֹל

יז א הֶהָמוֹן הָרָב וּשְׁאָר מְעַט מִזְעָר לוֹא כַבִּיר: מַשָּׂא דַּמָּשֶׂק הִנֵּה
ב דַמֶּשֶׂק מוּסָר מֵעִיר וְהָיְתָה מְעִי מַפָּלָה: עֲזֻבוֹת עָרֵי עֲרֹעֵר לַעֲדָרִים
ג תִּהְיֶינָה וְרָבְצוּ וְאֵין מַחֲרִיד: וְנִשְׁבַּת מִבְצָר מֵאֶפְרַיִם וּמַמְלָכָה מִדַּמֶּשֶׂק
ד וּשְׁאָר אֲרָם כִּכְבוֹד בְּנֵי־יִשְׂרָאֵל יִהְיוּ נְאֻם יהוה צְבָאוֹת: וְהָיָה
ה בַּיּוֹם הַהוּא יִדַּל כְּבוֹד יַעֲקֹב וּמִשְׁמַן בְּשָׂרוֹ יֵרָזֶה: וְהָיָה כֶּאֱסֹף קָצִיר קָמָה
ו וּזְרֹעוֹ שִׁבֳּלִים יִקְצוֹר וְהָיָה כִּמְלַקֵּט שִׁבֳּלִים בְּעֵמֶק רְפָאִים: וְנִשְׁאַר־בּוֹ
עוֹלֵלֹת כְּנֹקֶף זַיִת שְׁנַיִם שְׁלֹשָׁה גַּרְגְּרִים בְּרֹאשׁ אָמִיר אַרְבָּעָה חֲמִשָּׁה

15:9. A play on words: The name of the river דִימוֹן, "Dimon," is cognate with דָם, "blood" (*Rashi*).

16:1. In earlier times, these Moabite areas would submit a yearly tribute of fatted sheep to their Israelite overlords (*II Kings* 3:4). Thus, the formerly subordinate Moabites are being reprimanded for their arrogance.

16:3-4. Isaiah chastises Moab for not helping the fugitive Jews even after Nebuchadnezzar's army had departed. This was a lack of gratitude, for Abraham was Moab's ancestor. Moab risked his life to rescue Lot, Moab's ancestor. Moab should have provided hiding places, as if making the noontime become dark, so as to hinder Assyrian pursuit (*Radak*).

16:9-10. "*Hedad*" is a battle cry and also the cry of wine pressers (see *Jeremiah* 25:30 and 51:14).

16:14. A hired man counts the days and will not work a single extra day; i.e., the prophecy will come about in exactly three years, without delay (*Radak*).

17:1. The prophecy concerns Aram, of which Damascus was the capital.

17:2-3. By the time this prophecy was uttered the tribes of Reuben and Gad had already been exiled from their lands. Isaiah warns Aram that it would be exiled by Sennacherib, just as he had exiled the Jewish city of Aroer and then the rest of the Ten Tribes (*Rashi*).

⁸ *For the outcry envelops the boundary of Moab; until Eglaim is her wailing, until Beer-elim is her wailing.* ⁹ *For the waters of Dimon are filled with blood, for I will pour more [of it] into Dimon.* * *Upon the survivors of Moab there will come a lion, upon the remnant of the land.*

16
¹ *Send fatted sheep, O ruler of the land, from the Rock of the Wilderness to the Mountain of the Daughter of Zion.* * ² *Like a wandering bird, chased from the nest, will the daughters of Moab be at the crossings of the Arnon.* ³ *Render counsel, execute justice; during the noontime make your shade [as dark] as the night, hide the refugees;* * *do not reveal the wanderer.* ⁴ *Let My refugees live among you, O Moab; be a shelter for them from the pillager, for the oppressor is gone, the persecutor is finished, the tramplers are terminated from the land.*

Moab's death throes

⁵ *The throne [of Hezekiah] will then be established with kindness, and he will sit upon it in truthfulness in the tent of David, judging and striving for justice and being zealous for righteousness.* ⁶ *We have heard of Moab's pride — exceedingly proud — his haughtiness and pride and scorn are untrue deceptions.* ⁷ *Therefore, Moab will wail for Moab; everyone will wail; moan for the foundations of Kir-hareseth, O distressed ones,* ⁸ *for the fields of Heshbon are enfeebled; as for the vine of Sibmah — the kings of the nations have beaten down their shoots; they have reached until Jazer and become lost in the wilderness; her branches have spread out and crossed the sea.* ⁹ *Therefore, I cry with the weeping of Jazer, the vine of Sibmah; I will drench you with my tears, O Heshbon and Elealeh; for the cry of 'Hedad'* * *has descended over your summer fruits and harvest.* ¹⁰ *Gladness and joy will cease from fertile field, and in the vineyards there will be no rejoicing nor shouting for joy. The treader will not tread out wine in the winepresses; I have ended 'Hedad.'*

¹¹ *Therefore, my insides moan like a harp for Moab, and my innards for Kir-heres.* ¹² *And it shall be when Moab seems to be weary of the high place, and they will come to their sanctuary to pray, they will not be able.* ¹³ *This is the prophecy that HASHEM had spoken for Moab before,* ¹⁴ *but now HASHEM has spoken, saying:*

In three years, like the term of a hired hand, * *the honor of Moab will turn to disgrace, and there will be a very small remainder, not many.*

17
¹ A *prophecy concerning Damascus:* *

Breakup of Ephramite-Aramean alliance

Behold, Damascus will be negated from being a city, and it will be a heap of rubble. ² *Deserted will be the cities of Aroer; they will be for flocks, that will lie down with none to disturb them.* ³ *The stronghold will cease from Ephraim, and monarchy from Damascus and the rest of Aram;* * *they will be like the glory of the Children of Israel — the word of HASHEM, Master of Legions.*

⁴ *It shall be on that day that the honor of Jacob will diminish and the fatness of his flesh grow lean.* ⁵ *He will be as when the harvester gathers grain and his arm cuts the ears,* * *and he will be as when one gleans ears in the Valley of Rephaim.* ⁶ *Only gleanings will remain on him, like a picked olive tree, with but two or three olives on the top of the highest branch, or four or five*

17:5. Israel will be as uninhabited as a field that has been harvested and then gleaned by the poor. The Valley of Rephaim was near Jerusalem; thus, Sennacherib's butchery would extend up to Jerusalem (*Rashi*).

ז בִּסְעַפֶּיהָ פְּרִיָּה נְאֻם־יהוה אֱלֹהֵי יִשְׂרָאֵל׃ בַּיּוֹם הַהוּא יִשְׁעֶה

ח הָֽאָדָם עַל־עֹשֵׂהוּ וְעֵינָיו אֶל־קְדוֹשׁ יִשְׂרָאֵל תִּרְאֶינָה׃ וְלֹא יִשְׁעֶה אֶל־

הַֽמִּזְבְּחוֹת מַעֲשֵׂה יָדָיו וַאֲשֶׁר עָשׂוּ אֶצְבְּעֹתָיו לֹא יִרְאֶה וְהָאֲשֵׁרִים

ט וְהָחַמָּנִים׃ בַּיּוֹם הַהוּא יִהְיוּ ׀ עָרֵי מָעֻזּוֹ כַּעֲזוּבַת הַחֹרֶשׁ

י וְהָאָמִיר אֲשֶׁר עָזְבוּ מִפְּנֵי בְּנֵי יִשְׂרָאֵל וְהָיְתָה שְׁמָמָה׃ כִּי שָׁכַחַתְּ אֱלֹהֵי

יִשְׁעֵךְ וְצוּר מָעֻזֵּךְ לֹא זָכָרְתְּ עַל־כֵּן תִּטְּעִי נִטְעֵי נַעֲמָנִים וּזְמֹרַת זָר

יא תִּזְרָעֶנּוּ׃ בְּיוֹם נִטְעֵךְ תְּשַׂגְשֵׂגִי וּבַבֹּקֶר זַרְעֵךְ תַּפְרִיחִי נֵד קָצִיר בְּיוֹם נַחֲלָה

יב וּכְאֵב אָנוּשׁ׃ הוֹי הֲמוֹן עַמִּים רַבִּים כַּהֲמוֹת יַמִּים יֶהֱמָיוּן

יג וּשְׁאוֹן לְאֻמִּים כִּשְׁאוֹן מַיִם כַּבִּירִים יִשָּׁאוּן׃ לְאֻמִּים כִּשְׁאוֹן מַיִם רַבִּים

יִשָּׁאוּן וְגָעַר בּוֹ וְנָס מִמֶּרְחָק וְרֻדַּף כְּמֹץ הָרִים לִפְנֵי־רוּחַ וּכְגַלְגַּל לִפְנֵי

יד סוּפָה׃ לְעֵת עֶרֶב וְהִנֵּה בַלָּהָה בְּטֶרֶם בֹּקֶר אֵינֶנּוּ זֶה חֵלֶק שׁוֹסֵינוּ וְגוֹרָל

יח לְבֹזְזֵינוּ׃ הוֹי אֶרֶץ צִלְצַל כְּנָפָיִם אֲשֶׁר מֵעֵבֶר לְנַהֲרֵי־כוּשׁ׃

ב הַשֹּׁלֵחַ בַּיָּם צִירִים וּבִכְלֵי־גֹמֶא עַל־פְּנֵי־מַיִם לְכוּ ׀ מַלְאָכִים קַלִּים אֶל־

גּוֹי מְמֻשָּׁךְ וּמוֹרָט אֶל־עַם נוֹרָא מִן־הוּא וָהָלְאָה גּוֹי קַו־קָו וּמְבוּסָה אֲשֶׁר־

ג בָּזְאוּ נְהָרִים אַרְצוֹ׃ כָּל־יֹשְׁבֵי תֵבֵל וְשֹׁכְנֵי אָרֶץ כִּנְשֹׂא־נֵס הָרִים תִּרְאוּ

ד וְכִתְקֹעַ שׁוֹפָר תִּשְׁמָעוּ׃ כִּי כֹה אָמַר יהוה אֵלַי °אֶשְׁקוֹטָה

[°אֶשְׁקֳטָה ק׳] וְאַבִּיטָה בִמְכוֹנִי כְּחֹם צַח עֲלֵי־אוֹר כְּעָב טַל בְּחֹם קָצִיר׃

ה כִּי־לִפְנֵי קָצִיר כְּתָם־פֶּרַח וּבֹסֶר גֹּמֵל יִהְיֶה נִצָּה וְכָרַת הַזַּלְזַלִּים בַּמַּזְמֵרוֹת

ו וְאֶת־הַנְּטִישׁוֹת הֵסִיר הֵתַז׃ יֵעָזְבוּ יַחְדָּו לְעֵיט הָרִים וּלְבֶהֱמַת הָאָרֶץ

ז וְקָץ עָלָיו הָעַיִט וְכָל־בֶּהֱמַת הָאָרֶץ עָלָיו תֶּחֱרָף׃ בָּעֵת

הַהִיא יֽוּבַל־שַׁי לַיהוה צְבָאוֹת עַם מְמֻשָּׁךְ וּמוֹרָט וּמֵעַם נוֹרָא מִן־הוּא

וָהָלְאָה גּוֹי ׀ קַו־קָו וּמְבוּסָה אֲשֶׁר בָּזְאוּ נְהָרִים אַרְצוֹ אֶל־מְקוֹם שֵׁם־יהוה

יט צְבָאוֹת הַר־צִיּוֹן׃ מַשָּׂא מִצְרָיִם הִנֵּה יהוה רֹכֵב עַל־

עָב קַל וּבָא מִצְרַיִם וְנָעוּ אֱלִילֵי מִצְרַיִם מִפָּנָיו וּלְבַב מִצְרַיִם יִמַּס

ב בְּקִרְבּוֹ׃ וְסִכְסַכְתִּי מִצְרַיִם בְּמִצְרַיִם וְנִלְחֲמוּ אִישׁ־בְּאָחִיו וְאִישׁ בְּרֵעֵהוּ

ג עִיר בְּעִיר מַמְלָכָה בְּמַמְלָכָה׃ וְנָבְקָה רֽוּחַ־מִצְרַיִם בְּקִרְבּוֹ וַעֲצָתוֹ אֲבַלֵּעַ

17:9. The desertion of the country in the wake of Sennacherib will be reminiscent of the evacuation of many of the Canaanite cities when Moses and Joshua conquered the land (*Rashi*).

17:10. You had illustrious ancestors, but you fall short of their standard.

18:1. Isaiah envisions the onset of the Messianic era, and speaks to the nations involved in the wars of "Gog and Magog." The prophet refers to their country as a land of clamorous wings, because its warm climate attracts migratory birds (*Rashi*).

Alternatively: This prophecy concerns Sennacherib (*Kara*).

18:2-3. The nations send agents to see if it is true that

Israel has been returned to its ancestral land, but God says that when that time comes, the banner and shofar that will muster the scattered Israelites will be manifest for all to see (*Rashi*).

18:4. Though God will not be at ease as long as Israel is in exile (see 62:1), the salvation will yet come, and the Foundation, i.e., the Temple, will be rebuilt (*Radak*). He will refresh His nation just as pleasant weather refreshes people.

18:5. The aggressors against Israel will flourish temporarily, but before their evil designs come to fruition, God will stop them.

18:7. Having been punished by God, the peoples of the world will bring Him an offering; the offering will be the *on its flourishing boughs — the word of HASHEM, God of Israel.*

Abandonment of idolatry

⁷ *On that day, man will turn to his Maker and his eyes will look to the Holy One of Israel.* ⁸ *He will not turn to the altars of his own handiwork; and to what his fingers made he will not look, nor [to] the Asherah-trees or the sun-images.*

⁹ *On that day his fortified cities will be like the abandonment of forests and woodlands, which they abandoned before the Children of Israel;* * *and it will be desolate.* ¹⁰ *For you have forgotten the God of your salvation, and have not remembered the Rock of your stronghold; because you had been planted as pleasant saplings, but you sow strange shoots.* * ¹¹ *On the day you were planted you flourished, and at dawn your seed flowered; but your branch is removed, on a day of affliction and acute pain.*

Rebuke for the nations

¹² *Woe to the tumult of the many nations, who are as tumultuous as the tumult of the seas; and to the uproar of the nations, who roar like the uproar of powerful waters.* ¹³ *Nations roar like the roar of many waters, but He will rebuke them and they will flee far away; they will be pursued like the chaff of mountains before the wind, and like pollen before a stormy wind.* ¹⁴ *At evening time, behold there is fright; before the morning dawn, he is no more. This is the lot of our assailants and the due of our spoilers!*

18

Trans-Cushite emissaries

¹ *Woe to the land of clamorous wings,* * *on the other side of the rivers of Cush,* ² *which sends agents into the sea, in papyrus vessels upon the surface of the water. 'Go, fleet messengers, to the nation that is dragged and plucked, to the people that inspired awe from the day it came into being and onward, the nation that is detested and trampled, whose land was ravished by kings.'* ³ *All you inhabitants of the world and dwellers of the earth — you will see when the banner is hoisted up upon the mountains, and when the shofar sounds you will hear!* * ⁴ *For thus said HASHEM to me: 'I will be at ease* * *and I will look after My Place of Foundation; like crisp warmth after the rain, like a mist of dew in the heat of the harvest.'* ⁵ *For before the harvest, when the flower is finished and the bud turns to grapes approaching ripeness, He will cut down the young branches with pruning hooks and He will remove and chop off all the twigs.* * ⁶ *They will be left together for the bird of prey of the mountains and for the beast of the earth; and the bird of prey will [feast in] summer on them, and every beast of the earth will [feast in] winter on them.*

⁷ *At that time an offering* * *will be brought to HASHEM, Master of Legions — [namely,] the people that is dragged and plucked, and some of the people that inspired awe from the day it came into being and onward, the nation that is oppressed and trampled, whose land was ravished by rivers;* * *to the place [wherein rests] the Name of HASHEM, Master of Legions — Mount Zion.*

19

Downfall of Egypt

¹ *A prophecy concerning Egypt:*

Behold, HASHEM is riding upon a swift cloud and coming to Egypt; the Egyptian false gods will tremble before Him, and the heart of Egypt will melt within it. ² *I will cause Egyptians to fight Egyptians; each one will battle his brother and each his fellow; city against city; kingdom against kingdom.* ³ *The spirit of Egypt will be emptied within it, and I will confound their counsel;*

Jewish people (see 66:20) which is described here in the same terms as those used in verse 2 where the nation was

described at the time of its degradation.
Rivers is a metaphor for foreign invaders (*Targum*).

ד וְדָרְשׁוּ אֶל־הָאֱלִילִים וְאֶל־הָאִטִּים וְאֶל־הָאֹבוֹת וְאֶל־הַיִּדְּעֹנִים: וְסִכַּרְתִּי
אֶת־מִצְרַיִם בְּיַד אֲדֹנִים קָשֶׁה וּמֶלֶךְ עַז יִמְשָׁל־בָּם נְאֻם הָאָדוֹן יהוה

ה צְבָאוֹת: וְנִשְּׁתוּ־מַיִם מֵהַיָּם וְנָהָר יֶחֱרַב וְיָבֵשׁ: וְהֶאֶזְנִיחוּ נְהָרוֹת דַּלֲלוּ

ז וְחָרְבוּ יְאֹרֵי מָצוֹר קָנֶה וָסוּף קָמֵלוּ: עָרוֹת עַל־יְאוֹר עַל־פִּי יְאוֹר וְכֹל

ח מִזְרַע יְאוֹר יִיבַשׁ נִדַּף וְאֵינֶנּוּ: וְאָנוּ הַדַּיָּגִים וְאָבְלוּ כָּל־מַשְׁלִיכֵי בַיְאוֹר

ט חַכָּה וּפֹרְשֵׂי מִכְמֹרֶת עַל־פְּנֵי־מַיִם אֻמְלָלוּ: וּבֹשׁוּ עֹבְדֵי פִשְׁתִּים שְׂרִיקוֹת

י־יא וְאֹרְגִים חוֹרָי: וְהָיוּ שָׁתֹתֶיהָ מְדֻכָּאִים כָּל־עֹשֵׂי שֶׂכֶר אַגְמֵי־נָפֶשׁ: אַךְ־
אֱוִלִים שָׂרֵי צֹעַן חַכְמֵי יֹעֲצֵי פַרְעֹה עֵצָה נִבְעָרָה אֵיךְ תֹּאמְרוּ אֶל־פַּרְעֹה

יב בֶּן־חֲכָמִים אֲנִי בֶּן־מַלְכֵי־קֶדֶם: אַיָּם אֵפוֹא חֲכָמֶיךָ וְיַגִּידוּ נָא לָךְ וְיֵדְעוּ

יג מַה־יָּעַץ יהוה צְבָאוֹת עַל־מִצְרָיִם: נוֹאֲלוּ שָׂרֵי צֹעַן נִשְּׁאוּ שָׂרֵי נֹף הִתְעוּ

יד אֶת־מִצְרַיִם פִּנַּת שְׁבָטֶיהָ: יהוה מָסַךְ בְּקִרְבָּהּ רוּחַ עִוְעִים וְהִתְעוּ אֶת־

טו מִצְרַיִם בְּכָל־מַעֲשֵׂהוּ כְּהִתָּעוֹת שִׁכּוֹר בְּקִיאוֹ: וְלֹא־יִהְיֶה לְמִצְרַיִם

טז מַעֲשֶׂה אֲשֶׁר יַעֲשֶׂה רֹאשׁ וְזָנָב כִּפָּה וְאַגְמוֹן: בַּיּוֹם
הַהוּא יִהְיֶה מִצְרַיִם כַּנָּשִׁים וְחָרַד | וּפָחַד מִפְּנֵי תְּנוּפַת יַד־יהוה

יז צְבָאוֹת אֲשֶׁר־הוּא מֵנִיף עָלָיו: וְהָיְתָה אַדְמַת יְהוּדָה לְמִצְרַיִם לְחָגָּא
כֹּל אֲשֶׁר יַזְכִּיר אֹתָהּ אֵלָיו יִפְחָד מִפְּנֵי עֲצַת יהוה צְבָאוֹת אֲשֶׁר־הוּא

יח יוֹעֵץ עָלָיו: בַּיּוֹם הַהוּא יִהְיוּ חָמֵשׁ עָרִים בְּאֶרֶץ
מִצְרַיִם מְדַבְּרוֹת שְׂפַת כְּנַעַן וְנִשְׁבָּעוֹת לַיהוה צְבָאוֹת עִיר הַהֶרֶס יֵאָמֵר

יט לְאֶחָת: בַּיּוֹם הַהוּא יִהְיֶה מִזְבֵּחַ לַיהוה בְּתוֹךְ אֶרֶץ

כ מִצְרָיִם וּמַצֵּבָה אֵצֶל־גְּבוּלָהּ לַיהוה: וְהָיָה לְאוֹת וּלְעֵד לַיהוה צְבָאוֹת
בְּאֶרֶץ מִצְרָיִם כִּי־יִצְעֲקוּ אֶל־יהוה מִפְּנֵי לֹחֲצִים וְיִשְׁלַח לָהֶם מוֹשִׁיעַ

כא וָרָב וְהִצִּילָם: וְנוֹדַע יהוה לְמִצְרַיִם וְיָדְעוּ מִצְרַיִם אֶת־יהוה בַּיּוֹם הַהוּא
וְעָבְדוּ זֶבַח וּמִנְחָה וְנָדְרוּ־נֵדֶר לַיהוה וְשִׁלֵּמוּ: וְנָגַף יהוה אֶת־מִצְרַיִם

כג נָגֹף וְרָפוֹא וְשָׁבוּ עַד־יהוה וְנֶעְתַּר לָהֶם וּרְפָאָם: בַּיּוֹם הַהוּא
תִּהְיֶה מְסִלָּה מִמִּצְרַיִם אַשּׁוּרָה וּבָא־אַשּׁוּר בְּמִצְרַיִם וּמִצְרַיִם בְּאַשּׁוּר

כד וְעָבְדוּ מִצְרַיִם אֶת־אַשּׁוּר: בַּיּוֹם הַהוּא יִהְיֶה יִשְׂרָאֵל שְׁלִישִׁיָּה

כה לְמִצְרַיִם וּלְאַשּׁוּר בְּרָכָה בְּקֶרֶב הָאָרֶץ: אֲשֶׁר בֵּרֲכוֹ יהוה צְבָאוֹת

19:5. Lit., "the river." Arid Egypt depends on the Nile for its sustenance; therefore the drying of the Nile is a metaphor for the country's downfall (*Rashi*).

19:9. Since fishing will come to a standstill, those whose livelihood depends on it will be chagrined.

19:10. Fishermen used to dam the waters to trap fish in calm pools. Now all that will be useless (*Rashi*).

19:11. A royal Egyptian city (see 30:4).

19:13. Another Egyptian city, identified by *Targum* as Memphis.

19:15. The "head" and "tail" refer to the major and minor government advisers, as do the "canopied tree"

and the "reed"; that is, the strong, self-assured advisers and the weaker, more pliant ones (*Radak*).

19:17. When Egypt hears that the army of Sennacherib, its conqueror, was miraculously wiped out at the gates of Jerusalem, the Egyptians will realize that both their defeat and Judah's salvation were Divinely ordained, and they will fear God.

19:18. I.e., Hebrew. Egyptian eyewitnesses to the miracle in Jerusalem will set up, in Egypt, communities of people who are faithful to God.

One of those five communities was called City of the Sun (*Kara*); it was later destroyed (*Targum*; *Rashi*; see *Jeremiah* 43:13).

they will inquire of the false gods, of the sorcerers, of the necromancers, and of the diviners.

The Nile will dry up

⁴ I will deliver Egypt into the hands of a harsh master, and a strong king will rule them — the word of the Lord, HASHEM, Master of Legions. ⁵ The waters of the sea will recede, and the Nile* will dry out and be parched. ⁶ The rivers will become foul and [waters in] the moats will be diminished and dry up; the reeds and the bulrushes will wither. ⁷ The vegetation near the Nile, on the bank of the Nile, and everything planted alongside the Nile, will dry up, wither, and be no more. ⁸ The fishermen will mourn, and all those who cast their hooks into the Nile will lament; those who spread nets on the water will be bereaved. ⁹ Ashamed will be those who work at combing flax and weaving nets. * ¹⁰ The foundations of its fish pools will be battered, all who dammed calm pools will be depressed in spirit. *

¹¹ The officers of Zoan* are but fools, Pharaoh's wisest advisers offer boorish counsel. How can you tell Pharaoh, 'I am the son of wise men, the descendant of the kings of yore'? ¹² Where are they? Where are your wise men? Let them tell you now, let them try to know what HASHEM, Master of Legions, has planned for Egypt. ¹³ The officers of Zoan have become foolish, the officers of Noph* have become misguided. The cornerstones of her tribes have caused Egypt to stray. ¹⁴ HASHEM has poured out into her midst a spirit of insanity and they have caused Egypt to stray in all their actions, as a drunkard strays into his vomit. ¹⁵ There will be nothing that the Egyptians can do — the 'head' or the 'tail,'* the 'canopied tree' or the 'reed.' ¹⁶ On that day Egypt will be like women; it will tremble and fear before the wave of the hand of HASHEM, Master of Legions, which He will wave at it. ¹⁷ The land of Judah will be a source of fright for Egypt; when anyone mentions it to [Egypt], it will fear, * because of the counsel of HASHEM, Master of Legions, that He devises against it.

Egypt's worship of the true God, and its deliverance

¹⁸ On that day, there will be five cities in Egypt that speak the language of Canaan* and that swear by [the Name of] HASHEM, Master of Legions; one of them will be called 'the City of the Sun.'*

¹⁹ On that day there will be an altar [dedicated] to HASHEM in the midst of the land of Egypt, and a pillar [dedicated] to HASHEM near its border; ²⁰ and it will be a sign and a witness to HASHEM, Master of Legions, in the land of Egypt, that when they cry out to HASHEM because of oppressors, He will send them a savior and a leader and deliver them. ²¹ And HASHEM will become known to Egypt, for the Egyptians will know HASHEM on that day; and they will worship with sacrifice and meal-offering, and they will make a vow to HASHEM and fulfill it. ²² HASHEM will strike Egypt, striking and healing; they will repent to HASHEM, He will be appeased to them and heal them.

²³ On that day there will be a road from Egypt to Assyria; Assyrian will come into Egypt and Egyptian into Assyria, and Egypt will serve [HASHEM] with Assyria. *

²⁴ On that day Israel will be the third party with Egypt and with Assyria, a blessing in the midst of the land, ²⁵ for HASHEM, Master of Legions, will bless

---

19:23-25. Egypt and Assyria will make peace when they realize that God controls their fate. Israel will be their third partner in the worship of God (*Radak*).

Malbim cites three views of when this prophecy will take place: It will be in the future; it happened at the time of Simeon the Righteous during the early years of the Second Temple; it happened in Hezekiah's time, after the miracle at Jerusalem.

כ

א לֵאמֹר בָּרוּךְ עַמִּי מִצְרַיִם וּמַעֲשֵׂה יָדַי אַשּׁוּר וְנַחֲלָתִי יִשְׂרָאֵל: בִּשְׁנַת בֹּא תַרְתָּן אַשְׁדּוֹדָה בִּשְׁלֹחַ אֹתוֹ סַרְגוֹן מֶלֶךְ אַשּׁוּר וַיִּלָּחֶם בְּאַשְׁדּוֹד

ב וַיִּלְכְּדָהּ: בָּעֵת הַהִיא דִּבֶּר יהוה בְּיַד יְשַׁעְיָהוּ בֶן־אָמוֹץ לֵאמֹר לֵךְ וּפִתַּחְתָּ הַשַּׂק מֵעַל מָתְנֶיךָ וְנַעַלְךָ תַחֲלֹץ מֵעַל רַגְלֶיךָ וַיַּעַשׂ כֵּן הָלֹךְ עָרוֹם

ג וְיָחֵף: וַיֹּאמֶר יהוה כַּאֲשֶׁר הָלַךְ עַבְדִּי יְשַׁעְיָהוּ עָרוֹם וְיָחֵף

ד שָׁלֹשׁ שָׁנִים אוֹת וּמוֹפֵת עַל־מִצְרַיִם וְעַל־כּוּשׁ: כֵּן יִנְהַג מֶלֶךְ־אַשּׁוּר אֶת־שְׁבִי מִצְרַיִם וְאֶת־גָּלוּת כּוּשׁ נְעָרִים וּזְקֵנִים עָרוֹם וְיָחֵף וַחֲשׂוּפַי שֵׁת

ה־ו עֶרְוַת מִצְרָיִם: וְחַתּוּ וָבֹשׁוּ מִכּוּשׁ מַבָּטָם וּמִן־מִצְרַיִם תִּפְאַרְתָּם: וְאָמַר יֹשֵׁב הָאִי הַזֶּה בַּיּוֹם הַהוּא הִנֵּה־כֹה מַבָּטֵנוּ אֲשֶׁר־נַסְנוּ שָׁם לְעֶזְרָה לְהִנָּצֵל מִפְּנֵי מֶלֶךְ אַשּׁוּר וְאֵיךְ נִמָּלֵט אֲנָחְנוּ:

כא

א מַשָּׂא מִדְבַּר־

ב יָם כְּסוּפוֹת בַּנֶּגֶב לַחֲלֹף מִמִּדְבָּר בָּא מֵאֶרֶץ נוֹרָאָה: חָזוּת קָשָׁה הֻגַּד־לִי הַבּוֹגֵד | בּוֹגֵד וְהַשּׁוֹדֵד | שׁוֹדֵד עֲלִי עֵילָם צוּרִי מָדַי כָּל־אַנְחָתָה הִשְׁבַּתִּי:

ג עַל־כֵּן מָלְאוּ מָתְנַי חַלְחָלָה צִירִים אֲחָזוּנִי כְּצִירֵי יוֹלֵדָה נַעֲוֵיתִי מִשְּׁמֹעַ

ד נִבְהַלְתִּי מֵרְאוֹת: תָּעָה לְבָבִי פַּלָּצוּת בִּעֲתָתְנִי אֵת נֶשֶׁף חִשְׁקִי שָׂם לִי

ה לַחֲרָדָה: עָרֹךְ הַשֻּׁלְחָן צָפֹה הַצָּפִית אָכוֹל שָׁתֹה קוּמוּ הַשָּׂרִים מִשְׁחוּ

ו מָגֵן: כִּי כֹה אָמַר אֵלַי אֲדֹנָי לֵךְ הַעֲמֵד הַמְצַפֶּה אֲשֶׁר יִרְאֶה

ז יַגִּיד: וְרָאָה רֶכֶב צֶמֶד פָּרָשִׁים רֶכֶב חֲמוֹר רֶכֶב גָּמָל וְהִקְשִׁיב קֶשֶׁב רַב־

ח קָשֶׁב: וַיִּקְרָא אַרְיֵה עַל־מִצְפֶּה | אֲדֹנָי אָנֹכִי עֹמֵד תָּמִיד יוֹמָם וְעַל־

ט מִשְׁמַרְתִּי אָנֹכִי נִצָּב כָּל־הַלֵּילוֹת: וְהִנֵּה־זֶה בָא רֶכֶב אִישׁ צֶמֶד פָּרָשִׁים

י וַיַּעַן וַיֹּאמֶר נָפְלָה נָפְלָה בָּבֶל וְכָל־פְּסִילֵי אֱלֹהֶיהָ שִׁבַּר לָאָרֶץ: מְדֻשָׁתִי וּבֶן־גָּרְנִי אֲשֶׁר שָׁמַעְתִּי מֵאֵת יהוה צְבָאוֹת אֱלֹהֵי יִשְׂרָאֵל הִגַּדְתִּי

יא לָכֶם: מַשָּׂא דּוּמָה אֵלַי קֹרֵא מִשֵּׂעִיר שֹׁמֵר מַה־מִּלַּיְלָה

יב שֹׁמֵר מַה־מִּלֵּיל: אָמַר שֹׁמֵר אָתָה בֹקֶר וְגַם־לָיְלָה אִם־תִּבְעָיוּן בְּעָיוּ שֻׁבוּ

יג אֵתָיוּ: מַשָּׂא בַּעְרָב בַּיַּעַר בַּעְרַב תָּלִינוּ אֹרְחוֹת דְּדָנִים:

20:1. The commentators note that Sargon was Sennacherib. The conquest of Ashdod mentioned in this verse took place either the year he besieged Jerusalem or three years before.

20:2. I.e., he was wearing only sackcloth.

20:6. A reference to the people of Judah [which was like an island surrounded by Assyrian forces, yet] relying on Egypt (*Rashi*). *Radak* renders coastland, since Judah was on the Mediterranean.

21:1. This prophecy is addressed to Babylonia, as seen from v. 9. The prophet calls it Wilderness of the West, because he foretells a destruction that will come like a windstorm from the Persians and Medes, Babylonia's eastern neighbors (*Radak*).

21:2. Babylonia will be so vulnerable that anyone will be able to attack her (*Ibn Ezra*). God will end all the sighs of those who were mistreated by Babylonia, because the tyrant will be vanquished (*Rashi*).

21:3-5. The prophet laments as he empathizes with the fallen Babylonians. Alternatively: The prophet now speaks for the last Babylonian king, Belshazzar, who was killed during the course of a lavish banquet (*Daniel* Ch. 5). The feast (v. 5) was interrupted by the invasion of the Persians and Medes.

21:5. Shields were greased so that arrows would glance off rather than pierce them.

21:8. Understanding the lookout (v. 6) to refer to himself, Isaiah longs to be shown a vision concerning the wicked Babylonians (*Ibn Ezra*).

21:11. The name Duma is a reference to Edom (*Rashi*). In this prophecy, God says that Israel cries out to God, its Watchman, because of the oppression of the night, i.e., exile, inflicted by Edom, whose homeland was Seir.

21:12. Deliverance is at hand, but the night will continue for the wicked. Only repentance will bring the long-awaited salvation.

them, saying, 'Blessed is My people, Egypt; and the work of My hands, Assyria; and My heritage, Israel.'

20 ¹ In the year that Tartan came to Ashdod, when Sargon, king of Assyria, sent him, and he fought against Ashdod and captured it, * ² at that time HASHEM spoke through Isaiah son of Amoz, saying, ³ "Go and don sackcloth upon your loins and remove your shoe from your foot." He did so, going unclothed* and barefoot. ³ HASHEM said:

Exile of Egypt and Cush

Just as My servant Isaiah has gone unclothed and barefoot for three years, as a sign and a symbol for Egypt and Cush, ⁴ so will the king of Assyria lead away the captivity of Egypt and the exile of Cush — young and old — unclothed and barefoot, with exposed buttocks, the nakedness of Egypt. ⁵ Devastated and ashamed will be those whose longing was for Cush and whose splendor was from Egypt. ⁶ The inhabitant of this island* will say on that day, 'Behold, if such [was the defeat of] the one for whom we longed — to where we ran for help to be rescued from the king of Assyria — how can we hope to escape?'

21 ¹ A prophecy concerning the Wilderness of the West:*

Downfall of Baby-lonia . . .

Like windstorms sweeping through the desert, it will come from the wilderness, from a fearful land. ² A harsh vision has been told to me: The treacherous one may act treacherously, * and the pillager may pillage. 'Go up, O Elam! Besiege, O Media!' I have brought an end to every sigh.

³ Therefore, my* loins are full of anguish; pains have gripped me like the pains of a woman in childbirth. I have become confounded from hearing it; terrified from seeing it. ⁴ My heart has become disoriented; panic has terror-ized me. He has turned my festive evening into a horror. ⁵ Setting the table, lighting the candelabrum, eating and drinking, 'Arise, O officers; anoint the shield.'*

⁶ For thus said my Lord to me: Go, station the lookout, and let him tell what he sees. ⁷ He will see a chariot, a pair of horsemen, a donkey chariot, a camel chariot; and he will listen intently, with much to hear, ⁸ and he will call out like a lion.

My Lord, I stand on the lookout constantly* during the day, and I am stationed at my post all the nights. ⁹ Behold, it is coming: a chariot with a man, a pair of horsemen. Each says loudly, 'It has fallen! Babylonia has fallen! All the statues of its gods have been shattered on the ground! ¹⁰ It is [like] grain of the threshing floor, for me to thresh!'

What I have heard from HASHEM, Master of Legions, God of Israel, I have told you.

. . . Duma [Edom] . . .

¹¹ A prophecy concerning Duma:*

He calls out to Me because of Seir: 'Watchman, what of the night? Watch-man, what of the night?' ¹² The Watchman said, 'Morning is coming, but also night. * If you really desire it, repent and come.'

. . . and Arabia

¹³ A prophecy concerning Arabia:

In the forest in Arabia shall you lodge, [you] caravans of Dedanites. *

21:13. The Dedanites, who had availed themselves of the hospitality of the Arabs whenever they traveled through   the desert, would now lodge in the forests, because the Arabs would be driven from their land.

יד-טו לִקְרַאת צָמֵא הֵתָיוּ מָיִם יֹשְׁבֵי אֶרֶץ תֵּימָא בְּלַחְמוֹ קִדְּמוּ נֹדֵד: כִּי־
מִפְּנֵי חֲרָבוֹת נָדָדוּ מִפְּנֵי ׀ חֶרֶב נְטוּשָׁה וּמִפְּנֵי קֶשֶׁת דְּרוּכָה וּמִפְּנֵי כֹּבֶד
טז מִלְחָמָה: כִּי־כֹה אָמַר אֲדֹנָי אֵלָי בְּעוֹד שָׁנָה כִּשְׁנֵי שָׂכִיר וְכָלָה
יז כָּל־כְּבוֹד קֵדָר: וּשְׁאָר מִסְפַּר־קֶשֶׁת גִּבּוֹרֵי בְנֵי־קֵדָר יִמְעָטוּ כִּי יהוה אֱלֹהֵי־

כב א יִשְׂרָאֵל דִּבֵּר: מַשָּׂא גֵּיא חִזָּיוֹן מַה־לָּךְ אֵפוֹא כִּי־עָלִית כֻּלָּךְ
ב לַגַּגּוֹת: תְּשֻׁאוֹת ׀ מְלֵאָה עִיר הוֹמִיָּה קִרְיָה עַלִּיזָה חֲלָלַיִךְ לֹא חַלְלֵי־חֶרֶב
ג וְלֹא מֵתֵי מִלְחָמָה: כָּל־קְצִינַיִךְ נָדְדוּ־יַחַד מִקֶּשֶׁת אֻסָּרוּ כָּל־נִמְצָאַיִךְ
ד אֻסְּרוּ יַחְדָּו מֵרָחוֹק בָּרָחוּ: עַל־כֵּן אָמַרְתִּי שְׁעוּ מִנִּי אֲמָרֵר בַּבֶּכִי אַל־
ה תָּאִיצוּ לְנַחֲמֵנִי עַל־שֹׁד בַּת־עַמִּי: כִּי יוֹם מְהוּמָה וּמְבוּסָה וּמְבוּכָה לַאדֹנָי
ו יהוה צְבָאוֹת בְּגֵיא חִזָּיוֹן מְקַרְקַר קִר וְשׁוֹעַ אֶל־הָהָר: וְעֵילָם נָשָׂא אַשְׁפָּה
ז בְּרֶכֶב אָדָם פָּרָשִׁים וְקִיר עֵרָה מָגֵן: וַיְהִי מִבְחַר־עֲמָקַיִךְ מָלְאוּ רָכֶב
ח וְהַפָּרָשִׁים שֹׁת שָׁתוּ הַשָּׁעְרָה: וַיְגַל אֵת מָסַךְ יְהוּדָה וַתַּבֵּט בַּיּוֹם הַהוּא אֶל־
ט נֶשֶׁק בֵּית־הַיָּעַר: וְאֵת בְּקִיעֵי עִיר־דָּוִד רְאִיתֶם כִּי־רָבּוּ וַתְּקַבְּצוּ אֶת־מֵי
י הַבְּרֵכָה הַתַּחְתּוֹנָה: וְאֶת־בָּתֵּי יְרוּשָׁלַ͏ִם סְפַרְתֶּם וַתִּתְצוּ הַבָּתִּים לְבַצֵּר
יא הַחוֹמָה: וּמִקְוָה ׀ עֲשִׂיתֶם בֵּין הַחֹמֹתַיִם לְמֵי הַבְּרֵכָה הַיְשָׁנָה וְלֹא הִבַּטְתֶּם
יב אֶל־עֹשֶׂיהָ וְיֹצְרָהּ מֵרָחוֹק לֹא רְאִיתֶם: וַיִּקְרָא אֲדֹנָי יהוה צְבָאוֹת בַּיּוֹם
יג הַהוּא לִבְכִי וּלְמִסְפֵּד וּלְקָרְחָה וְלַחֲגֹר שָׂק: וְהִנֵּה ׀ שָׂשׂוֹן וְשִׂמְחָה הָרֹג ׀
יד בָּקָר וְשָׁחֹט צֹאן אָכֹל בָּשָׂר וְשָׁתוֹת יָיִן אָכוֹל וְשָׁתוֹ כִּי מָחָר נָמוּת: וְנִגְלָה
בְאָזְנָי יהוה צְבָאוֹת אִם־יְכֻפַּר הֶעָוֹן הַזֶּה לָכֶם עַד־תְּמֻתוּן אָמַר אֲדֹנָי יהוה
טו צְבָאוֹת: כֹּה אָמַר אֲדֹנָי יהוה צְבָאוֹת לֶךְ־בֹּא אֶל־הַסֹּכֵן
טז הַזֶּה עַל־שֶׁבְנָא אֲשֶׁר עַל־הַבָּיִת: מַה־לְּךָ פֹה וּמִי לְךָ פֹה כִּי־חָצַבְתָּ לְּךָ פֹּה
יז קֶבֶר חֹצְבִי מָרוֹם קִבְרוֹ חֹקְקִי בַסֶּלַע מִשְׁכָּן לוֹ: הִנֵּה יהוה מְטַלְטֶלְךָ
יח טַלְטֵלָה גָּבֶר וְעֹטְךָ עָטֹה: צָנוֹף יִצְנָפְךָ צְנֵפָה כַּדּוּר אֶל־אֶרֶץ רַחֲבַת יָדָיִם
יט שָׁמָּה תָמוּת וְשָׁמָּה מַרְכְּבוֹת כְּבוֹדֶךָ קְלוֹן בֵּית אֲדֹנֶיךָ: וַהֲדַפְתִּיךָ מִמַּצָּבֶךָ

21:14. The Arabs, who will be captured and led into exile, will be starving and thirsty, dependent on the good will of their neighbors for survival.

21:16. The timing will be exact, just as a wage earner does not work a moment longer than he is required to.

The Arab nation is called Kedar after Ishmael's second son (see *Genesis* 25:13).

22:1. I.e., Jerusalem, where many prophetic visions were seen (*Rashi*). Though it is on a hilltop, its sins brought it down to a spiritual valley.

The people went to the roofs to seek shelter from invaders, or to fight from a vantage point (*Radak*).

22:4. The prophet rejected his comforters.

22:5. Alternatively: "Kir breaching [the wall] and Shoa upon the mountain" (*Kara*). Among the allies of Babylonia were Kir (see *II Kings* 16:9), Shoa (see *Ezekiel* 23:23), and Elam (v. 6).

22:7. Isaiah now speaks to Jerusalem's inhabitants.

22:8-11. Isaiah decries the misplaced confidence of the Jews. They were sure that the Temple — the shelter of Judah — would protect them. When the enemy prevailed anyway, the people turned to a building called the House of the Forest [of Lebanon] (see *I Kings* 10:16) where King Solomon had stored shields and armaments. Seeing that the enemy had breached the wall, they gathered water to make mortar and tore down houses to acquire building blocks for repairs. The people drew the wrong conclusions. They trusted in external protection, but failed to turn to the only One Who could help them.

22:12. God called upon the people, through the agency of His prophets, to repent, bemoan their short-comings and return to Him.

22:15-25. Isaiah condemns Shebna, a deputy of King Hezekiah (see *II Kings* Chs. 18,19), who led a rebel

¹⁴ *Bring forth water for the thirsty!* * *Those who dwell in the land of Tema greeted the wanderer with food.* ¹⁵ *For they will wander because of swords; because of the outstretched sword, because of the drawn bow and because of the severity of the war.* ¹⁶ *For thus said my Lord to me: In one more year, like the years of a wage earner,* * *all the glory of Kedar* * *will be ended;* ¹⁷ *and the remainder of the numbers of archers, the mighty heroes of the sons of Kedar, will be diminished, for* HASHEM, *the God of Israel, has spoken.*

22

Downfall of Jerusalem

¹ A *prophecy concerning the Valley of Vision:* * *What happened to you now, that you have all gone up to the roofs,* * ² *you who had been full of commotion, a tumultuous city, an exuberant town? Your slain are not slain by the sword, nor did they die in war.* ³ *All of your officers wandered off together, but were confined by the bow; all those found within you were confined together, [as well as] those who had fled afar.*

⁴ *I said, therefore,* * '*Leave me alone; I will weep bitterly; do not insist on comforting me for the calamity of my people.'* ⁵ *For it is a day of turmoil and trampling and confusion unto my Lord,* HASHEM/ELOHIM, *Master of Legions, in the Valley of Vision, of breaching [the] wall and of crying out upon the mountain.* * ⁶ *Elam has taken up its quiver, with chariots of men and horsemen, and Kir bared its shield.*

⁷ * *The choicest of your valleys became filled with chariots, and horsemen positioned themselves toward your gate.* ⁸ *He uncovered the shelter of Judah, but on that day you looked to the armaments in the House of the Forest.* ⁹ *You saw that the breaches of the City of David were numerous, so you collected the waters of the Lower Pool.* ¹⁰ *You counted the houses of Jerusalem, and you demolished the houses to reinforce the wall.* ¹¹ *You made a water reservoir between the two walls, by the water of the Old Pool. But you did not look towards the One Who made this happen, nor did you consider the One Who formed it in the distant past.* * ¹² *My Lord* HASHEM/ELOHIM, *Master of Legions, declared that day to be for crying and lamenting,* * *for baldness and for the donning of sackcloth;* ¹³ *yet behold! there is joy and gladness, slaying of cattle and slaughtering of sheep, eating meat and drinking wine, [saying,] 'Eat and drink, for tomorrow we die.'*

¹⁴ *This became revealed in My ears, [I,]* HASHEM, *Master of Legions, that this sin will never be atoned for you until you die — said my Lord,* HASHEM/ELOHIM, *Master of Legions.*

Shebna's degradation

¹⁵ *Thus said my Lord,* HASHEM/ELOHIM, *Master of Legions: Go and approach that manager, Shebna,* * *who is in charge of the [king's] house.* ¹⁶ *[Tell him:] What have you here and whom have you here, that you have hewn yourself a grave here,* * *you who digs his grave on high and carves out in the rock an abode for himself?* ¹⁷ *Behold,* HASHEM *is going to make you wander an intense wandering, and He will send you circling afar.* ¹⁸ *He will wind you around like a turban, [and hurl you like] a ball to a land without obstacles;* * *there you will die and there [will die] your chariots of honor — O shame of your master's house.* ¹⁹ * *I will oust you from your position,*

---

party that wanted to capitulate to Sennacherib.

22:16. So sure was Shebna that he was irreplaceable, that he hewed out a grave for himself in the royal section [on high] of the burial ground (*Radak*).

22:18. Where the ball would keep rolling endlessly, with nothing to stop it (*Metzudos*).

22:19-23. Until now the prophet has been speaking in his own voice, referring to God in the third person. In

כ וּמִמַּעֲמָדְךָ יֶהֶרְסֶךָ: וְהָיָה בַּיּוֹם הַהוּא וְקָרָאתִי לְעַבְדִּי לְאֶלְיָקִים בֶּן־

כא חִלְקִיָּהוּ: וְהִלְבַּשְׁתִּיו כֻּתָּנְתֶּךָ וְאַבְנֵטְךָ אֲחַזְּקֶנּוּ וּמֶמְשַׁלְתְּךָ אֶתֵּן בְּיָדוֹ וְהָיָה

כב לְאָב לְיוֹשֵׁב יְרוּשָׁלַם וּלְבֵית יְהוּדָה: וְנָתַתִּי מַפְתֵּחַ בֵּית־דָּוִד עַל־שִׁכְמוֹ

כג וּפָתַח וְאֵין סֹגֵר וְסָגַר וְאֵין פֹּתֵחַ: וּתְקַעְתִּיו יָתֵד בְּמָקוֹם נֶאֱמָן וְהָיָה לְכִסֵּא

כד כָבוֹד לְבֵית אָבִיו: וְתָלוּ עָלָיו כֹּל ׀ כְּבוֹד בֵּית־אָבִיו הַצֶּאֱצָאִים וְהַצְּפִעוֹת

כה כֹּל כְּלֵי הַקָּטָן מִכְּלֵי הָאַגָּנוֹת וְעַד כָּל־כְּלֵי הַנְּבָלִים: בַּיּוֹם הַהוּא נְאֻם יְהוָה

צְבָאוֹת תָּמוּשׁ הַיָּתֵד הַתְּקוּעָה בְּמָקוֹם נֶאֱמָן וְנִגְדְּעָה וְנָפְלָה וְנִכְרַת

כג א הַמַּשָּׂא אֲשֶׁר עָלֶיהָ כִּי יְהוָה דִּבֵּר: מַשָּׂא צֹר הֵילִילוּ ׀ אֳנִיּוֹת

ב תַּרְשִׁישׁ כִּי־שֻׁדַּד מִבַּיִת מִבּוֹא מֵאֶרֶץ כִּתִּים נִגְלָה־לָמוֹ: דֹּמּוּ יֹשְׁבֵי אִי

ג סֹחֵר צִידוֹן עֹבֵר יָם מִלְאוּךְ: וּבְמַיִם רַבִּים זֶרַע שִׁחֹר קְצִיר יְאוֹר תְּבוּאָתָהּ

ד וַתְּהִי סְחַר גּוֹיִם: בּוֹשִׁי צִידוֹן כִּי־אָמַר יָם מָעוֹז הַיָּם לֵאמֹר לֹא־חַלְתִּי

ה וְלֹא־יָלַדְתִּי וְלֹא גִדַּלְתִּי בַּחוּרִים רוֹמַמְתִּי בְתוּלוֹת: כַּאֲשֶׁר־שֵׁמַע

ו לְמִצְרַיִם יָחִילוּ כְּשֵׁמַע צֹר: עִבְרוּ תַּרְשִׁישָׁה הֵילִילוּ יֹשְׁבֵי אִי: הֲזֹאת לָכֶם

ז עַלִּיזָה מִימֵי־קֶדֶם קַדְמָתָהּ יֹבִלוּהָ רַגְלֶיהָ מֵרָחוֹק לָגוּר: מִי יָעַץ זֹאת עַל־

ח צֹר הַמַּעֲטִירָה אֲשֶׁר סֹחֲרֶיהָ שָׂרִים כִּנְעָנֶיהָ נִכְבַּדֵּי־אָרֶץ: יְהוָה צְבָאוֹת

ט יְעָצָהּ לְחַלֵּל גְּאוֹן כָּל־צְבִי לְהָקֵל כָּל־נִכְבַּדֵּי־אָרֶץ: עָבְרִי אַרְצֵךְ כַּיְאֹר

י בַּת־תַּרְשִׁישׁ אֵין מֵזַח עוֹד: יָדוֹ נָטָה עַל־הַיָּם הִרְגִּיז מַמְלָכוֹת יְהוָה צִוָּה

יא אֶל־כְּנַעַן לַשְׁמִד מָעֻזְנֶיהָ: וַיֹּאמֶר לֹא־תוֹסִיפִי עוֹד לַעְלוֹז הַמְעֻשָּׁקָה

יב בְּתוּלַת בַּת־צִידוֹן °כתים [°כִּתִּים ק] קוּמִי עֲבֹרִי גַּם־שָׁם לֹא־יָנוּחַ לָךְ:

יג הֵן ׀ אֶרֶץ כַּשְׂדִּים זֶה הָעָם לֹא הָיָה אַשּׁוּר יְסָדָהּ לְצִיִּים הֵקִימוּ °בחיניו [°בַחוּנָיו ק]

יד עֹרְרוּ אַרְמְנוֹתֶיהָ שָׂמָהּ לְמַפֵּלָה: הֵילִילוּ אֳנִיּוֹת תַּרְשִׁישׁ כִּי

טו שֻׁדַּד מָעֻזְּכֶן: וְהָיָה בַּיּוֹם הַהוּא וְנִשְׁכַּחַת צֹר שִׁבְעִים שָׁנָה

טז כִּימֵי מֶלֶךְ אֶחָד מִקֵּץ שִׁבְעִים שָׁנָה יִהְיֶה לְצֹר כְּשִׁירַת הַזּוֹנָה: קְחִי

יז כִנּוֹר סֹבִּי עִיר זוֹנָה נִשְׁכָּחָה הֵיטִיבִי נַגֵּן הַרְבִּי־שִׁיר לְמַעַן תִּזָּכֵרִי: וְהָיָה

מִקֵּץ ׀ שִׁבְעִים שָׁנָה יִפְקֹד יְהוָה אֶת־צֹר וְשָׁבָה לְאֶתְנַנָּהּ וְזָנְתָה אֶת־כָּל־

---

verse 19 he speaks in God's voice using the first person, then switches back to the third person. For the remainder of the passage he reverts to the first person. This shifting of person and voice is not uncommon in prophecy (*Radak*).

22:22. I.e., the affairs of the royal house will be arranged through him.

22:24. Continuing the metaphor of the sturdy peg, Isaiah says that Eliakim will be trusted by all classes of people, who will rely (hang) on him for all their needs.

23:1. Tarshish ships are long-distance cargo vessels. The impending destruction of Tyre and Sidon would deprive the Tarshish ships of their principal destinations, and the ships' other ports of call would lack the merchandise that used to fill their docks and stores.

23:3. The Tyrians would import fine Egyptian grain.

23:4. The fortress is Tyre. Sidon, which was dependent on Tyre, will be ashamed when it hears vanquished Tyre lament, "All my children are gone forever, as if I had never borne or raised them."

23:5. When Egypt hears what Babylonia did to Tyre, they will tremble, as Tyre had when it learned that Nebuchadnezzar's forces were on the way (*Radak*).

23:6. You inhabitants of Tyre, flee for your lives to Tarshish (*Targum*).

23:8-9. Who could have devised a plan to destroy such a thriving, distinguished city? The answer follows: God decreed it and, as it were, ordered Tyre's citizens to flee into exile.

23:11. God decreed that ships with lucrative cargo would not reach Tyre (*Radak*). He also decreed destruc-

<table>
<tr><td>

Eliakim's
elevation

</td><td>

and He will bring you down from your post. ²⁰ It shall be on that day that I will call upon My servant, upon Eliakim son of Hilkiah; ²¹ I will dress him with your tunic and gird him with your belt, and I will deliver your dominion into his hand; and he will be a father to the inhabitants of Jerusalem and to the House of Judah. ²² I will place the key to the House of David on his shoulder; * he will open and no one will close, he will close and no one will open. ²³ I will affix him as a peg in a secure place, and he will be like a throne of honor for his father's house. ²⁴ They will hang upon him the entire honor of his father's house, the sons and the daughters, every small article, from various bowls to all kinds of stringed instruments. *

</td></tr>
</table>

²⁵ On that day — the word of HASHEM, Master of Legions — the peg [of Shebna] that is affixed in a secure place will move away, and the load that is upon it will be plucked off and fall and be destroyed, for HASHEM has spoken.

23

¹ **A** prophecy concerning Tyre:

Downfall of Tyre . . .

Wail, O ships of Tarshish, * for [Tyre] has been too sacked from within to be able to enter it. From the land of Kittim has [the invader] been revealed to it. ² Fall silent, you island dwellers, [for] the seafaring merchants of Sidon used to fill you. ³ Through many waters [came] the seed of the Nile, the harvest of the river as her produce; * she was the marketplace for all the nations. ⁴ Be ashamed, O Sidon, for the sea has spoken, the fortress on the sea, * saying, 'I have not gone into labor and I have not given birth, nor have I raised youths or reared maidens.' ⁵ When the news reaches Egypt, they will tremble, as when Tyre heard the news. * ⁶ Move on to Tarshish! * Wail, O dwellers of the island! ⁷ Is this happening to you, O exultant one, whose origins were in ancient days, but whose legs lead her to dwell in far-off [exile]? ⁸ Who devised this against Tyre, * the magnificent, whose merchants were princes and whose traders were the elite of the land? ⁹ HASHEM, Master of Legions, devised it, to defile pride in every delight, to suppress all the elite of the land. ¹⁰ Pass away from your land, like a [flowing] river, O daughter of Tarshish; you have no more power. ¹¹ [God] stretched out His hand over the sea, He incited kingdoms; HASHEM has issued a command against Canaan, * to destroy its source of strength. ¹² And He said, 'Exult no longer, O oppressed virgin daughter of Sidon, get up and cross over to Kittim; but even there there will be no rest for you.' ¹³ Behold, this is the land of the Chaldeans, * for this nation never used to be [here]. Assyria founded it for its fleets, they erected its towers; [now] they destroyed its palaces, it has been made a ruin. ¹⁴ Wail, O ships of Tarshish, for your source of strength has been sacked!

. . . and its restoration

¹⁵ It shall be on that day that Tyre will be forgotten for seventy years, like the lifetime of a unique king; * at the end of seventy years there will be for Tyre something like the song of a harlot. ¹⁶ Take a harp and circle the city, O forgotten harlot; play well, sing a lot, so that you may be remembered. ¹⁷ And it shall be at the end of seventy years that HASHEM will remember Tyre, and she will resume her harlot's hire, and she will engage in harlotry with all

---

tion on the Phoenician coast, which was inhabited by Canaanites (*Genesis* 10:19).

23:13. Tyre was founded by Chaldeans and Assyrians. The Phoenicians (*Canaanites*) who now populated the area arrived only afterwards (*Radak*). The newcomers

should not be surprised now when they are driven from this land.

23:15. I.e., King David, who lived for seventy years. Then, Tyre will be like a harlot past her prime, who sings a seductive song to call attention to herself.

יח מַמְלְכוֹת הָאָרֶץ עַל־פְּנֵי הָאֲדָמָה: וְהָיָה סַחְרָהּ וְאֶתְנַנָּהּ קֹדֶשׁ לַיהוָה לֹא יֵאָצֵר וְלֹא יֵחָסֵן כִּי לַיֹּשְׁבִים לִפְנֵי יהוה יִהְיֶה סַחְרָהּ לֶאֱכֹל לְשָׂבְעָה וְלִמְכַסֶּה עָתִיק:

כד

א הִנֵּה יהוה בּוֹקֵק הָאָרֶץ וּבוֹלְקָהּ וְעִוָּה פָנֶיהָ וְהֵפִיץ יֹשְׁבֶיהָ: וְהָיָה כָעָם כַּכֹּהֵן כַּעֶבֶד כַּאדֹנָיו כַּשִּׁפְחָה

ב כַּגְבִרְתָּהּ כַּקּוֹנֶה כַּמּוֹכֵר כַּמַּלְוֶה כַּלֹּוֶה כַּנֹּשֶׁה כַּאֲשֶׁר נֹשֶׁא בוֹ: הִבּוֹק |

ג תִּבּוֹק הָאָרֶץ וְהִבּוֹז | תִּבּוֹז כִּי יהוה דִּבֶּר אֶת־הַדָּבָר הַזֶּה: אָבְלָה נָבְלָה

ד הָאָרֶץ אֻמְלְלָה נָבְלָה תֵּבֵל אֻמְלָלוּ מְרוֹם עַם־הָאָרֶץ: וְהָאָרֶץ חָנְפָה

ה תַּחַת יֹשְׁבֶיהָ כִּי־עָבְרוּ תוֹרֹת חָלְפוּ חֹק הֵפֵרוּ בְּרִית עוֹלָם: עַל־כֵּן אָלָה

ו אָכְלָה אֶרֶץ וַיֶּאְשְׁמוּ יֹשְׁבֵי בָהּ עַל־כֵּן חָרוּ יֹשְׁבֵי אֶרֶץ וְנִשְׁאַר אֱנוֹשׁ

ז-ח מִזְעָר: אָבַל תִּירוֹשׁ אֻמְלְלָה־גָפֶן נֶאֶנְחוּ כָּל־שִׂמְחֵי־לֵב: שָׁבַת מְשׂוֹשׂ

ט תֻּפִּים חָדַל שְׁאוֹן עַלִּיזִים שָׁבַת מְשׂוֹשׂ כִּנּוֹר: בַּשִּׁיר לֹא יִשְׁתּוּ־יָיִן יֵמַר

י-יא שֵׁכָר לְשֹׁתָיו: נִשְׁבְּרָה קִרְיַת־תֹּהוּ סֻגַּר כָּל־בַּיִת מִבּוֹא: צְוָחָה עַל־הַיַּיִן

יב בַּחוּצוֹת עָרְבָה כָּל־שִׂמְחָה גָּלָה מְשׂוֹשׂ הָאָרֶץ: נִשְׁאַר בָּעִיר שַׁמָּה

יג וּשְׁאִיָּה יֻכַּת־שָׁעַר: כִּי כֹה יִהְיֶה בְּקֶרֶב הָאָרֶץ בְּתוֹךְ הָעַמִּים כְּנֹקֶף

יד זַיִת כְּעוֹלֵלֹת אִם־כָּלָה בָצִיר: הֵמָּה יִשְׂאוּ קוֹלָם יָרֹנּוּ בִּגְאוֹן יהוה

טו צָהֲלוּ מִיָּם: עַל־כֵּן בָּאֻרִים כַּבְּדוּ יהוה בְּאִיֵּי הַיָּם שֵׁם יהוה אֱלֹהֵי

טז יִשְׂרָאֵל: מִכְּנַף הָאָרֶץ זְמִרֹת שָׁמַעְנוּ צְבִי לַצַּדִּיק וָאֹמַר רָזִי־לִי רָזִי־לִי אוֹי לִי בֹּגְדִים בָּגָדוּ וּבֶגֶד בּוֹגְדִים בָּגָדוּ: פַּחַד וָפַחַת וָפָח

יז-יח עָלֶיךָ יוֹשֵׁב הָאָרֶץ: וְהָיָה הַנָּס מִקּוֹל הַפַּחַד יִפֹּל אֶל־הַפַּחַת וְהָעוֹלֶה מִתּוֹךְ הַפַּחַת יִלָּכֵד בַּפָּח כִּי־אֲרֻבּוֹת מִמָּרוֹם נִפְתָּחוּ וַיִּרְעֲשׁוּ מוֹסְדֵי

יט אָרֶץ: רֹעָה הִתְרֹעֲעָה הָאָרֶץ פּוֹר הִתְפּוֹרְרָה אֶרֶץ מוֹט הִתְמוֹטְטָה אָרֶץ:

כ נוֹעַ תָּנוּעַ אֶרֶץ כַּשִּׁכּוֹר וְהִתְנוֹדְדָה כַּמְּלוּנָה וְכָבַד עָלֶיהָ פִּשְׁעָהּ וְנָפְלָה

כא וְלֹא־תֹסִיף קוּם: וְהָיָה בַּיּוֹם הַהוּא יִפְקֹד יהוה עַל־

כב צְבָא הַמָּרוֹם בַּמָּרוֹם וְעַל־מַלְכֵי הָאֲדָמָה עַל־הָאֲדָמָה: וְאֻסְּפוּ אֲסֵפָה

כג אַסִּיר עַל־בּוֹר וְסֻגְּרוּ עַל־מַסְגֵּר וּמֵרֹב יָמִים יִפָּקֵדוּ: וְחָפְרָה הַלְּבָנָה וּבוֹשָׁה הַחַמָּה כִּי־מָלַךְ יהוה צְבָאוֹת בְּהַר צִיּוֹן וּבִירוּשָׁלַם וְנֶגֶד זְקֵנָיו

23:17. Tyre will again be a prosperous trader. Its profits and commerce are contemptuously referred to as "harlot's wages" and "harlotry."

24:1. This prophecy concerns the end of days (*Rashi*).

24:5. Because the people had been unfaithful to God, the land will act in kind; it will not bring forth produce when they cultivate it.

24:13. Few people will remain in the land, as few as the remaining olives or grapes after the harvest.

24:16. Upon seeing the vision that the wicked would be vanquished, Isaiah expresses consternation, for he knows that many Jews will perish for their unfaithfulness to God (*Radak*). Alternatively, Isaiah's words mean, "My secret is with me! My secret is with me!" God has revealed two secrets to the prophet: the secret of Israel's downfall and the secret of Israel's salvation. "Woe is me!" for I have been shown that five periods of subjugation will precede the final salvation [alluded to by the fivefold mention of treachery] (*Rashi*).

24:18. Misfortunes will follow one another as swiftly as if tragedy is raining down from the windows of Heaven (*Radak*).

24:21. The guardian angels of the nations (see *Daniel* 10:13) will be eliminated, and their earthly constituencies will follow them to oblivion (*Rashi*).

24:23. They will no longer be worshiped once the glory of God becomes clear for all to see (*Targum*).

the kingdoms of the land on the face of the earth. * [18] And her merchandise and harlot's wages will [one day] become holy to HASHEM; it shall not be stored nor accumulated, for her merchandise will belong to those who sit before HASHEM, to eat and be sated and for elegant clothing.

24

The desolation of the land

[1] **B**ehold, * HASHEM is emptying the land and making it deserted; He will distort its appearance and scatter its inhabitants: [2] as with the people, so with the priest; as with the slave, so with his master; as with the maidservant, so with her mistress; as with the buyer, so with the seller; as with the lender, so with the borrower; as with the creditor, so with the one who owes him. [3] The land will be utterly emptied and utterly despoiled, for HASHEM has spoken this word. [4] The land will become desolate and withered; the world will be wretched and withered; the exalted of the people of the land will be wretched. [5] The land will be unfaithful because of its inhabitants, * for they have transgressed commandments and have violated laws; they have abrogated the everlasting Covenant. [6] Because of [false] oath, the land is consumed and those who inhabit it have become decimated; for this, the inhabitants of the land have become parched, and few people remain. [7] The grapes are desolate, the vine is forlorn; all glad-hearted people groan. [8] Rejoicing with timbrels has ceased; the noise of revelers has stopped; the joy of the harp has ceased. [9] They do not drink wine with song; liquor has become bitter to those who drink it. [10] The chaotic city has been broken; every house has been closed against entry. [11] There was crying for wine in the streets; all gladness is dimmed; the joy of the land has been exiled. [12] Desolation has remained in the city, and the gate is stricken with desertion. [13] For thus shall it be in the midst of the land, among the nations: as [after] the beating of an olive tree, * like solitary grapes when the harvest is completed. [14] They will yet raise their voice, they will shout; over the greatness of HASHEM, they will shout [with] greater [joy] than at the Sea [of Reeds]. [15] Therefore, honor HASHEM in the valleys, in the islands of the sea, [honor] the Name of HASHEM, the God of Israel.

Expectant exuberance

[16] From the edge of the earth we have heard songs, "Glory for the righteous." But I say, "My lot is to waste away! My lot is to waste away! Woe is me! The treacherous have dealt with treachery; with the treachery of the treacherous have they dealt treacherously!" *

God's judgment

[17] Fear and pitfall and snare [will be] upon you, O inhabitant of the land; [18] it shall be that whoever flees the sound of the fear will fall into the pit, and whoever rises from within the pit will be trapped in the snare; for windows will be opened from above, * and the foundations of the earth will quake. [19] Broken, broken will be the land; crumbled, crumbled will be the land; trembling, trembling will be the land; [20] tottering, the land will totter like a drunkard, and sway like a shack; and its sins will weigh heavily upon it, and it will fall, never to rise again.

[21] It shall be on that day that HASHEM will deal with the hosts of heaven in heaven, * and with the kings of the earth on the earth. [22] They will be gathered together in a gathering, a captive in a dungeon, and they will be imprisoned in a prison; and [their sins] of many days will be recalled. [23] The moon will be humiliated and the sun will be shamed, * for HASHEM, Master of Legions, will have reigned in Mount Zion and in Jerusalem, and there will be honor for His elders.

כה
א יְהֹוָה אֱלֹהַי אַתָּה אֲרוֹמִמְךָ אוֹדֶה שִׁמְךָ כִּי עָשִׂיתָ פֶּלֶא עֵצוֹת מֵרָחֹק אֱמוּנָה אֹמֶן: כִּי שַׂמְתָּ מֵעִיר לַגָּל כָּבוֹד:
ב קִרְיָה בְּצוּרָה לְמַפֵּלָה אַרְמוֹן זָרִים מֵעִיר לְעוֹלָם לֹא יִבָּנֶה: עַל־כֵּן
ג יְכַבְּדוּךָ עַם־עָז קִרְיַת גּוֹיִם עָרִיצִים יִירָאוּךָ: כִּי־הָיִיתָ מָעוֹז לַדָּל
ד מָעוֹז לָאֶבְיוֹן בַּצַּר־לוֹ מַחְסֶה מִזֶּרֶם צֵל מֵחֹרֶב כִּי רוּחַ עָרִיצִים
ה כְּזֶרֶם קִיר: כְּחֹרֶב בְּצָיוֹן שְׁאוֹן זָרִים תַּכְנִיעַ חֹרֶב בְּצֵל עָב זְמִיר עָרִיצִים
ו יַעֲנֶה: וְעָשָׂה יְהֹוָה צְבָאוֹת לְכָל־הָעַמִּים בָּהָר הַזֶּה
ז מִשְׁתֵּה שְׁמָנִים מִשְׁתֵּה שְׁמָרִים שְׁמָנִים מְמֻחָיִם שְׁמָרִים מְזֻקָּקִים: וּבִלַּע בָּהָר הַזֶּה פְּנֵי־הַלּוֹט ׀ הַלּוֹט עַל־כָּל־הָעַמִּים וְהַמַּסֵּכָה הַנְּסוּכָה עַל־כָּל־
ח הַגּוֹיִם: בִּלַּע הַמָּוֶת לָנֶצַח וּמָחָה אֲדֹנָי יֱהֹוִה דִּמְעָה מֵעַל כָּל־פָּנִים וְחֶרְפַּת עַמּוֹ יָסִיר מֵעַל כָּל־הָאָרֶץ כִּי יְהֹוָה דִּבֵּר: וְאָמַר
ט בַּיּוֹם הַהוּא הִנֵּה אֱלֹהֵינוּ זֶה קִוִּינוּ לוֹ וְיוֹשִׁיעֵנוּ זֶה יְהֹוָה קִוִּינוּ לוֹ נָגִילָה
י וְנִשְׂמְחָה בִּישׁוּעָתוֹ: כִּי־תָנוּחַ יַד־יְהֹוָה בָּהָר הַזֶּה וְנָדוֹשׁ מוֹאָב תַּחְתָּיו
יא כְּהִדּוּשׁ מַתְבֵּן [°בְּמוֹ ק] °בְמִי מַדְמֵנָה: וּפֵרַשׂ יָדָיו בְּקִרְבּוֹ כַּאֲשֶׁר יְפָרֵשׂ
יב הַשֹּׁחֶה לִשְׂחוֹת וְהִשְׁפִּיל גַּאֲוָתוֹ עִם אָרְבּוֹת יָדָיו: וּמִבְצַר מִשְׂגַּב חוֹמֹתֶיךָ הֵשַׁח הִשְׁפִּיל הִגִּיעַ לָאָרֶץ עַד־עָפָר:

כו
א בַּיּוֹם הַהוּא יוּשַׁר הַשִּׁיר־הַזֶּה בְּאֶרֶץ יְהוּדָה עִיר עָז־לָנוּ יְשׁוּעָה יָשִׁית
ב־ג חוֹמוֹת וָחֵל: פִּתְחוּ שְׁעָרִים וְיָבֹא גוֹי־צַדִּיק שֹׁמֵר אֱמֻנִים: יֵצֶר סָמוּךְ
ד תִּצֹּר שָׁלוֹם ׀ שָׁלוֹם כִּי בְךָ בָּטוּחַ: בִּטְחוּ בַיהֹוָה עֲדֵי־עַד כִּי בְּיָהּ
ה יְהֹוָה צוּר עוֹלָמִים: כִּי הֵשַׁח יֹשְׁבֵי מָרוֹם קִרְיָה נִשְׂגָּבָה יַשְׁפִּילֶנָּה
ו יַשְׁפִּילָהּ עַד־אֶרֶץ יַגִּיעֶנָּה עַד־עָפָר: תִּרְמְסֶנָּה רָגֶל רַגְלֵי עָנִי פַּעֲמֵי
ז־ח דַלִּים: אֹרַח לַצַּדִּיק מֵישָׁרִים יָשָׁר מַעְגַּל צַדִּיק תְּפַלֵּס: אַף אֹרַח מִשְׁפָּטֶיךָ יְהֹוָה קִוִּינוּךָ לְשִׁמְךָ וּלְזִכְרְךָ תַּאֲוַת־נָפֶשׁ: נַפְשִׁי אִוִּיתִךָ
ט בַּלַּיְלָה אַף־רוּחִי בְקִרְבִּי אֲשַׁחֲרֶךָּ כִּי כַּאֲשֶׁר מִשְׁפָּטֶיךָ לָאָרֶץ צֶדֶק
י לָמְדוּ יֹשְׁבֵי תֵבֵל: יֻחַן רָשָׁע בַּל־לָמַד צֶדֶק בְּאֶרֶץ נְכֹחוֹת יְעַוֵּל וּבַל־
יא יִרְאֶה גֵּאוּת יְהֹוָה: יְהֹוָה רָמָה יָדְךָ בַּל־יֶחֱזָיוּן

25:1. When he received the prophecy of salvation, Isaiah burst forth with praise (*Ibn Ezra*). Alternatively: These are the words of those who will witness God's salvation described in Chapter 24 (*Radak*).

25:4. A reference to Israel, which suffered tribulations from the mighty during their exile.

25:5. God in His mercy protected Israel from the oppressive heat of their persecutors.

25:6. On Mount Zion, the final judgment of the nations will take place. God will serve a rich repast of retribution, like a feast of concentrated, potent, filling and intoxicating foods and spirits.

25:7. That is, He will take away their protection of veils and masks, and allow them to be routed.

25:8. Jews will no longer be killed by their persecutors, but death from natural causes will of course continue to occur (*Radak*). Alternatively: All death will be eliminated (*Rashi*).

26:1. The day of the future deliverance.

26:5. I.e., the fortified cities of Israel's enemies.

26:8. Even when You punished us for our sins, we kept faith and turned to You for assistance (*Radak*).

26:11. They believe that everything occurs by chance, not by God's intervention.

25

Praise for God's salvation

¹ H ASHEM, You are my * God; I will exalt You, I will give thanks to Your Name, for You have done wondrously; [Your] plans from the distant [past were kept] with firm faithfulness. ² For You have made [the oppressor's] city into a heap, [his] fortified town into a ruin; the palace of foreigners [removed] from each city, not to be rebuilt. ³ Therefore, [even] a strong people will honor You; the city of mighty nations will fear You. ⁴ For You were a stronghold for the meek, * a stronghold for the destitute when he was in distress; a shelter from downpour, a shade from the scorching heat, when the fury of the mighty was like a downpour against a wall. ⁵ [Though they were] like a scorching heat in the wasteland, You diminished the tumult of the foreigners; * [like] a scorching heat [is] shaded by a cloud, [so] the breaking of the mighty humbled [them].

A triumphal feast

⁶ HASHEM, Master of Legions, will make for all the nations on this moun-tain * a feast of fats, a feast of lees — rich fats and concentrated lees. ⁷ On this mountain He will eliminate the faces [wearing] veils, that are veiled, of all the nations, and the masks that mask all the nations. * ⁸ He will eliminate death forever, * and my Lord HASHEM/ELOHIM will erase tears from all faces; He will remove the shame of His nation from upon the entire earth, for HASHEM has spoken.

⁹ And they will say on that day, 'Behold, this is our God; we hoped to Him that He would save us; this is HASHEM to Whom we hoped, let us exult and be glad in His salvation.' ¹⁰ For the hand of HASHEM will descend upon this mountain, and Moab will be crushed in its place, as straw is crushed into a pile of refuse. ¹¹ And He will stretch out His hand in its midst, as a swimmer stretches out to swim, and He will put down its pride, with its places of ambush. ¹² And the stronghold of your powerful walls He will topple, He will lower; it will reach the ground, until the dust.

26

A song of thanksgiving

¹ On that day * this song will be sung in the land of Judah:
    The City is a stronghold for us;
        He will grant salvation to its high walls and outer wall.
² Open the gates, so the righteous nation, keeper of the faith, may enter!
³ The being that relied [on You], protect him with peace, peace;
        for in You did he trust.
⁴ Trust in HASHEM forever, for in God, HASHEM, is the strength of the worlds.
⁵ For He has brought down those who dwell on high, [in] an exalted city; *
He has lowered it, He has lowered it to the ground;
        He has brought it down to the dust.
⁶ It is trampled underfoot: the feet of the poor, the soles of the meek.

Righteousness

⁷ The way of uprightness is for the righteous;
        O Upright One, straighten the circuit of the righteous!
⁸ Even on the path of Your judgments, HASHEM, we put our hopes in You; *
        Your Name and Your mention, the yearning of [our] soul.
⁹ My soul desired You during the night;
        as long as my spirit is within me I seek You out,
    for when Your judgments are against the land,
        the inhabitants of the world learn righteousness.
¹⁰ Shall grace be granted the wicked one who did not learn righteousness?
He acts with corruption in the land of the upright;
        and does not see the exaltedness of HASHEM.
¹¹ HASHEM, when Your hand is raised, [the wicked] do not see it. *

יב יֶחֱזוּ וְיֵבֹשׁוּ קִנְאַת־עָם אַף־אֵשׁ צָרֶיךָ תֹאכְלֵם: יְהֹוָה תִּשְׁפֹּת שָׁלוֹם לָנוּ כִּי

יג גַּם כָּל־מַעֲשֵׂינוּ פָּעַלְתָּ לָּנוּ: יְהֹוָה אֱלֹהֵינוּ בְּעָלוּנוּ אֲדֹנִים זוּלָתֶךָ לְבַד־בְּךָ

יד נַזְכִּיר שְׁמֶךָ: מֵתִים בַּל־יִחְיוּ רְפָאִים בַּל־יָקֻמוּ לָכֵן פָּקַדְתָּ וַתַּשְׁמִידֵם

טו וַתְּאַבֵּד כָּל־זֵכֶר לָמוֹ: יָסַפְתָּ לַגּוֹי יְהֹוָה יָסַפְתָּ לַגּוֹי נִכְבָּדְתָּ רִחַקְתָּ כָּל־

טז קַצְוֵי־אָרֶץ: יְהֹוָה בַּצַּר פְּקָדוּךָ צָקוּן לַחַשׁ מוּסָרְךָ לָמוֹ: כְּמוֹ הָרָה

יח תַּקְרִיב לָלֶדֶת תָּחִיל תִּזְעַק בַּחֲבָלֶיהָ כֵּן הָיִינוּ מִפָּנֶיךָ יְהֹוָה: הָרִינוּ חַלְנוּ

יט כְּמוֹ יָלַדְנוּ רוּחַ יְשׁוּעֹת בַּל־נַעֲשֶׂה אֶרֶץ וּבַל־יִפְּלוּ יֹשְׁבֵי תֵבֵל: יִחְיוּ מֵתֶיךָ

נְבֵלָתִי יְקוּמוּן הָקִיצוּ וְרַנְּנוּ שֹׁכְנֵי עָפָר כִּי טַל אוֹרֹת טַלֶּךָ וָאָרֶץ רְפָאִים

כ תַּפִּיל: לֵךְ עַמִּי בֹּא בַחֲדָרֶיךָ וּסְגֹר דְּלָתֶיךָ [°דְּלָתְךָ ק] בַּעֲדֶךָ

כא חֲבִי כִמְעַט־רֶגַע עַד־יַעֲבוֹר [°יַעֲבָר־ ק] זָעַם: כִּי־הִנֵּה יְהֹוָה יֹצֵא מִמְּקוֹמוֹ

לִפְקֹד עֲוֹן יֹשֵׁב־הָאָרֶץ עָלָיו וְגִלְּתָה הָאָרֶץ אֶת־דָּמֶיהָ וְלֹא־תְכַסֶּה עוֹד

כז א עַל־הֲרוּגֶיהָ: בַּיּוֹם הַהוּא יִפְקֹד יְהֹוָה בְּחַרְבוֹ הַקָּשָׁה וְהַגְּדוֹלָה וְהַחֲזָקָה עַל לִוְיָתָן נָחָשׁ בָּרִחַ וְעַל לִוְיָתָן נָחָשׁ עֲקַלָּתוֹן וְהָרַג אֶת־הַתַּנִּין

ב־ג אֲשֶׁר בַּיָּם: בַּיּוֹם הַהוּא כֶּרֶם חֶמֶר עַנּוּ־לָהּ: אֲנִי יְהֹוָה נֹצְרָהּ

ד לִרְגָעִים אַשְׁקֶנָּה פֶּן יִפְקֹד עָלֶיהָ לַיְלָה וָיוֹם אֶצֳּרֶנָּה: חֵמָה אֵין לִי מִי־יִתְּנֵנִי

ה שָׁמִיר שַׁיִת בַּמִּלְחָמָה אֶפְשְׂעָה בָהּ אֲצִיתֶנָּה יָּחַד: אוֹ יַחֲזֵק בְּמָעוּזִּי יַעֲשֶׂה

HAFTARAS SHEMOS
Ashkenazim:
27:6-28:13;
29:22-23

ו שָׁלוֹם לִי שָׁלוֹם יַעֲשֶׂה־לִּי: הַבָּאִים יַשְׁרֵשׁ יַעֲקֹב יָצִיץ וּפָרַח יִשְׂרָאֵל

ז וּמָלְאוּ פְנֵי־תֵבֵל תְּנוּבָה: הַכְּמַכַּת מַכֵּהוּ הִכָּהוּ אִם־כְּהֶרֶג הֲרֻגָיו

ח־ט הֹרָג: בְּסַאסְּאָה בְּשַׁלְחָהּ תְּרִיבֶנָּה הָגָה בְּרוּחוֹ הַקָּשָׁה בְּיוֹם קָדִים: לָכֵן בְּזֹאת יְכֻפַּר עֲוֹן־יַעֲקֹב וְזֶה כָּל־פְּרִי הָסִר חַטָּאתוֹ בְּשׂוּמוֹ | כָּל־אַבְנֵי מִזְבֵּחַ

י כְּאַבְנֵי־גִר מְנֻפָּצוֹת לֹא־יָקֻמוּ אֲשֵׁרִים וְחַמָּנִים: כִּי עִיר בְּצוּרָה בָּדָד נָוֶה

יא מְשֻׁלָּח וְנֶעֱזָב כַּמִּדְבָּר שָׁם יִרְעֶה עֵגֶל וְשָׁם יִרְבָּץ וְכִלָּה סְעִפֶיהָ: בִּיבֹשׁ קְצִירָהּ תִּשָּׁבַרְנָה נָשִׁים בָּאוֹת מְאִירוֹת אוֹתָהּ כִּי לֹא עַם־בִּינוֹת הוּא

26:13. Although we were often pressed to renounce our faith and worship the gods of other nations, we remained steadfast in our dedication to You (*Radak*).

26:15. Israel honors You even when its sins force You to exile them to the ends of the earth (*Rashi; Radak*).

26:17-18. Our pain may be compared to that of a woman in false labor. She is not relieved when the pain subsides, because she knows she will repeat the ordeal when she goes into true labor. So, too, in our exile, we hoped each persecution would be the final one, only to realize that the ordeal was not over (*Rashi*).

26:19. The dead among Your [God's] righteous people and the corpses of my [Isaiah's] people, Israel. This is an allusion to the resurrection of the dead (*Ibn Ezra*).

Just as Your dew revives plants, so You will send a "dew" that will revive the dead (*Radak*).

26:21. In the Biblical idiom, murder that goes unavenged is described as "blood covered up by the earth." Now, when God punishes evildoers, all the innocent blood will be "uncovered" by the earth (*Radak*).

27:1. Leviathan, the giant, earth-girdling serpent-fish symbolizes the great world powers. Isaiah uses the death of the Leviathan to allude to the eventual downfall of all the enemies of Israel (*Radak*). The three descriptions — bar-like, twisting, in the sea — allude to the different natures of the world powers (*Rashi*).

27:4. God says that He withholds His total wrath from the nations — the weeds and thorns — because Israel, too, is sinful; if He were to punish the nations as they deserved, justice would dictate that He do the same to Israel. In order to save Israel from fearsome punishment, God relaxes His Attribute of Justice for everyone (*Rashi*).

27:5. If only Israel would hold fast to My Torah!

27:7. God does not punish Israel as severely as He punishes its enemies, such as Pharaoh or Sennacherib, as set forth in v. 4 (*Radak*).

27:10. The cities of Israel's enemies (*Rashi*).

May they see vengeance for [Your] people and be ashamed;
   and also the fire that will consume Your enemies.
¹² HASHEM, arrange peace for us,
   even as You brought about whatever happened to us.

*Evildoers
are dead*

¹³ HASHEM, our God, lords other than You have ruled over us.
But it is only You Whose Name we mention. *
¹⁴ [They are] dead, never to live; lifeless, never to arise.
Therefore You punished and destroyed them,
   and eradicated any memory of them.
¹⁵ You have exalted [Your] nation, HASHEM;
You have exalted the nation by whom You are honored
   [even] when You distanced them to all the edges of the earth. *
¹⁶ HASHEM, in their trouble they turned to You;
   they poured out their silent prayer when You reproached them.
¹⁷ Like a pregnant woman* close to giving birth — she is in travail,
   she screams in her pangs. So were we before You, HASHEM.
¹⁸ We have conceived and gone into travail, as if we had borne wind.
Salvations were not performed in the land
   and the [wicked] who dwell on the earth did not fall.

*Resurrection
of the dead*

¹⁹ May Your dead* come to life, may my corpses arise.
   Awake and shout for joy, you who rest in the dust!
For Your dew* is like the dew that [revives] vegetation.
   May You topple the lifeless [wicked] to the ground!
²⁰ Go, my people, enter your rooms and close your door behind you; hide for a brief moment until the wrath has passed. ²¹ For behold, HASHEM is going forth from His place, to bring punishment for the sin of the inhabitant of the world upon him; and the land will reveal its blood, and no longer cover over its slain. *

27

¹ On that day HASHEM will bring punishment with His harsh, great, mighty sword, upon Leviathan, * the bar-like serpent, and upon Leviathan, the twisting serpent, and He will kill the great fish that is in the sea.

*God's
vineyard*

² On that day [people] will sing about [Israel], 'A vineyard of fine wine.' ³ I am HASHEM, Who guards it; I water it frequently; lest [an enemy] attack it, night and day I will guard it. ⁴ I have no wrath;* if only I were at war with the weeds and thorns, I would then trample it and set it altogether afire. ⁵ If [Israel] would grasp My stronghold, * then he would make peace with Me; peace would he make with Me. ⁶ [Days] are coming when Jacob will take root; Israel will bud and blossom and fill the face of the earth like fruit.

⁷ Did He strike him* as He struck those who struck him? Was he slain like the slaying of his [enemies]? ⁸ According to its measure [of sin] He contended against her farmland, stripping it with His harsh wind on the day of the east wind. ⁹ Therefore, through this shall Jacob's iniquity be atoned for, and this shall be the fruit of his sin's removal: When he makes all the altar stones like ground chalk stones, and Asherah-trees and sun-idols arise no more. ¹⁰ For the fortified city* will be lonely, habitations depopulated and forlorn like the wilderness; there a calf will graze, there it will lie and consume its branches. ¹¹ When its boughs wither they will break; women will come and set it aflame, for it is not a nation of understanding;

עַל כֵּן לֹא־יְרַחֲמֶנּוּ עֹשֵׂהוּ וְיֹצְרוֹ לֹא יְחֻנֶּנּוּ: וְהָיָה בַּיּוֹם הַהוּא יַחְבֹּט יהוה מִשִּׁבֹּלֶת הַנָּהָר עַד־נַחַל מִצְרָיִם וְאַתֶּם תְּלֻקְּטוּ לְאַחַד אֶחָד בְּנֵי יִשְׂרָאֵל: וְהָיָה ׀ בַּיּוֹם הַהוּא יִתָּקַע בְּשׁוֹפָר גָּדוֹל וּבָאוּ הָאֹבְדִים בְּאֶרֶץ אַשּׁוּר וְהַנִּדָּחִים בְּאֶרֶץ מִצְרָיִם וְהִשְׁתַּחֲווּ לַיהוה בְּהַר הַקֹּדֶשׁ

כח א בִּירוּשָׁלָהִם: הוֹי עֲטֶרֶת גֵּאוּת שִׁכֹּרֵי אֶפְרַיִם וְצִיץ נֹבֵל צְבִי תִפְאַרְתּוֹ אֲשֶׁר עַל־רֹאשׁ גֵּיא־שְׁמָנִים הֲלוּמֵי יָיִן: הִנֵּה חָזָק וְאַמִּץ לַאדֹנָי כְּזֶרֶם בָּרָד שַׂעַר קָטֶב כְּזֶרֶם מַיִם כַּבִּירִים שֹׁטְפִים הִנִּיחַ לָאָרֶץ בְּיָד: בְּרַגְלַיִם תֵּרָמַסְנָה עֲטֶרֶת גֵּאוּת שִׁכֹּרֵי אֶפְרָיִם: וְהָיְתָה צִיצַת נֹבֵל צְבִי תִפְאַרְתּוֹ אֲשֶׁר עַל־רֹאשׁ גֵּיא שְׁמָנִים כְּבִכּוּרָהּ בְּטֶרֶם קַיִץ אֲשֶׁר יִרְאֶה הָרֹאֶה אוֹתָהּ בְּעוֹדָהּ בְּכַפּוֹ יִבְלָעֶנָּה: בַּיּוֹם הַהוּא יִהְיֶה יהוה צְבָאוֹת לַעֲטֶרֶת צְבִי וְלִצְפִירַת תִּפְאָרָה לִשְׁאָר עַמּוֹ: וּלְרוּחַ מִשְׁפָּט לַיּוֹשֵׁב עַל־הַמִּשְׁפָּט וְלִגְבוּרָה מְשִׁיבֵי מִלְחָמָה שָׁעְרָה: וְגַם־אֵלֶּה בַּיַּיִן שָׁגוּ וּבַשֵּׁכָר תָּעוּ כֹּהֵן וְנָבִיא שָׁגוּ בַשֵּׁכָר נִבְלְעוּ מִן־הַיַּיִן תָּעוּ מִן־הַשֵּׁכָר שָׁגוּ בָּרֹאֶה פָּקוּ פְּלִילִיָּה:

ח-ט כִּי כָּל־שֻׁלְחָנוֹת מָלְאוּ קִיא צֹאָה בְּלִי מָקוֹם: אֶת־מִי יוֹרֶה דֵעָה וְאֶת־מִי יָבִין שְׁמוּעָה גְּמוּלֵי מֵחָלָב עַתִּיקֵי מִשָּׁדָיִם: כִּי צַו לָצָו צַו לָצָו קַו לָקָו קַו לָקָו זְעֵיר שָׁם זְעֵיר שָׁם: כִּי בְּלַעֲגֵי שָׂפָה וּבְלָשׁוֹן אַחֶרֶת יְדַבֵּר אֶל־הָעָם הַזֶּה: אֲשֶׁר ׀ אָמַר אֲלֵיהֶם זֹאת הַמְּנוּחָה הָנִיחוּ לֶעָיֵף וְזֹאת הַמַּרְגֵּעָה וְלֹא אָבוּא שְׁמוֹעַ: וְהָיָה לָהֶם דְּבַר־יהוה צַו לָצָו צַו לָצָו קַו לָקָו קַו לָקָו זְעֵיר שָׁם זְעֵיר שָׁם לְמַעַן יֵלְכוּ וְכָשְׁלוּ אָחוֹר וְנִשְׁבָּרוּ וְנוֹקְשׁוּ וְנִלְכָּדוּ: ◀ לָכֵן שִׁמְעוּ דְבַר־יהוה אַנְשֵׁי לָצוֹן מֹשְׁלֵי הָעָם הַזֶּה אֲשֶׁר בִּירוּשָׁלָהִם: כִּי אֲמַרְתֶּם כָּרַתְנוּ בְרִית אֶת־מָוֶת וְעִם־שְׁאוֹל עָשִׂינוּ חֹזֶה °שיט [°שׁוֹט ק׳] שׁוֹטֵף כִּי־°עבר [°יַעֲבֹר ק׳] לֹא יְבוֹאֵנוּ כִּי שַׂמְנוּ כָזָב מַחְסֵנוּ וּבַשֶּׁקֶר נִסְתָּרְנוּ: לָכֵן כֹּה אָמַר אֲדֹנָי יֱהֹוִה הִנְנִי יִסַּד בְּצִיּוֹן אָבֶן אֶבֶן בֹּחַן פִּנַּת יִקְרַת מוּסָד מוּסָּד הַמַּאֲמִין לֹא יָחִישׁ: וְשַׂמְתִּי מִשְׁפָּט לְקָו וּצְדָקָה לְמִשְׁקָלֶת וְיָעָה בָרָד מַחְסֵה כָזָב וְסֵתֶר מַיִם יִשְׁטֹפוּ:

Haftarah
continues
on p. 1002

27:12-13. Lit., beat, as one beats an olive tree to release its fruit; i.e., the Israelites will be gathered together like an olive harvest. God will "beat" the "trees" from Assyria to Egypt, to release the Jews (*Rashi*).

27:13. A figure of speech. The sounding of the shofar was used to assemble a town's population (*Radak*).

28:1. Speaking of his own time, Isaiah condemns the hedonism of Ephraim, the Northern Kingdom of Israel. Their glory is a delusion. Oil cannot undo the battering suffered by a drunkard.

28:4. The occasional fig that ripens before the season is snatched and eaten by passersby. So too, the opulence of Ephraim would be consumed swiftly by the enemy.

28:5-13. After the Ten Tribes are defeated and exiled, God will turn to the deficiencies of King Hezekiah's

subjects, the tribes of Judah and Benjamin (*Radak*).

28:9. Given the general state of degeneracy, only small children are pure enough to hear the prophet's message.

28:10. The people can be taught only one message at a time, since they lack the sense to comprehend anything more complex than that. A mason uses a taut line to assure that his bricks are horizontally aligned; and he must reset his line for every new row of bricks. So must the prophet teach his message one step at a time (*Radak*).

28:11. To boors, the prophet's message is unintelligible, as if he were talking incoherently.

28:12-13. Though the prophet's teachings were for their own good, his words fell on deaf ears; therefore, the tragedies foretold by God would befall them one at a time *therefore, its Maker will not show it mercy, and its Creator will not be gracious unto it.*

The great ingathering

¹² *It shall be on that day that HASHEM will thresh,* * from the surging [Euphrates] River to the Brook of Egypt, and you will be gathered up one by one, O Children of Israel.*

¹³ *It shall be on that day that a great shofar will be blown,* * and those who are lost in the land of Assyria and those cast away in the land of Egypt will come [together], and they will prostrate themselves to HASHEM on the holy mountain in Jerusalem.*

28

A lesson for the debauched

¹ **W**oe to the crown of pride of Ephraim's drunkards;* * the delight of his glory is a fading blossom; it is [like] a valley of oil upon the head of those battered by wine. ² Behold, my Lord has a strong and powerful [wind], like a downpour of hail, a destructive tempest; like a downpour of mighty, surging waters He will lay [that crown] to the ground with [His] hand.* ³ Trodden underfoot will be the crown of pride of Ephraim's drunkards; ⁴ and the withering blossom, the delight of his glory that is like a valley of oil upon [his] head, will be like a fig that ripens before summer: as soon as an observer sees it, while it is yet in his hand, he swallows it. *

⁵ *On that day,* * HASHEM, Master of Legions, will be the crown of delight and a diadem of glory for the remnant of His people,* ⁶ *and a spirit of judgment for he who sits in judgment, and a source of strength for those who return from war to the gate.* ⁷ *For they, too, have erred because of wine and strayed because of liquor; the Kohen and the [false] prophet have erred because of liquor and were corrupted by wine; they have strayed because of liquor, erred in vision, perverted justice.* ⁸ *For all tables are full of vomit, filth, with no [clean] place.* ⁹ *To whom shall one teach knowledge? To whom shall one explain a message? [To] those weaned from [mother's] milk, removed from the breasts?* * ¹⁰ For it is commandment by commandment, commandment by commandment; line by line, line by line; a bit here and a bit there. * ¹¹ For as if with unintelligible speech and in another tongue* does one speak to this nation. ¹² Though he tells them, 'This is the [true] rest, "Give rest to the weary"; and this is the [true] satisfaction!' yet they would not consent to listen. ¹³ The word of HASHEM shall befall them commandment by commandment, commandment by commandment; line by line, line by line; a bit here and a bit there;* * so that they will go and stumble backward and be broken, and be tripped up and caught.*

Covenant with Death

¹⁴ *Therefore, hear the word of HASHEM, O scoffing men, O rulers of this people who are in Jerusalem.* ¹⁵ *For you say, 'We have sealed a covenant with Death and made a compact with the Grave; when the surging staff [of punishment] passes through it will not come to us, for we have made Deceit our shelter and taken refuge in Falsehood.'*

¹⁶ *Therefore, thus said my Lord HASHEM/ELOHIM: Behold, I am laying a stone for a foundation in Zion: a sturdy stone, a precious cornerstone, a secure foundation. Let the believer not expect it soon.* * ¹⁷ I shall use judgment as a [measuring] line, and righteousness as a plumb bob. Hail will sweep away the shelter of Deceit,* * and water will wash away the refuge [of False-*

---

time, in punishment for their refusal to heed the prophecies that were given them one at a time (*Radak*).

28:16. Hezekiah (*Radak*) or the Messiah (*Rashi*) — will

weed out the wicked, but it will not happen in the immediate future.

28:17. Idolatry will be swept away by invaders.

יח וְכֻפַּר בְּרִיתְכֶם אֶת־מָוֶת וְחָזוּתְכֶם אֶת־שְׁאוֹל לֹא תָקוּם שׁוֹט שׁוֹטֵף כִּי

יט יַעֲבֹר וִהְיִיתֶם לוֹ לְמִרְמָס: מִדֵּי עָבְרוֹ יִקַּח אֶתְכֶם כִּי־בַבֹּקֶר בַּבֹּקֶר יַעֲבֹר

כ בַּיּוֹם וּבַלָּיְלָה וְהָיָה רַק־זְוָעָה הָבִין שְׁמוּעָה: כִּי־קָצַר הַמַּצָּע מֵהִשְׂתָּרֵעַ

כא וְהַמַּסֵּכָה צָרָה כְּהִתְכַּנֵּס: כִּי כְהַר־פְּרָצִים יָקוּם יהוה כְּעֵמֶק בְּגִבְעוֹן יִרְגָּז

כב לַעֲשׂוֹת מַעֲשֵׂהוּ זָר מַעֲשֵׂהוּ וְלַעֲבֹד עֲבֹדָתוֹ נָכְרִיָּה עֲבֹדָתוֹ: וְעַתָּה אַל־

תִּתְלוֹצָצוּ פֶּן־יֶחְזְקוּ מוֹסְרֵיכֶם כִּי־כָלָה וְנֶחֱרָצָה שָׁמַעְתִּי מֵאֵת אֲדֹנָי

כג יֱהוִֹה צְבָאוֹת עַל־כָּל־הָאָרֶץ: הַאֲזִינוּ וְשִׁמְעוּ קוֹלִי הַקְשִׁיבוּ

כד וְשִׁמְעוּ אִמְרָתִי: הֲכֹל הַיּוֹם יַחֲרֹשׁ הַחֹרֵשׁ לִזְרֹעַ יְפַתַּח וִישַׂדֵּד אַדְמָתוֹ:

כה הֲלוֹא אִם־שִׁוָּה פָנֶיהָ וְהֵפִיץ קֶצַח וְכַמֹּן יִזְרֹק וְשָׂם חִטָּה שׂוֹרָה וּשְׂעֹרָה

כו-כז נִסְמָן וְכֻסֶּמֶת גְּבֻלָתוֹ: וְיִסְּרוֹ לַמִּשְׁפָּט אֱלֹהָיו יוֹרֶנּוּ: כִּי לֹא בֶחָרוּץ

יוּדַשׁ קֶצַח וְאוֹפַן עֲגָלָה עַל־כַּמֹּן יוּסָּב כִּי בַמַּטֶּה יֵחָבֶט קֶצַח וְכַמֹּן

כח בַּשָּׁבֶט: לֶחֶם יוּדָק כִּי לֹא לָנֶצַח אָדוֹשׁ יְדוּשֶׁנּוּ וְהָמַם גִּלְגַּל עֶגְלָתוֹ

כט וּפָרָשָׁיו לֹא־יְדֻקֶּנּוּ: גַּם־זֹאת מֵעִם יהוה צְבָאוֹת יָצָאָה הִפְלִיא עֵצָה

א הִגְדִּיל תּוּשִׁיָּה: הוֹי אֲרִיאֵל אֲרִיאֵל קִרְיַת חָנָה דָוִד סְפוּ

כט

ב שָׁנָה עַל־שָׁנָה חַגִּים יִנְקֹפוּ: וַהֲצִיקוֹתִי לַאֲרִיאֵל וְהָיְתָה תַאֲנִיָּה וַאֲנִיָּה

ג וְהָיְתָה לִּי כַּאֲרִיאֵל: וְחָנִיתִי כַדּוּר עָלָיִךְ וְצַרְתִּי עָלַיִךְ מֻצָּב וַהֲקִימֹתִי

ד עָלַיִךְ מְצֻרֹת: וְשָׁפַלְתְּ מֵאֶרֶץ תְּדַבֵּרִי וּמֵעָפָר תִּשַּׁח אִמְרָתֵךְ וְהָיָה כְּאוֹב

ה מֵאֶרֶץ קוֹלֵךְ וּמֵעָפָר אִמְרָתֵךְ תְּצַפְצֵף: וְהָיָה כְּאָבָק דַּק הֲמוֹן זָרָיִךְ וּכְמֹץ

ו עֹבֵר הֲמוֹן עָרִיצִים וְהָיָה לְפֶתַע פִּתְאֹם: מֵעִם יהוה צְבָאוֹת תִּפָּקֵד בְּרַעַם

ז וּבְרַעַשׁ וְקוֹל גָּדוֹל סוּפָה וּסְעָרָה וְלַהַב אֵשׁ אוֹכֵלָה: וְהָיָה כַּחֲלוֹם חֲזוֹן

לַיְלָה כָּל־הַגּוֹיִם הַצֹּבְאִים עַל־אֲרִיאֵל וְכָל־צֹבֶיהָ וּמְצֹדָתָהּ

ח וְהַמְּצִיקִים לָהּ: וְהָיָה כַּאֲשֶׁר יַחֲלֹם הָרָעֵב וְהִנֵּה אוֹכֵל וְהֵקִיץ וְרֵיקָה

נַפְשׁוֹ וְכַאֲשֶׁר יַחֲלֹם הַצָּמֵא וְהִנֵּה שֹׁתֶה וְהֵקִיץ וְהִנֵּה עָיֵף וְנַפְשׁוֹ שׁוֹקֵקָה

ט כֵּן יִהְיֶה הֲמוֹן כָּל־הַגּוֹיִם הַצֹּבְאִים עַל־הַר צִיּוֹן: הִתְמַהְמְהוּ

י וּתְמָהוּ הִשְׁתַּעַשְׁעוּ וָשֹׁעוּ שָׁכְרוּ וְלֹא־יַיִן נָעוּ וְלֹא שֵׁכָר: כִּי־נָסַךְ עֲלֵיכֶם

28:20. A metaphor. When the Assyrians invade, the Jews will be left with only the city of Jerusalem (*Radak*).

28:21. David defeated the Philistines that attacked him at Perazim (*II Samuel* 5:17-21); Joshua defeated a confederation of five Amorite kings at Gibeon (*Joshua* 10:8-11).

28:23-29. The prophet gives a parable and explains it. God's admonitions are likened to plowing, and His punishments to sowing. Just as a farmer will not plow continuously without planting, so God will not warn unless He is ready to carry out His threats. However, the purpose of punishment is to prompt repentance, and its degree varies according to the receptivity of the sinner. Some sinners are like cumin and caraway seeds; they require a minimum of "threshing," i.e., punishment, to achieve results. Others are like wheat, and require more

"threshing" to make them repent. But even wheat is not threshed endlessly, for threshing alone can damage the grain without producing flour, so the threshing must have reasonable limits. So too, even though God may punish Israel harshly, His purpose is to improve, not destroy (*Rashi*).

28:29. God created this difference between herbs and grains and the way in which they must be threshed in order to teach Israel the lesson implied by their differing natures.

29:1-3. Ariel is a name for the Temple Altar (see *Ezekiel* Ch. 43). Here it is used to symbolize the entire city of Jerusalem, saying that Assyria will besiege it (see *II Kings*, Chs. 18,19), and that the multitudes of slain people will be reminiscent of the Altar, which is surrounded by slaughtered animals (*Rashi*).

hood]. ¹⁸ *And your covenant with Death will be annulled, and your compact with the Grave will not be binding; when the surging staff passes through, you will be crushed by it.* ¹⁹ *Whenever it passes through it will take you, for it will pass through every morning, by day and by night; understanding of this report will bring sheer horror.* ²⁰ *For the mat will be too short for stretching out, and the cover too small for getting into.* *

²¹ *For HASHEM will rise up as at the mountain of Perazim; He will become enraged as at the valley in Gibeon;* * *to perform His deed, unusual is His deed — and doing His work, strange is His work.* ²² *So now, do not scoff, lest your affliction become more severe, for of total annihilation have I heard from my Lord, HASHEM/ELOHIM, Master of Legions, concerning the entire land.*

Parable of the farmer   ²³ *Give ear and listen to my voice; be attentive and hear my speech:* * ²⁴ *If one plows to sow, does he plow all day, [endlessly] opening and furrowing his land?* ²⁵ *Surely, when he smooths its surface he will scatter black caraway and throw around cumin; he will place wheat by measure and barley where designated and spelt at its border!* ²⁶ *[So too] one will be rebuked with judgment by his God Who teaches him.* ²⁷ *For not with a threshing board is black caraway threshed, nor does a wagon wheel roll over cumin; rather it is with a staff that black caraway is beaten, and cumin with a stick.* ²⁸ *[Wheat for] bread is pounded; but not forever does one thresh it, for even if he rolls his wagon wheel with its implements until they fall apart, he will not have milled the wheat.* ²⁹ *This, too, has issued from HASHEM, Master of Legions; His counsel is wondrous and His wisdom abundant.* *

29

Chastisement and deliverance of Jerusalem

¹ *Oh, Ariel, Ariel,* * *city where David encamped! You add [sins] year after year, until your holidays will be terminated.* ² *I will bring distress to Ariel; there will be agony and grief, and it will be for Me like Ariel.* ³ *I will encamp against you like a ring, and I will lay siege against you with a scaffold and set up a mound against you.* ⁴ *You will sink down; from the ground will you speak; downtrodden from the dust will your speech be; like a ghost from the ground will your voice be; and from the dust your speech will chirp.* *

⁵ *Then* * *your multitude of foreigners will become like fine dust, and the multitude of powerful ones will be like passing chaff; it will happen with quick suddenness.* ⁶ *By HASHEM, Master of Legions, will you be remembered, with thunder and with earthquake and loud sound, storm and tempest and consuming flame of fire.* ⁷ *Like a dream,* * *a vision of the night will be, the multitude of all the nations who muster themselves against Ariel along with all those who besiege her and beleaguer her and cause her distress.* ⁸ *It will be as when the hungry man dreams and, behold, he is eating, but he wakes up and his soul is empty; and as when the thirsty man dreams and, behold, he is drinking, but he wakes up and, behold, he is weary and his soul craves drink. So will be the multitude of all the nations that muster themselves against Mount Zion.*

⁹ *Ponder it and be astonished* * *— they have been utterly blinded; they were drunk, but not from wine; they staggered, but not from liquor.* ¹⁰ *For HASHEM has*

29:4. In a series of similar metaphors, the prophet speaks of defeated Israel as if it had sunken into the earth, and its prayers of contrition sounded as if they were emerging from underground.

29:5. Hearing your contrite prayers, God will wipe away

the attackers and they will vanish.

29:7-8. In retrospect, the frightening Assyrian invasion will prove to be no more than a fleeting dream.

29:9-12. Isaiah reprimands the people for rejecting the word of God and following false prophets (*Rashi*).

יְהוָֹה רוּחַ תַּרְדֵּמָה וַיְעַצֵּם אֶת־עֵינֵיכֶם אֶת־הַנְּבִיאִים וְאֶת־רָאשֵׁיכֶם

יא הַחֹזִים כִּסָּה: וַתְּהִי לָכֶם חָזוּת הַכֹּל כְּדִבְרֵי הַסֵּפֶר הֶחָתוּם אֲשֶׁר־יִתְּנוּ
אֹתוֹ אֶל־יוֹדֵעַ °הַסֵּפֶר [°סֵפֶר ק] לֵאמֹר קְרָא נָא־זֶה וְאָמַר לֹא אוּכַל כִּי

יב חָתוּם הוּא: וְנִתַּן הַסֵּפֶר עַל אֲשֶׁר לֹא־יָדַע סֵפֶר לֵאמֹר קְרָא נָא־זֶה וְאָמַר

יג לֹא יָדַעְתִּי סֵפֶר: וַיֹּאמֶר אֲדֹנָי יַעַן כִּי נִגַּשׁ הָעָם הַזֶּה בְּפִיו
וּבִשְׂפָתָיו כִּבְּדוּנִי וְלִבּוֹ רִחַק מִמֶּנִּי וַתְּהִי יִרְאָתָם אֹתִי מִצְוַת אֲנָשִׁים

יד מְלֻמָּדָה: לָכֵן הִנְנִי יוֹסִף לְהַפְלִיא אֶת־הָעָם־הַזֶּה הַפְלֵא וָפֶלֶא וְאָבְדָה
חָכְמַת חֲכָמָיו וּבִינַת נְבֹנָיו תִּסְתַּתָּר: הוֹי הַמַּעֲמִיקִים מֵיהוָֹה

טו לַסְתִּר עֵצָה וְהָיָה בְמַחְשָׁךְ מַעֲשֵׂיהֶם וַיֹּאמְרוּ מִי רֹאֵנוּ וּמִי יוֹדְעֵנוּ: הַפְכְּכֶם
אִם־כְּחֹמֶר הַיֹּצֵר יֵחָשֵׁב כִּי־יֹאמַר מַעֲשֶׂה לְעֹשֵׂהוּ לֹא עָשָׂנִי וְיֵצֶר אָמַר

יז לְיוֹצְרוֹ לֹא הֵבִין: הֲלוֹא־עוֹד מְעַט מִזְעָר וְשָׁב לְבָנוֹן לַכַּרְמֶל וְהַכַּרְמֶל

יח לַיַּעַר יֵחָשֵׁב: וְשָׁמְעוּ בַיּוֹם־הַהוּא הַחֵרְשִׁים דִּבְרֵי־סֵפֶר וּמֵאֹפֶל וּמֵחֹשֶׁךְ

יט עֵינֵי עִוְרִים תִּרְאֶינָה: וְיָסְפוּ עֲנָוִים בַּיהוָֹה שִׂמְחָה וְאֶבְיוֹנֵי אָדָם בִּקְדוֹשׁ

כ-כא יִשְׂרָאֵל יָגִילוּ: כִּי־אָפֵס עָרִיץ וְכָלָה לֵץ וְנִכְרְתוּ כָּל־שֹׁקְדֵי אָוֶן: מַחֲטִיאֵי
אָדָם בְּדָבָר וְלַמּוֹכִיחַ בַּשַּׁעַר יְקֹשׁוּן וַיַּטּוּ בַתֹּהוּ צַדִּיק: ◄ לָכֵן

כב כֹּה־אָמַר יְהוָֹה אֶל־בֵּית יַעֲקֹב אֲשֶׁר פָּדָה אֶת־אַבְרָהָם לֹא־עַתָּה יֵבוֹשׁ

כג יַעֲקֹב וְלֹא עַתָּה פָּנָיו יֶחֱוָרוּ: כִּי בִרְאֹתוֹ יְלָדָיו מַעֲשֵׂה יָדַי בְּקִרְבּוֹ יַקְדִּישׁוּ

כד שְׁמִי וְהִקְדִּישׁוּ אֶת־קְדוֹשׁ יַעֲקֹב וְאֶת־אֱלֹהֵי יִשְׂרָאֵל יַעֲרִיצוּ: ◄ וְיָדְעוּ
תֹעֵי־רוּחַ בִּינָה וְרוֹגְנִים יִלְמְדוּ־לֶקַח:

ל   א הוֹי בָּנִים סוֹרְרִים נְאֻם־
יְהוָֹה לַעֲשׂוֹת עֵצָה וְלֹא מִנִּי וְלִנְסֹךְ מַסֵּכָה וְלֹא רוּחִי לְמַעַן סְפוֹת חַטָּאת

ב עַל־חַטָּאת: הַהֹלְכִים לָרֶדֶת מִצְרַיִם וּפִי לֹא שָׁאָלוּ לָעוֹז בְּמָעוֹז

ג פַּרְעֹה וְלַחְסוֹת בְּצֵל מִצְרָיִם: וְהָיָה לָכֶם מָעוֹז פַּרְעֹה לְבֹשֶׁת וְהֶחָסוּת

ד-ה בְּצֵל־מִצְרַיִם לִכְלִמָּה: כִּי־הָיוּ בְצֹעַן שָׂרָיו וּמַלְאָכָיו חָנֵס יַגִּיעוּ: כֹּל
הֹבִאישׁ עַל־עַם לֹא־יוֹעִילוּ לָמוֹ לֹא לְעֵזֶר וְלֹא לְהוֹעִיל כִּי לְבֹשֶׁת וְגַם־

ו לְחֶרְפָּה: מַשָּׂא בַּהֲמוֹת נֶגֶב בְּאֶרֶץ צָרָה וְצוּקָה לָבִיא וָלַיִשׁ
מֵהֶם אֶפְעֶה וְשָׂרָף מְעוֹפֵף יִשְׂאוּ עַל־כֶּתֶף עֲיָרִים חֵילֵהֶם וְעַל־דַּבֶּשֶׁת

ז גְּמַלִּים אוֹצְרֹתָם עַל־עַם לֹא יוֹעִילוּ: וּמִצְרַיִם הֶבֶל וָרִיק יַעְזֹרוּ לָכֵן

ח קָרָאתִי לָזֹאת רַהַב הֵם שָׁבֶת: עַתָּה בּוֹא כָתְבָהּ עַל־לוּחַ אִתָּם וְעַל־

Haftaras Shemos continues here: 29:22-23

29:11-12. Isaiah illustrates the futility of the situation: Intelligent people would not try to decipher the prophecy, saying that the message was sealed, i.e., too vague. Unintelligent people were truly incapable of understanding the message. Thus no one paid attention to the prophecy (*Radak*).

29:17-18. The Lebanon is a forest with great cedar trees. When God judges people, the haughty will be brought down and the meek elevated, all to their appropriate places. Then, those who had been blind and deaf to God's word will see and hear (*Metzudos*).

29:20. The false prophets, described in v. 21, who use words to mislead the people.

29:22. Jacob will be able to face Abraham proudly when he sees his descendants following the way of God (*Rashi*).

30:1. The prophet chastises King Hoshea of Israel (*Rashi*) or King Hezekiah of Judah (*Radak*), both of whom sought to ally with Egypt against Assyria (*II Kings* 17:4; 18:21).

30:4. Israel's emissaries were in Zoan and Hanes, two major Egyptian cities.

30:6. They carry treasure in the direction of Egypt, to pay

Parable of the document

poured upon you a spirit of deep sleep and He has closed your eyes; He has covered the [false] prophets and your chiefs, the seers. ¹¹ To you all the [true] prophecy is like the words of a sealed document, which one gives to a literate person, saying, "Please read this," and he says, "I cannot, for it is sealed." ¹² Then the document is given to an illiterate person, saying, "Please read this," and he says, "I am not literate." *

Lip service

¹³ The Lord said: Inasmuch as this people has drawn close, with its mouth and with its lips it has honored Me, yet it has distanced its heart from Me — their fear of Me is like rote learning of human commands — ¹⁴ therefore, behold, I will continue to perform more wonders against this people — wonder upon wonder; the wisdom of its wise men will be lost and the understanding of its sages will become concealed.

¹⁵ Woe to those who try to hide in depths to conceal counsel from HASHEM, and their deeds are [done] in darkness; they say, 'Who sees us and who knows of us?' ¹⁶ Shall your contrariness be considered like the potter's clay? Can a product say of its maker, 'He did not make me'? Or a molded thing say of its molder, 'He does not understand'? ¹⁷ Behold, in just a little while the Lebanon will become farmland and the farmland will be considered like

Judgment

forest. ¹⁸ On that day the deaf will hear the words of a book and from darkness and blackness the eyes of blind people will see. * ¹⁹ The meek will increase their joy in HASHEM, and the poor among the people will rejoice in the Holy One of Israel; ²⁰ for the fierce man is no more and the scoffer has ceased to be; and all who strive for iniquity * will be cut off: ²¹ those who with a word cause man to sin and ensnare the one who gives rebuke at the city gate, and mislead the righteous with falsehood.

Redemption

²² Therefore, thus said HASHEM, Who redeemed Abraham, to the House of Jacob: Jacob will not be ashamed now, * and his face will not pale now, ²³ when he sees his children, My handiwork in their midst, who will sanctify My Name, they will sanctify the Holy One of Jacob and revere the God of Israel! ²⁴ Those of misguided spirit will attain understanding, and complainers will learn [God's] instruction.

30

Castigating Israel for its reliance on Egypt

¹ **W**oe, O wayward sons — the word of HASHEM — who take counsel, but not from Me, and who accept a ruler, * but not of My spirit, in order to add sin upon sin; ² who are going to descend to Egypt but did not inquire of My mouth, to seek strength in Pharaoh's stronghold and to take shelter in Egypt's shade. ³ Pharaoh's stronghold will be a shame for you and the shelter in Egypt's shade will be a humiliation! ⁴ For its * officers were in Zoan; its messengers have reached Hanes. ⁵ Everyone has been shamed by this people who cannot benefit them; not of assistance and not of benefit, but for shame and even for disgrace. ⁶ They load animals * [to travel] to the south, through a land of affliction and adversity, mature lion and young lion, among them, viper and flying serpent; they carry their wealth upon the shoulder of young donkeys and their riches upon the camels' hump, to a people who cannot provide benefit. ⁷ As for Egypt, they will help with vanity and emptiness; therefore I say of this, 'They are arrogant, sitting idle.'

⁸ Now, go and write this [prophecy] on a tablet in their presence, and

---

for unavailing protection (*Targum; Rashi*). Alternatively: מַשָּׂא means "prophecy," as in 22:1, and נֶגֶב means "dry,

arid." Thus, "A prophecy regarding animals in the desert" which will attack them on the way to Egypt (*Radak*).

ט סְפֶר חֲקֵה וְתִהִי לְיוֹם אַחֲרוֹן לָעַד עַד־עוֹלָם: כִּי עַם מְרִי הוּא בָּנִים
י כֶּחָשִׁים בָּנִים לֹא־אָבוּ שְׁמוֹעַ תּוֹרַת יהוה: אֲשֶׁר אָמְרוּ לָרֹאִים לֹא תִרְאוּ
יא וְלַחֹזִים לֹא תֶחֱזוּ־לָנוּ נְכֹחוֹת דַּבְּרוּ־לָנוּ חֲלָקוֹת חֲזוּ מַהֲתַלּוֹת: סוּרוּ מִנֵּי־
יב דֶרֶךְ הַטּוּ מִנֵּי־אֹרַח הַשְׁבִּיתוּ מִפָּנֵינוּ אֶת־קְדוֹשׁ יִשְׂרָאֵל: לָכֵן
יג כֹּה אָמַר קְדוֹשׁ יִשְׂרָאֵל יַעַן מָאָסְכֶם בַּדָּבָר הַזֶּה וַתִּבְטְחוּ בְּעֹשֶׁק וְנָלוֹז
יד וַתִּשָּׁעֲנוּ עָלָיו: לָכֵן יִהְיֶה לָכֶם הֶעָוֹן הַזֶּה כְּפֶרֶץ נֹפֵל נִבְעֶה בְּחוֹמָה נִשְׂגָּבָה
אֲשֶׁר־פִּתְאֹם לְפֶתַע יָבוֹא שִׁבְרָהּ: וּשְׁבָרָהּ כְּשֵׁבֶר נֵבֶל יוֹצְרִים כָּתוּת
טו לֹא יַחְמֹל וְלֹא־יִמָּצֵא בִמְכִתָּתוֹ חֶרֶשׂ לַחְתּוֹת אֵשׁ מִיָּקוּד וְלַחְשֹׂף מַיִם
מִגֶּבֶא: כִּי כֹה־אָמַר אֲדֹנָי יֱהוִֹה קְדוֹשׁ יִשְׂרָאֵל בְּשׁוּבָה וָנַחַת
טז תִּוָּשֵׁעוּן בְּהַשְׁקֵט וּבְבִטְחָה תִּהְיֶה גְּבוּרַתְכֶם וְלֹא אֲבִיתֶם: וַתֹּאמְרוּ לֹא־כִי
יז עַל־סוּס נָנוּס עַל־כֵּן תְּנוּסוּן וְעַל־קַל נִרְכָּב עַל־כֵּן יִקַּלּוּ רֹדְפֵיכֶם: אֶלֶף
אֶחָד מִפְּנֵי גַּעֲרַת אֶחָד מִפְּנֵי גַּעֲרַת חֲמִשָּׁה תָּנֻסוּ עַד אִם־נוֹתַרְתֶּם כַּתֹּרֶן
יח עַל־רֹאשׁ הָהָר וְכַנֵּס עַל־הַגִּבְעָה: וְלָכֵן יְחַכֶּה יהוה לַחֲנַנְכֶם וְלָכֵן יָרוּם
יט לְרַחֶמְכֶם כִּי־אֱלֹהֵי מִשְׁפָּט יהוה אַשְׁרֵי כָּל־חוֹכֵי לוֹ: כִּי־עַם
בְּצִיּוֹן יֵשֵׁב בִּירוּשָׁלִָם בָּכוֹ לֹא־תִבְכֶּה חָנוֹן יָחְנְךָ לְקוֹל זַעֲקֶךָ כְּשָׁמְעָתוֹ
כ עָנָךְ: וְנָתַן לָכֶם אֲדֹנָי לֶחֶם צָר וּמַיִם לָחַץ וְלֹא־יִכָּנֵף עוֹד מוֹרֶיךָ וְהָיוּ עֵינֶיךָ
כא רֹאוֹת אֶת־מוֹרֶיךָ: וְאָזְנֶיךָ תִּשְׁמַעְנָה דָבָר מֵאַחֲרֶיךָ לֵאמֹר זֶה הַדֶּרֶךְ לְכוּ
כב בוֹ כִּי תַאֲמִינוּ וְכִי תַשְׂמְאִילוּ: וְטִמֵּאתֶם אֶת־צִפּוּי פְּסִילֵי כַסְפֶּךָ וְאֶת־
כג אֲפֻדַּת מַסֵּכַת זְהָבֶךָ תִּזְרֵם כְּמוֹ דָוָה צֵא תֹּאמַר לוֹ: וְנָתַן מְטַר זַרְעֲךָ אֲשֶׁר־
תִּזְרַע אֶת־הָאֲדָמָה וְלֶחֶם תְּבוּאַת הָאֲדָמָה וְהָיָה דָשֵׁן וְשָׁמֵן יִרְעֶה מִקְנֶיךָ
כד בַּיּוֹם הַהוּא כַּר נִרְחָב: וְהָאֲלָפִים וְהָעֲיָרִים עֹבְדֵי הָאֲדָמָה בְּלִיל חָמִיץ
כה יֹאכֵלוּ אֲשֶׁר־זֹרֶה בָרַחַת וּבַמִּזְרֶה: וְהָיָה עַל־כָּל־הַר גָּבֹהַּ וְעַל כָּל־גִּבְעָה
כו נִשָּׂאָה פְּלָגִים יִבְלֵי־מָיִם בְּיוֹם הֶרֶג רָב בִּנְפֹל מִגְדָּלִים: וְהָיָה אוֹר־הַלְּבָנָה
כְּאוֹר הַחַמָּה וְאוֹר הַחַמָּה יִהְיֶה שִׁבְעָתַיִם כְּאוֹר שִׁבְעַת הַיָּמִים בְּיוֹם חֲבֹשׁ
כז יהוה אֶת־שֶׁבֶר עַמּוֹ וּמַחַץ מַכָּתוֹ יִרְפָּא: הִנֵּה שֵׁם־יהוה בָּא
מִמֶּרְחָק בֹּעֵר אַפּוֹ וְכֹבֶד מַשָּׂאָה שְׂפָתָיו מָלְאוּ זַעַם וּלְשׁוֹנוֹ כְּאֵשׁ אֹכָלֶת:
כח וְרוּחוֹ כְּנַחַל שׁוֹטֵף עַד־צַוָּאר יֶחֱצֶה לַהֲנָפָה גוֹיִם בְּנָפַת שָׁוְא וְרֶסֶן מַתְעֶה

30:8-14. God commanded Isaiah to inscribe this prophecy in order to bear witness that although Israel had been warned of the consequences of their misdeeds, they nevertheless depended on dishonest gains to buy security from Egypt, but Egypt was like a high wall — filled with cracks (*Radak*).

30:15-16. If you had followed My will, you would have been safeguarded from your enemies without recourse to foreign alliances. You preferred to have horses for flight in case of war; your punishment will be that you will indeed be forced to flee!

30:19. This prophecy refers to the end of days (*Rashi*).

30:20. You will stop craving a hedonistic life-style and be content with simple necessities, being attuned, instead, to spiritual pursuits (*Rashi*).

30:21. Unlike your present scornful attitude towards the word of God (vv. 10-11), you will be so anxious to obey Him that you will avidly heed even an overheard prophecy that is addressed to others (*Rashi*).

30:25. In the end of days, or at the time of Sennacherib's downfall (*Ibn Ezra*). The "great ones" refers to the lofty defense towers (*Kara*) or the leaders (*Targum*).

30:27. God will come to fulfill His ancient promise (*Rashi*).

inscribe it in a book; * and let it remain until the final day, forever, for eternity. ⁹ For it is a rebellious people, dishonest children; children who are not willing to hear the teaching of HASHEM; ¹⁰ who say to the seers, "Do not see," and to the prophets, "Do not see true visions for us! Speak pleasant things to us; see fantasies for us. ¹¹ Veer from the way, stray from the path. Remove from our presence [the word of] the Holy One of Israel!"

Like a fallen wall

¹² Therefore, thus said the Holy One of Israel: Since you have despised this word and you trusted in robbery and waywardness, and have depended on it — ¹³ therefore, this sin will be for you like the breach of a fallen [wall], like a bulge in a lofty wall, whose collapse comes with quick suddenness. ¹⁴ [God] will break it as one breaks the potters' flask into fragments, He will have no pity; there will not be found among the fragments a shard to scrape a burning coal from a fire or to scoop water from a cistern.

¹⁵ For thus said my Lord HASHEM/ELOHIM, the Holy One of Israel: 'In stillness and peacefulness will you be saved, in quiet and in confidence will be your might,' but you did not consent. ¹⁶ And you said, 'Not so! We will flee on a horse,'* therefore you will flee; and, 'We will ride upon swift animals,' therefore your pursuers will be swifter. ¹⁷ One thousand [will flee] from the shout of one, and from the shout of five you will [all] flee; until you will be left like a mast on the top of a mountain and like a pole atop a hill. ¹⁸ Therefore, HASHEM will delay in showing you grace, and therefore He will be aloof from showing you mercy. For HASHEM is a God of justice; praiseworthy are those who yearn for Him.

Another prophecy about the end of days

¹⁹ For a people will dwell in Zion, in Jerusalem. * You will not have to weep; He will surely show you grace at the sound of your outcry, when He hears, He will answer you. ²⁰ The Lord will give you meager bread and scant water;* your Teacher will no longer be hidden behind His garment, and your eyes will behold your Teacher. ²¹ And your ears will listen [even] to a word spoken from behind you, * saying, 'This is the path; walk in it, whether you go to your right or to your left.' ²² You will contaminate the coating of your silver graven idols and the embellishment of your golden molten images; you will cast them away like someone unclean; you will tell it, 'Be gone!'

²³ [God] will give rain for your seed that you will sow in the ground, and bread from the produce of the ground; it will be rich and fat; your livestock will graze in a broad pasture on that day. ²⁴ The oxen and the young donkeys that work the land will eat enriched fodder, which has been winnowed with a shovel and a fan. ²⁵ On every high mountain and on every exalted hill there will be pools, rivulets of water, on the day of the great killing, when great ones fall. * ²⁶ The light of the moon will be like the light of the sun, and the light of the sun will be seven times as strong, like the light of seven days, on the day that HASHEM bandages the injury of His people and heals the wound of His blow.

God's mighty vengeance

²⁷ Behold, the Name of HASHEM is coming from afar;* His anger is flaring, and the burden is heavy; His lips are full of rage and His tongue is like a consuming fire. ²⁸ His breath is like a raging stream that reaches up to the neck, to sift the nations in a faulty sieve, * and to be a diverting bridle

---

30:28. The sinful actions will not deserve mercy, so God will pour them all into a faulty sieve that lets everything slip through the holes, so that none of the nations will be spared. So too, He will put upon them a bridle that will direct them toward the course of their own destruction (*Radak*).

כט הַשִּׁיר֙ יִֽהְיֶ֣ה לָכֶ֔ם כְּלֵ֖יל הִתְקַדֶּשׁ־חָ֑ג וְשִׂמְחַ֣ת לֵבָ֗ב   עַל לְחַיֵּ֣י עַמִּֽים:

ל כַּֽהֲלֵ֣ךְ בֶּֽחָלִ֔יל לָב֥וֹא בְהַר־יְהֹוָ֖ה אֶל־צ֣וּר יִשְׂרָאֵ֑ל: וְהִשְׁמִ֣יעַ יְהֹוָ֗ה אֶת־
הוֹד֮ קוֹלוֹ֒ וְנַ֤חַת זְרוֹעוֹ֙ יַרְאֶ֔ה בְּזַ֣עַף אַ֔ף וְלַ֖הַב אֵ֣שׁ אוֹכֵלָ֑ה נֶ֥פֶץ וָזֶ֖רֶם וְאֶ֥בֶן

לא-לב בָּרָֽד: כִּֽי־מִקּ֥וֹל יְהֹוָ֖ה יֵחַ֣ת אַשּׁ֑וּר בַּשֵּׁ֖בֶט יַכֶּֽה: וְהָיָ֗ה כֹּ֚ל מַֽעֲבַר֙ מַטֵּ֣ה
מֽוּסָדָ֔ה אֲשֶׁ֨ר יָנִ֤יחַ יְהֹוָה֙ עָלָ֔יו בְּתֻפִּ֖ים וּבְכִנֹּר֑וֹת וּבְמִלְחֲמ֥וֹת תְּנוּפָ֖ה

לג נִלְחַם־ °בָּ֥ה [°בָּֽם ק]: כִּֽי־עָר֤וּךְ מֵֽאֶתְמוּל֙ תָּפְתֶּ֔ה גַּם־ °ה֖וּא [°הִ֥יא ק]
לַמֶּ֣לֶךְ הוּכָ֑ן הֶעְמִ֤יק הִרְחִב֙ מְדֻ֣רָתָ֗הּ אֵ֤שׁ וְעֵצִים֙ הַרְבֵּ֔ה נִשְׁמַ֤ת יְהֹוָה֙ כְּנַ֣חַל
גׇּפְרִ֔ית בֹּעֲרָ֖ה בָּֽהּ:

לא   א ה֣וֹי הַיֹּֽרְדִ֤ים מִצְרַ֨יִם֙ לְעֶזְרָ֔ה עַל־סוּסִ֖ים
יִשָּׁעֵ֑נוּ וַיִּבְטְח֨וּ עַל־רֶ֜כֶב כִּ֣י רָ֗ב וְעַ֤ל פָּֽרָשִׁים֙ כִּֽי־עָצְמ֣וּ מְאֹ֔ד וְלֹ֤א שָׁעוּ֙ עַל־
ב קְד֣וֹשׁ יִשְׂרָאֵ֔ל וְאֶת־יְהֹוָ֖ה לֹ֥א דָרָֽשׁוּ: וְגַם־ה֤וּא חָכָם֙ וַיָּ֣בֵא רָ֔ע וְאֶת־דְּבָרָ֖יו
ג לֹ֣א הֵסִ֑יר וְקָם֙ עַל־בֵּ֣ית מְרֵעִ֔ים וְעַל־עֶזְרַ֖ת פֹּ֥עֲלֵי אָֽוֶן: וּמִצְרַ֤יִם אָדָם֙ וְלֹא־
אֵ֔ל וְסֽוּסֵיהֶ֥ם בָּשָׂ֖ר וְלֹא־ר֑וּחַ וַֽיהֹוָ֞ה יַטֶּ֣ה יָד֗וֹ וְכָשַׁ֤ל עוֹזֵר֙ וְנָפַ֣ל עָזֻ֔ר וְיַחְדָּ֖ו
ד כֻּלָּ֥ם יִכְלָיֽוּן: כִּ֣י כֹ֣ה אָֽמַר־יְהֹוָ֣ה ׀ אֵלַ֗י כַּֽאֲשֶׁ֨ר יֶהְגֶּ֜ה הָֽאַרְיֵ֤ה
וְהַכְּפִיר֙ עַל־טַרְפּ֔וֹ אֲשֶׁ֨ר יִקָּרֵ֤א עָלָיו֙ מְלֹ֣א רֹעִ֔ים מִקּוֹלָם֙ לֹ֣א יֵחָ֔ת
ה וּמֵֽהֲמוֹנָ֖ם לֹ֣א יַֽעֲנֶ֑ה כֵּ֣ן יֵרֵ֞ד יְהֹוָ֤ה צְבָאוֹת֙ לִצְבֹּ֣א עַל־הַר־צִיּ֔וֹן וְעַל־
גִּבְעָתָֽהּ: כְּצִֽפֳּרִ֣ים עָפ֔וֹת כֵּ֗ן יָגֵ֛ן יְהֹוָ֥ה צְבָא֖וֹת עַל־יְרֽוּשָׁלָ֑͏ִם גָּנ֥וֹן וְהִצִּ֖יל
ו-ז פָּס֥וֹחַ וְהִמְלִֽיט: שׁ֗וּבוּ לַֽאֲשֶׁ֛ר הֶעְמִ֥יקוּ סָרָ֖ה בְּנֵ֥י יִשְׂרָאֵֽל: כִּ֚י בַּיּ֣וֹם הַה֔וּא
יִמְאָס֗וּן אִ֚ישׁ אֱלִ֣ילֵי כַסְפּ֔וֹ וֶֽאֱלִילֵ֖י זְהָב֑וֹ אֲשֶׁ֨ר עָשׂ֥וּ לָכֶ֛ם יְדֵיכֶ֖ם חֵֽטְא:
ח וְנָפַ֤ל אַשּׁוּר֙ בְּחֶ֣רֶב לֹא־אִ֔ישׁ וְחֶ֥רֶב לֹֽא־אָדָ֖ם תֹּֽאכְלֶ֑נּוּ וְנָ֥ס לוֹ֙ מִפְּנֵי־חֶ֔רֶב
ט וּבַֽחוּרָ֖יו לָמַ֥ס יִֽהְי֑וּ: וְסַלְעוֹ֙ מִמָּג֣וֹר יַֽעֲב֔וֹר וְחַתּ֥וּ מִנֵּ֖ס שָׂרָ֑יו נְאֻם־יְהֹוָ֗ה

לב   א אֲשֶׁר־א֥וּר לוֹ֙ בְּצִיּ֔וֹן וְתַנּ֥וּר ל֖וֹ בִּירֽוּשָׁלָֽ͏ִם: הֵ֥ן לְצֶ֖דֶק
ב יִמְלׇךְ־מֶ֑לֶךְ וּלְשָׂרִ֖ים לְמִשְׁפָּ֥ט יָשֹֽׂרוּ: וְהָיָֽה־אִ֥ישׁ כְּמַֽחֲבֵא־ר֖וּחַ וְסֵ֣תֶר
ג זָ֑רֶם כְּפַלְגֵי־מַ֣יִם בְּצָי֔וֹן כְּצֵ֥ל סֶֽלַע־כָּבֵ֖ד בְּאֶ֥רֶץ עֲיֵפָֽה: וְלֹ֥א תִשְׁעֶ֖ינָה
ד עֵינֵ֣י רֹאִ֑ים וְאׇזְנֵ֥י שֹֽׁמְעִ֖ים תִּקְשַֽׁבְנָה: וּלְבַ֥ב נִמְהָרִ֖ים יָבִ֣ין לָדָ֑עַת וּלְשׁ֣וֹן
ה עִלְּגִ֔ים תְּמַהֵ֖ר לְדַבֵּ֥ר צָחֽוֹת: לֹֽא־יִקָּרֵ֥א ע֛וֹד לְנָבָ֖ל נָדִ֑יב וּלְכִילַ֖י לֹ֥א
ו יֵֽאָמֵ֖ר שֽׁוֹעַ: כִּ֤י נָבָל֙ נְבָלָ֣ה יְדַבֵּ֔ר וְלִבּ֖וֹ יַֽעֲשֶׂה־אָ֑וֶן לַֽעֲשׂ֣וֹת חֹ֗נֶף וּלְדַבֵּ֤ר אֶל־
ז יְהֹוָה֙ תּוֹעָ֔ה לְהָרִיק֙ נֶ֣פֶשׁ רָעֵ֔ב וּמַשְׁקֶ֥ה צָמֵ֖א יַחְסִֽיר: וְכֵלַ֖י כֵּלָ֣יו רָעִ֑ים

30:29. I.e., the night of the first Passover.

30:32. When the wicked perish there is joy (*Proverbs* 11:10). The war will be fought as a conductor waves his hand to maintain the correct musical beat (*Radak*).

30:33. Isaiah describes the Hell that will accommodate all the wicked who would perish on that day.

31:2. Sarcastically, Isaiah tells his fellow Jews that they thought they could avert Divine punishment by seeking aid from foreign powers, but God is "also" wise and can easily circumvent their plans (*Metzudos; Malbim*).

31:5. Like birds appearing from nowhere, so will God's help arrive suddenly (*Radak*). As in the plague of the firstborn in Egypt, God will pass over the camp of Israel and decimate that of Assyria.

31:9. When the hand of God is displayed so manifestly through the miraculous defeat of Assyria, its king will flee and the rock of his confidence will disintegrate in fright, for he will realize that there is no escape from God's wrath.

32:1-8. Isaiah describes the noble goals of King Hezekiah and the sort of behavior that made him stand out and which elevated the people of his realm. He established a reign of justice and righteousness, and his kingdom was protected because of it. Justice and fairness were the rule in his days and people had no need to ingratiate themselves with degenerate overlords.

upon the cheeks of the nations. [29] The song will be yours like the night of the festival's consecration, * and heartfelt gladness like one who walks with a flute, to come onto the mountain of HASHEM, to the Rock of Israel. [30] HASHEM will make heard the majesty of His voice, and He will show the potency of His arm, with raging anger and with the flame of a consuming fire, with smashing, torrent, and hailstone. [31] For Assyria will become devastated by the voice of HASHEM, as if He struck with the stick. [32] And it shall be that with every passage of the firm staff that HASHEM will place upon him there will be timbrels and harps, and He will fight wars against them like a waving of the hand. * [33] For Hell* has been prepared from yesterday; it has been readied even for the king; [God] has deepened and widened it; its inferno has much fire and wood, and the breath of HASHEM is like a stream of sulfur burning within it.

The inferno of Hell

31

Egypt versus God

[1] **W**oe to those who go down to Egypt for help and who rely on horses; they trust in chariots because they are many and in horsemen because they are very strong, and they did not turn to the Holy One of Israel and did not seek out HASHEM. [2] But He is also wise, * and He has brought calamity, and He did not retract His words; He will rise up against the house of evildoers and against the assistance of those who commit sin. [3] Egypt is man and not god, and their horses are of flesh and not of spirit! HASHEM will stretch out His hand and the helper will stumble and the helped will fall; they will all perish together. [4] For thus said HASHEM to me: Just as when a lion or a lion cub roars over his prey and a gathering of shepherds assembles against him, it is not frightened by their voice and is not humbled by their noise, so shall HASHEM, Master of Legions, descend to do battle upon Mount Zion and upon its hill. [5] Like flying birds, * so will HASHEM, Master of Legions, protect Jerusalem, protecting and rescuing, passing over and delivering. [6] Return to the One from Whom you have profoundly turned away, O Children of Israel. [7] For on that day everyone will despise his false gods of silver and his false gods of gold, which your hands have made for you in sin, [8] when Assyria will fall by the sword of one who is not a man, and the sword of one who is not human will devour him. He will flee from the sword and his young men will become bondsmen. [9] His rock* will pass away in terror and his officers will be devastated by a miracle — the word of HASHEM — Who has a fire in Zion and a furnace in Jerusalem!

God, Defender of Jerusalem

32

Righteous-ness versus corruption

[1] **B**ehold, the king* will rule for the sake of righteousness and the officers will govern for justice. [2] Man will be like a hideout from the wind and a cover from a downpour, like pools of water in an arid area, like the shade of a large rock in a thirsty land. [3] The eyes of seeing people will no longer be closed and the ears of the hearing people will pay heed. [4] The heart of the impetuous will understand knowledge and the tongue of stammerers will hasten to speak fluently. [5] A vile person will no longer be called generous, and it will not be said that a miser is magnanimous. [6] For the vile person speaks villainy and his heart plans iniquity, to act with hypocrisy and to speak falsehood about HASHEM, * to empty the soul of the hungry and to diminish the drink of the thirsty. [7] As for the miser, his implements are evil; *

32:6. To say that God does not know or care about his evil deeds (*Radak*).

32:7. He cheats his customers by using false weights and measures (*Radak*).

הוּא זִמּוֹת יָעָץ לְחַבֵּל ענוים [עֲנָוִים °ק] בְּאִמְרֵי־שֶׁקֶר וּבְדַבֵּר אֶבְיוֹן

ח-ט מִשְׁפָּט: וְנָדִיב נְדִיבוֹת יָעָץ וְהוּא עַל־נְדִיבוֹת יָקוּם: נָשִׁים

י שַׁאֲנַנּוֹת קֹמְנָה שְׁמַעְנָה קוֹלִי בָּנוֹת בֹּטְחוֹת הַאְזֵנָּה אִמְרָתִי: יָמִים

יא עַל־שָׁנָה תִּרְגַּזְנָה בֹּטְחוֹת כִּי כָּלָה בָצִיר אֹסֶף בְּלִי יָבוֹא: חִרְדוּ שַׁאֲנַנּוֹת

יב רְגָזָה בֹּטְחוֹת פְּשֹׁטָה וְעֹרָה וַחֲגוֹרָה עַל־חֲלָצָיִם: עַל־שָׁדַיִם סֹפְדִים עַל־

יג שְׂדֵי־חֶמֶד עַל־גֶּפֶן פֹּרִיָּה: עַל אַדְמַת עַמִּי קוֹץ שָׁמִיר תַּעֲלֶה כִּי עַל־

יד כָּל־בָּתֵּי מָשׂוֹשׂ קִרְיָה עַלִּיזָה: כִּי־אַרְמוֹן נֻטָּשׁ הֲמוֹן עִיר עֻזָּב עֹפֶל

טו וָבַחַן הָיָה בְעַד מְעָרוֹת עַד־עוֹלָם מְשׂוֹשׂ פְּרָאִים מִרְעֵה עֲדָרִים: עַד־

יֵעָרֶה עָלֵינוּ רוּחַ מִמָּרוֹם וְהָיָה מִדְבָּר לַכַּרְמֶל וכרמל [וְהַכַּרְמֶל °ק]

טז-יז לַיַּעַר יֵחָשֵׁב: וְשָׁכַן בַּמִּדְבָּר מִשְׁפָּט וּצְדָקָה בַּכַּרְמֶל תֵּשֵׁב: וְהָיָה מַעֲשֵׂה

יח הַצְּדָקָה שָׁלוֹם וַעֲבֹדַת הַצְּדָקָה הַשְׁקֵט וָבֶטַח עַד־עוֹלָם: וְיָשַׁב עַמִּי בִּנְוֵה

יט שָׁלוֹם וּבְמִשְׁכְּנוֹת מִבְטַחִים וּבִמְנוּחֹת שַׁאֲנַנּוֹת: וּבָרַד בְּרֶדֶת הַיָּעַר

כ וּבַשִּׁפְלָה תִּשְׁפַּל הָעִיר: אַשְׁרֵיכֶם זֹרְעֵי עַל־כָּל־מָיִם מְשַׁלְּחֵי רֶגֶל־הַשּׁוֹר

וְהַחֲמוֹר: הוֹי שׁוֹדֵד וְאַתָּה לֹא שָׁדוּד וּבוֹגֵד וְלֹא־בָגְדוּ בוֹ

לג °נ"א בָּךְ

א

ב כַּהֲתִמְךָ שׁוֹדֵד תּוּשַּׁד כַּנְּלֹתְךָ לִבְגֹּד יִבְגְּדוּ־בָךְ: יהוה

ג חָנֵּנוּ לְךָ קִוִּינוּ הֱיֵה זְרֹעָם לַבְּקָרִים אַף־יְשׁוּעָתֵנוּ בְּעֵת צָרָה: מִקּוֹל

ד הָמוֹן נָדְדוּ עַמִּים מֵרוֹמְמֻתֶךָ נָפְצוּ גּוֹיִם: וְאֻסַּף שְׁלַלְכֶם אֹסֶף הֶחָסִיל

ה כְּמַשַּׁק גֵּבִים שׁוֹקֵק בּוֹ: נִשְׂגָּב יהוה כִּי שֹׁכֵן מָרוֹם מִלֵּא צִיּוֹן מִשְׁפָּט

ו וּצְדָקָה: וְהָיָה אֱמוּנַת עִתֶּיךָ חֹסֶן יְשׁוּעֹת חָכְמַת וָדָעַת יִרְאַת יהוה הִיא

ז אוֹצָרוֹ: הֵן אֶרְאֶלָּם צָעֲקוּ חֻצָה מַלְאֲכֵי שָׁלוֹם מַר יִבְכָּיוּן:

ח נָשַׁמּוּ מְסִלּוֹת שָׁבַת עֹבֵר אֹרַח הֵפֵר בְּרִית מָאַס עָרִים לֹא חָשַׁב אֱנוֹשׁ:

ט אָבַל אֻמְלְלָה אָרֶץ הֶחְפִּיר לְבָנוֹן קָמַל הָיָה הַשָּׁרוֹן כָּעֲרָבָה וְנֹעֵר בָּשָׁן

י-יא וְכַרְמֶל: עַתָּה אָקוּם יֹאמַר יהוה עַתָּה אֵרוֹמָם עַתָּה אֶנָּשֵׂא: תַּהֲרוּ חֲשַׁשׁ

יב תֵּלְדוּ קַשׁ רוּחֲכֶם אֵשׁ תֹּאכַלְכֶם: וְהָיוּ עַמִּים מִשְׂרְפוֹת שִׂיד קוֹצִים

יג כְּסוּחִים בָּאֵשׁ יִצַּתּוּ: שִׁמְעוּ רְחוֹקִים אֲשֶׁר עָשִׂיתִי וּדְעוּ

יד קְרוֹבִים גְּבֻרָתִי: פָּחֲדוּ בְצִיּוֹן חַטָּאִים אָחֲזָה רְעָדָה חֲנֵפִים מִי יָגוּר

טו לָנוּ אֵשׁ אוֹכֵלָה מִי־יָגוּר לָנוּ מוֹקְדֵי עוֹלָם: הֹלֵךְ צְדָקוֹת וְדֹבֵר מֵישָׁרִים

32:9. The women and daughters are metaphors for nations and city-states (*Targum*).

32:10. Their confidence will be shattered when the enemy robs them of their grape vintage and their grain harvest (*Rashi*).

32:13. I.e., Jerusalem (*Rashi*).

32:19. God will protect the peace of populated areas by letting hail fall only on the forests and by making the people so secure that houses will be built even in the vulnerable lowlands (*Ibn Ezra*).

33:1. This verse is addressed to Sennacherib (*Kara*).

33:2-3. This is Israel's prayer for God's help. The chapter then continues with God's response.

33:4. The spoils from the defeated Assyrian army.

33:7-9. Isaiah now describes the frightening situation when messengers brought the news that Sennacherib had overrun Judah and was headed for Jerusalem (*Radak*).

33:11. Isaiah tells the Assyrians that they have conceived and given birth to plans that are as worthless as stubble and straw (*Radak*), and that their own spirit, i.e., plans, would rebound against them.

33:12. Sennacherib's allies will be as quickly and easily destroyed as lime in a blazing furnace and as dry thorns.

he plans schemes to destroy the poor with words of falsehood and when the destitute speaks justly. ⁸ But a generous man plans generous acts, and stands for generous acts.

Parable of the complacent women

⁹ O complacent women, rise up and hear my voice! O confident daughters, * give ear to my speech! ¹⁰ Days upon years the confident women will shudder, when the vintage is finished, the harvest does not come in. * ¹¹ Tremble, O complacent women; shudder, O confident women; disrobe and bare yourselves, and don [sackcloth] on your loins. ¹²Beating upon [their] breasts in mourning over the lovely fields, over the fruitful vine. ¹³ Over the land of my people, thistles and weeds will sprout; over all the houses of merrymaking, over the exultant city. * ¹⁴ For the palace has been abandoned, the city's multitude forsaken; the fortification and stronghold have become ruins forever, a joy for wild asses, pasture for flocks; ¹⁵ until a spirit from on high will be poured out upon us, and the desert will become a fertile field and the fertile field will be reckoned like forest. ¹⁶ Justice will dwell in the wilderness and righteousness will live in the fertile field. ¹⁷ The product of righteousness shall be peace; and the effect of righteousness, quiet and security forever. ¹⁸ My people will live in a peaceful domain and in secure dwellings and in tranquil resting places. ¹⁹ Hail will come down on the forest * and the city will extend down to the valley. ²⁰ You will be so fortunate to sow upon all waters, sending the ox and the donkey to roam freely.

33

¹ Woe to you, pillager* but you have not been pillaged! Traitor, who has not been betrayed! When you finish pillaging, you will be pillaged; when you end your treachery, they will be treacherous with you.

Israel's prayer

² "HASHEM, grant us favor; * we have hoped for You! Be their [strong] arm every morning, also our salvation in time of distress. ³ At the noise of [Your] tumult, peoples have wandered; from Your exaltedness, nations have scattered."

The enemy will fall

⁴ Your spoils * will be gathered like the gathering of locusts, as the march of grasshoppers shall he march in it. ⁵ HASHEM is exalted, for He dwells on high; He has filled Zion with justice and righteousness. ⁶ The faith of your times will be the strength of your salvations, wisdom and knowledge; fear of HASHEM — that is [man's] treasure.

⁷ Behold, their herald cried out outside; * messengers of peace wept bitterly: ⁸ 'Roads are desolate, wayfarer has ceased! He has annulled the treaty, despised cities, respected no man. ⁹ The land is mournful and forlorn; Lebanon is shamed and cut down; Sharon has become a desert; Bashan and Carmel have become denuded.'

¹⁰ Now I shall arise — HASHEM will say — now I shall ascend; now I shall be exalted! ¹¹ Conceive stubble and give birth to straw; * your spirit is a fire that will consume you. ¹² Nations will be like burnings for lime; * like cut thorns set aflame. ¹³ Hear, O faraway people, * what I have done; and you who are close by, recognize My might.

¹⁴ Sinners were afraid in Zion; trembling seized hypocrites. 'Which of us can live with the consuming fire? Which of us can live with the eternal conflagration?' ¹⁵ One who walks with righteousness and speaks with truthful-

---

33:13. Those who hear how God demolished Assyria's army and caused its downfall will wonder who can live in the presence of such a powerful, terrifying force (*Targum*). Alternatively: The Jews will wonder who can stand up to Assyria (*Radak*). Either way, the answer is given in verse 15.

מֹאֵס בְּבֶצַע מַעֲשַׁקּוֹת נֹעֵר כַּפָּיו מִתְּמֹךְ בַּשֹּׁחַד אֹטֵם אָזְנוֹ מִשְּׁמֹעַ דָּמִים

טז וְעֹצֵם עֵינָיו מֵרְאוֹת בְּרָע: הוּא מְרוֹמִים יִשְׁכֹּן מְצָדוֹת סְלָעִים מִשְׂגַּבּוֹ

יז לַחְמוֹ נִתָּן מֵימָיו נֶאֱמָנִים: מֶלֶךְ בְּיָפְיוֹ תֶּחֱזֶינָה עֵינֶיךָ תִּרְאֶינָה אֶרֶץ

יח מַרְחַקִּים: לִבְּךָ יֶהְגֶּה אֵימָה אַיֵּה סֹפֵר אַיֵּה שֹׁקֵל אַיֵּה סֹפֵר אֶת־הַמִּגְדָּלִים:

יט אֶת־עַם נוֹעָז לֹא תִרְאֶה עַם עִמְקֵי שָׂפָה מִשְּׁמוֹעַ נִלְעַג לָשׁוֹן אֵין

כ בִּינָה: חֲזֵה צִיּוֹן קִרְיַת מוֹעֲדֵנוּ עֵינֶיךָ תִרְאֶינָה יְרוּשָׁלַ͏ִם נָוֶה שַׁאֲנָן אֹהֶל

כא בַּל־יִצְעָן בַּל־יִסַּע יְתֵדֹתָיו לָנֶצַח וְכָל־חֲבָלָיו בַּל־יִנָּתֵקוּ: כִּי אִם־שָׁם

אַדִּיר יְהוָה לָנוּ מְקוֹם־נְהָרִים יְאֹרִים רַחֲבֵי יָדָיִם בַּל־תֵּלֶךְ בּוֹ אֳנִי־שַׁיִט

כב וְצִי אַדִּיר לֹא יַעַבְרֶנּוּ: כִּי יְהוָה שֹׁפְטֵנוּ יְהוָה מְחֹקְקֵנוּ יְהוָה מַלְכֵּנוּ הוּא

כג יוֹשִׁיעֵנוּ: נִטְּשׁוּ חֲבָלָיִךְ בַּל־יְחַזְּקוּ כֵן־תָּרְנָם בַּל־פָּרְשׂוּ נֵס אָז חֻלַּק עַד־

כד שָׁלָל מַרְבֶּה פִסְחִים בָּזְזוּ בַז: וּבַל־יֹאמַר שָׁכֵן חָלִיתִי הָעָם הַיֹּשֵׁב בָּהּ נְשֻׂא

לד א עָוֹן: קִרְבוּ גוֹיִם לִשְׁמֹעַ וּלְאֻמִּים הַקְשִׁיבוּ תִּשְׁמַע הָאָרֶץ

ב וּמְלֹאָהּ תֵּבֵל וְכָל־צֶאֱצָאֶיהָ: כִּי קֶצֶף לַיהוָה עַל־כָּל־הַגּוֹיִם וְחֵמָה עַל־

ג כָּל־צְבָאָם הֶחֱרִימָם נְתָנָם לַטָּבַח: וְחַלְלֵיהֶם יֻשְׁלָכוּ וּפִגְרֵיהֶם יַעֲלֶה

ד בָאְשָׁם וְנָמַסּוּ הָרִים מִדָּמָם: וְנָמַקּוּ כָּל־צְבָא הַשָּׁמַיִם וְנָגֹלּוּ כַסֵּפֶר הַשָּׁמָיִם

ה וְכָל־צְבָאָם יִבּוֹל כִּנְבֹל עָלֶה מִגֶּפֶן וּכְנֹבֶלֶת מִתְּאֵנָה: כִּי־רִוְּתָה בַשָּׁמַיִם

ו חַרְבִּי הִנֵּה עַל־אֱדוֹם תֵּרֵד וְעַל־עַם חֶרְמִי לְמִשְׁפָּט: חֶרֶב לַיהוָה מָלְאָה

דָם הֻדַּשְׁנָה מֵחֵלֶב מִדַּם כָּרִים וְעַתּוּדִים מֵחֵלֶב כִּלְיוֹת אֵילִים כִּי זֶבַח

ז לַיהוָה בְּבָצְרָה וְטֶבַח גָּדוֹל בְּאֶרֶץ אֱדוֹם: וְיָרְדוּ רְאֵמִים עִמָּם וּפָרִים עִם־

ח אַבִּירִים וְרִוְּתָה אַרְצָם מִדָּם וַעֲפָרָם מֵחֵלֶב יְדֻשָּׁן: כִּי יוֹם נָקָם לַיהוָה שְׁנַת

ט שִׁלּוּמִים לְרִיב צִיּוֹן: וְנֶהֶפְכוּ נְחָלֶיהָ לְזֶפֶת וַעֲפָרָהּ לְגָפְרִית וְהָיְתָה אַרְצָהּ

י לְזֶפֶת בֹּעֵרָה: לַיְלָה וְיוֹמָם לֹא תִכְבֶּה לְעוֹלָם יַעֲלֶה עֲשָׁנָהּ מִדּוֹר לָדוֹר

יא תֶּחֱרָב לָנֶצַח נְצָחִים אֵין עֹבֵר בָּהּ: וִירֵשׁוּהָ קָאַת וְקִפּוֹד וְיַנְשׁוֹף וְעֹרֵב

יב יִשְׁכְּנוּ־בָהּ וְנָטָה עָלֶיהָ קַו־תֹהוּ וְאַבְנֵי־בֹהוּ: חֹרֶיהָ וְאֵין־שָׁם מְלוּכָה יִקְרָאוּ

יג וְכָל־שָׂרֶיהָ יִהְיוּ אָפֶס: וְעָלְתָה אַרְמְנֹתֶיהָ סִירִים קִמּוֹשׂ וָחוֹחַ בְּמִבְצָרֶיהָ

יד וְהָיְתָה נְוֵה תַנִּים חָצִיר לִבְנוֹת יַעֲנָה: וּפָגְשׁוּ צִיִּים אֶת־אִיִּים וְשָׂעִיר

טו עַל־רֵעֵהוּ יִקְרָא אַךְ־שָׁם הִרְגִּיעָה לִּילִית וּמָצְאָה לָהּ מָנוֹחַ: שָׁמָּה קִנְּנָה

קִפּוֹז וַתְּמַלֵּט וּבָקְעָה וְדָגְרָה בְצִלָּהּ אַךְ־שָׁם נִקְבְּצוּ דַיּוֹת אִשָּׁה רְעוּתָהּ:

33:15. He does not let unsubstantiated talk incite him to bloodshed (*Radak*).

33:17-22. Isaiah addresses the righteous people described above, even those in faraway lands (*Rashi*).

33:23. Isaiah likens the Assyrian foe to a disabled ship.

34:5. The sword has slain the Heavenly advocates of the nations God has condemned (*Rashi*).

34:6-7. The animals are metaphors for the kings and officers of God's enemy nations (*Targum*).

34:9. I.e., the land of Edom.

34:11. Commentaries differ widely regarding the identifications of the birds and animals mentioned here.

The line and the plumb bob are builder's tools used to ensure the horizontality and verticality of layers of stones or bricks (see 28:10). The metaphor means that Edom's total destruction will be thoroughly planned and executed.

34:14. The name of a female demon (*Rashi*) or a nocturnal bird (*Ibn Ezra*).

ness, who spurns extortionate profit and shakes off his hands from holding a bribe, who seals his ears from hearing of bloodshed* and shuts his eyes from seeing evil. ¹⁶ *He shall dwell in heights; in rocky fortresses is his stronghold; his bread will be granted, his water assured.*

Consolation
for Israel

¹⁷ *Your eyes will behold the King in His splendor; they will see Him from a faraway land.** ¹⁸ *Your heart will muse in dread, 'Where is the one who counts? Where is the one who weighs? Where is the one who counts the towers?'* ¹⁹ *You will not see bold people, the people whose speech is too difficult to understand, of garbled tongue, without comprehension.* ²⁰ *Behold Zion, the city of our festivals; your eyes will see Jerusalem, the tranquil abode, the tent that will not be displaced, whose stakes will not be uprooted forever, and none of whose ropes will be severed.* ²¹ *For only there will* HASHEM *be our Mighty One; [it will be like] a place of wide rivers and channels; a boat cannot traverse it, and a mighty vessel cannot cross it.* ²² *For* HASHEM *is our Judge;* HASHEM *is our Lawgiver;* HASHEM *is our King; He will save us.* ²³ *Your* ropes have been abandoned; they will not firmly secure their mast; they will not spread sail. Then abundant spoils and plunder will be distributed; [even] the lame will take booty.* ²⁴ *A dweller [of Jerusalem] will not say, 'I am sick'; the people dwelling there shall be forgiven of sin.*

34

*An end to
the ungodly
nations*

¹ **C**ome close, O nations, to hear, and regimes be attentive; let the earth and its fullness hear, the world and all its offspring.* ² *For* HASHEM *has a fury against all the nations and a wrath against all their legions; He has destroyed them, He has delivered them to the slaughter.* ³ *Their slain will be thrown aside and their corpses will bring up stench; the mountains will melt from their blood.* ⁴ *All the host of the heavens will dissolve and the heavens will be rolled up like a scroll; all their host will shrivel as a leaf of a grapevine shrivels and like a shriveled leaf of a fig tree.* ⁵ *For my sword has been sated in the heavens;* behold, it shall descend upon Edom and for judgment upon the people of My destruction.* ⁶ *The sword of* HASHEM *is full of blood, greased with fat, with the blood of fatted sheep* and he-goats, with the fat of the kidneys of rams; for* HASHEM *is making a sacrifice at Bozrah and a great slaughter in the land of Edom.* ⁷ *The wild oxen will go down [to the slaughter] with them, and bulls and fatted bulls; their land will be sated with blood and their soil enriched with fat.* ⁸ *For it is a day of vengeance for* HASHEM; *a year of retribution for the grievance of Zion.* ⁹ *Its* rivers will turn to tar and its soil to sulfur; its land will become burning tar.* ¹⁰ *Night and day it will not be extinguished; its smoke will ascend forever. From generation to generation [the land] will be desolate, for all eternity no one traverses it.* ¹¹ *Owls* and bitterns will occupy it, great owls and ravens will dwell in it; and He will draw against it a line* of emptiness and plumb bobs of void.* ¹² *Their noblemen would call out, 'There is no dominion [except us]'; but all its leaders will become nothingness.* ¹³ *Its palaces will sprout weeds, thorns and thistles in its fortresses. It will be an abode for jackals, a place for ostriches.* ¹⁴ *Martens will encounter cats, and one satyr will call out to another; there Lilith* also will relax and find rest for herself.* ¹⁵ *There the bittern will nest and lay her eggs, gathering them together under her shade and hatching them; there kites also will congregate with one another.*

דִּרְשׁ֤וּ מֵֽעַל־סֵ֨פֶר יְהֹוָ֜ה וּֽקְרָ֗אוּ אַחַ֤ת מֵהֵ֨נָּה֙ לֹ֣א נֶעְדָּ֔רָה אִשָּׁ֥ה רְעוּתָ֖הּ טז

לֹ֣א פָקָ֑דוּ כִּֽי־פִי֙ ה֣וּא צִוָּ֔ה וְרוּח֖וֹ ה֣וּא קִבְּצָֽן: וְהֽוּא־הִפִּ֤יל לָהֶן֙ יז

גּוֹרָ֔ל וְיָד֛וֹ חִלְּקַ֥תָּה לָהֶ֖ם בַּקָּ֑ו עַד־עוֹלָם֙ יִֽירָשׁ֔וּהָ לְד֥וֹר וָד֖וֹר יִשְׁכְּנוּ־

בָֽהּ: יְשֻׂשׂ֥וּם מִדְבָּ֖ר וְצִיָּ֑ה וְתָגֵ֧ל עֲרָבָ֛ה וְתִפְרַ֖ח כַּחֲבַצָּֽלֶת: א לה

פָּרֹ֣חַ תִּפְרַח֮ וְתָגֵל֒ אַ֣ף גִּילַ֣ת וְרַנֵּ֔ן כְּב֤וֹד הַלְּבָנוֹן֙ נִתַּן־לָ֔הּ הֲדַ֖ר הַכַּרְמֶ֣ל ב

וְהַשָּׁר֑וֹן הֵ֛מָּה יִרְא֥וּ כְבוֹד־יְהֹוָ֖ה הֲדַ֥ר אֱלֹהֵֽינוּ:   חַזְּק֖וּ יָדַ֣יִם ג

רָפ֑וֹת וּבִרְכַּ֥יִם כֹּשְׁל֖וֹת אַמֵּֽצוּ: אִמְרוּ֙ לְנִמְהֲרֵי־לֵ֔ב חִזְק֖וּ אַל־תִּירָ֑אוּ הִנֵּ֤ה ד

אֱלֹֽהֵיכֶם֙ נָקָ֣ם יָב֔וֹא גְּמ֖וּל אֱלֹהִ֑ים ה֥וּא יָב֖וֹא וְיֹֽשַׁעֲכֶֽם: אָ֥ז תִּפָּקַ֖חְנָה עֵינֵ֣י ה

עִוְרִ֑ים וְאׇזְנֵ֥י חֵֽרְשִׁ֖ים תִּפָּתַֽחְנָה: אָ֣ז יְדַלֵּ֤ג כָּֽאַיָּל֙ פִּסֵּ֔חַ וְתָרֹ֖ן לְשׁ֣וֹן אִלֵּ֑ם כִּֽי־ ו

נִבְקְע֤וּ בַמִּדְבָּר֙ מַ֔יִם וּנְחָלִ֖ים בָּֽעֲרָבָֽה: וְהָיָ֤ה הַשָּׁרָב֙ לַֽאֲגַ֔ם וְצִמָּא֖וֹן לְמַבּ֣וּעֵי ז

מָ֑יִם בִּנְוֵ֤ה תַנִּים֙ רִבְצָ֔הּ חָצִ֖יר לְקָנֶ֥ה וָגֹֽמֶא: וְהָֽיָה־שָׁ֞ם מַסְל֣וּל וָדֶ֗רֶךְ וְדֶ֣רֶךְ ח

הַקֹּ֘דֶשׁ֮ יִקָּ֣רֵא לָהּ֒ לֹֽא־יַעַבְרֶ֣נּוּ טָמֵ֔א וְהוּא־לָ֑מוֹ הֹלֵ֥ךְ דֶּ֛רֶךְ וֶאֱוִילִ֖ים לֹ֥א

יִתְעֽוּ: לֹא־יִֽהְיֶ֨ה שָׁ֜ם אַרְיֵ֗ה וּפְרִ֤יץ חַיּוֹת֙ בַּֽל־יַ֣עֲלֶ֔נָּה לֹ֥א תִמָּצֵ֖א שָׁ֑ם וְהָֽלְכ֖וּ ט

גְּאוּלִֽים: וּפְדוּיֵ֨י יְהֹוָ֜ה יְשֻׁב֗וּן וּבָ֤אוּ צִיּוֹן֙ בְּרִנָּ֔ה וְשִׂמְחַ֥ת עוֹלָ֖ם עַל־רֹאשָׁ֑ם י

שָׂשׂ֤וֹן וְשִׂמְחָה֙ יַשִּׂ֔יגוּ וְנָ֖סוּ יָג֥וֹן וַֽאֲנָחָֽה:

וַיְהִ֡י בְּאַרְבַּע֩ עֶשְׂרֵ֨ה שָׁנָ֜ה לַמֶּ֣לֶךְ חִזְקִיָּ֗הוּ עָלָ֞ה סַנְחֵרִ֤יב מֶֽלֶךְ־אַשּׁוּר֙ עַל א לו

כׇּל־עָרֵ֧י יְהוּדָ֛ה הַבְּצֻר֖וֹת וַֽיִּתְפְּשֵֽׂם: וַיִּשְׁלַ֣ח מֶֽלֶךְ־אַשּׁ֣וּר ׀ אֶת־רַב־שָׁקֵ֨ה ב

מִלָּכִ֥ישׁ יְרֽוּשָׁלַ֛͏ְמָה אֶל־הַמֶּ֥לֶךְ חִזְקִיָּ֖הוּ בְּחֵ֣יל כָּבֵ֑ד וַֽיַּעֲמֹ֗ד בִּתְעָלַת֙ הַבְּרֵכָ֣ה

הָעֶלְיוֹנָ֔ה בִּמְסִלַּ֖ת שְׂדֵ֥ה כוֹבֵֽס: וַיֵּצֵ֥א אֵלָ֛יו אֶלְיָקִ֥ים בֶּן־חִלְקִיָּ֖הוּ אֲשֶׁ֣ר עַל־ ג

הַבָּ֑יִת וְשֶׁבְנָא֙ הַסֹּפֵ֔ר וְיוֹאָ֥ח בֶּן־אָסָ֖ף הַמַּזְכִּֽיר: וַיֹּ֤אמֶר אֲלֵיהֶם֙ רַב־שָׁקֵ֔ה ד

אִמְרוּ־נָ֖א אֶל־חִזְקִיָּ֑הוּ כֹּֽה־אָמַ֞ר הַמֶּ֣לֶךְ הַגָּד֗וֹל מֶ֚לֶךְ אַשּׁ֔וּר מָ֧ה הַבִּטָּח֛וֹן

הַזֶּ֖ה אֲשֶׁ֥ר בָּטָֽחְתָּ: אָמַ֙רְתִּי֙ אַךְ־דְּבַר־שְׂפָתַ֔יִם עֵצָ֥ה וּגְבוּרָ֖ה לַמִּלְחָמָ֑ה ה

עַתָּה֙ עַל־מִ֣י בָטַ֔חְתָּ כִּ֥י מָרַ֖דְתָּ בִּֽי: הִנֵּ֣ה בָטַ֡חְתָּ עַל־מִשְׁעֶ֩נֶת֩ הַקָּנֶ֨ה הָֽרָצ֜וּץ ו

הַזֶּה֙ עַל־מִצְרַ֔יִם אֲשֶׁ֨ר יִסָּמֵ֥ךְ אִישׁ֙ עָלָ֔יו וּבָ֥א בְכַפּ֖וֹ וּנְקָבָ֑הּ כֵּ֚ן פַּרְעֹ֣ה מֶֽלֶךְ־

מִצְרַ֔יִם לְכׇל־הַבֹּֽטְחִ֖ים עָלָֽיו: וְכִֽי־תֹאמַ֣ר אֵלַ֔י אֶל־יְהֹוָ֥ה אֱלֹהֵ֖ינוּ בָּטָ֑חְנוּ ז

הֲלוֹא־ה֗וּא אֲשֶׁ֨ר הֵסִ֤יר חִזְקִיָּ֨הוּ֙ אֶת־בָּמֹתָ֣יו וְאֶת־מִזְבְּחֹתָ֔יו וַיֹּ֤אמֶר

לִֽיהוּדָה֙ וְלִיר֣וּשָׁלַ֔͏ִם לִפְנֵ֞י הַמִּזְבֵּ֧חַ הַזֶּ֛ה תִּֽשְׁתַּחֲוֽוּ: וְעַתָּה֙ הִתְעָ֣רֶב נָ֔א אֶת־ ח

אֲדֹנִ֖י הַמֶּ֣לֶךְ אַשּׁ֑וּר וְאֶתְּנָ֤ה לְךָ֙ אַלְפַּ֣יִם סוּסִ֔ים אִם־תּוּכַ֕ל לָ֥תֶת לְךָ֖ רֹֽכְבִ֥ים

עֲלֵיהֶֽם: וְאֵ֣יךְ תָּשִׁ֗יב אֵ֠ת פְּנֵ֨י פַחַ֥ת אַחַ֛ד עַבְדֵ֥י אֲדֹנִ֖י הַקְּטַנִּ֑ים וַתִּבְטַ֤ח לְךָ֙ ט

עַל־מִצְרַ֔יִם לְרֶ֖כֶב וּלְפָֽרָשִֽׁים: וְעַתָּ֗ה הֲמִבַּלְעֲדֵ֤י יְהֹוָה֙ עָלִ֖יתִי עַל־הָאָ֥רֶץ י

הַזֹּ֖את לְהַשְׁחִיתָ֑הּ יְהֹוָה֙ אָמַ֣ר אֵלַ֔י עֲלֵ֛ה אֶל־הָאָ֥רֶץ הַזֹּ֖את וְהַשְׁחִיתָֽהּ:

34:16. I.e., this book of prophecies. All the creatures mentioned above will prowl in the destroyed city (*Radak*).

35:1. Having concluded the prophecy of Edom's downfall, Isaiah turns to the Land of Israel. It had been desolate and forsaken, but now it will rejoice over Edom's fate as a precursor of its own rejuvenation (*Rashi*).

35:3. Isaiah urges faithful Jews to encourage one another's faith that salvation will come.

35:8. The road will be for the use of Israel (*Radak; Kara*), or for the lame and mute mentioned in vv. 5-6 (*Rashi*).

¹⁶ *Search in the Book of HASHEM* * and read it — not one of them is lacking; not one is missing its fellow. For My mouth has commanded it and its spirit has gathered them together.* ¹⁷ *He has cast lots for them, and His hand has distributed [the land] for them with a [measuring] line; they will inherit it forever, they will dwell in it from generation to generation.*

35

The return to Jerusalem

¹ **T**he wilderness and the wasteland* will rejoice over them; the desert will be glad and blossom like a lily. ² It will blossom abundantly and will rejoice, with joyousness and glad song; the glory of Lebanon has been given to her, the majesty of the Carmel and the Sharon; they will see the glory of HASHEM, the majesty of our God.

³ *Strengthen* * weak hands and give support to failing knees.* ⁴ *Say to those of impatient heart, 'Be strong; do not fear. Behold, your God will come with revenge, with Divine retribution; He will come and save you.'* ⁵ *Then the eyes of the blind will be opened and the ears of the deaf will be unstopped.* ⁶ *Then the lame man will skip like a gazelle and the tongue of the mute will sing glad song; for water will have broken out in the wilderness, and streams in the desert.* ⁷ *The scorched place will become a pond and the parched place springs of water; the abode where jackals rested will become grassland with reeds and bulrushes.* ⁸ *There will be a path and a road there; it will be called 'The Road of Holiness,' and no impure person will traverse it. It will be for them;* * the wayfarer, even ignorant ones, will not go astray [there].* ⁹ *There will be no lion there; the boldest of animals will not ascend it, will not be found there; the redeemed will walk there.* ¹⁰ *Then the redeemed of HASHEM will return and come to Zion with glad song, with eternal gladness on their heads. They will attain joy and gladness, and sadness and sighing will flee.*

36

Assyria wants conquest

¹ **I**t happened in the fourteenth year of King Hezekiah that Sennacherib king of Assyria attacked all the fortified cities of Judah, and captured them. ² *The king of Assyria sent Rabshakeh from Lachish to Jerusalem, to King Hezekiah, with a great army. He stood at the channel of the upper pool, in the road of the launderer's field. ³ Eliakim son of Hilkiah, who was in charge of the palace, went out, with Shebna the scribe, and Joah son of Asaph the recorder.

Assyria's ultimatum
. . .

⁴ Rabshakeh said to them, "Say now to Hezekiah: Thus said the great king, the king of Assyria: What is this confidence of which you are so confident? ⁵ I say [that you have spoken] but [idle] word of the lips, [claiming that you had] strategy and power for battle! Now — upon whom have you placed your trust, that you have rebelled against me? ⁶ Behold! You have relied upon the support of this splintered cane, upon Egypt, which, if a man leans on it, it will enter his palm and puncture it; so is Pharaoh king of Egypt to all who rely on him. ⁷ And if you will tell me, 'We trust in HASHEM our God' — is He not the One Whose high places and altars Hezekiah has removed; and he said to Judah and Jerusalem, '[Only] before this Altar may you prostrate yourselves'? ⁸ So now, provide a security guarantee to my master the king of Assyria, and I will give you two thousand horses — if you can put riders on them! ⁹ How dare you turn away even a single minor captain from among the servants of my master, and depend on Egypt for chariots and horsemen! ¹⁰ And now, is it without [the consent of] HASHEM that I have come up to this land to destroy it? HASHEM told me, 'Go up against this land and destroy it!' "

This way to Zion will be accessible to all deserving people, even to those who are unfamiliar with it.

36:2. With minor differences, 36:1-38:8 is a restatement of *II Kings* 18:13-20:9. See commentary there.

יא וַיֹּ֣אמֶר אֶלְיָקִ֣ים וְשֶׁבְנָ֣א וְיוֹאָ֡ח אֶל־רַב־שָׁקֵה֩ דַּבֶּר־נָ֨א אֶל־עֲבָדֶ֜יךָ אֲרָמִ֗ית
כִּ֤י שֹׁמְעִים֙ אֲנָ֔חְנוּ וְאַל־תְּדַבֵּ֥ר אֵלֵ֛ינוּ יְהוּדִ֖ית בְּאָזְנֵ֣י הָעָ֑ם אֲשֶׁ֖ר עַל־
יב הַחוֹמָֽה: וַיֹּ֣אמֶר רַב־שָׁקֵ֗ה הַאֶ֨ל אֲדֹנֶ֤יךָ וְאֵלֶ֙יךָ֙ שְׁלָחַ֣נִי אֲדֹנִ֔י לְדַבֵּ֖ר אֶת־
הַדְּבָרִ֣ים הָאֵ֑לֶּה הֲלֹ֣א עַל־הָאֲנָשִׁ֗ים הַיֹּֽשְׁבִים֙ עַל־הַ֣חוֹמָ֔ה לֶאֱכֹ֣ל אֶת־
°חֳרֵיהֶ֛ם [°צוֹאָתָ֛ם ק] וְלִשְׁתּ֥וֹת אֶת־°שֵׁינֵיהֶ֖ם [°מֵימֵ֥י רַגְלֵיהֶ֖ם ק]
יג עִמָּכֶֽם: וַיַּֽעֲמֹד֙ רַב־שָׁקֵ֔ה וַיִּקְרָ֥א בְקוֹל־גָּד֖וֹל יְהוּדִ֑ית וַיֹּ֕אמֶר שִׁמְע֖וּ אֶת־
יד דִּבְרֵ֥י הַמֶּ֖לֶךְ הַגָּד֣וֹל מֶ֣לֶךְ אַשּֽׁוּר: כֹּ֚ה אָמַ֣ר הַמֶּ֔לֶךְ אַל־יַשִּׁ֥א לָכֶ֖ם חִזְקִיָּ֑הוּ
טו כִּ֥י לֹֽא־יוּכַ֖ל לְהַצִּ֥יל אֶתְכֶֽם: וְאַל־יַבְטַ֨ח אֶתְכֶ֤ם חִזְקִיָּ֙הוּ֙ אֶל־יְהוָ֣ה לֵאמֹ֔ר
טז הַצֵּ֥ל יַצִּילֵ֖נוּ יְהוָ֑ה לֹ֤א תִנָּתֵן֙ הָעִ֣יר הַזֹּ֔את בְּיַ֖ד מֶ֥לֶךְ אַשּֽׁוּר: אַֽל־תִּשְׁמְע֖וּ אֶל־
חִזְקִיָּ֑הוּ כִּי֩ כֹ֨ה אָמַ֜ר הַמֶּ֣לֶךְ אַשּׁ֗וּר עֲשֽׂוּ־אִתִּ֤י בְרָכָה֙ וּצְא֣וּ אֵלַ֔י וְאִכְל֤וּ אִישׁ־
יז גַּפְנוֹ֙ וְאִ֣ישׁ תְּאֵֽנָת֔וֹ וּשְׁת֖וּ אִ֣ישׁ מֵֽי־בוֹר֑וֹ: עַד־בֹּאִ֕י וְלָקַחְתִּ֥י אֶתְכֶ֖ם אֶל־אֶ֑רֶץ
יח כְּאַרְצְכֶ֔ם אֶ֤רֶץ דָּגָן֙ וְתִיר֔וֹשׁ אֶ֥רֶץ לֶ֖חֶם וּכְרָמִֽים: פֶּן־יַסִּ֨ית אֶתְכֶ֤ם חִזְקִיָּ֙הוּ֙
לֵאמֹ֔ר יְהוָ֖ה יַצִּילֵ֑נוּ הַהִצִּ֜ילוּ אֱלֹהֵ֤י הַגּוֹיִם֙ אִ֣ישׁ אֶת־אַרְצ֔וֹ מִיַּ֖ד מֶ֥לֶךְ אַשּֽׁוּר:
יט אַיֵּ֞ה אֱלֹהֵ֤י חֲמָת֙ וְאַרְפָּ֔ד אַיֵּ֖ה אֱלֹהֵ֣י סְפַרְוָ֑יִם וְכִֽי־הִצִּ֥ילוּ אֶת־שֹׁמְר֖וֹן מִיָּדִֽי:
כ מִ֗י בְּכָל־אֱלֹהֵ֤י הָֽאֲרָצוֹת֙ הָאֵ֔לֶּה אֲשֶׁר־הִצִּ֥ילוּ אֶת־אַרְצָ֖ם מִיָּדִ֑י כִּֽי־יַצִּ֥יל
כא יְהוָ֖ה אֶת־יְרֽוּשָׁלַ֥͏ִם מִיָּדִֽי: וַֽיַּחֲרִ֔ישׁוּ וְלֹֽא־עָנ֥וּ אֹת֖וֹ דָּבָ֑ר כִּֽי־מִצְוַ֨ת הַמֶּ֧לֶךְ
כב הִ֛יא לֵאמֹ֖ר לֹ֥א תַעֲנֻֽהוּ: וַיָּבֹ֣א אֶלְיָקִ֣ים בֶּן־חִלְקִיָּ֣הוּ אֲשֶׁר־עַל־הַבַּ֡יִת
וְשֶׁבְנָ֣א הַסּוֹפֵר֩ וְיוֹאָ֨ח בֶּן־אָסָ֜ף הַמַּזְכִּ֗יר אֶל־חִזְקִיָּ֛הוּ קְרוּעֵ֥י בְגָדִ֖ים וַיַּגִּ֥ידוּ

לז א ל֖וֹ אֵ֥ת דִּבְרֵ֥י רַב־שָׁקֵֽה:　וַיְהִ֗י כִּשְׁמֹ֙עַ֙ הַמֶּ֣לֶךְ חִזְקִיָּ֔הוּ וַיִּקְרַ֖ע אֶת־
ב בְּגָדָ֑יו וַיִּתְכַּ֣ס בַּשָּׂ֔ק וַיָּבֹ֖א בֵּ֥ית יְהוָֽה: וַ֠יִּשְׁלַח אֶת־אֶלְיָקִ֨ים אֲשֶׁר־עַל־הַבַּ֜יִת
וְאֵ֣ת ׀ שֶׁבְנָ֣א הַסּוֹפֵ֗ר וְאֵת֙ זִקְנֵ֣י הַכֹּהֲנִ֔ים מִתְכַּסִּ֖ים בַּשַּׂקִּ֑ים אֶל־יְשַֽׁעְיָ֥הוּ בֶן־
ג אָמ֖וֹץ הַנָּבִֽיא: וַיֹּאמְר֣וּ אֵלָ֗יו כֹּ֚ה אָמַ֣ר חִזְקִיָּ֔הוּ יוֹם־צָרָ֧ה וְתוֹכֵחָ֛ה וּנְאָצָ֖ה
ד הַיּ֣וֹם הַזֶּ֑ה כִּ֣י בָ֤אוּ בָנִים֙ עַד־מַשְׁבֵּ֔ר וְכֹ֥חַ אַ֖יִן לְלֵדָֽה: אוּלַ֡י יִשְׁמַע֩ יְהוָ֨ה
אֱלֹהֶ֜יךָ אֵ֣ת ׀ דִּבְרֵ֣י רַב־שָׁקֵ֗ה אֲשֶׁר֩ שְׁלָח֨וֹ מֶֽלֶךְ־אַשּׁ֤וּר ׀ אֲדֹנָיו֙ לְחָרֵף֙
אֱלֹהִ֣ים חַ֔י וְהוֹכִ֙יחַ֙ בַּדְּבָרִ֔ים אֲשֶׁ֥ר שָׁמַ֖ע יְהוָ֣ה אֱלֹהֶ֑יךָ וְנָשָׂ֣אתָ תְפִלָּ֔ה בְּעַ֥ד
ה הַשְּׁאֵרִ֖ית הַנִּמְצָאָֽה: וַיָּבֹ֗אוּ עַבְדֵ֛י הַמֶּ֥לֶךְ חִזְקִיָּ֖הוּ אֶל־יְשַֽׁעְיָֽהוּ: וַיֹּ֤אמֶר
ו אֲלֵיהֶם֙ יְשַֽׁעְיָ֔הוּ כֹּ֥ה תֹאמְר֖וּן אֶל־אֲדֹֽנֵיכֶ֑ם כֹּ֣ה ׀ אָמַ֣ר יְהוָ֗ה אַל־תִּירָא֙
ז מִפְּנֵ֤י הַדְּבָרִים֙ אֲשֶׁ֣ר שָׁמַ֔עְתָּ אֲשֶׁ֧ר גִּדְּפ֛וּ נַעֲרֵ֥י מֶֽלֶךְ־אַשּׁ֖וּר אוֹתִֽי: הִנְנִ֨י נוֹתֵ֥ן
ח בּ֣וֹ ר֗וּחַ וְשָׁמַ֤ע שְׁמוּעָה֙ וְשָׁ֣ב אֶל־אַרְצ֔וֹ וְהִפַּלְתִּ֥יו בַּחֶ֖רֶב בְּאַרְצֽוֹ: וַיָּ֙שָׁב֙ רַב־
שָׁקֵ֔ה וַיִּמְצָא֙ אֶת־מֶ֣לֶךְ אַשּׁ֔וּר נִלְחָ֖ם עַל־לִבְנָ֑ה כִּ֣י שָׁמַ֔ע כִּ֥י נָסַ֖ע מִלָּכִֽישׁ:
ט וַיִּשְׁמַ֗ע עַל־תִּרְהָ֤קָה מֶֽלֶךְ־כּוּשׁ֙ לֵאמֹ֔ר יָצָ֖א לְהִלָּחֵ֣ם אִתָּ֑ךְ וַיִּשְׁמַע֙ וַיִּשְׁלַ֣ח
י מַלְאָכִ֔ים אֶל־חִזְקִיָּ֖הוּ לֵאמֹֽר: כֹּ֣ה תֹאמְר֗וּן אֶל־חִזְקִיָּ֤הוּ מֶֽלֶךְ־יְהוּדָה֙ לֵאמֹ֔ר
אַל־יַשִּׁאֲךָ֣ אֱלֹהֶ֔יךָ אֲשֶׁ֥ר אַתָּ֖ה בּוֹטֵ֣חַ בּ֑וֹ לֵאמֹ֔ר לֹ֤א תִנָּתֵן֙ יְר֣וּשָׁלַ֔͏ִם בְּיַ֖ד

37:3. Referring to Rabshakeh's rebuke of Hezekiah for betraying Assyria. Alternatively, this dreadful situation is God's rebuke to us because of our sins *(Radak)*.

[11] *Eliakim as well as Shebna and Joah, then said to Rabshakeh, "Please speak to your servants in Aramaic, for we understand it, and do not speak Hebrew with us within earshot of the people on the wall."*

[12] *But Rabshakeh said, "Is it to your master and to you that my master has sent me to speak these words? Is it not to the people sitting on the wall, who will eat their own excrement and drink their own urine with you?"*

[13] *Rabshakeh then stood up and called out in a loud voice in Hebrew; he said,*

... is intended to terrorize the people

[13] *"Hear the words of the great king, the king of Assyria!* [14] *Thus said the king: Let not Hezekiah delude you, for he cannot save you!* [15] *And let not Hezekiah reassure you with HASHEM, saying, 'HASHEM will surely save us, and this city shall not be delivered into the hand of the king of Assyria!'* [16] *Do not listen to Hezekiah, for thus said the king of Assyria: Make peace with me and come out to me, and each man will be able to eat [the fruits of] his grapevine and each man [the fruits of] his fig tree, and each man will drink the water of his well,* [17] *until I come and I bring you to a land like your land — a land of grain and wine, a land of bread and vineyards —* [18] *lest Hezekiah tries to entice you, saying, 'HASHEM will save us!' Did the gods of the nations save any person in his land from the hand of the king of Assyria?* [19] *Where are the gods of Hamath and Arpad? Where are the gods of Sepharvaim? Did they save Samaria from my hand?* [20] *Which among all the gods of the lands saved their land from my hand, that HASHEM should save Jerusalem from my hand?"*

Grief-stricken report to Hezekiah

[21] *The people remained silent and did not answer him a word, for there was a command from the king, saying, "Do not answer him."* [22] *Eliakim son of Hilkiah, who was in charge of the palace, came, as well as Shebna the scribe and Joah son of Asaph the recorder, to Hezekiah with rent garments, and told him the words of Rabshakeh.*

37

A distressed Hezekiah asks Isaiah to pray

[1] *It happened when King Hezekiah heard this: He rent his garments; he donned sackcloth and went to the Temple of HASHEM.* [2] *He sent Eliakim, who was in charge of the palace, and Shebna the scribe and the elders of the Kohanim, all dressed in sackcloth, to Isaiah son of Amoz, the prophet.* [3] *They said to him, "Thus said Hezekiah: Today is a day of distress, rebuke, and sacrilege.* [We are like] babies who have entered the birth canal, but [the mother] has no strength to give birth.* [4] *If only HASHEM, your God, will hear all the words of Rabshakeh, whom the king of Assyria, his master, sent to insult the living God, and He will punish him for those words that HASHEM your God heard. And may you offer a prayer for the remnant [of the people] that is still here!"*

Isaiah promises victory

[5] *King Hezekiah's servants came to Isaiah,* [6] *and Isaiah said to them, "Thus shall you say to your master: Thus said HASHEM: Do not be frightened by the words that you have heard, by which the attendants of the king of Assyria have blasphemed Me.* [7] *Behold, I am instilling a desire within him. He will hear a report and return to his land, and I will strike him down by the sword in his own land."**

Sennacherib withdraws to fight a war ...

... but sends an abusive threat

[8] *Rabshakeh went back and found the king of Assyria fighting against Libnah, because [Rabshakeh] had heard that he had journeyed from Lachish.* [9] *Then [Sennacherib] heard a report about Tirhakah, the king of Cush saying, "He has gone out to do battle against you."*

But he heard and he sent messengers to Hezekiah, saying, [10] *"Thus shall you speak unto Hezekiah king of Judah, saying: Do not let your God, in Whom you trust, persuade you, saying, 'Jerusalem will not be delivered into the hand of*

We must act swiftly and decisively, for even a short delay is certain to have tragic consequences.

37:7. For the sequence of events, see *II Kings* Ch. 19. Sennacherib heard that King Tirhakah of Cush was

יא מֶ֣לֶךְ אַשּׁ֑וּר הִנֵּ֣ה ׀ אַתָּ֣ה שָׁמַ֗עְתָּ אֲשֶׁ֨ר עָשׂ֜וּ מַלְכֵ֥י אַשּׁ֛וּר לְכָל־הָאֲרָצ֖וֹת

יב לְהַֽחֲרִימָ֑ם וְאַתָּ֖ה תִּנָּצֵֽל: הַהִצִּ֨ילוּ אוֹתָ֜ם אֱלֹהֵ֣י הַגּוֹיִ֗ם אֲשֶׁ֣ר הִשְׁחִ֣יתוּ

יג אֲבוֹתַ֔י אֶת־גּוֹזָ֖ן וְאֶת־חָרָ֑ן וְרֶ֥צֶף וּבְנֵי־עֶ֖דֶן אֲשֶׁ֥ר בִּתְלַשָּֽׂר: אַיֵּ֤ה מֶֽלֶךְ־

יד חֲמָ֔ת וּמֶ֖לֶךְ אַרְפָּ֑ד וּמֶ֖לֶךְ לָעִ֥יר סְפַרְוַ֖יִם הֵנַ֥ע וְעִוָּֽה: וַיִּקַּ֨ח חִזְקִיָּ֤הוּ אֶת־

הַסְּפָרִ֛ים מִיַּ֥ד הַמַּלְאָכִ֖ים וַיִּקְרָאֵ֑הוּ וַיַּ֙עַל֙ בֵּ֣ית יְהֹוָ֔ה וַיִּפְרְשֵׂ֥הוּ חִזְקִיָּ֖הוּ לִפְנֵ֥י

טו-טז יְהֹוָֽה: וַיִּתְפַּלֵּ֣ל חִזְקִיָּ֔הוּ אֶל־יְהֹוָ֖ה לֵאמֹֽר: יְהֹוָ֨ה צְבָא֜וֹת אֱלֹהֵ֣י יִשְׂרָאֵ֗ל יֹשֵׁ֣ב

הַכְּרֻבִ֔ים אַתָּה־ה֤וּא הָֽאֱלֹהִים֙ לְבַדְּךָ֔ לְכֹ֖ל מַמְלְכ֣וֹת הָאָ֑רֶץ אַתָּ֣ה עָשִׂ֔יתָ

יז אֶת־הַשָּׁמַ֖יִם וְאֶת־הָאָֽרֶץ: הַטֵּ֣ה יְהֹוָ֤ה ׀ אָזְנְךָ֙ וּֽשֲׁמָ֔ע פְּקַ֧ח יְהֹוָ֛ה עֵינֶ֖ךָ וּרְאֵ֑ה

יח וּשְׁמַ֗ע אֵ֣ת כָּל־דִּבְרֵ֣י סַנְחֵרִ֔יב אֲשֶׁ֣ר שָׁלַ֔ח לְחָרֵ֖ף אֱלֹהִ֥ים חָֽי: אָמְנָ֖ם יְהֹוָ֑ה

יט הֶחֱרִ֜יבוּ מַלְכֵ֥י אַשּׁ֛וּר אֶת־כָּל־הָאֲרָצ֖וֹת וְאֶת־אַרְצָֽם: וְנָתֹ֥ן אֶת־אֱלֹֽהֵיהֶ֖ם

בָּאֵ֑שׁ כִּ֣י לֹ֤א אֱלֹהִים֙ הֵ֔מָּה כִּ֣י אִם־מַֽעֲשֵׂ֧ה יְדֵֽי־אָדָ֛ם עֵ֥ץ וָאֶ֖בֶן וַֽיְאַבְּדֽוּם:

כ וְעַתָּה֙ יְהֹוָ֣ה אֱלֹהֵ֔ינוּ הֽוֹשִׁיעֵ֖נוּ מִיָּד֑וֹ וְיֵֽדְעוּ֙ כָּל־מַמְלְכ֣וֹת הָאָ֔רֶץ כִּֽי־אַתָּ֥ה

כא יְהֹוָ֖ה לְבַדֶּֽךָ: וַיִּשְׁלַח֙ יְשַֽׁעְיָ֣הוּ בֶן־אָמ֔וֹץ אֶל־חִזְקִיָּ֖הוּ לֵאמֹ֑ר כֹּֽה־אָמַ֥ר יְהֹוָ֖ה

כב אֱלֹהֵ֣י יִשְׂרָאֵ֔ל אֲשֶׁ֥ר הִתְפַּלַּ֖לְתָּ אֵלַ֑י אֶל־סַנְחֵרִ֖יב מֶ֥לֶךְ אַשּֽׁוּר: זֶ֣ה הַדָּבָ֔ר

אֲשֶׁר־דִּבֶּ֥ר יְהֹוָ֖ה עָלָ֑יו בָּזָ֨ה לְךָ֜ לָֽעֲגָ֤ה לְךָ֙ בְּתוּלַת֙ בַּת־צִיּ֔וֹן אַֽחֲרֶ֙יךָ֙ רֹ֣אשׁ

כג הֵנִ֔יעָה בַּ֖ת יְרֽוּשָׁלָֽ͏ִם: אֶת־מִ֤י חֵרַ֙פְתָּ֙ וְגִדַּ֔פְתָּ וְעַל־מִ֖י הֲרִימ֣וֹתָה קּ֑וֹל וַתִּשָּׂ֥א

כד מָר֛וֹם עֵינֶ֖יךָ אֶל־קְד֥וֹשׁ יִשְׂרָאֵֽל: בְּיַ֣ד עֲבָדֶ֘יךָ֘ חֵרַ֣פְתָּ ׀ אֲדֹנָי֒ וַתֹּ֗אמֶר בְּרֹ֥ב

רִכְבִּ֛י אֲנִ֥י עָלִ֛יתִי מְר֥וֹם הָרִ֖ים יַרְכְּתֵ֣י לְבָנ֑וֹן וְאֶכְרֹ֞ת קוֹמַ֤ת אֲרָזָיו֙ מִבְחַ֣ר

כה בְּרֹשָׁ֔יו וְאָבוֹא֙ מְר֣וֹם קִצּ֔וֹ יַ֖עַר כַּרְמִלּֽוֹ: אֲנִ֥י קַ֖רְתִּי וְשָׁתִ֣יתִי מָ֑יִם וְאַחְרִב֙

כו בְּכַף־פְּעָמַ֔י כֹּ֖ל יְאֹרֵ֥י מָצֽוֹר: הֲלֽוֹא־שָׁמַ֤עְתָּ לְמֵֽרָחוֹק֙ אוֹתָ֣הּ עָשִׂ֔יתִי מִ֤ימֵי

קֶ֙דֶם֙ וִֽיצַרְתִּ֔יהָ עַתָּ֣ה הֲבֵאתִ֑יהָ וּתְהִ֗י לְהַשְׁא֛וֹת גַּלִּ֥ים נִצִּ֖ים עָרִ֥ים בְּצֻרֽוֹת:

כז וְיֹֽשְׁבֵיהֶן֙ קִצְרֵי־יָ֔ד חַ֖תּוּ וָבֹ֑שׁוּ הָי֞וּ עֵ֤שֶׂב שָׂדֶה֙ וִ֣ירַק דֶּ֔שֶׁא חֲצִ֣יר גַּגּ֔וֹת

כח-כט וּשְׁדֵמָ֖ה לִפְנֵ֥י קָמָֽה: וְשִׁבְתְּךָ֛ וְצֵֽאתְךָ֥ וּבֽוֹאֲךָ֖ יָדָ֑עְתִּי וְאֵ֖ת הִֽתְרַגֶּזְךָ֥ אֵלָֽי: יַ֚עַן

הִֽתְרַגֶּזְךָ֣ אֵלַ֔י וְשַֽׁאֲנַנְךָ֖ עָלָ֣ה בְאָזְנָ֑י וְשַׂמְתִּ֨י חַחִ֜י בְּאַפֶּ֗ךָ וּמִתְגִּי֙ בִּשְׂפָתֶ֔יךָ

ל וַֽהֲשִֽׁיבֹתִ֔יךָ בַּדֶּ֖רֶךְ אֲשֶׁר־בָּ֥אתָ בָּֽהּ: וְזֶה־לְּךָ֣ הָא֔וֹת אָכ֤וֹל הַשָּׁנָה֙ סָפִ֔יחַ

וּבַשָּׁנָ֥ה הַשֵּׁנִ֖ית שָׁחִ֑יס וּבַשָּׁנָ֣ה הַשְּׁלִישִׁ֗ית זִרְע֧וּ וְקִצְר֛וּ וְנִטְע֥וּ כְרָמִ֖ים

לא °וְאָכ֣וֹל [וְאִכְל֨וּ ק] פִּרְיָֽם: וְיָ֨סְפָ֜ה פְּלֵיטַ֧ת בֵּֽית־יְהוּדָ֛ה הַנִּשְׁאָרָ֖ה שֹׁ֑רֶשׁ

לב לְמָ֑טָּה וְעָשָׂ֥ה פְרִ֖י לְמָֽעְלָה: כִּ֤י מִירֽוּשָׁלִַ֙ם֙ תֵּצֵ֣א שְׁאֵרִ֔ית וּפְלֵיטָ֖ה מֵהַ֣ר צִיּ֑וֹן

לג קִנְאַ֛ת יְהֹוָ֥ה צְבָא֖וֹת תַּֽעֲשֶׂה־זֹּֽאת:

---

attacking Assyria, so he went to defend Assyria, after
which he returned to his siege of Jerusalem. After the miracle that saved Jerusalem, Sennacherib returned to his
land, where he was killed.

37:16. Hezekiah refutes Sennacherib; Hashem is not the
God of only Israel.

37:24. I.e., having conquered the rest of Judah, I will now
take the ultimate prize — Jerusalem and the Holy Temple.

37:25. I.e., my armies and their animals are so vast that
they have depleted the known water sources of the countries they have invaded.

37:26. God says that Sennacherib's remarkable victories
were not his own doing. It was Divinely ordained that he
destroy the fortified cities of sinful nations, leaving them
as deserted heaps of debris, from which vegetation would
eventually grow (Rashi).

37:30. God now addresses Hezekiah saying that the

the king of Assyria.' [11] Behold, you have heard what the kings of Assyria have done to all the lands, laying them waste; will you be spared? [12] Did the gods of the nations rescue those whom my fathers destroyed — Gozan, Haran, Rezeph, and people of Eden who are in Telassar? [13] Where is the king of Hamath or the king of Arpad or the king of the city of Sepharvaim, or [of] Hena, or [of] Ivvah?"

Hezekiah sends the letters to Isaiah [14] Hezekiah took the letters from the hand of the messengers and read each [of them], and he went up to the Temple of HASHEM, and Hezekiah spread out each [of them] before HASHEM. [15] Hezekiah then prayed before HASHEM, and said, [16] "HASHEM, Master of Legions, God of Israel, Who dwells atop the Cherubim: You alone are God of all the kingdoms of the world;* You made heaven and earth. [17] Incline Your ear, HASHEM, and hear; open Your eyes, HASHEM, and see! Hear all the words of Sennacherib that he has sent to insult the living God! [18] Indeed, HASHEM, the kings of Assyria have destroyed all the countries and their land, [19] and placed their gods into the fire — for they are not gods, but the work of man's hands, wood and stone — so they destroyed them. [20] So now, HASHEM, our God, save us from his hand, then all the kingdoms of the world shall know that You alone are HASHEM."

Isaiah's encouraging prophecy . . . [21] Isaiah son of Amoz sent [word] to Hezekiah saying, "Thus said HASHEM, God of Israel: [Regarding] what you prayed to Me concerning Sennacherib king of Assyria, [22] this is the word that HASHEM has spoken about him:

The maiden daughter of Zion — she scorns you, she mocks you;
    the daughter of Jerusalem — she shakes her head at you.
[23] Whom have you insulted and blasphemed;
    against Whom have you raised a voice, and lifted your eyes on high?
    Against the Holy One of Israel!
[24] By the hand of your servants you have insulted my Lord, and said,
    'With my multitude of chariots I climbed the highest mountains,
    [to] the ends of the Lebanon [forest];
    I shall cut down its tallest cedars, its choicest cypresses,
    and I shall enter His ultimate height, the forest of His fruitful field. *
[25] I dug and drank waters,
    for the soles of my feet dried up all the rivers of the besieged area.'*
[26] Have you not heard from the distant [past that] I have done it?
    From earliest days [that] I have formed it?
    Now I have brought it about,
    to raze [into] desolate heaps [your] fortified cities.*
[27] Their inhabitants were short of power, crushed and ashamed;
    they were [like] herbage of the field and grassy vegetation,
    like grass on rooftops, like stalks wind-blasted, before standing [full].
. . . about Hezekiah's success . . . [28] Your sitting [in counsel], your going forth, and your coming in —
    I know [them]; and [also] your provocation against Me.
[29] Because you provoked Me, and your arrogance has risen unto My ears,
    I shall place My hook into your nose and My bridle into your lips,
    and I shall make you return by the route on which you came.
. . . and Sennacherib's downfall [30] And this shall be the sign for you: You will eat this year of the after-crop;* the second year fruits from tree stumps; and in the third year — sow and harvest, and plant vineyards and eat their fruits. [31] And the survivors that remained of the House of Judah shall take root below and produce fruit above. [32] For from Jerusalem shall emerge a remnant, and survivors from Mount Zion. The zeal of HASHEM, Master of Legions, shall do this!

כֹּה־אָמַר יְהוָה אֶל־מֶלֶךְ אַשּׁוּר לֹא יָבוֹא אֶל־הָעִיר הַזֹּאת וְלֹא־יוֹרֶה שָׁם

לד חֵץ וְלֹא־יְקַדְּמֶנָּה מָגֵן וְלֹא־יִשְׁפֹּךְ עָלֶיהָ סֹלְלָה: בַּדֶּרֶךְ אֲשֶׁר־בָּא בָּהּ יָשׁוּב

לה וְאֶל־הָעִיר הַזֹּאת לֹא יָבוֹא נְאֻם־יְהוָה: וְגַנּוֹתִי עַל־הָעִיר הַזֹּאת לְהוֹשִׁיעָהּ

לו לְמַעֲנִי וּלְמַעַן דָּוִד עַבְדִּי: וַיֵּצֵא | מַלְאַךְ יְהוָה וַיַּכֶּה בְּמַחֲנֵה

אַשּׁוּר מֵאָה וּשְׁמֹנִים וַחֲמִשָּׁה אָלֶף וַיַּשְׁכִּימוּ בַבֹּקֶר וְהִנֵּה כֻלָּם פְּגָרִים

לז-לח מֵתִים: וַיִּסַּע וַיֵּלֶךְ וַיָּשָׁב סַנְחֵרִיב מֶלֶךְ־אַשּׁוּר וַיֵּשֶׁב בְּנִינְוֵה: וַיְהִי הוּא

מִשְׁתַּחֲוֶה בֵּית | נִסְרֹךְ אֱלֹהָיו וְאַדְרַמֶּלֶךְ וְשַׂרְאֶצֶר בָּנָיו הִכֻּהוּ בַחֶרֶב

לח א וְהֵמָּה נִמְלְטוּ אֶרֶץ אֲרָרָט וַיִּמְלֹךְ אֵסַר־חַדֹּן בְּנוֹ תַּחְתָּיו: בַּיָּמִים

הָהֵם חָלָה חִזְקִיָּהוּ לָמוּת וַיָּבוֹא אֵלָיו יְשַׁעְיָהוּ בֶן־אָמוֹץ הַנָּבִיא וַיֹּאמֶר

ב אֵלָיו כֹּה־אָמַר יְהוָה צַו לְבֵיתֶךָ כִּי מֵת אַתָּה וְלֹא תִחְיֶה: וַיַּסֵּב חִזְקִיָּהוּ

ג פָּנָיו אֶל־הַקִּיר וַיִּתְפַּלֵּל אֶל־יְהוָה: וַיֹּאמַר אָנָּה יְהוָה זְכָר־נָא אֵת אֲשֶׁר

הִתְהַלַּכְתִּי לְפָנֶיךָ בֶּאֱמֶת וּבְלֵב שָׁלֵם וְהַטּוֹב בְּעֵינֶיךָ עָשִׂיתִי וַיֵּבְךְּ חִזְקִיָּהוּ

ד-ה בְּכִי גָדוֹל: וַיְהִי דְּבַר־יְהוָה אֶל־יְשַׁעְיָהוּ לֵאמֹר: הָלוֹךְ וְאָמַרְתָּ

אֶל־חִזְקִיָּהוּ כֹּה־אָמַר יְהוָה אֱלֹהֵי דָּוִד אָבִיךָ שָׁמַעְתִּי אֶת־תְּפִלָּתֶךָ רָאִיתִי

ו אֶת־דִּמְעָתֶךָ הִנְנִי יוֹסִף עַל־יָמֶיךָ חֲמֵשׁ עֶשְׂרֵה שָׁנָה: וּמִכַּף מֶלֶךְ־אַשּׁוּר

ז אַצִּילְךָ וְאֵת הָעִיר הַזֹּאת וְגַנּוֹתִי עַל־הָעִיר הַזֹּאת: וְזֶה־לְּךָ הָאוֹת מֵאֵת

ח יְהוָה אֲשֶׁר יַעֲשֶׂה יְהוָה אֶת־הַדָּבָר הַזֶּה אֲשֶׁר דִּבֵּר: הִנְנִי מֵשִׁיב אֶת־צֵל

הַמַּעֲלוֹת אֲשֶׁר יָרְדָה בְמַעֲלוֹת אָחָז בַּשֶּׁמֶשׁ אֲחֹרַנִּית עֶשֶׂר מַעֲלוֹת וַתָּשָׁב

ט הַשֶּׁמֶשׁ עֶשֶׂר מַעֲלוֹת בַּמַּעֲלוֹת אֲשֶׁר יָרָדָה: מִכְתָּב לְחִזְקִיָּהוּ

מֶלֶךְ־יְהוּדָה בַּחֲלֹתוֹ וַיְחִי מֵחָלְיוֹ: אֲנִי אָמַרְתִּי בִּדְמִי יָמַי אֵלֵכָה בְּשַׁעֲרֵי

י-יא שְׁאוֹל פֻּקַּדְתִּי יֶתֶר שְׁנוֹתָי: אָמַרְתִּי לֹא־אֶרְאֶה יָהּ יָהּ בְּאֶרֶץ הַחַיִּים לֹא־

יב אַבִּיט אָדָם עוֹד עִם־יוֹשְׁבֵי חָדֶל: דּוֹרִי נִסַּע וְנִגְלָה מִנִּי כְּאֹהֶל רֹעִי קִפַּדְתִּי

יג כָאֹרֵג חַיַּי מִדַּלָּה יְבַצְּעֵנִי מִיּוֹם עַד־לַיְלָה תַּשְׁלִימֵנִי: שִׁוִּיתִי עַד־בֹּקֶר

יד כָּאֲרִי כֵּן יְשַׁבֵּר כָּל־עַצְמוֹתָי מִיּוֹם עַד־לַיְלָה תַּשְׁלִימֵנִי: כְּסוּס עָגוּר כֵּן

אֲצַפְצֵף אֶהְגֶּה כַּיּוֹנָה דַּלּוּ עֵינַי לַמָּרוֹם אֲדֹנָי עָשְׁקָה־לִּי עָרְבֵנִי: מָה־אֲדַבֵּר

טז וְאָמַר־לִי וְהוּא עָשָׂה אֶדַּדֶּה כָל־שְׁנוֹתַי עַל־מַר נַפְשִׁי: אֲדֹנָי עֲלֵיהֶם יִחְיוּ

Assyrian downfall will be a portent of another miracle: The siege had prevented the people from plowing and sowing, thus threatening the starving populace with wholesale famine. This year, God said, there would be sufficient aftergrowth, i.e., wild growth, to feed them all, and the same would happen the following year, until the nation's agricultural capability recovered fully. This would symbolize the recovery of Judah into a strong, vibrant nation (*Rashi*).

38:8. The sun-clock built by Hezekiah's father, King Ahaz, is described at *II Kings* 20:9.

38:10. Hezekiah was thirty-nine years old when he took sick.

38:11. One "sees" God when he recognizes Divine kindness and thanks Him — but the dead are prevented from doing so (*Radak*).

38:12-13. Like a weaver cutting off the rough edges of his fabric. Hezekiah was in such pain that he was sure he would die before evening; and when he survived the night, he thought he would die during the next day (*Radak*).

38:16. God has declared that the dead will return to life.

The
fateful
night

³³ Therefore, thus says HASHEM about the king of Assyria: He will not enter this city, and will not shoot there an arrow; he will not approach it with a shield, and will not pour a ramp against it. ³⁴ On the route by which he came he will retreat, but he will not enter this city — the word of HASHEM. ³⁵ And I shall protect this city, to save it, for My sake and for the sake of My servant David."

³⁶ An angel of HASHEM went out and struck down one hundred eighty-five thousand [people] of the Assyrian camp. The rest arose [early], in the morning and behold — they were all dead corpses!

³⁷ So Sennacherib king of Assyria journeyed forth, went and returned; and he settled in Nineveh. ³⁸ It happened that he was worshiping in the Temple of his god Nisroch: His sons Adrammelech and Sarezer struck him down by the sword; they then fled to the land of Ararat, and Esar-haddon his son reigned in his place.

38

Hezekiah's
illness

¹ In those days Hezekiah became deathly ill. Isaiah son of Amoz, the prophet, came to him, and he said to him, "Thus said HASHEM: Instruct your household, for you shall die; and you shall not live."

² [Hezekiah] then turned his face to the wall and prayed to HASHEM. ³ He said, "Please, HASHEM, remember now that I have always walked before You faithfully and wholeheartedly, and I have done what is good in Your eyes." And Hezekiah wept an intense weeping.

Isaiah
prophesies
recovery,
and gives
a sign

⁴ The word of HASHEM then came to Isaiah, saying, ⁵ "Go and tell Hezekiah: Thus said HASHEM, the God of David, your forefather: I have heard your prayer; I have seen your tears. Behold, I am going to add fifteen years to your days. ⁶ I will also rescue you and this city from the grip of the king of Assyria, and I will protect this city. ⁷ And this is the sign for you from HASHEM that HASHEM will do the deed of which He spoke: ⁸ Behold, I shall turn back the shade over the degrees which it had already descended on the degrees of the sun-clock of Ahaz, * ten degrees backwards." And the sun went back ten degrees, over the degrees that it had already descended.

⁹ A composition written by Hezekiah, the king of Judah, when he was sick and recuperated from his illness:

Hezekiah's
song of
thanksgiving

¹⁰ I had said [to myself]: 'With my days cut short, *
    I will go to the gates of the Grave deprived of the rest of my years.'
¹¹ I had said, 'I will not see God* — God is in the land of the living;
    I will not again behold a man with the inhabitants of the earth.
¹² My dwelling was removed and exiled from me like a shepherd's tent;
    like a weaver I have shortened my life. *
He will end [my life] with sickness;
    from morning to night You will put an end to me.'
¹³ I waited until morning — as [if it] were a lion,
    so [my sickness] would shatter all my bones;
    from morning to night You will put an end to me.
¹⁴ Like a swallow and a crane, so do I chirp; I moan like a pigeon.
    My eyes were raised on high:
'My Lord, snatch away my [illness], be my surety.'
¹⁵ What can I say? He said to me [that He would heal me] and He did!
    All my sleep had left me because of my soul's bitterness!
¹⁶ My Lord, about them [You said], 'They shall live'; *

יז וּלְכָל־בָּהֶן חַיַּי רוּחִי וְתַחֲלִימֵנִי וְהַחֲיֵנִי: הִנֵּה לְשָׁלוֹם מַר־לִי מָר וְאַתָּה

יח חָשַׁקְתָּ נַפְשִׁי מִשַּׁחַת בְּלִי כִּי הִשְׁלַכְתָּ אַחֲרֵי גֵוְךָ כָּל־חֲטָאָי: כִּי לֹא

יט שְׁאוֹל תּוֹדֶךָּ מָוֶת יְהַלְלֶךָּ לֹא־יְשַׂבְּרוּ יוֹרְדֵי־בוֹר אֶל־אֲמִתֶּךָ: חַי חַי הוּא

כ יוֹדֶךָ כָּמוֹנִי הַיּוֹם אָב לְבָנִים יוֹדִיעַ אֶל־אֲמִתֶּךָ: יהוה לְהוֹשִׁיעֵנִי וּנְגִנוֹתַי

כא נְנַגֵּן כָּל־יְמֵי חַיֵּינוּ עַל־בֵּית יהוה: וַיֹּאמֶר יְשַׁעְיָהוּ יִשְׂאוּ דְּבֶלֶת תְּאֵנִים

כב וְיִמְרְחוּ עַל־הַשְּׁחִין וְיֶחִי: וַיֹּאמֶר חִזְקִיָּהוּ מָה אוֹת כִּי אֶעֱלֶה בֵּית

לט א יהוה: בָּעֵת הַהִוא שָׁלַח מְרֹאדַךְ בַּלְאֲדָן בֶּן־בַּלְאֲדָן מֶלֶךְ־

ב בָּבֶל סְפָרִים וּמִנְחָה אֶל־חִזְקִיָּהוּ וַיִּשְׁמַע וַיַּחֲזַק: וַיִּשְׂמַח עֲלֵיהֶם

חִזְקִיָּהוּ וַיַּרְאֵם אֶת־בֵּית °נכתה [נְכֹתוֹ ק] אֶת־הַכֶּסֶף וְאֶת־הַזָּהָב וְאֶת־

הַבְּשָׂמִים וְאֵת | הַשֶּׁמֶן הַטּוֹב וְאֵת כָּל־בֵּית כֵּלָיו וְאֵת כָּל־אֲשֶׁר נִמְצָא

בְּאֹצְרֹתָיו לֹא־הָיָה דָבָר אֲשֶׁר לֹא־הֶרְאָם חִזְקִיָּהוּ בְּבֵיתוֹ וּבְכָל־

ג מֶמְשַׁלְתּוֹ: וַיָּבֹא יְשַׁעְיָהוּ הַנָּבִיא אֶל־הַמֶּלֶךְ חִזְקִיָּהוּ וַיֹּאמֶר אֵלָיו מָה

אָמְרוּ | הָאֲנָשִׁים הָאֵלֶּה וּמֵאַיִן יָבֹאוּ אֵלֶיךָ וַיֹּאמֶר חִזְקִיָּהוּ מֵאֶרֶץ רְחוֹקָה

ד בָּאוּ אֵלַי מִבָּבֶל: וַיֹּאמֶר מָה רָאוּ בְּבֵיתֶךָ וַיֹּאמֶר חִזְקִיָּהוּ אֵת כָּל־אֲשֶׁר

ה בְּבֵיתִי רָאוּ לֹא־הָיָה דָבָר אֲשֶׁר לֹא־הִרְאִיתִים בְּאוֹצְרֹתָי: וַיֹּאמֶר

ו יְשַׁעְיָהוּ אֶל־חִזְקִיָּהוּ שְׁמַע דְּבַר־יהוה צְבָאוֹת: הִנֵּה יָמִים בָּאִים וְנִשָּׂא |

כָּל־אֲשֶׁר בְּבֵיתֶךָ וַאֲשֶׁר אָצְרוּ אֲבֹתֶיךָ עַד־הַיּוֹם הַזֶּה בָּבֶל לֹא־יִוָּתֵר

ז דָּבָר אָמַר יהוה: וּמִבָּנֶיךָ אֲשֶׁר יֵצְאוּ מִמְּךָ אֲשֶׁר תּוֹלִיד יִקָּחוּ וְהָיוּ

ח סָרִיסִים בְּהֵיכַל מֶלֶךְ בָּבֶל: וַיֹּאמֶר חִזְקִיָּהוּ אֶל־יְשַׁעְיָהוּ טוֹב דְּבַר־יהוה

מ א אֲשֶׁר דִּבַּרְתָּ וַיֹּאמֶר כִּי יִהְיֶה שָׁלוֹם וֶאֱמֶת בְּיָמָי: ◄ נַחֲמוּ נַחֲמוּ

ב עַמִּי יֹאמַר אֱלֹהֵיכֶם: דַּבְּרוּ עַל־לֵב יְרוּשָׁלַ͏ִם וְקִרְאוּ אֵלֶיהָ כִּי

מָלְאָה צְבָאָהּ כִּי נִרְצָה עֲוֹנָהּ כִּי לָקְחָה מִיַּד יהוה כִּפְלַיִם בְּכָל־

ג חַטֹּאתֶיהָ: קוֹל קוֹרֵא בַּמִּדְבָּר פַּנּוּ דֶּרֶךְ יהוה יַשְּׁרוּ

ד בָּעֲרָבָה מְסִלָּה לֵאלֹהֵינוּ: כָּל־גֶּיא יִנָּשֵׂא וְכָל־הַר וְגִבְעָה יִשְׁפָּלוּ וְהָיָה

ה הֶעָקֹב לְמִישׁוֹר וְהָרְכָסִים לְבִקְעָה: וְנִגְלָה כְּבוֹד יהוה וְרָאוּ כָל־בָּשָׂר

ו יַחְדָּו כִּי פִּי יהוה דִּבֵּר: קוֹל אֹמֵר קְרָא וְאָמַר מָה אֶקְרָא

38:17. During my illness, the more I longed for peace, the more my suffering was intensified (*Radak*).

38:19. Since only the living can praise You and pass on Your tradition, You should let man live and raise a family.

38:21-22. Chronologically, these two verses belong after verse 7 (see *II Kings* 20:7-11).

39:1. With minor word differences, Chapter 39 is a restatement of *II Kings* 20:12-19.

39:6. The reason for God's anger at Hezekiah is explained in *II Chronicles* (32:31): The king of Babylonia had sent this delegation because he had heard of the miraculous sign that God had performed for Hezekiah. Since they came to inquire about the glory of God,

Hezekiah should not have seized this opportunity to distract his guests from the purpose of their mission by trying to impress them with his own personal wealth and grandeur.

40:1. God speaks to the prophets of Israel, commanding them to comfort the suffering people (*Targum*). Until this point, Isaiah's prophecies have been mostly visions of retribution and destruction. The remaining ones speak words of consolation, and future Messianic redemption. This passage serves as a divider between the two types of prophecy (*Rashi*).

40:2. *Double* punishment cannot mean that Israel was punished more than it deserved. Various interpretations are offered: Her punishment was two pronged, she suf-

and therein is the life of my spirit, may You heal me and cure me.
[17] *Behold, [my longing] for peace, bitterness intensified against me.* *
But You desired that my soul not waste away in the netherworld,
for You have cast all my sins behind Yourself.
[18] *For the Grave cannot thank You nor can Death laud You;*
those who descend to the pit cannot hope for Your truth.
[19] *A living person, a living person, he shall thank you, as I do today!*
A father can make Your truth known to children. *
[20] HASHEM *[said] he would save me;*
let us play my songs all the days of our lives, in the Temple of HASHEM.

[21] Isaiah said, * "Let them lift a cake of figs and smear it on the abscess, and it will heal." [22] Hezekiah said, "What is the sign that I will [ever be able to] go up to the Temple of HASHEM?"

39

Hezekiah flatters the king of Babylonia . . .

[1] * At that time Merodach-baladan son of Baladan, the king of Babylonia, sent letters and a gift to Hezekiah, for he had heard that he was ill and had recuperated. [12] Hezekiah rejoiced with them and showed [the messengers] his whole treasure house — the silver, the gold, the spices, the fine oil, his entire warehouse, and everything that was found in his treasuries; there was nothing that Hezekiah did not show them in his palace and in all his realm.

[3] Isaiah the prophet came to King Hezekiah and said to him, "What did these men say, and from where did they come to you?"

Hezekiah said, "They came to me from a faraway land, from Babylonia."

[4] He said, "And what did they see in your house?"

Hezekiah said, "They saw everything in my house; there was nothing that I did not show them in my treasuries."

. . . and God rebukes him

[5] Isaiah then said to Hezekiah, "Hear the word of HASHEM, Master of Legions: [6] Behold, the days are coming when everything in your house, and whatever your forefathers have accumulated until this day, will be carried off to Babylonia. Not a thing will be left, said HASHEM. * [7] And they will also take some of your children who will issue from you, whom you will beget, and they shall become officers in the palace of the king of Babylonia."

[8] Hezekiah said to Isaiah, "The word of HASHEM that you have spoken is good"; and he said [to himself], "For there shall be peace and truth in my own days."

40

Prophecy of the end of the exile

[1] "Comfort, comfort My people,'* says your God. [2] 'Speak consolingly of Jerusalem and proclaim to her that her period [of exile] has been completed, that her iniquity has been forgiven; for she has received double for all her sins* from the hand of HASHEM.'

[3] A voice* calls out, In the wilderness, clear the way of HASHEM; make a straight path in the desert, a road for our God.' [4] Every valley will be raised, and every mountain and hill will be lowered; the crooked will become straight and heights will become valley. [5] The glory of HASHEM will be revealed, and all flesh together will see that the mouth of HASHEM has spoken.

[6] A voice says, 'Proclaim!' and [the prophet] asks, 'What shall I proclaim?'

---

fered two exiles (*Radak*); she embraced her ancestors' sins as her own, thus doubling her iniquity (*Rashi* to *Jeremiah* 16:18); God's consolation was as great as if she had suffered double what she actually had (*Targum*).

40:3. The *voice* proclaims that the return to Jerusalem is imminent and the road should be cleared and prepared. It is "the way of HASHEM," that leads to His holy city (*Ibn Ezra*).

ז   כָּל־הַבָּשָׂר חָצִיר וְכָל־חַסְדּוֹ כְּצִיץ הַשָּׂדֶה: יָבֵשׁ חָצִיר נָבֵל צִיץ כִּי רוּחַ

ח   יהוה נָשְׁבָה בּוֹ אָכֵן חָצִיר הָעָם: יָבֵשׁ חָצִיר נָבֵל צִיץ וּדְבַר־אֱלֹהֵינוּ יָקוּם

ט   לְעוֹלָם: עַל הַר־גָּבֹהַ עֲלִי־לָךְ מְבַשֶּׂרֶת צִיּוֹן הָרִימִי בַכֹּחַ

קוֹלֵךְ מְבַשֶּׂרֶת יְרוּשָׁלָ͏ִם הָרִימִי אַל־תִּירָאִי אִמְרִי לְעָרֵי יְהוּדָה הִנֵּה

י   אֱלֹהֵיכֶם: הִנֵּה אֲדֹנָי יֱהֹוִה בְּחָזָק יָבוֹא וּזְרֹעוֹ מֹשְׁלָה לוֹ הִנֵּה שְׂכָרוֹ אִתּוֹ

יא   וּפְעֻלָּתוֹ לְפָנָיו: כְּרֹעֶה עֶדְרוֹ יִרְעֶה בִּזְרֹעוֹ יְקַבֵּץ טְלָאִים וּבְחֵיקוֹ יִשָּׂא

עָלוֹת יְנַהֵל: מִי־מָדַד בְּשָׁעֳלוֹ מַיִם וְשָׁמַיִם בַּזֶּרֶת תִּכֵּן וְכָל

יב   בַּשָּׁלִשׁ עֲפַר הָאָרֶץ וְשָׁקַל בַּפֶּלֶס הָרִים וּגְבָעוֹת בְּמֹאזְנָיִם: מִי־תִכֵּן אֶת־

יג   רוּחַ יהוה וְאִישׁ עֲצָתוֹ יוֹדִיעֶנּוּ: אֶת־מִי נוֹעַץ וַיְבִינֵהוּ וַיְלַמְּדֵהוּ בְּאֹרַח

יד   מִשְׁפָּט וַיְלַמְּדֵהוּ דַעַת וְדֶרֶךְ תְּבוּנוֹת יוֹדִיעֶנּוּ: הֵן גּוֹיִם כְּמַר מִדְּלִי וּכְשַׁחַק

טו   מֹאזְנַיִם נֶחְשָׁבוּ הֵן אִיִּים כַּדַּק יִטּוֹל: וּלְבָנוֹן אֵין דֵּי בָּעֵר וְחַיָּתוֹ אֵין דֵּי

טז   עוֹלָה: כָּל־הַגּוֹיִם כְּאַיִן נֶגְדּוֹ מֵאֶפֶס וָתֹהוּ נֶחְשְׁבוּ־לוֹ: וְאֶל־

יז-יח   מִי תְּדַמְּיוּן אֵל וּמַה־דְּמוּת תַּעַרְכוּ־לוֹ: הַפֶּסֶל נָסַךְ חָרָשׁ וְצֹרֵף בַּזָּהָב

יט   יְרַקְּעֶנּוּ וּרְתֻקוֹת כֶּסֶף צוֹרֵף: הַמְסֻכָּן תְּרוּמָה עֵץ לֹא־יִרְקַב יִבְחָר חָרָשׁ

כ   חָכָם יְבַקֶּשׁ־לוֹ לְהָכִין פֶּסֶל לֹא יִמּוֹט: הֲלוֹא תֵדְעוּ הֲלוֹא תִשְׁמָעוּ

כא   הֲלוֹא הֻגַּד מֵרֹאשׁ לָכֶם הֲלוֹא הֲבִינֹתֶם מוֹסְדוֹת הָאָרֶץ: הַיֹּשֵׁב עַל־חוּג

כב   הָאָרֶץ וְיֹשְׁבֶיהָ כַּחֲגָבִים הַנּוֹטֶה כַדֹּק שָׁמַיִם וַיִּמְתָּחֵם כָּאֹהֶל לָשָׁבֶת:

כג-כד   הַנּוֹתֵן רוֹזְנִים לְאָיִן שֹׁפְטֵי אֶרֶץ כַּתֹּהוּ עָשָׂה: אַף בַּל־נִטָּעוּ אַף בַּל־

זֹרָעוּ אַף בַּל־שֹׁרֵשׁ בָּאָרֶץ גִּזְעָם וְגַם־נָשַׁף בָּהֶם וַיִּבָשׁוּ וּסְעָרָה כַּקַּשׁ

כה-כו   תִּשָּׂאֵם: וְאֶל־מִי תְדַמְּיוּנִי וְאֶשְׁוֶה יֹאמַר קָדוֹשׁ: שְׂאוּ־מָרוֹם

עֵינֵיכֶם וּרְאוּ מִי־בָרָא אֵלֶּה הַמּוֹצִיא בְמִסְפָּר צְבָאָם לְכֻלָּם בְּשֵׁם יִקְרָא

מֵרֹב אוֹנִים וְאַמִּיץ כֹּחַ אִישׁ לֹא נֶעְדָּר: ◀ ▶   לָמָּה תֹאמַר יַעֲקֹב

כז   וּתְדַבֵּר יִשְׂרָאֵל נִסְתְּרָה דַרְכִּי מֵיהוה וּמֵאֱלֹהַי מִשְׁפָּטִי יַעֲבוֹר: הֲלוֹא

כח   יָדַעְתָּ אִם־לֹא שָׁמַעְתָּ אֱלֹהֵי עוֹלָם ׀ יהוה בּוֹרֵא קְצוֹת הָאָרֶץ לֹא יִיעַף

כט   וְלֹא יִיגָע אֵין חֵקֶר לִתְבוּנָתוֹ: נֹתֵן לַיָּעֵף כֹּחַ וּלְאֵין אוֹנִים עָצְמָה יַרְבֶּה:

ל-לא   וְיִעֲפוּ נְעָרִים וְיִגָעוּ וּבַחוּרִים כָּשׁוֹל יִכָּשֵׁלוּ: וְקֹוֵי יהוה יַחֲלִיפוּ כֹחַ יַעֲלוּ

מא   אֵבֶר כַּנְּשָׁרִים יָרוּצוּ וְלֹא יִיגָעוּ יֵלְכוּ וְלֹא יִיעָפוּ:

א   הַחֲרִישׁוּ

HAFTARAS
LECH
LECHA
40:27-
41:16

40:6-8. The veracity of God's promise is contrasted with the unreliability of human promises (*Rashi*).

40:12-17. The prophet lyrically depicts God's greatness and absolute power.

40:12. The One Who created such a perfectly balanced natural order can surely fulfill His promises to His people.

40:15. "Islands" is often used as a metaphor for all of humanity, including even those living in remote places.

40:18-26. Isaiah asks incredulously how the idolaters could mistake their man-made toys for the omnipotent God. How can anyone fail to realize that the world in all its grandeur must have a Creator?

40:20. The poor man, who cannot afford the ornate idol of v. 19, chooses wood (*Radak*). Others interpret: "The expert (*Rashi*) or the curator (*Ibn Ezra*) makes a selection"; and "The laurel is selected" (*Targum*).

40:26. "By number" and "by name" mean that God assigns a specific purpose to each of the heavenly bodies (*Radak*).

40:27-31. Jews should never despair, thinking that God ignores or forsakes them. If He withholds His help, it is because His wisdom decrees that to be the best course.

40:31. All these metaphors mean that when God wills it, the return to Zion will be swift and without obstacle.

— 'All flesh is [like] grass,* and all its kindness like a blossom in the field. [7] Grass withers and blossom fades when the breath of HASHEM blows upon it; indeed the people is grass. [8] Grass withers and blossom fades, but the word of our God shall stand forever.'

The herald of Zion

[9] Ascend upon a high mountain, O herald of Zion; raise your voice with strength, O herald of Jerusalem! Raise it, fear not; say to the cities of Judah, 'Behold, your God!' [10] Behold, my Lord, HASHEM/ELOHIM, will come with [a] strong [arm], and His arm will dominate for Him; behold, His reward is with Him, and His wage is before Him. [11] [He is] like a shepherd who grazes his flock, who gathers the lambs in his arm, who carries them in his bosom, who guides the nursing ewes.

God, the Creator

[12] Who measured the waters in His palm,* gauged the Heavens with a span, measured in a huge vessel the dust of the earth, and weighed mountains with a scale and hills with a balance?* [13] Who can appraise the spirit of HASHEM, His man of counsel who informs Him? [14] From whom did He seek counsel? [Who] gave Him insight? [Who] taught Him about the path of justice? [Who] taught Him wisdom? [Who] explained the way of knowledge to Him? [15] Behold, all the nations are like a drop from a bucket and are reckoned like the dust rubbing off a scale; behold, He will cast away the islands like dust.* [16] The Lebanon is insufficient kindling, and its beasts are insufficient elevation-offerings. [17] All the nations are like nothing before Him; as nothingness and emptiness are they reckoned by Him.

Foolishness of idolatry

[18] *To whom can you liken God, and what likeness can you attribute to Him? [19] [To] the idol cast by a blacksmith, [which] a goldsmith overlays with gold and a silversmith with silver chains? [20] The poor man* [makes a] selection; he chooses wood that will not rot, he seeks for himself a wise woodworker to prepare an idol that will not fall apart. [21] Do you not realize? Have you not heard? Has it not been told to you from the beginning? Have

God, the Master of nature and history

you not contemplated the foundations of the earth? [22] It is He Who sits on the circumference of the earth, with its inhabitants like grasshoppers; Who spreads the heavens like a thin curtain, and stretches them like a tent to dwell in; [23] Who turns governors into nothingness; Who makes judges of the land into naught — [24] as if they were not even planted, as if they were not even sown, as if their stock was not even rooted in the ground; even if He were to blow on them they would wither, and a storm wind would carry them away like stubble. [25] 'To whom can you liken Me that I should be [his] equal?' says the Holy One. [26] Raise your eyes on high and see Who created these [things]! He brings forth their legions by number; He calls to each of them by name;* by the abundance of His power and by vigor of His strength, not one is missing!

God, the Eternal

[27] Why do you say, O Jacob, and declare, O Israel, — 'My way is hidden from HASHEM, and my cause has passed by my God'?* [28] Did you not know? Did you not hear? HASHEM is the eternal God, the Creator of the ends of the earth; He does not weary, He does not tire; there is no calculating His understanding. [29] He gives strength to the weary, and grants abundant might to the powerless. [30] Youths may weary and tire and young men may constantly falter, [31] but those whose hope is in HASHEM will have renewed strength; they will grow a wing, like eagles;* they will run and not grow tired, they will walk and not grow weary.

ב אֵלַי אִיִּים וּלְאֻמִּים יַחֲלִיפוּ כֹחַ יִגְּשׁוּ אָז יְדַבֵּרוּ יַחְדָּו לַמִּשְׁפָּט נִקְרָבָה: מִי

הֵעִיר מִמִּזְרָח צֶדֶק יִקְרָאֵהוּ לְרַגְלוֹ יִתֵּן לְפָנָיו גּוֹיִם וּמְלָכִים יַרְדְּ יִתֵּן

ג כֶּעָפָר חַרְבּוֹ כְּקַשׁ נִדָּף קַשְׁתּוֹ: יִרְדְּפֵם יַעֲבוֹר שָׁלוֹם אֹרַח בְּרַגְלָיו לֹא

ד יָבוֹא: מִי־פָעַל וְעָשָׂה קֹרֵא הַדֹּרוֹת מֵרֹאשׁ אֲנִי יהוה רִאשׁוֹן וְאֶת־

ה אַחֲרֹנִים אֲנִי־הוּא: רָאוּ אִיִּים וְיִירָאוּ קְצוֹת הָאָרֶץ יֶחֱרָדוּ קָרְבוּ וַיֶּאֱתָיוּן:

ו-ז אִישׁ אֶת־רֵעֵהוּ יַעְזֹרוּ וּלְאָחִיו יֹאמַר חֲזָק: וַיְחַזֵּק חָרָשׁ אֶת־צֹרֵף מַחֲלִיק

פַּטִּישׁ אֶת־הוֹלֶם פָּעַם אֹמֵר לַדֶּבֶק טוֹב הוּא וַיְחַזְּקֵהוּ בְמַסְמְרִים לֹא

ח יִמּוֹט: וְאַתָּה יִשְׂרָאֵל עַבְדִּי יַעֲקֹב אֲשֶׁר בְּחַרְתִּיךָ זֶרַע

ט אַבְרָהָם אֹהֲבִי: אֲשֶׁר הֶחֱזַקְתִּיךָ מִקְצוֹת הָאָרֶץ וּמֵאֲצִילֶיהָ קְרָאתִיךָ

י וָאֹמַר לְךָ עַבְדִּי־אַתָּה בְּחַרְתִּיךָ וְלֹא מְאַסְתִּיךָ: אַל־תִּירָא כִּי־עִמְּךָ אָנִי

אַל־תִּשְׁתָּע כִּי־אֲנִי אֱלֹהֶיךָ אִמַּצְתִּיךָ אַף־עֲזַרְתִּיךָ אַף־תְּמַכְתִּיךָ בִּימִין

יא צִדְקִי: הֵן יֵבֹשׁוּ וְיִכָּלְמוּ כֹּל הַנֶּחֱרִים בָּךְ יִהְיוּ כְאַיִן וְיֹאבְדוּ אַנְשֵׁי רִיבֶךָ:

יב תְּבַקְשֵׁם וְלֹא תִמְצָאֵם אַנְשֵׁי מַצֻּתֶךָ יִהְיוּ כְאַיִן וּכְאֶפֶס אַנְשֵׁי מִלְחַמְתֶּךָ:

יג כִּי אֲנִי יהוה אֱלֹהֶיךָ מַחֲזִיק יְמִינֶךָ הָאֹמֵר לְךָ אַל־תִּירָא אֲנִי

יד עֲזַרְתִּיךָ: אַל־תִּירְאִי תּוֹלַעַת יַעֲקֹב מְתֵי יִשְׂרָאֵל אֲנִי

טו עֲזַרְתִּיךְ נְאֻם־יהוה וְגֹאֲלֵךְ קְדוֹשׁ יִשְׂרָאֵל: הִנֵּה שַׂמְתִּיךְ לְמוֹרַג חָרוּץ

טז חָדָשׁ בַּעַל פִּיפִיּוֹת תָּדוּשׁ הָרִים וְתָדֹק וּגְבָעוֹת כַּמֹּץ תָּשִׂים: תִּזְרֵם

וְרוּחַ תִּשָּׂאֵם וּסְעָרָה תָּפִיץ אֹתָם וְאַתָּה תָּגִיל בַּיהוה בִּקְדוֹשׁ יִשְׂרָאֵל

יז תִּתְהַלָּל: ◄ הָעֲנִיִּים וְהָאֶבְיוֹנִים מְבַקְשִׁים מַיִם וָאַיִן לְשׁוֹנָם

בַּצָּמָא נָשָׁתָּה אֲנִי יהוה אֶעֱנֵם אֱלֹהֵי יִשְׂרָאֵל לֹא אֶעֶזְבֵם: אֶפְתַּח עַל־

יח שְׁפָיִים נְהָרוֹת וּבְתוֹךְ בְּקָעוֹת מַעְיָנוֹת אָשִׂים מִדְבָּר לַאֲגַם־מַיִם וְאֶרֶץ

יט צִיָּה לְמוֹצָאֵי מָיִם: אֶתֵּן בַּמִּדְבָּר אֶרֶז שִׁטָּה וַהֲדַס וְעֵץ שָׁמֶן אָשִׂים

כ בָּעֲרָבָה בְּרוֹשׁ תִּדְהָר וּתְאַשּׁוּר יַחְדָּו: לְמַעַן יִרְאוּ וְיֵדְעוּ וְיָשִׂימוּ וְיַשְׂכִּילוּ

כא יַחְדָּו כִּי יַד־יהוה עָשְׂתָה זֹּאת וּקְדוֹשׁ יִשְׂרָאֵל בְּרָאָהּ: קָרְבוּ

כב רִיבְכֶם יֹאמַר יהוה הַגִּישׁוּ עֲצֻמוֹתֵיכֶם יֹאמַר מֶלֶךְ יַעֲקֹב: יַגִּישׁוּ וְיַגִּידוּ

לָנוּ אֵת אֲשֶׁר תִּקְרֶינָה הָרִאשֹׁנוֹת | מָה הֵנָּה הַגִּידוּ וְנָשִׂימָה לִבֵּנוּ

כג וְנֵדְעָה אַחֲרִיתָן אוֹ הַבָּאוֹת הַשְׁמִיעֻנוּ: הַגִּידוּ הָאֹתִיּוֹת לְאָחוֹר וְנֵדְעָה כִּי

אֱלֹהִים אַתֶּם אַף־תֵּיטִיבוּ וְתָרֵעוּ וְנִשְׁתָּעָה °וְנִשְׁתָּעָה °וּנְרָא [°וְנִרְאֶה ק] יַחְדָּו:

41:2. A reference to Abraham who came to Canaan from Aram to the east. His war against the kings is discussed in *Genesis* Ch. 14 (*Rashi* based on *Taanis* 21a). Although the Hebrew verbs in this passage are in the future tense, prophecy is often spoken in a mixture of tenses. Such usage implies that just as God helped Abraham in the past, so will He help Abraham's offspring in the future (*Radak*).

41:4. God chose Abraham for He knew that his progeny would be worthy of this calling (see *Genesis* 18:19). Since He knows about all generations, past and future, Israel may feel assured that He will come to its salvation.

41:5-7. Despite Abraham's greatness, other nations opposed him and called upon their artisans to make more and better idols (*Radak*). So will some nations refuse to acknowledge Israel's pre-eminence in the future (*Rashi*).

41:14. I will transform you from the lowly worm that you are now into a mighty, formidable force.

41:18. Another metaphor depicting the transformation of Israel from a wretched band of exiles into a thriving, vibrant community (*Abarbanel*).

41:21. The prophet invites the enemies of Israel to present their grievances against God and His people.

41

TRIAL
OF THE
NATIONS
41:1-29

The lesson
of Abraham

Israel is
My servant

Fear not,
O Jacob

Parable of
the thirsty

Appeal
to history

¹ Be silent to [hear] Me, O islands, and let regimes renew strength. Let them approach, then let them speak; together let us approach for judgment. ² Who inspired [the one] from the east, * at whose [every] footstep righteousness attended? [Who] delivered nations to him, and subdued kings [before him]? [Who] made [his enemies] like dust [before] his sword; like straw blown about [before] his bow? ³ He pursued them and emerged unhurt, on a path where his feet had never gone. ⁴ Who brought about and accomplished [this]? He Who proclaimed the generations from the beginning: * I, HASHEM, am the first, and I am He Who will be with the last [generations]. ⁵ The islands saw and feared, * the ends of the earth shuddered; they approached and came. ⁶ Each man would help his fellow [worship idols] and to his brother he would say 'Be strong!' ⁷ The woodworker would encourage the goldsmith, the finishing hammerer [would encourage] the one who pounds from the start; he would say of the glue, 'This is good,' and he would strengthen it with nails so that it should not loosen.

⁸ But you, O Israel, My servant, Jacob, you whom I have chosen, offspring of Abraham who loved Me — ⁹ you whom I shall grasp from the ends of the earth and shall summon from among all its noblemen, and to whom I shall say, 'You are my servant' — I have chosen you and not rejected you. ¹⁰ Fear not for I am with you; be not dismayed, for I am your God; I have strengthened you, even helped you, and even sustained you with My righteous right hand. ¹¹ Behold, all who become angry with you will be shamed and humiliated; those who fight with you shall be like nothingness and shall perish. ¹² The men who struggle with you, you shall seek them but not find them; the men who fight you, they shall be like nothingness and naught. ¹³ For I am HASHEM, your God, Who grasps your right hand, Who says to you: 'Fear not, [for] I help you!'

¹⁴ Fear not, O worm of Jacob, * O men of Israel, [for] I help you — the word of HASHEM and your Redeemer, the Holy One of Israel. ¹⁵ Behold, I have made you like a new, sharp threshing iron with many blades; you will thresh and pulverize mountains, and you will make the hills like chaff. ¹⁶ You will winnow them and the wind will carry them off, a storm will scatter them — but you will rejoice in HASHEM; in the Holy One of Israel you will glory!

¹⁷ The poor and the destitute beg for water but there is none, their tongue withers from thirst; I, HASHEM, will answer them; the God of Israel, I will not forsake them. ¹⁸ I will open up rivers upon the hilltops and springs in the midst of valleys; I will turn the desert into a pond of water and a parched land into sources of water. * ¹⁹ In the wilderness I will set cedar, acacia, myrtle and pine tree; I will place cypress, fir and box tree together in a desert, ²⁰ so that they should see and know and consider and understand together that the hand of HASHEM has done this, and the Holy One of Israel has brought it about.

²¹ 'Bring your quarrel forward,' * says HASHEM. 'Present your accusations,' says the King of Jacob. ²² Let them bring forth [their prophets] and let them tell us what will happen, what primeval events signified. Tell it, that we may take to heart and know their end; or inform us about the future. ²³ Tell us the signs that will come in later times, and then we will know that you are gods and that you can do good or evil; together we will discuss and decide.

כד-כה הֶן־אַתֶּם מֵאַ֫יִן וּפָעָלְכֶ֣ם מֵאָ֑פַע תּוֹעֵבָ֖ה יִבְחַ֣ר בָּכֶֽם: הַעִירֹ֣תִי
מִצָּפ֣וֹן וַיַּ֗את מִמִּזְרַח־שֶׁ֙מֶשׁ֙ יִקְרָ֣א בִשְׁמִ֔י וְיָבֹ֥א סְגָנִ֖ים כְּמוֹ־חֹ֑מֶר וּכְמ֥וֹ
כו יוֹצֵ֖ר יִרְמָס־טִֽיט: מִֽי־הִגִּ֤יד מֵרֹאשׁ֙ וְנֵדָ֔עָה וּמִלְּפָנִ֖ים וְנֹאמַ֣ר צַדִּ֑יק אַ֣ף
כז אֵֽין־מַגִּ֗יד אַ֚ף אֵ֣ין מַשְׁמִ֔יעַ אַ֥ף אֵין־שֹׁמֵ֖עַ אִמְרֵיכֶֽם: רִאשׁ֥וֹן לְצִיּ֖וֹן הִנֵּ֣ה
כח הִנָּ֑ם וְלִירוּשָׁלַ֖͏ִם מְבַשֵּׂ֥ר אֶתֵּֽן: וְאֵ֙רֶא֙ וְאֵ֣ין אִ֔ישׁ וּמֵאֵ֖לֶּה וְאֵ֣ין יוֹעֵ֑ץ
כט וְאֶשְׁאָלֵ֖ם וְיָשִׁ֥יבוּ דָבָֽר: הֵ֣ן כֻּלָּ֗ם אָ֚וֶן אֶ֣פֶס מַֽעֲשֵׂיהֶ֔ם ר֥וּחַ וָתֹ֖הוּ
נִסְכֵּיהֶֽם:

מב   א הֵ֤ן עַבְדִּי֙ אֶתְמָךְ־בּ֔וֹ בְּחִירִ֖י רָֽצְתָ֣ה נַפְשִׁ֑י
נָתַ֤תִּי רוּחִי֙ עָלָ֔יו מִשְׁפָּ֖ט לַגּוֹיִ֥ם יוֹצִֽיא: ב לֹ֥א יִצְעַ֖ק וְלֹ֣א יִשָּׂ֑א וְלֹֽא־
ג יַשְׁמִ֥יעַ בַּח֖וּץ קוֹלֽוֹ: קָנֶ֤ה רָצוּץ֙ לֹ֣א יִשְׁבּ֔וֹר וּפִשְׁתָּ֥ה כֵהָ֖ה לֹ֣א יְכַבֶּ֑נָּה
ד לֶֽאֱמֶ֖ת יוֹצִ֥יא מִשְׁפָּֽט: לֹ֤א יִכְהֶה֙ וְלֹ֣א יָר֔וּץ עַד־יָשִׂ֥ים בָּאָ֖רֶץ מִשְׁפָּ֑ט
ה וּלְתֽוֹרָת֖וֹ אִיִּ֥ים יְיַחֵֽלוּ: ◄ כֹּֽה־אָמַ֞ר הָאֵ֣ל ׀ יְהֹוָ֗ה
בּוֹרֵ֤א הַשָּׁמַ֙יִם֙ וְנ֣וֹטֵיהֶ֔ם רֹקַ֥ע הָאָ֖רֶץ וְצֶֽאֱצָאֶ֑יהָ נֹתֵ֤ן נְשָׁמָה֙ לָעָ֣ם עָלֶ֔יהָ
ו וְר֖וּחַ לַהֹֽלְכִ֥ים בָּֽהּ: אֲנִ֧י יְהֹוָ֛ה קְרָאתִ֥יךָ בְצֶ֖דֶק וְאַחְזֵ֣ק בְּיָדֶ֑ךָ וְאֶצָּרְךָ֗
ז וְאֶתֶּנְךָ֛ לִבְרִ֥ית עָ֖ם לְא֥וֹר גּוֹיִֽם: לִפְקֹ֖חַ עֵינַ֣יִם עִוְר֑וֹת לְהוֹצִ֤יא מִמַּסְגֵּר֙
ח אַסִּ֔יר מִבֵּ֥ית כֶּ֖לֶא יֹ֥שְׁבֵי חֹֽשֶׁךְ: אֲנִ֥י יְהֹוָ֖ה ה֣וּא שְׁמִ֑י וּכְבוֹדִי֙ לְאַחֵ֣ר
ט לֹֽא־אֶתֵּ֔ן וּתְהִלָּתִ֖י לַפְּסִילִֽים: הָרִאשֹׁנ֖וֹת הִנֵּה־בָ֑אוּ וַֽחֲדָשׁוֹת֙ אֲנִ֣י מַגִּ֔יד
י בְּטֶ֥רֶם תִּצְמַ֖חְנָה אַשְׁמִ֥יע אֶתְכֶֽם: שִׁ֤ירוּ לַֽיהֹוָה֙
שִׁ֣יר חָדָ֔שׁ תְּהִלָּת֖וֹ מִקְצֵ֣ה הָאָ֑רֶץ יוֹרְדֵ֤י הַיָּם֙ וּמְלֹא֔וֹ אִיִּ֖ים וְיֹֽשְׁבֵיהֶֽם:
יא יִשְׂא֤וּ מִדְבָּר֙ וְעָרָ֔יו חֲצֵרִ֖ים תֵּשֵׁ֣ב קֵדָ֑ר יָרֹ֙נּוּ֙ יֹ֣שְׁבֵי סֶ֔לַע מֵרֹ֥אשׁ
יב-יג הָרִ֖ים יִצְוָֽחוּ: יָשִׂ֥ימוּ לַֽיהֹוָ֖ה כָּב֑וֹד וּתְהִלָּת֖וֹ בָּֽאִיִּ֥ים יַגִּֽידוּ: יְהֹוָה֙ כַּגִּבּ֣וֹר
יֵצֵ֔א כְּאִ֥ישׁ מִלְחָמ֖וֹת יָעִ֣יר קִנְאָ֑ה יָרִ֙יעַ֙ אַף־יַצְרִ֔יחַ עַל־אֹֽיְבָ֖יו
יד יִתְגַּבָּֽר: הֶֽחֱשֵׁ֙יתִי֙ מֵֽעוֹלָ֔ם אַֽחֲרִ֖ישׁ אֶתְאַפָּ֑ק כַּיּֽוֹלֵדָ֣ה
טו אֶפְעֶ֔ה אֶשֹּׁ֥ם וְאֶשְׁאַ֖ף יָֽחַד: אַֽחֲרִ֤יב הָרִים֙ וּגְבָע֔וֹת וְכָל־עֶשְׂבָּ֖ם אוֹבִ֑ישׁ
טז וְשַׂמְתִּ֤י נְהָרוֹת֙ לָֽאִיִּ֔ים וַֽאֲגַמִּ֖ים אוֹבִֽישׁ: וְהֽוֹלַכְתִּ֣י עִוְרִ֗ים בְּדֶ֘רֶךְ֮ לֹ֣א יָדָ֒עוּ֒
בִּנְתִיב֥וֹת לֹֽא־יָֽדְע֖וּ אַדְרִיכֵ֑ם אָשִׂים֩ מַחְשָׁ֨ךְ לִפְנֵיהֶ֜ם לָא֗וֹר וּמַֽעֲקַשִּׁים֙
יז לְמִישׁ֔וֹר אֵ֚לֶּה הַדְּבָרִ֔ים עֲשִׂיתִ֖ם וְלֹ֣א עֲזַבְתִּֽים: נָסֹ֤גוּ אָחוֹר֙ יֵבֹ֣שׁוּ בֹ֔שֶׁת

HAFTARAS BEREISHIS
Ashkenazim:
42:5-43:10
Sephardim:
42:5-21

41:25. A savior will arise from the northeast. According to most commentators it was Cyrus, the benevolent king of Persia, who initiated the return to Zion in the days of Ezra. According to some, the reference is to the Messiah, who will gather together the exiled Ten Tribes, who had inhabited mostly the northeast of Israel.

41:27. The first Jews who return to Zion will announce that the rest of the exiles are returning.

41:28. Who can respond to the challenge of vv. 21-23.

42:1. The Messiah (*Targum*).

42:2-3. He will be accepted by all and will have no need to proclaim his judgments loudly or demonstrate his power (*Radak*).

42:5. Isaiah refutes those who claim that the universe came into being without a Creator (*Radak*). Literally, the verse is in the present tense, because God renews His Creation constantly.

42:8. By not punishing the wicked, God indirectly encourages idolaters to believe in the potency of their gods. That will soon change.

42:15. Metaphorically, God will destroy the mighty kings and their followers (*Rashi*).

42:16. That is, the redeemed Jewish nation, which had been "blinded" by its suffering (*Radak*).

Judgment

²⁴ But behold, you are made from nothing and your deeds are naught; [only] an abominable one would choose you.

²⁵ I have inspired someone * from the north, and he has come; he calls out in My Name from where the sun rises. He will come upon rulers as [one treads on] mortar, as a potter trampling clay. ²⁶ Who [of the pagans] has told anything in advance that we may know; from beforehand, that we may say he was right? There is no one who tells, nor anyone who informs, nor is there anyone who hears your words! ²⁷ The first ones to come to Zion [will announce], 'Behold! They are here!'* and I will send a herald for Jerusalem. ²⁸ I see that there is no man, * and that among them there is no counselor whom I may ask and who can respond with a word. ²⁹ Behold, all of them: Their deeds are worthless and naught; their molten images are but wind and nothingness.

42

The Messiah, God's servant

¹ Behold My servant, * whom I shall uphold; My chosen one, whom My soul desired; I have placed My spirit upon him so he can bring forth justice to the nations. ² He will not shout* nor raise his voice, nor make his voice heard in the street. ³ He will not break [even] a bruised reed nor extinguish even flickering flax; but he will administer justice in truth. ⁴ He will not slacken nor tire until he sets justice in the land and islands will long for his teaching.

A light to the nations

⁵ Thus said the God, HASHEM, Who created the heavens and stretched them forth; * Who firmed the earth and its produce, Who gave a soul to the people upon it, and a spirit to those who walk on it: ⁶ I am HASHEM; I have called you with righteousness; I will strengthen your hand; I will protect you; I will set you for a covenant to the people, for a light to the nations; ⁷ to open blind eyes; to remove a prisoner from confinement, dwellers in darkness from a dungeon. ⁸ I am HASHEM; that is My Name; I shall not give My glory to another, nor My praise to graven idols. * ⁹ Behold, the early [prophecies] have come about; now I relate new ones; before they sprout I shall let you hear [them].

Hymn of redemption

¹⁰ Sing to HASHEM a new song, His praise from the end of the earth,
　　those who go down to the sea and those that fill it,
　　the islands and their inhabitants.
¹¹ The wilderness and its cities will lift [their voices],
　　the open cities where Kedar dwells;
those who dwell on bedrock will sing out,
　　they will shout from mountain peaks.
¹² They will render glory to HASHEM, and relate His praise in the islands.
¹³ HASHEM will go forth like a mighty warrior,
　　He will arouse vengeance like a man of war;
He will shout triumphantly, even roar; He will overpower his enemies.

God's intervention

¹⁴ I have long kept silent, I have been still, I have restrained myself; [but now] I will cry out like a woman in childbirth; I will both lay waste and swallow up. ¹⁵ I will destroy mountains and hills; * I will wither all their herbage; I will turn rivers into islands and I will dry up marshes. ¹⁶ I will lead the blind * on a way they never knew; on paths they did not know I will have them walk; I will turn darkness into light before them, and make the crooked places straight. These are the things I shall have done and not have neglected them. ¹⁷ They will withdraw to the rear and be deeply shamed,

יח הַחֵרְשִׁים הַבִּטְחִים בַּפֶּסֶל הָאֹמְרִים לְמַסֵּכָה אַתֶּם אֱלֹהֵינוּ:

יט שִׁמְעוּ וְהַעִוְרִים הַבִּיטוּ לִרְאוֹת: מִי עִוֵּר כִּי אִם־עַבְדִּי וְחֵרֵשׁ כְּמַלְאָכִי

כ אֶשְׁלָח מִי עִוֵּר כִּמְשֻׁלָּם וְעִוֵּר כְּעֶבֶד יְהוָה: רֹאית [°רָאוֹת ק] רַבּוֹת וְלֹא

כא תִשְׁמֹר פָּקוֹחַ אָזְנַיִם וְלֹא יִשְׁמָע: יְהוָה חָפֵץ לְמַעַן צִדְקוֹ יַגְדִּיל תּוֹרָה

כב וְיַאְדִּיר: ▶וְהוּא עַם־בָּזוּז וְשָׁסוּי הָפֵחַ בַּחוּרִים כֻּלָּם וּבְבָתֵּי כְלָאִים הָחְבָּאוּ

כג הָיוּ לָבַז וְאֵין מַצִּיל מְשִׁסָּה וְאֵין־אֹמֵר הָשַׁב: מִי בָכֶם יַאֲזִין זֹאת יַקְשִׁב

כד וְיִשְׁמַע לְאָחוֹר: מִי־נָתַן °לִמְשׁוֹסָה [°לִמְשִׁסָּה ק] יַעֲקֹב וְיִשְׂרָאֵל לְבֹזְזִים

הֲלוֹא יְהוָה זוּ חָטָאנוּ לוֹ וְלֹא־אָבוּ בִדְרָכָיו הָלוֹךְ וְלֹא שָׁמְעוּ בְּתוֹרָתוֹ:

כה וַיִּשְׁפֹּךְ עָלָיו חֵמָה אַפּוֹ וֶעֱזוּז מִלְחָמָה וַתְּלַהֲטֵהוּ מִסָּבִיב וְלֹא יָדָע

מג א וַתִּבְעַר־בּוֹ וְלֹא־יָשִׂים עַל־לֵב: וְעַתָּה כֹּה־אָמַר יְהוָה בֹּרַאֲךָ

יַעֲקֹב וְיֹצֶרְךָ יִשְׂרָאֵל אַל־תִּירָא כִּי גְאַלְתִּיךָ קָרָאתִי בְשִׁמְךָ לִי־אָתָּה: כִּי־

ב תַעֲבֹר בַּמַּיִם אִתְּךָ אָנִי וּבַנְּהָרוֹת לֹא יִשְׁטְפוּךָ כִּי־תֵלֵךְ בְּמוֹ־אֵשׁ לֹא

ג תִכָּוֶה וְלֶהָבָה לֹא תִבְעַר־בָּךְ: כִּי אֲנִי יְהוָה אֱלֹהֶיךָ קְדוֹשׁ יִשְׂרָאֵל מוֹשִׁיעֶךָ

ד נָתַתִּי כָפְרְךָ מִצְרַיִם כּוּשׁ וּסְבָא תַחְתֶּיךָ: מֵאֲשֶׁר יָקַרְתָּ בְעֵינַי נִכְבַּדְתָּ וַאֲנִי

ה אֲהַבְתִּיךָ וְאֶתֵּן אָדָם תַּחְתֶּיךָ וּלְאֻמִּים תַּחַת נַפְשֶׁךָ: אַל־תִּירָא כִּי־אִתְּךָ־

ו אָנִי מִמִּזְרָח אָבִיא זַרְעֶךָ וּמִמַּעֲרָב אֲקַבְּצֶךָּ: אֹמַר לַצָּפוֹן תֵּנִי וּלְתֵימָן אַל־

ז תִּכְלָאִי הָבִיאִי בָנַי מֵרָחוֹק וּבְנוֹתַי מִקְצֵה הָאָרֶץ: כֹּל הַנִּקְרָא בִשְׁמִי

ח וְלִכְבוֹדִי בְּרָאתִיו יְצַרְתִּיו אַף־עֲשִׂיתִיו: הוֹצִיא עַם־עִוֵּר וְעֵינַיִם יֵשׁ

ט וְחֵרְשִׁים וְאָזְנַיִם לָמוֹ: כָּל־הַגּוֹיִם נִקְבְּצוּ יַחְדָּו וְיֵאָסְפוּ לְאֻמִּים מִי בָהֶם

יַגִּיד זֹאת וְרִאשֹׁנוֹת יַשְׁמִיעֻנוּ יִתְּנוּ עֵדֵיהֶם וְיִצְדָּקוּ וְיִשְׁמְעוּ וְיֹאמְרוּ אֱמֶת:

י אַתֶּם עֵדַי נְאֻם־יְהוָה וְעַבְדִּי אֲשֶׁר בָּחָרְתִּי לְמַעַן תֵּדְעוּ וְתַאֲמִינוּ לִי

וְתָבִינוּ כִּי־אֲנִי הוּא לְפָנַי לֹא־נוֹצַר אֵל וְאַחֲרַי לֹא יִהְיֶה: ▶אָנֹכִי

יא אָנֹכִי יְהוָה וְאֵין מִבַּלְעָדַי מוֹשִׁיעַ: אָנֹכִי הִגַּדְתִּי וְהוֹשַׁעְתִּי וְהִשְׁמַעְתִּי וְאֵין

יב בָּכֶם זָר וְאַתֶּם עֵדַי נְאֻם־יְהוָה וַאֲנִי־אֵל: גַּם־מִיּוֹם אֲנִי הוּא וְאֵין מִיָּדִי

יג מַצִּיל אֶפְעַל וּמִי יְשִׁיבֶנָּה: כֹּה־אָמַר יְהוָה גֹּאַלְכֶם קְדוֹשׁ

יד יִשְׂרָאֵל לְמַעַנְכֶם שִׁלַּחְתִּי בָבֶלָה וְהוֹרַדְתִּי בָרִיחִים כֻּלָּם וְכַשְׂדִּים בָּאֳנִיּוֹת

טו-טז רִנָּתָם: אֲנִי יְהוָה קְדוֹשְׁכֶם בּוֹרֵא יִשְׂרָאֵל מַלְכְּכֶם: כֹּה

42:18-20. Those who were formerly blind and deaf to God's will will repent and become His servants and messengers (*Targum*). Alternatively: The Jews in exile turn a blind eye and a deaf ear to those who taunt and persecute them (*Kara*). Alternatively: The prophet is repeating the words of those whom he is admonishing. "[You deride the prophets and the righteous, saying,] 'Who is blinder than God's servants and messengers!' " (*Ibn Ezra, Radak*).

42:21. Israel's suffering in exile was ordained by God to cleanse them of their sins, just as the Torah was given to them for that purpose (*Kara*).

42:22-25. Isaiah describes the depredations of the exile, and criticizes the people for not returning to God to alleviate their frightful situation.

43:1. Isaiah now speaks of Jerusalem's delivery from Sennacherib (*Radak*).

43:3. Sennacherib went to war with Cush and put off attacking Jerusalem (37:9).

43:12. I told Israel of My salvation before it occurred (*Radak*) because they shunned idol-worship.

43:14. I sent Cyrus to conquer Babylonia, several decades after the Jews had been exiled there, to release you from your Babylonian captors (*Rashi*). According to *Targum*, the verse is addressed to the Jewish exiles themselves: "Because of *your* [sins] I sent [you] to Babylonia."

those who trust in graven idols; those who say to molten idols, 'You are our gods.'

[18] *O deaf ones, listen; and blind ones, gaze to see!* * [19] *Who is blind but My servant and deaf as My messenger whom I send? Who is blind like the perfected man? Blind like the servant of HASHEM?* [20] *Seeing much, but heeding not; opening ears, but hearing not?* [21] *HASHEM desired for the sake of [Israel's] righteousness that the Torah* * be made great and glorious.*

[22] *But it is a looted, downtrodden people,* * all of them trapped in holes, and hidden away in prisons; they are looted and there is no rescuer; plundered with none to say, 'Give it back!'* [23] *Who among you will give ear to this, will hearken and hear the outcome?* [24] *Who delivered Jacob to plunder and Israel to looters? Was it not HASHEM, He against Whom we have sinned? They did not wish to go in His ways and did not listen to His Torah.* [25] *So He poured out His fiery wrath upon him, and the power of war; it burned him from all around, but he would not know; it burned within him, but he did not take it to heart.*

43

[1] **A**nd now, * *thus says HASHEM, your Creator, O Jacob; the One Who fashioned you, O Israel: Fear not, for I have redeemed you; I have called [you] by name; you are Mine.* [2] *When you pass through water, I am with you; through rivers, they will not wash you away; when you walk through fire, you will not be singed, and no flame will burn you.* [3] *For I am HASHEM your God, the Holy One of Israel, your Savior; I gave Egypt as your ransom, and Cush* * and Seba in your place.* [4] *Because you were precious in My eyes you were honored and I loved you; I put people in your place and regimes in place of your soul.*

[5] *Fear not, for I am with you; from the East I will bring your offspring and from the West I will gather you.* [6] *I will say to the North, 'Give [them] over!' and to the South, 'Do not withhold! Bring My sons from afar and My daughters from the ends of the earth,* [7] *everyone who is called by My Name and whom I have created for My glory, whom I have fashioned, even perfected';* [8] *to liberate the people who are blind though they have eyes, and deaf though they have ears.*

[9] *Were all the nations gathered together and all the regimes assembled, who among them could have declared this and let us hear the early [prophecies]? Let them bring their witnesses and they will be vindicated; or else let them hear them say, 'It is true.'* [10] *You are My witnesses — the word of HASHEM — and My servant whom I have chosen, so that you will know and believe in Me, and understand that I am He; before Me nothing was created by a god nor will there be after Me!*

[11] *I, only I, am HASHEM, and there is no deliverer aside from Me.* [12] *I have foretold and brought salvation and informed you;* * there was no strange [god] in your midst. You are My witnesses — the word of HASHEM — and I am God.* [13] *Even before there was a day, I was He, and there is none who can save from My hand; when I act, who can reverse it?*

[14] *Thus said HASHEM, your Redeemer, the Holy One of Israel: Because of you I sent [him]* * to Babylonia and I took down all of their bolted gates and the Chaldeans [fled] in boats amid their shouting.* [15] *I am HASHEM, your holy One; the Creator of Israel, your King.*

יז אָמַר יְהֹוָה הַנּוֹתֵן בַּיָּם דָּרֶךְ וּבְמַיִם עַזִּים נְתִיבָה: הַמּוֹצִיא רֶכֶב־וָסוּס חַיִל

יח וְעִזּוּז יַחְדָּו יִשְׁכְּבוּ בַּל־יָקוּמוּ דָּעֲכוּ כַּפִּשְׁתָּה כָבוּ: אַל־תִּזְכְּרוּ רִאשֹׁנוֹת

יט וְקַדְמֹנִיּוֹת אַל־תִּתְבֹּנָנוּ: הִנְנִי עֹשֶׂה חֲדָשָׁה עַתָּה תִצְמָח הֲלוֹא תֵדָעוּהָ אַף

כ אָשִׂים בַּמִּדְבָּר דֶּרֶךְ בִּישִׁמוֹן נְהָרוֹת: תְּכַבְּדֵנִי חַיַּת הַשָּׂדֶה תַּנִּים וּבְנוֹת

HAFTARAS VAYIKRA 43:21-44:23

כא יַעֲנָה כִּי־נָתַתִּי בַמִּדְבָּר מַיִם נְהָרוֹת בִּישִׁימֹן לְהַשְׁקוֹת עַמִּי בְחִירִי: ◄ עַם־

כב זוּ יָצַרְתִּי לִי תְּהִלָּתִי יְסַפֵּרוּ: וְלֹא־אֹתִי קָרָאתָ יַעֲקֹב כִּי־יָגַעְתָּ בִּי יִשְׂרָאֵל:

כג לֹא־הֵבֵיאתָ לִּי שֵׂה עֹלֹתֶיךָ וּזְבָחֶיךָ לֹא כִבַּדְתָּנִי לֹא הֶעֱבַדְתִּיךָ בְּמִנְחָה

כד וְלֹא הוֹגַעְתִּיךָ בִּלְבוֹנָה: לֹא־קָנִיתָ לִּי בַכֶּסֶף קָנֶה וְחֵלֶב זְבָחֶיךָ לֹא

כה הִרְוִיתָנִי אַךְ הֶעֱבַדְתַּנִי בְּחַטֹּאותֶיךָ הוֹגַעְתַּנִי בַּעֲוֹנֹתֶיךָ: אָנֹכִי אָנֹכִי הוּא

כו מֹחֶה פְשָׁעֶיךָ לְמַעֲנִי וְחַטֹּאתֶיךָ לֹא אֶזְכֹּר: הַזְכִּירֵנִי נִשָּׁפְטָה יָחַד סַפֵּר

כז-כח אַתָּה לְמַעַן תִּצְדָּק: אָבִיךָ הָרִאשׁוֹן חָטָא וּמְלִיצֶיךָ פָּשְׁעוּ בִי: וַאֲחַלֵּל שָׂרֵי

א קֹדֶשׁ וְאֶתְּנָה לַחֵרֶם יַעֲקֹב וְיִשְׂרָאֵל לְגִדּוּפִים: וְעַתָּה שְׁמַע

מד

ב יַעֲקֹב עַבְדִּי וְיִשְׂרָאֵל בָּחַרְתִּי בוֹ: כֹּה־אָמַר יְהֹוָה עֹשֶׂךָ וְיֹצֶרְךָ מִבֶּטֶן יַעְזְרֶךָּ

ג אַל־תִּירָא עַבְדִּי יַעֲקֹב וִישֻׁרוּן בָּחַרְתִּי בוֹ: כִּי אֶצָּק־מַיִם עַל־צָמֵא וְנֹזְלִים

ד עַל־יַבָּשָׁה אֶצֹּק רוּחִי עַל־זַרְעֶךָ וּבִרְכָתִי עַל־צֶאֱצָאֶיךָ: וְצָמְחוּ בְּבֵין חָצִיר

ה כַּעֲרָבִים עַל־יִבְלֵי־מָיִם: זֶה יֹאמַר לַיהֹוָה אָנִי וְזֶה יִקְרָא בְשֵׁם־יַעֲקֹב וְזֶה

ו יִכְתֹּב יָדוֹ לַיהֹוָה וּבְשֵׁם יִשְׂרָאֵל יְכַנֶּה: כֹּה־אָמַר יְהֹוָה

מֶלֶךְ־יִשְׂרָאֵל וְגֹאֲלוֹ יְהֹוָה צְבָאוֹת אֲנִי רִאשׁוֹן וַאֲנִי אַחֲרוֹן וּמִבַּלְעָדַי אֵין

ז אֱלֹהִים: וּמִי־כָמוֹנִי יִקְרָא וְיַגִּידֶהָ וְיַעְרְכֶהָ לִי מִשּׂוּמִי עַם־עוֹלָם וְאֹתִיּוֹת

ח וַאֲשֶׁר תָּבֹאנָה יַגִּידוּ לָמוֹ: אַל־תִּפְחֲדוּ וְאַל־תִּרְהוּ הֲלֹא מֵאָז הִשְׁמַעְתִּיךָ

ט וְהִגַּדְתִּי וְאַתֶּם עֵדָי הֲיֵשׁ אֱלוֹהַּ מִבַּלְעָדַי וְאֵין צוּר בַּל־יָדָעְתִּי: יֹצְרֵי־פֶסֶל

כֻּלָּם תֹּהוּ וַחֲמוּדֵיהֶם בַּל־יוֹעִילוּ וְעֵדֵיהֶם הֵמָּה בַּל־יִרְאוּ וּבַל־יֵדְעוּ לְמַעַן

נקוד על המה

י-יא יֵבֹשׁוּ: מִי־יָצַר אֵל וּפֶסֶל נָסָךְ לְבִלְתִּי הוֹעִיל: הֵן כָּל־חֲבֵרָיו יֵבֹשׁוּ

יב וְחָרָשִׁים הֵמָּה מֵאָדָם יִתְקַבְּצוּ כֻלָּם יַעֲמֹדוּ יִפְחֲדוּ יֵבֹשׁוּ יָחַד: חָרַשׁ בַּרְזֶל

מַעֲצָד וּפָעַל בַּפֶּחָם וּבַמַּקָּבוֹת יִצְּרֵהוּ וַיִּפְעָלֵהוּ בִּזְרוֹעַ כֹּחוֹ גַּם־רָעֵב וְאֵין

יג כֹּחַ לֹא־שָׁתָה מַיִם וַיִּיעָף: חָרַשׁ עֵצִים נָטָה קָו יְתָאֲרֵהוּ בַשֶּׂרֶד יַעֲשֵׂהוּ

בַּמַּקְצֻעוֹת וּבַמְּחוּגָה יְתָאֲרֵהוּ וַיַּעֲשֵׂהוּ כְּתַבְנִית אִישׁ כְּתִפְאֶרֶת אָדָם

43:16-18. God recalls the Splitting of the Sea (*Exodus* 14:15-15:21), but says that the miracles of the future redemption will eclipse those of the Exodus.

43:20. Even the beasts of the field will rejoice over the bountiful greening of the desert, which will take place when My people returns.

43:23. Spoken sarcastically. Since you brought your sacrifices to your idols and not to Me, I was not a burden to you (*Radak*).

43:26. Of all your merits, if you think I have assessed you unfairly (*Radak*).

43:28. I.e., the Kohanim of the Temple (*Ibn Ezra*), or the religious leaders. Even the righteous suffer when God punishes the wicked (*Radak*).

44:2. This name for Israel, from יָשָׁר, *upright,* appears only here and in *Deuteronomy* 32:15 and 33:5, 26.

44:5. The prophet describes the enthusiastic attitude the redeemed people of Israel will assume.

44:8. No power can operate without My sanction (*Targum*).

44:9. Their worshipers.

44:12-20. Isaiah derides the foolish zeal of idolaters. So enthusiastic were people to create idols that they would even make carpenter's tools and work to the point of exhaustion (*Radak*). He goes on to describe their strenuous efforts to plant trees to be fashioned into useless idols.

¹⁶ Thus said HASHEM, He Who made a way through the Sea* and a path amid the mighty waters, ¹⁷ Who brought out chariot and horse, army and force, which all lie together, never to rise, extinguished and snuffed out like a piece of [burning] flax: ¹⁸ Do not recall former occurrences and do not contemplate earlier events. ¹⁹ [For] behold, I am bringing forth a new [miracle]! Now it will sprout, you will surely know it: I will make a road in the desert and in the wilderness rivers. ²⁰ The beasts of the field will honor Me* — the jackals and the ostriches — for I have put water in the desert and rivers in the wilderness, to provide drink for My chosen people, ²¹ this people which I fashioned for Myself that they might declare My praise.

²² But you did not call out to Me, O Jacob, for you grew weary of Me, O Israel. ²³ You did not bring Me sheep for your elevation-offerings, nor did you honor Me with your peace-offerings; I did not burden you with meal-offering,* nor did I weary you with frankincense. ²⁴ You spent no money buying Me fragrant cane, nor did you satiate Me with the fat of your offerings — rather, you burdened Me with your sins, you wearied Me with your iniquities. ²⁵ I, only I, am He Who wipes away your willful sins for My sake, and I shall not recall your sins. ²⁶ Remind Me;* let us go together for judgment; tell your [side first] that you may be vindicated. ²⁷ Your first ancestor sinned, and your advocates betrayed Me. ²⁸ Therefore I have profaned the holy princes;* I handed Jacob over to devastation and Israel to rebukes.

44

¹ But hear now, Jacob, My servant, and Israel, whom I have chosen! ² Thus said HASHEM Who made you and fashioned you from the womb, Who will help you: Fear not, My servant Jacob and Jeshurun,* whom I have chosen. ³ Just as I pour out water upon the thirsty [land] and flowing water upon the dry ground, so shall I pour out My spirit upon your offspring and My blessing upon your progeny, ⁴ and they will flourish among the grass like willows by streams of water. ⁵ This one will say: 'I am HASHEM's,'* and the other one will call [himself] by the name of Jacob; this one will sign his allegiance to HASHEM, and adopt the name of Israel.

⁶ Thus said HASHEM, King of Israel and its Redeemer, HASHEM, Master of Legions: I am the first and I am the last, and aside from Me there is no God. ⁷ Whoever will declare that he is like Me, let him proclaim it and set forth [all the events] since I emplaced the people of antiquity! And let them tell us coming events and what is yet to happen. ⁸ Be not afraid and be not terrified! Did I not make you hear of yore and tell you; and you are My witnesses: Is there a god aside from Me? There is no rock I do not know!*

⁹ All who fashion statues are empty, and the objects of their adoration will not avail; they bear witness on themselves, for they see not and they know not, so that they* should be ashamed. ¹⁰ Who fashioned a god or a molten idol? It is to no avail! ¹¹ Behold, all who join it will be shamed; and the artisans, they are but human! Let them all gather together and stand; let them be frightened and ashamed together! ¹² The ironsmith [makes] an adze; he works with charcoal and fashions it with hammers. He works on it with his strong arm, though he is hungry and without strength, though he drinks no water and grows faint. * ¹³ The woodworker stretches a line and marks [the wood] with chalk; he works on it with planes and marks it with a compass; he makes it like a man's form, like human splendor,

יד לָשֶׁבֶת בָּיִת: לִכְרָת־לוֹ אֲרָזִים וַיִּקַּח תִּרְזָה וְאַלּוֹן וַיְאַמֶּץ־לוֹ בַּעֲצֵי־יָעַר

טו נָטַע אֹרֶן וְגֶשֶׁם יְגַדֵּל: וְהָיָה לְאָדָם לְבָעֵר וַיִּקַּח מֵהֶם וַיָּחָם אַף־יַשִּׂיק וְאָפָה

טז לָחֶם אַף־יִפְעַל־אֵל וַיִּשְׁתָּחוּ עָשָׂהוּ פֶסֶל וַיִּסְגָּד־לָמוֹ: חֶצְיוֹ שָׂרַף בְּמוֹ־

אֵשׁ עַל־חֶצְיוֹ בָּשָׂר יֹאכֵל יִצְלֶה צָלִי וְיִשְׂבָּע אַף־יָחֹם וְיֹאמַר הֶאָח

יז חַמּוֹתִי רָאִיתִי אוּר: וּשְׁאֵרִיתוֹ לְאֵל עָשָׂה לְפִסְלוֹ °יִסְגוֹד [°יִסְגָּד־ ק'] לוֹ

יח וְיִשְׁתַּחוּ וְיִתְפַּלֵּל אֵלָיו וְיֹאמַר הַצִּילֵנִי כִּי אֵלִי אָתָּה: לֹא יָדְעוּ וְלֹא יָבִינוּ

יט כִּי טַח מֵרְאוֹת עֵינֵיהֶם מֵהַשְׂכִּיל לִבֹּתָם: וְלֹא־יָשִׁיב אֶל־לִבּוֹ וְלֹא דַעַת

וְלֹא־תְבוּנָה לֵאמֹר חֶצְיוֹ שָׂרַפְתִּי בְמוֹ־אֵשׁ וְאַף אָפִיתִי עַל־גֶּחָלָיו

כ לֶחֶם אֶצְלֶה בָשָׂר וְאֹכֵל וְיִתְרוֹ לְתוֹעֵבָה אֶעֱשֶׂה לְבוּל עֵץ אֶסְגּוֹד: רֹעֶה

אֵפֶר לֵב הוּתַל הִטָּהוּ וְלֹא־יַצִּיל אֶת־נַפְשׁוֹ וְלֹא יֹאמַר הֲלוֹא שֶׁקֶר

כא בִּימִינִי: זְכָר־אֵלֶּה יַעֲקֹב וְיִשְׂרָאֵל כִּי עַבְדִּי־אָתָּה יְצַרְתִּיךָ

כב עֶבֶד־לִי אַתָּה יִשְׂרָאֵל לֹא תִנָּשֵׁנִי: מָחִיתִי כָעָב פְּשָׁעֶיךָ וְכֶעָנָן חַטֹּאותֶיךָ

כג שׁוּבָה אֵלַי כִּי גְאַלְתִּיךָ: רָנּוּ שָׁמַיִם כִּי־עָשָׂה יְהוָֹה הָרִיעוּ תַּחְתִּיּוֹת אָרֶץ

פִּצְחוּ הָרִים רִנָּה יַעַר וְכָל־עֵץ בּוֹ כִּי־גָאַל יְהוָֹה יַעֲקֹב וּבְיִשְׂרָאֵל

כד יִתְפָּאָר: ◀ כֹּה־אָמַר יְהוָֹה גֹּאַלֶךָ וְיֹצֶרְךָ מִבָּטֶן אָנֹכִי יְהוָֹה

כה עֹשֶׂה כֹּל נֹטֶה שָׁמַיִם לְבַדִּי רֹקַע הָאָרֶץ °מי אתי [°מֵאִתִּי ק']: מֵפֵר אֹתוֹת

כו בַּדִּים וְקֹסְמִים יְהוֹלֵל מֵשִׁיב חֲכָמִים אָחוֹר וְדַעְתָּם יְשַׂכֵּל: מֵקִים דְּבַר

עַבְדּוֹ וַעֲצַת מַלְאָכָיו יַשְׁלִים הָאֹמֵר לִירוּשָׁלִַם תּוּשָׁב וּלְעָרֵי יְהוּדָה

כז תִּבָּנֶינָה וְחָרְבוֹתֶיהָ אֲקוֹמֵם: הָאֹמֵר לַצּוּלָה חֳרָבִי וְנַהֲרֹתַיִךְ אוֹבִישׁ:

כח הָאֹמֵר לְכוֹרֶשׁ רֹעִי וְכָל־חֶפְצִי יַשְׁלִם וְלֵאמֹר לִירוּשָׁלִַם תִּבָּנֶה וְהֵיכָל

מה א תִּוָּסֵד: כֹּה־אָמַר יְהוָֹה לִמְשִׁיחוֹ לְכוֹרֶשׁ אֲשֶׁר־הֶחֱזַקְתִּי

בִימִינוֹ לְרַד־לְפָנָיו גּוֹיִם וּמָתְנֵי מְלָכִים אֲפַתֵּחַ לִפְתֹּחַ לְפָנָיו דְּלָתַיִם

ב וּשְׁעָרִים לֹא יִסָּגֵרוּ: אֲנִי לְפָנֶיךָ אֵלֵךְ וַהֲדוּרִים °אושר [°אֲיַשֵּׁר ק'] דַּלְתוֹת

ג נְחוּשָׁה אֲשַׁבֵּר וּבְרִיחֵי בַרְזֶל אֲגַדֵּעַ: וְנָתַתִּי לְךָ אוֹצְרוֹת חֹשֶׁךְ וּמַטְמֻנֵי

מִסְתָּרִים לְמַעַן תֵּדַע כִּי־אֲנִי יְהוָֹה הַקּוֹרֵא בְשִׁמְךָ אֱלֹהֵי יִשְׂרָאֵל:

ד לְמַעַן עַבְדִּי יַעֲקֹב וְיִשְׂרָאֵל בְּחִירִי וָאֶקְרָא לְךָ בִּשְׁמֶךָ אֲכַנְּךָ וְלֹא יְדַעְתָּנִי:

ה־ו אֲנִי יְהוָֹה וְאֵין עוֹד זוּלָתִי אֵין אֱלֹהִים אֲאַזֶּרְךָ וְלֹא יְדַעְתָּנִי: לְמַעַן

יֵדְעוּ מִמִּזְרַח־שֶׁמֶשׁ וּמִמַּעֲרָבָה כִּי־אֶפֶס בִּלְעָדָי אֲנִי יְהוָֹה וְאֵין עוֹד:

44:27. A metaphor for Babylonia, which was known for its many waterways (*Rashi*).

44:28. Cyrus was the Persian conqueror of Babylonia, who generously allowed his Jewish subjects to rebuild the Temple. Although these events occurred two centuries after Isaiah's time, such is the gift of prophecy that he was able to foretell future events and even to mention the names of those who would be involved in them.

45:1-7. God, through Isaiah, addresses Cyrus (the anointed king of Persia), who will be His agent in bringing

Israel back to its land (*Radak*). According to the Talmud, "His anointed one" refers to the Messiah to whom God complained about Cyrus, "I commanded him to rebuild My Temple in Jerusalem (see *Ezra* 1:2), but instead of building it himself, he merely allowed those who wished to build it to do so (*Ezra* 1:3). Had he built it himself it would have stood forever and you, Messiah, would have been revealed now for the final redemption. However, because he did not follow My word exactly, this Temple will also be destroyed and the nation will once again go into exile" (*Megillah* 12a, as explained by *Rashba*).

Wood: god
or fuel?

to stay inside a house. ¹⁴ Cutting cedars for it; he takes laurel and oak and reinforces it with trees of the forest; he plants a fir tree and the rain makes it grow. ¹⁵ It will be fuel for man; he will take from it and warm himself, or even kindle a fire and bake bread. Yet he also makes a god and prostrates himself; he makes it a graven idol and bows to them! ¹⁶ He burns half of it in fire, or with half [he prepares] meat to eat, roasting it and sating himself, or he warms himself and says, 'Ah, I have warmed myself, I see the flame.' ¹⁷ Then the rest of it he makes into a god as his graven image; he will bow to it and prostrate himself and pray to it, and say, 'Rescue me, for you are my god!' ¹⁸ They do not know and they do not understand; for their eyes are smeared, [prevented] from seeing and their hearts from comprehending. ¹⁹ He does not take it to his heart; [he has] neither wisdom nor insight to say, 'I have burned half of it in the fire and I have baked bread on its coals; I have roasted meat and eaten it. Shall I make the remainder into an abomination? Shall I bow to stock of a tree?' ²⁰ The shepherd is but ash! A foolish heart deceived him, and he does not save his soul, and he does not say: 'Is there not falsehood in my right hand?!'

God grants
forgiveness

²¹ Remember these things, Jacob and Israel, for you are My servant: I fashioned you to be My servant; Israel, do not forget Me! ²² I will have wiped away your willful sins like a thick mist and your transgressions like a cloud; return to me, for I will have redeemed you! ²³ Sing glad song, O heavens, for HASHEM has done [wonders]; shout for joy, O foundations of the earth; break out with glad song, O mountains, O forest and all its trees; for HASHEM has redeemed Jacob, and He will glorify Himself through Israel.

The Temple
shall be
established

²⁴ Thus said HASHEM, your Redeemer and the One Who formed you from the womb: I am HASHEM, Who has made everything; Who spread out the heavens by Myself, and firmed the earth of My own accord; ²⁵ Who abrogates the omens of the stargazers and makes fools of the astrologers; Who makes wise men retreat and makes their knowledge foolish; ²⁶ Who confirms the words of His servant, and fulfills the counsel of His messengers; Who says of Jerusalem, 'It shall be settled,' and of the cities of Judah, 'They shall be built up, and I will rebuild its ruins'; ²⁷ Who says to the depths,* 'Dry up' and 'I shall dry out your rivers'; ²⁸ Who says of Cyrus,* 'He is My shepherd, He will fulfill all My desires,' to say of Jerusalem, 'It shall be built,' and of the Temple, 'It shall be established.'

45

Cyrus
is made
God's agent

¹ Thus said HASHEM to His anointed one, to Cyrus,* whose right hand I have grasped, to subdue nations before him, that I might loosen the loins of kings,* to open doors before him, and that gateways not be shut. ² "I will go before you and straighten the twisting paths; I will smash copper doors and sever iron bolts; ³ and I will grant you the treasures of darkness* and hidden riches of secret places, in order that you should know that I am HASHEM Who has proclaimed your name — [I,] the God of Israel — ⁴ for the sake of My servant Jacob and Israel, My chosen one; I have proclaimed you by name; I dubbed you, though you did not know Me. ⁵ I am HASHEM and there is no other; other than Me there is no God; I will gird you, though you did not know Me, ⁶ in order that those from east and west would know that there is nothing besides Me; I am HASHEM, and there is no other.

45:1. Just as "girding the loins" implies mustering strength or courage, "loosening the loins" denotes the loss of courage.

45:3. That is, riches that the Babylonians had hidden in dark places.

יוֹצֵר אוֹר וּבוֹרֵא חֹשֶׁךְ עֹשֶׂה שָׁלוֹם וּבוֹרֵא רָע אֲנִי יהוה עֹשֶׂה כָל־ ז
אֵלֶּה: הַרְעִיפוּ שָׁמַיִם מִמַּעַל וּשְׁחָקִים יִזְּלוּ־צֶדֶק תִּפְתַּח־ ח
אֶרֶץ וְיִפְרוּ־יֶשַׁע וּצְדָקָה תַצְמִיחַ יַחַד אֲנִי יהוה בְּרָאתִיו: הוֹי ט
רָב אֶת־יֹצְרוֹ חֶרֶשׂ אֶת־חַרְשֵׂי אֲדָמָה הֲיֹאמַר חֹמֶר לְיֹצְרוֹ מַה־תַּעֲשֶׂה
וּפָעָלְךָ אֵין־יָדַיִם לוֹ:   הוֹי אֹמֵר לְאָב מַה־תּוֹלִיד וּלְאִשָּׁה מַה־ י
תְּחִילִין: כֹּה־אָמַר יהוה קְדוֹשׁ יִשְׂרָאֵל וְיֹצְרוֹ הָאֹתִיּוֹת יא
שְׁאָלוּנִי עַל־בָּנַי וְעַל־פֹּעַל יָדַי תְּצַוֻּנִי: אָנֹכִי עָשִׂיתִי אֶרֶץ וְאָדָם עָלֶיהָ יב
בָרָאתִי אֲנִי יָדַי נָטוּ שָׁמַיִם וְכָל־צְבָאָם צִוֵּיתִי: אָנֹכִי הַעִירֹתִהוּ בְצֶדֶק יג
וְכָל־דְּרָכָיו אֲיַשֵּׁר הוּא־יִבְנֶה עִירִי וְגָלוּתִי יְשַׁלֵּחַ לֹא בִמְחִיר וְלֹא בְשֹׁחַד
אָמַר יהוה צְבָאוֹת: כֹּה ׀ אָמַר יהוה יְגִיעַ מִצְרַיִם וּסְחַר־ יד
כּוּשׁ וּסְבָאִים אַנְשֵׁי מִדָּה עָלַיִךְ יַעֲבֹרוּ וְלָךְ יִהְיוּ אַחֲרַיִךְ יֵלֵכוּ בַּזִּקִּים
יַעֲבֹרוּ וְאֵלַיִךְ יִשְׁתַּחֲווּ אֵלַיִךְ יִתְפַּלָּלוּ אַךְ בָּךְ אֵל וְאֵין עוֹד אֶפֶס אֱלֹהִים:
אָכֵן אַתָּה אֵל מִסְתַּתֵּר אֱלֹהֵי יִשְׂרָאֵל מוֹשִׁיעַ: בּוֹשׁוּ וְגַם־נִכְלְמוּ כֻּלָּם טו-טז
יַחְדָּו הָלְכוּ בַכְּלִמָּה חָרָשֵׁי צִירִים: יִשְׂרָאֵל נוֹשַׁע בַּיהוה תְּשׁוּעַת עוֹלָמִים יז
לֹא־תֵבֹשׁוּ וְלֹא־תִכָּלְמוּ עַד־עוֹלְמֵי עַד: כִּי־כֹה אָמַר־יהוה יח
בּוֹרֵא הַשָּׁמַיִם הוּא הָאֱלֹהִים יֹצֵר הָאָרֶץ וְעֹשָׂהּ הוּא כוֹנְנָהּ לֹא־תֹהוּ
בְרָאָהּ לָשֶׁבֶת יְצָרָהּ אֲנִי יהוה וְאֵין עוֹד: לֹא בַסֵּתֶר דִּבַּרְתִּי בִּמְקוֹם אֶרֶץ יט
חֹשֶׁךְ לֹא אָמַרְתִּי לְזֶרַע יַעֲקֹב תֹּהוּ בַקְּשׁוּנִי אֲנִי יהוה דֹּבֵר צֶדֶק מַגִּיד
מֵישָׁרִים: הִקָּבְצוּ וָבֹאוּ הִתְנַגְּשׁוּ יַחְדָּו פְּלִיטֵי הַגּוֹיִם לֹא יָדְעוּ הַנֹּשְׂאִים כ
אֶת־עֵץ פִּסְלָם וּמִתְפַּלְלִים אֶל־אֵל לֹא יוֹשִׁיעַ: הַגִּידוּ וְהַגִּישׁוּ אַף יִוָּעֲצוּ כא
יַחְדָּו מִי הִשְׁמִיעַ זֹאת מִקֶּדֶם מֵאָז הִגִּידָהּ הֲלוֹא אֲנִי יהוה וְאֵין־עוֹד
אֱלֹהִים מִבַּלְעָדַי אֵל־צַדִּיק וּמוֹשִׁיעַ אַיִן זוּלָתִי: פְּנוּ־אֵלַי וְהִוָּשְׁעוּ כָּל־ כב
אַפְסֵי־אָרֶץ כִּי אֲנִי־אֵל וְאֵין עוֹד: בִּי נִשְׁבַּעְתִּי יָצָא מִפִּי צְדָקָה דָּבָר וְלֹא כג
יָשׁוּב כִּי־לִי תִּכְרַע כָּל־בֶּרֶךְ תִּשָּׁבַע כָּל־לָשׁוֹן: אַךְ בַּיהוה לִי אָמַר צִדְקוֹת כד
וָעֹז עָדַי יָבוֹא יָבֹאוּ וְיֵבֹשׁוּ כֹּל הַנֶּחֱרִים בּוֹ: בַּיהוה יִצְדְּקוּ וְיִתְהַלְלוּ כָּל־זֶרַע כה
יִשְׂרָאֵל: כָּרַע בֵּל קֹרֵס נְבוֹ הָיוּ עֲצַבֵּיהֶם לַחַיָּה וְלַבְּהֵמָה נְשֻׂאֹתֵיכֶם א
עֲמוּסוֹת מַשָּׂא לַעֲיֵפָה: קָרְסוּ כָרְעוּ יַחְדָּו לֹא יָכְלוּ מַלֵּט מַשָּׂא וְנַפְשָׁם ב
בַּשְּׁבִי הָלָכָה: שִׁמְעוּ אֵלַי בֵּית יַעֲקֹב וְכָל־שְׁאֵרִית בֵּית ג

מו

45:11. Let the nations of the world ask Me what I have in store for My people!

45:14. This begins a prophecy. It refers to Sennacherib's attack on Jerusalem (*Rashi*), and reverts to the theme of 43:1-4. Sennacherib would bring hoards of spoils and prisoners when he returns to Jerusalem from an expedition to Cush (see Ch. 37). When God ends the siege, the Jews would take the property and set the captives free.

45:19. I did not keep My prophecies a secret; My proph-

ets revealed them to the peoples of the world (*Ibn Ezra*).

45:21. Who prophesied the salvation of Israel from Sennacherib or the Babylonians (*Radak*).

46:1. Bitingly and sarcastically, the chapter contrasts the omnipotence of God with the helplessness of idols and the foolishness of idolaters in general. It begins by speaking figuratively of Bel and Nebo, the Babylonian deities, which double over and collapse when their country is conquered, and are then ignominiously carted off by the victors.

⁷ *[I am the One] Who forms light and creates darkness; Who makes peace and creates evil; I am HASHEM, Maker of all these.*

⁸ *"Pour out, O heavens, from above, and let the upper heights drip righeousness; let the earth open up and salvation and goodness will flourish; let it make them sprout together; I am HASHEM, Who created this.*

God is sovereign ⁹ *"Woe to him who argues with his Creator, a shard among the shards of the earth! Does clay say to the one who forms it, 'What are you doing? Your creation is without [skilled] hands'?* ¹⁰ *Woe to he who says to a father, 'What have you begotten?' or to a woman, 'For what have you gone into labor?'* ¹¹ *Thus said HASHEM, the Holy One of Israel and the One Who formed it: Ask Me about the future events, about My sons and about the actions of My hands shall you command Me.* * ¹² *I made the earth and I created mankind upon it; it is I, My hands spread out the heavens and I commanded all its hosts [to come into existence].* ¹³ *I aroused [Cyrus] with righteousness and smoothed out all his paths; he will build My city and set My exiles free, not with a price and not with a bribe, said HASHEM, Master of Legions."*

The nations will confess ¹⁴ *Thus said HASHEM:* * *The toil of Egypt and the merchandise of Cush and the Sabeans, men of stature, will pass to you and will become yours; they will follow after you and pass in chains. They will prostrate themselves before you; they will pray before you, 'Only with you [Jerusalem] is God, and there is none other, except for God';* ¹⁵ *[and before God,] 'Indeed, You are a God Who conceals Himself, the God of Israel is the Savior!'* ¹⁶ *They will all be ashamed and humiliated; together the artisans of idolatrous forms will walk in shame.* ¹⁷ *But Israel is saved through HASHEM, an eternal salvation; you will not be ashamed nor humiliated for all eternity.*

God, the Creator ¹⁸ *For thus said HASHEM, Creator of the heavens; He is the God, the One Who fashioned the earth and its Maker; He established it; He did not create it for emptiness; He fashioned it to be inhabited: I am HASHEM and there is no other.* ¹⁹ *I did not speak in secrecy, some place in a land of darkness;* * *I did not tell the descendants of Jacob to seek Me for nothing; I am HASHEM Who speaks righteousness, Who declares upright things.* ²⁰ *Gather yourselves, come and approach together, O survivors of the nations, who do not know, who carry about the wood of their graven image, and pray to a god who cannot save.* ²¹ *Proclaim and approach; even let [your leaders] take counsel together: Who let this be heard from aforetimes, or related it from of old?* * *Is it not I, HASHEM? There is no other god besides Me; there is no righteous god besides Me and no savior other than Me.* ²² *Turn to Me and be saved, all ends of the earth, for I am God and there is no other.* ²³ *I swear by Myself, righteousness has gone forth from My mouth, a word that will not be rescinded: that to Me shall every knee kneel and every tongue swear.*

²⁴ *Only in HASHEM, Who spoke to me, is there righteousness and strength; all those who anger Him will come to Him and be ashamed.* ²⁵ *All the seed of Israel will be vindicated and will glory in HASHEM.*

46

Collapse of the idols ¹ Bel* *is kneeling; Nebo is doubled over. Their idols [were loaded] on the beast and animal; your bearers are overloaded, it is a burden on the weary [beast].* ² *They have doubled over and fallen on their knees together; they could not escape being carried off; and have themselves gone into captivity.* ³ *Listen to Me, O House of Jacob, and all the remnant of the House*

ד יִשְׂרָאֵל הַעֲמֻסִים מִנִּי־בֶטֶן הַנְּשֻׂאִים מִנִּי־רָחַם: וְעַד־זִקְנָה אֲנִי הוּא וְעַד־

ה שֵׂיבָה אֲנִי אֶסְבֹּל אֲנִי עָשִׂיתִי וַאֲנִי אֶשָּׂא וַאֲנִי אֶסְבֹּל וַאֲמַלֵּט: לְמִי

ו תְדַמְּיוּנִי וְתַשְׁווּ וְתַמְשִׁלוּנִי וְנִדְמֶה: הַזָּלִים זָהָב מִכִּיס וְכֶסֶף בַּקָּנֶה יִשְׁקֹלוּ

ז יִשְׂכְּרוּ צוֹרֵף וְיַעֲשֵׂהוּ אֵל יִסְגְּדוּ אַף־יִשְׁתַּחֲווּ: יִשָּׂאֻהוּ עַל־כָּתֵף יִסְבְּלֻהוּ

וְיַנִּיחֻהוּ תַחְתָּיו וְיַעֲמֹד מִמְּקוֹמוֹ לֹא יָמִישׁ אַף־יִצְעַק אֵלָיו וְלֹא יַעֲנֶה

ח מִצָּרָתוֹ לֹא יוֹשִׁיעֶנּוּ: זִכְרוּ־זֹאת וְהִתְאֹשָׁשׁוּ הָשִׁיבוּ פוֹשְׁעִים

ט עַל־לֵב: זִכְרוּ רִאשֹׁנוֹת מֵעוֹלָם כִּי אָנֹכִי אֵל וְאֵין עוֹד אֱלֹהִים וְאֶפֶס

י כָּמוֹנִי: מַגִּיד מֵרֵאשִׁית אַחֲרִית וּמִקֶּדֶם אֲשֶׁר לֹא־נַעֲשׂוּ אֹמֵר עֲצָתִי

יא תָקוּם וְכָל־חֶפְצִי אֶעֱשֶׂה: קֹרֵא מִמִּזְרָח עַיִט מֵאֶרֶץ מֶרְחָק אִישׁ °עֲצָתוֹ

יב [עֲצָתִי ק׳] אַף־דִּבַּרְתִּי אַף־אֲבִיאֶנָּה יָצַרְתִּי אַף־אֶעֱשֶׂנָּה: שִׁמְעוּ

יג אֵלַי אַבִּירֵי לֵב הָרְחוֹקִים מִצְּדָקָה: קֵרַבְתִּי צִדְקָתִי לֹא תִרְחָק וּתְשׁוּעָתִי

מז

א לֹא תְאַחֵר וְנָתַתִּי בְצִיּוֹן תְּשׁוּעָה לְיִשְׂרָאֵל תִּפְאַרְתִּי: רְדִי | וּשְׁבִי

עַל־עָפָר בְּתוּלַת בַּת־בָּבֶל שְׁבִי־לָאָרֶץ אֵין־כִּסֵּא בַּת־כַּשְׂדִּים כִּי לֹא

ב תוֹסִיפִי יִקְרְאוּ־לָךְ רַכָּה וַעֲנֻגָּה: קְחִי רֵחַיִם וְטַחֲנִי קָמַח גַּלִּי צַמָּתֵךְ

ג חֶשְׂפִּי־שֹׁבֶל גַּלִּי־שׁוֹק עִבְרִי נְהָרוֹת: תִּגָּל עֶרְוָתֵךְ גַּם תֵּרָאֶה חֶרְפָּתֵךְ

ד נָקָם אֶקָּח וְלֹא אֶפְגַּע אָדָם: גֹּאֲלֵנוּ יְהוָה צְבָאוֹת שְׁמוֹ קְדוֹשׁ

ה יִשְׂרָאֵל: שְׁבִי דוּמָם וּבֹאִי בַחֹשֶׁךְ בַּת־כַּשְׂדִּים כִּי לֹא תוֹסִיפִי יִקְרְאוּ־לָךְ

ו גְּבֶרֶת מַמְלָכוֹת: קָצַפְתִּי עַל־עַמִּי חִלַּלְתִּי נַחֲלָתִי וָאֶתְּנֵם בְּיָדֵךְ לֹא־

ז שַׂמְתְּ לָהֶם רַחֲמִים עַל־זָקֵן הִכְבַּדְתְּ עֻלֵּךְ מְאֹד: וַתֹּאמְרִי לְעוֹלָם אֶהְיֶה

ח גְּבָרֶת עַד לֹא־שַׂמְתְּ אֵלֶּה עַל־לִבֵּךְ לֹא זָכַרְתְּ אַחֲרִיתָהּ: וְעַתָּה

שִׁמְעִי־זֹאת עֲדִינָה הַיּוֹשֶׁבֶת לָבֶטַח הָאֹמְרָה בִּלְבָבָהּ אֲנִי וְאַפְסִי עוֹד

ט לֹא אֵשֵׁב אַלְמָנָה וְלֹא אֵדַע שְׁכוֹל: וְתָבֹאנָה לָּךְ שְׁתֵּי־אֵלֶּה רֶגַע בְּיוֹם

אֶחָד שְׁכוֹל וְאַלְמֹן כְּתֻמָּם בָּאוּ עָלַיִךְ בְּרֹב כְּשָׁפַיִךְ בְּעָצְמַת חֲבָרַיִךְ

י מְאֹד: וַתִּבְטְחִי בְרָעָתֵךְ אָמַרְתְּ אֵין רֹאָנִי חָכְמָתֵךְ וְדַעְתֵּךְ הִיא

יא שׁוֹבְבָתֶךְ וַתֹּאמְרִי בְלִבֵּךְ אֲנִי וְאַפְסִי עוֹד: וּבָא עָלַיִךְ רָעָה לֹא תֵדְעִי

שַׁחְרָהּ וְתִפֹּל עָלַיִךְ הֹוָה לֹא תוּכְלִי כַּפְּרָהּ וְתָבֹא עָלַיִךְ פִּתְאֹם שׁוֹאָה

יב לֹא תֵדָעִי: עִמְדִי־נָא בַחֲבָרַיִךְ וּבְרֹב כְּשָׁפַיִךְ בַּאֲשֶׁר יָגַעַתְּ מִנְּעוּרָיִךְ

יג אוּלַי תּוּכְלִי הוֹעִיל אוּלַי תַּעֲרוֹצִי: נִלְאֵית בְּרֹב עֲצָתָיִךְ יַעַמְדוּ־נָא

וְיוֹשִׁיעֻךְ °הֹבְרוּ [הֹבְרֵי ק׳] שָׁמַיִם הַחֹזִים בַּכּוֹכָבִים מוֹדִיעִם לֶחֳדָשִׁים

46:4. In contrast to the helpless idols, which are hauled off as looted baggage, God is not borne but bears His people and rescues them from all their difficulties (*Rashi*).

46:11. A reference to Cyrus, who would swoop down upon Babylonia from Persia (*Ibn Ezra*), and be the instrument to carry out God's plan.

46:12. The prophet is addressing the Babylonians who cruelly oppressed the Jews (*Radak*).

47:2. As a slave would. Your days as a member of the nobility are over; you will cross your river and go into exile.

47:4. The prophet interjects that all this will be caused by God (*Rashi*).

of Israel, who are borne [by Me] from birth, who are carried from the womb.
⁴ Until [your] old age I am unchanged, and until [your] hoary years I will carry [you]; I made [you] and I will bear [you], I will carry [you] and I will rescue [you]. * ⁵ To whom can you liken Me, or consider equal, or compare Me that we should seem alike? ⁶ — to those who pour gold from the purse and weigh silver in a balance-scale; who hire a goldsmith to make it into a god; who bow and even prostrate themselves; ⁷ who carry it on their shoulders and bear it; and when they set it down, it remains in its place, it does not budge from its place? He even cries out to it, but it does not answer; it does not save him from his distress.

God of history

⁸ Remember this and strengthen yourselves; take it to heart, O evildoers: ⁹ Recall the early events of ancient times, [see] that I am God and there is no other; [I am] God and there is none like Me. ¹⁰ From the beginning I foretell the outcome; and from earlier times, what has not yet been; [but] I say and My plan will stand, and I will carry out My every desire. ¹¹ I have summoned the vulture * from the east, from a distant land, [he is] the man of My counsel. I also spoke; I also will carry out. I formed [it]; I also will accomplish it.

¹² Listen to Me, O fierce-hearted ones, * who are far from righteousness: ¹³ I have brought My righteousness close, it will not be far; and My salvation, it will not delay; I will establish My salvation in Zion, My splendor for Israel.

47

The exile of the Babylonians

¹ **G**et down and sit on the dirt, O virgin daughter of Babylonia; sit on the ground without a chair, O daughter of Chaldeans; for they will no longer call you 'delicate and dainty.' ² Get a millstone and grind flour; * expose your hair and bare a leg; expose a thigh to cross through rivers. ³ Your nakedness will be exposed and your embarrassment will be seen; I will take revenge and I will not be entreated by man.

⁴ Our Redeemer, * Whose Name is HASHEM, Master of Legions, the Holy One of Israel!

⁵ Sit silently, then go into the darkness, O daughter of Chaldeans, for they will no longer call you 'the mistress of kingdoms.' ⁶ I became angry at My people; I degraded My heritage and delivered them into your hand. You showed them no compassion; you made your yoke very heavy upon the aged. ⁷ You said [to yourself], 'Forever will I be a mistress!' so you did not take these upon your heart; you did not remember [My heritage's] end.

From security to tragedy

⁸ Now, hear this, O pampered one, who dwells securely, who says in her heart, 'Only I and none but me! I shall not sit as a widow, and I shall not know bereavement': ⁹ Both of these will come upon you in a moment, on the same day — bereavement and widowhood; in their fullness will they come upon you, despite the abundance of your witchcraft and the great intensity of your enchantments. ¹⁰ You trusted in your evil; you said, 'No one sees me.' Your wisdom and your knowledge — that is what emboldened you; you said in your heart, 'Only I and none but me!' ¹¹ Misfortune will befall you, you will not know how to pray; tragedy will befall you, you will be unable to remove it; there will come upon you a sudden disaster such as you have never known. ¹² Stand fast now with your enchantments and with the abundance of your witchcraft, with which you have toiled from your youth; perhaps you will be able to avail, perhaps you will gain strength! ¹³ You have wearied yourself with your many counselors; let them stand up for you now and save you — the astrologers, the stargazers, who foretell by new moons —

יד מֵאֲשֶׁר יָגָעַתְּ: מִמַּד לָךְ-הָיוּ כֵּן נֶגְדּוֹ לָשֶׁבֶת אוֹר לַחְמָם אֵין-גַּחֶלֶת לְהָבָה מִד

מֵאֲשֶׁר יָבָאוּ עָלָיִךְ: הִנֵּה הָיוּ כְקַשׁ אֵשׁ שְׂרָפָתַם לֹא-יַצִּילוּ אֶת-נַפְשָׁם

טו סֹחֲרַיִךְ מִנְּעוּרַיִךְ אִישׁ לְעֶבְרוֹ תָּעוּ אֵין מוֹשִׁיעֵךְ: שִׁמְעוּ-זֹאת

מח א בֵּית-יַעֲקֹב הַנִּקְרָאִים בְּשֵׁם יִשְׂרָאֵל וּמִמֵּי יְהוּדָה יָצָאוּ הַנִּשְׁבָּעִים | בְּשֵׁם

ב יהוה וּבֵאלֹהֵי יִשְׂרָאֵל יַזְכִּירוּ לֹא בֶאֱמֶת וְלֹא בִצְדָקָה: כִּי-מֵעִיר הַקֹּדֶשׁ

ג נִקְרָאוּ וְעַל-אֱלֹהֵי יִשְׂרָאֵל נִסְמָכוּ יהוה צְבָאוֹת שְׁמוֹ: הָרִאשֹׁנוֹת

ד מֵאָז הִגַּדְתִּי וּמִפִּי יָצְאוּ וְאַשְׁמִיעֵם פִּתְאֹם עָשִׂיתִי וַתָּבֹאנָה: מִדַּעְתִּי כִּי

ה קָשֶׁה אָתָּה וְגִיד בַּרְזֶל עָרְפֶּךָ וּמִצְחֲךָ נְחוּשָׁה: וָאַגִּיד לְךָ מֵאָז בְּטֶרֶם תָּבוֹא

ו הִשְׁמַעְתִּיךָ פֶּן-תֹּאמַר עָצְבִּי עָשָׂם וּפִסְלִי וְנִסְכִּי צִוָּם: שָׁמַעְתָּ חֲזֵה כֻלָּהּ

ז וְאַתֶּם הֲלוֹא תַגִּידוּ הִשְׁמַעְתִּיךָ חֲדָשׁוֹת מֵעַתָּה וּנְצֻרוֹת וְלֹא יְדַעְתָּם: עַתָּה נִבְרְאוּ וְלֹא מֵאָז וְלִפְנֵי-יוֹם וְלֹא שְׁמַעְתָּם פֶּן-תֹּאמַר הִנֵּה יְדַעְתִּין:

ח גַּם לֹא-שָׁמַעְתָּ גַּם לֹא יָדַעְתָּ גַּם מֵאָז לֹא-פִתְּחָה אָזְנֶךָ כִּי יָדַעְתִּי בָּגוֹד

ט תִּבְגּוֹד וּפֹשֵׁעַ מִבֶּטֶן קֹרָא לָךְ: לְמַעַן שְׁמִי אַאֲרִיךְ אַפִּי וּתְהִלָּתִי אֶחֱטָם-

י-יא לָךְ לְבִלְתִּי הַכְרִיתֶךָ: הִנֵּה צְרַפְתִּיךָ וְלֹא בְכָסֶף בְּחַרְתִּיךָ בְּכוּר עֹנִי: לְמַעֲנִי

יב לְמַעֲנִי אֶעֱשֶׂה כִּי אֵיךְ יֵחָל וּכְבוֹדִי לְאַחֵר לֹא-אֶתֵּן: שְׁמַע

יג אֵלַי יַעֲקֹב וְיִשְׂרָאֵל מְקֹרָאִי אֲנִי-הוּא אֲנִי רִאשׁוֹן אַף אֲנִי אַחֲרוֹן: אַף-יָדִי

יד יָסְדָה אֶרֶץ וִימִינִי טִפְּחָה שָׁמָיִם קֹרֵא אֲנִי אֲלֵיהֶם יַעַמְדוּ יַחְדָּו: הִקָּבְצוּ

כֻלְּכֶם וְשַׁמָעוּ מִי בָהֶם הִגִּיד אֶת-אֵלֶּה יהוה אֲהֵבוֹ יַעֲשֶׂה חֶפְצוֹ בְּבָבֶל

טו וּזְרֹעוֹ כַּשְׂדִים: אֲנִי אֲנִי דִבַּרְתִּי אַף-קְרָאתִיו הֲבִיאֹתִיו וְהִצְלִיחַ דַּרְכּוֹ:

טז קִרְבוּ אֵלַי שִׁמְעוּ-זֹאת לֹא מֵרֹאשׁ בַּסֵּתֶר דִּבַּרְתִּי מֵעֵת הֱיוֹתָהּ שָׁם אָנִי

יז וְעַתָּה אֲדֹנָי יֱהוִֹה שְׁלָחַנִי וְרוּחוֹ: כֹּה-אָמַר יהוה גֹּאַלְךָ

קְדוֹשׁ יִשְׂרָאֵל אֲנִי יהוה אֱלֹהֶיךָ מְלַמֶּדְךָ לְהוֹעִיל מַדְרִיכֲךָ בְּדֶרֶךְ

יח תֵּלֵךְ: לוּא הִקְשַׁבְתָּ לְמִצְוֹתָי וַיְהִי כַנָּהָר שְׁלוֹמֶךָ וְצִדְקָתְךָ כְּגַלֵּי הַיָּם:

יט וַיְהִי כַחוֹל זַרְעֶךָ וְצֶאֱצָאֵי מֵעֶיךָ כִּמְעֹתָיו לֹא-יִכָּרֵת וְלֹא-יִשָּׁמֵד שְׁמוֹ

כ מִלְּפָנָי: צְאוּ מִבָּבֶל בִּרְחוּ מִכַּשְׂדִּים בְּקוֹל רִנָּה הַגִּידוּ הַשְׁמִיעוּ

כא זֹאת הוֹצִיאוּהָ עַד-קְצֵה הָאָרֶץ אִמְרוּ גָּאַל יהוה עַבְדּוֹ יַעֲקֹב: וְלֹא צָמְאוּ

47:14. Your obsession with astrology was as useless as straw, which leaves nothing of benefit after it is burned.

47:15. All the foreigners with whom you had had business dealings will desert you and flee for home when you come under attack (*Radak*).

48:1-3. They profane God's Name by using it to swear falsely (*Rashi*), or they hypocritically swear by His Name, but do not do His will (*Radak, Ibn Ezra*). Nevertheless, I shall redeem them, for they are known as "the people of the Holy City," and they rely on Me to save them. Thus, if I would not save them, My glory would be profaned. Therefore, God prophesied that He would save Hezekiah's kingdom from Sennacherib (*Rashi*).

48:6. Will you not proclaim that God carried out His promise to destroy the Assyrian army?

48:10. I will punish you, but not with the full severity you deserve, as one would smelt silver over the flaming fire, for then there would be nothing left of you.

48:11. If God permitted Israel to be vanquished, the victor would credit his own prowess or his gods.

48:14. Having proclaimed God's omnipotence, the prophet calls upon the idolaters to gather and declare that He has sent Cyrus, the one "whom HASHEM loves," carry out His will against Babylonia.

48:16. The prophet declares that he had spoken his prophecy regarding Sennacherib's downfall for all to hear from the very first time it was revealed to him (*Radak*). He then issues a new prophecy.

48:19. Your descendants will be as numerous as the fish in the ocean (*Rashi*).

from what will happen to you! [14] *Behold, they have become like straw:* * *fire burned them, they could not save themselves from the power of the flame; no coal remains by which to warm up; no fire by which to sit —* [15] *so were [those advisers] with whom you toiled. The merchants with whom you dealt since your youth have scattered,* * *each one in his own direction; there is no one to save you.*

48

Retrospective of prophecy

[1] **H**ear this, O House of Jacob, who are called by the name of Israel, and who emerged from the fount of Judah, who swear by the Name of HASHEM and make mention of the God of Israel — but not in truth and not in righteousness* — [2] rather because they are called after the Holy City and they rely on the God of Israel, HASHEM, Master of Legions, is His Name. [3] I foretold the earliest events beforehand; they emerged from My mouth and I announced them; I acted with suddenness and they came about. [4] Because of My knowledge that you are difficult, and that your neck is an iron sinew and your forehead is brazen, [5] I told you beforehand, and when it had not yet happened I informed you, lest you say, 'My deity accomplished them; my graven image and my molten idol have ordained them.' [6] You have heard it; now see it all [happen]! Now you — will you not tell it?* Now I will inform you of new events, hidden things that you did not know about. [7] They were created just now, not long ago and not before today, and you have never heard of them — lest you say, 'Behold, I already know them.' [8] You have neither heard nor have you known, nor was your ear opened to them from before. For I know that you would deal very treacherously, and you have been called a rebel from birth. [9] For My Name's sake I shall restrain My wrath; for My praise I shall withhold My anger from you, not to cut you down. [10] Behold, I refine you, but not like silver; I have chosen for you the crucible of hardship. * [11] For My sake, for My sake I will do [it], for how can I let [My Name] be profaned? I will not cede My glory to another!*

[12] Listen to Me, O Jacob, and Israel, as he was called by Me: I am He; I am the first, also I am the last. [13] Also, My hand has laid the foundation of the earth, and My right hand has measured out the heavens; I call to them and they stand together. [14] Gather together, all of you, and listen, who among them has related these things:* HASHEM loves him who does His will in Babylonia, and [shows] His arm against the Chaldeans. [15] I, only I, have spoken and even summoned him; I have brought him, and his path is successful.

[16] Approach me, hear this: I did not speak in secrecy at first;* from the time [the decree] was issued I was there. And now, My Lord, HASHEM/ELOHIM, has sent me with His spirit.

Reward for obedience

[17] Thus said HASHEM, your Redeemer, the Holy One of Israel: I am HASHEM, your God, Who instructs you for [your] benefit, Who guides you in the way you should follow. [18] If you had hearkened to My commandments, your peace would [flow] like a river and your righteousness like the waves of the sea. [19] Your offspring would be like the sand and those that emerge from your innards like [the sea's] innards. * Its name will not be cut off and will not be destroyed before Me.

[20] Go forth from Babylonia; hurry from Chaldea. With glad song relate, announce this; bring forth [the message] to the ends of the earth; say, 'HASHEM has redeemed His servant Jacob.' [21] They did not thirst,

כב בָּחֳרָבוֹת֙ הוֹלִיכָ֔ם מַ֥יִם מִצּ֖וּר הִזִּ֣יל לָ֑מוֹ וַיִּ֤בְקַע־צוּר֙ וַיָּזֻ֣בוּ מָ֔יִם: אֵ֥ין שָׁל֖וֹם

מט א אָמַ֥ר יְהוָ֖ה לָֽרְשָׁעִֽים: שִׁמְע֤וּ אִיִּים֙ אֵלַ֔י וְהַקְשִׁ֥יבוּ לְאֻמִּ֖ים מֵרָח֑וֹק

ב יְהוָה֙ מִבֶּ֣טֶן קְרָאָ֔נִי מִמְּעֵ֥י אִמִּ֖י הִזְכִּ֣יר שְׁמִֽי: וַיָּ֤שֶׂם פִּי֙ כְּחֶ֣רֶב חַדָּ֔ה בְּצֵ֥ל

ג יָד֖וֹ הֶחְבִּיאָ֑נִי וַיְשִׂימֵ֙נִי֙ לְחֵ֣ץ בָּר֔וּר בְּאַשְׁפָּת֖וֹ הִסְתִּירָ֑נִי: וַיֹּ֥אמֶר לִ֖י עַבְדִּי־

ד אַ֑תָּה יִשְׂרָאֵ֕ל אֲשֶׁר־בְּךָ֖ אֶתְפָּאָֽר: וַאֲנִ֤י אָמַ֙רְתִּי֙ לְרִ֣יק יָגַ֔עְתִּי לְתֹ֥הוּ וְהֶ֖בֶל

ה כֹּחִ֣י כִלֵּ֑יתִי אָכֵן֙ מִשְׁפָּטִ֣י אֶת־יְהוָ֔ה וּפְעֻלָּתִ֖י אֶת־אֱלֹהָֽי: וְעַתָּ֣ה ׀

אָמַ֣ר יְהוָ֗ה יֹצְרִ֤י מִבֶּ֙טֶן֙ לְעֶ֣בֶד ל֔וֹ לְשׁוֹבֵ֤ב יַֽעֲקֹב֙ אֵלָ֔יו וְיִשְׂרָאֵ֖ל °לֹ֣א

ו [ל֣וֹ ק] יֵֽאָסֵ֑ף וְאֶכָּבֵד֙ בְּעֵינֵ֣י יְהוָ֔ה וֵאלֹהַ֖י הָיָ֣ה עֻזִּֽי: וַיֹּ֗אמֶר נָקֵ֨ל מִֽהְיוֹתְךָ֥

לִי֙ עֶ֔בֶד לְהָקִים֙ אֶת־שִׁבְטֵ֣י יַעֲקֹ֔ב °וּנְצירֵ֥י [וּנְצוּרֵ֖י ק] יִשְׂרָאֵ֖ל לְהָשִׁ֑יב

ז וּנְתַתִּ֙יךָ֙ לְא֣וֹר גּוֹיִ֔ם לִֽהְי֥וֹת יְשֽׁוּעָתִ֖י עַד־קְצֵ֥ה הָאָֽרֶץ: כֹּ֣ה אָמַר־

יְהוָה֩ גֹּאֵ֨ל יִשְׂרָאֵ֜ל קְדוֹשׁ֗וֹ לִבְזֹה־נֶ֜פֶשׁ לִמְתָ֤עֵֽב גּוֹי֙ לְעֶ֣בֶד מֹֽשְׁלִ֔ים מְלָכִ֤ים

יִרְאוּ֙ וָקָ֔מוּ שָׂרִ֖ים וְיִֽשְׁתַּחֲו֑וּ לְמַ֤עַן יְהוָה֙ אֲשֶׁ֣ר נֶאֱמָ֔ן קְדֹ֥שׁ יִשְׂרָאֵ֖ל

ח וַיִּבְחָרֶֽךָּ:   כֹּ֣ה ׀ אָמַ֣ר יְהוָ֗ה בְּעֵ֤ת רָצוֹן֙ עֲנִיתִ֔יךָ וּבְי֥וֹם יְשׁוּעָ֖ה

עֲזַרְתִּ֑יךָ וְאֶצָּרְךָ֗ וְאֶתֶּנְךָ֙ לִבְרִ֣ית עָ֔ם לְהָקִ֣ים אֶ֔רֶץ לְהַנְחִ֖יל נְחָל֥וֹת

ט שֹׁמֵמֽוֹת: לֵאמֹ֤ר לַֽאֲסוּרִים֙ צֵ֔אוּ לַאֲשֶׁ֥ר בַּחֹ֖שֶׁךְ הִגָּל֑וּ עַל־דְּרָכִ֣ים יִרְע֔וּ

י וּבְכָל־שְׁפָיִ֖ים מַרְעִיתָֽם: לֹ֤א יִרְעָ֙בוּ֙ וְלֹ֣א יִצְמָ֔אוּ וְלֹֽא־יַכֵּ֥ם שָׁרָ֖ב וָשָׁ֑מֶשׁ

יא כִּֽי־מְרַחֲמָ֣ם יְנַהֲגֵ֔ם וְעַל־מַבּ֥וּעֵי מַ֖יִם יְנַהֲלֵֽם: וְשַׂמְתִּ֥י כָל־הָרַ֖י לַדָּ֑רֶךְ

יב וּמְסִלֹּתַ֖י יְרֻמֽוּן: הִנֵּה־אֵ֙לֶּה֙ מֵרָח֣וֹק יָבֹ֔אוּ וְהִנֵּה־אֵ֖לֶּה מִצָּפ֣וֹן וּמִיָּ֑ם וְאֵ֖לֶּה

יג מֵאֶ֥רֶץ סִינִֽים: רָנּ֤וּ שָׁמַ֙יִם֙ וְגִ֣ילִי אָ֔רֶץ °יפצחו [וּפִצְח֥וּ ק] הָרִ֖ים רִנָּ֑ה כִּֽי־

יד נִחַ֤ם יְהוָה֙ עַמּ֔וֹ וַעֲנִיָּ֖ו יְרַחֵֽם: וַתֹּ֥אמֶר צִיּ֖וֹן עֲזָבַ֣נִי יְהוָ֑ה וַאדֹנָ֖י

HAFTARAS EIKEV 49:14-51:3

טו שְׁכֵחָֽנִי: הֲתִשְׁכַּ֤ח אִשָּׁה֙ עוּלָ֔הּ מֵרַחֵ֖ם בֶּן־בִּטְנָ֑הּ גַּם־אֵ֣לֶּה תִשְׁכַּ֔חְנָה

טז-יז וְאָנֹכִ֖י לֹ֥א אֶשְׁכָּחֵֽךְ: הֵ֥ן עַל־כַּפַּ֖יִם חַקֹּתִ֑יךְ חוֹמֹתַ֥יִךְ נֶגְדִּ֖י תָּמִֽיד: מִֽהֲר֖וּ

בָּנָ֑יִךְ מְהָֽרְסַ֥יִךְ וּמַחֲרִבַ֖יִךְ מִמֵּ֥ךְ יֵצֵֽאוּ: שְׂאִֽי־סָבִ֤יב עֵינַ֙יִךְ֙ וּרְאִ֔י כֻּלָּ֖ם

יח נִקְבְּצ֣וּ בָֽאוּ־לָ֑ךְ חַי־אָ֣נִי נְאֻם־יְהוָ֗ה כִּ֤י כֻלָּם֙ כָּעֲדִ֣י תִלְבָּ֔שִׁי וּֽתְקַשְּׁרִ֖ים

יט כַּכַּלָּֽה: כִּ֤י חָרְבֹתַ֙יִךְ֙ וְשֹׁ֣מְמֹתַ֔יִךְ וְאֶ֖רֶץ הֲרִסֻתֵ֑ךְ כִּ֤י עַתָּה֙ תֵּצְרִ֣י מִיּוֹשֵׁ֔ב

כ וְרָחֲק֖וּ מְבַלְּעָֽיִךְ: ע֚וֹד יֹאמְר֣וּ בְאָזְנַ֔יִךְ בְּנֵ֖י שִׁכֻּלָ֑יִךְ צַר־לִ֥י הַמָּק֖וֹם גְּשָׁה־

כא לִּ֥י וְאֵשֵֽׁבָה: וְאָמַ֣רְתְּ בִּלְבָבֵ֗ךְ מִ֤י יָֽלַד־לִי֙ אֶת־אֵ֔לֶּה וַאֲנִ֥י שְׁכוּלָ֖ה

וְגַלְמוּדָ֑ה גֹּלָ֣ה ׀ וְסוּרָ֗ה וְאֵ֙לֶּה֙ מִ֣י גִדֵּ֔ל הֵ֤ן אֲנִי֙ נִשְׁאַ֣רְתִּי לְבַדִּ֔י אֵ֖לֶּה אֵיפֹ֥ה

48:22. The Babylonian victims of Cyrus's conquest.

49:1. As he prepares to prophesy regarding many countries, Isaiah stresses that God selected him for this purpose.

49:4. I was frustrated when I saw that people ignored my preaching, but God knows that I put all my effort into it, and that the failure was not my fault.

49:7. According to most commentators, this verse begins a new prophecy: When God redeems Israel, which has been "despised . . . loathed . . . a servant," its disgrace

will be ended and it will be honored by kings and rulers, who will recognize that the redemption came about "because of Hashem." Alternatively: The prophet is still speaking of himself and the contempt with which his prophecies have been treated (*Ibn Ezra*).

49:10-11. When the exiles return, they will find ample provisions; highlands and lowlands along the way will be leveled and easily traversed.

49:21. With her children driven from her, Zion regards herself as an exile.

though He led them through parched deserts; He made water flow for them from a rock; He split a rock and water gushed. ²² '[But] there is no peace for the wicked,'* said HASHEM.

49

Designated a prophet from the womb

¹ Listen to me, O islands, and hearken, O distant regimes: HASHEM summoned me from the belly; He mentioned my name from my mother's womb. * ² He made my mouth like a sharp sword; in the shadow of His hand He hid me; He made me like a smooth arrow, in His quiver He concealed me. ³ He said to me: "You are My servant, Israel, in whom I take glory." ⁴ But I said, "I have toiled in vain and used up my strength for nothingness and naught;* however, my judgment is with HASHEM and [the reward for] my accomplishment is with My God." ⁵ And now HASHEM, Who formed me from the belly to be a servant to Him, said [I should] return Jacob to Him, so that Israel would be gathered to Him; so I was honored in God's eyes and my God was my strength. ⁶ He said: It is insufficient that you be a servant for Me [only] to raise up the tribes of Jacob and

A light for the nations

to restore the ruins of Israel; I will make you a light for the nations, so that My salvation may extend to the ends of the earth.

⁷ Thus said HASHEM, the Redeemer of Israel and their Holy One, to the despised soul, to the one loathed by nations, to the servant of rulers: Kings will see [you] and arise;* officers will prostrate themselves, because of HASHEM, Who is faithful, and the Holy One of Israel, Who has chosen you.

⁸ Thus said HASHEM: In a time of favor I answer you, and on a day of salvation I assist you; I will protect you, and I will make you the people of the covenant, to restore the land and to cause you to inherit desolate heritages, ⁹ to say to prisoners 'Go out' and to those in the darkness, 'Be

Return from exile

revealed'; they will graze along the roads, and upon all the hilltops will be their pasture. ¹⁰ They will not hunger and they will not thirst; heat and sun will not afflict them, for their Merciful One will lead them, and along streams of water will He guide them. ¹¹ I will make all My mountains into roads, and all My paths will be uplifted. * ¹² Behold, these [will come] from afar; and behold, these [will come] from the north and from the west, and these from the land of the Sinites. ¹³ Sing glad song, O heavens, and rejoice, O earth; O mountains, break out in glad song; for HASHEM will have comforted His people and been merciful to His meek ones.

God did not forget

¹⁴ Zion said, 'HASHEM has forsaken me; my Lord has forgotten me.' ¹⁵ Can a woman forget her baby, or not feel compassion for the child of her womb? Even these may forget, but I would not forget you. ¹⁶ Behold, I have engraved you upon My palms; your walls are before Me always. ¹⁷ Your children will hasten [to return], and your ruiners and your destroyers will leave you. ¹⁸ Raise your eyes all around and see: They have all gathered, they have come to you. As I live — the word of HASHEM — [I swear] that you will clothe yourself with them all like jewelry and adorn yourself like a bride.

Jerusalem rebuilt and resettled

¹⁹ As for your ruins and desolations and your devastated land — you will now become crowded with inhabitants, and those who would devour you will be distanced. ²⁰ The children from whom you had been bereaved will yet say in your ears, 'The place is too crowded for me; move aside for me that I may dwell.' ²¹ And you will say in your heart, 'Who has begotten me these? For I have been bereaved and alone, an exile* and a wanderer — so who has reared these? Behold, I had been left by myself; where are these from?'

כב כֹּה־אָמַר אֲדֹנָי יֱהוִֹה הִנֵּה אֶשָּׂא אֶל־גּוֹיִם יָדִי וְאֶל־עַמִּים אָרִים נִסִּי וְהֵבִיאוּ בָנַיִךְ בְּחֹצֶן וּבְנֹתַיִךְ עַל־כָּתֵף תִּנָּשֶׂאנָה: וְהָיוּ מְלָכִים

כג אֹמְנַיִךְ וְשָׂרוֹתֵיהֶם מֵינִיקֹתַיִךְ אַפַּיִם אֶרֶץ יִשְׁתַּחֲווּ־לָךְ וַעֲפַר רַגְלַיִךְ יְלַחֵכוּ וְיָדַעַתְּ כִּי־אֲנִי יהוה אֲשֶׁר לֹא־יֵבֹשׁוּ קֹוָי: הֲיֻקַּח מִגִּבּוֹר

כד מַלְקוֹחַ וְאִם־שְׁבִי צַדִּיק יִמָּלֵט: כִּי־כֹה | אָמַר יהוה גַּם־שְׁבִי גִבּוֹר יֻקָּח

כה וּמַלְקוֹחַ עָרִיץ יִמָּלֵט וְאֶת־יְרִיבֵךְ אָנֹכִי אָרִיב וְאֶת־בָּנַיִךְ אָנֹכִי אוֹשִׁיעַ:

כו וְהַאֲכַלְתִּי אֶת־מוֹנַיִךְ אֶת־בְּשָׂרָם וְכֶעָסִיס דָּמָם יִשְׁכָּרוּן וְיָדְעוּ כָל־בָּשָׂר

נ א כִּי אֲנִי יהוה מוֹשִׁיעֵךְ וְגֹאֲלֵךְ אֲבִיר יַעֲקֹב: כֹּה | אָמַר יהוה אֵי זֶה סֵפֶר כְּרִיתוּת אִמְּכֶם אֲשֶׁר שִׁלַּחְתִּיהָ אוֹ מִי מִנּוֹשַׁי אֲשֶׁר־מָכַרְתִּי אֶתְכֶם לוֹ הֵן בַּעֲוֹנֹתֵיכֶם נִמְכַּרְתֶּם וּבְפִשְׁעֵיכֶם שֻׁלְּחָה אִמְּכֶם:

ב מַדּוּעַ בָּאתִי וְאֵין אִישׁ קָרָאתִי וְאֵין עוֹנֶה הֲקָצוֹר קָצְרָה יָדִי מִפְּדוּת וְאִם־אֵין־בִּי כֹחַ לְהַצִּיל הֵן בְּגַעֲרָתִי אַחֲרִיב יָם אָשִׂים נְהָרוֹת מִדְבָּר

ג תִּבְאַשׁ דְּגָתָם מֵאֵין מַיִם וְתָמֹת בַּצָּמָא: אַלְבִּישׁ שָׁמַיִם קַדְרוּת וְשַׂק אָשִׂים כְּסוּתָם: אֲדֹנָי יֱהוִֹה נָתַן לִי לְשׁוֹן לִמּוּדִים לָדַעַת

ד לָעוּת אֶת־יָעֵף דָּבָר יָעִיר | בַּבֹּקֶר בַּבֹּקֶר יָעִיר לִי אֹזֶן לִשְׁמֹעַ כַּלִּמּוּדִים:

ה אֲדֹנָי יֱהוִֹה פָּתַח־לִי אֹזֶן וְאָנֹכִי לֹא מָרִיתִי אָחוֹר לֹא נְסוּגֹתִי: גֵּוִי נָתַתִּי

ז לְמַכִּים וּלְחָיַי לְמֹרְטִים פָּנַי לֹא הִסְתַּרְתִּי מִכְּלִמּוֹת וָרֹק: וַאדֹנָי יֱהוִֹה יַעֲזָר־לִי עַל־כֵּן לֹא נִכְלָמְתִּי עַל־כֵּן שַׂמְתִּי פָנַי כַּחַלָּמִישׁ וָאֵדַע כִּי־לֹא

ח אֵבוֹשׁ: קָרוֹב מַצְדִּיקִי מִי־יָרִיב אִתִּי נַעַמְדָה יָּחַד מִי־בַעַל מִשְׁפָּטִי יִגַּשׁ

ט אֵלָי: הֵן אֲדֹנָי יֱהוִֹה יַעֲזָר־לִי מִי־הוּא יַרְשִׁיעֵנִי הֵן כֻּלָּם כַּבֶּגֶד יִבְלוּ עָשׁ

י יֹאכְלֵם: מִי בָכֶם יְרֵא יהוה שֹׁמֵעַ בְּקוֹל עַבְדּוֹ אֲשֶׁר | הָלַךְ

יא חֲשֵׁכִים וְאֵין נֹגַהּ לוֹ יִבְטַח בְּשֵׁם יהוה וְיִשָּׁעֵן בֵּאלֹהָיו: הֵן כֻּלְּכֶם קֹדְחֵי אֵשׁ מְאַזְּרֵי זִיקוֹת לְכוּ | בְּאוּר אֶשְׁכֶם וּבְזִיקוֹת בִּעַרְתֶּם מִיָּדִי הָיְתָה־זֹּאת לָכֶם לְמַעֲצֵבָה תִּשְׁכָּבוּן: שִׁמְעוּ אֵלַי רֹדְפֵי

נא א צֶדֶק מְבַקְשֵׁי יהוה הַבִּיטוּ אֶל־צוּר חֻצַּבְתֶּם וְאֶל־מַקֶּבֶת בּוֹר נֻקַּרְתֶּם:

ב הַבִּיטוּ אֶל־אַבְרָהָם אֲבִיכֶם וְאֶל־שָׂרָה תְּחוֹלֶלְכֶם כִּי־אֶחָד קְרָאתִיו

ג וַאֲבָרְכֵהוּ וְאַרְבֵּהוּ: כִּי־נִחַם יהוה צִיּוֹן נִחַם כָּל־חָרְבֹתֶיהָ וַיָּשֶׂם מִדְבָּרָהּ כְּעֵדֶן וְעַרְבָתָהּ כְּגַן־יהוה שָׂשׂוֹן וְשִׂמְחָה יִמָּצֵא בָהּ תּוֹדָה וְקוֹל

49:22. As signals that they should release the Jews in their midst.

49:24-26. The nations argue that they are justified in conquering and exiling Israel as a fair punishment for their sins, but God rejects their claim.

50:1. God says that even though He exiles the *mother*, i.e., the congregation of Israel, His relationship with her is intact because He never gave her a figurative *bill of divorce*.

50:2. Why do you not respond when I call upon you to repent? (*Radak*).

50:3. A reference to dark rain clouds (*Ibn Ezra*).

50:4-9. Isaiah speaks of both his own readiness to be God's spokesman and God's readiness to inspire him. Every morning, God inspires him anew with teachings and prophecies, and does it in such a way that he can understand them clearly (*Radak*).

50:11. Isaiah rebukes those whose sins have *ignited the fire* of God's rage, and tells them that they will suffer the consequences.

51:1. Isaiah speaks to the righteous ones, those who believe the words of the prophet (*Ibn Ezra*).

The captives returned

²² For thus said my Lord, HASHEM/ELOHIM: Behold I will raise My hand toward nations, and I will hoist my banner towards peoples, * and they will bring your children in [their] arms, and your daughters will be carried on [their] shoulder. ²³ Kings will be your nurturers and their princesses your wet nurses. With faces to the ground they will prostrate themselves to you; they will lick the dust of your feet. Then you will know that I am HASHEM, and those Who put their hopes in Me shall not be ashamed.

²⁴ [The nations ask,]* 'Should loot be retrieved from a warrior? Should a justly captured person be allowed to escape?' ²⁵ Yet thus said HASHEM: Even the captives of a warrior can be retrieved, and the booty of fierce men can escape; I Myself will take up your cause, and I Myself will save your children. ²⁶ And I will feed your tormentors their own flesh, and they will become drunk on their own blood as on sweet wine; then all flesh will know that I am HASHEM, your Savior and your Redeemer, the Mighty One of Jacob.

50

Encouraged to repent

¹ Thus said HASHEM: What is your mother's bill of divorce by which I sent her away?* Or to which of My creditors have I sold you? Behold, it is for your iniquities that you have been sold, and for your rebellious sins that your mother has been sent away. ² Why is it that I have come and there is no man?* [Why is it that] I have called and there is no one who answers? Is My hand too limited to grant redemption? Is there no strength in Me to rescue? Behold, by My rebuke I dry the sea; I make rivers into a desert; their fish become putrid for lack of water and die of thirst. ³ I clothe the heavens in blackness and make sackcloth their garment!*

The prophet's sacrifice

⁴ My Lord, HASHEM/ELOHIM, has granted me a tongue for teaching, to understand the need of the times in conveying matters to those who thirst [for knowledge]; He arouses [me] morning after morning; He arouses [my] ear for me to understand as disciples are taught.* ⁵ My Lord, HASHEM/ELOHIM, has opened [my] ear for me, and I did not resist; I did not retreat to the rear. ⁶ I submitted my body to those who smite and my cheeks to those who pluck; I did not hide my face from humiliation and spit. ⁷ For my Lord, HASHEM/ELOHIM, helps me; therefore, I was not humiliated; therefore, I made my face [as hard] as flint and knew that I would not be ashamed. ⁸ My Champion is near; whoever would contend with me, let us stand together; whoever is my adversary, let him approach me. ⁹ Behold, my Lord, HASHEM/ELOHIM, will help me; who is he that will condemn me? Behold, they will all wear out like a garment; a moth will devour them.

¹⁰ Who among you fears HASHEM, listening to the voice of His servant? Though he may have walked in darkness with no light for himself, let him trust in the Name of HASHEM, and rely upon his God. ¹¹ Behold, all of you are igniters of fire, * kindlers of sparks. Go in the flame of your fire, and in the sparks you have lit; from My hand has this [decree] come upon you, that you should die in sorrow.

51

Zion comforted

¹ Listen to me, O pursuers of righteousness, * O seekers of HASHEM: Look to the rock from which you were hewn, and at the hollow of the pit from which you were dug; ² look to Abraham your forefather and to Sarah who bore you, for when he was yet one alone did I summon him and bless him and make him many. ³ For HASHEM will comfort Zion, He will comfort all her ruins; He will make her wilderness like Eden and her wasteland like a garden of HASHEM; joy and gladness will be found there, thanksgiving and the sound of music.

ד הַקְשִׁיבוּ אֵלַי עַמִּי וּלְאוּמִּי אֵלַי הַאֲזִינוּ כִּי תוֹרָה ◀ זִמְרָה׃

ה מֵאִתִּי תֵצֵא וּמִשְׁפָּטִי לְאוֹר עַמִּים אַרְגִּיעַ קָרוֹב צִדְקִי יָצָא יִשְׁעִי וּזְרֹעַי

ו עַמִּים יִשְׁפֹּטוּ אֵלַי אִיִּים יְקַוּוּ וְאֶל־זְרֹעִי יְיַחֵלוּן׃ שְׂאוּ לַשָּׁמַיִם עֵינֵיכֶם וְהַבִּיטוּ אֶל־הָאָרֶץ מִתַּחַת כִּי־שָׁמַיִם כֶּעָשָׁן נִמְלָחוּ וְהָאָרֶץ כַּבֶּגֶד תִּבְלֶה וְיֹשְׁבֶיהָ כְּמוֹ־כֵן יְמוּתוּן וִישׁוּעָתִי לְעוֹלָם תִּהְיֶה וְצִדְקָתִי לֹא

ז תֵחָת׃ שִׁמְעוּ אֵלַי יֹדְעֵי צֶדֶק עַם תּוֹרָתִי בְלִבָּם אַל־תִּירְאוּ

ח חֶרְפַּת אֱנוֹשׁ וּמִגִּדֻּפֹתָם אַל־תֵּחָתּוּ׃ כִּי כַבֶּגֶד יֹאכְלֵם עָשׁ וְכַצֶּמֶר יֹאכְלֵם

ט סָס וְצִדְקָתִי לְעוֹלָם תִּהְיֶה וִישׁוּעָתִי לְדוֹר דּוֹרִים׃ עוּרִי עוּרִי לִבְשִׁי־עֹז זְרוֹעַ יְהוָה עוּרִי כִּימֵי קֶדֶם דֹּרוֹת עוֹלָמִים הֲלוֹא אַתְּ־

י הִיא הַמַּחְצֶבֶת רַהַב מְחוֹלֶלֶת תַּנִּין׃ הֲלוֹא אַתְּ־הִיא הַמַּחֲרֶבֶת יָם מֵי

יא תְּהוֹם רַבָּה הַשָּׂמָה מַעֲמַקֵּי־יָם דֶּרֶךְ לַעֲבֹר גְּאוּלִים׃ וּפְדוּיֵי יְהוָה יְשׁוּבוּן וּבָאוּ צִיּוֹן בְּרִנָּה וְשִׂמְחַת עוֹלָם עַל־רֹאשָׁם שָׂשׂוֹן וְשִׂמְחָה יַשִּׂיגוּן נָסוּ

יב יָגוֹן וַאֲנָחָה׃ ◀ אָנֹכִי אָנֹכִי הוּא מְנַחֶמְכֶם מִי־אַתְּ וַתִּירְאִי

יג מֵאֱנוֹשׁ יָמוּת וּמִבֶּן־אָדָם חָצִיר יִנָּתֵן׃ וַתִּשְׁכַּח יְהוָה עֹשֶׂךָ נוֹטֶה שָׁמַיִם וְיֹסֵד אָרֶץ וַתְּפַחֵד תָּמִיד כָּל־הַיּוֹם מִפְּנֵי חֲמַת הַמֵּצִיק כַּאֲשֶׁר כּוֹנֵן

יד לְהַשְׁחִית וְאַיֵּה חֲמַת הַמֵּצִיק׃ מִהַר צֹעֶה לְהִפָּתֵחַ וְלֹא־יָמוּת לַשַּׁחַת

טו וְלֹא יֶחְסַר לַחְמוֹ׃ וְאָנֹכִי יְהוָה אֱלֹהֶיךָ רֹגַע הַיָּם וַיֶּהֱמוּ גַּלָּיו יְהוָה צְבָאוֹת

טז שְׁמוֹ׃ וָאָשִׂים דְּבָרַי בְּפִיךָ וּבְצֵל יָדִי כִּסִּיתִיךָ לִנְטֹעַ שָׁמַיִם וְלִיסֹד אָרֶץ וְלֵאמֹר לְצִיּוֹן עַמִּי־אָתָּה׃

יז הִתְעוֹרְרִי הִתְעוֹרְרִי קוּמִי יְרוּשָׁלִַם אֲשֶׁר שָׁתִית מִיַּד יְהוָה אֶת־כּוֹס חֲמָתוֹ אֶת־קֻבַּעַת כּוֹס

יח הַתַּרְעֵלָה שָׁתִית מָצִית׃ אֵין־מְנַהֵל לָהּ מִכָּל־בָּנִים יָלָדָה וְאֵין מַחֲזִיק

יט בְּיָדָהּ מִכָּל־בָּנִים גִּדֵּלָה׃ שְׁתַּיִם הֵנָּה קֹרְאֹתַיִךְ מִי יָנוּד לָךְ הַשֹּׁד וְהַשֶּׁבֶר

כ וְהָרָעָב וְהַחֶרֶב מִי אֲנַחֲמֵךְ׃ בָּנַיִךְ עֻלְּפוּ שָׁכְבוּ בְּרֹאשׁ כָּל־חוּצוֹת כְּתוֹא מִכְמָר הַמְלֵאִים חֲמַת־יְהוָה גַּעֲרַת אֱלֹהָיִךְ׃ לָכֵן שִׁמְעִי־נָא זֹאת עֲנִיָּה

כא וּשְׁכֻרַת וְלֹא מִיָּיִן׃ כֹּה־אָמַר אֲדֹנַיִךְ יְהוָה וֵאלֹהַיִךְ יָרִיב

כב עַמּוֹ הִנֵּה לָקַחְתִּי מִיָּדֵךְ אֶת־כּוֹס הַתַּרְעֵלָה אֶת־קֻבַּעַת כּוֹס חֲמָתִי לֹא־

כג תוֹסִיפִי לִשְׁתּוֹתָהּ עוֹד׃ וְשַׂמְתִּיהָ בְּיַד־מוֹגַיִךְ אֲשֶׁר־אָמְרוּ לְנַפְשֵׁךְ שְׁחִי

נב א וְנַעֲבֹרָה וַתָּשִׂימִי כָאָרֶץ גֵּוֵךְ וְכַחוּץ לַעֹבְרִים׃ עוּרִי עוּרִי לִבְשִׁי עֻזֵּךְ צִיּוֹן לִבְשִׁי בִּגְדֵי תִפְאַרְתֵּךְ יְרוּשָׁלִַם עִיר הַקֹּדֶשׁ כִּי

ב לֹא יוֹסִיף יָבֹא־בָךְ עוֹד עָרֵל וְטָמֵא׃ הִתְנַעֲרִי מֵעָפָר קוּמִי שְּׁבִי יְרוּשָׁלִָם

HAFTARAS SHOFTIM 51:12-52:12

51:9. This is Isaiah's prayer to God that He display His strength in aid of Israel, as He did when He destroyed "the haughty one," i.e., Egypt (see 30:7), and "the sea serpent," i.e., Pharaoh (*Ezekiel* 29:3).

51:13. The enemy's fury has vanished with its perpetrator!

51:16. I.e., to prophesy that Israel will be restored to its

land (*Ibn Ezra*).

Israel's return from exile will be tantamount to a new creation (*Radak*).

51:19. No other nation has suffered so much that I could use its example to comfort you (*Rashi*).

51:21. Your senses have been dulled through endless suffering, not by alcohol.

⁴ *Pay attention to Me, my people; give ear to Me, My nation; for instruction will come forth from Me and My judgment will be a light for peoples, to whom I will give rest.* ⁵ *My righteousness is near; My salvation has gone forth; My arms will chastise nations; the islands will put their hope in Me and will trust in My arm.* ⁶ *Lift up your eyes to the heavens, look at the earth below — for the heavens will dissipate like smoke, and the earth will wear out like a garment and its inhabitants will die, as well; but My salvation will be forever and My righteousness will not be broken.*

⁷ *Listen to Me, you who know righteousness, the nation with My Torah in its heart: Do not fear from the disparagement of man, and do not be broken by their insults;* ⁸ *for like a garment, a moth will eat them, and like wool, a worm will eat them; but My righteousness will be forever, and My salvation for all generations.*

A call for God to intervene ⁹ *Awaken!* * *Awaken! Don strength, O arm of HASHEM! Awaken as in the days of old, as in previous generations. Are You not the One Who decimated the haughty, Who terrified the sea serpent?* ¹⁰ *Are You not the One Who dried up the sea, the waters of the great deep; Who made the depths of the sea a path for the redeemed ones to cross?* ¹¹ *Then the redeemed of HASHEM will return and come to Zion with glad song, with eternal gladness upon their head. They will attain joy and gladness; sadness and sighing will flee.*

The Creator, God of Israel ¹² *I, only I, am He Who comforts you; who are you that you should be afraid of mortal humans and of men who will be made as grass?* ¹³ *You have forgotten HASHEM, your Maker, Who spread out the heavens and set the foundations of the earth, and you are terrified continually, all day long, because of the oppressor's fury when he prepares to destroy — but where is the oppressor's fury?* * ¹⁴ *The wanderer will soon be released, and will not die in the pit, nor will his bread be lacking.* ¹⁵ *I am HASHEM, your God, Who stirs up the sea and its waves rage, Whose Name is HASHEM, Master of Legions.* ¹⁶ *And I have placed My words in your mouth — and with the shade of My hand have I covered you — to implant the heavens and to set a foundation for the earth* * *and to say unto Zion, "You are My people!"*

The cup of bewilderment ¹⁷ *Awaken yourself! Awaken yourself! Arise, O Jerusalem, you who have drunk from the hand of HASHEM the cup of His fury. You have drunk from and drained the sediments of the cup of bewilderment.* ¹⁸ *Among all the children she has borne there is no one to guide her; among all the children she has reared there is no one to hold her hand.* ¹⁹ *There are two [calamities] that have befallen you — who will bewail you? — the plunder and the calamity, the hunger and the sword. With whom can I comfort you?* * ²⁰ *Your children have fainted, they lie at the head of all the streets like a wild bull trapped in a net; they are full of HASHEM's fury, with your God's rebuke.*

²¹ *Therefore, hear this now, O afflicted one, drunk, but not from wine.* * ²² *Thus said your Lord, HASHEM, and your God, Who will defend His people: Behold, I have removed the cup of bewilderment from your hand; from the sediments of the cup of My fury shall you no longer drink any more.* ²³ *But I will put it into the hand of your tormentors, who have said to your soul, 'Prostrate yourself so that we may pass over you,' for whom you have made your body like the ground and like a street for passersby.*

52

The final redemption ¹ **A**waken, awaken! *Don your strength, O Zion; don your garments of splendor, O Jerusalem, the holy city, for uncircumcised and defiled people will no longer enter you.* ² *Shake the dust from yourself; arise and sit, O Jeru-*

ג °הִתְפַּתְּחוּ [°הִתְפַּתְּחִי ק] מוֹסְרֵי צַוָּארֵךְ שְׁבִיָּה בַּת־צִיּוֹן: כִּי־
ד כֹה אָמַר יהוה חִנָּם נִמְכַּרְתֶּם וְלֹא בְכֶסֶף תִּגָּאֵלוּ:   כִּי כֹה אָמַר
   אֲדֹנָי יהוה מִצְרַיִם יָרַד־עַמִּי בָרִאשֹׁנָה לָגוּר שָׁם וְאַשּׁוּר בְּאֶפֶס עֲשָׁקוֹ:
ה וְעַתָּה מַה־לִּי־פֹה נְאֻם־יהוה כִּי־לֻקַּח עַמִּי חִנָּם °מֹשְׁלָו [°מֹשְׁלָיו ק]
ו יְהֵילִילוּ נְאֻם־יהוה וְתָמִיד כָּל־הַיּוֹם שְׁמִי מִנֹּאָץ: לָכֵן יֵדַע עַמִּי שְׁמִי לָכֵן
ז בַּיּוֹם הַהוּא כִּי־אֲנִי־הוּא הַמְדַבֵּר הִנֵּנִי: מַה־נָּאווּ עַל־
   הֶהָרִים רַגְלֵי מְבַשֵּׂר מַשְׁמִיעַ שָׁלוֹם מְבַשֵּׂר טוֹב מַשְׁמִיעַ יְשׁוּעָה אֹמֵר
ח לְצִיּוֹן מָלַךְ אֱלֹהָיִךְ: קוֹל צֹפַיִךְ נָשְׂאוּ קוֹל יַחְדָּו יְרַנֵּנוּ כִּי עַיִן בְּעַיִן יִרְאוּ
ט בְּשׁוּב יהוה צִיּוֹן: פִּצְחוּ רַנְּנוּ יַחְדָּו חָרְבוֹת יְרוּשָׁלָ‍ִם כִּי־נִחַם יהוה עַמּוֹ
י גָּאַל יְרוּשָׁלָ‍ִם: חָשַׂף יהוה אֶת־זְרוֹעַ קָדְשׁוֹ לְעֵינֵי כָּל־הַגּוֹיִם וְרָאוּ כָּל־
יא אַפְסֵי־אָרֶץ אֵת יְשׁוּעַת אֱלֹהֵינוּ:   סוּרוּ סוּרוּ צְאוּ מִשָּׁם
   טָמֵא אַל־תִּגָּעוּ צְאוּ מִתּוֹכָהּ הִבָּרוּ נֹשְׂאֵי כְּלֵי יהוה: כִּי לֹא בְחִפָּזוֹן
יב תֵּצֵאוּ וּבִמְנוּסָה לֹא תֵלֵכוּן כִּי־הֹלֵךְ לִפְנֵיכֶם יהוה וּמְאַסִּפְכֶם אֱלֹהֵי
יג יִשְׂרָאֵל: ▸   הִנֵּה יַשְׂכִּיל עַבְדִּי יָרוּם וְנִשָּׂא וְגָבַהּ מְאֹד:
יד כַּאֲשֶׁר שָׁמְמוּ עָלֶיךָ רַבִּים כֵּן־מִשְׁחַת מֵאִישׁ מַרְאֵהוּ וְתֹאֲרוֹ מִבְּנֵי אָדָם:
טו כֵּן יַזֶּה גּוֹיִם רַבִּים עָלָיו יִקְפְּצוּ מְלָכִים פִּיהֶם כִּי אֲשֶׁר לֹא־סֻפַּר לָהֶם רָאוּ
נג א וַאֲשֶׁר לֹא־שָׁמְעוּ הִתְבּוֹנָנוּ: מִי הֶאֱמִין לִשְׁמֻעָתֵנוּ וּזְרוֹעַ יהוה עַל־מִי
ב נִגְלָתָה: וַיַּעַל כַּיּוֹנֵק לְפָנָיו וְכַשֹּׁרֶשׁ מֵאֶרֶץ צִיָּה לֹא־תֹאַר לוֹ וְלֹא הָדָר
ג וְנִרְאֵהוּ וְלֹא־מַרְאֶה וְנֶחְמְדֵהוּ: נִבְזֶה וַחֲדַל אִישִׁים אִישׁ מַכְאֹבוֹת וִידוּעַ
ד חֹלִי וּכְמַסְתֵּר פָּנִים מִמֶּנּוּ נִבְזֶה וְלֹא חֲשַׁבְנֻהוּ: אָכֵן חֳלָיֵנוּ הוּא נָשָׂא
ה וּמַכְאֹבֵינוּ סְבָלָם וַאֲנַחְנוּ חֲשַׁבְנֻהוּ נָגוּעַ מֻכֵּה אֱלֹהִים וּמְעֻנֶּה: וְהוּא
   מְחֹלָל מִפְּשָׁעֵנוּ מְדֻכָּא מֵעֲוֹנֹתֵינוּ מוּסַר שְׁלוֹמֵנוּ עָלָיו וּבַחֲבֻרָתוֹ נִרְפָּא־
ו לָנוּ: כֻּלָּנוּ כַּצֹּאן תָּעִינוּ אִישׁ לְדַרְכּוֹ פָּנִינוּ וַיהוה הִפְגִּיעַ בּוֹ אֵת עֲוֹן כֻּלָּנוּ:
ז נִגַּשׂ וְהוּא נַעֲנֶה וְלֹא יִפְתַּח־פִּיו כַּשֶּׂה לַטֶּבַח יוּבָל וּכְרָחֵל לִפְנֵי גֹזְזֶיהָ
ח נֶאֱלָמָה וְלֹא יִפְתַּח פִּיו: מֵעֹצֶר וּמִמִּשְׁפָּט לֻקָּח וְאֶת־דּוֹרוֹ מִי יְשׂוֹחֵחַ כִּי
ט נִגְזַר מֵאֶרֶץ חַיִּים מִפֶּשַׁע עַמִּי נֶגַע לָמוֹ: וַיִּתֵּן אֶת־רְשָׁעִים קִבְרוֹ וְאֶת־

52:3. You were *sold* to your enemies only in punishment for your sins, and you can be redeemed from their subjugation through repentance.

52:4-5. Egypt's guilt was not so great, because the Jews arrived there of their own accord and were given permission to live there. But Assyria oppressed and exiled the Israelites without any justification. Therefore, God asks, why should He permit Himself and His children to remain there? (*Rashi*).

52:6. When I redeem them.

52:11. Leave the lands of your dispersion. The redeemed Jews should cleanse themselves spiritually, for their *armor* must be their dedication to God and the Torah (*Ibn Ezra*, *Radak*).

52:13. I.e., God's servant, the people of Israel (*Rashi*).

52:15. Just as Israel had once been astonishingly degraded, so it will astonish the nations by its exaltedness when the time of redemption arrives.

53:1-3. This is a prophecy foretelling what the nations and their kings will exclaim when they witness Israel's rejuvenation. The nations will contrast their former scornful attitude toward the Jews (vv. 1-3) with their new realization of Israel's grandeur (vv. 4-7).

53:5. We brought suffering upon Israel for our own selfish purposes; it was not, as we had claimed, that God was punishing Israel for its own evil behavior.

53:6. We sinned by inflicting punishment upon Israel. Such oppression is often described as "Hashem's punish-

salem; *undo the straps on your neck, O captive daughter of Zion.* ³ *For thus said* HASHEM: *For naught were you sold, and without money will you be redeemed.* *

⁴ *For thus said my Lord,* HASHEM/ELOHIM: *As for Egypt, My people went down originally to sojourn there. But Assyria oppressed them without justification;* * ⁵ *so now, why should I [remain] here? — the word of* HASHEM — *where My people was taken for naught? Their rulers glorify themselves — the word of* HASHEM — *and constantly, all day, My Name is blasphemed.* ⁶ *Therefore, My people shall know My Name — therefore, on that day,* * *that it is I Who speaks, here I am!*

"Your God has reigned!"

⁷ *How pleasant are the footsteps of the herald upon the mountains announcing peace, heralding good tidings, announcing salvation, saying unto Zion, 'Your God has reigned!'* ⁸ *The voice of your lookouts, they raise their voice, they sing glad song in unison; with their own eyes they will see that* HASHEM *returns to Zion.* ⁹ *Burst out, sing glad song in unison, O ruins of Jerusalem, for* HASHEM *will have comforted His people; He will have redeemed Jerusalem.* ¹⁰ HASHEM *has bared His holy arm before the eyes of all the nations; all ends of the earth will see the salvation of our God!* ¹¹ *Turn away! Turn away! Get out from there!* * *It is defiled; do not touch it! Get out from inside it! Cleanse yourselves, O bearers of* HASHEM'S *armor.* ¹² *You will not leave in chaos, nor will you go in flight; for* HASHEM *will go before you, and the God of Israel will be your rear guard.*

Success of the righteous

¹³ *Behold, My servant* * *will succeed; he will be exalted and become high and exceedingly lofty.* ¹⁴ *Just as multitudes were astonished over you, [saying,] 'His appearance is too marred to be a man's, and his visage to be human,'* ¹⁵ *so will the many nations exclaim about him,* * *and kings will shut their mouths [in amazement], for they will see that which had never been told to them, and will perceive things they had never heard.*

53

The nations' wonderment at Israel's redemption

¹ **W**ho *would believe what we have heard!* * *For whom has the arm of* HASHEM *been revealed!* ² *Formerly he grew like a sapling or like a root from arid ground; he had neither form nor grandeur; we saw him, but without such visage that we could desire him.* ³ *He was despised and isolated from men, a man of pains and accustomed to illness. As one from whom we would hide our faces; he was despised, and we had no regard for him.* ⁴ *But in truth, it was our ills that he bore, and our pains that he carried — but we had regarded him diseased, stricken by God, and afflicted!* ⁵ *He was pained because of our rebellious sins and oppressed through our iniquities; the chastisement upon him was for our benefit,* * *and through his wounds, we were healed.* ⁶ *We have all strayed like sheep, each of us turning his own way, and* HASHEM *inflicted upon him the iniquity of us all.* * ⁷ *He was persecuted and afflicted, but he did not open his mouth; like a sheep being led to the slaughter or a ewe that is silent before her shearers, he did not open his mouth.* ⁸ *Now that he has been released from captivity and judgment, who could have imagined such a generation? For he had been removed from the land of the living, an affliction upon them that was my people's sin.* * ⁹ *He submitted himself to his grave like wicked men; and*

---

ment" (see 10:5, *Habakkuk* 1:12), for He decreed that it should happen (*Abarbanel*).

53:8. When Israel's exile is finally ended, the nations will

marvel that such a generation could have survived the expulsion from "the land of the living," i.e., the Land of Israel, that the nations had sinfully inflicted upon it.

עָשִׁיר בְּמֹתָיו עַל לֹא־חָמָס עָשָׂה וְלֹא מִרְמָה בְּפִיו: וַיהוָה חָפֵץ דַּכְּאוֹ
הֶחֱלִי אִם־תָּשִׂים אָשָׁם נַפְשׁוֹ יִרְאֶה זֶרַע יַאֲרִיךְ יָמִים וְחֵפֶץ יְהוָה בְּיָדוֹ
יִצְלָח: מֵעֲמַל נַפְשׁוֹ יִרְאֶה יִשְׂבָּע בְּדַעְתּוֹ יַצְדִּיק צַדִּיק עַבְדִּי לָרַבִּים
וַעֲוֺנֹתָם הוּא יִסְבֹּל: לָכֵן אֲחַלֶּק־לוֹ בָרַבִּים וְאֶת־עֲצוּמִים יְחַלֵּק שָׁלָל תַּחַת
אֲשֶׁר הֶעֱרָה לַמָּוֶת נַפְשׁוֹ וְאֶת־פֹּשְׁעִים נִמְנָה וְהוּא חֵטְא־רַבִּים נָשָׂא
וְלַפֹּשְׁעִים יַפְגִּיעַ: רָנִּי עֲקָרָה לֹא יָלָדָה פִּצְחִי רִנָּה

נד

HAFTARAS
NOACH
Ashkenazim:
54:1-55:5
Sephardim:
54:1-10

HAFTARAS
KI SEITZEI
54:1-10

וְצַהֲלִי לֹא־חָלָה כִּי־רַבִּים בְּנֵי־שׁוֹמֵמָה מִבְּנֵי בְעוּלָה אָמַר יְהוָה: הַרְחִיבִי |
מְקוֹם אָהֳלֵךְ וִירִיעוֹת מִשְׁכְּנוֹתַיִךְ יַטּוּ אַל־תַּחְשֹׂכִי הַאֲרִיכִי מֵיתָרַיִךְ
וִיתֵדֹתַיִךְ חַזֵּקִי: כִּי־יָמִין וּשְׂמֹאול תִּפְרֹצִי וְזַרְעֵךְ גּוֹיִם יִירָשׁ וְעָרִים נְשַׁמּוֹת
יוֹשִׁיבוּ: אַל־תִּירְאִי כִּי־לֹא תֵבוֹשִׁי וְאַל־תִּכָּלְמִי כִּי־לֹא תַחְפִּירִי כִּי בֹשֶׁת
עֲלוּמַיִךְ תִּשְׁכָּחִי וְחֶרְפַּת אַלְמְנוּתַיִךְ לֹא תִזְכְּרִי־
עוֹד: כִּי בֹעֲלַיִךְ עֹשַׂיִךְ יְהוָה צְבָאוֹת שְׁמוֹ וְגֹאֲלֵךְ קְדוֹשׁ יִשְׂרָאֵל אֱלֹהֵי כָל־
הָאָרֶץ יִקָּרֵא: כִּי־כְאִשָּׁה עֲזוּבָה וַעֲצוּבַת רוּחַ קְרָאָךְ יְהוָה וְאֵשֶׁת נְעוּרִים
כִּי תִמָּאֵס אָמַר אֱלֹהָיִךְ: בְּרֶגַע קָטֹן עֲזַבְתִּיךְ וּבְרַחֲמִים גְּדֹלִים אֲקַבְּצֵךְ:
בְּשֶׁצֶף קֶצֶף הִסְתַּרְתִּי פָנַי רֶגַע מִמֵּךְ וּבְחֶסֶד עוֹלָם רִחַמְתִּיךְ אָמַר גֹּאֲלֵךְ
יְהוָה: כִּי־מֵי נֹחַ זֹאת לִי אֲשֶׁר נִשְׁבַּעְתִּי
מֵעֲבֹר מֵי־נֹחַ עוֹד עַל־הָאָרֶץ כֵּן נִשְׁבַּעְתִּי מִקְּצֹף עָלַיִךְ וּמִגְּעָר־בָּךְ: כִּי
הֶהָרִים יָמוּשׁוּ וְהַגְּבָעוֹת תְּמוּטֶנָה וְחַסְדִּי מֵאִתֵּךְ לֹא־יָמוּשׁ וּבְרִית שְׁלוֹמִי
לֹא תָמוּט אָמַר מְרַחֲמֵךְ יְהוָה: עֲנִיָּה סֹעֲרָה

HAFTARAS
RE'EH
54:11-55:5

לֹא נֻחָמָה הִנֵּה אָנֹכִי מַרְבִּיץ בַּפּוּךְ אֲבָנַיִךְ וִיסַדְתִּיךְ בַּסַּפִּירִים:
וְשַׂמְתִּי כַּדְכֹד שִׁמְשֹׁתַיִךְ וּשְׁעָרַיִךְ לְאַבְנֵי אֶקְדָּח וְכָל־גְּבוּלֵךְ לְאַבְנֵי־חֵפֶץ:
וְכָל־בָּנַיִךְ לִמּוּדֵי יְהוָה וְרַב שְׁלוֹם בָּנָיִךְ: בִּצְדָקָה תִּכּוֹנָנִי רַחֲקִי מֵעֹשֶׁק כִּי־
לֹא תִירָאִי וּמִמְּחִתָּה כִּי לֹא־תִקְרַב אֵלָיִךְ: הֵן גּוֹר יָגוּר אֶפֶס מֵאוֹתִי מִי־גָר
אִתָּךְ עָלַיִךְ יִפּוֹל: °הן [הִנֵּה ק] אָנֹכִי בָּרָאתִי חָרָשׁ נֹפֵחַ בְּאֵשׁ פֶּחָם
וּמוֹצִיא כְלִי לְמַעֲשֵׂהוּ וְאָנֹכִי בָּרָאתִי מַשְׁחִית לְחַבֵּל: כָּל־כְּלִי יוּצַר עָלַיִךְ
לֹא יִצְלָח וְכָל־לָשׁוֹן תָּקוּם־אִתָּךְ לַמִּשְׁפָּט תַּרְשִׁיעִי זֹאת נַחֲלַת עַבְדֵי
יְהוָה וְצִדְקָתָם מֵאִתִּי נְאֻם־יְהוָה: הוֹי

נה

53:9. Ordinary Jews chose to die like common criminals, rather than renounce their faith; and wealthy Jews
were killed for no reason other than to enable their
wicked conquerors to confiscate their riches (*Radak*).

53:10. That is, Israel. God replies to the nations that
Israel's suffering was a punishment for its own sins; and
when the people realize this and repent, they will be
redeemed and rewarded.

53:11. Israel will teach the nations of God's righteousness.

53:12. In exile, Jews prayed for the welfare of their
host nations.

54:1. Zion, who is now without children (*Targum*).

54:4. At the time of your final redemption, there will
be none of the humiliations your ancestors encountered when they returned from exile in the days of Ezra
(*Radak*).

54:6. You are not like a widow, but like an unfaithful
woman whose husband has left her, but eventually
returns to her (*Radak*).

54:16. You need not fear weapons, for I am the One
Who created the producers of those weapons, and
I have also created the power to annihilate them
(*Radak*).

the wealthy [submitted] to his executions, for committing no crime and with no deceit in his mouth. *

God's will was done

¹⁰ HASHEM desired to oppress him * and He afflicted him; if his soul would acknowledge guilt, he would see offspring and live long days and the desire of HASHEM would succeed in his hand. ¹¹ He would see [the purpose] and be satisfied with his soul's distress. With his knowledge My servant will vindicate the Righteous One to multitudes; * it is their iniquities that he will carry. ¹² Therefore, I will assign him a portion from the multitudes and he will divide the mighty as spoils — in return for having poured out his soul for death and being counted among the wicked, for he bore the sin of the multitudes, and prayed for the wicked. *

54

The many children of the barren one

¹ Sing out, O barren one * who has not given birth; break into glad song and be jubilant, you who have not been in birth travail. For the children of the desolate [Jerusalem] will outnumber the children of the inhabited one, said HASHEM. ² Broaden the place of your tent and let the curtains of your dwellings stretch out, stint not; lengthen your cords and strengthen your pegs. ³ For you will burst out to the right and to the left; your offspring will inherit nations, and they will settle desolate cities. ⁴ Fear not, for you will not be shamed; * do not feel humiliated, for you will not be disgraced; for you will forget the shame of your youth and you will no longer recall the disgrace of your widowhood. ⁵ For your Master is your Maker, HASHEM, Master of Legions, is His Name; your Redeemer is the Holy One of Israel; God of all the world will He be called. ⁶ For like a wife who had been forsaken and melancholy has HASHEM called you, * and like a wife of one's youth who had become despised, said your God. ⁷ For but a brief moment have I forsaken you, and with abundant mercy will I gather you in. ⁸ With a slight wrath have I concealed My countenance from you for a moment, but with eternal kindness shall I show you mercy, said your Redeemer, HASHEM.

Eternal mercy and kindness

⁹ For [like] the waters of Noah this shall be to Me: Just as I swore that the waters of Noah would never again pass over the earth, so have I sworn not to be wrathful with you nor to rebuke you. ¹⁰ For the mountains may be moved and the hills may falter, but My kindness shall not be removed from you and My covenant of peace shall not falter, said the One Who shows you mercy, HASHEM.

The new glory of Jerusalem

¹¹ O afflicted, storm-tossed one, who has not been consoled: Behold, I will set down gems as your [flooring] stones and lay your foundation with sapphires. ¹² I will set your window [frames] with ruby and [make] your gates of carbuncle stones, and your entire boundary of precious stones. ¹³ All your children will be students of HASHEM, and your children's peace will be abundant. ¹⁴ Establish yourself through righteousness, distance yourself from oppression, for you need not fear it, and from devastation, for it will not come near you. ¹⁵ Behold, they may indeed gather together, but it is without My consent. Whoever will gather against you will fall because of you. ¹⁶ Behold, I created the smith, who fans his charcoal flame and withdraws a tool for his labor, but I have [also] created the destroyer to demolish. * ¹⁷ Any weapon sharpened against you will not succeed, and any tongue that will rise against you in judgment, you will condemn. This is the heritage of the servants of HASHEM, and their righteousness from Me — the word of HASHEM.

כָּל־צָמֵא לְכוּ לַמַּיִם וַאֲשֶׁר אֵין־לוֹ כָּסֶף לְכוּ שִׁבְרוּ וֶאֱכֹלוּ וּלְכוּ שִׁבְרוּ

ב בְּלוֹא־כֶסֶף וּבְלוֹא מְחִיר יַיִן וְחָלָב: לָמָּה תִשְׁקְלוּ־כֶסֶף בְּלוֹא־לֶחֶם
וִיגִיעֲכֶם בְּלוֹא לְשָׂבְעָה שִׁמְעוּ שָׁמוֹעַ אֵלַי וְאִכְלוּ־טוֹב וְתִתְעַנַּג בַּדֶּשֶׁן

ג נַפְשְׁכֶם: הַטּוּ אָזְנְכֶם וּלְכוּ אֵלַי שִׁמְעוּ וּתְחִי נַפְשְׁכֶם וְאֶכְרְתָה לָכֶם בְּרִית

ד-ה עוֹלָם חַסְדֵי דָוִד הַנֶּאֱמָנִים: הֵן עֵד לְאוּמִּים נְתַתִּיו נָגִיד וּמְצַוֵּה לְאֻמִּים: הֵן
גּוֹי לֹא־תֵדַע תִּקְרָא וְגוֹי לֹא־יְדָעוּךָ אֵלֶיךָ יָרוּצוּ לְמַעַן יהוה אֱלֹהֶיךָ

ו וְלִקְדוֹשׁ יִשְׂרָאֵל כִּי פֵאֲרָךְ: ◀ דִּרְשׁוּ יהוה בְּהִמָּצְאוֹ קְרָאֻהוּ

ז בִּהְיוֹתוֹ קָרוֹב: יַעֲזֹב רָשָׁע דַּרְכּוֹ וְאִישׁ אָוֶן מַחְשְׁבֹתָיו וְיָשֹׁב אֶל־יהוה

ח וִירַחֲמֵהוּ וְאֶל־אֱלֹהֵינוּ כִּי־יַרְבֶּה לִסְלוֹחַ: כִּי לֹא מַחְשְׁבוֹתַי מַחְשְׁבוֹתֵיכֶם

ט וְלֹא דַרְכֵיכֶם דְּרָכָי נְאֻם יהוה: כִּי־גָבְהוּ שָׁמַיִם מֵאָרֶץ כֵּן גָּבְהוּ דְרָכַי

י מִדַּרְכֵיכֶם וּמַחְשְׁבֹתַי מִמַּחְשְׁבֹתֵיכֶם: כִּי כַּאֲשֶׁר יֵרֵד הַגֶּשֶׁם וְהַשֶּׁלֶג מִן־
הַשָּׁמַיִם וְשָׁמָּה לֹא יָשׁוּב כִּי אִם־הִרְוָה אֶת־הָאָרֶץ וְהוֹלִידָהּ וְהִצְמִיחָהּ

יא וְנָתַן זֶרַע לַזֹּרֵעַ וְלֶחֶם לָאֹכֵל: כֵּן יִהְיֶה דְבָרִי אֲשֶׁר יֵצֵא מִפִּי לֹא־יָשׁוּב אֵלַי

יב רֵיקָם כִּי אִם־עָשָׂה אֶת־אֲשֶׁר חָפַצְתִּי וְהִצְלִיחַ אֲשֶׁר שְׁלַחְתִּיו: כִּי־
בְשִׂמְחָה תֵצֵאוּ וּבְשָׁלוֹם תּוּבָלוּן הֶהָרִים וְהַגְּבָעוֹת יִפְצְחוּ לִפְנֵיכֶם

יג רִנָּה וְכָל־עֲצֵי הַשָּׂדֶה יִמְחֲאוּ־כָף: תַּחַת הַנַּעֲצוּץ יַעֲלֶה בְרוֹשׁ ׳תַחַת
[׳וְתַחַת ק] הַסִּרְפַּד יַעֲלֶה הֲדַס וְהָיָה לַיהוה לְשֵׁם לְאוֹת עוֹלָם לֹא

נו
א יִכָּרֵת: כֹּה אָמַר יהוה שִׁמְרוּ מִשְׁפָּט וַעֲשׂוּ צְדָקָה כִּי־קְרוֹבָה

ב יְשׁוּעָתִי לָבוֹא וְצִדְקָתִי לְהִגָּלוֹת: אַשְׁרֵי אֱנוֹשׁ יַעֲשֶׂה־זֹּאת וּבֶן־אָדָם
יַחֲזִיק בָּהּ שֹׁמֵר שַׁבָּת מֵחַלְּלוֹ וְשֹׁמֵר יָדוֹ מֵעֲשׂוֹת כָּל־רָע: וְאַל־יֹאמַר בֶּן־

ג הַנֵּכָר הַנִּלְוָה אֶל־יהוה לֵאמֹר הַבְדֵּל יַבְדִּילַנִי יהוה מֵעַל עַמּוֹ וְאַל־יֹאמַר
הַסָּרִיס הֵן אֲנִי עֵץ יָבֵשׁ:   כִּי־כֹה ׀ אָמַר יהוה לַסָּרִיסִים אֲשֶׁר

ד יִשְׁמְרוּ אֶת־שַׁבְּתוֹתַי וּבָחֲרוּ בַּאֲשֶׁר חָפָצְתִּי וּמַחֲזִיקִים בִּבְרִיתִי: וְנָתַתִּי

ה לָהֶם בְּבֵיתִי וּבְחוֹמֹתַי יָד וָשֵׁם טוֹב מִבָּנִים וּמִבָּנוֹת שֵׁם עוֹלָם אֶתֶּן־לוֹ

ו אֲשֶׁר לֹא יִכָּרֵת: וּבְנֵי הַנֵּכָר הַנִּלְוִים עַל־יהוה לְשָׁרְתוֹ וּלְאַהֲבָה
אֶת־שֵׁם יהוה לִהְיוֹת לוֹ לַעֲבָדִים כָּל־שֹׁמֵר שַׁבָּת מֵחַלְּלוֹ וּמַחֲזִיקִים

ז בִּבְרִיתִי: וַהֲבִיאוֹתִים אֶל־הַר קָדְשִׁי וְשִׂמַּחְתִּים בְּבֵית תְּפִלָּתִי עוֹלֹתֵיהֶם
וְזִבְחֵיהֶם לְרָצוֹן עַל־מִזְבְּחִי כִּי בֵיתִי בֵּית־תְּפִלָּה יִקָּרֵא לְכָל־הָעַמִּים:

ח נְאֻם אֲדֹנָי יֱהֹוִה מְקַבֵּץ נִדְחֵי יִשְׂרָאֵל עוֹד אֲקַבֵּץ עָלָיו לְנִקְבָּצָיו: ◀

HAFTARAH
MINCHAH
OF PUBLIC
FAST DAY
55:6-56:8

55:1. The free "water, wine, and milk" are metaphors for the teachings of God. Torah knowledge is available without cost.

55:3. The promise (II Samuel 7:11-16) that the Messiah will be David's descendant (Ibn Ezra).

55:6. Before He seals the evil decree against you (Rashi). According to the Sages, the days when God is most accessible are the ten days between Rosh Hashanah and Yom Kippur.

55:8. God forgives without reservation, unlike human beings (Radak).

55:11. God's promises of redemption and forgiveness will not go unfulfilled.

55:12. You will leave your exile joyously and the mountains and the trees will welcome you back to your land with abundant produce (Rashi).

55:13. A description of the blooming of the barren wilderness upon the return of Israel to its land (Radak); or,

55

*Come,
study Torah!*

¹ Ho, everyone who is thirsty, go to the water, even one with no money, go, buy and eat; go and buy wine and milk without money and without price. * ² Why do you weigh out money without getting bread and [exert] your efforts for that which does not satisfy? Listen well to Me and you will eat well, and your soul will delight in rich food. ³ Incline your ear and come to Me; listen, and your soul will be rejuvenated; I will make an eternal

*Davidic
covenant*

covenant with you, the enduring kindnesses [promised to] David. * ⁴ Behold, I have appointed him as a witness over the regimes, a prince and a commander to the regimes. ⁵ Behold, you will summon a nation you had not known, and a nation that had not known you will run to you, for the sake of HASHEM, your God, for the Holy One of Israel, Who has glorified you.

*Seek God
and return
to Him*

⁶ Seek HASHEM when He can be found; * call upon Him when He is near. ⁷ Let the wicked one forsake his way and the iniquitous man his thoughts; let him return to HASHEM and He will show him mercy; to our God, for He is abundantly forgiving. ⁸ For My thoughts are not your thoughts and your ways are not My ways* — the word of HASHEM. ⁹ As high as the heavens over the earth, so are My ways higher than your ways, and My thoughts than your thoughts. ¹⁰ For just as the rain and snow descend from heaven and will not return there, rather it waters the earth and causes it to produce and sprout, and gives seed to the sower and food to the eater, ¹¹ so shall be My word that emanates from My mouth, it will not return to Me unfulfilled unless it will have accomplished what I desired and brought success where I sent it. * ¹² For in gladness shall you go out and in peace shall you arrive, the mountains and hills will break out in glad song before you, and all the trees of the field will clap hands. * ¹³ In place of the thornbush, a cypress will rise; and in place of the nettle, a myrtle will rise. * This will be a monument to HASHEM, an eternal sign never to be cut down.

56

*Keep
the law*

¹ Thus said HASHEM: Observe justice and perform righteousness, for My salvation is soon to come and My righteousness to be revealed. ² Praiseworthy is the man who does this and the person who grasps it tightly: who guards the Sabbath against desecrating it and guards his hand against doing any evil.

*The
foreigner,
the barren
one . . .*

³ Let not the foreigner, who has joined himself to HASHEM, speak, saying, 'HASHEM will utterly separate me from His people'; and let not the barren one say, 'Behold I am a shriveled tree.' ⁴ For thus said HASHEM to the barren ones who observe My Sabbaths and choose what I desire, and grasp My covenant tightly: ⁵ In My house and within My walls I will give them a place of honor and renown, which is better than sons and daughters; eternal renown will I give them, which will never be terminated. ⁶ And the foreigners who join themselves to HASHEM to serve Him and to love the Name of HASHEM to become servants unto Him, all who guard the Sabbath against desecration, and grasp My covenant tightly — ⁷ I will bring them to My holy mountain, and I will gladden them in My house of prayer; their elevation-offerings and their feast-offerings will find favor on My Altar, for My House will be called a house of prayer for all the peoples. ⁸ The word of my Lord,

*. . . and the
dispersed*

HASHEM/ELOHIM, Who gathers in the dispersed of Israel: I shall gather to him even more than those already gathered to him. *

---

a metaphor for the replacement of the wicked with the righteous (*Targum*).

56:8. In addition to the exiled Jews, many gentile converts will rally to Messiah (*Rashi*).

נו
כָּל־חַיְתוֹ שָׂדָי אֵתָיוּ לֶאֱכֹל כָּל־חַיְתוֹ בַּיָּעַר: °צפו [°צָפָיו ק] ט

עִוְרִים כֻּלָּם לֹא יָדָעוּ כֻּלָּם כְּלָבִים אִלְּמִים לֹא יוּכְלוּ לִנְבֹּחַ הֹזִים שֹׁכְבִים

אֹהֲבֵי לָנוּם: וְהַכְּלָבִים עַזֵּי־נֶפֶשׁ לֹא יָדְעוּ שָׂבְעָה וְהֵמָּה רֹעִים לֹא יָדָעוּ יא

הָבִין כֻּלָּם לְדַרְכָּם פָּנוּ אִישׁ לְבִצְעוֹ מִקָּצֵהוּ: אֵתָיוּ אֶקְחָה־יַיִן וְנִסְבְּאָה יב

נז שֵׁכָר וְהָיָה כָזֶה יוֹם מָחָר גָּדוֹל יֶתֶר מְאֹד: הַצַּדִּיק אָבָד וְאֵין אִישׁ שָׂם עַל־ א

לֵב וְאַנְשֵׁי־חֶסֶד נֶאֱסָפִים בְּאֵין מֵבִין כִּי־מִפְּנֵי הָרָעָה נֶאֱסַף הַצַּדִּיק: יָבוֹא ב

שָׁלוֹם יָנוּחוּ עַל־מִשְׁכְּבוֹתָם הֹלֵךְ נְכֹחוֹ: וְאַתֶּם קִרְבוּ־הֵנָּה ג

בְּנֵי עֹנְנָה זֶרַע מְנָאֵף וַתִּזְנֶה: עַל־מִי תִּתְעַנָּגוּ עַל־מִי תַּרְחִיבוּ פֶה תַּאֲרִיכוּ ד

לָשׁוֹן הֲלוֹא־אַתֶּם יִלְדֵי־פֶשַׁע זֶרַע שָׁקֶר: הַנֵּחָמִים בָּאֵלִים תַּחַת כָּל־עֵץ ה

רַעֲנָן שֹׁחֲטֵי הַיְלָדִים בַּנְּחָלִים תַּחַת סְעִפֵי הַסְּלָעִים: בְּחַלְּקֵי־נַחַל חֶלְקֵךְ ו

הֵם הֵם גּוֹרָלֵךְ גַּם־לָהֶם שָׁפַכְתְּ נֶסֶךְ הֶעֱלִית מִנְחָה הַעַל אֵלֶּה אֶנָּחֵם: עַל־ ז

הַר־גָּבֹהַּ וְנִשָּׂא שַׂמְתְּ מִשְׁכָּבֵךְ גַּם־שָׁם עָלִית לִזְבֹּחַ זָבַח: וְאַחַר הַדֶּלֶת ח

וְהַמְּזוּזָה שַׂמְתְּ זִכְרוֹנֵךְ כִּי מֵאִתִּי גִּלִּית וַתַּעֲלִי הִרְחַבְתְּ מִשְׁכָּבֵךְ וַתִּכְרָת־

לָךְ מֵהֶם אָהַבְתְּ מִשְׁכָּבָם יָד חָזִית: וַתָּשֻׁרִי לַמֶּלֶךְ בַּשֶּׁמֶן וַתַּרְבִּי רִקֻּחָיִךְ ט

וַתְּשַׁלְּחִי צִירַיִךְ עַד־מֵרָחֹק וַתַּשְׁפִּילִי עַד־שְׁאוֹל: בְּרֹב דַּרְכֵּךְ יָגַעַתְּ לֹא י

אָמַרְתְּ נוֹאָשׁ חַיַּת יָדֵךְ מָצָאת עַל־כֵּן לֹא חָלִית: וְאֶת־מִי דָּאַגְתְּ וַתִּירְאִי יא

כִּי תְכַזֵּבִי וְאוֹתִי לֹא זָכַרְתְּ לֹא־שַׂמְתְּ עַל־לִבֵּךְ הֲלֹא אֲנִי מַחְשֶׁה וּמֵעֹלָם

וְאוֹתִי לֹא תִירָאִי: אֲנִי אַגִּיד צִדְקָתֵךְ וְאֶת־מַעֲשַׂיִךְ וְלֹא יוֹעִילוּךְ: בְּזַעֲקֵךְ יב-יג

יַצִּילֵךְ קִבּוּצַיִךְ וְאֶת־כֻּלָּם יִשָּׂא־רוּחַ יִקַּח־הָבֶל וְהַחוֹסֶה בִי יִנְחַל־

אֶרֶץ וְיִירַשׁ הַר־קָדְשִׁי: ◄ וְאָמַר סֹלּוּ־סֹלּוּ פַּנּוּ־דָרֶךְ הָרִימוּ מִכְשׁוֹל מִדֶּרֶךְ יד

HAFTARAS
YOM
KIPPUR
SHACHARIS
57:14-
58:14

עַמִּי: כִּי כֹה אָמַר רָם וְנִשָּׂא שֹׁכֵן עַד וְקָדוֹשׁ שְׁמוֹ מָרוֹם טו

וְקָדוֹשׁ אֶשְׁכּוֹן וְאֶת־דַּכָּא וּשְׁפַל־רוּחַ לְהַחֲיוֹת רוּחַ שְׁפָלִים וּלְהַחֲיוֹת

לֵב נִדְכָּאִים: כִּי לֹא לְעוֹלָם אָרִיב וְלֹא לָנֶצַח אֶקְצוֹף כִּי־רוּחַ מִלְּפָנַי טז

יַעֲטוֹף וּנְשָׁמוֹת אֲנִי עָשִׂיתִי: בַּעֲוֹן בִּצְעוֹ קָצַפְתִּי וְאַכֵּהוּ הַסְתֵּר וְאֶקְצֹף יז

וַיֵּלֶךְ שׁוֹבָב בְּדֶרֶךְ לִבּוֹ: דְּרָכָיו רָאִיתִי וְאֶרְפָּאֵהוּ וְאַנְחֵהוּ וַאֲשַׁלֵּם נִחֻמִים יח

לוֹ וְלַאֲבֵלָיו: בּוֹרֵא °נוב [°נִיב ק] שְׂפָתָיִם שָׁלוֹם שָׁלוֹם לָרָחוֹק יט

וְלַקָּרוֹב אָמַר יהוה וּרְפָאתִיו: וְהָרְשָׁעִים כַּיָּם נִגְרָשׁ כִּי הַשְׁקֵט לֹא יוּכָל כ

56:9. "Beasts of the field" is a metaphor for the converts, while "beasts in the forest" is a metaphor for their more powerful enemies, the opponents of Israel. At the time of the redemption, the erstwhile weaklings will devour those who try to deter them from joining Israel (*Rashi*).

56:10. In contrast to those who seek God (55:6), the "watchmen" — leaders — are too blind to see and too mute to arouse the people from their spiritual slumber (*Rashi*).

56:12. This is what the gluttonous men of power would say to each other (*Rashi*).

57:1-2. Isaiah addresses the wicked people of his generation, and explains that at a time when righteous people are not respected, they may die so that they should not witness the evil that is about to come upon the world.

57:4. How dare you take delight in deriding the prophets of God, as the verse now describes? (*Radak*).

57:5. Idols were often located under trees or on hilltops.

57:6. The prophet often speaks in the first person as if God were speaking.

57:9-11. In addition to putting your spiritual trust in idols, you sought to ingratiate yourself with foreign powers, such as Assyria, going to great lengths to woo them, and never losing hope despite their failure to help you. God showed forbearance, but you ignored Him (*Radak*).

57:12. You ignore My teachings (*Metzudos*).

⁹ *All beasts of the field, come to eat all the beasts in the forest.* *

The blind, ¹⁰ *Their watchmen* * *are all blind; they do not comprehend. They are all dumb*
greedy *dogs who cannot bark, who doze off and lie down and love to sleep.* ¹¹ *And the*
leaders *dogs are greedy; they do not know satiation. These are the shepherds who cannot*
understand; they have all gone off on their own ways, each from his own corner,
for his own dishonest gain, [saying:] ¹² *"Come,* * *I will get wine and we will guzzle*
liquor together; and tomorrow will also be like this, and even much greater!"

57

¹ **T**he righteous one perishes, and no man takes it to heart; men of kindness
The *are gathered in with no one understanding that because of the impending evil*
righteous one *the righteous one was gathered in.* * ² *He will come in peace; they will rest on their*
will rest *resting places — he who walks in his integrity.*

³ *And now come near to here, you children of the astrologer, seed of the*
Adulterous *adulterer and the adulteress.* ⁴ *Against whom do you take delight;* * *against whom*
idolaters *do you open wide a mouth [and] stick out a tongue? Are you not children of sin,*
seed of falsehood, ⁵ *you who indulge your lusts at the elm trees,* * *under every*
leafy tree, who slaughter children in the valleys, under the crags of the rocks?
⁶ *Smooth stones of the valley are your portion, only they are your lot. Even to*
them have you poured out libation and offered up meal-offering. Can I * *relent*
regarding these deeds? ⁷ *On the high, lofty mountain you have set up your bed;*
even there you went up to slaughter a sacrifice. ⁸ *Behind the door and the door-*
post you placed your remembrance[-idol]; for you exiled yourself from Me and
went up [to those hills]; you expanded your bed and you made covenants with
[the idols] for yourself; you loved their bed in every place you saw. ⁹ *You sent a*
tribute of oil to the king * *and prepared numerous spice mixtures [for him]; you*
dispatched your agents afar, and you demeaned yourself as low as the grave.
¹⁰ *You wearied yourself with the length of your journey; you did not say, "I am*
discouraged"; you found your source of strength and therefore did not become ill.
¹¹ *Whom did you dread and fear, that you should have been deceitful [to Me]? You*
did not remember Me; you did not take [Me] to your heart. Behold, I have been
silent, as always — but you did not fear Me. ¹² *I proclaim how you should be*
righteous and what deeds you should do, but they shall not avail you. * ¹³ *When*
you cry out let your cohorts rescue you! But the wind will carry them all off;
nothingness will take them. But the one who trusts in Me will have a portion in the
earth and will inherit My holy mountain. ¹⁴ *He will say, "Pave, pave! Clear the*
road! Remove the obstacle from My people's path." *

God's abode ¹⁵ *For thus said the exalted and uplifted One, Who abides forever and*
Whose Name is holy: I abide in exaltedness and holiness, but I am with the
despondent and lowly of spirit, to revive the spirit of the lowly and to revive
the heart of the despondent. ¹⁶ *For not forever will I contend, nor will I be*
eternally wrathful, when the spirit that envelops [them] is from Me, and I made
[their] souls. ¹⁷ *I became angry because of his sinful thievery; I struck him, I*
hid Myself * *and became angry, because he continued waywardly in the path*
Contrition, *of his heart.* ¹⁸ *But when I see his [contrite] ways, I will heal him; I will guide*
healing, *him and recompense him and his mourners with consolations.* ¹⁹ *I create the*
consolation *speech of the lips: 'Peace, peace, for the far and near,'* * *said* HASHEM, *'and*
I will heal him.' ²⁰ *But the wicked will be like the driven sea that cannot rest,*

57:14. Remove the Evil Inclination that prevents us from   **57:17.** Not coming to their aid in times of need.
repenting (*Rashi*), or remove the physical obstacles that   **57:19.** People will no longer know war in the Messianic
prevent My people's return from exile (*Ibn Ezra*).   era.

נח
כא‑א וַיִּגְרְשׁוּ מֵימָיו רֶפֶשׁ וָטִיט: אֵין שָׁלוֹם אָמַר אֱלֹהַי לָרְשָׁעִים: קְרָא
בְגָרוֹן אַל‑תַּחְשֹׂךְ כַּשּׁוֹפָר הָרֵם קוֹלֶךָ וְהַגֵּד לְעַמִּי פִּשְׁעָם וּלְבֵית יַעֲקֹב
ב חַטֹּאתָם: וְאוֹתִי יוֹם יוֹם יִדְרֹשׁוּן וְדַעַת דְּרָכַי יֶחְפָּצוּן כְּגוֹי אֲשֶׁר‑צְדָקָה
עָשָׂה וּמִשְׁפַּט אֱלֹהָיו לֹא עָזָב יִשְׁאָלוּנִי מִשְׁפְּטֵי‑צֶדֶק קִרְבַת אֱלֹהִים
ג יֶחְפָּצוּן: לָמָּה צַּמְנוּ וְלֹא רָאִיתָ עִנִּינוּ נַפְשֵׁנוּ וְלֹא תֵדָע הֵן בְּיוֹם צֹמְכֶם
ד תִּמְצְאוּ‑חֵפֶץ וְכָל‑עַצְּבֵיכֶם תִּנְגֹּשׂוּ: הֵן לְרִיב וּמַצָּה תָּצוּמוּ וּלְהַכּוֹת
ה בְּאֶגְרֹף רֶשַׁע לֹא‑תָצוּמוּ כַיּוֹם לְהַשְׁמִיעַ בַּמָּרוֹם קוֹלְכֶם: הֲכָזֶה יִהְיֶה צוֹם
אֶבְחָרֵהוּ יוֹם עַנּוֹת אָדָם נַפְשׁוֹ הֲלָכֹף כְּאַגְמֹן רֹאשׁוֹ וְשַׂק וָאֵפֶר יַצִּיעַ
ו הֲלָזֶה תִּקְרָא‑צוֹם וְיוֹם רָצוֹן לַיהוָה: הֲלוֹא זֶה צוֹם אֶבְחָרֵהוּ פַּתֵּחַ
חַרְצֻבּוֹת רֶשַׁע הַתֵּר אֲגֻדּוֹת מוֹטָה וְשַׁלַּח רְצוּצִים חָפְשִׁים וְכָל‑מוֹטָה
ז תְּנַתֵּקוּ: הֲלוֹא פָרֹס לָרָעֵב לַחְמֶךָ וַעֲנִיִּים מְרוּדִים תָּבִיא בָיִת כִּי‑תִרְאֶה
ח עָרֹם וְכִסִּיתוֹ וּמִבְּשָׂרְךָ לֹא תִתְעַלָּם: אָז יִבָּקַע כַּשַּׁחַר אוֹרֶךָ וַאֲרֻכָתְךָ
ט מְהֵרָה תִצְמָח וְהָלַךְ לְפָנֶיךָ צִדְקֶךָ כְּבוֹד יהוה יַאַסְפֶךָ: אָז תִּקְרָא וַיהוָה
יַעֲנֶה תְּשַׁוַּע וְיֹאמַר הִנֵּנִי אִם‑תָּסִיר מִתּוֹכְךָ מוֹטָה שְׁלַח אֶצְבַּע וְדַבֶּר‑
י אָוֶן: וְתָפֵק לָרָעֵב נַפְשֶׁךָ וְנֶפֶשׁ נַעֲנָה תַּשְׂבִּיעַ וְזָרַח בַּחֹשֶׁךְ אוֹרֶךָ וַאֲפֵלָתְךָ
יא כַּצָּהֳרָיִם: וְנָחֲךָ יהוה תָּמִיד וְהִשְׂבִּיעַ בְּצַחְצָחוֹת נַפְשֶׁךָ וְעַצְמֹתֶיךָ יַחֲלִיץ
יב וְהָיִיתָ כְּגַן רָוֶה וּכְמוֹצָא מַיִם אֲשֶׁר לֹא‑יְכַזְּבוּ מֵימָיו: וּבָנוּ מִמְּךָ חָרְבוֹת
עוֹלָם מוֹסְדֵי דוֹר‑וָדוֹר תְּקוֹמֵם וְקֹרָא לְךָ גֹּדֵר פֶּרֶץ מְשֹׁבֵב נְתִיבוֹת לָשָׁבֶת:
יג אִם‑תָּשִׁיב מִשַּׁבָּת רַגְלֶךָ עֲשׂוֹת חֲפָצֶךָ בְּיוֹם קָדְשִׁי וְקָרָאתָ לַשַּׁבָּת עֹנֶג
לִקְדוֹשׁ יהוה מְכֻבָּד וְכִבַּדְתּוֹ מֵעֲשׂוֹת דְּרָכֶיךָ מִמְּצוֹא חֶפְצְךָ וְדַבֵּר דָּבָר:
יד אָז תִּתְעַנַּג עַל‑יְהוָה וְהִרְכַּבְתִּיךָ עַל‑בָּמֳתֵי [°במותי ק] אָרֶץ וְהַאֲכַלְתִּיךָ
נַחֲלַת יַעֲקֹב אָבִיךָ כִּי פִּי יהוה דִּבֵּר: ◄   הֵן לֹא‑קָצְרָה יַד‑יהוָה

נט
א מֵהוֹשִׁיעַ וְלֹא‑כָבְדָה אָזְנוֹ מִשְּׁמוֹעַ: כִּי אִם‑עֲוֹנֹתֵיכֶם הָיוּ מַבְדִּלִים בֵּינֵכֶם
ב לְבֵין אֱלֹהֵיכֶם וְחַטֹּאותֵיכֶם הִסְתִּירוּ פָנִים מִכֶּם מִשְּׁמוֹעַ: כִּי כַפֵּיכֶם
ג נְגֹאֲלוּ בַדָּם וְאֶצְבְּעוֹתֵיכֶם בֶּעָוֹן שִׂפְתוֹתֵיכֶם דִּבְּרוּ‑שֶׁקֶר לְשׁוֹנְכֶם עַוְלָה
ד תֶהְגֶּה: אֵין‑קֹרֵא בְצֶדֶק וְאֵין נִשְׁפָּט בֶּאֱמוּנָה בָּטוֹחַ עַל‑תֹּהוּ וְדַבֶּר‑שָׁוְא
ה הָרוֹ עָמָל וְהוֹלֵיד אָוֶן: בֵּיצֵי צִפְעוֹנִי בִּקֵּעוּ וְקוּרֵי עַכָּבִישׁ יֶאֱרֹגוּ הָאֹכֵל
ו מִבֵּיצֵיהֶם יָמוּת וְהַזּוּרֶה תִּבָּקַע אֶפְעֶה: קוּרֵיהֶם לֹא‑יִהְיוּ לְבֶגֶד וְלֹא

58:1. God addresses Isaiah.

58:2. Why the wicked prosper and the righteous (among whom they count themselves) suffer (*Abarbanel*).

58:3. God tells Isaiah to give the following reply to the nation's question.

58:8. Your good deeds will be a source of merit throughout your life and also when you are *gathered in*, i.e., when you die (*Abarbanel*).

58:10. Take a genuine interest in his plight (*Radak*).

58:11. He will give you good health.

59:1. In the previous chapter, the prophet elaborated on the proper behavior that will save Israel; he reverts to chastising them for their previous actions (*Radak*).

59:4. Spiritual leaders do not rebuke the people, their judges are unjust, and people are deceitful with one another; hence they always rely on empty promises (*Ibn Ezra*).

and whose waters disgorge mire and mud. ²¹ 'There is no peace,' said my God, 'for the wicked.'

58

Insincere fasting

¹ Cry out vociferously, * do not restrain yourself; raise your voice like a shofar — proclaim to My people their willful sins, to the House of Jacob their transgressions. ² They [pretend to] seek Me every day and to desire to know My ways, like a nation that acts righteously and has not forsaken the justice of its God; they inquire of Me about the laws of justice, * as if they desire the nearness of God, [asking,] ³ "Why did we fast and You did not see? Why did we afflict our souls and You did not know?"

Behold* on your fast day you seek out personal gain and you extort all your debts. ⁴ Because you fast for grievance and strife, to strike [each other] with a wicked fist; you do not fast as befits this day, to make your voice heard above. ⁵ Can such be the fast I choose, a day when man merely afflicts himself? Can it be merely bowing one's head like a bulrush and spreading [a mattress of] sackcloth and ashes? Do you call this a fast and a day of favor to Hashem? ⁶ Surely, this is the fast I choose: To break open the shackles of wickedness, to undo the bonds of injustice, and to let the

Sincere fasting

oppressed go free, and annul all perversion. ⁷ Surely you should break your bread for the hungry, and bring the moaning poor [to your] home; when you see a naked person, clothe him; and do not hide yourself from your kin. ⁸ Then your light will burst out like the dawn and your healing will speedily sprout; your righteous deed will precede you and the glory of Hashem will gather you in. * ⁹ Then you will call and Hashem will respond; you will cry out and He will say, 'Here I am!' If you remove from your midst perversion, finger-pointing, and evil speech, ¹⁰ and offer your soul to the hungry* and satisfy the afflicted soul; then your light will shine [even] in the darkness, and your deepest gloom will be like the noon. ¹¹ Then Hashem will guide you always, sate your soul in times of drought and strengthen your bones; * and you will be like a well-watered garden and a spring of water whose waters never fail. ¹² Ancient ruins will be rebuilt through you, and you will restore generations-old foundations; and they will call you, 'repairer of the breach' and 'restorer of paths for habitation.'

The Sabbath and its reward

¹³ If you restrain your foot because it is the Sabbath; refrain from accomplishing your own needs on My holy day; if you proclaim the Sabbath 'a delight,' and the holy [day] of Hashem 'honored,' and you honor it by not engaging in your own affairs, from seeking your own needs or discussing the forbidden — ¹⁴ then you will delight in Hashem, and I will mount you astride the heights of the world; I will provide you the heritage of your forefather Jacob, for the mouth of Hashem has spoken.

59

Iniquity distances man from God

¹ Surely, * the hand of Hashem is not short, [preventing Him] from saving, nor is His ear heavy, [preventing Him] from hearing; ² rather, your iniquities have separated between you and your God, and your transgressions have caused [Him] to hide [His] countenance from you, from hearing [you]. ³ For your palms are stained with blood and your fingers with iniquity; your lips speak falsehood, your tongues utter wickedness. ⁴ No one calls out in righteousness* and no one is judged truthfully; trusting in emptiness and speaking vanity, conceiving wrongdoing and giving birth to wickedness. ⁵ They hatch adder's eggs and weave spider webs: Whoever eats of their eggs will die, and when [the eggs] are squeezed a viper is hatched. ⁶ Their webs will not become a garment, and people will not

ז יִתְבַּסּוּ בְּמַעֲשֵׂיהֶם מַעֲשֵׂיהֶם מַעֲשֵׂי־אָוֶן וּפֹעַל חָמָס בְּכַפֵּיהֶם: רַגְלֵיהֶם לָרַע יָרֻצוּ וִימַהֲרוּ לִשְׁפֹּךְ דָּם נָקִי מַחְשְׁבוֹתֵיהֶם מַחְשְׁבוֹת אָוֶן שֹׁד וָשֶׁבֶר

ח בִּמְסִלּוֹתָם: דֶּרֶךְ שָׁלוֹם לֹא יָדָעוּ וְאֵין מִשְׁפָּט בְּמַעְגְּלוֹתָם נְתִיבוֹתֵיהֶם

ט עִקְּשׁוּ לָהֶם כֹּל דֹּרֵךְ בָּהּ לֹא יָדַע שָׁלוֹם: עַל־כֵּן רָחַק מִשְׁפָּט מִמֶּנּוּ וְלֹא תַשִּׂיגֵנוּ צְדָקָה נְקַוֶּה לָאוֹר וְהִנֵּה־חֹשֶׁךְ לִנְגֹהוֹת בָּאֲפֵלוֹת נְהַלֵּךְ:

י נְגַשְׁשָׁה כַעִוְרִים קִיר וּכְאֵין עֵינַיִם נְגַשֵּׁשָׁה כָּשַׁלְנוּ בַצָּהֳרַיִם כַּנֶּשֶׁף בָּאַשְׁמַנִּים

יא כַּמֵּתִים: נֶהֱמֶה כַדֻּבִּים כֻּלָּנוּ וְכַיּוֹנִים הָגֹה נֶהְגֶּה נְקַוֶּה לַמִּשְׁפָּט וָאַיִן

יב לִישׁוּעָה רָחֲקָה מִמֶּנּוּ: כִּי־רַבּוּ פְשָׁעֵינוּ נֶגְדֶּךָ וְחַטֹּאותֵינוּ עָנְתָה בָּנוּ כִּי־

יג פְשָׁעֵינוּ אִתָּנוּ וַעֲוֺנֹתֵינוּ יְדַעֲנוּם: פָּשֹׁעַ וְכַחֵשׁ בַּיהוָה וְנָסוֹג מֵאַחַר

יד אֱלֹהֵינוּ דַּבֶּר־עֹשֶׁק וְסָרָה הֹרוֹ וְהֹגוֹ מִלֵּב דִּבְרֵי־שָׁקֶר: וְהֻסַּג אָחוֹר מִשְׁפָּט וּצְדָקָה מֵרָחוֹק תַּעֲמֹד כִּי־כָשְׁלָה בָרְחוֹב אֱמֶת וּנְכֹחָה לֹא־תוּכַל

טו לָבוֹא: וַתְּהִי הָאֱמֶת נֶעְדֶּרֶת וְסָר מֵרָע מִשְׁתּוֹלֵל וַיַּרְא יְהוָה וַיֵּרַע בְּעֵינָיו

טז כִּי־אֵין מִשְׁפָּט: וַיַּרְא כִּי־אֵין אִישׁ וַיִּשְׁתּוֹמֵם כִּי אֵין מַפְגִּיעַ וַתּוֹשַׁע לוֹ

יז זְרֹעוֹ וְצִדְקָתוֹ הִיא סְמָכָתְהוּ: וַיִּלְבַּשׁ צְדָקָה כַּשִּׁרְיָן וְכוֹבַע יְשׁוּעָה בְּרֹאשׁוֹ

יח וַיִּלְבַּשׁ בִּגְדֵי נָקָם תִּלְבֹּשֶׁת וַיַּעַט כַּמְעִיל קִנְאָה: כְּעַל גְּמֻלוֹת כְּעַל

יט יְשַׁלֵּם חֵמָה לְצָרָיו גְּמוּל לְאֹיְבָיו לָאִיִּים גְּמוּל יְשַׁלֵּם: וְיִירְאוּ מִמַּעֲרָב אֶת־שֵׁם יְהוָה וּמִמִּזְרַח־שֶׁמֶשׁ אֶת־כְּבוֹדוֹ כִּי־יָבוֹא כַנָּהָר צָר רוּחַ יְהוָה

כ-כא נֹסְסָה בוֹ: וּבָא לְצִיּוֹן גּוֹאֵל וּלְשָׁבֵי פֶשַׁע בְּיַעֲקֹב נְאֻם יְהוָה: וַאֲנִי זֹאת בְּרִיתִי אוֹתָם אָמַר יְהוָה רוּחִי אֲשֶׁר עָלֶיךָ וּדְבָרַי אֲשֶׁר־שַׂמְתִּי בְּפִיךָ לֹא־יָמוּשׁוּ מִפִּיךָ וּמִפִּי זַרְעֲךָ וּמִפִּי זֶרַע זַרְעֲךָ אָמַר יְהוָה מֵעַתָּה וְעַד־

א עוֹלָם: ◄ קוּמִי אוֹרִי כִּי־בָא אוֹרֵךְ וּכְבוֹד יְהוָה עָלַיִךְ

ס

HAFTARAS KI SAVO 60:1-22

ב זָרָח: כִּי־הִנֵּה הַחֹשֶׁךְ יְכַסֶּה־אֶרֶץ וַעֲרָפֶל לְאֻמִּים וְעָלַיִךְ יִזְרַח יְהוָה

ג-ד וּכְבוֹדוֹ עָלַיִךְ יֵרָאֶה: וְהָלְכוּ גוֹיִם לְאוֹרֵךְ וּמְלָכִים לְנֹגַהּ זַרְחֵךְ: שְׂאִי־סָבִיב עֵינַיִךְ וּרְאִי כֻּלָּם נִקְבְּצוּ בָאוּ־לָךְ בָּנַיִךְ מֵרָחוֹק יָבֹאוּ וּבְנֹתַיִךְ עַל־צַד

ה תֵּאָמַנָה: אָז תִּרְאִי וְנָהַרְתְּ וּפָחַד וְרָחַב לְבָבֵךְ כִּי־יֵהָפֵךְ עָלַיִךְ הֲמוֹן יָם

ו חֵיל גּוֹיִם יָבֹאוּ לָךְ: שִׁפְעַת גְּמַלִּים תְּכַסֵּךְ בִּכְרֵי מִדְיָן וְעֵיפָה כֻּלָּם מִשְּׁבָא

ז יָבֹאוּ זָהָב וּלְבוֹנָה יִשָּׂאוּ וּתְהִלֹּת יְהוָה יְבַשֵּׂרוּ: כָּל־צֹאן קֵדָר יִקָּבְצוּ לָךְ אֵילֵי נְבָיוֹת יְשָׁרְתוּנֶךְ יַעֲלוּ עַל־רָצוֹן מִזְבְּחִי וּבֵית תִּפְאַרְתִּי אֲפָאֵר:

59:9. Isaiah now speaks the thoughts of the chastened and contrite nation (*Radak*).

59:16. When God sees that His people are not worthy on their own, He relies on His attribute of benevolence to bring about their redemption.

59:18. Just as He meted out retribution to Pharaoh, Sennacherib and others of their ilk, so shall He mete out retribution to the oppressor nation when He returns Israel from its final exile (*Radak*).

59:21. No matter how bitter the tribulations of exile and oppression, the Torah will never be forgotten from the Jewish people (*Rashi*).

60:1. Isaiah addresses Jerusalem, assuring her that the redemption is at hand, and that never again will she be deprived of her children.

60:4. They will be cared for by the kings mentioned in verse 3 (see 49:23).

clothe themselves with their work; their work is the work of wickedness and an act of corruption is in their palms. ⁷ Their feet run to evil, and they rush to shed innocent blood; their thoughts are thoughts of wickedness; plunder and calamity are in their roads. ⁸ They know not the way of peace and there is no justice in their circuits; they have made their paths crooked; all who walk them do not know peace.

Israel's lament and confession

⁹ "That is why justice has become distant from us * and righteousness has not reached us; we hope for light, but, behold, there is darkness; for brightness, but we walk in deep darkness. ¹⁰ We grope the wall like the blind; and like the eyeless we grope; we stumble at noon as in the dark of night; as if in graves like the dead. ¹¹ We all growl like bears and moan like doves. We hope for justice, but there is none; for salvation, but it is distant from us. ¹² For our willful sins have increased before You and our transgressions have testified against us; for our willful sins are with us and we are aware of our iniquities: ¹³ defiance and denial of HASHEM and withdrawal from after our God, speaking of oppression and rebellion, conceiving and contemplating words of falsehood from the heart. ¹⁴ Thus justice has been withdrawn and righteousness stands at a distance; because truth has stumbled in the street, and integrity cannot enter. ¹⁵ Truth became lacking and refraining from evil seemed foolish. HASHEM saw all this and it was evil in His eyes that there is no justice."

¹⁶ But He saw that there was no [worthy] man and was astounded that there was no one to entreat, so His arm wrought salvation to him and it was His benevolence that was his support. * ¹⁷ He donned righteousness like armor and a helmet of salvation on His head; and He donned garments of vengeance as His attire and clothed Himself in zealousness like a coat. ¹⁸ Just as [His earlier] retributions, so shall He repay * wrath to His enemies, retribution to His adversaries; He will pay retribution to the islands. ¹⁹ From the west [people] will fear the name of HASHEM, and from the rising of the sun His glory; for travail will come like a river, the spirit of HASHEM will gnaw at them.

Israel's redeemer will come

²⁰ A redeemer will come to Zion, and to those of Jacob who repent from willful sin — the word of HASHEM. ²¹ And as for Me, this is My covenant with them, said HASHEM, My spirit which is upon you and My words that I have placed in your mouth will not be withdrawn from your mouth nor from the mouth of your offspring nor from the mouth of your offspring's offspring, said HASHEM, from this moment and forever. *

60

God's glory arrives

¹ **A**rise! Shine!* for your light has arrived, and the glory of HASHEM shines upon you. ² For, behold, darkness may cover the earth and a thick cloud [may cover] the kingdoms, but upon you HASHEM will shine, and His glory will be seen upon you. ³ Nations will walk by your light and kings by the brilliance of your shine. ⁴ Lift up your eyes all around and see, they are all assembling and coming to you; your sons will arrive from afar and your daughters will be raised at [their] side. * ⁵ Then you will see and be radiant, your heart will be startled and broadened, for the affluence of the West will be turned over to you, and the wealth of nations will come to you. ⁶ An abundance of camels will envelop you, camel colts of Midian and Ephah, and all of them will come from Sheba; gold and frankincense will they bear, and the praises of HASHEM will they proclaim. ⁷ All the flocks of Kedar will be gathered unto you, the rams of Nebaioth will serve you; they will be brought up with favor upon My Altar, and I will glorify the House of My Splendor.

The wealth of nations

ח-ט מִי־אֵ֙לֶּה֙ כָּעָ֣ב תְּעוּפֶ֔ינָה וְכַיּוֹנִ֖ים אֶל־אֲרֻבֹּֽתֵיהֶֽם: כִּי־לִ֣י ׀ אִיִּ֣ים יְקַוּ֗וּ וָאֳנִיּ֤וֹת
תַּרְשִׁישׁ֙ בָּרִ֣אשֹׁנָ֔ה לְהָבִ֤יא בָנַ֙יִךְ֙ מֵֽרָח֔וֹק כַּסְפָּ֥ם וּזְהָבָ֖ם אִתָּ֑ם לְשֵׁם֙ יְהוָ֣ה

י אֱלֹהַ֔יִךְ וְלִקְד֥וֹשׁ יִשְׂרָאֵ֖ל כִּ֥י פֵֽאֲרָֽךְ: וּבָנ֤וּ בְנֵֽי־נֵכָר֙ חֹֽמֹתַ֔יִךְ וּמַלְכֵיהֶ֖ם

יא יְשָׁרְת֑וּנֶךְ כִּ֤י בְקִצְפִּי֙ הִכִּיתִ֔יךְ וּבִרְצוֹנִ֖י רִֽחַמְתִּֽיךְ: וּפִתְּח֨וּ שְׁעָרַ֜יִךְ תָּמִ֗יד

יב יוֹמָ֤ם וָלַ֙יְלָה֙ לֹ֣א יִסָּגֵ֔רוּ לְהָבִ֤יא אֵלַ֙יִךְ֙ חֵ֣יל גּוֹיִ֔ם וּמַלְכֵיהֶ֖ם נְהוּגִֽים: כִּֽי־הַגּ֧וֹי

יג וְהַמַּמְלָכָ֛ה אֲשֶׁ֥ר לֹֽא־יַֽעַבְד֖וּךְ יֹאבֵ֑דוּ וְהַגּוֹיִ֖ם חָרֹ֥ב יֶֽחֱרָֽבוּ: כְּב֤וֹד הַלְּבָנוֹן֙
אֵלַ֣יִךְ יָב֔וֹא בְּר֛וֹשׁ תִּדְהָ֥ר וּתְאַשּׁ֖וּר יַחְדָּ֑ו לְפָאֵר֙ מְק֣וֹם מִקְדָּשִׁ֔י וּמְק֥וֹם רַגְלַ֖י

יד אֲכַבֵּֽד: וְהָֽלְכ֨וּ אֵלַ֤יִךְ שְׁח֙וֹחַ֙ בְּנֵ֣י מְעַנַּ֔יִךְ וְהִֽשְׁתַּֽחֲו֛וּ עַל־כַּפּ֥וֹת רַגְלַ֖יִךְ כָּל־

טו מְנַֽאֲצָ֑יִךְ וְקָ֤רְאוּ לָךְ֙ עִ֣יר יְהוָ֔ה צִיּ֖וֹן קְד֥וֹשׁ יִשְׂרָאֵֽל: תַּ֧חַת הֱיוֹתֵ֛ךְ עֲזוּבָ֥ה

טז וּשְׂנוּאָ֖ה וְאֵ֣ין עוֹבֵ֑ר וְשַׂמְתִּיךְ֙ לִגְא֣וֹן עוֹלָ֔ם מְשׂ֖וֹשׂ דּ֥וֹר וָדֽוֹר: וְיָנַ֙קְתְּ֙ חֲלֵ֣ב
גּוֹיִ֔ם וְשֹׁ֥ד מְלָכִ֖ים תִּינָ֑קִי וְיָדַ֗עַתְּ כִּ֣י אֲנִ֤י יְהוָה֙ מֽוֹשִׁיעֵ֔ךְ וְגֹֽאֲלֵ֖ךְ אֲבִ֥יר יַֽעֲקֹֽב:

יז תַּ֣חַת הַנְּחֹ֜שֶׁת אָבִ֣יא זָהָ֗ב וְתַ֤חַת הַבַּרְזֶל֙ אָבִ֣יא כֶ֔סֶף וְתַ֥חַת הָֽעֵצִ֖ים
נְחֹ֔שֶׁת וְתַ֥חַת הָֽאֲבָנִ֖ים בַּרְזֶ֑ל וְשַׂמְתִּ֤י פְקֻדָּתֵךְ֙ שָׁל֔וֹם וְנֹֽגְשַׂ֖יִךְ צְדָקָֽה: לֹֽא־

יח יִשָּׁמַ֨ע ע֤וֹד חָמָס֙ בְּאַרְצֵ֔ךְ שֹׁ֥ד וָשֶׁ֖בֶר בִּגְבוּלָ֑יִךְ וְקָרָ֤את יְשׁוּעָה֙ חֽוֹמֹתַ֔יִךְ

יט וּשְׁעָרַ֖יִךְ תְּהִלָּֽה: לֹא־יִֽהְיֶה־לָּ֨ךְ ע֤וֹד הַשֶּׁ֙מֶשׁ֙ לְא֣וֹר יוֹמָ֔ם וּלְנֹ֕גַהּ הַיָּרֵ֖חַ לֹֽא־
יָאִ֣יר לָ֑ךְ וְהָֽיָה־לָ֤ךְ יְהוָה֙ לְא֣וֹר עוֹלָ֔ם וֵֽאלֹהַ֖יִךְ לְתִפְאַרְתֵּֽךְ: לֹֽא־יָב֨וֹא עוֹד֙

כ שִׁמְשֵׁ֔ךְ וִֽירֵחֵ֖ךְ לֹ֣א יֵֽאָסֵ֑ף כִּ֣י יְהוָ֗ה יִֽהְיֶה־לָּךְ֙ לְא֣וֹר עוֹלָ֔ם וְשָֽׁלְמ֖וּ יְמֵ֥י

כא אֶבְלֵֽךְ: וְעַמֵּךְ֙ כֻּלָּ֣ם צַדִּיקִ֔ים לְעוֹלָ֖ם יִ֣ירְשׁוּ אָ֑רֶץ נֵ֧צֶר [°מַטָּעַ֛י ק] מטעו

כב מַֽעֲשֵׂ֥ה יָדַ֖י לְהִתְפָּאֵֽר: הַקָּטֹן֙ יִֽהְיֶ֣ה לָאֶ֔לֶף וְהַצָּעִ֖יר לְג֣וֹי עָצ֑וּם אֲנִ֤י יְהוָה֙

סא א בְּעִתָּ֖הּ אֲחִישֶֽׁנָּה: ▶ ר֛וּחַ אֲדֹנָ֥י יֱהֹוִ֖ה עָלָ֑י יַ֡עַן מָשַׁח֩ יְהוָ֨ה אֹתִ֜י
לְבַשֵּׂ֣ר עֲנָוִ֗ים שְׁלָחַ֙נִי֙ לַֽחֲבֹ֣שׁ לְנִשְׁבְּרֵי־לֵ֔ב לִקְרֹ֤א לִשְׁבוּיִם֙ דְּר֔וֹר

ב וְלַֽאֲסוּרִ֖ים פְּקַח־קֽוֹחַ: לִקְרֹ֤א שְׁנַת־רָצוֹן֙ לַֽיהוָ֔ה וְי֥וֹם נָקָ֖ם לֵֽאלֹהֵ֑ינוּ לְנַחֵ֖ם

ג כָּל־אֲבֵלִֽים: לָשׂ֣וּם ׀ לַֽאֲבֵלֵ֣י צִיּ֗וֹן לָתֵת֩ לָהֶ֨ם פְּאֵ֜ר תַּ֣חַת אֵ֗פֶר שֶׁ֤מֶן שָׂשׂוֹן֙
תַּ֣חַת אֵ֗בֶל מַֽעֲטֵ֤ה תְהִלָּה֙ תַּ֣חַת ר֣וּחַ כֵּהָ֔ה וְקֹרָ֤א לָהֶם֙ אֵילֵ֣י הַצֶּ֔דֶק

ד מַטַּ֥ע יְהוָ֖ה לְהִתְפָּאֵֽר: וּבָנוּ֙ חָרְב֣וֹת עוֹלָ֔ם שֹֽׁמְמ֥וֹת רִֽאשֹׁנִ֖ים יְקוֹמֵ֑מוּ

ה וְחִדְּשׁוּ֙ עָ֣רֵי חֹ֔רֶב שֹֽׁמְמ֖וֹת דּ֣וֹר וָד֑וֹר: וְעָֽמְד֤וּ זָרִים֙ וְרָע֣וּ צֹֽאנְכֶ֔ם וּבְנֵ֥י

ו נֵכָ֖ר אִכָּֽרֵיכֶ֥ם וְכֹֽרְמֵיכֶֽם: וְאַתֶּ֗ם כֹּֽהֲנֵ֤י יְהוָה֙ תִּקָּרֵ֔אוּ מְשָֽׁרְתֵ֥י אֱלֹהֵ֖ינוּ
יֵֽאָמֵ֣ר לָכֶ֔ם חֵ֥יל גּוֹיִ֖ם תֹּאכֵ֑לוּ וּבִכְבוֹדָ֖ם תִּתְיַמָּֽרוּ: תַּ֤חַת בָּשְׁתְּכֶם֙ מִשְׁנֶ֔ה

ז וּכְלִמָּ֖ה יָרֹ֣נּוּ חֶלְקָ֑ם לָכֵ֤ן בְּאַרְצָם֙ מִשְׁנֶ֣ה יִירָ֔שׁוּ שִׂמְחַ֥ת עוֹלָ֖ם תִּֽהְיֶ֥ה לָהֶֽם:

60:8. This question will be asked by the startled and astonished city of Jerusalem.

60:9. As in the days of Solomon (see *I Kings* 10:22).

60:13. The Temple is called the "place of God's feet," as if God sits on His throne in heaven and His feet reach the earth at this holy site (*Radak*).

60:16. You will have the possessions of the nations and the spoils of kings.

60:17. Whatever was plundered from you years ago will be returned many times over, as if copper is being replaced with gold.

60:18. You will not need walls and gateways for defense; instead you will rely on God.

60:22. Tribe or family (*Radak*).

61:2. "Favor" for His people and "vengeance" for their enemies.

61:6. For they will bring you lavish gifts, as described several times in this and preceding chapters.

⁸ 'Who are these, * who fly like a cloud, like doves to their cote-windows?'

⁹ For the islands will place their hope in Me, with the ships of Tarshish in earlier times, * to bring your children from afar with their gold and silver with them, for the Name of HASHEM, your God, and for the Holy One of Israel, for He will have glorified you. ¹⁰ Then the sons of foreigners will build your walls and their kings will serve you. Though I struck you in My indignation, in My favor have I been compassionate to you. ¹¹ Your gates will be opened continuously, day and night they will not be closed; for [them] to bring you the wealth of nations, and their kings under escort. ¹² For the nation and kingdom that does not serve you will perish, and those nations will be utterly destroyed. ¹³ The glory of the Lebanon [forest] will come to you — cypress, fir, and box tree together — to glorify the place of My Sanctuary; and I will bring honor to the place of My feet. * ¹⁴ The sons of your oppressors will go to you submissively, and all who scorned you will prostrate themselves at the soles of your feet; they will call you 'City of HASHEM, Zion of the Holy One of Israel.'

The Temple will be rebuilt

Zion, eternal city

¹⁵ Instead of your being forsaken and despised, without wayfarers, I will make you into an eternal pride, a joy for generation after generation. ¹⁶ You will nurse from the milk of the nations and from the breast of kings will you nurse; * then you will realize that I, HASHEM, am your Savior and your Redeemer, the Mighty One of Jacob. ¹⁷ In place of the copper I will bring gold; * and in place of the iron I will bring silver; in place of the wood, copper; and in place of the stones, iron. I will designate your appointed officials for peace and your overlords for righteousness. ¹⁸ No longer will violence be heard of in your land, nor plunder and calamity in your borders. You will call [God's] salvation your protective walls, and [His] praise to be your gateways. * ¹⁹ The sun will no longer be for you the light of day and brightness and the moon will not illuminate for you. HASHEM will be an eternal light for you, and your God will be your splendor. ²⁰ Never again will your sun set, and your moon will not be withdrawn; for HASHEM will be unto you an eternal light, and the days of your mourning will be ended. ²¹ Your people will all be righteous; they will inherit the land forever; a shoot of My planting, My handiwork, in which to glory. ²² The smallest * will increase a thousandfold, and the youngest into a mighty nation. I am HASHEM, in its time I will hasten it.

The splendor of God

61

Joyful tidings to the humbled

¹ The spirit of my Lord, HASHEM/ELOHIM, is upon me, because HASHEM has anointed me to bring tidings to the humbled; He has sent me to bind up the brokenhearted, to proclaim freedom for captives and release from bondage for the imprisoned, ² to proclaim a year of favor unto HASHEM and a day of vengeance * for our God, to comfort all mourners, ³ to bring about for the mourners of Zion to give them splendor instead of ashes, oil of joy instead of mourning, a cloak of praise instead of a dim spirit. They will then be called "elms of righteousness, the planting of HASHEM in which to glory." ⁴ They will rebuild the ancient ruins, the wastelands of former times they will restore; they will renew ruined cities, generations-old wastelands. ⁵ Foreigners will stand and tend your flocks and the sons of the stranger will be your plowmen and your vineyard workers. ⁶ And you will be called "priests of HASHEM"; "ministers of our God" will be said of you. You will eat of the wealth of nations * and will pride yourselves in their glory. ⁷ Instead of your shame which was double and disgrace which they would bemoan as their portion; therefore, they will inherit a double portion in their land, and eternal gladness will be theirs.

Spiritual preeminence

ח כִּי אֲנִי יהוה אֹהֵב מִשְׁפָּט שֹׂנֵא גָזֵל בְּעוֹלָה וְנָתַתִּי פְעֻלָּתָם בֶּאֱמֶת
ט וּבְרִית עוֹלָם אֶכְרוֹת לָהֶם: וְנוֹדַע בַּגּוֹיִם זַרְעָם וְצֶאֱצָאֵיהֶם בְּתוֹךְ
י הָעַמִּים כָּל־רֹאֵיהֶם יַכִּירוּם כִּי הֵם זֶרַע בֵּרַךְ יהוה:

שׁוֹשׂ ◀

HAFTARAS
NITZAVIM
61:10-63:9

אָשִׂישׂ בַּיהוה תָּגֵל נַפְשִׁי בֵּאלֹהַי כִּי הִלְבִּישַׁנִי בִּגְדֵי־יֶשַׁע מְעִיל צְדָקָה
יא יְעָטָנִי כֶּחָתָן יְכַהֵן פְּאֵר וְכַכַּלָּה תַּעְדֶּה כֵלֶיהָ: כִּי כָאָרֶץ תּוֹצִיא צִמְחָהּ
וּכְגַנָּה זֵרוּעֶיהָ תַצְמִיחַ כֵּן ׀ אֲדֹנָי יהוה יַצְמִיחַ צְדָקָה וּתְהִלָּה נֶגֶד כָּל־

סב

א הַגּוֹיִם: לְמַעַן צִיּוֹן לֹא אֶחֱשֶׁה וּלְמַעַן יְרוּשָׁלַםִ לֹא אֶשְׁקוֹט עַד־יֵצֵא
ב כַנֹּגַהּ צִדְקָהּ וִישׁוּעָתָהּ כְּלַפִּיד יִבְעָר: וְרָאוּ גוֹיִם צִדְקֵךְ וְכָל־מְלָכִים
ג כְּבוֹדֵךְ וְקֹרָא לָךְ שֵׁם חָדָשׁ אֲשֶׁר פִּי יהוה יִקֳּבֶנּוּ: וְהָיִית עֲטֶרֶת תִּפְאֶרֶת
ד בְּיַד־יהוה °וּצְנוֹף [°וּצְנִיף ק] מְלוּכָה בְּכַף־אֱלֹהָיִךְ: לֹא־יֵאָמֵר לָךְ עוֹד
עֲזוּבָה וּלְאַרְצֵךְ לֹא־יֵאָמֵר עוֹד שְׁמָמָה כִּי לָךְ יִקָּרֵא חֶפְצִי־בָהּ וּלְאַרְצֵךְ
ה בְּעוּלָה כִּי־חָפֵץ יהוה בָּךְ וְאַרְצֵךְ תִּבָּעֵל: כִּי־יִבְעַל בָּחוּר בְּתוּלָה
ו יִבְעָלוּךְ בָּנָיִךְ וּמְשׂוֹשׂ חָתָן עַל־כַּלָּה יָשִׂישׂ עָלַיִךְ אֱלֹהָיִךְ: עַל־חוֹמֹתַיִךְ
יְרוּשָׁלַםִ הִפְקַדְתִּי שֹׁמְרִים כָּל־הַיּוֹם וְכָל־הַלַּיְלָה תָּמִיד לֹא יֶחֱשׁוּ
ז הַמַּזְכִּרִים אֶת־יהוה אַל־דֳּמִי לָכֶם: וְאַל־תִּתְּנוּ דֳמִי לוֹ עַד־יְכוֹנֵן
ח וְעַד־יָשִׂים אֶת־יְרוּשָׁלַםִ תְּהִלָּה בָּאָרֶץ: נִשְׁבַּע יהוה בִּימִינוֹ וּבִזְרוֹעַ
עֻזּוֹ אִם־אֶתֵּן אֶת־דְּגָנֵךְ עוֹד מַאֲכָל לְאֹיְבַיִךְ וְאִם־יִשְׁתּוּ בְנֵי־נֵכָר
ט תִּירוֹשֵׁךְ אֲשֶׁר יָגַעַתְּ בּוֹ: כִּי מְאַסְפָיו יֹאכְלֻהוּ וְהִלְלוּ אֶת־יהוה וּמְקַבְּצָיו
י יִשְׁתֻּהוּ בְּחַצְרוֹת קָדְשִׁי: עִבְרוּ עִבְרוּ בַּשְּׁעָרִים
פַּנּוּ דֶּרֶךְ הָעָם סֹלּוּ סֹלּוּ הַמְסִלָּה סַקְּלוּ מֵאֶבֶן הָרִימוּ נֵס עַל־הָעַמִּים:
יא הִנֵּה יהוה הִשְׁמִיעַ אֶל־קְצֵה הָאָרֶץ אִמְרוּ לְבַת־צִיּוֹן הִנֵּה יִשְׁעֵךְ בָּא
יב הִנֵּה שְׂכָרוֹ אִתּוֹ וּפְעֻלָּתוֹ לְפָנָיו: וְקָרְאוּ לָהֶם עַם־הַקֹּדֶשׁ גְּאוּלֵי יהוה

סג

א וְלָךְ יִקָּרֵא דְרוּשָׁה עִיר לֹא נֶעֱזָבָה: מִי־זֶה ׀
בָּא מֵאֱדוֹם חֲמוּץ בְּגָדִים מִבָּצְרָה זֶה הָדוּר בִּלְבוּשׁוֹ צֹעֶה בְּרֹב כֹּחוֹ
ב אֲנִי מְדַבֵּר בִּצְדָקָה רַב לְהוֹשִׁיעַ: מַדּוּעַ אָדֹם לִלְבוּשֶׁךָ וּבְגָדֶיךָ כְּדֹרֵךְ
ג בְּגַת: פּוּרָה ׀ דָּרַכְתִּי לְבַדִּי וּמֵעַמִּים אֵין־אִישׁ אִתִּי וְאֶדְרְכֵם בְּאַפִּי
ד וְאֶרְמְסֵם בַּחֲמָתִי וְיֵז נִצְחָם עַל־בְּגָדַי וְכָל־מַלְבּוּשַׁי אֶגְאָלְתִּי: כִּי יוֹם
ה נָקָם בְּלִבִּי וּשְׁנַת גְּאוּלַי בָּאָה: וְאַבִּיט וְאֵין עֹזֵר וְאֶשְׁתּוֹמֵם וְאֵין

61:10. Zion responds to the words of comfort spoken to her thus far.

62:6. You need not fear that I have forgotten you. I encourage those who mourn and pray for the restoration of Zion's ruined walls and exhort the guardians never to stop their prayers for Zion (*Radak*).

62:10. Enter the gates of other cities to proclaim the ingathering of the exiles (*Ibn Ezra*), and raise a banner to signal the scattered Jews to return to their land (*Rashi*).

62:11. To apportion reward to those who deserve it.

63:1. God's vengeance for Edom's persecution of His people is described through a dialogue between an anonymous onlooker and God Himself, as if He were a warrior coming from a destructive attack on the Edomite city of Bozrah.

63:5. To save Israel from Edom.

8 For I am HASHEM, Who loves justice and hates a burnt-offering [bought] with robbery; and I will repay their deeds in truth and I will seal an eternal covenant with them. 9 Their offspring will be known among the nations, and their descendants amid the peoples; all who see them will recognize them, that they are the seed that HASHEM has blessed.

Hymn of   10 "I * will rejoice intensely with HASHEM, my soul will exult with my God, for He
thanksgiving has dressed me in the raiment of salvation, in a robe of righteousness has He cloaked me, like a bridegroom who exalts [himself] with splendor, like a bride who bedecks herself with her jewelry. 11 For, as the earth sends forth its growth and as a garden sprouts forth its seedlings, so will my Lord, HASHEM/ELOHIM, cause righteousness and praise to sprout in the presence of all the nations."

62

1 For or Zion's sake I will not be silent, and for Jerusalem's sake I will not be still, until her righteousness emanates like bright light, and her salvation blazes like a torch. 2 Nations will perceive your righteousness and all the kings your honor; and you will be called by a new name, which the mouth of HASHEM will pronounce. 3 Then you will be a crown of splendor in the hand of HASHEM and a royal diadem in the palm of your God. 4 It will no longer be said of you "Forsaken One," and of your land it will no longer be said "Desolate Place"; for you will be called "My Desire Is In Her," and your land "Inhabited," for HASHEM's desire is in you, and your land will become inhabited. 5 As a young man takes a maiden in marriage, so will your children settle in you; and like a bridegroom's rejoicing over his bride, so will your God rejoice over you.

The   6 Upon your walls, O Jerusalem, have I posted guardians; * all the day and
guardians all the night, continuously, they will never be silent. 'You who remind
on the HASHEM, be not silent! 7 Do not give Him silence, until He establishes and until
walls He makes Jerusalem a source of praise in the Land.' 8 HASHEM has sworn by His right hand and by His powerful arm: 'I will no longer give your grain as food for your enemies; and the sons of strangers will not drink your wine for which you have toiled. 9 For those who have harvested it will eat it, and will praise HASHEM; and those who have gathered it in will drink it in My holy courtyards.'

The   10 Go through, go through the gates; * clear the way for the people; pave,
Holy People pave the road; clear it of stones; raise a banner over the peoples. 11 Behold, HASHEM has announced to the ends of the earth: Say to the daughter of Zion, 'Behold, your Savior has come!' Behold, His reward is with Him, and His wage is before Him. * 12 People will call them, 'the Holy People, the Redeemed of HASHEM'; and you will be called, 'Sought After,' 'The City Not Forsaken.'

63

1 'Who ho is this coming from Edom, * with sullied garments, from Bozrah?
The This One Who is majestic in His raiment, girded with His abundant
Conqueror strength?'
of Edom 'It is I, Who speaks with righteousness, abundantly able to save!'
2 'Why is there red on Your raiment, and [why are] Your garments like those of someone treading in a wine vat?'
3 'I alone have trodden a winepress, not a man from the nations was with Me; I trod on them in My anger and trampled them in My wrath, and their lifeblood spurted out on My garments, so I soiled all My garments. 4 For a day of vengeance is in My heart, and the year of My redemption has come. 5 I looked, but there was no helper; * I was astounded that there was no

ו סוֹמֵךְ וַתּוֹשַׁע לִי זְרֹעִי וַחֲמָתִי הִיא סְמָכָתְנִי: וְאָבוּס עַמִּים בְּאַפִּי

ז וַאֲשַׁכְּרֵם בַּחֲמָתִי וְאוֹרִיד לָאָרֶץ נִצְחָם: חַסְדֵי יהוה ׀ אַזְכִּיר
תְּהִלֹּת יהוה כְּעַל כֹּל אֲשֶׁר־גְּמָלָנוּ יהוה וְרַב־טוּב לְבֵית יִשְׂרָאֵל אֲשֶׁר־

ח גְּמָלָם כְּרַחֲמָיו וּכְרֹב חֲסָדָיו: וַיֹּאמֶר אַךְ־עַמִּי הֵמָּה בָּנִים לֹא יְשַׁקֵּרוּ וַיְהִי

ט לָהֶם לְמוֹשִׁיעַ: בְּכָל־צָרָתָם ׀ לֹא [°לוֹ ק] צָר וּמַלְאַךְ פָּנָיו הוֹשִׁיעָם
בְּאַהֲבָתוֹ וּבְחֶמְלָתוֹ הוּא גְאָלָם וַיְנַטְּלֵם וַיְנַשְּׂאֵם כָּל־יְמֵי עוֹלָם: ◄

י וְהֵמָּה מָרוּ וְעִצְּבוּ אֶת־רוּחַ קָדְשׁוֹ וַיֵּהָפֵךְ לָהֶם לְאוֹיֵב הוּא נִלְחַם־בָּם:

יא וַיִּזְכֹּר יְמֵי־עוֹלָם מֹשֶׁה עַמּוֹ אַיֵּה ׀ הַמַּעֲלֵם מִיָּם אֵת °רֹעֵי צֹאנוֹ אַיֵּה   °נ״א רֹעֵה
הַשָּׂם בְּקִרְבּוֹ אֶת־רוּחַ קָדְשׁוֹ:

יב מוֹלִיךְ לִימִין מֹשֶׁה זְרוֹעַ תִּפְאַרְתּוֹ בּוֹקֵעַ
מַיִם מִפְּנֵיהֶם לַעֲשׂוֹת לוֹ שֵׁם עוֹלָם: מוֹלִיכָם בַּתְּהֹמוֹת כַּסּוּס בַּמִּדְבָּר לֹא

יג יִכָּשֵׁלוּ:

יד כַּבְּהֵמָה בַּבִּקְעָה תֵרֵד רוּחַ יהוה תְּנִיחֶנּוּ כֵּן נִהַגְתָּ עַמְּךָ לַעֲשׂוֹת
לְךָ שֵׁם תִּפְאָרֶת: הַבֵּט מִשָּׁמַיִם וּרְאֵה מִזְּבֻל קָדְשְׁךָ וְתִפְאַרְתֶּךָ אַיֵּה

טו קִנְאָתְךָ וּגְבוּרֹתֶךָ הֲמוֹן מֵעֶיךָ וְרַחֲמֶיךָ אֵלַי הִתְאַפָּקוּ: כִּי־אַתָּה אָבִינוּ כִּי

טז אַבְרָהָם לֹא יְדָעָנוּ וְיִשְׂרָאֵל לֹא יַכִּירָנוּ אַתָּה יהוה אָבִינוּ גֹּאֲלֵנוּ מֵעוֹלָם

יז שְׁמֶךָ: לָמָּה תַתְעֵנוּ יהוה מִדְּרָכֶיךָ תַּקְשִׁיחַ לִבֵּנוּ מִיִּרְאָתֶךָ שׁוּב לְמַעַן
עֲבָדֶיךָ שִׁבְטֵי נַחֲלָתֶךָ: לַמִּצְעָר יָרְשׁוּ עַם־קָדְשֶׁךָ צָרֵינוּ בּוֹסְסוּ מִקְדָּשֶׁךָ:

יח

יט הָיִינוּ מֵעוֹלָם לֹא־מָשַׁלְתָּ בָּם לֹא־נִקְרָא שִׁמְךָ עֲלֵיהֶם לוּא־קָרַעְתָּ שָׁמַיִם

סד

א יָרַדְתָּ מִפָּנֶיךָ הָרִים נָזֹלּוּ: כִּקְדֹחַ אֵשׁ הֲמָסִים מַיִם תִּבְעֶה־אֵשׁ לְהוֹדִיעַ

ב שִׁמְךָ לְצָרֶיךָ מִפָּנֶיךָ גּוֹיִם יִרְגָּזוּ: בַּעֲשׂוֹתְךָ נוֹרָאוֹת לֹא נְקַוֶּה יָרַדְתָּ מִפָּנֶיךָ

ג הָרִים נָזֹלּוּ: וּמֵעוֹלָם לֹא־שָׁמְעוּ לֹא הֶאֱזִינוּ עַיִן לֹא־רָאָתָה אֱלֹהִים

ד זוּלָתְךָ יַעֲשֶׂה לִמְחַכֵּה־לוֹ: פָּגַעְתָּ אֶת־שָׂשׂ וְעֹשֵׂה צֶדֶק בִּדְרָכֶיךָ יִזְכְּרוּךָ

ה הֵן־אַתָּה קָצַפְתָּ וַנֶּחֱטָא בָּהֶם עוֹלָם וְנִוָּשֵׁעַ: וַנְּהִי כַטָּמֵא כֻּלָּנוּ וּכְבֶגֶד

ו עִדִּים כָּל־צִדְקֹתֵינוּ וַנָּבֶל כֶּעָלֶה כֻּלָּנוּ וַעֲוֹנֵנוּ כָּרוּחַ יִשָּׂאֻנוּ: וְאֵין־קוֹרֵא
בְשִׁמְךָ מִתְעוֹרֵר לְהַחֲזִיק בָּךְ כִּי־הִסְתַּרְתָּ פָנֶיךָ מִמֶּנּוּ וַתְּמוּגֵנוּ בְּיַד־

ז עֲוֹנֵנוּ: וְעַתָּה יהוה אָבִינוּ אָתָּה אֲנַחְנוּ הַחֹמֶר וְאַתָּה יֹצְרֵנוּ וּמַעֲשֵׂה

ח יָדְךָ כֻּלָּנוּ: אַל־תִּקְצֹף יהוה עַד־מְאֹד וְאַל־לָעַד תִּזְכֹּר עָוֹן הֵן הַבֶּט־נָא

ט עַמְּךָ כֻּלָּנוּ: עָרֵי קָדְשְׁךָ הָיוּ מִדְבָּר צִיּוֹן מִדְבָּר הָיָתָה יְרוּשָׁלַ͏ִם שְׁמָמָה:

י בֵּית קָדְשֵׁנוּ וְתִפְאַרְתֵּנוּ אֲשֶׁר הִלְלוּךָ אֲבֹתֵינוּ הָיָה לִשְׂרֵפַת אֵשׁ וְכָל־

יא מַחֲמַדֵּינוּ הָיָה לְחָרְבָּה: הַעַל־אֵלֶּה תִתְאַפַּק יהוה תֶּחֱשֶׁה וּתְעַנֵּנוּ עַד־

63:7. This commences a prayer of the prophet, which continues until the end of Chapter 64.

63:10. By enabling Israel's enemies to subjugate them, and it was as if God Himself were fighting against them (*Radak*).

63:13. A horse gallops easily in the desert, where there are few natural impediments to block its path (*Rashi*). So too, the bed of the split sea was dry and easy to traverse.

63:14. That is, slowly and with great care (*Ibn Ezra*).

63:17. Although we are unworthy, return to us for the sake of your faithful servants, the Patriarchs and the progenitors of the twelve tribes (*Radak*).

64:1-2. The verses refer to the revelation at Mount Sinai (see *Exodus* 19:18).

64:4. We had always been redeemed thanks to the prayers of the righteous, but now You have taken them away and we are left helpless (see 57:1, 59:16).

supporter; so My arm wrought salvation for Me and My wrath was a support for Me. ⁶ I stepped on peoples in My anger and made them drunk with My wrath, and I threw their lifeblood to the ground.'

The prophet praises God ⁷ HASHEM's kindnesses will I proclaim* as the praises of HASHEM, in accordance with all that HASHEM has bestowed upon us and the abundant goodness to the House of Israel that He has bestowed upon them in His compassion and in His abundant kindness. ⁸ For He said, "Indeed they are My people, children who will not be false," and He became their Savior. ⁹ In all their troubles He was troubled, so an angel from before Him saved them. With His love and with His compassion He redeemed them; He lifted them and bore them all the days of the world.

¹⁰ But they rebelled and distressed His holy spirit; so He changed toward them into an enemy; He fought them.* ¹¹ They [then] remembered the days of old, of *Kindness through the centuries* Moses [with] His people: Where is the One Who brought [the Israelites] out of the Sea together with the shepherds of His flock? Where is the One who infused His holy spirit in their midst? ¹² Who caused His splendrous arm to go at Moses' right side? Who split the Sea before them to make Himself eternal renown? ¹³ Who led them through the depths as a horse in the desert,* so they would not falter? ¹⁴ As an animal descends into a valley, so the spirit of HASHEM led them;* thus did You guide Your people along, to make a splendrous Name for Yourself. ¹⁵ Look down from Heaven and see, from Your abode of holiness and splendor! Where is Your zealousness and Your might? Your inner yearning and Your mercy have been held back from me! ¹⁶ For You are our Father; though Abraham may not know us and Israel may not recognize us, You, HASHEM, are our Father; "our Eternal Redeemer" *Return!* is Your Name. ¹⁷ Why, HASHEM, do You let us stray from Your paths, letting our heart become hardened from fearing You? Return [to us] for the sake of Your servants,* the tribes of Your heritage! ¹⁸ For but a short time did Your holy people possess [it]; our enemies have trampled Your Temple. ¹⁹ We have become as if You had never ruled over them, as if Your Name had not been called upon them. If only You would tear open the heavens and descend, the mountains would melt

64 before You! ¹ As a melting fire burned* — a fire that caused water to bubble — *Knowledge of God* to make Your Name known to Your enemies, so that nations would tremble before You, ² when You performed awesome wonders that we had not expected, You descended and the mountains melted because of You. ³ [People] had never heard, never observed, no eye had ever seen a god — except for You — that acted for those who trust in Him.

⁴ You have eliminated those who rejoiced in doing righteousness, who would invoke Your ways [in prayer]; You became enraged because we had sinned. We *Confessed guilt* had always [relied] on them and been saved.* ⁵ We have all become defiled and all our righteousness is like a worn-out garment; we all wither like a leaf; and like a wind, our sins carry us off. ⁶ There is no one to call out in Your Name, who arouses himself to hold fast to You when You hide Your face from us and melt us away because of our iniquities.

⁷ So now, HASHEM, You are our Father. We are the clay and You are our Potter, and we are all Your handiwork. ⁸ O HASHEM, do not become greatly enraged and do not remember iniquity forever; behold, see now, all of us are Your people. ⁹ Your holy cities have become a wilderness; Zion has become a wilderness, Jerusalem a wasteland. ¹⁰ The Temple of our holiness and our splendor, where our fathers praised You, has become a fiery conflagration, and all that we desired has become a ruin. ¹¹ Will You restrain Yourself in the face of all these, HASHEM, and be silent and let us suffer so much?

סה

א נִדְרַשְׁתִּי לְלוֹא שָׁאָלוּ נִמְצֵאתִי לְלֹא בִקְשֻׁנִי אָמַרְתִּי ‏ מְאָד:
הִנֵּנִי הִנֵּנִי אֶל־גּוֹי לֹא־קֹרָא בִשְׁמִי: פֵּרַשְׂתִּי יָדַי כָּל־הַיּוֹם אֶל־עַם סוֹרֵר ב
הַהֹלְכִים הַדֶּרֶךְ לֹא־טוֹב אַחַר מַחְשְׁבֹתֵיהֶם: הָעָם הַמַּכְעִיסִים אוֹתִי עַל־ ג
פָּנַי תָּמִיד זֹבְחִים בַּגַּנּוֹת וּמְקַטְּרִים עַל־הַלְּבֵנִים: הַיֹּשְׁבִים בַּקְּבָרִים ד
וּבַנְּצוּרִים יָלִינוּ הָאֹכְלִים בְּשַׂר הַחֲזִיר °וּפְרַק [°וּמְרַק ק] פִּגֻּלִים כְּלֵיהֶם:
הָאֹמְרִים קְרַב אֵלֶיךָ אַל־תִּגַּשׁ־בִּי כִּי קְדַשְׁתִּיךָ אֵלֶּה עָשָׁן בְּאַפִּי אֵשׁ ה
יֹקֶדֶת כָּל־הַיּוֹם: הִנֵּה כְתוּבָה לְפָנָי לֹא אֶחֱשֶׂה כִּי אִם־שִׁלַּמְתִּי וְשִׁלַּמְתִּי ו
עַל־חֵיקָם: ‏ עֲוֺנֹתֵיכֶם וַעֲוֺנֹת אֲבוֹתֵיכֶם יַחְדָּו אָמַר יהוה אֲשֶׁר קִטְּרוּ עַל־ ז
הֶהָרִים וְעַל־הַגְּבָעוֹת חֵרְפוּנִי וּמַדֹּתִי פְעֻלָּתָם רִאשֹׁנָה °עַל־ [°אֶל־ ק]
חֵיקָם: ‏ כֹּה ׀ אָמַר יהוה כַּאֲשֶׁר יִמָּצֵא הַתִּירוֹשׁ בָּאֶשְׁכּוֹל ח
וְאָמַר אַל־תַּשְׁחִיתֵהוּ כִּי בְרָכָה בּוֹ כֵּן אֶעֱשֶׂה לְמַעַן עֲבָדַי לְבִלְתִּי הַשְׁחִית
הַכֹּל: וְהוֹצֵאתִי מִיַּעֲקֹב זֶרַע וּמִיהוּדָה יוֹרֵשׁ הָרָי וִירֵשׁוּהָ בְחִירַי וַעֲבָדַי ט
יִשְׁכְּנוּ־שָׁמָּה: וְהָיָה הַשָּׁרוֹן לִנְוֵה־צֹאן וְעֵמֶק עָכוֹר לְרֵבֶץ בָּקָר לְעַמִּי י
אֲשֶׁר דְּרָשׁוּנִי: וְאַתֶּם עֹזְבֵי יהוה הַשְּׁכֵחִים אֶת־הַר קָדְשִׁי הַעֹרְכִים לַגַּד יא
שֻׁלְחָן וְהַמְמַלְאִים לַמְנִי מִמְסָךְ: וּמָנִיתִי אֶתְכֶם לַחֶרֶב וְכֻלְּכֶם לַטֶּבַח יב
תִּכְרָעוּ יַעַן קָרָאתִי וְלֹא עֲנִיתֶם דִּבַּרְתִּי וְלֹא שְׁמַעְתֶּם וַתַּעֲשׂוּ הָרַע בְּעֵינַי
וּבַאֲשֶׁר לֹא־חָפַצְתִּי בְּחַרְתֶּם: ‏ לָכֵן כֹּה־אָמַר ׀ אֲדֹנָי יֱהֹוִה יג
הִנֵּה עֲבָדַי ׀ יֹאכֵלוּ וְאַתֶּם תִּרְעָבוּ הִנֵּה עֲבָדַי יִשְׁתּוּ וְאַתֶּם תִּצְמָאוּ
הִנֵּה עֲבָדַי יִשְׂמָחוּ וְאַתֶּם תֵּבֹשׁוּ: הִנֵּה עֲבָדַי יָרֹנּוּ מִטּוּב לֵב וְאַתֶּם תִּצְעֲקוּ יד
מִכְּאֵב לֵב וּמִשֵּׁבֶר רוּחַ תְּיֵלִילוּ: וְהִנַּחְתֶּם שִׁמְכֶם לִשְׁבוּעָה לִבְחִירַי טו
וֶהֱמִיתְךָ אֲדֹנָי יֱהֹוִה וְלַעֲבָדָיו יִקְרָא שֵׁם אַחֵר: אֲשֶׁר הַמִּתְבָּרֵךְ בָּאָרֶץ טז
יִתְבָּרֵךְ בֵּאלֹהֵי אָמֵן וְהַנִּשְׁבָּע בָּאָרֶץ יִשָּׁבַע בֵּאלֹהֵי אָמֵן כִּי נִשְׁכְּחוּ
הַצָּרוֹת הָרִאשֹׁנוֹת וְכִי נִסְתְּרוּ מֵעֵינָי: כִּי־הִנְנִי בוֹרֵא שָׁמַיִם חֲדָשִׁים יז
וָאָרֶץ חֲדָשָׁה וְלֹא תִזָּכַרְנָה הָרִאשֹׁנוֹת וְלֹא תַעֲלֶינָה עַל־לֵב: כִּי־אִם־ יח
שִׂישׂוּ וְגִילוּ עֲדֵי־עַד אֲשֶׁר אֲנִי בוֹרֵא כִּי הִנְנִי בוֹרֵא אֶת־יְרוּשָׁלַ͏ִם גִּילָה
וְעַמָּהּ מָשׂוֹשׂ: וְגַלְתִּי בִירוּשָׁלַ͏ִם וְשַׂשְׂתִּי בְעַמִּי וְלֹא־יִשָּׁמַע בָּהּ עוֹד קוֹל יט
בְּכִי וְקוֹל זְעָקָה: לֹא־יִהְיֶה מִשָּׁם עוֹד עוּל יָמִים וְזָקֵן אֲשֶׁר לֹא־יְמַלֵּא כ
אֶת־יָמָיו כִּי הַנַּעַר בֶּן־מֵאָה שָׁנָה יָמוּת וְהַחוֹטֶא בֶּן־מֵאָה שָׁנָה יְקֻלָּל:
וּבָנוּ בָתִּים וְיָשָׁבוּ וְנָטְעוּ כְרָמִים וְאָכְלוּ פִּרְיָם: לֹא יִבְנוּ וְאַחֵר יֵשֵׁב כא-כב

65:1. Here begins God's reply to Israel's just concluded prayer. He was accessible even to those who neither called to Him nor wished to be called by His Name (*Rashi*).

65:3. By setting up idols even in Jerusalem, and even in the Temple itself (*Radak*).

65:4. To communicate with spirits, which, they believe, frequent such places (*Radak*).

65:5. After defiling themselves, they have the audacity to say that they are purer than others who do not follow their practices.

65:6. Their sin is inscribed before Me and I will not delay their punishment till a future generation; the punishment will fall into their own *bosoms*.

65:10. Lit., the "Valley of Repugnance," so called because of the abhorrent events that took place there (see *Joshua* 7:24). Even this place will now become lush grazing land.

65

God is accessible

¹ I * was accessible to those who did not ask; I could be found by those who did not seek Me. I said, 'Here I am! Here I am!' to a nation not called by My Name. ² I stretched out My hands all day to a straying people, who walk the road that is not good, following after their own thoughts; ³ the people who continually anger Me to My face; * who sacrifice in their gardens and burn incense on the bricks; ⁴ who sit in graves and sleep with corpses; * who eat the flesh of the swine and have the sauce of forbidden foods in their

Idolatry punished

utensils; ⁵ who say, 'Keep to yourself; do not come near me, for I am holier than thou.' * These are the smoke of My wrath, like a fire burning all the day. ⁶ Behold, it is inscribed before Me; I will not be silent until I repay; I will repay into their bosom. * ⁷ for your sins and the sins of your fathers together, said HASHEM, who burned incense on the mountains and blasphemed Me on the hills. First I will mete out the payment of their actions into their bosom.

Reward . . .

⁸ Thus said HASHEM: Just as when the wine is found in a cluster, and someone says, 'Do not destroy it, for there is blessing in it,' so will I do for My servants, not to destroy everything. ⁹ I will bring forth offspring from Jacob, and from Judah the heir of My mountains; My chosen ones will inherit it and My servants will dwell there. ¹⁰ The Sharon will become a fold for the sheep and the Valley of Achor* will become fit for cattle to lie down, for My people who have sought Me out. ¹¹ But you who have forsaken

. . . and punishment

HASHEM, who have forgotten My holy mountain, who set a table for Gad, * who fill a libation to Meni* — ¹² I will consign you to the sword and all of you will slump down in slaughter, because I called and you did not answer; I spoke and you did not hear; you did what is evil in My eyes, and what I did not desire you chose.

¹³ Therefore, thus said my Lord, HASHEM/ELOHIM: Behold, My servants will eat and you will starve; behold, My servants will drink and you will thirst; behold, My servants will rejoice and you will be ashamed; ¹⁴ behold, My servants will exult from goodheartedness, and you will cry out from pain of heart and wail from a broken spirit. ¹⁵ You will leave your name as an oath for My chosen ones, and the Lord, HASHEM/ELOHIM, will put you to death; but He will call His servants a different name. *

¹⁶ Whoever blesses himself in the land will bless himself by the God of Truth, and whoever takes an oath in the land will take an oath by the God of Truth, for the earlier travails will have been forgotten and concealed from My eyes. ¹⁷ For behold, I am creating new heavens and a new earth; the former [events] will no longer be recalled and will not be taken to heart.

An age of peace

¹⁸ Only rejoice and be happy forever for what I am creating; for behold, I am recreating Jerusalem as 'Gladness,' and its people as 'Joy'; ¹⁹ for I will rejoice over Jerusalem and exult with My people, and there will no longer be heard in it the sound of weeping and the sound of outcry. ²⁰ Never again will come from there a young child or old man who will not fill his days; for the youth of one hundred years will die and a sinner at the age of one hundred years will be cursed. * ²¹ They will build houses and inhabit [them], they will plant vineyards and eat their fruit; ²² they will not build and have another inhabit,

---

65:11. *Gad* and *Meni* are either names of deities (*Kara*); the planets Jupiter and Mercury (*R' Moshe HaKohen*); or general names for the stars and constellations (*Ibn Ezra*).
65:15. Your name will become a curse, but His servants

will be recalled as a blessing (*Rashi*).
65:20. People will have such longevity that dying at the age of one hundred will be considered as dying young, or it will be considered as a punishment to die at that age.

לֹא יִטְעוּ וְאַחֵר יֹאכֵל כִּי־כִימֵי הָעֵץ יְמֵי עַמִּי וּמַעֲשֵׂה יְדֵיהֶם יְבַלּוּ בְחִירָי:
כג לֹא יִיגְעוּ לָרִיק וְלֹא יֵלְדוּ לַבֶּהָלָה כִּי זֶרַע בְּרוּכֵי יהוה הֵמָּה וְצֶאֱצָאֵיהֶם
כד-כה אִתָּם: וְהָיָה טֶרֶם יִקְרָאוּ וַאֲנִי אֶעֱנֶה עוֹד הֵם מְדַבְּרִים וַאֲנִי אֶשְׁמָע: זְאֵב
וְטָלֶה יִרְעוּ כְאֶחָד וְאַרְיֵה כַּבָּקָר יֹאכַל־תֶּבֶן וְנָחָשׁ עָפָר לַחְמוֹ לֹא־יָרֵעוּ

א וְלֹא־יַשְׁחִיתוּ בְּכָל־הַר קָדְשִׁי אָמַר יהוה: ◀ כֹּה אָמַר יהוה
הַשָּׁמַיִם כִּסְאִי וְהָאָרֶץ הֲדֹם רַגְלָי אֵי־זֶה בַיִת אֲשֶׁר תִּבְנוּ־לִי וְאֵי־זֶה מָקוֹם
ב מְנוּחָתִי: וְאֶת־כָּל־אֵלֶּה יָדִי עָשָׂתָה וַיִּהְיוּ כָל־אֵלֶּה נְאֻם־יהוה וְאֶל־זֶה
ג אַבִּיט אֶל־עָנִי וּנְכֵה־רוּחַ וְחָרֵד עַל־דְּבָרִי: שׁוֹחֵט הַשּׁוֹר מַכֵּה־אִישׁ זוֹבֵחַ
הַשֶּׂה עֹרֵף כֶּלֶב מַעֲלֵה מִנְחָה דַּם־חֲזִיר מַזְכִּיר לְבֹנָה מְבָרֵךְ אָוֶן גַּם־הֵמָּה
ד בָּחֲרוּ בְּדַרְכֵיהֶם וּבְשִׁקּוּצֵיהֶם נַפְשָׁם חָפֵצָה: גַּם־אֲנִי אֶבְחַר בְּתַעֲלוּלֵיהֶם
וּמְגוּרֹתָם אָבִיא לָהֶם יַעַן קָרָאתִי וְאֵין עוֹנֶה דִּבַּרְתִּי וְלֹא שָׁמֵעוּ וַיַּעֲשׂוּ
ה הָרַע בְּעֵינַי וּבַאֲשֶׁר לֹא־חָפַצְתִּי בָּחָרוּ: שִׁמְעוּ דְּבַר־יהוה
הַחֲרֵדִים אֶל־דְּבָרוֹ אָמְרוּ אֲחֵיכֶם שֹׂנְאֵיכֶם מְנַדֵּיכֶם לְמַעַן שְׁמִי יִכְבַּד
ו יהוה וְנִרְאֶה בְשִׂמְחַתְכֶם וְהֵם יֵבֹשׁוּ: קוֹל שָׁאוֹן מֵעִיר קוֹל מֵהֵיכָל קוֹל
ז יהוה מְשַׁלֵּם גְּמוּל לְאֹיְבָיו: בְּטֶרֶם תָּחִיל יָלָדָה בְּטֶרֶם יָבוֹא חֵבֶל
ח לָהּ וְהִמְלִיטָה זָכָר: מִי־שָׁמַע כָּזֹאת מִי רָאָה כָּאֵלֶּה הֲיוּחַל אֶרֶץ בְּיוֹם
אֶחָד אִם־יִוָּלֵד גּוֹי פַּעַם אֶחָת כִּי־חָלָה גַּם־יָלְדָה צִיּוֹן אֶת־בָּנֶיהָ:
ט הַאֲנִי אַשְׁבִּיר וְלֹא אוֹלִיד יֹאמַר יהוה אִם־אֲנִי הַמּוֹלִיד וְעָצַרְתִּי אָמַר
י אֱלֹהָיִךְ: שִׂמְחוּ אֶת־יְרוּשָׁלַ͏ִם וְגִילוּ בָהּ כָּל־אֹהֲבֶיהָ שִׂישׂוּ אִתָּהּ
יא מָשׂוֹשׂ כָּל־הַמִּתְאַבְּלִים עָלֶיהָ: לְמַעַן תִּינְקוּ וּשְׂבַעְתֶּם מִשֹּׁד תַּנְחֻמֶיהָ
יב לְמַעַן תָּמֹצּוּ וְהִתְעַנַּגְתֶּם מִזִּיז כְּבוֹדָהּ: כִּי־כֹה ׀ אָמַר יהוה הִנְנִי
נֹטֶה־אֵלֶיהָ כְּנָהָר שָׁלוֹם וּכְנַחַל שׁוֹטֵף כְּבוֹד גּוֹיִם וִינַקְתֶּם עַל־צַד תִּנָּשֵׂאוּ
יג וְעַל־בִּרְכַּיִם תְּשָׁעֳשָׁעוּ: כְּאִישׁ אֲשֶׁר אִמּוֹ תְּנַחֲמֶנּוּ כֵּן אָנֹכִי אֲנַחֶמְכֶם
יד וּבִירוּשָׁלַ͏ִם תְּנֻחָמוּ: וּרְאִיתֶם וְשָׂשׂ לִבְּכֶם וְעַצְמוֹתֵיכֶם כַּדֶּשֶׁא תִפְרַחְנָה
טו וְנוֹדְעָה יַד־יהוה אֶת־עֲבָדָיו וְזָעַם אֶת־אֹיְבָיו: כִּי־הִנֵּה יהוה בָּאֵשׁ יָבוֹא
טז וְכַסּוּפָה מַרְכְּבֹתָיו לְהָשִׁיב בְּחֵמָה אַפּוֹ וְגַעֲרָתוֹ בְּלַהֲבֵי־אֵשׁ: כִּי בָאֵשׁ יהוה
יז נִשְׁפָּט וּבְחַרְבּוֹ אֶת־כָּל־בָּשָׂר וְרַבּוּ חַלְלֵי יהוה: הַמִּתְקַדְּשִׁים וְהַמִּטַּהֲרִים
אֶל־הַגַּנּוֹת אַחַר אַחַד [°אַחַת ק] בַּתָּוֶךְ אֹכְלֵי בְּשַׂר הַחֲזִיר וְהַשֶּׁקֶץ

65:22. They will outlive that which they produce.

66:1. This prophecy admonishes the Israelites for their belief that they could do whatever evil deeds they wished and then gain atonement by bringing a gift to the Temple.

66:2-3. It is obedience to My words that is important to Me, not perfunctory acts of sacrifice without remorse and contrition.

66:5. They believe that they are the ones who truly bring glory to God (*Rashi*).

66:7. Zion's redemption will come quickly and painlessly.

66:9. When the process of redemption begins, you may be sure that it will be carried through to its culmination.

66:11-12. Jerusalem and Israel are likened to a mother nursing her child. Just as a baby is nursed without any effort on his part, so will you enjoy the endless prosperity that will be bestowed upon you (*Radak*).

66:17. Where their idols were set up for worship (*Rashi*).

they will not plant and have another eat. For the lifetime of My people will be like the lifetime of the tree, and My chosen ones will wear out their handiwork. * ²³ *They will not struggle in vain nor produce for futility; for they are the offspring of the blessed ones of* HASHEM, *and their descendants will be with them.* ²⁴ *It will be that before they call I will answer; while they yet speak I will hear.* ²⁵ *Wolf and lamb will graze as one, a lion — like cattle — will eat straw, a snake's food will be dirt; they will not inflict harm nor destruction in all My holy mountain, says* HASHEM.

66

Corrupt offerings

¹ **T**hus said HASHEM: *The Heaven is My throne and the earth is My footstool; what house could you build for Me, and what place could be My resting place?* ² *My hand created all these things and thus all these things came into being — the word of* HASHEM *— but it is to this that I look: to the poor and broken-spirited person who is zealous regarding My word.* * ³ *He who slaughters an ox [is as if he] slays a man; he who offers a sheep [is as if he] breaks a dog's neck; he who brings up a meal-offering [is as if he offers] a swine's blood; he who brings a frankincense remembrance [is as if he] brings a gift of wickedness. They have even chosen their ways and their souls have desired their abominations.*

⁴ *I, too, will choose to mock them and what they dread I will bring upon them — because I called but no one answered; I spoke but they did not hear. They did what is wrong in My eyes and what I did not desire, they chose.*

The sound of retribution

⁵ *Listen to the word of* HASHEM, *you who are zealous regarding His word: Your brethren, who hate you and shun you, say, 'HASHEM is glorified because of my reputation.'* * *— but we will see your gladness, while they will be shamed!* ⁶ *The sound of tumult comes from the city, a sound from the Sanctuary: the sound of* HASHEM *dealing retribution to His enemies.* ⁷ *Before she* * *even feels her labor pains she will give birth; before any travail comes to her she will deliver a son!* ⁸ *Who has heard such as this? Who has seen such as these? Has a land ever gone through its labor in one day? Has a nation ever been born at one time, as Zion went through her labor and gave*

Repopulated Zion

birth to her children? ⁹ *Shall I bring [a woman] to the birthstool and not have her give birth?* * *says* HASHEM. *Shall I, Who causes birth, hold it back? says your God.*

¹⁰ *Be glad with Jerusalem and rejoice in her, all you who love her; exult with her in exultation, all you who mourned for her;* ¹¹ *so that you may nurse and be sated from the breast of her consolations;* * *so that you may suck and delight from the*

Motherly consolation

glow of her glory. ¹² *For thus said* HASHEM: *Behold, I will extend peace to her like a river and the wealth of nations like a surging stream, and you will suckle; you will be carried on the side and dandled on the knees.* ¹³ *Like a man whose mother consoled him, so will I console you, and in Jerusalem will you be consoled.* ¹⁴ *You will see and your heart will exult, and your bones will flourish like grass; the hand of* HASHEM *will be known to His servants, and He will show anger to His enemies.* ¹⁵ *For behold,* HASHEM *will arrive in fire and His chariots like the whirlwind, to vent His anger with wrath, and His rebuke with flaming fire.* ¹⁶ *For* HASHEM *will enter into judgment with fire and with His sword against all mankind; there will be many who will be slain by* HASHEM. ¹⁷ *Those who prepare and purify themselves [to go] to the gardens,* * *going one [group] after another to its midst, and those who eat the flesh of the swine, the abominable creature,*

יח וְהָעֹכְבָּר יַחְדָּו יָסֻפוּ נְאֻם־יהוה: וְאָנֹכִי מַעֲשֵׂיהֶם וּמַחְשְׁבֹתֵיהֶם בָּאָה

יט לְקַבֵּץ אֶת־כָּל־הַגּוֹיִם וְהַלְּשֹׁנוֹת וּבָאוּ וְרָאוּ אֶת־כְּבוֹדִי: וְשַׂמְתִּי בָהֶם אוֹת וְשִׁלַּחְתִּי מֵהֶם ׀ פְּלֵיטִים אֶל־הַגּוֹיִם תַּרְשִׁישׁ פּוּל וְלוּד מֹשְׁכֵי קֶשֶׁת תֻּבַל וְיָוָן הָאִיִּים הָרְחֹקִים אֲשֶׁר לֹא־שָׁמְעוּ אֶת־שִׁמְעִי וְלֹא־רָאוּ אֶת־

כ כְּבוֹדִי וְהִגִּידוּ אֶת־כְּבוֹדִי בַּגּוֹיִם: וְהֵבִיאוּ אֶת־כָּל־אֲחֵיכֶם מִכָּל־הַגּוֹיִם ׀ מִנְחָה ׀ לַיהוה בַּסּוּסִים וּבָרֶכֶב וּבַצַּבִּים וּבַפְּרָדִים וּבַכִּרְכָּרוֹת עַל הַר קָדְשִׁי יְרוּשָׁלַ͏ִם אָמַר יהוה כַּאֲשֶׁר יָבִיאוּ בְנֵי יִשְׂרָאֵל אֶת־הַמִּנְחָה בִּכְלִי

כא-כב טָהוֹר בֵּית יהוה: וְגַם־מֵהֶם אֶקַּח לַכֹּהֲנִים לַלְוִיִּם אָמַר יהוה: כִּי כַאֲשֶׁר הַשָּׁמַיִם הַחֲדָשִׁים וְהָאָרֶץ הַחֲדָשָׁה אֲשֶׁר אֲנִי עֹשֶׂה עֹמְדִים לְפָנַי נְאֻם־

כג יהוה כֵּן יַעֲמֹד זַרְעֲכֶם וְשִׁמְכֶם: וְהָיָה מִדֵּי־חֹדֶשׁ בְּחָדְשׁוֹ וּמִדֵּי שַׁבָּת

כד בְּשַׁבַּתּוֹ יָבוֹא כָל־בָּשָׂר לְהִשְׁתַּחֲוֺת לְפָנַי אָמַר יהוה: וְיָצְאוּ וְרָאוּ בְּפִגְרֵי הָאֲנָשִׁים הַפֹּשְׁעִים בִּי כִּי תוֹלַעְתָּם לֹא תָמוּת וְאִשָּׁם לֹא תִכְבֶּה וְהָיוּ דֵרָאוֹן לְכָל־בָּשָׂר:

וְהָיָה מִדֵּי־חֹדֶשׁ בְּחָדְשׁוֹ וּמִדֵּי שַׁבָּת בְּשַׁבַּתּוֹ

◀ יָבוֹא כָל־בָּשָׂר לְהִשְׁתַּחֲוֺת לְפָנַי אָמַר יהוה:

סכום הפסוקים של ישעיה אלף ומאתים ותשעים וחמשה. אמת **ארצה** סימן. בריח ניחח **ארצה** אתכם סימן.

and the mouse will all be consumed together — the word of HASHEM.

[18] I [know] their actions and their thoughts; [the time] has come to gather all the nations and tongues, * they will come and see My glory. [19] I will put a sign upon them and send some of them as survivors* to the nations — Tarshish, Pul, Lud, the Archers, Tubal and Javan, the distant islands who have not heard of My fame and not seen My glory — and they will declare My glory among the nations. [20] They will bring all your brethren from all the nations as an offering to HASHEM — with horses and with chariots and with covered wagons and with mules — with joyous dances, to My holy mountain, Jerusalem, says HASHEM; just as the Children of Israel bring the offering in a pure vessel to the House of HASHEM. [21] From them, too, I will take men to be Kohanim and Levites, * says HASHEM. [22] For just as the new heavens and the new earth that I will make will endure before Me — the word of HASHEM — so will your offspring and your name endure.

[23] It shall be that at every New Moon and on every Sabbath all mankind will come to prostrate themselves before Me, says HASHEM. [24] And they will go out and see the corpses of the men who rebelled against Me, for their decay will not cease and their fire* will not be extinguished, and they will lie in disgrace before all mankind.

* It shall be that at every New Moon and on every Sabbath
all mankind will come to prostrate themselves before Me, says HASHEM.

Jeremiah ירמיה

Of all the prophets charged to remonstrate with the Jewish people to stop their plunge to destruction, none had a more difficult task than Jeremiah. He was still a young man when he was given his mission, and he spent the rest of his life gamely and vainly trying to persuade a people convinced of its rectitude and the invincibility of its Temple to change their ways. Jeremiah began his prophetic career under Josiah, one of the most righteous of all the kings of Judah, the one who restored the Temple and its service to their previous glory. Ironically, that made Jeremiah's task even harder, because the people insisted that the Temple would save them — despite their private worship of idols.

Jeremiah was opposed by false prophets who insisted that night was day and day was night. Nebuchadnezzar had conquered and sacked Jerusalem — could there be greater proof of God's wrath? But charlatans "prophesied" that the conqueror would soon return the Temple's looted treasures and go down to defeat. The mendacious priests of the Temple, in the service of their supporters rather than of the truth, disputed him at every turn. The masses, always hungry for reassurance and outraged at Jeremiah's refusal to say the popular thing, demanded that he be put to death, as the prophet Uriah had been. King Jehoiakim disobeyed him and burned the scroll of his prophecies. When Jeremiah refused to be silenced, King Zedekiah had him hurled into a dungeon, where he remained until the sun set on Jerusalem.

Ultimately Jeremiah had the bitter taste of vindication, as Jerusalem was destroyed and he was set free, not by his own people but by the plunderers. Consumed by his love for Israel, Jeremiah wept and grieved for his tormented brethren as they were led into exile. He encouraged them, telling them that they should bear their ordeal in a hostile, foreign land with fortitude, because they would become the foundation upon which the new commonwealth would be built.

Jeremiah bemoaned his own fate. Why had he been the one chosen to not only foretell the horrors but to witness them, and even to be at the mercy of the brethren he had been trying to save? But there is no doubt that the exiles in Babylon found strength in his prophecy that there would be redemption and glory seventy years after the Destruction. Jeremiah did not live to see his prophecy fulfilled, but many of those who had heard his prophecies were among the ones who returned with Ezra and Nehemiah to inaugurate the Second Temple.

א

א   דִּבְרֵי יִרְמְיָהוּ בֶּן־חִלְקִיָּהוּ מִן־הַכֹּהֲנִים אֲשֶׁר בַּעֲנָתוֹת בְּאֶרֶץ בִּנְיָמִן:

ב   אֲשֶׁר הָיָה דְבַר־יְהֹוָה אֵלָיו בִּימֵי יֹאשִׁיָּהוּ בֶן־אָמוֹן מֶלֶךְ יְהוּדָה בִּשְׁלֹשׁ־

ג   עֶשְׂרֵה שָׁנָה לְמָלְכוֹ: וַיְהִי בִּימֵי יְהוֹיָקִים בֶּן־יֹאשִׁיָּהוּ מֶלֶךְ יְהוּדָה עַד־תֹּם עַשְׁתֵּי־עֶשְׂרֵה שָׁנָה לְצִדְקִיָּהוּ בֶן־יֹאשִׁיָּהוּ מֶלֶךְ יְהוּדָה עַד־גְּלוֹת יְרוּשָׁלַ͏ִם

ד-ה   בַּחֹדֶשׁ הַחֲמִישִׁי: וַיְהִי דְבַר־יְהֹוָה אֵלַי לֵאמֹר: בְּטֶרֶם °אֶצּוֹרְךָ [°אֶצָּרְךָ ק] בַבֶּטֶן יְדַעְתִּיךָ וּבְטֶרֶם תֵּצֵא מֵרֶחֶם הִקְדַּשְׁתִּיךָ נָבִיא לַגּוֹיִם

ו   נְתַתִּיךָ: וָאֹמַר אֲהָהּ אֲדֹנָי יֱהֹוִה הִנֵּה לֹא־יָדַעְתִּי דַּבֵּר כִּי־נַעַר אָנֹכִי:

ז   וַיֹּאמֶר יְהֹוָה אֵלַי אַל־תֹּאמַר נַעַר אָנֹכִי כִּי עַל־כָּל־אֲשֶׁר אֶשְׁלָחֲךָ תֵּלֵךְ וְאֵת

ח   כָּל־אֲשֶׁר אֲצַוְּךָ תְּדַבֵּר: אַל־תִּירָא מִפְּנֵיהֶם כִּי־אִתְּךָ אֲנִי לְהַצִּלֶךָ נְאֻם־יְהֹוָה:

ט   וַיִּשְׁלַח יְהֹוָה אֶת־יָדוֹ וַיַּגַּע עַל־פִּי וַיֹּאמֶר יְהֹוָה אֵלַי הִנֵּה נָתַתִּי דְבָרַי בְּפִיךָ:

י   רְאֵה הִפְקַדְתִּיךָ | הַיּוֹם הַזֶּה עַל־הַגּוֹיִם וְעַל־הַמַּמְלָכוֹת לִנְתוֹשׁ וְלִנְתוֹץ

יא   וּלְהַאֲבִיד וְלַהֲרוֹס לִבְנוֹת וְלִנְטוֹעַ: וַיְהִי דְבַר־יְהֹוָה אֵלַי לֵאמֹר

יב   מָה־אַתָּה רֹאֶה יִרְמְיָהוּ וָאֹמַר מַקֵּל שָׁקֵד אֲנִי רֹאֶה: וַיֹּאמֶר יְהֹוָה אֵלַי

יג   הֵיטַבְתָּ לִרְאוֹת כִּי־שֹׁקֵד אֲנִי עַל־דְּבָרִי לַעֲשֹׂתוֹ: וַיְהִי דְבַר־יְהֹוָה | אֵלַי שֵׁנִית לֵאמֹר מָה אַתָּה רֹאֶה וָאֹמַר סִיר נָפוּחַ אֲנִי רֹאֶה וּפָנָיו מִפְּנֵי

יד-טו   צָפוֹנָה: וַיֹּאמֶר יְהֹוָה אֵלָי מִצָּפוֹן תִּפָּתַח הָרָעָה עַל כָּל־יֹשְׁבֵי הָאָרֶץ: כִּי | הִנְנִי קֹרֵא לְכָל־מִשְׁפְּחוֹת מַמְלְכוֹת צָפוֹנָה נְאֻם־יְהֹוָה וּבָאוּ וְנָתְנוּ אִישׁ כִּסְאוֹ פֶּתַח | שַׁעֲרֵי יְרוּשָׁלַ͏ִם וְעַל כָּל־חוֹמֹתֶיהָ סָבִיב וְעַל כָּל־עָרֵי יְהוּדָה:

טז   וְדִבַּרְתִּי מִשְׁפָּטַי אוֹתָם עַל כָּל־רָעָתָם אֲשֶׁר עֲזָבוּנִי וַיְקַטְּרוּ לֵאלֹהִים

יז   אֲחֵרִים וַיִּשְׁתַּחֲווּ לְמַעֲשֵׂי יְדֵיהֶם: וְאַתָּה תֶּאְזֹר מָתְנֶיךָ וְקַמְתָּ וְדִבַּרְתָּ אֲלֵיהֶם אֵת כָּל־אֲשֶׁר אָנֹכִי אֲצַוֶּךָּ אַל־תֵּחַת מִפְּנֵיהֶם פֶּן־אֲחִתְּךָ לִפְנֵיהֶם:

יח   וַאֲנִי הִנֵּה נְתַתִּיךָ הַיּוֹם לְעִיר מִבְצָר וּלְעַמּוּד בַּרְזֶל וּלְחֹמוֹת נְחֹשֶׁת עַל־

יט   כָּל־הָאָרֶץ לְמַלְכֵי יְהוּדָה לְשָׂרֶיהָ לְכֹהֲנֶיהָ וּלְעַם הָאָרֶץ: וְנִלְחֲמוּ אֵלֶיךָ

ב

א   וְלֹא־יוּכְלוּ לָךְ כִּי־אִתְּךָ אֲנִי נְאֻם־יְהֹוָה לְהַצִּילֶךָ: וַיְהִי דְבַר־

ב   יְהֹוָה אֵלַי לֵאמֹר: הָלֹךְ וְקָרָאתָ בְאָזְנֵי יְרוּשָׁלַ͏ִם לֵאמֹר כֹּה אָמַר יְהֹוָה זָכַרְתִּי לָךְ חֶסֶד נְעוּרַיִךְ אַהֲבַת כְּלוּלֹתָיִךְ לֶכְתֵּךְ אַחֲרַי בַּמִּדְבָּר בְּאֶרֶץ

ג   לֹא זְרוּעָה: קֹדֶשׁ יִשְׂרָאֵל לַיהֹוָה רֵאשִׁית תְּבוּאָתֹה כָּל־אֹכְלָיו יֶאְשָׁמוּ

ד   רָעָה תָּבֹא אֲלֵיהֶם נְאֻם־יְהֹוָה: שִׁמְעוּ דְבַר־יְהֹוָה בֵּית יַעֲקֹב

ה   וְכָל־מִשְׁפְּחוֹת בֵּית יִשְׂרָאֵל: כֹּה | אָמַר יְהֹוָה מַה־מָּצְאוּ אֲבוֹתֵיכֶם

HAFTARAS PINCHAS OR MATTOS SHEMOS *Sephardim:* 1:1-2:3

HAFTARAS MASEI *Ashkenazim:* 2:4-28; 3:4 *Sephardim:* 2:4-28; 4:1-2

1:5. Knowing that Jeremiah would protest that he was not worthy of his prophetic mission, God began by saying that Jeremiah had been destined for this calling even before he was born. Furthermore, for a person to have the potential to be a great prophet, his parents would have had to conduct themselves in a pure and holy manner even before he was conceived (*Radak; Rambam*).

1:12. The almond tree symbolizes swift, efficient action

because it blossoms well before other trees in the spring. This is a play on words: The Hebrew words for "almond" (שָׁקֵד) and "hasten" (שֹׁקֵד) are linguistically related.

1:19. The leaders of Judah will dispute your message and even try to kill you; but they will be helpless, for I shall protect you.

2:1-3. God recalls the early days of Israel's national history — when the nation displayed total faith by following Him into a desolate wilderness — in order to tell the

1

Call to prophecy
(See Appendix A, timeline 4)

¹ The words of Jeremiah son of Hilkiah, of the Kohanim who were in Anathoth, in the land of Benjamin, ² to whom the word of HASHEM came in the days of Josiah son of Amon, king of Judah, in the thirteenth year of his reign. ³ [The word of HASHEM] came to him [also] in the days of Jehoiakim son of Josiah, king of Judah, until the end of the eleventh year of Zedekiah son of Josiah, king of Judah, until Jerusalem was exiled in the fifth month.

⁴ The word of HASHEM came to me, saying, ⁵ "Before I formed you in the belly I knew you, and before you left the womb I sanctified you; I established you as a prophet unto the nations."*

⁶ But I said, "Alas, my Lord HASHEM/ELOHIM, see, I do not know how to speak, for I am just a youth!"

⁷ Then HASHEM said to me, "Do not say, 'I am just a youth'; rather, wherever I shall send you, you shall go, and whatever I shall command you, you shall speak. ⁸ Do not fear them, for I am with you to rescue you — the word of HASHEM." ⁹ Then HASHEM extended His hand and touched my mouth, and HASHEM said to me, "Behold! I have placed My words in your mouth. ¹⁰ See, I have appointed you this day over the nations and over the kingdoms, to uproot and to smash, and to destroy and to overthrow, to build and to plant."

Vision of the almond

¹¹ The word of HASHEM then came to me, saying, "What do you see, Jeremiah?"

And I said, "I see a staff of an almond tree."

¹² HASHEM said to me, "You have seen well, for I hasten* to fulfill My word."

Vision of the bubbling pot

¹³ The word of HASHEM came to me a second time, saying, "What do you see?"

And I said, "I see a bubbling pot, and its spout is facing north."

¹⁴ HASHEM said to me, "From the North the evil will be released upon all the inhabitants of the land. ¹⁵ For behold, I am calling all the families of the kingdoms of the North — the word of HASHEM — and they shall come and each of them shall place his throne at the entrance of Jerusalem's gates and by all its walls roundabout, and by all the cities of Judah. ¹⁶ I shall pronounce My judgments against [Judah] for all their evil, for they have forsaken Me and burned incense to the gods of others and prostrated themselves to their own handiwork.

¹⁷ "And as for you, you shall gird your loins, and get up and speak to them all that I command you; do not be frightened of them, lest I let you be broken before them. ¹⁸ For behold, I have set you this day as a fortified city, an iron pillar and copper walls against the entire land — against the kings of Judah, against its leaders, against its priests and against the people of the land. ¹⁹ They will wage war against you, but will be unable to [defeat] you, for I am with you — the word of HASHEM — to rescue you!"*

2

Your early loyalty . . .

¹ The word of HASHEM came to me, saying, ² "Go and call out in the ears of Jerusalem, saying:

Thus said HASHEM: I recall for you the kindness of your youth, the love of your nuptials, your following Me into the Wilderness, into an unsown land. ³ Israel is holy to HASHEM, the first of His crop; all who devour it will be held guilty; evil shall come upon them — the word of HASHEM. *

⁴ Hear the word of HASHEM, O House of Jacob and all families of the House of Israel: ⁵ Thus said HASHEM: What wrong did your forefathers find

---

people that the heartrending prophecies of Jeremiah would not be fulfilled if the people returned to their earlier faith. God's love for Israel remains intact, and He longs to forgive them, but only if they repent.

בִּי עָ֗וֶל כִּ֤י רָֽחֲקוּ֙ מֵֽעָלַ֔י וַיֵּ֛לְכ֥וּ אַֽחֲרֵ֥י הַהֶ֖בֶל וַיֶּהְבָּֽלוּ׃ וְלֹ֣א אָֽמְר֔וּ אַיֵּ֣ה יְהֹוָ֔ה
הַמַּֽעֲלֶ֥ה אֹתָ֖נוּ מֵאֶ֣רֶץ מִצְרָ֑יִם הַמּוֹלִ֨יךְ אֹתָ֜נוּ בַּמִּדְבָּ֗ר בְּאֶ֨רֶץ עֲרָבָ֤ה
וְשׁוּחָה֙ בְּאֶ֣רֶץ צִיָּ֣ה וְצַלְמָ֔וֶת בְּאֶ֗רֶץ לֹא־עָ֤בַר בָּהּ֙ אִ֔ישׁ וְלֹֽא־יָשַׁ֥ב אָדָ֖ם
שָֽׁם׃ וָֽאָבִ֤יא אֶתְכֶם֙ אֶל־אֶ֣רֶץ הַכַּרְמֶ֔ל לֶֽאֱכֹ֥ל פִּרְיָ֖הּ וְטוּבָ֑הּ וַתָּבֹ֨אוּ֙
וַתְּטַמְּא֣וּ אֶת־אַרְצִ֔י וְנַֽחֲלָתִ֥י שַׂמְתֶּ֖ם לְתֽוֹעֵבָֽה׃ הַכֹּֽהֲנִ֗ים לֹ֤א אָֽמְרוּ֙ אַיֵּ֣ה
יְהֹוָ֔ה וְתֹֽפְשֵׂ֤י הַתּוֹרָה֙ לֹ֣א יְדָע֔וּנִי וְהָֽרֹעִ֖ים פָּ֣שְׁעוּ בִ֑י וְהַנְּבִיאִים֙ נִבְּא֣וּ
בַבַּ֔עַל וְאַֽחֲרֵ֥י לֹֽא־יוֹעִ֖לוּ הָלָֽכוּ׃ לָכֵ֗ן עֹ֛ד אָרִ֥יב אִתְּכֶ֖ם נְאֻם־יְהֹוָ֑ה
וְאֶת־בְּנֵ֥י בְנֵיכֶ֖ם אָרִֽיב׃ כִּ֣י עִבְר֞וּ אִיֵּ֤י כִתִּיִּים֙ וּרְא֔וּ וְקֵדָ֛ר שִׁלְח֥וּ וְהִֽתְבּֽוֹנְנ֖וּ
מְאֹ֑ד וּרְא֕וּ הֵ֥ן הָֽיְתָ֖ה כָּזֹֽאת׃ הַהֵימִ֥יר גּוֹי֙ אֱלֹהִ֔ים וְהֵ֖מָּה לֹ֣א אֱלֹהִ֑ים
וְעַמִּ֛י הֵמִ֥יר כְּבוֹד֖וֹ בְּל֥וֹא יוֹעִֽיל׃ שֹׁ֤מּוּ שָׁמַ֨יִם֙ עַל־זֹ֔את וְשַֽׂעֲר֛וּ חׇֽרְב֥וּ
מְאֹ֖ד נְאֻם־יְהֹוָֽה׃ כִּֽי־שְׁתַּ֥יִם רָע֖וֹת עָשָׂ֣ה עַמִּ֑י אֹתִ֨י עָֽזְב֜וּ מְק֣וֹר ׀ מַ֣יִם
חַיִּ֗ים לַחְצֹ֤ב לָהֶם֙ בֹּאר֔וֹת בֹּארֹת֙ נִשְׁבָּרִ֔ים אֲשֶׁ֥ר לֹֽא־יָכִ֖לוּ הַמָּֽיִם׃
הַעֶ֨בֶד֙ יִשְׂרָאֵ֔ל אִם־יְלִ֥יד בַּ֖יִת ה֑וּא מַדּ֖וּעַ הָיָ֥ה לָבַֽז׃ עָלָיו֙ יִשְׁאֲג֣וּ כְפִרִ֔ים
נָֽתְנ֖וּ קוֹלָ֑ם וַיָּשִׁ֤יתוּ אַרְצוֹ֙ לְשַׁמָּ֔ה עָרָ֥יו °נצתה [נִצְּת֖וּ ק׳] מִבְּלִ֥י יֹשֵֽׁב׃
גַּם־בְּנֵי־נֹ֖ף °ותחפנס [וְתַחְפַּנְחֵ֑ס ק׳] יִרְע֖וּךְ קׇדְקֹֽד׃ הֲלוֹא־זֹ֖את
תַּֽעֲשֶׂה־לָּ֑ךְ עׇזְבֵ֛ךְ אֶת־יְהֹוָ֥ה אֱלֹהַ֖יִךְ בְּעֵ֣ת מֽוֹלִכֵ֥ךְ בַּדָּֽרֶךְ׃ וְעַתָּ֗ה מַה־
לָּךְ֙ לְדֶ֣רֶךְ מִצְרַ֔יִם לִשְׁתּ֖וֹת מֵ֣י שִׁח֑וֹר וּמַה־לָּךְ֙ לְדֶ֣רֶךְ אַשּׁ֔וּר לִשְׁתּ֖וֹת
מֵ֣י נָהָֽר׃ תְּיַסְּרֵ֣ךְ רָעָתֵ֗ךְ וּמְשֻֽׁבוֹתַ֨יִךְ֙ תּֽוֹכִחֻ֔ךְ וּדְעִ֤י וּרְאִי֙ כִּי־רַ֣ע וָמָ֔ר
עׇזְבֵ֖ךְ אֶת־יְהֹוָ֣ה אֱלֹהָ֑יִךְ וְלֹ֤א פַחְדָּתִי֙ אֵלַ֔יִךְ נְאֻם־אֲדֹנָ֥י יְהֹוִ֖ה צְבָאֽוֹת׃
כִּ֣י מֵֽעוֹלָ֞ם שָׁבַ֣רְתִּי עֻלֵּ֗ךְ נִתַּ֨קְתִּי֙ מֽוֹסְרוֹתַ֔יִךְ וַתֹּֽאמְרִ֖י לֹ֣א °אעבוד [אֶֽעֱב֑וֹר ק׳]
כִּ֤י עַֽל־כׇּל־גִּבְעָ֣ה גְּבֹהָ֗ה וְתַ֨חַת֙ כׇּל־עֵ֣ץ רַֽעֲנָ֔ן אַ֖תְּ צֹעָ֥ה
זֹנָֽה׃ וְאָֽנֹכִי֙ נְטַעְתִּ֣יךְ שֹׂרֵ֔ק כֻּלֹּ֖ה זֶ֣רַע אֱמֶ֑ת וְאֵיךְ֙ נֶהְפַּ֣כְתְּ לִ֔י סוּרֵ֖י
הַגֶּ֥פֶן נׇכְרִיָּֽה׃ כִּ֤י אִם־תְּכַבְּסִי֙ בַּנֶּ֔תֶר וְתַרְבִּי־לָ֖ךְ בֹּרִ֑ית נִכְתָּ֤ם עֲוֺנֵךְ֙
לְפָנַ֔י נְאֻ֖ם אֲדֹנָ֥י יְהֹוִֽה׃ אֵ֣יךְ תֹּֽאמְרִ֞י לֹ֣א נִטְמֵ֗אתִי אַֽחֲרֵ֤י הַבְּעָלִים֙ לֹ֣א
הָלַ֔כְתִּי רְאִ֤י דַרְכֵּךְ֙ בַּגַּ֔יְא דְּעִ֖י מֶ֣ה עָשִׂ֑ית בִּכְרָ֥ה קַלָּ֖ה מְשָׂרֶ֥כֶת דְּרָכֶֽיהָ׃
פֶּ֣רֶה ׀ לִמֻּ֣ד מִדְבָּ֗ר בְּאַוַּ֤ת °נפשו [נַפְשָׁהּ֙ ק׳] שָֽׁאֲפָ֣ה ר֔וּחַ תַּֽאֲנָתָ֖הּ מִ֣י
יְשִׁיבֶ֑נָּה כׇּל־מְבַקְשֶׁ֨יהָ֙ לֹ֣א יִיעָ֔פוּ בְּחׇדְשָׁ֖הּ יִמְצָאֽוּנְהָ׃ מִנְעִ֤י רַגְלֵךְ֙ מִיָּחֵ֔ף
°וגורנך [וּגְרוֹנֵ֖ךְ ק׳] מִצִּמְאָ֑ה וַתֹּֽאמְרִ֣י נוֹאָ֔שׁ ל֕וֹא כִּֽי־אָהַ֥בְתִּי זָרִ֖ים
וְאַֽחֲרֵיהֶ֥ם אֵלֵֽךְ׃ כְּבֹ֤שֶׁת גַּנָּב֙ כִּ֣י יִמָּצֵ֔א כֵּ֥ן הֹבִ֖ישׁוּ בֵּ֣ית יִשְׂרָאֵ֑ל
הֵ֤מָּה מַלְכֵיהֶם֙ שָֽׂרֵיהֶ֔ם וְכֹֽהֲנֵיהֶ֖ם וּנְבִֽיאֵיהֶֽם׃ אֹֽמְרִ֧ים לָעֵ֣ץ אָ֣בִי אַ֗תָּה

2:6. Instead of pursuing their idolatrous cults, the people should have sought out God.

2:13. Israel's actions involve a double indignity: the abandonment of God *per se,* and the choice of such an inferior substitute.

2:16. These were Egyptian cities. When the Israelites abrogated their treaty with Assyria and Babylonia, they relied upon Egypt to protect them, but the "protectors" became persecutors.

2:24. Just as the wild beast can easily be caught during her final month of gestation, so will Israel become easy prey for the enemy when the month of its retribution will arrive (*Metzudos*).

. . . evapo-
rated and . . .

in Me, that they distanced themselves from Me and pursued futility, and became futile? ⁶ But they did not say, * 'Where is HASHEM, Who brought us up from the land of Egypt, Who led us in the Wilderness, in a land of desert and pit, in a land of waste and the shadow of death, in a land through which no man passed and where no person settled?' ⁷ I brought you into a fruitful land, to eat its fruit and bounty; but you came and contaminated My land, and made My heritage into an abomination. ⁸ The Kohanim did not say, 'Where is HASHEM?'; those charged with teaching the Torah did not know Me; the shepherds rebelled against Me; the prophets prophesied by the Baal; and they went after those that cannot avail.

. . . turned
to idolatry

⁹ Therefore I will yet contend with you — the word of HASHEM — and with your children's children I will contend. ¹⁰ Traverse the isles of the Kittites and observe, send forth unto Kedar and consider deeply — and see whether there has [ever] been such a thing. ¹¹ Has a nation [ever] exchanged its gods, though they are not [genuine] gods? Yet My people has exchanged its Glory for something of no avail. ¹² Be astounded, O heavens, over this; rage forth in storm, be greatly devastated — the word of HASHEM. ¹³ For My people has committed two evils: They have forsaken Me, the Source of living waters, to dig for themselves cisterns, broken cisterns that cannot hold the water. *

You ignored
God's chas-
tening . . .

¹⁴ Is Israel a slave? Is he born to a house [maid]? Why has he become prey? ¹⁵ Young lions have roared over him, they have raised their voice. They have made his land wasteland; his cities have been devastated, without inhabitant. ¹⁶ Even the people of Noph and Tahpanhes* smash your skull. ¹⁷ Has this not been done to you [because] you forsake HASHEM, your God, when He leads you on the path? ¹⁸ And now, what is there for you on the road to Egypt, to drink the waters of the Nile? And what is there for you on the road to Assyria to drink the water of the Euphrates? ¹⁹ Your evil shall castigate you; your waywardness shall chasten you; realize and understand that your forsaking of HASHEM, your God, is evil and bitter, and that My awe was not upon you — the word of my Lord, HASHEM/ELOHIM, Master of Legions.

. . . and
rejected His
salvation . . .

²⁰ For I have always broken your yoke and torn off your straps, and you have said, 'I will not transgress!' Yet upon every lofty hill and under every leafy tree you wander like a harlot. ²¹ I had planted you from a choice vine, entirely of faithful seed; how, then, have you turned yourself into an inferior, alien vine before Me? ²² Even if you were to wash with niter and use much soap, your iniquity has become a stain before Me — the word of my Lord, HASHEM/ELOHIM.

. . . preferring
the
Baalim . . .

²³ How can you say, 'I have not become contaminated; I have not gone after the Baalim'? See your pathway in the valley and recognize what you have done, [like] a young camel, careening in her ways. ²⁴ [Like] a wild donkey accustomed to the wilderness — at her soul's desire she sucks in air; who can restrain her serpentine manner? All who seek her should not weary themselves, [for] in her month they will find her. *

. . . and
wood and
stone

²⁵ Withhold your foot from barefootedness and your throat from thirst! But you have said, 'It is hopeless! No! For I am in love with strangers and after them will I go.' ²⁶ Like the shame of a thief when he is discovered, so has the House of Israel been shamed — they, their kings, their princes, their priests and their prophets. ²⁷ They say to the wood, 'You are my father,'

וְלָאֶבֶן אַתְּ °יְלַדְתָּנִי [°יְלִדְתָּנוּ ק] כִּי־פָנוּ אֵלַי עֹרֶף וְלֹא פָנִים וּבְעֵת רָעָתָם

כח יֹאמְרוּ קוּמָה וְהוֹשִׁיעֵנוּ: וְאַיֵּה אֱלֹהֶיךָ אֲשֶׁר עָשִׂיתָ לָּךְ יָקוּמוּ אִם־יוֹשִׁיעוּךָ

כט בְּעֵת רָעָתֶךָ כִּי מִסְפַּר עָרֶיךָ הָיוּ אֱלֹהֶיךָ יְהוּדָה: ▶ לָמָּה תָרִיבוּ

ל אֵלַי כֻּלְּכֶם פְּשַׁעְתֶּם בִּי נְאֻם־יְהוָה: לַשָּׁוְא הִכֵּיתִי אֶת־בְּנֵיכֶם מוּסָר לֹא

לא לָקָחוּ אָכְלָה חַרְבְּכֶם נְבִיאֵיכֶם כְּאַרְיֵה מַשְׁחִית: הַדּוֹר אַתֶּם רְאוּ דְבַר־

יְהוָה הֲמִדְבָּר הָיִיתִי לְיִשְׂרָאֵל אִם־אֶרֶץ מַאְפֵּלְיָה מַדּוּעַ אָמְרוּ עַמִּי רַדְנוּ

לב לוֹא־נָבוֹא עוֹד אֵלֶיךָ: הֲתִשְׁכַּח בְּתוּלָה עֶדְיָהּ כַּלָּה קִשֻּׁרֶיהָ וְעַמִּי שְׁכֵחוּנִי

לג יָמִים אֵין מִסְפָּר: מַה־תֵּיטִבִי דַּרְכֵּךְ לְבַקֵּשׁ אַהֲבָה לָכֵן גַּם אֶת־הָרָעוֹת

לד °לִמַּדְתִּי [°לִמַּדְתְּ ק] אֶת־דְּרָכָיִךְ: גַּם בִּכְנָפַיִךְ נִמְצְאוּ דַּם נַפְשׁוֹת אֶבְיוֹנִים

לה נְקִיִּם לֹא־בַמַּחְתֶּרֶת מְצָאתִים כִּי עַל־כָּל־אֵלֶּה: וַתֹּאמְרִי כִּי נִקֵּיתִי אַךְ

לו שָׁב אַפּוֹ מִמֶּנִּי הִנְנִי נִשְׁפָּט אוֹתָךְ עַל־אָמְרֵךְ לֹא חָטָאתִי: מַה־תֵּזְלִי מְאֹד

לז לְשַׁנּוֹת אֶת־דַּרְכֵּךְ גַּם מִמִּצְרַיִם תֵּבוֹשִׁי כַּאֲשֶׁר־בֹּשְׁתְּ מֵאַשּׁוּר: גַּם מֵאֵת

זֶה תֵּצְאִי וְיָדַיִךְ עַל־רֹאשֵׁךְ כִּי־מָאַס יְהוָה בְּמִבְטַחַיִךְ וְלֹא תַצְלִיחִי לָהֶם:

Haftaras Masei for Ashkenazim continues below; for Sephardim on p. 1078

ג א לֵאמֹר הֵן יְשַׁלַּח אִישׁ אֶת־אִשְׁתּוֹ וְהָלְכָה מֵאִתּוֹ וְהָיְתָה לְאִישׁ־אַחֵר

הֲיָשׁוּב אֵלֶיהָ עוֹד הֲלוֹא חָנוֹף תֶּחֱנַף הָאָרֶץ הַהִיא וְאַתְּ זָנִית רֵעִים רַבִּים

ב וְשׁוֹב אֵלַי נְאֻם־יְהוָה: שְׂאִי־עֵינַיִךְ עַל־שְׁפָיִם וּרְאִי אֵיפֹה לֹא °שֻׁגַּלְתְּ

[°שֻׁכַּבְתְּ ק] עַל־דְּרָכִים יָשַׁבְתְּ לָהֶם כַּעֲרָבִי בַּמִּדְבָּר וַתַּחֲנִיפִי אֶרֶץ

ג בִּזְנוּתַיִךְ וּבְרָעָתֵךְ: וַיִּמָּנְעוּ רְבִבִים וּמַלְקוֹשׁ לוֹא הָיָה וּמֵצַח אִשָּׁה זוֹנָה הָיָה

ד לָךְ מֵאַנְתְּ הִכָּלֵם: ▶ הֲלוֹא מֵעַתָּה °קָרָאתי [°קָרָאת ק] לִי אָבִי אַלּוּף נְעֻרַי

ה אָתָּה: ▶ הֲיִנְטֹר לְעוֹלָם אִם־יִשְׁמֹר לָנֶצַח הִנֵּה °דִבַּרְתִּי [°דִבַּרְתְּ ק] וַתַּעֲשִׂי

Haftaras Masei for Ashkenazim continues here: 3:4

הָרָעוֹת וַתּוּכָל: וַיֹּאמֶר יְהוָה אֵלַי בִּימֵי יֹאשִׁיָּהוּ הַמֶּלֶךְ הֲרָאִיתָ

ו אֲשֶׁר עָשְׂתָה מְשֻׁבָה יִשְׂרָאֵל הֹלְכָה הִיא עַל־כָּל־הַר גָּבֹהַּ וְאֶל־תַּחַת כָּל־

ז עֵץ רַעֲנָן וַתִּזְנִי־שָׁם: וָאֹמַר אַחֲרֵי עֲשׂוֹתָהּ אֶת־כָּל־אֵלֶּה אֵלַי תָּשׁוּב וְלֹא־

ח שָׁבָה °וַתֵּרֶא [°וַתֵּרֶא ק] בָּגוֹדָה אֲחוֹתָהּ יְהוּדָה: וָאֵרֶא כִּי עַל־כָּל־

אֹדוֹת אֲשֶׁר נִאֲפָה מְשֻׁבָה יִשְׂרָאֵל שִׁלַּחְתִּיהָ וָאֶתֵּן אֶת־סֵפֶר כְּרִיתֻתֶיהָ

ט אֵלֶיהָ וְלֹא יָרְאָה בֹּגֵדָה יְהוּדָה אֲחוֹתָהּ וַתֵּלֶךְ וַתִּזֶן גַּם־הִיא: וְהָיָה מִקֹּל

י זְנוּתָהּ וַתֶּחֱנַף אֶת־הָאָרֶץ וַתִּנְאַף אֶת־הָאֶבֶן וְאֶת־הָעֵץ: וְגַם־בְּכָל־זֹאת

לֹא־שָׁבָה אֵלַי בָּגוֹדָה אֲחוֹתָהּ יְהוּדָה בְּכָל־לִבָּהּ כִּי אִם־בְּשֶׁקֶר נְאֻם־

יא יְהוָה: וַיֹּאמֶר יְהוָה אֵלַי צִדְּקָה נַפְשָׁהּ מְשֻׁבָה יִשְׂרָאֵל מִבֹּגֵדָה

2:33. Like an immodest woman, you beautify yourself to seek the approval and companionship of other nations, and you adopt their worst practices.

2:34. You cannot justify such murders on the grounds of self-defense. (See *Exodus* 22:1.)

2:36. See *II Chronicles* 28:16-21.

3:1. See *Deuteronomy* 24:1-2.

Throughout Scripture, the prophets use adultery as a metaphor for idolatry.

3:2. An Arab merchant in the desert constantly awaits passing caravans with whom to trade.

3:6. This refers to the wayward Ten Tribes of the Kingdom of Israel (Samaria), who had been conquered and exiled by Assyria more than a century earlier.

3:7. Alternatively: "And I said [to Myself], 'Even after she has done all these things, she would return to Me.' "

3:9. Judah committed "adultery" by betraying God and worshiping idols made of stone and wood.

and to the stone, 'You have borne us.' To Me they turned their backs and not their faces; but in their time of distress they will say, 'Arise and save us!' ²⁸ Now where are your gods that you made for yourself? Let them arise if they can save you in the time of your distress; for as the number of your cities were your gods, O Judah.

Wasted castigation

²⁹ Why should you contend with Me? You have all rebelled against Me — the word of HASHEM. ³⁰ In vain did I strike your children, for they did not accept rebuke; your sword has devoured your prophets like a destructive lion. ³¹ O generation, contemplate the word of HASHEM. Have I been a wilderness to Israel, or a land of deep darkness? Why have My people said, 'We separate ourselves [from You]; we will no longer come to You'? ³² Can a maiden forget her jewelry? A bride her adornments? Yet My people have forgotten Me for days without number. ³³ How you adorned your way to seek love!* Indeed, to the [greatest] evils have you accustomed your ways. ³⁴ Even on your hems is found the blood of poor, innocent souls; you did not discover them in a break-in!* For all these [I condemn you]: ³⁵ that you say, 'No, I am pure; His anger will subside from me!' Behold, I am [entering] into judgment with you because of your saying, 'I have not sinned.' ³⁶ How very much you demean yourself to change your way! You will be shamed even by Egypt, as you were shamed by Assyria;* ³⁷ from this [alliance] also you will emerge clapping your hands to your head; for HASHEM has rejected your guarantors — you will not succeed with them — ¹ saying: If a man divorces his wife, and she goes from him and marries another man, can he return to her again? Would that not bring profound guilt upon the land? Yet you have committed adultery with many lovers and would now return to Me* — the word of HASHEM. ² Lift your eyes to the hilltops and see; where have you not been lain with? On the roads you awaited [your lovers], like an Arab in the desert. * You have brought guilt upon the land with your adultery and with your evil; ³ the raindrops have been withheld and the late rain did not happen; yet you had the boldness of a harlot woman, you refused to be ashamed. ⁴ If only from now on you would call Me 'My Father! You are the Master of my youth.' ⁵ Would He bear a grudge forever, or keep it in mind eternally? Nevertheless — behold, you spoke and carried out evil deeds, as much as you could."

3

Idolatry equals adultery

⁶ HASHEM said to me in the days of King Josiah, "Have you seen what rebellious Israel* did? She went onto every high mountain and under every leafy tree, and committed adultery there. ⁷ I said, even after she had done all these things, 'Return to Me!'* but she did not return. And her unfaithful sister, Judah, saw [what befell her], ⁸ and I saw that despite the fact that I divorced wayward Israel because of her adultery and gave her bill of divorce to her, unfaithful Judah, her sister, was not afraid; she, too, went and committed adultery. ⁹ So it happened that with the frivolity of her adultery she brought guilt upon the land, because she committed adultery with stone and wood [idols]. * ¹⁰ Despite all this, the unfaithful one, her sister Judah, did not return to Me with all her heart, but only falsely* — the word of HASHEM."

Judah did not learn from Israel

¹¹ And HASHEM said to me, "Wayward Israel was more virtuous than unfaithful

---

3:10. Although King Josiah thoroughly purged all idolatrous practices (*II Kings* Ch. 23), the common people were less enthusiastic about his religious reforms (*Radak*).

יב יְהוּדָה: הָלֹךְ וְקָרָאתָ אֶת־הַדְּבָרִים הָאֵלֶּה צָפוֹנָה וְאָמַרְתָּ שׁוּבָה מְשֻׁבָה
יִשְׂרָאֵל נְאֻם־יְהוָה לֽוֹא־אַפִּיל פָּנַי בָּכֶם כִּי־חָסִיד אֲנִי נְאֻם־יְהוָה לֹא
יג אֶטּוֹר לְעוֹלָם: אַךְ דְּעִי עֲוֺנֵךְ כִּי בַּיהוָה אֱלֹהַיִךְ פָּשָׁעַתְּ וַתְּפַזְּרִי אֶת־
דְּרָכַיִךְ לַזָּרִים תַּחַת כָּל־עֵץ רַעֲנָן וּבְקוֹלִי לֹא־שְׁמַעְתֶּם נְאֻם־יְהוָֽה:
יד שׁוּבוּ בָנִים שׁוֹבָבִים נְאֻם־יְהוָה כִּי אָנֹכִי בָּעַלְתִּי בָכֶם וְלָקַחְתִּי אֶתְכֶם
טו אֶחָד מֵעִיר וּשְׁנַיִם מִמִּשְׁפָּחָה וְהֵבֵאתִי אֶתְכֶם צִיּוֹן: וְנָתַתִּי לָכֶם רֹעִים
טז כְּלִבִּי וְרָעוּ אֶתְכֶם דֵּעָה וְהַשְׂכֵּיל: וְהָיָה כִּי תִרְבּוּ וּפְרִיתֶם בָּאָרֶץ בַּיָּמִים
הָהֵמָּה נְאֻם־יְהוָה לֹא־יֹאמְרוּ עוֹד אֲרוֹן בְּרִית־יְהוָה וְלֹא יַעֲלֶה עַל־לֵב
יז וְלֹא יִזְכְּרוּ־בוֹ וְלֹא יִפְקֹדוּ וְלֹא יֵעָשֶׂה עוֹד: בָּעֵת הַהִיא יִקְרְאוּ לִירוּשָׁלִַם
כִּסֵּא יְהוָה וְנִקְווּ אֵלֶיהָ כָל־הַגּוֹיִם לְשֵׁם יְהוָה לִירוּשָׁלִָם וְלֹא־יֵלְכוּ עוֹד
יח אַחֲרֵי שְׁרִרוּת לִבָּם הָרָע: בַּיָּמִים הָהֵמָּה יֵלְכוּ בֵית־
יְהוּדָה עַל־בֵּית יִשְׂרָאֵל וְיָבֹאוּ יַחְדָּו מֵאֶרֶץ צָפוֹן עַל־הָאָרֶץ אֲשֶׁר
יט הִנְחַלְתִּי אֶת־אֲבֽוֹתֵיכֶם: וְאָנֹכִי אָמַרְתִּי אֵיךְ אֲשִׁיתֵךְ בַּבָּנִים וְאֶתֶּן־לָךְ
אֶרֶץ חֶמְדָּה נַחֲלַת צְבִי צִבְאוֹת גּוֹיִם וָאֹמַר אָבִי °תִּקְרְאוּ־ [°תִּקְרְאִי ק]
כ לִי וּמֵאַחֲרַי לֹא °תָשׁוּבוּ [°תָשׁוּבִי ק]: אָכֵן בָּגְדָה אִשָּׁה מֵרֵעָהּ כֵּן בְּגַדְתֶּם
כא בִּי בֵּית יִשְׂרָאֵל נְאֻם־יְהוָֽה: קוֹל עַל־שְׁפָיִים נִשְׁמָע בְּכִי תַחֲנוּנֵי בְּנֵי
כב יִשְׂרָאֵל כִּי הֶעֱווּ אֶת־דַּרְכָּם שָׁכְחוּ אֶת־יְהוָה אֱלֹהֵיהֶם: שׁוּבוּ בָּנִים
כג שׁוֹבָבִים אֶרְפָּה מְשׁוּבֹתֵיכֶם הִנְנוּ אָתָנוּ לָךְ כִּי אַתָּה יְהוָה אֱלֹהֵֽינוּ: אָכֵן
לַשֶּׁקֶר מִגְּבָעוֹת הָמוֹן הָרִים אָכֵן בַּיהוָה אֱלֹהֵינוּ תְּשׁוּעַת יִשְׂרָאֵֽל:
כד וְהַבֹּשֶׁת אָכְלָה אֶת־יְגִיעַ אֲבוֹתֵינוּ מִנְּעוּרֵינוּ אֶת־צֹאנָם וְאֶת־בְּקָרָם
כה אֶת־בְּנֵיהֶם וְאֶת־בְּנוֹתֵיהֶם: נִשְׁכְּבָה בְּבָשְׁתֵּנוּ וּתְכַסֵּנוּ כְּלִמָּתֵנוּ כִּי
לַיהוָה אֱלֹהֵינוּ חָטָאנוּ אֲנַחְנוּ וַאֲבוֹתֵינוּ מִנְּעוּרֵינוּ וְעַד־הַיּוֹם הַזֶּה וְלֹא
א שָׁמַעְנוּ בְּקוֹל יְהוָה אֱלֹהֵֽינוּ: ▸ אִם־תָּשׁוּב יִשְׂרָאֵל | נְאֻם־יְהוָה אֵלַי

ד

Haftaras Masei for *Sephardim* continues here: 4:1-2

ב תָּשׁוּב וְאִם־תָּסִיר שִׁקּוּצֶיךָ מִפָּנַי וְלֹא תָנֽוּד: וְנִשְׁבַּעְתָּ חַי־יְהוָה בֶּאֱמֶת
בְּמִשְׁפָּט וּבִצְדָקָה וְהִתְבָּרְכוּ בוֹ גּוֹיִם וּבוֹ יִתְהַלָּלוּ: ▸   כִּי־כֹה |
ג אָמַר יְהוָה לְאִישׁ יְהוּדָה וְלִירוּשָׁלִַם נִירוּ לָכֶם נִיר וְאַל־תִּזְרְעוּ אֶל־
ד קֹצִים: הִמֹּלוּ לַיהוָה וְהָסִרוּ עָרְלוֹת לְבַבְכֶם אִישׁ יְהוּדָה וְיֹשְׁבֵי
יְרוּשָׁלִָם פֶּן־תֵּצֵא כָאֵשׁ חֲמָתִי וּבָעֲרָה וְאֵין מְכַבֶּה מִפְּנֵי רֹעַ מַעַלְלֵיכֶֽם:

3:11. The ten exiled tribes of Israel had no previous example of the sentence of exile being carried out, but Judah should have taken Israel's exile to heart.

3:12. God sent Jeremiah to the lands of the North where the Israelite exiles were taken.

3:16-17. The entire people will be so imbued with a spirit of sanctity that God's Presence will rest upon them collectively, as if the congregation itself was the Ark of the Covenant (*Rashi*).

3:19. I did not want to place Israel, My special son, among

the other nations, so I gave him a unique land as a heritage (*Rashi*). All I asked was your loyalty and your recognition that I am your Father and Protector.

3:21. As a result of their infidelity, they were severely punished, and cried out to God.

4:1. If you repent I will accept you; the decree of exile can still be averted.

4:2. Jeremiah urges his brethren to take a sincere oath to repent, and if they would do so, they would enjoy such good fortune that people would bless each other, "May

Judah. * ¹² *Go and proclaim these words towards the North,* * *and say:*

God's reproach . . .

Return, O wayward Israel — the word of HASHEM — I will not cast down My anger upon you, for I am the Beneficent One — the word of HASHEM — and I will not bear a grudge forever. ¹³ *But [you must] recognize your sin, that you have rebelled against HASHEM, your God, and that you have spread out your ways to [seek] strange gods, under every leafy tree, and you did not heed My voice — the word of HASHEM.* ¹⁴ *Return, O wayward sons — the word of HASHEM — for I shall be your master. I shall take you, [even] one from a city and two from a family, and I shall bring you to Zion.* ¹⁵ *I shall appoint*

. . . and Messianic prophecy

shepherds for you according to My own heart, and they will care for you with knowledge and wisdom. ¹⁶ *And it shall be that when you multiply and become fruitful in the land, in those days — the word of HASHEM — they will no longer say, 'The Ark of the Covenant of HASHEM,' and it will not come to mind;* * they will not mention it and will not recall it, and it will not be used any more.* ¹⁷ *At that time people will call Jerusalem 'The Throne of HASHEM,' and all the nations will be gathered to her in the Name of HASHEM — to Jerusalem; they will no longer follow the visions of their evil heart.*

¹⁸ *In those days the House of Judah will walk with the House of Israel, and they will come together from the land of the North to the land that I have given as a possession to your fathers.* ¹⁹ *I had said, 'How can I place you*

Call to repentance

among the other children?' So I gave you a cherished land, the heritage coveted by the multitudes of nations. And I said, 'Call me "my Father," and do not turn away from behind Me.' * ²⁰ *But, like a woman who was unfaithful to her mate, you have been unfaithful to Me, O House of Israel — the word of HASHEM.* ²¹ *A voice is heard on the hilltops, the crying of the Children of Israel's supplications,* * for they have corrupted their ways, they have forgotten HASHEM, their God.* ²² *[But I say to them,] 'Return, O wayward sons, and I will heal your waywardness. [Say,] "Behold, we come to You, for You are HASHEM, our God.* ²³ *Truly it was falsehood [that we worshiped] from the hills, the multitude of mountains, for truly in HASHEM, our God, is the salvation of Israel.* ²⁴ *But the shameful idolatry has devoured the toil of our fathers from our youth — their sheep and their cattle, their sons and their daughters.* ²⁵ *We lie down in our shame and our humiliation covers us, for we have sinned to HASHEM our God, we and our forefathers, from our youth until this very day, and we have not heeded the voice of HASHEM, our God." '*

4

It is not too late . . .

¹ *If you repent, O Israel — the word of HASHEM — you will return to Me;* * if you remove your abominations from before Me, then you will not [have to] wander.* ² *If you swear, 'As HASHEM lives!' in truth, in justice, and in righteousness, the nations will bless themselves through [Israel], and will praise themselves through it."* *

³ *For thus said HASHEM to the people of Judah and to Jerusalem:*

Plow for yourselves a furrow, and do not sow upon thornbushes. ⁴ *Circum-*

. . . but you must listen . . .

cise yourselves unto HASHEM — remove the barriers of your hearts * — O people of Judah and inhabitants of Jerusalem, lest My wrath go forth like fire and burn with none to extinguish [it], because of the wickedness of your deeds.*

---

you be like an Israelite."
4:3-4. Just as a farmer plows to uproot all the unwanted weeds and thorns that would ruin his crop, so too, Jews

must circumcise their hearts, i.e., remove the impediments to total commitment to God's will, lest sinful thoughts ruin the efficacy of their supplications (*Rashi*).

ה הַגִּידוּ בִיהוּדָה וּבִירוּשָׁלַ֨͏ִם הַשְׁמִ֔יעוּ וְאִמְר֔וּ וֹתקעו [°תִּקְע֣וּ ק] שׁוֹפָ֖ר

ו בָּאָ֑רֶץ קִרְא֣וּ מַלְא֔וּ וְאִמְר֗וּ הֵאָסְפ֛וּ וְנָב֥וֹאָה אֶל־עָרֵ֖י הַמִּבְצָ֑ר: שְׂאוּ־נֵ֣ס

ז צִיּ֗וֹנָה הָעִ֙יזוּ֙ אַֽל־תַּעֲמֹ֔דוּ כִּ֣י רָעָ֗ה אָֽנֹכִ֛י מֵבִ֥יא מִצָּפ֖וֹן וְשֶׁ֥בֶר גָּד֑וֹל: עָלָ֤ה

אַרְיֵה֙ מִ֣סֻּבְּכ֔וֹ וּמַשְׁחִ֣ית גּוֹיִ֔ם נָסַ֖ע יָצָ֣א מִמְּקֹמ֑וֹ לָשׂ֤וּם אַרְצֵךְ֙ לְשַׁמָּ֔ה

ח עָרַ֥יִךְ תִּצֶּ֖ינָה מֵאֵ֣ין יוֹשֵֽׁב: עַל־זֹ֛את חִגְר֥וּ שַׂקִּ֖ים סִפְד֣וּ וְהֵילִ֑ילוּ כִּ֥י לֹא־

ט שָׁ֛ב חֲר֥וֹן אַף־יְהֹוָ֖ה מִמֶּֽנּוּ: וְהָיָ֤ה בַיּוֹם־הַהוּא֙ נְאֻם־

יְהֹוָ֔ה יֹאבַ֥ד לֵב־הַמֶּ֖לֶךְ וְלֵ֣ב הַשָּׂרִ֑ים וְנָשַׁ֙מּוּ֙ הַכֹּ֣הֲנִ֔ים וְהַנְּבִיאִ֖ים יִתְמָֽהוּ:

י וָאֹמַ֞ר אֲהָ֣הּ ׀ אֲדֹנָ֣י יֱהֹוִ֗ה אָכֵן֩ הַשֵּׁ֨א הִשֵּׁ֜אתָ לָעָ֤ם הַזֶּה֙ וְלִירוּשָׁלַ֙͏ִם֙ לֵאמֹ֔ר

יא שָׁל֖וֹם יִהְיֶ֣ה לָכֶ֑ם וְנָגְעָ֥ה חֶ֖רֶב עַד־הַנָּֽפֶשׁ: בָּעֵ֣ת הַהִ֗יא יֵאָמֵ֤ר לָֽעָם־

הַזֶּה֙ וְלִירֽוּשָׁלַ֔͏ִם ר֣וּחַ צַ֤ח שְׁפָיִים֙ בַּמִּדְבָּ֔ר דֶּ֖רֶךְ בַּת־עַמִּ֑י ל֥וֹא לִזְר֖וֹת

יב וְל֣וֹא לְהָבַֽר: ר֧וּחַ מָלֵ֛א מֵאֵ֖לֶּה יָ֣בוֹא לִ֑י עַתָּ֕ה גַּם־אֲנִ֛י אֲדַבֵּ֥ר מִשְׁפָּטִ֖ים

יג אוֹתָֽם: הִנֵּ֣ה ׀ כַּֽעֲנָנִ֣ים יַֽעֲלֶ֗ה וְכַסּוּפָה֙ מַרְכְּבוֹתָ֔יו קַלּ֥וּ מִנְּשָׁרִ֖ים סוּסָ֑יו

יד א֥וֹי לָ֖נוּ כִּ֣י שֻׁדָּֽדְנוּ: כַּבְּסִ֤י מֵרָעָה֙ לִבֵּ֔ךְ יְר֣וּשָׁלַ֔͏ִם לְמַ֖עַן תִּוָּשֵׁ֑עִי עַד־מָתַ֛י

תָּלִ֥ין בְּקִרְבֵּ֖ךְ מַחְשְׁב֥וֹת אוֹנֵֽךְ: כִּ֣י ק֥וֹל מַגִּ֛יד מִדָּ֖ן וּמַשְׁמִ֥יעַ אָ֖וֶן מֵהַ֥ר

טו אֶפְרָֽיִם: הַזְכִּ֣ירוּ לַגּוֹיִ֗ם הִנֵּה֙ הַשְׁמִ֣יעוּ עַל־יְר֣וּשָׁלַ֔͏ִם נֹֽצְרִ֥ים בָּאִ֖ים מֵאֶ֥רֶץ

טז הַמֶּרְחָ֑ק וַיִּתְּנ֥וּ עַל־עָרֵ֛י יְהוּדָ֖ה קוֹלָֽם: כְּשֹֽׁמְרֵ֣י שָׂדַ֔י הָי֥וּ עָלֶ֖יהָ מִסָּבִ֑יב

יז כִּֽי־אֹתִ֥י מָרָ֖תָה נְאֻם־יְהֹוָֽה: דַּרְכֵּ֣ךְ וּמַעֲלָלַ֔יִךְ עָשׂ֥וֹ אֵ֖לֶּה לָ֑ךְ זֹ֤את רָֽעָתֵךְ֙ כִּ֣י

יח מָ֔ר כִּ֥י נָגַ֖ע עַד־לִבֵּֽךְ: מֵעַ֣י ׀ מֵעַ֣י ׀ °אֹחִ֗ילָה [°אוֹחִ֗ילָה ק]

יט קִיר֤וֹת לִבִּי֙ הֹֽמֶה־לִּ֣י לִבִּ֔י לֹ֥א אַֽחֲרִ֖ישׁ כִּ֣י ק֤וֹל שׁוֹפָר֙ °שָׁמַ֔עְתִּי [°שָׁמַ֔עַתְּ ק]

נַפְשִׁ֔י תְּרוּעַ֖ת מִלְחָמָֽה: שֶׁ֤בֶר עַל־שֶׁ֙בֶר֙ נִקְרָ֔א כִּ֥י שֻׁדְּדָ֖ה

כ כׇל־הָאָ֑רֶץ פִּתְאֹם֙ שֻׁדְּד֣וּ אֹהָלַ֔י רֶ֖גַע יְרִֽיעֹתָֽי: עַד־מָתַ֖י אֶרְאֶה־נֵּ֑ס

כא אֶשְׁמְעָ֖ה ק֥וֹל שׁוֹפָֽר: כִּ֣י ׀ אֱוִ֣יל עַמִּ֗י אוֹתִי֙ לֹ֣א יָדָ֔עוּ

כב בָּנִ֤ים סְכָלִים֙ הֵ֔מָּה וְלֹ֥א נְבוֹנִ֖ים הֵ֑מָּה חֲכָמִ֥ים הֵ֙מָּה֙ לְהָרַ֔ע וּלְהֵיטִ֖יב

כג לֹ֥א יָדָֽעוּ: רָאִ֙יתִי֙ אֶת־הָאָ֔רֶץ וְהִנֵּה־תֹ֖הוּ וָבֹ֑הוּ וְאֶל־הַשָּׁמַ֖יִם וְאֵ֥ין

כד-כה אוֹרָֽם: רָאִ֙יתִי֙ הֶ֣הָרִ֔ים וְהִנֵּ֖ה רֹעֲשִׁ֑ים וְכׇל־הַגְּבָע֖וֹת הִתְקַלְקָֽלוּ: רָאִ֕יתִי

כו וְהִנֵּ֖ה אֵ֣ין הָאָדָ֑ם וְכׇל־ע֥וֹף הַשָּׁמַ֖יִם נָדָֽדוּ: רָאִ֕יתִי וְהִנֵּ֥ה הַכַּרְמֶ֖ל הַמִּדְבָּ֑ר

כז וְכׇל־עָרָ֗יו נִתְּצוּ֙ מִפְּנֵ֣י יְהֹוָ֔ה מִפְּנֵ֖י חֲר֣וֹן אַפּֽוֹ: כִּי־

כח כֹה֙ אָמַ֣ר יְהֹוָ֔ה שְׁמָמָ֥ה תִֽהְיֶ֖ה כׇל־הָאָ֑רֶץ וְכָלָ֖ה לֹ֣א אֶֽעֱשֶֽׂה: עַל־

זֹ֗את תֶּאֱבַ֤ל הָאָ֙רֶץ֙ וְקָֽדְר֥וּ הַשָּׁמַ֖יִם מִמָּ֑עַל עַ֣ל כִּֽי־דִבַּ֙רְתִּי֙ זַמֹּ֔תִי וְלֹ֥א

4:10. Jeremiah interjected a plea in defense of Israel: "By not preventing the false prophets from deceiving the people with vain assurances of peace, it is as if You agreed with them." But God did not reply; He just continued the prophecy.

4:11. The invading enemy will be like a fierce wind in the desert, where there are no obstacles to impede its force. It will not be a useful wind, such as one used for winnowing grain to rid it of its chaff, but a totally destructive one.

4:19-21. Again Jeremiah interrupts his prophecy to express his own feelings.

4:20. The stately buildings of Jerusalem fell as easily and swiftly as if they were mere tents or canopies (Radak).

⁵ Relate [it] in Judah and let [it] be heard in Jerusalem. Say, 'Sound the shofar in the land!' Call out, 'Assemble together!' Say, 'Gather together and let us go to the fortified cities!' ⁶ Hoist a banner over Zion; gather together, do not stand still, for I am bringing evil from the North, and great destruction.

... for the
Babylonian
lion is ready

⁷ The lion has left his den; the destroyer of nations has set out, has gone forth from his place, to lay your land waste; your cities will be desolate, without inhabitant. ⁸ For this, don sackcloth, lament and mourn; for the burning wrath of HASHEM has not receded from us!

⁹ And it shall be on that day — the word of HASHEM — that the heart of the king and the heart of the ministers will be lost, the Kohanim will be astounded and the prophets will be amazed.

¹⁰ I then said, "Alas, my Lord, HASHEM/ELOHIM, in truth, You have certainly misled this people and Jerusalem, saying, * 'You will have peace,' and yet the sword has reached the very soul!"

God's
warning

¹¹ At that time it will be said of this people and of Jerusalem: '[Like] a dry wind over the hilltops of the wilderness, so is the way of My people; not [a wind] for winnowing and not for separating chaff.'* ¹² One of those intense winds will come [upon them] for Me. Now, I will also speak words of judgment against them. ¹³ Behold, [the enemy] will rise up like the clouds, and his chariots like the storm, swifter than eagles are his horses.

'Woe to us, for we are vanquished!'

¹⁴ Cleanse your heart of evil, O Jerusalem, so that you may be saved; how long will you lodge your iniquitous thoughts within yourself? ¹⁵ For the voice of the herald comes from Dan, and announces misfortune from Mount Ephraim. ¹⁶ Mention to the nations, behold, let it be heard regarding Jerusalem: 'Besiegers are coming from a distant land; they raise their voice against the cities of Judah!' ¹⁷ Like watchmen of a field they are all around [Jerusalem], for she has rebelled against Me — the word of HASHEM. ¹⁸ Your path and your deeds have done these to you; this is your wickedness — it is bitter, for it has touched upon your heart.

The
prophet
laments

¹⁹* My innards, my innards — I shudder; the walls of my heart — my heart murmurs within me; I cannot be silent, for you have heard the sound of the shofar, O my soul, the shofar blast of war. ²⁰ Disaster upon disaster has occurred, for the entire land has been vanquished; suddenly my tents were vanquished, my canopies in an instant. * ²¹ How long will I see the banner [of the enemy] and hear the sound of the shofar?

²² For My people are stupid; they have not recognized Me. They are foolish children, and they are not discerning; they are wise at doing evil, but know not how to do good.

²³ I saw the land, and behold, it was void and empty; [I looked] to the heavens and their light was gone. ²⁴ I saw the mountains, and behold, they were trembling, and all the hills had crumbled. ²⁵ I saw, and behold, there was no man, and all the birds of the heavens had moved away. ²⁶ I saw, and behold, the fertile field had become a wilderness, and all its cities had been decimated before HASHEM, before His burning wrath.

The land
will mourn

²⁷ For thus said HASHEM: The entire land will become a wasteland, although I will not annihilate [the people]. ²⁸ For this the land will mourn, and the heavens above will become black — because I decreed and I planned; I did not

כט נִחַמְתִּי וְלֹא־אָשׁוּב מִמֶּנָּה: מִקּוֹל פָּרָשׁ וְרֹמֵה קֶשֶׁת בֹּרַחַת כָּל־הָעִיר
ל בָּאוּ בֶּעָבִים וּבַכֵּפִים עָלוּ כָּל־הָעִיר עֲזוּבָה וְאֵין־יוֹשֵׁב בָּהֵן אִישׁ: °וְאַתִּי
[°וְאַתְּ ק] שָׁדוּד מַה־תַּעֲשִׂי כִּי־תִלְבְּשִׁי שָׁנִי כִּי־תַעְדִּי עֲדִי־זָהָב כִּי־
לא תִקְרְעִי בַפּוּךְ עֵינַיִךְ לַשָּׁוְא תִּתְיַפִּי מָאֲסוּ־בָךְ עֹגְבִים נַפְשֵׁךְ יְבַקֵּשׁוּ: כִּי
קוֹל כְּחוֹלָה שָׁמַעְתִּי צָרָה כְּמַבְכִּירָה קוֹל בַּת־צִיּוֹן תִּתְיַפֵּחַ תְּפָרֵשׂ כַּפֶּיהָ
ה א אוֹי־נָא לִי כִּי־עָיְפָה נַפְשִׁי לְהֹרְגִים: שׁוֹטְטוּ בְּחוּצוֹת
יְרוּשָׁלַם וּרְאוּ־נָא וּדְעוּ וּבַקְשׁוּ בִרְחוֹבוֹתֶיהָ אִם־תִּמְצְאוּ אִישׁ אִם־יֵשׁ
ב עֹשֶׂה מִשְׁפָּט מְבַקֵּשׁ אֱמוּנָה וְאֶסְלַח לָהּ: וְאִם חַי־יְהוָֹה יֹאמֵרוּ לָכֵן
ג לַשֶּׁקֶר יִשָּׁבֵעוּ: יְהוָֹה עֵינֶיךָ הֲלוֹא לֶאֱמוּנָה הִכִּיתָה אֹתָם וְלֹא־חָלוּ
ד כִּלִּיתָם מֵאֲנוּ קַחַת מוּסָר חִזְּקוּ פְנֵיהֶם מִסֶּלַע מֵאֲנוּ לָשׁוּב: וַאֲנִי אָמַרְתִּי
ה אַךְ־דַּלִּים הֵם נוֹאֲלוּ כִּי לֹא יָדְעוּ דֶּרֶךְ יְהוָֹה מִשְׁפַּט אֱלֹהֵיהֶם: אֵלֲכָה־
לִּי אֶל־הַגְּדֹלִים וַאֲדַבְּרָה אוֹתָם כִּי הֵמָּה יָדְעוּ דֶּרֶךְ יְהוָֹה מִשְׁפַּט
ו אֱלֹהֵיהֶם אַךְ הֵמָּה יַחְדָּו שָׁבְרוּ עֹל נִתְּקוּ מוֹסֵרוֹת: עַל־כֵּן הִכָּם אַרְיֵה
מִיַּעַר זְאֵב עֲרָבוֹת יְשָׁדְדֵם נָמֵר שֹׁקֵד עַל־עָרֵיהֶם כָּל־הַיּוֹצֵא מֵהֵנָּה
ז יִטָּרֵף כִּי רַבּוּ פִּשְׁעֵיהֶם עָצְמוּ °מְשֻׁבוֹתֵיהֶם [°מְשׁוּבוֹתֵיהֶם ק]: אֵי
לָזֹאת °אֶסְלוֹחַ־ [°אֶסְלַח־ ק] לָךְ בָּנַיִךְ עֲזָבוּנִי וַיִּשָּׁבְעוּ בְּלֹא אֱלֹהִים
ח וָאַשְׂבִּעַ אוֹתָם וַיִּנְאָפוּ וּבֵית זוֹנָה יִתְגֹּדָדוּ: סוּסִים °מְזוּנִים [°מְיֻזָּנִים ק]
ט מַשְׁכִּים הָיוּ אִישׁ אֶל־אֵשֶׁת רֵעֵהוּ יִצְהָלוּ: הַעַל־אֵלֶּה לוֹא־אֶפְקֹד
י נְאֻם־יְהוָֹה וְאִם בְּגוֹי אֲשֶׁר־כָּזֶה לֹא תִתְנַקֵּם נַפְשִׁי: עֲלוּ
בְשָׁרוֹתֶיהָ וְשַׁחֵתוּ וְכָלָה אַל־תַּעֲשׂוּ הָסִירוּ נְטִישׁוֹתֶיהָ כִּי לוֹא לַיהוָֹה
יא-יב הֵמָּה: כִּי בָגוֹד בָּגְדוּ בִּי בֵּית יִשְׂרָאֵל וּבֵית יְהוּדָה נְאֻם־יְהוָֹה: כִּחֲשׁוּ
בַּיהוָֹה וַיֹּאמְרוּ לֹא־הוּא וְלֹא־תָבוֹא עָלֵינוּ רָעָה וְחֶרֶב וְרָעָב לוֹא נִרְאֶה:
יג-יד וְהַנְּבִיאִים יִהְיוּ לְרוּחַ וְהַדִּבֵּר אֵין בָּהֶם כֹּה יֵעָשֶׂה לָהֶם: לָכֵן
כֹּה־אָמַר יְהוָֹה אֱלֹהֵי צְבָאוֹת יַעַן דַּבֶּרְכֶם אֶת־הַדָּבָר הַזֶּה הִנְנִי נֹתֵן
טו דְּבָרַי בְּפִיךָ לְאֵשׁ וְהָעָם הַזֶּה עֵצִים וַאֲכָלָתַם: הִנְנִי מֵבִיא עֲלֵיכֶם גּוֹי
מִמֶּרְחָק בֵּית יִשְׂרָאֵל נְאֻם־יְהוָֹה גּוֹי אֵיתָן הוּא גּוֹי מֵעוֹלָם הוּא גּוֹי
טז לֹא־תֵדַע לְשֹׁנוֹ וְלֹא תִשְׁמַע מַה־יְדַבֵּר: אַשְׁפָּתוֹ כְּקֶבֶר פָּתוּחַ כֻּלָּם
יז גִּבּוֹרִים: וְאָכַל קְצִירְךָ וְלַחְמֶךָ יֹאכְלוּ בָּנֶיךָ וּבְנוֹתֶיךָ יֹאכַל צֹאנְךָ
וּבְקָרֶךָ יֹאכַל גַּפְנְךָ וּתְאֵנָתֶךָ יְרֹשֵׁשׁ עָרֵי מִבְצָרֶיךָ אֲשֶׁר אַתָּה בוֹטֵחַ
יח בָּהֵנָּה בֶּחָרֶב: וְגַם בַּיָּמִים הָהֵמָּה נְאֻם־יְהוָֹה לֹא־אֶעֱשֶׂה אִתְּכֶם כָּלָה:

5:4. Jeremiah tried to justify the stubbornness of those who spurned his admonitions. At first he thought that the recalcitrants must be intellectually and spiritually impoverished. But, as he later saw, leaders and commoners alike refused to accept God's yoke.

5:10. God now addresses the invading enemy, instructing them on how to do battle with Judah.
5:13. The false prophecies of peace and prosperity will not come to pass; the prophecies of invasion and destruction will.

relent, and I will not turn back from it. ²⁹ *From the sound of horseman and archer the entire city is fleeing; they have come into the thick forests and have gone up into the rocks. The whole city is abandoned; not a man dwells in it.* ³⁰ *And you, O plundered one, what will you do? If you wear scarlet, if you don a golden ornament, if you paint your eyes with mascara, you will be beautifying yourself in vain; your lovers have come to detest you, they seek your life.* ³¹ *For I have heard an outcry like that of a woman in labor, in pain like a woman giving birth for the first time. It is the voice of the daughter of Zion, [for] she will wail, she will wring her hands, 'Woe is me, now, for my soul has been wearied by the killers.'*

5   ¹ **W**alk *about in the streets of Jerusalem, see now and know, and seek in its plazas; if you will find a man [of authority], if there is one who dispenses justice and seeks truth, then I will forgive her.* ² *And even if they say, 'As* HASHEM *lives!' they will surely be swearing falsely!*

The prophet's advocacy

³ HASHEM, *are Your eyes not toward truth?! [Therefore] You have stricken them, but they have not felt sickened; You have [nearly] annihilated them, but they have refused to accept discipline. They made their countenances harder than rock; they refused to repent.* ⁴ *And as for me, I had said [to myself], " They must only be the impoverished ones;* * *they act foolishly, for they do not know the way of* HASHEM, *the law of their God.* ⁵ *I will go to the leaders and speak to them, for they know the way of* HASHEM, *the law of their God!" But [I saw that] together they have broken the yoke, snapped the straps.* ⁶ *Therefore the lion of the forest struck them, the wolf of the deserts vanquishes them; the leopard stalks their cities — whoever leaves them will be torn apart, for their sins are abundant and their waywardness is intense.*

God is not appeased

⁷ *Why should I forgive you for this? Your children have forsaken Me; they swear by non-gods. I made them affluent, but they acted adulterously; they converged upon a brothel.* ⁸ *They were like well-fed horses rising early, each man neighing to the wife of his acquaintance.* ⁹ *Shall I not punish for these things? — the word of* HASHEM. *And from a nation such as this, shall My soul not exact vengeance?*

¹⁰ * *Attack her plains and destroy — but do not completely annihilate; remove her shoots, for they are not [faithful] to* HASHEM. ¹¹ *For they have completely betrayed Me, the House of Israel and the House of Judah — the word of* HASHEM. ¹² *They have denied [the providence of]* HASHEM *and they have said, 'It is not so! No harm will come upon us, and we will never see sword or famine.'* ¹³ *The [false] prophets will become like the wind, for the word [of God] is not with them — so will be done with them!* *

¹⁴ *Therefore, thus said* HASHEM, *God of Legions, [to me,] because you [the people] have spoken these words: Behold, I am making My words in your mouth into fire, and this people will be like wood that it will consume.* ¹⁵ *Behold, I am bringing upon you a nation from afar, O House of Israel — the word of* HASHEM. *It is a powerful nation, an ancient nation, a nation whose lang- uage you will not know, so you will not understand what they say.* ¹⁶ *Their quiver is like an open grave; they are all mighty men.* ¹⁷ *They will consume your harvest and your bread; they will consume your sons and your daugh-ters; they will consume your sheep and your cattle; they will consume your vines and your fig trees; it will impoverish your fortified cities on which you depend, by the sword.* ¹⁸ *But even in those days — the word of* HASHEM — *I will not annihilate you.*

Very难

יט וְהָיָה כִּי תֹאמְרוּ תַּחַת מֶה עָשָׂה יהוה אֱלֹהֵינוּ לָנוּ אֶת־כָּל־אֵלֶּה וְאָמַרְתָּ
אֲלֵיהֶם כַּאֲשֶׁר עֲזַבְתֶּם אוֹתִי וַתַּעַבְדוּ אֱלֹהֵי נֵכָר בְּאַרְצְכֶם כֵּן תַּעַבְדוּ
כ זָרִים בְּאֶרֶץ לֹא לָכֶם: הַגִּידוּ זֹאת בְּבֵית יַעֲקֹב
כא וְהַשְׁמִיעוּהָ בִיהוּדָה לֵאמֹר: שִׁמְעוּ־נָא זֹאת עַם סָכָל וְאֵין לֵב עֵינַיִם
כב לָהֶם וְלֹא יִרְאוּ אָזְנַיִם לָהֶם וְלֹא יִשְׁמָעוּ: הַאוֹתִי לֹא־תִירָאוּ נְאֻם־יהוה
אִם מִפָּנַי לֹא תָחִילוּ אֲשֶׁר־שַׂמְתִּי חוֹל גְּבוּל לַיָּם חָק־עוֹלָם וְלֹא
כג יַעַבְרֶנְהוּ וַיִּתְגָּעֲשׁוּ וְלֹא יוּכָלוּ וְהָמוּ גַלָּיו וְלֹא יַעַבְרֻנְהוּ: וְלָעָם הַזֶּה הָיָה
כד לֵב סוֹרֵר וּמוֹרֶה סָרוּ וַיֵּלֵכוּ: וְלֹא־אָמְרוּ בִלְבָבָם נִירָא נָא אֶת־יהוה
אֱלֹהֵינוּ הַנֹּתֵן גֶּשֶׁם °וירה [°יוֹרֶה ק] וּמַלְקוֹשׁ בְּעִתּוֹ שְׁבֻעוֹת חֻקּוֹת קָצִיר
כה-כו יִשְׁמָר־לָנוּ: עֲוֹנוֹתֵיכֶם הִטּוּ־אֵלֶּה וְחַטֹּאותֵיכֶם מָנְעוּ הַטּוֹב מִכֶּם: כִּי־
נִמְצְאוּ בְעַמִּי רְשָׁעִים יָשׁוּר כְּשַׁךְ יְקוּשִׁים הִצִּיבוּ מַשְׁחִית אֲנָשִׁים יִלְכֹּדוּ:
כז-כח כִּכְלוּב מָלֵא עוֹף כֵּן בָּתֵּיהֶם מְלֵאִים מִרְמָה עַל־כֵּן גָּדְלוּ וַיַּעֲשִׁירוּ: שָׁמְנוּ
עָשְׁתוּ גַּם עָבְרוּ דִבְרֵי־רָע דִּין לֹא־דָנוּ דִּין יָתוֹם וְיַצְלִיחוּ וּמִשְׁפַּט
כט אֶבְיוֹנִים לֹא שָׁפָטוּ: הַעַל־אֵלֶּה לֹא־אֶפְקֹד נְאֻם־יהוה אִם בְּגוֹי אֲשֶׁר־
ל כָּזֶה לֹא תִתְנַקֵּם נַפְשִׁי: שַׁמָּה וְשַׁעֲרוּרָה נִהְיְתָה בָּאָרֶץ:
לא הַנְּבִיאִים נִבְּאוּ־בַשֶּׁקֶר וְהַכֹּהֲנִים יִרְדּוּ עַל־יְדֵיהֶם וְעַמִּי אָהֲבוּ כֵן וּמַה־
א תַּעֲשׂוּ לְאַחֲרִיתָהּ: הָעִזוּ בְּנֵי בִנְיָמִן מִקֶּרֶב יְרוּשָׁלַ͏ִם וּבִתְקוֹעַ תִּקְעוּ שׁוֹפָר ו
ב וְעַל־בֵּית הַכֶּרֶם שְׂאוּ מַשְׂאֵת כִּי רָעָה נִשְׁקְפָה מִצָּפוֹן וְשֶׁבֶר גָּדוֹל: הַנָּוָה
ג וְהַמְעֻנָּגָה דָּמִיתִי בַּת־צִיּוֹן: אֵלֶיהָ יָבֹאוּ רֹעִים וְעֶדְרֵיהֶם תָּקְעוּ עָלֶיהָ
ד אֹהָלִים סָבִיב רָעוּ אִישׁ אֶת־יָדוֹ: קַדְּשׁוּ עָלֶיהָ מִלְחָמָה קוּמוּ וְנַעֲלֶה
ה בַצָּהֳרַיִם אוֹי לָנוּ כִּי־פָנָה הַיּוֹם כִּי יִנָּטוּ צִלְלֵי־עָרֶב: קוּמוּ וְנַעֲלֶה בַלָּיְלָה
ו וְנַשְׁחִיתָה אַרְמְנוֹתֶיהָ: כִּי כֹה אָמַר יהוה צְבָאוֹת כִּרְתוּ
עֵצָה וְשִׁפְכוּ עַל־יְרוּשָׁלַ͏ִם סֹלְלָה הִיא הָעִיר הָפְקַד כֻּלָּהּ עֹשֶׁק בְּקִרְבָּהּ:
ז כְּהָקִיר °בור [°בַּיִר ק] מֵימֶיהָ כֵּן הֵקֵרָה רָעָתָהּ חָמָס וָשֹׁד יִשָּׁמַע בָּהּ עַל־
ח פָּנַי תָּמִיד חֳלִי וּמַכָּה: הִוָּסְרִי יְרוּשָׁלַ͏ִם פֶּן־תֵּקַע נַפְשִׁי מִמֵּךְ פֶּן־אֲשִׂימֵךְ
ט שְׁמָמָה אֶרֶץ לוֹא נוֹשָׁבָה: כֹּה אָמַר יהוה צְבָאוֹת
עוֹלֵל יְעוֹלְלוּ כַגֶּפֶן שְׁאֵרִית יִשְׂרָאֵל הָשֵׁב יָדְךָ כְּבוֹצֵר עַל־סַלְסִלּוֹת:

5:19. God addresses Jeremiah.

5:21. I.e., "without understanding." Scripture refers to the heart as the seat of the intellect.

5:22. Just as God established the beaches as boundaries of the seas so the raging waves cannot flood the continents, so too the rebellious people of Jerusalem should realize that they cannot succeed in defying Him.

5:24. Jeremiah reprimands the people for not recognizing the hand of God in the laws He has established for the agricultural cycle in the Land of Israel. For He does not allow rain to fall during the harvest season; thus, the grain can dry in the field for many weeks so that it can be

processed and ground easily.

5:31. The prophets lulled the people into thinking that all was well; their false prophecies conferred authority upon avaricious priests; and the people were content, refusing to realize that eventually they would have to face reality.

6:1. Jerusalem bordered the provinces of Benjamin and Judah; thus, Jeremiah was addressing its citizens, telling them that they would be forced to flee the invasion from the North.

6:4-5. The "shepherds" debate when to attack. Some say to wait until high noon of the next day, while others want

¹⁹* And it shall be, when they will say, "Because of what has HASHEM, our God, done all these things to us?" you shall say to them, "Just as you deserted Me and worshiped alien gods in your land, so will you serve foreigners in a land not your own."

²⁰ Proclaim this in the House of Jacob; announce it in Judah, saying:

²¹ Hear this, O nation that is foolish and without a heart. * They have eyes, but cannot see; they have ears, but cannot hear! ²² Will you not fear Me? — the word of HASHEM — Will you not tremble before Me? For I have set sand as boundary against the sea, as a permanent law that cannot be broken. Its waves rage forth but cannot succeed, they roar but cannot cross it. * ²³ But this people has a wayward and rebellious heart; they have turned astray and left, ²⁴ and they did not say in their hearts, 'Let us fear HASHEM our God, Who supplies rain — early rain and late rain — in its proper time, and Who preserves for us the weeks appointed for the harvest.'* ²⁵ Your sins have overturned these, and your transgressions have kept goodness away from you. ²⁶ For wicked men are found among My people, who lie in ambush like a trap that snaps shut; they set a snare; they trap people. ²⁷ Like a cage full of fowl, so their houses are full of deceit; thereby they have grown great and wealthy. ²⁸ They have grown fat and corpulent, and also transgressed through wicked deeds; they did not rule justly — [even] the claim of the orphan — to enable them to prosper; and they did not judge the judgment of the poor. ²⁹ Shall I not punish for [these] things? — the word of HASHEM. From a nation such as this shall My soul not exact vengeance?

A litany
of sin

³⁰ Astonishing and disgraceful things have taken place in the land: ³¹ The prophets prophesied falsely and the priests dominated [the people] by their hands — and My people liked it that way! But what will you do upon its climax?*

6

Take
heed, O
Benjamites

¹ Come together, O sons of Benjamin, out of the midst of Jerusalem; sound the shofar in Tekoa and hoist a flag over Beth-cherem, for evil can be espied from the North, and a major disaster. * ² I had compared the daughter of Zion to the beautiful and delicate woman. ³ Now shepherds come to her with their flocks; they have pitched tents roundabout her, each one grazing in his place, [saying,] ⁴ 'Devote yourselves to war against [Zion]; arise, let us attack at noon; woe to us for the day draws to a close, for the shadows of late afternoon grow longer!' ⁵ 'Arise, let us attack at night; let us destroy its palaces!'*

⁶ For thus said HASHEM, Master of Legions: Cut down wood, pour out a ramp against Jerusalem; * she — the city — is being brought to account, for oppression is in her midst. ⁷ As a spring issues forth its waters, so she issues forth her evil; corruption and thievery are heard in her before Me continuously — [hence] disease and affliction. ⁸ Be chastened, O Jerusalem, lest My soul become alienated from you, lest I make you a wasteland, [like] an uninhabited land.

⁹ Thus said HASHEM, Master of Legions: They will glean bare the remnant of Israel like a grapevine. [Tell the besiegers,] 'Send out your hand again, like a grape harvester over the shoots!'

---

to invade immediately, at night.
6:6. God calls upon the enemy, as it were, to build towers and scaffolds for the siege, and to pour a ramp against its wall (Radak).

י עַל־מִי אֲדַבְּרָה וְאָעִידָה וְיִשְׁמָעוּ הִנֵּה עֲרֵלָה אָזְנָם וְלֹא יוּכְלוּ לְהַקְשִׁיב
יא הִנֵּה דְבַר־יהוה הָיָה לָהֶם לְחֶרְפָּה לֹא יַחְפְּצוּ־בוֹ: וְאֵת חֲמַת יהוה |
מָלֵאתִי נִלְאֵיתִי הָכִיל שְׁפֹךְ עַל־עוֹלָל בַּחוּץ וְעַל סוֹד בַּחוּרִים יַחְדָּו
יב כִּי־גַם־אִישׁ עִם־אִשָּׁה יִלָּכֵדוּ זָקֵן עִם־מְלֵא יָמִים: וְנָסַבּוּ בָתֵּיהֶם
לַאֲחֵרִים שָׂדוֹת וְנָשִׁים יַחְדָּו כִּי־אַטֶּה אֶת־יָדִי עַל־יֹשְׁבֵי הָאָרֶץ נְאֻם־
יג יהוה: כִּי מִקְּטַנָּם וְעַד־גְּדוֹלָם כֻּלּוֹ בּוֹצֵעַ בָּצַע וּמִנָּבִיא וְעַד־כֹּהֵן כֻּלּוֹ
יד עֹשֶׂה שָּׁקֶר: וַיְרַפְּאוּ אֶת־שֶׁבֶר עַמִּי עַל־נְקַלָּה לֵאמֹר שָׁלוֹם | שָׁלוֹם וְאֵין
טו שָׁלוֹם: הֹבִישׁוּ כִּי תוֹעֵבָה עָשׂוּ גַּם־בּוֹשׁ לֹא־יֵבוֹשׁוּ גַּם־הַכְלִים לֹא יָדָעוּ
לָכֵן יִפְּלוּ בַנֹּפְלִים בְּעֵת־פְּקַדְתִּים יִכָּשְׁלוּ אָמַר יהוה: כֹּה
טז אָמַר יהוה עִמְדוּ עַל־דְּרָכִים וּרְאוּ וְשַׁאֲלוּ | לִנְתִבוֹת עוֹלָם אֵי־זֶה
יז דֶרֶךְ הַטּוֹב וּלְכוּ־בָהּ וּמִצְאוּ מַרְגּוֹעַ לְנַפְשְׁכֶם וַיֹּאמְרוּ לֹא נֵלֵךְ: וַהֲקִמֹתִי
יח עֲלֵיכֶם צֹפִים הַקְשִׁיבוּ לְקוֹל שׁוֹפָר וַיֹּאמְרוּ לֹא נַקְשִׁיב: לָכֵן שִׁמְעוּ
יט הַגּוֹיִם וּדְעִי עֵדָה אֶת־אֲשֶׁר־בָּם: שִׁמְעִי הָאָרֶץ הִנֵּה אָנֹכִי מֵבִיא רָעָה
אֶל־הָעָם הַזֶּה פְּרִי מַחְשְׁבוֹתָם כִּי עַל־דְּבָרַי לֹא הִקְשִׁיבוּ וְתוֹרָתִי
כ וַיִּמְאֲסוּ־בָהּ: לָמָּה־זֶּה לִי לְבוֹנָה מִשְּׁבָא תָבוֹא וְקָנֶה הַטּוֹב מֵאֶרֶץ
כא מֶרְחָק עֹלוֹתֵיכֶם לֹא לְרָצוֹן וְזִבְחֵיכֶם לֹא־עָרְבוּ לִי: לָכֵן
כֹּה אָמַר יהוה הִנְנִי נֹתֵן אֶל־הָעָם הַזֶּה מִכְשֹׁלִים וְכָשְׁלוּ בָם אָבוֹת
כב וּבָנִים יַחְדָּו שָׁכֵן וְרֵעוֹ [יֹאבְדוּ °יֹאבֵדוּ ק]: כֹּה אָמַר
כג יהוה הִנֵּה עַם בָּא מֵאֶרֶץ צָפוֹן וְגוֹי גָּדוֹל יֵעוֹר מִיַּרְכְּתֵי־אָרֶץ: קֶשֶׁת
וְכִידוֹן יַחֲזִיקוּ אַכְזָרִי הוּא וְלֹא יְרַחֵמוּ קוֹלָם כַּיָּם יֶהֱמֶה וְעַל־
כד סוּסִים יִרְכָּבוּ עָרוּךְ כְּאִישׁ לַמִּלְחָמָה עָלַיִךְ בַּת־צִיּוֹן: שָׁמַעְנוּ אֶת־
כה שָׁמְעוֹ רָפוּ יָדֵינוּ צָרָה הֶחֱזִיקַתְנוּ חִיל כַּיּוֹלֵדָה: אַל־°תֵּצְאִי [°תֵּצְאוּ ק]
הַשָּׂדֶה וּבַדֶּרֶךְ אַל־°תֵּלֵכִי [°תֵּלֵכוּ ק] כִּי חֶרֶב לְאֹיֵב מָגוֹר מִסָּבִיב:
כו בַּת־עַמִּי חִגְרִי־שָׂק וְהִתְפַּלְּשִׁי בָאֵפֶר אֵבֶל יָחִיד עֲשִׂי־לָךְ מִסְפַּד
כז תַּמְרוּרִים כִּי פִתְאֹם יָבֹא הַשֹּׁדֵד עָלֵינוּ: בָּחוֹן נְתַתִּיךָ בְעַמִּי מִבְצָר
כח וְתֵדַע וּבָחַנְתָּ אֶת־דַּרְכָּם: כֻּלָּם סָרֵי סוֹרְרִים הֹלְכֵי רָכִיל נְחֹשֶׁת וּבַרְזֶל
כט כֻּלָּם מַשְׁחִיתִים הֵמָּה: נָחַר מַפֻּחַ °מֵאֵשׁ [°מֵאִשָּׁתַם ק] תַּם עֹפָרֶת
ל לַשָּׁוְא צָרַף צָרוֹף וְרָעִים לֹא נִתָּקוּ: כֶּסֶף נִמְאָס קָרְאוּ לָהֶם כִּי־מָאַס
א יהוה בָּהֶם: הַדָּבָר אֲשֶׁר הָיָה אֶל־יִרְמְיָהוּ מֵאֵת יהוה **ז**
ב לֵאמֹר: עֲמֹד בְּשַׁעַר בֵּית יהוה וְקָרָאתָ שָּׁם אֶת־הַדָּבָר הַזֶּה וְאָמַרְתָּ

6:24. The prophet describes his reaction to the prophecy of doom that he was charged to deliver.

6:27. Here, God responds to Jeremiah's interjection by reiterating the theme of 1:17-19, that He would protect Jeremiah from those who would threaten him because of his scathing criticisms and bitter prophecies.

6:29. The task of the prophets is compared to the process of refining silver, which is purified by heating the ore (and fanning the fire with bellows) and adding bits of lead, which absorb much of the dross. But the prophetic attempt to purify the Israelites had become futile, as if the bellows were ruined and the lead depleted.

The people
are
unmoved

¹⁰ *To whom shall I speak and warn, that they will take heed? Behold, their ear is blocked and they are unable to listen! Behold, the word of HASHEM has become an object of ridicule to them; they have no desire for it.* ¹¹ *And I am filled with [prophecies of] the wrath of HASHEM; I am too weary to contain them!*

Pour [this wrath] onto little children in the street and onto the gathering of youths, for men and women alike will be captured, the elders with the very aged. ¹² *Their houses will be turned over to others, [and their] fields and women, at once, for I will stretch out My hand against the inhabitants of the land — the word of HASHEM.* ¹³ *For from their simplest to their greatest people, they all extort booty; from prophet to priest, all deal in falsehood.* ¹⁴ *They relieved the [impending] disaster of My people by making light of it, saying, 'Peace! Peace!' But there is no peace.* ¹⁵ *Were they ashamed that they had committed abominations? They will never feel shame; they will not know humiliation! Therefore, they will fall among the fallen; at the time I punish them they will stumble, said HASHEM.*

¹⁶ *Thus said HASHEM: Stand on the roads and see; ask about the various paths of history, which path is best, and walk on it and find solace for your soul.*

We will
not walk
nor hearken

But they said, 'We will not walk.'

¹⁷ *I appointed watchmen over you [who warned], 'Hearken to the sound of the shofar!'*

But they said, 'We will not hearken.'

¹⁸ *Therefore, hear, O nations; know, O congregation, [the evil] that is in them.* ¹⁹ *Listen, O Land: Behold, I am bringing evil upon this nation, the fruits of their schemes, for they did not hearken to My words or My teaching — they rejected it.* ²⁰ *Why do I need frankincense that comes from Sheba or the aromatic cane from a distant land? Your burnt-offerings do not find favor and your sacrifices are not pleasant to Me.* ²¹ *Therefore, thus said HASHEM: Behold, I am putting stumbling blocks before this people and they will stumble over them, fathers and sons together, as well as the neighbor and his acquaintance, and they will perish.*

The
Babylonian
bow and
spear

²² *Thus said HASHEM: Behold, a people is coming from the land of the North, a great nation will rouse itself from the ends of the earth.* ²³ *They will grasp bow and spear; it is [a] cruel [nation] and they will not have pity. Their sound will rage like the sea. They will be riding horses, equipped like a man setting out to battle — against you, O daughter of Zion.*

²⁴ *[When] we heard of its reputation, our hands grew weak,* * *anxiety took hold of us, pains like those of a woman in childbirth.* ²⁵ *Do not go out into the field, and do not venture forth on the road, for the enemy has a sword; [there is] terror all around!* ²⁶ *O daughter of my people, don sackcloth and wallow in the ashes; mourn as if for an only child, make yourself a bitter lament, for the plunderer will come upon us suddenly.*

²⁷ *I have made you a fortress among My people, a stronghold;* * *you shall observe and test their ways.* ²⁸ *They are all the ultimate rebels, gossipmongers, [brazen as] copper and iron; they are all destroyers.* ²⁹ *The bellows are singed by fire, the lead is spent. The smelter smelts in vain, for the dross is not removed.* * ³⁰ *People call them 'Rejected Silver,' for HASHEM has rejected them.*

Rejected
Silver

7 ¹ **T**he word that came to Jeremiah from HASHEM, saying: ² Stand in the gateway of the Temple of HASHEM and proclaim this message there. Say:

שִׁמְעוּ דְבַר־יְהֹוָה כָּל־יְהוּדָה הַבָּאִים בַּשְּׁעָרִים הָאֵלֶּה לְהִשְׁתַּחֲוֺת
ג   לַיהֹוָה: כֹּה־אָמַר יְהֹוָה צְבָאוֹת אֱלֹהֵי יִשְׂרָאֵל הֵיטִיבוּ דַרְכֵיכֶם
ד   וּמַעַלְלֵיכֶם וַאֲשַׁכְּנָה אֶתְכֶם בַּמָּקוֹם הַזֶּה: אַל־תִּבְטְחוּ לָכֶם אֶל־דִּבְרֵי
ה   הַשֶּׁקֶר לֵאמֹר הֵיכַל יְהֹוָה הֵיכַל יְהֹוָה הֵיכַל יְהֹוָה הֵמָּה: כִּי אִם־הֵיטֵיב
    תֵּיטִיבוּ אֶת־דַּרְכֵיכֶם וְאֶת־מַעַלְלֵיכֶם אִם־עָשׂוֹ תַעֲשׂוּ מִשְׁפָּט בֵּין אִישׁ
ו   וּבֵין רֵעֵהוּ: גֵּר יָתוֹם וְאַלְמָנָה לֹא תַעֲשֹׁקוּ וְדָם נָקִי אַל־תִּשְׁפְּכוּ בַּמָּקוֹם
ז   הַזֶּה וְאַחֲרֵי אֱלֹהִים אֲחֵרִים לֹא תֵלְכוּ לְרַע לָכֶם: וְשִׁכַּנְתִּי אֶתְכֶם בַּמָּקוֹם
ח   הַזֶּה בָּאָרֶץ אֲשֶׁר נָתַתִּי לַאֲבוֹתֵיכֶם לְמִן־עוֹלָם וְעַד־עוֹלָם: הִנֵּה אַתֶּם
ט   בֹּטְחִים לָכֶם עַל־דִּבְרֵי הַשֶּׁקֶר לְבִלְתִּי הוֹעִיל: הֲגָנֹב ׀ רָצֹחַ וְנָאֹף וְהִשָּׁבֵעַ
    לַשֶּׁקֶר וְקַטֵּר לַבָּעַל וְהָלֹךְ אַחֲרֵי אֱלֹהִים אֲחֵרִים אֲשֶׁר לֹא־יְדַעְתֶּם:
י   וּבָאתֶם וַעֲמַדְתֶּם לְפָנַי בַּבַּיִת הַזֶּה אֲשֶׁר נִקְרָא־שְׁמִי עָלָיו וַאֲמַרְתֶּם נִצַּלְנוּ
יא לְמַעַן עֲשׂוֹת אֵת כָּל־הַתּוֹעֵבוֹת הָאֵלֶּה: הַמְעָרַת פָּרִצִים הָיָה הַבַּיִת הַזֶּה
יב אֲשֶׁר־נִקְרָא־שְׁמִי עָלָיו בְּעֵינֵיכֶם גַּם אָנֹכִי הִנֵּה רָאִיתִי נְאֻם־יְהֹוָה: כִּי
    לְכוּ־נָא אֶל־מְקוֹמִי אֲשֶׁר בְּשִׁילוֹ אֲשֶׁר שִׁכַּנְתִּי שְׁמִי שָׁם בָּרִאשׁוֹנָה וּרְאוּ
יג אֵת אֲשֶׁר־עָשִׂיתִי לוֹ מִפְּנֵי רָעַת עַמִּי יִשְׂרָאֵל: וְעַתָּה יַעַן עֲשׂוֹתְכֶם אֶת־
    כָּל־הַמַּעֲשִׂים הָאֵלֶּה נְאֻם־יְהֹוָה וָאֲדַבֵּר אֲלֵיכֶם הַשְׁכֵּם וְדַבֵּר וְלֹא
יד שְׁמַעְתֶּם וָאֶקְרָא אֶתְכֶם וְלֹא עֲנִיתֶם: וְעָשִׂיתִי לַבַּיִת ׀ אֲשֶׁר נִקְרָא־שְׁמִי
    עָלָיו אֲשֶׁר אַתֶּם בֹּטְחִים בּוֹ וְלַמָּקוֹם אֲשֶׁר־נָתַתִּי לָכֶם וְלַאֲבוֹתֵיכֶם
טו כַּאֲשֶׁר עָשִׂיתִי לְשִׁלוֹ: וְהִשְׁלַכְתִּי אֶתְכֶם מֵעַל פָּנָי כַּאֲשֶׁר הִשְׁלַכְתִּי אֶת־
טז כָּל־אֲחֵיכֶם אֵת כָּל־זֶרַע אֶפְרָיִם: וְאַתָּה אַל־תִּתְפַּלֵּל ׀
    בְּעַד־הָעָם הַזֶּה וְאַל־תִּשָּׂא בַעֲדָם רִנָּה וּתְפִלָּה וְאַל־תִּפְגַּע־בִּי כִּי־אֵינֶנִּי
יז שֹׁמֵעַ אֹתָךְ: הַאֵינְךָ רֹאֶה מָה הֵמָּה עֹשִׂים בְּעָרֵי יְהוּדָה וּבְחֻצוֹת יְרוּשָׁלָ͏ִם:
יח הַבָּנִים מְלַקְּטִים עֵצִים וְהָאָבוֹת מְבַעֲרִים אֶת־הָאֵשׁ וְהַנָּשִׁים לָשׁוֹת
    בָּצֵק לַעֲשׂוֹת כַּוָּנִים לִמְלֶכֶת הַשָּׁמַיִם וְהַסֵּךְ נְסָכִים לֵאלֹהִים אֲחֵרִים
יט לְמַעַן הַכְעִסֵנִי: הַאֹתִי הֵם מַכְעִסִים נְאֻם־יְהֹוָה הֲלוֹא אֹתָם לְמַעַן בֹּשֶׁת
כ   פְּנֵיהֶם: לָכֵן כֹּה־אָמַר ׀ אֲדֹנָי יֱהֹוִה הִנֵּה אַפִּי וַחֲמָתִי נִתֶּכֶת
    אֶל־הַמָּקוֹם הַזֶּה עַל־הָאָדָם וְעַל־הַבְּהֵמָה וְעַל־עֵץ הַשָּׂדֶה וְעַל־פְּרִי
כא הָאֲדָמָה וּבָעֲרָה וְלֹא תִכְבֶּה: כֹּה אָמַר יְהֹוָה צְבָאוֹת אֱלֹהֵי
כב יִשְׂרָאֵל עֹלוֹתֵיכֶם סְפוּ עַל־זִבְחֵיכֶם וְאִכְלוּ בָשָׂר: כִּי לֹא־דִבַּרְתִּי אֶת־
    אֲבוֹתֵיכֶם וְלֹא צִוִּיתִים בְּיוֹם °הוֹצִיא [°הוֹצִיאִי ק] אוֹתָם מֵאֶרֶץ מִצְרָיִם
כג עַל־דִּבְרֵי עוֹלָה וָזָבַח: כִּי אִם־אֶת־הַדָּבָר הַזֶּה צִוִּיתִי אוֹתָם לֵאמֹר שִׁמְעוּ

HAFTARAS
TZAV
7:21-8:3;
9:22-23

7:4. Reiterating over and over that the Temple buildings were the Sanctuary of Hashem, the false prophets would assure the people that no harm could befall the Temple. Surely God would preserve it!
7:10. Jeremiah railed against a common human failing.

People often act as if they can commit every manner of sin, but expect Divine help because they mouth empty commitments to their faith.
7:13. Lit., "arising early and speaking"; i.e., I sent My prophets to remonstrate with you, at all times of the day.

Hear the word of HASHEM, *all [people of] Judah who come through these gates to prostrate themselves before* HASHEM.

^{Another call to repentance} ³ *Thus said* HASHEM, *Master of Legions, God of Israel: Improve your ways and your deeds and I will cause you to dwell in this place.* ⁴ *Do not trust the false statements that say, 'The Sanctuary of* HASHEM, *the Sanctuary of* HASHEM, *the Sanctuary of* HASHEM *are they!'** ⁵ *Only if you truly improve your ways and your deeds; if you truly do justice between man and his fellow;* ⁶ *do not oppress stranger, orphan and widow; and do not shed innocent blood in this place; and do not go after the gods of others, to your own harm —* ⁷ *then I will cause you to dwell in this place, in the land that I gave to your forefathers, forever and ever.* ⁸ *Behold, you trust the false statements that are of no use.* ⁹ *Can one steal, murder, and commit adultery and swear falsely and burn incense to the Baal and go after the gods of others that you never knew,* ¹⁰ *and then come and stand before Me in this Temple, upon which My Name is proclaimed, and say, 'We are saved!' — in order to [continue] committing all these abominations?** ¹¹ *Has this Temple, upon which My Name is proclaimed, become a cave of criminals in your eyes? Moreover — behold, I have seen it — the word of* HASHEM.

^{Learn from Shiloh} ¹² *For go to My shrine that is in Shiloh, where I caused My Name to dwell there at first, and see what I did to it because of the wickedness of My people Israel.* ¹³ *So now, since you do all these deeds — the word of* HASHEM — *and I have spoken to you, speaking repeatedly,* * *but you have not listened; I have called out to you but you did not respond,* ¹⁴ *I shall do to the Temple — upon which My Name is proclaimed, upon which you place your trust — and to the place that I have given to you and to your fathers, as I did to Shiloh.* ¹⁵ *I shall cast you from My presence, as I cast out all your brethren, all the seed of Ephraim.* *

^{Jeremiah, do not intercede} ¹⁶ *And you, [Jeremiah] — do not pray for this people; do not speak up for them with a cry and a prayer, and do not entreat Me, for I will not listen to you.* ¹⁷ *Do you not see what they do in the cities of Judah and in the streets of Jerusalem?* ¹⁸ *The sons gather wood, the fathers kindle the fire, and the women knead dough — to make pastries in honor of the queen of heaven** *and to pour out libations to the gods of others, in order to provoke Me.* ¹⁹ *Is it Me they are provoking? — the word of* HASHEM. *Is it not themselves, bringing shame upon themselves?*

²⁰ *Therefore, thus said my Lord* HASHEM/ELOHIM: *Behold, My anger and wrath will be poured out upon this place — upon the people and upon the animals, upon the trees of the field and upon the fruits of the earth; it shall burn and not be extinguished.*

²¹ *Thus said* HASHEM, *Master of Legions, God of Israel: Add your burnt-offerings to your peace-offerings and eat [their] meat!** ²² *For I did not speak with your forefathers, nor did I command them, on the day I took them out of the land of Egypt, concerning burnt- or peace-offerings.* ²³ *Rather, it was only this thing that I commanded them, saying: 'Hearken*

7:15. The prophets often refer to the Ten Tribes of the Northern Kingdom, whose inhabitants had been exiled by Assyria over a century before, by the collective name "Ephraim," because its first king, Jeroboam, was from that tribe (*Radak*).

7:18. That is, the sun.

7:21. Burnt-offerings are completely burned on the Altar, while the flesh of peace-offerings is eaten. God scathingly tells the people that they may as well not waste meat by bringing burnt-offerings — they should be brought rather as peace-offerings — because they are not acceptable to Him in any event (*Rashi*).

בְּקוֹלִ֗י וְהָיִ֤יתִי לָכֶם֙ לֵֽאלֹהִ֔ים וְאַתֶּ֖ם תִּֽהְיוּ־לִ֣י לְעָ֑ם וַהֲלַכְתֶּ֗ם בְּכָל־הַדֶּ֙רֶךְ֙

כד אֲשֶׁ֣ר אֲצַוֶּ֣ה אֶתְכֶ֔ם לְמַ֖עַן יִיטַ֥ב לָכֶֽם: וְלֹ֤א שָֽׁמְעוּ֙ וְלֹֽא־הִטּ֣וּ אֶת־אָזְנָ֔ם

כה וַיֵּֽלְכוּ֙ בְּמֹ֣עֵצ֔וֹת בִּשְׁרִר֖וּת לִבָּ֣ם הָרָ֑ע וַיִּֽהְי֥וּ לְאָח֖וֹר וְלֹ֥א לְפָנִֽים: לְמִן־הַיּ֗וֹם

אֲשֶׁ֨ר יָֽצְא֤וּ אֲבֽוֹתֵיכֶם֙ מֵאֶ֣רֶץ מִצְרַ֔יִם עַ֖ד הַיּ֣וֹם הַזֶּ֑ה וָֽאֶשְׁלַ֤ח אֲלֵיכֶם֙ אֶת־

כו כָּל־עֲבָדַ֣י הַנְּבִיאִ֔ים י֥וֹם הַשְׁכֵּ֖ם וְשָׁלֹֽחַ: וְל֤וֹא שָֽׁמְעוּ֙ אֵלַ֔י וְלֹ֥א הִטּ֖וּ אֶת־

כז אָזְנָ֑ם וַיַּקְשׁוּ֙ אֶת־עָרְפָּ֔ם הֵרֵ֖עוּ מֵֽאֲבוֹתָֽם: וְדִבַּרְתָּ֤ אֲלֵיהֶם֙ אֶת־כָּל־

כח הַדְּבָרִ֣ים הָאֵ֔לֶּה וְלֹ֥א יִשְׁמְע֖וּ אֵלֶ֑יךָ וְקָרָ֥אתָ אֲלֵיהֶ֖ם וְלֹ֣א יַֽעֲנ֑וּכָה: וְאָֽמַרְתָּ֣

אֲלֵיהֶ֗ם זֶ֤ה הַגּוֹי֙ אֲשֶׁ֣ר לֽוֹא־שָֽׁמְע֗וּ בְּקוֹל֙ יְהֹוָ֣ה אֱלֹהָ֔יו וְלֹ֥א לָֽקְח֖וּ מוּסָ֑ר

כט אָֽבְדָה֙ הָֽאֱמוּנָ֔ה וְנִכְרְתָ֖ה מִפִּיהֶֽם: גָּ֣זִּי נִזְרֵךְ֮ וְהַשְׁלִ֒יכִי֒ וּשְׂאִ֤י

עַל־שְׁפָיִ֙ם קִינָ֔ה כִּ֚י מָאַ֣ס יְהֹוָ֔ה וַיִּטֹּ֖שׁ אֶת־דּ֣וֹר עֶבְרָתֽוֹ: כִּֽי־עָ֨שׂוּ בְנֵֽי־יְהוּדָ֤ה

ל הָרַע֙ בְּעֵינַ֔י נְאֻם־יְהֹוָ֑ה שָׂ֣מוּ שִׁקּֽוּצֵיהֶ֗ם בַּבַּ֛יִת אֲשֶׁר־נִקְרָֽא־שְׁמִ֥י עָלָ֖יו אֶת־

לא לְטַמְּאֽוֹ: וּבָנ֞וּ בָּמ֣וֹת הַתֹּ֗פֶת אֲשֶׁר֙ בְּגֵ֣יא בֶן־הִנֹּ֔ם לִשְׂרֹ֛ף אֶת־בְּנֵיהֶ֥ם וְאֶת־

לב בְּנֹֽתֵיהֶ֖ם בָּאֵ֑שׁ אֲשֶׁר֙ לֹ֣א צִוִּ֔יתִי וְלֹ֥א עָֽלְתָ֖ה עַל־לִבִּֽי: לָכֵ֞ן

הִנֵּֽה־יָמִ֤ים בָּאִים֙ נְאֻם־יְהֹוָ֔ה וְלֹֽא־יֵֽאָמֵ֥ר ע֛וֹד הַתֹּ֖פֶת וְגֵ֣יא בֶן־הִנֹּ֑ם כִּ֧י

לג אִם־גֵּ֣יא הַֽהֲרֵגָ֗ה וְקָֽבְר֥וּ בְתֹ֛פֶת מֵאֵ֥ין מָק֖וֹם: וְהָֽיְתָ֡ה נִבְלַת֩ הָעָ֨ם הַזֶּ֜ה

לד לְמַֽאֲכָ֗ל לְע֤וֹף הַשָּׁמַ֙יִם֙ וּלְבֶֽהֱמַ֣ת הָאָ֔רֶץ וְאֵ֖ין מַֽחֲרִֽיד: וְהִשְׁבַּתִּ֣י | מֵֽעָרֵ֣י

יְהוּדָ֗ה וּמֵֽחֻצוֹת֙ יְר֣וּשָׁלַ֔͏ִם ק֤וֹל שָׂשׂוֹן֙ וְק֣וֹל שִׂמְחָ֔ה ק֥וֹל חָתָ֖ן וְק֣וֹל כַּלָּ֑ה

ח א כִּ֥י לְחָרְבָּ֖ה תִּֽהְיֶ֥ה הָאָֽרֶץ: בָּעֵ֣ת הַהִ֣יא נְאֻם־יְהֹוָ֗ה °ויציאו [י֠וֹצִ֡יאוּ ק]

אֶת־עַצְמ֣וֹת מַלְכֵֽי־יְהוּדָ֣ה וְאֶת־עַצְמוֹת־שָׂרָיו֮ וְאֶת־עַצְמ֣וֹת הַכֹּֽהֲנִים֒

וְאֵ֣ת | עַצְמ֣וֹת הַנְּבִיאִ֗ים וְאֵ֛ת עַצְמ֥וֹת יֽוֹשְׁבֵֽי־יְרֽוּשָׁלָ֖͏ִם מִקִּבְרֵיהֶֽם:

ב וּשְׁטָחוּם֩ לַשֶּׁ֨מֶשׁ וְלַיָּרֵ֜חַ וּלְכֹ֣ל | צְבָ֣א הַשָּׁמַ֗יִם אֲשֶׁ֨ר אֲהֵב֜וּם וַֽאֲשֶׁ֤ר עֲבָדוּם֙

וַֽאֲשֶׁר֙ הָֽלְכ֣וּ אַֽחֲרֵיהֶ֔ם וַֽאֲשֶׁ֥ר דְּרָשׁ֖וּם וַֽאֲשֶׁ֣ר הִשְׁתַּֽחֲו֣וּ לָהֶ֑ם לֹ֤א יֵאָֽסְפוּ֙

ג וְלֹ֣א יִקָּבֵ֔רוּ לְדֹ֛מֶן עַל־פְּנֵ֥י הָֽאֲדָמָ֖ה יִֽהְי֑וּ: וְנִבְחַ֥ר מָ֙וֶת֙ מֵֽחַיִּ֔ים לְכֹ֗ל

הַשְּׁאֵרִית֙ הַנִּשְׁאָרִ֔ים מִן־הַמִּשְׁפָּחָ֥ה הָֽרָעָ֖ה הַזֹּ֑את בְּכָ֤ל־הַמְּקֹמוֹת֙

ד הַנִּשְׁאָרִ֔ים אֲשֶׁ֣ר הִדַּחְתִּ֣ים שָׁ֔ם נְאֻ֖ם יְהֹוָ֥ה צְבָאֽוֹת: וְאָֽמַרְתָּ֣

אֲלֵיהֶ֗ם כֹּ֚ה אָמַ֣ר יְהֹוָ֔ה הֲיִפְּל֖וּ וְלֹ֣א יָק֑וּמוּ אִם־יָשׁ֖וּב וְלֹ֥א יָשֽׁוּב:

ה מַדּ֨וּעַ שֽׁוֹבְבָ֜ה הָעָ֥ם הַזֶּ֛ה יְרֽוּשָׁלַ֖͏ִם מְשֻׁבָ֣ה נִצַּ֑חַת הֶֽחֱזִ֙יקוּ֙ בַּתַּרְמִ֔ית

ו מֵֽאֲנ֖וּ לָשֽׁוּב: הִקְשַׁ֤בְתִּי וָֽאֶשְׁמָע֙ לוֹא־כֵ֣ן יְדַבֵּ֔רוּ אֵ֣ין אִ֗ישׁ נִחָם֙ עַל־

רָ֣עָת֔וֹ לֵאמֹ֖ר מֶ֣ה עָשִׂ֑יתִי כֻּלֹּ֗ה שָׁב֙ °במרצותם [בִּמְר֣וּצָתָ֔ם ק] כְּס֥וּס

ז שׁוֹטֵ֖ף בַּמִּלְחָמָֽה: גַּם־חֲסִידָ֣ה בַשָּׁמַ֗יִם יָֽדְעָה֙ מֽוֹעֲדֶ֔יהָ וְתֹ֨ר °וסיס

[וְסִ֤יס ק] וְעָגוּר֙ שָׁמְר֖וּ אֶת־עֵ֣ת בֹּאָ֑נָה וְעַמִּ֕י לֹ֣א יָֽדְע֔וּ אֵ֖ת מִשְׁפַּ֥ט יְהֹוָֽה:

7:29. Tearing out one's hair is an expression of grief. Here God addresses the Congregation of Israel.

7:31. It cannot be said that the Israelites abandoned the service of God because they found it to be too heavy a burden, for they have adopted religions which make demands such as child sacrifice, which God never commanded, nor even considered.

8:1. I.e., the invading enemy.

Haftaras Tzav continues on p. 1094

Backward, not foward

to My voice, that I will be your God and you will be My people; and you will go on the entire way that I command you, so that it will be well for you.' ²⁴ But they did not listen, and they did not incline their ear, but followed [their own] counsels and the visions of their evil heart; they went backward and not forward. ²⁵ From the day your forefathers left the land of Egypt until this day, I sent to you all My servants, the prophets, daily, rising early and sending forth. ²⁶ But they would not listen to Me, and they would not incline their ear; they stiffened their neck, and became worse than their forefathers.

²⁷ You will tell them all these things, but they will not listen to you; you will call out to them, but they will not answer you. ²⁸ Say unto them:

'This is the nation that would not listen to the voice of HASHEM, its God; and they would not accept rebuke! Faith is lost; it is detached from their speech.'

²⁹ Tear out your hair* and throw it away, proclaim lament from the hilltops; for HASHEM has rejected and forsaken the generation of His wrath. ³⁰ For the children of Judah have done what is evil in My eyes — the word of HASHEM; they have placed their abominations in the Temple upon which My Name is proclaimed, to contaminate it. ³¹ They have built the high places of the Topheth that are in the Valley of the Son of Hinnom, to burn their sons and their daughters in fire — which I had not commanded and had not entered My mind. *

³² Therefore, behold, days are coming — the word of HASHEM — when it will no longer be called the Topheth and the Valley of the Son of Hinnom, but the Valley of Killing, for they will bury in Topheth until there is no more room.

Disappearance of joy

³³ The corpses of this people will become food for the birds of the heavens and the animals of the earth, and none will make them afraid. ³⁴ I will eliminate from the cities of Judah and from the streets of Jerusalem the sound of joy and the sound of gladness, the sound of groom and the sound of bride; for the land will become ruin.

8

Posthumous punishment

¹ A t that time — the word of HASHEM — they* will remove the bones of the kings of Judah, the bones of its leaders, the bones of the priests, the bones of the prophets and the bones of Jerusalem's inhabitants from their graves, ² and spread them out under the sun and the moon and all the heavenly legion, which they loved and which they worshiped and which they followed and which they sought out, and to which they prostrated themselves. They will not be gathered together nor buried; they will be like dung upon the face of the earth. ³ Yet death will be preferable to life for the surviving remnant of this evil family, in all the places of the survivors where I will have driven them — the word of HASHEM, Master of Legions.

⁴ You shall say unto them:

Thus said HASHEM: Will they fall out and not rise? If he would repent, would He not return [to them]? ⁵ Then why is this rebellious people of Jerusalem eternally rebellious? They hold fast to guile; they refuse to repent. ⁶ I have listened and heard. They speak untruth; no man relents of his evil, saying, 'What have I done?' They all follow their course like a horse racing headlong in war. ⁷ Even the stork in the heavens knows its [migration] seasons, and the turtledove, the swift, and the crane keep the time of their arrival; but My people do not know the law of HASHEM.

ח אֵיכָה תֹאמְרוּ חֲכָמִים אֲנַחְנוּ וְתוֹרַת יְהֹוָה אִתָּנוּ אָכֵן הִנֵּה לַשֶּׁקֶר עָשָׂה

ט עֵט שֶׁקֶר סֹפְרִים: הֹבִישׁוּ חֲכָמִים חַתּוּ וַיִּלָּכֵדוּ הִנֵּה בִדְבַר־יְהֹוָה מָאָסוּ

י וְחָכְמַת מֶה לָהֶם: לָכֵן אֶתֵּן אֶת־נְשֵׁיהֶם לַאֲחֵרִים שְׂדוֹתֵיהֶם לְיוֹרְשִׁים

כִּי מִקָּטֹן וְעַד־גָּדוֹל כֻּלֹּה בֹּצֵעַ בָּצַע מִנָּבִיא וְעַד־כֹּהֵן כֻּלֹּה עֹשֶׂה שָּׁקֶר:

יא וַיְרַפְּאוּ אֶת־שֶׁבֶר בַּת־עַמִּי עַל־נְקַלָּה לֵאמֹר שָׁלוֹם ׀ שָׁלוֹם וְאֵין שָׁלוֹם:

יב הֹבִישׁוּ כִּי תוֹעֵבָה עָשׂוּ גַּם־בּוֹשׁ לֹא־יֵבֹשׁוּ וְהִכָּלֵם לֹא יָדָעוּ לָכֵן יִפְּלוּ

יג בַנֹּפְלִים בְּעֵת פְּקֻדָּתָם יִכָּשְׁלוּ אָמַר יְהֹוָה:

◀ אָסֹף

אֲסִיפֵם נְאֻם־יְהֹוָה אֵין עֲנָבִים בַּגֶּפֶן וְאֵין תְּאֵנִים בַּתְּאֵנָה וְהֶעָלֶה

יד נָבֵל וָאֶתֵּן לָהֶם יַעַבְרוּם: עַל־מָה אֲנַחְנוּ יֹשְׁבִים הֵאָסְפוּ וְנָבוֹא אֶל־

עָרֵי הַמִּבְצָר וְנִדְּמָה־שָּׁם כִּי יְהֹוָה אֱלֹהֵינוּ הֲדִמָּנוּ וַיַּשְׁקֵנוּ מֵי־

טו רֹאשׁ כִּי חָטָאנוּ לַיהֹוָה: קַוֵּה לְשָׁלוֹם וְאֵין טוֹב לְעֵת מַרְפֵּה וְהִנֵּה

טז בְעָתָה: מִדָּן נִשְׁמַע נַחְרַת סוּסָיו מִקּוֹל מִצְהֲלוֹת אַבִּירָיו רָעֲשָׁה

יז כָל־הָאָרֶץ וַיָּבוֹאוּ וַיֹּאכְלוּ אֶרֶץ וּמְלוֹאָהּ עִיר וְיֹשְׁבֵי בָהּ: כִּי הִנְנִי

מְשַׁלֵּחַ בָּכֶם נְחָשִׁים צִפְעֹנִים אֲשֶׁר אֵין־לָהֶם לָחַשׁ וְנִשְּׁכוּ אֶתְכֶם נְאֻם־

יח-יט יְהֹוָה: מַבְלִיגִיתִי עֲלֵי יָגוֹן עָלַי לִבִּי דַוָּי: הִנֵּה־קוֹל

שַׁוְעַת בַּת־עַמִּי מֵאֶרֶץ מַרְחַקִּים הַיהֹוָה אֵין בְּצִיּוֹן אִם־מַלְכָּהּ אֵין בָּהּ

כ מַדּוּעַ הִכְעִסוּנִי בִּפְסִלֵיהֶם בְּהַבְלֵי נֵכָר: עָבַר קָצִיר כָּלָה קָיִץ וַאֲנַחְנוּ

כא לוֹא נוֹשָׁעְנוּ: עַל־שֶׁבֶר בַּת־עַמִּי הָשְׁבָּרְתִּי קָדַרְתִּי שַׁמָּה הֶחֱזִקָתְנִי:

כב הַצֳרִי אֵין בְּגִלְעָד אִם־רֹפֵא אֵין שָׁם כִּי מַדּוּעַ לֹא עָלְתָה אֲרֻכַת בַּת־

כג עַמִּי: מִי־יִתֵּן רֹאשִׁי מַיִם וְעֵינִי מְקוֹר דִּמְעָה וְאֶבְכֶּה יוֹמָם

וָלַיְלָה אֵת חַלְלֵי בַת־עַמִּי: מִי־יִתְּנֵנִי בַמִּדְבָּר מְלוֹן אֹרְחִים וְאֶעֶזְבָה

ט א

ב אֶת־עַמִּי וְאֵלְכָה מֵאִתָּם כִּי כֻלָּם מְנָאֲפִים עֲצֶרֶת בֹּגְדִים: וַיַּדְרְכוּ אֶת־

לְשׁוֹנָם קַשְׁתָּם שֶׁקֶר וְלֹא לֶאֱמוּנָה גָּבְרוּ בָאָרֶץ כִּי מֵרָעָה אֶל־רָעָה ׀

ג יָצָאוּ וְאֹתִי לֹא־יָדָעוּ נְאֻם־יְהֹוָה: אִישׁ מֵרֵעֵהוּ הִשָּׁמֵרוּ וְעַל־כָּל־אָח

ד אַל־תִּבְטָחוּ כִּי כָל־אָח עָקוֹב יַעְקֹב וְכָל־רֵעַ רָכִיל יַהֲלֹךְ: וְאִישׁ בְּרֵעֵהוּ

ה יְהָתֵלּוּ וֶאֱמֶת לֹא יְדַבֵּרוּ לִמְּדוּ לְשׁוֹנָם דַּבֶּר־שֶׁקֶר הַעֲוֵה נִלְאוּ:

לָכֵן

ו בְּתוֹךְ מִרְמָה בְּמִרְמָה מֵאֲנוּ דַעַת־אוֹתִי נְאֻם־יְהֹוָה: כֹּה אָמַר יְהֹוָה צְבָאוֹת הִנְנִי צוֹרְפָם וּבְחַנְתִּים כִּי־אֵיךְ אֶעֱשֶׂה מִפְּנֵי בַּת־

ז עַמִּי: חֵץ °שׁוֹחֵט [°שָׁחוּט ק] לְשׁוֹנָם מִרְמָה דִבֵּר בְּפִיו שָׁלוֹם אֶת־

ח רֵעֵהוּ יְדַבֵּר וּבְקִרְבּוֹ יָשִׂים אָרְבּוֹ: הַעַל־אֵלֶּה לֹא־אֶפְקָד־בָּם נְאֻם־יְהֹוָה

HAFTARAH
TISHAH
B'AV
SHACHARIS
8:13-9:23

ט

8:14. An imagined conversation among the besieged Israelites.

8:22. Are there no merits or acts of righteousness that can advocate favorably on behalf of my people?

9:2. They use their tongue as a weapon to entrap others.

9:6. I will punish them to refine them of their impurities, for I cannot let My people continue their unabated wrongdoing.

Lives
of lies

⁸ How can you say, 'We are wise, and HASHEM's Torah is with us'? Indeed, they made the quill for falsehood, the scribes are false. ⁹ The wise men are ashamed, they are distraught and trapped; behold, they have rejected the word of HASHEM, so what wisdom is in them? ¹⁰ Therefore, I will give their wives to others and their fields to usurpers, for from the simplest to the most distinguished, they all extort booty; from prophet to priest, all deal in falsehood. ¹¹ They relieved the [impending] disaster of the daughter of My people by making light [of it], saying, 'Peace! Peace!' But there is no peace. ¹² Were they ashamed that they had committed abominations? They are not ashamed, nor do they know how to feel humiliated! Therefore they will fall among the fallen; at the time I attend to them they will stumble, said HASHEM.

¹³ I shall utterly destroy them — the word of HASHEM; there will be no grapes on the vine and no figs on the fig-tree; the leaf will wither, and what I have given to them will pass away. ¹⁴ 'Why do we remain [here]?* Let us gather together and go to the fortified cities, there to be silent; for HASHEM, our God, has caused us to be silent and has given us poisonous water to drink, for we have sinned to HASHEM. ¹⁵ We may hope for peace, but there is no goodness; [we hope] for a time of healing, but behold, there is terror.'

¹⁶ From Dan is heard the snorting of his steeds; at the sound of his mighty ones' footsteps the whole land quakes. They will come and devour the land and its fullness, the city and those who dwell in it. ¹⁷ For behold, I am inciting against you venomous serpents that cannot be charmed, and they will sting you — the word of HASHEM.

¹⁸ I seek strength to withstand the sorrow, but my heart is sick within me. ¹⁹ Behold, the sound of the cry of the daughter of my people from a distant land: "Is HASHEM not in Zion, is its king not within it?"

[But He replies,] "Why have they angered Me with their idols, with their alien vanities?"

²⁰ The harvest has passed, the summer has ended, but we have not been saved.

Jeremiah
laments

²¹ Over the disaster of the daughter of my people have I been shattered; I am blackened; desolation has gripped me. ²² Is there no balm in Gilead?* Is there no healer there? Why has the health of the daughter of my people not recovered?

²³ If only my head would be water and my eyes a spring of tears, so that I could

9

cry all day and night for the slain of the daughter of my people! ¹ If only someone would give me a travelers' lodge in the wilderness, then I would forsake my people and leave them, for they are all adulterers, a band of traitors. ² They draw their tongues, [but] their bow is falsehood. *

Not for good faith have they grown strong in the land, for they go forth from evil to evil, but Me they do not know — the word of HASHEM. ³ Let each man beware of his fellow; do not trust any kin! For every kinsman acts perversely and every acquaintance mongers slander. ⁴ Each man mocks his fellow and they do not speak truth; they train their tongue to speak false-

Their deceit
breeds their
punishment

hood, striving to be iniquitous. ⁵ Your dwelling is amid deceit; because of their deceit they refuse to know Me — the word of HASHEM.

⁶ Therefore, thus said HASHEM, Master of Legions: Behold, I shall purge them and I shall test them — for what [else] can I do for the daughter of My people?* ⁷ Their tongue is like a drawn arrow, speaking deceit; with his mouth one speaks peace with his fellow, but inside of him he lays his ambush. ⁸ Shall I not punish them for these [things]? — the word of HASHEM.

ט אִם בְּגוֹי אֲשֶׁר־כָּזֶה לֹא תִתְנַקֵּם נַפְשִׁי:
הֶהָרִים אֶשָּׂא בְכִי וָנֶהִי וְעַל־נְאוֹת מִדְבָּר קִינָה כִּי נִצְּתוּ מִבְּלִי־אִישׁ עֹבֵר
י וְלֹא שָׁמְעוּ קוֹל מִקְנֶה מֵעוֹף הַשָּׁמַיִם וְעַד־בְּהֵמָה נָדְדוּ הָלָכוּ: וְנָתַתִּי אֶת־
יְרוּשָׁלַ͏ִם לְגַלִּים מְעוֹן תַּנִּים וְאֶת־עָרֵי יְהוּדָה אֶתֵּן שְׁמָמָה מִבְּלִי
יא יוֹשֵׁב: מִי־הָאִישׁ הֶחָכָם וְיָבֵן אֶת־זֹאת וַאֲשֶׁר דִּבֶּר
פִּי־יְהוָה אֵלָיו וְיַגִּדָהּ עַל־מָה אָבְדָה הָאָרֶץ נִצְּתָה כַמִּדְבָּר מִבְּלִי
יב עֹבֵר: וַיֹּאמֶר יְהוָה עַל־עָזְבָם אֶת־תּוֹרָתִי אֲשֶׁר נָתַתִּי
יג לִפְנֵיהֶם וְלֹא־שָׁמְעוּ בְקוֹלִי וְלֹא־הָלְכוּ בָהּ: וַיֵּלְכוּ אַחֲרֵי שְׁרִרוּת לִבָּם
יד וְאַחֲרֵי הַבְּעָלִים אֲשֶׁר לִמְּדוּם אֲבוֹתָם: לָכֵן כֹּה־אָמַר
יהוָה צְבָאוֹת אֱלֹהֵי יִשְׂרָאֵל הִנְנִי מַאֲכִילָם אֶת־הָעָם הַזֶּה לַעֲנָה
טו וְהִשְׁקִיתִים מֵי־רֹאשׁ: וַהֲפִצוֹתִים בַּגּוֹיִם אֲשֶׁר לֹא יָדְעוּ הֵמָּה וַאֲבוֹתָם
טז וְשִׁלַּחְתִּי אַחֲרֵיהֶם אֶת־הַחֶרֶב עַד כַּלּוֹתִי אוֹתָם: כֹּה
אָמַר יְהוָה צְבָאוֹת הִתְבּוֹנְנוּ וְקִרְאוּ לַמְקוֹנְנוֹת וּתְבוֹאֶינָה וְאֶל־הַחֲכָמוֹת
יז שִׁלְחוּ וְתָבוֹאנָה: וּתְמַהֵרְנָה וְתִשֶּׂנָה עָלֵינוּ נֶהִי וְתֵרַדְנָה עֵינֵינוּ דִּמְעָה
יח וְעַפְעַפֵּינוּ יִזְּלוּ־מָיִם: כִּי קוֹל נְהִי נִשְׁמַע מִצִּיּוֹן אֵיךְ שֻׁדָּדְנוּ בֹּשְׁנוּ מְאֹד כִּי־
יט עָזַבְנוּ אָרֶץ כִּי הִשְׁלִיכוּ מִשְׁכְּנוֹתֵינוּ: כִּי־שְׁמַעְנָה
נָשִׁים דְּבַר־יְהוָה וְתִקַּח אָזְנְכֶם דְּבַר־פִּיו וְלַמֵּדְנָה בְנוֹתֵיכֶם נֶהִי וְאִשָּׁה
כ רְעוּתָהּ קִינָה: כִּי־עָלָה מָוֶת בְּחַלּוֹנֵינוּ בָּא בְּאַרְמְנוֹתֵינוּ לְהַכְרִית עוֹלָל
כא מִחוּץ בַּחוּרִים מֵרְחֹבוֹת: דַּבֵּר כֹּה נְאֻם־יְהוָה וְנָפְלָה נִבְלַת הָאָדָם כְּדֹמֶן
כב עַל־פְּנֵי הַשָּׂדֶה וּכְעָמִיר מֵאַחֲרֵי הַקֹּצֵר וְאֵין מְאַסֵּף: כֹּה ו

Haftaras
Tzav
continues
here:
9:22-23

אָמַר יְהוָה אַל־יִתְהַלֵּל חָכָם בְּחָכְמָתוֹ וְאַל־יִתְהַלֵּל הַגִּבּוֹר בִּגְבוּרָתוֹ
כג אַל־יִתְהַלֵּל עָשִׁיר בְּעָשְׁרוֹ: כִּי אִם־בְּזֹאת יִתְהַלֵּל הַמִּתְהַלֵּל הַשְׂכֵּל וְיָדֹעַ
אוֹתִי כִּי אֲנִי יְהוָה עֹשֶׂה חֶסֶד מִשְׁפָּט וּצְדָקָה בָּאָרֶץ כִּי־בְאֵלֶּה חָפַצְתִּי
כד נְאֻם־יְהוָה: הִנֵּה יָמִים בָּאִים נְאֻם־יְהוָה וּפָקַדְתִּי עַל־
כה כָּל־מוּל בְּעָרְלָה: עַל־מִצְרַיִם וְעַל־יְהוּדָה וְעַל־אֱדוֹם וְעַל־בְּנֵי עַמּוֹן
וְעַל־מוֹאָב וְעַל כָּל־קְצוּצֵי פֵאָה הַיֹּשְׁבִים בַּמִּדְבָּר כִּי כָל־הַגּוֹיִם עֲרֵלִים
א וְכָל־בֵּית יִשְׂרָאֵל עַרְלֵי־לֵב: שִׁמְעוּ אֶת־הַדָּבָר אֲשֶׁר
ב דִּבֶּר יְהוָה עֲלֵיכֶם בֵּית יִשְׂרָאֵל: כֹּה ו אָמַר יְהוָה אֶל־דֶּרֶךְ הַגּוֹיִם אַל־
ג תִּלְמָדוּ וּמֵאֹתוֹת הַשָּׁמַיִם אַל־תֵּחָתּוּ כִּי־יֵחַתּוּ הַגּוֹיִם מֵהֵמָּה: כִּי־חֻקּוֹת

9:16. Contemplate your dire situation and you will realize that it is time to call the professional dirge-women, who would cry and wail at funerals.

9:23. To know God is to imitate His ways by dealing with others with kindness, justice and righteousness, for such is "My desire" (*Radak*).

9:25. The circumcised Jews will be punished along with all their uncircumcised neighbors, because the physical sign of the covenant of circumcision is not enough — a Jew must be spiritually distinct as well. But the Jews to whom Jeremiah was speaking left their hearts uncircumcised — i.e., unpurified.

From a nation such as this, shall My soul not exact vengeance?

⁹ For the mountains I will raise [My voice] in weeping and wailing, and for the pastures of the wilderness a dirge, for they are parched, without a person passing by; and they will not hear the sound of cattle; from bird of heaven to animal, they have wandered off and gone. ¹⁰ I shall make Jerusalem heaps of rubble, a serpent's lair; the cities of Judah I shall make a wasteland, without inhabitant.

Exile . . .

¹¹ Who is the wise man who will understand this? Who is he to whom the mouth of HASHEM speaks, that he may explain this? 'For what reason did the land perish and become parched like the desert, without a passerby?'

¹² But HASHEM has said: Because of their forsaking My Torah that I put before them; moreover, they did not heed My voice nor follow it. ¹³ They followed the vision of their heart and [they followed] the Baalim, as their fathers taught them.

. . . for forsaking the Torah

¹⁴ Therefore, thus said HASHEM, Master of Legions, God of Israel: Behold, I am feeding this people wormwood and giving them poisonous water to drink. ¹⁵ I shall scatter them among nations that neither they nor their fathers have known; I shall send the sword after them until I annihilate them.

¹⁶ Thus said HASHEM, Master of Legions: Contemplate;* call upon the dirge-women to come, and send for the wise women to come. ¹⁷ Let them come quickly and raise up a lament for us; let our eyes run with tears and our eyelids flow with water, ¹⁸ for the sound of wailing is heard [coming] from Zion: 'How we have been plundered! How greatly we have been shamed, for we have forsaken the land, for our own dwellings have cast us out!'

¹⁹ Therefore, hearken, O women, to the word of HASHEM and let your ear absorb the word of His mouth; teach a lament to your daughters, each woman a dirge to her friend. ²⁰ For death has ascended through our windows, it has entered our palaces, to cut down the infant from the street, young men from the plazas.

²¹ Speak: Thus is the word of HASHEM: Human corpses will fall like dung on the open field, and like a sheaf behind the harvester, but there is none to gather.

²² Thus said HASHEM: Let not the wise man glorify himself with his wisdom, and let not the strong man glorify himself with his strength, let not the rich man glorify himself with his wealth. ²³ For only with this may one glorify himself — contemplating and knowing Me, for I am HASHEM Who does kindness, justice and righteousness in the land, for in these is My desire* — the word of HASHEM.

Idle glory

²⁴ Behold, days are coming — the word of HASHEM — when I shall deal with everyone who is circumcised for [his] uncircumcision: ²⁵ with Egypt, with Judah, with Edom, with the Children of Ammon and with Moab, and with all those who dwell in the remotest corners of the wilderness; for all the nations are uncircumcised, and the House of Israel is of uncircumcised heart.*

10 ¹ Hear the word that HASHEM has spoken concerning you, O House of Israel. ² Thus said HASHEM:

Do not learn from the way of the nations; do not be frightened by the signs of the heavens, though the nations are frightened by them. ³ For the practices

Foolishness of idolatry

ד הָעַמִּים הֶבֶל הוּא כִּי־עֵץ מִיַּעַר כְּרָתוֹ מַעֲשֵׂה יְדֵי־חָרָשׁ בַּמַּעֲצָד: בְּכֶסֶף

ה וּבְזָהָב יְיַפֵּהוּ בְּמַסְמְרוֹת וּבְמַקָּבוֹת יְחַזְּקוּם וְלוֹא יָפִיק: כְּתֹמֶר מִקְשָׁה הֵמָּה וְלֹא יְדַבֵּרוּ נָשׂוֹא יִנָּשׂוּא כִּי לֹא יִצְעָדוּ אַל־תִּירְאוּ מֵהֶם כִּי־לֹא

ו יָרֵעוּ וְגַם־הֵיטֵיב אֵין אוֹתָם: מֵאֵין כָּמוֹךָ יְהוָה גָּדוֹל אַתָּה

ז וְגָדוֹל שִׁמְךָ בִּגְבוּרָה: מִי לֹא יִרָאֲךָ מֶלֶךְ הַגּוֹיִם כִּי לְךָ יָאָתָה כִּי בְכָל־

ח חַכְמֵי הַגּוֹיִם וּבְכָל־מַלְכוּתָם מֵאֵין כָּמוֹךָ: וּבְאַחַת יִבְעֲרוּ וְיִכְסָלוּ מוּסַר

ט הֲבָלִים עֵץ הוּא: כֶּסֶף מְרֻקָּע מִתַּרְשִׁישׁ יוּבָא וְזָהָב מֵאוּפָז מַעֲשֵׂה חָרָשׁ

י וִידֵי צוֹרֵף תְּכֵלֶת וְאַרְגָּמָן לְבוּשָׁם מַעֲשֵׂה חֲכָמִים כֻּלָּם: וַיהוָה אֱלֹהִים אֱמֶת הוּא־אֱלֹהִים חַיִּים וּמֶלֶךְ עוֹלָם מִקִּצְפּוֹ תִּרְעַשׁ הָאָרֶץ וְלֹא־יָכִלוּ

יא גוֹיִם זַעְמוֹ:   כִּדְנָה תֵּאמְרוּן לְהוֹם אֱלָהַיָּא דִּי־שְׁמַיָּא וְאַרְקָא

יב לָא עֲבַדוּ יֵאבַדוּ מֵאַרְעָא וּמִן־תְּחוֹת שְׁמַיָּא אֵלֶּה: עֹשֵׂה אֶרֶץ בְּכֹחוֹ מֵכִין תֵּבֵל בְּחָכְמָתוֹ וּבִתְבוּנָתוֹ נָטָה שָׁמָיִם: לְקוֹל תִּתּוֹ הֲמוֹן

יג מַיִם בַּשָּׁמַיִם וַיַּעֲלֶה נְשִׂאִים מִקְצֵה ״אֶרֶץ ״הָאָרֶץ ק׳ [בְּרָקִים לַמָּטָר

יד עָשָׂה וַיּוֹצֵא רוּחַ מֵאֹצְרֹתָיו: נִבְעַר כָּל־אָדָם מִדַּעַת הֹבִישׁ כָּל־צוֹרֵף

טו מִפֶּסֶל כִּי שֶׁקֶר נִסְכּוֹ וְלֹא־רוּחַ בָּם: הֶבֶל הֵמָּה מַעֲשֵׂה תַּעְתֻּעִים בְּעֵת

טז פְּקֻדָּתָם יֹאבֵדוּ: לֹא־כְאֵלֶּה חֵלֶק יַעֲקֹב כִּי־יוֹצֵר הַכֹּל הוּא וְיִשְׂרָאֵל שֵׁבֶט

יז נַחֲלָתוֹ יְהוָה צְבָאוֹת שְׁמוֹ:   אִסְפִּי מֵאֶרֶץ כִּנְעָתֵךְ ״יֹשַׁבְתִּי

יח ״יֹשֶׁבֶת ק׳ [בַּמָּצוֹר: כִּי־כֹה אָמַר יְהֹוָה הִנְנִי קוֹלֵעַ אֶת־יוֹשְׁבֵי

יט הָאָרֶץ בַּפַּעַם הַזֹּאת וַהֲצֵרוֹתִי לָהֶם לְמַעַן יִמְצָאוּ: אוֹי לִי עַל־

כ שִׁבְרִי נַחְלָה מַכָּתִי וַאֲנִי אָמַרְתִּי אַךְ זֶה חֳלִי וְאֶשָּׂאֶנּוּ: אָהֳלִי שֻׁדָּד וְכָל־

כא מֵיתָרַי נִתָּקוּ בָּנַי יְצָאֻנִי וְאֵינָם אֵין־נֹטֶה עוֹד אָהֳלִי וּמֵקִים יְרִיעוֹתָי: כִּי נִבְעֲרוּ הָרֹעִים וְאֶת־יְהוָה לֹא דָרָשׁוּ עַל־כֵּן לֹא הִשְׂכִּילוּ וְכָל־מַרְעִיתָם

כב נָפוֹצָה: קוֹל שְׁמוּעָה הִנֵּה בָאָה וְרַעַשׁ גָּדוֹל מֵאֶרֶץ צָפוֹן לָשׂוּם

כג אֶת־עָרֵי יְהוּדָה שְׁמָמָה מְעוֹן תַּנִּים: יָדַעְתִּי יְהוָה כִּי לֹא לָאָדָם דַּרְכּוֹ

כד לֹא־לְאִישׁ הֹלֵךְ וְהָכִין אֶת־צַעֲדוֹ: יַסְּרֵנִי יְהוָה אַךְ־בְּמִשְׁפָּט אַל־בְּאַפְּךָ

כה פֶּן־תַּמְעִטֵנִי: שְׁפֹךְ חֲמָתְךָ עַל־הַגּוֹיִם אֲשֶׁר לֹא־יְדָעוּךָ וְעַל מִשְׁפָּחוֹת אֲשֶׁר בְּשִׁמְךָ לֹא קָרָאוּ כִּי־אָכְלוּ אֶת־יַעֲקֹב וַאֲכָלֻהוּ וַיְכַלֻּהוּ וְאֶת־נָוֵהוּ

יא א הֵשַׁמּוּ:   הַדָּבָר אֲשֶׁר הָיָה אֶל־יִרְמְיָהוּ מֵאֵת יְהוָה לֵאמֹר:

ב שִׁמְעוּ אֶת־דִּבְרֵי הַבְּרִית הַזֹּאת וְדִבַּרְתֶּם אֶל־אִישׁ יְהוּדָה וְעַל־יֹשְׁבֵי

10:5. *Kara* translates: like a scarecrow.

10:9. The silver and gold idols are clothed in precious royal garments.

10:11. This (vv. 11-16) is the text of a letter Jeremiah sent to the Jewish exiles in Babylonia, telling them what to answer the captors who would try to persuade them to worship their heathen gods (*Targum*).

The first verse of the letter is written in Aramaic, the language of Babylonia, to indicate that the re-sponse must be understood clearly by the oppressors (*Radak*).

10:22. I.e., news of the impending Babylonian invasion from the North, which will devastate the land.

10:23-24. Jeremiah acknowledges that Nebuchadnezzar's siege and destruction of Jerusalem must have been Divinely ordained (*Rashi*), and that man cannot control his fate, but he pleads that judgment be tempered with mercy and that Israel be spared.

of the nations are foolish; [for one takes] wood that he cut down from the forest, fashioned by an artisan with an adze, ⁴ embellishes it with silver and gold, fastens it with nails and with hammers so that it does not come apart. ⁵ They are like a sculpted palm tree* — they do not speak; they are carried about for they cannot walk. Do not fear them; for they can do no harm, nor can they do good.

Jeremiah speaks God's praises

⁶ There is none like You, O HASHEM! You are great and Your Name is great in might. ⁷ Who would not fear You, O King of the nations? For [kingship] befits You; for among all the wise men of the nations and in all their kingdoms [it is known that] there is none like You. ⁸ They are uniformly foolish and stupid, the vain [idols] for which they are punished; it is [but] wood. ⁹ Beaten silver is imported from Tarshish and gold from Uphaz, the work of an artisan and the hands of a goldsmith; turquoise and purple are their raiment, * all of them the work of skilled craftsmen. ¹⁰ But HASHEM, God, is True; He is the Living God and the Eternal King; from His anger the earth quakes, and nations cannot bear His wrath.

¹¹ Tell them this: *

Only the Creator is God

The gods who did not make the heavens and the earth shall vanish from the earth and from under these heavens! ¹² [But HASHEM] made the earth with His might, He established the world with His wisdom, and with His understanding spread out the heavens. ¹³ At the sound of His placement of a multitude of water in the heavens, He raised clouds from the end of the earth; He makes lightning bolts for the rain and brings forth wind from His treasuries. ¹⁴ Every man is bereft of wisdom, every smith is shamed by his graven image, for his molten idol is false, and there is no life in them. ¹⁵ They are vanity, the work of deception; when they are dealt with, they shall perish. ¹⁶ Unlike these is the Portion of Jacob, for He is the Molder of everything, and Israel is the tribe that is His heritage; His Name is HASHEM, Master of Legions.

¹⁷ Gather your possessions from the land, you who live under siege. ¹⁸ For thus said HASHEM:

Behold, this time I am slinging out the dwellers of the land, and I shall beleaguer them so that they may find [their just punishment].

Jerusalem's lament

¹⁹ "Woe is me for my disaster; my wound is acute. I said [to myself], 'It is but an ailment, I can bear it' — ²⁰ but my tent has been plundered and all my cords have been snapped. My sons have left me and are no more; there is no longer anyone to pitch my tent, to set up my curtains. ²¹ For the shepherds have been foolish and did not seek out HASHEM; therefore they did not succeed and all their flock was dispersed. ²² The news of a report — behold, it comes, and a resounding noise from a land of the North, * which will make the cities of Judah a wasteland, a serpents' lair."

²³ I know, HASHEM, that a man's path is not his own [doing]; nor can a man who walks direct his own steps. ²⁴ Chastise me, HASHEM, but with justice, not with Your anger, lest You diminish me. * ²⁵ Pour out Your wrath upon the nations that know You not and upon the families that do not call out in Your Name, for they have consumed Jacob — they have consumed him and annihilated him — and have devastated his abode.

11 ¹ The word that came to Jeremiah from HASHEM, saying: ² "Hear the words of this covenant, and speak them to the men of Judah and to the inhabitants

ג יְרוּשָׁלָ֑ם: וְאָמַרְתָּ֣ אֲלֵיהֶ֗ם כֹּֽה־אָמַ֤ר יהוה֙ אֱלֹהֵ֣י יִשְׂרָאֵ֔ל אָר֣וּר הָאִ֔ישׁ

ד אֲשֶׁר֙ לֹ֣א יִשְׁמַ֔ע אֶת־דִּבְרֵ֖י הַבְּרִ֣ית הַזֹּֽאת: אֲשֶׁ֣ר צִוִּ֣יתִי אֶת־אֲבֽוֹתֵיכֶ֗ם

בְּי֨וֹם הוֹצִיאִֽי־אוֹתָ֜ם מֵאֶֽרֶץ־מִצְרַ֘יִם֮ מִכּ֣וּר הַבַּרְזֶל֒ לֵאמֹ֔ר שִׁמְע֣וּ בְקוֹלִ֗י

וַעֲשִׂיתֶ֣ם אוֹתָ֔ם כְּכֹ֥ל אֲשֶׁר־אֲצַוֶּ֖ה אֶתְכֶ֑ם וִהְיִ֤יתֶם לִי֙ לְעָ֔ם וְאָ֣נֹכִ֔י אֶהְיֶ֥ה

ה לָכֶ֖ם לֵֽאלֹהִֽים: לְמַ֩עַן֩ הָקִ֨ים אֶת־הַשְּׁבוּעָ֜ה אֲשֶׁר־נִשְׁבַּ֣עְתִּי לַֽאֲבֽוֹתֵיכֶ֗ם

לָתֵ֤ת לָהֶם֙ אֶ֣רֶץ זָבַ֥ת חָלָ֖ב וּדְבַ֑שׁ כַּיּ֣וֹם הַזֶּ֑ה וָאַ֥עַן וָאֹמַ֖ר אָמֵ֥ן |

ו יהוֽה: וַיֹּ֤אמֶר יהוה֙ אֵלַ֔י קְרָ֣א אֶת־כָּל־הַדְּבָרִ֥ים הָאֵ֖לֶּה בְּעָרֵ֣י

יְהוּדָ֔ה וּבְחֻצ֖וֹת יְרֽוּשָׁלַ֣ם לֵאמֹ֑ר שִׁמְע֗וּ אֶת־דִּבְרֵי֙ הַבְּרִ֣ית הַזֹּ֔את וַעֲשִׂיתֶ֖ם

ז אוֹתָֽם: כִּי֩ הָעֵ֨ד הַעִדֹ֜תִי בַּֽאֲבֽוֹתֵיכֶ֗ם בְּיוֹם֩ הַעֲלוֹתִ֨י אוֹתָ֜ם מֵאֶ֣רֶץ מִצְרַ֗יִם

ח עַד־הַיּ֤וֹם הַזֶּה֙ הַשְׁכֵּ֣ם וְהָעֵ֔ד לֵאמֹ֖ר שִׁמְע֣וּ בְּקוֹלִֽי: וְלֹ֤א שָֽׁמְעוּ֙ וְלֹֽא־הִטּ֣וּ

אֶת־אָזְנָ֔ם וַיֵּ֣לְכ֔וּ אִ֕ישׁ בִּשְׁרִיר֖וּת לִבָּ֣ם הָרָ֑ע וָאָבִ֤יא עֲלֵיהֶם֙ אֶֽת־כָּל־דִּבְרֵ֤י

ט הַבְּרִֽית־הַזֹּ֔את אֲשֶׁר־צִוִּ֥יתִי לַעֲשׂ֖וֹת וְלֹ֥א עָשֽׂוּ:   וַיֹּ֤אמֶר

י יהוה֙ אֵלַ֔י נִמְצָא־קֶ֖שֶׁר בְּאִ֣ישׁ יְהוּדָ֑ה וּבְיֹֽשְׁבֵ֖י יְרֽוּשָׁלָֽ͏ִם: שָׁ֩בוּ֩ עַל־עֲוֺנֹ֨ת

אֲבוֹתָ֜ם הָרִֽאשֹׁנִ֗ים אֲשֶׁ֤ר מֵֽאֲנוּ֙ לִשְׁמ֣וֹעַ אֶת־דְּבָרַ֔י וְהֵ֣מָּה הָֽלְכ֗וּ אַחֲרֵ֛י

אֱלֹהִ֥ים אֲחֵרִ֖ים לְעָבְדָ֑ם הֵפֵ֤רוּ בֵּֽית־יִשְׂרָאֵל֙ וּבֵ֣ית יְהוּדָ֔ה אֶת־בְּרִיתִ֕י

יא אֲשֶׁ֥ר כָּרַ֖תִּי אֶת־אֲבוֹתָֽם: לָכֵ֗ן כֹּ֤ה אָמַ֤ר יהוה֙ הִנְנִ֨י מֵבִ֤יא

אֲלֵיהֶם֙ רָעָ֔ה אֲשֶׁ֥ר לֹֽא־יוּכְל֖וּ לָצֵ֣את מִמֶּ֑נָּה וְזָעֲק֣וּ אֵלַ֔י וְלֹ֥א אֶשְׁמַ֖ע

יב אֲלֵיהֶֽם: וְהָֽלְכ֞וּ עָרֵ֣י יְהוּדָ֗ה וְיֹשְׁבֵי֙ יְר֣וּשָׁלַ֔͏ִם וְזָֽעֲקוּ֙ אֶל־הָ֣אֱלֹהִ֔ים אֲשֶׁ֥ר הֵ֖ם

מְקַטְּרִ֣ים לָהֶ֑ם וְהוֹשֵׁ֛עַ לֹֽא־יוֹשִׁ֥יעוּ לָהֶ֖ם בְּעֵ֥ת רָעָתָֽם: כִּ֚י מִסְפַּ֣ר עָרֶ֔יךָ

יג הָי֥וּ אֱלֹהֶ֖יךָ יְהוּדָ֑ה וּמִסְפַּ֞ר חֻצ֣וֹת יְרֽוּשָׁלַ֗͏ִם שַׂמְתֶּ֤ם מִזְבְּחוֹת֙ לַבֹּ֔שֶׁת

מִזְבְּח֖וֹת לְקַטֵּ֥ר לַבָּֽעַל: וְאַתָּ֗ה אַל־תִּתְפַּלֵּל֙ בְּעַד־הָעָ֣ם הַזֶּ֔ה

יד וְאַל־תִּשָּׂ֧א בַעֲדָ֛ם רִנָּ֣ה וּתְפִלָּ֑ה כִּ֣י אֵינֶ֣נִּי שֹׁמֵ֗עַ בְּעֵ֛ת קָרְאָ֥ם אֵלַ֖י בְּעַ֥ד

טו רָעָתָֽם: מֶ֣ה לִֽידִידִ֞י בְּבֵיתִ֗י עֲשׂוֹתָ֤הּ הַֽמְזִמָּ֙תָה֙ הָרַבִּ֔ים וּבְשַׂר־

טז קֹ֖דֶשׁ יַעַבְר֣וּ מֵֽעָלָ֑יִךְ כִּ֥י רָעָתֵ֖כִי אָ֥ז תַּֽעֲלֹֽזִי: זַ֤יִת רַֽעֲנָן֙ יְפֵ֣ה פְרִי־תֹ֔אַר קָרָ֥א

יהוה֙ שְׁמֵ֔ךְ לְק֣וֹל | הֲמוּלָּ֣ה גְדֹלָ֗ה הִצִּ֥ית אֵשׁ֙ עָלֶ֔יהָ וְרָע֖וּ דָּלִיּוֹתָֽיו: וַֽיהֹוָ֧ה

יז צְבָא֛וֹת הַנּוֹטֵ֥עַ אוֹתָ֖ךְ דִּבֶּ֣ר עָלַ֣יִךְ רָעָ֑ה בִּ֠גְלַ֠ל רָעַ֨ת בֵּֽית־יִשְׂרָאֵ֜ל וּבֵ֣ית

יְהוּדָ֗ה אֲשֶׁ֨ר עָשׂ֤וּ לָהֶם֙ לְהַכְעִסֵ֔נִי לְקַטֵּ֖ר לַבָּֽעַל: וַֽיהֹוָ֥ה

יח הֽוֹדִיעַ֖נִי וָֽאֵדָ֑עָה אָ֖ז הִרְאִיתַ֥נִי מַעַלְלֵיהֶֽם: וַאֲנִ֕י כְּכֶ֥בֶשׂ אַלּ֖וּף יוּבַ֣ל

יט לִטְב֑וֹחַ וְלֹֽא־יָדַ֗עְתִּי כִּֽי־עָלַ֞י | חָֽשְׁב֣וּ מַחֲשָׁב֗וֹת נַשְׁחִ֤יתָה עֵץ֙ בְּלַחְמ֔וֹ

11:8. Whenever Jews sinned against God, He brought upon them whatever punishments they deserved, as related in the Admonition of *Deuteronomy* (Ch. 28). Now, too, Jeremiah was to warn them that their failure to obey the covenant would result in punishment; but this time, commensurate with the degree of their sins, the retribution would be more severe.

11:10. *Radak* suggests that this prophecy was spoken after the death of Josiah, when the effects of that king's immense spiritual revival quickly dissipated and the spiritual state of the people reverted to its previous sorry state (see *II Kings* Ch. 23).

11:15. God says, "Israel, My formerly cherished nation, should stop coming to My Temple, for even the leaders among her exult in their sinful schemes, going so far as to ignore the laws of circumcision which make their flesh sacred." Then He said to the people, "When you do evil . . ." (*Rashi*).

of Jerusalem. ³ *Say to them:*

Obey the
covenant . . .

Thus said HASHEM, God of Israel: Cursed is the man who will not listen to the words of this covenant ⁴ that I commanded your forefathers on the day I took them out from the land of Egypt, from the iron crucible, saying: Listen to My voice and fulfill [the commandments], according to all that I command you, so that you will be a people for Me and I will be a God for you, ⁵ in order to fulfill the oath that I swore to your forefathers to give them a land flowing with milk and honey, as this very day.

And I responded, saying, "Amen, HASHEM."

⁶ HASHEM then said to me, "Proclaim all these words in the cities of Judah and in the streets of Jerusalem, saying:

Hear the words of this covenant and fulfill them. ⁷ For I have repeatedly warned your forefathers on the day I brought them up from the land of Egypt, and until this very day, arising early and warning [them], saying: 'Listen to My voice!' ⁸ But they did not listen and did not incline their ear,

. . . or it
will turn
against you

and each man went after the vision of his evil heart; so I brought upon them all the words of this covenant* that I had commanded them to fulfill, but they did not fulfill."

⁹ HASHEM said to me, "A conspiracy can be found among the people of Judah and the inhabitants of Jerusalem. ¹⁰ They reverted to the sins of their forefathers,* the earlier ones, who refused to listen to My words, and they followed the gods of others to worship them; the House of Israel and the House of Judah have abrogated My covenant that I sealed with their forefathers.

¹¹ Therefore, thus said HASHEM: Behold, I bring against them an evil from which they will not be able to escape; and they will cry out to Me, but I will not listen to them. ¹² The [inhabitants of the] cities of Judah and the inhabitants of Jerusalem will then go and cry out to the gods to whom they burn offerings, but they will not save them at all at the time of their misfortune. ¹³ For the number of your cities was [the number of] your gods, O Judah, and like the number of streets in Jerusalem have you made altars to the shameful idol — altars to sacrifice to the Baal.

¹⁴ As for you [Jeremiah]: Do not pray for this people, and do not raise [your voice] in outcry and prayer on their behalf, for I do not listen when they call to Me because of their misfortune.

The broken
olive tree

¹⁵ What has My beloved [nation] to do in My Temple, while she — [her] great ones — carries out her evil schemes, while the sacred flesh is passed away from you?* When you do evil, only then do you rejoice! ¹⁶ HASHEM had called your name, 'A leafy olive tree, beautiful with shapely fruit'; [but now,] amid the sound of a great commotion He has set fire to it and its branches were broken. ¹⁷ And HASHEM, Master of Legions, the One Who planted you, has declared evil upon you, because of the evil of the House of Israel and the House of Judah, which they committed in order to anger Me, by sacrificing to the Baal."

¹⁸ HASHEM informed me, so I would know — then You showed me their deeds.

Threatened
prophet

¹⁹ I am like a choice sheep led to the slaughter; I did not know that they devised schemes against me: "Let us destroy [him by placing] tree-poison in his food

כ וַֽיהוָ֣ה צְבָא֗וֹת · · · · · · · · · · · · · · וְנִכְרְתֶ֤נּוּ מֵאֶ֙רֶץ֙ חַיִּ֔ים וּשְׁמ֖וֹ לֹֽא־יִזָּכֵ֥ר עֽוֹד:
שֹׁפֵ֣ט צֶ֔דֶק בֹּחֵ֥ן כְּלָי֖וֹת וָלֵ֑ב אֶרְאֶ֤ה נִקְמָֽתְךָ֙ מֵהֶ֔ם כִּ֥י אֵלֶ֖יךָ גִּלִּ֥יתִי אֶת־
כא רִיבִֽי: · · · · · · · · לָכֵ֗ן כֹּֽה־אָמַ֤ר יְהוָה֙ עַל־אַנְשֵׁ֣י עֲנָת֔וֹת הַֽמְבַקְשִׁ֖ים אֶת־
כב נַפְשְׁךָ֖ לֵאמֹ֑ר לֹ֤א תִנָּבֵא֙ בְּשֵׁ֣ם יְהוָ֔ה וְלֹ֥א תָמ֖וּת בְּיָדֵֽנוּ: · · · · · · · · לָכֵ֗ן כֹּ֤ה
אָמַר֙ יְהוָ֣ה צְבָא֔וֹת הִנְנִ֥י פֹקֵ֖ד עֲלֵיהֶ֑ם הַבַּֽחוּרִ֞ים יָמֻ֣תוּ בַחֶ֗רֶב בְּנֵיהֶ֤ם
כג וּבְנֽוֹתֵיהֶם֙ יָמֻ֣תוּ בָּֽרָעָֽב: וּשְׁאֵרִ֕ית לֹ֥א תִֽהְיֶ֖ה לָהֶ֑ם כִּֽי־אָבִ֥יא רָעָ֛ה אֶל־
אַנְשֵׁ֥י עֲנָת֖וֹת שְׁנַ֥ת פְּקֻדָּתָֽם: · · · · צַדִּ֤יק אַתָּה֙ יְהוָ֔ה כִּ֥י אָרִ֖יב אֵלֶ֑יךָ **יב** א
אַ֤ךְ מִשְׁפָּטִים֙ אֲדַבֵּ֣ר אוֹתָ֔ךְ מַדּ֗וּעַ דֶּ֤רֶךְ רְשָׁעִים֙ צָלֵ֔חָה שָׁל֖וּ כָּל־בֹּ֥גְדֵי בָֽגֶד:
ב נְטַעְתָּם֙ גַּם־שֹׁרָ֔שׁוּ יֵֽלְכ֖וּ גַּם־עָ֣שׂוּ פֶ֑רִי קָר֤וֹב אַתָּה֙ בְּפִיהֶ֔ם וְרָח֖וֹק
ג מִכִּלְיֽוֹתֵיהֶֽם: וְאַתָּ֤ה יְהוָה֙ יְדַעְתָּ֔נִי תִּרְאֵ֕נִי וּבָחַנְתָּ֥ לִבִּ֖י אִתָּ֑ךְ הַתִּקֵ֣ם כְּצֹ֔אן
ד לְטִבְחָ֔ה וְהַקְדִּשֵׁ֖ם לְי֥וֹם הֲרֵגָֽה: · · · · · עַד־מָתַי֙ תֶּאֱבַ֣ל הָאָ֔רֶץ וְעֵ֥שֶׂב
כָּל־הַשָּׂדֶ֖ה יִיבָ֑שׁ מֵרָעַ֣ת יֹֽשְׁבֵי־בָ֗הּ סָפְתָ֤ה בְהֵמוֹת֙ וָע֔וֹף כִּ֣י אָֽמְר֔וּ לֹ֥א יִרְאֶ֖ה
ה אֶת־אַֽחֲרִיתֵֽנוּ: כִּ֣י אֶת־רַגְלִ֤ים ׀ רַ֗צְתָּה וַיַּלְא֔וּךָ וְאֵ֥יךְ תְּתַֽחֲרֶ֖ה אֶת־הַסּוּסִ֑ים
ו וּבְאֶ֤רֶץ שָׁלוֹם֙ אַתָּ֣ה בוֹטֵ֔חַ וְאֵ֥יךְ תַּֽעֲשֶׂ֖ה בִּגְא֣וֹן הַיַּרְדֵּֽן: כִּ֧י גַם־אַחֶ֣יךָ וּבֵֽית־
אָבִ֗יךָ גַּם־הֵ֙מָּה֙ בָּ֣גְדוּ בָ֔ךְ גַּם־הֵ֖מָּה קָֽרְא֣וּ אַֽחֲרֶ֖יךָ מָלֵ֑א אַל־תַּֽאֲמֵ֣ן בָּ֔ם כִּֽי־
ז יְדַבְּר֥וּ אֵלֶ֖יךָ טוֹבֽוֹת: · · · · · · עָזַ֙בְתִּי֙ אֶת־בֵּיתִ֔י נָטַ֖שְׁתִּי אֶת־נַֽחֲלָתִ֑י
ח נָתַ֛תִּי אֶת־יְדִד֥וּת נַפְשִׁ֖י בְּכַ֥ף אֹֽיְבֶֽיהָ: הָֽיְתָה־לִּ֥י נַֽחֲלָתִ֖י כְּאַרְיֵ֣ה בַיָּ֑עַר נָֽתְנָ֥ה
ט עָלַ֛י בְּקוֹלָ֖הּ עַל־כֵּ֥ן שְׂנֵאתִֽיהָ: הַעַ֨יִט צָב֤וּעַ נַֽחֲלָתִי֙ לִ֔י הַעַ֖יִט סָבִ֣יב עָלֶ֑יהָ
י לְכ֣וּ אִסְפ֗וּ כָּל־חַיַּ֤ת הַשָּׂדֶה֙ הֵתָ֣יוּ לְאָכְלָֽה: רֹעִ֤ים רַבִּים֙ שִֽׁחֲת֣וּ כַרְמִ֔י בֹּֽסְס֖וּ
יא אֶת־חֶלְקָתִ֑י נָֽתְנ֛וּ אֶת־חֶלְקַ֥ת חֶמְדָּתִ֖י לְמִדְבַּ֥ר שְׁמָמָֽה: שָׂמָהּ֙ לִשְׁמָמָ֔ה
יב אָֽבְלָ֥ה עָלַ֖י שְׁמֵמָ֑ה נָשַׁ֙מָּה֙ כָּל־הָאָ֔רֶץ כִּ֛י אֵ֥ין אִ֖ישׁ שָׂ֥ם עַל־לֵֽב: עַל־כָּל־
שְׁפָיִ֣ם בַּמִּדְבָּ֗ר בָּ֚אוּ שֹֽׁדְדִ֔ים כִּ֣י חֶ֤רֶב לַֽיהוָה֙ אֹֽכְלָ֔ה מִקְצֵה־אֶ֖רֶץ וְעַד־קְצֵ֣ה
יג הָאָ֑רֶץ אֵ֥ין שָׁל֖וֹם לְכָל־בָּשָֽׂר: זָֽרְע֤וּ חִטִּים֙ וְקֹצִ֣ים קָצָ֔רוּ נֶֽחְל֖וּ לֹ֣א יוֹעִ֑לוּ
יד וּבֹ֙שׁוּ֙ מִתְּבֻ֣אֹֽתֵיכֶ֔ם מֵֽחֲר֖וֹן אַף־יְהוָֽה: · · · · · · כֹּ֣ה ׀ אָמַ֣ר יְהוָ֗ה עַל־
כָּל־שְׁכֵנַי֙ הָֽרָעִ֔ים הַנֹּֽגְעִים֙ בַּֽנַּֽחֲלָ֔ה אֲשֶׁר־הִנְחַ֖לְתִּי אֶת־עַמִּ֣י אֶת־יִשְׂרָאֵ֑ל
טו הִנְנִ֤י נֹֽתְשָׁם֙ מֵעַ֣ל אַדְמָתָ֔ם וְאֶת־בֵּ֥ית יְהוּדָ֖ה אֶתּ֣וֹשׁ מִתּוֹכָֽם: וְהָיָ֗ה אַֽחֲרֵי֙
נָֽתְשִׁ֣י אוֹתָ֔ם אָשׁ֖וּב וְרִֽחַמְתִּ֑ים וַֽהֲשִֽׁבֹתִים֙ אִ֣ישׁ לְנַֽחֲלָת֔וֹ וְאִ֖ישׁ לְאַרְצֽוֹ:

11:19. Jeremiah's townspeople plotted to kill him for his constant rebukes and prophecies of doom.

11:20. Literally, "kidneys and heart," an oft-used metaphor for thoughts and feelings.

12:1-4. Jeremiah is troubled by the age-old problem of why the wicked prosper while the righteous suffer. He prefaces his words by saying that he does not question God's justice; he wishes only to understand why such things are happening. Then he contrasts the insincerity of those who falsely proclaim homage to God with his own loyalty, and asks, "Why are they tranquil while I am persecuted? Furthermore, why are the sinners permitted to drag the country down to destruction?"

12:2. Lit., "kidneys"; see 11:20. Jeremiah accuses the betrayers of paying lip service, but not bringing God into their thoughts and emotions.

12:5-6. God responds to Jeremiah's query (*Targum*) with two metaphors to show Jeremiah that the answer to his question is beyond human comprehension. (a) An ordinary person becomes tired if he runs with faster people; surely he cannot keep up with horses. (b) Jeremiah should have expected to be safest with his kinsmen in Anathoth, yet they tried to poison him — how much more would the prophet be in danger from the antagonistic nobles of Jerusalem or the conquering Nebuchadnezzar (*Radak*).

and cut him off from the land of the living, so that his name will not be remembered any more."* 20 But HASHEM, Master of Legions, righteous Judge, Who examines innermost thoughts and feelings, * let me see Your vengeance against them, for I have revealed my grievance to You.

21 Therefore, thus said HASHEM, concerning the men of Anathoth who seek your life, saying: "Do not prophecy in the Name of HASHEM, so that you not die at our hand" — 22 Therefore, thus said HASHEM, Master of Legions: "Behold, I shall punish them; the young men will die by the sword, their sons and their daughters will die in the famine. 23 There will be no remnant of them, for I shall bring evil upon the men of Anathoth [in] the year of their punishment."

12

Why prosperity for the wicked?

1 **Y**ou are righteous, O HASHEM, though I may express a grievance to You; but I will speak with You of judgments:* Why does the way of the wicked prosper, and [why are] all the betrayers tranquil? 2 You have planted them and they have even taken root; they even produce fruit. You are close to their mouths, but distant from their thoughts. * 3 You, HASHEM, know me; You see me and You have determined that my heart is with You. Bring them out like sheep to the slaughter; prepare them for the day of killing! 4 How long must the land mourn and the vegetation of the entire field become withered? Because of the wickedness of its inhabitants even animals and birds have ceased [to live], because they said, "[God] sees not our end."

God replies . . .

5 If when you race with footmen they exhaust you, how can you compete with horses? [If] in peaceful territory, where you are secure, [you are endangered,] how will you cope in the heights of the Jordan? 6 Even your brothers and your father's household — even they have betrayed you! Even they called out against you in a full assemblage. Do not trust them, [even] when they speak kindnesses to you!*

. . . and describes the impending repercussions

7 I have forsaken My Temple, * I have abandoned My heritage; I have delivered the love of My soul into the palm of her enemies. 8 To Me, My heritage was like a lion in the forest; she raised up her voice* against Me; therefore I hated her. 9 Has My heritage become for Me like a bloodstained bird of prey which the other birds of prey surround [proclaiming]: "Go gather all the beasts of the field, let them come to eat"? 10 Many shepherds* have ravaged My vineyard; they have trampled My portion and turned the portion of My desire into a barren wasteland. 11 He made it a wasteland, the wasteland mourns before Me; the entire land has been laid waste, for no man took it to heart. 12 On all the wilderness hilltops have pillagers come, for HASHEM's sword consumes from one end of the land to the [other] end of the land; there is no peace for any flesh. 13 They sowed wheat but reaped thorns; they ached without relief. Be ashamed of your produce, [which is stricken] by the burning wrath of HASHEM!

But eventually Israel will return

14 Thus said HASHEM: Concerning all My evil neighbors* who damage the inheritance that I have caused My people Israel to inherit: Behold, I am uprooting them from their land, and I will uproot the House of Judah from among them. 15 And it shall be that after I uproot them I will pity them again, and I will return each man of them to his heritage and each man to his land.

12:7-13. These verses speak of the impending tragedy. God likens Himself to a man who has left everything dear to him because he was betrayed.

12:8. The raised voice refers to the cries and prayers of the oppressed Jews of Jerusalem (*Radak*).

12:10. "Shepherds" is a metaphor for kings.

12:14-17. Israel's antagonistic neighbors — e.g., Tyre, Egypt, Moab, etc. — will also be exiled by the Babylonians' conquest. The Jews who had been exiled among them will be uprooted from their homes and returned to the Land of Israel. If the nations learn from Israel to mend their ways, they, too, will be returned to their homelands (*Radak*).

טז וְהָיָ֗ה אִֽם־לָמֹ֤ד יִלְמְדוּ֙ אֶת־דַּרְכֵ֣י עַמִּ֔י לְהִשָּׁבֵ֤עַ בִּשְׁמִי֙ חַי־יְהֹוָ֔ה כַּאֲשֶׁ֥ר

יז לִמְּד֛וּ אֶת־עַמִּ֖י לְהִשָּׁבֵ֣עַ בַּבָּ֑עַל וְנִבְנ֖וּ בְּת֥וֹךְ עַמִּֽי: וְאִ֖ם לֹ֣א יִשְׁמָ֑עוּ וְנָתַשְׁתִּ֞י

יג א אֶת־הַגּ֣וֹי הַה֗וּא נָת֧וֹשׁ וְאַבֵּ֛ד נְאֻם־יְהֹוָֽה: כֹּֽה־אָמַ֨ר יְהֹוָ֜ה אֵלַ֗י

הָל֞וֹךְ וְקָנִ֤יתָ לְּךָ֙ אֵז֣וֹר פִּשְׁתִּ֔ים וְשַׂמְתּ֖וֹ עַל־מָתְנֶ֑יךָ וּבַמַּ֖יִם לֹ֥א תְבִאֵֽהוּ:

ב-ג וָאֶקְנֶ֤ה אֶת־הָֽאֵזוֹר֙ כִּדְבַ֣ר יְהֹוָ֔ה וָאָשִׂ֖ם עַל־מָתְנָֽי: וַיְהִ֧י דְבַר־

ד יְהֹוָ֛ה אֵלַ֖י שֵׁנִ֣ית לֵאמֹֽר: קַ֧ח אֶת־הָאֵז֛וֹר אֲשֶׁ֥ר קָנִ֖יתָ אֲשֶׁ֣ר עַל־מָתְנֶ֑יךָ וְק֗וּם

ה לֵ֣ךְ פְּרָ֔תָה וְטָמְנֵ֥הוּ שָׁ֖ם בִּנְקִ֥יק הַסָּֽלַע: וָאֵלֵ֕ךְ וָאֶטְמְנֵ֖הוּ בִּפְרָ֑ת כַּאֲשֶׁ֥ר צִוָּ֖ה

ו יְהֹוָ֥ה אוֹתִֽי: וַיְהִ֕י מִקֵּ֖ץ יָמִ֣ים רַבִּ֑ים וַיֹּ֤אמֶר יְהֹוָה֙ אֵלַ֔י ק֚וּם לֵ֣ךְ פְּרָ֔תָה וְקַ֤ח

ז מִשָּׁם֙ אֶת־הָ֣אֵז֔וֹר אֲשֶׁ֥ר צִוִּיתִ֖יךָ לְטׇמְנוֹ־שָׁ֑ם וָאֵלֵ֣ךְ פְּרָ֗תָה וָאֶחְפֹּר֙ וָֽאֶקַּח֙

אֶת־הָ֣אֵז֔וֹר מִן־הַמָּק֖וֹם אֲשֶׁר־טְמַנְתִּ֣יו שָׁ֑מָּה וְהִנֵּ֤ה נִשְׁחַת֙ הָאֵז֔וֹר לֹ֥א

ח-ט יִצְלַ֖ח לַכֹּֽל: וַיְהִ֥י דְבַר־יְהֹוָ֖ה אֵלַ֥י לֵאמֹֽר: כֹּ֚ה אָמַ֣ר יְהֹוָ֔ה כָּ֗כָה

י אַשְׁחִ֞ית אֶת־גְּא֤וֹן יְהוּדָה֙ וְאֶת־גְּא֥וֹן יְרוּשָׁלַ֖͏ִם הָרָֽב: הָעָם֩ הַזֶּ֨ה הָרָ֜ע

הַמֵּאֲנִ֣ים ׀ לִשְׁמ֣וֹעַ אֶת־דְּבָרַ֗י הַהֹֽלְכִים֙ בִּשְׁרִר֣וּת לִבָּ֔ם וַיֵּֽלְכ֗וּ אַחֲרֵי֙ אֱלֹהִ֣ים

אֲחֵרִ֔ים לְעׇבְדָ֖ם וּלְהִשְׁתַּחֲוֺ֣ת לָהֶ֑ם וִיהִי֙ כָּאֵז֣וֹר הַזֶּ֔ה אֲשֶׁ֥ר לֹֽא־יִצְלַ֖ח לַכֹּֽל:

יא כִּ֡י כַּאֲשֶׁר֩ יִדְבַּ֨ק הָאֵז֜וֹר אֶל־מׇתְנֵי־אִ֗ישׁ כֵּ֣ן הִדְבַּ֣קְתִּי אֵ֠לַ֠י אֶת־כׇּל־בֵּ֨ית

יִשְׂרָאֵ֜ל וְאֶת־כׇּל־בֵּ֤ית יְהוּדָה֙ נְאֻם־יְהֹוָ֔ה לִֽהְי֥וֹת לִי֙ לְעָ֔ם וּלְשֵׁ֥ם וְלִתְהִלָּ֖ה

יב וּלְתִפְאָ֑רֶת וְלֹ֖א שָׁמֵֽעוּ: וְאָמַרְתָּ֨ אֲלֵיהֶ֜ם אֶת־הַדָּבָ֣ר הַזֶּ֗ה כֹּֽה־אָמַ֤ר יְהֹוָה֙

אֱלֹהֵ֣י יִשְׂרָאֵ֔ל כׇּל־נֵ֖בֶל יִמָּ֣לֵא יָ֑יִן וְאָמְר֣וּ אֵלֶ֔יךָ הֲיָדֹ֙עַ֙ לֹ֣א נֵדַ֔ע כִּ֥י כׇל־נֵ֖בֶל

יג יִמָּ֥לֵא יָֽיִן: וְאָמַרְתָּ֨ אֲלֵיהֶ֜ם כֹּֽה־אָמַ֣ר יְהֹוָ֗ה הִנְנִ֣י מְמַלֵּ֣א אֶת־כׇּל־

יֹשְׁבֵ֣י הָאָ֣רֶץ הַזֹּ֡את וְאֶת־הַמְּלָכִ֣ים הַיֹּשְׁבִים֩ לְדָוִ֨ד עַל־כִּסְא֜וֹ וְאֶת־

יד הַכֹּהֲנִ֣ים וְאֶת־הַנְּבִיאִ֗ים וְאֵ֛ת כׇּל־יֹשְׁבֵ֥י יְרוּשָׁלָ֖͏ִם שִׁכָּרֽוֹן: וְנִפַּצְתִּים֩ אִ֨ישׁ

אֶל־אָחִ֜יו וְהָאָב֧וֹת וְהַבָּנִ֛ים יַחְדָּ֖ו נְאֻם־יְהֹוָ֑ה לֹֽא־אֶחְמ֣וֹל וְלֹֽא־אָח֛וּס

טו-טז וְלֹ֥א אֲרַחֵ֖ם מֵהַשְׁחִיתָֽם: שִׁמְע֤וּ וְהַאֲזִ֙ינוּ֙ אַל־תִּגְבָּ֔הוּ כִּ֥י יְהֹוָ֖ה דִּבֵּֽר: תְּנוּ֩

לַיהֹוָ֨ה אֱלֹהֵיכֶ֤ם כָּבוֹד֙ בְּטֶ֣רֶם יַחְשִׁ֔ךְ וּבְטֶ֛רֶם יִֽתְנַגְּפ֥וּ רַגְלֵיכֶ֖ם עַל־הָ֣רֵי נָ֑שֶׁף

וְקִוִּיתֶ֤ם לְאוֹר֙ וְשָׂמָ֣הּ לְצַלְמָ֔וֶת °יָשִׁ֖ית [יָשִׁ֖ית ק] לַעֲרָפֶֽל: וְאִם֙ לֹ֣א

יז תִשְׁמָע֔וּהָ בְּמִסְתָּרִ֥ים תִּבְכֶּה־נַפְשִׁ֖י מִפְּנֵ֣י גֵוָ֑ה וְדָמֹ֨עַ תִּדְמַ֜ע וְתֵרַ֤ד עֵינִי֙

יח דִּמְעָ֔ה כִּ֥י נִשְׁבָּ֖ה עֵ֥דֶר יְהֹוָֽה: אֱמֹ֥ר לַמֶּ֛לֶךְ וְלַגְּבִירָ֖ה הַשְׁפִּ֑ילוּ

יט שֵׁ֔בוּ כִּ֣י יָרַ֔ד מַרְאֲשֽׁוֹתֵיכֶ֔ם עֲטֶ֖רֶת תִּפְאַרְתְּכֶֽם: עָרֵ֥י הַנֶּ֛גֶב סֻגְּר֖וּ וְאֵ֣ין פֹּתֵ֑חַ

כ הׇגְלָ֤ת יְהוּדָה֙ כֻּלָּ֔הּ הׇגְלָ֖ת שְׁלוֹמִֽים: °שְׂאִי [°שְׂא֤וּ ק] עֵֽינֵיכֶם֙

°וּרְאִי [°וּרְאוּ֙ ק] הַבָּאִ֖ים מִצָּפ֑וֹן אַיֵּ֤ה הָעֵ֙דֶר֙ נִתַּן־לָ֔ךְ צֹ֖אן תִּפְאַרְתֵּֽךְ:

כא מַה־תֹּֽאמְרִי֙ כִּֽי־יִפְקֹ֣ד עָלַ֔יִךְ וְ֠אַ֠תְּ לִמַּ֨דְתְּ אֹתָ֥ם עָלַ֛יִךְ אַלֻּפִ֖ים לְרֹ֑אשׁ

13:1. God commanded Jeremiah to perform a symbolic act that would lend force to his prophecy about Israel's imminent downfall. By absorbing the sweat of his loins and not being laundered, the girdle would decay faster. **13:13-14.** The jugs are the dignitaries of Jerusalem, who will be "drunk" with calamity and misfortune, i.e., they will be so overwhelmed by troubles that they will be helpless as a drunkard to deal with them. And these crises will cause strife among the leaders, and they will be like earthenware jugs that shatter when they strike

¹⁶ It shall be if they learn well the ways of My people, to swear in My Name, 'As HASHEM lives,' just as they taught My people to swear by the Baal, then they shall be restored along with My people. ¹⁷ But if they do not listen, I shall uproot that nation, uprooting and destroying it — the word of HASHEM.

13

The parable of the linen belt

¹ Thus said HASHEM to me: "Go and buy for yourself a linen belt and place it on your loins, but do not bring it into water."* ² So I bought the belt, in accordance with the word of HASHEM, and placed it on my loins.

³ The word of HASHEM came to me once again, saying, ⁴ "Take the belt that you bought, which is upon your loins; arise and go to the Euphrates, and conceal it there in a cleft of the rock." ⁵ So I went and concealed it by the Euphrates, as HASHEM had commanded me. ⁶ It was at the end of many days, and HASHEM said to me: "Arise, go to the Euphrates and from there take the belt that I had commanded you to conceal there." ⁷ So I went to the Euphrates and I dug and took the belt from the place where I had concealed it, and behold the belt was ruined; it was not of any use.

⁸ The word of HASHEM then came to me, saying, ⁹ "Thus said HASHEM: So shall I destroy the pride of Judah and the immense pride of Jerusalem — ¹⁰ this evil nation, who refuse to hear My words, who follow the vision of their heart, who went after the gods of others, to worship them, to prostrate themselves to them — it will become like this belt, which is not of any use. ¹¹ For just as a belt is fastened to a man's loins, so I fastened to Myself the entire House of Israel and the entire House of Judah — the word of HASHEM — to be unto Me a people, and for renown, for praise, and for splendor, but they would not listen [to Me].

The parable of the wine jug

¹² "Tell them this declaration: Thus said HASHEM, God of Israel: 'Every wine jug should be filled with wine.' And when they say to you, 'Don't we know that every wine jug should be filled with wine?' ¹³ you will say to them, Thus said HASHEM: Behold, I am filling all the inhabitants of this land, as well as the kings who sit on the throne of David and the priests and the prophets and all the inhabitants of Jerusalem, with drunkenness. * ¹⁴ And I will smash them, each man against his brother, and fathers and sons together — the word of HASHEM; I shall not show mercy nor shall I pity nor shall I have compassion [to stop Me] from destroying them.

Honor God!

¹⁵ Listen and be attentive, do not be haughty; for HASHEM has spoken. ¹⁶ Give honor to HASHEM your God, before it gets dark, and before your feet stub themselves upon the mountains of night; you will then hope for light, but He will place deep darkness and will make it thickly clouded. ¹⁷ And if you do not heed this, my soul will cry in [its] hidden chambers because of [your] haughtiness; and if tears will flow freely, my eye will drip tears, for the flock of HASHEM will have been captured.

Humble yourself!

¹⁸ Say to the king and to the queen mother, * 'Humble yourselves, sit, for your dominions have collapsed, the crown of your glory.' ¹⁹ The cities of the South are shut, with no one to open [them]; all of Judah has been exiled — exiled completely.

²⁰ Lift your eyes and see those who are coming from the North; where is the flock that was given you, the sheep of your glory? ²¹ What will you say when He punishes you? You yourself have trained them as rulers over you; *

---

one another (*Radak*).

13:18. This refers to King Jehoiachin and his mother, who were among the first to be exiled by the Baby-

lonians (see *II Kings* 24:12).

13:21. The kings of Judah invited trouble by seeking alliances with foreign powers.

כב הֲלוֹא חֲבָלִים יֹאחֵזוּךְ כְּמוֹ אֵשֶׁת לֵדָה: וְכִי תֹאמְרִי בִּלְבָבֵךְ מַדּוּעַ קְרָאֻנִי

כג אֵלֶּה בְּרֹב עֲוֹנֵךְ נִגְלוּ שׁוּלַיִךְ נֶחְמְסוּ עֲקֵבָיִךְ: הֲיַהֲפֹךְ כּוּשִׁי עוֹרוֹ וְנָמֵר

כד חֲבַרְבֻּרֹתָיו גַּם־אַתֶּם תּוּכְלוּ לְהֵיטִיב לִמֻּדֵי הָרֵעַ: וַאֲפִיצֵם כְּקַשׁ־עוֹבֵר

כה לְרוּחַ מִדְבָּר: זֶה גוֹרָלֵךְ מְנָת־מִדַּיִךְ מֵאִתִּי נְאֻם־יְהוָה אֲשֶׁר שָׁכַחַתְּ אוֹתִי

כו-כז וַתִּבְטְחִי בַּשָּׁקֶר: וְגַם־אֲנִי חָשַׂפְתִּי שׁוּלַיִךְ עַל־פָּנָיִךְ וְנִרְאָה קְלוֹנֵךְ: נִאֻפַיִךְ

וּמִצְהֲלוֹתַיִךְ זִמַּת זְנוּתֵךְ עַל־גְּבָעוֹת בַּשָּׂדֶה רָאִיתִי שִׁקּוּצָיִךְ אוֹי לָךְ

יד א יְרוּשָׁלִַם לֹא תִטְהֲרִי אַחֲרֵי מָתַי עֹד: אֲשֶׁר הָיָה דְבַר־יְהוָה אֶל־

ב יִרְמְיָהוּ עַל־דִּבְרֵי הַבַּצָּרוֹת: אָבְלָה יְהוּדָה וּשְׁעָרֶיהָ אֻמְלְלוּ קָדְרוּ לָאָרֶץ

ג וְצִוְחַת יְרוּשָׁלִַם עָלָתָה: וְאַדִּרֵיהֶם שָׁלְחוּ °צעוריהם [°צְעִירֵיהֶם ק]

לַמָּיִם בָּאוּ עַל־גֵּבִים לֹא־מָצְאוּ מַיִם שָׁבוּ כְלֵיהֶם רֵיקָם בֹּשׁוּ וְהָכְלְמוּ

ד וְחָפוּ רֹאשָׁם: בַּעֲבוּר הָאֲדָמָה חַתָּה כִּי לֹא־הָיָה גֶשֶׁם בָּאָרֶץ בֹּשׁוּ אִכָּרִים

ה-ו חָפוּ רֹאשָׁם: כִּי גַם־אַיֶּלֶת בַּשָּׂדֶה יָלְדָה וְעָזוֹב כִּי לֹא־הָיָה דֶּשֶׁא: וּפְרָאִים

ז עָמְדוּ עַל־שְׁפָיִם שָׁאֲפוּ רוּחַ כַּתַּנִּים כָּלוּ עֵינֵיהֶם כִּי־אֵין עֵשֶׂב: אִם־עֲוֹנֵינוּ

ח עָנוּ בָנוּ יְהוָה עֲשֵׂה לְמַעַן שְׁמֶךָ כִּי־רַבּוּ מְשׁוּבֹתֵינוּ לְךָ חָטָאנוּ: מִקְוֵה

יִשְׂרָאֵל מוֹשִׁיעוֹ בְּעֵת צָרָה לָמָּה תִהְיֶה כְּגֵר בָּאָרֶץ וּכְאֹרֵחַ נָטָה לָלוּן:

ט לָמָּה תִהְיֶה כְּאִישׁ נִדְהָם כְּגִבּוֹר לֹא־יוּכַל לְהוֹשִׁיעַ וְאַתָּה בְקִרְבֵּנוּ יְהוָה

י וְשִׁמְךָ עָלֵינוּ נִקְרָא אַל־תַּנִּחֵנוּ: כֹּה־אָמַר יְהוָה לָעָם הַזֶּה

כֵּן אָהֲבוּ לָנוּעַ רַגְלֵיהֶם לֹא חָשָׂכוּ וַיהוָה לֹא רָצָם עַתָּה יִזְכֹּר עֲוֹנָם וְיִפְקֹד

יא חַטֹּאתָם: וַיֹּאמֶר יְהוָה אֵלָי אַל־תִּתְפַּלֵּל בְּעַד־הָעָם

יב הַזֶּה לְטוֹבָה: כִּי יָצֻמוּ אֵינֶנִּי שֹׁמֵעַ אֶל־רִנָּתָם וְכִי יַעֲלוּ עֹלָה וּמִנְחָה אֵינֶנִּי

יג רֹצָם כִּי בַּחֶרֶב וּבָרָעָב וּבַדֶּבֶר אָנֹכִי מְכַלֶּה אוֹתָם: וָאֹמַר אֲהָהּ אֲדֹנָי יְהוִֹה

הִנֵּה הַנְּבִאִים אֹמְרִים לָהֶם לֹא־תִרְאוּ חֶרֶב וְרָעָב לֹא־יִהְיֶה לָכֶם כִּי־

יד שָׁלוֹם אֱמֶת אֶתֵּן לָכֶם בַּמָּקוֹם הַזֶּה: וַיֹּאמֶר יְהוָה אֵלַי

שֶׁקֶר הַנְּבִאִים נִבְּאִים בִּשְׁמִי לֹא שְׁלַחְתִּים וְלֹא צִוִּיתִים וְלֹא דִבַּרְתִּי

אֲלֵיהֶם חֲזוֹן שֶׁקֶר וְקֶסֶם °ואלול ותרמות [°וֶאֱלִיל וְתַרְמִית ק] לָכֶם

טו הֵמָּה מִתְנַבְּאִים לָכֶם: לָכֵן כֹּה־אָמַר יְהוָה עַל־הַנְּבִאִים הַנִּבְּאִים

בִּשְׁמִי וַאֲנִי לֹא־שְׁלַחְתִּים וְהֵמָּה אֹמְרִים חֶרֶב וְרָעָב לֹא יִהְיֶה בָּאָרֶץ

טז בַּחֶרֶב וּבָרָעָב יִתַּמּוּ הַנְּבִאִים הָהֵמָּה: וְהָעָם אֲשֶׁר־הֵמָּה נִבְּאִים

לָהֶם יִהְיוּ מֻשְׁלָכִים בְּחֻצוֹת יְרוּשָׁלִַם מִפְּנֵי הָרָעָב וְהַחֶרֶב וְאֵין מְקַבֵּר

לָהֵמָּה הֵמָּה נְשֵׁיהֶם וּבְנֵיהֶם וּבְנֹתֵיהֶם וְשָׁפַכְתִּי עֲלֵיהֶם אֶת־רָעָתָם:

13:22. Because of adulterous behavior, they would suffer an adulteress' fate — her skirts pulled up over her head (*Rashi*), her limbs exposed to public humiliation (*Radak*).

13:23. Generally translated "Ethiopian." *Rashi* renders "Moor."

14:1. This refers to the hunger and thirst that will accompany the siege of Jerusalem (*II Kings 25:2-3*) and

which will culminate in the capture of the city and the destruction of the Temple (*Kara*).

14:7. Jeremiah pleads with God: "If You answer us, people will be inspired to believe in You."

14:8. A casual passerby is not concerned with the welfare of the cities he visits (*Kara*).

14:10. The leaders went from country to country seeking

surely pains will seize you like a woman in childbirth! [22] And if you say in your heart, 'Why have these things happened to me?' — through your multitude of sin the bottoms of your garments have been revealed, your heels have been uncovered. * [23] Can a Cushite* change his skin [color], or a leopard its spots? So too, can you — in whom evil is ingrained — do good? [24] Therefore I shall scatter them, like chaff blown about by a desert wind. [25] This is your lot, your portion measured out by Me — the word of HASHEM — for you have forgotten Me and relied on falsehood. [26] I have even exposed the bottoms of your garments, [throwing them] upon your face, so your shame is revealed. [27] Your adultery and your exultant neighings, your fantasies of immorality — upon the hills in the field I have seen your abominations. Woe to you, Jerusalem; you will not become purified after so long!"

Can a leopard change his spots?

14

[1] The word of HASHEM that came to Jeremiah concerning the droughts: * [2] Judah mourns; her cities are devastated, they are blackened like the ground; and the cry of Jerusalem has gone up. [3] Their officers send out their youngsters for water. They go to cisterns, but do not find water; they bring back their containers empty; they are embarrassed and ashamed and cover their head. [4] Because the ground is parched, for there has been no rain in the land, plowmen are embarrassed; they cover their head. [5] Even the hind in the field gives birth and then abandons [her young], for there is no vegetation. [6] The wild donkeys stand on the hilltops; they suck in the air like serpents; their eyes pine away because there is no herbage.

Prophecy concerning the droughts

[7] If our sins testify against us, O HASHEM, act for Your Name's sake; * for our rebelliousness is great; we have sinned to You. [8] O Hope of Israel, its Redeemer in time of trouble, why should You be like a stranger in the land, like a wayfarer who turns off [the road] to sleep over for the night?* [9] Why should You be like a man in shock, like a hero who cannot save? But You are in our midst, O HASHEM, and Your Name is proclaimed upon us; do not abandon us.

Jeremiah's supplication

[10] Thus said HASHEM concerning this people, "Indeed they liked to move about, they did not spare their legs; * so HASHEM found them undesirable. Now He will recall their iniquity, and He will punish [them for] their transgressions."

[11] And HASHEM said to me, "Do not pray for beneficence on behalf of this people. [12] If they fast, I will not listen to their call; if they sacrifice a burnt-offering or meal-offering I will not accept them. For I am going to annihilate them by the sword, by famine and by pestilence."

Pray not for them; blame the false prophets

[13] Then I said, "Alas, my Lord HASHEM/ELOHIM! Behold, the [false] prophets say to them, 'You will not see a sword, and famine will not befall you; for I will present you a true peace in this place!' "

[14] But HASHEM said to me, "These prophets prophesy falsehood in My Name! I did not send them nor command them nor speak to them. A false vision, divination, emptiness, and the deception of their heart are they prophesying to you.

[15] "Therefore, thus said HASHEM concerning the prophets who prophesy in My Name though I did not send them, yet they say, 'Sword and famine will never visit this land!': Those prophets shall perish by sword and by famine! [16] And the people to whom they prophesy will be strewn about in the streets of Jerusalem because of the famine and sword, and there will be no one to bury them — they, their wives and their sons and daughters — for I will have poured out their [own] evil upon

---

allies; now let them wander in search of food and refuge (*Radak*).

יז וְאָמַרְתָּ אֲלֵיהֶם אֶת־הַדָּבָר הַזֶּה תֵּרַדְנָה עֵינַי דִּמְעָה לַיְלָה וְיוֹמָם וְאַל־
תִּדְמֶינָה כִּי שֶׁבֶר גָּדוֹל נִשְׁבְּרָה בְּתוּלַת בַּת־עַמִּי מַכָּה נַחְלָה מְאֹד: אִם־
יז יָצָאתִי הַשָּׂדֶה וְהִנֵּה חַלְלֵי־חֶרֶב וְאִם בָּאתִי הָעִיר וְהִנֵּה תַּחֲלוּאֵי רָעָב
כִּי־גַם־נָבִיא גַם־כֹּהֵן סָחֲרוּ אֶל־אֶרֶץ וְלֹא יָדָעוּ: הֲמָאֹס
יט מָאַסְתָּ אֶת־יְהוּדָה אִם־בְּצִיּוֹן גָּעֲלָה נַפְשֶׁךָ מַדּוּעַ הִכִּיתָנוּ וְאֵין לָנוּ מַרְפֵּא
קַוֵּה לְשָׁלוֹם וְאֵין טוֹב וּלְעֵת מַרְפֵּא וְהִנֵּה בְעָתָה: יָדַעְנוּ יהוה רִשְׁעֵנוּ עֲוֹן
כא אֲבוֹתֵינוּ כִּי חָטָאנוּ לָךְ: אַל־תִּנְאַץ לְמַעַן שִׁמְךָ אַל־תְּנַבֵּל כִּסֵּא כְבוֹדֶךָ
כב זְכֹר אַל־תָּפֵר בְּרִיתְךָ אִתָּנוּ: הֲיֵשׁ בְּהַבְלֵי הַגּוֹיִם מַגְשִׁמִים וְאִם־הַשָּׁמַיִם
יִתְּנוּ רְבִבִים הֲלֹא אַתָּה־הוּא יהוה אֱלֹהֵינוּ וּנְקַוֶּה־לָּךְ כִּי־אַתָּה עָשִׂיתָ
אֶת־כָּל־אֵלֶּה: וַיֹּאמֶר יהוה אֵלַי אִם־יַעֲמֹד מֹשֶׁה וּשְׁמוּאֵל

טו
ב לְפָנַי אֵין נַפְשִׁי אֶל־הָעָם הַזֶּה שַׁלַּח מֵעַל־פָּנַי וְיֵצֵאוּ: וְהָיָה כִּי־יֹאמְרוּ
אֵלֶיךָ אָנָה נֵצֵא וְאָמַרְתָּ אֲלֵיהֶם כֹּה־אָמַר יהוה אֲשֶׁר לַמָּוֶת לַמָּוֶת וַאֲשֶׁר
ג לַחֶרֶב לַחֶרֶב וַאֲשֶׁר לָרָעָב לָרָעָב וַאֲשֶׁר לַשְּׁבִי לַשֶּׁבִי: וּפָקַדְתִּי עֲלֵיהֶם
אַרְבַּע מִשְׁפָּחוֹת נְאֻם־יהוה אֶת־הַחֶרֶב לַהֲרֹג וְאֶת־הַכְּלָבִים לִסְחֹב
ד וְאֶת־עוֹף הַשָּׁמַיִם וְאֶת־בֶּהֱמַת הָאָרֶץ לֶאֱכֹל וּלְהַשְׁחִית: וּנְתַתִּים °לִזְוָעָה
[לְזַעֲוָה ק] לְכֹל מַמְלְכוֹת הָאָרֶץ בִּגְלַל מְנַשֶּׁה בֶן־יְחִזְקִיָּהוּ מֶלֶךְ יְהוּדָה
ה עַל אֲשֶׁר־עָשָׂה בִּירוּשָׁלִָם: כִּי מִי־יַחְמֹל עָלַיִךְ יְרוּשָׁלִַם וּמִי יָנוּד לָךְ וּמִי
ו יָסוּר לִשְׁאֹל לְשָׁלֹם לָךְ: אַתְּ נָטַשְׁתְּ אֹתִי נְאֻם־יהוה אָחוֹר תֵּלֵכִי וָאַט
ז אֶת־יָדִי עָלַיִךְ וָאַשְׁחִיתֵךְ נִלְאֵיתִי הִנָּחֵם: וָאֶזְרֵם בְּמִזְרֶה בְּשַׁעֲרֵי הָאָרֶץ
ח שִׁכַּלְתִּי אִבַּדְתִּי אֶת־עַמִּי מִדַּרְכֵיהֶם לוֹא־שָׁבוּ: עָצְמוּ־לִי אַלְמְנֹתָו מֵחוֹל
יַמִּים הֵבֵאתִי לָהֶם עַל־אֵם בָּחוּר שֹׁדֵד בַּצָּהֳרָיִם הִפַּלְתִּי עָלֶיהָ פִּתְאֹם
ט עִיר וּבֶהָלוֹת: אֻמְלְלָה יֹלֶדֶת הַשִּׁבְעָה נָפְחָה נַפְשָׁהּ °בָאָה [בָּא ק]
שִׁמְשָׁהּ בְּעֹד יוֹמָם בּוֹשָׁה וְחָפֵרָה וּשְׁאֵרִיתָם לַחֶרֶב אֶתֵּן לִפְנֵי אֹיְבֵיהֶם
י נְאֻם־יהוה: אוֹי־לִי אִמִּי כִּי יְלִדְתִּנִי אִישׁ רִיב וְאִישׁ מָדוֹן
לְכָל־הָאָרֶץ לֹא־נָשִׁיתִי וְלֹא־נָשׁוּ־בִי כֻּלֹּה מְקַלְלַונִי: אָמַר יהוה אִם־לֹא
יא °שרותך [שֵׁרִיתִךָ ק] לְטוֹב אִם־לוֹא ׀ הִפְגַּעְתִּי בְךָ בְּעֵת־רָעָה וּבְעֵת
יב צָרָה אֶת־הָאֹיֵב: הֲיָרֹעַ בַּרְזֶל ׀ בַּרְזֶל מִצָּפוֹן וּנְחֹשֶׁת: חֵילְךָ וְאוֹצְרוֹתֶיךָ
יג-יד לָבַז אֶתֵּן לֹא בִמְחִיר וּבְכָל־חַטֹּאותֶיךָ וּבְכָל־גְּבוּלֶיךָ: וְהַעֲבַרְתִּי אֶת־אֹיְבֶיךָ
טו בְּאֶרֶץ לֹא יָדָעְתָּ כִּי־אֵשׁ קָדְחָה בְאַפִּי עֲלֵיכֶם תּוּקָד: אַתָּה

14:17. The virgin daughter of Israel represents the nation before it was ravished by the enemy (*Radak*).

15:1. Though Moses and Samuel prayed for Israel, they did so only after chastising them and convincing them to repent (*Rashi*).

15:4. See *II Kings* Ch. 21.

15:10. Jeremiah moans that he is hated for having proclaimed the word of God, and wishes he had never been born.

15:11. Lit., "If I do not make your end good. . .; if I will not make your enemy. . .!" This is an oath, and, in the manner of Scripture, the conclusion is left unstated. God assures Jeremiah that the destruction will not be total and that his opponents will beg him to pray for them (*Rashi*).

15:12. The iron weapons of Israel cannot beat the powerful invader from the North (*Rashi; Radak*).

them. ¹⁷ Tell them this thing:

My eyes drip tears night and day, and do not stop, for the virgin daughter of my people* is broken by a great disaster, a very sickening blow. ¹⁸ If I go out to the field, behold, there are the slain of the sword! And if I enter the city, behold, there are those ill from famine! For prophet and priest alike have mongered [falsehood] throughout the land, for they did not know [the word of God]."

Jeremiah supplicates again ¹⁹ Do You totally despise Judah; do You loathe Zion? Why did You strike us so that we have no cure? [We may] hope for peace, but there is no goodness; for a time of healing, but [instead] there is terror. ²⁰ We know, O HASHEM, of our wickedness, the transgression of our forefathers, for we have sinned against You. ²¹ Do not reject [us], for Your Name's sake; do not abominate the Throne of Your Glory. Remember, do not annul Your covenant with us. ²² Are there rainmakers among the follies of the nations? Will the heavens issue raindrops? Surely it is You, HASHEM, our God, and we place our hope in You, for You do all these [things].

15 ¹ HASHEM said to me, "Even if Moses and Samuel were to stand before Me, I would have no desire for this people. * Send [them] away from My Presence and let them go! ² And if they tell you, 'Where shall we go?' say to them, 'Thus said **Death, sword, famine, captivity** HASHEM: Whoever is [destined] for death, to death; whoever for the sword, to sword; whoever for famine, to famine; and whoever for captivity, to captivity. ³ I shall appoint over them four families [of punishment] — the word of HASHEM: the sword to kill; the dogs to drag off [corpses]; and the bird of the heavens and the animal of the earth to devour and destroy [the corpses]. ⁴ I shall make them a horror for all the kingdoms of the earth, because of Manasseh son of Hezekiah, king of Judah, for what he did in Jerusalem. * ⁵ Who will pity you, O Jerusalem, and who will shake [his head] for you, and who will turn aside to inquire after your welfare? ⁶ You abandoned Me — the word of HASHEM — you retreated; I shall stretch out My hand against you and I shall destroy you; I am weary of relenting. ⁷ I shall scatter them with a winnowing fork throughout the cities of the world; I bereaved and annihilated My people, but they did not turn back from their ways. ⁸ Their widows were more numerous before Me than the sand of the seas; I brought upon them — upon the mother-city — a youthful band that pillages at [high] noon; I cast this down upon her suddenly, an [enemy] city and turmoil. ⁹ She who gave birth to seven [children] is distressed, her soul is distraught; her sun set while it was still daytime; she was shamed and disgraced. Now I shall deliver their remnant to the sword before their enemies — the word of HASHEM."

¹⁰ *Woe is me, Mother, that you gave birth to me, a man of strife and a man of controversy for all the land; I did not lend money nor did anyone lend to me, yet everyone curses me.

¹¹ HASHEM replied, "A remnant will remain for good; good for you in the end; I will make your enemy entreat you at a time of distress and a time of travail. * ¹² Can ordinary iron smash northern iron alloyed with copper?* ¹³ I shall deliver your fortune and your treasuries as spoils, without payment, because of all your sins throughout your borders. ¹⁴ And I shall cause you to pass over to your enemies, into a land you do not know, for a fire has been kindled in My wrath, and it burns against you."

יָדַעְתָּ יהוה זָכְרֵנִי וּפָקְדֵנִי וְהִנָּקֶם לִי מֵרֹדְפַי אַל־לְאֶרֶךְ אַפְּךָ תִּקָּחֵנִי דַּע

טז שְׂאֵתִי עָלֶיךָ חֶרְפָּה: נִמְצְאוּ דְבָרֶיךָ וָאֹכְלֵם וַיְהִי °דבריך [אדְבָרְךָ ק] לִי

יז לְשָׂשׂוֹן וּלְשִׂמְחַת לְבָבִי כִּי־נִקְרָא שִׁמְךָ עָלַי יהוה אֱלֹהֵי צְבָאוֹת: לֹא־

יָשַׁבְתִּי בְסוֹד־מְשַׂחֲקִים וָאֶעְלֹז מִפְּנֵי יָדְךָ בָּדָד יָשַׁבְתִּי כִּי־זַעַם מִלֵּאתָנִי:

יח לָמָּה הָיָה כְאֵבִי נֶצַח וּמַכָּתִי אֲנוּשָׁה מֵאֲנָה הֵרָפֵא הָיוֹ תִהְיֶה לִי כְּמוֹ אַכְזָב

יט מַיִם לֹא נֶאֱמָנוּ: לָכֵן כֹּה־אָמַר יהוה אִם־תָּשׁוּב וַאֲשִׁיבְךָ לְפָנַי

תַּעֲמֹד וְאִם־תּוֹצִיא יָקָר מִזּוֹלֵל כְּפִי תִהְיֶה הֵמָּה יָשֻׁבוּ אֵלֶיךָ וְאַתָּה לֹא־

כ תָשׁוּב אֲלֵיהֶם: וּנְתַתִּיךָ לָעָם הַזֶּה לְחוֹמַת נְחֹשֶׁת בְּצוּרָה וְנִלְחֲמוּ אֵלֶיךָ

כא וְלֹא־יוּכְלוּ לָךְ כִּי־אִתְּךָ אֲנִי לְהוֹשִׁיעֲךָ וּלְהַצִּילֶךָ נְאֻם־יהוה: וְהִצַּלְתִּיךָ

מִיַּד רָעִים וּפְדִתִיךָ מִכַּף עָרִצִים: וַיְהִי דְבַר־יהוה אֵלַי לֵאמֹר:

טז א־ב לֹא־תִקַּח לְךָ אִשָּׁה וְלֹא־יִהְיוּ לְךָ בָּנִים וּבָנוֹת בַּמָּקוֹם הַזֶּה: כִּי־

ג כֹה ׀ אָמַר יהוה עַל־הַבָּנִים וְעַל־הַבָּנוֹת הַיִּלּוֹדִים בַּמָּקוֹם הַזֶּה וְעַל־

אִמֹּתָם הַיֹּלְדוֹת אוֹתָם וְעַל־אֲבוֹתָם הַמּוֹלִדִים אוֹתָם בָּאָרֶץ הַזֹּאת:

ד מְמוֹתֵי תַחֲלֻאִים יָמֻתוּ לֹא יִסָּפְדוּ וְלֹא יִקָּבֵרוּ לְדֹמֶן עַל־פְּנֵי הָאֲדָמָה יִהְיוּ

וּבַחֶרֶב וּבָרָעָב יִכְלוּ וְהָיְתָה נִבְלָתָם לְמַאֲכָל לְעוֹף הַשָּׁמַיִם וּלְבֶהֱמַת

ה הָאָרֶץ: כִּי־כֹה ׀ אָמַר יהוה אַל־תָּבוֹא בֵּית מַרְזֵחַ וְאַל־

תֵּלֵךְ לִסְפּוֹד וְאַל־תָּנֹד לָהֶם כִּי־אָסַפְתִּי אֶת־שְׁלוֹמִי מֵאֵת הָעָם הַזֶּה

ו נְאֻם־יהוה אֶת־הַחֶסֶד וְאֶת־הָרַחֲמִים: וּמֵתוּ גְדֹלִים וּקְטַנִּים בָּאָרֶץ הַזֹּאת

ז לֹא יִקָּבֵרוּ וְלֹא־יִסְפְּדוּ לָהֶם וְלֹא יִתְגֹּדַד וְלֹא יִקָּרֵחַ לָהֶם: וְלֹא־

יִפְרְסוּ לָהֶם עַל־אֵבֶל לְנַחֲמוֹ עַל־מֵת וְלֹא־יַשְׁקוּ אוֹתָם כּוֹס תַּנְחוּמִים

ח עַל־אָבִיו וְעַל־אִמּוֹ: וּבֵית־מִשְׁתֶּה לֹא־תָבוֹא לָשֶׁבֶת אוֹתָם לֶאֱכֹל

ט וְלִשְׁתּוֹת: כִּי כֹה אָמַר יהוה צְבָאוֹת אֱלֹהֵי יִשְׂרָאֵל הִנְנִי

מַשְׁבִּית מִן־הַמָּקוֹם הַזֶּה לְעֵינֵיכֶם וּבִימֵיכֶם קוֹל שָׂשׂוֹן וְקוֹל שִׂמְחָה

י קוֹל חָתָן וְקוֹל כַּלָּה: וְהָיָה כִּי תַגִּיד לָעָם הַזֶּה אֵת כָּל־הַדְּבָרִים הָאֵלֶּה

וְאָמְרוּ אֵלֶיךָ עַל־מֶה דִבֶּר יהוה עָלֵינוּ אֵת כָּל־הָרָעָה הַגְּדוֹלָה הַזֹּאת וּמֶה

יא עֲוֹנֵנוּ וּמֶה חַטָּאתֵנוּ אֲשֶׁר חָטָאנוּ לַיהוה אֱלֹהֵינוּ: וְאָמַרְתָּ אֲלֵיהֶם עַל

אֲשֶׁר־עָזְבוּ אֲבוֹתֵיכֶם אוֹתִי נְאֻם־יהוה וַיֵּלְכוּ אַחֲרֵי אֱלֹהִים אֲחֵרִים

יב וַיַּעַבְדוּם וַיִּשְׁתַּחֲווּ לָהֶם וְאֹתִי עָזָבוּ וְאֶת־תּוֹרָתִי לֹא שָׁמָרוּ: וְאַתֶּם

הֲרֵעֹתֶם לַעֲשׂוֹת מֵאֲבוֹתֵיכֶם וְהִנְּכֶם הֹלְכִים אִישׁ אַחֲרֵי שְׁרִרוּת לִבּוֹ־

יג הָרָע לְבִלְתִּי שְׁמֹעַ אֵלָי: וְהֵטַלְתִּי אֶתְכֶם מֵעַל הָאָרֶץ הַזֹּאת עַל־הָאָרֶץ

אֲשֶׁר לֹא יְדַעְתֶּם אַתֶּם וַאֲבוֹתֵיכֶם וַעֲבַדְתֶּם־שָׁם אֶת־אֱלֹהִים אֲחֵרִים

15:19. God tells Jeremiah that he has spoken irreverently to Him (v. 18) and must atone for his sacrilege (*Radak*); then he will continue to be God's prophet. If he succeeds in transforming people from figurative gluttons into righteous penitents, his wishes will be fulfilled, as if they had

been spoken by God's own mouth, and people will seek him out, instead of him having to pursue them.

16:2. Like other actions Jeremiah was commanded to take, this was meant as a symbolic act to impart a lesson to the people. When asked why he did not marry, Jere-

Persecution of Jeremiah	¹⁵ You know, HASHEM! Remember me, think of me, and avenge me of my pursuers; in Your patience [with them] do not take my life. Know that I have borne disgrace for You. ¹⁶ As soon as Your words come [to me] I devour them, for me Your word was the joy and gladness of my heart, for Your Name was proclaimed upon me, O HASHEM, God of Legions. ¹⁷ I did not sit in the company of revelers and celebrate; because of Your mission I sat alone, for You filled me with [prophecies of] fury. ¹⁸ Why has my pain become everlasting and my wound acute? It refuses to be healed. You have become like a disillusionment to me, like unfaithful waters.
God's reply	¹⁹ Therefore, thus said HASHEM: * "If you repent I will bring you back, let you stand before Me; if you bring forth an honorable person from a glutton, then you will be like My own mouth. They will return to you, and you will not have to return to them. ²⁰ And I shall make you like a fortified copper wall against this people; they will battle you but they will not be able to overcome you, for I am with you to save you and to rescue you — the word of HASHEM. ²¹ I shall rescue you from the hand of the wicked, and shall redeem you from the grip of the powerful."

16

Disassociate from the people . . .	¹ The word of HASHEM came to me, saying: ² "Do not take for yourself a wife, so that you do not have sons and daughters in this place. * ³ For thus said HASHEM concerning the sons and daughters who are born in this place, and concerning their mothers who give birth to them and their fathers who beget them in this land: ⁴ They will die as victims of diseases. They will not be eulogized nor buried; like dung upon the face of the earth will they be. By the sword and by famine will they perish, and their carcasses will be food for the bird of the heavens and the animal of the earth.
. . . do not grieve . . .	⁵ For thus said HASHEM: Do not go to a house of mourning * and do not go to eulogize nor to shake [your head] for them; for I have revoked My peace and kindness and mercy from this people — the word of HASHEM. ⁶ Great and small will die in this land and will not be buried; no one will eulogize them nor cut himself nor tear out his hair for them. * ⁷ No one will break bread for their bereavement to comfort them for the dead; no one will offer them a cup of consolations for their father and for their mother.
. . . or make merry with them	⁸ "Also, do not go to a house of merrymaking, to sit with them, to eat and to drink. ⁹ For thus said HASHEM, Master of Legions, God of Israel: Behold, I am abolishing from this place, before your eyes and in your days, the sound of joy and the sound of gladness, the sound of groom and the sound of bride. ¹⁰ And it shall be that when you tell all these things to this people, they will say to you, 'Why has HASHEM spoken all this great evil against us? What is our iniquity, what is our transgression that we have transgressed before HASHEM our God?' ¹¹ Say to them: It is because your forefathers have forsaken Me — the word of HASHEM — and they followed the gods of others; they worshiped them and prostrated themselves before them; but Me, they forsook; and My Torah they did not
They will be exiled . . .	observe. ¹² And you have acted worse than your forefathers, for each one of you follows the vision of his evil heart, in order not to listen to Me. ¹³ So I shall hurl you from upon this land into a land that you did not know — you or your forefathers — and there you will serve the gods of others,

---

miah would say that he did not wish to bring children into the world only to face a certain tragic end (*Abarbanel*).

16:5. Another symbolic act: When asked why he refused to comfort mourners, Jeremiah was to say because the time was coming when death would be so commonplace

that the few survivors would not bother to mourn (*Rashi*).

16:6. These acts of mourning are forbidden by the Torah (*Deuteronomy* 14:1); part of Jeremiah's rebuke was that some people did not heed this prohibition of the Torah (*Radak*).

יד   לָכֵן הִנֵּה יָמִים בָּאִים   יוֹמָם וָלַיְלָה אֲשֶׁר לֹא־אֶתֵּן לָכֶם חֲנִינָה:
נְאֻם־יהוה וְלֹא־יֵאָמֵר עוֹד חַי־יהוה אֲשֶׁר הֶעֱלָה אֶת־בְּנֵי יִשְׂרָאֵל מֵאֶרֶץ

טו   מִצְרָיִם: כִּי אִם־חַי־יהוה אֲשֶׁר הֶעֱלָה אֶת־בְּנֵי יִשְׂרָאֵל מֵאֶרֶץ צָפוֹן וּמִכֹּל
הָאֲרָצוֹת אֲשֶׁר הִדִּיחָם שָׁמָּה וַהֲשִׁבֹתִים עַל־אַדְמָתָם אֲשֶׁר נָתַתִּי

טז   לַאֲבוֹתָם: הִנְנִי שֹׁלֵחַ °לדוגים [°לְדַיָּגִים ק] רַבִּים נְאֻם־יהוה
וְדִיגוּם וְאַחֲרֵי־כֵן אֶשְׁלַח לְרַבִּים צַיָּדִים וְצָדוּם מֵעַל כָּל־הַר וּמֵעַל כָּל־

יז   גִּבְעָה וּמִנְּקִיקֵי הַסְּלָעִים: כִּי עֵינַי עַל־כָּל־דַּרְכֵיהֶם לֹא נִסְתְּרוּ מִלְּפָנָי
וְלֹא־נִצְפַּן עֲוֹנָם מִנֶּגֶד עֵינָי: וְשִׁלַּמְתִּי רִאשׁוֹנָה מִשְׁנֵה עֲוֹנָם וְחַטָּאתָם
עַל חַלְּלָם אֶת־אַרְצִי בְּנִבְלַת שִׁקּוּצֵיהֶם וְתוֹעֲבוֹתֵיהֶם מָלְאוּ אֶת־

יט   נַחֲלָתִי: ◀ יהוה עֻזִּי וּמָעֻזִּי וּמְנוּסִי בְּיוֹם צָרָה אֵלֶיךָ גּוֹיִם יָבֹאוּ

HAFTARAS
BECHU-
KOSAI
16:19-17:14

מֵאַפְסֵי־אָרֶץ וְיֹאמְרוּ אַךְ־שֶׁקֶר נָחֲלוּ אֲבוֹתֵינוּ הֶבֶל וְאֵין־בָּם מוֹעִיל:

כ־כא   הֲיַעֲשֶׂה־לּוֹ אָדָם אֱלֹהִים וְהֵמָּה לֹא אֱלֹהִים: לָכֵן הִנְנִי מוֹדִיעָם בַּפַּעַם
הַזֹּאת אוֹדִיעֵם אֶת־יָדִי וְאֶת־גְּבוּרָתִי וְיָדְעוּ כִּי־שְׁמִי יהוה: חַטַּאת

יז

א   יְהוּדָה כְּתוּבָה בְּעֵט בַּרְזֶל בְּצִפֹּרֶן שָׁמִיר חֲרוּשָׁה עַל־לוּחַ לִבָּם וּלְקַרְנוֹת

ב   מִזְבְּחוֹתֵיכֶם: כִּזְכֹּר בְּנֵיהֶם מִזְבְּחוֹתָם וַאֲשֵׁרֵיהֶם עַל־עֵץ רַעֲנָן עַל גְּבָעוֹת

ג   הַגְּבֹהוֹת: הֲרָרִי בַּשָּׂדֶה חֵילְךָ כָל־אוֹצְרוֹתֶיךָ לָבַז אֶתֵּן בָּמֹתֶיךָ בְּחַטָּאת

ד   בְּכָל־גְּבוּלֶיךָ: וְשָׁמַטְתָּה וּבְךָ מִנַּחֲלָתְךָ אֲשֶׁר נָתַתִּי לָךְ וְהַעֲבַדְתִּיךָ אֶת־
אֹיְבֶיךָ בָּאָרֶץ אֲשֶׁר לֹא־יָדָעְתָּ כִּי־אֵשׁ קְדַחְתֶּם בְּאַפִּי עַד־עוֹלָם

ה   תּוּקָד: כֹּה ׀ אָמַר יהוה אָרוּר הַגֶּבֶר אֲשֶׁר יִבְטַח בָּאָדָם וְשָׂם

ו   בָּשָׂר זְרֹעוֹ וּמִן־יהוה יָסוּר לִבּוֹ: וְהָיָה כְּעַרְעָר בָּעֲרָבָה וְלֹא יִרְאֶה כִּי־יָבוֹא

ז   טוֹב וְשָׁכַן חֲרֵרִים בַּמִּדְבָּר אֶרֶץ מְלֵחָה וְלֹא תֵשֵׁב: בָּרוּךְ הַגֶּבֶר

ח   אֲשֶׁר יִבְטַח בַּיהוה וְהָיָה יהוה מִבְטַחוֹ: וְהָיָה כְּעֵץ ׀ שָׁתוּל עַל־מַיִם וְעַל־
יוּבַל יְשַׁלַּח שָׁרָשָׁיו וְלֹא °יִרא [°יִרְאֶה ק] כִּי־יָבֹא חֹם וְהָיָה עָלֵהוּ רַעֲנָן

ט   וּבִשְׁנַת בַּצֹּרֶת לֹא יִדְאָג וְלֹא יָמִישׁ מֵעֲשׂוֹת פֶּרִי: עָקֹב הַלֵּב מִכֹּל וְאָנֻשׁ

י   הוּא מִי יֵדָעֶנּוּ: אֲנִי יהוה חֹקֵר לֵב בֹּחֵן כְּלָיוֹת וְלָתֵת לְאִישׁ °כדרכו
[°כִּדְרָכָיו ק] כִּפְרִי מַעֲלָלָיו: קֹרֵא דָגַר וְלֹא יָלָד עֹשֶׂה עֹשֶׁר

יא   וְלֹא בְמִשְׁפָּט בַּחֲצִי °ימו [°יָמָיו ק] יַעַזְבֶנּוּ וּבְאַחֲרִיתוֹ יִהְיֶה נָבָל: כִּסֵּא

יב   כָבוֹד מָרוֹם מֵרִאשׁוֹן מְקוֹם מִקְדָּשֵׁנוּ: מִקְוֵה יִשְׂרָאֵל יהוה כָּל־עֹזְבֶיךָ

יג   יֵבֹשׁוּ °יסורי [°וְסוּרַי ק] בָּאָרֶץ יִכָּתֵבוּ כִּי עָזְבוּ מְקוֹר מַיִם־חַיִּים אֶת־

16:13. According to *Targum*, "You will serve the worshipers of other gods day and night."

16:14. The redemption from the new exile will be so
much greater than the miracles of the Exodus from Egypt
that people will take oaths by the new redemption.

16:16. After an interlude of consolation, God resumes
His rebuke and prophecy of doom. The passage begins by
saying that there will be no escape from the coming retribution; God will seek out the Jews wherever they may be.

17:10. See 11:20.

17:11. A person with ill-gotten gains is like a partridge,
which sits on eggs laid by other birds. When the chicks
hatch, they soon leave the nest, and there is no attach-
ment between them and the bird that is not their real
mother (*Radak; Kara*). So too, a dishonest person may
prosper, but he will eventually lose it all.

17:12. God's Presence is as immanent on earth as in
heaven; He knows man's actions and thoughts (*Radak*).

day and night, * *for I will not grant you leniency.*

    ¹⁴ *However, behold — days are coming — the word of HASHEM — when it will no longer be said,* * *'As HASHEM lives, Who took out the Children of Israel from the land of Egypt,'* ¹⁵ *but rather, 'As HASHEM lives, Who took out the Children of Israel from the land of the North and from all the lands where He had scattered them'; and I shall return them to their land, which I gave to their forefathers.*

    ¹⁶ *Behold, I shall send many fishermen* * *— the word of HASHEM — and they will fish them out, and afterwards I shall send many trappers and they will trap them from atop every mountain and every hill and from the crevices in the rocks.* ¹⁷ *For My eyes are upon all their ways; they are not hidden from before Me, and their sin is not concealed from before My eyes.* ¹⁸ *I shall repay them first for the repetition of their [forefathers'] sin and transgression, for having desecrated My land; with their disgusting abominations and their detestations they have filled up My heritage."*

    ¹⁹ *HASHEM, my Strength, my Stronghold and my Refuge on the day of distress! To You nations will come from the ends of the earth and say: "It was all falsehood that our ancestors inherited, futility that has no purpose.* ²⁰ *Can a man make gods for himself? — they are not gods!"*

    ²¹ *Therefore, behold, I inform them at this time, I shall let them know of My hand and My strength; and they shall know that My Name is HASHEM!*

17

¹ *The sin of Judah is inscribed with an iron pen, with a hard metal fingernail; etched onto the tablet of their heart and into the corners of your altars.* ² *As they remember their children, [so they remember] their altars and their Asherah-trees, beside leafy trees and upon lofty hills.* ³ *O [idolaters] on mountains in the field: Your wealth, all your treasures, shall I make into booty, because of your high places [made] in sin throughout your boundaries.* ⁴ *You will be forced to withdraw from your heritage that I have given you, and I will enslave you to your enemies in a land that you knew not; for you have ignited a fire in My wrath, and it will burn forever.*

    ⁵ *Thus said HASHEM: Accursed is the man who trusts in people and makes flesh [and blood] his strength and turns his heart away from HASHEM.* ⁶ *He will be like a lone tree in the desert, and will not see when goodness comes; it dwells in parched lands in the wilderness, in an salty, uninhabited land.*

    ⁷ *Blessed is the man who trusts in HASHEM, then HASHEM will be his security.* ⁸ *He will be like a tree planted near water, which spreads out its roots along a brook and does not see when heat comes, whose foliage is ever fresh; it will not worry in a year of drought and will not stop producing fruit.* ⁹ *The heart is the most deceitful of all, and it is fragile — who can know it?* ¹⁰ *I, HASHEM, plumb the feelings and test the innermost thoughts,* * *to give to man according to his ways, the fruit of his deeds.*

    ¹¹ *[Like] a partridge summoning together [chicks] it did not bear, so is one who amasses wealth unjustly; in the middle of his days it will leave him, and at his end he will be considered a scoundrel.* *

    ¹² *Like the Throne of Glory, primevally exalted, is the place of our Sanctuary.* *
¹³ *O HASHEM, Hope of Israel! May all who forsake You be ashamed; may those who turn aside from my [teachings] be inscribed [for burial] in the earth; for they have forsaken HASHEM, the Source of fresh water.*

Side notes (left margin):

. . . *but will be redeemed*

Further rebuke

The cursedness of idolatry

The blessedness of faith in God

יד   רְפָאֵ֤נִי יהוה֙ וְאֵ֣רָפֵ֔א הֽוֹשִׁיעֵ֖נִי וְאִוָּשֵׁ֑עָה כִּ֥י תְהִלָּתִ֖י אָֽתָּה׃   ◀ יהוה:

טו-טז   הִנֵּה־הֵ֖מָּה אֹמְרִ֣ים אֵלָ֑י אַיֵּ֥ה דְבַר־יהוה יָב֖וֹא נָ֑א: וַאֲנִ֣י לֹא־אַ֠צְתִּי ׀ מֵֽרֹעֶ֤ה

אַחֲרֶ֙יךָ֙ וְי֥וֹם אָנ֖וּשׁ לֹ֣א הִתְאַוֵּ֑יתִי אַתָּ֣ה יָדָ֑עְתָּ מוֹצָ֣א שְׂפָתַ֔י נֹ֥כַח פָּנֶ֖יךָ הָיָֽה:

יז-יח   אַל־תִּֽהְיֵה־לִ֖י לִמְחִתָּ֑ה מַֽחֲסִי־אַ֖תָּה בְּי֥וֹם רָעָֽה: יֵבֹ֤שׁוּ רֹֽדְפַי֙ וְאַל־אֵבֹ֣שָׁה

אָ֔נִי יֵחַ֣תּוּ הֵ֔מָּה וְאַל־אֵחַ֖תָּה אָ֑נִי הָבִ֤יא עֲלֵיהֶם֙ י֣וֹם רָעָ֔ה וּמִשְׁנֶ֥ה שִׁבָּר֖וֹן

שָׁבְרֵֽם: יט   כֹּֽה־אָמַ֨ר יהוה אֵלַ֜י הָלֹ֣ךְ וְעָֽמַדְתָּ֗ בְּשַׁ֙עַר֙ בְּנֵֽי־°עם [הָעָ֣ם ק']

אֲשֶׁ֨ר יָבֹ֤אוּ בוֹ֙ מַלְכֵ֣י יְהוּדָ֔ה וַאֲשֶׁ֖ר יֵ֣צְאוּ ב֑וֹ וּבְכֹ֖ל שַׁעֲרֵ֥י יְרֽוּשָׁלָֽ͏ִם: וְאָֽמַרְתָּ֣

כ   אֲלֵיהֶ֡ם שִׁמְע֣וּ דְבַר־יהוה מַלְכֵ֤י יְהוּדָה֙ וְכׇל־יְהוּדָ֔ה וְכֹ֖ל יֹֽשְׁבֵ֣י יְרוּשָׁלָ֑͏ִם הַבָּאִ֖ים

כא   בַּשְּׁעָרִ֥ים הָאֵֽלֶּה: כֹּ֚ה אָמַ֣ר יהוה הִשָּׁמְר֖וּ בְּנַפְשֽׁוֹתֵיכֶ֑ם וְאַל־תִּשְׂא֤וּ

כב   מַשָּׂא֙ בְּי֣וֹם הַשַּׁבָּ֔ת וַֽהֲבֵאתֶ֖ם בְּשַׁעֲרֵ֣י יְרֽוּשָׁלָֽ͏ִם: וְלֹא־תוֹצִ֨יאוּ מַשָּׂ֤א

מִבָּֽתֵּיכֶם֙ בְּי֣וֹם הַשַּׁבָּ֔ת וְכׇל־מְלָאכָ֖ה לֹ֣א תַֽעֲשׂ֑וּ וְקִדַּשְׁתֶּם֙ אֶת־י֣וֹם הַשַּׁבָּ֔ת

כג   כַּֽאֲשֶׁ֥ר צִוִּ֖יתִי אֶת־אֲבֽוֹתֵיכֶֽם: וְלֹ֤א שָֽׁמְעוּ֙ וְלֹ֣א הִטּ֣וּ אֶת־אׇזְנָ֔ם וַיַּקְשׁוּ֙ אֶת־

כד   עׇרְפָּ֔ם לְבִלְתִּ֣י °שומע [שְׁמ֔וֹעַ ק'] וּלְבִלְתִּ֖י קַ֥חַת מוּסָֽר: וְ֠הָיָ֞ה אִם־שָׁמֹ֨עַ

תִּשְׁמְע֤וּן אֵלַי֙ נְאֻם־יהוה לְבִלְתִּ֣י ׀ הָבִ֣יא מַשָּׂ֡א בְּשַׁעֲרֵ֣י הָעִ֣יר הַזֹּאת֮ בְּי֣וֹם

הַשַּׁבָּת֒ וּלְקַדֵּשׁ֙ אֶת־י֣וֹם הַשַּׁבָּ֔ת לְבִלְתִּ֥י עֲשֽׂוֹת־°בה [ב֖וֹ ק'] כׇּל־מְלָאכָֽה:

כה   וּבָ֣אוּ בְשַׁעֲרֵ֣י הָעִ֣יר הַזֹּ֡את מְלָכִ֣ים ׀ וְשָׂרִ֡ים יֹֽשְׁבִים֩ עַל־כִּסֵּ֨א דָוִ֜ד רֹכְבִ֣ים ׀

בָּרֶ֣כֶב וּבַסּוּסִ֗ים הֵ֚מָּה וְשָׂ֣רֵיהֶ֔ם אִ֥ישׁ יְהוּדָ֖ה וְיֹֽשְׁבֵ֣י יְרֽוּשָׁלָ֑͏ִם וְיָֽשְׁבָ֥ה הָעִ֖יר

כו   הַזֹּ֥את לְעוֹלָֽם: וּבָ֣אוּ מֵעָרֵֽי־֠יְהוּדָ֠ה וּמִסְּבִיב֨וֹת יְרֽוּשָׁלַ֜͏ִם וּמֵאֶ֣רֶץ בִּנְיָמִ֗ן וּמִן־

הַשְּׁפֵלָ֤ה וּמִן־הָהָר֙ וּמִן־הַנֶּ֔גֶב מְבִאִ֛ים עוֹלָ֥ה וְזֶ֖בַח וּמִנְחָ֣ה וּלְבוֹנָ֑ה וּמְבִאֵ֥י

כז   תוֹדָ֖ה בֵּ֥ית יהוה: וְאִם־לֹ֨א תִשְׁמְע֜וּ אֵלַ֗י לְקַדֵּשׁ֙ אֶת־י֣וֹם הַשַּׁבָּ֔ת וּלְבִלְתִּ֣י ׀

שְׂאֵ֣ת מַשָּׂ֗א וּבֹ֛א בְּשַׁעֲרֵ֥י יְרֽוּשָׁלַ֖͏ִם בְּי֣וֹם הַשַּׁבָּ֑ת וְהִצַּ֧תִּי אֵ֣שׁ בִּשְׁעָרֶ֗יהָ

יח   א   וְאָֽכְלָ֛ה אַרְמְנ֥וֹת יְרֽוּשָׁלַ֖͏ִם וְלֹ֥א תִכְבֶּֽה: הַדָּבָר֙ אֲשֶׁ֣ר הָיָ֣ה אֶֽל־

ב   יִרְמְיָ֔הוּ מֵאֵ֥ת יהוה לֵאמֹֽר: ק֥וּם וְיָרַדְתָּ֖ בֵּ֣ית הַיּוֹצֵ֑ר וְשָׁ֖מָּה אַשְׁמִֽיעֲךָ֥ אֶת־

ג   דְּבָרָֽי: וָֽאֵרֵ֖ד בֵּ֣ית הַיּוֹצֵ֑ר °והנהו [וְהִנֵּה־ה֛וּא ק'] עֹשֶׂ֥ה מְלָאכָ֖ה עַל־

ד   הָֽאׇבְנָֽיִם: וְנִשְׁחַ֣ת הַכְּלִ֗י אֲשֶׁ֨ר ה֥וּא עֹשֶׂ֛ה בַּחֹ֖מֶר בְּיַ֣ד הַיּוֹצֵ֑ר וְשָׁ֣ב וַֽיַּעֲשֵׂ֙הוּ֙

ה   כְּלִ֣י אַחֵ֔ר כַּֽאֲשֶׁ֥ר יָשַׁ֛ר בְּעֵינֵ֥י הַיּוֹצֵ֖ר לַעֲשֽׂוֹת: וַיְהִ֥י דְבַר־יהוה

ו   אֵלַ֖י לֵאמֽוֹר: הֲכַיּוֹצֵ֨ר הַזֶּ֜ה לֹא־אוּכַ֧ל לַעֲשׂ֛וֹת לָכֶ֖ם בֵּ֣ית יִשְׂרָאֵ֑ל נְאֻם־

יהוה הִנֵּ֤ה כַחֹ֙מֶר֙ בְּיַ֣ד הַיּוֹצֵ֔ר כֵּן־אַתֶּ֥ם בְּיָדִ֖י בֵּ֥ית יִשְׂרָאֵֽל: רֶ֣גַע

ז   אֲדַבֵּ֣ר עַל־גּ֔וֹי וְעַל־מַמְלָכָ֑ה לִנְת֥וֹשׁ וְלִנְת֖וֹץ וּֽלְהַֽאֲבִֽיד: וְשָׁב֙ הַגּ֣וֹי הַה֔וּא

ח   מֵרָ֣עָת֔וֹ אֲשֶׁ֥ר דִּבַּ֖רְתִּי עָלָ֑יו וְנִֽחַמְתִּ֔י עַל־הָ֣רָעָ֔ה אֲשֶׁ֥ר חָשַׁ֖בְתִּי לַֽעֲשׂ֥וֹת

ט-י   לֽוֹ: וְרֶ֣גַע אֲדַבֵּ֔ר עַל־גּ֖וֹי וְעַל־מַמְלָכָ֑ה לִבְנֹ֖ת וְלִנְטֹֽעַ: וְעָשָׂ֤ה °הרעה

[הָרַע֙ ק'] בְּעֵינַ֔י לְבִלְתִּ֖י שְׁמֹ֣עַ בְּקוֹלִ֑י וְנִֽחַמְתִּי֙ עַל־הַטּוֹבָ֔ה אֲשֶׁ֥ר אָמַ֖רְתִּי

יא   לְהֵיטִ֥יב אוֹתֽוֹ: וְעַתָּ֡ה אֱמׇר־נָ֣א אֶל־אִישׁ־יְהוּדָ֣ה וְעַל־יֽוֹשְׁבֵ֣י יְרוּשָׁלַ֘͏ִם֮ לֵאמֹר֒

17:16. I did not seek to be a prophet, and I asked You (1:6) not to select me (Radak). Although the people accuse me of hating them, You know that I appealed to You on their behalf (Rashi).

Jeremiah prays for an end to his torment

¹⁴ *Heal me, HASHEM, and I will be healed; save me, and I will be saved; for You are my praise.* ¹⁵ *Behold, they say to me, "Where is the word of HASHEM? Let it come true!"* ¹⁶ *I was not anxious to become a shepherd for You and I did not lust for a day of distress; You know [this]! The words of my lips were directed to Your presence.* * ¹⁷ *May You not cause me dismay, for You are my shelter on a day of evil.* ¹⁸ *Let my pursuers be shamed, and let me not be shamed; let them be dismayed, but let me not be dismayed; bring upon them a day of evil and devastate them with double disaster.*

¹⁹ *Thus said HASHEM to me: "Go and stand in the Gate of the Children of the People, through which the kings of Judah enter and through which they exit, and in all the gates of Jerusalem.* ²⁰ *Say to them:*

Castigate the desecrators of the Sabbath!

Hear the word of HASHEM, O kings of Judah and all of Judah and all inhabitants of Jerusalem who enter through these gates: ²¹ *Thus said HASHEM: 'Beware for your souls; do not carry a burden on the Sabbath day to bring it into the gates of Jerusalem.* ²² *And do not bring a burden out from your houses on the Sabbath day; you shall not do any [manner of] work. Sanctify the Sabbath day as I commanded your forefathers.'* ²³ *But they did not listen and did not incline their ear; they stiffened their neck, in order not to hear and in order not to accept rebuke.* ²⁴ *And it shall be that if you truly listen to Me — the word of HASHEM — not to bring a burden into the gates of this city on the Sabbath day, and to sanctify the Sabbath day, not to do any [manner of] work on it,* ²⁵ *then, kings and princes who sit upon the throne of David will enter the gates of this city, riding chariots and horses — they and their officers, the men of Judah and the inhabitants of Jerusalem — and this city will be inhabited forever;* ²⁶ *and [people] will come from the cities of Judah and from the environs of Jerusalem, from the land of Benjamin, from the lowland, from the mountain, and from the South, bringing burnt-offerings, peace-offerings, meal-offerings and frankincense, and bringing thanksgiving-offerings to the Temple of HASHEM.* ²⁷ *But if you do not listen to Me, to sanctify the Sabbath Day and not to carry a burden and enter the gates of Jerusalem on the Sabbath day, then I shall set a fire to its gates, which will consume the palaces of Jerusalem and not be extinguished."*

18

The parable of the potter

¹ *The word which came to Jeremiah from HASHEM, saying:* ² *"Arise and go down to the potter's shop, and there I will let you hear My words."* ³ *So I went down to a potter's shop, and behold, he was working on the [potter's] wheels.* ⁴ *The vessel that he was making of the clay became ruined in the potter's hand, so he began again and made it into a different vessel, to do as was fitting in the eyes of the potter.*

⁵ *The word of HASHEM then came to me, saying:* ⁶ *"Can I not do to you, O House of Israel, what this potter does? — the word of HASHEM. Behold, just as clay is in the hand of the potter, so are you in My hand, O House of Israel.* ⁷ *One moment I may speak concerning a nation or a kingdom, to destroy, demolish or annihilate [it],* ⁸ *but if that nation repents of its evil deed of which I had spoken, then I relent of the evil [decree] that I had planned to carry out against it.* ⁹ *Or, one moment I may speak concerning a nation or a kingdom, to build and establish [it],* ¹⁰ *but if they do what is wrong in My eyes, not heeding My voice, then I relent of the goodness that I had said to bestow upon it.* ¹¹ *So now, please say to the people of Judah and to the inhabitants of Jerusalem saying:*

כֹּה אָמַ֣ר יְהֹוָ֗ה הִנֵּ֨ה אָנֹכִ֜י יוֹצֵ֤ר עֲלֵיכֶם֙ רָעָ֔ה וְחֹשֵׁ֥ב עֲלֵיכֶ֖ם מַחֲשָׁבָ֑ה

יב שׁ֣וּבוּ נָ֗א אִ֚ישׁ מִדַּרְכּ֣וֹ הָֽרָעָ֔ה וְהֵיטִ֥יבוּ דַרְכֵיכֶ֖ם וּמַ֥עַלְלֵיכֶֽם: וְאָמְר֣וּ נוֹאָ֔שׁ לָכֵ֑ן

יג כִּי־אַחֲרֵ֤י מַחְשְׁבוֹתֵ֙ינוּ֙ נֵלֵ֔ךְ וְאִ֕ישׁ שְׁרִיר֥וּת לִבּֽוֹ־הָרָ֖ע נַעֲשֶֽׂה: כֹּ֣ה אָמַ֣ר יְהֹוָ֗ה שַׁאֲלוּ־נָא֙ בַּגּוֹיִ֔ם מִ֥י שָׁמַ֖ע כָּאֵ֑לֶּה שַֽׁעֲרֻרִ֥ת עָשְׂתָ֖ה מְאֹ֑ד

יד בְּתוּלַ֖ת יִשְׂרָאֵֽל: הֲיַעֲזֹ֤ב מִצּוּר֙ שָׂדַ֔י שֶׁ֖לֶג לְבָנ֑וֹן אִם־יִנָּֽתְשׁ֗וּ מַ֥יִם זָרִ֖ים

טו קָרִ֖ים נוֹזְלִֽים: כִּֽי־שְׁכֵחֻ֣נִי עַמִּ֔י לַשָּׁ֖וְא יְקַטֵּ֑רוּ וַיַּכְשִׁל֤וּם בְּדַרְכֵיהֶם֙ שְׁבִילֵ֣י

טז עוֹלָ֔ם לָלֶ֣כֶת נְתִיב֔וֹת דֶּ֖רֶךְ לֹ֣א סְלוּלָֽה: לָשׂ֥וּם אַרְצָ֛ם לְשַׁמָּ֖ה שְׁרוּק֣וֹת °שְׁרוּקֹ֣ת ק׳

יז עוֹלָ֑ם כֹּ֚ל עוֹבֵ֣ר עָלֶ֔יהָ יִשֹּׁ֖ם וְיָנִ֥יד בְּרֹאשֽׁוֹ: כְּרֽוּחַ־קָדִ֣ים

יח אֲפִיצֵ֖ם לִפְנֵ֣י אוֹיֵ֑ב עֹ֧רֶף וְלֹֽא־פָנִ֛ים אֶרְאֵ֖ם בְּי֥וֹם אֵידָֽם: וַיֹּאמְר֞וּ לְכ֣וּ וְנַחְשְׁבָ֣ה עַֽל־יִרְמְיָ֘הוּ֮ מַחֲשָׁבוֹת֒ כִּ֣י לֹא־תֹאבַ֨ד תּוֹרָ֜ה מִכֹּהֵ֗ן וְעֵצָה֙ מֵֽחָכָ֔ם וְדָבָ֖ר מִנָּבִ֑יא לְכ֗וּ וְנַכֵּ֙הוּ֙ בַלָּשׁ֔וֹן וְאַל־נַקְשִׁ֖יבָה אֶל־כָּל־דְּבָרָֽיו:

יט–כ הַקְשִׁ֤יבָה יְהֹוָה֙ אֵלָ֔י וּשְׁמַ֖ע לְק֣וֹל יְרִיבָֽי: הַיְשֻׁלַּ֤ם תַּֽחַת־טוֹבָה֙ רָעָ֔ה כִּֽי־כָר֥וּ שׁוּחָ֖ה לְנַפְשִׁ֑י זְכֹ֣ר ׀ עָמְדִ֣י לְפָנֶ֗יךָ לְדַבֵּ֤ר עֲלֵיהֶם֙ טוֹבָ֔ה לְהָשִׁ֥יב אֶת־חֲמָֽתְךָ֖

כא מֵהֶֽם: לָכֵן֩ תֵּ֨ן אֶת־בְּנֵיהֶ֜ם לָֽרָעָ֗ב וְהַגִּרֵם֮ עַל־יְדֵי־חֶרֶב֒ וְתִֽהְיֶ֤נָה נְשֵׁיהֶם֙ שַׁכֻּל֣וֹת וְאַלְמָנ֔וֹת וְאַ֨נְשֵׁיהֶ֔ם יִֽהְי֖וּ הֲרֻ֣גֵי מָ֑וֶת בַּחֽוּרֵיהֶ֖ם מֻכֵּי־חֶ֥רֶב

כב בַּמִּלְחָמָֽה: תִּשָּׁמַ֤ע זְעָקָה֙ מִבָּ֣תֵּיהֶ֔ם כִּֽי־תָבִ֧יא עֲלֵיהֶ֛ם גְּד֖וּד פִּתְאֹ֑ם כִּֽי־כָר֤וּ

כג °שִׁיחָ֨ה °שׁוּחָ֜ה ק׳ לְלָכְדֵ֗נִי וּפַחִ֛ים טָמְנ֥וּ לְרַגְלָֽי: וְאַתָּ֣ה יְ֠הֹוָה יָדַ֜עְתָּ אֶת־ כָּל־עֲצָתָ֤ם עָלַי֙ לַמָּ֔וֶת אַל־תְּכַפֵּר֙ עַל־עֲוֺנָ֔ם וְחַטָּאתָ֖ם מִלְּפָנֶ֣יךָ אַל־תֶּ֑מְחִי

יט א °וְהָי֤וּ °וְיִֽהְי֤וּ ק׳ מֻכְשָׁלִים֙ לְפָנֶ֔יךָ בְּעֵ֥ת אַפְּךָ֖ עֲשֵׂ֥ה בָהֶֽם: כֹּ֣ה אָמַ֣ר

יב יְהֹוָ֗ה הָל֞וֹךְ וְקָנִ֤יתָ בַקְבֻּק֙ יוֹצֵ֣ר חָ֔רֶשׂ וּמִזִּקְנֵ֥י הָעָ֖ם וּמִזִּקְנֵ֥י הַכֹּהֲנִֽים: וְיָצָ֙אתָ֙ אֶל־גֵּ֣יא בֶן־הִנֹּ֔ם אֲשֶׁ֕ר פֶּ֖תַח שַׁ֣עַר °הַחֲרָס֑וּת °הַֽחַרְסִֽית ק׳ וְקָרָ֣אתָ שָּׁ֔ם

ג אֶת־הַדְּבָרִ֖ים אֲשֶׁר־אֲדַבֵּ֣ר אֵלֶֽיךָ: וְאָמַרְתָּ֙ שִׁמְע֣וּ דְבַר־יְהֹוָ֔ה מַלְכֵ֥י יְהוּדָ֖ה וְיֹשְׁבֵ֣י יְרֽוּשָׁלָ֑͏ִם כֹּֽה־אָמַ֞ר יְהֹוָ֤ה צְבָאוֹת֙ אֱלֹהֵ֣י יִשְׂרָאֵ֔ל הִנְנִ֨י מֵבִ֤יא רָעָה֙

ד עַל־הַמָּק֣וֹם הַזֶּ֔ה אֲשֶׁ֥ר כָּל־שֹׁמְעָ֖הּ תִּצַּ֣לְנָה אָזְנָֽיו: יַ֣עַן ׀ אֲשֶׁ֣ר עֲזָבֻ֗נִי וַֽיְנַכְּר֞וּ אֶת־הַמָּק֤וֹם הַזֶּה֙ וַיְקַטְּרוּ־בוֹ֙ לֵאלֹהִ֣ים אֲחֵרִ֔ים אֲשֶׁ֧ר לֹֽא־יְדָע֛וּם הֵ֖מָּה

ה וַאֲבֽוֹתֵיהֶ֖ם וּמַלְכֵ֣י יְהוּדָ֑ה וּמָֽלְא֛וּ אֶת־הַמָּק֥וֹם הַזֶּ֖ה דַּ֥ם נְקִיִּֽם: וּבָנ֞וּ אֶת־ בָּמ֣וֹת הַבַּ֗עַל לִשְׂרֹ֤ף אֶת־בְּנֵיהֶם֙ בָּאֵ֔שׁ עֹל֖וֹת לַבָּ֑עַל אֲשֶׁ֤ר לֹֽא־צִוִּ֙יתִי֙ וְלֹ֣א

ו דִבַּ֔רְתִּי וְלֹ֥א עָֽלְתָ֖ה עַל־לִבִּֽי: לָכֵ֞ן הִנֵּ֤ה יָמִים֙ בָּאִ֔ים נְאֻם־יְהֹוָ֑ה וְלֹא־יִקָּרֵ֩א לַמָּק֨וֹם הַזֶּ֥ה ע֛וֹד הַתֹּ֖פֶת וְגֵ֣יא בֶן־הִנֹּ֑ם כִּ֖י אִם־גֵּ֥יא הַהֲרֵגָֽה:

ז וּבַקֹּתִ֞י אֶת־עֲצַ֣ת יְהוּדָ֣ה וִירוּשָׁלַ֘͏ִם֮ בַּמָּק֣וֹם הַזֶּה֒ וְהִפַּלְתִּ֤ים בַּחֶ֙רֶב֙ לִפְנֵ֣י

18:13. God says that it is unprecedented that Israel should reject Him. If any rational person will welcome much-needed water though it comes from a distant unknown source, surely Israel should revere God! The people's defection happened only because the evil ways of the false prophets (v. 15) deceived them and led them astray.

18:18. Jeremiah once again beseeches God to spare him from the machinations of his opponents, who say that they should use slander to remove him from a position of influence. No one will suffer from his absence, since there are many other people just as wise, but whose messages will be more popular.

19:2. Later known as the Dung Gate.

Thus said HASHEM: *Behold, I am fashioning evil against you, and I am devising a plan against you. Repent now, each man from his evil way; improve your ways and your deeds.* [12] *But they will say, 'It is hopeless! For we shall follow our own ideas and each one of us will act according to the evil vision of his heart.'*

The land will be desolate

[13] *Therefore, thus said* HASHEM: *Inquire now of the nations whether anyone has heard such a thing; very often has the virgin of Israel done disgraceful things!* * [14] *Does one decline melting snows of Lebanon that flow over the rocks in the fields? Are refreshing, cool, flowing waters rejected?* [15] *Yet My people have forgotten Me; they burn incense to the nothings. They have been made to stumble in their ways, eternal paths, to walk in byways, an untrodden road;* [16] *to cause their land to become a wasteland, an eternal whistling; every passerby will be astonished and shake his head.* [17] *Like an east wind, I shall scatter them before the enemy: the back of [My] neck, and not [My] face will I show them on the day of their calamity."*

Hashem, protect me from adversity

[18] *They say, "Come and let us devise plans against Jeremiah,* * *for instruction will never be lost from the priest, nor advice from the wise man, nor prophecy from the prophet; come, let us assault him verbally, and let us not hear his many words."* [19] *Be attentive to me,* HASHEM, *and hear the voice of my adversaries!* [20] *Should good be repaid with evil? Yet they have dug a pit for my soul. Remember my standing before You to speak well of them, to turn Your anger away from them!* [21] *Therefore, give their sons over to hunger and fell them by the sword. Let their wives be bereaved [of children] and widowed; let their men be killed by a plague and their young men struck down by the sword in war.* [22] *Let a cry be heard from their houses when You bring a sudden troop upon them, for they have dug a pit to ensnare me, and concealed traps for my feet.* [23] *You,* HASHEM, *know all their counsel against me for death; do not pardon their sin and do not erase their transgression from before You. May they be caused to stumble before You. At the time of Your anger, act against them!*

19

The parable of the earthenware bottle

[1] *Thus said* HASHEM: *"Go, and buy a potter's earthenware bottle; and [take with you] some of the elders of the people and some of the elders of the Kohanim.* [2] *Then go out to the Valley of the Son of Hinnom, which is at the opening of the Potsherd Gate,* * *and proclaim there the words that I shall speak to you.* [3] *Say:*

Hear the word of HASHEM, *O kings of Judah and inhabitants of Jerusalem! Thus said* HASHEM, *Master of Legions, God of Israel: Behold, I am bringing such evil upon this place, that whoever hears of it, his ears will ring.* [4] *Because they forsook Me and estranged this place [from Me]; and they burned incense in it to the gods of other that they had not known — they and their forefathers and the kings of Judah; and they filled this place with the blood of innocent people;* [5] *and they built the high places of the Baal, [at which] to burn their sons in fire as burnt-offerings to the Baal, which I never commanded, nor spoke of, nor even considered in My heart.* [6] *Therefore, behold, days are coming — the word of* HASHEM — *when this place will no longer be called Topheth and the Valley of the Son of Hinnom, but the Valley of the Killing.* [7] *In this place I shall make void the counsel of Judah and Jerusalem, and I shall make them fall by the sword before*

The Valley of the Son of Hinnom

אֹיְבֵיהֶ֑ם וּבְיַ֖ד מְבַקְשֵׁ֣י נַפְשָׁ֑ם וְנָתַתִּ֤י אֶת־נִבְלָתָם֙ לְמַֽאֲכָ֔ל לְע֥וֹף הַשָּׁמַ֖יִם

ח וּלְבֶֽהֱמַ֥ת הָאָֽרֶץ: וְשַׂמְתִּי֙ אֶת־הָעִ֣יר הַזֹּ֔את לְשַׁמָּ֖ה וְלִשְׁרֵקָ֑ה כֹּ֚ל עֹבֵ֣ר

ט עָלֶ֔יהָ יִשֹּׁ֥ם וְיִשְׁרֹ֖ק עַל־כָּל־מַכֹּתֶֽהָ: וְהַֽאֲכַלְתִּ֗ים אֶת־בְּשַׂ֤ר בְּנֵיהֶם֙ וְאֵת֙

בְּשַׂ֣ר בְּנֹֽתֵיהֶ֔ם וְאִ֥ישׁ בְּשַׂר־רֵעֵ֖הוּ יֹאכֵ֑לוּ בְּמָצוֹר֙ וּבְמָצ֔וֹק אֲשֶׁ֤ר יָצִ֙יקוּ֙

י לָהֶ֣ם אֹֽיְבֵיהֶ֔ם וּמְבַקְשֵׁ֖י נַפְשָֽׁם: וְשָֽׁבַרְתָּ֙ הַבַּקְבֻּ֔ק לְעֵינֵי֙ הָֽאֲנָשִׁ֔ים הַהֹֽלְכִ֖ים

אוֹתָֽךְ: וְאָֽמַרְתָּ֣ אֲלֵיהֶ֗ם כֹּֽה־אָמַר֮ יְהֹוָ֣ה צְבָאוֹת֒ כָּ֣כָה אֶשְׁבֹּ֞ר אֶת־הָעָ֤ם

יא הַזֶּה֙ וְאֶת־הָעִ֣יר הַזֹּ֔את כַּֽאֲשֶׁ֤ר יִשְׁבֹּר֙ אֶת־כְּלִ֣י הַיּוֹצֵ֔ר אֲשֶׁ֥ר לֹֽא־יוּכַ֖ל

לְהֵֽרָפֵ֣ה ע֑וֹד וּבְתֹ֣פֶת יִקְבְּר֔וּ מֵאֵ֥ין מָק֖וֹם לִקְבּֽוֹר: כֵּֽן־אֶֽעֱשֶׂ֞ה לַמָּק֤וֹם הַזֶּה֙

יב נְאֻם־יְהֹוָ֔ה וּלְיֽוֹשְׁבָ֑יו וְלָתֵ֛ת אֶת־הָעִ֥יר הַזֹּ֖את כְּתֹֽפֶת: וְהָי֣וּ בָתֵּ֣י יְרֽוּשָׁלַ֡͏ִם

וּבָתֵּ֣י מַלְכֵֽי־יְהוּדָ֡ה כִּמְק֣וֹם הַתֹּ֩פֶת֩ הַטְּמֵאִ֨ים לְכֹ֤ל הַבָּתִּים֙ אֲשֶׁ֣ר קִטְּר֣וּ עַל־

יג גַּגֹּֽתֵיהֶ֗ם לְכֹל֙ צְבָ֣א הַשָּׁמַ֔יִם וְהַסֵּ֥ךְ נְסָכִ֖ים לֵֽאלֹהִ֥ים אֲחֵרִֽים: וַיָּבֹ֤א

יד יִרְמְיָ֙הוּ֙ מֵֽהַתֹּ֔פֶת אֲשֶׁ֨ר שְׁלָח֧וֹ יְהֹוָ֛ה שָׁ֖ם לְהִנָּבֵ֑א וַֽיַּֽעֲמֹד֙ בַּֽחֲצַ֣ר בֵּֽית־יְהֹוָ֔ה

טו וַיֹּ֖אמֶר אֶל־כָּל־הָעָֽם: כֹּֽה־אָמַ֞ר יְהֹוָ֤ה צְבָאוֹת֙ אֱלֹהֵ֣י יִשְׂרָאֵ֔ל

הִנְנִ֨י °מבי [°מֵבִ֤יא ק] אֶל־הָעִ֤יר הַזֹּאת֙ וְעַל־כָּל־עָרֶ֔יהָ אֵ֖ת כָּל־הָ֣רָעָ֑ה

אֲשֶׁ֖ר דִּבַּ֣רְתִּי עָלֶ֑יהָ כִּ֤י הִקְשׁוּ֙ אֶת־עָרְפָּ֔ם לְבִלְתִּ֖י שְׁמ֥וֹעַ אֶת־דְּבָרָֽי:

א וַיִּשְׁמַ֤ע פַּשְׁחוּר֙ בֶּן־אִמֵּ֣ר הַכֹּהֵ֔ן וְהֽוּא־פָקִ֥יד נָגִ֖יד בְּבֵ֣ית יְהֹוָ֑ה אֶֽת־יִרְמְיָ֖הוּ

ב נִבָּ֖א אֶת־הַדְּבָרִ֥ים הָאֵֽלֶּה: וַיַּכֶּ֣ה פַשְׁחוּר֔ אֵ֖ת יִרְמְיָ֣הוּ הַנָּבִ֑יא וַיִּתֵּ֤ן אֹתוֹ֙

ג עַל־הַמַּהְפֶּ֔כֶת אֲשֶׁ֛ר בְּשַׁ֥עַר בִּנְיָמִ֛ן הָֽעֶלְי֖וֹן אֲשֶׁ֣ר בְּבֵ֣ית יְהֹוָֽה: וַֽיְהִי֙

מִֽמָּחֳרָ֔ת וַיֹּצֵ֥א פַשְׁח֖וּר אֶת־יִרְמְיָ֣הוּ מִן־הַמַּהְפָּ֑כֶת וַיֹּ֨אמֶר אֵלָ֜יו יִרְמְיָ֗הוּ

ד לֹ֤א פַשְׁחוּר֙ קָרָ֤א יְהֹוָה֙ שְׁמֶ֔ךָ כִּ֖י אִם־מָג֥וֹר מִסָּבִֽיב: כִּ֣י כֹ֣ה

אָמַ֣ר יְהֹוָ֗ה הִנְנִ֤י נֹֽתֶנְךָ֙ לְמָגוֹר֙ לְ֔ךָ וּלְכָל־אֹֽהֲבֶ֔יךָ וְנָֽפְל֖וּ בְּחֶ֣רֶב אֹֽיְבֵיהֶ֑ם

וְעֵינֶ֣יךָ רֹא֑וֹת וְאֶת־כָּל־יְהוּדָ֗ה אֶתֵּן֙ בְּיַ֣ד מֶֽלֶךְ־בָּבֶ֔ל וְהִגְלָ֥ם בָּבֶ֖לָה

ה וְהִכָּ֣ם בֶּחָֽרֶב: וְנָֽתַתִּ֗י אֶת־כָּל־חֹ֨סֶן֙ הָעִ֣יר הַזֹּ֔את וְאֶת־כָּל־יְגִיעָ֖הּ וְאֶת־

כָּל־יְקָרָ֑הּ וְאֵ֨ת כָּל־אֽוֹצְר֜וֹת מַלְכֵ֤י יְהוּדָה֙ אֶתֵּן֙ בְּיַ֣ד אֹֽיְבֵיהֶ֔ם וּבְזָז֖וּם

ו וּלְקָח֑וּם וֶֽהֱבִיא֖וּם בָּבֶֽלָה: וְאַתָּ֣ה פַשְׁח֗וּר וְכֹל֙ יֹֽשְׁבֵ֣י בֵיתֶ֔ךָ תֵּֽלְכ֖וּ בַּשֶּׁ֑בִי

וּבָבֶ֣ל תָּב֗וֹא וְשָׁ֤ם תָּמוּת֙ וְשָׁ֣ם תִּקָּבֵ֔ר אַתָּה֙ וְכָל־אֹֽהֲבֶ֔יךָ אֲשֶׁר־נִבֵּ֥אתָ

ז לָהֶ֖ם בַּשָּֽׁקֶר: פִּתִּיתַ֤נִי יְהֹוָה֙ וָֽאֶפָּ֔ת חֲזַקְתַּ֖נִי וַתּוּכָ֑ל

הָיִ֤יתִי לִשְׂחוֹק֙ כָּל־הַיּ֔וֹם כֻּלֹּ֖ה לֹעֵ֣ג לִֽי: כִּֽי־מִדֵּ֤י אֲדַבֵּר֙ אֶזְעָ֔ק חָמָ֥ס

ח וָשֹׁ֖ד אֶקְרָ֑א כִּֽי־הָיָ֨ה דְבַר־יְהֹוָ֥ה לִ֛י לְחֶרְפָּ֥ה וּלְקֶ֖לֶס כָּל־הַיּֽוֹם: וְאָמַרְתִּ֞י

ט לֹֽא־אֶזְכְּרֶ֗נּוּ וְלֹֽא־אֲדַבֵּ֥ר עוֹד֙ בִּשְׁמ֔וֹ וְהָיָ֤ה בְלִבִּי֙ כְּאֵ֣שׁ בֹּעֶ֔רֶת עָצֻ֖ר

בְּעַצְמֹתָ֑י וְנִלְאֵ֥יתִי כַּֽלְכֵ֖ל וְלֹ֥א אוּכָֽל: כִּ֣י שָׁמַ֗עְתִּי דִּבַּ֤ת רַבִּים֙ מָג֣וֹר מִסָּבִ֔יב

19:12. Like Topheth, Jerusalem will be filled with corpses.

20:2. The jail was called Mahpechah (*Rashi*). Alternatively, the word means stocks or pillory (*Radak*).

20:3. Pashhur understood his name as a hybrid of פֶּשׁ

חוּר, *great noble*. But God considered it a contraction of פֶּשׁ סָחוּר, which means the same as מָגוֹר מִסָּבִיב, *a multitude [of marauders gathered] roundabout* (*Rashi*).

20:7. I did not wish to accept the mission of being a prophet, but You prevailed upon me to do so (see 1:4-10).

their enemies and at the hand of those who seek their lives; and I shall lay out their carcasses as food for the bird of the heavens and for the animal of the land. ⁸ I shall make this city a place of astonishment and whistling; anyone who passes it will be astonished and whistle over its calamities. ⁹ I shall feed them the flesh of their sons and the flesh of their daughters, and everyone will eat the flesh of his fellow, in the siege and in the misery that their enemies, and those who seek their lives, will suppress them with."

Break the bottle! ¹⁰ "Then break the bottle before the eyes of the men who go with you, ¹¹ and say to them:

Thus said HASHEM, Master of Legions: So shall I shatter this people and this city, just as one breaks a potter's vessel, which cannot be fixed any more; and they will bury in Topheth until there is no [more] room to bury. ¹² Thus shall I do to this place — the word of HASHEM — and to its inhabitants; and I shall make this city like Topheth. * ¹³ And the houses of Jerusalem and the houses of the kings of Judah — the contaminated ones — will be like the shrine of Topheth; all the houses upon whose rooftops they burnt incense to the entire host of the heavens, and poured libations to the gods of others."

¹⁴ Jeremiah then came from Topheth, where HASHEM had sent him to prophesy, and he stood in the courtyard of the Temple of HASHEM and said to all the people:

¹⁵ Thus said HASHEM, Master of Legions, God of Israel: Behold I am bringing upon this city — and upon all its [surrounding] cities — all the evil that I spoke concerning it, for they have stiffened their necks, not listening to My words.

20

Imprisoned, Jeremiah rails at his jailer

¹ **P**ashhur son of Immer the Kohen, who was the chief official of the Temple of HASHEM, heard Jeremiah prophesying these words; ² Pashhur struck Jeremiah the prophet and put him in the prison* that was at the Upper Gate of Benjamin which was in the Temple of HASHEM. ³ It was on the next day; Pashhur released Jeremiah from the prison, and Jeremiah said to him, "HASHEM did not call your name Pashhur, rather, Magor-missabib. * ⁴ For thus said HASHEM: Behold, I am delivering you to a [marauding] troop, you and all your loved ones, and they will fall by the sword of their enemies and your own eyes will see [it]; and I will deliver all of Judah into the hand of the king of Babylonia, who will exile [some] to Babylonia and strike down [others] by the sword. ⁵ And I shall deliver all the wealth of this city, all [the fruits of] its labor, and all its precious items; all the treasures of the kings of Judah I shall deliver into the hand of their enemies, and they will plunder them and take them away, and bring them to Babylonia. ⁶ And you, Pashhur, and all who dwell in your house, will go into captivity; you will come to Babylonia and there you will die and and there you will be buried, you and all your loved ones, to whom you prophesied falsehood."

Jeremiah complains of his role ⁷ You persuaded me, * HASHEM, and I was persuaded; You were more forceful than I and You prevailed. I have become a laughingstock all day long, and everyone ridicules me. ⁸ Whenever I speak [to them], I shout; "Corruption! Robbery!" do I proclaim, for the word of HASHEM has become a source of shame and derision to me all day long. ⁹ Yet if I would say, "I will not mention Him and not speak in His Name any more" — [His word] would be like a burning fire in my heart, stored in my bones, and though I might struggle to contain it, I could not. ¹⁰ For I have heard the slander of the many, the multitude gathered roundabout,

הַגִּידוּ וְנַגִּידֶנּוּ כֹּל אֱנוֹשׁ שְׁלוֹמִי שֹׁמְרֵי צַלְעִי אוּלַי יְפֻתֶּה וְנוּכְלָה לוֹ

יא וְנִקְחָה נִקְמָתֵנוּ מִמֶּנּוּ: וַיהוָה אוֹתִי כְּגִבּוֹר עָרִיץ עַל־כֵּן רֹדְפַי יִכָּשְׁלוּ וְלֹא

יב יָכֹלוּ בֹּשׁוּ מְאֹד כִּי־לֹא הִשְׂכִּילוּ כְּלִמַּת עוֹלָם לֹא תִשָּׁכֵחַ: וַיהוָה צְבָאוֹת

בֹּחֵן צַדִּיק רֹאֶה כְלָיוֹת וָלֵב אֶרְאֶה נִקְמָתְךָ מֵהֶם כִּי אֵלֶיךָ גִּלִּיתִי אֶת־

יג רִיבִי: שִׁירוּ לַיהוָה הַלְלוּ אֶת־יְהוָה כִּי הִצִּיל אֶת־נֶפֶשׁ אֶבְיוֹן

יד מִיַּד מְרֵעִים: אָרוּר הַיּוֹם אֲשֶׁר יֻלַּדְתִּי בּוֹ יוֹם אֲשֶׁר־יְלָדַתְנִי אִמִּי

טו אַל־יְהִי בָרוּךְ: אָרוּר הָאִישׁ אֲשֶׁר בִּשַּׂר אֶת־אָבִי לֵאמֹר יֻלַּד־לְךָ בֵּן זָכָר

טז שַׂמֵּחַ שִׂמֳּחָהוּ: וְהָיָה הָאִישׁ הַהוּא כֶּעָרִים אֲשֶׁר־הָפַךְ יְהוָה וְלֹא נִחָם

יז וְשָׁמַע זְעָקָה בַּבֹּקֶר וּתְרוּעָה בְּעֵת צָהֳרָיִם: אֲשֶׁר לֹא־מוֹתְתַנִי מֵרָחֶם

יח וַתְּהִי־לִי אִמִּי קִבְרִי וְרַחְמָה הֲרַת עוֹלָם: לָמָּה זֶּה מֵרֶחֶם יָצָאתִי לִרְאוֹת

א עָמָל וְיָגוֹן וַיִּכְלוּ בְּבֹשֶׁת יָמָי: הַדָּבָר אֲשֶׁר־הָיָה אֶל־יִרְמְיָהוּ מֵאֵת **כא**

יְהוָה בִּשְׁלֹחַ אֵלָיו הַמֶּלֶךְ צִדְקִיָּהוּ אֶת־פַּשְׁחוּר בֶּן־מַלְכִּיָּה וְאֶת־צְפַנְיָה

ב בֶן־מַעֲשֵׂיָה הַכֹּהֵן לֵאמֹר: דְּרָשׁ־נָא בַעֲדֵנוּ אֶת־יְהוָה כִּי נְבוּכַדְרֶאצַּר

מֶלֶךְ־בָּבֶל נִלְחָם עָלֵינוּ אוּלַי יַעֲשֶׂה יְהוָה אוֹתָנוּ כְּכָל־נִפְלְאֹתָיו וְיַעֲלֶה

ג מֵעָלֵינוּ: וַיֹּאמֶר יִרְמְיָהוּ אֲלֵיהֶם כֹּה תֹאמְרֻן אֶל־צִדְקִיָּהוּ: כֹּה־

ד אָמַר יְהוָה אֱלֹהֵי יִשְׂרָאֵל הִנְנִי מֵסֵב אֶת־כְּלֵי הַמִּלְחָמָה אֲשֶׁר בְּיֶדְכֶם

אֲשֶׁר אַתֶּם נִלְחָמִים בָּם אֶת־מֶלֶךְ בָּבֶל וְאֶת־הַכַּשְׂדִּים הַצָּרִים עֲלֵיכֶם

ה מִחוּץ לַחוֹמָה וְאָסַפְתִּי אוֹתָם אֶל־תּוֹךְ הָעִיר הַזֹּאת: וְנִלְחַמְתִּי אֲנִי אִתְּכֶם

ו בְּיָד נְטוּיָה וּבִזְרוֹעַ חֲזָקָה וּבְאַף וּבְחֵמָה וּבְקֶצֶף גָּדוֹל: וְהִכֵּיתִי אֶת־יוֹשְׁבֵי

ז הָעִיר הַזֹּאת וְאֶת־הָאָדָם וְאֶת־הַבְּהֵמָה בְּדֶבֶר גָּדוֹל יָמֻתוּ: וְאַחֲרֵי־כֵן

נְאֻם־יְהוָה אֶתֵּן אֶת־צִדְקִיָּהוּ מֶלֶךְ־יְהוּדָה וְאֶת־עֲבָדָיו וְאֶת־הָעָם

וְאֶת־הַנִּשְׁאָרִים בָּעִיר הַזֹּאת מִן־הַדֶּבֶר | מִן־הַחֶרֶב וּמִן־הָרָעָב בְּיַד

נְבוּכַדְרֶאצַּר מֶלֶךְ־בָּבֶל וּבְיַד אֹיְבֵיהֶם וּבְיַד מְבַקְשֵׁי נַפְשָׁם וְהִכָּם לְפִי־

ח חֶרֶב לֹא־יָחוּס עֲלֵיהֶם וְלֹא יַחְמֹל וְלֹא יְרַחֵם: וְאֶל־הָעָם הַזֶּה תֹּאמַר כֹּה

ט אָמַר יְהוָה הִנְנִי נֹתֵן לִפְנֵיכֶם אֶת־דֶּרֶךְ הַחַיִּים וְאֶת־דֶּרֶךְ הַמָּוֶת: הַיֹּשֵׁב

בָּעִיר הַזֹּאת יָמוּת בַּחֶרֶב וּבָרָעָב וּבַדָּבֶר וְהַיּוֹצֵא וְנָפַל עַל־הַכַּשְׂדִּים

י הַצָּרִים עֲלֵיכֶם °יִחְיֶה [יְקָ וְחָיָה] וְהָיְתָה־לּוֹ נַפְשׁוֹ לְשָׁלָל: כִּי־שַׂמְתִּי פָנַי

בָּעִיר הַזֹּאת לְרָעָה וְלֹא לְטוֹבָה נְאֻם־יְהוָה בְּיַד־מֶלֶךְ בָּבֶל תִּנָּתֵן וּשְׂרָפָהּ

יא-יב בָּאֵשׁ: וּלְבֵית מֶלֶךְ יְהוּדָה שִׁמְעוּ דְּבַר־יְהוָה: בֵּית דָּוִד כֹּה אָמַר

יְהוָה דִּינוּ לַבֹּקֶר מִשְׁפָּט וְהַצִּילוּ גָזוּל מִיַּד עוֹשֵׁק פֶּן־תֵּצֵא כָאֵשׁ חֲמָתִי

20:10. Jeremiah's detractors would surround him, urging each other to denounce him to the government because of his unpopular prophecies (see 18:18).

20:12. See 11:20.

20:13. Certain that God will help him, Jeremiah thanks Him now.

20:15. How could Jeremiah curse a man who surely

meant well? The Sages had a tradition that it was the wicked Pashhur son of Immer who had delivered the message of Jeremiah's birth to his father (*Radak*).

21:2. This variant spelling of Nebuchadnezzar appears only in the Books of *Jeremiah* and *Ezekiel*.

21:4. The Jews thought that their secret weapon was God, Who would surely help them — but they did not [saying,] "Tell it;* let us tell about him!" All the men [that I thought were] at peace with me wait for me to become hobbled; [they say,] "Perhaps he can be enticed, so that we will be able to overcome him and take our revenge against him." [11] But HASHEM is with me like a mighty hero, and therefore my pursuers stumble and cannot overcome [me]; they are exceedingly shamed for they did not succeed — with lasting disgrace that is not forgotten. [12] O HASHEM, Master of Legions, Who discerns the righteous one, for He sees innermost thoughts and feelings,* may I see Your vengeance against them, for I have revealed my grievance to You.

[13] Sing unto HASHEM, praise HASHEM, for He will have saved the life of the destitute from the hand of evildoers!*

He cursed the day of his birth

[14] Cursed be the day on which I was born; may the day on which my mother bore me be not blessed; [15] cursed be the man who brought the news to my father, saying, "A boy has been born to you," causing him to be gladdened.* [16] May that man be like cities that HASHEM overturned without relenting; may he hear moaning in the morning and wailing at noontime — [17] because no one killed me in the womb, so that my mother would be my grave and her womb a place of eternal gestation. [18] Why is it that I left the womb, only to see distress and grief and have my days end in shame?

21

Zedekiah's plea

[1] The word that came to Jeremiah from HASHEM when King Zedekiah sent Pashhur son of Malchiah and Zephaniah son of Maaseiah the Kohen to him, saying, [2] "Please inquire of HASHEM on our behalf, for Nebuchadrezzar,* king of Babylonia, is making war against us; perhaps HASHEM will act toward us in accordance with all of His [past] wonders, and [the king] will withdraw from us."

The city is doomed

[3] Jeremiah replied to them: Say thus to Zedekiah: [4] "Thus said HASHEM, God of Israel: Behold, I am turning about the weapons in your hands,* with which you [presume to] fight the king of Babylonia and the Chaldeans who are besieging you from outside the wall, and I shall gather [the invader] into this city. [5] And I Myself shall fight you with an outstretched hand and a strong arm, and with anger and wrath and great rage. [6] I shall strike down the inhabitants of this city — the people and the animals; they will all die in a great pestilence. [7] After this — the word of HASHEM — I will deliver Zedekiah, king of Judah, and his servants and the people and whoever in this city has survived the pestilence, the sword and the famine, into the hand of Nebuchadrezzar, king of Babylonia, into the hand of their enemies and into the hand of those who seek their lives. He will strike them down by the edge of the sword; he will not take pity, he will not show compassion, and he will not have mercy."

Let the citizenry capitulate

[8] And to this people, you shall say: "Thus said HASHEM: Behold, I place before you the path of life and the path of death: [9] Whoever remains in this city will die by the sword or by famine or by pestilence; but whoever leaves and surrenders to the Chaldeans who are besieging you will live, and his life will be his spoils.* [10] For I have directed My attention to this city, for evil and not for good — the word of HASHEM — and it shall be delivered into the hand of the king of Babylonia, and he will burn it down in fire."

O House of David, repent

[11] And to the house of the king of Judah [say]: "Hear the word of HASHEM: [12] O House of David, thus said HASHEM: Administer justice diligently and save the robbed from the hand of an oppressor, lest My anger rage forth like a fire,

---

deserve His help. God told them that He would assist not them — but their enemies.

21:9. Those who surrender will be destitute, but they will be content to escape with their lives.

יג וּבְעָרָה וְאֵין מְכַבֶּה מִפְּנֵי רֹעַ °מַעַלְלֵיהֶם [°מַעַלְלֵיכֶם ק]: הִנְנִי אֵלַיִךְ
יֹשֶׁבֶת הָעֵמֶק צוּר הַמִּישֹׁר נְאֻם־יהוה הָאֹמְרִים מִי־יֵחַת עָלֵינוּ וּמִי יָבוֹא
יד בִּמְעוֹנוֹתֵינוּ: וּפָקַדְתִּי עֲלֵיכֶם כִּפְרִי מַעַלְלֵיכֶם נְאֻם־יהוה וְהִצַּתִּי אֵשׁ

כב א בְּיַעְרָהּ וְאָכְלָה כָּל־סְבִיבֶיהָ: כֹּה אָמַר יהוה רֵד בֵּית־מֶלֶךְ
ב יְהוּדָה וְדִבַּרְתָּ שָׁם אֶת־הַדָּבָר הַזֶּה: וְאָמַרְתָּ שְׁמַע דְּבַר־יהוה מֶלֶךְ יְהוּדָה
ג הַיֹּשֵׁב עַל־כִּסֵּא דָוִד אַתָּה וַעֲבָדֶיךָ וְעַמְּךָ הַבָּאִים בַּשְּׁעָרִים הָאֵלֶּה: כֹּה |
אָמַר יהוה עֲשׂוּ מִשְׁפָּט וּצְדָקָה וְהַצִּילוּ גָזוּל מִיַּד עָשׁוֹק וְגֵר יָתוֹם וְאַלְמָנָה
ד אַל־תֹּנוּ אַל־תַּחְמֹסוּ וְדָם נָקִי אַל־תִּשְׁפְּכוּ בַּמָּקוֹם הַזֶּה: כִּי אִם־עָשׂוֹ
תַּעֲשׂוּ אֶת־הַדָּבָר הַזֶּה וּבָאוּ בְשַׁעֲרֵי הַבַּיִת הַזֶּה מְלָכִים יֹשְׁבִים לְדָוִד עַל־
ה כִּסְאוֹ רֹכְבִים בָּרֶכֶב וּבַסּוּסִים הוּא °וַעֲבָדוּ [°וַעֲבָדָיו ק] וְעַמּוֹ: וְאִם לֹא
תִשְׁמְעוּ אֶת־הַדְּבָרִים הָאֵלֶּה בִּי נִשְׁבַּעְתִּי נְאֻם־יהוה כִּי־לְחָרְבָּה יִהְיֶה
ו הַבַּיִת הַזֶּה: כִּי־כֹה | אָמַר יהוה עַל־בֵּית מֶלֶךְ יְהוּדָה גִּלְעָד אַתָּה
לִי רֹאשׁ הַלְּבָנוֹן אִם־לֹא אֲשִׁיתְךָ מִדְבָּר עָרִים לֹא °נוֹשָׁבָה [°נוֹשָׁבוּ ק]:
ז וְקִדַּשְׁתִּי עָלֶיךָ מַשְׁחִתִים אִישׁ וְכֵלָיו וְכָרְתוּ מִבְחַר אֲרָזֶיךָ וְהִפִּילוּ עַל־
ח הָאֵשׁ: וְעָבְרוּ גּוֹיִם רַבִּים עַל הָעִיר הַזֹּאת וְאָמְרוּ אִישׁ אֶל־רֵעֵהוּ עַל־מֶה
ט עָשָׂה יהוה כָּכָה לָעִיר הַגְּדוֹלָה הַזֹּאת: וְאָמְרוּ עַל אֲשֶׁר עָזְבוּ אֶת־בְּרִית
י יהוה אֱלֹהֵיהֶם וַיִּשְׁתַּחֲווּ לֵאלֹהִים אֲחֵרִים וַיַּעַבְדוּם: אַל־
תִּבְכּוּ לְמֵת וְאַל־תָּנֻדוּ לוֹ בְּכוּ בָכוֹ לַהֹלֵךְ כִּי לֹא יָשׁוּב עוֹד וְרָאָה אֶת־
יא אֶרֶץ מוֹלַדְתּוֹ: כִּי־כֹה אָמַר־יהוה אֶל־שַׁלֻּם בֶּן־יֹאשִׁיָּהוּ מֶלֶךְ
יְהוּדָה הַמֹּלֵךְ תַּחַת יֹאשִׁיָּהוּ אָבִיו אֲשֶׁר יָצָא מִן־הַמָּקוֹם הַזֶּה לֹא־יָשׁוּב
יב שָׁם עוֹד: כִּי בִּמְקוֹם אֲשֶׁר־הִגְלוּ אֹתוֹ שָׁם יָמוּת וְאֶת־הָאָרֶץ הַזֹּאת לֹא־
יג יִרְאֶה עוֹד: הוֹי בֹּנֶה בֵיתוֹ בְּלֹא־צֶדֶק וַעֲלִיּוֹתָיו בְּלֹא מִשְׁפָּט
יד בְּרֵעֵהוּ יַעֲבֹד חִנָּם וּפֹעֲלוֹ לֹא יִתֶּן־לוֹ: הָאֹמֵר אֶבְנֶה־לִּי בֵּית מִדּוֹת
וַעֲלִיּוֹת מְרֻוָּחִים וְקָרַע לוֹ חַלּוֹנָי וְסָפוּן בָּאָרֶז וּמָשׁוֹחַ בַּשָּׁשַׁר: הֲתִמְלֹךְ כִּי
טו אַתָּה מְתַחֲרֶה בָאָרֶז אָבִיךָ הֲלוֹא אָכַל וְשָׁתָה וְעָשָׂה מִשְׁפָּט וּצְדָקָה אָז
טז-יז טוֹב לוֹ: דָּן דִּין־עָנִי וְאֶבְיוֹן אָז טוֹב הֲלוֹא־הִיא הַדַּעַת אֹתִי נְאֻם־יהוה: כִּי
אֵין עֵינֶיךָ וְלִבְּךָ כִּי אִם־עַל־בִּצְעֶךָ וְעַל דַּם־הַנָּקִי לִשְׁפּוֹךְ וְעַל־הָעֹשֶׁק
יח וְעַל־הַמְּרוּצָה לַעֲשׂוֹת: לָכֵן כֹּה־אָמַר יהוה אֶל־יְהוֹיָקִים בֶּן־
יֹאשִׁיָּהוּ מֶלֶךְ יְהוּדָה לֹא־יִסְפְּדוּ לוֹ הוֹי אָחִי וְהוֹי אָחוֹת לֹא־יִסְפְּדוּ לוֹ הוֹי

21:13. Jeremiah addresses the people of Jerusalem, which is surrounded by valleys and is itself on a mountain. Its topography and defenses made its people confident that they were safe from attack (*Metzudos*).

21:14. Forest is a metaphor for Jerusalem's main buildings, the Temple, or the towns that surround it like a forest.

22:6. Even if you were as magnificent and attractive as the lush and fertile Gilead and Lebanon, I will transform you into a desolate, arid desert because of your sins (*Malbim*). Alternatively: Gilead, known for its healing balm, and Lebanon, which means "whitener," are metaphors for the Temple which, through the service and worship performed there, cures and whitens the effects of sinfulness (see *Rashi*).

22:11. See *I Chronicles* 3:15. There is no other mention in Scripture of Shallum inheriting Josiah's *it will burn, but there will be no one to extinguish it, due to the wickedness of your deeds.*

¹³ *"Behold, I am against you, O dweller [near] the valley, on the mountain of the plain* — the word of HASHEM — [you] who say, 'Who can attack us? Who can enter our abodes?'* ¹⁴ *I shall repay you according to the fruits of your deeds — the word of HASHEM — and I shall set fire to its forest, * which will consume all around it."*

22

Dire prophecy to Jehoiakim, king of Judah

¹ **T**hus said HASHEM: *"Go down to the palace of the king of Judah and speak this matter there.* ² *Say: Hear the word of HASHEM, O king of Judah, who sits upon the throne of David — you and your servants and your people who come through these gates.* ³ *Thus said HASHEM: Administer justice and righteousness, and save the robbed from the hand of the oppressor; do not taunt and do not cheat the stranger, the orphan and the widow; and do not spill innocent blood in this place.* ⁴ *For if you carry out this matter, then there will [continue to] come through the gates of this palace kings of [the line of] David sitting on his throne, riding chariot and horses — he and his servants and his people.* ⁵ *But if you do not heed these words, I swear by Myself — the word of HASHEM — that this palace will become a ruin.*

⁶ *"For thus said HASHEM concerning the palace of the king of Judah: [Even if] you are like Gilead to me, or the summit of Lebanon, I would transform you into a desert, like uninhabited cities.* * ⁷ *I would designate destroyers against you, each man with his implements, and they will cut down your choice cedars and fell them into the fire.* ⁸ *Many nations will pass by this city, and each man will say to his fellow, 'For what reason did HASHEM do this to this great city?'* ⁹ *And they will reply, 'It is because they forsook the covenant of HASHEM their God and prostrated themselves to the gods of others and worshiped them.'*

¹⁰ *"Do not weep for a dead man, and do not shake your head for him; weep rather for the one who went away, for he will never again return and see the land of his birthplace.* ¹¹ *For thus said HASHEM of Shallum son of Josiah, * who reigns in place of his father Josiah, who has left this place: He shall never again return there,* ¹² *for in the place where they exiled him, there he will die, and this land he will never again see.*

A house of injustice

¹³ *"Woe to him* who builds his house without righteousness and his upper stories without justice; who works his fellow without payment, and does not give him his wages;* ¹⁴ *who says, 'I shall build myself a house of large dimensions and spacious upper stories,' and he breaks open windows for himself, and it is paneled with cedar and painted with bright colors.* ¹⁵ *Shall you reign just because you flaunt your cedar? Behold, your father ate and drank, and practiced justice and righteousness — then it went well for him.* * ¹⁶ *If one does justice to the poor and destitute, then it is good; is this not 'knowing Me'? — the word of HASHEM.* ¹⁷ *But your eyes and heart focus on nothing but your profit, and upon innocent blood to shed, and to practice oppression and persecution.* ¹⁸ *Therefore, thus says HASHEM concerning Jehoiakim son of Josiah, king of Judah: They will not lament for him: 'Woe, my brother!' or 'Woe, sister!' They will not lament for him, 'Woe,*

---

throne. Therefore, the Sages (*Horayos* 11b) identify Shallum [lit., wholesome] as Zedekiah [lit., righteous of God] (*Rashi*). Alternatively, Shallum is Josiah's son Jehoiakim (see v. 18), or his grandson Jehoiachin (Coniah of v. 24). [See Appendix A, timeline 4.]

22:13. This begins a prophecy concerning King Jehoiakim, who is mentioned specifically in v. 18.

22:15. Josiah was successful because he was righteous.

יט   אָדוֹן וְהוֹי הֹדָה: קְבוּרַת חֲמוֹר יִקָּבֵר סָחוֹב וְהַשְׁלֵךְ מֵהָלְאָה לְשַׁעֲרֵי

כ   יְרוּשָׁלָ͏ִם: עֲלִי הַלְּבָנוֹן וּצְעָקִי וּבַבָּשָׁן תְּנִי קוֹלֵךְ וְצַעֲקִי מֵעֲבָרִים

כא   כִּי נִשְׁבְּרוּ כָּל־מְאַהֲבָיִךְ: דִּבַּרְתִּי אֵלַיִךְ בְּשַׁלְוֺתַיִךְ אָמַרְתְּ לֹא אֶשְׁמָע זֶה

כב   דַרְכֵּךְ מִנְּעוּרַיִךְ כִּי לֹא־שָׁמַעַתְּ בְּקוֹלִי: כָּל־רֹעַיִךְ תִּרְעֶה־רוּחַ וּמְאַהֲבַיִךְ

כג   בַּשֶּׁבִי יֵלֵכוּ כִּי אָז תֵּבֹשִׁי וְנִכְלַמְתְּ מִכֹּל רָעָתֵךְ: ׳יֹשַׁבְתִּי [°יֹשַׁבְתְּ ק]

   בַּלְּבָנוֹן °מְקֻנַּנְתִּי [°מְקֻנַּנְתְּ ק] בָּאֲרָזִים מַה־נֵּחַנְתְּ בְּבֹא־לָךְ חֲבָלִים חִיל

כד   כַּיֹּלֵדָה: חַי־אָנִי נְאֻם־יְהֹוָה כִּי אִם־יִהְיֶה כָּנְיָהוּ בֶן־יְהוֹיָקִים מֶלֶךְ יְהוּדָה

כה   חוֹתָם עַל־יַד יְמִינִי כִּי מִשָּׁם אֶתְּקֶנְךָּ: וּנְתַתִּיךָ בְּיַד מְבַקְשֵׁי נַפְשֶׁךָ וּבְיַד

   אֲשֶׁר־אַתָּה יָגוֹר מִפְּנֵיהֶם וּבְיַד נְבוּכַדְרֶאצַּר מֶלֶךְ־בָּבֶל וּבְיַד הַכַּשְׂדִּים:

כו   וְהֵטַלְתִּי אֹתְךָ וְאֶת־אִמְּךָ אֲשֶׁר יְלָדַתְךָ עַל הָאָרֶץ אַחֶרֶת אֲשֶׁר לֹא־

כז   יֻלַּדְתֶּם שָׁם וְשָׁם תָּמוּתוּ: וְעַל־הָאָרֶץ אֲשֶׁר־הֵם מְנַשְּׂאִים אֶת־נַפְשָׁם

כח   לָשׁוּב שָׁם שָׁמָּה לֹא יָשׁוּבוּ: הַעֶצֶב נִבְזֶה נָפוּץ הָאִישׁ הַזֶּה

   כָּנְיָהוּ אִם־כְּלִי אֵין חֵפֶץ בּוֹ מַדּוּעַ הוּטְלוּ הוּא וְזַרְעוֹ וְהֻשְׁלְכוּ עַל־הָאָרֶץ

כט־ל   אֲשֶׁר לֹא־יָדָעוּ: אֶרֶץ אֶרֶץ אָרֶץ שִׁמְעִי דְּבַר־יְהֹוָה: כֹּה ׀ אָמַר יְהֹוָה

   כִּתְבוּ אֶת־הָאִישׁ הַזֶּה עֲרִירִי גֶּבֶר לֹא־יִצְלַח בְּיָמָיו כִּי לֹא יִצְלַח מִזַּרְעוֹ

כג   א   אִישׁ יֹשֵׁב עַל־כִּסֵּא דָוִד וּמֹשֵׁל עוֹד בִּיהוּדָה: הוֹי רֹעִים

ב   מְאַבְּדִים וּמְפִצִים אֶת־צֹאן מַרְעִיתִי נְאֻם־יְהֹוָה: לָכֵן כֹּה־אָמַר יְהֹוָה

   אֱלֹהֵי יִשְׂרָאֵל עַל־הָרֹעִים הָרֹעִים אֶת־עַמִּי אַתֶּם הֲפִצֹתֶם אֶת־צֹאנִי

   וַתַּדִּחוּם וְלֹא פְקַדְתֶּם אֹתָם הִנְנִי פֹקֵד עֲלֵיכֶם אֶת־רֹעַ מַעַלְלֵיכֶם נְאֻם־

ג   יְהֹוָה: וַאֲנִי אֲקַבֵּץ אֶת־שְׁאֵרִית צֹאנִי מִכֹּל הָאֲרָצוֹת אֲשֶׁר־הִדַּחְתִּי אֹתָם

   שָׁם וַהֲשִׁבֹתִי אֶתְהֶן עַל־נְוֵהֶן וּפָרוּ וְרָבוּ: וַהֲקִמֹתִי עֲלֵיהֶם רֹעִים וְרָעוּם

ד

ה   וְלֹא־יִירְאוּ עוֹד וְלֹא־יֵחַתּוּ וְלֹא יִפָּקֵדוּ נְאֻם־יְהֹוָה: הִנֵּה

   יָמִים בָּאִים נְאֻם־יְהֹוָה וַהֲקִמֹתִי לְדָוִד צֶמַח צַדִּיק וּמָלַךְ מֶלֶךְ וְהִשְׂכִּיל

ו   וְעָשָׂה מִשְׁפָּט וּצְדָקָה בָּאָרֶץ: בְּיָמָיו תִּוָּשַׁע יְהוּדָה וְיִשְׂרָאֵל יִשְׁכֹּן לָבֶטַח

ז   וְזֶה־שְּׁמוֹ אֲשֶׁר־יִקְרְאוֹ יְהֹוָה ׀ צִדְקֵנוּ:   לָכֵן הִנֵּה־יָמִים

   בָּאִים נְאֻם־יְהֹוָה וְלֹא־יֹאמְרוּ עוֹד חַי־יְהֹוָה אֲשֶׁר הֶעֱלָה אֶת־בְּנֵי יִשְׂרָאֵל

ח   מֵאֶרֶץ מִצְרָיִם: כִּי אִם־חַי־יְהֹוָה אֲשֶׁר הֶעֱלָה וַאֲשֶׁר הֵבִיא אֶת־זֶרַע בֵּית

   יִשְׂרָאֵל מֵאֶרֶץ צָפוֹנָה וּמִכֹּל הָאֲרָצוֹת אֲשֶׁר הִדַּחְתִּים שָׁם וְיָשְׁבוּ עַל־

ט   אַדְמָתָם: לַנְּבִאִים נִשְׁבַּר לִבִּי בְקִרְבִּי רָחֲפוּ כָּל־עַצְמוֹתַי

   הָיִיתִי כְּאִישׁ שִׁכּוֹר וּכְגֶבֶר עֲבָרוֹ יָיִן מִפְּנֵי יְהֹוָה וּמִפְּנֵי דִּבְרֵי קָדְשׁוֹ:

22:20. This prophecy concerns King Jeconiah (see vv. 24-30), and is addressed to the royal house and to the inhabitants of Jerusalem. Their lovers, i.e., the nations they always relied on, Assyria and Egypt, had already been conquered by Babylonia.

22:24. Coniah is a derisive nickname for Jehoiakim's son Jeconiah (also known as Jehoiachin).

23:1. The kings of Judah are the shepherds; Israel is God's flock.

23:9. That is, because of the prophecies of doom that He has shown me (*Rashi*). Alternatively: Jeremiah castigates the liars and hypocritical leaders whose falsehoods have profaned and cheapened God's Name and His word among the people (*Radak*).

master!' or 'Woe, his majesty!' ¹⁹ With the burial of a donkey will he be buried — dragged and thrown beyond the gates of Jerusalem."

Foreign allies will not avail; Jeconiah will be exiled

²⁰ Go up to Lebanon and cry out, in Bashan raise your voice; cry out from [all] sides, for all your paramours have been crushed. * ²¹ I spoke to you while you were tranquil; you said, 'I will not listen.' This was your way since your youth — not to listen to My voice. ²² All your shepherds will be blasted by the wind, and your paramours will go into captivity; for then you will be embarrassed and ashamed because of all your wickedness. ²³ You dwell in Lebanon, you have nested in the cedars; what will all this charm avail you when pains come to you, [like] the travail of childbirth? ²⁴ As I live — the word of HASHEM — even if you, Coniah* son of Jehoiakim, king of Judah, would be a signet ring on My right hand, I would pull you off it. ²⁵ I will deliver you into the hand of those who seek your soul, into the hand of those you fear — into the hand of Nebuchadrezzar, king of Babylonia, and into the hand of the Chaldeans. ²⁶ I shall cast you and your mother who bore you into an alien land where you were not born, and there you shall die. ²⁷ And to the land, there to where their soul yearns to return — they shall not return there.

²⁸ Is this man Coniah a despised, shattered statue, or an unwanted vessel? Why have he and his descendants been displaced and thrown into a land they did not know? ²⁹ O land, land, land! Hear the word of HASHEM! ³⁰ Thus said HASHEM: Inscribe this man to become childless, a man who will not suceed in his life; for none of his descendants will ever succeed in being a man who sits on the throne of David, and ever to rule over Judah.

23

The wicked shepherd kings are castigated

¹ Woe to the shepherds who lose and scatter My sheep of pasture* — the word of HASHEM. ² Therefore, thus said HASHEM, God of Israel, concerning the shepherds who tend My people: You scattered My sheep and dispersed them, and you did not pay attention to them; behold, therefore, I visit upon you the wickedness of your deeds — the word of HASHEM. ³ And I shall gather together the remnant of My sheep from all the lands wherein I had dispersed them, and I shall bring them back to their cotes, and they will be fruitful and multiply. ⁴ I will establish shepherds for them who will tend them, and they will no longer be afraid nor be terrified nor suffer losses — the word of HASHEM.

The righteous Messiah

⁵ Behold, days are coming — the word of HASHEM — when I will establish a righteous sprout from David; a king will reign and prosper and he will administer justice and righteousness in the land. ⁶ In his days Judah will be saved, and Israel will dwell securely. This is the name people will call him: HASHEM is our righteousness.

⁷ Therefore, behold, days are coming — the word of HASHEM — when people will no longer swear, 'As HASHEM lives, Who brought the Children of Israel up from the land of Egypt,' ⁸ but rather, 'As HASHEM lives, Who brought up and brought back the offspring of the House of Israel from the land of the North and from all the lands wherein He had dispersed them'; and they will dwell in their [own] land.

⁹ Because of the [false] prophets My heart is broken within me, all my bones tremble; I am like a drunken man, like a man overcome by wine — because of HASHEM and because of His holy words. *

כִּי מְנָאֲפִים מָלְאָה הָאָ֔רֶץ כִּי־מִפְּנֵי אָלָה֙ אָבְלָ֣ה הָאָ֔רֶץ יָבְשׁ֖וּ נְאֽוֹת י

מִדְבָּ֑ר וַתְּהִ֤י מְרֽוּצָתָם֙ רָעָ֔ה וּגְבֽוּרָתָ֖ם לֹא־כֵֽן: כִּֽי־גַם־נָבִ֥יא גַם־כֹּהֵ֖ן חָנֵ֑פוּ יא

גַּם־בְּבֵיתִ֛י מָצָ֥אתִי רָעָתָ֖ם נְאֻם־יְהֹוָֽה: לָכֵן֩ יִֽהְיֶ֨ה דַרְכָּ֜ם לָהֶ֗ם כַּֽחֲלַקְלַקּוֹת֙ יב

בָּֽאֲפֵלָ֔ה יִדַּ֖חוּ וְנָ֣פְלוּ בָ֑הּ כִּֽי־אָבִ֨יא עֲלֵיהֶ֥ם רָעָ֛ה שְׁנַ֥ת פְּקֻדָּתָ֖ם נְאֻם־

יְהֹוָֽה: וּבִנְבִיאֵ֥י שֹֽׁמְר֖וֹן רָאִ֣יתִי תִפְלָ֑ה הִנַּבְּא֣וּ בַבַּ֔עַל וַיַּתְע֖וּ יג

אֶת־עַמִּ֣י אֶת־יִשְׂרָאֵֽל: וּבִנְבִיאֵ֨י יְרֽוּשָׁלִַ֜ם רָאִ֣יתִי שַֽׁעֲרוּרָ֗ה נָאוֹף֙ וְהָלֹ֣ךְ יד

בַּשֶּׁ֔קֶר וְחִזְּקוּ֙ יְדֵ֣י מְרֵעִ֔ים לְבִלְתִּי־שָׁ֖בוּ אִ֣ישׁ מֵרָֽעָת֑וֹ הָֽיוּ־לִ֤י כֻלָּם֙ כִּסְדֹ֔ם

וְיֹשְׁבֶ֖יהָ כַּֽעֲמֹרָֽה: לָכֵ֗ן כֹּֽה־אָמַ֞ר יְהֹוָ֤ה צְבָאוֹת֙ עַל־הַנְּבִאִ֔ים טו

הִנְנִ֨י מַֽאֲכִ֤יל אוֹתָם֙ לַֽעֲנָ֔ה וְהִשְׁקִתִ֖ים מֵי־רֹ֑אשׁ כִּ֗י מֵאֵת֙ נְבִיאֵ֣י יְרֽוּשָׁלִַ֔ם

יָֽצְאָ֥ה חֲנֻפָּ֖ה לְכָל־הָאָֽרֶץ: כֹּה־אָמַ֞ר יְהֹוָ֣ה צְבָא֗וֹת אַל־ טז

תִּשְׁמְע֞וּ עַל־דִּבְרֵ֤י הַנְּבִאִים֙ הַנִּבְּאִ֣ים לָכֶ֔ם מַהְבִּלִ֥ים הֵ֖מָּה אֶתְכֶ֑ם חֲז֤וֹן

לִבָּם֙ יְדַבֵּ֔רוּ לֹ֖א מִפִּ֥י יְהֹוָֽה: אֹֽמְרִ֤ים אָמוֹר֙ לִמְנַ֣אֲצַ֔י דִּבֶּ֣ר יְהֹוָ֔ה שָׁל֖וֹם יִֽהְיֶ֣ה יז

לָכֶ֑ם וְ֠כֹל הֹלֵ֞ךְ בִּשְׁרִר֤וּת לִבּוֹ֙ אָ֣מְר֔וּ לֹֽא־תָב֥וֹא עֲלֵיכֶ֖ם רָעָֽה: כִּ֣י מִ֤י יח

עָמַד֙ בְּס֣וֹד יְהֹוָ֔ה וְיֵ֖רֶא וְיִשְׁמַ֣ע אֶת־דְּבָר֑וֹ מִֽי־הִקְשִׁ֥יב [דְּבָרִ֖י ק] °דְּבָר֖וֹ

וַיִּשְׁמָֽע: הִנֵּ֣ה ׀ סַֽעֲרַ֣ת יְהֹוָ֗ה חֵמָה֙ יָֽצְאָ֔ה וְסַ֖עַר מִתְחוֹלֵ֑ל עַ֖ל יט

רֹ֣אשׁ רְשָׁעִ֖ים יָחֽוּל: לֹ֤א יָשׁוּב֙ אַף־יְהֹוָ֔ה עַד־עֲשֹׂת֥וֹ וְעַד־הֲקִימ֖וֹ מְזִמּ֣וֹת כ

לִבּ֑וֹ בְּאַֽחֲרִית֙ הַיָּמִ֔ים תִּתְבּֽוֹנְנוּ בָ֖הּ בִּינָֽה: לֹֽא־שָׁלַ֥חְתִּי אֶת־הַנְּבִאִ֖ים וְהֵ֣ם כא

רָ֑צוּ לֹֽא־דִבַּ֥רְתִּי אֲלֵיהֶ֖ם וְהֵ֥ם נִבָּֽאוּ: וְאִֽם־עָֽמְד֖וּ בְּסוֹדִ֑י וְיַשְׁמִ֤עוּ דְבָרַי֙ כב

אֶת־עַמִּ֔י וִֽישִׁבוּם֙ מִדַּרְכָּ֣ם הָרָ֔ע וּמֵרֹ֖עַ מַֽעַלְלֵיהֶֽם: הַֽאֱלֹהֵ֧י כג

מִקָּרֹ֛ב אָ֖נִי נְאֻם־יְהֹוָ֑ה וְלֹ֥א אֱלֹהֵ֖י מֵֽרָחֹֽק: אִם־יִסָּתֵ֨ר אִ֤ישׁ בַּמִּסְתָּרִים֙ כד

וַֽאֲנִ֥י לֹֽא־אֶרְאֶ֖נּוּ נְאֻם־יְהֹוָ֑ה הֲל֨וֹא אֶת־הַשָּׁמַ֧יִם וְאֶת־הָאָ֛רֶץ אֲנִ֥י מָלֵ֖א

נְאֻם־יְהֹוָֽה: שָׁמַ֗עְתִּי אֵ֤ת אֲשֶׁר־אָֽמְרוּ֙ הַנְּבִאִ֔ים הַנִּבְּאִ֥ים בִּשְׁמִ֖י שָׁ֣קֶר כה

לֵאמֹ֑ר חָלַ֖מְתִּי חָלָֽמְתִּי: עַד־מָתַ֗י הֲיֵ֛שׁ בְּלֵ֥ב הַנְּבִאִ֖ים נִבְּאֵ֣י הַשָּׁ֑קֶר וּנְבִיאֵ֖י כו

תַּרְמִ֥ת לִבָּֽם: הַחֹֽשְׁבִ֗ים לְהַשְׁכִּ֤יחַ אֶת־עַמִּי֙ שְׁמִ֔י בַּֽחֲל֣וֹמֹתָ֔ם אֲשֶׁ֥ר יְסַפְּר֖וּ כז

אִ֣ישׁ לְרֵעֵ֑הוּ כַּֽאֲשֶׁ֨ר שָֽׁכְח֧וּ אֲבוֹתָ֛ם אֶת־שְׁמִ֖י בַּבָּֽעַל: הַנָּבִ֞יא אֲשֶׁר־אִתּ֤וֹ כח

חֲלוֹם֙ יְסַפֵּ֣ר חֲל֔וֹם וַֽאֲשֶׁ֤ר דְּבָרִי֙ אִתּ֔וֹ יְדַבֵּ֥ר דְּבָרִ֖י אֱמֶ֑ת מַה־לַתֶּ֥בֶן אֶת־

הַבָּ֖ר נְאֻם־יְהֹוָֽה: הֲל֨וֹא כֹ֧ה דְבָרִ֛י כָּאֵ֖שׁ נְאֻם־יְהֹוָ֑ה וּכְפַטִּ֖ישׁ יְפֹ֥צֵֽץ כט

סָֽלַע: לָכֵ֛ן הִנְנִ֥י עַל־הַנְּבִאִ֖ים נְאֻם־יְהֹוָ֑ה מְגַנְּבֵ֣י דְבָרַ֔י אִ֖ישׁ מֵאֵ֥ת רֵעֵֽהוּ: ל

הִנְנִ֥י עַל־הַנְּבִיאִ֖ם נְאֻם־יְהֹוָ֑ה הַלֹּֽקְחִ֣ים לְשׁוֹנָ֔ם וַֽיִּנְאֲמ֖וּ נְאֻֽם: הִנְנִ֞י עַֽל־ לא-לב

נִבְּאֵ֣י חֲלֹמוֹת֮ שֶׁקֶר֒ נְאֻם־יְהֹוָ֔ה וַֽיְסַפְּרוּם֙ וַיַּתְע֣וּ אֶת־עַמִּ֔י בְּשִׁקְרֵיהֶ֖ם

וּבְפַֽחֲזוּתָ֑ם וְאָֽנֹכִ֨י לֹֽא־שְׁלַחְתִּ֜ים וְלֹ֣א צִוִּיתִ֗ים וְהוֹעֵ֛יל לֹֽא־יוֹעִ֥ילוּ לָֽעָם־

הַזֶּ֖ה נְאֻם־יְהֹוָֽה: וְכִֽי־יִשְׁאָֽלְךָ֩ הָעָ֨ם הַזֶּ֜ה אֽוֹ־הַנָּבִ֤יא אֽוֹ־כֹהֵן֙ לֵאמֹ֔ר מַה־ לג

23:16. Jeremiah now addresses the populace, urging them to ignore the false prophets who mislead them.

23:20. You will fully appreciate the import of this prophecy only in the end of days, when it is realized.

¹⁰ *For the land is full of adulterers; for due to [false] oaths the land has become desolate, and the pastures of the wilderness withered; their course is evil and their might is in untruth.* ¹¹ *For even the prophet and the priest are insincere; even in My Temple I find their evil — the word of* HASHEM. ¹² *Therefore, their way shall be for them like a slippery path in the dark; they will be pushed and fall on it; for I shall bring evil upon them, [it is] the year of their reckoning — the word of* HASHEM.

¹³ *I saw fraudulence in the prophets of Samaria; they prophesied by the Baal and misled My people Israel,* ¹⁴ *and I see disgrace among the prophets of Jerusalem, adultery and continuing falsehood; they encouraged the evildoers so that they not repent, each man of his wickedness; they were all like Sodom to me, and [Jerusalem's] inhabitants were like Gemorrah.* ¹⁵ *Therefore, thus said* HASHEM, *Master of Legions, concerning these prophets: Behold, I shall feed them wormwood and give them poisonous water to drink, for deceit has spread out over all the land from the prophets of Jerusalem.*

¹⁶ *Thus said* HASHEM, *Master of Legions:* * *Pay no heed to the words of the prophets who prophesy to you; they are deluding you. They speak the vision of their own heart, not of the mouth of* HASHEM. ¹⁷ *They always tell those who anger Me, '*HASHEM *has spoken: There will be peace for you'; and to all who follow the vision of his heart they say, 'No evil shall befall you.'* ¹⁸ *But which [of them] was exposed to the mystery of* HASHEM, *who has seen or heard His word? Who obeyed His word and heeded it?* ¹⁹ *Behold, the storm of* HASHEM: *A fury shall go forth; a tempest shall seek rest; it will rest upon the head of the wicked.* ²⁰ HASHEM's *wrath will not recede until He has accomplished it and upheld the plans of His heart. In the end of days you will have an understanding of it.* * ²¹ *I did not send those prophets, yet they ran; I did not speak to them, yet they prophesied.* ²² *If they were exposed to My mystery, let them proclaim My words to My people and bring them back from their evil way and from the wickedness of their deeds.*

²³ *Am I a God [only] from nearby — says* HASHEM — *and not a God from afar?* ²⁴ *Can a man hide in concealments and that I not see him? — the word of* HASHEM! *Do I not fill the heaven and the earth? — the word of* HASHEM. ²⁵ *I have heard what is said by the prophets who prophesy falsely in My Name, saying: 'I had a dream! I had a dream!'* ²⁶ *How long! Is anything in the heart of the prophets who prophesy falsehood, the prophets of their heart's deceit,* ²⁷ *who think to make My people forget My Name through their dreams that they tell to each other, just as their fathers forgot My Name through [worshiping] the Baal.* ²⁸ *The prophet with a dream tells [his] dream, but the one with My word speaks My word of truth. How can the chaff compare to the kernel? — the word of* HASHEM. ²⁹ *Behold, My word is like fire — the word of* HASHEM — *and like a hammer that shatters a rock.*

³⁰ *Therefore, behold I am [acting] against the prophets — the word of* HASHEM — *who steal My word, one from the other.* ³¹ *Behold, I am [acting] against the prophets — the word of* HASHEM — *who train their tongues and deliver an oration.* ³² *Behold, I am [acting] against those who prophesy with false dreams — says* HASHEM — *who tell them and mislead My people with their lies and with flippancy. I did not send them nor command them. They were of no benefit to this people — the word of* HASHEM.

³³ *If this people — or a prophet or a priest — should ask you, saying, 'What*

מַשָּׂא יְהֹוָה וְאָמַרְתָּ֤ אֲלֵיהֶם֙ אֶת־מַה־מַשָּׂ֔א וְנָטַשְׁתִּ֥י אֶתְכֶ֖ם נְאֻם־יְהֹוָֽה:

לד וְהַנָּבִ֣יא וְהַכֹּהֵ֗ן וְהָעָם֙ אֲשֶׁ֣ר יֹאמַ֔ר מַשָּׂ֖א יְהֹוָ֑ה וּפָקַדְתִּ֛י עַל־הָאִ֥ישׁ הַה֖וּא

לה וְעַל־בֵּיתֽוֹ: כֹּ֣ה תֹֽאמְר֞וּ אִ֤ישׁ עַל־רֵעֵ֙הוּ֙ וְאִ֣ישׁ אֶל־אָחִ֔יו מֶה־עָנָ֥ה יְהֹוָ֖ה

לו וּמַה־דִּבֶּ֥ר יְהֹוָֽה: וּמַשָּׂ֥א יְהֹוָ֖ה לֹ֣א תִזְכְּרוּ־ע֑וֹד כִּ֣י הַמַּשָּׂ֗א יִֽהְיֶה֙ לְאִ֣ישׁ דְּבָר֔וֹ

לז וַהֲפַכְתֶּ֗ם אֶת־דִּבְרֵ֛י אֱלֹהִ֥ים חַיִּ֖ים יְהֹוָ֣ה צְבָא֑וֹת אֱלֹהֵֽינוּ: כֹּ֥ה תֹאמַ֖ר אֶל־

לח הַנָּבִ֑יא מֶה־עָנָ֣ךְ יְהֹוָ֔ה וּמַה־דִּבֶּ֖ר יְהֹוָֽה: וְאִם־מַשָּׂ֣א יְהֹוָה֮ תֹּאמֵרוּ֒ לָכֵ֗ן כֹּ֚ה

אָמַ֣ר יְהֹוָ֔ה יַ֧עַן אֲמׇרְכֶ֛ם אֶת־הַדָּבָ֥ר הַזֶּ֖ה מַשָּׂ֣א יְהֹוָ֑ה וָאֶשְׁלַ֤ח אֲלֵיכֶם֙

לט לֵאמֹ֔ר לֹ֥א תֹֽאמְר֖וּ מַשָּׂ֣א יְהֹוָֽה: לָכֵ֣ן הִנְנִ֗י וְנָשִׁ֤יתִי אֶתְכֶם֙ נָשֹׁ֔א וְנָטַשְׁתִּ֣י

מ אֶתְכֶ֗ם וְאֶת־הָעִיר֙ אֲשֶׁ֨ר נָתַ֧תִּי לָכֶ֛ם וְלַאֲבֽוֹתֵיכֶ֖ם מֵעַ֣ל פָּנָֽי: וְנָתַתִּ֤י עֲלֵיכֶם֙

חֶרְפַּ֣ת עוֹלָ֑ם וּכְלִמּ֣וּת עוֹלָ֔ם אֲשֶׁ֖ר לֹ֥א תִשָּׁכֵֽחַ:   הִרְאַ֣נִי יְהֹוָ֗ה   **כד**

א וְהִנֵּ֞ה שְׁנֵ֣י דֽוּדָאֵ֣י תְאֵנִ֗ים מֽוּעָדִים֙ לִפְנֵי֙ הֵיכַ֣ל יְהֹוָ֔ה אַחֲרֵ֣י הַגְל֣וֹת

נְבֽוּכַדְרֶאצַּ֣ר מֶֽלֶךְ־בָּבֶ֡ל אֶת־יְכׇנְיָ֣ה בֶן־יְהֽוֹיָקִ֩ים מֶֽלֶךְ־יְהוּדָ֨ה וְאֶת־שָׂרֵ֤י

ב יְהוּדָה֙ וְאֶת־הֶֽחָרָ֣שׁ וְאֶת־הַמַּסְגֵּ֔ר מִירֽוּשָׁלִַ֖ם וַיְבִאֵ֣ם בָּבֶֽל: הַדּ֣וּד אֶחָ֗ד

תְּאֵנִים֙ טֹב֣וֹת מְאֹ֔ד כִּתְאֵנֵ֖י הַבַּכֻּר֑וֹת וְהַדּ֣וּד אֶחָ֗ד תְּאֵנִים֙ רָע֣וֹת מְאֹ֔ד אֲשֶׁ֥ר

ג לֹא־תֵֽאָכַ֖לְנָה מֵרֹֽעַ:   וַיֹּ֨אמֶר יְהֹוָ֜ה אֵלַ֗י מָֽה־אַתָּ֤ה רֹאֶה֙ יִרְמְיָ֔הוּ

וָאֹמַ֖ר תְּאֵנִ֑ים הַתְּאֵנִ֤ים הַטֹּבוֹת֙ טֹב֣וֹת מְאֹ֔ד וְהָֽרָעוֹת֙ רָע֣וֹת מְאֹ֔ד אֲשֶׁ֥ר

ד-ה לֹא־תֵֽאָכַ֖לְנָה מֵרֹֽעַ:   וַיְהִ֥י דְבַר־יְהֹוָ֖ה אֵלַ֥י לֵאמֹֽר: כֹּֽה־אָמַ֞ר

יְהֹוָה֙ אֱלֹהֵ֣י יִשְׂרָאֵ֔ל כַּתְּאֵנִ֥ים הַטֹּב֖וֹת הָאֵ֑לֶּה כֵּ֣ן אַכִּ֗יר אֶת־גָּל֤וּת יְהוּדָה֙

ו אֲשֶׁ֨ר שִׁלַּ֜חְתִּי מִן־הַמָּק֥וֹם הַזֶּ֛ה אֶ֥רֶץ כַּשְׂדִּ֖ים לְטוֹבָֽה: וְשַׂמְתִּ֨י עֵינִ֤י עֲלֵיהֶם֙

לְטוֹבָ֔ה וַהֲשִֽׁבֹתִ֖ים עַל־הָאָ֣רֶץ הַזֹּ֑את וּבְנִיתִים֙ וְלֹ֣א אֶהֱרֹ֔ס וּנְטַעְתִּ֖ים וְלֹ֥א

ז אֶתּֽוֹשׁ: וְנָתַתִּ֨י לָהֶ֥ם לֵב֙ לָדַ֣עַת אֹתִ֔י כִּ֥י אֲנִ֖י יְהֹוָ֑ה וְהָיוּ־לִ֣י לְעָ֗ם וְאָֽנֹכִי֙ אֶֽהְיֶ֣ה

ח לָהֶ֖ם לֵֽאלֹהִ֑ים כִּֽי־יָשֻׁ֥בוּ אֵלַ֖י בְּכׇל־לִבָּֽם: וְכַתְּאֵנִים֙ הָֽרָע֔וֹת

אֲשֶׁ֥ר לֹא־תֵֽאָכַ֖לְנָה מֵרֹ֑עַ כִּי־כֹ֣ה ׀ אָמַ֣ר יְהֹוָ֗ה כֵּ֣ן אֶתֵּ֞ן אֶת־צִדְקִיָּ֤הוּ מֶֽלֶךְ־

יְהוּדָה֙ וְאֶת־שָׂרָ֣יו וְאֵ֣ת ׀ שְׁאֵרִ֣ית יְרֽוּשָׁלַ֗͏ִם הַנִּשְׁאָרִים֙ בָּאָ֣רֶץ הַזֹּ֔את

ט וְהַיֹּשְׁבִ֖ים בְּאֶ֣רֶץ מִצְרָֽיִם: וּנְתַתִּ֣ים °לִזְוָעָה ק׳] [לְזַעֲוָ֣ה לְרָעָ֔ה לְכֹ֖ל

מַמְלְכ֣וֹת הָאָ֑רֶץ לְחֶרְפָּ֤ה וּלְמָשָׁל֙ לִשְׁנִינָ֣ה וְלִקְלָלָ֔ה בְּכׇל־הַמְּקֹמ֖וֹת אֲשֶֽׁר־

י אַדִּיחֵ֥ם שָֽׁם: וְשִׁלַּ֣חְתִּי בָ֗ם אֶת־הַחֶ֙רֶב֙ אֶת־הָֽרָעָ֣ב וְאֶת־הַדָּ֑בֶר עַד־תֻּמָּם֙

א מֵעַ֣ל הָֽאֲדָמָ֔ה אֲשֶׁר־נָתַ֥תִּי לָהֶ֖ם וְלַאֲבוֹתֵיהֶֽם: הַדָּבָ֞ר אֲשֶׁר־הָיָ֤ה   **כה**

עַֽל־יִרְמְיָ֙הוּ֙ עַל־כׇּל־עַ֣ם יְהוּדָ֔ה בַּשָּׁנָה֙ הָרְבִעִ֔ית לִיהוֹיָקִ֥ים בֶּן־יֹאשִׁיָּ֖הוּ

ב מֶ֣לֶךְ יְהוּדָ֑ה הִ֚יא הַשָּׁנָ֣ה הָרִֽאשֹׁנִ֔ית לִנְבֽוּכַדְרֶאצַּ֖ר מֶ֥לֶךְ בָּבֶֽל: אֲשֶׁ֣ר דִּבֶּ֗ר

ג יִרְמְיָ֤הוּ הַנָּבִיא֙ עַל־כׇּל־עַ֣ם יְהוּדָ֔ה וְאֶ֛ל כׇּל־יֹשְׁבֵ֥י יְרוּשָׁלַ֖͏ִם לֵאמֹֽר: מִן־

שְׁלֹ֣שׁ עֶשְׂרֵ֣ה שָׁנָ֡ה לְיֹאשִׁיָּ֣הוּ בֶן־אָמוֹן֩ מֶ֨לֶךְ יְהוּדָ֜ה וְעַ֣ד ׀ הַיּ֣וֹם הַזֶּ֗ה זֶ֚ה

23:33. These people refer to Jeremiah's prophecy sarcastically and insolently as a burden and an annoyance.

23:36. Although true prophets, the men of His word, are indeed privileged to receive the burden of God's prophecy and consider it an honor, you have turned

is the burden* of HASHEM?' Tell them, 'What is the burden? I shall reject you!
— the word of HASHEM!' ³⁴ And any prophet or priest or one of the populace
who says 'burden of HASHEM,' I shall deal with that person and with his
household. ³⁵ So shall you say to one another, and each man to his brother:
'What did HASHEM pronounce?' 'What did HASHEM speak?' ³⁶ Never again
mention 'burden of HASHEM,' for although a burden comes to a man of His
word,* you have perverted the words of the living God — HASHEM, Master
of Legions, our God. ³⁷ Say thus to the [true] prophet: 'What did HASHEM
pronounce to you?' 'What did HASHEM speak?' ³⁸ And if you still say 'burden
of HASHEM' — therefore, thus said HASHEM: Because you said this thing,
'burden of HASHEM!' — when I sent to you, saying, 'Do not say burden of
HASHEM' — ³⁹ therefore, behold, I am [acting], and I shall completely forget
you, and I shall discard you and the city that I gave to you and to your
fathers, from My presence. ⁴⁰ And I shall place upon you an everlasting
disgrace and everlasting humiliations, which will not be forgotten.

24

*Vision
of the
good figs
and the
bad figs*

¹ Hᴀꜱʜᴇᴍ showed me [a vision] and behold, two baskets of figs were prepared
before the Sanctuary of HASHEM — after Nebuchadrezzar king of Babylonia
had exiled Jeconiah son of Jehoiakim, king of Judah, and the officers of Judah
and the artisans and gatekeepers* from Jerusalem, and brought them to Babylonia — ² one basket [contained] very good figs, like early-ripening figs, and one
basket [contained] very bad figs, which were so bad they were inedible. ³ HASHEM
said to me, "What do you see, Jeremiah?"

And I said, "Figs. The good figs are very good, and the bad figs are so bad that
they are inedible."

⁴ The word of HASHEM then came to me, saying, ⁵ "Thus said HASHEM, God of
Israel: Like these good figs, so shall I recall the exile of Judah, whom I expelled
from this place to the land of the Chaldeans, for goodness. ⁶ I shall set My eye
upon them for goodness, and return them to this land, and I shall rebuild them and
not destroy; I shall replant them and not uproot. ⁷ And I shall grant them the heart
to know Me,* that I am HASHEM, and they will be a people unto Me, and I shall
be a God for them; for they will return to Me with all their heart. ⁸ And like the bad
figs, which are so bad that they are inedible — thus said HASHEM: So shall I give
over Zedekiah king of Judah and his officers and the remnant of Jerusalem who
remain in this land and who dwell in the land of Egypt, ⁹ I shall give them over to
all the kingdoms of the earth for horror and for evil, and they will be a [paradigm
of] shame and a parable and a lesson and a curse, in all the places to which I will
disperse them. ¹⁰ And I shall send after them the sword and famine and pestilence
until they are annihilated from upon the land which I gave them and their
forefathers."

25

¹ The word that came to Jeremiah concerning all the people of Judah, in the
fourth year of Jehoiakim son of Josiah, king of Judah, which was the first
year of Nebuchadrezzar king of Babylonia, ² that Jeremiah the prophet spoke to
all the people of Judah and to all the inhabitants of Jerusalem, saying: ³ "From the
thirteenth year of Josiah son of Amon, king of Judah, until this day — this was

---

around the lofty meaning of this expression and use it
to derogate God's word (*Rashi*).
24:1. See *II Kings* 24:14.

24:7. I will give them the spiritual strength to recognize Me and be dedicated to My service.

שָׁלֹשׁ וְעֶשְׂרִים שָׁנָה דִּבֶּר יְהֹוָה אֵלַי וָאֲדַבֵּר אֲלֵיכֶם אַשְׁכֵּים וְדַבֵּר

ד וְלֹא שְׁמַעְתֶּם: וְשָׁלַח יְהֹוָה אֲלֵיכֶם אֶת־כָּל־עֲבָדָיו הַנְּבִאִים הַשְׁכֵּם וְשָׁלֹחַ

ה וְלֹא שְׁמַעְתֶּם וְלֹא־הִטִּיתֶם אֶת־אָזְנְכֶם לִשְׁמֹעַ: לֵאמֹר שׁוּבוּ־נָא אִישׁ מִדַּרְכּוֹ הָרָעָה וּמֵרֹעַ מַעַלְלֵיכֶם וּשְׁבוּ עַל־הָאֲדָמָה אֲשֶׁר נָתַן יְהֹוָה לָכֶם

ו וְלַאֲבוֹתֵיכֶם לְמִן־עוֹלָם וְעַד־עוֹלָם: וְאַל־תֵּלְכוּ אַחֲרֵי אֱלֹהִים אֲחֵרִים לְעָבְדָם וּלְהִשְׁתַּחֲוֹת לָהֶם וְלֹא־תַכְעִיסוּ אוֹתִי בְּמַעֲשֵׂה יְדֵיכֶם וְלֹא אָרַע

ז לָכֶם: וְלֹא־שְׁמַעְתֶּם אֵלַי נְאֻם־יְהֹוָה לְמַעַן °הכעסוני [הַכְעִסֵנִי ק]

ח בְּמַעֲשֵׂה יְדֵיכֶם לְרַע לָכֶם: לָכֵן כֹּה אָמַר יְהֹוָה צְבָאוֹת יַעַן

ט אֲשֶׁר לֹא־שְׁמַעְתֶּם אֶת־דְּבָרָי: הִנְנִי שֹׁלֵחַ וְלָקַחְתִּי אֶת־כָּל־מִשְׁפְּחוֹת צָפוֹן נְאֻם־יְהֹוָה וְאֶל־נְבוּכַדְרֶאצַּר מֶלֶךְ־בָּבֶל עַבְדִּי וַהֲבִאֹתִים עַל־הָאָרֶץ הַזֹּאת וְעַל־יֹשְׁבֶיהָ וְעַל כָּל־הַגּוֹיִם הָאֵלֶּה סָבִיב וְהַחֲרַמְתִּים

י וְשַׂמְתִּים לְשַׁמָּה וְלִשְׁרֵקָה וּלְחָרְבוֹת עוֹלָם: וְהַאֲבַדְתִּי מֵהֶם קוֹל שָׂשׂוֹן

יא וְקוֹל שִׂמְחָה קוֹל חָתָן וְקוֹל כַּלָּה קוֹל רֵחַיִם וְאוֹר נֵר: וְהָיְתָה כָּל־הָאָרֶץ הַזֹּאת לְחָרְבָּה לְשַׁמָּה וְעָבְדוּ הַגּוֹיִם הָאֵלֶּה אֶת־מֶלֶךְ בָּבֶל שִׁבְעִים שָׁנָה:

יב וְהָיָה כִמְלֹאות שִׁבְעִים שָׁנָה אֶפְקֹד עַל־מֶלֶךְ־בָּבֶל וְעַל־הַגּוֹי הַהוּא נְאֻם־יְהֹוָה אֶת־עֲוֹנָם וְעַל־אֶרֶץ כַּשְׂדִּים וְשַׂמְתִּי אֹתוֹ לְשִׁמְמוֹת עוֹלָם:

יג °והבאתי [וְהֵבֵאתִי ק] עַל־הָאָרֶץ הַהִיא אֶת־כָּל־דְּבָרַי אֲשֶׁר־דִּבַּרְתִּי עָלֶיהָ אֵת כָּל־הַכָּתוּב בַּסֵּפֶר הַזֶּה אֲשֶׁר־נִבָּא יִרְמְיָהוּ עַל־כָּל־הַגּוֹיִם: כִּי

יד עָבְדוּ־בָם גַּם־הֵמָּה גּוֹיִם רַבִּים וּמְלָכִים גְּדוֹלִים וְשִׁלַּמְתִּי לָהֶם כְּפָעֳלָם

טו וּכְמַעֲשֵׂה יְדֵיהֶם: כִּי כֹה אָמַר יְהֹוָה אֱלֹהֵי יִשְׂרָאֵל אֵלַי קַח אֶת־כּוֹס הַיַּיִן הַחֵמָה הַזֹּאת מִיָּדִי וְהִשְׁקִיתָה אֹתוֹ אֶת־כָּל־הַגּוֹיִם אֲשֶׁר

טז אָנֹכִי שֹׁלֵחַ אוֹתְךָ אֲלֵיהֶם: וְשָׁתוּ וְהִתְגֹּעֲשׁוּ וְהִתְהֹלָלוּ מִפְּנֵי הַחֶרֶב אֲשֶׁר

יז אָנֹכִי שֹׁלֵחַ בֵּינֹתָם: וָאֶקַּח אֶת־הַכּוֹס מִיַּד יְהֹוָה וָאַשְׁקֶה אֶת־כָּל־הַגּוֹיִם

יח אֲשֶׁר־שְׁלָחַנִי יְהֹוָה אֲלֵיהֶם: אֶת־יְרוּשָׁלַ͏ִם וְאֶת־עָרֵי יְהוּדָה וְאֶת־מְלָכֶיהָ אֶת־שָׂרֶיהָ לָתֵת אֹתָם לְחָרְבָּה לְשַׁמָּה לִשְׁרֵקָה וְלִקְלָלָה כַּיּוֹם הַזֶּה: אֶת־

יט פַּרְעֹה מֶלֶךְ־מִצְרַיִם וְאֶת־עֲבָדָיו וְאֶת־שָׂרָיו וְאֶת־כָּל־עַמּוֹ: וְאֵת כָּל־

כ הָעֶרֶב וְאֵת כָּל־מַלְכֵי אֶרֶץ הָעוּץ וְאֵת כָּל־מַלְכֵי אֶרֶץ פְּלִשְׁתִּים וְאֶת־

כא אַשְׁקְלוֹן וְאֶת־עַזָּה וְאֶת־עֶקְרוֹן וְאֵת שְׁאֵרִית אַשְׁדּוֹד: אֶת־אֱדוֹם

כב וְאֶת־מוֹאָב וְאֶת־בְּנֵי עַמּוֹן: וְאֵת כָּל־מַלְכֵי־צֹר וְאֵת כָּל־מַלְכֵי צִידוֹן

כג וְאֵת מַלְכֵי הָאִי אֲשֶׁר בְּעֵבֶר הַיָּם: וְאֶת־דְּדָן וְאֶת־תֵּימָא וְאֶת־בּוּז וְאֵת

כד כָּל־קְצוּצֵי פֵאָה: וְאֵת כָּל־מַלְכֵי עֲרָב וְאֵת כָּל־מַלְכֵי הָעֶרֶב הַשֹּׁכְנִים

כה בַּמִּדְבָּר: וְאֵת ׀ כָּל־מַלְכֵי זִמְרִי וְאֵת כָּל־מַלְכֵי עֵילָם וְאֵת כָּל־מַלְכֵי מָדָי:

כו וְאֵת ׀ כָּל־מַלְכֵי הַצָּפוֹן הַקְּרֹבִים וְהָרְחֹקִים אִישׁ אֶל־אָחִיו וְאֵת כָּל־ הַמַּמְלְכוֹת הָאָרֶץ אֲשֶׁר עַל־פְּנֵי הָאֲדָמָה וּמֶלֶךְ שֵׁשַׁךְ יִשְׁתֶּה אַחֲרֵיהֶם:

twenty-three years — the word of HASHEM has been coming to me, and I have spoken to you, speaking from early [morning], but you have not listened. ⁴ *HASHEM has sent you all His servants the prophets, sending them from early [morning] — but you did not listen, and you did not incline your ear to hear —* ⁵ *saying, 'Repent now, each man from his evil way and from the wickedness of your deeds, so that you may remain on the land that HASHEM gave you and your fathers for ever and ever.* ⁶ *Do not follow the gods of others, worshiping them and prostrating yourselves to them, and do not anger Me with your handiwork, so that I not bring evil upon you.'* ⁷ *But you did not listen to Me — the word of HASHEM — in order to anger Me with your handiwork, to your own harm."*

The
Babylonian
king is
coming

⁸ *Therefore, thus says HASHEM, Master of Legions: Because you have not heeded My words,* ⁹ *behold I am sending and will take all the families of the North — the word of HASHEM — and [am sending] to Nebuchadrezzar king of Babylonia, My servant;* * *and I shall bring them upon this land and upon its inhabitants and upon all these surrounding nations, and I shall destroy them and make them places of desolation and whistling and eternal ruins.* ¹⁰ *I shall eliminate from them the sound of joy and the sound of gladness, the sound of the groom and the sound of the bride, the sound of the mill and the light of the candle.* * ¹¹ *This entire land shall be a ruin and desolation, and*

Seventy-year
exile
(See Appendix A,
timeline 5)

these nations will serve the king of Babylonia for seventy years. ¹² *Then, upon the completion of seventy years, I shall make an account of their sin for the king of Babylonia and for that nation — the word of HASHEM — and for the land of the Chaldeans; and I shall make it into eternal desolations.* ¹³ *And I shall bring upon that land all My words that I have spoken concerning it, all that is written in this book, which Jeremiah prophesied concerning all the nations.* ¹⁴ *For many nations and great kings will enslave [Babylonia] also; I shall repay them according to their action and according to their handiwork.*

The cup of
wrath

¹⁵ *For thus said HASHEM, God of Israel, to me: "Take this cup of the wine of wrath* * *from My hand, and make all the nations to whom I shall send you drink from it.* ¹⁶ *They will drink and they will quiver and become deranged, because of the sword that I am sending among them."* ¹⁷ *So I took the cup from the hand of HASHEM, and I made all the nations whom HASHEM had sent me drink from it —* ¹⁸ *Jerusalem and the cities of Judah, along with its kings and its officers — to turn them into places of ruin and of desolation, of whistling and of curse, as it is this very day;* ¹⁹ *and to Pharaoh, king of Egypt, and his servants and his officers and all his people,* ²⁰ *and all his allies; all the kings of the land of Uz; all the kings of the land of the Philistines: Ashkelon, Gaza, Ekron, and the remnant of Ashdod;* ²¹ *Edom, Moab and the Children of Ammon;* ²² *all the kings of Tyre and all the kings of Sidon; the kings of the island that is on the other side of the sea;* ²³ *Dedan, Tema and Buz and all the inhabitants of the remotest areas;* ²⁴ *all the kings of Arabia and all the kings of the allies, who dwell in the desert;* ²⁵ *all the kings of Zimri and all the kings of Elam and all the kings of Medea;* ²⁶ *and all the kings of the North, whether they are near or far from another, along with all the kingdoms of the land that are on the face of the earth; and the king of Sheshach* * *will drink after them.*

25:9. Nebuchadnezzar was God's servant in the sense that he would carry out God's decree against Israel.
25:10. So complete will the desolation be that even

everyday sights and sounds will be discontinued.
25:15. A metaphor for dire prophecy.
25:26. Sheshach is another name for Babylonia.

כז וְאָמַרְתָּ֣ אֲלֵיהֶ֗ם כֹּֽה־אָמַ֞ר יְהֹוָ֤ה צְבָאוֹת֙ אֱלֹהֵ֣י יִשְׂרָאֵ֔ל שְׁת֣וּ וְשִׁכְר֗וּ וּקְי֤וּ

כח וְנִפְל֨וּ וְלֹ֤א תָק֙וּמוּ֙ מִפְּנֵ֣י הַחֶ֔רֶב אֲשֶׁ֛ר אָנֹכִ֥י שֹׁלֵ֖חַ בֵּֽינֵיכֶֽם: וְהָיָ֗ה כִּ֤י יְמָֽאֲנוּ֙ לָקַֽחַת־הַכּ֤וֹס מִיָּֽדְךָ֙ לִשְׁתּ֔וֹת וְאָמַרְתָּ֣ אֲלֵיהֶ֔ם כֹּ֥ה אָמַ֖ר יְהֹוָ֣ה צְבָא֑וֹת שָׁת֥וֹ

כט תִשְׁתּֽוּ: כִּי֩ הִנֵּ֨ה בָעִ֜יר אֲשֶׁ֧ר נִקְרָא־שְׁמִ֣י עָלֶ֗יהָ אָֽנֹכִי֙ מֵחֵ֣ל לְהָרַ֔ע וְאַתֶּ֖ם הִנָּקֵ֣ה תִנָּק֑וּ לֹ֣א תִנָּ֔קוּ כִּ֣י חֶ֗רֶב אֲנִ֤י קֹרֵא֙ עַל־כָּל־יֹֽשְׁבֵ֣י הָאָ֔רֶץ נְאֻ֖ם יְהֹוָ֥ה

ל צְבָא֑וֹת: וְאַתָּה֙ תִּנָּבֵ֣א אֲלֵיהֶ֔ם אֵ֥ת כָּל־הַדְּבָרִ֖ים הָאֵ֑לֶּה וְאָמַרְתָּ֣ אֲלֵיהֶ֗ם יְהֹוָ֞ה מִמָּר֤וֹם יִשְׁאָג֙ וּמִמְּע֤וֹן קָדְשׁוֹ֙ יִתֵּ֣ן קוֹל֔וֹ שָׁאֹ֥ג יִשְׁאַ֖ג עַל־נָוֵ֑הוּ

לא הֵידָד֙ כְּדֹרְכִ֣ים יַֽעֲנֶ֔ה אֶ֥ל כָּל־יֹֽשְׁבֵ֖י הָאָֽרֶץ: בָּ֤א שָׁאוֹן֙ עַד־קְצֵ֣ה הָאָ֔רֶץ כִּ֣י רִ֤יב לַֽיהֹוָה֙ בַּגּוֹיִ֔ם נִשְׁפָּ֥ט ה֖וּא לְכָל־בָּשָׂ֑ר הָרְשָׁעִ֛ים נְתָנָ֥ם לַחֶ֖רֶב נְאֻם־

לב יְהֹוָֽה: כֹּ֤ה אָמַר֙ יְהֹוָ֣ה צְבָא֔וֹת הִנֵּ֥ה רָעָ֛ה יֹצֵ֖את מִגּ֣וֹי אֶל־גּ֑וֹי

לג וְסַ֣עַר גָּד֔וֹל יֵע֖וֹר מִיַּרְכְּתֵי־אָֽרֶץ: וְהָי֞וּ חַֽלְלֵ֤י יְהֹוָה֙ בַּיּ֣וֹם הַה֔וּא מִקְצֵ֥ה הָאָ֖רֶץ וְעַד־קְצֵ֣ה הָאָ֑רֶץ לֹ֣א יִסָּ֧פְדוּ וְלֹ֣א יֵאָֽסְפוּ֮ וְלֹ֣א יִקָּבֵ֒רוּ֒ לְדֹ֛מֶן עַל־

לד פְּנֵ֥י הָֽאֲדָמָ֖ה יִֽהְיֽוּ: הֵילִ֣ילוּ הָֽרֹעִ֗ים וְזַֽעֲקוּ֙ וְהִֽתְפַּלְּשׁוּ֙ אַדִּירֵ֣י הַצֹּ֔אן כִּֽי

לה מָֽלְא֥וּ יְמֵיכֶ֖ם לִטְב֑וֹחַ וּתְפוֹצ֣וֹתִיכֶ֔ם וּנְפַלְתֶּ֖ם כִּכְלִ֥י חֶמְדָּֽה: וְאָבַ֣ד מָנ֗וֹס

לו מִן־הָֽרֹעִ֔ים וּפְלֵיטָ֖ה מֵֽאַדִּירֵ֥י הַצֹּֽאן: ק֚וֹל צַֽעֲקַ֣ת הָֽרֹעִ֔ים וְיִלְלַ֖ת אַדִּירֵ֣י

לז הַצֹּ֑אן כִּֽי־שֹׁדֵ֥ד יְהֹוָ֖ה אֶת־מַרְעִיתָֽם: וְנָדַ֖מּוּ נְא֣וֹת הַשָּׁל֑וֹם מִפְּנֵ֖י חֲר֥וֹן אַף־

לח יְהֹוָֽה: עָזַ֤ב כַּכְּפִיר֙ סֻכּ֔וֹ כִּֽי־הָֽיְתָ֤ה אַרְצָם֙ לְשַׁמָּ֔ה מִפְּנֵי֙ חֲר֣וֹן הַיּוֹנָ֔ה וּמִפְּנֵ֖י חֲר֥וֹן אַפּֽוֹ:

כו א בְּרֵאשִׁ֗ית מַמְלְכ֛וּת יְהֽוֹיָקִ֥ים בֶּן־יֹֽאשִׁיָּ֖הוּ מֶ֣לֶךְ

ב יְהוּדָ֑ה הָיָה֙ הַדָּבָ֣ר הַזֶּ֔ה מֵאֵ֥ת יְהֹוָ֖ה לֵאמֹֽר: כֹּ֣ה ׀ אָמַ֣ר יְהֹוָ֗ה עֲמֹד֙ בַּֽחֲצַ֣ר בֵּֽית־יְהֹוָ֔ה וְדִבַּרְתָּ֞ עַל־כָּל־עָרֵ֣י יְהוּדָ֗ה הַבָּאִים֙ לְהִשְׁתַּֽחֲוֺ֣ת בֵּֽית־יְהֹוָ֔ה

ג אֵ֚ת כָּל־הַדְּבָרִ֔ים אֲשֶׁ֥ר צִוִּיתִ֖יךָ לְדַבֵּ֣ר אֲלֵיהֶ֑ם אַל־תִּגְרַ֖ע דָּבָֽר: אוּלַ֣י יִשְׁמְע֔וּ וְיָשֻׁ֕בוּ אִ֖ישׁ מִדַּרְכּ֣וֹ הָֽרָעָ֑ה וְנִֽחַמְתִּ֣י אֶל־הָֽרָעָ֔ה אֲשֶׁ֧ר אָֽנֹכִ֛י חֹשֵׁ֖ב

ד לַֽעֲשׂ֣וֹת לָהֶ֑ם מִפְּנֵ֖י רֹ֥עַ מַֽעַלְלֵיהֶֽם: וְאָמַרְתָּ֣ אֲלֵיהֶ֔ם כֹּ֖ה אָמַ֣ר יְהֹוָ֑ה אִם־

ה לֹ֤א תִשְׁמְעוּ֙ אֵלַ֔י לָלֶ֖כֶת בְּתֽוֹרָתִ֑י אֲשֶׁ֥ר נָתַ֖תִּי לִפְנֵיכֶֽם: לִשְׁמֹ֗עַ עַל־דִּבְרֵ֞י עֲבָדַ֣י הַנְּבִאִ֗ים אֲשֶׁ֤ר אָֽנֹכִי֙ שֹׁלֵ֣חַ אֲלֵיכֶ֔ם וְהַשְׁכֵּ֥ם וְשָׁלֹ֖חַ וְלֹ֥א שְׁמַעְתֶּֽם:

ו וְנָֽתַתִּ֛י אֶת־הַבַּ֥יִת הַזֶּ֖ה כְּשִׁלֹ֑ה וְאֶת־הָעִ֤יר °הָאתה [הַזֹּ֙את ק] אֶתֵּ֣ן

ז לִקְלָלָ֔ה לְכֹ֖ל גּוֹיֵ֥י הָאָֽרֶץ: וַיִּשְׁמְע֤וּ הַכֹּֽהֲנִים֙ וְהַנְּבִאִ֔ים

ח וְכָל־הָעָ֑ם אֶֽת־יִרְמְיָ֔הוּ מְדַבֵּ֖ר אֶת־הַדְּבָרִ֣ים הָאֵ֑לֶּה בְּבֵ֖ית יְהֹוָֽה: וַיְהִ֣י ׀ כְּכַלּ֣וֹת יִרְמְיָ֗הוּ לְדַבֵּר֙ אֵ֣ת כָּל־אֲשֶׁר־צִוָּ֣ה יְהֹוָ֔ה לְדַבֵּ֖ר אֶל־כָּל־הָעָ֑ם

25:30. Grape tramplers would chant "Hedad!" to urge each other on in their arduous task. Similarly, God will summon the nations to come and destroy the Temple (*Radak*).

25:38. Just as a young lion leaves the den of his birth when it can no longer provide him with sufficient food, so God leaves His Temple because it has been emptied of its spirituality.

26:6. The Tabernacle at Shiloh was destroyed by the Philistines (*I Samuel* 4:10-11).

²⁷ *"You shall say unto them:*

Thus said HASHEM, Master of Legions, God of Israel: Drink, become intoxicated and vomit; fall down and do not rise up again — because of the sword that I am sending against you.

²⁸ *"And it shall be if they refuse to take the cup from your hand to drink, that you shall say to them:*

Thus said HASHEM, Master of Legions: You will surely drink! ²⁹ *For behold, even in the city upon which My Name is proclaimed I have begun to bring evil — will you be exonerated? You will not be exonerated, for I am summoning the sword against all the inhabitants of the land — the word of HASHEM, Master of Legions.*

³⁰ *"So you, prophesy to them all these words, and say to them:*

HASHEM roars from on high and sends out His voice from His holy Abode; He is roaring over His Lodging, He shouts 'Hedad' — like those who trample the grapes at the winepress * *— to all the inhabitants of the land.* ³¹ *The commotion reaches the end of the world, for HASHEM is contending with the nations, He is passing judgment on all flesh; He has delivered the wicked to the sword — the word of HASHEM.*

Babylonia will dominate the entire world

³² *Thus said HASHEM, Master of Legions: Behold, evil is going out from nation to nation, and a great storm will be aroused from the edges of the earth.* ³³ *The slain of HASHEM on that day will cover from one end of the land to the other; they will not be eulogized nor gathered nor buried; they will remain like dung on the face of the earth.* ³⁴ *Wail, O shepherds, and shout! Wallow in the dirt, O leaders of the flock! For your days before slaughter are completed, and your dispersions, and you will fall [and shatter] like a precious vessel.* ³⁵ *Flight will be foreclosed from the shepherds, and escape from the leaders of the flock.* ³⁶ *The sound of the shepherds' outcry and the wailing of the leaders of the flock — for HASHEM is plundering their pasture!* ³⁷ *The peaceful cottages shall be destroyed before the burning wrath of HASHEM.* ³⁸ *Like a young lion, [God] has forsaken His Tabernacle,* * *for their land has become a desolation, because of the oppressor's anger, and because of His burning wrath.*

26

¹ *In the beginning of the reign of Jehoiakim son of Josiah, king of Judah, this word came from HASHEM, saying:*

Prophesy in the Temple Courtyard

² *Thus said HASHEM: "Stand in the Courtyard of the Temple of HASHEM and speak to all the cities of Judah who come to prostrate themselves in the Temple of HASHEM all the words that I shall command you to speak to them; do not omit a word.* ³ *Perhaps they will listen and repent, each man from his evil way, then I will relent of the evil that I am planning to do to them because of the wickedness of their deeds.* ⁴ *Say to them:*

Thus said HASHEM: If you do not listen to Me, to follow My Torah that I have placed before you, ⁵ *to listen to the words of My servants the prophets whom I send to you, sending them from early [morning] — but you did not listen!* ⁶ *So I shall make this Temple like Shiloh,* * *and I will make this city [the epitome of] a curse for all the nations of the land."*

⁷ *The priests and the [false] prophets and all the people heard Jeremiah speaking these words in the Temple of HASHEM.* ⁸ *It happened that as Jeremiah finished speaking everything that HASHEM had commanded him to speak to all the people,*

ט וַיִּתְפְּשׂוּ אֹתוֹ הַכֹּהֲנִים וְהַנְּבִאִים וְכָל־הָעָם לֵאמֹר מוֹת תָּמוּת: מַדּוּעַ נִבֵּיתָ
בְשֵׁם־יְהוָה לֵאמֹר כְּשִׁלוֹ יִהְיֶה הַבַּיִת הַזֶּה וְהָעִיר הַזֹּאת תֶּחֱרַב מֵאֵין
י יוֹשֵׁב וַיִּקָּהֵל כָּל־הָעָם אֶל־יִרְמְיָהוּ בְּבֵית יְהוָה: וַיִּשְׁמְעוּ | שָׂרֵי יְהוּדָה אֵת
הַדְּבָרִים הָאֵלֶּה וַיַּעֲלוּ מִבֵּית־הַמֶּלֶךְ בֵּית יְהוָה וַיֵּשְׁבוּ בְּפֶתַח שַׁעַר־יְהוָה
יא הֶחָדָשׁ: וַיֹּאמְרוּ הַכֹּהֲנִים וְהַנְּבִאִים אֶל־הַשָּׂרִים וְאֶל־כָּל־הָעָם לֵאמֹר
מִשְׁפַּט־מָוֶת לָאִישׁ הַזֶּה כִּי נִבָּא אֶל־הָעִיר הַזֹּאת כַּאֲשֶׁר שְׁמַעְתֶּם
יב בְּאָזְנֵיכֶם: וַיֹּאמֶר יִרְמְיָהוּ אֶל־כָּל־הַשָּׂרִים וְאֶל־כָּל־הָעָם לֵאמֹר יְהוָה
שְׁלָחַנִי לְהִנָּבֵא אֶל־הַבַּיִת הַזֶּה וְאֶל־הָעִיר הַזֹּאת אֵת כָּל־הַדְּבָרִים אֲשֶׁר
יג שְׁמַעְתֶּם: וְעַתָּה הֵיטִיבוּ דַרְכֵיכֶם וּמַעַלְלֵיכֶם וְשִׁמְעוּ בְּקוֹל יְהוָה אֱלֹהֵיכֶם
יד וְיִנָּחֵם יְהוָה אֶל־הָרָעָה אֲשֶׁר דִּבֶּר עֲלֵיכֶם: וַאֲנִי הִנְנִי בְיֶדְכֶם עֲשׂוּ־לִי
טו כַּטּוֹב וְכַיָּשָׁר בְּעֵינֵיכֶם: אַךְ | יָדֹעַ תֵּדְעוּ כִּי אִם־מְמִתִים אַתֶּם אֹתִי כִּי־דָם
נָקִי אַתֶּם נֹתְנִים עֲלֵיכֶם וְאֶל־הָעִיר הַזֹּאת וְאֶל־יֹשְׁבֶיהָ כִּי בֶאֱמֶת שְׁלָחַנִי
טז יְהוָה עֲלֵיכֶם לְדַבֵּר בְּאָזְנֵיכֶם אֵת כָּל־הַדְּבָרִים הָאֵלֶּה: וַיֹּאמְרוּ
הַשָּׂרִים וְכָל־הָעָם אֶל־הַכֹּהֲנִים וְאֶל־הַנְּבִאִים אֵין־לָאִישׁ הַזֶּה מִשְׁפַּט־
יז מָוֶת כִּי בְּשֵׁם יְהוָה אֱלֹהֵינוּ דִּבֶּר אֵלֵינוּ: וַיָּקֻמוּ אֲנָשִׁים מִזִּקְנֵי הָאָרֶץ
יח וַיֹּאמְרוּ אֶל־כָּל־קְהַל הָעָם לֵאמֹר: °מִיכָיָה [°מִיכָה ק'] הַמּוֹרַשְׁתִּי הָיָה
נִבָּא בִּימֵי חִזְקִיָּהוּ מֶלֶךְ־יְהוּדָה וַיֹּאמֶר אֶל־כָּל־עַם יְהוּדָה לֵאמֹר
כֹּה־אָמַר | יְהוָה צְבָאוֹת צִיּוֹן שָׂדֶה תֵחָרֵשׁ וִירוּשָׁלַיִם עִיִּים תִּהְיֶה וְהַר
יט הַבַּיִת לְבָמוֹת יָעַר: הֶהָמֵת הֱמִתֻהוּ חִזְקִיָּהוּ מֶלֶךְ־יְהוּדָה וְכָל־יְהוּדָה
הֲלֹא יָרֵא אֶת־יְהוָה וַיְחַל אֶת־פְּנֵי יְהוָה וַיִּנָּחֶם יְהוָה אֶל־הָרָעָה אֲשֶׁר־
כ דִּבֶּר עֲלֵיהֶם וַאֲנַחְנוּ עֹשִׂים רָעָה גְדוֹלָה עַל־נַפְשׁוֹתֵינוּ: וְגַם־אִישׁ הָיָה
מִתְנַבֵּא בְּשֵׁם יְהוָה אוּרִיָּהוּ בֶּן־שְׁמַעְיָהוּ מִקִּרְיַת הַיְּעָרִים וַיִּנָּבֵא עַל־הָעִיר
כא הַזֹּאת וְעַל־הָאָרֶץ הַזֹּאת כְּכֹל דִּבְרֵי יִרְמְיָהוּ: וַיִּשְׁמַע הַמֶּלֶךְ־יְהוֹיָקִים
וְכָל־גִּבּוֹרָיו וְכָל־הַשָּׂרִים אֶת־דְּבָרָיו וַיְבַקֵּשׁ הַמֶּלֶךְ הֲמִיתוֹ וַיִּשְׁמַע
כב אוּרִיָּהוּ וַיִּרָא וַיִּבְרַח וַיָּבֹא מִצְרָיִם: וַיִּשְׁלַח הַמֶּלֶךְ יְהוֹיָקִים אֲנָשִׁים מִצְרָיִם
כג אֵת־אֶלְנָתָן בֶּן־עַכְבּוֹר וַאֲנָשִׁים אִתּוֹ אֶל־מִצְרָיִם: וַיּוֹצִיאוּ אֶת־אוּרִיָּהוּ
מִמִּצְרַיִם וַיְבִאֻהוּ אֶל־הַמֶּלֶךְ יְהוֹיָקִים וַיַּכֵּהוּ בֶּחָרֶב וַיַּשְׁלֵךְ אֶת־נִבְלָתוֹ
כד אֶל־קִבְרֵי בְּנֵי הָעָם: אַךְ יַד אֲחִיקָם בֶּן־שָׁפָן הָיְתָה אֶת־יִרְמְיָהוּ לְבִלְתִּי
כז א תֵּת־אֹתוֹ בְיַד־הָעָם לַהֲמִיתוֹ: בְּרֵאשִׁית מַמְלֶכֶת יְהוֹיָקִם
בֶּן־יֹאושִׁיָּהוּ מֶלֶךְ יְהוּדָה הָיָה הַדָּבָר הַזֶּה אֶל־יִרְמְיָה מֵאֵת יְהוָה
ב לֵאמֹר: כֹּה־אָמַר יְהוָה אֵלַי עֲשֵׂה לְךָ מוֹסֵרוֹת וּמֹטוֹת וּנְתַתָּם עַל־
ג צַוָּארֶךָ: וְשִׁלַּחְתָּם אֶל־מֶלֶךְ אֱדוֹם וְאֶל־מֶלֶךְ מוֹאָב וְאֶל־מֶלֶךְ

26:10. When Jehoiachin was exiled by Nebuchadnezzar, his troops broke down the East Gate. When
Zedekiah subsequently rebuilt it, he called it the New

Gate (*Rashi*).
26:18. Micah 3:12.
26:20-23. The false prophets and priests respond to

The priests the priests and the prophets and all the people seized him, saying, "You shall die!
and false 9 Why have you prophesied in the Name of HASHEM, saying, 'This Temple will be
prophets like Shiloh, and this city will be destroyed, without an inhabitant'?" And all the
react people congregated around Jeremiah in the Temple of HASHEM.

10 The ministers of Judah heard these things and they went up from the king's palace to the Temple of HASHEM, and they sat at the entrance of the New Gate* [of the Temple] of HASHEM. 11 The priests and the prophets said to the officers and to all the people, saying, "A death judgment should be upon this man, for he has prophesied against this city as you have heard with your own ears."

12 Jeremiah said to all the ministers and all the people, saying, "HASHEM has sent me to prophesy about this Temple and about this city all the things that you have heard. 13 So now, correct your ways and your deeds and heed the voice of HASHEM your God, and HASHEM will relent of the evil that He has spoken about you. 14 As for me, here I am in your hand; do to me whatever is right and proper in your eyes! 15 But you must surely know that if you put me to death you will be putting innocent blood upon yourselves and upon this city and upon all its inhabitants, for in truth HASHEM sent me to you to speak all these things in your ears."

The people 16 The ministers and all the people then said to the priests and to the prophets,
defend "This man does not deserve death judgment, for he has spoken to us in the Name
Jeremiah of HASHEM our God!"

17 Then some of the elders of the land arose and said to the entire congregation of the people, 18 "Micah the Morashite used to prophesy in the days of Hezekiah, king of Judah, and he said to all the people of Judah: 'Thus said HASHEM, Master of Legions: Zion will be plowed over like a field; Jerusalem will become ruins and the Temple Mount will become like heaps [of rubble] in the forest.'* 19 Did Hezekiah king of Judah and all of Judah put him to death? Behold, he feared HASHEM and supplicated before HASHEM, and HASHEM relented of the evil that He had spoken concerning them! So we would be bringing great evil upon ourselves [if we would kill Jeremiah].

But what 20 "Now* there was another man who prophesied in the Name of HASHEM —
about Uriah? Uriah son of Shemaiah of Kiryath-jearim. He prophesied concerning this city and concerning this land exactly like all the words of Jeremiah. 21 When King Jehoiakim and all his soldiers and all the officers heard his words, the king attempted to have him killed; Uriah heard and became afraid and fled, going to Egypt. 22 King Jehoiakim sent men to Egypt — he sent Elnathan son of Achbor and some men with him to Egypt. 23 They removed Uriah from Egypt and brought him to King Jehoiakim, who struck him down by the sword and threw his body into the graves of the common people."

24 However, the power of Ahikam son of Shaphan was with Jeremiah, not to deliver him into the hand of the people to kill him.

27 ¹ In the beginning of the reign of Jehoiakim son of Josiah,* king of Judah, this word came to Jeremiah from HASHEM, saying:

Parable of ² Thus said HASHEM to me: "Make yourself straps and bars and put them on your
the yoke neck.* ³ Send [them] to the king of Edom, to the king of Moab, to the king of

---

Jeremiah's defenders.
27:1. Although the text of the prophecy was to be delivered to King Zedekiah (v. 3), who reigned some eleven years after his brother Jehoiakim, it was told to Jeremiah now so that he could let Jehoiakim know that

the king of Egypt, who had placed him upon the throne (*II Kings* 23:34), would soon lose power, and that Israel should not depend on him (*Radak*).

27:2. He would wear these yokes until the fourth year of Zedekiah's reign, fifteen years later (see 28:10).

בְּנֵי עַמּוֹן וְאֶל־מֶלֶךְ צֹר וְאֶל־מֶלֶךְ צִידוֹן בְּיַד מַלְאָכִים הַבָּאִים יְרוּשָׁלַ֫͏ִם

ד אֶל־צִדְקִיָּהוּ מֶלֶךְ יְהוּדָה: וְצִוִּיתָ אֹתָם אֶל־אֲדֹנֵיהֶם לֵאמֹר כֹּה־אָמַר

ה יְהוָֹה צְבָאוֹת אֱלֹהֵי יִשְׂרָאֵל כֹּה תֹאמְרוּ אֶל־אֲדֹנֵיכֶם: אָנֹכִי עָשִׂיתִי אֶת־הָאָרֶץ אֶת־הָאָדָם וְאֶת־הַבְּהֵמָה אֲשֶׁר עַל־פְּנֵי הָאָרֶץ בְּכֹחִי הַגָּדוֹל

ו וּבִזְרוֹעִי הַנְּטוּיָה וּנְתַתִּיהָ לַאֲשֶׁר יָשַׁר בְּעֵינָי: וְעַתָּה אָנֹכִי נָתַ֫תִּי אֶת־כָּל־הָאֲרָצוֹת הָאֵלֶּה בְּיַד נְבוּכַדְנֶאצַּר מֶלֶךְ־בָּבֶל עַבְדִּי וְגַם אֶת־חַיַּת הַשָּׂדֶה

ז נָתַ֫תִּי לוֹ לְעָבְדוֹ: וְעָבְדוּ אֹתוֹ כָּל־הַגּוֹיִם וְאֶת־בְּנוֹ וְאֶת־בֶּן־בְּנוֹ עַד בֹּא־עֵת אַרְצוֹ גַּם־הוּא וְעָבְדוּ בוֹ גּוֹיִם רַבִּים וּמְלָכִים גְּדֹלִים: וְהָיָה הַגּוֹי

ח וְהַמַּמְלָכָה אֲשֶׁר לֹא־יַעַבְדוּ אֹתוֹ אֶת־נְבוּכַדְנֶאצַּר מֶלֶךְ־בָּבֶל וְאֵת אֲשֶׁר לֹא־יִתֵּן אֶת־צַוָּארוֹ בְּעֹל מֶלֶךְ בָּבֶל בַּחֶ֫רֶב וּבָרָעָב וּבַדֶּ֫בֶר אֶפְקֹד עַל־

ט הַגּוֹי הַהוּא נְאֻם־יְהֹוָה עַד־תֻּמִּי אֹתָם בְּיָדוֹ: וְאַתֶּם אַל־תִּשְׁמְעוּ אֶל־נְבִיאֵיכֶם וְאֶל־קֹסְמֵיכֶם וְאֶל־חֲלֹמֹתֵיכֶם וְאֶל־עֹנְנֵיכֶם וְאֶל־כַּשָּׁפֵיכֶם

י אֲשֶׁר־הֵם אֹמְרִים אֲלֵיכֶם לֵאמֹר לֹא תַעַבְדוּ אֶת־מֶלֶךְ בָּבֶל: כִּי שֶׁ֫קֶר הֵם נִבְּאִים לָכֶם לְמַעַן הַרְחִיק אֶתְכֶם מֵעַל אַדְמַתְכֶם וְהִדַּחְתִּי אֶתְכֶם

יא וַאֲבַדְתֶּם: וְהַגּוֹי אֲשֶׁר יָבִיא אֶת־צַוָּארוֹ בְּעֹל מֶלֶךְ־בָּבֶל וַעֲבָדוֹ וְהִנַּחְתִּיו עַל־אַדְמָתוֹ נְאֻם־יְהֹוָה וַעֲבָדָהּ וְיָשַׁב בָּהּ: וְאֶל־צִדְקִיָּה מֶלֶךְ־יְהוּדָה

יב דִּבַּרְתִּי כְּכָל־הַדְּבָרִים הָאֵלֶּה לֵאמֹר הָבִיאוּ אֶת־צַוְּארֵיכֶם בְּעֹל מֶלֶךְ־

יג בָּבֶל וְעִבְדוּ אֹתוֹ וְעַמּוֹ וִחְיוּ: לָ֫מָּה תָמוּתוּ אַתָּה וְעַמֶּךָ בַּחֶ֫רֶב בָּרָעָב

יד וּבַדֶּבֶר כַּאֲשֶׁר דִּבֶּר יְהֹוָה אֶל־הַגּוֹי אֲשֶׁר לֹא־יַעֲבֹד אֶת־מֶלֶךְ בָּבֶל: וְאַל־תִּשְׁמְעוּ אֶל־דִּבְרֵי הַנְּבִאִים הָאֹמְרִים אֲלֵיכֶם לֵאמֹר לֹא תַעַבְדוּ אֶת־

טו מֶלֶךְ בָּבֶל כִּי שֶׁ֫קֶר הֵם נִבְּאִים לָכֶם: כִּי לֹא שְׁלַחְתִּים נְאֻם־יְהֹוָה וְהֵם נִבְּאִים בִּשְׁמִי לַשָּׁ֫קֶר לְמַעַן הַדִּיחִי אֶתְכֶם וַאֲבַדְתֶּם אַתֶּם וְהַנְּבִאִים

טז הַנִּבְּאִים לָכֶם: וְאֶל־הַכֹּהֲנִים וְאֶל־כָּל־הָעָם הַזֶּה דִּבַּרְתִּי לֵאמֹר כֹּה אָמַר יְהֹוָה אַל־תִּשְׁמְעוּ אֶל־דִּבְרֵי נְבִיאֵיכֶם הַנִּבְּאִים לָכֶם לֵאמֹר הִנֵּה כְלֵי בֵית־יְהֹוָה מוּשָׁבִים מִבָּבֶ֫לָה עַתָּה מְהֵרָה כִּי שֶׁ֫קֶר הֵ֫מָּה נִבְּאִים לָכֶם:

יז אַל־תִּשְׁמְעוּ אֲלֵיהֶם עִבְדוּ אֶת־מֶלֶךְ־בָּבֶל וִחְיוּ לָ֫מָּה תִהְיֶה הָעִיר הַזֹּאת

יח חָרְבָּה: וְאִם־נְבִאִים הֵם וְאִם־יֶשׁ דְּבַר־יְהֹוָה אִתָּם יִפְגְּעוּ־נָא בַּיהֹוָה צְבָאוֹת לְבִלְתִּי־בֹ֫אוּ הַכֵּלִים ׀ הַנּוֹתָרִים בְּבֵית־יְהֹוָה וּבֵית מֶלֶךְ יְהוּדָה

יט וּבִירוּשָׁלַ֫͏ִם בָּבֶ֫לָה: כִּי כֹה אָמַר יְהֹוָה צְבָאוֹת אֶל־הָעַמֻּדִים וְעַל־הַיָּם וְעַל־הַמְּכֹנוֹת וְעַל יֶ֫תֶר הַכֵּלִים הַנּוֹתָרִים בָּעִיר

כ הַזֹּאת: אֲשֶׁר לֹא־לְקָחָם נְבוּכַדְנֶאצַּר מֶלֶךְ בָּבֶל בַּגְלוֹתוֹ אֶת־°יְכוֹנְיָה
[°יְכָנְיָ֫ה ק] בֶּן־יְהוֹיָקִים מֶלֶךְ־יְהוּדָה מִירוּשָׁלַ֫͏ִם בָּבֶ֫לָה וְאֵת כָּל־חֹרֵי

27:3. Rashi cites a tradition of the Sages that Jeremiah was prophesying that Nebuchadnezzar would place these five kings under Zedekiah's author- | ity; and in the fourth year of Zedekiah's reign, this prophecy was fulfilled (see 28:1).
27:10. Their disastrous advice will cause you to be

Prophecy of the Children of Ammon, to the king of Tyre and to the king of Sidon, * by the
Nebuchad- hand of the messengers who come to Jerusalem to Zedekiah, king of Judah.
nezzar's ⁴ Instruct them [with a message] to their masters, saying: Thus said HASHEM,
dominion: to Master of Legions, God of Israel: Thus shall you say to your masters: ⁵ 'I made
the foreign the earth — with the man and the animal that are on the face of the earth — with
kings . . . My great strength and with My outstretched hand, and I gave it to whomever
was fitting in My eyes. ⁶ And now I have delivered all these lands into the hand
of Nebuchadnezzar, king of Babylonia, My servant; I have even delivered the
beast of the field to him to serve him. ⁷ All the nations will serve him and his son
and his son's son, until the time [of reckoning] of his land comes, as well, and
many nations and great kings will enslave him. ⁸ And it shall be that the nation or
the kingdom that does not serve him, Nebuchadnezzar king of Babylonia, and
that does not put its neck into the yoke of the king of Babylonia, I will attend to
that nation with the sword and with famine and with pestilence — the word of
HASHEM — until I have annihilated them through [Nebuchadnezzar's] hand. ⁹ You
should not listen to your prophets and to your magicians and to your dreamers
and to your wizards and sorcerers, who are telling you, "Do not serve the king of
Babylonia." ¹⁰ For they are prophesying falsehood to you, in order to distance
you far from upon your homeland; * for I shall then disperse you and you will be
lost. ¹¹ But any nation that puts its neck into the yoke of the king of Babylonia
and serves him — I shall allow them to stay upon their land — the word of
HASHEM — and they will work it and live there.' "

. . . to the ¹² And to Zedekiah, king of Judah, I spoke the same words, saying, "Put your
king of necks into the yoke of the king of Babylonia and serve him and his people, so
Judah . . . that you may live. ¹³ Why should you and your people die by the sword, by
famine and by pestilence as HASHEM spoke concerning the nation that will not
serve the king of Babylonia? ¹⁴ Do not listen to the words of the prophets who tell
you, saying, 'Do not serve the king of Babylonia,' for they are prophesying
falsely to you. ¹⁵ For I did not send them — the word of HASHEM — and they
prophesy falsely in My Name, in order that I should disperse you, so that you
and your prophets who prophesy to you will be lost."

. . . and to ¹⁶ And to the priests and to all this people I spoke, saying:
Jeremiah's
detractors   Thus said HASHEM: Do not listen to the words of your prophets who
prophesy to you, saying, 'Behold, the articles of the Temple of HASHEM *
are being returned from Babylonia — now, soon!' for they are prophesying
falsehood to you. ¹⁷ Do not listen to them! Serve the king of Babylonia and
live; why should this city become destroyed? ¹⁸ And if they are [really]
prophets and if the word of HASHEM is [really] with them, let them now
beseech HASHEM, Master of Legions, that the articles which remain in the
Temple of HASHEM and in the palace of the king of Judah and in Jerusalem
not be brought to Babylonia. ¹⁹ For thus said HASHEM, Master of Legions,
concerning the pillars and the sea and the stands * and the rest of
the articles that remain in this city, ²⁰ that Nebuchadnezzar king of
Babylonia did not take when he exiled Jeconiah son of Jehoiakim, king of
Judah, from Jerusalem to Babylonia, along with all the noblemen of

---

exiled from your land.
27:16. These are the articles that Nebuchadnezzar
had looted from the Temple when he exiled Jehoi-

achin, eleven years before the final Destruction (*II
Kings* 24:13).
27:19. See *I Kings* 7:27-40.

כא יְהוּדָה וִירוּשָׁלָ͏ִם: כִּי כֹה אָמַר יהוה צְבָאוֹת אֱלֹהֵי יִשְׂרָאֵל עַל־

כב הַכֵּלִים הַנּוֹתָרִים בֵּית יהוה וּבֵית מֶלֶךְ־יְהוּדָה וִירוּשָׁלָ͏ִם: בָּבֶלָה יוּבָאוּ וְשָׁמָּה יִהְיוּ עַד יוֹם פָּקְדִי אֹתָם נְאֻם־יהוה וְהַעֲלִיתִים וַהֲשִׁיבֹתִים אֶל־

כח א הַמָּקוֹם הַזֶּה: וַיְהִי | בַּשָּׁנָה הַהִיא בְּרֵאשִׁית מַמְלֶכֶת צִדְקִיָּה מֶלֶךְ־יְהוּדָה °בִּשְׁנַת [בַּשָּׁנָה ק°] הָרְבִעִית בַּחֹדֶשׁ הַחֲמִישִׁי אָמַר אֵלַי חֲנַנְיָה בֶן־עַזּוּר הַנָּבִיא אֲשֶׁר מִגִּבְעוֹן בְּבֵית יהוה לְעֵינֵי הַכֹּהֲנִים וְכָל־

ב הָעָם לֵאמֹר: כֹּה־אָמַר יהוה צְבָאוֹת אֱלֹהֵי יִשְׂרָאֵל לֵאמֹר שָׁבַרְתִּי אֶת־

ג עֹל מֶלֶךְ בָּבֶל: בְּעוֹד | שְׁנָתַיִם יָמִים אֲנִי מֵשִׁיב אֶל־הַמָּקוֹם הַזֶּה אֶת־כָּל־כְּלֵי בֵּית יהוה אֲשֶׁר לָקַח נְבוּכַדְנֶאצַּר מֶלֶךְ־בָּבֶל מִן־הַמָּקוֹם הַזֶּה

ד וַיְבִיאֵם בָּבֶל: וְאֶת־יְכָנְיָה בֶן־יְהוֹיָקִים מֶלֶךְ־יְהוּדָה וְאֶת־כָּל־גָּלוּת יְהוּדָה הַבָּאִים בָּבֶלָה אֲנִי מֵשִׁיב אֶל־הַמָּקוֹם הַזֶּה נְאֻם־יהוה כִּי אֶשְׁבֹּר אֶת־עֹל

ה מֶלֶךְ בָּבֶל: וַיֹּאמֶר יִרְמְיָה הַנָּבִיא אֶל־חֲנַנְיָה הַנָּבִיא לְעֵינֵי הַכֹּהֲנִים

ו וּלְעֵינֵי כָּל־הָעָם הָעֹמְדִים בְּבֵית יהוה: וַיֹּאמֶר יִרְמְיָה הַנָּבִיא אָמֵן כֵּן יַעֲשֶׂה יהוה יָקֵם יהוה אֶת־דְּבָרֶיךָ אֲשֶׁר נִבֵּאתָ לְהָשִׁיב כְּלֵי בֵית־יהוה

ז וְכָל־הַגּוֹלָה מִבָּבֶל אֶל־הַמָּקוֹם הַזֶּה: אַךְ־שְׁמַע־נָא הַדָּבָר הַזֶּה אֲשֶׁר

ח אָנֹכִי דֹּבֵר בְּאָזְנֶיךָ וּבְאָזְנֵי כָּל־הָעָם: הַנְּבִיאִים אֲשֶׁר הָיוּ לְפָנַי וּלְפָנֶיךָ מִן־הָעוֹלָם וַיִּנָּבְאוּ אֶל־אֲרָצוֹת רַבּוֹת וְעַל־מַמְלָכוֹת גְּדֹלוֹת לְמִלְחָמָה

ט וּלְרָעָה וּלְדָבֶר: הַנָּבִיא אֲשֶׁר יִנָּבֵא לְשָׁלוֹם בְּבֹא דְּבַר הַנָּבִיא יִוָּדַע הַנָּבִיא

י אֲשֶׁר־שְׁלָחוֹ יהוה בֶּאֱמֶת: וַיִּקַּח חֲנַנְיָה הַנָּבִיא אֶת־הַמּוֹטָה מֵעַל צַוַּאר

יא יִרְמְיָה הַנָּבִיא וַיִּשְׁבְּרֵהוּ: וַיֹּאמֶר חֲנַנְיָה לְעֵינֵי כָל־הָעָם לֵאמֹר כֹּה אָמַר יהוה כָּכָה אֶשְׁבֹּר אֶת־עֹל | נְבֻכַדְנֶאצַּר מֶלֶךְ־בָּבֶל בְּעוֹד שְׁנָתַיִם יָמִים מֵעַל צַוַּאר כָּל־הַגּוֹיִם וַיֵּלֶךְ יִרְמְיָה הַנָּבִיא לְדַרְכּוֹ: וַיְהִי דְבַר־

יב יהוה אֶל־יִרְמְיָהוּ אַחֲרֵי שְׁבוֹר חֲנַנְיָה הַנָּבִיא אֶת־הַמּוֹטָה מֵעַל צַוַּאר

יג יִרְמְיָה הַנָּבִיא לֵאמֹר: הָלוֹךְ וְאָמַרְתָּ אֶל־חֲנַנְיָה לֵאמֹר כֹּה אָמַר יהוה

יד מוֹטֹת עֵץ שָׁבָרְתָּ וְעָשִׂיתָ תַחְתֵּיהֶן מֹטוֹת בַּרְזֶל: כִּי כֹה־אָמַר יהוה צְבָאוֹת אֱלֹהֵי יִשְׂרָאֵל עֹל בַּרְזֶל נָתַתִּי עַל־צַוַּאר | כָּל־הַגּוֹיִם הָאֵלֶּה לַעֲבֹד אֶת־נְבֻכַדְנֶאצַּר מֶלֶךְ־בָּבֶל וַעֲבָדֻהוּ וְגַם אֶת־חַיַּת הַשָּׂדֶה נָתַתִּי

טו לוֹ: וַיֹּאמֶר יִרְמְיָה הַנָּבִיא אֶל־חֲנַנְיָה הַנָּבִיא שְׁמַע־נָא חֲנַנְיָה לֹא־שְׁלָחֲךָ

טז יהוה וְאַתָּה הִבְטַחְתָּ אֶת־הָעָם הַזֶּה עַל־שָׁקֶר: לָכֵן כֹּה אָמַר יהוה הִנְנִי מְשַׁלֵּחֲךָ מֵעַל פְּנֵי הָאֲדָמָה הַשָּׁנָה אַתָּה מֵת כִּי־סָרָה דִבַּרְתָּ אֶל־יהוה:

כט יז–א וַיָּמָת חֲנַנְיָה הַנָּבִיא בַּשָּׁנָה הַהִיא בַּחֹדֶשׁ הַשְּׁבִיעִי: וְאֵלֶּה

28:1. The first part of this verse concludes the narrative that began in 27:12 — Jeremiah delivered his message to Zedekiah et al., during Zedekiah's first year as king. The remainder of the verse introduces the narrative that follows it (Kara).

Alternatively: The phrase "in the beginning of the reign of Zedekiah" refers to the beginning of his reign over the five foreign kings (see 27:3), which was the fourth year of his reign over Judah (Rashi).

Judah and Jerusalem, ²¹ thus said HASHEM, Master of Legions, the God of Israel, concerning the articles that remain in the Temple of HASHEM and in the palace of the king of Judah and in Jerusalem: ²² They will be brought to Babylonia and they will be there until the day that I attend to them — the word of HASHEM — when I shall bring them up and return them to this place.

28

The charlatan prophecies

¹ It happened in that year, in the beginning of the reign of Zedekiah king of Judah, * in the fourth year, in the fifth month, that Hananiah son of Azzur the [false] prophet from Gibeon said to me in the Temple of HASHEM, before the eyes of the priests and all the people, saying, ² "Thus said HASHEM, Master of Legions, God of Israel, saying: 'I have broken the yoke of the king of Babylonia! ³ In another two years I shall return to this place all the articles of the Temple of HASHEM that Nebuchadnezzar king of Babylonia took from this place and brought them to Babylonia. ⁴ And I am returning Jeconiah son of Jehoiakim, king of Judah; and all the exile of Judah who have gone to Babylonia I shall return to this place — the word of HASHEM — for I shall break the yoke of the king of Babylonia.' "

Jeremiah's rebuttal

⁵ Jeremiah the prophet then spoke to Hananiah the prophet before the eyes of the priests and before the eyes of all the people standing in the Temple of HASHEM. ⁶ Jeremiah the prophet said, "Amen, may HASHEM do so! May HASHEM fulfill your words that you prophesied, to return the articles of the Temple of HASHEM and the entire exile from Babylonia to this place! ⁷ But hear now this statement that I am speaking in your ears and in the ears of all the people: ⁸ The prophets who were before me and before you, from ancient times, used to prophesy about many lands and about great kingdoms — for war and for evil and for pestilence. ⁹ When a prophet speaks of peace, it is [only] when the word of that prophet comes true that it is known that that prophet was indeed sent by HASHEM."*

The charlatan acts

¹⁰ Hananiah the prophet took the bar* from upon the neck of Jeremiah the prophet and broke it. ¹¹ Hananiah then said before the eyes of all the people, "Thus said HASHEM: This is how I will break off the yoke of Nebuchadnezzar king of Babylonia from the neck of all the nations in another two years!" Jeremiah the prophet then went on his way.

God responds

¹² The word of HASHEM came to Jeremiah after Hananiah the prophet had broken off the bar from the neck of Jeremiah the prophet, saying: ¹³ "Go and say to Hananiah: Thus said HASHEM: You have broken wooden bars, but you will make metal bars in their place! ¹⁴ For thus said HASHEM, Master of Legions, God of Israel: I have placed an iron yoke upon the neck of all these nations, to serve Nebuchadnezzar king of Babylonia, and they shall serve him; even the beast of the field have I given him."

The charlatan's end

¹⁵ Jeremiah the prophet then said to Hananiah the prophet, "Hear now, Hananiah! HASHEM did not send you, and you have reassured this people with a lie. ¹⁶ Therefore, thus said HASHEM: Behold, I am casting you off from the face of the earth. You shall die this year, for you have spoken a falsehood in the name of HASHEM."

¹⁷ Hananiah the prophet died that year, in the seventh month.

28:9. A prophecy of punishment can be rescinded if its subject repents; thus Jeremiah would not be discredited if Hananiah's prediction of goodness were to come true. But prophecies of peace and good fortune are never rescinded, even if the subject subsequently sins; thus Hananiah would be repudiated when his prophecy failed to come true.

28:10. The yoke mentioned in 27:2.

דִּבְרֵי הַסֵּפֶר אֲשֶׁר שָׁלַח יִרְמְיָה הַנָּבִיא מִירוּשָׁלָ͏ִם אֶל־יֶ֣תֶר זִקְנֵ֣י הַגּוֹלָ֗ה וְאֶל־הַכֹּהֲנִ֤ים וְאֶל־הַנְּבִיאִים֙ וְאֶל־כָּל־הָעָ֔ם אֲשֶׁ֨ר הֶגְלָ֧ה נְבֽוּכַדְנֶאצַּ֛ר

ב מִירוּשָׁלַ֖͏ִם בָּבֶֽלָה: אַחֲרֵ֣י צֵ֣את יְכָנְיָֽה־הַ֠מֶּ֠לֶךְ וְהַגְּבִירָ֨ה וְהַסָּרִיסִ֜ים שָׂרֵ֣י

ג יְהוּדָ֣ה וִירֽוּשָׁלַ֗͏ִם וְהֶחָרָ֤שׁ וְהַמַּסְגֵּר֙ מִירוּשָׁלָ͏ִ֔ם: בְּיַ֞ד אֶלְעָשָׂ֤ה בֶן־שָׁפָן֙

וּגְמַרְיָ֣ה בֶן־חִלְקִיָּ֔ה אֲשֶׁ֨ר שָׁלַ֜ח צִדְקִיָּ֣ה מֶֽלֶךְ־יְהוּדָ֗ה אֶל־נְבֽוּכַדְנֶאצַּ֛ר מֶ֥לֶךְ

ד בָּבֶ֖ל בָּבֶ֣לָה לֵאמֹֽר: כֹּ֣ה אָמַ֞ר יְהֹוָ֤ה צְבָאוֹת֙ אֱלֹהֵ֣י יִשְׂרָאֵ֔ל לְכָל־הַ֨גּוֹלָ֔ה

ה אֲשֶׁר־הִגְלֵ֥יתִי מִירוּשָׁלַ֖͏ִם בָּבֶֽלָה: בְּנ֥וּ בָתִּ֖ים וְשֵׁ֑בוּ וְנִטְע֣וּ גַנּ֔וֹת וְאִכְל֖וּ אֶת־

ו פִּרְיָֽן: קְח֣וּ נָשִׁ֗ים וְהֽוֹלִיד֘וּ֮ בָּנִ֣ים וּבָנוֹת֒ וּקְח֣וּ לִבְנֵיכֶ֜ם נָשִׁ֗ים וְאֶת־בְּנֽוֹתֵיכֶם֙

ז תְּנ֣וּ לַֽאֲנָשִׁ֔ים וְתֵלַ֖דְנָה בָּנִ֣ים וּבָנ֑וֹת וּרְבוּ־שָׁ֖ם וְאַל־תִּמְעָֽטוּ: וְדִרְשׁ֞וּ אֶת־

שְׁל֣וֹם הָעִ֗יר אֲשֶׁ֨ר הִגְלֵ֤יתִי אֶתְכֶם֙ שָׁ֔מָּה וְהִתְפַּֽלְל֥וּ בַֽעֲדָ֖הּ אֶל־יְהֹוָ֑ה כִּ֣י

ח בִשְׁלוֹמָ֔הּ יִהְיֶ֥ה לָכֶ֖ם שָׁלֽוֹם: כִּי֩ כֹ֨ה אָמַ֜ר יְהֹוָ֤ה צְבָאוֹת֙ אֱלֹהֵ֣י

יִשְׂרָאֵ֔ל אַל־יַשִּׁ֧יאוּ לָכֶ֛ם נְבִֽיאֵיכֶ֥ם אֲשֶׁר־בְּקִרְבְּכֶ֖ם וְקֹֽסְמֵיכֶ֑ם וְאַל־

ט תִּשְׁמְעוּ֙ אֶל־חֲלֹמֹ֣תֵיכֶ֔ם אֲשֶׁ֥ר אַתֶּ֖ם מַחְלְמִֽים: כִּ֣י בְשֶׁ֗קֶר הֵ֛ם נִבְּאִ֥ים לָכֶ֖ם

י בִּשְׁמִ֑י לֹ֥א שְׁלַחְתִּ֖ים נְאֻם־יְהֹוָֽה: כִּי־כֹה֙ אָמַ֣ר יְהֹוָ֔ה כִּ֠י לְפִ֞י

מְלֹ֧את לְבָבֶ֛ל שִׁבְעִ֥ים שָׁנָ֖ה אֶפְקֹ֣ד אֶתְכֶ֑ם וַהֲקִֽמֹתִ֤י עֲלֵיכֶם֙ אֶת־דְּבָרִ֣י

יא הַטּ֔וֹב לְהָשִׁ֣יב אֶתְכֶ֔ם אֶל־הַמָּק֖וֹם הַזֶּֽה: כִּ֣י אָֽנֹכִ֡י יָדַ֩עְתִּי֩ אֶת־הַמַּֽחֲשָׁבֹ֨ת

אֲשֶׁ֧ר אָֽנֹכִ֛י חֹשֵׁ֥ב עֲלֵיכֶ֖ם נְאֻם־יְהֹוָ֑ה מַחְשְׁב֤וֹת שָׁלוֹם֙ וְלֹ֣א לְרָעָ֔ה לָתֵ֥ת

יב לָכֶ֖ם אַֽחֲרִ֥ית וְתִקְוָֽה: וּקְרָאתֶ֤ם אֹתִי֙ וַֽהֲלַכְתֶּ֔ם וְהִתְפַּלַּלְתֶּ֖ם אֵלָ֑י וְשָֽׁמַעְתִּ֖י

יג-יד אֲלֵיכֶֽם: וּבִקַּשְׁתֶּ֥ם אֹתִ֖י וּמְצָאתֶ֑ם כִּ֥י תִדְרְשֻׁ֖נִי בְּכָל־לְבַבְכֶֽם: וְנִמְצֵ֨אתִ֜י

לָכֶ֣ם נְאֻם־יְהֹוָה֘ וְשַׁבְתִּ֣י אֶת־שְׁבִיתְכֶם֒ [שְׁבוּתְכֶ֣ם ק] וְקִבַּצְתִּ֣י אֶתְכֶ֗ם

מִֽכָּל־הַגּוֹיִ֞ם וּמִכָּל־הַמְּקוֹמ֗וֹת אֲשֶׁ֨ר הִדַּ֧חְתִּי אֶתְכֶ֛ם שָׁ֖ם נְאֻם־יְהֹוָ֑ה וַהֲשִֽׁבֹתִ֣י

טו אֶתְכֶ֔ם אֶל־הַ֨מָּק֔וֹם אֲשֶׁר־הִגְלֵ֥יתִי אֶתְכֶ֖ם מִשָּֽׁם: כִּ֥י אֲמַרְתֶּ֑ם הֵקִ֨ים לָ֤נוּ

טז יְהֹוָ֖ה נְבִאִ֥ים בָּבֶֽלָה: כִּי־כֹ֣ה ׀ אָמַ֣ר יְהֹוָ֗ה אֶל־הַמֶּ֨לֶךְ֙ הַיּוֹשֵׁב֙

אֶל־כִּסֵּ֣א דָוִ֔ד וְאֶל־כָּל־הָעָ֔ם הַיּוֹשֵׁ֖ב בָּעִ֣יר הַזֹּ֑את אֲחֵיכֶ֕ם אֲשֶׁ֥ר לֹֽא־יָֽצְא֖וּ

יז אִתְּכֶ֥ם בַּגּוֹלָֽה: כֹּ֤ה אָמַר֙ יְהֹוָ֣ה צְבָא֔וֹת הִנְנִ֨י מְשַׁלֵּ֜חַ בָּ֗ם אֶת־

הַחֶ֨רֶב֙ אֶת־הָ֣רָעָ֔ב וְאֶת־הַדָּ֑בֶר וְנָֽתַתִּ֣י אוֹתָ֗ם כַּתְּאֵנִים֙ הַשֹּׁ֣עָרִ֔ים אֲשֶׁ֥ר לֹֽא־

יח תֵאָכַ֖לְנָה מֵרֹֽעַ: וְרָֽדַפְתִּי֙ אַֽחֲרֵיהֶ֔ם בַּחֶ֖רֶב בָּֽרָעָ֣ב וּבַדָּ֑בֶר וּנְתַתִּ֨ים ׃לְזַֽעֲוָ֜ה

[לְזַֽעֲוָ֜ה ק] לְכֹ֣ל ׀ מַמְלְכ֣וֹת הָאָ֗רֶץ לְאָלָ֤ה וּלְשַׁמָּה֙ וְלִשְׁרֵקָ֣ה וּלְחֶרְפָּ֔ה

יט בְּכָל־הַגּוֹיִ֖ם אֲשֶׁ֣ר הִדַּחְתִּ֣ים שָֽׁם: תַּ֣חַת אֲשֶֽׁר־לֹֽא־שָֽׁמְע֣וּ אֶל־דְּבָרַ֣י נְאֻם־

יְהֹוָ֑ה אֲשֶׁר֩ שָׁלַ֨חְתִּי אֲלֵיהֶ֜ם אֶת־עֲבָדַ֤י הַנְּבִאִים֙ הַשְׁכֵּ֣ם וְשָׁלֹ֔חַ וְלֹ֥א

כ שְׁמַעְתֶּ֖ם נְאֻם־יְהֹוָֽה: וְאַתֶּ֖ם שִׁמְע֣וּ דְבַר־יְהֹוָ֑ה כָּל־הַ֨גּוֹלָ֔ה אֲשֶׁר־שִׁלַּ֥חְתִּי

כא מִירֽוּשָׁלַ֖͏ִם בָּבֶֽלָה: כֹּה־אָמַר֩ יְהֹוָ֨ה צְבָא֜וֹת אֱלֹהֵ֣י

יִשְׂרָאֵ֗ל אֶל־אַחְאָ֤ב בֶּן־קֽוֹלָיָה֙ וְאֶל־צִדְקִיָּ֣הוּ בֶן־מַֽעֲשֵׂיָ֔ה הַֽנִּבְּאִ֥ים לָכֶ֖ם

בִּשְׁמִ֣י שָׁ֑קֶר הִנְנִ֣י ׀ נֹתֵ֣ן אֹתָ֗ם בְּיַד֙ נְבֽוּכַדְרֶאצַּ֣ר מֶֽלֶךְ־בָּבֶ֔ל וְהִכָּ֖ם לְעֵֽינֵיכֶֽם:

29

Jeremiah's letter to the exiles in Babylonia

¹ These are the words of the letter that Jeremiah the prophet sent from Jerusalem to the rest of the elders of the exile, to the Kohanim, the prophets, and all the people whom Nebuchadnezzar had exiled from Jerusalem to Babylonia, ² after King Jeconiah and the queen mother and the servants, the officers of Judah and Jerusalem, and the artisans and the gatekeepers* left Jerusalem. ³ [He sent the letter] by the hand of Elasah son of Shaphan and Gemariah son of Hilkiah, whom Zedekiah king of Judah sent to Nebuchadnezzar king of Babylonia to Babylonia, saying:

⁴ Thus said HASHEM, Master of Legions, God of Israel, to all of the exile whom I have exiled from Jerusalem to Babylonia: ⁵ Build houses and settle; plant gardens and eat their produce. ⁶ Take wives and beget sons and daughters; take wives for your sons and give your daughters to men, and let them give birth to sons and daughters. Multiply there; do not [let your numbers] diminish. ⁷ Seek the peace of the city to which I have exiled you and pray for it to HASHEM, for through its peace will you have peace. ⁸ For thus said HASHEM, Master of Legions, God of Israel: Do not let your prophets who are in your midst and your magicians delude you; do not listen to your dreamers whom you appoint to dream. ⁹ For it is falsehood that they prophesy to you in My Name; I did not send them — the word of HASHEM. ¹⁰ For thus said HASHEM: After seventy years for Babylonia have been completed I will attend to you and I will fulfill for you My favorable promise, to return you to this place. ¹¹ For I know the thoughts that I am thinking for you — the word of HASHEM; thoughts of peace and not evil, to give you a future and a hope. ¹² You will then call out to Me and follow [Me]; you will pray to Me and I will listen to You. ¹³ You will seek Me and you will find [Me], if you search for Me with all your hearts. ¹⁴ I will make Myself available to you — the word of HASHEM — and I will return your captivity and I will gather you in from all the nations and from all the places where I have dispersed you — the word of HASHEM — and I will return you to the place from which I exiled you.

¹⁵ If you will say, 'HASHEM has established prophets for us in Babylonia!'* — ¹⁶ rather, thus said HASHEM concerning the king who sits on the throne of David and concerning all the people who dwell in this city, your brethren who did not go with you into exile; ¹⁷ thus said HASHEM, Master of Legions: Behold, I am sending against them the sword, the famine, and the pestilence, and I shall make them like detestable figs, which are so bad they are inedible. ¹⁸ I shall chase after them with the sword, the famine, and the pestilence, and I shall make them a horror for all the kingdoms of the earth, for a curse, for desolation, for a whistling, and for a shame among all the nations where I have dispersed them; ¹⁹ because they did not listen to My words — the word of HASHEM — which I sent to them with My servants the prophets, arising early and sending [them], but you did not listen — the word of HASHEM. ²⁰ So you must listen [to] the word of HASHEM, the entire exile that I have sent out from Jerusalem to Babylonia.

²¹ Thus said HASHEM, Master of Legions, God of Israel, concerning Ahab son of Kolaiah and Zedekiah son of Maaseiah, who prophesy falsely to you in My Name: Behold, I am delivering them into the hand of Nebuchadrezzar king of Babylonia, and he will strike them down before your eyes.

Do not believe the false prophets of hope
(See Appendix A, timeline 5)

The exile will last seventy years

Charlatans unmasked

29:2. See *II Kings* 24:14.
29:15. Lest you counter that there are "prophets" in Babylonia who assure us of a hasty deliverance and return to Jerusalem — do not believe them; they are false.

כב וְלָקַח מֵהֶם קְלָלָה לְכֹל גָּלוּת יְהוּדָה אֲשֶׁר בְּבָבֶל לֵאמֹר יְשִׂמְךָ יְהוָה
כְּצִדְקִיָּהוּ וּכְאֶחָב אֲשֶׁר־קָלָם מֶלֶךְ־בָּבֶל בָּאֵשׁ: יַעַן אֲשֶׁר עָשׂוּ נְבָלָה
כג בְּיִשְׂרָאֵל וַיְנַאֲפוּ אֶת־נְשֵׁי רֵעֵיהֶם וַיְדַבְּרוּ דָבָר בִּשְׁמִי שֶׁקֶר אֲשֶׁר לוֹא
כד צִוִּיתִם וְאָנֹכִי °הַיּוֹדֵעַ [°הַיֹּדֵעַ כ׳] וָעֵד נְאֻם־יְהוָה:
כה שְׁמַעְיָהוּ הַנֶּחֱלָמִי תֹּאמַר לֵאמֹר: כֹּה־אָמַר יְהוָה צְבָאוֹת אֱלֹהֵי יִשְׂרָאֵל
לֵאמֹר יַעַן אֲשֶׁר אַתָּה שָׁלַחְתָּ בְשִׁמְכָה סְפָרִים אֶל־כָּל־הָעָם אֲשֶׁר
כו בִּירוּשָׁלַם וְאֶל־צְפַנְיָה בֶן־מַעֲשֵׂיָה הַכֹּהֵן וְאֶל כָּל־הַכֹּהֲנִים לֵאמֹר: יְהוָה
נְתָנְךָ כֹהֵן תַּחַת יְהוֹיָדָע הַכֹּהֵן לִהְיוֹת פְּקִדִים בֵּית יְהוָה לְכָל־אִישׁ מְשֻׁגָּע
כז וּמִתְנַבֵּא וְנָתַתָּה אֹתוֹ אֶל־הַמַּהְפֶּכֶת וְאֶל־הַצִּינֹק: וְעַתָּה לָמָּה לֹא
כח גָעַרְתָּ בְּיִרְמְיָהוּ הָעֲנְתֹתִי הַמִּתְנַבֵּא לָכֶם: כִּי עַל־כֵּן שָׁלַח אֵלֵינוּ בָּבֶל
כט לֵאמֹר אֲרֻכָּה הִיא בְּנוּ בָתִּים וְשֵׁבוּ וְנִטְעוּ גַנּוֹת וְאִכְלוּ אֶת־פְּרִיהֶן: וַיִּקְרָא
ל צְפַנְיָה הַכֹּהֵן אֶת־הַסֵּפֶר הַזֶּה בְּאָזְנֵי יִרְמְיָהוּ הַנָּבִיא: וַיְהִי
לא דְבַר־יְהוָה אֶל־יִרְמְיָהוּ לֵאמֹר: שְׁלַח עַל־כָּל־הַגּוֹלָה לֵאמֹר כֹּה אָמַר יְהוָה
אֶל־שְׁמַעְיָה הַנֶּחֱלָמִי יַעַן אֲשֶׁר נִבָּא לָכֶם שְׁמַעְיָה וַאֲנִי לֹא שְׁלַחְתִּיו
לב וַיַּבְטַח אֶתְכֶם עַל־שָׁקֶר: לָכֵן כֹּה־אָמַר יְהוָה הִנְנִי פֹקֵד עַל־שְׁמַעְיָה
הַנֶּחֱלָמִי וְעַל־זַרְעוֹ לֹא־יִהְיֶה לוֹ אִישׁ יוֹשֵׁב בְּתוֹךְ־הָעָם הַזֶּה
וְלֹא־יִרְאֶה בַטּוֹב אֲשֶׁר־אֲנִי עֹשֶׂה לְעַמִּי נְאֻם־יְהוָה כִּי־סָרָה דִבֶּר עַל־
יְהוָה: הַדָּבָר אֲשֶׁר הָיָה אֶל־יִרְמְיָהוּ מֵאֵת יְהוָה לֵאמֹר: כֹּה־אָמַר
ל א

א יְהוָה אֱלֹהֵי יִשְׂרָאֵל לֵאמֹר כְּתָב־לְךָ אֵת כָּל־הַדְּבָרִים אֲשֶׁר־דִּבַּרְתִּי
ב אֵלֶיךָ אֶל־סֵפֶר: כִּי הִנֵּה יָמִים בָּאִים נְאֻם־יְהוָה וְשַׁבְתִּי אֶת־שְׁבוּת עַמִּי
ג יִשְׂרָאֵל וִיהוּדָה אָמַר יְהוָה וַהֲשִׁבֹתִים אֶל־הָאָרֶץ אֲשֶׁר־נָתַתִּי לַאֲבוֹתָם
ד וִירֵשׁוּהָ: וְאֵלֶּה הַדְּבָרִים אֲשֶׁר דִּבֶּר יְהוָה אֶל־יִשְׂרָאֵל וְאֶל־
ה יְהוּדָה: כִּי־כֹה אָמַר יְהוָה קוֹל חֲרָדָה שָׁמָעְנוּ פַּחַד וְאֵין שָׁלוֹם: שַׁאֲלוּ־נָא
ו וּרְאוּ אִם־יֹלֵד זָכָר מַדּוּעַ רָאִיתִי כָל־גֶּבֶר יָדָיו עַל־חֲלָצָיו כַּיּוֹלֵדָה וְנֶהֶפְכוּ
ז כָל־פָּנִים לְיֵרָקוֹן: הוֹי כִּי גָדוֹל הַיּוֹם הַהוּא מֵאַיִן כָּמֹהוּ וְעֵת־צָרָה הִיא
ח לְיַעֲקֹב וּמִמֶּנָּה יִוָּשֵׁעַ: וְהָיָה בַיּוֹם הַהוּא נְאֻם יְהוָה צְבָאוֹת אֶשְׁבֹּר עֻלּוֹ
ט מֵעַל צַוָּארֶךָ וּמוֹסְרוֹתֶיךָ אֲנַתֵּק וְלֹא־יַעַבְדוּ־בוֹ עוֹד זָרִים: וְעָבְדוּ אֵת יְהוָה
י אֱלֹהֵיהֶם וְאֵת דָּוִד מַלְכָּם אֲשֶׁר אָקִים לָהֶם: וְאַתָּה אַל־תִּירָא
עַבְדִּי יַעֲקֹב נְאֻם־יְהוָה וְאַל־תֵּחַת יִשְׂרָאֵל כִּי הִנְנִי מוֹשִׁיעֲךָ מֵרָחוֹק וְאֶת־
יא זַרְעֲךָ מֵאֶרֶץ שִׁבְיָם וְשָׁב יַעֲקֹב וְשָׁקַט וְשַׁאֲנַן וְאֵין מַחֲרִיד: כִּי־אִתְּךָ אֲנִי
נְאֻם־יְהוָה לְהוֹשִׁיעֶךָ כִּי אֶעֱשֶׂה כָלָה בְּכָל־הַגּוֹיִם אֲשֶׁר הֲפִצוֹתִיךָ שָּׁם
יב כִּי אַךְ אֹתְךָ לֹא־אֶעֱשֶׂה כָלָה וְיִסַּרְתִּיךָ לַמִּשְׁפָּט וְנַקֵּה לֹא אֲנַקֶּךָּ: כִּי

29:32. That is, the return to Jerusalem.

30:3. This is the reason for writing down the prophecies: They are intended for the future (see v. 24), when

the ultimate redemption will take place (*Radak*).

30:5. God is quoting the words of those people who will witness the momentous events of the future.

²² From them, a curse will be derived by all the exile of Judah that is in Babylonia, saying, 'May HASHEM make you like Zedekiah and like Ahab, whom the king of Babylonia roasted in fire.' ²³ Because they committed an abomination in Israel: They committed adultery with the wives of their fellows and they spoke false words in My Name, which I did not command them, and I am the One who knows and bears Witness — the word of HASHEM.

Jeremiah answers his opponents

²⁴ Concerning Shemaiah the Nehelamite speak, saying: ²⁵ Thus said HASHEM, Master of Legions, God of Israel, saying: Since you sent letters in your name to all the people in Jerusalem and to Zephaniah son of Maaseiah the Kohen and to all the other Kohanim, saying: ²⁶ 'HASHEM made you a Kohen in place of Jehoiada the Kohen so that there should be officials in the Temple of HASHEM in charge of every man who is mad and who prophesies, to put them into the prison or into the stocks. ²⁷ Why then have you not condemned Jeremiah of Anathoth, who prophesies to you, ²⁸ on the grounds that he has sent [messages] to us in Babylonia, saying: "It will be a long [exile]; build houses and settle, plant gardens and eat their produce"?' ²⁹ Zephaniah the Kohen read this letter in the ears of Jeremiah the prophet, ³⁰ and the word of HASHEM [came] to Jeremiah, saying: ³¹ Send a message to the entire exile, saying: Thus said HASHEM concerning Shemiaiah the Nehelamite: Because Shemaiah has prophesied to you although I did not send him, and he reassured you falsely, ³² therefore, thus said HASHEM: Behold, I shall deal with Shemaiah the Nehelamite and with his descendants; he will not have a person [from among his descendants] dwelling in the midst of this people, and they will not see the goodness * that I will be doing for My people — the word of HASHEM — for he spoke perversion about HASHEM.

30

A prophecy of Messianic times

¹ **T**his is the word that came to Jeremiah from HASHEM, saying:

² Thus said HASHEM, God of Israel, saying: "Write down for yourself all these things that I am telling you into a book. ³ For behold, days are coming * — the word of HASHEM — when I will return the captivity of My people Israel and Judah, said HASHEM, and I will return them to the land that I gave their forefathers, and they will possess it."

⁴ These are the things HASHEM spoke concerning Israel and concerning Judah:

⁵ For thus said HASHEM: 'A sound of terror have we * heard; of fear, and not peace.' ⁶ Ask now and see if a male has ever given birth. Why, [then], do I see that every man puts his hand upon his loins like a woman in childbirth, and all faces turn pallid? ⁷ Woe! For that day will be momentous, there is nothing like it; it will be a time of trouble for Jacob, but he shall be saved from it. ⁸ It shall be on that day — the word of HASHEM, Master of Legions — that I will break off the yoke [of the conqueror] from your neck and I will tear your straps, and foreigners will no longer enslave him. ⁹ They will serve HASHEM their God and David their king, whom I will establish over them.

Re-establishment of David's throne

¹⁰ But as for you, do not fear, My servant Jacob, the word of HASHEM, and do not be afraid, Israel; for behold, I am saving you from distant places, and your descendants from the land of their captivity, and Jacob will return and be at peace and tranquil, and none will make [him] afraid. ¹¹ For I am with you — the word of HASHEM — to save you; for I will bring annihilation upon all the nations among whom I have dispersed you, but upon you I will not bring annihilation; I will chastise you with justice, but I will never eliminate you completely.

יג כֹּה אָמַר יהוֹה אָנֵוּשׁ לְשִׁבְרֵךְ נַחְלָה מַכָּתֵךְ: אֵין־דָּן דִּינֵךְ לְמָזֵוֹר רְפֻאֵוֹת
יד תְּעָלָה אֵין לָךְ: כָּל־מְאַהֲבַיִךְ שְׁכֵחוּךְ אוֹתָךְ לֹא יִדְרֹשׁוּ כִּי מַכַּת אוֹיֵב
טו הִכִּיתִיךְ מוּסַר אַכְזָרִי עַל רֹב עֲוֹנֵךְ עָצְמוּ חַטֹּאתָיִךְ: מַה־תִּזְעַק עַל־
שִׁבְרֵךְ אָנֵוּשׁ מַכְאֹבֵךְ עַל | רֹב עֲוֹנֵךְ עָצְמוּ חַטֹּאתַיִךְ עָשִׂיתִי אֵלֶּה לָךְ:
טז לָכֵן כָּל־אֹכְלַיִךְ יֵאָכֵלוּ וְכָל־צָרַיִךְ כֻּלָּם בַּשְּׁבִי יֵלֵכוּ וְהָיוּ שֹׁאסַיִךְ
למְשִׁסָּה וְכָל־בֹּזְזַיִךְ אֶתֵּן לָבַז: כִּי אַעֲלֶה אֲרֻכָה לָךְ וּמִמַּכּוֹתַיִךְ אֶרְפָּאֵךְ
יז נְאֻם־יהוֹה כִּי נִדָּחָה קָרְאוּ לָךְ צִיּוֹן הִיא דֹּרֵשׁ אֵין לָהּ: כֹּה | כֹּה
יח אָמַר יהוֹה הִנְנִי־שָׁב שְׁבוּת אָהֳלֵי יַעֲקוֹב וּמִשְׁכְּנֹתָיו אֲרַחֵם וְנִבְנְתָה עִיר
יט עַל־תִּלָּהּ וְאַרְמוֹן עַל־מִשְׁפָּטוֹ יֵשֵׁב: וְיָצָא מֵהֶם תּוֹדָה וְקֹל מְשַׂחֲקִים
כ וְהִרְבִּתִים וְלֹא יִמְעָטוּ וְהִכְבַּדְתִּים וְלֹא יִצְעָרוּ: וְהָיוּ בָנָיו כְּקֶדֶם וַעֲדָתוֹ
כא לְפָנַי תִּכּוֹן וּפָקַדְתִּי עַל כָּל־לֹחֲצָיו: וְהָיָה אַדִּירוֹ מִמֶּנּוּ וּמֹשְׁלוֹ מִקִּרְבּוֹ
יֵצֵא וְהִקְרַבְתִּיו וְנִגַּשׁ אֵלָי כִּי מִי הוּא־זֶה עָרַב אֶת־לִבּוֹ לָגֶשֶׁת אֵלַי נְאֻם־
כב-כג יהוֹה: וִהְיִיתֶם לִי לְעָם וְאָנֹכִי אֶהְיֶה לָכֶם לֵאלֹהִים: הִנֵּה |
כד סַעֲרַת יהוֹה חֵמָה יָצְאָה סַעַר מִתְגּוֹרֵר עַל רֹאשׁ רְשָׁעִים יָחוּל: לֹא יָשׁוּב
חֲרוֹן אַף־יהוֹה עַד־עֲשֹׂתוֹ וְעַד־הֲקִימוֹ מְזִמּוֹת לִבּוֹ בְּאַחֲרִית הַיָּמִים
כה תִּתְבּוֹנְנוּ בָהּ: בָּעֵת הַהִיא נְאֻם־יהוֹה אֶהְיֶה לֵאלֹהִים לְכֹל מִשְׁפְּחוֹת

לא

HAFTARAH
SECOND
DAY ROSH
HASHANAH
31:1-19

א יִשְׂרָאֵל וְהֵמָּה יִהְיוּ־לִי לְעָם: ◀ כֹּה אָמַר יהוֹה מָצָא חֵן בַּמִּדְבָּר
ב עַם שְׂרִידֵי חָרֶב הָלוֹךְ לְהַרְגִּיעוֹ יִשְׂרָאֵל: מֵרָחוֹק יהוֹה נִרְאָה לִי וְאַהֲבַת
ג עוֹלָם אֲהַבְתִּיךְ עַל־כֵּן מְשַׁכְתִּיךְ חָסֶד: עוֹד אֶבְנֵךְ וְנִבְנֵית בְּתוּלַת
ד יִשְׂרָאֵל עוֹד תַּעְדִּי תֻפַּיִךְ וְיָצָאת בִּמְחוֹל מְשַׂחֲקִים: עוֹד תִּטְּעִי כְרָמִים
ה בְּהָרֵי שֹׁמְרוֹן נָטְעוּ נֹטְעִים וְחִלֵּלוּ: כִּי יֶשׁ־יוֹם קָרְאוּ נֹצְרִים בְּהַר אֶפְרָיִם
ו קוּמוּ וְנַעֲלֶה צִיּוֹן אֶל־יהוֹה אֱלֹהֵינוּ: כִּי־כֹה | אָמַר יהוֹה רָנּוּ
לְיַעֲקֹב שִׂמְחָה וְצַהֲלוּ בְּרֹאשׁ הַגּוֹיִם הַשְׁמִיעוּ הַלְלוּ וְאִמְרוּ הוֹשַׁע יהוֹה
ז אֶת־עַמְּךָ אֵת שְׁאֵרִית יִשְׂרָאֵל: הִנְנִי מֵבִיא אוֹתָם מֵאֶרֶץ צָפוֹן וְקִבַּצְתִּים
מִיַּרְכְּתֵי־אָרֶץ בָּם עִוֵּר וּפִסֵּחַ הָרָה וְיֹלֶדֶת יַחְדָּו קָהָל גָּדוֹל יָשׁוּבוּ הֵנָּה:
ח בִּבְכִי יָבֹאוּ וּבְתַחֲנוּנִים אוֹבִילֵם אוֹלִיכֵם אֶל־נַחֲלֵי מַיִם בְּדֶרֶךְ יָשָׁר לֹא
ט יִכָּשְׁלוּ בָּהּ כִּי־הָיִיתִי לְיִשְׂרָאֵל לְאָב וְאֶפְרַיִם בְּכֹרִי הוּא: שָׁמְעוּ

30:13. You were considered so hopelessly ill that no medications were prescribed; no one believed that you could be saved after so many years of neglect (*Rashi*).

30:21. Who would dare approach Me unless I Myself draw him near?

30:24. You may not appreciate the import of this prophecy now, but in the end of days, when it is realized, it will become clear to you (see 23:19-10).

31:1-2. The translation follows *Radak*. When God began to speak of the nation's early days, the people cried out, "We have found favor with You in the past, but now You have removed Yourself from our presence!"

Alternatively: This clause is part of the prophecy. The prophet explains that when God speaks of the time when Israel left Egypt, it is to stress that His love for them never abated since it first began, despite the people's sins and His decision to exile them (*Kara*).

31:4. See *Leviticus* 19:24.

31:5. That is, prophets.

31:8. God refers to the nation as Ephraim, because ten of the twelve tribes had lived in the Northern Kingdom, which was led originally by Ephraimite kings. The entire nation is called God's firstborn, and Ephraim had the status of Joseph's firstborn (*Radak*).

*When
everything
looks
bleakest . . .*

¹² *For thus said* HASHEM: *Your injury is grave, your wound is acute.* ¹³ *No one judges your wound to have a cure; medications or remedy do not exist for you.* * ¹⁴ *All your paramours have forgotten you, they do not inquire after you. For I struck you the blow of an enemy, with a cruel reproof, because of your many sins, your transgressions that were so numerous.* ¹⁵ *How can you cry out over your injury, over your pain that is grave? It is because of your many sins, your transgressions that were so numerous, that I inflicted these upon you!* ¹⁶ *Nevertheless, all who devoured you shall themselves be devoured; all who oppressed you will all go into captivity; who trampled you*

*. . . God will
heal you*

will be trampled; and all who despoiled you, I shall deliver to become spoils. ¹⁷ *For I will make a cure for you, and I will heal you from your wounds — the word of* HASHEM; *for they called you 'Discarded!' [saying,] 'She is Zion — no one cares about her!'*

¹⁸ *Thus said* HASHEM: *Behold, I am returning the captivity of the tents of Jacob and I will have mercy on his abodes, and the City will be built upon its hill, and the Palace will sit in its proper place.* ¹⁹ *The sound of thanksgiving and the sound of merrymakers will emanate from them; I will multiply them, and they will not be diminished; and I will make them heavy [of number], and they will not dwindle.* ²⁰ *His sons will be [beloved] as in the past, and his assembly will be established before Me, and I shall deal with all his oppressors.* ²¹ *His leader will be from his midst and his ruler will emerge from within him. I will bring him close and then he will be able to approach Me; for who then would embolden his heart to approach Me?* * — *the word of* HASHEM.

*Israel unto
God; God
unto Israel*

²² *You will be a people unto Me, and I will be a God unto you.*

²³ *Behold, the storm of* HASHEM: *A rage shall go forth, a tempest shall seek rest; it will rest upon the head of the wicked.* ²⁴ HASHEM's *burning wrath will not recede until He has accomplished it, and until He has upheld the plans of his heart. In the end of days you will be able to understand it.* * ²⁵ *At that time* — *the word of* HASHEM — *I will be a God for all the families of Israel, and they will be a people for Me.*

31 ¹ T*hus said* HASHEM: *"This people that survived the sword found favor in the wilderness, as I led Israel to its place of tranquility."*

² *[Israel interjects,] "From the distant past* HASHEM *appeared to me."* *

*Ingathering
of the exiles*

[God continues:] And I have loved you with an eternal love, therefore I have extended kindness to you. ³ *I shall yet rebuild you and you shall be rebuilt, O Maiden of Israel; you will yet adorn yourself with drums and go forth in the dance of merrymakers.* ⁴ *You will yet plant vineyards in the mountains of Samaria; the planters will plant and redeem.* * ⁵ *For there will be a day when watchmen* * *will call out on Mount Ephraim, 'Arise, let us ascend to Zion, to* HASHEM *our God.* ⁶ *For thus said* HASHEM: *Sing, O Jacob, with gladness, exult on the peaks of the nations; announce, laud [God], and say, "O* HASHEM, *save Your people, the remnant of Israel!"'* ⁷ *Behold, I will bring them from the land of the North and gather them from the ends of the earth. Among them will be the blind and the lame, the pregnant and the birthing together; a great congregation will return here.* ⁸ *With weeping they will come and through supplications I will bring them; I will guide them on streams of water, on a direct path in which they will not stumble; for I have been a father to Israel, and Ephraim is My firstborn.* *

יא דְּבַר־יְהֹוָה גּוֹיִם וְהַגִּידוּ בָאִיִּים מִמֶּרְחָק וְאִמְרוּ מְזָרֵה יִשְׂרָאֵל יְקַבְּצֶנּוּ וּשְׁמָרוֹ כְּרֹעֶה עֶדְרוֹ: כִּי־פָדָה יְהֹוָה אֶת־יַעֲקֹב וּגְאָלוֹ מִיַּד חָזָק מִמֶּנּוּ: וּבָאוּ וְרִנְּנוּ בִמְרוֹם־צִיּוֹן וְנָהֲרוּ אֶל־טוּב יְהֹוָה עַל־דָּגָן וְעַל־תִּירֹשׁ וְעַל־יִצְהָר

יב וְעַל־בְּנֵי־צֹאן וּבָקָר וְהָיְתָה נַפְשָׁם כְּגַן רָוֶה וְלֹא־יוֹסִיפוּ לְדַאֲבָה עוֹד: אָז תִּשְׂמַח בְּתוּלָה בְּמָחוֹל וּבַחֻרִים וּזְקֵנִים יַחְדָּו וְהָפַכְתִּי אֶבְלָם לְשָׂשׂוֹן

יג וְנִחַמְתִּים וְשִׂמַּחְתִּים מִיגוֹנָם: וְרִוֵּיתִי נֶפֶשׁ הַכֹּהֲנִים דָּשֶׁן וְעַמִּי אֶת־טוּבִי יִשְׂבָּעוּ נְאֻם־יְהֹוָה:

יד כֹּה ׀ אָמַר יְהֹוָה קוֹל בְּרָמָה נִשְׁמָע נְהִי בְּכִי תַמְרוּרִים רָחֵל מְבַכָּה עַל־בָּנֶיהָ מֵאֲנָה לְהִנָּחֵם עַל־בָּנֶיהָ כִּי אֵינֶנּוּ:

טו כֹּה ׀ אָמַר יְהֹוָה מִנְעִי קוֹלֵךְ מִבֶּכִי וְעֵינַיִךְ מִדִּמְעָה כִּי יֵשׁ שָׂכָר לִפְעֻלָּתֵךְ נְאֻם־יְהֹוָה וְשָׁבוּ מֵאֶרֶץ אוֹיֵב: וְיֵשׁ־תִּקְוָה לְאַחֲרִיתֵךְ נְאֻם־

טז יְהֹוָה וְשָׁבוּ בָנִים לִגְבוּלָם: שָׁמוֹעַ שָׁמַעְתִּי אֶפְרַיִם מִתְנוֹדֵד יִסַּרְתַּנִי וָאִוָּסֵר

יז כְּעֵגֶל לֹא לֻמָּד הֲשִׁיבֵנִי וְאָשׁוּבָה כִּי אַתָּה יְהֹוָה אֱלֹהָי: כִּי־אַחֲרֵי שׁוּבִי

יח נִחַמְתִּי וְאַחֲרֵי הִוָּדְעִי סָפַקְתִּי עַל־יָרֵךְ בֹּשְׁתִּי וְגַם־נִכְלַמְתִּי כִּי נָשָׂאתִי

יט חֶרְפַּת נְעוּרָי: הֲבֵן יַקִּיר לִי אֶפְרַיִם אִם יֶלֶד שַׁעֲשֻׁעִים כִּי־מִדֵּי דַבְּרִי בּוֹ זָכֹר אֶזְכְּרֶנּוּ עוֹד עַל־כֵּן הָמוּ מֵעַי לוֹ רַחֵם אֲרַחֲמֶנּוּ נְאֻם־יְהֹוָה:

כ הַצִּיבִי לָךְ צִיֻּנִים שִׂמִי לָךְ תַּמְרוּרִים שִׁתִי לִבֵּךְ לַמְסִלָּה דֶּרֶךְ °הָלָכְתְּ [°הָלָכְתִּי ק]

כא שׁוּבִי בְּתוּלַת יִשְׂרָאֵל שֻׁבִי אֶל־עָרַיִךְ אֵלֶּה: עַד־מָתַי תִּתְחַמָּקִין הַבַּת

כב הַשּׁוֹבֵבָה כִּי־בָרָא יְהֹוָה חֲדָשָׁה בָּאָרֶץ נְקֵבָה תְּסוֹבֵב גָּבֶר: כֹּה־ אָמַר יְהֹוָה צְבָאוֹת אֱלֹהֵי יִשְׂרָאֵל עוֹד יֹאמְרוּ אֶת־הַדָּבָר הַזֶּה בְּאֶרֶץ יְהוּדָה וּבְעָרָיו בְּשׁוּבִי אֶת־שְׁבוּתָם יְבָרֶכְךָ יְהֹוָה נְוֵה־צֶדֶק הַר הַקֹּדֶשׁ:

כג-כב וְיָשְׁבוּ בָהּ יְהוּדָה וְכָל־עָרָיו יַחְדָּו אִכָּרִים וְנָסְעוּ בַּעֵדֶר: כִּי הִרְוֵיתִי נֶפֶשׁ

כה עֲיֵפָה וְכָל־נֶפֶשׁ דָּאֲבָה מִלֵּאתִי: עַל־זֹאת הֱקִיצֹתִי וָאֶרְאֶה וּשְׁנָתִי עָרְבָה לִי: הִנֵּה יָמִים בָּאִים נְאֻם־יְהֹוָה וְזָרַעְתִּי אֶת־בֵּית יִשְׂרָאֵל

כו וְאֶת־בֵּית יְהוּדָה זֶרַע אָדָם וְזֶרַע בְּהֵמָה: וְהָיָה כַּאֲשֶׁר שָׁקַדְתִּי עֲלֵיהֶם

כז לִנְתוֹשׁ וְלִנְתוֹץ וְלַהֲרֹס וּלְהַאֲבִיד וּלְהָרֵעַ כֵּן אֶשְׁקֹד עֲלֵיהֶם לִבְנוֹת

כח וְלִנְטוֹעַ נְאֻם־יְהֹוָה: בַּיָּמִים הָהֵם לֹא־יֹאמְרוּ עוֹד אָבוֹת אָכְלוּ בֹסֶר וְשִׁנֵּי

כט בָנִים תִּקְהֶינָה: כִּי אִם־אִישׁ בַּעֲוֺנוֹ יָמוּת כָּל־הָאָדָם הָאֹכֵל הַבֹּסֶר תִּקְהֶינָה

31:14-16. The Midrash relates that all the Patriarchs and Matriarchs attempted to appease God when King Menasseh introduced idolatry into the Temple (*II Kings* 21:4-5). But He rejected all their pleas until Rachel recalled her own magnanimity to her sister Leah. When Leah was fraudulently married to Jacob in place of Rachel, Rachel did not let jealous resentment lead her to protest. Why, then, should God be so zealous in punishing His children for bringing idols into His Temple? God accepted her plea and promised that Israel would be redeemed eventually, in her merit (*Rashi*).

31:19. God wonders, as it were, why He feels such compassion for wayward Ephraim. Nevertheless, He does love him, and therefore pledges to redeem him.

31:20. As you go into exile, mark your route, for you will come back home.

31:21. God is often portrayed as Israel's "husband." Although the man commonly courts his mate, eventually Israel will repent and seek out God.

31:25. Jeremiah interjects a personal note. Unlike many other visions, in which he was shown prophecies of retribution and exile, this one reassuring vision allowed him to sleep peacefully.

31:28. In the perfect future, children will no longer suffer for the sins of their parents.

⁹ *Hear the word of HASHEM, O nations, relate it in distant islands, and say, 'The One Who scattered Israel, He shall gather him in and guard him as a shepherd [guards] his flock.'* ¹⁰ *For HASHEM will have redeemed Jacob and delivered him from the hand of one mightier than he.* ¹¹ *And they will come and sing joyously on the height of Zion; they will stream to HASHEM's bounty — upon grain, upon wine, upon oil, and upon young sheep and cattle; then their soul shall be like a well-watered garden, and they shall not continue to agonize any more.* ¹² *Then the maiden shall rejoice with dance, and young men and old men [will rejoice] together; I shall transform their mourning into joy and I shall comfort them and gladden them from their grief.* ¹³ *I shall satisfy the desire of the Kohanim with the fat [of offerings], and My people will be sated with My bounty — the word of HASHEM.*

Redemption of Jacob

God appeases Rachel

¹⁴ *Thus said HASHEM: A voice is heard on high, wailing, bitter weeping, Rachel* weeps for her children; she refuses to be consoled for her children, for they are gone.* ¹⁵ *Thus said HASHEM: Restrain your voice from weeping and your eyes from tears; for there is reward for your accomplishment — the word of HASHEM — and they will return from the enemy's land.* ¹⁶ *There is hope for your future — the word of HASHEM — and your children will return to their border.*

¹⁷ *I have indeed heard Ephraim moaning, 'You have chastised me and I have become chastened, like an untrained calf; bring me back [to You] and I shall return, for You are HASHEM, my God.* ¹⁸ *For after my returning, I regretted; and after my being made aware [of my sinfulness], I slapped [my] thigh [in anguish]; I was ashamed and also humiliated, for I bore the disgrace of my youth.'* ¹⁹ *Is Ephraim My favorite son or a delightful child, that whenever I speak of him I remember him more and more?* Therefore, My inner self yearns for him; I will surely take pity on him — the word of HASHEM.*

Remember the road home

²⁰ *Make road markers for yourself, set up landmarks for yourself; set [the thoughts of] your heart upon the road, the route that you are walking. * Return, O Maiden of Israel, return to these cities of yours!* ²¹ *How long will you slip away, O wayward daughter? For HASHEM has created something new in the world — that the woman will court the man. **

²² *Thus said HASHEM, Master of Legions, God of Israel: People will again say this thing in the land of Judah and in its cities, when I return their captivity: 'May HASHEM bless you, O Abode of Righteousness, O Holy Mountain!'* ²³ *Judah will dwell in it and in its cities together — plowmen and those who travel with the herd.* ²⁴ *For I have quenched the thirsty soul and have replenished every distraught soul.*

²⁵ *Because of this [vision], when I woke up after I saw it, my sleep was pleasant to me!**

²⁶ *Behold, days are coming — the word of HASHEM — when I shall sow the House of Israel and the House of Judah — the seed of man and the seed of animal.* ²⁷ *And it shall be that just as I was diligent concerning them, to uproot, to smash, to destroy, to annihilate and to bring evil, so will I be diligent concerning them to build and to plant — the word of HASHEM.* ²⁸ *In those days it will no longer be said, 'The fathers ate sour grapes, but the teeth of the sons are set on edge.'** ²⁹ *Rather, every man will die for his own sin, and the man who eats the sour grapes, his own teeth will be set on edge.*

ל שָׁנָיו: הִנֵּה יָמִים בָּאִים נְאֻם־יְהֹוָה וְכָרַתִּי אֶת־בֵּית יִשְׂרָאֵל וְאֶת־

לא בֵּית יְהוּדָה בְּרִית חֲדָשָׁה: לֹא כַבְּרִית אֲשֶׁר כָּרַתִּי אֶת־אֲבוֹתָם בְּיוֹם

הֶחֱזִיקִי בְיָדָם לְהוֹצִיאָם מֵאֶרֶץ מִצְרָיִם אֲשֶׁר־הֵמָּה הֵפֵרוּ אֶת־בְּרִיתִי

לב וְאָנֹכִי בָּעַלְתִּי בָם נְאֻם־יְהֹוָה: כִּי זֹאת הַבְּרִית אֲשֶׁר אֶכְרֹת אֶת־בֵּית

יִשְׂרָאֵל אַחֲרֵי הַיָּמִים הָהֵם נְאֻם־יְהֹוָה נָתַתִּי אֶת־תּוֹרָתִי בְּקִרְבָּם וְעַל־

לג לִבָּם אֶכְתֳּבֶנָּה וְהָיִיתִי לָהֶם לֵאלֹהִים וְהֵמָּה יִהְיוּ־לִי לְעָם: וְלֹא יְלַמְּדוּ

עוֹד אִישׁ אֶת־רֵעֵהוּ וְאִישׁ אֶת־אָחִיו לֵאמֹר דְּעוּ אֶת־יְהֹוָה כִּי־כוּלָּם יֵדְעוּ

אוֹתִי לְמִקְּטַנָּם וְעַד־גְּדוֹלָם נְאֻם־יְהֹוָה כִּי אֶסְלַח לַעֲוֹנָם וּלְחַטָּאתָם לֹא

לד אֶזְכָּר־עוֹד: כֹּה ׀ אָמַר יְהֹוָה נֹתֵן שֶׁמֶשׁ לְאוֹר יוֹמָם חֻקֹּת יָרֵחַ

לה וְכוֹכָבִים לְאוֹר לָיְלָה רֹגַע הַיָּם וַיֶּהֱמוּ גַלָּיו יְהֹוָה צְבָאוֹת שְׁמוֹ: אִם־יָמֻשׁוּ

הַחֻקִּים הָאֵלֶּה מִלְּפָנַי נְאֻם־יְהֹוָה גַּם זֶרַע יִשְׂרָאֵל יִשְׁבְּתוּ מִהְיוֹת גּוֹי לְפָנַי

לו כָּל־הַיָּמִים: כֹּה ׀ אָמַר יְהֹוָה אִם־יִמַּדּוּ שָׁמַיִם מִלְמַעְלָה וְיֵחָקְרוּ

מוֹסְדֵי־אֶרֶץ לְמָטָּה גַּם־אֲנִי אֶמְאַס בְּכָל־זֶרַע יִשְׂרָאֵל עַל־כָּל־אֲשֶׁר עָשׂוּ

לז נְאֻם־יְהֹוָה: הִנֵּה יָמִים [בָּאִים ק׳ ולא כ׳] נְאֻם־יְהֹוָה וְנִבְנְתָה הָעִיר

לח לַיהֹוָה מִמִּגְדַּל חֲנַנְאֵל עַד־שַׁעַר הַפִּנָּה: וְיָצָא עוֹד [קָו ק׳] °קוה הַמִּדָּה

לט נֶגְדּוֹ עַל גִּבְעַת גָּרֵב וְנָסַב גֹּעָתָה: וְכָל־הָעֵמֶק הַפְּגָרִים ׀ וְהַדֶּשֶׁן וְכָל־

°הַשְּׁרֵמוֹת [הַשְּׁדֵמוֹת ק׳] עַד־נַחַל קִדְרוֹן עַד־פִּנַּת שַׁעַר הַסּוּסִים

לב
א מִזְרָחָה קֹדֶשׁ לַיהֹוָה לֹא־יִנָּתֵשׁ וְלֹא־יֵהָרֵס עוֹד לְעוֹלָם: הַדָּבָר אֲשֶׁר־

הָיָה אֶל־יִרְמְיָהוּ מֵאֵת יְהֹוָה °בשנת [בַּשָּׁנָה ק׳] הָעֲשִׂרִית לְצִדְקִיָּהוּ מֶלֶךְ־

ב יְהוּדָה הִיא הַשָּׁנָה שְׁמֹנֶה־עֶשְׂרֵה שָׁנָה לִנְבֻכַדְרֶאצַּר: וְאָז חֵיל מֶלֶךְ בָּבֶל

צָרִים עַל־יְרוּשָׁלָ͏ִם וְיִרְמְיָהוּ הַנָּבִיא הָיָה כָלוּא בַּחֲצַר הַמַּטָּרָה אֲשֶׁר בֵּית־

ג מֶלֶךְ יְהוּדָה: אֲשֶׁר כְּלָאוֹ צִדְקִיָּהוּ מֶלֶךְ־יְהוּדָה לֵאמֹר מַדּוּעַ אַתָּה נִבָּא

לֵאמֹר כֹּה אָמַר יְהֹוָה הִנְנִי נֹתֵן אֶת־הָעִיר הַזֹּאת בְּיַד מֶלֶךְ־בָּבֶל וּלְכָדָהּ:

ד וְצִדְקִיָּהוּ מֶלֶךְ יְהוּדָה לֹא יִמָּלֵט מִיַּד הַכַּשְׂדִּים כִּי־הִנָּתֹן יִנָּתֵן בְּיַד מֶלֶךְ־

ה בָּבֶל וְדִבֶּר־פִּיו עִם־פִּיו וְעֵינָיו אֶת־עֵינָיו תִּרְאֶינָה: וּבָבֶל יוֹלִךְ אֶת־

צִדְקִיָּהוּ וְשָׁם יִהְיֶה עַד־פָּקְדִי אֹתוֹ נְאֻם־יְהֹוָה כִּי תִלָּחֲמוּ אֶת־הַכַּשְׂדִּים

לֹא תַצְלִיחוּ:   ◀ וַיֹּאמֶר יִרְמְיָהוּ הָיָה דְּבַר־יְהֹוָה

אֵלַי לֵאמֹר: הִנֵּה חֲנַמְאֵל בֶּן־שַׁלֻּם דֹּדְךָ בָּא אֵלֶיךָ לֵאמֹר קְנֵה לְךָ אֶת־

ח שָׂדִי אֲשֶׁר בַּעֲנָתוֹת כִּי לְךָ מִשְׁפַּט הַגְּאֻלָּה לִקְנוֹת: וַיָּבֹא אֵלַי חֲנַמְאֵל בֶּן־

דֹּדִי כִּדְבַר יְהֹוָה אֶל־חֲצַר הַמַּטָּרָה וַיֹּאמֶר אֵלַי קְנֵה נָא אֶת־שָׂדִי אֲשֶׁר־

בַּעֲנָתוֹת אֲשֶׁר ׀ בְּאֶרֶץ בִּנְיָמִין כִּי־לְךָ מִשְׁפַּט הַיְרֻשָּׁה וּלְךָ הַגְּאֻלָּה

ט קְנֵה־לָךְ וָאֵדַע כִּי דְבַר־יְהֹוָה הוּא: וָאֶקְנֶה אֶת־הַשָּׂדֶה מֵאֵת חֲנַמְאֵל

HAFTARAS
BEHAR
Ashkenazim:
32:6-27
Sephardim:
32:6-22

לב

32:1-15. The actual prophecy begins in verse 6. But the prophet interrupts his narrative with four verses that describe the circumstances under which Jeremiah re- ceived this message of hope from God.
32:5. That is, until Zedekiah dies (*Rashi*).
32:7. See *Leviticus* 25:25.

³⁰ Behold, days are coming — the word of HASHEM — when I will seal a new covenant with the House of Israel and with the House of Judah: ³¹ not like the covenant that I sealed with their forefathers on the day that I took hold of their hand to take them out of the land of Egypt, for they abrogated My covenant, although I became their Master — the word of HASHEM. ³² For this is the covenant that I shall seal with the House of Israel after those days — the word of HASHEM — I will place My Torah within them and I will write it onto their heart; I will be a God for them and they will be a people for Me. ³³ They will no longer teach — each man his fellow, each man his brother — saying, 'Know HASHEM!' For all of them will know Me, from their smallest to their greatest — the word of HASHEM — when I will forgive their iniquity and will no longer recall their sin.

The Creator's promise

³⁴ Thus said HASHEM, Who gives the sun as a light by day and the laws of the moon and the stars as a light by night; Who agitates the sea so that its waves roar; HASHEM, Master of Legions, is His Name: ³⁵ If these laws could be removed from before Me — the word of HASHEM — so could the seed of Israel cease from being a people before Me forever. ³⁶ Thus said HASHEM: If the heavens above could be measured or the foundations of the earth plumbed below, so too would I reject the entire seed of Israel because of everything they did — the word of HASHEM.

Rebuilt Jerusalem

³⁷ Behold, days are coming — the word of HASHEM — when the City will be built up unto HASHEM, from the Tower of Hananel until the Corner Gate. ³⁸ The measuring line will once again be stretched out over Gareb Hill and around to Goah. ³⁹ And all the valley of the corpses and the place of the ashes and all the fields up to the Kidron Valley until the corner of the Horses' Gate to the east will be holy unto HASHEM; it will not be abandoned nor destroyed again forever.

32

Prophecy from prison to Zedekiah

¹ The word that came to Jeremiah from HASHEM, * in the tenth year of Zedekiah, king of Judah, that year was the eighteenth year of Nebuchadrezzar: ² (At that time the army of the king of Babylonia was besieging Jerusalem, and Jeremiah the prophet was being detained in the Courtyard of Confinement that was at the palace of the king of Judah, ³ where Zedekiah king of Judah had imprisoned him, saying, "Why do you prophesy, saying, 'Thus said HASHEM: Behold, I am giving this city into the hand of the king of Babylonia, and he will capture it; ⁴ and Zedekiah, king of Judah, will not escape the hand of the Chaldeans, for he will certainly be delivered into the hand of the king of Babylonia, and he will speak with him mouth to mouth and see his eye to eye; ⁵ and he will lead Zedekiah off to Babylonia, and he will remain there until I attend to him. * — the word of HASHEM. Even if you try to fight against the Chaldeans you will not succeed'?")

The purchased field

⁶ Jeremiah said: The word of HASHEM came to me, saying: ⁷ "Behold, Hanamel, the son of your uncle Shallum, is coming to you to say: 'Buy for yourself my field that is in Anathoth, for upon you is the law of redemption, * to buy it.' "

⁸ My cousin Hanamel came to me, according to the word of HASHEM, to the Courtyard of Confinement, and he said to me, "Please buy for yourself my field that is in Anathoth, that is in the territory of Benjamin, for yours is the law of inheritance and yours is the [law of] redemption; buy [it] for yourself." And I knew that it was the word of HASHEM. ⁹ So I bought the field that was in Anathoth from Hanamel,

בֶּן־דֹּדִי בַּעֲנָתוֹת וָאֶשְׁקֲלָה־לּוֹ אֶת־הַכֶּסֶף שִׁבְעָה שְׁקָלִים וַעֲשָׂרָה

י הַכָּסֶף: וָאֶכְתֹּב בַּסֵּפֶר וָאֶחְתֹּם וָאָעֵד עֵדִים וָאֶשְׁקֹל הַכֶּסֶף בְּמֹאזְנָיִם:

יא־יב וָאֶקַּח אֶת־סֵפֶר הַמִּקְנָה אֶת־הֶחָתוּם הַמִּצְוָה וְהַחֻקִּים וְאֶת־הַגָּלוּי: וָאֶתֵּן אֶת־הַסֵּפֶר הַמִּקְנָה אֶל־בָּרוּךְ בֶּן־נֵרִיָּה בֶּן־מַחְסֵיָה לְעֵינֵי חֲנַמְאֵל דֹּדִי וּלְעֵינֵי הָעֵדִים הַכֹּתְבִים בְּסֵפֶר הַמִּקְנָה לְעֵינֵי כָּל־הַיְּהוּדִים הַיֹּשְׁבִים

יג־יד בַּחֲצַר הַמַּטָּרָה: וָאֲצַוֶּה אֶת־בָּרוּךְ לְעֵינֵיהֶם לֵאמֹר: כֹּה־אָמַר יְהֹוָה צְבָאוֹת אֱלֹהֵי יִשְׂרָאֵל לָקוֹחַ אֶת־הַסְּפָרִים הָאֵלֶּה אֵת סֵפֶר הַמִּקְנָה הַזֶּה וְאֵת הֶחָתוּם וְאֵת סֵפֶר הַגָּלוּי הַזֶּה וּנְתַתָּם בִּכְלִי־חָרֶשׂ לְמַעַן יַעַמְדוּ

טו יָמִים רַבִּים: כִּי כֹה אָמַר יְהֹוָה צְבָאוֹת אֱלֹהֵי יִשְׂרָאֵל עוֹד

טז יִקָּנוּ בָתִּים וְשָׂדוֹת וּכְרָמִים בָּאָרֶץ הַזֹּאת: וָאֶתְפַּלֵּל אֶל־

יז יְהֹוָה אַחֲרֵי תִתִּי אֶת־סֵפֶר הַמִּקְנָה אֶל־בָּרוּךְ בֶּן־נֵרִיָּה לֵאמֹר: אֲהָהּ אֲדֹנָי יֱהֹוִה הִנֵּה אַתָּה עָשִׂיתָ אֶת־הַשָּׁמַיִם וְאֶת־הָאָרֶץ בְּכֹחֲךָ הַגָּדוֹל

יח וּבִזְרֹעֲךָ הַנְּטוּיָה לֹא־יִפָּלֵא מִמְּךָ כָּל־דָּבָר: עֹשֶׂה חֶסֶד לַאֲלָפִים וּמְשַׁלֵּם עֲוֹן אָבוֹת אֶל־חֵיק בְּנֵיהֶם אַחֲרֵיהֶם הָאֵל הַגָּדוֹל הַגִּבּוֹר יְהֹוָה צְבָאוֹת

יט שְׁמוֹ: גְּדֹל הָעֵצָה וְרַב הָעֲלִילִיָּה אֲשֶׁר־עֵינֶיךָ פְקֻחוֹת עַל־כָּל־דַּרְכֵי בְּנֵי אָדָם לָתֵת לְאִישׁ כִּדְרָכָיו וְכִפְרִי מַעֲלָלָיו: אֲשֶׁר־שַׂמְתָּ אֹתוֹת וּמֹפְתִים

כ בְּאֶרֶץ־מִצְרַיִם עַד־הַיּוֹם הַזֶּה וּבְיִשְׂרָאֵל וּבָאָדָם וַתַּעֲשֶׂה־לְּךָ שֵׁם כַּיּוֹם

כא הַזֶּה: וַתֹּצֵא אֶת־עַמְּךָ אֶת־יִשְׂרָאֵל מֵאֶרֶץ מִצְרָיִם בְּאֹתוֹת וּבְמוֹפְתִים

כב וּבְיָד חֲזָקָה וּבְאֶזְרוֹעַ נְטוּיָה וּבְמוֹרָא גָּדוֹל: וַתִּתֵּן לָהֶם אֶת־הָאָרֶץ הַזֹּאת

כג אֲשֶׁר־נִשְׁבַּעְתָּ לַאֲבוֹתָם לָתֵת לָהֶם אֶרֶץ זָבַת חָלָב וּדְבָשׁ: ◄ וַיָּבֹאוּ וַיִּרְשׁוּ אֹתָהּ וְלֹא־שָׁמְעוּ בְקוֹלֶךָ °וּבְתֹרֹותֶךָ [°וּבְתוֹרָתְךָ ק] לֹא־הָלָכוּ אֵת כָּל־ אֲשֶׁר צִוִּיתָה לָהֶם לַעֲשׂוֹת לֹא עָשׂוּ וַתַּקְרֵא אֹתָם אֵת כָּל־הָרָעָה הַזֹּאת:

כד הִנֵּה הַסֹּלְלוֹת בָּאוּ הָעִיר לְלָכְדָהּ וְהָעִיר נִתְּנָה בְּיַד הַכַּשְׂדִּים הַנִּלְחָמִים

כה עָלֶיהָ מִפְּנֵי הַחֶרֶב וְהָרָעָב וְהַדָּבֶר וַאֲשֶׁר דִּבַּרְתָּ הָיָה וְהִנְּךָ רֹאֶה: וְאַתָּה אָמַרְתָּ אֵלַי אֲדֹנָי יֱהֹוִה קְנֵה־לְךָ הַשָּׂדֶה בַּכֶּסֶף וְהָעֵד עֵדִים וְהָעִיר נִתְּנָה

כו בְּיַד הַכַּשְׂדִּים: וַיְהִי דְּבַר־יְהֹוָה אֶל־יִרְמְיָהוּ

כז־כח לֵאמֹר: הִנֵּה אֲנִי יְהֹוָה אֱלֹהֵי כָּל־בָּשָׂר הֲמִמֶּנִּי יִפָּלֵא כָּל־דָּבָר: לָכֵן כֹּה אָמַר יְהֹוָה הִנְנִי נֹתֵן אֶת־הָעִיר הַזֹּאת בְּיַד הַכַּשְׂדִּים וּבְיַד נְבוּכַדְרֶאצַּר

כט מֶלֶךְ־בָּבֶל וּלְכָדָהּ: וּבָאוּ הַכַּשְׂדִּים הַנִּלְחָמִים עַל־הָעִיר הַזֹּאת וְהִצִּיתוּ אֶת־הָעִיר הַזֹּאת בָּאֵשׁ וּשְׂרָפוּהָ וְאֵת הַבָּתִּים אֲשֶׁר קִטְּרוּ עַל־גַּגּוֹתֵיהֶם

ל לַבַּעַל וְהִסִּכוּ נְסָכִים לֵאלֹהִים אֲחֵרִים לְמַעַן הַכְעִסֵנִי: כִּי־הָיוּ בְנֵי־ יִשְׂרָאֵל וּבְנֵי יְהוּדָה אַךְ עֹשִׂים הָרַע בְּעֵינַי מִנְּעֻרֹתֵיהֶם כִּי בְנֵי־יִשְׂרָאֵל

לא אַךְ מַכְעִסִים אֹתִי בְּמַעֲשֵׂה יְדֵיהֶם נְאֻם־יְהֹוָה: כִּי עַל־אַפִּי וְעַל־ חֲמָתִי הָיְתָה לִּי הָעִיר הַזֹּאת לְמִן־הַיּוֹם אֲשֶׁר בָּנוּ אוֹתָהּ וְעַד הַיּוֹם הַזֶּה

my cousin. I weighed out the money for him: seven shekels and ten silver pieces. ¹⁰ *I wrote out the deed and sealed [it], and I designated witnesses; I then weighed out the money on a scale.* ¹¹ *I took the bill of sale, the one that was sealed [according to] the ordinance and the decrees, and the unsealed [bill],* * ¹² *and I gave the bill of sale to Baruch son of Neriah son of Mahseiah before the eyes of Hanamel, [son of] my uncle, and before the eyes of the witnesses who signed the bill of sale and before the eyes of all the Jews who were sitting in the Courtyard of Confinement.*

Lasting proof ¹³ *I instructed Baruch before their eyes, saying,* ¹⁴ *"Thus said HASHEM, Master of Legions, God of Israel: 'Take these documents — this bill of sale, the sealed one and this unsealed document — and place them in an earthenware vessel, so that they will endure for many years.'* ¹⁵ *For thus said HASHEM, Master of Legions, God of Israel: 'Houses, fields and vineyards will yet be bought in this land.'"*

Jeremiah praises God; yet a question remains ¹⁶ *I then prayed to HASHEM, after giving the bill of sale to Baruch son of Neriah, saying:* ¹⁷ *"Alas, my Lord, HASHEM/ELOHIM! Behold, You made the heavens and the earth with Your great strength and Your outstretched arm, and nothing can be hidden from You;* ¹⁸ *You are the One Who deals kindly with thousands [of generations] and repays the sin of parents into the bosom of their children after them; the great and mighty God, His Name is HASHEM, Master of Legions;* ¹⁹ *great in counsel and mighty in deed, Your eyes are cognizant to all the ways of mankind, to grant each man according to his ways and the consequences of his deeds;* ²⁰ *it is You Who placed signs and wonders in the land of Egypt [that are remembered] until this day, and among Israel and other people; You made a reputation for Yourself, to this very day;* ²¹ *You took Your people Israel out of the land of Egypt with signs and wonders, with a strong hand and an outstretched arm, and with great awe;* ²² *and You gave them this land that You swore to their forefathers to give them, a land flowing with milk and honey.* ²³ *They came and possessed it, but they did not heed Your voice and did not follow Your teaching; everything that You commanded them to do, they did not do; so You caused all this evil to befall them!* ²⁴ *Behold, the ramps, they have come to the city to capture it, and the city has been delivered into the hand of the Chaldeans who are attacking it, due to the sword, the famine and the pestilence.* * *What You declared has happened, and You see it!* ²⁵ *Yet You said to me, my Lord HASHEM/ELOHIM, 'Buy a field for yourself with money and designate witnesses.' Yet the city has been handed over to the Chaldeans!"*

God's answer: Israel and Judah strayed after idolatry . . . ²⁶ *Then the word of HASHEM came to Jeremiah, saying:* ²⁷ *"Behold! I am HASHEM, the God of all flesh; can anything be hidden from Me?* ²⁸ *Therefore, thus said HASHEM: Behold, I am delivering this city into the hand of the Chaldeans and into the hand of Nebuchadrezzar, king of Babylonia, and he will capture it;* ²⁹ *and the Chaldeans who are attacking this city will come and ignite this city with fire and burn it down, along with the houses upon whose roofs the people used to burn incense to the Baal and pour out libations to the gods of others, in order to anger Me.* ³⁰ *For the Children of Israel and the Children of Judah have been doing only what is wrong in My eyes since their youth; for the Children of Israel only anger Me with their handiwork — the word of HASHEM.* ³¹ *For this city has aroused My anger and My wrath in Me from the day that they built it until this day,*

32:11. Two documents were drawn up to attest to the sale: one, the sealed document that transferred ownership; the second, an unsealed document attesting that

the sale was legal and uncontested (*Metzudos*).
32:24. See *II Kings* 25:3-4.

לב הַסִירָהּ מֵעַל פָּנָי: עַל כָּל־רָעַת בְּנֵי־יִשְׂרָאֵל וּבְנֵי יְהוּדָה אֲשֶׁר עָשׂוּ
לְהַכְעִסֵנִי הֵמָּה מַלְכֵיהֶם שָׂרֵיהֶם כֹּהֲנֵיהֶם וּנְבִיאֵיהֶם וְאִישׁ יְהוּדָה וְיֹשְׁבֵי
לג יְרוּשָׁלָ͏ִם: וַיִּפְנוּ אֵלַי עֹרֶף וְלֹא פָנִים וְלַמֵּד אֹתָם הַשְׁכֵּם וְלַמֵּד וְאֵינָם
לד שֹׁמְעִים לָקַחַת מוּסָר: וַיָּשִׂימוּ שִׁקּוּצֵיהֶם בַּבַּיִת אֲשֶׁר־נִקְרָא־שְׁמִי עָלָיו
לה לְטַמְּאוֹ: וַיִּבְנוּ אֶת־בָּמוֹת הַבַּעַל אֲשֶׁר | בְּגֵיא בֶן־הִנֹּם לְהַעֲבִיר אֶת־בְּנֵיהֶם
וְאֶת־בְּנוֹתֵיהֶם לַמֹּלֶךְ אֲשֶׁר לֹא־צִוִּיתִים וְלֹא עָלְתָה עַל־לִבִּי לַעֲשׂוֹת
לו הַתּוֹעֵבָה הַזֹּאת לְמַעַן °הַחֲטִי [°הַחֲטִיא ק] אֶת־יְהוּדָה: וְעַתָּה
לָכֵן כֹּה־אָמַר יהוה אֱלֹהֵי יִשְׂרָאֵל אֶל־הָעִיר הַזֹּאת אֲשֶׁר | אַתֶּם אֹמְרִים
לז נִתְּנָה בְּיַד מֶלֶךְ־בָּבֶל בַּחֶרֶב וּבָרָעָב וּבַדָּבֶר: הִנְנִי מְקַבְּצָם מִכָּל־הָאֲרָצוֹת
אֲשֶׁר הִדַּחְתִּים שָׁם בְּאַפִּי וּבַחֲמָתִי וּבְקֶצֶף גָּדוֹל וַהֲשִׁבֹתִים אֶל־הַמָּקוֹם
לח-לט הַזֶּה וְהֹשַׁבְתִּים לָבֶטַח: וְהָיוּ לִי לְעָם וַאֲנִי אֶהְיֶה לָהֶם לֵאלֹהִים: וְנָתַתִּי
לָהֶם לֵב אֶחָד וְדֶרֶךְ אֶחָד לְיִרְאָה אוֹתִי כָּל־הַיָּמִים לְטוֹב לָהֶם וְלִבְנֵיהֶם
מ אַחֲרֵיהֶם: וְכָרַתִּי לָהֶם בְּרִית עוֹלָם אֲשֶׁר לֹא־אָשׁוּב מֵאַחֲרֵיהֶם
מא לְהֵיטִיבִי אוֹתָם וְאֶת־יִרְאָתִי אֶתֵּן בִּלְבָבָם לְבִלְתִּי סוּר מֵעָלָי: וְשַׂשְׂתִּי
עֲלֵיהֶם לְהֵטִיב אוֹתָם וּנְטַעְתִּים בָּאָרֶץ הַזֹּאת בֶּאֱמֶת בְּכָל־לִבִּי וּבְכָל־
מב נַפְשִׁי: כִּי־כֹה אָמַר יהוה כַּאֲשֶׁר הֵבֵאתִי אֶל־הָעָם הַזֶּה אֵת כָּל־
הָרָעָה הַגְּדוֹלָה הַזֹּאת כֵּן אָנֹכִי מֵבִיא עֲלֵיהֶם אֶת־כָּל־הַטּוֹבָה אֲשֶׁר אָנֹכִי
מג דֹּבֵר עֲלֵיהֶם: וְנִקְנָה הַשָּׂדֶה בָּאָרֶץ הַזֹּאת אֲשֶׁר | אַתֶּם אֹמְרִים שְׁמָמָה הִיא
מד מֵאֵין אָדָם וּבְהֵמָה נִתְּנָה בְּיַד הַכַּשְׂדִּים: שָׂדוֹת בַּכֶּסֶף יִקְנוּ וְכָתוֹב בַּסֵּפֶר |
וְחָתוֹם וְהָעֵד עֵדִים בְּאֶרֶץ בִּנְיָמִן וּבִסְבִיבֵי יְרוּשָׁלַ͏ִם וּבְעָרֵי יְהוּדָה
וּבְעָרֵי הָהָר וּבְעָרֵי הַשְּׁפֵלָה וּבְעָרֵי הַנֶּגֶב כִּי־אָשִׁיב אֶת־שְׁבוּתָם נְאֻם־
לג א יהוה: וַיְהִי דְבַר־יהוה אֶל־יִרְמְיָהוּ שֵׁנִית וְהוּא עוֹדֶנּוּ עָצוּר בַּחֲצַר
ב הַמַּטָּרָה לֵאמֹר: כֹּה־אָמַר יהוה עֹשָׂהּ יהוה יוֹצֵר אוֹתָהּ לַהֲכִינָהּ יהוה |
ג שְׁמוֹ: קְרָא אֵלַי וְאֶעֱנֶךָּ וְאַגִּידָה לְּךָ גְּדֹלוֹת וּבְצֻרוֹת לֹא יְדַעְתָּם: כִּי
ד כֹה אָמַר יהוה אֱלֹהֵי יִשְׂרָאֵל עַל־בָּתֵּי הָעִיר הַזֹּאת וְעַל־בָּתֵּי מַלְכֵי
ה יְהוּדָה הַנְּתֻצִים אֶל־הַסֹּלְלוֹת וְאֶל־הֶחָרֶב: בָּאִים לְהִלָּחֵם אֶת־הַכַּשְׂדִּים
וּלְמַלְאָם אֶת־פִּגְרֵי הָאָדָם אֲשֶׁר־הִכֵּיתִי בְאַפִּי וּבַחֲמָתִי וַאֲשֶׁר הִסְתַּרְתִּי
ו פָנַי מֵהָעִיר הַזֹּאת עַל כָּל־רָעָתָם: הִנְנִי מַעֲלֶה־לָּהּ אֲרֻכָה וּמַרְפֵּא
ז וּרְפָאתִים וְגִלֵּיתִי לָהֶם עֲתֶרֶת שָׁלוֹם וֶאֱמֶת: וַהֲשִׁבֹתִי אֶת־שְׁבוּת יְהוּדָה
ח וְאֵת שְׁבוּת יִשְׂרָאֵל וּבְנִתִים כְּבָרִאשֹׁנָה: וְטִהַרְתִּים מִכָּל־עֲוֺנָם אֲשֶׁר
חָטְאוּ־לִי וְסָלַחְתִּי °לְכוֹל [°לְכָל־ ק] עֲוֺנוֹתֵיהֶם אֲשֶׁר חָטְאוּ־לִי וַאֲשֶׁר
ט פָּשְׁעוּ בִי: וְהָיְתָה לִי לְשֵׁם שָׂשׂוֹן לִתְהִלָּה וּלְתִפְאֶרֶת לְכֹל גּוֹיֵי הָאָרֶץ

32:33. I sent My prophets to teach them, but to no avail. **33:5.** Their hopeless resistance is producing nothing
33:2. That is, Jerusalem's Maker. but an abundance of corpses.

so that I should remove it from My presence, [32] because of all the evil of the Children of Israel and the Children of Judah that they committed to anger Me — they and their kings and their officers, their priests and their prophets, and the people of Judah and the inhabitants of Jerusalem. [33] To Me they turned their back and not their face, and, though I taught them, arising early and teaching, * they do not listen to accept rebuke. [34] They placed their detestations into the Temple, upon which My Name is proclaimed, to contaminate it; [35] and they built the high places of the Baal that are in the Valley of the Son of Hinnom, at which to pass their sons and their daughters to the Molech — which I never commanded them, nor did I ever contemplate performing this abomination — in order to cause Judah to sin.

... turning their back on God ...

[36] "And now, nevertheless, thus said HASHEM, God of Israel, concerning this city, which you say is given over into the hand of the king of Babylonia, due to the sword, the famine and the pestilence: [37] Behold, I shall gather them back from all the lands to which I have dispersed them in My anger, in My wrath and in great fury; and I shall return them to this place, and cause them to dwell in security. [38] They will be a people unto Me and I will be a God unto them; [39] and I will give them a single heart and a single path — to fear Me all the days, so that it will be well for them and their children after them. [40] I will seal an everlasting covenant with them: that I shall never depart from them, to bestow goodness upon them; and I will place My fear in their hearts, so that they not turn away from Me. [41] And I will rejoice over them, to bestow goodness upon them; and I will plant them steadfastly in this land, with all My heart and with all My soul.

... nevertheless, God will return them ...

[42] "For thus said HASHEM: Just as I brought upon this people all this great evil, so will I bring upon them all the goodness that I speak of concerning them. [43] And fields will be bought in this land that you say is desolate without man or beast, delivered into the hand of the Chaldeans. [44] They will buy fields with money and write it in a document and seal [it] and designate witnesses — in the land of Benjamin, in the surroundings of Jerusalem, in the cities of Judah, in the cities of the mountain, in the cities of the lowland, and in the cities of the South — for I will return their captivity — the word of HASHEM!"

... to their fields and cities

33

[1] The word of HASHEM came to Jeremiah a second time, while he was still being detained in the Courtyard of Confinement, saying: [2] "Thus said HASHEM its* Maker, HASHEM is fashioning it to establish it, HASHEM is His Name: [3] Call to Me and I will answer you; and I will tell you great and mighty things that you do not know. [4] For thus said HASHEM, God of Israel, concerning the houses of this city and concerning the palaces of the kings of Judah, which are being shattered by the ramps and by the sword, [5] because they are coming to fight the Chaldeans and to fill [their houses] with human corpses, * whom I have struck down in My anger and in My wrath, for I have concealed My Presence from this city because of all their wickedness: [6] Behold, I am bringing it a remedy and a cure, and I shall heal them, and I shall reveal to them an abundance of peace and truth. [7] I will return the captivity of Judah and the captivity of Israel, and will rebuild them as at first. [8] I will cleanse them of all their sins that they committed against Me, and I will forgive all their iniquities that they committed against Me, and that they transgressed before Me. [9] And this will be for Me for the sake of rejoicing, for praise and for splendor before all the nations of the earth

Another prophecy from prison:

The people will return ...

אֲשֶׁ֣ר יִשְׁמְע֗וּ אֶת־כָּל־הַטּוֹבָ֞ה אֲשֶׁ֤ר אָֽנֹכִי֙ עֹשֶׂ֣ה אֹתָ֔ם וּפָחֲד֣וּ וְרָֽגְז֗וּ עַ֤ל
כָּל־הַטּוֹבָה֙ וְעַ֣ל כָּל־הַשָּׁל֔וֹם אֲשֶׁ֥ר אָֽנֹכִ֖י עֹ֥שֶׂה לָּֽהּ׃   כֹּ֣ה | **י**
אָמַ֣ר יהו֮ה עוֹד֒ יִשָּׁמַ֣ע בַּמָּקֽוֹם־הַזֶּ֗ה אֲשֶׁ֤ר אַתֶּם֙ אֹֽמְרִ֔ים חָרֵ֥ב ה֖וּא מֵאֵ֣ין
אָדָ֣ם וּמֵאֵ֣ין בְּהֵמָ֑ה בְּעָרֵ֤י יְהוּדָה֙ וּבְחֻצ֣וֹת יְרֽוּשָׁלִַ֔ם הַֽנְשַׁמּ֛וֹת מֵאֵ֥ין אָדָ֖ם
וּמֵאֵ֥ין יוֹשֵׁ֖ב וּמֵאֵ֥ין בְּהֵמָֽה׃ ק֣וֹל שָׂשׂ֣וֹן וְק֣וֹל שִׂמְחָ֗ה ק֤וֹל חָתָן֙ וְק֣וֹל כַּלָּ֔ה **יא**
ק֣וֹל אֹמְרִ֡ים הוֹד֣וּ אֶת־יהו֣ה צְבָאוֹת֮ כִּֽי־ט֣וֹב יהו֣ה כִּֽי־לְעוֹלָ֣ם חַסְדּוֹ֒
מְבִאִ֥ים תּוֹדָ֖ה בֵּ֣ית יהו֑ה כִּֽי־אָשִׁ֧יב אֶת־שְׁבֽוּת־הָאָ֛רֶץ כְּבָרִֽאשֹׁנָ֖ה אָמַ֥ר
יהוֽה׃   כֹּֽה־אָמַר֮ יהו֣ה צְבָאוֹת֒ ע֞וֹד יִֽהְיֶ֣ה | בַּמָּק֣וֹם הַזֶּ֣ה הֶחָרֵ֗ב **יב**
מֵֽאֵין־אָדָ֣ם וְעַד־בְּהֵמָה֒ וּבְכָל־עָרָ֑יו נְוֵ֣ה רֹעִ֔ים מַרְבִּצִ֖ים צֹֽאן׃ בְּעָרֵ֣י הָהָ֡ר **יג**
בְּעָרֵ֣י הַשְּׁפֵלָה֩ וּבְעָרֵ֨י הַנֶּ֜גֶב וּבְאֶ֣רֶץ בִּנְיָמִ֗ן וּבִסְבִיבֵ֤י יְרֽוּשָׁלִַ֨ם֙ וּבְעָרֵ֣י
יְהוּדָ֑ה עֹ֣ד תַּעֲבֹ֧רְנָה הַצֹּ֛אן עַל־יְדֵ֥י מוֹנֶ֖ה אָמַ֥ר יהוֽה׃   הִנֵּ֛ה **יד**
יָמִ֥ים בָּאִ֖ים נְאֻם־יהו֑ה וַהֲקִֽמֹתִי֙ אֶת־הַדָּבָ֣ר הַטּ֔וֹב אֲשֶׁ֥ר דִּבַּ֖רְתִּי אֶל־בֵּ֥ית
יִשְׂרָאֵ֖ל וְעַל־בֵּ֥ית יְהוּדָֽה׃ בַּיָּמִ֤ים הָהֵם֙ וּבָעֵ֣ת הַהִ֔יא אַצְמִ֥יחַ לְדָוִ֖ד צֶ֣מַח **טו**
צְדָקָ֑ה וְעָשָׂ֛ה מִשְׁפָּ֥ט וּצְדָקָ֖ה בָּאָֽרֶץ׃ בַּיָּמִ֤ים הָהֵם֙ תִּוָּשַׁ֣ע יְהוּדָ֔ה וִירֽוּשָׁלִַ֖ם **טז**
תִּשְׁכּ֣וֹן לָבֶ֑טַח וְזֶ֥ה אֲשֶׁר־יִקְרָא־לָ֖הּ יהו֥ה | צִדְקֵֽנוּ׃   כִּי־כֹ֖ה **יז**
אָמַ֣ר יהו֑ה לֹֽא־יִכָּרֵ֣ת לְדָוִ֔ד אִ֕ישׁ יֹשֵׁ֖ב עַל־כִּסֵּ֥א בֵֽית־יִשְׂרָאֵֽל׃ וְלַכֹּהֲנִ֣ים
הַלְוִיִּ֗ם לֹֽא־יִכָּרֵ֥ת אִ֛ישׁ מִלְּפָנָ֑י מַעֲלֶ֣ה עוֹלָ֗ה וּמַקְטִ֥יר מִנְחָ֛ה וְעֹֽשֶׂה־זֶּ֖בַח
כָּל־הַיָּמִֽים׃   וַֽיְהִי֙ דְּבַר־יהו֔ה אֶֽל־יִרְמְיָ֖הוּ לֵאמֽוֹר׃   כֹּ֚ה אָמַ֣ר **יח** **יט-כ**
יהו֔ה אִם־תָּפֵ֨רוּ֙ אֶת־בְּרִיתִ֣י הַיּ֔וֹם וְאֶת־בְּרִיתִ֖י הַלָּ֑יְלָה וּלְבִלְתִּ֛י הֱי֥וֹת
יֽוֹמָם־וָלַ֖יְלָה בְּעִתָּֽם׃ גַּם־בְּרִיתִ֣י תֻפַר֩ אֶת־דָּוִ֨ד עַבְדִּ֜י מִֽהְיֽוֹת־ל֥וֹ בֵ֛ן מֹלֵ֖ךְ **כא**
עַל־כִּסְא֑וֹ וְאֶת־הַלְוִיִּ֖ם הַכֹּהֲנִ֥ים מְשָׁרְתָֽי׃ אֲשֶׁ֤ר לֹֽא־יִסָּפֵר֙ צְבָ֣א הַשָּׁמַ֔יִם **כב**
וְלֹ֥א יִמַּ֖ד ח֣וֹל הַיָּ֑ם כֵּ֣ן אַרְבֶּ֗ה אֶת־זֶ֨רַע֙ דָּוִ֣ד עַבְדִּ֔י וְאֶת־הַלְוִיִּ֖ם מְשָׁ֥רְתֵ֥י
אֹתִֽי׃   וַֽיְהִי֙ דְּבַר־יהו֔ה אֶֽל־יִרְמְיָ֖הוּ לֵאמֹֽר׃ הֲל֣וֹא רָאִ֗יתָ מָֽה־ **כג-כד**
הָעָ֤ם הַזֶּה֙ דִּבְּר֣וּ לֵאמֹ֔ר שְׁתֵּ֣י הַמִּשְׁפָּח֗וֹת אֲשֶׁ֨ר בָּחַ֧ר יהו֛ה בָּהֶ֖ם וַיִּמְאָסֵ֑ם
וְאֶת־עַמִּי֙ יִנְאָצ֔וּן מִֽהְי֥וֹת ע֖וֹד גּ֥וֹי לִפְנֵיהֶֽם׃   ◀ כֹּ֣ה אָמַ֣ר יהו֗ה **כה**

Haftaras Mishpatim continues here: 33:25-26

אִם־לֹ֤א בְרִיתִי֙ יוֹמָ֣ם וָלָ֔יְלָה חֻקּ֛וֹת שָׁמַ֥יִם וָאָ֖רֶץ לֹא־שָׂ֑מְתִּי׃ גַּם־זֶ֡רַע **כו**
יַעֲקוֹב֩ וְדָוִ֨ד עַבְדִּ֜י אֶמְאַ֗ס מִקַּ֤חַת מִזַּרְעוֹ֙ מֹֽשְׁלִ֔ים אֶל־זֶ֥רַע אַבְרָהָ֖ם
יִשְׂחָ֣ק וְיַֽעֲקֹ֑ב כִּֽי־°אשוב [°אָשִׁ֥יב ק] אֶת־שְׁבוּתָ֖ם וְרִֽחַמְתִּֽים׃   הַדָּבָ֞ר **א** **לד**
אֲשֶׁר־הָיָ֤ה אֶֽל־יִרְמְיָ֨הוּ֙ מֵאֵ֣ת יהו֔ה וּנְבֽוּכַדְרֶאצַּ֣ר מֶֽלֶךְ־בָּבֶ֣ל | וְכָל־
חֵיל֡וֹ וְכָל־מַמְלְכ֣וֹת אֶ֩רֶץ֩ מֶמְשֶׁ֨לֶת יָד֜וֹ וְכָל־הָֽעַמִּ֗ים נִלְחָמִ֛ים עַל־
יְרֽוּשָׁלִַ֖ם וְעַל־כָּל־עָרֶ֑יהָ לֵאמֹֽר׃ כֹּֽה־אָמַ֤ר יהו֙ה אֱלֹהֵ֣י יִשְׂרָאֵ֔ל הָלֹ֞ךְ **ב**
וְאָֽמַרְתָּ֗ אֶל־צִדְקִיָּ֨הוּ֙ מֶ֣לֶךְ יְהוּדָ֔ה וְאָֽמַרְתָּ֣ אֵלָ֔יו כֹּ֚ה אָמַ֣ר יהו֔ה הִנְנִ֣י

33:12. Shepherds and flocks are a metaphor for Israel and their leaders.
33:24. By claiming that God has rejected the Davidic and Levitic lines, individuals encourage their fellow Jews not to submit to the leadership of these two families (*Radak*).

who will hear about all the goodness that I will be doing for them, and who will fear and tremble over all the goodness and all the peace that I will do for it.

^{... gladness will return ...} ¹⁰ "Thus said HASHEM: There will again be heard in this place about which you say, 'It is destroyed, without man and without animal,' in the cities of Judah and in the streets of Jerusalem that are desolate, without man and without inhabitant and without animal, ¹¹ the sound of joy and the sound of gladness, the sound of groom and the sound of bride, the sound of people saying, 'Praise HASHEM, Master of Legions, for HASHEM is good, for His mercy is forever,' bringing thanksgiving offerings to the Temple of HASHEM; for I will return the captivity of the land as at first, said HASHEM.

^{... flocks will return ...} ¹² "Thus said HASHEM, Master of Legions: There will yet again be in this place, which is desolate without man or animal, and in all its cities, a cote for shepherds who rest their flocks;* ¹³ in the cities of the mountain, in the cities of the lowland, in the cities of the South, in the land of Benjamin, in the surroundings of Jerusalem, and in the cities of Judah, the sheep will again pass before the hands of a counter, says HASHEM.

^{... the Davidic dynasty will return ...} ¹⁴ "Behold, days are coming — the word of HASHEM — when I will fulfill the favorable matter that I spoke concerning the House of Israel and the House of Judah. ¹⁵ In those days, at that time, I will cause a sprout of righteousness to sprout forth for David, and he will administer justice and righteousness in the land. ¹⁶ In those days Judah will be saved and Jerusalem will dwell in security; and this is what people will call [Jerusalem]: 'HASHEM Is Our Righteous One.' ¹⁷ For thus said HASHEM: There shall not be cut off from David a man who sits on the throne of the House of Israel. ¹⁸ And for the Kohanim, the Levites, there will never be cut off a man from before Me who offers elevation-offerings and burns meal-offerings and performs feast-offerings all the days."

^{... the Levites and Kohanim will return}

¹⁹ The word of HASHEM came to Jeremiah, saying:

²⁰ Thus said HASHEM: If you could annul My covenant with the day and My covenant with the night, so that day and night would not come in their proper times, ²¹ so too could My covenant be annulled with David, My servant, so that he would not have a descendant reigning on his throne, or [My covenant] with the Levites and the Kohanim, My attendants. ²² Just as the hosts of heaven cannot be counted nor the sand of the shore measured, so will I multiply the seed of My servant David and the Levites, My attendants.

²³ The word of HASHEM came to Jeremiah, saying: ²⁴ "Surely you have observed what this people have spoken, saying, 'The two families that HASHEM had chosen, He has rejected them,' thereby causing My people to renounce being a nation before them anymore.* ²⁵ Thus said HASHEM: If My covenant with the night and with the day would not be; had I not set up the laws of heaven and earth, ²⁶ so too would I reject the seed of Jacob and My servant David, from selecting from his descendants rulers over the seed of Abraham, Isaac, and Jacob; for I will return their captivity, and I will show them mercy."

34

Prophecy of Zedekiah's peaceful end

¹ The word that came to Jeremiah from HASHEM, while Nebuchadrezzar king of Babylonia and his entire army and all the kingdoms of the land under the rule of his hand and all the nations were fighting against Jerusalem and against all its [surrounding] cities, saying: ² "Thus said HASHEM, God of Israel: Go and speak to Zedekiah, king of Judah, and say to him: Thus said HASHEM: Behold, I am

ג נָתֹן אֶת־הָעִיר הַזֹּאת בְּיַד מֶלֶךְ־בָּבֶל וּשְׂרָפָהּ בָּאֵשׁ: וְאַתָּה לֹא תִמָּלֵט מִיָּדוֹ
כִּי תָּפֹשׂ תִּתָּפֵשׂ וּבְיָדוֹ תִּנָּתֵן וְעֵינֶיךָ אֶת־עֵינֵי מֶלֶךְ־בָּבֶל תִּרְאֶינָה וּפִיהוּ
אֶת־פִּיךָ יְדַבֵּר וּבָבֶל תָּבוֹא: אַךְ שְׁמַע דְּבַר־יְהוָה צִדְקִיָּהוּ מֶלֶךְ יְהוּדָה כֹּה־
ד אָמַר יְהוָה עָלֶיךָ לֹא תָמוּת בֶּחָרֶב: בְּשָׁלוֹם תָּמוּת וּבְמִשְׂרְפוֹת אֲבוֹתֶיךָ
ה הַמְּלָכִים הָרִאשֹׁנִים אֲשֶׁר־הָיוּ לְפָנֶיךָ כֵּן יִשְׂרְפוּ־לָךְ וְהוֹי אָדוֹן יִסְפְּדוּ־לָךְ
כִּי־דָבָר אֲנִי־דִבַּרְתִּי נְאֻם־יְהוָה: וַיְדַבֵּר יִרְמְיָהוּ הַנָּבִיא
ו אֶל־צִדְקִיָּהוּ מֶלֶךְ יְהוּדָה אֵת כָּל־הַדְּבָרִים הָאֵלֶּה בִּירוּשָׁלָ͏ִם: וְחֵיל מֶלֶךְ־
ז בָּבֶל נִלְחָמִים עַל־יְרוּשָׁלַ͏ִם וְעַל כָּל־עָרֵי יְהוּדָה הַנּוֹתָרֹת אֶל־לָכִישׁ וְאֶל־
עֲזֵקָה כִּי הֵנָּה נִשְׁאֲרוּ בְּעָרֵי יְהוּדָה עָרֵי מִבְצָר: ◄ הַדָּבָר אֲשֶׁר־

HAFTARAS MISHPATIM 34:8-22; 33:25-26

ח הָיָה אֶל־יִרְמְיָהוּ מֵאֵת יְהוָה אַחֲרֵי כְּרֹת הַמֶּלֶךְ צִדְקִיָּהוּ בְּרִית אֶת־כָּל־
ט הָעָם אֲשֶׁר בִּירוּשָׁלַ͏ִם לִקְרֹא לָהֶם דְּרוֹר: לְשַׁלַּח אִישׁ אֶת־עַבְדּוֹ וְאִישׁ
אֶת־שִׁפְחָתוֹ הָעִבְרִי וְהָעִבְרִיָּה חָפְשִׁים לְבִלְתִּי עֲבָד־בָּם בִּיהוּדִי אָחִיהוּ
י אִישׁ: וַיִּשְׁמְעוּ כָל־הַשָּׂרִים וְכָל־הָעָם אֲשֶׁר־בָּאוּ בַבְּרִית לְשַׁלַּח אִישׁ אֶת־
עַבְדּוֹ וְאִישׁ אֶת־שִׁפְחָתוֹ חָפְשִׁים לְבִלְתִּי עֲבָד־בָּם עוֹד וַיִּשְׁמְעוּ וַיְשַׁלֵּחוּ:
יא וַיָּשׁוּבוּ אַחֲרֵי־כֵן וַיָּשִׁבוּ אֶת־הָעֲבָדִים וְאֶת־הַשְּׁפָחוֹת אֲשֶׁר שִׁלְּחוּ חָפְשִׁים
יב °וַיִּכְבִּישׁוּם [וַיִּכְבְּשׁוּם ק] לַעֲבָדִים וְלִשְׁפָחוֹת: וַיְהִי
יג דְבַר־יְהוָה אֶל־יִרְמְיָהוּ מֵאֵת יְהוָה לֵאמֹר: כֹּה־אָמַר יְהוָה אֱלֹהֵי יִשְׂרָאֵל
אָנֹכִי כָּרַתִּי בְרִית אֶת־אֲבוֹתֵיכֶם בְּיוֹם הוֹצִאִי אוֹתָם מֵאֶרֶץ מִצְרַיִם מִבֵּית
יד עֲבָדִים לֵאמֹר: מִקֵּץ שֶׁבַע שָׁנִים תְּשַׁלְּחוּ אִישׁ אֶת־אָחִיו הָעִבְרִי אֲשֶׁר־
יִמָּכֵר לְךָ וַעֲבָדְךָ שֵׁשׁ שָׁנִים וְשִׁלַּחְתּוֹ חָפְשִׁי מֵעִמָּךְ וְלֹא־שָׁמְעוּ אֲבוֹתֵיכֶם
טו אֵלַי וְלֹא הִטּוּ אֶת־אָזְנָם: וַתָּשֻׁבוּ אַתֶּם הַיּוֹם וַתַּעֲשׂוּ אֶת־
הַיָּשָׁר בְּעֵינַי לִקְרֹא דְרוֹר אִישׁ לְרֵעֵהוּ וַתִּכְרְתוּ בְרִית לְפָנַי בַּבַּיִת אֲשֶׁר־
טז נִקְרָא שְׁמִי עָלָיו: וַתָּשֻׁבוּ וַתְּחַלְּלוּ אֶת־שְׁמִי וַתָּשִׁבוּ אִישׁ אֶת־עַבְדּוֹ
וְאִישׁ אֶת־שִׁפְחָתוֹ אֲשֶׁר־שִׁלַּחְתֶּם חָפְשִׁים לְנַפְשָׁם וַתִּכְבְּשׁוּ אֹתָם
יז לִהְיוֹת לָכֶם לַעֲבָדִים וְלִשְׁפָחוֹת: לָכֵן כֹּה־אָמַר יְהוָה
אַתֶּם לֹא־שְׁמַעְתֶּם אֵלַי לִקְרֹא דְרוֹר אִישׁ לְאָחִיו וְאִישׁ לְרֵעֵהוּ הִנְנִי
קֹרֵא לָכֶם דְּרוֹר נְאֻם־יְהוָה אֶל־הַחֶרֶב אֶל־הַדֶּבֶר וְאֶל־הָרָעָב וְנָתַתִּי
יח אֶתְכֶם °לְזַועָה [לְזַעֲוָה ק] לְכֹל מַמְלְכוֹת הָאָרֶץ: וְנָתַתִּי אֶת־הָאֲנָשִׁים
הָעֹבְרִים אֶת־בְּרִיתִי אֲשֶׁר לֹא־הֵקִימוּ אֶת־דִּבְרֵי הַבְּרִית אֲשֶׁר כָּרְתוּ
יט לְפָנָי הָעֵגֶל אֲשֶׁר כָּרְתוּ לִשְׁנַיִם וַיַּעַבְרוּ בֵּין בְּתָרָיו: שָׂרֵי יְהוּדָה וְשָׂרֵי
יְרוּשָׁלַ͏ִם הַסָּרִסִים וְהַכֹּהֲנִים וְכֹל עַם הָאָרֶץ הָעֹבְרִים בֵּין בִּתְרֵי

34:5. Although Zedekiah would be blinded and placed in chains by Nebuchadnezzar (*II Kings* 24:7), he is said to have died in peace. The Talmud (*Moed Kattan* 28b) interprets this to mean that Zedekiah outlived Nebuchadnezzar. *Rashi* cites a tradition that on the day Nebuchadnez- zar died, all his prisoners were released. Zedekiah died on the next day and was buried with proper honors, includ- ing the burning of the king's bedding and private utensils at his funeral — so that no commoner could ever make use of these objects (*Rashi*) — and the burning of incense delivering this city into the hand of the king of Babylonia, and he will burn it in fire. ³ You will not escape from his hand, for you will certainly be captured and will be delivered into his hand; your eyes will see the eyes of the king of Babylonia and his mouth will speak to your mouth, and you shall come to Babylonia. ⁴ But hear the word of HASHEM, Zedekiah king of Judah! Thus said HASHEM concerning you: You will not die by the sword. ⁵ You will die peacefully, * and like the burnings performed for your forefathers, the earlier kings who were before you, so will they burn for you; and they will lament for you, [saying,] 'Woe, master!' For I have spoken this word — the word of HASHEM."

⁶ So Jeremiah the prophet spoke all these things to Zedekiah, king of Judah, in Jerusalem, ⁷ while the army of the king of Babylonia was besieging Jerusalem and all the remaining cities of Judah — Lachish and Azekah — for they remained of the fortified cities among the cities of Judah.

Covenant of emancipa- tion sealed ...

⁸ The word that came to Jeremiah from HASHEM, after King Zedekiah sealed a covenant with all the people who were in Jerusalem, to proclaim freedom for them, ⁹ that every man send forth his bondsman and his bondswoman — a Hebrew man or a Hebrew woman — as freemen, so that no man should enslave his fellow Jew. ¹⁰ All the leaders and all the people who entered into the covenant hearkened — that every man should send forth his bondsman and every man his bondswoman as freemen, not to enslave them further — they hearkened and they sent them off. ¹¹ But they reneged after that and brought back the bondsmen and bondswomen whom they had sent forth as freemen and subjugated them as bondsmen and bondswomen.

... and abrogated

¹² The word of HASHEM then came to Jeremiah from HASHEM, saying:

¹³ Thus said HASHEM, God of Israel: I sealed a covenant with your forefathers on the day I took them out of the land of Egypt, from the house of slaves, saying, ¹⁴ 'At the outset of the seventh year, * each of you shall send forth his Hebrew brother who will have been be sold to you; he shall serve you for six years and then you shall send him forth free from yourself'; but your forefathers did not hearken to Me, nor incline their ear. ¹⁵ Today you repented and did what is just in My eyes, for every man to proclaim freedom for his fellow, and you sealed a covenant before Me in the Temple upon which My Name is proclaimed. ¹⁶ But then you reneged and desecrated My Name, and every man brought back his bondsman and every man his bondswoman whom you had sent forth free on their own, and you subjugated them to be bondsmen and bondswomen to you.

Punishment for violating the covenant

¹⁷ Therefore, thus said HASHEM: You did not hearken to Me to proclaim freedom, every man for his brother and every man for his fellow; behold, I proclaim you to be free — the word of HASHEM — for the sword, for pestilence and for famine; and I shall make you an object of horror for all the kingdoms of the earth. ¹⁸ I shall deliver the people who violated My covenant, who did not uphold the words of the covenant that they sealed before Me through the calf that they cut in two and passed between its parts, * ¹⁹ the leaders of Judah and the leaders of Jerusalem, the officers, the Kohanim and all the people of the land, who passed through the parts of

---

around his body (*Kara*). See *II Chronicles* 16:14.

34:14. See *Exodus* 21:2 and *Deuteronomy* 15:12, where the Torah prescribes that a Jewish bondsman or bondswoman works for six years and then goes free.

Thus, the deadline beyond which servitude may not continue is the start of the seventh year.

34:18. The customary way of making a covenant; see *Genesis* 15:17-18.

כ הָעֵגֶל: וְנָתַתִּי אוֹתָם בְּיַד אֹיְבֵיהֶם וּבְיַד מְבַקְשֵׁי נַפְשָׁם וְהָיְתָה נִבְלָתָם

כא לְמַאֲכָל לְעוֹף הַשָּׁמַיִם וּלְבֶהֱמַת הָאָרֶץ: וְאֶת־צִדְקִיָּהוּ מֶלֶךְ־יְהוּדָה
וְאֶת־שָׂרָיו אֶתֵּן בְּיַד אֹיְבֵיהֶם וּבְיַד מְבַקְשֵׁי נַפְשָׁם וּבְיַד חֵיל מֶלֶךְ בָּבֶל

כב הָעֹלִים מֵעֲלֵיכֶם: הִנְנִי מְצַוֶּה נְאֻם־יהוה וַהֲשִׁבֹתִים אֶל־הָעִיר הַזֹּאת
וְנִלְחֲמוּ עָלֶיהָ וּלְכָדוּהָ וּשְׂרָפֻהָ בָאֵשׁ וְאֶת־עָרֵי יְהוּדָה אֶתֵּן שְׁמָמָה מֵאֵין

לה א יֹשֵׁב: ◄ הַדָּבָר אֲשֶׁר־הָיָה אֶל־יִרְמְיָהוּ מֵאֵת יהוה בִּימֵי יְהוֹיָקִים

לה

Haftaras
Mishpatim
continues
on p. 1152

ב בֶּן־יֹאשִׁיָּהוּ מֶלֶךְ יְהוּדָה לֵאמֹר: הָלוֹךְ אֶל־בֵּית הָרֵכָבִים וְדִבַּרְתָּ אוֹתָם

ג וַהֲבִאוֹתָם בֵּית יהוה אֶל־אַחַת הַלְּשָׁכוֹת וְהִשְׁקִיתָ אוֹתָם יָיִן: וָאֶקַּח אֶת־
יַאֲזַנְיָה בֶן־יִרְמְיָהוּ בֶּן־חֲבַצִּנְיָה וְאֶת־אֶחָיו וְאֶת־כָּל־בָּנָיו וְאֵת כָּל־בֵּית

ד הָרֵכָבִים: וָאָבִא אֹתָם בֵּית יהוה אֶל־לִשְׁכַּת בְּנֵי חָנָן בֶּן־יִגְדַּלְיָהוּ אִישׁ
הָאֱלֹהִים אֲשֶׁר־אֵצֶל לִשְׁכַּת הַשָּׂרִים אֲשֶׁר מִמַּעַל לְלִשְׁכַּת מַעֲשֵׂיָהוּ בֶן־

ה שַׁלֻּם שֹׁמֵר הַסַּף: וָאֶתֵּן לִפְנֵי ׀ בְּנֵי בֵית־הָרֵכָבִים גְּבִעִים מְלֵאִים יַיִן וְכֹסוֹת

ו וָאֹמַר אֲלֵיהֶם שְׁתוּ־יָיִן: וַיֹּאמְרוּ לֹא נִשְׁתֶּה־יָּיִן כִּי יוֹנָדָב בֶּן־רֵכָב אָבִינוּ

ז צִוָּה עָלֵינוּ לֵאמֹר לֹא תִשְׁתּוּ־יַיִן אַתֶּם וּבְנֵיכֶם עַד־עוֹלָם: וּבַיִת לֹא־תִבְנוּ
וְזֶרַע לֹא־תִזְרָעוּ וְכֶרֶם לֹא־תִטָּעוּ וְלֹא יִהְיֶה לָכֶם כִּי בָּאֹהָלִים תֵּשְׁבוּ כָּל־
יְמֵיכֶם לְמַעַן תִּחְיוּ יָמִים רַבִּים עַל־פְּנֵי הָאֲדָמָה אֲשֶׁר אַתֶּם גָּרִים שָׁם:

ח וַנִּשְׁמַע בְּקוֹל יְהוֹנָדָב בֶּן־רֵכָב אָבִינוּ לְכֹל אֲשֶׁר צִוָּנוּ לְבִלְתִּי שְׁתוֹת־יַיִן

ט כָּל־יָמֵינוּ אֲנַחְנוּ נָשֵׁינוּ בָּנֵינוּ וּבְנֹתֵינוּ: וּלְבִלְתִּי בְּנוֹת בָּתִּים לְשִׁבְתֵּנוּ

י וְכֶרֶם וְשָׂדֶה וָזֶרַע לֹא יִהְיֶה־לָּנוּ: וַנֵּשֶׁב בָּאֹהָלִים וַנִּשְׁמַע וַנַּעַשׂ כְּכֹל

יא אֲשֶׁר־צִוָּנוּ יוֹנָדָב אָבִינוּ: וַיְהִי בַּעֲלוֹת נְבוּכַדְרֶאצַּר מֶלֶךְ־בָּבֶל אֶל־הָאָרֶץ
וַנֹּאמֶר בֹּאוּ וְנָבוֹא יְרוּשָׁלַ͏ִם מִפְּנֵי חֵיל הַכַּשְׂדִּים וּמִפְּנֵי חֵיל אֲרָם וַנֵּשֶׁב

יב-יג בִּירוּשָׁלָ͏ִם: וַיְהִי דְּבַר־יהוה אֶל־יִרְמְיָהוּ לֵאמֹר: כֹּה־אָמַר יהוה
צְבָאוֹת אֱלֹהֵי יִשְׂרָאֵל הָלֹךְ וְאָמַרְתָּ לְאִישׁ יְהוּדָה וּלְיוֹשְׁבֵי יְרוּשָׁלָ͏ִם

יד הֲלוֹא תִקְחוּ מוּסָר לִשְׁמֹעַ אֶל־דְּבָרַי נְאֻם־יהוה: הוּקַם אֶת־דִּבְרֵי יְהוֹנָדָב
בֶּן־רֵכָב אֲשֶׁר־צִוָּה אֶת־בָּנָיו לְבִלְתִּי שְׁתוֹת־יַיִן וְלֹא שָׁתוּ עַד־הַיּוֹם הַזֶּה
כִּי שָׁמְעוּ אֵת מִצְוַת אֲבִיהֶם וְאָנֹכִי דִּבַּרְתִּי אֲלֵיכֶם הַשְׁכֵּם וְדַבֵּר וְלֹא

טו שְׁמַעְתֶּם אֵלָי: וָאֶשְׁלַח אֲלֵיכֶם אֶת־כָּל־עֲבָדַי הַנְּבִאִים ׀ הַשְׁכֵּים וְשָׁלֹחַ ׀
לֵאמֹר שֻׁבוּ־נָא אִישׁ מִדַּרְכּוֹ הָרָעָה וְהֵיטִיבוּ מַעַלְלֵיכֶם וְאַל־תֵּלְכוּ אַחֲרֵי
אֱלֹהִים אֲחֵרִים לְעָבְדָם וּשְׁבוּ אֶל־הָאֲדָמָה אֲשֶׁר־נָתַתִּי לָכֶם וְלַאֲבֹתֵיכֶם

טז וְלֹא הִטִּיתֶם אֶת־אָזְנְכֶם וְלֹא שְׁמַעְתֶּם אֵלָי: כִּי הֵקִימוּ בְּנֵי יְהוֹנָדָב בֶּן־

יז רֵכָב אֶת־מִצְוַת אֲבִיהֶם אֲשֶׁר צִוָּם וְהָעָם הַזֶּה לֹא שָׁמְעוּ אֵלָי: לָכֵן

34:21. These events took place during the Babylonian retreat; see 37:5.

35:2. The Rechabites, descendants of Jehonadab (see *II Kings* 10:15), were Kenites (see *I Chronicles* 2:55), a tribe that converted to Judaism and

which was known for its piety and loyalty to the Israelites.

35:7. A nomadic lifestyle enables one to relocate easily, in case of famine or other local calamity, and thus is conducive to long life.

the calf; [20] I shall deliver them into the hand of their enemies and into the hand of those who seek their soul; their corpses will be food for the bird of the heavens and the beast of the land. [21] And I shall deliver Zedekiah, king of Judah, and his leaders into the hand of their enemies and into the hand of those who seek their soul and into the hand of the army of the king of Babylonia, who have retreated from you. * [22] Behold, I am commanding — the word of HASHEM: I shall return them to this city and they shall make war against it, conquer it, and burn it in fire; and I shall make the cities of Judah desolate, without an inhabitant.

35 [1] The word that came to Jeremiah from HASHEM, during the days of Jehoiakim son of Josiah king of Judah, saying: [2] "Go to the house of the Rechabites* and speak to them. Bring them to the Temple of HASHEM, to one of the chambers, and give them wine to drink."

[3] So I took Jaazaniah son of Jeremiah son of Habazziniah and his brothers and all his sons, and the entire house of the Rechabites, [4] and brought them to the Temple of HASHEM, to the Chamber of the Sons of Hanan son of Igdaliah the man of God, which is next to the Chamber of the Officers, which is above the Chamber of Maaseiah son of Shallum the Gatekeeper. [5] Before the members of the house of the Rechabites I placed drinking bowls full of wine and cups, and I said to them, "Drink wine!"

The Rechabites' loyalty to their ancestor

[6] But they said, "We do not drink wine, for Jehonadab son of Rechab, our ancestor, commanded us, saying, 'You shall not drink wine, you or your descendants, forever; [7] and a house you shall not build, seed you shall not sow, a vineyard you shall not plant, nor shall there [even] be [any] for you. Rather live in tents all your days, so that you may live many years upon the land in which you sojourn.'* [8] We heeded the voice of Jehonadab son of Rechab, our ancestor, according to all that he commanded us, not to drink wine all our days — we, our wives, our sons, and our daughters; [9] and not to build houses as our dwellings; and there will not be for us vineyard or field or seed. [10] Rather, we live in tents, for we hearkened and acted according to everything that Jehonadab our ancestor commanded us. [11] But it happened that when Nebuchadrezzar king of Babylonia attacked the land, we said, 'Come, let us go to Jerusalem because of the army of the Chaldeans and because of the army of Aram,' and we settled in Jerusalem."

[12] The word of HASHEM then came to Jeremiah, saying: [13] "Thus said HASHEM, Master of Legions, the God of Israel: Go and say to the men of Judah and to the inhabitants of Jerusalem:

The lesson to be learned

Will you not learn a lesson, to hearken to My words? — the word of HASHEM. [14] Upheld were the words of Jehonadab son of Rechab, who commanded his children not to drink wine, and they have not drunk wine until this day, for they obey the commandment of their ancestor. Yet I have spoken to you, arising early and speaking, and you have not listened to Me. [15] I sent all My servants the prophets, arising early and sending [them], saying, 'Repent now, each of you from his evil way; improve your deeds! Do not go after the gods of others to worship them, so that you may settle upon the land that I have given to you and your forefathers.' But you did not incline your ear and you did not listen to Me. [16] For the children of Jehonadab son of Rechab have upheld the word of their ancestor that he commanded them, but this people have not listened to Me!

כֹּה־אָמַר יְהֹוָה אֱלֹהֵי צְבָאוֹת אֱלֹהֵי יִשְׂרָאֵל הִנְנִי מֵבִיא אֶל־יְהוּדָה וְאֶל
כָּל־יֽוֹשְׁבֵי יְרוּשָׁלַם אֵת כָּל־הָרָעָה אֲשֶׁר דִּבַּרְתִּי עֲלֵיהֶם יַעַן דִּבַּרְתִּי

יח אֲלֵיהֶם וְלֹא שָׁמֵעוּ וָאֶקְרָא לָהֶם וְלֹא עָנוּ: וּלְבֵית הָרֵכָבִים אָמַר יִרְמְיָהוּ
כֹּה־אָמַר יְהֹוָה צְבָאוֹת אֱלֹהֵי יִשְׂרָאֵל יַעַן אֲשֶׁר שְׁמַעְתֶּם עַל־מִצְוַת
יְהוֹנָדָב אֲבִיכֶם וַתִּשְׁמְרוּ אֶת־כָּל־מִצְוֹתָיו וַתַּעֲשׂוּ כְּכֹל אֲשֶׁר־צִוָּה

יט אֶתְכֶם: לָכֵן כֹּה־אָמַר יְהֹוָה צְבָאוֹת אֱלֹהֵי יִשְׂרָאֵל לֹא־יִכָּרֵת אִישׁ
לְיוֹנָדָב בֶּן־רֵכָב עֹמֵד לְפָנַי כָּל־הַיָּמִים: וַיְהִי בַּשָּׁנָה **לו**

א הָרְבִיעִת לִיהוֹיָקִים בֶּן־יֹאשִׁיָּהוּ מֶלֶךְ יְהוּדָה הָיָה הַדָּבָר הַזֶּה אֶל־יִרְמְיָהוּ

ב מֵאֵת יְהֹוָה לֵאמֹר: קַח־לְךָ מְגִלַּת־סֵפֶר וְכָתַבְתָּ אֵלֶיהָ אֵת כָּל־הַדְּבָרִים
אֲשֶׁר־דִּבַּרְתִּי אֵלֶיךָ עַל־יִשְׂרָאֵל וְעַל־יְהוּדָה וְעַל־כָּל־הַגּוֹיִם מִיּוֹם

ג דִּבַּרְתִּי אֵלֶיךָ מִימֵי יֹאשִׁיָּהוּ וְעַד הַיּוֹם הַזֶּה: אוּלַי יִשְׁמְעוּ בֵּית יְהוּדָה
אֵת כָּל־הָרָעָה אֲשֶׁר אָנֹכִי חֹשֵׁב לַעֲשׂוֹת לָהֶם לְמַעַן יָשׁוּבוּ אִישׁ מִדַּרְכּוֹ

ד הָרָעָה וְסָלַחְתִּי לַעֲוֹנָם וּלְחַטָּאתָם: וַיִּקְרָא יִרְמְיָהוּ
אֶת־בָּרוּךְ בֶּן־נֵרִיָּה וַיִּכְתֹּב בָּרוּךְ מִפִּי יִרְמְיָהוּ אֵת כָּל־דִּבְרֵי יְהֹוָה

ה אֲשֶׁר־דִּבֶּר אֵלָיו עַל־מְגִלַּת־סֵפֶר: וַיְצַוֶּה יִרְמְיָהוּ אֶת־בָּרוּךְ לֵאמֹר אֲנִי
ו עָצוּר לֹא אוּכַל לָבוֹא בֵּית יְהֹוָה: וּבָאתָ אַתָּה וְקָרָאתָ בַמְּגִלָּה אֲשֶׁר־
כָּתַבְתָּ מִפִּי אֶת־דִּבְרֵי יְהֹוָה בְּאָזְנֵי הָעָם בֵּית יְהֹוָה בְּיוֹם צוֹם וְגַם בְּאָזְנֵי

ז כָל־יְהוּדָה הַבָּאִים מֵעָרֵיהֶם תִּקְרָאֵם: אוּלַי תִּפֹּל תְּחִנָּתָם לִפְנֵי יְהֹוָה
וְיָשֻׁבוּ אִישׁ מִדַּרְכּוֹ הָרָעָה כִּי־גָדוֹל הָאַף וְהַחֵמָה אֲשֶׁר־דִּבֶּר יְהֹוָה

ח אֶל־הָעָם הַזֶּה: וַיַּעַשׂ בָּרוּךְ בֶּן־נֵרִיָּה כְּכֹל אֲשֶׁר־צִוָּהוּ יִרְמְיָהוּ הַנָּבִיא

ט לִקְרֹא בַסֵּפֶר דִּבְרֵי יְהֹוָה בֵּית יְהֹוָה: וַיְהִי בַשָּׁנָה
הַחֲמִשִׁית לִיהוֹיָקִים בֶּן־יֹאשִׁיָּהוּ מֶלֶךְ־יְהוּדָה בַּחֹדֶשׁ הַתְּשִׁעִי קָרְאוּ
צוֹם לִפְנֵי יְהֹוָה כָּל־הָעָם בִּירוּשָׁלָם וְכָל־הָעָם הַבָּאִים מֵעָרֵי יְהוּדָה

י בִּירוּשָׁלָם: וַיִּקְרָא בָרוּךְ בַּסֵּפֶר אֶת־דִּבְרֵי יִרְמְיָהוּ בֵּית יְהֹוָה בְּלִשְׁכַּת
גְּמַרְיָהוּ בֶן־שָׁפָן הַסֹּפֵר בֶּחָצֵר הָעֶלְיוֹן פֶּתַח שַׁעַר בֵּית־יְהֹוָה הֶחָדָשׁ

יא בְּאָזְנֵי כָּל־הָעָם: וַיִּשְׁמַע מִכָיְהוּ בֶן־גְּמַרְיָהוּ בֶּן־שָׁפָן אֶת־כָּל־דִּבְרֵי

יב יְהֹוָה מֵעַל־הַסֵּפֶר: וַיֵּרֶד בֵּית־הַמֶּלֶךְ עַל־לִשְׁכַּת הַסֹּפֵר וְהִנֵּה־שָׁם כָּל־
הַשָּׂרִים יוֹשְׁבִים אֱלִישָׁמָע הַסֹּפֵר וּדְלָיָהוּ בֶן־שְׁמַעְיָהוּ וְאֶלְנָתָן בֶּן־

יג עַכְבּוֹר וּגְמַרְיָהוּ בֶן־שָׁפָן וְצִדְקִיָּהוּ בֶן־חֲנַנְיָהוּ וְכָל־הַשָּׂרִים: וַיַּגֵּד לָהֶם
מִכָיְהוּ אֵת כָּל־הַדְּבָרִים אֲשֶׁר שָׁמֵעַ בִּקְרֹא בָרוּךְ בַּסֵּפֶר בְּאָזְנֵי הָעָם:

יד וַיִּשְׁלְחוּ כָל־הַשָּׂרִים אֶל־בָּרוּךְ אֶת־יְהוּדִי בֶּן־נְתַנְיָהוּ בֶּן־שֶׁלֶמְיָהוּ
בֶן־כּוּשִׁי לֵאמֹר הַמְּגִלָּה אֲשֶׁר קָרָאתָ בָּהּ בְּאָזְנֵי הָעָם קָחֶנָּה בְיָדְךָ

טו וָלֵךְ וַיִּקַּח בָּרוּךְ בֶּן־נֵרִיָּהוּ אֶת־הַמְּגִלָּה בְּיָדוֹ וַיָּבֹא אֲלֵיהֶם: וַיֹּאמְרוּ אֵלָיו
טז שֵׁב נָא וּקְרָאֶנָּה בְּאָזְנֵינוּ וַיִּקְרָא בָרוּךְ בְּאָזְנֵיהֶם: וַיְהִי כְּשָׁמְעָם אֶת־כָּל־

¹⁷ *Therefore, thus says HASHEM, God of Legions, God of Israel: Behold, I am bringing to Judah and to all the inhabitants of Jerusalem all the evil that I have spoken concerning them, because I spoke to them and they did not listen, and I called out to them but they would not answer."*

¹⁸ *And to the house of the Rechabites Jeremiah said, "Thus said HASHEM, Master of Legions, God of Israel: Because you have heeded the commandment of your ancestor Jehonadab, and you have kept all his commandments and have done according to all that he commanded you, ¹⁹ therefore, thus said HASHEM, Master of Legions, God of Israel: There will not be cut off from Jehonadab son of Rechab's [descendants] a man who stands before Me* all of the days."*

36

Jeremiah writes his prophecies in a scroll

¹ *It happened during the fourth year of Jehoiakim the son of Josiah, king of Judah, that this word came to Jeremiah from HASHEM, saying: ² "Take a scroll book and write on it all the words that I have spoken to you concerning Israel, concerning Judah and concerning all the nations, from the day that I [first] spoke to you, from the days of Josiah, until this day. ³ Perhaps the House of Judah will hear of all the evil that I intend to do to them, so that they will repent, each man from his evil way, and then I can forgive their sin and transgression."*

⁴ *Jeremiah then summoned Baruch son of Neriah, and Baruch wrote from the mouth of Jeremiah all the words of HASHEM that He had spoken to him on a scroll book. ⁵ And Jeremiah commanded Baruch, saying, "I am detained;* I cannot go to the Temple of HASHEM. ⁶ So you go and read from the scroll, on which you have written the words of HASHEM from my mouth, in the ears of the people in the Temple of HASHEM on a fast day; and also in the ears of all of Judah, who come from their cities, shall you read them. ⁷ Perhaps their supplication will fall before HASHEM and they will repent, each man from his evil way, for great is the anger and wrath that HASHEM spoke concerning this people."*

Baruch reads Jeremiah's words in the Temple

⁸ *Baruch son of Neriah did everything just as Jeremiah the prophet had commanded him, to read the words of HASHEM from the book, in the Temple of HASHEM. ⁹ It happened in the fifth year of Jehoiakim son of Josiah, king of Judah, in the ninth month, that a fast was declared before HASHEM in Jerusalem, all the people in Jerusalem and all the people coming from the cities of Judah into Jerusalem. ¹⁰ And Baruch read the words of Jeremiah from the book in the Temple of HASHEM, in the chamber of Gemariah son of Shaphan the scribe, in the Upper Courtyard, at the opening of the New Gate* of the Temple of HASHEM, in the presence of all the people. ¹¹ Micaiah son of Gemariah son of Shaphan heard all the words of HASHEM being read from the book, ¹² and he went down to the king's palace, to the scribe's chamber, and behold, all the officers were sitting there: Elishama the scribe, Delaiah son of Shemaiah, Elnathan son of Achbor, Gemariah son of Shaphan, Zedekiah son of Hananiah, and all the [other] officers. ¹³ Micaiah told them all the things that he had heard when Baruch was reading the book in the ears of the people.*

¹⁴ *All the officers then sent Jehudi son of Nethaniah son of Shelemiah son of Cushi to Baruch, saying, "The scroll from which you have read in the ears of the people — take it in your hand and go." So Baruch son of Neriah took the scroll in his hand and came to them. ¹⁵ They said to him, "Sit now and read it in our ears." So Baruch read it in their ears. ¹⁶ It happened when they heard all the*

35:19. They will be members of the Sanhedrin, or their daughters will marry Kohanim and their grandsons will serve in the Temple (*Radak*).

36:5. As often happened, Jeremiah had been arrested for his "demoralizing and seditious" statements.
36:10. See 26:10.

הַדְּבָרִים פָּחֲדוּ אִישׁ אֶל־רֵעֵהוּ וַיֹּאמְרוּ אֶל־בָּרוּךְ הַגֵּיד נַגִּיד לַמֶּלֶךְ אֵת

כָּל־הַדְּבָרִים הָאֵלֶּה: וְאֶת־בָּרוּךְ שָׁאֲלוּ לֵאמֹר הַגֶּד־נָא לָנוּ אֵיךְ כָּתַבְתָּ

יז

אֶת־כָּל־הַדְּבָרִים הָאֵלֶּה מִפִּיו: וַיֹּאמֶר לָהֶם בָּרוּךְ מִפִּיו יִקְרָא אֵלַי אֵת

יח

כָּל־הַדְּבָרִים הָאֵלֶּה וַאֲנִי כֹּתֵב עַל־הַסֵּפֶר בַּדְּיוֹ:   וַיֹּאמְרוּ

יט

הַשָּׂרִים אֶל־בָּרוּךְ לֵךְ הִסָּתֵר אַתָּה וְיִרְמְיָהוּ וְאִישׁ אַל־יֵדַע אֵיפֹה אַתֶּם:

וַיָּבֹאוּ אֶל־הַמֶּלֶךְ חָצֵרָה וְאֶת־הַמְּגִלָּה הִפְקִדוּ בְּלִשְׁכַּת אֱלִישָׁמָע הַסֹּפֵר

כ

וַיַּגִּידוּ בְּאָזְנֵי הַמֶּלֶךְ אֵת כָּל־הַדְּבָרִים: וַיִּשְׁלַח הַמֶּלֶךְ אֶת־יְהוּדִי לָקַחַת

כא

אֶת־הַמְּגִלָּה וַיִּקָּחֶהָ מִלִּשְׁכַּת אֱלִישָׁמָע הַסֹּפֵר וַיִּקְרָאֶהָ יְהוּדִי בְּאָזְנֵי

הַמֶּלֶךְ וּבְאָזְנֵי כָּל־הַשָּׂרִים הָעֹמְדִים מֵעַל הַמֶּלֶךְ: וְהַמֶּלֶךְ יוֹשֵׁב בֵּית

כב

הַחֹרֶף בַּחֹדֶשׁ הַתְּשִׁיעִי וְאֶת־הָאָח לְפָנָיו מְבֹעָרֶת: וַיְהִי ׀ כִּקְרוֹא יְהוּדִי

כג

שָׁלֹשׁ דְּלָתוֹת וְאַרְבָּעָה יִקְרָעֶהָ בְּתַעַר הַסֹּפֵר וְהַשְׁלֵךְ אֶל־הָאֵשׁ אֲשֶׁר

אֶל־הָאָח עַד־תֹּם כָּל־הַמְּגִלָּה עַל־הָאֵשׁ אֲשֶׁר עַל־הָאָח: וְלֹא פָחֲדוּ

כד

וְלֹא קָרְעוּ אֶת־בִּגְדֵיהֶם הַמֶּלֶךְ וְכָל־עֲבָדָיו הַשֹּׁמְעִים אֵת כָּל־הַדְּבָרִים

הָאֵלֶּה: וְגַם אֶלְנָתָן וּדְלָיָהוּ וּגְמַרְיָהוּ הִפְגִּעוּ בַמֶּלֶךְ לְבִלְתִּי שְׂרֹף אֶת־

כה

הַמְּגִלָּה וְלֹא שָׁמַע אֲלֵיהֶם: וַיְצַוֶּה הַמֶּלֶךְ אֶת־יְרַחְמְאֵל בֶּן־הַמֶּלֶךְ וְאֶת־

כו

שְׂרָיָהוּ בֶן־עַזְרִיאֵל וְאֶת־שֶׁלֶמְיָהוּ בֶּן־עַבְדְּאֵל לָקַחַת אֶת־בָּרוּךְ הַסֹּפֵר

וְאֵת יִרְמְיָהוּ הַנָּבִיא וַיַּסְתִּרֵם יְהוָה: וַיְהִי דְבַר־יְהוָה

כז

אֶל־יִרְמְיָהוּ אַחֲרֵי ׀ שְׂרֹף הַמֶּלֶךְ אֶת־הַמְּגִלָּה וְאֶת־הַדְּבָרִים אֲשֶׁר כָּתַב

בָּרוּךְ מִפִּי יִרְמְיָהוּ לֵאמֹר: שׁוּב קַח־לְךָ מְגִלָּה אַחֶרֶת וּכְתֹב עָלֶיהָ אֵת

כח

כָּל־הַדְּבָרִים הָרִאשֹׁנִים אֲשֶׁר הָיוּ עַל־הַמְּגִלָּה הָרִאשֹׁנָה אֲשֶׁר שָׂרַף

יְהוֹיָקִים מֶלֶךְ־יְהוּדָה: וְעַל־יְהוֹיָקִים מֶלֶךְ־יְהוּדָה תֹאמַר כֹּה אָמַר יְהוָה

כט

אַתָּה שָׂרַפְתָּ אֶת־הַמְּגִלָּה הַזֹּאת לֵאמֹר מַדּוּעַ כָּתַבְתָּ עָלֶיהָ לֵאמֹר בֹּא־

יָבוֹא מֶלֶךְ־בָּבֶל וְהִשְׁחִית אֶת־הָאָרֶץ הַזֹּאת וְהִשְׁבִּית מִמֶּנָּה אָדָם

וּבְהֵמָה: לָכֵן כֹּה־אָמַר יְהוָה עַל־יְהוֹיָקִים מֶלֶךְ יְהוּדָה לֹא־

ל

יִהְיֶה־לּוֹ יוֹשֵׁב עַל־כִּסֵּא דָוִד וְנִבְלָתוֹ תִּהְיֶה מֻשְׁלֶכֶת לַחֹרֶב בַּיּוֹם וְלַקֶּרַח

בַּלָּיְלָה: וּפָקַדְתִּי עָלָיו וְעַל־זַרְעוֹ וְעַל־עֲבָדָיו אֶת־עֲוֹנָם וְהֵבֵאתִי עֲלֵיהֶם

לא

וְעַל־יֹשְׁבֵי יְרוּשָׁלַם וְאֶל־אִישׁ יְהוּדָה אֵת כָּל־הָרָעָה אֲשֶׁר־דִּבַּרְתִּי

אֲלֵיהֶם וְלֹא שָׁמֵעוּ:   וְיִרְמְיָהוּ לָקַח ׀ מְגִלָּה אַחֶרֶת וַיִּתְּנָהּ אֶל־

לב

בָּרוּךְ בֶּן־נֵרִיָּהוּ הַסֹּפֵר וַיִּכְתֹּב עָלֶיהָ מִפִּי יִרְמְיָהוּ אֵת כָּל־דִּבְרֵי הַסֵּפֶר

אֲשֶׁר שָׂרַף יְהוֹיָקִים מֶלֶךְ־יְהוּדָה בָּאֵשׁ וְעוֹד נוֹסַף עֲלֵיהֶם דְּבָרִים רַבִּים

כָּהֵמָּה: וַיִּמְלָךְ־מֶלֶךְ צִדְקִיָּהוּ בֶּן־יֹאשִׁיָּהוּ תַּחַת כָּנְיָהוּ בֶּן־

א

לז

יְהוֹיָקִים אֲשֶׁר הִמְלִיךְ נְבוּכַדְרֶאצַּר מֶלֶךְ בָּבֶל בְּאֶרֶץ יְהוּדָה: וְלֹא שָׁמַע

ב

הוּא וַעֲבָדָיו וְעַם הָאָרֶץ אֶל־דִּבְרֵי יְהוָה אֲשֶׁר דִּבֶּר בְּיַד יִרְמְיָהוּ הַנָּבִיא:

וַיִּשְׁלַח הַמֶּלֶךְ צִדְקִיָּהוּ אֶת־יְהוּכַל בֶּן־שֶׁלֶמְיָה וְאֶת־צְפַנְיָהוּ בֶן־מַעֲשֵׂיָה

ג

words, they expressed fear to one another, and they said to Baruch, "We must tell the king all these things." [17] They asked Baruch, saying, "Tell us now how it is that you wrote down all these things from [Jeremiah's] mouth."

[18] Baruch replied to them, "From his own mouth he would dictate all these words to me and I would write on the book with the ink."

[19] The officers then said to Baruch, "Go into hiding, you and Jeremiah, and let no man know where you are."*

The king burns the scroll [20] They came to the king's courtyard, and deposited the scroll in the chamber of Elishama the scribe; and they related all its words into the ears of the king. [21] The king sent Jehudi to get the scroll, and he took it from the chamber of Elishama the scribe; Jehudi then read it in the ears of the king and in the ears of all the officers who were standing before the king. [22] Now the king was sitting in his winter house, for it was the ninth month,* and the fireplace was burning before him. [23] It happened that whenever Jehudi would read three or four columns, [the king] would cut it out with a scribe's razor and throw it into the fire that was in the fireplace, until the entire scroll was burnt up by the fire that was in the fireplace. [24] The king and all his servants who heard all these words did not fear and they did not tear their clothes. [25] Elnathan and Delaiah and Gemariah even begged the king not to burn the scroll, but he did not listen to them. [26] The king commanded Jerahmeel, the king's son, and Seraiah son of Azriel and Shelemiah son of Abdeel to apprehend Baruch the scribe and Jeremiah the prophet, but HASHEM had hidden them.

[27] The word of HASHEM came to Jeremiah, after the king had burned the scroll with the words that Baruch had written from the mouth of Jeremiah, saying: *Jeremiah rewrites the scroll* [28] "Once again, take another scroll and write down on it all the original words that were on the first scroll that Jehoiakim king of Judah burned. [29] And to Jehoiakim king of Judah say: Thus said HASHEM: You burned this scroll, saying, 'Why did you write in it, saying: The king of Babylonia will definitely come here, and he will destroy this land and eliminate man and beast from it?' [30] Therefore, thus said HASHEM concerning Jehoiakim king of Judah: He will not have anyone who will sit upon the throne of David; and his corpse shall be cast out into the heat of the day and to the frost of the night. [31] I will recall their sin upon him and his descendants and his servants, and I will bring upon them and upon the inhabitants of Jerusalem and upon the people of Judah all the evil that I have spoken concerning them, yet they would not listen."

[32] So Jeremiah took another scroll and gave it to Baruch son of Neriah the scribe, and he wrote upon it, from the mouth of Jeremiah, all the words of the book that Jehoiakim king of Judah had burned in the fire, and many more similar words were added to them.*

37 [1] **K**ing Zedekiah son of Josiah, whom Nebuchadrezzar, king of Babylonia, enthroned in the land of Judah, reigned in place of Coniah* son of Jehoiakim. [2] He did not listen, [neither] he [nor] his servants [nor] the people of the land, to the words of HASHEM, which He spoke through Jeremiah the prophet. [3] King Zedekiah sent Jehucal son of Shelemiah and Zephaniah son of Maaseiah

---

36:19. The officers respected Jeremiah and Baruch, and wanted to protect them in case the king would try to punish them for daring to voice these prophecies.

36:22. Kislev, corresponding roughly to December.

36:32. The original scroll contained Chapters 1, 2 and 4

of *Lamentations.* Each chapter comprises twenty-two verses whose initial letters form the *aleph-beis.* A new chapter (Ch. 3) was added, this one containing three verses for each letter of the alphabet (*Rashi*).

37:1. See 22:24.

הַכֹּהֵן אֶל־יִרְמְיָהוּ הַנָּבִיא לֵאמֹר הִתְפַּלֶּל־נָא בַעֲדֵנוּ אֶל־יהוה אֱלֹהֵינוּ:

ד וְיִרְמְיָהוּ בָּא וְיֹצֵא בְּתוֹךְ הָעָם וְלֹא־נָתְנוּ אֹתוֹ בֵּית °הַכְּלִיא [הַכְּלוּא ק]:

ה וְחֵיל פַּרְעֹה יָצָא מִמִּצְרָיִם וַיִּשְׁמְעוּ הַכַּשְׂדִּים הַצָּרִים עַל־יְרוּשָׁלַ͏ִם אֶת־

ו שִׁמְעָם וַיֵּעָלוּ מֵעַל יְרוּשָׁלָ͏ִם: וַיְהִי דְּבַר־יהוה אֶל־יִרְמְיָהוּ

ז הַנָּבִיא לֵאמֹר: כֹּה־אָמַר יהוה אֱלֹהֵי יִשְׂרָאֵל כֹּה תֹאמְרוּ אֶל־מֶלֶךְ יְהוּדָה הַשֹּׁלֵחַ אֶתְכֶם אֵלַי לְדָרְשֵׁנִי הִנֵּה ׀ חֵיל פַּרְעֹה הַיֹּצֵא לָכֶם לְעֶזְרָה שָׁב

ח לְאַרְצוֹ מִצְרָיִם: וְשָׁבוּ הַכַּשְׂדִּים וְנִלְחֲמוּ עַל־הָעִיר הַזֹּאת וּלְכָדֻהָ וּשְׂרָפֻהָ

ט בָאֵשׁ:   כֹּה ׀ אָמַר יהוה אַל־תַּשִּׁאוּ נַפְשֹׁתֵיכֶם לֵאמֹר הָלֹךְ

י יֵלְכוּ מֵעָלֵינוּ הַכַּשְׂדִּים כִּי־לֹא יֵלֵכוּ: כִּי אִם־הִכִּיתֶם כָּל־חֵיל כַּשְׂדִּים הַנִּלְחָמִים אִתְּכֶם וְנִשְׁאֲרוּ־בָם אֲנָשִׁים מְדֻקָּרִים אִישׁ בְּאָהֳלוֹ יָקוּמוּ וְשָׂרְפוּ

יא אֶת־הָעִיר הַזֹּאת בָּאֵשׁ: וְהָיָה בְּהֵעָלוֹת חֵיל הַכַּשְׂדִּים מֵעַל יְרוּשָׁלָ͏ִם מִפְּנֵי

יב חֵיל פַּרְעֹה: וַיֵּצֵא יִרְמְיָהוּ מִירוּשָׁלַ͏ִם לָלֶכֶת אֶרֶץ בִּנְיָמִן

יג לַחֲלִק מִשָּׁם בְּתוֹךְ הָעָם: וַיְהִי־הוּא בְּשַׁעַר בִּנְיָמִן וְשָׁם בַּעַל פְּקִדֻת וּשְׁמוֹ יִרְאִיָּיה בֶּן־שֶׁלֶמְיָה בֶּן־חֲנַנְיָה וַיִּתְפֹּשׂ אֶת־יִרְמְיָהוּ הַנָּבִיא לֵאמֹר אֶל־

יד הַכַּשְׂדִּים אַתָּה נֹפֵל: וַיֹּאמֶר יִרְמְיָהוּ שֶׁקֶר אֵינֶנִּי נֹפֵל עַל־הַכַּשְׂדִּים וְלֹא

טו שָׁמַע אֵלָיו וַיִּתְפֹּשׂ יִרְאִיָּיה בְּיִרְמְיָהוּ וַיְבִאֵהוּ אֶל־הַשָּׂרִים: וַיִּקְצְפוּ הַשָּׂרִים עַל־יִרְמְיָהוּ וְהִכּוּ אֹתוֹ וְנָתְנוּ אוֹתוֹ בֵּית הָאֵסוּר בֵּית יְהוֹנָתָן הַסֹּפֵר כִּי־

טז אֹתוֹ עָשׂוּ לְבֵית הַכֶּלֶא: כִּי בָא יִרְמְיָהוּ אֶל־בֵּית הַבּוֹר וְאֶל־הַחֲנֻיוֹת

יז וַיֵּשֶׁב־שָׁם יִרְמְיָהוּ יָמִים רַבִּים: וַיִּשְׁלַח הַמֶּלֶךְ צִדְקִיָּהוּ וַיִּקָּחֵהוּ וַיִּשְׁאָלֵהוּ הַמֶּלֶךְ בְּבֵיתוֹ בַּסֵּתֶר וַיֹּאמֶר הֲיֵשׁ דָּבָר מֵאֵת יהוה וַיֹּאמֶר יִרְמְיָהוּ יֵשׁ

יח וַיֹּאמֶר בְּיַד מֶלֶךְ־בָּבֶל תִּנָּתֵן: וַיֹּאמֶר יִרְמְיָהוּ אֶל־הַמֶּלֶךְ צִדְקִיָּהוּ מֶה

יט חָטָאתִי לְךָ וְלַעֲבָדֶיךָ וְלָעָם הַזֶּה כִּי־נְתַתֶּם אוֹתִי אֶל־בֵּית הַכֶּלֶא: °וְאַיּוֹ [וְאַיֵּה ק] נְבִיאֵיכֶם אֲשֶׁר־נִבְּאוּ לָכֶם לֵאמֹר לֹא־יָבֹא מֶלֶךְ־בָּבֶל עֲלֵיכֶם

כ וְעַל הָאָרֶץ הַזֹּאת: וְעַתָּה שְׁמַע־נָא אֲדֹנִי הַמֶּלֶךְ תִּפָּל־נָא תְחִנָּתִי לְפָנֶיךָ

כא וְאַל־תְּשִׁבֵנִי בֵּית יְהוֹנָתָן הַסֹּפֵר וְלֹא אָמוּת שָׁם: וַיְצַוֶּה הַמֶּלֶךְ צִדְקִיָּהוּ וַיַּפְקִדוּ אֶת־יִרְמְיָהוּ בַּחֲצַר הַמַּטָּרָה וְנָתֹן לוֹ כִכַּר־לֶחֶם לַיּוֹם מִחוּץ הָאֹפִים עַד־תֹּם כָּל־הַלֶּחֶם מִן־הָעִיר וַיֵּשֶׁב יִרְמְיָהוּ בַּחֲצַר הַמַּטָּרָה:

לח

א וַיִּשְׁמַע שְׁפַטְיָה בֶן־מַתָּן וּגְדַלְיָהוּ בֶּן־פַּשְׁחוּר וְיוּכַל בֶּן־שֶׁלֶמְיָהוּ וּפַשְׁחוּר

ב בֶּן־מַלְכִּיָּה אֶת־הַדְּבָרִים אֲשֶׁר יִרְמְיָהוּ מְדַבֵּר אֶל־כָּל־הָעָם לֵאמֹר: כֹּה אָמַר יהוה הַיֹּשֵׁב בָּעִיר הַזֹּאת יָמוּת בַּחֶרֶב בָּרָעָב וּבַדָּבֶר וְהַיֹּצֵא אֶל־

ג הַכַּשְׂדִּים °יִחְיֶה [וְחָיָה ק] וְהָיְתָה־לּוֹ נַפְשׁוֹ לְשָׁלָל וָחָי: כֹּה

37:4. Zedekiah had freed Jeremiah upon ascending the throne (*Rashi*), although he was incarcerated subsequently (see vv. 15-16).

37:5. To aid their allies, the Judeans (*Rashi*).

37:12. Taking advantage of the lull in the fighting to go to his home in the land of Benjamin, Jeremiah tried to slip out of the city undetected, with the throngs of people. Apparently his latest prophecy (vv. 6-10) had upset the authorities and he was afraid of being recognized and arrested (*Radak*).

the Kohen to Jeremiah the prophet, saying, "Please pray on our behalf unto HASHEM, our God." [4] Now Jeremiah was coming and going among the people; they had not [yet] put him into prison. * [5] The army of Pharaoh had departed from Egypt; * the Chaldeans who were besieging Jerusalem heard the news about them and withdrew from Jerusalem.

The Chaldeans withdraw

[6] The word of HASHEM came to Jeremiah the prophet, saying, [7] "Thus said HASHEM, God of Israel: Say thus to the king of Judah, who sends you to Me to inquire of Me:

Prophecy that the Chaldeans would return

Behold, the army of Pharaoh that left to assist you is returning to its land, Egypt; [8] and the Chaldeans will return and fight against this city, and they will capture it and burn it [down].

[9] Thus said HASHEM: Do not delude yourselves, saying, 'The Chaldeans will surely depart from us,' for they will not depart! [10] For even if you would strike the entire Chaldean army that is fighting against you, and only wounded men will remain of them, each man would rise up from his tent and burn [down] this city in fire."

Jeremiah arrested . . .

[11] It happened when the Chaldean army was withdrawn from Jerusalem because of Pharaoh's army: [12] Jeremiah left Jerusalem to go to the land of Benjamin, to slip out from there among the people. * [13] He was in the Benjamin Gate, but an official was there — his name, Irijah son of Shelemiah son of Hananiah — and he seized Jeremiah the prophet, saying, "You are deserting to the Chaldeans!"

[14] Jeremiah replied, "Falsehood! I am not deserting to the Chaldeans!" But he did not listen to him, and Irijah seized Jeremiah and brought him to the officers. [15] The officers became enraged with Jeremiah and struck him; and they put him into a house of confinement, in the house of Jonathan the scribe, which they had made into a prison. [16] So Jeremiah was put into the dungeon which was behind the shops, and Jeremiah stayed there many days.

. . . then brought before Zedekiah

[17] Then King Zedekiah sent [a messenger] and took him out; and the king questioned him in his house, secretly, and said, "Is there word from HASHEM?" Jeremiah answered, "There is!" And he said [further], "You will be delivered into the hand of the king of Babylonia!" [18] Jeremiah then said to King Zedekiah, "In what way have I sinned to you and to your servants and to this people, that you have put me into prison? [19] And where are your prophets that prophesied to you, saying, 'The king of Babylonia will not come upon you and upon this land'? [20] And now, please hear me, my lord, the king! Please let my supplication be acceptable before you, and do not return me to the house of Jonathan the scribe, and let me not die there."

[21] So King Zedekiah issued a command, and they consigned Jeremiah to the Courtyard of Confinement, and gave him a loaf of bread every day from the bakers' market, until all the bread had been depleted from the city; and Jeremiah remained in the Courtyard of Confinement.

38   [1] Shephatiah son of Mattan, Gedaliah son of Pashhur, Jehucal son of She-lemiah, and Pashhur son of Malchiah heard the things that Jeremiah was speaking to all the people, saying:

[2] Thus said HASHEM: Whoever remains in this city will die by the sword, by the famine or by the pestilence, whereas whoever goes out [in surrender] to the Chaldeans will live; he will have his life as a booty, and he will live. [3] Thus

ד אָמַר יְהֹוָה הִנָּתֹן תִּנָּתֵן הָעִיר הַזֹּאת בְּיַד חֵיל מֶלֶךְ־בָּבֶל וּלְכָדָהּ: וַיֹּאמְרוּ
הַשָּׂרִים אֶל־הַמֶּלֶךְ יוּמַת נָא אֶת־הָאִישׁ הַזֶּה כִּי־עַל־כֵּן הֽוּא־מְרַפֵּא אֶת־
יְדֵי אַנְשֵׁי הַמִּלְחָמָה הַנִּשְׁאָרִים ׀ בָּעִיר הַזֹּאת וְאֵת יְדֵי כָל־הָעָם לְדַבֵּר
אֲלֵיהֶם כַּדְּבָרִים הָאֵלֶּה כִּי ׀ הָאִישׁ הַזֶּה אֵינֶנּוּ דֹרֵשׁ לְשָׁלוֹם לָעָם הַזֶּה כִּי
ה אִם־לְרָעָה: וַיֹּאמֶר הַמֶּלֶךְ צִדְקִיָּהוּ הִנֵּה־הוּא בְּיֶדְכֶם כִּי־אֵין הַמֶּלֶךְ יוּכַל
ו אֶתְכֶם דָּבָר: וַיִּקְחוּ אֶת־יִרְמְיָהוּ וַיַּשְׁלִכוּ אֹתוֹ אֶל־הַבּוֹר ׀ מַלְכִּיָּהוּ בֶן־
הַמֶּלֶךְ אֲשֶׁר בַּחֲצַר הַמַּטָּרָה וַיְשַׁלְּחוּ אֶת־יִרְמְיָהוּ בַּחֲבָלִים וּבַבּוֹר אֵין־
ז מַיִם כִּי אִם־טִיט וַיִּטְבַּע יִרְמְיָהוּ בַּטִּיט: וַיִּשְׁמַע עֶבֶד־מֶלֶךְ הַכּוּשִׁי אִישׁ
סָרִיס וְהוּא בְּבֵית הַמֶּלֶךְ כִּי־נָתְנוּ אֶת־יִרְמְיָהוּ אֶל־הַבּוֹר וְהַמֶּלֶךְ יוֹשֵׁב
ח בְּשַׁעַר בִּנְיָמִן: וַיֵּצֵא עֶבֶד־מֶלֶךְ מִבֵּית הַמֶּלֶךְ וַיְדַבֵּר אֶל־הַמֶּלֶךְ לֵאמֹר:
ט אֲדֹנִי הַמֶּלֶךְ הֵרֵעוּ הָאֲנָשִׁים הָאֵלֶּה אֵת כָּל־אֲשֶׁר עָשׂוּ לְיִרְמְיָהוּ הַנָּבִיא
אֵת אֲשֶׁר־הִשְׁלִיכוּ אֶל־הַבּוֹר וַיָּמָת תַּחְתָּיו מִפְּנֵי הָרָעָב כִּי אֵין הַלֶּחֶם עוֹד
י בָּעִיר: וַיְצַוֶּה הַמֶּלֶךְ אֵת עֶבֶד־מֶלֶךְ הַכּוּשִׁי לֵאמֹר קַח בְּיָדְךָ מִזֶּה שְׁלֹשִׁים
יא אֲנָשִׁים וְהַעֲלִיתָ אֶת־יִרְמְיָהוּ הַנָּבִיא מִן־הַבּוֹר בְּטֶרֶם יָמוּת: וַיִּקַּח ׀ עֶבֶד־
מֶלֶךְ אֶת־הָאֲנָשִׁים בְּיָדוֹ וַיָּבֹא בֵית־הַמֶּלֶךְ אֶל־תַּחַת הָאוֹצָר וַיִּקַּח מִשָּׁם
בְּלוֹיֵ °הַסְּחָבוֹת [סְחָבוֹת ק] וּבְלוֹיֵ מְלָחִים וַיְשַׁלְּחֵם אֶל־יִרְמְיָהוּ אֶל־
יב הַבּוֹר בַּחֲבָלִים: וַיֹּאמֶר עֶבֶד־מֶלֶךְ הַכּוּשִׁי אֶל־יִרְמְיָהוּ שִׂים נָא בְּלוֹאֵי
הַסְּחָבוֹת וְהַמְּלָחִים תַּחַת אַצִּלוֹת יָדֶיךָ מִתַּחַת לַחֲבָלִים וַיַּעַשׂ יִרְמְיָהוּ כֵּן:
יג וַיִּמְשְׁכוּ אֶת־יִרְמְיָהוּ בַּחֲבָלִים וַיַּעֲלוּ אֹתוֹ מִן־הַבּוֹר וַיֵּשֶׁב יִרְמְיָהוּ בַּחֲצַר
יד הַמַּטָּרָה: וַיִּשְׁלַח הַמֶּלֶךְ צִדְקִיָּהוּ וַיִּקַּח אֶת־יִרְמְיָהוּ הַנָּבִיא
אֵלָיו אֶל־מָבוֹא הַשְּׁלִישִׁי אֲשֶׁר בְּבֵית יְהֹוָה וַיֹּאמֶר הַמֶּלֶךְ אֶל־יִרְמְיָהוּ
טו שֹׁאֵל אֲנִי אֹתְךָ דָּבָר אַל־תְּכַחֵד מִמֶּנִּי דָּבָר: וַיֹּאמֶר יִרְמְיָהוּ אֶל־צִדְקִיָּהוּ
טז כִּי אַגִּיד לְךָ הֲלוֹא הָמֵת תְּמִיתֵנִי וְכִי אִיעָצְךָ לֹא תִשְׁמַע אֵלָי: וַיִּשָּׁבַע
הַמֶּלֶךְ צִדְקִיָּהוּ אֶל־יִרְמְיָהוּ בַּסֵּתֶר לֵאמֹר חַי־יְהֹוָה [°אֵת כ ולא ק] אֲשֶׁר
עָשָׂה־לָנוּ אֶת־הַנֶּפֶשׁ הַזֹּאת אִם־אֲמִיתֶךָ וְאִם־אֶתֶּנְךָ בְּיַד הָאֲנָשִׁים הָאֵלֶּה
יז אֲשֶׁר מְבַקְשִׁים אֶת־נַפְשֶׁךָ:   וַיֹּאמֶר יִרְמְיָהוּ אֶל־צִדְקִיָּהוּ כֹּה־
אָמַר יְהֹוָה אֱלֹהֵי צְבָאוֹת אֱלֹהֵי יִשְׂרָאֵל אִם־יָצֹא תֵצֵא אֶל־שָׂרֵי
מֶלֶךְ־בָּבֶל וְחָיְתָה נַפְשֶׁךָ וְהָעִיר הַזֹּאת לֹא תִשָּׂרֵף בָּאֵשׁ וְחָיִתָה אַתָּה
יח וּבֵיתֶךָ: וְאִם לֹא־תֵצֵא אֶל־שָׂרֵי מֶלֶךְ בָּבֶל וְנִתְּנָה הָעִיר הַזֹּאת בְּיַד
הַכַּשְׂדִּים וּשְׂרָפוּהָ בָּאֵשׁ וְאַתָּה לֹא־תִמָּלֵט מִיָּדָם: וַיֹּאמֶר הַמֶּלֶךְ
יט צִדְקִיָּהוּ אֶל־יִרְמְיָהוּ אֲנִי דֹאֵג אֶת־הַיְּהוּדִים אֲשֶׁר נָפְלוּ אֶל־הַכַּשְׂדִּים פֶּן־
כ יִתְּנוּ אֹתִי בְּיָדָם וְהִתְעַלְּלוּ־בִי: וַיֹּאמֶר יִרְמְיָהוּ לֹא יִתֵּנוּ
כא שְׁמַע־נָא ׀ בְּקוֹל יְהֹוָה לַאֲשֶׁר אֲנִי דֹּבֵר אֵלֶיךָ וְיִיטַב לְךָ וּתְחִי נַפְשֶׁךָ: וְאִם־
כב מָאֵן אַתָּה לָצֵאת זֶה הַדָּבָר אֲשֶׁר הִרְאַנִי יְהֹוָה: וְהִנֵּה כָל־הַנָּשִׁים אֲשֶׁר
נִשְׁאֲרוּ בְּבֵית מֶלֶךְ־יְהוּדָה מוּצָאוֹת אֶל־שָׂרֵי מֶלֶךְ בָּבֶל וְהֵנָּה אֹמְרוֹת

said HASHEM: This city will surely be delivered into the hand of the army of the king of Babylonia, and he will capture it.

⁴ And the[se] officers said to the king, "Let this man be put to death now, because he is weakening the hands of the soldiers who remain in this city, and the hands of all the people, by speaking to them such things. For this man does not seek the welfare of this people, but rather [their] detriment."

Jeremiah cast into the pit ⁵ King Zedekiah then said, "Behold, he is in your hands; for the king has no word to dispute you." ⁶ So they took Jeremiah and threw him into the pit of Malchiah son of the king which was in the Courtyard of Confinement; they lowered Jeremiah with ropes. In the pit there was no water, only mud; and Jeremiah sank [partially] into the mud.

⁷ Ebed-melech the Cushite, a senior officer, who was in the king's house, heard that they had put Jeremiah into the pit, while the king was sitting at the Benjamin Gate. ⁸ So Ebed-melech left the king's house and spoke to the king, saying, ⁹ "My lord, the king, these men have acted wickedly in all that they have done to Jeremiah the prophet, in that they have thrown him into the pit. He will die of hunger where he is now, for there is no more bread in the city."

¹⁰ So the king commanded Ebed-melech the Cushite, saying, "Take thirty men from here with you and raise Jeremiah the prophet from the pit before he dies!"

Ebed-melech rescues Jeremiah ¹¹ So Ebed-melech took the men with him and went to the king's palace, under the treasury, and from there he took worn out rags and worn-out scraps, and sent them down with ropes to Jeremiah, into the pit. ¹² Ebed-melech the Cushite then said to Jeremiah, "Put the worn-out rags and the scraps under your armpits, under the ropes," and Jeremiah did so. ¹³ They then pulled out Jeremiah with the ropes and raised him out of the pit; and Jeremiah remained in the Courtyard of Confinement.

¹⁴ King Zedekiah then sent [a messenger] and summoned Jeremiah the prophet [to come] to him, to the third entrance of the Temple of HASHEM. The king said to Jeremiah, "I am asking you something; do not withhold anything from me!"

¹⁵ Jeremiah answered Zedekiah, "If I answer you, will you not have me put to death? And if I give you advice, you will not listen to me!"

¹⁶ King Zedekiah swore to Jeremiah secretly, saying, "As HASHEM lives, Who created this soul, [I swear that] I shall not put you to death nor turn you over to those people who seek your soul!"

Prophecy to Zedekiah: Surrender and live ¹⁷ So Jeremiah said to Zedekiah, "Thus said HASHEM, God of Legions, God of Israel: If you go forth [in surrender] to the officers of the king of Babylonia, your soul will live, and this city will not be burnt [down] in fire; rather you and your household will survive. ¹⁸ But if you do not go forth to the officers of the king of Babylonia, this city will be delivered into the hand of the Chaldeans, and they will burn it [down] in fire. And you will not escape from their hand!"

¹⁹ King Zedekiah said to Jeremiah, "I fear the Jews who have deserted to the Chaldeans, lest they give me over into their hand and they abuse me."

²⁰ But Jeremiah said, "They will not give you over; hearken to the voice of HASHEM, to what I am telling you, and it will be well for you and you will live. ²¹ But if you refuse to go forth [in surrender], this is the matter that HASHEM has shown me: ²² Behold, all the women who remain in the house of the king of Judah are being brought out to the officers of the king of Babylonia, and they are saying,

הִסִּיתוּךָ וְיָכְלוּ לְךָ אַנְשֵׁי שְׁלֹמֶךָ הָטְבְּעוּ בַבֹּץ רַגְלֶךָ נָסֹגוּ אָחוֹר: וְאֶת־כָּל־ כג
נָשֶׁיךָ וְאֶת־בָּנֶיךָ מוֹצִאִים אֶל־הַכַּשְׂדִּים וְאַתָּה לֹא־תִמָּלֵט מִיָּדָם כִּי בְיַד־
מֶלֶךְ־בָּבֶל תִּתָּפֵשׂ וְאֶת־הָעִיר הַזֹּאת תִּשְׂרֹף בָּאֵשׁ:   וַיֹּאמֶר כד
צִדְקִיָּהוּ אֶל־יִרְמְיָהוּ אִישׁ אַל־יֵדַע בַּדְּבָרִים־הָאֵלֶּה וְלֹא תָמוּת: וְכִי־ כה
יִשְׁמְעוּ הַשָּׂרִים כִּי־דִבַּרְתִּי אִתָּךְ וּבָאוּ אֵלֶיךָ וְאָמְרוּ אֵלֶיךָ הַגִּידָה־נָּא לָנוּ
מַה־דִּבַּרְתָּ אֶל־הַמֶּלֶךְ אַל־תְּכַחֵד מִמֶּנּוּ וְלֹא נְמִיתֶךָ וּמַה־דִּבֶּר אֵלֶיךָ
הַמֶּלֶךְ: וְאָמַרְתָּ אֲלֵיהֶם מַפִּיל־אֲנִי תְחִנָּתִי לִפְנֵי הַמֶּלֶךְ לְבִלְתִּי הֲשִׁיבֵנִי כו
בֵּית יְהוֹנָתָן לָמוּת שָׁם: וַיָּבֹאוּ כָל־הַשָּׂרִים אֶל־יִרְמְיָהוּ וַיִּשְׁאֲלוּ כז
אֹתוֹ וַיַּגֵּד לָהֶם כְּכָל־הַדְּבָרִים הָאֵלֶּה אֲשֶׁר צִוָּה הַמֶּלֶךְ וַיַּחֲרִשׁוּ מִמֶּנּוּ כִּי
לֹא־נִשְׁמַע הַדָּבָר: וַיֵּשֶׁב יִרְמְיָהוּ בַּחֲצַר הַמַּטָּרָה עַד־יוֹם כח
אֲשֶׁר־נִלְכְּדָה יְרוּשָׁלָ͏ִם   וְהָיָה כַּאֲשֶׁר נִלְכְּדָה יְרוּשָׁלָ͏ִם: בַּשָּׁנָה לט כט/א
הַתְּשִׁעִית לְצִדְקִיָּהוּ מֶלֶךְ־יְהוּדָה בַּחֹדֶשׁ הָעֲשִׂרִי בָּא נְבוּכַדְרֶאצַּר מֶלֶךְ־
בָּבֶל וְכָל־חֵילוֹ אֶל־יְרוּשָׁלַ͏ִם וַיָּצֻרוּ עָלֶיהָ: בְּעַשְׁתֵּי־עֶשְׂרֵה שָׁנָה לְצִדְקִיָּהוּ ב
בַּחֹדֶשׁ הָרְבִיעִי בְּתִשְׁעָה לַחֹדֶשׁ הָבְקְעָה הָעִיר: וַיָּבֹאוּ כֹּל שָׂרֵי מֶלֶךְ־ ג
בָּבֶל וַיֵּשְׁבוּ בְּשַׁעַר הַתָּוֶךְ נֵרְגַל שַׂר־אֶצֶר סַמְגַּר־נְבוּ שַׂר־סְכִים רַב־
סָרִיס נֵרְגַל שַׂר־אֶצֶר רַב־מָג וְכָל־שְׁאֵרִית שָׂרֵי מֶלֶךְ־בָּבֶל: וַיְהִי כַּאֲשֶׁר ד
רָאָם צִדְקִיָּהוּ מֶלֶךְ־יְהוּדָה וְכָל ׀ אַנְשֵׁי הַמִּלְחָמָה וַיִּבְרְחוּ וַיֵּצְאוּ לַיְלָה
מִן־הָעִיר דֶּרֶךְ גַּן הַמֶּלֶךְ בְּשַׁעַר בֵּין הַחֹמֹתָיִם וַיֵּצֵא דֶּרֶךְ הָעֲרָבָה: וַיִּרְדְּפוּ ה
חֵיל־כַּשְׂדִּים אַחֲרֵיהֶם וַיַּשִּׂגוּ אֶת־צִדְקִיָּהוּ בְּעַרְבוֹת יְרֵחוֹ וַיִּקְחוּ אֹתוֹ
וַיַּעֲלֻהוּ אֶל־נְבוּכַדְרֶאצַּר מֶלֶךְ־בָּבֶל רִבְלָתָה בְּאֶרֶץ חֲמָת וַיְדַבֵּר אִתּוֹ
מִשְׁפָּטִים: וַיִּשְׁחַט מֶלֶךְ בָּבֶל אֶת־בְּנֵי צִדְקִיָּהוּ בְּרִבְלָה לְעֵינָיו וְאֵת כָּל־ ו
חֹרֵי יְהוּדָה שָׁחַט מֶלֶךְ בָּבֶל: וְאֶת־עֵינֵי צִדְקִיָּהוּ עִוֵּר וַיַּאַסְרֵהוּ בַּנְחֻשְׁתַּיִם ז
לָבִיא אֹתוֹ בָּבֶלָה: וְאֶת־בֵּית הַמֶּלֶךְ וְאֶת־בֵּית הָעָם שָׂרְפוּ הַכַּשְׂדִּים ח
בָּאֵשׁ וְאֶת־חֹמוֹת יְרוּשָׁלַ͏ִם נָתָצוּ: וְאֵת יֶתֶר הָעָם הַנִּשְׁאָרִים בָּעִיר וְאֶת־ ט
הַנֹּפְלִים אֲשֶׁר נָפְלוּ עָלָיו וְאֵת יֶתֶר הָעָם הַנִּשְׁאָרִים הֶגְלָה נְבוּזַרְאֲדָן
רַב־טַבָּחִים בָּבֶל: וּמִן־הָעָם הַדַּלִּים אֲשֶׁר אֵין־לָהֶם מְאוּמָה הִשְׁאִיר י
נְבוּזַרְאֲדָן רַב־טַבָּחִים בְּאֶרֶץ יְהוּדָה וַיִּתֵּן לָהֶם כְּרָמִים וִיגֵבִים בַּיּוֹם הַהוּא:
וַיְצַו נְבוּכַדְרֶאצַּר מֶלֶךְ־בָּבֶל עַל־יִרְמְיָהוּ בְּיַד נְבוּזַרְאֲדָן רַב־טַבָּחִים יא
לֵאמֹר: קָחֶנּוּ וְעֵינֶיךָ שִׂים עָלָיו וְאַל־תַּעַשׂ לוֹ מְאוּמָה רָע כִּי °אִם כ׳ ולא ק׳] יב
כַּאֲשֶׁר יְדַבֵּר אֵלֶיךָ כֵּן עֲשֵׂה עִמּוֹ: וַיִּשְׁלַח נְבוּזַרְאֲדָן רַב־טַבָּחִים יג
וּנְבוּשַׁזְבָּן רַב־סָרִיס וְנֵרְגַל שַׂר־אֶצֶר רַב־מָג וְכֹל רַבֵּי מֶלֶךְ־בָּבֶל:

38:22. The advisers and false prophets, who encouraged you to rebel against Babylonian rule (see *II Kings* 24:20). Your position was immeasurably worsened by their advice — and then they abandoned you.

38:23. You are at fault for the burning of the city.

38:27. No one knew the content of the king's conversation with Jeremiah, so the officers believed Jeremiah's story.

38:28. What happened is told in 39:3.
The familiar numbered chapters of Scriptures are

'Your allies have persuaded you and overcome you; your feet have been sunken into the mire, they have retreated backwards.'* [23] *And all your wives and children are being brought out to the Chaldeans; you [yourself] will not escape from their hand, for you will be seized by the hand of the king of Babylonia; and you will burn this city [down] in fire."**

The king swears Jeremiah to secrecy

[24] *Zedekiah told Jeremiah, "Let no man know about this conversation, and you will not die.* [25] *But if the officers hear that I have spoken to you, and they come to you and ask you, 'Tell us now what you spoke to the king — do not withhold it from us and then we will not kill you — and what did the king speak to you?'* [26] *Say to them, 'I was pouring out my supplication before the king, that he not send me back to the house of Jonathan to die there.'"*

[27] *All the officers came to Jeremiah and asked him; he told them according to all these words that the king had commanded [him], and they left him alone, for the matter had not been heard.** [28] *Jeremiah remained in the Courtyard of Confinement until the day Jerusalem was captured.*

39

Jerusalem falls
(See Appendix A, timelines 4-5)

*It happened when Jerusalem was captured** [1] *(in the ninth year of Zedekiah,* king of Judah, in the tenth month, Nebuchadrezzar king of Babylonia and all his army came to Jerusalem and laid siege to it;* [2] *and in the eleventh year of Zedekiah, in the fourth month, on the ninth of the month, the city was breached)* [3] *— all the officers of the king of Babylonia came and sat in the Middle Gate: Nargel-sarezer, Samgar-nebu, Sarsachim the chief captain, Nergal-sarezer the chief officer, and all the rest of the officers of the king of Babylonia.* [4] *It happened when Zedekiah king of Judah and all the men of war saw them: They fled and went forth from the city at night, by way of the king's garden, through the gate between the walls; [the king] went forth by way of the Arabah.* [5] *The Chaldean army pursued them and overtook Zedekiah at the plains of Jericho; they took him and brought him up to Nebuchadrezzar king of Babylonia at Riblah, in the land of Hamath, and he spoke [words of] judgment to him.* [6] *The king of Babylonia slaughtered Zedekiah's sons in Riblah before his eyes; and the king of Babylonia slaughtered all the noblemen*

Zedekiah is blinded and chained by Nebuchadnezzar

of Judah. [7] *He [also] blinded Zedekiah's eyes and bound him in leg-irons to bring him to Babylonia.* [8] *The Chaldeans burned [down] the king's palace and the houses of the people in fire, and they smashed the walls of Jerusalem.* [9] *The remainder of the people who were left in the city, the defectors who had surrendered to him, and the rest of the people who remained,** Nebuzaradan, the chief executioner, exiled to Babylonia.* [10] *But some of the poor people who owned nothing, Nebuzaradan the chief executioner left in the land of Judah, and he gave them vineyards and fields on that day.*

[11] *Nebuchadrezzar king of Babylonia gave charge of Jeremiah in the hand of Nebuzaradan the chief executioner saying,* [12] *"Take him, keep your eyes on him, and do not do him any harm; rather, as he says to you, so shall you do for him."*

Jeremiah in the hand of Nebuzaradan

[13] *So Nebuzaradan the chief executioner sent — as well as Nebushazban the chief captain and Nergal-sarezer the chief officer and all the officers of Babylonia —*

---

not of Jewish origin, but were devised by Christian Bible scholars and introduced into Hebrew editions by non-Jewish Venetian printers during the sixteenth century. Their use is limited to identification of verses, and is never considered authoritative regarding the beginning or ending of a topic in Scripture. Thus,

despite the new chapter number, the second clause of 38:28 and verses 1-3 of Ch. 39 form one continuous sentence with verses 1 and 2 being parenthetic.

39:1-10. This passage is very similar to *II Kings* 25:1-12. See also 52:4-16 below.

39:9. Those remaining outside the city (*Metzudos*).

יד וַיִּשְׁלְחוּ וַיִּקְחוּ אֶת־יִרְמְיָהוּ מֵחֲצַר הַמַּטָּרָה וַיִּתְּנוּ אֹתוֹ אֶל־גְּדַלְיָהוּ בֶּן־

טו אֲחִיקָם בֶּן־שָׁפָן לְהוֹצִאֵהוּ אֶל־הַבָּיִת וַיֵּשֶׁב בְּתוֹךְ הָעָם: וְאֶל־

טז יִרְמְיָהוּ הָיָה דְבַר־יְהוָה בִּהְיֹתוֹ עָצוּר בַּחֲצַר הַמַּטָּרָה לֵאמֹר: הָלוֹךְ וְאָמַרְתָּ

לְעֶבֶד־מֶלֶךְ הַכּוּשִׁי לֵאמֹר כֹּה־אָמַר יְהוָה צְבָאוֹת אֱלֹהֵי יִשְׂרָאֵל הִנְנִי

°מבי [°מֵבִיא ק] אֶת־דְּבָרַי אֶל־הָעִיר הַזֹּאת לְרָעָה וְלֹא לְטוֹבָה וְהָיוּ

יז לְפָנֶיךָ בַּיּוֹם הַהוּא: וְהִצַּלְתִּיךָ בַיּוֹם־הַהוּא נְאֻם־יְהוָה וְלֹא תִנָּתֵן בְּיַד

יח הָאֲנָשִׁים אֲשֶׁר־אַתָּה יָגוֹר מִפְּנֵיהֶם: כִּי מַלֵּט אֲמַלֶּטְךָ וּבַחֶרֶב לֹא תִפֹּל

מ א וְהָיְתָה לְךָ נַפְשְׁךָ לְשָׁלָל כִּי־בָטַחְתָּ בִּי נְאֻם־יְהוָה: הַדָּבָר אֲשֶׁר־הָיָה אֶל־

יִרְמְיָהוּ מֵאֵת יְהוָה אַחַר ׀ שַׁלַּח אֹתוֹ נְבוּזַרְאֲדָן רַב־טַבָּחִים מִן־הָרָמָה

בְּקַחְתּוֹ אֹתוֹ וְהוּא־אָסוּר בָּאזִקִּים בְּתוֹךְ כָּל־גָּלוּת יְרוּשָׁלַם וִיהוּדָה

ב הַמֻּגְלִים בָּבֶלָה: וַיִּקַּח רַב־טַבָּחִים לְיִרְמְיָהוּ וַיֹּאמֶר אֵלָיו יְהוָה אֱלֹהֶיךָ

ג דִּבֶּר אֶת־הָרָעָה הַזֹּאת אֶל־הַמָּקוֹם הַזֶּה: וַיָּבֵא וַיַּעַשׂ יְהוָה כַּאֲשֶׁר דִּבֵּר

כִּי־חֲטָאתֶם לַיהוָה וְלֹא־שְׁמַעְתֶּם בְּקוֹלוֹ וְהָיָה לָכֶם °דבר [°הַדָּבָר ק]

ד הַזֶּה: וְעַתָּה הִנֵּה פִתַּחְתִּיךָ הַיּוֹם מִן־הָאזִקִּים אֲשֶׁר עַל־יָדֶךָ אִם־טוֹב

בְּעֵינֶיךָ לָבוֹא אִתִּי בָבֶל בֹּא וְאָשִׂים אֶת־עֵינִי עָלֶיךָ וְאִם־רַע בְּעֵינֶיךָ

לָבוֹא־אִתִּי בָבֶל חֲדָל רְאֵה כָּל־הָאָרֶץ לְפָנֶיךָ אֶל־טוֹב וְאֶל־הַיָּשָׁר

ה בְּעֵינֶיךָ לָלֶכֶת שָׁמָּה לֵךְ: וְעוֹדֶנּוּ לֹא־יָשׁוּב וְשֻׁבָה אֶל־גְּדַלְיָה בֶן־אֲחִיקָם

בֶּן־שָׁפָן אֲשֶׁר הִפְקִיד מֶלֶךְ־בָּבֶל בְּעָרֵי יְהוּדָה וְשֵׁב אִתּוֹ בְּתוֹךְ הָעָם אוֹ

אֶל־כָּל־הַיָּשָׁר בְּעֵינֶיךָ לָלֶכֶת לֵךְ וַיִּתֶּן־לוֹ רַב־טַבָּחִים אֲרֻחָה וּמַשְׂאֵת

ו וַיְשַׁלְּחֵהוּ: וַיָּבֹא יִרְמְיָהוּ אֶל־גְּדַלְיָה בֶן־אֲחִיקָם הַמִּצְפָּתָה וַיֵּשֶׁב אִתּוֹ

ז בְּתוֹךְ הָעָם הַנִּשְׁאָרִים בָּאָרֶץ: וַיִּשְׁמְעוּ כָל־שָׂרֵי הַחֲיָלִים אֲשֶׁר

בַּשָּׂדֶה הֵמָּה וְאַנְשֵׁיהֶם כִּי־הִפְקִיד מֶלֶךְ־בָּבֶל אֶת־גְּדַלְיָהוּ בֶן־אֲחִיקָם

בָּאָרֶץ וְכִי ׀ הִפְקִיד אִתּוֹ אֲנָשִׁים וְנָשִׁים וָטָף וּמִדַּלַּת הָאָרֶץ מֵאֲשֶׁר לֹא־

ח הָגְלוּ בָּבֶלָה: וַיָּבֹאוּ אֶל־גְּדַלְיָה הַמִּצְפָּתָה וְיִשְׁמָעֵאל בֶּן־נְתַנְיָהוּ וְיוֹחָנָן

וְיוֹנָתָן בְּנֵי־קָרֵחַ וּשְׂרָיָה בֶן־תַּנְחֻמֶת וּבְנֵי ׀ °עופי [°עֵיפַי ק] הַנְּטֹפָתִי

ט וִיזַנְיָהוּ בֶּן־הַמַּעֲכָתִי הֵמָּה וְאַנְשֵׁיהֶם: וַיִּשָּׁבַע לָהֶם גְּדַלְיָהוּ בֶן־אֲחִיקָם

בֶּן־שָׁפָן וּלְאַנְשֵׁיהֶם לֵאמֹר אַל־תִּירְאוּ מֵעֲבוֹד הַכַּשְׂדִּים שְׁבוּ בָאָרֶץ

י וְעִבְדוּ אֶת־מֶלֶךְ בָּבֶל וְיִטַב לָכֶם: וַאֲנִי הִנְנִי יֹשֵׁב בַּמִּצְפָּה לַעֲמֹד לִפְנֵי

הַכַּשְׂדִּים אֲשֶׁר יָבֹאוּ אֵלֵינוּ וְאַתֶּם אִסְפוּ יַיִן וְקַיִץ וְשֶׁמֶן וְשִׂמוּ בִּכְלֵיכֶם

יא וּשְׁבוּ בְּעָרֵיכֶם אֲשֶׁר־תְּפַשְׂתֶּם: וְגַם כָּל־הַיְּהוּדִים אֲשֶׁר־בְּמוֹאָב ׀ וּבִבְנֵי

עַמּוֹן וּבֶאֱדוֹם וַאֲשֶׁר בְּכָל־הָאֲרָצוֹת שָׁמְעוּ כִּי־נָתַן מֶלֶךְ־בָּבֶל שְׁאֵרִית

39:14. Though Nebuzaradan sent for Jeremiah, the prophet had already been removed from the Courtyard of Confinement and taken away in chains (40:1). Later, Nebuzaradan found him among the exiles and carried out Nebuchadnezzar's orders, as our verse states (*Radak*).

40:1. This prophecy is not related until 42:7. Until then, Scripture describes the historical background of the prophecy (*Rashi*).

Regarding Jeremiah's being bound in chains, see 39:14.

¹⁴ they sent [for him]; but [others] had already taken Jeremiah out of the Courtyard of Confinement. * They gave him over to Gedaliah son of Ahikam son of Shaphan, to remove him to [Gedaliah's] house, and he dwelt among the people.

¹⁵ The word of HASHEM had come to Jeremiah while he was in the Courtyard of *Ebed-* Confinement, saying, ¹⁶ "Go and say to Ebed-melech the Cushite, saying: Thus *melech's* said HASHEM, Master of Legions, the God of Israel: Behold, I am bringing about *reward* the fulfillment of My words concerning this city, for evil and not for good, and they will [take place] before you on that day. ¹⁷ But I will rescue you on that day — the word of HASHEM — and you will not be given over into the hand of the men of whom you are afraid. ¹⁸ For I shall surely rescue you; you will not fall by the sword and you will have your life for booty, for you trusted in Me — the word of HASHEM."

40 ¹ The word that came to Jeremiah from HASHEM, * after Nebuzaradan, the chief executioner, sent him off from Ramah, when he had taken him [from where he had been] bound in chains * among all the exile of Jerusalem and Judah who were being exiled to Babylonia:

² The chief executioner took Jeremiah [aside] and said to him, "HASHEM, your God, foretold this evil concerning this place; ³ and HASHEM brought it about and did as He said, because you sinned to HASHEM and did not heed His voice, so this *Jeremiah* matter befell you. ⁴ Now, behold, I have released you today from the chains that *unchained* were on your arm. If it is proper in your eyes to come with me to Babylonia, come, and I will set my eye on you; * but if it is improper in your eyes to come with me to Babylonia, refrain [from doing so]. See, the entire land is before you; to wherever it is good and proper in your eyes to go, there shall you go!" ⁵ He had *Gedaliah* not yet turned back [when he was told], * "Turn back to Gedaliah son of Ahikam *appointed* son of Shaphan, whom the king of Babylonia has appointed over the cities of *governor* Judah, and stay with him among the people; or go to wherever it is proper in your eyes to go." The chief executioner then gave him a grant and a gift and sent him off. ⁶ Jeremiah came to Gedaliah son of Ahikam at Mizpah, and he settled with him, in the midst of the people who remained in the land.

⁷ All the officers of the army that were in the field — they and their men — heard that the king of Babylonia had appointed Gedaliah son of Ahikam over the land, and that he had entrusted him with men, women and children, and some of the *The people* poor people of the land who were not exiled to Babylonia, ⁸ so they came to *rally to* Gedaliah at Mizpah, along with Ishmael son of Nethaniah, Johanan and Jonathan *Gedaliah* the sons of Kareah, Seraiah son of Tanhumeth, the sons of Ephai the Netophathite, and Jezaniah son of the Maacathite, they and their men. ⁹ Gedaliah son of Ahikam son of Shaphan swore to them and their men, saying, "Do not be afraid of serving the Chaldeans; settle in the land and serve the king of Babylonia and it will be well for you. ¹⁰ As for me, behold I will stay in Mizpah, standing before the Chaldeans * who will come to us; and as for you, gather wine, dried fruits, and oil and store it in your containers, and settle in your cities that you have occupied."

¹¹ Also all the Jews who were in Moab and with the Children of Ammon and in Edom and in all the lands heard that the king of Babylonia had left a remnant

---

40:4. That is, I will look after you.
40:5. Though Jeremiah had not answered him, Nebuzaradan saw that he was inclined to return to Judah, and suggested that he join Gedaliah's community, though he was free to settle wherever he wished (*Radak*). According

to the Sages, Jeremiah couldn't decide what would be best for the Jews, so God told him, "Go to Gedaliah."
40:10. I will deal with the Chaldean occupiers, while you reestablish your normal routines, beginning with the preparations for the winter.

יב לִֽיהוּדָ֗ה וְכִֽי־הִפְקִ֤יד עֲלֵיהֶם֙ אֶת־גְּדַלְיָ֨הוּ֙ בֶּן־אֲחִיקָ֣ם בֶּן־שָׁפָ֔ן וַיֵּ֥שְׁבוּ כׇל־
הַיְּהוּדִ֗ים מִכׇּל־הַמְּקֹמוֹת֙ אֲשֶׁ֣ר נִדְּחוּ־שָׁ֔ם וַיָּבֹ֥אוּ אֶֽרֶץ־יְהוּדָ֛ה אֶל־גְּדַלְיָ֖הוּ
יג הַמִּצְפָּ֑תָה וַיַּאַסְפ֛וּ יַ֥יִן וָקַ֖יִץ הַרְבֵּ֥ה מְאֹֽד׃

יד וְכׇל־שָׂרֵ֤י הַחֲיָלִים֙ אֲשֶׁ֣ר בַּשָּׂדֶ֔ה בָּ֥אוּ אֶל־גְּדַלְיָ֖הוּ הַמִּצְפָּ֑תָה וַיֹּאמְר֣וּ אֵלָ֗יו
הֲיָדֹ֣עַ תֵּדַ֔ע כִּ֞י בַּעְלִ֣יס ׀ מֶ֣לֶךְ בְּנֵֽי־עַמּ֗וֹן שָׁלַ֛ח אֶת־יִשְׁמָעֵ֥אל בֶּן־נְתַנְיָ֖ה
טו לְהַכֹּתְךָ֣ נָ֑פֶשׁ וְלֹא־הֶאֱמִ֥ין לָהֶ֖ם גְּדַלְיָ֥הוּ בֶּן־אֲחִיקָֽם׃ וְיֽוֹחָנָ֣ן בֶּן־קָרֵ֡חַ אָמַ֣ר
אֶל־גְּדַלְיָ֩הוּ֩ בַסֵּ֨תֶר בַּמִּצְפָּ֜ה לֵאמֹ֗ר אֵ֤לְכָה נָּא֙ וְאַכֶּה֙ אֶת־יִשְׁמָעֵ֣אל
בֶּן־נְתַנְיָ֔ה וְאִ֖ישׁ לֹ֣א יֵדָ֑ע לָ֣מָּה יַכֶּ֣כָּה נֶּ֗פֶשׁ וְנָפֹ֙צוּ֙ כׇּל־יְהוּדָה֙ הַנִּקְבָּצִ֣ים
טז אֵלֶ֔יךָ וְאָבְדָ֖ה שְׁאֵרִ֥ית יְהוּדָֽה׃ וַיֹּ֩אמֶר֩ גְּדַלְיָ֨הוּ בֶן־אֲחִיקָ֜ם אֶל־יוֹחָנָ֣ן בֶּן־
קָרֵ֗חַ אַל־°תַּעֲשֵׂ אֶת־הַדָּבָ֣ר הַזֶּ֑ה כִּֽי־שֶׁ֛קֶר אַתָּ֥ה דֹבֵ֖ר אֶל־
יִשְׁמָעֵֽאל׃   וַיְהִ֣י ׀ בַּחֹ֣דֶשׁ הַשְּׁבִיעִ֗י בָּ֣א יִשְׁמָעֵ֣אל בֶּן־נְתַנְיָ֣ה   **מא**

מא א בֶן־אֱלִ֠ישָׁמָ֠ע מִזֶּ֨רַע הַמְּלוּכָ֜ה וְרַבֵּ֤י הַמֶּ֙לֶךְ֙ וַעֲשָׂרָ֤ה אֲנָשִׁים֙ אִתּ֔וֹ אֶל־
ב גְּדַלְיָ֥הוּ בֶן־אֲחִיקָ֖ם הַמִּצְפָּ֑תָה וַיֹּ֨אכְלוּ שָׁ֥ם לֶ֛חֶם יַחְדָּ֖ו בַּמִּצְפָּֽה׃ וַיָּ֩קׇם֩
יִשְׁמָעֵ֨אל בֶּן־נְתַנְיָ֜ה וַעֲשֶׂ֥רֶת הָאֲנָשִׁ֣ים ׀ אֲשֶׁר־הָי֣וּ אִתּ֗וֹ וַ֠יַּכּ֠וּ אֶת־גְּדַלְיָ֨הוּ
בֶן־אֲחִיקָ֧ם בֶּן־שָׁפָ֛ן בַּחֶ֖רֶב וַיָּ֣מֶת אֹת֑וֹ אֲשֶׁר־הִפְקִ֥יד מֶֽלֶךְ־בָּבֶ֖ל בָּאָֽרֶץ׃
ג וְאֵ֣ת כׇּל־הַיְּהוּדִ֗ים אֲשֶׁר־הָי֨וּ אִתּ֤וֹ אֶת־גְּדַלְיָ֙הוּ֙ בַּמִּצְפָּ֔ה וְאֶת־הַכַּשְׂדִּ֖ים
ד אֲשֶׁ֣ר נִמְצְאוּ־שָׁ֑ם אֵ֚ת אַנְשֵׁ֣י הַמִּלְחָמָ֔ה הִכָּ֖ה יִשְׁמָעֵֽאל׃ וַיְהִ֗י בַּיּ֥וֹם הַשֵּׁנִ֛י
ה לְהָמִ֥ית אֶת־גְּדַלְיָ֖הוּ וְאִ֥ישׁ לֹ֥א יָדָֽע׃ וַיָּבֹ֣אוּ אֲ֠נָשִׁ֠ים מִשְּׁכֶ֞ם מִשִּׁל֤וֹ
וּמִשֹּֽׁמְרוֹן֙ שְׁמֹנִ֣ים אִ֔ישׁ מְגֻלְּחֵ֥י זָקָ֛ן וּקְרֻעֵ֥י בְגָדִ֖ים וּמִתְגֹּדְדִ֑ים וּמִנְחָ֤ה
ו וּלְבוֹנָה֙ בְּיָדָ֔ם לְהָבִ֖יא בֵּ֥ית יְהֹוָֽה׃ וַ֠יֵּצֵ֠א יִשְׁמָעֵ֨אל בֶּן־נְתַנְיָ֤ה לִקְרָאתָם֙ מִן־
הַמִּצְפָּ֔ה הֹלֵ֥ךְ הָלֹ֖ךְ וּבֹכֶ֑ה וַֽיְהִי֙ כִּפְגֹ֣שׁ אֹתָ֔ם וַיֹּ֣אמֶר אֲלֵיהֶ֔ם בֹּ֖אוּ אֶל־
ז גְּדַלְיָ֥הוּ בֶן־אֲחִיקָֽם׃ וַיְהִ֕י כְּבוֹאָ֖ם אֶל־תּ֣וֹךְ הָעִ֑יר וַיִּשְׁחָטֵ֞ם יִשְׁמָעֵ֤אל בֶּן־
ח נְתַנְיָה֙ אֶל־תּ֣וֹךְ הַבּ֔וֹר ה֖וּא וְהָאֲנָשִׁ֥ים אֲשֶׁר־אִתּֽוֹ׃ וַעֲשָׂרָ֨ה אֲנָשִׁ֜ים נִמְצְאוּ־
בָ֗ם וַיֹּאמְר֤וּ אֶל־יִשְׁמָעֵאל֙ אַל־תְּמִתֵ֔נוּ כִּֽי־יֶשׁ־לָ֤נוּ מַטְמֹנִים֙ בַּשָּׂדֶ֔ה חִטִּ֣ים
ט וּשְׂעֹרִ֗ים וְשֶׁ֤מֶן וּדְבָ֔שׁ וַיֶּחְדַּ֕ל וְלֹ֥א הֱמִיתָ֖ם בְּת֣וֹךְ אֲחֵיהֶֽם׃ וְהַבּ֗וֹר אֲשֶׁ֣ר
הִשְׁלִ֤יךְ שָׁם֙ יִשְׁמָעֵ֔אל אֵ֣ת ׀ כׇּל־פִּגְרֵ֣י הָאֲנָשִׁ֗ים אֲשֶׁ֤ר הִכָּה֙ בְּיַד־גְּדַלְיָ֔הוּ
ה֗וּא אֲשֶׁ֤ר עָשָׂה֙ הַמֶּ֣לֶךְ אָסָ֔א מִפְּנֵ֖י בַּעְשָׁ֣א מֶֽלֶךְ־יִשְׂרָאֵ֑ל אֹת֣וֹ מִלֵּ֛א
י יִשְׁמָעֵ֥אל בֶּן־נְתַנְיָ֖הוּ חֲלָלִֽים׃ וַיִּ֣שְׁבְּ ׀ יִ֠שְׁמָעֵ֠אל אֶת־כׇּל־שְׁאֵרִ֨ית הָעָ֜ם
אֲשֶׁ֣ר בַּמִּצְפָּ֗ה אֶת־בְּנ֤וֹת הַמֶּ֙לֶךְ֙ וְאֶת־כׇּל־הָעָם֙ הַנִּשְׁאָרִ֣ים בַּמִּצְפָּ֔ה אֲשֶׁ֣ר
הִפְקִ֗יד נְבֽוּזַרְאֲדָן֙ רַב־טַבָּחִ֔ים אֶת־גְּדַלְיָ֖הוּ בֶּן־אֲחִיקָ֑ם וַיִּשְׁבֵּם֙ יִשְׁמָעֵ֣אל
יא בֶּן־נְתַנְיָ֔ה וַיֵּ֕לֶךְ לַעֲבֹ֖ר אֶל־בְּנֵ֥י עַמּֽוֹן׃   וַיִּשְׁמַ֤ע יֽוֹחָנָן֙ בֶּן־
קָרֵ֔חַ וְכׇל־שָׂרֵ֥י הַחֲיָלִ֖ים אֲשֶׁ֣ר אִתּ֑וֹ אֵ֤ת כׇּל־הָרָעָה֙ אֲשֶׁ֣ר עָשָׂ֔ה יִשְׁמָעֵ֖אל
יב בֶּן־נְתַנְיָֽה׃ וַיִּקְחוּ֙ אֶת־כׇּל־הָ֣אֲנָשִׁ֔ים וַיֵּ֣לְכ֔וּ לְהִלָּחֵ֖ם עִם־יִשְׁמָעֵ֣אל בֶּן־
יג נְתַנְיָ֑ה וַיִּמְצְא֣וּ אֹת֔וֹ אֶל־מַ֥יִם רַבִּ֖ים אֲשֶׁ֣ר בְּגִבְע֑וֹן וַיְהִ֗י כִּרְא֤וֹת כׇּל־הָעָם֙

for Judah, and that he had appointed Gedaliah son of Ahikam son of Shaphan over them. ¹² So the Jews returned from all the places where they had been dispersed; and they came to the land of Judah, to Gedaliah in Mizpah, and they gathered together a great deal of wine and dried fruit.

Unheeded ¹³ Johanan son of Kareah and all the officers of the army that had been in the **warning** field came to Gedaliah at Mizpah. ¹⁴ They said to him, "Do you know that Baalis, king of the Children of Ammon, has sent Ishmael son of Nethaniah to assassinate you?" But Gedaliah son of Ahikam did not believe them.

¹⁵ Johanan son of Kareah spoke to Gedaliah secretly in Mizpah, saying, "Let me go and kill Ishmael son of Nethaniah, and no one will know! Why should he kill you, and then all of Judah who have gathered to you will be scattered, and the remnant of Judah lost?"

¹⁶ But Gedaliah son of Ahikam said to Johanan son of Kareah, "Do not do this thing, for you are speaking falsely about Ishmael!"

41 ¹ It happened in the seventh month that Ishmael son of Nethaniah son of
Gedaliah's Elishama, who was of the royal family, came to Gedaliah son of Ahikam at
assassination Mizpah, and with him the king's captains* and ten [other] men; and they ate a meal together there at Mizpah. ² Ishmael son of Nethaniah arose, along with the ten men who were with him, and struck Gedaliah son of Ahikam son of Shaphan by the sword, and killed him, the one whom the king of Babylonia had appointed over the land. ³ And Ishmael struck down all the Jews who were with him, with Gedaliah in Mizpah and the Chaldeans who were found there, the men of war.

⁴ It happened on the second day after Gedaliah's assassination, when no one knew about it [yet], ⁵ that men came from Shechem, from Shiloh and from Samaria, eighty men, with shaven beards and torn clothing, and having cut [their flesh]; offering and frankincense were in their hand to bring to the Temple of
Ishmael's HASHEM. * ⁶ Ishmael son of Nethaniah went out towards them from Mizpah,
further weeping as he went. When he met them he said to them, "Come to Gedaliah son
treachery of Ahikam!" ⁷ As soon as they came inside the city, Ishmael son of Nethaniah, he and the men who were with him, slaughtered them into the pit. ⁸ Ten men were found among them who said to Ishmael, "Do not kill us, for we have treasures hidden in the countryside — wheat, barley, oil, and honey." So [Ishmael] refrained from killing them along with their brethren. ⁹ (The pit into which Ishmael threw all the bodies of the men he had struck in the wake of Gedaliah's [murder] was the [same pit] that King Asa had made on account of Baasa king of Israel;* Ishmael son of Nethaniah filled that one with corpses.)

¹⁰ Ishmael took captive all the remnant of the people who were in Mizpah, the king's daughters and all the people who remained in Mizpah, over whom Nebuzaradan, the chief executioner, had appointed Gedaliah son of Ahikam; Ishmael son of Nethaniah took them captive and went to cross over [the Jordan] to the Children of Ammon.

¹¹ Johanan son of Kareah and all the army officers who were with him heard of all the evil that Ishmael son of Nethaniah had done. ¹² They took all the people and went to fight against Ishmael son of Nethaniah. They encountered him at the Great Water [Pool] that is in Gibeon. ¹³ It happened that as soon as all the captives

---

41:1. The advisers and ministers of Zedekiah who escaped execution and exile.

41:5. And on the way to Jerusalem they heard of the destruction of the Temple, which was the cause of their outward signs of deep anguish.

41:9. Asa had fortified Mizpah during the course of the unceasing warfare between these two kings. See *I Kings* 15:22.

אֲשֶׁר אֶת־יִשְׁמָעֵאל אֶת־יוֹחָנָן בֶּן־קָרֵחַ וְאֵת כָּל־שָׂרֵי הַחֲיָלִים אֲשֶׁר
יד אִתּוֹ וַיִּשְׂמָחוּ: וַיָּסֹבּוּ כָּל־הָעָם אֲשֶׁר־שָׁבָה יִשְׁמָעֵאל מִן־הַמִּצְפָּה וַיָּשֻׁבוּ
טו וַיֵּלְכוּ אֶל־יוֹחָנָן בֶּן־קָרֵחַ: וְיִשְׁמָעֵאל בֶּן־נְתַנְיָה נִמְלַט בִּשְׁמֹנָה אֲנָשִׁים
טז מִפְּנֵי יוֹחָנָן וַיֵּלֶךְ אֶל־בְּנֵי עַמּוֹן: וַיִּקַּח יוֹחָנָן בֶּן־קָרֵחַ וְכָל־שָׂרֵי
הַחֲיָלִים אֲשֶׁר־אִתּוֹ אֵת כָּל־שְׁאֵרִית הָעָם אֲשֶׁר הֵשִׁיב מֵאֵת יִשְׁמָעֵאל
בֶּן־נְתַנְיָה מִן־הַמִּצְפָּה אַחַר הִכָּה אֶת־גְּדַלְיָה בֶּן־אֲחִיקָם גְּבָרִים אַנְשֵׁי
יז הַמִּלְחָמָה וְנָשִׁים וְטַף וְסָרִסִים אֲשֶׁר הֵשִׁיב מִגִּבְעוֹן: וַיֵּלְכוּ וַיֵּשְׁבוּ בְּגֵרוּת
יח °כְּמוֹהֶם [°כִּמְהָם ק] אֲשֶׁר־אֵצֶל בֵּית לָחֶם לָלֶכֶת לָבוֹא מִצְרָיִם: מִפְּנֵי
הַכַּשְׂדִּים כִּי יָרְאוּ מִפְּנֵיהֶם כִּי־הִכָּה יִשְׁמָעֵאל בֶּן־נְתַנְיָה אֶת־גְּדַלְיָהוּ בֶּן־
מב **א** אֲחִיקָם אֲשֶׁר־הִפְקִיד מֶלֶךְ־בָּבֶל בָּאָרֶץ: וַיִּגְּשׁוּ כָּל־שָׂרֵי
הַחֲיָלִים וְיוֹחָנָן בֶּן־קָרֵחַ וִיזַנְיָה בֶּן־הוֹשַׁעְיָה וְכָל־הָעָם מִקָּטֹן וְעַד־גָּדוֹל:
ב וַיֹּאמְרוּ אֶל־יִרְמְיָהוּ הַנָּבִיא תִּפָּל־נָא תְחִנָּתֵנוּ לְפָנֶיךָ וְהִתְפַּלֵּל בַּעֲדֵנוּ
אֶל־יְהוָה אֱלֹהֶיךָ בְּעַד כָּל־הַשְּׁאֵרִית הַזֹּאת כִּי־נִשְׁאַרְנוּ מְעַט מֵהַרְבֵּה
ג כַּאֲשֶׁר עֵינֶיךָ רֹאוֹת אֹתָנוּ: וְיַגֶּד־לָנוּ יְהוָה אֱלֹהֶיךָ אֶת־הַדֶּרֶךְ אֲשֶׁר נֵלֶךְ־
ד בָּהּ וְאֶת־הַדָּבָר אֲשֶׁר נַעֲשֶׂה: וַיֹּאמֶר אֲלֵיהֶם יִרְמְיָהוּ הַנָּבִיא שָׁמַעְתִּי הִנְנִי
מִתְפַּלֵּל אֶל־יְהוָה אֱלֹהֵיכֶם כְּדִבְרֵיכֶם וְהָיָה כָּל־הַדָּבָר אֲשֶׁר־יַעֲנֶה יְהוָה
ה אֶתְכֶם אַגִּיד לָכֶם לֹא־אֶמְנַע מִכֶּם דָּבָר: וְהֵמָּה אָמְרוּ אֶל־יִרְמְיָהוּ יְהִי
יְהוָה בָּנוּ לְעֵד אֱמֶת וְנֶאֱמָן אִם־לֹא כְּכָל־הַדָּבָר אֲשֶׁר יִשְׁלָחֲךָ יְהוָה
ו אֱלֹהֶיךָ אֵלֵינוּ כֵּן נַעֲשֶׂה: אִם־טוֹב וְאִם־רָע בְּקוֹל ׀ יְהוָה אֱלֹהֵינוּ אֲשֶׁר
°אֲנוּ [°אֲנַחְנוּ ק] שֹׁלְחִים אֹתְךָ אֵלָיו נִשְׁמָע לְמַעַן אֲשֶׁר יִיטַב־לָנוּ כִּי
ז נִשְׁמַע בְּקוֹל יְהוָה אֱלֹהֵינוּ: וַיְהִי מִקֵּץ עֲשֶׂרֶת יָמִים וַיְהִי דְבַר־
ח יְהוָה אֶל־יִרְמְיָהוּ: וַיִּקְרָא אֶל־יוֹחָנָן בֶּן־קָרֵחַ וְאֶל כָּל־שָׂרֵי הַחֲיָלִים אֲשֶׁר
ט אִתּוֹ וּלְכָל־הָעָם לְמִקָּטֹן וְעַד־גָּדוֹל: וַיֹּאמֶר אֲלֵיהֶם כֹּה־אָמַר יְהוָה אֱלֹהֵי
י יִשְׂרָאֵל אֲשֶׁר שְׁלַחְתֶּם אֹתִי אֵלָיו לְהַפִּיל תְּחִנַּתְכֶם לְפָנָיו: אִם־שׁוֹב תֵּשְׁבוּ
בָּאָרֶץ הַזֹּאת וּבָנִיתִי אֶתְכֶם וְלֹא אֶהֱרֹס וְנָטַעְתִּי אֶתְכֶם וְלֹא אֶתּוֹשׁ כִּי
יא נִחַמְתִּי אֶל־הָרָעָה אֲשֶׁר עָשִׂיתִי לָכֶם: אַל־תִּירְאוּ מִפְּנֵי מֶלֶךְ בָּבֶל אֲשֶׁר־
אַתֶּם יְרֵאִים מִפָּנָיו אַל־תִּירְאוּ מִמֶּנּוּ נְאֻם־יְהוָה כִּי־אִתְּכֶם אָנִי לְהוֹשִׁיעַ
יב אֶתְכֶם וּלְהַצִּיל אֶתְכֶם מִיָּדוֹ: וְאֶתֵּן לָכֶם רַחֲמִים וְרִחַם אֶתְכֶם וְהֵשִׁיב
יג אֶתְכֶם אֶל־אַדְמַתְכֶם: וְאִם־אֹמְרִים אַתֶּם לֹא נֵשֵׁב בָּאָרֶץ הַזֹּאת לְבִלְתִּי
יד שְׁמֹעַ בְּקוֹל יְהוָה אֱלֹהֵיכֶם: לֵאמֹר לֹא כִּי אֶרֶץ מִצְרַיִם נָבוֹא אֲשֶׁר לֹא־
נִרְאֶה מִלְחָמָה וְקוֹל שׁוֹפָר לֹא נִשְׁמָע וְלַלֶּחֶם לֹא־נִרְעָב וְשָׁם נֵשֵׁב:
טו וְעַתָּה לָכֵן שִׁמְעוּ דְבַר־יְהוָה שְׁאֵרִית יְהוּדָה כֹּה־אָמַר יְהוָה צְבָאוֹת
אֱלֹהֵי יִשְׂרָאֵל אִם־אַתֶּם שׂוֹם תְּשִׂמוּן פְּנֵיכֶם לָבֹא מִצְרַיִם וּבָאתֶם לָגוּר
טז שָׁם: וְהָיְתָה הַחֶרֶב אֲשֶׁר אַתֶּם יְרֵאִים מִמֶּנָּה שָׁם תַּשִּׂיג אֶתְכֶם בְּאֶרֶץ

who were with Ishmael saw Johanan son of Kareah and all the army officers with him, they rejoiced. [14] *And all the people whom Ishmael had taken captive from Mizpah turned back and went over to Johanan son of Kareah.* [15] *Ishmael son of Nethaniah escaped from Johanan with eight men, and he went to the Children of Ammon.*

In the aftermath [16] *Johanan son of Kareah and all the army officers with him then took the entire remnant of the people, whom he had brought back from Ishmael son of Nethaniah, from Mizpah, after he had struck down Gedaliah son of Ahikam, men who were warriors, women, children, and officials whom he had brought back from Gibeon,* [17] *and they went and settled in Chimham's Dwelling, which is near Beth-lehem, intending to go on to Egypt,* [18] *away from the Chaldeans, for they feared them, for Ishmael son of Nethaniah had murdered Gedaliah son of Ahikam, whom the king of Babylonia had appointed over the land.*

42

Jeremiah is asked to pray

[1] **A**ll the army officers and Johanan son of Kareah and Jezaniah son of Hoshaiah and all the people, from the smallest to the greatest, approached, [2] and said to Jeremiah the prophet, "May our supplication please be acceptable to you, and may you pray on our behalf, to HASHEM your God, on behalf of all this remnant, for we are left as few out of many, as your eyes see us. [3] And may HASHEM your God tell us the way in which we should go and the thing we should do."

[4] Jeremiah the prophet said to them, "I have heard. Behold, I will pray to HASHEM your God, as you have said; and it shall be that whatever HASHEM will answer you, I will tell you; I will not withhold anything from you."

[5] They said to Jeremiah, "Let HASHEM be a true and faithful witness against us, if we do not act according to everything that HASHEM your God tells you concerning us. [6] Whether for better or for worse, we will obey the voice of HASHEM our God, to Whom we are sending you, in order that it should be good for us when we listen to the voice of HASHEM our God."

[7] It happened at the end of ten days, that the word of HASHEM came to Jeremiah. [8] He called Johanan son of Kareah, all the army officers who were with him and all the people, from the smallest to the greatest, [9] and he said to them: "Thus said HASHEM, God of Israel, before Whom you have sent me to pour forth your supplications:

Stay here; do not seek refuge in Egypt

[10] If you stay in this land, I will build you [up] and I will not destroy, and I will plant you and not uproot; for I have relented of the misfortune that I have brought upon you. [11] Do not be afraid of the king of Babylonia of whom you are afraid; do not be afraid of him — the word of HASHEM — for I am with you to save you and rescue you from his hand. [12] I will show you mercy, and he will have mercy on you and return you* to your land. [13] But if you say, 'We shall not stay in this land,' not heeding the voice of HASHEM your God, [14] saying, 'No, but to the land of Egypt shall we go, so that we will not see war nor hear the sound of the shofar [in battle] nor hunger for bread, and there shall we settle' — [15] then hear now the word of HASHEM, O remnant of Judah! Thus said HASHEM, Master of Legions, God of Israel: If you would turn your face to go to Egypt and you will come to sojourn there, [16] the very sword of which you are afraid will reach you there in the land of

---

42:12. That is, Nebuchadnezzar will return the majority of the Jewish people from Babylonia back to *Eretz Yisrael.*

מִצְרַ֔יִם וְהָרָעָ֑ב אֲשֶׁר־אַתֶּ֣ם ׀ דְּאָגִ֣ים מִמֶּ֑נּוּ שָׁ֣ם יִדְבַּ֧ק אַחֲרֵיכֶ֛ם מִצְרַ֖יִם

יז וְשָׁ֣ם תָּמֻֽתוּ: וְיִֽהְי֣וּ כָל־הָאֲנָשִׁ֗ים אֲשֶׁר־שָׂ֤מוּ אֶת־פְּנֵיהֶם֙ לָב֣וֹא מִצְרַ֔יִם לָג֣וּר שָׁ֔ם יָמ֕וּתוּ בַּחֶ֖רֶב בָּרָעָ֣ב וּבַדָּ֑בֶר וְלֹא־יִהְיֶ֤ה לָהֶם֙ שָׂרִ֣יד וּפָלִ֔יט מִפְּנֵ֣י

יח הָ֣רָעָ֔ה אֲשֶׁ֥ר אֲנִ֖י מֵבִ֥יא עֲלֵיהֶֽם: כִּי֩ כֹ֨ה אָמַ֜ר יְהוָ֣ה צְבָא֗וֹת אֱלֹהֵ֣י יִשְׂרָאֵ֔ל כַּאֲשֶׁר֩ נִתַּ֨ךְ אַפִּ֜י וַחֲמָתִ֗י עַל־יֹֽשְׁבֵי֙ יְר֣וּשָׁלִַ֔ם כֵּ֣ן תִּתַּ֤ךְ חֲמָתִי֙ עֲלֵיכֶ֔ם בְּבֹאֲכֶ֖ם מִצְרָ֑יִם וִהְיִיתֶ֞ם לְאָלָ֤ה וּלְשַׁמָּה֙ וְלִקְלָלָ֣ה וּלְחֶרְפָּ֔ה וְלֹֽא־תִרְא֥וּ

יט ע֖וֹד אֶת־הַמָּק֥וֹם הַזֶּֽה: דִּבֶּ֨ר יְהוָ֤ה עֲלֵיכֶם֙ שְׁאֵרִ֣ית יְהוּדָ֔ה אַל־תָּבֹ֖אוּ מִצְרָ֑יִם יָדֹ֙עַ֙ תֵּֽדְע֔וּ כִּֽי־הַעִידֹ֥תִי בָכֶ֖ם הַיּֽוֹם: כִּ֣י °הִתְעֵתֶם֮ [°הִתְעֵיתֶם֮ ק]

כ בְּנַפְשֽׁוֹתֵיכֶם֒ כִּֽי־אַתֶּ֞ם שְׁלַחְתֶּ֣ם אֹתִ֗י אֶל־יְהוָ֤ה אֱלֹֽהֵיכֶם֙ לֵאמֹ֔ר הִתְפַּלֵּ֣ל בַּעֲדֵ֗נוּ אֶל־יְהוָ֣ה אֱלֹהֵ֔ינוּ וּכְכֹל֩ אֲשֶׁ֨ר יֹאמַ֜ר יְהוָ֧ה אֱלֹהֵ֛ינוּ כֵּ֥ן הַגֶּד־לָ֖נוּ

כא וְעָשִֽׂינוּ: וָאַגִּ֥ד לָכֶ֖ם הַיּ֑וֹם וְלֹ֣א שְׁמַעְתֶּ֗ם בְּקוֹל֙ יְהוָ֣ה אֱלֹֽהֵיכֶ֔ם וּלְכֹ֖ל אֲשֶׁר־

כב שְׁלָחַ֥נִי אֲלֵיכֶֽם: וְעַתָּ֖ה יָדֹ֣עַ תֵּֽדְע֑וּ כִּ֗י בַּחֶ֛רֶב בָּרָעָ֥ב וּבַדֶּ֖בֶר תָּמ֑וּתוּ בַּמָּקוֹם֙

מג א אֲשֶׁ֣ר חֲפַצְתֶּ֔ם לָב֖וֹא לָג֥וּר שָֽׁם: וַיְהִי֙ כְּכַלּ֣וֹת יִרְמְיָ֔הוּ לְדַבֵּ֣ר אֶל־ כָּל־הָעָ֗ם אֶת־כָּל־דִּבְרֵי֙ יְהוָ֣ה אֱלֹֽהֵיהֶ֔ם אֲשֶׁ֧ר שְׁלָח֛וֹ יְהוָ֥ה אֱלֹהֵיהֶ֖ם

ב אֲלֵיהֶ֑ם אֵ֥ת כָּל־הַדְּבָרִ֖ים הָאֵֽלֶּה: וַיֹּ֨אמֶר עֲזַרְיָ֤ה בֶן־הוֹשַֽׁעְיָה֙ וְיֽוֹחָנָ֣ן בֶּן־קָרֵ֔חַ וְכָל־הָאֲנָשִׁ֖ים הַזֵּדִ֑ים אֹֽמְרִ֣ים אֶֽל־יִרְמְיָ֔הוּ שֶׁ֣קֶר אַתָּ֣ה

ג מְדַבֵּ֑ר לֹ֣א שְׁלָחֲךָ֞ יְהוָ֤ה אֱלֹהֵ֙ינוּ֙ לֵאמֹ֔ר לֹֽא־תָבֹ֥אוּ מִצְרַ֖יִם לָג֥וּר שָֽׁם: כִּ֗י בָּר֙וּךְ֙ בֶּן־נֵ֣רִיָּ֔ה מַסִּ֥ית אֹֽתְךָ֖ בָּ֑נוּ לְמַ֩עַן֩ תֵּ֨ת אֹתָ֤נוּ בְיַד־הַכַּשְׂדִּים֙ לְהָמִ֣ית

ד אֹתָ֔נוּ וּלְהַגְל֥וֹת אֹתָ֖נוּ בָּבֶֽל: וְלֹא־שָׁמַ֞ע יֽוֹחָנָ֤ן בֶּן־קָרֵ֙חַ֙ וְכָל־שָׂרֵ֣י הַחֲיָלִ֔ים

ה וְכָל־הָעָ֑ם בְּק֖וֹל יְהוָ֑ה לָשֶׁ֖בֶת בְּאֶ֥רֶץ יְהוּדָֽה: וַיִּקַּ֞ח יֽוֹחָנָ֤ן בֶּן־קָרֵ֙חַ֙ וְכָל־ שָׂרֵ֣י הַחֲיָלִ֔ים אֵ֥ת כָּל־שְׁאֵרִ֖ית יְהוּדָ֑ה אֲשֶׁר־שָׁ֗בוּ מִכָּל־הַגּוֹיִם֙ אֲשֶׁ֣ר נִדְּחוּ־

ו שָׁ֔ם לָג֖וּר בְּאֶ֥רֶץ יְהוּדָֽה: אֶֽת־הַגְּבָרִ֞ים וְאֶת־הַנָּשִׁ֣ים וְאֶת־הַטַּ֗ף וְאֶת־בְּנ֣וֹת הַמֶּ֙לֶךְ֙ וְאֵ֣ת כָּל־הַנֶּ֔פֶשׁ אֲשֶׁ֣ר הִנִּ֗יחַ נְבוּזַרְאֲדָן֙ רַב־טַבָּחִ֔ים אֶת־גְּדַלְיָ֖הוּ בֶּן־

ז אֲחִיקָ֣ם בֶּן־שָׁפָ֑ן וְאֵת֙ יִרְמְיָ֣הוּ הַנָּבִ֔יא וְאֶת־בָּר֖וּךְ בֶּן־נֵרִיָּֽהוּ: וַיָּבֹ֙אוּ֙ אֶ֣רֶץ

ח מִצְרַ֔יִם כִּ֛י לֹ֥א שָֽׁמְע֖וּ בְּק֣וֹל יְהוָ֑ה וַיָּבֹ֖אוּ עַד־תַּחְפַּנְחֵֽס: וַיְהִ֤י

ט דְבַר־יְהוָה֙ אֶֽל־יִרְמְיָ֔הוּ בְּתַחְפַּנְחֵ֖ס לֵאמֹֽר: קַ֣ח בְּיָדְךָ֞ אֲבָנִ֣ים גְּדֹל֗וֹת וּטְמַנְתָּ֤ם בַּמֶּ֙לֶט֙ בַּמַּלְבֵּ֔ן אֲשֶׁ֛ר בְּפֶ֥תַח בֵּית־פַּרְעֹ֖ה בְּתַחְפַּנְחֵ֑ס לְעֵינֵ֖י

י אֲנָשִׁ֥ים יְהוּדִֽים: וְאָמַרְתָּ֣ אֲלֵיהֶ֡ם כֹּֽה־אָמַר֩ יְהוָ֨ה צְבָא֜וֹת אֱלֹהֵ֣י יִשְׂרָאֵ֗ל הִנְנִ֤י שֹׁלֵ֙חַ֙ וְ֠לָקַחְתִּי אֶת־נְבֽוּכַדְרֶאצַּ֤ר מֶֽלֶךְ־בָּבֶל֙ עַבְדִּ֔י וְשַׂמְתִּ֣י כִסְא֔וֹ מִמַּ֛עַל לָאֲבָנִ֥ים הָאֵ֖לֶּה אֲשֶׁ֣ר טָמָ֑נְתִּי וְנָטָ֥ה אֶת־°שַׁפְרוּרוֹ [°שַׁפְרִירֽוֹ ק]

יא עֲלֵיהֶֽם: °וּבָאָה [°וּבָ֙א ק] וְהִכָּ֖ה אֶת־אֶ֣רֶץ מִצְרָ֑יִם אֲשֶׁ֧ר לַמָּ֣וֶת לַמָּ֗וֶת

יב וַאֲשֶׁ֤ר לַשְּׁבִי֙ לַשֶּׁ֔בִי וַאֲשֶׁ֥ר לַחֶ֖רֶב לֶחָֽרֶב: וְהִצַּ֣תִּי אֵ֗שׁ בְּבָתֵּי֙ אֱלֹהֵ֣י מִצְרַ֔יִם וּשְׂרָפָ֖ם וְשָׁבָ֑ם וְעָטָה֩ אֶת־אֶ֨רֶץ מִצְרַ֜יִם כַּאֲשֶׁר־יַעְטֶ֤ה הָֽרֹעֶה֙ אֶת־בִּגְד֔וֹ

יג וְיָצָ֥א מִשָּׁ֖ם בְּשָׁלֽוֹם: וְשִׁבַּ֗ר אֶת־מַצְּבוֹת֙ בֵּ֣ית שֶׁ֔מֶשׁ אֲשֶׁ֖ר בְּאֶ֣רֶץ מִצְרָ֑יִם

Egypt, and the very hunger about which you worry will pursue you in Egypt, and there you will die. [17] And all the men who turn their faces to go to Egypt to live there will die by the sword, by the famine and by the pestilence; there will not be any remnant or survivor among them from the evil that I am bringing upon them. [18] For thus said HASHEM, Master of Legions, God of Israel: Just as My anger and My wrath were poured out against the inhabitants of Jerusalem, so will My wrath be poured out upon you if you go to Egypt, and you will be [an example for] an oath, * an astonishment, a curse and a disgrace, and you will never see this place again."

But you will not listen [19] HASHEM has spoken to you, O remnant of Judah — do not go to Egypt! Know for certain that I have warned you today! [20] For you have deceived me about your true thoughts, * for you sent me to HASHEM your God, saying, "Pray on our behalf to HASHEM our God, and whatever HASHEM our God says, tell us, and we will do it"; [21] and I told you this day, but you did not listen to the voice of HASHEM, your God, and to all that he has sent me to [tell] you. [22] Know now for certain that you will die by the sword, by the famine and by the pestilence in the place in which you desire to go to live.

43 [1] It happened when Jeremiah finished speaking all the words of HASHEM, their God, to all the people to whom HASHEM, their God, had sent him — [2] that Azariah son of Hoshaiah and Johanan son of Kareah and all the arrogant men said to Jeremiah, "You speak falsehood! HASHEM, our God, did not send you to say, 'Do not go to Egypt to sojourn there.' [3] Rather, Baruch son of Neriah is inciting you against us, in order to deliver us into the hand of the Chaldeans, and to exile us to Babylonia." [4] So Johanan son of Kareah, all the army officers and all the people did not listen to the voice of HASHEM, to settle in the land of Judah. [5] Johanan son of Kareah and all the army officers took all the remnant of Judah that had returned from all the countries to which they had been dispersed to sojourn in the land of Judah [6] (the men, the women, the children, the daughters of the king; all the people whom Nebuzaradan, the chief executioner, had left with Gedaliah son of Ahikam son of Shaphan; and Jeremiah the prophet and Baruch son of Neriah) [7] and they came to the land of Egypt, for they did not listen to the voice of HASHEM; and they came to Tahpanhes.

[8] The word of HASHEM came to Jeremiah in Tahpanhes, saying, [9] "Take in your hand large stones and cover them with mortar at the brick kiln that is near the entryway to the palace of Pharaoh in Tahpanhes, in the presence of Jewish men, [10] and say to them: Thus said HASHEM, Master of Legions, the God of Israel: Behold, I am sending to take Nebuchadrezzar king of Babylonia, My servant, and I am placing his throne above these stones that I have covered, and he will spread his tent over them. [11] And he will come and strike the land of Egypt: Whoever is destined for death will go to death, for captivity to captivity, and for the sword to the sword. [12] And I shall set fire to all the temples of the gods of Egypt, and he will burn them and plunder them; he will wrap up [the booty of] the land of Egypt as a shepherd wraps [things in] his garment, and he will leave there in peace. [13] He will shatter the pillars of the temple of the sun that is in the land of Egypt,

---

42:18. When taking an oath, people will say, "May I be like these men if I am not telling the truth."
42:20. The people claimed to be seeking counsel; but

Jeremiah saw in their reaction to his prophecy that what they really sought was an automatic endorsement of the course of action they had already decided upon.

מד א וְאֵת־בָּתֵּי אֱלֹהֵי מִצְרַיִם יִשְׂרֹף בָּאֵשׁ:   הַדָּבָר אֲשֶׁר הָיָה
אֶל־יִרְמְיָ֔הוּ אֶל כָּל־הַיְּהוּדִ֔ים הַיֹּשְׁבִים בְּאֶרֶץ מִצְרָיִם הַיֹּשְׁבִים בְּמִגְדֹּל
ב וּבְתַחְפַּנְחֵס וּבְנֹף וּבְאֶרֶץ פַּתְרוֹס לֵאמֹר: כֹּה־אָמַר יְהוָה צְבָאוֹת אֱלֹהֵי
יִשְׂרָאֵל אַתֶּם רְאִיתֶם אֵת כָּל־הָרָעָה אֲשֶׁר הֵבֵאתִי עַל־יְרוּשָׁלַ֔ם וְעַל
ג כָּל־עָרֵי יְהוּדָה וְהִנָּם חָרְבָּה הַיּוֹם הַזֶּה וְאֵין בָּהֶם יוֹשֵׁב: מִפְּנֵי רָעָתָם
אֲשֶׁר עָשׂוּ לְהַכְעִסֵ֔נִי לָלֶכֶת לְקַטֵּר לַעֲבֹד לֵאלֹהִים אֲחֵרִים אֲשֶׁר לֹא
ד יְדָעוּם הֵמָּה אַתֶּם וַאֲבֹתֵיכֶם: וָאֶשְׁלַח אֲלֵיכֶם אֶת־כָּל־עֲבָדַי הַנְּבִיאִים
הַשְׁכֵּים וְשָׁלֹחַ לֵאמֹר אַל־נָא תַעֲשׂוּ אֵת דְּבַר־הַתֹּעֵבָה הַזֹּאת אֲשֶׁר
ה שָׂנֵאתִי: וְלֹא שָׁמְעוּ וְלֹא־הִטּוּ אֶת־אָזְנָ֔ם לָשׁוּב מֵרָעָתָם לְבִלְתִּי קַטֵּר
ו לֵאלֹהִים אֲחֵרִים: וַתִּתַּךְ חֲמָתִי וְאַפִּי וַתִּבְעַר בְּעָרֵי יְהוּדָה וּבְחֻצוֹת
ז יְרוּשָׁלָ֔ם וַתִּהְיֶינָה לְחָרְבָּה לִשְׁמָמָה כַּיּוֹם הַזֶּה: וְעַתָּה
כֹּה־אָמַר יְהוָה אֱלֹהֵי צְבָאוֹת אֱלֹהֵי יִשְׂרָאֵל לָמָה אַתֶּם עֹשִׂים רָעָה
גְדוֹלָה אֶל־נַפְשֹׁתֵכֶם לְהַכְרִית לָכֶם אִישׁ־וְאִשָּׁה עוֹלֵל וְיוֹנֵק מִתּוֹךְ
ח יְהוּדָה לְבִלְתִּי הוֹתִיר לָכֶם שְׁאֵרִית: לְהַכְעִסֵ֫נִי בְּמַעֲשֵׂי יְדֵיכֶם לְקַטֵּר
לֵאלֹהִים אֲחֵרִים בְּאֶרֶץ מִצְרַיִם אֲשֶׁר־אַתֶּם בָּאִים לָגוּר שָׁם לְמַעַן
הַכְרִית לָכֶם וּלְמַעַן הֱיוֹתְכֶם לִקְלָלָה וּלְחֶרְפָּה בְּכֹל גּוֹיֵי הָאָרֶץ:
ט הַשְׁכַחְתֶּם אֶת־רָעוֹת אֲבוֹתֵיכֶם וְאֶת־רָעוֹת | מַלְכֵי יְהוּדָה וְאֵת רָעוֹת
נָשָׁיו וְאֵת רָעֹתֵכֶם וְאֵת רָעֹת נְשֵׁיכֶם אֲשֶׁר עָשׂוּ בְּאֶרֶץ יְהוּדָה וּבְחֻצוֹת
י יְרוּשָׁלָ֔ם: לֹא דֻכְּאוּ עַד הַיּוֹם הַזֶּה וְלֹא יָרְאוּ וְלֹא־הָלְכוּ בְתוֹרָתִי
יא וּבְחֻקֹּתַי אֲשֶׁר־נָתַתִּי לִפְנֵיכֶם וְלִפְנֵי אֲבוֹתֵיכֶם: לָכֵן
כֹּה־אָמַר יְהוָה צְבָאוֹת אֱלֹהֵי יִשְׂרָאֵל הִנְנִי שָׂם פָּנַי בָּכֶם לְרָעָה
יב וּלְהַכְרִית אֶת־כָּל־יְהוּדָה: וְלָקַחְתִּי אֶת־שְׁאֵרִית יְהוּדָה אֲשֶׁר־שָׂמוּ
פְנֵיהֶם לָבוֹא אֶרֶץ־מִצְרַיִם לָגוּר שָׁם וְתַמּוּ כֹל בְּאֶרֶץ מִצְרַיִם יִפֹּלוּ
בַּחֶרֶב בָּרָעָב יִתַּמּוּ מִקָּטֹן וְעַד־גָּדוֹל בַּחֶרֶב וּבָרָעָב יָמֻתוּ וְהָיוּ לְאָלָה
יג לְשַׁמָּה וְלִקְלָלָה וּלְחֶרְפָּה: וּפָקַדְתִּי עַל הַיּוֹשְׁבִים בְּאֶרֶץ מִצְרַיִם כַּאֲשֶׁר
יד פָּקַדְתִּי עַל־יְרוּשָׁלָ֔ם בַּחֶרֶב בָּרָעָב וּבַדָּבֶר: וְלֹא יִהְיֶה פָּלִיט וְשָׂרִיד
לִשְׁאֵרִית יְהוּדָה הַבָּאִים לָגוּר־שָׁם בְּאֶרֶץ מִצְרָיִם וְלָשׁוּב | אֶרֶץ יְהוּדָה
אֲשֶׁר־הֵמָּה מְנַשְּׂאִים אֶת־נַפְשָׁם לָשׁוּב לָשֶׁבֶת שָׁם כִּי לֹא־יָשׁוּבוּ כִּי
טו אִם־פְּלֵטִים: וַיַּעֲנוּ אֶת־יִרְמְיָ֔הוּ כָּל־הָאֲנָשִׁים הַיֹּדְעִים
כִּי־מְקַטְּרוֹת נְשֵׁיהֶם לֵאלֹהִים אֲחֵרִים וְכָל־הַנָּשִׁים הָעֹמְדוֹת קָהָל גָּדוֹל
טז וְכָל־הָעָם הַיֹּשְׁבִים בְּאֶרֶץ־מִצְרַיִם בְּפַתְרוֹס לֵאמֹר: הַדָּבָר אֲשֶׁר־דִּבַּרְתָּ
יז אֵלֵינוּ בְּשֵׁם יְהוָה אֵינֶנּוּ שֹׁמְעִים אֵלֶיךָ: כִּי עָשֹׂה נַעֲשֶׂה אֶת־כָּל־הַדָּבָר |
אֲשֶׁר־יָצָא מִפִּינוּ לְקַטֵּר לִמְלֶכֶת הַשָּׁמַיִם וְהַסֵּיךְ־לָהּ נְסָכִים כַּאֲשֶׁר
עָשִׂינוּ אֲנַחְנוּ וַאֲבֹתֵינוּ מְלָכֵינוּ וְשָׂרֵינוּ בְּעָרֵי יְהוּדָה וּבְחֻצוֹת יְרוּשָׁלַ֔ם

and he will burn [down] the temples of the Egyptian gods in fire."

44 ¹ The word that came to Jeremiah, concerning all the Jews who were living in the land of Egypt — who were living in Migdol, in Tahpanhes, in Noph and in the land of Pathros — saying:

Jeremiah warns the Jews in Egypt against idolatry

² Thus said HASHEM, Master of Legions, God of Israel: You have seen all the misfortune that I have brought upon Jerusalem and upon all the cities of Judah, and behold, they are a ruin to this day, there is no inhabitant in them, ³ because of their evil that they did to anger Me, to go to burn incense to worship the gods of others, whom they did not know — they, you and your fathers. ⁴ I sent all My servants the prophets to you, arising early and sending, saying, 'Do not perform this act of abomination that I detest.' ⁵ But they did not listen nor incline their ear, to repent from their evil, not to burn incense to the gods of others. ⁶ So My wrath, My anger was poured out, and it burned in the cities of Judah and in the streets of Jerusalem, so that they became ruined and desolate, as this day. ⁷ And now, thus said HASHEM, the God of Legions, the God of Israel: Why are you doing great evil to your souls: to cut off from yourselves man and woman, child and infant, from the midst of Judah, not to leave yourselves a remnant; ⁸ to anger Me with the deeds of your hands, to burn incense to the gods of others in the land Egypt, where you have gone to sojourn; so that you will cut yourselves off, and so that you will be a curse and a disgrace among all the nations of the earth? ⁹ Have you forgotten the evils of your forefathers, the evils of [each of] the kings of Judah and the evils of his wives, your own evils and the evils of your wives, that they committed in the land of Judah and in the streets of Jerusalem? ¹⁰ They have not been subdued to this day; they have not feared and have not followed My teaching and My decrees that I placed before you and before your fathers. ¹¹ Therefore, thus said HASHEM, Master of Legions, God of Israel: Behold, I am turning My attention to you for adversity, to cut off all of Judah. ¹² And I will take the remnant of Judah, who have set their faces to come to the land of Egypt to sojourn there, and they will all perish; they will fall in the land of Egypt; they will perish by the sword and by the famine — from the smallest to the greatest — they will die by the sword and by the famine, and they will be an [example for an] oath, an astonishment, a curse, and a disgrace. ¹³ I shall deal with those who dwell in the land of Egypt as I dealt with Jerusalem — with the sword, with the famine and with the pestilence. ¹⁴ There will be no fugitive nor survivor from the remnant of Judah who have come to sojourn there in the land of Egypt, to return to the land of Judah, to where they lift their hopes to return to settle; for they will not return, except as fugitives.

The peole refuse to obey

¹⁵ They answered Jeremiah — all the people who knew that their wives were burning incense to the gods of others, and all the women who stood in a great assembly, and all the people who dwelled in the land of Egypt, in Pathros — saying, ¹⁶ "Concerning the word that you have spoken to us in the name of HASHEM — we do not listen to you! ¹⁷ Rather, we will indeed continue to fulfill everything that came from our mouths, to burn incense to the queen of the heavens* and pour out libations to her, as we did — we and our fathers, our kings and our officers — in the cities of Judah and in the streets of Jerusalem,

---

44:17. That is, the sun (see 43:13).

יח וַנִּשְׂבַּע־לֶחֶם וַנִּהְיֶה טוֹבִים וְרָעָה לֹא רָאִינוּ: וּמִן־אָז חָדַלְנוּ לְקַטֵּר
יט לִמְלֶכֶת הַשָּׁמַיִם וְהַסֵּךְ־לָהּ נְסָכִים חָסַרְנוּ כֹל וּבַחֶרֶב וּבָרָעָב תָּמְנוּ: וְכִי־
אֲנַחְנוּ מְקַטְּרִים לִמְלֶכֶת הַשָּׁמַיִם וּלְהַסֵּךְ לָהּ נְסָכִים הֲמִבַּלְעֲדֵי אֲנָשֵׁינוּ
כ עָשִׂינוּ לָהּ כַּוָּנִים לְהַעֲצִבָה וְהַסֵּךְ לָהּ נְסָכִים: וַיֹּאמֶר יִרְמְיָהוּ
אֶל־כָּל־הָעָם עַל־הַגְּבָרִים וְעַל־הַנָּשִׁים וְעַל־כָּל־הָעָם הָעֹנִים אֹתוֹ דָּבָר
כא לֵאמֹר: הֲלוֹא אֶת־הַקִּטֵּר אֲשֶׁר קִטַּרְתֶּם בְּעָרֵי יְהוּדָה וּבְחֻצוֹת יְרוּשָׁלַ͏ִם
אַתֶּם וַאֲבוֹתֵיכֶם מַלְכֵיכֶם וְשָׂרֵיכֶם וְעַם הָאָרֶץ אֹתָם זָכַר יְהוָה וַתַּעֲלֶה
כב עַל־לִבּוֹ: וְלֹא־יוּכַל יְהוָה עוֹד לָשֵׂאת מִפְּנֵי רֹעַ מַעַלְלֵיכֶם מִפְּנֵי הַתּוֹעֵבֹת
אֲשֶׁר עֲשִׂיתֶם וַתְּהִי אַרְצְכֶם לְחָרְבָּה וּלְשַׁמָּה וְלִקְלָלָה מֵאֵין יוֹשֵׁב כְּהַיּוֹם
כג הַזֶּה: מִפְּנֵי אֲשֶׁר קִטַּרְתֶּם וַאֲשֶׁר חֲטָאתֶם לַיהוָה וְלֹא שְׁמַעְתֶּם בְּקוֹל יְהוָה
וּבְתֹרָתוֹ וּבְחֻקֹּתָיו וּבְעֵדְוֹתָיו לֹא הֲלַכְתֶּם עַל־כֵּן קָרָאת אֶתְכֶם הָרָעָה
כד כַּזֹּאת כַּיּוֹם הַזֶּה: וַיֹּאמֶר יִרְמְיָהוּ אֶל־כָּל־הָעָם וְאֶל כָּל־
כה הַנָּשִׁים שִׁמְעוּ דְּבַר־יְהוָה כָּל־יְהוּדָה אֲשֶׁר בְּאֶרֶץ מִצְרָיִם: כֹּה־אָמַר
יְהוָה־צְבָאוֹת אֱלֹהֵי יִשְׂרָאֵל לֵאמֹר אַתֶּם וּנְשֵׁיכֶם וַתְּדַבֵּרְנָה בְּפִיכֶם
וּבִידֵיכֶם מִלֵּאתֶם ׀ לֵאמֹר עָשֹׂה נַעֲשֶׂה אֶת־נְדָרֵינוּ אֲשֶׁר נָדַרְנוּ לְקַטֵּר
לִמְלֶכֶת הַשָּׁמַיִם וּלְהַסֵּךְ לָהּ נְסָכִים הָקֵים תָּקִימְנָה אֶת־נִדְרֵיכֶם וְעָשֹׂה
כו תַעֲשֶׂינָה אֶת־נִדְרֵיכֶם: לָכֵן שִׁמְעוּ דְבַר־יְהוָה כָּל־יְהוּדָה הַיֹּשְׁבִים בְּאֶרֶץ
מִצְרָיִם הִנְנִי נִשְׁבַּעְתִּי בִּשְׁמִי הַגָּדוֹל אָמַר יְהוָה אִם־יִהְיֶה עוֹד שְׁמִי
נִקְרָא ׀ בְּפִי ׀ כָּל־אִישׁ יְהוּדָה אֹמֵר חַי־אֲדֹנָי יֱהוִֹה בְּכָל־אֶרֶץ מִצְרָיִם:
כז הִנְנִי שֹׁקֵד עֲלֵיהֶם לְרָעָה וְלֹא לְטוֹבָה וְתַמּוּ כָל־אִישׁ יְהוּדָה אֲשֶׁר בְּאֶרֶץ־
כח מִצְרַיִם בַּחֶרֶב וּבָרָעָב עַד־כְּלוֹתָם: וּפְלִיטֵי חֶרֶב יְשֻׁבוּן מִן־אֶרֶץ מִצְרַיִם
אֶרֶץ יְהוּדָה מְתֵי מִסְפָּר וְיָדְעוּ כָּל־שְׁאֵרִית יְהוּדָה הַבָּאִים לְאֶרֶץ־מִצְרַיִם
כט לָגוּר שָׁם דְּבַר־מִי יָקוּם מִמֶּנִּי וּמֵהֶם: וְזֹאת־לָכֶם הָאוֹת נְאֻם־יְהוָה
כִּי־פֹקֵד אֲנִי עֲלֵיכֶם בַּמָּקוֹם הַזֶּה לְמַעַן תֵּדְעוּ כִּי קוֹם יָקוּמוּ דְבָרַי עֲלֵיכֶם
ל לְרָעָה: כֹּה ׀ אָמַר יְהוָה הִנְנִי נֹתֵן אֶת־פַּרְעֹה חָפְרַע מֶלֶךְ־
מִצְרַיִם בְּיַד אֹיְבָיו וּבְיַד מְבַקְשֵׁי נַפְשׁוֹ כַּאֲשֶׁר נָתַתִּי אֶת־צִדְקִיָּהוּ מֶלֶךְ־
מה א יְהוּדָה בְּיַד נְבוּכַדְרֶאצַּר מֶלֶךְ־בָּבֶל אֹיְבוֹ וּמְבַקֵּשׁ נַפְשׁוֹ: הַדָּבָר
אֲשֶׁר דִּבֶּר יִרְמְיָהוּ הַנָּבִיא אֶל־בָּרוּךְ בֶּן־נֵרִיָּה בְּכָתְבוֹ אֶת־הַדְּבָרִים
הָאֵלֶּה עַל־סֵפֶר מִפִּי יִרְמְיָהוּ בַּשָּׁנָה הָרְבִעִית לִיהוֹיָקִים בֶּן־יֹאשִׁיָּהוּ
ב־ג מֶלֶךְ יְהוּדָה לֵאמֹר: כֹּה־אָמַר יְהוָה אֱלֹהֵי יִשְׂרָאֵל עָלֶיךָ בָּרוּךְ: אָמַרְתָּ
אוֹי־נָא לִי כִּי־יָסַף יְהוָה יָגוֹן עַל־מַכְאֹבִי יָגַעְתִּי בְּאַנְחָתִי וּמְנוּחָה
ד לֹא מָצָאתִי: תֹּאמַר אֵלָיו כֹּה אָמַר יְהוָה הִנֵּה אֲשֶׁר־בָּנִיתִי אֲנִי הֹרֵס

44:24. The women are singled out here for it was they who performed the incense service about which Jeremiah was berating the people.

44:26. Since they rejected Me, they will no longer be able to swear in My Name, because they will be annihilated.

when we were sated with food, lived well and saw no misfortune. [18] For ever since we stopped burning incense to the queen of the heavens and pouring out libations to her, we have lacked everything and we have perished by the sword and by the famine. [19] Furthermore, when we burn offerings to the queen of the heavens and pour out libations to her, is it without our husbands' [consent] that we make her delicacies to gladden her and pour out the libations?"

[20] Jeremiah then spoke to the people — to the men and to the women and to all the people who had given him this answer — saying, [21] "Is it not [because of] the incense that you and your fathers and your kings and your officers and the general populace burned in the cities of Judah and in the streets of Jerusalem? They are what HASHEM recalled, and they came to His attention. [22] HASHEM could no longer forbear in the face of the wickedness of your deeds, in the face of the abominations that you had committed, so your land became a ruin and a desolation and a curse, without inhabitant, as this very day! [23] Because you burned incense and sinned to HASHEM and did not heed the voice of HASHEM, and you did not follow His teaching, His decrees and His testimonies, therefore this evil has befallen you, as this very day."

Jeremiah prophesies the destruction of Egypt and its Jewish population

[24] Jeremiah then said to all the people and [especially] to all the women: *

Hear the word of HASHEM, all of Judah who are in the land of Egypt! [25] Thus said HASHEM, Master of Legions, the God of Israel: You and your wives have spoken with your mouths and have performed with your hands, saying, 'We will surely fulfill our vows that we have vowed to burn incense to the queen of the heavens and to pour out libations to her'; indeed, you continue to fulfill your vows and to carry out your vows. [26] Therefore, hear the word of HASHEM, all of Judah who dwelled in the land of Egypt: Behold, I swear by My great Name, said HASHEM, that My Name will no longer be mentioned in the mouths of any man of Judah, saying, 'As my Lord, HASHEM/ELOHIM lives,' in the entire land of Egypt. * [27] Behold I shall be diligent towards them for evil and not for good, and all the men of Judah who are in the land of Egypt will perish by the sword and by the famine, until they are annihilated. [28] And fugitives from the sword will return from the land of Egypt to the land of Judah, few in number; and all the remnant of Judah who have come to the land of Egypt to sojourn there will know whose word will prevail, Mine or theirs. [29] This will be the sign for you — the word of HASHEM — that I will attend to you in this place, in order that you may know that My words concerning you, for evil, will surely come about: [30] Thus said HASHEM: Behold, I am delivering Pharaoh Hophra king of Egypt into the hand of his enemies and into the hand of those who seek his soul, just as I delivered Zedekiah king of Judah into the hand of Nebuchadrezzar king of Babylonia, his enemy who sought his soul.

45

Prophecy to Baruch

[1] The word that Jeremiah the Prophet spoke to Baruch son of Neriah, when he wrote down these prophecies into a book by the mouth of Jeremiah, * in the fourth year of Jehoiakim son of Josiah, king of Judah, saying: [2] "Thus said HASHEM, God of Israel, concerning you, Baruch: [3] You said, 'Woe is me, for HASHEM has added grief upon my pain. I have grown weary from my groaning, and have found no rest.' * [4] Say thus to him: Thus said HASHEM: Behold, that which I built I am destroying,

---

45:1. See 36:1-4.
45:3. The Sages explain that Baruch was disappointed that despite his devotion to Jeremiah, he did not merit the prophetic spirit himself.

ה וְאֵת אֲשֶׁר־נָטַעְתִּי אֲנִי נֹתֵשׁ וְאֶת־כָּל־הָאָרֶץ הִיא: וְאַתָּה תְּבַקֶּשׁ־לְךָ
גְדֹלוֹת אַל־תְּבַקֵּשׁ כִּי הִנְנִי מֵבִיא רָעָה עַל־כָּל־בָּשָׂר נְאֻם־יהוה וְנָתַתִּי
א לְךָ אֶת־נַפְשְׁךָ לְשָׁלָל עַל כָּל־הַמְּקֹמוֹת אֲשֶׁר תֵּלֶךְ־שָׁם: מו אֲשֶׁר
ב הָיָה דְבַר־יהוה אֶל־יִרְמְיָהוּ הַנָּבִיא עַל־הַגּוֹיִם: לְמִצְרַיִם עַל־חֵיל פַּרְעֹה
נְכוֹ מֶלֶךְ מִצְרַיִם אֲשֶׁר־הָיָה עַל־נְהַר־פְּרָת בְּכַרְכְּמִשׁ אֲשֶׁר הִכָּה
נְבוּכַדְרֶאצַּר מֶלֶךְ בָּבֶל בִּשְׁנַת הָרְבִיעִית לִיהוֹיָקִים בֶּן־יֹאשִׁיָּהוּ מֶלֶךְ
ג-ד יְהוּדָה: עִרְכוּ מָגֵן וְצִנָּה וּגְשׁוּ לַמִּלְחָמָה: אִסְרוּ הַסּוּסִים וַעֲלוּ הַפָּרָשִׁים
ה וְהִתְיַצְּבוּ בְּכוֹבָעִים מִרְקוּ הָרְמָחִים לִבְשׁוּ הַסִּרְיֹנֹת: מַדּוּעַ רָאִיתִי הֵמָּה
חַתִּים נְסֹגִים אָחוֹר וְגִבּוֹרֵיהֶם יֻכַּתּוּ וּמָנוֹס נָסוּ וְלֹא הִפְנוּ מָגוֹר מִסָּבִיב
ו נְאֻם־יהוה: אַל־יָנוּס הַקַּל וְאַל־יִמָּלֵט הַגִּבּוֹר צָפוֹנָה עַל־יַד נְהַר־פְּרָת
ז-ח כָּשְׁלוּ וְנָפָלוּ: מִי־זֶה כַּיְאֹר יַעֲלֶה כַּנְּהָרוֹת יִתְגָּעֲשׁוּ מֵימָיו: מִצְרַיִם כַּיְאֹר
יַעֲלֶה וְכַנְּהָרוֹת יִתְגֹּעֲשׁוּ מָיִם וַיֹּאמֶר אַעֲלֶה אֲכַסֶּה־אֶרֶץ אֹבִידָה עִיר
ט וְיֹשְׁבֵי בָהּ: עֲלוּ הַסּוּסִים וְהִתְהֹלְלוּ הָרֶכֶב וְיֵצְאוּ הַגִּבּוֹרִים כּוּשׁ וּפוּט
י תֹּפְשֵׂי מָגֵן וְלוּדִים תֹּפְשֵׂי דֹּרְכֵי קָשֶׁת: וְהַיּוֹם הַהוּא לַאדֹנָי יהוה צְבָאוֹת
יוֹם נְקָמָה לְהִנָּקֵם מִצָּרָיו וְאָכְלָה חֶרֶב וְשָׂבְעָה וְרָוְתָה מִדָּמָם כִּי זֶבַח
יא לַאדֹנָי יהוה צְבָאוֹת בְּאֶרֶץ צָפוֹן אֶל־נְהַר־פְּרָת: עֲלִי גִלְעָד וּקְחִי צֳרִי
בְּתוּלַת בַּת־מִצְרָיִם לַשָּׁוְא °הִרְבֵּיתי [°הִרְבֵּית ק] רְפֻאוֹת תְּעָלָה אֵין לָךְ:
יב שָׁמְעוּ גוֹיִם קְלוֹנֵךְ וְצִוְחָתֵךְ מָלְאָה הָאָרֶץ כִּי־גִבּוֹר בְּגִבּוֹר כָּשָׁלוּ יַחְדָּו
יג נָפְלוּ שְׁנֵיהֶם: ◀ הַדָּבָר אֲשֶׁר דִּבֶּר יהוה אֶל־יִרְמְיָהוּ הַנָּבִיא

HAFTARAS BO 46:13-28

יד לָבוֹא נְבוּכַדְרֶאצַּר מֶלֶךְ בָּבֶל לְהַכּוֹת אֶת־אֶרֶץ מִצְרָיִם: הַגִּידוּ בְמִצְרַיִם
וְהַשְׁמִיעוּ בְמִגְדּוֹל וְהַשְׁמִיעוּ בְנֹף וּבְתַחְפַּנְחֵס אִמְרוּ הִתְיַצֵּב וְהָכֵן לָךְ כִּי־
טו-טז אָכְלָה חֶרֶב סְבִיבֶיךָ: מַדּוּעַ נִסְחַף אַבִּירֶיךָ לֹא עָמַד כִּי יהוה הֲדָפוֹ: הִרְבָּה
כּוֹשֵׁל גַּם־נָפַל אִישׁ אֶל־רֵעֵהוּ וַיֹּאמְרוּ קוּמָה וְנָשֻׁבָה אֶל־עַמֵּנוּ וְאֶל־
יז אֶרֶץ מוֹלַדְתֵּנוּ מִפְּנֵי חֶרֶב הַיּוֹנָה: קָרְאוּ שָׁם פַּרְעֹה מֶלֶךְ־מִצְרַיִם שָׁאוֹן
יח הֶעֱבִיר הַמּוֹעֵד: חַי־אָנִי נְאֻם־הַמֶּלֶךְ יהוה צְבָאוֹת שְׁמוֹ כִּי כְּתָבוֹר בֶּהָרִים
יט וּכְכַרְמֶל בַּיָּם יָבוֹא: כְּלֵי גוֹלָה עֲשִׂי לָךְ יוֹשֶׁבֶת בַּת־מִצְרָיִם כִּי־נֹף לְשַׁמָּה
כ תִהְיֶה וְנִצְּתָה מֵאֵין יוֹשֵׁב: עֶגְלָה יְפֵה־פִיָּה מִצְרָיִם קֶרֶץ מִצָּפוֹן
כא בָּא בָא: גַּם־שְׂכִרֶיהָ בְקִרְבָּהּ כְּעֶגְלֵי מַרְבֵּק כִּי־גַם־הֵמָּה הִפְנוּ נָסוּ יַחְדָּיו
כב לֹא עָמָדוּ כִּי יוֹם אֵידָם בָּא עֲלֵיהֶם עֵת פְּקֻדָּתָם: קוֹלָהּ כַּנָּחָשׁ יֵלֵךְ כִּי־

45:5. God informed Baruch that his lack of prophecy was not due to his own shortcoming but to the fact that the chaotic conditions prevailing among the Jewish people did not warrant it. In the words of the Sages, "If there are no sheep, is there a shepherd?" (*Rashi*).

46:9. Jeremiah sarcastically calls upon Pharaoh and his allies to charge into battle against the Babylonians.

46:10. There, at Carchemish, God would avenge Pharaoh's killing of the righteous King Josiah on the way to

that place [see *II Kings* 23:29] (*Radak*).

46:13. This event took place several decades after Pharaoh Neco's defeat at Carchemish (*Rashi*).

46:17. The Chaldean army taunted Pharaoh for failing to confront Nebuchadnezzar's army when the challenge was issued.

46:21. When they realized that it was hopeless to fight Nebuchadnezzar's army, they fled, preferring their peaceful lives at home to honoring their commitment to Egypt.

and that which I have planted I am uprooting, and this is so throughout all the land; ⁵ yet you seek great things for yourself?* Do not seek [them]! For behold, I am bringing misfortune upon all flesh — the word of HASHEM — and I will give you your soul as booty, in all the places where you go."

46 ¹ The word of HASHEM that came to Jeremiah the prophet concerning the nations, ² concerning Egypt, concerning the army of Pharaoh Neco king of Egypt, which was at the Euphrates River, in Carchemish, which Nebuchadrezzar king of Babylonia defeated in the fourth year of Jehoiakim son of Josiah, king of Judah:

Prophecy of Pharaoh Neco's fall to Nebuchadnezzar

³ Prepare the buckler and the shield, and approach the battle. ⁴ Harness the horses and mount [them], O cavalrymen; stand [ready] in helmets; sharpen the spears; don the mail-armor. ⁵ Why do I see them panicking and retreating, their strongmen crushed, fleeing in haste without turning around? There is terror all around — the word of HASHEM. ⁶ The swift cannot flee and the strongman cannot escape; up north, by the Euphrates, they stumble and fall. ⁷ Who is this who rises up like the Nile; like rivers, its waters would surge? ⁸ It is Egypt that rises like the Nile; and like rivers, its waters would surge. It said, 'I will rise up and cover the land, I will destroy city and those who inhabit it.' ⁹ Go up, O horses; drive in a frenzy, O chariot; let the strongmen go forth — [the men of] Cush and Put, graspers of the shield, and the Ludites, graspers and drawers of the bow!* ¹⁰ That day will be a day of revenge for my Lord, HASHEM/ELOHIM, Master of Legions, a day of vengeance to avenge Himself of His enemies;* and the sword shall consume and be sated, [its thirst] quenched by their blood, for it is a slaughter for my Lord, HASHEM/ELOHIM, Master of Legions, in the land of the North, on the Euphrates River. ¹¹ You may go up to Gilead to get balm, O virgin daughter of Egypt, in vain have you increased remedies; there is no cure for you. ¹² The nations hear of your debacle, and your outcry fills the land, for warrior will stumble over warrior; both of them will fall together.

¹³ The word that HASHEM spoke to Jeremiah the prophet, that Nebuchadnezzar, king of Babylonia, would come to strike the land of Egypt:*

Another prophecy regarding Nebuchadnezzar's conquest of Egypt

¹⁴ Proclaim it in Egypt! Make it heard in Midgol! Make it heard in Noph and Tahpanhes! Say: 'Stand erect and prepare yourself.' For the sword will devour all your surroundings. ¹⁵ Why are all your warriors swept away? None could stand, because HASHEM thrust him down. ¹⁶ He caused much stumbling; indeed, each man fell against his fellow, and they said, 'Arise and let us return to our people and the land of our birth, from before the sword of the oppressor.' ¹⁷ [The Chaldeans] called out there, 'Pharaoh, the blustery king of Egypt, has let the appointed time go by.'*

¹⁸ As I live, the word of the King, Whose Name is HASHEM, Master of Legions, [I swear that] like Tabor among the mountains and Carmel by the sea, so shall [Nebuchadnezzar] come! ¹⁹ Make yourself gear for exile, O daughter who dwells in Egypt, for Noph shall be a desolation and a wasteland without an inhabitant. ²⁰ Egypt is a beautiful calf, but a slaughterer from the North is surely coming. ²¹ Even its mercenaries within it are like fatted calves, for they, too, have turned and fled together, they did not stand;* for the day of their tragedy has come upon them, the time of their accounting. ²² [Egypt's] voice will travel like a snake's, for [the Babylonians]

כג בְּחַ֤יִל יֵלֵ֨כוּ֙ וּבְקַרְדֻּמּ֔וֹת בָּ֥אוּ לָ֖הּ כְּחֹטְבֵ֣י עֵצִ֑ים כָּרְת֤וּ יַעְרָהּ֙ נְאֻם־יְהֹוָ֔ה כִּ֣י

כד לֹ֣א יֵֽחָקֵ֔ר כִּ֥י רַבּ֖וּ מֵֽאַרְבֶּ֑ה וְאֵ֥ין לָהֶ֖ם מִסְפָּֽר: הֹבִ֖ישָׁה בַּת־מִצְרָ֑יִם נִתְּנָ֖ה

כה בְּיַ֥ד עַם־צָפֽוֹן: אָמַר֩ יְהֹוָ֨ה צְבָא֜וֹת אֱלֹהֵ֣י יִשְׂרָאֵ֗ל הִנְנִ֤י פוֹקֵד֙ אֶל־אָמ֣וֹן מִנֹּ֔א וְעַל־פַּרְעֹה֙ וְעַל־מִצְרַ֔יִם וְעַל־אֱלֹהֶ֖יהָ וְעַל־מְלָכֶ֑יהָ וְעַל־פַּרְעֹ֖ה וְעַ֥ל

כו הַבֹּֽטְחִ֥ים בּֽוֹ: וּנְתַתִּ֗ים בְּיַד֙ מְבַקְשֵׁ֣י נַפְשָׁ֔ם וּבְיַ֛ד נְבֽוּכַדְרֶאצַּ֥ר מֶֽלֶךְ־בָּבֶ֖ל

כז וּבְיַד־עֲבָדָ֑יו וְאַֽחֲרֵי־כֵ֛ן תִּשְׁכֹּ֥ן כִּֽימֵי־קֶ֖דֶם נְאֻם־יְהֹוָֽה: וְ֠אַתָּ֠ה אַל־תִּירָ֨א עַבְדִּ֤י יַֽעֲקֹב֙ וְאַל־תֵּחַ֣ת יִשְׂרָאֵ֔ל כִּ֠י הִנְנִ֤י מֽוֹשִֽׁיעֲךָ֙ מֵֽרָח֔וֹק וְאֶֽת־זַרְעֲךָ֖

כח מֵאֶ֣רֶץ שִׁבְיָ֑ם וְשָׁ֧ב יַֽעֲק֛וֹב וְשָׁקַ֥ט וְשַֽׁאֲנַ֖ן וְאֵ֥ין מַֽחֲרִֽיד: אַ֠תָּ֠ה אַל־תִּירָ֞א עַבְדִּ֤י יַֽעֲקֹב֙ נְאֻם־יְהֹוָ֔ה כִּ֥י אִתְּךָ֖ אָ֑נִי כִּי֩ אֶעֱשֶׂ֨ה כָלָ֜ה בְּכָֽל־הַגּוֹיִ֣ם ׀ אֲשֶׁ֧ר הִדַּחְתִּ֣יךָ שָּׁ֗מָּה וְאֹֽתְךָ֙ לֹֽא־אֶֽעֱשֶׂ֣ה כָלָ֔ה וְיִסַּרְתִּ֨יךָ֙ לַמִּשְׁפָּ֔ט וְנַקֵּ֖ה לֹ֥א אֲנַקֶּֽךָּ:

מז א אֲשֶׁ֨ר הָיָ֧ה דְבַר־יְהֹוָ֛ה אֶל־יִרְמְיָ֥הוּ הַנָּבִ֖יא אֶל־פְּלִשְׁתִּ֑ים בְּטֶ֛רֶם יַכֶּ֥ה פַרְעֹ֖ה אֶת־עַזָּֽה:

ב כֹּ֣ה ׀ אָמַ֣ר יְהֹוָ֗ה הִנֵּה־מַ֜יִם עֹלִ֤ים מִצָּפוֹן֙ וְהָיוּ֙ לְנַ֣חַל שׁוֹטֵ֔ף וְיִשְׁטְפוּ֙ אֶ֣רֶץ וּמְלוֹאָ֔הּ עִ֖יר וְיֹ֣שְׁבֵי בָ֑הּ וְזָֽעֲקוּ֙ הָֽאָדָ֔ם וְהֵילִ֕ל כֹּ֖ל יוֹשֵׁ֥ב הָאָֽרֶץ:

ג מִקּ֞וֹל שַֽׁעֲטַ֤ת פַּרְסוֹת֙ אַבִּירָ֔יו מֵרַ֣עַשׁ לְרִכְבּ֔וֹ הֲמ֖וֹן גַּלְגִּלָּ֑יו לֹֽא־הִפְנ֤וּ אָבוֹת֙ אֶל־בָּנִ֔ים מֵֽרִפְי֖וֹן יָדָֽיִם:

ד עַל־הַיּ֗וֹם הַבָּא֙ לִשְׁד֣וֹד אֶת־כָּל־פְּלִשְׁתִּ֔ים לְהַכְרִ֣ית לְצֹ֔ר וּלְצִיד֔וֹן כֹּ֖ל שָׂרִ֣יד עֹזֵ֑ר כִּֽי־שֹׁדֵ֤ד יְהֹוָה֙ אֶת־פְּלִשְׁתִּ֔ים שְׁאֵרִ֖ית אִ֥י כַפְתּֽוֹר:

ה בָּ֤אָה קָרְחָה֙ אֶל־עַזָּ֔ה נִדְמְתָ֖ה אַשְׁקְל֑וֹן שְׁאֵרִ֣ית עִמְקָ֔ם עַד־מָתַ֖י תִּתְגּֽוֹדָֽדִי:

ו ה֗וֹי חֶ֚רֶב לַֽיהֹוָ֔ה עַד־אָ֖נָה לֹ֣א תִשְׁקֹ֑טִי הֵאָֽסְפִי֙ אֶל־תַּעְרֵ֔ךְ הֵרָֽגְעִ֖י וָדֹֽמִּי:

ז אֵ֣יךְ תִּשְׁקֹ֔טִי וַֽיהֹוָ֖ה צִוָּה־לָ֑הּ אֶֽל־אַשְׁקְל֛וֹן וְאֶל־ח֥וֹף הַיָּ֖ם שָׁ֥ם יְעָדָֽהּ:

מח א לְמוֹאָ֡ב כֹּה־אָמַר֩ יְהֹוָ֨ה צְבָא֜וֹת אֱלֹהֵ֣י יִשְׂרָאֵ֗ל ה֤וֹי אֶל־נְבוֹ֙ כִּ֣י שֻׁדָּ֔דָה הֹבִ֥ישָׁה נִלְכְּדָ֖ה קִרְיָתָ֑יִם הֹבִ֥ישָׁה הַמִּשְׂגָּ֖ב וָחָֽתָּה:

ב אֵ֣ין עוֹד֮ תְּהִלַּ֣ת מוֹאָב֒ בְּחֶשְׁבּ֗וֹן חָֽשְׁב֤וּ עָלֶ֨יהָ֙ רָעָ֔ה לְכ֖וּ וְנַכְרִיתֶ֣נָּה מִגּ֑וֹי גַּם־מַדְמֵ֣ן תִּדֹּ֔מִּי אַֽחֲרַ֖יִךְ תֵּ֥לֶךְ חָֽרֶב:

ג ק֥וֹל צְעָקָ֖ה מֵֽחֹֽרוֹנָ֑יִם שֹׁ֖ד וָשֶׁ֥בֶר גָּדֽוֹל:

ד נִשְׁבְּרָ֖ה מוֹאָ֑ב הִשְׁמִ֥יעוּ זְּעָקָ֖ה °צְעוֹרֶֽיהָ °[צְעִירֶ֥יהָ ק]:

ה כִּ֚י מַֽעֲלֵ֣ה °הַלֻּח֔וֹת °[הַלֻּחִ֔ית ק] בִּבְכִ֖י יַֽעֲלֶה־בֶּ֑כִי כִּ֚י בְּמוֹרַ֣ד חֽוֹרֹנַ֔יִם צָרֵ֥י צַֽעֲקַת־שֶׁ֖בֶר שָׁמֵֽעוּ:

ו נֻ֖סוּ מַלְּט֣וּ נַפְשְׁכֶ֑ם וְתִֽהְיֶ֕ינָה כַּֽעֲרוֹעֵ֖ר בַּמִּדְבָּֽר:

ז כִּ֠י יַ֚עַן בִּטְחֵ֣ךְ בְּמַֽעֲשַׂ֔יִךְ וּבְאֽוֹצְרוֹתַ֖יִךְ גַּם־אַ֣תְּ תִּלָּכֵ֑דִי

46:25. **Amon** is variously interpreted as: "multitude" (*Targum*); the name of the prince (*Rashi*) or king (*Radak*) of the city of No; or "metropolis" (*Kara*). Alternatively: Amon was originally a minor deity in No, but eventually was adopted as the chief god of Egypt.

47:1. Gaza, the main Philistine city, was first attacked by Pharaoh Hophra and then by the Chaldeans (*Radak*).

47:4. The progenitors of the Philistines and Caphtorites were brothers (see *Genesis* 10:14). The Philistine nation originated in Caphtorean territory (see *Amos* 9:7).

47:5. The baldness resulted from pulling out their hair in grief. Cutting the flesh is likewise a sign of grief.

48:1. Jeremiah now begins a series of prophecies (Chs.

48-51) concerning the final judgments of the nations: Moab, Ammon, Edom, Damascus, Keder, Elam, and Babylonia. The place names mentioned in the respective passages are usually cities in the land under discussion. Often cities in different countries would bear the same name; or a border city or a contested city may be spoken of in more than one passage.

48:1. Alternatively, the word המשגב is not a proper noun, but means "the fortress" (as in *Psalms* 9:10, etc.).

48:6. Aroer was an isolated desert outpost. If you flee, you may be able to save yourself and be one of the few, isolated survivors (*Targum*). Alternatively: "Aroer" is a solitary desert shrub (see 17:6).

will come against them with an army; they arrive against her with axes, like woodcutters. [23] They will cut down her forest — the word of HASHEM — for they are beyond calculation, for they are more numerous than locusts, and there is no number for them. [24] The daughter of Egypt shall be humiliated, delivered into the hand of the Northern people.

[25] HASHEM, Master of Legions, the God of Israel, said: Behold, I am attending to Amon of No, * to Pharaoh, to Egypt and its gods and its kings; and to Pharaoh and to those who trust in him. [26] And I shall deliver them into the hand of those who seek their souls, and into the hand of Nebuchadrezzar king of Babylonia and into the hand of his servants; but thereafter you shall have rest, as in days of old — the word of HASHEM.

Words of hope

[27] But as for you, do not be afraid, My servant Jacob, and do not be frightened, O Israel, for behold, I am saving you from afar, and your offspring from the land of their captivity; and Jacob shall return and be tranquil and complacent, and none will make [him] afraid. [28] You, do not be afraid, My servant Jacob — the word of HASHEM — for I am with you; though I shall make an end of all the nations where I have dispersed you, but of you I shall not make an end; I shall punish you with justice, but I shall not destroy you utterly.

47

The fate of Philistia

[1] The word of HASHEM that came to Jeremiah the prophet concerning the Philistines, before Pharaoh attacked Gaza: *

[2] Thus said HASHEM: Behold, waters are rising from the North and will become a swift stream; they will sweep away the land and all that is in it, the city and all who dwell in it. The people will cry out and all the inhabitants of the land will wail. [3] Because of the sound of the galloping hooves of his mighty [steeds], because of the noise of his chariots and the tumult of his wheels, fathers will not attend to [their] children because of the feebleness of [their] hands, [4] on the day that is approaching for the plunder of all the Philistines, to cut off any remaining help from Tyre and Sidon, for HASHEM is plundering the Philistines, the remnant of the isle of Caphtor. * [5] Baldness * comes to Gaza, and Ashkelon is demolished, the remnant of their lowland; how long will you cut your flesh? [6] Alas, sword of HASHEM! How long will you not be quiet? Gather yourself into your scabbard; be at ease and be still! [7] But how could it be quiet, when HASHEM has sent it on a mission against Ashkelon and against the seashore, that is where He directed it?

48

The fate of Moab

[1] Concerning Moab: *

Thus said HASHEM, Master of Legions, God of Israel: Alas unto Nebo, for it has been plundered; shamed, captured was Kiriathaim; shamed was Misgab* and devastated. [2] The glory of Moab is no more; in Heshbon [its enemies] have devised evil against it: 'Let us go and eliminate it from nationhood.' Madmein, also be still, for the sword will come after you. [3] The sound of outcry comes from Horonaim, plunder and a great calamity. [4] Moab has been shattered; its youths have let out a cry. [5] For people will go up the ascent of Luhith with weeping, ascending weeping; for in the descent of Horonaim, adversaries heard the cries of calamity. [6] Flee, save yourselves; be like Aroer* in the desert! [7] For, because you put your trust in your accomplishments and in your treasures, you, too, will be conquered.

ח וַיָּבֹא °כמיש [°כְמוֹשׁ ק] בַּגוֹלָה כֹּהֲנָיו וְשָׂרָיו °יַחַד [°יַחְדָּיו ק]: וְיָבֹא
שֹׁדֵד אֶל־כָּל־עִיר וְעִיר לֹא תִמָּלֵט וְאָבַד הָעֵמֶק וְנִשְׁמַד הַמִּישֹׁר אֲשֶׁר

ט אָמַר יְהוָה: תְּנוּ־צִיץ לְמוֹאָב כִּי נָצֹא תֵּצֵא וְעָרֶיהָ לְשַׁמָּה תִהְיֶינָה מֵאֵין
י-יא יוֹשֵׁב בָּהֵן: אָרוּר עֹשֶׂה מְלֶאכֶת יְהוָה רְמִיָּה וְאָרוּר מֹנֵעַ חַרְבּוֹ מִדָּם: שַׁאֲנַן
מוֹאָב מִנְּעוּרָיו וְשֹׁקֵט הוּא אֶל־שְׁמָרָיו וְלֹא־הוּרַק מִכְּלִי אֶל־כֶּלִי וּבַגּוֹלָה

יב לֹא הָלָךְ עַל־כֵּן עָמַד טַעְמוֹ בּוֹ וְרֵיחוֹ לֹא נָמָר: לָכֵן הִנֵּה־יָמִים
בָּאִים נְאֻם־יְהוָה וְשִׁלַּחְתִּי־לוֹ צֹעִים וְצֵעֻהוּ וְכֵלָיו יָרִיקוּ וְנִבְלֵיהֶם יְנַפֵּצוּ:

יג-יד וּבֹשׁ מוֹאָב מִכְּמוֹשׁ כַּאֲשֶׁר־בֹּשׁוּ בֵּית יִשְׂרָאֵל מִבֵּית אֵל מִבְטֶחָם: אֵיךְ
תֹּאמְרוּ גִּבּוֹרִים אֲנָחְנוּ וְאַנְשֵׁי־חַיִל לַמִּלְחָמָה: שֻׁדַּד מוֹאָב וְעָרֶיהָ עָלָה

טו-טז וּמִבְחַר בַּחוּרָיו יָרְדוּ לַטָּבַח נְאֻם־הַמֶּלֶךְ יְהוָה צְבָאוֹת שְׁמוֹ: קָרוֹב אֵיד־
מוֹאָב לָבוֹא וְרָעָתוֹ מִהֲרָה מְאֹד: נֻדוּ לוֹ כָּל־סְבִיבָיו וְכֹל יֹדְעֵי שְׁמוֹ אִמְרוּ

יז-יח אֵיכָה נִשְׁבַּר מַטֵּה־עֹז מַקֵּל תִּפְאָרָה: רְדִי מִכָּבוֹד °ישבי [°וּשְׁבִי ק] בַּצָּמָא
יט יֹשֶׁבֶת בַּת־דִּיבוֹן כִּי־שֹׁדֵד מוֹאָב עָלָה בָךְ שִׁחֵת מִבְצָרָיִךְ: אֶל־דֶּרֶךְ עִמְדִי
כ וְצַפִּי יוֹשֶׁבֶת עֲרוֹעֵר שַׁאֲלִי־נָס וְנִמְלָטָה אִמְרִי מַה־נִּהְיָתָה: הֹבִישׁ מוֹאָב
כִּי־חַתָּה °הילילי [°הֵילִילוּ ק] וזעקי [°וּזְעָקוּ ק] הַגִּידוּ בְאַרְנוֹן כִּי שֻׁדַּד

כא מוֹאָב: וּמִשְׁפָּט בָּא אֶל־אֶרֶץ הַמִּישֹׁר אֶל־חֹלוֹן וְאֶל־יַהְצָה וְעַל־°מופעת
כב-כג [°מֵיפָעַת ק]: וְעַל־דִּיבוֹן וְעַל־נְבוֹ וְעַל־בֵּית דִּבְלָתָיִם: וְעַל־קִרְיָתַיִם וְעַל־
כד בֵּית גָּמוּל וְעַל־בֵּית מְעוֹן: וְעַל־קְרִיּוֹת וְעַל־בָּצְרָה וְעַל כָּל־עָרֵי אֶרֶץ
כה מוֹאָב הָרְחֹקוֹת וְהַקְּרֹבוֹת: נִגְדְּעָה קֶרֶן מוֹאָב וּזְרֹעוֹ נִשְׁבָּרָה נְאֻם יְהוָה:
כו הַשְׁכִּירֻהוּ כִּי עַל־יְהוָה הִגְדִּיל וְסָפַק מוֹאָב בְּקִיאוֹ וְהָיָה לִשְׂחֹק גַּם־הוּא:
כז וְאִם ׀ לוֹא הַשְּׂחֹק הָיָה לְךָ יִשְׂרָאֵל אִם־בְּגַנָּבִים °נמצאה [°נִמְצָא ק]
כח כִּי־מִדֵּי דְבָרֶיךָ בּוֹ תִּתְנוֹדָד: עִזְבוּ עָרִים וְשִׁכְנוּ בַּסֶּלַע יֹשְׁבֵי מוֹאָב
כט וִהְיוּ כְיוֹנָה תְּקַנֵּן בְּעֶבְרֵי פִי־פָחַת: שָׁמַעְנוּ גְאוֹן־מוֹאָב גֵּאֶה מְאֹד גָּבְהוֹ
ל וּגְאוֹנוֹ וְגַאֲוָתוֹ וְרֻם לִבּוֹ: אֲנִי יָדַעְתִּי נְאֻם־יְהוָה עֶבְרָתוֹ וְלֹא־כֵן בַּדָּיו
לא לֹא־כֵן עָשׂוּ: עַל־כֵּן עַל־מוֹאָב אֲיֵלִיל וּלְמוֹאָב כֻּלֹּה אֶזְעָק אֶל־אַנְשֵׁי
לב קִיר־חֶרֶשׂ יֶהְגֶּה: מִבְּכִי יַעְזֵר אֶבְכֶּה־לָּךְ הַגֶּפֶן שִׂבְמָה נְטִישֹׁתַיִךְ עָבְרוּ
לג יָם עַד יָם יַעְזֵר נָגָעוּ עַל־קֵיצֵךְ וְעַל־בְּצִירֵךְ שֹׁדֵד נָפָל: וְנֶאֶסְפָה
שִׂמְחָה וָגִיל מִכַּרְמֶל וּמֵאֶרֶץ מוֹאָב וְיַיִן מִיקָבִים הִשְׁבַּתִּי לֹא־יִדְרֹךְ
לד הֵידָד הֵידָד לֹא הֵידָד: מִזַּעֲקַת חֶשְׁבּוֹן עַד־אֶלְעָלֵה עַד־יַהַץ נָתְנוּ קוֹלָם

48:7. The Moabite deity.

48:11. Moab's tranquility and complacence is compared to a barrel of fine wine that has sat undisturbed in the same place for many years.

48:13. Moab will be as ashamed of its idol, Chemosh, as Israel was of its idol at Beth-el.

48:26-27. When Israel was defeated, the Moabites derided them as well as God, for not having saved His people (Radak).

48:29. In this verse, Jeremiah prophesies the reaction of other nations to Moab's defeat.

48:30. Abraham saved Lot, the ancestor of Moab, yet the Moabites showed gross ingratitude (Rashi).

48:31. Here, Jeremiah prophesies the Moabites' reaction to their nation's downfall.

48:33. See 25:30.

Chemosh* will leave for exile, his priests and officials together. ⁸ A plunderer will come to every city; no city will be spared. The valley will be lost and the plain laid waste, for HASHEM has spoken. ⁹ Give Moab a wing, for they will be flying away! Its cities will become desolate, without an inhabitant in them. ¹⁰ Cursed be the one who carries out the mission of HASHEM deceitfully! Cursed be the one who withholds his sword from bloodshed. ¹¹ Moab was complacent from its youth, tranquil on its lees and not being poured from container to container, * and did not go into exile; therefore its taste has stayed in it, and its scent was not diminished.

Moabite
and Israelite
idolatry
compared

¹² Therefore, behold, days are coming — the word of HASHEM — when I will send against it pourers and they will pour it out; they will empty [Moab's] containers and smash its barrels. ¹³ Moab will be ashamed of Chemosh, just as the House of Israel was ashamed of Beth-el, * in which they trusted. ¹⁴ How can you say, 'We are mighty men, brave men of war'? ¹⁵ Moab has been plundered and its cities obliterated; and its best young men have gone to the slaughter — the word of the King, HASHEM, Master of Legions, is His Name. ¹⁶ Moab's disaster is near to come; its misfortune hurries fast. ¹⁷ Mourn for it, all who are around it and all who know of its renown; say, 'How has the staff of strength, the rod of splendor, been shattered?' ¹⁸ Descend from glory and sit in thirst, O daughter who dwells in Dibon! For the despoiler of Moab has come upon you and has destroyed all your strongholds. ¹⁹ Stand and watch by the road, O dweller of Aroer! Ask him that flees and her that escapes; say, 'What happened?' ²⁰ Moab has become ashamed, for they have been devastated. Wail and cry out! Announce in Arnon that Moab has been plundered.

The
judgment
of Moab

²¹ Judgment is coming to the land of the plain; to Holon, to Jahzah and to Mephaath; ²² to Dibon, to Nebo and to Beth-diblathaim; ²³ to Kiriathaim, to Beth-gamul and to Beth-meon; ²⁴ to Kerioth, to Bozrah and to all the cities of the land of Moab, the far ones and the near ones. ²⁵ The horn of Moab has been nipped, and its arm broken — the word of HASHEM.

²⁶ Get him drunk, for he has been arrogant to HASHEM; let Moab wallow in his vomit, and him too become a laughingstock. ²⁷ For, was Israel not a laughingstock to you? Was he found among thieves? Yet whenever you speak of him you wag your head. * ²⁸ Leave the cities and reside in the rock, O dwellers of Moab; be like a dove who nests in the sides of the pit.

²⁹ 'We* have heard of the pride of Moab, it was excessively prideful: his conceit, his pride, his haughtiness and the arrogance of his heart.'

³⁰ I know his fury — the word of HASHEM — and it is unfounded; his heroes acted improperly. *

³¹ 'Therefore, for Moab will I wail, * and for all of Moab will I cry out; moan for the men of Kir-heres. ³² I will weep for you like the weeping of Jazer, O vine of Sibmah; your shoots have gone over the sea, reaching the sea of Jazer; upon your fruits and upon your grape harvest has the plunderer descended.'

³³ Joy and happiness will cease from the fertile field and from the land of Moab. I have abolished wine from the winepresses; they will no longer trample [the grapes with cries of] 'Hedad!'* — no [more] 'Hedad!' ³⁴ An outcry from Heshbon to Elealeh, as far as Jahaz have they raised their voice;

מִצְעָר עַד־חֹרֹנַ֫יִם עֶגְלַ֤ת שְׁלִשִׁיָּ֔ה כִּ֚י גַּם־מֵ֣י נִמְרִ֔ים לִמְשַׁמּ֖וֹת יִהְיֽוּ׃

לה-לו וְהִשְׁבַּתִּ֤י לְמוֹאָב֙ נְאֻם־יְהֹוָ֔ה מַעֲלֶ֥ה בָמָ֖ה וּמַקְטִ֥יר לֵֽאלֹהָֽיו׃ עַל־כֵּ֞ן לִבִּ֤י לְמוֹאָב֙ כַּחֲלִלִ֣ים יֶהֱמֶ֔ה וְלִבִּ֛י אֶל־אַנְשֵׁ֥י קִֽיר־חֶ֖רֶשׂ כַּחֲלִילִ֣ים יֶהֱמֶ֑ה עַל־כֵּ֛ן

לו יִתְרַ֥ת עָשָׂ֖ה אָבָֽדוּ׃ כִּ֤י כׇל־רֹאשׁ֙ קׇרְחָ֔ה וְכׇל־זָקָ֖ן גְּרֻעָ֑ה עַל־כׇּל־

לז יָדַ֣יִם גְּדֻדֹ֔ת וְעַל־מׇתְנַ֖יִם שָֽׂק׃ עַ֣ל כׇּל־גַּגּ֥וֹת מוֹאָ֛ב וּבִרְחֹבֹתֶ֖יהָ כֻּלֹּ֣ה מִסְפֵּ֑ד

לח כִּֽי־שָׁבַ֤רְתִּי אֶת־מוֹאָב֙ כִּכְלִ֣י אֵֽין־חֵ֣פֶץ בּ֔וֹ נְאֻם־יְהֹוָֽה׃ אֵ֥יךְ

לט חַ֙תָּה֙ הֵילִ֔ילוּ אֵ֛יךְ הִפְנָה־עֹ֥רֶף מוֹאָ֖ב בּ֑וֹשׁ וְהָיָ֥ה מוֹאָ֛ב לִשְׂחֹ֥ק וְלִמְחִתָּ֖ה לְכׇל־סְבִיבָֽיו׃ כִּי־כֹה֙ אָמַ֣ר יְהֹוָ֔ה הִנֵּ֥ה כַנֶּ֖שֶׁר יִדְאֶ֑ה וּפָרַ֥שׂ

מ כְּנָפָ֖יו אֶל־מוֹאָֽב׃ נִלְכְּדָה֙ הַקְּרִיּ֔וֹת וְהַמְּצָד֖וֹת נִתְפָּ֑שָׂה וְֽהָיָ֞ה לֵ֣ב גִּבּוֹרֵ֤י

מא מוֹאָב֙ בַּיּ֣וֹם הַה֔וּא כְּלֵ֖ב אִשָּׁ֥ה מְצֵרָֽה׃ וְנִשְׁמַ֥ד מוֹאָ֖ב מֵעָ֑ם כִּ֥י עַל־יְהֹוָ֖ה

מב הִגְדִּֽיל׃ פַּ֥חַד וָפַ֖חַת וָפָ֑ח עָלֶ֛יךָ יוֹשֵׁ֥ב מוֹאָ֖ב נְאֻם־יְהֹוָֽה׃ °הַנִּיס [הַנָּ֞ס ק]

מג-מד מִפְּנֵ֤י הַפַּ֙חַד֙ יִפֹּ֣ל אֶל־הַפַּ֔חַת וְהָֽעֹלֶה֙ מִן־הַפַּ֔חַת יִלָּכֵ֖ד בַּפָּ֑ח כִּֽי־אָבִ֨יא אֵלֶ֧יהָ אֶל־מוֹאָ֛ב שְׁנַ֥ת פְּקֻדָּתָ֖ם נְאֻם־יְהֹוָֽה׃ בְּצֵ֥ל חֶשְׁבּ֖וֹן עָמְד֣וּ מִכֹּ֑חַ

מה נָסִ֗ים כִּי־אֵ֞שׁ יָצָ֤א מֵֽחֶשְׁבּוֹן֙ וְלֶ֣הָבָ֔ה מִבֵּ֖ין סִיח֑וֹן וַתֹּ֙אכַל֙ פְּאַ֣ת מוֹאָ֔ב

מו וְקׇדְקֹ֖ד בְּנֵ֥י שָׁאֽוֹן׃ אוֹי־לְךָ֣ מוֹאָ֔ב אָבַ֖ד עַם־כְּמ֑וֹשׁ כִּֽי־לֻקְּח֤וּ בָנֶ֙יךָ֙ בַּשֶּׁ֔בִי

מז וּבְנֹתֶ֖יךָ בַּשִּׁבְיָֽה׃ וְשַׁבְתִּ֧י שְׁבוּת־מוֹאָ֛ב בְּאַחֲרִ֥ית הַיָּמִ֖ים נְאֻם־יְהֹוָ֑ה עַד־הֵ֖נָּה מִשְׁפַּ֥ט מוֹאָֽב׃

מט   א לִבְנֵ֣י עַמּ֗וֹן כֹּ֚ה אָמַ֣ר יְהֹוָ֔ה הֲבָנִ֥ים אֵין֙ לְיִשְׂרָאֵ֔ל אִם־יוֹרֵ֖שׁ אֵ֣ין ל֑וֹ מַדּ֗וּעַ יָרַ֤שׁ מַלְכָּם֙ אֶת־גָּ֔ד וְעַמּ֖וֹ

ב בְּעָרָ֥יו יָשָֽׁב׃ לָכֵ֡ן הִנֵּה֩ יָמִ֨ים בָּאִ֜ים נְאֻם־יְהֹוָ֗ה וְהִשְׁמַעְתִּ֤י אֶל־רַבַּ֤ת בְּנֵֽי־עַמּוֹן֙ תְּרוּעַ֣ת מִלְחָמָ֔ה וְהָֽיְתָה֙ לְתֵ֣ל שְׁמָמָ֔ה וּבְנֹתֶ֖יהָ בָּאֵ֣שׁ תִּצַּ֑תְנָה

ג וְיָרַ֧שׁ יִשְׂרָאֵ֛ל אֶת־יֹרְשָׁ֖יו אָמַ֥ר יְהֹוָֽה׃ הֵילִ֨ילִי חֶשְׁבּ֜וֹן כִּ֣י שֻׁדְּדָה־עַ֗י צְעַקְנָה֮ בְּנ֣וֹת רַבָּה֒ חֲגֹ֣רְנָה שַׂקִּ֔ים סְפֹ֕דְנָה וְהִתְשׁוֹטַ֖טְנָה בַּגְּדֵר֑וֹת

ד כִּ֤י מַלְכָּם֙ בַּגּוֹלָ֣ה יֵלֵ֔ךְ כֹּהֲנָ֥יו וְשָׂרָ֖יו יַחְדָּֽיו׃ מַה־תִּתְהַֽלְלִי֙ בָּֽעֲמָקִ֔ים זָ֣ב

ה עִמְקֵ֔ךְ הַבַּ֖ת הַשּׁוֹבֵבָ֑ה הַבֹּֽטְחָה֙ בְּאֹ֣צְרֹתֶ֔יהָ מִ֖י יָב֣וֹא אֵלָ֑י הִנְנִי֩ מֵבִ֨יא עָלַ֜יִךְ פַּ֗חַד נְאֻם־אֲדֹנָ֧י יֱהֹוִ֛ה צְבָא֖וֹת מִכׇּל־סְבִיבָ֑יִךְ וְנִדַּחְתֶּם֙ אִ֣ישׁ

ו לְפָנָ֔יו וְאֵ֥ין מְקַבֵּ֖ץ לַנֹּדֵֽד׃ וְאַֽחֲרֵי־כֵ֗ן אָשִׁ֛יב אֶת־שְׁב֥וּת בְּנֵֽי־עַמּ֖וֹן נְאֻם־

ז יְהֹוָֽה׃ לֶאֱד֗וֹם כֹּ֤ה אָמַר֙ יְהֹוָ֣ה צְבָא֔וֹת הַאֵ֥ין ע֛וֹד חׇכְמָ֖ה בְּתֵימָ֑ן

48:34. A cow's third calf is considered its choicest offspring. The metaphor applies to either Moab in general (*Metzudos*), Horonaim (*Kara*) or Zoar (see *Isaiah* 15:5).

48:36. Once again, Jeremiah prophesies the words that the Moabites will speak when they meet their national doom.

48:39. The prophet quotes the reaction of the neighboring peoples who will witness the horrible fate of Moab, and who will first mock Moab and then be frightened that they might suffer the same way.

48:45. Sihon was the Amorite conqueror and rebuilder of Heshbon many centuries earlier (see *Numbers* 21:26).

49:1. The Ammonite deity was Malcam, and its followers annexed the territory of Gad after that tribe was driven from the land.

49:3. This prophecy describes Nebuchadnezzar's defeat of the Ammonites, before he conquered Moab and Judah. Jeremiah warns Moabite Heshbon to shudder when hearing of the fall of the Ammonite Ai, for Moab would soon meet the same fate (*Radak*).

[outcries come] from Zoar to Horonaim, a third-born calf; * *for even the waters of Nimrim will become desolate.* ³⁵ *I will abolish for Moab — the word of HASHEM — whoever sacrifices at high places and whoever burns incense to his god.*

³⁶ *'Therefore, my heart* * *moans for Moab like flutes, and my heart moans like flutes for the men of Kir-heres; therefore, the prosperity that they had amassed has been lost.'*

³⁷ *For every head is bald and every beard is plucked; on every hand there are cuts, and on the loins is sackcloth.* ³⁸ *On every rooftop of Moab and in its streets there is lamenting everywhere; for I have shattered Moab like a useless vessel — the word of HASHEM.* ³⁹ *'How have you been devastated!' they wailed. 'How has Moab, in shame, turned its back [in flight]?' For Moab will become a laughingstock and a source of fright* * *for all those around it.*

Woe
unto
Moab

⁴⁰ *For thus said HASHEM: Behold, like an eagle [the enemy] will swoop down and spread its wings against Moab.* ⁴¹ *Kerioth is captured, and the strongholds seized; on that day the hearts of Moab's warriors will be like the heart of a woman in childbirth.* ⁴² *Moab shall be destroyed as a people, for they have been arrogant to HASHEM.* ⁴³ *Terror and pit and snare be upon you, O dweller of Moab! — the word of HASHEM.* ⁴⁴ *Whoever escapes the terror will fall into the pit, and whoever emerges from the pit will be caught in the trap, for I shall bring against Moab the year of their accounting — the word of HASHEM.* ⁴⁵ *Those who flee stand in the shadow of Heshbon, without strength; but a fire has come forth from Heshbon, a flame from the city of Sihon,* * *which consumes the uttermost corner of Moab and the skull of the tumultuous people.* ⁴⁶ *Woe to you, Moab! The people of Chemosh are lost! For your sons are taken into captivity and your daughters into captivity.* ⁴⁷ *However, I will bring back the captivity of Moab in the end of days — the word of HASHEM.*

Until this point is the judgment of Moab.

49

The fate
of Ammon

¹ Concerning the Children of Ammon:

Thus said HASHEM: Does Israel have no children? Does he have no heir? Why, then, has Malcam * *inherited Gad, his people dwelling in its cities?* ² *Therefore, behold, days are coming — the word of HASHEM — when I will make the alarm of war heard in Rabbah [capital] of the Children of Ammon; it will become a heap of ruins and its surrounding towns will be burned down in fire; then Israel will inherit its inheritors, said HASHEM.* ³ *Wail, Heshbon, for Ai has been plundered!* * *Cry out, you daughters of Rabbah; gird yourselves with sackcloth, lament and wander about in the sheepfolds; for Malcam will go out into exile, his priests and his officers together.* ⁴ *Why do you pride yourselves on the valleys? Your valley flows [with blood], O wayward daughter, who trusts in her treasures, [saying,] 'Who could ever attack me?'* ⁵ *Behold, I am bringing a fright upon you from your entire surroundings — the word of my Lord, HASHEM/ELOHIM, Master of Legions — you will scatter, everyone in his own direction, and there will be no one to bring together those who are wandering about.* ⁶ *But afterwards I will return the captivity of the Children of Ammon — the word of HASHEM.*

The fate
of Edom

⁷ Concerning Edom:

Thus said HASHEM, Master of Legions: Is there no more wisdom in Teman?

ח אָבְדָה עֵצָה מִבָּנִים נִסְרְחָה חָכְמָתָם נָסוּ הָפְנוּ הֶעְמִיקוּ לָשֶׁבֶת יֹשְׁבֵי

ט דְּדָן כִּי אֵיד עֵשָׂו הֵבֵאתִי עָלָיו עֵת פְּקַדְתִּיו אִם־בֹּצְרִים בָּאוּ לָךְ לֹא

י יַשְׁאִרוּ עוֹלֵלוֹת אִם־גַּנָּבִים בַּלַּיְלָה הִשְׁחִיתוּ דַיָּם כִּי־אֲנִי חָשַׂפְתִּי אֶת־
עֵשָׂו גִּלֵּיתִי אֶת־מִסְתָּרָיו וְנֶחְבָּה לֹא יוּכָל שֻׁדַּד זַרְעוֹ וְאֶחָיו וּשְׁכֵנָיו

יא־יב וְאֵינֶנּוּ עָזְבָה יְתֹמֶיךָ אֲנִי אֲחַיֶּה וְאַלְמְנֹתֶיךָ עָלַי תִּבְטָחוּ׃ כִּי־
כֹה אָמַר יהוה הִנֵּה אֲשֶׁר־אֵין מִשְׁפָּטָם לִשְׁתּוֹת הַכּוֹס שָׁתוֹ יִשְׁתּוּ

יג וְאַתָּה הוּא נָקֹה תִנָּקֶה לֹא תִנָּקֶה כִּי שָׁתֹה תִּשְׁתֶּה כִּי בִי נִשְׁבַּעְתִּי
נְאֻם־יהוה כִּי־לְשַׁמָּה לְחֶרְפָּה לְחֹרֶב וְלִקְלָלָה תִּהְיֶה בָצְרָה וְכָל־

יד עָרֶיהָ תִהְיֶינָה לְחָרְבוֹת עוֹלָם שְׁמוּעָה שָׁמַעְתִּי מֵאֵת יהוה וְצִיר בַּגּוֹיִם
שָׁלוּחַ הִתְקַבְּצוּ וּבֹאוּ עָלֶיהָ וְקוּמוּ לַמִּלְחָמָה׃ כִּי־הִנֵּה קָטֹן נְתַתִּיךָ

טו בַּגּוֹיִם בָּזוּי בָּאָדָם׃ תִּפְלַצְתְּךָ הִשִּׁיא אֹתָךְ זְדוֹן לִבֶּךָ שֹׁכְנִי בְּחַגְוֵי הַסֶּלַע

טז תֹּפְשִׂי מְרוֹם גִּבְעָה כִּי־תַגְבִּיהַ כַּנֶּשֶׁר קִנֶּךָ מִשָּׁם אוֹרִידְךָ נְאֻם־יהוה׃

יז וְהָיְתָה אֱדוֹם לְשַׁמָּה כֹּל עֹבֵר עָלֶיהָ יִשֹּׁם וְיִשְׁרֹק עַל־כָּל־מַכּוֹתֶהָ׃

יח כְּמַהְפֵּכַת סְדֹם וַעֲמֹרָה וּשְׁכֵנֶיהָ אָמַר יהוה לֹא־יֵשֵׁב שָׁם אִישׁ וְלֹא־
יָגוּר בָּהּ בֶּן־אָדָם׃ הִנֵּה כְּאַרְיֵה יַעֲלֶה מִגְּאוֹן הַיַּרְדֵּן אֶל־נְוֵה אֵיתָן

יט כִּי־אַרְגִּיעָה אֲרִיצֶנּוּ מֵעָלֶיהָ וּמִי בָחוּר אֵלֶיהָ אֶפְקֹד כִּי מִי כָמוֹנִי וּמִי
יֹעִידֶנִּי וּמִי־זֶה רֹעֶה אֲשֶׁר יַעֲמֹד לְפָנָי׃ לָכֵן שִׁמְעוּ עֲצַת־יהוה אֲשֶׁר

כ יָעַץ אֶל־אֱדוֹם וּמַחְשְׁבוֹתָיו אֲשֶׁר חָשַׁב אֶל־יֹשְׁבֵי תֵימָן אִם־לֹא
יִסְחָבוּם צְעִירֵי הַצֹּאן אִם־לֹא־יַשִּׁים עֲלֵיהֶם נְוֵהֶם׃ מִקּוֹל נִפְלָם רָעֲשָׁה

כא הָאָרֶץ צְעָקָה בְּיַם־סוּף נִשְׁמַע קוֹלָהּ׃ הִנֵּה כַנֶּשֶׁר יַעֲלֶה וְיִדְאֶה וְיִפְרֹשׂ

כב כְּנָפָיו עַל־בָּצְרָה וְהָיָה לֵב גִּבּוֹרֵי אֱדוֹם בַּיּוֹם הַהוּא כְּלֵב אִשָּׁה
מְצֵרָה׃

כג לְדַמֶּשֶׂק בּוֹשָׁה חֲמָת וְאַרְפָּד כִּי־שְׁמֻעָה רָעָה

כד שָׁמְעוּ נָמֹגוּ בַּיָּם דְּאָגָה הַשְׁקֵט לֹא יוּכָל׃ רָפְתָה דַמֶּשֶׂק הִפְנְתָה לָנוּס

כה וְרֶטֶט הֶחֱזִיקָה צָרָה וַחֲבָלִים אֲחָזַתָּה כַּיּוֹלֵדָה׃ אֵיךְ לֹא־עֻזְּבָה עִיר

כו °תְּהִלָּה [תְּהִלָּת ק] קִרְיַת מְשׂוֹשִׂי׃ לָכֵן יִפְּלוּ בַחוּרֶיהָ בִּרְחֹבֹתֶיהָ וְכָל־

כז אַנְשֵׁי הַמִּלְחָמָה יִדַּמּוּ בַּיּוֹם הַהוּא נְאֻם יהוה צְבָאוֹת׃ וְהִצַּתִּי אֵשׁ
בְּחוֹמַת דַּמָּשֶׂק וְאָכְלָה אַרְמְנוֹת בֶּן־הֲדָד׃　　　　　　　　לְקֵדָר |

כח וּלְמַמְלְכוֹת חָצוֹר אֲשֶׁר הִכָּה °נְבוּכַדְרֶאצוֹר [נְבוּכַדְרֶאצַּר ק] מֶלֶךְ־בָּבֶל

49:9. But the Babylonians caused utter and complete devastation.

49:12. If the alien nations, who perhaps thought to justify their hostility to Israel because they viewed Israel as a foreign invader, were nevertheless made to drink from the cup of retribution, will you, Edom (Esau), brother of Israel (Jacob), be absolved?

49:14. This verse is Jeremiah's own comment.

49:20. The enemy, who was earlier compared to a ferocious lion (v. 19), is here likened to the youngest sheep, because Edom will be conquered by Israel, which is regarded lightly by all its enemies (Kara).

49:25. Jeremiah prophesies the words of the king of Damascus at its downfall.

49:28. These were nomadic tribes, like today's Bedouins (Rashi).

Counsel has been lost from the children; their wisdom has turned putrid. ⁸ Flee, be evacuated, dwell in the depths, O inhabitants of Dedan; for I have brought Esau's calamity upon him, the time when I will call him to account. ⁹ If grape harvesters would come to you, would they not leave over gleanings? If thieves in the night, would they damage after they were satisfied?* ¹⁰ For I have uncovered Esau; I have exposed his hidden places, and he cannot hide. Plundered were his offspring, his brothers and his neighbors, and there is no one [to say,] ¹¹ 'Leave your orphans; I will sustain [them]; your widows can depend on me.'

¹² For thus said HASHEM: Behold, if those who did not deserve to drink of the cup have drunk, will you be absolved?* You will not be absolved, but you shall most certainly drink! ¹³ For I swear by Myself — the word of HASHEM — that Bozrah will be made desolate, a shame, a ruin and a curse; and all its towns will suffer eternal destruction.

¹⁴ *I have heard the tidings from HASHEM, and a messenger has been sent among the nations: [saying,] "Gather together and come against it, and rise up to battle!"

Edom's inferiority ¹⁵ For behold, I have made you inferior among the nations, despised among men. ¹⁶ Your awe-inspiring presence has misled you, the wickedness of your heart, [you] who dwells in the crags of the rock, who has seized the height of the hill. Even if you raise your nest as high as the eagle, I will bring you down from there — the word of HASHEM. ¹⁷ Edom shall be desolate; everyone who passes by it will be astonished and whistle over all its afflictions, ¹⁸ like the overturning of Sodom and Gomorrah and its neighbors — said HASHEM — where no man shall dwell and no human shall sojourn. ¹⁹ Behold, [the enemy] will ascend as a lion from the heights of the Jordan to a secure pasture land; for I shall bring [the enemy] suddenly and make him overrun her, and he who is chosen I shall charge against her. For who is like Me? Who can challenge Me? And who is the shepherd who can stand before Me?

²⁰ Therefore, hear the counsel of HASHEM that He has devised against Edom, and His thoughts that he has conceived against the dwellers of Teman: the youngest of the flock will indeed drag them off;* he will indeed devastate their pasture. ²¹ From the sound of their fall the earth quakes; a cry, at the Sea of Reeds their voice is heard. ²² Behold, [the enemy] will ascend like an eagle and swoop down and spread out his wings over Bozrah. On that day, the hearts of the mighty men of Edom will be like the heart of a woman in travail.

The fate of Damascus ²³ Concerning Damascus:

Hamath and Arpad are ashamed, for they have heard an ominous report and have melted in fear. There is trouble in the sea, it cannot be calm. ²⁴ Damascus is weakened; she has turned aside to flee and trembling has overpowered her; agony and pains have seized her like a woman in childbirth. ²⁵ 'How was the city of glory not spared, the city of my delight?'* ²⁶ Indeed, her young men will fall in her streets, and all the soldiers will fall silent on that day — the word of HASHEM, Master of Legions. ²⁷ And I will set fire to the wall of Damascus, and it will consume the palaces of Ben-hadad.

²⁸ Concerning Kedar and the kingdoms of Hazor,* whom Nebuchadrezzar king of Babylonia struck:

כט כֹּ֣ה אָמַ֣ר יְהֹוָ֗ה ק֤וּמוּ עֲלוּ֙ אֶל־קֵדָ֔ר וְשָׁדְד֖וּ אֶת־בְּנֵי־קֶ֑דֶם אׇהֳלֵיהֶ֤ם
וְצֹאנָם֙ יִקָּ֔חוּ יְרִיעוֹתֵיהֶ֤ם וְכׇל־כְּלֵיהֶם֙ וּגְמַלֵּיהֶ֔ם יִשְׂא֖וּ לָהֶ֑ם וְקָרְא֧וּ
ל עֲלֵיהֶ֛ם מָג֖וֹר מִסָּבִֽיב׃ נֻ֣סוּ נֻּדוּ֩ מְאֹ֨ד הֶעְמִ֜יקוּ לָשֶׁ֗בֶת יֹשְׁבֵי֙ חָצ֔וֹר נְאֻם־
יְהֹוָ֑ה כִּֽי־יָעַ֨ץ עֲלֵיכֶ֜ם נְבוּכַדְרֶאצַּ֤ר מֶֽלֶךְ־בָּבֶל֙ עֵצָ֔ה וְחָשַׁ֥ב °עֲלֵיהֶם
לא [°עֲלֵיכֶ֖ם ק׳] מַחֲשָׁבָֽה׃ ק֣וּמוּ עֲל֗וּ אֶל־גּ֥וֹי שְׁלֵ֛יו יוֹשֵׁ֥ב לָבֶ֖טַח נְאֻם־יְהֹוָ֑ה
לב לֹֽא־דְלָתַ֧יִם וְלֹֽא־בְרִ֛יחַ ל֖וֹ בָּדָ֥ד יִשְׁכֹּֽנוּ׃ וְהָי֨וּ גְמַלֵּיהֶ֜ם לָבַ֗ז וַהֲמ֤וֹן מִקְנֵיהֶם֙
לְשָׁלָ֔ל וְזֵרִתִ֥ים לְכׇל־ר֖וּחַ קְצוּצֵ֣י פֵאָ֑ה וּמִכׇּל־עֲבָרָ֛יו אָבִ֥יא אֶת־אֵידָ֖ם
לג נְאֻם־יְהֹוָֽה׃ וְהָיְתָ֨ה חָצ֜וֹר לִמְע֥וֹן תַּנִּ֛ים שְׁמָמָ֖ה עַד־עוֹלָ֑ם לֹֽא־יֵשֵׁ֥ב שָׁם֙
לד אִ֔ישׁ וְלֹֽא־יָג֥וּר בָּ֖הּ בֶּן־אָדָֽם׃   אֲשֶׁ֨ר הָיָ֤ה דְבַר־יְהֹוָה֙ אֶל־יִרְמְיָ֣הוּ
לה הַנָּבִ֔יא אֶל־עֵילָ֑ם בְּרֵאשִׁ֗ית מַלְכ֛וּת צִדְקִיָּ֥ה מֶלֶךְ־יְהוּדָ֖ה לֵאמֹֽר׃ כֹּ֤ה אָמַר֙
לו יְהֹוָ֣ה צְבָא֔וֹת הִנְנִ֤י שֹׁבֵר֙ אֶת־קֶ֣שֶׁת עֵילָ֔ם רֵאשִׁ֖ית גְּבוּרָתָֽם׃ וְהֵבֵאתִ֨י אֶל־
עֵילָ֜ם אַרְבַּ֣ע רוּח֗וֹת מֵֽאַרְבַּע֙ קְצ֣וֹת הַשָּׁמַ֔יִם וְזֵ֣רִתִ֔ים לְכֹ֖ל הָרֻח֣וֹת הָאֵ֑לֶּה
לז וְלֹֽא־יִהְיֶ֣ה הַגּ֔וֹי אֲשֶׁ֛ר לֹֽא־יָב֥וֹא שָׁ֖ם נִדְחֵ֥י °עוֹלָם [°עֵילָ֑ם ק׳]׃ וְהַחְתַּתִּ֣י
אֶת־עֵ֠ילָ֠ם לִפְנֵ֨י אֹיְבֵיהֶ֜ם וְלִפְנֵ֣י ׀ מְבַקְשֵׁ֣י נַפְשָׁ֗ם וְהֵבֵאתִ֨י עֲלֵיהֶ֤ם ׀ רָעָה֙
אֶת־חֲר֣וֹן אַפִּ֔י נְאֻם־יְהֹוָ֑ה וְשִׁלַּחְתִּ֤י אַחֲרֵיהֶם֙ אֶת־הַחֶ֔רֶב עַ֥ד כַּלּוֹתִ֖י
לח אוֹתָֽם׃ וְשַׂמְתִּ֥י כִסְאִ֖י בְּעֵילָ֑ם וְהַאֲבַדְתִּ֥י מִשָּׁ֛ם מֶ֥לֶךְ וְשָׂרִ֖ים נְאֻם־יְהֹוָֽה׃
לט וְהָיָ֣ה ׀ בְּאַחֲרִ֣ית הַיָּמִ֗ים °אָשׁוּב [°אָשִׁ֞יב ק׳] אֶת־°שבית [°שְׁב֤וּת ק׳]
א עֵילָ֖ם נְאֻם־יְהֹוָֽה׃   הַדָּבָ֗ר אֲשֶׁ֨ר דִּבֶּ֧ר יְהֹוָ֛ה אֶל־בָּבֶ֖ל אֶל־אֶ֣רֶץ   **נ**

ב כַּשְׂדִּ֑ים בְּיַ֖ד יִרְמְיָ֥הוּ הַנָּבִֽיא׃ הַגִּ֨ידוּ בַגּוֹיִ֤ם וְהַשְׁמִ֙יעוּ֙ וּֽשְׂאוּ־נֵ֔ס הַשְׁמִ֖יעוּ
אַל־תְּכַחֵ֑דוּ אִמְרוּ֩ נִלְכְּדָ֨ה בָבֶ֜ל הֹבִ֣ישׁ בֵּ֗ל חַת֙ מְרֹדָ֔ךְ הֹבִ֙ישׁוּ֙ עֲצַבֶּ֔יהָ
ג חַ֖תּוּ גִּלּוּלֶֽיהָ׃ כִּ֣י עָלָה֩ עָלֶ֨יהָ גּ֜וֹי מִצָּפ֗וֹן הֽוּא־יָשִׁ֤ית אֶת־אַרְצָהּ֙ לְשַׁמָּ֔ה
ד וְלֹֽא־יִהְיֶ֥ה יוֹשֵׁ֖ב בָּ֑הּ מֵאָדָ֥ם וְעַד־בְּהֵמָ֖ה נָ֥דוּ הָלָֽכוּ׃ בַּיָּמִ֨ים הָהֵ֤מָּה וּבָעֵ֣ת
הַהִיא֙ נְאֻם־יְהֹוָ֔ה יָבֹ֧אוּ בְנֵֽי־יִשְׂרָאֵ֛ל הֵ֥מָּה וּבְנֵֽי־יְהוּדָ֖ה יַחְדָּ֑ו הָל֤וֹךְ וּבָכוֹ֙
ה יֵלֵ֔כוּ וְאֶת־יְהֹוָ֥ה אֱלֹהֵיהֶ֖ם יְבַקֵּֽשׁוּ׃ צִיּ֣וֹן יִשְׁאָ֔לוּ דֶּ֖רֶךְ הֵ֣נָּה פְנֵיהֶ֑ם בֹּ֚אוּ
ו וְנִלְו֣וּ אֶל־יְהֹוָ֔ה בְּרִ֥ית עוֹלָ֖ם לֹ֥א תִשָּׁכֵֽחַ׃ צֹ֤אן אֹֽבְדוֹת֙ °היה [°הָיוּ֙ ק׳] עַמִּ֔י
רֹעֵיהֶ֣ם הִתְע֔וּם הָרִ֖ים °שובבים [°שֽׁוֹבְב֑וּם ק׳]
ז מֵהַ֤ר אֶל־גִּבְעָה֙ הָלָ֔כוּ שָׁכְח֖וּ רִבְצָֽם׃ כׇּל־מוֹצְאֵיהֶ֣ם אֲכָל֔וּם וְצָרֵיהֶ֖ם
אָמְר֣וּ לֹ֣א נֶאְשָׁ֑ם תַּ֗חַת אֲשֶׁ֨ר חָטְא֤וּ לַֽיהֹוָה֙ נְוֵה־צֶ֔דֶק וּמִקְוֵ֥ה אֲבֽוֹתֵיהֶ֖ם
ח יְהֹוָֽה׃ נֻ֚דוּ מִתּ֣וֹךְ בָּבֶ֔ל וּמֵאֶ֥רֶץ כַּשְׂדִּ֖ים °יצאו [°צֵ֑אוּ ק׳] וִהְי֕וּ
ט כְּעַתּוּדִ֖ים לִפְנֵי־צֹֽאן׃ כִּ֣י הִנֵּ֣ה אָנֹכִ֡י מֵעִיר֩ וּמַעֲלֶ֨ה עַל־בָּבֶ֜ל קְהַ֣ל
גּוֹיִ֤ם גְּדֹלִים֙ מֵאֶ֣רֶץ צָפ֔וֹן וְעָ֣רְכוּ לָ֔הּ מִשָּׁ֖ם תִּלָּכֵ֑ד חִצָּיו֙ כְּגִבּ֣וֹר מַשְׁכִּ֔יל

50:2. Bel and Merodach were principal Babylonian deities.

50:3. Persia and Medea came from the North to conquer Babylonia from Nebuchadnezzar's son (*Rashi*).

50:4. The Jews will cry with joy when the conquer-

ing Persians allow them to return to *Eretz Yisrael* (*Radak*).

50:8. Jeremiah urges the "flock" of Israel to escape from Babylonia, to avoid the slaughter that the invaders would inflict on anyone they would find.

The fate of Kedar and Hazor

Thus said HASHEM: Get up and attack Kedar; plunder the people of the East! [29] *They will take away their tents and their flocks; their curtains and all their vessels and their camels they will carry off for themselves; there will be for them terror from all around.* [30] *Flee! Wander exceedingly! Go stay in deep, hidden places, you inhabitants of Hazor!* — *the word of HASHEM* — *for Nebuchadrezzar king of Babylonia has devised counsel against you and has conceived a thought against you.* [31] *Get up and attack the tranquil nation that dwells securely* — *the word of HASHEM* — *it has no gates and no bolt, they live in isolation.* [32] *Their camels will become spoils and the multitude of their livestock will become booty. I will scatter them in all directions, the remotest corners; from all sides I will bring their calamity* — *the word of HASHEM.* [33] *And Hazor will be a lair of serpents, desolate forever, where no man will dwell and no human will sojourn.*

[34] *The word of HASHEM that came to Jeremiah the prophet concerning Elam, in the beginning of the reign of Zedekiah king of Judah, saying:*

The fate of Elam

[35] *Thus said HASHEM, Master of Legions: Behold, I am breaking the bow of Elam, the apex of their might.* [36] *And I will bring upon Elam four winds from the four corners of the heavens, and I will scatter them to all these directions; there will be no nation where the exiles of Elam will not come.* [37] *I will devastate Elam before their enemies and before those who seek their soul, and I will bring upon them evil, My burning wrath* — *the word of HASHEM; I will send the sword after them, until I make an end of them.* [38] *I will place My throne in Elam; and I will cause king and officers to cease from there* — *the word of HASHEM.* [39] *But it will be, in the end of days, that I will return the captivity of Elam* — *the word of HASHEM.*

50

The fate of Babylonia

[1] *T*he word that HASHEM spoke concerning Babylonia, concerning the land of the Chaldeans, through the hand of Jeremiah the prophet:

[2] *Proclaim it among the nations, announce it and hoist up a banner; make it heard, do not hold back. Say, 'Babylonia is captured! Bel is ashamed, Merodach* is devastated; her idols are ashamed, her gods are devastated;* [3] *for a nation from the North* has attacked it.' They will lay their land waste and there will be no inhabitant in it; from man to beast, they have all wandered and gone off.*

[4] *In those days and at that time* — *the word of HASHEM* — *the Children of Israel will come, they together with the Children of Judah; they will walk along crying,* they will seek out HASHEM, their God.* [5] *They will ask about Zion; their faces will be turned toward it; [and they will say,] 'Come, be joined to HASHEM, with an eternal covenant, never to be forgotten.'* [6] *My people were [like] lost sheep; their shepherds caused them to go astray, aimless in the mountains. They went from mountain to hilltop, they forgot their pasture.* [7] *All who found them devoured them, and their enemies said, 'We feel no guilt; because they sinned against HASHEM, the Abode of righteousness, the Hope of their forefathers, HASHEM.'*

Babylonia will be plundered

[8] *Now wander forth from amid Babylonia, and leave the land of the Chaldeans;* be like male goats in front of the flock.* [9] *For behold, I am arousing and raising up against Babylonia an assembly of great nations from the land of the North and they will array themselves for battle against her; from there they will be captured. His arrows are like a deadly warrior,*

לֹא יָשׁוּב רֵיקָם: וְהָיְתָה כַשְׂדִּים לְשָׁלָל כָּל־שֹׁלְלֶיהָ יִשְׂבָּעוּ נְאֻם־יְהֹוָה: כִּי
°תִשְׂמְחִי [°תִּשְׂמְחוּ ק] כִּי °תַעַלְזִי [°תַעֲלֹזוּ ק] שֹׂסֵי נַחֲלָתִי כִּי °תָפוּשִׁי
[°תָפוֹשׁוּ ק] כְּעֶגְלָה דָשָׁה °וּתִצְהֲלִי [°וְתִצְהֲלוּ ק] כָּאַבִּירִים: בּוֹשָׁה
אִמְּכֶם מְאֹד חָפְרָה יוֹלַדְתְּכֶם הִנֵּה אַחֲרִית גּוֹיִם מִדְבָּר צִיָּה וַעֲרָבָה:
מִקֶּצֶף יְהֹוָה לֹא תֵשֵׁב וְהָיְתָה שְׁמָמָה כֻּלָּהּ כֹּל עֹבֵר עַל־בָּבֶל יִשֹּׁם וְיִשְׁרֹק
עַל־כָּל־מַכּוֹתֶיהָ: עִרְכוּ עַל־בָּבֶל ׀ סָבִיב כָּל־דֹּרְכֵי קֶשֶׁת יְדוּ אֵלֶיהָ אַל־
תַּחְמְלוּ אֶל־חֵץ כִּי לַיהֹוָה חָטָאָה: הָרִיעוּ עָלֶיהָ סָבִיב נָתְנָה יָדָהּ נָפְלוּ
°אָשְׁוִיתֶהָ [°אָשְׁיוֹתֶיהָ ק] נֶהֶרְסוּ חוֹמוֹתֶיהָ כִּי נִקְמַת יְהֹוָה הִיא הִנָּקְמוּ
בָהּ כַּאֲשֶׁר עָשְׂתָה עֲשׂוּ־לָהּ: כִּרְתוּ זוֹרֵעַ מִבָּבֶל וְתֹפֵשׂ מַגָּל בְּעֵת קָצִיר
מִפְּנֵי חֶרֶב הַיּוֹנָה אִישׁ אֶל־עַמּוֹ יִפְנוּ וְאִישׁ לְאַרְצוֹ יָנֻסוּ: שֶׂה
פְזוּרָה יִשְׂרָאֵל אֲרָיוֹת הִדִּיחוּ הָרִאשׁוֹן אֲכָלוֹ מֶלֶךְ אַשּׁוּר וְזֶה הָאַחֲרוֹן
עִצְּמוֹ נְבוּכַדְרֶאצַּר מֶלֶךְ בָּבֶל: לָכֵן כֹּה־אָמַר יְהֹוָה צְבָאוֹת אֱלֹהֵי
יִשְׂרָאֵל הִנְנִי פֹקֵד אֶל־מֶלֶךְ בָּבֶל וְאֶל־אַרְצוֹ כַּאֲשֶׁר פָּקַדְתִּי אֶל־מֶלֶךְ
אַשּׁוּר: וְשֹׁבַבְתִּי אֶת־יִשְׂרָאֵל אֶל־נָוֵהוּ וְרָעָה הַכַּרְמֶל וְהַבָּשָׁן וּבְהַר
אֶפְרַיִם וְהַגִּלְעָד תִּשְׂבַּע נַפְשׁוֹ: בַּיָּמִים הָהֵם וּבָעֵת הַהִיא נְאֻם־יְהֹוָה
יְבֻקַּשׁ אֶת־עֲוֺן יִשְׂרָאֵל וְאֵינֶנּוּ וְאֶת־חַטֹּאת יְהוּדָה וְלֹא תִמָּצֶאינָה כִּי
אֶסְלַח לַאֲשֶׁר אַשְׁאִיר: עַל־הָאָרֶץ מְרָתַיִם עֲלֵה עָלֶיהָ
וְאֶל־יוֹשְׁבֵי פְּקוֹד חֲרֹב וְהַחֲרֵם אַחֲרֵיהֶם נְאֻם־יְהֹוָה וַעֲשֵׂה כְּכֹל אֲשֶׁר
צִוִּיתִיךָ: קוֹל מִלְחָמָה בָּאָרֶץ וְשֶׁבֶר גָּדוֹל: אֵיךְ נִגְדַּע וַיִּשָּׁבֵר פַּטִּישׁ כָּל־
הָאָרֶץ אֵיךְ הָיְתָה לְשַׁמָּה בָּבֶל בַּגּוֹיִם: יָקֹשְׁתִּי לָךְ וְגַם־נִלְכַּדְתְּ בָּבֶל וְאַתְּ
לֹא יָדַעַתְּ נִמְצֵאת וְגַם־נִתְפַּשְׂתְּ כִּי בַיהֹוָה הִתְגָּרִית: פָּתַח יְהֹוָה אֶת־
אוֹצָרוֹ וַיּוֹצֵא אֶת־כְּלֵי זַעְמוֹ כִּי־מְלָאכָה הִיא לַאדֹנָי יֱהֹוִה צְבָאוֹת בְּאֶרֶץ
כַּשְׂדִּים: בֹּאוּ־לָהּ מִקֵּץ פִּתְחוּ מַאֲבֻסֶיהָ סָלּוּהָ כְמוֹ־עֲרֵמִים וְהַחֲרִימוּהָ
אַל־תְּהִי־לָהּ שְׁאֵרִית: חִרְבוּ כָּל־פָּרֶיהָ יֵרְדוּ לַטָּבַח הוֹי עֲלֵיהֶם כִּי־בָא
יוֹמָם עֵת פְּקֻדָּתָם: קוֹל נָסִים וּפְלֵטִים מֵאֶרֶץ בָּבֶל לְהַגִּיד בְּצִיּוֹן אֶת־
נִקְמַת יְהֹוָה אֱלֹהֵינוּ נִקְמַת הֵיכָלוֹ: הַשְׁמִיעוּ אֶל־בָּבֶל ׀ רַבִּים כָּל־דֹּרְכֵי
קֶשֶׁת חֲנוּ עָלֶיהָ סָבִיב אַל־יְהִי־[לָהּ ק ולֹא כ] פְּלֵטָה שַׁלְּמוּ־לָהּ כְּפָעֳלָהּ
כְּכֹל אֲשֶׁר עָשְׂתָה עֲשׂוּ־לָהּ כִּי אֶל־יְהֹוָה זָדָה אֶל־קְדוֹשׁ יִשְׂרָאֵל: לָכֵן
יִפְּלוּ בַחוּרֶיהָ בִּרְחֹבֹתֶיהָ וְכָל־אַנְשֵׁי מִלְחַמְתָּהּ יִדַּמּוּ בַּיּוֹם הַהוּא נְאֻם־
יְהֹוָה: הִנְנִי אֵלֶיךָ זָדוֹן נְאֻם־אֲדֹנָי יֱהֹוִה צְבָאוֹת כִּי בָּא יוֹמְךָ עֵת
פְּקַדְתִּיךָ: וְכָשַׁל זָדוֹן וְנָפַל וְאֵין לוֹ מֵקִים וְהִצַּתִּי אֵשׁ בְּעָרָיו וְאָכְלָה כָּל־

they will not return empty-handed. ¹⁰ The Chaldeans will become plunder; all its plunderers will be sated — the word of HASHEM. ¹¹ because you are glad, because you exult, you tramplers of My heritage; because you fatten yourselves like a calf in the grass and neigh like mighty steeds; ¹² your mother is very shamed; the one who bore you is embarrassed; behold, the final outcome of the nations is as a wilderness, a wasteland and a desert. * ¹³ Out of the rage of HASHEM it will not be inhabited, and all of it will be desolate; whoever passes Babylonia will be astonished and whistle over all its afflictions. ¹⁴ Array yourselves for battle against Babylonia all around, all you who draw the bow; shoot at her, do not spare arrows; for she has sinned to HASHEM. ¹⁵ Shout [the battle cry] against her, she puts her hand [out for help] all around. The foundations of her wall have fallen, her walls were cast down. Because it is the vengeance of HASHEM; be avenged against her! Do to her as she did! ¹⁶ Eliminate the sower from Babylonia, as well as the bearer of a sickle at harvest time; from before the oppressor's sword, every man will turn toward his people and every man will flee to his country. *

¹⁷ Israel is [like] scattered sheep — lions have dispersed them; the first one, the king of Assyria, devoured him, and this last one, Nebuchadrezzar king of Babylonia, chewed up the bones. ¹⁸ Therefore, thus said HASHEM, Master of Legions, God of Israel: Behold, I will punish the king of Babylonia and his land, just as I punished the king of Assyria. ¹⁹ And I will return Israel to its abode, and he will graze in the Carmel and in the Bashan; and in Mount Ephraim and in the Gilead his soul will be satiated. ²⁰ In those days and at that time — the word of HASHEM — the iniquity of Israel will be sought but it will not be there, and the transgressions of Judah, but they will not be found; for I will forgive those whom I will leave over.

²¹ Attack the rebellious land* and the inhabitants of Pekod; destroy and demolish them, the word of HASHEM, and do according to all that I command you! ²² There is a sound of war in the land and a great disaster. ²³ How has the hammer for the whole world been snapped and broken? How has Babylonia become desolate among the nations? ²⁴ I laid a snare for you and you were trapped in it, O Babylonia, and you were unaware. You have been found and even seized, for you provoked HASHEM. ²⁵ HASHEM has opened up His arsenal and has taken out the weapons of His wrath, for it is a task for my Lord, HASHEM/ELOHIM, Master of Legions, in the land of the Chaldeans. ²⁶ Come to her from [every] side; open up her storehouses, trample her like piles of grain and decimate her; leave her no remnant. ²⁷ Destroy all her bulls, * let them go down to the slaughter; woe to them, for their day is coming, the time of their reckoning. ²⁸ There is a sound of fleeing people and fugitives from the land of Babylonia to relate in Zion the revenge of HASHEM, our God, the revenge of His Sanctuary. ²⁹ Mobilize against Babylonia, you marksmen, all who draw the bow, encamp against her all around; let her not have any survivor. Repay her according to her actions; do unto her according to all that she has done, for she has acted wickedly toward HASHEM, toward the Holy One of Israel. ³⁰ Therefore, her young men will fall in her streets, and all her men of war will fall silent on that day — the word of HASHEM. ³¹ Behold, I am against you, O wicked one — the word of my Lord, HASHEM/ELOHIM, Master of Legions — for your day has arrived, the time for Me to punish you. ³² The wicked one will stumble and fall, and there will be no one to lift it up. And I will set fire to its cities, and it will consume all

Like Assyria, Babylonia

Babylonia despoiled

לג	סְבִיבֹתָיו:　　כֹּה אָמַר יהוה צְבָאוֹת עֲשׁוּקִים בְּנֵי־יִשְׂרָאֵל
לד	וּבְנֵי־יְהוּדָה יַחְדָּו וְכָל־שֹׁבֵיהֶם הֶחֱזִיקוּ בָם מֵאֲנוּ שַׁלְּחָם: גֹּאֲלָם	חָזָק
	יהוה צְבָאוֹת שְׁמוֹ רִיב יָרִיב אֶת־רִיבָם לְמַעַן הִרְגִּיעַ אֶת־הָאָרֶץ וְהִרְגִּיז
לה	לְיֹשְׁבֵי בָבֶל: חֶרֶב עַל־כַּשְׂדִּים נְאֻם־יהוה וְאֶל־יֹשְׁבֵי בָבֶל וְאֶל־שָׂרֶיהָ
לו-לז	וְאֶל־חֲכָמֶיהָ: חֶרֶב אֶל־הַבַּדִּים וְנֹאָלוּ חֶרֶב אֶל־גִּבּוֹרֶיהָ וָחָתּוּ: חֶרֶב
	אֶל־סוּסָיו וְאֶל־רִכְבּוֹ וְאֶל־כָּל־הָעֶרֶב אֲשֶׁר בְּתוֹכָהּ וְהָיוּ לְנָשִׁים
לח	חֶרֶב אֶל־אוֹצְרֹתֶיהָ וּבֻזָּזוּ: חֹרֶב אֶל־מֵימֶיהָ וְיָבֵשׁוּ כִּי אֶרֶץ פְּסִלִים
לט	הִיא וּבָאֵימִים יִתְהֹלָלוּ: לָכֵן יֵשְׁבוּ צִיִּים אֶת־אִיִּים וְיָשְׁבוּ בָהּ בְּנוֹת
מ	יַעֲנָה וְלֹא־תֵשֵׁב עוֹד לָנֶצַח וְלֹא תִשְׁכּוֹן עַד־דּוֹר וָדוֹר: כְּמַהְפֵּכַת
	אֱלֹהִים אֶת־סְדֹם וְאֶת־עֲמֹרָה וְאֶת־שְׁכֵנֶיהָ נְאֻם־יהוה לֹא־יֵשֵׁב שָׁם
מא	אִישׁ וְלֹא־יָגוּר בָּהּ בֶּן־אָדָם: הִנֵּה עַם בָּא מִצָּפוֹן וְגוֹי גָּדוֹל וּמְלָכִים
מב	רַבִּים יֵעֹרוּ מִיַּרְכְּתֵי־אָרֶץ: קֶשֶׁת וְכִידֹן יַחֲזִיקוּ אַכְזָרִי הֵמָּה וְלֹא
	יְרַחֵמוּ קוֹלָם כַּיָּם יֶהֱמֶה וְעַל־סוּסִים יִרְכָּבוּ עָרוּךְ כְּאִישׁ לַמִּלְחָמָה עָלַיִךְ
מג	בַּת־בָּבֶל: שָׁמַע מֶלֶךְ־בָּבֶל אֶת־שִׁמְעָם וְרָפוּ יָדָיו צָרָה הֶחֱזִיקַתְהוּ
מד	חִיל כַּיּוֹלֵדָה: הִנֵּה כְּאַרְיֵה יַעֲלֶה מִגְּאוֹן הַיַּרְדֵּן אֶל־נְוֵה אֵיתָן כִּי־אַרְגִּעָה
	֯אֲרוּצֵם [°אֲרִיצֵם ק] מֵעָלֶיהָ וּמִי בָחוּר אֵלֶיהָ אֶפְקֹד כִּי מִי כָמוֹנִי
מה	וּמִי יוֹעִדֶנִּי וּמִי־זֶה רֹעֶה אֲשֶׁר יַעֲמֹד לְפָנָי: לָכֵן שִׁמְעוּ עֲצַת־יהוה אֲשֶׁר
	יָעַץ אֶל־בָּבֶל וּמַחְשְׁבוֹתָיו אֲשֶׁר חָשַׁב אֶל־אֶרֶץ כַּשְׂדִּים אִם־לֹא
מו	יִסְחָבוּם צְעִירֵי הַצֹּאן אִם־לֹא יַשִּׁים עֲלֵיהֶם נָוֶה: מִקּוֹל נִתְפְּשָׂה בָבֶל

א	נִרְעֲשָׁה הָאָרֶץ וּזְעָקָה בַּגּוֹיִם נִשְׁמָע:　　כֹּה אָמַר יהוה	נא
ב	הִנְנִי מֵעִיר עַל־בָּבֶל וְאֶל־יֹשְׁבֵי לֵב קָמָי רוּחַ מַשְׁחִית: וְשִׁלַּחְתִּי	
	לְבָבֶל	זָרִים וְזֵרוּהָ וִיבֹקְקוּ אֶת־אַרְצָהּ כִּי־הָיוּ עָלֶיהָ מִסָּבִיב בְּיוֹם	
ג	רָעָה: אֶל־יִדְרֹךְ °יִדְרֹךְ [°ולא ק] הַדֹּרֵךְ קַשְׁתּוֹ וְאֶל־יִתְעַל בְּסִרְיֹנוֹ	
ד	וְאַל־תַּחְמְלוּ אֶל־בַּחֻרֶיהָ הַחֲרִימוּ כָּל־צְבָאָהּ: וְנָפְלוּ חֲלָלִים בְּאֶרֶץ	
ה	כַּשְׂדִּים וּמְדֻקָּרִים בְּחוּצוֹתֶיהָ: °כִּי לֹא־אַלְמָן יִשְׂרָאֵל וִיהוּדָה מֵאֱלֹהָיו	
ו	מֵיהוה צְבָאוֹת כִּי אַרְצָם מָלְאָה אָשָׁם מִקְּדוֹשׁ יִשְׂרָאֵל: נֻסוּ	מִתּוֹךְ	
	בָּבֶל וּמַלְּטוּ אִישׁ נַפְשׁוֹ אַל־תִּדַּמּוּ בַּעֲוֹנָהּ כִּי עֵת נְקָמָה הִיא לַיהוה	
ז	גְּמוּל הוּא מְשַׁלֵּם לָהּ: כּוֹס־זָהָב בָּבֶל בְּיַד־יהוה מְשַׁכֶּרֶת כָּל־הָאָרֶץ	
ח	מִיֵּינָהּ שָׁתוּ גוֹיִם עַל־כֵּן יִתְהֹלְלוּ גוֹיִם: פִּתְאֹם נָפְלָה בָבֶל וַתִּשָּׁבֵר	

50:37. The foreigners who joined in the Babylonian despotism and barbarism (Radak). Let them be as helpless in battle as women against well-armed, well-trained warriors.

51:1. Lit., "the heart of those who rise against Me," i.e.,

the Chaldean people. In the reversed alphabet code known as *at-bash*, לב קמי, *Leb-kamei*, is the coded form of כשדים, *Chaldea* (Rashi).

51:5. Despite the exile, God's people are not alone; He will surely rise to their aid.

its surroundings.

*God will
redeem
Israel*

³³ Thus said HASHEM, Master of Legions: The Children of Israel and the Children of Judah are oppressed together; all their captors hold them fast and refuse to let them free. ³⁴ Their mighty Redeemer, HASHEM, Master of Legions is His Name, will certainly take up their grievance, in order to calm the land and cause trembling for the inhabitants of Babylonia. ³⁵ A sword against the Chaldeans — the word of HASHEM — and against the inhabitants of Babylonia and against its officers and against its wise men! ³⁶ A sword against the sorcerers; let them be shown to be fools! A sword against its mighty men; let them be devastated! ³⁷ A sword against its horses and chariots and against all the foreigners in its midst; let them be like women!* A sword against its treasuries; let them be sacked! ³⁸ A dry heat against its waters; let them evaporate! For it is a land of graven idols, and they are mad over dread idols. ³⁹ Therefore, the martens will inhabit it together with the cats, and owls will dwell there; and it will never again be settled, and it will not be inhabited for generation after generation, ⁴⁰ like HASHEM's overthrow of Sodom and Gomorrah and its neighbors — the word of HASHEM — where no man shall live and no human shall sojourn. ⁴¹ Behold, a people is coming from the North; a great nation and many kings will arouse themselves from the ends of the earth. ⁴² They will be holding bow and spear; they are cruel and will show no mercy; their voice will roar like the sea, and they will ride upon horses. Armed, like a man [going] to war, against you, O daughter of Babylonia. ⁴³ The king of Babylonia heard of their renown and his hands weakened; consternation seizes him, and pains like a woman in childbirth. ⁴⁴ Behold, [the enemy] will ascend like a lion from the heights of the Jordan to a secure pasture land, for I shall bring [the enemy] suddenly and I shall make him overrun them, and I shall charge the designated [enemy] to deal with them. For who is like Me? Who can challenge Me? And who is the shepherd who can stand before Me? ⁴⁵ Therefore, hear the counsel of HASHEM that He has devised against Babylonia, and His thoughts that he has conceived against the land of the Chaldeans: [The enemy] will indeed drag them off, the youngest of the flock; he will indeed destroy their abode. ⁴⁶ The earth quakes from the sound of Babylonia's being seized, and the outcry is heard among the nations.

*No mercy
for Babylonia*

51

¹ Thus said HASHEM: Behold, I am stirring up a spirit of destruction against Babylonia and against the inhabitants of Leb-kamai.* ² I shall send foreigners to Babylonia, who will scatter her and empty her land; for they will descend upon her from all around on the day of evil. ³ To the archer who draws his bow and to the one who goes forth boldly in his armor [I say]: 'Do not have compassion upon her young men; destroy all her legions!' ⁴ The slain will fall in the land of the Chaldeans, and the pierced in her streets. ⁵ For Israel is not widowed, [nor is] Judah, from his God, HASHEM, Master of Legions;* for the [Chaldean] land is full of guilt toward the Holy One of Israel. ⁶ Flee from the midst of Babylonia; everyone save his soul; do not be annihilated for their sin. For it is a time of vengeance for HASHEM; He is paying [Babylonia] her due.

*The golden
cup will
be broken*

⁷ A golden cup was Babylonia in the hand of HASHEM, which intoxicated all the land; nations would drink from its wine, and the nations would thus become crazed. ⁸ But suddenly Babylonia has fallen and become broken.

ט הֵילִ֣ילוּ עָלֶ֗יהָ קְח֤וּ צֳרִי֙ לְמַכְאוֹבָ֔הּ אוּלַ֖י תֵּרָפֵֽא: רְפִאנ֣וּ אֶת־בָּבֶל֮ וְלֹ֣א נִרְפָּ֒תָה֒ עִזְב֕וּהָ וְנֵלֵ֖ךְ אִ֣ישׁ לְאַרְצ֑וֹ כִּֽי־נָגַ֤ע אֶל־הַשָּׁמַ֙יִם֙ מִשְׁפָּטָ֔הּ וְנִשָּׂ֖א

י עַד־שְׁחָקִֽים: הוֹצִ֥יא יהו֖ה אֶת־צִדְקֹתֵ֑ינוּ בֹּ֚אוּ וּנְסַפְּרָ֣ה בְצִיּ֔וֹן אֶת־מַעֲשֵׂ֖ה

יא יהו֥ה אֱלֹהֵֽינוּ: הָבֵ֣רוּ הַחִצִּים֮ מִלְא֣וּ הַשְּׁלָטִים֒ הֵעִ֣יר יהו֗ה אֶת־ר֙וּחַ֙ מַלְכֵ֣י מָדַ֔י כִּי־עַל־בָּבֶ֥ל מְזִמָּת֖וֹ לְהַשְׁחִיתָ֑הּ כִּֽי־נִקְמַ֤ת יהוה֙ הִ֔יא נִקְמַ֖ת

יב הֵיכָלֽוֹ: אֶל־חוֹמֹ֨ת בָּבֶ֜ל שְׂאוּ־נֵ֗ס הַֽחֲזִ֙יקוּ֙ הַמִּשְׁמָ֔ר הָקִ֙ימוּ֙ שֹׁ֣מְרִ֔ים הָכִ֖ינוּ הָאֹֽרְבִ֑ים כִּ֚י גַּם־זָמַ֣ם יהו֔ה גַּם־עָשָׂ֕ה אֵ֛ת אֲשֶׁר־דִּבֶּ֖ר אֶל־יֹשְׁבֵ֥י בָבֶֽל:

יג שֹׁכַנְתְּ֙ [שֹׁכַנְתְּ֙ ק] עַל־מַ֣יִם רַבִּ֔ים רַבַּ֖ת אֽוֹצָרֹ֑ת בָּ֥א קִצֵּ֖ךְ אַמַּ֥ת

יד בִּצְעֵֽךְ: נִשְׁבַּ֛ע יהו֥ה צְבָא֖וֹת בְּנַפְשׁ֑וֹ כִּ֣י אִם־מִלֵּ֤אתִיךְ֙ אָדָם֙ כַּיֶּ֔לֶק וְעָנ֥וּ עָלַ֖יִךְ הֵידָֽד:

טו עֹשֵׂ֥ה אֶ֙רֶץ֙ בְּכֹח֔וֹ מֵכִ֥ין תֵּבֵ֖ל בְּחָכְמָת֑וֹ

טז וּבִתְבוּנָת֖וֹ נָטָ֣ה שָׁמָ֑יִם לְק֨וֹל תִּתּ֜וֹ הֲמ֥וֹן מַ֙יִם֙ בַּשָּׁמַ֔יִם וַיַּ֙עַל֙ נְשִׂאִ֔ים מִקְצֵה־אָ֑רֶץ בְּרָקִ֤ים לַמָּטָר֙ עָשָׂ֔ה וַיּ֥וֹצֵא ר֖וּחַ מֵאֹצְרֹתָֽיו:

יז נִבְעַ֤ר כָּל־אָדָם֙ מִדַּ֔עַת הֹבִ֥ישׁ כָּל־צֹרֵ֖ף מִפָּ֑סֶל כִּ֛י שֶׁ֥קֶר נִסְכּ֖וֹ וְלֹא־ר֥וּחַ בָּֽם: הֶ֣בֶל הֵ֔מָּה

יח מַעֲשֵׂ֖ה תַּעְתֻּעִ֑ים בְּעֵ֥ת פְּקֻדָּתָ֖ם יֹאבֵֽדוּ: לֹֽא־כְאֵ֜לֶּה חֵ֣לֶק יַעֲקֹ֗ב כִּֽי־

יט יוֹצֵ֤ר הַכֹּל֙ ה֔וּא וְשֵׁ֖בֶט נַחֲלָת֑וֹ יהו֥ה צְבָא֖וֹת שְׁמֽוֹ: מַפֵּץ־

כ אַתָּ֣ה לִ֔י כְּלֵ֖י מִלְחָמָ֑ה וְנִפַּצְתִּ֤י בְךָ֙ גּוֹיִ֔ם וְהִשְׁחַתִּ֥י בְךָ֖ מַמְלָכֽוֹת: וְנִפַּצְתִּ֤י

כא בְךָ֙ ס֣וּס וְרֹֽכְב֔וֹ וְנִפַּצְתִּ֥י בְךָ֖ רֶ֥כֶב וְרֹכְבֽוֹ: וְנִפַּצְתִּ֤י בְךָ֙ אִ֣ישׁ וְאִשָּׁ֔ה

כב וְנִפַּצְתִּ֥י בְךָ֖ זָקֵ֣ן וָנָ֑עַר וְנִפַּצְתִּ֥י בְךָ֖ בָּח֥וּר וּבְתוּלָֽה: וְנִפַּצְתִּ֤י בְךָ֙ רֹעֶ֣ה וְעֶדְר֔וֹ

כג וְנִפַּצְתִּ֤י בְךָ֙ אִכָּ֣ר וְצִמְדּ֔וֹ וְנִפַּצְתִּ֥י בְךָ֖ פַּח֣וֹת וּסְגָנִֽים: וְשִׁלַּמְתִּ֨י לְבָבֶ֜ל

כד וּלְכֹ֣ל ׀ יוֹשְׁבֵ֣י כַשְׂדִּ֗ים אֵ֧ת כָּל־רָעָתָ֛ם אֲשֶׁר־עָשׂ֥וּ בְצִיּ֖וֹן לְעֵינֵיכֶ֑ם נְאֻ֖ם יהוֽה:

כה הִנְנִ֤י אֵלֶ֙יךָ֙ הַ֣ר הַמַּשְׁחִ֔ית נְאֻם־יהו֔ה הַמַּשְׁחִ֖ית אֶת־כָּל־הָאָ֑רֶץ וְנָטִ֤יתִי אֶת־יָדִי֙ עָלֶ֔יךָ וְגִלְגַּלְתִּ֙יךָ֙ מִן־הַסְּלָעִ֔ים וּנְתַתִּ֖יךָ

כו לְהַ֥ר שְׂרֵפָֽה: וְלֹֽא־יִקְח֤וּ מִמְּךָ֙ אֶ֣בֶן לְפִנָּ֔ה וְאֶ֖בֶן לְמֽוֹסָד֑וֹת כִּֽי־שִׁמְמ֥וֹת עוֹלָ֖ם תִּֽהְיֶ֣ה נְאֻם־יהוֽה: שְׂאוּ־נֵ֣ס בָּאָ֗רֶץ תִּקְע֙וּ שׁוֹפָ֜ר בַּגּוֹיִם֙ קַדְּשׁ֤וּ

כז עָלֶ֙יהָ֙ גּוֹיִ֔ם הַשְׁמִ֧יעוּ עָלֶ֛יהָ מַמְלְכ֥וֹת אֲרָרַ֖ט מִנִּ֣י וְאַשְׁכְּנָ֑ז פִּקְד֤וּ עָלֶ֙יהָ֙

כח טִפְסָ֔ר הַעֲלוּ־ס֖וּס כְּיֶ֥לֶק סָמָֽר: קַדְּשׁ֙וּ עָלֶ֤יהָ גוֹיִם֙ אֶת־מַלְכֵ֣י מָדַ֔י אֶת־

כט פַּחוֹתֶ֖יהָ וְאֶת־כָּל־סְגָנֶ֑יהָ וְאֵ֖ת כָּל־אֶ֥רֶץ מֶמְשַׁלְתּֽוֹ: וַתִּרְעַ֤שׁ הָאָ֙רֶץ֙ וַתָּחֹ֔ל כִּ֛י קָ֥מָה עַל־בָּבֶ֖ל מַחְשְׁב֣וֹת יהו֑ה לָשׂ֞וּם אֶת־אֶ֧רֶץ בָּבֶ֛ל לְשַׁמָּ֖ה

ל מֵאֵ֣ין יוֹשֵֽׁב: חָדְלוּ֩ גִבּוֹרֵ֨י בָבֶ֜ל לְהִלָּחֵ֗ם יָֽשְׁבוּ֙ בַּמְּצָד֔וֹת נָשְׁתָ֥ה

לא גְבוּרָתָ֖ם הָי֣וּ לְנָשִׁ֑ים הִצִּ֥יתוּ מִשְׁכְּנֹתֶ֖יהָ נִשְׁבְּר֥וּ בְרִיחֶֽיהָ: רָ֤ץ לִקְרַאת־רָץ֙ יָר֔וּץ וּמַגִּ֖יד לִקְרַ֣את מַגִּ֑יד לְהַגִּיד֙ לְמֶ֣לֶךְ בָּבֶ֔ל כִּֽי־נִלְכְּדָ֥ה עִיר֖וֹ

51:9. Babylonia's allies would say this when they saw that she could not be helped.

51:10. He has brought our cause to mind and wrought vengeance for us.

51:14. A common battle cry.

51:25. Babylonia is referred to as a "mountain" because of its great strength and apparent invincibility.

*Babylonia
will not
be healed*

Wail for her; get balm for her pain; perhaps she can be healed. ⁹ *'We tried to heal Babylonia, but she could not be healed; leave her, and let each of us go back to his land!'* For her judgment reaches the very heavens, and rises to the highest heavens.* ¹⁰ HASHEM *has brought out our [deeds of] righteousness;* come let us relate in Zion the action of* HASHEM *our God.* ¹¹ *Prepare the arrows, fill the quivers; for* HASHEM *has stirred up the spirit of the kings of Medea, for His thoughts are directed against Babylonia, to destroy it; for it is the vengeance of* HASHEM, *vengeance for His Sanctuary.* ¹² *Hoist up a banner against the walls of Babylon; strengthen the watch, set up guards, prepare the ambush, for* HASHEM *has also planned, and is also carrying out, what He had spoken concerning the inhabitants of Babylonia.* ¹³ *You who dwell upon many waters, who have many treasures, your end has come, the measure of your violence.* ¹⁴ HASHEM, *Master of Legions, has sworn by Himself, 'I shall fill you with men as [numerous] as locusts, and they will call out against you, "Hedad!" '**

*The
Creator*

¹⁵ *He made the earth with His might, He established the world with His wisdom, and with His understanding spread out the heavens.* ¹⁶ *At the sound of His placement of a multitude of water in the heavens, He raised clouds from the end of the earth; He made lightning bolts for the rain and brings forth wind from His treasuries.* ¹⁷ *Every man is bereft of wisdom, every smith is shamed by [his] graven image, for his molten idol is false, and there is no life in it.* ¹⁸ *They are vanity, the work of deception; when they are called to account, they shall perish.* ¹⁹ *Unlike these is the Portion of Jacob, for He is the Molder of everything, and [Israel] is the tribe of His heritage; His Name is* HASHEM, *Master of Legions.*

²⁰ *You [Babylonia] were a mallet for Me, a tool of war; I smashed nations through you and destroyed kingdoms through you.* ²¹ *Through you I smashed the horse and its rider; through you I smashed the chariot and its rider;* ²² *through you I smashed man and woman, and through you I smashed elder and youth; through you I smashed young man and maiden;* ²³ *through you I smashed the shepherd and his flock; through you I smashed the plowman with his yoke of oxen; through you I smashed governors and deputies.* ²⁴ *Now I shall repay to Babylonia and to all the inhabitants of Chaldea all their evil that they did in Zion before your eyes — the word of* HASHEM.

²⁵ *Behold, I am against you, O Mount of Destruction* — the word of* HASHEM *— that destroys the entire land; I shall stretch out My hand against you; I shall roll you down from the rocks and make you into a burnt mountain.* ²⁶ *They will not take from you a stone for a corner or a stone for foundations, for you will be an eternal wasteland — the word of* HASHEM. ²⁷ *Raise a banner in the land, sound the shofar among the nations; summon nations against it, muster against it the kingdoms of Ararat, Minni and Ashkenaz; appoint a commander against it; bring up the horse, as the bristling locust.* ²⁸ *Prepare nations against it: the kings of Media, its governors and all its dep-*

*Babylonia
desolated*

uties and the entire land of its dominion. ²⁹ *The land quaked and shuddered; for the thoughts of* HASHEM *arose against Babylonia, to lay the land of Babylonia desolate, without inhabitant.* ³⁰ *The warriors of Babylonia have ceased to fight; they settled into the fortresses. Their might has slipped away; they have become [weak] like women. [The enemies] have set fire to its dwellings and its bolts have been broken.* ³¹ *Runner after runner will run, herald after herald to report to the king of Babylonia that his city has been taken*

לב מִקְצֵה: וְהַמַּעְבְּרוֹת נִתְפָּשׂוּ וְאֶת־הָאֲגַמִּים שָׂרְפוּ בָאֵשׁ וְאַנְשֵׁי הַמִּלְחָמָה
לג נִבְהָלוּ:   כִּי כֹה אָמַר יְהֹוָה צְבָאוֹת אֱלֹהֵי יִשְׂרָאֵל בַּת־בָּבֶל
לד כְּגֹרֶן עֵת הִדְרִיכָהּ עוֹד מְעַט וּבָאָה עֵת־הַקָּצִיר לָהּ: °אכלנו [°אֲכָלַנִי ק]
°הממנו [°הֲמָמַנִי ק] נְבוּכַדְרֶאצַּר מֶלֶךְ בָּבֶל °הציגנו [°הִצִּיגַנִי ק]
כְּלִי רִיק °בלענו [°בְּלָעַנִי ק] כַּתַּנִּין מִלָּא כְרֵשׂוֹ מֵעֲדָנָי °הדיחנו
לה [°הֱדִיחָנִי ק]: חֲמָסִי וּשְׁאֵרִי עַל־בָּבֶל תֹּאמַר יֹשֶׁבֶת צִיּוֹן וְדָמִי אֶל־יֹשְׁבֵי
לו כַשְׂדִּים תֹּאמַר יְרוּשָׁלָ͏ִם: לָכֵן כֹּה אָמַר יְהֹוָה הִנְנִי־רָב אֶת־רִיבֵךְ
לז וְנִקַּמְתִּי אֶת־נִקְמָתֵךְ וְהַחֲרַבְתִּי אֶת־יַמָּהּ וְהֹבַשְׁתִּי אֶת־מְקוֹרָהּ: וְהָיְתָה
לח בָבֶל ׀ לְגַלִּים ׀ מְעוֹן־תַּנִּים שַׁמָּה וּשְׁרֵקָה מֵאֵין יוֹשֵׁב: יַחְדָּו כַּכְּפִרִים
לט יִשְׁאָגוּ נָעֲרוּ כְּגוֹרֵי אֲרָיוֹת: בְּחֻמָּם אָשִׁית אֶת־מִשְׁתֵּיהֶם וְהִשְׁכַּרְתִּים
מ לְמַעַן יַעֲלֹזוּ וְיָשְׁנוּ שְׁנַת־עוֹלָם וְלֹא יָקִיצוּ נְאֻם יְהֹוָה: אוֹרִידֵם כְּכָרִים
מא לִטְבוֹחַ כְּאֵילִים עִם־עַתּוּדִים: אֵיךְ נִלְכְּדָה שֵׁשַׁךְ וַתִּתָּפֵשׂ תְּהִלַּת כָּל־
מב הָאָרֶץ אֵיךְ הָיְתָה לְשַׁמָּה בָּבֶל בַּגּוֹיִם: עָלָה עַל־בָּבֶל הַיָּם בַּהֲמוֹן גַּלָּיו
מג נִכְסָתָה: הָיוּ עָרֶיהָ לְשַׁמָּה אֶרֶץ צִיָּה וַעֲרָבָה אֶרֶץ לֹא־יֵשֵׁב בָּהֵן כָּל־אִישׁ
מד וְלֹא־יַעֲבֹר בָּהֵן בֶּן־אָדָם: וּפָקַדְתִּי עַל־בֵּל בְּבָבֶל וְהֹצֵאתִי אֶת־בִּלְעוֹ
מה מִפִּיו וְלֹא־יִנְהֲרוּ אֵלָיו עוֹד גּוֹיִם גַּם־חוֹמַת בָּבֶל נָפָלָה: צְאוּ מִתּוֹכָהּ עַמִּי
מו וּמַלְּטוּ אִישׁ אֶת־נַפְשׁוֹ מֵחֲרוֹן אַף־יְהֹוָה: וּפֶן־יֵרַךְ לְבַבְכֶם וְתִירְאוּ
בַשְּׁמוּעָה הַנִּשְׁמַעַת בָּאָרֶץ וּבָא בַשָּׁנָה הַשְּׁמוּעָה וְאַחֲרָיו בַּשָּׁנָה
מז הַשְּׁמוּעָה וְחָמָס בָּאָרֶץ וּמֹשֵׁל עַל־מֹשֵׁל: לָכֵן הִנֵּה יָמִים בָּאִים וּפָקַדְתִּי
מח עַל־פְּסִילֵי בָבֶל וְכָל־אַרְצָהּ תֵּבוֹשׁ וְכָל־חֲלָלֶיהָ יִפְּלוּ בְתוֹכָהּ: וְרִנְּנוּ עַל־
בָּבֶל שָׁמַיִם וָאָרֶץ וְכֹל אֲשֶׁר בָּהֶם כִּי מִצָּפוֹן יָבוֹא־לָהּ הַשּׁוֹדְדִים נְאֻם־
מט יְהֹוָה: גַּם־בָּבֶל לִנְפֹּל חַלְלֵי יִשְׂרָאֵל גַּם־לְבָבֶל נָפְלוּ חַלְלֵי כָל־הָאָרֶץ:
נ פְּלֵטִים מֵחֶרֶב הִלְכוּ אַל־תַּעֲמֹדוּ זִכְרוּ מֵרָחוֹק אֶת־יְהֹוָה וִירוּשָׁלַ͏ִם
נא תַּעֲלֶה עַל־לְבַבְכֶם: בֹּשְׁנוּ כִּי־שָׁמַעְנוּ חֶרְפָּה כִּסְּתָה כְלִמָּה פָּנֵינוּ כִּי
נב בָּאוּ זָרִים עַל־מִקְדְּשֵׁי בֵּית יְהֹוָה: לָכֵן הִנֵּה־יָמִים בָּאִים
נג נְאֻם־יְהֹוָה וּפָקַדְתִּי עַל־פְּסִילֶיהָ וּבְכָל־אַרְצָהּ יֶאֱנֹק חָלָל: כִּי־תַעֲלֶה
בָבֶל הַשָּׁמַיִם וְכִי תְבַצֵּר מְרוֹם עֻזָּהּ מֵאִתִּי יָבֹאוּ שֹׁדְדִים לָהּ נְאֻם־
נד-נה יְהֹוָה: קוֹל זְעָקָה מִבָּבֶל וְשֶׁבֶר גָּדוֹל מֵאֶרֶץ כַּשְׂדִּים: כִּי־שֹׁדֵד יְהֹוָה אֶת־
בָּבֶל וְאִבַּד מִמֶּנָּה קוֹל גָּדוֹל וְהָמוּ גַלֵּיהֶם כְּמַיִם רַבִּים נִתַּן שְׁאוֹן קוֹלָם:

51:39. A reference to King Belshazzar's drunken orgy, huge royal banquet and assassination (*Daniel* Ch. 5).

51:41. In the reverse alphabet code known as *at-bash*, שׁשׁך, *Sheshach*, is the coded form of בבל, *Babylonia* (*Rashi*).

51:44. Bel was the chief deity of Babylonia. The metaphor means, "I will take away the wealth that Babylonia has accumulated from its vassal nations" (*Kara*).

51:46. There will be a report of the impending Persian invasion (*Radak*). After the Persian conquest, Darius, the conqueror, and Cyrus will reign in quick succession (*Rashi*).

51:50. Jeremiah urges the Jewish survivors in Babylonia to take advantage of Cyrus's future offer to rebuild the Temple.

51:51. Israel responds.

from end [to end]. ³² And the river crossings have been seized and the fortresses burned with fire; and the soldiers have become overwhelmed.

³³ For thus said HASHEM, Master of Legions, the God of Israel: The daughter of Babylonia is like a threshing floor at the time of its threshing; in a little while the harvest time will have come for her.

³⁴ 'Nebuchadrezzar, the king of Babylonia, devoured me and demolished me; he left me like an empty vessel; he swallowed me like a serpent; he filled his stomach with my delicacies; he washed me out. ³⁵ May the violence done against me and my sustenance be upon Babylonia,' says the inhabitant of Zion; 'and my blood upon the inhabitants of the Chaldeans,' says Jerusalem.

Babylonia will be a heap

³⁶ Therefore, thus said HASHEM: Behold, I take up your grievance and avenge your vengeance, and I will dry out its sea and I will dry up its source. ³⁷ Babylonia will be a heap, a lair for jackals, desolate and a source of whistling, without inhabitant. ³⁸ Together the [enemies] will roar like lion whelps; they growl like lion cubs. ³⁹ During their drunkenness I will spoil their drinking parties; I will intoxicate them so that they become merry; they will sleep an eternal sleep and never awaken — the word of HASHEM. * ⁴⁰ I will bring them down like fatted sheep for the slaughter, like rams and goats. ⁴¹ How has Sheshach* been captured, and the glory of the whole world seized? How has Babylonia become a desolation among the nations? ⁴² The sea has risen against Babylonia; she has been covered over by the multitude of its waves. ⁴³ Its cities have become desolate, an arid land and a desert; a land in which no man lives and through which no human passes. ⁴⁴ I will deal with Bel in Babylonia and I will remove from his mouth what he has swallowed, * and nations will no longer be drawn to him; even the wall of Babylonia will tumble.

⁴⁵ Go out from its midst, My people, and let each man save his soul from the burning anger of HASHEM. ⁴⁶ Lest you be disheartened and frightened by the report that will be heard in the land, a report will come that year and after it a report the next year: Violence in the land, and one ruler after another. *

⁴⁷ Therefore, behold, days are coming when I will deal with the graven idols of Babylonia, and its entire land will be ashamed; and all its slain will

Plundered from the north

fall in its midst. ⁴⁸ Heaven and earth and all that is in them will rejoice over Babylonia, for the plunderers will come to it from the North — the word of HASHEM — ⁴⁹ because Babylonia caused the slain of Israel to fall; and because of Babylonia the slain of the entire land fell. ⁵⁰ O survivors of the sword* — go forth, do not stand still; remember HASHEM from the distance and let Jerusalem come up in your hearts!

⁵¹ "We* were shamed, for we heard words of disgrace; embarrassment covered our faces; for foreigners set upon the sanctuaries of HASHEM's Temple."

⁵² Therefore, behold, days are coming — the word of HASHEM — when I will attend to their graven idols, and in all their land the mortally wounded will groan. ⁵³ Even if Babylonia were to ascend to the heavens, and even if she were to fortify the height of her strongholds, pillagers would come to her from Me — the word of HASHEM. ⁵⁴ A sound, a cry from Babylonia, and of a great calamity from the land of the Chaldeans, ⁵⁵ for HASHEM is plundering Babylonia and He will end the loud sound from it; their waves roared like many waters; the din of their voices went forth.

נו כִּי בָא עָלֶיהָ עַל־בָּבֶל שׁוֹדֵד וְנִלְכְּדוּ גִּבּוֹרֶיהָ חִתְּתָה קַשְּׁתוֹתָם כִּי אֵל

נז גְּמֻלוֹת יְהֹוָה שַׁלֵּם יְשַׁלֵּם: וְהִשְׁכַּרְתִּי שָׂרֶיהָ וַחֲכָמֶיהָ פַּחוֹתֶיהָ וּסְגָנֶיהָ וְגִבּוֹרֶיהָ וְיָשְׁנוּ שְׁנַת־עוֹלָם וְלֹא יָקִיצוּ נְאֻם־הַמֶּלֶךְ יְהֹוָה צְבָאוֹת

נח שְׁמוֹ: כֹּה־אָמַר יְהֹוָה צְבָאוֹת חֹמוֹת בָּבֶל הָרְחָבָה עַרְעֵר תִּתְעַרְעָר וּשְׁעָרֶיהָ הַגְּבֹהִים בָּאֵשׁ יִצַּתּוּ וְיִגְעוּ עַמִּים בְּדֵי־רִיק וּלְאֻמִּים

נט בְּדֵי־אֵשׁ וְיָעֵפוּ: הַדָּבָר אֲשֶׁר־צִוָּה ׀ יִרְמְיָהוּ הַנָּבִיא אֶת־ שְׂרָיָה בֶן־נֵרִיָּה בֶּן־מַחְסֵיָה בְּלֶכְתּוֹ אֶת־צִדְקִיָּהוּ מֶלֶךְ־יְהוּדָה בָּבֶל בִּשְׁנַת הָרְבִעִית לְמָלְכוֹ וּשְׂרָיָה שַׂר מְנוּחָה: וַיִּכְתֹּב יִרְמְיָהוּ אֵת כָּל־הָרָעָה

ס אֲשֶׁר־תָּבוֹא אֶל־בָּבֶל אֶל־סֵפֶר אֶחָד אֵת כָּל־הַדְּבָרִים הָאֵלֶּה הַכְּתֻבִים

סא אֶל־בָּבֶל: וַיֹּאמֶר יִרְמְיָהוּ אֶל־שְׂרָיָה כְּבֹאֲךָ בָבֶל וְרָאִיתָ וְקָרָאתָ אֵת כָּל־

סב הַדְּבָרִים הָאֵלֶּה: וְאָמַרְתָּ יְהֹוָה אַתָּה דִבַּרְתָּ אֶל־הַמָּקוֹם הַזֶּה לְהַכְרִיתוֹ לְבִלְתִּי הֱיוֹת־בּוֹ יוֹשֵׁב לְמֵאָדָם וְעַד־בְּהֵמָה כִּי־שִׁמְמוֹת עוֹלָם תִּהְיֶה:

סג וְהָיָה כְּכַלֹּתְךָ לִקְרֹא אֶת־הַסֵּפֶר הַזֶּה תִּקְשֹׁר עָלָיו אֶבֶן וְהִשְׁלַכְתּוֹ אֶל־

סד תּוֹךְ פְּרָת: וְאָמַרְתָּ כָּכָה תִּשְׁקַע בָּבֶל וְלֹא־תָקוּם מִפְּנֵי הָרָעָה אֲשֶׁר אָנֹכִי מֵבִיא עָלֶיהָ וְיָעֵפוּ עַד־הֵנָּה דִּבְרֵי יִרְמְיָהוּ:

נב א בֶּן־עֶשְׂרִים וְאַחַת שָׁנָה צִדְקִיָּהוּ בְמָלְכוֹ וְאַחַת עֶשְׂרֵה שָׁנָה מָלַךְ בִּירוּשָׁלִָם וְשֵׁם אִמּוֹ

ב °חֲמִיטַל [°חֲמוּטַל ק] בַּת־יִרְמְיָהוּ מִלִּבְנָה: וַיַּעַשׂ הָרַע בְּעֵינֵי יְהֹוָה כְּכֹל

ג אֲשֶׁר־עָשָׂה יְהוֹיָקִים: כִּי ׀ עַל־אַף יְהֹוָה הָיְתָה בִּירוּשָׁלִַם וִיהוּדָה עַד־

ד הִשְׁלִיכוֹ אוֹתָם מֵעַל פָּנָיו וַיִּמְרֹד צִדְקִיָּהוּ בְּמֶלֶךְ בָּבֶל: וַיְהִי בַשָּׁנָה הַתְּשִׁעִית לְמָלְכוֹ בַּחֹדֶשׁ הָעֲשִׂירִי בֶּעָשׂוֹר לַחֹדֶשׁ בָּא נְבוּכַדְרֶאצַּר מֶלֶךְ־בָּבֶל הוּא וְכָל־חֵילוֹ עַל־יְרוּשָׁלִַם וַיַּחֲנוּ עָלֶיהָ וַיִּבְנוּ

ה עָלֶיהָ דָּיֵק סָבִיב: וַתָּבֹא הָעִיר בַּמָּצוֹר עַד עַשְׁתֵּי עֶשְׂרֵה שָׁנָה לַמֶּלֶךְ

ו צִדְקִיָּהוּ: בַּחֹדֶשׁ הָרְבִיעִי בְּתִשְׁעָה לַחֹדֶשׁ וַיֶּחֱזַק הָרָעָב בָּעִיר וְלֹא־הָיָה

ז לֶחֶם לְעַם הָאָרֶץ: וַתִּבָּקַע הָעִיר וְכָל־אַנְשֵׁי הַמִּלְחָמָה יִבְרְחוּ וַיֵּצְאוּ מֵהָעִיר לַיְלָה דֶּרֶךְ שַׁעַר בֵּין־הַחֹמֹתַיִם אֲשֶׁר עַל־גַּן הַמֶּלֶךְ וְכַשְׂדִּים עַל־

ח הָעִיר סָבִיב וַיֵּלְכוּ דֶּרֶךְ הָעֲרָבָה: וַיִּרְדְּפוּ חֵיל־כַּשְׂדִּים אַחֲרֵי הַמֶּלֶךְ

ט וַיַּשִּׂיגוּ אֶת־צִדְקִיָּהוּ בְּעַרְבֹת יְרֵחוֹ וְכָל־חֵילוֹ נָפֹצוּ מֵעָלָיו: וַיִּתְפְּשׂוּ אֶת־הַמֶּלֶךְ וַיַּעֲלוּ אֹתוֹ אֶל־מֶלֶךְ בָּבֶל רִבְלָתָה בְּאֶרֶץ חֲמָת וַיְדַבֵּר אִתּוֹ

י מִשְׁפָּטִים: וַיִּשְׁחַט מֶלֶךְ־בָּבֶל אֶת־בְּנֵי צִדְקִיָּהוּ לְעֵינָיו וְגַם אֶת־כָּל־שָׂרֵי

יא יְהוּדָה שָׁחַט בְּרִבְלָתָה: וְאֶת־עֵינֵי צִדְקִיָּהוּ עִוֵּר וַיַּאַסְרֵהוּ בַנְחֻשְׁתַּיִם וַיְבִאֵהוּ מֶלֶךְ־בָּבֶל בָּבֶלָה וַיִּתְּנֵהוּ °בבית [°בֵית ק] הַפְּקֻדֹּת עַד־יוֹם

יב מוֹתוֹ: וּבַחֹדֶשׁ הַחֲמִישִׁי בֶּעָשׂוֹר לַחֹדֶשׁ הִיא שְׁנַת תְּשַׁע־עֶשְׂרֵה

52:1-27. Aside from a few minor differences, this passage is identical to *II Kings* 24:18-25:21.

52:3. Because of Israel's many sins, God decided to bring an end to the Jewish presence in the land. Therefore He incited Zedekiah to rebel against Nebuchadnezzar.

52:9. Nebuchadnezzar reprimanded Zedekiah for break-

⁵⁶ *For upon her, upon Babylonia, a plunderer is coming; her warriors will be captured and their bows will be smashed, for HASHEM is a God of retribution; He will surely exact recompense.* ⁵⁷ *I will intoxicate her officers and her wise men, her governors, her deputies and her warriors; they will sleep an eternal sleep and never awaken — the word of the King, HASHEM, Master of Legions, is His Name.*

⁵⁸ *Thus said HASHEM, Master of Legions: The broad walls of Babylonia will be completely uprooted and her tall gates will be set on fire; the peoples will toil in great futility and nations shall become exhausted through much fire.*

Jeremiah's charge to Seraiah ⁵⁹ *[This is] the word that Jeremiah the prophet commanded to Seraiah son of Neriah son of Mahseiah, when he went with Zedekiah king of Judah to Babylonia, in the fourth year of his reign. (Seraiah was in charge of tribute.)* ⁶⁰ *Jeremiah wrote down all the misfortunes that were to come upon Babylonia in one book, all these prophecies that are written about Babylonia;* ⁶¹ *and Jeremiah said to Seraiah, "When you arrive in Babylonia, you shall see and read all these words,* ⁶² *and say, 'HASHEM, You have spoken of destroying this place, so that there should no longer be an inhabitant in it, from man to beast, for it shall be an eternal wasteland!'* ⁶³ *And then, when you finish reading this book, tie a stone onto it and throw it into the midst of the Euphrates,* ⁶⁴ *and say, 'Thus shall Babylonia sink and not rise, because of the evil that I am bringing against it; and they will grow exhausted.'"*

Until this point are the prophecies of Jeremiah.

52
Zedekiah's reign
(See Appendix A, timelines 4-5)

¹ * Zedekiah *was twenty-one years old when he became king, and he reigned for eleven years in Jerusalem. His mother's name was Hamutal daughter of Jeremiah of Libnah.* ² *He did what was evil in the eyes of HASHEM, like everything that Jehoiakim had done.* ³ *It was because the wrath of HASHEM was upon Jerusalem and Judah, until He would cast them away from His presence, that Zedekiah rebelled against the king of Babylonia.* *

The siege and breaching of the walls
⁴ *It happened in the ninth year of [Zedekiah's] reign, in the tenth month, on the tenth of the month, that Nebuchadrezzar king of Babylonia, he and his entire army, came [to wage war] against Jerusalem and encamped near it, and built a siege tower around it.* ⁵ *The city came under siege until the eleventh year of King Zedekiah.* ⁶ *In the fourth month, on the ninth of the month, the famine in the city became critical; there was no food for the people of the land.* ⁷ *The city was breached, and all the men of war fled and left the city during the night, by way of the gate between the walls, which was near the king's garden, although the Chaldeans were upon the city all around; and they went by way of the Arabah.* ⁸ *The Chaldean army pursued the king and overtook Zedekiah at the plains of Jericho and his entire army dispersed from him.* ⁹ *They seized the king and brought him up to the king of Babylonia at Riblah, in the land of Hamath, and he spoke [words of] judgment to him.* * ¹⁰ *The king of Babylonia slaughtered*

Zedekiah's capture
Zedekiah's sons before his eyes; he also slaughtered the officers of Judah in Riblah; ¹¹ *and he blinded Zedekiah's eyes, then they bound him in copper chains; the king of Babylonia brought him to Babylonia, where he was put in the place of detention until the day of his death.*

¹² *In the fifth month, on the tenth of the month,* * *which was the nineteenth year*

---

ing his pledge of loyalty to Babylonia (*Rashi*).
52:12-13. The Temple was actually set afire in the late

afternoon of the ninth of the month, Tishah B'Av, but the fire did most of the damage on the tenth (*Taanis* 29a).

שָׁנָה֙ לַמֶּ֣לֶךְ נְבֻכַדְרֶאצַּ֔ר מֶ֥לֶךְ־בָּבֶ֖ל בָּ֣א נְבֽוּזַרְאֲדָ֧ן רַב־טַבָּחִ֛ים עָמַ֖ד
יג לִפְנֵ֥י מֶֽלֶךְ־בָּבֶ֖ל בִּירֽוּשָׁלִָֽם: וַיִּשְׂרֹ֤ף אֶת־בֵּית־יְהוָֹה֙ וְאֶת־בֵּ֣ית הַמֶּ֔לֶךְ וְאֵ֖ת
יד כָּל־בָּתֵּ֧י יְרֽוּשָׁלַ֛ם וְאֶת־כָּל־בֵּ֥ית הַגָּד֖וֹל שָׂרַ֥ף בָּאֵֽשׁ: וְאֶת־כָּל־חֹמ֣וֹת
טו יְרֽוּשָׁלַ֣ם סָבִ֔יב נָֽתְצ֕וּ כָּל־חֵ֥יל כַּשְׂדִּ֖ים אֲשֶׁ֣ר אֶת־רַב־טַבָּחִֽים: וּמִדַּלּ֣וֹת
הָעָ֗ם וְאֶת־יֶ֤תֶר הָעָם֙ הַנִּשְׁאָרִ֣ים בָּעִ֔יר וְאֶת־הַנֹּֽפְלִ֗ים אֲשֶׁ֤ר נָֽפְלוּ֙ אֶל־
טז מֶ֣לֶךְ בָּבֶ֔ל וְאֵ֖ת יֶ֣תֶר הָֽאָמ֑וֹן הֶגְלָ֕ה נְבֽוּזַרְאֲדָ֖ן רַב־טַבָּחִֽים: וּמִדַּלּ֣וֹת הָאָ֗רֶץ
יז הִשְׁאִ֛יר נְבֽוּזַרְאֲדָ֥ן רַב־טַבָּחִ֖ים לְכֹֽרְמִ֥ים וּלְיֹֽגְבִֽים: וְאֶת־עַמּוּדֵ֣י הַנְּחֹ֡שֶׁת
אֲשֶׁ֣ר לְבֵית־יְהוָֹ֡ה וְֽאֶת־הַמְּכֹנ֣וֹת וְאֶת־יָ֣ם הַנְּחֹ֣שֶׁת אֲשֶׁ֣ר בְּבֵֽית־יְהוָֹ֗ה
יח שִׁבְּר֤וּ כַשְׂדִּים֙ וַיִּשְׂא֥וּ אֶת־כָּל־נְחֻשְׁתָּ֖ם בָּבֶֽלָה: וְאֶת־הַסִּר֤וֹת וְאֶת־הַיָּעִים֙
וְאֶת־הַֽמְזַמְּרוֹת֙ וְאֶת־הַמִּזְרָקֹ֔ת וְאֶת־הַכַּפּ֖וֹת וְאֵ֥ת כָּל־כְּלֵ֥י הַנְּחֹ֖שֶׁת
יט אֲשֶׁר־יְשָֽׁרְתוּ־בָהֶ֖ם לָקָֽחוּ: וְאֶת־הַסִּפִּ֨ים וְאֶת־הַמַּחְתּ֜וֹת וְאֶת־הַמִּזְרָק֣וֹת
וְאֶת־הַסִּיר֣וֹת וְאֶת־הַמְּנֹר֗וֹת וְאֶת־הַכַּפּוֹת֙ וְאֶת־הַמְּנַקִּיּ֔וֹת אֲשֶׁ֤ר זָהָב֙ זָהָ֔ב
כ וַֽאֲשֶׁר־כֶּ֣סֶף כָּ֑סֶף לָקַ֖ח רַב־טַבָּחִֽים: הָֽעַמּוּדִ֣ים ׀ שְׁנַ֗יִם הַיָּ֤ם אֶחָד֙ וְהַבָּקָ֤ר
שְׁנֵים־עָשָׂ֨ר נְחֹ֜שֶׁת אֲשֶׁר־תַּ֣חַת הַמְּכֹנ֗וֹת אֲשֶׁ֤ר עָשָׂה֙ הַמֶּ֣לֶךְ שְׁלֹמֹ֔ה
כא לְבֵ֣ית יְהוָֹ֑ה לֹֽא־הָיָ֣ה מִשְׁקָ֔ל לִֽנְחֻשְׁתָּ֖ם כָּל־הַכֵּלִ֥ים הָאֵֽלֶּה: וְהָֽעַמּוּדִ֗ים
שְׁמֹנֶ֨ה עֶשְׂרֵ֤ה אַמָּה֙ °קוֹמָה [קוֹמַת֙ ק] הָֽעַמֻּ֣ד הָֽאֶחָ֔ד וְח֥וּט שְׁתֵּֽים־
כב עֶשְׂרֵ֤ה אַמָּה֙ יְסֻבֶּ֔נּוּ וְעָבְי֛וֹ אַרְבַּ֥ע אַצְבָּע֖וֹת נָבֽוּב: וְכֹתֶ֨רֶת עָלָ֜יו נְחֹ֗שֶׁת
וְקוֹמַ֣ת הַכֹּתֶ֣רֶת הָֽאַחַת֩ חָמֵ֨שׁ אַמּ֜וֹת וּשְׂבָכָ֧ה וְרִמּוֹנִ֛ים עַל־הַכּוֹתֶ֖רֶת
כג סָבִ֣יב הַכֹּ֣ל נְחֹ֑שֶׁת וְכָאֵ֛לֶּה לַֽעַמּ֥וּד הַשֵּׁנִ֖י וְרִמּוֹנִֽים: וַיִּֽהְי֤וּ הָֽרִמֹּנִים֙
כד תִּשְׁעִ֣ים וְשִׁשָּׁ֔ה ר֖וּחָה כָּל־הָֽרִמּוֹנִ֥ים מֵאָ֛ה עַל־הַשְּׂבָכָ֖ה סָבִֽיב: וַיִּקַּ֣ח רַב־
טַבָּחִ֗ים אֶת־שְׂרָיָה֙ כֹּהֵ֣ן הָרֹ֔אשׁ וְאֶת־צְפַנְיָ֖ה כֹּהֵ֣ן הַמִּשְׁנֶ֑ה וְאֶת־שְׁלֹ֖שֶׁת
כה שֹֽׁמְרֵ֥י הַסַּֽף: וּמִן־הָעִ֡יר לָקַח֩ סָרִ֨יס אֶחָ֜ד אֲשֶׁר־הָיָ֥ה פָקִ֣יד ׀ עַל־אַנְשֵׁ֣י
הַמִּלְחָמָ֗ה וְשִׁבְעָ֨ה אֲנָשִׁ֜ים מֵֽרֹאֵ֤י פְנֵֽי־הַמֶּ֨לֶךְ֙ אֲשֶׁ֣ר נִמְצְא֣וּ בָעִ֔יר וְאֵ֗ת
סֹפֵ֨ר שַׂ֤ר הַצָּבָא֙ הַמַּצְבִּ֖א אֶת־עַ֣ם הָאָ֑רֶץ וְשִׁשִּׁ֥ים אִישׁ֙ מֵעַ֣ם הָאָ֔רֶץ
כו הַֽנִּמְצְאִ֖ים בְּת֣וֹךְ הָעִֽיר: וַיִּקַּ֣ח אוֹתָ֔ם נְבֽוּזַרְאֲדָ֖ן רַב־טַבָּחִ֑ים וַיֹּ֧לֶךְ אוֹתָ֛ם
כז אֶל־מֶ֥לֶךְ בָּבֶ֖ל רִבְלָֽתָה: וַיַּכֶּ֣ה אוֹתָ֩ם מֶ֨לֶךְ בָּבֶ֤ל וַיְמִתֵם֙ בְּרִבְלָ֔ה בְּאֶ֖רֶץ
כח חֲמָ֑ת וַיִּ֥גֶל יְהוּדָ֖ה מֵעַ֥ל אַדְמָתֽוֹ: זֶ֣ה הָעָ֔ם אֲשֶׁ֥ר הֶגְלָ֖ה נְבֽוּכַדְרֶאצַּ֑ר
בִּשְׁנַת־שֶׁ֕בַע יְהוּדִ֕ים שְׁלֹ֥שֶׁת אֲלָפִ֖ים וְעֶשְׂרִ֥ים וּשְׁלֹשָֽׁה: בִּשְׁנַ֣ת שְׁמוֹנֶ֤ה
כט עֶשְׂרֵה֙ לִנְבֽוּכַדְרֶאצַּ֔ר מִירֽוּשָׁלִַ֔ם נֶ֕פֶשׁ שְׁמֹנֶ֥ה מֵא֖וֹת שְׁלֹשִׁ֥ים וּשְׁנָֽיִם:
ל בִּשְׁנַ֨ת שָׁלֹ֣שׁ וְעֶשְׂרִים֮ לִנְבֽוּכַדְרֶאצַּר֒ הֶגְלָ֗ה נְבֽוּזַרְאֲדָ֣ן רַב־טַבָּחִ֔ים
יְהוּדִ֕ים נֶ֕פֶשׁ שְׁבַ֥ע מֵא֖וֹת אַרְבָּעִ֣ים וַֽחֲמִשָּׁ֑ה כָּל־נֶ֕פֶשׁ אַרְבַּ֥עַת אֲלָפִ֖ים
לא וְשֵׁ֥שׁ מֵאֽוֹת: וַיְהִי֩ בִשְׁלֹשִׁ֨ים וָשֶׁ֜בַע שָׁנָ֗ה לְגָלוּ֙ת
יְהוֹיָכִ֣ין מֶֽלֶךְ־יְהוּדָ֔ה בִּשְׁנֵ֤ים עָשָׂר֙ חֹ֔דֶשׁ בְּעֶשְׂרִ֥ים וַֽחֲמִשָּׁ֖ה לַחֹ֑דֶשׁ
נָשָׂא֩ אֱוִ֨יל מְרֹדַ֜ךְ מֶ֣לֶךְ בָּבֶ֗ל בִּשְׁנַת֙ מַלְכֻת֔וֹ אֶת־רֹ֖אשׁ יְהוֹיָכִ֣ין מֶֽלֶךְ־

The city in flames of Nebuchadrezzar king of Babylonia, Nebuzaradan, the chief executioner, [who] was in the service of the king of Babylonia, came to Jerusalem. ¹³ He burned the Temple of HASHEM, the king's palace and all the buildings of Jerusalem; and every great house * he burned in fire. ¹⁴ And all the walls of Jerusalem all around, the entire Chaldean army that was with the chief executioner smashed. ¹⁵ And some of the poor people, the remainder of the people who were left in the city, the defectors who had surrendered to the king of Babylonia, and the rest of the masses, Nebuzaradan, the chief executioner, sent into exile. ¹⁶ But the chief executioner left some of the poor people of the land, to be workers in vineyards and in fields.

Sack of the Temple ¹⁷ The copper pillars of the Temple of HASHEM, and the laver-stands * and the copper sea that were in the Temple of HASHEM, the Chaldeans shattered and carried off their copper to Babylonia. ¹⁸ The pots, the shovels, the musical instruments, the bowls, the spoons and all the copper utensils with which [the Kohanim] served, [the Chaldeans] took away. ¹⁹ The basins, the pans, the bowls, the pots, the candelabra, the spoons and the table-rods, whether of gold or of silver, the chief executioner took away. ²⁰ The two pillars, the one sea, the twelve copper oxen that were near the laver-stands that King Solomon had made for the Temple of HASHEM — there was no weight [with which to measure] the copper of all these items. ²¹ [This is a description of] the pillars: eighteen cubits the height of the one pillar, a twelve-cubit line would encircle it, its thickness four finger-breadths, and [it was] hollow; ²² a copper capital upon it, the height of the single capital five cubits; and a netting and pomegranate figures upon the capital all around, all of copper; the same [ornaments] for the second pillar, with pomegranates. ²³ There were ninety-six pomegranates facing outside; altogether there were one hundred pomegranates all around the netting.

²⁴ The chief executioner took Seraiah the chief Kohen and Zephaniah the deputy Kohen and the three gatekeepers. ²⁵ From the city he took one officer who was in charge of the men of war; seven men from those [advisers] who see the king's face, who were found in the city; the secretary of the general of the army, who would marshal the common people for war; and sixty men of the common *Death and exile* people who were found inside the city. ²⁶ Nebuzaradan, the chief executioner, took them and brought them to the king of Babylonia at Riblah, ²⁷ and the king of Babylonia struck them down and killed them at Riblah, in the land of Hamath. And Judah was exiled from its land.

²⁸ This is the people whom Nebuchadnezzar exiled: In the seventh year, * three thousand and twenty-three Jews; ²⁹ in Nebuchadrezzar's eighteenth year, * from Jerusalem, eight hundred and thirty-two souls; ³⁰ and in Nebuchadrezzar's twenty-third year, Nebuzaradan the chief executioner exiled seven hundred and forty-five Jewish souls — altogether four thousand and six hundred souls.

(See Appendix A, timelines 4-5) ³¹ *It happened in the thirty-seventh year of the exile of Jehoiachin king of Judah, in the twelfth month, on the twenty-fifth of the month: Evil-merodach, * the king of Babylonia, in the year of his coronation, elevated Jehoiachin king of

---

52:13. The Sages interpret that they burned the synagogues and study halls, which are the major buildings of the Jewish people (*Rashi*).

52:17. These parts of the Temple are described in *I Kings* Ch. 7.

52:28. When Jehoiachin was exiled (*II Kings* 24:10-

16).

52:29. The year of Zedekiah's exile and the destruction of the Temple.

52:31-34. Aside from a few minor differences, this passage is identical to *II Kings* 25:27-30.

52:31. Nebuchadnezzar's son.

לב יְהוּדָה וַיֹּצֵא אֹתוֹ מִבֵּית °הַכְּלִיא [°הַכְּלוּא ק]: וַיְדַבֵּר אִתּוֹ טֹבוֹת וַיִּתֵּן

לג אֶת־כִּסְאוֹ מִמַּעַל לְכִסֵּא °מְלָכִים [°הַמְּלָכִים ק] אֲשֶׁר אִתּוֹ בְּבָבֶל: וְשִׁנָּה

לד אֵת בִּגְדֵי כִלְאוֹ וְאָכַל לֶחֶם לְפָנָיו תָּמִיד כָּל־יְמֵי חַיָּיו: וַאֲרֻחָתוֹ אֲרֻחַת

תָּמִיד נִתְּנָה־לּוֹ מֵאֵת מֶלֶךְ מֶלֶךְ־בָּבֶל דְּבַר־יוֹם בְּיוֹמוֹ עַד־יוֹם מוֹתוֹ כָּל יְמֵי

חַיָּיו:

סכום הפסוקים של ירמיהו אלף ושלש מאות ושלשים וחמשה. וכל **אַנְשֵׁיָה** גברים סימן. אנכי **אֶשְׂמַח בֹּה** סימן.

Jehoiachin's Judah and released him from prison. [32] He spoke kindly with him, and set his
release seat above the seats of the [other] kings who were with him in Babylonia. [33] He
changed [from] his prison clothing, and he ate [his] meal before him regularly, all
the days of his life. [34] His allowance was a regular allowance given to him from
the king, each day's portion on its day, until the day of his death, all the days of
his life.

Ezekiel יְחֶזְקֵאל

*T*he sins of Israel had become irreparable. The Temple would be destroyed, as the somber narratives of the later chapters of Kings and Chronicles detail. The people looked up the hill at their Temple, confident that it would protect itself and them from King Nebuchadnezzar of Babylon and his conquering army. No human king could destroy the habitat of God's Presence! But, as the Talmud describes it, the Divine Presence was receding from the Temple, stage by stage, in ten stages. Holiness had been there because of the people; when they lost their merit, it lost its holiness. The building on the hill was no longer a "Temple," it was merely a grand edifice, a shell, devoid of its sanctity. And then, it was reduced to a flaming ruin, with its people dead or driven off to exile and slavery.

Such was the world of the prophet Ezekiel. His primary mission was directed not to the Jews of a dying Land of Israel, but to the Jews of Babylon, the exiled Jews who thought that they had lost their share in the God of Israel. They reasoned; Does a husband have a claim to his wife's loyalty after he divorced her? Does a master have a claim to his slave's services after he sent him away? And can God still claim us as His people after abandoning us to Nebuchadnezzar?

To these forlorn Jews, Ezekiel was a prophet of hope, as well as rebuke. Most of his prophecy was to the exiles, although he had much to say to the unheeding Jews of Jerusalem, as well. He showed them that he truly shared their suffering, becoming the very symbol of their plight — as he pounded his hand and stamped his foot in despair, and lost his own beloved wife in a plague, to symbolize for them that even one's most cherished possession — a wife, a Temple — could be stripped away.

But ultimately, Ezekiel is the prophet of hope and triumph. He foretells the time when God will pluck Israel from the nations and sprinkle purifying waters upon it, and replace its stubborn heart with a warm, feeling heart of flesh; when Israel — a humble, battered "vine" — would rise to dwarf the haughty cedars and redwoods. Ezekiel is the prophet who was shown the vision of the "dry bones" rising and coming back to life. In his prophecy, despair disappears; death turns to life; the "corpse" of Israel becomes a vibrant new nation. Judah and Ephraim are united again with a scion of David as their king, with the Land of Israel as their home, and with Hashem as their God.

The Book of Ezekiel is surely a book of tragedy, but not a book of despair, for Israel will rise again and return to its home. There, in Jerusalem, it will assume a new and eternal name: ה' שָׁמָּה, Hashem is there (48:35).

א וַיְהִ֣י ׀ בִּשְׁלֹשִׁ֣ים שָׁנָ֗ה בָּֽרְבִיעִי֙ בַּֽחֲמִשָּׁ֣ה לַחֹ֔דֶשׁ וַֽאֲנִ֥י בְתֽוֹךְ־הַגּוֹלָ֖ה עַל־
ב נְהַר־כְּבָ֑ר נִפְתְּחוּ֙ הַשָּׁמַ֔יִם וָֽאֶרְאֶ֖ה מַרְא֥וֹת אֱלֹהִֽים: בַּֽחֲמִשָּׁ֣ה לַחֹ֔דֶשׁ הִ֖יא
ג הַשָּׁנָ֣ה הַֽחֲמִישִׁ֑ית לְגָל֖וּת הַמֶּ֥לֶךְ יֽוֹיָכִֽין: הָיֹ֣ה הָיָ֣ה דְבַר־יְהֹוָ֡ה אֶל־יְחֶזְקֵאל֩
בֶּן־בּוּזִ֨י הַכֹּהֵ֜ן בְּאֶ֤רֶץ כַּשְׂדִּים֙ עַל־נְהַר־כְּבָ֔ר וַתְּהִ֥י עָלָ֛יו שָׁ֖ם יַד־יְהֹוָֽה:
ד וָאֵ֣רֶא וְהִנֵּה֩ ר֨וּחַ סְעָרָ֜ה בָּאָ֣ה מִן־הַצָּפ֗וֹן עָנָ֤ן גָּדוֹל֙ וְאֵ֣שׁ מִתְלַקַּ֔חַת וְנֹ֥גַֽהּ
ה ל֖וֹ סָבִ֑יב וּמִ֨תּוֹכָ֔הּ כְּעֵ֥ין הַחַשְׁמַ֖ל מִתּ֥וֹךְ הָאֵֽשׁ: וּמִ֨תּוֹכָ֔הּ דְּמ֖וּת אַרְבַּ֣ע
ו חַיּ֑וֹת וְזֶה֙ מַרְאֵֽיהֶ֔ן דְּמ֥וּת אָדָ֖ם לָהֵֽנָּה: וְאַרְבָּעָ֥ה פָנִ֖ים לְאֶחָ֑ת וְאַרְבַּ֥ע
ז כְּנָפַ֖יִם לְאַחַ֥ת לָהֶֽם: וְרַגְלֵיהֶ֖ם רֶ֣גֶל יְשָׁרָ֑ה וְכַ֣ף רַגְלֵיהֶ֗ם כְּכַף֙ רֶ֣גֶל עֵ֔גֶל
ח וְנֹ֣צְצִ֔ים כְּעֵ֖ין נְחֹ֥שֶׁת קָלָֽל: °וְיָדוֹ [°וִידֵ֣י ק] אָדָ֗ם מִתַּ֨חַת֙ כַּנְפֵיהֶ֔ם עַ֖ל
ט אַרְבַּ֣עַת רִבְעֵיהֶ֑ם וּפְנֵיהֶ֥ם וְכַנְפֵיהֶ֖ם לְאַרְבַּעְתָּֽם: חֹֽבְרֹ֛ת אִשָּׁ֥ה אֶל־
י אֲחוֹתָ֖הּ כַּנְפֵיהֶ֑ם לֹֽא־יִסַּ֣בּוּ בְלֶכְתָּ֔ן אִ֛ישׁ אֶל־עֵ֥בֶר פָּנָ֖יו יֵלֵֽכוּ: וּדְמ֣וּת
פְּנֵיהֶם֮ פְּנֵ֣י אָדָם֒ וּפְנֵ֨י אַרְיֵ֤ה אֶל־הַיָּמִין֙ לְאַרְבַּעְתָּ֔ם וּפְנֵי־שׁ֥וֹר מֵֽהַשְּׂמֹ֖אול
יא לְאַרְבַּעְתָּ֑ן וּפְנֵי־נֶ֖שֶׁר לְאַרְבַּעְתָּֽן: וּפְנֵיהֶ֕ם וְכַנְפֵיהֶ֥ם פְּרֻד֖וֹת מִלְמָ֑עְלָה
יב לְאִ֗ישׁ שְׁתַּ֨יִם֙ חֹֽבְר֣וֹת אִ֔ישׁ וּשְׁתַּ֣יִם מְכַסּ֔וֹת אֵ֖ת גְּוִיֹֽתֵיהֶֽנָה: וְאִ֛ישׁ אֶל־עֵ֥בֶר
פָּנָ֖יו יֵלֵ֑כוּ אֶ֣ל אֲשֶׁר֩ יִֽהְיֶה־שָּׁ֨מָּה הָר֤וּחַ לָלֶ֨כֶת֙ יֵלֵ֔כוּ לֹ֥א יִסַּ֖בּוּ בְּלֶכְתָּֽן:
יג וּדְמ֨וּת הַֽחַיּ֜וֹת מַרְאֵיהֶ֣ם כְּגַֽחֲלֵי־אֵ֗שׁ בֹּֽעֲרוֹת֙ כְּמַרְאֵ֣ה הַלַּפִּדִ֔ים הִ֕יא
יד מִתְהַלֶּ֖כֶת בֵּ֣ין הַֽחַיּ֑וֹת וְנֹ֣גַהּ לָאֵ֔שׁ וּמִן־הָאֵ֖שׁ יוֹצֵ֥א בָרָֽק: וְהַֽחַיּ֖וֹת רָצ֣וֹא
טו וָשׁ֑וֹב כְּמַרְאֵ֖ה הַבָּזָֽק: וָאֵ֖רֶא הַֽחַיּ֑וֹת וְהִנֵּה֩ אוֹפַ֨ן אֶחָ֥ד בָּאָ֛רֶץ אֵ֥צֶל הַֽחַיּ֖וֹת
טז לְאַרְבַּ֥עַת פָּנָֽיו: מַרְאֵ֨ה הָאֽוֹפַנִּ֤ים וּמַֽעֲשֵׂיהֶם֙ כְּעֵ֣ין תַּרְשִׁ֔ישׁ וּדְמ֥וּת אֶחָ֖ד
לְאַרְבַּעְתָּ֑ן וּמַרְאֵיהֶם֙ וּמַ֣עֲשֵׂיהֶ֔ם כַּֽאֲשֶׁ֛ר יִֽהְיֶ֥ה הָֽאוֹפַ֖ן בְּת֥וֹךְ הָֽאוֹפָֽן: עַל־
יז אַרְבַּ֤עַת רִבְעֵיהֶן֙ בְּלֶכְתָּ֣ם יֵלֵ֔כוּ לֹ֥א יִסַּ֖בּוּ בְּלֶכְתָּֽן: וְגַבֵּיהֶ֕ן וְגֹ֥בַהּ לָהֶ֖ם
יח וְיִרְאָ֣ה לָהֶ֑ם וְגַבֹּתָ֗ם מְלֵאֹ֥ת עֵינַ֛יִם סָבִ֖יב לְאַרְבַּעְתָּֽן: וּבְלֶ֨כֶת֙ הַֽחַיּ֔וֹת יֵֽלְכ֥וּ
יט הָאֽוֹפַנִּ֖ים אֶצְלָ֑ם וּבְהִנָּשֵׂ֤א הַֽחַיּוֹת֙ מֵעַ֣ל הָאָ֔רֶץ יִנָּֽשְׂא֖וּ הָאֽוֹפַנִּֽים: עַ֣ל אֲשֶׁר֩
כ יִֽהְיֶה־שָּׁ֨ם הָר֤וּחַ לָלֶ֨כֶת֙ יֵלֵ֔כוּ שָׁ֥מָּה הָר֖וּחַ לָלֶ֑כֶת וְהָאֽוֹפַנִּ֗ים יִנָּֽשְׂאוּ֙
כא לְעֻמָּתָ֔ם כִּ֛י ר֥וּחַ הַֽחַיָּ֖ה בָּאֽוֹפַנִּֽים: בְּלֶכְתָּ֣ם יֵלֵ֔כוּ וּבְעָמְדָ֖ם יַֽעֲמֹ֑דוּ
וּבְהִנָּֽשְׂאָ֞ם מֵעַ֣ל הָאָ֗רֶץ יִנָּֽשְׂא֤וּ הָאֽוֹפַנִּים֙ לְעֻמָּתָ֔ם כִּ֛י ר֥וּחַ הַֽחַיָּ֖ה
כב בָּֽאוֹפַנִּֽים: וּדְמ֞וּת עַל־רָאשֵׁ֤י הַֽחַיָּה֙ רָקִ֔יעַ כְּעֵ֖ין הַקֶּ֣רַח הַנּוֹרָ֑א נָט֥וּי עַל־
כג רָֽאשֵׁיהֶ֖ם מִלְמָֽעְלָה: וְתַ֨חַת֙ הָֽרָקִ֔יעַ כַּנְפֵיהֶ֣ם יְשָׁר֔וֹת אִשָּׁ֖ה אֶל־אֲחוֹתָ֑הּ
לְאִ֗ישׁ שְׁתַּ֚יִם מְכַסּוֹת֙ לָהֵ֔נָּה וּלְאִ֗ישׁ שְׁתַּ֣יִם מְכַסּ֔וֹת לָהֵ֕נָּה אֵ֖ת גְּוִיֹּֽתֵיהֶֽם:

Chapter 1. This chapter is referred to by the Sages as *Maaseh Merkavah*, "The Account of the Chariot." The first three verses give the time and place of the vision, and the remaining verses describe the vision itself. In this account, Ezekiel speaks of the workings of the Heavenly Throne, a topic so far removed from human comprehension that even the Sages of the Talmud felt inadequate to interpret it, and sharply limited the permissibility of expounding its teachings. It describes supernatural con-

cepts in human terms, but they cannot be understood literally nor are we equipped even to attempt a glimpse at their inner meaning.

1:1. This was in the thirtieth year of the fifty-year Jubilee cycle *(Rashi)*, during the month of Tammuz; as explained in verse 2, this was the fifth year of King Jehoiachin's exile to Babylonia.

1:4. According to the Sages, the *Chashmal* is a type of angel that at times stands silent (חַשׁ) and at times speaks

1

EZEKIEL'S VISION OF THE MERKAVAH/ CHARIOT

1:1-3:13

[1] *It happened in the thirtieth year, in the fourth [month],* * *on the fifth of the month, as I was among the exile by the River Chebar; the heavens opened and I saw visions of God.* [2] *On the fifth of the month, which was in the fifth year of the exile of King Jehoiachin,* [3] *the word of HASHEM came to Ezekiel son of Buzi, the Kohen, in the land of the Chaldeans, by the River Chebar; and the hand of HASHEM came upon him there.*

[4] *I saw, and behold! there was a stormy wind coming from the north, a great cloud with flashing fire and a brilliance surrounding it; and from its midst, like the color of the Chashmal* * *from the midst of the fire;* [5] *and in its midst there was a likeness of four Chayos.* * *This was their appearance: They had the likeness of a man;* [6] *each one had four faces, and each one of them had four wings;* [7] *their legs were a straight leg, and the sole of their feet was like the sole of a rounded foot, and they glittered with the color of burnished copper;* [8] *there were human hands under their wings on their four sides. Their faces and their wings [were alike] on the four of them;* [9] *their wings were joined to one another. They did not turn as they went; each in the direction of its faces would they go.* [10] *As for the likeness of their faces: There was a human face; and a lion's face to the right for the four of them; and an ox's face to the left for the four of them, and an eagle's face for the four of them.* [11] *As for their faces: Their wings extended upward [over them]; for each [face] two [wings] were joined to each other;* * *and two [wings] were covering their bodies.* [12] *Each in the direction of its faces would they go; toward wherever there was the spirit to go, they would go; they did not turn as they went.* [13] *As for the likeness of the Chayos: Their appearance was like fiery coals, burning like the appearance of torches; it* * *spread about among the Chayos; there was a brilliance to the fire, and from the fire went forth lightning.* [14] *The Chayos ran to and fro like the appearance of a flash.* [15] *I saw the Chayos — and behold! one Ofan* * *was on the surface near [each of] the Chayos by its four faces.* [16] *The appearance of the Ofanim and their nature were like the color of tarshish,* * *with the same likeness for the four of them; and their appearance and their works were as if there would be a wheel within a wheel.* [17] *When they went, they would go toward their four sides; they did not turn as they went.* * [18] *They had backs, and they were tall, and they were fearsome. Their backs were full of eyes surrounding the four of them.* [19] *When the Chayos would go, the Ofanim would go next to them, and when the Chayos were lifted from upon the surface, the Ofanim were lifted.* [20] *Toward wherever there was the spirit to go, they would go, [for] there was the spirit to go; the Ofanim were lifted facing them, for the spirit in the Chayah was [also] in the Ofanim.* [21] *When [the Chayos] would go, [the Ofanim] would go, and when they halted, they halted; and when they were lifted from upon the surface, the Ofanim were lifted facing them, for the spirit in the Chayah was [also] in the Ofanim.* [22] *There was a likeness of an expanse above the heads of the Chayah, like the color of the awesome ice, spread out over their heads from above.* [23] *And beneath the expanse, their wings were even one with the other;* * *for each [of them] two [wings] covered them, and for each [of them] two covered them, their bodies.*

(מְמַלֵּל) God's praises (*Chagigah* 13a).

1:5. Lit., living beings (singular, *Chayah*). These were the angels who bore the Heavenly Chariot.

1:11. Two wings touched one another in front of their faces, so that they would not gaze at God's glory (*Rashi*).

1:13. The above appearance (*Rashi*); or the fire (*Targum*).

1:15. An *Ofan* (lit., wheel) is a type of celestial being.

1:16. Rock crystal or beryl.

1:17. See 10:11.

1:23. The wings of each *Chayah* were paired — two to cover its face and two to cover its body (*Kara*).

כד וָאֶשְׁמַע אֶת־ק֣וֹל כַּנְפֵיהֶ֡ם כְּקוֹל֩ מַ֨יִם רַבִּ֤ים כְּקוֹל־שַׁדַּי֙ בְּלֶכְתָּ֔ם ק֥וֹל
כה הֲמֻלָּ֖ה כְּק֣וֹל מַחֲנֶ֑ה בְּעׇמְדָ֖ם תְּרַפֶּ֥ינָה כַנְפֵיהֶֽן׃ וַֽיְהִי־ק֕וֹל מֵעַ֕ל לָרָקִ֖יעַ אֲשֶׁ֣ר
כו עַל־רֹאשָׁ֑ם בְּעׇמְדָ֖ם תְּרַפֶּ֥ינָה כַנְפֵיהֶֽן׃ וּמִמַּ֗עַל לָרָקִ֙יעַ֙ אֲשֶׁ֣ר עַל־רֹאשָׁ֔ם
כְּמַרְאֵ֥ה אֶֽבֶן־סַפִּ֖יר דְּמ֣וּת כִּסֵּ֑א וְעַל֙ דְּמ֣וּת הַכִּסֵּ֔א דְּמ֞וּת כְּמַרְאֵ֥ה אָדָ֛ם
כז עָלָ֖יו מִלְמָֽעְלָה׃ וָאֵ֣רֶא ׀ כְּעֵ֣ין חַשְׁמַ֗ל כְּמַרְאֵה־אֵ֤שׁ בֵּֽית־לָהּ֙ סָבִ֔יב
מִמַּרְאֵ֥ה מׇתְנָ֖יו וּלְמָ֑עְלָה וּמִמַּרְאֵ֤ה מׇתְנָיו֙ וּלְמַ֔טָּה רָאִ֙יתִי֙ כְּמַרְאֵה־אֵ֔שׁ
כח וְנֹ֥גַֽהּ ל֖וֹ סָבִֽיב׃ כְּמַרְאֵ֣ה הַקֶּ֡שֶׁת אֲשֶׁר֩ יִהְיֶ֨ה בֶעָנָ֜ן בְּי֣וֹם הַגֶּ֗שֶׁם כֵּ֣ן מַרְאֵ֤ה
הַנֹּ֙גַהּ֙ סָבִ֔יב ה֕וּא מַרְאֵ֖ה דְּמ֣וּת כְּבוֹד־יְהֹוָ֑ה וָֽאֶרְאֶה֙ וָאֶפֹּ֣ל עַל־פָּנַ֔י וָֽאֶשְׁמַ֖ע

ב
Haftarah
continues
on p. 1212

א ק֥וֹל מְדַבֵּֽר׃ ◄ וַיֹּ֖אמֶר אֵלָ֑י בֶּן־אָדָם֙ עֲמֹ֣ד עַל־רַגְלֶ֔יךָ וַאֲדַבֵּ֖ר
אֹתָֽךְ׃ וַתָּ֧בֹא בִ֣י ר֗וּחַ כַּֽאֲשֶׁר֙ דִּבֶּ֣ר אֵלַ֔י וַתַּֽעֲמִדֵ֖נִי עַל־רַגְלָ֑י וָֽאֶשְׁמַ֖ע אֵ֥ת
ג מְדַבֵּ֥ר אֵלָֽי׃ וַיֹּ֣אמֶר אֵלַ֗י בֶּן־אָדָם֙ שׁוֹלֵ֨חַ אֲנִ֤י אוֹתְךָ֙ אֶל־בְּנֵ֣י
יִשְׂרָאֵ֔ל אֶל־גּוֹיִ֥ם הַמּוֹרְדִ֖ים אֲשֶׁ֣ר מָֽרְדוּ־בִ֑י הֵ֤מָּה וַאֲבוֹתָם֙ פָּ֣שְׁעוּ בִ֔י עַד־
ד עֶ֖צֶם הַיּ֥וֹם הַזֶּֽה׃ וְהַבָּנִ֗ים קְשֵׁ֤י פָנִים֙ וְחׅזְקֵי־לֵ֔ב אֲנִ֛י שׁוֹלֵ֥חַ אוֹתְךָ֖ אֲלֵיהֶ֑ם
ה וְאָמַרְתָּ֣ אֲלֵיהֶ֔ם כֹּ֥ה אָמַ֖ר אֲדֹנָ֥י יֱהֹוִֽה׃ וְהֵ֙מָּה֙ אִם־יִשְׁמְעוּ֙ וְאִם־יֶחְדָּ֔לוּ כִּ֛י
ו בֵּ֥ית מְרִ֖י הֵ֑מָּה וְיָ֣דְע֔וּ כִּ֥י נָבִ֖יא הָיָ֥ה בְתוֹכָֽם׃ וְאַתָּ֣ה בֶן־אָ֠דָ֠ם
אַל־תִּירָ֨א מֵהֶ֜ם וּמִדִּבְרֵיהֶ֣ם אַל־תִּירָ֗א כִּ֣י סָרָבִ֤ים וְסַלּוֹנִים֙ אוֹתָ֔ךְ וְאֶל־
עַקְרַבִּ֖ים אַתָּ֣ה יוֹשֵׁ֑ב מִדִּבְרֵיהֶ֤ם אַל־תִּירָא֙ וּמִפְּנֵיהֶ֣ם אַל־תֵּחָ֔ת כִּ֛י בֵּ֥ית
ז מְרִ֖י הֵֽמָּה׃ וְדִבַּרְתָּ֤ אֶת־דְּבָרַי֙ אֲלֵיהֶ֔ם אִֽם־יִשְׁמְע֖וּ וְאִם־יֶחְדָּ֑לוּ כִּ֥י מְרִ֖י
ח הֵֽמָּה׃ וְאַתָּ֣ה בֶן־אָדָ֗ם שְׁמַע֙ אֵ֤ת אֲשֶׁר־אֲנִי֙ מְדַבֵּ֣ר אֵלֶ֔יךָ אַל־
ט תְּהִי־מֶ֙רִי֙ כְּבֵ֣ית הַמֶּ֔רִי פְּצֵ֣ה פִ֔יךָ וֶאֱכֹ֕ל אֵ֥ת אֲשֶׁר־אֲנִ֖י נֹתֵ֥ן אֵלֶֽיךָ׃ וָאֶרְאֶ֕ה
י וְהִנֵּה־יָ֖ד שְׁלוּחָ֣ה אֵלָ֑י וְהִנֵּה־ב֖וֹ מְגִלַּת־סֵֽפֶר׃ וַיִּפְרֹ֤שׂ אוֹתָהּ֙ לְפָנַ֔י וְהִ֥יא

ג

א כְתוּבָ֖ה פָּנִ֣ים וְאָח֑וֹר וְכָת֣וּב אֵלֶ֔יהָ קִנִ֥ים וָהֶ֖גֶה וָהִֽי׃ וַיֹּ֣אמֶר אֵלַ֔י
בֶּן־אָדָ֕ם אֵ֥ת אֲשֶׁר־תִּמְצָ֖א אֱכ֑וֹל אֱכוֹל֙ אֶת־הַמְּגִלָּ֣ה הַזֹּ֔את וְלֵ֥ךְ דַּבֵּ֖ר אֶל־
ב־ג בֵּ֥ית יִשְׂרָאֵֽל׃ וָאֶפְתַּ֖ח אֶת־פִּ֑י וַיַּ֣אֲכִלֵ֔נִי אֵ֖ת הַמְּגִלָּ֥ה הַזֹּֽאת׃ וַיֹּ֣אמֶר אֵלַ֗י
בֶּן־אָדָם֙ בִּטְנְךָ֣ תַֽאֲכֵ֔ל וּמֵעֶ֙יךָ֙ תְמַלֵּ֔א אֵ֚ת הַמְּגִלָּ֣ה הַזֹּ֔את אֲשֶׁ֥ר אֲנִ֖י נֹתֵ֣ן
ד אֵלֶ֑יךָ וָאֹ֣כְלָ֔ה וַתְּהִ֥י בְּפִ֖י כִּדְבַ֥שׁ לְמָתֽוֹק׃ וַיֹּ֖אמֶר אֵלָ֑י בֶּן־אָדָ֖ם לֶךְ־
ה בֹּ֤א אֶל־בֵּ֣ית יִשְׂרָאֵ֔ל וְדִבַּרְתָּ֥ בִדְבָרַ֖י אֲלֵיהֶֽם׃ כִּ֡י לֹא֩ אֶל־עַ֨ם עִמְקֵ֤י שָׂפָה֙
ו וְכִבְדֵ֣י לָשׁ֔וֹן אַתָּ֥ה שָׁל֖וּחַ אֶל־בֵּ֣ית יִשְׂרָאֵ֑ל לֹ֣א ׀ אֶל־עַמִּ֣ים רַבִּ֗ים עִמְקֵ֤י
שָׂפָה֙ וְכִבְדֵ֣י לָשׁ֔וֹן אֲשֶׁ֥ר לֹֽא־תִשְׁמַ֖ע דִּבְרֵיהֶ֑ם אִם־לֹ֤א אֲלֵיהֶם֙ שְׁלַחְתִּ֔יךָ
ז הֵ֖מָּה יִשְׁמְע֥וּ אֵלֶֽיךָ׃ וּבֵ֣ית יִשְׂרָאֵ֗ל לֹ֤א יֹאבוּ֙ לִשְׁמֹ֣עַ אֵלֶ֔יךָ כִּֽי־אֵינָ֥ם אֹבִ֖ים

1:24. The Divine Name SHADDAI (usually translated "the Almighty") indicates God's might and His control over nature. See also 10:5.

1:27. See v. 4.

2:1. Throughout this Book, God addresses Ezekiel as "Son of *Adam*," i.e. of Man, and speaks of Israel collectively as "Adam" (34:31, 36:10). The reference is to Adam, the first man, and the mission for which he was created. By use of these names, God suggests to Ezekiel that he and his nation, despite their severe shortcomings, are still expected to live up to God's hopes for humanity, the mission that was originally given to Adam and then transferred to Abraham and his offspring (*R' M. Eisemann*).

²⁴ *I heard the sound of their wings, like the sound of great waters, like the sound of* SHADDAI, * *as they moved, the sound of a commotion, like the sound of a camp; when they would halt, they would release their wings.* ²⁵ *There was a voice from above the expanse that was over their heads; when they would halt, they would release their wings.* ²⁶ *Above the expanse that was over their heads was the appearance of sapphire stone in the likeness of a throne, and upon the likeness of the throne there was a likeness like the appearance of a man upon it, from above.* ²⁷ *And I saw the color of Chashmal,* * *like the appearance of fire inside it all around, from the appearance of his loins and upward; and from the appearance of his loins and downward I saw something like the appearance of fire, and a brilliance surrounding it.* ²⁸ *Like the appearance of a bow that would be in the clouds on a rainy day, so was the appearance of the brilliance all around. That was the appearance of the likeness of the glory of* HASHEM!

When I saw, I fell upon my face, and I heard a voice speaking.

2

"Son of Man"

Ezekiel's Mission

¹ Then He said to me, *"Son of Man,* * *stand on your feet and I will speak to you."* ² *A spirit entered into me as He spoke to me and it stood me on my feet, and I heard that which was being spoken to me.*

³ *He said to me, "Son of Man, I send you to the Children of Israel, to the rebellious nations* * *that have rebelled against Me; they and their fathers have defiantly sinned against Me to this very day;* ⁴ *and the children are brazen-faced and hard-hearted — I send you to them. You shall say to them, 'Thus said the Lord* HASHEM/ELOHIM.'* * ⁵ *Now they, whether they will heed, whether they will refrain* * *— for a rebellious house are they — they will know that a prophet has been among them.*

⁶ *"But you, Son of Man, fear not them and fear not their words, though they are thorns and thistles to you, and among scorpions do you dwell; fear not their words and be not intimidated before them, though they are a rebellious house.* ⁷ *Speak My words to them, whether they will obey, whether they will refrain — for they are rebellious!*

⁸ *"And you, Son of Man, heed that which I speak to you: Be not rebellious like the rebellious house. Open your mouth and eat that which I give you."* ⁹ *Then I saw, and behold! a hand was outstretched to me; and behold! in it was a scroll of parchment.* ¹⁰ *He spread it out before me; it was inscribed within and without, and in it was inscribed lamentations, moaning, and woe.*

3

"Eat this scroll!"

¹ *He then said to me, "Son of Man, that which you find, eat; eat this scroll* * *then go speak to the House of Israel!"* ² *So I opened my mouth and He fed me that scroll.* ³ *And He said to me, "Son of Man, feed your stomach and fill your innards with this scroll that I give to you." So I ate; and it was as sweet as honey in my mouth.*

⁴ *He said to me, "Son of Man, go and approach the House of Israel and speak to them with My words.* ⁵ *For not to a people of incoherent language and difficult speech are you being sent, [but] to the House of Israel.* ⁶ *It is not to numerous peoples of incoherent language and difficult speech whose words you cannot understand; surely, had I sent you to them they would have heeded you!* ⁷ *But the House of Israel will not wish to heed you for they do not wish*

2:3. The tribes of Israel are called nations (*Radak*).

2:4. The combined Name HASHEM/ELOHIM represents God's love showing itself in justice, meaning that even when He denies or punishes, His underlying purpose is merciful. Since Ezekiel, more than any other, was the

prophet of exile, he uses this Name far more than any other prophet (*R' S. R. Hirsch*).

2:5. From sinning (*Targum*); from obeying (*Rashi*).

3:1. This is a metaphor, meaning that he had internalized the mission with which he had been charged (*Targum*).

ח לִשְׁמֹעַ אֵלֶיךָ כִּי כָּל־בֵּית יִשְׂרָאֵל חִזְקֵי־מֵצַח וּקְשֵׁי־לֵב הֵמָּה: הִנֵּה נָתַתִּי

ט אֶת־פָּנֶיךָ חֲזָקִים לְעֻמַּת פְּנֵיהֶם וְאֶת־מִצְחֲךָ חָזָק לְעֻמַּת מִצְחָם: כְּשָׁמִיר חָזָק מִצֹּר נָתַתִּי מִצְחֶךָ לֹא־תִירָא אוֹתָם וְלֹא־תֵחַת מִפְּנֵיהֶם כִּי בֵּית מְרִי

י הֵמָּה: וַיֹּאמֶר אֵלָי בֶּן־אָדָם אֶת־כָּל־דְּבָרַי אֲשֶׁר אֲדַבֵּר אֵלֶיךָ

יא קַח בִּלְבָבְךָ וּבְאָזְנֶיךָ שְׁמָע: וְלֵךְ בֹּא אֶל־הַגּוֹלָה אֶל־בְּנֵי עַמֶּךָ וְדִבַּרְתָּ אֲלֵיהֶם וְאָמַרְתָּ אֲלֵיהֶם כֹּה אָמַר אֲדֹנָי יֱהֹוִה אִם־יִשְׁמְעוּ וְאִם־יֶחְדָּלוּ:

יב וַתִּשָּׂאֵנִי רוּחַ וָאֶשְׁמַע אַחֲרַי קוֹל רַעַשׁ גָּדוֹל בָּרוּךְ כְּבוֹד־יהוה

יג מִמְּקוֹמוֹ: וְקוֹל ׀ כַּנְפֵי הַחַיּוֹת מַשִּׁיקוֹת אִשָּׁה אֶל־אֲחוֹתָהּ וְקוֹל הָאוֹפַנִּים

יד לְעֻמָּתָם וְקוֹל רַעַשׁ גָּדוֹל: וְרוּחַ נְשָׂאַתְנִי וַתִּקָּחֵנִי וָאֵלֵךְ מַר בַּחֲמַת רוּחִי

טו וְיַד־יהוה עָלַי חָזָקָה: וָאָבוֹא אֶל־הַגּוֹלָה תֵּל אָבִיב הַיֹּשְׁבִים אֶל־נְהַר־כְּבָר °וָאֵשֵׁב [ק וָאֵשֵׁב] הֵמָּה יוֹשְׁבִים שָׁם וָאֵשֵׁב שָׁם שִׁבְעַת יָמִים

טז מַשְׁמִים בְּתוֹכָם: וַיְהִי מִקְצֵה שִׁבְעַת יָמִים וַיְהִי דְבַר־יהוה

יז אֵלַי לֵאמֹר: בֶּן־אָדָם צֹפֶה נְתַתִּיךָ לְבֵית יִשְׂרָאֵל וְשָׁמַעְתָּ מִפִּי דָּבָר

יח וְהִזְהַרְתָּ אוֹתָם מִמֶּנִּי: בְּאָמְרִי לָרָשָׁע מוֹת תָּמוּת וְלֹא הִזְהַרְתּוֹ וְלֹא דִבַּרְתָּ לְהַזְהִיר רָשָׁע מִדַּרְכּוֹ הָרְשָׁעָה לְחַיֹּתוֹ הוּא רָשָׁע בַּעֲוֹנוֹ יָמוּת וְדָמוֹ מִיָּדְךָ

יט אֲבַקֵּשׁ: וְאַתָּה כִּי־הִזְהַרְתָּ רָשָׁע וְלֹא־שָׁב מֵרִשְׁעוֹ וּמִדַּרְכּוֹ הָרְשָׁעָה הוּא בַּעֲוֹנוֹ יָמוּת וְאַתָּה אֶת־נַפְשְׁךָ הִצַּלְתָּ: וּבְשׁוּב צַדִּיק מִצִּדְקוֹ

כ וְעָשָׂה עָוֶל וְנָתַתִּי מִכְשׁוֹל לְפָנָיו הוּא יָמוּת כִּי לֹא הִזְהַרְתּוֹ בְּחַטָּאתוֹ יָמוּת וְלֹא תִזָּכַרְןָ צִדְקֹתָו אֲשֶׁר עָשָׂה וְדָמוֹ מִיָּדְךָ אֲבַקֵּשׁ: וְאַתָּה כִּי

כא הִזְהַרְתּוֹ צַדִּיק לְבִלְתִּי חֲטֹא צַדִּיק וְהוּא לֹא־חָטָא חָיוֹ יִחְיֶה כִּי נִזְהָר

כב וְאַתָּה אֶת־נַפְשְׁךָ הִצַּלְתָּ: וַתְּהִי עָלַי שָׁם יַד־יהוה וַיֹּאמֶר אֵלַי

כג קוּם צֵא אֶל־הַבִּקְעָה וְשָׁם אֲדַבֵּר אוֹתָךְ: וָאָקוּם וָאֵצֵא אֶל־הַבִּקְעָה וְהִנֵּה־

כד שָׁם כְּבוֹד־יהוה עֹמֵד כַּכָּבוֹד אֲשֶׁר רָאִיתִי עַל־נְהַר־כְּבָר וָאֶפֹּל עַל־פָּנָי: וַתָּבֹא־בִי רוּחַ וַתַּעֲמִדֵנִי עַל־רַגְלָי וַיְדַבֵּר אֹתִי וַיֹּאמֶר אֵלַי בֹּא הִסָּגֵר

כה בְּתוֹךְ בֵּיתֶךָ: וְאַתָּה בֶן־אָדָם הִנֵּה נָתְנוּ עָלֶיךָ עֲבוֹתִים וַאֲסָרוּךָ

כו בָּהֶם וְלֹא תֵצֵא בְּתוֹכָם: וּלְשׁוֹנְךָ אַדְבִּיק אֶל־חִכֶּךָ וְנֶאֱלַמְתָּ וְלֹא־תִהְיֶה

כז לָהֶם לְאִישׁ מוֹכִיחַ כִּי בֵּית מְרִי הֵמָּה: וּבְדַבְּרִי אוֹתְךָ אֶפְתַּח אֶת־פִּיךָ וְאָמַרְתָּ אֲלֵיהֶם כֹּה אָמַר אֲדֹנָי יֱהֹוִה ׀ הַשֹּׁמֵעַ ׀ יִשְׁמָע וְהֶחָדֵל ׀ יֶחְדָּל כִּי

א בֵּית מְרִי הֵמָּה: וְאַתָּה בֶן־אָדָם קַח־לְךָ לְבֵנָה וְנָתַתָּה **ד**

ב אוֹתָהּ לְפָנֶיךָ וְחַקּוֹתָ עָלֶיהָ עִיר אֶת־יְרוּשָׁלָ‍ִם: וְנָתַתָּה עָלֶיהָ מָצוֹר וּבָנִיתָ עָלֶיהָ דָּיֵק וְשָׁפַכְתָּ עָלֶיהָ סֹלְלָה וְנָתַתָּה עָלֶיהָ מַחֲנֹת וְשִׂים־

◄ Haftarah for
first day of
Shavuos
continues
here: 3:12

3:8. I have given you greater fortitude than they have.
3:11. See 2:5.
3:13. Celestial beings described in Chapter 1.
3:17. You became responsible for the welfare of the people who will rely on you to warn them of danger.

3:24. Ezekiel was not to rebuke the people until he had received the complete prophecy (*Radak*).

4:1. God commanded Ezekiel to perform an act that would symbolize the impending siege of Jerusalem. Jeremiah had been foretelling it, but the people ignored to heed Me, for the entire House of Israel is hard-browed and brazen-hearted. [8] Behold, I have made your face hard against their face, and your brow hard against their brow. * [9] Like a metal stronger than flint have I made your brow; fear them not and be not intimidated before them, though they are a rebellious house."

[10] Then He said to me, "Son of Man, all My words that I will speak to you, take into your heart and hearken with your ears; [11] and go, come to the exile, to the children of your people, and speak to them. Say to them, 'Thus says the Lord, HASHEM/ELOHIM' whether they will heed or whether they will refrain."*

[12] Then a wind lifted me and I heard behind me the sound of a great noise, [saying,] "Blessed be the glory of HASHEM from His place," [13] and the sound of the wings of the Chayos* knocking against one another, and the sound of the Ofanim* opposite them, and the sound of a great noise.

Among the exiles [14] Thus a wind lifted me and took me and I went in bitterness, in the wrath of my spirit, and the hand of HASHEM was strong upon me. [15] Then I came to the exiles, to Tel-abib, who were dwelling along the River Chebar, and I dwelt where they were dwelling. I dwelt there for a seven-day period, silently among them.

[16] It happened at the end of [the] seven-day period that the word of HASHEM came to me, saying, [17] "Son of Man, I have appointed you a sentinel* for the House of Israel; when you hear a matter from My mouth, you shall warn them on My behalf. [18] When I say of a wicked one, 'You shall surely die!' and you do not warn him, and do not speak up to warn the wicked one concerning his evil way, to save his life, then he, the wicked one, will die for his iniquity and I will demand his blood from your hand. [19] But if you did warn the wicked one, yet he does not turn away from his wickedness and from his evil way, he will die for his iniquity. And as for you, you will have saved your soul.

The prophet as sentinel

[20] "And when a righteous person turns from his righteousness and acts corruptly and I place a stumbling block before him, he will die. Because you did not warn him he will die for his sin, and his righteousness that he did will not be remembered, and I will demand his blood from your hand. [21] But you, if you did warn him, the righteous man, that the righteous man should not sin, and he did not sin; he will surely live because he was careful. And as for you, you will have saved your soul."

Another vision of God's glory [22] The hand of HASHEM came upon me there, and He said to me, "Arise and go out to the valley and there I will speak with you." [23] So I arose and went out to the valley and behold — the glory of HASHEM was standing there, like the glory that I saw by the River Chebar, and I fell upon my face. [24] Then a spirit entered into me and stood me on my feet; and He spoke to me, and said to me, "Come, shut yourself inside your house. * [25] And you, Son of Man, behold, [it is as if] they had put ropes upon you and bound you with them; you shall not go out among them. [26] I will make your tongue cleave to your palate and you will become mute, and you will not be a man of rebuke unto them, for they are a rebellious house. [27] But when I will have spoken to you I will open your mouth, and you will say to them, 'Thus said the Lord, HASHEM/ELOHIM.' Whoever hears will hear and whoever refrains will refrain, for they are a rebellious house.

4

[1] "Now you, Son of Man, take for yourself a brick, place it before you, and engrave on it a city — Jerusalem. * [2] Then lay siege against it — erect a siege tower against it, pour a ramp against it, place camps against it and set up

Acting out the siege

---

his prophecies, deluding themselves that the Temple was immune to attack. Ezekiel would now try to convince them otherwise by symbolically besieging the city with his arm bared (v. 7), like a warrior.

ג עָלֶיהָ כָּרִים סָבִיב: וְאַתָּה קַח־לְךָ מַחֲבַת בַּרְזֶל וְנָתַתָּה אוֹתָהּ קִיר בַּרְזֶל
בֵּינְךָ וּבֵין הָעִיר וַהֲכִינֹתָה אֶת־פָּנֶיךָ אֵלֶיהָ וְהָיְתָה בַמָּצוֹר וְצַרְתָּ עָלֶיהָ

ד אוֹת הִיא לְבֵית יִשְׂרָאֵל: וְאַתָּה שְׁכַב עַל־צִדְּךָ הַשְּׂמָאלִי
וְשַׂמְתָּ אֶת־עֲוֹן בֵּית־יִשְׂרָאֵל עָלָיו מִסְפַּר הַיָּמִים אֲשֶׁר תִּשְׁכַּב עָלָיו תִּשָּׂא

ה אֶת־עֲוֹנָם: וַאֲנִי נָתַתִּי לְךָ אֶת־שְׁנֵי עֲוֹנָם לְמִסְפַּר יָמִים שְׁלֹשׁ־מֵאוֹת

ו וְתִשְׁעִים יוֹם וְנָשָׂאתָ עֲוֹן בֵּית־יִשְׂרָאֵל: וְכִלִּיתָ אֶת־אֵלֶּה וְשָׁכַבְתָּ עַל־
צִדְּךָ °הַיְמִינִי [°הַיְמָנִי ק] שֵׁנִית וְנָשָׂאתָ אֶת־עֲוֹן בֵּית־יְהוּדָה אַרְבָּעִים יוֹם

ז יוֹם לַשָּׁנָה יוֹם לַשָּׁנָה נְתַתִּיו לָךְ: וְאֶל־מְצוֹר יְרוּשָׁלַ͏ִם תָּכִין פָּנֶיךָ וּזְרֹעֲךָ

ח חֲשׂוּפָה וְנִבֵּאתָ עָלֶיהָ: וְהִנֵּה נָתַתִּי עָלֶיךָ עֲבוֹתִים וְלֹא־תֵהָפֵךְ מִצִּדְּךָ אֶל־

ט צִדֶּךָ עַד־כַּלּוֹתְךָ יְמֵי מְצוּרֶךָ: וְאַתָּה קַח־לְךָ חִטִּין וּשְׂעֹרִים וּפוֹל וַעֲדָשִׁים
וְדֹחַן וְכֻסְּמִים וְנָתַתָּה אוֹתָם בִּכְלִי אֶחָד וְעָשִׂיתָ אוֹתָם לְךָ לְלָחֶם
מִסְפַּר הַיָּמִים אֲשֶׁר־אַתָּה | שׁוֹכֵב עַל־צִדְּךָ שְׁלֹשׁ־מֵאוֹת וְתִשְׁעִים יוֹם

י תֹּאכֲלֶנּוּ: וּמַאֲכָלְךָ אֲשֶׁר תֹּאכֲלֶנּוּ בְּמִשְׁקוֹל עֶשְׂרִים שֶׁקֶל לַיּוֹם מֵעֵת

יא עַד־עֵת תֹּאכֲלֶנּוּ: וּמַיִם בִּמְשׂוּרָה תִשְׁתֶּה שִׁשִּׁית הַהִין מֵעֵת עַד־עֵת

יב תִּשְׁתֶּה: וְעֻגַת שְׂעֹרִים תֹּאכֲלֶנָּה וְהִיא בְּגֶלְלֵי צֵאַת הָאָדָם תְּעֻגֶנָה

יג לְעֵינֵיהֶם: וַיֹּאמֶר יְהוָֹה כָּכָה יֹאכְלוּ בְנֵי־יִשְׂרָאֵל אֶת־לַחְמָם

יד טָמֵא בַּגּוֹיִם אֲשֶׁר אַדִּיחֵם שָׁם: וָאֹמַר אֲהָהּ אֲדֹנָי יֱהֹוִה הִנֵּה נַפְשִׁי לֹא
מְטֻמָּאָה וּנְבֵלָה וּטְרֵפָה לֹא־אָכַלְתִּי מִנְּעוּרַי וְעַד־עַתָּה וְלֹא־בָא בְּפִי

טו בְּשַׂר פִּגּוּל: וַיֹּאמֶר אֵלַי רְאֵה נָתַתִּי לְךָ אֶת־°צְפוּעֵי [°צְפִיעֵי ק]

טז הַבָּקָר תַּחַת גֶּלְלֵי הָאָדָם וְעָשִׂיתָ אֶת־לַחְמְךָ עֲלֵיהֶם: וַיֹּאמֶר
אֵלַי בֶּן־אָדָם הִנְנִי שֹׁבֵר מַטֵּה־לֶחֶם בִּירוּשָׁלַ͏ִם וְאָכְלוּ־לֶחֶם בְּמִשְׁקָל

יז וּבִדְאָגָה וּמַיִם בִּמְשׂוּרָה וּבְשִׁמָּמוֹן יִשְׁתּוּ: לְמַעַן יַחְסְרוּ לֶחֶם וָמָיִם וְנָשַׁמּוּ
א אִישׁ וְאָחִיו וְנָמַקּוּ בַּעֲוֹנָם: ה   וְאַתָּה בֶן־אָדָם קַח־לְךָ | חֶרֶב חַדָּה
תַּעַר הַגַּלָּבִים תִּקָּחֶנָּה לָּךְ וְהַעֲבַרְתָּ עַל־רֹאשְׁךָ וְעַל־זְקָנֶךָ וְלָקַחְתָּ לְךָ

ב מֹאזְנֵי מִשְׁקָל וְחִלַּקְתָּם: שְׁלִשִׁית בָּאוּר תַּבְעִיר בְּתוֹךְ הָעִיר כִּמְלֹאת יְמֵי
הַמָּצוֹר וְלָקַחְתָּ אֶת־הַשְּׁלִשִׁית תַּכֶּה בַחֶרֶב סְבִיבוֹתֶיהָ וְהַשְּׁלִשִׁית תִּזְרֶה

ג לָרוּחַ וְחֶרֶב אָרִיק אַחֲרֵיהֶם: וְלָקַחְתָּ מִשָּׁם מְעַט בְּמִסְפָּר וְצַרְתָּ אוֹתָם

ד בִּכְנָפֶיךָ: וּמֵהֶם עוֹד תִּקָּח וְהִשְׁלַכְתָּ אוֹתָם אֶל־תּוֹךְ הָאֵשׁ וְשָׂרַפְתָּ אֹתָם
בָּאֵשׁ מִמֶּנּוּ תֵצֵא־אֵשׁ אֶל־כָּל־בֵּית יִשְׂרָאֵל: כֹּה אָמַר אֲדֹנָי

ה יֱהֹוִה זֹאת יְרוּשָׁלַ͏ִם בְּתוֹךְ הַגּוֹיִם שַׂמְתִּיהָ וּסְבִיבוֹתֶיהָ אֲרָצוֹת: וַתֶּמֶר אֶת־

4:4. Ezekiel would lie on his side for a long period — 390 days — to symbolize 390 years of Israel's general sinfulness, and another forty days because the Kingdom of Judah had continued to sin for forty years after the Ten Tribes had been exiled. His suffering would atone somewhat for Israel's sins, so that the people would not be eradicated entirely (*Rashi*).

4:10. This represented the severe rationing system that would be imposed during the siege (*Rashi*), twenty *shekels* weighing between two and three pounds for each 24-hour period.

4:11. Between twenty-five and thirty fluid ounces.

4:12. To emphasize the desperate nature of the siege, the people would eat barley, which was usually used as battering rams all around. ³ Now you, take for yourself an iron pan and place it as an iron wall between yourself and the city, and set your face against it; thus it will be under siege, for you will lay siege to it. It is a sign to the House of Israel.

⁴ "Then lie upon your left side, and place the iniquity of the House of Israel upon it; * according to the number of days that you lie upon it you will bear their iniquity.

390 days and 40 days ⁵ I have given you the years of their iniquity as a number of days — three hundred and ninety days — and you shall bear the iniquity of the House of Israel. ⁶ "When you complete these, then lie upon your right side a second time and bear the iniquity of the House of Judah for forty days; a day for a year, a day for a year have I assigned it for you. ⁷ Direct your face toward the siege of Jerusalem, with your arm bared; and you shall prophesy against it. ⁸ Behold, [it is as if] I had placed ropes upon you so that you not turn from your one side to your other side until you have completed the days of your siege.

The food of siege ⁹ "Now you, take for yourself wheat, barley, beans, lentils, millet, and spelt; put them into one vessel and prepare them as food for yourself. According to the number of days that you lie on your side — three hundred and ninety days — are you to eat it. ¹⁰ Now, your food that you eat shall be twenty shekels per day by weight, * you shall eat [this amount] from this time [one day] to the same time [the next day]. ¹¹ And water by measure shall you drink; a sixth of a hin * from this time to the same time shall you drink [it]. ¹² You shall eat it as a barley cake, * and you shall bake it with pieces of human excrement, before their eyes."

¹³ HASHEM said, "Thus will the Children of Israel eat their food: unclean, among the nations where I will banish them."

¹⁴ But I said, "Alas, Lord HASHEM/ELOHIM! Behold, my soul has not been defiled; I have never eaten carrion nor meat from a wounded animal from my youth until now, nor has loathsome meat ever come into my mouth." *

¹⁵ So He said to me, "See, I have permitted you the dung of cattle instead of human excrement; you may prepare your food upon them."

¹⁶ Then He said to me, "Son of Man, behold, I am breaking the staff of bread in Jerusalem, and people will eat bread by weight and with worry, and drink water by measure and with consternation; ¹⁷ for they will lack bread and water, and every man and his brother will be confounded, and they will pine away in their iniquity."

5

The sword, the fire, and the wind ¹ "You, Son of Man, take for yourself a sharp sword, take for yourself a barber's razor, and pass it over your head and over your beard; then take for yourself the scales of a balance and divide them. * ² Burn one third in a fire inside the city * upon completion of the days of the siege, take one third and strike [it] with a sword all around it, and scatter one third to the wind, and I will unsheathe a sword after them. ³ Then take from there a numbered few and bind them into your hems. ⁴ Then take from them once again and throw them into the middle of the fire, and burn them in the fire; from it a fire will go forth to the entire House of Israel. *

⁵ Thus said the Lord, HASHEM/ELOHIM: This is Jerusalem! Among the nations have I placed her, and all around her are countries. ⁶ She exchanged

---

fodder, and for fuel they would be forced to use human excrement.
4:14. I cannot bear to eat such repulsive food.
5:1. I.e., divide your hairs.

5:2. Burn it in the "city" etched into the brick (4:1).
5:4. That is, these symbolic acts that you perform will portend actual events in the real world, as described in v. 12, where God addresses Jerusalem.

מִשְׁפָּטַי לְרִשְׁעָה מִן־הַגּוֹיִם וְאֶת־חֻקּוֹתַי מִן־הָאֲרָצוֹת אֲשֶׁר סְבִיבוֹתֶיהָ
כִּי בְמִשְׁפָּטַי מָאָסוּ וְחֻקּוֹתַי לֹא־הָלְכוּ בָהֶם: לָכֵן כֹּה־אָמַר ׀ ז
אֲדֹנָי יֱהוִֹה יַעַן הֲמָנְכֶם מִן־הַגּוֹיִם אֲשֶׁר סְבִיבוֹתֵיכֶם בְּחֻקּוֹתַי לֹא הֲלַכְתֶּם
וְאֶת־מִשְׁפָּטַי לֹא עֲשִׂיתֶם וּכְמִשְׁפְּטֵי הַגּוֹיִם אֲשֶׁר סְבִיבוֹתֵיכֶם לֹא
עֲשִׂיתֶם: לָכֵן כֹּה אָמַר אֲדֹנָי יֱהוִֹה הִנְנִי עָלַיִךְ גַּם־אָנִי וְעָשִׂיתִי ח
בְתוֹכֵךְ מִשְׁפָּטִים לְעֵינֵי הַגּוֹיִם: וְעָשִׂיתִי בָךְ אֵת אֲשֶׁר לֹא־עָשִׂיתִי ט
וְאֵת אֲשֶׁר־לֹא־אֶעֱשֶׂה כָמֹהוּ עוֹד יַעַן כָּל־תּוֹעֲבֹתָיִךְ: לָכֵן י
אָבוֹת יֹאכְלוּ בָנִים בְּתוֹכֵךְ וּבָנִים יֹאכְלוּ אֲבוֹתָם וְעָשִׂיתִי בָךְ שְׁפָטִים
וְזֵרִיתִי אֶת־כָּל־שְׁאֵרִיתֵךְ לְכָל־רוּחַ: לָכֵן חַי־אָנִי נְאֻם אֲדֹנָי יֱהוִֹה אִם־ יא
לֹא יַעַן אֶת־מִקְדָּשִׁי טִמֵּאת בְּכָל־שִׁקּוּצַיִךְ וּבְכָל־תּוֹעֲבֹתָיִךְ וְגַם־אֲנִי
אֶגְרַע וְלֹא־תָחוֹס עֵינִי וְגַם־אֲנִי לֹא אֶחְמוֹל: שְׁלִשִׁתֵיךְ בַּדֶּבֶר יָמוּתוּ יב
וּבָרָעָב יִכְלוּ בְתוֹכֵךְ וְהַשְּׁלִשִׁית בַּחֶרֶב יִפְּלוּ סְבִיבוֹתָיִךְ וְהַשְּׁלִישִׁית לְכָל־
רוּחַ אֱזָרֶה וְחֶרֶב אָרִיק אַחֲרֵיהֶם: וְכָלָה אַפִּי וַהֲנִחוֹתִי חֲמָתִי בָּם יג
וְהִנֶּחָמְתִּי וְיָדְעוּ כִּי־אֲנִי יהוה דִּבַּרְתִּי בְּקִנְאָתִי בְּכַלּוֹתִי חֲמָתִי בָּם: וְאֶתְּנֵךְ יד
לְחָרְבָּה וּלְחֶרְפָּה בַּגּוֹיִם אֲשֶׁר סְבִיבוֹתָיִךְ לְעֵינֵי כָּל־עוֹבֵר: וְהָיְתָה טו
חֶרְפָּה וּגְדוּפָה מוּסָר וּמְשַׁמָּה לַגּוֹיִם אֲשֶׁר סְבִיבוֹתָיִךְ בַּעֲשׂוֹתִי בָךְ
שְׁפָטִים בְּאַף וּבְחֵמָה וּבְתֹכְחוֹת חֵמָה אֲנִי יהוה דִּבַּרְתִּי: בְּשַׁלְּחִי אֶת־ טז
חִצֵּי הָרָעָב הָרָעִים בָּהֶם אֲשֶׁר הָיוּ לְמַשְׁחִית אֲשֶׁר־אֲשַׁלַּח אוֹתָם
לְשַׁחֶתְכֶם וְרָעָב אֹסֵף עֲלֵיכֶם וְשָׁבַרְתִּי לָכֶם מַטֵּה־לָחֶם: וְשִׁלַּחְתִּי יז
עֲלֵיכֶם רָעָב וְחַיָּה רָעָה וְשִׁכְּלֻךְ וְדֶבֶר וָדָם יַעֲבָר־בָּךְ וְחֶרֶב אָבִיא עָלַיִךְ
אֲנִי יהוה דִּבַּרְתִּי: וַיְהִי דְבַר־יהוה אֵלַי לֵאמֹר: בֶּן־אָדָם א-ב ו
שִׂים פָּנֶיךָ אֶל־הָרֵי יִשְׂרָאֵל וְהִנָּבֵא אֲלֵיהֶם: וְאָמַרְתָּ הָרֵי יִשְׂרָאֵל שִׁמְעוּ ג
דְּבַר־אֲדֹנָי יֱהוִֹה כֹּה־אָמַר אֲדֹנָי יֱהוִֹה לֶהָרִים וְלַגְּבָעוֹת לָאֲפִיקִים
וְלַגֵּאָיוֹת [° וְלַגֵּאָיֹת ק] הִנְנִי אֲנִי מֵבִיא עֲלֵיכֶם חֶרֶב וְאִבַּדְתִּי בָּמוֹתֵיכֶם:
וְנָשַׁמּוּ מִזְבְּחוֹתֵיכֶם וְנִשְׁבְּרוּ חַמָּנֵיכֶם וְהִפַּלְתִּי חַלְלֵיכֶם לִפְנֵי גִלּוּלֵיכֶם: ד
וְנָתַתִּי אֶת־פִּגְרֵי בְּנֵי יִשְׂרָאֵל לִפְנֵי גִּלּוּלֵיהֶם וְזֵרִיתִי אֶת־עַצְמוֹתֵיכֶם ה
סְבִיבוֹת מִזְבְּחוֹתֵיכֶם: בְּכֹל מוֹשְׁבוֹתֵיכֶם הֶעָרִים תֶּחֱרַבְנָה וְהַבָּמוֹת ו
תִּישַׁמְנָה לְמַעַן יֶחֶרְבוּ וְיֶאְשְׁמוּ מִזְבְּחוֹתֵיכֶם וְנִשְׁבְּרוּ וְנִשְׁבְּתוּ גִּלּוּלֵיכֶם
וְנִגְדְּעוּ חַמָּנֵיכֶם וְנִמְחוּ מַעֲשֵׂיכֶם: וְנָפַל חָלָל בְּתוֹכְכֶם וִידַעְתֶּם כִּי־ ז
אֲנִי יהוה: וְהוֹתַרְתִּי בִּהְיוֹת לָכֶם פְּלִיטֵי חֶרֶב בַּגּוֹיִם בְּהִזָּרוֹתֵיכֶם ח
בָּאֲרָצוֹת: וְזָכְרוּ פְלִיטֵיכֶם אוֹתִי בַּגּוֹיִם אֲשֶׁר נִשְׁבּוּ־שָׁם אֲשֶׁר נִשְׁבַּרְתִּי ט
אֶת־לִבָּם הַזּוֹנֶה אֲשֶׁר־סָר מֵעָלַי וְאֵת עֵינֵיהֶם הַזֹּנוֹת אַחֲרֵי גִּלּוּלֵיהֶם

5:7. Instead of following the decent practices of your neighbors, you copied those that are contemptible.

5:11. Just as you showed no compunction about desecrating My glory, I will show no compassion to you.

My laws for wickedness more than the nations did, and [exchanged] My decrees more than the countries that are around her; for they spurned My laws and did not follow My decrees. [7] *Therefore, thus said the Lord HASHEM/ ELOHIM: Because you readied yourselves [for sin] more than the nations around you — you did not follow My decrees, you did not fulfill My laws; you did not even act according to the laws of the nations around you* * — [8] *therefore, thus said the Lord HASHEM/ELOHIM: Behold, I too am against you, and I will execute judgments in your midst, before the eyes of the nations.* [9] *I will do with you what I have never done, and the likes of which I will never do again, because of all your abominations.* [10] *Therefore, fathers will eat sons in your midst, and sons will eat their fathers; and I will execute judgments among you and scatter your entire remnant to every direction.* [11] *Therefore, as I live — the word of the Lord HASHEM/ELOHIM — I swear that because you have defiled My Sanctuary with all your detestations and all your abominations, also I will diminish [you]; My eye will have no pity, and I, too, will show no compassion.* * [12] *One third of you will die by the plague and be consumed by the famine in your midst; one third will fall around you by the sword; and one third I will scatter to every direction, and I will unsheathe the sword after them.* [13] *My anger will be spent and I will put My wrath to rest through [punishing] them and so I will find consolation. Then they will know that I, HASHEM, have spoken in My zeal, when I spend My wrath upon them.* [14] *I will make you into a ruin and a disgrace among the nations that are around you, before the eyes of every passerby.* [15] *[Jerusa-lem] will be a disgrace and a taunt, a lesson and an astonishment to the nations that are around you when I execute judgments on you in anger, in wrath and with wrathful rebuke; I am HASHEM, I have spoken.* [16] *When I dis-patch against them the evil arrows of famine that are for destruction, which I will dispatch to destroy you, then I will intensify the famine upon you and I will break your staff of bread;* [17] *I will send against you famine and harmful beast, and they will bereave you; and plague and bloodshed will pass among you; and I will bring the sword against you. I, HASHEM, have spoken."*

6

[1] The word of HASHEM came to me, saying, [2] "Son of Man, direct your face toward the mountains of Israel and prophesy to them: [3] Say,

Mountains of Israel, hear the word of the Lord HASHEM/ELOHIM! Thus said the Lord HASHEM/ELOHIM to the mountains and to the hills, to the ravines and to the valleys: Behold, I am bringing the sword against you and I will destroy your high places. [4] *Desolate will your altars be, and broken will your sun-images be, and I will cast down your slain before your idols.* [5] *I will set the corpses of the Children of Israel before their idols, and I will scatter your bones around your altars.* [6] *In all your habitations the cities will be destroyed and the high places made desolate, so that your altars be destroyed and desolated, your idols broken and nullified, your sun-images cut down, and your deeds eradicated.* [7] *Corpses will fall in your midst, and you will know that I am HASHEM.* [8] *But I will leave a remnant, so that you will have some survivors from the sword among the nations when you become scattered among the lands;* [9] *and your survivors will remember Me among the nations where they were taken captive, how I was anguished by their straying heart that turned away from Me and by their eyes that strayed after their idols;*

וְנָקֹ֙טוּ֙ בִּפְנֵיהֶ֔ם אֶל־הָרָעוֹת֙ אֲשֶׁ֣ר עָשׂ֔וּ לְכֹ֖ל תּוֹעֲבֹֽתֵיהֶ֑ם וְיָדְע֖וּ כִּֽי־אֲנִ֥י י   כֹּֽה־
יְהֹוָ֕ה לֹ֥א אֶל־חִנָּ֖ם דִּבַּ֑רְתִּי לַעֲשׂ֥וֹת לָהֶ֖ם הָרָעָ֥ה הַזֹּֽאת: יא
אָמַ֞ר אֲדֹנָ֣י יֱהֹוִ֗ה הַכֵּ֤ה בְכַפְּךָ֙ וּרְקַ֣ע בְּרַגְלְךָ֔ וֶאֱמָר־אָ֕ח אֶ֥ל כָּל־תּוֹעֲב֖וֹת
רָע֣וֹת בֵּֽית־יִשְׂרָאֵ֑ל אֲשֶׁ֗ר בַּחֶ֙רֶב֙ בָּרָעָ֣ב וּבַדֶּ֔בֶר יִפֹּֽלוּ: הָרָח֞וֹק בַּדֶּ֣בֶר יָמ֗וּת   יב
וְהַקָּרוֹב֙ בַּחֶ֣רֶב יִפּ֔וֹל וְהַנִּשְׁאָר֙ וְהַנָּצ֔וּר בָּרָעָ֖ב יָמ֑וּת וְכִלֵּיתִ֥י חֲמָתִ֖י בָּֽם:
וִֽידַעְתֶּם֙ כִּֽי־אֲנִ֣י יְהֹוָ֔ה בִּֽהְי֣וֹת חַלְלֵיהֶ֗ם בְּתוֹךְ֙ גִּלּ֣וּלֵיהֶ֔ם סְבִיב֖וֹת   יג
מִזְבְּחֽוֹתֵיהֶ֑ם אֶ֣ל כָּל־גִּבְעָ֣ה רָמָ֡ה בְּכֹל֩ ׀ רָאשֵׁ֨י הֶהָרִ֜ים וְתַ֣חַת כָּל־עֵ֣ץ
רַעֲנָ֗ן וְתַ֙חַת֙ כָּל־אֵלָ֣ה עֲבֻתָּ֔ה מְק֗וֹם אֲשֶׁ֤ר נָֽתְנוּ־שָׁם֙ רֵ֣יחַ נִיחֹ֔חַ לְכֹ֖ל
גִּלּֽוּלֵיהֶ֑ם: וְנָטִ֤יתִי אֶת־יָדִי֙ עֲלֵיהֶ֔ם וְנָתַתִּ֤י אֶת־הָאָ֙רֶץ֙ שְׁמָמָ֣ה וּמְשַׁמָּ֔ה   יד
מִמִּדְבַּ֣ר דִּבְלָ֔תָה בְּכֹ֖ל מֽוֹשְׁבֽוֹתֵיהֶ֑ם וְיָדְע֖וּ כִּֽי־אֲנִ֥י יְהֹוָֽה: **ז**

וַיְהִ֥י   א
דְבַר־יְהֹוָ֖ה אֵלַ֥י לֵאמֹֽר: וְאַתָּ֣ה בֶן־אָדָ֗ם כֹּֽה־אָמַ֞ר אֲדֹנָ֤י יֱהֹוִה֙ לְאַדְמַ֣ת   ב
יִשְׂרָאֵ֔ל קֵ֣ץ בָּ֔א הַקֵּ֥ץ עַל־[°אַרְבַּעַת ק] ׀ ״אַרְבַּע ק] כַּנְפ֣וֹת הָאָֽרֶץ: עַתָּה֙ הַקֵּ֣ץ   ג
עָלַ֔יִךְ וְשִׁלַּחְתִּ֤י אַפִּי֙ בָּ֔ךְ וּשְׁפַטְתִּ֖יךְ כִּדְרָכָ֑יִךְ וְנָתַתִּ֣י עָלַ֔יִךְ אֵ֖ת כָּל־
תּוֹעֲבֹתָֽיִךְ: וְלֹא־תָח֥וֹס עֵינִ֛י עָלַ֖יִךְ וְלֹ֣א אֶחְמ֑וֹל כִּ֣י דְרָכַ֜יִךְ עָלַ֙יִךְ֙ אֶתֵּ֔ן   ד
וְתוֹעֲבוֹתַ֛יִךְ בְּתוֹכֵ֥ךְ תִּֽהְיֶ֖יןָ וִֽידַעְתֶּ֥ם כִּֽי־אֲנִ֥י יְהֹוָֽה: כֹּ֥ה אָמַר֙   ה
אֲדֹנָ֣י יֱהֹוִ֔ה רָעָ֛ה אַחַ֥ת רָעָ֖ה הִנֵּ֥ה בָאָֽה: קֵ֣ץ בָּ֔א בָּ֥א הַקֵּ֖ץ הֵקִ֣יץ אֵלָ֑יִךְ   ו
הִנֵּ֖ה בָּאָֽה: בָּ֧אָה הַצְּפִירָ֛ה אֵלַ֖יִךְ יוֹשֵׁ֣ב הָאָ֑רֶץ בָּ֣א הָעֵ֗ת קָר֛וֹב הַיּ֥וֹם   ז
מְהוּמָ֖ה וְלֹא־הֵ֥ד הָרִֽים: עַתָּ֣ה מִקָּר֗וֹב אֶשְׁפּ֤וֹךְ חֲמָתִי֙ עָלַ֔יִךְ וְכִלֵּיתִ֤י   ח
אַפִּי֙ בָּ֔ךְ וּשְׁפַטְתִּ֖יךְ כִּדְרָכָ֑יִךְ וְנָתַתִּ֣י עָלַ֔יִךְ אֵ֖ת כָּל־תּוֹעֲבֹתָֽיִךְ: וְלֹא־   ט
תָח֥וֹס עֵינִ֛י וְלֹ֣א אֶחְמ֑וֹל כִּדְרָכַ֜יִךְ עָלַ֣יִךְ אֶתֵּ֗ן וְתוֹעֲבוֹתַ֛יִךְ בְּתוֹכֵ֥ךְ תִּֽהְיֶ֑יןָ
וִֽידַעְתֶּ֕ם כִּ֛י אֲנִ֥י יְהֹוָ֖ה מַכֶּֽה: הִנֵּ֥ה הַיּ֖וֹם הִנֵּ֣ה בָאָ֑ה יָֽצְאָה֙ הַצְּפִרָ֔ה צָ֥ץ   י
הַמַּטֶּ֖ה פָּרַ֥ח הַזָּדֽוֹן: הֶחָמָ֣ס ׀ קָ֚ם לְמַטֵּה־רֶ֔שַׁע לֹא־מֵהֶ֥ם וְלֹ֛א מֵהֲמוֹנָ֖ם   יא
וְלֹ֣א מֵהֶ֑מֶהם וְלֹא־נֹ֖הַּ בָּהֶֽם: בָּ֤א הָעֵת֙ הִגִּ֣יעַ הַיּ֔וֹם הַקּוֹנֶה֙ אַל־יִשְׂמָ֔ח   יב
וְהַמּוֹכֵ֖ר אַל־יִתְאַבָּ֑ל כִּ֥י חָר֖וֹן אֶל־כָּל־הֲמוֹנָֽהּ: כִּ֣י הַמּוֹכֵ֗ר אֶל־הַמִּמְכָּר֙   יג
לֹ֣א יָשׁ֔וּב וְע֥וֹד בַּחַיִּ֖ים חַיָּתָ֑ם כִּֽי־חָז֤וֹן אֶל־כָּל־הֲמוֹנָהּ֙ לֹ֣א יָשׁ֔וּב
וְאִ֧ישׁ בַּעֲוֺנ֛וֹ חַיָּת֖וֹ לֹ֥א יִתְחַזָּֽקוּ: תָּקְע֤וּ בַתָּק֙וֹעַ֙ וְהָכִ֣ין הַכֹּ֔ל וְאֵ֥ין הֹלֵ֖ךְ   יד
לַמִּלְחָמָ֑ה כִּ֥י חֲרוֹנִ֖י אֶל־כָּל־הֲמוֹנָֽהּ: הַחֶ֣רֶב בַּח֔וּץ וְהַדֶּ֥בֶר וְהָרָעָ֖ב   טו
מִבָּ֑יִת אֲשֶׁ֤ר בַּשָּׂדֶה֙ בַּחֶ֣רֶב יָמ֔וּת וַאֲשֶׁ֣ר בָּעִ֔יר רָעָ֥ב וָדֶ֖בֶר יֹֽאכְלֶֽנּוּ:
וּפָֽלְטוּ֙ פְּלִ֣יטֵיהֶ֔ם וְהָי֣וּ אֶל־הֶהָרִ֗ים כְּיוֹנֵ֧י הַגֵּאָי֛וֹת כֻּלָּ֖ם הֹמ֑וֹת אִ֖ישׁ   טז
בַּעֲוֺנֽוֹ: כָּל־הַיָּדַ֖יִם תִּרְפֶּ֑ינָה וְכָל־בִּרְכַּ֖יִם תֵּלַ֥כְנָה מָּֽיִם: וְחָגְר֣וּ שַׂקִּ֗ים   יז-יח

6:9. Realizing that it was their own fault that they had been exiled, they will be ashamed for not having heeded the exhortations of the prophets (*Rashi*).

7:10. The rod of punishment is ready to strike.

7:12-13. Whether or not a deal was profitable will be immaterial because total destruction is at hand. The seller will be exiled too far away from his former field to be reminded of its forfeiture (*Rashi*).

7:13. Morally or spiritually.

7:14. They will be overwhelmed by the enemy.

then they will be disgusted with themselves* for the evils they did through all their abominations. ¹⁰ Then they will know that I am HASHEM, that I did not speak in vain about doing this evil to them.

¹¹ Thus said the Lord HASHEM/ELOHIM: Clap with your hand and stamp with your foot and say, 'Alas!' because of all the evil abominations of the House of Israel, who will fall by the sword, by the famine and by the plague. ¹² He who is far [from the battlefield] will die by the plague, and he who is near will fall by the sword, and he that remains and is besieged will die by the famine; and I will spend My wrath upon them. ¹³ Then you will know that I am HASHEM, when their corpses will be among their idols around their altars, on every high hill, on all the mountaintops and under every leafy tree and under every thick elm — the place where they offered the savor of pleasing aroma to all their idols. ¹⁴ And I will stretch out My hand over them and lay the land waste and desolate, from the wilderness of Diblah throughout all their habitations; then they will know that I am HASHEM.

7

Retribution
is inherent
in the evil
itself

¹ The word of HASHEM came to me, saying: ² You, Son of Man, thus said the Lord HASHEM/ELOHIM to [those who dwell upon] the soil of Israel: An end! The end has come upon the four corners of the land! ³ Now the end is upon you, and I will send My anger against you and I will judge you according to your ways, and I will place upon you [punishment for] all your abominations; ⁴ My eye will not spare you and I will not have compassion; for I will place upon you [punishment for] your ways and [punishment for] your abominations will be in your midst; then you will know that I am HASHEM.

⁵ Thus said the Lord HASHEM/ELOHIM: An evil, a singular evil — behold, it is coming. ⁶ An end has come; the end has come! It is aroused against you. Behold, it comes.

⁷ The dawn has come against you, O dweller of the land. The time has come; the day of tumult is near — and it is not the [joyous] shout of the mountains. ⁸ Now, speedily, I will pour My wrath upon you, and I will spend My anger against you, and I will judge you according to your ways; and I will place upon you [punishment for] all your abominations. ⁹ And My eye will not spare and I will not have compassion. I will place upon you [punishment for] your ways, and [punishment for] your abominations will be in your midst; then you will know that I am HASHEM Who smites. ¹⁰ Behold the day! Behold, it comes! The dawn has gone forth, the rod has sprouted fruit,* wantonness has blossomed. ¹¹ Violence has arisen to become a rod of wickedness; there is not among them, nor among their multitude nor among their offspring, anyone among them who yearns [for Me].

¹² The time has come, the day has arrived; let the buyer not be glad nor the seller mourn; for fury is upon her entire multitude. * ¹³ For the seller — he will not return to that which was sold as long as his soul is alive; for there was a prophetic vision for her entire multitude, it will not return. Each man — his very being remains with his iniquity; they will not fortify themselves. *

¹⁴ They will blow the horn and prepare everything, but no one will go to war,* for My fury is upon all her multitude. ¹⁵ The sword is outside and plague and famine are inside; whoever is in the field will die by the sword, and whoever is in the city, famine and plague will consume him. ¹⁶ Their fugitives will flee; and they will be in the mountains, all of them moaning like pigeons of the valleys, each man in his iniquity. ¹⁷ All hands will be weak and all knees will melt [like] water. ¹⁸ They will gird themselves in sackcloth

וְכִסְּתָה אוֹתָם פַּלָּצוּת וְאֶל כָּל־פָּנִים בּוּשָׁה וּבְכָל־רָאשֵׁיהֶם קָרְחָה:

יט כַּסְפָּם בַּחוּצוֹת יַשְׁלִיכוּ וּזְהָבָם לְנִדָּה יִהְיֶה כַּסְפָּם וּזְהָבָם לֹא־יוּכַל לְהַצִּילָם בְּיוֹם עֶבְרַת יהוה נַפְשָׁם לֹא יְשַׂבֵּעוּ וּמֵעֵיהֶם לֹא יְמַלֵּאוּ כִּי־

כ מִכְשׁוֹל עֲוֹנָם הָיָה: וּצְבִי עֶדְיוֹ לְגָאוֹן שָׂמָהוּ וְצַלְמֵי תוֹעֲבֹתָם שִׁקּוּצֵיהֶם

כא עָשׂוּ בוֹ עַל־כֵּן נְתַתִּיו לָהֶם לְנִדָּה: וּנְתַתִּיו בְּיַד־הַזָּרִים לָבַז וּלְרִשְׁעֵי הָאָרֶץ לְשָׁלָל °וְחִלְּלוּהָ [°וְחִלְּלוּהוּ ק]: וַהֲסִבּוֹתִי פָנַי מֵהֶם וְחִלְּלוּ אֶת־

כג צְפוּנִי וּבָאוּ־בָהּ פָּרִיצִים וְחִלְּלוּהָ: עֲשֵׂה הָרַתּוֹק כִּי הָאָרֶץ

כד מָלְאָה מִשְׁפַּט דָּמִים וְהָעִיר מָלְאָה חָמָס: וְהֵבֵאתִי רָעֵי גוֹיִם וְיָרְשׁוּ אֶת־ בָּתֵּיהֶם וְהִשְׁבַּתִּי גְּאוֹן עַזִּים וְנִחֲלוּ מְקַדְשֵׁיהֶם: קְפָדָה בָא וּבִקְשׁוּ שָׁלוֹם

כו וָאָיִן: הֹוָה עַל־הֹוָה תָּבוֹא וּשְׁמֻעָה אֶל־שְׁמוּעָה תִּהְיֶה וּבִקְשׁוּ חָזוֹן מִנָּבִיא

כז וְתוֹרָה תֹּאבַד מִכֹּהֵן וְעֵצָה מִזְּקֵנִים: הַמֶּלֶךְ יִתְאַבָּל וְנָשִׂיא יִלְבַּשׁ שְׁמָמָה וִידֵי עַם־הָאָרֶץ תִּבָּהַלְנָה מִדַּרְכָּם אֶעֱשֶׂה אוֹתָם וּבְמִשְׁפְּטֵיהֶם אֶשְׁפְּטֵם וְיָדְעוּ כִּי־אֲנִי יהוה:

ח

א וַיְהִי ׀ בַּשָּׁנָה הַשִּׁשִּׁית בַּשִּׁשִּׁי בַּחֲמִשָּׁה לַחֹדֶשׁ אֲנִי יוֹשֵׁב בְּבֵיתִי וְזִקְנֵי יְהוּדָה יוֹשְׁבִים לְפָנָי וַתִּפֹּל עָלַי שָׁם יַד אֲדֹנָי

ב יֱהוִה: וָאֶרְאֶה וְהִנֵּה דְמוּת כְּמַרְאֵה־אֵשׁ מִמַּרְאֵה מָתְנָיו וּלְמַטָּה אֵשׁ וּמִמָּתְנָיו וּלְמַעְלָה כְּמַרְאֵה־זֹהַר כְּעֵין הַחַשְׁמַלָה: וַיִּשְׁלַח תַּבְנִית יָד וַיִּקָּחֵנִי בְּצִיצִת רֹאשִׁי וַתִּשָּׂא אֹתִי רוּחַ ׀ בֵּין־הָאָרֶץ וּבֵין הַשָּׁמַיִם וַתָּבֵא אֹתִי יְרוּשָׁלַ͏ְמָה בְּמַרְאוֹת אֱלֹהִים אֶל־פֶּתַח שַׁעַר הַפְּנִימִית הַפּוֹנֶה צָפוֹנָה

ד אֲשֶׁר־שָׁם מוֹשַׁב סֵמֶל הַקִּנְאָה הַמַּקְנֶה: וְהִנֵּה־שָׁם כְּבוֹד אֱלֹהֵי יִשְׂרָאֵל

ה כַּמַּרְאֶה אֲשֶׁר רָאִיתִי בַּבִּקְעָה: וַיֹּאמֶר אֵלַי בֶּן־אָדָם שָׂא־נָא עֵינֶיךָ דֶּרֶךְ צָפוֹנָה וָאֶשָּׂא עֵינַי דֶּרֶךְ צָפוֹנָה וְהִנֵּה מִצָּפוֹן לְשַׁעַר הַמִּזְבֵּחַ סֵמֶל הַקִּנְאָה

ו הַזֶּה בַּבִּאָה: וַיֹּאמֶר אֵלַי בֶּן־אָדָם הֲרֹאֶה אַתָּה °מהם [°מָה הֵם ק] עֹשִׂים תּוֹעֵבוֹת גְּדֹלוֹת אֲשֶׁר בֵּית־יִשְׂרָאֵל ׀ עֹשִׂים פֹּה לְרָחֳקָה מֵעַל מִקְדָּשִׁי

ז וְעוֹד תָּשׁוּב תִּרְאֶה תּוֹעֵבוֹת גְּדֹלוֹת: וַיָּבֵא אֹתִי אֶל־פֶּתַח הֶחָצֵר וָאֶרְאֶה

ח וְהִנֵּה חֹר־אֶחָד בַּקִּיר: וַיֹּאמֶר אֵלַי בֶּן־אָדָם חֲתָר־נָא בַקִּיר וָאֶחְתֹּר בַּקִּיר

ט וְהִנֵּה פֶּתַח אֶחָד: וַיֹּאמֶר אֵלַי בֹּא וּרְאֵה אֶת־הַתּוֹעֵבוֹת הָרָעוֹת אֲשֶׁר הֵם

י עֹשִׂים פֹּה: וָאָבוֹא וָאֶרְאֶה וְהִנֵּה כָל־תַּבְנִית רֶמֶשׂ וּבְהֵמָה שֶׁקֶץ וְכָל־

יא גִּלּוּלֵי בֵּית יִשְׂרָאֵל מְחֻקֶּה עַל־הַקִּיר סָבִיב ׀ סָבִיב: וְשִׁבְעִים אִישׁ מִזִּקְנֵי בֵית־יִשְׂרָאֵל וְיַאֲזַנְיָהוּ בֶן־שָׁפָן עֹמֵד בְּתוֹכָם עֹמְדִים לִפְנֵיהֶם וְאִישׁ

7:18. They will have pulled out their hair in grief.

7:20. The Temple.

7:22. When God turns away from Israel, the enemy will be enabled to enter and profane the Temple, where His Presence had been concealed.

7:23. Ezekiel was commanded to make a chain as a sign that the people would soon be led into exile in fetters.

8:1. This vision occurred in the month of Elul of the sixth year of Jehoiachin's exile, exactly fourteen months after the vision described in Chapter 1 (see 1:2). In this prophetic vision, Ezekiel is transported to Jerusalem and shown its destruction.

8:2. See note to 1:4.

8:3. This was the name of an idol.

8:8. Ezekiel enlarged the hole to symbolize that enemies would soon break down the walls of the Temple because of the sins that were taking place there (*Radak*).

and terror will cover them; on every face will be shame, and on all their heads baldness. * ¹⁹ They will throw their silver in the streets and their gold will become repulsive, for their silver and their gold will be unable to rescue them on the day of HASHEM's fury; they will not satisfy their souls and they will not fill their stomachs, for it was the stumbling block of their iniquity. ²⁰ The beauty of His ornament* He had set for majesty, yet they made their abominable and detestable images within it; therefore, I have made it into a repulsive thing for them. ²¹ And I will give it into the hand of strangers for plunder, and unto the wicked of the earth for spoils, and they will profane it. ²² I will turn My face away from them and they will profane the place where I am hidden, * and into it will come lawless people and profane it.

²³ Make the chain, * for the land is full of blood guilt and the city is full of injustice. ²⁴ So I will bring the wickedest nations and they will inherit their houses; and I will put an end to the pride of the mighty; and their holy places will be profaned.

²⁵ A cutting off is coming; they will seek peace, but there will be none. ²⁶ Disaster will come upon disaster, and report will be upon report; [in vain] will they seek vision from the prophet, and teaching will be lost from the Kohen, and counsel from the elders. ²⁷ The king will mourn and the leader will be clothed with consternation, and the hands of the people of the land will be confounded; I will act with them according to their ways, and by the judgments they deserve I will judge them. Then they will know that I am HASHEM."

8

Idolatry in the Temple itself

¹ It happened in the sixth year, in the sixth [month], * on the fifth of the month, I was sitting in my house and the elders of Judah were sitting before me, and the hand of the Lord HASHEM/ELOHIM fell upon me there. ² I saw and behold! there was a likeness like the appearance of fire; from the appearance of his loins and downward there was fire; from his loins and upward was like the appearance of a radiance like the color of the Chashmal. * ³ Then he stretched forth the form of a hand and took me by a lock of my head; and a wind carried me between the earth and the heavens and brought me to Jerusalem in Divine visions, to the entrance of the inner gate that faces northward, where the seat of the provocative Image of Provocation [stood]. * ⁴ And behold, the glory of the God of Israel was there, like the appearance that I had seen in the valley.

⁵ He said to me, "Son of Man, lift your eyes now to the way northward." So I lifted up my eyes to the way northward, and behold, north of the altar gate, this Image of Provocation [was] in the entryway. ⁶ Then He said to me, "Son of Man, do you see what they do? Great abominations are [the people of] the House of Israel committing here, to cause Me to distance Myself from My Sanctuary. And now you will yet again see great abominations."

⁷ He then brought me to the entrance of the courtyard. I saw that behold, there was a single hole in the wall. ⁸ Then He said to me, "Son of Man, tunnel through the wall now."* So I tunneled through the wall, and behold, [there was] an entrance. ⁹ Then He said to me, "Enter and see the evil abominations that they commit here!"

¹⁰ So I entered and I saw, and behold, every sort of image — disgusting creeping things and animals and all the idols of the House of Israel — were carved upon the wall all around. ¹¹ And seventy men of the elders of the House of Israel, with Jaazaniah son of Shaphan standing among them, were standing before them, each man

יב מִקְטַרְתּוֹ בְּיָדוֹ וַעֲתַר עֲנַן־הַקְּטֹרֶת עֹלֶה: וַיֹּאמֶר אֵלַי הֲרָאִיתָ בֶן־אָדָם
אֲשֶׁר זִקְנֵי בֵית־יִשְׂרָאֵל עֹשִׂים בַּחֹשֶׁךְ אִישׁ בְּחַדְרֵי מַשְׂכִּיתוֹ כִּי אֹמְרִים
יג אֵין יְהֹוָה רֹאֶה אֹתָנוּ עֹזֵב יְהֹוָה אֶת־הָאָרֶץ: וַיֹּאמֶר אֵלַי עוֹד תָּשׁוּב
יד תִּרְאֶה תּוֹעֵבוֹת גְּדֹלוֹת אֲשֶׁר־הֵמָּה עֹשִׂים: וַיָּבֵא אֹתִי אֶל־פֶּתַח שַׁעַר
בֵּית־יְהֹוָה אֲשֶׁר אֶל־הַצָּפוֹנָה וְהִנֵּה־שָׁם הַנָּשִׁים יֹשְׁבוֹת מְבַכּוֹת אֶת־
טו הַתַּמּוּז: וַיֹּאמֶר אֵלַי הֲרָאִיתָ בֶן־אָדָם עוֹד תָּשׁוּב תִּרְאֶה
טז תּוֹעֵבוֹת גְּדֹלוֹת מֵאֵלֶּה: וַיָּבֵא אֹתִי אֶל־חֲצַר בֵּית־יְהֹוָה הַפְּנִימִית וְהִנֵּה־
פֶּתַח הֵיכַל יְהֹוָה בֵּין הָאוּלָם וּבֵין הַמִּזְבֵּחַ כְּעֶשְׂרִים וַחֲמִשָּׁה אִישׁ
אֲחֹרֵיהֶם אֶל־הֵיכַל יְהֹוָה וּפְנֵיהֶם קֵדְמָה וְהֵמָּה מִשְׁתַּחֲוִיתֶם קֵדְמָה
יז לַשָּׁמֶשׁ: וַיֹּאמֶר אֵלַי הֲרָאִיתָ בֶן־אָדָם הֲנָקֵל לְבֵית יְהוּדָה מֵעֲשׂוֹת אֶת־
הַתּוֹעֵבוֹת אֲשֶׁר עָשׂוּ־פֹה כִּי־מָלְאוּ אֶת־הָאָרֶץ חָמָס וַיָּשֻׁבוּ לְהַכְעִיסֵנִי
יח וְהִנָּם שֹׁלְחִים אֶת־הַזְּמוֹרָה אֶל־אַפָּם: וְגַם־אֲנִי אֶעֱשֶׂה בְחֵמָה לֹא־תָחוֹס
א עֵינִי וְלֹא אֶחְמֹל וְקָרְאוּ בְאָזְנַי קוֹל גָּדוֹל וְלֹא אֶשְׁמַע אוֹתָם: וַיִּקְרָא בְאָזְנַי

ב קוֹל גָּדוֹל לֵאמֹר קָרְבוּ פְּקֻדּוֹת הָעִיר וְאִישׁ כְּלִי מַשְׁחֵתוֹ בְּיָדוֹ: וְהִנֵּה שִׁשָּׁה
אֲנָשִׁים בָּאִים | מִדֶּרֶךְ־שַׁעַר הָעֶלְיוֹן אֲשֶׁר | מָפְנֶה צָפוֹנָה וְאִישׁ כְּלִי מַפָּצוֹ
בְּיָדוֹ וְאִישׁ־אֶחָד בְּתוֹכָם לָבֻשׁ בַּדִּים וְקֶסֶת הַסֹּפֵר בְּמָתְנָיו וַיָּבֹאוּ וַיַּעַמְדוּ
ג אֵצֶל מִזְבַּח הַנְּחֹשֶׁת: וּכְבוֹד | אֱלֹהֵי יִשְׂרָאֵל נַעֲלָה מֵעַל הַכְּרוּב אֲשֶׁר הָיָה
עָלָיו אֶל מִפְתַּן הַבָּיִת וַיִּקְרָא אֶל־הָאִישׁ הַלָּבֻשׁ הַבַּדִּים אֲשֶׁר קֶסֶת הַסֹּפֵר
ד בְּמָתְנָיו: וַיֹּאמֶר יְהֹוָה °אֵלוֹ [°אֵלָיו ק] עֲבֹר בְּתוֹךְ הָעִיר בְּתוֹךְ
יְרוּשָׁלִָם וְהִתְוִיתָ תָּו עַל־מִצְחוֹת הָאֲנָשִׁים הַנֶּאֱנָחִים וְהַנֶּאֱנָקִים עַל כָּל־
ה הַתּוֹעֵבוֹת הַנַּעֲשׂוֹת בְּתוֹכָהּ: וּלְאֵלֶּה אָמַר בְּאָזְנַי עִבְרוּ בָעִיר אַחֲרָיו וְהַכּוּ
ו °עַל [°אַל ק] תָּחֹס °עֵינֵיכֶם [°עֵינְכֶם ק] וְאַל־תַּחְמֹלוּ: זָקֵן בָּחוּר
וּבְתוּלָה וְטַף וְנָשִׁים תַּהַרְגוּ לְמַשְׁחִית וְעַל־כָּל־אִישׁ אֲשֶׁר־עָלָיו הַתָּו אַל־
תִּגַּשׁוּ וּמִמִּקְדָּשִׁי תָּחֵלּוּ וַיָּחֵלּוּ בָּאֲנָשִׁים הַזְּקֵנִים אֲשֶׁר לִפְנֵי הַבָּיִת:
ז וַיֹּאמֶר אֲלֵיהֶם טַמְּאוּ אֶת־הַבַּיִת וּמַלְאוּ אֶת־הַחֲצֵרוֹת חֲלָלִים צֵאוּ וְיָצְאוּ
ח וְהִכּוּ בָעִיר: וַיְהִי כְּהַכּוֹתָם וְנֵאשֲׁאֵר אָנִי וָאֶפְּלָה עַל־פָּנַי וָאֶזְעַק וָאֹמַר
אֲהָהּ אֲדֹנָי יֱהֹוִה הֲמַשְׁחִית אַתָּה אֵת כָּל־שְׁאֵרִית יִשְׂרָאֵל בְּשָׁפְכְּךָ
ט אֶת־חֲמָתְךָ עַל־יְרוּשָׁלִָם: וַיֹּאמֶר אֵלַי עֲוֹן בֵּית־יִשְׂרָאֵל וִיהוּדָה גָּדוֹל
בִּמְאֹד מְאֹד וַתִּמָּלֵא הָאָרֶץ דָּמִים וְהָעִיר מָלְאָה מֻטֶּה כִּי אָמְרוּ עָזַב
י יְהֹוָה אֶת־הָאָרֶץ וְאֵין יְהֹוָה רֹאֶה: וְגַם־אֲנִי לֹא־תָחוֹס עֵינִי וְלֹא אֶחְמֹל

8:12. I.e., paved surfaces for prostration and worship (see *Leviticus* 26:1).

8:14. The Tammuz was an idol made in such a way as to create the optical illusion that it was crying, as if begging for offerings (*Rashi*).

8:17. The scent of their incense is referred to derogatorily as the foul odor of expelled flatulence. In deference to

God's honor, the odor is described as going into their nose, rather than into God's nose.

9:1. Ezekiel heard as God summoned the forces that were to destroy the city.

9:2. The man clothed in linen was the angel Gabriel, the angel of fire, who, in Ezekiel's vision, was to cast fire upon Jerusalem. From his loins hung scribal implements (rep-

with his censer in his hand, with a thick cloud of incense rising.

¹² *Then He said to me, "Have you seen, O Son of Man, what the elders of the House of Israel do in the darkness, each man in his paved rooms?* * *For they say, 'HASHEM does not see us,' [and] 'HASHEM has forsaken the land.' "* ¹³ *And He said to me, "Now you will see yet again great abominations that they do."*

¹⁴ *He then brought me to the entrance of the gate of the Temple of HASHEM that is to the north, and behold, there were women sitting, causing Tammuz to cry.* * ¹⁵ *And He said to me, "Do you see, Son of Man? Now you will see yet again even greater abominations than these."* ¹⁶ *Then He brought me to the inner courtyard of the Temple of HASHEM, and behold, at the entrance of the Sanctuary of HASHEM, between the Entrance-hall and the Altar, were some twenty-five men, with their backs to the Sanctuary of HASHEM, with their faces turned eastward; they were bowing eastward to the sun.* ¹⁷ *He said to me, "Do you see, Son of Man? Were [their other sins] too trivial for the House of Judah that they had to commit the abominations that they have committed here? For they have filled the Land with injustice, and yet they return to anger Me [in My own House], for here they are, they are sending their foul odor into their nose.* * ¹⁸ *I, too, will react with wrath; My eye will not spare and I will not have compassion; though they cry in My ears with a loud voice, I will not hearken to them."*

9 ¹ **H**e then called within my earshot [with] a loud voice, saying, "Bring near those appointed over the city, * each with his weapon of destruction in his hand." ² And behold, six men were coming from the direction of the Upper Gate that faces northward, each man with his sledgehammer in his hand; but one man among them was clothed in linen, with a scribe's slate at his loins. * They came and stood by the Copper Altar.

³ *Then the glory of the God of Israel ascended from atop the Cherub on which it had been, going to the threshold of the Temple; and He called to the man clothed in linen, on whose loins was the scribe's slate.* ⁴ *And HASHEM said to him, "Pass through the midst of the city, through the midst of Jerusalem, and mark a sign on the foreheads of the men who sigh and moan for all the abominations that are done within it."* *

⁵ *Then He said to those within my earshot, "Pass through the city behind him and smite; let your eye not spare and do not have compassion.* ⁶ *Old man, young man and maiden, children and women, shall you slay, to utter destruction; but do not approach any man upon whom is the sign. Begin from My Sanctuary!" So they began with the elders who were before the Temple.* ⁷ *He said to them, "Defile the Temple* * *and fill the courtyards with the slain. Go forth!" So they went forth and smote throughout the city.*

⁸ *And it was while they were smiting: I remained and I fell upon my face and I cried out and said, "Alas, Lord HASHEM/ELOHIM! Are You destroying the entire remnant of Israel as You pour out Your wrath on Jerusalem?"*

⁹ *Then He said to me, "The iniquity of the House of Israel and Judah is very, very great — the land has been filled with bloodshed and the city has been filled with injustice, for they have said, 'HASHEM has forsaken the land,' and HASHEM does not see.'* ¹⁰ *So I, too, My eye will not spare nor will I have compassion;*

---

resented in the verse by the slate) with which to inscribe on the foreheads of the righteous the mark that would spare them from death (*Radak*).

9:4. The prophecy goes on to say that the sinners were

about to be wiped out. This sign on the forehead of the righteous was to protect them from the fate of the sinners.

9:7. Do not be concerned that corpses will defile the Temple grounds.

י

יא דַרְכָּם בְּרֹאשָׁם נָתָתִי: וְהִנֵּה הָאִישׁ ׀ לְבֻשׁ הַבַּדִּים אֲשֶׁר הַקֶּסֶת בְּמָתְנָיו
א מֵשִׁיב דָּבָר לֵאמֹר עָשִׂיתִי °כַּאֲשֶׁר [°כְּכֹל אֲשֶׁר ק] צִוִּיתָנִי: וָאֶרְאֶה
וְהִנֵּה אֶל־הָרָקִיעַ אֲשֶׁר עַל־רֹאשׁ הַכְּרֻבִים כְּאֶבֶן סַפִּיר כְּמַרְאֵה דְּמוּת
ב כִּסֵּא נִרְאָה עֲלֵיהֶם: וַיֹּאמֶר אֶל־הָאִישׁ ׀ לְבֻשׁ הַבַּדִּים וַיֹּאמֶר בֹּא אֶל־
בֵּינוֹת לַגַּלְגַּל אֶל־תַּחַת לַכְּרוּב וּמַלֵּא חָפְנֶיךָ גַחֲלֵי־אֵשׁ מִבֵּינוֹת לַכְּרֻבִים
ג וּזְרֹק עַל־הָעִיר וַיָּבֹא לְעֵינָי: וְהַכְּרֻבִים עֹמְדִים מִימִין לַבַּיִת בְּבֹאוֹ הָאִישׁ
ד וְהֶעָנָן מָלֵא אֶת־הֶחָצֵר הַפְּנִימִית: וַיָּרָם כְּבוֹד־יהוה מֵעַל הַכְּרוּב עַל
מִפְתַּן הַבָּיִת וַיִּמָּלֵא הַבַּיִת אֶת־הֶעָנָן וְהֶחָצֵר מָלְאָה אֶת־נֹגַהּ כְּבוֹד יהוה:
ה וְקוֹל כַּנְפֵי הַכְּרוּבִים נִשְׁמַע עַד־הֶחָצֵר הַחִיצֹנָה כְּקוֹל אֵל־שַׁדַּי בְּדַבְּרוֹ:
ו וַיְהִי בְּצַוֹּתוֹ אֶת־הָאִישׁ לְבֻשׁ־הַבַּדִּים לֵאמֹר קַח אֵשׁ מִבֵּינוֹת לַגַּלְגַּל
ז מִבֵּינוֹת לַכְּרוּבִים וַיָּבֹא וַיַּעֲמֹד אֵצֶל הָאוֹפָן: וַיִּשְׁלַח הַכְּרוּב אֶת־יָדוֹ
מִבֵּינוֹת לַכְּרוּבִים אֶל־הָאֵשׁ אֲשֶׁר בֵּינוֹת הַכְּרֻבִים וַיִּשָּׂא וַיִּתֵּן אֶל־חָפְנֵי
ח לְבֻשׁ הַבַּדִּים וַיִּקַּח וַיֵּצֵא: וַיֵּרָא לַכְּרֻבִים תַּבְנִית יַד־אָדָם תַּחַת כַּנְפֵיהֶם:
ט וָאֶרְאֶה וְהִנֵּה אַרְבָּעָה אוֹפַנִּים אֵצֶל הַכְּרוּבִים אוֹפַן אֶחָד אֵצֶל הַכְּרוּב
אֶחָד וְאוֹפַן אֶחָד אֵצֶל הַכְּרוּב אֶחָד וּמַרְאֵה הָאוֹפַנִּים כְּעֵין אֶבֶן תַּרְשִׁישׁ:
י וּמַרְאֵיהֶם דְּמוּת אֶחָד לְאַרְבַּעְתָּם כַּאֲשֶׁר יִהְיֶה הָאוֹפַן בְּתוֹךְ הָאוֹפָן:
יא בְּלֶכְתָּם אֶל־אַרְבַּעַת רִבְעֵיהֶם יֵלֵכוּ לֹא יִסַּבּוּ בְּלֶכְתָּם כִּי הַמָּקוֹם אֲשֶׁר־
יב יִפְנֶה הָרֹאשׁ אַחֲרָיו יֵלֵכוּ לֹא יִסַּבּוּ בְּלֶכְתָּם: וְכָל־בְּשָׂרָם וְגַבֵּהֶם וִידֵיהֶם
יג וְכַנְפֵיהֶם וְהָאוֹפַנִּים מְלֵאִים עֵינַיִם סָבִיב לְאַרְבַּעְתָּם אוֹפַנֵּיהֶם: לָאוֹפַנִּים
יד לָהֶם קוֹרָא הַגַּלְגַּל בְּאָזְנָי: וְאַרְבָּעָה פָנִים לְאֶחָד פְּנֵי הָאֶחָד פְּנֵי הַכְּרוּב
טו וּפְנֵי הַשֵּׁנִי פְּנֵי אָדָם וְהַשְּׁלִישִׁי פְּנֵי אַרְיֵה וְהָרְבִיעִי פְּנֵי־נָשֶׁר: וַיֵּרֹמּוּ
טז הַכְּרוּבִים הִיא הַחַיָּה אֲשֶׁר רָאִיתִי בִּנְהַר־כְּבָר: וּבְלֶכֶת הַכְּרוּבִים יֵלְכוּ
הָאוֹפַנִּים אֶצְלָם וּבִשְׂאֵת הַכְּרוּבִים אֶת־כַּנְפֵיהֶם לָרוּם מֵעַל הָאָרֶץ לֹא־
יז יִסַּבּוּ הָאוֹפַנִּים גַּם־הֵם מֵאֶצְלָם: בְּעָמְדָם יַעֲמֹדוּ וּבְרוֹמָם יֵרוֹמּוּ אוֹתָם כִּי
יח רוּחַ הַחַיָּה בָּהֶם: וַיֵּצֵא כְּבוֹד יהוה מֵעַל מִפְתַּן הַבָּיִת וַיַּעֲמֹד עַל־הַכְּרוּבִים:
יט וַיִּשְׂאוּ הַכְּרוּבִים אֶת־כַּנְפֵיהֶם וַיֵּרוֹמּוּ מִן־הָאָרֶץ לְעֵינַי בְּצֵאתָם
וְהָאוֹפַנִּים לְעֻמָּתָם וַיַּעֲמֹד פֶּתַח שַׁעַר בֵּית־יהוה הַקַּדְמוֹנִי וּכְבוֹד אֱלֹהֵי־
כ יִשְׂרָאֵל עֲלֵיהֶם מִלְמָעְלָה: הִיא הַחַיָּה אֲשֶׁר רָאִיתִי תַּחַת אֱלֹהֵי־יִשְׂרָאֵל
כא בִּנְהַר־כְּבָר וָאֵדַע כִּי כְרוּבִים הֵמָּה: אַרְבָּעָה אַרְבָּעָה פָנִים לְאֶחָד וְאַרְבַּע
כב כְּנָפַיִם לְאֶחָד וּדְמוּת יְדֵי אָדָם תַּחַת כַּנְפֵיהֶם: וּדְמוּת פְּנֵיהֶם הֵמָּה הַפָּנִים
אֲשֶׁר רָאִיתִי עַל־נְהַר־כְּבָר מַרְאֵיהֶם וְאוֹתָם אִישׁ אֶל־עֵבֶר פָּנָיו יֵלֵכוּ:

9:10. I.e., the consequences of their sins.

10:1-2. Much of the vision here is similar to the *Merkavah* vision in Chapter 1, and is generally beyond human comprehension. The *Cherubim* here are called *Chayos* in that vision (see 1:5 and vv. 14-15 below), and the *Galgalim* here

are called *Ofanim* there (see 1:15 and v. 13 below).

10:5. See 1:24.

10:14. The ox's face in the first vision (1:10) had been changed to a cherub's face. Ezekiel had entreated God not to have the ox remain as a constant reminder of the

I have placed their way upon their head." * [11] *Just then the man clothed in linen, with the slate upon his loins, brought back an answer, saying, "I have done according to all that You have commanded me."*

10 [1] *Then I saw that behold, on top of the expanse that was above the heads of the Cherubim* something like a sapphire stone, like the appearance of the likeness of a throne, could be seen over them.*

[2] *Then He said to the man clothed in linen, "Come between the Galgal,* beneath the Cherub, and fill your cupped hands with fire-coals from among the Cherubim, and throw [them] upon the city!" He entered before my eyes.*

[3] *The Cherubim were standing to the right of the Temple when the man came; and a cloud filled the inner courtyard.* [4] *Then the glory of HASHEM rose up from upon the Cherub [and rested] upon the threshold of the Temple; and the Temple was filled with the cloud, and the courtyard was filled with the glow of the Glory of HASHEM.* [5] *And the sound of the wings of the Cherubim was heard up to the outer courtyard, like the voice of EL SHADDAI* when He speaks.*

[6] *It happened when He commanded the man clothed in linen saying, "Take fire from between the Galgal, from between the Cherubim," that he came and stood near the Ofan.* [7] *The Cherub stretched out his hand from between the Cherubim to the fire that was between the Cherubim, and he carried [it] and put [it] into the cupped hands of the one clothed in linen. Then he took [it] and went out.* [8] *There could be seen on the Cherubim the form of a human hand, under their wings.*

[9] *Then I saw and behold, there were four Ofanim beside the Cherubim, one Ofan beside one Cherub, and another Ofan beside another Cherub; the appearance of the Ofanim was like the color of tarshish stone.* [10] *As for their appearances, there was one likeness for all four of them, as if there would be a wheel within a wheel.* [11] *When they went, they would go toward their four sides; they did not turn as they went; for whichever place the head faced, they went after it; they did not turn as they went,* [12] *with their whole body, and their backs and their hands and their wings. The Ofanim were full of eyes all around, for all four of the Ofanim.* [13] *As for the Ofanim, they were called "The Galgal" within my earshot.* [14] *Each one had four faces: the one face, the face of the Cherub;* the second face, the face of a man; the third, the face of a lion; and the fourth, the face of an eagle.* [15] *Then the Cherubim rose up; it was the Chayah that I had seen at the River Chebar.* [16] *When the Cherubim would go, the Ofanim would go next to them and when the Cherubim lifted their wings to rise from upon the surface, the Ofanim did not turn away from beside them.* [17] *When they stood still, they stood still, and when they rose, they rose with them; for the spirit in the Chayah was [also] in them.*

[18] *The glory of HASHEM then went forth from upon the threshold of the Temple and stood upon the Cherubim.* [19] *The Cherubim then lifted their wings and rose from the surface before my eyes as they went forth, with the Ofanim opposite them, and it* stood at the entrance of the eastern gate of the Temple of HASHEM; and the glory of the God of Israel was upon them from above.* [20] *This was the Chayah that I had seen beneath the God of Israel at the River Chebar; I realized that they were Cherubim.** [21] *Each one had four faces, and each one had four wings, and there was the form of human hands beneath their wings.* [22] *As for the likeness of their faces: They were the faces which I saw by the River Chebar — their appearances were the same as theirs; each one went in the direction he faced.*

Golden Calf [see *Exodus* Ch. 32]; (*Chagigah* 13b).
10:19. I.e., the *Merkavah* chariot.

10:20. When I heard them called by that name (*Kara*).

יא

א וַתִּשָּׂא אֹתִי ר֗וּחַ וַתָּבֵ֣א אֹתִ֣י אֶל־שַׁ֩עַר֩ בֵּית־יְהֹוָ֨ה הַקַּדְמוֹנִ֜י הַפּוֹנֶ֣ה קָדִ֗ימָה וְהִנֵּה֙ בְּפֶ֣תַח הַשַּׁ֔עַר עֶשְׂרִ֥ים וַחֲמִשָּׁ֖ה אִ֑ישׁ וָאֶרְאֶ֨ה בְתוֹכָ֜ם אֶת־יַֽאֲזַנְיָ֤ה

ב בֶן־עַזֻּר֙ וְאֶת־פְּלַטְיָ֣הוּ בֶן־בְּנָיָ֔הוּ שָׂרֵ֖י הָעָֽם: וַיֹּ֖אמֶר אֵלָ֑י בֶּן־אָדָ֕ם

ג אֵ֣לֶּה הָֽאֲנָשִׁ֗ים הַחֹֽשְׁבִ֥ים אָ֛וֶן וְהַיֹּֽעֲצִ֥ים עֲצַת־רָ֖ע בָּעִ֥יר הַזֹּֽאת: הָאֹ֣מְרִ֔ים

ד לֹ֥א בְקָר֖וֹב בְּנ֣וֹת בָּתִּ֑ים הִ֣יא הַסִּ֔יר וַֽאֲנַ֖חְנוּ הַבָּשָֽׂר: לָכֵ֖ן הִנָּבֵ֣א

ה עֲלֵיהֶ֑ם הִנָּבֵ֖א בֶּן־אָדָֽם: וַתִּפֹּ֨ל עָלַ֜י ר֣וּחַ יְהֹוָ֗ה וַיֹּ֤אמֶר אֵלַי֙ כֹּ֣ה אָמַ֣ר

ו יְהֹוָ֔ה כֵּ֥ן אֲמַרְתֶּ֖ם בֵּ֣ית יִשְׂרָאֵ֑ל וּמַֽעֲל֥וֹת רֽוּחֲכֶ֖ם אֲנִ֥י יְדַעְתִּֽיהָ: הִרְבֵּיתֶ֣ם

ז חַלְלֵיכֶ֔ם בָּעִ֖יר הַזֹּ֑את וּמִלֵּאתֶ֥ם חֽוּצֹתֶ֖יהָ חָלָֽל: לָכֵ֗ן כֹּֽה־אָמַ֞ר

אֲדֹנָ֣י יֱהֹוִ֗ה חַלְלֵיכֶם֙ אֲשֶׁ֣ר שַׂמְתֶּ֣ם בְּתוֹכָ֔הּ הֵ֥מָּה הַבָּשָׂ֖ר וְהִ֣יא הַסִּ֑יר

ח וְאֶתְכֶ֖ם הוֹצִ֥יא מִתּוֹכָֽהּ: חֶ֖רֶב יְרֵאתֶ֑ם וְחֶ֨רֶב֙ אָבִ֣יא עֲלֵיכֶ֔ם נְאֻ֖ם אֲדֹנָ֥י יֱהֹוִֽה:

ט וְהֽוֹצֵאתִ֤י אֶתְכֶם֙ מִתּוֹכָ֔הּ וְנָֽתַתִּ֥י אֶתְכֶ֖ם בְּיַד־זָרִ֑ים וְעָשִׂ֥יתִי בָכֶ֖ם שְׁפָטִֽים:

י בַּחֶ֣רֶב תִּפֹּ֔לוּ עַל־גְּב֥וּל יִשְׂרָאֵ֖ל אֶשְׁפּ֣וֹט אֶתְכֶ֑ם וִֽידַעְתֶּ֖ם כִּֽי־אֲנִ֥י יְהֹוָֽה:

יא הִ֗יא לֹֽא־תִֽהְיֶ֤ה לָכֶם֙ לְסִ֔יר וְאַתֶּ֛ם תִּֽהְי֥וּ בְתוֹכָ֖הּ לְבָשָׂ֑ר אֶל־גְּב֥וּל יִשְׂרָאֵ֖ל

יב אֶשְׁפֹּ֥ט אֶתְכֶֽם: וִֽידַעְתֶּ֗ם כִּֽי־אֲנִ֤י יְהֹוָה֙ אֲשֶׁ֤ר בְּחֻקַּי֙ לֹ֣א הֲלַכְתֶּ֔ם וּמִשְׁפָּטַ֖י

יג לֹ֣א עֲשִׂיתֶ֑ם וּֽכְמִשְׁפְּטֵ֧י הַגּוֹיִ֛ם אֲשֶׁ֥ר סְבִיבֽוֹתֵיכֶ֖ם עֲשִׂיתֶֽם: וַיְהִי֙ כְּהִנָּ֣בְאִ֔י וּפְלַטְיָ֥הוּ בֶן־בְּנָיָ֖ה מֵ֑ת וָֽאֶפֹּ֨ל עַל־פָּנַ֜י וָֽאֶזְעַ֤ק קוֹל־גָּדוֹל֙ וָֽאֹמַ֔ר אֲהָהּ֙ אֲדֹנָ֣י

יד יֱהֹוִ֔ה כָּלָ֣ה אַתָּ֣ה עֹשֶׂ֔ה אֵ֖ת שְׁאֵרִ֥ית יִשְׂרָאֵֽל: וַֽיְהִ֥י דְבַר־יְהֹוָ֖ה

טו אֵלַ֥י לֵאמֹֽר: בֶּן־אָדָ֗ם אַחֶ֤יךָ אַחֶ֨יךָ֙ אַנְשֵׁ֣י גְאֻלָּתֶ֔ךָ וְכָל־בֵּ֥ית יִשְׂרָאֵ֖ל כֻּלֹּ֑ה אֲשֶׁר֩ אָֽמְר֨וּ לָהֶ֜ם יֹֽשְׁבֵ֣י יְרֽוּשָׁלַ֗͏ִם רַֽחֲקוּ֙ מֵעַ֣ל יְהֹוָ֔ה לָ֥נוּ הִ֛יא נִתְּנָ֥ה הָאָ֖רֶץ

טז לְמֽוֹרָשָֽׁה: לָכֵ֣ן אֱמֹ֗ר כֹּֽה־אָמַר֘ אֲדֹנָ֣י יֱהֹוִה֒ כִּ֤י הִרְחַקְתִּים֙ בַּגּוֹיִ֔ם וְכִ֥י הֲפִֽיצוֹתִ֖ים בָּֽאֲרָצ֑וֹת וָֽאֱהִ֤י לָהֶם֙ לְמִקְדָּ֣שׁ מְעַ֔ט בָּֽאֲרָצ֖וֹת אֲשֶׁר־

יז בָּ֥אוּ שָֽׁם: לָכֵ֣ן אֱמֹ֗ר כֹּֽה־אָמַר֘ אֲדֹנָ֣י יֱהֹוִה֒ וְקִבַּצְתִּ֤י אֶתְכֶם֙ מִן־הָ֣עַמִּ֔ים וְאָֽסַפְתִּ֣י אֶתְכֶ֔ם מִן־הָ֣אֲרָצ֔וֹת אֲשֶׁ֥ר נְפֹֽצוֹתֶ֖ם בָּהֶ֑ם וְנָֽתַתִּ֥י לָכֶ֖ם

יח אֶת־אַדְמַ֥ת יִשְׂרָאֵֽל: וּבָ֖אוּ שָׁ֑מָּה וְהֵסִ֥ירוּ אֶת־כָּל־שִׁקּוּצֶ֛יהָ וְאֶת־כָּל־

יט תּֽוֹעֲבוֹתֶ֖יהָ מִמֶּֽנָּה: וְנָֽתַתִּ֤י לָהֶם֙ לֵ֣ב אֶחָ֔ד וְר֥וּחַ חֲדָשָׁ֖ה אֶתֵּ֣ן °בְּקִרְבְּכֶ֑ם °נ״א בְּקִרְבָּ֑ם

כ וַֽהֲסִ֨רֹתִ֜י לֵ֤ב הָאֶ֨בֶן֙ מִבְּשָׂרָ֔ם וְנָֽתַתִּ֥י לָהֶ֖ם לֵ֥ב בָּשָֽׂר: לְמַ֨עַן֙ בְּחֻקֹּתַ֣י יֵלֵ֔כוּ וְאֶת־מִשְׁפָּטַ֥י יִשְׁמְר֖וּ וְעָשׂ֣וּ אֹתָ֑ם וְהָֽיוּ־לִ֣י לְעָ֔ם וַֽאֲנִ֕י אֶֽהְיֶ֥ה לָהֶ֖ם לֵֽאלֹהִֽים:

כא וְאֶל־לֵ֧ב שִׁקּֽוּצֵיהֶ֛ם וְתֽוֹעֲבֽוֹתֵיהֶ֖ם לִבָּ֣ם הֹלֵ֑ךְ דַּרְכָּם֙ בְּרֹאשָׁ֣ם נָתַ֔תִּי

כב נְאֻ֖ם אֲדֹנָ֥י יֱהֹוִֽה: וַיִּשְׂא֤וּ הַכְּרוּבִים֙ אֶת־כַּנְפֵיהֶ֔ם וְהָאֽוֹפַנִּ֖ים לְעֻמָּתָ֑ם

11:3. The false prophets likened Jerusalem to a pot in which meat is being cooked, as if to say: "Just as meat is not removed from the pot until it is fully cooked, so we shall not be forced to leave Jerusalem before our time. We will stay here until we die a natural death!"

11:5. Your metaphor of the pot and the meat will come true, not as you mean it, but as explained in v. 7 (*Radak*).

11:11. You will be "cooked" (beaten and attacked) in the city, but you will be taken out of it before you are "done," to be slaughtered elsewhere (*Rashi*). See *II Kings* 25:18.

11:15. The triple expression alludes to the three waves of exiles from the land: first the two tribes on the eastern bank of the River Jordan (*II Kings* 15:29-30), then the remainder of the Ten Tribes (*II Kings* 17:6), and finally Jehoiachin's exile to Babylon (*Radak*).

11:16. "I have given them small sanctuaries, in the form of synagogues, which are second to My Temple" (*Tar-*

11

The false prophets

¹ **A** wind then lifted me up and brought me to the East Gate of the Temple of HASHEM, which faces eastward; and behold, at the entrance of the gate, were twenty-five men; in their midst I saw Jaazaniah son of Azzur and Pelatiah son of Benaiah, the leaders of the people. ² Then He said to me, "Son of Man, these are the men who connive iniquity and who give evil counsel in this city, ³ who say, '[The end] is not near! Build houses! [The city] is the caldron and we

False prophecy refuted

are the meat.'* ⁴ Therefore, prophesy against them! Prophesy, O Son of Man!" ⁵ Then the spirit of HASHEM fell upon me and He said to me, "Say:

Thus said HASHEM: This is what you have said, O House of Israel, and I know what thoughts enter your mind. * ⁶ You have multiplied your slain in this city

Their fate is Sealed

and filled its streets with the slain. ⁷ Therefore, thus said the Lord HASHEM/ELOHIM: Your slain that you have placed within it — they are the meat, and [the city] is the pot; but I will withdraw you from within it. ⁸ You have feared the sword, and the sword shall I bring against you — the word of the Lord HASHEM/ELOHIM. ⁹ I will take you out from within it and deliver you into the hands of foreigners, and I will execute judgments upon you. ¹⁰ You will fall by the sword; I will execute judgment against you on the border of Israel; then you will know that I am HASHEM. ¹¹ [The city] will not be a pot for you, but you will be like meat within it;* I will execute judgment against you at the border of Israel. ¹² Then you will know that I am HASHEM, Whose decrees you did not follow and Whose laws you did not carry out; for you acted according to the laws of the nations who are around you."

The prophet's plea

¹³ As I was prophesying, Pelatiah son of Benaiah died; and I fell upon my face and I cried out in a loud voice, and said, "Alas, Lord HASHEM/ELOHIM! Are You making an end of the remnant of Israel?"

¹⁴ The word of HASHEM came to me, saying, ¹⁵ "Son of Man, your brothers, your brothers, your kinsmen, * and the entire House of Israel, about whom the inhabitants of Jerusalem say, 'Distance yourselves from HASHEM; the Land is given to us for a heritage'; ¹⁶ therefore, say:

Thus said the Lord HASHEM/ELOHIM: Though I have removed them far away among the nations, and though I have scattered them among the lands, yet I have been for them a small sanctuary* in the lands where they arrived."

¹⁷ "Therefore, say:

The exiles will return

Thus said the Lord HASHEM/ELOHIM: I will assemble you from the nations and gather you in from the lands where you have been scattered, and give you the Land of Israel. ¹⁸ They will come there and remove all its detestations and all its abominations from it. ¹⁹ I will give them an undivided heart and I will place a new spirit in them; I will remove the heart of stone from their flesh and give them a heart of flesh, * ²⁰ so that they may walk in My decrees and observe My laws and fulfill them. Then they will be a people unto Me, and I will be a God for them. ²¹ But those whose heart follows the heart of their detestations and abominations, I will place [the consequences of] their way upon their head — the word of the Lord HASHEM/ELOHIM."

²² Then the Cherubim raised their wings, with the Ofanim opposite them,

---

gum); even in the darkest exile, the Jews can find the Divine Presence in their synagogues and study halls.

11:19. I will replace their tendency toward obstinacy with a frame of mind that is receptive to spiritual matters.

כג וּכְבוֹד אֱלֹהֵי־יִשְׂרָאֵל עֲלֵיהֶם מִלְמָעְלָה: וַיַּעַל כְּבוֹד יהוה מֵעַל תּוֹךְ הָעִיר

כד וַיַּעֲמֹד עַל־הָהָר אֲשֶׁר מִקֶּדֶם לָעִיר: וְרוּחַ נְשָׂאַתְנִי וַתְּבִיאֵנִי כַשְׂדִּימָה
אֶל־הַגּוֹלָה בַּמַּרְאֶה בְּרוּחַ אֱלֹהִים וַיַּעַל מֵעָלַי הַמַּרְאֶה אֲשֶׁר רָאִיתִי: וָאֲדַבֵּר

כה:א אֶל־הַגּוֹלָה אֵת כָּל־דִּבְרֵי יהוה אֲשֶׁר הֶרְאָנִי: וַיְהִי

יב דְּבַר־יהוה אֵלַי לֵאמֹר: בֶּן־אָדָם בְּתוֹךְ בֵּית־הַמֶּרִי אַתָּה יֹשֵׁב אֲשֶׁר
עֵינַיִם לָהֶם לִרְאוֹת וְלֹא רָאוּ אָזְנַיִם לָהֶם לִשְׁמֹעַ וְלֹא שָׁמֵעוּ כִּי בֵּית

ג מְרִי הֵם: וְאַתָּה בֶן־אָדָם עֲשֵׂה לְךָ כְּלֵי גוֹלָה וּגְלֵה יוֹמָם
לְעֵינֵיהֶם וְגָלִיתָ מִמְּקוֹמְךָ אֶל־מָקוֹם אַחֵר לְעֵינֵיהֶם אוּלַי יִרְאוּ כִּי בֵּית

ד מְרִי הֵמָּה: וְהוֹצֵאתָ כֵלֶיךָ כִּכְלֵי גוֹלָה יוֹמָם לְעֵינֵיהֶם וְאַתָּה תֵּצֵא
בָעֶרֶב לְעֵינֵיהֶם כְּמוֹצָאֵי גּוֹלָה: לְעֵינֵיהֶם חֲתָר־לְךָ בַקִּיר וְהוֹצֵאתָ בּוֹ:

ו לְעֵינֵיהֶם עַל־כָּתֵף תִּשָּׂא בָּעֲלָטָה תוֹצִיא פָּנֶיךָ תְכַסֶּה וְלֹא תִרְאֶה

ז אֶת־הָאָרֶץ כִּי־מוֹפֵת נְתַתִּיךָ לְבֵית יִשְׂרָאֵל: וָאַעַשׂ כֵּן כַּאֲשֶׁר צֻוֵּיתִי כֵּלַי
הוֹצֵאתִי כִּכְלֵי גוֹלָה יוֹמָם וּבָעֶרֶב חָתַרְתִּי־לִי בַקִּיר בְּיָד בָּעֲלָטָה הוֹצֵאתִי

ח עַל־כָּתֵף נָשָׂאתִי לְעֵינֵיהֶם: וַיְהִי דְבַר־יהוה אֵלַי

ט בַּבֹּקֶר לֵאמֹר: בֶּן־אָדָם הֲלֹא אָמְרוּ אֵלֶיךָ בֵּית יִשְׂרָאֵל בֵּית הַמֶּרִי מָה
י אַתָּה עֹשֶׂה: אֱמֹר אֲלֵיהֶם כֹּה אָמַר אֲדֹנָי יֱהֹוִה הַנָּשִׂיא הַמַּשָּׂא הַזֶּה
יא בִירוּשָׁלַ͏ִם וְכָל־בֵּית יִשְׂרָאֵל אֲשֶׁר־הֵמָּה בְתוֹכָם: אֱמֹר אֲנִי מוֹפֶתְכֶם
יב כַּאֲשֶׁר עָשִׂיתִי כֵּן יֵעָשֶׂה לָהֶם בַּגּוֹלָה בַשְּׁבִי יֵלֵכוּ: וְהַנָּשִׂיא אֲשֶׁר־בְּתוֹכָם
אֶל־כָּתֵף יִשָּׂא בָּעֲלָטָה וְיֵצֵא בַּקִּיר יַחְתְּרוּ לְהוֹצִיא בוֹ פָּנָיו יְכַסֶּה יַעַן
יג אֲשֶׁר לֹא־יִרְאֶה לַעַיִן הוּא אֶת־הָאָרֶץ: וּפָרַשְׂתִּי אֶת־רִשְׁתִּי עָלָיו
וְנִתְפַּשׂ בִּמְצוּדָתִי וְהֵבֵאתִי אֹתוֹ בָבֶלָה אֶרֶץ כַּשְׂדִּים וְאוֹתָהּ לֹא־יִרְאֶה
יד וְשָׁם יָמוּת: וְכֹל אֲשֶׁר סְבִיבֹתָיו °עֶזְרֹה [°עֶזְרוֹ ק] וְכָל־אֲגַפָּיו אֱזָרֶה
טו לְכָל־רוּחַ וְחֶרֶב אָרִיק אַחֲרֵיהֶם: וְיָדְעוּ כִּי־אֲנִי יהוה בַּהֲפִיצִי אוֹתָם
טז בַּגּוֹיִם וְזֵרִיתִי אוֹתָם בָּאֲרָצוֹת: וְהוֹתַרְתִּי מֵהֶם אַנְשֵׁי מִסְפָּר מֵחֶרֶב
מֵרָעָב וּמִדָּבֶר לְמַעַן יְסַפְּרוּ אֶת־כָּל־תּוֹעֲבוֹתֵיהֶם בַּגּוֹיִם אֲשֶׁר־בָּאוּ
יז-יח שָׁם וְיָדְעוּ כִּי־אֲנִי יהוה: וַיְהִי דְבַר־יהוה אֵלַי לֵאמֹר: בֶּן־
יט אָדָם לַחְמְךָ בְּרַעַשׁ תֹּאכֵל וּמֵימֶיךָ בְּרָגְזָה וּבִדְאָגָה תִּשְׁתֶּה: וְאָמַרְתָּ
אֶל־עַם הָאָרֶץ כֹּה־אָמַר אֲדֹנָי יֱהֹוִה לְיוֹשְׁבֵי יְרוּשָׁלַ͏ִם אֶל־אַדְמַת
יִשְׂרָאֵל לַחְמָם בִּדְאָגָה יֹאכֵלוּ וּמֵימֵיהֶם בְּשִׁמָּמוֹן יִשְׁתּוּ לְמַעַן תֵּשַׁם
כ אַרְצָהּ מִמְּלֹאָהּ מֵחֲמַס כָּל־הַיֹּשְׁבִים בָּהּ: וְהֶעָרִים הַנּוֹשָׁבוֹת תֶּחֱרַבְנָה
כא וְהָאָרֶץ שְׁמָמָה תִהְיֶה וִידַעְתֶּם כִּי־אֲנִי יהוה: וַיְהִי

12:3. Ezekiel was to go into a symbolic exile, in the hope that it might shock the people out of their spiritual stupor (*Radak*).
12:6. Acting out the embarrassment of the refugee.
12:10. King Zedekiah.

12:13. He will not see the land because he will be blinded before he arrives (see *II Kings* 25:7).
12:19. This was to be said to the Jews remaining in Jerusalem, as opposed to those who were in exile in Babylonia (*Metzudos*).

The Divine and the glory of the God of Israel was upon them from above. ²³ And the glory of
Presence HASHEM ascended from over the midst of the city and stood upon the mountain
withdraws that is east of the city. ²⁴ Then a wind lifted me and brought me to Chaldea, to the
completely exiles — in the vision, by the spirit of God — then the vision that I had seen
departed from upon me.
²⁵ Then I told the exiles all the things of HASHEM that He had shown me.

12 ¹ The word of HASHEM came to me, saying, ² "Son of Man, you dwell in the midst
of the rebellious house, who have eyes to see but do not see, who have ears
to hear but do not hear, for they are a rebellious house. ³ And you, Son of Man,
make for yourself implements of exile, and go into exile by day before their eyes;
exile yourself from your place to another place before their eyes; perhaps they will
understand, for they are a rebellious house. * ⁴ Take out your implements, like
implements of exile, during the day before their eyes. Then depart in the evening
before their eyes, like the departures of an exile. ⁵ Before their eyes tunnel through
the wall, and bring out [your implements] through it. ⁶ Before their eyes bear
[them] on [your] shoulder; bring [them] out in the darkness; cover your face * that
you not see the ground; for I have made you a symbol to the House of Israel."

⁷ I did so, as I was commanded. I brought out my implements as implements
of exile by day; and in the evening I tunneled through the wall with my hand; in
the darkness I brought [them] out, bearing them on [my] shoulder before their eyes.

⁸ The word of HASHEM came to me in the morning, saying, ⁹ "Son of Man, has
not the House of Israel, the rebellious house, said to you, 'What are you doing?'
¹⁰ Say to them:

Thus said the Lord HASHEM/ELOHIM: This prophecy concerns the prince *
who is in Jerusalem and all the House of Israel that is in its midst.

¹¹ Say:

I am a sign for you. As I have done, so shall be done to them. Into exile, into
captivity, will they go. ¹² The prince who is among them will bear [his belong-
ings] on his shoulder in the darkness and go out; they will tunnel through the
wall to bring out [their belongings] through it; he will cover his face so as not
to see the ground with [his] eye. ¹³ I will spread My net over him and he will
be caught in My snare; then I will bring him to Babylonia, the land of the
Chaldeans, yet he will not see [it], * and there he will die. ¹⁴ Then I will scatter
all who are around him, his aide and all his officers, in every direction, and
I will unsheathe the sword after them. ¹⁵ Then they will know that I am
HASHEM, when I disperse them among the nations and scatter them among
the countries. ¹⁶ But from them I will leave over a few men from the sword,
the famine, and the plague, so that they may relate all their abominations
among the nations where they arrive; and they will know that I am HASHEM."

¹⁷ The word of HASHEM came to me, saying, ¹⁸ "Son of Man, eat your bread with
quaking, and drink your water with trembling and anxiety; ¹⁹ and say to the people
of the land:

Thus said the Lord HASHEM/ELOHIM concerning the inhabitants of Jerusalem
on the soil of Israel: * They will eat their bread with anxiety and drink their
water in desolation, because their land will be desolate of all that fills it, on
account of the injustice of all who dwell in it. ²⁰ The inhabited cities will be
laid waste, and the land will be a desolation; then you will know that I am
HASHEM."

כב וַיְהִי דְבַר־יְהוָה אֵלַי לֵאמֹר: בֶּן־אָדָם מָה־הַמָּשָׁל הַזֶּה לָכֶם עַל־אַדְמַת יִשְׂרָאֵל
כג לֵאמֹר יַאַרְכוּ הַיָּמִים וְאָבַד כָּל־חָזוֹן: לָכֵן אֱמֹר אֲלֵיהֶם כֹּה־אָמַר אֲדֹנָי
יֱהֹוִה הִשְׁבַּתִּי אֶת־הַמָּשָׁל הַזֶּה וְלֹא־יִמְשְׁלוּ אֹתוֹ עוֹד בְּיִשְׂרָאֵל כִּי אִם־
כד דַּבֵּר אֲלֵיהֶם קָרְבוּ הַיָּמִים וּדְבַר כָּל־חָזוֹן: כִּי לֹא יִהְיֶה עוֹד כָּל־חֲזוֹן שָׁוְא
כה וּמִקְסַם חָלָק בְּתוֹךְ בֵּית יִשְׂרָאֵל: כִּי | אֲנִי יְהוָה אֲדַבֵּר אֵת אֲשֶׁר אֲדַבֵּר
דָּבָר וְיֵעָשֶׂה לֹא תִמָּשֵׁךְ עוֹד כִּי בִימֵיכֶם בֵּית הַמֶּרִי אֲדַבֵּר דָּבָר וַעֲשִׂיתִיו
כו־כז נְאֻם אֲדֹנָי יֱהֹוִה: וַיְהִי דְבַר־יְהוָה אֵלַי לֵאמֹר: בֶּן־אָדָם הִנֵּה בֵית־יִשְׂרָאֵל
אֹמְרִים הֶחָזוֹן אֲשֶׁר־הוּא חֹזֶה לְיָמִים רַבִּים וּלְעִתִּים רְחוֹקוֹת הוּא
כח נִבָּא: לָכֵן אֱמֹר אֲלֵיהֶם כֹּה אָמַר אֲדֹנָי יֱהֹוִה לֹא־תִמָּשֵׁךְ עוֹד כָּל־

יג
א דְּבָרַי אֲשֶׁר אֲדַבֵּר דָּבָר וְיֵעָשֶׂה נְאֻם אֲדֹנָי יֱהֹוִה: וַיְהִי דְבַר־יְהוָה
ב אֵלַי לֵאמֹר: בֶּן־אָדָם הִנָּבֵא אֶל־נְבִיאֵי יִשְׂרָאֵל הַנִּבָּאִים וְאָמַרְתָּ לִנְבִיאֵי
ג מִלִּבָּם שִׁמְעוּ דְּבַר־יְהוָה: כֹּה אָמַר אֲדֹנָי יֱהֹוִה הוֹי עַל־הַנְּבִיאִים הַנְּבָלִים
ד אֲשֶׁר הֹלְכִים אַחַר רוּחָם וּלְבִלְתִּי רָאוּ: כְּשֻׁעָלִים בָּחֳרָבוֹת נְבִיאֶיךָ
ה יִשְׂרָאֵל הָיוּ: לֹא עֲלִיתֶם בַּפְּרָצוֹת וַתִּגְדְּרוּ גָדֵר עַל־בֵּית יִשְׂרָאֵל לַעֲמֹד
ו בַּמִּלְחָמָה בְּיוֹם יְהוָה: חָזוּ שָׁוְא וְקֶסֶם כָּזָב הָאֹמְרִים נְאֻם־יְהוָה וַיהוָה לֹא
ז שְׁלָחָם וְיִחֲלוּ לְקַיֵּם דָּבָר: הֲלוֹא מַחֲזֵה־שָׁוְא חֲזִיתֶם וּמִקְסַם כָּזָב אֲמַרְתֶּם
ח וְאֹמְרִים נְאֻם־יְהוָה וַאֲנִי לֹא דִבַּרְתִּי: לָכֵן כֹּה אָמַר אֲדֹנָי
יֱהֹוִה יַעַן דַּבֶּרְכֶם שָׁוְא וַחֲזִיתֶם כָּזָב לָכֵן הִנְנִי אֲלֵיכֶם נְאֻם אֲדֹנָי יֱהֹוִה:
ט וְהָיְתָה יָדִי אֶל־הַנְּבִיאִים הַחֹזִים שָׁוְא וְהַקֹּסְמִים כָּזָב בְּסוֹד עַמִּי לֹא־יִהְיוּ
וּבִכְתָב בֵּית־יִשְׂרָאֵל לֹא יִכָּתֵבוּ וְאֶל־אַדְמַת יִשְׂרָאֵל לֹא יָבֹאוּ וִידַעְתֶּם
י כִּי אֲנִי אֲדֹנָי יֱהֹוִה: יַעַן וּבְיַעַן הִטְעוּ אֶת־עַמִּי לֵאמֹר שָׁלוֹם וְאֵין שָׁלוֹם |
יא וְהוּא בֹּנֶה חַיִץ וְהִנָּם טָחִים אֹתוֹ תָּפֵל: אֱמֹר אֶל־טָחֵי תָפֵל וְיִפֹּל הָיָה |
יב גֶּשֶׁם שׁוֹטֵף וְאַתֵּנָה אַבְנֵי אֶלְגָּבִישׁ תִּפֹּלְנָה וְרוּחַ סְעָרוֹת תְּבַקֵּעַ: וְהִנֵּה נָפַל
יג הַקִּיר הֲלוֹא יֵאָמֵר אֲלֵיכֶם אַיֵּה הַטִּיחַ אֲשֶׁר טַחְתֶּם: לָכֵן
כֹּה אָמַר אֲדֹנָי יֱהֹוִה וּבִקַּעְתִּי רוּחַ־סְעָרוֹת בַּחֲמָתִי וְגֶשֶׁם שֹׁטֵף בְּאַפִּי יִהְיֶה
יד וְאַבְנֵי אֶלְגָּבִישׁ בְּחֵמָה לְכָלָה: וְהָרַסְתִּי אֶת־הַקִּיר אֲשֶׁר־טַחְתֶּם תָּפֵל
וְהִגַּעְתִּיהוּ אֶל־הָאָרֶץ וְנִגְלָה יְסֹדוֹ וְנָפְלָה וּכְלִיתֶם בְּתוֹכָהּ וִידַעְתֶּם כִּי־
טו אֲנִי יְהוָה: וְכִלֵּיתִי אֶת־חֲמָתִי בַּקִּיר וּבַטָּחִים אֹתוֹ תָּפֵל וְאֹמַר לָכֶם אֵין

12:22-25. God lashed out against the heretical parable which claimed that Ezekiel's prophecies would not come true. Instead, God assured him that the time would yet come when the facile visions of the false prophets would forever be discredited and silenced.

13:2. Ezekiel was now to discredit the false prophets, whose soothing lies were preventing repentance.

13:4. Who scurry off at the sound of any man's approach (*Rashi*).

13:5. You did not mend the breaches of the people's actions, which would have served them well in the day of God's wrath.

13:9. They will not be included with the rest of God's people when they receive their reward in the World to Come (*Targum*).

13:10. The false prophets are as destructive as someone who builds a flimsy partition and fortifies it with weak plaster instead of strong cement.

13:14. I.e., the verbal wall of false security with which you surrounded Jerusalem.

[21] *The word of* HASHEM *came to me, saying,* [22] *"Son of Man, what is this parable of yours regarding the soil of Israel, saying, 'The days will draw out and all the visions will become null'?* * [23] *Therefore, say to them:*

> *Thus said the Lord* HASHEM/ELOHIM*: I will put an end to this proverb and they will no longer say it as a proverb in Israel. Rather, say to them, 'The days are near for [the fulfillment of] the word of every vision.* [24] *For there will be no more vain vision nor smooth divination within the House of Israel.* [25] *For I am* HASHEM*; I speak whatever word I speak, and it is carried out; it will be delayed no longer; for in your days, O rebellious house, I will speak a word and carry it out — the word of the Lord* HASHEM/ELOHIM*.' "*

[26] *The word of* HASHEM *came to me, saying:* [27] *"Son of Man, behold, the House of Israel says, 'The vision which he sees is many days off and he prophesies concerning distant times.'* [28] *Therefore, say to them:*

> *Thus said the Lord* HASHEM/ELOHIM*: No longer will [the fulfillment of] all My words be delayed; the word that I speak shall be done — the word of the Lord* HASHEM/ELOHIM*."*

13

Prophecy against false prophecy

[1] *The word of* HASHEM *came to me, saying,* [2] *"Son of Man, prophesy against the prophets of Israel* * *who prophesy, and say to those who prophesy out of their own hearts:*

> *Hear the word of* HASHEM*!* [3] *Thus said the Lord* HASHEM/ELOHIM*: Woe unto the foolish prophets, who follow their own spirit, and things they have not seen.* [4] *Like foxes among the ruins,* * *so are your prophets, O Israel.* [5] *You did not ascend into the breaches nor build a fence for the House of Israel, which could stand up in battle on the day of* HASHEM*.* * [6] *They saw a worthless [vision] and false divination; they say, 'The word of* HASHEM*!' but* HASHEM *did not send them, yet they expect that their word will be confirmed.* [7] *Have you not envisioned a worthless vision and uttered a false divination? You say, 'The word of* HASHEM*,' when I have not spoken!*
>
> [8] *Therefore, thus said the Lord* HASHEM/ELOHIM*: Because you have spoken worthless words and have seen a false vision, therefore, behold, I am against you — the word of the Lord* HASHEM/ELOHIM*;* [9] *and My hand will be against the prophets who see worthless [visions] and who divine falsehood; they will not be among the counsel of My people, nor will they be inscribed in the record of the House of Israel,* * *nor will they enter upon the soil of Israel. Then you will know that I am the Lord* HASHEM/ELOHIM*.* [10] *Because — and again because — they led My people astray, saying, 'Peace,' but there is no peace; it is building a partition, and they are even smearing it with plaster.* *

Wall of illusion; veneer of hope

> [11] *Say to those who smear with plaster: 'It will collapse! There will be pouring rain.' And as for you, O huge hailstones, you shall fall and a stormy wind shall break forth.* [12] *Then behold, the wall will fall! Surely it will be said to you, 'Where is the daub that you smeared?'* [13] *Therefore, thus said the Lord* HASHEM/ELOHIM*: I will cause a stormy wind to break out in My wrath, and there will be pouring rain in My anger, with huge hailstones in My wrath, to cause annihilation;* [14] *and I will break down the wall that you smeared with plaster* * *and bring it down to the ground, and its foundation will be bared; it will fall and you will be annihilated within. Then you will know that I am* HASHEM*.* [15] *Thus I will spend My wrath upon the wall and upon those who smear it with plaster, and I will say to you, 'The wall is no more,*

טז הַקִּיר וְאֵין הַטָּחִים אֹתוֹ: נְבִיאֵי יִשְׂרָאֵל הַנִּבְּאִים אֶל־יְרוּשָׁלַ͏ִם וְהַחֹזִים לָהּ

חֲזוֹן שָׁלֹם וְאֵין שָׁלֹם נְאֻם אֲדֹנָי יֱהֹוִה: וְאַתָּה בֶן־אָדָם שִׂים

יז פָּנֶיךָ אֶל־בְּנוֹת עַמְּךָ הַמִּתְנַבְּאוֹת מִלִּבְּהֶן וְהִנָּבֵא עֲלֵיהֶן: וְאָמַרְתָּ כֹּה־

אָמַר | אֲדֹנָי יֱהֹוִה הוֹי לִמְתַפְּרוֹת כְּסָתוֹת עַל | כָּל־אַצִּילֵי יָדַי וְעֹשׂוֹת

הַמִּסְפָּחוֹת עַל־רֹאשׁ כָּל־קוֹמָה לְצוֹדֵד נְפָשׁוֹת הַנְּפָשׁוֹת תְּצוֹדֵדְנָה לְעַמִּי

יח וּנְפָשׁוֹת לָכֶנָה תְחַיֶּינָה: וַתְּחַלֶּלְנָה אֹתִי אֶל־עַמִּי בְּשַׁעֲלֵי שְׂעֹרִים

וּבִפְתוֹתֵי לֶחֶם לְהָמִית נְפָשׁוֹת אֲשֶׁר לֹא־תְמוּתֶנָה וּלְחַיּוֹת נְפָשׁוֹת אֲשֶׁר

כ לֹא־תִחְיֶינָה בְּכַזֶּבְכֶם לְעַמִּי שֹׁמְעֵי כָזָב: לָכֵן כֹּה־אָמַר |

אֲדֹנָי יֱהֹוִה הִנְנִי אֶל־כִּסְּתוֹתֵיכֶנָה אֲשֶׁר אַתֵּנָה מְצֹדְדוֹת שָׁם אֶת־

הַנְּפָשׁוֹת לְפֹרְחוֹת וְקָרַעְתִּי אֹתָם מֵעַל זְרוֹעֹתֵיכֶם וְשִׁלַּחְתִּי אֶת־הַנְּפָשׁוֹת

כא אֲשֶׁר אַתֶּם מְצֹדְדוֹת אֶת־נְפָשִׁים לְפֹרְחֹת: וְקָרַעְתִּי אֶת־מִסְפְּחֹתֵיכֶם

וְהִצַּלְתִּי אֶת־עַמִּי מִיֶּדְכֶן וְלֹא־יִהְיוּ עוֹד בְּיֶדְכֶן לִמְצוּדָה וִידַעְתֶּן כִּי־אֲנִי

כב יְהֹוָה: יַעַן הַכְאוֹת לֵב־צַדִּיק שֶׁקֶר וַאֲנִי לֹא הִכְאַבְתִּיו וּלְחַזֵּק יְדֵי רָשָׁע

כג לְבִלְתִּי־שׁוּב מִדַּרְכּוֹ הָרָע לְהַחֲיֹתוֹ: לָכֵן שָׁוְא לֹא תֶחֱזֶינָה וְקֶסֶם לֹא־

יד א תִקְסַמְנָה עוֹד וְהִצַּלְתִּי אֶת־עַמִּי מִיֶּדְכֶן וִידַעְתֶּן כִּי־אֲנִי יְהֹוָה: וַיָּבוֹא אֵלַי

ב אֲנָשִׁים מִזִּקְנֵי יִשְׂרָאֵל וַיֵּשְׁבוּ לְפָנָי: וַיְהִי דְבַר־יְהֹוָה אֵלַי

ג לֵאמֹר: בֶּן־אָדָם הָאֲנָשִׁים הָאֵלֶּה הֶעֱלוּ גִלּוּלֵיהֶם עַל־לִבָּם וּמִכְשׁוֹל

ד עֲוֺנָם נָתְנוּ נֹכַח פְּנֵיהֶם הַאִדָּרֹשׁ אִדָּרֵשׁ לָהֶם: לָכֵן דַּבֵּר־אוֹתָם וְאָמַרְתָּ

אֲלֵיהֶם כֹּה־אָמַר | אֲדֹנָי יֱהֹוִה אִישׁ אִישׁ מִבֵּית יִשְׂרָאֵל אֲשֶׁר יַעֲלֶה אֶת־

גִּלּוּלָיו אֶל־לִבּוֹ וּמִכְשׁוֹל עֲוֺנוֹ יָשִׂים נֹכַח פָּנָיו וּבָא אֶל־הַנָּבִיא אֲנִי

ה יְהֹוָה נַעֲנֵיתִי לוֹ °בָה [°בָא ק] בְּרֹב גִּלּוּלָיו: לְמַעַן תְּפֹשׂ אֶת־בֵּית־

ו יִשְׂרָאֵל בְּלִבָּם אֲשֶׁר נָזֹרוּ מֵעָלַי בְּגִלּוּלֵיהֶם כֻּלָּם: לָכֵן אֱמֹר |

אֶל־בֵּית יִשְׂרָאֵל כֹּה אָמַר אֲדֹנָי יֱהֹוִה שׁוּבוּ וְהָשִׁיבוּ מֵעַל גִּלּוּלֵיכֶם

ז וּמֵעַל כָּל־תּוֹעֲבֹתֵיכֶם הָשִׁיבוּ פְנֵיכֶם: כִּי־אִישׁ אִישׁ מִבֵּית יִשְׂרָאֵל וּמֵהַגֵּר

אֲשֶׁר־יָגוּר בְּיִשְׂרָאֵל וְיִנָּזֵר מֵאַחֲרַי וְיַעַל גִּלּוּלָיו אֶל־לִבּוֹ וּמִכְשׁוֹל עֲוֺנוֹ

יָשִׂים נֹכַח פָּנָיו וּבָא אֶל־הַנָּבִיא לִדְרָשׁ־לוֹ בִי אֲנִי יְהֹוָה נַעֲנֶה־לּוֹ בִּי:

ח וְנָתַתִּי פָנַי בָּאִישׁ הַהוּא וַהֲשִׂמֹתִיהוּ לְאוֹת וְלִמְשָׁלִים וְהִכְרַתִּיו מִתּוֹךְ

ט עַמִּי וִידַעְתֶּם כִּי־אֲנִי יְהֹוָה: וְהַנָּבִיא כִי־יְפֻתֶּה וְדִבֶּר דָּבָר

אֲנִי יְהֹוָה פִּתֵּיתִי אֵת הַנָּבִיא הַהוּא וְנָטִיתִי אֶת־יָדִי עָלָיו וְהִשְׁמַדְתִּיו

י מִתּוֹךְ עַמִּי יִשְׂרָאֵל: וְנָשְׂאוּ עֲוֺנָם כַּעֲוֺן הַדֹּרֵשׁ כַּעֲוֺן הַנָּבִיא יִהְיֶה: לְמַעַן
יא

13:18. These were types of magical practices.

13:19. A reference to the charlatans' practice of predicting life for their followers and death for their detractors.

13:20. By ensnaring people with your magical rites you cause their souls to lose their rightful reward in the World to Come (*Rashi*).

14:1. Chastened, perhaps, by Ezekiel's rebuke in the previous chapters, the elders came to him for guidance, but God revealed to him that their fervent devotion to idolatry had not changed.

14:9. Many of the false prophets posed as God-fearing people, while secretly living immorally and sinfully. In order to expose them, God will entice them to prophecy, so that their wickedness will become apparent when their *nor those who smeared it,'* [16] *[you] prophets of Israel who prophesy con-cerning Jerusalem and envision for it a vision of peace when there is no peace — the word of the Lord HASHEM/ELOHIM."*

Against the [17] *"And now you, Son of Man, direct your face towards the daughters of your*
sorceresses *people who prophesy out of their own heart, and prophesy against them.* [18] *Say:*

Thus said the Lord HASHEM/ELOHIM: Woe to those who sew cushions near all armpits * and make kerchiefs for the head of anyone who stands erect, in order to trap souls. Would you trap souls of My people, souls for your own livelihood?* [19] *You have profaned Me among My people for handfuls of barley and for crumbs of bread, to slay souls who should not die and to preserve souls who should not live,* * by your lying to My people, who listen to lies.* [20] *Therefore, thus said the Lord HASHEM/ELOHIM: Behold, I am turning against your cushions with which you trap souls to make them fly off,* * and I will tear them from upon your arms; I will send free the souls whom you trap, the souls you cause to fly off.* [21] *I will tear your kerchiefs and I will save My people from your hand and they will no longer be in your hand to be trapped; then you will know that I am HASHEM.* [22] *Because you cowed the heart of the righteous one with lies when I did not wish to pain him, and strengthened the hands of the wicked one that he not repent from his evil way to preserve his life,* [23] *therefore, you will see neither a worthless vision nor a divine divination any longer. Thus I will save My people from your hand; and then you will know that I am HASHEM."*

14   [1] **M**en came to me from the elders of Israel, and they sat before me. * [2] *The*
Feigned   *word of HASHEM came to me, saying,* [3] *"Son of Man, these men have*
repentance *brought up their idols upon their heart, and have placed the stumbling block of their iniquity opposite their faces; shall I then make Myself accessible to them?* [4] *Therefore, speak with them and say to them, 'Thus said the Lord HASHEM/ELOHIM: Any man of the House of Israel who brings up his idols upon his heart and places the stumbling block of his iniquity opposite his face, and comes to the prophet — I, HASHEM, will respond to him, though he comes with the multitude of his idols;* [5] *in order to seize the House of Israel for what is in their heart, although they have withdrawn themselves from Me with their idols, all of them.'*

[6] *"Therefore say to the House of Israel:*

Thus said the Lord HASHEM/ELOHIM: Return and turn away from your idols, and turn away your faces from all your abominations. [7] *For any man of the House of Israel or of the stranger who sojourns in Israel who withdraws himself from Me and brings up his idols upon his heart and sets the stumbling block of his iniquity opposite his face, and yet he comes to the prophet to seek an answer of Me through him, I, HASHEM, will respond to him for My sake.* [8] *And I will set My anger against that man and set him for a sign and for parables, and I will cut him off from amid My people; then you will know that I am HASHEM.*

[9] *And if a [false] prophet is enticed and makes a declaration, I, HASHEM, have enticed that prophet, and I will stretch out My hand against him and destroy him from amid My people Israel.* * [10] *They will bear their iniquity; like the iniquity of the inquirer shall be the iniquity of the prophet,* [11] *so that the*

predictions are shown to be false (*Radak*).

לֹא־יִתְעוּ עוֹד בֵּית־יִשְׂרָאֵל מֵאַחֲרַי וְלֹא־יִטַּמְּאוּ עוֹד בְּכָל־פִּשְׁעֵיהֶם

יב וְהָיוּ־לִי לְעָם וַאֲנִי אֶהְיֶה לָהֶם לֵאלֹהִים נְאֻם אֲדֹנָי יֱהֹוִה: וַיְהִי

יג דְבַר־יְהֹוָה אֵלַי לֵאמֹר: בֶּן־אָדָם אֶרֶץ כִּי תֶחֱטָא־לִי לִמְעָל־מַעַל וְנָטִיתִי יָדִי עָלֶיהָ וְשָׁבַרְתִּי לָהּ מַטֵּה־לָחֶם וְהִשְׁלַחְתִּי־בָהּ רָעָב וְהִכְרַתִּי

יד מִמֶּנָּה אָדָם וּבְהֵמָה: וְהָיוּ שְׁלֹשֶׁת הָאֲנָשִׁים הָאֵלֶּה בְּתוֹכָהּ נֹחַ °דָנִאל

טו [°דָנִיֵּאל ק] וְאִיּוֹב הֵמָּה בְצִדְקָתָם יְנַצְּלוּ נַפְשָׁם נְאֻם אֲדֹנָי יֱהֹוִה: לוּ־חַיָּה רָעָה אַעֲבִיר בָּאָרֶץ וְשִׁכְּלָתָּה וְהָיְתָה שְׁמָמָה מִבְּלִי עוֹבֵר מִפְּנֵי הַחַיָּה:

טז שְׁלֹשֶׁת הָאֲנָשִׁים הָאֵלֶּה בְּתוֹכָהּ חַי־אָנִי נְאֻם אֲדֹנָי יֱהֹוִה אִם־בָּנִים

יז וְאִם־בָּנוֹת יַצִּילוּ הֵמָּה לְבַדָּם יִנָּצֵלוּ וְהָאָרֶץ תִּהְיֶה שְׁמָמָה: אוֹ חֶרֶב אָבִיא עַל־הָאָרֶץ הַהִיא וְאָמַרְתִּי חֶרֶב תַּעֲבֹר בָּאָרֶץ וְהִכְרַתִּי מִמֶּנָּה

יח אָדָם וּבְהֵמָה: וּשְׁלֹשֶׁת הָאֲנָשִׁים הָאֵלֶּה בְּתוֹכָהּ חַי־אָנִי נְאֻם אֲדֹנָי

יט יֱהֹוִה לֹא יַצִּילוּ בָּנִים וּבָנוֹת כִּי הֵם לְבַדָּם יִנָּצֵלוּ: אוֹ דֶבֶר אֲשַׁלַּח אֶל־ הָאָרֶץ הַהִיא וְשָׁפַכְתִּי חֲמָתִי עָלֶיהָ בְּדָם לְהַכְרִית מִמֶּנָּה אָדָם וּבְהֵמָה:

כ וְנֹחַ °דָנִאל [°דָנִיֵּאל ק] וְאִיּוֹב בְּתוֹכָהּ חַי־אָנִי נְאֻם אֲדֹנָי יֱהֹוִה אִם־ בֵּן אִם־בַּת יַצִּילוּ הֵמָּה בְצִדְקָתָם יַצִּילוּ נַפְשָׁם: כִּי כֹה

כא אָמַר אֲדֹנָי יֱהֹוִה אַף כִּי־אַרְבַּעַת שְׁפָטַי ׀ הָרָעִים חֶרֶב וְרָעָב וְחַיָּה רָעָה

כב וָדֶבֶר שִׁלַּחְתִּי אֶל־יְרוּשָׁלִָם לְהַכְרִית מִמֶּנָּה אָדָם וּבְהֵמָה: וְהִנֵּה נוֹתְרָה־ בָּהּ פְּלֵטָה הַמּוּצָאִים בָּנִים וּבָנוֹת הִנָּם יוֹצְאִים אֲלֵיכֶם וּרְאִיתֶם אֶת־ דַּרְכָּם וְאֶת־עֲלִילוֹתָם וְנִחַמְתֶּם עַל־הָרָעָה אֲשֶׁר הֵבֵאתִי עַל־יְרוּשָׁלִָם

כג אֵת כָּל־אֲשֶׁר הֵבֵאתִי עָלֶיהָ: וְנִחֲמוּ אֶתְכֶם כִּי־תִרְאוּ אֶת־דַּרְכָּם וְאֶת־ עֲלִילוֹתָם וִידַעְתֶּם כִּי לֹא חִנָּם עָשִׂיתִי אֵת כָּל־אֲשֶׁר־עָשִׂיתִי בָהּ נְאֻם אֲדֹנָי יֱהֹוִה:

טו א-ב וַיְהִי דְבַר־יְהֹוָה אֵלַי לֵאמֹר: בֶּן־אָדָם

ג מַה־יִּהְיֶה עֵץ־הַגֶּפֶן מִכָּל־עֵץ הַזְּמוֹרָה אֲשֶׁר הָיָה בַּעֲצֵי הַיָּעַר: הֲיֻקַּח מִמֶּנּוּ עֵץ לַעֲשׂוֹת לִמְלָאכָה אִם־יִקְחוּ מִמֶּנּוּ יָתֵד לִתְלוֹת עָלָיו כָּל־כֶּלִי:

ד הִנֵּה לָאֵשׁ נִתַּן לְאָכְלָה אֵת שְׁנֵי קְצוֹתָיו אָכְלָה הָאֵשׁ וְתוֹכוֹ נָחָר הֲיִצְלַח

ה לִמְלָאכָה: הִנֵּה בִּהְיוֹתוֹ תָמִים לֹא יֵעָשֶׂה לִמְלָאכָה אַף כִּי־אֵשׁ אֲכָלָתְהוּ

ו וַיֵּחָר וְנַעֲשָׂה עוֹד לִמְלָאכָה: לָכֵן כֹּה אָמַר אֲדֹנָי יֱהֹוִה כַּאֲשֶׁר עֵץ־הַגֶּפֶן בְּעֵץ הַיַּעַר אֲשֶׁר־נְתַתִּיו לָאֵשׁ לְאָכְלָה כֵּן

ז נָתַתִּי אֶת־יֹשְׁבֵי יְרוּשָׁלִָם: וְנָתַתִּי אֶת־פָּנַי בָּהֶם מֵהָאֵשׁ יָצָאוּ וְהָאֵשׁ

ח תֹּאכְלֵם וִידַעְתֶּם כִּי־אֲנִי יְהֹוָה בְּשׂוּמִי אֶת־פָּנַי בָּהֶם: וְנָתַתִּי אֶת־

14:14. These three men had survived in the face of general collapse: Noah of the whole world, Daniel of his country, and Job of his family (*Abarbanel*). Ezekiel warns the nation not to rely on the merits of the few righteous people living in Jerusalem to save the populace at large.

14:22. When the Jews in Babylonia see the exiles coming to join them, they will realize that by right there

should have been no survivors at all.

15:1. In this prophecy, Israel is likened to a vine, but not to a grapevine flourishing in the vineyard; rather, a fruitless vine growing among the trees of the forest. Unlike other barren trees that can be used for lumber, this vine has no practical use for man except as fuel for his fire. Similarly, if Israel produces no spiritual fruits, it is

House of Israel will no longer stray from following Me, and no longer be defiled by all their sins. Then they will be a people for Me and I will be a God for them — the word of the Lord HASHEM/ELOHIM."

The prayers of the righteous ¹² *The word of HASHEM came to me, saying,* ¹³ *"Son of Man, when a country sins against Me, acting with treachery, and I stretch out My hand against it, and break its staff of bread, and dispatch famine against it, and eliminate man and beast from it,* ¹⁴ *then even if these three men would be in its midst — Noah, Daniel and Job* — they, by their righteousness, would save [only] their own souls — the word of the Lord HASHEM/ELOHIM.*

¹⁵ *"If I cause a ferocious beast to traverse a country and bereave it, and it becomes desolate, without wayfarers, because of the beast,* ¹⁶ *if these three men would be in its midst, as I live — the word of the Lord HASHEM/ELOHIM — [I swear] that they would save neither sons nor daughters; they alone would be saved, but the land would be desolate.*

¹⁷ *"Or if I bring the sword against that country, and I say, 'Let the sword traverse the land,' and I cut off from it man and animal,* ¹⁸ *if these three men would be in its midst, as I live — the word of the Lord HASHEM/ELOHIM — [I swear] that they would save neither sons nor daughters, for they alone would be saved.*

¹⁹ *"Or if I send pestilence to that country, and I pour My fury upon it in blood, to eliminate off from it man and animal,* ²⁰ *even if Noah, Daniel and Job would be in it, as I live — says the Lord HASHEM/ELOHIM — [I swear] that they not save neither son nor daughter; they, in their righteousness, would save [only] their own souls.*

²¹ *"For thus said the Lord HASHEM/ELOHIM: How much more when I send [all of] My four evil judgments — sword, hunger, ferocious beast, and pestilence — against Jerusalem, to cut off from it man and animal!* ²² *And yet behold, a remnant has been left in it, who are being taken out, sons and daughters; behold, they are coming out to you. You will see their way and their deeds and you will be consoled* over the evil that I brought upon Jerusalem, over all that I brought upon it.* ²³ *They will be a comfort for you when you see their way and their deeds; and you will know that it is not for nothing that I did all that I did in it — the word of the Lord HASHEM/ELOHIM."*

15

God's vine

¹ **T**he word of HASHEM came to me, saying, ² *"Son of Man, what will become of the vine-tree compared to any [other] tree, the branch that was among the trees of the forest?** ³ *Can wood be taken from it to use for productive work? Can one take a peg from it upon which to hang any article?* ⁴ *Behold, if it were put into the fire for fuel, and the fire consumed its two ends,* and its inside were charred — would it be useful for productive work?* ⁵ *Behold, when it was whole it could not be used for productive work; how much more so when fire consumed it and it became charred — could it yet be put to productive work?*

⁶ *"Therefore, thus said the Lord HASHEM/ELOHIM: Like a vine-tree [compared] to another tree of the forest, which I have put into the fire for fuel, so have I made the inhabitants of Jerusalem.* ⁷ *I will direct My attention against them; they have emerged from the fire, but [now] fire will consume them;* then you will know that I am HASHEM, when I set My attention against them.* ⁸ *I will make the*

---

doomed to the "flames" of exile.

15:4. The two final phases of Jerusalem's destruction were the exiles of Jehoiakim (*Daniel* 1:2) and Jehoiachin (*II Kings* 24:14), which included the great Torah

scholars (*Rashi*).

15:7. Though Jerusalem was saved from the destruction of Sennacherib, it will be consumed by the Babylonians (*Metzudos*).

טז

א וַיְהִי דְבַר־ הָאָרֶץ שְׁמֵמָה יַעַן מַעַל מֹעֲלוּ נְאֻם אֲדֹנָי יֱהוִֹה:

ב־ג יְהוָה אֵלַי לֵאמֹר: בֶּן־אָדָם הוֹדַע אֶת־יְרוּשָׁלַ͏ִם אֶת־תּוֹעֲבֹתֶיהָ: וְאָמַרְתָּ כֹּה־אָמַר אֲדֹנָי יֱהוִֹה לִירוּשָׁלַ͏ִם מְכֹרֹתַיִךְ וּמֹלְדֹתַיִךְ מֵאֶרֶץ הַכְּנַעֲנִי אָבִיךְ

ד הָאֱמֹרִי וְאִמֵּךְ חִתִּית: וּמוֹלְדוֹתַיִךְ בְּיוֹם הוּלֶּדֶת אֹתָךְ לֹא־כָרַּת שָׁרֵּךְ וּבְמַיִם לֹא־רֻחַצְתְּ לְמִשְׁעִי וְהָמְלֵחַ לֹא הֻמְלַחַתְּ וְהָחְתֵּל לֹא חֻתָּלְתְּ:

ה לֹא־חָסָה עָלַיִךְ עַיִן לַעֲשׂוֹת לָךְ אַחַת מֵאֵלֶּה לְחֻמְלָה עָלָיִךְ וַתֻּשְׁלְכִי אֶל־

ו פְּנֵי הַשָּׂדֶה בְּגֹעַל נַפְשֵׁךְ בְּיוֹם הֻלֶּדֶת אֹתָךְ: וָאֶעֱבֹר עָלַיִךְ וָאֶרְאֵךְ

ז מִתְבּוֹסֶסֶת בְּדָמָיִךְ וָאֹמַר לָךְ בְּדָמַיִךְ חֲיִי וָאֹמַר לָךְ בְּדָמַיִךְ חֲיִי: רְבָבָה כְּצֶמַח הַשָּׂדֶה נְתַתִּיךְ וַתִּרְבִּי וַתִּגְדְּלִי וַתָּבֹאִי בַּעֲדִי עֲדָיִים שָׁדַיִם נָכֹנוּ

ח וּשְׂעָרֵךְ צִמֵּחַ וְאַתְּ עֵרֹם וְעֶרְיָה: וָאֶעֱבֹר עָלַיִךְ וָאֶרְאֵךְ וְהִנֵּה עִתֵּךְ עֵת דֹּדִים וָאֶפְרֹשׂ כְּנָפִי עָלַיִךְ וָאֲכַסֶּה עֶרְוָתֵךְ וָאֶשָּׁבַע לָךְ וָאָבוֹא בִבְרִית אֹתָךְ

ט נְאֻם אֲדֹנָי יֱהוִֹה וַתִּהְיִי־לִי: וָאֶרְחָצֵךְ בַּמַּיִם וָאֶשְׁטֹף דָּמַיִךְ מֵעָלָיִךְ וָאֲסֻכֵךְ

י בַּשָּׁמֶן: וָאַלְבִּישֵׁךְ רִקְמָה וָאֶנְעֲלֵךְ תָּחַשׁ וָאֶחְבְּשֵׁךְ בַּשֵּׁשׁ וַאֲכַסֵּךְ מֶשִׁי:

יא־יב וָאֶעְדֵּךְ עֶדִי וָאֶתְּנָה צְמִידִים עַל־יָדַיִךְ וְרָבִיד עַל־גְּרוֹנֵךְ: וָאֶתֵּן נֶזֶם עַל־

יג אַפֵּךְ וַעֲגִילִים עַל־אָזְנָיִךְ וַעֲטֶרֶת תִּפְאֶרֶת בְּרֹאשֵׁךְ: וַתַּעְדִּי זָהָב וָכֶסֶף וּמַלְבּוּשֵׁךְ °שֵׁשִׁי [°שֵׁשׁ ק׳] וָמֶשִׁי וְרִקְמָה סֹלֶת וּדְבַשׁ וָשֶׁמֶן °אָכָלְתִּי

יד [°אָכָלְתְּ ק׳] וַתִּיפִי בִּמְאֹד מְאֹד וַתִּצְלְחִי לִמְלוּכָה: וַיֵּצֵא לָךְ שֵׁם בַּגּוֹיִם בְּיָפְיֵךְ כִּי | כָּלִיל הוּא בַּהֲדָרִי אֲשֶׁר־שַׂמְתִּי עָלַיִךְ נְאֻם אֲדֹנָי יֱהוִֹה: וַתִּבְטְחִי

טו בְיָפְיֵךְ וַתִּזְנִי עַל־שְׁמֵךְ וַתִּשְׁפְּכִי אֶת־תַּזְנוּתַיִךְ עַל־כָּל־עוֹבֵר לוֹ־יֶהִי:

טז וַתִּקְחִי מִבְּגָדַיִךְ וַתַּעֲשִׂי־לָךְ בָּמוֹת טְלֻאוֹת וַתִּזְנִי עֲלֵיהֶם לֹא בָאוֹת

יז וְלֹא יִהְיֶה: וַתִּקְחִי כְּלֵי תִפְאַרְתֵּךְ מִזְּהָבִי וּמִכַּסְפִּי אֲשֶׁר נָתַתִּי לָךְ

יח וַתַּעֲשִׂי־לָךְ צַלְמֵי זָכָר וַתִּזְנִי־בָם: וַתִּקְחִי אֶת־בִּגְדֵי רִקְמָתֵךְ וַתְּכַסִּים

יט וְשַׁמְנִי וּקְטָרְתִּי °נָתַתִּי [°נָתַתְּ ק׳] לִפְנֵיהֶם: וְלַחְמִי אֲשֶׁר־נָתַתִּי לָךְ סֹלֶת וָשֶׁמֶן וּדְבַשׁ הֶאֱכַלְתִּיךְ וּנְתַתִּיהוּ לִפְנֵיהֶם לְרֵיחַ נִיחֹחַ וַיֶּהִי נְאֻם

כ אֲדֹנָי יֱהוִֹה: וַתִּקְחִי אֶת־בָּנַיִךְ וְאֶת־בְּנוֹתַיִךְ אֲשֶׁר יָלַדְתְּ לִי וַתִּזְבָּחִים

כא לָהֶם לֶאֱכוֹל הַמְעַט °מִתַּזְנוּתֵךְ [°מִתַּזְנוּתַיִךְ ק׳]: וַתִּשְׁחֲטִי אֶת־בָּנָי

כב וַתִּתְּנִים בְּהַעֲבִיר אוֹתָם לָהֶם: וְאֵת כָּל־תּוֹעֲבֹתַיִךְ וְתַזְנֻתַיִךְ לֹא °זָכַרְתִּי [°זָכַרְתְּ ק׳] אֶת־יְמֵי נְעוּרָיִךְ בִּהְיוֹתֵךְ עֵרֹם וְעֶרְיָה מִתְבּוֹסֶסֶת בְּדָמֵךְ הָיִית:

16:3. You act as if you were Canaanites, born of heathen parents (*Radak*).

16:4-8. Allegorically, Israel is likened to a newborn baby girl, abandoned and neglected, who is saved by a benefactor. This refers to Israel's inception as a nation, when it was enslaved to Egypt and in a very downtrodden spiritual and physical state, but nevertheless had a miraculously high birth rate.

16:4. A newborn would be salted in order to firm its tender flesh (*Rashi*).

16:8. The time had come for God to make the covenant with Israel at Mount Sinai. I then gave you great prosperity in the Land of Israel.

16:9-14. God lavished affection upon Israel as a benefactor would upon his bride.

16:10. See *Exodus* 25:5.

16:15. Adultery and licentiousness are common Scriptural metaphors for idolatry.

16:16. You set up magnificent shrines for your idolatrous worship.

16:20. As sacrifices for your deities.

land desolate, because you have acted treacherously — the word of the Lord HASHEM/ELOHIM."

16 ¹ The word of HASHEM came to me, saying, ² "Son of Man, inform Jerusalem of her abominations. ³ Say:

Prophesy unto Jerusalem

Thus said the Lord HASHEM/ELOHIM to Jerusalem: Your dwelling place and your birthplace are of the land of the Canaanites; your father was an Amorite and your mother a Hittite. * ⁴ And as for your birth:* On the day you were born your umbilical cord was not cut, nor were you washed with water to smooth [your skin], nor were you salted, * nor were you swaddled. ⁵ No eye pitied you to do any one of these things for you, to show you compassion; you were cast out upon the open field because of the loathsomeness of your being, on the day you were born. ⁶ Then I passed you and saw you wallowing in your blood, and I said to you, 'In your blood you shall live'; I said to you, 'In your blood you shall live.' ⁷ I made you as numerous as the plants of the field; you increased and grew, and you came to have great charm, breasts developed and your hair sprouting, but you were naked and bare. ⁸ I passed by you and saw you, and behold, your time was the time of love; * and I spread the hems of My garment over you and covered your nakedness; and I took an oath to you and entered into a covenant with you — the word of the Lord HASHEM/ELOHIM — and you became Mine. ⁹ I bathed you with water and washed away your blood from upon you, and I anointed you with oil;* ¹⁰ I clothed you in embroidered garments, I shod you in tachash* leather, I bound you with linen, I covered you with silk, ¹¹ I decked you with ornaments, I put bracelets on your hands and a necklace on your neck, ¹² and I placed a ring on your nose, earrings on your ears and a crown of beauty on your head. ¹³ You decked yourself with gold and silver, and your garments were linen, silk and embroidery; you ate fine flour, honey and oil. You became exceedingly beautiful, and you became fit for royalty. ¹⁴ Your fame went forth among the nations for your beauty, for it was perfect, through My splendor which I placed upon you — the word of the Lord HASHEM/ELOHIM.

The neglected infant

Redemption

Idolatry as adultery

¹⁵ But you trusted in your beauty, and you became licentious because of your fame; you poured forth your harlotries upon every passerby, * to be his. ¹⁶ So you took of your garments and made for yourself harlequin platforms, and were licentious upon them.* This should not have been and shall not recur. ¹⁷ Then you took your beautiful objects, from My gold and My silver that I gave you, and made for yourself male images and were licentious with them; ¹⁸ you took your embroidered garments and covered them; and My oil and My incense you placed before them; ¹⁹ My bread that I gave you — I had fed you fine flour, oil and honey — you placed before them for a satisfying aroma, and so it was! — the word of the Lord HASHEM/ELOHIM. ²⁰ Then you took your sons and your daughters whom you begot for Me, and these you slaughtered for them* to devour! Was your harlotry so trivial ²¹ that you slew My children and gave them away by passing them over before [your idols]? ²² And with all your abominations and your harlotries you did not remember the days of your youth, when you were naked and bare, when you were wallowing in your blood.

כג־כד וַיְהִי אַחֲרֵי כָּל־רָעָתֵךְ אוֹי אוֹי לָךְ נְאֻם אֲדֹנָי יֱהֹוִה: וַתִּבְנִי־לָךְ גֶּב

כה וַתַּעֲשִׂי־לָךְ רָמָה בְּכָל־רְחוֹב: אֶל־כָּל־רֹאשׁ דֶּרֶךְ בָּנִית רָמָתֵךְ וַתְּתַעֲבִי

אֶת־יָפְיֵךְ וַתְּפַשְּׂקִי אֶת־רַגְלַיִךְ לְכָל־עוֹבֵר וַתַּרְבִּי אֶת־[°תַּזְנוּתֵךְ

כו °תַּזְנוּתָיִךְ ק]: וַתִּזְנִי אֶל־בְּנֵי־מִצְרַיִם שְׁכֵנַיִךְ גִּדְלֵי בָשָׂר וַתַּרְבִּי אֶת־

כז תַּזְנֻתֵךְ לְהַכְעִיסֵנִי: וְהִנֵּה נָטִיתִי יָדִי עָלַיִךְ וָאֶגְרַע חֻקֵּךְ וָאֶתְּנֵךְ בְּנֶפֶשׁ

כח שֹׂנְאוֹתַיִךְ בְּנוֹת פְּלִשְׁתִּים הַנִּכְלָמוֹת מִדַּרְכֵּךְ זִמָּה: וַתִּזְנִי אֶל־בְּנֵי אַשּׁוּר

כט מִבִּלְתִּי שָׂבְעָתֵךְ וַתִּזְנִים וְגַם לֹא שָׂבָעַתְּ: וַתַּרְבִּי אֶת־תַּזְנוּתֵךְ אֶל־אֶרֶץ

ל כְּנַעַן כַּשְׂדִּימָה וְגַם־בְּזֹאת לֹא שָׂבָעַתְּ: מָה אֲמֻלָה לִבָּתֵךְ נְאֻם אֲדֹנָי יֱהֹוִה

לא בַּעֲשׂוֹתֵךְ אֶת־כָּל־אֵלֶּה מַעֲשֵׂה אִשָּׁה־זוֹנָה שַׁלָּטֶת: בִּבְנוֹתַיִךְ גַּבֵּךְ

בְּרֹאשׁ כָּל־דֶּרֶךְ וְרָמָתֵךְ [°עָשִׂיתִי °עָשִׂית ק] בְּכָל־רְחוֹב וְלֹא־°הָיִיתִי

לב [°הָיִית ק] כַּזּוֹנָה לְקַלֵּס אֶתְנָן: הָאִשָּׁה הַמְּנָאָפֶת תַּחַת אִישָׁהּ תִּקַּח

לג אֶת־זָרִים: לְכָל־זֹנוֹת יִתְּנוּ־נֵדֶה וְאַתְּ נָתַתְּ אֶת־נְדָנַיִךְ לְכָל־מְאַהֲבַיִךְ

לד וַתִּשְׁחֲדִי אוֹתָם לָבוֹא אֵלַיִךְ מִסָּבִיב בְּתַזְנוּתָיִךְ: וַיְהִי־בָךְ הֵפֶךְ מִן־הַנָּשִׁים

בְּתַזְנוּתַיִךְ וְאַחֲרַיִךְ לֹא זוּנָּה וּבְתִתֵּךְ אֶתְנָן וְאֶתְנַן לֹא נִתַּן־לָךְ וַתְּהִי

לה־לו לְהֶפֶךְ: לָכֵן זוֹנָה שִׁמְעִי דְּבַר־יְהֹוָה: כֹּה־אָמַר

אֲדֹנָי יֱהֹוִה יַעַן הִשָּׁפֵךְ נְחֻשְׁתֵּךְ וַתִּגָּלֶה עֶרְוָתֵךְ בְּתַזְנוּתַיִךְ עַל־מְאַהֲבָיִךְ

לז וְעַל כָּל־גִּלּוּלֵי תוֹעֲבוֹתַיִךְ וְכִדְמֵי בָנַיִךְ אֲשֶׁר נָתַתְּ לָהֶם: לָכֵן הִנְנִי מְקַבֵּץ

אֶת־כָּל־מְאַהֲבַיִךְ אֲשֶׁר עָרַבְתְּ עֲלֵיהֶם וְאֵת כָּל־אֲשֶׁר אָהַבְתְּ עַל כָּל־

אֲשֶׁר שָׂנֵאת וְקִבַּצְתִּי אֹתָם עָלַיִךְ מִסָּבִיב וְגִלֵּיתִי עֶרְוָתֵךְ אֲלֵהֶם וְרָאוּ

לח אֶת־כָּל־עֶרְוָתֵךְ: וּשְׁפַטְתִּיךְ מִשְׁפְּטֵי נֹאֲפוֹת וְשֹׁפְכֹת דָּם וּנְתַתִּיךְ דַּם

לט חֵמָה וְקִנְאָה: וְנָתַתִּי אֹתָךְ בְּיָדָם וְהָרְסוּ גַבֵּךְ וְנִתְּצוּ רָמֹתַיִךְ וְהִפְשִׁיטוּ

מ אוֹתָךְ בְּגָדַיִךְ וְלָקְחוּ כְּלֵי תִפְאַרְתֵּךְ וְהִנִּיחוּךְ עֵירֹם וְעֶרְיָה: וְהֶעֱלוּ עָלַיִךְ

מא קָהָל וְרָגְמוּ אוֹתָךְ בָּאָבֶן וּבִתְּקוּךְ בְּחַרְבוֹתָם: וְשָׂרְפוּ בָתַּיִךְ בָּאֵשׁ

וְעָשׂוּ־בָךְ שְׁפָטִים לְעֵינֵי נָשִׁים רַבּוֹת וְהִשְׁבַּתִּיךְ מִזּוֹנָה וְגַם־אֶתְנַן לֹא

מב תִתְּנִי־עוֹד: וַהֲנִחֹתִי חֲמָתִי בָּךְ וְסָרָה קִנְאָתִי מִמֵּךְ וְשָׁקַטְתִּי וְלֹא

מג אֶכְעַס עוֹד: יַעַן אֲשֶׁר לֹא־°זָכַרְתִּי [°זָכַרְתְּ ק] אֶת־יְמֵי נְעוּרַיִךְ וַתִּרְגְּזִי־

לִי בְּכָל־אֵלֶּה וְגַם־אֲנִי הֵא אֲנִי דַּרְכֵּךְ ׀ בְּרֹאשׁ נָתַתִּי נְאֻם אֲדֹנָי יֱהֹוִה

מד וְלֹא °עָשִׂיתִי [°עָשִׂית ק] אֶת־הַזִּמָּה עַל כָּל־תּוֹעֲבֹתָיִךְ: הִנֵּה כָּל־

מה הַמֹּשֵׁל עָלַיִךְ יִמְשֹׁל לֵאמֹר כְּאִמָּה כְּבִתָּהּ: בַּת־אִמֵּךְ אַתְּ גֹּעֶלֶת אִישָׁהּ

וּבָנֶיהָ וַאֲחוֹת אֲחוֹתֵךְ אַתְּ אֲשֶׁר גָּעֲלוּ אַנְשֵׁיהֶן וּבְנֵיהֶן אִמְּכֶן חִתִּית

16:24. Temples for your idolatrous cults.

16:27. I brought famine upon you.

16:31. A typical harlot will rejoice over a gift given as her

hire. To you the gift was of no importance; you were
attracted by the licentious act.

16:43. You had no thoughts of remorse or repentance.

²³ And now, after all your wickedness — woe, woe unto you — the word of the Lord HASHEM/ELOHIM.

²⁴ You built for yourself an eminent place* and made for yourself a lofty place in every street. ²⁵ At every crossroad you built your lofty place; you profaned your beauty and opened your legs to every passerby, and you multiplied your harlotries; ²⁶ you were licentious with the sons of Egypt, your neighbors, great of flesh; and you multiplied your harlotry to provoke Me. ²⁷ Then, behold, I stretched out My hand against you and diminished your allotment;* then I delivered you to the whim of those who hate you, the daughters of the Philistines, who were ashamed of your lewd way. ²⁸ You were licentious with the sons of Assyria, because you were not sated; you were licentious with them, yet you were still not sated. ²⁹ Then you multiplied your harlotry toward the land of the merchants, toward Chaldea; but even with this you were not sated. ³⁰ How degenerate is your heart — the word of the Lord HASHEM/ELOHIM — when you do all these things, the deed of an aggressive, adulterous woman; ³¹ when you build your eminent place at every crossroad and make your lofty place in every street. You were not like a harlot, who cherishes her fee;* ³² O adulterous wife, who takes strangers in place of her husband! ³³ To all [other] harlots gifts are given, but you — you have given your gifts to all your paramours, and bribed them to come to you from all around, with your harlotries. ³⁴ So with you it was the opposite of other women in your harlotries, and after you will never be such harlotry, in that you gave a fee, and a fee was not given to you; thus have you become the opposite.

³⁵ Therefore, O harlot, hear the word of HASHEM! ³⁶ Thus said the Lord HASHEM/ELOHIM: Because your shame was poured out and your nakedness was uncovered by all your harlotries with your paramours, and because of all your abominable idols, and in accordance with the blood of your children whom you gave to them; ³⁷ therefore, behold, I will gather all your paramours to whom you have been pleasant, and all whom you love together with all whom you hate; I will gather them to you from all around and uncover your nakedness to them, and they will see all your nakedness. ³⁸ I will administer upon you the judgments of adulteresses and spillers of blood, and deliver you to the blood of wrath and jealousy. ³⁹ Then I will place you in their hand; they will tear down your eminent place and smash your lofty places; they will strip you of your clothes and take your beautiful vessels and leave you naked and bare. ⁴⁰ They will bring up an assemblage against you; they will pelt you with stone and pierce you with their swords; ⁴¹ they will burn down your houses in fire; and they will execute judgments against you before the eyes of many women. I will stop you from being a harlot, and you will nevermore pay a fee. ⁴² Then I will relieve My fury [that had been] upon you, and My jealousy will turn away from you; then I will be at rest and not be angry any more.

⁴³ [This will befall you] because you did not remember the days of your youth, but have angered Me with all these things; so, behold, I also will place your way upon [your] head — the word of the Lord HASHEM/ELOHIM — but you did not consider this, concerning all your abominations.*

Like mother, like daughter

⁴⁴ Behold, all those who speak in parables will use this parable about you, saying, 'Like mother, [so] her daughter.' ⁴⁵ You are your mother's daughter, spewing forth her husband and her children; you are your sister's sister, who spewed forth their husbands and children, [as if] your mother was a Hittite

מו וַאֲבִיכֶן אֱמֹרִי: וַאֲחוֹתֵךְ הַגְּדוֹלָה שֹׁמְרוֹן הִיא וּבְנוֹתֶיהָ הַיּוֹשֶׁבֶת עַל־
מז שְׂמֹאולֵךְ וַאֲחוֹתֵךְ הַקְּטַנָּה מִמֵּךְ הַיּוֹשֶׁבֶת מִימִינֵךְ סְדֹם וּבְנוֹתֶיהָ: וְלֹא
בִדְרָכֵיהֶן הָלַכְתְּ וּכְתוֹעֲבוֹתֵיהֶן °עָשִׂיתי [°עָשִׂית ק] כִּמְעַט קָט וַתַּשְׁחִתִי
מח מֵהֵן בְּכָל־דְּרָכָיִךְ: חַי־אָנִי נְאֻם אֲדֹנָי יֱהוִֹה אִם־עָשְׂתָה סְדֹם אֲחוֹתֵךְ הִיא
מט וּבְנוֹתֶיהָ כַּאֲשֶׁר עָשִׂית אַתְּ וּבְנוֹתָיִךְ: הִנֵּה־זֶה הָיָה עֲוֹן סְדֹם אֲחוֹתֵךְ גָּאוֹן
שִׂבְעַת־לֶחֶם וְשַׁלְוַת הַשְׁקֵט הָיָה לָהּ וְלִבְנוֹתֶיהָ וְיַד־עָנִי וְאֶבְיוֹן לֹא
נ הֶחֱזִיקָה: וַתִּגְבְּהֶינָה וַתַּעֲשֶׂינָה תוֹעֵבָה לְפָנָי וָאָסִיר אֶתְהֶן כַּאֲשֶׁר
נא רָאִיתִי: וְשֹׁמְרוֹן כַּחֲצִי חַטֹּאתַיִךְ לֹא חָטָאָה וַתַּרְבִּי אֶת־
תוֹעֲבוֹתַיִךְ מֵהֵנָּה וַתְּצַדְּקִי אֶת־°אֲחוֹתֵךְ [°אֲחוֹתַיִךְ ק] בְּכָל־תּוֹעֲבוֹתַיִךְ
נב אֲשֶׁר °עָשִׂיתי [°עָשִׂית ק]: גַּם־אַתְּ | שְׂאִי כְלִמָּתֵךְ אֲשֶׁר פִּלַּלְתְּ לַאֲחוֹתֵךְ
בְּחַטֹּאתַיִךְ אֲשֶׁר־הִתְעַבְתְּ מֵהֵן תִּצְדַּקְנָה מִמֵּךְ וְגַם־אַתְּ בּוֹשִׁי וּשְׂאִי
נג כְלִמָּתֵךְ בְּצַדֶּקְתֵּךְ אַחְיוֹתֵךְ: וְשַׁבְתִּי אֶת־שְׁבִיתְהֶן אֶת־°שבית
[°שְׁבוּת ק] סְדֹם וּבְנוֹתֶיהָ וְאֶת־°שבית [°שְׁבוּת ק] שֹׁמְרוֹן וּבְנוֹתֶיהָ
נד °ושבית [°וּשְׁבוּת ק] שְׁבִיתַיִךְ בְּתוֹכָהֵנָה: לְמַעַן תִּשְׂאִי כְלִמָּתֵךְ וְנִכְלַמְתְּ
נה מִכֹּל אֲשֶׁר עָשִׂית בְּנַחֲמֵךְ אֹתָן: וַאֲחוֹתַיִךְ סְדֹם וּבְנוֹתֶיהָ תָּשֹׁבְןָ לְקַדְמָתָן
וְשֹׁמְרוֹן וּבְנוֹתֶיהָ תָּשֹׁבְןָ לְקַדְמָתָן וְאַתְּ וּבְנוֹתַיִךְ תְּשֻׁבֶינָה לְקַדְמַתְכֶן:
נו-נז וְלוֹא הָיְתָה סְדֹם אֲחוֹתֵךְ לִשְׁמוּעָה בְּפִיךְ בְּיוֹם גְּאוֹנָיִךְ: בְּטֶרֶם תִּגָּלֶה
רָעָתֵךְ כְּמוֹ עֵת חֶרְפַּת בְּנוֹת־אֲרָם וְכָל־סְבִיבוֹתֶיהָ בְּנוֹת פְּלִשְׁתִּים
נח הַשָּׁאטוֹת אוֹתָךְ מִסָּבִיב: אֶת־זִמָּתֵךְ וְאֶת־תּוֹעֲבוֹתַיִךְ אַתְּ נְשָׂאתִים נְאֻם
נט יְהוָה: כִּי כֹה אָמַר אֲדֹנָי יֱהוִֹה °ועשיתי [°וְעָשִׂית ק] אוֹתָךְ
ס כַּאֲשֶׁר עָשִׂית אֲשֶׁר־בָּזִית אָלָה לְהָפֵר בְּרִית: וְזָכַרְתִּי אֲנִי אֶת־בְּרִיתִי
סא אוֹתָךְ בִּימֵי נְעוּרָיִךְ וַהֲקִמוֹתִי לָךְ בְּרִית עוֹלָם: וְזָכַרְתְּ אֶת־דְּרָכַיִךְ וְנִכְלַמְתְּ
בְּקַחְתֵּךְ אֶת־אֲחוֹתַיִךְ הַגְּדֹלוֹת מִמֵּךְ אֶל־הַקְּטַנּוֹת מִמֵּךְ וְנָתַתִּי אֶתְהֶן לָךְ
סב לְבָנוֹת וְלֹא מִבְּרִיתֵךְ: וַהֲקִימוֹתִי אֲנִי אֶת־בְּרִיתִי אִתָּךְ וְיָדַעַתְּ כִּי־אֲנִי
סג יְהוָה: לְמַעַן תִּזְכְּרִי וָבֹשְׁתְּ וְלֹא יִהְיֶה־לָּךְ עוֹד פִּתְחוֹן פֶּה מִפְּנֵי כְּלִמָּתֵךְ
א בְּכַפְּרִי־לָךְ לְכָל־אֲשֶׁר עָשִׂית נְאֻם אֲדֹנָי יֱהוִֹה: וַיְהִי דְבַר־   **יז**
ב יְהוָה אֵלַי לֵאמֹר: בֶּן־אָדָם חוּד חִידָה וּמְשֹׁל מָשָׁל אֶל־בֵּית יִשְׂרָאֵל:
ג וְאָמַרְתָּ כֹּה־אָמַר | אֲדֹנָי יֱהוִֹה הַנֶּשֶׁר הַגָּדוֹל גְּדוֹל הַכְּנָפַיִם אֶרֶךְ הָאֵבֶר
מָלֵא הַנּוֹצָה אֲשֶׁר־לוֹ הָרִקְמָה בָּא אֶל־הַלְּבָנוֹן וַיִּקַּח אֶת־צַמֶּרֶת הָאָרֶז:
ד אֵת רֹאשׁ יְנִיקוֹתָיו קָטָף וַיְבִיאֵהוּ אֶל־אֶרֶץ כְּנַעַן בְּעִיר רֹכְלִים שָׂמוֹ:

16:46. Lit., "your left." Compass directions in Scripture are oriented to the person facing east; thus, north is left, south is right, east is before, and west is behind.

Samaria and Sodom refer to the metropolises; their "daughters" are their surrounding villages.

16:53. In the case of Sodom, "returning her captivity" means again making her an inhabitable place (*Rashi*).

16:54. Israel was so sinful that Sodom and Samaria looked at her and felt comfort, thinking that they were not that bad after all (*Rashi*).

16:56. A "metaphor" for evil and the destruction it brings.

17:2. This chapter opens with a parable, then proceeds to explain it.

and your father an Amorite. ⁴⁶ *Your older sister is Samaria — she and her daughters — who dwells to your north,* * *and your sister who is younger than you, who dwells to your south, is Sodom and its daughters.* ⁴⁷ *If only you had gone in their ways, and acted like their abominations, it would have been a small trifle! But you were even more corrupt than they in all your ways.* ⁴⁸ *As I live — the word of the Lord HASHEM/ELOHIM — [I swear that] Sodom, your sister — she and her daughters — have not done as you and your daughters did.* ⁴⁹ *Behold, this was the sin of Sodom, your sister: She and her daughters had pride, surfeit of bread and peaceful serenity, but she did not strengthen the hand of the poor and the needy.* ⁵⁰ *And they were haughty, and they committed an abomination before Me, so I removed them in accordance with what I saw.* ⁵¹ *And as for Samaria, she did not sin even half of your sins. For you have increased your abominations beyond them; you have vindicated your sisters with all your abominations that you have committed!* ⁵² *Now you, too, bear your humiliation that you had judged appropriate for your sister; through your sins by which you acted more abominably than they, they are more righteous than you! You, too, feel ashamed and bear your humiliation, as you vindicate your sisters.*

⁵³ *And I will return their captivity, the captivity of Sodom* * *and her daughters, and the captivity of Samaria and her daughters, and the captivity of your captives in their midst,* ⁵⁴ *so that you bear your humiliation and be humiliated for all you have done by comforting them.* * ⁵⁵ *And your sisters, Sodom and her daughters, will return to their former state, and Samaria and her daughters, will return to their former state, and you and your daughters will return to your former state.*

⁵⁶ *Was not your sister Sodom a saying* * *in your mouth, in your day of pride,* ⁵⁷ *before your wickedness was revealed, as at the time of the disgrace of the daughters of Aram and all who are around her, and the daughters of the Philistines, who demean you from all around?* ⁵⁸ *You have borne your scheming and your abominations — the word of HASHEM.*

⁵⁹ *For thus said the Lord HASHEM/ELOHIM: I will do to you as you have*

done, for you have scorned an oath, breaking [our] covenant. ⁶⁰ *But I will remember My covenant [made] with you in the days of your youth, and I will establish for you an everlasting covenant.* ⁶¹ *Then you will remember your [evil] ways and be humiliated, when you take your sisters who are older than you with those who are younger than you and I give them to you as daughters, but not because [you kept] your covenant.* ⁶² *Then I will establish My covenant with you, and you will know that I am HASHEM,* ⁶³ *in order that you remember and be ashamed, and so that you no longer have an excuse because of your humiliation, when I forgive you for all that you have done — the word of the Lord HASHEM/ELOHIM."*

17

¹ The word of HASHEM came to me, saying, ² *"Son of Man, propose a riddle and relate a parable to the House of Israel.* * ³ *You shall say:*

Thus said the Lord HASHEM/ELOHIM: The great eagle — great of wings and long of pinion, full of plumage — which has many colors, came to the Lebanon and took the crown of the cedar. ⁴ *He cropped the top of the young twigs and brought it to the land of the merchants, placing it in the city of traders.*

ה וַיִּקַּח מִזֶּרַע הָאָרֶץ וַיִּתְּנֵהוּ בִּשְׂדֵה־זָרַע קַח עַל־מַיִם רַבִּים צַפְצָפָה שָׂמוֹ:

ו וַיִּצְמַח וַיְהִי לְגֶפֶן סֹרַחַת שִׁפְלַת קוֹמָה לִפְנוֹת דָּלִיּוֹתָיו אֵלָיו וְשָׁרָשָׁיו

ז תַּחְתָּיו יִהְיוּ וַתְּהִי לְגֶפֶן וַתַּעַשׂ בַּדִּים וַתְּשַׁלַּח פֹּארוֹת: וַיְהִי נֶשֶׁר־אֶחָד גָּדוֹל גְּדוֹל כְּנָפַיִם וְרַב־נוֹצָה וְהִנֵּה הַגֶּפֶן הַזֹּאת כָּפְנָה שָׁרָשֶׁיהָ עָלָיו

ח וְדָלִיּוֹתָיו שִׁלְּחָה־לּוֹ לְהַשְׁקוֹת אוֹתָהּ מֵעֲרֻגוֹת מַטָּעָהּ: אֶל־שָׂדֶה טּוֹב אֶל־מַיִם רַבִּים הִיא שְׁתוּלָה לַעֲשׂוֹת עָנָף וְלָשֵׂאת פֶּרִי לִהְיוֹת לְגֶפֶן אַדָּרֶת:

ט אֱמֹר כֹּה אָמַר אֲדֹנָי יֱהוִה תִּצְלָח הֲלוֹא אֶת־שָׁרָשֶׁיהָ יְנַתֵּק וְאֶת־פִּרְיָהּ ׀ יְקוֹסֵס וְיָבֵשׁ כָּל־טַרְפֵּי צִמְחָהּ תִּיבָשׁ וְלֹא־בִזְרֹעַ גְּדוֹלָה וּבְעַם־רָב לְמַשְׂאוֹת אוֹתָהּ מִשָּׁרָשֶׁיהָ: וְהִנֵּה שְׁתוּלָה הֲתִצְלָח הֲלֹא כְגַעַת בָּהּ רוּחַ

י הַקָּדִים תִּיבַשׁ יָבֹשׁ עַל־עֲרֻגֹת צִמְחָהּ תִּיבָשׁ:   וַיְהִי דְבַר־יְהוָה אֵלַי

יא לֵאמֹר: אֱמָר־נָא לְבֵית הַמֶּרִי הֲלֹא יְדַעְתֶּם מָה־אֵלֶּה אֱמֹר הִנֵּה־בָא מֶלֶךְ־

יב בָּבֶל יְרוּשָׁלַ͏ִם וַיִּקַּח אֶת־מַלְכָּהּ וְאֶת־שָׂרֶיהָ וַיָּבֵא אוֹתָם אֵלָיו בָּבֶלָה: וַיִּקַּח

יג מִזֶּרַע הַמְּלוּכָה וַיִּכְרֹת אִתּוֹ בְּרִית וַיָּבֵא אֹתוֹ בְּאָלָה וְאֶת־אֵילֵי הָאָרֶץ

יד לָקָח: לִהְיוֹת מַמְלָכָה שְׁפָלָה לְבִלְתִּי הִתְנַשֵּׂא לִשְׁמֹר אֶת־בְּרִיתוֹ לְעָמְדָהּ:

טו וַיִּמְרָד־בּוֹ לִשְׁלֹחַ מַלְאָכָיו מִצְרַיִם לָתֶת־לוֹ סוּסִים וְעַם־רָב הֲיִצְלָח

טז הֲיִמָּלֵט הָעֹשֵׂה אֵלֶּה וְהֵפֵר בְּרִית וְנִמְלָט: חַי־אָנִי נְאֻם אֲדֹנָי יֱהוִה אִם־לֹא בִּמְקוֹם הַמֶּלֶךְ הַמַּמְלִיךְ אֹתוֹ אֲשֶׁר בָּזָה אֶת־אָלָתוֹ וַאֲשֶׁר הֵפֵר אֶת־בְּרִיתוֹ

יז אִתּוֹ בְתוֹךְ־בָּבֶל יָמוּת: וְלֹא בְחַיִל גָּדוֹל וּבְקָהָל רָב יַעֲשֶׂה אוֹתוֹ פַרְעֹה

יח בַּמִּלְחָמָה בִּשְׁפֹּךְ סֹלְלָה וּבִבְנוֹת דָּיֵק לְהַכְרִית נְפָשׁוֹת רַבּוֹת: וּבָזָה אָלָה

יט לְהָפֵר בְּרִית וְהִנֵּה נָתַן יָדוֹ וְכָל־אֵלֶּה עָשָׂה לֹא יִמָּלֵט: לָכֵן כֹּה־אָמַר אֲדֹנָי יֱהוִה חַי־אָנִי אִם־לֹא אָלָתִי אֲשֶׁר בָּזָה וּבְרִיתִי אֲשֶׁר הֵפִיר וּנְתַתִּיו

כ בְרֹאשׁוֹ: וּפָרַשְׂתִּי עָלָיו רִשְׁתִּי וְנִתְפַּשׂ בִּמְצוּדָתִי וַהֲבִיאוֹתִיהוּ בָבֶלָה

כא וְנִשְׁפַּטְתִּי אִתּוֹ שָׁם מַעֲלוֹ אֲשֶׁר מָעַל־בִּי: וְאֵת כָּל־°מברחו [°מִבְרָחָיו ק] בְּכָל־אֲגַפָּיו בַּחֶרֶב יִפֹּלוּ וְהַנִּשְׁאָרִים לְכָל־רוּחַ יִפָּרֵשׂוּ וִידַעְתֶּם כִּי אֲנִי

כב יְהוָה דִּבַּרְתִּי: כֹּה אָמַר אֲדֹנָי יֱהוִה וְלָקַחְתִּי אָנִי מִצַּמֶּרֶת הָאֶרֶז הָרָמָה וְנָתָתִּי מֵרֹאשׁ יֹנְקוֹתָיו רַךְ אֶקְטֹף וְשָׁתַלְתִּי אָנִי עַל הַר־גָּבֹהַ וְתָלוּל:

כג בְּהַר מְרוֹם יִשְׂרָאֵל אֶשְׁתֳּלֶנּוּ וְנָשָׂא עָנָף וְעָשָׂה פֶרִי וְהָיָה לְאֶרֶז אַדִּיר

כד וְשָׁכְנוּ תַחְתָּיו כֹּל צִפּוֹר כָּל־כָּנָף בְּצֵל דָּלִיּוֹתָיו תִּשְׁכֹּנָּה: וְיָדְעוּ כָּל־עֲצֵי

17:12. Nebuchadnezzar is the great eagle (v. 3); Jerusalem, the crown (v. 3); Jehoiachin, the young twigs (v. 4); Babylonia, the land of the merchants (v. 4; 16:29); and Babylonia's attack, the east wind (v. 10). The second eagle (v. 7) is Pharaoh.

17:13. Zedekiah, brother of Jehoiachin.

17:15. The subject is Zedekiah's rebellion against King Nebuchadnezzar, for which Zedekiah was blinded and exiled. This rebellion is mentioned very briefly in *II Kings*

24:20 and *Jeremiah* 52:3, and here in some detail.

17:18. Zedekiah had given his hand to Nebuchadnezzar to validate his oath.

17:19. Zedekiah had taken his oath in the Name of God.

17:22. In place of Zedekiah, God will give the throne to Zerubbabel, who led the people's return from the Babylonian exile (*Radak*).

17:23. All Israel will dwell securely under the protection of the new leader (*Radak*).

⁵ He then took from the seed of the land and placed it in a fertile field; he took [it to a place] of abundant waters; he set it up to be [as lush as] a mountain willow. ⁶ It sprouted and became a spreading vine, low of stature, with its tendrils turned inward with its roots underneath it; it became a vine and produced branches and sent out boughs.

⁷ There was a[nother] great eagle — great of wings and abundant of plumage. And behold, this vine's roots yearned toward him, and it extended its tendrils toward him from the furrows of its bed, that he should water it — ⁸ [though] it had been planted in a fertile field, by abundant waters, to produce branches and bear fruit, to become a stately vine.

⁹ "Say:

Thus said the Lord HASHEM/ELOHIM: Shall it prosper? Will [the first eagle] not tear out its roots and cut off its fruits so that it will wither and all its sprouting leaves wither? And no great arm nor multitude of people can prevent its being ripped out by the roots. ¹⁰ Behold, it had been firmly planted; can it prosper? When the east wind touches it, will it not completely wither? In the very furrows of its sprouting it will wither."

¹¹ The word of HASHEM came to me, saying, ¹² "Say now to the rebellious house: Do you not know what this [parable] represents?

Say:

The interpretation — Behold, the king of Babylonia* came to Jerusalem, and he took its king and princes, and brought them to him to Babylonia. ¹³ Then he took someone from the royal seed* and sealed a covenant with him and had him take an oath, and he took away the mighty of the land, ¹⁴ so that it would be a lowly kingdom that could not rise up, and so that it should keep his covenant, that it might endure. ¹⁵ But he rebelled against him,* sending his agents to Egypt to provide them with horses and great multitude. Shall one who does such things succeed; shall he escape? Shall he annul a covenant and escape? ¹⁶ As I live — the word of the Lord, HASHEM/ELOHIM — [I swear] that at the place of the king who installed him, whose oath he spurned and whose covenant he broke — with him, in the midst of Babylonia, he shall die. ¹⁷ And Pharaoh will not aid him in war with a large army or a great assembly, when ramps are poured and siege towers built to cut down numerous lives. ¹⁸ And as for the one who spurned an oath to annul [his] covenant — behold, he had given his hand* yet he did all of these [things]; he shall not escape!

¹⁹ Therefore, thus said the Lord HASHEM/ELOHIM: As I live, [I swear that] I shall place on his head [the punishment for] My oath* that he has spurned, and My covenant that he has broken. ²⁰ I will spread My net over him and he will be caught in My trap; I will bring him to Babylonia, and I will contend with him there for his treachery that he has committed against Me. ²¹ And all his fugitives together with all his officers will fall by the sword, and the remaining ones will spread out in every direction; then you will know that I, HASHEM, have spoken.

The redemption — ²² Thus said the Lord HASHEM/ELOHIM: Then I will take from the crown of the lofty cedar and establish it; from the head of the young twigs I will crop a tender one* and plant it on a high and eminent mountain. ²³ I will plant it on the mountain of the height of Israel, and it will bear branches and produce fruit and become a stately cedar; and every bird of every kind of wing will dwell under it;* they will dwell in the shade of its tendrils. ²⁴ And all the trees

הַשָּׁרֶה כִּי אֲנִי יהוה הִשְׁפַּלְתִּי ׀ עֵץ גָּבֹהַ הִגְבַּהְתִּי עֵץ שָׁפָל הוֹבַשְׁתִּי עֵץ

יח לָח וְהִפְרַחְתִּי עֵץ יָבֵשׁ אֲנִי יהוה דִּבַּרְתִּי וְעָשִׂיתִי: **וַיְהִי** א

ב דְבַר־יהוה אֵלַי לֵאמֹר: מַה־לָכֶם אַתֶּם מֹשְׁלִים אֶת־הַמָּשָׁל הַזֶּה עַל־

ג אַדְמַת יִשְׂרָאֵל לֵאמֹר אָבוֹת יֹאכְלוּ בֹסֶר וְשִׁנֵּי הַבָּנִים תִּקְהֶינָה: חַי־אָנִי

ד נְאֻם אֲדֹנָי יֱהוִֹה אִם־יִהְיֶה לָכֶם עוֹד מְשֹׁל הַמָּשָׁל הַזֶּה בְּיִשְׂרָאֵל: הֵן כָּל־

הַנְּפָשׁוֹת לִי הֵנָּה כְּנֶפֶשׁ הָאָב וּכְנֶפֶשׁ הַבֵּן לִי־הֵנָּה הַנֶּפֶשׁ הַחֹטֵאת הִיא

ה תָמוּת: וְאִישׁ כִּי־יִהְיֶה צַדִּיק וְעָשָׂה מִשְׁפָּט וּצְדָקָה:

ו אֶל־הֶהָרִים לֹא אָכָל וְעֵינָיו לֹא נָשָׂא אֶל־גִּלּוּלֵי בֵּית יִשְׂרָאֵל וְאֶת־אֵשֶׁת

ז רֵעֵהוּ לֹא טִמֵּא וְאֶל־אִשָּׁה נִדָּה לֹא יִקְרָב: וְאִישׁ לֹא יוֹנֶה חֲבֹלָתוֹ חוֹב

ח יָשִׁיב גְּזֵלָה לֹא יִגְזֹל לַחְמוֹ לְרָעֵב יִתֵּן וְעֵירֹם יְכַסֶּה־בָּגֶד: בַּנֶּשֶׁךְ לֹא־יִתֵּן

וְתַרְבִּית לֹא יִקָּח מֵעָוֶל יָשִׁיב יָדוֹ מִשְׁפַּט אֱמֶת יַעֲשֶׂה בֵּין אִישׁ לְאִישׁ:

ט בְּחֻקּוֹתַי יְהַלֵּךְ וּמִשְׁפָּטַי שָׁמַר לַעֲשׂוֹת אֱמֶת צַדִּיק הוּא חָיֹה יִחְיֶה נְאֻם

יא-י אֲדֹנָי יֱהוִֹה: וְהוֹלִיד בֵּן־פָּרִיץ שֹׁפֵךְ דָּם וְעָשָׂה אָח מֵאַחַד מֵאֵלֶּה: וְהוּא

אֶת־כָּל־אֵלֶּה לֹא עָשָׂה כִּי גַם אֶל־הֶהָרִים אָכָל וְאֶת־אֵשֶׁת רֵעֵהוּ טִמֵּא:

יב עָנִי וְאֶבְיוֹן הוֹנָה גְּזֵלוֹת גָּזָל חֲבֹל לֹא יָשִׁיב וְאֶל־הַגִּלּוּלִים נָשָׂא עֵינָיו

יג תּוֹעֵבָה עָשָׂה: בַּנֶּשֶׁךְ נָתַן וְתַרְבִּית לָקַח וָחָי לֹא יִחְיֶה אֵת כָּל־הַתּוֹעֵבוֹת

יד הָאֵלֶּה עָשָׂה מוֹת יוּמָת דָּמָיו בּוֹ יִהְיֶה: וְהִנֵּה הוֹלִיד בֵּן וַיַּרְא אֶת־כָּל־

טו חַטֹּאת אָבִיו אֲשֶׁר עָשָׂה °וַיִּרְאֶה [וַיִּרְאֶה ק] וְלֹא יַעֲשֶׂה כָּהֵן: עַל־הֶהָרִים

לֹא אָכָל וְעֵינָיו לֹא נָשָׂא אֶל־גִּלּוּלֵי בֵּית יִשְׂרָאֵל אֶת־אֵשֶׁת רֵעֵהוּ לֹא

טז טִמֵּא: וְאִישׁ לֹא הוֹנָה חֲבֹל לֹא חָבָל וּגְזֵלָה לֹא גָזָל לַחְמוֹ לְרָעֵב נָתָן

יז וְעֵרוֹם כִּסָּה־בָגֶד: מֵעָנִי הֵשִׁיב יָדוֹ נֶשֶׁךְ וְתַרְבִּית לֹא לָקָח מִשְׁפָּטַי עָשָׂה

יח בְּחֻקּוֹתַי הָלָךְ הוּא לֹא יָמוּת בַּעֲוֹן אָבִיו חָיֹה יִחְיֶה: אָבִיו כִּי־עָשַׁק עֹשֶׁק

גָּזַל גֵּזֶל אָח וַאֲשֶׁר לֹא־טוֹב עָשָׂה בְּתוֹךְ עַמָּיו וְהִנֵּה־מֵת בַּעֲוֹנוֹ: וַאֲמַרְתֶּם

יט מַדֻּעַ לֹא־נָשָׂא הַבֵּן בַּעֲוֹן הָאָב וְהַבֵּן מִשְׁפָּט וּצְדָקָה עָשָׂה אֵת כָּל־חֻקּוֹתַי

שָׁמַר וַיַּעֲשֶׂה אֹתָם חָיֹה יִחְיֶה: הַנֶּפֶשׁ הַחֹטֵאת הִיא תָמוּת

כ בֵּן לֹא־יִשָּׂא ׀ בַּעֲוֹן הָאָב וְאָב לֹא יִשָּׂא בַּעֲוֹן הַבֵּן צִדְקַת הַצַּדִּיק עָלָיו

כא תִּהְיֶה וְרִשְׁעַת °רשע [הָרָשָׁע ק] עָלָיו תִּהְיֶה: וְהָרָשָׁע

כִּי יָשׁוּב מִכָּל־°חטאתו [חַטֹּאתָיו ק] אֲשֶׁר עָשָׂה וְשָׁמַר אֶת־כָּל־חֻקּוֹתַי

כב וְעָשָׂה מִשְׁפָּט וּצְדָקָה חָיֹה יִחְיֶה לֹא יָמוּת: כָּל־פְּשָׁעָיו אֲשֶׁר עָשָׂה לֹא

כג יִזָּכְרוּ לוֹ בְּצִדְקָתוֹ אֲשֶׁר־עָשָׂה יִחְיֶה: הֶחָפֹץ אֶחְפֹּץ מוֹת רָשָׁע נְאֻם

18:2. The people felt that they were being punished unfairly for the sins of their fathers, but Ezekiel rejected this contention (v. 4), saying that punishment is exacted only of those who deserve it. **18:7.** See *Exodus* 22:25.

18:19. Since Ezekiel's listeners thought they were being punished only for the wickedness of such evil predecessors as King Manasseh, they would wonder why the righteous son of Ezekiel's parable went unscathed.

of the field will know that I, HASHEM, have lowered a high tree, and have raised a low tree; I have dried up a moist tree and made blossom a dry tree — I am HASHEM; I have spoken and I shall carry it out."

18 | Fathers and sons | The righteous father | The violent son | The righteous grandson | The soul that sins | The penitent

¹ T he word of HASHEM came to me, saying:

Fathers and sons ² Why do you relate this parable upon the land of Israel, saying, 'The fathers eat sour grapes, but the teeth of the sons are set on edge!'* ³ As I live — the word of the Lord HASHEM/ELOHIM — [I swear] that there will no longer be anyone among you who uses this parable in Israel. ⁴ Behold, all souls are Mine; like the soul of the father, so the soul of the son, they are Mine. The soul that sins — it shall die.

The righteous father ⁵ If a man is righteous and practices justice and righteousness: ⁶ he does not partake [of idolatrous sacrifices] upon the mountains; does not lift his eyes towards the idols of the House of Israel; does not defile his neighbor's wife nor approach an impure woman; ⁷ does not oppress any man; returns a collateral for a debt;* does not rob any loot; gives his bread to the hungry and covers the naked with clothing; ⁸ does not give [loans] with usury nor take interest; withholds his hand from corruption; executes true justice between man and man; ⁹ goes according to My decrees and observes My ordinances to practice truth — he is a righteous man; he shall surely live — the word of the Lord, HASHEM/ELOHIM.

The violent son ¹⁰ If he begets a violent son, who sheds blood, who does any of these [sins] to [his] brother, ¹¹ who does not do all these [good deeds]: for he even partakes [of idolatrous sacrifices] upon the mountains; defiles his neighbor's wife; ¹² oppresses the poor and the needy; robs loot; does not return collateral; lifts his eyes towards the idols; commits abomination; ¹³ gives [loans] with usury and takes interest — should he live? He shall not live! He has committed all these abominations; he shall surely die and his blood will be upon himself.

The righteous grandson ¹⁴ Then if he begets a son who sees all the sins of his father that he had done; he sees, but does not do [acts] like them: ¹⁵ He does not partake [of idolatrous sacrifices] upon the mountains; does not lift his eyes towards the idols of the House of Israel; does not defile his neighbor's wife; ¹⁶ does not oppress any man; does not keep collateral; does not rob any loot; gives his bread to the hungry and covers the naked with clothing; ¹⁷ withholds his hand from [harming] the poor; does not take usury or interest; obeys My ordinances and follows My decrees — he shall not die for his father's iniquity; he shall surely live.

¹⁸ His father, because he has cruelly oppressed [others], has robbed loot from [his] brother and did that which is not good among his people — behold, he died for his sin. ¹⁹ Yet you say, 'Why did the son not bear the iniquity of the father?'* But the son performed justice and righteousness, and observed all My decrees and performed them; he should surely live! ²⁰ **The soul that sins** The soul that sins, it shall die! A son shall not bear the iniquity of [his] father and a father shall not bear the iniquity of [his] son; the righteousness of the righteous person shall be upon him and the wickedness of the wicked person shall be upon him.

The penitent ²¹ As for the wicked man, if he repents from all his sins that he committed, and he observes all My decrees and practices justice and righteousness, he shall surely live, he shall not die. ²² All his transgressions that he committed will not be remembered against him; he shall live because of the righteousness that he did. ²³ Do I desire at all the death of the wicked man? — the word

כד אֲדֹנָ֣י יֱהֹוִ֗ה הֲלֹ֨א בְּשׁ֣וּב מִדְּרָכָ֖יו וְחָיָֽה: וּבְשׁ֨וּב צַדִּ֤יק מִצִּדְקָתוֹ֙
וְעָ֣שָׂה עָ֔וֶל כְּכֹ֤ל הַתּֽוֹעֵבוֹת֙ אֲשֶׁר־עָשָׂ֣ה הָֽרָשָׁ֔ע יַֽעֲשֶׂ֖ה וָחָ֑י כָּל־°צִדְקֹתָו֙
[צִדְקֹתָ֤יו ק] אֲשֶׁר־עָשָׂה֙ לֹ֣א תִזָּכַ֔רְנָה בְּמַֽעֲל֧וֹ אֲשֶׁר־מָעַ֛ל וּבְחַטָּאת֥וֹ
כה אֲשֶׁר־חָטָ֖א בָּ֣ם יָמֽוּת: וַֽאֲמַרְתֶּ֔ם לֹ֥א יִתָּכֵ֖ן דֶּ֣רֶךְ אֲדֹנָ֑י שִׁמְעוּ־נָא֙ בֵּ֣ית
כו יִשְׂרָאֵ֔ל הֲדַרְכִּ֣י לֹ֣א יִתָּכֵ֔ן הֲלֹ֥א דַרְכֵיכֶ֖ם לֹ֥א יִתָּכֵֽנוּ: בְּשׁוּב־צַדִּ֧יק מִצִּדְקָת֛וֹ
וְעָ֥שָׂה עָ֖וֶל וּמֵ֣ת עֲלֵיהֶ֑ם בְּעַוְל֥וֹ אֲשֶׁר־עָשָׂ֖ה יָמֽוּת: וּבְשׁ֣וּב
כז רָשָׁ֗ע מֵֽרִשְׁעָתוֹ֙ אֲשֶׁ֣ר עָשָׂ֔ה וַיַּ֥עַשׂ מִשְׁפָּ֖ט וּצְדָקָ֑ה ה֖וּא אֶת־נַפְשׁ֥וֹ יְחַיֶּֽה:
כח וַיִּרְאֶ֣ה °וישוב [וַיָּ֗שׁב ק] מִכָּל־פְּשָׁעָיו֙ אֲשֶׁ֣ר עָשָׂ֔ה חָי֥וֹ יִחְיֶ֖ה לֹ֥א יָמֽוּת:
כט וְאָֽמְרוּ֙ בֵּ֣ית יִשְׂרָאֵ֔ל לֹ֥א יִתָּכֵ֖ן דֶּ֣רֶךְ אֲדֹנָ֑י הַדְּרָכַ֞י לֹ֤א יִתָּֽכְנוּ֙ בֵּ֣ית יִשְׂרָאֵ֔ל
ל הֲלֹ֥א דַרְכֵיכֶ֖ם לֹ֣א יִתָּכֵֽן: לָכֵן֩ אִ֨ישׁ כִּדְרָכָ֜יו אֶשְׁפֹּ֤ט אֶתְכֶם֙ בֵּ֣ית יִשְׂרָאֵ֔ל
נְאֻ֖ם אֲדֹנָ֣י יֱהֹוִ֑ה שׁ֧וּבוּ וְהָשִׁ֛יבוּ מִכָּל־פִּשְׁעֵיכֶ֖ם וְלֹֽא־יִֽהְיֶ֥ה לָכֶ֖ם לְמִכְשׁ֥וֹל
לא עָוֺֽן: הַשְׁלִ֣יכוּ מֵֽעֲלֵיכֶ֗ם אֶת־כָּל־פִּשְׁעֵיכֶם֙ אֲשֶׁ֣ר פְּשַׁעְתֶּ֣ם בָּ֔ם וַֽעֲשׂ֥וּ לָכֶ֛ם
לב לֵ֥ב חָדָ֖שׁ וְר֣וּחַ חֲדָשָׁ֑ה וְלָ֥מָּה תָמֻ֖תוּ בֵּ֥ית יִשְׂרָאֵֽל: כִּ֣י לֹ֤א אֶחְפֹּץ֙ בְּמ֣וֹת
א הַמֵּ֔ת נְאֻ֖ם אֲדֹנָ֣י יֱהֹוִ֑ה וְהָשִׁ֖יבוּ וִֽחְיֽוּ:   וְאַתָּה֙ שָׂ֣א קִינָ֔ה אֶל־   **יט**
ב נְשִׂיאֵ֖י יִשְׂרָאֵֽל: וְאָֽמַרְתָּ֗ מָ֤ה אִמְּךָ֙ לְבִיָּ֔א בֵּ֥ין אֲרָי֖וֹת רָבָ֑צָה בְּת֥וֹךְ כְּפִרִ֖ים
ג רִבְּתָ֥ה גוּרֶֽיהָ: וַתַּ֛עַל אֶחָ֥ד מִגֻּרֶ֖יהָ כְּפִ֣יר הָיָ֑ה וַיִּלְמַ֥ד לִטְרָף־טֶ֖רֶף אָדָ֥ם
ד אָכָֽל: וַיִּשְׁמְע֥וּ אֵלָ֛יו גּוֹיִ֖ם בְּשַׁחְתָּ֣ם נִתְפָּ֑שׂ וַיְבִאֻ֥הוּ בַחַחִ֖ים אֶל־אֶ֥רֶץ
ה מִצְרָֽיִם: וַתֵּ֨רֶא֙ כִּ֣י נֽוֹחֲלָ֔ה אָֽבְדָ֖ה תִּקְוָתָ֑הּ וַתִּקַּ֛ח אֶחָ֥ד מִגֻּרֶ֖יהָ כְּפִ֥יר
ו שָׂמָֽתְהוּ: וַיִּתְהַלֵּ֥ךְ בְּתֽוֹךְ־אֲרָי֖וֹת כְּפִ֣יר הָיָ֑ה וַיִּלְמַ֣ד לִטְרָף־טֶ֔רֶף אָדָ֥ם אָכָֽל:
ז-ח וַיֵּ֨דַע֙ אַלְמְנוֹתָ֔יו וְעָֽרֵיהֶ֖ם הֶֽחֱרִ֑יב וַתֵּ֤שַׁם אֶ֨רֶץ֙ וּמְלֹאָ֔הּ מִקּ֖וֹל שַֽׁאֲגָתֽוֹ: וַיִּתְּנ֨וּ
ט עָלָ֤יו גּוֹיִם֙ סָבִ֣יב מִמְּדִינ֔וֹת וַיִּפְרְשׂ֥וּ עָלָ֖יו רִשְׁתָּ֑ם בְּשַׁחְתָּ֖ם נִתְפָּֽשׂ: וַֽיִּתְּנֻ֤הוּ
בַסּוּגַר֙ בַּֽחַחִ֔ים וַיְבִאֻ֖הוּ אֶל־מֶ֣לֶךְ בָּבֶ֑ל יְבִאֻ֨הוּ֙ בַּמְּצֹד֔וֹת לְמַ֨עַן֙ לֹֽא־יִשָּׁמַ֤ע
י קוֹלוֹ֙ ע֔וֹד אֶל־הָרֵ֖י יִשְׂרָאֵֽל: אִמְּךָ֣ כַגֶּ֔פֶן בְּדָֽמְךָ֖ עַל־מַ֑יִם
יא שְׁתוּלָ֑ה פֹּֽרִיָּה֙ וַֽעֲנֵפָ֔ה הָֽיְתָ֖ה מִמַּ֥יִם רַבִּֽים: וַיִּֽהְיוּ־לָ֣הּ מַטּ֣וֹת עֹ֗ז אֶל־שִׁבְטֵי֙
יב מֹֽשְׁלִ֔ים וַתִּגְבַּ֥הּ קֽוֹמָת֖וֹ עַל־בֵּ֣ין עֲבֹתִ֑ים וַיֵּרָ֥א בְגָבְה֖וֹ בְּרֹ֥ב דָּֽלִיֹּתָֽיו: וַתֻּתַּ֨שׁ
בְּחֵמָ֜ה לָאָ֣רֶץ הֻשְׁלָ֗כָה וְר֤וּחַ הַקָּדִים֙ הוֹבִ֣ישׁ פִּרְיָ֔הּ הִתְפָּֽרְק֥וּ וְיָבֵ֖שׁוּ מַטֵּ֥ה
יג-יד עֻזָּ֖הּ אֵ֥שׁ אֲכָלָֽתְהוּ: וְעַתָּ֖ה שְׁתוּלָ֣ה בַמִּדְבָּ֑ר בְּאֶ֖רֶץ צִיָּ֥ה וְצָמָֽא: וַתֵּצֵ֨א אֵ֜שׁ
מִמַּטֵּ֤ה בַדֶּ֨יהָ֙ פִּרְיָ֣הּ אָכָ֔לָה וְלֹֽא־הָ֥יָה בָ֛הּ מַטֵּה־עֹ֖ז שֵׁ֣בֶט לִמְשׁ֑וֹל קִ֥ינָה הִ֖יא
וַתְּהִ֥י לְקִינָֽה:

18:24. If a sinner repudiates the good deeds of his past, he loses credit for them.

18:26. "Them" is plural: He deserves to die for regretting his good deeds and for committing sins (*Radak*).

19:2. The mother is the Congregation of Israel; her two cubs are Kings Jehoahaz and Jehoiakim, sons of Josiah.

19:3. Young King Jehoahaz betrayed and robbed from his fellow Jews (*Rashi*).

19:7. (*Targum*). Alternatively: He ravished their widows (*Rashi*). The ruinous policies of King Jehoiakim brought about the destruction of much of Judah at the hands of the surrounding nations (*Radak; see II Kings* 24:1-2).

19:10. Israel is likened to the reigns of David and Solomon, which were blessed with success (*Radak*).

19:12. See 17:10,12.

19:14. Now it is only prophecy, but soon it will be reality.

of the Lord HASHEM/ELOHIM. Is it not rather his return from his ways, that he might live?

²⁴ And when a righteous man turns away from his righteousness and practices corruption, shall he do like all the abominations that the wicked man did, and live? All his righteousness that he had done will not be remembered* because of his treachery with which he betrayed and because of his sin that he sinned. Because of them, he shall die!

²⁵ And if you should say, 'The way of my Lord is not proper' — hear now, O House of Israel! Is My way not proper? Surely it is your ways that are not proper! ²⁶ When the righteous man turns away from his righteousness and practices corruption, he shall die for them;* for the corruption that he practiced he shall die. ²⁷ And if the wicked man turns away from his wickedness that he did and performs justice and righteousness, he will cause his soul to live. ²⁸ Because he contemplated and repented from all his transgressions that he did he shall surely live; he shall not die. ²⁹ Yet the House of Israel says, 'The way of my Lord is not proper.' Are My ways not proper, O House of Israel? Surely it is your ways that are not proper! ³⁰ Therefore, I will judge you, each man according to his ways, O House of Israel — the word of the Lord HASHEM/ELOHIM. Return and bring [others] back from all your transgressions, so that they not be for you an obstacle of iniquity. ³¹ Cast off from upon yourselves all your transgressions through which you have transgressed, and make for yourselves a new heart and a new spirit. Why should you die, O House of Israel? ³² For I do not desire the death of the one who should die — the word of the Lord HASHEM/ELOHIM. Turn [yourselves] back and live!

19 ¹ "Now take up a lamentation for the princes of Israel, ² and say:

Oh, how your mother* was a lioness, crouching among lions, rearing her cubs among young lions. ³ She raised one of her cubs, and he became a young lion; he learned to tear prey, and he devoured men. * ⁴ So the nations were mustered against him, and he was caught in their pit; and they brought him with hooks to the land of Egypt.

⁵ She saw herself disillusioned, her hope was lost; so she took another one of her cubs and made him into a young lion. ⁶ He roamed among the lions; he became a young lion. He learned to tear prey; he devoured men. ⁷ He destroyed their palaces and their cities he laid waste;* the land and all that fills it then became desolate through the noise of his roar. ⁸ So all the nations of the surrounding countries set themselves against him; they spread their net over him, and he was caught in their pit. ⁹ They put him in a collar with hooks and brought him to the king of Babylonia; they brought him into fortresses in order that his voice be no longer heard upon the mountains of Israel.

¹⁰ You are likened to one whose mother* was a vine planted by waters, that was fruitful and full-branched from the abundant waters. ¹¹ It had strong rods for scepters of sovereigns, and its stature grew high among the tallest branches, and it became visible by its height and by its many tendrils. ¹² But then it was uprooted in wrath and cast down to the ground; the east wind* withered its fruit; dismembered and withered were its strong rods; fire devoured it. ¹³ And now it is planted in the desert, in a parched and thirsty land. ¹⁴ And a fire went forth from the rod of its branches and devoured its fruit; it no longer had in it a strong rod, a scepter to rule.

It is a lamentation, and it will be a lamentation."*

Marginal notes:

Your mother, a lioness

The first cub

The second cub

Your mother, a vine

כ

א וַיְהִי ׀ בַּשָּׁנָה הַשְּׁבִיעִית בַּחֲמִשִׁי בֶּעָשׂוֹר לַחֹדֶשׁ בָּאוּ אֲנָשִׁים מִזִּקְנֵי יִשְׂרָאֵל
לִדְרֹשׁ אֶת־יְהֹוָה וַיֵּשְׁבוּ לְפָנָי: ◄ וַיְהִי דְבַר־יְהֹוָה אֵלַי לֵאמֹר:
ב בֶּן־אָדָם דַּבֵּר אֶת־זִקְנֵי יִשְׂרָאֵל וְאָמַרְתָּ אֲלֵהֶם כֹּה אָמַר אֲדֹנָי יֱהֹוִה
ג הֲלִדְרֹשׁ אֹתִי אַתֶּם בָּאִים חַי־אָנִי אִם־אִדָּרֵשׁ לָכֶם נְאֻם אֲדֹנָי יֱהֹוִה:
ד-ה הֲתִשְׁפֹּט אֹתָם הֲתִשְׁפּוֹט בֶּן־אָדָם אֶת־תּוֹעֲבֹת אֲבוֹתָם הוֹדִיעֵם: וְאָמַרְתָּ
אֲלֵיהֶם כֹּה־אָמַר אֲדֹנָי יֱהֹוִה בְּיוֹם בָּחֳרִי בְיִשְׂרָאֵל וָאֶשָּׂא יָדִי לְזֶרַע בֵּית
יַעֲקֹב וָאִוָּדַע לָהֶם בְּאֶרֶץ מִצְרָיִם וָאֶשָּׂא יָדִי לָהֶם לֵאמֹר אֲנִי יְהֹוָה
ו אֱלֹהֵיכֶם: בַּיּוֹם הַהוּא נָשָׂאתִי יָדִי לָהֶם לְהוֹצִיאָם מֵאֶרֶץ מִצְרָיִם אֶל־אֶרֶץ
ז אֲשֶׁר־תַּרְתִּי לָהֶם זָבַת חָלָב וּדְבַשׁ צְבִי הִיא לְכָל־הָאֲרָצוֹת: וָאֹמַר אֲלֵהֶם
אִישׁ שִׁקּוּצֵי עֵינָיו הַשְׁלִיכוּ וּבְגִלּוּלֵי מִצְרַיִם אַל־תִּטַּמָּאוּ אֲנִי יְהֹוָה
ח אֱלֹהֵיכֶם: וַיַּמְרוּ־בִי וְלֹא אָבוּ לִשְׁמֹעַ אֵלַי אִישׁ אֶת־שִׁקּוּצֵי עֵינֵיהֶם לֹא
הִשְׁלִיכוּ וְאֶת־גִּלּוּלֵי מִצְרַיִם לֹא עָזָבוּ וָאֹמַר לִשְׁפֹּךְ חֲמָתִי עֲלֵיהֶם לְכַלּוֹת
ט אַפִּי בָּהֶם בְּתוֹךְ אֶרֶץ מִצְרָיִם: וָאַעַשׂ לְמַעַן שְׁמִי לְבִלְתִּי הֵחֵל לְעֵינֵי הַגּוֹיִם
אֲשֶׁר־הֵמָּה בְתוֹכָם אֲשֶׁר נוֹדַעְתִּי אֲלֵיהֶם לְעֵינֵיהֶם לְהוֹצִיאָם מֵאֶרֶץ
י-יא מִצְרָיִם: וָאוֹצִיאֵם מֵאֶרֶץ מִצְרָיִם וָאֲבִאֵם אֶל־הַמִּדְבָּר: וָאֶתֵּן לָהֶם אֶת־
חֻקּוֹתַי וְאֶת־מִשְׁפָּטַי הוֹדַעְתִּי אוֹתָם אֲשֶׁר יַעֲשֶׂה אוֹתָם הָאָדָם וָחַי בָּהֶם:
יב וְגַם אֶת־שַׁבְּתוֹתַי נָתַתִּי לָהֶם לִהְיוֹת לְאוֹת בֵּינִי וּבֵינֵיהֶם לָדַעַת כִּי אֲנִי
יג יְהֹוָה מְקַדְּשָׁם: וַיַּמְרוּ־בִי בֵית־יִשְׂרָאֵל בַּמִּדְבָּר בְּחֻקּוֹתַי לֹא־הָלָכוּ וְאֶת־
מִשְׁפָּטַי מָאָסוּ אֲשֶׁר יַעֲשֶׂה אֹתָם הָאָדָם וָחַי בָּהֶם וְאֶת־שַׁבְּתֹתַי חִלְּלוּ
יד מְאֹד וָאֹמַר לִשְׁפֹּךְ חֲמָתִי עֲלֵיהֶם בַּמִּדְבָּר לְכַלּוֹתָם: וָאֶעֱשֶׂה לְמַעַן שְׁמִי
טו לְבִלְתִּי הֵחֵל לְעֵינֵי הַגּוֹיִם אֲשֶׁר הוֹצֵאתִים לְעֵינֵיהֶם: וְגַם־אֲנִי נָשָׂאתִי
יָדִי לָהֶם בַּמִּדְבָּר לְבִלְתִּי הָבִיא אוֹתָם אֶל־הָאָרֶץ אֲשֶׁר־נָתַתִּי זָבַת חָלָב
טז וּדְבַשׁ צְבִי הִיא לְכָל־הָאֲרָצוֹת: יַעַן בְּמִשְׁפָּטַי מָאָסוּ וְאֶת־חֻקּוֹתַי לֹא־
יז הָלְכוּ בָהֶם וְאֶת־שַׁבְּתוֹתַי חִלֵּלוּ כִּי אַחֲרֵי גִלּוּלֵיהֶם לִבָּם הֹלֵךְ: וַתָּחָס
יח עֵינִי עֲלֵיהֶם מִשַּׁחֲתָם וְלֹא־עָשִׂיתִי אוֹתָם כָּלָה בַּמִּדְבָּר: וָאֹמַר אֶל־בְּנֵיהֶם
בַּמִּדְבָּר בְּחוּקֵּי אֲבוֹתֵיכֶם אַל־תֵּלֵכוּ וְאֶת־מִשְׁפְּטֵיהֶם אַל־תִּשְׁמֹרוּ
יט וּבְגִלּוּלֵיהֶם אַל־תִּטַּמָּאוּ: אֲנִי יְהֹוָה אֱלֹהֵיכֶם בְּחֻקּוֹתַי לֵכוּ וְאֶת־מִשְׁפָּטַי
כ שִׁמְרוּ וַעֲשׂוּ אוֹתָם: וְאֶת־שַׁבְּתוֹתַי קַדֵּשׁוּ וְהָיוּ לְאוֹת בֵּינִי וּבֵינֵיכֶם
כא לָדַעַת כִּי אֲנִי יְהֹוָה אֱלֹהֵיכֶם: ◄ וַיַּמְרוּ־בִי הַבָּנִים בְּחֻקּוֹתַי לֹא־הָלָכוּ

20:3. The elders were in shock that God had apparently
spurned Israel, and they asked whether they still owed
Him allegiance. If they were no longer His Chosen People, why couldn't they be like all the other nations?
Ezekiel responded that they were wrong. Even their exile
and oppression were functions of their chosenness; Israel
was being punished because it had fallen short of its
mission. But, as Ezekiel says in verses 32-33, Israel is not
free to join the nations.

20:4. God instructed Ezekiel to tell the protesting elders
of the national shortcomings over the course of history,
in Egypt, the Wilderness, and in *Eretz Yisrael.*

20:13. They worshiped the Golden Calf and rebelled
against the manna.

20:15. At the incident of the Spies (*Numbers* Chs.
13-14).

20:21. At Baal Peor (*Numbers* Ch. 25).

20 ¹ It was in the seventh year, in the fifth [month], on the tenth of the month:
An Some men of the elders of Israel came to inquire of HASHEM, and they sat
inquiry of before me. ² Then the word of HASHEM came to me, saying, ³ "Son of Man, speak
Ezekiel to the elders of Israel and say to them:

Thus said the Lord HASHEM/ELOHIM: Is it to inquire of Me that you come?*
As I live, [I swear] that I will not relate to your inquiries — the word of the
Lord HASHEM/ELOHIM.' "

A rebuke ⁴ "Won't you rebuke them? Won't you rebuke, Son of Man? Inform them of the
abominations of their fathers!* ⁵ Say to them:

Thus said the Lord HASHEM/ELOHIM: On the day I chose Israel, I raised My
hand [in oath] for the seed of the House of Jacob and made Myself known
Mercy in to them in the land of Egypt, I raised My hand for them, saying, 'I am
Egypt . . . HASHEM, your God.' ⁶ On that day I raised My hand for them, [swearing] to
take them out from the land of Egypt to the Land that I had sought out for
them — [a land that] flows with milk and honey, a splendor for all the lands.
⁷ And I said to them, 'Every man, cast away the detestable [idols] of his
eyes; do not defile youselves with the idols of Egypt; I am HASHEM, your
God.'

. . . repaid ⁸ But they rebelled against Me and did not want to listen to Me; no man of
with them cast away the detestable [idols] of their eyes, and they did not forsake
rebellion . . . the idols of Egypt. So I had thought to pour out My wrath upon them, to
spend My anger on them, in the midst of the land of Egypt. ⁹ But I acted for
the sake of My Name, that it not be desecrated in the eyes of the nations in
whose midst they were, before whose eyes I made Myself known to them,
[promising] to take them out of the land of Egypt.

¹⁰ So I took them out of the land of Egypt and brought them to the
Wilderness. ¹¹ I gave them My decrees and My laws I made known to them,
through which, if a man fulfills them, he will live through them. ¹² I also gave
them My Sabbaths, to be a sign between Me and them, to know that I am
HASHEM Who sanctifies them.

¹³ But the House of Israel rebelled against Me in the Wilderness: They did
not follow My decrees and they spurned My laws,* through which, if a man
fulfills them, he will live through them; and they desecrated My Sabbaths
Even after exceedingly. So I had thought to pour out My wrath upon them in the
the Exodus Wilderness, to make an end of them. ¹⁴ But I acted for the sake of My Name,
that it should not be desecrated in the eyes of the nations before whose eyes
I had taken them out. ¹⁵ I also raised My hand [in oath] against them in the
Wilderness,* not to bring them to the land that I had given them — [a land
that] flows with milk and honey, a splendor for all the lands. ¹⁶ [All this]
because they spurned My laws and did not follow My decrees and they
desecrated My Sabbaths, because their heart kept going after their idols.
¹⁷ But My eye pitied them, rather than destroying them, so I did not put an
end to them in the Wilderness.

Warning ¹⁸ I said to their children in the Wilderness, 'Do not follow the practices of
to the your fathers and do not observe their laws, and do not defile yourselves
children . . . with their idols. ¹⁹ I am HASHEM your God; follow My decrees and observe
My laws and fulfill them. ²⁰ Sanctify My Sabbaths; and they shall be a sign
between Me and you, for you to know that I am HASHEM, your God.'
²¹ But the children rebelled against Me:* They did not follow My decrees

וְאֶת־מִשְׁפָּטַי לֹא־שָׁמְרוּ לַעֲשׂוֹת אוֹתָם אֲשֶׁר יַעֲשֶׂה אוֹתָם הָאָדָם וָחַי
בָּהֶם אֶת־שַׁבְּתוֹתַי חִלֵּלוּ וָאֹמַר לִשְׁפֹּךְ חֲמָתִי עֲלֵיהֶם לְכַלּוֹת אַפִּי בָּם
כב בַּמִּדְבָּר: וַהֲשִׁבֹתִי אֶת־יָדִי וָאַעַשׂ לְמַעַן שְׁמִי לְבִלְתִּי הֵחֵל לְעֵינֵי הַגּוֹיִם
כג אֲשֶׁר־הוֹצֵאתִי אוֹתָם לְעֵינֵיהֶם: גַּם־אֲנִי נָשָׂאתִי אֶת־יָדִי לָהֶם בַּמִּדְבָּר
כד לְהָפִיץ אֹתָם בַּגּוֹיִם וּלְזָרוֹת אוֹתָם בָּאֲרָצוֹת: יַעַן מִשְׁפָּטַי לֹא־עָשׂוּ
וְחֻקּוֹתַי מָאָסוּ וְאֶת־שַׁבְּתוֹתַי חִלֵּלוּ וְאַחֲרֵי גִּלּוּלֵי אֲבוֹתָם הָיוּ עֵינֵיהֶם:
כה-כו וְגַם־אֲנִי נָתַתִּי לָהֶם חֻקִּים לֹא טוֹבִים וּמִשְׁפָּטִים לֹא יִחְיוּ בָּהֶם: וָאֲטַמֵּא
אוֹתָם בְּמַתְּנוֹתָם בְּהַעֲבִיר כָּל־פֶּטֶר רָחַם לְמַעַן אֲשִׁמֵּם לְמַעַן אֲשֶׁר
כז יֵדְעוּ אֲשֶׁר אֲנִי יְהוָה: לָכֵן דַּבֵּר אֶל־בֵּית יִשְׂרָאֵל בֶּן־אָדָם
וְאָמַרְתָּ אֲלֵיהֶם כֹּה אָמַר אֲדֹנָי יְהוִה עוֹד זֹאת גִּדְּפוּ אוֹתִי אֲבוֹתֵיכֶם
כח בְּמַעֲלָם בִּי מָעַל: וָאֲבִיאֵם אֶל־הָאָרֶץ אֲשֶׁר נָשָׂאתִי אֶת־יָדִי לָתֵת אוֹתָהּ
לָהֶם וַיִּרְאוּ כָל־גִּבְעָה רָמָה וְכָל־עֵץ עָבֹת וַיִּזְבְּחוּ־שָׁם אֶת־זִבְחֵיהֶם
וַיִּתְּנוּ־שָׁם כַּעַס קָרְבָּנָם וַיָּשִׂימוּ שָׁם רֵיחַ נִיחוֹחֵיהֶם וַיַּסִּיכוּ שָׁם אֶת־
כט נִסְכֵּיהֶם: וָאֹמַר אֲלֵהֶם מָה הַבָּמָה אֲשֶׁר־אַתֶּם הַבָּאִים שָׁם וַיִּקָּרֵא שְׁמָהּ
ל בָּמָה עַד הַיּוֹם הַזֶּה: לָכֵן אֱמֹר ׀ אֶל־בֵּית יִשְׂרָאֵל כֹּה אָמַר
אֲדֹנָי יְהוִה הַבְּדֶרֶךְ אֲבוֹתֵיכֶם אַתֶּם נִטְמְאִים וְאַחֲרֵי שִׁקּוּצֵיהֶם אַתֶּם
לא זֹנִים: וּבִשְׂאֵת מַתְּנֹתֵיכֶם בְּהַעֲבִיר בְּנֵיכֶם בָּאֵשׁ אַתֶּם נִטְמְאִים לְכָל־
גִּלּוּלֵיכֶם עַד־הַיּוֹם וַאֲנִי אִדָּרֵשׁ לָכֶם בֵּית יִשְׂרָאֵל חַי־אָנִי נְאֻם אֲדֹנָי
לב יְהוִה אִם־אִדָּרֵשׁ לָכֶם: וְהָעֹלָה עַל־רוּחֲכֶם הָיוֹ לֹא תִהְיֶה אֲשֶׁר ׀ אַתֶּם
לג אֹמְרִים נִהְיֶה כַגּוֹיִם כְּמִשְׁפְּחוֹת הָאֲרָצוֹת לְשָׁרֵת עֵץ וָאָבֶן: חַי־אָנִי נְאֻם
אֲדֹנָי יְהוִה אִם־לֹא בְּיָד חֲזָקָה וּבִזְרוֹעַ נְטוּיָה וּבְחֵמָה שְׁפוּכָה אֶמְלוֹךְ
לד עֲלֵיכֶם: וְהוֹצֵאתִי אֶתְכֶם מִן־הָעַמִּים וְקִבַּצְתִּי אֶתְכֶם מִן־הָאֲרָצוֹת אֲשֶׁר
לה נְפוֹצֹתֶם בָּם בְּיָד חֲזָקָה וּבִזְרוֹעַ נְטוּיָה וּבְחֵמָה שְׁפוּכָה: וְהֵבֵאתִי אֶתְכֶם
אֶל־מִדְבַּר הָעַמִּים וְנִשְׁפַּטְתִּי אִתְּכֶם שָׁם פָּנִים אֶל־פָּנִים: כַּאֲשֶׁר
לו נִשְׁפַּטְתִּי אֶת־אֲבוֹתֵיכֶם בְּמִדְבַּר אֶרֶץ מִצְרָיִם כֵּן אִשָּׁפֵט אִתְּכֶם נְאֻם
לז אֲדֹנָי יְהוִה: וְהַעֲבַרְתִּי אֶתְכֶם תַּחַת הַשָּׁבֶט וְהֵבֵאתִי אֶתְכֶם בְּמָסֹרֶת
לח הַבְּרִית: וּבָרוֹתִי מִכֶּם הַמֹּרְדִים וְהַפּוֹשְׁעִים בִּי מֵאֶרֶץ מְגוּרֵיהֶם אוֹצִיא
לט אוֹתָם וְאֶל־אַדְמַת יִשְׂרָאֵל לֹא יָבוֹא וִידַעְתֶּם כִּי־אֲנִי יְהוָה: וְאַתֶּם בֵּית־
יִשְׂרָאֵל כֹּה־אָמַר ׀ אֲדֹנָי יְהוִה אִישׁ גִּלּוּלָיו לְכוּ עֲבֹדוּ וְאַחַר אִם־אֵינְכֶם
שֹׁמְעִים אֵלָי וְאֶת־שֵׁם קָדְשִׁי לֹא תְחַלְּלוּ־עוֹד בְּמַתְּנוֹתֵיכֶם וּבְגִלּוּלֵיכֶם:

20:25. In punishment, I let them be subjugated by the bitter, impossible decrees of their enemies (*Radak*).

20:29. The term "high place" should signify spiritual elevation, yet you give this title to a place of degradation.

20:35. You will be punished in a deserted area, so that your enemies do not witness your downfall (*Radak*).

20:37. I will force you to submit to My authority (*Rashi*).

20:39. You desecrate My Name when you come to My prophet, only to ignore his words, and when you bring Me your offerings, but continue worshiping your idols. There would be less desecration if you adopted idolatry completely and abandoned your hypocrisy! (*Rashi*; *Radak*).

...unheeded

and did not observe My laws, to fulfill them, through which, if a man fulfills them, he will live through them; and they desecrated My Sabbaths; so I spoke [to myself] to pour out My wrath upon them, to spend My anger on them in the Wilderness, ²² but I restrained My hand and acted for the sake of My Name, that it not be desecrated in the eyes of the nations before whose eyes I had taken them out.

An oath in the Wilderness

²³ I also raised up My hand [in oath] against them in the Wilderness to scatter them among the nations and to disperse them among the lands, ²⁴ because they did not fulfill My laws, they spurned My decrees, desecrated My Sabbaths, and their eyes went after the idols of their fathers. ²⁵ So I too gave them decrees that were not good* and laws by which they could not live. ²⁶ I profaned them because of their gifts — of passing every firstborn [before Molech] — so that I might destroy them, so that they should know that I am HASHEM."

Blasphemy in the land

²⁷ "Therefore, speak to the House of Israel, Son of Man, and say to them: Thus said the Lord HASHEM/ELOHIM: Your fathers blasphemed Me further even with this, when they acted treacherously against Me. ²⁸ I had brought them to the land that I had raised up My hand [in oath] to give to them, and they saw every high hill and every thick-branched tree — they slaughtered their sacrifices there and they offered their offerings of provocation there; they placed their satisfying aromas there, and poured out their libations there. ²⁹ Then I said to them, 'What is this high place to which only you come?' Yet it is called a high place until this day." *

³⁰ "Therefore, say to the House of Israel:

Attempts at assimilation

Thus said the Lord HASHEM/ELOHIM: Do you defile yourselves in the manner of your fathers and go astray after their abominations? ³¹ And by giving your gifts — by passing your children through fire — you defile yourselves unto all your idols to this day, should I relate to your inquiries, O House of Israel? As I live — the word of the Lord HASHEM/ELOHIM — [I swear that] I will not relate to your inquiries! ³² As for what enters your minds — it shall not be! As for what you say, 'We will be like the nations, like the families of the lands, to worship wood and stone,' ³³ as I live — the word of the Lord

God will not permit it

HASHEM/ELOHIM — [I swear that] I will rule over you with a strong hand and with an outstretched arm and with outpoured wrath. ³⁴ I will take you out from the nations and gather you from the lands to which you were scattered, with a strong hand and with an outstretched arm and with outpoured wrath; ³⁵ and I will bring you to the Wilderness of the Nations* and I will contend with you there, face to face. ³⁶ Just as I contended with your forefathers in the Wilderness of the land of Egypt, so will I contend with you

Retribution

— the word of the Lord HASHEM/ELOHIM. ³⁷ I will make you pass under the rod* and bring you into the bond of the covenant. ³⁸ I will separate from among you those who rebel and those who transgress against Me; I will take them out of the land of their sojourning, but they will not come to the soil of Israel; then you will know that I am HASHEM.

³⁹ And you, O House of Israel, thus said the Lord HASHEM/ELOHIM: Let every man go serve his idols, since you do not listen to Me; and do not profane My holy Name any longer with your gifts and with your idols. *

מ כִּי בְהַר־קָדְשִׁי בְּהַר ׀ מְרַוֹם יִשְׂרָאֵל נְאֻם אֲדֹנָי יֱהֹוִה שָׁם יַעַבְדֻנִי כָּל־בֵּית יִשְׂרָאֵל כֻּלֹּה בָּאָרֶץ שָׁם אֶרְצֵם וְשָׁם אֶדְרַוֹשׁ אֶת־תְּרוּמֹתֵיכֶם וְאֶת־

מא רֵאשִׁית מַשְׂאוֹתֵיכֶם בְּכָל־קָדְשֵׁיכֶם: בְּרֵיחַ נִיחֹחַ אֶרְצֶה אֶתְכֶם בְּהוֹצִיאִי אֶתְכֶם מִן־הָעַמִּים וְקִבַּצְתִּי אֶתְכֶם מִן־הָאֲרָצוֹת אֲשֶׁר נְפֹצֹתֶם בָּם

מב וְנִקְדַּשְׁתִּי בָכֶם לְעֵינֵי הַגּוֹיִם: וִידַעְתֶּם כִּי־אֲנִי יְהוָה בַּהֲבִיאִי אֶתְכֶם אֶל־אַדְמַת יִשְׂרָאֵל אֶל־הָאָרֶץ אֲשֶׁר נָשָׂאתִי אֶת־יָדִי לָתֵת אוֹתָהּ לַאֲבוֹתֵיכֶם:

מג וּזְכַרְתֶּם־שָׁם אֶת־דַּרְכֵיכֶם וְאֵת כָּל־עֲלִילוֹתֵיכֶם אֲשֶׁר נִטְמֵאתֶם בָּם וּנְקֹטֹתֶם בִּפְנֵיכֶם בְּכָל־רָעוֹתֵיכֶם אֲשֶׁר עֲשִׂיתֶם: וִידַעְתֶּם כִּי־אֲנִי יְהוָה

מד בַּעֲשׂוֹתִי אִתְּכֶם לְמַעַן שְׁמִי לֹא כְדַרְכֵיכֶם הָרָעִים וְכַעֲלִילוֹתֵיכֶם הַנִּשְׁחָתוֹת בֵּית יִשְׂרָאֵל נְאֻם אֲדֹנָי יֱהֹוִה:

כא א   וַיְהִי דְבַר־יְהוָה
ב אֵלַי לֵאמֹר: בֶּן־אָדָם שִׂים פָּנֶיךָ דֶּרֶךְ תֵּימָנָה וְהַטֵּף אֶל־דָּרוֹם וְהִנָּבֵא
ג אֶל־יַעַר הַשָּׂדֶה נֶגֶב: וְאָמַרְתָּ לְיַעַר הַנֶּגֶב שְׁמַע דְּבַר־יְהוָה כֹּה־אָמַר אֲדֹנָי יֱהֹוִה הִנְנִי מַצִּית־בְּךָ ׀ אֵשׁ וְאָכְלָה בְךָ כָל־עֵץ־לַח וְכָל־עֵץ יָבֵשׁ

ד לֹא־תִכְבֶּה לַהֶבֶת שַׁלְהֶבֶת וְנִצְרְבוּ־בָהּ כָּל־פָּנִים מִנֶּגֶב צָפוֹנָה: וְרָאוּ

ה כָל־בָּשָׂר כִּי אֲנִי יְהוָה בִּעַרְתִּיהָ לֹא תִכְבֶּה: וָאֹמַר אֲהָהּ אֲדֹנָי יֱהֹוִה
ו   הֵמָּה אֹמְרִים לִי הֲלֹא מְמַשֵּׁל מְשָׁלִים הוּא: וַיְהִי דְבַר־יְהוָה

ז אֵלַי לֵאמֹר: בֶּן־אָדָם שִׂים פָּנֶיךָ אֶל־יְרוּשָׁלַ͏ִם וְהַטֵּף אֶל־מִקְדָּשִׁים וְהִנָּבֵא
ח אֶל־אַדְמַת יִשְׂרָאֵל: וְאָמַרְתָּ לְאַדְמַת יִשְׂרָאֵל כֹּה אָמַר יְהוָה הִנְנִי

ט אֵלַיִךְ וְהוֹצֵאתִי חַרְבִּי מִתַּעְרָהּ וְהִכְרַתִּי מִמֵּךְ צַדִּיק וְרָשָׁע: יַעַן אֲשֶׁר הִכְרַתִּי מִמֵּךְ צַדִּיק וְרָשָׁע לָכֵן תֵּצֵא חַרְבִּי מִתַּעְרָהּ אֶל־כָּל־בָּשָׂר מִנֶּגֶב

י צָפוֹן: וְיָדְעוּ כָּל־בָּשָׂר כִּי אֲנִי יְהוָה הוֹצֵאתִי חַרְבִּי מִתַּעְרָהּ לֹא תָשׁוּב
יא עוֹד: וְאַתָּה בֶן־אָדָם הֵאָנַח בְּשִׁבְרוֹן מָתְנַיִם וּבִמְרִירוּת

יב תֵּאָנַח לְעֵינֵיהֶם: וְהָיָה כִּי־יֹאמְרוּ אֵלֶיךָ עַל־מָה אַתָּה נֶאֱנָח וְאָמַרְתָּ אֶל־שְׁמוּעָה כִי־בָאָה וְנָמֵס כָּל־לֵב וְרָפוּ כָל־יָדַיִם וְכִהֲתָה כָל־רוּחַ וְכָל־

יג בִּרְכַּיִם תֵּלַכְנָה מַּיִם הִנֵּה בָאָה וְנִהְיָתָה נְאֻם אֲדֹנָי יֱהֹוִה: וַיְהִי

יד דְבַר־יְהוָה אֵלַי לֵאמֹר: בֶּן־אָדָם הִנָּבֵא וְאָמַרְתָּ כֹּה אָמַר אֲדֹנָי אֱמֹר חֶרֶב חֶרֶב הוּחַדָּה וְגַם־מְרוּטָה: לְמַעַן טְבֹחַ טֶבַח הוּחַדָּה לְמַעַן־

טו הֱיֵה־לָהּ בָּרָק מֹרָטָּה אוֹ נָשִׂישׂ שֵׁבֶט בְּנִי מֹאֶסֶת כָּל־עֵץ: וַיִּתֵּן אֹתָהּ

טז לְמָרְטָה לִתְפֹּשׂ בַּכָּף הִיא־הוּחַדָּה חֶרֶב וְהִיא מֹרָטָּה לָתֵת אוֹתָהּ

יז בְּיַד־הוֹרֵג: זְעַק וְהֵילֵל בֶּן־אָדָם כִּי־הִיא הָיְתָה בְעַמִּי הִיא בְּכָל־נְשִׂיאֵי

21:2. This parable (vv. 1-4) is explained later (vv. 7-10).

21:7. Jerusalem, the victim, is south of Babylonia, the fire, and is filled with both righteous and wicked people, as a forest has different types of trees (*Rashi*).

21:9. After destroying Israel, the sword will annihilate other peoples.

21:12. The report that Jerusalem has fallen.

21:14. The twice-mentioned sword alludes to the sword of Nebuchadnezzar against Jerusalem and the sword of Ammon against Gedaliah (*Jeremiah* 40:13-41:3).

21:15. The staff with which God punished the Jews is so lethal and strong that it scorns every type of wood. This being so, how can we ever rejoice again?

21:16. The staff took the form of the sword with which

You will come to My holy mountain

⁴⁰ *But on My holy mountain, on the mountain of the height of Israel — the word of the Lord HASHEM/ELOHIM — there the entire House of Israel, all of it, will serve Me in the land; there I will accept them favorably, and there I will seek your tributes and the finest of your offerings, with all your consecrated things.* ⁴¹ *Through a satisfying aroma I will accept you favorably, when I remove you from the peoples and gather you from the lands where you were scattered; and I will be sanctified through you in the eyes of the nations.* ⁴² *Then you will know that I am HASHEM, when I bring you to the soil of Israel, to the land about which I raised My hand [in oath] to give to your forefathers.* ⁴³ *And there you will remember your ways and all your deeds by which you became defiled; and you will be disgusted with yourselves for all your evils that you have done.* ⁴⁴ *Then you will know that I am HASHEM, when I act with you for My Name's sake, and not in accord with your evil ways and your corrupt deeds, O House of Israel — the word of the Lord HASHEM/ELOHIM."*

21

A fire is coming

¹ The word of HASHEM came to me, saying, ² "Son of Man, direct your face toward the south and proclaim southward; prophesy against the forest-field of the south. * ³ Say to the forest of the south, 'Hear the word of HASHEM! Thus said the Lord HASHEM/ELOHIM: Behold, I am igniting a fire within you that will consume within you every fresh tree and every dry tree, an intense flame that will not be extinguished, and every face from south to north will be singed by it. ⁴ Then all flesh will see that I, HASHEM, have kindled it; it shall not be extinguished.' "

⁵ I then said, "Ah, Lord HASHEM/ELOHIM! They say about me, 'Behold, he invents parables!' "

God's sword against Jerusalem

⁶ So the word of HASHEM came to me, saying, ⁷ "Son of Man, direct your face toward Jerusalem * and proclaim to the Sanctuaries, and prophesy against the soil of Israel. ⁸ Say to the soil of Israel, 'Thus said HASHEM: Behold, I am against you! I will draw My sword from its scabbard and I will cut off righteous and wicked from [among] you. ⁹ Because I have cut off righteous and wicked from [among] you, therefore My sword will come out of its scabbard against all flesh from south [to] north. * ¹⁰ Then all flesh will know that I, HASHEM, have drawn My sword from its scabbard; it will never again return.'

The prophet's groan

¹¹ "And you, Son of Man, groan! With a shattering of the loins and with bitterness, groan before their eyes. ¹² And it shall be that when they say to you, 'For what are you groaning?' you shall say, 'Because of the report that is coming, * when every heart will melt, all hands will weaken, every spirit will grow faint and all knees will melt [like] water! Behold, it is coming; it will happen — the word of the Lord HASHEM/ELOHIM.' "

Prophecies of the swords

¹³ The word of HASHEM came to me, saying, ¹⁴ "Son of Man, prophesy and say: Thus said the Lord: Say: A sword, a sword* has been sharpened and even burnished. ¹⁵ That it may make a slaughter has it been sharpened, and that it may have a flash has it been burnished. Can we rejoice? The staff [that beats] My son scorns every wood!* ¹⁶ He gave it to be burnished, [the better] to hold in the hand; it* is the sword that has been sharpened and burnished, to place in the killer's hand.

¹⁷ "Cry out and wail, Son of Man, for it will come against My people, against all

---

the invaders slaughtered Israel.

יח יִשְׂרָאֵל אֶל־חֶרֶב הָיוּ אֶת־עַמִּי לָכֵן סְפֹק אֶל־יָרֵךְ: כִּי בֹחַן וּמָה אִם־

יט גַּם־שֵׁבֶט מֹאֶסֶת לֹא יִהְיֶה נְאֻם אֲדֹנָי יֱהֹוִה: וְאַתָּה בֶן־אָדָם
הִנָּבֵא וְהַךְ כַּף אֶל־כָּף וְתִכָּפֵל חֶרֶב שְׁלִישָׁתָה חֶרֶב חֲלָלִים הִיא חֶרֶב חָלָל

כ הַגָּדוֹל הַחֹדֶרֶת לָהֶם: לְמַעַן ׀ לָמוּג לֵב וְהַרְבֵּה הַמִּכְשֹׁלִים עַל כָּל־

כא שַׁעֲרֵיהֶם נָתַתִּי אִבְחַת־חָרֶב אָח עֲשׂוּיָה לְבָרָק מְעֻטָּה לְטָבַח: הִתְאַחֲדִי

כב הֵימִנִי הָשִׂימִי הַשְׂמִילִי אָנָה פָּנַיִךְ מֻעָדוֹת: וְגַם־אֲנִי אַכֶּה כַפִּי אֶל־כַּפִּי

כג וַהֲנִחֹתִי חֲמָתִי אֲנִי יְהֹוָה דִּבַּרְתִּי: וַיְהִי דְבַר־יְהֹוָה אֵלַי לֵאמֹר:

כד וְאַתָּה בֶן־אָדָם שִׂים־לְךָ ׀ שְׁנַיִם דְּרָכִים לָבוֹא חֶרֶב מֶלֶךְ־בָּבֶל מֵאֶרֶץ אֶחָד

כה יֵצְאוּ שְׁנֵיהֶם וְיָד בָּרֵא בְּרֹאשׁ דֶּרֶךְ־עִיר בָּרֵא: דֶּרֶךְ תָּשִׂים לָבוֹא חֶרֶב אֶת

כו רַבַּת בְּנֵי־עַמּוֹן וְאֶת־יְהוּדָה בִירוּשָׁלַ‍ִם בְּצוּרָה: כִּי־עָמַד מֶלֶךְ־בָּבֶל אֶל־
אֵם הַדֶּרֶךְ בְּרֹאשׁ שְׁנֵי הַדְּרָכִים לִקְסָם־קָסֶם קִלְקַל בַּחִצִּים שָׁאַל בַּתְּרָפִים

כז רָאָה בַּכָּבֵד: בִּימִינוֹ הָיָה ׀ הַקֶּסֶם יְרוּשָׁלַ‍ִם לָשׂוּם כָּרִים לִפְתֹּחַ פֶּה בְּרֶצַח
לְהָרִים קוֹל בִּתְרוּעָה לָשׂוּם כָּרִים עַל־שְׁעָרִים לִשְׁפֹּךְ סֹלְלָה לִבְנוֹת דָּיֵק:

כח וְהָיָה לָהֶם °כְּקֶסוֹם־ [°כִּקְסָם־ ק] שָׁוְא בְּעֵינֵיהֶם שְׁבֻעֵי שְׁבֻעוֹת לָהֶם וְהוּא־

כט מַזְכִּיר עָוֹן לְהִתָּפֵשׂ: לָכֵן כֹּה־אָמַר אֲדֹנָי יֱהֹוִה יַעַן הַזְכַּרְכֶם
עֲוֹנְכֶם בְּהִגָּלוֹת פִּשְׁעֵיכֶם לְהֵרָאוֹת חַטֹּאותֵיכֶם בְּכֹל עֲלִילוֹתֵיכֶם יַעַן

ל הִזָּכֶרְכֶם בַּכַּף תִּתָּפֵשׂוּ: וְאַתָּה חָלָל רָשָׁע נְשִׂיא יִשְׂרָאֵל

לא אֲשֶׁר־בָּא יוֹמוֹ בְּעֵת עֲוֹן קֵץ: כֹּה אָמַר אֲדֹנָי יֱהֹוִה הָסִיר
הַמִּצְנֶפֶת וְהָרִים הָעֲטָרָה זֹאת לֹא־זֹאת הַשָּׁפָלָה הַגְבֵּהַ וְהַגָּבֹהַ הַשְׁפִּיל:

לב עַוָּה עַוָּה עַוָּה אֲשִׂימֶנָּה גַּם־זֹאת לֹא הָיָה עַד־בֹּא אֲשֶׁר־לוֹ הַמִּשְׁפָּט

לג וּנְתַתִּיו: וְאַתָּה בֶן־אָדָם הִנָּבֵא וְאָמַרְתָּ כֹּה אָמַר אֲדֹנָי יֱהֹוִה אֶל־
בְּנֵי עַמּוֹן וְאֶל־חֶרְפָּתָם וְאָמַרְתָּ חֶרֶב חֶרֶב פְּתוּחָה לְטֶבַח מְרוּטָה לְהָכִיל

לד לְמַעַן בָּרָק: בַּחֲזוֹת לָךְ שָׁוְא בִּקְסָם־לָךְ כָּזָב לָתֵת אוֹתָךְ אֶל־צַוְּארֵי חַלְלֵי

לה רְשָׁעִים אֲשֶׁר־בָּא יוֹמָם בְּעֵת עֲוֹן קֵץ: הָשַׁב אֶל־תַּעְרָהּ בִּמְקוֹם אֲשֶׁר־

לו נִבְרֵאת בְּאֶרֶץ מְכֻרוֹתַיִךְ אֶשְׁפֹּט אֹתָךְ: וְשָׁפַכְתִּי עָלַיִךְ זַעְמִי בְּאֵשׁ עֶבְרָתִי

לז אָפִיחַ עָלָיִךְ וּנְתַתִּיךְ בְּיַד אֲנָשִׁים בֹּעֲרִים חָרָשֵׁי מַשְׁחִית: לָאֵשׁ תִּהְיֶה

21:17. A gesture of grief.

21:18. The burnished sword — a metaphor for the warnings of the prophets — was meant to frighten the people to repent. But what good would that be if the sword refrains from punishing the Jewish *rod*, i.e., nation? So, all the warnings will have been wasted (*Radak*).

21:19. After the two swords of verse 13, the people will be subjected to a third sword, which will be as powerful as the other two combined (*Rashi*).

20:20. It has been polished and sheathed to retain its sharpness.

21:21. You, Nebuchadnezzar's sword, are you headed south toward Judah or north toward Rabbah of Ammon?

21:26. Nebuchadnezzar shot arrows skyward to see whether they would turn towards Rabbah or Jerusalem, and looked to his magic charms for guidance.

21:27. See 4:2.

21:28. Despite the fact that all forty-nine divinations cast by Nebuchadnezzar pointed to Jerusalem as his target, the people of Judah attached no importance to those results (*Rashi*). Alternatively: The last phrase does not speak of numbers (שֶׁבַע, *seven*) but of oaths (שְׁבוּעָה, *oath*), and means: "[as if the Babylonians had] sworn oaths [not] to [harm] them" (*Radak*).

21:30. That is, the sin that finally brought about his ruination.

21:31. The crown of King Zedekiah will not remain with him much longer. King Jehoiachin, who has already been the princes of Israel; an assemblage with swords came against My people. There-fore, clap [hand] against thigh. * ¹⁸ For it is testing; what will be if [the sword] scorns even this rod?* It will not be — the word of the Lord HASHEM/ELOHIM.

¹⁹ "And you, Son of Man, prophesy and pound hand to hand: The third sword will be doubled, * the sword of the slain; it is the sword of the great massacre that will penetrate to them. ²⁰ In order to melt heart and increase obstacles, I have brought the dread of the sword to all their gates. Alas! It is readied to flash; it is sheathed for the slaughter. * ²¹ Concentrate yourself to the south, set yourself to the north — which way is your face destined?* ²² I, too, will pound My hand upon My hand, and I will put My wrath to rest; I, HASHEM, have spoken."

Two roads

²³ The word of HASHEM came to me, saying, ²⁴ "You, Son of Man, depict for yourself two paths on which the king of Babylonia's sword may come; both should emerge from one land. And choose a place; choose it at the crossroad near the city. ²⁵ Depict a road for the sword to go to Rabbah of the Children of Ammon, and to Judah, to the fortified Jerusalem. ²⁶ For the king of Babylonia stood at the crossroads, at the head of the two roads, to practice divination — he shot ar-rows, * inquired of the teraphim and looked into the liver. ²⁷ In his right hand the divination indicated Jerusalem, to set up battering rams, to give the order to mur-der, to raise the voice with shouting, to set up battering rams at the gates, to pour out a ramp, to build a siege tower. * ²⁸ But it was for them a meaningless divination in their eyes, [even though they had cast] seven times seven [divinations, and all pointed] to them; * and this recalled [their] iniquity, that they might be captured.

²⁹ Therefore, thus said the Lord HASHEM/ELOHIM: Since you cause your iniquity to be recalled, as your sins are revealed, as your transgressions are seen through all your deeds, because you are recalled [for your evilness], you will be captured by the hand [of Nebuchadnezzar].

Zedekiah is castigated

³⁰ And you, defiled and wicked one, prince of Israel, whose day has come, at the time of the final iniquity * — ³¹ thus said the Lord HASHEM/ELOHIM: Re-move the turban, lift off the crown! This will not remain as such: The de-graded will be exalted and the exalted will be degraded. * ³² Desolate, deso-late, desolate will I make [Jerusalem]. Such a thing had never been, * until the coming of the executor of judgment, when I will deliver him [into his hands]."

³³ "Now you, Son of Man, prophesy and say:

Thus said the Lord HASHEM/ELOHIM concerning the Children of Ammon and concerning their scorn.'* Say, 'A sword, an open sword, is burnished for slaughter, to consume, in order to flash * — ³⁴ while worthless [prophecies] are seen for you, while falsehood is divined for you — to place you with the necks of the slain wicked ones * whose day has come at the time of the final iniquity. ³⁵ [After the sword] has been returned to its scabbard, * in the place where you originated, in your native land, I shall punish you! ³⁶ I will pour out My fury upon you; I will fan the fire of My fury against you; I will place you in the hand of brutish men, artisans of destruction. ³⁷ You will be given to the

---

exiled, will be shown clemency (see *II Kings* 25:27-30), while Zedekiah, who currently occupies the throne, will be disgraced, being forced to watch all his sons slaugh-tered. Then he will be blinded and led off to Babylonia (*Radak*).

21:32. Although Zedekiah's predecessors were far from righteous, they were not punished with such degra-dation.

21:33. They rejoiced and taunted the Israelites when Nebuchadnezzar decided to attack Jerusalem instead of Rabbah.

The flashing sword would frighten its intended victims.

21:34. Despite the false prophecies that reassure you of your immunity to Nebuchadnezzar's sword, your turn for the slaughter will come soon after that of the Jews.

21:35. After the slaughter in Jerusalem.

כב

HAFTARAS
ACHREI
for
Sephardim

HAFTARAS
KEDOSHIM
for
Ashkenazim
22:1-16

א לְאָכְלָ֤ה דָּמֵךְ֙ יִהְיֶ֣ה בְּת֣וֹךְ הָאָ֔רֶץ לֹ֥א תִזָּכֵ֖רִי כִּ֛י אֲנִ֥י יהו֖ה דִּבַּֽרְתִּי: וַיְהִ֥י

ב דְבַר־יהו֖ה אֵלַ֥י לֵאמֹֽר: וְאַתָּ֣ה בֶן־אָדָ֔ם הֲתִשְׁפֹּ֥ט הֲתִשְׁפֹּ֖ט אֶת־עִ֣יר

ג הַדָּמִ֑ים וְה֣וֹדַעְתָּ֔הּ אֵ֖ת כָּל־תּוֹעֲבוֹתֶֽיהָ: וְאָמַרְתָּ֗ כֹּ֤ה אָמַר֙ אֲדֹנָ֣י יֱהֹוִ֔ה
עִ֣יר שֹׁפֶ֥כֶת דָּ֖ם בְּתוֹכָ֑הּ לָב֣וֹא עִתָּ֑הּ וְעָשְׂתָ֧ה גִלּוּלִ֛ים עָלֶ֖יהָ לְטָמְאָֽה:

ד בְּדָמֵ֤ךְ אֲשֶׁר־שָׁפַכְתְּ֙ אָשַׁ֔מְתְּ וּבְגִלּוּלַ֥יִךְ אֲשֶׁר־עָשִׂ֖ית טָמֵ֑את וַתַּקְרִ֣יבִי
יָמַ֔יִךְ וַתָּב֖וֹא עַד־שְׁנוֹתָ֑יִךְ עַל־כֵּ֗ן נְתַתִּ֤יךְ חֶרְפָּה֙ לַגּוֹיִ֔ם וְקַלָּסָ֖ה לְכָל־

ה הָאֲרָצֽוֹת: הַקְּרֹב֛וֹת וְהָרְחֹק֖וֹת מִמֵּ֑ךְ יִתְקַלְּסוּ־בָ֔ךְ טְמֵאַ֥ת הַשֵּׁ֖ם רַבַּ֥ת

ו הַמְּהוּמָֽה: הִנֵּה֙ נְשִׂיאֵ֣י יִשְׂרָאֵ֔ל אִ֥ישׁ לִזְרֹע֖וֹ הָ֥יוּ בָ֖ךְ לְמַ֥עַן שְׁפָךְ־דָּֽם:

ז אָ֤ב וָאֵם֙ הֵקַ֣לּוּ בָ֔ךְ לַגֵּ֛ר עָשׂ֥וּ בַעֹ֖שֶׁק בְּתוֹכֵ֑ךְ יָת֥וֹם וְאַלְמָנָ֖ה ה֥וֹנוּ בָֽךְ:

ח-ט קׇדָשַׁ֣י בָּזִ֔ית וְאֶת־שַׁבְּתֹתַ֖י חִלָּֽלְתְּ: אַנְשֵׁ֥י רָכִ֛יל הָ֥יוּ בָ֖ךְ לְמַ֣עַן שְׁפׇךְ־דָּ֑ם

י וְאֶל־הֶֽהָרִים֙ אָ֣כְלוּ בָ֔ךְ זִמָּ֖ה עָשׂ֥וּ בְתוֹכֵֽךְ: עֶרְוַת־אָ֖ב גִּלָּה־בָ֑ךְ טְמֵאַ֥ת

יא הַנִּדָּ֖ה עִנּוּ־בָֽךְ: וְאִ֣ישׁ ׀ אֶת־אֵ֣שֶׁת רֵעֵ֗הוּ עָשָׂה֙ תּֽוֹעֵבָ֔ה וְאִ֗ישׁ אֶת־כַּלָּתוֹ֙

יב טִמֵּ֣א בְזִמָּ֔ה וְאִ֛ישׁ אֶת־אֲחֹת֥וֹ בַת־אָבִ֖יו עִנָּה־בָֽךְ: שֹׁ֣חַד לָֽקְחוּ־בָ֖ךְ לְמַ֣עַן
שְׁפׇךְ־דָּ֑ם נֶ֧שֶׁךְ וְתַרְבִּ֣ית לָקַ֗חַתְּ וַתְּבַצְּעִ֤י רֵעַ֙יִךְ֙ בַּעֹ֔שֶׁק וְאֹתִ֣י שָׁכַ֔חַתְּ

יג נְאֻ֖ם אֲדֹנָ֥י יֱהֹוִֽה: וְהִנֵּה֙ הִכֵּ֣יתִי כַפִּ֔י אֶל־בִּצְעֵ֖ךְ אֲשֶׁ֣ר עָשִׂ֑ית וְעַל־דָּמֵ֔ךְ

יד אֲשֶׁ֥ר הָי֖וּ בְּתוֹכֵֽךְ: הֲיַעֲמֹ֤ד לִבֵּךְ֙ אִם־תֶּחֱזַ֣קְנָה יָדַ֔יִךְ לַיָּמִ֕ים אֲשֶׁ֥ר אֲנִ֖י

טו עֹשֶׂ֣ה אוֹתָ֑ךְ אֲנִ֧י יהו֛ה דִּבַּ֖רְתִּי וְעָשִֽׂיתִי: וַהֲפִיצוֹתִ֤י אוֹתָךְ֙ בַּגּוֹיִ֔ם

טז וְזֵֽרִיתִ֖יךְ בָּאֲרָצ֑וֹת וַהֲתִמֹּתִ֥י טֻמְאָתֵ֖ךְ מִמֵּֽךְ: וְנִחַ֥לְתְּ בָּ֖ךְ לְעֵינֵ֣י גוֹיִ֑ם
וְיָדַ֖עַתְּ כִּֽי־אֲנִ֥י יהוֽה: ◄ וַיְהִ֥י דְבַר־יהו֖ה אֵלַ֥י לֵאמֹֽר:

יז בֶּן־אָדָ֗ם הָֽיוּ־לִ֥י בֵֽית־יִשְׂרָאֵ֖ל לְסוֹג [לְ֟סִיג ק] כֻּלָּ֗ם נְחֹ֤שֶׁת וּבְדִיל֙

יח וּבַרְזֶ֣ל וְעוֹפֶ֔רֶת בְּת֣וֹךְ כּ֔וּר סִגִ֥ים כֶּ֖סֶף הָיֽוּ: לָכֵ֗ן כֹּ֤ה אָמַר֙

יט אֲדֹנָ֣י יֱהֹוִ֔ה יַ֛עַן הֱי֥וֹת כֻּלְּכֶ֖ם לְסִגִ֑ים לָכֵ֗ן הִנְנִ֤י קֹבֵץ֙ אֶתְכֶ֔ם אֶל־תּ֖וֹךְ

כ יְרוּשָׁלָֽ͏ִם: קְבֻצַ֣ת כֶּ֡סֶף וּ֠נְחֹ֠שֶׁת וּבַרְזֶ֨ל וְעוֹפֶ֜רֶת וּבְדִ֗יל אֶל־תּ֣וֹךְ כּ֔וּר
לָפַֽחַת־עָלָ֥יו אֵ֖שׁ לְהַנְתִּ֑יךְ כֵּ֤ן אֶקְבֹּץ֙ בְּאַפִּ֣י וּבַחֲמָתִ֔י וְהִנַּחְתִּ֥י וְהִתַּכְתִּ֖י

כא אֶתְכֶֽם: וְכִנַּסְתִּ֣י אֶתְכֶ֔ם וְנָפַחְתִּ֥י עֲלֵיכֶ֖ם בְּאֵ֣שׁ עֶבְרָתִ֑י וְנִתַּכְתֶּ֖ם בְּתוֹכָֽהּ:

כב כְּהִתּ֥וּךְ כֶּ֙סֶף֙ בְּת֣וֹךְ כּ֔וּר כֵּ֖ן תֻּתְּכ֣וּ בְתוֹכָ֑הּ וִֽידַעְתֶּם֙ כִּֽי־אֲנִ֣י יהו֔ה

כג שָׁפַ֥כְתִּי חֲמָתִ֖י עֲלֵיכֶֽם: וַיְהִ֥י דְבַר־יהו֖ה אֵלַ֥י לֵאמֹֽר:

כד בֶּן־אָדָ֕ם אֱמׇר־לָ֕הּ אַ֣תְּ אֶ֔רֶץ לֹ֥א מְטֹהָרָ֖ה הִ֑יא לֹ֥א גֻשְׁמָ֖הּ בְּי֥וֹם זָֽעַם:

21:37. It will be forgotten and unavenged (*Radak*).

22:5. You will be taunted as a result of your catastrophic defeat (*Radak*).

22:9-12. This list of transgressions is a mixture of sins between man and God and man and his fellow man. This is to show that man's obligations to God and man cannot be independent of one another (*Rabbi J. Breuer*).

22:10. A euphemism for incest with one's mother or stepmother.

22:11-12. Moses warned Israel that imitation of the sexual perversions of the Canaanites would cause them to be evicted from the land (see *Leviticus* 18:28).

22:13. An expression of consternation, as it were.

22:24. That is, cleansed. You were found to be sullied with sin on the day of God's fury (*Rashi*).

fire to consume; your blood will be [swallowed] into the midst of the land; *
you will not be remembered; for I, HASHEM, have spoken."

22

*The
denunciation
of Jerusalem*

¹ The word of HASHEM came to me, saying, ² "Now you, Son of Man, won't
you rebuke? Won't you rebuke the city of bloodshed, and inform her of all her
abominations? ³ Say:

Thus said the Lord HASHEM/ELOHIM: O city that sheds blood in her midst,
hastening her time [of judgment], that fashioned idols within herself for
contamination: ⁴ Through the blood that you shed have you become guilty,
and through your idols that you fashioned you have become contaminated;
[thus] you brought your [judgment] days near and reached the limit of your
years. Therefore, I have made you a shame to the nations, and a disgrace
for all the lands. ⁵ Those near and those far from you will degrade you [as]

*Selfish
leaders*

'contaminated of name, great of confusion.'* ⁶ Behold, the princes of Israel:
Each [acted] within you for the sake of his own power, in order to shed blood.
⁷ Father and mother have they disparaged within you; toward the stranger
in your midst have they acted oppressively; orphan and widow have they
wronged within you. ⁸ My sanctities have you scorned and My Sabbaths
have you desecrated. ⁹ Talebearers were among you, in order to shed
blood; * they partook [of idolatrous sacrifices] upon the mountains within
you; they plotted evil schemes in your midst. ¹⁰ They uncovered a father's
nakedness * within you; they coerced women among you during their

*Pervasive
immorality*

menstrual impurity. ¹¹ A man would commit abominations against his
neighbor's wife; * a man would defile his daughter-in-law with licentiousness; a man would coerce his sister, his father's daughter, within you.
¹² They took bribery within you in order to shed blood; you took usury and
interest, and enriched your friends with extorted money. You have forgotten
Me — the word of the Lord HASHEM/ELOHIM.

¹³ Now, behold, I have pounded My hand* because of your robbery that
you committed and because of your bloodshed that was in your midst.
¹⁴ Will your heart endure, will your hands be strong, in the days when I shall
deal with you? I am HASHEM; I have spoken and I shall carry it out. ¹⁵ I will
scatter you among the nations and disperse you among the lands; and I will
eliminate your contamination from you. ¹⁶ You will be caused to tremble
before the eyes of the nations; then you will know that I am HASHEM."

¹⁷ The word of HASHEM came to me, saying, ¹⁸ "Son of Man, the House of Israel
has become dross to Me; they are all copper, tin, iron, and lead in the midst of a

*Dross in the
furnace*

smelting furnace; they are the dross of silver.

¹⁹ Therefore, thus said the Lord HASHEM/ELOHIM: Because you have all
become dross, therefore, behold, I am gathering you into the midst of
Jerusalem, ²⁰ like the gathering of silver, copper, iron, lead and tin into the
midst of a smelting furnace, to fan the fire onto it to melt [it] down; so will
I gather you in My anger and in My wrath, and I will emplace you and melt
you down. ²¹ I will gather you and fan the fire of My fury upon you, and you
will be melted down within it. ²² As silver is melted down in the midst of a
furnace, so will you be melted down in its midst; then you will know that I,
HASHEM, have poured out My wrath upon you."

²³ The word of HASHEM came to me, saying, ²⁴ "Son of Man, say to her:

*The sins of
the land*

You are a land that has not been cleansed, that has not been rained upon *
on the day of fury.

כה קֶשֶׁר נְבִיאֶיהָ בְּתוֹכָהּ כַּאֲרִי שׁוֹאֵג טֹרֵף טָרֶף נֶפֶשׁ אָכָלוּ חֹסֶן וִיקָר יִקָּחוּ

כו אַלְמְנוֹתֶיהָ הִרְבּוּ בְתוֹכָהּ: כֹּהֲנֶיהָ חָמְסוּ תוֹרָתִי וַיְחַלְּלוּ קָדָשַׁי בֵּין־קֹדֶשׁ לְחֹל לֹא הִבְדִּילוּ וּבֵין־הַטָּמֵא לְטָהוֹר לֹא הוֹדִיעוּ וּמִשַּׁבְּתוֹתַי הֶעְלִימוּ

כז עֵינֵיהֶם וָאֵחַל בְּתוֹכָם: שָׂרֶיהָ בְקִרְבָּהּ כִּזְאֵבִים טֹרְפֵי טָרֶף לִשְׁפָּךְ־דָּם

כח לְאַבֵּד נְפָשׁוֹת לְמַעַן בְּצֹעַ בָּצַע: וּנְבִיאֶיהָ טָחוּ לָהֶם תָּפֵל חֹזִים שָׁוְא

כט וְקֹסְמִים לָהֶם כָּזָב אֹמְרִים כֹּה אָמַר אֲדֹנָי יֱהֹוִה וַיהֹוָה לֹא דִבֵּר: עַם הָאָרֶץ עָשְׁקוּ עֹשֶׁק וְגָזְלוּ גָּזֵל וְעָנִי וְאֶבְיוֹן הוֹנוּ וְאֶת־הַגֵּר עָשְׁקוּ בְּלֹא מִשְׁפָּט:

ל וָאֲבַקֵּשׁ מֵהֶם אִישׁ גֹּדֵר־גָּדֵר וְעֹמֵד בַּפֶּרֶץ לְפָנַי בְּעַד הָאָרֶץ לְבִלְתִּי

לא שַׁחֲתָהּ וְלֹא מָצָאתִי: וָאֶשְׁפֹּךְ עֲלֵיהֶם זַעְמִי בְּאֵשׁ עֶבְרָתִי כִּלִּיתִים דַּרְכָּם בְּרֹאשָׁם נָתַתִּי נְאֻם אֲדֹנָי יֱהֹוִה:

כג א וַיְהִי דְבַר־יְהֹוָה אֵלַי לֵאמֹר:

ב־ג בֶּן־אָדָם שְׁתַּיִם נָשִׁים בְּנוֹת אֵם־אַחַת הָיוּ: וַתִּזְנֶינָה בְמִצְרַיִם בִּנְעוּרֵיהֶן זָנוּ

ד שָׁמָּה מֹעֲכוּ שְׁדֵיהֶן וְשָׁם עִשּׂוּ דַּדֵּי בְּתוּלֵיהֶן: וּשְׁמוֹתָן אָהֳלָה הַגְּדוֹלָה וְאָהֳלִיבָה אֲחוֹתָהּ וַתִּהְיֶינָה לִי וַתֵּלַדְנָה בָּנִים וּבָנוֹת וּשְׁמוֹתָן שֹׁמְרוֹן

ה אָהֳלָה וִירוּשָׁלַ‍ִם אָהֳלִיבָה: וַתִּזֶן אָהֳלָה תַּחְתָּי וַתַּעְגַּב עַל־מְאַהֲבֶיהָ אֶל־

ו אַשּׁוּר קְרוֹבִים: לְבֻשֵׁי תְכֵלֶת פַּחוֹת וּסְגָנִים בַּחוּרֵי חֶמֶד כֻּלָּם פָּרָשִׁים

ז רֹכְבֵי סוּסִים: וַתִּתֵּן תַּזְנוּתֶיהָ עֲלֵיהֶם מִבְחַר בְּנֵי־אַשּׁוּר כֻּלָּם וּבְכֹל אֲשֶׁר־

ח עָגְבָה בְּכָל־גִּלּוּלֵיהֶם נִטְמָאָה: וְאֶת־תַּזְנוּתֶיהָ מִמִּצְרַיִם לֹא עָזָבָה כִּי אוֹתָהּ שָׁכְבוּ בִנְעוּרֶיהָ וְהֵמָּה עִשּׂוּ דַּדֵּי בְתוּלֶיהָ וַיִּשְׁפְּכוּ תַזְנוּתָם עָלֶיהָ:

ט־י לָכֵן נְתַתִּיהָ בְּיַד־מְאַהֲבֶיהָ בְּיַד בְּנֵי אַשּׁוּר אֲשֶׁר עָגְבָה עֲלֵיהֶם: הֵמָּה גִּלּוּ עֶרְוָתָהּ בָּנֶיהָ וּבְנוֹתֶיהָ לָקָחוּ וְאוֹתָהּ בַּחֶרֶב הָרָגוּ וַתְּהִי־שֵׁם לַנָּשִׁים וּשְׁפוּטִים עָשׂוּ בָהּ:

יא וַתֵּרֶא אֲחוֹתָהּ אָהֳלִיבָה וַתַּשְׁחֵת עַגְבָתָהּ

יב מִמֶּנָּה וְאֶת־תַּזְנוּתֶיהָ מִזְּנוּנֵי אֲחוֹתָהּ: אֶל־בְּנֵי אַשּׁוּר עָגָבָה פַּחוֹת וּסְגָנִים

יג קְרֹבִים לְבֻשֵׁי מִכְלוֹל פָּרָשִׁים רֹכְבֵי סוּסִים בַּחוּרֵי חֶמֶד כֻּלָּם: וָאֵרֶא כִּי

יד נִטְמָאָה דֶּרֶךְ אֶחָד לִשְׁתֵּיהֶן: וַתּוֹסֶף אֶל־תַּזְנוּתֶיהָ וַתֵּרֶא אַנְשֵׁי מְחֻקֶּה עַל־

טו הַקִּיר צַלְמֵי כַשְׂדִּיים [כַשְׂדִּים ק] חֲקֻקִים בַּשָּׁשַׁר: חֲגוֹרֵי אֵזוֹר בְּמָתְנֵיהֶם סְרוּחֵי טְבוּלִים בְּרָאשֵׁיהֶם מַרְאֵה שָׁלִישִׁים כֻּלָּם דְּמוּת בְּנֵי־בָבֶל

טז כַּשְׂדִּים אֶרֶץ מוֹלַדְתָּם: וַתַּעְגַּב [וַתַּעְגְּבָה ק] עֲלֵיהֶם לְמַרְאֵה עֵינֶיהָ

22:25. After a lion frightens his prey with a roar, he kills and devours it. Similarly the false prophets would shout out their false messages, which would lead to the deaths of those who heeded them (*Radak*).

22:26. The *Kohanim* had been charged with instructing the people in the ways of the Torah (see *Leviticus* 10:10-11), but they ignored their duty, thus depriving the people of the privilege of studying the Torah.

22:28. See 13:8-12.

23:3. In a slashing indictment of Israel's betrayal of Him, God likens the nation to prostitutes, whose infidelity earns the contempt of all, even their paramours.

Israel's two branches, Judah and Ephraim, began as a united nation in Egypt. But even there they were promiscuous, as described in the following metaphor, i.e., they learned from the idolatrous practices of Egypt.

23:8. King Hoshea's political alliance with Egypt [*II Kings* 17:4] maintained Israel's ancient affinity to Egypt (*Rashi*).

23:9. See *II Kings* 17:4-6.

23:10. She became an example of the consequences of disloyalty and the hatred it engenders among others.

23:12. King Ahaz of Judah ingratiated himself to Assyria, using the Temple treasury to purchase Assyria's military assistance [*II Kings* 16:7-8] (*Rashi*).

²⁵ *"There is a conspiracy of her prophets in her midst, like a roaring lion that tears [its] prey;* for they have devoured souls, they have taken away [Jerusalem's] treasure and worth, they have increased her widows in her midst. ²⁶ Her priests robbed My Torah* and desecrated My sanctities; they did not distinguish between holy and profane, and they did not make known the difference between contaminated and purified; they hid their eyes from My Sabbaths, and I became profaned among them. ²⁷ Her officers within her are like wolves who tear prey — to shed blood, to destroy souls, for the sake of unjust gain. ²⁸ And her prophets smeared plaster for them,* for they see worthless [visions] and they divine falsehood for them. They say, 'Thus said the Lord HASHEM/ELOHIM,' when HASHEM did not speak.*

²⁹ "The people of the land have perpetrated oppression and robbed loot; they have wronged the poor and the needy and oppressed the stranger without justice. ³⁰ From among them I sought a man who could build a fence and stand in the breach before Me, for the sake of the land, so that it might not be destroyed, but I did not find [anyone]. ³¹ So I poured out My wrath over them, and consumed them with the flame of My fury; I have placed [the consequences of] their [evil] way upon their head — the word of the Lord HASHEM/ELOHIM."*

23

The two sisters

¹ The word of HASHEM came to me, saying, ² "Son of Man: There were two women, who were daughters of one mother. ³ They indulged in promiscuity in Egypt; they were promiscuous in their youth.* There their bosoms were pressed and there their virgin breasts were squeezed. ⁴ Their names were Oholah, the older one, and Oholibah, her sister. They became Mine and bore sons and daughters. As for their [true] names: Samaria is Oholah and Jerusalem is Oholibah.

Oholah's adulteries

⁵ "Now Oholah was adulterous under Me, for she lusted for her paramours, for neighboring Assyria, ⁶ [who were] clothed in royal blue, governors and rulers, pleasant young men all of them, horsemen riding horses. ⁷ And she bestowed her adulterous favors upon them, the choicest of Assyria's sons all of them; and for whomever she lusted, with all their idols she became defiled. ⁸ But she did not forsake her promiscuity with Egypt,* for they had lain with her in her youth; they had squeezed her virgin breasts and they had poured their *Oholah's* philandering upon her. ⁹ Therefore, I delivered her into the hand of her *punishment* paramours, into the hands of Assyria's sons for whom she lusted.* ¹⁰ They uncovered her nakedness — they took her sons and daughters, and they killed her by the sword. Thus she became a byword among women, and they executed punishments against her.*

Oholibah's adulteries

¹¹ "Now her sister Oholibah observed and was even more corrupt in her lusting than she, and in her adulteries more than her sister's adulteries. ¹² She lusted for Assyria's sons,* neighboring governors and rulers, clothed in splendor, horsemen riding horses, pleasant young men all of them.

¹³ "Then I saw that she [also] had become defiled, the two of them [had taken] the same way, ¹⁴ and that she had even added to her adulteries — for she saw engraved men upon the wall, images of Chaldeans engraved in bright color, ¹⁵ girded with belts upon their loins, with hanging turbans upon their heads, all of them resembling captains, the likeness of Babylonia's children, the Chaldeans, [from] the land of their birth; ¹⁶ she lusted for them because of what her eyes had seen,

יז וַתִּשְׁלַ֨ח מַלְאָכִ֤ים אֲלֵיהֶם֙ כַּשְׂדִּ֔ימָה וַיָּבֹ֧אוּ אֵלֶ֛יהָ בְנֵֽי־בָבֶ֖ל לְמִשְׁכַּ֣ב

יח דֹּדִ֑ים וַיְטַמְּא֥וּ אוֹתָ֖הּ בְּתַזְנוּתָ֑ם וַתִּטְמָא־בָ֔ם וַתֵּ֥קַע נַפְשָׁ֖הּ מֵהֶֽם: וַתְּגַ֖ל תַּזְנוּתֶ֑יהָ וַתְּגַ֖ל אֶת־עֶרְוָתָ֑הּ וַתֵּ֤קַע נַפְשִׁי֙ מֵֽעָלֶ֔יהָ כַּאֲשֶׁ֛ר נָקְעָ֥ה נַפְשִׁ֖י

יט מֵעַ֥ל אֲחוֹתָֽהּ: וַתַּרְבֶּ֖ה אֶת־תַּזְנוּתֶ֑יהָ לִזְכֹּר֙ אֶת־יְמֵ֣י נְעוּרֶ֔יהָ אֲשֶׁ֥ר זָנְתָ֖ה

כ בְּאֶ֥רֶץ מִצְרָֽיִם: וַתַּעְגְּבָ֖ה עַ֣ל פִּֽלַגְשֵׁיהֶ֑ם אֲשֶׁ֤ר בְּשַׂר־חֲמוֹרִים֙ בְּשָׂרָ֔ם

כא וְזִרְמַ֥ת סוּסִ֖ים זִרְמָתָֽם: וַתִּפְקְדִ֕י אֵ֖ת זִמַּ֣ת נְעוּרָ֑יִךְ בַּעְשׂ֤וֹת מִמִּצְרַ֙יִם֙

כב דַּדַּ֔יִךְ לְמַ֖עַן שְׁדֵ֥י נְעוּרָֽיִךְ: לָכֵ֣ן אָהֳלִיבָ֗ה כֹּֽה־אָמַר֮ אֲדֹנָ֣י

יְהֹוִה֒ הִנְנִ֨י מֵעִ֤יר אֶת־מְאַהֲבַ֙יִךְ֙ עָלַ֔יִךְ אֵ֥ת אֲשֶׁר־נָקְעָ֖ה נַפְשֵׁ֣ךְ מֵהֶ֑ם

כג וַהֲבֵאתִ֥ים עָלַ֖יִךְ מִסָּבִֽיב: בְּנֵ֧י בָבֶ֣ל וְכׇל־כַּשְׂדִּ֗ים פְּק֤וֹד וְשׁ֙וֹעַ֙ וְק֔וֹעַ כׇּל־ בְּנֵ֥י אַשּׁ֖וּר אוֹתָ֑ם בַּח֤וּרֵי חֶ֙מֶד֙ פַּחוֹ֤ת וּסְגָנִים֙ כֻּלָּ֔ם שָֽׁלִשִׁ֖ים וּקְרוּאִ֑ים

כד רֹכְבֵ֥י סוּסִ֖ים כֻּלָּֽם: וּבָ֣אוּ עָלַ֗יִךְ הֹ֚צֶן רֶ֣כֶב וְגַלְגַּ֔ל וּבִקְהַ֣ל עַמִּ֔ים צִנָּ֥ה וּמָגֵ֖ן וְקוֹבַ֛ע יָשִׂ֥ימוּ עָלַ֖יִךְ סָבִ֑יב וְנָתַתִּ֤י לִפְנֵיהֶם֙ מִשְׁפָּ֔ט וּשְׁפָט֖וּךְ בְּמִשְׁפְּטֵיהֶֽם:

כה וְנָתַתִּ֨י קִנְאָתִ֜י בָּ֗ךְ וְעָשׂ֤וּ אוֹתָךְ֙ בְּחֵמָ֔ה אַפֵּ֥ךְ וְאׇזְנַ֖יִךְ יָסִ֑ירוּ וְאַחֲרִיתֵ֖ךְ בַּחֶ֣רֶב תִּפּ֑וֹל הֵ֗מָּה בָּנַ֤יִךְ וּבְנוֹתַ֙יִךְ֙ יִקָּ֔חוּ וְאַחֲרִיתֵ֖ךְ תֵּאָכֵ֥ל בָּאֵֽשׁ:

כו-כז וְהִפְשִׁיט֖וּךְ אֶת־בְּגָדָ֑יִךְ וְלָקְח֖וּ כְּלֵ֥י תִפְאַרְתֵּֽךְ: וְהִשְׁבַּתִּ֤י זִמָּתֵךְ֙ מִמֵּ֔ךְ וְאֶת־ זְנוּתֵ֖ךְ מֵאֶ֣רֶץ מִצְרָ֑יִם וְלֹֽא־תִשְׂאִ֤י עֵינַ֙יִךְ֙ אֲלֵיהֶ֔ם וּמִצְרַ֖יִם לֹ֥א תִזְכְּרִי־

כח ע֖וֹד: כִּ֣י כֹ֤ה אָמַר֙ אֲדֹנָ֣י יְהֹוִ֔ה הִנְנִי֙ נֹֽתְנָ֔ךְ בְּיַ֖ד אֲשֶׁ֣ר

כט שָׂנֵ֑את בְּיַ֖ד אֲשֶׁר־נָקְעָ֥ה נַפְשֵׁ֖ךְ מֵהֶֽם: וְעָשׂ֨וּ אוֹתָ֤ךְ בְּשִׂנְאָה֙ וְלָקְח֣וּ כׇּל־ יְגִיעֵ֔ךְ וַעֲזָב֖וּךְ עֵירֹ֣ם וְעֶרְיָ֑ה וְנִגְלָה֙ עֶרְוַ֣ת זְנוּנַ֔יִךְ וְזִמָּתֵ֖ךְ וְתַזְנוּתָֽיִךְ: עָשֹׂ֥ה

ל-לא אֵ֖לֶּה לָ֑ךְ בִּזְנוֹתֵ֣ךְ אַחֲרֵ֣י גוֹיִ֔ם עַ֥ל אֲשֶׁר־נִטְמֵ֖את בְּגִלּֽוּלֵיהֶֽם: בְּדֶ֤רֶךְ אֲחוֹתֵ֖ךְ הָלָ֑כְתְּ וְנָתַתִּ֥י כוֹסָ֖הּ בְּיָדֵֽךְ: כֹּ֥ה אָמַר֮ אֲדֹנָ֣י

לב יְהֹוִה֒ כּ֤וֹס אֲחוֹתֵךְ֙ תִּשְׁתִּ֔י הָעֲמֻקָּ֖ה וְהָרְחָבָ֑ה תִּֽהְיֶ֥ה לִצְחֹ֖ק וּלְלַ֑עַג

לג מִרְבָּ֖ה לְהָכִֽיל: שִׁכָּר֤וֹן וְיָגוֹן֙ תִּמָּלֵ֔אִי כּ֖וֹס שַׁמָּ֣ה וּשְׁמָמָ֑ה כּ֖וֹס אֲחוֹתֵ֥ךְ

לד שֹׁמְרֽוֹן: וְשָׁתִ֨ית אוֹתָ֜הּ וּמָצִ֗ית וְאֶת־חֲרָשֶׂ֛יהָ תְּגָרֵ֖מִי וְשָׁדַ֣יִךְ תְּנַתֵּ֑קִי כִּ֚י אֲנִ֣י

לה דִבַּ֔רְתִּי נְאֻ֖ם אֲדֹנָ֥י יְהֹוִֽה: לָכֵ֗ן כֹּ֤ה אָמַר֙ אֲדֹנָ֣י יְהֹוִ֔ה יַ֚עַן שָׁכַ֣חַתְּ אוֹתִ֔י וַתַּשְׁלִ֥יכִי אוֹתִ֖י אַחֲרֵ֣י גַוֵּ֑ךְ וְגַם־אַ֛תְּ שְׂאִ֥י

לו זִמָּתֵ֖ךְ וְאֶת־תַּזְנוּתָֽיִךְ: וַיֹּ֤אמֶר יְהֹוָה֙ אֵלַ֔י בֶּן־אָדָ֕ם הֲתִשְׁפּ֥וֹט אֶת־אׇהֳלָ֖ה וְאֶת־אׇהֳלִיבָ֑ה וְהַגֵּ֣ד לָהֶ֔ן אֵ֖ת תּוֹעֲבוֹתֵיהֶֽן:

לז כִּ֣י נִאֵ֗פוּ וְדָם֙ בִּֽידֵיהֶ֔ן וְאֶת־גִּלּֽוּלֵיהֶ֖ן נִאֵ֑פוּ וְגַ֤ם אֶת־בְּנֵיהֶן֙ אֲשֶׁ֣ר יָֽלְדוּ־לִ֔י הֶעֱבִ֥ירוּ

לח לָהֶ֖ם לְאׇכְלָֽה: ע֥וֹד זֹ֖את עָ֣שׂוּ לִ֑י טִמְּא֤וּ אֶת־מִקְדָּשִׁי֙ בַּיּ֣וֹם הַה֔וּא

23:17. King Hezekiah enthusiastically received a Babylonian delegation (*II Kings* 20:12-13), but generations later the kings Jehoiachin and Zedekiah rebelled against Babylonia (*Rashi*).

23:19. Zedekiah sent to Egypt seeking military assistance [17:15] (*Rashi*).

23:25. The heathen nations punished unfaithful wives by mutilating their faces. This is used as a metaphor for Israel's high priesthood and the monarchy, which will cease as a result of the nation's sins (*Rashi*).

sending emissaries to them, to Chaldea; [17] and Babylonia's sons came to her for a bed of love, defiling her with their philandering; she became defiled through them, but then her soul became repulsed from them. * [18] She revealed her harlotries, and she revealed her nakedness — so My soul became repulsed from her as My soul had become repulsed from her sister.

[19] "Then she increased her adulteries, remembering the days of her youth, when she was promiscuous in the land of Egypt. * [20] She lusted for the concubinage of those whose flesh is the flesh of donkeys and whose issue is the issue of horses.

Oholibah's punishment

[21] You recalled the licentiousness of your youth, when your breasts were squeezed by Egypt, for the sake of your youthful bosom. [22] Therefore, O Oholibah, thus said the Lord HASHEM/ELOHIM: Behold, I am inciting your paramours against you, those from whom your soul has become repulsed, and I will bring them against you from round about — [23] Babylonia's sons and all the Chaldeans, Pekod and Shoa and Koa, and all of Assyria's sons with them, pleasant young men, governors and rulers all of them; captains and appointees, all of them riding horses. [24] They will come against you with weaponry, with chariot and wheel, and with an assemblage of nations; with buckler, shield and helmet they will set upon you all around. I will place justice at their disposal and they will punish you with their judgments. [25] I will set My jealousy against you, and they will act upon you with fury — they will remove your nose and your ears * and your final remainder will fall by the sword; they will take your sons and daughters, and your final remainder will be consumed by fire; [26] they will strip you of your clothes and take your splendid articles. [27] I will cause you to cease your licentiousness and your Egyptian promiscuity; you will not raise your eyes to them, and you will no longer remember Egypt.

[28] For thus said the Lord HASHEM/ELOHIM: Behold, I am delivering you into the hand of those you hated, into the hand of those from whom your soul was repulsed. [29] They will act toward you with hatred and take away all your toil, leaving you naked and bare, so that the shame of your adulteries, your licentiousness and your promiscuity will be uncovered. [30] These things will be done to you because of your straying after the nations, because you became defiled with their idols. [31] You followed the way of your sister; therefore I placed her cup in your hand.

The cup of desolation

[32] Thus said the Lord HASHEM/ELOHIM: You will drink of your sister's deep and wide cup; it will be a cause of scorn and derision [for you], of ample volume. [33] You will be filled with drunkenness and sadness [from] the cup of astonishment and bewilderment, the cup of your sister, Samaria. [34] You will drink it and suck it out and chew its shards, and you will tear at your bosom, for I have spoken — the word of the Lord HASHEM/ELOHIM. [35] Therefore, thus said the Lord HASHEM/ELOHIM: Because you have forgotten Me and cast Me behind your back, therefore you too will bear your licentiousness and your promiscuity."

[36] HASHEM said to me, "Son of Man, won't you rebuke Oholah and Oholibah and tell them of their abominations?

[37] For they have committed adultery and there is blood on their hands and they have committed adultery with their idols; and even their children, whom they had borne for Me, they passed before them to be consumed. [38] Moreover, they have done this to Me: They defiled My Sanctuary on that day,

לט וְאֶת־שַׁבְּתוֹתַי חִלֵּלוּ: וּבְשַׁחֲטָם אֶת־בְּנֵיהֶם לְגִלּוּלֵיהֶם וַיָּבֹאוּ אֶל־מִקְדָּשִׁי
מ בַּיּוֹם הַהוּא לְחַלְּלוֹ וְהִנֵּה־כֹה עָשׂוּ בְּתוֹךְ בֵּיתִי: וְאַף כִּי תִשְׁלַחְנָה
לַאֲנָשִׁים בָּאִים מִמֶּרְחָק אֲשֶׁר מַלְאָךְ שָׁלוּחַ אֲלֵיהֶם וְהִנֵּה־בָאוּ לַאֲשֶׁר
מא רָחַצְתְּ כָּחַלְתְּ עֵינַיִךְ וְעָדִית עֶדִי: וְיָשַׁבְתְּ עַל־מִטָּה כְבוּדָּה וְשֻׁלְחָן עָרוּךְ
מב לְפָנֶיהָ וּקְטָרְתִּי וְשַׁמְנִי שַׂמְתְּ עָלֶיהָ: וְקוֹל הָמוֹן שָׁלֵו בָהּ וְאֶל־אֲנָשִׁים מֵרֹב
אָדָם מוּבָאִים °סוֹבָאִים [°סָבָאִים ק] מִמִּדְבָּר וַיִּתְּנוּ צְמִידִים אֶל־יְדֵיהֶן
מג וַעֲטֶרֶת תִּפְאֶרֶת עַל־רָאשֵׁיהֶן: וָאֹמַר לַבָּלָה נִאוּפִים °עת [°עַתָּה ק]
מד °יזנה [°יִזְנוּ ק] תַזְנוּתֶיהָ וָהִיא: וַיָּבוֹא אֵלֶיהָ כְּבוֹא אֶל־אִשָּׁה זוֹנָה כֵּן
מה בָּאוּ אֶל־אׇהֳלָה וְאֶל־אׇהֳלִיבָה אִשֹּׁת הַזִּמָּה: וַאֲנָשִׁים צַדִּיקִם הֵמָּה
יִשְׁפְּטוּ אוֹתְהֶם מִשְׁפַּט נֹאֲפוֹת וּמִשְׁפַּט שֹׁפְכוֹת דָּם כִּי נֹאֲפֹת הֵנָּה וְדָם
מו בִּידֵיהֶן: כִּי כֹּה אָמַר אֲדֹנָי יֱהֹוִה הַעֲלֵה עֲלֵיהֶם קָהָל וְנָתֹן
מז אֶתְהֶן לְזַעֲוָה וְלָבַז: וְרָגְמוּ עֲלֵיהֶן אֶבֶן קָהָל וּבָרֵא אוֹתְהֶן בְּחַרְבוֹתָם
מח בְּנֵיהֶם וּבְנוֹתֵיהֶם יַהֲרֹגוּ וּבָתֵּיהֶן בָּאֵשׁ יִשְׂרֹפוּ: וְהִשְׁבַּתִּי זִמָּה מִן־הָאָרֶץ
מט וְנִוַּסְּרוּ כָּל־הַנָּשִׁים וְלֹא תַעֲשֶׂינָה כְּזִמַּתְכֶנָה: וְנָתְנוּ זִמַּתְכֶנָה עֲלֵיכֶן
וַחֲטָאֵי גִלּוּלֵיכֶן תִּשֶּׂאינָה וִידַעְתֶּם כִּי אֲנִי אֲדֹנָי יֱהֹוִה: וַיְהִי

כד א דְבַר־יֱהֹוָה אֵלַי בַּשָּׁנָה הַתְּשִׁיעִית בַּחֹדֶשׁ הָעֲשִׂירִי בֶּעָשׂוֹר לַחֹדֶשׁ לֵאמֹר:
ב בֶּן־אָדָם °כתוב [°כְּתׇב־ ק] לְךָ אֶת־שֵׁם הַיּוֹם אֶת־עֶצֶם הַיּוֹם הַזֶּה סָמַךְ
ג מֶלֶךְ־בָּבֶל אֶל־יְרוּשָׁלַ͏ִם בְּעֶצֶם הַיּוֹם הַזֶּה: וּמְשֹׁל אֶל־בֵּית־הַמֶּרִי מָשָׁל
וְאָמַרְתָּ אֲלֵיהֶם כֹּה אָמַר אֲדֹנָי יֱהֹוִה שְׁפֹת הַסִּיר שְׁפֹת וְגַם־יְצֹק בּוֹ מָיִם:
ד-ה אֱסֹף נְתָחֶיהָ אֵלֶיהָ כָּל־נֵתַח טוֹב יָרֵךְ וְכָתֵף מִבְחַר עֲצָמִים מַלֵּא: מִבְחַר
הַצֹּאן לָקוֹחַ וְגַם דּוּר הָעֲצָמִים תַּחְתֶּיהָ רַתַּח רְתָחֶיהָ גַּם־בָּשְׁלוּ עֲצָמֶיהָ
ו בְּתוֹכָהּ:   לָכֵן כֹּה־אָמַר אֲדֹנָי יֱהֹוִה אוֹי עִיר הַדָּמִים סִיר
אֲשֶׁר חֶלְאָתָה בָהּ וְחֶלְאָתָהּ לֹא יָצְאָה מִמֶּנָּה לִנְתָחֶיהָ לִנְתָחֶיהָ הוֹצִיאָהּ
ז לֹא־נָפַל עָלֶיהָ גּוֹרָל: כִּי דָמָהּ בְּתוֹכָהּ הָיָה עַל־צְחִיחַ סֶלַע שָׂמָתְהוּ לֹא
ח שְׁפָכַתְהוּ עַל־הָאָרֶץ לְכַסּוֹת עָלָיו עָפָר: לְהַעֲלוֹת חֵמָה לִנְקֹם נָקָם נָתַתִּי
ט אֶת־דָּמָהּ עַל־צְחִיחַ סֶלַע לְבִלְתִּי הִכָּסוֹת: לָכֵן כֹּה אָמַר אֲדֹנָי
י יֱהֹוִה אוֹי עִיר הַדָּמִים גַּם־אֲנִי אַגְדִּיל הַמְּדוּרָה: הַרְבֵּה הָעֵצִים הַדְלֵק
יא הָאֵשׁ הָתֵם הַבָּשָׂר וְהַרְקַח הַמֶּרְקָחָה וְהָעֲצָמוֹת יֵחָרוּ: וְהַעֲמִידֶהָ עַל־
גֶּחָלֶיהָ רֵקָה לְמַעַן תֵּחַם וְחָרָה נְחֻשְׁתָּהּ וְנִתְּכָה בְתוֹכָהּ טֻמְאָתָהּ תִּתֻּם
יב חֶלְאָתָהּ: תְּאֻנִים הֶלְאָת וְלֹא־תֵצֵא מִמֶּנָּה רַבַּת חֶלְאָתָהּ בָּאֵשׁ חֶלְאָתָהּ:

23:40. To import their degenerate cultures to the people of Israel (*Radak*).

23:42. Many foreigners had been invited to Jerusalem, and Oholah and Oholibah made themselves attractive for the lovers they had summoned.

23:45. Compared to Oholah and Oholibah, the Babylonians were righteous, because Zedekiah had violated his

oath of loyalty to Nebuchadnezzar.

24:3. The prophet describes the siege of Jerusalem in terms of a pot on the stove.

24:4. All the notables would stream to Jerusalem (the pot) to seek shelter from the invasion (*Rashi*).

24:5. The bones symbolize the warriors, who would take the brunt of the suffering to protect the rest of the and they desecrated My Sabbaths, [39] when they slaughtered their children for their idols they would come to My Sanctuary on that very day to defile it! Behold, they have done this in My Temple! [40] And even more, they sent for men who came from afar, * to whom a messenger had been sent, and they came to where [you were waiting], having washed, daubed your eyes and donned ornaments. [41] You sat on a stately couch with a table prepared before it, and you set My incense and My oil upon it. [42] The sound of a peaceful multitude was within [Jerusalem], that of men, of many people, who were brought from the surrounding wilderness; they placed bracelets on their hands and splendid crowns upon their heads. * [43] And I thought of this one who had become worn out through adulteries, 'Now surely her harlotries will depart [from her]!' But she [is still the same]. [44] [People] came to her as one comes to a harlot; so they came to Oholah and to Oholibah, the women of licentiousness. [45] Righteous men * will judge them with the judgment of adulteresses and the judgment of those who spill blood; for they are adulteresses, and there is blood on their hands.

[46] For thus said the Lord HASHEM/ELOHIM: I will bring up an assemblage against them and make them into a horror and into plunder. [47] And the assemblage will pelt them with stones and cut them down with their swords; they will kill their sons and daughters and burn down their houses in fire.

[48] Then I will cause licentiousness to cease from the land, and all the women will be chastised, and they will not imitate your licentiousness. [49] They will place your licentiousness upon you and you will bear the sins of your idols; then you will know that I am the Lord HASHEM/ELOHIM."

24

The tenth of Teves

[1] The word of HASHEM came to me in the ninth year, in the tenth month, on the tenth of the month, saying, [2] "Son of Man, write for yourself the name of this day — this very day; the king of Babylonia has reached Jerusalem on this very day. [3] Tell a parable to the rebellious house. Say to them:

Thus said the Lord HASHEM/ELOHIM: Set the pot, * set it! And also pour water into it! [4] Gather its cuts into it, all the good cuts — thigh and shoulder; * fill [it] with the choicest bones. [5] Take the choicest of the flock; and also arrange the bones at its bottom; * then boil it well, so that even its bones become cooked within it.

The seething blood

[6] Therefore, thus said the Lord HASHEM/ELOHIM: Woe, O city of bloodshed, the pot in which there is filth, whose filth has not gone out of it! Empty it cut by cut; no lot has been cast over it. * [7] For her blood was within her; she placed it upon a smooth rock. She did not pour it upon the ground to cover it with dirt. * [8] So that it might stir up [My] wrath to take vengeance, I have placed her blood upon the smooth rock, that it not be covered.

Attempted cleansing

[9] Therefore, thus said the Lord HASHEM/ELOHIM: Woe, O city of bloodshed! I too will enlarge the pyre, [10] increase the wood, kindle the fire, consume the meat, and mix the spices, so that the bones become scorched — [11] and then stand it empty upon its coals, so that its bottom becomes hot and scorched, its contamination melted within it, its filth consumed. [12] She has become weary with her deceptions, thus her abundant filth cannot come out of it; [only] by fire [can] her filth [be purged].

---

populace (Rashi).

24:6. The people will be killed gradually, through starvation, disease, battle, etc. Death will strike randomly, with-

out any lots, i.e., systematic pattern (Radak).

24:7. People committed murder publicly, shamelessly, not trying to hide their heinous acts (Metzudos).

יג בְּטֻמְאָתֵךְ זִמָּה יַעַן טִהַרְתִּיךְ וְלֹא טָהַרְתְּ מִטֻּמְאָתֵךְ לֹא תִטְהֲרִי־עוֹד
יד עַד־הֲנִיחִי אֶת־חֲמָתִי בָּךְ: אֲנִי יהוה דִּבַּרְתִּי בָּאָה וְעָשִׂיתִי לֹא־אֶפְרַע
וְלֹא־אָחוּס וְלֹא אֶנָּחֵם כִּדְרָכַיִךְ וְכַעֲלִילוֹתַיִךְ שְׁפָטוּךְ נְאֻם אֲדֹנָי
טו־טז יֱהוִֹה: וַיְהִי דְבַר־יהוה אֵלַי לֵאמֹר: בֶּן־אָדָם הִנְנִי לֹקֵחַ
מִמְּךָ אֶת־מַחְמַד עֵינֶיךָ בְּמַגֵּפָה וְלֹא תִסְפֹּד וְלֹא תִבְכֶּה וְלוֹא תָבוֹא
יז דִּמְעָתֶךָ: הֵאָנֵק ׀ דֹּם מֵתִים אֵבֶל לֹא־תַעֲשֶׂה פְּאֵרְךָ חֲבוֹשׁ עָלֶיךָ וּנְעָלֶיךָ
יח תָּשִׂים בְּרַגְלֶיךָ וְלֹא תַעְטֶה עַל־שָׂפָם וְלֶחֶם אֲנָשִׁים לֹא תֹאכֵל: וָאֲדַבֵּר
אֶל־הָעָם בַּבֹּקֶר וַתָּמָת אִשְׁתִּי בָּעָרֶב וָאַעַשׂ בַּבֹּקֶר כַּאֲשֶׁר צֻוֵּיתִי:
יט־כ וַיֹּאמְרוּ אֵלַי הָעָם הֲלֹא־תַגִּיד לָנוּ מָה־אֵלֶּה לָּנוּ כִּי אַתָּה עֹשֶׂה: וָאֹמַר
כא אֲלֵיהֶם דְּבַר־יהוה הָיָה אֵלַי לֵאמֹר: אֱמֹר ׀ לְבֵית יִשְׂרָאֵל כֹּה־אָמַר אֲדֹנָי
יֱהוִֹה הִנְנִי מְחַלֵּל אֶת־מִקְדָּשִׁי גְּאוֹן עֻזְּכֶם מַחְמַד עֵינֵיכֶם וּמַחְמַל
כב נַפְשְׁכֶם וּבְנֵיכֶם וּבְנוֹתֵיכֶם אֲשֶׁר עֲזַבְתֶּם בַּחֶרֶב יִפֹּלוּ: וַעֲשִׂיתֶם כַּאֲשֶׁר
כג עָשִׂיתִי עַל־שָׂפָם לֹא תַעְטוּ וְלֶחֶם אֲנָשִׁים לֹא תֹאכֵלוּ: וּפְאֵרֵכֶם עַל־
רָאשֵׁיכֶם וְנַעֲלֵיכֶם בְּרַגְלֵיכֶם לֹא תִסְפְּדוּ וְלֹא תִבְכּוּ וּנְמַקֹּתֶם בַּעֲוֹנֹתֵיכֶם
כד וּנְהַמְתֶּם אִישׁ אֶל־אָחִיו: וְהָיָה יְחֶזְקֵאל לָכֶם לְמוֹפֵת כְּכֹל אֲשֶׁר־
עָשָׂה תַּעֲשׂוּ בְּבֹאָהּ וִידַעְתֶּם כִּי אֲנִי אֲדֹנָי יֱהוִֹה:
כה בֶּן־אָדָם הֲלוֹא בְּיוֹם קַחְתִּי מֵהֶם אֶת־מָעוּזָּם מְשׂוֹשׂ תִּפְאַרְתָּם אֶת־
מַחְמַד עֵינֵיהֶם וְאֶת־מַשָּׂא נַפְשָׁם בְּנֵיהֶם וּבְנוֹתֵיהֶם: בַּיּוֹם הַהוּא
כו־כז יָבוֹא הַפָּלִיט אֵלֶיךָ לְהַשְׁמָעוּת אָזְנָיִם: בַּיּוֹם הַהוּא יִפָּתַח פִּיךָ
אֶת־הַפָּלִיט וּתְדַבֵּר וְלֹא תֵאָלֵם עוֹד וְהָיִיתָ לָהֶם לְמוֹפֵת וְיָדְעוּ כִּי־אֲנִי
כה א־ב יהוה: וַיְהִי דְבַר־יהוה אֵלַי לֵאמֹר: בֶּן־אָדָם שִׂים פָּנֶיךָ
ג אֶל־בְּנֵי עַמּוֹן וְהִנָּבֵא עֲלֵיהֶם: וְאָמַרְתָּ לִבְנֵי עַמּוֹן שִׁמְעוּ דְּבַר־אֲדֹנָי
יֱהוִֹה כֹּה־אָמַר אֲדֹנָי יֱהוִֹה יַעַן אָמְרֵךְ הֶאָח אֶל־מִקְדָּשִׁי כִי־נִחָל וְאֶל־
ד אַדְמַת יִשְׂרָאֵל כִּי נָשַׁמָּה וְאֶל־בֵּית יְהוּדָה כִּי הָלְכוּ בַּגּוֹלָה: לָכֵן הִנְנִי
נֹתְנָךְ לִבְנֵי־קֶדֶם לְמוֹרָשָׁה וְיִשְּׁבוּ טִירוֹתֵיהֶם בָּךְ וְנָתְנוּ בָךְ מִשְׁכְּנֵיהֶם
ה הֵמָּה יֹאכְלוּ פִרְיֵךְ וְהֵמָּה יִשְׁתּוּ חֲלָבֵךְ: וְנָתַתִּי אֶת־רַבָּה לִנְוֵה גְמַלִּים
ו וְאֶת־בְּנֵי עַמּוֹן לְמִרְבַּץ־צֹאן וִידַעְתֶּם כִּי־אֲנִי יהוה: כֹּה אָמַר אֲדֹנָי יֱהוִֹה יַעַן מַחְאֲךָ יָד וְרַקְעֲךָ בְּרָגֶל וַתִּשְׂמַח בְּכָל־
ז שָׁאטְךָ בְּנֶפֶשׁ אֶל־אַדְמַת יִשְׂרָאֵל: לָכֵן הִנְנִי נָטִיתִי אֶת־יָדִי עָלֶיךָ

24:14. The nations who have attacked you, at My behest (Radak).

24:16. Ezekiel's own beloved wife would be among the victims.

24:17. Ezekiel was commanded to refrain from all the customary practices of mourners. *Rashi* (v. 22) explains that mourners find comfort only when there are others to console them, but the loss of the beloved Temple, now

symbolized by Ezekiel's personal bereavement, was universal and beyond consolation.

24:26. See 33:21-22.

24:27. When the herald brings the disastrous news about Jerusalem, Ezekiel's audiences will no longer be unreceptive; the people will have complete faith in his words.

25:4. The Chaldeans and Arameans (*Rashi*).

¹³ [You remain] in your licentious contamination. Because I [tried to] cleanse you but you would not be cleansed, you will not again be cleansed of your contamination until I place My wrath upon you. ¹⁴ I, HASHEM, have spoken; it is coming, and I shall carry it out; I will not hinder, I will not pity, I will not relent; they * have judged you according to your ways and according to your deeds — the word of the Lord HASHEM/ELOHIM."

The
prophet's
bereavement

¹⁵ The word of HASHEM came to me, saying, ¹⁶ "Son of Man, behold, I am taking from you the darling of your eyes in a plague: * You shall not lament and you shall not weep, and your tears shall not come forth. ¹⁷ Be silent from groaning; do not practice rites of mourning for the dead; don your headgear upon yourself and place your shoes upon your feet; do not veil yourself to the lips, and do not eat the bread of [other] people." *

¹⁸ I told [this] to the people in the morning. In the evening my wife died, and in the morning I did as I had been commanded.

¹⁹ The people said to me, "Won't you tell us what these acts that you are doing [mean] for us?"

²⁰ So I said to them, "The word of HASHEM came to me, saying, ²¹ 'Say to the House of Israel:

No overt
grief

Thus said the Lord HASHEM/ELOHIM: Behold, I am profaning My Sanctuary, the pride of your strength, the darling of your eyes, and the yearning of your soul; and your sons and daughters, whom you have left behind, will fall by the sword. ²² And you will do as I have done; you will not veil yourselves to the lips, and you will not eat the bread [of] other people; ²³ your headgear will be upon your heads and your shoes upon your feet; you shall not lament and you shall not weep; and you will pine away because of your iniquities; and each of you will moan to his brother. ²⁴ Ezekiel will be a sign for you; you will do according to everything that he has done; and when this comes [to pass], you will know that I am the Lord HASHEM/ELOHIM.'

²⁵ And you, Son of Man, behold, on the day that I take their stronghold from them, the joy of their glory, the darling of their eyes, and the exaltation of their soul, their sons and their daughters — ²⁶ on that day, a fugitive will come to you, to let your ears hear. ²⁷ On that day, your mouth will be opened with the fugitive's [arrival], and you will speak and no longer be dumb; * then you will be a sign to them, and they will know that I am HASHEM."

25

¹ The word of HASHEM came to me, saying, ² "Son of Man, direct your face towards the Children of Ammon and prophesy against them. ³ Say to the Children of Ammon:

Prophecy
against
Ammon

Hear the word of the Lord HASHEM/ELOHIM! Thus said the Lord HASHEM/ELOHIM: Because you said 'Hurrah!' of My Sanctuary when it was desecrated, and of the soil of Israel when it was laid waste, and of the House of Judah when they went into exile, ⁴ therefore, behold, I am delivering you to the people of the East * as a heritage, and they will establish their palaces within you and place their dwelling places within you; they will eat your fruits and they will drink your milk. ⁵ I will make Rabbah an abode for camels and the [land of the] Children of Ammon a resting place for flocks; then you will know that I am HASHEM.

⁶ For thus said the Lord, HASHEM/ELOHIM: Because you clapped [your] hand and stamped with [your] foot and rejoiced with all your rashness of soul over the soil of Israel, ⁷ therefore, behold, I will extend My hand against you

וּנְתַתִּיךְ °לְבַג [°לְבַז ק] לַגּוֹיִם וְהִכְרַתִּיךָ מִן־הָעַמִּים וְהַאֲבַדְתִּיךָ מִן־
הָאֲרָצוֹת אַשְׁמִידְךָ וְיָדַעְתָּ כִּי־אֲנִי יְהוָה: כֹּה אָמַר אֲדֹנָי יְהוִה ח
יַעַן אָמַר מוֹאָב וְשֵׂעִיר הִנֵּה כְּכָל־הַגּוֹיִם בֵּית יְהוּדָה: לָכֵן הִנְנִי פֹתֵחַ אֶת־ ט
כֶּתֶף מוֹאָב מֵהֶעָרִים מֵעָרָיו מִקָּצֵהוּ צְבִי אֶרֶץ בֵּית הַיְשִׁימֹת בַּעַל מְעוֹן
°וְקִרְיָתְמה [°וְקִרְיָתָיְמָה ק]: לִבְנֵי־קֶדֶם עַל־בְּנֵי עַמּוֹן וּנְתַתִּיהָ לְמוֹרָשָׁה י
לְמַעַן לֹא־תִזָּכֵר בְּנֵי־עַמּוֹן בַּגּוֹיִם: וּבְמוֹאָב אֶעֱשֶׂה שְׁפָטִים וְיָדְעוּ כִּי־אֲנִי יא
יְהוָה: כֹּה אָמַר אֲדֹנָי יְהוִה יַעַן עֲשׂוֹת אֱדוֹם בִּנְקֹם נָקָם לְבֵית יב
יְהוּדָה וַיֶּאְשְׁמוּ אָשׁוֹם וְנִקְּמוּ בָהֶם: לָכֵן כֹּה אָמַר אֲדֹנָי יְהוִה וְנָטִתִי יג
יָדִי עַל־אֱדוֹם וְהִכְרַתִּי מִמֶּנָּה אָדָם וּבְהֵמָה וּנְתַתִּיהָ חָרְבָּה מִתֵּימָן
וּדְדָנֶה בַּחֶרֶב יִפֹּלוּ: וְנָתַתִּי אֶת־נִקְמָתִי בֶּאֱדוֹם בְּיַד עַמִּי יִשְׂרָאֵל וְעָשׂוּ יד
בֶאֱדוֹם כְּאַפִּי וְכַחֲמָתִי וְיָדְעוּ אֶת־נִקְמָתִי נְאֻם אֲדֹנָי יְהוִה: כֹּה טו
אָמַר אֲדֹנָי יְהוִה יַעַן עֲשׂוֹת פְּלִשְׁתִּים בִּנְקָמָה וַיִּנָּקְמוּ נָקָם בִּשְׁאָט
בְּנֶפֶשׁ לְמַשְׁחִית אֵיבַת עוֹלָם: לָכֵן כֹּה אָמַר אֲדֹנָי יְהוִה הִנְנִי נוֹטֶה יָדִי טז
עַל־פְּלִשְׁתִּים וְהִכְרַתִּי אֶת־כְּרֵתִים וְהַאֲבַדְתִּי אֶת־שְׁאֵרִית חוֹף הַיָּם:
וְעָשִׂיתִי בָם נְקָמוֹת גְּדֹלוֹת בְּתוֹכְחוֹת חֵמָה וְיָדְעוּ כִּי־אֲנִי יְהוָה בְּתִתִּי יז
אֶת־נִקְמָתִי בָּם:

כו וַיְהִי בְּעַשְׁתֵּי־עֶשְׂרֵה שָׁנָה בְּאֶחָד לַחֹדֶשׁ הָיָה דְבַר־יְהוָה אֵלַי לֵאמֹר: א
בֶּן־אָדָם יַעַן אֲשֶׁר־אָמְרָה צֹּר עַל־יְרוּשָׁלִַם הֶאָח נִשְׁבְּרָה דַּלְתוֹת ב
הָעַמִּים נָסֵבָּה אֵלָי אִמָּלְאָה הָחֳרָבָה: לָכֵן כֹּה אָמַר אֲדֹנָי יְהוִה הִנְנִי ג
עָלַיִךְ צֹר וְהַעֲלֵיתִי עָלַיִךְ גּוֹיִם רַבִּים כְּהַעֲלוֹת הַיָּם לְגַלָּיו: וְשִׁחֲתוּ חֹמוֹת ד
צֹר וְהָרְסוּ מִגְדָּלֶיהָ וְסִחֵיתִי עֲפָרָהּ מִמֶּנָּה וְנָתַתִּי אוֹתָהּ לִצְחִיחַ סָלַע:
מִשְׁטַח חֲרָמִים תִּהְיֶה בְּתוֹךְ הַיָּם כִּי אֲנִי דִבַּרְתִּי נְאֻם אֲדֹנָי יְהוִה וְהָיְתָה ה
לְבַז לַגּוֹיִם: וּבְנוֹתֶיהָ אֲשֶׁר בַּשָּׂדֶה בַּחֶרֶב תֵּהָרַגְנָה וְיָדְעוּ כִּי־אֲנִי ו
יְהוָה: כִּי כֹה אָמַר אֲדֹנָי יְהוִה הִנְנִי מֵבִיא אֶל־צֹר נְבוּכַדְרֶאצַּר ז
מֶלֶךְ־בָּבֶל מִצָּפוֹן מֶלֶךְ מְלָכִים בְּסוּס וּבְרֶכֶב וּבְפָרָשִׁים וְקָהָל וְעַם־רָב:
בְּנוֹתַיִךְ בַּשָּׂדֶה בַּחֶרֶב יַהֲרֹג וְנָתַן עָלַיִךְ דָּיֵק וְשָׁפַךְ עָלַיִךְ סֹלְלָה וְהֵקִים ח
עָלַיִךְ צִנָּה: וּמְחִי קָבָלּוֹ יִתֵּן בְּחֹמוֹתָיִךְ וּמִגְדְּלֹתַיִךְ יִתֹּץ בְּחַרְבוֹתָיו: ט
מִשִּׁפְעַת סוּסָיו יְכַסֵּךְ אֲבָקָם מִקּוֹל פָּרַשׁ וְגַלְגַּל וָרֶכֶב תִּרְעַשְׁנָה חוֹמוֹתַיִךְ י
בְּבֹאוֹ בִּשְׁעָרַיִךְ כִּמְבוֹאֵי עִיר מְבֻקָּעָה: בְּפַרְסוֹת סוּסָיו יִרְמֹס אֶת־כָּל־ יא

25:8. They have lost God's special favor; they share the fate of all other nations.

25:10. When the Babylonians go to attack the Ammonites they will invade Moab on the way (*Rashi*).

25:13. A major Edomite city.

25:16. An area of the Philistine nation (*Rashi*), situated along the Mediterranean coast (see *Zephaniah* 2:5).

26:1. The month is not specified. According to a

responsum of *Rashi*, it was Tishrei, the beginning of the year. According to *Radak*, since this was the year of the Destruction, this was the month of Av, when the tragedy took place.

26:2. The gateways of commerce, which had heretofore been directed toward Jerusalem, will now turn to Tyre.

26:6. This refers to the surrounding villages that were under Tyre's domain (*Rashi*).

and present you as spoils to the nations; I will eliminate you from the peoples and make you perish from among the lands. I will destroy you; then you will know that I am HASHEM.

⁸ Thus said the Lord HASHEM/ELOHIM: Because Moab and Seir say, 'Behold, the House of Judah is like all the nations'; * ⁹ therefore, behold, I will expose the flank of Moab, from the cities, from its cities at its border — the splendor of the land of Beth-jeshimoth, Baal-meon, and Kiriathaim — ¹⁰ to the children of the East [as they march] against the Children of Ammon, * I will present it as a heritage, so that the Children of Ammon will not be remembered among the nations. ¹¹ Then I will execute punishments against Moab; and they will know that I am HASHEM.

¹² Thus said the Lord HASHEM/ELOHIM: Because Edom acted in wreaking vengeance against the House of Judah, and has incurred guilt by taking vengeance against them, ¹³ therefore, thus said the Lord HASHEM/ELOHIM: I will extend My hand against Edom and eliminate from it man and animal, and I will make it desolate from the south, and the inhabitants of Dedan * will fall by the sword. ¹⁴ Then I will place My vengeance in Edom by the hand of My people Israel, and they will deal with Edom in accordance with My anger and My wrath; then they will know My vengeance — the word of the Lord HASHEM/ELOHIM.

¹⁵ Thus said the Lord HASHEM/ELOHIM: Because the Philistines have acted with vengeance, and they wreaked vengeance with rashness of soul, to destroy with everlasting hatred, ¹⁶ therefore, thus said the Lord HASHEM/ELOHIM: Behold, I am extending My hand against the Philistines, and I will eliminate the Cherethites * and destroy the remnant by the seashore. ¹⁷ I will execute great vengeance against them with rebukes of wrath; and they will know that I am HASHEM, when I place My vengeance upon them.

26

¹ It happened in the eleventh year, on the first of the month, * that the word of HASHEM came to me, saying, ² "Son of Man: Because Tyre has said of Jerusalem, 'Hurrah! The gateways of the nations have been broken; it is turned toward me! * I will be filled, for she was destroyed!' — ³ therefore, thus said the
Lord HASHEM/ELOHIM: Behold, I am against you, O Tyre, and I will bring up many nations against you, as the sea brings up its waves. ⁴ They will destroy the walls of Tyre and break down her towers. I will scrape away her soil from her and make her into a bare rock. ⁵ She will be a spreading-place for nets, in the midst of the sea; for I have spoken — the word of the Lord HASHEM/ELOHIM — and she will become plunder for the nations. ⁶ Her daughters that are in the field * will be killed by the sword; then they will know that I am HASHEM.

⁷ For thus said the Lord HASHEM/ELOHIM: Behold, I am bringing Nebuchadrezzar king of Babylonia against Tyre from the north, a king of kings, with horse, with chariot and with riders, an assembly and a multitude of people. ⁸ He will kill your daughters in the field by the sword; he will build a siege tower against you and pour a ramp against you and set his buckler[ed warriors] against you. ⁹ He will set his catapults at your walls, and he will dismantle your towers with his swords. ¹⁰ From the abundance of his horses their dust will cover you; your walls will tremble from the noise of rider, wheel and chariot, when he enters your gates as people enter a breached city. ¹¹ With the hooves of his horses he will trample all

יב חוּצוֹתַ֫יִךְ עַמֵּ֤ךְ בַּחֶ֙רֶב֙ יַהֲרֹ֔ג וּמַצְּב֥וֹת עֻזֵּ֖ךְ לָאָ֣רֶץ תֵּרֵ֑ד וְשָׁלְל֤וּ חֵילֵךְ֙ וּבָֽזְז֣וּ רְכֻלָּתֵ֔ךְ וְהָֽרְסוּ֙ חֽוֹמוֹתַ֔יִךְ וּבָתֵּ֥י חֶמְדָּתֵ֖ךְ יִתֹּ֑צוּ וַאֲבָנַ֤יִךְ וְעֵצַ֙יִךְ֙

יג וַעֲפָרֵ֔ךְ בְּת֥וֹךְ מַ֖יִם יָשִֽׂימוּ: וְהִשְׁבַּתִּ֖י הֲמ֣וֹן שִׁירָ֑יִךְ וְק֣וֹל כִּנּוֹרַ֔יִךְ לֹ֥א

יד יִשָּׁמַ֖ע עֽוֹד: וּנְתַתִּ֞יךְ לִצְחִ֣יחַ סֶ֗לַע מִשְׁטַ֤ח חֲרָמִים֙ תִּֽהְיֶ֔ה לֹ֥א תִבָּנֶ֖ה

טו ע֑וֹד כִּ֚י אֲנִ֣י יְהוָ֣ה דִּבַּ֔רְתִּי נְאֻ֖ם אֲדֹנָ֥י יֱהֹוִֽה: כֹּ֥ה אָמַ֛ר אֲדֹנָ֥י יֱהֹוִ֖ה לְצ֑וֹר הֲלֹ֣א | מִקּ֤וֹל מַפַּלְתֵּךְ֙ בֶּאֱנֹ֣ק חָלָ֔ל בֵּהָֽרֵ֥ג הֶ֙רֶג֙

טז בְּתוֹכֵ֔ךְ יִרְעֲשׁ֖וּ הָֽאִיִּֽים: וְֽיָרְד֞וּ מֵעַ֣ל כִּסְאוֹתָ֗ם כֹּ֚ל נְשִׂיאֵ֣י הַיָּ֔ם וְהֵסִ֙ירוּ֙ אֶת־מְעִ֣ילֵיהֶ֔ם וְאֶת־בִּגְדֵ֥י רִקְמָתָ֖ם יִפְשֹׁ֑טוּ חֲרָד֤וֹת | יִלְבָּ֙שׁוּ֙ עַל־הָאָ֣רֶץ

יז יֵשֵׁ֔בוּ וְחָֽרְדוּ֙ לִרְגָעִ֔ים וְשָֽׁמְמ֖וּ עָלָֽיִךְ: וְנָשְׂא֨וּ עָלַ֤יִךְ קִינָה֙ וְאָ֣מְרוּ לָ֔ךְ אֵ֣יךְ אָבַ֗דְתְּ נוֹשֶׁ֙בֶת֙ מִיַּמִּ֔ים הָעִ֖יר הַהֻלָּ֑לָה אֲשֶׁר֩ הָֽיְתָ֨ה חֲזָקָ֤ה בַיָּם֙ הִ֣יא

יח וְיֹֽשְׁבֶ֔יהָ אֲשֶׁר־נָתְנ֥וּ חִתִּיתָ֖ם לְכָל־יֽוֹשְׁבֶֽיהָ: עַתָּה֙ יֶחְרְד֣וּ הָֽאִיִּ֔ן י֖וֹם

יט מַפַּלְתֵּ֑ךְ וְנִבְהֲל֧וּ הָאִיִּ֛ים אֲשֶׁר־בַּיָּ֖ם מִצֵּאתֵֽךְ: כֹּ֤ה אָמַר֙ אֲדֹנָ֣י יֱהֹוִ֔ה בְּתִתִּ֤י אֹתָךְ֙ עִ֣יר נֶחֱרֶ֔בֶת כֶּֽעָרִ֖ים אֲשֶׁ֣ר לֹֽא־נוֹשָׁ֑בוּ

כ בְּהַעֲל֨וֹת עָלַ֜יִךְ אֶת־תְּה֗וֹם וְכִסּ֛וּךְ הַמַּ֥יִם הָֽרַבִּֽים: וְהֽוֹרַדְתִּיךְ֩ אֶת־יֽוֹרְדֵ֨י ב֜וֹר אֶל־עַ֣ם עוֹלָ֗ם וְ֠הֽוֹשַׁבְתִּיךְ בְּאֶ֨רֶץ תַּחְתִּיּ֜וֹת כׇּחֳרָב֤וֹת מֵֽעוֹלָם֙ אֶת־י֣וֹרְדֵי ב֔וֹר לְמַ֖עַן לֹ֣א תֵשֵׁ֑בִי וְנָתַתִּ֥י צְבִ֖י בְּאֶ֥רֶץ חַיִּֽים:

כא בַּלָּה֥וֹת אֶתְּנֵ֖ךְ וְאֵינֵ֑ךְ וּֽתְבֻקְשִׁ֗י וְלֹֽא־תִמָּצְאִ֥י עוֹד֙ לְעוֹלָ֔ם נְאֻ֖ם אֲדֹנָ֥י יֱהֹוִֽה: וַיְהִ֥י דְבַר־יְהוָ֖ה אֵלַ֥י לֵאמֹֽר:

כז א-ב וְאַתָּ֣ה בֶן־אָדָ֔ם שָׂ֥א עַל־צֹ֖ר קִינָֽה: וְאָֽמַרְתָּ֣ לְצ֗וֹר °הַיּשֶׁ֙בֶת֙ [°הַיֹּשֶׁ֙בֶת֙ ק] עַל־מְבוֹאֹ֣ת

ג יָ֔ם רֹכֶ֙לֶת֙ הָֽעַמִּ֔ים אֶל־אִיִּ֖ים רַבִּ֑ים כֹּ֤ה אָמַר֙ אֲדֹנָ֣י יֱהֹוִ֔ה צ֕וֹר אַ֣תְּ

ד-ה אָמַ֔רְתְּ אֲנִ֖י כְּלִ֥ילַת יֹֽפִי: בְּלֵ֥ב יַמִּ֖ים גְּבֽוּלָ֑יִךְ בֹּנַ֕יִךְ כָּֽלְל֖וּ יׇפְיֵֽךְ: בְּרוֹשִׁ֤ים מִשְּׂנִיר֙ בָּ֣נוּ לָ֔ךְ אֵ֖ת כָּל־לֻֽחֹתָ֑יִם אֶ֤רֶז מִלְּבָנוֹן֙ לָקָ֔חוּ לַעֲשׂ֥וֹת תֹּ֖רֶן

ו עָלָֽיִךְ: אַלּוֹנִים֙ מִבָּ֔שָׁן עָשׂ֖וּ מִשּׁוֹטָ֑יִךְ קַרְשֵׁ֤ךְ עָֽשׂוּ־שֵׁן֙ בַּת־אֲשֻׁרִ֔ים

ז מֵאִיֵּ֖י °כתים [°כִתִּיֽם ק]: שֵׁשׁ־בְּרִקְמָ֤ה מִמִּצְרַ֙יִם֙ הָיָ֣ה מִפְרָשֵׂ֔ךְ לִֽהְי֥וֹת

ח לָ֖ךְ לְנֵ֑ס תְּכֵ֧לֶת וְאַרְגָּמָ֛ן מֵֽאִיֵּ֥י אֱלִישָׁ֖ה הָיָ֥ה מְכַסֵּֽךְ: יֹֽשְׁבֵ֤י צִידוֹן֙ וְאַרְוַ֔ד הָי֥וּ שָׁטִ֖ים לָ֑ךְ חֲכָמַ֤יִךְ צוֹר֙ הָ֣יוּ בָ֔ךְ הֵ֖מָּה חֹֽבְלָֽיִךְ:

ט זִקְנֵ֨י גְבַ֤ל וַֽחֲכָמֶ֙יהָ֙ הָ֣יוּ בָ֔ךְ מַחֲזִיקֵ֖י בִּדְקֵ֑ךְ כָּל־אֳנִיּ֤וֹת הַיָּם֙ וּמַלָּ֣חֵיהֶ֔ם הָ֥יוּ בָ֖ךְ לַעֲרֹ֥ב מַעֲרָבֵֽךְ:

26:12. The Babylonians will utterly demolish Tyre, so that it will figuratively fall into the Mediterranean.

26:15-18. Although Tyre was a relatively small city-state, its economic power was such that it had an influence over much larger countries. Thus, Ezekiel prophesies that its downfall would cause widespread tremors.

26:16. Having seen the fall of once-mighty Tyre, they will fear for their own safety.

26:20. I.e., the Land of Israel in contrast to Tyre's arrogant conviction (v. 2) that "[Tyre] will become filled for

[Jerusalem] was destroyed" (*Metzudos*).

27:3. In its arrogance Tyre had taken for itself this title, which had formerly been applied to Jerusalem (*Lamentations* 2:15).

27:5. Since Tyre was known for its maritime enterprises, it is described here as a magnificent ship (*Rashi*).

27:8. The professional sailors were natives of Tyre, while the lowly oarsmen were from other nations.

27:9. The Gebalites were expert builders (see *I Kings* 5:32).

your streets; he will kill your people by the sword, and your pillars of strength will descend to the ground. ¹² Then they will plunder your wealth and despoil your merchandise; they will break down your walls and smash your houses of delight; and they will throw down your walls and dismantle the houses of your delight. Your stones, your wood and your dust they will place into the midst of the water . * ¹³ I will put an end to the multitude of your songs, and the sound of your harps will be heard no more. ¹⁴ I will make you into a bare rock; you will be a spreading-place for nets, never to be rebuilt again, for I, HASHEM, have spoken — the word of the Lord HASHEM/ELOHIM.

¹⁵ Thus said the Lord HASHEM/ELOHIM to Tyre: Will not the islands tremble from the noise of your downfall, * with the groan of the slain, as slaughter is perpetrated in your midst? ¹⁶ Then all the princes of the sea will descend from their thrones, remove their robes, and remove their embroidered garments; * they will garb themselves with trembling and sit on the ground; they will tremble for fear of destruction and be astonished because of you. ¹⁷ They will take up a lament for you and say of you:

How have you perished, [you who are] settled by the seas,
The lauded city that was mighty in the sea, she and her inhabitants,
Who had set their terror upon all [the sea's] inhabitants.
¹⁸ Now the open places will tremble on the day of your downfall
And the islands of the sea will be confounded by your exile.

¹⁹ For thus said the Lord HASHEM/ELOHIM: When I make you a devastated city, as cities that have never been inhabited, when I raise the depths of the sea over you and the abundant waters cover you, ²⁰ then I will bring you down with those who descend to the pit, to the people of antiquity, and I will settle you in the nethermost depths of the earth, like the cities that were devastated in antiquity, with those who descend to the pit, so that you will not be inhabited. But I will bestow splendor upon the Land of Life. * ²¹ I will make you into a fright and you will be no more; you will be sought, but you will never be found again, forever! — the word of the Lord HASHEM/ELOHIM."

27

A lament
for Tyre

¹ The word of HASHEM came to me, saying: ² "Now you, Son of Man, take up a lament for Tyre; ³ and say to Tyre, which dwells at the harbors of the sea, merchant of the peoples to many islands:

Thus said the Lord HASHEM/ELOHIM:
Tyre, you have said, 'I am perfect in beauty.'*

Tyre's
beauty

⁴ In the heart of the seas are your borders;
Your builders perfected your beauty.
⁵ Of cypress wood from Senir they built you, all the planks;
Cedar from Lebanon they took, to make a mast upon you. *
⁶ Of oaks from Bashan they made your oars;
Your rudder they made of ivory-inlaid ebony from the Kittite isles.
⁷ Of embroidered Egyptian linen was your sail, to be an ensign for you;
Of turquoise and purple from the isles of Elishah was your awning.
⁸ The inhabitants of Sidon and Arvad were oarsmen for you;
Your wise men, O Tyre, were within you; * they were your sailors.
⁹ The elders of Gebal* and its wise men were within you,
caulkers of your cracks.
All the ships of the sea and their rowers were within you,
to provide your merchandise.

י פָּרַס וְלוּד וּפוּט הָיוּ בְחֵילֵךְ אַנְשֵׁי מִלְחַמְתֵּךְ מָגֵן וְכוֹבַע תִּלּוּ־בָךְ הֵמָּה
נָתְנוּ הֲדָרֵךְ: יא בְּנֵי אַרְוַד וְחֵילֵךְ עַל־חוֹמוֹתַיִךְ סָבִיב וְגַמָּדִים בְּמִגְדְּלוֹתַיִךְ
היָ הָיוּ שִׁלְטֵיהֶם תִּלּוּ עַל־חוֹמוֹתַיִךְ סָבִיב הֵמָּה כָּלְלוּ יָפְיֵךְ: יב תַּרְשִׁישׁ
סֹחַרְתֵּךְ מֵרֹב כָּל־הוֹן בְּכֶסֶף בַּרְזֶל בְּדִיל וְעוֹפֶרֶת נָתְנוּ עִזְבוֹנָיִךְ: יג יָוָן
תֻּבַל וָמֶשֶׁךְ הֵמָּה רֹכְלָיִךְ בְּנֶפֶשׁ אָדָם וּכְלֵי נְחֹשֶׁת נָתְנוּ מַעֲרָבֵךְ:
יד-טו מִבֵּית תּוֹגַרְמָה סוּסִים וּפָרָשִׁים וּפְרָדִים נָתְנוּ עִזְבוֹנָיִךְ: בְּנֵי דְדָן רֹכְלַיִךְ
אִיִּים רַבִּים סְחֹרַת יָדֵךְ קַרְנוֹת שֵׁן °והובנים [וְהָבְנִים ק] הֵשִׁיבוּ
אֶשְׁכָּרֵךְ: טז אֲרָם סֹחַרְתֵּךְ מֵרֹב מַעֲשָׂיִךְ בְּנֹפֶךְ אַרְגָּמָן וְרִקְמָה וּבוּץ
וְרָאמֹת וְכַדְכֹּד נָתְנוּ בְּעִזְבוֹנָיִךְ: יז יְהוּדָה וְאֶרֶץ יִשְׂרָאֵל הֵמָּה רֹכְלָיִךְ
בְּחִטֵּי מִנִּית וּפַנַּג וּדְבַשׁ וָשֶׁמֶן וָצֹרִי נָתְנוּ מַעֲרָבֵךְ: יח דַּמֶּשֶׂק סֹחַרְתֵּךְ
בְּרֹב מַעֲשַׂיִךְ מֵרֹב כָּל־הוֹן בְּיֵין חֶלְבּוֹן וְצֶמֶר צָחַר: יט וְדָן וְיָוָן מְאוּזָּל
בְּעִזְבוֹנַיִךְ נָתָנּוּ בַּרְזֶל עָשׁוֹת קִדָּה וְקָנֶה בְּמַעֲרָבֵךְ הָיָה: כ דְּדָן רֹכַלְתֵּךְ
בְּבִגְדֵי־חֹפֶשׁ לְרִכְבָּה: כא עֲרַב וְכָל־נְשִׂיאֵי קֵדָר הֵמָּה סֹחֲרֵי יָדֵךְ בְּכָרִים
וְאֵילִם וְעַתּוּדִים בָּם סֹחֲרָיִךְ: כב רֹכְלֵי שְׁבָא וְרַעְמָה הֵמָּה רֹכְלָיִךְ
בְּרֹאשׁ כָּל־בֹּשֶׂם וּבְכָל־אֶבֶן יְקָרָה וְזָהָב נָתְנוּ עִזְבוֹנָיִךְ: כג חָרָן וְכַנֵּה
וָעֶדֶן רֹכְלֵי שְׁבָא אַשּׁוּר כִּלְמַד רֹכַלְתֵּךְ: כד הֵמָּה רֹכְלַיִךְ בְּמַכְלֻלִים
בִּגְלוֹמֵי תְּכֵלֶת וְרִקְמָה וּבְגִנְזֵי בְּרֹמִים בַּחֲבָלִים חֲבֻשִׁים וַאֲרֻזִים
בְּמַרְכֻלְתֵּךְ: כה אֳנִיּוֹת תַּרְשִׁישׁ שָׁרוֹתַיִךְ מַעֲרָבֵךְ וַתִּמָּלְאִי וַתִּכְבְּדִי מְאֹד
בְּלֵב יַמִּים: כו בְּמַיִם רַבִּים הֱבִיאוּךְ הַשָּׁטִים אֹתָךְ רוּחַ הַקָּדִים שְׁבָרֵךְ
בְּלֵב יַמִּים: כז הוֹנֵךְ וְעִזְבוֹנַיִךְ מַעֲרָבֵךְ מַלָּחַיִךְ וְחֹבְלָיִךְ מַחֲזִיקֵי בִדְקֵךְ
וְעֹרְבֵי מַעֲרָבֵךְ וְכָל־אַנְשֵׁי מִלְחַמְתֵּךְ אֲשֶׁר־בָּךְ וּבְכָל־קְהָלֵךְ אֲשֶׁר
בְּתוֹכֵךְ יִפְּלוּ בְּלֵב יַמִּים בְּיוֹם מַפַּלְתֵּךְ: כח לְקוֹל זַעֲקַת חֹבְלָיִךְ יִרְעֲשׁוּ
מִגְרֹשׁוֹת: כט וְיָרְדוּ מֵאֳנִיּוֹתֵיהֶם כֹּל תֹּפְשֵׂי מָשׁוֹט מַלָּחִים כֹּל חֹבְלֵי הַיָּם
אֶל־הָאָרֶץ יַעֲמֹדוּ: ל וְהִשְׁמִיעוּ עָלַיִךְ בְּקוֹלָם וְיִזְעֲקוּ מָרָה וְיַעֲלוּ עָפָר
עַל־רָאשֵׁיהֶם בָּאֵפֶר יִתְפַּלָּשׁוּ: לא וְהִקְרִיחוּ אֵלַיִךְ קָרְחָה וְחָגְרוּ שַׂקִּים

27:11. Another name for the Cappadocians (*Targum*). *Metzudos* renders this word as "dwarfs." They would be stationed as lookouts because they could hide more easily from the enemy.

27:12. Tarshish exported these raw materials to Tyre, which processed them and became wealthy selling them (*Metzudos*).

27:13. Nations engaged in the slave trade.

27:14. They brought valuable goods in boxes and chests.

27:28-31. With the downfall of Tyre, the sailors will lose their livelihood and grieve.

27:25. Like an overloaded vessel heading for doom on the high seas, your pride and wealth brought about your downfall (*Radak*).

27:29. All maritime commerce will stop when Tyre is destroyed.

¹⁰ Persia, Lud, and Put were in your army — your men of war;
They hung shield and helmet in you; they provided your beauty.
¹¹ The sons of Arvad and your army, up on your walls all around;
And Gammadim* were in your towers.
They hung their shields upon your walls all around,
they perfected your beauty.

Tyre's trading partners

¹² Tarshish was your merchant because of the multitude of every richness:*
With silver, iron, tin, and lead they provided your wares.
¹³ Javan, Tubal, and Meshech,* they were your peddlers:
With human soul and copper vessels, they provided your merchandise.
¹⁴ From the house of Togarmah, horses, riders, and mules,*
they provided your wares.
¹⁵ The men of Dedan were your peddlers; many islands traded with you;
Ivory tusks and peacocks they brought as your tribute.
¹⁶ Aram was your merchant because of your great wealth:
With carbuncle, purple wool, and embroidery,
Fine linen, coral, and pearl, they provided your wares.
¹⁷ Judah and the Land of Israel, they were your peddlers:
With wheat from Minnith, and balsam oil, honey, oil, and balm,
they provided your merchandise.
¹⁸ Damascus was your merchant because of your great wealth,
Because of the multitude of every richness:
with wine from Helbon and white wool.
¹⁹ Vedan and Javan provided your wares with fine yarn,
Iron bars, cassia, and cane were among your merchandise.
²⁰ Dedan was your peddler, with exquisite clothes for riding.
²¹ Arabia and all of Kedar's princes, they were your local merchants:
With fatted sheep, rams, and he-goats, with these they were your merchants.
²² The peddlers of Sheba and Raamah, they were your peddlers;
With the best of every spice, and every precious stone and gold,
they provided your wares.
²³ Haran, Canneh, and Eden, the peddlers of Sheba, Asshur, and Media,
were your peddlers.
²⁴ They were your peddlers in objects of perfection:
In wraps of blue wool and embroidery; in treasures kept in chests,
fastened with bands and cedar boxed, for your wares.
²⁵ The ships of Tarshish were your caravans for your merchandise.
Thus you were filled and made very heavy in the heart of the seas. *

Tyre's downfall

²⁶ Into many waters your oarsmen brought you;
The east wind has broken you in the heart of the seas.
²⁷ Your riches, and your wares, your merchandise; your rowers and your sailors,
The caulkers of your cracks and the providers of your merchandise,
And all your men of war who are within you,
And with your entire assembly that is in your midst,
They will fall in the heart of the seas on the day of your downfall.
²⁸ At the sound of your sailors' cries,* the surrounding areas will tremble;
²⁹ They will descend from their boats: All who grasp an oar,
rowers and all sailors of the sea; they will stand upon the ground. *
³⁰ They will let their voices to be heard about you, and they will cry out bitterly.
They will put dust upon their heads and wallow in the ashes.
³¹ They will tear out their hair for you, and gird themselves in sackcloth;

לב וּבָכ֤וּ אֵלַ֙יִךְ֙ בְּמַ֔ר נֶ֖פֶשׁ מִסְפֵּ֣ד מָ֑ר וְנָשְׂא֨וּ אֵלַ֤יִךְ בְּנִיהֶם֙ קִינָ֔ה וְקוֹנְנ֖וּ עָלָֽיִךְ׃

לג מִ֣י כְצ֔וֹר כְּדֻמָּ֖ה בְּת֣וֹךְ הַיָּ֑ם בְּצֵ֤את עִזְבוֹנַ֙יִךְ֙ מִיַּמִּ֔ים הִשְׂבַּ֖עַתְּ עַמִּ֣ים

לג רַבִּ֑ים בְּרֹ֧ב הוֹנַ֛יִךְ וּמַעֲרָבַ֖יִךְ הֶעֱשַׁ֣רְתְּ מַלְכֵי־אָֽרֶץ׃ עֵ֚ת נִשְׁבֶּ֣רֶת מִיַּמִּ֔ים

לה בְּמַֽעֲמַקֵּי־מָ֑יִם מַעֲרָבֵ֥ךְ וְכָל־קְהָלֵ֖ךְ בְּתוֹכֵ֣ךְ נָפָ֑לוּ׃ כֹּ֚ל יֹשְׁבֵ֣י הָֽאִיִּ֔ים

לו שָֽׁמְמ֣וּ עָלָ֔יִךְ וּמַלְכֵיהֶ֙ם֙ שָׂ֣עֲרוּ שַׂ֔עַר רָעֲמ֖וּ פָּנִ֑ים סֹחֲרִים֙ בָּֽעַמִּ֔ים שָׁרְק֣וּ

כח א עָלָ֔יִךְ בַּלָּה֣וֹת הָיִ֔ית וְאֵינֵ֖ךְ עַד־עוֹלָֽם׃　　　　וַיְהִ֥י דְבַר־

ב יְהֹוָ֖ה אֵלַ֣י לֵאמֹֽר׃ בֶּן־אָדָ֡ם אֱמֹר֩ לִנְגִ֨יד צֹ֜ר כֹּֽה־אָמַ֣ר ׀ אֲדֹנָ֣י יֱהֹוִ֗ה

יַ֣עַן גָּבַ֤הּ לִבְּךָ֙ וַתֹּ֔אמֶר אֵ֣ל אָ֔נִי מוֹשַׁ֧ב אֱלֹהִ֛ים יָשַׁ֖בְתִּי בְּלֵ֣ב יַמִּ֑ים וְאַתָּ֤ה

ג אָדָם֙ וְלֹא־אֵ֔ל וַתִּתֵּ֥ן לִבְּךָ֖ כְּלֵ֣ב אֱלֹהִֽים׃ הִנֵּ֥ה חָכָ֛ם אַתָּ֖ה °מִדָּֽנִאֵל

ד [°מִדָּֽנִיֵּ֖אל ק] כָּל־סָת֖וּם לֹ֣א עֲמָמ֑וּךָ׃ בְּחׇכְמָֽתְךָ֙ וּבִתְבֽוּנָתְךָ֔ עָשִׂ֥יתָ לְּךָ֖

ה חָ֑יִל וַתַּ֛עַשׂ זָהָ֥ב וָכֶ֖סֶף בְּאוֹצְרוֹתֶֽיךָ׃ בְּרֹ֤ב חׇכְמָֽתְךָ֙ בִּרְכֻלָּ֣תְךָ֔ הִרְבִּ֖יתָ

ו חֵילֶ֑ךָ וַיִּגְבַּ֥הּ לְבָבְךָ֖ בְּחֵילֶֽךָ׃　　　　לָכֵ֗ן כֹּ֤ה אָמַר֙ אֲדֹנָ֣י

ז יֱהֹוִ֔ה יַ֛עַן תִּתְּךָ֥ אֶת־לְבָבְךָ֖ כְּלֵ֣ב אֱלֹהִֽים׃ לָכֵ֗ן הִנְנִ֨י מֵבִ֤יא עָלֶ֙יךָ֙ זָרִ֔ים

ח עָרִיצֵ֖י גּוֹיִ֑ם וְהֵרִ֤יקוּ חַרְבוֹתָם֙ עַל־יְפִ֣י חׇכְמָתֶ֔ךָ וְחִלְּל֖וּ יִפְעָתֶֽךָ׃ לַשַּׁ֣חַת

ט יֽוֹרִד֔וּךָ וָמַ֛תָּה מְמוֹתֵ֥י חָלָ֖ל בְּלֵ֥ב יַמִּֽים׃ הֶאָמֹ֤ר תֹּאמַר֙ אֱלֹהִ֣ים אָ֔נִי לִפְנֵ֖י

י הֹֽרְגֶ֑ךָ וְאַתָּ֥ה אָדָ֛ם וְלֹא־אֵ֖ל בְּיַ֥ד מְחַלְלֶֽיךָ׃ מוֹתֵ֧י עֲרֵלִ֛ים תָּמ֖וּת בְּיַד־

יא זָרִ֑ים כִּ֥י אֲנִ֛י דִּבַּ֖רְתִּי נְאֻ֥ם אֲדֹנָ֥י יֱהֹוִֽה׃　　　　וַיְהִ֥י

יב דְבַר־יְהֹוָ֖ה אֵלַ֣י לֵאמֹֽר׃ בֶּן־אָדָ֕ם שָׂ֥א קִינָ֖ה עַל־מֶ֣לֶךְ צ֑וֹר וְאָמַ֣רְתָּ לּ֗וֹ

כֹּ֤ה אָמַר֙ אֲדֹנָ֣י יֱהֹוִ֔ה אַתָּה֙ חוֹתֵ֣ם תׇּכְנִ֔ית מָלֵ֥א חׇכְמָ֖ה וּכְלִ֥יל יֹֽפִי׃

יג בְּעֵ֨דֶן גַּן־אֱלֹהִ֜ים הָיִ֗יתָ כָּל־אֶ֨בֶן יְקָרָ֤ה מְסֻכָתֶ֙ךָ֙ אֹ֣דֶם פִּטְדָה֙ וְיָ֣הֲלֹ֔ם

תַּרְשִׁ֥ישׁ שֹׁ֙הַם֙ וְיָ֣שְׁפֵ֔ה סַפִּ֣יר נֹ֔פֶךְ וּבָרְקַ֖ת וְזָהָ֑ב מְלֶ֨אכֶת תֻּפֶּ֤יךָ וּנְקָבֶ֙יךָ֙

יד בָּ֔ךְ בְּי֥וֹם הִבָּרַֽאֲךָ֖ כּוֹנָֽנוּ׃ אַ֨תְּ־כְּר֔וּב מִמְשַׁ֖ח הַסּוֹכֵ֑ךְ וּנְתַתִּ֗יךָ בְּהַ֤ר קֹ֙דֶשׁ֙

טו אֱלֹהִים֙ הָיִ֔יתָ בְּת֥וֹךְ אַבְנֵי־אֵ֖שׁ הִתְהַלָּֽכְתָּ׃ תָּמִ֤ים אַתָּה֙ בִּדְרָכֶ֔יךָ

טז מִיּ֖וֹם הִבָּֽרְאָ֑ךְ עַד־נִמְצָ֥א עַוְלָ֖תָה בָּֽךְ׃ בְּרֹ֣ב רְכֻלָּֽתְךָ֗ מָל֧וּ תֽוֹכְךָ֛ חָמָ֖ס

וַֽתֶּחֱטָ֑א וָאֲחַלֶּלְךָ֩ מֵהַ֨ר אֱלֹהִ֜ים וָאַבֶּדְךָ֙ כְּר֣וּב הַסֹּכֵ֔ךְ מִתּ֖וֹךְ אַבְנֵי־אֵֽשׁ׃

27:36. In astonishment. According to *Rashi*, this was a passing phenomenon. After the initial astonishment at Tyre's downfall, its former trading partners forgot about it and and found other ways to conduct their business.

28:3. The question is meant sarcastically. Nebuchadnezzar had wanted to proclaim Daniel to be a God, but Daniel refused (*Rashi*). See 14:14 above and *Daniel* 2:46.

28:10. This refers to those of uncircumcised heart, meaning that they persist in their wickedness and refuse to accept the truth. See 44:7.

28:12. Are you as perfect as the first man, Adam, the die from which all mankind was cast? (*Midrash*)

28:13. These precious stones formed a canopy over Adam's head in the Garden of Eden (*Talmud; Bava Basra* 75a). See note to *Exodus* 28:17-20 regarding the identity of these gemstones.

28:14. You were a leader of very great stature. God blessed you because your predecessor, King Hiram of Tyre, played a major role in the building of Solomon's Temple, upon the mountain of God (see *I Kings* Ch. 15), in cooperation with the fiery stones, i.e., David and Solomon, the great kings of Israel (*Rashi*).

They will weep for you with embittered soul, bitter lamentation.

The lament ³² *They will take up for you a lament in their wailing, and lament over you:*
'Who is like Tyre! Who can compare to her in the midst of the sea?'
³³ *When your wares went forth from the seas you satiated many peoples;*
With your abundant riches and your merchandise,
you enriched the kings of the earth.
³⁴ *When you were broken by the seas, in the depths of the waters,*
your merchandise and all your assembly fell in your midst.
³⁵ *All inhabitants of the islands became astonished over you.*
Their kings shook with trembling; their faces showing anguish.
³⁶ *Merchants among the peoples whistled over you;* *
You were a terror, but you shall be no more, forever."

28   ¹ **T**he word of HASHEM came to me, saying, ² "Son of Man, say to the prince

Prophecy
against the
king of Tyre of Tyre:

Thus said the Lord HASHEM/ELOHIM: Because your heart has grown proud
and you have said, 'I am a god; I occupy the seat of God in the heart of the
seas!' — but you are a man and not a god, though you set your heart like
the heart of God! ³ *Are you wiser than Daniel?* * *Does no mystery perplex*
you? ⁴ *Through your wisdom and discernment you have acquired wealth for*
yourself and amassed gold and silver in your treasuries. ⁵ *Through your*
abundant wisdom in your commerce, you have increased your wealth, and
your heart became proud with your wealth.

⁶ *Therefore, thus said the Lord HASHEM/ELOHIM: Because you have set*
your heart like the heart of God, ⁷ *therefore, behold, I am bringing foreigners*
upon you, the fiercest of the nations, and they will draw their swords against
the beauty of your wisdom, and they will defile your splendor. ⁸ *They will*
bring you down to the grave, and you will die the death of the slain, in the
heart of the seas. ⁹ *Will you say, 'I am a God,' before your killer? You are a*
man and not a god in the hand of your slayer! ¹⁰ *You will die the death of the*
uncircumcised * *by the hand of foreigners, for I have spoken — the word of*
the Lord HASHEM/ELOHIM.' "

A lament
over the king
of Tyre ¹¹ *The word of HASHEM came to me, saying,* ¹² "Son of Man, take up a lamentation over the king of Tyre. Say of him:

Thus said the Lord HASHEM/ELOHIM:
Are you [Adam] the culmination of perfection, *
full of wisdom, perfect in beauty?
¹³ *Were you in Eden, the garden of God;*
Was your canopy of every precious stone —
Odem, pitdah and yahalom; tarshish, shoham and yashfeh;
sapir, nophech and barkas — and gold? *
The work of your drums and wind instruments was in you;
They were established on the day of your creation.
¹⁴ *You were a great sheltering cherub,* * *and it is I [who] granted you this;*
You were upon the holy mountain of God; you walked among fiery stones;
¹⁵ *Perfect were you in your ways from the day of your creation —*
until wrongdoing was found in you.
¹⁶ *Because of your abundant commerce,*
your midst filled with injustice and you sinned;
So I desecrated you from the mountain of God
And destroyed you, O sheltering cherub, from among the fiery stones.

יח גָּבַהּ לִבְּךָ֙ בְּיָפְיֶ֔ךָ שִׁחַ֥תָּ חָכְמָתְךָ֖ עַל־יִפְעָתֶ֑ךָ עַל־אֶ֨רֶץ֙ הִשְׁלַכְתִּ֔יךָ לִפְנֵ֥י

מְלָכִ֖ים נְתַתִּ֣יךָ לְרַ֣אֲוָה בָֽךְ: מֵרֹ֣ב עֲוֺנֶ֗יךָ בְּעֶ֨וֶל֙ רְכֻלָּ֣תְךָ֔ חִלַּ֖לְתָּ מִקְדָּשֶׁ֑יךָ

וָאֽוֹצִא־אֵ֤שׁ מִתּֽוֹכְךָ֙ הִ֣יא אֲכָלַ֔תְךָ וָאֶתֶּנְךָ֤ לְאֵ֨פֶר֙ עַל־הָאָ֔רֶץ לְעֵינֵ֖י

יט כָּל־רֹאֶֽיךָ: כָּל־יֽוֹדְעֶ֨יךָ֙ בָּֽעַמִּ֔ים שָֽׁמְמ֖וּ עָלֶ֑יךָ בַּלָּה֣וֹת הָיִ֔יתָ וְאֵֽינְךָ֖ עַד־

כ-כא עוֹלָֽם: וַיְהִ֥י דְבַר־יְהֺוָ֖ה אֵלַ֥י לֵאמֹֽר: בֶּן־אָדָ֕ם שִׂ֥ים פָּנֶ֖יךָ

כב אֶל־צִיד֑וֹן וְהִנָּבֵ֖א עָלֶֽיהָ: וְאָֽמַרְתָּ֗ כֹּ֤ה אָמַר֙ אֲדֹנָ֣י יֱהֺוִ֔ה הִנְנִ֤י עָלַ֨יִךְ֙ צִיד֔וֹן

וְנִכְבַּדְתִּ֖י בְּתוֹכֵ֑ךְ וְיָֽדְע֞וּ כִּֽי־אֲנִ֣י יְהֺוָ֗ה בַּֽעֲשׂ֥וֹתִי בָ֛הּ שְׁפָטִ֖ים וְנִקְדַּ֥שְׁתִּי בָֽהּ:

כג וְשִׁלַּחְתִּי־בָ֞הּ דֶּ֤בֶר וָדָם֙ בְּח֣וּצוֹתֶ֔יהָ וְנִפְלַ֤ל חָלָל֙ בְּתוֹכָ֔הּ בְּחֶ֖רֶב עָלֶ֣יהָ

כד מִסָּבִ֑יב וְיָֽדְע֖וּ כִּֽי־אֲנִ֥י יְהֺוָֽה: וְלֹֽא־יִהְיֶ֣ה ע֠וֹד לְבֵ֨ית יִשְׂרָאֵ֜ל סִלּ֤וֹן מַמְאִיר֙

וְק֣וֹץ מַכְאִ֔ב מִכֹּל֙ סְבִ֣יבֹתָ֔ם הַשָּׁאטִ֖ים אוֹתָ֑ם וְיָ֣דְע֔וּ כִּ֥י אֲנִ֖י אֲדֹנָ֥י

כה יֱהֺוִֽה: ◀ כֹּֽה־אָמַר֮ אֲדֹנָ֣י יֱהֺוִה֒ בְּקַבְּצִ֣י ׀ אֶת־בֵּ֣ית יִשְׂרָאֵ֗ל

מִן־הָֽעַמִּים֙ אֲשֶׁ֣ר נָפֹ֣צוּ בָ֔ם וְנִקְדַּ֥שְׁתִּי בָ֖ם לְעֵינֵ֣י הַגּוֹיִ֑ם וְיָֽשְׁב֣וּ עַל־

כו אַדְמָתָ֔ם אֲשֶׁ֥ר נָתַ֖תִּי לְעַבְדִּ֣י לְיַֽעֲקֹֽב: וְיָֽשְׁב֣וּ עָלֶיהָ֮ לָבֶטַח֒ וּבָנ֤וּ בָתִּים֙

וְנָֽטְע֣וּ כְרָמִ֔ים וְיָֽשְׁב֖וּ לָבֶ֑טַח בַּֽעֲשׂוֹתִ֣י שְׁפָטִ֗ים בְּכֹ֤ל הַשָּׁאטִים֙ אֹתָ֔ם

א מִסְּבִֽיבוֹתָ֔ם וְיָ֣דְע֔וּ כִּ֛י אֲנִ֥י יְהֺוָ֖ה אֱלֹֽהֵיהֶֽם:

**HAFTARAS
VA'EIRA**
28:25-29:21

כט

הָעֲשִׂירִ֗ית בִּשְׁנֵ֤ים עָשָׂר֙ חֹ֔דֶשׁ בַּֽחֲדַ֖שׁ הָיָ֥ה דְבַר־יְהֺוָ֖ה אֵלַ֥י לֵאמֹֽר: בֶּן־

ב אָדָ֕ם שִׂ֣ים פָּנֶ֔יךָ עַל־פַּרְעֹ֖ה מֶ֣לֶךְ מִצְרָ֑יִם וְהִנָּבֵ֣א עָלָ֔יו וְעַל־מִצְרַ֖יִם כֻּלָּֽהּ:

ג דַּבֵּ֨ר וְאָֽמַרְתָּ֜ כֹּֽה־אָמַ֣ר ׀ אֲדֹנָ֣י יֱהֺוִ֗ה הִנְנִ֤י עָלֶ֨יךָ֙ פַּרְעֹ֣ה מֶֽלֶךְ־מִצְרַ֔יִם

הַתַּנִּים֙ הַגָּד֔וֹל הָֽרֹבֵ֖ץ בְּת֣וֹךְ יְאֹרָ֑יו אֲשֶׁ֥ר אָמַ֛ר לִ֥י יְאֹרִ֖י וַֽאֲנִ֥י עֲשִׂיתִֽנִי:

ד וְנָֽתַתִּ֣י °חַחִיים [°חַחִ֣ים ק] בִּלְחָיֶ֔יךָ וְהִדְבַּקְתִּ֥י דְגַת־יְאֹרֶ֖יךָ בְּקַשְׂקְשֹׂתֶ֑יךָ

וְהַֽעֲלִיתִ֨יךָ֙ מִתּ֣וֹךְ יְאֹרֶ֔יךָ וְאֵת֙ כָּל־דְּגַ֣ת יְאֹרֶ֔יךָ בְּקַשְׂקְשֹׂתֶ֖יךָ תִּדְבָּֽק:

ה וּנְטַשְׁתִּ֣יךָ הַמִּדְבָּ֗רָה אֽוֹתְךָ֙ וְאֵת֙ כָּל־דְּגַ֣ת יְאֹרֶ֔יךָ עַל־פְּנֵ֤י הַשָּׂדֶה֙ תִּפּ֔וֹל

לֹ֥א תֵֽאָסֵ֖ף וְלֹ֣א תִקָּבֵ֑ץ לְחַיַּ֥ת הָאָ֛רֶץ וּלְע֥וֹף הַשָּׁמַ֖יִם נְתַתִּ֥יךָ לְאָכְלָֽה:

ו וְיָֽדְעוּ֙ כָּל־יֽוֹשְׁבֵ֣י מִצְרַ֔יִם כִּ֖י אֲנִ֣י יְהֺוָ֑ה יַ֛עַן הֱיוֹתָ֥ם מִשְׁעֶ֥נֶת קָנֶ֖ה לְבֵ֥ית

ז יִשְׂרָאֵֽל: בְּתָפְשָׂ֤ם בְּךָ֙ °בכפך [°בַכַּ֣ף ק] תֵּר֔וֹץ וּבָֽקַעְתָּ֥ לָהֶ֖ם כָּל־כָּתֵ֑ף וּבְהִֽשָּׁעֲנָ֤ם

עָלֶ֨יךָ֙ תִּשָּׁבֵ֔ר וְהַֽעֲמַדְתָּ֥ לָהֶ֖ם כָּל־מָתְנָֽיִם:

ח לָכֵ֗ן כֹּ֤ה אָמַר֙ אֲדֹנָ֣י יֱהֺוִ֔ה הִנְנִ֛י מֵבִ֥יא עָלַ֖יִךְ חָ֑רֶב וְהִכְרַתִּ֥י מִמֵּ֖ךְ אָדָ֥ם

ט וּבְהֵמָֽה: וְהָֽיְתָ֤ה אֶֽרֶץ־מִצְרַ֨יִם֙ לִשְׁמָמָ֣ה וְחָרְבָּ֔ה וְיָֽדְע֖וּ כִּֽי־אֲנִ֣י יְהֺוָ֑ה

י יַ֧עַן אָמַ֛ר יְאֹ֥ר לִ֖י וַֽאֲנִ֣י עָשִֽׂיתִי: לָכֵ֛ן הִנְנִ֥י אֵלֶ֖יךָ וְאֶל־יְאֹרֶ֑יךָ וְנָֽתַתִּ֞י אֶת־

28:18. You will be consumed because of your own sins (*Targum*).

28:24. A metaphor for menacing neighbors.

29:1. This prophecy came to Ezekiel on the twelfth of Teves, in the tenth year of Jehoiachin's exile and Zedekiah's reign.

29:3. Because Egypt is completely dependent upon the Nile, Pharaoh is compared to the largest and fiercest denizen of the Nile, and his people to fish (*Rashi*).

29:7. Egypt disappointed those who depended on its support. It broke like a reed, injuring those who relied upon it, or forcing them to stand erect without the needed aid.

¹⁷ *Your heart became proud because of your beauty;*
You corrupted your wisdom because of your splendor.
So I have thrown you to the ground
And I have set you before kings to gaze upon you.
¹⁸ *By the multitude of your iniquities, by the dishonesty of your commerce,*
You desecrated your sanctities; so I drew out a fire from within you.
It consumed you; * *thus I made you into ashes upon the earth in the eyes of*
all who see you.
¹⁹ *All who knew you among the peoples were astonished over you;*
You were a terror, but you shall be no more, forever."

Prophecy
against
Zidon ²⁰ *The word of* HASHEM *came to me, saying,* ²¹ *"Son of Man, direct your face towards Sidon and prophesy against it.* ²² *Say:*

Thus said the Lord HASHEM/ELOHIM: *Behold, I am against you, O Sidon; I will be honored within you, and they will know that I am* HASHEM, *when I execute judgments upon her and I become sanctified through her.* ²³ *I will send pestilence and blood into her, into her streets; and the slain will fall within her when the sword comes upon her from all around; then they will know that I am* HASHEM. ²⁴ *Then there will no longer be for the House of Israel any harmful briar nor painful thorn* * *among all their surroundings, who despoil them; and they will know that I am the Lord HASHEM/ELOHIM.*

The
ingathering
of Israel ²⁵ *Thus said the Lord HASHEM/ELOHIM: When I gather in the House of Israel from the peoples among whom they were scattered, then I will be sanctified through them in the eyes of the nations, and they will dwell on their land that I gave to My servant, to Jacob.* ²⁶ *They will dwell upon it in security and build houses and plant vineyards and dwell in security, when I execute judgments upon all those who despoil them from all their surroundings; then they will know that I am* HASHEM, *their God.*

29   ¹ *In the tenth year, in the tenth [month], on the twelfth of the month,* * *the word* Prophecy
against
Pharaoh
and Egypt *of* HASHEM *came to me, saying,* ² *"Son of Man, direct your face towards Pharaoh, king of Egypt, and prophesy concerning him and concerning all of Egypt.* ³ *Speak and say:*

Thus said the Lord HASHEM/ELOHIM: *Behold, I am against you, Pharaoh, king of Egypt, the great serpent* * *that crouches within its rivers, who has said, 'Mine is my river, and I have made myself [powerful].'* ⁴ *I will attach hooks to your cheeks, and I will cause the fish of your rivers to cling to your scales; I will draw you out from within your rivers, and all the fish of your rivers will cling to your scales,* ⁵ *and I will cast you into the wilderness, you and all the fish of your rivers. You will fall upon the surface of the open field; you will not be gathered in and not be collected together; I will present you as food to the beast of the land and to the bird of the heavens.* ⁶ *Then all the inhabitants of Egypt will know that I am* HASHEM, *because they were a reed-like support for the House of Israel —* ⁷ *whenever they held you in their hand you would snap, piercing their every shoulder, and whenever they leaned upon you, you would break and make their loins stand upright.* *

⁸ *Therefore, thus said the Lord HASHEM/ELOHIM: Behold, I am bringing a sword against you and I will eliminate from you man and animal.* ⁹ *The land of Egypt will become desolate and a ruin; then they will know that I am* HASHEM *— because he said, 'The river is mine and I have made [it].'* ¹⁰ *Therefore, behold, I am against you and against your rivers, and I will make the*

יא אֶרֶץ מִצְרַיִם לַחֳרָבוֹת חָרֵב שְׁמָמָה מִמִּגְדֹּל סְוֵנֵה וְעַד־גְּבוּל כּוּשׁ: לֹא תַעֲבָר־בָּהּ רֶגֶל אָדָם וְרֶגֶל בְּהֵמָה לֹא תַעֲבָר־בָּהּ וְלֹא תֵשֵׁב אַרְבָּעִים שָׁנָה: יב וְנָתַתִּי אֶת־אֶרֶץ מִצְרַיִם שְׁמָמָה בְּתוֹךְ ׀ אֲרָצוֹת נְשַׁמּוֹת וְעָרֶיהָ בְּתוֹךְ עָרִים מַחֳרָבוֹת תִּהְיֶיןָ שְׁמָמָה אַרְבָּעִים שָׁנָה וַהֲפִצֹתִי אֶת־מִצְרַיִם בַּגּוֹיִם וְזֵרִיתִים בָּאֲרָצוֹת: יג כִּי כֹּה אָמַר אֲדֹנָי יֱהֹוִה מִקֵּץ אַרְבָּעִים שָׁנָה אֲקַבֵּץ אֶת־מִצְרַיִם מִן־הָעַמִּים אֲשֶׁר־נָפֹצוּ שָׁמָּה: יד וְשַׁבְתִּי אֶת־שְׁבוּת מִצְרַיִם וַהֲשִׁבֹתִי אֹתָם אֶרֶץ פַּתְרוֹס עַל־אֶרֶץ מְכוּרָתָם וְהָיוּ שָׁם מַמְלָכָה שְׁפָלָה: טו מִן־הַמַּמְלָכוֹת תִּהְיֶה שְׁפָלָה וְלֹא־תִתְנַשֵּׂא עוֹד עַל־הַגּוֹיִם וְהִמְעַטְתִּים לְבִלְתִּי רְדוֹת בַּגּוֹיִם: טז וְלֹא יִהְיֶה־עוֹד לְבֵית יִשְׂרָאֵל לְמִבְטָח מַזְכִּיר עָוֹן בִּפְנוֹתָם אַחֲרֵיהֶם וְיָדְעוּ כִּי אֲנִי אֲדֹנָי יֱהֹוִה: יז וַיְהִי בְּעֶשְׂרִים וָשֶׁבַע שָׁנָה בָּרִאשׁוֹן בְּאֶחָד לַחֹדֶשׁ הָיָה דְבַר־יְהֹוָה אֵלַי לֵאמֹר: יח בֶּן־אָדָם נְבוּכַדְרֶאצַּר מֶלֶךְ־בָּבֶל הֶעֱבִיד אֶת־חֵילוֹ עֲבֹדָה גְדוֹלָה אֶל־צֹר כָּל־רֹאשׁ מֻקְרָח וְכָל־כָּתֵף מְרוּטָה וְשָׂכָר לֹא־הָיָה לוֹ וּלְחֵילוֹ מִצֹּר עַל־הָעֲבֹדָה אֲשֶׁר־עָבַד עָלֶיהָ: יט לָכֵן כֹּה אָמַר אֲדֹנָי יֱהֹוִה הִנְנִי נֹתֵן לִנְבוּכַדְרֶאצַּר מֶלֶךְ־בָּבֶל אֶת־אֶרֶץ מִצְרָיִם וְנָשָׂא הֲמֹנָהּ וְשָׁלַל שְׁלָלָהּ וּבָזַז בִּזָּהּ וְהָיְתָה שָׂכָר לְחֵילוֹ: כ פְּעֻלָּתוֹ אֲשֶׁר־עָבַד בָּהּ נָתַתִּי לוֹ אֶת־אֶרֶץ מִצְרָיִם אֲשֶׁר עָשׂוּ לִי נְאֻם אֲדֹנָי יֱהֹוִה: כא בַּיּוֹם הַהוּא אַצְמִיחַ קֶרֶן לְבֵית יִשְׂרָאֵל וּלְךָ אֶתֵּן פִּתְחוֹן־פֶּה בְּתוֹכָם וְיָדְעוּ כִּי־אֲנִי יְהֹוָה: ◄

ל

א וַיְהִי דְבַר־יְהֹוָה אֵלַי לֵאמֹר: ב בֶּן־אָדָם הִנָּבֵא וְאָמַרְתָּ כֹּה אָמַר אֲדֹנָי יֱהֹוִה הֵילִילוּ הָהּ לַיּוֹם: ג כִּי־קָרוֹב יוֹם וְקָרוֹב יוֹם לַיהֹוָה יוֹם עָנָן עֵת גּוֹיִם יִהְיֶה: ד וּבָאָה חֶרֶב בְּמִצְרַיִם וְהָיְתָה חַלְחָלָה בְּכוּשׁ בִּנְפֹל חָלָל בְּמִצְרָיִם וְלָקְחוּ הֲמוֹנָהּ וְנֶהֶרְסוּ יְסוֹדֹתֶיהָ: ה כּוּשׁ וּפוּט וְלוּד וְכָל־הָעֶרֶב וְכוּב וּבְנֵי אֶרֶץ הַבְּרִית אִתָּם בַּחֶרֶב יִפֹּלוּ: ו כֹּה אָמַר יְהֹוָה וְנָפְלוּ סֹמְכֵי מִצְרַיִם וְיָרַד גְּאוֹן עֻזָּהּ מִמִּגְדֹּל סְוֵנֵה בַּחֶרֶב יִפְּלוּ־בָהּ נְאֻם אֲדֹנָי יֱהֹוִה: ז וְנָשַׁמּוּ בְּתוֹךְ אֲרָצוֹת נְשַׁמּוֹת וְעָרָיו בְּתוֹךְ־עָרִים נַחֳרָבוֹת תִּהְיֶינָה: ח-ט וְיָדְעוּ כִּי־אֲנִי יְהֹוָה בְּתִתִּי־אֵשׁ בְּמִצְרַיִם וְנִשְׁבְּרוּ כָּל־עֹזְרֶיהָ: בַּיּוֹם הַהוּא יֵצְאוּ מַלְאָכִים מִלְּפָנַי בַּצִּים לְהַחֲרִיד אֶת־כּוּשׁ בֶּטַח וְהָיְתָה חַלְחָלָה בָהֶם °בְּיוֹם מִצְרַיִם כִּי הִנֵּה בָּאָה: י כֹּה אָמַר אֲדֹנָי יֱהֹוִה וְהִשְׁבַּתִּי אֶת־הֲמוֹן מִצְרַיִם בְּיַד נְבוּכַדְרֶאצַּר מֶלֶךְ־בָּבֶל: יא הוּא

°נ״א כְּיוֹם

29:10. Ethiopia.

29:16. It was a sin for Israel to put its faith in Egypt, instead of turning to God.

29:17. Of Nebuchadnezzar's reign (*Seder Olam*), which was eight years after the Destruction of the Temple and the seventeenth year of Jehoiachin's exile. Thus, this prophecy was not recorded in its chronological setting.

29:18. From the immense amount of war materiel the soldiers hauled on their heads and shoulders. But the spoils of Tyre were not commensurate with the immense amount of labor invested in its siege.

29:20. Egypt's betrayal of Israel is considered a sin against God Himself.

29:21. When Egypt's forty-year exile is over (*Rashi*),

land of Egypt into destroyed and desolate ruins, from Migdol to Aswan to the border of Cush. * [11] The foot of a man will not traverse it, and the foot of an animal will not traverse it; and it will not be inhabited for forty years. [12] I will make the land of Egypt desolate among desolate lands, and its cities will be desolate among destroyed cities for forty years; and I will scatter Egypt among the nations and disperse them through the lands.

[13] For thus said the Lord HASHEM/ELOHIM: At the end of forty years I will gather Egypt from the nations where they were scattered, [14] and I will return the captivity of Egypt and bring them back to the land of Pathros, upon their native land, and they will be a lowly kingdom there. [15] It will be the lowest of the kingdoms, and it will not exalt itself again above nations; and I will diminish them, so that they not dominate nations. [16] They will no longer be a guarantor for the House of Israel, recalling their iniquity, when they looked to them [for help]; * then they will know that I am the Lord HASHEM/ELOHIM.

Nebuchad-
rezzar's
reward
[17] It happened in the twenty-seventh year, * in the first [month], on the first of the month, that the word of HASHEM came to me, saying, [18] "Son of Man: Nebuchadrezzar, king of Babylonia, has pressed his army to perform a difficult labor against Tyre; every head was made bald and every shoulder peeled; * and he and his army had no reward from Tyre for the labor that they had performed against her. [19] Therefore, thus said the Lord HASHEM/ELOHIM: Behold, I am giving the land of Egypt to Nebuchadrezzar, king of Babylonia; he will carry off its multitude and seize its booty and take its plunder, and that will be the reward for his army. [20] In return for the labor that he did there, I have given him the land of Egypt, because of what they did to Me* — the word of the Lord HASHEM/ELOHIM.

[21] "On that day* I will cause the might of the House of Israel to sprout, and I will thus grant you an opening of the mouth in their midst, * and they will know that I am HASHEM."

30

Prophecies
against
Egypt and
her allies

[1] The word of HASHEM came to me, saying, [2] "Son of Man, prophesy and say: Thus said the Lord HASHEM/ELOHIM: Wail, 'Woe for the day!' [3] For the day is close, the day of HASHEM is close, a cloudy day; it will be a time for the nations. [4] The sword will come against Egypt, and there will be a trembling in Cush when the slain fall in Egypt, * when they take away her multitude and her foundations are broken. [5] Cush, Put, Lud and all the people of mixed blood, and Cub and the inhabitants of [Egypt's] allied lands will fall with them by the sword.

[6] Thus said HASHEM: The supporters of Egypt will fall and the pride of its power will collapse; from Migdol to Aswan they will fall by the sword in her — the word of the Lord HASHEM/ELOHIM. [7] They will become desolate among desolate lands; and its cities will be among ruined cities. [8] Then they will know that I am HASHEM, when I place a fire in Egypt and all its helpers are smashed. [9] On that day messengers from Me* will go out in ships to frighten secure Cush, and there will be a trembling among them on the day of Egypt, for it is coming!

[10] For thus said the Lord HASHEM/ELOHIM: I will cause the multitude of Egypt to cease by the hand of Nebuchadrezzar, king of Babylonia. [11] He

---

Ezekiel's prophecy will be confirmed and he will be able to open his mouth to a receptive audience.

30:4. For they will fear for their own fate.

30:9. Since they are carrying out God's will, the destroyers are called God's messengers (*Radak*).

וְעַמּוֹ אִתּוֹ עָרִיצֵי גוֹיִם מוּבָאִים לְשַׁחֵת הָאָרֶץ וְהֵרִיקוּ חַרְבוֹתָם
יב עַל־מִצְרַיִם וּמָלְאוּ אֶת־הָאָרֶץ חָלָל: וְנָתַתִּי יְאֹרִים חָרָבָה וּמָכַרְתִּי
אֶת־הָאָרֶץ בְּיַד־רָעִים וַהֲשִׁמֹּתִי אֶרֶץ וּמְלֹאָהּ בְּיַד־זָרִים אֲנִי יְהוָה
יג דִּבַּרְתִּי: כֹּה־אָמַר אֲדֹנָי יֱהֹוִה וְהַאֲבַדְתִּי גִלּוּלִים וְהִשְׁבַּתִּי
אֱלִילִים מִנֹּף וְנָשִׂיא מֵאֶרֶץ־מִצְרַיִם לֹא יִהְיֶה־עוֹד וְנָתַתִּי יִרְאָה בְּאֶרֶץ
יד מִצְרָיִם: וַהֲשִׁמֹּתִי אֶת־פַּתְרוֹס וְנָתַתִּי אֵשׁ בְּצֹעַן וְעָשִׂיתִי שְׁפָטִים בְּנֹא:
טו-טז וְשָׁפַכְתִּי חֲמָתִי עַל־סִין מָעוֹז מִצְרָיִם וְהִכְרַתִּי אֶת־הֲמוֹן נָא: וְנָתַתִּי אֵשׁ
בְּמִצְרַיִם חוּל [°תָּחוּל ק] °תָּחִיל סִין וְנֹא תִּהְיֶה לְהִבָּקֵעַ וְנֹף צָרֵי יוֹמָם:
יז-יח בַּחוּרֵי אָוֶן וּפִי־בֶסֶת בַּחֶרֶב יִפֹּלוּ וְהֵנָּה בַּשְּׁבִי תֵלַכְנָה: וּבִתְחַפְנְחֵס חָשַׂךְ
הַיּוֹם בְּשִׁבְרִי־שָׁם אֶת־מֹטוֹת מִצְרַיִם וְנִשְׁבַּת־בָּהּ גְּאוֹן עֻזָּהּ הִיא עָנָן
יט יְכַסֶּנָּה וּבְנוֹתֶיהָ בַּשְּׁבִי תֵלַכְנָה: וְעָשִׂיתִי שְׁפָטִים בְּמִצְרָיִם וְיָדְעוּ כִּי־אֲנִי
יהוָה: וַיְהִי בְּאַחַת עֶשְׂרֵה שָׁנָה בָּרִאשׁוֹן בְּשִׁבְעָה לַחֹדֶשׁ הָיָה
כא דְבַר־יְהוָה אֵלַי לֵאמֹר: בֶּן־אָדָם אֶת־זְרוֹעַ פַּרְעֹה מֶלֶךְ־מִצְרַיִם שָׁבָרְתִּי
וְהִנֵּה לֹא־חֻבְּשָׁה לָתֵת רְפֻאוֹת לָשׂוּם חִתּוּל לְחָבְשָׁהּ לְחָזְקָהּ לִתְפֹּשׂ
כב בֶּחָרֶב: לָכֵן כֹּה־אָמַר ׀ אֲדֹנָי יֱהֹוִה הִנְנִי אֶל־פַּרְעֹה מֶלֶךְ־
מִצְרַיִם וְשָׁבַרְתִּי אֶת־זְרֹעֹתָיו אֶת־הַחֲזָקָה וְאֶת־הַנִּשְׁבָּרֶת וְהִפַּלְתִּי אֶת־
כג-כד הַחֶרֶב מִיָּדוֹ: וַהֲפִצוֹתִי אֶת־מִצְרַיִם בַּגּוֹיִם וְזֵרִיתִם בָּאֲרָצוֹת: וְחִזַּקְתִּי אֶת־
זְרֹעוֹת מֶלֶךְ בָּבֶל וְנָתַתִּי אֶת־חַרְבִּי בְּיָדוֹ וְשָׁבַרְתִּי אֶת־זְרֹעוֹת פַּרְעֹה וְנָאַק
כה נַאֲקוֹת חָלָל לְפָנָיו: וְהַחֲזַקְתִּי אֶת־זְרֹעוֹת מֶלֶךְ בָּבֶל וּזְרֹעוֹת פַּרְעֹה
תִּפֹּלְנָה וְיָדְעוּ כִּי־אֲנִי יְהוָה בְּתִתִּי חַרְבִּי בְּיַד מֶלֶךְ־בָּבֶל וְנָטָה אוֹתָהּ אֶל־
כו אֶרֶץ מִצְרָיִם: וַהֲפִצוֹתִי אֶת־מִצְרַיִם בַּגּוֹיִם וְזֵרִיתִי אוֹתָם בָּאֲרָצוֹת וְיָדְעוּ
א כִּי־אֲנִי יְהוָה: וַיְהִי בְּאַחַת עֶשְׂרֵה שָׁנָה בַּשְּׁלִישִׁי בְּאֶחָד לַחֹדֶשׁ   לא
ב הָיָה דְבַר־יְהוָה אֵלַי לֵאמֹר: בֶּן־אָדָם אֱמֹר אֶל־פַּרְעֹה מֶלֶךְ־מִצְרַיִם
ג וְאֶל־הֲמוֹנוֹ אֶל־מִי דָּמִיתָ בְגָדְלֶךָ: הִנֵּה אַשּׁוּר אֶרֶז בַּלְּבָנוֹן יְפֵה עָנָף וְחֹרֶשׁ
ד מֵצַל וּגְבַהּ קוֹמָה וּבֵין עֲבֹתִים הָיְתָה צַמַּרְתּוֹ: מַיִם גִּדְּלוּהוּ תְּהוֹם רֹמְמָתְהוּ
אֶת־נַהֲרֹתֶיהָ הֹלֵךְ סְבִיבוֹת מַטָּעָהּ וְאֶת־תְּעָלֹתֶיהָ שִׁלְּחָה אֶל כָּל־עֲצֵי
ה הַשָּׂדֶה: עַל־כֵּן גָּבְהָא קֹמָתוֹ מִכֹּל עֲצֵי הַשָּׂדֶה וַתִּרְבֶּינָה סַרְעַפֹּתָיו
ו וַתֶּאֱרַכְנָה °פֹארֹתוֹ [°פֹארֹתָיו ק] מִמַּיִם רַבִּים בְּשַׁלְּחוֹ: בִּסְעַפֹּתָיו קִנְנוּ
כָּל־עוֹף הַשָּׁמַיִם וְתַחַת פֹּארֹתָיו יָלְדוּ כֹּל חַיַּת הַשָּׂדֶה וּבְצִלּוֹ יֵשְׁבוּ כֹּל
ז גּוֹיִם רַבִּים: וַיִּיף בְּגָדְלוֹ בְּאֹרֶךְ דָּלִיּוֹתָיו כִּי־הָיָה שָׁרְשׁוֹ אֶל־מַיִם רַבִּים:

30:13. No Egyptian will rule over other lands (*Radak*).

30:20. The seventh of Nissan, in the eleventh year of Jehoiachin's exile and Zedekiah's reign, five months before Nebuchadnezzer destroyed the Temple.

30:21. Egypt had ceased to be a world power some eighteen years before this prophecy, in the fourth year of Jehoiakim's reign (*Rashi*).

31:1. The first of Sivan, in Zedekiah's eleventh year.

31:2. Despite your haughty delusions, you will fall as did Assyria, whose power is described in the following verses.

31:4. Nineveh, the Assyrian capital, flourished to the point where its rule spread over other nations (*Targum*).

Pharaoh defeated by Nebuchad-rezzar

and his people with him, the fiercest of nations, are being brought to destroy the land; they will draw their swords against Egypt and fill the land with slain. ¹² I will make the rivers dry and deliver the land into the hand of evil people; and I will make the land and all that fills it desolate by the hand of foreigners. I, HASHEM, have spoken.

¹³ Thus said the Lord HASHEM/ELOHIM: I will destroy the idols and cause the false gods to cease from Noph; there will never again be a ruler from the land of Egypt,* and I will instill fear over the land of Egypt. ¹⁴ I will make Pathros desolate and set a fire in Zoan, and I will execute punishments in No; ¹⁵ I will pour out My wrath upon Sin, the stronghold of Egypt; and I will cut off the multitudes of No. ¹⁶ I will set a fire in Egypt; Sin will tremble greatly, No will be split asunder and Noph beset by enemies daily. ¹⁷ The young men of Aven and Pi-beseth will fall by the sword, and [their wives] will go into captivity. ¹⁸ In Tehaphnehes the day will withhold [light], when I break the rods of Egypt there, and the pride of her power will cease in her; a cloud will cover it, and its daughters will go into captivity. ¹⁹ I will execute judgments in Egypt; then they will know that I am HASHEM."

²⁰ It happened in the eleventh year, in the first [month], on the seventh of the month,* that the word of HASHEM came to me, saying, ²¹ "Son of Man: I have [already] broken an arm of Pharaoh, king of Egypt,* and behold, it has not been bound up to provide healing, to place a bandage, to bind it up, to strengthen it, so that it might grasp a sword.

Egypt's arms broken

²² "Therefore, thus said the Lord HASHEM/ELOHIM: Behold, I am against Pharaoh, king of Egypt, and I will break his arms, the strong one and the broken one, and I will make the sword drop from his hand; ²³ I will scatter Egypt among the nations and disperse them among the lands. ²⁴ I will strengthen the arms of the king of Babylonia and put My sword in his hand; and I will break the arms of Pharaoh, and he will groan before him with the groans of the slain. ²⁵ I will support the arms of the king of Babylonia, but the arms of Pharaoh will drop; then they will know that I am HASHEM, when I put My sword in the hand of Babylonia's king and he stretches it out over the land of Egypt. ²⁶ I will scatter Egypt among the nations and disperse them among the lands; then they will know that I am HASHEM."

Babylon's arms strengthened

31

Egypt, learn from Assyria, the giant of the forest

¹ It happened in the eleventh year, in the third [month], on the first of the month,* that the word of HASHEM came to me, saying, ² "Son of Man, say to Pharaoh, king of Egypt, and to his multitude:

To whom do you liken yourself in your greatness?* ³ Behold Assyria, a cedar in the Lebanon [forest] with beautiful branches and a shady thickness, tall of stature, with its crown among the thick branches; ⁴ water nourished it, the depths elevated it, its rivers flowed around its bed, and it sent forth its streams to all the trees of the field.* ⁵ Thus its height surpassed all the trees of the field; its boughs multiplied and its branches grew long when it sent them forth, because of the abundant waters. ⁶ In its boughs every fowl of the heavens nested, and under its branches every beast of the field gave birth; in its shade dwelt all the many nations. ⁷ It became beautiful in its greatness, in the length of its tendrils, for its roots were upon abundant waters.

ח אֲרָזִ֤ים לֹֽא־עֲמָמֻ֨הוּ֙ בְּגַן־אֱלֹהִ֔ים בְּרוֹשִׁ֗ים לֹ֤א דָמוּ֙ אֶל־סְעַפֹּתָ֔יו
וְעַרְמֹנִ֖ים לֹא־הָי֣וּ כְּפֹארֹתָ֑יו כָּל־עֵץ֙ בְּגַן־אֱלֹהִ֔ים לֹא־דָמָ֥ה אֵלָ֖יו
ט בְּיָפְי֑וֹ: יָפֶ֣ה עֲשִׂיתִ֔יו בְּרֹ֖ב דָּֽלִיּוֹתָ֑יו וַֽיְקַנְאֻ֙הוּ֙ כָּל־עֲצֵי־עֵ֔דֶן אֲשֶׁ֖ר בְּגַ֥ן
י הָֽאֱלֹהִֽים: לָכֵ֗ן כֹּ֤ה אָמַר֙ אֲדֹנָ֣י יֱהוִ֔ה יַ֕עַן אֲשֶׁ֥ר גָּבַ֖הְתָּ בְּקוֹמָ֑ה
יא וַיִּתֵּ֤ן צַמַּרְתּוֹ֙ אֶל־בֵּ֣ין עֲבוֹתִ֔ים וְרָ֥ם לְבָב֖וֹ בְּגָבְה֑וֹ: וְאֶתְּנֵ֗הוּ בְּיַד֙ אֵ֣יל גּוֹיִ֔ם
יב עָשׂ֤וֹ יַֽעֲשֶׂה֙ ל֔וֹ °כְּרִשְׁע֖וֹ גֵּֽרַשְׁתִּֽהוּ: וַיִּכְרְתֻ֣הוּ זָרִ֡ים עָֽרִיצֵ֣י גוֹיִם֮ וַֽיִּטְּשֻׁ֒הוּ֒   נ״א בְּרִשְׁעוֹ
אֶל־הֶֽהָרִ֣ים וּבְכָל־גֵּֽאָי֗וֹת נָֽפְל֤וּ דָֽלִיּוֹתָיו֙ וַתִּשָּׁבַ֣רְנָה פֹֽארֹתָ֔יו בְּכֹ֖ל אֲפִיקֵ֣י
יג הָאָ֑רֶץ וַיֵּֽרְד֧וּ מִצִּלּ֛וֹ כָּל־עַמֵּ֥י הָאָ֖רֶץ וַֽיִּטְּשֻֽׁהוּ: עַל־מַפַּלְתּ֖וֹ יִשְׁכְּנ֣וּ כָּל־ע֣וֹף
יד הַשָּׁמָ֑יִם וְאֶל־פֹּֽארֹתָ֣יו הָי֔וּ כֹּ֖ל חַיַּ֥ת הַשָּׂדֶֽה: לְמַ֡עַן אֲשֶׁ֣ר לֹֽא־יִגְבְּה֣וּ
בְקוֹמָתָ֣ם כָּל־עֲצֵי־מַ֗יִם וְלֹֽא־יִתְּנ֤וּ אֶת־צַמַּרְתָּם֙ אֶל־בֵּ֣ין עֲבֹתִ֔ים וְלֹֽא־
יַֽעַמְד֧וּ אֵֽלֵיהֶ֛ם בְּגָבְהָ֖ם כָּל־שֹׁ֣תֵי מָ֑יִם כִּֽי־כֻלָּם֩ נִתְּנ֨וּ לַמָּ֜וֶת אֶל־אֶ֣רֶץ
טו תַּחְתִּ֗ית בְּת֛וֹךְ בְּנֵ֥י אָדָ֖ם אֶל־י֥וֹרְדֵי בֽוֹר: כֹּֽה־אָמַ֞ר אֲדֹנָ֣י
יֱהוִ֗ה בְּי֨וֹם רִדְתּ֤וֹ שְׁא֨וֹלָה֙ הֶֽאֱבַ֔לְתִּי כִּסֵּ֧תִי עָלָ֛יו אֶת־תְּה֖וֹם וָֽאֶמְנַ֑ע
נַֽהֲרוֹתֶ֗יהָ וַיִּכָּֽלְאוּ֙ מַ֣יִם רַבִּ֔ים וָֽאַקְדִּ֤ר עָלָיו֙ לְבָנ֔וֹן וְכָל־עֲצֵ֥י הַשָּׂדֶ֖ה עָלָ֥יו
טז עֻלְּפֶֽה: מִקּ֤וֹל מַפַּלְתּוֹ֙ הִרְעַ֣שְׁתִּי גוֹיִ֔ם בְּהֽוֹרִדִ֥י אֹת֛וֹ שְׁא֖וֹלָה אֶת־י֣וֹרְדֵי
ב֑וֹר וַיִּנָּ֨חֲמ֜וּ בְּאֶ֤רֶץ תַּחְתִּית֙ כָּל־עֲצֵי־עֵ֔דֶן מִבְחַ֥ר וְטֽוֹב־לְבָנ֖וֹן כָּל־שֹׁ֥תֵי
יז מָֽיִם: גַּם־הֵ֗ם אִתּ֛וֹ יָֽרְד֥וּ שְׁא֖וֹלָה אֶל־חַלְלֵי־חָ֑רֶב וּזְרֹע֛וֹ יָֽשְׁב֥וּ בְצִלּ֖וֹ בְּת֥וֹךְ
יח גּוֹיִֽם: אֶל־מִ֨י דָמִ֥יתָ כָּ֛כָה בְּכָב֖וֹד וּבְגֹ֑דֶל בַּֽעֲצֵי־עֵ֔דֶן וְהֽוֹרַדְתָּ֞ אֶת־עֲצֵי־
עֵ֣דֶן אֶל־אֶ֣רֶץ תַּחְתִּ֗ית בְּת֨וֹךְ עֲרֵלִ֤ים תִּשְׁכַּב֙ אֶת־חַלְלֵי־חֶ֔רֶב ה֥וּא פַרְעֹ֛ה
א וְכָל־°הֲמוֹנֹ֖ה [°הֲמוֹנ֖וֹ ק] נְאֻ֥ם אֲדֹנָ֥י יֱהוִֽה: לב   וַֽיְהִי֙ בִּשְׁתֵּ֣י עֶשְׂרֵ֣ה
ב שָׁנָ֔ה בִּשְׁנֵֽי־עָשָׂ֥ר חֹ֖דֶשׁ בְּאֶחָ֣ד לַחֹ֑דֶשׁ הָיָ֥ה דְבַר־יְהֹוָ֖ה אֵלַ֥י לֵאמֹֽר: בֶּן־
אָדָ֗ם שָׂ֤א קִינָה֙ עַל־פַּרְעֹ֣ה מֶֽלֶךְ־מִצְרַ֔יִם וְאָֽמַרְתָּ֣ אֵלָ֔יו כְּפִ֥יר גּוֹיִ֖ם נִדְמֵ֑יתָ
וְאַתָּה֙ כַּתַּנִּ֣ים בַּיַּמִּ֔ים וַתָּ֣גַח בְּנַֽהֲרוֹתֶ֔יךָ וַתִּדְלַח־מַ֨יִם֙ בְּרַגְלֶ֔יךָ וַתִּרְפֹּ֖ס
ג נַֽהֲרוֹתָֽם: כֹּ֤ה אָמַר֙ אֲדֹנָ֣י יֱהוִ֔ה וּפָֽרַשְׂתִּ֤י עָלֶ֨יךָ֙ אֶת־רִשְׁתִּ֔י
ד בִּקְהַ֖ל עַמִּ֣ים רַבִּ֑ים וְהֶֽעֱל֖וּךָ בְּחֶרְמִֽי: וּנְטַשְׁתִּ֣יךָ בָאָ֗רֶץ עַל־פְּנֵ֤י הַשָּׂדֶה֙
אֲטִילֶ֔ךָ וְהִשְׁכַּנְתִּ֥י עָלֶ֖יךָ כָּל־ע֣וֹף הַשָּׁמַ֑יִם וְהִשְׂבַּעְתִּ֥י מִמְּךָ֖ חַיַּ֥ת כָּל־
ה הָאָֽרֶץ: וְנָֽתַתִּ֥י אֶת־בְּשָׂרְךָ֖ עַל־הֶֽהָרִ֑ים וּמִלֵּאתִ֥י הַגֵּֽאָי֖וֹת רָֽמוּתֶֽךָ:
ו-ז וְהִשְׁקֵיתִ֨י אֶ֧רֶץ צָֽפָתְךָ֛ מִדָּֽמְךָ֖ אֶל־הֶֽהָרִ֑ים וַֽאֲפִקִ֖ים יִמָּֽלְא֥וּן מִמֶּֽךָּ: וְכִסֵּיתִ֤י
בְכַבּֽוֹתְךָ֙ שָׁמַ֔יִם וְהִקְדַּרְתִּ֖י אֶת־כֹּֽכְבֵיהֶ֑ם שֶׁ֚מֶשׁ בֶּֽעָנָ֣ן אֲכַסֶּ֔נּוּ וְיָרֵ֖חַ לֹא־

31:10-11. Scripture often shifts from second person to third and vice versa, even in the same verse. Thus, "you," "it," and "him" of this passage all refer to Assyria.

31:11. Assyria was conquered by Babylonia under the rule of Nebuchadnezzar.

31:15. Assyria.

31:16. When they saw that the great Assyria ultimately shared their fate.

31:18. Pharaoh; see verse 1.

32:1. On the first of Adar, in the twelfth year after the exile of Jechoniah and reign of Zedekiah, nineteen months after the Temple was destroyed.

32:2. A sea serpent has no dominion outside his marine habitat. So too, Pharaoh should never have gone out of Egypt to invade other lands (*Rashi*).

8 [Even] cedars could not obscure it in God's garden, cypresses could not compare to its boughs, and chestnut trees were nothing like its branches; no tree in God's garden could compare to it in its beauty. 9 I made it so beautiful with its abundant tendrils that it was envied by all the trees of Eden that were in God's garden.

The penalty for Assyria's haughtiness

10 Therefore, thus said the Lord HASHEM/ELOHIM: Because you* grew haughty in stature and put its* crown among the thick branches, and its heart became proud of its height, 11 I delivered him into the hand of the strongest of nations;* who dealt freely with him, commensurate with his wickedness, and I drove him out. 12 Strangers, the fiercest of the nations, cut it down and abandoned it; its tendrils fell upon the mountains and in all the valleys, and its branches lay broken in all the channels of the earth, and all the nations of the earth departed from its shade and forsook it. 13 Upon its ruins every bird of heaven rested, and upon its branches was every beast of the field. 14 [I did this] so that none of all the water-nourished trees should become haughty with their stature and they should not place their crown among the thick branches; and the elms, [as well as] all [other trees] that drink water, should not stand tall in their height, for they are all given over to death, into the nethermost earth, in the midst of the children of man, among those who descend to the pit.

The nations mourn Assyria

15 Thus said the Lord HASHEM/ELOHIM: On the day he* descended to the grave I caused mourning; I constrained the depths because of him and withheld its rivers, and the abundant waters ceased; I darkened the Lebanon because of him, and all the trees of the field grew faint because of him. 16 I made the nations tremble at the sound of his fall, when I brought him down to the grave with those who descend to the pit; then all the trees of Eden were comforted* in the nethermost earth, the choicest and best of the Lebanon, all those that drink water. 17 They, too, descended with him to the grave, to those slain by the sword, along with his supporter[s] who had dwelled in his protection among the nations.

18 To whom did you* thus liken yourself in glory and size among Eden's trees? Now you will be brought down with Eden's trees into the nethermost earth; you will lay among the uncircumcised, with the slain of the sword; this is Pharaoh and all his multitude! — the word of the Lord HASHEM/ELOHIM."

32

1 It happened in the twelfth year, in the twelfth month, on the first of the month, * the word of HASHEM came to me, saying, 2 "Son of Man, take up a lament for Pharaoh, king of Egypt, and say to him:

A lament for Pharaoh and Egypt

You imagined yourself a young lion among the nations, but you are like a serpent in the seas. * You emerged with your rivers and you churned waters with your feet and fouled their rivers.

3 Thus said the Lord HASHEM/ELOHIM: I will spread My net over you with an assemblage of many nations, and they will lift you in My web. 4 I will leave you abandoned upon the earth; I will hurl you upon the open field; I will cause all the fowl of the heavens to settle upon you, and I will sate every beast of the land with you. 5 I will place your flesh upon the mountains and fill the valleys with your decay. 6 The land where you swam I will inundate with your blood until the mountains, and the channels will be filled from you. 7 With [the smoke of] your extinguishment I will cover the heavens and I will darken their stars; I will cover the sun with a cloud and the moon will not

ח יָאִיר אוֹרְךָ: כָּל־מְאוֹרֵי אוֹר בַּשָּׁמַיִם אַקְדִּירֵם עָלֶיךָ וְנָתַתִּי חֹשֶׁךְ עַל־

ט אַרְצֶךָ נְאֻם אֲדֹנָי יֱהֹוִה: וְהִכְעַסְתִּי לֵב עַמִּים רַבִּים בַּהֲבִיאִי שִׁבְרְךָ בַּגּוֹיִם

י עַל־אֲרָצוֹת אֲשֶׁר לֹא־יְדַעְתָּם: וַהֲשִׁמּוֹתִי עָלֶיךָ עַמִּים רַבִּים וּמַלְכֵיהֶם יִשְׂעֲרוּ עָלֶיךָ שַׂעַר בְּעוֹפְפִי חַרְבִּי עַל־פְּנֵיהֶם וְחָרְדוּ לִרְגָעִים אִישׁ

יא לְנַפְשׁוֹ בְּיוֹם מַפַּלְתֶּךָ: כִּי כֹּה אָמַר אֲדֹנָי יֱהֹוִה חֶרֶב מֶלֶךְ־בָּבֶל

יב תְּבוֹאֶךָ: בְּחַרְבוֹת גִּבּוֹרִים אַפִּיל הֲמוֹנֶךָ עָרִיצֵי גוֹיִם כֻּלָּם וְשָׁדְדוּ אֶת־

יג גְּאוֹן מִצְרַיִם וְנִשְׁמַד כָּל־הֲמוֹנָהּ: וְהַאֲבַדְתִּי אֶת־כָּל־בְּהֶמְתָּהּ מֵעַל מַיִם

יד רַבִּים וְלֹא תִדְלָחֵם רֶגֶל־אָדָם עוֹד וּפַרְסוֹת בְּהֵמָה לֹא תִדְלָחֵם: אָז

טו אַשְׁקִיעַ מֵימֵיהֶם וְנַהֲרוֹתָם כַּשֶּׁמֶן אוֹלִיךְ נְאֻם אֲדֹנָי יֱהֹוִה: בְּתִתִּי אֶת־ אֶרֶץ מִצְרַיִם שְׁמָמָה וּנְשַׁמָּה אֶרֶץ מִמְּלֹאָהּ בְּהַכּוֹתִי אֶת־כָּל־יוֹשְׁבֵי בָהּ

טז וְיָדְעוּ כִּי־אֲנִי יְהֹוָה: קִינָה הִיא וְקוֹנְנוּהָ בְּנוֹת הַגּוֹיִם תְּקוֹנֵנָּה אוֹתָהּ עַל־ מִצְרַיִם וְעַל־כָּל־הֲמוֹנָהּ תְּקוֹנֵנָּה אוֹתָהּ נְאֻם אֲדֹנָי יֱהֹוִה:

יז וַיְהִי בִּשְׁתֵּי עֶשְׂרֵה שָׁנָה בַּחֲמִשָּׁה עָשָׂר לַחֹדֶשׁ הָיָה דְבַר־יְהֹוָה אֵלַי

יח לֵאמֹר: בֶּן־אָדָם נְהֵה עַל־הֲמוֹן מִצְרַיִם וְהוֹרִדֵהוּ אוֹתָהּ וּבְנוֹת גּוֹיִם אַדִּרִם אֶל־אֶרֶץ תַּחְתִּיּוֹת אֶת־יוֹרְדֵי בוֹר: מִמִּי נָעָמְתָּ רְדָה וְהָשְׁכְּבָה אֶת־

כ עֲרֵלִים: בְּתוֹךְ חַלְלֵי־חֶרֶב יִפֹּלוּ חֶרֶב נִתָּנָה מָשְׁכוּ אוֹתָהּ וְכָל־הֲמוֹנֶיהָ:

כא יְדַבְּרוּ־לוֹ אֵלֵי גִבּוֹרִים מִתּוֹךְ שְׁאוֹל אֶת־עֹזְרָיו יָרְדוּ שָׁכְבוּ הָעֲרֵלִים

כב חַלְלֵי־חָרֶב: שָׁם אַשּׁוּר וְכָל־קְהָלָהּ סְבִיבוֹתָיו קִבְרֹתָיו כֻּלָּם חֲלָלִים

כג הַנֹּפְלִים בֶּחָרֶב: אֲשֶׁר נִתְּנוּ קִבְרֹתֶיהָ בְּיַרְכְּתֵי־בוֹר וַיְהִי קְהָלָהּ סְבִיבוֹת

כד קְבֻרָתָהּ כֻּלָּם חֲלָלִים נֹפְלִים בַּחֶרֶב אֲשֶׁר־נָתְנוּ חִתִּית בְּאֶרֶץ חַיִּים: שָׁם עֵילָם וְכָל־הֲמוֹנָהּ סְבִיבוֹת קְבֻרָתָהּ כֻּלָּם חֲלָלִים הַנֹּפְלִים בַּחֶרֶב אֲשֶׁר־ יָרְדוּ עֲרֵלִים ׀ אֶל־אֶרֶץ תַּחְתִּיּוֹת אֲשֶׁר נָתְנוּ חִתִּיתָם בְּאֶרֶץ חַיִּים וַיִּשְׂאוּ

כה כְלִמָּתָם אֶת־יוֹרְדֵי בוֹר: בְּתוֹךְ חֲלָלִים נָתְנוּ מִשְׁכָּב לָהּ בְּכָל־הֲמוֹנָהּ סְבִיבוֹתָיו קִבְרֹתֶהָ כֻּלָּם עֲרֵלִים חַלְלֵי־חֶרֶב כִּי־נִתַּן חִתִּיתָם בְּאֶרֶץ חַיִּים

כו וַיִּשְׂאוּ כְלִמָּתָם אֶת־יוֹרְדֵי בוֹר בְּתוֹךְ חֲלָלִים נִתָּן: שָׁם מֶשֶׁךְ תֻּבַל וְכָל־ הֲמוֹנָהּ סְבִיבוֹתָיו קִבְרוֹתֶיהָ כֻּלָּם עֲרֵלִים מְחֻלְלֵי חֶרֶב כִּי־נָתְנוּ חִתִּיתָם

כז בְּאֶרֶץ חַיִּים: וְלֹא יִשְׁכְּבוּ אֶת־גִּבּוֹרִים נֹפְלִים מֵעֲרֵלִים אֲשֶׁר יָרְדוּ שְׁאוֹל בִּכְלֵי־מִלְחַמְתָּם וַיִּתְּנוּ אֶת־חַרְבוֹתָם תַּחַת רָאשֵׁיהֶם וַתְּהִי עֲוֺנֹתָם עַל־עַצְמוֹתָם כִּי־חִתִּית גִּבּוֹרִים בְּאֶרֶץ חַיִּים: וְאַתָּה בְּתוֹךְ עֲרֵלִים

כח תִּשָּׁבַר וְתִשְׁכַּב אֶת־חַלְלֵי־חָרֶב: שָׁמָּה אֱדוֹם מְלָכֶיהָ וְכָל־נְשִׂיאֶיהָ

32:14. As clear as pure oil, with no sediment.

32:17. The month is not mentioned, so this prophecy presumably came in Adar, as did the prophecy of verse 1.

32:22. In the netherworld, i.e., Gehinnom (*Rashi*).

32:22-27. The masculine and feminine pronouns refer to Egypt and Assyria, but it is not clear which pronoun

refers to which country.

32:23. That is, the Land of Israel (*Targum*).

32:25. For Elam.

32:27. It was customary for warriors killed in battle to be buried with their weapons.

32:28. Addressed to Pharaoh.

radiate its light. ⁸ *I will darken all the bright lights of heaven because of you, and I will place darkness upon your land — the word of the Lord* HASHEM/ELOHIM. ⁹ *Then I will vex the heart of many peoples, when I announce your destruction among the nations, to lands that you never knew;* ¹⁰ *I will cause many peoples to be astonished by you, and their kings will shake with trembling concerning you, when I brandish My sword in their presence; and each man will quake constantly on the day of your downfall.*

   ¹¹ *For thus said the Lord* HASHEM/ELOHIM: *The sword of the king of Babylonia will come upon you.* ¹² *I will topple your multitude by the swords of the mighty, the fiercest of the nations all of them; they will despoil the pride of Egypt, and all her multitude will be destroyed.* ¹³ *I will annihilate her every animal from beside her abundant waters, and the foot of man will not muddy them again, and the hooves of animals will not muddy them.* ¹⁴ *Then I will make their waters settle and cause their rivers to run like oil** — *says the Lord* HASHEM/ELOHIM. ¹⁵ *When I lay waste to the land of Egypt, making the land desolate and waste from its fullness, when I smite all who dwell in it, then they will know that I am* HASHEM.'

   ¹⁶ *It is a lament, and they will lament it, the daughters of the nations will lament it; they will lament it for Egypt and for all her multitude — the word of the Lord* HASHEM/ELOHIM."

   ¹⁷ *It happened in the twelfth year, on the fifteenth of the month,* the word of* HASHEM *came to me, saying,* ¹⁸ *"Son of Man, sigh for the multitude of Egypt, and cast it down — it and the daughters of mighty nations — to the nethermost earth, to those who descend to the pit.* ¹⁹ [*Say*]:

A lament for Egypt and her allies . . .

Whom have you surpassed in beauty? Descend and be laid to rest with the uncircumcised! ²⁰ *They will fall amid those slain by the sword; they will be delivered to the sword. Drag her and all her multitudes away!* ²¹ *The mightiest warriors will speak about [Pharaoh] and his supporters from the grave, 'They have descended, the uncircumcised lie [dead], victims of the sword.'*

. . . Assyria

²² *Assyria and all its assemblage are there,* his* graves are all around him; all of them slain, those fallen by the sword* ²³ *Her* graves are placed at the depths of the pit; her assemblage is all around her burial place, all of them slain, fallen by the sword, because they instilled terror in the Land of Life.* * ²⁴ *There are Elam and all of her multitude around her grave, all of them*

. . . Elam

slain, those fallen by the sword, who descended uncircumcised to the nethermost earth, because they instilled their terror in the Land of Life and they bore their shame with those who descend to the pit. ²⁵ *They set a resting place among the slain for her* and all her multitude, her graves all around him; all of them uncircumcised, slain by the sword; for their terror was instilled in the Land of Life and they bore their shame with those who*

. . . Meshech Tubal

descend to the pit; they were placed among the slain. ²⁶ *There Meshech, Tubal and all her multitude, her graves surrounding him, all of them uncircumcised, slain by the sword, because they instilled their terror in the Land of Life.* ²⁷ *They will not lie with the mighty, for they are inferior to those uncircumcised who have descended to the grave with their weapons of war,* and they placed their swords under their heads; for their iniquities remain upon them, for the terror of [these] warriors was in the Land of Life.* ²⁸ *And as for you, * you will be broken among the uncircumcised and lie with*

. . . Edom

those slain by the sword. ²⁹ *There is Edom, her kings and all her princes,*

אֲשֶׁר־נִתְּנוּ בִגְבוּרָתָם אֶת־חַלְלֵי־חֶרֶב הֵמָּה אֶת־עֲרֵלִים יִשְׁכָּבוּ

ל וְאֶת־יֹרְדֵי בוֹר: שָׁמָּה נְסִיכֵי צָפוֹן כֻּלָּם וְכָל־צִדֹנִי אֲשֶׁר־יָרְדוּ אֶת־
חֲלָלִים בְּחִתִּיתָם מִגְבוּרָתָם בּוֹשִׁים וַיִּשְׁכְּבוּ עֲרֵלִים אֶת־חַלְלֵי־חֶרֶב

לא וַיִּשְׂאוּ כְלִמָּתָם אֶת־יוֹרְדֵי בוֹר: אוֹתָם יִרְאֶה פַרְעֹה וְנִחַם עַל־כָּל־

לב °הֲמוֹנוֹ [הֲמוֹנוֹ ק] חַלְלֵי־חֶרֶב פַּרְעֹה וְכָל־חֵילוֹ נְאֻם אֲדֹנָי יֱהוֹה: כִּי־
נָתַתִּי אֶת־°חִתִּיתו [חִתִּיתִי ק] בְּאֶרֶץ חַיִּים וְהֻשְׁכַּב בְּתוֹךְ עֲרֵלִים אֶת־

לג א חַלְלֵי־חֶרֶב פַּרְעֹה וְכָל־°הֲמוֹנה [הֲמוֹנוֹ ק] נְאֻם אֲדֹנָי יֱהוֹה: וַיְהִי

ב דְבַר־יְהֹוָה אֵלַי לֵאמֹר: בֶּן־אָדָם דַּבֵּר אֶל־בְּנֵי־עַמְּךָ וְאָמַרְתָּ אֲלֵיהֶם
אֶרֶץ כִּי־אָבִיא עָלֶיהָ חָרֶב וְלָקְחוּ עַם־הָאָרֶץ אִישׁ אֶחָד מִקְצֵיהֶם וְנָתְנוּ

ג אֹתוֹ לָהֶם לְצֹפֶה: וְרָאָה אֶת־הַחֶרֶב בָּאָה עַל־הָאָרֶץ וְתָקַע בַּשּׁוֹפָר

ד וְהִזְהִיר אֶת־הָעָם: וְשָׁמַע הַשֹּׁמֵעַ אֶת־קוֹל הַשּׁוֹפָר וְלֹא נִזְהָר וַתָּבוֹא

ה חֶרֶב וַתִּקָּחֵהוּ דָּמוֹ בְרֹאשׁוֹ יִהְיֶה: אֵת קוֹל הַשּׁוֹפָר שָׁמַע וְלֹא נִזְהָר דָּמוֹ

ו בּוֹ יִהְיֶה וְהוּא נִזְהָר נַפְשׁוֹ מִלֵּט: וְהַצֹּפֶה כִּי־יִרְאֶה אֶת־הַחֶרֶב בָּאָה וְלֹא־
תָקַע בַּשּׁוֹפָר וְהָעָם לֹא־נִזְהָר וַתָּבוֹא חֶרֶב וַתִּקַּח מֵהֶם נָפֶשׁ הוּא בַּעֲוֹנוֹ

ז נִלְקָח וְדָמוֹ מִיַּד־הַצֹּפֶה אֶדְרֹשׁ: וְאַתָּה
בֶן־אָדָם צֹפֶה נְתַתִּיךָ לְבֵית יִשְׂרָאֵל וְשָׁמַעְתָּ מִפִּי דָּבָר וְהִזְהַרְתָּ אֹתָם

ח מִמֶּנִּי: בְּאָמְרִי לָרָשָׁע רָשָׁע מוֹת תָּמוּת וְלֹא דִבַּרְתָּ לְהַזְהִיר רָשָׁע

ט מִדַּרְכּוֹ הוּא רָשָׁע בַּעֲוֹנוֹ יָמוּת וְדָמוֹ מִיָּדְךָ אֲבַקֵּשׁ: וְאַתָּה כִּי־הִזְהַרְתָּ
רָשָׁע מִדַּרְכּוֹ לָשׁוּב מִמֶּנָּה וְלֹא־שָׁב מִדַּרְכּוֹ הוּא בַּעֲוֹנוֹ יָמוּת וְאַתָּה

י נַפְשְׁךָ הִצַּלְתָּ: וְאַתָּה בֶן־אָדָם אֱמֹר אֶל־בֵּית
יִשְׂרָאֵל כֵּן אֲמַרְתֶּם לֵאמֹר כִּי־פְשָׁעֵינוּ וְחַטֹּאתֵינוּ עָלֵינוּ וּבָם אֲנַחְנוּ

יא נְמַקִּים וְאֵיךְ נִחְיֶה: אֱמֹר אֲלֵיהֶם חַי־אָנִי נְאֻם אֲדֹנָי יֱהוֹה אִם־אֶחְפֹּץ
בְּמוֹת הָרָשָׁע כִּי אִם־בְּשׁוּב רָשָׁע מִדַּרְכּוֹ וְחָיָה שׁוּבוּ שׁוּבוּ מִדַּרְכֵיכֶם

יב הָרָעִים וְלָמָּה תָמוּתוּ בֵּית יִשְׂרָאֵל: וְאַתָּה
בֶן־אָדָם אֱמֹר אֶל־בְּנֵי־עַמְּךָ צִדְקַת הַצַּדִּיק לֹא תַצִּילֶנּוּ בְּיוֹם
פִּשְׁעוֹ וְרִשְׁעַת הָרָשָׁע לֹא־יִכָּשֶׁל בָּהּ בְּיוֹם שׁוּבוֹ מֵרִשְׁעוֹ וְצַדִּיק לֹא

יג יוּכַל לִחְיוֹת בָּהּ בְּיוֹם חֲטָאתוֹ: בְּאָמְרִי לַצַּדִּיק חָיֹה יִחְיֶה וְהוּא־
בָטַח עַל־צִדְקָתוֹ וְעָשָׂה עָוֶל כָּל־°צִדְקֹתו [צִדְקֹתָיו ק] לֹא תִזָּכַרְנָה

יד וּבְעַוְלוֹ אֲשֶׁר־עָשָׂה בּוֹ יָמוּת: וּבְאָמְרִי לָרָשָׁע מוֹת תָּמוּת וְשָׁב מֵחַטָּאתוֹ

טו וְעָשָׂה מִשְׁפָּט וּצְדָקָה: חֲבֹל יָשִׁיב רָשָׁע גְּזֵלָה יְשַׁלֵּם בְּחֻקּוֹת הַחַיִּים הָלַךְ

33:10. The people believed their situation was hopeless, beyond atonement (*Rashi*).　　**33:15.** In accordance with *Exodus* 22:25.

who were laid, despite their might, with the victims of the sword; they will lie with the uncircumcised, together with those who descend to the pit. ³⁰ There are princes of the North, all of them, and every Sidonian, those who descended with the slain, when they were broken from their might in shame; they lie uncircumcised with those slain by the sword, bearing their shame with those who descend to the pit. ³¹ Pharaoh will see them and be consoled with all his multitude, Pharaoh and all his army, slain by the sword — the word of the Lord HASHEM/ELOHIM. ³² For I have instilled My terror in the Land of Life; and Pharaoh and all his multitude will be laid in the midst of the uncircumcised, with those slain by the sword — the word of the Lord HASHEM/ELOHIM.' "

33

¹ The word of HASHEM came to me, saying, ² "Son of Man, speak to the children of your people and say to them:

When I bring the sword [of war] upon a land, the people of the land take one man from among them and set him as a sentinel for themselves. ³ If, when he sees the sword coming upon the land, he blows the shofar and warns the people, ⁴ and a listener hears the sound of the shofar but does not take heed and the sword comes and takes him, his blood will be upon his head. ⁵ He heard the sound of the shofar but did not take heed, so his blood will be upon him; had he taken heed, he would have saved his soul. ⁶ But if the sentinel saw the sword coming and he did not blow the shofar and the people were not warned, and a sword came and took a soul from among them — he was taken for his own iniquity, but I will seek his blood from the sentinel's hand."

⁷ "Now you, Son of Man, I have made you a sentinel for the House of Israel; when you hear a matter from My mouth, you must warn them for Me. ⁸ If I say of a wicked person, 'Wicked one, you shall surely die!' and you do not speak up to warn the wicked one concerning his way — he is wicked and will die for his iniquity, but I will demand his blood from your hand. ⁹ But you, if you did warn the wicked one concering his way to repent from it, but he did not repent from his way, he will die for his iniquity, and you will have saved your soul."

¹⁰ "Now you, Son of Man, say to the House of Israel,

'Thus have you spoken, saying, 'Since our sins and our iniquities are upon us and we are wasting away because of them, how can we live?'*

¹¹ Say to them:

'As I live — the word of the Lord HASHEM/ELOHIM — [I swear] that I do not desire the death of the wicked one, but rather the wicked one's return from his way, that he may live. Repent, repent from your evil ways! Why should you die, O House of Israel?' "

¹² "Now you, Son of Man, say to the children of your people:

The righteousness of the righteous person shall not rescue him on the day of his rebellious sin; and as for the wickedness of the wicked person — he shall not stumble over it on the day of his repentance from his wickedness; but the righteous person cannot live because of [his righteousness] on the day he sins. ¹³ If I say of a righteous person that he shall surely live, and he relies on his righteousness yet practices corruption, all his righteousness will not be recalled, rather because of his corruption that he practiced, for that he will die. ¹⁴ And if I say to a wicked person, 'You shall surely die,' and he repents from his sin and acts with justice and righteousness — ¹⁵ the wicked person returns a pledge, * repays for his theft, follows the life-giving decrees,

טז לְבִלְתִּי עֲשׂוֹת עָ֑וֶל חָי֣וֹ יִֽחְיֶ֖ה לֹ֣א יָמֽוּת: כָּל־°חטאתו [°חַטֹּאתָ֗יו ק]
יז אֲשֶׁ֣ר חָטָ֔א לֹ֥א תִזָּכַ֖רְנָה ל֑וֹ מִשְׁפָּ֧ט וּצְדָקָ֛ה עָשָׂ֖ה חָי֥וֹ יִֽחְיֶֽה: וְאָֽמְרוּ֙ בְּנֵ֣י
יח עַמְּךָ֔ לֹ֥א יִתָּכֵ֖ן דֶּ֣רֶךְ אֲדֹנָ֑י וְהֵ֥מָּה דַּרְכָּ֖ם לֹֽא־יִתָּכֵֽן: בְּשׁוּב־צַדִּ֥יק מִצִּדְקָת֖וֹ
יט וְעָ֣שָׂה עָ֑וֶל וּמֵ֖ת בָּהֶֽם: וּבְשׁ֣וּב רָשָׁ֗ע מֵֽרִשְׁעָתוֹ֙ וְעָשָׂ֣ה מִשְׁפָּ֣ט וּצְדָקָ֔ה
כ עֲלֵיהֶ֖ם ה֥וּא יִֽחְיֶֽה: וַאֲמַרְתֶּ֕ם לֹ֥א יִתָּכֵ֖ן דֶּ֣רֶךְ אֲדֹנָ֑י אִ֧ישׁ כִּדְרָכָ֛יו אֶשְׁפּ֥וֹט
כא אֶתְכֶ֖ם בֵּ֥ית יִשְׂרָאֵֽל: וַיְהִ֞י בִּשְׁתֵּ֧י עֶשְׂרֵ֣ה שָׁנָ֗ה בָּֽעֲשִׂרִי֙ בַּֽחֲמִשָּׁ֣ה
כב לַחֹ֔דֶשׁ לְגָֽלוּתֵ֑נוּ בָּא־אֵלַ֨י הַפָּלִ֤יט מִ֣ירֽוּשָׁלַ֨͏ִם֙ לֵאמֹ֔ר הֻכְּתָ֖ה הָעִֽיר: וְיַד־
יְהוָה֩ הָֽיְתָ֨ה אֵלַ֜י בָּעֶ֗רֶב לִפְנֵי֙ בּ֣וֹא הַפָּלִ֔יט וַיִּפְתַּ֣ח אֶת־פִּ֔י עַד־בּ֥וֹא אֵלַ֖י
כג בַּבֹּ֑קֶר וַיִּפָּ֣תַח פִּ֔י וְלֹ֥א נֶֽאֱלַ֖מְתִּי עֽוֹד: וַיְהִ֥י דְבַר־יְהוָ֖ה אֵלַ֥י
כד לֵאמֹֽר: בֶּן־אָדָ֗ם יֹֽשְׁבֵי֙ הֶחֳרָב֣וֹת הָאֵ֔לֶּה עַל־אַדְמַ֥ת יִשְׂרָאֵ֖ל אֹֽמְרִ֣ים
לֵאמֹ֑ר אֶחָד֙ הָיָ֣ה אַבְרָהָ֔ם וַיִּירַ֖שׁ אֶת־הָאָ֑רֶץ וַֽאֲנַ֣חְנוּ רַבִּ֔ים לָ֥נוּ נִתְּנָ֛ה
כה הָאָ֖רֶץ לְמֽוֹרָשָֽׁה: לָכֵן֩ אֱמֹ֨ר אֲלֵיהֶ֜ם כֹּֽה־אָמַ֣ר ׀ אֲדֹנָ֣י יֱהֹוִ֗ה
עַל־הַדָּ֣ם ׀ תֹּאכֵ֡לוּ וְעֵֽינֵכֶ֞ם תִּשְׂא֤וּ אֶל־גִּלּֽוּלֵיכֶם֙ וְדָ֣ם תִּשְׁפֹּ֔כוּ וְהָאָ֖רֶץ
כו תִּירָֽשׁוּ: עֲמַדְתֶּ֤ם עַל־חַרְבְּכֶם֙ עֲשִׂיתֶ֣ן תּֽוֹעֵבָ֔ה וְאִ֛ישׁ אֶת־אֵ֥שֶׁת רֵעֵ֖הוּ
כז טִמֵּאתֶ֑ם וְהָאָ֖רֶץ תִּירָֽשׁוּ: כֹּֽה־תֹאמַ֨ר אֲלֵהֶ֜ם כֹּה־אָמַ֨ר אֲדֹנָ֣י יֱהֹוִה֮ חַי־
אָ֒נִי֒ אִם־לֹ֠א אֲשֶׁ֨ר בֶּֽחֳרָב֤וֹת בַּחֶ֨רֶב֙ יִפֹּ֔לוּ וַֽאֲשֶׁר֙ עַל־פְּנֵ֣י הַשָּׂדֶ֔ה לַֽחַיָּ֥ה
כח נְתַתִּ֖יו לְאָכְל֑וֹ וַֽאֲשֶׁ֛ר בַּמְּצָד֥וֹת וּבַמְּעָר֖וֹת בַּדֶּ֥בֶר יָמֽוּתוּ: וְנָֽתַתִּ֤י אֶת־
הָאָ֨רֶץ֙ שְׁמָמָ֣ה וּמְשַׁמָּ֔ה וְנִשְׁבַּ֖ת גְּא֣וֹן עֻזָּ֑הּ וְשָֽׁמְמ֛וּ הָרֵ֥י יִשְׂרָאֵ֖ל מֵאֵ֥ין
כט עוֹבֵֽר: וְיָֽדְע֖וּ כִּֽי־אֲנִ֣י יְהוָ֑ה בְּתִתִּ֤י אֶת־הָאָ֨רֶץ֙ שְׁמָמָ֣ה וּמְשַׁמָּ֔ה עַ֥ל כָּל־
ל תּֽוֹעֲבֹתָ֖ם אֲשֶׁ֥ר עָשֽׂוּ: וְאַתָּ֣ה בֶן־אָדָ֗ם בְּנֵ֤י עַמְּךָ֙ הַנִּדְבָּרִ֣ים
בְּךָ֔ אֵ֥צֶל הַקִּיר֖וֹת וּבְפִתְחֵ֣י הַבָּתִּ֑ים וְדִבֶּר־חַ֣ד אֶת־אַחַ֗ד אִ֤ישׁ אֶת־אָחִיו֙
לא לֵאמֹ֔ר בֹּֽאוּ־נָ֣א וְשִׁמְע֔וּ מָ֣ה הַדָּבָ֔ר הַיּוֹצֵ֖א מֵאֵ֣ת יְהוָֽה: וְיָב֣וֹאוּ אֵ֠לֶיךָ
כִּמְבוֹא־עָ֜ם וְיֵֽשְׁב֤וּ לְפָנֶ֨יךָ֙ עַמִּ֔י וְשָֽׁמְעוּ֙ אֶת־דְּבָרֶ֔יךָ וְאוֹתָ֖ם לֹ֣א יַֽעֲשׂ֑וּ כִּֽי־
לב עֲגָבִ֤ים בְּפִיהֶם֙ הֵ֣מָּה עֹשִׂ֔ים אַֽחֲרֵ֥י בִצְעָ֖ם לִבָּ֥ם הֹלֵֽךְ: וְהִנְּךָ֤ לָהֶם֙ כְּשִׁ֣יר
עֲגָבִ֗ים יְפֵ֥ה ק֙וֹל֙ וּמֵטִ֣ב נַגֵּ֔ן וְשָֽׁמְעוּ֙ אֶת־דְּבָרֶ֔יךָ וְעֹשִׂ֥ים אֵינָ֖ם אוֹתָֽם:
לד וּבְבֹאָ֕הּ הִנֵּ֣ה בָאָ֑ה וְיָ֣דְע֔וּ כִּ֥י נָבִ֖יא הָיָ֥ה בְתוֹכָֽם: וַיְהִ֥י דְבַר־
לג:א-ב
יְהוָ֖ה אֵלַ֥י לֵאמֹֽר: בֶּן־אָדָ֕ם הִנָּבֵ֖א עַל־רוֹעֵ֣י יִשְׂרָאֵ֑ל הִנָּבֵ֣א וְאָֽמַרְתָּ֣
אֲלֵיהֶם֩ לָֽרֹעִ֨ים כֹּ֣ה אָמַ֣ר ׀ אֲדֹנָ֣י יֱהֹוִ֗ה ה֤וֹי רֹֽעֵֽי־יִשְׂרָאֵל֙ אֲשֶׁ֤ר הָיוּ֙ רֹעִ֣ים
ג אוֹתָ֔ם הֲל֥וֹא הַצֹּ֖אן יִרְע֣וּ הָֽרֹעִ֑ים אֶת־הַחֵ֤לֶב תֹּאכֵ֨לוּ֙ וְאֶת־הַצֶּ֣מֶר
ד תִּלְבָּ֔שׁוּ הַבְּרִיאָ֖ה תִּזְבָּ֑חוּ הַצֹּ֖אן לֹ֥א תִרְעֽוּ: אֶת־הַנַּחְלוֹת֙ לֹ֣א חִזַּקְתֶּם֙

33:21. Teves.

33:22. As foretold in 24:26-27.

33:24. Although the country has been conquered, we can rely on the Divine guarantee that the land is ours.

33:25. The reference is to an idolatrous ritual, in which

the meat of a slaughtered animal was eaten near its blood (*Radak*). Alternatively, the reference is to the sin of murdering wealthy people in order to buy expensive food with their money (*Rashi*).

33:33. When they see your prophecies begin to materialize, as when the fugitive comes.

without practicing corruption — he will surely live; he will not die. [16] *All his sins that he had committed will not be remembered for him; he has practiced justice and righteousness, he shall surely live.*

[17] *Now the members of your people say, 'The way of the Lord is not proper'; but them, it is their ways that are not proper.* [18] *If a righteous person turns back from his righteousness and practices corruption, he shall die for [his acts];* [19] *and if a wicked person turns back from his wickedness and acts with justice and righteousness, he shall live for [his acts].* [20] *Yet you say, 'The way of the Lord is not proper'! I shall judge you, each man according to his ways, O House of Israel!"*

The fugitive's report

[21] *It happened in the twelfth year of our exile, in the tenth [month],* * *on the fifth of the month: A fugitive came to me from Jerusalem, saying, "The City has been conquered."* [22] *Now the hand of HASHEM had come upon me on the evening before the arrival of the fugitive, and He had opened my mouth before his coming to me in the morning; my mouth was opened and I was dumb no more.* *

Shall you inherit?

[23] *The word of HASHEM came to me, saying,* [24] *"Son of Man, the inhabitants of these ruins upon the ground of Israel speak, saying, 'Abraham was [but] one, yet he inherited the land; we are many, so the land is given us as a heritage.'* *

[25] *Therefore, say to them:*

Thus said the Lord HASHEM/ELOHIM: You eat over the blood, * *you lift up your eyes to your idols and you shed blood; shall you then inherit the land?* [26] *You relied upon your sword, you committed abomination, a man has defiled his fellow's wife; shall you then inherit the land?*

[27] *Say thus to them:*

Thus said the Lord HASHEM/ELOHIM: As I live, [I swear] that those who are in the ruined cities will fall by the sword; and whoever is out in the open field I have given over to the beast to devour him; and those in the strongholds and in the caves will die by the plague. [28] *I will make the land desolate and a waste, and its prideful power will cease; and the mountains of Israel will be desolate, without passerby.* [29] *Then they will know that I am HASHEM, when I make the land desolate and a waste because of all their abominations that they have committed."*

Ignoring the prophet

[30] *"Now you, Son of Man, the children of your people who speak against you near the walls and in the entrances of the houses, and speak to one another, each man to his brother, saying, 'Come now and hear what is the word that comes forth from HASHEM.'* [31] *They come to you as a people comes, and My people sits before you and they hear your words, but they do not fulfill [them], for they relegate them to ridicule with their mouths, and their heart lusts for unjust gain.* [32] *You are like a love song to them, with a beautiful voice, skillfully sung; they hear your words, but do not fulfill them.* [33] *But when it comes,* * *for it will come, they will know that a prophet was among them."*

34

[1] **T**he word of HASHEM came to me, saying, [2] *"Son of Man, prophesy against the shepherds of Israel; prophesy and say to them, to the shepherds:*

Woe to the shepherds/ kings

Thus said the Lord HASHEM/ELOHIM: Woe to the shepherds of Israel who have tended themselves! Is it not the flock that the shepherds should tend? [3] *The choicest you eat; the wool you wear; and the healthiest you slaughter; [but] the [rest of the] flock you do not tend!* [4] *The frail you did not strengthen;*

וְאֶת־הַחוֹלָה לְא־רִפֵּאתֶם וְלַנִּשְׁבֶּרֶת לְא חֲבַשְׁתֶּם וְאֶת־הַנִּדַּחַת לֹא הֲשֵׁבֹתֶם וְאֶת־הָאֹבֶדֶת לֹא בִקַּשְׁתֶּם וּבְחׇזְקָה רְדִיתֶם אֹתָם וּבְפָרֶךְ:

ה וַתְּפוּצֶינָה מִבְּלִי רֹעֶה וַתִּהְיֶינָה לְאׇכְלָה לְכׇל־חַיַּת הַשָּׂדֶה וַתְּפוּצֶינָה:

ו יִשְׁגּוּ צֹאנִי בְּכׇל־הֶהָרִים וְעַל כׇּל־גִּבְעָה רָמָה וְעַל כׇּל־פְּנֵי הָאָרֶץ נָפֹצוּ

ז-ח צֹאנִי וְאֵין דּוֹרֵשׁ וְאֵין מְבַקֵּשׁ: לָכֵן רֹעִים שִׁמְעוּ אֶת־דְּבַר יְהֹוָה: חַי־אָנִי נְאֻם ׀ אֲדֹנָי יֱהֹוִה אִם־לֹא יַעַן הֱיוֹת־צֹאנִי ׀ לָבַז וַתִּהְיֶינָה צֹאנִי לְאׇכְלָה לְכׇל־חַיַּת הַשָּׂדֶה מֵאֵין רֹעֶה וְלֹא־דָרְשׁוּ רֹעַי אֶת־צֹאנִי וַיִּרְעוּ הָרֹעִים

ט אוֹתָם וְאֶת־צֹאנִי לֹא רָעוּ: לָכֵן הָרֹעִים שִׁמְעוּ דְּבַר־יְהֹוָה: כה כֹּה־ אָמַר אֲדֹנָי יֱהֹוִה הִנְנִי אֶל־הָרֹעִים וְדָרַשְׁתִּי אֶת־צֹאנִי מִיָּדָם וְהִשְׁבַּתִּים מֵרְעוֹת צֹאן וְלֹא־יִרְעוּ עוֹד הָרֹעִים אוֹתָם וְהִצַּלְתִּי צֹאנִי מִפִּיהֶם וְלֹא־

יא תִהְיֶיןָ לָהֶם לְאׇכְלָה: כִּי כֹּה אָמַר אֲדֹנָי יֱהֹוִה הִנְנִי־אָנִי

יב וְדָרַשְׁתִּי אֶת־צֹאנִי וּבִקַּרְתִּים: כְּבַקָּרַת רֹעֶה עֶדְרוֹ בְּיוֹם־הֱיוֹתוֹ בְתוֹךְ־ צֹאנוֹ נִפְרָשׁוֹת כֵּן אֲבַקֵּר אֶת־צֹאנִי וְהִצַּלְתִּי אֶתְהֶם מִכׇּל־הַמְּקוֹמֹת אֲשֶׁר

יג נָפֹצוּ שָׁם בְּיוֹם עָנָן וַעֲרָפֶל: וְהוֹצֵאתִים מִן־הָעַמִּים וְקִבַּצְתִּים מִן־ הָאֲרָצוֹת וַהֲבִיאֹתִים אֶל־אַדְמָתָם וּרְעִיתִים אֶל־הָרֵי יִשְׂרָאֵל בָּאֲפִיקִים

יד וּבְכֹל מוֹשְׁבֵי הָאָרֶץ: בְּמִרְעֶה־טּוֹב אֶרְעֶה אֹתָם וּבְהָרֵי מְרוֹם־יִשְׂרָאֵל יִהְיֶה נְוֵהֶם שָׁם תִּרְבַּצְנָה בְּנָוֶה טּוֹב וּמִרְעֶה שָׁמֵן תִּרְעֶינָה אֶל־הָרֵי

טו-טז יִשְׂרָאֵל: אֲנִי אֶרְעֶה צֹאנִי וַאֲנִי אַרְבִּיצֵם נְאֻם אֲדֹנָי יֱהֹוִה: אֶת־הָאֹבֶדֶת אֲבַקֵּשׁ וְאֶת־הַנִּדַּחַת אָשִׁיב וְלַנִּשְׁבֶּרֶת אֶחֱבֹשׁ וְאֶת־הַחוֹלָה אֲחַזֵּק וְאֶת־ הַשְּׁמֵנָה וְאֶת־הַחֲזָקָה אַשְׁמִיד אֶרְעֶנָּה בְמִשְׁפָּט: וְאַתֵּנָה צֹאנִי כֹּה אָמַר

יז-יח אֲדֹנָי יֱהֹוִה הִנְנִי שֹׁפֵט בֵּין־שֶׂה לָשֶׂה לָאֵילִים וְלָעַתּוּדִים: הַמְעַט מִכֶּם הַמִּרְעֶה הַטּוֹב תִּרְעוּ וְיֶתֶר מִרְעֵיכֶם תִּרְמְסוּ בְּרַגְלֵיכֶם וּמִשְׁקַע־מַיִם

יט תִּשְׁתּוּ וְאֵת הַנּוֹתָרִים בְּרַגְלֵיכֶם תִּרְפֹּשׂוּן: וְצֹאנִי מִרְמַס רַגְלֵיכֶם תִּרְעֶינָה וּמִרְפַּשׂ רַגְלֵיכֶם תִּשְׁתֶּינָה: לָכֵן כֹּה אָמַר אֲדֹנָי יֱהֹוִה

כא אֲלֵיהֶם הִנְנִי־אָנִי וְשָׁפַטְתִּי בֵּין־שֶׂה בִרְיָה וּבֵין שֶׂה רָזֶה: יַעַן בְּצַד וּבְכָתֵף תֶּהְדֹּפוּ וּבְקַרְנֵיכֶם תְּנַגְּחוּ כׇּל־הַנַּחְלוֹת עַד אֲשֶׁר הֲפִיצוֹתֶם

כב אוֹתָנָה אֶל־הַחוּצָה: וְהוֹשַׁעְתִּי לְצֹאנִי וְלֹא־תִהְיֶינָה עוֹד לָבַז וְשָׁפַטְתִּי

כג בֵּין שֶׂה לָשֶׂה: וַהֲקִמֹתִי עֲלֵיהֶם רֹעֶה אֶחָד וְרָעָה אֶתְהֶן אֵת עַבְדִּי

כד דָוִיד הוּא יִרְעֶה אֹתָם וְהוּא־יִהְיֶה לָהֶן לְרֹעֶה: וַאֲנִי יְהֹוָה אֶהְיֶה לָהֶם

כה לֵאלֹהִים וְעַבְדִּי דָוִד נָשִׂיא בְתוֹכָם אֲנִי יְהֹוָה דִּבַּרְתִּי: וְכָרַתִּי לָהֶם בְּרִית שָׁלוֹם וְהִשְׁבַּתִּי חַיָּה־רָעָה מִן־הָאָרֶץ וְיָשְׁבוּ בַמִּדְבָּר לָבֶטַח

כו וְיָשְׁנוּ בַּיְּעָרִים: וְנָתַתִּי אוֹתָם וּסְבִיבוֹת גִּבְעָתִי בְּרָכָה וְהוֹרַדְתִּי הַגֶּשֶׁם

34:17. This parable is explained in verse 20.
34:25. Because of the total lack of fear.

34:26. The Temple (*Targum*), or the Land of Israel (*Metzudos*).

the ill you did not cure; the broken you did not bind; the banished you did not retrieve; for the lost you did not search — rather, you subjugated them with force and with rigor. [5] Thus they became scattered for lack of a shepherd and became food for every beast of the field; they became scattered. [6] My sheep wander on all the mountains and upon every high hill; My sheep have scattered upon the whole face of the earth, but no one seeks and no one searches.

[7] Therefore, O shepherds, hear the word of HASHEM: [8] As I live — the word of the Lord HASHEM/ELOHIM — [I swear] that because My sheep have become spoils, and My sheep have become food for every beast of the field for lack of a shepherd, and My shepherds did not seek out My sheep, for the shepherds tended themselves, but did not tend My flock — [9] therefore, shepherds, hear the word of HASHEM!

I will seek My flock . . .

[10] Thus said the Lord HASHEM/ELOHIM: Behold, I am against the shepherds, and I will seek out My flock from their hand, and I will cause them to cease herding sheep, and the shepherds will no longer tend themselves; thus I will rescue My sheep from their mouths, and they will no longer be food for them. [11] For thus said the Lord HASHEM/ELOHIM: Behold, I am here, and I will seek out My sheep and I will tend them. [12] As a shepherd tends his flock on the day he is among his separated sheep, so I will tend to My sheep and rescue them from all the places where they were scattered on the day of cloud and thick cloud. [13] I will remove them from the peoples and gather them from the lands and bring them to their soil, and I will tend them upon the mountains of Israel, in the streams and in all the land's habitations. [14] I will shepherd them upon a good pasture and their fold will be upon the heights of Israel's mountains; there they will lie down in a good fold and graze upon fat pastures, on the mountains of Israel. [15] I will care for My sheep and I will lay them down — the word of the Lord HASHEM/ELOHIM. [16] For the lost I will search; the banished I will retrieve; the broken I will bind; the ill I will strengthen; but the fat one and the strong one I will destroy. I will tend them with justice.

. . . and gather in My sheep

I will separate the guilty from the innocent

[17] And as for you, My sheep, thus said the Lord HASHEM/ELOHIM: Behold, I am judging between lamb and lamb * and the rams and the he-goats. [18] Is it not enough for you that you graze in the good pasture, that you must also trample the rest of your pasture underfoot? [Is it not enough] that you drink settled waters, that you must also befoul the rest with your feet? [19] And My flock, must they graze the tramplings of your feet and drink the befoulment of your feet?

[20] Therefore, thus said the Lord HASHEM/ELOHIM to them: Behold, I am here, and I shall judge between the robust lamb and the famished lamb; [21] because you push with flank and shoulder and you gore all the frail ones with your horns until you have scattered them away. [22] So I will save My sheep, and they will no longer be for spoils, and I will judge between lamb and lamb. [23] I will establish over them a single shepherd and he will tend them — My servant David; he will tend them and he will be a shepherd unto them. [24] And I, HASHEM, I will be a God to them, and My servant David a prince among them. I, HASHEM, have spoken. [25] I will seal a covenant of peace with them and abolish evil beast from the land; and they will dwell securely in the wilderness, and sleep in the forests. * [26] Then I will make them and the surroundings of My hill* into a blessing, and I will bring the rain

A covenant of peace

כז בְּעִתּוֹ גִּשְׁמֵי בְרָכָה יִהְיוּ: וְנָתַן עֵץ הַשָּׂדֶה אֶת־פִּרְיוֹ וְהָאָרֶץ תִּתֵּן יְבוּלָהּ
וְהָיוּ עַל־אַדְמָתָם לָבֶטַח וְיָדְעוּ כִּי־אֲנִי יהוה בְּשִׁבְרִי אֶת־מֹטוֹת עֻלָּם
כח וְהִצַּלְתִּים מִיַּד הָעֹבְדִים בָּהֶם: וְלֹא־יִהְיוּ עוֹד בַּז לַגּוֹיִם וְחַיַּת הָאָרֶץ לֹא
כט תֹאכְלֵם וְיָשְׁבוּ לָבֶטַח וְאֵין מַחֲרִיד: וַהֲקִמֹתִי לָהֶם מַטָּע לְשֵׁם וְלֹא־יִהְיוּ
ל עוֹד אֲסֻפֵי רָעָב בָּאָרֶץ וְלֹא־יִשְׂאוּ עוֹד כְּלִמַּת הַגּוֹיִם: וְיָדְעוּ כִּי אֲנִי יהוה
לא אֱלֹהֵיהֶם אִתָּם וְהֵמָּה עַמִּי בֵּית יִשְׂרָאֵל נְאֻם אֲדֹנָי יֱהוִֹה: וְאַתֵּן צֹאנִי צֹאן
לה א מַרְעִיתִי אָדָם אַתֶּם אֲנִי אֱלֹהֵיכֶם נְאֻם אֲדֹנָי יֱהוִֹה: וַיְהִי
ב דְבַר־יהוה אֵלַי לֵאמֹר: בֶּן־אָדָם שִׂים פָּנֶיךָ עַל־הַר שֵׂעִיר וְהִנָּבֵא
ג עָלָיו: וְאָמַרְתָּ לּוֹ כֹּה אָמַר אֲדֹנָי יֱהוִֹה הִנְנִי אֵלֶיךָ הַר־שֵׂעִיר וְנָטִיתִי יָדִי
ד עָלֶיךָ וּנְתַתִּיךָ שְׁמָמָה וּמְשַׁמָּה: עָרֶיךָ חָרְבָּה אָשִׂים וְאַתָּה שְׁמָמָה תִהְיֶה
ה וְיָדַעְתָּ כִּי־אֲנִי יהוה: יַעַן הֱיוֹת לְךָ אֵיבַת עוֹלָם וַתַּגֵּר אֶת־בְּנֵי־יִשְׂרָאֵל
ו עַל־יְדֵי־חָרֶב בְּעֵת אֵידָם בְּעֵת עֲוֹן קֵץ: לָכֵן חַי־אָנִי נְאֻם אֲדֹנָי יֱהוִֹה כִּי־
ז לְדָם אֶעֶשְׂךָ וְדָם יִרְדְּפֶךָ אִם־לֹא דָם שָׂנֵאתָ וְדָם יִרְדְּפֶךָ: וְנָתַתִּי אֶת־הַר
ח שֵׂעִיר לְשִׁמְמָה וּשְׁמָמָה וְהִכְרַתִּי מִמֶּנּוּ עֹבֵר וָשָׁב: וּמִלֵּאתִי אֶת־הָרָיו
ט חֲלָלָיו גִּבְעוֹתֶיךָ וְגֵאוֹתֶיךָ וְכָל־אֲפִיקֶיךָ חַלְלֵי־חֶרֶב יִפְּלוּ בָהֶם: שִׁמְמוֹת
עוֹלָם אֶתֶּנְךָ וְעָרֶיךָ לֹא °תִשֹׁבְנָה [תֵשַׁבְנָה ק] וִידַעְתֶּם כִּי־אֲנִי יהוה:
י יַעַן אֲמָרְךָ אֶת־שְׁנֵי הַגּוֹיִם וְאֶת־שְׁתֵּי הָאֲרָצוֹת לִי תִהְיֶינָה וִירַשְׁנוּהָ
יא וַיהוה שָׁם הָיָה: לָכֵן חַי־אָנִי נְאֻם אֲדֹנָי יֱהוִֹה וְעָשִׂיתִי כְּאַפְּךָ וּכְקִנְאָתְךָ
יב אֲשֶׁר עָשִׂיתָה מִשִּׂנְאָתֶיךָ בָּם וְנוֹדַעְתִּי בָם כַּאֲשֶׁר אֶשְׁפְּטֶךָ: וְיָדַעְתָּ כִּי־
אֲנִי יהוה שָׁמַעְתִּי ׀ אֶת־כָּל־נָאָצוֹתֶיךָ אֲשֶׁר אָמַרְתָּ עַל־הָרֵי יִשְׂרָאֵל
יג לֵאמֹר ׀ °שממה [שָׁמֵמוּ ק] לָנוּ נִתְּנוּ לְאָכְלָה: וַתַּגְדִּילוּ עָלַי בְּפִיכֶם
יד וְהַעְתַּרְתֶּם עָלַי דִּבְרֵיכֶם אֲנִי שָׁמָעְתִּי: כֹּה אָמַר
טו אֲדֹנָי יֱהוִֹה כִּשְׂמֹחַ כָּל־הָאָרֶץ שְׁמָמָה אֶעֱשֶׂה־לָּךְ: כְּשִׂמְחָתְךָ לְנַחֲלַת
בֵּית־יִשְׂרָאֵל עַל אֲשֶׁר־שָׁמֵמָה כֵּן אֶעֱשֶׂה־לָּךְ שְׁמָמָה תִהְיֶה הַר־
לו א שֵׂעִיר וְכָל־אֱדוֹם כֻּלָּהּ וְיָדְעוּ כִּי־אֲנִי יהוה: וְאַתָּה
בֶן־אָדָם הִנָּבֵא אֶל־הָרֵי יִשְׂרָאֵל וְאָמַרְתָּ הָרֵי יִשְׂרָאֵל שִׁמְעוּ דְּבַר־יהוה:
ב כֹּה אָמַר אֲדֹנָי יֱהוִֹה יַעַן אָמַר הָאוֹיֵב עֲלֵיכֶם הֶאָח וּבָמוֹת עוֹלָם
ג לְמוֹרָשָׁה הָיְתָה לָּנוּ: לָכֵן הִנָּבֵא וְאָמַרְתָּ כֹּה אָמַר אֲדֹנָי יֱהוִֹה יַעַן ׀ בְּיַעַן

34:29. I will plant them firmly in their land.

35:2. Seir was the home of Esau/Edom, so that this prophecy was directed against Israel's historic arch-enemy.

35:5. That is, the sin that finally brought about their ruination.

35:6. You hated the murderers who would try to kill you, but they will pursue and apprehend you.

35:10. The northern Kingdom of Israel and the Kingdom of Judah. However, since God's presence rests in the land, He would not permit you to succeed (*Metzudos*).

35:11. By repaying Seir in kind for its hatred and vengefulness against Israel, God will cause His greatness and justice to be acknowledged by Israel (*Radak*).

35:14. At the end of days (*Rashi*).

in its time; they will be rains of blessing. [27] *The tree of the field will yield its fruit, and the earth will yield its produce, and they will be secure upon their land. Then they will know that I am* HASHEM, *when I break the rods of their yoke and rescue them from the hand of those who enslave them.* [28] *They will no longer be spoils for the nations, and the beast of the land will no longer devour them; they will dwell securely, and none will make [them] afraid.* [29] *I will establish for them a planting of renown,* * *and they will no longer be decimated by famine in the land, and they will no longer bear the shame of the nations.* [30] *Then they will know that I,* HASHEM *their God, am with them, and that they are My people, the House of Israel — the word of the Lord* HASHEM/ELOHIM.

You are man
[31] *Now, you are My sheep, the sheep of My pasture, you are Man; I am your God — the word of the Lord* HASHEM/ELOHIM."

35

Another prophecy against Edom . . .

[1] T*he word of* HASHEM *came to me, saying,* [2] *"Son of Man, direct your face toward Mount Seir* * *and prophesy against it.* [3] *Say to it:*

Thus said the Lord HASHEM/ELOHIM: *Behold, I am against you, Mount Seir; I will stretch out My hand against you and make you desolate and a waste.* [4] *I will make your cities into ruins, and you will be desolate; then you will know that I am* HASHEM. [5] *Because you have eternal hatred, and you caused the [blood of the] Children of Israel to stream forth by the sword at the moment of their disaster, at the time of the climactic sin,* * [6] *therefore, as I live — the word of the Lord* HASHEM/ELOHIM — *[I swear] that I will turn you to blood, and blood will pursue you. Surely though you have hated bloodshed,* * *bloodshed will pursue you.* [7] *I will make Mount Seir desolate and a waste, and I will cut off from it those who come and go.* [8] *I will fill his mountains with his corpses; your hills and your valleys and all your streams. Those slain by the sword will fall in them.* [9] *I will make you an eternal desolation, that your cities will never be restored; then you will know that I am* HASHEM.

. . . because of its vengefulness
[10] *Because you said, 'The two nations and the two lands* * *shall be mine and we shall inherit them' — but* HASHEM *was there!* [11] *Therefore, as I live — the word of the Lord* HASHEM/ELOHIM — *I will act according to your anger and according to your vengefulness, for what you have done because of your hatred of them; then I will become known among them,* * *when I judge you.* [12] *Then you will know that I am* HASHEM. *I have heard all your provocations that you have spoken against the mountains of Israel, saying, 'They are desolate; they are presented to us to devour.'* [13] *You have exalted yourselves against Me with your mouths and have spoken your words excessively against Me; I have heard!*

[14] *Thus said the Lord* HASHEM/ELOHIM: *When all the earth rejoices,* * *I will make you desolate.* [15] *In accordance with your rejoicing that the heritage of the House of Israel had become desolate, so will I do to you; you shall be desolate, Mount Seir and every bit of Edom! Then they will know that I am* HASHEM.' "

36

Prophecy of renewal

[1] "N*ow you, Son of Man, prophesy to the mountains of Israel and say:*

Mountains of Israel, hear the word of HASHEM! [2] *Thus said the Lord* HASHEM/ELOHIM: *Because the enemy has said against you, 'Hurrah! The heights of the world have become a heritage for us!' —* [3] *therefore, prophesy and say, 'Thus said the Lord* HASHEM/ELOHIM: *Because, and again because,*

שַׁמּוֹת וְשָׁאָף אֶתְכֶם מִסָּבִיב לִהְיֽוֹתְכֶם מֽוֹרָשָׁה לִשְׁאֵרִית הַגּוֹיִם וַתֵּֽעֲלוּ

ד עַל־שְׂפַת לָשׁוֹן וְדִבַּת־עָם: לָכֵן הָרֵי יִשְׂרָאֵל שִׁמְעוּ דְּבַר־אֲדֹנָי יֱהֹוִה כֹּה־

אָמַר אֲדֹנָי יֱהֹוִה לֶהָרִים וְלַגְּבָעוֹת לָאֲפִיקִים וְלַגֵּֽאָיוֹת וְלֶחֳרָבוֹת

הַשֹּֽׁמְמוֹת וְלֶעָרִים הַנֶּֽעֱזָבוֹת אֲשֶׁר הָיוּ לְבַז וּלְלַעַג לִשְׁאֵרִית הַגּוֹיִם אֲשֶׁר

ה מִסָּבִיב: לָכֵן כֹּה־אָמַר אֲדֹנָי יֱהֹוִה אִם־לֹא בְּאֵשׁ קִנְאָתִי

דִבַּרְתִּי עַל־שְׁאֵרִית הַגּוֹיִם וְעַל־אֱדוֹם כֻּלָּא אֲשֶׁר נָֽתְנוּ־אֶת־אַרְצִי ׀ לָהֶם

לְמֽוֹרָשָׁה בְּשִׂמְחַת כָּל־לֵבָב בִּשְׁאָט נֶפֶשׁ לְמַעַן מִגְרָשָׁהּ לָבַז: ו לָכֵן הִנָּבֵא

עַל־אַדְמַת יִשְׂרָאֵל וְאָֽמַרְתָּ לֶהָרִים וְלַגְּבָעוֹת לָֽאֲפִיקִים וְלַגֵּֽאָיוֹת כֹּה־

אָמַר ׀ אֲדֹנָי יֱהֹוִה הִנְנִי בְקִנְאָתִי וּבַֽחֲמָתִי דִּבַּרְתִּי יַעַן כְּלִמַּת גּוֹיִם נְשָׂאתֶם:

ז לָכֵן כֹּה אָמַר אֲדֹנָי יֱהֹוִה אֲנִי נָשָׂאתִי אֶת־יָדִי אִם־לֹא הַגּוֹיִם אֲשֶׁר לָכֶם

ח מִסָּבִיב הֵמָּה כְּלִמָּתָם יִשָּֽׂאוּ: וְאַתֶּם הָרֵי יִשְׂרָאֵל עַנְפְּכֶם תִּתֵּנוּ וּפֶרְיְכֶם

ט תִּשְׂאוּ לְעַמִּי יִשְׂרָאֵל כִּי קֵֽרְבוּ לָבֽוֹא: כִּי הִנְנִי אֲלֵיכֶם וּפָנִיתִי אֲלֵיכֶם

י וְנֶֽעֱבַדְתֶּם וְנִזְרַעְתֶּם: וְהִרְבֵּיתִי עֲלֵיכֶם אָדָם כָּל־בֵּית יִשְׂרָאֵל כֻּלֹּה וְנֹֽשְׁבוּ

יא הֶֽעָרִים וְהֶֽחֳרָבוֹת תִּבָּנֶֽינָה: וְהִרְבֵּיתִי עֲלֵיכֶם אָדָם וּבְהֵמָה וְרָבוּ וּפָרוּ

וְהֽוֹשַׁבְתִּי אֶתְכֶם כְּקַדְמֽוֹתֵיכֶם וְהֵֽטִבֹתִי מֵרִֽאשֹׁתֵיכֶם וִֽידַעְתֶּם כִּי־אֲנִי

יב יְהֹוָה: וְהֽוֹלַכְתִּי עֲלֵיכֶם אָדָם אֶת־עַמִּי יִשְׂרָאֵל וִירֵשׁוּךָ וְהָיִיתָ לָהֶם

יג לְנַֽחֲלָה וְלֹֽא־תוֹסִף עוֹד לְשַׁכְּלָֽם: כֹּה אָמַר אֲדֹנָי יֱהֹוִה

יַעַן אֹֽמְרִים לָכֶם אֹכֶלֶת אָדָם °אָתִי [°אָתְּ ק] וּמְשַׁכֶּלֶת °גּוֹיַךְ [°גּוֹיַיִךְ ק]

יד הָיִית: לָכֵן אָדָם לֹא־תֹ֣אכְלִי עוֹד °וְגוֹיַךְ [°וְגוֹיַיִךְ ק] לֹא °תְכַשְׁלִי־

טו °תְשַׁכְּלִי־ ק] עוֹד נְאֻם אֲדֹנָי יֱהֹוִה: וְלֹֽא־אַשְׁמִיעַ אֵלַיִךְ עוֹד כְּלִמַּת

הַגּוֹיִם וְחֶרְפַּת עַמִּים לֹא תִשְׂאִי־עוֹד °וְגוֹיַךְ [°וְגוֹיַיִךְ ק] לֹֽא־תַכְשִׁלִי עוֹד

טז נְאֻם אֲדֹנָי יֱהֹוִה: וַיְהִי דְבַר־יְהֹוָה אֵלַי לֵאמֹֽר:

יז בֶּן־אָדָם בֵּית יִשְׂרָאֵל יֹֽשְׁבִים עַל־אַדְמָתָם וַיְטַמְּאוּ אוֹתָהּ בְּדַרְכָּם

וּבַֽעֲלִֽילוֹתָם כְּטֻמְאַת הַנִּדָּה הָֽיְתָה דַרְכָּם לְפָנָי: וָֽאֶשְׁפֹּךְ חֲמָתִי עֲלֵיהֶם

יח עַל־הַדָּם אֲשֶׁר־שָֽׁפְכוּ עַל־הָאָרֶץ וּבְגִלּֽוּלֵיהֶם טִמְּאֽוּהָ: וָֽאָפִיץ אֹתָם בַּגּוֹיִם

יט וַיִּזָּרוּ בָּֽאֲרָצוֹת כְּדַרְכָּם וְכַֽעֲלִֽילוֹתָם שְׁפַטְתִּים: וַיָּבוֹא אֶל־הַגּוֹיִם אֲשֶׁר־

כ בָּאוּ שָׁם וַֽיְחַלְּלוּ אֶת־שֵׁם קָדְשִׁי בֶּֽאֱמֹר לָהֶם עַם־יְהֹוָה אֵלֶּה וּמֵֽאַרְצוֹ

יָצָֽאוּ: וָֽאֶחְמֹל עַל־שֵׁם קָדְשִׁי אֲשֶׁר חִלְּלֻהוּ בֵּית יִשְׂרָאֵל בַּגּוֹיִם אֲשֶׁר־בָּאוּ

כא שָֽׁמָּה: לָכֵן אֱמֹר לְבֵֽית־יִשְׂרָאֵל כֹּה אָמַר אֲדֹנָי יֱהֹוִה

כב לֹא לְמַֽעַנְכֶם אֲנִי עֹשֶׂה בֵּית יִשְׂרָאֵל כִּי אִם־לְשֵׁם־קָדְשִׁי אֲשֶׁר חִלַּלְתֶּם

HAFTARAS
PARASHAS
PARAH
Ashkenazim:
36:16-38
Sephardim:
36:16-36

36:13. The Canaanite nations were spewed out of the land, and now Israel has been driven from the land (*Rashi*).
36:17. She must be separated from her husband until the purification process is completed (*Radak*).

36:20. People assumed that God's people were forced into exile because He lacked the power to save them. When weakness can be ascribed to God, His Name is desecrated.

there was astonishment and craving for you from all around, for you to become a heritage for the rest of the nations, and you were taken up on [every] lip of each nation as the subject of the people's disparagement, ⁴ therefore, mountains of Israel, hear the word of the Lord HASHEM/ELOHIM! Thus said the Lord HASHEM/ELOHIM to the mountains and to the hills, to the streams and to the valleys, to the desolate ruins and to the forlorn cities, which have become a scorn and a derision for the remaining nations all around — ⁵ therefore, thus said the Lord HASHEM/ELOHIM: [I swear] that I have spoken in the fire of My vengefulness against the remaining nations and against all of Edom, who have arrogated My land to themselves as a heritage with the joy of all their heart, with contempt of soul, because of [Israel's] expulsion in scorn.

⁶ "Therefore, prophesy concerning the Land of Israel and say to the mountains and to the hills, to the streams and to the valleys,

'Thus said the Lord HASHEM/ELOHIM: Behold, I have spoken in My vengeful-ness and in My wrath, because you bore the shame of the nations. ⁷ There-fore, thus said the Lord HASHEM/ELOHIM: I have lifted My hand, [swearing] that the nations surrounding you will bear their shame, ⁸ but you, O moun-tains of Israel, will give forth your branch and bear your fruit for My people Israel, for they are soon to come. ⁹ For behold, I am with you; and I will turn [My attention] to you, and you will be tilled and you will be sown. ¹⁰ I will make people numerous upon you — the entire House of Israel, all of it; the cities will be inhabited and the ruins will be rebuilt. ¹¹ I will multiply man and animal upon you, and they will multiply and be fruitful; I will make you inhabited as in your earlier times, and I will make it better than it was at your beginning; then you will know that I am HASHEM. ¹² I will cause man to walk upon you — My people Israel — and they will inherit you. Then you will be theirs for a possession, and you will no longer be bereaved of them.

¹³ Thus said the Lord HASHEM/ELOHIM: Because people say of you, 'You devour man, and you have become one who drives out your nations'* — ¹⁴ therefore, you will no longer devour people, and you will never again drive out your nations — the word of the Lord HASHEM/ELOHIM. ¹⁵ I will no longer allow the derision of nations to be heard about you, and you will no longer bear the shame of the peoples, and you will never again cause your nations to falter — the word of the Lord HASHEM/ELOHIM.'"

What was . . .

¹⁶ The word of HASHEM came to me, saying, ¹⁷ "Son of Man, the House of Israel dwell on their land, and they have contaminated it with their way and with their acts; their way has become like the contamination of a menstruous woman* before Me. ¹⁸ So I poured My wrath upon them, because of the blood that they had shed in the land, and [because] they had defiled it with their idols. ¹⁹ I scattered them among the nations and they were dispersed among the lands; according to their way and according to their acts did I judge them. ²⁰ They came among the nations where they came, and they desecrated My holy Name when it was said of them, 'These are the people of HASHEM, but they departed His land.'* ²¹ I took pity on My holy Name, which the House of Israel had desecrated among the nations where they came. ²² Therefore, say to the House of Israel:

. . . and what will be

Thus said the Lord HASHEM/ELOHIM: It is not for your sake that I act, O House of Israel, but for My holy Name that you have desecrated

כג בַּגּוֹיִם אֲשֶׁר־בָּאתֶם שָׁם: וְקִדַּשְׁתִּי אֶת־שְׁמִי הַגָּדוֹל הַמְחֻלָּל בַּגּוֹיִם אֲשֶׁר
חִלַּלְתֶּם בְּתוֹכָם וְיָדְעוּ הַגּוֹיִם כִּי־אֲנִי יהוה נְאֻם אֲדֹנָי יֱהוִה בְּהִקָּדְשִׁי בָכֶם
כד לְעֵינֵיהֶם: וְלָקַחְתִּי אֶתְכֶם מִן־הַגּוֹיִם וְקִבַּצְתִּי אֶתְכֶם מִכָּל־הָאֲרָצוֹת
כה וְהֵבֵאתִי אֶתְכֶם אֶל־אַדְמַתְכֶם: וְזָרַקְתִּי עֲלֵיכֶם מַיִם טְהוֹרִים וּטְהַרְתֶּם
כו מִכֹּל טֻמְאוֹתֵיכֶם וּמִכָּל־גִּלּוּלֵיכֶם אֲטַהֵר אֶתְכֶם: וְנָתַתִּי לָכֶם לֵב חָדָשׁ
וְרוּחַ חֲדָשָׁה אֶתֵּן בְּקִרְבְּכֶם וַהֲסִרֹתִי אֶת־לֵב הָאֶבֶן מִבְּשַׂרְכֶם וְנָתַתִּי לָכֶם
כז לֵב בָּשָׂר: וְאֶת־רוּחִי אֶתֵּן בְּקִרְבְּכֶם וְעָשִׂיתִי אֵת אֲשֶׁר־בְּחֻקַּי תֵּלֵכוּ
כח וּמִשְׁפָּטַי תִּשְׁמְרוּ וַעֲשִׂיתֶם: וִישַׁבְתֶּם בָּאָרֶץ אֲשֶׁר נָתַתִּי לַאֲבֹתֵיכֶם
כט וִהְיִיתֶם לִי לְעָם וְאָנֹכִי אֶהְיֶה לָכֶם לֵאלֹהִים: וְהוֹשַׁעְתִּי אֶתְכֶם מִכֹּל
טֻמְאוֹתֵיכֶם וְקָרָאתִי אֶל־הַדָּגָן וְהִרְבֵּיתִי אֹתוֹ וְלֹא־אֶתֵּן עֲלֵיכֶם רָעָב:
ל וְהִרְבֵּיתִי אֶת־פְּרִי הָעֵץ וּתְנוּבַת הַשָּׂדֶה לְמַעַן אֲשֶׁר לֹא־תִקְחוּ עוֹד חֶרְפַּת
לא רָעָב בַּגּוֹיִם: וּזְכַרְתֶּם אֶת־דַּרְכֵיכֶם הָרָעִים וּמַעַלְלֵיכֶם אֲשֶׁר לֹא־טוֹבִים
לב וּנְקֹטֹתֶם בִּפְנֵיכֶם עַל עֲוֹנֹתֵיכֶם וְעַל תּוֹעֲבוֹתֵיכֶם: לֹא לְמַעַנְכֶם אֲנִי־עֹשֶׂה
נְאֻם אֲדֹנָי יֱהוִה יִוָּדַע לָכֶם בּוֹשׁוּ וְהִכָּלְמוּ מִדַּרְכֵיכֶם בֵּית יִשְׂרָאֵל:
לג כֹּה אָמַר אֲדֹנָי יֱהוִה בְּיוֹם טַהֲרִי אֶתְכֶם מִכֹּל עֲוֹנוֹתֵיכֶם וְהוֹשַׁבְתִּי אֶת־
לד הֶעָרִים וְנִבְנוּ הֶחֳרָבוֹת: וְהָאָרֶץ הַנְּשַׁמָּה תֵּעָבֵד תַּחַת אֲשֶׁר הָיְתָה שְׁמָמָה
לה לְעֵינֵי כָּל־עוֹבֵר: וְאָמְרוּ הָאָרֶץ הַלֵּזוּ הַנְּשַׁמָּה הָיְתָה כְּגַן־עֵדֶן וְהֶעָרִים
לו הֶחֳרֵבוֹת וְהַנְּשַׁמּוֹת וְהַנֶּהֱרָסוֹת בְּצוּרוֹת יָשָׁבוּ: וְיָדְעוּ הַגּוֹיִם אֲשֶׁר יִשָּׁאֲרוּ
סְבִיבוֹתֵיכֶם כִּי | אֲנִי יהוה בָּנִיתִי הַנֶּהֱרָסוֹת נָטַעְתִּי הַנְּשַׁמָּה אֲנִי יהוה
לז דִּבַּרְתִּי וְעָשִׂיתִי: ◀   כֹּה אָמַר אֲדֹנָי יֱהוִה עוֹד זֹאת
לח אִדָּרֵשׁ לְבֵית־יִשְׂרָאֵל לַעֲשׂוֹת לָהֶם אַרְבֶּה אֹתָם כַּצֹּאן אָדָם: כְּצֹאן
קָדָשִׁים כְּצֹאן יְרוּשָׁלַ͏ִם בְּמוֹעֲדֶיהָ כֵּן תִּהְיֶינָה הֶעָרִים הֶחֳרֵבוֹת מְלֵאוֹת
צֹאן אָדָם וְיָדְעוּ כִּי־אֲנִי יהוה: ◀

א הָיְתָה עָלַי יַד־יהוה וַיּוֹצִאֵנִי בְרוּחַ יהוה וַיְנִיחֵנִי בְּתוֹךְ הַבִּקְעָה
ב וְהִיא מְלֵאָה עֲצָמוֹת: וְהֶעֱבִירַנִי עֲלֵיהֶם סָבִיב | סָבִיב וְהִנֵּה רַבּוֹת מְאֹד
ג עַל־פְּנֵי הַבִּקְעָה וְהִנֵּה יְבֵשׁוֹת מְאֹד: וַיֹּאמֶר אֵלַי בֶּן־אָדָם הֲתִחְיֶינָה
ד הָעֲצָמוֹת הָאֵלֶּה וָאֹמַר אֲדֹנָי יֱהוִה אַתָּה יָדָעְתָּ: וַיֹּאמֶר אֵלַי הִנָּבֵא
עַל־הָעֲצָמוֹת הָאֵלֶּה וְאָמַרְתָּ אֲלֵיהֶם הָעֲצָמוֹת הַיְבֵשׁוֹת שִׁמְעוּ דְּבַר־
ה יהוה: כֹּה אָמַר אֲדֹנָי יֱהוִה לָעֲצָמוֹת הָאֵלֶּה הִנֵּה אֲנִי מֵבִיא בָכֶם
ו רוּחַ וִחְיִיתֶם: וְנָתַתִּי עֲלֵיכֶם גִּדִים וְהַעֲלֵתִי עֲלֵיכֶם בָּשָׂר וְקָרַמְתִּי
ז עֲלֵיכֶם עוֹר וְנָתַתִּי בָכֶם רוּחַ וִחְיִיתֶם וִידַעְתֶּם כִּי־אֲנִי יהוה: וְנִבֵּאתִי
כַּאֲשֶׁר צֻוֵּיתִי וַיְהִי־קוֹל כְּהִנָּבְאִי וְהִנֵּה־רַעַשׁ וַתִּקְרְבוּ עֲצָמוֹת עֶצֶם

36:38. At festival times, huge numbers of animals were brought to Jerusalem for offerings.
37:1. That is, in a prophetic vision, not physically (*Radak*).

There are two points of view in the Talmud as to whether this prophecy is a parable or whether the bones in the valley actually came to life (*Sanhedrin* 92b). In either among the nations where you came. ²³ I will sanctify My great Name that is desecrated among the nations, that you have desecrated among them; then the nations will know that I am HASHEM — the word of the Lord HASHEM/ELO-HIM — when I become sanctified through you before their eyes. ²⁴ I will take you from [among] the nations and gather you from all the lands, and I will bring you to your own soil. ²⁵ Then I will sprinkle pure water upon you, that you may become cleansed; I will cleanse you from all your contamination

A new heart and a new spirit   and from all your idols. ²⁶ I will give you a new heart and put a new spirit within you; I will remove the heart of stone from your flesh and give you a heart of flesh. ²⁷ I will put My spirit within you, and I will make it so that you will follow My decrees and guard My ordinances and fulfill them. ²⁸ You will dwell in the land that I gave to your forefathers; you will be a people to Me, and I will be a God to you. ²⁹ I will save you from all your contaminations; I will summon the grain and increase it, and I will not inflict famine upon you. ³⁰ I will increase the fruit of the tree and the produce of the field, so that you will no longer be subject to the shame of hunger among the nations. ³¹ Then you will remember your evil ways and your deeds that were not good, and you will be disgusted with yourselves in your own sight because of your iniquities and because of your abominations. ³² Not for your sake do I act — the word of the Lord HASHEM/ELOHIM — let this be known to you! Be embarrassed and ashamed of your ways, O House of Israel!

Rebuilding the desolate   ³³ Thus said the Lord HASHEM/ELOHIM: On the day when I cleanse you from all your iniquities, I will cause the cities to be inhabited and the ruins will be built. ³⁴ The desolated land will be tilled, instead of having been desolate in the eyes of every passerby. ³⁵ People will say, 'This very land, which had been desolate, has become like the Garden of Eden; and the ruined, desolate and demolished cities have been fortified, inhabited!' ³⁶ The nations that remain around you will know that I, HASHEM, have rebuilt the ruins and I have replanted the wasteland; I, HASHEM, have spoken and I shall act.

³⁷ Thus said the Lord HASHEM/ELOHIM: With this also I will relate to the inquiries of the House of Israel, to act for them. I will multiply them, the people, like sheep. ³⁸ Like consecrated sheep, like the sheep of Jerusalem on her festivals, * so will the destroyed cities be filled with flocks of people; then they will know that I am HASHEM."

37

The dry bones   ¹ The hand of HASHEM was upon me; it took me out by the spirit of HASHEM* and set me down in the midst of the valley — and it was filled with bones. ² He passed me over them all around and around; and behold, they were very numerous upon the face of the valley, and behold, they were very dry. ³ Then He said to me: "Son of Man, can these bones come to life?"

And I said, "Lord HASHEM/ELOHIM, You know!"

⁴ He said to me, "Prophesy over these bones! Say to them, 'O dry bones, hear the word of HASHEM! ⁵ Thus said the Lord HASHEM/ELOHIM to these bones: Behold, I bring a spirit into you, and you will come to life. ⁶ I will put sinews upon you, I will bring up flesh upon you, and I will coat you with skin; then I will put a spirit into you and you will come to life; then you will know that I am HASHEM.' "

⁷ So I prophesied as I had been commanded. There was a sound as I was prophesying. Then behold, there was a noise, and the bones drew near, each bone

---

case, it is understood by the commentators as a source of hope for Israel in its exile and as a reinforcement of the   principle that the dead will come to life again in Messianic times.

ח אֶל־עַצְמֽוֹ: וְרָאִ֗יתִי וְהִנֵּֽה־עֲלֵיהֶ֤ם גִּדִים֙ וּבָשָׂ֣ר עָלָ֔ה וַיִּקְרַ֧ם עֲלֵיהֶ֛ם ע֖וֹר
ט מִלְמָ֑עְלָה וְר֖וּחַ אֵ֣ין בָּהֶֽם: וַיֹּ֣אמֶר אֵלַ֔י הִנָּבֵ֖א אֶל־הָר֑וּחַ הִנָּבֵ֣א בֶן־אָדָ֗ם
וְאָמַרְתָּ֣ אֶל־הָר֡וּחַ כֹּֽה־אָמַר֩ ׀ אֲדֹנָ֨י יֱהֹוִ֜ה מֵאַרְבַּ֤ע רוּחוֹת֙ בֹּ֣אִי הָר֔וּחַ וּפְחִ֛י
י בַּהֲרוּגִ֥ים הָאֵ֖לֶּה וְיִחְיֽוּ: וְהִנַּבֵּ֙אתִי֙ כַּֽאֲשֶׁ֣ר צִוָּ֔נִי וַתָּבוֹא֩ בָהֶ֨ם הָר֜וּחַ וַיִּֽחְי֗וּ
יא וַיַּֽעַמְדוּ֙ עַל־רַגְלֵיהֶ֔ם חַ֖יִל גָּד֣וֹל מְאֹ֥ד מְאֹֽד: וַיֹּאמֶר֮ אֵלַי֒ בֶּן־אָדָ֔ם הָעֲצָמ֣וֹת
הָאֵ֔לֶּה כׇּל־בֵּ֥ית יִשְׂרָאֵ֖ל הֵ֑מָּה הִנֵּ֣ה אֹֽמְרִ֗ים יָבְשׁ֧וּ עַצְמוֹתֵ֛ינוּ וְאָבְדָ֥ה
יב תִקְוָתֵ֖נוּ נִגְזַ֥רְנוּ לָֽנוּ: לָכֵן֩ הִנָּבֵ֨א וְאָֽמַרְתָּ֜ אֲלֵיהֶ֗ם כֹּֽה־אָמַר֮ אֲדֹנָ֣י יֱהֹוִה֒ הִנֵּה֩
אֲנִ֨י פֹתֵ֜חַ אֶת־קִבְרוֹֽתֵיכֶ֗ם וְהַעֲלֵיתִ֥י אֶתְכֶ֛ם מִקִּבְרוֹתֵיכֶ֖ם עַמִּ֑י וְהֵבֵאתִ֥י
יג אֶתְכֶ֖ם אֶל־אַדְמַ֥ת יִשְׂרָאֵֽל: וִֽידַעְתֶּ֖ם כִּֽי־אֲנִ֣י יְהֹוָ֑ה בְּפִתְחִ֣י אֶת־קִבְרֽוֹתֵיכֶ֗ם
יד וּבְהַעֲלוֹתִ֥י אֶתְכֶ֛ם מִקִּבְרֽוֹתֵיכֶ֖ם עַמִּֽי: וְנָֽתַתִּ֨י רוּחִ֤י בָכֶם֙ וִֽחְיִיתֶ֔ם וְהִנַּחְתִּ֥י
אֶתְכֶ֖ם עַל־אַדְמַתְכֶ֑ם וִֽידַעְתֶּ֞ם כִּֽי־אֲנִ֧י יְהֹוָ֛ה דִּבַּ֥רְתִּי וְעָשִׂ֖יתִי נְאֻם־

טו־טז יְהֹוָֽה: ◀ וַיְהִ֥י דְבַר־יְהֹוָ֖ה אֵלַ֥י לֵאמֹֽר: וְאַתָּ֣ה בֶן־אָדָ֗ם קַ֣ח־

HAFTARAS
VAYIGASH
37:15-28

לְךָ֙ עֵ֣ץ אֶחָ֔ד וּכְתֹ֤ב עָלָיו֙ לִֽיהוּדָ֔ה וְלִבְנֵ֥י יִשְׂרָאֵ֖ל °חֲבֵרָ֑ו [°חֲבֵרָ֑יו ק] וּלְקַח֙
עֵ֣ץ אֶחָ֔ד וּכְת֣וֹב עָלָ֗יו לְיוֹסֵף֙ עֵ֣ץ אֶפְרַ֔יִם וְכׇל־בֵּ֥ית יִשְׂרָאֵ֖ל °חֲבֵרָ֑ו
יז [°חֲבֵרָ֑יו ק]: וְקָרַ֨ב אֹתָ֜ם אֶחָ֧ד אֶל־אֶחָ֛ד לְךָ֖ לְעֵ֣ץ אֶחָ֑ד וְהָי֥וּ לַֽאֲחָדִ֖ים
יח בְּיָדֶֽךָ: וְכַֽאֲשֶׁר֙ יֹֽאמְר֣וּ אֵלֶ֔יךָ בְּנֵ֥י עַמְּךָ֖ לֵאמֹ֑ר הֲלֽוֹא־תַגִּ֥יד לָ֖נוּ מָה־אֵ֥לֶּה
יט לָּֽךְ: דַּבֵּ֣ר אֲלֵהֶ֗ם כֹּֽה־אָמַר֮ אֲדֹנָ֣י יֱהֹוִה֒ הִנֵּה֩ אֲנִ֨י לֹקֵ֜חַ אֶת־עֵ֤ץ יוֹסֵף֙ אֲשֶׁ֣ר
בְּיַד־אֶפְרַ֔יִם וְשִׁבְטֵ֥י יִשְׂרָאֵ֖ל °חֲבֵרָ֑ו [°חֲבֵרָ֑יו ק] וְנָֽתַתִּי֩ אוֹתָ֨ם עָלָ֜יו אֶת־
כ עֵ֣ץ יְהוּדָ֗ה וַֽעֲשִׂיתִם֙ לְעֵ֣ץ אֶחָ֔ד וְהָי֥וּ אֶחָ֖ד בְּיָדִֽי: וְהָי֨וּ הָעֵצִ֜ים אֲֽשֶׁר־תִּכְתֹּ֧ב
כא עֲלֵיהֶ֛ם בְּיָדְךָ֖ לְעֵינֵיהֶֽם: וְדַבֵּ֣ר אֲלֵהֶ֗ם כֹּֽה־אָמַר֮ אֲדֹנָ֣י יֱהֹוִה֒ הִנֵּ֨ה אֲנִ֤י לֹקֵ֙חַ֙
אֶת־בְּנֵ֣י יִשְׂרָאֵ֔ל מִבֵּ֥ין הַגּוֹיִ֖ם אֲשֶׁ֣ר הָֽלְכוּ־שָׁ֑ם וְקִבַּצְתִּ֤י אֹתָם֙ מִסָּבִ֔יב
כב וְהֵֽבֵאתִ֥י אוֹתָ֖ם אֶל־אַדְמָתָֽם: וְעָשִׂ֣יתִי אֹ֠תָ֠ם לְג֨וֹי אֶחָ֤ד בָּאָ֙רֶץ֙ בְּהָרֵ֣י
יִשְׂרָאֵ֔ל וּמֶ֧לֶךְ אֶחָ֛ד יִֽהְיֶ֥ה לְכֻלָּ֖ם לְמֶ֑לֶךְ וְלֹ֤א °יִֽהְיֶה [°יִֽהְיוּ ק] ע֖וֹד לִשְׁנֵ֣י
כג גוֹיִ֔ם וְלֹ֨א יֵחָ֤צוּ עוֹד֙ לִשְׁתֵּ֣י מַמְלָכ֔וֹת ע֑וֹד: וְלֹ֧א יִֽטַּמְּא֣וּ ע֗וֹד בְּגִלּֽוּלֵיהֶם֙
וּבְשִׁקֻּ֣צֵיהֶ֔ם וּבְכֹ֖ל פִּשְׁעֵיהֶ֑ם וְהוֹשַׁעְתִּ֣י אֹתָ֗ם מִכֹּ֤ל מוֹשְׁבֹֽתֵיהֶם֙ אֲשֶׁ֣ר
חָֽטְא֣וּ בָהֶ֔ם וְטִהַרְתִּ֣י אוֹתָ֔ם וְהָיוּ־לִ֣י לְעָ֑ם וַֽאֲנִ֕י אֶֽהְיֶ֥ה לָהֶ֖ם לֵֽאלֹהִֽים:
כד וְעַבְדִּ֤י דָוִד֙ מֶ֣לֶךְ עֲלֵיהֶ֔ם וְרוֹעֶ֥ה אֶחָ֖ד יִֽהְיֶ֣ה לְכֻלָּ֑ם וּבְמִשְׁפָּטַ֣י יֵלֵ֔כוּ
כה וְחֻקֹּתַ֥י יִשְׁמְר֖וּ וְעָשׂ֥וּ אוֹתָֽם: וְיָֽשְׁב֣וּ עַל־הָאָ֗רֶץ אֲשֶׁ֤ר נָתַ֙תִּי֙ לְעַבְדִּ֣י לְיַֽעֲקֹ֔ב
אֲשֶׁ֥ר יָֽשְׁבוּ־בָ֖הּ אֲבֽוֹתֵיכֶ֑ם וְיָֽשְׁב֣וּ עָלֶ֡יהָ הֵ֠מָּה וּבְנֵיהֶ֞ם וּבְנֵ֤י בְנֵיהֶם֙ עַד־
כו עוֹלָ֔ם וְדָוִ֣ד עַבְדִּ֔י נָשִׂ֥יא לָהֶ֖ם לְעוֹלָֽם: וְכָֽרַתִּ֤י לָהֶם֙ בְּרִ֣ית שָׁל֔וֹם בְּרִ֥ית
עוֹלָ֖ם יִֽהְיֶ֣ה אוֹתָ֑ם וּנְתַתִּים֙ וְהִרְבֵּיתִ֣י אוֹתָ֔ם וְנָֽתַתִּ֧י אֶת־מִקְדָּשִׁ֛י בְּתוֹכָ֖ם
כז לְעוֹלָֽם: וְהָיָ֤ה מִשְׁכָּנִי֙ עֲלֵיהֶ֔ם וְהָיִ֥יתִי לָהֶ֖ם לֵֽאלֹהִ֑ים וְהֵ֖מָּה יִֽהְיוּ־לִ֥י לְעָֽם:
כח וְיָֽדְעוּ֙ הַגּוֹיִ֔ם כִּ֚י אֲנִ֣י יְהֹוָ֔ה מְקַדֵּ֖שׁ אֶת־יִשְׂרָאֵ֑ל בִּֽהְי֧וֹת מִקְדָּשִׁ֛י בְּתוֹכָ֖ם

37:16. The tribe of Benjamin, which had allied itself with the Judean Kingdom (see *I Kings* 12:21).

The bones
come alive

to its [matching] bone. [8] Then I looked, and behold, upon them were sinews, and flesh had come up and skin had covered them over; but there was no spirit in them. [9] Then He said to me, "Prophesy to the spirit! Prophesy, O Son of Man, and say to the spirit, 'Thus said the Lord HASHEM/ELOHIM: Come from the four directions, O spirit, and blow into these slain people, that they may come to life!' " [10] I prophesied as I had been commanded and the spirit entered them and they came to life. They stood upon their feet, a very, very great legion.

[11] He said to me, "Son of Man, these bones — they are the whole House of Israel. Behold, they are saying, 'Our bones are dried out and our hope is lost; we are doomed!' [12] Therefore, prophesy and say to them:

Thus said the Lord HASHEM/ELOHIM: Behold, I am opening your graves and raising you up from your graves, My people, and I will bring you to the soil of Israel. [13] Then you will know that I am HASHEM, when I open your graves and when I raise you up from your graves, My people, [14] and when I put My spirit into you, and you come to life, and I set you on your soil. Then you will know that I HASHEM have spoken and I have fulfilled — the word of HASHEM."

Two tablets
— Judah
and Joseph

[15] The word of HASHEM came to me, saying, [16] "Now you, Son of Man, take for yourself one piece of wood and write upon it, 'For Judah and for the Children of Israel, his comrades'; * and take one piece of wood and write upon it, 'For Joseph, the wood of Ephraim and all the House of Israel, his comrades.' [17] Then bring them close to yourself, one to the other, like one piece of wood, and they will become united in your hand. [18] Now when the children of your people say to you, saying, 'Will you not tell us what these things are to you,' [19] say to them:

Thus said the Lord HASHEM/ELOHIM: Behold, I am taking the wood of Joseph which is in the hand of Ephraim, and the tribes of Israel, his comrades, and I am placing them and him together with the wood of Judah; and I will make them into one piece of wood, and they will become one in My hand.

One tablet —
one nation

[20] The pieces of wood upon which you will write shall be in your hand, before their eyes. [21] Say to them,

'Thus said the Lord HASHEM/ELOHIM: Behold, I am taking the Children of Israel from among the nations to which they have gone; I will gather them from all around and I will bring them to their soil; [22] I will make them into one nation in the land, upon the mountains of Israel, and one king will be a king for them all; they will no longer be two nations, and they will no longer be divided into two kingdoms, ever again. [23] They will no longer be contaminated with their idols and with their abhorrent things and with all their sins. I will save them [taking them] from all their dwelling places in which they had sinned, and I will purify them; they will be a nation to Me, and I will be a God to them. [24] My servant David will be king over them, and there will be one shepherd for all of them; they will follow My ordinances and keep My decrees and fulfill them. [25] They will dwell on the land that I gave to My servant Jacob, within which your fathers dwelled; they and their children and their children's children will dwell upon it forever; and My servant David

An eternal
covenant
of peace

will be a leader for them forever. [26] I will seal a covenant of peace with them; it will be an eternal covenant with them; and I will emplace them and increase them, and I will place My Sanctuary among them forever. [27] My dwelling place will be among them; I will be a God to them and they will be a people to Me. [28] Then the nations will know that I am HASHEM Who sanctifies Israel, when My sanctuary will be among them forever.' "

לח א-ב וַיְהִי דְבַר־יְהֹוָה אֵלַי לֵאמֹר: בֶּן־אָדָם שִׂים פָּנֶיךָ לְעוֹלָם: ◀

ג אֶל־גּוֹג אֶרֶץ הַמָּגוֹג נְשִׂיא רֹאשׁ מֶשֶׁךְ וְתֻבָל וְהִנָּבֵא עָלָיו: וְאָמַרְתָּ כֹּה

ד אָמַר אֲדֹנָי יֱהֹוִה הִנְנִי אֵלֶיךָ גּוֹג נְשִׂיא רֹאשׁ מֶשֶׁךְ וְתֻבָל: וְשֽׁוֹבַבְתִּיךָ וְנָתַתִּי חַחִים בִּלְחָיֶיךָ וְהוֹצֵאתִי אוֹתְךָ וְאֶת־כָּל־חֵילֶךָ סוּסִים וּפָרָשִׁים

ה לְבֻשֵׁי מִכְלוֹל כֻּלָּם קָהָל רָב צִנָּה וּמָגֵן תֹּפְשֵׂי חֲרָבוֹת כֻּלָּם: פָּרַס כּוּשׁ וּפוּט

ו אִתָּם כֻּלָּם מָגֵן וְכוֹבָע: גֹּמֶר וְכָל־אֲגַפֶּיהָ בֵּית תּֽוֹגַרְמָה יַרְכְּתֵי צָפוֹן וְאֶת־

ז כָּל־אֲגַפָּיו עַמִּים רַבִּים אִתָּךְ: הִכֹּן וְהָכֵן לְךָ אַתָּה וְכָל־קְהָלֶךָ הַנִּקְהָלִים

ח עָלֶיךָ וְהָיִיתָ לָהֶם לְמִשְׁמָר: מִיָּמִים רַבִּים תִּפָּקֵד בְּאַחֲרִית הַשָּׁנִים תָּבוֹא ׀ אֶל־אֶרֶץ ׀ מְשׁוֹבֶבֶת מֵחֶרֶב מְקֻבֶּצֶת מֵעַמִּים רַבִּים עַל הָרֵי יִשְׂרָאֵל

ט אֲשֶׁר־הָיוּ לְחָרְבָּה תָּמִיד וְהִיא מֵעַמִּים הוּצָאָה וְיָשְׁבוּ לָבֶטַח כֻּלָּם: וְעָלִיתָ כַּשֹּׁאָה תָבוֹא כֶּעָנָן לְכַסּוֹת הָאָרֶץ תִּהְיֶה אַתָּה וְכָל־אֲגַפֶּיךָ וְעַמִּים רַבִּים

י אוֹתָךְ: כֹּה אָמַר אֲדֹנָי יֱהֹוִה ׀ וְהָיָה ׀ בַּיּוֹם הַהוּא יַעֲלוּ דְבָרִים

יא עַל־לְבָבְךָ וְחָשַׁבְתָּ מַחֲשֶׁבֶת רָעָה: וְאָמַרְתָּ אֶעֱלֶה עַל־אֶרֶץ פְּרָזוֹת אָבוֹא הַשֹּׁקְטִים יֹשְׁבֵי לָבֶטַח כֻּלָּם יֹשְׁבִים בְּאֵין חוֹמָה וּבְרִיחַ וּדְלָתַיִם אֵין לָהֶם:

יב לִשְׁלֹל שָׁלָל וְלָבֹז בַּז לְהָשִׁיב יָדְךָ עַל־חֳרָבוֹת נוֹשָׁבֹת וְאֶל־עַם מְאֻסָּף

יג מִגּוֹיִם עֹשֶׂה מִקְנֶה וְקִנְיָן יֹשְׁבֵי עַל־טַבּוּר הָאָרֶץ: שְׁבָא וּדְדָן וְסֹחֲרֵי תַרְשִׁישׁ וְכָל־כְּפִרֶיהָ יֹאמְרוּ לְךָ הֲלִשְׁלֹל שָׁלָל אַתָּה בָא הֲלָבֹז בַּז הִקְהַלְתָּ קְהָלֶךָ לָשֵׂאת ׀ כֶּסֶף וְזָהָב לָקַחַת מִקְנֶה וְקִנְיָן לִשְׁלֹל שָׁלָל

יד גָּדוֹל: לָכֵן הִנָּבֵא בֶן־אָדָם וְאָמַרְתָּ לְגוֹג כֹּה אָמַר אֲדֹנָי יֱהֹוִה

טו הֲלוֹא ׀ בַּיּוֹם הַהוּא בְּשֶׁבֶת עַמִּי יִשְׂרָאֵל לָבֶטַח תֵּדָע: וּבָאתָ מִמְּקוֹמְךָ מִיַּרְכְּתֵי צָפוֹן אַתָּה וְעַמִּים רַבִּים אִתָּךְ רֹכְבֵי סוּסִים כֻּלָּם קָהָל גָּדוֹל וְחַיִל

טז רָב: וְעָלִיתָ עַל־עַמִּי יִשְׂרָאֵל כֶּעָנָן לְכַסּוֹת הָאָרֶץ בְּאַחֲרִית הַיָּמִים תִּהְיֶה וַהֲבִאוֹתִיךָ עַל־אַרְצִי לְמַעַן דַּעַת הַגּוֹיִם אֹתִי בְּהִקָּדְשִׁי בְךָ לְעֵינֵיהֶם

יז גּוֹג: כֹּה־אָמַר אֲדֹנָי יֱהֹוִה הַאַתָּה־הוּא אֲשֶׁר־דִּבַּרְתִּי בְּיָמִים קַדְמוֹנִים בְּיַד עֲבָדַי נְבִיאֵי יִשְׂרָאֵל הַנִּבְּאִים בַּיָּמִים הָהֵם שָׁנִים לְהָבִיא

יח אֹתְךָ עֲלֵיהֶם: וְהָיָה ׀ בַּיּוֹם הַהוּא בְּיוֹם בּוֹא גוֹג עַל־אַדְמַת

יט יִשְׂרָאֵל נְאֻם אֲדֹנָי יֱהֹוִה תַּעֲלֶה חֲמָתִי בְּאַפִּי: וּבְקִנְאָתִי בְאֵשׁ־עֶבְרָתִי דִּבַּרְתִּי אִם־לֹא ׀ בַּיּוֹם הַהוּא יִהְיֶה רַעַשׁ גָּדוֹל עַל אַדְמַת יִשְׂרָאֵל:

כ וְרָעֲשׁוּ מִפָּנַי דְּגֵי הַיָּם וְעוֹף הַשָּׁמַיִם וְחַיַּת הַשָּׂדֶה וְכָל־הָרֶמֶשׂ הָרֹמֵשׂ עַל־הָאֲדָמָה וְכֹל הָאָדָם אֲשֶׁר עַל־פְּנֵי הָאֲדָמָה וְנֶהֶרְסוּ הֶהָרִים

HAFTARAH
SABBATH
OF CHOL
HAMOED
SUCCOS
38:18-39:16

38:1. Chapters 38-39 foretell the climactic War of Gog and Magog, which will introduce the End of Days and the Messianic era. In it, Gog, from the land of Magog — allied with a multitude of nations — will advance to attack Israel in its own land. The war will end with the destruction of Israel's enemies and the promised Messianic era of bliss. *Rambam* cautions against attempting to pinpoint the time

and identity of the kingdoms discussed in this prophecy. **38:7.** Take responsibility for protecting them during the siege (*Rashi*). **38:8.** Only recently had the land been resettled by its people. **38:12.** The land of Israel is considered the *navel*, or center, of the world (*Radak*).

38

Gog, prince of Magog, and his allies

¹ The word of HASHEM came to me, saying, ² "Son of Man, direct your face towards Gog of the land of Magog, the prince, leader of Meshech and Tubal, and prophesy concerning him. ³ Say:

Thus said the Lord HASHEM/ELOHIM: Behold, I am against you, Gog, the prince, leader of Meshech and Tubal. ⁴ I will lead you astray, and I will place hooks into your cheeks and bring you out with your entire army, horses and riders, all of them clothed in splendor, a vast assembly with buckler and shield, all of them wielding swords. ⁵ Persia, Cush, and Put will be with them, all of them with shield and helmet; ⁶ Gomer and all her cohorts, the house of Togarmah in the uttermost parts of the north, and all its cohorts — many peoples will be with you. ⁷ Prepare and make ready for yourself, you and all your hordes that are mustered about you, and be a guardian for them. *
⁸ You will be repaid for [your sins] of ancient times; in the end of years you will come to a land restored from the sword, gathered from many nations, upon the mountains of Israel that had lain desolate continuously, * [to people] who had been brought out from the nations, all of them dwelling in security. ⁹ You will attack; like a storm you will come; you will be like a cloud covering the earth, you and all your cohorts and the many nations with you.

¹⁰ Thus said the Lord HASHEM/ELOHIM: It shall be on that day that ideas will arise in your heart, and you will conceive a wicked design. ¹¹ You will say, 'I will advance against a land of open towns, I will come up against the tranquil people who dwell securely, all of them living without a [protective] wall; they have neither bars nor doors' — ¹² to seize booty and to take spoils, to turn your hand against resettled ruins, against a people gathered from the nations, which possesses livestock and property, who dwell upon the navel of the earth. * ¹³ Sheba, Dedan and the merchants of Tarshish and all its officers will say to you, 'Have you come to seize booty? Is it to take spoils that you have assembled your hordes, to carry off silver and gold, to take livestock and property, to seize great booty?'

¹⁴ "Therefore, prophesy, Son of Man, and say to Gog:

The first war of Gog and Magog . . .

Thus said the Lord HASHEM/ELOHIM: Surely on that day, when My people Israel dwells securely, you will come to know, ¹⁵ when you come from your place in the uttermost parts of the north, you and many peoples with you, all of them riding horses, a vast horde, a mighty army, ¹⁶ and you advance against My people Israel like a cloud covering the earth. It will be at the End of Days that I will bring you upon My land, in order that the nations may know Me, when I become sanctified through you before their eyes, O Gog!

. . . had already ben prophesied

¹⁷ Thus said the Lord HASHEM/ELOHIM: Are you the one of whom I spoke in earlier days, through My servants, the prophets of Israel, * who prophesied in those days, years [ago], that I would bring you against them? ¹⁸ It shall be on that day that on the day that Gog comes against the soil of Israel — the word of the Lord HASHEM/ELOHIM — My raging anger will flare up; ¹⁹ for in My vengefulness, in the fire of My fury, I have spoken: [I swear] that on that day a great earthquake will take place upon the soil of Israel. ²⁰ They will quake before Me — the fish of the sea, the bird of the heavens, the beast of the field, every creeping thing that creeps on the ground and every human being that is on the face of the earth; the mountains will be broken apart

---

38:17. The verse refers to this prophecy of Ezekiel and to that of Zechariah (14:2), among others. When Gog attacks the land of Israel, these prophecies will already have been uttered "in those days, years ago."

כא וְנָפְלוּ הַמַּדְרֵגוֹת וְכָל־חוֹמָה לָאָרֶץ תִּפּוֹל: וְקָרָאתִי עָלָיו לְכָל־הָרַי חֶרֶב

כב נְאֻם אֲדֹנָי יֱהֹוִה חֶרֶב אִישׁ בְּאָחִיו תִּהְיֶה: וְנִשְׁפַּטְתִּי אִתּוֹ בְּדֶבֶר וּבְדָם

וְגֶשֶׁם שׁוֹטֵף וְאַבְנֵי אֶלְגָּבִישׁ אֵשׁ וְגָפְרִית אַמְטִיר עָלָיו וְעַל־אֲגַפָּיו וְעַל־

כג עַמִּים רַבִּים אֲשֶׁר אִתּוֹ: וְהִתְגַּדִּלְתִּי וְהִתְקַדִּשְׁתִּי וְנוֹדַעְתִּי לְעֵינֵי גּוֹיִם

א רַבִּים וְיָדְעוּ כִּי־אֲנִי יְהֹוָה: וְאַתָּה בֶן־אָדָם הִנָּבֵא עַל־גּוֹג   לט

וְאָמַרְתָּ כֹּה אָמַר אֲדֹנָי יֱהֹוִה הִנְנִי אֵלֶיךָ גּוֹג נְשִׂיא רֹאשׁ מֶשֶׁךְ וְתֻבָל:

ב וְשֹׁבַבְתִּיךָ וְשִׁשֵּׁאתִיךָ וְהַעֲלִיתִיךָ מִיַּרְכְּתֵי צָפוֹן וַהֲבִאוֹתִיךָ עַל־הָרֵי

ג יִשְׂרָאֵל: וְהִכֵּיתִי קַשְׁתְּךָ מִיַּד שְׂמֹאולֶךָ וְחִצֶּיךָ מִיַּד יְמִינְךָ אַפִּיל:

ד עַל־הָרֵי יִשְׂרָאֵל תִּפּוֹל אַתָּה וְכָל־אֲגַפֶּיךָ וְעַמִּים אֲשֶׁר אִתָּךְ לְעֵיט צִפּוֹר כָּל־כָּנָף

ה וְחַיַּת הַשָּׂדֶה נְתַתִּיךָ לְאָכְלָה: עַל־פְּנֵי הַשָּׂדֶה תִּפּוֹל כִּי אֲנִי דִבַּרְתִּי נְאֻם

ו אֲדֹנָי יֱהֹוִה: וְשִׁלַּחְתִּי־אֵשׁ בְּמָגוֹג וּבְיֹשְׁבֵי הָאִיִּים לָבֶטַח וְיָדְעוּ כִּי־אֲנִי

ז יְהֹוָה: וְאֶת־שֵׁם קָדְשִׁי אוֹדִיעַ בְּתוֹךְ עַמִּי יִשְׂרָאֵל וְלֹא־אַחֵל אֶת־שֵׁם־

ח קָדְשִׁי עוֹד וְיָדְעוּ הַגּוֹיִם כִּי־אֲנִי יְהֹוָה קָדוֹשׁ בְּיִשְׂרָאֵל: הִנֵּה בָאָה וְנִהְיָתָה

ט נְאֻם אֲדֹנָי יֱהֹוִה הוּא הַיּוֹם אֲשֶׁר דִּבַּרְתִּי: וְיָצְאוּ יֹשְׁבֵי עָרֵי יִשְׂרָאֵל וּבִעֲרוּ

וְהִשִּׂיקוּ בְּנֶשֶׁק וּמָגֵן וְצִנָּה בְּקֶשֶׁת וּבְחִצִּים וּבְמַקֵּל יָד וּבְרֹמַח וּבִעֲרוּ בָהֶם

י אֵשׁ שֶׁבַע שָׁנִים: וְלֹא־יִשְׂאוּ עֵצִים מִן־הַשָּׂדֶה וְלֹא יַחְטְבוּ מִן־הַיְּעָרִים כִּי

בַנֶּשֶׁק יְבַעֲרוּ־אֵשׁ וְשָׁלְלוּ אֶת־שֹׁלְלֵיהֶם וּבָזְזוּ אֶת־בֹּזְזֵיהֶם נְאֻם אֲדֹנָי

יא יֱהֹוִה: וְהָיָה בַיּוֹם הַהוּא אֶתֵּן לְגוֹג | מְקוֹם־שָׁם קֶבֶר בְּיִשְׂרָאֵל

גֵּי הָעֹבְרִים קִדְמַת הַיָּם וְחֹסֶמֶת הִיא אֶת־הָעֹבְרִים וְקָבְרוּ שָׁם אֶת־גּוֹג

יב וְאֶת־כָּל־הֲמוֹנֹה וְקָרְאוּ גֵּיא הֲמוֹן גּוֹג: וּקְבָרוּם בֵּית יִשְׂרָאֵל לְמַעַן טַהֵר

יג אֶת־הָאָרֶץ שִׁבְעָה חֳדָשִׁים: וְקָבְרוּ כָּל־עַם הָאָרֶץ וְהָיָה לָהֶם לְשֵׁם יוֹם

יד הִכָּבְדִי נְאֻם אֲדֹנָי יֱהֹוִה: וְאַנְשֵׁי תָמִיד יַבְדִּילוּ עֹבְרִים בָּאָרֶץ מְקַבְּרִים

אֶת־הָעֹבְרִים אֶת־הַנּוֹתָרִים עַל־פְּנֵי הָאָרֶץ לְטַהֲרָהּ מִקְצֵה שִׁבְעָה־

טו חֳדָשִׁים יַחְקֹרוּ: וְעָבְרוּ הָעֹבְרִים בָּאָרֶץ וְרָאָה עֶצֶם אָדָם וּבָנָה אֶצְלוֹ צִיּוּן

טז עַד קָבְרוּ אֹתוֹ הַמְקַבְּרִים אֶל־גֵּיא הֲמוֹן גּוֹג: וְגַם שֶׁם־עִיר הֲמוֹנָה וְטִהֲרוּ

יז הָאָרֶץ: וְאַתָּה בֶן־אָדָם כֹּה־אָמַר | אֲדֹנָי יֱהֹוִה אֱמֹר לְצִפּוֹר

כָּל־כָּנָף וּלְכֹל | חַיַּת הַשָּׂדֶה הִקָּבְצוּ וָבֹאוּ הֵאָסְפוּ מִסָּבִיב עַל־זִבְחִי

אֲשֶׁר אֲנִי זֹבֵחַ לָכֶם זֶבַח גָּדוֹל עַל הָרֵי יִשְׂרָאֵל וַאֲכַלְתֶּם בָּשָׂר וּשְׁתִיתֶם

יח דָם: בְּשַׂר גִּבּוֹרִים תֹּאכֵלוּ וְדַם־נְשִׂיאֵי הָאָרֶץ תִּשְׁתּוּ אֵילִים כָּרִים

יט וְעַתּוּדִים פָּרִים מְרִיאֵי בָשָׁן כֻּלָּם: וַאֲכַלְתֶּם־חֵלֶב לְשָׂבְעָה וּשְׁתִיתֶם

39:7. By allowing My people to be subjugated and humiliated.

39:11. There will be so many corpses that they will block passage through the valley.

39.13. Israel will be praised for according honor to the bodies of their mortal enemies.

39:14. After the corpses that are visible are buried, the people will search for corpses in hidden places (*Rashi*).

39:16. In the vicinity of the valley (*Radak*).

39:18. The named animals are metaphors for Gog's officers.

and the cliffs will topple, and every wall will topple to the ground. ²¹ I will summon the sword against him to all My mountains — the word of the Lord HASHEM/ELOHIM — each man's sword will be against his brother. ²² I will punish him with pestilence and with blood; torrential rain and hailstones, fire and sulfur will I rain down upon him and upon his cohorts and upon the many peoples who are with him. ²³ I will be exalted and I will be sanctified, and I will make Myself known before the eyes of many nations; then they will know that I am HASHEM."

39

¹ "**N**ow you, Son of Man, prophesy against Gog. Say:

The second war of Gog and Magog

Thus said the Lord HASHEM/ELOHIM: Behold, I am against you, Gog, the prince, leader of Meshech and Tubal! ² I will lead you astray and seduce you; I will cause you to ascend from the uttermost north and bring you upon the mountains of Israel. ³ I will strike your bow from your left hand, and cast down your arrows from your right hand. ⁴ You will fall upon the mountains of Israel, you and all your cohorts and the peoples that are with you; I will give you to the bird of prey, to every winged bird, and to the beast of the field as food. ⁵ You will fall upon the open field, for I have spoken — the word of the Lord HASHEM/ELOHIM. ⁶ I will dispatch a fire against Magog and against those who dwell confidently in the islands, and they will know that I am HASHEM. ⁷ I will make My holy Name known among My people Israel, and I will not desecrate My holy Name * any longer; then the nations will know that I am HASHEM, the Holy One in Israel. ⁸ Behold, it is coming and it will happen — the word of the Lord HASHEM/ELOHIM — that is the day of which I have spoken.

⁹ Then the inhabitants of the cities of Israel will go out and kindle fires and fuel them with their weaponry — shield and buckler, with bow and with arrows, with mace and with spear; they will fuel fires with them for seven years. ¹⁰ They will not carry wood from the field, and they will not cut it from the forests, for they will fuel fires with the weaponry. They will plunder those who had plundered them and despoil those who had despoiled them — the word of the Lord HASHEM/ELOHIM.

A grave for Gog

¹¹ It shall be on that day that I will assign Gog a burial site there in Israel — the Valley of the Passersby, east of the Sea; it will block the passersby, * and there they will bury Gog and all his multitude, and call it the Valley of Hamon-gog (Gog's Multitude). ¹² The House of Israel will bury them in order to cleanse the land, for seven months. ¹³ All the people of the land will bury, and it will bring them renown; * on the day that I manifest My glory — the word of the Lord HASHEM/ELOHIM. ¹⁴ They will designate permanent officials to pass through the land, burying, together with the passersby, those that remain upon the open field, to cleanse [the land]. After seven months, they will [begin to] search. * ¹⁵ The passersby will traverse the land and when they see a human bone, they will build a marker near it, until the buriers bury it in the Valley of Hamon-gog. ¹⁶ There will also be a city * called Hamonah (Her Multitude). Thus they will cleanse the land.

Feasting on Gog's multitude

¹⁷ Now you, Son of Man, thus said the Lord HASHEM/ELOHIM: Say to every winged bird and to every beast of the field, 'Assemble and come, gather together from all around for My feast that I slaughter for you, a great feast upon the mountains of Israel; eat flesh and drink blood! ¹⁸ Eat the flesh of warriors and drink the blood of the earth's princes — all of them like rams, lambs and he-goats, bulls [and] fatlings of Bashan. * ¹⁹ Eat fat to satiety and drink

כ דָּם לְשֻׁבְּרוֹן מִזְבְּחִי אֲשֶׁר־זָבַחְתִּי לָכֶם: וּשְׂבַעְתֶּם עַל־שֻׁלְחָנִי סוּס וָרֶכֶב
כא גִּבּוֹר וְכָל־אִישׁ מִלְחָמָה נְאֻם אֲדֹנָי יֱהוִֹה: וְנָתַתִּי אֶת־כְּבוֹדִי בַּגּוֹיִם וְרָאוּ
כב כָל־הַגּוֹיִם אֶת־מִשְׁפָּטִי אֲשֶׁר עָשִׂיתִי וְאֶת־יָדִי אֲשֶׁר־שַׂמְתִּי בָהֶם: וְיָדְעוּ
כג בֵּית יִשְׂרָאֵל כִּי אֲנִי יהוה אֱלֹהֵיהֶם מִן־הַיּוֹם הַהוּא וָהָלְאָה: וְיָדְעוּ הַגּוֹיִם
כִּי בַעֲוֹנָם גָּלוּ בֵית־יִשְׂרָאֵל עַל אֲשֶׁר מָעֲלוּ־בִי וָאַסְתִּר פָּנַי מֵהֶם וָאֶתְּנֵם
כד בְּיַד צָרֵיהֶם וַיִּפְּלוּ בַחֶרֶב כֻּלָּם: כְּטֻמְאָתָם וּכְפִשְׁעֵיהֶם עָשִׂיתִי אֹתָם
כה וָאַסְתִּר פָּנַי מֵהֶם: לָכֵן כֹּה אָמַר אֲדֹנָי יֱהוִֹה עַתָּה אָשִׁיב אֶת־
°שְׁבִית [°שְׁבוּת ק] יַעֲקֹב וְרִחַמְתִּי כָּל־בֵּית יִשְׂרָאֵל וְקִנֵּאתִי לְשֵׁם קָדְשִׁי:
כו וְנָשׂוּ אֶת־כְּלִמָּתָם וְאֶת־כָּל־מַעֲלָם אֲשֶׁר מָעֲלוּ־בִי בְּשִׁבְתָּם עַל־אַדְמָתָם
כז לָבֶטַח וְאֵין מַחֲרִיד: בְּשׁוֹבְבִי אוֹתָם מִן־הָעַמִּים וְקִבַּצְתִּי אֹתָם מֵאַרְצוֹת
כח אֹיְבֵיהֶם וְנִקְדַּשְׁתִּי בָם לְעֵינֵי הַגּוֹיִם רַבִּים: וְיָדְעוּ כִּי אֲנִי יהוה אֱלֹהֵיהֶם
בְּהַגְלוֹתִי אֹתָם אֶל־הַגּוֹיִם וְכִנַּסְתִּים °אֶל־אַדְמָתָם וְלֹא־אוֹתִיר עוֹד מֵהֶם
כט שָׁם: וְלֹא־אַסְתִּיר עוֹד פָּנַי מֵהֶם אֲשֶׁר שָׁפַכְתִּי אֶת־רוּחִי עַל־בֵּית יִשְׂרָאֵל

°נ"א עַל־

מ א נְאֻם אֲדֹנָי יֱהוִֹה: בְּעֶשְׂרִים וְחָמֵשׁ שָׁנָה לְגָלוּתֵנוּ בְּרֹאשׁ הַשָּׁנָה
בֶּעָשׂוֹר לַחֹדֶשׁ בְּאַרְבַּע עֶשְׂרֵה שָׁנָה אַחַר אֲשֶׁר הֻכְּתָה הָעִיר בְּעֶצֶם הַיּוֹם
ב הַזֶּה הָיְתָה עָלַי יַד־יהוה וַיָּבֵא אֹתִי שָׁמָּה: בְּמַרְאוֹת אֱלֹהִים הֱבִיאַנִי אֶל־
ג אֶרֶץ יִשְׂרָאֵל וַיְנִיחֵנִי אֶל־הַר גָּבֹהַּ מְאֹד וְעָלָיו כְּמִבְנֵה־עִיר מִנֶּגֶב: וַיָּבִיא
אוֹתִי שָׁמָּה וְהִנֵּה־אִישׁ מַרְאֵהוּ כְּמַרְאֵה נְחֹשֶׁת וּפְתִיל־פִּשְׁתִּים בְּיָדוֹ וּקְנֵה
ד הַמִּדָּה וְהוּא עֹמֵד בַּשָּׁעַר: וַיְדַבֵּר אֵלַי הָאִישׁ בֶּן־אָדָם רְאֵה בְעֵינֶיךָ וּבְאָזְנֶיךָ
שְׁמָע וְשִׂים לִבְּךָ לְכֹל אֲשֶׁר־אֲנִי מַרְאֶה אוֹתָךְ כִּי לְמַעַן הַרְאוֹתְכָה
ה הֻבָאתָה הֵנָּה הַגֵּד אֶת־כָּל־אֲשֶׁר־אַתָּה רֹאֶה לְבֵית יִשְׂרָאֵל: וְהִנֵּה חוֹמָה
מִחוּץ לַבַּיִת סָבִיב ׀ סָבִיב וּבְיַד הָאִישׁ קְנֵה הַמִּדָּה שֵׁשׁ־אַמּוֹת בָּאַמָּה
ו וָטֹפַח וַיָּמָד אֶת־רֹחַב הַבִּנְיָן קָנֶה אֶחָד וְקוֹמָה קָנֶה אֶחָד: וַיָּבוֹא אֶל־שַׁעַר
אֲשֶׁר פָּנָיו דֶּרֶךְ הַקָּדִימָה וַיַּעַל °בְמַעֲלוֹתָו [°בְּמַעֲלוֹתָיו ק] וַיָּמָד ׀ אֶת־סַף
ז הַשַּׁעַר קָנֶה אֶחָד רֹחַב וְאֵת סַף אֶחָד קָנֶה אֶחָד רֹחַב: וְהַתָּא קָנֶה אֶחָד
אֹרֶךְ וְקָנֶה אֶחָד רֹחַב וּבֵין הַתָּאִים חָמֵשׁ אַמּוֹת וְסַף הַשַּׁעַר מֵאֵצֶל אוּלָם
ח-ט הַשַּׁעַר מֵהַבַּיִת קָנֶה אֶחָד: וַיָּמָד אֶת־אֻלָם הַשַּׁעַר קָנֶה אֶחָד: וַיָּמָד
אֶת־אֻלָם הַשַּׁעַר שְׁמֹנֶה אַמּוֹת °וְאֵילוֹ [°וְאֵילָיו ק] שְׁתַּיִם אַמּוֹת וְאֻלָם

39:23. The fate of Gog will prove that Israel's weakness was not because of God's weakness.

◄§ **Chapters 40-48** are unique in Scripture. At the very moment when Jerusalem lay in ruin and the nation was weeping in its Babylonian exile, Ezekiel proclaimed a very detailed plan for the construction of the future Temple, the laws that would govern it, and the respective roles of the *Kohanim*, king and people in the renewed Temple service. Thus, Ezekiel ends his dirges with concrete chapters of consolation.

[For diagrams on the plans, see the appendix, "Floor Plan of Ezekiel's Temple," at the end of this volume.

40:1. The Talmud (*Arachin* 12a) explains that this vision took place in a Jubilee year [*Yovel*]. The special laws of *Yovel* take effect on the tenth of Tishrei [Yom Kippur]; the prophet therefore calls that day Rosh Hashanah, literally, "the beginning of the year."

40:2. Ezekiel saw a vision of the future city. In ancient times, most of Jerusalem was south of the Temple Mount.

40:3. This description of angelic beings also appears in 1:7.

blood to intoxication from My feast that I have slaughtered for you; [20] sate yourselves at My table with horse and rider, warrior and every man of war — the word of the Lord HASHEM/ELOHIM.'

[21] I will manifest My glory among the nations, and all the nations will see My judgment that I have executed and My hand that I have placed upon them. [22] Then the House of Israel will know that I am HASHEM, their God, from that day and onward. [23] Then the nations will know that because of their iniquity the House of Israel was exiled, * because they betrayed Me and I hid My countenance from them; and I delivered them into the hand of their enemies, and they fell by the sword, all of them. [24] I dealt with them in accordance with their contamination and their sins, and I hid My counte- nance from them.

The true cause of exile

[25] Therefore, thus said the Lord HASHEM/ELOHIM: Now I will bring back the captivity of Jacob and show mercy to the entire House of Israel and be zealous for My holy Name. [26] They will bear their shame and all their betrayal that they committed against Me when they dwelt securely upon their soil, and none will make [them] afraid, [27] when I return them from the peoples and gather them in from the land of their enemies and I become sanctified through them in the eyes of the many nations. [28] Then they will know that I am HASHEM, their God, for I have exiled them to the nations, and I will bring them to their land, and will not leave any of them there. [29] Then I will not hide My countenance from them again, for I will pour out My spirit upon the House of Israel — the word of the Lord HASHEM/ELOHIM."

Return of Jacob's captivity

40

[1] In the twenty-fifth year of our exile, at the beginning of the year, on the tenth of the month, * in the fourteenth year after the City was conquered — on that very day the hand of HASHEM came upon me and He brought me there. [2] In a Divine vision He brought me to the Land of Israel; He set me down on a very high mountain, near which there was something like the structure of a city to the south. * [3] He brought me there, and behold, there was a man whose appearance was like that of copper, * with a linen cord and a measuring rod in his hand; he was standing by the gate.

A new vision . . .

[4] The man said to me, "Son of Man, see with your eyes and hear with your ears and set your heart to all that I am showing you, for it was in order to show you that you have been brought here. Relate all that you see to the House of Israel."

[5] Behold, there was a wall outside the Temple, surrounding it. In the man's hand was a measuring rod of six cubits, each [cubit] being a cubit and a handbreadth. * He measured the thickness of the [wall's] structure as one [measuring] rod; and its height as one rod. [6] Then he went to a gate that faced eastward and went up its steps; he measured the doorpost of the gate as one rod in width and the other doorpost as one rod in width. [7] Each cell* [was] one rod in length and one rod in width; and between the cells [were walls of] five cubits. The doorpost of the gate, inside the hall of the gate, was one rod [thick]. [8] He measured the [walls of the] inside hall of the gate as one rod. [9] Then he measured the hall of the gate as eight cubits [long], and its pillars* as two cubits. The hall of

. . . of the future Temple

(See Appendix C, illustration 19)

40:5. Not all Scriptural cubits are the same: Some are five handbreadths long, others are six (*Keilim* 7:10; *Menachos* 97a). The cubits of our passage were the longer ones; each was "a [five-handbreadth] cubit and a[n additional] hand- breadth." A handbreadth is 3-4 inches.

40:7. Rooms — the cells mentioned here — were built along the outside of the courtyard wall, flanking the gate on either side.

40:9. Decorative columns, placed just outside of the eight-cubit long hall of the gate.

י הַשַּׁעַר מֵהַבָּיִת: וְתָאֵי הַשַּׁעַר דֶּרֶךְ הַקָּדִים שְׁלֹשָׁה מִפֹּה וּשְׁלֹשָׁה מִפֹּה
יא מִדָּה אַחַת לִשְׁלָשְׁתָּם וּמִדָּה אַחַת לָאֵילִם מִפֹּה וּמִפּוֹ: וַיָּמָד אֶת־רֹחַב
יב פֶּתַח־הַשַּׁעַר עֶשֶׂר אַמּוֹת אֹרֶךְ הַשַּׁעַר שְׁלוֹשׁ עֶשְׂרֵה אַמּוֹת: וּגְבוּל לִפְנֵי
הַתָּאוֹת אַמָּה אֶחָת וְאַמָּה־אַחַת גְּבוּל מִפֹּה וְהַתָּא שֵׁשׁ־אַמּוֹת מִפּוֹ וְשֵׁשׁ
יג אַמּוֹת מִפּוֹ: וַיָּמָד אֶת־הַשַּׁעַר מִגַּג הַתָּא לְגַגּוֹ רֹחַב עֶשְׂרִים וְחָמֵשׁ אַמּוֹת
יד פֶּתַח נֶגֶד פָּתַח: וַיַּעַשׂ אֶת־אֵילִים שִׁשִּׁים אַמָּה וְאֶל־אֵיל הֶחָצֵר הַשַּׁעַר
טו סָבִיב ׀ סָבִיב: וְעַל פְּנֵי הַשַּׁעַר °הַיאתון [הָאִיתוֹן ק] עַל־לִפְנֵי אֻלָם
טז הַשַּׁעַר הַפְּנִימִי חֲמִשִּׁים אַמָּה: וְחַלּוֹנוֹת אֲטֻמוֹת אֶל־הַתָּאִים וְאֶל
אֵלֵיהֵמָה לִפְנִימָה לַשַּׁעַר סָבִיב ׀ סָבִיב וְכֵן לָאֵלַמּוֹת וְחַלּוֹנוֹת סָבִיב ׀
יז סָבִיב לִפְנִימָה וְאֶל־אַיִל תִּמֹרִים: וַיְבִיאֵנִי אֶל־הֶחָצֵר הַחִיצוֹנָה וְהִנֵּה
לְשָׁכוֹת וְרִצְפָה עָשׂוּי לֶחָצֵר סָבִיב ׀ סָבִיב שְׁלֹשִׁים לְשָׁכוֹת אֶל־הָרִצְפָה:
יח וְהָרִצְפָה אֶל־כֶּתֶף הַשְּׁעָרִים לְעֻמַּת אֹרֶךְ הַשְּׁעָרִים הָרִצְפָה הַתַּחְתּוֹנָה:
יט וַיָּמָד רֹחַב מִלִּפְנֵי הַשַּׁעַר הַתַּחְתּוֹנָה לִפְנֵי הֶחָצֵר הַפְּנִימִי מִחוּץ מֵאָה
כ אַמָּה הַקָּדִים וְהַצָּפוֹן: וְהַשַּׁעַר אֲשֶׁר פָּנָיו דֶּרֶךְ הַצָּפוֹן לֶחָצֵר הַחִיצוֹנָה
כא מָדַד אָרְכּוֹ וְרָחְבּוֹ: °ותאו [וְתָאָיו ק] שְׁלוֹשָׁה מִפּוֹ וּשְׁלֹשָׁה מִפּוֹ °ואילו
[וְאֵילָו ק] °ואלמו [וְאֵלַמָּו ק] הָיָה כְּמִדַּת הַשַּׁעַר הָרִאשׁוֹן חֲמִשִּׁים אַמָּה
כב אָרְכּוֹ וְרֹחַב חָמֵשׁ וְעֶשְׂרִים בָּאַמָּה: °וחלונו [וְחַלּוֹנָו ק] ואלמו ותמרו [וְאֵלַמָּו וְתִמֹרָו ק]
כְּמִדַּת הַשַּׁעַר אֲשֶׁר פָּנָיו דֶּרֶךְ הַקָּדִים וּבְמַעֲלוֹת שֶׁבַע
כג יַעֲלוּ־בוֹ °ואילמו [וְאֵילַמָּו ק] לִפְנֵיהֶם: וְשַׁעַר לֶחָצֵר הַפְּנִימִי נֶגֶד
כד הַשַּׁעַר לַצָּפוֹן וְלַקָּדִים וַיָּמָד מִשַּׁעַר אֶל־שַׁעַר מֵאָה אַמָּה: וַיּוֹלִכֵנִי דֶּרֶךְ
הַדָּרוֹם וְהִנֵּה־שַׁעַר דֶּרֶךְ הַדָּרוֹם וּמָדַד °אילו ואלמו [אֵילָו וְאֵלַמָּו ק] °ואיליו [וְאֵילָו וְאֵלַמָּו ק]
כה כְּמִדּוֹת הָאֵלֶּה: וְחַלּוֹנִים לוֹ °ולאילמו [וּלְאֵלַמָּו ק] סָבִיב ׀ סָבִיב
כְּהַחֲלֹנוֹת הָאֵלֶּה חֲמִשִּׁים אַמָּה אֹרֶךְ וְרֹחַב חָמֵשׁ וְעֶשְׂרִים אַמָּה:
כו וּמַעֲלוֹת שִׁבְעָה °עלותו [עֹלוֹתָו ק] ואלמו [וְאֵלַמָּו ק] לִפְנֵיהֶם וְתִמֹרִים לוֹ
כז אֶחָד מִפּוֹ וְאֶחָד מִפּוֹ אֶל־°אילו [אֵילָו ק]: וְשַׁעַר לֶחָצֵר הַפְּנִימִי דֶּרֶךְ
כח הַדָּרוֹם וַיָּמָד מִשַּׁעַר אֶל־הַשַּׁעַר דֶּרֶךְ הַדָּרוֹם מֵאָה אַמּוֹת: וַיְבִיאֵנִי אֶל־
חָצֵר הַפְּנִימִי בְּשַׁעַר הַדָּרוֹם וַיָּמָד אֶת־הַשַּׁעַר הַדָּרוֹם כַּמִּדּוֹת הָאֵלֶּה:
כט °ותאו ואלו ואלמו [וְתָאָיו וְאֵילָו וְאֵלַמָּו ק] כַּמִּדּוֹת הָאֵלֶּה וְחַלּוֹנוֹת
לוֹ °ולאלמו [וּלְאֵלַמָּו ק] סָבִיב ׀ סָבִיב חֲמִשִּׁים אַמָּה אֹרֶךְ וְרֹחַב
ל עֶשְׂרִים וְחָמֵשׁ אַמּוֹת: וְאֵלַמּוֹת סָבִיב ׀ סָבִיב אֹרֶךְ חָמֵשׁ וְעֶשְׂרִים
לא אַמָּה וְרֹחַב חָמֵשׁ אַמּוֹת: °ואלמו [וְאֵלַמָּו ק] אֶל־חָצֵר הַחִיצוֹנָה
וְתִמֹרִים אֶל־°אילו [אֵילָו ק] °ואלמיו [וְאֵילָו ק] וּמַעֲלוֹת שְׁמוֹנֶה °מעלו [מַעֲלָיו ק]:

40:16. These windows were narrow on the inside (thus restricting the light that could enter the Temple) and wide on the outside, symbolizing that the Temple did not require outside illumination; on the contrary, it shed spiritual light to the outside world.

40:19. This was the eastern gate, the subject of the

The cells
(See Appendix C,
illustration 19)

the gate faced inward. ¹⁰ The cells of the eastern gate were three on the one side and three on the other, the same size for the three of them; and the same size for the pillars on the one side and on the other. ¹¹ Then he measured the width of the opening of the gate as ten cubits; the length of the gate was thirteen cubits. ¹² There was a space of one cubit before the cells [on the one side], and a space of one cubit on the other. The cell was six cubits on the one side and six cubits on the other side. ¹³ Then he measured the gate from the roof of the one cell to the roof of [the opposite cell] as twenty-five cubits in width; an entrance opposite an entrance.

Pillars

¹⁴ Then he made pillars sixty cubits [high]; and so it was for every pillar of the courtyard, at the gates all around. ¹⁵ The height of the entry gate, as well as the height of the inner hall of the gate, was fifty cubits. ¹⁶ There were narrowing windows* for the cells and for their side walls, facing inward towards the gate all around; also the halls had windows all around, facing inward. Each pillar had a date-palm capital.

The outer
courtyard

¹⁷ Then he brought me into the outer courtyard, and behold, chambers and a balcony were provided for the courtyard all around; thirty chambers on the balcony. ¹⁸ The balcony was off to the sides of the gates; the bottom of the balcony was flush with the top of the gates. ¹⁹ Then he measured the width from the front of the lower gate* to the front of the inner courtyard, on its outside, as one hundred cubits; [this was the distance] in the east and in the north.

²⁰ Then he measured the gate of the outer courtyard that faced northward, its length and its width. ²¹ Its cells — three on the one side and three on the other side — its pillars and its hall were like the size of the first gate; its height was fifty cubits, and its width was twenty-five cubits. ²² Its windows, its hall and its date-palm capitals were like the size of the gate that faced east. They would ascend to it by seven steps, its halls being before them. *

²³ There was a gate to the inner courtyard opposite the gate to the north and to the east; he measured from [the outer] gate to [the inner] gate as one hundred cubits.

The southern
gate

²⁴ Then he took me towards the south, and behold, there was a gate at the south. He measured its pillars and halls; [they were] of the same dimensions as those.* ²⁵ There were windows for it and for its halls all around, like those windows;* fifty cubits in height and twenty-five cubits in width. ²⁶ Its stairway was of seven steps, with its halls before them; it had date-palm capitals, one on the one side and one on the other, on its pillars. ²⁷ There was a gate to the inner courtyard toward the south. He measured from [the outer] gate to [the inner] gate of the south as one hundred cubits.

The inner
courtyard

²⁸ Then he brought me to the inner courtyard through the southern gate and he measured the southern gate; [it was] of the same dimensions as those. ²⁹ Its cells, its pillars and its halls [were] of the same dimension as those, and there were windows for it and for its halls all around; fifty cubits in height and twenty-five cubits in width. ³⁰ There were halls all around,* twenty-five cubits in length and five cubits in width. ³¹ Its halls faced toward the outer courtyard. There were date-palm capitals on its pillars, and its stairway was of eight steps.

---

discussion since the beginning of the chapter.
40:22. The halls of the gate were situated at the top of the stairway.

40:24-25. They had the same dimensions as those described earlier.
40:30. Along the inside of the inner courtyard's wall.

לב וַיְבִיאֵ֗נִי אֶל־הֶֽחָצֵר֙ הַפְּנִימִי֙ דֶּ֣רֶךְ הַקָּדִ֔ים וַיָּ֣מָד אֶת־הַשַּׁ֔עַר כַּמִּדּ֖וֹת הָאֵֽלֶּה:

לג °וְתָאָו֙ ואלו ואלמו [וְאֵלָמָ֤יו ק] כַּמִּדּ֣וֹת הָאֵ֔לֶּה וְחַלּוֹנ֥וֹת ל֛וֹ °ולאלמו [וּלְאֵלַמָּ֖יו ק] סָבִ֣יב ׀ סָבִ֑יב אֹ֚רֶךְ חֲמִשִּׁ֣ים אַמָּ֔ה וְרֹ֖חַב חָמֵ֥שׁ

לד וְעֶשְׂרִ֥ים אַמָּֽה: °ואלמו [וְאֵלַמָּ֗יו ק] לֶֽחָצֵר֙ הַחִ֣יצוֹנָ֔ה וְתִֽמֹרִ֥ים אֶל־°אֵלָ֖ו [אֵלָ֑יו ק] מַֽעֲל֣וֹת °מַֽעֲל֖וֹ [מַֽעֲלָ֑יו ק]: וַיְבִיאֵ֖נִי אֶל־

לה שַׁ֣עַר הַצָּפ֑וֹן וּמָדַ֖ד כַּמִּדּ֥וֹת הָאֵֽלֶּה: תָּאָ֤ו אֵלָו֙ ואלמו [תָּאָ֤יו אֵלָיו֙ וְאֵֽלַמָּ֔יו ק]

לו וְחַלּוֹנ֥וֹת ל֛וֹ סָבִ֣יב ׀ סָבִ֑יב אֹ֚רֶךְ חֲמִשִּׁ֣ים אַמָּ֔ה וְרֹ֖חַב חָמֵ֥שׁ וְעֶשְׂרִ֥ים אַמָּֽה: °ואילו [וְאֵילָ֗יו ק] לֶֽחָצֵר֙ הַחִ֣יצוֹנָ֔ה וְתִֽמֹרִ֥ים אֶל־°אֵלָ֖ו [אֵילָ֑יו ק]

לז °אֵלָ֖ו [אֵילָ֑יו ק] מִפּ֤וֹ וּמִפּוֹ֙ וּשְׁמֹנֶ֣ה מַֽעֲל֔וֹת מַֽעֲל֖וֹ °מַֽעֲלָ֑יו ק]: וְלִשְׁכָּ֣ה וּפִתְחָ֔הּ

לח בְּאֵילִ֣ים הַשְּׁעָרִ֑ים שָׁ֥ם יָדִ֖יחוּ אֶת־הָֽעֹלָֽה: וּבְאֵלָ֣ם הַשַּׁ֗עַר שְׁנַ֤יִם שֻׁלְחָנוֹת֙

לט מִפּ֣וֹ וּשְׁנַ֤יִם שֻׁלְחָנוֹת֙ מִפֹּ֔ה לִשְׁח֣וֹט אֲלֵיהֶ֗ם הָֽעוֹלָ֛ה וְהַֽחַטָּ֖את וְהָֽאָשָֽׁם:

מ וְאֶל־הַכָּתֵ֣ף מִח֡וּצָה לָֽעוֹלֶה֩ לְפֶ֨תַח הַשַּׁ֜עַר הַצָּפ֗וֹנָה שְׁנַ֣יִם שֻׁלְחָנ֔וֹת וְאֶל־

מא הַכָּתֵ֣ף הָֽאַחֶ֗רֶת אֲשֶׁר֙ לְאֵלָ֣ם הַשַּׁ֔עַר שְׁנַ֖יִם שֻׁלְחָנ֑וֹת אַרְבָּעָ֣ה שֻׁלְחָנ֗וֹת מִפּ֤וֹ וְאַרְבָּעָ֤ה שֻׁלְחָנוֹת֙ מִפֹּ֔ה לְכֶ֣תֶף הַשַּׁ֔עַר שְׁמוֹנָ֖ה שֻׁלְחָנ֑וֹת אֲלֵיהֶ֖ם

מב יִשְׁחָֽטוּ: וְאַרְבָּעָ֣ה שֻׁלְחָנ֩וֹת לָֽעוֹלָ֨ה אַבְנֵ֜י גָזִ֗ית אֹ֣רֶךְ אַמָּ֤ה אַחַת֙ וָחֵ֔צִי וְרֹ֨חַב אַמָּ֤ה אַחַת֙ וָחֵ֔צִי וְגֹ֖בַהּ אַמָּ֣ה אֶחָ֑ת אֲלֵיהֶ֗ם וְיַנִּ֙יחוּ֙ אֶת־הַכֵּלִ֔ים

מג אֲשֶׁ֨ר יִשְׁחֲט֧וּ אֶת־הָֽעוֹלָ֛ה בָּ֖ם וְהַזָּ֑בַח: וְהַֽשְׁפַתַּ֗יִם טֹ֧פַח אֶחָ֛ד מֽוּכָנִ֖ים

מד בַּבַּ֣יִת סָבִ֣יב ׀ סָבִ֑יב וְאֶל־הַשֻּׁלְחָנ֖וֹת בְּשַׂ֥ר הַקָּרְבָּֽן: וּמִח֡וּצָה לַשַּׁ֩עַר֩ הַפְּנִימִ֨י לִשְׁכ֤וֹת שָׁרִים֙ בֶּחָצֵ֣ר הַפְּנִימִ֔י אֲשֶׁ֗ר אֶל־כֶּ֨תֶף֙ שַׁ֣עַר הַצָּפ֔וֹן וּפְנֵיהֶ֖ם דֶּ֥רֶךְ

מה הַדָּר֑וֹם אֶחָ֗ד אֶל־כֶּ֨תֶף֙ שַׁ֣עַר הַקָּדִ֔ים פְּנֵ֖י דֶּ֥רֶךְ הַצָּפֹֽן: וַיְדַבֵּ֖ר אֵלָ֑י זֹ֣ה הַלִּשְׁכָּ֗ה אֲשֶׁ֤ר פָּנֶ֙יהָ֙ דֶּ֣רֶךְ הַדָּר֔וֹם לַכֹּ֣הֲנִ֔ים שֹׁמְרֵ֖י מִשְׁמֶ֥רֶת הַבָּֽיִת: וְהַלִּשְׁכָּ֗ה

מו אֲשֶׁ֤ר פָּנֶ֙יהָ֙ דֶּ֣רֶךְ הַצָּפ֔וֹן לַכֹּ֣הֲנִ֔ים שֹׁמְרֵ֖י מִשְׁמֶ֣רֶת הַמִּזְבֵּ֑חַ הֵ֣מָּה בְנֵֽי־צָד֗וֹק הַקְּרֵבִ֧ים מִבְּנֵֽי־לֵוִ֛י אֶל־יְהוָ֖ה לְשָֽׁרְתֽוֹ: וַיָּ֣מָד אֶת־הֶֽחָצֵ֗ר אֹ֚רֶךְ ׀ מֵאָ֣ה אַמָּ֔ה

מז וְרֹ֖חַב מֵאָ֣ה אַמָּ֑ה מְרֻבָּ֑עַת וְהַמִּזְבֵּ֖חַ לִפְנֵ֥י הַבָּֽיִת: וַיְבִיאֵ֘נִי֮ אֶל־אֻלָ֣ם הַבַּ֒יִת֒

מח וַיָּ֙מָד֙ אֵ֣ל אֻלָ֔ם חָמֵ֤שׁ אַמּוֹת֙ מִפֹּ֔ה וְחָמֵ֥שׁ אַמּ֖וֹת מִפֹּ֑ה וְרֹ֣חַב הַשַּׁ֔עַר שָׁלֹ֥שׁ אַמּ֛וֹת מִפּ֖וֹ וְשָׁלֹ֥שׁ אַמּ֖וֹת מִפֹּֽה: אֹ֣רֶךְ הָֽאֻלָ֗ם עֶשְׂרִ֤ים אַמָּה֙ וְרֹ֔חַב עַשְׁתֵּ֥י

מט עֶשְׂרֵ֖ה אַמָּ֑ה וּבַֽמַּעֲל֔וֹת אֲשֶׁ֥ר יַעֲל֖וּ אֵלָ֑יו וְעַמֻּדִים֙ אֶל־הָ֣אֵילִ֔ים אֶחָ֥ד מִפּ֖וֹ

מא א וְאֶחָ֥ד מִפֹּֽה: וַיְבִיאֵ֖נִי אֶל־הַֽהֵיכָ֑ל וַיָּ֣מָד אֶת־הָֽאֵילִ֗ים שֵׁשׁ־אַמּ֤וֹת רֹ֙חַב֙

ב מִפּ֔וֹ וְשֵֽׁשׁ־אַמּ֥וֹת רֹ֖חַב מִפּ֑וֹ רֹ֣חַב הָאֹֽהֶל: וְרֹ֣חַב הַפֶּ֔תַח עֶ֥שֶׂר אַמּ֖וֹת

40:40. There was a recess on each side of the inner part of the gate, before it opened into the hall. These recesses are called "shoulders."

40:43. A slaughtered offering was hung on the hooks in order to flay its hide.

40:44. The text specifies neither the dimensions nor the exact location of these chambers.

40:45. Since verse 44 was speaking of the choristers,

who were Levites, Rashi interprets that these *kohanim* [lit., "ministers"] were Levites who assisted the *Kohanim* in the Temple service.

40:46. The first high priest in Solomon's Temple.

41:1. The main Temple building was divided into two parts: the Sanctuary, which was forty cubits long, and the Inner Sanctum (Holy of Holies, or Most Holy), which was twenty cubits long. Besides these there was

(See Appendix C, illustration 19)

³² Then he brought me to the inner courtyard through the east [gate] and he measured the gate; [it was] of the same dimensions as those. ³³ Its cells, its pillars and its halls [were] of the same dimensions of those, and there were windows for it and its halls all around; it was fifty cubits in height, and twenty-five cubits in width. ³⁴ Its halls faced toward the outer courtyard. There were date-palm capitals on its pillars on the one side and on the other, and its stairway was of eight steps.

The northern gate

³⁵ Then he brought me to the northern gate and measured it; [it was] the same dimensions as those. ³⁶ It had cells, pillars and halls, and windows for it all around; fifty cubits in height and twenty-five cubits in width. ³⁷ Its halls faced the outer courtyard and there were date-palm capitals on its pillars on the one side and on the other; its stairway was of eight steps.

Washing chamber

³⁸ There was a chamber there with its entrance facing the side walls of the gates; there they would rinse the burnt-offering. ³⁹ In the hall of this gate were two tables on the one side and two tables on the other, near which to slaughter the burnt-offering, the sin-offering and the guilt-offering. ⁴⁰ Along the shoulder* [of the gate], outside [the hall], as one ascended into the opening of the northern gate, there were two tables; and along the other shoulder of the gate's hall were two tables — ⁴¹ [altogether] four tables on the one side and four tables on the other side along the shoulder of the gate; eight tables near which they would slaughter. ⁴² There were also four tables for the burnt-offering, of hewn stone, one cubit and a half in length, one cubit and a half in width, and one cubit in height; upon them they would lay the implements with which they would slaughter the burnt-offering and [any other] sacrifice. ⁴³ There were also hooks* of one handbreadth, set up inside [the inner courtyard] all around; and the flesh of the offerings [was prepared] upon the tables.

⁴⁴ Outside the inner gate were chambers* for the choristers, in the inner courtyard, along the flank of the northern gate, facing towards the south, and there was also one [chamber]* along the flank of the eastern gate, facing towards the north. ⁴⁵ He said to me, "This chamber, which faces south, is for the kohanim,* the guardians of the charge of the House; ⁴⁶ and the chamber that faces north is for the Kohanim, the guardians of the charge of the Altar. They, who are the descendants of Zadok,* are the ones from among the sons of Levi who approach HASHEM, to serve Him."

The Hall

⁴⁷ Then he measured the [inner] courtyard; [it was] one hundred cubits in length and one hundred cubits in width, square. The Altar was before the Temple. ⁴⁸ Then he brought me to the Hall of the Temple. He measured the [thickness of the] side wall of the Hall as five cubits on the one side and five cubits on the other, and the width of the gate was three cubits on the one side and three cubits on the other. ⁴⁹ The length of the Hall was twenty cubits, and its width was eleven cubits. There were steps by which one ascended to [the Hall]; and there were pillars for the doorposts, one on the one side and one on the other.

41

¹ Then he brought me to the Sanctuary.* He measured the side walls [of the entrance] as six cubits wide on the one side and six cubits wide on the other — the width of the tent. ² The width of the entrance was ten cubits,

---

the Hall in front of the Sanctuary that was eleven cubits long (see 40:49). All these components were twenty cubits wide.

The Sanctuary was entered from the Hall through a ten-cubit (v. 2) by six-cubit passageway, referred to here as "the tent."

וְכִתְפוֹת הַפֶּתַח חָמֵשׁ אַמּוֹת מִפּוֹ וְחָמֵשׁ אַמּוֹת מִפּוֹ וַיָּמָד אָרְכּוֹ
ג אַרְבָּעִים אַמָּה וְרֹחַב עֶשְׂרִים אַמָּה: וּבָא לִפְנִימָה וַיָּמָד אֵיל־הַפֶּתַח
ד שְׁתַּיִם אַמּוֹת וְהַפֶּתַח שֵׁשׁ אַמּוֹת וְרֹחַב הַפֶּתַח שֶׁבַע אַמּוֹת: וַיָּמָד אֶת־
אָרְכּוֹ עֶשְׂרִים אַמָּה וְרֹחַב עֶשְׂרִים אַמָּה אֶל־פְּנֵי הַהֵיכָל וַיֹּאמֶר אֵלַי זֶה
ה קֹדֶשׁ הַקֳּדָשִׁים: וַיָּמָד קִיר־הַבַּיִת שֵׁשׁ אַמּוֹת וְרֹחַב הַצֵּלָע אַרְבַּע אַמּוֹת
ו סָבִיב ׀ סָבִיב לַבַּיִת סָבִיב: וְהַצְּלָעוֹת צֵלָע אֶל־צֵלָע שָׁלוֹשׁ וּשְׁלֹשִׁים
פְּעָמִים וּבָאוֹת בַּקִּיר אֲשֶׁר־לַבַּיִת לַצְּלָעוֹת סָבִיב ׀ סָבִיב לִהְיוֹת אֲחוּזִים
ז וְלֹא־יִהְיוּ אֲחוּזִים בְּקִיר הַבָּיִת: וְרָחֲבָה וְנָסְבָה לְמַעְלָה לְמַעְלָה לַצְּלָעוֹת
כִּי מֽוּסַב־הַבַּיִת לְמַעְלָה לְמַעְלָה סָבִיב ׀ סָבִיב לַבַּיִת עַל־כֵּן רֹחַב־לַבַּיִת
ח לְמָעְלָה וְכֵן הַתַּחְתּוֹנָה יַעֲלֶה עַל־הָעֶלְיוֹנָה לַתִּיכוֹנָה: וְרָאִיתִי לַבַּיִת גֹּבַהּ
סָבִיב ׀ סָבִיב °מְיֻסְּדֹת [°מוּסְדוֹת ק] הַצְּלָעוֹת מְלוֹ הַקָּנֶה שֵׁשׁ אַמּוֹת
ט אַצִּילָה: רֹחַב הַקִּיר אֲשֶׁר־לַצֵּלָע אֶל־הַחוּץ חָמֵשׁ אַמּוֹת וַאֲשֶׁר מֻנָּח
י בֵּית צְלָעוֹת אֲשֶׁר לַבָּיִת: וּבֵין הַלְּשָׁכוֹת רֹחַב עֶשְׂרִים אַמָּה סָבִיב לַבַּיִת
יא סָבִיב ׀ סָבִיב: וּפֶתַח הַצֵּלָע לַמֻּנָּח פֶּתַח אֶחָד דֶּרֶךְ הַצָּפוֹן וּפֶתַח אֶחָד
יב לַדָּרוֹם וְרֹחַב מְקוֹם הַמֻּנָּח חָמֵשׁ אַמּוֹת סָבִיב ׀ סָבִיב: וְהַבִּנְיָן אֲשֶׁר אֶל־
פְּנֵי הַגִּזְרָה פְּאַת דֶּרֶךְ־הַיָּם רֹחַב שִׁבְעִים אַמָּה וְקִיר הַבִּנְיָן חָמֵשׁ־אַמּוֹת
יג רֹחַב סָבִיב ׀ סָבִיב וְאָרְכּוֹ תִּשְׁעִים אַמָּה: וּמָדַד אֶת־הַבַּיִת אֹרֶךְ מֵאָה
יד אַמָּה וְהַגִּזְרָה וְהַבִּנְיָה וְקִירוֹתֶיהָ אֹרֶךְ מֵאָה אַמָּה: וְרֹחַב פְּנֵי הַבַּיִת
טו וְהַגִּזְרָה לַקָּדִים מֵאָה אַמָּה: וּמָדַד אֹרֶךְ־הַבִּנְיָן אֶל־פְּנֵי הַגִּזְרָה אֲשֶׁר עַל־
אַחֲרֶיהָ °וְאַתּוּקֵיהָא [°וְאַתִּיקֶיהָ ק] מִפּוֹ וּמִפּוֹ מֵאָה אַמָּה וְהַהֵיכָל
טז הַפְּנִימִי וְאֻלַמֵּי הֶחָצֵר: הַסִּפִּים וְהַחַלּוֹנִים הָאֲטֻמוֹת וְהָאַתִּיקִים ׀ סָבִיב
לִשְׁלָשְׁתָּם נֶגֶד הַסַּף שְׂחִיף עֵץ סָבִיב ׀ סָבִיב וְהָאָרֶץ עַד־הַחַלֹּנוֹת
יז וְהַחַלֹּנוֹת מְכֻסּוֹת: עַל־מֵעַל הַפֶּתַח וְעַד־הַבַּיִת הַפְּנִימִי וְלַחוּץ וְאֶל־כָּל־
יח הַקִּיר סָבִיב ׀ סָבִיב בַּפְּנִימִי וּבַחִיצוֹן מִדּוֹת: וְעָשׂוּי כְּרוּבִים וְתִמֹרִים
יט וְתִֽמֹרָה בֵּין־כְּרוּב לִכְרוּב וּשְׁנַיִם פָּנִים לַכְּרוּב: וּפְנֵי אָדָם אֶל־הַתִּמֹרָה

41:5. Along the walls, there were three levels of cells, one on top of the other, each level consisting of eleven cells — five on the northern side of the Temple building, five on the south, and one on the west.

41:6. Although the cells were along the outer wall of the Temple building, they were not anchored to the wall by means of pegs; due to the sanctity of the Temple, no holes were bored into this wall to anchor the ceiling beams of the cells. (See also *I Kings 6:6*.)

41:7. There were three levels of cells, each level wider than the one below it, and a spiral staircase went from the lowest up to the highest.

41:9. Below ground-level the wall's foundation was six cubits (v. 8), but it narrowed to five cubits above the ground.

41:12. Counting from west to east: The back wall of the structure, which was the outer wall of the western cell, was 6 cubits thick (v. 8); the cell itself was 4 cubits wide (v. 5); the Temple wall was 6 cubits thick (v. 5); the Inner Sanctum's interior was 20 cubits (v. 4); the dividing wall between the Sanctuary and the Inner Sanctum was 2 cubits thick (v. 3); the Sanctuary was 40 cubits long (v. 2); the wall dividing the Sanctuary from the Hall was 6 cubits thick (v. 1); the Hall's interior was 11 cubits (40:49), and its front wall was 5 cubits thick (40:48). This yields a total of 100 (6 + 4 + 6 + 20 + 2 + 40 + 6 + 11 + 5 = 100) cubits (see next verse). In this verse, the easternmost 10 cubits are not counted — thus yielding a total of 90 — because, there, the otherwise straight wall jutted out considerably, as explained below.

41:14. At the front of the Temple building a structure jutted out to the north and south, fifteen cubits in each and [the walls on the] shoulders of the entrance were five cubits on the one side and five cubits on the other. He measured its length as forty cubits and [it was] twenty cubits in width.

The Inner Sanctum
(See Appendix C, illustration 19)

³ Then he entered the Inner [Sanctum]. He measured the side walls of the entrance as two cubits [wide]; the entrance was six cubits [in height], and the width of the entrance was seven cubits. ⁴ He measured its length as twenty cubits, and its width as twenty cubits, along the Sanctuary. He said to me, "This is the Holy of Holies."

The Temple wall

⁵ Then he measured the [thickness of the] wall of the Temple as six cubits. The width of each cell* was four cubits, surrounding the Temple all around. ⁶ The cells [were arranged] cell upon cell, thirty-three in number. They rested upon the inner wall of the cells all around, and were anchored there, but they were not anchored into the wall of the Temple building. * ⁷ [The cells] became broader and there was a spiral [stairway] for the [levels of] cells proceeding upward; * for the Temple was surrounded by successive levels, all around the [cell-]structure. Thus, the widest part of the [cell-]structure was at the top [level]. And thus one would ascend from the lowest to the highest through the middle [cells].

⁸ I saw the height of the Temple all around.

The foundations of the cells were a full rod [thick], a six-cubit space. ⁹ The width of the cell's wall toward the outside was five cubits. * There was also an open space at the end of the Temple's cells.

¹⁰ Between the chambers [and the Temple building] there was a twenty-cubit-wide space around the Temple, all around.

The open space

¹¹ The entrance to the cells-[structure] was by the open space; one entrance to the north and one entrance to the south. The width of the open space was five cubits, all around. ¹² The [entire] structure that was built alongside the main Temple building was seventy cubits in width on its western side, the [outer] wall of the structure was five cubits in width all around; and its length was ninety cubits. * ¹³ Then he measured the Temple building as one hundred cubits in length; the main Temple building, the [cell-]structure and its walls were one hundred cubits in length. ¹⁴ The width of the front of the building and the main Temple

The building

building on the east was one hundred cubits. * ¹⁵ He measured the length of the structure, * along the main Temple building, going towards its rear, including its corner structures on the one side and the other, as one hundred cubits. Now the Sanctuary [and] the Inner [Sanctum] and the halls of the courtyard — ¹⁶ there were doorposts, narrowing windows and square pillars all around for all three of the [areas]. Opposite the doorpost was wood paneling* all around, as well as [on the wall from] the ground to the windows — the windows were [partly] covered — ¹⁷ to above the doorway, and until the Inner Sanctum and outward, and to the entire wall all around, in the Inner [Sanctum] and in the outer [room], the panels were of [the same] dimensions. ¹⁸ [The panels] were engraved with cherubim and date palms, with a date palm between cherub and cherub. Each cherub had two faces: ¹⁹ There was the face of a person toward the date palm

---

direction and ten cubits wide. Adding these 30 cubits to the 70 of verse 12 and the ten to the 90 of verse 12 yields 100 cubits in each direction.

41:15. The measurement in verse 13 was taken on the northern side of the building, going from its back towards

its front to the east, while this measurement was taken on the southern side, going towards its rear to the west (Rashi).

41:16. The wood paneling was a base on which to affix gold plating (see I Kings 6:14-22).

מִפּוֹ וּפְנֵי־כְפִיר אֶל־הַתִּמֹרָה מִפּוֹ עָשׂוּי אֶל־כָּל־הַבַּיִת סָבִיב ׀ סָבִיב:

כ מֵהָאָרֶץ עַד־מֵעַל הַפֶּתַח הַכְּרוּבִים וְהַתִּמֹרִים עֲשׂוּיִם וְקִיר הַהֵיכָל:

כא-כב הַהֵיכָל מְזוּזַת רְבֻעָה וּפְנֵי הַקֹּדֶשׁ הַמַּרְאֶה כַּמַּרְאֶה: הַמִּזְבֵּחַ עֵץ שָׁלוֹשׁ אַמּוֹת גָּבֹהַּ וְאָרְכּוֹ שְׁתַּיִם־אַמּוֹת וּמִקְצֹעוֹתָיו לוֹ וְאָרְכּוֹ וְקִירֹתָיו עֵץ

כג וַיְדַבֵּר אֵלַי זֶה הַשֻּׁלְחָן אֲשֶׁר לִפְנֵי יְהוָה: וּשְׁתַּיִם דְּלָתוֹת לַהֵיכָל וְלַקֹּדֶשׁ:

כד וּשְׁתַּיִם דְּלָתוֹת לַדְּלָתוֹת שְׁתַּיִם מוּסַבּוֹת דְּלָתוֹת שְׁתַּיִם לְדֶלֶת אֶחָת

כה וּשְׁתֵּי דְלָתוֹת לָאַחֶרֶת: וַעֲשׂוּיָה אֲלֵיהֶן אֶל־דַּלְתוֹת הַהֵיכָל כְּרוּבִים וְתִמֹרִים כַּאֲשֶׁר עֲשׂוּיִם לַקִּירוֹת וְעָב עֵץ אֶל־פְּנֵי הָאוּלָם מֵהַחוּץ:

כו וְחַלּוֹנִים אֲטֻמוֹת וְתִמֹרִים מִפּוֹ וּמִפּוֹ אֶל־כִּתְפוֹת הָאוּלָם וְצַלְעוֹת הַבַּיִת

מב

א וְהָעֻבִּים: וַיּוֹצִיאֵנִי אֶל־הֶחָצֵר הַחִיצוֹנָה הַדֶּרֶךְ דֶּרֶךְ הַצָּפוֹן וַיְבִאֵנִי אֶל־

ב הַלִּשְׁכָּה אֲשֶׁר נֶגֶד הַגִּזְרָה וַאֲשֶׁר־נֶגֶד הַבִּנְיָן אֶל־הַצָּפוֹן: אֶל־פְּנֵי אֹרֶךְ

ג אַמּוֹת הַמֵּאָה פֶּתַח הַצָּפוֹן וְהָרֹחַב חֲמִשִּׁים אַמּוֹת: נֶגֶד הָעֶשְׂרִים אֲשֶׁר לֶחָצֵר הַפְּנִימִי וְנֶגֶד רִצְפָה אֲשֶׁר לֶחָצֵר הַחִיצוֹנָה אַתִּיק אֶל־פְּנֵי־אַתִּיק

ד בַּשְּׁלִשִׁים: וְלִפְנֵי הַלְּשָׁכוֹת מַהֲלַךְ עֶשֶׂר אַמּוֹת רֹחַב אֶל־הַפְּנִימִית דֶּרֶךְ

ה אַמָּה אֶחָת וּפִתְחֵיהֶם לַצָּפוֹן: וְהַלְּשָׁכוֹת הָעֶלְיוֹנֹת קְצֻרוֹת כִּי־יוֹכְלוּ

ו אַתִּיקִים מֵהֵנָּה מֵהַתַּחְתֹּנוֹת וּמֵהַתִּכֹנוֹת בִּנְיָן: כִּי מְשֻׁלָּשׁוֹת הֵנָּה וְאֵין לָהֶן עַמּוּדִים כְּעַמּוּדֵי הַחֲצֵרוֹת עַל־כֵּן נֶאֱצַל מֵהַתַּחְתֹּנוֹת וּמֵהַתִּיכֹנוֹת

ז מֵהָאָרֶץ: וְגָדֵר אֲשֶׁר־לַחוּץ לְעֻמַּת הַלְּשָׁכוֹת דֶּרֶךְ הֶחָצֵר הַחִצוֹנָה אֶל־

ח פְּנֵי הַלְּשָׁכוֹת אָרְכּוֹ חֲמִשִּׁים אַמָּה: כִּי־אֹרֶךְ הַלְּשָׁכוֹת אֲשֶׁר לֶחָצֵר

ט הַחִיצוֹנָה חֲמִשִּׁים אַמָּה וְהִנֵּה עַל־פְּנֵי הַהֵיכָל מֵאָה אַמָּה: °וּמִתַּחְתָּה לשכת [°וּמִתַּחַת הַלְּשָׁכוֹת ק] הָאֵלֶּה °הַמֵּבוֹא [°הַמֵּבִיא ק] מֵהַקָּדִים

י בְּבֹאוֹ לָהֵנָּה מֵהֶחָצֵר הַחִצֹנָה: בְּרֹחַב ׀ גֶּדֶר הֶחָצֵר דֶּרֶךְ הַקָּדִים אֶל־

יא פְּנֵי הַגִּזְרָה וְאֶל־פְּנֵי הַבִּנְיָן לְשָׁכוֹת: וְדֶרֶךְ לִפְנֵיהֶם כְּמַרְאֵה הַלְּשָׁכוֹת אֲשֶׁר דֶּרֶךְ הַצָּפוֹן כְּאָרְכָּן כֵּן רָחְבָּן וְכֹל מוֹצָאֵיהֶן וּכְמִשְׁפְּטֵיהֶן

יב וּכְפִתְחֵיהֶן: וּכְפִתְחֵי הַלְּשָׁכוֹת אֲשֶׁר דֶּרֶךְ הַדָּרוֹם פֶּתַח בְּרֹאשׁ דָּרֶךְ דֶּרֶךְ בִּפְנֵי הַגְּדֶרֶת הַהֲגִינָה דֶּרֶךְ הַקָּדִים בְּבוֹאָן: וַיֹּאמֶר אֵלַי לִשְׁכוֹת הַצָּפוֹן

יג לִשְׁכוֹת הַדָּרוֹם אֲשֶׁר אֶל־פְּנֵי הַגִּזְרָה הֵנָּה ׀ לִשְׁכוֹת הַקֹּדֶשׁ אֲשֶׁר יֹאכְלוּ־שָׁם הַכֹּהֲנִים אֲשֶׁר־קְרוֹבִים לַיהוָה קָדְשֵׁי הַקֳּדָשִׁים שָׁם יַנִּיחוּ ׀

41:21. I saw the same appearance of God's Glory that I had seen in the Account of the Chariot [see Ch. 1] (*Rashi*). This first inkling of the return of God's Glory to the Temple took Ezekiel by suprise. He was filled with yearning to know if it was true, yet dared not confirm it to himself. Thus, he left his words dangling (*R' Yosef Breuer*).

41:25. This beam extended from the Sanctuary's eastern wall to the Hall's eastern wall. It helped secure the enormously high facade of the Hall (*Rashi*, from

Middos 3:8).

41:26. See 40:48.

42:2. There were fifty cubits between the chamber and the end of the courtyard.

42:3. A balcony ran alongside the interior of the outer courtyard's wall (40:17).

42:6. The pillars that reinforced the courtyard walls (see 41:16) were not as thick or as numerous as the ones in the chamber complex. The lower stories required more supportive pillars than the uppermost story, which had on the one side and the face of a young lion toward the date palm on the other side; so it was engraved for the entire interior all around. ²⁰ The cherubim and date palms were engraved from the ground until above the entrance; and [so it was for] the wall of the Sanctuary.

²¹ The Sanctuary had a square doorpost; and from the entrance to the Holy [of Holies] the appearance was like the appearance . . . *

The Inner   ²² The Altar was of wood, three cubits tall and its length was two cubits
Altar including its corners; its surface and its sides were of wood. He said to me, "This is the Table that is before HASHEM."

Doors   ²³ There were two doors to the Sanctuary and to the Holy [of Holies]. ²⁴ Each set of doors had two doors, two swinging doors: two comprised one door and two doors comprised the other. ²⁵ Engraved upon them, upon the doors of the Sanctuary, were cherubim and date palms, just as they were engraved on the walls. There was a thick wooden beam going into the front wall of the Hall, towards the outside. *

²⁶ There were narrowing windows and date palms on the one side and on the other, on the shoulders of the Hall; * [he also showed me] the casings of the Temple and the beams.

42   ¹ Then he took me out to the outer courtyard, in the direction going to the north,
Northern and he brought me to the chamber that was opposite the main Temple
courtyard building and the structure to the north, ² facing the hundred-cubit length by the
(See Appendix C, northern entrance, and the [courtyard's] width was fifty cubits. * ³ It was opposite
illustration 19) the twenty [cubits] of the inner courtyard and opposite the balcony of the outer courtyard; * pillar faced pillar in the three-storied [complex]. ⁴ In front of the chambers was a passageway ten cubits in width leading to the inner space, through a one-cubit path; and their entrances faced north. ⁵ The upper chambers were narrowed because the pillars took up space from them, from the lower and middle ones of the structure. ⁶ For they were three storied, so they did not have pillars like the pillars of the courtyards; * hence, the lower and middle [chambers] were deprived of floor space. ⁷ The wall that faced the outside, opposite the chambers, toward the direction of the outer courtyard in front of the chambers, its length was fifty cubits. ⁸ For the length of the chambers, which were adjacent to the outer courtyard, was fifty cubits, and there before the Temple building was a hundred cubits [long].

Holy   ⁹ Downhill from these chambers, as one comes from the east, coming towards
chambers them from the outer courtyard, ¹⁰ along the width of the eastern wall of the [inner] courtyard, opposite the main Temple building and the structure, were chambers. ¹¹ There was a passage before them. [Theirs was] like the appearance of northern chambers: like their length, like their width, and [like] all their exits, their measurements, and their entrances, ¹² and like the entrances of the chambers that were to the south. * There was an entrance at the main approach, an approach that led to the platform of the singers, the easterly path as they entered.

¹³ Then he said to me: "The northern chambers and southern chambers that face the main Temple building are the holy chambers where the Kohanim who approach HASHEM may eat the most-holy offerings; there they may put down the

---

to support only the roof.   the main Temple building, symmetrical to the one on
42:12. There was a chamber complex on the south of   the north (*Rashi*).

יד קָדְשֵׁי הַקֳּדָשִׁים וְהַמִּנְחָה וְהַחַטָּאת וְהָאָשָׁם כִּי הַמָּקוֹם קָדֹשׁ: בְּבֹאָם
הַכֹּהֲנִים וְלֹא־יֵצְאוּ מֵהַקֹּדֶשׁ אֶל־הֶחָצֵר הַחִיצוֹנָה וְשָׁם יַנִּיחוּ בִגְדֵיהֶם
אֲשֶׁר־יְשָׁרְתוּ בָהֶן כִּי־קֹדֶשׁ הֵנָּה °יִלְבְּשׁוּ [וְלָבְשׁוּ ק] בְּגָדִים אֲחֵרִים
טו וְקָרְבוּ אֶל־אֲשֶׁר לָעָם: וְכִלָּה אֶת־מִדּוֹת הַבַּיִת הַפְּנִימִי וְהוֹצִיאַנִי דֶּרֶךְ
טז הַשַּׁעַר אֲשֶׁר פָּנָיו דֶּרֶךְ הַקָּדִים וּמְדָדוֹ סָבִיב ׀ סָבִיב: מָדַד רוּחַ הַקָּדִים
בִּקְנֵה הַמִּדָּה חֲמֵשׁ־°אמות [מֵאוֹת ק] קָנִים בִּקְנֵה הַמִּדָּה סָבִיב: מָדַד
יז רוּחַ הַצָּפוֹן חֲמֵשׁ־מֵאוֹת קָנִים בִּקְנֵה הַמִּדָּה סָבִיב: אֵת רוּחַ הַדָּרוֹם מָדַד
יח חֲמֵשׁ־מֵאוֹת קָנִים בִּקְנֵה הַמִּדָּה: סָבַב אֶל־רוּחַ הַיָּם מָדַד חֲמֵשׁ־מֵאוֹת
יט קָנִים בִּקְנֵה הַמִּדָּה: לְאַרְבַּע רוּחוֹת מְדָדוֹ חוֹמָה לוֹ סָבִיב ׀ סָבִיב אֹרֶךְ
כ חֲמֵשׁ מֵאוֹת וְרֹחַב חֲמֵשׁ מֵאוֹת לְהַבְדִּיל בֵּין הַקֹּדֶשׁ לְחֹל: וַיּוֹלִכֵנִי אֶל־

מג
א הַשַּׁעַר שַׁעַר אֲשֶׁר פֹּנֶה דֶּרֶךְ הַקָּדִים: וְהִנֵּה כְּבוֹד אֱלֹהֵי יִשְׂרָאֵל בָּא מִדֶּרֶךְ
ב הַקָּדִים וְקוֹלוֹ כְּקוֹל מַיִם רַבִּים וְהָאָרֶץ הֵאִירָה מִכְּבֹדוֹ: וּכְמַרְאֵה הַמַּרְאֶה
ג אֲשֶׁר רָאִיתִי כַּמַּרְאֶה אֲשֶׁר־רָאִיתִי בְּבֹאִי לְשַׁחֵת אֶת־הָעִיר וּמַרְאוֹת
ד כַּמַּרְאֶה אֲשֶׁר רָאִיתִי אֶל־נְהַר־כְּבָר וָאֶפֹּל אֶל־פָּנָי: וּכְבוֹד יהוה בָּא אֶל־
ה הַבָּיִת דֶּרֶךְ שַׁעַר אֲשֶׁר פָּנָיו דֶּרֶךְ הַקָּדִים: וַתִּשָּׂאֵנִי רוּחַ וַתְּבִיאֵנִי אֶל־
ו הֶחָצֵר הַפְּנִימִי וְהִנֵּה מָלֵא כְבוֹד־יהוה הַבָּיִת: וָאֶשְׁמַע מִדַּבֵּר אֵלַי מֵהַבָּיִת
ז וְאִישׁ הָיָה עֹמֵד אֶצְלִי: וַיֹּאמֶר אֵלַי בֶּן־אָדָם אֶת־מְקוֹם כִּסְאִי וְאֶת־מְקוֹם
כַּפּוֹת רַגְלַי אֲשֶׁר אֶשְׁכָּן־שָׁם בְּתוֹךְ בְּנֵי־יִשְׂרָאֵל לְעוֹלָם וְלֹא יְטַמְּאוּ עוֹד
בֵּית־יִשְׂרָאֵל שֵׁם קָדְשִׁי הֵמָּה וּמַלְכֵיהֶם בִּזְנוּתָם וּבְפִגְרֵי מַלְכֵיהֶם בָּמוֹתָם:
ח בְּתִתָּם סִפָּם אֶת־סִפִּי וּמְזוּזָתָם אֵצֶל מְזוּזָתִי וְהַקִּיר בֵּינִי וּבֵינֵיהֶם וְטִמְּאוּ ׀
ט אֶת־שֵׁם קָדְשִׁי בְּתוֹעֲבוֹתָם אֲשֶׁר עָשׂוּ וָאֲכַל אֹתָם בְּאַפִּי: עַתָּה יְרַחֲקוּ אֶת־
זְנוּתָם וּפִגְרֵי מַלְכֵיהֶם מִמֶּנִּי וְשָׁכַנְתִּי בְתוֹכָם לְעוֹלָם: אַתָּה בֶן־אָדָם

HAFTARAS
TETZAVEH
43:10-27

י הַגֵּד אֶת־בֵּית־יִשְׂרָאֵל אֶת־הַבַּיִת וְיִכָּלְמוּ מֵעֲוֺנוֹתֵיהֶם וּמָדְדוּ אֶת־תָּכְנִית:
יא וְאִם־נִכְלְמוּ מִכֹּל אֲשֶׁר־עָשׂוּ צוּרַת הַבַּיִת וּתְכוּנָתוֹ וּמוֹצָאָיו וּמוֹבָאָיו
וְכָל־°צורתו [צוּרֹתָיו ק] וְאֵת כָּל־חֻקֹּתָיו וְכָל־°צורתו [צוּרֹתָיו ק]
וְכָל־°תורתו [תּוֹרֹתָיו ק] הוֹדַע אוֹתָם וּכְתֹב לְעֵינֵיהֶם וְיִשְׁמְרוּ אֶת־
יב כָּל־צוּרָתוֹ וְאֶת־כָּל־חֻקֹּתָיו וְעָשׂוּ אוֹתָם: זֹאת תּוֹרַת הַבָּיִת עַל־רֹאשׁ
הָהָר כָּל־גְּבֻלוֹ סָבִיב ׀ סָבִיב קֹדֶשׁ קָדָשִׁים הִנֵּה־זֹאת תּוֹרַת הַבָּיִת:
יג וְאֵלֶּה מִדּוֹת הַמִּזְבֵּחַ בָּאַמּוֹת אַמָּה אַמָּה וָטֹפַח וְחֵיק הָאַמָּה וְאַמָּה־

42:16. According to *Rashi* this was the same measuring rod that had been used in measuring the Temple's other dimensions, so that the Temple Mount enclosure was 3,000 cubits square. According to *Radak* the rod used here was only one cubit long, yielding an enclosure of 500 cubits square.

43:7. Several kings had been buried on the grounds of the royal residence, adjacent to the Temple (*Rashi*).

43:9. Because of the large perimeter of the sacred Temple Mount enclosure surrounding the Temple.

43:12. The laws mentioned in these passages.

43:13. Although for most purposes the Temple and its appurtenances were measured in cubits of six hand-breadths (see 40:5), this verse now mentions some exceptions to that rule. Among them are certain parts of the Altar that were measured in five-handbreadth cubits: the *base* that jutted out one cubit at the bottom; a *most-holy offerings, the meal-offering, the sin-offering and the guilt-offering, for the place is holy.* [14] *When the Kohanim arrive there, they shall not leave the holy place [directly] to the outer courtyard; [rather] they shall leave their garments in which they minister, for they are holy; they shall don other garments and then approach the domain of the people."*

The eastern side
(See Appendix C, illustration 19)

[15] *When he finished the measurements of the inner House, he took me out by way of the gate that faced eastward, and then measured it all around.* [16] *He measured the eastern side with the measuring rod;* * *it was five hundred rods with the measuring rod all around.* [17] *He measured the northern side as five hundred rods with the measuring rod all around.* [18] *He measured the southern side as five hundred rods with the measuring rod.* [19] *Circling around to the western side he measured five hundred rods with the measuring rod.* [20] *On four sides he measured it — it had a wall all around it — five hundred [rods] in length and five hundred in width, to separate between the holy and the common [areas].*

43

The Glory enters

[1] Then he led me to the gate — a gate that faces east — [2] *and behold, the glory of the God of Israel was coming from the east. Its sound was like the sound of a multitude of waters, and the earth shone with His glory.* [3] *It was a vision like the vision I had seen [before] — like the vision that I had seen when I came to [prophetically] destroy the city, and visions like the vision I had seen at the River Chebar — and I fell upon my face.* [4] *The glory of* HASHEM *then entered the Temple by way of the gate that faced east.* [5] *Then a wind lifted me up and brought me into the inner courtyard; and behold, the glory of* HASHEM *filled the Temple.*

God speaks

[6] *I heard Him addressing Himself to me from the Temple; and there was a man standing next to me.* [7] *He said to me, "Son of Man, [this is] the place of My throne and the place of My footstool, where I will dwell amid the Children of Israel forever. The House of Israel will no longer defile My holy Name, they and their kings with their promiscuous idolatry, and with the corpses of their kings,* * *and with their high places,* [8] *by their placing their threshold near My threshold and their doorpost next to My doorpost, with but a wall between Me and them, whereby they defiled My holy Name with the abominations they committed, so that I consumed them in My anger.* [9] *Now they will distance their promiscuous idolatry and the corpses of their kings from Me,* * *that I may dwell among them forever.*

Tell Israel

[10] *"You, Son of Man! Tell the House of Israel about the Temple, and let them be ashamed of their iniquities and calculate the [Temple's] design.* [11] *If they become ashamed of all that they have done, then make known to them the form of the Temple and its design, its exits and its entrances and all its [buildings'] forms, all its laws, all its designs and all its teachings, and write [all this] down before their eyes, so that they may safeguard its entire form and all its rules and fulfill them.*

[12] *"This* * *is the teaching regarding the Temple: Atop the mountain, its entire boundary all around, shall be most holy; behold, this is the teaching regarding the Temple.*

[13] *"Now these are the dimensions of the Altar in cubits, each cubit being a cubit and a handbreadth* * *— except for the base of one cubit [wide]; the cubit of the*

---

one-cubit ledge located six cubits above the ground; *the border pieces upon its edge,* i.e., the "horns," which were the four one-cubit cubic projections jutting up from the four corners of the Altar's roof. The Inner, or Golden,

Altar was also measured with the shorter cubit.

The "horns" were measured from the midpoint of a side to its outer edge. This came to one *zeres,* or "span," i.e., half a cubit.

יד רֹחַב וּגְבוּלָהּ אֶל־שְׂפָתָהּ סָבִיב זֶרֶת הָאֶחָד וְזֶה גַּב הַמִּזְבֵּחַ: וּמֵחֵיק הָאָרֶץ
עַד־הָעֲזָרָה הַתַּחְתּוֹנָה שְׁתַּיִם אַמּוֹת וְרֹחַב אַמָּה אֶחָת וּמֵהָעֲזָרָה הַקְּטַנָּה

טו עַד־הָעֲזָרָה הַגְּדוֹלָה אַרְבַּע אַמּוֹת וְרֹחַב הָאַמָּה: וְהָהַרְאֵל אַרְבַּע אַמּוֹת

טז °וּמֵהָאַרְאֵיל [וּמֵהָאֲרִיאֵל ק'] וּלְמַעְלָה הַקְּרָנוֹת אַרְבַּע: °וְהָאַרְאֵיל
[וְהָאֲרִיאֵ֗ל ק'] שְׁתֵּים עֶשְׂרֵה אֹרֶךְ בִּשְׁתֵּים עֶשְׂרֵה רֹחַב רָבוּעַ אֶל

יז אַרְבַּעַת רְבָעָיו: וְהָעֲזָרָה אַרְבַּע עֶשְׂרֵה אֹרֶךְ בְּאַרְבַּע עֶשְׂרֵה רֹחַב אֶל־
אַרְבַּעַת רְבָעֶיהָ וְהַגְּבוּל סָבִיב אוֹתָהּ חֲצִי הָאַמָּה וְהַחֵיק־לָהּ אַמָּה סָבִיב

יח וּמַעֲלֹתֵהוּ פְּנוֹת קָדִים: וַיֹּאמֶר אֵלַי בֶּן־אָדָם כֹּה אָמַר אֲדֹנָי יֱהוִֹה אֵלֶּה
חֻקּוֹת הַמִּזְבֵּחַ בְּיוֹם הֵעָשׂוֹתוֹ לְהַעֲלוֹת עָלָיו עוֹלָה וְלִזְרֹק עָלָיו דָּם:

יט וְנָתַתָּה אֶל־הַכֹּהֲנִים הַלְוִיִּם אֲשֶׁר הֵם מִזֶּרַע צָדוֹק הַקְּרֹבִים אֵלַי נְאֻם אֲדֹנָי

כ יֱהוִֹה לְשָׁרְתֵנִי פַּר בֶּן־בָּקָר לְחַטָּאת: וְלָקַחְתָּ מִדָּמוֹ וְנָתַתָּה עַל־אַרְבַּע
קַרְנֹתָיו וְאֶל־אַרְבַּע פִּנּוֹת הָעֲזָרָה וְאֶל־הַגְּבוּל סָבִיב וְחִטֵּאתָ אוֹתוֹ

כא וְכִפַּרְתָּהוּ: וְלָקַחְתָּ אֵת הַפָּר הַחַטָּאת וּשְׂרָפוֹ בְּמִפְקַד הַבַּיִת מִחוּץ לַמִּקְדָּשׁ:

כב וּבַיּוֹם הַשֵּׁנִי תַּקְרִיב שְׂעִיר־עִזִּים תָּמִים לְחַטָּאת וְחִטְּאוּ אֶת־הַמִּזְבֵּחַ

כג כַּאֲשֶׁר חִטְּאוּ בַּפָּר: בְּכַלּוֹתְךָ מֵחַטֵּא תַּקְרִיב פַּר בֶּן־בָּקָר תָּמִים וְאַיִל מִן־

כד הַצֹּאן תָּמִים: וְהִקְרַבְתָּם לִפְנֵי יְהוָה וְהִשְׁלִיכוּ הַכֹּהֲנִים עֲלֵיהֶם מֶלַח וְהֶעֱלוּ

כה אוֹתָם עֹלָה לַיהוָה: שִׁבְעַת יָמִים תַּעֲשֶׂה שְׂעִיר־חַטָּאת לַיּוֹם וּפַר בֶּן־בָּקָר

כו וְאַיִל מִן־הַצֹּאן תְּמִימִם יַעֲשׂוּ: שִׁבְעַת יָמִים °יְכַפְּרוּ [יְכַפְּרוּ ק'] אֶת־
הַמִּזְבֵּחַ וְטִהֲרוּ אֹתוֹ וּמִלְאוּ °יָדוֹ [יָדָיו ק']: וִיכַלּוּ אֶת־הַיָּמִים וְהָיָה בַיּוֹם

כז הַשְּׁמִינִי וָהָלְאָה יַעֲשׂוּ הַכֹּהֲנִים עַל־הַמִּזְבֵּחַ אֶת־עוֹלוֹתֵיכֶם וְאֶת־

מד א שַׁלְמֵיכֶם וְרָצִאתִי אֶתְכֶם נְאֻם אֲדֹנָי יֱהוִֹה: ◄ וַיָּשֶׁב אֹתִי

ב דֶּרֶךְ שַׁעַר הַמִּקְדָּשׁ הַחִיצוֹן הַפֹּנֶה קָדִים וְהוּא סָגוּר: וַיֹּאמֶר אֵלַי יְהוָה
הַשַּׁעַר הַזֶּה סָגוּר יִהְיֶה לֹא יִפָּתֵחַ וְאִישׁ לֹא־יָבֹא בוֹ כִּי יְהוָה אֱלֹהֵי־

ג יִשְׂרָאֵל בָּא בוֹ וְהָיָה סָגוּר: אֶת־הַנָּשִׂיא נָשִׂיא הוּא יֵשֶׁב־בּוֹ °לֶאֱכוֹל
[לֶאֱכָל ק'] לֶחֶם לִפְנֵי יְהוָה מִדֶּרֶךְ אֻלָם הַשַּׁעַר יָבוֹא וּמִדַּרְכּוֹ יֵצֵא:

ד וַיְבִיאֵנִי דֶּרֶךְ־שַׁעַר הַצָּפוֹן אֶל־פְּנֵי הַבַּיִת וָאֵרֶא וְהִנֵּה מָלֵא כְבוֹד־יְהוָה

ה אֶת־בֵּית יְהוָה וָאֶפֹּל אֶל־פָּנָי: וַיֹּאמֶר אֵלַי יְהוָה בֶּן־אָדָם שִׂים לִבְּךָ וּרְאֵה
בְעֵינֶיךָ וּבְאָזְנֶיךָ שְּׁמָע אֵת כָּל־אֲשֶׁר אֲנִי מְדַבֵּר אֹתָךְ לְכָל־חֻקּוֹת בֵּית־

43:14. The Altar consisted of three large blocks, centered one on top of the other. The lowest block was 32 cubits square and two cubits high. The middle block was narrower by two cubits and so it covered the entire top of the lowest block, except for a one-cubit shelf that protruded all around; this block was called the base (v. 17) and was four cubits high. The top block was also four cubits high, and was two cubits narrower than the middle block; it thus left a second one-cubit shelf all around.

43:15. See verse 17.

43:16-17. It was 24 cubits squared, yielding four quadrants of 12x12 cubits. Circling the quadrants was a one-cubit walkway for the *Kohanim*, which was indented another cubit from the very edge of the Altar's top. Thus, the entire top of the Altar comprised four fourteen-cubit square quadrants for a total area of 28x28 cubits.

43:17. The uppermost shelf refers to the top of the Altar; from the border pieces to the horns (see v. 20). From the very center of each side of a horn to the center of each outer edge was a half-cubit, so that the full horn was a one-cubit cube.

[ledge's] width; and the border [pieces] upon its edge all around of one span each; and this [too] for the top of the [Inner] Altar. ¹⁴ From the foundation upon the ground up to the lower shelf* is two cubits; [the shelf being] one cubit in width. From the smaller shelf to the larger shelf is four cubits; [the shelf being] one cubit in width. ¹⁵ The [block of the] hearth area is four cubits [high]; and from the hearth area four horns [project] upwards. * ¹⁶ The hearth area is twelve [cubits] long by twelve wide, square, for its four quadrants. * ¹⁷ The [uppermost] shelf* is fourteen cubits long by fourteen cubits wide, for its four quadrants. The border [pieces] all around it are a half-cubit. Its base is a cubit [wide] all around. [Whoever ascends] its ramp would face eastward."*

Altar's **18** Then He said to me, "Son of Man, thus said the Lord HASHEM/ELOHIM: These
inauguration are the laws of the Altar on the day that it is made, to offer a burnt-offering on it and to sprinkle blood on it. ¹⁹ You shall give to the Kohanim, the Levites, who are from the seed of Zadok, who approach Me — the word of the Lord HASHEM/ELO-HIM — to serve Me, a young bull for a sin-offering. ²⁰ You shall take some of its blood and place it upon its four horns and upon the four corners of the [uppermost] shelf and upon the border all around; thus you will cleanse it and purify it. ²¹ Then you shall take the bull of the sin-offering and burn it at the edge of the Temple, outside the Sanctuary. ²² On the second day you shall offer an unblemished he-goat for a sin-offering, and they shall cleanse the Altar as they had cleansed it with the bull.

²³ "When you have finished cleansing, you shall offer an unblemished young bull, and an unblemished ram from the flock; ²⁴ you shall offer them before HASHEM. The Kohanim shall throw salt upon them and offer them up as a burnt-offering to HASHEM. ²⁵ For seven days you shall prepare a he-goat as a sin-offering for each day, and they shall prepare an unblemished young bull and ram from the flock. ²⁶ For seven days they shall purify the Altar, and they shall cleanse it and inaugurate it. ²⁷ When these days have passed, it shall be that from the eighth day onward the Kohanim may prepare on the Altar your burnt-offerings and your peace-offerings, and I will accept you with favor — the word of the Lord HASHEM/ELOHIM."

44 ¹ Then He returned me towards the outer gate of the Sanctuary which faces
The prince's   eastward, and it was closed. ² HASHEM said to me, "This gate shall be closed;
gate it shall not be opened; no man may come through it, * because HASHEM, the God of Israel, has come through it; it shall be closed. ³ It is for the prince, * he is the leader, so he will sit within it to eat food before HASHEM; he shall come in by way of the Hall of the [eastern] gate, and by that way he shall depart."

⁴ Then He brought me toward the northern gate, to the front of the Temple building and, behold, I saw that the glory of HASHEM filled the House of HASHEM! I fell upon my face.

⁵ HASHEM said to me, "Son of Man, set your heart and see with your eyes and hear with your ears all that I am saying to you about all the laws of the Temple

---

The ramp leading up to the Altar was on its south. Since the Temple practice was that one turned to the right rather than the left, anyone going up the ramp (facing north) would turn eastward when he reached the top of the Altar (Rashi).

44:2. Next to this small door, which would remain closed,

was a larger one for the use of the Kohanim (Rashi).

44:3. The prince of this and the following chapters is either the Kohen Gadol (Rashi); the king (R' Menachem cited by Rashi to 45:17); or the Messiah (Metzudos). He may sit in the doorway of the sealed gate and eat the sacrificial foods.

יְהֹוָה וּלְכׇל־°תּוֹרֹתוֹ [תּוֹרֹתָ֖יו ק] וְשַׂמְתָּ֤ לְּךָ֙ לִמְב֣וֹא הַבַּ֔יִת בְּכֹ֖ל מוֹצָאֵ֥י

ו הַמִּקְדָּֽשׁ: וְאָמַרְתָּ֞ אֶל־מֶ֣רִי אֶל־בֵּ֣ית יִשְׂרָאֵ֗ל כֹּ֤ה אָמַר֙ אֲדֹנָ֣י יֱהֹוִ֔ה רַב־

ז לָכֶ֛ם מִֽכׇּל־תּוֹעֲבֽוֹתֵיכֶ֖ם בֵּ֣ית יִשְׂרָאֵֽל: בַּהֲבִיאֲכֶ֣ם בְּנֵֽי־נֵכָ֗ר עַרְלֵי־לֵ֤ב

וְעַרְלֵ֣י בָשָׂ֔ר לִֽהְי֥וֹת בְּמִקְדָּשִׁ֖י לְחַלְּל֣וֹ אֶת־בֵּיתִ֑י בְּהַקְרִֽיבְכֶ֤ם אֶת־לַחְמִי֙

ח חֵ֣לֶב וָדָ֔ם וַיָּפֵ֙רוּ֙ אֶת־בְּרִיתִ֔י אֶ֖ל כׇּל־תּוֹעֲבֽוֹתֵיכֶֽם: וְלֹ֣א שְׁמַרְתֶּ֔ם מִשְׁמֶ֖רֶת

ט קׇדָשָׁ֑י וַתְּשִׂימ֗וּן לְשֹֽׁמְרֵ֧י מִשְׁמַרְתִּ֛י בְּמִקְדָּשִׁ֖י לָכֶֽם: כֹּה־ כה

אָמַ֞ר אֲדֹנָ֣י יֱהֹוִ֗ה כׇּל־בֶּן־נֵכָר֙ עֶ֣רֶל לֵ֔ב וְעֶ֖רֶל בָּשָׂ֑ר לֹ֤א יָבוֹא֙ אֶל־מִקְדָּשִׁ֔י

י לְכׇל־בֶּן־נֵכָ֔ר אֲשֶׁ֖ר בְּת֥וֹךְ בְּנֵ֥י יִשְׂרָאֵֽל: כִּ֣י אִם־הַלְוִיִּ֗ם אֲשֶׁ֤ר רָֽחֲקוּ֙ מֵֽעָלַ֔י

יא בִּתְע֤וֹת יִשְׂרָאֵל֙ אֲשֶׁ֤ר תָּעוּ֙ מֵֽעָלַ֔י אַחֲרֵ֖י גִּלּֽוּלֵיהֶ֑ם וְנָשְׂא֖וּ עֲוֺנָֽם: וְהָי֤וּ

בְּמִקְדָּשִׁי֙ מְשָׁ֣רְתִ֔ים פְּקֻדּוֹת֙ אֶל־שַֽׁעֲרֵ֣י הַבַּ֔יִת וּֽמְשָֽׁרְתִ֖ים אֶת־הַבָּ֑יִת הֵ֣מָּה

יב יִשְׁחֲט֧וּ אֶת־הָעֹלָ֛ה וְאֶת־הַזֶּ֖בַח לָעָ֑ם וְהֵ֛מָּה יַֽעַמְד֥וּ לִפְנֵיהֶ֖ם לְשָֽׁרְתָֽם: יַ֣עַן

אֲשֶׁ֨ר יְשָֽׁרְת֤וּ אוֹתָם֙ לִפְנֵ֣י גִלּֽוּלֵיהֶ֔ם וְהָי֥וּ לְבֵֽית־יִשְׂרָאֵ֖ל לְמִכְשׁ֣וֹל עָוֺ֑ן עַל־

יג כֵּן֩ נָשָׂ֨אתִי יָדִ֜י עֲלֵיהֶ֗ם נְאֻם֙ אֲדֹנָ֣י יֱהֹוִ֔ה וְנָשְׂא֖וּ עֲוֺנָֽם: וְלֹֽא־יִגְּשׁ֤וּ אֵלַי֙ לְכַהֵ֣ן

לִ֔י וְלָגֶ֙שֶׁת֙ עַל־כׇּל־קׇדָשַׁ֔י אֶל־קׇדְשֵׁ֖י הַקֳּדָשִׁ֑ים וְנָֽשְׂאוּ֙ כְּלִמָּתָ֔ם וְתוֹעֲבוֹתָ֖ם

יד אֲשֶׁ֥ר עָשֽׂוּ: וְנָתַתִּ֣י אוֹתָ֔ם שֹֽׁמְרֵ֖י מִשְׁמֶ֣רֶת הַבָּ֑יִת לְכֹל֙ עֲבֹ֣דָת֔וֹ וּלְכֹ֖ל אֲשֶׁ֥ר

טו יֵעָ֥שֶׂה בּֽוֹ: ◄ וְהַכֹּהֲנִ֨ים הַלְוִיִּ֜ם בְּנֵ֣י צָד֗וֹק אֲשֶׁ֨ר שָֽׁמְר֜וּ אֶת־

HAFTARAS
EMOR
44:15-31

מִשְׁמֶ֤רֶת מִקְדָּשִׁי֙ בִּתְע֤וֹת בְּנֵֽי־יִשְׂרָאֵל֙ מֵֽעָלַ֔י הֵ֛מָּה יִקְרְב֥וּ אֵלַ֖י לְשָֽׁרְתֵ֑נִי

טז וְעָמְד֣וּ לְפָנַ֗י לְהַקְרִ֥יב לִי֙ חֵ֣לֶב וָדָ֔ם נְאֻ֖ם אֲדֹנָ֣י יֱהֹוִֽה: הֵ֜מָּה יָבֹ֣אוּ אֶל־

מִקְדָּשִׁ֗י וְהֵ֛מָּה יִקְרְב֥וּ אֶל־שֻׁלְחָנִ֖י לְשָֽׁרְתֵ֑נִי וְשָׁמְר֖וּ אֶת־מִשְׁמַרְתִּֽי:

יז וְהָיָ֗ה בְּבוֹאָם֙ אֶל־שַֽׁעֲרֵי֙ הֶֽחָצֵ֣ר הַפְּנִימִ֔ית בִּגְדֵ֥י פִשְׁתִּ֖ים יִלְבָּ֑שׁוּ וְלֹֽא־

יח יַעֲלֶ֤ה עֲלֵיהֶם֙ צֶ֔מֶר בְּשָֽׁרְתָ֗ם בְּשַֽׁעֲרֵ֛י הֶֽחָצֵ֥ר הַפְּנִימִ֖ית וָבָֽיְתָה: פַּֽאֲרֵ֤י

פִשְׁתִּים֙ יִהְי֣וּ עַל־רֹאשָׁ֔ם וּמִכְנְסֵ֣י פִשְׁתִּ֔ים יִהְי֖וּ עַל־מׇתְנֵיהֶ֑ם לֹ֥א יַחְגְּר֖וּ

יט בַּיָּֽזַע: וּבְצֵאתָ֞ם אֶל־הֶחָצֵ֣ר הַחִ֣יצוֹנָ֗ה אֶל־הֶחָצֵ֤ר הַחִֽיצוֹנָה֙ אֶל־הָעָ֔ם

יִפְשְׁט֣וּ אֶת־בִּגְדֵיהֶ֗ם אֲשֶׁר־הֵ֙מָּה֙ מְשָֽׁרְתִ֣ם בָּ֔ם וְהִנִּ֥יחוּ אוֹתָ֖ם בְּלִֽשְׁכֹ֣ת

כ הַקֹּ֑דֶשׁ וְלָֽבְשׁוּ֙ בְּגָדִ֣ים אֲחֵרִ֔ים וְלֹֽא־יְקַדְּשׁ֥וּ אֶת־הָעָ֖ם בְּבִגְדֵיהֶֽם: וְרֹאשָׁם֙

כא לֹ֣א יְגַלֵּ֔חוּ וּפֶ֖רַע לֹ֣א יְשַׁלֵּ֑חוּ כָּס֥וֹם יִכְסְמ֖וּ אֶת־רָֽאשֵׁיהֶֽם: וְיַ֥יִן לֹֽא־יִשְׁתּ֖וּ

כב כׇּל־כֹּהֵ֑ן בְּבוֹאָ֖ם אֶל־הֶחָצֵ֥ר הַפְּנִימִֽית: וְאַלְמָנָה֙ וּגְרוּשָׁ֔ה לֹֽא־יִקְח֤וּ לָהֶם֙

44:7. People with impure, unholy hearts.

"Fat and blood" refers to the portions of sacrificial animals placed on the Altar fire or sprinkled on the Altar wall.

44:8. Your criteria for appointing officials in My Temple were not based on their fitness for the task, but on the benefits that would accrue to you as a result of those appointments (*Rashi*). Alternatively: You appointed those who had been priests "for yourselves," i.e., for your idolatrous worship, to be priests in My Temple (*Radak*).

44:11. Although these erstwhile wayward *Kohanim* have been disqualified from the priesthood, they nevertheless will retain their status as Levites. Thus, they may perform the Levitical duty of gatekeeping; they may also slaughter sacrificial animals, an act that may be performed by a non-*Kohen*.

44:12. In oath.

44:13. In those capacities that require a *Kohen*.

44:15. See v. 7.

44:17. The following series of verses seem to contradict the laws pertaining to the *Kohanim* that appear in *Leviticus*. The commentaries view these verses in two ways. According to *Rashi*, the prophet is describing, in cryptic form, the precise laws as stated in *Leviticus*; to under-of HASHEM and all its teachings; set your heart toward the entrance of the Temple, and to all the exits of the Sanctuary. [6] Then say to the [House of] Rebellion, to the House of Israel:

God's warning

Thus said the Lord HASHEM/ELOHIM: You have indulged too much in all your abominations, O House of Israel, [7] by bringing in strangers of uncircumcised heart* and uncircumcised flesh to be in My Sanctuary to defile My Temple when you offer My food — fat and blood* — and they have violated My covenant, in addition to all your abominations. [8] You did not safeguard the charge of My holy places; you set as guardians of My charge in My Sanctuary [those who were] for yourselves." *

Traitors stay away

[9] Thus said the Lord HASHEM/ELOHIM: Any estranged person of uncircumcised heart or uncircumcised flesh shall not enter My Sanctuary — any estranged person among the Children of Israel. [10] But those Levites who distanced themselves from Me during Israel's straying, when they strayed from Me after their idols, they shall bear their iniquity. [11] They may be attendants in My Sanctuary, responsible for the gates of the Temple, serving the Temple; they may slaughter* the burnt-offering and feast-offering of the people, and they may stand before them to serve them. [12] But because they ministered to [the people] before their idols, and they became a stumbling-block of iniquity for the House of Israel, therefore, I have raised My hand* against them — the word of the Lord HASHEM/ELOHIM — and they shall bear their iniquity. [13] They shall not approach Me to serve Me, * or to approach My holy places, to the Holy of Holies; but they shall bear their shame and their abominations that they have committed. [14] Yet I will make them guardians of the charge of the House, for all its service and for everything that is done in it.

Loyal ones draw near

[15] "But the Kohanim, the Levites, descendants of Zadok, who safeguarded the charge of My Sanctuary when the Children of Israel strayed from Me, let them draw near to Me to serve Me; let them stand before Me to offer to Me fat and blood* — the word of the Lord HASHEM/ELOHIM. [16] They will come to My Sanctuary and they will draw near to My Table to serve Me, and they will safeguard My charge.

[17] "It shall be that when they come to the gates of the inner courtyard, they shall wear linen clothes;* wool shall not be upon them when they serve inside the gates of the inner courtyard, within. [18] Linen turbans shall be on their heads and linen breeches shall be on their loins. They shall not gird themselves where one perspires. * [19] When they go out to the outer [part of the] courtyard* — to the outer courtyard to the people — they shall remove the clothes in which they had ministered and leave them in the holy chambers, and they shall don other garments; they shall not mingle with the people while wearing their clothes.

Laws of the Kohanim

[20] "They shall not shave their heads, nor shall they allow them to grow wild; they shall keep their heads trimmed. [21] No Kohen shall drink wine when they enter the inner courtyard. [22] They shall not take a widow or a divorcee unto themselves

---

stand these verses we cannot rely on the *p'shat,* simple meanings of the words, but must rely on *derash,* exegesis of a non-literal level. According to *Radak* the increased sanctity of both Israel and the Temple of future times will be reflected in higher standards imposed on the ordinary *Kohanim;* thus, the service described here will enhance the service ordained in *Leviticus,* but will not replace any of its components.

Although couched in the plural, this passage speaks of

the *Kohen Gadol* entering the Inner Sanctum on Yom Kippur; he then wears garments of pure linen (*Rashi*).

44:18. The belt worn over the robe should be above the hips and below the armpits, at elbow level (*Rashi*).

44:19. When the *Kohen Gadol* would leave the section of the courtyard reserved for the *Kohanim,* he would remove his linen garments and don his regular garb (*Rashi*).

לְנָשִׁים כִּי אִם־בְּתוּלֹת מִזֶּרַע בֵּית יִשְׂרָאֵל וְהָאַלְמָנָה אֲשֶׁר תִּהְיֶה אַלְמָנָה
מִכֹּהֵן יִקָּחוּ: וְאֶת־עַמִּי יוֹרוּ בֵּין קֹדֶשׁ לְחֹל וּבֵין־טָמֵא לְטָהוֹר יוֹדִעֻם: וְעַל־   כג-כד
רִיב הֵמָּה יַעַמְדוּ לִשְׁפֹּט [לְמִשְׁפָּט ק] בְּמִשְׁפָּטַי [וּשְׁפָטֻהוּ ק] יִשְׁפְּטֻהוּ
וְאֶת־תּוֹרֹתַי וְאֶת־חֻקֹּתַי בְּכָל־מוֹעֲדַי יִשְׁמֹרוּ וְאֶת־שַׁבְּתוֹתַי יְקַדֵּשׁוּ:
וְאֶל־מֵת אָדָם לֹא יָבוֹא לְטָמְאָה כִּי אִם־לְאָב וּלְאֵם וּלְבֵן וּלְבַת לְאָח   כה
וּלְאָחוֹת אֲשֶׁר־לֹא־הָיְתָה לְאִישׁ יִטַּמָּאוּ: וְאַחֲרֵי טָהֳרָתוֹ שִׁבְעַת יָמִים   כו
יִסְפְּרוּ־לוֹ: וּבְיוֹם בֹּאוֹ אֶל־הַקֹּדֶשׁ אֶל־הֶחָצֵר הַפְּנִימִית לְשָׁרֵת בַּקֹּדֶשׁ   כז
יַקְרִיב חַטָּאתוֹ נְאֻם אֲדֹנָי יֱהֹוִה: וְהָיְתָה לָהֶם לְנַחֲלָה אֲנִי נַחֲלָתָם וַאֲחֻזָּה   כח
לֹא־תִתְּנוּ לָהֶם בְּיִשְׂרָאֵל אֲנִי אֲחֻזָּתָם: הַמִּנְחָה וְהַחַטָּאת וְהָאָשָׁם הֵמָּה   כט
יֹאכְלוּם וְכָל־חֵרֶם בְּיִשְׂרָאֵל לָהֶם יִהְיֶה: וְרֵאשִׁית כָּל־בִּכּוּרֵי כֹל וְכָל־   ל
תְּרוּמַת כֹּל מִכֹּל תְּרוּמוֹתֵיכֶם לַכֹּהֲנִים יִהְיֶה וְרֵאשִׁית עֲרִסוֹתֵיכֶם
תִּתְּנוּ לַכֹּהֵן לְהָנִיחַ בְּרָכָה אֶל־בֵּיתֶךָ: כָּל־נְבֵלָה וּטְרֵפָה מִן־הָעוֹף וּמִן־   לא
הַבְּהֵמָה לֹא יֹאכְלוּ הַכֹּהֲנִים: ▸

מה   וּבְהַפִּילְכֶם אֶת־הָאָרֶץ   א
בְּנַחֲלָה תָּרִימוּ תְרוּמָה לַיהֹוָה | קֹדֶשׁ מִן־הָאָרֶץ אֹרֶךְ חֲמִשָּׁה וְעֶשְׂרִים
אֶלֶף אֹרֶךְ וְרֹחַב עֲשָׂרָה אָלֶף קֹדֶשׁ־הוּא בְכָל־גְּבוּלָהּ סָבִיב: יִהְיֶה מִזֶּה   ב
אֶל־הַקֹּדֶשׁ חֲמֵשׁ מֵאוֹת בַּחֲמֵשׁ מֵאוֹת מְרֻבָּע סָבִיב וַחֲמִשִּׁים אַמָּה מִגְרָשׁ
לוֹ סָבִיב: וּמִן־הַמִּדָּה הַזֹּאת תָּמוֹד אֹרֶךְ [חָמֵשׁ ק] חֲמִשָּׁה וְעֶשְׂרִים   ג
אֶלֶף וְרֹחַב עֲשֶׂרֶת אֲלָפִים וּבוֹ־יִהְיֶה הַמִּקְדָּשׁ קֹדֶשׁ קָדָשִׁים: קֹדֶשׁ מִן־   ד
הָאָרֶץ הוּא לַכֹּהֲנִים מְשָׁרְתֵי הַמִּקְדָּשׁ יִהְיֶה הַקְּרֵבִים לְשָׁרֵת אֶת־יְהֹוָה
וְהָיָה לָהֶם מָקוֹם לְבָתִּים וּמִקְדָּשׁ לַמִּקְדָּשׁ: וַחֲמִשָּׁה וְעֶשְׂרִים אֶלֶף אֹרֶךְ   ה
וַעֲשֶׂרֶת אֲלָפִים רֹחַב יהיה [וְהָיָה ק] לַלְוִיִּם מְשָׁרְתֵי הַבַּיִת לָהֶם
לַאֲחֻזָּה עֶשְׂרִים לְשָׁכֹת: וַאֲחֻזַּת הָעִיר תִּתְּנוּ חֲמֵשֶׁת אֲלָפִים רֹחַב   ו
וְאֹרֶךְ חֲמִשָּׁה וְעֶשְׂרִים אָלֶף לְעֻמַּת תְּרוּמַת הַקֹּדֶשׁ לְכָל־בֵּית יִשְׂרָאֵל
יִהְיֶה: וְלַנָּשִׂיא מִזֶּה וּמִזֶּה לִתְרוּמַת הַקֹּדֶשׁ וְלַאֲחֻזַּת הָעִיר אֶל־פְּנֵי   ז
תְרוּמַת־הַקֹּדֶשׁ וְאֶל־פְּנֵי אֲחֻזַּת הָעִיר מִפְּאַת־יָם יָמָּה וּמִפְּאַת קֵדְמָה
קָדִימָה וְאֹרֶךְ לְעֻמּוֹת אַחַד הַחֲלָקִים מִגְּבוּל יָם אֶל־גְּבוּל קָדִימָה: לָאָרֶץ   ח
יִהְיֶה־לּוֹ לַאֲחֻזָּה בְּיִשְׂרָאֵל וְלֹא־יוֹנוּ עוֹד נְשִׂיאַי אֶת־עַמִּי וְהָאָרֶץ
יִתְּנוּ לְבֵית־יִשְׂרָאֵל לְשִׁבְטֵיהֶם: ט

44:22. This prohibition applies to a sitting, acting, or former *Kohen Gadol,* and to the *Kohen* who addressed the troops before battle (see *Deuteronomy* 20:2). Other *Kohanim* may marry widows *who are only widowed*, i.e., they are not divorcees.

44:26. After which he becomes fully purified, as in *Numbers* Ch. 19.

44:27. As in *Leviticus* 6:13 (*Rashi*).

44:28. *Kohanim* did not receive land in Israel so that they could devote themselves to the service of God.

44:30. A portion of the produce that must be given to the *Kohen* (see *Deuteronomy* 18:4).

44:31. This refers to the meat of an animal that died without *shechitah,* ritual slaughter.

45:1. This "inheritance," i.e., the portions to be allotted to the tribes, is given in Chapter 48.

45:2-3. Verse 1 did not clarify in what unit the 25,000 x 10,000 area should be measured, but the area mentioned in verse 2 as the Sanctuary enclosure was in the six-cubit rods (see 40:5), as stated in 42:15-20. By stating in verse for wives, * but only virgins from the offspring of the House of Israel; but a widow who is only widowed, some Kohanim may marry. ²³ They shall instruct My people concerning [the difference] between holy and ordinary, and they shall inform them of [the difference] between contaminated and clean. ²⁴ Concerning a disagreement, they shall stand in judgment, and shall adjudicate them according to My laws; they shall safeguard My teachings and My decrees regarding all My appointed times and they shall sanctify My Sabbaths. ²⁵ They shall not approach a human corpse to become contaminated, except that each of them may become contaminated to [the corpse of his] father, mother, son, daughter, brother or sister who had never been married to a man. ²⁶ And then, after his cleansing, they shall count seven days for him. *

²⁷ "On the day of his entry into the Sanctuary, to the inner courtyard, to minister in the Sanctuary, he shall bring his sin-offering * — the word of the Lord HASHEM/ELOHIM.

Heritage of the Kohanim   ²⁸ "[The priesthood] will be a heritage for them; I am their heritage. For you shall not give them a possession in Israel; I am their possession. * ²⁹ They shall eat the meal-offering, the sin-offering and the guilt-offering; and any consecrated property in Israel will be for them. ³⁰ All the first fruits of every kind and all terumah * of any kind, of all your terumah gifts, shall be for the Kohanim; and you shall give the first portion of your dough to the Kohen, to bring a blessing to rest upon your home. ³¹ The Kohanim shall not eat any carrion * nor meat from a fatally wounded animal, of fowl or of livestock."

45

Division of the land   ¹ "When you allot the land as an inheritance * you shall set aside a sacred portion to HASHEM from the land, in length, twenty-five thousand long and in width ten thousand; it shall be holy within its entire boundary all around. ² From this shall come for the Sanctuary [enclosure] five hundred by five hundred * square all around, and fifty cubits of open space all around [it]. ³ By this same measure you shall measure a length of twenty-five thousand and a width of ten thousand; within it shall be the Sanctuary, Holy of Holies. ⁴ It * is a sacred portion from the land; for the Kohanim, the ministrants of the Sanctuary, shall it be, those who approach to minister before HASHEM; it shall be for them a place for houses, and as holy ground for the Sanctuary.

Levite portion   ⁵ "And [another strip] of twenty-five thousand long and ten thousand wide shall be for the Levites, the ministers of the Temple, as their possession — with twenty chambers. * ⁶ As the possession of the city, you shall allot five thousand wide by a length of twenty-five thousand alongside the sacred portion; for the entire House of Israel shall it be.

Princely portion   ⁷ "And [as the portion] for the prince, * on the one and the other sides of the sacred portion and the possession of the city, facing the sacred portion and facing the possession of the city, from the western side extending westward and from the eastern side extending eastward, the length corresponding to each of the [tribal] portions from the western border to the eastern border. ⁸ It shall be his as a possession in Israel, that My princes shall not again extort from My people, * rather they shall give the land to the House of Israel according to their tribes.

---

3 that the large enclosure of verse 1 was in the *same measure,* Scripture informs us that the unit of all the measurements was the six-cubit rod.

45:4. I.e., the sacred portion of verse 1.

45:5. These chambers are left unexplained. *Radak* sug-

gests that they were alongside the strip of the *Kohanim,* so that the Levites could be near the Temple area.

45:7. See 44:3.

45:8. Since he will have such a large estate, he will not be tempted to seize property unjustly from the people.

אָמַר אֲדֹנָי יֱהֹוִה רַב־לָכֶם נְשִׂיאֵי יִשְׂרָאֵל חָמָס וָשֹׁד הָסִירוּ וּמִשְׁפָּט
י וּצְדָקָה עֲשׂוּ הָרִימוּ גְרֻשֹׁתֵיכֶם מֵעַל עַמִּי נְאֻם אֲדֹנָי יֱהֹוִה: מֹאזְנֵי־צֶדֶק
יא וְאֵיפַת־צֶדֶק וּבַת־צֶדֶק יְהִי לָכֶם: הָאֵיפָה וְהַבַּת תֹּכֶן אֶחָד יִהְיֶה לָשֵׂאת
מַעְשַׂר הַחֹמֶר הַבַּת וַעֲשִׂירִת הַחֹמֶר הָאֵיפָה אֶל־הַחֹמֶר יִהְיֶה מַתְכֻּנְתּוֹ:
יב וְהַשֶּׁקֶל עֶשְׂרִים גֵּרָה עֶשְׂרִים שְׁקָלִים חֲמִשָּׁה וְעֶשְׂרִים שְׁקָלִים עֲשָׂרָה
יג וַחֲמִשָּׁה שֶׁקֶל הַמָּנֶה יִהְיֶה לָכֶם: זֹאת הַתְּרוּמָה אֲשֶׁר תָּרִימוּ שִׁשִּׁית
יד הָאֵיפָה מֵחֹמֶר הַחִטִּים וְשִׁשִּׁיתֶם הָאֵיפָה מֵחֹמֶר הַשְּׂעֹרִים: וְחֹק הַשֶּׁמֶן
הַבַּת הַשֶּׁמֶן מַעְשַׂר הַבַּת מִן־הַכֹּר עֲשֶׂרֶת הַבַּתִּים חֹמֶר כִּי־עֲשֶׂרֶת
טו הַבַּתִּים חֹמֶר: וְשֶׂה־אַחַת מִן־הַצֹּאן מִן־הַמָּאתַיִם מִמַּשְׁקֵה יִשְׂרָאֵל כָּל ◀
טז לְמִנְחָה וּלְעוֹלָה וְלִשְׁלָמִים לְכַפֵּר עֲלֵיהֶם נְאֻם אֲדֹנָי יֱהֹוִה:

HAFTARAS PARASHAS HACHODESH
Ashkenazim: 45:16-46:18
Sephardim: 45:18-46:15

הָעָם הָאָרֶץ אֶל־הַתְּרוּמָה הַזֹּאת לַנָּשִׂיא בְּיִשְׂרָאֵל: וְעַל־הַנָּשִׂיא
יז יִהְיֶה הָעוֹלוֹת וְהַמִּנְחָה וְהַנֵּסֶךְ בַּחַגִּים וּבֶחֳדָשִׁים וּבַשַּׁבָּתוֹת בְּכָל־
מוֹעֲדֵי בֵּית יִשְׂרָאֵל הוּא־יַעֲשֶׂה אֶת־הַחַטָּאת וְאֶת־הַמִּנְחָה וְאֶת־
הָעוֹלָה וְאֶת־הַשְּׁלָמִים לְכַפֵּר בְּעַד בֵּית־יִשְׂרָאֵל: כֹּה־אָמַר ◀
יח אֲדֹנָי יֱהֹוִה בָּרִאשׁוֹן בְּאֶחָד לַחֹדֶשׁ תִּקַּח פַּר־בֶּן־בָּקָר תָּמִים וְחִטֵּאתָ
יט אֶת־הַמִּקְדָּשׁ: וְלָקַח הַכֹּהֵן מִדַּם הַחַטָּאת וְנָתַן אֶל־מְזוּזַת הַבַּיִת וְאֶל־
אַרְבַּע פִּנּוֹת הָעֲזָרָה לַמִּזְבֵּחַ וְעַל־מְזוּזַת שַׁעַר הֶחָצֵר הַפְּנִימִית: וְכֵן
כ תַּעֲשֶׂה בְּשִׁבְעָה בַחֹדֶשׁ מֵאִישׁ שֹׁגֶה וּמִפֶּתִי וְכִפַּרְתֶּם אֶת־הַבָּיִת:
כא בָּרִאשׁוֹן בְּאַרְבָּעָה עָשָׂר יוֹם לַחֹדֶשׁ יִהְיֶה לָכֶם הַפָּסַח חָג שְׁבֻעוֹת יָמִים
כב מַצּוֹת יֵאָכֵל: וְעָשָׂה הַנָּשִׂיא בַּיּוֹם הַהוּא בַּעֲדוֹ וּבְעַד כָּל־עַם הָאָרֶץ פַּר
כג חַטָּאת: וְשִׁבְעַת יְמֵי־הֶחָג יַעֲשֶׂה עוֹלָה לַיהֹוָה שִׁבְעַת פָּרִים וְשִׁבְעַת
כד אֵילִים תְּמִימִם לַיּוֹם שִׁבְעַת הַיָּמִים וְחַטָּאת שְׂעִיר עִזִּים לַיּוֹם: וּמִנְחָה
כה אֵיפָה לַפָּר וְאֵיפָה לָאַיִל יַעֲשֶׂה וְשֶׁמֶן הִין לָאֵיפָה: בַּשְּׁבִיעִי בַּחֲמִשָּׁה
עָשָׂר יוֹם לַחֹדֶשׁ בֶּחָג יַעֲשֶׂה כָאֵלֶּה שִׁבְעַת הַיָּמִים כַּחַטָּאת כָּעֹלָה
א וְכַמִּנְחָה וְכַשָּׁמֶן: כֹּה־אָמַר אֲדֹנָי יֱהֹוִה שַׁעַר הֶחָצֵר הַפְּנִימִית מו
הַפֹּנֶה קָדִים יִהְיֶה סָגוּר שֵׁשֶׁת יְמֵי הַמַּעֲשֶׂה וּבְיוֹם הַשַּׁבָּת יִפָּתֵחַ וּבְיוֹם
ב הַחֹדֶשׁ יִפָּתֵחַ: וּבָא הַנָּשִׂיא דֶּרֶךְ אוּלָם הַשַּׁעַר מִחוּץ וְעָמַד עַל־מְזוּזַת
הַשַּׁעַר וְעָשׂוּ הַכֹּהֲנִים אֶת־עוֹלָתוֹ וְאֶת־שְׁלָמָיו וְהִשְׁתַּחֲוָה עַל־מִפְתַּן
ג הַשַּׁעַר וְיָצָא וְהַשַּׁעַר לֹא־יִסָּגֵר עַד־הָעָרֶב: וְהִשְׁתַּחֲווּ עַם־הָאָרֶץ

45:10-12. The prince must maintain societal honesty by enforcing honest weights. The *ephah* is a dry measure and the *bas* is a liquid measure, but both are the volume of a tenth of a *chomer*. Verse 12 gives three different *shekel* weights that add up to a *maneh*. Each of those weights is a separate commercial unit of weight and of coinage, since the value of ancient coins depended on their precious metal content.

45:13. This was a mandatory contribution toward the

dedication ceremony of the Third Temple.

45:14. The *kor* and the *chomer* are of the same volume.

45:16. This refers either to the gift of land (vv. 7-8) to be given to the prince (*Rashi*); or to the gifts mentioned above (vv. 13-14) which were to be brought as a communal offering from which the prince was exempt (*Radak*) or were to be an additional gift for the prince (*Malbim*).

45:18. The offerings now enumerated were ordained

⁹ Thus said the Lord HASHEM/ELOHIM: It is too much for you, O princes of Israel! Set aside lawlessness and rapine, and do justice and righteousness; desist from your evictions of My people — the word of the Lord HASHEM/ELOHIM."

Honest dealings ¹⁰ "Honest scales, * an honest ephah, and an honest bas shall you have. ¹¹ The ephah and the bas shall be the same volume: the bas shall contain a tenth part of a chomer, and the ephah is a tenth of a chomer; relative to the chomer shall their volume be. ¹² The shekel shall be twenty gerah. Twenty shekels [plus] twenty-five shekels [plus] fifteen shekels shall comprise a maneh for you.

Contribution for the Temple ¹³ "This is the portion that you shall set aside: * a sixth of an ephah from a chomer of wheat and you shall take a sixth of an ephah from a chomer of barley. ¹⁴ The law of the oil: The bas [is the measure for] the oil; the bas shall be a tenth of the kor* [which is] ten bas, a chomer, for ten bas are a chomer. ¹⁵ And one lamb from the flock out of two hundred, from Israel's fatted animals. [These are all] for a meal-offering, a burnt-offering and a peace-offering to atone for you — the word of the Lord, HASHEM/ELOHIM. ¹⁶ The entire people of the land shall join in this donation* with the prince in Israel.

¹⁷ "Upon the prince shall be [the responsibility for] the burnt-offerings, the meal-offering and the libation, on the festivals, on the New Moons, and on the Sabbaths, on all the appointed times of the House of Israel; he shall prepare the sin-offering, the meal-offering, the burnt-offering, and the peace-offering to atone on behalf of the House of Israel."

Inauguration offerings ¹⁸ Thus said the Lord HASHEM/ELOHIM: "In the first [month], on the first of the month, * you shall take an unblemished bull of the herd, and you shall cleanse the Sanctuary. ¹⁹ The Kohen shall take from the blood of the sin-offering and put it on the doorpost of the Temple and on the four corners of the Altar's shelf and on the doorpost of the gate of the inner courtyard. ²⁰ And so you shall do for a week* in the month — [to atone for contamination caused by] an unwitting or ignorant person, you shall purify the House. ²¹ In the first [month] on the fourteenth day of the month you shall have the pesach-offering; a festival of seven days, when unleavened bread shall be eaten. ²² On that day, the prince shall bring a bull sin-offering for himself and for the entire people of the land. ²³ During the seven days of the festival he shall bring a burnt-offering for HASHEM: seven bulls and seven rams, unblemished, each day for the seven days, and a sin-offering, a goat for each day; ²⁴ and he shall bring a meal-offering, an ephah for each bull and an ephah for each ram, and a hin of oil for each ephah. ²⁵ In the seventh [month] on the fifteenth day of the month, during the [Succos] festival, he shall do the same for the seven days, like the sin-offering, like the burnt-offering, like the meal-offering and like the oil."

46

Sabbath and New Moon ¹ Thus said the Lord HASHEM/ELOHIM: "The gate of the inner courtyard that faces eastward shall be closed during the six days of labor, but on the Sabbath day it shall be opened, and on the day of the New Moon it shall be opened. ² Then the prince shall enter by way of the hall of the gate from without, and stand before the doorpost of the gate; * the Kohanim will prepare his burnt-offering and his peace-offerings, and he will then prostrate himself at the threshold of the gate and depart; but the gate shall not be closed until the evening. ³ The people of the land

---

especially for the dedication of the Temple (*Rashi*).
45:20. See 43:26.

46:2. The gate's hall projected out of the gate into the outer courtyard.

ד פֶּתַח הַשַּׁעַר הַהוּא בַּשַּׁבָּתוֹת וּבֶחֳדָשִׁים לִפְנֵי יהוה: וְהָעֹלָה אֲשֶׁר־יַקְרִב

ה הַנָּשִׂיא לַיהוה בְּיוֹם הַשַּׁבָּת שִׁשָּׁה כְבָשִׂים תְּמִימִם וְאַיִל תָּמִים: וּמִנְחָה

ו אֵיפָה לָאַיִל וְלַכְּבָשִׂים מִנְחָה מַתַּת יָדוֹ וְשֶׁמֶן הִין לָאֵיפָה: וּבְיוֹם הַחֹדֶשׁ

פַּר בֶּן־בָּקָר תְּמִימִם וְשֵׁשֶׁת כְּבָשִׂים וָאַיִל תְּמִימִם יִהְיוּ: וְאֵיפָה לַפָּר

וְאֵיפָה לָאַיִל יַעֲשֶׂה מִנְחָה וְלַכְּבָשִׂים כַּאֲשֶׁר תַּשִּׂיג יָדוֹ וְשֶׁמֶן הִין לָאֵיפָה:

ח-ט וּבְבוֹא הַנָּשִׂיא דֶּרֶךְ אוּלָם הַשַּׁעַר יָבוֹא וּבְדַרְכּוֹ יֵצֵא: וּבְבוֹא עַם־הָאָרֶץ

לִפְנֵי יהוה בַּמּוֹעֲדִים הַבָּא דֶּרֶךְ־שַׁעַר צָפוֹן לְהִשְׁתַּחֲוֹת יֵצֵא דֶּרֶךְ־שַׁעַר

נֶגֶב וְהַבָּא דֶּרֶךְ־שַׁעַר נֶגֶב יֵצֵא דֶּרֶךְ־שַׁעַר צָפוֹנָה לֹא יָשׁוּב דֶּרֶךְ הַשַּׁעַר

י אֲשֶׁר־בָּא בּוֹ כִּי נִכְחוֹ °יצאו [°יֵצֵא ק]: וְהַנָּשִׂיא בְּתוֹכָם בְּבוֹאָם יָבוֹא

יא וּבְצֵאתָם יֵצֵאוּ: וּבַחַגִּים וּבַמּוֹעֲדִים תִּהְיֶה הַמִּנְחָה אֵיפָה לַפָּר וְאֵיפָה

יב לָאַיִל וְלַכְּבָשִׂים מַתַּת יָדוֹ וְשֶׁמֶן הִין לָאֵיפָה: וְכִי־יַעֲשֶׂה

הַנָּשִׂיא נְדָבָה עוֹלָה אוֹ־שְׁלָמִים נְדָבָה לַיהוה וּפָתַח לוֹ אֶת־הַשַּׁעַר

הַפֹּנֶה קָדִים וְעָשָׂה אֶת־עֹלָתוֹ וְאֶת־שְׁלָמָיו כַּאֲשֶׁר יַעֲשֶׂה בְּיוֹם הַשַּׁבָּת

יג וְיָצָא וְסָגַר אֶת־הַשַּׁעַר אַחֲרֵי צֵאתוֹ: וְכֶבֶשׂ בֶּן־שְׁנָתוֹ תָּמִים תַּעֲשֶׂה

יד עוֹלָה לַיּוֹם לַיהוה בַּבֹּקֶר בַּבֹּקֶר תַּעֲשֶׂה אֹתוֹ: וּמִנְחָה תַעֲשֶׂה עָלָיו בַּבֹּקֶר

בַּבֹּקֶר שִׁשִּׁית הָאֵיפָה וְשֶׁמֶן שְׁלִישִׁית הַהִין לָרֹס אֶת־הַסֹּלֶת מִנְחָה

טו לַיהוה חֻקּוֹת עוֹלָם תָּמִיד: °ועשו [°יַעֲשׂוּ ק] אֶת־הַכֶּבֶשׂ וְאֶת־הַמִּנְחָה

טז וְאֶת־הַשֶּׁמֶן בַּבֹּקֶר בַּבֹּקֶר עוֹלַת תָּמִיד: ▸ כֹּה־אָמַר אֲדֹנָי

יהוה כִּי־יִתֵּן הַנָּשִׂיא מַתָּנָה לְאִישׁ מִבָּנָיו נַחֲלָתוֹ הִיא לְבָנָיו תִּהְיֶה

יז אֲחֻזָּתָם הִיא בְּנַחֲלָה: וְכִי־יִתֵּן מַתָּנָה מִנַּחֲלָתוֹ לְאַחַד מֵעֲבָדָיו וְהָיְתָה לּוֹ

עַד־שְׁנַת הַדְּרוֹר וְשָׁבַת לַנָּשִׂיא אַךְ נַחֲלָתוֹ בָּנָיו לָהֶם תִּהְיֶה: וְלֹא־יִקַּח

יח הַנָּשִׂיא מִנַּחֲלַת הָעָם לְהוֹנֹתָם מֵאֲחֻזָּתָם מֵאֲחֻזָּתוֹ יַנְחִל אֶת־בָּנָיו לְמַעַן

יט אֲשֶׁר לֹא־יָפֻצוּ עַמִּי אִישׁ מֵאֲחֻזָּתוֹ: ▸ וַיְבִיאֵנִי בַמָּבוֹא אֲשֶׁר עַל־כֶּתֶף

הַשַּׁעַר אֶל־הַלִּשְׁכוֹת הַקֹּדֶשׁ אֶל־הַכֹּהֲנִים הַפֹּנוֹת צָפוֹנָה וְהִנֵּה־שָׁם

כ מָקוֹם °בירכתם [°בַּיַּרְכָתַיִם ק] יָמָּה: וַיֹּאמֶר אֵלַי זֶה הַמָּקוֹם אֲשֶׁר

יְבַשְּׁלוּ־שָׁם הַכֹּהֲנִים אֶת־הָאָשָׁם וְאֶת־הַחַטָּאת אֲשֶׁר יֹאפוּ אֶת־הַמִּנְחָה

כא לְבִלְתִּי הוֹצִיא אֶל־הֶחָצֵר הַחִיצוֹנָה לְקַדֵּשׁ אֶת־הָעָם: וַיּוֹצִיאֵנִי אֶל־

הֶחָצֵר הַחִיצֹנָה וַיַּעֲבִירֵנִי אֶל־אַרְבַּעַת מִקְצוֹעֵי הֶחָצֵר וְהִנֵּה חָצֵר

כב בְּמִקְצֹעַ הֶחָצֵר חָצֵר בְּמִקְצֹעַ הֶחָצֵר: בְּאַרְבַּעַת מִקְצֹעוֹת הֶחָצֵר חֲצֵרוֹת

קְטֻרוֹת אַרְבָּעִים אֹרֶךְ וּשְׁלֹשִׁים רֹחַב מִדָּה אַחַת לְאַרְבַּעְתָּם מְהֻקְצָעוֹת:

46:9. The three pilgrimage festivals.

46:13. This offering was to enhance the daily continual offering [the *tamid*] during the seven-month period of the inauguration services (*Abarbanel*).

46:15. This is the daily continual offering (*Abarbanel*).

46:16. From the tract described in 45:7-8.

shall prostrate themselves before HASHEM at the entrance of that gate on the Sabbaths and on the New Moons.

Prince's offerings ⁴ "And [this is] the burnt-offering that the prince shall bring for HASHEM: on the Sabbath day, six unblemished sheep and an unblemished ram, ⁵ and a meal-offering of one ephah for the ram and a meal-offering of whatever his hand gives for the sheep, with a hin of oil for each ephah; ⁶ on the day of the New Moon an unblemished bull from the herd and six sheep and a ram, they shall be unblemished, ⁷ and he shall make an ephah for the bull and an ephah for the ram as a meal-offering, and for the sheep according to his means, with a hin of oil per ephah.

⁸ "When the prince enters, he shall enter by way of the hall of the gate, and by the same way he shall leave. ⁹ But when the populace comes before HASHEM on the appointed days, * whoever comes in by way of the northern gate to prostrate himself shall go out by way of the southern gate, and whoever comes in by way of the southern gate shall go out by way of the northern gate. He shall not return by way of the gate through which he came in; rather he shall go out opposite it. ¹⁰ And the prince: He shall enter among them when they enter, and when they leave he shall leave. ¹¹ On the festivals and at the appointed times, the meal-offering shall be an ephah for a bull and an ephah for a ram; and for the sheep, whatever his hand gives, with a hin of oil per ephah.

¹² "When the prince makes a free-will offering, a burnt-offering or a peace-offering as a free-will offering for HASHEM, they shall open for him the gate that faces eastward, and he shall make his burnt-offering and his peace-offerings as he does on the Sabbath day, then he shall go out, and they shall close the gate after his departure.

¹³ "You shall prepare a sheep in its first year, unblemished, as a daily burnt-offering for HASHEM; you shall make it every morning. * ¹⁴ And you shall bring a meal-offering with it every morning, a sixth of an ephah, a third of a hin of oil with which to mix the flour; it is a meal-offering to HASHEM. As an eternal portion [to be offered] continually, ¹⁵ they shall make the sheep and the meal-offering and the oil every morning as a continual burnt-offering. * "

Prince's inheritance ¹⁶ Thus said the Lord HASHEM/ELOHIM: "If the prince makes a gift* to one of his sons, since it is his inheritance that will belong to his sons, it is their possession by inheritance. ¹⁷ But if he makes a gift from his inheritance to any of his servants, it shall remain his until the Jubilee Year; then it shall revert to the prince; His inheritance shall be only for his sons. ¹⁸ The prince may not take from the inheritance of the people to extort their possession from them; he shall bequeath to his sons from his own possession, so that My people will not be scattered, each man from his possession."

Kohanim's chambers ¹⁹ Then he brought me through the passage that was at the side of the [western] gate, to the sacred chambers of the Kohanim that faced northward, and, behold, there was a place at its western ends. ²⁰ He said to me, "This is the place where the Kohanim shall cook the guilt-offering and the sin-offering, and where they shall bake the meal-offering, so as not to bring [them] into the outer courtyard to mingle with the people."

Enclosures ²¹ Then he brought me out into the outer courtyard and led me past the four corners of the courtyard, and, behold, an enclosure at one corner of the courtyard [and] an enclosure at the other end of the courtyard. ²² At the four corners of the courtyard were open enclosures, forty [cubits] in length and thirty [cubits] in width; there was one measurement for the four of them situated in the corners.

כג וְטוּר סָבִיב בָּהֶם סָבִיב סָבִיב לְאַרְבַּעְתָּם וּמְבַשְּׁלוֹת עָשׂוּי מִתַּחַת הַטִּירוֹת

כד סָבִיב: וַיֹּאמֶר אֵלַי אֵלֶּה בֵּית הַמְבַשְּׁלִים אֲשֶׁר יְבַשְּׁלוּ־שָׁם מְשָׁרְתֵי הַבַּיִת

מז א אֶת־זֶבַח הָעָם: וַיְשִׁבֵנִי אֶל־פֶּתַח הַבַּיִת וְהִנֵּה־מַיִם יֹצְאִים מִתַּחַת מִפְתַּן הַבַּיִת קָדִימָה כִּי־פְנֵי הַבַּיִת קָדִים וְהַמַּיִם יֹרְדִים מִתַּחַת מִכֶּתֶף הַבַּיִת

ב הַיְמָנִית מִנֶּגֶב לַמִּזְבֵּחַ: וַיּוֹצִאֵנִי דֶּרֶךְ־שַׁעַר צָפוֹנָה וַיְסִבֵּנִי דֶּרֶךְ חוּץ אֶל־ שַׁעַר הַחוּץ דֶּרֶךְ הַפּוֹנֶה קָדִים וְהִנֵּה־מַיִם מְפַכִּים מִן־הַכָּתֵף הַיְמָנִית:

ג בְּצֵאת־הָאִישׁ קָדִים וְקָו בְּיָדוֹ וַיָּמָד אֶלֶף בָּאַמָּה וַיַּעֲבִרֵנִי בַמַּיִם מֵי

ד אָפְסָיִם: וַיָּמָד אֶלֶף וַיַּעֲבִרֵנִי בַמַּיִם מַיִם בִּרְכָּיִם וַיָּמָד אֶלֶף וַיַּעֲבִרֵנִי מֵי

ה מָתְנָיִם: וַיָּמָד אֶלֶף נַחַל אֲשֶׁר לֹא־אוּכַל לַעֲבֹר כִּי־גָאוּ הַמַּיִם מֵי שָׂחוּ

ו נַחַל אֲשֶׁר לֹא־יֵעָבֵר: וַיֹּאמֶר אֵלַי הֲרָאִיתָ בֶן־אָדָם וַיּוֹלִכֵנִי וַיְשִׁבֵנִי שְׂפַת

ז-ח הַנָּחַל: בְּשׁוּבֵנִי וְהִנֵּה אֶל־שְׂפַת הַנַּחַל עֵץ רַב מְאֹד מִזֶּה וּמִזֶּה: וַיֹּאמֶר אֵלַי הַמַּיִם הָאֵלֶּה יוֹצְאִים אֶל־הַגְּלִילָה הַקַּדְמוֹנָה וְיָרְדוּ עַל־הָעֲרָבָה וּבָאוּ

ט הַיָּמָּה אֶל־הַיָּמָּה הַמּוּצָאִים וְנִרְפְּאוּ הַמָּיִם: וְהָיָה כָל־נֶפֶשׁ חַיָּה ‖ אֲשֶׁר־ יִשְׁרֹץ אֶל כָּל אֲשֶׁר יָבוֹא שָׁם נַחֲלַיִם יִחְיֶה וְהָיָה הַדָּגָה רַבָּה מְאֹד כִּי בָאוּ

י שָׁמָּה הַמַּיִם הָאֵלֶּה וְיֵרָפְאוּ וָחָי כֹּל אֲשֶׁר־יָבוֹא שָׁמָּה הַנָּחַל: וְהָיָה יעמדו [°עָמְדוּ ק] עָלָיו דַּוָּגִים מֵעֵין גֶּדִי וְעַד־עֵין עֶגְלַיִם מִשְׁטוֹחַ

יא לַחֲרָמִים יִהְיוּ לְמִינָה תִּהְיֶה דְגָתָם כִּדְגַת הַיָּם הַגָּדוֹל רַבָּה מְאֹד: °בצאתו [בִּצֹּאתָיו ק]

יב וּגְבָאָיו וְלֹא יֵרָפְאוּ לְמֶלַח נִתָּנוּ: וְעַל־הַנַּחַל יַעֲלֶה עַל־ שְׂפָתוֹ מִזֶּה ‖ וּמִזֶּה ‖ כָּל־עֵץ־מַאֲכָל לֹא־יִבּוֹל עָלֵהוּ וְלֹא־יִתֹּם פִּרְיוֹ לָחֳדָשָׁיו יְבַכֵּר כִּי מֵימָיו מִן־הַמִּקְדָּשׁ הֵמָּה יוֹצְאִים °והיו [וְהָיָה ק] פִרְיוֹ

יג לְמַאֲכָל וְעָלֵהוּ לִתְרוּפָה: כֹּה אָמַר אֲדֹנָי יֱהֹוִה גֵּה גְבוּל אֲשֶׁר

יד תִּתְנַחֲלוּ אֶת־הָאָרֶץ לִשְׁנֵי עָשָׂר שִׁבְטֵי יִשְׂרָאֵל יוֹסֵף חֲבָלִים: וּנְחַלְתֶּם אוֹתָהּ אִישׁ כְּאָחִיו אֲשֶׁר נָשָׂאתִי אֶת־יָדִי לְתִתָּהּ לַאֲבֹתֵיכֶם וְנָפְלָה הָאָרֶץ

טו הַזֹּאת לָכֶם בְּנַחֲלָה: וְזֶה גְּבוּל הָאָרֶץ לִפְאַת צָפוֹנָה מִן־הַיָּם הַגָּדוֹל הַדֶּרֶךְ

טז חֶתְלֹן לְבוֹא צְדָדָה: חֲמָת ‖ בֵּרוֹתָה סִבְרַיִם אֲשֶׁר בֵּין־גְּבוּל דַּמֶּשֶׂק וּבֵין

יז גְּבוּל חֲמָת חָצֵר הַתִּיכוֹן אֲשֶׁר אֶל־גְּבוּל חַוְרָן: וְהָיָה גְבוּל מִן־הַיָּם חֲצַר עֵינוֹן גְּבוּל דַּמֶּשֶׂק וְצָפוֹן ‖ צָפוֹנָה וּגְבוּל חֲמָת וְאֵת פְּאַת צָפוֹן: וּפְאַת

יח קָדִים מִבֵּין חַוְרָן וּמִבֵּין־דַּמֶּשֶׂק וּמִבֵּין הַגִּלְעָד וּמִבֵּין אֶרֶץ יִשְׂרָאֵל הַיַּרְדֵּן

יט מִגְּבוּל עַל־הַיָּם הַקַּדְמוֹנִי תָּמֹדּוּ וְאֵת פְּאַת קָדִימָה: וּפְאַת נֶגֶב תֵּימָנָה מִתָּמָר עַד־מֵי מְרִיבוֹת קָדֵשׁ נַחֲלָה אֶל־הַיָּם הַגָּדוֹל וְאֵת פְּאַת־תֵּימָנָה

כ נֶגְבָּה: וּפְאַת־יָם הַיָּם הַגָּדוֹל מִגְּבוּל עַד־נֹכַח לְבוֹא חֲמָת זֹאת פְּאַת־יָם:

46:23. The masonry functioned as stoves, and fires were lit under them.

²³ *There was a row [of masonry protruding] all around for the four of them,* * *and hearths were made beneath these rows all around.* ²⁴ *He said to me, "These are the cooking places where the Temple ministers shall cook the sacrifice of the people."*

47

Water under the threshold

¹ T*hen he returned me to the entrance of the Temple and water was emerging from under the threshold of the Temple, [going] eastward — for the House faced eastward. The water ran down from under the right side of the Temple, south of the Altar.* ² *Then he took me out through the northern gate and led me around the outside to the outer gate by the way [of the gate] that faced east, and there was water trickling out from the right side.* ³ *As the man left to the east with a measuring rod in his hand, he measured one thousand cubits and led me across the water, ankle-deep water;* ⁴ *he measured [another] thousand and led me across the water, knee-deep water; he measured [another] thousand and led me across waist-deep water.* ⁵ *He measured [another] thousand, [and it became] a stream that I could not cross, for the water had swollen into water for swimming, a stream that could not be crossed!*

Streams from the Temple

⁶ *He said to me, "Have you seen, O Son of Man?" He then led me and returned me to the bank of the stream.* ⁷ *Upon my return, behold, along the bank of the stream were very many trees on one side and on the other.* ⁸ *He said to me, "These waters go out to the eastern region; they descend to the Arabah and go to the Sea, to the spreading sea, and the water will become sweetened.* ⁹ *And it will be that any living thing that will swarm, wherever these streams flow, will live, and the fish will be exceedingly abundant; for these waters will come there and they will become sweetened, so that [the fish] may live, wherever the stream comes.* ¹⁰ *It will happen that fisherman will stand by it, from En-gedi to En-eglaim; they will be spreading places for nets. Their fish will be of as many species as the fish of the Great Sea, exceedingly abundant.* ¹¹ *But its swamps and pools will not become sweetened; they will be set aside to provide salt.* ¹² *Along the stream will grow every [species of] food tree on its banks on one side and the other, its leaf will not wither and its fruit will not fail; every month it will yield new fruit. For its waters will go forth from the Sanctuary, so its fruit will be for food and its leaves for healing."*

Portions of the tribes

¹³ *Thus said the Lord HASHEM/ELOHIM: "This is the boundary by which you shall allot the land for inheritance to the twelve tribes of Israel, two portions for Joseph.* ¹⁴ *You shall inherit [the land], each tribe equal to his brother, about which I raised My hand to give it to your forefathers; this land shall become yours as an inheritance.*

¹⁵ *"This is the boundary of the land. On the north side: From the Great Sea, by way of Hethlon, to the approach to Zedad,* ¹⁶ *Hamath, Berothah, and Sibraim which is between the border of Damascus and the border of Hamath, [and] Hazer-hatticon which is on the border of Hauran.* ¹⁷ *The border shall thus go from the Sea to Hazar-enon by the border of Damascus, with the northern [border] extending northward to the border of Hamath. [This is] the northern side.*

¹⁸ *"The eastern side: Between Hauran and Damascus, between Gilead and the Land of Israel, the Jordan, you shall measure from the [northern] border to the Eastern Sea. [This is] the eastern side.*

¹⁹ *"The southern side southward: From Tamar until the waters of Meriboth-kadesh, to the stream, to the Great Sea. [This is] the southern side southward.*

²⁰ *"And the western side: The Great Sea, from the [southern] border until opposite the approach to Hamath. This is the western side.*

כא-כב　וְחִלַּקְתֶּ֞ם אֶת־הָאָ֧רֶץ הַזֹּ֛את לָכֶ֖ם לְשִׁבְטֵ֣י יִשְׂרָאֵ֑ל וְהָיָ֗ה תַּפִּ֣לוּ אוֹתָ֜הּ
בְּנַחֲלָ֗ה לָכֶ֤ם וּלְהַגֵּרִים֙ הַגָּרִ֣ים בְּתוֹכְכֶ֔ם אֲשֶׁר־הוֹלִ֥דוּ בָנִ֖ים בְּתוֹכְכֶ֑ם
וְהָי֣וּ לָכֶ֗ם כְּאֶזְרָח֙ בִּבְנֵ֣י יִשְׂרָאֵ֔ל אִתְּכֶם֙ יִפְּל֣וּ בְנַחֲלָ֔ה בְּת֖וֹךְ שִׁבְטֵ֥י

כג　יִשְׂרָאֵֽל׃ וְהָיָ֣ה בַשֵּׁ֔בֶט אֲשֶׁר־גָּ֥ר הַגֵּ֖ר אִתּ֑וֹ שָׁ֚ם תִּתְּנ֣וּ נַחֲלָת֔וֹ נְאֻ֖ם אֲדֹנָ֥י

מח　א　יֱהֹוִֽה׃　וְאֵ֖לֶּה שְׁמ֣וֹת הַשְּׁבָטִ֑ים מִקְצֵ֣ה צָפ֡וֹנָה אֶל־יַ֣ד דֶּֽרֶךְ־
חֶתְלֹ֣ן ׀ לְֽבוֹא־חֲמָ֡ת חֲצַ֣ר עֵינָ֩ן֩ גְּב֨וּל דַּמֶּ֤שֶׂק צָפ֙וֹנָה֙ אֶל־יַ֣ד חֲמָ֔ת וְהָיוּ־ל֧וֹ

ב　פְאַת־קָדִ֛ים הַיָּ֖ם דָּ֣ן אֶחָֽד׃ וְעַ֣ל ׀ גְּב֣וּל דָּ֗ן מִפְּאַ֥ת קָדִ֛ים עַד־פְּאַת־יָ֖מָּה אָשֵׁ֥ר

ג-ד　אֶחָֽד׃ וְעַ֣ל ׀ גְּב֣וּל אָשֵׁ֔ר מִפְּאַ֥ת קָדִ֖ימָה וְעַד־פְּאַת־יָ֑מָּה נַפְתָּלִ֖י אֶחָֽד׃ וְעַ֣ל ׀

ה　גְּב֣וּל נַפְתָּלִ֔י מִפְּאַ֥ת קָדִ֖מָה עַד־פְּאַת־יָ֑מָּה מְנַשֶּׁ֖ה אֶחָֽד׃ וְעַ֖ל ׀ גְּב֣וּל מְנַשֶּׁ֑ה

ו　מִפְּאַ֥ת קָדִ֖מָה עַד־פְּאַת־יָ֑מָּה אֶפְרַ֖יִם אֶחָֽד׃ וְעַ֣ל ׀ גְּב֣וּל אֶפְרַ֔יִם מִפְּאַ֥ת

ז　קָדִ֖ים וְעַד־פְּאַת־יָ֑מָּה רְאוּבֵ֖ן אֶחָֽד׃ וְעַ֣ל ׀ גְּב֣וּל רְאוּבֵ֔ן מִפְּאַ֥ת קָדִ֖ים עַד־

ח　פְּאַת־יָ֑מָּה יְהוּדָ֖ה אֶחָֽד׃ וְעַל֙ גְּב֣וּל יְהוּדָ֔ה מִפְּאַ֥ת קָדִ֖ים עַד־פְּאַת־יָ֑מָּה
תִּהְיֶ֣ה הַתְּרוּמָ֣ה אֲשֶׁר־תָּרִ֡ימוּ חֲמִשָּׁה֩ וְעֶשְׂרִ֨ים אֶ֜לֶף רֹ֗חַב וְאֹ֜רֶךְ כְּאַחַ֤ד

ט　הַחֲלָקִים֙ מִפְּאַ֣ת קָדִ֔ימָה עַד־פְּאַת־יָ֑מָּה וְהָיָ֥ה הַמִּקְדָּ֖שׁ בְּתוֹכֽוֹ׃ הַתְּרוּמָ֕ה
אֲשֶׁ֥ר תָּרִ֖ימוּ לַיהֹוָ֑ה אֹ֗רֶךְ חֲמִשָּׁ֤ה וְעֶשְׂרִים֙ אֶ֔לֶף וְרֹ֖חַב עֲשֶׂ֥רֶת אֲלָפִֽים׃

י*　וּ֠לְאֵ֠לֶּה תִּהְיֶ֞ה תְּרֽוּמַת־הַקֹּ֣דֶשׁ לַכֹּהֲנִ֗ים צָפ֜וֹנָה חֲמִשָּׁ֧ה וְעֶשְׂרִ֣ים אֶ֗לֶף
וְיָ֙מָּה֙ רֹ֣חַב עֲשֶׂ֣רֶת אֲלָפִ֔ים וְקָדִ֗ימָה רֹ֚חַב עֲשֶׂ֣רֶת אֲלָפִ֔ים וְנֶ֙גְבָּה֙ אֹ֔רֶךְ

יא　חֲמִשָּׁ֥ה וְעֶשְׂרִ֖ים אָ֑לֶף וְהָיָ֥ה מִקְדַּשׁ־יְהֹוָ֖ה בְּתוֹכֽוֹ׃ לַכֹּהֲנִ֤ים הַֽמְקֻדָּשׁ֙ מִבְּנֵ֣י
צָד֔וֹק אֲשֶׁ֥ר שָׁמְר֖וּ מִשְׁמַרְתִּ֑י אֲשֶׁ֣ר לֹֽא־תָעוּ֗ בִּתְעוֹת֙ בְּנֵ֣י יִשְׂרָאֵ֔ל כַּאֲשֶׁ֥ר

יב　תָּע֖וּ הַלְוִיִּֽם׃ וְהָ֨יְתָ֤ה לָהֶם֙ תְּרֽוּמִיָּ֔ה מִתְּרוּמַ֖ת הָאָ֑רֶץ קֹ֥דֶשׁ קָדָשִׁ֖ים אֶל־

יג　גְּב֣וּל הַלְוִיִּֽם׃ וְהַלְוִיִּ֗ם לְעֻמַּת֙ גְּב֣וּל הַכֹּהֲנִ֔ים חֲמִשָּׁ֥ה וְעֶשְׂרִ֛ים אֶ֖לֶף אֹ֑רֶךְ
וְרֹ֖חַב עֲשֶׂ֣רֶת אֲלָפִ֑ים כָּל־אֹ֗רֶךְ חֲמִשָּׁ֤ה וְעֶשְׂרִים֙ אֶ֔לֶף וְרֹ֖חַב עֲשֶׂ֥רֶת

יד　אֲלָפִֽים׃ וְלֹא־יִמְכְּר֣וּ מִמֶּ֗נּוּ וְלֹ֥א יָמֵ֛ר וְלֹ֥א °יַעֲבוֹר [°יַעֲבִ֖יר ק] רֵאשִׁ֣ית

טו　הָאָ֑רֶץ כִּי־קֹ֖דֶשׁ לַיהֹוָֽה׃ וַחֲמֵ֨שֶׁת אֲלָפִ֜ים הַנּוֹתָ֣ר בָּרֹ֗חַב עַל־פְּנֵ֞י חֲמִשָּׁ֤ה
וְעֶשְׂרִים֙ אֶ֔לֶף חֹֽל־ה֣וּא לָעִ֔יר לְמוֹשָׁ֖ב וּלְמִגְרָ֑שׁ וְהָיְתָ֥ה הָעִ֖יר °בְּתוֹכֹה

טז　[°בְּתוֹכֽוֹ ק]׃ וְאֵ֖לֶּה מִדּוֹתֶ֑יהָ פְּאַ֤ת צָפוֹן֙ חֲמֵ֣שׁ מֵא֣וֹת וְאַרְבַּ֣עַת אֲלָפִ֔ים
וּפְאַת־נֶ֤גֶב חֲמֵ֣שׁ °חמש [°וַלֹא ק] מֵאוֹת֙ וְאַרְבַּ֣עַת אֲלָפִ֔ים וּמִפְּאַ֣ת קָדִ֗ים
חֲמֵ֤שׁ מֵאוֹת֙ וְאַרְבַּ֣עַת אֲלָפִ֔ים וּפְאַת־יָ֗מָּה חֲמֵ֥שׁ מֵא֖וֹת וְאַרְבַּ֥עַת אֲלָפִֽים׃

יז　וְהָיָ֣ה מִגְרָשׁ֮ לָעִיר֒ צָפ֙וֹנָה֙ חֲמִשִּׁ֣ים וּמָאתַ֔יִם וְנֶ֖גְבָּה חֲמִשִּׁ֣ים וּמָאתָ֑יִם

יח　וְקָדִ֙ימָה֙ חֲמִשִּׁ֣ים וּמָאתַ֔יִם וְיָ֖מָּה חֲמִשִּׁ֣ים וּמָאתָֽיִם׃ וְהַנּוֹתָ֨ר בָּאֹ֜רֶךְ לְעֻמַּ֣ת ׀
תְּרוּמַ֣ת הַקֹּ֗דֶשׁ עֲשֶׂ֤רֶת אֲלָפִים֙ קָדִ֔ימָה וַעֲשֶׂ֤רֶת אֲלָפִים֙ יָ֔מָּה וְהָיָ֞ה לְעֻמַּ֣ת
תְּרוּמַ֣ת הַקֹּ֗דֶשׁ וְהָיְתָ֤ה °תְבוּאָתֹה [°תְבוּאָתֹ֙ו ק] לְלֶ֖חֶם לְעֹבְדֵ֥י הָעִֽיר׃

יט-כ　וְהָעֹבֵ֖ד הָעִ֑יר יַעַבְד֕וּהוּ מִכֹּ֖ל שִׁבְטֵ֥י יִשְׂרָאֵֽל׃ כָּל־הַתְּרוּמָ֗ה חֲמִשָּׁ֤ה וְעֶשְׂרִים֙
אֶ֔לֶף בַּחֲמִשָּׁ֥ה וְעֶשְׂרִ֖ים אָ֑לֶף רְבִיעִ֗ית תָּרִ֙ימוּ֙ אֶת־תְּרוּמַ֣ת הַקֹּ֔דֶשׁ אֶל־

* הקורא יטעים
האלף גרש
קודם התלישא

²¹ You shall divide this land among yourselves, according to the tribes of Israel. ²² It shall be that you shall allot it as an inheritance, for yourselves and for the strangers who dwell among you, who will bear children in your midst; they shall be for you like the natives among the Children of Israel; they are to be allotted an inheritance with you, among the tribes of Israel. ²³ It shall be that the tribe within which the stranger has settled, there shall you allot his inheritance — the word of the Lord HASHEM/ELOHIM."

48

Names of the tribes

¹ "These are the names of the tribes:
At the northern end, near the way to Hethlon to the approach of Hamath to Hazar-enan, to the northern border of Damascus near Hamath, this shall be for him [from] the eastern side to the west — Dan, one [portion]. ² Next to Dan's border, from the eastern side to the western side — Asher, one [portion]. ³ Next to Asher's border, from the eastern side to the western side — Naphtali, one [portion]. ⁴ Next to Naphtali's border, from the eastern side to the western side — Manasseh, one [portion]. ⁵ Next to Manasseh's border, from the eastern side to the western side — Ephraim, one [portion]. ⁶ Next to Ephraim's border, from the eastern side to the western side — Reuben, one [portion]. ⁷ Next to Reuben's border, from the eastern side to the western side — Judah, one [portion].

⁸ "Next to Judah's border, from the eastern side to the western side, shall be the [sacred] portion* that you shall set aside, twenty-five thousand wide, with a length equal to one of the other portions from the eastern side to the western side; the Sanctuary shall be within it. ⁹ The [sacred] portion that you set aside for HASHEM shall have a length of twenty-five thousand long and a width of ten thousand. ¹⁰ This shall be the sacred portion for the Kohanim, twenty-five thousand on the north, ten thousand wide on the west, ten thousand in width on the east and twenty-five thousand long on the south; the Sanctuary of HASHEM shall

Kohanim and Levites

be within it. ¹¹ This hallowed place shall belong to the Kohanim of the sons of Zadok, who safeguarded My charge, who did not stray when the Children of Israel strayed, as the Levites had strayed. ¹² It shall be a separated portion for them, out of the [sacred] portion of the land, holy of holies, next to the border of the Levites. ¹³ Now for the Levites: opposite the border of the Kohanim, twenty-five thousand long and ten thousand wide, the entire length being twenty-five thousand and the width ten thousand. ¹⁴ They shall not sell any of it, nor exchange nor transfer this choicest of the land, for it is sacred to HASHEM. ¹⁵ The remaining five thousand in width by twenty-five thousand in length shall be secular, for the city, for settlement and for open space; the city shall be within it. ¹⁶ These are its dimensions: the northern side four thousand five hundred, the southern side four thousand five hundred, the eastern side four thousand five hundred, and the western side four thousand five hundred. ¹⁷ And the city shall have an open space, two hundred and fifty to the north; two hundred and fifty to the south; two hundred and fifty to the east and two hundred and fifty to the west. ¹⁸ The remainder of the [twenty-five thousand] length alongside the sacred portion — ten thousand towards the east, and ten thousand towards the west, which runs alongside the sacred portion — its produce shall be food for those that serve the city. * ¹⁹ The worker of the city shall serve it on behalf of all the tribes of Israel. ²⁰ The entire [sacred] portion — twenty-five thousand by twenty-five thousand, square — you shall set aside as the sacred portion and

---

48:8. See 45:1-4.   **48:18.** I.e., the city's residents, who work at its upkeep.

כא אֲחֻזַּ֣ת הָעִ֑יר: וְהַנּוֹתָ֣ר לַנָּשִׂ֣יא מִזֶּ֣ה ׀ וּמִזֶּ֣ה ׀ לִתְרֽוּמַת־הַקֹּ֣דֶשׁ וְלַאֲחֻזַּ֣ת הָעִ֗יר אֶל־פְּנֵ֞י חֲמִשָּׁ֤ה וְעֶשְׂרִים֙ אֶ֔לֶף ׀ תְּרוּמָה֙ עַד־גְּב֣וּל קָדִ֔ימָה וְיָ֡מָּה עַל־פְּנֵי֩ חֲמִשָּׁ֨ה וְעֶשְׂרִ֥ים אֶ֙לֶף֙ עַל־גְּב֣וּל יָ֔מָּה לְעֻמַּ֥ת חֲלָקִ֖ים לַנָּשִׂ֑יא

כב וְהָ֥יְתָה תְּרוּמַ֖ת הַקֹּ֑דֶשׁ וּמִקְדַּ֤שׁ הַבַּ֙יִת֙ בְּתוֹכֹ֔ה [בְּתוֹכ֖וֹ ק]: וּמֵאֲחֻזַּ֣ת הַלְוִיִּ֗ם וּמֵאֲחֻזַּ֤ת הָעִיר֙ בְּת֗וֹךְ אֲשֶׁ֤ר לַנָּשִׂיא֙ יִֽהְיֶ֔ה בֵּ֣ין ׀ גְּב֣וּל יְהוּדָ֗ה וּבֵין֙

כג גְּב֣וּל בִּנְיָמִ֔ן לַנָּשִׂ֖יא יִֽהְיֶֽה: וְיֶ֖תֶר הַשְּׁבָטִ֑ים מִפְּאַ֤ת קָדִ֙ימָה֙ עַד־פְּאַת־יָ֔מָּה

כד בִּנְיָמִ֖ן אֶחָֽד: וְעַ֣ל ׀ גְּב֣וּל בִּנְיָמִ֗ן מִפְּאַ֤ת קָדִ֙ימָה֙ עַד־פְּאַת־יָ֔מָּה שִׁמְע֖וֹן

כה אֶחָֽד: וְעַ֣ל ׀ גְּב֣וּל שִׁמְע֗וֹן מִפְּאַ֤ת קָדִ֙ימָה֙ עַד־פְּאַת־יָ֔מָּה יִשָּׂשכָ֖ר אֶחָֽד:

כו-כז וְעַ֣ל ׀ גְּב֣וּל יִשָּׂשכָ֗ר מִפְּאַ֤ת קָדִ֙ימָה֙ עַד־פְּאַת־יָ֔מָּה זְבוּלֻ֖ן אֶחָֽד: וְעַ֣ל ׀

כח גְּב֣וּל זְבוּלֻ֗ן מִפְּאַ֤ת קָדִ֙מָה֙ עַד־פְּאַת־יָ֔מָּה גָּ֖ד אֶחָֽד: וְעַל֙ גְּב֣וּל גָּ֔ד אֶל־ פְּאַ֖ת נֶ֣גֶב תֵּימָ֑נָה וְהָיָ֨ה גְב֜וּל מִתָּמָ֗ר מֵ֚י מְרִיבַ֣ת קָדֵ֔שׁ נַחֲלָ֖ה עַל־הַיָּ֥ם

כט הַגָּדֽוֹל: זֹ֣את הָאָ֗רֶץ אֲשֶׁר־תַּפִּ֧ילוּ מִנַּחֲלָ֛ה לְשִׁבְטֵ֥י יִשְׂרָאֵ֖ל וְאֵ֣לֶּה

ל מַחְלְקוֹתָ֑ם נְאֻ֖ם אֲדֹנָ֥י יֱהֹוִֽה: וְאֵ֖לֶּה תּוֹצְאֹ֣ת הָעִ֑יר מִפְּאַ֣ת

לא צָפ֗וֹן חֲמֵ֥שׁ מֵא֛וֹת וְאַרְבַּ֥עַת אֲלָפִ֖ים מִדָּֽה: וְשַׁעֲרֵ֣י הָעִ֗יר עַל־שְׁמוֹת֙ שִׁבְטֵ֣י יִשְׂרָאֵ֔ל שְׁעָרִ֖ים שְׁלוֹשָׁ֑ה צָפ֜וֹנָה שַׁ֣עַר רְאוּבֵ֣ן אֶחָ֗ד שַׁ֤עַר יְהוּדָה֙

לב אֶחָ֔ד שַׁ֥עַר לֵוִ֖י אֶחָֽד: וְאֶל־פְּאַ֣ת קָדִ֗ימָה חֲמֵ֤שׁ מֵאוֹת֙ וְאַרְבַּ֣עַת אֲלָפִ֔ים וּשְׁעָרִ֖ים שְׁלֹשָׁ֑ה וְשַׁ֣עַר יוֹסֵ֣ף אֶחָ֗ד שַׁ֤עַר בִּנְיָמִן֙ אֶחָ֔ד שַׁ֥עַר דָּ֖ן אֶחָֽד:

לג וּפְאַת־נֶ֙גְבָּה֙ חֲמֵ֥שׁ מֵא֛וֹת וְאַרְבַּ֥עַת אֲלָפִ֖ים מִדָּ֑ה וּשְׁעָרִ֣ים שְׁלֹשָׁ֑ה שַׁ֣עַר שִׁמְע֞וֹן אֶחָ֗ד שַׁ֤עַר יִשָּׂשכָר֙ אֶחָ֔ד שַׁ֥עַר זְבוּלֻ֖ן אֶחָֽד: פְּאַת־יָ֙מָּה֙ חֲמֵ֣שׁ

לד-לה מֵא֔וֹת וְאַרְבַּ֖עַת אֲלָפִ֑ים שַׁעֲרֵיהֶ֣ם שְׁלֹשָׁ֑ה שַׁ֣עַר גָּ֗ד אֶחָ֗ד שַׁ֤עַר אָשֵׁר֙ אֶחָ֔ד שַׁ֥עַר נַפְתָּלִ֖י אֶחָֽד: סָבִ֕יב שְׁמֹנָ֥ה עָשָׂ֖ר אָ֑לֶף וְשֵׁם־הָעִ֛יר מִיּ֖וֹם יְהֹוָ֥ה ׀ שָֽׁמָּה:

סכום הפסוקים של ספר יחזקאל אלף ומאתים ושבעים ושלשה.
וסימנו כאיל תערג על אפיקי **מים כן נפשי תערג** אליך אלקים.

48:28. The Nile (*Rashi* to *Joshua* 13:3); or, Wadi El Arish (*Kaftor VaFerach*).

the property of the city. [21] And the remaining area [of the strip] shall be for the prince, on the one side and on the other of the sacred portion and the property of the city; alongside the twenty-five thousand of the [sacred] portion to the eastern border, and westward, along the twenty-five thousand to the western border — parallel to the [tribal] portions, shall be for the prince; the sacred portion and the Sanctuary of the Temple shall be within it. [22] And the property of the Levites and the property of the city shall be within that which belongs to the prince; between the border of Judah and the border of Benjamin shall be for the prince.

The other tribes [23] "As for the rest of the tribes: from the eastern side to the western side — Benjamin, one [portion]. [24] Next to Benjamin's border, from the eastern side to the western side — Simeon, one [portion]. [25] Next to Simeon's border, from the eastern side to the western side — Issachar, one [portion]. [26] Next to Issachar's border, from the eastern side to the western side — Zebulun, one [portion]. [27] Next to Zebulun's border from the eastern side to the western side — Gad, one [portion]. [28] Along Gad's border, on its southern side southward, the boundary shall be from Tamar to the waters of Meribath-kadesh, to the Brook [of Egypt]* to the Great Sea.

[29] "This is the land that you shall allot as an inheritance to the tribes of Israel and these are their divisions — the word of the Lord HASHEM/ELOHIM.

The Holy City [30] "These are the exits of the city: On the northern side, a measure of four thousand five hundred, [31] the gates of the city shall be [called] by the names of the tribes of Israel, three gates to the north: the gate of Reuben, one; the gate of Judah, one; the gate of Levi, one. [32] And the eastern side, [a measure] of four thousand five hundred and three gates: the gate of Joseph, one; the gate of Benjamin, one; the gate of Dan, one. [33] And the southern side, a measure four thousand five hundred and three gates: the gate of Simeon, one; the gate of Issachar, one; the gate of Zebulun, one. [34] The western side, [a measure of] four thousand five hundred, and their three gates: the gate of Gad, one; the gate of Asher, one; the gate of Naphtali, one.

[35] "The circumference [of the city] is thus eighteen thousand. And the name of the city from that day shall be "HASHEM-Is-There!' "

The Twelve Prophets תרי עשר

*T*his Book contains the words of men whose prophecies spanned over three hundred and fifty years (beginning 700 B.C.E.), from the middle of the First Temple era to the the the early years of the Second Temple. Since the prophecies of these disparate individuals were comparatively brief — some only a single chapter — they were collected in one Book, so that they would not be lost (Bava Basra 14b). As Rashi explains, seeing that the era of prophecy was ending and that they would be the last prophets, Haggai, Zechariah, and Malachi wrote down their own prophecies and appended the other small books to them.

We should not be deceived by the brevity of these books, for, like all prophecies recorded in Scripture, they have a message for every generation. Non-Jewish Bibles refer to The Twelve Prophets as "The Minor Prophets," which is not only degrading, but a gross misnomer. In fact, Hosea, a contemporary of Isaiah, was, according to the Sages, the greatest prophet of his time.

The Book is a panorama of Jewish history. It begins at the time when there were two Jewish kingdoms, and the Ten Tribes of the North seemed to be by far the more powerful. It concludes with the Northern Kingdom in oblivion, and the tribes of the South, primarily Judah and Benjamin, on the way back to their land, to build the Second Temple. The intervening years were a time of strife and disappointment, as prophet after prophet begged and warned, foretold and chastised about the impending doom — all in vain.

The Book of Hosea is perhaps the starkest of the twelve. In admonishing his people, he called them God's "estranged wife." For his harshness, he incurred God's wrath. To demonstrate the eternal truth that Israel remains His Chosen People despite its major shortcomings, God commanded Hosea to undergo one of Scriptures most difficult ordeals, a personal torture that mirrored God's own anguish and loyalty.

Fittingly and inspiringly, The Twelve Prophets ends the era of prophecy with the exhortation:

> Remember the Torah of Moses My servant, which I commanded him at Horeb for all of Israel — [its] decrees and [its] statutes. Behold, I send you Elijah the prophet before the coming of the great and awesome day of HASHEM. And he will turn back [to God] the hearts of fathers with [their] sons and the hearts of sons with their fathers …

א

א דְּבַר־יהוה ׀ אֲשֶׁר הָיָה אֶל־הוֹשֵׁעַ בֶּן־בְּאֵרִי בִּימֵי עֻזִּיָּה יוֹתָם אָחָז יְחִזְקִיָּה
ב מַלְכֵי יְהוּדָה וּבִימֵי יָרׇבְעָם בֶּן־יוֹאָשׁ מֶלֶךְ יִשְׂרָאֵל: תְּחִלַּת דִּבֶּר־יהוה
בְּהוֹשֵׁעַ וַיֹּאמֶר יהוה אֶל־הוֹשֵׁעַ לֵךְ קַח־לְךָ אֵשֶׁת זְנוּנִים וְיַלְדֵי זְנוּנִים כִּי־
ג זָנֹה תִזְנֶה הָאָרֶץ מֵאַחֲרֵי יהוה: וַיֵּלֶךְ וַיִּקַּח אֶת־גֹּמֶר בַּת־דִּבְלָיִם וַתַּהַר
ד וַתֵּלֶד־לוֹ בֵּן: וַיֹּאמֶר יהוה אֵלָיו קְרָא שְׁמוֹ יִזְרְעֶאל כִּי־עוֹד מְעַט וּפָקַדְתִּי
ה אֶת־דְּמֵי יִזְרְעֶאל עַל־בֵּית יֵהוּא וְהִשְׁבַּתִּי מַמְלְכוּת בֵּית יִשְׂרָאֵל: וְהָיָה
ו בַּיּוֹם הַהוּא וְשָׁבַרְתִּי אֶת־קֶשֶׁת יִשְׂרָאֵל בְּעֵמֶק יִזְרְעֶאל: וַתַּהַר עוֹד וַתֵּלֶד
בַּת וַיֹּאמֶר לוֹ קְרָא שְׁמָהּ לֹא רֻחָמָה כִּי לֹא אוֹסִיף עוֹד אֲרַחֵם אֶת־בֵּית
ז יִשְׂרָאֵל כִּי־נָשֹׂא אֶשָּׂא לָהֶם: וְאֶת־בֵּית יְהוּדָה אֲרַחֵם וְהוֹשַׁעְתִּים בַּיהוה
אֱלֹהֵיהֶם וְלֹא אוֹשִׁיעֵם בְּקֶשֶׁת וּבְחֶרֶב וּבְמִלְחָמָה בְּסוּסִים וּבְפָרָשִׁים:
ח-ט וַתִּגְמֹל אֶת־לֹא רֻחָמָה וַתַּהַר וַתֵּלֶד בֵּן: וַיֹּאמֶר קְרָא שְׁמוֹ לֹא עַמִּי כִּי

ב

אַתֶּם לֹא עַמִּי וְאָנֹכִי לֹא־אֶהְיֶה לָכֶם: ◀ וְהָיָה מִסְפַּר בְּנֵי־

HAFTARAS
BAMIDBAR
2:1-22

יִשְׂרָאֵל כְּחוֹל הַיָּם אֲשֶׁר לֹא־יִמַּד וְלֹא יִסָּפֵר וְהָיָה בִּמְקוֹם אֲשֶׁר־יֵאָמֵר
ב לָהֶם לֹא־עַמִּי אַתֶּם יֵאָמֵר לָהֶם בְּנֵי אֵל־חָי: וְנִקְבְּצוּ בְּנֵי־יְהוּדָה וּבְנֵי־
יִשְׂרָאֵל יַחְדָּו וְשָׂמוּ לָהֶם רֹאשׁ אֶחָד וְעָלוּ מִן־הָאָרֶץ כִּי גָדוֹל יוֹם
ג יִזְרְעֶאל: אִמְרוּ לַאֲחֵיכֶם עַמִּי וְלַאֲחוֹתֵיכֶם רֻחָמָה: רִיבוּ בְאִמְּכֶם רִיבוּ
כִּי־הִיא לֹא אִשְׁתִּי וְאָנֹכִי לֹא אִישָׁהּ וְתָסֵר זְנוּנֶיהָ מִפָּנֶיהָ וְנַאֲפוּפֶיהָ מִבֵּין
ד-ה שָׁדֶיהָ: פֶּן־אַפְשִׁיטֶנָּה עֲרֻמָּה וְהִצַּגְתִּיהָ כְּיוֹם הִוָּלְדָהּ וְשַׂמְתִּיהָ כַמִּדְבָּר
ו וְשַׁתִּהָ כְּאֶרֶץ צִיָּה וַהֲמִתִּיהָ בַּצָּמָא: וְאֶת־בָּנֶיהָ לֹא אֲרַחֵם כִּי־בְנֵי זְנוּנִים
ז הֵמָּה: כִּי זָנְתָה אִמָּם הֹבִישָׁה הוֹרָתָם כִּי אָמְרָה אֵלְכָה אַחֲרֵי מְאַהֲבַי נֹתְנֵי
ח לַחְמִי וּמֵימַי צַמְרִי וּפִשְׁתִּי שַׁמְנִי וְשִׁקּוּיָי: לָכֵן הִנְנִי־שָׂךְ אֶת־דַּרְכֵּךְ
ט בַּסִּירִים וְגָדַרְתִּי אֶת־גְּדֵרָהּ וּנְתִיבוֹתֶיהָ לֹא תִמְצָא: וְרִדְּפָה אֶת־מְאַהֲבֶיהָ
וְלֹא־תַשִּׂיג אֹתָם וּבִקְשָׁתַם וְלֹא תִמְצָא וְאָמְרָה אֵלְכָה וְאָשׁוּבָה אֶל־
י אִישִׁי הָרִאשׁוֹן כִּי טוֹב לִי אָז מֵעָתָּה: וְהִיא לֹא יָדְעָה כִּי אָנֹכִי נָתַתִּי
לָהּ הַדָּגָן וְהַתִּירוֹשׁ וְהַיִּצְהָר וְכֶסֶף הִרְבֵּיתִי לָהּ וְזָהָב עָשׂוּ לַבָּעַל:

1:1. Uzziah (also called Azariah) reigned fifty-two years, beginning in the twenty-seventh year of Jeroboam's forty-one-year reign; Jotham and Ahaz each reigned sixteen years; and Hezekiah reigned twenty-nine years. Their histories are recorded in *II Kings* Chs. 15-20 and *II Chronicles* Chs. 26-32. Hosea prophesied for ninety of those years (*Seder Olam*). According to the Talmud (*Pesachim* 87a) he was a greater prophet than any of his contemporaries, which included Isaiah, Amos and Micah. Nevertheless, Hosea's words were not accorded a book of their own, as were the prophecies of Isaiah, Jeremiah, and Ezekiel, because his prophecies were far fewer than theirs (*Bava Basra* 14b).

1:2. This prophecy was to depict Israel's unfaithfulness to God as the equivalent of a harlot's infidelity to her husband. There are two general views among the com-

mentators: Either this command's implementation took place only in the prophetic vision, but not in real life; or, it was an actual command — הוֹרָאַת שָׁעָה, *a ruling for the moment* — by which God overrode the law of the Torah, and the marriage and subsequent births actually took place.

1:4. The name Jezreel has a double meaning. First, as the verse states, it refers to the valley in which Jeroboam's ancestor Jehu spilled considerable blood (see *II Kings* Ch. 10). Although Jehu's killings marked the fulfillment of Elijah's prophecy against the house of Ahab and the destruction of the Baal worship, his motivation was not inspired by a desire to fulfill God's will, rather it was to intensify the calf worship (see 10:5) at Beth-el (Beth-aven) and Dan (*Rashi*). Second, the name Jezreel means "seeded by God" and is a reference to the exile by

1

(See Appendix A, timeline 4)

¹ The word of HASHEM that came to Hosea son of Beeri in the days of Uzziah, Jotham, Ahaz [and] Hezekiah, * the kings of Judah, and in the days of Jeroboam son of Joash, king of Israel.

² The initial speech of HASHEM with Hosea:

A harlot and her children　HASHEM said to Hosea, "Go take unto yourself a wife of harlotry and [beget] children of harlotry. * For the land is straying completely from following HASHEM."
³ So he went and took Gomer daughter of Diblaim, and she conceived and bore him a son. ⁴ HASHEM said to him, "Call his name Jezreel, * for, in a short while, I will avenge the blood of Jezreel upon the house of Jehu, and I will terminate the monarchy of the House of Israel. ⁵ It will happen on that day that I will break the bow of Israel in the Valley of Jezreel."

⁶ She conceived again and bore a daughter, and [God] said to him, "Call her name Lo-ruhamah (Not Pitied); for I will no longer pity the House of Israel, that I should show them forbearance. ⁷ But upon the House of Judah I will have mercy and I will save them through HASHEM their God; * I will not save them with bow, with sword, with warfare, with steeds or with riders."

⁸ She weaned Lo-ruhamah, and she conceived and bore a son. ⁹ [God] said, "Call his name Lo-ammi (Not My People); for you are not My people, and I will not be yours. ¹ Yet the number of the Children of Israel will be like the sand of the sea,

2

Growth and unity　which can neither be measured nor counted; and it will happen that in the place [of their exile] where it was said to them, 'You are not My people,' it will be said to them, 'Children of the living God.' ² The Children of Judah and the Children of Israel will be assembled together, and they will appoint for themselves one head and ascend from the land, for the day of Jezreel is great. * ³ Say to your brothers 'Ammi' (My People) and your sisters 'Ruhamah' (Pitied).

A disloyal wife . . .　⁴ Contend with your mother, * contend; for she is not My wife and I am not her husband; and have her remove her harlotries from her face and her adulteries from between her breasts; ⁵ lest I strip her bare and stand her as on the day she was born, and make her like a wilderness and render her like a parched land and cause her to die of thirst. ⁶ And upon her children I will not have mercy, for they are children of harlotry. ⁷ For their mother has committed harlotry; she who conceived them has shamed herself; for she said, 'I will go after my paramours, those who provide my bread and my water, my wool and my linen, my oil and my drink.' * ⁸ Therefore, behold, I will hedge your way with thorns, and I will hem her in with a fence, and she will not find her paths. ⁹ And she will pursue her paramours, but not reach
. . . returns remorsefully . . .　them; she will seek them, but not find [them]. Then she will say, 'I will go and return to my first husband, for it was better for me then than it is now.' ¹⁰ For she did not realize that it was I who gave her the grain and the wine and the oil; I lavished silver and gold upon her, [but] they used it for the Baal.

---

which Israel will be strewn, like sown seeds, among the hostile nations.

1:7. God intervened to save Jerusalem from being overrun by Sennacherib (see *II Kings* 19:32-35).

2:2. The "day of Jezreel" (1:4-5) will ultimately result in a long exile, after which Israel will leave the lands of their dispersion and ascend to Israel (*Radak*). The name Jezreel also may be rendered "God will gather seed" (*Rashi*).

2:4. After tempering rebuke with words of love and comfort, the prophet returns to castigation and urges the righteous people of Israel to rebuke their "mother," the Congregation of Israel, for she had been unfaithful to God, just as Hosea's wife was unfaithful to him. Such a "wife" cannot expect her "husband" to be loyal.

2:7. Israel attributed its prosperity not to God, but to its false deities (*Radak*), as she is quoted in verse 14.

יא לָכֵ֣ן אָשׁ֗וּב וְלָקַחְתִּ֤י דְגָנִי֙ בְּעִתּ֔וֹ וְתִירוֹשִׁ֖י בְּמֽוֹעֲד֑וֹ וְהִצַּלְתִּי֙ צַמְרִ֣י וּפִשְׁתִּ֔י
לְכַסּ֖וֹת אֶת־עֶרְוָתָֽהּ: יב וְעַתָּ֛ה אֲגַלֶּ֥ה אֶת־נַבְלֻתָ֖הּ לְעֵינֵ֣י מְאַֽהֲבֶ֑יהָ וְאִ֖ישׁ לֹא־
יג יַצִּילֶ֥נָּה מִיָּדִֽי: וְהִשְׁבַּתִּי֙ כָּל־מְשׂוֹשָׂ֔הּ חַגָּ֖הּ חָדְשָׁ֣הּ וְשַׁבַּתָּ֑הּ וְכֹ֖ל מֽוֹעֲדָֽהּ:
יד וַֽהֲשִׁמֹּתִ֤י גַּפְנָהּ֙ וּתְאֵ֣נָתָ֔הּ אֲשֶׁ֣ר אָֽמְרָ֗ה אֶתְנָ֥ה הֵ֨מָּה֙ לִ֔י אֲשֶׁ֥ר נָֽתְנוּ־לִ֖י
טו מְאַֽהֲבָ֑י וְשַׂמְתִּ֣ים לְיַ֔עַר וַֽאֲכָלָ֖תַם חַיַּ֥ת הַשָּׂדֶֽה: וּפָֽקַדְתִּ֣י עָלֶ֗יהָ אֶת־יְמֵ֣י
הַבְּעָלִ֜ים אֲשֶׁ֣ר תַּקְטִ֣יר לָהֶ֗ם וַתַּ֤עַד נִזְמָהּ֙ וְחֶלְיָתָ֔הּ וַתֵּ֖לֶךְ אַֽחֲרֵ֣י מְאַֽהֲבֶ֑יהָ
טז וְאֹתִ֥י שָֽׁכְחָ֖ה נְאֻם־יְהוָֽה: לָכֵ֗ן הִנֵּ֤ה אָֽנֹכִי֙ מְפַתֶּ֔יהָ וְהֹֽלַכְתִּ֖יהָ
יז הַמִּדְבָּ֑ר וְדִבַּרְתִּ֖י עַל־לִבָּֽהּ: וְנָתַ֨תִּי לָ֤הּ אֶת־כְּרָמֶ֨יהָ֙ מִשָּׁ֔ם וְאֶת־עֵ֖מֶק
עָכ֖וֹר לְפֶ֣תַח תִּקְוָ֑ה וְעָ֤נְתָה שָּׁ֨מָּה֙ כִּימֵ֣י נְעוּרֶ֔יהָ וּכְי֖וֹם עֲלוֹתָ֥הּ מֵֽאֶֽרֶץ־
יח מִצְרָֽיִם: וְהָיָ֤ה בַיּֽוֹם־הַהוּא֙ נְאֻם־יְהוָ֔ה תִּקְרְאִ֖י אִישִׁ֑י וְלֹֽא־תִקְרְאִי־
יט לִ֥י ע֖וֹד בַּעְלִֽי: וַֽהֲסִֽרֹתִ֛י אֶת־שְׁמ֥וֹת הַבְּעָלִ֖ים מִפִּ֑יהָ וְלֹֽא־יִזָּֽכְר֥וּ ע֖וֹד בִּשְׁמָֽם:
כ וְכָֽרַתִּ֨י לָהֶ֤ם בְּרִית֙ בַּיּ֣וֹם הַה֔וּא עִם־חַיַּ֤ת הַשָּׂדֶה֙ וְעִם־ע֣וֹף הַשָּׁמַ֔יִם וְרֶ֖מֶשׂ
הָֽאֲדָמָ֑ה וְקֶ֨שֶׁת וְחֶ֤רֶב וּמִלְחָמָה֙ אֶשְׁבּ֣וֹר מִן־הָאָ֔רֶץ וְהִשְׁכַּבְתִּ֖ים לָבֶֽטַח:
כא וְאֵֽרַשְׂתִּ֥יךְ לִ֖י לְעוֹלָ֑ם וְאֵֽרַשְׂתִּ֥יךְ לִי֙ בְּצֶ֣דֶק וּבְמִשְׁפָּ֔ט וּבְחֶ֖סֶד וּבְרַֽחֲמִֽים:
כב-כג וְאֵֽרַשְׂתִּ֥יךְ לִ֖י בֶּאֱמוּנָ֑ה וְיָדַ֖עַתְּ אֶת־יְהוָֽה: ◀ וְהָיָ֣ה ׀ בַּיּ֣וֹם הַה֗וּא
כד אֶֽעֱנֶה֙ נְאֻם־יְהֹוָ֔ה אֶֽעֱנֶ֖ה אֶת־הַשָּׁמָ֑יִם וְהֵ֖ם יַֽעֲנ֥וּ אֶת־הָאָֽרֶץ: וְהָאָ֣רֶץ תַּֽעֲנֶ֗ה
כה אֶת־הַדָּגָן֙ וְאֶת־הַתִּיר֣וֹשׁ וְאֶת־הַיִּצְהָ֔ר וְהֵ֖ם יַֽעֲנ֥וּ אֶֽת־יִזְרְעֶֽאל: וּזְרַעְתִּ֤יהָ
לִּי֙ בָּאָ֔רֶץ וְרִֽחַמְתִּ֖י אֶת־לֹ֣א רֻחָ֑מָה וְאָֽמַרְתִּ֤י לְלֹֽא־עַמִּי֙ עַמִּי־אַ֔תָּה וְה֖וּא
ג א יֹאמַ֥ר אֱלֹהָֽי: וַיֹּ֨אמֶר יְהֹוָ֜ה אֵלַ֗י ע֚וֹד לֵ֣ךְ אֱֽהַב־אִשָּׁ֔ה אֲהֻ֥בַת רֵ֖עַ
וּמְנָאָ֑פֶת כְּאַֽהֲבַ֤ת יְהוָה֙ אֶת־בְּנֵ֣י יִשְׂרָאֵ֔ל וְהֵ֗ם פֹּנִים֙ אֶל־אֱלֹהִ֣ים אֲחֵרִ֔ים
ב וְאֹֽהֲבֵ֖י אֲשִׁישֵׁ֥י עֲנָבִֽים: וָֽאֶכְּרֶ֣הָ לִּ֔י בַּֽחֲמִשָּׁ֥ה עָשָׂ֖ר כָּ֑סֶף וְחֹ֥מֶר שְׂעֹרִ֖ים
ג וְלֵ֥תֶךְ שְׂעֹרִֽים: וָֽאֹמַ֣ר אֵלֶ֗יהָ יָמִ֤ים רַבִּים֙ תֵּ֣שְׁבִי לִ֔י לֹ֤א תִזְנִי֙ וְלֹ֣א תִֽהְיִ֔י
ד לְאִ֖ישׁ וְגַם־אֲנִ֥י אֵלָֽיִךְ: כִּ֣י ׀ יָמִ֣ים רַבִּ֗ים יֵֽשְׁבוּ֙ בְּנֵ֣י יִשְׂרָאֵ֔ל אֵ֥ין מֶ֨לֶךְ֙ וְאֵ֣ין שָׂ֔ר
ה וְאֵ֥ין זֶ֨בַח֙ וְאֵ֣ין מַצֵּבָ֔ה וְאֵ֥ין אֵפ֖וֹד וּתְרָפִֽים: אַחַ֗ר יָשֻׁ֨בוּ֙ בְּנֵ֣י יִשְׂרָאֵ֔ל וּבִקְשׁוּ֙
אֶת־יְהֹוָ֣ה אֱלֹֽהֵיהֶ֔ם וְאֵ֖ת דָּוִ֣ד מַלְכָּ֑ם וּפָֽחֲד֧וּ אֶל־יְהוָ֛ה וְאֶל־טוּב֖וֹ בְּאַֽחֲרִ֥ית
ד א הַיָּמִֽים: שִׁמְע֥וּ דְבַר־יְהוָ֖ה בְּנֵ֣י יִשְׂרָאֵ֑ל כִּ֣י רִ֤יב לַֽיהוָה֙ עִם־
ב יֽוֹשְׁבֵ֣י הָאָ֔רֶץ כִּ֠י אֵֽין־אֱמֶ֧ת וְאֵֽין־חֶ֛סֶד וְאֵֽין־דַּ֥עַת אֱלֹהִ֖ים בָּאָֽרֶץ: אָלֹ֣ה
ג וְכַחֵ֔שׁ וְרָצֹ֥חַ וְגָנֹ֖ב וְנָאֹ֑ף פָּרָ֕צוּ וְדָמִ֥ים בְּדָמִ֖ים נָגָֽעוּ: עַל־כֵּ֣ן ׀ תֶּֽאֱבַ֣ל הָאָ֗רֶץ

2:16. In exile, she will realize in her heart how wrong she had been (*Rashi*).

2:17. From the desert of exile, I will restore her to her fertile land. For Valley of Achor see *Joshua 7:24-26* and *Isaiah 65:10*.

2:18. *Ishi* and *Baali* both mean "my husband," but with different connotations. *Ishi*, literally, "my man," implies a relationship based on love; but *Baali*, literally, "my master," can also refer to a relationship based on fear of a superior (*Rashi*).

2:20. That they no longer harm the people in the land (cf. *Isaiah 11:9*).

2:23. The heavens "desire," as it were, to provide their moisture; God will now accede to their "request" (*Radak*).

2:24. The exiles who had been strewn like sown seed (1:4) and gathered like grown seed (2:2).

3:2. A *chomer* is equal to ten *ephah* (or about 8 bushels), and a *lesech* is equal to five *ephah*.

3:4. *Ephod* refers to the *Urim VeTumim* (see *Exodus*

. . . but too late

[11] *Therefore, I will return and take My grain in its time and My wine in its season, and I will remove My wool and My linen [that I gave her] to cover her nakedness.* [12] *And now I will reveal her repulsiveness before the eyes of her paramours, and no man will save her from My hand.* [13] *I will terminate her every rejoicing, her festival, her New Moon, her Sabbath and her every appointed season.* [14] *I will lay waste her vine and her fig tree, [about] which she said, 'They are a payment for me that my paramours have given me'; and I will make them like a forest, and the beasts of the field will devour them.* [15] *And I will repay her for all the days of the Baalim to which she burns incense; and she adorned herself with her earrings and her jewelry and followed after her paramours, but Me she forgot — the word of* HASHEM.

God will relent

[16] *Therefore, behold, I will seduce her, and I will lead her to the desert and I will speak to her heart.* * [17] *And I will give to her her vineyards from there,* * *and [make] the Valley of Achor (Troubling)* * *into a portal of hope; she will dwell* * *there as in the days of her youth, and as on the day of her ascent from the land of Egypt.* [18] *And it shall be on that day — the word of* HASHEM — *that you will call [Me] Ishi (my husband) and you will no longer call Me Baali (my master).* * [19] *I will remove the names of the Baalim from her mouth and they will not be mentioned again by their name.* [20] *And I will seal a covenant for them on that day with the beast of the field and the bird of the heavens and the creeping thing of the ground;* * *I will banish bow and sword and warfare from the land; and I will lay them down in safety.* [21] *I will betroth you to Me forever; and I will betroth you to Me with righteousness, with justice, with kindness and with mercy;* [22] *and I will betroth you to Me with fidelity, and you will know* HASHEM. [23] *And it shall be on that day that I will respond — the word of* HASHEM — *I will respond to the heavens,* * *and they will respond to the earth.* [24] *And the earth will respond with the grain and the wine and the oil, and they will respond to Jezreel.* * [25] *I will sow her for Myself in the land, and I will pity Lo-ruhamah (Not Pitied), and I will say to Lo-ammi (Not My People), 'You are Ammi (My People),' and he will say '[You are] my God.' "*

3

Another faithless wife

[1] **H**ASHEM *said to me, "Go again, love a woman who was the beloved of [her] companion, yet an adulteress — like* HASHEM's *love for the Children of Israel, yet they turn to the gods of others and cherish goblets of grape [wine]."*

[2] *So I acquired her for myself for fifteen [pieces of] silver and a chomer* * *of barley and a lesech* * *of barley.* [3] *And I said to her, "Wait for me for many days; do not act the harlot and do not marry a[nother] man, and so will I be [faithful] to you."* [4] *For many days the Children of Israel will sit with no king, no officer, no sacrifice, no pillar, and no ephod or teraphim.* * [5] *Afterward the Children of Israel will return and seek out* HASHEM *their God and David their king, and they will tremble for* HASHEM *and for His goodness in the end of days.*

4

A chilling condemnation

[1] **H**ear the words of HASHEM, O Children of Israel! For HASHEM has a grievance with the inhabitants of the land, for there is no truth nor kindness nor knowledge of God in the land. [2] [Rather,] swearing, lying, murdering, robbing, and adultery; they have breached [standards], and blood reaches [more] blood.* [3] Therefore, the land will be destroyed

---

28:30); *Teraphim are among the divining tools of the sorcerers.* **4:2.** *There is so much bloodshed that the blood of one victim mingles with the blood of the next (Rashi).*

וְאֻמְלַ֗ל כָּל־יוֹשֵׁ֣ב בָּ֔הּ בְּחַיַּ֤ת הַשָּׂדֶה֙ וּבְע֣וֹף הַשָּׁמָ֔יִם וְגַם־דְּגֵ֥י הַיָּ֖ם יֵאָסֵֽפוּ׃

ד-ה אַ֥ךְ אִ֛ישׁ אַל־יָרֵ֖ב וְאַל־יוֹכַ֣ח אִ֑ישׁ וְעַמְּךָ֖ כִּמְרִיבֵ֥י כֹהֵֽן׃ וְכָשַׁלְתָּ֣ הַיּ֔וֹם

ו וְכָשַׁ֧ל גַּם־נָבִ֛יא עִמְּךָ֖ לָ֑יְלָה וְדָמִ֖יתִי אִמֶּֽךָ׃ נִדְמ֥וּ עַמִּ֖י מִבְּלִ֣י הַדָּ֑עַת כִּֽי־אַתָּ֞ה הַדַּ֣עַת מָאַ֗סְתָּ °וּאמאסאך [וְאֶמְאָֽסְךָ֙ ק] מִכַּהֵ֣ן לִ֔י וַתִּשְׁכַּח֙ תּוֹרַ֣ת

ז אֱלֹהֶ֔יךָ אֶשְׁכַּ֥ח בָּנֶ֖יךָ גַּם־אָֽנִי׃ כְּרֻבָּ֖ם כֵּ֣ן חָֽטְאוּ־לִ֑י כְּבוֹדָ֖ם בְּקָל֥וֹן אָמִֽיר׃

ח-ט חַטַּ֥את עַמִּ֖י יֹאכֵ֑לוּ וְאֶל־עֲוֺנָ֖ם יִשְׂא֥וּ נַפְשֽׁוֹ׃ וְהָיָ֥ה כָעָ֖ם כַּכֹּהֵ֑ן וּפָקַדְתִּ֤י עָלָיו֙

י דְּרָכָ֔יו וּמַעֲלָלָ֖יו אָשִׁ֥יב לֽוֹ׃ וְאָֽכְלוּ֙ וְלֹ֣א יִשְׂבָּ֔עוּ הִזְנ֖וּ וְלֹ֣א יִפְרֹ֑צוּ כִּֽי־אֶת־

יא-יב יְהוָ֥ה עָֽזְב֖וּ לִשְׁמֹֽר׃ זְנ֛וּת וְיַ֥יִן וְתִיר֖וֹשׁ יִ֥קַּֽח־לֵֽב׃ עַמִּי֙ בְּעֵצ֣וֹ יִשְׁאָ֔ל וּמַקְל֖וֹ

יג יַגִּ֣יד ל֑וֹ כִּ֣י ר֤וּחַ זְנוּנִים֙ הִתְעָ֔ה וַיִּזְנ֖וּ מִתַּ֥חַת אֱלֹֽהֵיהֶֽם׃ עַל־רָאשֵׁ֨י הֶהָרִ֜ים יְזַבֵּ֗חוּ וְעַל־הַגְּבָעוֹת֙ יְקַטֵּ֔רוּ תַּ֣חַת אַלּ֧וֹן וְלִבְנֶ֛ה וְאֵלָ֖ה כִּ֣י ט֣וֹב צִלָּ֑הּ עַל־כֵּ֗ן

יד תִּזְנֶ֙ינָה֙ בְּנ֣וֹתֵיכֶ֔ם וְכַלּֽוֹתֵיכֶ֖ם תְּנָאַֽפְנָה׃ לֹֽא־אֶפְק֨וֹד עַל־בְּנוֹתֵיכֶ֜ם כִּ֣י תִזְנֶ֗ינָה וְעַל־כַּלּֽוֹתֵיכֶם֙ כִּ֣י תְנָאַ֔פְנָה כִּי־הֵם֙ עִם־הַזֹּנ֣וֹת יְפָרֵ֔דוּ וְעִם־הַקְּדֵשׁ֖וֹת יְזַבֵּ֑חוּ

טו וְעָ֥ם לֹֽא־יָבִ֖ין יִלָּבֵֽט׃ אִם־זֹנֶ֤ה אַתָּה֙ יִשְׂרָאֵ֔ל אַל־יֶאְשַׁ֖ם יְהוּדָ֑ה וְאַל־תָּבֹ֣אוּ

טז הַגִּלְגָּ֗ל וְאַֽל־תַּעֲלוּ֙ בֵּ֣ית אָ֔וֶן וְאַל־תִּשָּֽׁבְע֖וּ חַי־יְהוָֽה׃ כִּ֚י כְּפָרָ֣ה סֹֽרֵרָ֔ה סָרַ֖ר

יז יִשְׂרָאֵ֑ל עַתָּה֙ יִרְעֵ֣ם יְהוָ֔ה כְּכֶ֖בֶשׂ בַּמֶּרְחָֽב׃ חֲב֥וּר עֲצַבִּ֖ים אֶפְרָ֑יִם הַֽנַּֽח־לֽוֹ׃

יח-יט סָ֖ר סָבְאָ֑ם הַזְנֵ֣ה הִזְנ֔וּ אָהֲב֥וּ הֵב֛וּ קָל֖וֹן מָגִנֶּֽיהָ׃ צָרַ֥ר ר֛וּחַ אוֹתָ֖הּ בִּכְנָפֶ֑יהָ

ה א וְיֵבֹ֖שׁוּ מִזִּבְחוֹתָֽם׃ שִׁמְעוּ־זֹ֣את הַכֹּהֲנִ֗ים וְהַקְשִׁ֙יבוּ֙ ׀ בֵּ֣ית יִשְׂרָאֵ֔ל וּבֵ֤ית הַמֶּ֙לֶךְ֙ הַאֲזִ֔ינוּ כִּ֥י לָכֶ֖ם הַמִּשְׁפָּ֑ט כִּֽי־פַח֙ הֱיִיתֶ֣ם לְמִצְפָּ֔ה וְרֶ֖שֶׁת

ב-ג פְּרוּשָׂ֥ה עַל־תָּבֽוֹר׃ וְשַׁחֲטָ֥ה שֵׂטִ֖ים הֶעְמִ֑יקוּ וַאֲנִ֖י מוּסָ֥ר לְכֻלָּֽם׃ אֲנִ֤י יָדַ֙עְתִּי֙ אֶפְרַ֔יִם וְיִשְׂרָאֵ֖ל לֹֽא־נִכְחַ֣ד מִמֶּ֑נִּי כִּ֤י עַתָּה֙ הִזְנֵ֣יתָ אֶפְרַ֔יִם נִטְמָ֖א יִשְׂרָאֵֽל׃

ד לֹ֤א יִתְּנוּ֙ מַ֣עַלְלֵיהֶ֔ם לָשׁ֖וּב אֶל־אֱלֹֽהֵיהֶ֑ם כִּ֣י ר֤וּחַ זְנוּנִים֙ בְּקִרְבָּ֔ם וְאֶת־

ה יְהוָ֖ה לֹ֥א יָדָֽעוּ׃ וְעָנָ֥ה גְאֽוֹן־יִשְׂרָאֵ֖ל בְּפָנָ֑יו וְיִשְׂרָאֵ֣ל וְאֶפְרַ֗יִם יִכָּֽשְׁלוּ֙ בַּעֲוֺנָ֔ם

ו כָּשַׁ֥ל גַּם־יְהוּדָ֖ה עִמָּֽם׃ בְּצֹאנָ֣ם וּבִבְקָרָ֗ם יֵֽלְכ֛וּ לְבַקֵּ֥שׁ אֶת־יְהוָ֖ה וְלֹ֣א

ז יִמְצָ֑אוּ חָלַ֖ץ מֵהֶֽם׃ בַּֽיהוָ֣ה בָּגָ֔דוּ כִּֽי־בָנִ֥ים זָרִ֖ים יָלָ֑דוּ עַתָּ֛ה יֹאכְלֵ֥ם חֹ֖דֶשׁ

4:4. The wrongdoers forewarn the prophets not to rebuke them, yet they rebuke the righteous *Kohanim* who are supposed to teach them righteously (*Rashi*). Alternatively: No one can rebuke the wrongdoers, because all are equally wicked (*Radak*).

4:5. Israel's "mother" is a metaphor for the nation. Individuals will be exiled and the "Congregation" of Israel will cease to exist (*Radak*).

4:6-9. Hosea turns his rebuke to the *Kohanim*, who not only failed to live up to their calling, but encouraged the sins of the masses.

4:8. Instead of discouraging sin, the *Kohen* eagerly anticipates it, in order to eat from additional sin-offerings (*Radak*).

4:9. The populace and the *Kohanim* were equally sinful, so they will be equally punished (*Radak*).

4:12. The people believe in idols made of wood and rods.

4:13. Because the men are disloyal to God, the women are disloyal to their husbands (*Malbim*).

4:15. Gilgal and Beth-el (House of God) — here contemptuously called "Beth-aven" (house of iniquity) — were centers of idol worship.

4:16. An untended lamb is helpless and panicky on an open range.

4:17. It is futile to rebuke Ephraim, the leading tribe of the Northern Kingdom.

4:19. Like a bird blown off course by a strong wind, you will be driven into exile (*Rashi*), ashamed that your gods could not save you.

5:1. God asked the *Kohanim,* "Why do you not offer sacrifices on the Altar?" They replied, "Because Israel does not avail us any." Then God said to Israel, "Why do you not bring offerings?" They replied, "Because the king has blockaded the roads to Jerusalem." So God rebuked the royal household, "The sentence of punishments is upon you" (*Rashi; Kara*). Alternatively: Instead of admin-

and all who dwell in it will be enfeebled, along with the beast of the field and the bird of the heavens and even the fish of the sea will be annihilated. [4] Indeed [you say,] 'Let no one contend; let no one reprimand!' Yet your people contends with the Kohen!* [5] You will stumble by day and the [false] prophet who is with you will also stumble, as if by night; and I will silence your mother. *

Measure for measure

[6] My people has been eliminated for lack of knowledge;* for you have spurned knowledge, and I will spurn you from serving Me; and as you have forgotten the Torah of your God, I, too, will forget your children. [7] As much as they have increased, so have they sinned against Me; [therefore] I will exchange their honor for disgrace. [8] The sin-offerings of My people they consume; and for their iniquities, his soul yearns. * [9] So it shall be — like people, like Kohen;* I will visit his ways upon him, and I will requite him for his deeds. [10] They will eat but not be sated; they will be promiscuous but will not proliferate, for they have abandoned HASHEM, [ceasing] to keep [His ways]. [11] Harlotry and wine and fresh wine capture the heart.

Saturated with idolatry

[12] My people asks of its wood, and its rod relates to it;* for a spirit of harlotry has misled [them] and they have strayed from under their God. [13] They slaughter sacrifices upon the mountaintops and they burn incense upon the hills, under oak and poplar, and elm, for their shade is good. Therefore, * your daughters commit harlotry and your daughters-in-law commit adultery. [14] I will not punish your daughters when they commit harlotry, [nor] your daughters-in-law when they commit adultery, for [the men] are secluded with harlots and sacrifice with prostitutes; and the people that does not understand will stumble.

[15] If you have turned astray, O Israel, let Judah not become guilty! Do not come to Gilgal, do not ascend to Beth-aven, * and do not swear [falsely, saying], 'As HASHEM lives.' [16] For Israel has strayed like a wayward cow; now HASHEM will graze them like a lamb on the broad range. * [17] Ephraim is attached to idols; let him be. *

[18] Their adulterous drinking orgies have become foreign [to Me]; her rulers love to invite disgrace. [19] The wind has bound her by her wings;* they will be ashamed of their sacrifices.

5

The monarchy rebuked

[1] Hear this, O Kohanim. Hearken, O House of Israel. O royal house, give ear, for the judgment is yours; you have been a snare to Mizpah and a net extended over Tabor. * [2] [By preventing] the slaughter [of offerings] the deviants deepened [iniquity], and I castigate them all. [3] I knew Ephraim, and Israel was not hidden from Me; for now you have committed harlotry, Ephraim; Israel has been defiled. [4] They will not abandon their deeds to return to their God, for a spirit of harlotries is in their midst, and HASHEM they do not know. [5] The pride of Israel will be humbled before Him, and Israel and Ephraim will stumble over their iniquity, [and] Judah, too, will stumble with them. [6] With their sheep and with their cattle* they will go to seek HASHEM, but they will not find [Him]; He has withdrawn from them. [7] They betrayed HASHEM, for they begot alien children; now a month will devour them*

---

istering justice you were a snare to the populace, who followed your example of corruption and perversion. Tabor and Mizpah were high mountains where hunters often set up traps and nets (*Radak*).

5:6. This refers to their sacrificial animals.
5:7. Because they begot gentile children through intermarriage, their downfall will come in the month of Av (*Rashi*).

תִּקְע֤וּ שׁוֹפָר֙ בַּגִּבְעָ֔ה חֲצֹצְרָ֖ה בָּרָמָ֑ה הָרִ֙יעוּ֙ אֶת־חֶלְקֵיהֶֽם: ח

בֵּ֣ית אָ֔וֶן אַחֲרֶ֖יךָ בִּנְיָמִֽין: אֶפְרַ֙יִם֙ לְשַׁמָּ֣ה תִֽהְיֶ֔ה בְּי֖וֹם תּֽוֹכֵחָ֑ה בְּשִׁבְטֵי֙ ט

יִשְׂרָאֵ֔ל הוֹדַ֖עְתִּי נֶֽאֱמָנָֽה: הָי֙וּ֙ שָׂרֵ֣י יְהוּדָ֔ה כְּמַסִּיגֵ֖י גְּב֑וּל עֲלֵיהֶ֕ם אֶשְׁפּ֥וֹךְ י

כַּמַּ֖יִם עֶבְרָתִֽי: עָשׁ֤וּק אֶפְרַ֙יִם֙ רְצ֣וּץ מִשְׁפָּ֔ט כִּ֣י הוֹאִ֔יל הָלַ֖ךְ אַחֲרֵי־צָֽו: יא

וַאֲנִ֥י כָעָ֖שׁ לְאֶפְרָ֑יִם וְכָרָקָ֖ב לְבֵ֥ית יְהוּדָֽה: וַיַּ֨רְא אֶפְרַ֜יִם אֶת־חׇלְי֗וֹ וִיהוּדָה֙ יב־יג

אֶת־מְזֹר֔וֹ וַיֵּ֤לֶךְ אֶפְרַ֙יִם֙ אֶל־אַשּׁ֔וּר וַיִּשְׁלַ֖ח אֶל־מֶ֣לֶךְ יָרֵ֑ב וְה֗וּא לֹ֤א יוּכַל֙

לִרְפֹּ֣א לָכֶ֔ם וְלֹא־יִגְהֶ֥ה מִכֶּ֖ם מָזֽוֹר: כִּ֣י אָנֹכִ֤י כַשַּׁ֙חַל֙ לְאֶפְרַ֔יִם וְכַכְּפִ֖יר יד

לְבֵ֣ית יְהוּדָ֑ה אֲנִ֣י אֲנִ֤י אֶטְרֹף֙ וְאֵלֵ֔ךְ אֶשָּׂ֖א וְאֵ֥ין מַצִּֽיל: אֵלֵ֤ךְ אָשׁ֙וּבָה֙ אֶל־ טו

מְקוֹמִ֔י עַ֥ד אֲשֶֽׁר־יֶאְשְׁמ֖וּ וּבִקְשׁ֣וּ פָנָ֑י בַּצַּ֥ר לָהֶ֖ם יְשַֽׁחֲרֻֽנְנִי: לְכוּ֙ וְנָשׁ֣וּבָה א **ו**

אֶל־יְהֹוָ֔ה כִּ֛י ה֥וּא טָרָ֖ף וְיִרְפָּאֵ֑נוּ יַ֖ךְ וְיַחְבְּשֵֽׁנוּ: יְחַיֵּ֖נוּ מִיֹּמָ֑יִם בַּיּוֹם֙ הַשְּׁלִישִׁ֔י ב

יְקִמֵ֖נוּ וְנִחְיֶ֥ה לְפָנָֽיו: וְנֵדְעָ֗ה נִרְדְּפָ֞ה לָדַ֙עַת֙ אֶת־יְהֹוָ֔ה כְּשַׁ֖חַר נָכ֣וֹן מֽוֹצָא֑וֹ ג

וְיָב֤וֹא כַגֶּ֙שֶׁם֙ לָ֔נוּ כְּמַלְק֖וֹשׁ י֥וֹרֶה אָֽרֶץ: מָ֤ה אֶֽעֱשֶׂה־לְּךָ֙ אֶפְרַ֔יִם מָ֥ה אֶעֱשֶׂה־ ד

לְּךָ֖ יְהוּדָ֑ה וְחַסְדְּכֶם֙ כַּעֲנַן־בֹּ֔קֶר וְכַטַּ֖ל מַשְׁכִּ֥ים הֹלֵֽךְ: עַל־כֵּ֗ן חָצַ֙בְתִּי֙ ה

בַּנְּבִיאִ֔ים הֲרַגְתִּ֖ים בְּאִמְרֵי־פִ֑י וּמִשְׁפָּטֶ֖יךָ א֥וֹר יֵצֵֽא: כִּ֛י חֶ֥סֶד חָפַ֖צְתִּי ו

וְלֹא־זָ֑בַח וְדַ֥עַת אֱלֹהִ֖ים מֵעֹלֽוֹת: וְהֵ֕מָּה כְּאָדָ֖ם עָבְר֣וּ בְרִ֑ית שָׁ֖ם בָּ֥גְדוּ בִֽי: ז

גִּלְעָ֗ד קִרְיַת֙ פֹּ֣עֲלֵי אָ֔וֶן עֲקֻבָּ֖ה מִדָּֽם: וּכְחַכֵּ֨י אִ֜ישׁ גְּדוּדִ֗ים חֶ֚בֶר כֹּֽהֲנִ֔ים דֶּ֖רֶךְ ח־ט

יְרַצְּחוּ־שֶׁ֑כְמָה כִּ֥י זִמָּ֖ה עָשֽׂוּ: בְּבֵית֙ יִשְׂרָאֵ֔ל רָאִ֖יתִי °שַׁעֲרִ֑יָּה י

[שַׁעֲרֻרִיָּ֖ה ק] שָׁ֚ם זְנ֣וּת לְאֶפְרַ֔יִם נִטְמָ֖א יִשְׂרָאֵֽל: גַּם־יְהוּדָ֕ה שָׁ֥ת קָצִ֖יר יא

לָ֑ךְ בְּשׁוּבִ֖י שְׁב֥וּת עַמִּֽי: כְּרׇפְאִ֣י לְיִשְׂרָאֵ֗ל וְנִגְלָ֞ה א **ז**

עֲוֺ֤ן אֶפְרַ֙יִם֙ וְרָע֣וֹת שֹׁמְר֔וֹן כִּ֥י פָעֲל֖וּ שָׁ֑קֶר וְגַנָּ֣ב יָב֔וֹא פָּשַׁ֥ט גְּד֖וּד בַּחֽוּץ:

וּבַל־יֹאמְרוּ֙ לִלְבָבָ֔ם כׇּל־רָעָתָ֖ם זָכָ֑רְתִּי עַתָּה֙ סְבָב֣וּם מַֽעַלְלֵיהֶ֔ם נֶ֥גֶד פָּנַ֖י ב

הָיֽוּ: בְּרָעָתָ֖ם יְשַׂמְּחוּ־מֶ֑לֶךְ וּבְכַחֲשֵׁיהֶ֖ם שָׂרִֽים: כֻּלָּם֙ מְנָ֣אֲפִ֔ים כְּמ֣וֹ תַנּ֔וּר ג־ד

בֹּעֵ֙רָה֙ מֵֽאֹפֶ֔ה יִשְׁבּ֣וֹת מֵעִ֔יר מִלּ֥וּשׁ בָּצֵ֖ק עַד־חֻמְצָתֽוֹ: י֣וֹם מַלְכֵּ֔נוּ הֶחֱל֥וּ ה

שָׂרִ֖ים חֲמַ֣ת מִיָּ֑יִן מָשַׁ֥ךְ יָד֖וֹ אֶת־לֹצְצִֽים: כִּֽי־קֵרְב֧וּ כַתַּנּ֛וּר לִבָּ֖ם בְּאׇרְבָּ֑ם ו

כׇּל־הַלַּ֙יְלָה֙ יָשֵׁ֣ן אֹֽפֵהֶ֔ם בֹּ֕קֶר ה֥וּא בֹעֵ֖ר כְּאֵ֣שׁ לֶהָבָֽה: כֻּלָּ֤ם יֵחַ֙מּוּ֙ ז

כַּתַּנּ֔וּר וְאָכְל֖וּ אֶת־שֹׁפְטֵיהֶ֑ם כׇּל־מַלְכֵיהֶ֖ם נָפָ֑לוּ אֵֽין־קֹרֵ֥א בָהֶ֖ם אֵלָֽי:

5:9. In the Torah I informed them that they would be punished if they sinned (*Radak*).

5:10. See *Deuteronomy* 19:14.

5:11. The bidding of the idolatrous priests (*Rashi*) and the wicked kings (*Radak*).

5:12. A moth devours clothing and rot destroys timber, gradually, but thoroughly.

5:13. Literally, "king of Contention"; Jareb is another name for Assyria.

6:2. Even if our misfortune is prolonged and "incurable," He will heal us in a matter of days (*Kara*).

6:5. I sent a clear-cut message to you through My prophets; you heard and refused to repent, so My offer resulted in your death sentence. How could I vindicate you

after such defiance? (*Rashi*).

6:7. In the magnificent land that I had given them (*Radak*).

6:11. Hearing Israel's remorse-filled statement (vv. 1-3), God considers ending their exile. But, by following Ephraim's example, Judah planted a branch of Ephraim's sinfulness, and in doing so made God reconsider His plan to return them from their captivity (*Ibn Ezra*).

7:1. Whenever I want to bring salvation to the Northern Kingdom, the sins of Ephraim, its leader, and the other tribes of Samaria prevent Me from doing so.

7:3. Rather than protesting injustice, their king rejoices in it, because he, too, is corrupt (*Radak*).

7:4. The Inciter — the evil inclination — devises its plan and rests until the time is ripe to bring it to fruition.

with their portions.

Forewarned

⁸ Sound a shofar in Gibeah, a trumpet in Ramah; shout in Beth-aven, '[The enemy is coming] after you, Benjamin!' ⁹ Ephraim will be bewildered on the day of rebuke; among the tribes of Israel I made the truth known. * ¹⁰ The officers of Judah were like those who shift the boundaries; * upon them I will pour out My wrath like water. ¹¹ Ephraim is plundered, shattered by his judgment; for he has willingly followed after their bidding. * ¹² I will be like a moth to Ephraim, like rot to the House of Judah. *

¹³ Ephraim saw his ailment and Judah his wound; and Ephraim went to Assyria and [Judah] sent [tribute] to the king of Jareb * — but he will not be able to cure you nor to heal your wound. ¹⁴ For I am like a lion to Ephraim and like a lion's whelp to the House of Judah. As for Me, Me, I will mangle and I will go; I will carry off and no one will rescue. ¹⁵ I will go, I will return to My place until they will acknowledge their guilt and seek My face; in their distress they will seek Me. ¹ [They will say,] 'Come, let us return to HASHEM, for He has mangled [us] and He will heal us; He has smitten and He will bandage us. ² He will heal us after two days; * on the third day He will raise us up and we will live before Him. ³ Let us know, let us strive to know HASHEM like the dawn whose emergence is certain; then He will come to us like the rain, like the late rain that satiates the earth.'

6

Thoughts of return . . .

. . . that were ephemeral

⁴ What can I do for you, Ephraim? What can I do for you, Judah, when your kindness is like a morning cloud and like the dew that departs in early morning? ⁵ Because I have [made My words] clear-cut through the prophets, I have slain [the sinners] through the utterances of My mouth — can your judgment be [favorable] as the light? * ⁶ For I desire kindness, not sacrifice; and knowledge of God more than burnt-offerings. ⁷ But they, like Adam, transgressed the covenant; there * they betrayed Me. ⁸ Gilead is a city of evildoers, of those who waylay for blood. ⁹ Like gangs awaiting a man [to rob], a band of priests murders on the road with one will, for they devised a plot. ¹⁰ In the House of Israel I have seen a disgrace; the harlotry of Ephraim is there; Israel has been defiled. ¹¹ Judah, too, has planted a branch of yours, * when I [sought to] return the captivity of My people. ¹ When I would have healed Israel, the iniquity of Ephraim became revealed, along with the evils of Samaria; * for they have wrought falsehood — a thief comes, a gang spreads out outside. ² They do not say in their hearts that I remember all their evils; now their deeds have surrounded them; they were before My face. ³ With their evil they gladden the king; * and with their falsehoods, officers. ⁴ They are all adulterers, [their passions burning] like an oven fired by a baker. The Inciter * rests from the kneading of the dough until its leavening. ⁵ On the day of our king, * the officers became ill from the heat of wine; and he withdrew his hand [to be] with scoffers. ⁶ For they have prepared their heart with their ambush-plot like an oven; all night their 'Baker' sleeps, and in the morning he burns like a blazing fire. * ⁷ They have all become heated like an oven and they have devoured their judges; all their kings have fallen, [yet] no one among them calls out to Me. *

7

Unmitigated falsehood

7:5. On the day of the king's coronation, when he should have been concerned with the welfare of his people, he joined the revelry of his drunken officials.

7:6. Just as a baker goes to sleep after he fires the oven for the morning's work, so their Baker (called the Inciter in

v.4) devises plans and rests until it is time to carry them out (Rashi).

7:7. Their passionate wickedness has brought Divine retribution upon their judges and kings, but they have not learned their lesson (Rashi).

ח-ט אֶפְרַ֕יִם בָּעַמִּ֖ים ה֣וּא יִתְבּוֹלָ֑ל אֶפְרַ֕יִם הָיָ֥ה עֻגָ֖ה בְּלִ֥י הֲפוּכָֽה: אָכְל֤וּ זָרִ֨ים

י כֹּח֙וֹ וְה֣וּא לֹ֣א יָדָ֔ע גַּם־שֵׂיבָה֙ זָ֣רְקָה בּ֔וֹ וְה֖וּא לֹ֣א יָדָֽע: וְעָנָ֥ה גְאֽוֹן־יִשְׂרָאֵל֙

יא בְּפָנָ֔יו וְלֹא־שָׁ֥בוּ אֶל־יְהֹוָ֖ה אֱלֹֽהֵיהֶ֑ם וְלֹ֥א בִקְשֻׁ֖הוּ בְּכׇל־זֹֽאת: וַיְהִ֣י אֶפְרַ֗יִם

יב כְּיוֹנָ֥ה פוֹתָ֖ה אֵ֣ין לֵ֑ב מִצְרַ֥יִם קָרָ֖אוּ אַשּׁ֥וּר הָלָֽכוּ: כַּאֲשֶׁ֣ר יֵלֵ֔כוּ אֶפְר֤וֹשׂ

יג עֲלֵיהֶם֙ רִשְׁתִּ֔י כְּע֥וֹף הַשָּׁמַ֖יִם אֽוֹרִידֵ֑ם אַיְסִירֵ֕ם כְּשֵׁ֖מַע לַעֲדָתָֽם: א֤וֹי

לָהֶם֙ כִּֽי־נָדְד֣וּ מִמֶּ֔נִּי שֹׁ֥ד לָהֶ֖ם כִּי־פָ֣שְׁעוּ בִ֑י וְאָנֹכִ֣י אֶפְדֵּ֔ם וְהֵ֕מָּה דִּבְּר֥וּ עָלַ֖י

יד כְּזָבִֽים: וְלֹֽא־זָעֲק֤וּ אֵלַי֙ בְּלִבָּ֔ם כִּ֥י יְיֵלִ֖ילוּ עַל־מִשְׁכְּבוֹתָ֑ם עַל־דָּגָ֤ן וְתִירוֹשׁ֙

טו-טז יִתְגּוֹרָ֔רוּ יָס֖וּרוּ בִֽי: וַאֲנִ֣י יִסַּ֔רְתִּי חִזַּ֖קְתִּי זְרֽוֹעֹתָ֑ם וְאֵלַ֖י יְחַשְּׁבוּ־רָֽע: יָשׁ֣וּבוּ ׀

א לֹ֣א עָ֗ל הָיוּ֙ כְּקֶ֣שֶׁת רְמִיָּ֔ה יִפְּל֤וּ בַחֶ֨רֶב֙ שָֽׂרֵיהֶ֔ם מִזַּ֖עַם לְשׁוֹנָ֑ם ז֥וֹ לַעְגָּ֖ם

ח בְּאֶ֥רֶץ מִצְרָֽיִם: אֶל־חִכְּךָ֣ שֹׁפָ֔ר כַּנֶּ֖שֶׁר עַל־בֵּ֣ית יְהֹוָ֑ה יַ֚עַן עָבְר֣וּ בְרִיתִ֔י

ב-ג וְעַל־תּוֹרָתִ֖י פָּשָֽׁעוּ: לִ֖י יִזְעָ֑קוּ אֱלֹהַ֖י יְדַעֲנ֥וּךָ יִשְׂרָאֵֽל: זָנַ֥ח יִשְׂרָאֵ֖ל ט֑וֹב אוֹיֵ֖ב

ד יִרְדְּפֽוֹ: הֵ֤ם הִמְלִ֨יכוּ֙ וְלֹ֣א מִמֶּ֔נִּי הֵשִׂ֖ירוּ וְלֹ֣א יָדָ֑עְתִּי כַּסְפָּ֣ם וּזְהָבָ֗ם עָשׂ֤וּ לָהֶם֙

ה עֲצַבִּ֔ים לְמַ֖עַן יִכָּרֵֽת: זָנַח֙ עֶגְלֵ֣ךְ שֹֽׁמְר֔וֹן חָרָ֥ה אַפִּ֖י בָּ֑ם עַד־מָתַ֕י לֹ֥א

ו יֽוּכְל֖וּ נִקָּיֹֽן: כִּ֤י מִיִּשְׂרָאֵל֙ וְה֔וּא חָרָ֖שׁ עָשָׂ֑הוּ וְלֹ֥א אֱלֹהִ֖ים ה֑וּא כִּֽי־שְׁבָבִ֣ים

ז יִֽהְיֶ֔ה עֵ֖גֶל שֹׁמְרֽוֹן: כִּ֤י ר֨וּחַ֙ יִזְרָ֔עוּ וְסוּפָ֖תָה יִקְצֹ֑רוּ קָמָ֣ה אֵֽין־ל֗וֹ צֶ֚מַח בְּלִ֣י

ח יַֽעֲשֶׂה־קֶּ֔מַח אוּלַ֣י יַֽעֲשֶׂ֔ה זָרִ֖ים יִבְלָעֻֽהוּ: נִבְלַ֖ע יִשְׂרָאֵ֑ל עַתָּה֙ הָי֣וּ בַגּוֹיִ֔ם

ט כִּכְלִ֥י אֵֽין־חֵ֖פֶץ בּֽוֹ: כִּי־הֵ֨מָּה֙ עָל֣וּ אַשּׁ֔וּר פֶּ֖רֶא בּוֹדֵ֣ד ל֑וֹ אֶפְרַ֖יִם הִתְנ֥וּ

י אֲהָבִֽים: גַּ֛ם כִּֽי־יִתְנ֥וּ בַגּוֹיִ֖ם עַתָּ֣ה אֲקַבְּצֵ֑ם וַיָּחֵ֣לּוּ מְעָ֔ט מִמַּשָּׂ֖א מֶ֥לֶךְ שָׂרִֽים:

יא-יב כִּֽי־הִרְבָּ֥ה אֶפְרַ֛יִם מִזְבְּחֹ֖ת לַחֲטֹ֑א הָֽיוּ־ל֥וֹ מִזְבְּח֖וֹת לַחֲטֹֽא: °אֶכְתׇּב־

[אֶכְתׇּב־ ק] ל֔וֹ °רֻבּ֖וֹ [רֻבֵּ֖י ק] תּֽוֹרָתִ֑י כְּמוֹ־זָ֖ר נֶחְשָֽׁבוּ: זִבְחֵ֣י הַבְהָבַ֗י

יג יִזְבְּחוּ֙ בָשָׂ֣ר וַיֹּאכֵ֔לוּ יְהֹוָ֖ה לֹ֣א רָצָ֑ם עַתָּ֞ה יִזְכֹּ֤ר עֲוֹנָם֙ וְיִפְקֹ֣ד חַטֹּאותָ֔ם הֵ֖מָּה

יד מִצְרַ֥יִם יָשֽׁוּבוּ: וַיִּשְׁכַּ֤ח יִשְׂרָאֵל֙ אֶת־עֹשֵׂ֔הוּ וַיִּ֖בֶן הֵֽיכָל֑וֹת וִיהוּדָ֕ה הִרְבָּ֖ה

א עָרִ֣ים בְּצֻר֑וֹת וְשִׁלַּחְתִּי־אֵ֣שׁ בְּעָרָ֔יו וְאָכְלָ֖ה אַרְמְנֹתֶֽיהָ: אַל־

ט תִּשְׂמַ֨ח יִשְׂרָאֵ֤ל ׀ אֶל־גִּיל֙ כָּֽעַמִּ֔ים כִּ֥י זָנִ֖יתָ מֵעַ֣ל אֱלֹהֶ֑יךָ אָהַ֣בְתָּ אֶתְנַ֔ן עַ֖ל

ב-ג כׇּל־גׇּרְנ֥וֹת דָּגָֽן: גֹּ֥רֶן וָיֶ֖קֶב לֹ֣א יִרְעֵ֑ם וְתִיר֖וֹשׁ יְכַ֣חֶשׁ בָּֽהּ: לֹ֤א יֵשְׁבוּ֙ בְּאֶ֣רֶץ

7:8. Like a cake eaten before it is fully baked, they will be annihilated before their time (*Targum*).

7:9. Ephraim failed to realize that his ills were a punishment for his sins.

7:11. Like birds, they foolishly flew into the trap of reliance on foreign powers (*Radak*).

7:13. They denied that I direct and control events (*Radak*).

7:15. I afflicted them only to strengthen their resolve so that they would repent — but they do not realize this (*Rashi*).

7:16. Like a bow that seems to aim in one direction but shoots in another, Israel's fidelity to Me was mercurial and short-lived (*Radak*).

Their impudence in seeking help from Egypt caused their downfall, and made them a laughingstock in Egypt (*Radak*).

8:1. Nebuchadnezzar, king of Babylonia (see *Ezekiel* 17:3, 12).

8:4. Their gold and silver (*Rashi*).

8:5. The calves worshiped by Samaria, the Northern Kingdom, did not help them (*Radak*). Alternatively: The verse reads, "He [i.e., God] has forsaken [you because of] your calf" (*Rashi*).

8:6. The calf was not merely commissioned by King Jeroboam; it was made of gold donated by the people (*Rashi*).

8:9. They tried to buy alliances with powerful nations (*Radak*).

8:10. Despite their faith in other nations, I will gather in the Jewish people, but first they will be humbled by the burdens of exile (*Rashi*).

8:11. Beyond the many altars built by their ancestors,

Foolish
Ephraim . . .

⁸ Ephraim will be intermingled with the nations. Ephraim was like a cake that was not turned over. * ⁹ Strangers have consumed his strength, but he did not know; also old age was cast upon him but he did not know. * ¹⁰ The glory of Israel was humbled before him, but they did not turn back to HASHEM their God and they did not seek Him despite all this. ¹¹ Ephraim was like a foolish dove* with no understanding: They have called to Egypt, they have gone to Assyria. ¹² When they go, I will spread My net over them, I will bring them down like the birds of the sky; I will afflict them, as has been heard by their congregation.

¹³ Woe to them for they have moved away from Me; plunder upon them for they have rebelled against Me. I would redeem them, but they have spoken lies about Me. * ¹⁴ They did not cry out to Me in their hearts when they wailed on their beds. They gather together for grain and wine, yet they turn away from Me. ¹⁵ As for Me, I afflicted [them; I] strengthened their arms, * but they think evil of Me. ¹⁶ They turn, but not to the One Above; they

. . . is
doomed

are like a deceptive bow. * Their officers will fall by the sword because of the fury of their tongues; this was their derision in the land of Egypt. *

8

Instead of
returning to
God . . .

¹ To your palate [put] a shofar; [the enemy swoops] like an eagle* upon the Temple of HASHEM, because they have violated My covenant, and they have rebelled against My Torah. ² To Me Israel should cry out, 'My God, we acknowledge you!' ³ Israel has forsaken the Benevolent One; so the enemy will pursue him. ⁴ They enthroned kings, but not from Me; they ordained officers but I did not know. [From] their silver and gold they made themselves idols, for it* to be eliminated. ⁵ Your calf has forsaken [you], Samaria!* My anger burns against them; how long will they be incapable of cleansing? ⁶ For [it is] from Israel;* a craftsman made it, and it is not a god; for the calf of Samaria will be splinters. ⁷ For they sow wind and they will reap a tempest; it has no standing stalks, a sprout that will produce no flour; [and] if it should somehow produce, strangers will swallow it. ⁸ Israel has been swallowed up; now they have become among the nations like a useless vessel. ⁹ For they ascended to Assyria like a wild donkey on its own;

. . . Ephraim
tried to buy
allies

Ephraim has paid tribute for friendship. * ¹⁰ Although they pay tribute to the nations, now I will gather them; but [first] they will be humbled somewhat by the burden of the king and officers. * ¹¹ For Ephraim has increased the [number of] altars* to sin, [even though] he had altars to sin! ¹² I wrote for them the great principles of My Torah, but they were regarded as something alien. ¹³ The sacrifices for My burnt-offerings let them slaughter for meat and let them eat!* HASHEM does not desire them! Now He will remember their iniquity and punish their sins, and they will return to Egypt. ¹⁴ Israel has forgotten his Maker and he has built temples, and Judah has proliferated fortified cities; I will send a fire into his cities and it will consume his palaces.

9

No reason
to rejoice

¹ Rejoice not, Israel, like the exultation of the peoples, for you have strayed from your God; you have loved a harlot's fee on all the threshing floors of grain. * ² The threshing floor and wine pit will not provide food for them, and wine will betray them. ³ They will not dwell in the land of

---

Ephraim built even more (*Radak*).
8:13. You try to appease God by bringing burnt-offerings, but you are insincere and God rejects them. Instead of

bogus offerings, slaughter those animals for meat (*Rashi*).
9:1. Like a harlot taking her fee in grain, you have prostituted yourself before the nations.

ד יהוֹה וְשָׁב אֶפְרַיִם מִצְרַיִם וּבְאַשּׁוּר טָמֵא יֹאכֵלוּ: לֹא־יִסְכוּ לַיהוֹה יַיִן וְלֹא
יֶעֶרְבוּ־לוֹ זִבְחֵיהֶם כְּלֶחֶם אוֹנִים לָהֶם כָּל־אֹכְלָיו יִטַּמָּאוּ כִּי־לַחְמָם
ה-ו לְנַפְשָׁם לֹא יָבוֹא בֵּית יהוֹה: מַה־תַּעֲשׂוּ לְיוֹם מוֹעֵד וּלְיוֹם חַג־יהוֹה: כִּי־
הִנֵּה הָלְכוּ מִשֹּׁד מִצְרַיִם תְּקַבְּצֵם מֹף תְּקַבְּרֵם מַחְמַד לְכַסְפָּם קִמּוֹשׂ
ז יִירָשֵׁם חוֹחַ בְּאָהֳלֵיהֶם: בָּאוּ | יְמֵי הַפְּקֻדָּה בָּאוּ יְמֵי הַשִּׁלֻּם יֵדְעוּ יִשְׂרָאֵל
ח אֱוִיל הַנָּבִיא מְשֻׁגָּע אִישׁ הָרוּחַ עַל רֹב עֲוֹנְךָ וְרַבָּה מַשְׂטֵמָה: צֹפֶה אֶפְרַיִם
ט עִם־אֱלֹהָי נָבִיא פַּח יָקוֹשׁ עַל־כָּל־דְּרָכָיו מַשְׂטֵמָה בְּבֵית אֱלֹהָיו: הֶעְמִיקוּ
י שִׁחֵתוּ כִּימֵי הַגִּבְעָה יִזְכּוֹר עֲוֹנָם יִפְקוֹד חַטֹּאותָם: כַּעֲנָבִים
בַּמִּדְבָּר מָצָאתִי יִשְׂרָאֵל כְּבִכּוּרָה בִתְאֵנָה בְּרֵאשִׁיתָהּ רָאִיתִי אֲבוֹתֵיכֶם
יא הֵמָּה בָּאוּ בַעַל־פְּעוֹר וַיִּנָּזְרוּ לַבֹּשֶׁת וַיִּהְיוּ שִׁקּוּצִים כְּאָהֳבָם: אֶפְרַיִם
יב כָּעוֹף יִתְעוֹפֵף כְּבוֹדָם מִלֵּדָה וּמִבֶּטֶן וּמֵהֵרָיוֹן: כִּי אִם־יְגַדְּלוּ אֶת־בְּנֵיהֶם
יג וְשִׁכַּלְתִּים מֵאָדָם כִּי־גַם־אוֹי לָהֶם בְּשׂוּרִי מֵהֶם: אֶפְרַיִם כַּאֲשֶׁר־רָאִיתִי
יד לְצוֹר שְׁתוּלָה בְנָוֶה וְאֶפְרַיִם לְהוֹצִיא אֶל־הֹרֵג בָּנָיו: תֵּן־לָהֶם יהוֹה מַה־
טו תִּתֵּן תֵּן־לָהֶם רֶחֶם מַשְׁכִּיל וְשָׁדַיִם צֹמְקִים: כָּל־רָעָתָם בַּגִּלְגָּל כִּי־שָׁם
שְׂנֵאתִים עַל רֹעַ מַעַלְלֵיהֶם מִבֵּיתִי אֲגָרְשֵׁם לֹא אוֹסֵף אַהֲבָתָם כָּל־
טז שָׂרֵיהֶם סֹרְרִים: הֻכָּה אֶפְרַיִם שָׁרְשָׁם יָבֵשׁ פְּרִי °בְלִי־ [°בַל־ ק] יַעֲשׂוּן גַּם
יז כִּי יֵלֵדוּן וְהֵמַתִּי מַחֲמַדֵּי בִטְנָם: יִמְאָסֵם אֱלֹהַי כִּי לֹא שָׁמְעוּ לוֹ וְיִהְיוּ
א נֹדְדִים בַּגּוֹיִם: גֶּפֶן בּוֹקֵק יִשְׂרָאֵל פְּרִי יְשַׁוֶּה־לּוֹ כְּרֹב לְפִרְיוֹ **י**
ב הִרְבָּה לַמִּזְבְּחוֹת כְּטוֹב לְאַרְצוֹ הֵיטִיבוּ מַצֵּבוֹת: חָלַק לִבָּם עַתָּה יֶאְשָׁמוּ
ג הוּא יַעֲרֹף מִזְבְּחוֹתָם יְשֹׁדֵד מַצֵּבוֹתָם: כִּי עַתָּה יֹאמְרוּ אֵין מֶלֶךְ לָנוּ כִּי
ד לֹא יָרֵאנוּ אֶת־יהוֹה וְהַמֶּלֶךְ מַה־יַּעֲשֶׂה־לָּנוּ: דִּבְּרוּ דְבָרִים אָלוֹת שָׁוְא
ה כָּרֹת בְּרִית וּפָרַח כָּרֹאשׁ מִשְׁפָּט עַל תַּלְמֵי שָׂדָי: לְעֶגְלוֹת בֵּית אָוֶן יָגוּרוּ
שְׁכַן שֹׁמְרוֹן כִּי־אָבַל עָלָיו עַמּוֹ וּכְמָרָיו עָלָיו יָגִילוּ עַל־כְּבוֹדוֹ כִּי־גָלָה
ו מִמֶּנּוּ: גַּם־אוֹתוֹ לְאַשּׁוּר יוּבָל מִנְחָה לְמֶלֶךְ יָרֵב בָּשְׁנָה אֶפְרַיִם יִקָּח וְיֵבוֹשׁ
ז-ח יִשְׂרָאֵל מֵעֲצָתוֹ: נִדְמֶה שֹׁמְרוֹן מַלְכָּהּ כְּקֶצֶף עַל־פְּנֵי־מָיִם: וְנִשְׁמְדוּ בָמוֹת

9:4. Because they are brought without feelings of sincere contrition, God considers their offerings like food that is defiled by people who have had contact with the dead (*Radak*). They might as well save their money and eat the food themselves rather than offer it to God, Who does not accept it (*Rashi*).

9:5. A euphemism for the day He has set for a great slaughter (see *Zephaniah* 1:7).

9:6. An Egyptian city, usually identified as Memphis.

9:8. Ephraim set up prophets who claim that they were "with my God," but they were false prophets, as the verse goes on to explain (*Abarbanel*).

9:9. See *Judges* Chs. 19-20.

9:10. When Israel first became My people, I regarded them as enthusiastically as a traveler in the desert who

encounters a rare grapevine. At Baal-peor (see *Numbers* 25:1-9), their love for the Midianite women drew them into idolatry.

9:11. That is, their progeny who are commanded to honor them [see *Exodus* 20:12] (*Radak*).

9:12. They will not live to reach manhood.

9:13. Tyre was once prosperous and secure, but it was destroyed. Ephraim, too, will send its young men out to defend the country, only to be slain in battle (*Radak*).

9:15. A center of idolatrous worship (see 4:15).

10:1. Israel was once a fruitful, bountiful nation, but lost its prosperity because they wasted their good fortune on idol worship (*Rashi*).

10:4. A poisonous plant.

HASHEM, but Ephraim will return to Egypt and eat unclean food in Assyria. ⁴ They should not pour out wine [libations] to HASHEM for they will not be pleasing to Him; * their sacrifices will be to them like the bread of mourners, of which all who partake are defiled; rather, let their bread be for themselves, let it not come to the Temple of HASHEM. ⁵ What will you do on the appointed day, and on the day of HASHEM's feast? * ⁶ For behold, they have gone away because of plunder; Egypt will gather them in, Moph* will bury them. As for the treasure houses of their silver — thistles will inherit them; briars [will grow] in their tents. ⁷ The days of punishment have come; the days of requital have come; let Israel know — the [false] prophet is a fool; the man of spirit is mad — because of the abundance of your iniquity; the enmity is great. ⁸ The prophet of Ephraim is with my God; * the prophet is a net that ensnares [him] in all his ways and who causes enmity in the house of his God. ⁹ They deepened, they corrupted themselves as in the days of Gibeah; * He will remember their iniquity; He will punish their sins.

False prophets

¹⁰ 'I found Israel like grapes in the desert; * like a ripe fruit on a fig tree in its beginning did I view your fathers; but they came to Baal-peor and dedicated themselves to shamefulness; and they became loathsome by their love. ¹¹ [As for] Ephraim: their honor* will fly away like a bird, [perishing] from birth or from the womb or from conception. ¹² For even if they rear their children I will bereave them before manhood, * for woe is to them, as well, when I turn away from them! ¹³ Ephraim is as I saw Tyre, * implanted in [its] dwelling place; but Ephraim will [seek] to take his children out to the slayer.'

Frustrated hope

¹⁴ Give them, HASHEM, what You will give; give them a bereaving womb and shriveled breasts.

¹⁵ 'All their evil is in Gilgal, * where I hated them; for the evil of their deeds I will banish them from My house. I will not continue to love them; all their officers are rebellious. ¹⁶ Ephraim has been smitten; their root is withered, they will not produce fruit; even if they give birth I will slay the treasures of their wombs.'

¹⁷ My God will spurn them, for they have not obeyed Him, and they will wander about among the nations.

10

Bitter fruit

¹ Israel is [like] a vine that has shed the fruit that befits it; * when his fruit was abundant, he increased altars; when his land was bountiful, they improved pillars. ² Their hearts have become detached [from God]; now they will become desolate. He will destroy their altars and will lay waste to their pillars. ³ For now they will say, 'We have no king, for since we did not fear HASHEM, what can the king do for us?' ⁴ They have spoken words, swearing falsely, sealing covenants, so [their] judgment will sprout up like hemlock* on the furrows of the field. ⁵ Because of the calves of Beth-aven, * the inhabitants of Samaria will be frightened; for its people will mourn over it, as well as its priests who used to rejoice over its glory which has been exiled from it. ⁶ It, too, will be brought to Assyria, a gift to the king of Jareb; * Ephraim will take shame, and Israel will be ashamed for its counsel. * ⁷ Samaria's king has been silenced; he is like foam upon the water. ⁸ And the high places of

---

10:5. The calves were idols set up by Jeroboam son of Nebat, first king of the Northern Kingdom (*I Kings* 12:26-29).

10:6. For Jareb, see 5:13.
Ephraim and Israel will be ashamed for having set up the calves for worship (*Rashi*).

אָ֣וֶן חַטַּ֣את יִשְׂרָאֵ֗ל ק֤וֹץ וְדַרְדַּר֙ יַֽעֲלֶ֣ה עַל־מִזְבְּחוֹתָ֔ם וְאָֽמְר֤וּ לֶֽהָרִים֙
כַּסּ֔וּנוּ וְלַגְּבָע֖וֹת נִפְל֥וּ עָלֵֽינוּ: מִימֵי֙ הַגִּבְעָ֣ה חָטָ֔אתָ ט

יִשְׂרָאֵ֔ל שָׁ֖ם עָמָ֑דוּ לֹֽא־תַשִּׂיגֵ֧ם בַּגִּבְעָ֛ה מִלְחָמָ֖ה עַל־בְּנֵ֥י עַלְוָֽה: בְּאַוָּתִ֖י י
וְאֶסֳרֵ֑ם וְאֻסְּפ֤וּ עֲלֵיהֶם֙ עַמִּ֔ים בְּאָסְרָ֖ם לִשְׁתֵּ֥י °עֵינֹתָ֖ם [°עֽוֹנֹתָ֖ם ק]:

וְאֶפְרַ֨יִם֙ עֶגְלָ֣ה מְלֻמָּדָ֔ה אֹהַ֖בְתִּי לָד֑וּשׁ וַאֲנִ֣י עָבַ֗רְתִּי עַל־ט֣וּב צַוָּארָ֔הּ יא
אַרְכִּ֤יב אֶפְרַ֨יִם֙ יַֽחֲר֣וֹשׁ יְהוּדָ֔ה יְשַׂדֶּד־ל֖וֹ יַֽעֲקֹֽב: זִרְע֨וּ לָכֶ֤ם לִצְדָקָה֙ קִצְר֣וּ יב
לְפִי־חֶ֔סֶד נִ֥ירוּ לָכֶ֖ם נִ֑יר וְעֵת֙ לִדְר֣וֹשׁ אֶת־יְהֹוָ֔ה עַד־יָב֕וֹא וְיֹרֶ֥ה צֶ֖דֶק
לָכֶֽם: חֲרַשְׁתֶּם־רֶ֛שַׁע עַוְלָ֥תָה קְצַרְתֶּ֖ם אֲכַלְתֶּ֣ם פְּרִי־כָ֑חַשׁ כִּֽי־בָטַ֥חְתָּ יג
בְדַרְכְּךָ֖ בְּרֹ֣ב גִּבּוֹרֶ֑יךָ: וְקָ֣אם שָׁאוֹן֮ בְּעַמֶּךָ֒ וְכָל־מִבְצָרֶ֖יךָ יוּשַּׁ֑ד כְּשֹׁ֧ד יד
שַׁלְמַ֛ן בֵּ֥ית אַֽרְבֵ֖אל בְּי֣וֹם מִלְחָמָ֑ה אֵ֥ם עַל־בָּנִ֖ים רֻטָּֽשָׁה: כָּ֗כָה עָשָׂ֤ה לָכֶם֙ טו
בֵּֽית־אֵ֔ל מִפְּנֵ֖י רָעַ֣ת רָֽעַתְכֶ֑ם בַּשַּׁ֕חַר נִדְמֹ֥ה נִדְמָ֖ה מֶ֥לֶךְ יִשְׂרָאֵֽל: יא א כִּ֛י
נַ֥עַר יִשְׂרָאֵ֖ל וָֽאֹֽהֲבֵ֑הוּ וּמִמִּצְרַ֖יִם קָרָ֥אתִי לִבְנִֽי: קָֽרְא֖וּ לָהֶ֑ם כֵּ֚ן הָֽלְכ֣וּ ב
מִפְּנֵיהֶ֔ם לַבְּעָלִ֣ים יְזַבֵּ֔חוּ וְלַפְּסִלִ֖ים יְקַטֵּרֽוּן: וְאָֽנֹכִ֤י תִרְגַּ֨לְתִּי֙ לְאֶפְרַ֔יִם ג
קָחָ֖ם עַל־זְרֽוֹעֹתָ֑יו וְלֹ֥א יָֽדְע֖וּ כִּ֥י רְפָאתִֽים: בְּחַבְלֵ֨י אָדָ֤ם אֶמְשְׁכֵם֙ ד
בַּֽעֲבֹת֣וֹת אַֽהֲבָ֔ה וָֽאֶהְיֶ֥ה לָהֶ֛ם כִּמְרִ֥ימֵי עֹ֖ל עַ֣ל לְחֵיהֶ֑ם וְאַ֥ט אֵלָ֖יו
אוֹכִֽיל: לֹ֤א יָשׁוּב֙ אֶל־אֶ֣רֶץ מִצְרַ֔יִם וְאַשּׁ֖וּר ה֣וּא מַלְכּ֑וֹ כִּ֥י מֵֽאֲנ֖וּ ה
לָשֽׁוּב: וְחָֽלָ֥ה חֶ֨רֶב֙ בְּעָרָ֔יו וְכִלְּתָ֥ה בַדָּ֖יו וְאָכָ֑לָה מִמֹּֽעֲצֽוֹתֵיהֶֽם: וְעַמִּ֥י ו-ז
תְלוּאִ֖ים לִמְשֽׁוּבָתִ֑י וְאֶל־עַל֙ יִקְרָאֻ֔הוּ יַ֖חַד לֹ֥א יְרוֹמֵֽם: אֵ֣יךְ אֶתֶּנְךָ֣ אֶפְרַ֗יִם ח
אֲמַגֶּנְךָ֣ יִשְׂרָאֵ֔ל אֵ֚יךְ אֶתֶּנְךָ֣ כְאַדְמָ֔ה אֲשִֽׂימְךָ֖ כִּצְבֹאיִ֑ם נֶֽהְפַּ֤ךְ עָלַי֙
לִבִּ֔י יַ֖חַד נִכְמְר֥וּ נִֽחוּמָֽי: לֹ֤א אֶֽעֱשֶׂה֙ חֲר֣וֹן אַפִּ֔י לֹ֥א אָשׁ֖וּב לְשַׁחֵ֣ת ט
אֶפְרָ֑יִם כִּ֣י אֵ֤ל אָֽנֹכִי֙ וְלֹא־אִ֔ישׁ בְּקִרְבְּךָ֖ קָד֑וֹשׁ וְלֹ֥א אָב֖וֹא בְּעִֽיר: אַֽחֲרֵ֧י י
יְהֹוָ֣ה יֵֽלְכ֗וּ כְּאַרְיֵ֣ה יִשְׁאָ֔ג כִּי־ה֥וּא יִשְׁאַ֖ג וְיֶֽחֶרְד֥וּ בָנִ֖ים מִיָּֽם: יֶֽחֶרְד֤וּ יא
כְצִפּוֹר֙ מִמִּצְרַ֔יִם וּכְיוֹנָ֖ה מֵאֶ֣רֶץ אַשּׁ֑וּר וְהֽוֹשַׁבְתִּ֥ים עַל־בָּֽתֵּיהֶ֖ם נְאֻם־ יב א
יְהֹוָֽה: סְבָבֻ֤נִי בְכַ֨חַשׁ֙ אֶפְרַ֔יִם וּבְמִרְמָ֖ה בֵּ֣ית יִשְׂרָאֵ֑ל וִֽיהוּדָ֗ה עֹ֥ד
רָ֤ד עִם־אֵל֙ וְעִם־קְדוֹשִׁ֣ים נֶֽאֱמָ֔ן: אֶפְרַ֜יִם רֹעֶ֥ה ר֨וּחַ֙ וְרֹדֵ֣ף קָדִ֔ים כָּל־הַיּ֕וֹם ב

HAFTARAS
VAYEITZEI
Sephardim:
11:7-12:12;
some
continue
until 13:6.
Ashkenazim
begin on
p. 1346

10:8. Israel (*Rashi*), or the altars (*Ibn Ezra*), will beg to be covered, because of their great shame.

10:9. Idolatry was introduced to Israel at the time of the concubine at Gibeah (see *Judges* Chs. 19-20). Because of the idols, the campaign against the Gibeonites was not blessed with immediate success.

10:10. God used the nations to exact retribution against Israel. Both Ephraim and Judah were subjugated, like oxen plowing separate furrows.

10:11. Like a cow that would rather thresh than plow, because it can eat while it threshes, Ephraim preferred immediate pleasures to the "yoke" of the commandments. I took pity on its "neck," and gave it a Torah that was easily within its capability (*Radak*). If only the leaders of both Ephraim and Judah would carry out their responsibilities, the nation of Jacob would break up the clumps

of soil that impede their spiritual progress.

10:12. Set aside time for Torah study, and God will help you harvest an abundant spiritual crop.

10:15. At dawn, when most people go about their business, the king of Israel will be silenced, stunned in powerlessness by the presence of the king of Assyria (*Rashi*).

11:1-3. God reviews Israel's beginnings, when the nation was but a "lad" in Egypt. He sent Moses to redeem them, but "Ephraim," representing the future idolaters, failed to recognize that it was God who had saved them.

11:2. The prophets.

11:4. The kind of rope one would use to gently prod a person, as opposed to an animal's leash, which *forces* it to move along (*Rashi*).

11:7. The prophets.

Aven — the sin of Israel — will be destroyed; thorn and thistle will sprout up on their altars; they * will say to the mountains, 'Cover us!' and to the hills, 'Fall upon us!'

Dividends of sin

⁹ Since the days of Gibeah you have sinned, O Israel; there they stood. The war against men of iniquity did not overtake them in Gibeah. * ¹⁰ By My will I afflicted them, then the nations gathered against them when they bound them [to plow] two furrows. * ¹¹ Ephraim is a trained calf who loves to thresh; * and I passed over the goodliness of her neck; I joined Ephraim to plow [with] Judah, that Jacob should harrow. ¹² [I said,] 'Sow for yourselves righteousness and you will reap according to kindness; till for yourselves a tilling and [set] a time to seek HASHEM* until He comes and teaches you righteousness.' ¹³ But you have plowed wickedness, and you have reaped iniquity and eaten the fruit of denial; for you relied on your [evil] way, on your many mighty men. ¹⁴ And there will arise a din among your people, and all your fortresses will be plundered, like Shalman plundered Beth-arbel on the day of war, [when] mother and children were torn asunder. ¹⁵ So has Beth-el done to you because of your greatest evil; at dawn, * the king of Israel will be utterly silenced.

11

God reached out . . .

¹ **W**hen Israel was a lad* I loved him, and since Egypt I have been calling out to My son. ² [As much as] they * called to them, so did they turn away from them; they sacrificed to the Baalim and burnt incense to the idols. ³ I sent [a leader] to Ephraim who took them upon his arms and they did not know that I healed them. ⁴ With the cords of man I drew them, * with bonds of love, and I acted towards them like [farmers] who raise the yoke [from] upon their [animals'] jaws, and I provided food for them. ⁵ He will not return to the land of Egypt, but now Assyria is his king, for they refused to repent. ⁶ The sword will alight upon his cities, and it will destroy and devour his villages, because of their own designs. ⁷ And yet My people waver about returning to Me; and [though] they * call them to the Supreme One, they are together in not exalting [Him].

. . . Ephraim spurned Him

⁸ How can I hand you over, Ephraim, or deliver you, Israel?* How can I render you like Admah [or] make you like Zeboim? My heart has been over-turned; My mercies have been kindled together. ⁹ I will not carry out My burning wrath; I will not recant and destroy Ephraim, for I am God and not a man; the Holy One is in your midst, and I will not enter a city. * ¹⁰ They will follow after HASHEM, like a lion He will roar; * for He will roar and [His] children will stir from the west, ¹¹ they will stir like a bird from Egypt and like a dove from the land of Assyria, and I will settle them in their homes — the word of HASHEM.

12

Judah re-mained loyal

¹ **E**phraim has surrounded Me with falsehood, and the House of Israel with deceit, but Judah still ruled with God* and was faithful with the Holy One. ² Ephraim embraces the wind* and pursues the east wind; all day

---

11:8. Despite your sins, I cannot hand you over to the full punishments you deserve. I cannot destroy you like Admah and Zeboim (see *Deuteronomy* 29:22).

11:9. To destroy it like Admah and Zeboim (*Kara*). Alternatively: I will never choose another city over Jerusalem (*Targum*).

11:10. That is, He will declare His will — to gather in the

exiles — plainly and clearly, through the prophets (*Radak*).

12:1. When the schism among the tribes of Israel originally took place, Judah remained loyal to God [see *I Kings* Ch. 12] (*Radak*).

12:2. "Wind," signifying nothingness, refers to Ephraim's idol worship.

ג כָּזָב וָשֹׁד יַרְבֶּה וּבְרִית עִם־אַשּׁוּר יִכְרֹתוּ וְשֶׁמֶן לְמִצְרַיִם יוּבָל: ◀ וְרִיב
ד לַיהוָה עִם־יְהוּדָה וְלִפְקֹד עַל־יַעֲקֹב כִּדְרָכָיו כְּמַעֲלָלָיו יָשִׁיב לוֹ: בַּבֶּטֶן
ה עָקַב אֶת־אָחִיו וּבְאוֹנוֹ שָׂרָה אֶת־אֱלֹהִים: וַיָּשַׂר אֶל־מַלְאָךְ וַיֻּכָל בָּכָה
ו וַיִּתְחַנֶּן־לוֹ בֵּית־אֵל יִמְצָאֶנּוּ וְשָׁם יְדַבֵּר עִמָּנוּ: וַיהוָה אֱלֹהֵי הַצְּבָאוֹת
ז יְהוָה זִכְרוֹ: וְאַתָּה בֵּאלֹהֶיךָ תָשׁוּב חֶסֶד וּמִשְׁפָּט שְׁמֹר וְקַוֵּה אֶל־אֱלֹהֶיךָ
ח־ט תָּמִיד: כְּנַעַן בְּיָדוֹ מֹאזְנֵי מִרְמָה לַעֲשֹׁק אָהֵב: וַיֹּאמֶר אֶפְרַיִם אַךְ עָשַׁרְתִּי
י מָצָאתִי אוֹן לִי כָּל־יְגִיעַי לֹא יִמְצְאוּ־לִי עָוֹן אֲשֶׁר־חֵטְא: וְאָנֹכִי יְהוָה
יא אֱלֹהֶיךָ מֵאֶרֶץ מִצְרָיִם עֹד אוֹשִׁיבְךָ בָאֳהָלִים כִּימֵי מוֹעֵד: וְדִבַּרְתִּי עַל־
יב הַנְּבִיאִים וְאָנֹכִי חָזוֹן הִרְבֵּיתִי וּבְיַד הַנְּבִיאִים אֲדַמֶּה: אִם־גִּלְעָד אָוֶן אַךְ־
שָׁוְא הָיוּ בַּגִּלְגָּל שְׁוָרִים זִבֵּחוּ גַּם מִזְבְּחוֹתָם כְּגַלִּים עַל תַּלְמֵי שָׂדָי:

HAFTARAS VAYEITZEI
Ashkenazim:
12:13-14:10
יג

יג ◀ וַיִּבְרַח יַעֲקֹב שְׂדֵה אֲרָם וַיַּעֲבֹד יִשְׂרָאֵל בְּאִשָּׁה וּבְאִשָּׁה שָׁמָר: וּבְנָבִיא
טו הֶעֱלָה יְהוָה אֶת־יִשְׂרָאֵל מִמִּצְרָיִם וּבְנָבִיא נִשְׁמָר: הִכְעִיס אֶפְרַיִם
א תַּמְרוּרִים וְדָמָיו עָלָיו יִטּוֹשׁ וְחֶרְפָּתוֹ יָשִׁיב לוֹ אֲדֹנָיו: כְּדַבֵּר אֶפְרַיִם רְתֵת
ב נָשָׂא הוּא בְּיִשְׂרָאֵל וַיֶּאְשַׁם בַּבַּעַל וַיָּמֹת: וְעַתָּה | יוֹסִפוּ לַחֲטֹא וַיַּעֲשׂוּ
לָהֶם מַסֵּכָה מִכַּסְפָּם כִּתְבוּנָם עֲצַבִּים מַעֲשֵׂה חָרָשִׁים כֻּלֹּה לָהֶם הֵם
ג אֹמְרִים זֹבְחֵי אָדָם עֲגָלִים יִשָּׁקוּן: לָכֵן יִהְיוּ כַּעֲנַן־בֹּקֶר וְכַטַּל מַשְׁכִּים
ד הֹלֵךְ כְּמֹץ יְסֹעֵר מִגֹּרֶן וּכְעָשָׁן מֵאֲרֻבָּה: וְאָנֹכִי יְהוָה אֱלֹהֶיךָ מֵאֶרֶץ
ה מִצְרָיִם וֵאלֹהִים זוּלָתִי לֹא תֵדָע וּמוֹשִׁיעַ אַיִן בִּלְתִּי: אֲנִי יְדַעְתִּיךָ בַּמִּדְבָּר
ו בְּאֶרֶץ תַּלְאֻבוֹת: ◀ כְּמַרְעִיתָם וַיִּשְׂבָּעוּ שָׂבְעוּ וַיָּרָם לִבָּם עַל־כֵּן שְׁכֵחוּנִי:
ז־ח וָאֱהִי לָהֶם כְּמוֹ־שָׁחַל כְּנָמֵר עַל־דֶּרֶךְ אָשׁוּר: אֶפְגְּשֵׁם כְּדֹב שַׁכּוּל וְאֶקְרַע
ט סְגוֹר לִבָּם וְאֹכְלֵם שָׁם כְּלָבִיא חַיַּת הַשָּׂדֶה תְּבַקְּעֵם: שִׁחֶתְךָ יִשְׂרָאֵל כִּי־
י בִי בְעֶזְרֶךָ: אֱהִי מַלְכְּךָ אֵפוֹא וְיוֹשִׁיעֲךָ בְּכָל־עָרֶיךָ וְשֹׁפְטֶיךָ אֲשֶׁר אָמַרְתָּ
יא־יב תְּנָה־לִּי מֶלֶךְ וְשָׂרִים: אֶתֶּן־לְךָ מֶלֶךְ בְּאַפִּי וְאֶקַּח בְּעֶבְרָתִי: צָרוּר
יג עֲוֹן אֶפְרָיִם צְפוּנָה חַטָּאתוֹ: חֶבְלֵי יוֹלֵדָה יָבֹאוּ לוֹ הוּא־בֵן לֹא
יד חָכָם כִּי־עֵת לֹא־יַעֲמֹד בְּמִשְׁבַּר בָּנִים: מִיַּד שְׁאוֹל אֶפְדֵּם מִמָּוֶת
טו אֶגְאָלֵם אֱהִי דְבָרֶיךָ מָוֶת אֱהִי קָטָבְךָ שְׁאוֹל נֹחַם יִסָּתֵר מֵעֵינָי: כִּי הוּא

12:3. The entire nation, Ephraim and Judah together (*Ibn Ezra*).

12:4. See *Genesis* 25:26; 32:25-31.

12:5. Jacob did not release the angel until he promised him that God would appear in Beth-el and bless Jacob in person (*Rashi*).

12:6. He is remembered by His holy Name, the Tetragrammaton, which indicates His mastery over everything (*Metzudos*).

12:7. By dint of His promise and His support, you can return to Him (*Rashi*).

12:9. Instead of "hoping to God," they attribute their prosperity to their own doing and deny that wrongdoing had a part in amassing their fortunes.

12:10. Just as I provided your every need in the wilderness for forty years, I can do so today (*Ibn Ezra*).

12:12. Gilead was destroyed because the deeds of its people were vain and worthless.

12:14. During the forty years in the wilderness, God, through Moses, protected them from all their enemies. But instead of showing gratitude, Ephraim angered Him.

13:2. They made silver copies of Jeroboam's calf-idols, and the priests said that any parents who sacrifice their children will have the honor of kissing the calves, in reward for their devotion (*Rashi*).

13:6. The fruitful Land of Israel (*Rashi*).

13:8. I will force them to open their hearts to Me (*Rashi*).

13:13. A "wise" baby emerges from the womb quickly,

he increases falsehood and plunder; they seal a covenant with Assyria and oil is transported to Egypt. ³ HASHEM has a contention with Judah, to visit upon Jacob* according to his [evil] ways; He will requite him in accordance with his deeds. ⁴ In the womb he seized his brother's heel, and with his strength he struggled with [an angel of] God;* ⁵ he struggled with an angel and prevailed; [the angel] wept and beseeched him: 'In Beth-el He will find us and there He will speak with us.'* ⁶ HASHEM is the God of Legions; HASHEM is His remembrance.* ⁷ And as for you, return by your God;* observe kindness and justice, and always hope to your God. ⁸ [But you are instead] a trader with scales of deceit in his hand, who loves to cheat.

Ephraim was
arrogant ⁹ Ephraim said, 'Indeed I have become rich; I have found power for myself,* for in all my toil they will not find for me any iniquity which [contains] sin.' ¹⁰ I am HASHEM your God since the land of Egypt; I will yet settle you in tents as in the days of [early] times.* ¹¹ I spoke with the prophets and provided numerous visions, and through the prophets I conveyed allegories. ¹² If Gilead [suffered] destruction, they were but vanity,* in Gilgal they slaughtered oxen; indeed, their altars are like heaps upon the furrows of the field.

¹³ Jacob fled to the field of Aram; Israel worked for a wife, and for a wife he guarded [sheep]. ¹⁴ And by a prophet HASHEM brought Israel up from Egypt, and through a prophet they were safeguarded.* ¹⁵ Ephraim has angered [God] bitterly, and his blood guilt will be spread upon him, and his Lord will repay him for his scorn.

13

Plunging to
their doom ¹ When Ephraim spoke there was trembling; he was exalted in Israel, but he became guilty through Baal and he died. ² Now they continue to sin and they have made for themselves a molten image from their silver according to their design, idols, wholly the work of craftsmen. [The priests] say to them, 'Those who slaughter man shall kiss the calves.'* ³ Therefore, they shall become like the morning cloud, like the early dew that departs, like chaff that is blown from the threshing floor, and like smoke from a skylight. ⁴ I am HASHEM your God since the land of Egypt, and you should not have known any god besides Me, for there is no savior but Me. ⁵ I knew you in the wilderness, in a parched land. ⁶ With their pasture* they became sated; they were sated and their hearts grew haughty; therefore they forgot Me. ⁷ I will be like a lion to them; like a leopard I will lurk on the road. ⁸ I will encounter them like a bereaved bear and rip open the enclosure of their heart;* I will devour them there like a lion; the beast of the field will split them open. ⁹ You have destroyed yourself, Israel! For [you rebelled] against Me, your help. ¹⁰ I will be; [but] where is your king, that he may save you in all your cities, and your judges, of whom you said, 'Give me a king and officers'? ¹¹ I gave you a king in My anger, and I will take [him] away in My fury.

Ephraim's
foolishness ¹² Ephraim's iniquity is bound up; his sin is hidden away. ¹³ The pangs of childbirth will come upon him; he is an unwise child,* for he should not stay long at the children's birthstool. ¹⁴ From the clutches of the grave I would have ransomed them; I would have redeemed them from death; [but now,] I will be your words of death; I will be the One Who decrees the grave upon you; remorse will be hidden from My eyes. ¹⁵ For [though] he

---

thus avoiding a lengthy trauma at birth. The people of Ephraim are "unwise," for by repenting they could

shorten the pain that is imposed on them for their sins, but they refuse to do so (Radak).

בֵּין אַחִים יַפְרִיא יָבוֹא קָדִים רוּחַ יהוה מִמִּדְבָּר עֹלֶה וְיֵבוֹשׁ מְקוֹרוֹ

וְיֶחֱרַב מַעְיָנוֹ הוּא יִשְׁסֶה אוֹצַר כָּל־כְּלִי חֶמְדָּה: תֶּאְשַׁם שֹׁמְרוֹן

כִּי מָרְתָה בֵּאלֹהֶיהָ בַּחֶרֶב יִפֹּלוּ עֹלְלֵיהֶם יְרֻטָּשׁוּ וְהָרִיּוֹתָיו

יְבֻקָּעוּ:   ◄שׁוּבָה יִשְׂרָאֵל עַד יהוה אֱלֹהֶיךָ כִּי כָשַׁלְתָּ

בַּעֲוֹנֶךָ: קְחוּ עִמָּכֶם דְּבָרִים וְשׁוּבוּ אֶל־יהוה אִמְרוּ אֵלָיו כָּל־תִּשָּׂא עָוֹן

וְקַח־טוֹב וּנְשַׁלְּמָה פָרִים שְׂפָתֵינוּ: אַשּׁוּר ׀ לֹא יוֹשִׁיעֵנוּ עַל־סוּס לֹא

נִרְכָּב וְלֹא־נֹאמַר עוֹד אֱלֹהֵינוּ לְמַעֲשֵׂה יָדֵינוּ אֲשֶׁר־בְּךָ יְרֻחַם יָתוֹם:

אֶרְפָּא מְשׁוּבָתָם אֹהֲבֵם נְדָבָה כִּי שָׁב אַפִּי מִמֶּנּוּ: אֶהְיֶה כַטַּל לְיִשְׂרָאֵל

יִפְרַח כַּשּׁוֹשַׁנָּה וְיַךְ שָׁרָשָׁיו כַּלְּבָנוֹן: יֵלְכוּ יוֹנְקוֹתָיו וִיהִי כַזַּיִת הוֹדוֹ וְרֵיחַ

לוֹ כַּלְּבָנוֹן: יָשֻׁבוּ יֹשְׁבֵי בְצִלּוֹ יְחַיּוּ דָגָן וְיִפְרְחוּ כַגָּפֶן זִכְרוֹ כְּיֵין לְבָנוֹן:

אֶפְרַיִם מַה־לִּי עוֹד לָעֲצַבִּים אֲנִי עָנִיתִי וַאֲשׁוּרֶנּוּ אֲנִי כִּבְרוֹשׁ רַעֲנָן מִמֶּנִּי

פֶּרְיְךָ נִמְצָא: מִי חָכָם וְיָבֵן אֵלֶּה נָבוֹן וְיֵדָעֵם כִּי־יְשָׁרִים דַּרְכֵי יהוה

וְצַדִּקִים יֵלְכוּ בָם וּפֹשְׁעִים יִכָּשְׁלוּ בָם:◄

יד

HAFTARAS
SHABBAS
SHUVAH
(ALSO
HAFTARAH
MINCHAH
OF TISHAH
B'AV FOR
SEPHARDIM)
14:2-10

Haftarah
for Shabbos
Shuvah
continues:
Ashkenazim
on p. 1352,
Sephardim
on p. 1384

13:15. A metaphor for the kings of Assyria, who attacked, and eventually conquered, the Northern Kingdom.

14:3. An essential part of repentance is that one feel remorse for his past failings and sincerely resolve to improve. Thus the penitent begins by begging God to look favorably upon his good intentions and to accept the prayers, confession, and pledges of his lips in place of, and as more worthy than, fatted bulls as offerings, which may look superficially impressive but are lacking in inner content.

14:4. We will no longer put our faith in military might,

14

flourishes among the marshes, an east wind* will come, a wind of HASHEM ascending from the wilderness, and his fountainhead will become parched and his spring will dry up; and it will plunder the treasure of every splendid article. [1] *Samaria will be laid waste, for she has rebelled against her God. They will fall by the sword; their infants will be dashed and their pregnant women split open.*

Appeal for repentance

[2] *Return, Israel, unto HASHEM your God, for you have stumbled in your iniquity.* [3] *Take words with you and return to HASHEM; say to Him, 'May You forgive all iniquity and accept good [intentions], and let our lips substitute for bulls.* * [4] *Assyria will not save us; we will not ride upon horses,* * *and we will no longer say, "O our gods!" to the work of our hands; for it is with You that an orphan finds mercy.'*

Ephraim's rejuvenation

[5] *I* will rectify their waywardness; I will love them gratuitously; for My anger has turned away from them.* [6] *I will be to Israel like the dew, and he will blossom like a rosebush, and his roots will strike out like the [cedars of] Lebanon.* [7] *His tender branches will go forth, and his glory will be like [that of] the olive tree and his fragrance like that of Lebanon.* [8] *Those who dwell in His shade will return; they will revive [like] grain and blossom like a vine; their repute [will be] like the wine of Lebanon.* [9] *Ephraim [will say], 'What more need have I of idols?' I will respond and I will gaze upon him. I am like an ever-fresh cypress tree; your fruit will be provided from Me.*

[10] *Who is wise and will understand these things; [who is] understanding and will know them? For the ways of HASHEM are straight; the righteous will walk in them and sinners will stumble over them.*

---

for You alone are the champion of the oppressed, and the source of mercy.

14:5. God responds to Israel's contrition.

א א-ב דְּבַר־יהוה אֲשֶׁר הָיָה אֶל־יוֹאֵל בֶּן־פְּתוּאֵל: שִׁמְעוּ־זֹאת הַזְּקֵנִים וְהַאֲזִינוּ
ג כָּל יוֹשְׁבֵי הָאָרֶץ הֶהָיְתָה זֹּאת בִּימֵיכֶם וְאִם בִּימֵי אֲבֹתֵיכֶם: עָלֶיהָ לִבְנֵיכֶם
ד סַפֵּרוּ וּבְנֵיכֶם לִבְנֵיהֶם וּבְנֵיהֶם לְדוֹר אַחֵר: יֶתֶר הַגָּזָם אָכַל הָאַרְבֶּה וְיֶתֶר
ה הָאַרְבֶּה אָכַל הַיֶּלֶק וְיֶתֶר הַיֶּלֶק אָכַל הֶחָסִיל: הָקִיצוּ שִׁכּוֹרִים וּבְכוּ
ו וְהֵילִלוּ כָּל־שֹׁתֵי יָיִן עַל־עָסִיס כִּי נִכְרַת מִפִּיכֶם: כִּי־גוֹי עָלָה עַל־אַרְצִי
ז עָצוּם וְאֵין מִסְפָּר שִׁנָּיו שִׁנֵּי אַרְיֵה וּמְתַלְּעוֹת לָבִיא לוֹ: שָׂם גַּפְנִי לְשַׁמָּה
ח וּתְאֵנָתִי לִקְצָפָה חָשֹׂף חֲשָׂפָהּ וְהִשְׁלִיךְ הִלְבִּינוּ שָׂרִיגֶיהָ: אֱלִי כִּבְתוּלָה
ט חֲגֻרַת־שַׂק עַל־בַּעַל נְעוּרֶיהָ: הָכְרַת מִנְחָה וָנֶסֶךְ מִבֵּית יהוה אָבְלוּ
י הַכֹּהֲנִים מְשָׁרְתֵי יהוה: שֻׁדַּד שָׂדֶה אָבְלָה אֲדָמָה כִּי שֻׁדַּד דָּגָן הוֹבִישׁ
יא תִּירוֹשׁ אֻמְלַל יִצְהָר: הֹבִישׁוּ אִכָּרִים הֵילִילוּ כֹּרְמִים עַל־חִטָּה וְעַל־שְׂעֹרָה
יב כִּי אָבַד קְצִיר שָׂדֶה: הַגֶּפֶן הוֹבִישָׁה וְהַתְּאֵנָה אֻמְלָלָה רִמּוֹן גַּם־תָּמָר חָגְרוּ
יג וְתַפּוּחַ כָּל־עֲצֵי הַשָּׂדֶה יָבֵשׁוּ כִּי־הֹבִישׁ שָׂשׂוֹן מִן־בְּנֵי אָדָם:
    וְסִפְדוּ הַכֹּהֲנִים הֵילִילוּ מְשָׁרְתֵי מִזְבֵּחַ בֹּאוּ לִינוּ בַשַּׂקִּים מְשָׁרְתֵי אֱלֹהָי
יד כִּי נִמְנַע מִבֵּית אֱלֹהֵיכֶם מִנְחָה וָנָסֶךְ: קַדְּשׁוּ־צוֹם קִרְאוּ עֲצָרָה אִסְפוּ
טו זְקֵנִים כֹּל יֹשְׁבֵי הָאָרֶץ בֵּית יהוה אֱלֹהֵיכֶם וְזַעֲקוּ אֶל־יהוה: אֲהָהּ לַיּוֹם כִּי
טז קָרוֹב יוֹם יהוה וּכְשֹׁד מִשַּׁדַּי יָבוֹא: הֲלוֹא נֶגֶד עֵינֵינוּ אֹכֶל נִכְרָת מִבֵּית
יז אֱלֹהֵינוּ שִׂמְחָה וָגִיל: עָבְשׁוּ פְרֻדוֹת תַּחַת מֶגְרְפֹתֵיהֶם נָשַׁמּוּ אֹצָרוֹת
יח נֶהֶרְסוּ מַמְּגֻרוֹת כִּי הֹבִישׁ דָּגָן: מַה־נֶּאֶנְחָה בְהֵמָה נָבֹכוּ עֶדְרֵי בָקָר כִּי אֵין
יט מִרְעֶה לָהֶם גַּם־עֶדְרֵי הַצֹּאן נֶאְשָׁמוּ: אֵלֶיךָ יהוה אֶקְרָא כִּי אֵשׁ אָכְלָה
כ נְאוֹת מִדְבָּר וְלֶהָבָה לִהֲטָה כָּל־עֲצֵי הַשָּׂדֶה: גַּם־בַּהֲמוֹת שָׂדֶה תַּעֲרוֹג

ב א אֵלֶיךָ כִּי יָבְשׁוּ אֲפִיקֵי מָיִם וְאֵשׁ אָכְלָה נְאוֹת הַמִּדְבָּר: תִּקְעוּ
    שׁוֹפָר בְּצִיּוֹן וְהָרִיעוּ בְּהַר קָדְשִׁי יִרְגְּזוּ כֹּל יֹשְׁבֵי הָאָרֶץ כִּי־בָא יוֹם־
ב יהוה כִּי קָרוֹב: יוֹם חֹשֶׁךְ וַאֲפֵלָה יוֹם עָנָן וַעֲרָפֶל כְּשַׁחַר פָּרֻשׂ עַל־הֶהָרִים
    עַם רַב וְעָצוּם כָּמֹהוּ לֹא נִהְיָה מִן־הָעוֹלָם וְאַחֲרָיו לֹא יוֹסֵף עַד־שְׁנֵי
ג דּוֹר וָדוֹר: לְפָנָיו אָכְלָה אֵשׁ וְאַחֲרָיו תְּלַהֵט לֶהָבָה כְּגַן־עֵדֶן הָאָרֶץ
ד לְפָנָיו וְאַחֲרָיו מִדְבַּר שְׁמָמָה וְגַם־פְּלֵיטָה לֹא־הָיְתָה לּוֹ: כְּמַרְאֵה סוּסִים
ה מַרְאֵהוּ וּכְפָרָשִׁים כֵּן יְרוּצוּן: כְּקוֹל מַרְכָּבוֹת עַל־רָאשֵׁי הֶהָרִים יְרַקֵּדוּן

1:1. Scripture does not indicate when Joel prophesied. *Rashi* cites three opinions regarding his identity: He was the son of Samuel, see *I Samuel* 8:2 (*Midrash Rabbah*); he was a contemporary of Elisha (*Taanis* 5a); and Joel, Nahum and Habakkuk all prophesied during the reign of Manasseh (*Halachos Gedolos; Seder Olam*).

1:2. The Talmud (*Taanis* 5a) explains that Joel was sent to elaborate upon the seven-year famine foretold by Elisha (*II Kings* 8:1). Joel prophesied about a devastating plague of locusts, in the hope that the people would take the impending disaster to heart and avert it by repenting, as he exhorts them in the next chapter (*Rashi*).

1:6. The swarms of locusts are depicted as invading armies. *Abarbanel* interprets the four species of locusts as an allegory for the four conquerors of the land: Babylonia, Persia, Greece and Rome.

1:10. By the locusts.

1:17. Because they were not refilled.

1:19. The total destruction wrought by the locusts is compared to the ravages of a raging fire (*Radak*).

2:2. The swarms of locusts are depicted as an invading army.

2:3. The locusts will cause total destruction, as if they had been preceded and followed by raging fire.

2:4. The swarms.

1

**The terrible
locust plague**

¹ The word of HASHEM, which came to Joel son of Pethuel: *

² Hear this, O elders, and give ear, all inhabitants of the land! Was there such a thing in your days or in the days of your forefathers? * ³ Tell your children about it, and your children to their children, and their children to another generation: ⁴ What remained from the cutting-locust the abundant-locust has devoured; what remained from the abundant-locust the chewing-locust has devoured; and what remained from the chewing-locust the demolishing-locust has devoured. ⁵ Awaken, you drunkards, and weep, and wail all you wine-drinkers, over the fine wine that has been eliminated from your mouths. ⁶ For a nation * has come up against My land, mighty and without number; its teeth are the teeth of a lion, and it has the molars of a lion cub. ⁷ It has rendered my vine desolate and my fig tree a source of despair; it has stripped it [of its bark] and discarded [it]; its branches have turned white. ⁸ Lament like a maiden girded with sackcloth for the husband of her youth! ⁹ Meal-offering and libation have been eliminated from the Temple of HASHEM; the Kohanim, the ministers of HASHEM, mourn. ¹⁰ The field has been plundered, * the land destroyed; for the grain has been robbed, the wine dried up, and the oil devastated. ¹¹ Be ashamed, O plowmen; wail, O vine dressers — over wheat and over barley, for the harvest of the field has been lost; ¹² the vine has dried up and the fig tree has been devastated; the pomegranate tree as well as the date tree and the apple tree — all the trees of the field — have dried up, for rejoicing has dried up from among the sons of man.

**Lament the
plunder**

**Fast and
wail**

¹³ Gird yourselves [with sackcloth] and lament, O Kohanim; wail, O ministers of the Altar; come spend the night in sackcloth, O ministers of my God, for meal-offering and libation have been withheld from the Temple of your God. ¹⁴ Decree a fast; declare an assembly; gather the elders [and] all the inhabitants of the land to the Temple of HASHEM your God, and cry out to HASHEM. ¹⁵ Woe for that day! For the day of HASHEM is near, and like [sudden] plunder it will come from the Almighty. ¹⁶ Is not food cut off from before our eyes, and happiness and exultation from the Temple of our God? ¹⁷ Casks of wine have become moldy under their lids; * storehouses are laid desolate and silos destroyed, for the grain has withered. ¹⁸ How the animals groan; herds of cattle are bewildered, for there is no pasture for them; also flocks of sheep were made desolate. ¹⁹ To You, HASHEM, I call out, for fire * has consumed the dwellings of the wilderness, and flame has scorched the trees of the field. ²⁰ Also the animals of the field cry out to You, for the springs of water have dried up and fire has consumed the dwellings of the wilderness.

2

**An army
of locusts**

¹ Blow the shofar in Zion and sound the trumpet on My holy mountain! Let all the inhabitants of the land tremble; for the day of HASHEM has come; it is near — ² a day of darkness and thick darkness, a day of cloud and thick cloud, spreading over the mountains like the dawn — a numerous and mighty people; * its like has not been from eternity, and after it there will never again be, until the years of generation after generation. ³ Before it a fire consumes and after it a flame scorches; * before it the land was like the Garden of Eden, but after it a desolate desert; there is no remnant from it. ⁴ Like the appearance of horses is its * appearance; and like horsemen, so do they run. ⁵ With a noise like chariots they leap on the mountaintops,

ו   כְּקוֹל לַהַב אֵשׁ אֹכְלָה קָשׁ כְּעַם עָצוּם עֱרוּךְ מִלְחָמָה: מִפָּנָיו יָחִילוּ עַמִּים

ז   כָּל־פָּנִים קִבְּצוּ פָארוּר: כְּגִבּוֹרִים יְרֻצוּן כְּאַנְשֵׁי מִלְחָמָה יַעֲלוּ חוֹמָה וְאִישׁ

ח   בִּדְרָכָיו יֵלֵכוּן וְלֹא יְעַבְּטוּן אֹרְחוֹתָם: וְאִישׁ אָחִיו לֹא יִדְחָקוּן גֶּבֶר

ט   בִּמְסִלָּתוֹ יֵלֵכוּן וּבְעַד הַשֶּׁלַח יִפֹּלוּ לֹא יִבְצָעוּ: בָּעִיר יָשֹׁקּוּ בַּחוֹמָה יְרֻצוּן

י   בַּבָּתִּים יַעֲלוּ בְּעַד הַחַלּוֹנִים יָבֹאוּ כַּגַּנָּב: לְפָנָיו רָגְזָה אֶרֶץ רָעֲשׁוּ שָׁמָיִם

יא   שֶׁמֶשׁ וְיָרֵחַ קָדָרוּ וְכוֹכָבִים אָסְפוּ נָגְהָם: ◀וַיהוָה נָתַן קוֹלוֹ לִפְנֵי חֵילוֹ כִּי

   רַב מְאֹד מַחֲנֵהוּ כִּי עָצוּם עֹשֵׂה דְבָרוֹ כִּי־גָדוֹל יוֹם־יהוה וְנוֹרָא מְאֹד וּמִי

יב   יְכִילֶנּוּ: וְגַם־עַתָּה נְאֻם־יהוה שֻׁבוּ עָדַי בְּכָל־לְבַבְכֶם וּבְצוֹם וּבִבְכִי וּבְמִסְפֵּד:

יג   וְקִרְעוּ לְבַבְכֶם וְאַל־בִּגְדֵיכֶם וְשׁוּבוּ אֶל־יהוה אֱלֹהֵיכֶם כִּי־חַנּוּן וְרַחוּם

יד   הוּא אֶרֶךְ אַפַּיִם וְרַב־חֶסֶד וְנִחָם עַל־הָרָעָה: מִי יוֹדֵעַ יָשׁוּב וְנִחָם וְהִשְׁאִיר

טו   אַחֲרָיו בְּרָכָה מִנְחָה וָנֶסֶךְ לַיהוה אֱלֹהֵיכֶם: תִּקְעוּ שׁוֹפָר בְּצִיּוֹן

טז   קַדְּשׁוּ־צוֹם קִרְאוּ עֲצָרָה: אִסְפוּ־עָם קַדְּשׁוּ קָהָל קִבְצוּ זְקֵנִים אִסְפוּ עוֹלָלִים

יז   וְיֹנְקֵי שָׁדָיִם יֵצֵא חָתָן מֵחֶדְרוֹ וְכַלָּה מֵחֻפָּתָהּ: בֵּין הָאוּלָם וְלַמִּזְבֵּחַ יִבְכּוּ

   הַכֹּהֲנִים מְשָׁרְתֵי יהוה וְיֹאמְרוּ חוּסָה יהוה עַל־עַמֶּךָ וְאַל־תִּתֵּן נַחֲלָתְךָ

יח   לְחֶרְפָּה לִמְשָׁל־בָּם גּוֹיִם לָמָּה יֹאמְרוּ בָעַמִּים אַיֵּה אֱלֹהֵיהֶם: וַיְקַנֵּא יהוה

יט   לְאַרְצוֹ וַיַּחְמֹל עַל־עַמּוֹ: וַיַּעַן יהוה וַיֹּאמֶר לְעַמּוֹ הִנְנִי שֹׁלֵחַ לָכֶם אֶת־הַדָּגָן

   וְהַתִּירוֹשׁ וְהַיִּצְהָר וּשְׂבַעְתֶּם אֹתוֹ וְלֹא־אֶתֵּן אֶתְכֶם עוֹד חֶרְפָּה בַּגּוֹיִם:

כ   וְאֶת־הַצְּפוֹנִי אַרְחִיק מֵעֲלֵיכֶם וְהִדַּחְתִּיו אֶל־אֶרֶץ צִיָּה וּשְׁמָמָה אֶת־פָּנָיו

   אֶל־הַיָּם הַקַּדְמֹנִי וְסֹפוֹ אֶל־הַיָּם הָאַחֲרוֹן וְעָלָה בָאְשׁוֹ וְתַעַל צַחֲנָתוֹ כִּי

כא   הִגְדִּיל לַעֲשׂוֹת: אַל־תִּירְאִי אֲדָמָה גִּילִי וּשְׂמָחִי כִּי־הִגְדִּיל יהוה לַעֲשׂוֹת:

כב   אַל־תִּירְאוּ בַּהֲמוֹת שָׂדַי כִּי דָשְׁאוּ נְאוֹת מִדְבָּר כִּי־עֵץ נָשָׂא פִרְיוֹ תְּאֵנָה

כג   וָגֶפֶן נָתְנוּ חֵילָם: וּבְנֵי צִיּוֹן גִּילוּ וְשִׂמְחוּ בַּיהוה אֱלֹהֵיכֶם כִּי־נָתַן לָכֶם אֶת־

   הַמּוֹרֶה לִצְדָקָה וַיּוֹרֶד לָכֶם גֶּשֶׁם מוֹרֶה וּמַלְקוֹשׁ בָּרִאשׁוֹן: וּמָלְאוּ הַגֳּרָנוֹת

כד   בָּר וְהֵשִׁיקוּ הַיְקָבִים תִּירוֹשׁ וְיִצְהָר: וְשִׁלַּמְתִּי לָכֶם אֶת־הַשָּׁנִים אֲשֶׁר אָכַל

כה   הָאַרְבֶּה הַיֶּלֶק וְהֶחָסִיל וְהַגָּזָם חֵילִי הַגָּדוֹל אֲשֶׁר שִׁלַּחְתִּי בָּכֶם: וַאֲכַלְתֶּם

כו   אָכוֹל וְשָׂבוֹעַ וְהִלַּלְתֶּם אֶת־שֵׁם יהוה אֱלֹהֵיכֶם אֲשֶׁר־עָשָׂה עִמָּכֶם עִמָּכֶם

כז   לְהַפְלִיא וְלֹא־יֵבֹשׁוּ עַמִּי לְעוֹלָם: וִידַעְתֶּם כִּי בְקֶרֶב יִשְׂרָאֵל אָנִי וַאֲנִי

ג א   יהוה אֱלֹהֵיכֶם וְאֵין עוֹד וְלֹא־יֵבֹשׁוּ עַמִּי לְעוֹלָם: ▶ וְהָיָה אַחֲרֵי־

   כֵן אֶשְׁפּוֹךְ אֶת־רוּחִי עַל־כָּל־בָּשָׂר וְנִבְּאוּ בְּנֵיכֶם וּבְנוֹתֵיכֶם זִקְנֵיכֶם

Haftaras Shabbas Shuvah for Ashkenazim continues here: 2:11-27

Haftaras Shabbas Shuvah concludes on p. 1384

2:6. In consternation.

2:8. Even if the locusts were to fall upon swords, they would be unharmed; a sword is ineffectual against this enemy.

2:11. God's prophets forewarned the people of the impending disaster.

2:12. It is never too late to repent, even though God's decree has been issued (*Metzudos*).

2:14. There will be a blessing after the plague of locusts.

2:17. The Hall at the entrance of the Sanctuary building (see *I Kings* 6:3 and *Ezekiel* 40:48-49).

2:20. The northern one is the locust swarm; the Eastern Sea is either the Kinnereth or the Dead Sea; and the Western Sea is the Mediterranean (*Radak*).

2:23. A reference to the prophets (*Targum*).

3:1. In the End of Days, as explained in 4:1.

like the sound of a flaming fire consuming straw; like a mighty people arrayed for battle. ⁶ Peoples tremble before it; all faces become blackened. * ⁷ They run like mighty men; they scale the wall like men of war; everyone goes in his set way, and they do not corrupt their paths. ⁸ A man does not press his fellow, each one walks his course; they fall upon the sword, but are not wounded. * ⁹ They stride in the city; they run on the wall; they ascend into the houses; they come through the windows like a thief. ¹⁰ Before it the land trembles, the heavens quake; the sun and moon become blackened and the stars withdraw their shine.

God sent warnings

¹¹ HASHEM has emitted His voice before [the advent of] His army, * for His camp is very numerous, for those who carry out His word are mighty. For the day of HASHEM is great and very awesome; who will be able to bear it? ¹² 'Even now * — the word of HASHEM — return to Me with all your heart, with fasting, with weeping, and with lamentation.' ¹³ Rend your hearts and not your garments, and return to HASHEM your God, for He is gracious and merciful, slow to anger and of great kindness, and He relents of evil. ¹⁴ Whoever knows, let him repent and regret, and it will leave a blessing behind it, * for meal-offering and libation to HASHEM your God.

Get the people to respond . . .

¹⁵ Blow the shofar in Zion; decree a fast; call an assembly; ¹⁶ gather the people; summon the congregation; assemble the elders; gather the young children and sucklings; let the bridegroom go forth from his chamber and the bride from her canopy. ¹⁷ Between the Hall* and the Altar let the Kohanim, the ministers of HASHEM, weep; and let them say, 'Have pity, HASHEM, upon Your people, let not Your heritage be an object of scorn, for nations to dominate them. Why should they say among the peoples, "Where is their God?"'

¹⁸ Then HASHEM will take up the cause of His land and take pity on His people. ¹⁹ HASHEM will reply and say to His people: Behold, I am sending you the grain and the wine and the oil, and you will be sated from it, and I will no longer make you a disgrace among the nations. ²⁰ I will distance the northern one * from you and I will banish it to an arid and desolate land, its face to the Eastern Sea * and its rear to the Western Sea; * its foul odor will ascend, and its stench will go out, for it has done great [evil].

. . . and God will bless them

²¹ Fear not, O land; exult and be glad, for HASHEM has done great [kindness]. ²² Fear not, animals of the field, for the dwellings of the wilderness have become covered with grass; for the tree has borne its fruit; the fig tree and the vine have given forth their wealth. ²³ Children of Zion, exult and be glad with HASHEM your God, for He has given you a teacher for righteousness, * and He has brought down the rain for you — the early rain and the late rain — in the first [month]. ²⁴ The granaries will be filled with grain, and the vats will overflow with wine and oil. ²⁵ I will repay you for the years that the abundant-locust, the chewing-locust and the demolishing-locust and the cutting-locust — My great army that I sent among you — consumed. ²⁶ And you will eat, eating and being satisfied, and you will praise the name of HASHEM your God who has acted wondrously with you; and My people will not be shamed evermore. ²⁷ Then you will know that in the midst of Israel am I, and that I am HASHEM your God, there is none other; and My people will not be shamed evermore.

3

¹ And it will happen after this, * that I will pour out My spirit upon all flesh, and your sons and daughters will prophesy; your elders

ג חֲלֹמוֹת יַחֲלֹמוּן בַּחוּרֵיכֶם חֶזְיֹנוֹת יִרְאוּ: וְגַם עַל־הָעֲבָדִים וְעַל־הַשְּׁפָחוֹת

ג בַּיָּמִים הָהֵמָּה אֶשְׁפּוֹךְ אֶת־רוּחִי: וְנָתַתִּי מוֹפְתִים בַּשָּׁמַיִם וּבָאָרֶץ דָּם וָאֵשׁ

ד וְתִימֲרוֹת עָשָׁן: הַשֶּׁמֶשׁ יֵהָפֵךְ לְחֹשֶׁךְ וְהַיָּרֵחַ לְדָם לִפְנֵי בּוֹא יוֹם יהוה

ה הַגָּדוֹל וְהַנּוֹרָא: וְהָיָה כֹּל אֲשֶׁר־יִקְרָא בְּשֵׁם יהוה יִמָּלֵט כִּי בְּהַר־צִיּוֹן

וּבִירוּשָׁלִַם תִּהְיֶה פְלֵיטָה כַּאֲשֶׁר אָמַר יהוה וּבַשְּׂרִידִים אֲשֶׁר יהוה קֹרֵא:

ד א כִּי הִנֵּה בַּיָּמִים הָהֵמָּה וּבָעֵת הַהִיא אֲשֶׁר °אָשׁוּב [°אָשִׁיב ק] אֶת־שְׁבוּת

ב יְהוּדָה וִירוּשָׁלִָם: וְקִבַּצְתִּי אֶת־כָּל־הַגּוֹיִם וְהוֹרַדְתִּים אֶל־עֵמֶק יְהוֹשָׁפָט

וְנִשְׁפַּטְתִּי עִמָּם שָׁם עַל־עַמִּי וְנַחֲלָתִי יִשְׂרָאֵל אֲשֶׁר פִּזְּרוּ בַגּוֹיִם וְאֶת־

ג אַרְצִי חִלֵּקוּ: וְאֶל־עַמִּי יַדּוּ גוֹרָל וַיִּתְּנוּ הַיֶּלֶד בַּזּוֹנָה וְהַיַּלְדָּה מָכְרוּ בַיַּיִן

ד וַיִּשְׁתּוּ: וְגַם מָה־אַתֶּם לִי צֹר וְצִידוֹן וְכֹל גְּלִילוֹת פְּלָשֶׁת הַגְּמוּל אַתֶּם

מְשַׁלְּמִים עָלָי וְאִם־גֹּמְלִים אַתֶּם עָלַי קַל מְהֵרָה אָשִׁיב גְּמֻלְכֶם בְּרֹאשְׁכֶם:

ה-ו אֲשֶׁר־כַּסְפִּי וּזְהָבִי לְקַחְתֶּם וּמַחֲמַדַּי הַטֹּבִים הֲבֵאתֶם לְהֵיכְלֵיכֶם: וּבְנֵי

יְהוּדָה וּבְנֵי יְרוּשָׁלִַם מְכַרְתֶּם לִבְנֵי הַיְּוָנִים לְמַעַן הַרְחִיקָם מֵעַל גְּבוּלָם:

ז הִנְנִי מְעִירָם מִן־הַמָּקוֹם אֲשֶׁר־מְכַרְתֶּם אֹתָם שָׁמָּה וַהֲשִׁבֹתִי גְמֻלְכֶם

ח בְּרֹאשְׁכֶם: וּמָכַרְתִּי אֶת־בְּנֵיכֶם וְאֶת־בְּנוֹתֵיכֶם בְּיַד בְּנֵי יְהוּדָה וּמְכָרוּם

ט לִשְׁבָאיִם אֶל־גּוֹי רָחוֹק כִּי יהוה דִּבֵּר:　　　קִרְאוּ־זֹאת בַּגּוֹיִם קַדְּשׁוּ

י מִלְחָמָה הָעִירוּ הַגִּבּוֹרִים יִגְּשׁוּ יַעֲלוּ כֹּל אַנְשֵׁי הַמִּלְחָמָה: כֹּתּוּ אִתֵּיכֶם

יא לַחֲרָבוֹת וּמַזְמְרֹתֵיכֶם לִרְמָחִים הַחַלָּשׁ יֹאמַר גִּבּוֹר אָנִי: עוּשׁוּ וָבֹאוּ כָל־

יב הַגּוֹיִם מִסָּבִיב וְנִקְבָּצוּ שָׁמָּה הַנְחַת יהוה גִּבּוֹרֶיךָ: יֵעוֹרוּ וְיַעֲלוּ הַגּוֹיִם אֶל־

יג עֵמֶק יְהוֹשָׁפָט כִּי שָׁם אֵשֵׁב לִשְׁפֹּט אֶת־כָּל־הַגּוֹיִם מִסָּבִיב: שִׁלְחוּ מַגָּל כִּי

בָשַׁל קָצִיר בֹּאוּ רְדוּ כִּי־מָלְאָה גַּת הֵשִׁיקוּ הַיְקָבִים כִּי רַבָּה רָעָתָם:

יד-טו הֲמוֹנִים הֲמוֹנִים בְּעֵמֶק הֶחָרוּץ כִּי קָרוֹב יוֹם יהוה בְּעֵמֶק הֶחָרוּץ: שֶׁמֶשׁ

טז וְיָרֵחַ קָדָרוּ וְכוֹכָבִים אָסְפוּ נָגְהָם: וַיהוה מִצִּיּוֹן יִשְׁאָג וּמִירוּשָׁלִַם יִתֵּן קוֹלוֹ

יז וְרָעֲשׁוּ שָׁמַיִם וָאָרֶץ וַיהוה מַחֲסֶה לְעַמּוֹ וּמָעוֹז לִבְנֵי יִשְׂרָאֵל: וִידַעְתֶּם כִּי

אֲנִי יהוה אֱלֹהֵיכֶם שֹׁכֵן בְּצִיּוֹן הַר־קָדְשִׁי וְהָיְתָה יְרוּשָׁלִַם קֹדֶשׁ וְזָרִים לֹא־

יח יַעַבְרוּ־בָהּ עוֹד:　　　וְהָיָה בַיּוֹם הַהוּא יִטְּפוּ הֶהָרִים עָסִיס וְהַגְּבָעוֹת

תֵּלַכְנָה חָלָב וְכָל־אֲפִיקֵי יְהוּדָה יֵלְכוּ מָיִם וּמַעְיָן מִבֵּית יהוה יֵצֵא וְהִשְׁקָה

יט אֶת־נַחַל הַשִּׁטִּים: מִצְרַיִם לִשְׁמָמָה תִהְיֶה וֶאֱדוֹם לְמִדְבַּר שְׁמָמָה תִּהְיֶה

כ מֵחֲמַס בְּנֵי יְהוּדָה אֲשֶׁר־שָׁפְכוּ דָם־נָקִיא בְּאַרְצָם: וִיהוּדָה לְעוֹלָם תֵּשֵׁב

כא וִירוּשָׁלִַם לְדוֹר וָדוֹר: וְנִקֵּיתִי דָּמָם לֹא־נִקֵּיתִי וַיהוה שֹׁכֵן בְּצִיּוֹן:

3:4. Perhaps a metaphor for the great cataclysms and upheavals of that day (Rambam).

4:2. Alternatively: "the Valley of God's Judgment" (Rashi).

4:4. Israel has done you no harm, so you cannot claim that you are repaying them (or Me) for past wrongs.

4:10. Even erstwhile weaklings will be strong enough to join the army.

4:13. God is speaking to His agents of destruction, who are now to "harvest the crops" of Divine vengeance.

4:18. See *Ezekiel* 47:1-12.

4:21. Though I will cleanse the nations by forgiving many of their sins, I will not forgive them for the bloodshed they perpetrated against Israel. When "HASHEM dwells in Zion," i.e., at the End of Days, they will be punished.

Those who
repent
will be safe

will dream [prophetic] dreams, and your young men will see visions. ² Even also upon the slaves and upon the maidservants in those days I will pour out My spirit. ³ I will set wonders in the heavens and on earth: blood and fire and pillars of smoke; ⁴ the sun will turn to darkness and the moon to blood [red], * before the coming of the great and awesome Day of HASHEM. ⁵ And it will be that anyone who calls in the Name of HASHEM will escape, for on the mountain of Zion and in Jerusalem there will be refuge as HASHEM said, and among the survivors whom HASHEM summons.

4

Ingathering
of exiles

¹ "**F**or behold, in those days and at that time, when I will bring back the captivity of Judah and Jerusalem, ² I will gather all of the nations and bring them down to the Valley of Jehoshaphat * and I will contend with them there concerning My people and My possession, Israel, that they dispersed among the nations, and they divided up My land, ³ and they cast lots upon My people; they gave boys for harlot's [fee], and they sold girls for wine and drank [it]. ⁴ Also, what are you to Me, O Tyre and Sidon and all the districts of Philistia? Are you paying requital to Me?* And if you are requiting Me, swiftly and soon will I return your requital upon your head — ⁵ for you have taken My silver and My gold and you have brought My desirable and good possessions to your palaces; ⁶ and you have sold the children of Judah and the children of Jerusalem to the children of the Greeks in order to distance them from their border. ⁷ Behold, I will rouse them from the place to which you sold them, and I will return your requital upon your head. ⁸ And I will sell your sons and daughters into the hands of the children of Judah, and they will sell them to Sabaeans, to a distant people, for HASHEM has spoken.

Beat plows
into
swords . . .

⁹ Announce this among the nations; prepare for war; arouse the mighty men; let all the men of war approach and ascend. ¹⁰ Beat your plows into swords and your pruning forks into spears; even the weak one will say, 'I am mighty.'* ¹¹ Let all the surrounding nations hurry and come, and let them gather together; there HASHEM will demolish your warriors. ¹² Let the nations rouse themselves and go up to the Valley of Jehoshaphat, for there I will sit to judge all the nations from all around.

. . . bring on
destruction

¹³ 'Extend the sickle, * for the harvest has ripened! Come and trample [the grapes], for the winepress is full, the vats have overflowed!' — for their evil is great. ¹⁴ Multitudes upon multitudes [will fall] in the Valley of the [Final] Decision, for the day of HASHEM is near in the Valley of the [Final] Decision. ¹⁵ The sun and moon have become blackened, and the stars have withdrawn their shine. ¹⁶ And HASHEM will roar from Zion and will emit His voice from Jerusalem; and the heavens and earth will tremble. But HASHEM will be a shelter for His people and a stronghold for the Children of Israel. ¹⁷ Thus you will know that I am HASHEM your God, Who dwells in Zion, My holy mountain; Jerusalem will be holy, and aliens will no longer pass through her.

But
Judah will
ultimately
triumph

¹⁸ And it shall be on that day that the mountains will drip with wine, the hills will flow with milk, and all the watercourses of Judah will flow with water, and a spring will go out from the House of HASHEM and water the Valley of Shittim. * ¹⁹ Egypt will become a desolation and Edom will become a desolate wilderness; because of the robbery of the children of Judah, for they shed innocent blood in their land. ²⁰ Judah will exist forever, and Jerusalem from generation to generation. ²¹ Though I cleanse, their blood-shed I will not cleanse, * when HASHEM dwells in Zion.

א דִּבְרֵי עָמוֹס אֲשֶׁר־הָיָה בַנֹּקְדִים מִתְּקוֹעַ אֲשֶׁר חָזָה עַל־יִשְׂרָאֵל בִּימֵי ו עֻזִּיָּה מֶלֶךְ־יְהוּדָה וּבִימֵי יָרָבְעָם בֶּן־יוֹאָשׁ מֶלֶךְ יִשְׂרָאֵל שְׁנָתַיִם לִפְנֵי

ב הָרָעַשׁ: וַיֹּאמַר יְהוָה מִצִּיּוֹן יִשְׁאָג וּמִירוּשָׁלַ͏ִם יִתֵּן קוֹלוֹ וְאָבְלוּ נְאוֹת

ג הָרֹעִים וְיָבֵשׁ רֹאשׁ הַכַּרְמֶל: כֹּה אָמַר יְהוָה עַל־ שְׁלֹשָׁה פִּשְׁעֵי דַמֶּשֶׂק וְעַל־אַרְבָּעָה לֹא אֲשִׁיבֶנּוּ עַל־דּוּשָׁם בַּחֲרֻצוֹת

ד הַבַּרְזֶל אֶת־הַגִּלְעָד: וְשִׁלַּחְתִּי אֵשׁ בְּבֵית חֲזָאֵל וְאָכְלָה אַרְמְנוֹת בֶּן־הֲדָד:

ה וְשָׁבַרְתִּי בְּרִיחַ דַּמֶּשֶׂק וְהִכְרַתִּי יוֹשֵׁב מִבִּקְעַת־אָוֶן וְתוֹמֵךְ שֵׁבֶט מִבֵּית עֶדֶן וְגָלוּ עַם־אֲרָם קִירָה אָמַר יְהוָה: כֹּה אָמַר יְהוָה

ו עַל־שְׁלֹשָׁה פִּשְׁעֵי עַזָּה וְעַל־אַרְבָּעָה לֹא אֲשִׁיבֶנּוּ עַל־הַגְלוֹתָם גָּלוּת

ז שְׁלֵמָה לְהַסְגִּיר לֶאֱדוֹם: וְשִׁלַּחְתִּי אֵשׁ בְּחוֹמַת עַזָּה וְאָכְלָה אַרְמְנֹתֶיהָ:

ח וְהִכְרַתִּי יוֹשֵׁב מֵאַשְׁדּוֹד וְתוֹמֵךְ שֵׁבֶט מֵאַשְׁקְלוֹן וַהֲשִׁיבוֹתִי יָדִי עַל־עֶקְרוֹן

ט וְאָבְדוּ שְׁאֵרִית פְּלִשְׁתִּים אָמַר אֲדֹנָי יְהוִה: כֹּה אָמַר יְהוָה עַל־שְׁלֹשָׁה פִּשְׁעֵי־צֹר וְעַל־ אַרְבָּעָה לֹא אֲשִׁיבֶנּוּ עַל־הַסְגִּירָם גָּלוּת

י שְׁלֵמָה לֶאֱדוֹם וְלֹא זָכְרוּ בְּרִית אַחִים: וְשִׁלַּחְתִּי אֵשׁ בְּחוֹמַת צֹר וְאָכְלָה אַרְמְנֹתֶיהָ: כֹּה אָמַר יְהוָה עַל־שְׁלֹשָׁה פִּשְׁעֵי אֱדוֹם וְעַל־

יא אַרְבָּעָה לֹא אֲשִׁיבֶנּוּ עַל־רָדְפוֹ בַחֶרֶב אָחִיו וְשִׁחֵת רַחֲמָיו וַיִּטְרֹף לָעַד

יב אַפּוֹ וְעֶבְרָתוֹ שְׁמָרָה נֶצַח: וְשִׁלַּחְתִּי אֵשׁ בְּתֵימָן וְאָכְלָה אַרְמְנוֹת בָּצְרָה: כֹּה אָמַר יְהוָה עַל־שְׁלֹשָׁה פִּשְׁעֵי בְנֵי־עַמּוֹן וְעַל־

יג אַרְבָּעָה לֹא אֲשִׁיבֶנּוּ עַל־בִּקְעָם הָרוֹת הַגִּלְעָד לְמַעַן הַרְחִיב אֶת־ גְּבוּלָם:

יד וְהִצַּתִּי אֵשׁ בְּחוֹמַת רַבָּה וְאָכְלָה אַרְמְנוֹתֶיהָ בִּתְרוּעָה בְּיוֹם מִלְחָמָה

טו בְּסַעַר בְּיוֹם סוּפָה: וְהָלַךְ מַלְכָּם בַּגּוֹלָה הוּא וְשָׂרָיו יַחְדָּו אָמַר

א יְהוָה: כֹּה אָמַר יְהוָה עַל־שְׁלֹשָׁה פִּשְׁעֵי מוֹאָב וְעַל־אַרְבָּעָה ב

ב לֹא אֲשִׁיבֶנּוּ עַל־שָׂרְפוֹ עַצְמוֹת מֶלֶךְ־אֱדוֹם לַשִּׂיד: וְשִׁלַּחְתִּי־אֵשׁ בְּמוֹאָב וְאָכְלָה אַרְמְנוֹת הַקְּרִיּוֹת וּמֵת בְּשָׁאוֹן מוֹאָב בִּתְרוּעָה בְּקוֹל שׁוֹפָר: כֹּה

ג וְהִכְרַתִּי שׁוֹפֵט מִקִּרְבָּהּ וְכָל־שָׂרֶיהָ אֶהֱרוֹג עִמּוֹ אָמַר יְהוָה: אָמַר יְהוָה עַל־שְׁלֹשָׁה פִּשְׁעֵי יְהוּדָה וְעַל־אַרְבָּעָה לֹא אֲשִׁיבֶנּוּ

ד עַל־מָאֳסָם אֶת־תּוֹרַת יְהוָה וְחֻקָּיו לֹא שָׁמָרוּ וַיַּתְעוּם כִּזְבֵיהֶם אֲשֶׁר־הָלְכוּ אֲבוֹתָם אַחֲרֵיהֶם: וְשִׁלַּחְתִּי אֵשׁ בִּיהוּדָה וְאָכְלָה אַרְמְנוֹת ה

1:1. Also known as Azariah (see *II Kings* 15:17; *II Chronicles* Ch. 26).

This earthquake is mentioned also in *Zechariah* 14:5.

1:2. This verse is an allegorical prophecy concerning the downfall of the wicked nations, and may be seen as an introduction to the series of prophecies that follow (*Radak*).

1:3. In each of the prophecies that follow, the three transgressions are: the three cardinal sins — idolatry, adultery and murder (*Abarbanel*); or three [or more] other incidents in the history of the nation being ad-

dressed (*Radak*).

1:3-4. Ben-hadad and Hazael, kings of Damascus (Aram), oppressed the residents of Gilead physically (*Targum*). See *II Kings* 8:12 and 10:32.

1:5. See *II Kings* 16:9.

1:9. The covenant of friendship between King Solomon and King Hiram of Tyre (*I Kings* 5:26, 9:13).

1:11. A reference to *Numbers* 20:14-21 (*Rashi*), or to the Roman destruction of the Second Temple and Jerusalem (*Radak*).

1

(See Appendix A, timeline 4)

The four
sins of
Damascus . . .

¹ The words of Amos, who was one of the herders of Tekoa, who saw visions concerning Israel, in the days of Uzziah* king of Judah and in the days of Jeroboam son of Joash king of Israel, two years before the earthquake.* ² He said:

HASHEM will roar from Zion and emit His voice from Jerusalem, and the pastures of the shepherds will wither and the best of the fertile fields will dry up.*

³ Thus said HASHEM: For three transgressions of Damascus [I have looked away], but for four I will not pardon them — for their threshing the Gilead with rods of iron.* ⁴ I will send fire into the house of Hazael and it will consume the palaces of Ben-hadad. ⁵ I will break the bolt of Damascus, and I will eliminate inhabitants from Bikath-aven and the one who holds the scepter from Beth-eden, and the nation of Aram will be exiled to Kir* — said HASHEM.

. . . of Gaza

⁶ Thus said HASHEM: For three transgressions of Gaza [I have looked away], but for four I will not pardon them — for their effecting a total exile by handing over [escapees] to Edom. ⁷ I will send fire into the wall of Gaza and it will consume its palaces. ⁸ I will eliminate inhabitants from Ashdod and the one who holds the scepter from Ashkelon; I will turn My hand repeatedly against Ekron, and the remnant of the Philistines will perish — said the Lord HASHEM/ELOHIM.

. . . of Tyre

⁹ Thus said HASHEM: For three transgressions of Tyre [I have looked away], but for four I will not pardon them — for their delivering a total exile to Edom, not remembering the covenant of brothers.* ¹⁰ I will send fire into the wall of Tyre, and it will consume its palaces.

. . . of Edom

¹¹ Thus said HASHEM: For three transgressions of Edom [I have looked away], but for four I will not pardon them — for their pursuing his brother with the sword* and suppressing his mercy; his anger has slaughtered incessantly and he has kept his fury forever. ¹² I will send fire into Teman and it will consume the palaces of Bozrah.

. . . of Ammon

¹³ Thus said HASHEM: For three transgressions of the Children of Ammon [I have looked away], but for four I will not pardon them — for their splitting open the pregnant women of the Gilead* in order to broaden their own border. ¹⁴ I will kindle a fire in the wall of Rabbah and it will consume its palaces amidst trumpeting on the day of battle, with a whirlwind, on the day of the tempest. ¹⁵ Their king will go into exile, he and his officers together — said HASHEM.

2

The four sins
of Moab . . .

¹ Thus said HASHEM: For three transgressions of Moab [I have looked away], but for four I will not pardon them — for their burning the bones of the king of Edom into lime.* ² I will send fire into Moab and it will consume the palaces of Kerioth, and Moab will die in a tumult, amidst trumpeting and the sound of the shofar. ³ I will eliminate any judge from its midst, and I will kill all of its officers along with them — said HASHEM.

. . . and of
Judah

⁴ Thus said HASHEM: For three transgressions of Judah [I have looked away], but for four I will not pardon them — for their despising the Torah of HASHEM and not observing His statutes; their falsehoods that their fathers followed have corrupted them. ⁵ I will send fire into Judah and it will consume the palaces of Jerusalem.

1:13. So ruthless were they in their drive to eliminate the Jewish population there.

2:1. This gruesome act is not recorded in Scripture (Rashi).

יְרוּשָׁלָ͏ִם: ◄ כֹּה אָמַר יהוה עַל־שְׁלֹשָׁה פִּשְׁעֵי יִשְׂרָאֵל וְעַל־אַרְבָּעָה
ז לֹא אֲשִׁיבֶנּוּ עַל־מִכְרָם בַּכֶּסֶף צַדִּיק וְאֶבְיוֹן בַּעֲבוּר נַעֲלָיִם: הַשֹּׁאֲפִים עַל־
עֲפַר־אֶרֶץ בְּרֹאשׁ דַּלִּים וְדֶרֶךְ עֲנָוִים יַטּוּ וְאִישׁ וְאָבִיו יֵלְכוּ אֶל־הַנַּעֲרָה
ח לְמַעַן חַלֵּל אֶת־שֵׁם קָדְשִׁי: וְעַל־בְּגָדִים חֲבֻלִים יַטּוּ אֵצֶל כָּל־מִזְבֵּחַ וְיֵין
ט עֲנוּשִׁים יִשְׁתּוּ בֵּית אֱלֹהֵיהֶם: וְאָנֹכִי הִשְׁמַדְתִּי אֶת־הָאֱמֹרִי מִפְּנֵיהֶם אֲשֶׁר
כְּגֹבַהּ אֲרָזִים גָּבְהוֹ וְחָסֹן הוּא כָּאַלּוֹנִים וָאַשְׁמִיד פִּרְיוֹ מִמַּעַל וְשָׁרָשָׁיו
י מִתָּחַת: וְאָנֹכִי הֶעֱלֵיתִי אֶתְכֶם מֵאֶרֶץ מִצְרָיִם וָאוֹלֵךְ אֶתְכֶם בַּמִּדְבָּר
יא אַרְבָּעִים שָׁנָה לָרֶשֶׁת אֶת־אֶרֶץ הָאֱמֹרִי: וָאָקִים מִבְּנֵיכֶם לִנְבִיאִים
יב וּמִבַּחוּרֵיכֶם לִנְזִרִים הַאַף אֵין־זֹאת בְּנֵי יִשְׂרָאֵל נְאֻם־יהוה: וַתַּשְׁקוּ אֶת־
יג הַנְּזִרִים יָיִן וְעַל־הַנְּבִיאִים צִוִּיתֶם לֵאמֹר לֹא תִּנָּבְאוּ: הִנֵּה אָנֹכִי מֵעִיק
יד תַּחְתֵּיכֶם כַּאֲשֶׁר תָּעִיק הָעֲגָלָה הַמְלֵאָה לָהּ עָמִיר: וְאָבַד מָנוֹס מִקָּל וְחָזָק
טו לֹא־יְאַמֵּץ כֹּחוֹ וְגִבּוֹר לֹא־יְמַלֵּט נַפְשׁוֹ: וְתֹפֵשׂ הַקֶּשֶׁת לֹא יַעֲמֹד וְקַל
טז בְּרַגְלָיו לֹא יְמַלֵּט וְרֹכֵב הַסּוּס לֹא יְמַלֵּט נַפְשׁוֹ: וְאַמִּיץ לִבּוֹ בַּגִּבּוֹרִים
ג א עָרוֹם יָנוּס בַּיּוֹם־הַהוּא נְאֻם־יהוה: שִׁמְעוּ אֶת־הַדָּבָר הַזֶּה
אֲשֶׁר דִּבֶּר יהוה עֲלֵיכֶם בְּנֵי יִשְׂרָאֵל עַל כָּל־הַמִּשְׁפָּחָה אֲשֶׁר הֶעֱלֵיתִי
ב מֵאֶרֶץ מִצְרַיִם לֵאמֹר: רַק אֶתְכֶם יָדַעְתִּי מִכֹּל מִשְׁפְּחוֹת הָאֲדָמָה עַל־כֵּן
ג אֶפְקֹד עֲלֵיכֶם אֵת כָּל־עֲוֺנֹתֵיכֶם: הֲיֵלְכוּ שְׁנַיִם יַחְדָּו בִּלְתִּי אִם־נוֹעָדוּ:
ד הֲיִשְׁאַג אַרְיֵה בַּיַּעַר וְטֶרֶף אֵין לוֹ הֲיִתֵּן כְּפִיר קוֹלוֹ מִמְּעֹנָתוֹ בִּלְתִּי אִם־
ה לָכָד: הֲתִפֹּל צִפּוֹר עַל־פַּח הָאָרֶץ וּמוֹקֵשׁ אֵין לָהּ הֲיַעֲלֶה־פַּח מִן־הָאֲדָמָה
ו וְלָכוֹד לֹא יִלְכּוֹד: אִם־יִתָּקַע שׁוֹפָר בְּעִיר וְעָם לֹא יֶחֱרָדוּ אִם־תִּהְיֶה רָעָה
ז בְּעִיר וַיהוה לֹא עָשָׂה: כִּי לֹא יַעֲשֶׂה אֲדֹנָי יֱהוִֹה דָּבָר כִּי אִם־גָּלָה סוֹדוֹ
ח אֶל־עֲבָדָיו הַנְּבִיאִים: אַרְיֵה שָׁאָג מִי לֹא יִירָא אֲדֹנָי יֱהוִֹה דִּבֶּר מִי לֹא
ט יִנָּבֵא: ▸ הַשְׁמִיעוּ עַל־אַרְמְנוֹת בְּאַשְׁדּוֹד וְעַל־אַרְמְנוֹת בְּאֶרֶץ מִצְרָיִם
וְאִמְרוּ הֵאָסְפוּ עַל־הָרֵי שֹׁמְרוֹן וּרְאוּ מְהוּמֹת רַבּוֹת בְּתוֹכָהּ וַעֲשׁוּקִים
י בְּקִרְבָּהּ: וְלֹא־יָדְעוּ עֲשׂוֹת־נְכֹחָה נְאֻם־יהוה הָאוֹצְרִים חָמָס וָשֹׁד
יא בְּאַרְמְנוֹתֵיהֶם: לָכֵן כֹּה אָמַר אֲדֹנָי יֱהוִֹה צַר וּסְבִיב הָאָרֶץ
יב וְהוֹרִד מִמֵּךְ עֻזֵּךְ וְנָבֹזּוּ אַרְמְנוֹתָיִךְ: כֹּה אָמַר יהוה כַּאֲשֶׁר יַצִּיל הָרֹעֶה מִפִּי
הָאֲרִי שְׁתֵּי כְרָעַיִם אוֹ בְדַל־אֹזֶן כֵּן יִנָּצְלוּ בְּנֵי יִשְׂרָאֵל הַיֹּשְׁבִים בְּשֹׁמְרוֹן
יג בִּפְאַת מִטָּה וּבִדְמֶשֶׁק עָרֶשׂ: שִׁמְעוּ וְהָעִידוּ בְּבֵית יַעֲקֹב נְאֻם־

2:6. Their judges accepted bribes to exonerate the highest bidder (Radak).

2:7. For immoral purposes.

2:11. People who would withdraw from physical pleasure in order to teach the Torah to others (Targum, Rashi).

3:1. The subject is God. The prophet often speaks of God in the first and third persons interchangeably.

3:3. The following prophecy, which begins with verse 9,

is introduced by a series of rhetorical questions. Their theme is that just as events can be understood only if one knows their cause, so too, the calamities that befall Israel must be understood as punishment for sin, never as coincidence.

3:6. By the sentries.

3:7. So when you are warned of imminent punishment, why do you fail to repent?

The sins of Israel

⁶ Thus said HASHEM: For three transgressions of Israel [I have looked away], but for four I will not pardon them — for their selling a righteous man for money, and a poor man for shoes. * ⁷ They aspire [as they walk on] the dust of the earth for the head of the poor and they twist the judgment of the humble; a man and his father go to a maiden* in order to desecrate My holy Name. ⁸ They recline on pawned garments beside every altar and they drink the wine of victims they penalized in the temple of their gods. ⁹ Yet I destroyed the Amorite from before them — [the Amorite] whose height was like the height of cedar trees and who were mighty as oaks — and I destroyed his fruit from above and his roots from below. ¹⁰ I brought you up from the land of Egypt and I led you through the wilderness for forty years, to take possession of the land of the Amorite. ¹¹ I established some of your sons as prophets and some of your young men as nazirites;* is this not also so, O Children of Israel? — the word of HASHEM. ¹² But you gave the nazirites wine to drink and you commanded the prophets, saying, 'Do not prophesy.' ¹³ Behold, I will encumber [you] in your place just as a wagon full of sheaves is encumbered. ¹⁴ Escape will elude the swift one; the strong one will not muster his strength; and the mighty one will not save his soul. ¹⁵ He who holds the bow will not stand; the swift of foot will not save himself; the rider of the horse will not save his soul; ¹⁶ and the bold-hearted among the mighty will flee naked on that day — the word of HASHEM.

Ungrateful nation

3

¹ Hear this prophecy that HASHEM has spoken concerning you, Children of Israel, concerning the entire family that I* brought up from the land of Egypt, saying:

Not a coincidence

² You alone did I know from among all the families of the earth; therefore I will hold you to account for all your inquities. ³ Do two people walk together, unless they had [so] arranged?* ⁴ Does a lion roar in the forest, if it has no kill? Does a young lion send forth his voice from his lair, unless he has captured [prey]? ⁵ Does a bird fall into a trap on the ground, if it does not have a snare? Does the trap rise from the ground, unless it has entrapped? ⁶ Is the shofar ever sounded* in a city and the people not tremble? Can there be misfortune in a city, if HASHEM had not brought it? ⁷ For the Lord HASHEM/ELOHIM will not do anything unless He has revealed His secret to His servants the prophets. * ⁸ A lion has roared; who will not fear? The Lord HASHEM/ELOHIM has spoken; who will not prophesy?*

Observe the destruction

⁹ Announce atop the palaces of Ashdod and atop the palaces in the land of Egypt; say, 'Gather together on the mountains of Samaria and observe the great turmoils within it and the oppressed people in its midst.' ¹⁰ They do not know how to do right — the word of HASHEM — they store up violence and plunder in their palaces. ¹¹ Therefore, thus said the Lord HASHEM/ELOHIM: An enemy, encircling the land, and he will take your might down from you, and your palaces will be plundered. ¹² Thus said HASHEM: Just as a shepherd can rescue from the mouth of a lion [but] two legs or the cartilage of an ear, so shall be rescued from the Children of Israel who dwell in Samaria [but] the corner of a bed and the edge of a couch. ¹³ Listen and testify in the House of Jacob* — the word of the

---

3:8. Just as one cannot ignore a lion's roar, so the prophets cannot ignore the command to prophesy (Rashi).

3:13. God commands the prophets to hear and convey His words to the people.

יד אֲדֹנָי יֱהֹוִה אֱלֹהֵי הַצְּבָאוֹת: כִּי בְּיוֹם פׇּקְדִי פִשְׁעֵי־יִשְׂרָאֵל עָלָיו וּפָקַדְתִּי
טו עַל־מִזְבְּחוֹת בֵּית־אֵל וְנִגְדְּעוּ קַרְנוֹת הַמִּזְבֵּחַ וְנָפְלוּ לָאָרֶץ: וְהִכֵּיתִי
בֵית־הַחֹרֶף עַל־בֵּית הַקָּיִץ וְאָבְדוּ בָּתֵּי הַשֵּׁן וְסָפוּ בָּתִּים רַבִּים נְאֻם־

ד א יְהֹוָה: שִׁמְעוּ הַדָּבָר הַזֶּה פָּרוֹת הַבָּשָׁן אֲשֶׁר בְּהַר שֹׁמְרוֹן
הָעֹשְׁקוֹת דַּלִּים הָרֹצְצוֹת אֶבְיוֹנִים הָאֹמְרֹת לַאֲדֹנֵיהֶם הָבִיאָה וְנִשְׁתֶּה:
ב נִשְׁבַּע אֲדֹנָי יֱהֹוִה בְּקׇדְשׁוֹ כִּי הִנֵּה יָמִים בָּאִים עֲלֵיכֶם וְנִשָּׂא אֶתְכֶם
ג בְּצִנּוֹת וְאַחֲרִיתְכֶן בְּסִירוֹת דּוּגָה: וּפְרָצִים תֵּצֶאנָה אִשָּׁה נֶגְדָּהּ
ד וְהִשְׁלַכְתֶּנָה הַהַרְמוֹנָה נְאֻם־יְהֹוָה: בֹּאוּ בֵית־אֵל וּפִשְׁעוּ הַגִּלְגָּל הַרְבּוּ
ה לִפְשֹׁעַ וְהָבִיאוּ לַבֹּקֶר זִבְחֵיכֶם לִשְׁלֹשֶׁת יָמִים מַעְשְׂרֹתֵיכֶם: וְקַטֵּר מֵחָמֵץ
תּוֹדָה וְקִרְאוּ נְדָבוֹת הַשְׁמִיעוּ כִּי כֵן אֲהַבְתֶּם בְּנֵי יִשְׂרָאֵל נְאֻם אֲדֹנָי יֱהֹוִה:
ו וְגַם־אֲנִי נָתַתִּי לָכֶם נִקְיוֹן שִׁנַּיִם בְּכׇל־עָרֵיכֶם וְחֹסֶר לֶחֶם בְּכֹל
ז מְקוֹמֹתֵיכֶם וְלֹא־שַׁבְתֶּם עָדַי נְאֻם־יְהֹוָה: וְגַם אָנֹכִי מָנַעְתִּי מִכֶּם אֶת־
הַגֶּשֶׁם בְּעוֹד שְׁלֹשָׁה חֳדָשִׁים לַקָּצִיר וְהִמְטַרְתִּי עַל־עִיר אֶחָת וְעַל־עִיר
אַחַת לֹא אַמְטִיר חֶלְקָה אַחַת תִּמָּטֵר וְחֶלְקָה אֲשֶׁר־לֹא־תַמְטִיר עָלֶיהָ
ח תִּיבָשׁ: וְנָעוּ שְׁתַּיִם שָׁלֹשׁ עָרִים אֶל־עִיר אַחַת לִשְׁתּוֹת מַיִם וְלֹא יִשְׂבָּעוּ
ט וְלֹא־שַׁבְתֶּם עָדַי נְאֻם־יְהֹוָה: הִכֵּיתִי אֶתְכֶם בַּשִּׁדָּפוֹן וּבַיֵּרָקוֹן הַרְבּוֹת
גַּנּוֹתֵיכֶם וְכַרְמֵיכֶם וּתְאֵנֵיכֶם וְזֵיתֵיכֶם יֹאכַל הַגָּזָם וְלֹא־שַׁבְתֶּם עָדַי
י נְאֻם־יְהֹוָה: שִׁלַּחְתִּי בָכֶם דֶּבֶר בְּדֶרֶךְ מִצְרַיִם הָרַגְתִּי בַחֶרֶב בַּחוּרֵיכֶם
עִם שְׁבִי סוּסֵיכֶם וָאַעֲלֶה בְּאֹשׁ מַחֲנֵיכֶם וּבְאַפְּכֶם וְלֹא־שַׁבְתֶּם עָדַי
יא נְאֻם־יְהֹוָה: הָפַכְתִּי בָכֶם כְּמַהְפֵּכַת אֱלֹהִים אֶת־סְדֹם וְאֶת־עֲמֹרָה וַתִּהְיוּ
יב כְּאוּד מֻצָּל מִשְּׂרֵפָה וְלֹא־שַׁבְתֶּם עָדַי נְאֻם־יְהֹוָה: לָכֵן
כֹּה אֶעֱשֶׂה־לְּךָ יִשְׂרָאֵל עֵקֶב כִּי־זֹאת אֶעֱשֶׂה־לָּךְ הִכּוֹן לִקְרַאת־
יג אֱלֹהֶיךָ יִשְׂרָאֵל: כִּי הִנֵּה יוֹצֵר הָרִים וּבֹרֵא רוּחַ וּמַגִּיד לְאָדָם מַה־
שֵּׂחוֹ עֹשֵׂה שַׁחַר עֵיפָה וְדֹרֵךְ עַל־בָּמֳתֵי אָרֶץ יְהֹוָה אֱלֹהֵי־צְבָאוֹת

ה א שְׁמוֹ:   שִׁמְעוּ אֶת־הַדָּבָר הַזֶּה אֲשֶׁר אָנֹכִי נֹשֵׂא עֲלֵיכֶם קִינָה
ב בֵּית יִשְׂרָאֵל: נָפְלָה לֹא־תוֹסִיף קוּם בְּתוּלַת יִשְׂרָאֵל נִטְּשָׁה עַל־אַדְמָתָהּ
ג אֵין מְקִימָהּ: כִּי כֹה אָמַר אֲדֹנָי יֱהֹוִה הָעִיר הַיֹּצֵאת אֶלֶף
ד תַּשְׁאִיר מֵאָה וְהַיּוֹצֵאת מֵאָה תַּשְׁאִיר עֲשָׂרָה לְבֵית יִשְׂרָאֵל: כִּי

4:1. A reference to the wives of the nobles, whose desire for a luxurious life-style drove their husbands to unjust monetary practices (*Rashi*).

4:2. These were small boats that were shield-like in appearance and were used to transport slaves (*Metzudos*). Alternatively: The verse speaks not of boats, but of hooks: "You will be dragged off with grappling hooks, and your children with fish hooks" (*Ibn Ezra*).

4:3. The walls will be breached in so many places that the women will have many avenues of escape.

4:6. From lack of rich foods (*Rashi*).

4:10. When you sent your youths to buy food in Egypt, I brought death and pillage upon their caravans, but still you did not repent (*Radak*).

4:11. See *Genesis* 19:24-25.

4:13. Metaphorically, He humbles the haughty (*Rashi*).

5:2. The Talmud relates that this phrase may be repunctuated as a message of encouragement: *She has fallen, but will no longer; rise up, O virgin of Israel!* (*Berachos* 4b).

Lord HASHEM/ELOHIM, the God of Legions. [14] For on the day that I visit the transgressions of Israel against them, I will avenge the altars of Beth-el; the corners of the altar will be cut off and they will fall to the ground. [15] I will strike the winter house along with the summer house; the houses of ivory will be lost, and many houses will be destroyed — the word of HASHEM.

4 [1] Hear this prophecy, you cows of Bashan* who are on the mountain of Samaria, who oppress the poor, who crush the destitute, who say to their lords, "Bring, so we may drink!"

Warning to the women

[2] The Lord HASHEM/ELOHIM has sworn by His Holiness that there are days coming upon you when you will be carried off on shields,* and your posterity in fishing boats. [3] Through breaches [in the wall] they flee, every woman straight ahead,* and you will cast off your haughtiness — the word of HASHEM.

[4] Come to Beth-el and rebel; in Gilgal rebel greatly! Bring your sacrifices every morning, your tithes for three days; [5] burn thanksgiving-offerings of leavened bread, and announce and publicize voluntary offerings; for this is what you have loved to do, O Children of Israel — the word of the Lord HASHEM/ELOHIM. [6] Also, I have given you cleanness of teeth* in all your cities and lack of bread in all your places; yet you have not returned to Me — the word of HASHEM.

Blind to the truth

[7] Also, I have withheld the rain from you three months before the harvest; and I brought down rain upon one city, but upon another city I did not bring rain; one area was rained upon, and the area that did not receive rain will wither. [8] And two or three cities traveled to one city to drink water, but they were not sated; yet you have not returned to Me — the word of HASHEM.

[9] I have smitten your [crops] with wind blast and withering; the increase of your gardens and your vineyards and your fig trees and your olive trees the locusts will consume; yet you have not returned to Me — the word of HASHEM.

[10] I have sent against you pestilence on the way to Egypt;* I have killed your youths by the sword and carried away your horses; I have raised the stench of your camps even into your own nostrils; yet you have not returned to Me — the word of HASHEM.

[11] I have overturned among you as God overturned Sodom and Gomorrah;* you were like a brand salvaged from burning; yet you did not return to Me — the word of HASHEM.

[12] Therefore, thus will I do to you, O Israel; [and] because I do this to you, prepare [to go] towards your God, O Israel.

[13] For behold, He forms mountains and creates winds; He recounts to a person what were his deeds; He turns the dawn into darkness and tramples upon the heights of the earth;* HASHEM, God of Legions, is His Name.

5 [1] Hear this pronouncement that I recite over you in lamentation, O House of Israel:

Final fall

[2] She has fallen and will no longer rise — virgin of Israel;* she has been abandoned upon her soil, with no one to lift her up. [3] For thus said the Lord HASHEM/ELOHIM: The city from which a thousand [people] go forth will be left with a hundred, and one from which a hundred [people] go forth will be left with ten of the House of Israel.

ה כֹּה אָמַר יְהוָה לְבֵית יִשְׂרָאֵל דִּרְשׁוּנִי וֽחְיֽוּ: וְאַֽל־תִּדְרְשׁוּ בֵּֽית־אֵל וְהַגִּלְגָּל לֹא תָבֹאוּ וּבְאֵר שֶׁבַע לֹא תַעֲבֹרוּ כִּי הַגִּלְגָּל גָּלֹה יִגְלֶה וּבֵֽית־

ו אֵל יִהְיֶה לְאָֽוֶן: דִּרְשׁוּ אֶת־יְהוָה וֽחְיֽוּ פֶּן־יִצְלַח כָּאֵשׁ בֵּית יוֹסֵף וְאָֽכְלָה וְאֵֽין־מְכַבֶּה לְבֵֽית־אֵל:

ז הַהֹפְכִים לְלַֽעֲנָה מִשְׁפָּט וּצְדָקָה לָאָרֶץ הִנִּֽיחוּ:

ח עֹשֵׂה כִימָה וּכְסִיל וְהֹפֵךְ לַבֹּקֶר צַלְמָוֶת וְיוֹם לַיְלָה הֶחְשִׁיךְ הַקּוֹרֵא לְמֵֽי־ הַיָּם וַיִּשְׁפְּכֵם עַל־פְּנֵי הָאָרֶץ יְהוָה שְׁמֽוֹ:

ט הַמַּבְלִיג שֹׁד עַל־עָז וְשֹׁד עַל־ מִבְצָר יָבֽוֹא:

י שָׂנְאוּ בַשַּׁעַר מוֹכִיחַ וְדֹבֵר תָּמִים יְתָעֵֽבוּ: לָכֵן יַעַן בּוֹשַׁסְכֶם עַל־דָּל וּמַשְׂאַת־בַּר תִּקְחוּ מִמֶּנּוּ בָּתֵּי גָזִית בְּנִיתֶם וְלֹא־תֵשְׁבוּ בָם כַּרְמֵֽי־

יא חֶמֶד נְטַעְתֶּם וְלֹא תִשְׁתּוּ אֶת־יֵינָֽם: כִּי יָדַעְתִּי רַבִּים פִּשְׁעֵיכֶם וַעֲצֻמִים

יב חַטֹּֽאתֵיכֶם צֹרְרֵי צַדִּיק לֹקְחֵי כֹפֶר וְאֶבְיוֹנִים בַּשַּׁעַר הִטּֽוּ: לָכֵן הַמַּשְׂכִּיל

יג בָּעֵת הַהִיא יִדֹּם כִּי עֵת רָעָה הִֽיא: דִּרְשׁוּ־טוֹב וְאַל־רָע לְמַעַן תִּֽחְיוּ

יד וִֽיהִי־כֵן יְהוָה אֱלֹהֵֽי־צְבָאוֹת אִתְּכֶם כַּאֲשֶׁר אֲמַרְתֶּם: שִׂנְאוּ־רָע וְאֶֽהֱבוּ

טו טוֹב וְהַצִּיגוּ בַשַּׁעַר מִשְׁפָּט אוּלַי יֶחֱנַן יְהוָה אֱלֹהֵֽי־צְבָאוֹת שְׁאֵרִית יוֹסֵֽף:

טז לָכֵן כֹּה־אָמַר יְהֹוָה אֱלֹהֵי צְבָאוֹת אֲדֹנָי בְּכָל־רְחֹבוֹת מִסְפֵּד וּבְכָל־חוּצוֹת יֹאמְרוּ הוֹ־הוֹ וְקָרְאוּ אִכָּר אֶל־אֵבֶל וּמִסְפֵּד אֶל־יֽוֹדְעֵי

יז נֶֽהִי: וּבְכָל־כְּרָמִים מִסְפֵּד כִּֽי־אֶעֱבֹר בְּקִרְבְּךָ אָמַר יְהוָֽה: הוֹי

יח הַמִּתְאַוִּים אֶת־יוֹם יְהוָה לָמָּה־זֶּה לָכֶם יוֹם יְהוָה הוּא־חֹשֶׁךְ וְלֹא־אֽוֹר:

יט כַּאֲשֶׁר יָנוּס אִישׁ מִפְּנֵי הָאֲרִי וּפְגָעוֹ הַדֹּב וּבָא הַבַּיִת וְסָמַךְ יָדוֹ עַל־הַקִּיר

כ וּנְשָׁכוֹ הַנָּחָֽשׁ: הֲלֹא־חֹשֶׁךְ יוֹם יְהוָה וְלֹא־אוֹר וְאָפֵל וְלֹא־נֹגַֽהּ לֽוֹ:

כא-כב שָׂנֵאתִי מָאַסְתִּי חַגֵּיכֶם וְלֹא אָרִיחַ בְּעַצְּרֹֽתֵיכֶם: כִּי אִם־תַּֽעֲלוּ־לִי עֹלוֹת וּמִנְחֹתֵיכֶם לֹא אֶרְצֶה וְשֶׁלֶם מְרִיאֵיכֶם לֹא אַבִּֽיט: הָסֵר מֵעָלַי הֲמוֹן

כג שִׁרֶיךָ וְזִמְרַת נְבָלֶיךָ לֹא אֶשְׁמָֽע: וְיִגַּל כַּמַּיִם מִשְׁפָּט וּצְדָקָה כְּנַחַל אֵיתָֽן:

כד הַזְּבָחִים וּמִנְחָה הִגַּשְׁתֶּם־לִי בַמִּדְבָּר אַרְבָּעִים שָׁנָה בֵּית יִשְׂרָאֵֽל:

כה וּנְשָׂאתֶם אֵת סִכּוּת מַלְכְּכֶם וְאֵת כִּיּוּן צַלְמֵיכֶם כּוֹכַב אֱלֹהֵיכֶם אֲשֶׁר

כו עֲשִׂיתֶם לָכֶֽם: וְהִגְלֵיתִי אֶתְכֶם מֵהָלְאָה לְדַמָּשֶׂק אָמַר יְהוָה אֱלֹהֵֽי־

כז צְבָאוֹת שְׁמֽוֹ: הוֹי הַשַּׁאֲנַנִּים בְּצִיּוֹן וְהַבֹּטְחִים בְּהַר

ו א שֹׁמְרוֹן נְקֻבֵי רֵאשִׁית הַגּוֹיִם וּבָאוּ לָהֶם בֵּית יִשְׂרָאֵֽל: עִבְרוּ כַלְנֵה וּרְאוּ

ב וּלְכוּ מִשָּׁם חֲמַת רַבָּה וּרְדוּ גַת־פְּלִשְׁתִּים הֲטוֹבִים מִן־הַמַּמְלָכוֹת

ג הָאֵלֶּה אִם־רַב גְּבוּלָם מִגְּבֻלְכֶֽם: הַֽמְנַדִּים לְיוֹם רָע וַתַּגִּישׁוּן שֶׁבֶת חָמָֽס:

5:13. Prudent people refrain from speaking out, for fear that you will harm them (*Ibn Ezra*).

5:16. He will mourn for his lost crops (*Ibn Ezra*).

5:18. The Day of Judgment.

5:19. So too, on the Day of Judgment one tragedy will come upon the heels of the other.

5:25. The Israelites were not required to bring personal offerings during their forty years in the Wilderness (ex-cept for one *pesach* offering; see *Numbers* Ch. 9). This shows that God desires righteousness and justice more than offerings (*Rashi*).

5:26. These were the names of idols.

6:1. Jews mingled with the nations and adopted their degenerate ways.

6:2. Were the cities of your neighbors better than those God gave you?

Seek Hashem and live

⁴ *For thus said HASHEM to the House of Israel: Seek Me and live!* ⁵ *Do not seek Beth-el and do not go to Gilgal and do not traverse Beer-sheba, for Gilgal will be completely exiled and Beth-el will become nothingness.* ⁶ *Seek HASHEM and live, lest He burn through the house of Joseph like a fire and consume Beth-el, with none to extinguish it,* ⁷ *O you who turn justice to wormwood and lay righteousness upon the ground.* ⁸ *[He is] the One Who made Pleiades and Orion; Who turns blackness to morning and darkens the day into night; Who summons the waters of the sea and pours them upon the face of the earth, HASHEM is His Name.* ⁹ *[He is] the One Who grants a robbed one power over the mighty, and a robbed one will prevail over a fortress.*

They hate the righteous

¹⁰ *They despise the one who admonishes by the gate, and the one who speaks purely they detest.* ¹¹ *Therefore, because you trample upon the poor and exact a burden of grain from him — you have built houses of hewn stone, but you will not dwell in them; you have planted delightful vineyards, but you will not drink their wine.* ¹² *For I know that your transgressions are many and your sins are substantial, O oppressors of the righteous person, takers of ransom, who distort the [justice of] the destitute by the gate.* ¹³ *Therefore, the prudent man keeps silent at that time,* * *for it is a time of evil.* ¹⁴ *Seek good and not evil, so that you may live, and HASHEM, God of Legions, will indeed be with you as you said.* ¹⁵ *Despise evil and love good, and establish justice by the gate; then perhaps HASHEM, God of Legions, will grant favor to the remnant of Joseph.*

¹⁶ *Therefore, thus said HASHEM, God of Legions, the Lord:*

God loathes insincere offerings

In all the plazas will be mourning and in all the streets they will exclaim, 'Woe! Woe!'; they will call the plowman to mourning * *and those skilled in wailing to lamentation,* ¹⁷ *and in all the vineyards there will be lamentation, for I will pass through your midst, said HASHEM.*

¹⁸ *Woe to those who desire the day of HASHEM.* * *Why do you [seek] this day of HASHEM? It is darkness and not light —* ¹⁹ *as when a man flees from before the lion and a bear encounters him; and he comes home and leans his hand on the wall and a snake bites him.* * ²⁰ *Behold, the day of HASHEM is darkness and not light, blackness without glimmer!* ²¹ *I hate and loathe your festive offerings, and I will not be appeased by your assemblies.* ²² *For even if you offer up to Me burnt-offerings and your meal-offerings, I will not be appeased, and I will not regard the peace-offering from your fatlings.* ²³ *Remove from before Me the multitude of your songs, and the music of your lutes I will not hear.* ²⁴ *Rather, let justice be revealed like water, and righteousness like a mighty stream.* ²⁵ *Did you bring sacrifices and meal-offerings to Me for forty years in the Wilderness,* * *O House of Israel?* ²⁶ *You will carry off Siccuth your king* * *and your images of Chiun, and the Kochav your god, which you made for yourselves;* ²⁷ *and I will exile you to beyond Damascus, said HASHEM, God of Legions is His Name.*

6

Woe to the overconfident

¹ **W**oe *to the serene people in Zion and the secure people in Mount Samaria! They are called the foremost of the nations, but the House of Israel came among them.* * ² *Cross over to Calneh and see, and go from there to Great Hamath and descend to Gath of the Philistines — are they better than these kingdoms?* * *Is their border greater than your border?* ³ *[Woe to you] who spurn the day of evil, while you convene sessions of injustice;*

ד הַשֹּׁכְבִים עַל־מִטּוֹת שֵׁן וּסְרֻחִים עַל־עַרְשׂוֹתָם וְאֹכְלִים כָּרִים מִצֹּאן
ה וַעֲגָלִים מִתּוֹךְ מַרְבֵּק: הַפֹּרְטִים עַל־פִּי הַנָּבֶל כְּדָוִיד חָשְׁבוּ לָהֶם כְּלֵי־
ו שִׁיר: הַשֹּׁתִים בְּמִזְרְקֵי יַיִן וְרֵאשִׁית שְׁמָנִים יִמְשָׁחוּ וְלֹא נֶחְלוּ עַל־שֵׁבֶר
ז יוֹסֵף: לָכֵן עַתָּה יִגְלוּ בְּרֹאשׁ גֹּלִים וְסָר מִרְזַח סְרוּחִים: נִשְׁבַּע אֲדֹנָי יֱהֹוִה
בְּנַפְשׁוֹ נְאֻם־יְהֹוָה אֱלֹהֵי צְבָאוֹת מְתָאֵב אָנֹכִי אֶת־גְּאוֹן יַעֲקֹב וְאַרְמְנֹתָיו
ט שָׂנֵאתִי וְהִסְגַּרְתִּי עִיר וּמְלֹאָהּ: וְהָיָה אִם־יִוָּתְרוּ עֲשָׂרָה אֲנָשִׁים בְּבַיִת
י אֶחָד וָמֵתוּ: וּנְשָׂאוֹ דּוֹדוֹ וּמְסָרְפוֹ לְהוֹצִיא עֲצָמִים מִן־הַבַּיִת וְאָמַר
לַאֲשֶׁר בְּיַרְכְּתֵי הַבַּיִת הַעוֹד עִמָּךְ וְאָמַר אָפֶס וְאָמַר הָס כִּי לֹא לְהַזְכִּיר
יא בְּשֵׁם יְהֹוָה: כִּי־הִנֵּה יְהֹוָה מְצַוֶּה וְהִכָּה הַבַּיִת הַגָּדוֹל
רְסִיסִים וְהַבַּיִת הַקָּטֹן בְּקִעִים: הַיְרֻצוּן בַּסֶּלַע סוּסִים אִם־יַחֲרוֹשׁ בַּבְּקָרִים
יב כִּי־הֲפַכְתֶּם לְרֹאשׁ מִשְׁפָּט וּפְרִי צְדָקָה לְלַעֲנָה: הַשְּׂמֵחִים לְלֹא דָבָר
יג הָאֹמְרִים הֲלוֹא בְחָזְקֵנוּ לָקַחְנוּ לָנוּ קַרְנָיִם: כִּי הִנְנִי מֵקִים עֲלֵיכֶם בֵּית
יד יִשְׂרָאֵל נְאֻם־יְהֹוָה אֱלֹהֵי הַצְּבָאוֹת גּוֹי וְלָחֲצוּ אֶתְכֶם מִלְּבוֹא חֲמָת עַד־
נַחַל הָעֲרָבָה:

ז

א כֹּה הִרְאַנִי אֲדֹנָי יֱהֹוִה וְהִנֵּה יוֹצֵר גֹּבַי
ב בִּתְחִלַּת עֲלוֹת הַלָּקֶשׁ וְהִנֵּה־לֶקֶשׁ אַחַר גִּזֵּי הַמֶּלֶךְ: וְהָיָה אִם־כִּלָּה
לֶאֱכוֹל אֶת־עֵשֶׂב הָאָרֶץ וָאֹמַר אֲדֹנָי יֱהֹוִה סְלַח־נָא מִי יָקוּם יַעֲקֹב כִּי
ג–ד קָטֹן הוּא: נִחַם יְהֹוָה עַל־זֹאת לֹא תִהְיֶה אָמַר יְהֹוָה: כֹּה
הִרְאַנִי אֲדֹנָי יֱהֹוִה וְהִנֵּה קֹרֵא לָרִב בָּאֵשׁ אֲדֹנָי יֱהֹוִה וַתֹּאכַל אֶת־תְּהוֹם
ה רַבָּה וְאָכְלָה אֶת־הַחֵלֶק: וָאֹמַר אֲדֹנָי יֱהֹוִה חֲדַל־נָא מִי יָקוּם יַעֲקֹב
ו כִּי קָטֹן הוּא: נִחַם יְהֹוָה עַל־זֹאת גַּם־הִיא לֹא תִהְיֶה אָמַר אֲדֹנָי
ז יֱהֹוִה: כֹּה הִרְאַנִי וְהִנֵּה אֲדֹנָי נִצָּב עַל־חוֹמַת אֲנָךְ וּבְיָדוֹ אֲנָךְ:
ח וַיֹּאמֶר יְהֹוָה אֵלַי מָה־אַתָּה רֹאֶה עָמוֹס וָאֹמַר אֲנָךְ וַיֹּאמֶר אֲדֹנָי הִנְנִי שָׂם
אֲנָךְ בְּקֶרֶב עַמִּי יִשְׂרָאֵל לֹא־אוֹסִיף עוֹד עֲבוֹר לוֹ: וְנָשַׁמּוּ בָּמוֹת יִשְׂחָק
י וּמִקְדְּשֵׁי יִשְׂרָאֵל יֶחֱרָבוּ וְקַמְתִּי עַל־בֵּית יָרָבְעָם בֶּחָרֶב: וַיִּשְׁלַח
אֲמַצְיָה כֹּהֵן בֵּית־אֵל אֶל־יָרָבְעָם מֶלֶךְ־יִשְׂרָאֵל לֵאמֹר קָשַׁר עָלֶיךָ
עָמוֹס בְּקֶרֶב בֵּית יִשְׂרָאֵל לֹא־תוּכַל הָאָרֶץ לְהָכִיל אֶת־כָּל־דְּבָרָיו:
יא כִּי־כֹה אָמַר עָמוֹס בַּחֶרֶב יָמוּת יָרָבְעָם וְיִשְׂרָאֵל גָּלֹה יִגְלֶה מֵעַל
יב אַדְמָתוֹ: וַיֹּאמֶר אֲמַצְיָה אֶל־עָמוֹס חֹזֶה לֵךְ בְּרַח־לְךָ אֶל־אֶרֶץ
יג יְהוּדָה וֶאֱכָל־שָׁם לֶחֶם וְשָׁם תִּנָּבֵא: וּבֵית־אֵל לֹא־תוֹסִיף עוֹד לְהִנָּבֵא

6:8. The Temple in Jerusalem (*Rashi*).

6:9. Even if they survive the enemy onslaught, they will die of disease.

6:10. Having been told that there were no living survivors, the kinsman will order the corpses removed, and will declare that they died because they did not serve God.

7:1. The later growth is the regrowth that sprouted after the early growth had been cut for the king's animals' food (*Targum*).

7:2. The swarm.

7:4. The fire devoured the king's property, to indicate that the king is responsible for the social and religious shortcomings of the community.

7:8. Symbolizing strict, measured judgment.

7:10. From the site of his idolatrous temple (see *I Kings* 12:29), Amaziah complained that even the populace is upset with Amos' prophecies (*Ibn Ezra*).

4 who lie on ivory couches, stretched out on their beds, eating the fattened sheep of the flock and calves from inside the stall; 5 who sing along to the tune of the lute, considering themselves like David with [their] musical instruments; 6 who drink wine out of bowls, anoint themselves with choicest oils, and are not pained by the destruction of Joseph. 7 Therefore, they will now be exiled at the head of the exiles, and the banquets of the haughty will cease. 8 The Lord HASHEM/ELOHIM has sworn by Himself — the word of HASHEM the Lord of Legions — 'I loathe the Glory of Jacob * and I detest his palaces; and I will deliver the city and its inhabitants.' 9 It will happen that even if ten men remain in one house, they will die. * 10 And his kinsman who saves him from burning will carry him to take the bones from the house, and he will say to the one who is at the far end of the house, 'Are there any more [live people] near you?' and he will say, 'None'; and he will say, 'Remove them, for [they] were not [wont] to mention the Name of HASHEM.'* 11 For behold, HASHEM commands, and He will shatter the large house into fragments and small houses into chips.

God has come to hate them

12 Do horses gallop on a rock; can one plow [it] with cattle, that you have turned justice into hemlock and the fruit of righteousness into wormwood — 13 you who rejoice over nothingness, [you] who say, 'Behold, with our strength we have taken power for ourselves'? 14 For behold, I am bringing up a nation against you, O House of Israel — the word of HASHEM, God of Legions — and they will distress you, from the approach to Hamath to the Arabah Brook.

7

God relented

1 Thus did the Lord HASHEM/ELOHIM show me: Behold, He was forming [a swarm of] locusts as the later growth was beginning to sprout; and behold the later growth appeared after the king's reaping. * 2 It was when it * was finished devouring the grass of the earth, that I said, "Lord HASHEM/ELOHIM, please forgive! How will Jacob survive, for he is small?" 3 So HASHEM relented concerning this: "It shall not be," said HASHEM.

4 Thus did the Lord HASHEM/ELOHIM show me: Behold, the Lord HASHEM/ELOHIM was summoning [His legions] to contend [with Israel] by fire; and it consumed the great depths and devoured the portion of land. * 5 And I said, "Lord HASHEM/ELOHIM, please refrain! How will Jacob survive, for he is small?" 6 So HASHEM relented concerning this: "It too shall not be," said the Lord HASHEM/ELOHIM.

The end of forbearance

7 Thus did He show me: Behold, the Lord standing on a plumbed wall with a plumb line in His hand. 8 And HASHEM said to me, "What do you see, Amos?" I said, "A plumb line." The Lord then said, "Behold, I am placing a plumb line in the midst of My nation Israel; * I will no longer continue to forbear them. 9 The high places of Isaac will be made desolate and the sanctuaries of Israel destroyed; and I will rise up against the house of Jeroboam with the sword."

Amaziah accuses Amos

10 Amaziah, the priest of Beth-el, sent word to Jeroboam, king of Israel, saying, "Amos has conspired against you in the midst of the House of Israel; the land cannot tolerate all his words. * 11 For thus did Amos say, 'Jeroboam will die by the sword, and Israel will be exiled from upon its land.' "

12 Amaziah then said to Amos, "Seer, go flee to the land of Judah! Eat bread there and there you may prophesy. * 13 But do not continue to prophesy in Beth-el,

---

7:12. The people of Judah will be eager to hear your prophecies of doom against Jeroboam's Northern Kingdom, and they will even give you bread as your wage!

יד כִּי מִקְדַּשׁ־מֶלֶךְ הוּא וּבֵית מַמְלָכָה הוּא: וַיַּעַן עָמוֹס וַיֹּאמֶר אֶל־אֲמַצְיָה
טו לֹא־נָבִיא אָנֹכִי וְלֹא בֶן־נָבִיא אָנֹכִי כִּי־בוֹקֵר אָנֹכִי וּבוֹלֵס שִׁקְמִים: וַיִּקָּחֵנִי
טז יְהוָה מֵאַחֲרֵי הַצֹּאן וַיֹּאמֶר אֵלַי יְהוָה לֵךְ הִנָּבֵא אֶל־עַמִּי יִשְׂרָאֵל: וְעַתָּה
שְׁמַע דְּבַר־יְהוָה אַתָּה אֹמֵר לֹא תִנָּבֵא עַל־יִשְׂרָאֵל וְלֹא תַטִּיף עַל־בֵּית
יז יִשְׂחָק: לָכֵן כֹּה־אָמַר יְהוָה אִשְׁתְּךָ בָּעִיר תִּזְנֶה וּבָנֶיךָ וּבְנֹתֶיךָ בַּחֶרֶב יִפֹּלוּ
וְאַדְמָתְךָ בַּחֶבֶל תְּחֻלָּק וְאַתָּה עַל־אֲדָמָה טְמֵאָה תָמוּת וְיִשְׂרָאֵל גָּלֹה
ח א יִגְלֶה מֵעַל אַדְמָתוֹ:   כֹּה הִרְאַנִי אֲדֹנָי יְהוִה וְהִנֵּה כְּלוּב קָיִץ:
ב וַיֹּאמֶר מָה־אַתָּה רֹאֶה עָמוֹס וָאֹמַר כְּלוּב קָיִץ וַיֹּאמֶר יְהוָה אֵלַי בָּא הַקֵּץ
ג אֶל־עַמִּי יִשְׂרָאֵל לֹא־אוֹסִיף עוֹד עֲבוֹר לוֹ: וְהֵילִילוּ שִׁירוֹת הֵיכָל בַּיּוֹם
ד הַהוּא נְאֻם אֲדֹנָי יְהוִה רַב הַפֶּגֶר בְּכָל־מָקוֹם הִשְׁלִיךְ הָס: שִׁמְעוּ־
ה זֹאת הַשֹּׁאֲפִים אֶבְיוֹן וְלַשְׁבִּית °עֲנִוֵּי [עֲנִיֵּי ק] אָרֶץ: לֵאמֹר מָתַי יַעֲבֹר
הַחֹדֶשׁ וְנַשְׁבִּירָה שֶּׁבֶר וְהַשַּׁבָּת וְנִפְתְּחָה־בָּר לְהַקְטִין אֵיפָה וּלְהַגְדִּיל
ו שֶׁקֶל וּלְעַוֵּת מֹאזְנֵי מִרְמָה: לִקְנוֹת בַּכֶּסֶף דַּלִּים וְאֶבְיוֹן בַּעֲבוּר נַעֲלָיִם
ז וּמַפַּל בַּר נַשְׁבִּיר: נִשְׁבַּע יְהוָה בִּגְאוֹן יַעֲקֹב אִם־אֶשְׁכַּח לָנֶצַח כָּל־
ח מַעֲשֵׂיהֶם: הַעַל זֹאת לֹא־תִרְגַּז הָאָרֶץ וְאָבַל כָּל־יוֹשֵׁב בָּהּ וְעָלְתָה כָאֹר
ט כֻּלָּהּ וְנִגְרְשָׁה °וְנִשְׁקָה [וְנִשְׁקְעָה ק] כִּיאוֹר מִצְרָיִם: וְהָיָה ׀
בַּיּוֹם הַהוּא נְאֻם אֲדֹנָי יְהוִה וְהֵבֵאתִי הַשֶּׁמֶשׁ בַּצָּהֳרָיִם וְהַחֲשַׁכְתִּי לָאָרֶץ
י בְּיוֹם אוֹר: וְהָפַכְתִּי חַגֵּיכֶם לְאֵבֶל וְכָל־שִׁירֵיכֶם לְקִינָה וְהַעֲלֵיתִי עַל־כָּל־
מָתְנַיִם שָׂק וְעַל־כָּל־רֹאשׁ קָרְחָה וְשַׂמְתִּיהָ כְּאֵבֶל יָחִיד וְאַחֲרִיתָהּ כְּיוֹם
יא מָר: הִנֵּה ׀ יָמִים בָּאִים נְאֻם אֲדֹנָי יְהוִה וְהִשְׁלַחְתִּי רָעָב בָּאָרֶץ
לֹא־רָעָב לַלֶּחֶם וְלֹא־צָמָא לַמַּיִם כִּי אִם־לִשְׁמֹעַ אֵת דִּבְרֵי יְהוָה: וְנָעוּ
יב מִיָּם עַד־יָם וּמִצָּפוֹן וְעַד־מִזְרָח יְשׁוֹטְטוּ לְבַקֵּשׁ אֶת־דְּבַר־יְהוָה וְלֹא יִמְצָאוּ:
יג-יד בַּיּוֹם הַהוּא תִּתְעַלַּפְנָה הַבְּתוּלֹת הַיָּפוֹת וְהַבַּחוּרִים בַּצָּמָא: הַנִּשְׁבָּעִים
בְּאַשְׁמַת שֹׁמְרוֹן וְאָמְרוּ חֵי אֱלֹהֶיךָ דָּן וְחֵי דֶּרֶךְ בְּאֵר־שָׁבַע וְנָפְלוּ וְלֹא־
ט א יָקוּמוּ עוֹד: רָאִיתִי אֶת־אֲדֹנָי נִצָּב עַל־הַמִּזְבֵּחַ וַיֹּאמֶר הַךְ
הַכַּפְתּוֹר וְיִרְעֲשׁוּ הַסִּפִּים וּבְצַעַם בְּרֹאשׁ כֻּלָּם וְאַחֲרִיתָם בַּחֶרֶב אֶהֱרֹג
ב לֹא־יָנוּס לָהֶם נָס וְלֹא־יִמָּלֵט לָהֶם פָּלִיט: אִם־יַחְתְּרוּ בִשְׁאוֹל מִשָּׁם יָדִי
ג תִקָּחֵם וְאִם־יַעֲלוּ הַשָּׁמַיִם מִשָּׁם אוֹרִידֵם: וְאִם־יֵחָבְאוּ בְּרֹאשׁ הַכַּרְמֶל
מִשָּׁם אֲחַפֵּשׂ וּלְקַחְתִּים וְאִם־יִסָּתְרוּ מִנֶּגֶד עֵינַי בְּקַרְקַע הַיָּם מִשָּׁם אֲצַוֶּה

7:14. I do not profit from my prophecies as you insinuated; I am a cattleman and a timber consultant, as it were.

7:17. That is, outside the Land of Israel.

8:2. The prophecy is a play on the words קַיִץ, *summer,* and קֵץ, *end.*

8:4-6. The prophet mentions various ways that the unprincipled wealthy cheat the poor: withholding crops from the market, then charging exorbitant prices; hoard-

ing crops until after the Sabbatical Year; falsifying weights; and demanding heavier coins.

8:8. When the Nile overflows its banks, it pushes the soil aside as it inundates the area around it.

8:9. A metaphor for sudden disaster, during prosperous times (*Rashi*).

8:11. Because the people spurned Amos' prophecies, the time will come when they will desperately seek prophecy, but not be able to find it (*Radak*).

for it is the sanctuary of the king and the seat of royalty!"

Amos responds   [14] *Amos replied and said to Amaziah, "I am not a prophet nor am I the son of a prophet, but I am a cattle herder and an examiner of sycamores.* * [15] *HASHEM took me from behind the flock, and HASHEM said to me, 'Go prophesy to My people, Israel.'* [16] *And now, hear the word of HASHEM! You say, 'Do not prophesy concerning Israel nor preach about the house of Isaac.'* [17] *Therefore, thus said HASHEM, 'Your wife will be promiscuous in the city and your sons and daughters will fall by the sword, and your land will be divided up by lot; you will die on contaminated soil,* * and Israel will surely be exiled from its land.'"*

8

A vision of fruit   [1] *Thus did the Lord HASHEM/ELOHIM show me: Behold, a basket of summer fruits,* [2] *and He said, "What do you see, Amos?" I replied, "A basket of summer fruits." HASHEM then said to me, "The end* * has come for My people Israel; I will no longer continue to forbear them.* [3] *They will wail the songs of the banquet hall on that day — the word of the Lord HASHEM/ELOHIM. There will be many corpses; in every place, 'Cast away! Remove!'*

Against those who persecute the poor   [4] *Hear this, you who devour the needy,* * decimating the poor of the land,* [5] *saying, 'When will the month pass, so that we can sell grain; the Sabbatical [Year], so we can open the [stores of] grain; reduce the ephah and increase the shekel, and distort scales of deceit,* [6] *to purchase the poor with silver and the destitute for shoes; and we will sell the refuse of grain?'* [7] *HASHEM has sworn by the Glory of Jacob, 'I will never forget all their deeds.'* [8] *Should not the land quake for this, and all its inhabitants will be destroyed? [Water] will rise like the river over all of it, and it will push aside and submerge [the land] as does the River of Egypt.* *

Sunset at midday   [9] *And it shall be on that day — the word of the Lord HASHEM/ELOHIM — that I will bring down the sun at midday* * and I will darken the land on a day of light.* [10] *I will turn your festivals into mourning, and all your songs into lamentation; and I will bring sackcloth upon all loins and baldness upon every head; and I will make [the land] as if in mourning for an only [son], and its end like a bitter day.*

Hunger for Hashem   [11] *Behold, days are coming — the word of the Lord HASHEM/ELOHIM — when I will send hunger into the land; not a hunger for bread nor a thirst for water, but to hear the words of HASHEM.* * [12] *[People] will travel from sea to sea, and from north to east; they will wander about to seek the word of HASHEM, but they will not find it.* [13] *On that day the beautiful virgins and the young men will faint from thirst —* [14] *those who swear by the idol of Samaria and say, 'By the life of your god, Dan,' and 'By the life of the Beer-sheba rites';* * and they will fall and will not rise again."*

9

Vision against the Temple   [1] *I saw the Lord standing upon the Altar, and He said:*

Strike the lintel and the side posts will quake; and shatter the head of them all, * and the rest of them I will slay by the sword; no fugitive among them will flee and no refugee among them will escape.* [2] *If they dig down into the grave, from there My hand will take them; and if they ascend to the heavens, from there I will bring them down.* [3] *If they hide on the top of Carmel, from there I will seek [them] out and take them, and if they conceal themselves from My eyes on the floor of the sea, from there I will command*

8:14. Dan and Beer-sheba were the sites of idolatrous shrines, at both ends of the country.

9:1. God commanded an angel to strike at the Temple building and the leaders of the people.

ד אֶת־הַנָּחָשׁ וּנְשָׁכָם: וְאִם־יֵלְכוּ בַשְּׁבִי לִפְנֵי אֹיְבֵיהֶם מִשָּׁם אֲצַוֶּה אֶת־
ה הַחֶרֶב וַהֲרָגָתַם וְשַׂמְתִּי עֵינִי עֲלֵיהֶם לְרָעָה וְלֹא לְטוֹבָה: וַאדֹנָי יֱהֹוִה
הַצְּבָאוֹת הַנּוֹגֵעַ בָּאָרֶץ וַתָּמוֹג וְאָבְלוּ כָּל־יוֹשְׁבֵי בָהּ וְעָלְתָה כַיְאֹר
ו כֻּלָּהּ וְשָׁקְעָה כִּיאֹר מִצְרָיִם: הַבּוֹנֶה בַשָּׁמַיִם °מַעֲלוֹתוֹ [°מַעֲלוֹתָיו ק]
וַאֲגֻדָּתוֹ עַל־אֶרֶץ יְסָדָהּ הַקֹּרֵא לְמֵי־הַיָּם וַיִּשְׁפְּכֵם עַל־פְּנֵי הָאָרֶץ יְהֹוָה
ז שְׁמוֹ: ◂ הֲלוֹא כִבְנֵי כֻשִׁיִּים אַתֶּם לִי בְּנֵי יִשְׂרָאֵל נְאֻם־יְהֹוָה

הֲלוֹא אֶת־יִשְׂרָאֵל הֶעֱלֵיתִי מֵאֶרֶץ מִצְרַיִם וּפְלִשְׁתִּיִּים מִכַּפְתּוֹר וַאֲרָם
ח מִקִּיר: הִנֵּה עֵינֵי ׀ אֲדֹנָי יֱהֹוִה בַּמַּמְלָכָה הַחַטָּאָה וְהִשְׁמַדְתִּי אֹתָהּ מֵעַל
ט פְּנֵי הָאֲדָמָה אֶפֶס כִּי לֹא הַשְׁמֵיד אַשְׁמִיד אֶת־בֵּית יַעֲקֹב נְאֻם־יְהֹוָה: כִּי־
הִנֵּה אָנֹכִי מְצַוֶּה וַהֲנִעוֹתִי בְכָל־הַגּוֹיִם אֶת־בֵּית יִשְׂרָאֵל כַּאֲשֶׁר יִנּוֹעַ
י בַּכְּבָרָה וְלֹא־יִפּוֹל צְרוֹר אָרֶץ: בַּחֶרֶב יָמוּתוּ כֹּל חַטָּאֵי עַמִּי הָאֹמְרִים
יא לֹא־תַגִּישׁ וְתַקְדִּים בַּעֲדֵינוּ הָרָעָה: בַּיּוֹם הַהוּא אָקִים אֶת־סֻכַּת דָּוִיד
יב הַנֹּפֶלֶת וְגָדַרְתִּי אֶת־פִּרְצֵיהֶן וַהֲרִסֹתָיו אָקִים וּבְנִיתִיהָ כִּימֵי עוֹלָם: לְמַעַן
יִירְשׁוּ אֶת־שְׁאֵרִית אֱדוֹם וְכָל־הַגּוֹיִם אֲשֶׁר־נִקְרָא שְׁמִי עֲלֵיהֶם נְאֻם־
יג יְהֹוָה עֹשֶׂה זֹּאת: הִנֵּה יָמִים בָּאִים נְאֻם־יְהֹוָה וְנִגַּשׁ חוֹרֵשׁ
בַּקֹּצֵר וְדֹרֵךְ עֲנָבִים בְּמֹשֵׁךְ הַזָּרַע וְהִטִּיפוּ הֶהָרִים עָסִיס וְכָל־הַגְּבָעוֹת
יד תִּתְמוֹגַגְנָה: וְשַׁבְתִּי אֶת־שְׁבוּת עַמִּי יִשְׂרָאֵל וּבָנוּ עָרִים נְשַׁמּוֹת וְיָשָׁבוּ
וְנָטְעוּ כְרָמִים וְשָׁתוּ אֶת־יֵינָם וְעָשׂוּ גַנּוֹת וְאָכְלוּ אֶת־פְּרִיהֶם: וּנְטַעְתִּים
טו עַל־אַדְמָתָם וְלֹא יִנָּתְשׁוּ עוֹד מֵעַל אַדְמָתָם אֲשֶׁר נָתַתִּי לָהֶם אָמַר יְהֹוָה
אֱלֹהֶיךָ: ◂

9:5. When the Nile overflows its banks it completely inundates the area around it.

9:6. The living creatures.

9:7. I liberated you from Egypt to become My servants. Now that you have rebelled, you are no better than other nations (*Kara*).

9:9-10. Just as large items do not fall through the sieve, so the House of Israel, though they will be shaken from place to place, will never "fall to the ground" completely. The sinners, however, will perish.

9:11. The royal house of David (*Targum*), or the Temple, for which David made preparations (*Kara*).

the serpent and it will bite them. ⁴ If they go into captivity before their enemies, from there I will command the sword and it will slay them; and I will fix My eye upon them for evil and not for good.

⁵ The Lord HASHEM/ELOHIM, the Master of Legions, He touches the land and it melts and all its inhabitants are destroyed, and [water] rises like the River over it and it becomes submerged, as [under] the River of Egypt; * ⁶ Who built His strata in the Heavens and founded His group* upon the earth; Who calls to the waters of the sea and pours them out upon the face of the earth — HASHEM is His Name.

Like an alien people

⁷ Behold, you are like the children of the Cushites to Me, O Children of Israel — the word of HASHEM. Did I not bring up Israel from the land of Egypt, as well as the Philistines from Caphtor and Aram from Kir? * ⁸ Behold, the eyes of the Lord HASHEM/ELOHIM are upon the sinful kingdom, and I will destroy it from upon the face of the earth; but I will not totally destroy the house of Jacob — the word of HASHEM. ⁹ For behold, I decree that I will shake out the House of Israel among all the nations, as [grain] is shaken in a sieve, and not a pebble falls to the ground. * ¹⁰ They will perish by the sword, all the sinners of My people, those who say, 'Not because of us will the evil approach any sooner.' ¹¹ On that day I will raise up the fallen booth of David; * I will repair their breaches and raise up its ruins, and I will build it up as in days of old, ¹² so that they upon whom My Name is called may inherit the remnant of Edom and all the nations — the word of HASHEM, Who shall do this.

Bountiful future

¹³ Behold, days are coming — the word of HASHEM — when the plowman will meet the reaper, * and the treader of grapes [will meet] the one who carries the seed; the mountains will drip juice and all the hills will melt. ¹⁴ I will return the captivity of My people Israel, and they will rebuild desolate cities and settle them; they will plant vineyards and drink their wine; they will cultivate gardens and eat their fruits. ¹⁵ I will plant them upon their land and they will never again be uprooted from their land that I have given them, said HASHEM, your God.

9:13. The crops will be so bountiful that seasons will overlap, the plowing season and reaping season, and the | grape-squeezing and planting. The fertile soil, softened by the rain, will look as if it is "melting" (*Rashi*).

א ◀ חֲזוֹן עֹבַדְיָה כֹּה־אָמַר אֲדֹנָי יֱהֹוִה לֶאֱדוֹם שְׁמוּעָה שָׁמַעְנוּ מֵאֵת יהוה
וְצִיר בַּגּוֹיִם שֻׁלָּח קוּמוּ וְנָקוּמָה עָלֶיהָ לַמִּלְחָמָה: הִנֵּה קָטֹן נְתַתִּיךָ בַּגּוֹיִם

ב בָּזוּי אַתָּה מְאֹד: זְדוֹן לִבְּךָ הִשִּׁיאֶךָ שֹׁכְנִי בְחַגְוֵי־סֶלַע מְרוֹם שִׁבְתּוֹ אֹמֵר

ג בְּלִבּוֹ מִי יוֹרִדֵנִי אָרֶץ: אִם־תַּגְבִּיהַּ כַּנֶּשֶׁר וְאִם־בֵּין כּוֹכָבִים שִׂים קִנֶּךָ

ד מִשָּׁם אוֹרִידְךָ נְאֻם־יהוה: אִם־גַּנָּבִים בָּאוּ־לְךָ אִם־שׁוֹדְדֵי לַיְלָה אֵיךְ

ה נִדְמֵיתָה הֲלוֹא יִגְנְבוּ דַּיָּם אִם־בֹּצְרִים בָּאוּ לָךְ הֲלוֹא יַשְׁאִירוּ עֹלֵלוֹת:

ו אֵיךְ נֶחְפְּשׂוּ עֵשָׂו נִבְעוּ מַצְפֻּנָיו: עַד־הַגְּבוּל שִׁלְּחוּךָ כֹּל אַנְשֵׁי בְרִיתֶךָ

ז הִשִּׁיאוּךָ יָכְלוּ לְךָ אַנְשֵׁי שְׁלֹמֶךָ לַחְמְךָ יָשִׂימוּ מָזוֹר תַּחְתֶּיךָ אֵין תְּבוּנָה

ח בּוֹ: הֲלוֹא בַּיּוֹם הַהוּא נְאֻם־יהוה וְהַאֲבַדְתִּי חֲכָמִים מֵאֱדוֹם וּתְבוּנָה מֵהַר

ט עֵשָׂו: וְחַתּוּ גִבּוֹרֶיךָ תֵּימָן לְמַעַן יִכָּרֶת־אִישׁ מֵהַר עֵשָׂו מִקָּטֶל: מֵחֲמַס

יא אָחִיךָ יַעֲקֹב תְּכַסְּךָ בוּשָׁה וְנִכְרַתָּ לְעוֹלָם: בְּיוֹם עֲמָדְךָ מִנֶּגֶד בְּיוֹם שְׁבוֹת
זָרִים חֵילוֹ וְנָכְרִים בָּאוּ °שְׁעָרָו [°שְׁעָרָיו ק] וְעַל־יְרוּשָׁלַםִ יַדּוּ גוֹרָל גַּם־

יב אַתָּה כְּאַחַד מֵהֶם: וְאַל־תֵּרֶא בְיוֹם־אָחִיךָ בְּיוֹם נָכְרוֹ וְאַל־תִּשְׂמַח לִבְנֵי־

יג יְהוּדָה בְּיוֹם אָבְדָם וְאַל־תַּגְדֵּל פִּיךָ בְּיוֹם צָרָה: אַל־תָּבוֹא בְשַׁעַר־עַמִּי
בְּיוֹם אֵידָם אַל־תֵּרֶא גַם־אַתָּה בְּרָעָתוֹ בְּיוֹם אֵידוֹ וְאַל־תִּשְׁלַחְנָה בְחֵילוֹ

יד בְּיוֹם אֵידוֹ: וְאַל־תַּעֲמֹד עַל־הַפֶּרֶק לְהַכְרִית אֶת־פְּלִיטָיו וְאַל־תַּסְגֵּר
שְׂרִידָיו בְּיוֹם צָרָה: כִּי־קָרוֹב יוֹם־יהוה עַל־כָּל־הַגּוֹיִם כַּאֲשֶׁר עָשִׂיתָ

טו יֵעָשֶׂה לָּךְ גְּמֻלְךָ יָשׁוּב בְּרֹאשֶׁךָ: כִּי כַּאֲשֶׁר שְׁתִיתֶם עַל־הַר קָדְשִׁי יִשְׁתּוּ

טז כָל־הַגּוֹיִם תָּמִיד וְשָׁתוּ וְלָעוּ וְהָיוּ כְּלוֹא הָיוּ: וּבְהַר צִיּוֹן תִּהְיֶה פְלֵיטָה

יז וְהָיָה קֹדֶשׁ וְיָרְשׁוּ בֵּית יַעֲקֹב אֵת מוֹרָשֵׁיהֶם: וְהָיָה בֵית־יַעֲקֹב אֵשׁ וּבֵית

יח יוֹסֵף לֶהָבָה וּבֵית עֵשָׂו לְקַשׁ וְדָלְקוּ בָהֶם וַאֲכָלוּם וְלֹא־יִהְיֶה שָׂרִיד לְבֵית
עֵשָׂו כִּי יהוה דִּבֵּר: וְיָרְשׁוּ הַנֶּגֶב אֶת־הַר עֵשָׂו וְהַשְּׁפֵלָה אֶת־פְּלִשְׁתִּים

יט וְיָרְשׁוּ אֶת־שְׂדֵה אֶפְרַיִם וְאֵת שְׂדֵה שֹׁמְרוֹן וּבִנְיָמִן אֶת־הַגִּלְעָד: וְגָלֻת

כ הַחֵל־הַזֶּה לִבְנֵי יִשְׂרָאֵל אֲשֶׁר־כְּנַעֲנִים עַד־צָרְפַת וְגָלֻת יְרוּשָׁלַםִ אֲשֶׁר

כא בִּסְפָרַד יִרְשׁוּ אֵת עָרֵי הַנֶּגֶב: וְעָלוּ מוֹשִׁעִים בְּהַר צִיּוֹן לִשְׁפֹּט אֶת־הַר
עֵשָׂו וְהָיְתָה לַיהוה הַמְּלוּכָה: ◀

Obadiah was a proselyte from Edom, who became a high official in the court of Ahab and Jezebel. When the latter set out to murder all the prophets of God, Obadiah, at great personal risk, hid and sustained one hundred of them (*I Kings* Ch. 18). In this merit, he was rewarded with this prophecy.

1:1. "We," quoting the nations; alternatively, quoting Obadiah and his fellow prophets (*Radak*).

1:2. Obadiah addresses Edom (see *Jeremiah* 49:14-16).

1:5-7. The prophet describes the disaster that will befall Edom/Esau. Ordinary robbers leave incidentals and gleanings behind, but Edom will be stripped bare, and betrayed by her allies.

1:7. Esau naively failed to realize that these dangers were imminent.

1:11-14. The prophet chastises Edom for joining Israel's enemies in looting and delighting in her misfortune.

1:12. Israel.

1:14. Into the hands of the enemy.

1

Prophecy against Edom

¹ The vision of Obadiah; thus said the Lord HASHEM/ELOHIM concerning Edom: We* have heard tidings from HASHEM and a messenger has been sent among the nations [saying], 'Arise, and let us rise up against her for battle.'

² 'Behold, I have made you* inferior among the nations; you are very despised. ³ The wickedness of your heart has misled you, [you] who dwells in the clefts of the rocks [in] his lofty abode, who says in his heart, 'Who can bring me down to earth?' ⁴ Even if you raise [your nest] like an eagle or if you place your nest among the stars, I will bring you down from there — the word of HASHEM. ⁵ If thieves had come upon you, if plunderers of the night — how utterly you are cut off! — would they not steal [only] until they had enough for themselves?* If grape harvesters would come to you, would they not leave over gleanings? ⁶ How has Esau been searched, his hoards revealed? ⁷ All the men of your covenant escorted you until the border; the men at peace with you misled you [and] prevailed over you; [those who eat] your bread made a wound in your place. There is no understanding in him. *

Esau is revealed . . .

⁸ Behold, on that day — the word of HASHEM — I will eradicate wise men from Edom and understanding from the Mountain of Esau. ⁹ Your mighty ones to the south will be broken, so that every man will be cut off from the Mountain of Esau by the slaughter. ¹⁰ For the oppression of your brother Jacob, disgrace will envelop you and you will be cut off forever. ¹¹ On the day that you stood from afar, on the day that strangers captured his wealth, and foreigners came to his gates and cast a lottery on Jerusalem, you too were like one of them. * ¹² Gaze not on the day of your brother,* the day of his estrangement; and rejoice not over the Children of Judah on the day of their destruction; and do not expand your mouth on the day of misfortune. ¹³ Enter not the gate of My people on the day of their calamity; gaze not, you too, upon his evil on the day of his calamity, and do not extend [your hands] to his wealth on his day of his calamity. ¹⁴ Stand not by the crossroads to cut off his fugitives; and deliver not his survivors on the day of misfortune.

. . . because he oppressed Jacob

Retribution is coming

¹⁵ For the day of HASHEM upon all the nations is close; as you have done, [so] shall be done to you; your requital shall return upon your head. ¹⁶ For just as you drank on My holy mountain, so will all the nations drink ceaselessly; they will drink and be confounded, and become as if they never were.

¹⁷ On Mount Zion there will be refuge, and it will be holy; and the house of Jacob will inherit those who had dispossessed them. ¹⁸ The house of Jacob will be fire, the house of Joseph a flame, and the house of Esau for straw; and they will ignite them and devour them. There will be no survivor to the house of Esau, for HASHEM has spoken. ¹⁹ And [those of] the southland will inherit the Mountain of Esau; and [those of] the lowlands [will inherit] the Philistines, and they will inherit the fields of Ephraim and the fields of Samaria; and Benjamin [will inherit] Gilead. ²⁰ This exiled host of the Children of Israel who are among the Canaanites until Zarephath, and the exile of Jerusalem which is in Sepharad will inherit the cities of the South. ²¹ And saviors* will ascend Mount Zion to judge the Mountain of Esau, and the kingdom will be HASHEM's.

Israel's exiles will return

1:21. Messiah and his colleagues (see *Micah* 5:4) will exact retribution from the Edomites for their cruelty, and then God will be recognized as the Sovereign of the entire universe (*Radak*).

**HAFTARAS
YOM
KIPPUR
MINCHAH**
1:1-4:11;
Micah
7:18-20

א

א־ב וַיְהִי֙ דְּבַר־יְהֹוָ֔ה אֶל־יוֹנָ֥ה בֶן־אֲמִתַּ֖י לֵאמֹֽר: ק֠וּם לֵ֧ךְ אֶל־נִֽינְוֵ֛ה הָעִ֥יר
ג הַגְּדוֹלָ֖ה וּקְרָ֣א עָלֶ֑יהָ כִּֽי־עָלְתָ֥ה רָעָתָ֖ם לְפָנָֽי: וַיָּ֤קׇם יוֹנָה֙ לִבְרֹ֣חַ תַּרְשִׁ֔ישָׁה
מִלִּפְנֵ֖י יְהֹוָ֑ה וַיֵּ֨רֶד יָפ֜וֹ וַיִּמְצָ֥א אֳנִיָּ֣ה ׀ בָּאָ֣ה תַרְשִׁ֗ישׁ וַיִּתֵּ֨ן שְׂכָרָ֜הּ וַיֵּ֤רֶד בָּהּ֙
ד לָב֤וֹא עִמָּהֶם֙ תַּרְשִׁ֔ישָׁה מִלִּפְנֵ֖י יְהֹוָֽה: וַֽיהֹוָ֗ה הֵטִ֤יל רֽוּחַ־גְּדוֹלָה֙ אֶל־הַיָּ֔ם
ה וַיְהִ֥י סַֽעַר־גָּד֖וֹל בַּיָּ֑ם וְהָ֣אֳנִיָּ֔ה חִשְּׁבָ֖ה לְהִשָּׁבֵֽר: וַיִּֽירְא֣וּ הַמַּלָּחִ֗ים וַֽיִּזְעֲקוּ֮
אִ֣ישׁ אֶל־אֱלֹהָיו֒ וַיָּטִ֨לוּ אֶת־הַכֵּלִ֜ים אֲשֶׁ֤ר בָּֽאֳנִיָּה֙ אֶל־הַיָּ֔ם לְהָקֵ֖ל
ו מֵֽעֲלֵיהֶ֑ם וְיוֹנָ֗ה יָרַד֙ אֶל־יַרְכְּתֵ֣י הַסְּפִינָ֔ה וַיִּשְׁכַּ֖ב וַיֵּֽרָדַֽם: וַיִּקְרַ֤ב אֵלָיו֙ רַ֣ב
הַחֹבֵ֔ל וַיֹּ֥אמֶר ל֖וֹ מַה־לְּךָ֣ נִרְדָּ֑ם ק֚וּם קְרָ֣א אֶל־אֱלֹהֶ֔יךָ אוּלַ֞י יִתְעַשֵּׁ֧ת
ז הָאֱלֹהִ֛ים לָ֖נוּ וְלֹ֥א נֹאבֵֽד: וַיֹּאמְר֞וּ אִ֣ישׁ אֶל־רֵעֵ֗הוּ לְכוּ֙ וְנַפִּ֣ילָה גֽוֹרָל֔וֹת
וְנֵ֣דְעָ֔ה בְּשֶׁלְּמִ֛י הָרָעָ֥ה הַזֹּ֖את לָ֑נוּ וַיַּפִּ֙לוּ֙ גּֽוֹרָל֔וֹת וַיִּפֹּ֥ל הַגּוֹרָ֖ל עַל־יוֹנָֽה:
ח וַיֹּאמְר֣וּ אֵלָ֗יו הַגִּֽידָה־נָּ֣א לָ֔נוּ בַּאֲשֶׁ֛ר לְמִֽי־הָרָעָ֥ה הַזֹּ֖את לָ֑נוּ מַה־מְּלַאכְתְּךָ֙
ט וּמֵאַ֣יִן תָּב֔וֹא מָ֥ה אַרְצֶ֖ךָ וְאֵֽי־מִזֶּ֥ה עַ֥ם אָֽתָּה: וַיֹּ֥אמֶר אֲלֵיהֶ֖ם עִבְרִ֣י אָנֹ֑כִי
וְאֶת־יְהֹוָ֞ה אֱלֹהֵ֤י הַשָּׁמַ֙יִם֙ אֲנִ֣י יָרֵ֔א אֲשֶׁר־עָשָׂ֥ה אֶת־הַיָּ֖ם וְאֶת־הַיַּבָּשָֽׁה:
י וַיִּֽירְא֤וּ הָֽאֲנָשִׁים֙ יִרְאָ֣ה גְדוֹלָ֔ה וַיֹּאמְר֥וּ אֵלָ֖יו מַה־זֹּ֣את עָשִׂ֑יתָ כִּֽי־יָדְע֣וּ
יא הָֽאֲנָשִׁ֗ים כִּֽי־מִלִּפְנֵ֤י יְהֹוָה֙ ה֣וּא בֹרֵ֔חַ כִּ֥י הִגִּ֖יד לָהֶֽם: וַיֹּאמְר֤וּ אֵלָיו֙ מַה־
נַּ֣עֲשֶׂה לָּ֔ךְ וְיִשְׁתֹּ֥ק הַיָּ֖ם מֵֽעָלֵ֑ינוּ כִּ֥י הַיָּ֖ם הוֹלֵ֥ךְ וְסֹעֵֽר: וַיֹּ֣אמֶר אֲלֵיהֶ֗ם שָׂא֙וּנִי֙
יב וַהֲטִילֻ֣נִי אֶל־הַיָּ֔ם וְיִשְׁתֹּ֥ק הַיָּ֖ם מֵֽעֲלֵיכֶ֑ם כִּ֚י יוֹדֵ֣עַ אָ֔נִי כִּ֣י בְשֶׁלִּ֔י הַסַּ֧עַר
יג הַגָּד֛וֹל הַזֶּ֖ה עֲלֵיכֶֽם: וַיַּחְתְּר֣וּ הָֽאֲנָשִׁ֗ים לְהָשִׁ֛יב אֶל־הַיַּבָּשָׁ֖ה וְלֹ֣א יָכֹ֑לוּ כִּ֣י
יד הַיָּ֔ם הוֹלֵ֥ךְ וְסֹעֵ֖ר עֲלֵיהֶֽם: וַיִּקְרְא֣וּ אֶל־יְהֹוָ֗ה וַיֹּאמְרוּ֒ אָנָּ֤ה יְהֹוָה֙ אַל־נָ֣א
נֹֽאבְדָ֗ה בְּנֶ֙פֶשׁ֙ הָאִ֣ישׁ הַזֶּ֔ה וְאַל־תִּתֵּ֥ן עָלֵ֖ינוּ דָּ֣ם נָקִ֑יא כִּֽי־אַתָּ֣ה יְהֹוָ֔ה
טו כַּאֲשֶׁ֥ר חָפַ֖צְתָּ עָשִֽׂיתָ: וַיִּשְׂאוּ֙ אֶת־יוֹנָ֔ה וַיְטִלֻ֖הוּ אֶל־הַיָּ֑ם וַיַּעֲמֹ֥ד הַיָּ֖ם
טז מִזַּעְפּֽוֹ: וַיִּֽירְא֧וּ הָאֲנָשִׁ֛ים יִרְאָ֥ה גְדוֹלָ֖ה אֶת־יְהֹוָ֑ה וַיִּזְבְּחוּ־זֶ֙בַח֙ לַֽיהֹוָ֔ה וַיִּדְּר֖וּ

ב

א נְדָרִֽים: וַיְמַ֤ן יְהֹוָה֙ דָּ֣ג גָּד֔וֹל לִבְלֹ֖עַ אֶת־יוֹנָ֑ה וַיְהִ֤י יוֹנָה֙ בִּמְעֵ֣י הַדָּ֔ג שְׁלֹשָׁ֥ה
ב־ג יָמִ֖ים וּשְׁלֹשָׁ֥ה לֵילֽוֹת: וַיִּתְפַּלֵּ֣ל יוֹנָ֔ה אֶל־יְהֹוָ֖ה אֱלֹהָ֑יו מִמְּעֵ֖י הַדָּגָֽה: וַיֹּ֗אמֶר
קָ֠רָ֠אתִי מִצָּ֥רָה לִ֛י אֶל־יְהֹוָ֖ה וַֽיַּעֲנֵ֑נִי מִבֶּ֧טֶן שְׁא֛וֹל שִׁוַּ֖עְתִּי שָׁמַ֥עְתָּ קוֹלִֽי:
ד וַתַּשְׁלִיכֵ֤נִי מְצוּלָה֙ בִּלְבַ֣ב יַמִּ֔ים וְנָהָ֖ר יְסֹֽבְבֵ֑נִי כׇּל־מִשְׁבָּרֶ֥יךָ וְגַלֶּ֖יךָ עָלַ֥י
ה עָבָֽרוּ: וַאֲנִ֣י אָמַ֔רְתִּי נִגְרַ֖שְׁתִּי מִנֶּ֣גֶד עֵינֶ֑יךָ אַ֚ךְ אוֹסִ֣יף לְהַבִּ֔יט אֶל־הֵיכַ֖ל
ו קׇדְשֶֽׁךָ: אֲפָפ֤וּנִי מַ֙יִם֙ עַד־נֶ֔פֶשׁ תְּה֖וֹם יְסֹבְבֵ֑נִי ס֖וּף חָב֥וּשׁ לְרֹאשִֽׁי: לְקִצְבֵ֤י
ז הָרִים֙ יָרַ֔דְתִּי הָאָ֛רֶץ בְּרִחֶ֥יהָ בַעֲדִ֖י לְעוֹלָ֑ם וַתַּ֧עַל מִשַּׁ֛חַת חַיַּ֖י יְהֹוָ֥ה אֱלֹהָֽי:

1:1. Jonah prophesied during the reign of Jeroboam son of Joash (*II Kings* 14:25); and (according to *Seder Olam* 19) was the prophet sent by Elisha to anoint Jehu (*II Kings* 9:1).

1:2. The capital of Assyria.

1:3. Tarshish is either a distant sea (*Rashi*) or city (*Ibn Ezra*), or is a generic term for the sea (*Targum*).

Jonah did not want to carry out God's command to prophesy. He was afraid that if the people of Nineveh repented, as indeed they did, it would be an implied condemnation of the people of Israel, who had defied the warnings and exhortations of the prophets.

1:13. The sailors were honorable people. Despite the lots and Jonah's own admission, they tried to row to safety without throwing him overboard.

1:16. They pledged to offer sacrifices when they would arrive on land (*Targum*); and they vowed to convert (*Rashi*), or to help the poor (*Radak*).

2:3. A figurative reference to the fish.

1

Go to
Nineveh

¹ **A**nd the word of HASHEM came to Jonah* son of Amittai saying: ² "Arise! Go to Nineveh,* the great city, and call out against her, for their wickedness has ascended before Me." ³ But Jonah arose to flee to Tarshish* from before HASHEM.* He went down to Jaffa and found a ship bound for Tarshish; he paid its fare, and boarded it to travel with them to Tarshish from before HASHEM.

The tempest

⁴ Then HASHEM cast a mighty wind toward the sea; there was a great tempest in the sea and the ship threatened to be broken. ⁵ The sailors became frightened and they cried out, each to his god; they cast the wares that were on the ship into the sea to lighten it for them. But Jonah had descended to the ship's holds and he lay down and fell fast asleep.

⁶ The ship's master approached him, and said to him, "How can you sleep so soundly? Arise! Call to your God! Perhaps God will think of us and we will not perish."

Who is
responsible?

⁷ Then they said one to another, "Come, let us cast lots that we may determine because of whom this calamity is upon us." So they cast lots and the lot fell on Jonah. ⁸ They said to him, "Tell us now, because of whom has this evil befallen us? What is your trade? And from where do you come? What is your land? And of what people are you?"

⁹ He said to them, "I am a Hebrew and I fear HASHEM, the God of the Heavens, Who made the sea and the dry land."

¹⁰ The men were frightened with great fear and they said to him, "What is this that you have done?" For the men knew that it was from before HASHEM that he was fleeing, for he had told them. ¹¹ They said to him, "What must we do to you so that the sea will subside from upon us? — for the sea grows stormier!"

Jonah is
heaved into
the sea

¹² He said to them, "Pick me up and heave me into the sea and the sea will calm down from upon you; for I know that it is because of me that this great tempest is upon you." ¹³ [Nevertheless,] the men rowed hard to return to the shore,* but they could not, because the sea was growing stormier upon them.

¹⁴ They called out to HASHEM, and said, "Please, HASHEM, let us not perish now on account of this man's soul and do not reckon it against us as innocent blood, for You, HASHEM, as You wished, so have You done." ¹⁵ So they lifted Jonah and heaved him into the sea, and the sea stopped its raging. ¹⁶ Then the men felt a great fear of HASHEM; they slaughtered a sacrifice* to HASHEM and took vows.*

2

Prayer
from the
innards of
the fish

¹ **H**ASHEM designated a large fish to swallow Jonah, and Jonah remained in the fish's innards for three days and three nights. ² Jonah prayed to HASHEM, his God, from the fish's innards, ³ and said:

I called, in my distress, to HASHEM, and He answered me;
From the belly of the grave* I cried out — You heard my voice.
⁴ You cast me into the depth in the heart of the seas, the river surrounded me;
All Your breakers and your waves passed over me.
⁵ Then I said [to myself], 'I was driven from before Your eyes,
but I will again gaze at Your Holy Temple!' *
⁶ Waters encompassed me to the soul, the deep whirled around me;
Reeds were tangled about my head.
⁷ I descended to the bases of the mountains;
The earth — its bars [were closed] against me forever. *
Yet, You lifted my life from the pit, O HASHEM, my God.

2:5. The miracle of the fish convinced Jonah that God wanted to save his life (*Rashi*).

2:7. While plunging deep into the water Jonah thought that he was "barred" from ever seeing dry land again.

ח בְּהִתְעַטֵּף עָלַי נַפְשִׁי אֶת־יהוה זָכָרְתִּי וַתָּבוֹא אֵלֶיךָ תְּפִלָּתִי אֶל־הֵיכַל

ט קָדְשֶׁךָ: מְשַׁמְּרִים הַבְלֵי־שָׁוְא חַסְדָּם יַעֲזֹבוּ: וַאֲנִי בְּקוֹל תּוֹדָה אֶזְבְּחָה־לָּךְ

יא אֲשֶׁר נָדַרְתִּי אֲשַׁלֵּמָה יְשׁוּעָתָה לַיהוָה: וַיֹּאמֶר יהוה לַדָּג וַיָּקֵא

אֶת־יוֹנָה אֶל־הַיַּבָּשָׁה:

ג א־ב וַיְהִי דְבַר־יהוה אֶל־יוֹנָה שֵׁנִית לֵאמֹר: קוּם

לֵךְ אֶל־נִינְוֵה הָעִיר הַגְּדוֹלָה וּקְרָא אֵלֶיהָ אֶת־הַקְּרִיאָה אֲשֶׁר אָנֹכִי דֹּבֵר

ג אֵלֶיךָ: וַיָּקָם יוֹנָה וַיֵּלֶךְ אֶל־נִינְוֵה כִּדְבַר יהוה וְנִינְוֵה הָיְתָה עִיר־גְּדוֹלָה

ד לֵאלֹהִים מַהֲלַךְ שְׁלֹשֶׁת יָמִים: וַיָּחֶל יוֹנָה לָבוֹא בָעִיר מַהֲלַךְ יוֹם אֶחָד

ה וַיִּקְרָא וַיֹּאמַר עוֹד אַרְבָּעִים יוֹם וְנִינְוֵה נֶהְפָּכֶת: וַיַּאֲמִינוּ אַנְשֵׁי נִינְוֵה

ו בֵּאלֹהִים וַיִּקְרְאוּ־צוֹם וַיִּלְבְּשׁוּ שַׂקִּים מִגְּדוֹלָם וְעַד־קְטַנָּם: וַיִּגַּע הַדָּבָר

אֶל־מֶלֶךְ נִינְוֵה וַיָּקָם מִכִּסְאוֹ וַיַּעֲבֵר אַדַּרְתּוֹ מֵעָלָיו וַיְכַס שַׂק וַיֵּשֶׁב עַל־

ז הָאֵפֶר: וַיַּזְעֵק וַיֹּאמֶר בְּנִינְוֵה מִטַּעַם הַמֶּלֶךְ וּגְדֹלָיו לֵאמֹר הָאָדָם וְהַבְּהֵמָה

ח הַבָּקָר וְהַצֹּאן אַל־יִטְעֲמוּ מְאוּמָה אַל־יִרְעוּ וּמַיִם אַל־יִשְׁתּוּ: וְיִתְכַּסּוּ שַׂקִּים

הָאָדָם וְהַבְּהֵמָה וְיִקְרְאוּ אֶל־אֱלֹהִים בְּחָזְקָה וְיָשֻׁבוּ אִישׁ מִדַּרְכּוֹ הָרָעָה

ט וּמִן־הֶחָמָס אֲשֶׁר בְּכַפֵּיהֶם: מִי־יוֹדֵעַ יָשׁוּב וְנִחַם הָאֱלֹהִים וְשָׁב מֵחֲרוֹן אַפּוֹ

י וְלֹא נֹאבֵד: וַיַּרְא הָאֱלֹהִים אֶת־מַעֲשֵׂיהֶם כִּי־שָׁבוּ מִדַּרְכָּם הָרָעָה וַיִּנָּחֶם

הָאֱלֹהִים עַל־הָרָעָה אֲשֶׁר־דִּבֶּר לַעֲשׂוֹת־לָהֶם וְלֹא עָשָׂה: וַיֵּרַע אֶל־יוֹנָה

ד א רָעָה גְדוֹלָה וַיִּחַר לוֹ: וַיִּתְפַּלֵּל אֶל־יהוה וַיֹּאמַר אָנָּה יהוה הֲלוֹא־זֶה דְבָרִי

ב עַד־הֱיוֹתִי עַל־אַדְמָתִי עַל־כֵּן קִדַּמְתִּי לִבְרֹחַ תַּרְשִׁישָׁה כִּי יָדַעְתִּי כִּי אַתָּה

ג אֵל־חַנּוּן וְרַחוּם אֶרֶךְ אַפַּיִם וְרַב־חֶסֶד וְנִחָם עַל־הָרָעָה: וְעַתָּה יהוה קַח־

ד נָא אֶת־נַפְשִׁי מִמֶּנִּי כִּי טוֹב מוֹתִי מֵחַיָּי: וַיֹּאמֶר יהוה הַהֵיטֵב חָרָה לָךְ:

ה וַיֵּצֵא יוֹנָה מִן־הָעִיר וַיֵּשֶׁב מִקֶּדֶם לָעִיר וַיַּעַשׂ לוֹ שָׁם סֻכָּה וַיֵּשֶׁב תַּחְתֶּיהָ

ו בַּצֵּל עַד אֲשֶׁר יִרְאֶה מַה־יִּהְיֶה בָּעִיר: וַיְמַן יהוה־אֱלֹהִים קִיקָיוֹן וַיַּעַל ׀

מֵעַל לְיוֹנָה לִהְיוֹת צֵל עַל־רֹאשׁוֹ לְהַצִּיל לוֹ מֵרָעָתוֹ וַיִּשְׂמַח יוֹנָה עַל־

ז הַקִּיקָיוֹן שִׂמְחָה גְדוֹלָה: וַיְמַן הָאֱלֹהִים תּוֹלַעַת בַּעֲלוֹת הַשַּׁחַר לַמָּחֳרָת

ח וַתַּךְ אֶת־הַקִּיקָיוֹן וַיִּיבָשׁ: וַיְהִי ׀ כִּזְרֹחַ הַשֶּׁמֶשׁ וַיְמַן אֱלֹהִים רוּחַ קָדִים

חֲרִישִׁית וַתַּךְ הַשֶּׁמֶשׁ עַל־רֹאשׁ יוֹנָה וַיִּתְעַלָּף וַיִּשְׁאַל אֶת־נַפְשׁוֹ לָמוּת

ט וַיֹּאמֶר טוֹב מוֹתִי מֵחַיָּי: וַיֹּאמֶר אֱלֹהִים אֶל־יוֹנָה הַהֵיטֵב חָרָה־לְךָ עַל־

הַקִּיקָיוֹן וַיֹּאמֶר הֵיטֵב חָרָה־לִי עַד־מָוֶת: וַיֹּאמֶר יהוה אַתָּה חַסְתָּ עַל־

הַקִּיקָיוֹן אֲשֶׁר לֹא־עָמַלְתָּ בּוֹ וְלֹא גִדַּלְתּוֹ שֶׁבִּן־לַיְלָה הָיָה וּבִן־לַיְלָה אָבָד:

יא וַאֲנִי לֹא אָחוּס עַל־נִינְוֵה הָעִיר הַגְּדוֹלָה אֲשֶׁר יֶשׁ־בָּהּ הַרְבֵּה מִשְׁתֵּים־

עֶשְׂרֵה רִבּוֹ אָדָם אֲשֶׁר לֹא־יָדַע בֵּין־יְמִינוֹ לִשְׂמֹאלוֹ וּבְהֵמָה רַבָּה: ▶

Haftaras Yom Kippur Minchah continues on p. 1384

2:9. During the storm, the sailors had observed the futility of praying to their gods, so they vowed to turn to HASHEM, and no longer bestow their kindness on idols (*Midrash*).

3:3-4. So large was the city that it would have taken three days to walk across it. Jonah walked a third of the way into it and made his announcement (*Radak*).

3:10. The Talmud notes that the verse does not read "and God saw their sackcloth and their fasting," but that He saw "their deeds" — that they repented of their evil ways.

4:2-3. Jonah felt from the start that the Ninevites would repent, thus gaining God's mercy — and thus reflecting badly upon Israel (see note to 1:3). Now he prayed that he

I will fulfill my vows

⁸ When my soul was faint within me, I remembered HASHEM;
My prayer came to You, to Your Holy Temple.
⁹ They watch false vanities, they forsake their kindness. *
¹⁰ And as for me, with a voice of thanksgiving I will make sacrifices to You. What I have vowed I will fulfill for the salvation which is HASHEM's.

¹¹ Then HASHEM addressed the fish and it spewed out Jonah onto dry land.

3

The second prophecy

¹ The word of HASHEM came to Jonah a second time, saying: ² "Arise! Go to Nineveh the great city, and call out against her the proclamation that I tell you." ³ So Jonah arose and went to Nineveh, in accordance with God's word. Now Nineveh was an enormously great city, a three-day journey. * ⁴ Jonah commenced to enter the city, a distance of one day's journey, then he called out and said, "Forty days more and Nineveh shall be overturned!"

Nineveh heeds Jonah . . .

⁵ The people of Nineveh believed in God, so they proclaimed a fast and donned sackcloth, from their great to their small. ⁶ The matter reached the king of Nineveh; he rose from his throne, removed his robe from upon himself, covered himself with sackcloth and sat on the ashes, ⁷ and had it promulgated and declared in Nineveh by the counsel of the king and his nobles, saying: "The man and the animal, the herd and the flock shall not taste anything; they shall neither graze, nor drink water. ⁸ Both man and animal shall cover themselves with sackcloth; and they shall call out mightily to God. Every man shall turn back from his evil way, and from the robbery that is in their hands. ⁹ He who knows shall repent and God will relent; He will turn away from His burning wrath so that we not perish."

. . . and God sees their needs

4

¹⁰ And God saw their deeds, * that they repented from their evil way; and God relented concerning the evil He had said He would bring upon them, and did not do it. ¹ And it displeased Jonah greatly and angered him. ² He prayed to HASHEM, and said, "Please, HASHEM, was this not my contention when I was still on my own soil? Because of this I had hastened to flee to Tarshish for I knew that You are a gracious and merciful God, slow to anger, abundant in kindness, and relent from doing harm. ³ So now, HASHEM, please take my soul from me, for better is my death than my life." *

⁴ And HASHEM said, "Are you so deeply grieved?" *

Jonah is grieved

⁵ Jonah left the city and sat at the east of the city. He made himself a booth there, and sat under it in the shade until he would see what would occur in the city.
⁶ HASHEM, God, designated a kikayon, * which rose up above Jonah to form a shade over his head, to relieve him from his discomfort. Jonah rejoiced over the kikayon, a great joy. ⁷ Then God designated a worm at the dawn of the next day, and it attacked the kikayon so that it withered. ⁸ And it was when the sun shone that God designated a stifling east wind; the sun beat upon Jonah's head and he felt faint. He asked for his soul's death, and said, "Better is my death than my life!"
⁹ And God said to Jonah, "Are you so deeply grieved over the kikayon?" *
And he said, "I am greatly grieved to death."

Misplaced pity

¹⁰ HASHEM said, "You took pity on the kikayon for which you did not labor, nor did you make it grow; it lived [one] night and perished after one night. ¹¹ And I — shall I not take pity upon Nineveh the great city, in which there are more than a hundred and twenty thousand persons who do not know their right hand from their left, and many animals as well?"

---

not live to see Israel's destruction (*Ibn Ezra; Radak*).
4:4. A rhetorical question.
4:6. A leafy, shady plant (*Rashi*).

4:9-11. God showed Jonah how wrong he had been by being apathetic to the horrible fate that could have befallen a great city with its huge population.

א דְּבַר־יְהֹוָה l אֲשֶׁר הָיָה אֶל־מִיכָה הַמֹּרַשְׁתִּי בִּימֵי יוֹתָם אָחָז יְחִזְקִיָּה מַלְכֵי
ב יְהוּדָה אֲשֶׁר־חָזָה עַל־שֹׁמְרוֹן וִירוּשָׁלָ͏ִם: שִׁמְעוּ עַמִּים כֻּלָּם הַקְשִׁיבִי אֶרֶץ
ג וּמְלֹאָהּ וִיהִי אֲדֹנָי יֱהֹוִה בָּכֶם לְעֵד אֲדֹנָי מֵהֵיכַל קָדְשׁוֹ: כִּי־הִנֵּה יְהֹוָה יֹצֵא
ד מִמְּקוֹמוֹ וְיָרַד וְדָרַךְ עַל־°בָּמוֹתֵי [°בָּ֥מֳתֵי ק] אָרֶץ: וְנָמַסּוּ הֶהָרִים תַּחְתָּיו
ה וְהָעֲמָקִים יִתְבַּקָּעוּ כַּדּוֹנַג מִפְּנֵי הָאֵשׁ כְּמַיִם מֻגָּרִים בְּמוֹרָד: בְּפֶשַׁע יַעֲקֹב
כָּל־זֹאת וּבְחַטֹּאות בֵּית יִשְׂרָאֵל מִי־פֶשַׁע יַעֲקֹב הֲלוֹא שֹׁמְרוֹן וּמִי בָּמוֹת
ו יְהוּדָה הֲלוֹא יְרוּשָׁלָ͏ִם: וְשַׂמְתִּי שֹׁמְרוֹן לְעִי הַשָּׂדֶה לְמַטָּעֵי כָרֶם וְהִגַּרְתִּי
ז לַגַּי אֲבָנֶיהָ וִיסֹדֶיהָ אֲגַלֶּה: וְכָל־פְּסִילֶיהָ יֻכַּתּוּ וְכָל־אֶתְנַנֶּיהָ יִשָּׂרְפוּ בָאֵשׁ
וְכָל־עֲצַבֶּיהָ אָשִׂים שְׁמָמָה כִּי מֵאֶתְנַן זוֹנָה קִבָּצָה וְעַד־אֶתְנַן זוֹנָה יָשׁוּבוּ:
ח עַל־זֹאת אֶסְפְּדָה וְאֵילִילָה אֵילְכָה °שֵׁילָל [°שׁוֹלָ֥ל ק] וְעָרוֹם אֶעֱשֶׂה
ט מִסְפֵּד כַּתַּנִּים וְאֵבֶל כִּבְנוֹת יַעֲנָה: כִּי אֲנוּשָׁה מַכּוֹתֶיהָ כִּי־בָאָה עַד־יְהוּדָה
י נָגַע עַד־שַׁעַר עַמִּי עַד־יְרוּשָׁלָ͏ִם: בְּגַת אַל־תַּגִּידוּ בָּכוֹ אַל־תִּבְכּוּ בְּבֵית
יא לְעַפְרָה עָפָר °הִתְפַּלָּשְׁתִּי [°הִתְפַּלָּ֖שִׁי ק]: עִבְרִי לָכֶם יוֹשֶׁבֶת שָׁפִיר
עֶרְיָה־בֹשֶׁת לֹא יָצְאָה יוֹשֶׁבֶת צַאֲנָן מִסְפַּד בֵּית הָאֵצֶל יִקַּח מִכֶּם עֶמְדָּתוֹ:
יב כִּי־חָלָה לְטוֹב יוֹשֶׁבֶת מָרוֹת כִּי־יָרַד רָע מֵאֵת יְהֹוָה לְשַׁעַר יְרוּשָׁלָ͏ִם:
יג רְתֹם הַמֶּרְכָּבָה לָרֶכֶשׁ יוֹשֶׁבֶת לָכִישׁ רֵאשִׁית חַטָּאת הִיא לְבַת־צִיּוֹן כִּי־
יד בָךְ נִמְצְאוּ פִּשְׁעֵי יִשְׂרָאֵל: לָכֵן תִּתְּנִי שִׁלּוּחִים עַל מוֹרֶשֶׁת גַּת בָּתֵּי אַכְזִיב
טו לְאַכְזָב לְמַלְכֵי יִשְׂרָאֵל: עֹד הַיֹּרֵשׁ אָבִי לָךְ יוֹשֶׁבֶת מָרֵשָׁה עַד־עֲדֻלָּם
טז יָבוֹא כְּבוֹד יִשְׂרָאֵל: קָרְחִי וָגֹזִּי עַל־בְּנֵי תַּעֲנוּגָיִךְ הַרְחִבִי קָרְחָתֵךְ כַּנֶּשֶׁר כִּי גָלוּ מִמֵּךְ:

ב א הוֹי חֹשְׁבֵי־אָוֶן וּפֹעֲלֵי רָע עַל־
ב מִשְׁכְּבוֹתָם בְּאוֹר הַבֹּקֶר יַעֲשׂוּהָ כִּי יֶשׁ־לְאֵל יָדָם: וְחָמְדוּ שָׂדוֹת וְגָזָלוּ
ג וּבָתִּים וְנָשָׂאוּ וְעָשְׁקוּ גֶּבֶר וּבֵיתוֹ וְאִישׁ וְנַחֲלָתוֹ: לָכֵן כֹּה אָמַר
יְהֹוָה הִנְנִי חֹשֵׁב עַל־הַמִּשְׁפָּחָה הַזֹּאת רָעָה אֲשֶׁר לֹא־תָמִישׁוּ מִשָּׁם
ד צַוְּארֹתֵיכֶם וְלֹא תֵלְכוּ רוֹמָה כִּי עֵת רָעָה הִיא: בַּיּוֹם הַהוּא יִשָּׂא עֲלֵיכֶם
מָשָׁל וְנָהָה נְהִי נִהְיָה אָמַר שָׁדוֹד נְשַׁדֻּנוּ חֵלֶק עַמִּי יָמִיר אֵיךְ יָמִישׁ לִי
ה לְשׁוֹבֵב שָׂדֵינוּ יְחַלֵּק: לָכֵן לֹא־יִהְיֶה לְךָ מַשְׁלִיךְ חֶבֶל בְּגוֹרָל בִּקְהַל יְהֹוָה:

1:1. See *Hosea* 1:1.

1:2. That you have been warned.

1:5. The rulers of Samaria and Jerusalem were responsible for the proliferation of idolatry in the Northern Kingdom and in Judah.

1:7. As a betrayal of God, idolatry is comparable to idolatry. Its lavish shrines, built with treasures collected for idolatry, will be looted by other idolaters (*Radak*).

1:9. After conquering the Northern Kingdom and most of Judah, the mighty Assyrian army reached the gates of Jerusalem, where it was miraculously decimated [see *II Kings* 18:9-19:35] (*Ibn Ezra*).

1:10-16. After expressing the hope that the Philistines of Gath not be given the opportunity to gloat over our

downfall, the prophet gives poignant expression to the mourning of various Jewish cities.

1:11. When the residents of Beth-ezel are exiled, the people of Zaanan will not console them, for they will be awaiting the same fate. The conquerors of hapless, abandoned Beth-ezel will plunder its possessions as a "payment" for their protracted siege of the city (*Radak*).

1:13. Micah turns his anger to Lachish, urging its people to flee. Lachish was the first city in Judah that imported the Samarian worship of Baal (*Radak*).

1:14. Scornfully, Micah suggests that the people send gifts to the Philistines in Moresheth-gath, in the vain hope that they would come to Judah's defense against Assyria (*Ibn Ezra*).

1

¹ The word of HASHEM that came to Micah the Morashite, in the days of Jotham, Ahaz [and] Hezekiah, * kings of Judah — that he saw concerning Samaria and Jerusalem:

Samaria and Jerusalem — sinners both

² Hear, O peoples, all of them! Listen, O Land and its fullness! Let the Lord HASHEM/ELOHIM be a witness* against you, the Lord from His holy Sanctuary. ³ For behold, HASHEM is going forth from His place; He will descend and trample the heights of the land. ⁴ The mountains will melt away under Him and the valleys will split open, like wax before a fire, like water flowing down a slope. ⁵ All this because of the sin of Jacob, because of the transgressions of the House of Israel. Who [caused] the sin of Jacob; was it not Samaria? Who [caused] the high places of Judah; was it not Jerusalem?* ⁶ I will make Samaria into a mound in the field, a place to plant vineyards. I will roll away its stones to the valley and lay bare its foundations. ⁷ All of its graven images will be smashed and all of its [idolatrous] gifts will be burned in fire, and I will make all of its idols desolate. For they were collected as harlot's hire, and they will revert to harlot's hire. *

The prophet's grief

⁸ For this I will lament and wail; I will go about delirious and naked; I will make lamentation like the jackals and mourning like owls. ⁹ For her wound is grievous; for it has come to Judah; it has extended to the gate of My people, up to Jerusalem. * ¹⁰ Tell it not in Gath;* weep not at all; in each house of Aphrah wallow in the dirt. ¹¹ Pass on [to exile], O inhabitant of Saphir, with nakedness uncovered. The inhabitant of Zaanan did not go forth in lamentation for Beth-ezel;* [the enemy] will seize [the cost of] his stay from you. ¹² For the inhabitants of Maroth hoped for the best, but evil came down from before HASHEM, to the gate of Jerusalem. ¹³ Fasten the chariot to the swift steed, O inhabitant of Lachish; that was the origin of sin for the people of Zion,* for it was in you that the sins of Israel were found. ¹⁴ Therefore, send gifts to Moresheth-gath!* The houses of Achzib will become a lost cause to the kings of Israel. ¹⁵ I will yet bring a dispossessor against you, O inhabitant of Mareshah; the glory of Israel will withdraw to Adullam. * ¹⁶ Make yourself bald and pull out your hair* for the children of your delight; make your baldness broad like an eagle's, for they have departed from you.

No hope

2

¹ Woe to those who devise iniquity and plan evil upon their beds; at the morning's light they carry it out, for there is power in their hand. ² They covet fields and they rob [them], [they covet] houses and they take [them]; they oppress a man and his household, a person and his heritage.

³ Therefore, thus said HASHEM:

False prophets are exposed

Behold, I am devising evil against this family, from which you will not extricate your necks; you will not walk erect, for it will be a bad time. ⁴ On that day he* will recite a parable about you; he will lament, 'A lament has come to be!' He will say, 'We have been utterly plundered! [God] is exchanging the portion of my people! How could He return what was mine when our field is apportioned to the enemy?'

⁵ Therefore, there shall not be for you one who casts [the surveyor's] line for the lot* in the congregation of HASHEM.

1:15. The Assyrian conqueror will push the "glory of Israel" back from city after city.

1:16. A sign of mourning and distress.

2:4. A false prophet will lament, in the obscure wording of a parable, because his prophecies will not be fulfilled and his advice will come to naught (*Radak*).

2:5. Micah responds to the false prophet that *he* will not have any heirs to divide up his inheritance.

ו-ז אַל־תַּטִּפוּ יַטִּיפוּן לֹא־יַטִּפוּ לָאֵלֶּה לֹא יִסַּג כְּלִמְּוֹת: הֶאָמוּר בֵּית־יַעֲקֹב הֲקָצַר רוּחַ יהוה אִם־אֵלֶּה מַעֲלָלָיו הֲלוֹא דְבָרַי יֵיטִיבוּ עִם הַיָּשָׁר הוֹלֵךְ:

ח וְאֶתְמוּל עַמִּי לְאוֹיֵב יְקוֹמֵם מִמּוּל שַׂלְמָה אֶדֶר תַּפְשִׁטוּן מֵעֹבְרִים בֶּטַח

ט שׁוּבֵי מִלְחָמָה: נְשֵׁי עַמִּי תְּגָרְשׁוּן מִבֵּית תַּעֲנֻגֶיהָ מֵעַל עֹלָלֶיהָ תִּקְחוּ

י הֲדָרִי לְעוֹלָם: קוּמוּ וּלְכוּ כִּי לֹא־זֹאת הַמְּנוּחָה בַּעֲבוּר טָמְאָה תְּחַבֵּל

יא וְחֶבֶל נִמְרָץ: לוּ־אִישׁ הֹלֵךְ רוּחַ וָשֶׁקֶר כִּזֵּב אַטִּף לְךָ לַיַּיִן וְלַשֵּׁכָר וְהָיָה

יב מַטִּיף הָעָם הַזֶּה: אָסֹף אֶאֱסֹף יַעֲקֹב כֻּלָּךְ קַבֵּץ אֲקַבֵּץ שְׁאֵרִית יִשְׂרָאֵל

יג יַחַד אֲשִׂימֶנּוּ כְּצֹאן בָּצְרָה כְּעֵדֶר בְּתוֹךְ הַדָּבְרוֹ תְּהִימֶנָה מֵאָדָם: עָלָה הַפֹּרֵץ לִפְנֵיהֶם פָּרְצוּ וַיַּעֲבֹרוּ שַׁעַר וַיֵּצְאוּ בוֹ וַיַּעֲבֹר מַלְכָּם לִפְנֵיהֶם

ג   א וַיהוה בְּרֹאשָׁם: וָאֹמַר שִׁמְעוּ־נָא רָאשֵׁי יַעֲקֹב וּקְצִינֵי בֵּית

ב יִשְׂרָאֵל הֲלוֹא לָכֶם לָדַעַת אֶת־הַמִּשְׁפָּט: שֹׂנְאֵי טוֹב וְאֹהֲבֵי °רעה

ג [רָע ק] גֹּזְלֵי עוֹרָם מֵעֲלֵיהֶם וּשְׁאֵרָם מֵעַל עַצְמוֹתָם: וַאֲשֶׁר אָכְלוּ שְׁאֵר עַמִּי וְעוֹרָם מֵעֲלֵיהֶם הִפְשִׁיטוּ וְאֶת־עַצְמֹתֵיהֶם פִּצֵּחוּ וּפָרְשׂוּ כַּאֲשֶׁר

ד בַּסִּיר וּכְבָשָׂר בְּתוֹךְ קַלָּחַת: אָז יִזְעֲקוּ אֶל־יהוה וְלֹא יַעֲנֶה אוֹתָם וְיַסְתֵּר

ה פָּנָיו מֵהֶם בָּעֵת הַהִיא כַּאֲשֶׁר הֵרֵעוּ מַעַלְלֵיהֶם: כֹּה אָמַר יהוה עַל־הַנְּבִיאִים הַמַּתְעִים אֶת־עַמִּי הַנֹּשְׁכִים בְּשִׁנֵּיהֶם וְקָרְאוּ שָׁלוֹם וַאֲשֶׁר

ו לֹא־יִתֵּן עַל־פִּיהֶם וְקִדְּשׁוּ עָלָיו מִלְחָמָה: לָכֵן לַיְלָה לָכֶם מֵחָזוֹן וְחָשְׁכָה

ז לָכֶם מִקְּסֹם וּבָאָה הַשֶּׁמֶשׁ עַל־הַנְּבִיאִים וְקָדַר עֲלֵיהֶם הַיּוֹם: וּבֹשׁוּ הַחֹזִים וְחָפְרוּ הַקֹּסְמִים וְעָטוּ עַל־שָׂפָם כֻּלָּם כִּי אֵין מַעֲנֵה אֱלֹהִים:

ח וְאוּלָם אָנֹכִי מָלֵאתִי כֹחַ אֶת־רוּחַ יהוה וּמִשְׁפָּט וּגְבוּרָה לְהַגִּיד לְיַעֲקֹב

ט פִּשְׁעוֹ וּלְיִשְׂרָאֵל חַטָּאתוֹ:   שִׁמְעוּ־נָא זֹאת רָאשֵׁי בֵּית יַעֲקֹב

י וּקְצִינֵי בֵּית יִשְׂרָאֵל הַמְתַעֲבִים מִשְׁפָּט וְאֵת כָּל־הַיְשָׁרָה יְעַקֵּשׁוּ: בֹּנֶה

יא צִיּוֹן בְּדָמִים וִירוּשָׁלַ͏ִם בְּעַוְלָה: רָאשֶׁיהָ בְּשֹׁחַד יִשְׁפֹּטוּ וְכֹהֲנֶיהָ בִּמְחִיר יוֹרוּ וּנְבִיאֶיהָ בְּכֶסֶף יִקְסֹמוּ וְעַל־יהוה יִשָּׁעֵנוּ לֵאמֹר הֲלוֹא יהוה בְּקִרְבֵּנוּ

יב לֹא־תָבוֹא עָלֵינוּ רָעָה: לָכֵן בִּגְלַלְכֶם צִיּוֹן שָׂדֶה תֵחָרֵשׁ וִירוּשָׁלַ͏ִם

ד   א עִיִּין תִּהְיֶה וְהַר הַבַּיִת לְבָמוֹת יָעַר: וְהָיָה ׀ בְּאַחֲרִית הַיָּמִים יִהְיֶה הַר בֵּית־יהוה נָכוֹן בְּרֹאשׁ הֶהָרִים וְנִשָּׂא הוּא מִגְּבָעוֹת וְנָהֲרוּ עָלָיו

ב עַמִּים: וְהָלְכוּ גּוֹיִם רַבִּים וְאָמְרוּ לְכוּ ׀ וְנַעֲלֶה אֶל־הַר־יהוה וְאֶל־בֵּית

2:6. But the false prophets shout that the true agents of God should not preach to the people.

2:7. Is it proper to spurn God's word? Is God so impatient — "short-spirited" — that He cannot show us mercy as He did in the past (*Rashi*).

2:10. The Land of Israel, which is called "the Resting Place" (*Deuteronomy* 12:9), was not meant for you to contaminate with your degenerate actions.

2:11. The people deserved to be exiled, because they were so receptive to false prophets.

2:13. The Messiah will break through all the barriers that have been restraining Israel's return to its land (*Kara*).

3:1. You are responsible to know whether the law is being enforced (*Radak*).

3:4. When the enemy comes (*Radak*).

3:5. When they are well fed, i.e., paid to their satisfaction, they foretell peace; otherwise, they announce war.

3:7. A veiled face was the traditional sign of mourning and anguish. The "prophets" will have been revealed as charlatans, to whom God had never spoken.

False hope

⁶ 'Do not preach!'* they preach, 'They shall not preach to these [people], [so that] shame shall not overtake them.'⁷ Should this be said by the House of Jacob?* Has HASHEM become short-spirited? Are these His deeds? Behold, My ways are benevolent with the one who walks with uprightness. ⁸ Yesterday My people arose as an enemy [to its fellows]; for the sake of a garment, a mantle, you would strip them, [making] innocent passersby fugitives of war. ⁹ You evict [each of] the women of My people from the home of her delight; from her young children you remove My glory forever. ¹⁰ Arise and go [into exile], because not for this [purpose] is the Resting Place* [given to you]. Because it has become defiled, it will destroy you absolutely. ¹¹ If a man would be going about, deceiving with wind and falsehood, [and would say,] 'I will preach to you to [drink] wine and liquor,' he would be an [approved] preacher for this people!*

¹² I will surely gather all of you, O Jacob. I will surely assemble the remnant of Israel; I will place them together like a flock in a fold; like a herd in its pen, they will teem with people. ¹³ The one who breaks forth* will go before them; they will break forth and pass through; they will go out through the gates; their king will pass in front of them, with HASHEM at their head.

3

Indictment of oppressive rulers

¹ I said, "Listen, now, you leaders of Jacob and officers of the House of Israel! Is it not up to you to know the law?*² [But you] hate good and love evil; you rob [people's] skin from upon them and their flesh from upon their bones; ³ [you] have eaten the flesh of My people, you have stripped their skin from upon them, you have broken open their bones; and you have sliced them like that which is in the pot and like meat in a cauldron. ⁴ Then* they will cry out to HASHEM, but He will not answer them; He will hide His face from them at that time, just as they had done evil with their deeds."

⁵ Thus said HASHEM about the prophets who mislead My nation, who chew with their teeth and declare peace, but whoever does not put [food] into their mouths, they prepare war against him:*

Misleading prophets

⁶ Therefore, it shall be night for you because of such vision, and it shall be dark for you because of such divination; the sun will set upon the prophets and the daylight will be blackened for them. ⁷ The seers will be ashamed and the diviners disgraced and all of them will wear veils over their lips,* for [they] had no word of God.

⁸ But as for me, I was filled with strength by the spirit of HASHEM, and [with] justice and might, to inform Jacob of his transgression and Israel of his sin.

⁹ Listen, now, to this, O leaders of the House of Jacob and officers of the House of Israel, who detest justice and who twist all that is straight, ¹⁰ who build Zion with blood and Jerusalem with iniquity:

Wholesale corruption

¹¹ Her leaders judge for bribes and her Kohanim teach for a fee and her prophets divine for money — yet they rely on HASHEM, saying, 'Behold, HASHEM is in our midst; no evil can befall us!' ¹² Therefore, because of you, Zion will be plowed over like a field; Jerusalem will become heaps of rubble and the Temple Mount will become like stone heaps in the forest.

4

Return to the Temple

¹ It will be in the end of days that the mountain of the Temple of HASHEM will be firmly established as the most prominent of the mountains, and it will be exalted up above the hills, and peoples will stream to it. ² Many nations will go and say, 'Come, let us go up to the Mountain of HASHEM and to the Temple

אֱלֹהֵי יַעֲקֹב וְיוֹרֵנוּ מִדְּרָכָיו וְנֵלְכָה בְּאֹרְחֹתָיו כִּי מִצִּיּוֹן תֵּצֵא תוֹרָה וּדְבַר־

ג יהוה מִירוּשָׁלָ͏ִם: וְשָׁפַט בֵּין עַמִּים רַבִּים וְהוֹכִיחַ לְגוֹיִם עֲצֻמִים עַד־רָחוֹק

וְכִתְּתוּ חַרְבֹתֵיהֶם לְאִתִּים וַחֲנִיתֹתֵיהֶם לְמַזְמֵרוֹת לֹא־יִשְׂאוּ גּוֹי אֶל־גּוֹי

ד חֶרֶב וְלֹא־יִלְמְדוּן עוֹד מִלְחָמָה: וְיָשְׁבוּ אִישׁ תַּחַת גַּפְנוֹ וְתַחַת תְּאֵנָתוֹ

ה וְאֵין מַחֲרִיד כִּי־פִי יהוה צְבָאוֹת דִּבֵּר: כִּי כָּל־הָעַמִּים יֵלְכוּ אִישׁ בְּשֵׁם

ו אֱלֹהָיו וַאֲנַחְנוּ נֵלֵךְ בְּשֵׁם־יהוה אֱלֹהֵינוּ לְעוֹלָם וָעֶד:

ז בַּיּוֹם הַהוּא נְאֻם־יהוה אֹסְפָה הַצֹּלֵעָה וְהַנִּדָּחָה אֲקַבֵּצָה וַאֲשֶׁר הֲרֵעֹתִי: וְשַׂמְתִּי

אֶת־הַצֹּלֵעָה לִשְׁאֵרִית וְהַנַּהֲלָאָה לְגוֹי עָצוּם וּמָלַךְ יהוה עֲלֵיהֶם בְּהַר

ח צִיּוֹן מֵעַתָּה וְעַד־עוֹלָם: וְאַתָּה מִגְדַּל־עֵדֶר עֹפֶל בַּת־צִיּוֹן

ט עָדֶיךָ תֵּאתֶה וּבָאָה הַמֶּמְשָׁלָה הָרִאשֹׁנָה מַמְלֶכֶת לְבַת־יְרוּשָׁלָ͏ִם: עַתָּה

לָמָּה תָרִיעִי רֵעַ הֲמֶלֶךְ אֵין־בָּךְ אִם־יוֹעֲצֵךְ אָבָד כִּי־הֶחֱזִיקֵךְ חִיל

י כַּיּוֹלֵדָה: חוּלִי וָגֹחִי בַּת־צִיּוֹן כַּיּוֹלֵדָה כִּי־עַתָּה תֵצְאִי מִקִּרְיָה וְשָׁכַנְתְּ

יא בַּשָּׂדֶה וּבָאת עַד־בָּבֶל שָׁם תִּנָּצֵלִי שָׁם יִגְאָלֵךְ יהוה מִכַּף אֹיְבָיִךְ: וְעַתָּה

יב נֶאֶסְפוּ עָלַיִךְ גּוֹיִם רַבִּים הָאֹמְרִים תֶּחֱנָף וְתַחַז בְּצִיּוֹן עֵינֵינוּ: וְהֵמָּה לֹא

יג יָדְעוּ מַחְשְׁבוֹת יהוה וְלֹא הֵבִינוּ עֲצָתוֹ כִּי קִבְּצָם כֶּעָמִיר גֹּרְנָה: קוּמִי

וָדוֹשִׁי בַת־צִיּוֹן כִּי־קַרְנֵךְ אָשִׂים בַּרְזֶל וּפַרְסֹתַיִךְ אָשִׂים נְחוּשָׁה וַהֲדִקּוֹת

יד עַמִּים רַבִּים וְהַחֲרַמְתִּי לַיהוה בִּצְעָם וְחֵילָם לַאֲדוֹן כָּל־הָאָרֶץ: עַתָּה

תִּתְגֹּדְדִי בַת־גְּדוּד מָצוֹר שָׂם עָלֵינוּ בַּשֵּׁבֶט יַכּוּ עַל־הַלְּחִי אֵת שֹׁפֵט

א יִשְׂרָאֵל: וְאַתָּה בֵּית־לֶחֶם אֶפְרָתָה צָעִיר לִהְיוֹת בְּאַלְפֵי

ה

יְהוּדָה מִמְּךָ לִי יֵצֵא לִהְיוֹת מוֹשֵׁל בְּיִשְׂרָאֵל וּמוֹצָאֹתָיו מִקֶּדֶם מִימֵי

ב עוֹלָם: לָכֵן יִתְּנֵם עַד־עֵת יוֹלֵדָה יָלָדָה וְיֶתֶר אֶחָיו יְשׁוּבוּן עַל־בְּנֵי יִשְׂרָאֵל:

ג וְעָמַד וְרָעָה בְּעֹז יהוה בִּגְאוֹן שֵׁם יהוה אֱלֹהָיו וְיָשָׁבוּ כִּי־עַתָּה יִגְדַּל

ד עַד־אַפְסֵי־אָרֶץ: וְהָיָה זֶה שָׁלוֹם אַשּׁוּר כִּי־יָבוֹא בְאַרְצֵנוּ וְכִי יִדְרֹךְ

ה בְּאַרְמְנֹתֵינוּ וַהֲקֵמֹנוּ עָלָיו שִׁבְעָה רֹעִים וּשְׁמֹנָה נְסִיכֵי אָדָם: וְרָעוּ

אֶת־אֶרֶץ אַשּׁוּר בַּחֶרֶב וְאֶת־אֶרֶץ נִמְרֹד בִּפְתָחֶיהָ וְהִצִּיל מֵאַשּׁוּר כִּי־

יָבוֹא בְאַרְצֵנוּ וְכִי יִדְרֹךְ בִּגְבוּלֵנוּ: ▸ וְהָיָה ׀ שְׁאֵרִית יַעֲקֹב

בְּקֶרֶב עַמִּים רַבִּים כְּטַל מֵאֵת יהוה כִּרְבִיבִים עֲלֵי־עֵשֶׂב אֲשֶׁר לֹא־

HAFTARAS
BALAK
5:6-6:8

4:3. The judge who will preside at the Temple Mount, i.e., the Messiah (*Ibn Ezra*). Nations will accept his judgments, and never again resort to war (*Radak*).

4:8. Having compared the ingathering of the exiles to the collecting of lost sheep, the prophet refers to the "Ophel," one of Jerusalem's fortifications, as the "Tower of the Flock."

4:10. Having failed to serve God, you will be dragged off to Babylonian captivity, but God will redeem you from there.

4:11-13. At the time of the war of Gog and Magog, before the ultimate redemption, the conquerors will exult

in Zion's obvious guilt, and the enemies of Israel will gloat over her degradation. However, they will not realize that God is bringing them together to be trampled.

4:14. This is addressed to the foreign invaders, who will attack Israel (*Rashi*).

5:1. Another name for Bethlehem of Judah (see *Genesis* 48:7). As the city of Ruth, a convert from Moab, Bethlehem was an unlikely source of leadership, but it produced David, the ancestor of the Messiah.

5:2. The hardships of exile will become as intense as labor pains, but it will end with the rebirth of the Jewish nation (*Kara*), and the return of the Messiah's brethren.

of the God of Jacob, and He will teach us of His ways and we will walk in His paths.' For from Zion shall go forth the Torah, and the word of HASHEM from Jerusalem. ³ *He* will judge between many peoples, and will settle the*

Swords into plowshares

arguments of mighty nations from far away. They will beat their swords into plowshares and their spears into pruning knives; nation will not lift sword against nation, nor will they learn war anymore. ⁴ *They will sit, each man under his vine and under his fig tree, and none will make them afraid, for the mouth of HASHEM, Master of Legions, has spoken.* ⁵ *For all the peoples will go forth, each man in the name of his god, but we go forth with the Name of HASHEM, our God, forever and ever.*

Even the handicapped

⁶ *On that day — the word of HASHEM — I will assemble the lame one and gather in the one driven away and whomever I have harmed,* ⁷ *and I will make the lame one into a remnant and the one forced to wander into a mighty nation; and HASHEM will reign over them at Mount Zion, from now and forever.* ⁸ *And you, Migdal-eder (Tower of the Flock), Ophel of the daughter of Zion,* they will come [back] to you; and the original kingdom will arrive, the kingdom of the daughter of Jerusalem.* ⁹ *Now, why do you seek [foreign] alliance? Is there not a king in your midst? Has your counselor become lost, that pains have gripped you like a woman in childbirth?*

Saved from the enemy

¹⁰ *Be in pain and groan like a woman in childbirth, O daughter of Zion;* for now you will leave the city and dwell in the field; you will come to Babylonia and there you will be rescued; there HASHEM will redeem you from the palms of your enemies.* ¹¹ *And now, many nations have assembled against you; they say, 'Let her be [proclaimed] guilty, and let our eyes behold Zion!'** ¹² *But they do not know the thoughts of HASHEM and do not understand His counsel — for He has gathered them like sheaves to the threshing floor.* ¹³ *Arise and thresh, O daughter of Zion! For I will make your horn [like] iron and I will make your hooves [like] copper, and you will grind many peoples. I will consecrate unto HASHEM all their ill-gotten riches, and their wealth unto the Lord of the entire land.*

¹⁴ *'Now, muster yourself,* O daughter of the armed band!' He has laid siege against us; with a stick they strike on the cheek the judges of Israel.*

5

Jewish rulers emerge

¹**B**ethlehem — Ephratah* — *you are too small to be among the thousands of Judah, but from you someone will emerge for Me to be a ruler over Israel; and his origins will be from early times, from days of old.* ² *Therefore, He will deliver them [to their enemies] until the time that a woman in childbirth gives birth; then the rest of his brothers will return with the Children of Israel.* * ³ *He will stand up and lead with the strength of HASHEM, with the majesty of the Name of HASHEM his God. They will settle [in peace], for at that time he will be great to the ends of the earth,* ⁴ *and this will [assure] peace. If Assyria will come into our land, and if he will tread upon our palaces, we will set up seven shepherds or eight officers against him,* ⁵ *and they will pound the land of Assyria with the sword, and the land of Nimrod* at its gateways; and he will rescue [us] from Assyria when they enter our land and when they tread onto our borders.* ⁶ *The remnant of Jacob will be in the midst of many peoples like dew from HASHEM,* like raindrops upon grass, which is not*

5:5. See *Genesis* 10:8-11.
5:6. When the redemption is imminent and the forces of Gog converge upon Jerusalem, the remnant of Israel will

be among them. And that will be as God-given a phenomenon as dew and rain, because no human being would or could have brought it about (Radak).

ז יְקַוֶּה לְאִישׁ וְלֹא יְיַחֵל לִבְנֵי אָדָם: וְהָיָה שְׁאֵרִית יַעֲקֹב בַּגּוֹיִם בְּקֶרֶב עַמִּים רַבִּים כְּאַרְיֵה בְּבַהֲמוֹת יַעַר כִּכְפִיר בְּעֶדְרֵי־צֹאן אֲשֶׁר אִם־עָבַר וְרָמַס

ח-ט וְטָרַף וְאֵין מַצִּיל: תָּרֹם יָדְךָ עַל־צָרֶיךָ וְכָל־אֹיְבֶיךָ יִכָּרֵתוּ: וְהָיָה בַיּוֹם־הַהוּא נְאֻם־יְהוָה וְהִכְרַתִּי סוּסֶיךָ מִקִּרְבֶּךָ וְהַאֲבַדְתִּי מַרְכְּבֹתֶיךָ:

יא-יב וְהִכְרַתִּי עָרֵי אַרְצֶךָ וְהָרַסְתִּי כָּל־מִבְצָרֶיךָ: וְהִכְרַתִּי כְשָׁפִים מִיָּדֶךָ וּמְעוֹנְנִים לֹא יִהְיוּ־לָךְ: וְהִכְרַתִּי פְסִילֶיךָ וּמַצֵּבוֹתֶיךָ מִקִּרְבֶּךָ וְלֹא־

יג תִשְׁתַּחֲוֶה עוֹד לְמַעֲשֵׂה יָדֶיךָ: וְנָתַשְׁתִּי אֲשֵׁירֶיךָ מִקִּרְבֶּךָ וְהִשְׁמַדְתִּי עָרֶיךָ:

יד-ו:א וְעָשִׂיתִי בְּאַף וּבְחֵמָה נָקָם אֶת־הַגּוֹיִם אֲשֶׁר לֹא שָׁמֵעוּ: שִׁמְעוּ־

נָא אֵת אֲשֶׁר־יְהוָה אֹמֵר קוּם רִיב אֶת־הֶהָרִים וְתִשְׁמַעְנָה הַגְּבָעוֹת

ב קוֹלֶךָ: שִׁמְעוּ הָרִים אֶת־רִיב יְהוָה וְהָאֵתָנִים מֹסְדֵי אָרֶץ כִּי רִיב לַיהוָה

ג עִם־עַמּוֹ וְעִם־יִשְׂרָאֵל יִתְוַכָּח: עַמִּי מֶה־עָשִׂיתִי לְךָ וּמָה הֶלְאֵתִיךָ עֲנֵה

ד בִי: כִּי הֶעֱלִתִיךָ מֵאֶרֶץ מִצְרַיִם וּמִבֵּית עֲבָדִים פְּדִיתִיךָ וָאֶשְׁלַח

ה לְפָנֶיךָ אֶת־מֹשֶׁה אַהֲרֹן וּמִרְיָם: עַמִּי זְכָר־נָא מַה־יָּעַץ בָּלָק מֶלֶךְ מוֹאָב וּמֶה־עָנָה אֹתוֹ בִּלְעָם בֶּן־בְּעוֹר מִן־הַשִּׁטִּים עַד־הַגִּלְגָּל לְמַעַן

ו דַּעַת צִדְקוֹת יְהוָה: בַּמָּה אֲקַדֵּם יְהוָה אִכַּף לֵאלֹהֵי מָרוֹם הַאֲקַדְּמֶנּוּ

ז בְעוֹלוֹת בַּעֲגָלִים בְּנֵי שָׁנָה: הֲיִרְצֶה יְהוָה בְּאַלְפֵי אֵילִים בְּרִבְבוֹת

ח נַחֲלֵי־שָׁמֶן הַאֶתֵּן בְּכוֹרִי פִּשְׁעִי פְּרִי בִטְנִי חַטַּאת נַפְשִׁי: הִגִּיד לְךָ אָדָם מַה־טּוֹב וּמָה־יְהוָה דּוֹרֵשׁ מִמְּךָ כִּי אִם־עֲשׂוֹת מִשְׁפָּט וְאַהֲבַת חֶסֶד

ט וְהַצְנֵעַ לֶכֶת עִם־אֱלֹהֶיךָ: ◀ קוֹל יְהוָה לָעִיר יִקְרָא וְתוּשִׁיָּה

י יִרְאֶה שְׁמֶךָ שִׁמְעוּ מַטֶּה וּמִי יְעָדָהּ: עוֹד הַאִשׁ בֵּית רָשָׁע אֹצְרוֹת רֶשַׁע

יא-יב וְאֵיפַת רָזוֹן זְעוּמָה: הַאֶזְכֶּה בְּמֹאזְנֵי רֶשַׁע וּבְכִיס אַבְנֵי מִרְמָה: אֲשֶׁר עֲשִׁירֶיהָ מָלְאוּ חָמָס וְיֹשְׁבֶיהָ דִּבְּרוּ־שָׁקֶר וּלְשׁוֹנָם רְמִיָּה בְּפִיהֶם: וְגַם־אֲנִי

יג-יד הֶחֱלֵיתִי הַכּוֹתֶךָ הַשְׁמֵם עַל־חַטֹּאתֶךָ: אַתָּה תֹאכַל וְלֹא תִשְׂבָּע וְיֶשְׁחֲךָ בְּקִרְבֶּךָ וְתַסֵּג וְלֹא תַפְלִיט וַאֲשֶׁר תְּפַלֵּט לַחֶרֶב אֶתֵּן: אַתָּה תִזְרַע וְלֹא

טו תִקְצוֹר אַתָּה תִדְרֹךְ־זַיִת וְלֹא־תָסוּךְ שֶׁמֶן וְתִירוֹשׁ וְלֹא תִשְׁתֶּה־יָּיִן:

טז וְיִשְׁתַּמֵּר חֻקּוֹת עָמְרִי וְכֹל מַעֲשֵׂה בֵית־אַחְאָב וַתֵּלְכוּ בְּמֹעֲצוֹתָם לְמַעַן

ז תִּתִּי אֹתְךָ לְשַׁמָּה וְיֹשְׁבֶיהָ לִשְׁרֵקָה וְחֶרְפַּת עַמִּי תִּשָּׂאוּ:

5:9-10. There will be no need for weapons or defenses, for there will be no more wars (*Radak*).

6:5. To hire Balaam to pronounce a curse against Israel (see *Numbers* 22:1-25:9 and *Joshua* 4:19).

Balaam's plan to seduce Israel into immorality and idolatry met with a measure of success in Shittim. Nevertheless, God did not allow that waywardness to prevent the nation from entering the Land of Israel where they first encamped in Gilgal (*Rashi*).

6:7. Olive oil is a part of the meal-offering (*Rashi*).

6:8. God's definition of good is different from yours.

6:10. Even after the exhortations of the prophets, how can people behave wickedly and retain fraudulent weights which they use to cheat their customers?

6:13. Measure for measure, just as you have hurt the poor and defenseless, I have punished you.

6:16. Omri and his son Ahab were exceedingly wicked kings of Israel (see *II Kings* 16:23-34). Because Israel did not repudiate the precedent they set, people will whistle in amazement at the destruction you will suffer for defrauding the poor (vv. 10-11).

hoped for from man and not awaited from a human being.

Lion-like Jacob

⁷ And the remnant of Jacob will be among the nations, in the midst of many peoples, like a lion among the animals of the forest and like a lion's whelp among flocks of sheep, who, when he passes by, tramples and tears apart, and there is no rescuer. ⁸ Your hand will be raised over your enemies, and all your adversaries will be eliminated.

Danger eliminated

⁹ It will be on that day — the word of HASHEM — I will eliminate your horses from your midst and I will destroy your chariots. * ¹⁰ I will eliminate the [walled] cities from your land and I will tear down all your fortifications. ¹¹ I will eliminate witchcraft from your domain, and there will be no diviners among you. ¹² I will eliminate your graven idols and your pillars from your midst, and you will no longer prostrate yourselves to your own handiwork. ¹³ I will uproot your Asherah trees from your midst, and I will destroy those who hate you. ¹⁴ And with anger and wrath I will carry out revenge against the nations, because they did not listen.

6

¹ Listen, now, what HASHEM says [to me]: "Arise and contend before the mountains, and let the hills hear your voice!" ² Listen, you mountains, to the grievance of HASHEM, and you bedrock, the foundations of the earth! For HASHEM has a grievance with His people, and He will contend with Israel:

Defend your ingratitude

³ My people, what [wrong] did I do to you and how did I tire you? Testify against Me! ⁴ For I brought you up from the land of Egypt and redeemed you from the house of bondage; and I sent Moses, Aaron and Miriam before you. ⁵ My people, hear, now, what Balak, king of Moab, schemed, * and what Balaam son of Beor answered him, [and all the events] from Shittim to Gilgal * — in order to recognize the righteous acts of HASHEM.

⁶ [You ask,] With what shall I approach HASHEM, humble myself before God on high? Shall I approach Him with burnt-offerings, or with calves in their first year? ⁷ Will HASHEM be appeased by thousands of rams or with tens of thousands of streams of oil? * Shall I give over my firstborn [to atone for] my transgression, or the fruit of my belly [for] the sin of my soul?'

What does God ask?

⁸ He has told you, O man, what is good! * What does HASHEM require of you but to do justice, to love kindness and to walk humbly with your God?

How can you rebel?

⁹ The voice of HASHEM calls out to the [people of the] city; the [man of] wisdom recognizes Your Name: Listen [O Israel,] to the rod [of punishment] and to the One Who has ordained it! ¹⁰ Are there still stores of wickedness in the house of the wicked one, or a lean measure * that angers [God]? ¹¹ Can I be judged righteous with scales of wickedness, or with a pouch of deceitful weights? ¹² For its rich men are full of thievery, and its inhabitants speak falsehood; their tongue is guile in their mouth. ¹³ I have hurt you, * as well, by smiting you, bringing desolation for your sins. ¹⁴ You will eat but not be satisfied, and you will stoop over because of [sickness in] your innards; you will conceive but you will not deliver, and those you do deliver I will give to the sword. ¹⁵ You will sow, but not reap; you will trample olives, but not smear oil; [trample] wine-grapes, but not drink wine. ¹⁶ The decrees of Omri * and all the deeds of the house of Ahab are preserved, and you follow their counsels, so that I will give you over to [be an] astonishment, and its inhabitants [to be a cause for] whistling; and you will bear [the punishment of] the shame of My people.

לִי כִּי הָיִ֙יתִי֙ כְּאׇסְפֵּי־קַ֔יִץ כְּעֹלְלֹ֖ת בָּצִ֑יר אֵין־אֶשְׁכּ֣וֹל לֶאֱכ֔וֹל בִּכּוּרָ֖ה

ב אִוְּתָ֥ה נַפְשִֽׁי: אָבַ֤ד חָסִיד֙ מִן־הָאָ֔רֶץ וְיָשָׁ֥ר בָּאָדָ֖ם אָ֑יִן כֻּלָּם֙ לְדָמִ֣ים יֶאֱרֹ֔בוּ

ג אִ֥ישׁ אֶת־אָחִ֖יהוּ יָצ֥וּדוּ חֵֽרֶם: עַל־הָרַ֣ע כַּפַּ֜יִם לְהֵיטִ֗יב הַשַּׂ֤ר שֹׁאֵל֙

ד וְהַשֹּׁפֵ֣ט בַּשִּׁלּ֔וּם וְהַגָּד֗וֹל דֹּבֵ֛ר הַוַּ֥ת נַפְשׁ֖וֹ ה֑וּא וַֽיְעַבְּתֽוּהָ: טוֹבָ֣ם כְּחֵ֔דֶק יָשָׁ֖ר

ה מִמְּסוּכָ֑ה י֥וֹם מְצַפֶּ֛יךָ פְּקֻדָּתְךָ֥ בָ֖אָה עַתָּ֥ה תִהְיֶ֖ה מְבוּכָתָֽם: אַל־תַּאֲמִ֣ינוּ

ו בְרֵ֗עַ אַֽל־תִּבְטְח֖וּ בְּאַלּ֑וּף מִשֹּׁכֶ֣בֶת חֵיקֶ֔ךָ שְׁמֹ֖ר פִּתְחֵי־פִֽיךָ: כִּי־בֵן֙ מְנַבֵּ֣ל

ז אָ֗ב בַּ֚ת קָמָ֣ה בְאִמָּ֔הּ כַּלָּ֖ה בַּחֲמֹתָ֑הּ אֹיְבֵ֥י אִ֖ישׁ אַנְשֵׁ֥י בֵיתֽוֹ: וַאֲנִי֙ בַּֽיהֹוָ֣ה

ח אֲצַפֶּ֔ה אוֹחִ֖ילָה לֵאלֹהֵ֣י יִשְׁעִ֑י יִשְׁמָעֵ֖נִי אֱלֹהָֽי: אַֽל־תִּשְׂמְחִ֤י אֹיַ֨בְתִּי֙ לִ֔י כִּ֥י

ט נָפַ֖לְתִּי קָ֑מְתִּי כִּֽי־אֵשֵׁ֣ב בַּחֹ֔שֶׁךְ יְהֹוָ֖ה א֥וֹר לִֽי: זַ֤עַף

יְהֹוָה֙ אֶשָּׂ֔א כִּ֥י חָטָ֖אתִי ל֑וֹ עַ֤ד אֲשֶׁר֙ יָרִ֣יב רִיבִ֗י וְעָשָׂה֙ מִשְׁפָּטִ֔י יוֹצִיאֵ֣נִי

י לָא֔וֹר אֶרְאֶ֖ה בְּצִדְקָתֽוֹ: וְתֵרֶ֤א אֹיַ֨בְתִּי֙ וּתְכַסֶּ֣הָ בוּשָׁ֔ה הָאֹמְרָ֣ה אֵלַ֔י אַיּ֖וֹ

יא יְהֹוָ֣ה אֱלֹהָ֑יִךְ עֵינַי֙ תִּרְאֶ֣ינָה בָּ֔הּ עַתָּ֛ה תִּֽהְיֶ֥ה לְמִרְמָ֖ס כְּטִ֥יט חוּצֽוֹת: י֖וֹם

יב לִבְנ֣וֹת גְּדֵרָ֑יִךְ י֥וֹם הַה֖וּא יִרְחַק־חֹֽק: י֥וֹם הוּא֙ וְעָדֶ֣יךָ יָב֔וֹא לְמִנִּ֥י אַשּׁ֖וּר

יג וְעָרֵ֣י מָצ֑וֹר וּלְמִנִּ֤י מָצוֹר֙ וְעַד־נָהָ֔ר וְיָ֥ם מִיָּ֖ם וְהַ֥ר הָהָֽר: וְהָיְתָ֤ה הָאָ֨רֶץ֙

יד לִשְׁמָמָ֔ה עַל־יֹשְׁבֶ֖יהָ מִפְּרִ֥י מַֽעַלְלֵיהֶֽם: רְעֵ֧ה עַמְּךָ֣ בְשִׁבְטֶ֗ךָ

צֹ֤אן נַֽחֲלָתֶ֨ךָ֙ שֹׁכְנִ֤י לְבָדָד֙ יַ֔עַר בְּת֖וֹךְ כַּרְמֶ֑ל יִרְע֥וּ בָשָׁ֛ן וְגִלְעָ֖ד כִּימֵ֥י עוֹלָֽם:

טו-טז כִּימֵ֥י צֵאתְךָ֖ מֵאֶ֣רֶץ מִצְרָ֑יִם אַרְאֶ֖נּוּ נִפְלָאֽוֹת: יִרְא֤וּ גוֹיִם֙ וְיֵבֹ֔שׁוּ מִכֹּ֖ל

יז גְּבֽוּרָתָ֑ם יָשִׂ֤ימוּ יָד֙ עַל־פֶּ֔ה אׇזְנֵיהֶ֖ם תֶּחֱרַֽשְׁנָה: יְלַחֲכ֤וּ עָפָר֙ כַּנָּחָ֔שׁ כְּזֹחֲלֵ֣י

יח אֶ֔רֶץ יִרְגְּז֖וּ מִמִּסְגְּרֹֽתֵיהֶ֑ם אֶל־יְהֹוָ֤ה אֱלֹהֵ֨ינוּ֙ יִפְחָ֔דוּ וְיִֽרְא֖וּ מִמֶּֽךָּ: ◀ מִי־אֵ֣ל

כָּמ֗וֹךָ נֹשֵׂ֤א עָוֺן֙ וְעֹבֵ֣ר עַל־פֶּ֔שַׁע לִשְׁאֵרִ֖ית נַחֲלָת֑וֹ לֹא־הֶחֱזִ֤יק לָעַד֙ אַפּ֔וֹ

יט כִּֽי־חָפֵ֥ץ חֶ֖סֶד הֽוּא: יָשׁ֣וּב יְרַֽחֲמֵ֔נוּ יִכְבֹּ֖שׁ עֲוֺֽנֹתֵ֑ינוּ וְתַשְׁלִ֣יךְ בִּמְצֻל֥וֹת

כ יָ֖ם כָּל־חַטֹּאתָֽם: תִּתֵּ֤ן אֱמֶת֙ לְיַֽעֲקֹ֔ב חֶ֖סֶד לְאַבְרָהָ֑ם אֲשֶׁר־נִשְׁבַּ֥עְתָּ

לַאֲבֹתֵ֖ינוּ מִ֥ימֵי קֶֽדֶם: ◀

Conclusion of *Haftaros of Shabbas Shuvah* and Yom Kippur *Minchah:* 7:18-20

7:1. That is, the leftover fruit after the yield has been harvested. Micah bemoans his role as a prophet to an unreceptive, unrighteous nation.

7:3. The official, the judge and the nobleman braid their strands of evil into a strong rope of iniquity (*Rashi*).

7:4. On the very day when you expect good fortune (*Rashi*), as predicted by your false prophets (*Radak*).

7:7. Despite the shortcomings of the people to whom I must prophesy, I remain steadfast in my allegiance to God.

7:8. Micah now prophesies the exchange that will take place between a contrite Israel and its oppressor nations (*Rashi*).

7:11. The oppressor chides Israel, "The day of your salvation will never come!" (*Rashi*).

7:12. The prophet replies on Israel's behalf, "That day is real! And on it your enemies will come against you" (*Rashi*).

7:14. The prophet now asks God's blessing and protection for Israel.

7:15-16. God responds with a pledge of great miracles.

7:17. The prophet describes the final humbling of the

7

Goodness has vanished

¹ **W**oe is me, for I am like the last pickings of the summer fruits, * like the glean-ings of the grape harvest; there is no cluster to eat; my soul yearns for a ripe fruit. ² The devout one has disappeared from the land; and one upright among men is no more. They all lie in ambush [to shed] blood; they trap, each man his brother, with a net. ³ [They expect] to benefit from the evil of their hands: the official asks [for bribes]; the judge [has a share] in the payment; and the nobleman expresses his selfish desires; and they * plait them together. ⁴ The best of them is like a thorn, the upright one, like a hedge of thistles. On the day of your expectation, your punishment will come; * now you will become perplexed. ⁵ Do not trust a friend; do not rely on an official; guard the doorways of your mouth from the one who lies in your bosom. ⁶ For a son disparages [his] father; a daughter rises up against her mother, a daughter-in-law against her mother-in-law; a man's enemies are the people of his household. ⁷ As for me, * I put my hope in HASHEM and await the God of my salvation; my God will hear me.

Enemy — do not rejoice!

⁸ 'Do not rejoice over me, * my enemy, for though I fell, I will rise! Though I sit in the darkness, HASHEM is a light unto me! ⁹ I shall bear the fury of HASHEM for I have sinned unto Him, until He will take up my cause and execute judgment for me; He will bring me out into the light; I will behold His righteousness. ¹⁰ Then my enemy will see and shame will cover her, she who said to me, "Where is HASHEM your God?" My eyes will behold her: now she will be for trampling, like mud in the streets.'

Your day will come . . .

¹¹ 'The day to rebuild your fences, that day is far away in a distant time.'* ¹² 'That day exists!* And he will come against you: from Assyria to the fortified cities; from Egypt to the [Euphrates] River; from the Western (Mediterranean) Sea; and from mountain to mountain. ¹³ And the land will be desolate with its inhabitants, as the fruit of their actions.

¹⁴ Shepherd Your people * with Your staff, the flock of Your heritage; let them dwell [in secure] isolation, in forest as in fertile field; let them graze in Bashan and Gilead as in days of old.'

. . . but Israel will be redeemed . . .

¹⁵ 'As in the days when you left the land of Egypt I will show it wonders. * ¹⁶ The nations will see and be ashamed of all their [unavailing] power; they will place a hand over [their] mouth; their ears will become deaf.'

¹⁷ 'They will lick the dirt like the snake and like creatures that crawl on the ground; they will tremble from their places of confinement; they will fear HASHEM our God and be afraid of you.'*

. . . as of old

¹⁸ Who is a God like You, Who pardons iniquity and overlooks transgression for the remnant of His heritage? He does not maintain His wrath forever, for He desires kindness. ¹⁹ He will once again show us mercy, He will suppress our iniquities. You will cast all their sins into the depths of the sea. ²⁰ Grant truth to Jacob, * kindness to Abraham, as you swore to our forefathers in days of old.

---

nations, and their awe and reverence for God and Israel (*Radak*).

7:20. Fulfill your promise to the Patriarchs to preserve their descendants and give them the Land of Israel.

א

א-ב מַשָּׂא נִינְוֵה סֵפֶר חֲזוֹן נַחוּם הָאֶלְקֹשִׁי: אֵל קַנּוֹא וְנֹקֵם יְהוָה נֹקֵם יְהוָה
ג וּבַעַל חֵמָה נֹקֵם יְהוָה לְצָרָיו וְנוֹטֵר הוּא לְאֹיְבָיו: יְהוָה אֶרֶךְ אַפַּיִם
°וגדול- [°וּגְדָל- ק] כֹּחַ וְנַקֵּה לֹא יְנַקֶּה יְהוָה בְּסוּפָה וּבִשְׂעָרָה דַּרְכּוֹ וְעָנָן
ד אֲבַק רַגְלָיו: גּוֹעֵר בַּיָּם וַיַּבְּשֵׁהוּ וְכָל-הַנְּהָרוֹת הֶחֱרִיב אֻמְלַל בָּשָׁן וְכַרְמֶל
ה וּפֶרַח לְבָנוֹן אֻמְלָל: הָרִים רָעֲשׁוּ מִמֶּנּוּ וְהַגְּבָעוֹת הִתְמֹגָגוּ וַתִּשָּׂא הָאָרֶץ
ו מִפָּנָיו וְתֵבֵל וְכָל-יֹשְׁבֵי בָהּ: לִפְנֵי זַעְמוֹ מִי יַעֲמוֹד וּמִי יָקוּם בַּחֲרוֹן אַפּוֹ
ז חֲמָתוֹ נִתְּכָה כָאֵשׁ וְהַצֻּרִים נִתְּצוּ מִמֶּנּוּ: טוֹב יְהוָה לְמָעוֹז בְּיוֹם צָרָה וְיֹדֵעַ
ח-ט חֹסֵי בוֹ: וּבְשֶׁטֶף עֹבֵר כָּלָה יַעֲשֶׂה מְקוֹמָהּ וְאֹיְבָיו יְרַדֶּף-חֹשֶׁךְ: מַה-
י תְּחַשְּׁבוּן אֶל-יְהוָה כָּלָה הוּא עֹשֶׂה לֹא-תָקוּם פַּעֲמַיִם צָרָה: כִּי עַד-
יא סִירִים סְבֻכִים וּכְסָבְאָם סְבוּאִים אֻכְּלוּ כְּקַשׁ יָבֵשׁ מָלֵא: מִמֵּךְ יָצָא חֹשֵׁב
יב עַל-יְהוָה רָעָה יֹעֵץ בְּלִיָּעַל: כֹּה ׀ אָמַר יְהוָה אִם-שְׁלֵמִים וְכֵן
יג רַבִּים וְכֵן נָגֹזּוּ וְעָבָר וְעִנִּתִךְ לֹא אֲעַנֵּךְ עוֹד: וְעַתָּה אֶשְׁבֹּר מֹטֵהוּ מֵעָלָיִךְ
יד וּמוֹסְרֹתַיִךְ אֲנַתֵּק: וְצִוָּה עָלֶיךָ יְהוָה לֹא-יִזָּרַע מִשִּׁמְךָ עוֹד מִבֵּית אֱלֹהֶיךָ

ב

א אַכְרִית פֶּסֶל וּמַסֵּכָה אָשִׂים קִבְרֶךָ כִּי קַלּוֹתָ:   הִנֵּה עַל-הֶהָרִים
רַגְלֵי מְבַשֵּׂר מַשְׁמִיעַ שָׁלוֹם חָגִּי יְהוּדָה חַגַּיִךְ שַׁלְּמִי נְדָרָיִךְ כִּי לֹא יוֹסִיף
ב עוֹד °לעבור- [°לַעֲבָר- ק] בָּךְ בְּלִיַּעַל כֻּלֹּה נִכְרָת: עָלָה מֵפִיץ עַל-פָּנַיִךְ
ג נָצוֹר מְצֻרָה צַפֵּה-דֶרֶךְ חַזֵּק מָתְנַיִם אַמֵּץ כֹּחַ מְאֹד: כִּי שָׁב יְהוָה אֶת-גְּאוֹן
ד יַעֲקֹב כִּגְאוֹן יִשְׂרָאֵל כִּי בְקָקוּם בֹּקְקִים וּזְמֹרֵיהֶם שִׁחֵתוּ: מָגֵן גִּבֹּרֵיהוּ
מְאָדָּם אַנְשֵׁי-חַיִל מְתֻלָּעִים בְּאֵשׁ-פְּלָדוֹת הָרֶכֶב בְּיוֹם הֲכִינוֹ וְהַבְּרֹשִׁים
ה הָרְעָלוּ: בַּחוּצוֹת יִתְהוֹלְלוּ הָרֶכֶב יִשְׁתַּקְשְׁקוּן בָּרְחֹבוֹת מַרְאֵיהֶן כַּלַּפִּידִם
ו כַּבְּרָקִים יְרוֹצֵצוּ: יִזְכֹּר אַדִּירָיו יִכָּשְׁלוּ °בהלכותם [°בַּהֲלִיכָתָם ק]
ז-ח יְמַהֲרוּ חוֹמָתָהּ וְהֻכַן הַסֹּכֵךְ: שַׁעֲרֵי הַנְּהָרוֹת נִפְתָּחוּ וְהַהֵיכָל נָמוֹג: וְהֻצַּב
גֻּלְּתָה הֹעֲלָתָה וְאַמְהֹתֶיהָ מְנַהֲגוֹת כְּקוֹל יוֹנִים מְתֹפְפֹת עַל-לִבְבֵהֶן:
ט וְנִינְוֵה כִבְרֵכַת-מַיִם מִימֵי הִיא וְהֵמָּה נָסִים עִמְדוּ עֲמֹדוּ וְאֵין מַפְנֶה:

1:1. Scripture does not indicate when Nahum prophesied. According to *Seder Olam*, Joel, Nahum and Habakkuk prophesied in the time of King Manasseh of Judah. Manasseh's name is omitted, however, because of his wickedness (*Radak*).

1:3. He administers justice swiftly, like a storm wind or a swiftly moving cloud (*Ibn Ezra*).

1:4-6. The verses are metaphorical: God destroys mighty nations and lays waste populated areas (*Rashi*).

1:7. Even when wrathful to His enemies, God shows kindness to those who trust in Him.

1:8. Nineveh, mentioned in verse 1.

1:9. Destruction will be total the first time.

1:10. Fully developed and firmly rooted; i.e., their downfall will come suddenly and swiftly (*Rashi*).

1:11. Sennacherib.

1:14. God scorns Sennacherib, saying that he will have no ruling descendants, and will die in his own temple (see *II Kings* 19:37).

2:1. Having foretold the downfall of Assyria, Nahum addresses the jubilant Judeans, who were miraculously delivered from the "lawless" Sennacherib (see *II Kings*, Chs. 18-19).

2:2. Eventually, the Assyrian Empire will be besieged and conquered by the Babylonians. Nahum exhorts the people of Judah to "look out" at the rout of the Assyrians, from which they will receive much satisfaction and strength (*Rashi*).

2:3. The Assyrians.

2:4. The fierce Babylonian army that conquered Assyria.

2:6. The king of Assyria at the time of the Babylonian onslaught.

The "covering" was a protective roof to shield the besiegers from the projectiles of the defenders (*Radak*).

1

Hashem is vengeful

¹ **A** prophecy regarding Nineveh. The book of the vision of Nahum the Elkoshite: *

² HASHEM is a jealous and vengeful God; HASHEM is vengeful and full of wrath; HASHEM is vengeful to His adversaries and reserves hostility for His enemies. ³ HASHEM is slow to anger, but He has great power and He will not absolve [iniquity]. HASHEM — His path is in a storm and in a tempest, and clouds are the dust of His feet. * ⁴ He rebukes the sea and makes it dry, and makes all the rivers parched. * Bashan and Carmel become devastated, and the flower of Lebanon becomes devastated. ⁵ Mountains quake because of Him and the hills melt; the earth smolders from before Him, the world and all who dwell

Terrible devastation

in it. ⁶ Who can stand before His fury, and who can rise against His burning wrath? His wrath is poured out like fire and rocks become shattered because of Him. ⁷ HASHEM is beneficent, a stronghold on the day of distress, * and mindful of those who take refuge in Him. ⁸ With a sweeping flood, He puts an end to its place, * and He pursues His enemies with darkness. ⁹ What can you devise against HASHEM? He is making an end [of you]; misfortune will not arise twice. * ¹⁰ While they are still like tangled thorns * and while they are drunk in their swilling, they will be consumed like fully grown dried straw. ¹¹ From you has come forth a plotter of evil* against HASHEM, a lawless counselor.

¹² Thus said HASHEM [to Nineveh]: Even if [your troops] are united and also numerous — even so they will be cut down and pass on. I will afflict you, and I will not [need to] afflict you again.

Israel will be freed

¹³ And now, I will break his yoke from upon you, [O Israel,] and I will snap your bonds. ¹⁴ And HASHEM will decree upon you that your name will never again be sown. * I will eliminate idol and molten image from the temple of your gods; I will make your grave [there], because you have become abhorrent [to Me].

2

The herald proclaims

¹ **B**ehold on the mountains the feet of the herald proclaiming peace!* Celebrate your feasts, O Judah, fulfill your vows; for the lawless one will never pass by you again; he is completely cut off. ² The scatterer has left your presence, he is beset with a siege. Look out at the road; gird your loins and gather much strength. * ³ For HASHEM has restored the pride of Jacob like the [former] pride of Israel; for plunderers have laid them* bare and have destroyed their vine branches. ⁴ The shields of his* warriors are reddened; his soldiers are colored scarlet; the chariots [glisten] with the fire of torches on the day he is readied; his cypress [spears] are poisoned. ⁵ The chariots careen in the streets; they clang in the city squares; their appearance is like flames; they dash like lightning. ⁶ He* will [then] remember his mighty men — but they will stumble as they go. They will hasten [to defend] its wall, but the covering* will have been set up.

The evil flee from Nineveh

⁷ The gates of the rivers * have been opened, and the palace is melting. ⁸ The queen has been exposed and carried off [into captivity]; her handmaids moan, like the sounding of doves, beating upon their hearts. ⁹ Nineveh had been like a pool of [still] water, from her [earliest] days — but now they flee! 'Halt! Halt!'* but no one pays attention.

2:7. Those of Nineveh's gates that opened to the banks of the Tigris River (*Rashi*).

2:9. Her officers try to stop their fleeing troops, but to no avail.

יא בְּזוּ כֶסֶף בְּזוּ זָהָב וְאֵין קֵצֶה לַתְּכוּנָה כָּבֹד מִכֹּל כְּלִי חֶמְדָּה: בּוּקָה וּמְבוּקָה
וּמְבֻלָּקָה וְלֵב נָמֵס וּפִק בִּרְכַּיִם וְחַלְחָלָה בְּכָל־מָתְנַיִם וּפְנֵי כֻלָּם קִבְּצוּ
יב פָארוּר: אַיֵּה מְעוֹן אֲרָיוֹת וּמִרְעֶה הוּא לַכְּפִרִים אֲשֶׁר הָלַךְ אַרְיֵה לָבִיא
יג שָׁם גּוּר אַרְיֵה וְאֵין מַחֲרִיד: אַרְיֵה טֹרֵף בְּדֵי גְרוֹתָיו וּמְחַנֵּק לְלִבְאֹתָיו
יד וַיְמַלֵּא־טֶרֶף חֹרָיו וּמְעֹנֹתָיו טְרֵפָה: הִנְנִי אֵלַיִךְ נְאֻם יהוה צְבָאוֹת
וְהִבְעַרְתִּי בֶעָשָׁן רִכְבָּהּ וּכְפִירַיִךְ תֹּאכַל חָרֶב וְהִכְרַתִּי מֵאֶרֶץ טַרְפֵּךְ וְלֹא־
ג א יִשָּׁמַע עוֹד קוֹל מַלְאָכֵכֵה: הוֹי עִיר דָּמִים כֻּלָּהּ כַּחַשׁ פֶּרֶק
ב מְלֵאָה לֹא יָמִישׁ טָרֶף: קוֹל שׁוֹט וְקוֹל רַעַשׁ אוֹפָן וְסוּס דֹּהֵר וּמֶרְכָּבָה
ג מְרַקֵּדָה: פָּרָשׁ מַעֲלֶה וְלַהַב חֶרֶב וּבְרַק חֲנִית וְרֹב חָלָל וְכֹבֶד פָּגֶר וְאֵין
ד קֵצֶה לַגְּוִיָּה °יִכְשְׁלוּ [°וְכָשְׁלוּ ק] בִּגְוִיָּתָם: מֵרֹב זְנוּנֵי זוֹנָה טוֹבַת חֵן בַּעֲלַת
ה כְּשָׁפִים הַמֹּכֶרֶת גּוֹיִם בִּזְנוּנֶיהָ וּמִשְׁפָּחוֹת בִּכְשָׁפֶיהָ: הִנְנִי אֵלַיִךְ נְאֻם יהוה
צְבָאוֹת וְגִלֵּיתִי שׁוּלַיִךְ עַל־פָּנָיִךְ וְהַרְאֵיתִי גוֹיִם מַעְרֵךְ וּמַמְלָכוֹת קְלוֹנֵךְ:
ו וְהִשְׁלַכְתִּי עָלַיִךְ שִׁקֻּצִים וְנִבַּלְתִּיךְ וְשַׂמְתִּיךְ כְּרֹאִי: וְהָיָה כָל־רֹאַיִךְ יִדּוֹד
ז מִמֵּךְ וְאָמַר שָׁדְּדָה נִינְוֵה מִי יָנוּד לָהּ מֵאַיִן אֲבַקֵּשׁ מְנַחֲמִים לָךְ: הֲתֵיטְבִי
ח מִנֹּא אָמוֹן הַיֹּשְׁבָה בַּיְאֹרִים מַיִם סָבִיב לָהּ אֲשֶׁר־חֵיל יָם מִיָּם חוֹמָתָהּ:
ט כּוּשׁ עָצְמָה וּמִצְרַיִם וְאֵין קֵצֶה פּוּט וְלוּבִים הָיוּ בְּעֶזְרָתֵךְ: גַּם־הִיא לַגֹּלָה
י הָלְכָה בַשֶּׁבִי גַּם עֹלָלֶיהָ יְרֻטְּשׁוּ בְּרֹאשׁ כָּל־חוּצוֹת וְעַל־נִכְבַּדֶּיהָ יַדּוּ גוֹרָל
יא וְכָל־גְּדוֹלֶיהָ רֻתְּקוּ בַזִּקִּים: גַּם־אַתְּ תִּשְׁכְּרִי תְּהִי נַעֲלָמָה גַּם־אַתְּ תְּבַקְשִׁי
יב מָעוֹז מֵאוֹיֵב: כָּל־מִבְצָרַיִךְ תְּאֵנִים עִם־בִּכּוּרִים אִם־יִנּוֹעוּ וְנָפְלוּ עַל־פִּי
יג אוֹכֵל: הִנֵּה עַמֵּךְ נָשִׁים בְּקִרְבֵּךְ לְאֹיְבַיִךְ פָּתוֹחַ נִפְתְּחוּ שַׁעֲרֵי אַרְצֵךְ אָכְלָה
יד אֵשׁ בְּרִיחָיִךְ: מֵי מָצוֹר שַׁאֲבִי־לָךְ חַזְּקִי מִבְצָרָיִךְ בֹּאִי בַטִּיט וְרִמְסִי בַחֹמֶר
טו הַחֲזִיקִי מַלְבֵּן: שָׁם תֹּאכְלֵךְ אֵשׁ תַּכְרִיתֵךְ חֶרֶב תֹּאכְלֵךְ כַּיָּלֶק הִתְכַּבֵּד
טז כַּיֶּלֶק הִתְכַּבְּדִי כָּאַרְבֶּה: הִרְבֵּית רֹכְלַיִךְ מִכּוֹכְבֵי הַשָּׁמָיִם יֶלֶק פָּשַׁט וַיָּעֹף:
יז מִנְּזָרַיִךְ כָּאַרְבֶּה וְטַפְסְרַיִךְ כְּגוֹב גֹּבָי הַחוֹנִים בַּגְּדֵרוֹת בְּיוֹם קָרָה שֶׁמֶשׁ
יח זָרְחָה וְנוֹדַד וְלֹא־נוֹדַע מְקוֹמוֹ אַיָּם: נָמוּ רֹעֶיךָ מֶלֶךְ אַשּׁוּר יִשְׁכְּנוּ אַדִּירֶיךָ
יט נָפֹשׁוּ עַמְּךָ עַל־הֶהָרִים וְאֵין מְקַבֵּץ: אֵין־כֵּהָה לְשִׁבְרֶךָ נַחְלָה מַכָּתֶךָ כֹּל ׀
שֹׁמְעֵי שִׁמְעֲךָ תָּקְעוּ כַף עָלֶיךָ כִּי עַל־מִי לֹא־עָבְרָה רָעָתְךָ תָּמִיד:

2:10. Nahum addresses Nineveh's Babylonian conquerors.

2:12. Nahum "laments" the downfall of the great and powerful Nineveh.

2:14. See *II Kings* 18:17-35.

3:1. Nineveh.

3:4. The Assyrians would seduce nations into making pacts with them, and then dishonor the treaty and conquer their unsuspecting allies (*Rashi*).

3:8. See *Jeremiah* 46:25.

3:9. The forebears of these nations were all relatives of

Ashur, the founder of Nineveh and progenitor of Assyria (see *Genesis* 10:6-13).

3:11. From the "cup of God's wrath" (*Radak*), a common Scriptural metaphor.

3:13. They have become physically weak and defenseless against attack.

3:14. A city under siege must produce brick and mortar to repair breaches in its defenses.

3:16-19. Despite their abundance, in the end they fly away and are gone.

Babylon
plunders
Nineveh

¹⁰ 'Plunder silver, plunder gold; * the amount is limitless! To sweep [it] clean of every precious vessel!' ¹¹ She is emptied, emptied and breached; with melted heart, buckled knees, pain in all the loins, and faces [there], and all their faces have gathered blackness. ¹² Where is the lion's den, * which was the feeding place of the young lions, where the lion, the awesome lion, and lion whelp would go, with none to make them afraid? ¹³ The lion would tear prey to provide for his cubs, choking [prey] for his lionesses. He would fill up his lairs with prey and his dens with torn carcasses. ¹⁴ Behold, I am against you — the word of HASHEM, Master of Legions — I will burn your chariots in smoke, and the sword will devour your cubs. I will eliminate your prey from the earth, and the voice of your messengers * will be heard no more!

3

Woe to
Nineveh

¹ **W**oe to the City of Blood; * it is all deceit, full of robbery; prey departs not [from it]; ² the sound of the whip and the sound of rattling wheel; galloping horse and bounding chariot; ³ the horseman raises flashing sword and glittering spear; numerous slain and heaps of corpses; there is no end to the bodies, and they stumble over their bodies. ⁴ [All this] because of the many harlotries of the harlot, rich in grace, practitioner of witchcraft, who sells nations through her harlotries * and families through her witchcraft.

It will be
humiliated

⁵ Behold, I am against you — the word of HASHEM, Master of Legions — and I will pull up your skirts over your face; and I will show the nations your nakedness and the kingdoms your shame. ⁶ I will cast repulsive things upon you and make you disgusting; I will make you like dung. ⁷ And it will be that all who see you will move away from you and say, 'Nineveh has been ravaged; who will bemoan her?' From where can I seek comforters for you?

⁸ Are you better than No-amon, * which sits by the rivers, with water surrounding it, whose rampart was the sea, and whose wall of the sea? ⁹ Powerful Cush and endless Egypt, Put and Lubim were your helpers. *

Its allies
exiled

¹⁰ Yet each of them too went into exile in captivity, its babies were also smashed at the head of every street; they cast lots over her noblemen, and all her great men were bound in chains. ¹¹ You, too, will become drunk; * you will become unknown; you will also seek refuge from the enemy. ¹² All your fortresses will be [like] fig trees with newly ripened fruit, when they are shaken, they fall into the mouth of the eater. ¹³ Behold, your nation is [like] women * in your midst. The gates of your land have been opened wide to your enemies; fire has consumed your bolts. ¹⁴ Draw water for the siege, bolster your fortresses. Come into the clay and trample the mortar; grasp the brick mold. * ¹⁵ There fire will consume you; a sword will cut you down. It

It will be
consumed

will consume you like the chewing-locust — you will be swept away as [by] the chewing-locust; you will be swept as [by] the abundant-locust. ¹⁶ You had more merchants than the stars of the sky, [like] the chewing-locust that spreads out and then flies away. * ¹⁷ Your princes are like abundant-locusts and your captains are like a swarm of great locusts which settle on the fences on a cold day; when the sun shines they move away, and their place is unknown — Where are they? ¹⁸ Your shepherds are asleep, O king of Assyria, your mighty men are at rest. Your nation is scattered upon the mountains with no one to gather them. ¹⁹ There is no one in pain over your fracture [though] your wound is grievous. All who hear the report about you clap their hands over you; for over whom has your wickedness not passed constantly?

א

א-ב הַמַּשָּׂא אֲשֶׁר חָזָה חֲבַקּוּק הַנָּבִיא: עַד־אָנָה יהוה שִׁוַּעְתִּי וְלֹא תִשְׁמָע

ג אֶזְעַק אֵלֶיךָ חָמָס וְלֹא תוֹשִׁיעַ: לָמָּה תַרְאֵנִי אָוֶן וְעָמָל תַּבִּיט וְשֹׁד וְחָמָס

ד לְנֶגְדִּי וַיְהִי רִיב וּמָדוֹן יִשָּׂא: עַל־כֵּן תָּפוּג תּוֹרָה וְלֹא־יֵצֵא לָנֶצַח מִשְׁפָּט

ה כִּי רָשָׁע מַכְתִּיר אֶת־הַצַּדִּיק עַל־כֵּן יֵצֵא מִשְׁפָּט מְעֻקָּל: רְאוּ בַגּוֹיִם

ו וְהַבִּיטוּ וְהִתַּמְּהוּ תְּמָהוּ כִּי־פֹעַל פֹּעֵל בִּימֵיכֶם לֹא תַאֲמִינוּ כִּי יְסֻפָּר: כִּי־הִנְנִי מֵקִים אֶת־הַכַּשְׂדִּים הַגּוֹי הַמַּר וְהַנִּמְהָר הַהוֹלֵךְ לְמֶרְחֲבֵי־אֶרֶץ

ז לָרֶשֶׁת מִשְׁכָּנוֹת לֹא־לוֹ: אָיֹם וְנוֹרָא הוּא מִמֶּנּוּ מִשְׁפָּטוֹ וּשְׂאֵתוֹ יֵצֵא:

ח וְקַלּוּ מִנְּמֵרִים סוּסָיו וְחַדּוּ מִזְּאֵבֵי עֶרֶב וּפָשׁוּ פָּרָשָׁיו וּפָרָשָׁיו מֵרָחוֹק

ט יָבֹאוּ יָעֻפוּ כְּנֶשֶׁר חָשׁ לֶאֱכוֹל: כֻּלֹּה לְחָמָס יָבוֹא מְגַמַּת פְּנֵיהֶם קָדִימָה

י וַיֶּאֱסֹף כַּחוֹל שֶׁבִי: וְהוּא בַּמְּלָכִים יִתְקַלָּס וְרֹזְנִים מִשְׂחָק לוֹ הוּא לְכָל־

יא מִבְצָר יִשְׂחָק וַיִּצְבֹּר עָפָר וַיִּלְכְּדָהּ: אָז חָלַף רוּחַ וַיַּעֲבֹר וְאָשֵׁם זוּ כֹחוֹ

יב לֵאלֹהוֹ: הֲלוֹא אַתָּה מִקֶּדֶם יהוה אֱלֹהַי קְדֹשִׁי לֹא נָמוּת יהוה לְמִשְׁפָּט

יג שַׂמְתּוֹ וְצוּר לְהוֹכִיחַ יְסַדְתּוֹ: טְהוֹר עֵינַיִם מֵרְאוֹת רָע וְהַבִּיט אֶל־עָמָל

יד לֹא תוּכָל לָמָּה תַבִּיט בּוֹגְדִים תַּחֲרִישׁ בְּבַלַּע רָשָׁע צַדִּיק מִמֶּנּוּ: וַתַּעֲשֶׂה

טו אָדָם כִּדְגֵי הַיָּם כְּרֶמֶשׂ לֹא־מֹשֵׁל בּוֹ: כֻּלֹּה בְּחַכָּה הֵעֲלָה יְגֹרֵהוּ בְחֶרְמוֹ

טז וְיַאַסְפֵהוּ בְּמִכְמַרְתּוֹ עַל־כֵּן יִשְׂמַח וְיָגִיל: עַל־כֵּן יְזַבֵּחַ לְחֶרְמוֹ וִיקַטֵּר

יז לְמִכְמַרְתּוֹ כִּי בָהֵמָּה שָׁמֵן חֶלְקוֹ וּמַאֲכָלוֹ בְּרִאָה: הַעַל כֵּן יָרִיק חֶרְמוֹ

ב

א וְתָמִיד לַהֲרֹג גּוֹיִם לֹא יַחְמוֹל: עַל־מִשְׁמַרְתִּי אֶעֱמֹדָה וְאֶתְיַצְּבָה עַל־מָצוֹר וַאֲצַפֶּה לִרְאוֹת מַה־יְדַבֶּר־בִּי וּמָה אָשִׁיב עַל־

ב תּוֹכַחְתִּי: וַיַּעֲנֵנִי יהוה וַיֹּאמֶר כְּתוֹב חָזוֹן וּבָאֵר עַל־הַלֻּחוֹת לְמַעַן יָרוּץ

ג קוֹרֵא בוֹ: כִּי עוֹד חָזוֹן לַמּוֹעֵד וְיָפֵחַ לַקֵּץ וְלֹא יְכַזֵּב אִם־יִתְמַהְמָהּ חַכֵּה־

ד לוֹ כִּי־בֹא יָבֹא לֹא יְאַחֵר: הִנֵּה עֻפְּלָה לֹא־יָשְׁרָה נַפְשׁוֹ בּוֹ וְצַדִּיק

ה בֶּאֱמוּנָתוֹ יִחְיֶה: וְאַף כִּי־הַיַּיִן בּוֹגֵד גֶּבֶר יָהִיר וְלֹא יִנְוֶה אֲשֶׁר הִרְחִיב כִּשְׁאוֹל נַפְשׁוֹ וְהוּא כַמָּוֶת וְלֹא יִשְׂבָּע וַיֶּאֱסֹף אֵלָיו כָּל־הַגּוֹיִם וַיִּקְבֹּץ

ו אֵלָיו כָּל־הָעַמִּים: הֲלוֹא־אֵלֶּה כֻלָּם עָלָיו מָשָׁל יִשָּׂאוּ וּמְלִיצָה חִידוֹת

ז לוֹ וְיֹאמַר הוֹי הַמַּרְבֶּה לֹּא־לוֹ עַד־מָתַי וּמַכְבִּיד עָלָיו עַבְטִיט: הֲלוֹא

ח פֶתַע יָקוּמוּ נֹשְׁכֶיךָ וְיִקְצוּ מְזַעְזְעֶיךָ וְהָיִיתָ לִמְשִׁסּוֹת לָמוֹ: כִּי־אַתָּה

1:1. According to *Seder Olam*, Habakkuk prophesied in the time of the very wicked King Manasseh of Judah (see *Nahum* 1:1). The prophet alternates between prayer on behalf of the persecuted Jews and prophecy of the downfall of their future Babylonian conqueror.

1:10. The Babylonian army builds a mound from which it storms the fortress.

1:12. The conqueror may attribute his success to an idol; we, however, know that You have allowed Babylonia to punish us; but let us not be wiped out!

1:16. He sacrifices to his idols, whom he credits with

granting him the means ("nets") of his success.

2:1. Habakkuk anticipates an answer to those who challenge him with the questions raised in Chapter 1.

2:4. The Babylonian king's.

2:5. Like a man whose confidence is bolstered by alcohol, Nebuchadnezzar continuously leaves home to embark on ambitious expeditions of conquest and pillage in foreign lands (*Ibn Ezra*).

2:6. His ill-gained fortune will prove to be nothing but a heavy burden of sin (*Rashi*).

1

Why do you distort justice?

[1] The prophecy that Habakkuk the prophet saw: * [2] How long, O HASHEM, will I cry out and You not hear me; [how long] will I cry out to You [regarding] injustice and You not save? [3] Why do You allow me to see iniquity and You look at evil deeds, with robbery and injustice before me, while the one who carries strife and contention still remains? [4] That is why the Torah is weakened and justice never emerges. Since the wicked surround the righteous, therefore justice emerges distorted.

The terrible Chaldeans

[5] Look among the nations and observe, and be utterly astounded; for [God] is bringing about an occurrence in your days that you will not believe when it is related. [6] For behold, I am establishing the Chaldeans, that bitter and impetuous nation that will go across the breadth of the earth to possess dwelling places that are not its own. [7] It is awesome and terrifying; its judgment and its burden go forth from it. [8] Its horses are swifter than leopards and fiercer than wolves of the evening, and its horsemen are fleet. Its horsemen will come from afar; they will fly like an eagle hastening to eat. [9] It comes entirely for plunder; the eagerness of their faces is like the east wind; and it will gather captives like the sand. [10] It scoffs at kings, and officers are its sport. It laughs at every stronghold; heaping up earth and capturing it. * [11] Then a spirit will come and pass over it, and it will incur guilt [by saying] that its god gave it strength.

A plea to God

[12] Are You not from the beginning of time, O HASHEM my God, my Holy One? Let us not die! O HASHEM, You have ordained him for judgment; O Stronghold, You have established him to chasten [us]. * [13] [Your eyes] are too pure to see evil and You cannot look upon wrongdoing. Why, then, do You look upon betrayers? [Why do] You remain silent when a wicked man swallows up one more righteous than he? [14] You have made man like the [helpless] fish of the sea, like creeping things without a ruler. [15] He brings them all up with a fishhook; He catches them in his net and he gathers them in his trawl; therefore he rejoices and exults. [16] Therefore, he sacrifices to his net * and burns incense to his trawl, for through them his portion is fat and his food is plentiful. [17] Shall he therefore empty his net, to slay nations continuously, without compassion?

2

God answers

[1] I will stand upon my watch and take my place at the siege, and I will wait to see what He will speak to me and what I can answer my reproof. *

[2] And HASHEM answered me and said, "Write the vision and clarify it upon tablets, so that a reader may read it swiftly. [3] For there is yet another vision about the appointed time; it will speak of the End and it will not deceive. Though it may tarry, await it, for it will surely come; it will not delay.

Nebuchad-nezzar advances

[4] Behold, his* soul is defiant; it is unsettled in him. But the righteous person shall live through his faith. [5] The [man of] wine * also acts treacherously; he is an arrogant man and does not stay at home. He has widened his soul like the grave and, like death, he is not satisfied. He gathered unto himself all the nations and assembled unto himself all the peoples. [6] Shall all of these not take up a parable about him and a metaphor; [and] riddles regarding him? One will say, 'Woe to him who amasses that which is not his. How long [can he go on]? He burdens himself heavily with thick mud.'* [7] Will those who would bite you not rise up suddenly? And [will] those who would cause you to tremble [not] awaken? You will be plunder for them! [8] Because you have

שַׁלּוֹתָ גּוֹיִם רַבִּים יְשָׁלּוּךָ כָּל־יֶתֶר עַמִּים מִדְּמֵי אָדָם וַחֲמַס־אֶרֶץ קִרְיָה

ט   וְכָל־יֹשְׁבֵי בָהּ:   הוֹי בֹּצֵעַ בֶּצַע רָע לְבֵיתוֹ לָשׂוּם בַּמָּרוֹם

י   קִנּוֹ לְהִנָּצֵל מִכַּף־רָע: יָעַצְתָּ בֹּשֶׁת לְבֵיתֶךָ קְצוֹת־עַמִּים רַבִּים וְחוֹטֵא

   נַפְשֶׁךָ: כִּי־אֶבֶן מִקִּיר תִּזְעָק וְכָפִיס מֵעֵץ יַעֲנֶנָּה: הוֹי   יא-יב

יג   בֹּנֶה עִיר בְּדָמִים וְכוֹנֵן קִרְיָה בְּעַוְלָה: הֲלוֹא הִנֵּה מֵאֵת יהוה צְבָאוֹת

יד   וְיִיגְעוּ עַמִּים בְּדֵי־אֵשׁ וּלְאֻמִּים בְּדֵי־רִיק יִעָפוּ: כִּי תִּמָּלֵא הָאָרֶץ לָדַעַת

טו   אֶת־כְּבוֹד יהוה כַּמַּיִם יְכַסּוּ עַל־יָם: הוֹי מַשְׁקֶה רֵעֵהוּ

טז   מְסַפֵּחַ חֲמָתְךָ וְאַף שַׁכֵּר לְמַעַן הַבִּיט עַל־מְעוֹרֵיהֶם: שָׂבַעְתָּ קָלוֹן מִכָּבוֹד

   שְׁתֵה גַם־אַתָּה וְהֵעָרֵל תִּסּוֹב עָלֶיךָ כּוֹס יְמִין יהוה וְקִיקָלוֹן עַל־כְּבוֹדֶךָ:

יז   כִּי חֲמַס לְבָנוֹן יְכַסֶּךָּ וְשֹׁד בְּהֵמוֹת יְחִיתַן מִדְּמֵי אָדָם וַחֲמַס־אֶרֶץ

יח   קִרְיָה וְכָל־יֹשְׁבֵי בָהּ:   מָה־הוֹעִיל פֶּסֶל כִּי פְסָלוֹ

   יֹצְרוֹ מַסֵּכָה וּמוֹרֶה שָּׁקֶר כִּי בָטַח יֹצֵר יִצְרוֹ עָלָיו לַעֲשׂוֹת אֱלִילִים

יט   אִלְּמִים: הוֹי אֹמֵר לָעֵץ הָקִיצָה עוּרִי לְאֶבֶן דּוּמָם הוּא יוֹרֶה

כ   הִנֵּה־הוּא תָּפוּשׂ זָהָב וָכֶסֶף וְכָל־רוּחַ אֵין בְּקִרְבּוֹ: ◄ וַיהוה בְּהֵיכַל קָדְשׁוֹ

ג   הַס מִפָּנָיו כָּל־הָאָרֶץ: תְּפִלָּה לַחֲבַקּוּק הַנָּבִיא עַל שִׁגְיֹנוֹת: א

ב   יהוה שָׁמַעְתִּי שִׁמְעֲךָ יָרֵאתִי יהוה פָּעָלְךָ בְּקֶרֶב שָׁנִים חַיֵּיהוּ בְּקֶרֶב שָׁנִים

ג   תּוֹדִיעַ בְּרֹגֶז רַחֵם תִּזְכּוֹר: אֱלוֹהַּ מִתֵּימָן יָבוֹא וְקָדוֹשׁ מֵהַר־פָּארָן סֶלָה

ד   כִּסָּה שָׁמַיִם הוֹדוֹ וּתְהִלָּתוֹ מָלְאָה הָאָרֶץ: וְנֹגַהּ כָּאוֹר תִּהְיֶה קַרְנַיִם

ה-ו   מִיָּדוֹ לוֹ וְשָׁם חֶבְיוֹן עֻזֹּה: לְפָנָיו יֵלֶךְ דָּבֶר וְיֵצֵא רֶשֶׁף לְרַגְלָיו: עָמַד |

   וַיְמֹדֶד אֶרֶץ רָאָה וַיַּתֵּר גּוֹיִם וַיִּתְפֹּצְצוּ הַרְרֵי־עַד שַׁחוּ גִּבְעוֹת עוֹלָם

ז   הֲלִיכוֹת עוֹלָם לוֹ: תַּחַת אָוֶן רָאִיתִי אָהֳלֵי כוּשָׁן יִרְגְּזוּן יְרִיעוֹת אֶרֶץ

ח   מִדְיָן: הֲבִנְהָרִים חָרָה יהוה אִם בַּנְּהָרִים אַפֶּךָ אִם־בַּיָּם עֶבְרָתֶךָ

ט   כִּי תִרְכַּב עַל־סוּסֶיךָ מַרְכְּבֹתֶיךָ יְשׁוּעָה: עֶרְיָה תֵעוֹר קַשְׁתֶּךָ שְׁבֻעוֹת

י   מַטּוֹת אֹמֶר סֶלָה נְהָרוֹת תְּבַקַּע־אָרֶץ: רָאוּךָ יָחִילוּ הָרִים זֶרֶם מַיִם עָבָר

HAFTARAH
SECOND
DAY
SHAVUOS
2:20-3:19

ג

2:8. Jerusalem (*Targum*).

2:11-12. The very stones and beams of your house testify that you built your house through bloodshed and plunder.

2:13. The retribution.

2:15-16. The enemy gained the friendship of Israel, and then treacherously "intoxicated" her with a potent brew of suffering. His intent was not for gain, but to gloat over the "shame" imposed upon Israel.

2:17. A poetic name for the Land of Israel (*Radak*) or the Temple (*Targum*).

3:1. Habakkuk had protested God's strict judgment against the sinners of Israel (1:4,14). Now he expresses his regret for those "erroneous utterances" (*Rashi*).

3:2. During the long years of exile, keep Israel alive, for the nation is Your "accomplishment" on earth. "Make

known" Your promise to preserve them (*Leviticus 26:44*) no matter how grievously they may have sinned (*Radak*).

3:3. Mount Seir which is south of Israel. The verse speaks of the giving of the Torah at Sinai (see *Deuteronomy 33:2*).

3:5. When the Israelites entered their land, pestilence and disease helped them subdue the Canaanite nations (*Ibn Ezra*).

3:6. God assigned portions of the land to the Jews (*Ibn Ezra*).

3:7. See *Judges 3:7-11* and Chs. 6-7.

3:8. A reference to the splitting of the Sea of Reeds (*Exodus Ch. 14*) and the Jordan (*Joshua Ch. 3*). God split the waters as if He were a Savior riding to save Israel.

3:9. In the Wilderness, God provided water to the Israelites.

pillaged many nations, all the remnants of the nations will pillage you, for the blood of men [that you spilt] and the robbery of the land, the city * and all its inhabitants.

Israel has earned its punishment

⁹ Woe to him who gains evil profit for his house, so that he may set his nest up high to be rescued from the grasp of evil. ¹⁰ You have counseled shame for your house by cutting off many peoples, and you have sinned against your soul. ¹¹ For a stone will cry out from the wall and a sliver will answer it from the beams. *

¹² Woe to him who builds a city with bloodshed and establishes a city with iniquity. ¹³ Behold, is it * not from HASHEM, Master of Legions, that the peoples will toil for the fire, and the nations will weary themselves for nothingness? ¹⁴ For the earth will be filled with knowledge of HASHEM's glory, as the waters cover the seabed.

Treacherous enemy

¹⁵ Woe to him who gives his fellow to drink: * You gather your anger and intoxicate [them] so that you may look upon their nakedness. ¹⁶ You are sated more with shame than with glory. You too will drink and become confounded; the cup of HASHEM's right hand is turned upon you, and the vomit of shame will cover your glory. ¹⁷ For the robbery of Lebanon * will inundate you, and the plunder [done] by [your] animals will destroy you, because of the blood of men [that you spilt] and the robbery of the land, the city and all its inhabitants.

¹⁸ Of what avail is the graven image that its maker has carved, the molten image or teacher of falsehood, that its maker should place his trust in it to make mute idols?

¹⁹ Woe to him who says to wood, 'Wake up!' and to silent stone, 'Arise!' Will it teach? Behold, it is coated with gold and silver and there is no spirit within it. ²⁰ But HASHEM is in His holy Sanctuary; let all the world be silent before Him."

3

Habakkuk's prayer

¹ A prayer of Habakkuk the prophet, for erroneous utterances: *

² O HASHEM, I have heard Your news [of impending exile]; I was afraid.
O HASHEM, in the midst of the years, keep Your accomplishment alive;
    in the midst of the years, make it known. *
    In wrath, remember to be merciful.
³ God came from the south; the Holy One from Mount Paran, Selah! *
    His glory covered the heavens His praise filled the earth.
⁴ A glow was like the light [of day]; rays of light [came] from His hand
    to [Israel]; and there His hidden strength [was revealed].

God's wrath

⁵ Before Him went a plague; pestilence went forth as He advanced. *
⁶ He stood and measured out the land; * He looked and dispersed nations.
Everlasting mountains were smashed, eternal hills were laid low;
    for the ways of the world are His.
⁷ Because of [our] iniquity I saw the tents of Cushan;
    the curtains of the land of Midian trembled. *
⁸ Was HASHEM angry with the rivers;
    was Your wrath with the rivers, or Your fury against the Sea?
Rather You rode upon Your horses, Your chariots were [our] salvation. *
⁹ Your bow bared itself; the oaths to the tribes, an enduring word.
You split open the earth with rivers. *
¹⁰ Mountains saw You and shuddered; a stream of water flowed.

יא נָתַן תְּהוֹם קוֹלוֹ רוֹם יָדֵיהוּ נָשָׂא: שֶׁמֶשׁ יָרֵחַ עָמַד זְבֻלָה לְאוֹר חִצֶּיךָ
יב-יג יְהַלֵּכוּ לְנֹגַהּ בְּרַק חֲנִיתֶךָ: בְּזַעַם תִּצְעַד־אָרֶץ בְּאַף תָּדוּשׁ גּוֹיִם: יָצָאתָ
לְיֵשַׁע עַמֶּךָ לְיֵשַׁע אֶת־מְשִׁיחֶךָ מָחַצְתָּ רֹּאשׁ מִבֵּית רָשָׁע עָרוֹת יְסוֹד
יד עַד־צַוָּאר סֶלָה: נָקַבְתָּ בְמַטָּיו רֹאשׁ °פְּרָזָו [פְּרָזוֹ ק׳]
טו יִסְעָרוּ לַהֲפִיצֵנִי עֲלִיצֻתָם כְּמוֹ־לֶאֱכֹל עָנִי בַּמִּסְתָּר: דָּרַכְתָּ בַיָּם סוּסֶיךָ
טז חֹמֶר מַיִם רַבִּים: שָׁמַעְתִּי ׀ וַתִּרְגַּז בִּטְנִי לְקוֹל צָלֲלוּ שְׂפָתַי יָבוֹא רָקָב
יז בַּעֲצָמַי וְתַחְתַּי אֶרְגָּז אֲשֶׁר אָנוּחַ לְיוֹם צָרָה לַעֲלוֹת לְעַם יְגוּדֶנּוּ: כִּי־
תְאֵנָה לֹא־תִפְרָח וְאֵין יְבוּל בַּגְּפָנִים כִּחֵשׁ מַעֲשֵׂה־זַיִת וּשְׁדֵמוֹת לֹא־
יח עָשָׂה אֹכֶל גָּזַר מִמִּכְלָה צֹאן וְאֵין בָּקָר בָּרְפָתִים: וַאֲנִי בַּיהֹוָה אֶעְלוֹזָה
יט אָגִילָה בֵּאלֹהֵי יִשְׁעִי: יְהֹוִה אֲדֹנָי חֵילִי וַיָּשֶׂם רַגְלַי כָּאַיָּלוֹת וְעַל בָּמוֹתַי
יְדַרִכֵנִי לַמְנַצֵּחַ בִּנְגִינוֹתָי: ◀

3:10. God's glorious deeds were praised on earth and in Heaven.

3:11. At Gibeon (see *Joshua* Ch. 10).

3:13. You toppled their walls and their tall "neck"-like towers.

3:16. About the events alluded to in the next verse.

The depth raised its voice, and the heights [of Heaven] raised their hands. *
¹¹ The sun and the moon stood still in their abodes. *
[Israel] would travel by the light of Your arrows,
    by the lightning flash of Your spear.

God comes to save Israel . . .

¹² In fury You trod the earth; in anger You trampled nations.
¹³ You went forth to save Your people, to save Your anointed one.
You crushed the head of the house of the wicked,
    laying bare from the foundation to the neck, * Selah!
¹⁴ With his own staffs You pierced the head of his outspread troops,
    who came storming to scatter me.
Their joy came when they could devour a poor man in secret.
¹⁵ You trampled [them] in the sea with Your steed-like [clouds],
    with mountains of abundant water.
¹⁶ I heard and my innards shuddered; my lips quivered at the report. *
Rot came into my bones and I shuddered in my place;
    because the time I should have rested will become a day of distress,
    for a people to come up with its troops.
¹⁷ For the fig tree blossoms not; there is no fruit on the grapevines;
    the labor of the olive trees has failed and the fields do not yield food; *
    the sheep are cut off from the fold and no cattle are in the stall.

. . . and it will rejoice in Him

¹⁸ But as for me, in HASHEM will I rejoice;
    I will exult in the God of my salvation.
¹⁹ HASHEM/ELOHIM, the Lord, is my strength.
He makes my legs [as swift] as harts;
    and He leads me upon my high places.
To the conductor, [for accompaniment] with my songs.

3:17. This famine represents the distress that will prevail at the time described by Habakkuk. This is either the time of the downfall of Babylonia (*Targum*), or the Messianic-age war of Gog and Magog (*Radak*), or the Roman destruction of the Second Temple (*Abarbanel*).

א א דְּבַר־יְהֹוָה ׀ אֲשֶׁר הָיָה אֶל־צְפַנְיָה בֶּן־כּוּשִׁי בֶן־גְּדַלְיָה בֶּן־אֲמַרְיָה בֶּן־
ב חִזְקִיָּה בִּימֵי יֹאשִׁיָּהוּ בֶן־אָמוֹן מֶלֶךְ יְהוּדָה: אָסֹף אָסֵף כֹּל מֵעַל פְּנֵי
ג הָאֲדָמָה נְאֻם־יְהֹוָה: אָסֵף אָדָם וּבְהֵמָה אָסֵף עוֹף־הַשָּׁמַיִם וּדְגֵי הַיָּם
וְהַמַּכְשֵׁלוֹת אֶת־הָרְשָׁעִים וְהִכְרַתִּי אֶת־הָאָדָם מֵעַל פְּנֵי הָאֲדָמָה נְאֻם־
ד יְהֹוָה: וְנָטִיתִי יָדִי עַל־יְהוּדָה וְעַל כָּל־יוֹשְׁבֵי יְרוּשָׁלָ͏ִם וְהִכְרַתִּי מִן־הַמָּקוֹם
ה הַזֶּה אֶת־שְׁאָר הַבַּעַל אֶת־שֵׁם הַכְּמָרִים עִם־הַכֹּהֲנִים: וְאֶת־הַמִּשְׁתַּחֲוִים
עַל־הַגַּגּוֹת לִצְבָא הַשָּׁמָיִם וְאֶת־הַמִּשְׁתַּחֲוִים הַנִּשְׁבָּעִים לַיהֹוָה וְהַנִּשְׁבָּעִים
ו בְּמַלְכָּם: וְאֶת־הַנְּסוֹגִים מֵאַחֲרֵי יְהֹוָה וַאֲשֶׁר לֹא־בִקְשׁוּ אֶת־יְהֹוָה וְלֹא
ז דְרָשֻׁהוּ: הַס מִפְּנֵי אֲדֹנָי יֱהֹוִה כִּי קָרוֹב יוֹם יְהֹוָה כִּי־הֵכִין יְהֹוָה זֶבַח
ח הִקְדִּישׁ קְרֻאָיו: וְהָיָה בְּיוֹם זֶבַח יְהֹוָה וּפָקַדְתִּי עַל־הַשָּׂרִים וְעַל־
ט בְּנֵי הַמֶּלֶךְ וְעַל כָּל־הַלֹּבְשִׁים מַלְבּוּשׁ נָכְרִי: וּפָקַדְתִּי עַל כָּל־הַדּוֹלֵג עַל־
י הַמִּפְתָּן בַּיּוֹם הַהוּא הַמְמַלְאִים בֵּית אֲדֹנֵיהֶם חָמָס וּמִרְמָה: וְהָיָה
בַיּוֹם הַהוּא נְאֻם־יְהֹוָה קוֹל צְעָקָה מִשַּׁעַר הַדָּגִים וִילָלָה מִן־הַמִּשְׁנֶה
יא וְשֶׁבֶר גָּדוֹל מֵהַגְּבָעוֹת: הֵילִילוּ יֹשְׁבֵי הַמַּכְתֵּשׁ כִּי נִדְמָה כָּל־עַם כְּנַעַן
יב נִכְרְתוּ כָּל־נְטִילֵי כָסֶף: וְהָיָה בָּעֵת הַהִיא אֲחַפֵּשׂ אֶת־יְרוּשָׁלַ͏ִם
בַּנֵּרוֹת וּפָקַדְתִּי עַל־הָאֲנָשִׁים הַקֹּפְאִים עַל־שִׁמְרֵיהֶם הָאֹמְרִים בִּלְבָבָם
יג לֹא־יֵיטִיב יְהֹוָה וְלֹא יָרֵעַ: וְהָיָה חֵילָם לִמְשִׁסָּה וּבָתֵּיהֶם לִשְׁמָמָה וּבָנוּ
יד בָתִּים וְלֹא יֵשֵׁבוּ וְנָטְעוּ כְרָמִים וְלֹא יִשְׁתּוּ אֶת־יֵינָם: קָרוֹב יוֹם־יְהֹוָה
טו הַגָּדוֹל קָרוֹב וּמַהֵר מְאֹד קוֹל יוֹם יְהֹוָה מַר צֹרֵחַ שָׁם גִּבּוֹר: יוֹם עֶבְרָה
הַיּוֹם הַהוּא יוֹם צָרָה וּמְצוּקָה יוֹם שֹׁאָה וּמְשׁוֹאָה יוֹם חֹשֶׁךְ וַאֲפֵלָה יוֹם
טז עָנָן וַעֲרָפֶל: יוֹם שׁוֹפָר וּתְרוּעָה עַל הֶעָרִים הַבְּצֻרוֹת וְעַל הַפִּנּוֹת הַגְּבֹהוֹת:
יז וַהֲצֵרֹתִי לָאָדָם וְהָלְכוּ כַּעִוְרִים כִּי לַיהֹוָה חָטָאוּ וְשֻׁפַּךְ דָּמָם כֶּעָפָר
יח וּלְחֻמָם כַּגְּלָלִים: גַּם־כַּסְפָּם גַּם־זְהָבָם לֹא־יוּכַל לְהַצִּילָם בְּיוֹם עֶבְרַת
יְהֹוָה וּבְאֵשׁ קִנְאָתוֹ תֵּאָכֵל כָּל־הָאָרֶץ כִּי־כָלָה אַךְ־נִבְהָלָה יַעֲשֶׂה אֵת כָּל־
ב א־ב יֹשְׁבֵי הָאָרֶץ: הִתְקוֹשְׁשׁוּ וָקוֹשּׁוּ הַגּוֹי לֹא נִכְסָף:
בְּטֶרֶם לֶדֶת חֹק
כְּמֹץ עָבַר יוֹם בְּטֶרֶם ׀ לֹא־יָבוֹא עֲלֵיכֶם חֲרוֹן אַף־יְהֹוָה בְּטֶרֶם לֹא־יָבוֹא
ג עֲלֵיכֶם יוֹם אַף־יְהֹוָה: בַּקְּשׁוּ אֶת־יְהֹוָה כָּל־עַנְוֵי הָאָרֶץ אֲשֶׁר מִשְׁפָּטוֹ פָּעָלוּ
ד בַּקְּשׁוּ־צֶדֶק בַּקְּשׁוּ עֲנָוָה אוּלַי תִּסָּתְרוּ בְּיוֹם אַף־יְהֹוָה: כִּי עַזָּה עֲזוּבָה תִהְיֶה

1:1. During Josiah's reign (*II Kings* 21:24-22:30), Jeremiah prophesied in the public marketplaces, Zephaniah in the synagogues, and Huldah (see *II Kings* 22:14) for the women (*Radak*).

1:3. That is, their false deities (*Rashi*).

1:5. "Their king" refers to their idols, whose name they used to lend credence to their oath (*Rashi*).

1:8. In imitation of the ways of idolaters (*Rashi*).

1:9. An idolatrous ritual [see *I Samuel* 5:5] (*Targum*).

1:10. A gate in the wall of Jerusalem; the second gate was called the Birds' Gate (*Rashi*).

1:11. The Jews, who have adopted the degenerate practices of their Canaanite predecessors (*Targum*).

1:12. Like wine sitting tranquilly on its lees, complacent people sit around and say that God does not reward or punish.

1:17. They will wander aimlessly, vainly seeking shelter.

2:1. You lack desire to become closer to God.

1

¹ The word of HASHEM that came to Zephaniah, son of Cushi, son of Gedaliah, son of Amariah, son of Hezekiah, in the days of Josiah son of Amon, * king of Judah:

God threatens . . .

² I will utterly destroy everything from upon the face of the land — the word of HASHEM. ³ I will destroy man and animal; I will destroy the bird of the sky and the fish of the sea and the stumbling blocks of the wicked; * and I will cut off mankind from the face of the land — the word of HASHEM. ⁴ I will stretch out My hand against Judah and against all the inhabitants of Jerusalem; and I will cut off from this place any remnant of the Baal and the memory of the ministers with the priests; ⁵ and those who prostrate themselves on the roofs to the heavenly host, and those who bow down and swear to HASHEM and [then] swear by their king; * ⁶ and those who have turned back from following HASHEM and those who have not sought HASHEM nor inquired after Him.

. . . a day of destruction

⁷ Be silent before the Lord HASHEM/ELOHIM, for the day of HASHEM is near! For HASHEM has prepared a slaughter; He has invited His guests. ⁸ And it will happen on the day of HASHEM's slaughter that I will deal with the officials and the king's sons and all who wear foreign garments. * ⁹ And I will deal with all those who leap over the threshold* on that day, [and with] those who fill the houses of their masters with injustice and deceit.

¹⁰ On that day — the word of HASHEM — there will be a sound of an outcry from the Fish Gate* and a wail from the second gate, and of a great catastrophe from the hills. ¹¹ Wail, O inhabitants of Maktesh, for the entire people of Canaan* has been destroyed; all those laden with silver have been cut off.

Searching out the sinners

¹² It will be at that time that I will search Jerusalem with candles and I will deal with the men who are settled on their lees, * who say in their heart, 'HASHEM will not do good, and will not do evil.' ¹³ Their wealth will give way to plunder and their houses to desolation; they will build houses, but will not dwell in them; they will plant vineyards, but not drink their wine. ¹⁴ The great day of HASHEM is near, it is near and hastens greatly, the sound of the day of HASHEM, when the mighty warrior cries out bitterly. ¹⁵ A day of fury is that day, a day of trouble and distress, a day of destruction and desolation, a day of darkness and blackness, a day of cloud and thick cloud, ¹⁶ a day of trumpet and battle cries against the fortified cities and against the high towers. ¹⁷ I will lay siege against the people, and they will go about like the blind* for they have sinned against HASHEM. Their blood will be spilled out like dust and their flesh like dung. ¹⁸ Even their silver, even their gold will not be able to rescue them on the day of HASHEM's fury; in the fire of His zeal the entire land will be consumed; for He will make an end, an abrupt one, of all the inhabitants of the land.

2

Improve before it is too late

¹ Improve yourselves and improve each other, O nation without desire: * ² before the decree is born, the day you will become like chaff; before HASHEM's burning wrath comes upon you; before the day of HASHEM's anger comes upon you. ³ Seek HASHEM, all you humble of the land who have fulfilled His law; seek righteousness, seek humility. Perhaps you will be concealed on the day of HASHEM's anger. ⁴ For Gaza will be deserted;

ה וְאַשְׁקְלוֹן לִשְׁמָמָה אַשְׁדּוֹד בַּצָּהֳרַיִם יְגָרְשׁוּהָ וְעֶקְרוֹן תֵּעָקֵר: הוֹי
יֹשְׁבֵי חֶבֶל הַיָּם גּוֹי כְּרֵתִים דְּבַר־יהוה עֲלֵיכֶם כְּנַעַן אֶרֶץ פְּלִשְׁתִּים

ו וְהַאֲבַדְתִּיךְ מֵאֵין יוֹשֵׁב: וְהָיְתָה חֶבֶל הַיָּם נְוֹת כְּרֹת רֹעִים וְגִדְרוֹת צֹאן:

ז וְהָיָה חֶבֶל לִשְׁאֵרִית בֵּית יְהוּדָה עֲלֵיהֶם יִרְעוּן בְּבָתֵּי אַשְׁקְלוֹן בָּעֶרֶב
יִרְבָּצוּן כִּי יִפְקְדֵם יהוה אֱלֹהֵיהֶם וְשָׁב °שבותם [°שְׁבִיתָם ק]: שָׁמַעְתִּי

ח חֶרְפַּת מוֹאָב וְגִדּוּפֵי בְּנֵי עַמּוֹן אֲשֶׁר חֵרְפוּ אֶת־עַמִּי וַיַּגְדִּילוּ עַל־גְּבוּלָם:

ט לָכֵן חַי־אָנִי נְאֻם יהוה צְבָאוֹת אֱלֹהֵי יִשְׂרָאֵל כִּי־מוֹאָב כִּסְדֹם תִּהְיֶה
וּבְנֵי עַמּוֹן כַּעֲמֹרָה מִמְשַׁק חָרוּל וּמִכְרֵה־מֶלַח וּשְׁמָמָה עַד־עוֹלָם

י שְׁאֵרִית עַמִּי יְבָזּוּם וְיֶתֶר °גוי [°גּוֹיַ ק] יִנְחָלוּם: זֹאת לָהֶם תַּחַת גְּאוֹנָם

יא כִּי חֵרְפוּ וַיַּגְדִּלוּ עַל־עַם יהוה צְבָאוֹת: נוֹרָא יהוה עֲלֵיהֶם כִּי רָזָה אֵת
כָּל־אֱלֹהֵי הָאָרֶץ וְיִשְׁתַּחֲווּ־לוֹ אִישׁ מִמְּקוֹמוֹ כֹּל אִיֵּי הַגּוֹיִם: גַּם־אַתֶּם

יב כּוּשִׁים חַלְלֵי חַרְבִּי הֵמָּה: וְיֵט יָדוֹ עַל־צָפוֹן וִיאַבֵּד אֶת־אַשּׁוּר וְיָשֵׂם אֶת־

יג נִינְוֵה לִשְׁמָמָה צִיָּה כַּמִּדְבָּר: וְרָבְצוּ בְתוֹכָהּ עֲדָרִים כָּל־חַיְתוֹ־גוֹי גַּם־
קָאַת גַּם־קִפֹּד בְּכַפְתֹּרֶיהָ יָלִינוּ קוֹל יְשׁוֹרֵר בַּחַלּוֹן חֹרֶב בַּסַּף כִּי אַרְזָה

טו עֵרָה: *זֹאת הָעִיר הָעַלִּיזָה הַיּוֹשֶׁבֶת לָבֶטַח הָאֹמְרָה בִּלְבָבָהּ אֲנִי וְאַפְסִי
עוֹד אֵיךְ ׀ הָיְתָה לְשַׁמָּה מַרְבֵּץ לַחַיָּה כֹּל עוֹבֵר עָלֶיהָ יִשְׁרֹק יָנִיעַ

ג א־ב יָדוֹ:   הוֹי מֹרְאָה וְנִגְאָלָה הָעִיר הַיּוֹנָה: לֹא שָׁמְעָה בְּקוֹל לֹא

ג לָקְחָה מוּסָר בַּיהוה לֹא בָטָחָה אֶל־אֱלֹהֶיהָ לֹא קָרֵבָה: שָׂרֶיהָ בְקִרְבָּהּ

ד אֲרָיוֹת שֹׁאֲגִים שֹׁפְטֶיהָ זְאֵבֵי עֶרֶב לֹא גָרְמוּ לַבֹּקֶר: נְבִיאֶיהָ פֹּחֲזִים אַנְשֵׁי

ה בֹגְדוֹת כֹּהֲנֶיהָ חִלְּלוּ־קֹדֶשׁ חָמְסוּ תוֹרָה: יהוה צַדִּיק בְּקִרְבָּהּ לֹא יַעֲשֶׂה
עַוְלָה בַּבֹּקֶר בַּבֹּקֶר מִשְׁפָּטוֹ יִתֵּן לָאוֹר לֹא נֶעְדָּר וְלֹא־יוֹדֵעַ עַוָּל בֹּשֶׁת:

ו הִכְרַתִּי גוֹיִם נָשַׁמּוּ פִּנּוֹתָם הֶחֱרַבְתִּי חוּצוֹתָם מִבְּלִי עוֹבֵר נִצְדּוּ עָרֵיהֶם

ז מִבְּלִי־אִישׁ מֵאֵין יוֹשֵׁב: אָמַרְתִּי אַךְ־תִּירְאִי אוֹתִי תִּקְחִי מוּסָר וְלֹא־
יִכָּרֵת מְעוֹנָהּ כֹּל אֲשֶׁר־פָּקַדְתִּי עָלֶיהָ אָכֵן הִשְׁכִּימוּ הִשְׁחִיתוּ כֹּל

ח עֲלִילוֹתָם: לָכֵן חַכּוּ־לִי נְאֻם־יהוה לְיוֹם קוּמִי לְעַד כִּי מִשְׁפָּטִי לֶאֱסֹף
גּוֹיִם לְקָבְצִי מַמְלָכוֹת לִשְׁפֹּךְ עֲלֵיהֶם זַעְמִי כֹּל חֲרוֹן אַפִּי כִּי בְּאֵשׁ קִנְאָתִי

ט תֵּאָכֵל כָּל־הָאָרֶץ: כִּי־אָז אֶהְפֹּךְ אֶל־עַמִּים שָׂפָה בְרוּרָה לִקְרֹא כֻלָּם

*הקורא יטעים
הגרשיים
קודם התלישא

2:4. The verse mentions the four main Philistine cities. God's wrath will be poured out against them, as well, on the Day of Judgment (*Radak*).

2:5. See Joshua 13:3.

2:7. The Jewish people, portrayed here as sheep of a flock (*Radak*).

2:11. A metaphor for far-flung places.

2:15. Nineveh.

   "And wave his hand" in gestures of amazement.

3:1. Zephaniah reverts to the topic of Jerusalem.

3:3. Preying on the underprivileged.

3:4. By not fulfilling their duty to teach the people.

3:5. The dishonest judges of Jerusalem are not ashamed to corrupt justice, despite God's presence in its midst.

3:7. Jerusalem's Temple and all the other blessings God ordained for it.

3:8. Because of the sins listed above, salvation will not come for a long time, and you will have to wait for the day when God plunders the nations that oppressed Israel (*Abarbanel*).

3:9. They will no longer speak of idols (*Radak*). Alternatively, they will speak Hebrew, the pure and holy tongue (*Ibn Ezra*).

and Ashkelon become a wasteland; they will drive out Ashdod's residents at noon; and Ekron will be uprooted. *

⁵ Woe to the inhabitants of the seacoast, the nation of the Cherethites! The word of HASHEM is against you, O Canaan, land of the Philistines, * and I will destroy you, without an inhabitant. ⁶ The seacoast will be an abode for shepherds and sheepfolds. ⁷ It will be a portion for the remnant of the House of Judah; upon which they * will graze. In the houses of Ashkelon they will lie down in the evening, for HASHEM, their God, will remember them and will return their captivity.

⁸ I have heard the taunt of Moab and the jeers of the Children of Ammon who taunted My people, and expanded [their territory] along their border. ⁹ Therefore, as I live — the word of HASHEM, Master of Legions, God of Israel — [I swear] that Moab will be like Sodom and the Children of Ammon like Gomorrah, a rustling thornbush, a salt mine, a desolate wasteland forever. The remnant of My people will loot them and the remainder of My nation will inherit them. ¹⁰ This they shall have in place of their haughtiness, for they taunted and boasted over the people of ʰHASHEM, Master of Legions. ¹¹ HASHEM will be fearsome unto them, for He will enfeeble all the powers of the earth. And they will prostrate themselves to Him, each man from his place, all the islands * of the nations.

¹² You, too, Cushites, you are slain by My sword.

¹³ He will stretch out His hand towards the north, and He will destroy Assyria; he will make Nineveh a wasteland, arid as the desert. ¹⁴ Herds will lie down in its midst, every nation's beasts; both owls and bitterns will lodge in its capitals, [their] voice will sing out in the window; desolation will be in its doorway, for the cedarwork will be removed. ¹⁵ This * is the exultant city that dwelt in security; that said in its heart, 'Only I, and besides me, nothing.' How did it become desolate, a resting place for the beast? Everyone who passes by it will whistle and wave his hand. *

3

¹ **W**oe to the filthy and polluted one, the City of Oppression. * ² It did not listen to the voice [of the prophets]; it did not accept chastisement; it did not trust HASHEM; it did not draw near to its God. ³ Its princes in its midst are roaring lions; * its judges are wolves of the evening, they do not leave a bone for the morning; ⁴ its prophets are impetuous, men of rebellion; its priests have desecrated the sacred; they have robbed the Torah. * ⁵ HASHEM, the Righteous One, is within it; He commits no corruption. Morning after morning, He brings His judgment to light, it does not fail, but the corrupt one * knows no shame. ⁶ I have eliminated nations, their towers have become desolate; I have destroyed their streets without passerby; their cities have become ruins, without people, so there is no inhabitant. ⁷ I said, 'Just fear Me, accept chastisement,' so that her Abode * would not be terminated, despite all that I have ordained upon her. But [instead] they arose early and corrupted all their deeds.

⁸ Therefore, wait for Me * — the word of HASHEM — for the day when I will arise to plunder [them]. For My judgment will be to assemble nations, to gather kingdoms, to pour My fury upon them, all My burning wrath; for with the fire of My jealousy the entire earth will be consumed. ⁹ For then I will change the nations [to speak] a pure language, * so that they all will proclaim

בְּשֵׁם יהוה לְעָבְדוֹ שְׁכֶם אֶחָד: מֵעֵבֶר לְנַהֲרֵי־כוּשׁ עֲתָרַי בַּת־פּוּצַי י
יוֹבִלוּן מִנְחָתִי: בַּיּוֹם הַהוּא לֹא תֵבוֹשִׁי מִכֹּל עֲלִילֹתַיִךְ אֲשֶׁר פָּשַׁעַתְּ בִּי יא
כִּי־אָז | אָסִיר מִקִּרְבֵּךְ עַלִּיזֵי גַּאֲוָתֵךְ וְלֹא־תוֹסִפִי לְגָבְהָה עוֹד בְּהַר
קָדְשִׁי: וְהִשְׁאַרְתִּי בְקִרְבֵּךְ עַם עָנִי וָדָל וְחָסוּ בְּשֵׁם יהוה: שְׁאֵרִית יִשְׂרָאֵל יב־יג
לֹא־יַעֲשׂוּ עַוְלָה וְלֹא־יְדַבְּרוּ כָזָב וְלֹא־יִמָּצֵא בְּפִיהֶם לְשׁוֹן תַּרְמִית כִּי־
הֵמָּה יִרְעוּ וְרָבְצוּ וְאֵין מַחֲרִיד: רָנִּי בַּת־צִיּוֹן הָרִיעוּ יִשְׂרָאֵל יד
שִׂמְחִי וְעָלְזִי בְּכָל־לֵב בַּת יְרוּשָׁלָ͏ִם: הֵסִיר יהוה מִשְׁפָּטַיִךְ פִּנָּה אֹיְבֵךְ טו
מֶלֶךְ יִשְׂרָאֵל | יהוה בְּקִרְבֵּךְ לֹא־תִירְאִי רָע עוֹד: בַּיּוֹם טז
הַהוּא יֵאָמֵר לִירוּשָׁלַ͏ִם אַל־תִּירָאִי צִיּוֹן אַל־יִרְפּוּ יָדָיִךְ: יהוה אֱלֹהַיִךְ יז
בְּקִרְבֵּךְ גִּבּוֹר יוֹשִׁיעַ יָשִׂישׂ עָלַיִךְ בְּשִׂמְחָה יַחֲרִישׁ בְּאַהֲבָתוֹ יָגִיל עָלַיִךְ
בְּרִנָּה: נוּגֵי מִמּוֹעֵד אָסַפְתִּי מִמֵּךְ הָיוּ מַשְׂאֵת עָלֶיהָ חֶרְפָּה: הִנְנִי עֹשֶׂה יח־יט
אֶת־כָּל־מְעַנַּיִךְ בָּעֵת הַהִיא וְהוֹשַׁעְתִּי אֶת־הַצֹּלֵעָה וְהַנִּדָּחָה אֲקַבֵּץ
וְשַׂמְתִּים לִתְהִלָּה וּלְשֵׁם בְּכָל־הָאָרֶץ בָּשְׁתָּם: בָּעֵת הַהִיא אָבִיא אֶתְכֶם כ
וּבָעֵת קַבְּצִי אֶתְכֶם כִּי־אֶתֵּן אֶתְכֶם לְשֵׁם וְלִתְהִלָּה בְּכֹל עַמֵּי הָאָרֶץ
בְּשׁוּבִי אֶת־שְׁבוּתֵיכֶם לְעֵינֵיכֶם אָמַר יהוה:

3:17. He will ignore your past sins and not punish you for them.

3:18. Those who mourned for the long-delayed festival of the Redemption (*Radak*); or who mourned Jerusalem's loss of the pilgrimage festivals (*Rashi*).

the Name of HASHEM, to worship Him with a united resolve. [10] From the other side of the rivers of Cush, My supplicants, groups of My scattered ones, will bring My tribute. [11] On that day, you will not be ashamed of all your deeds by which you have wantonly sinned against Me. For then I will remove from your midst those who exult in your arrogance, and you will no longer continue to be haughty on My holy mountain. [12] And I will leave in your midst a humble and destitute people, and they will take shelter in the Name of HASHEM. [13] The remnant of Israel will not commit corruption, they will not speak falsehood, and a deceitful tongue will not be found in their mouth; for they will graze and lie down with none to make them afraid.

But Zion will yet exult

[14] Sing, O daughter of Zion! Sound the trumpet, O Israel! Be glad and exult with all your heart, O daughter of Jerusalem! [15] HASHEM has removed your judgments; He has cleared away your enemy. The King of Israel, HASHEM, is in your midst, you will never again fear evil.

[16] On that day, it will be said to Jerusalem, 'Have no fear! O Zion, do not despair!' [17] HASHEM, your God, is in your midst, the Mighty One Who will save. He will rejoice over you with gladness; He will be silent* with His love; He will be joyful over you with glad song. [18] I have gathered together those who have mourned for the appointed time, * they came from you, who had carried a burden of shame for it. [19] Behold, at that time I will crush all those who afflict you. I will save the cripple, and gather the castoff; and I will make them for praise and a good name throughout the land of their shame. [20] At that time I will bring you [in], and at [that] time I will gather you; for I will make you into a good name and praise among all the peoples of the earth, when I return your captives before your eyes, said HASHEM.

א   א בִּשְׁנַ֣ת שְׁתַּ֗יִם לְדָרְיָ֙וֶשׁ֙ הַמֶּ֔לֶךְ בַּחֹ֙דֶשׁ֙ הַשִּׁשִּׁ֔י בְּי֥וֹם אֶחָ֖ד לַחֹ֑דֶשׁ הָיָ֣ה דְבַר־
יְהֹוָ֗ה בְּיַד־חַגַּי֙ הַנָּבִ֔יא אֶל־זְרֻבָּבֶ֤ל בֶּן־שְׁאַלְתִּיאֵל֙ פַּחַ֣ת יְהוּדָ֔ה וְאֶל־
ב יְהוֹשֻׁ֧עַ בֶּן־יְהוֹצָדָ֛ק הַכֹּהֵ֥ן הַגָּד֖וֹל לֵאמֹֽר: כֹּ֥ה אָמַ֛ר יְהֹוָ֥ה צְבָא֖וֹת לֵאמֹ֑ר
הָעָ֤ם הַזֶּה֙ אָֽמְר֔וּ לֹ֥א עֶת־בֹּ֖א עֶת־בֵּ֥ית יְהֹוָ֖ה לְהִבָּנֽוֹת: ג וַֽיְהִי֙ דְּבַר־
ד יְהֹוָ֔ה בְּיַד־חַגַּ֥י הַנָּבִ֖יא לֵאמֹֽר: הַעֵ֤ת לָכֶם֙ אַתֶּ֔ם לָשֶׁ֖בֶת בְּבָתֵּיכֶ֣ם סְפוּנִ֑ים
ה וְהַבַּ֥יִת הַזֶּ֖ה חָרֵֽב: וְעַתָּ֗ה כֹּ֤ה אָמַר֙ יְהֹוָ֣ה צְבָא֔וֹת שִׂ֥ימוּ לְבַבְכֶ֖ם עַל־דַּרְכֵיכֶֽם:
ו זְרַעְתֶּ֤ם הַרְבֵּה֙ וְהָבֵ֣א מְעָ֔ט אָכ֖וֹל וְאֵ֣ין לְשָׂבְעָ֑ה שָׁת֣וֹ וְאֵֽין־לְשָׁכְרָ֗ה לָב֙וֹשׁ֙
ז וְאֵֽין־לְחֹ֣ם ל֔וֹ וְהַ֙מִּשְׂתַּכֵּ֔ר מִשְׂתַּכֵּ֖ר אֶל־צְר֥וֹר נָקֽוּב: כֹּ֥ה אָמַ֖ר יְהֹוָ֣ה
ח צְבָא֑וֹת שִׂ֥ימוּ לְבַבְכֶ֖ם עַל־דַּרְכֵיכֶֽם: עֲל֥וּ הָהָ֛ר וַֽהֲבֵאתֶ֥ם עֵ֖ץ וּבְנ֣וּ הַבָּ֑יִת
ט וְאֶרְצֶה־בּ֥וֹ °וְאֶכָּבֵ֖דָה [וְאֶכָּבְדָ֖ה ק] אָמַ֥ר יְהֹוָֽה: פָּנֹ֤ה אֶל־הַרְבֵּה֙ וְהִנֵּ֣ה
לִמְעָ֔ט וַֽהֲבֵאתֶ֥ם הַבַּ֖יִת וְנָפַ֣חְתִּי ב֑וֹ יַ֣עַן מֶ֗ה נְאֻם֙ יְהֹוָ֣ה צְבָא֔וֹת יַ֣עַן בֵּיתִ֗י
י אֲשֶׁר־ה֣וּא חָרֵ֔ב וְאַתֶּ֥ם רָצִ֖ים אִ֣ישׁ לְבֵיתֽוֹ: עַל־כֵּ֗ן עֲלֵיכֶ֛ם כָּֽלְא֥וּ שָׁמַ֖יִם
יא מִטָּ֑ל וְהָאָ֖רֶץ כָּֽלְאָ֥ה יְבוּלָֽהּ: וָֽאֶקְרָ֨א חֹ֜רֶב עַל־הָאָ֣רֶץ וְעַל־הֶֽהָרִ֗ים וְעַל־
הַדָּגָן֙ וְעַל־הַתִּיר֣וֹשׁ וְעַל־הַיִּצְהָ֔ר וְעַ֖ל אֲשֶׁ֣ר תּוֹצִ֣יא הָֽאֲדָמָ֑ה וְעַל־הָֽאָדָם֙
יב וְעַל־הַבְּהֵמָ֔ה וְעַ֖ל כָּל־יְגִ֥יעַ כַּפָּֽיִם: וַיִּשְׁמַ֣ע זְרֻבָּבֶ֣ל ׀ בֶּן־שַׁלְתִּיאֵ֡ל
וִֽיהוֹשֻׁ֣עַ בֶּן־יְהוֹצָדָק֩ הַכֹּהֵ֨ן הַגָּד֜וֹל וְכֹ֣ל ׀ שְׁאֵרִ֣ית הָעָ֗ם בְּקוֹל֙ יְהֹוָ֣ה אֱלֹֽהֵיהֶ֔ם
וְעַל־דִּבְרֵי֙ חַגַּ֣י הַנָּבִ֔יא כַּֽאֲשֶׁ֥ר שְׁלָח֖וֹ יְהֹוָ֣ה אֱלֹֽהֵיהֶ֑ם וַיִּֽירְא֥וּ הָעָ֖ם מִפְּנֵ֥י
יג יְהֹוָֽה: וַ֠יֹּ֠אמֶר חַגַּ֞י מַלְאַ֤ךְ יְהֹוָה֙ בְּמַלְאֲכ֣וּת יְהֹוָ֔ה לָעָ֖ם לֵאמֹ֑ר
יד אֲנִ֥י אִתְּכֶ֖ם נְאֻם־יְהֹוָֽה: וַיָּ֣עַר יְהֹוָ֡ה אֶת־ר֠וּחַ זְרֻבָּבֶ֨ל בֶּן־שַׁלְתִּיאֵ֜ל פַּחַ֣ת
יְהוּדָ֗ה וְאֶת־ר֙וּחַ֙ יְהוֹשֻׁ֤עַ בֶּן־יְהוֹצָדָק֙ הַכֹּהֵ֣ן הַגָּד֔וֹל וְאֶת־ר֕וּחַ כֹּ֖ל שְׁאֵרִ֣ית
טו הָעָ֑ם וַיָּבֹ֙אוּ֙ וַיַּֽעֲשׂ֣וּ מְלָאכָ֔ה בְּבֵית־יְהֹוָ֥ה צְבָא֖וֹת אֱלֹֽהֵיהֶֽם: בְּי֨וֹם

ב   עֶשְׂרִ֧ים וְאַרְבָּעָ֛ה לַחֹ֖דֶשׁ בַּשִּׁשִּׁ֑י בִּשְׁנַ֥ת שְׁתַּ֖יִם לְדָרְיָ֥וֶשׁ הַמֶּֽלֶךְ: א בַּשְּׁבִיעִ֗י
ב בְּעֶשְׂרִ֤ים וְאֶחָד֙ לַחֹ֔דֶשׁ הָיָה֙ דְּבַר־יְהֹוָ֔ה בְּיַד־חַגַּ֥י הַנָּבִ֖יא לֵאמֹֽר: אֱמָר־נָ֗א
אֶל־זְרֻבָּבֶ֤ל בֶּן־שַׁלְתִּיאֵל֙ פַּחַ֣ת יְהוּדָ֔ה וְאֶל־יְהוֹשֻׁ֖עַ בֶּן־יְהוֹצָדָ֣ק הַכֹּהֵ֣ן
ג הַגָּד֑וֹל וְאֶל־שְׁאֵרִ֥ית הָעָ֖ם לֵאמֹֽר: מִ֤י בָכֶם֙ הַנִּשְׁאָ֔ר אֲשֶׁ֤ר רָאָה֙ אֶת־הַבַּ֣יִת
הַזֶּ֔ה בִּכְבוֹד֖וֹ הָֽרִאשׁ֑וֹן וּמָ֨ה אַתֶּ֜ם רֹאִ֤ים אֹתוֹ֙ עַ֔תָּה הֲל֥וֹא כָמֹ֛הוּ כְּאַ֖יִן
ד בְּעֵֽינֵיכֶֽם: וְעַתָּ֣ה חֲזַ֣ק זְרֻבָּבֶ֣ל ׀ נְאֻם־יְהֹוָ֡ה וַֽחֲזַ֣ק יְהוֹשֻׁ֣עַ בֶּן־יְהוֹצָדָק֩
הַכֹּהֵ֨ן הַגָּד֜וֹל וַֽחֲזַ֨ק כָּל־עַ֥ם הָאָ֛רֶץ נְאֻם־יְהֹוָ֖ה וַֽעֲשׂ֑וּ כִּֽי־אֲנִ֣י אִתְּכֶ֔ם נְאֻ֖ם

◄§ Haggai, Zechariah and Malachi, the last three prophets, were among the one hundred and twenty members of
the Great Assembly [אַנְשֵׁי כְּנֶסֶת הַגְּדוֹלָה], the body that led
the Jewish people during the early years of the Second
Temple era. The Assembly was headed by Ezra and
included other such Scriptural leaders as Zerubbabel and
Joshua the Kohen Gadol (a nephew of Ezra); Nehemiah,
Seraiah, Reelaiah and Mordechai-bilsham [see Ezra 2:2];
and Daniel, Chananiah, Mishael and Azariah [see Daniel
1:6] (Rambam, Intro.; Rashi, Avos 1:1).
1:1. Darius was the king of Persia (see Ezra 4:24-5:1).

According to the Midrash, he was the son of Ahasuerus
and Esther (Vayikra Rabbah 13:4). He sanctioned and
encouraged the construction of the Second Temple,
which had begun in the days of Cyrus (Ezra Ch. 3), but was
subsequently discontinued for eighteen years. This Darius should not be confused with Darius the Mede, who
conquered Babylonia and ended the dynasty of Nebuchadnezzar.

The sixth month is Elul.

1:3. The prophecy of verse 2 was intended solely for the

1

(See Appendix A,
timeline 5)

¹ In the second year of King Darius, * in the sixth month, * on the first day of the month, the word of HASHEM came by the hand of Haggai the prophet to Zerubbabel son of Shealtiel, governor of Judea, and to Joshua son of Jehozadak, the Kohen Gadol, saying: ² "Thus said HASHEM, Master of Legions: This nation has said, 'The time has not yet come!' [But I say] 'It is the time for the Temple of HASHEM to be rebuilt!' "

³ And the word of HASHEM came by the hand of Haggai the prophet, saying: *

Resume the construc-
tion . . .

⁴ Is this a time for you yourselves to sit in your paneled houses, while this House is in ruins? * ⁵ So now, thus said HASHEM, Master of Legions: Set your heart to [consider] your ways! ⁶ You have sown much but bring in little; eating without being satisfied, drinking without quenching thirst, dressing, yet no one is warmed; and whoever earns money earns it for a purse with a hole.

⁷ Thus said HASHEM, Master of Legions: Set your heart to your ways! ⁸ Go up to the mountain and bring wood and build the Temple; I will be pleased with it and I will be honored — said HASHEM. ⁹ You looked for much [produce] but, behold, it is little; you bring it home and I blow * upon it. Why is this?! — the word of HASHEM, Master of Legions — because of My Temple which is ruined, while you run, each to his own house. ¹⁰ Therefore, because of you,

. . . or suffer
drought

the heavens withhold from [giving] dew, and the land withholds its produce. ¹¹ I have declared a drought upon the land and upon the mountains and upon the grain and upon the wine and upon the oil and upon whatever the earth brings forth and upon the [many] people and upon the animal and upon all the toil of [your] hands.

Zerubbabel
and Joshua
obey

¹² And so Zerubbabel son of Shealtiel and Joshua son of Jehozadak, the Kohen Gadol, and the entire remnant of the people listened to the voice of HASHEM their God and to the words of Haggai the prophet, according to what HASHEM their God had sent him [to prophesy], and the people feared before HASHEM. ¹³ And Haggai, the agent of HASHEM, in the agency of HASHEM, spoke to the people, saying, "I am with you — the word of HASHEM."

¹⁴ HASHEM aroused the spirit of Zerubbabel son of Shealtiel, the governor of Judea, and the spirit of Joshua son of Jehozadak, the Kohen Gadol, and the spirit of the entire remnant of the people, and they came and did work on the Temple of HASHEM, Master of Legions, their God, ¹⁵ on the twenty-fourth day of the month, in the sixth [month], in the second year of King Darius.

2

¹ In the seventh [month], * on the twenty-first of the month, the word of HASHEM came through Haggai the prophet, saying: ² "Speak, now, to Zerubbabel son of Shealtiel, governor of Judea, and to Joshua son of Jehozadak, the Kohen Gadol, and to the rest of the people, saying:

Be
encouraged

³ Who is left among you who remembers this Temple in its original glory, * and how do you view it now? Is it not like nothing in your eyes? ⁴ So now, be strong, O Zerubbabel — the word of HASHEM — and be strong, Joshua son of Jehozadak, the Kohen Gadol, and be strong, the entire people of the land — the word of HASHEM — and fulfill, for I am with you — the word of

leaders. This prophecy is for the people.

1:4. Since the construction of the Temple had been stopped for a long time, the people had given up hope of reversing that status. Haggai's prophecy was meant to put an end to this lethargy.

1:9. I will scorch the grain with hot winds.

2:1. The month of Tishrei. The twenty-first of Tishrei is the seventh day of the Succos festival.

2:3. The First Temple, prior to its destruction by the Babylonians, seventy years ago.

ה יהוה צְבָאוֹת: אֶת־הַדָּבָ֨ר אֲשֶׁר־כָּרַ֤תִּי אִתְּכֶם֙ בְּצֵאתְכֶ֣ם מִמִּצְרַ֔יִם וְרוּחִ֖י
ו עֹמֶ֣דֶת בְּתוֹכְכֶ֑ם אַל־תִּירָֽאוּ: כִּ֣י כֹ֤ה אָמַר֙ יהוה צְבָא֔וֹת ע֖וֹד
אַחַ֣ת מְעַ֣ט הִ֑יא וַאֲנִ֗י מַרְעִישׁ֙ אֶת־הַשָּׁמַ֣יִם וְאֶת־הָאָ֔רֶץ וְאֶת־הַיָּ֖ם וְאֶת־
ז הֶחָרָבָֽה: וְהִרְעַשְׁתִּי֙ אֶת־כָּל־הַגּוֹיִ֔ם וּבָ֖אוּ חֶמְדַּ֣ת כָּל־הַגּוֹיִ֑ם וּמִלֵּאתִ֞י
ח אֶת־הַבַּ֤יִת הַזֶּה֙ כָּב֔וֹד אָמַ֖ר יהוה צְבָאֽוֹת: לִ֥י הַכֶּ֖סֶף וְלִ֣י הַזָּהָ֑ב נְאֻ֖ם יהוה
ט צְבָאֽוֹת: גָּד֣וֹל יִֽהְיֶ֡ה כְּבוֹד֩ הַבַּ֨יִת הַזֶּ֤ה הָאַֽחֲרוֹן֙ מִן־הָ֣רִאשׁ֔וֹן אָמַ֖ר יהוה
י צְבָא֑וֹת וּבַמָּק֤וֹם הַזֶּה֙ אֶתֵּ֣ן שָׁל֔וֹם נְאֻ֖ם יהוה צְבָאֽוֹת: {פ}

וְאַרְבָּעָ֞ה לַתְּשִׁיעִ֗י בִּשְׁנַ֤ת שְׁתַּ֨יִם֙ לְדָרְיָ֔וֶשׁ הָיָה֙ דְּבַר־יהוה ֯אֶל־חַגַּ֧י
יא הַנָּבִ֛יא לֵאמֹֽר: כֹּ֤ה אָמַר֙ יהוה צְבָא֔וֹת שְׁאַל־נָ֧א אֶת־הַכֹּהֲנִ֛ים תּוֹרָ֖ה
יב לֵאמֹֽר: הֵ֣ן ׀ יִשָּׂא־אִ֣ישׁ בְּשַׂר־קֹ֗דֶשׁ בִּכְנַ֣ף בִּגְד֔וֹ וְנָגַ֣ע בִּ֠כְנָפ֠וֹ אֶל־הַלֶּ֜חֶם
וְאֶל־הַנָּזִ֧יד וְאֶל־הַיַּ֛יִן וְאֶל־שֶׁ֥מֶן וְאֶל־כָּל־מַאֲכָ֖ל הֲיִקְדָּ֑שׁ וַיַּעֲנ֧וּ הַכֹּהֲנִ֛ים
יג וַיֹּאמְר֖וּ לֹֽא: וַיֹּ֣אמֶר חַגַּ֗י אִם־יִגַּ֧ע טְמֵא־נֶ֛פֶשׁ בְּכָל־אֵ֖לֶּה הֲיִטְמָ֑א וַיַּעֲנ֧וּ
יד הַכֹּהֲנִ֛ים וַיֹּאמְר֖וּ יִטְמָֽא: וַיַּ֨עַן חַגַּ֜י וַיֹּ֗אמֶר כֵּ֣ן הָֽעָם־הַזֶּ֩ה וְכֵ֨ן־הַגּ֤וֹי הַזֶּה֙
לְפָנַ֣י נְאֻם־יהוה וְכֵ֖ן כָּל־מַעֲשֵׂ֣ה יְדֵיהֶ֑ם וַאֲשֶׁ֥ר יַקְרִ֛יבוּ שָׁ֖ם טָמֵ֥א הֽוּא:
טו וְעַתָּה֙ שִֽׂימוּ־נָ֣א לְבַבְכֶ֔ם מִן־הַיּ֥וֹם הַזֶּ֖ה וָמָ֑עְלָה מִטֶּ֧רֶם שֽׂוּם־אֶ֛בֶן אֶל־אֶ֖בֶן
טז בְּהֵיכַ֥ל יהוה: מִֽהְיוֹתָ֔ם בָּ֛א אֶל־עֲרֵמַ֥ת עֶשְׂרִ֖ים וְהָיְתָ֣ה עֲשָׂרָ֑ה בָּ֣א אֶל־
יז הַיֶּ֗קֶב לַחְשֹׂף֙ חֲמִשִּׁ֣ים פּוּרָ֔ה וְהָיְתָ֖ה עֶשְׂרִֽים: הִכֵּ֨יתִי אֶתְכֶ֤ם בַּשִּׁדָּפוֹן֙
וּבַיֵּרָק֔וֹן וּבַבָּרָ֔ד אֵ֖ת כָּל־מַעֲשֵׂ֣ה יְדֵיכֶ֑ם וְאֵין־אֶתְכֶ֥ם אֵלַ֖י נְאֻם־יהוֽה:
יח שִֽׂימוּ־נָ֣א לְבַבְכֶ֔ם מִן־הַיּ֥וֹם הַזֶּ֖ה וָמָ֑עְלָה מִיּוֹם֩ עֶשְׂרִ֨ים וְאַרְבָּעָ֜ה לַתְּשִׁיעִ֗י
יט לְמִן־הַיּ֛וֹם אֲשֶׁר־יֻסַּ֥ד הֵֽיכַל־יהוה שִׂ֥ימוּ לְבַבְכֶֽם: הַע֤וֹד הַזֶּ֨רַע֙ בַּמְּגוּרָ֔ה
וְעַד־הַגֶּ֧פֶן וְהַתְּאֵנָ֛ה וְהָרִמּ֥וֹן וְעֵ֥ץ הַזַּ֖יִת לֹ֣א נָשָׂ֑א מִן־הַיּ֥וֹם הַזֶּ֖ה
אֲבָרֵֽךְ: {פ}

כ וַיְהִ֨י דְבַר־יהוה ׀ שֵׁנִית֙ אֶל־חַגַּ֔י בְּעֶשְׂרִ֥ים וְאַרְבָּעָ֖ה
כא לַחֹ֣דֶשׁ לֵאמֹֽר: אֱמֹ֕ר אֶל־זְרֻבָּבֶ֥ל פַּֽחַת־יְהוּדָ֖ה לֵאמֹ֑ר אֲנִ֣י מַרְעִ֔ישׁ אֶת־
כב הַשָּׁמַ֖יִם וְאֶת־הָאָֽרֶץ: וְהָֽפַכְתִּי֙ כִּסֵּ֣א מַמְלָכ֔וֹת וְהִ֨שְׁמַדְתִּ֔י חֹ֖זֶק מַמְלְכ֣וֹת
הַגּוֹיִ֑ם וְהָפַכְתִּ֤י מֶרְכָּבָה֙ וְרֹ֣כְבֶ֔יהָ וְיָרְד֤וּ סוּסִים֙ וְרֹ֣כְבֵיהֶ֔ם אִ֖ישׁ בְּחֶ֥רֶב
כג אָחִֽיו: בַּיּ֣וֹם הַה֣וּא נְאֻם־יהוה צְבָא֗וֹת אֶקָּֽחֲךָ֞ זְרֻבָּבֶ֤ל בֶּן־שְׁאַלְתִּיאֵ֤ל
עַבְדִּי֙ נְאֻם־יהוה וְשַׂמְתִּ֖יךָ כַּֽחוֹתָ֑ם כִּֽי־בְךָ֣ בָחַ֔רְתִּי נְאֻ֖ם יהוה צְבָאֽוֹת: {פ}

֯נ״א בְּיַד

2:6. One more nation will subdue you, the Greeks; but their domination will last only a short time (*Rashi*). During the Greek rule, I will cause a major upheaval in the land — a reference to the Hasmonean revolt against the Greeks and the miracle of Chanukah.

2:7. People of all nations will bring offerings to the Temple at that time.

2:10. The month of Kislev.

2:12-13. Since knowledge of the complex laws of ritually purity are essential to the functioning of the Temple, Haggai tested the Kohanim to see if they had forgotten the laws as a result of the exile in Babylonia, when many of the laws had not been relevant. Indeed, they did not answer all the questions correctly.

2:14. Haggai reprimanded the Kohanim for being insufficiently versed in the laws of ritual purity, thus causing defilement of sacrificial foods in the Temple.

2:15. Despite the above shortcoming, Haggai urged, consider what happened before you resumed construction of the Temple (*Rashi*).

2:16. Haggai repeats the description of the lack of prosperity, mentioned in 1:6 and 1:9 above.

HASHEM, Master of Legions — [5] the matter [of the covenant] that I sealed with you when you went forth from Egypt. My spirit remains in your midst; do not be afraid. [6] For thus said HASHEM, Master of Legions: There will be one

God will glorify the Temple

more; it is a small one. * I will shake the heavens and the earth and the sea and the dry land. [7] I will shake all the nations, and the precious things of all the nations will arrive here, * and I will fill this Temple with glory, said HASHEM, Master of Legions. [8] Mine is the silver and mine is the gold — the word of HASHEM, Master of Legions. [9] The glory of this latter Temple will be greater than [that of] the first, said HASHEM, Master of Legions; and I will grant peace to this place — the word of HASHEM, Master of Legions."

[10] On the twenty-fourth of the ninth [month], * in the second year of Darius, the word of HASHEM came to Haggai the prophet, saying: [11] "Thus said HASHEM, Master of Legions: Inquire, now, for a ruling from the Kohanim, saying, [12] 'If a person

Is it defiled?

carries ritually defiled flesh in the corner of his garment, and then he touches bread with his [garment's] corner, and [the bread touches] stew, and [the stew touches] wine or oil or any other food — does [that food] become defiled?' "*

The Kohanim answered and said, "No."

[13] Haggai said, "If one who touched a dead person would touch all of these, would it become defiled?"

And the Kohanim answered and said, "It would become defiled."

[14] Haggai spoke up and said:

New beginning

So is this people and so is this nation before Me — the word of HASHEM — and so is all their handiwork: what they offer there will be defiled. * [15] But nevertheless, * consider [the situation] from this day and previously, before stone was placed upon stone in the Sanctuary of HASHEM, [16] when they would come to a grain heap of [what should have been] twenty [units] but was [only] ten; * [when one would] come to the winepress to draw out fifty [units] from the pit, but there were [only] twenty. [17] I had struck you with blast and blight and hail, upon all your handiwork, yet you are not [returning] to Me — the word of HASHEM. [18] Set now your heart [to consider] from this day and before, from the twenty-fourth of the ninth [month], [back] to the day when the foundations of the Sanctuary were laid; * set your heart [to consider]: [19] Is there any more seed in the silo? Even the grapevine and the fig tree and the pomegranate tree and the olive tree have not borne [their fruit]. But from this day on I will provide blessing. *

Zerubbabel is chosen

[20] The word of HASHEM came to Haggai a second time on the twenty-fourth of the month, saying, [21] "Speak to Zerubbabel, governor of Judea, saying:

I am shaking the heavens and the earth. [22] I will upset the thrones of kingdoms and destroy the strength of kingdoms of the nations; * I will turn over a chariot and its drivers, and horses and their riders will fall down, one by the sword of the other. [23] On that day — the word of HASHEM, Master of Legions — I will take you, Zerubbabel son of Shealtiel, my servant — the word of HASHEM — and I will make you like [My] signet ring; * for you have I chosen — the word of HASHEM, Master of Legions."

2:18. In the days of Cyrus — see note to 1:1.

2:19. Because you have resumed the building of the Temple.

2:22. Referring to the downfall of the Persian empire at

the hands of the Greeks a few years after this prophecy (Rashi).

2:23. A signet ring never leaves the hand of its owner (Radak).

א

א בַּחֹדֶשׁ הַשְּׁמִינִי בִּשְׁנַת שְׁתַּיִם לְדָרְיָוֶשׁ הָיָה דְבַר־יהוה אֶל־זְכַרְיָה בֶּן־

ב־ג בֶּרֶכְיָה בֶּן־עִדּוֹ הַנָּבִיא לֵאמֹר: קָצַף יהוה עַל־אֲבוֹתֵיכֶם קָצֶף: וְאָמַרְתָּ אֲלֵהֶם כֹּה אָמַר יהוה צְבָאוֹת שׁוּבוּ אֵלַי נְאֻם יהוה צְבָאוֹת וְאָשׁוּב

ד אֲלֵיכֶם אָמַר יהוה צְבָאוֹת: אַל־תִּהְיוּ כַאֲבֹתֵיכֶם אֲשֶׁר קָרְאוּ־אֲלֵיהֶם הַנְּבִיאִים הָרִאשֹׁנִים לֵאמֹר כֹּה אָמַר יהוה צְבָאוֹת שׁוּבוּ נָא מִדַּרְכֵיכֶם הָרָעִים °וּמַעֲלִילֵיכֶם [°וּמַעַלְלֵיכֶם ק] וְלֹא שָׁמְעוּ וְלֹא־הִקְשִׁיבוּ

ה־ו אֵלַי נְאֻם־יהוה: אֲבוֹתֵיכֶם אַיֵּה־הֵם וְהַנְּבִאִים הַלְעוֹלָם יִחְיוּ: אַךְ ׀ דְּבָרַי וְחֻקַּי אֲשֶׁר צִוִּיתִי אֶת־עֲבָדַי הַנְּבִיאִים הֲלוֹא הִשִּׂיגוּ אֲבֹתֵיכֶם וַיָּשׁוּבוּ וַיֹּאמְרוּ כַּאֲשֶׁר זָמַם יהוה צְבָאוֹת לַעֲשׂוֹת לָנוּ כִּדְרָכֵינוּ וּכְמַעֲלָלֵינוּ כֵּן עָשָׂה אִתָּנוּ: בְּיוֹם עֶשְׂרִים וְאַרְבָּעָה לְעַשְׁתֵּי־עָשָׂר

ז חֹדֶשׁ הוּא־חֹדֶשׁ שְׁבָט בִּשְׁנַת שְׁתַּיִם לְדָרְיָוֶשׁ הָיָה דְבַר־יהוה אֶל־זְכַרְיָה

ח בֶּן־בֶּרֶכְיָהוּ בֶּן־עִדּוֹא הַנָּבִיא לֵאמֹר: רָאִיתִי ׀ הַלַּיְלָה וְהִנֵּה־אִישׁ רֹכֵב עַל־סוּס אָדֹם וְהוּא עֹמֵד בֵּין הַהֲדַסִּים אֲשֶׁר בַּמְּצֻלָה וְאַחֲרָיו סוּסִים

ט אֲדֻמִּים שְׂרֻקִּים וּלְבָנִים: וָאֹמַר מָה־אֵלֶּה אֲדֹנִי וַיֹּאמֶר אֵלַי הַמַּלְאָךְ

י הַדֹּבֵר בִּי אֲנִי אַרְאֶךָּ מָה־הֵמָּה אֵלֶּה: וַיַּעַן הָאִישׁ הָעֹמֵד בֵּין־הַהֲדַסִּים

יא וַיֹּאמַר אֵלֶּה אֲשֶׁר שָׁלַח יהוה לְהִתְהַלֵּךְ בָּאָרֶץ: וַיַּעֲנוּ אֶת־מַלְאַךְ יהוה הָעֹמֵד בֵּין הַהֲדַסִּים וַיֹּאמְרוּ הִתְהַלַּכְנוּ בָאָרֶץ וְהִנֵּה כָל־הָאָרֶץ יֹשֶׁבֶת

יב וְשֹׁקָטֶת: וַיַּעַן מַלְאַךְ־יהוה וַיֹּאמַר יהוה צְבָאוֹת עַד־מָתַי אַתָּה לֹא־תְרַחֵם אֶת־יְרוּשָׁלַ͏ִם וְאֵת עָרֵי יְהוּדָה אֲשֶׁר זָעַמְתָּה זֶה שִׁבְעִים שָׁנָה:

יג־יד וַיַּעַן יהוה אֶת־הַמַּלְאָךְ הַדֹּבֵר בִּי דְּבָרִים טוֹבִים דְּבָרִים נִחֻמִים: וַיֹּאמֶר אֵלַי הַמַּלְאָךְ הַדֹּבֵר בִּי קְרָא לֵאמֹר כֹּה אָמַר יהוה צְבָאוֹת קִנֵּאתִי

טו לִירוּשָׁלַ͏ִם וּלְצִיּוֹן קִנְאָה גְדוֹלָה: וְקֶצֶף גָּדוֹל אֲנִי קֹצֵף עַל־הַגּוֹיִם הַשַּׁאֲנַנִּים אֲשֶׁר אֲנִי קָצַפְתִּי מְּעָט וְהֵמָּה עָזְרוּ לְרָעָה:

טז לָכֵן כֹּה־אָמַר יהוה שַׁבְתִּי לִירוּשָׁלַ͏ִם בְּרַחֲמִים בֵּיתִי יִבָּנֶה בָּהּ נְאֻם יהוה צְבָאוֹת °וְקָוָה [°וְקָו ק] יִנָּטֶה עַל־יְרוּשָׁלָ͏ִם: עוֹד ׀ קְרָא לֵאמֹר

יח כֹּה אָמַר יהוה צְבָאוֹת עוֹד תְּפוּצֶינָה עָרַי מִטּוֹב וְנִחַם יהוה עוֹד אֶת־צִיּוֹן וּבָחַר עוֹד בִּירוּשָׁלָ͏ִם:

ב

א וָאֶשָּׂא אֶת־עֵינַי

ב וָאֵרֶא וְהִנֵּה אַרְבַּע קְרָנוֹת: וָאֹמַר אֶל־הַמַּלְאָךְ הַדֹּבֵר בִּי מָה־אֵלֶּה

◄§ Zechariah was a contemporary of Haggai (see *Haggai* 1:1). Zechariah chastised the people for their lack of alacrity in rebuilding the Temple, even though King Darius of Persia had given his permission and even support to enable them to do so. His prophecies deal with the entire period from his own day until the End of Days. The commentaries agree that Zechariah's prophetic visions are so esoteric that many will not be fully understood until the coming of Elijah the Prophet.

1:1. The month of Cheshvan.

1:2. That is, the Jews who lived at the time of the destruction of the Temple.

1:5. When I ask you, "Where are your fathers now?" you may counter, "The prophets died, as well!" My answer is that the prophets died natural deaths. But your forefathers suffered brutal death and exile, exactly as the prophets had foretold (*Rashi*).

1:7. That is, he was "to say" (to relate) his vision to the people.

1:8-9. Either the "man" (v. 8) and the "angel" (v. 9) are

1   ¹ In the eighth month, * in the second year of Darius, the word of HASHEM came to Zechariah son of Berechiah son of Iddo, the prophet, saying: ² HASHEM became wrathful with your forefathers, * wrath. ³ Say to [the people]:

Return to God   Thus said HASHEM, Master of Legions: Return unto Me — the word of HASHEM, Master of Legions — and I will return unto you, said HASHEM, Master of Legions. ⁴ Do not be like your fathers, to whom the prophets of old called out, saying, 'Thus said HASHEM, Master of Legions: Return, now, from your evil ways and from your evil deeds,' but they did not listen nor pay attention to Me — the word of HASHEM. ⁵ Your forefathers, where are they? And as for the prophets, could they live forever?* ⁶ However, My words and My decrees, which I commanded My servants the prophets, did they not befall your fathers? They repented and said, 'Just as HASHEM, Master of Legions, thought to do to us, according to our ways and our deeds, so did He with us.'

A strange vision   ⁷ On the twenty-fourth day of the eleventh month, which is the month of Shevat, in the second year of Darius, the word of HASHEM came to Zechariah son of Berechiah son of Iddo, the prophet, saying. * ⁸ I saw [a vision in] the night. There was a man* riding upon a red horse, and he was standing among myrtle bushes that were in a pool of water; behind him were horses: red, sorrel and white. ⁹ I said, "What are these, my lord?"

The angel* who was speaking to me said to me, "I will show you what these are!" ¹⁰ And the man who was standing among the myrtles spoke up and said, "These are the ones whom HASHEM has sent to travel about the earth."

¹¹ Then they* spoke up to the angel of HASHEM who was standing among the myrtles and said, "We have traveled about the earth, and behold, all the earth sits still and is at rest."

Plea for Jerusalem   ¹² The angel of HASHEM then spoke up and said, "HASHEM, Master of Legions, until when will You not have mercy upon Jerusalem and upon the cities of Judah, which You have spurned for these seventy years?" ¹³ HASHEM then answered favorable things to the angel who was speaking to me, words of comfort. *

¹⁴ The angel who was speaking to me then said to me:

Reassurance   Call out, saying, 'Thus said HASHEM, Master of Legions: I have become zealous for Jerusalem and for Zion, a great zeal; ¹⁵ and I am wrathful, a great wrath against the complacent nations, who, when I became slightly wrathful, augmented the evil. * ¹⁶ Therefore, thus said HASHEM: I have returned to Jerusalem in mercy; My Temple will be rebuilt in it — the word of HASHEM, Master of Legions — and a plumb line* will be stretched out over Jerusalem.'

¹⁷ Call out again, saying, 'Thus said HASHEM, Master of Legions: My cities will once again spread out with bounty; HASHEM will have mercy on Zion once again and He will choose Jerusalem once again.'

2   ¹ Then I lifted my eyes and looked, and behold four horns. ² I said to the angel who was speaking to me, "What are these?"

---

one and the same (*Kara; Ibn Ezra*); or they are two different angels (*Radak; Metzudos*).

1:11. They, the other horsemen, told their leader who was standing among the myrtles that while Jerusalem and the Land of Israel were in ruins, the rest of the world was dwelling in tranquility.

1:13. That message is recorded in verses 14-17 (*Radak*).

1:15. When I decreed that a nation be a "rod of punishment" for My people, they exceeded their mandate and magnified the ordained punishment many times over.

1:16. References to builders' tools will be used throughout. The sense of the verse is that Jerusalem will be rebuilt.

וַיֹּ֣אמֶר אֵלַ֔י אֵ֚לֶּה הַקְּרָנ֔וֹת אֲשֶׁ֥ר זֵר֖וּ אֶת־יְהוּדָ֖ה אֶת־יִשְׂרָאֵ֑ל

ג־ד וִירוּשָׁלָ֑͏ִם: וַיַּרְאֵ֣נִי יְהֹוָ֔ה אַרְבָּעָ֖ה חָרָשִֽׁים: וָאֹמַ֕ר מָ֛ה אֵ֥לֶּה בָאִ֖ים

לַעֲשׂ֑וֹת וַיֹּ֣אמֶר לֵאמֹ֔ר אֵ֣לֶּה הַקְּרָנ֗וֹת אֲשֶׁר־זֵר֤וּ אֶת־יְהוּדָה֙ כְּפִי־אִ֔ישׁ

לֹא־נָשָׂ֣א רֹאשׁ֔וֹ וַיָּבֹ֣אוּ אֵ֔לֶּה לְהַחֲרִ֣יד אֹתָ֔ם לְיַדּ֕וֹת אֶת־קַרְנ֥וֹת הַגּוֹיִ֖ם

ה הַנֹּשְׂאִ֥ים קֶ֛רֶן אֶל־אֶ֥רֶץ יְהוּדָ֖ה לְזָרוֹתָֽהּ: וָאֶשָּׂ֥א עֵינַ֖י וָאֵ֑רֶא

ו וְהִנֵּה־אִ֑ישׁ וּבְיָד֖וֹ חֶ֥בֶל מִדָּֽה: וָאֹמַ֕ר אָ֥נָה אַתָּ֖ה הֹלֵ֑ךְ וַיֹּ֣אמֶר אֵלַ֔י לָמֹ֖ד אֶת־

ז יְרוּשָׁלַ֔͏ִם לִרְא֥וֹת כַּמָּה־רָחְבָּ֖הּ וְכַמָּ֥ה אׇרְכָּֽהּ: וְהִנֵּ֗ה הַמַּלְאָ֛ךְ הַדֹּבֵ֥ר בִּ֖י יֹצֵ֑א

ח וּמַלְאָ֣ךְ אַחֵ֔ר יֹצֵ֖א לִקְרָאתֽוֹ: וַיֹּ֣אמֶר אֵלָ֔ו רֻ֗ץ דַּבֵּ֛ר אֶל־הַנַּ֥עַר הַלָּ֖ז לֵאמֹ֑ר

ט פְּרָז֖וֹת תֵּשֵׁ֣ב יְרוּשָׁלַ֑͏ִם מֵרֹ֥ב אָדָ֛ם וּבְהֵמָ֖ה בְּתוֹכָֽהּ: וַאֲנִ֨י אֶֽהְיֶה־לָּ֜הּ נְאֻם־

י יְהֹוָ֗ה חֽוֹמַת אֵ֣שׁ סָבִ֔יב וּלְכָב֖וֹד אֶֽהְיֶ֥ה בְתוֹכָֽהּ: ה֣וֹי ה֗וֹי וְנֻ֤סוּ

מֵאֶ֣רֶץ צָפ֔וֹן נְאֻם־יְהֹוָ֑ה כִּ֠י כְּאַרְבַּ֞ע רוּח֧וֹת הַשָּׁמַ֛יִם פֵּרַ֥שְׂתִּי אֶתְכֶ֖ם נְאֻם־

יא־יב יְהֹוָֽה: ה֥וֹי צִיּ֖וֹן הִמָּלְטִ֑י יוֹשֶׁ֖בֶת בַּת־בָּבֶֽל: כִּ֣י כֹ֣ה אָמַר֮ יְהֹוָ֣ה

צְבָאוֹת֒ אַחַ֣ר כָּב֔וֹד שְׁלָחַ֔נִי אֶל־הַגּוֹיִ֖ם הַשֹּׁלְלִ֣ים אֶתְכֶ֑ם כִּ֚י הַנֹּגֵ֣עַ בָּכֶ֔ם נֹגֵ֖עַ

יג בְּבָבַ֥ת עֵינֽוֹ: כִּ֠י הִנְנִ֨י מֵנִ֤יף אֶת־יָדִי֙ עֲלֵיהֶ֔ם וְהָי֥וּ שָׁלָ֖ל לְעַבְדֵיהֶ֑ם וִֽידַעְתֶּ֕ם

יד כִּֽי־יְהֹוָ֥ה צְבָא֖וֹת שְׁלָחָֽנִי: ◀ רׇנִּ֥י וְשִׂמְחִ֖י בַּת־צִיּ֑וֹן כִּ֧י הִנְנִי־בָ֛א

טו וְשָׁכַנְתִּ֥י בְתוֹכֵ֖ךְ נְאֻם־יְהֹוָֽה: וְנִלְו֩וּ גוֹיִ֨ם רַבִּ֤ים אֶל־יְהֹוָה֙ בַּיּ֣וֹם הַה֔וּא וְהָ֥יוּ לִ֖י

טז לְעָ֑ם וְשָׁכַנְתִּ֣י בְתוֹכֵ֔ךְ וְיָדַ֕עַתְּ כִּֽי־יְהֹוָ֥ה צְבָא֖וֹת שְׁלָחַ֣נִי אֵלָֽיִךְ: וְנָחַ֨ל יְהֹוָ֤ה

יז אֶת־יְהוּדָה֙ חֶלְק֔וֹ עַ֖ל אַדְמַ֣ת הַקֹּ֑דֶשׁ וּבָחַ֥ר ע֖וֹד בִּירֽוּשָׁלָֽ͏ִם: הַ֥ס כׇּל־בָּשָׂ֖ר

ג מִפְּנֵ֣י יְהֹוָ֑ה כִּ֥י נֵע֖וֹר מִמְּע֥וֹן קׇדְשֽׁוֹ: וַיַּרְאֵ֗נִי אֶת־יְהוֹשֻׁ֙עַ֙

א הַכֹּהֵ֣ן הַגָּד֔וֹל עֹמֵ֕ד לִפְנֵ֖י מַלְאַ֣ךְ יְהֹוָ֑ה וְהַשָּׂטָ֛ן עֹמֵ֥ד עַל־יְמִינ֖וֹ לְשִׂטְנֽוֹ:

ב וַיֹּ֣אמֶר יְהֹוָ֣ה אֶל־הַשָּׂטָ֡ן יִגְעַ֣ר יְהֹוָה֩ בְּךָ֨ הַשָּׂטָ֜ן וְיִגְעַ֤ר יְהֹוָה֙ בְּךָ֔ הַבֹּחֵ֖ר

ג בִּירֽוּשָׁלָ֑͏ִם הֲל֧וֹא זֶ֦ה א֖וּד מֻצָּ֣ל מֵאֵֽשׁ: וִיהוֹשֻׁ֕עַ הָיָ֥ה לָבֻ֖שׁ בְּגָדִ֣ים צוֹאִ֑ים

ד וְעֹמֵ֖ד לִפְנֵ֥י הַמַּלְאָֽךְ: וַיַּ֣עַן וַיֹּ֗אמֶר אֶל־הָעֹמְדִ֤ים לְפָנָיו֙ לֵאמֹ֔ר הָסִ֛ירוּ

הַבְּגָדִ֥ים הַצֹּאִ֖ים מֵֽעָלָ֑יו וַיֹּ֣אמֶר אֵלָ֗יו רְאֵ֨ה הֶעֱבַ֤רְתִּי מֵעָלֶ֙יךָ֙ עֲוֺנֶ֔ךָ וְהַלְבֵּ֥שׁ

ה אֹתְךָ֖ מַחֲלָצֽוֹת: וָאֹמַ֕ר יָשִׂ֛ימוּ צָנִ֥יף טָה֖וֹר עַל־רֹאשׁ֑וֹ וַיָּשִׂ֩ימוּ֩ הַצָּנִ֨יף

ו הַטָּה֜וֹר עַל־רֹאשׁ֗וֹ וַיַּלְבִּשֻׁ֙הוּ֙ בְּגָדִ֔ים וּמַלְאַ֥ךְ יְהֹוָ֖ה עֹמֵֽד: וַיָּ֙עַד֙ מַלְאַ֣ךְ יְהֹוָ֔ה

HAFTARAS
BEHA'ALOS-
CHA AND
SHABBAS
CHANUKAH
2:14-4:7

2:4. The four horns represent the "Four Kingdoms" — Babylonia, Persia-Media, Greece, Rome — that would persecute Israel, until the final Messianic Redemption. The four carpenters are the successive conquerors who would conquer those kingdoms. The fourth and final carpenter will be King Messiah (*Radak*).

2:7. The "man" with the line (*Rashi*).

2:8-9. The "new" angel told the one with the rope to measure Jerusalem, and to explain to the young man, i.e., Zechariah, that there was no reason to know the city's dimensions, because its population would grow continuously, and expand beyond its walls. Instead of an actual wall, the people would be protected by a Divine wall of fire.

2:10. Babylonia (see *Jeremiah* 1:14).

2:12. After God gives you the glory described in verse 9, He will send His prophet to punish your former persecutors.

2:17. Be silent, all wicked nations, for HASHEM is coming to avenge your oppression of Israel.

3:1. The confrontation between Joshua and Satan represents the contention between the Jews who were trying to rebuild the Temple and the local chieftains, who tried to halt the construction, as described in the fourth chapter of *Ezra* (*Radak*).

3:2. Joshua survived the Babylonian exile and, against all odds, returned to Jerusalem. This is an indication of his holiness and righteousness, and hence you should not

Horns of dispersion And he said to me, "These are the horns that dispersed Judah, Israel and Jerusalem."

³ HASHEM then showed me four carpenters. ⁴ I asked, "What are they coming to do?"

And He spoke, saying, "These horns that dispersed Judah, [humiliating them] until no man could raise his head — so these [carpenters] have come to terrify them, to cast down the horns of the nations who raise a horn against the [populace of the] land of Judah, to disperse it."*

Measuring Jerusalem . . . ⁵ Then I raised my eyes and looked, and behold, there was a man, and in his hand was a measuring line. ⁶ I asked, "Where are you going?"

And he answered me, "To measure Jerusalem, to see how wide its breadth and how long its length." ⁷ Just then the angel* who was speaking to me was going forth, and another angel was going forth toward him. ⁸ He said to him, "Run, speak to that young man over there, saying:

. . . growth beyond measure Jerusalem will be settled beyond its walls, because of the multitude of people and livestock within it.* ⁹ And I will be for it — the word of HASHEM — a wall of fire all around and for glory will I be in its midst. ¹⁰ Woe! Woe! Flee from the land of the north!* — the word of HASHEM — for I have scattered you like the four directions of the heavens — the word of HASHEM. ¹¹ Woe! O [exiles of] Zion. Escape, O you who dwell with the daughter Babylonia! ¹² For thus said HASHEM, Master of Legions, after glory,* He will send me to the nations who despoil you, for whoever touches you touches the pupil of his own eye. ¹³ For behold, I am waving My hand against them, and they will become spoils to those who had served them; then you will know that HASHEM, Master of Legions, has sent me.

The nations will join in ¹⁴ Sing and be glad, O daughter of Zion! For behold, I am coming and I will dwell in your midst — the word of HASHEM. ¹⁵ Many nations will join themselves to HASHEM on that day, and they will become a people unto Me; and I will dwell in your midst. Then you will know that HASHEM, Master of Legions, has sent me to you. ¹⁶ HASHEM will take Judah as His heritage, His portion upon the Holy Land, and He will choose Jerusalem again. ¹⁷ Be silent, all flesh,* before HASHEM, for He is aroused from His holy abode!"

3

Protection against the Satan ¹ Then He showed me Joshua, the Kohen Gadol, standing before the angel of HASHEM, and the Satan was standing on his right to accuse him.* ² [The angel of] HASHEM said to the Satan, "May HASHEM denounce you, O Satan! May HASHEM, Who chooses Jerusalem, denounce you! Indeed, this [man] is like a firebrand saved from a fire!"* ³ But Joshua was dressed in filthy garments* as he stood before the angel. ⁴ [The angel] spoke up and spoke to those standing before him, saying, "Remove the filthy garments from upon him!" Then he said to [Joshua], "See, I have removed your iniquity from upon you, and dressed you with clean attire."* ⁵ Then I said, "Let them put a pure turban on his head." So they put a pure turban on his head and they dressed him in [clean] garments, while the angel of HASHEM [remained] standing. ⁶ The angel of HASHEM then warned

---

harass him (*Rashi*).

3:3. There was a "stain" on Joshua's family — his own sons had married non-Jewish wives [see *Ezra* 10:18] (*Targum, Radak*).

3:4. The angel commanded that Joshua's sons leave their forbidden wives; with the filthy garments removed from him, Joshua's innate righteousness was no longer blemished (*Rashi*).

בְּיהוֹשֻׁעַ לֵאמֹר: כֹּה־אָמַר יהוה צְבָאוֹת אִם־בִּדְרָכַי תֵּלֵךְ וְאִם אֶת־ ז
מִשְׁמַרְתִּי תִשְׁמֹר וְגַם־אַתָּה תָּדִין אֶת־בֵּיתִי וְגַם תִּשְׁמֹר אֶת־חֲצֵרָי
וְנָתַתִּי לְךָ מַהְלְכִים בֵּין הָעֹמְדִים הָאֵלֶּה: שְׁמַע־נָא יְהוֹשֻׁעַ ׀ הַכֹּהֵן הַגָּדוֹל ח
אַתָּה וְרֵעֶיךָ הַיֹּשְׁבִים לְפָנֶיךָ כִּי־אַנְשֵׁי מוֹפֵת הֵמָּה כִּי־הִנְנִי מֵבִיא אֶת־
עַבְדִּי צֶמַח: כִּי ׀ הִנֵּה הָאֶבֶן אֲשֶׁר נָתַתִּי לִפְנֵי יְהוֹשֻׁעַ עַל־אֶבֶן אַחַת ט
שִׁבְעָה עֵינָיִם הִנְנִי מְפַתֵּחַ פִּתֻּחָהּ נְאֻם יהוה צְבָאוֹת וּמַשְׁתִּי אֶת־עֲוֹן
הָאָרֶץ־הַהִיא בְּיוֹם אֶחָד: בַּיּוֹם הַהוּא נְאֻם יהוה צְבָאוֹת תִּקְרְאוּ אִישׁ י
לְרֵעֵהוּ אֶל־תַּחַת גֶּפֶן וְאֶל־תַּחַת תְּאֵנָה:

ד וַיָּשָׁב הַמַּלְאָךְ א
הַדֹּבֵר בִּי וַיְעִירֵנִי כְּאִישׁ אֲשֶׁר־יֵעוֹר מִשְּׁנָתוֹ: וַיֹּאמֶר אֵלַי מָה אַתָּה רֹאֶה ב
°וָאֹמַר [וָאֹמַר קרי] רָאִיתִי וְהִנֵּה מְנוֹרַת זָהָב כֻּלָּהּ וְגֻלָּהּ עַל־רֹאשָׁהּ
וְשִׁבְעָה נֵרֹתֶיהָ עָלֶיהָ שִׁבְעָה וְשִׁבְעָה מוּצָקוֹת לַנֵּרוֹת אֲשֶׁר עַל־רֹאשָׁהּ:
וּשְׁנַיִם זֵיתִים עָלֶיהָ אֶחָד מִימִין הַגֻּלָּה וְאֶחָד עַל־שְׂמֹאלָהּ: וָאַעַן וָאֹמַר ג-ד
אֶל־הַמַּלְאָךְ הַדֹּבֵר בִּי לֵאמֹר מָה אֵלֶּה אֲדֹנִי: וַיַּעַן הַמַּלְאָךְ הַדֹּבֵר בִּי ה
וַיֹּאמֶר אֵלַי הֲלוֹא יָדַעְתָּ מָה־הֵמָּה אֵלֶּה וָאֹמַר לֹא אֲדֹנִי: וַיַּעַן וַיֹּאמֶר ו
אֵלַי לֵאמֹר זֶה דְּבַר־יהוה אֶל־זְרֻבָּבֶל לֵאמֹר לֹא בְחַיִל וְלֹא בְכֹחַ כִּי
אִם־בְּרוּחִי אָמַר יהוה צְבָאוֹת: מִי־אַתָּה הַר־הַגָּדוֹל לִפְנֵי זְרֻבָּבֶל ז
לְמִישֹׁר וְהוֹצִיא אֶת־הָאֶבֶן הָרֹאשָׁה תְּשֻׁאוֹת חֵן חֵן לָהּ: ◂ וַיְהִי ח
דְבַר־יהוה אֵלַי לֵאמֹר: יְדֵי זְרֻבָּבֶל יִסְּדוּ הַבַּיִת הַזֶּה וְיָדָיו תְּבַצַּעְנָה ט
וְיָדַעְתָּ כִּי־יהוה צְבָאוֹת שְׁלָחַנִי אֲלֵכֶם: כִּי מִי בַז לְיוֹם קְטַנּוֹת וְשָׂמְחוּ י
וְרָאוּ אֶת־הָאֶבֶן הַבְּדִיל בְּיַד זְרֻבָּבֶל שִׁבְעָה־אֵלֶּה עֵינֵי יהוה הֵמָּה
מְשׁוֹטְטִים בְּכָל־הָאָרֶץ: וָאַעַן וָאֹמַר אֵלָיו מַה־שְׁנֵי הַזֵּיתִים הָאֵלֶּה יא
עַל־יְמִין הַמְּנוֹרָה וְעַל־שְׂמֹאוֹלָהּ: וָאַעַן שֵׁנִית וָאֹמַר אֵלָיו מַה־שְׁתֵּי יב
שִׁבֲּלֵי הַזֵּיתִים אֲשֶׁר בְּיַד שְׁנֵי צַנְתְּרוֹת הַזָּהָב הַמְרִיקִים מֵעֲלֵיהֶם הַזָּהָב:
וַיֹּאמֶר אֵלַי לֵאמֹר הֲלוֹא יָדַעְתָּ מָה־אֵלֶּה וָאֹמַר לֹא אֲדֹנִי: וַיֹּאמֶר אֵלֶּה יג-יד
ה שְׁנֵי בְנֵי־הַיִּצְהָר הָעֹמְדִים עַל־אֲדוֹן כָּל־הָאָרֶץ: א
וָאָשׁוּב וָאֶשָּׂא עֵינַי וָאֶרְאֶה וְהִנֵּה מְגִלָּה עָפָה: וַיֹּאמֶר אֵלַי מָה אַתָּה רֹאֶה ב

3:7. You will be granted eternal life among the angels in the afterworld (*Targum*).

3:8. To Joshua and his great companions, the angel gave the welcome assurance that God's flourishing servant — either Zerubbabel (*Ibn Ezra; Radak*) or the Messiah (*Targum*) — will complete the rebuilding of the Temple.

3:9. When God brings about the construction of the Temple, its cornerstone will, figuratively, have all eyes upon it and be adorned with beautiful engravings.

3:10. An indication of the prosperity and tranquility that will prevail at that time.

4:2. The oil from the bowl flowed through seven ducts into each of the lamps.

4:6. Just as the olive trees in the vision produce oil because that is what God created them to do, so Israel would rebuild the Temple because that is what God wanted. They did not succeed because of their army or their strength, but because God inspired Darius with a spirit of kindness that provided the initiative for the construction and a major part of the needed supplies (*Rashi*).

4:7. All obstacles and opponents facing Zerubbabel will be cleared away, and the people will cheer him on as he puts his tools of construction to work (*Rashi*).

4:10. The Second Temple was a humble structure compared to the Temple of Solomon. Laying its foundation was a disappointing experience for those who

The Kohen Gadol at his post

Joshua, saying, ⁷ "Thus said HASHEM, Master of Legions: If you go in My ways, and if you will safeguard My watch, and you also administer My Temple, and you will also guard My courtyards, then I will grant you strides among these [angels] who stand here.* ⁸ Listen, now, O, Joshua, the Kohen Gadol: you and your companions who are sitting before you, for they are men [worthy] of a miracle — for behold, I am bringing My servant, Zemah [the flourishing one].* ⁹ For behold, the [foundation] stone that I have placed before Joshua — seven eyes toward one stone;* behold I am engraving its adornment — the word of HASHEM, Master of Legions — and I will remove the iniquity of that land on one day. ¹⁰ On that day — the word of HASHEM, Master of Legions — each man will invite his fellow beneath the vine and beneath the fig tree."*

4

Vision of the menorah

¹ Then the angel who was speaking with me returned and woke me, as a man is awakened from his sleep. ² He said to me, "What do you see?"

I said, "I see and behold — there is a menorah [made] entirely of gold with its bowl on its top; its seven lamps are upon it, and there are seven ducts for [each of] the lamps on its top.* ³ There are two olive trees over it, one at the right of the bowl and one on its left." ⁴ I spoke up and said to the angel who was speaking to me, saying, "What are these, my lord?"

⁵ The angel who was speaking to me answered, and said to me, "Do you not know what these are?"

And I said, "No, my lord!"

Only through My spirit

⁶ He spoke up and said to me, saying, "This is the word of HASHEM to Zerubbabel, saying, 'Not through army and not through strength, but through My spirit,' said HASHEM, Master of Legions.'* ⁷ Who are you, O great mountain? Before Zerubbabel [you will] become a plain! He will bring out the cornerstone, with cheers of 'Grace! Grace!' for it."*

⁸ The word of HASHEM then came to me, saying, ⁹ "The hands of Zerubbabel laid the foundations of this Temple and his hands will complete it; then you will know that HASHEM, Master of Legions, has sent me to you. ¹⁰ For who is scornful on the day of small things?* They will rejoice when they see the stone of the plumb line in the hand of Zerubbabel, [building] seven times as much. The eyes of HASHEM — they scan the whole world!"*

¹¹ I then spoke up and said to him, "What are these two olive trees, on the right of the menorah and on its left?" ¹² I spoke up a second time and said to him, "What are the two clusters of olives that are next to the two golden presses, which are pouring golden [oil] from themselves?"

¹³ He spoke to me, saying, "Do you not know what these are?"

And I said, "No, my lord!"

The two anointed men

¹⁴ He said, "These are the two anointed men who are standing by the Lord of all the land."*

5

¹ Once again I raised my eyes and looked, and behold, a scroll was flying. ² He said to me, "What do you see?"

---

remembered the magnificence of the First Temple (see *Ezra* 3:12, *Haggai* 2:3), but eventually, the building would be seven times more imposing than it is now (*Rashi*).

And its builder is Zerubbabel, whom God has chosen

from all people of the world, as the one fit to execute this task (*Rashi*).

4:14. Zerubbabel (scion of King David) and Joshua the Kohen Gadol. Originally, both a king and a *Kohen Gadol* were anointed.

וָאֹמַר אֲנִי רֹאֶה מְגִלָּה עָפָה אָרְכָּהּ עֶשְׂרִים בָּאַמָּה וְרָחְבָּהּ עֶשֶׂר בָּאַמָּה:

ג וַיֹּאמֶר אֵלַי זֹאת הָאָלָה הַיּוֹצֵאת עַל־פְּנֵי כָל־הָאָרֶץ כִּי כָל־הַגֹּנֵב מִזֶּה

ד כָּמוֹהָ נִקָּה וְכָל־הַנִּשְׁבָּע מִזֶּה כָּמוֹהָ נִקָּה: הוֹצֵאתִיהָ נְאֻם יְהוָה צְבָאוֹת

וּבָאָה אֶל־בֵּית הַגַּנָּב וְאֶל־בֵּית הַנִּשְׁבָּע בִּשְׁמִי לַשָּׁקֶר וְלָנֶה בְּתוֹךְ בֵּיתוֹ

ה וְכִלַּתּוּ וְאֶת־עֵצָיו וְאֶת־אֲבָנָיו: וַיֵּצֵא הַמַּלְאָךְ הַדֹּבֵר בִּי וַיֹּאמֶר אֵלַי שָׂא

ו נָא עֵינֶיךָ וּרְאֵה מָה הַיּוֹצֵאת הַזֹּאת: וָאֹמַר מַה־הִיא וַיֹּאמֶר זֹאת הָאֵיפָה

ז הַיּוֹצֵאת וַיֹּאמֶר זֹאת עֵינָם בְּכָל־הָאָרֶץ: וְהִנֵּה כִּכַּר עֹפֶרֶת נִשֵּׂאת וְזֹאת

ח אִשָּׁה אַחַת יוֹשֶׁבֶת בְּתוֹךְ הָאֵיפָה: וַיֹּאמֶר זֹאת הָרִשְׁעָה וַיַּשְׁלֵךְ אֹתָהּ

ט אֶל־תּוֹךְ הָאֵיפָה וַיַּשְׁלֵךְ אֶת־אֶבֶן הָעֹפֶרֶת אֶל־פִּיהָ: וָאֶשָּׂא

עֵינַי וָאֵרֶא וְהִנֵּה שְׁתַּיִם נָשִׁים יוֹצְאוֹת וְרוּחַ בְּכַנְפֵיהֶם וְלָהֵנָּה

כְנָפַיִם כְּכַנְפֵי הַחֲסִידָה וַתִּשֶּׂאנָה אֶת־הָאֵיפָה בֵּין הָאָרֶץ וּבֵין הַשָּׁמָיִם:

י וָאֹמַר אֶל־הַמַּלְאָךְ הַדֹּבֵר בִּי אָנָה הֵמָּה מוֹלִכוֹת אֶת־הָאֵיפָה:

יא וַיֹּאמֶר אֵלַי לִבְנוֹת־לָהּ בַיִת בְּאֶרֶץ שִׁנְעָר וְהוּכַן וְהֻנִּיחָה שָּׁם עַל־

א מְכֻנָתָהּ:   וָאָשֻׁב וָאֶשָּׂא עֵינַי וָאֶרְאֶה וְהִנֵּה אַרְבַּע מַרְכָּבוֹת

ו

ב יֹצְאוֹת מִבֵּין שְׁנֵי הֶהָרִים וְהֶהָרִים הָרֵי נְחֹשֶׁת: בַּמֶּרְכָּבָה הָרִאשֹׁנָה

ג סוּסִים אֲדֻמִּים וּבַמֶּרְכָּבָה הַשֵּׁנִית סוּסִים שְׁחֹרִים: וּבַמֶּרְכָּבָה הַשְּׁלִשִׁית

ד סוּסִים לְבָנִים וּבַמֶּרְכָּבָה הָרְבִעִית סוּסִים בְּרֻדִּים אֲמֻצִּים: וָאַעַן וָאֹמַר

ה אֶל־הַמַּלְאָךְ הַדֹּבֵר בִּי מָה־אֵלֶּה אֲדֹנִי: וַיַּעַן הַמַּלְאָךְ וַיֹּאמֶר אֵלַי אֵלֶּה

ו אַרְבַּע רֻחוֹת הַשָּׁמַיִם יוֹצְאוֹת מֵהִתְיַצֵּב עַל־אֲדוֹן כָּל־הָאָרֶץ: אֲשֶׁר־בָּהּ

הַסּוּסִים הַשְּׁחֹרִים יֹצְאִים אֶל־אֶרֶץ צָפוֹן וְהַלְּבָנִים יָצְאוּ אֶל־אַחֲרֵיהֶם

ז וְהַבְּרֻדִּים יָצְאוּ אֶל־אֶרֶץ הַתֵּימָן: וְהָאֲמֻצִּים יָצְאוּ וַיְבַקְשׁוּ לָלֶכֶת

ח לְהִתְהַלֵּךְ בָּאָרֶץ וַיֹּאמֶר לְכוּ הִתְהַלְּכוּ בָאָרֶץ וַתִּתְהַלַּכְנָה בָּאָרֶץ: וַיַּזְעֵק

אֹתִי וַיְדַבֵּר אֵלַי לֵאמֹר רְאֵה הַיּוֹצְאִים אֶל־אֶרֶץ צָפוֹן הֵנִיחוּ אֶת־רוּחִי

ט בְּאֶרֶץ צָפוֹן: וַיְהִי דְבַר־יְהוָה אֵלַי לֵאמֹר: לָקוֹחַ מֵאֵת הַגּוֹלָה

מֵחֶלְדַּי וּמֵאֵת טוֹבִיָּה וּמֵאֵת יְדַעְיָה וּבָאתָ אַתָּה בַּיּוֹם הַהוּא וּבָאתָ בֵּית

יא יֹאשִׁיָּה בֶן־צְפַנְיָה אֲשֶׁר־בָּאוּ מִבָּבֶל: וְלָקַחְתָּ כֶסֶף־וְזָהָב וְעָשִׂיתָ עֲטָרוֹת

יב וְשַׂמְתָּ בְּרֹאשׁ יְהוֹשֻׁעַ בֶּן־יְהוֹצָדָק הַכֹּהֵן הַגָּדוֹל: וְאָמַרְתָּ אֵלָיו לֵאמֹר

כֹּה אָמַר יְהוָה צְבָאוֹת לֵאמֹר הִנֵּה־אִישׁ צֶמַח שְׁמוֹ וּמִתַּחְתָּיו יִצְמָח

5:2. These are the dimensions of the Sanctuary doorway, from which the scroll was emerging (*Rashi*).

5:3. Up to now, I have been lenient with sinners, but now I will begin to carry out the curses written in this scroll.

5:5. Something else was emerging from the Temple (*Rashi*).

5:6. A large measuring vessel, to measure out punishment to the wicked, because their greed has caused them to covet whatever they could see (*Rashi*).

5:7-11. The *ephah* and the lead symbolize the sin of false weights and measures that led to the exile, in which the people were carried off from their land to Babylonia [see v. 11] (*Kara*).

The woman of "Wickedness" symbolized the state of the nation. She would be carried off by an alliance of Babylonia and Chaldea, and her very sins would become the basis of her seventy-year Babylonian exile (*Rashi*).

5:11. Another name for Babylonia (see *Genesis* 10:10).

6:1. To carry the decrees of Heaven out to the four corners of the earth (*Ibn Ezra*). According to *Targum* and

I answered, "I see a flying scroll: twenty cubits its width and ten cubits its length." *

Retribution to the wicked

³ *He said to me, "This is the curse that is going out over the surface of the whole land. For [heretofore] anyone who steals has been absolved of such a curse;* * *and everyone who swears [falsely] has been absolved of such a curse.* ⁴ *I have taken it out [the curse] — the word of* HASHEM, *Master of Legions — and it shall enter the house of the thief and the house of the one who swears falsely in My Name, and it shall lodge within his house and annihilate it, with its wood and stones."*

⁵ *Then the angel who was speaking to me went forth and said to me, "Raise your eyes and see what this emerging thing is."* *

⁶ *I said, "What is it?"*

And he said, "This is an ephah * *that is emerging." And he said, "This, [because] their [greedy] eyes are in all the land."* ⁷ *Then, behold, a block of lead was being lifted,* * *and this one woman was sitting inside the ephah.* ⁸ *And he said, "This [woman] is Wickedness," and he threw her into the ephah and threw the lead weight into her mouth.*

⁹ *Then I raised my eyes and looked, and behold two women were emerging with wind in their wings, for they had wings like a stork's wings, and they lifted the ephah between the earth and the heavens.* ¹⁰ *I said to the angel who was speaking to me, "Where are they taking the ephah?"* ¹¹ *He said to me, "To build her a house in the land of Shinar;* * *it will be established, and she will be set down there on her base."*

6

Vision of the chariots

¹ *Once again I raised up my eyes and saw, and behold, four chariots* * *were emerging from between two mountains, and the mountains were mountains of copper.* ² *In the first chariot there were red horses, in the second chariot there were black horses,* ³ *in the third chariot there were white horses, and in the fourth chariot there were spotted, gray horses.* ⁴ *I spoke up and said to the angel who was speaking to me, "What are these, my lord?"*

⁵ *The angel answered and said to me, "These are going out [to] the four directions of the heavens, from standing before the Lord of all the earth.* ⁶ *[The chariot] within which are the black horses . . . they are going forth to the land of the north, and the white ones went forth after them; the spotted ones went forth to the land of the south.* ⁷ *The gray ones went forth and asked to go, to travel, through the world: He said, 'Go, travel through the world,' so they traveled through the world."*

⁸ *He then summoned me and he spoke to me, saying, "See, the ones going out to the land of the north have allayed My anger in the land of the north."* *

Let the exiles contribute . . .

⁹ *The word of* HASHEM *came to me, saying,* ¹⁰ *"Take from the exiles — from Heldai, from Tobijah and from Jedaiah. Come on that day; come to the household of Josiah son of Zephaniah, who have come from Babylonia,* * ¹¹ *and take silver and gold and make crowns, and place [one of them] on the head of Joshua son of Jehozadak, the Kohen Gadol.* * ¹² *Say to him, 'Thus said* HASHEM, *Master of Legions: Behold, there is a man, his name is Zemah,* * *and he will flourish in his place;*

---

many commentators, they represent the four kingdoms that had dominion over Israel after the destruction of the Temple — Babylonia, Persia-Media, Greece and Rome.

6:8. They brought punishment upon the land of the north, i.e., Babylonia, thus alleviating My anger against them. Then, Jews in that realm would be safe (*Ibn Ezra*).

6:10. All those mentioned in this verse come from Babylonia.

6:11. These men had contributed gold and silver for the Temple. Zechariah was to use it to make two crowns (*Radak*).

6:12. Lit., flourishing (see 3:8).

יג וּבָנָה אֶת־הֵיכַל יהוה וְהוּא־יִבְנֶה אֶת־הֵיכַל יהוה וְהוּא־יִשָּׂא הוֹד וְיָשַׁב
וּמָשַׁל עַל־כִּסְאוֹ וְהָיָה כֹהֵן עַל־כִּסְאוֹ וַעֲצַת שָׁלוֹם תִּהְיֶה בֵּין שְׁנֵיהֶם:
יד וְהָעֲטָרֹת תִּהְיֶה לְחֵלֶם וּלְטוֹבִיָּה וְלִידַעְיָה וּלְחֵן בֶּן־צְפַנְיָה לְזִכָּרוֹן בְּהֵיכַל
יהוה: טו וּרְחוֹקִים ׀ יָבֹאוּ וּבָנוּ בְּהֵיכַל יהוה וִידַעְתֶּם כִּי־יהוה צְבָאוֹת שְׁלָחַנִי

ז א אֲלֵיכֶם וְהָיָה אִם־שָׁמוֹעַ תִּשְׁמְעוּן בְּקוֹל יהוה אֱלֹהֵיכֶם: וַיְהִי
בִּשְׁנַת אַרְבַּע לְדָרְיָוֶשׁ הַמֶּלֶךְ הָיָה דְבַר־יהוה אֶל־זְכַרְיָה בְּאַרְבָּעָה
ב לַחֹדֶשׁ הַתְּשִׁעִי בְּכִסְלֵו: וַיִּשְׁלַח בֵּית־אֵל שַׂר־אֶצֶר וְרֶגֶם מֶלֶךְ וַאֲנָשָׁיו
ג לְחַלּוֹת אֶת־פְּנֵי יהוה: לֵאמֹר אֶל־הַכֹּהֲנִים אֲשֶׁר לְבֵית־יהוה צְבָאוֹת
וְאֶל־הַנְּבִיאִים לֵאמֹר הַאֶבְכֶּה בַּחֹדֶשׁ הַחֲמִשִׁי הִנָּזֵר כַּאֲשֶׁר עָשִׂיתִי זֶה
ד-ה כַּמֶּה שָׁנִים: וַיְהִי דְּבַר־יהוה צְבָאוֹת אֵלַי לֵאמֹר: אֱמֹר אֶל־
כָּל־עַם הָאָרֶץ וְאֶל־הַכֹּהֲנִים לֵאמֹר כִּי־צַמְתֶּם וְסָפוֹד בַּחֲמִישִׁי וּבַשְּׁבִיעִי
ו וְזֶה שִׁבְעִים שָׁנָה הֲצוֹם צַמְתֻּנִי אָנִי: וְכִי תֹאכְלוּ וְכִי תִשְׁתּוּ הֲלוֹא אַתֶּם
ז הָאֹכְלִים וְאַתֶּם הַשֹּׁתִים: הֲלוֹא אֶת־הַדְּבָרִים אֲשֶׁר קָרָא יהוה בְּיַד
הַנְּבִיאִים הָרִאשֹׁנִים בִּהְיוֹת יְרוּשָׁלַ͏ִם יֹשֶׁבֶת וּשְׁלֵוָה וְעָרֶיהָ סְבִיבֹתֶיהָ
ח-ט וְהַנֶּגֶב וְהַשְּׁפֵלָה יֹשֵׁב: וַיְהִי דְּבַר־יהוה אֶל־זְכַרְיָה לֵאמֹר: כֹּה
אָמַר יהוה צְבָאוֹת לֵאמֹר מִשְׁפַּט אֱמֶת שְׁפֹטוּ וְחֶסֶד וְרַחֲמִים עֲשׂוּ אִישׁ
י אֶת־אָחִיו: וְאַלְמָנָה וְיָתוֹם גֵּר וְעָנִי אַל־תַּעֲשֹׁקוּ וְרָעַת אִישׁ אָחִיו אַל־
יא תַּחְשְׁבוּ בִּלְבַבְכֶם: וַיְמָאֲנוּ לְהַקְשִׁיב וַיִּתְּנוּ כָתֵף סֹרָרֶת וְאָזְנֵיהֶם הִכְבִּידוּ
יב מִשְּׁמוֹעַ: וְלִבָּם שָׂמוּ שָׁמִיר מִשְּׁמוֹעַ אֶת־הַתּוֹרָה וְאֶת־הַדְּבָרִים אֲשֶׁר
שָׁלַח יהוה צְבָאוֹת בְּרוּחוֹ בְּיַד הַנְּבִיאִים הָרִאשֹׁנִים וַיְהִי קֶצֶף גָּדוֹל מֵאֵת
יג יהוה צְבָאוֹת: וַיְהִי כַאֲשֶׁר־קָרָא וְלֹא שָׁמֵעוּ כֵּן יִקְרְאוּ וְלֹא אֶשְׁמָע אָמַר
יד יהוה צְבָאוֹת: וְאֵסָעֲרֵם עַל כָּל־הַגּוֹיִם אֲשֶׁר לֹא־יְדָעוּם וְהָאָרֶץ נָשַׁמָּה
ח א אַחֲרֵיהֶם מֵעֹבֵר וּמִשָּׁב וַיָּשִׂימוּ אֶרֶץ־חֶמְדָּה לְשַׁמָּה: וַיְהִי
ב דְּבַר־יהוה צְבָאוֹת לֵאמֹר: כֹּה אָמַר יהוה צְבָאוֹת קִנֵּאתִי לְצִיּוֹן קִנְאָה
ג גְדוֹלָה וְחֵמָה גְדוֹלָה קִנֵּאתִי לָהּ: כֹּה אָמַר יהוה שַׁבְתִּי אֶל־צִיּוֹן וְשָׁכַנְתִּי

6:13. Zerubbabel will wear the other crown (*Ibn Ezra*; *Radak*).

Though the governor and the *Kohen Gadol* will each have his own separate throne, there will not be animosity between them (*Ibn Ezra*; *Radak*).

6:14. The crowns were later placed inside the Sanctuary, where they memorialized the generosity of these men who had contributed the gold and silver from which they were fashioned (*Radak*).

7:2-3. These were righteous Jews in the diaspora who asked whether they were still required to observe the fast of the fifth month [i.e., the Ninth of Av; the question included the other fasts that commemorate the Destruction (see v. 5), but only the day of the worst tragedy is mentioned], to mourn the destruction of the First Temple. Since a new Temple was being built, was it still

appropriate to fast? (*Rashi*). Alternatively: They doubted that the construction would be completed (*Radak*). Alternatively: Despite the new construction, they were still subjects of Persia (*Metzudos*).

Zechariah's answer, which continues until 8:19, is rather vague. The Talmud (*Rosh Hashanah* 18b) explains that when the Temple is functioning, then: (a) If the land is under oppressive foreign domination, all the fasts remain in force; (b) if the land is under benign foreign domination, the Ninth of Av remains a fast day, but the other fasts are voluntary; (c) if the land is free of foreign domination, the former fast days are celebrated as festive days.

7:3. From those pleasures prohibited by the mourning of that day.

7:5. The Fast of Gedaliah is on the third day of Tish-

<table>
<tr><td>

... to build
the Temple

</td><td>

he will build the Sanctuary of HASHEM. [13] He will build the Sanctuary of HASHEM; he will bear majesty, * and he will sit and rule upon his throne. The Kohen will be upon his own throne, and there will be a disposition of peace between the two of them. * [14] The crowns will be a remembrance for Helem, for Tobijah, for Jedaiah and for Hen son of Zephaniah in the Sanctuary of HASHEM.'* [15] People from far away will come and build the Sanctuary of HASHEM, and then you will know that HASHEM, Master of Legions, has sent me to you. This will happen if you truly listen to the voice of HASHEM your God."

</td></tr>
</table>

7

Should we
still mourn?

[1] It happened in the fourth year of King Darius that the word of HASHEM came to Zechariah, on the fourth day of the ninth month, in Kislev. [2] Sarezer, as well as Regem-melech and his associates, had sent a message to Beth-el, * to beseech HASHEM, [3] [and] to speak [their question] to the Kohanim of the Temple of HASHEM, Master of Legions, and to the prophets, saying, "Should I weep in the fifth month, abstaining [from pleasures], * as I have been doing for many years?"

[4] So the word of HASHEM, Master of Legions, came to me, saying:

Why did
you fast?

[5] Speak to all the people of the land and the Kohanim, saying, 'When you fasted and mourned in the fifth [month] and in the seventh * for these seventy years, was the fasting that you fasted for My honor? [Was it] for Me?* [6] And when you eat and when you drink, is it not you who are the eaters and you who are the drinkers? [7] Behold, [consider] the prophecies that HASHEM pronounced through the earliest prophets, when Jerusalem and its surrounding cities were settled and peaceful, and the south and the lowlands were settled.'

[8] The word of HASHEM came to Zechariah, saying:

God
demanded
kindness ...

[9] Thus spoke HASHEM, Master of Legions, saying: 'Judge with truthful justice, and perform kindness and mercy towards one another. [10] Do not oppress the widow and the orphan, the stranger and the poor, and do not think in your hearts of wronging one another.' [11] But they refused to heed, and they turned a rebellious shoulder, they made their ears hard of hearing. [12] They made their hearts like hard iron, rather than hear the teaching and the words that HASHEM, Master of Legions, had sent by His spirit through the earliest prophets, and there was a great rage from HASHEM, Master of Legions.

... but they
refused

[13] And it happened that just as He had called, but they did not listen, 'So will they call out and I will not listen,' said HASHEM, Master of Legions; [14] 'and I will cause them to be storm-tossed among all the nations that they did not know. After that the land became deserted from any who come and go; they made an exquisite land into a desolation.

8

Zeal
for Zion

[1] The word of HASHEM, Master of Legions, came [to me], saying:

[2] Thus said HASHEM, Master of Legions: I have become zealous with great zeal on behalf of Zion; I have become zealous with great wrath on its behalf. * [3] Thus said HASHEM: I have returned to Zion, and I have made My dwelling

---

rei, the seventh month. It commemorates the assassination of Gedaliah, whom Nebuchadnezzar had appointed as governor of the Jewish community after the Destruction. After Gedaliah was assassinated, the remnant still in Jerusalem was exiled (see *Jeremiah*, Chs. 40-41).

7:5-7. God replies that He did not decide that they should fast. They had to fast because of the disaster

brought about by their sins, and because they ignored the exhortations of the prophets when the nation was still secure, when repentance could have saved them. If they would put an end to their sins, they would have no reason to fast (*Radak*).

8:2. This is a chapter of comfort. At the end of the exile, God will direct His zeal to the defense of Jerusalem and vengeance against its enemies.

בְּתוֹךְ יְרוּשָׁלָ֑ם וְנִקְרְאָ֧ה יְרוּשָׁלַ֛ם עִ֥יר הָאֱמֶ֖ת וְהַר־יְהֹוָ֥ה צְבָא֖וֹת הַ֥ר

ד הַקֹּֽדֶשׁ:   כֹּ֤ה אָמַר֙ יְהֹוָ֣ה צְבָא֔וֹת עֹ֥ד יֵֽשְׁב֛וּ זְקֵנִ֥ים וּזְקֵנ֖וֹת בִּרְחֹב֣וֹת

ה יְרֽוּשָׁלָ֑ם וְאִ֧ישׁ מִשְׁעַנְתּ֛וֹ בְּיָד֖וֹ מֵרֹ֥ב יָמִֽים: וּרְחֹב֤וֹת הָעִיר֙ יִמָּ֣לְא֔וּ יְלָדִ֖ים

ו וִֽילָד֑וֹת מְשַׂחֲקִ֖ים בִּרְחֹֽבֹתֶֽיהָ:   כֹּ֤ה אָמַר֙ יְהֹוָ֣ה צְבָא֔וֹת כִּ֣י

יִפָּלֵ֗א בְּעֵינֵי֙ שְׁאֵרִית֙ הָעָ֣ם הַזֶּ֔ה בַּיָּמִ֖ים הָהֵ֑ם גַּם־בְּעֵינַי֙ יִפָּלֵ֔א נְאֻ֖ם יְהֹוָ֥ה

ז צְבָאֽוֹת: כֹּ֤ה אָמַר֙ יְהֹוָ֣ה צְבָא֔וֹת הִנְנִ֥י מוֹשִׁ֛יעַ אֶת־עַמִּ֖י מֵאֶ֥רֶץ

ח מִזְרָ֑ח וּמֵאֶ֖רֶץ מְב֣וֹא הַשָּֽׁמֶשׁ: וְהֵבֵאתִ֣י אֹתָ֔ם וְשָֽׁכְנ֖וּ בְּת֣וֹךְ יְרֽוּשָׁלָ֑ם וְהָֽיוּ־

ט לִ֣י לְעָ֗ם וַֽאֲנִי֙ אֶֽהְיֶ֤ה לָהֶם֙ לֵֽאלֹהִ֔ים בֶּֽאֱמֶ֖ת וּבִצְדָקָֽה: כֹּ֤ה־אָמַר֙

יְהֹוָ֣ה צְבָא֔וֹת תֶּֽחֱזַ֣קְנָה יְדֵיכֶ֔ם הַשֹּֽׁמְעִים֙ בַּיָּמִ֣ים הָאֵ֔לֶּה אֵ֖ת הַדְּבָרִ֣ים

הָאֵ֑לֶּה מִפִּי֙ הַנְּבִיאִ֔ים אֲשֶׁ֗ר בְּי֛וֹם יֻסַּ֥ד בֵּֽית־יְהֹוָ֥ה צְבָא֖וֹת הַהֵיכָ֥ל לְהִבָּנֽוֹת:

י כִּ֗י לִפְנֵי֙ הַיָּמִ֣ים הָהֵ֔ם שְׂכַ֤ר הָֽאָדָם֙ לֹ֣א נִֽהְיָ֔ה וּשְׂכַ֥ר הַבְּהֵמָ֖ה אֵינֶ֑נָּה וְלַיּוֹצֵ֨א

וְלַבָּ֜א אֵֽין־שָׁל֗וֹם מִן־הַצָּ֔ר וַֽאֲשַׁלַּ֥ח אֶת־כָּל־הָֽאָדָ֖ם אִ֥ישׁ בְּרֵעֵֽהוּ: וְעַתָּ֗ה

יא יב לֹ֣א כַיָּמִ֤ים הָרִֽאשֹׁנִים֙ אֲנִ֔י לִשְׁאֵרִ֛ית הָעָ֥ם הַזֶּ֖ה נְאֻ֥ם יְהֹוָ֥ה צְבָאֽוֹת: כִּֽי־

זֶ֣רַע הַשָּׁל֗וֹם הַגֶּ֜פֶן תִּתֵּ֤ן פִּרְיָהּ֙ וְהָאָ֨רֶץ֙ תִּתֵּ֣ן אֶת־יְבוּלָ֔הּ וְהַשָּׁמַ֖יִם יִתְּנ֣וּ

יג טַלָּ֑ם וְהִנְחַלְתִּ֗י אֶת־שְׁאֵרִ֛ית הָעָ֥ם הַזֶּ֖ה אֶת־כָּל־אֵֽלֶּה: וְהָיָ֡ה כַּֽאֲשֶׁר֩

הֱיִיתֶ֨ם קְלָלָ֜ה בַּגּוֹיִ֗ם בֵּ֤ית יְהוּדָה֙ וּבֵ֣ית יִשְׂרָאֵ֔ל כֵּ֖ן אוֹשִׁ֣יעַ אֶתְכֶ֑ם וִֽהְיִיתֶ֖ם

יד בְּרָכָ֑ה אַל־תִּירָ֖אוּ תֶּֽחֱזַ֥קְנָה יְדֵיכֶֽם: כִּ֣י כֹ֤ה אָמַר֙ יְהֹוָ֣ה צְבָא֔וֹת

כַּֽאֲשֶׁ֨ר זָמַ֜מְתִּי לְהָרַ֣ע לָכֶ֗ם בְּהַקְצִ֤יף אֲבֹֽתֵיכֶם֙ אֹתִ֔י אָמַ֖ר יְהֹוָ֣ה צְבָא֑וֹת

טו וְלֹ֣א נִחָֽמְתִּי: כֵּ֣ן שַׁ֤בְתִּי זָמַ֨מְתִּי֙ בַּיָּמִ֣ים הָאֵ֔לֶּה לְהֵיטִ֥יב אֶת־יְרֽוּשָׁלַ֖ם וְאֶת־

טז בֵּ֣ית יְהוּדָ֑ה אַל־תִּירָֽאוּ: אֵ֥לֶּה הַדְּבָרִ֖ים אֲשֶׁ֣ר תַּֽעֲשׂ֑וּ דַּבְּר֤וּ אֱמֶת֙ אִ֣ישׁ

אֶת־רֵעֵ֔הוּ אֱמֶת֙ וּמִשְׁפַּ֣ט שָׁל֔וֹם שִׁפְט֖וּ בְּשַֽׁעֲרֵיכֶֽם: וְאִ֣ישׁ ׀ אֶת־רָעַ֣ת

יז רֵעֵ֗הוּ אַל־תַּחְשְׁבוּ֙ בִּלְבַבְכֶ֔ם וּשְׁבֻ֥עַת שֶׁ֖קֶר אַל־תֶּֽאֱהָ֑בוּ כִּ֧י אֶת־כָּל־

יח אֵ֛לֶּה אֲשֶׁ֥ר שָׂנֵ֖אתִי נְאֻם־יְהֹוָֽה: וַֽיְהִ֛י דְּבַר־יְהֹוָ֥ה

יט אֵלַ֖י לֵֽאמֹֽר: כֹּֽה־אָמַ֞ר יְהֹוָ֣ה צְבָא֗וֹת צ֣וֹם הָֽרְבִיעִ֡י וְצ֣וֹם הַֽחֲמִישִׁי֩ וְצ֨וֹם

הַשְּׁבִיעִ֜י וְצ֣וֹם הָֽעֲשִׂירִ֗י יִֽהְיֶ֤ה לְבֵית־יְהוּדָה֙ לְשָׂשׂ֣וֹן וּלְשִׂמְחָ֔ה וּלְמֹֽעֲדִ֖ים

כ טוֹבִ֑ים וְהָֽאֱמֶ֥ת וְהַשָּׁל֖וֹם אֱהָֽבוּ:   כֹּ֥ה אָמַ֖ר יְהֹוָ֣ה צְבָא֑וֹת עֹ֚ד

כא אֲשֶׁ֣ר יָבֹ֣אוּ עַמִּ֔ים וְיֹֽשְׁבֵ֖י עָרִ֥ים רַבּֽוֹת: וְהָֽלְכ֡וּ יֹֽשְׁבֵי֩ אַחַ֨ת אֶל־אַחַ֜ת

לֵאמֹ֗ר נֵֽלְכָ֤ה הָלוֹךְ֙ לְחַלּוֹת֙ אֶת־פְּנֵ֣י יְהֹוָ֔ה וּלְבַקֵּ֖שׁ אֶת־יְהֹוָ֣ה צְבָא֑וֹת

כב אֵֽלְכָ֖ה גַּם־אָֽנִי: וּבָ֨אוּ עַמִּ֤ים רַבִּים֙ וְגוֹיִ֣ם עֲצוּמִ֔ים לְבַקֵּ֛שׁ אֶת־יְהֹוָ֥ה

כג צְבָא֖וֹת בִּירֽוּשָׁלָ֑ם וּלְחַלּ֖וֹת אֶת־פְּנֵ֥י יְהֹוָֽה: כֹּ֥ה אָמַ֖ר יְהֹוָ֣ה

צְבָא֑וֹת בַּיָּמִ֣ים הָהֵ֔מָּה אֲשֶׁ֤ר יַֽחֲזִ֨יקוּ֙ עֲשָׂרָ֣ה אֲנָשִׁ֔ים מִכֹּ֖ל לְשֹׁנ֣וֹת הַגּוֹיִ֑ם

8:6. The miracles that I will perform at that time will be greater than any I had ever done before (*Ibn Ezra*).

8:9,13. The word "hands" is a metaphor for "resolve."

8:10. Before Darius gave permission to resume construction of the Temple, there was a curse in the land; people

had no earnings from their own labor or from their livestock. See *Haggai* 1:5-6, 1:9-11, 2:15-19.

8:19. The Babylonians breached the walls of Jerusalem in the fourth month [17 Tammuz] (see *Jeremiah* 39:2); they destroyed the Temple in the fifth month [9 Av];

in the midst of Jerusalem; Jerusalem will be called 'The City of Truth' and the mountain of HASHEM, Master of Legions, 'The Holy Mountain.'

Young and
old will
rejoice . . .

⁴ *Thus said HASHEM, Master of Legions: Old men and old women will once again sit in the streets of Jerusalem, each with his staff in his hand because of advanced age;* ⁵ *and the streets of the city will be filled with boys and girls playing in its streets.*

⁶ *Thus said HASHEM, Master of Legions: Just as it will be wondrous in the eyes of the remnant of this people in those days, so will it be wondrous in My eyes* — the word of HASHEM, Master of Legions.*

⁷ *Thus said HASHEM, Master of Legions: Behold, I am saving My people from the land of the east and from the land where the sun sets;* ⁸ *and I will bring them and they will dwell within Jerusalem. They will be a people unto Me, and I will be a God unto them, in truth and in righteousness.*

. . . for God
will bring
prosperity

⁹ *Thus said HASHEM, Master of Legions: Let your hands* be strong, you who hear these days these words from the mouths of the prophets, which [were spoken] on the day that the foundation was laid for the Temple of HASHEM, Master of Legions — the Sanctuary — to be built.* ¹⁰ *For before those days, people had no earnings, * nor were there earnings from animals; those who travel back and forth had no peace because of the enemy; and I set everyone, man against his neighbor.* ¹¹ *But now, not as in earlier days am I toward the remnant of this people — the word of HASHEM, Master of Legions.* ¹² *For [now] the seed is of peace: The vine gives forth its fruit, the land gives forth its produce, and the heavens give forth their dew. I have bestowed all these upon the remnant of this people.* ¹³ *And it will happen that just as you, O House of Judah and House of Israel, had been a curse for the nations, so will I save you and you will be a blessing. Do not fear, and let your hands* be strong!* ¹⁴ *For thus said HASHEM, Master of Legions: Just as I had planned to bring misfortune upon you when your forefathers angered Me — said HASHEM, Master of Legions — and I did not relent [from doing so],* ¹⁵ *so have I turned back these days and planned to benefit Jerusalem and the House of Judah. Do not fear!* ¹⁶ *These are the things that you should do: Speak the truth with one another; and in your gates judge with truth, justice and peace.* ¹⁷ *Do not think evil toward one another in your hearts and do not love false oaths, for all these are what I hate — the word of HASHEM.*

¹⁸ *The word of HASHEM, Master of Legions, came to me, saying:*

Fast turned
to joy . . .

¹⁹ *Thus said HASHEM, Master of Legions: The fast of the fourth [month], the fast of the fifth, the fast of the seventh and the fast of the tenth* will be to the House of Judah for joy and for gladness and for happy festivals. [Only] love truth and peace!*

²⁰ *Thus said HASHEM, Master of Legions: It will yet be that peoples will come, as well as inhabitants of many cities.* ²¹ *The dwellers of one [city] will go to [those of] the other, saying, 'Let us go and supplicate before HASHEM and seek out HASHEM, Master of Legions!' [They will answer,] 'I, too, will go!'* ²² *Many peoples and mighty nations will come to seek out HASHEM, Master of Legions, in Jerusalem, and to supplicate before HASHEM.*

. . . and the
nations
will join

²³ *Thus said HASHEM, Master of Legions: In those days it will happen that ten men, of all the [different] languages of the nations, will take hold,*

Gedaliah was murdered in the seventh month [3 Tishrei] (see 7:5); and the siege began in the tenth month [10   Teves]. And those days became days of fasting and mourning.

ט
וְהֶחֱזִיקוּ בִּכְנַף אִישׁ יְהוּדִי לֵאמֹר נֵלְכָה עִמָּכֶם כִּי שָׁמַעְנוּ אֱלֹהִים

א עִמָּכֶם: מַשָּׂא דְבַר־יְהוָֹה בְּאֶרֶץ חַדְרָךְ וְדַמֶּשֶׂק מְנֻחָתוֹ כִּי לַיהוָֹה
ב עֵין אָדָם וְכֹל שִׁבְטֵי יִשְׂרָאֵל: וְגַם־חֲמָת תִּגְבָּל־בָּהּ צֹר וְצִידוֹן כִּי חָכְמָה
ג־ד מְאֹד: וַתִּבֶן צֹר מָצוֹר לָהּ וַתִּצְבָּר־כֶּסֶף כֶּעָפָר וְחָרוּץ כְּטִיט חוּצוֹת: הִנֵּה
ה אֲדֹנָי יוֹרִשֶׁנָּה וְהִכָּה בַיָּם חֵילָהּ וְהִיא בָּאֵשׁ תֵּאָכֵל: תֵּרֶא אַשְׁקְלוֹן וְתִירָא
וְעַזָּה וְתָחִיל מְאֹד וְעֶקְרוֹן כִּי־הֹבִישׁ מֶבָּטָהּ וְאָבַד מֶלֶךְ מֵעַזָּה וְאַשְׁקְלוֹן
ו־ז לֹא תֵשֵׁב: וְיָשַׁב מַמְזֵר בְּאַשְׁדּוֹד וְהִכְרַתִּי גְּאוֹן פְּלִשְׁתִּים: וַהֲסִרֹתִי דָמָיו
מִפִּיו וְשִׁקֻּצָיו מִבֵּין שִׁנָּיו וְנִשְׁאַר גַּם־הוּא לֵאלֹהֵינוּ וְהָיָה כְּאַלֻּף בִּיהוּדָה
ח וְעֶקְרוֹן כִּיבוּסִי: וְחָנִיתִי לְבֵיתִי מִצָּבָה מֵעֹבֵר וּמִשָּׁב וְלֹא־יַעֲבֹר עֲלֵיהֶם
ט עוֹד נֹגֵשׂ כִּי עַתָּה רָאִיתִי בְעֵינָי: גִּילִי מְאֹד בַּת־צִיּוֹן הָרִיעִי בַּת
יְרוּשָׁלִַם הִנֵּה מַלְכֵּךְ יָבוֹא לָךְ צַדִּיק וְנוֹשָׁע הוּא עָנִי וְרֹכֵב עַל־חֲמוֹר וְעַל־
י עַיִר בֶּן־אֲתֹנוֹת: וְהִכְרַתִּי־רֶכֶב מֵאֶפְרַיִם וְסוּס מִירוּשָׁלִַם וְנִכְרְתָה קֶשֶׁת
מִלְחָמָה וְדִבֶּר שָׁלוֹם לַגּוֹיִם וּמָשְׁלוֹ מִיָּם עַד־יָם וּמִנָּהָר עַד־אַפְסֵי־אָרֶץ:
יא־יב גַּם־אַתְּ בְּדַם־בְּרִיתֵךְ שִׁלַּחְתִּי אֲסִירַיִךְ מִבּוֹר אֵין מַיִם בּוֹ: שׁוּבוּ לְבִצָּרוֹן
יג אֲסִירֵי הַתִּקְוָה גַּם־הַיּוֹם מַגִּיד מִשְׁנֶה אָשִׁיב לָךְ: כִּי־דָרַכְתִּי לִי יְהוּדָה
קֶשֶׁת מִלֵּאתִי אֶפְרַיִם וְעוֹרַרְתִּי בָנַיִךְ צִיּוֹן עַל־בָּנַיִךְ יָוָן וְשַׂמְתִּיךְ כְּחֶרֶב
יד גִּבּוֹר: וַיהוָֹה עֲלֵיהֶם יֵרָאֶה וְיָצָא כַבָּרָק חִצּוֹ וַאדֹנָי יֱהוִֹה בַּשּׁוֹפָר יִתְקָע
טו וְהָלַךְ בְּסַעֲרוֹת תֵּימָן: יְהוָֹה צְבָאוֹת יָגֵן עֲלֵיהֶם וְאָכְלוּ וְכָבְשׁוּ אַבְנֵי־קֶלַע
טז וְשָׁתוּ הָמוּ כְּמוֹ־יָיִן וּמָלְאוּ כַּמִּזְרָק כְּזָוִיּוֹת מִזְבֵּחַ: וְהוֹשִׁיעָם יְהוָֹה אֱלֹהֵיהֶם
יז בַּיּוֹם הַהוּא כְּצֹאן עַמּוֹ כִּי אַבְנֵי־נֵזֶר מִתְנוֹסְסוֹת עַל־אַדְמָתוֹ: כִּי מַה־טּוּבוֹ
י
א וּמַה־יָּפְיוֹ דָּגָן בַּחוּרִים וְתִירוֹשׁ יְנוֹבֵב בְּתֻלוֹת: שַׁאֲלוּ מֵיְהוָֹה מָטָר בְּעֵת
ב מַלְקוֹשׁ יְהוָֹה עֹשֶׂה חֲזִיזִים וּמְטַר־גֶּשֶׁם יִתֵּן לָהֶם לְאִישׁ עֵשֶׂב בַּשָּׂדֶה: כִּי
הַתְּרָפִים דִּבְּרוּ־אָוֶן וְהַקּוֹסְמִים חָזוּ שֶׁקֶר וַחֲלֹמוֹת הַשָּׁוְא יְדַבֵּרוּ הֶבֶל
ג יְנַחֵמוּן עַל־כֵּן נָסְעוּ כְמוֹ־צֹאן יַעֲנוּ כִּי־אֵין רֹעֶה: עַל־

9:1. The prophecy was given in Hadrach, near Damascus, and it would rest, i.e., occur, in Damascus (*Ibn Ezra*).

9:2. These places, even Tyre, which considered itself too wise to be conquered, will become part of the Land of Israel.

9:4. The sea will inundate Tyre and carry away all her possessions and merchandise [see *Ezekiel* 26:3,19; 27:34], and then a fire will destroy her buildings [*Ezekiel* 28:18] (*Radak*).

9:6. Namely Israel, whom the Philistines had derided as foreigners (*Targum*).

9:7. The Philistines will stop their bloodthirsty and idolatrous practices, and join the people of Israel in worshiping God. Then, even the Philistines will be like the leaders of Judah, and Ekron will be as Jewish as the former Jebusite city of Jerusalem.

9:9. The Messiah will be a humble man riding a donkey rather than an ostentatious horse (*Rashi*).

9:11. Not only the Messiah, but all Jews will be protected and snatched from the waterless pit of exile by merit of the blood of circumcision covenant (*Radak*) and the blood of the covenant of Sinai [*Exodus* 24:8] (*Rashi*).

9:12. Jerusalem (*Ibn Ezra*). Alternatively: Although you are in exile, return to your original strength and glory (*Rashi*). This is the first announcement (see v. 13).

9:13. God will use Judah and Ephraim as His weapons against their oppressor. He will "draw" Judah like a bow, pulling Ephraim taut to fire His arrow against the Greeks who will conquer Persia, thus gaining control of the Land of Israel. This is the second announcement (*Rashi*).

9:15. An appellation for the Greeks, whose warriors were skilled at directing stones against their enemies (*Rashi*).

9:16. The priestly Hasmoneans who will reclaim the land from the Greek oppressors (*Rashi*).

10:1. The time of which the prophet has been speaking will be a time of Divine favor. Even if at the end of the *they will take hold of the corner of the garment of a Jewish man, saying, 'Let us go with you, for we have heard that God is with you!'*

9

A prophecy against enemy cities

¹ *T*he prophecy of the word of HASHEM for the land of Hadrach, with Damascus its resting place: *

Toward HASHEM will be the eyes of mankind, and all the tribes of Israel. ² *Also Hamath will be in its borders, as well as Tyre and Sidon, though she is very wise.* * ³ *Tyre built herself a fortification; she amassed silver like dirt, and fine gold like the mud of the street.* ⁴ *Behold, the Lord will impoverish her, and He will strike her wealth with the sea, and it will be consumed by fire.* * ⁵ *Ashkelon will see this and fear, and Gaza [will see] and tremble greatly, and Ekron, for the one to whom she looked [for protection] has been humiliated. A king will perish from Gaza, and Ashkelon will not be inhabited.* ⁶ *A stranger* will dwell in Ashdod, and I will eliminate the pride of the Philistines.* ⁷ *I will remove his blood from his mouth and his abominations from between his teeth, and then he too will remain for our God. He, will be like a master in Judah, and Ekron will be like the Jebusite.* * ⁸ *I will encamp at My home [to protect it] against any army and from any [enemy] who comes and goes, and an oppressor will never again pass through them; for now I have seen [their suffering] with My eyes.*

Messiah comes to Zion

⁹ *Rejoice greatly, O daughter of Zion! Shout for joy, O daughter of Jerusalem! For behold, your king will come to you, righteous and victorious is he, a humble man riding upon a donkey,* * upon a foal, a calf of she-donkeys.* ¹⁰ *I will eliminate any [battle]-chariot from Ephraim and any [war] horse from Jerusalem, and the bow of warfare will be eliminated; and he will speak peace to the nations. His dominion will be from sea to sea and from the river to the ends of the earth.*

Freedom, unity, celebration

¹¹ *Also you,* * through the blood of your covenant I will have released your prisoners from the pit in which there is no water.* ¹² *Return to the fortress,* * O prisoners of hope! Today, too, a second announcement, 'I will return to you.'* ¹³ *For I will bend Judah [as a bow] for Me;* * I will fill [the hand of] Ephraim with a bow; and I will stir up your children, O Zion, against your children, O Greece; and I will make you like the sword of a warrior.* ¹⁴ *HASHEM will appear to them, and His arrow will go forth like the lightning; and the Lord HASHEM/ELOHIM will blow with a shofar and go forth in southern tempests.* ¹⁵ *HASHEM, Master of Legions, will protect them, and they will devour and conquer the 'stones of the slingshot.'* * They will drink and be boisterous as from wine; they will be filled up like a bowl, and like the corners of the altar.* ¹⁶ *HASHEM their God will save His people like sheep on that day, for the 'stones of the crown'* * will be exalted on His land.* ¹⁷ *How goodly and how beautiful will be the grain of young men and the wine that will make maidens sing.*

10

False oracles and leaders

¹ *R*equest rain of HASHEM in the season of the late rains, [of] HASHEM Who makes rainclouds; and He will provide them a shower of rain,* * for each man, herbage in the field.* ² *For the teraphim* * speak words of nothingness, the diviners see falsehoods, and dreamers speak lies; they comfort with meaningless words. Therefore, they have wandered off like sheep; they are humbled, for there is no shepherd.*

---

season you pray for unusually heavy rain, God will provide it (*Radak*).

10:2. Oracles used by idolaters to divine the future.
10:3. A metaphor for the leaders of the community.

הָרֵעִים חָרָה אַפִּי וְעַל־הָעַתּוּדִים אֶפְק֑וֹד כִּי־פָקַד יהוה צְבָאוֹת אֶת־עֶדְרוֹ

ד אֶת־בֵּית יְהוּדָה וְשָׂם אוֹתָם כְּסוּס הוֹדוֹ בַּמִּלְחָמָֽה׃ מִמֶּנּוּ פִנָּה מִמֶּנּוּ יָתֵד

ה מִמֶּנּוּ קֶשֶׁת מִלְחָמָה מִמֶּנּוּ יֵצֵא כָל־נוֹגֵשׂ יַחְדָּ֑ו וְהָיוּ כְגִבֹּרִים בּוֹסִים בְּטִיט

ו חוּצוֹת בַּמִּלְחָמָה וְנִלְחֲמוּ כִּי יהוה עִמָּם וְהֹבִישׁוּ רֹכְבֵי סוּסִֽים׃ וְגִבַּרְתִּי |

אֶת־בֵּית יְהוּדָה וְאֶת־בֵּית יוֹסֵף אוֹשִׁיעַ וְהוֹשְׁבוֹתִים כִּי רִחַמְתִּים וְהָיוּ

ז כַּאֲשֶׁר לֹא־זְנַחְתִּים כִּי אֲנִי יהוה אֱלֹהֵיהֶם וְאֶעֱנֵֽם׃ וְהָיוּ כְגִבּוֹר אֶפְרַיִם

ח וְשָׂמַח לִבָּם כְּמוֹ־יָ֑יִן וּבְנֵיהֶם יִרְאוּ וְשָׂמֵחוּ יָגֵל לִבָּם בַּֽיהוָֽה׃ אֶשְׁרְקָה לָהֶם

ט וַאֲקַבְּצֵם כִּי פְדִיתִים וְרָבוּ כְּמוֹ רָבֽוּ׃ וְאֶזְרָעֵם בָּעַמִּים וּבַמֶּרְחַקִּים יִזְכְּרוּנִי

י וְחָיוּ אֶת־בְּנֵיהֶם וָשָֽׁבוּ׃ וַהֲשִׁיבוֹתִים מֵאֶרֶץ מִצְרַיִם וּמֵאַשּׁוּר אֲקַבְּצֵם וְאֶל־

יא אֶרֶץ גִּלְעָד וּלְבָנוֹן אֲבִיאֵם וְלֹא יִמָּצֵא לָהֶֽם׃ וְעָבַר בַּיָּם צָרָה וְהִכָּה בַיָּם

גַּלִּים וְהֹבִישׁוּ כֹּל מְצוּלוֹת יְאֹר וְהוּרַד גְּאוֹן אַשּׁוּר וְשֵׁבֶט מִצְרַיִם יָסֽוּר׃

פְּתַח לְבָנוֹן דְּלָתֶיךָ

יב-יא־א וְגִבַּרְתִּים בַּֽיהוָה וּבִשְׁמוֹ יִתְהַלָּכוּ נְאֻם יהוָֽה׃

יא

ב וְתֹאכַל אֵשׁ בַּאֲרָזֶֽיךָ׃ הֵילֵל בְּרוֹשׁ כִּי־נָפַל אֶרֶז אֲשֶׁר אַדִּרִים שֻׁדָּ֑דוּ הֵילִילוּ

ג אַלּוֹנֵי בָשָׁן כִּי יָרַד יַעַר הבצור[הַבָּצִיר ק]׃ קוֹל יִלְלַת הָרֹעִים כִּי שֻׁדְּדָה

ד אַדַּרְתָּם קוֹל שַׁאֲגַת כְּפִירִים כִּי שֻׁדַּד גְּאוֹן הַיַּרְדֵּֽן׃ כֹּה אָמַר יהוה

ה אֱלֹהָ֑י רְעֵה אֶת־צֹאן הַהֲרֵגָֽה׃ אֲשֶׁר קֹנֵיהֶן יַהֲרֹגָן וְלֹא יֶאְשָׁמוּ וּמֹכְרֵיהֶן

ו יֹאמַר בָּרוּךְ יהוה וַאעְשִׁר וְרֹעֵיהֶם לֹא יַחְמוֹל עֲלֵיהֶֽן׃ כִּי לֹא אֶחְמוֹל עוֹד

עַל־יֹשְׁבֵי הָאָרֶץ נְאֻם־יהוָ֑ה וְהִנֵּה אָנֹכִי מַמְצִיא אֶת־הָאָדָם אִישׁ בְּיַד־

ז רֵעֵהוּ וּבְיַד מַלְכּוֹ וְכִתְּתוּ אֶת־הָאָרֶץ וְלֹא אַצִּיל מִיָּדָֽם׃ וָאֶרְעֶה אֶת־צֹאן

הַהֲרֵגָה לָכֵן עֲנִיֵּי הַצֹּ֑אן וָאֶקַּח־לִי שְׁנֵי מַקְלוֹת לְאַחַד קָרָאתִי נֹעַם וּלְאַחַד

ח קָרָאתִי חֹֽבְלִים וָאֶרְעֶה אֶת־הַצֹּֽאן׃ וָאַכְחִד אֶת־שְׁלֹשֶׁת הָרֹעִים

ט בְּיֶרַח אֶחָד וַתִּקְצַר נַפְשִׁי בָּהֶם וְגַם־נַפְשָׁם בָּחֲלָה בִֽי׃ וָאֹמַר לֹא אֶרְעֶה

אֶתְכֶם הַמֵּתָה תָמוּת וְהַנִּכְחֶדֶת תִּכָּחֵד וְהַנִּשְׁאָרוֹת תֹּאכַלְנָה אִשָּׁה אֶת־

י בְּשַׂר רְעוּתָֽהּ׃ וָאֶקַּח אֶת־מַקְלִי אֶת־נֹעַם וָאֶגְדַּע אֹתוֹ לְהָפֵיר אֶת־בְּרִיתִי

יא אֲשֶׁר כָּרַתִּי אֶת־כָּל־הָעַמִּֽים׃ וַתֻּפַר בַּיּוֹם הַה֑וּא וַיֵּדְעוּ כֵן עֲנִיֵּי הַצֹּאן

יב הַשֹּׁמְרִים אֹתִי כִּי דְבַר־יהוה הֽוּא׃ וָאֹמַר אֲלֵיהֶם אִם־טוֹב בְּעֵינֵיכֶם הָבוּ

10:8. As one whistles to get the attention of a lost person (*Rashi*).

10:11. The nations are likened to the waves of the sea and turbulent rivers. God will quell them all (*Radak*).

11:1-3. These verses metaphorically portray the downfall of the mighty nations and their subordinates, who had oppressed Israel (*Targum*). Lebanon is the great forest in the north of the land.

11:4. A reference to the persecuted people of Israel.

11:5. The Jews are sold like animals; the seller is happy because he has received his money and the buyer is cruel to them.

11:7. "*Hobelim*" means "destroyers" and alludes to the

Kingdom of Judah, whose first king, Rehoboam, ruled with a destructive iron hand (see *I Kings* Ch.12); "*Noam*" means "pleasantness" and alludes to the Northern Kingdom of Israel, whose first king, Jeroboam, used pleasant words to lure ten of the tribes into his camp (*Rashi*). Alternatively: The two staffs represent the two different manners by which God tended His flock: "pleasantness" when the kings were righteous and the people obedient to God; "destroyers" when their kings were wicked and the people were not obedient to God (*Radak*).

11:8. The three are King Jehoram, of the Northern Kingdom; King Ahaziah, of Judah; and Ahaziah's potential successors, all of whom were murdered at the same time [*II Kings*, Chs. 9,11] (*Rashi*). Alternatively: They are

³ My anger is kindled against the shepherds, and I will punish the he-goats. * For HASHEM, Master of Legions, has remembered his flock, the House of Judah, and He will make them like a horse whose glory is in war. ⁴ From themselves the cornerstone; from themselves the peg; from themselves the bow of war; — from themselves all the leaders will come forth together. ⁵ They will be like warriors trampling [their enemies] in the mud of the streets in war; they will wage war, for HASHEM will be with them; and the [enemy] riders of horses will be put to shame. ⁶ I will give power to the House of Judah and I will save the house of Joseph; I will settle them, for I will have mercy upon them, and they will be as if I had not rejected them; for I am HASHEM their God, and I will answer them. ⁷ Ephraim will be like a mighty warrior, and their heart will be glad as [with] wine. Their children will see and be glad; their heart will rejoice in HASHEM. ⁸ I will whistle to them* and gather them, for I have redeemed them; and they will become as numerous as they had been numerous. ⁹ I had sown them among the nations, and they remembered Me in faraway places; so they will live, with their children, and they will return.

¹⁰ I will bring them back from the land of Egypt; I will gather them in from Assyria; I will bring them to the land of Gilead and Lebanon; there will not be enough [room] for them. ¹¹ Misfortune will pass through the sea, and [God] will strike the waves in the sea; * all the deep waters of the river will dry up; the pride of Assyria will be brought down, and the staff of Egypt will depart. ¹² I will give [Israel] power through HASHEM, and they will walk with His Name — the word of HASHEM.

11

¹ Open your doors, O Lebanon, * and let fire consume your cedars! ² Wail, O cypress, for the cedar has fallen, for the mighty ones have been vanquished; wail, O oaks of Bashan, because the impregnable forest has come down. ³ There is a sound of the shepherds' wailing, for their power has been vanquished; there is a sound of young lions' roar, for the heights of the Jordan have been vanquished.

⁴ Thus said HASHEM, My God: Tend the flock meant to be slain, * ⁵ whom their buyers slay and they are not guilty and those who sell them say, 'Blessed be HASHEM! Now I am rich!' and whose shepherds do not pity them. * ⁶ For I will no longer pity the inhabitants of the land — the word of HASHEM. Behold, I am giving over the people, each one into the hand of his fellow and into the hand of his king; they will crush the land, and I will not save [them] from their hand. ⁷ I had tended the flock meant to be slain, because they were the meekest of the flock. I took for Myself two staffs — one I called "Noam" and the other I called "Hobelim"* and I tended the flock. ⁸ I removed the three shepherds in one month, * and My soul became impatient with them, for their soul also found Me repulsive. ⁹ I said, 'I will not tend you! Let the dying one die and let the decimated one be decimated; and as for the remaining ones, let each devour the other's flesh!'

¹⁰ And I took My staff Noam and broke it, to annul My covenant that I had sealed with the peoples. * ¹¹ So it became annulled on that day; and the meek of the flock, all who paid heed to Me, recognized that it was so, that it was the word of HASHEM. ¹² I said to [the people], 'If it is proper in your eyes, give Me

---

the three sons of Josiah who reigned after him: Jehoa-haz, Jehoiakim and Zedekiah [II Kings, Chs. 23-25], who died within several years of each other. Accordingly,

"one month" is figurative (Radak).]
11:10. God had made a covenant, as it were, with the nations that they should not harm Israel.

יג שְׂכָרִי וְאִם־לֹא ׀ חֲדָלוּ וַיִּשְׁקְלוּ אֶת־שְׂכָרִי שְׁלֹשִׁים כָּסֶף: וַיֹּאמֶר יְהוָֹה אֵלַי הַשְׁלִיכֵהוּ אֶל־הַיּוֹצֵר אֶדֶר הַיְקָר אֲשֶׁר יָקַרְתִּי מֵעֲלֵיהֶם וָאֶקְחָה שְׁלֹשִׁים הַכֶּסֶף וָאַשְׁלִיךְ אֹתוֹ בֵּית יְהוָֹה אֶל־הַיּוֹצֵר: וָאֶגְדַּע אֶת־מַקְלִי הַשֵּׁנִי אֶת

יד הַחֹבְלִים לְהָפֵר אֶת־הָאַחֲוָה בֵּין יְהוּדָה וּבֵין יִשְׂרָאֵל: וַיֹּאמֶר

טו יְהוָֹה אֵלַי עוֹד קַח־לְךָ כְּלִי רֹעֶה אֱוִלִי: כִּי הִנֵּה־אָנֹכִי מֵקִים רֹעֶה בָּאָרֶץ הַנִּכְחָדוֹת לֹא־יִפְקֹד הַנַּעַר לֹא־יְבַקֵּשׁ וְהַנִּשְׁבֶּרֶת לֹא יְרַפֵּא

טז הַנִּצָּבָה לֹא יְכַלְכֵּל וּבְשַׂר הַבְּרִיאָה יֹאכַל וּפַרְסֵיהֶן יְפָרֵק: הוֹי רֹעִי

יז הָאֱלִיל עֹזְבִי הַצֹּאן חֶרֶב עַל־זְרוֹעוֹ וְעַל־עֵין יְמִינוֹ זְרֹעוֹ יָבוֹשׁ תִּיבָשׁ וְעֵין יְמִינוֹ כָּהֹה תִכְהֶה:

יב   א מַשָּׂא דְבַר־יְהוָֹה עַל־יִשְׂרָאֵל נְאֻם־יְהוָֹה

ב נֹטֶה שָׁמַיִם וְיֹסֵד אָרֶץ וְיֹצֵר רוּחַ־אָדָם בְּקִרְבּוֹ: הִנֵּה אָנֹכִי שָׂם אֶת־ יְרוּשָׁלַ͏ִם סַף־רַעַל לְכָל־הָעַמִּים סָבִיב וְגַם עַל־יְהוּדָה יִהְיֶה בַמָּצוֹר עַל־

ג יְרוּשָׁלָ͏ִם: וְהָיָה בַיּוֹם־הַהוּא אָשִׂים אֶת־יְרוּשָׁלַ͏ִם אֶבֶן מַעֲמָסָה לְכָל־ הָעַמִּים כָּל־עֹמְסֶיהָ שָׂרוֹט יִשָּׂרֵטוּ וְנֶאֶסְפוּ עָלֶיהָ כֹּל גּוֹיֵי הָאָרֶץ: בַּיּוֹם

ד הַהוּא נְאֻם־יְהוָֹה אַכֶּה כָל־סוּס בַּתִּמָּהוֹן וְרֹכְבוֹ בַּשִּׁגָּעוֹן וְעַל־בֵּית יְהוּדָה אֶפְקַח אֶת־עֵינַי וְכֹל סוּס הָעַמִּים אַכֶּה בַּעִוָּרוֹן: וְאָמְרוּ אַלֻּפֵי יְהוּדָה

ה בְּלִבָּם אַמְצָה לִי יֹשְׁבֵי יְרוּשָׁלַ͏ִם בַּיהוָֹה צְבָאוֹת אֱלֹהֵיהֶם: בַּיּוֹם הַהוּא

ו אָשִׂים אֶת־אַלֻּפֵי יְהוּדָה כְּכִיּוֹר אֵשׁ בְּעֵצִים וּכְלַפִּיד אֵשׁ בְּעָמִיר וְאָכְלוּ עַל־יָמִין וְעַל־שְׂמֹאול אֶת־כָּל־הָעַמִּים סָבִיב וְיָשְׁבָה יְרוּשָׁלַ͏ִם עוֹד

ז תַּחְתֶּיהָ בִּירוּשָׁלָ͏ִם: וְהוֹשִׁיעַ יְהוָֹה אֶת־אָהֳלֵי יְהוּדָה בָּרִאשֹׁנָה לְמַעַן לֹא־

ח תִגְדַּל תִּפְאֶרֶת בֵּית־דָּוִיד וְתִפְאֶרֶת יֹשֵׁב יְרוּשָׁלַ͏ִם עַל־יְהוּדָה: בַּיּוֹם הַהוּא יָגֵן יְהוָֹה בְּעַד יוֹשֵׁב יְרוּשָׁלַ͏ִם וְהָיָה הַנִּכְשָׁל בָּהֶם בַּיּוֹם הַהוּא כְּדָוִיד

ט וּבֵית דָּוִיד כֵּאלֹהִים כְּמַלְאַךְ יְהוָֹה לִפְנֵיהֶם: וְהָיָה בַּיּוֹם הַהוּא אֲבַקֵּשׁ

י לְהַשְׁמִיד אֶת־כָּל־הַגּוֹיִם הַבָּאִים עַל־יְרוּשָׁלָ͏ִם: וְשָׁפַכְתִּי עַל־בֵּית־ דָּוִיד וְעַל ׀ יוֹשֵׁב יְרוּשָׁלַ͏ִם רוּחַ חֵן וְתַחֲנוּנִים וְהִבִּיטוּ אֵלַי אֵת אֲשֶׁר־ דָּקָרוּ וְסָפְדוּ עָלָיו כְּמִסְפֵּד עַל־הַיָּחִיד וְהָמֵר עָלָיו כְּהָמֵר עַל־הַבְּכוֹר:

יא בַּיּוֹם הַהוּא יִגְדַּל הַמִּסְפֵּד בִּירוּשָׁלַ͏ִם כְּמִסְפַּד הֲדַדְרִמּוֹן בְּבִקְעַת מְגִדּוֹן:

11:12. If you want Me to be your Shepherd, you must pay My fee, namely, you must righteously observe My laws. But, as the verse goes on, only thirty people were truly righteous (*Rashi*).

11:13. The Temple. By throwing the deeds of these thirty righteous people into the Temple, Zechariah symbolized that the Temple would be rebuilt because of their merits (*Rashi*).

11:14. A reference to the destruction of Judah, two centuries after that of the Northern Kingdom. The destruction of Judah ended the idolatrous practices that the Judeans had learned through their ties with their northern brethren (*Rashi*).

11:16. Edom (the Roman empire), in whose lands the exiled Jews would settle and be maltreated (*Rashi*). Alternatively: Herod, the notorious king, who reigned towards the end of the Second Temple period (*Radak*).

12:2. Before the End of Days, the nations will besiege Jerusalem, and even force Jews to join them, but the enemies will be destroyed instead (*Targum*).

12:3. A heavy stone that a taskmaster puts on a laborer's shoulders.

12:4. To protect the Jews who had been forced to join the siege.

12:6. When the Judeans compelled to fight their brethren see that they were miraculously spared, they will turn against their enemies who forced them to join their ranks. Then Jerusalem will be restored to its former status.

My fee, * and if not, refrain.' So they weighed out My fee: thirty silver coins.
¹³ HASHEM said to me, "Throw it to the treasurer of the Precious Stronghold, *
which I have divested from them." So I took (full amount of) thirty silver coins and
I threw it into the Temple of HASHEM, to the treasurer.

¹⁴ Then I broke My second staff, Hobelim, to annul the brotherhood between
Judah and Israel. *

¹⁵ HASHEM said to me:

An evil ruler

Again take for yourself the implement[s] of a foolish shepherd. ¹⁶ For behold,
I am setting up a shepherd* in the land: He will not pay attention to the
decimated ones; he will not seek out the youth; he will not heal the broken
one; and he will not nurture the weak one; but he will eat the flesh of the
healthy one and break their hooves. ¹⁷ Woe to the worthless shepherd who
abandons the flock! A sword upon his arm and upon his right eye! May his
arm utterly wither and his right eye go completely blind!

12 ¹ The prophecy of the word of HASHEM concerning Israel:

*God will
protect
Jerusalem*

The word of HASHEM, Who stretches out the heavens and lays the foundation
of the earth, and Who fashions the spirit of man within him: ² Behold, I am
making Jerusalem a cup of poison for all the peoples all around; * also Judah
will take part in the siege of Jerusalem. ³ It shall be on that day that I will
make Jerusalem for all the peoples a burdensome stone, * all whose bearers
become lacerated; and all the nations of the world will gather against it. ⁴ On
that day — the word of HASHEM — I will strike every horse with confusion
and its rider with madness. But I will open My eyes to the House of Judah, *
while I strike every horse of the peoples with blindness. ⁵ Then the captains
of Judah will say in their hearts, 'The inhabitants of Jerusalem are a source
of strength for me, [in their prayers] to HASHEM, Master of Legions, their God!'

*Jews will
rebel against
alien masters*

⁶ On that day I will make the captains of Judah like a stove, fire [burning]
wood, and like a fiery torch [burning] sheaf, and they will consume on the
right and on the left all the peoples all around; * and Jerusalem will again
settle in its place, in Jerusalem. ⁷ HASHEM will save the tents of Judah first,
so that the splendor of the house of David and the splendor of the inhabitants
of Jerusalem should not overwhelm Judah. ⁸ On that day HASHEM will protect the inhabitant of Jerusalem; on that day even the weakest among them
will be like David, and the house of David will be like divine beings, like an
angel of HASHEM before them. ⁹ It shall be on that day that I will seek to destroy
all the nations that come upon Jerusalem. ¹⁰ I will pour out upon the house
of David and upon the inhabitant of Jerusalem a spirit of grace and supplications. They will look toward Me because of those whom they have
stabbed; * they will mourn over him as one mourns over an only [child], and
be embittered over him like the embitterment over a [deceased] firstborn.
¹¹ On that day the mourning will become intense in Jerusalem, like the
mourning of Hadadrimmon [and the mourning] at the Valley of Megiddon. *

12:10. The salvation will be so complete that people will
be astonished if even one man is killed by the enemy
(*Radak*).

12:11. According to *Targum* and the Talmud (*Moed
Katan* 28b), two events are alluded to here: the mourning

over Ahab son of Omri, king of Israel, who was killed in
battle (*I Kings* Ch. 22) by Hadadrimmon son of Tabrimmon; and the mourning for Josiah, king of Judah, who
was slain in the Valley of Megiddon (*Megiddo;* see *II
Chronicles* 36:20-25).

יב וְסָפְדָה הָאָרֶץ מִשְׁפָּחוֹת מִשְׁפָּחוֹת לְבָד מִשְׁפַּחַת בֵּית־דָּוִיד לְבָד וּנְשֵׁיהֶם

יג לְבָד מִשְׁפַּחַת בֵּית־נָתָן לְבָד וּנְשֵׁיהֶם לְבָד: מִשְׁפַּחַת בֵּית־לֵוִי לְבָד

יד וּנְשֵׁיהֶם לְבָד מִשְׁפַּחַת הַשִּׁמְעִי לְבָד וּנְשֵׁיהֶם לְבָד: כֹּל הַמִּשְׁפָּחוֹת

יג א הַנִּשְׁאָרוֹת מִשְׁפָּחֹת מִשְׁפָּחֹת לְבָד וּנְשֵׁיהֶם לְבָד: בַּיּוֹם הַהוּא יִהְיֶה מָקוֹר

ב נִפְתָּח לְבֵית דָּוִיד וּלְיֹשְׁבֵי יְרוּשָׁלִָם לְחַטַּאת וּלְנִדָּה: וְהָיָה בַיּוֹם הַהוּא

נְאֻם | יהוה צְבָאוֹת אַכְרִית אֶת־שְׁמוֹת הָעֲצַבִּים מִן־הָאָרֶץ וְלֹא יִזָּכְרוּ

ג עוֹד וְגַם אֶת־הַנְּבִיאִים וְאֶת־רוּחַ הַטֻּמְאָה אַעֲבִיר מִן־הָאָרֶץ: וְהָיָה כִּי־

יִנָּבֵא אִישׁ עוֹד וְאָמְרוּ אֵלָיו אָבִיו וְאִמּוֹ יֹלְדָיו לֹא תִחְיֶה כִּי שֶׁקֶר דִּבַּרְתָּ

ד בְּשֵׁם יהוה וּדְקָרֻהוּ אָבִיהוּ וְאִמּוֹ יֹלְדָיו בְּהִנָּבְאוֹ: וְהָיָה | בַּיּוֹם הַהוּא

יֵבֹשׁוּ הַנְּבִיאִים אִישׁ מֵחֶזְיֹנוֹ בְּהִנָּבְאֹתוֹ וְלֹא יִלְבְּשׁוּ אַדֶּרֶת שֵׂעָר לְמַעַן

ה כַּחֵשׁ: וְאָמַר לֹא נָבִיא אָנֹכִי אִישׁ־עֹבֵד אֲדָמָה אָנֹכִי כִּי אָדָם הִקְנַנִי

ו מִנְּעוּרָי: וְאָמַר אֵלָיו מָה הַמַּכּוֹת הָאֵלֶּה בֵּין יָדֶיךָ וְאָמַר אֲשֶׁר הֻכֵּיתִי בֵּית

ז מְאַהֲבָי: חֶרֶב עוּרִי עַל־רֹעִי וְעַל־גֶּבֶר עֲמִיתִי נְאֻם יהוה

צְבָאוֹת הַךְ אֶת־הָרֹעֶה וּתְפוּצֶיןָ הַצֹּאן וַהֲשִׁבֹתִי יָדִי עַל־הַצֹּעֲרִים: וְהָיָה

ח בְכָל־הָאָרֶץ נְאֻם־יהוה פִּי־שְׁנַיִם בָּהּ יִכָּרְתוּ יִגְוָעוּ וְהַשְּׁלִשִׁית יִוָּתֶר בָּהּ:

ט וְהֵבֵאתִי אֶת־הַשְּׁלִשִׁית בָּאֵשׁ וּצְרַפְתִּים כִּצְרֹף אֶת־הַכֶּסֶף וּבְחַנְתִּים

כִּבְחֹן אֶת־הַזָּהָב הוּא | יִקְרָא בִשְׁמִי וַאֲנִי אֶעֱנֶה אֹתוֹ אָמַרְתִּי עַמִּי הוּא

יד א וְהוּא יֹאמַר יהוה אֱלֹהָי: ◀ הִנֵּה יוֹם־בָּא לַיהוה וְחֻלַּק

שְׁלָלֵךְ בְּקִרְבֵּךְ: וְאָסַפְתִּי אֶת־כָּל־הַגּוֹיִם | אֶל־יְרוּשָׁלִַם לַמִּלְחָמָה

וְנִלְכְּדָה הָעִיר וְנָשַׁסּוּ הַבָּתִּים וְהַנָּשִׁים °תִּשָּׁגַלְנָה [תִּשָּׁכַבְנָה ק] וְיָצָא

ג חֲצִי הָעִיר בַּגּוֹלָה וְיֶתֶר הָעָם לֹא יִכָּרֵת מִן־הָעִיר: וְיָצָא יהוה וְנִלְחַם

ד בַּגּוֹיִם הָהֵם כְּיוֹם הִלָּחֲמוֹ בְּיוֹם קְרָב: וְעָמְדוּ רַגְלָיו בַּיּוֹם־הַהוּא עַל־הַר

הַזֵּיתִים אֲשֶׁר עַל־פְּנֵי יְרוּשָׁלִַם מִקֶּדֶם וְנִבְקַע הַר הַזֵּיתִים מֵחֶצְיוֹ מִזְרָחָה

ה וָיָמָּה גֵּיא גְּדוֹלָה מְאֹד וּמָשׁ חֲצִי הָהָר צָפוֹנָה וְחֶצְיוֹ־נֶגְבָּה: וְנַסְתֶּם גֵּיא־

הָרַי כִּי־יַגִּיעַ גֵּי־הָרִים אֶל־אָצַל וְנַסְתֶּם כַּאֲשֶׁר נַסְתֶּם מִפְּנֵי הָרַעַשׁ בִּימֵי

ו עֻזִּיָּה מֶלֶךְ־יְהוּדָה וּבָא יהוה אֱלֹהַי כָּל־קְדֹשִׁים עִמָּךְ: וְהָיָה בַּיּוֹם הַהוּא

HAFTARAH
FIRST DAY
SUCCOS
14:1-21

12:12-13. Nathan and Shimei were sons of David, whose descendants formed distinct groups within the royal family (*Rashi*).

13:1. The water will be used for purposes of ritual purification. According to some commentators, this prophecy is meant to be understood as a metaphor: People will become "cleansed" of their sins (*Targum*, *Kara*, etc.).

13:3. His parents will injure him to prevent him from prophesying falsely (*Radak*).

13:4. A garment signifying great piety, which false prophets wore to give their messages an aura of acceptability (*Rashi*).

13:5-6. He will be forced to admit that he was not a

prophet but a mere shepherd, and that his parents tried to stop him (*Kara*).

13:7. The kings and leaders of the nations were the shepherds, God's colleagues, to whom He entrusted the fate of His "flock" Israel. When they harm instead of help, God will unleash the sword against them (*Rashi*). Then, the flock will be free to escape, and God will turn His vengeance against the subordinates who helped molest Israel (*Kara*).

14:1-3. At the End of Days, in the War of Gog and Magog, the nations will conquer Jerusalem and divide its spoils, but God will save the people, as He did when the Egyptians pursued them to the Sea of Reeds (*Radak*).

14:4. An anthropomorphism indicating the cataclysmic

¹² *The land will mourn each of the families by itself: the family of the house of David by itself, and their wives by themselves; the family of the house of Nathan* by itself and their wives by themselves;* ¹³ *the family of the house of Levi by itself and their wives by themselves; the family of Shimei* by itself and their wives by themselves;* ¹⁴ *and all the families who remain, each of the families by itself and their wives by themselves.*

13

Removal of impurity

¹ On *that day there will be a spring opened up for the house of David and for the inhabitants of Jerusalem, for cleansing and for purification.* * ² *It will happen on that day — the word of HASHEM, Master of Legions — that I will eliminate the names of the idols from the land, and they will not be mentioned again; I will also remove the [false] prophets and the spirit of impurity from the land.* ³ *It will happen when a man will prophesy [falsely] in the future, that his father and his mother, those who bore him, will say to him, 'You should not live, for you have spoken falsehood in the name of HASHEM!' His father and mother, those who bore him, will stab him when he prophesies.* * ⁴ *It will happen on that day, the prophets will be ashamed, each one of his vision when he prophesies it, and they will no longer wear the fur cloak* in order to declare their lies.* ⁵ *Rather, he will say, 'I am not a prophet! I am a worker of the land, for a person took me as a herdsman since my youth.'* * ⁶ *And [if] someone will say to him, 'What are these scars between your arms?' He will say, 'It is from when I was beaten in the house of those who loved me.'*

A sword turned against enemies

⁷ *O sword, arouse yourself against My shepherd and against the man who is My colleague!* * — *the word of HASHEM, Master of Legions. Strike the shepherd and let the flock disperse! And I will turn My hand against the lesser leaders.* ⁸ *There will be in all the land — the word of HASHEM — two portions [of the population] will be cut off and perish, and the third will be left in it.* ⁹ *I will bring that third into fire and purify it as one purifies silver, and I will refine it as one refines gold; it will call out in My Name, and I will answer it. I have said, 'It is My people,' and it will say, 'HASHEM is my God.'*

14

War against Jerusalem

¹ Behold, *a day is coming for HASHEM,* * *when your spoils will be divided up in your midst.* ² *I will gather all the nations to Jerusalem for the war; the city will be captured, the houses will be pillaged and the women will be violated; half of the city will go out into exile, but the rest of the people will not be eliminated from the city.* ³ *HASHEM will go out and wage war with those nations, as He waged war on the day of battle.* ⁴ *His feet will stand* on that day on the Mount of Olives, which faces Jerusalem on the east, and the Mount of Olives will split open at its middle, east to west, [forming] a very wide valley; half of the mountain will move to the north and half of it to the south.* ⁵ *And you will flee to the valley of the mountains, for the valley of the mountains will reach to Azal,* * *and you will flee as you fled from the earthquake that was in the days of Uzziah, king of Judah. And HASHEM, My God, will come; all of His Holy Ones will be with you.* ⁶ *It will be on that day,*

The Mount of Olives will split

---

events that will occur. *Radak* suggests that the splitting of the Mount of Olives is to be understood as a metaphor for the total routing of the invading armies.

14:5. That is, you will flee in the valley created by the fissure of the Mount of Olives, all the way to a place called Azal, to escape the earthquake.

ז לֹא־יִהְיֶה אוֹר יְקָרוֹת °יִקְפָּאוֹן [°וְקִפָּאוֹן ק]: וְהָיָה יוֹם־אֶחָד הוּא יִוָּדַע
ח לַיהוֹה לֹא־יוֹם וְלֹא־לָיְלָה וְהָיָה לְעֵת־עֶרֶב יִהְיֶה־אוֹר: וְהָיָה ׀ בַּיּוֹם
הַהוּא יֵצְאוּ מַיִם־חַיִּים מִירוּשָׁלַ͏ִם חֶצְיָם אֶל־הַיָּם הַקַּדְמוֹנִי וְחֶצְיָם אֶל־
ט הַיָּם הָאַחֲרוֹן בַּקַּיִץ וּבַחֹרֶף יִהְיֶה: וְהָיָה יהוֹה לְמֶלֶךְ עַל־כָּל־הָאָרֶץ בַּיּוֹם
י הַהוּא יִהְיֶה יהוֹה אֶחָד וּשְׁמוֹ אֶחָד: יִסּוֹב כָּל־הָאָרֶץ כָּעֲרָבָה מִגֶּבַע
לְרִמּוֹן נֶגֶב יְרוּשָׁלָ͏ִם וְרָאֲמָה וְיָשְׁבָה תַחְתֶּיהָ לְמִשַּׁעַר בִּנְיָמִן עַד־מְקוֹם
יא שַׁעַר הָרִאשׁוֹן עַד־שַׁעַר הַפִּנִּים וּמִגְדַּל חֲנַנְאֵל עַד יִקְבֵי הַמֶּלֶךְ: וְיָשְׁבוּ
יב בָהּ וְחֵרֶם לֹא יִהְיֶה־עוֹד וְיָשְׁבָה יְרוּשָׁלַ͏ִם לָבֶטַח: וְזֹאת ׀
תִּהְיֶה הַמַּגֵּפָה אֲשֶׁר יִגֹּף יהוה אֶת־כָּל־הָעַמִּים אֲשֶׁר צָבְאוּ עַל־יְרוּשָׁלָ͏ִם
הָמֵק ׀ בְּשָׂרוֹ וְהוּא עֹמֵד עַל־רַגְלָיו וְעֵינָיו תִּמַּקְנָה בְחֹרֵיהֶן וּלְשׁוֹנוֹ תִּמַּק
יג בְּפִיהֶם: וְהָיָה בַּיּוֹם הַהוּא תִּהְיֶה מְהוּמַת־יהוֹה רַבָּה בָּהֶם וְהֶחֱזִיקוּ אִישׁ
יד יַד רֵעֵהוּ וְעָלְתָה יָדוֹ עַל־יַד רֵעֵהוּ: וְגַם־יְהוּדָה תִּלָּחֵם בִּירוּשָׁלָ͏ִם וְאֻסַּף
טו חֵיל כָּל־הַגּוֹיִם סָבִיב זָהָב וָכֶסֶף וּבְגָדִים לָרֹב מְאֹד: וְכֵן תִּהְיֶה מַגֵּפַת
הַסּוּס הַפֶּרֶד הַגָּמָל וְהַחֲמוֹר וְכָל־הַבְּהֵמָה אֲשֶׁר יִהְיֶה בַּמַּחֲנוֹת הָהֵמָּה
טז כַּמַּגֵּפָה הַזֹּאת: וְהָיָה כָּל־הַנּוֹתָר מִכָּל־הַגּוֹיִם הַבָּאִים עַל־יְרוּשָׁלָ͏ִם וְעָלוּ
מִדֵּי שָׁנָה בְשָׁנָה לְהִשְׁתַּחֲוֹת לְמֶלֶךְ יהוֹה צְבָאוֹת וְלָחֹג אֶת־חַג הַסֻּכּוֹת:
יז וְהָיָה אֲשֶׁר לֹא־יַעֲלֶה מֵאֵת מִשְׁפְּחוֹת הָאָרֶץ אֶל־יְרוּשָׁלַ͏ִם לְהִשְׁתַּחֲוֹת
יח לְמֶלֶךְ יהוֹה צְבָאוֹת וְלֹא עֲלֵיהֶם יִהְיֶה הַגָּשֶׁם: וְאִם־מִשְׁפַּחַת מִצְרַיִם
לֹא־תַעֲלֶה וְלֹא בָאָה וְלֹא עֲלֵיהֶם תִּהְיֶה הַמַּגֵּפָה אֲשֶׁר יִגֹּף יהוה אֶת־
יט הַגּוֹיִם אֲשֶׁר לֹא יַעֲלוּ לָחֹג אֶת־חַג הַסֻּכּוֹת: זֹאת תִּהְיֶה חַטַּאת מִצְרָיִם
כ וְחַטַּאת כָּל־הַגּוֹיִם אֲשֶׁר לֹא יַעֲלוּ לָחֹג אֶת־חַג הַסֻּכּוֹת: בַּיּוֹם הַהוּא
יִהְיֶה עַל־מְצִלּוֹת הַסּוּס קֹדֶשׁ לַיהוֹה וְהָיָה הַסִּירוֹת בְּבֵית יהוֹה כַּמִּזְרָקִים
כא לִפְנֵי הַמִּזְבֵּחַ: וְהָיָה כָּל־סִיר בִּירוּשָׁלַ͏ִם וּבִיהוּדָה קֹדֶשׁ לַיהוֹה צְבָאוֹת
וּבָאוּ כָּל־הַזֹּבְחִים וְלָקְחוּ מֵהֶם וּבִשְּׁלוּ בָהֶם וְלֹא־יִהְיֶה כְנַעֲנִי עוֹד
בְּבֵית־יהוֹה צְבָאוֹת בַּיּוֹם הַהוּא: ◀

14:7. It will become famous as the unique day when God revealed His might and His wonders. When the tragedy of exile is about to begin (vv. 2-3), there will be great light, i.e., God's salvation, as described in the preceding verses.

14:8. The Dead Sea to the east, and the Mediterranean to the west.

14:9. There will be no more idolatry in the world.

14:10. Which was outside the city limits (*Rashi*); thus Jerusalem would expand beyond its present borders.

14:14. The verse refers to the war mentioned above (12:2ff), when Jerusalem will be plundered by an army that includes people of Judah.

14:15. When God strikes Jerusalem's attackers (v. 12), He will do the same to their army's animals.

14:16. The people who repented when they saw the catastrophe that was befalling their camp will mark the anniversary of the miracle on the Succos festival (*Radak*).

14:17. Because they spurned the Succos festival, which is a time of petition for rainfall for the coming year (*Rashi*).

14:18. Egypt is not irrigated by rainfall, rather the flooding Nile supplies its water; therefore, instead of being deprived of rainfall, Egypt will be deprived of the Nile's waters (*Rashi*).

14:20. Even the metal bells of the horses will be used to *the light will not be either very bright or very dim.* ⁷ *It will be a unique day; it will be known as* HASHEM's *[day], neither day nor night, but it will happen towards evening time that there will be light.* * ⁸ *It shall be on that day, spring water will flow out of Jerusalem; half of it [will flow] to the Eastern Sea* * *and half of it to the Western Sea.* * *This will be in summer and in winter.* ⁹ HASHEM *will be the King over all the land; on that day* HASHEM *will be One and His Name will be One.* * ¹⁰ *The entire land will change to a plain, from Geba to Rimmon, south of Jerusalem, and [Jerusalem] will become lofty and it will be settled in its place, from the Gate of Benjamin to the place of the first gate, to the Corner Gate, and [from] the Tower of Hananel up to the king's winery.* * ¹¹ *People will live in it, and there will be no more devastation; and Jerusalem will settle in security.*

¹² *This will be the plague with which* HASHEM *will strike all the peoples that have organized against Jerusalem: Each one's flesh will melt away while he is standing on his feet; each one's eyes will melt away in their sockets; and each one's tongue will melt away in their mouths.* ¹³ *It shall be on that day that there will be a great panic of* HASHEM *among them; each one will grab the hand of his fellow, and his hand will be raised up against the hand of his fellow.* ¹⁴ *Also Judah will wage war against Jerusalem;* * *and the wealth of all the nations all around will be gathered — gold, silver and garments in great abundance.* ¹⁵ *And similarly* * *will be the plague of the horse, the mule, the camel and the donkey, all the animals that will be in those camps, just like this plague.*

¹⁶ *It shall be that all who are left over from all the nations who had invaded Jerusalem will come up every year to worship the King* HASHEM, *Master of Legions, and to celebrate the festival of Succos.* * ¹⁷ *And it shall be that whichever of the families of the land does not go up to Jerusalem to bow down before the King,* HASHEM, *Master of Legions, there will be no rain upon them.* * ¹⁸ *But if it is the family of Egypt that does not go up and does not come [to Jerusalem], there will be no [water] for them;* * *the same plague will come to pass with which* HASHEM *will strike the nations that do not go up to celebrate the festival of Succos.* ¹⁹ *This will be the punishment of the Egyptians and the punishment of all the nations that will not go up to celebrate the festival of Succos.*

²⁰ *On that day will be [written] on the horse's bells, 'Holy unto* HASHEM';* *and the pots in the Temple of* HASHEM *will be as [numerous] as the bowls before the Altar.* ²¹ *And it will happen that every pot in Jerusalem and in Judah will be holy unto* HASHEM, *Master of Legions;* * *all those who sacrifice will come and take from them and cook in them; and there will no longer be any merchants in the Temple of* HASHEM, *Master of Legions, on that day.*

Spring flowing from Jerusalem

Plague against the besiegers

Nations celebrating Succos

Multitudes of offerings

---

produce vessels with which to bring offerings to God and pots in which to cook them, so numerous will those sacrifices be (*Rashi*).

14:21. So many offerings will be brought that all the vessels of Jerusalem will be needed to cook them. And there will be so many vessels that there will be no need for merchants who sell cooking utensils.

Thus, Zechariah ends his prophecy with a vision of Jerusalem at the zenith of its redemption and holiness.

א

א־ב מַשָּׂא דְבַר־יְהֹוָה אֶל־יִשְׂרָאֵל בְּיַד מַלְאָכִי: אָהַבְתִּי אֶתְכֶם אָמַר יְהֹוָה
וַאֲמַרְתֶּם בַּמֶּה אֲהַבְתָּנוּ הֲלוֹא־אָח עֵשָׂו לְיַעֲקֹב נְאֻם־יְהֹוָה וָאֹהַב אֶת־

HAFTARAS
TOLDOS
1:1-2:7

ג יַעֲקֹב: וְאֶת־עֵשָׂו שָׂנֵאתִי וָאָשִׂים אֶת־הָרָיו שְׁמָמָה וְאֶת־נַחֲלָתוֹ לְתַנּוֹת
ד מִדְבָּר: כִּי־תֹאמַר אֱדוֹם רֻשַּׁשְׁנוּ וְנָשׁוּב וְנִבְנֶה חֳרָבוֹת כֹּה אָמַר יְהֹוָה
צְבָאוֹת הֵמָּה יִבְנוּ וַאֲנִי אֶהֱרוֹס וְקָרְאוּ לָהֶם גְּבוּל רִשְׁעָה וְהָעָם אֲשֶׁר־
ה זָעַם יְהֹוָה עַד־עוֹלָם: וְעֵינֵיכֶם תִּרְאֶינָה וְאַתֶּם תֹּאמְרוּ יִגְדַּל יְהֹוָה מֵעַל
ו לִגְבוּל יִשְׂרָאֵל: בֵּן יְכַבֵּד אָב וְעֶבֶד אֲדֹנָיו וְאִם־אָב אָנִי אַיֵּה כְבוֹדִי וְאִם־
אֲדוֹנִים אָנִי אַיֵּה מוֹרָאִי אָמַר | יְהֹוָה צְבָאוֹת לָכֶם הַכֹּהֲנִים בּוֹזֵי שְׁמִי
ז וַאֲמַרְתֶּם בַּמֶּה בָזִינוּ אֶת־שְׁמֶךָ: מַגִּישִׁים עַל־מִזְבְּחִי לֶחֶם מְגֹאָל
ח וַאֲמַרְתֶּם בַּמֶּה גֵאַלְנוּךָ בֶּאֱמָרְכֶם שֻׁלְחַן יְהֹוָה נִבְזֶה הוּא: וְכִי־תַגִּשׁוּן
עִוֵּר לִזְבֹּחַ אֵין רָע וְכִי תַגִּישׁוּ פִּסֵּחַ וְחֹלֶה אֵין רָע הַקְרִיבֵהוּ נָא לְפֶחָתֶךָ
ט הֲיִרְצְךָ אוֹ הֲיִשָּׂא פָנֶיךָ אָמַר יְהֹוָה צְבָאוֹת: וְעַתָּה חַלּוּ־נָא פְנֵי־אֵל
י וִיחָנֵּנוּ מִיֶּדְכֶם הָיְתָה זֹּאת הֲיִשָּׂא מִכֶּם פָּנִים אָמַר יְהֹוָה צְבָאוֹת: מִי גַם־
בָּכֶם וְיִסְגֹּר דְּלָתַיִם וְלֹא־תָאִירוּ מִזְבְּחִי חִנָּם אֵין־לִי חֵפֶץ בָּכֶם אָמַר
יא יְהֹוָה צְבָאוֹת וּמִנְחָה לֹא־אֶרְצֶה מִיֶּדְכֶם: כִּי מִמִּזְרַח־שֶׁמֶשׁ וְעַד־מְבוֹאוֹ
גָּדוֹל שְׁמִי בַּגּוֹיִם וּבְכָל־מָקוֹם מֻקְטָר מֻגָּשׁ לִשְׁמִי וּמִנְחָה טְהוֹרָה כִּי־
יב גָדוֹל שְׁמִי בַּגּוֹיִם אָמַר יְהֹוָה צְבָאוֹת: וְאַתֶּם מְחַלְּלִים אוֹתוֹ בֶּאֱמָרְכֶם
שֻׁלְחַן אֲדֹנָי מְגֹאָל הוּא וְנִיבוֹ נִבְזֶה אָכְלוֹ: וַאֲמַרְתֶּם הִנֵּה מַתְּלָאָה
יג וְהִפַּחְתֶּם אוֹתוֹ אָמַר יְהֹוָה צְבָאוֹת וַהֲבֵאתֶם גָּזוּל וְאֶת־הַפִּסֵּחַ וְאֶת־
יד הַחוֹלֶה וַהֲבֵאתֶם אֶת־הַמִּנְחָה הַאֶרְצֶה אוֹתָהּ מִיֶּדְכֶם אָמַר יְהֹוָה: וְאָרוּר
נוֹכֵל וְיֵשׁ בְּעֶדְרוֹ זָכָר וְנֹדֵר וְזֹבֵחַ מָשְׁחָת לַאדֹנָי כִּי מֶלֶךְ גָּדוֹל אָנִי אָמַר

ב

א יְהֹוָה צְבָאוֹת וּשְׁמִי נוֹרָא בַגּוֹיִם: וְעַתָּה אֲלֵיכֶם הַמִּצְוָה הַזֹּאת הַכֹּהֲנִים:
ב אִם־לֹא תִשְׁמְעוּ וְאִם־לֹא תָשִׂימוּ עַל־לֵב לָתֵת כָּבוֹד לִשְׁמִי אָמַר יְהֹוָה
צְבָאוֹת וְשִׁלַּחְתִּי בָכֶם אֶת־הַמְּאֵרָה וְאָרוֹתִי אֶת־בִּרְכוֹתֵיכֶם וְגַם
ג אָרוֹתִיהָ כִּי אֵינְכֶם שָׂמִים עַל־לֵב: הִנְנִי גֹעֵר לָכֶם אֶת־הַזֶּרַע וְזֵרִיתִי
פֶרֶשׁ עַל־פְּנֵיכֶם פֶּרֶשׁ חַגֵּיכֶם וְנָשָׂא אֶתְכֶם אֵלָיו: וִידַעְתֶּם כִּי שִׁלַּחְתִּי
ד אֲלֵיכֶם אֵת הַמִּצְוָה הַזֹּאת לִהְיוֹת בְּרִיתִי אֶת־לֵוִי אָמַר יְהֹוָה צְבָאוֹת:
ה בְּרִיתִי | הָיְתָה אִתּוֹ הַחַיִּים וְהַשָּׁלוֹם וָאֶתְּנֵם־לוֹ מוֹרָא וַיִּירָאֵנִי וּמִפְּנֵי
ו שְׁמִי נִחַת הוּא: תּוֹרַת אֱמֶת הָיְתָה בְּפִיהוּ וְעַוְלָה לֹא־נִמְצָא בִשְׂפָתָיו

1:7. The people showed disrespect to the Altar by deriding it as full of blood and fats (*Radak*).

1:8. If a human governor would not accept such offerings, surely it is scornful to bring them to God!

1:10. I would rather have no sacrifices at all than invalid ones.

1:13. You bring an inferior offering and exclaim falsely how hard it is for you to afford it (*Rashi*).

2:2. I will send a curse instead of the blessings you currently enjoy (*Radak*).

2:3. God will command seeds not to sprout. In a further manifestation of God's anger, He will cast the filth of your invalid offerings in your faces, as it were, and all of this will be brought about by your own sins (*Radak*).

2:5. God made a covenant with the founders of the priestly line of Levi, Aaron and his great-grandson Phinehas. See *Numbers* 25:12-13 (*Ibn Ezra*).

1

(See Appendix A,
timeline 4)

*Loving
Jacob,
not Esau*

*National
disrespect*

*Repulsive
offerings*

¹ **T**he prophecy of the word of HASHEM to Israel, by the hand of Malachi:

² *I loved you, says HASHEM; but you say, 'How have You loved us?' Was not Esau the brother of Jacob — the word of HASHEM — yet I loved Jacob.* ³ *But I hated Esau; I made his mountains a desolation and [gave] his heritage to the desert serpents.* ⁴ *Though Edom will say, 'We have become destitute, but we will return and rebuild the ruins,' thus says HASHEM, Master of Legions: They may build, but I will tear down! They will be called 'the boundary of wickedness' and 'the people whom HASHEM has condemned forever.'* ⁵ *And your eyes will behold it, and you will say upon the territory of Israel, 'May HASHEM be glorified!'*

⁶ *A son will honor his father and a servant his master. If I am a Father where is my honor? And if I am a Master where is My fear? says HASHEM, Master of Legions, to you, the Kohanim who scorn My Name. Yet you say, 'How have we scorned Your Name?'* ⁷ *You present on My Altar loathsome food, and you say, 'How have we loathed You?' By your saying, 'The table of HASHEM is repulsive.'* * ⁸ *When you present a blind animal for sacrifice, is nothing wrong? And when you present a lame or sick [animal], is nothing wrong? Present it, if you please, to your governor:* * *Would he be pleased with you or show you favor? said HASHEM, Master of Legions.* ⁹ *And now, if you now entreat God, will He be gracious unto us? This [sin] comes from your hand; will He show you favor? says HASHEM, Master of Legions.*

¹⁰ *If only there were someone among you who would shut the [Temple] doors, so that you could not kindle upon My Altar in vain!* * *I have no desire for you, said HASHEM, Master of Legions, and I will not accept an offering from your hand.* ¹¹ *For from the rising of the sun to its setting, My Name is great among the nations, and in every place [where offerings] are presented to My Name, and also pure meal-offerings; for My Name is great among the nations, says HASHEM, Master of Legions.* ¹² *But you defile it, by your saying, 'The table of the Lord is loathsome'; and by [your] description of it as 'Its food is repulsive.'* ¹³ *You say, 'Behold, this [offering] is so burdensome,'* * *and so you vex Him, says HASHEM, Master of Legions. You bring the stolen and the lame, and the sick [animal], and bring [it] as an offering — shall I accept it from your hand? says HASHEM.* ¹⁴ *Cursed be the charlatan who has a [superior] ram in his flock, but vows and sacrifices a blemished [animal] to the Lord! For I am a great King, says HASHEM, Master of Legions, and My Name is awesome among the nations.*

2

*Obedience
or curse*

*Levi's
covenant*

¹ **A**nd now, this commandment is upon you, O Kohanim. ² *If you do not listen and do not take it to heart to render honor to My Name, says HASHEM, Master of Legions, I will send the curse among you and I will curse your blessings.* * *Indeed I have already cursed it, for you do not take to heart.* ³ *Behold, I am suppressing the seed because of you;* * *and I will scatter filth upon your faces, the filth of your festive offerings; [your sin] will carry you to this.*

⁴ *Know that I have sent this commandment to you, so that My covenant should be with Levi, says HASHEM, Master of Legions.* ⁵ *My covenant was with him, life and peace;* * *I gave these to him for the sake of the fear with which he feared Me, for he was in awe of My Name.* ⁶ *The teaching of truth was in his mouth, and injustice was not found on his lips;*

בְּשָׁלוֹם וּבְמִישׁוֹר הָלַךְ אִתִּי וְרַבִּים הֵשִׁיב מֵעָוֺן: כִּי־שִׂפְתֵי כֹהֵן יִשְׁמְרוּ־ ז

דַעַת וְתוֹרָה יְבַקְשׁוּ מִפִּיהוּ כִּי מַלְאַךְ יהוה־צְבָאוֹת הוּא: ◀ וְאַתֶּם סַרְתֶּם ח

מִן־הַדֶּרֶךְ הִכְשַׁלְתֶּם רַבִּים בַּתּוֹרָה שִׁחַתֶּם בְּרִית הַלֵּוִי אָמַר יהוה צְבָאוֹת:

וְגַם־אֲנִי נָתַתִּי אֶתְכֶם נִבְזִים וּשְׁפָלִים לְכָל־הָעָם כְּפִי אֲשֶׁר אֵינְכֶם שֹׁמְרִים ט

אֶת־דְּרָכַי וְנֹשְׂאִים פָּנִים בַּתּוֹרָה: הֲלוֹא אָב אֶחָד לְכֻלָּנוּ הֲלוֹא אֵל אֶחָד י

בְּרָאָנוּ מַדּוּעַ נִבְגַּד אִישׁ בְּאָחִיו לְחַלֵּל בְּרִית אֲבֹתֵינוּ: בָּגְדָה יְהוּדָה יא

וְתוֹעֵבָה נֶעֶשְׂתָה בְיִשְׂרָאֵל וּבִירוּשָׁלָ‍ִם כִּי ׀ חִלֵּל יְהוּדָה קֹדֶשׁ יהוה אֲשֶׁר

אָהֵב וּבָעַל בַּת־אֵל נֵכָר: יַכְרֵת יהוה לָאִישׁ אֲשֶׁר יַעֲשֶׂנָּה עֵר וְעֹנֶה יב

מֵאָהֳלֵי יַעֲקֹב וּמַגִּישׁ מִנְחָה לַיהוה צְבָאוֹת: וְזֹאת שֵׁנִית תַּעֲשׂוּ יג

כַּסּוֹת דִּמְעָה אֶת־מִזְבַּח יהוה בְּכִי וַאֲנָקָה מֵאֵין עוֹד פְּנוֹת אֶל־הַמִּנְחָה

וְלָקַחַת רָצוֹן מִיֶּדְכֶם: וַאֲמַרְתֶּם עַל־מָה עַל כִּי־יהוה הֵעִיד בֵּינְךָ וּבֵין ׀ אֵשֶׁת יד

נְעוּרֶיךָ אֲשֶׁר אַתָּה בָּגַדְתָּה בָּהּ וְהִיא חֲבֶרְתְּךָ וְאֵשֶׁת בְּרִיתֶךָ: וְלֹא־אֶחָד טו

עָשָׂה וּשְׁאָר רוּחַ לוֹ וּמָה הָאֶחָד מְבַקֵּשׁ זֶרַע אֱלֹהִים וְנִשְׁמַרְתֶּם בְּרוּחֲכֶם

וּבְאֵשֶׁת נְעוּרֶיךָ אַל־יִבְגֹּד: כִּי־שָׂנֵא שַׁלַּח אָמַר יהוה אֱלֹהֵי יִשְׂרָאֵל טז

וְכִסָּה חָמָס עַל־לְבוּשׁוֹ אָמַר יהוה צְבָאוֹת וְנִשְׁמַרְתֶּם בְּרוּחֲכֶם וְלֹא

תִבְגֹּדוּ: הוֹגַעְתֶּם יהוה בְּדִבְרֵיכֶם וַאֲמַרְתֶּם בַּמֶּה הוֹגָעְנוּ בֶּאֱמָרְכֶם יז

כָּל־עֹשֵׂה רָע טוֹב ׀ בְּעֵינֵי יהוה וּבָהֶם הוּא חָפֵץ אוֹ אַיֵּה אֱלֹהֵי הַמִּשְׁפָּט:

הִנְנִי שֹׁלֵחַ מַלְאָכִי וּפִנָּה־דֶרֶךְ לְפָנָי וּפִתְאֹם יָבוֹא אֶל־הֵיכָלוֹ הָאָדוֹן ׀ א   **ג**

אֲשֶׁר־אַתֶּם מְבַקְשִׁים וּמַלְאַךְ הַבְּרִית אֲשֶׁר־אַתֶּם חֲפֵצִים הִנֵּה־בָא אָמַר

יהוה צְבָאוֹת: וּמִי מְכַלְכֵּל אֶת־יוֹם בּוֹאוֹ וּמִי הָעֹמֵד בְּהֵרָאוֹתוֹ כִּי־הוּא ב

כְּאֵשׁ מְצָרֵף וּכְבֹרִית מְכַבְּסִים: וְיָשַׁב מְצָרֵף וּמְטַהֵר כֶּסֶף וְטִהַר אֶת־בְּנֵי־ ג

לֵוִי וְזִקַּק אֹתָם כַּזָּהָב וְכַכָּסֶף וְהָיוּ לַיהוה מַגִּישֵׁי מִנְחָה בִּצְדָקָה: ◀ וְעָרְבָה ד

לַיהוה מִנְחַת יְהוּדָה וִירוּשָׁלָ‍ִם כִּימֵי עוֹלָם וּכְשָׁנִים קַדְמֹנִיּוֹת: וְקָרַבְתִּי ה

אֲלֵיכֶם לַמִּשְׁפָּט וְהָיִיתִי ׀ עֵד מְמַהֵר בַּמְכַשְּׁפִים וּבַמְנָאֲפִים וּבַנִּשְׁבָּעִים

לַשֶּׁקֶר וּבְעֹשְׁקֵי שְׂכַר־שָׂכִיר אַלְמָנָה וְיָתוֹם וּמַטֵּי־גֵר וְלֹא יְרֵאוּנִי אָמַר

יהוה צְבָאוֹת: כִּי אֲנִי יהוה לֹא שָׁנִיתִי וְאַתֶּם בְּנֵי־יַעֲקֹב לֹא כְלִיתֶם: ו

HAFTARAS
SHABBAS
HAGADOL
3:4-24

2:9. When an important person brings an unacceptable offering, you defer to his status and allow it to be brought.

2:10. Malachi now addresses himself to the men of his day who betrayed their Jewish wives during the exile and married local heathen women.

2:11. By betraying the daughters of Israel.

2:12. If that man is a *Kohen,* may he have no children to serve in the Temple (*Rashi*).

2:13. Your additional sin of marrying heathen women compounds the sin of bringing inferior sacrifices to the Temple (*Radak*). Your betrayal of your Jewish wives caused them to flood the Altar with their tears.

2:15. An allusion to Abraham (see *Ezekiel* 33:24). The treacherous husbands retorted, "The exalted Abraham

did the same thing: Did he not take Hagar while he was married to Sarah?" To this the prophet responded, "Abraham's motive was holy; he had not had any children with Sarah and his only reason for taking Hagar was to raise a family faithful to God. But you have no such higher purpose; how dare you betray your Jewish wives?" (*Kara*).

2:16. A man who insists on retaining the wife he hates is concealing his dislike, as if covering injustice with his garment. You should at least divorce the wives you dislike so that they would be free to remarry (*Rashi*).

2:17. You see that wicked people prosper and you conclude that either God loves the wicked or there is no justice in the world (*Rashi*).

3:1. The prophet Elijah, God's messenger of the

he walked with Me in peace and with fairness, and turned many away from iniquity.

Lips of the
Kohen

⁷ *For the lips of the Kohen should safeguard knowledge, and people should seek teaching from his mouth; for he is an agent of* HASHEM, *Master of Legions.* ⁸ *But you have veered from the path; you have caused many people to stumble through [your] teaching. You have corrupted the covenant of Levi, says* HASHEM, *Master of Legions.* ⁹ *Therefore, I have also made you repulsive and lowly to all the people, because you do not observe My ways and you show favoritism in [your] teaching.* *

Denunciation
of
intermarriage

¹⁰ *"Have we not all one Father?* * *Did not one God create us [all]? Why, then, is one person betrayed by another, in order to defile the covenant of our forefathers?* ¹¹ *Judah has betrayed, and an abomination has been done in Israel and in Jerusalem. For Judah has defiled the holy [nation]* * *of* HASHEM, *which He loved, and has taken in marriage the daughter of a foreign god.* ¹² *May* HASHEM *eliminate from the man who does this any child and descendant from the tents of Jacob, and anyone who might present an offering* * *to* HASHEM, *Master of Legions.* ¹³ *And this is a second [sin] that you commit:* * *covering the altar of* HASHEM *with tears, crying and moaning, so that He will no longer turn to [your] offering, or take it with favor from your hand.* ¹⁴ *You say, "Why [is this]?" It is because* HASHEM *has testified between you and the wife of your youth whom you have betrayed, though she is your companion and the wife of your covenant.* ¹⁵ *[You ask,] "But did not the unique one* * *do [so], and he had an extraordinary spirit?" And what did the unique one seek? Godly offspring! However, you should guard your spirit and let it not betray the wife of your youth!*

¹⁶ *For he who hates [his wife] should divorce [her], says* HASHEM, *God of Israel! He covers injustice with his garment,* * *says* HASHEM, *Master of Legions! Guard your spirit and do not commit betrayal.*

Questioning
God's justice

¹⁷ *You have wearied* HASHEM *with your words, but you say, "How have we wearied Him?" By your saying, "Everyone who does wrong is good in the eyes of* HASHEM, *and He favors them; or else where is the God of justice?"* *

3

God's
messenger
brings justice

¹ *Behold, I am sending My messenger, and he will clear a path before Me;* * *suddenly the Lord Whom you seek will come to His Sanctuary, and the messenger of the covenant for whom you yearn, behold, he comes, says* HASHEM, *Master of Legions.* ² *Who can bear the day of his coming and who can survive when he appears? For he will be like the smelter's fire and like the launderers' soap.* ³ *He will sit smelting and purifying silver; he will purify the children of Levi and refine them like gold and like silver, and they will be for* HASHEM *presenters of offerings in righteousness.* ⁴ *Then the offering of Judah and Jerusalem will be pleasing to* HASHEM *as in the days of old and in previous years.* ⁵ *I will draw near to you for the judgment, and I will be a swift witness against the sorcerers; against the adulterers; against those who swear falsely; against those who extort the wage of the worker, the widow and the orphan; and [against] those who wrong the stranger and do not fear Me, says* HASHEM, *Master of Legions.* ⁶ *For I,* HASHEM, *have not changed;* * *and you, the sons of Jacob, you have not perished.*

---

covenant (*Radak*), will eliminate the wicked from the land in preparation for the Messianic era (*Rashi*).
3:6. Although I let the wicked prosper, it is not because I

have changed (as you suggested in 2:17), but because I am merciful and patient with sinners (*Rashi*). So too, is your existence as a people guaranteed forever (*Radak*).

ז לְמִימֵי אֲבֹתֵיכֶם סַרְתֶּם מֵחֻקַּי וְלֹא שְׁמַרְתֶּם שׁוּבוּ אֵלַי וְאָשׁוּבָה אֲלֵיכֶם

ח אָמַר יהוה צְבָאוֹת וַאֲמַרְתֶּם בַּמֶּה נָשׁוּב: הֲיִקְבַּע אָדָם אֱלֹהִים כִּי אַתֶּם

ט קֹבְעִים אֹתִי וַאֲמַרְתֶּם בַּמֶּה קְבַעֲנוּךָ הַמַּעֲשֵׂר וְהַתְּרוּמָה: בַּמְּאֵרָה אַתֶּם

י נֵאָרִים וְאֹתִי אַתֶּם קֹבְעִים הַגּוֹי כֻּלּוֹ: הָבִיאוּ אֶת־כָּל־הַמַּעֲשֵׂר אֶל־בֵּית הָאוֹצָר וִיהִי טֶרֶף בְּבֵיתִי וּבְחָנוּנִי נָא בָּזֹאת אָמַר יהוה צְבָאוֹת אִם־לֹא אֶפְתַּח לָכֶם אֵת אֲרֻבּוֹת הַשָּׁמַיִם וַהֲרִיקֹתִי לָכֶם בְּרָכָה עַד־בְּלִי־דָי:

יא וְגָעַרְתִּי לָכֶם בָּאֹכֵל וְלֹא־יַשְׁחִת לָכֶם אֶת־פְּרִי הָאֲדָמָה וְלֹא־תְשַׁכֵּל לָכֶם הַגֶּפֶן בַּשָּׂדֶה אָמַר יהוה צְבָאוֹת: וְאִשְּׁרוּ אֶתְכֶם כָּל־הַגּוֹיִם כִּי־תִהְיוּ

יב

יג אַתֶּם אֶרֶץ חֵפֶץ אָמַר יהוה צְבָאוֹת: חָזְקוּ עָלַי דִּבְרֵיכֶם

יד אָמַר יהוה וַאֲמַרְתֶּם מַה־נִּדְבַּרְנוּ עָלֶיךָ: אֲמַרְתֶּם שָׁוְא עֲבֹד אֱלֹהִים וּמַה־

טו בֶּצַע כִּי שָׁמַרְנוּ מִשְׁמַרְתּוֹ וְכִי הָלַכְנוּ קְדֹרַנִּית מִפְּנֵי יהוה צְבָאוֹת: וְעַתָּה אֲנַחְנוּ מְאַשְּׁרִים זֵדִים גַּם־נִבְנוּ עֹשֵׂי רִשְׁעָה גַּם בָּחֲנוּ אֱלֹהִים וַיִּמָּלֵטוּ: אָז

טז נִדְבְּרוּ יִרְאֵי יהוה אִישׁ אֶל־רֵעֵהוּ וַיַּקְשֵׁב יהוה וַיִּשְׁמָע וַיִּכָּתֵב סֵפֶר זִכָּרוֹן לְפָנָיו לְיִרְאֵי יהוה וּלְחֹשְׁבֵי שְׁמוֹ: וְהָיוּ לִי אָמַר יהוה צְבָאוֹת לַיּוֹם

יז אֲשֶׁר אֲנִי עֹשֶׂה סְגֻלָּה וְחָמַלְתִּי עֲלֵיהֶם כַּאֲשֶׁר יַחְמֹל אִישׁ עַל־בְּנוֹ

יח הָעֹבֵד אֹתוֹ: וְשַׁבְתֶּם וּרְאִיתֶם בֵּין צַדִּיק לְרָשָׁע בֵּין עֹבֵד אֱלֹהִים לַאֲשֶׁר

יט לֹא עֲבָדוֹ: כִּי־הִנֵּה הַיּוֹם בָּא בֹּעֵר כַּתַּנּוּר וְהָיוּ כָל־ זֵדִים וְכָל־עֹשֵׂה רִשְׁעָה קַשׁ וְלִהַט אֹתָם הַיּוֹם הַבָּא אָמַר יהוה צְבָאוֹת

כ אֲשֶׁר לֹא־יַעֲזֹב לָהֶם שֹׁרֶשׁ וְעָנָף: וְזָרְחָה לָכֶם יִרְאֵי שְׁמִי שֶׁמֶשׁ צְדָקָה וּמַרְפֵּא בִּכְנָפֶיהָ וִיצָאתֶם וּפִשְׁתֶּם כְּעֶגְלֵי מַרְבֵּק: וְעַסּוֹתֶם רְשָׁעִים

כא כִּי־יִהְיוּ אֵפֶר תַּחַת כַּפּוֹת רַגְלֵיכֶם בַּיּוֹם אֲשֶׁר אֲנִי עֹשֶׂה אָמַר יהוה צְבָאוֹת: זִכְרוּ תּוֹרַת מֹשֶׁה עַבְדִּי אֲשֶׁר צִוִּיתִי אוֹתוֹ

כב

כג בְחֹרֵב עַל־כָּל־יִשְׂרָאֵל חֻקִּים וּמִשְׁפָּטִים: הִנֵּה אָנֹכִי שֹׁלֵחַ לָכֶם אֵת

כד אֵלִיָּה הַנָּבִיא לִפְנֵי בּוֹא יוֹם יהוה הַגָּדוֹל וְהַנּוֹרָא: וְהֵשִׁיב לֵב־אָבוֹת עַל־ בָּנִים וְלֵב בָּנִים עַל־אֲבוֹתָם פֶּן־אָבוֹא וְהִכֵּיתִי אֶת־הָאָרֶץ חֵרֶם:

הִנֵּה אָנֹכִי שֹׁלֵחַ לָכֶם אֵת אֵלִיָּה הַנָּבִיא לִפְנֵי בּוֹא יוֹם יהוה הַגָּדוֹל וְהַנּוֹרָא: ◀

סכום פסוקי תרי עשר: הושע מאה ותשעים ושבעה. יואל שבעים ושלושה. שלחו מג״ל סימן. ורגלך לא שבעים סימן. בצק״ה סימן. עמוס מאה וארבעים וששה. קמ״ו בניה סימן. עובדיה עשרים ואחד. א״ך טוב לישראל סימן. יונה ארבעים ושמונה. ישראל עשרה חי״ל סימן. מיכה מאה וחמשה. על״ה אלקים בתרועה סימן. נחום ארבעים ושבעה מים סימן. חבקוק חמשים וששה. ול״ך תהיה צדקה סימן. צפניה חמשים ושלשה. ג״ן נעול סימן. חגי שלשים ושמונה. כי אם גל״ה סודו סימן. זכריה מאתים ואחד עשר. אשרי כל יר״א סימן. מלאכי חמשים וחמשה. הל״ך לדרכו סימן. סכום הפסוקים של כל שנים עשר נביאים אלף וחמשים ב״י שרי״ת ע״ם אלהים סימן.

3:9. You were not chastened by the punishments I meted out to you, and you continue to commit the same sin.

3:11. Locusts and other crop-destroying creatures.

3:16. Refuting the just quoted blasphemies of the impious (Radak).

3:17. On the day when God judges the wicked, the

*Return
to Me!*

⁷ Since the days of your forefathers you have veered away from My laws and you have not observed them. Return to Me and I will return to you! says HASHEM, Master of Legions; but you say, 'For what should we repent?' ⁸ Should a person steal from God, as you steal from Me? And you say, 'How have we stolen from you?' [By withholding] the tithes and the terumah-offerings! ⁹ You are cursed with a curse, yet you [continue to] steal from Me, the entire nation!* ¹⁰ Bring all the tithes into the storage house, and let it be sustenance in My Temple. Test Me, if you will, with this, says HASHEM, Master of Legions, [see] if I do not open up for you the windows of the heavens and pour out upon you blessing without end. ¹¹ And I will rebuke the devourer* for you, and they will not destroy for you the produce of the ground, and the vine will not cast off its fruit for you in the field, says HASHEM, Master of Legions. ¹² All the nations will praise you, for you will be a land of desire, says HASHEM, Master of Legions.

*Your words
were harsh*

¹³ Your words have become harsh against Me, says HASHEM; but you say, 'How have we spoken against You?' ¹⁴ You have said, 'It is useless to serve God! What gain is there for us that we have kept His watch, and that we walk submissively before HASHEM, Master of Legions? ¹⁵ So now we praise the wicked. Evildoers are built up; they have even tested God and escaped.' ¹⁶ Then those who fear HASHEM spoke to one another, * and HASHEM listened and heard, and a book of remembrance was written before Him for those who fear HASHEM and those who give thought to His Name. ¹⁷ They will be a precious treasure for Me, says HASHEM, Master of Legions, on the day which I bring about;* and I will have mercy on them as a man has mercy on his son who serves him. ¹⁸ Then you will return and see the difference between the righteous and the wicked, between one who serves God and one who does not serve Him.

*A great
day is
coming . . .*

¹⁹ For behold, the day* is coming, burning like an oven, when all the wicked people and all the evildoers will be like straw; and that coming day* will burn them up, says HASHEM, Master of Legions, so that it will not leave them a root or branch. ²⁰ But a sun of righteousness will shine for you who fear My Name, with healing in its rays, and you will go out and flourish like calves [fattened] in the stall. ²¹ And you will trample the wicked, for they will be ashes under the soles of your feet, on that day that I bring about, says HASHEM, Master of Legions. ²² Remember the Torah of Moses My servant, * which I commanded him at Horeb for all of Israel — [its] decrees and [its] statutes.

*. . . when
God will
send Elijah*

²³ Behold, I send you Elijah the prophet before the coming of the great and awesome day of HASHEM. ²⁴ And he will turn back [to God] the hearts of fathers with [their] sons and the hearts of sons with their fathers, lest I come and strike the land with utter destruction."*

*Behold, * I send you Elijah the prophet before the coming
of the great and awesome day of HASHEM.*

---

righteous people will be His treasure (*Radak*).

3:19. A metaphor for the sun.

3:22. Observe the Torah, so that you will be spared on Judgment Day.

3:24. Elijah will draw people's hearts back to God before Judgment Day, to increase the number of people who will

survive His judgment.

It is customary, during public readings of *Malachi*, to repeat the *penultimate* verse. This is done to end the reading on a positive note. The same custom is also followed at the conclusion of *Isaiah, Lamentations* and *Ecclesiastes* (*Rashi*).

כתובים
The Writings

תהלים	❖	*Psalms / Tehillim*
משלי	❖	*Proverbs / Mishlei*
איוב	❖	*Job / Iyov*
שיר השירים	❖	*The Song of Songs / Shir HaShirim*
רות	❖	*Ruth / Rus*
איכה	❖	*Lamentations / Eichah*
קהלת	❖	*Ecclesiastes / Koheles*
אסתר	❖	*Esther / Esther*
דניאל	❖	*Daniel / Daniel*
עזרא־נחמיה	❖	*Ezra-Nehemiah / Ezra-Nechemiah*
דברי הימים	❖	*Chronicles / Divrei HaYamim*

כתובים / The Writings

Psalms / תְּהִלִּים

For nearly three thousand years, every situation in a Jew's life has been reflected in King David's Book of Psalms. Referring to this Book, God said to David, "One day of your songs and praises is more precious to Me than the thousands of offerings that will be brought by your son Solomon." In illness and in strife, in triumph and in success, the Jew opens his Book of Psalms and lets David become the harp upon which his own emotions sing or weep. Small wonder that when the Chofetz Chaim, as an old man, was presented with his mother's ancient Book of Psalms, its pages swollen with her lifetime of tears, he was overcome with emotion. Who can assess the worth of the little Book that has been the chariot bearing countless tears to the Heavenly Throne?

Upon reading of King David's many ordeals, one can begin to understand how he could compose the psalms that capture every person's joy and grief, thanksgiving and remorse, cries from the heart and songs of happiness. He was the Sweet Singer of Israel; more than that, however, he experienced the travail of every person, and that is why everyone can see himself mirrored in David's psalms.

Many of the psalms were composed to be sung by the Levites in the Temple, with musical accompaniment, and such psalms generally begin by naming the instrument upon which they would be played. Many of the psalms are attributed to authors other than David, but according to one view in the Talmud, he was the author of them all, presumably drawing upon ideas or texts and weaving them into his own compositions.

Whatever the authorship of the psalms, one thing is certain: Since the day it was composed, the Book of Psalms has become interwoven with the souls of countless Jews. The psalms are part of the daily prayers. They are recited at moments of illness and crisis. They are chanted joyously in times of good fortune and when heartfelt prayers have been answered. The last verse of the Book proclaims: "Let all souls [כָּל הַנְּשָׁמָה] praise God, Hallelujah!" The Sages expound homiletically that the verse also means to teach: "Praise God for every breath [עַל כָּל נְשִׁימָה וּנְשִׁימָה] that you are privileged to take." This degree of gratitude that sees everything — even as automatic an act as drawing a breath — as a Divine gift is one of the countless teachings of David. It is the soul that permeates the entire Book of Psalms.

ספר ראשון

א

א אַשְׁרֵי־הָאִישׁ אֲשֶׁר ׀ לֹא הָלַךְ בַּעֲצַת רְשָׁעִים וּבְדֶרֶךְ חַטָּאִים לֹא עָמָד

ב וּבְמוֹשַׁב לֵצִים לֹא יָשָׁב: כִּי אִם בְּתוֹרַת יהוה חֶפְצוֹ וּבְתוֹרָתוֹ יֶהְגֶּה יוֹמָם

ג וָלָיְלָה: וְהָיָה כְּעֵץ שָׁתוּל עַל־פַּלְגֵי מָיִם אֲשֶׁר פִּרְיוֹ ׀ יִתֵּן בְּעִתּוֹ וְעָלֵהוּ לֹא־

ד יִבּוֹל וְכֹל אֲשֶׁר־יַעֲשֶׂה יַצְלִיחַ: לֹא־כֵן הָרְשָׁעִים כִּי אִם־כַּמֹּץ אֲשֶׁר־

ה תִּדְּפֶנּוּ רוּחַ: עַל־כֵּן ׀ לֹא־יָקֻמוּ רְשָׁעִים בַּמִּשְׁפָּט וְחַטָּאִים בַּעֲדַת צַדִּיקִים:

ו כִּי־יוֹדֵעַ יהוה דֶּרֶךְ צַדִּיקִים וְדֶרֶךְ רְשָׁעִים תֹּאבֵד:

ב

א־ב לָמָּה רָגְשׁוּ גוֹיִם וּלְאֻמִּים יֶהְגּוּ־רִיק: יִתְיַצְּבוּ ׀ מַלְכֵי־אֶרֶץ וְרוֹזְנִים נוֹסְדוּ־

ג יַחַד עַל־יהוה וְעַל־מְשִׁיחוֹ: נְנַתְּקָה אֶת־מוֹסְרוֹתֵימוֹ וְנַשְׁלִיכָה מִמֶּנּוּ

ד־ה עֲבֹתֵימוֹ: יוֹשֵׁב בַּשָּׁמַיִם יִשְׂחָק אֲדֹנָי יִלְעַג־לָמוֹ: אָז יְדַבֵּר אֵלֵימוֹ בְאַפּוֹ

ו־ז וּבַחֲרוֹנוֹ יְבַהֲלֵמוֹ: וַאֲנִי נָסַכְתִּי מַלְכִּי עַל־צִיּוֹן הַר־קָדְשִׁי: אֲסַפְּרָה אֶל חֹק

ח יהוה אָמַר אֵלַי בְּנִי אַתָּה אֲנִי הַיּוֹם יְלִדְתִּיךָ: שְׁאַל מִמֶּנִּי וְאֶתְּנָה גוֹיִם

ט נַחֲלָתֶךָ וַאֲחֻזָּתְךָ אַפְסֵי־אָרֶץ: תְּרֹעֵם בְּשֵׁבֶט בַּרְזֶל כִּכְלִי יוֹצֵר תְּנַפְּצֵם:

י־יא וְעַתָּה מְלָכִים הַשְׂכִּילוּ הִוָּסְרוּ שֹׁפְטֵי אָרֶץ: עִבְדוּ אֶת־יהוה בְּיִרְאָה וְגִילוּ

יב בִּרְעָדָה: נַשְּׁקוּ־בַר פֶּן־יֶאֱנַף ׀ וְתֹאבְדוּ דֶרֶךְ כִּי־יִבְעַר כִּמְעַט אַפּוֹ אַשְׁרֵי

כָּל־חוֹסֵי בוֹ:

ג

א־ב מִזְמוֹר לְדָוִד בְּבָרְחוֹ מִפְּנֵי ׀ אַבְשָׁלוֹם בְּנוֹ: יהוה מָה־רַבּוּ צָרָי רַבִּים קָמִים

ג־ד עָלָי: רַבִּים אֹמְרִים לְנַפְשִׁי אֵין יְשׁוּעָתָה לּוֹ בֵאלֹהִים סֶלָה: וְאַתָּה יהוה מָגֵן

ה בַּעֲדִי כְּבוֹדִי וּמֵרִים רֹאשִׁי: קוֹלִי אֶל־יהוה אֶקְרָא וַיַּעֲנֵנִי מֵהַר קָדְשׁוֹ סֶלָה:

ו־ז אֲנִי שָׁכַבְתִּי וָאִישָׁנָה הֱקִיצוֹתִי כִּי יהוה יִסְמְכֵנִי: לֹא־אִירָא מֵרִבְבוֹת עָם

ח אֲשֶׁר סָבִיב שָׁתוּ עָלָי: קוּמָה יהוה ׀ הוֹשִׁיעֵנִי אֱלֹהַי כִּי־הִכִּיתָ אֶת־כָּל־אֹיְבַי

ט לֶחִי שִׁנֵּי רְשָׁעִים שִׁבַּרְתָּ: לַיהוה הַיְשׁוּעָה עַל־עַמְּךָ בִרְכָתֶךָ סֶּלָה:

ד

א־ב לַמְנַצֵּחַ בִּנְגִינוֹת מִזְמוֹר לְדָוִד: בְּקָרְאִי עֲנֵנִי ׀ אֱלֹהֵי צִדְקִי בַּצָּר הִרְחַבְתָּ לִּי

ג חָנֵּנִי וּשְׁמַע תְּפִלָּתִי: בְּנֵי אִישׁ עַד־מֶה כְבוֹדִי לִכְלִמָּה תֶּאֱהָבוּן רִיק

ד תְּבַקְשׁוּ כָזָב סֶלָה: וּדְעוּ כִּי־הִפְלָה יהוה חָסִיד לוֹ יהוה יִשְׁמַע בְּקָרְאִי

ה־ו אֵלָיו: רִגְזוּ וְאַל־תֶּחֱטָאוּ אִמְרוּ בִלְבַבְכֶם עַל־מִשְׁכַּבְכֶם וְדֹמּוּ סֶלָה: זִבְחוּ

ז זִבְחֵי־צֶדֶק וּבִטְחוּ אֶל־יהוה: רַבִּים אֹמְרִים מִי־יַרְאֵנוּ טוֹב נְסָה־עָלֵינוּ

ח־ט אוֹר פָּנֶיךָ יהוה: נָתַתָּה שִׂמְחָה בְלִבִּי מֵעֵת דְּגָנָם וְתִירוֹשָׁם רָבּוּ: בְּשָׁלוֹם

יַחְדָּו אֶשְׁכְּבָה וְאִישָׁן כִּי־אַתָּה יהוה לְבָדָד לָבֶטַח תּוֹשִׁיבֵנִי:

1:2. At first it is called "the Torah of HASHEM," but after one has toiled to understand it, he has acquired it as his own, and it is called "his *own* Torah" (*Rashi*).

1:6. God "attends the way of the righteous," protecting and rewarding it (*Radak*), "but the way of the wicked," lacking God's loving care, "will perish" on its own (*R' Hirsch*).

2:2. Since the Philistines knew that David was God's

chosen one, their attack against him was an attack against God (*Radak*).

2:10-11. If gentile kings and judges turn away from sin, they too will rejoice when the wicked tremble in fear of God's wrath (*Rashi*).

3:1. See *II Samuel*, Chapters 15-19.

3:3. This word is variously rendered as: "forever" (*Eruvin* 54a; *Targum*); "true and certain" (*Ibn Ezra*); an instruction

BOOK ONE

1

The Book of Psalms begins by asserting that the keys to good fortune are to shun evil influences and to study the Torah.

¹ **P**raiseworthy is the man who walked not in the counsel of the wicked, and stood not in the path of the sinful, and sat not in the session of scorners. ² But his desire is in the Torah of HASHEM, and in His Torah* he meditates day and night. ³ He shall be like a tree deeply rooted alongside brooks of water, that yields its fruit in its season, and whose leaf never withers; and everything that he does will succeed. ⁴ Not so the wicked; rather [they are] like the chaff that the wind drives away. ⁵ Therefore the wicked shall not be vindicated in judgment, nor the sinful in the assembly of the righteous — ⁶ for HASHEM attends the way of the righteous, while the way of the wicked will perish. *

2

No matter how powerful the force, nothing can thwart God's will. Rashi comments that the psalm alludes to the encounter between the nations and the Messiah.

¹ **W**hy do nations gather, and regimes talk in vain? ² The kings of the earth take their stand and the princes conspire secretly, against HASHEM* and against His anointed: ³ "Let us cut their cords and let us cast off their ropes from ourselves." ⁴ He Who sits in heaven will laugh, the Lord will mock them. ⁵ Then He will speak to them in His anger, and in His wrath He will terrify them: ⁶ "I Myself have anointed My king, over Zion, My holy mountain!" ⁷ I am obliged to proclaim that HASHEM said to me, "You are My son, I have begotten you this day. ⁸ Ask of Me and I will make nations your inheritance, and the ends of the earth your possession. ⁹ You will smash them with an iron rod; you will shatter them like a potter's vessel." ¹⁰ And now, O kings, * be wise; be disciplined, O judges of the earth. ¹¹ Serve HASHEM with awe that you may rejoice when there is trembling. ¹² Yearn for purity, lest He grow wrathful and your way be doomed, for in a brief moment His anger will blaze; praiseworthy are all who trust in Him.

3

Despite the apparent hopelessness of one's situation, trust in God will bring peace and security.

¹ **A** psalm by David, as he fled from Absalom his son. * ² HASHEM, how numerous are my tormentors! The great rise up against me! ³ The great say of my soul, "There is no salvation for him from God, Selah!" * ⁴ But You, HASHEM, are a shield for me, for my soul, and the One Who raises my head. ⁵ With my voice I call out to HASHEM, and He answers me from His holy mountain, Selah. ⁶ I lay down* and slept, yet I awoke, for HASHEM supports me. ⁷ I fear not the myriads of people deployed against me all around. ⁸ Rise up, HASHEM; save me, my God, for You struck all of my enemies on the cheek. You broke the teeth of the wicked. ⁹ Salvation is HASHEM's, upon Your people is Your blessing, Selah.

4

When sinners abandon the deceptiveness of temporary glory and recognize the truth, they will repent and find true happiness.

¹ **F**or the conductor, on the neginos, * a psalm by David. ² When I call, answer me, O God of my vindication. You have relieved me in my distress; be gracious to me and hear my prayer. ³ O sons of [great] men, how long will you put my honor to shame, love futility, and seek deception? Selah. ⁴ Be aware that HASHEM has set aside the devout one for Himself; so HASHEM will listen when I call to Him. ⁵ Tremble, and sin not; reflect in your hearts while on your beds and be utterly silent, Selah. ⁶ Slaughter offerings of righteousness, and trust in HASHEM. ⁷ Many say, "Who will show us good? Let the light of Your face shine upon us, HASHEM." ⁸ [But] You put gladness in my heart that is greater than theirs at the time that their grain and wine abound. ⁹ In peace, in harmony, I lie down and sleep; * for You, HASHEM, will make me dwell solitary and secure.

---

to the choristers to raise their voices (*Radak*); and a notation that directs one to reflect upon the preceding thought (*R' Hirsch*).

3:6. Crushed under a burden of worry and fear (*Rashi*).

4:1. Many psalms begin with a direction to the conductor

of the Temple orchestra. The *neginos* is a type of musical instrument (see *Radak*).

4:9. Even when I am threatened by my enemies, I sleep calmly as if I were enveloped in peace and harmony, for God places me in safety and security (*R' Hirsch*).

ה

א-ב לַמְנַצֵּחַ אֶל־הַנְּחִילוֹת מִזְמוֹר לְדָוִד: אֲמָרַי הַאֲזִינָה ׀ יהוה בִּינָה הֲגִיגִי:

ג-ד הַקְשִׁיבָה ׀ לְקוֹל שַׁוְעִי מַלְכִּי וֵאלֹהָי כִּי־אֵלֶיךָ אֶתְפַּלָּל: יהוה בֹּקֶר

ה תִּשְׁמַע קוֹלִי בֹּקֶר אֶעֱרָךְ־לְךָ וַאֲצַפֶּה: כִּי ׀ לֹא אֵל־חָפֵץ רֶשַׁע ׀ אָתָּה לֹא

ו-ז יְגֻרְךָ רָע: לֹא־יִתְיַצְּבוּ הוֹלְלִים לְנֶגֶד עֵינֶיךָ שָׂנֵאתָ כָּל־פֹּעֲלֵי אָוֶן: תְּאַבֵּד

ח דֹּבְרֵי כָזָב אִישׁ־דָּמִים וּמִרְמָה יְתָעֵב ׀ יהוה: וַאֲנִי בְּרֹב חַסְדְּךָ אָבוֹא

ט בֵיתֶךָ אֶשְׁתַּחֲוֶה אֶל־הֵיכַל־קָדְשְׁךָ בְּיִרְאָתֶךָ: יהוה ׀ נְחֵנִי בְצִדְקָתֶךָ לְמַעַן

י שׁוֹרְרָי °הוֹשַׁר [הַיְשַׁר ק] לְפָנַי דַּרְכֶּךָ: כִּי אֵין בְּפִיהוּ נְכוֹנָה קִרְבָּם

יא הַוּוֹת קֶבֶר־פָּתוּחַ גְּרוֹנָם לְשׁוֹנָם יַחֲלִיקוּן: הַאֲשִׁימֵם ׀ אֱלֹהִים יִפְּלוּ

יב מִמֹּעֲצוֹתֵיהֶם בְּרֹב פִּשְׁעֵיהֶם הַדִּיחֵמוֹ כִּי־מָרוּ בָךְ: וְיִשְׂמְחוּ כָל־חוֹסֵי בָךְ

יג לְעוֹלָם יְרַנֵּנוּ וְתָסֵךְ עָלֵימוֹ וְיַעְלְצוּ בְךָ אֹהֲבֵי שְׁמֶךָ: כִּי־אַתָּה תְּבָרֵךְ צַדִּיק

יהוה כַּצִּנָּה רָצוֹן תַּעְטְרֶנּוּ:

ו

א-ב לַמְנַצֵּחַ בִּנְגִינוֹת עַל־הַשְּׁמִינִית מִזְמוֹר לְדָוִד: יהוה אַל־בְּאַפְּךָ תוֹכִיחֵנִי

ג וְאַל־בַּחֲמָתְךָ תְיַסְּרֵנִי: חָנֵּנִי יהוה כִּי אֻמְלַל אָנִי רְפָאֵנִי יהוה כִּי נִבְהֲלוּ

ד-ה עֲצָמָי: וְנַפְשִׁי נִבְהֲלָה מְאֹד °ואת [וְאַתָּ ק] יהוה עַד־מָתָי: שׁוּבָה יהוה

ו-ז חַלְּצָה נַפְשִׁי הוֹשִׁיעֵנִי לְמַעַן חַסְדֶּךָ: כִּי אֵין בַּמָּוֶת זִכְרֶךָ בִּשְׁאוֹל מִי יוֹדֶה־

ח לָךְ: יָגַעְתִּי ׀ בְּאַנְחָתִי אַשְׂחֶה בְכָל־לַיְלָה מִטָּתִי בְּדִמְעָתִי עַרְשִׂי אַמְסֶה:

ט עָשְׁשָׁה מִכַּעַס עֵינִי עָתְקָה בְּכָל־צוֹרְרָי: סוּרוּ מִמֶּנִּי כָּל־פֹּעֲלֵי אָוֶן כִּי־

י-יא שָׁמַע יהוה קוֹל בִּכְיִי: שָׁמַע יהוה תְּחִנָּתִי יהוה תְּפִלָּתִי יִקָּח: יֵבֹשׁוּ ׀

וְיִבָּהֲלוּ מְאֹד כָּל־אֹיְבָי יָשֻׁבוּ יֵבֹשׁוּ רָגַע:

ז

א-ב שִׁגָּיוֹן לְדָוִד אֲשֶׁר־שָׁר לַיהוה עַל־דִּבְרֵי־כוּשׁ בֶּן־יְמִינִי: יהוה אֱלֹהַי בְּךָ

ג חָסִיתִי הוֹשִׁיעֵנִי מִכָּל־רֹדְפַי וְהַצִּילֵנִי: פֶּן־יִטְרֹף כְּאַרְיֵה נַפְשִׁי פֹּרֵק

ד-ה וְאֵין מַצִּיל: יהוה אֱלֹהַי אִם־עָשִׂיתִי זֹאת אִם־יֶשׁ־עָוֶל בְּכַפָּי: אִם־גָּמַלְתִּי

ו שׁוֹלְמִי רָע וָאֲחַלְּצָה צוֹרְרִי רֵיקָם: יִרַדֹּף אוֹיֵב ׀ נַפְשִׁי וְיַשֵּׂג וְיִרְמֹס

ז לָאָרֶץ חַיַּי וּכְבוֹדִי ׀ לֶעָפָר יַשְׁכֵּן סֶלָה: קוּמָה יהוה ׀ בְּאַפֶּךָ הִנָּשֵׂא בְּעַבְרוֹת

ח צוֹרְרָי וְעוּרָה אֵלַי מִשְׁפָּט צִוִּיתָ: וַעֲדַת לְאֻמִּים תְּסוֹבְבֶךָּ וְעָלֶיהָ לַמָּרוֹם

ט-י שׁוּבָה: יהוה יָדִין עַמִּים שָׁפְטֵנִי יהוה כְּצִדְקִי וּכְתֻמִּי עָלָי: יִגְמָר־נָא

יא רַע ׀ רְשָׁעִים וּתְכוֹנֵן צַדִּיק וּבֹחֵן לִבּוֹת וּכְלָיוֹת אֱלֹהִים צַדִּיק: מָגִנִּי עַל־

יב-יג אֱלֹהִים מוֹשִׁיעַ יִשְׁרֵי־לֵב: אֱלֹהִים שׁוֹפֵט צַדִּיק וְאֵל זֹעֵם בְּכָל־יוֹם: אִם־

יד לֹא יָשׁוּב חַרְבּוֹ יִלְטוֹשׁ קַשְׁתּוֹ דָרַךְ וַיְכוֹנְנֶהָ: וְלוֹ הֵכִין כְּלֵי־מָוֶת חִצָּיו

5:1. A type of musical instrument *(Rashi)*.

6:1. *Neginos* and *sheminis* are types of musical instruments.

6:2. Even if I deserve to be punished, do so gradually, not *in anger*, for then it would be beyond my endurance *(Radak)*.

6:4. How long will You let me suffer?

7:1. A type of musical instrument.

Kush ben Yemini was an enemy of David (see *Rashi*).

7:5. Without any expectation of reward, David restrained his followers from killing his pursuer, Saul (see *I Samuel* 24:8; 26:8-9).

7:8. An attack on Your anointed king is an attack against You *(Radak)*.

7:10. God knows the true character of each person and metes out His justice accordingly.

5

When beset by enemies, pray for deliverance, not merely to alleviate physical suffering, but to be free to serve God without distraction.

¹ For the conductor, on the nechilos,* a psalm by David. ² Hear my words, HASHEM, perceive my thoughts. ³ Hearken to the sound of my outcry, my King and my God, for to You do I pray. ⁴ HASHEM, at dawn hear my voice, at dawn as I arrange [my prayer] before You, and I wait expectantly. ⁵ For You are not a God who desires wickedness, no evil sojourns with You. ⁶ Roisterers cannot stand firm before Your eyes, You despise all evildoers. ⁷ May You doom the speakers of deception; HASHEM abhors a bloodthirsty and deceitful man. ⁸ But I, through Your abundant kindness I will enter Your house; I will prostrate myself toward Your Holy Sanctuary in awe of You. ⁹ HASHEM, guide me in Your righteousness, because of my watchful enemies; make Your way straight before me. ¹⁰ For there is no sincerity in the mouth of any of them, their inner [thought] is treacherous; their throat an open grave, their tongue is glib. ¹¹ Declare them guilty, O God, may they fall short in their schemes; cast them away because of their many sins, for they have rebelled against You. ¹² But all who take refuge in You will rejoice, they will sing joyously forever, You will shelter them; and those who love Your Name will exult in You. ¹³ When You will bless the righteous, HASHEM, You will envelop him with favor like a shield.

6

A prayer for when the community or individual suffers oppression and deprivation, sickness and distress.

¹ For the conductor, with the neginos; on the sheminis.* A psalm by David. ² HASHEM, do not rebuke me in Your anger, nor chastise me in Your wrath.* ³ Favor me, HASHEM, for I am feeble; heal me, HASHEM, for my bones shudder with terror. ⁴ My soul is utterly terrified, and You, HASHEM, how long?* ⁵ Desist, HASHEM, release my soul; save me as befits Your kindness. ⁶ For in death there is no mention of You; in the grave who will praise You? ⁷ I am wearied with my sigh, every night I drench my bed, with my tears I soak my couch. ⁸ My eye is dimmed because of anger, aged by all my tormentors. ⁹ Depart from me, all evildoers, for HASHEM has heard the sound of my weeping. ¹⁰ HASHEM has heard my plea, HASHEM will accept my prayer. ¹¹ Let all my foes be shamed and utterly confounded, they will regret and be shamed in an instant.

7

The righteous take heart in knowing that they will prevail over the wicked, while their enemies will fall victim to their own schemes.

¹ A [song of the] shiggayon,* by David; which he sang to HASHEM concerning Kush ben Yemini.* ² HASHEM, my God, in You I seek refuge, save me from all my pursuers and rescue me — ³ lest, like a lion, he tear my soul asunder, dismembering with none to rescue. ⁴ HASHEM, my God, if I have done this, if there is injustice in my hands; ⁵ if I have paid with evil those who were at peace with me — I, who rescued my tormentors gratuitously* — ⁶ then let the enemy pursue my soul and overtake it, let him trample my life to the ground, and lay my soul in the dust, Selah. ⁷ Rise up, HASHEM, in Your anger, be lifted in fury against my tormentors, and awaken on my behalf [according to] the decree You commanded. ⁸ When the assembly of nations surrounds You,* then rise above it — return to the heights. ⁹ HASHEM will punish the peoples; judge me, HASHEM, reward me according to my righteousness and my integrity. ¹⁰ Let the evil of the wicked destroy them, but You will sustain the righteous one; for the Searcher of hearts and minds is the righteous God.* ¹¹ My protection lies with God Who saves the upright of heart. ¹² God is a righteous Judge, and God is angered every day.* ¹³ If one does not repent, He will sharpen His sword; He has bent his bow and aimed it. ¹⁴ And for him He prepared the instruments of death, He will use His arrows

---

7:12-13. God is ever mindful of evil and holds the instruments of retribution in readiness.

טו־טז לְדֹלְקִים יִפְעָל: הִנֵּה יְחַבֶּל־אָוֶן וְהָרָה עָמָל וְיָלַד שָׁקֶר: בּוֹר כָּרָה

יז וַיַּחְפְּרֵהוּ וַיִּפֹּל בְּשַׁחַת יִפְעָל: יָשׁוּב עֲמָלוֹ בְרֹאשׁוֹ וְעַל קָדְקֳדוֹ חֲמָסוֹ יֵרֵד:

יח אוֹדֶה יְהוָה כְּצִדְקוֹ וַאֲזַמְּרָה שֵׁם־יְהוָה עֶלְיוֹן:

ח

א־ב לַמְנַצֵּחַ עַל־הַגִּתִּית מִזְמוֹר לְדָוִד: יְהוָה אֲדֹנֵינוּ מָה־אַדִּיר שִׁמְךָ בְּכָל־

ג הָאָרֶץ אֲשֶׁר תְּנָה הוֹדְךָ עַל־הַשָּׁמָיִם: מִפִּי עוֹלְלִים ׀ וְיֹנְקִים יִסַּדְתָּ עֹז

ד לְמַעַן צוֹרְרֶיךָ לְהַשְׁבִּית אוֹיֵב וּמִתְנַקֵּם: כִּי־אֶרְאֶה שָׁמֶיךָ מַעֲשֵׂי

ה אֶצְבְּעֹתֶיךָ יָרֵחַ וְכוֹכָבִים אֲשֶׁר כּוֹנָנְתָּה: מָה־אֱנוֹשׁ כִּי־תִזְכְּרֶנּוּ וּבֶן־אָדָם

ו־ז כִּי תִפְקְדֶנּוּ: וַתְּחַסְּרֵהוּ מְּעַט מֵאֱלֹהִים וְכָבוֹד וְהָדָר תְּעַטְּרֵהוּ: תַּמְשִׁילֵהוּ

ח בְּמַעֲשֵׂי יָדֶיךָ כֹּל שַׁתָּה תַחַת־רַגְלָיו: צֹנֶה וַאֲלָפִים כֻּלָּם וְגַם בַּהֲמוֹת שָׂדָי:

ט צִפּוֹר שָׁמַיִם וּדְגֵי הַיָּם עֹבֵר אָרְחוֹת יַמִּים: יְהוָה אֲדֹנֵינוּ מָה־אַדִּיר שִׁמְךָ

יא בְּכָל־הָאָרֶץ:

ט

א־ב לַמְנַצֵּחַ עַל־מוּת לַבֵּן מִזְמוֹר לְדָוִד: אוֹדֶה יְהוָה בְּכָל־לִבִּי אֲסַפְּרָה כָּל־

ג נִפְלְאוֹתֶיךָ: אֶשְׂמְחָה וְאֶעֶלְצָה בָךְ אֲזַמְּרָה שִׁמְךָ עֶלְיוֹן: בְּשׁוּב־אוֹיְבַי

ה אָחוֹר יִכָּשְׁלוּ וְיֹאבְדוּ מִפָּנֶיךָ: כִּי־עָשִׂיתָ מִשְׁפָּטִי וְדִינִי יָשַׁבְתָּ לְכִסֵּא

ו־ז שׁוֹפֵט צֶדֶק: גָּעַרְתָּ גוֹיִם אִבַּדְתָּ רָשָׁע שְׁמָם מָחִיתָ לְעוֹלָם וָעֶד: הָאוֹיֵב ׀

ח תַּמּוּ חֳרָבוֹת לָנֶצַח וְעָרִים נָתַשְׁתָּ אָבַד זִכְרָם הֵמָּה: וַיהוָה לְעוֹלָם יֵשֵׁב

ט כּוֹנֵן לַמִּשְׁפָּט כִּסְאוֹ: וְהוּא יִשְׁפֹּט־תֵּבֵל בְּצֶדֶק יָדִין לְאֻמִּים בְּמֵישָׁרִים:

י־יא וִיהִי יְהוָה מִשְׂגָּב לַדָּךְ מִשְׂגָּב לְעִתּוֹת בַּצָּרָה: וְיִבְטְחוּ בְךָ יוֹדְעֵי שְׁמֶךָ כִּי

יב לֹא־עָזַבְתָּ דֹרְשֶׁיךָ יְהוָה: זַמְּרוּ לַיהוָה יֹשֵׁב צִיּוֹן הַגִּידוּ בָעַמִּים עֲלִילוֹתָיו:

יג־יד כִּי־דֹרֵשׁ דָּמִים אוֹתָם זָכָר לֹא־שָׁכַח צַעֲקַת °עניים [°עֲנָוִים ק]: חָנְנֵנִי

טו יְהוָה רְאֵה עָנְיִי מִשֹּׂנְאָי מְרוֹמְמִי מִשַּׁעֲרֵי מָוֶת: לְמַעַן אֲסַפְּרָה כָּל־

טז תְּהִלָּתֶיךָ בְּשַׁעֲרֵי בַת־צִיּוֹן אָגִילָה בִּישׁוּעָתֶךָ: טָבְעוּ גוֹיִם בְּשַׁחַת עָשׂוּ

יז בְּרֶשֶׁת־זוּ טָמָנוּ נִלְכְּדָה רַגְלָם: נוֹדַע ׀ יְהוָה מִשְׁפָּט עָשָׂה בְּפֹעַל כַּפָּיו

יח נוֹקֵשׁ רָשָׁע הִגָּיוֹן סֶלָה: יָשׁוּבוּ רְשָׁעִים לִשְׁאוֹלָה כָּל־גּוֹיִם שְׁכֵחֵי אֱלֹהִים:

יט־כ כִּי לֹא לָנֶצַח יִשָּׁכַח אֶבְיוֹן תִּקְוַת °ענוים [°עֲנִיִּים ק] תֹּאבַד לָעַד: קוּמָה

כא יְהוָה אַל־יָעֹז אֱנוֹשׁ יִשָּׁפְטוּ גוֹיִם עַל־פָּנֶיךָ: שִׁיתָה יְהוָה ׀ מוֹרָה לָהֶם

יֵדְעוּ גוֹיִם אֱנוֹשׁ הֵמָּה סֶּלָה:

י

א־ב לָמָה יְהוָה תַּעֲמֹד בְּרָחוֹק תַּעְלִים לְעִתּוֹת בַּצָּרָה: בְּגַאֲוַת רָשָׁע יִדְלַק עָנִי

יום ב לחדש

ג יִתָּפְשׂוּ ׀ בִּמְזִמּוֹת זוּ חָשָׁבוּ: כִּי־הִלֵּל רָשָׁע עַל־תַּאֲוַת נַפְשׁוֹ וּבֹצֵעַ בֵּרֵךְ

ד נִאֵץ ׀ יְהוָה: רָשָׁע כְּגֹבַהּ אַפּוֹ בַּל־יִדְרֹשׁ אֵין אֱלֹהִים כָּל־מְזִמּוֹתָיו:

8:1. A type of musical instrument.

8:3. With uncorrupted intelligence, even children can perceive God's hand in Creation. Such intelligence is the "strength" God has "established" for man, so that he can refute and silence enemies of truth.

9:1. An enemy of David.

10:4. Wicked people assume that God will not punish misdeeds.

against those in hot pursuit. [15] *Behold, he conceives iniquity, is pregnant with evil schemes, but he gives birth to failure.* [16] *He has dug a pit, and dug it deep, only to fall into a trap of his making.* [17] *His mischief will recoil upon his [own] head, and upon his [own] skull will his violence descend.* [18] *[Then] I will thank HASHEM according to his righteousness, and sing praises to the Name of HASHEM the Supreme.*

8

One with clarity of vision perceives God's handiwork everywhere and realizes that all man's accomplishments are His gifts.

[1] *For the conductor, on the gittis,* * *a psalm by David.* [2] *HASHEM, our Master, how mighty is Your Name throughout the earth, [You] Who places Your majesty on the heavens.* [3] *Out of the mouths of babes and sucklings You have established strength, because of Your enemies, to silence foe and avenger.* * [4] *When I behold Your heavens, the work of Your fingers, the moon and the stars that You have set in place, [I think,]* [5] *"What is frail man that You should remember him, and the son of mortal man that You should be mindful of him?"* [6] *Yet, You have made him but slightly less than the angels, and crowned him with soul and splendor.* [7] *You give him dominion over Your handiwork, You placed everything under his feet:* [8] *sheep and cattle, all of them, even the beasts of the field;* [9] *the birds of the sky and the fish of the sea; for [man] even traverses the lanes of the sea.* [10] *HASHEM, our Master, how mighty is Your Name throughout the earth!*

9

Despite their dazzling successes, the wicked will fade into oblivion; only the Godly will prevail.

[1] *For the conductor, upon the death of Labben,* * *a psalm by David.* [2] *I will thank HASHEM with all my heart, I will proclaim all Your wondrous deeds.* [3] *I will rejoice and exult in You, I will sing praise to Your Name, Most High.* [4] *When my enemies turn backward, they stumble and perish from before You.* [5] *For You executed my judgment and my cause; You sat on the throne, O righteous Judge.* [6] *You destroyed nations and doomed the wicked; You blotted out their name for all eternity.* [7] *The enemy, [his] ruins are forever gone; and the cities that You uprooted, their memory is lost.* [8] *For HASHEM is enthroned forever, He prepares His throne for judgment.* [9] *And He will judge the world in righteousness, He will judge the regimes with fairness.* [10] *HASHEM will be a fortress for the oppressed, a fortress in times of distress.* [11] *And those who know Your Name will trust in You, for You have not forsaken those who seek You, HASHEM.* [12] *Sing to HASHEM Who dwells in Zion, proclaim His deeds among the peoples.* [13] *That the Avenger of blood has remembered them, He has not forgotten the cry of the humble.* [14] *Have mercy on me, O HASHEM, see my affliction by my foes, You Who raises me above the gates of death;* [15] *so that I may proclaim all Your praises, in the gates of the daughter of Zion I will rejoice in Your salvation:* [16] *"The nations sank in their self-made pit, in the very trap they concealed, their own foot was ensnared.* [17] *HASHEM became known through the judgment that He executed; through his own handiwork was the wicked person entrapped, reflect on this, Selah."* [18] *The wicked will return to the depths of the grave, all the nations that forget God;* [19] *for the pauper shall not be forgotten eternally, nor the hope of the afflicted forever perish.* [20] *Arise, HASHEM, let not frail man feel invincible! Let the peoples be judged before You.* [21] *HASHEM, place [Your] mastery over them, that the peoples may know they are but frail men, Selah!*

10

God punishes the wicked and champions the downtrodden.

[1] *Why, HASHEM, do You stand aloof, do You conceal Yourself in times of distress?* [2] *In the wicked one's haughtiness, he hunts down the poor, who are caught in the schemes they have contrived.* [3] *[Why do You stand aloof] when the wicked man glories in his personal desire, and the robber praises himself that he has blasphemed HASHEM?* [4] *The wicked man, in the pride of his countenance, [says]: "He will not avenge!" All his schemes are: "There is no Divine Judge."* *

ה יָחִילוּ °דרכו [°דְּרָכָיו ק״] ׀ בְּכָל־עֵת מָרוֹם מִשְׁפָּטֶיךָ מִנֶּגְדּוֹ כָּל־צוֹרְרָיו

ו־ז יָפִיחַ בָּהֶם: אָמַר בְּלִבּוֹ בַּל־אֶמּוֹט לְדֹר וָדֹר אֲשֶׁר לֹא־בְרָע: אָלָה ׀ פִּיהוּ

ח מָלֵא וּמִרְמוֹת וָתֹךְ תַּחַת לְשׁוֹנוֹ עָמָל וָאָוֶן: יֵשֵׁב ׀ בְּמַאְרַב חֲצֵרִים

ט בַּמִּסְתָּרִים יַהֲרֹג נָקִי עֵינָיו לְחֵלְכָה יִצְפֹּנוּ: יֶאֱרֹב בַּמִּסְתָּר ׀ כְּאַרְיֵה בְסֻכֹּה

י יֶאֱרֹב לַחֲטוֹף עָנִי יַחְטֹף עָנִי בְּמָשְׁכוֹ בְרִשְׁתּוֹ: °ודכה [°יִדְכֶּה ק״] יָשֹׁחַ

יא וְנָפַל בַּעֲצוּמָיו °חלכאים [°חֵל כָּאִים ק״]: אָמַר בְּלִבּוֹ שָׁכַח אֵל הִסְתִּיר

יב פָּנָיו בַּל־רָאָה לָנֶצַח: קוּמָה יְהוָה אֵל נְשָׂא יָדֶךָ אַל־תִּשְׁכַּח °עניים

יג־יד [°עֲנָוִים ק״]: עַל־מֶה ׀ נִאֵץ רָשָׁע ׀ אֱלֹהִים אָמַר בְּלִבּוֹ לֹא תִדְרֹשׁ: רָאִתָה

כִּי־אַתָּה ׀ עָמָל וָכַעַס ׀ תַּבִּיט לָתֵת בְּיָדֶךָ עָלֶיךָ יַעֲזֹב חֵלְכָה יָתוֹם אַתָּה ׀

טו־טז הָיִיתָ עוֹזֵר: שְׁבֹר זְרוֹעַ רָשָׁע וָרָע תִּדְרוֹשׁ־רִשְׁעוֹ בַל־תִּמְצָא: יְהוָה מֶלֶךְ

יז עוֹלָם וָעֶד אָבְדוּ גוֹיִם מֵאַרְצוֹ: תַּאֲוַת עֲנָוִים שָׁמַעְתָּ יְהוָה תָּכִין לִבָּם

יח תַּקְשִׁיב אָזְנֶךָ: לִשְׁפֹּט יָתוֹם וָדָךְ בַּל־יוֹסִיף עוֹד לַעֲרֹץ אֱנוֹשׁ מִן־הָאָרֶץ:

יא א לַמְנַצֵּחַ לְדָוִד בַּיהוָה ׀ חָסִיתִי אֵיךְ תֹּאמְרוּ לְנַפְשִׁי °נודו [°נוּדִי ק״] הַרְכֶם

ב צִפּוֹר: כִּי הִנֵּה הָרְשָׁעִים יִדְרְכוּן קֶשֶׁת כּוֹנְנוּ חִצָּם עַל־יֶתֶר לִירוֹת בְּמוֹ־

ג־ד אֹפֶל לְיִשְׁרֵי־לֵב: כִּי הַשָּׁתוֹת יֵהָרֵסוּן צַדִּיק מַה־פָּעָל: יְהוָה ׀ בְּהֵיכַל קָדְשׁוֹ

ה יְהוָה בַּשָּׁמַיִם כִּסְאוֹ עֵינָיו יֶחֱזוּ עַפְעַפָּיו יִבְחֲנוּ בְּנֵי אָדָם: יְהוָה צַדִּיק יִבְחָן

ו וְרָשָׁע וְאֹהֵב חָמָס שָׂנְאָה נַפְשׁוֹ: יַמְטֵר עַל־רְשָׁעִים פַּחִים אֵשׁ וְגָפְרִית

ז וְרוּחַ זִלְעָפוֹת מְנָת כּוֹסָם: כִּי־צַדִּיק יְהוָה צְדָקוֹת אָהֵב יָשָׁר יֶחֱזוּ פָנֵימוֹ:

יב א־ב לַמְנַצֵּחַ עַל־הַשְּׁמִינִית מִזְמוֹר לְדָוִד: הוֹשִׁיעָה יְהוָה כִּי־גָמַר חָסִיד כִּי־

ג פַסּוּ אֱמוּנִים מִבְּנֵי אָדָם: שָׁוְא ׀ יְדַבְּרוּ אִישׁ אֶת־רֵעֵהוּ שְׂפַת חֲלָקוֹת בְּלֵב

ד־ה וָלֵב יְדַבֵּרוּ: יַכְרֵת יְהוָה כָּל־שִׂפְתֵי חֲלָקוֹת לָשׁוֹן מְדַבֶּרֶת גְּדֹלוֹת: אֲשֶׁר

ו אָמְרוּ ׀ לִלְשֹׁנֵנוּ נַגְבִּיר שְׂפָתֵינוּ אִתָּנוּ מִי אָדוֹן לָנוּ: מִשֹּׁד עֲנִיִּים מֵאֶנְקַת

ז אֶבְיוֹנִים עַתָּה אָקוּם יֹאמַר יְהוָה אָשִׁית בְּיֵשַׁע יָפִיחַ לוֹ: אִמְרוֹת יְהוָה

ח אֲמָרוֹת טְהֹרוֹת כֶּסֶף צָרוּף בַּעֲלִיל לָאָרֶץ מְזֻקָּק שִׁבְעָתָיִם: אַתָּה־יְהוָה

ט תִּשְׁמְרֵם תִּצְּרֶנּוּ ׀ מִן־הַדּוֹר זוּ לְעוֹלָם: סָבִיב רְשָׁעִים יִתְהַלָּכוּן כְּרֻם זֻלּוּת

לִבְנֵי אָדָם:

יג א־ב לַמְנַצֵּחַ מִזְמוֹר לְדָוִד: עַד־אָנָה יְהוָה תִּשְׁכָּחֵנִי נֶצַח עַד־אָנָה ׀ תַּסְתִּיר אֶת־

ג פָּנֶיךָ מִמֶּנִּי: עַד־אָנָה אָשִׁית עֵצוֹת בְּנַפְשִׁי יָגוֹן בִּלְבָבִי יוֹמָם עַד־אָנָה ׀ יָרוּם

ד־ה אֹיְבִי עָלָי: הַבִּיטָה עֲנֵנִי יְהוָה אֱלֹהָי הָאִירָה עֵינַי פֶּן־אִישַׁן הַמָּוֶת: פֶּן־יֹאמַר

10:15. When you will break the power of the wicked, those tempted to emulate them will repent.

10:17. Life's hardships make it difficult to pray properly. Therefore, we entreat God to guide our heart in prayer, so that we will be worthy of His attentiveness (*Radak*).

11:1. David confronts the scoffers who urge him to abandon his trust in God (*Malbim*).

11:4. This answers the scoffers: Although God is infinitely exalted, He is thoroughly cognizant of human affairs.

11:5. It is specifically the righteous whom God chastises in order to purify them (*Rashi*).

12:3. Literally, with two hearts. Outwardly they display friendship, but their hearts harbor animosity.

12:8. The aforementioned poor and needy.

13:2. David speaks prophetically on behalf of Israel in exile.

13:3. How long must I continue to devise schemes to extricate myself from my distress?

⁵ His ways are always successful, Your judgments are far removed from him; all his foes — he puffs at them! ⁶ He says in his heart: "I shall not falter, throughout generations I will be without adversity." ⁷ His mouth is filled with [false] oaths, with deception and malice; under his tongue are mischief and iniquity. ⁸ He waits in ambush near open cities, in hidden places he murders the innocent, his eyes spy on the helpless. ⁹ He lurks in hiding like a lion in his lair, he lurks to seize the poor; then he seizes the poor when he draws his net. ¹⁰ He lowers himself; he crouches; and the helpless fall prey to his mighty limbs. ¹¹ He says in his heart: "God has forgotten, He has hidden His face, He will never see."

¹² Arise, O HASHEM! O God, raise Your hand, do not forget the humble! ¹³ Why does the wicked man blaspheme God? Because he says in his heart: "You will not avenge." ¹⁴ But You do see! For You observe mischief and vexation, to dispense [punishment] is in Your power; the helpless rely upon You. The orphan — You were the helper. ¹⁵ Break the power of the wicked; and the bad one — You will search for his wickedness and find it not. * ¹⁶ HASHEM is King forever and ever, when the nations have perished from His earth. ¹⁷ The desire of the humble You have heard, HASHEM; guide their heart; let Your ear be attentive: * ¹⁸ to champion the orphan and the downtrodden, so that he shall no longer be terrified of an earthly mortal.

11

The righteous suffer to atone for sin, but are rewarded in the World to Come. Evildoers are rewarded in this world.

¹ For the conductor, by David. In HASHEM I have taken refuge. How dare you* say to me, "Flee from your mountain like a bird! ² For, behold, the wicked bend the bow, ready their arrow on the bowstring, to shoot in the dark at the upright of heart. ³ When the foundations are destroyed, what has the righteous man accomplished?"

⁴ HASHEM is in the abode of His holiness, HASHEM's Throne is in heaven; His eyes behold, His eyelids scrutinize mankind. * ⁵ HASHEM examines the righteous one, * but He despises the wicked and the lover of violence. ⁶ He will rain down coals upon the wicked; fire and brimstone and a burning blast is their allotted portion. ⁷ For HASHEM is righteous, He loves those of righteous deeds — those whose faces behold uprightness.

12

Human friendship and loyalty are often suspect; but God's assurances are pure and enduring.

¹ For the conductor, on the sheminis, a psalm by David. ² Save, O HASHEM, for the devout one is no more, for truthful people have vanished from mankind. ³ Each man speaks untruth to his neighbor; a lip of smooth talk, with an insincere heart* do they speak. ⁴ May HASHEM excise all lips of smooth talk, the tongue which speaks boastfully. ⁵ Those who have said, "Because of our tongues we shall prevail, our lips are with us, who is master over us?" ⁶ Because of the plundering of the poor, because of the cry of the needy — "Now I will arise!" HASHEM will say. "I will grant safety," He will speak regarding him. ⁷ The words of HASHEM are pure words; like purified silver, clear to the world, refined sevenfold. ⁸ You, HASHEM, will guard them, * You will preserve each one forever from such a generation, ⁹ [in which] the wicked walk on every side, when baseness is exalted among the sons of men.

13

Exile is like a long, dark, seemingly endless night.

¹ For the conductor, a psalm by David. ² How long, HASHEM, will You endlessly forget me?* How long will You hide Your countenance from me? ³ How long must I set schemes* within myself? My heart is melancholy even by day. How long will my enemy triumph over me? ⁴ Look! Answer me, HASHEM, my God! Enlighten my eyes, lest I sleep the sleep of death. ⁵ Lest my enemy boast,

ו אֹיְבַי יְכַלְּתֶֽיהָ צָרַי יָגִילוּ כִּי אֶמּוֹט: וַאֲנִי ׀ בְּחַסְדְּךָ בָטַחְתִּי יָגֵל לִבִּי
בִּישׁוּעָתֶךָ אָשִׁירָה לַיהֹוָה כִּי גָמַל עָלָֽי:

יד א לַמְנַצֵּחַ לְדָוִד אָמַר נָבָל בְּלִבּוֹ אֵין אֱלֹהִים הִשְׁחִיתוּ הִתְעִיבוּ עֲלִילָה אֵין
ב עֹֽשֵׂה־טֽוֹב: יְהֹוָה מִשָּׁמַיִם הִשְׁקִיף עַל־בְּנֵי־אָדָם לִרְאוֹת הֲיֵשׁ מַשְׂכִּיל
ג דֹּרֵשׁ אֶת־אֱלֹהִים: הַכֹּל סָר יַחְדָּו נֶאֱלָחוּ אֵין עֹֽשֵׂה־טוֹב אֵין גַּם־
ד אֶחָֽד: הֲלֹא יָֽדְעוּ כָּל־פֹּעֲלֵי אָוֶן אֹכְלֵי עַמִּי אָכְלוּ לֶחֶם יְהֹוָה לֹא קָרָֽאוּ:
ה־ו שָׁם ׀ פָּֽחֲדוּ פָחַד כִּי־אֱלֹהִים בְּדוֹר צַדִּיק: עֲצַת־עָנִי תָבִישׁוּ כִּי יְהֹוָה
ז מַחְסֵֽהוּ: מִי יִתֵּן מִצִּיּוֹן יְשׁוּעַת יִשְׂרָאֵל בְּשׁוּב יְהֹוָה שְׁבוּת עַמּוֹ יָגֵל יַעֲקֹב
יִשְׂמַח יִשְׂרָאֵֽל:

טו א־ב מִזְמוֹר לְדָוִד יְהֹוָה מִי־יָגוּר בְּאָֽהֳלֶךָ מִי־יִשְׁכֹּן בְּהַר קָדְשֶֽׁךָ: הוֹלֵךְ תָּמִים
ג וּפֹעֵל צֶדֶק וְדֹבֵר אֱמֶת בִּלְבָבֽוֹ: לֹֽא־רָגַל ׀ עַל־לְשֹׁנוֹ לֹא־עָשָׂה לְרֵעֵהוּ
ד רָעָה וְחֶרְפָּה לֹא־נָשָׂא עַל־קְרֹבֽוֹ: נִבְזֶה ׀ בְּעֵינָיו נִמְאָס וְאֶת־יִרְאֵי יְהֹוָה
ה יְכַבֵּד נִשְׁבַּע לְהָרַע וְלֹא יָמִֽר: כַּסְפּוֹ ׀ לֹא־נָתַן בְּנֶשֶׁךְ וְשֹׁחַד עַל־נָקִי לֹא
לָקָח עֹֽשֵׂה־אֵלֶּה לֹא יִמּוֹט לְעוֹלָֽם:

טז א־ב מִכְתָּם לְדָוִד שָׁמְרֵנִי אֵל כִּי־חָסִיתִי בָֽךְ: אָמַרְתְּ לַיהֹוָה אֲדֹנָי אָתָּה טוֹבָתִי
ג־ד בַּל־עָלֶֽיךָ: לִקְדוֹשִׁים אֲשֶׁר־בָּאָרֶץ הֵמָּה וְאַדִּירֵי כָּל־חֶפְצִי־בָֽם: יִרְבּוּ
עַצְּבוֹתָם אַחֵר מָהָרוּ בַּל־אַסִּיךְ נִסְכֵּיהֶם מִדָּם וּבַל־אֶשָּׂא אֶת־שְׁמוֹתָם
ה־ו עַל־שְׂפָתָֽי: יְהֹוָה מְנָת־חֶלְקִי וְכוֹסִי אַתָּה תּוֹמִיךְ גּוֹרָלִֽי: חֲבָלִים נָֽפְלוּ־לִי
ז בַּנְּעִמִים אַף־נַחֲלָת שָֽׁפְרָה עָלָֽי: אֲבָרֵךְ אֶת־יְהֹוָה אֲשֶׁר יְעָצָנִי אַף־לֵילוֹת
ח־ט יִסְּרוּנִי כִלְיוֹתָֽי: שִׁוִּיתִי יְהֹוָה לְנֶגְדִּי תָמִיד כִּי מִֽימִינִי בַּל־אֶמּֽוֹט: לָכֵן ׀
י שָׂמַח לִבִּי וַיָּגֶל כְּבוֹדִי אַף־בְּשָׂרִי יִשְׁכֹּן לָבֶֽטַח: כִּי ׀ לֹא־תַעֲזֹב נַפְשִׁי
יא לִשְׁאוֹל לֹא־תִתֵּן °חֲסִידְךָ [°חֲסִידֶיךָ ק] לִרְאוֹת שָֽׁחַת: תּוֹדִיעֵנִי אֹרַח
חַיִּים שֹׂבַע שְׂמָחוֹת אֶת־פָּנֶיךָ נְעִמוֹת בִּימִינְךָ נֶֽצַח:

יז א תְּפִלָּה לְדָוִד שִׁמְעָה יְהֹוָה ׀ צֶדֶק הַקְשִׁיבָה רִנָּתִי הַאֲזִינָה תְפִלָּתִי
ב בְּלֹא שִׂפְתֵי מִרְמָֽה: מִלְּפָנֶיךָ מִשְׁפָּטִי יֵצֵא עֵינֶיךָ תֶּחֱזֶינָה מֵישָׁרִֽים:
ג בָּחַנְתָּ לִבִּי ׀ פָּקַדְתָּ לַּיְלָה צְרַפְתַּנִי בַל־תִּמְצָא זַמֹּתִי בַּל־יַעֲבָר־פִּֽי:
ד־ה לִפְעֻלּוֹת אָדָם בִּדְבַר שְׂפָתֶיךָ אֲנִי שָׁמַרְתִּי אָרְחוֹת פָּרִֽיץ: תָּמֹךְ אֲשֻׁרַי
בְּמַעְגְּלוֹתֶיךָ בַּל־נָמוֹטּוּ פְעָמָֽי: אֲנִי־קְרָאתִיךָ כִֽי־תַעֲנֵנִי אֵל הַֽט־אָזְנְךָ לִּי
ו שְׁמַע אִמְרָתִֽי: הַפְלֵה חֲסָדֶיךָ מוֹשִׁיעַ חוֹסִים מִמִּתְקוֹמְמִים בִּימִינֶֽךָ:

13:6. My enemies declare that I have no savior, but I know that I have one in You.

14:3. No one from among the nations protests the atrocities perpetrated by its leaders against Israel (*Rashi*).

15:4. He does not insincerely flatter those who are contemptible (*Metzudos*).

16:1. A musical instrument.

16:2. David addresses his soul: You, my soul, have said . . .

16:3. You have given me everything in the merit of my righteous ancestors (*Rashi*).

17:3. You examined my thoughts at night, when, free from distraction, a person can think, but You found nothing improper in me (*Ibn Ezra*).

"I have overcome him!"; lest my tormentors rejoice when I falter. [6] But as for me, I trust in Your kindness;* my heart will exult in Your salvation. I will sing to HASHEM, for He has dealt kindly with me.

14

The entire world may have gone astray, but God will yet redeem His nation and Israel will rejoice.

[1] **F**or the conductor, by David. The degraded one says in his heart, "There is no God!" They have acted corruptly and abominably [in their] action; there is no doer of good. [2] From heaven HASHEM gazed down upon mankind, to see if there exists a reflective person who seeks out God. [3] Everyone has gone astray,* together they have become depraved; there is no doer of good, there is not even one. [4] Do they not realize — all those evildoers, who devour my people as they would devour bread, who do not call upon HASHEM — [5] [that] there they will be struck with terror, for God is with the righteous generation? [6] You shame the poor man's counsel, that HASHEM is his refuge. [7] O, that out of Zion would come Israel's salvation! When HASHEM restores the captivity of His people, Jacob will exult, Israel will rejoice.

15

The way to come closer to God is to be generous and honest toward man.

[1] **A** psalm by David. HASHEM, who may sojourn in Your Tent? Who may dwell on Your Holy Mountain? [2] One who walks in perfect innocence, and does what is right, and speaks the truth from his heart; [3] who has no slander on his tongue, who has done his fellow no evil, nor cast disgrace upon his close one; [4] in whose eyes a contemptible person is repulsive,* but who honors those who fear HASHEM; who can swear to his detriment without retracting; [5] who lends not his money on interest; and takes not a bribe against the innocent. The doer of these shall not falter forever.

16

Talent and external forces are merely the Creator's tools in guiding history.

[1] **A** [song of the] michtam* by David. Protect me O God, for I have sought refuge in You. [2] You* have said to HASHEM, "You are my Master, I have no claim to Your benefit." [3] For the sake of the holy ones who are [interred] in the earth and for the mighty* — all my desires are fulfilled because of them. [4] Their sorrows will multiply, those who rush after other [gods]; I shall not pour their libations of blood; I shall not carry their names upon my lips. [5] HASHEM is my allotted portion and my share, You guide my destiny. [6] Portions have fallen to me in pleasant places, even the inheritance is beautiful to me. [7] I will bless HASHEM Who has advised me, also in the nights my intellect instructs me. [8] I have set HASHEM before me always; because He is at my right hand I shall not falter. [9] For this reason my heart rejoices and my soul is elated; my flesh, too, rests in confidence: [10] Because You will not abandon my soul to the grave, You will not allow Your devout one to witness destruction. [11] You will make known to me the path of life, the fullness of joys in Your Presence, the delights that are in Your right hand for eternity.

17

The righteous person beseeches God to examine his deeds, to protect him from his enemies, and to allow him to enjoy God's glory.

[1] **A** prayer of David: Hear, HASHEM, what is righteous, be attentive to my entreaty; give ear to my prayer, which is from lips without deceit. [2] May my judgment go out from before You, Your eyes behold uprightness. [3] You examined my heart, You searched at night; You tested me — You found not;* my thoughts do not transgress the words of my mouth. [4] So that [my] human deeds would accord with the word of Your lips, I guarded myself from the paths of the lawless; [5] supporting my strides in Your pathways, my footsteps did not falter. [6] I have called out to You, because You will answer me, O God; incline Your ear to me, hear my utterance. [7] Demonstrate clearly Your kindnesses, [You] Who saves with Your right hand those who seek refuge [in You] from those who arise [against

ח-ט שָׁמְרֵנִי כְּאִישׁוֹן בַּת־עָיִן בְּצֵל כְּנָפֶיךָ תַּסְתִּירֵנִי: מִפְּנֵי רְשָׁעִים זוּ שַׁדּוּנִי

י-יא אֹיְבַי בְּנֶפֶשׁ יַקִּיפוּ עָלָי: חֶלְבָּמוֹ סָגְרוּ פִּימוֹ דִּבְּרוּ בְגֵאוּת: אַשֻּׁרֵינוּ עַתָּה

יב סְבָבוּנִי [סְבָבוּנוּ ק׳] עֵינֵיהֶם יָשִׁיתוּ לִנְטוֹת בָּאָרֶץ: דִּמְיֹנוֹ כְּאַרְיֵה יִכְסוֹף

יג לִטְרֹף וְכִכְפִיר יֹשֵׁב בְּמִסְתָּרִים: קוּמָה יְהוָה קַדְּמָה פָנָיו הַכְרִיעֵהוּ פַּלְּטָה

יד נַפְשִׁי מֵרָשָׁע חַרְבֶּךָ: מִמְתִים יָדְךָ ׀ יְהוָה מִמְתִים מֵחֶלֶד חֶלְקָם בַּחַיִּים

טו וּצְפוּנְךָ [וּצְפִינְךָ ק׳] תְּמַלֵּא בִטְנָם יִשְׂבְּעוּ בָנִים וְהִנִּיחוּ יִתְרָם

לְעוֹלְלֵיהֶם: אֲנִי בְּצֶדֶק אֶחֱזֶה פָנֶיךָ אֶשְׂבְּעָה בְהָקִיץ תְּמוּנָתֶךָ:

יח א לַמְנַצֵּחַ ׀ לְעֶבֶד יְהוָה לְדָוִד אֲשֶׁר דִּבֶּר ׀ לַיהוָה אֶת־דִּבְרֵי הַשִּׁירָה הַזֹּאת
יום ג לחדש
ב בְּיוֹם הִצִּיל־יְהוָה אוֹתוֹ מִכַּף כָּל־אֹיְבָיו וּמִיַּד שָׁאוּל: וַיֹּאמַר אֶרְחָמְךָ

ג יְהוָה חִזְקִי: יְהוָה ׀ סַלְעִי וּמְצוּדָתִי וּמְפַלְטִי אֵלִי צוּרִי אֶחֱסֶה־בּוֹ מָגִנִּי

ד-ה וְקֶרֶן־יִשְׁעִי מִשְׂגַּבִּי: מְהֻלָּל אֶקְרָא יְהוָה וּמִן־אֹיְבַי אִוָּשֵׁעַ: אֲפָפוּנִי חֶבְלֵי

ו מָוֶת וְנַחֲלֵי בְלִיַּעַל יְבַעֲתוּנִי: חֶבְלֵי שְׁאוֹל סְבָבוּנִי קִדְּמוּנִי מוֹקְשֵׁי מָוֶת:

ז בַּצַּר־לִי ׀ אֶקְרָא יְהוָה וְאֶל־אֱלֹהַי אֲשַׁוֵּעַ יִשְׁמַע מֵהֵיכָלוֹ קוֹלִי וְשַׁוְעָתִי

ח לְפָנָיו ׀ תָּבוֹא בְאָזְנָיו: וַתִּגְעַשׁ וַתִּרְעַשׁ ׀ הָאָרֶץ וּמוֹסְדֵי הָרִים יִרְגָּזוּ

ט וַיִּתְגָּעֲשׁוּ כִּי־חָרָה לוֹ: עָלָה עָשָׁן ׀ בְּאַפּוֹ וְאֵשׁ־מִפִּיו תֹּאכֵל גֶּחָלִים בָּעֲרוּ

י-יא מִמֶּנּוּ: וַיֵּט שָׁמַיִם וַיֵּרַד וַעֲרָפֶל תַּחַת רַגְלָיו: וַיִּרְכַּב עַל־כְּרוּב וַיָּעֹף וַיֵּדֶא

יב עַל־כַּנְפֵי־רוּחַ: יָשֶׁת חֹשֶׁךְ ׀ סִתְרוֹ סְבִיבוֹתָיו סֻכָּתוֹ חֶשְׁכַת־מַיִם עָבֵי

יג-יד שְׁחָקִים: מִנֹּגַהּ נֶגְדּוֹ עָבָיו עָבְרוּ בָּרָד וְגַחֲלֵי־אֵשׁ: וַיַּרְעֵם בַּשָּׁמַיִם ׀ יְהוָה

טו וְעֶלְיוֹן יִתֵּן קֹלוֹ בָּרָד וְגַחֲלֵי־אֵשׁ: וַיִּשְׁלַח חִצָּיו וַיְפִיצֵם וּבְרָקִים רָב

טז וַיְהֻמֵּם: וַיֵּרָאוּ ׀ אֲפִיקֵי מַיִם וַיִּגָּלוּ מוֹסְדוֹת תֵּבֵל מִגַּעֲרָתְךָ יְהוָה מִנִּשְׁמַת

יז-יח רוּחַ אַפֶּךָ: יִשְׁלַח מִמָּרוֹם יִקָּחֵנִי יַמְשֵׁנִי מִמַּיִם רַבִּים: יַצִּילֵנִי מֵאֹיְבִי עָז

יט וּמִשֹּׂנְאַי כִּי־אָמְצוּ מִמֶּנִּי: יְקַדְּמוּנִי בְיוֹם־אֵידִי וַיְהִי־יְהוָה לְמִשְׁעָן לִי:

כ-כא וַיּוֹצִיאֵנִי לַמֶּרְחָב יְחַלְּצֵנִי כִּי חָפֵץ בִּי: יִגְמְלֵנִי יְהוָה כְּצִדְקִי כְּבֹר יָדַי

כב-כג יָשִׁיב לִי: כִּי־שָׁמַרְתִּי דַּרְכֵי יְהוָה וְלֹא־רָשַׁעְתִּי מֵאֱלֹהָי: כִּי כָל־מִשְׁפָּטָיו

כד-כה לְנֶגְדִּי וְחֻקֹּתָיו לֹא־אָסִיר מֶנִּי: וָאֱהִי תָמִים עִמּוֹ וָאֶשְׁתַּמֵּר מֵעֲוֺנִי: וַיָּשֶׁב־

כו יְהוָה לִי כְצִדְקִי כְּבֹר יָדַי לְנֶגֶד עֵינָיו: עִם־חָסִיד תִּתְחַסָּד עִם־גְּבַר תָּמִים

כז-כח תִּתַּמָּם: עִם־נָבָר תִּתְבָּרָר וְעִם־עִקֵּשׁ תִּתְפַּתָּל: כִּי־אַתָּה עַם־עָנִי תוֹשִׁיעַ

כט-ל וְעֵינַיִם רָמוֹת תַּשְׁפִּיל: כִּי־אַתָּה תָּאִיר נֵרִי יְהוָה אֱלֹהַי יַגִּיהַּ חָשְׁכִּי: כִּי־בְךָ

17:10. Their prosperity has blocked their hearts and eyes from any awareness and fear of God.

17:13. The wicked are merely God's tools to execute His judgments.

17:15. I will enjoy the true bliss of perceiving God when I awake to the life and clarity of the World to Come (*R' Hirsch*).

18:1. With minor differences this psalm appears as Chapter 22 of *II Samuel*.

18:8-16. These verses contain allegorical depictions of the disasters that God visited upon Israel's mighty enemies (*Radak*).

18:10. God intervened in the course of human affairs (*Ralbag*).

18:11. God's punishment of the enemy came swiftly (*Ibn Ezra*).

18:22. If I did sin, it was unintentional (*Radak*).

them]. ⁸ *Guard me like the apple of the eye; shelter me in the shadow of Your wings,* ⁹ *from the wicked who have plundered me, my mortal enemies who surround me.* ¹⁰ *In their fat they enclose themselves;* * their mouths speak with arrogance.* ¹¹ *As we step forth they immediately surround us, they fix their gaze to spread over the land.* ¹² *His appearance is like a lion that yearns to tear asunder and like a young lion lurking in hiding.* ¹³ *Rise up, HASHEM, confront him and bring him to his knees; rescue my soul from the wicked one, who is Your sword.* * ¹⁴ *Oh to be among those who die by Your hand, HASHEM, who die of old age — whose portion is eternal life, and whose belly You fill with Your concealed treasure; they are sated with sons and they bequeath their abundance to their babes.* ¹⁵ *And I — in righteousness I shall behold Your face; upon awakening I will be sated by Your image.* *

18

David earned
the right to
sing God's
praises by
perceiving
the Divine
hand in all
the trials and
triumphs of
his long and
varied career.

¹ *For the conductor; by the servant of HASHEM, by David; who spoke the words of this song* * to HASHEM on the day that HASHEM delivered him from the hand of all his enemies and from the hand of Saul.* ² *He said: I will love You, HASHEM, my Strength.* ³ *HASHEM is my Rock, my Fortress, and my Rescuer; my God, my Rock in Whom I take shelter, my Shield, and the Horn of my Salvation, my Stronghold.* ⁴ *With praises I call unto HASHEM, and I am saved from my enemies.* ⁵ *The pains of death encircled me, and torrents of godless men would frighten me.* ⁶ *The pains of the grave surrounded me, the snares of death confronted me.* ⁷ *In my distress I would call upon HASHEM, and to my God I would cry [for salvation]. From His abode He would hear my voice, my cry to Him would reach His ears.* ⁸ *And the earth quaked and roared,* * the foundations of the mountains shook; they quaked when His wrath flared.* ⁹ *Smoke rose up in His nostrils, a devouring fire from His mouth, flaming coals blazed forth from Him.* ¹⁰ *He bent down the heavens and descended,* * with thick cloud beneath His feet.* ¹¹ *He mounted a cherub and flew; He swooped on the wings of the wind.* * ¹² *He made darkness His concealment, around Him His shelter — the darkness of water, the clouds of heaven.* ¹³ *From out of the brilliance that is before Him, His clouds passed over, with hail and fiery coals.* ¹⁴ *And HASHEM thundered in the heavens, the Most High gave forth His voice — hail and fiery coals.* ¹⁵ *He sent forth His arrows and scattered them; many lightning bolts, and He terrified them.* ¹⁶ *And the depths of the water became visible, the foundations of the earth were laid bare; by Your rebuke, HASHEM, by the blowing of the breath of Your nostrils.* ¹⁷ *He sent from on high and took me, He drew me out of deep waters.* ¹⁸ *He saved me from my mighty foe, and from my enemies when they overpowered me.* ¹⁹ *They confronted me on the day of my misfortune, but HASHEM was a support unto me.* ²⁰ *He brought me out into a broad space, He released me for He desired me.* ²¹ *HASHEM recompensed me according to my righteousness; He repaid me befitting the cleanliness of my hands.* ²² *For I have kept the ways of HASHEM, and I have not departed wickedly* * from my God.* ²³ *For all His judgments are before me, and I shall not remove His decrees from myself.* ²⁴ *I was perfectly innocent with Him, and I was vigilant against my sin.* ²⁵ *HASHEM repaid me in accordance with my righteousness, according to the purity of my hands before His eyes.* ²⁶ *With the devout You act devoutly, with the wholehearted man You act wholeheartedly.* ²⁷ *With the pure You act purely, and with the crooked You act perversely.* ²⁸ *For it is You Who saves a humble people, and haughty eyes You bring down.* ²⁹ *For it is You Who will light my lamp, HASHEM, my God, illuminates my darkness.* ³⁰ *For with You*

לא אֶרֶץ גָּדוֹד וּבֵאלֹהַי אֲדַלֶּג־שׁוּר: הָאֵל תָּמִים דַּרְכּוֹ אִמְרַת־יהוה צְרוּפָה
לב מָגֵן הוּא לְכֹל | הַחֹסִים בּוֹ: כִּי מִי אֱלוֹהַּ מִבַּלְעֲדֵי יהוה וּמִי צוּר זוּלָתִי
לג-לד אֱלֹהֵינוּ: הָאֵל הַמְאַזְּרֵנִי חָיִל וַיִּתֵּן תָּמִים דַּרְכִּי: מְשַׁוֶּה רַגְלַי כָּאַיָּלוֹת וְעַל
לה בָּמֹתַי יַעֲמִידֵנִי: מְלַמֵּד יָדַי לַמִּלְחָמָה וְנִחֲתָה קֶשֶׁת־נְחוּשָׁה זְרוֹעֹתָי:
לו-לז וַתִּתֶּן־לִי מָגֵן יִשְׁעֶךָ וִימִינְךָ תִסְעָדֵנִי וְעַנְוַתְךָ תַרְבֵּנִי: תַּרְחִיב צַעֲדִי תַחְתָּי
לח וְלֹא מָעֲדוּ קַרְסֻלָּי: אֶרְדּוֹף אוֹיְבַי וְאַשִּׂיגֵם וְלֹא־אָשׁוּב עַד־כַּלּוֹתָם:
לט-מ אֶמְחָצֵם וְלֹא־יֻכְלוּ קוּם יִפְּלוּ תַּחַת רַגְלָי: וַתְּאַזְּרֵנִי חַיִל לַמִּלְחָמָה
מא-מב תַּכְרִיעַ קָמַי תַּחְתָּי: וְאֹיְבַי נָתַתָּה לִּי עֹרֶף וּמְשַׂנְאַי אַצְמִיתֵם: יְשַׁוְּעוּ וְאֵין
מג מוֹשִׁיעַ עַל־יהוה וְלֹא עָנָם: וְאֶשְׁחָקֵם כְּעָפָר עַל־פְּנֵי־רוּחַ כְּטִיט חוּצוֹת
מד אֲרִיקֵם: תְּפַלְּטֵנִי מֵרִיבֵי עָם תְּשִׂימֵנִי לְרֹאשׁ גּוֹיִם עַם לֹא־יָדַעְתִּי יַעַבְדוּנִי:
מה-מו לְשֵׁמַע אֹזֶן יִשָּׁמְעוּ לִי בְּנֵי־נֵכָר יְכַחֲשׁוּ־לִי: בְּנֵי־נֵכָר יִבֹּלוּ וְיַחְרְגוּ
מז-מח מִמִּסְגְּרוֹתֵיהֶם: חַי־יהוה וּבָרוּךְ צוּרִי וְיָרוּם אֱלוֹהֵי יִשְׁעִי: הָאֵל הַנּוֹתֵן
מט נְקָמוֹת לִי וַיַּדְבֵּר עַמִּים תַּחְתָּי: מְפַלְּטִי מֵאֹיְבָי אַף מִן־קָמַי תְּרוֹמְמֵנִי
נ-נא מֵאִישׁ חָמָס תַּצִּילֵנִי: עַל־כֵּן | אוֹדְךָ בַגּוֹיִם | יהוה וּלְשִׁמְךָ אֲזַמֵּרָה: מַגְדִּל
יְשׁוּעוֹת מַלְכּוֹ וְעֹשֶׂה חֶסֶד | לִמְשִׁיחוֹ לְדָוִד וּלְזַרְעוֹ עַד־עוֹלָם:

יט א-ב לַמְנַצֵּחַ מִזְמוֹר לְדָוִד: הַשָּׁמַיִם מְסַפְּרִים כְּבוֹד־אֵל וּמַעֲשֵׂה יָדָיו מַגִּיד
ג-ד הָרָקִיעַ: יוֹם לְיוֹם יַבִּיעַ אֹמֶר וְלַיְלָה לְּלַיְלָה יְחַוֶּה־דָּעַת: אֵין־אֹמֶר וְאֵין
ה דְּבָרִים בְּלִי נִשְׁמָע קוֹלָם: בְּכָל־הָאָרֶץ | יָצָא קַוָּם וּבִקְצֵה תֵבֵל מִלֵּיהֶם
ו לַשֶּׁמֶשׁ שָׂם־אֹהֶל בָּהֶם: וְהוּא כְּחָתָן יֹצֵא מֵחֻפָּתוֹ יָשִׂישׂ כְּגִבּוֹר לָרוּץ
ז אֹרַח: מִקְצֵה הַשָּׁמַיִם | מוֹצָאוֹ וּתְקוּפָתוֹ עַל־קְצוֹתָם וְאֵין נִסְתָּר מֵחַמָּתוֹ:
ח תּוֹרַת יהוה תְּמִימָה מְשִׁיבַת נָפֶשׁ עֵדוּת יהוה נֶאֱמָנָה מַחְכִּימַת פֶּתִי:
ט-י פִּקּוּדֵי יהוה יְשָׁרִים מְשַׂמְּחֵי־לֵב מִצְוַת יהוה בָּרָה מְאִירַת עֵינָיִם: יִרְאַת
יא יהוה | טְהוֹרָה עוֹמֶדֶת לָעַד מִשְׁפְּטֵי־יהוה אֱמֶת צָדְקוּ יַחְדָּו: הַנֶּחֱמָדִים
יב מִזָּהָב וּמִפַּז רָב וּמְתוּקִים מִדְּבַשׁ וְנֹפֶת צוּפִים: גַּם־עַבְדְּךָ נִזְהָר בָּהֶם
יג-יד בְּשָׁמְרָם עֵקֶב רָב: שְׁגִיאוֹת מִי־יָבִין מִנִּסְתָּרוֹת נַקֵּנִי: גַּם מִזֵּדִים | חֲשֹׂךְ
טו עַבְדֶּךָ אַל־יִמְשְׁלוּ־בִי אָז אֵיתָם וְנִקֵּיתִי מִפֶּשַׁע רָב: יִהְיוּ לְרָצוֹן | אִמְרֵי־פִי
וְהֶגְיוֹן לִבִּי לְפָנֶיךָ יהוה צוּרִי וְגֹאֲלִי:

כ א-ב לַמְנַצֵּחַ מִזְמוֹר לְדָוִד: יַעַנְךָ יהוה בְּיוֹם צָרָה יְשַׂגֶּבְךָ שֵׁם | אֱלֹהֵי
ג-ד יַעֲקֹב: יִשְׁלַח־עֶזְרְךָ מִקֹּדֶשׁ וּמִצִּיּוֹן יִסְעָדֶךָּ: יִזְכֹּר כָּל־מִנְחֹתֶךָ
ה-ו וְעוֹלָתְךָ יְדַשְּׁנֶה סֶלָה: יִתֶּן־לְךָ כִלְבָבֶךָ וְכָל־עֲצָתְךָ יְמַלֵּא: נְרַנְּנָה |

18:36. You condescended to pay special attention to me, although I am unworthy.

19:3. Each day brings to light more and more of the Divine wisdom in Creation (*Malbim*).

19:4. Yet man's soul discerns their message clearly.

19:8. God's Torah directs man to his true place in the scheme of Creation.

19:14. Do not let my evil inclination overpower me. God assists those who yearn to do what is right and proper (*Yoma* 38b).

20:3. David prayed that his aid come from the Sanctuary, based in holiness, and not from unholy sources such as the hands of gentile kings and armies.

I smash a troop, and with my God I leap over a wall. [31] The God! His way is perfect; the promise of HASHEM is flawless, He is a shield for all who take refuge in Him. [32] For who is God besides HASHEM, and who is a Rock except for our God? [33] The God Who girds me with strength and Who made my way perfect, [34] Who straightened my feet like the hinds, and stood me upon my heights, [35] Who trained my hands for battle so that a copper bow could be bent by my arms. [36] You have given me the shield of Your salvation; and Your right hand has sustained me, and Your humility* made me great. [37] You have widened my stride beneath me, and my ankles have not faltered. [38] I pursued my foes and overtook them, and returned not until they were destroyed. [39] I struck them down and they could not rise, they fell beneath my feet. [40] You girded me with strength for battle, You brought my adversaries to their knees beneath me. [41] And my enemies — You gave to me in retreat; and my antagonists — I cut them down. [42] They cried out, but there was no savior; to HASHEM, but He answered them not. [43] I pulverized them like dust in the face of the storm, like mud of the streets I poured them out. [44] You rescued me from the strife of the people; You have made me the head of the nations, a people I did not know serves me. [45] At the ear's hearing they obey me, foreigners lie to me. [46] Foreigners are withered and terrified [even] from within their fortified enclosures. [47] HASHEM lives! Blessed is my Rock, and the God of my salvation is exalted! [48] The God Who grants me vengeance, and subjugates nations beneath me; [49] You rescue me from my foes; even above my adversaries You raise me; from the man of violence You rescue me. [50] Therefore, I shall give thanks to You among the nations, HASHEM, and to Your Name I will sing. [51] Who magnifies the salvations of His king, and does kindness to His anointed one, to David and his offspring, forever.

19

Contemplation of nature and study of Torah will teach man to relate to God and to achieve spiritual fulfillment.

[1] **F**or the conductor, a psalm by David. [2] The heavens declare the glory of God, and the firmament tells of His handiwork. [3] Day following day utters speech,* and night following night declares knowledge. [4] There is no speech and there are no words; their sound is not heard.* [5] [But] their precision goes forth throughout the earth, and their words reach the end of the inhabited world. In their midst He has set up a tent for the sun, [6] which is like a groom emerging from his bridal chamber, it rejoices like a powerful warrior to run the course. [7] Its source is the end of the heavens and its circuit is to their end; nothing is hidden from its heat. [8] The Torah of HASHEM is perfect, restoring the soul;* the testimony of HASHEM is trustworthy, making the simple one wise; [9] the orders of HASHEM are upright, gladdening the heart; the command of HASHEM is clear, enlightening the eyes; [10] the fear of HASHEM is pure, enduring forever; the judgments of HASHEM are true, altogether righteous. [11] They are more desirable than gold, than even much fine gold; and sweeter than honey, and drippings from the combs. [12] Also, when Your servant is scrupulous in them, in observing them there is great reward. [13] Who can discern mistakes? Cleanse me from unperceived faults. [14] Also from intentional sins restrain Your servant; let them not rule me,* then I shall be perfect; and I will be cleansed of great transgression. [15] May the expressions of my mouth and the thoughts of my heart find favor before You, HASHEM, my Rock and my Redeemer.

20

God responds in times of distress.

[1] **F**or the conductor, a psalm by David. [2] May HASHEM answer you on the day of distress; may the Name of Jacob's God make you impregnable. [3] May He dispatch your help from the Sanctuary,* and support you from Zion. [4] May He remember all your offerings, and consider your burnt-offerings generous, Selah. [5] May He grant you your heart's [desire], and fulfill your every plan. [6] May we sing

ז   בִּישׁוּעָתֶךָ וּבְשֵׁם־אֱלֹהֵינוּ נִדְגֹּל יְמַלֵּא יהוה כָּל־מִשְׁאֲלוֹתֶיךָ: עַתָּה יָדַעְתִּי

ח   כִּי הוֹשִׁיעַ ׀ יהוה מְשִׁיחוֹ יַעֲנֵהוּ מִשְּׁמֵי קָדְשׁוֹ בִּגְבֻרוֹת יֵשַׁע יְמִינוֹ: אֵלֶּה

ט   בָרֶכֶב וְאֵלֶּה בַסּוּסִים וַאֲנַחְנוּ ׀ בְּשֵׁם־יהוה אֱלֹהֵינוּ נַזְכִּיר: הֵמָּה כָּרְעוּ

וְנָפָלוּ וַאֲנַחְנוּ קַּמְנוּ וַנִּתְעוֹדָד: יהוה הוֹשִׁיעָה הַמֶּלֶךְ יַעֲנֵנוּ בְיוֹם־קָרְאֵנוּ:

כא   א-ב   לַמְנַצֵּחַ מִזְמוֹר לְדָוִד: יהוה בְּעָזְּךָ יִשְׂמַח־מֶלֶךְ וּבִישׁוּעָתְךָ מַה־יָּגֶיל

ג-ד   [יָּגֶל ק] מְאֹד: תַּאֲוַת לִבּוֹ נָתַתָּה לּוֹ וַאֲרֶשֶׁת שְׂפָתָיו בַּל־מָנַעְתָּ סֶּלָה: כִּי־

ה   תְקַדְּמֶנּוּ בִּרְכוֹת טוֹב תָּשִׁית לְרֹאשׁוֹ עֲטֶרֶת פָּז: חַיִּים ׀ שָׁאַל מִמְּךָ נָתַתָּה

ו   לּוֹ אֹרֶךְ יָמִים עוֹלָם וָעֶד: גָּדוֹל כְּבוֹדוֹ בִּישׁוּעָתֶךָ הוֹד וְהָדָר תְּשַׁוֶּה עָלָיו:

ז-ח   כִּי־תְשִׁיתֵהוּ בְרָכוֹת לָעַד תְּחַדֵּהוּ בְשִׂמְחָה אֶת־פָּנֶיךָ: כִּי־הַמֶּלֶךְ בֹּטֵחַ

ט   בַּיהוה וּבְחֶסֶד עֶלְיוֹן בַּל־יִמּוֹט: תִּמְצָא יָדְךָ לְכָל־אֹיְבֶיךָ יְמִינְךָ תִּמְצָא

י   שֹׂנְאֶיךָ: תְּשִׁיתֵמוֹ ׀ כְּתַנּוּר אֵשׁ לְעֵת פָּנֶיךָ יהוה בְּאַפּוֹ יְבַלְּעֵם וְתֹאכְלֵם

יא-יב   אֵשׁ: פִּרְיָמוֹ מֵאֶרֶץ תְּאַבֵּד וְזַרְעָם מִבְּנֵי אָדָם: כִּי־נָטוּ עָלֶיךָ רָעָה חָשְׁבוּ

יג-יד   מְזִמָּה בַּל־יוּכָלוּ: כִּי תְּשִׁיתֵמוֹ שֶׁכֶם בְּמֵיתָרֶיךָ תְּכוֹנֵן עַל־פְּנֵיהֶם: רוּמָה

יהוה בְעֻזֶּךָ נָשִׁירָה וּנְזַמְּרָה גְּבוּרָתֶךָ:

כב   א-ב   לַמְנַצֵּחַ עַל־אַיֶּלֶת הַשַּׁחַר מִזְמוֹר לְדָוִד: אֵלִי אֵלִי לָמָה עֲזַבְתָּנִי רָחוֹק

ג   מִישׁוּעָתִי דִּבְרֵי שַׁאֲגָתִי: אֱלֹהַי אֶקְרָא יוֹמָם וְלֹא תַעֲנֶה וְלַיְלָה וְלֹא־

ד-ה   דֻמִיָּה לִי: וְאַתָּה קָדוֹשׁ יוֹשֵׁב תְּהִלּוֹת יִשְׂרָאֵל: בְּךָ בָּטְחוּ אֲבֹתֵינוּ בָּטְחוּ

ו-ז   וַתְּפַלְּטֵמוֹ: אֵלֶיךָ זָעֲקוּ וְנִמְלָטוּ בְּךָ בָטְחוּ וְלֹא־בוֹשׁוּ: וְאָנֹכִי תוֹלַעַת וְלֹא־

ח   אִישׁ חֶרְפַּת אָדָם וּבְזוּי עָם: כָּל־רֹאַי יַלְעִגוּ לִי יַפְטִירוּ בְשָׂפָה יָנִיעוּ רֹאשׁ:

ט-י   גֹּל אֶל־יהוה יְפַלְּטֵהוּ יַצִּילֵהוּ כִּי חָפֵץ בּוֹ: כִּי־אַתָּה גֹחִי מִבָּטֶן מַבְטִיחִי

יא-יב   עַל־שְׁדֵי אִמִּי: עָלֶיךָ הָשְׁלַכְתִּי מֵרָחֶם מִבֶּטֶן אִמִּי אֵלִי אָתָּה: אַל־תִּרְחַק

יג   מִמֶּנִּי כִּי־צָרָה קְרוֹבָה כִּי־אֵין עוֹזֵר: סְבָבוּנִי פָּרִים רַבִּים אַבִּירֵי בָשָׁן

יד-טו   כִּתְּרוּנִי: פָּצוּ עָלַי פִּיהֶם אַרְיֵה טֹרֵף וְשֹׁאֵג: כַּמַּיִם נִשְׁפַּכְתִּי וְהִתְפָּרְדוּ כָּל־

טז   עַצְמוֹתָי הָיָה לִבִּי כַּדּוֹנָג נָמֵס בְּתוֹךְ מֵעָי: יָבֵשׁ כַּחֶרֶשׂ ׀ כֹּחִי וּלְשׁוֹנִי מֻדְבָּק

יז   מַלְקוֹחָי וְלַעֲפַר־מָוֶת תִּשְׁפְּתֵנִי: כִּי סְבָבוּנִי כְּלָבִים עֲדַת מְרֵעִים הִקִּיפוּנִי

יח-יט   כָּאֲרִי יָדַי וְרַגְלָי: אֲסַפֵּר כָּל־עַצְמוֹתָי הֵמָּה יַבִּיטוּ יִרְאוּ־בִי: יְחַלְּקוּ בְגָדַי

כ   לָהֶם וְעַל־לְבוּשִׁי יַפִּילוּ גוֹרָל: וְאַתָּה יהוה אַל־תִּרְחָק אֱיָלוּתִי לְעֶזְרָתִי

כא-כב   חוּשָׁה: הַצִּילָה מֵחֶרֶב נַפְשִׁי מִיַּד־כֶּלֶב יְחִידָתִי: הוֹשִׁיעֵנִי מִפִּי אַרְיֵה

כג-כד   וּמִקַּרְנֵי רֵמִים עֲנִיתָנִי: אֲסַפְּרָה שִׁמְךָ לְאֶחָי בְּתוֹךְ קָהָל אֲהַלְלֶךָּ: יִרְאֵי

21:2. David speaks of himself in the third person: "I do not rejoice in my own strength, but in Yours."

21:5. Even if the chain of Jewish sovereignty is interrupted, the monarchy will be restored to the seed of David (*Meiri*).

21:7. People will bless each other with the wish, "May God make you like him" (*Radak*).

22:1. *Aiyeles hashachar* is a musical instrument.

22:13. Powerful empires.

22:17. Frenzied mobs comprised of the base people.

22:19. They wish to take my mantle of royalty for themselves (*Ibn Ezra*).

22:22. The *reimim* are exceptionally powerful, horned beasts (see below 29:6), variously identified as buffaloes, rhinoceroses, unicorns, etc.

for joy at your salvation, and raise our banner in the Name of our God; may HASHEM fulfill all your requests. 7 Now I know that HASHEM has saved His anointed one; He will answer him from His sacred heaven, with the omnipotent victories of His right arm. 8 Some with chariots, and some with horses; but we, in the Name of HASHEM, our God, call out. 9 They slumped and fell, but we arose and were invigorated. 10 HASHEM save! May the King answer us on the day we call.

21

More than anyone else, kings and powerful people must set an example by acknowledging God's kindness.

1 For the conductor, a psalm by David. 2 HASHEM, in Your might the king* rejoices, and in Your salvation how greatly does he exult. 3 You have granted him his heart's desire, and the utterance of his lips You have not withheld, Selah! 4 For You anticipate him with blessings of good; You place on his head a crown of pure gold. 5 Life he requested of You, You gave it to him; length of days forever and ever. * 6 Great is his glory in Your salvation; majesty and splendor You confer upon him. 7 For You set him for blessings* forever; You gladden him with the joy of Your Presence. 8 For the king trusts in HASHEM, and in the kindness of the Most High, that he will not falter. 9 Your hand will suffice for all Your foes, Your right hand will find Your enemies. 10 You will make them like a fiery furnace at the time of Your anger; may HASHEM consume them in His wrath, and let a fire devour them. 11 Wipe their progeny from the earth, and their offspring from mankind. 12 For they have directed evil against You, they have concocted a scheme they cannot carry out. 13 For You shall place them as a portion [apart]; with Your bowstrings You will aim at their faces. 14 Be exalted, HASHEM, in Your might; we shall sing and chant the praise of Your omnipotence.

22

Speaking as an individual, the Jew prays for a final end to Israel's long exile from its land and its Temple.

1 For the conductor, on the aiyeles hashachar, * a psalm by David. 2 My God, my God, why have You forsaken me; why so far from saving me, from the words of my roar? 3 O my God! I call out by day, but You answer not; and by night, but there is no respite for me. 4 Yet You are the Holy One, enthroned upon the praises of Israel! 5 In You our fathers trusted, they trusted and You delivered them. 6 To You they cried out and they were rescued; in You they trusted and they were not shamed. 7 But I am a worm and not a man, scorn of humanity, despised of people. 8 All who see me, deride me; they open wide with [their] lip, they wag [their] head. 9 If one commits himself to HASHEM, He will deliver him! He will rescue him, for He desires him! 10 For You are the One Who drew me forth from the womb, and made me secure on my mother's breasts. 11 I was cast upon You from birth, from my mother's womb You have been my God. 12 Be not aloof from me for distress is near, for there is none to help. 13 Many bulls* surround me, Bashan's mighty ones encircle me. 14 They open their mouths against me like a tearing, roaring lion. 15 I am poured out like water, and all my bones became disjointed; my heart is like wax, melted within my innards. 16 My strength is dried up like baked clay, and my tongue cleaves to my palate; in the dust of death You set me down. 17 For dogs* have surrounded me; a pack of evildoers has enclosed me, like the [prey of a] lion are my hands and my feet. 18 I can count all my bones; they look on and gloat over me. 19 They divide my garments among themselves, and cast lots for my clothing. * 20 But You, HASHEM, be not far. O my Strength, hasten to my assistance! 21 Rescue my soul from the sword, my essence from the grip of the dog. 22 Save me from the lion's mouth as You have answered me from the horns of the reimim. * 23 I will proclaim Your Name to my brethren; in the midst of the congregation I will praise You. 24 You who fear

כה כִּי יהוה ׀ הָלְלוּהוּ כָּל־זֶרַע יַעֲקֹב כַּבְּדוּהוּ וְגוּרוּ מִמֶּנּוּ כָּל־זֶרַע יִשְׂרָאֵל: כִּי לֹא־בָזָה וְלֹא שִׁקַּץ עֱנוּת עָנִי וְלֹא־הִסְתִּיר פָּנָיו מִמֶּנּוּ וּבְשַׁוְּעוֹ אֵלָיו שָׁמֵעַ:

כו-כז מֵאִתְּךָ תְהִלָּתִי בְּקָהָל רָב נְדָרַי אֲשַׁלֵּם נֶגֶד יְרֵאָיו: יֹאכְלוּ עֲנָוִים ׀ וְיִשְׂבָּעוּ

כח יְהַלְלוּ יהוה דֹּרְשָׁיו יְחִי לְבַבְכֶם לָעַד: יִזְכְּרוּ ׀ וְיָשֻׁבוּ אֶל־יהוה כָּל־אַפְסֵי־

כט אָרֶץ וְיִשְׁתַּחֲווּ לְפָנֶיךָ כָּל־מִשְׁפְּחוֹת גּוֹיִם: כִּי לַיהוה הַמְּלוּכָה וּמֹשֵׁל

ל בַּגּוֹיִם: אָכְלוּ וַיִּשְׁתַּחֲווּ ׀ כָּל־דִּשְׁנֵי־אֶרֶץ לְפָנָיו יִכְרְעוּ כָּל־יוֹרְדֵי עָפָר

לא-לב וְנַפְשׁוֹ לֹא חִיָּה: זֶרַע יַעַבְדֶנּוּ יְסֻפַּר לַאדֹנָי לַדּוֹר: יָבֹאוּ וְיַגִּידוּ צִדְקָתוֹ לְעַם נוֹלָד כִּי עָשָׂה:

א מִזְמוֹר לְדָוִד יהוה רֹעִי לֹא אֶחְסָר: בִּנְאוֹת דֶּשֶׁא יַרְבִּיצֵנִי עַל־מֵי מְנֻחוֹת

יום ד לחדש

ג-ד יְנַהֲלֵנִי: נַפְשִׁי יְשׁוֹבֵב יַנְחֵנִי בְמַעְגְּלֵי־צֶדֶק לְמַעַן שְׁמוֹ: גַּם כִּי־אֵלֵךְ בְּגֵיא צַלְמָוֶת לֹא־אִירָא רָע כִּי־אַתָּה עִמָּדִי שִׁבְטְךָ וּמִשְׁעַנְתֶּךָ הֵמָּה יְנַחֲמֻנִי:

ה-ו תַּעֲרֹךְ לְפָנַי ׀ שֻׁלְחָן נֶגֶד צֹרְרָי דִּשַּׁנְתָּ בַשֶּׁמֶן רֹאשִׁי כּוֹסִי רְוָיָה: אַךְ ׀ טוֹב וָחֶסֶד יִרְדְּפוּנִי כָּל־יְמֵי חַיָּי וְשַׁבְתִּי בְּבֵית־יהוה לְאֹרֶךְ יָמִים:

א-ב לְדָוִד מִזְמוֹר לַיהוה הָאָרֶץ וּמְלוֹאָהּ תֵּבֵל וְיֹשְׁבֵי בָהּ: כִּי־הוּא עַל־יַמִּים

ג יְסָדָהּ וְעַל־נְהָרוֹת יְכוֹנְנֶהָ: מִי־יַעֲלֶה בְהַר־יהוה וּמִי־יָקוּם בִּמְקוֹם קָדְשׁוֹ:

ד נְקִי כַפַּיִם וּבַר־לֵבָב אֲשֶׁר ׀ לֹא־נָשָׂא לַשָּׁוְא °נַפְשִׁי [°נַפְשׁוֹ ק] וְלֹא נִשְׁבַּע

ה לְמִרְמָה: יִשָּׂא בְרָכָה מֵאֵת יהוה וּצְדָקָה מֵאֱלֹהֵי יִשְׁעוֹ: זֶה דּוֹר °דֹּרְשׁוֹ

ז [°דֹּרְשָׁיו ק] מְבַקְשֵׁי פָנֶיךָ יַעֲקֹב סֶלָה: שְׂאוּ שְׁעָרִים ׀ רָאשֵׁיכֶם וְהִנָּשְׂאוּ

ח פִּתְחֵי עוֹלָם וְיָבוֹא מֶלֶךְ הַכָּבוֹד: מִי זֶה מֶלֶךְ הַכָּבוֹד יהוה עִזּוּז וְגִבּוֹר יהוה

ט גִּבּוֹר מִלְחָמָה: שְׂאוּ שְׁעָרִים ׀ רָאשֵׁיכֶם וּשְׂאוּ פִּתְחֵי עוֹלָם וְיָבֹא מֶלֶךְ

י הַכָּבוֹד: מִי הוּא זֶה מֶלֶךְ הַכָּבוֹד יהוה צְבָאוֹת הוּא מֶלֶךְ הַכָּבוֹד סֶלָה:

א-ב לְדָוִד אֵלֶיךָ יהוה נַפְשִׁי אֶשָּׂא: אֱלֹהַי בְּךָ בָטַחְתִּי אַל־אֵבוֹשָׁה אַל־יַעַלְצוּ

ג-ד אֹיְבַי לִי: גַּם כָּל־קֹוֶיךָ לֹא יֵבֹשׁוּ יֵבֹשׁוּ הַבּוֹגְדִים רֵיקָם: דְּרָכֶיךָ יהוה

ה הוֹדִיעֵנִי אֹרְחוֹתֶיךָ לַמְּדֵנִי: הַדְרִיכֵנִי בַאֲמִתֶּךָ ׀ וְלַמְּדֵנִי כִּי־אַתָּה אֱלֹהֵי

ו יִשְׁעִי אוֹתְךָ קִוִּיתִי כָּל־הַיּוֹם: זְכֹר־רַחֲמֶיךָ יהוה וַחֲסָדֶיךָ כִּי מֵעוֹלָם

ז הֵמָּה: חַטֹּאות נְעוּרַי ׀ וּפְשָׁעַי אַל־תִּזְכֹּר כְּחַסְדְּךָ זְכָר־לִי־אַתָּה לְמַעַן

ח-ט טוּבְךָ יהוה: טוֹב־וְיָשָׁר יהוה עַל־כֵּן יוֹרֶה חַטָּאִים בַּדָּרֶךְ: יַדְרֵךְ עֲנָוִים

י בַּמִּשְׁפָּט וִילַמֵּד עֲנָוִים דַּרְכּוֹ: כָּל־אָרְחוֹת יהוה חֶסֶד וֶאֱמֶת לְנֹצְרֵי

יא-יב בְרִיתוֹ וְעֵדֹתָיו: לְמַעַן־שִׁמְךָ יהוה וְסָלַחְתָּ לַעֲוֹנִי כִּי רַב־הוּא: מִי־זֶה

22:30. The prosperous nations, who were all destined for the grave and for mortality, will return to God [and their repentance will be accepted] (*Meiri*). But there are those among them who will descend to the grave and whose souls He will not revive even though they now kneel before Him. These are the ones whose hands are stained with Jewish blood (*Radak*).

22:31. Even though all of mankind will eventually return to God, Israel will remain foremost among them (*Radak; Meiri*).

23:4. The morbid "valley" is a characterization of all exiles. Alternatively, it is a place so dangerous that it is as dark and forbidding as the grave.

24:3-4. One who wishes to enjoy spiritual elevation must refine his behavior.

24:4. Honest in his dealings with man; reverent in his attitude toward God.

HASHEM, praise Him! All of you, seed of Jacob, glorify Him! Be in awe of Him, all you seed of Israel. [25] For He has neither despised nor loathed the supplication of the poor, nor has He concealed His face from him; but when he cried to Him, He heard. [26] From You is my praise in the great congregation; I will fulfill my vows before those who fear Him. [27] The humble will eat and be satisfied, those who seek HASHEM will praise Him — your hearts will live forever. [28] All the ends of the earth will remember and turn back to HASHEM; all the families of nations will bow before You. [29] For the kingship belongs to HASHEM, and He rules the nations. [30] All the fat ones of the earth will eat and bow down; all who descend to the dust will kneel before Him, but He will not revive each one's soul. * [31] About the seed of those who have served Him, * it will be told of the Lord to the latter generation. [32] They will come and relate His righteousness, to the newborn nation that which He has done.

23

Whether in a verdant meadow or a parched desert, God provides man's every need.

[1] A psalm by David. HASHEM is my shepherd, I shall not lack. [2] In lush meadows He lays me down, beside tranquil waters He leads me. [3] He restores my soul. He leads me on paths of righteousness for His Name's sake. [4] Though I walk in the valley overshadowed by death, * I will fear no evil, for You are with me. Your rod and Your staff, they comfort me. [5] You prepare a table before me in view of my tormentors. You anointed my head with oil, my cup overflows. [6] May only goodness and kindness pursue me all the days of my life, and I shall dwell in the House of HASHEM for long days.

24

More than the land, brick and mortar, only the personal qualities of the worshipers can build God's Temple.

[1] By David, a psalm. HASHEM's is the earth and its fullness, the inhabited land and those who dwell in it. [2] For He founded it upon seas, and established it upon rivers. [3] Who may ascend the mountain of HASHEM, * and who may stand in the place of His sanctity? [4] One with clean hands and pure heart; who has not sworn in vain by My soul, and has not sworn deceitfully. * [5] He will receive a blessing from HASHEM and just kindness from the God of his salvation. [6] This is the generation of those who seek Him, those who strive for Your Presence, [the nation of] Jacob, Selah. [7] Raise up your heads, O gates, and be uplifted, you everlasting entrances, so that the King of Glory may enter. [8] Who is this King of Glory? HASHEM, the mighty and strong; HASHEM, the strong in battle. [9] Raise up your heads, O gates, and raise up, you everlasting entrances, so that the King of Glory may enter. [10] Who is He, this King of Glory? HASHEM, Master of Legions, He is the King of Glory, Selah!

25

The righteous person seeks closeness to God and salvation from distress by repenting and extolling God's kindness to those who seek Him.

[1] By David: To You HASHEM I lift up my soul. * [2] My God, in You I have trusted, let me not be shamed; let not my enemies exult over me. [3] Also, let none who hope in You be shamed; let those who betray without cause be shamed. [4] Make Your ways known to me, HASHEM; teach me Your paths. [5] Lead me in Your truth and teach me, for You are the God of my salvation, to You I have hoped all the day. [6] Remember Your mercies, * HASHEM, and Your kindnesses, for they are eternal. [7] Remember not the sins of my youth and my rebellions; may You remember for me [the deeds] worthy of Your kindness, because of Your goodness, HASHEM. [8] Good and upright is HASHEM, therefore He guides sinners on the way. * [9] He leads the humble with justice, and teaches His way to the humble. [10] All the ways of HASHEM are kindness and truth, to those who guard His covenant and testimonies. [11] For Your Name's sake, HASHEM, pardon my guilt for it is great. [12] Whosoever is

---

25:1. I dedicate it to Your service *(Ibn Ezra)*.
25:6. To bestow them upon me now as You have

always done previously.
25:8. Toward repentance.

יג הָאִישׁ יָרֵא יְהוָֹה יוֹרֶנּוּ בְּדֶרֶךְ יִבְחָר: נַפְשׁוֹ בְּטוֹב תָּלִין וְזַרְעוֹ יִירַשׁ אָרֶץ:

יד־טו סוֹד יְהוָֹה לִירֵאָיו וּבְרִיתוֹ לְהוֹדִיעָם: עֵינַי תָּמִיד אֶל־יְהוָֹה כִּי הוּא־יוֹצִיא

טז־יז מֵרֶשֶׁת רַגְלָי: פְּנֵה־אֵלַי וְחָנֵּנִי כִּי־יָחִיד וְעָנִי אָנִי: צָרוֹת לְבָבִי הִרְחִיבוּ

יח־יט מִמְּצוּקוֹתַי הוֹצִיאֵנִי: רְאֵה עָנְיִי וַעֲמָלִי וְשָׂא לְכָל־חַטֹּאותָי: רְאֵה־אוֹיְבַי

כ כִּי־רָבּוּ וְשִׂנְאַת חָמָס שְׂנֵאוּנִי: שָׁמְרָה נַפְשִׁי וְהַצִּילֵנִי אַל־אֵבוֹשׁ כִּי־

כא־כב חָסִיתִי בָךְ: תֹּם־וָיֹשֶׁר יִצְּרוּנִי כִּי קִוִּיתִיךָ: פְּדֵה אֱלֹהִים אֶת־יִשְׂרָאֵל מִכֹּל צָרוֹתָיו:

כו א לְדָוִד שָׁפְטֵנִי יְהוָֹה כִּי־אֲנִי בְּתֻמִּי הָלַכְתִּי וּבַיהוָֹה בָּטַחְתִּי לֹא אֶמְעָד:

ב־ג בְּחָנֵנִי יְהוָֹה וְנַסֵּנִי °צרופה [°צָרְפָה ק] כִלְיוֹתַי וְלִבִּי: כִּי־חַסְדְּךָ לְנֶגֶד עֵינָי

ד וְהִתְהַלַּכְתִּי בַּאֲמִתֶּךָ: לֹא־יָשַׁבְתִּי עִם־מְתֵי־שָׁוְא וְעִם נַעֲלָמִים לֹא

ה־ו אָבוֹא: שָׂנֵאתִי קְהַל מְרֵעִים וְעִם־רְשָׁעִים לֹא אֵשֵׁב: אֶרְחַץ בְּנִקָּיוֹן כַּפָּי

ז־ח וַאֲסֹבְבָה אֶת־מִזְבַּחֲךָ יְהוָֹה: לַשְׁמִעַ בְּקוֹל תּוֹדָה וּלְסַפֵּר כָּל־נִפְלְאוֹתֶיךָ:

ט יְהוָֹה אָהַבְתִּי מְעוֹן בֵּיתֶךָ וּמְקוֹם מִשְׁכַּן כְּבוֹדֶךָ: אַל־תֶּאֱסֹף עִם־חַטָּאִים

י־יא נַפְשִׁי וְעִם־אַנְשֵׁי דָמִים חַיָּי: אֲשֶׁר־בִּידֵיהֶם זִמָּה וִימִינָם מָלְאָה שֹּׁחַד: וַאֲנִי

יב בְּתֻמִּי אֵלֵךְ פְּדֵנִי וְחָנֵּנִי: רַגְלִי עָמְדָה בְמִישׁוֹר בְּמַקְהֵלִים אֲבָרֵךְ יְהוָֹה:

כז א־ב לְדָוִד יְהוָֹה אוֹרִי וְיִשְׁעִי מִמִּי אִירָא יְהוָֹה מָעוֹז־חַיַּי מִמִּי אֶפְחָד: בִּקְרֹב

ג עָלַי מְרֵעִים לֶאֱכֹל אֶת־בְּשָׂרִי צָרַי וְאֹיְבַי לִי הֵמָּה כָשְׁלוּ וְנָפָלוּ: אִם־

תַּחֲנֶה עָלַי מַחֲנֶה לֹא־יִירָא לִבִּי אִם־תָּקוּם עָלַי מִלְחָמָה בְּזֹאת אֲנִי

ד בוֹטֵחַ: אַחַת שָׁאַלְתִּי מֵאֵת־יְהוָֹה אוֹתָהּ אֲבַקֵּשׁ שִׁבְתִּי בְּבֵית־יְהוָֹה כָּל־

ה יְמֵי חַיַּי לַחֲזוֹת בְּנֹעַם־יְהוָֹה וּלְבַקֵּר בְּהֵיכָלוֹ: כִּי יִצְפְּנֵנִי בְּסֻכֹּה בְּיוֹם רָעָה

ו יַסְתִּרֵנִי בְּסֵתֶר אָהֳלוֹ בְּצוּר יְרוֹמְמֵנִי: וְעַתָּה יָרוּם רֹאשִׁי עַל אֹיְבַי

ז סְבִיבוֹתַי וְאֶזְבְּחָה בְאָהֳלוֹ זִבְחֵי תְרוּעָה אָשִׁירָה וַאֲזַמְּרָה לַיהוָֹה: שְׁמַע־

ח יְהוָֹה קוֹלִי אֶקְרָא וְחָנֵּנִי וַעֲנֵנִי: לְךָ אָמַר לִבִּי בַּקְּשׁוּ פָנָי אֶת־פָּנֶיךָ יְהוָֹה

ט אֲבַקֵּשׁ: אַל־תַּסְתֵּר פָּנֶיךָ מִמֶּנִּי אַל־תַּט־בְּאַף עַבְדֶּךָ עֶזְרָתִי הָיִיתָ אַל־

י תִּטְּשֵׁנִי וְאַל־תַּעַזְבֵנִי אֱלֹהֵי יִשְׁעִי: כִּי־אָבִי וְאִמִּי עֲזָבוּנִי וַיהוָֹה יַאַסְפֵנִי:

יא־יב הוֹרֵנִי יְהוָֹה דַּרְכֶּךָ וּנְחֵנִי בְּאֹרַח מִישׁוֹר לְמַעַן שׁוֹרְרָי: אַל־תִּתְּנֵנִי בְּנֶפֶשׁ

יג צָרָי כִּי קָמוּ־בִי עֵדֵי־שֶׁקֶר וִיפֵחַ חָמָס: לוּלֵא הֶאֱמַנְתִּי לִרְאוֹת בְּטוּב־יְהוָֹה

יד בְּאֶרֶץ חַיִּים: קַוֵּה אֶל־יְהוָֹה חֲזַק וְיַאֲמֵץ לִבֶּךָ וְקַוֵּה אֶל־יְהוָֹה:

כח א לְדָוִד אֵלֶיךָ יְהוָֹה אֶקְרָא צוּרִי אַל־תֶּחֱרַשׁ מִמֶּנִּי פֶּן־תֶּחֱשֶׁה מִמֶּנִּי

ב וְנִמְשַׁלְתִּי עִם־יוֹרְדֵי בוֹר: שְׁמַע קוֹל תַּחֲנוּנַי בְּשַׁוְּעִי אֵלֶיךָ בְּנָשְׂאִי יָדַי אֶל־

26:3. I have been loyal to You because my goal was not to ingratiate myself to men, only to be worthy of Your kindness (see *Radak; R' Hirsch*).

26:6. I come to worship God not sullied by sin but in true repentance.

27:4. This request embodies all of my desires: to serve God and understand His ways (*Malbim*).

27:10. After my adolescence, they sent me out on my own (*Sforno*).

27:13. The conclusion of this exclamation is implied: If not for my faith, the relentless attacks of such false witnesses would have overwhelmed me long ago (*Rashi; Radak*). The "land of life" is the World to Come (*Berachos 4a*).

the man who fears HASHEM, He will teach him the way that he should choose. [13] His soul will repose in goodness, and his offspring will inherit the land. [14] The secret of HASHEM is to those who fear Him, and His covenant to inform them. [15] My eyes are constantly toward HASHEM, for He will remove my feet from the snare. [16] Turn to me and show me favor, for I am alone and afflicted. [17] The troubles of my heart have broadened, release me from my distresses. [18] See my afflictions and my toil, and forgive all my sins. [19] See my foes, that they have become many, and they hate me with violent animosity. [20] Protect my soul and rescue me; let me not be ashamed, for I take refuge in You. [21] Perfect innocence and uprightness will guard me, for I hope to You. [22] Redeem Israel, O God, from all its distresses.

26

A righteous person walks in purity and vigilance, and prays for Divine help in avoiding life's pitfalls.

[1] By David. Judge me, HASHEM, for I — I have walked in my perfect innocence; and I have trusted in HASHEM, I shall not waver. [2] Examine me, HASHEM, and test me; scrutinize my intellect and my heart. [3] For Your kindness is before my eyes, * and I have walked in Your truth. [4] I did not sit with dishonest people, nor did I associate with hypocrites. [5] I hated the gathering of evildoers, and I did not sit with the wicked. [6] I wash my hands in purity * and circle around Your altar, HASHEM. [7] To proclaim thanksgiving in a loud voice and to recount all Your wondrous deeds. [8] HASHEM, I love the shelter of Your House and the place of Your glory's residence. [9] Gather not my soul with sinners; nor my life with men of bloodshed, [10] in whose hands is conspiracy, and whose right hand is full of bribery. [11] As for me, I will walk in my perfect innocence, redeem me and show me favor. [12] My foot is set on the straight path, in assemblies I will bless HASHEM.

27

The House of God provides the sole island of constancy amid life's swirling waters of pain and disappoint-ment. To dwell in it is David's constant goal.

[1] By David. HASHEM is my light and my salvation, whom shall I fear? HASHEM is my life's strength, whom shall I dread? [2] When evildoers approach me to devour my flesh, my tormentors and my foes against me, it is they who stumble and fall. [3] Though an army would besiege me, my heart would not fear; though war would arise against me, in this I trust. [4] One thing * I asked of HASHEM, that shall I seek: Would that I dwell in the House of HASHEM all the days of my life, to behold the sweetness of HASHEM and to contemplate in His Sanctuary. [5] Indeed, He will hide me in His Shelter on the day of evil; He will conceal me in the concealment of His Tent; He will lift me upon a rock. [6] Now my head is raised above my enemies around me, and I will slaughter offerings in His Tent accompa-nied by joyous song; I will sing and chant praise to HASHEM. [7] HASHEM, hear my voice when I call, be gracious toward me and answer me. [8] In Your behalf, my heart has said, "Seek My Presence." Your Presence, HASHEM, do I seek. [9] Conceal not Your Presence from me, repel not Your servant in anger. You have been my Helper, abandon me not, forsake me not, O God of my salvation. [10] Though my father and mother have forsaken me, * HASHEM will gather me in. [11] Teach me Your way, HASHEM; and lead me on the path of integrity, because of my watchful foes. [12] Deliver me not to the wishes of my tormentors, for there have arisen against me false witnesses who breathe out violence. [13] Had I not trusted that I would see the goodness of HASHEM in the land of life! * [14] Hope to HASHEM; strengthen yourself and He will give you courage, and hope to HASHEM.

28

[1] By David. To You, HASHEM, I call, my Rock, be not deaf to me; for should You be silent to me I would be likened to those who descend to the grave. [2] Hear the sound of my supplications when I cry to You; when I lift my hands towards

ג דְּבִיר קָדְשֶׁךָ: אַל־תִּמְשְׁכֵנִי עִם־רְשָׁעִים וְעִם־פֹּעֲלֵי אָוֶן דֹּבְרֵי שָׁלוֹם עִם־

ד רֵעֵיהֶם וְרָעָה בִּלְבָבָם: תֶּן־לָהֶם כְּפָעֳלָם וּכְרֹעַ מַעַלְלֵיהֶם כְּמַעֲשֵׂה יְדֵיהֶם

ה תֵּן לָהֶם הָשֵׁב גְּמוּלָם לָהֶם: כִּי לֹא יָבִינוּ אֶל־פְּעֻלֹּת יְהוָה וְאֶל־מַעֲשֵׂה

ו־ז יָדָיו יֶהֶרְסֵם וְלֹא יִבְנֵם: בָּרוּךְ יְהוָה כִּי־שָׁמַע קוֹל תַּחֲנוּנָי: יְהוָה עֻזִּי וּמָגִנִּי

ח בּוֹ בָטַח לִבִּי וְנֶעֱזָרְתִּי וַיַּעֲלֹז לִבִּי וּמִשִּׁירִי אֲהוֹדֶנּוּ: יְהוָה עֹז־לָמוֹ וּמָעוֹז

ט יְשׁוּעוֹת מְשִׁיחוֹ הוּא: הוֹשִׁיעָה אֶת־עַמֶּךָ וּבָרֵךְ אֶת־נַחֲלָתֶךָ וּרְעֵם

וְנַשְּׂאֵם עַד־הָעוֹלָם:

כט   א־ב מִזְמוֹר לְדָוִד הָבוּ לַיהוָה בְּנֵי אֵלִים הָבוּ לַיהוָה כָּבוֹד וָעֹז: הָבוּ לַיהוָה
יום ה לחדש

ג כְּבוֹד שְׁמוֹ הִשְׁתַּחֲווּ לַיהוָה בְּהַדְרַת־קֹדֶשׁ: קוֹל יְהוָה עַל־הַמָּיִם אֵל־

ד הַכָּבוֹד הִרְעִים יְהוָה עַל־מַיִם רַבִּים: קוֹל־יְהוָה בַּכֹּחַ קוֹל יְהוָה בֶּהָדָר:

ה־ו קוֹל יְהוָה שֹׁבֵר אֲרָזִים וַיְשַׁבֵּר יְהוָה אֶת־אַרְזֵי הַלְּבָנוֹן: וַיַּרְקִידֵם כְּמוֹ־עֵגֶל

ז־ח לְבָנוֹן וְשִׂרְיֹן כְּמוֹ בֶן־רְאֵמִים: קוֹל־יְהוָה חֹצֵב לַהֲבוֹת אֵשׁ: קוֹל יְהוָה

ט יָחִיל מִדְבָּר יָחִיל יְהוָה מִדְבַּר קָדֵשׁ: קוֹל יְהוָה יְחוֹלֵל אַיָּלוֹת וַיֶּחֱשֹׂף

י יְעָרוֹת וּבְהֵיכָלוֹ כֻּלּוֹ אֹמֵר כָּבוֹד: יְהוָה לַמַּבּוּל יָשָׁב וַיֵּשֶׁב יְהוָה מֶלֶךְ

יא לְעוֹלָם: יְהוָה עֹז לְעַמּוֹ יִתֵּן יְהוָה יְבָרֵךְ אֶת־עַמּוֹ בַשָּׁלוֹם:

ל   א־ב מִזְמוֹר שִׁיר־חֲנֻכַּת הַבַּיִת לְדָוִד: אֲרוֹמִמְךָ יְהוָה כִּי דִלִּיתָנִי וְלֹא־שִׂמַּחְתָּ
יום שני

ג־ד אֹיְבַי לִי: יְהוָה אֱלֹהָי שִׁוַּעְתִּי אֵלֶיךָ וַתִּרְפָּאֵנִי: יְהוָה הֶעֱלִיתָ מִן־שְׁאוֹל

ה נַפְשִׁי חִיִּיתַנִי °מִיּוֹרְדִי [מִיָּרְדִי ק] בוֹר: זַמְּרוּ לַיהוָה חֲסִידָיו וְהוֹדוּ

ו לְזֵכֶר קָדְשׁוֹ: כִּי רֶגַע בְּאַפּוֹ חַיִּים בִּרְצוֹנוֹ בָּעֶרֶב יָלִין בֶּכִי וְלַבֹּקֶר רִנָּה:

ז־ח וַאֲנִי אָמַרְתִּי בְשַׁלְוִי בַּל־אֶמּוֹט לְעוֹלָם: יְהוָה בִּרְצוֹנְךָ הֶעֱמַדְתָּה לְהַרְרִי

ט עֹז הִסְתַּרְתָּ פָנֶיךָ הָיִיתִי נִבְהָל: אֵלֶיךָ יְהוָה אֶקְרָא וְאֶל־אֲדֹנָי אֶתְחַנָּן: מַה־

י־יא בֶּצַע בְּדָמִי בְּרִדְתִּי אֶל־שָׁחַת הֲיוֹדְךָ עָפָר הֲיַגִּיד אֲמִתֶּךָ: שְׁמַע־יְהוָה

יב וְחָנֵּנִי יְהוָה הֱיֵה־עֹזֵר לִי: הָפַכְתָּ מִסְפְּדִי לְמָחוֹל לִי פִּתַּחְתָּ שַׂקִּי וַתְּאַזְּרֵנִי

יג שִׂמְחָה: לְמַעַן יְזַמֶּרְךָ כָבוֹד וְלֹא יִדֹּם יְהוָה אֱלֹהַי לְעוֹלָם אוֹדֶךָּ:

לא   א־ב לַמְנַצֵּחַ מִזְמוֹר לְדָוִד: בְּךָ־יְהוָה חָסִיתִי אַל־אֵבוֹשָׁה לְעוֹלָם בְּצִדְקָתְךָ

ג פַלְּטֵנִי: הַטֵּה אֵלַי אָזְנְךָ מְהֵרָה הַצִּילֵנִי הֱיֵה לִי לְצוּר־מָעוֹז לְבֵית מְצוּדוֹת

ד לְהוֹשִׁיעֵנִי: כִּי־סַלְעִי וּמְצוּדָתִי אָתָּה וּלְמַעַן שִׁמְךָ תַּנְחֵנִי וּתְנַהֲלֵנִי:

ה־ו תּוֹצִיאֵנִי מֵרֶשֶׁת זוּ טָמְנוּ לִי כִּי־אַתָּה מָעוּזִּי: בְּיָדְךָ אַפְקִיד רוּחִי פָּדִיתָה

28:6. Such was David's trust that he speaks as if he had already been answered (*Meiri*).

29:1. Abraham, Isaac, and Jacob, who were "powerful" in their righteousness.

29:6. See 22:22.

29:7. When God pronounced the Ten Commandments, the very words sprang forth like fire, so to speak, and seared their way into the Tablets of the Law (*Midrash*).

29:8. "Kadesh," cognate with *kadosh*, "holy," is another name for the Wilderness of Sinai, where Israel became

sanctified by accepting the Torah.

29:10. In Messianic times God's reign will be as absolute as it was during the Flood, when nearly all life was washed away.

30:4. The flames of frustration, anguish, and melancholy are the equivalent of the fires of *Gehinnom*, "the nether-world." Thus, the Talmud (*Nedarim* 22a) teaches, "Whoever becomes angry is subjected to all types of *Gehinnom*" (*R' Yerucham Levovitz*).

31:2. David composed this psalm while in flight from Saul's relentless pursuit. Time and again his whereabouts

When He favors the righteous and rejects those unmindful of Him, God assists man in remaining on His chosen path.

Your Holy Sanctuary. ³ Do not cause me to be drawn with the wicked and with the doers of iniquity, who speak peace with their companions though evil is in their hearts. ⁴ Give them according to their deeds and according to the evil of their actions; according to their handiwork give them, render their recompense to them. ⁵ For they do not contemplate the deeds of HASHEM or His handiwork; may He tear them down and not rebuild them. ⁶ Blessed is HASHEM, for He has heard* the sound of my supplications. ⁷ HASHEM is my strength and my shield, in Him my heart trusted and I was helped; and my heart exulted, with my song I praise Him: ⁸ "HASHEM is strength to them; and the stronghold of salvations for His anointed is He." ⁹ Save Your nation, and bless Your inheritance; tend them and elevate them forever.

29

God's power and glory pervade all of creation. It functions solely according to His will, as has been manifested by His intervention in history.

¹ A psalm of David: Render unto HASHEM, you sons of the powerful,* render unto HASHEM honor and might. ² Render unto HASHEM the honor due His Name, bow to HASHEM in the beauty of holiness. ³ The voice of HASHEM is upon the waters, the God of Glory thunders; HASHEM is upon vast waters. ⁴ The voice of HASHEM [comes] in power! The voice of HASHEM [comes] in majesty! ⁵ The voice of HASHEM breaks the cedars, HASHEM shatters the cedars of Lebanon! ⁶ He makes them prance about like a calf; Lebanon and Siryon like young re'eimim. * ⁷ The voice of HASHEM cleaves with shafts of fire. * ⁸ The voice of HASHEM convulses the wilderness; HASHEM convulses the wilderness of Kadesh. * ⁹ The voice of HASHEM frightens the hinds, and strips the forests bare; while in His Temple all will proclaim, "Glory!" ¹⁰ HASHEM sat enthroned at the Flood;* HASHEM sits enthroned as King forever. ¹¹ HASHEM will give might to His nation, HASHEM will bless His nation with peace.

30

As darkness precedes dawn, so travail should be accepted as a prerequisite for success.

¹ A psalm, a song for the inauguration of the Temple, by David. ² I will exalt You, HASHEM, for You have drawn me up, and not let my foes rejoice over me. ³ HASHEM, my God, I cried out to You and You healed me. ⁴ HASHEM, You have raised up my soul from the lower world;* You have preserved me from my descent to the pit. ⁵ Sing to HASHEM, His devout ones, and give thanks to His holy Name. ⁶ For His anger endures but a moment; life results from His favor. In the evening one lies down weeping, but with dawn — a cry of joy! ⁷ I had said in my serenity, "I would never falter." ⁸ But, HASHEM, all is through Your favor — You supported my greatness with might; should You but conceal Your face, I would be confounded. ⁹ To You, HASHEM, I would call and to the Lord I would appeal. ¹⁰ What gain is there in my death, in my descent to the pit? Will the dust acknowledge You? Will it declare Your truth? ¹¹ Hear, HASHEM, and favor me; HASHEM, be my Helper! ¹² You have transformed my lament into dancing for me, You undid my sackcloth and girded me with gladness. ¹³ So that my soul might sing to You and not be stilled, HASHEM, my God, forever will I thank You.

31

¹ For the conductor, a song by David. ² In You, HASHEM, I have taken refuge,* let me not be shamed ever; in Your righteousness liberate me. ³ Incline to me Your ear, quickly rescue me; be for me a stronghold rock, a fortress to save me. ⁴ For my Rock and my Fortress are You, for Your Name's sake guide me and lead me. ⁵ Remove me from this net that they have hidden for me, for You are my stronghold. ⁶ In Your hand I entrust my spirit; You redeemed

were betrayed to Saul, and time and again God rescued him (see I Samuel Chs. 22-24).

ז אוֹתִי יהוה אֵל אֱמֶת: שָׂנֵאתִי הַשֹּׁמְרִים הַבְלֵי־שָׁוְא וַאֲנִי אֶל־יהוה

ח בָּטַחְתִּי: אָגִילָה וְאֶשְׂמְחָה בְּחַסְדֶּךָ אֲשֶׁר רָאִיתָ אֶת־עָנְיִי יָדַעְתָּ בְּצָרוֹת

ט נַפְשִׁי: וְלֹא הִסְגַּרְתַּנִי בְּיַד־אוֹיֵב הֶעֱמַדְתָּ בַמֶּרְחָב רַגְלָי: חָנֵּנִי יהוה כִּי

י צַר־לִי עָשְׁשָׁה בְכַעַס עֵינִי נַפְשִׁי וּבִטְנִי: כִּי כָלוּ בְיָגוֹן חַיַּי וּשְׁנוֹתַי

יא בַּאֲנָחָה כָּשַׁל בַּעֲוֹנִי כֹחִי וַעֲצָמַי עָשֵׁשׁוּ: מִכָּל־צֹרְרַי הָיִיתִי חֶרְפָּה

יב וְלִשְׁכֵנַי ׀ מְאֹד וּפַחַד לִמְיֻדָּעָי רֹאַי בַּחוּץ נָדְדוּ מִמֶּנִּי: נִשְׁכַּחְתִּי כְּמֵת

יג מִלֵּב הָיִיתִי כִּכְלִי אֹבֵד: כִּי שָׁמַעְתִּי ׀ דִּבַּת רַבִּים מָגוֹר מִסָּבִיב בְּהִוָּסְדָם

יד יַחַד עָלַי לָקַחַת נַפְשִׁי זָמָמוּ: וַאֲנִי ׀ עָלֶיךָ בָטַחְתִּי יהוה אָמַרְתִּי אֱלֹהַי

טו אָתָּה: בְּיָדְךָ עִתֹּתָי הַצִּילֵנִי מִיַּד־אוֹיְבַי וּמֵרֹדְפָי: הָאִירָה פָנֶיךָ עַל־עַבְדֶּךָ

טז-יז הוֹשִׁיעֵנִי בְחַסְדֶּךָ: יהוה אַל־אֵבוֹשָׁה כִּי קְרָאתִיךָ יֵבֹשׁוּ רְשָׁעִים יִדְּמוּ

יח לִשְׁאוֹל: תֵּאָלַמְנָה שִׂפְתֵי שָׁקֶר הַדֹּבְרוֹת עַל־צַדִּיק עָתָק בְּגַאֲוָה וָבוּז: מָה

יט רַב־טוּבְךָ אֲשֶׁר־צָפַנְתָּ לִּירֵאֶיךָ פָּעַלְתָּ לַחֹסִים בָּךְ נֶגֶד בְּנֵי אָדָם:

כא-כב תַּסְתִּירֵם ׀ בְּסֵתֶר פָּנֶיךָ מֵרֻכְסֵי אִישׁ תִּצְפְּנֵם בְּסֻכָּה מֵרִיב לְשֹׁנוֹת: בָּרוּךְ

כג יהוה כִּי הִפְלִיא חַסְדּוֹ לִי בְּעִיר מָצוֹר: וַאֲנִי ׀ אָמַרְתִּי בְחָפְזִי נִגְרַזְתִּי

כד מִנֶּגֶד עֵינֶיךָ אָכֵן שָׁמַעְתָּ קוֹל תַּחֲנוּנַי בְּשַׁוְּעִי אֵלֶיךָ: אֶהֱבוּ אֶת־יהוה כָּל־

כה חֲסִידָיו אֱמוּנִים נֹצֵר יהוה וּמְשַׁלֵּם עַל־יֶתֶר עֹשֵׂה גַאֲוָה: חִזְקוּ וְיַאֲמֵץ

לְבַבְכֶם כָּל־הַמְיַחֲלִים לַיהוה:

א-ב לְדָוִד מַשְׂכִּיל אַשְׁרֵי נְשׂוּי־פֶּשַׁע כְּסוּי חֲטָאָה: אַשְׁרֵי אָדָם לֹא יַחְשֹׁב **לב**

ג יהוה לוֹ עָוֹן וְאֵין בְּרוּחוֹ רְמִיָּה: כִּי־הֶחֱרַשְׁתִּי בָּלוּ עֲצָמָי בְּשַׁאֲגָתִי

ד כָּל־הַיּוֹם: כִּי ׀ יוֹמָם וָלַיְלָה תִּכְבַּד עָלַי יָדֶךָ נֶהְפַּךְ לְשַׁדִּי בְּחַרְבֹנֵי קַיִץ

ה סֶלָה: חַטָּאתִי אוֹדִיעֲךָ וַעֲוֹנִי לֹא־כִסִּיתִי אָמַרְתִּי אוֹדֶה עֲלֵי פְשָׁעַי

ו לַיהוה וְאַתָּה נָשָׂאתָ עֲוֹן חַטָּאתִי סֶלָה: עַל־זֹאת יִתְפַּלֵּל כָּל־חָסִיד ׀

ז אֵלֶיךָ לְעֵת מְצֹא רַק לְשֵׁטֶף מַיִם רַבִּים אֵלָיו לֹא יַגִּיעוּ: אַתָּה ׀ סֵתֶר

ח לִי מִצַּר תִּצְּרֵנִי רָנֵּי פַלֵּט תְּסוֹבְבֵנִי סֶלָה: אַשְׂכִּילְךָ ׀ וְאוֹרְךָ בְּדֶרֶךְ־

ט זוּ תֵלֵךְ אִיעֲצָה עָלֶיךָ עֵינִי: אַל־תִּהְיוּ ׀ כְּסוּס כְּפֶרֶד אֵין הָבִין

י בְּמֶתֶג־וָרֶסֶן עֶדְיוֹ לִבְלוֹם בַּל קְרֹב אֵלֶיךָ: רַבִּים מַכְאוֹבִים לָרָשָׁע

יא וְהַבּוֹטֵחַ בַּיהוה חֶסֶד יְסוֹבְבֶנּוּ: שִׂמְחוּ בַיהוה וְגִילוּ צַדִּיקִים וְהַרְנִינוּ

כָּל־יִשְׁרֵי־לֵב:

31:7. By relying upon diviners and soothsayers (Ibn Ezra).

31:12. So many enemies have risen up against me that people have come to question my character (R' Hirsch).

31:21. "Countenance" is used in Scripture to denote God's attention to man, whether for reward or for punishment (Radak).

32:1. Literally, "a wise man." A psalm introduced in this way was explained by a wise orator, who would retell it in the vernacular for the benefit of the unlearned of the congregation (Pesachim 117a).

32:6. Let the devout one pray at the first intimation of misfortune, so that a flood of suffering not overtake him (Sforno).

32:9. When ornaments are placed on an animal it reacts by biting, not understanding that they are intended for its benefit (Metzudos).

32:10. To one who trusts in Hashem, "kindness surrounds him," i.e., he knows the pain of his suffering is relieved by his awareness that the suffering is intended for his benefit (Malbim).

David was relentlessly pursued, but always rescued. So too, we should entrust ourselves to God's mercy.

me, O HASHEM, God of truth. [7] I despise those who await worthless vanities; * as for me, I trust HASHEM! [8] I will exult and rejoice in Your kindness; that You have seen my affliction, You have known of the troubles of my soul; [9] and You have not delivered me into the hand of the foe, but stood my feet in a broad place. [10] Favor me, HASHEM, for I am distressed; my eyes are wasted away in grief, my soul and my belly. [11] For my life is spent in sorrow and my years in sighing; because of my iniquity my strength has failed and my bones are wasted away. [12] Because of all my tormentors I have become a disgrace, * especially to my neighbors, and a fright to those who know me; those who see me outside move away from me. [13] I have become forgotten as the dead from the heart, I have become like a decaying vessel. [14] For I have heard the slander of the multitude, terror all around; when they conspired together against me, they have plotted to take my soul. [15] But as for me, in You have I trusted, HASHEM. I have said, "You are my God." [16] In Your hand are my times, rescue me from the hand of my foes and from my pursuers. [17] Shine Your face upon Your servant, save me in Your kindness. [18] O HASHEM, let me not be ashamed, for I have called upon You! Let the wicked ones be shamed, let them be stilled to the grave. [19] May the lying lips be silenced, which speak falsehood about a righteous one with arrogance and contempt. [20] How abundant is Your goodness that You have stored away for those who fear You, that You have performed for those who seek refuge in You in the presence of men. [21] Shelter them in the cover of Your countenance * from the haughtiness of man; protect them in a shelter from the strife of tongues. [22] Blessed is HASHEM, for He has been wondrously kind to me in the besieged city. [23] I had said in my panic, "I am cut off from before Your eyes!" But in truth, You heard the sound of my supplications when I cried to You. [24] Love HASHEM, all His devout ones! HASHEM safeguards the faithful, but He repays for his haughtiness one who acts with arrogance. [25] Be strong, and let your hearts take courage, all who wait longingly for HASHEM.

32

God sends suffering and misfortune to help man reach the state of true repentance and its accompanying joy.

[1] **B**y David, a maskil. * Praiseworthy is one whose transgression is forgiven, whose sin is covered over. [2] Praiseworthy is the man to whom HASHEM does not ascribe iniquity, and in whose spirit there is no deceit. [3] When I was silent my bones deteriorated because of my anguished roar all day long. [4] For day and night Your hand was heavily upon me; my freshness was transformed [as] by summer droughts, Selah. [5] My sin I make known to You, my iniquity I do not hide. I said, "I will confess my transgressions to HASHEM," and You have [always] forgiven my iniquitous sin, Selah. [6] For this let every devout one pray to You at a time when [misfortune] befalls: Only that the flooding, mighty waters not overtake him. * [7] You are a shelter for me, from distress You preserve me; with glad song of rescue You envelop me, Selah! [8] I will educate you and enlighten you in which path to go, I will advise you with [what] my eye [has seen]. [9] Be not like a horse, like a mule, uncomprehending; to restrain it with muzzle and bridle when it is adorned, * so that it not approach you. [10] Many are the agonies of the wicked, but as for one who trusts in HASHEM, kindness surrounds him. * [11] Be glad in HASHEM and rejoice, O righteous. Cry out in joy, all upright of heart.

לג   א-ב   רַנְּנוּ צַדִּיקִים בַּיהוה לַיְשָׁרִים נָאוָה תְהִלָּה: הוֹדוּ לַיהוה בְּכִנּוֹר בְּנֵבֶל

ג-ד   עָשׂוֹר זַמְּרוּ־לוֹ: שִׁירוּ־לוֹ שִׁיר חָדָשׁ הֵיטִיבוּ נַגֵּן בִּתְרוּעָה: כִּי־יָשָׁר דְּבַר־

ה   יהוה וְכָל־מַעֲשֵׂהוּ בֶּאֱמוּנָה: אֹהֵב צְדָקָה וּמִשְׁפָּט חֶסֶד יהוה מָלְאָה

ו-ז   הָאָרֶץ: בִּדְבַר יהוה שָׁמַיִם נַעֲשׂוּ וּבְרוּחַ פִּיו כָּל־צְבָאָם: כֹּנֵס כַּנֵּד מֵי הַיָּם

ח   נֹתֵן בְּאֹצָרוֹת תְּהוֹמוֹת: יִירְאוּ מֵיהוה כָּל־הָאָרֶץ מִמֶּנּוּ יָגוּרוּ כָּל־יֹשְׁבֵי

ט-י   תֵבֵל: כִּי הוּא אָמַר וַיֶּהִי הוּא־צִוָּה וַיַּעֲמֹד: יהוה הֵפִיר עֲצַת־גּוֹיִם הֵנִיא

יא   מַחְשְׁבוֹת עַמִּים: עֲצַת יהוה לְעוֹלָם תַּעֲמֹד מַחְשְׁבוֹת לִבּוֹ לְדֹר וָדֹר:

יב-יג   אַשְׁרֵי הַגּוֹי אֲשֶׁר־יהוה אֱלֹהָיו הָעָם | בָּחַר לְנַחֲלָה לוֹ: מִשָּׁמַיִם הִבִּיט

יד   יהוה רָאָה אֶת־כָּל־בְּנֵי הָאָדָם: מִמְּכוֹן־שִׁבְתּוֹ הִשְׁגִּיחַ אֶל כָּל־יֹשְׁבֵי

טו-טז   הָאָרֶץ: הַיֹּצֵר יַחַד לִבָּם הַמֵּבִין אֶל־כָּל־מַעֲשֵׂיהֶם: אֵין־הַמֶּלֶךְ נוֹשָׁע

יז   בְּרָב־חָיִל גִּבּוֹר לֹא־יִנָּצֵל בְּרָב־כֹּחַ: שֶׁקֶר הַסּוּס לִתְשׁוּעָה וּבְרֹב חֵילוֹ

יח-יט   לֹא יְמַלֵּט: הִנֵּה עֵין יהוה אֶל־יְרֵאָיו לַמְיַחֲלִים לְחַסְדּוֹ: לְהַצִּיל מִמָּוֶת

כ-כא   נַפְשָׁם וּלְחַיּוֹתָם בָּרָעָב: נַפְשֵׁנוּ חִכְּתָה לַיהוה עֶזְרֵנוּ וּמָגִנֵּנוּ הוּא: כִּי־

כב   בוֹ יִשְׂמַח לִבֵּנוּ כִּי בְשֵׁם קָדְשׁוֹ בָטָחְנוּ: יְהִי־חַסְדְּךָ יהוה עָלֵינוּ כַּאֲשֶׁר

יִחַלְנוּ לָךְ:

לד   א-ב   לְדָוִד בְּשַׁנּוֹתוֹ אֶת־טַעְמוֹ לִפְנֵי אֲבִימֶלֶךְ וַיְגָרְשֵׁהוּ וַיֵּלַךְ: אֲבָרֲכָה אֶת־

ג   יהוה בְּכָל־עֵת תָּמִיד תְּהִלָּתוֹ בְּפִי: בַּיהוה תִּתְהַלֵּל נַפְשִׁי יִשְׁמְעוּ עֲנָוִים

ד-ה   וְיִשְׂמָחוּ: גַּדְּלוּ לַיהוה אִתִּי וּנְרוֹמְמָה שְׁמוֹ יַחְדָּו: דָּרַשְׁתִּי אֶת־יהוה וְעָנָנִי

ו-ז   וּמִכָּל־מְגוּרוֹתַי הִצִּילָנִי: הִבִּיטוּ אֵלָיו וְנָהָרוּ וּפְנֵיהֶם אַל־יֶחְפָּרוּ: זֶה עָנִי

ח   קָרָא וַיהוה שָׁמֵעַ וּמִכָּל־צָרוֹתָיו הוֹשִׁיעוֹ: חֹנֶה מַלְאַךְ־יהוה סָבִיב

ט   לִירֵאָיו וַיְחַלְּצֵם: טַעֲמוּ וּרְאוּ כִּי־טוֹב יהוה אַשְׁרֵי הַגֶּבֶר יֶחֱסֶה־בּוֹ: יְראוּ

י   אֶת־יהוה קְדֹשָׁיו כִּי־אֵין מַחְסוֹר לִירֵאָיו: כְּפִירִים רָשׁוּ וְרָעֵבוּ וְדֹרְשֵׁי

יא   יְהוָה לֹא־יַחְסְרוּ כָל־טוֹב: לְכוּ־בָנִים שִׁמְעוּ־לִי יִרְאַת יהוה אֲלַמֶּדְכֶם:

יב-יג   מִי־הָאִישׁ הֶחָפֵץ חַיִּים אֹהֵב יָמִים לִרְאוֹת טוֹב: נְצֹר לְשׁוֹנְךָ מֵרָע

יד-טו   וּשְׂפָתֶיךָ מִדַּבֵּר מִרְמָה: סוּר מֵרָע וַעֲשֵׂה־טוֹב בַּקֵּשׁ שָׁלוֹם וְרָדְפֵהוּ: עֵינֵי

טז   יהוה אֶל־צַדִּיקִים וְאָזְנָיו אֶל־שַׁוְעָתָם: פְּנֵי יהוה בְּעֹשֵׂי רָע לְהַכְרִית

יז-יח   מֵאֶרֶץ זִכְרָם: צָעֲקוּ וַיהוה שָׁמֵעַ וּמִכָּל־צָרוֹתָם הִצִּילָם: קָרוֹב יהוה

יט-כ   לְנִשְׁבְּרֵי־לֵב וְאֶת־דַּכְּאֵי־רוּחַ יוֹשִׁיעַ: רַבּוֹת רָעוֹת צַדִּיק וּמִכֻּלָּם יַצִּילֶנּוּ

כא   יהוה: שֹׁמֵר כָּל־עַצְמוֹתָיו אַחַת מֵהֵנָּה לֹא נִשְׁבָּרָה: תְּמוֹתֵת רָשָׁע רָעָה

כב-כג   וְשֹׂנְאֵי צַדִּיק יֶאְשָׁמוּ: פּוֹדֶה יהוה נֶפֶשׁ עֲבָדָיו וְלֹא יֶאְשְׁמוּ כָּל־הַחֹסִים בּוֹ:

33:5. Though God loves righteousness and justice, He tempers it with merciful kindness.

33:7. God set limits for the powerful seas so that they would not flood the dry land.

34:1. When forced to flee from King Saul, David found refuge with the Philistines. But when some of them threatened him with death, he pretended to be insane, and King Abimelech, disgusted by David's lunatic behavior, drove him out (see *I Samuel* 21:11-16).

34:7. In his humility, David looks upon himself as poor and undeserving (*Radak*).

33

Just as God created the physical world to function according to consistent laws, so His moral demands are constant and inviolable.

[1] Sing joyfully, O righteous, because of HASHEM; for the upright, praise is fitting. [2] Give thanks to HASHEM with a harp, with a ten-stringed lyre make music to Him. [3] Sing Him a new song, play well with sounds of deep emotion. [4] For the word of HASHEM is upright, and all His deeds [are done] with faithfulness. [5] He loves righteousness and justice; the kindness of HASHEM fills the earth. * [6] By the word of HASHEM the heavens were made, and by the breath of His mouth all their host. [7] He assembles the waters of the sea like a mound, He places the deep waters in vaults. * [8] Fear HASHEM, all the earth; be in dread of Him all inhabitants of the world. [9] For He spoke and it came to be, He commanded and it stood firm. [10] HASHEM annuls the counsel of nations, he thwarts the designs of peoples. [11] The counsel of HASHEM will endure forever, the designs of His heart from generation to generation. [12] Praiseworthy is the nation that HASHEM is their God, the people He chose for His own heritage. [13] From heaven HASHEM looks down, He sees all mankind. [14] From His dwelling place He oversees all inhabitants of the earth, [15] He Who fashions their hearts together, Who comprehends all their deeds. [16] A king is not saved by a great army, nor is a hero rescued by great strength. [17] Illusory is the horse for salvation; despite its great strength it provides no escape. [18] Behold, the eye of HASHEM is on those who fear Him, upon those who await His kindness. [19] To rescue their soul from death, and to sustain them in famine. [20] Our soul longed for HASHEM; He is our help and our shield. [21] For in Him will our hearts be glad; for in His Holy Name we trusted. [22] May Your kindness, HASHEM, be upon us, just as we awaited You.

34

David conquered despair by composing this alphabetical hymn, to show that our every faculty, from aleph to tav, should be dedicated to God.

[1] By David: When he disguised his sanity before Abimelech, * who drove him out and he left. [2] א I shall bless HASHEM at all times, always shall His praise be in my mouth. [3] ב In HASHEM does my soul glory, may humble ones hear and be glad. [4] ג Declare the greatness of HASHEM with me, and let us exalt His name together. [5] ד I sought out HASHEM and He answered me, and from all my terrors He delivered me. [6] ה Those who looked to Him became radiant, ו and their faces will not be shamed. [7] ז This poor man * calls and HASHEM hears, and from all his troubles He saves him. [8] ח The angel of HASHEM encamps around His reverent ones and he releases them. [9] ט Contemplate and see that HASHEM is good; praiseworthy is the man who takes refuge in Him. [10] י Fear HASHEM, O [you] His holy ones, for there is no deprivation for His reverent ones. [11] כ Young lions may want and hunger, but those who seek HASHEM will not lack any good. [12] ל Go, O sons, heed me, I will teach you the fear of HASHEM. [13] מ Who is the man who desires life, who loves days of seeing good? [14] נ Guard your tongue from evil, and your lips from speaking deceit. [15] ס Turn from evil and do good, seek peace and pursue it. [16] ע The eyes of HASHEM are toward the righteous, and His ears to their cry. [17] פ The face of HASHEM is against evildoers, to cut off their memory from earth. [18] צ They [the righteous] cried out and HASHEM heeds, and from all their troubles He rescues them. [19] ק HASHEM is close to the brokenhearted; and those crushed in spirit, He saves. [20] ר Many are the mishaps of the righteous, * but from them all HASHEM rescues him. [21] ש He guards all his bones, even one of them was not broken. [22] ת The death blow of the wicked is evil, * and the haters of the righteous will be condemned. [23] HASHEM redeems the soul of His servants, and all those who take refuge in Him will not be condemned.

34:20. No one becomes truly righteous and great without his share of mishaps *(Sfas Emes).*

34:22. Wicked people will be destroyed by the very evil they set in motion *(Radak).*

א-ב לְדָוִד ׀ רִיבָה יְהוָה אֶת־יְרִיבַי לְחַם אֶת־לֹחֲמָי: הַחֲזֵק מָגֵן וְצִנָּה

ג וְקוּמָה בְּעֶזְרָתִי: וְהָרֵק חֲנִית וּסְגֹר לִקְרַאת רֹדְפָי אֱמֹר לְנַפְשִׁי יְשֻׁעָתֵךְ

ד-ה אָנִי: יֵבֹשׁוּ וְיִכָּלְמוּ מְבַקְשֵׁי נַפְשִׁי יִסֹּגוּ אָחוֹר וְיַחְפְּרוּ חֹשְׁבֵי רָעָתִי: יִהְיוּ

ו כְּמֹץ לִפְנֵי־רוּחַ וּמַלְאַךְ יְהוָה דּוֹחֶה: יְהִי־דַרְכָּם חֹשֶׁךְ וַחֲלַקְלַקֹּת

ז וּמַלְאַךְ יְהוָה רֹדְפָם: כִּי־חִנָּם טָמְנוּ־לִי שַׁחַת רִשְׁתָּם חִנָּם חָפְרוּ לְנַפְשִׁי:

ח תְּבוֹאֵהוּ שׁוֹאָה לֹא־יֵדָע וְרִשְׁתּוֹ אֲשֶׁר־טָמַן תִּלְכְּדוֹ בְּשׁוֹאָה יִפָּל־בָּהּ:

ט-י וְנַפְשִׁי תָּגִיל בַּיהוָה תָּשִׂישׂ בִּישׁוּעָתוֹ: כָּל עַצְמוֹתַי ׀ תֹּאמַרְנָה יְהוָה

יא מִי כָמוֹךָ מַצִּיל עָנִי מֵחָזָק מִמֶּנּוּ וְעָנִי וְאֶבְיוֹן מִגֹּזְלוֹ: יְקוּמוּן עֵדֵי חָמָס

יב אֲשֶׁר לֹא־יָדַעְתִּי יִשְׁאָלוּנִי: יְשַׁלְּמוּנִי רָעָה תַּחַת טוֹבָה שְׁכוֹל לְנַפְשִׁי:

יג וַאֲנִי ׀ בַּחֲלוֹתָם לְבוּשִׁי שָׂק עִנֵּיתִי בַצּוֹם נַפְשִׁי וּתְפִלָּתִי עַל־חֵיקִי

יד-טו תָשׁוּב: כְּרֵעַ־כְּאָח לִי הִתְהַלָּכְתִּי כַּאֲבֶל־אֵם קֹדֵר שַׁחוֹתִי: וּבְצַלְעִי

טו שָׂמְחוּ וְנֶאֱסָפוּ נֶאֶסְפוּ עָלַי נֵכִים וְלֹא יָדַעְתִּי קָרְעוּ וְלֹא־דָמּוּ: בְּחַנְפֵי

יז לַעֲגֵי מָעוֹג חָרֹק עָלַי שִׁנֵּימוֹ: אֲדֹנָי כַּמָּה תִרְאֶה הָשִׁיבָה נַפְשִׁי

יח מִשֹּׁאֵיהֶם מִכְּפִירִים יְחִידָתִי: אוֹדְךָ בְּקָהָל רָב בְּעַם עָצוּם אֲהַלְלֶךָּ:

יט-כ אַל־יִשְׂמְחוּ־לִי אֹיְבַי שֶׁקֶר שֹׂנְאַי חִנָּם יִקְרְצוּ־עָיִן: כִּי לֹא שָׁלוֹם

כא יְדַבֵּרוּ וְעַל רִגְעֵי־אֶרֶץ דִּבְרֵי מִרְמוֹת יַחֲשֹׁבוּן: וַיַּרְחִיבוּ עָלַי פִּיהֶם

כב אָמְרוּ הֶאָח ׀ הֶאָח רָאֲתָה עֵינֵינוּ: רָאִיתָה יְהוָה אַל־תֶּחֱרַשׁ אֲדֹנָי

כג אַל־תִּרְחַק מִמֶּנִּי: הָעִירָה וְהָקִיצָה לְמִשְׁפָּטִי אֱלֹהַי וַאדֹנָי לְרִיבִי:

כד-כה שָׁפְטֵנִי כְצִדְקְךָ יְהוָה אֱלֹהָי וְאַל־יִשְׂמְחוּ־לִי: אַל־יֹאמְרוּ בְלִבָּם הֶאָח

כו נַפְשֵׁנוּ אַל־יֹאמְרוּ בִּלַּעֲנוּהוּ: יֵבֹשׁוּ וְיַחְפְּרוּ ׀ יַחְדָּו שְׂמֵחֵי רָעָתִי

כז יִלְבְּשׁוּ־בֹשֶׁת וּכְלִמָּה הַמַּגְדִּילִים עָלָי: יָרֹנּוּ וְיִשְׂמְחוּ חֲפֵצֵי צִדְקִי וְיֹאמְרוּ

כח תָמִיד יִגְדַּל יְהוָה הֶחָפֵץ שְׁלוֹם עַבְדּוֹ: וּלְשׁוֹנִי תֶּהְגֶּה צִדְקֶךָ כָּל־הַיּוֹם

תְּהִלָּתֶךָ:

א-ב לַמְנַצֵּחַ ׀ לְעֶבֶד־יְהוָה לְדָוִד: נְאֻם־פֶּשַׁע לָרָשָׁע בְּקֶרֶב לִבִּי אֵין־פַּחַד

ג אֱלֹהִים לְנֶגֶד עֵינָיו: כִּי־הֶחֱלִיק אֵלָיו בְּעֵינָיו לִמְצֹא עֲוֹנוֹ לִשְׂנֹא: דִּבְרֵי־

ה פִיו אָוֶן וּמִרְמָה חָדַל לְהַשְׂכִּיל לְהֵיטִיב: אָוֶן ׀ יַחְשֹׁב עַל־מִשְׁכָּבוֹ יִתְיַצֵּב

ו עַל־דֶּרֶךְ לֹא־טוֹב רָע לֹא יִמְאָס: יְהוָה בְּהַשָּׁמַיִם חַסְדֶּךָ אֱמוּנָתְךָ עַד־

ז שְׁחָקִים: צִדְקָתְךָ ׀ כְּהַרְרֵי־אֵל מִשְׁפָּטֶךָ תְּהוֹם רַבָּה אָדָם וּבְהֵמָה תוֹשִׁיעַ

ח-ט יְהוָה: מַה־יָּקָר חַסְדְּךָ אֱלֹהִים וּבְנֵי אָדָם בְּצֵל כְּנָפֶיךָ יֶחֱסָיוּן: יִרְוְיֻן מִדֶּשֶׁן

י בֵּיתֶךָ וְנַחַל עֲדָנֶיךָ תַשְׁקֵם: כִּי־עִמְּךָ מְקוֹר חַיִּים בְּאוֹרְךָ נִרְאֶה־אוֹר:

35:11. David now describes the machinations of his enemies.
35:17. See 22:21.
35:19. In gleeful mockery of my downfall.

36:2. The Evil Inclination is personified as "Transgression." It claims that God is unconcerned with this world, so man is free to do as he pleases (*Rashi*).

35

David appeals for help against friends turned traitors; so too, Israel in exile appeals against nations that repay Israel's contributions with oppression.

¹ By David: O HASHEM, fight my adversaries, battle those who do battle with me. ² Take hold of shield and buckler, and rise up in my defense. ³ And draw the spear, and bar the way before my pursuers; say to my soul, "I am your salvation." ⁴ May they be shamed and disgraced, those who seek my life; let them retreat and be humiliated, those who plot my harm. ⁵ May they be like chaff before the wind, with the angel of HASHEM thrusting away. ⁶ May their way be dark and exceedingly slippery, with the angel of HASHEM pursuing them. ⁷ For without cause they have hidden for me the snare of their net, without cause they have dug [pits] to kill me. ⁸ May disaster come upon each of them unawares; and may his own net which he concealed ensnare him, may he fall into it in disaster. ⁹ Then my soul will exult in HASHEM, rejoice in His salvation. ¹⁰ All my limbs will say, "HASHEM, who is like You? Deliverer of the poor from one mightier than he, of the poor and the destitute from the one who robs him." ¹¹ False witnesses rise up, * for that of which I know nothing they call me to account. ¹² They repay me evil for good, bereavement for my soul. ¹³ But as for me, when they were ill, my clothing was sackcloth, and I afflicted myself with fasting, may my prayer return upon my own bosom. ¹⁴ As for a friend, as for my own brother, I went about; like a mother in mourning, I bent over in gloom. ¹⁵ But when I limped they rejoiced and gathered; the wretched gathered against me — I know not why, they tore at me and would not be silenced. ¹⁶ With flattery and mockery, for the sake of a loaf, they gnash their teeth at me. ¹⁷ O Lord, how long will You look on? Rescue my soul from their destruction, my essence * from the young lions. ¹⁸ [Then] I will thank You in a great congregation, before a mighty throng I will praise You. ¹⁹ Let them not rejoice over me, those who oppose me for false cause, nor those who hate me without reason wink an eye. * ²⁰ For it is not peace that they speak; rather against the broken people of the earth they scheme deceitful matters. ²¹ They opened their mouths broadly against me; they said, "Aha! Aha! Our own eyes have seen [his misfortune]!" ²² You have seen, HASHEM, do not be mute; O Lord be not far from me. ²³ Arouse Yourself and awaken to my judgment; my God and the Lord to my cause. ²⁴ Judge me according to Your righteousness, HASHEM, my God, and let them not rejoice over me. ²⁵ Let them not say in their hearts, "Aha! Our souls!" Let them not say, "We have swallowed him." ²⁶ May they be shamed and humiliated together, those who are glad over my misfortune; may they be clothed in shame and disgrace, those who lift themselves up haughtily over me. ²⁷ May they sing in joy and be glad, those who desire my vindication; let them always say, "Be glorified, HASHEM, Who desires the peace of His servant!" ²⁸ Then my tongue will express Your righteousness; Your praise all day long.

36

Sin entices with false illusions; man can dispel them only with the objective light of truth.

¹ For the conductor, by the servant of HASHEM, by David. ² Transgression's * word to the wicked is in my heart, that there should be no dread of God before his eyes. ³ For it smoothed the way before him in his eyes, that He should find his iniquity to hate [him]. ⁴ The words of his mouth are iniquity and deceit; he has ceased contemplating to do good. ⁵ On his bed he devises iniquity; he stations himself on a path of no good, he does not disdain evil. ⁶ HASHEM, unto the heavens is Your kindness; Your faithfulness is till the upper heights; ⁷ Your righteousness is like the mighty mountains; Your judgments are like the vast deep waters; You save both man and beast, O HASHEM. ⁸ How precious is Your kindness, O God! Mankind takes refuge in the shelter of Your wings. ⁹ They will be sated from the abundance of Your house; and from the stream of Your delights You give them to drink. ¹⁰ For with You is the source of life; by Your light may we see light.

יא-יב מְשֹׁךְ חַסְדְּךָ לְיֹדְעֶיךָ וְצִדְקָתְךָ לְיִשְׁרֵי־לֵב: אַל־תְּבוֹאֵנִי רֶגֶל גַּאֲוָה וְיַד־
רְשָׁעִים אַל־תְּנִדֵנִי: שָׁם נָפְלוּ פֹּעֲלֵי אָוֶן דֹּחוּ וְלֹא־יָכְלוּ קוּם:

לז א-ב לְדָוִד ׀ אַל־תִּתְחַר בַּמְּרֵעִים אַל־תְּקַנֵּא בְּעֹשֵׂי עַוְלָה: כִּי כֶחָצִיר מְהֵרָה
ג יִמָּלוּ וּכְיֶרֶק דֶּשֶׁא יִבּוֹלוּן: בְּטַח בַּיהוה וַעֲשֵׂה־טוֹב שְׁכָן־אֶרֶץ וּרְעֵה
ד-ה אֱמוּנָה: וְהִתְעַנַּג עַל־יהוה וְיִתֶּן־לְךָ מִשְׁאֲלֹת לִבֶּךָ: גּוֹל עַל־יהוה דַּרְכֶּךָ
ו וּבְטַח עָלָיו וְהוּא יַעֲשֶׂה: וְהוֹצִיא כָאוֹר צִדְקֶךָ וּמִשְׁפָּטֶךָ כַּצָּהֳרָיִם:
ז דּוֹם ׀ לַיהוה וְהִתְחוֹלֵל לוֹ אַל־תִּתְחַר בְּמַצְלִיחַ דַּרְכּוֹ בְּאִישׁ עֹשֶׂה
ח-ט מְזִמּוֹת: הֶרֶף מֵאַף וַעֲזֹב חֵמָה אַל־תִּתְחַר אַךְ־לְהָרֵעַ: כִּי־מְרֵעִים
י יִכָּרֵתוּן וְקֹוֵי יהוה הֵמָּה יִירְשׁוּ־אָרֶץ: וְעוֹד מְעַט וְאֵין רָשָׁע וְהִתְבּוֹנַנְתָּ
יא-יב עַל־מְקוֹמוֹ וְאֵינֶנּוּ: וַעֲנָוִים יִירְשׁוּ־אָרֶץ וְהִתְעַנְּגוּ עַל־רֹב שָׁלוֹם: זֹמֵם
יג רָשָׁע לַצַּדִּיק וְחֹרֵק עָלָיו שִׁנָּיו: אֲדֹנָי יִשְׂחַק־לוֹ כִּי־רָאָה כִּי־יָבֹא יוֹמוֹ:
יד חֶרֶב ׀ פָּתְחוּ רְשָׁעִים וְדָרְכוּ קַשְׁתָּם לְהַפִּיל עָנִי וְאֶבְיוֹן לִטְבוֹחַ יִשְׁרֵי־
טו-טז דָרֶךְ: חַרְבָּם תָּבוֹא בְלִבָּם וְקַשְּׁתוֹתָם תִּשָּׁבַרְנָה: טוֹב־מְעַט לַצַּדִּיק
יז מֵהֲמוֹן רְשָׁעִים רַבִּים: כִּי זְרוֹעוֹת רְשָׁעִים תִּשָּׁבַרְנָה וְסוֹמֵךְ צַדִּיקִים
יח-יט יהוה: יוֹדֵעַ יהוה יְמֵי תְמִימִם וְנַחֲלָתָם לְעוֹלָם תִּהְיֶה: לֹא־יֵבֹשׁוּ בְּעֵת
כ רָעָה וּבִימֵי רְעָבוֹן יִשְׂבָּעוּ: כִּי רְשָׁעִים ׀ יֹאבֵדוּ וְאֹיְבֵי יהוה כִּיקַר כָּרִים
כא-כב כָּלוּ בֶעָשָׁן כָּלוּ: לֹוֶה רָשָׁע וְלֹא יְשַׁלֵּם וְצַדִּיק חוֹנֵן וְנוֹתֵן: כִּי מְבֹרָכָיו
כג יִירְשׁוּ אָרֶץ וּמְקֻלָּלָיו יִכָּרֵתוּ: מֵיהוה מִצְעֲדֵי־גֶבֶר כּוֹנָנוּ וְדַרְכּוֹ יֶחְפָּץ:
כד-כה כִּי־יִפֹּל לֹא־יוּטָל כִּי־יהוה סוֹמֵךְ יָדוֹ: נַעַר ׀ הָיִיתִי גַּם־זָקַנְתִּי וְלֹא־
כו רָאִיתִי צַדִּיק נֶעֱזָב וְזַרְעוֹ מְבַקֶּשׁ־לָחֶם: כָּל־הַיּוֹם חוֹנֵן וּמַלְוֶה וְזַרְעוֹ
כז-כח לִבְרָכָה: סוּר מֵרָע וַעֲשֵׂה־טוֹב וּשְׁכֹן לְעוֹלָם: כִּי יהוה ׀ אֹהֵב מִשְׁפָּט
כט וְלֹא־יַעֲזֹב אֶת־חֲסִידָיו לְעוֹלָם נִשְׁמָרוּ וְזֶרַע רְשָׁעִים נִכְרָת: צַדִּיקִים
ל יִירְשׁוּ־אָרֶץ וְיִשְׁכְּנוּ לָעַד עָלֶיהָ: פִּי־צַדִּיק יֶהְגֶּה חָכְמָה וּלְשׁוֹנוֹ תְּדַבֵּר
לא-לב מִשְׁפָּט: תּוֹרַת אֱלֹהָיו בְּלִבּוֹ לֹא תִמְעַד אֲשֻׁרָיו: צוֹפֶה רָשָׁע לַצַּדִּיק
לג וּמְבַקֵּשׁ לַהֲמִיתוֹ: יהוה לֹא־יַעַזְבֶנּוּ בְיָדוֹ וְלֹא יַרְשִׁיעֶנּוּ בְּהִשָּׁפְטוֹ:
לד קַוֵּה אֶל־יהוה ׀ וּשְׁמֹר דַּרְכּוֹ וִירוֹמִמְךָ לָרֶשֶׁת אָרֶץ בְּהִכָּרֵת רְשָׁעִים
לה-לו תִּרְאֶה: רָאִיתִי רָשָׁע עָרִיץ וּמִתְעָרֶה כְּאֶזְרָח רַעֲנָן: וַיַּעֲבֹר וְהִנֵּה אֵינֶנּוּ
לז וָאֲבַקְשֵׁהוּ וְלֹא נִמְצָא: שְׁמָר־תָּם וּרְאֵה יָשָׁר כִּי־אַחֲרִית לְאִישׁ שָׁלוֹם:
לח-לט וּפֹשְׁעִים נִשְׁמְדוּ יַחְדָּו אַחֲרִית רְשָׁעִים נִכְרָתָה: וּתְשׁוּעַת צַדִּיקִים מֵיהוה
מ מָעוּזָּם בְּעֵת צָרָה: וַיַּעְזְרֵם יהוה וַיְפַלְּטֵם יְפַלְּטֵם מֵרְשָׁעִים וְיוֹשִׁיעֵם
כִּי־חָסוּ בוֹ:

36:13. In prophetic vision, future events are described as having already transpired (*Radak*).

37:1. Do not try to achieve prosperity through the sinful ways of the wicked (*Rashi*).

37:16. More enjoyable are the meager resources of the

righteous than the fabulous wealth of the wicked, for they are never satisfied (*Ibn Ezra*).

37:33. Regarding the false charges that the wicked schemer has brought against him.

¹¹ Extend Your kindness to those who know You, and Your charity to the upright of heart. ¹² Let not the foot of arrogance come to me, and let not the hand of the wicked move me. ¹³ There they fell, the practitioners of iniquity; they were thrust down and unable to rise. *

37

Do not be lured by the external trappings of prosperity of the wicked, for it is God's blessed ones who will inherit the earth.

¹ By David: Do not compete with the evildoers, * be not envious of the doers of injustice, ² for like grass will they be cut down swiftly, and like green vegetation they will wither. ³ Trust in HASHEM and do good; dwell in the land and nourish [yourself] with faithfulness. ⁴ And rely upon HASHEM for your enjoyments, for He will grant you the desires of your heart. ⁵ Commit your way to HASHEM, rely on Him and He will act. ⁶ He will bring forth your righteousness like a light, and your justice like the high noon. ⁷ Wait silently for [the salvation of] HASHEM and wait longingly for Him; do not compete with him who prospers, with the man who executes malicious plans. ⁸ Desist from anger and forsake wrath; do not compete, it brings but harm. ⁹ For the evildoers shall be cut off, but those who hope to HA-SHEM, they shall inherit the earth. ¹⁰ Just a little longer and there will be no wicked one; you will contemplate his place and he will not be there. ¹¹ But the humble shall inherit the earth, and delight in abundant peace. ¹² The wicked man plots against the righteous person and gnashes his teeth at him. ¹³ The Lord laughs at him, for He has seen that his day approaches. ¹⁴ The wicked drew a sword and bent their bows, to bring down the poor and the destitute, to slaughter those of upright ways. ¹⁵ Their sword will pierce their own heart, and their bows will be broken. ¹⁶ Better is the little of the righteous than the great multitude of the wicked. * ¹⁷ For the arms of the wicked will be broken, but the support of the righteous is HASHEM. ¹⁸ HASHEM knows the days of the perfect, their inheritance will be forever. ¹⁹ They will not be shamed in time of calamity; and in days of famine they will be satisfied. ²⁰ For the wicked will perish, and the foes of HASHEM are like the glory of fattened sheep: Consumed! In smoke they are consumed. ²¹ The wicked one borrows but repays not, while the righteous one is generous and gives. ²² For His blessed ones shall inherit the earth, while His accursed ones will be cut off. ²³ By HASHEM are a man's footsteps established, and He shall favor his way. ²⁴ Should he totter, he will not be cast down, for HASHEM supports his hand. ²⁵ I have been a youth and also aged; but I have not seen a righteous man forsaken, nor his children begging for bread. ²⁶ All day long he is gracious and lends, and his children are a blessing. ²⁷ Turn from evil and do good, that you may dwell forever. ²⁸ For HASHEM loves justice and does not forsake His devout ones — they will be eternally protected, but the offspring of the wicked are cut off. ²⁹ The righteous will inherit the earth and dwell forever upon it. ³⁰ The mouth of the righteous man utters wisdom, and his tongue speaks justice. ³¹ The Torah of his God is in his heart; his footsteps will not falter. ³² The wicked one watches for the righteous and seeks to kill him. ³³ But HASHEM will not forsake him to his hand, nor let him be condemned when he is judged. * ³⁴ Hope to HASHEM and safeguard His way, and He will raise you high to inherit the earth; you will witness the excision of the wicked. ³⁵ I have seen a wicked man powerful, well rooted like a native evergreen. ³⁶ Yet he vanished, and behold! he was no more; and I sought him, but he was not to be found. ³⁷ Guard the perfect and watch the upright, for there is a destiny for the man of peace. ³⁸ But the sinners are destroyed together, the destiny of the wicked is to be cut off. ³⁹ And the salvation of the righteous is from HASHEM, their might in time of distress. ⁴⁰ HASHEM helped them and caused them to escape; He will cause them to escape from the wicked and He will save them, for they took refuge in Him.

לח א-ג מִזְמוֹר לְדָוִד לְהַזְכִּיר: יְהוָה אַל-בְּקֶצְפְּךָ תוֹכִיחֵנִי וּבַחֲמָתְךָ תְיַסְּרֵנִי: כִּי-

ד חִצֶּיךָ נִחֲתוּ בִי וַתִּנְחַת עָלַי יָדֶךָ: אֵין-מְתֹם בִּבְשָׂרִי מִפְּנֵי זַעְמֶךָ אֵין-

ה שָׁלוֹם בַּעֲצָמַי מִפְּנֵי חַטָּאתִי: כִּי עֲוֺנֹתַי עָבְרוּ רֹאשִׁי כְּמַשָּׂא כָבֵד יִכְבְּדוּ

ו-ז מִמֶּנִּי: הִבְאִישׁוּ נָמַקּוּ חַבּוּרֹתָי מִפְּנֵי אִוַּלְתִּי: נַעֲוֵיתִי שַׁחֹתִי עַד-מְאֹד כָּל-

ח-ט הַיּוֹם קֹדֵר הִלָּכְתִּי: כִּי-כְסָלַי מָלְאוּ נִקְלֶה וְאֵין מְתֹם בִּבְשָׂרִי: נְפוּגוֹתִי

י וְנִדְכֵּיתִי עַד-מְאֹד שָׁאַגְתִּי מִנַּהֲמַת לִבִּי: אֲדֹנָי נֶגְדְּךָ כָל-תַּאֲוָתִי וְאַנְחָתִי

יא מִמְּךָ לֹא-נִסְתָּרָה: לִבִּי סְחַרְחַר עֲזָבַנִי כֹחִי וְאוֹר-עֵינַי גַּם-הֵם אֵין אִתִּי:

יב-יג אֹהֲבַי | וְרֵעַי מִנֶּגֶד נִגְעִי יַעֲמֹדוּ וּקְרוֹבַי מֵרָחֹק עָמָדוּ: וַיְנַקְשׁוּ | מְבַקְשֵׁי

יד נַפְשִׁי וְדֹרְשֵׁי רָעָתִי דִּבְּרוּ הַוּוֹת וּמִרְמוֹת כָּל-הַיּוֹם יֶהְגּוּ: וַאֲנִי כְחֵרֵשׁ לֹא

טו אֶשְׁמָע וּכְאִלֵּם לֹא יִפְתַּח-פִּיו: וָאֱהִי כְּאִישׁ אֲשֶׁר לֹא-שֹׁמֵעַ וְאֵין בְּפִיו

טז-יז תּוֹכָחוֹת: כִּי-לְךָ יְהוָה הוֹחָלְתִּי אַתָּה תַעֲנֶה אֲדֹנָי אֱלֹהָי: כִּי-אָמַרְתִּי פֶּן-

יח יִשְׂמְחוּ-לִי בְּמוֹט רַגְלִי עָלַי הִגְדִּילוּ: כִּי-אֲנִי לְצֶלַע נָכוֹן וּמַכְאוֹבִי נֶגְדִּי

יט-כ תָמִיד: כִּי-עֲוֺנִי אַגִּיד אֶדְאַג מֵחַטָּאתִי: וְאֹיְבַי חַיִּים עָצֵמוּ וְרַבּוּ שֹׂנְאַי

כא שָׁקֶר: וּמְשַׁלְּמֵי רָעָה תַּחַת טוֹבָה יִשְׂטְנוּנִי תַּחַת °רדופי [רָדְפִי-ק°]

כב-כג טוֹב: אַל-תַּעַזְבֵנִי יְהוָה אֱלֹהַי אַל-תִּרְחַק מִמֶּנִּי: חוּשָׁה לְעֶזְרָתִי אֲדֹנָי

תְּשׁוּעָתִי:

לט א-ב לַמְנַצֵּחַ °לידיתון [°לִידוּתוּן-ק°] מִזְמוֹר לְדָוִד: אָמַרְתִּי אֶשְׁמְרָה דְרָכַי יום ז לחדש

ג מֵחֲטוֹא בִלְשׁוֹנִי אֶשְׁמְרָה לְפִי מַחְסוֹם בְּעֹד רָשָׁע לְנֶגְדִּי: נֶאֱלַמְתִּי דוּמִיָּה

ד הֶחֱשֵׁיתִי מִטּוֹב וּכְאֵבִי נֶעְכָּר: חַם-לִבִּי | בְּקִרְבִּי בַּהֲגִיגִי תִבְעַר-אֵשׁ

ה דִּבַּרְתִּי בִּלְשׁוֹנִי: הוֹדִיעֵנִי יְהוָה | קִצִּי וּמִדַּת יָמַי מַה-הִיא אֵדְעָה מֶה-

ו חָדֵל אָנִי: הִנֵּה טְפָחוֹת | נָתַתָּה יָמַי וְחֶלְדִּי כְאַיִן נֶגְדֶּךָ אַךְ כָּל-הֶבֶל כָּל-

ז אָדָם נִצָּב סֶלָה: אַךְ-בְּצֶלֶם | יִתְהַלֶּךְ-אִישׁ אַךְ-הֶבֶל יֶהֱמָיוּן יִצְבֹּר וְלֹא-

ח-ט יֵדַע מִי-אֹסְפָם: וְעַתָּה מַה-קִּוִּיתִי אֲדֹנָי תּוֹחַלְתִּי לְךָ הִיא: מִכָּל-פְּשָׁעַי

י-יא הַצִּילֵנִי חֶרְפַּת נָבָל אַל-תְּשִׂימֵנִי: נֶאֱלַמְתִּי לֹא אֶפְתַּח-פִּי כִּי אַתָּה

יב עָשִׂיתָ: הָסֵר מֵעָלַי נִגְעֶךָ מִתִּגְרַת יָדְךָ אֲנִי כָלִיתִי: בְּתוֹכָחוֹת עַל-עָוֺן |

יג יִסַּרְתָּ אִישׁ וַתֶּמֶס כָּעָשׁ חֲמוּדוֹ אַךְ הֶבֶל כָּל-אָדָם סֶלָה: שִׁמְעָה-תְפִלָּתִי

| יְהוָה וְשַׁוְעָתִי | הַאֲזִינָה אֶל-דִּמְעָתִי אַל-תֶּחֱרַשׁ כִּי גֵר אָנֹכִי עִמָּךְ תּוֹשָׁב

יד כְּכָל-אֲבוֹתָי: הָשַׁע מִמֶּנִּי וְאַבְלִיגָה בְּטֶרֶם אֵלֵךְ וְאֵינֶנִּי:

מ א-ב לַמְנַצֵּחַ לְדָוִד מִזְמוֹר: קַוֺּה קִוִּיתִי יְהוָה וַיֵּט אֵלַי וַיִּשְׁמַע שַׁוְעָתִי:

ג וַיַּעֲלֵנִי | מִבּוֹר שָׁאוֹן מִטִּיט הַיָּוֵן וַיָּקֶם עַל-סֶלַע רַגְלַי כּוֹנֵן אֲשֻׁרָי:

38:2. Although I deserve punishment, do not send upon me the full intensity of Your wrath.

39:1. A leader of the Temple choristers; also the name of a musical instrument (*Rashi*).

39:2. I will not question God's ways, even while the wicked one inflicts pain and suffering (*Rashi*).

39:3. I refrained even from saying comforting things,

lest my pain cause me to let slip a word of complaint.

39:14. Only in this world can man earn reward. The World to Come is solely for receiving the fruits of the deeds performed in life (*Radak*).

40:3. The critical illness which engulfed me and threatened to kill me (*Radak*).

38

Suffering must be recognized as chastisement for sin. One must repent and look to God for salvation.

¹ **A** psalm by David, to proclaim: ² HASHEM, do not rebuke me in Your rage, nor chasten me in Your wrath. * ³ For Your arrows have been shot into me, and Your hand has come down upon me. ⁴ There is no soundness in my flesh because of Your fury, no peace in my bones because of my sin. ⁵ For my iniquities have inundated me; like a heavy load, they are burdensome beyond me. ⁶ Putrid and rotted are my sores, because of my folly. ⁷ I am bent and exceedingly bowed, all day long in bleakness I go about. ⁸ For my loins are full of a loathsome affliction and there is no soundness in my flesh. ⁹ I am faint and exceedingly crushed. I roar from the groaning of my heart. ¹⁰ O Lord, before You is all my yearning, my sighing is not concealed from You. ¹¹ My heart is engulfed, my strength has forsaken me; and the light of my eyes — they, too — is no longer with me. ¹² My friends and companions stand aloof from my affliction, and my close ones stand at a distance. ¹³ And the seekers of my life have laid snares, those who seek my harm speak treacheries, all day long they contemplate deceit. ¹⁴ But I am like a deaf man, I do not hear, like a mute who does not open his mouth. ¹⁵ I was like a man who does not hear, and in whose mouth there are no rebuttals. ¹⁶ Because for You, HASHEM, do I wait; You will answer, O Lord, my God. ¹⁷ For I said, "Lest they will be glad about me, at the faltering of my foot they will magnify themselves over me!" ¹⁸ For I am prone to crippling pain, and my ache is always before me. ¹⁹ Because I admit my iniquity, I worry because of my sin. ²⁰ But my foes abound with life, and those who hate me without cause grow great. ²¹ Those who repay evil for good harass me for my pursuit of good. ²² Forsake me not, O HASHEM, my God, be not far from me. ²³ Hasten to my assistance, O Lord, my Salvation.

39

Suffering makes man aware of human frailty and transience. One should pray for the ability to devote oneself to Torah and mitzvos.

¹ **F**or the conductor, for Jeduthun, * a psalm by David. ² I said, "I will guard my ways from sinning with my tongue, I will guard my mouth with a muzzle, even while the wicked one stands before me."* ³ I became mute with stillness, I was silent [even] from good, though my pain was intense. * ⁴ My heart grew hot within me, in my contemplations a fire blazed; then I spoke out with my tongue: ⁵ "Let me know my end, O HASHEM, and the measure of my days, what it is; that I may know when I will cease." ⁶ Behold, like handbreadths have You made my days, and my lifetime is as naught before You; all is but total futility — ⁷ all human existence, Selah. Only in shadowy darkness does man make his way, it is but futility for which they are in turmoil; he amasses [riches], but he knows not who will harvest them. ⁸ And now, for what do I hope, O Lord? My longing is to You. ⁹ From all my transgressions rescue me; do not make me a disgrace before the degenerate! ¹⁰ I am mute, I open not my mouth, because it is You Who has done it. ¹¹ Remove from me Your plague; from the attack of Your hand am I devastated. ¹² With rebukes for iniquity You have chastened man, You have worn away like a moth his precious health. All mankind is but futility, Selah. ¹³ Hear my prayer, HASHEM, give ear to my outcry, be not mute to my tears; for I am a sojourner with You, a settler like all my forefathers. ¹⁴ Turn [Your punishment] from me that I may recover my strength, before I depart and I am no more. *

40

¹ **F**or the conductor, by David, a psalm. ² I have greatly hoped for HASHEM; He inclined to me, and heard my cry. ³ He raised me from the pit of raging waters, from the slimy mud. * He set my feet upon a rock, firmly establishing my steps.

ד וַיִּתֵּן בְּפִי | שִׁיר חָדָשׁ תְּהִלָּה לֵאלֹהֵינוּ יִרְאוּ רַבִּים וְיִירָאוּ וְיִבְטְחוּ

ה בַּיהוָה: אַשְׁרֵי הַגֶּבֶר אֲשֶׁר־שָׂם יְהוָה מִבְטַחוֹ וְלֹא־פָנָה אֶל־רְהָבִים

ו וְשָׂטֵי כָזָב: רַבּוֹת עָשִׂיתָ | אַתָּה | יְהוָה אֱלֹהַי נִפְלְאֹתֶיךָ וּמַחְשְׁבֹתֶיךָ

ז אֵלֵינוּ אֵין | עֲרֹךְ אֵלֶיךָ אַגִּידָה וַאֲדַבֵּרָה עָצְמוּ מִסַּפֵּר: זֶבַח וּמִנְחָה |

ח לֹא־חָפַצְתָּ אָזְנַיִם כָּרִיתָ לִּי עוֹלָה וַחֲטָאָה לֹא שָׁאָלְתָּ: אָז אָמַרְתִּי

ט הִנֵּה־בָאתִי בִּמְגִלַּת־סֵפֶר כָּתוּב עָלָי: לַעֲשׂוֹת־רְצוֹנְךָ אֱלֹהַי חָפָצְתִּי

י וְתוֹרָתְךָ בְּתוֹךְ מֵעָי: בִּשַּׂרְתִּי צֶדֶק | בְּקָהָל רָב הִנֵּה שְׂפָתַי לֹא אֶכְלָא

יא יְהוָה אַתָּה יָדָעְתָּ: צִדְקָתְךָ לֹא־כִסִּיתִי | בְּתוֹךְ לִבִּי אֱמוּנָתְךָ וּתְשׁוּעָתְךָ

יב אָמַרְתִּי לֹא־כִחַדְתִּי חַסְדְּךָ וַאֲמִתְּךָ לְקָהָל רָב: אַתָּה יְהוָה לֹא־

יג תִכְלָא רַחֲמֶיךָ מִמֶּנִּי חַסְדְּךָ וַאֲמִתְּךָ תָּמִיד יִצְּרוּנִי: כִּי אָפְפוּ־עָלַי | רָעוֹת

עַד־אֵין מִסְפָּר הִשִּׂיגוּנִי עֲוֹנֹתַי וְלֹא־יָכֹלְתִּי לִרְאוֹת עָצְמוּ מִשַּׂעֲרוֹת

יד-טו רֹאשִׁי וְלִבִּי עֲזָבָנִי: רְצֵה יְהוָה לְהַצִּילֵנִי יְהוָה לְעֶזְרָתִי חוּשָׁה: יֵבֹשׁוּ

וְיַחְפְּרוּ | יַחַד מְבַקְשֵׁי נַפְשִׁי לִסְפּוֹתָהּ יִסֹּגוּ אָחוֹר וְיִכָּלְמוּ חֲפֵצֵי

טז-יז רָעָתִי: יָשֹׁמּוּ עַל־עֵקֶב בָּשְׁתָּם הָאֹמְרִים לִי הֶאָח | הֶאָח: יָשִׂישׂוּ

וְיִשְׂמְחוּ | בְּךָ כָּל־מְבַקְשֶׁיךָ יֹאמְרוּ תָמִיד יִגְדַּל יְהוָה אֹהֲבֵי תְּשׁוּעָתֶךָ:

יח וַאֲנִי | עָנִי וְאֶבְיוֹן אֲדֹנָי יַחֲשָׁב לִי עֶזְרָתִי וּמְפַלְטִי אַתָּה אֱלֹהַי אַל־

תְּאַחַר:

מא א-ב לַמְנַצֵּחַ מִזְמוֹר לְדָוִד: אַשְׁרֵי מַשְׂכִּיל אֶל־דָּל בְּיוֹם רָעָה יְמַלְּטֵהוּ יְהוָה:

ג יְהוָה | יִשְׁמְרֵהוּ וִיחַיֵּהוּ °יֻאֻשַּׁר [וְאֻשַּׁר ק] בָּאָרֶץ וְאַל־תִּתְּנֵהוּ

ד בְּנֶפֶשׁ אֹיְבָיו: יְהוָה יִסְעָדֶנּוּ עַל־עֶרֶשׂ דְּוָי כָּל־מִשְׁכָּבוֹ הָפַכְתָּ בְחָלְיוֹ:

ה אֲנִי־אָמַרְתִּי יְהוָה חָנֵּנִי רְפָאָה נַפְשִׁי כִּי־חָטָאתִי לָךְ: אוֹיְבַי | יֹאמְרוּ

ו רַע לִי מָתַי יָמוּת וְאָבַד שְׁמוֹ: וְאִם־בָּא לִרְאוֹת | שָׁוְא יְדַבֵּר לִבּוֹ |

ז יִקְבָּץ־אָוֶן לוֹ יֵצֵא לַחוּץ יְדַבֵּר: יַחַד עָלַי יִתְלַחֲשׁוּ כָּל־שֹׂנְאָי עָלַי |

ח יַחְשְׁבוּ רָעָה לִי: דְּבַר־בְּלִיַּעַל יָצוּק בּוֹ וַאֲשֶׁר שָׁכַב לֹא־יוֹסִיף לָקוּם:

ט-י גַּם־אִישׁ שְׁלוֹמִי | אֲשֶׁר־בָּטַחְתִּי בוֹ אוֹכֵל לַחְמִי הִגְדִּיל עָלַי עָקֵב:

יא וְאַתָּה יְהוָה חָנֵּנִי וַהֲקִימֵנִי וַאֲשַׁלְּמָה לָהֶם: בְּזֹאת יָדַעְתִּי כִּי־חָפַצְתָּ

יא-יב בִּי כִּי לֹא־יָרִיעַ אֹיְבִי עָלָי: וַאֲנִי בְּתֻמִּי תָּמַכְתָּ בִּי וַתַּצִּיבֵנִי לְפָנֶיךָ

יג לְעוֹלָם: בָּרוּךְ יְהוָה | אֱלֹהֵי יִשְׂרָאֵל מֵהָעוֹלָם וְעַד הָעוֹלָם אָמֵן |

יד וְאָמֵן:

40:4. I sing praise for every new kindness (*Radak*).

40:8-10. I show my gratitude not with offerings, but I present myself holding the Torah, resolved to obey everything in it (*Ibn Ezra*).

40:18. Although I am a king, I am totally dependent upon God's constant care and attention (*Radak*).

41:2. To learn what assistance to offer (*Rashi*), or to see

from their experiences how God helps the poor and sick (*Ibn Ezra*).

41:5. A person should pray that his spiritual shortcoming be cured, not only its physical symptoms (*Radak*).

41:11. My vengeance against them will be that You disappoint their hopes for my downfall (*R' Hirsch*).

4 He put a new song* into my mouth, a hymn to our God; multitudes shall see and be awed, and they shall trust in HASHEM. **5** Praiseworthy is the man who has made HASHEM his trust, and turned not to the arrogant, and to strayers after falsehood. **6** Much have You done, O You HASHEM, my God, Your wonders and Your thoughts are for us — none can compare to You — were I to relate or speak [of them], they are too overwhelming to recount. **7** Neither feast-offering nor meal-offering did You desire, but You opened ears for me; burnt-offering and sin-offering You did not request. **8** Then I said, "Behold I have come!" with the Scroll of the Book that is written for me.* **9** To fulfill Your will, my God, do I desire, and Your Torah is in my innards. **10** I pro-claimed [Your] righteousness in a vast assembly, behold I will never restrain my lips; HASHEM, You know [it]. **11** Your righteousness I have not concealed within my heart, of Your faithfulness and Your salvation have I spoken; I have not concealed Your kindness and Your truth from the vast assembly. **12** You, HASHEM, do not withhold Your mercy from me; may Your kindness and Your truth always protect me. **13** For innumerable evils have encircled me, my sins have overtaken me and I am unable to see; they have become more numerous than the hairs on my head and my courage has abandoned me. **14** May it be Your will, HASHEM, to rescue me; HASHEM, hasten to my assistance. **15** May they be put to shame and disgrace, all together, those who seek my soul to put an end to it; may they draw back and be humi-liated, those who desire my misfortune. **16** May they be desolate as a result of their shaming, those who say about me, "Aha! Aha!" **17** May they rejoice and be glad in You, all who seek You; may they always say, "HASHEM be magnified!" those who love Your salvation. **18** As for me, I am poor and destitute,* the Lord will think of me. You are my Help and my Rescuer, my God, do not delay.

41

1 For the conductor, a psalm by David. **2** Praiseworthy is he who contemplates the needy,* on the day of evil HASHEM will deliver him. **3** HASHEM will preserve him and restore him to life, and he will be happy on earth, and You will not give him over to the desire of his foes. **4** HASHEM will fortify him on the bed of misery, even when You have upset all his restfulness by his illness. **5** As for me [when I was sick], I said, "O HASHEM, show me favor! Heal my soul* for I have sinned against You!" **6** My foes speak evil of me, "When will he die and his name perish?" **7** And if one comes to visit, insincerely does he speak, his heart gathers iniquity for himself; upon going out he speaks [it]. **8** Together, all my enemies whisper against me, against me they devise my harm [saying], **9** "The result of his lawlessness is poured over him; and now that he lies ill, he will rise no more!" **10** Even my ally in whom I trusted, who ate my bread, has raised his heel to trample me. **11** But as for You, HASHEM, show me favor and raise me up, then I shall repay them.* **12** By this I shall know that You desire me; that You will not let my foe shout gleefully over me. **13** And I, because of my integrity You have supported me, and You have stood me erect before You forever. **14** Blessed is HASHEM, the God of Israel, from all times past to all times to come, Amen and Amen!

ספר שני

מב א־ב לַמְנַצֵּחַ מַשְׂכִּיל לִבְנֵי־קֹרַח: כְּאַיָּל תַּעֲרֹג עַל־אֲפִיקֵי־מָיִם כֵּן נַפְשִׁי תַעֲרֹג
ג אֵלֶיךָ אֱלֹהִים: צָמְאָה נַפְשִׁי ׀ לֵאלֹהִים לְאֵל חָי מָתַי אָבוֹא וְאֵרָאֶה פְּנֵי
ד אֱלֹהִים: הָיְתָה־לִּי דִמְעָתִי לֶחֶם יוֹמָם וָלָיְלָה בֶּאֱמֹר אֵלַי כָּל־הַיּוֹם אַיֵּה
ה אֱלֹהֶיךָ: אֵלֶּה אֶזְכְּרָה ׀ וְאֶשְׁפְּכָה עָלַי ׀ נַפְשִׁי כִּי אֶעֱבֹר ׀ בַּסָּךְ ׀ אֶדַּדֵּם עַד־
ו בֵּית אֱלֹהִים בְּקוֹל־רִנָּה וְתוֹדָה הָמוֹן חוֹגֵג: מַה־תִּשְׁתּוֹחֲחִי ׀ נַפְשִׁי וַתֶּהֱמִי
ז עָלַי הוֹחִילִי לֵאלֹהִים כִּי־עוֹד אוֹדֶנּוּ יְשׁוּעוֹת פָּנָיו: אֱלֹהַי עָלַי נַפְשִׁי
ח תִשְׁתּוֹחָח עַל־כֵּן אֶזְכָּרְךָ מֵאֶרֶץ יַרְדֵּן וְחֶרְמוֹנִים מֵהַר מִצְעָר: תְּהוֹם־אֶל־
ט תְּהוֹם קוֹרֵא לְקוֹל צִנּוֹרֶיךָ כָּל־מִשְׁבָּרֶיךָ וְגַלֶּיךָ עָלַי עָבָרוּ: יוֹמָם ׀ יְצַוֶּה
י יְהוָה ׀ חַסְדּוֹ וּבַלַּיְלָה שִׁירֹה עִמִּי תְּפִלָּה לְאֵל חַיָּי: אוֹמְרָה ׀ לְאֵל סַלְעִי
יא לָמָה שְׁכַחְתָּנִי לָמָּה־קֹדֵר אֵלֵךְ בְּלַחַץ אוֹיֵב: בְּרֶצַח ׀ בְּעַצְמוֹתַי חֵרְפוּנִי
יב צוֹרְרָי בְּאָמְרָם אֵלַי כָּל־הַיּוֹם אַיֵּה אֱלֹהֶיךָ: מַה־תִּשְׁתּוֹחֲחִי ׀ נַפְשִׁי וּמַה־
תֶּהֱמִי עָלָי הוֹחִילִי לֵאלֹהִים כִּי־עוֹד אוֹדֶנּוּ יְשׁוּעֹת פָּנַי וֵאלֹהָי:

מג א שָׁפְטֵנִי אֱלֹהִים ׀ וְרִיבָה רִיבִי מִגּוֹי לֹא־חָסִיד מֵאִישׁ־מִרְמָה וְעַוְלָה
ב תְפַלְּטֵנִי: כִּי־אַתָּה ׀ אֱלֹהֵי מָעוּזִּי לָמָה זְנַחְתָּנִי לָמָּה־קֹדֵר אֶתְהַלֵּךְ בְּלַחַץ
ג אוֹיֵב: שְׁלַח־אוֹרְךָ וַאֲמִתְּךָ הֵמָּה יַנְחוּנִי יְבִיאוּנִי אֶל־הַר־קָדְשְׁךָ וְאֶל־
ד מִשְׁכְּנוֹתֶיךָ: וְאָבוֹאָה ׀ אֶל־מִזְבַּח אֱלֹהִים אֶל־אֵל שִׂמְחַת גִּילִי וְאוֹדְךָ
ה בְכִנּוֹר אֱלֹהִים אֱלֹהָי: מַה־תִּשְׁתּוֹחֲחִי ׀ נַפְשִׁי וּמַה־תֶּהֱמִי עָלָי הוֹחִילִי
לֵאלֹהִים כִּי־עוֹד אוֹדֶנּוּ יְשׁוּעֹת פָּנַי וֵאלֹהָי:

מד א־ב לַמְנַצֵּחַ לִבְנֵי־קֹרַח מַשְׂכִּיל: אֱלֹהִים ׀ בְּאָזְנֵינוּ שָׁמַעְנוּ אֲבוֹתֵינוּ סִפְּרוּ־לָנוּ
יום ח לחדש   ג פֹּעַל פָּעַלְתָּ בִימֵיהֶם בִּימֵי קֶדֶם: אַתָּה ׀ יָדְךָ גּוֹיִם הוֹרַשְׁתָּ וַתִּטָּעֵם תָּרַע
ד לְאֻמִּים וַתְּשַׁלְּחֵם: כִּי לֹא בְחַרְבָּם יָרְשׁוּ אָרֶץ וּזְרוֹעָם לֹא־הוֹשִׁיעָה לָּמוֹ
ה כִּי־יְמִינְךָ וּזְרוֹעֲךָ וְאוֹר פָּנֶיךָ כִּי רְצִיתָם: אַתָּה־הוּא מַלְכִּי אֱלֹהִים צַוֵּה
ו־ז יְשׁוּעוֹת יַעֲקֹב: בְּךָ צָרֵינוּ נְנַגֵּחַ בְּשִׁמְךָ נָבוּס קָמֵינוּ: כִּי לֹא בְקַשְׁתִּי אֶבְטָח
ח־ט וְחַרְבִּי לֹא תוֹשִׁיעֵנִי: כִּי הוֹשַׁעְתָּנוּ מִצָּרֵינוּ וּמְשַׂנְאֵינוּ הֱבִישׁוֹתָ: בֵּאלֹהִים
י הִלַּלְנוּ כָל־הַיּוֹם וְשִׁמְךָ ׀ לְעוֹלָם נוֹדֶה סֶלָה: אַף־זָנַחְתָּ וַתַּכְלִימֵנוּ וְלֹא־
יא־יב תֵצֵא בְּצִבְאוֹתֵינוּ: תְּשִׁיבֵנוּ אָחוֹר מִנִּי־צָר וּמְשַׂנְאֵינוּ שָׁסוּ לָמוֹ: תִּתְּנֵנוּ
יג כְּצֹאן מַאֲכָל וּבַגּוֹיִם זֵרִיתָנוּ: תִּמְכֹּר־עַמְּךָ בְלֹא־הוֹן וְלֹא־רִבִּיתָ
יד־טו בִּמְחִירֵיהֶם: תְּשִׂימֵנוּ חֶרְפָּה לִשְׁכֵנֵינוּ לַעַג וָקֶלֶס לִסְבִיבוֹתֵינוּ: תְּשִׂימֵנוּ
טז מָשָׁל בַּגּוֹיִם מְנוֹד־רֹאשׁ בַּלְאֻמִּים: כָּל־הַיּוֹם כְּלִמָּתִי נֶגְדִּי וּבֹשֶׁת פָּנַי

42:1. Twelve psalms (42-49, 84-85, 87-88) were "by the sons of Korah." They were either the sons of the Korah who rebelled against Moses (*Numbers* Ch. 16) or his descendants, who were Levite choristers during David's reign.

42:3. "When will I return to the Land of Israel and go up

to Jerusalem for the Three Pilgrimage Festivals?"

42:8. One misfortune follows another in rapid succession.

42:9. "Day" represents redemption; "night," exile.

44:3. The first "them" refers to "our fathers"; the second to the Canaanite nations.

BOOK TWO

42

The exiled individual or nation calls longingly to God to be brought home.

¹ For the conductor, a maskil by the sons of Korah.* ² As the deer longs for brooks of water, so my soul longs for You, O God. ³ My soul thirsts for God, for the living God, "When shall I come and appear before God?"* ⁴ For me my tears were sustenance day and night, when [they] say to me all day long, "Where is your God?" ⁵ These do I recall and pour out my soul for [what has befallen] me: how I passed with the throng, walking slowly with them up to the Temple of God; with joyous song and thanks, a celebrating multitude. ⁶Why are you downcast, my soul, and why are you disturbed on my account? Hope to God! For I shall yet thank Him for the salvations of His countenance. ⁷ O my God, my soul is downcast over me, because I remember You from the land of Jordan and Hermon's peaks, from Mount Mizar. ⁸ Watery deep calls out to watery deep* to the roar of Your water channels, all Your breakers and Your waves have swept over me. ⁹ In the day* HASHEM will command His lovingkindness, even by night His resting place is with me; a prayer to the God of my life! ¹⁰ I will say to God, my Rock, "Why have You forgotten me? Why must I walk in gloom under the foe's oppression?" ¹¹ With a murderous dagger in my bones have my tormentors taunted me, when they say to me all day long, "Where is your God?" ¹² Why are you downcast, my soul, and why are you disturbed on my account? Hope to God! For I shall yet thank Him for the salvations of my countenance and because He is my God.

43

When God sends forth His light, the exiles will return to their land.

¹ Avenge me, O God, and champion my cause against an unkind nation; deliver me from a man of deceit and iniquity. ² For You are the God of my strength, why have You abandoned me? Why must I walk in gloom because of the foe's oppression? ³ Dispatch Your light and Your truth, they will guide me, they will bring me to Your holy mountain and to Your dwellings. ⁴ That I may come to the altar of God, to God, the gladness of my joy; and praise You on the harp, O God, my God. ⁵ Why are you downcast, my soul, and why are you disturbed on my account? Hope to God, for I shall yet thank Him for the salvations of my countenance and because He is my God.

44

Vividly portraying the recurring oppressions and persecutions of exile, Israel pleads for strength to endure until it is redeemed.

¹ For the conductor, by the sons of Korah, a maskil. ² God, with our ears we have heard, our fathers have recounted to us, the work that You wrought in their days, in days of old. ³ You, with Your own hand, drove out nations, and You implanted them;* You afflicted regimes and banished them. * ⁴ For not by their sword did they possess the land, nor did their own arm help them; but by Your right hand, Your arm, and the light of Your Countenance — for You favored them. ⁵ It is You Who are my King, O God; command the salvations of Jacob! ⁶ Through You we shall gore our foes; by Your Name we will trample our opponents. ⁷ For I do not trust in my bow, nor does my sword save me. ⁸ For You have saved us from our oppressors, and You shamed those who hate us. ⁹ In God we glory all the day, and Your Name we forever thank, Selah! — ¹⁰ Even though You abandon and disgrace us, and You do not go forth with our armies; ¹¹ You cause us to retreat from the oppressor, and our haters plunder for themselves; ¹² You deliver us like sheep to be eaten, and have scattered us among the nations; ¹³ You sell Your nation for no fortune, and You did not inflate their price; ¹⁴ You make us a disgrace to our neighbors, the mockery and scorn of those around us; ¹⁵ You make us a byword among the nations, a cause for the regimes to shake their heads. ¹⁶ All day long my humiliation is before me and my shamefacedness

יז-יח   כִּסָּתְנִי: מִקּוֹל מְחָרֵף וּמְגַדֵּף מִפְּנֵי אוֹיֵב וּמִתְנַקֵּם: כָּל־זֹאת בָּאַתְנוּ וְלֹא

יט   שְׁכַחֲנוּךָ וְלֹא־שִׁקַּרְנוּ בִּבְרִיתֶךָ: לֹא־נָסוֹג אָחוֹר לִבֵּנוּ וַתֵּט אֲשֻׁרֵינוּ מִנִּי

כ-כא   אָרְחֶךָ: כִּי דִכִּיתָנוּ בִּמְקוֹם תַּנִּים וַתְּכַס עָלֵינוּ בְצַלְמָוֶת: אִם־שָׁכַחְנוּ שֵׁם

כב   אֱלֹהֵינוּ וַנִּפְרֹשׂ כַּפֵּינוּ לְאֵל זָר: הֲלֹא אֱלֹהִים יַחֲקָר־זֹאת כִּי־הוּא יֹדֵעַ

כג-כד   תַּעֲלֻמוֹת לֵב: כִּי־עָלֶיךָ הֹרַגְנוּ כָל־הַיּוֹם נֶחְשַׁבְנוּ כְּצֹאן טִבְחָה: עוּרָה |

כה   לָמָּה תִישַׁן | אֲדֹנָי הָקִיצָה אַל־תִּזְנַח לָנֶצַח: לָמָּה־פָנֶיךָ תַסְתִּיר תִּשְׁכַּח

כו-כז   עָנְיֵנוּ וְלַחֲצֵנוּ: כִּי שָׁחָה לֶעָפָר נַפְשֵׁנוּ דָּבְקָה לָאָרֶץ בִּטְנֵנוּ: קוּמָה עֶזְרָתָה

  לָּנוּ וּפְדֵנוּ לְמַעַן חַסְדֶּךָ:

מה   א-ב   לַמְנַצֵּחַ עַל־שֹׁשַׁנִּים לִבְנֵי־קֹרַח מַשְׂכִּיל שִׁיר יְדִידֹת: רָחַשׁ לִבִּי | דָּבָר

ג   טוֹב אֹמֵר אָנִי מַעֲשַׂי לְמֶלֶךְ לְשׁוֹנִי עֵט | סוֹפֵר מָהִיר: יָפְיָפִיתָ מִבְּנֵי אָדָם

ד   הוּצַק חֵן בְּשִׂפְתוֹתֶיךָ עַל־כֵּן בֵּרַכְךָ אֱלֹהִים לְעוֹלָם: חֲגוֹר־חַרְבְּךָ עַל־

ה   יָרֵךְ גִּבּוֹר הוֹדְךָ וַהֲדָרֶךָ: וַהֲדָרְךָ | צְלַח רְכַב עַל־דְּבַר־אֱמֶת וְעַנְוָה־צֶדֶק

ו   וְתוֹרְךָ נוֹרָאוֹת יְמִינֶךָ: חִצֶּיךָ שְׁנוּנִים עַמִּים תַּחְתֶּיךָ יִפְּלוּ בְּלֵב אוֹיְבֵי

ז-ח   הַמֶּלֶךְ: כִּסְאֲךָ אֱלֹהִים עוֹלָם וָעֶד שֵׁבֶט מִישֹׁר שֵׁבֶט מַלְכוּתֶךָ: אָהַבְתָּ

  צֶּדֶק וַתִּשְׂנָא רֶשַׁע עַל־כֵּן | מְשָׁחֲךָ אֱלֹהִים אֱלֹהֶיךָ שֶׁמֶן שָׂשׂוֹן מֵחֲבֵרֶיךָ:

ט   מֹר־וַאֲהָלוֹת קְצִיעוֹת כָּל־בִּגְדֹתֶיךָ מִן־הֵיכְלֵי שֵׁן מִנִּי שִׂמְּחוּךָ: בְּנוֹת

י   מְלָכִים בְּיִקְּרוֹתֶיךָ נִצְּבָה שֵׁגַל לִימִינְךָ בְּכֶתֶם אוֹפִיר: שִׁמְעִי־בַת וּרְאִי

יא   וְהַטִּי אָזְנֵךְ וְשִׁכְחִי עַמֵּךְ וּבֵית אָבִיךְ: וְיִתְאָו הַמֶּלֶךְ יָפְיֵךְ כִּי־הוּא אֲדֹנַיִךְ

יב   וְהִשְׁתַּחֲוִי־לוֹ: וּבַת־צֹר | בְּמִנְחָה פָּנַיִךְ יְחַלּוּ עֲשִׁירֵי עָם: כָּל־כְּבוּדָּה בַת־

יג-יד   מֶלֶךְ פְּנִימָה מִמִּשְׁבְּצוֹת זָהָב לְבוּשָׁהּ: לִרְקָמוֹת תּוּבַל לַמֶּלֶךְ בְּתוּלוֹת

טו   אַחֲרֶיהָ רֵעוֹתֶיהָ מוּבָאוֹת לָךְ: תּוּבַלְנָה בִּשְׂמָחֹת וָגִיל תְּבֹאֶינָה בְּהֵיכַל

טז   מֶלֶךְ: תַּחַת אֲבֹתֶיךָ יִהְיוּ בָנֶיךָ תְּשִׁיתֵמוֹ לְשָׂרִים בְּכָל־הָאָרֶץ: אַזְכִּירָה

יז-יח   שִׁמְךָ בְּכָל־דֹּר וָדֹר עַל־כֵּן עַמִּים יְהוֹדֻךָ לְעֹלָם וָעֶד:

מו   א-ב   לַמְנַצֵּחַ לִבְנֵי־קֹרַח עַל־עֲלָמוֹת שִׁיר: אֱלֹהִים לָנוּ מַחֲסֶה וָעֹז עֶזְרָה

ג   בְצָרוֹת נִמְצָא מְאֹד: עַל־כֵּן לֹא־נִירָא בְּהָמִיר אָרֶץ וּבְמוֹט הָרִים בְּלֵב

ד-ה   יַמִּים: יֶהֱמוּ יֶחְמְרוּ מֵימָיו יִרְעֲשׁוּ הָרִים בְּגַאֲוָתוֹ סֶלָה: נָהָר פְּלָגָיו יְשַׂמְּחוּ

ו   עִיר־אֱלֹהִים קְדֹשׁ מִשְׁכְּנֵי עֶלְיוֹן: אֱלֹהִים בְּקִרְבָּהּ בַּל־תִּמּוֹט יַעְזְרֶהָ

ז   אֱלֹהִים לִפְנוֹת בֹּקֶר: הָמוּ גוֹיִם מָטוּ מַמְלָכוֹת נָתַן בְּקוֹלוֹ תָּמוּג אָרֶץ:

ח-ט   יְהוָה צְבָאוֹת עִמָּנוּ מִשְׂגָּב־לָנוּ אֱלֹהֵי יַעֲקֹב סֶלָה: לְכוּ־חֲזוּ מִפְעֲלוֹת

44:23. When one performs the *mitzvos* in the face of jeers and humiliation that cause one's face to blanch, it is as if one is sacrificing his life for God's commandments (*R' Yehudah HaChasid*).

45:4. Although the Messianic era will bring peace, it will begin with the war of Gog and Magog (*Radak*).

45:10-16. These verses describe with vivid imagery the subservience of the nations to the Messiah.

45:11. Repudiate false religions and sincerely embrace the Torah (*Meiri*).

45:15. The secondary nations who are in the spheres of influence of the "princesses," the primary nations (*Meiri*).

46:1. A musical instrument.

46:3. The violent upheavals of powerful nations are described in the imagery of natural calamities.

46:6. The dawn of the final redemption (*Radak*).

covers me — ¹⁷ *at the voice of the reviler and blasphemer, because of the enemy and avenger.* ¹⁸ *All this came upon us yet we have not forgotten You, and we have not been false to Your covenant.* ¹⁹ *Our heart has not turned back, nor have our footsteps strayed from Your path,* ²⁰ *even when You crushed us in the place of serpents and shrouded us in the shadow of death.* ²¹ *Have we forgotten the Name of our God and extended our hands to a strange god?* ²² *Is it not so that God can examine this, for He knows the secrets of the heart?* ²³ *Because for Your sake we are killed all the time,* * *we are considered as sheep for slaughter.* ²⁴ *Awaken, why do You seem to sleep, O Lord? Arouse Yourself, forsake not forever!* ²⁵ *Why do You conceal Your face, do You forget our affliction and oppression?* ²⁶ *For prostrated to the dust is our soul, stuck to the earth is our belly.* ²⁷ *Arise! Assist us! And redeem us for the sake of Your kindness!*

45

A song of praise, describing the splendor and sovereignty of the king Messiah.

¹ For the conductor, on the shoshannim, by the sons of Korah, a Maskil, a song of endearment.* ² *My heart is astir with a good theme, I say, "My works are for a king, my tongue is like the pen of a skillful scribe."* ³ *You are beautiful beyond other men, charm is poured upon your lips, therefore God has blessed you for eternity.* ⁴ *Gird your sword* * *upon [your] thigh, O mighty one, your majesty and your splendor.* ⁵ *And with your splendor, overcome and ride [over your enemies], for the sake of truth and righteous humility; may your right hand guide you to awesome deeds.* ⁶ *Your arrows are sharp — nations fall beneath you, in the heart of the foes of the king.* ⁷ *Your throne is from God, it is forever and ever, [for] the scepter of fairness is the scepter of your kingdom.* ⁸ *You love righteousness and hate wickedness; therefore has God, your God, anointed you, with oil of joy from among your peers.* ⁹ *Myrrh, aloes, and cassia, are [the fragrance of] all your garments — from ivory palaces, from those which have gladdened you.* ¹⁰ **Daughters of kings are your visitors, the queen stands erect at your right in the golden jewelry of Ophir.* ¹¹ *Hear, O daughter, and see, and incline your ear; forget your people and your father's house,* * *then the king will desire your beauty; for he is your master, so bow to him.* ¹³ *And daughter of Tyre, you whose favor has been sought with homage by the richest of the nation;* ¹⁴ *[as well as] every honorable princess dwelling within, whose raiment is of golden settings;* ¹⁵ *in embroidered apparel she will be brought to the king; the virgins in her train,* * *her companions, are [also] led to you.* ¹⁶ *They are brought with gladness and joy, they enter the palace of the king.* ¹⁷ *Succeeding your fathers will be your sons; you will appoint them leaders throughout the land.* ¹⁸ *I will make your name remembered in all generations, therefore the nations will acknowledge you forever and ever.*

46

In the upheavals of the Messianic era, God will shield Israel, as He shields all distraught people who seek His support.

¹ For the conductor, by the sons of Korah, on the alamos,* * *a song.* ² *God is a refuge and strength for us, a help in distress, very accessible.* ³ *Therefore, we shall not be afraid when the earth is transformed, and at mountains' collapse in the heart of the seas;* * ⁴ *when its waters rage and are muddied, mountains quake in His majesty, Selah.* ⁵ *A river: Its streams will gladden the City of God, the most sacred of the dwellings of the Most High.* ⁶ *God is in its midst, it shall not falter; God will help it towards morning.* * ⁷ *Nations are in turmoil, kingdoms totter; He has raised His voice, the earth dissolves.* ⁸ HASHEM, *Master of Legions, is with us, a stronghold for us is the God of Jacob, Selah.* ⁹ *Go and see the works*

י　יְהוָה אֲשֶׁר־שָׂם שַׁמּוֹת בָּאָרֶץ: מַשְׁבִּית מִלְחָמוֹת עַד־קְצֵה הָאָרֶץ קֶשֶׁת
יא　יְשַׁבֵּר וְקִצֵּץ חֲנִית עֲגָלוֹת יִשְׂרֹף בָּאֵשׁ: הַרְפּוּ וּדְעוּ כִּי־אָנֹכִי אֱלֹהִים אָרוּם
יב　בַּגּוֹיִם אָרוּם בָּאָרֶץ: יְהוָה צְבָאוֹת עִמָּנוּ מִשְׂגָּב־לָנוּ אֱלֹהֵי יַעֲקֹב סֶלָה:

א-ב　לַמְנַצֵּחַ | לִבְנֵי־קֹרַח מִזְמוֹר: כָּל־הָעַמִּים תִּקְעוּ־כָף הָרִיעוּ לֵאלֹהִים בְּקוֹל
ג-ד　רִנָּה: כִּי־יְהוָה עֶלְיוֹן נוֹרָא מֶלֶךְ גָּדוֹל עַל־כָּל־הָאָרֶץ: יַדְבֵּר עַמִּים תַּחְתֵּינוּ
ה　וּלְאֻמִּים תַּחַת רַגְלֵינוּ: יִבְחַר־לָנוּ אֶת־נַחֲלָתֵנוּ אֶת גְּאוֹן יַעֲקֹב אֲשֶׁר־
ו　אָהֵב סֶלָה: עָלָה אֱלֹהִים בִּתְרוּעָה יְהוָה בְּקוֹל שׁוֹפָר: זַמְּרוּ אֱלֹהִים זַמֵּרוּ
ז-ח　זַמְּרוּ לְמַלְכֵּנוּ זַמֵּרוּ: כִּי מֶלֶךְ כָּל־הָאָרֶץ אֱלֹהִים זַמְּרוּ מַשְׂכִּיל: מָלַךְ
ט　אֱלֹהִים עַל־גּוֹיִם אֱלֹהִים יָשַׁב עַל־כִּסֵּא קָדְשׁוֹ: נְדִיבֵי עַמִּים | נֶאֱסָפוּ עַם
י　אֱלֹהֵי אַבְרָהָם כִּי לֵאלֹהִים מָגִנֵּי־אֶרֶץ מְאֹד נַעֲלָה:

א-ב　שִׁיר מִזְמוֹר לִבְנֵי־קֹרַח: גָּדוֹל יְהוָה וּמְהֻלָּל מְאֹד בְּעִיר אֱלֹהֵינוּ הַר־קָדְשׁוֹ:
ג-ד　יְפֵה נוֹף מְשׂוֹשׂ כָּל־הָאָרֶץ הַר־צִיּוֹן יַרְכְּתֵי צָפוֹן קִרְיַת מֶלֶךְ רָב: אֱלֹהִים
ה-ו　בְּאַרְמְנוֹתֶיהָ נוֹדַע לְמִשְׂגָּב: כִּי־הִנֵּה הַמְּלָכִים נוֹעֲדוּ עָבְרוּ יַחְדָּו: הֵמָּה רָאוּ
ז-ח　כֵּן תָּמָהוּ נִבְהֲלוּ נֶחְפָּזוּ: רְעָדָה אֲחָזָתַם שָׁם חִיל כַּיּוֹלֵדָה: בְּרוּחַ קָדִים
ט　תְּשַׁבֵּר אֳנִיּוֹת תַּרְשִׁישׁ: כַּאֲשֶׁר שָׁמַעְנוּ | כֵּן רָאִינוּ בְּעִיר־יְהוָה צְבָאוֹת בְּעִיר
י　אֱלֹהֵינוּ אֱלֹהִים יְכוֹנְנֶהָ עַד־עוֹלָם סֶלָה: דִּמִּינוּ אֱלֹהִים חַסְדֶּךָ בְּקֶרֶב הֵיכָלֶךָ:
יא　כְּשִׁמְךָ אֱלֹהִים כֵּן תְּהִלָּתְךָ עַל־קַצְוֵי־אֶרֶץ צֶדֶק מָלְאָה יְמִינֶךָ: יִשְׂמַח | הַר־
יב-יג　צִיּוֹן תָּגֵלְנָה בְּנוֹת יְהוּדָה לְמַעַן מִשְׁפָּטֶיךָ: סֹבּוּ צִיּוֹן וְהַקִּיפוּהָ סִפְרוּ מִגְדָּלֶיהָ:
יד　שִׁיתוּ לִבְּכֶם | לְחֵילָה פַּסְּגוּ אַרְמְנוֹתֶיהָ לְמַעַן תְּסַפְּרוּ לְדוֹר אַחֲרוֹן: כִּי זֶה |
טו　אֱלֹהִים אֱלֹהֵינוּ עוֹלָם וָעֶד הוּא יְנַהֲגֵנוּ עַל־מוּת:

א-ב　לַמְנַצֵּחַ | לִבְנֵי־קֹרַח מִזְמוֹר: שִׁמְעוּ־זֹאת כָּל־הָעַמִּים הַאֲזִינוּ כָּל־יֹשְׁבֵי
ג　חָלֶד: גַּם־בְּנֵי אָדָם גַּם־בְּנֵי־אִישׁ יַחַד עָשִׁיר וְאֶבְיוֹן: פִּי יְדַבֵּר חָכְמוֹת
ד-ה　וְהָגוּת לִבִּי תְבוּנוֹת: אַטֶּה לְמָשָׁל אָזְנִי אֶפְתַּח בְּכִנּוֹר חִידָתִי: לָמָּה אִירָא
ו-ז　בִּימֵי רָע עֲוֹן עֲקֵבַי יְסוּבֵּנִי: הַבֹּטְחִים עַל־חֵילָם וּבְרֹב עָשְׁרָם יִתְהַלָּלוּ: אָח
ח	לֹא־פָדֹה יִפְדֶּה אִישׁ לֹא־יִתֵּן לֵאלֹהִים כָּפְרוֹ: וְיֵקַר פִּדְיוֹן נַפְשָׁם וְחָדַל
ט-י	לְעוֹלָם: וִיחִי־עוֹד לָנֶצַח לֹא יִרְאֶה הַשָּׁחַת: כִּי יִרְאֶה | חֲכָמִים יָמוּתוּ יַחַד
יא	כְּסִיל וָבַעַר יֹאבֵדוּ וְעָזְבוּ לַאֲחֵרִים חֵילָם: קִרְבָּם בָּתֵּימוֹ | לְעוֹלָם מִשְׁכְּנֹתָם
יב-יג	לְדֹר וָדֹר קָרְאוּ בִשְׁמוֹתָם עֲלֵי אֲדָמוֹת: וְאָדָם בִּיקָר בַּל־יָלִין נִמְשַׁל
יד-טו	כַּבְּהֵמוֹת נִדְמוּ: זֶה דַרְכָּם כֵּסֶל לָמוֹ | וְאַחֲרֵיהֶם | בְּפִיהֶם יִרְצוּ סֶלָה: כַּצֹּאן |
　　לִשְׁאוֹל שַׁתּוּ מָוֶת יִרְעֵם וַיִּרְדּוּ בָם יְשָׁרִים | לַבֹּקֶר °וצירם [°וְצוּרָם ק]

47:2. The nations will blow the *shofar* when they acknowledge God as their sovereign (*Malbim*).

47:10. Gentiles who converted or otherwise made sacrifices for the sake of God will be gathered under His protection. Like Abraham they left their family and heritage to follow God (*Rashi*).

48:5-7. Whenever kings assembled to attack Jerusalem,

they saw that God was its "stronghold." They were astounded and fled (*Radak*).

48:8. A major seaport, Tarshish represents invading fleets that were dispatched against the Land of Israel.

49:6. If I misuse my limited time in this world, I will feel pain and anguish "in days of evil" — when I will have to account for "the injunctions that I trod upon."

of HASHEM, Who has wrought devastation in the land. ¹⁰ He causes wars to cease to the end of the earth; He will break the bow, and cut the spear, He will burn chariots in fire. ¹¹ Desist and know that I am God; I shall be exalted among the nations; I shall be exalted upon the earth. ¹² HASHEM, Master of Legions, is with us, a stronghold for us is the God of Jacob, Selah.

47

God's sovereignty will ultimately be recognized and accepted by all mankind.

¹ For the conductor, by the sons of Korah, a psalm. ² All you nations, join hands; sound the shofar* to God with a cry of joy. ³ For HASHEM is supreme, awesome; a great King over all the earth. ⁴ He shall lead nations under us and regimes beneath our feet. ⁵ He will choose our heritage for us, the pride of Jacob that He loves, Selah. ⁶ God has ascended with the blast; HASHEM, with the sound of the shofar. ⁷ Make music for God, make music; make music for our King, make music. ⁸ For God is King of all the earth; make music, O enlightened one! ⁹ God reigns over the nations; God sits upon His holy throne. ¹⁰ The nobles of the peoples gathered, the people of the God of Abraham;* for the protectors of the earth are God's, He is exceedingly exalted.

48

Jerusalem is eternally beautiful and glorious because God chose it for the abode of His Presence.

¹ A song, a psalm, by the sons of Korah. ² Great is HASHEM and much praised, in the city of our God, mount of His Holiness, ³ fairest of sites, joy of all the earth, Mount Zion, by the northern side of the great king's city. ⁴ In her palaces God is known as the Stronghold. ⁵ For behold the kings assembled,* they came together. ⁶ They saw and were indeed astounded, they were confounded and fled in haste. ⁷ Trembling gripped them there, convulsions like a woman in birth travail. ⁸ With an east wind You smashed the ships of Tarshish.* ⁹ As we heard, so we saw in the city of HASHEM, Master of Legions, in the city of our God, may God establish it to eternity, Selah! ¹⁰ We hoped, O God, for Your kindness in the midst of Your Sanctuary. ¹¹ Like Your Name, O God, so is Your praise: to the ends of the earth. Righteousness fills Your right hand. ¹² May Mount Zion be glad, may the daughters of Judah rejoice, because of Your judgments. ¹³ Walk about Zion and encircle her, count her towers. ¹⁴ Mark well in your hearts her ramparts, raise up her palaces, that you may recount it to the succeeding generation. ¹⁵ For this is God, our God, forever and ever, He will guide us forever.

49

Man should use his sojourn on earth to enhance his spiritual development and prepare for the World to Come.

¹ For the conductor, by the sons of Korah, a psalm. ² Hear this all you peoples, give ear all you dwellers of decaying earth; ³ sons of Adam and sons of man alike; rich and poor together. ⁴ My mouth will speak wisdom, and the meditations of my heart are insightful. ⁵ I will incline my ear to the parable; with a harp I will solve my riddle. ⁶ Why should I be fearful in days of evil, when the injunctions that I trod upon will surround me?* ⁷ Those who rely on their possessions, and they are boastful of their great wealth — ⁸ yet a man cannot redeem a brother, he cannot give his ransom to God. ⁹ Too costly is their soul's redemption and unattainable forever. ¹⁰ Can one live eternally, never to see the pit? ¹¹ Though he sees that wise men die, that the foolish and boorish perish together and leave their possessions to others, ¹² [nevertheless,] in their imagination their houses are forever, their dwellings for generation after generation; they have proclaimed their names throughout the lands. ¹³ But as for man: In glory he shall not repose, he is likened to the silenced animals. ¹⁴ This is their way, folly is theirs, yet of their destiny their mouths speak soothingly, Selah! ¹⁵ Like sheep, they are destined for the Lower World, death shall consume them; and the upright shall dominate them at daybreak, their form

יז לִבְל֣וֹת שְׁא֣וֹל מִזְּבֻ֣ל ל֑וֹ: אַךְ־אֱ֭לֹהִים יִפְדֶּ֣ה נַ֭פְשִׁי מִיַּד־שְׁא֑וֹל כִּ֖י יִקָּחֵ֣נִי
יז־יח סֶֽלָה: אַל־תִּ֭ירָא כִּֽי־יַֽעֲשִׁ֣ר אִ֑ישׁ כִּֽי־יִרְבֶּ֝֗ה כְּב֣וֹד בֵּיתֽוֹ: כִּ֤י לֹ֣א בְ֭מוֹתוֹ יִקַּ֣ח
יט הַכֹּ֑ל לֹא־יֵרֵ֖ד אַֽחֲרָ֣יו כְּבוֹדֽוֹ: כִּֽי־נַ֭פְשׁוֹ בְּחַיָּ֣יו יְבָרֵ֑ךְ וְ֝יוֹדֻ֗ךָ כִּי־תֵיטִ֥יב לָֽךְ:
כ־כא תָּ֭בוֹא עַד־דּ֣וֹר אֲבוֹתָ֑יו עַד־נֵ֝֗צַח לֹ֣א יִרְאוּ־אֽוֹר: אָדָ֣ם בִּ֭יקָר וְלֹ֣א יָבִ֑ין
נִמְשַׁ֖ל כַּבְּהֵמ֣וֹת נִדְמֽוּ:

נ
א מִזְמ֗וֹר לְאָ֫סָ֥ף אֵ֤ל ׀ אֱֽלֹהִ֡ים יְהֹוָ֗ה דִּבֶּ֥ר וַיִּקְרָא־אָ֑רֶץ מִמִּזְרַח־שֶׁ֝֗מֶשׁ עַד־
ב־ג מְבֹאֽוֹ: מִצִּיּ֥וֹן מִכְלַל־יֹ֗פִי אֱלֹהִ֥ים הוֹפִֽיעַ: יָ֤בֹ֣א אֱלֹהֵינוּ֮ וְֽאַל־יֶ֫חֱרַ֥שׁ אֵשׁ־
ד לְפָנָ֥יו תֹּאכֵ֑ל וּ֝סְבִיבָ֗יו נִשְׂעֲרָ֥ה מְאֹֽד: יִקְרָ֣א אֶל־הַשָּׁמַ֣יִם מֵעָ֑ל וְאֶל־הָ֝אָ֗רֶץ
ה לָדִ֥ין עַמּֽוֹ: אִסְפוּ־לִ֥י חֲסִידָ֑י כֹּֽרְתֵ֖י בְרִיתִ֣י עֲלֵי־זָֽבַח: וַיַּגִּ֖ידוּ שָׁמַ֣יִם צִדְק֑וֹ
ה־ו כִּֽי־אֱלֹהִ֓ים ׀ שֹׁפֵ֖ט ה֣וּא סֶֽלָה: שִׁמְעָ֤ה עַמִּ֨י ׀ וַֽאֲדַבֵּ֗רָה יִ֭שְׂרָאֵל וְאָעִ֣ידָה בָּ֑ךְ
ז־ח אֱלֹהִ֖ים אֱלֹהֶ֣יךָ אָנֹֽכִי: לֹ֣א עַל־זְ֭בָחֶיךָ אוֹכִיחֶ֑ךָ וְעוֹלֹתֶ֖יךָ לְנֶגְדִּ֣י תָמִֽיד:
ט לֹא־אֶקַּ֣ח מִבֵּֽיתְךָ֣ פָ֑ר מִ֝מִּכְלְאֹתֶ֗יךָ עַתּוּדִֽים: כִּי־לִ֥י כָל־חַיְתוֹ־יָ֑עַר
י־יא בְּ֝הֵמ֗וֹת בְּהַֽרְרֵי־אָֽלֶף: יָ֭דַעְתִּי כָּל־ע֣וֹף הָרִ֑ים וְזִ֥יז שָׂ֝דַ֗י עִמָּדִֽי: אִם־אֶרְעַ֥ב
יב לֹא־אֹ֣מַר לָ֑ךְ כִּי־לִ֥י תֵ֝בֵ֗ל וּמְלֹאָֽהּ: הַֽאוֹכַ֗ל בְּשַׂ֥ר אַבִּירִ֑ים וְדַ֖ם עַתּוּדִ֣ים
יג־יד אֶשְׁתֶּֽה: זְבַ֣ח לֵֽאלֹהִ֣ים תּוֹדָ֑ה וְשַׁלֵּ֖ם לְעֶלְי֣וֹן נְדָרֶֽיךָ: וּ֭קְרָאֵנִי בְּי֣וֹם צָרָ֑ה
יד־טו אֲ֝חַלֶּצְךָ֗ וּֽתְכַבְּדֵֽנִי: וְלָֽרָשָׁ֨ע ׀ אָ֘מַ֤ר אֱלֹהִ֗ים מַה־לְּ֭ךָ לְסַפֵּ֣ר חֻקָּ֑י וַתִּשָּׂ֖א
טז־יז בְרִיתִ֣י עֲלֵי־פִֽיךָ: וְ֭אַתָּה שָׂנֵ֣אתָ מוּסָ֑ר וַתַּשְׁלֵ֖ךְ דְּבָרַ֣י אַֽחֲרֶֽיךָ: אִם־רָאִ֣יתָ
יח־יט גַ֭נָּב וַתִּ֣רֶץ עִמּ֑וֹ וְעִ֖ם מְנָֽאֲפִ֣ים חֶלְקֶֽךָ: פִּ֭יךָ שָׁלַ֣חְתָּ בְרָעָ֑ה וּ֝לְשֽׁוֹנְךָ֗ תַּצְמִ֥יד
כ־כא מִרְמָֽה: תֵּ֭שֵׁב בְּאָחִ֣יךָ תְדַבֵּ֑ר בְּבֶֽן־אִ֝מְּךָ֗ תִּתֶּן־דֹּֽפִי: אֵ֤לֶּה עָשִׂ֨יתָ ׀
כב וְֽהֶֽחֱרַ֗שְׁתִּי דִּמִּ֗יתָ הֱיֽוֹת־אֶֽהְיֶ֥ה כָמ֑וֹךָ אוֹכִיחֲךָ֖ וְאֶֽעֶרְכָ֣ה לְעֵינֶֽיךָ: בִּֽינוּ־נָ֣א
כג זֹ֭את שֹֽׁכְחֵ֣י אֱל֑וֹהַּ פֶּן־אֶ֝טְרֹ֗ף וְאֵ֣ין מַצִּֽיל: זֹבֵ֥חַ תּוֹדָ֗ה יְֽכַ֫בְּדָ֥נְנִי וְשָׂ֥ם דֶּ֑רֶךְ
אַ֝רְאֶ֗נּוּ בְּיֵ֣שַׁע אֱלֹהִֽים:

נא
א־ב לַמְנַצֵּ֗חַ מִזְמ֥וֹר לְדָוִֽד: בְּֽבוֹא־אֵ֭לָיו נָתָ֣ן הַנָּבִ֑יא כַּֽאֲשֶׁר־בָּ֝֗א אֶל־בַּת־שָֽׁבַע:
ג־ד חָנֵּ֣נִי אֱלֹהִ֣ים כְּחַסְדֶּ֑ךָ כְּרֹ֥ב רַ֝חֲמֶ֗יךָ מְחֵ֣ה פְשָׁעָֽי: [הַרְבֵּ֣ה ק] הרבה
ה כַּבְּסֵ֣נִי מֵֽעֲוֹנִ֑י וּֽמֵחַטָּאתִ֥י טַֽהֲרֵֽנִי: כִּֽי־פְ֭שָׁעַי אֲנִ֣י אֵדָ֑ע וְחַטָּאתִ֖י נֶגְדִּ֣י תָמִֽיד:
ו לְךָ֤ לְבַדְּךָ֨ ׀ חָטָאתִי֮ וְהָרַ֥ע בְּעֵינֶ֗יךָ עָ֫שִׂ֥יתִי לְמַ֖עַן תִּצְדַּ֣ק בְּדָבְרֶ֑ךָ תִּזְכֶּ֥ה
ז־ח בְשָׁפְטֶֽךָ: הֵן־בְּעָו֥וֹן חוֹלָ֑לְתִּי וּ֝בְחֵ֗טְא יֶֽחֱמַ֥תְנִי אִמִּֽי: הֵן־אֱ֭מֶת חָפַ֣צְתָּ
ט בַטֻּח֑וֹת וּ֝בְסָתֻ֗ם חָכְמָ֥ה תֽוֹדִיעֵֽנִי: תְּחַטְּאֵ֣נִי בְאֵז֣וֹב וְאֶטְהָ֑ר תְּ֝כַבְּסֵ֗נִי

49:19. The greedy are confident that they are above criticism, but sincere praise is earned if you "improve" yourself (*Rashi*).

49:20. The soul of the evildoer, as the souls of his wicked ancestors, will not see the light of redemption (*Rashi*).

50:1. Asaph was the leading Levite musician of David's time and, like David, he composed while endowed with a spirit of prophecy (*I Chronicles* 16:5-7, 25:2). In all, he wrote twelve psalms, this one and Psalms 73-83.

Although couched in the past tense, this psalm refers to the era of the final redemption when God will judge all of mankind.

50:5. Devout Jews — learned and simple — have renewed this covenant through the sacrifice of their own lives and that of their children, rather than repudiate God and His Torah (*Mahara Azulai*).

50:14. Sincerely repent your misdeeds; only then will God favorably accept "your vows" (*Rashi*).

50:21. Because I let you go unpunished, you thought I sanctioned your behavior.

51:2. This incident is found in *II Samuel* Chs. 12-13.

is doomed to rot in the grave, each from his dwelling. [16] But God will redeem my soul from the hand of the Lower World, for He will take me, Selah! [17] Fear not when a man grows rich, when he increases the glory of his house, [18] for upon his death he will not take anything, his glory will not descend after him. [19] Though he may bless himself in his lifetime, others will praise you if you improve yourself. * [20] It shall come to the generation of its fathers; unto eternity they shall see no light. * [21] Man is glorious but [if he] understands not, he is likened to the silenced animals.

50

God desires not only external adherence to His commandments, but purity of spirit.

[1] A song by Asaph. * O Almighty God, HASHEM, spoke and called to the earth from the rising of the sun to its setting. [2] Out of Zion, consummation of beauty, God appeared. [3] Our God will come and not be silent; a fire will consume before Him, and His surroundings are exceedingly turbulent. [4] He will call to the heavens above and to the earth to avenge His people. [5] Gather My devout ones unto me, sealers of My covenant through sacrifice. * [6] Then the heavens proclaimed His righteousness, for God is the Judge, Selah! [7] Pay heed, My people, and I shall speak; Israel, and I shall bear witness against you; God, your God, am I. [8] I shall not rebuke you for your sacrifices,nor are your burnt-offerings my constant concern. [9] I take not from your household any bull, nor from your pens any goats. [10] For Mine is every beast of the forest, the cattle of a thousand mountains. [11] I know every bird of the mountains, and what creeps upon My fields is with Me. [12] Even were I hungry I would not tell you, for Mine is the world and its fullness. [13] Do I eat the flesh of bulls or drink the blood of goats? [14] Offer God confession, * then redeem your vows to the Most High. [15] And call upon Me in the day of distress, I will release you and you will honor Me. [16] But to the wicked, God said, "To what purpose do you recount My decrees and bear My covenant upon your lips?" [17] For you hate discipline and you threw My words behind you. [18] If you saw a thief you agreed to be with him, and with adulterers was your lot. [19] You dispatched your mouth for evil, and your tongue adheres to deceit. [20] You sit and speak against your brother, you slander your mother's son. [21] These have you done and I kept silent, You thought that I was like you; * I will rebuke you and lay it clearly before your eyes! [22] Understand this now, you who have forgotten God, lest I tear you asunder and there be none to rescue. [23] He who offers confession honors Me; and one who orders [his] way, I will show him the salvation of God.

51

David's psalm of remorse includes the principles of repentance. Thus, it is a fitting prayer for any penitent.

[1] For the conductor, a song by David. [2] When Nathan the Prophet came to him, when he came to Bath-sheba. * [3] Show me favor, O God, according to Your kindness, according to Your vast compassion erase my transgressions. [4] Abundantly cleanse me from my iniquity, and from my sin purify me. [5] For I recognize my transgressions, and my sin is before me always. [6] Against You alone did I sin, * and that which is evil in Your eyes did I do; therefore, You are justified when You speak, and faultless when You judge. [7] Behold, in iniquity was I fashioned, * and in sin did my mother conceive me. [8] Behold, the truth which You desire is in the concealed parts, * and in the covered part is the wisdom that You teach me. [9] Purge me of sin with hyssop * and I shall be pure, cleanse me

---

Although technically David did not sin, his remorseful reaction is the paradigm of repentance.

51:6. That David sinned *only* against God corroborates the Sages' assertion that David's conduct, though wrong, did not violate the *letter* of the law.

51:7. The impulses which can cause man to sin are

present in him from his very inception. It is man's duty to control and channel them properly (*Ibn Ezra*).

51:8. The part of us that perceives truth and wisdom is "concealed" by thick layers of physical desires (*Malbim*).

51:9. Hyssop was used in certain purification rituals. See *Leviticus* 14:4-6 and *Numbers* 19:6,18.

יא־יא וּמִשֶּׁלֶג אַלְבִּין: תַּשְׁמִיעֵנִי שָׂשׂוֹן וְשִׂמְחָה תָּגֵלְנָה עֲצָמוֹת דִּכִּיתָ: הַסְתֵּר

יב פָּנֶיךָ מֵחֲטָאָי וְכָל־עֲוֺנֹתַי מְחֵה: לֵב טָהוֹר בְּרָא־לִי אֱלֹהִים וְרוּחַ נָכוֹן

יג־יד חַדֵּשׁ בְּקִרְבִּי: אַל־תַּשְׁלִיכֵנִי מִלְּפָנֶיךָ וְרוּחַ קָדְשְׁךָ אַל־תִּקַּח מִמֶּנִּי:

יה הָשִׁיבָה לִּי שְׂשׂוֹן יִשְׁעֶךָ וְרוּחַ נְדִיבָה תִסְמְכֵנִי: אֲלַמְּדָה פֹשְׁעִים דְּרָכֶיךָ

יז וְחַטָּאִים אֵלֶיךָ יָשׁוּבוּ: הַצִּילֵנִי מִדָּמִים ׀ אֱלֹהִים אֱלֹהֵי תְּשׁוּעָתִי תְּרַנֵּן

יז־יח לְשׁוֹנִי צִדְקָתֶךָ: אֲדֹנָי שְׂפָתַי תִּפְתָּח וּפִי יַגִּיד תְּהִלָּתֶךָ: כִּי ׀ לֹא־תַחְפֹּץ

יט זֶבַח וְאֶתֵּנָה עוֹלָה לֹא תִרְצֶה: זִבְחֵי אֱלֹהִים רוּחַ נִשְׁבָּרָה לֵב־נִשְׁבָּר

כ־כא וְנִדְכֶּה אֱלֹהִים לֹא תִבְזֶה: הֵיטִיבָה בִרְצוֹנְךָ אֶת־צִיּוֹן תִּבְנֶה חוֹמוֹת

יְרוּשָׁלָ͏ִם: אָז תַּחְפֹּץ זִבְחֵי־צֶדֶק עוֹלָה וְכָלִיל אָז יַעֲלוּ עַל־מִזְבַּחֲךָ פָרִים:

נב א־ב לַמְנַצֵּחַ מַשְׂכִּיל לְדָוִד: בְּבוֹא ׀ דּוֹאֵג הָאֲדֹמִי וַיַּגֵּד לְשָׁאוּל וַיֹּאמֶר לוֹ בָּא

ג דָוִד אֶל־בֵּית אֲחִימֶלֶךְ: מַה־תִּתְהַלֵּל בְּרָעָה הַגִּבּוֹר חֶסֶד אֵל כָּל־הַיּוֹם:

ד־ה הַוּוֹת תַּחְשֹׁב לְשׁוֹנֶךָ כְּתַעַר מְלֻטָּשׁ עֹשֵׂה רְמִיָּה: אָהַבְתָּ רָּע מִטּוֹב שֶׁקֶר ׀

ו־ז מִדַּבֵּר צֶדֶק סֶלָה: אָהַבְתָּ כָל־דִּבְרֵי־בָלַע לְשׁוֹן מִרְמָה: גַּם־אֵל יִתָּצְךָ

ח לָנֶצַח יַחְתְּךָ וְיִסָּחֲךָ מֵאֹהֶל וְשֵׁרֶשְׁךָ מֵאֶרֶץ חַיִּים סֶלָה: וְיִרְאוּ צַדִּיקִים

ט וְיִירָאוּ וְעָלָיו יִשְׂחָקוּ: הִנֵּה הַגֶּבֶר לֹא יָשִׂים אֱלֹהִים מָעוּזּוֹ וַיִּבְטַח בְּרֹב

י עָשְׁרוֹ יָעֹז בְּהַוָּתוֹ: וַאֲנִי ׀ כְּזַיִת רַעֲנָן בְּבֵית אֱלֹהִים בָּטַחְתִּי בְחֶסֶד־אֱלֹהִים

יא עוֹלָם וָעֶד: אוֹדְךָ לְעוֹלָם כִּי עָשִׂיתָ וַאֲקַוֶּה שִׁמְךָ כִי־טוֹב נֶגֶד חֲסִידֶיךָ:

נג א־ב לַמְנַצֵּחַ עַל־מָחֲלַת מַשְׂכִּיל לְדָוִד: אָמַר נָבָל בְּלִבּוֹ אֵין אֱלֹהִים הִשְׁחִיתוּ

ג וְהִתְעִיבוּ עָוֶל אֵין עֹשֵׂה־טוֹב: אֱלֹהִים מִשָּׁמַיִם הִשְׁקִיף עַל־בְּנֵי־אָדָם

ד לִרְאוֹת הֲיֵשׁ מַשְׂכִּיל דֹּרֵשׁ אֶת־אֱלֹהִים: כֻּלּוֹ סָג יַחְדָּו נֶאֱלָחוּ אֵין עֹשֵׂה־

ה טוֹב אֵין גַּם־אֶחָד: הֲלֹא יָדְעוּ פֹּעֲלֵי אָוֶן אֹכְלֵי עַמִּי אָכְלוּ לֶחֶם אֱלֹהִים

ו לֹא קָרָאוּ: שָׁם ׀ פָּחֲדוּ פַחַד לֹא־הָיָה פָחַד כִּי־אֱלֹהִים פִּזַּר עַצְמוֹת חֹנָךְ

ז הֱבִשֹׁתָה כִּי־אֱלֹהִים מְאָסָם: מִי יִתֵּן מִצִּיּוֹן יְשֻׁעוֹת יִשְׂרָאֵל בְּשׁוּב אֱלֹהִים

שְׁבוּת עַמּוֹ יָגֵל יַעֲקֹב יִשְׂמַח יִשְׂרָאֵל:

נד א־ב לַמְנַצֵּחַ בִּנְגִינֹת מַשְׂכִּיל לְדָוִד: בְּבוֹא הַזִּיפִים וַיֹּאמְרוּ לְשָׁאוּל הֲלֹא דָוִד

ג־ד מִסְתַּתֵּר עִמָּנוּ: אֱלֹהִים בְּשִׁמְךָ הוֹשִׁיעֵנִי וּבִגְבוּרָתְךָ תְדִינֵנִי: אֱלֹהִים

ה שְׁמַע תְּפִלָּתִי הַאֲזִינָה לְאִמְרֵי־פִי: כִּי זָרִים ׀ קָמוּ עָלַי וְעָרִיצִים בִּקְשׁוּ

ו נַפְשִׁי לֹא שָׂמוּ אֱלֹהִים לְנֶגְדָּם סֶלָה: הִנֵּה אֱלֹהִים עֹזֵר לִי אֲדֹנָי בְּסֹמְכֵי

ז־ח נַפְשִׁי: °יָשׁוּב [יָשִׁיב ק׳] הָרַע לְשֹׁרְרָי בַּאֲמִתְּךָ הַצְמִיתֵם: בִּנְדָבָה

ט אֶזְבְּחָה־לָּךְ אוֹדֶה שִּׁמְךָ יְהֹוָה כִּי־טוֹב: כִּי מִכָּל־צָרָה הִצִּילָנִי וּבְאֹיְבַי

רָאֲתָה עֵינִי:

51:10. *Fear of Your Divine retribution caused my body to deteriorate (Radak).*

52:2. See *I Samuel* Chs. 21-22.

52:4. Like a sharp, "deceptive" razor, an evil tongue cuts far deeper than originally intended.

53:1. *The machalas* is a musical instrument. Alternatively, it means "*affliction*." This psalm discusses the affliction that will be brought about by the Temple's destruction (*Rashi*).

54:2. See *I Samuel* 23:19-29.

and I shall be whiter than snow. [10] Make me hear joy and gladness, may the bones that You crushed* exult. [11] Hide Your face from my sins, and erase all my iniquities. [12] Create a pure heart for me, O God, and a steadfast spirit renew within me. [13] Cast me not away from Your Presence, and take not Your Holy Spirit from me. [14] Restore to me the joy of Your salvation, and with a generous spirit sustain me. [15] I will teach transgressors Your ways, and sinners will return to You. [16] Rescue me from blood-guilt, O God, God of my salvation, let my tongue sing joyously of Your righteousness. [17] O Lord, open my lips, that my mouth may declare Your praise. [18] For You do not desire a sacrifice, else I would give it; a burnt-offering You do not want. [19] The sacrifices God desires are a broken spirit; a heart broken and humbled, O God, You will not despise. [20] Do good in Your favor unto Zion; build the walls of Jerusalem. [21] Then You will desire the offerings of righteousness, burnt-offering, and whole offering; then will bulls go up upon Your altar.

52

Doeg's fate exemplifies the tragedy that results when one turns one's talents to evil.

[1] For the conductor, a maskil by David. [2] When Doeg the Edomite* came and informed Saul, and said to him, "David came to the house of Ahimelech." [3] Why do you pride yourself with evil, O mighty warrior? The kindness of God is all day long. [4] Your tongue devises treachery, like a sharpened razor* that works deceit. [5] You loved evil more than good, falsehood more than speaking righteousness, Selah. [6] You have loved all devouring words, a tongue of deceit. [7] Likewise, God will shatter you for eternity; He will break you and tear you from the tent, and uproot you from the land of life, Selah. [8] The righteous will see and be awed, and they will laugh at him: [9] "Behold, the man who did not make God his stronghold; but he trusted in his abundance of wealth, he drew strength from his treachery." [10] But I am like an ever-fresh olive tree in the House of God, I trust in the kindness of God forever and ever. [11] I will thank You forever because You have done [it], and in the presence of Your devout ones I will hope to Your Name, for it is good.

53

Alluding prophetically to the destruction of the land and the Temple, this psalm also assures Israel's eventual restoration.

[1] For the conductor on the machalas, * a maskil by David. [2] The degraded one says in his heart, "There is no God!" They have acted corruptly and despicably [with] iniquity; there is no doer of good. [3] From heaven God gazed down upon mankind, to see if there exists a reflective person who seeks out God. [4] Everyone is dross, together they have become depraved; there is no doer of good, there is not even one. [5] Do they not realize — those evildoers who devour my people as they would devour bread, who do not call upon God — [6] [that] there they will be stricken with terror, a terror such as never was; for God scatters the bones of those encamped against you? You shamed [them], for God has rejected them. [7] O, that out of Zion would come Israel's salvations! When God restores the captivity of His people, Jacob will exult, Israel will be glad.

54

Pursued by foes, one must pray for God's salvation.

[1] For the conductor with the neginos, a maskil by David. [2] When the Ziphites* came and said to Saul, "Is not David in hiding among us?" [3] O God, by Your Name save me, and by Your might vindicate me. [4] O God, hear my prayer, give ear to the utterances of my mouth. [5] For strangers have risen up against me and oppressors have sought my soul, they have not set God before themselves, Selah. [6] Behold! God is my Helper, the Lord is with the supporters of my soul. [7] May He repay the evil to my watchful enemies, in Your truth cut them down! [8] With a free-will offering I will sacrifice to You; I will thank Your Name, HASHEM, for it is good. [9] For from every distress He has rescued me, and upon my foes my eye has looked.

א-ב לַמְנַצֵּחַ בִּנְגִינֹת מַשְׂכִּיל לְדָוִד: הַאֲזִינָה אֱלֹהִים תְּפִלָּתִי וְאַל־תִּתְעַלַּם

ג-ד מִתְּחִנָּתִי: הַקְשִׁיבָה לִּי וַעֲנֵנִי אָרִיד בְּשִׂיחִי וְאָהִימָה: מִקּוֹל אוֹיֵב מִפְּנֵי

ה עָקַת רָשָׁע כִּי־יָמִיטוּ עָלַי אָוֶן וּבְאַף יִשְׂטְמוּנִי: לִבִּי יָחִיל בְּקִרְבִּי וְאֵימוֹת

ו-ז מָוֶת נָפְלוּ עָלָי: יִרְאָה וָרַעַד יָבֹא בִי וַתְּכַסֵּנִי פַּלָּצוּת: וָאֹמַר מִי־יִתֶּן־לִי

ח אֵבֶר כַּיּוֹנָה אָעוּפָה וְאֶשְׁכֹּנָה: הִנֵּה אַרְחִיק נְדֹד אָלִין בַּמִּדְבָּר סֶלָה:

ט אָחִישָׁה מִפְלָט לִי מֵרוּחַ סֹעָה מִסָּעַר: בַּלַּע אֲדֹנָי פַּלַּג לְשׁוֹנָם כִּי־רָאִיתִי

י חָמָס וְרִיב בָּעִיר: יוֹמָם וָלַיְלָה יְסוֹבְבֻהָ עַל־חוֹמֹתֶיהָ וְאָוֶן וְעָמָל בְּקִרְבָּהּ:

יא-יג הַוּוֹת בְּקִרְבָּהּ וְלֹא־יָמִישׁ מֵרְחֹבָהּ תֹּךְ וּמִרְמָה: כִּי לֹא־אוֹיֵב יְחָרְפֵנִי

יד וְאֶשָּׂא לֹא־מְשַׂנְאִי עָלַי הִגְדִּיל וְאֶסָּתֵר מִמֶּנּוּ: וְאַתָּה אֱנוֹשׁ כְּעֶרְכִּי אַלּוּפִי

טו-טז וּמְיֻדָּעִי: אֲשֶׁר יַחְדָּו נַמְתִּיק סוֹד בְּבֵית אֱלֹהִים נְהַלֵּךְ בְּרָגֶשׁ: °יַשִּׁימוֹת

[°יַשִּׁי מָוֶת ק] | עָלֵימוֹ יֵרְדוּ שְׁאוֹל חַיִּים כִּי־רָעוֹת בִּמְגוּרָם בְּקִרְבָּם:

יז-יח אֲנִי אֶל־אֱלֹהִים אֶקְרָא וַיהוה יוֹשִׁיעֵנִי: עֶרֶב וָבֹקֶר וְצָהֳרַיִם אָשִׂיחָה

יט וְאֶהֱמֶה וַיִּשְׁמַע קוֹלִי: פָּדָה בְשָׁלוֹם נַפְשִׁי מִקְּרָב־לִי כִּי־בְרַבִּים הָיוּ עִמָּדִי:

כ יִשְׁמַע | אֵל | וְיַעֲנֵם וְיֹשֵׁב קֶדֶם סֶלָה אֲשֶׁר אֵין חֲלִיפוֹת לָמוֹ וְלֹא יָרְאוּ

כא-כב אֱלֹהִים: שָׁלַח יָדָיו בִּשְׁלֹמָיו חִלֵּל בְּרִיתוֹ: חָלְקוּ | מַחְמָאֹת פִּיו וּקֲרָב־לִבּוֹ

כג רַכּוּ דְבָרָיו מִשֶּׁמֶן וְהֵמָּה פְתִחוֹת: הַשְׁלֵךְ עַל־יהוה | יְהָבְךָ וְהוּא יְכַלְכְּלֶךָ

כד לֹא־יִתֵּן לְעוֹלָם מוֹט לַצַּדִּיק: וְאַתָּה אֱלֹהִים | תּוֹרִדֵם | לִבְאֵר שַׁחַת אַנְשֵׁי

דָמִים וּמִרְמָה לֹא־יֶחֱצוּ יְמֵיהֶם וַאֲנִי אֶבְטַח־בָּךְ:

א לַמְנַצֵּחַ | עַל־יוֹנַת אֵלֶם רְחֹקִים לְדָוִד מִכְתָּם בֶּאֱחֹז אֹתוֹ פְלִשְׁתִּים בְּגַת:

ב-ג חָנֵּנִי אֱלֹהִים כִּי־שְׁאָפַנִי אֱנוֹשׁ כָּל־הַיּוֹם לֹחֵם יִלְחָצֵנִי: שָׁאֲפוּ שׁוֹרְרַי כָּל־

ד-ה הַיּוֹם כִּי־רַבִּים לֹחֲמִים לִי מָרוֹם: יוֹם אִירָא אֲנִי אֵלֶיךָ אֶבְטָח: בֵּאלֹהִים

ו אֲהַלֵּל דְּבָרוֹ בֵּאלֹהִים בָּטַחְתִּי לֹא אִירָא מַה־יַּעֲשֶׂה בָשָׂר לִי: כָּל־הַיּוֹם

ז דְּבָרַי יְעַצֵּבוּ עָלַי כָּל־מַחְשְׁבֹתָם לָרָע: יָגוּרוּ | °יצפינו [°יִצְפּוֹנוּ ק] הֵמָּה

ח עֲקֵבַי יִשְׁמֹרוּ כַּאֲשֶׁר קִוּוּ נַפְשִׁי: עַל־אָוֶן פַּלֶּט־לָמוֹ בְּאַף עַמִּים | הוֹרֵד

ט אֱלֹהִים: נֹדִי סָפַרְתָּה אָתָּה שִׂימָה דִמְעָתִי בְנֹאדֶךָ הֲלֹא בְּסִפְרָתֶךָ: אָז

י יָשׁוּבוּ אוֹיְבַי אָחוֹר בְּיוֹם אֶקְרָא זֶה־יָדַעְתִּי כִּי־אֱלֹהִים לִי: בֵּאלֹהִים

יא-יב אֲהַלֵּל דָּבָר בַּיהוה אֲהַלֵּל דָּבָר: בֵּאלֹהִים בָּטַחְתִּי לֹא אִירָא מַה־יַּעֲשֶׂה

יג אָדָם לִי: עָלַי אֱלֹהִים נְדָרֶיךָ אֲשַׁלֵּם תּוֹדֹת לָךְ: כִּי הִצַּלְתָּ נַפְשִׁי מִמָּוֶת

יד הֲלֹא רַגְלַי מִדֶּחִי לְהִתְהַלֵּךְ לִפְנֵי אֱלֹהִים בְּאוֹר הַחַיִּים:

55:7. David is overcome by a desire to flee the company of men and dwell in isolation (*R' Hirsch*).

55:11. Violence and strife.

55:14-15. David speaks of Ahithophel, who had been his friend and adviser, and then betrayed him.

55:16. Ahithophel and his cohorts.

55:20. They persist in their evil ways, and never repent and return to God (*Meiri*).

55:21. The treacherous Ahithophel (*Rashi*).

56:1. "The distant dove of silence" is David himself, who was then far from his land, defenseless before his Philistine captors like a silent dove [see *I Samuel* 21:11-16] (*Rashi*).

56:8. Until now, they have escaped the consequences of their iniquity. Therefore, I implore You now, O God, to cast them down (*Meiri*).

55

Despite the revolt of his son Absalom and the defection of his intimate friend and adviser Ahithophel, David was unwavering in his faith that God would enable him to prevail.

¹ For the conductor with the neginos, a maskil by David. ² Listen, O God, to my prayer, do not disregard my pleas. ³ Pay heed to me and answer me; I lament as I speak, and I moan; ⁴ because of the shout of the foe, on account of the oppression of the wicked; for they accuse me of evil and hate me with passion. ⁵ My heart shudders within me, and the terrors of death have befallen me. ⁶ Fear and trembling penetrate me, and I am overcome with horror. ⁷ Then I said, "O that I had a wing like the dove! I would fly off and find rest!* ⁸ Behold! I would wander afar; I would dwell in the wilderness, Selah. ⁹ I would speedily obtain deliverance for myself from violent wind, from tempest." ¹⁰ Consume, O Lord, and confuse their tongue; for I have seen violence and strife in the city. ¹¹ Day and night they* encircle it upon its walls; iniquity and mischief are within it. ¹² Treachery is within it; never leaving its square are fraud and deception. ¹³ For it is not my foe who reviles me, that I could endure; it is not my enemy who has magnified himself against me that I could hide from him. ¹⁴ But it is you,* a man of my measure, my guide, and my intimate friend; ¹⁵ together we would take sweet counsel; in the House of God we would walk in company. ¹⁶ May He incite death against them,* may they descend to the grave alive; for evil is in their dwelling, within them. ¹⁷ As for me, I shall call unto God, and HASHEM will save me. ¹⁸ Evening, morning, and noon, I supplicate and moan; and He has heard my voice. ¹⁹ He redeemed my soul in peace from battles against me, for with many they were against me. ²⁰ May God hear and humble them — He Who is enthroned from days of old, Selah — those in whom there is no change* and they fear not God. ²¹ He* stretched out his hands against those who were at peace with him, he profaned his covenant. ²² Smooth were the buttery words of his mouth, but his heart was at war; his words were softer than oil, yet they were curses. ²³ Cast upon HASHEM your burden and He will sustain you; He will never allow the faltering of the righteous. ²⁴ And You, O God, You will lower them into the well of destruction, men of bloodshed and deceit shall not live out half their days; but as for me, I will trust in You.

56

Though his situation seemed hopeless, David's trust in God was unshaken, an attitude to be emulated by anyone in distress.

¹ For the conductor, regarding the distant dove of silence,* by David, a michtam, when the Philistines seized him in Gath. ² Show me favor, O God, for men yearn to swallow me; all the day, warlike, they oppress me. ³ Each day my watchful foes yearn to swallow [me], for many battle me, O Most High! ⁴ On the day that I fear, I trust in You. ⁵ In God — I will praise His word — in God I have trusted, I shall not fear; what can mortal flesh do to me? ⁶ All the day they make my words sorrowful; about me all their thoughts are for evil. ⁷ They assemble, they lie in ambush, they watch my every step, as they anticipate my life. ⁸ Despite iniquity, escape has been theirs; cast the peoples down in anger, O God!* ⁹ You Yourself have counted my wanderings; place my tears in Your flask, are they not in Your record? ¹⁰ Then my foes will retreat on the day I cry out; this I know: that God is with me. ¹¹ In God — I will praise the Word; in HASHEM — I will praise the Word. ¹² In God I have trusted, I shall not fear; what can man do to me? ¹³ Upon me, O God, are [my] vows unto You; I shall render thanksgiving offerings to You. ¹⁴ For You rescued my soul from death, even my feet from stumbling; to walk before God in the light of life.

נז

א-ב לַמְנַצֵּחַ אַל־תַּשְׁחֵת לְדָוִד מִכְתָּם בְּבָרְחוֹ מִפְּנֵי־שָׁאוּל בַּמְּעָרָה: חָנֵּנִי
אֱלֹהִים ׀ חָנֵּנִי כִּי בְךָ חָסָיָה נַפְשִׁי וּבְצֵל־כְּנָפֶיךָ אֶחְסֶה עַד יַעֲבֹר הַוּוֹת:
ג-ד אֶקְרָא לֵאלֹהִים עֶלְיוֹן לָאֵל גֹּמֵר עָלָי: יִשְׁלַח מִשָּׁמַיִם ׀ וְיוֹשִׁיעֵנִי חֵרֵף
ה שֹׁאֲפִי סֶלָה יִשְׁלַח אֱלֹהִים חַסְדּוֹ וַאֲמִתּוֹ: נַפְשִׁי ׀ בְּתוֹךְ לְבָאִם אֶשְׁכְּבָה
ו לֹהֲטִים בְּנֵי־אָדָם שִׁנֵּיהֶם חֲנִית וְחִצִּים וּלְשׁוֹנָם חֶרֶב חַדָּה: רוּמָה עַל־
ז הַשָּׁמַיִם אֱלֹהִים עַל כָּל־הָאָרֶץ כְּבוֹדֶךָ: רֶשֶׁת ׀ הֵכִינוּ לִפְעָמַי כָּפַף נַפְשִׁי
ח כָּרוּ לְפָנַי שִׁיחָה נָפְלוּ בְתוֹכָהּ סֶלָה: נָכוֹן לִבִּי אֱלֹהִים נָכוֹן לִבִּי אָשִׁירָה
ט-י וַאֲזַמֵּרָה: עוּרָה כְבוֹדִי עוּרָה הַנֵּבֶל וְכִנּוֹר אָעִירָה שָּׁחַר: אוֹדְךָ בָעַמִּים ׀
יא אֲדֹנָי אֲזַמֶּרְךָ בַּלְאֻמִּים: כִּי־גָדֹל עַד־שָׁמַיִם חַסְדֶּךָ וְעַד־שְׁחָקִים אֲמִתֶּךָ:
יב רוּמָה עַל־שָׁמַיִם אֱלֹהִים עַל כָּל־הָאָרֶץ כְּבוֹדֶךָ:

נח

א-ב לַמְנַצֵּחַ אַל־תַּשְׁחֵת לְדָוִד מִכְתָּם: הַאֻמְנָם אֵלֶם צֶדֶק תְּדַבֵּרוּן מֵישָׁרִים
ג תִּשְׁפְּטוּ בְּנֵי אָדָם: אַף־בְּלֵב עוֹלֹת תִּפְעָלוּן בָּאָרֶץ חֲמַס יְדֵיכֶם תְּפַלֵּסוּן:
ד-ה זֹרוּ רְשָׁעִים מֵרָחֶם תָּעוּ מִבֶּטֶן דֹּבְרֵי כָזָב: חֲמַת־לָמוֹ כִּדְמוּת חֲמַת־נָחָשׁ
ו כְּמוֹ־פֶתֶן חֵרֵשׁ יַאְטֵם אָזְנוֹ: אֲשֶׁר לֹא־יִשְׁמַע לְקוֹל מְלַחֲשִׁים חוֹבֵר
ז חֲבָרִים מְחֻכָּם: אֱלֹהִים הֲרָס־שִׁנֵּימוֹ בְּפִימוֹ מַלְתְּעוֹת כְּפִירִים נְתֹץ ׀
ח-ט יְהוָה: יִמָּאֲסוּ כְמוֹ־מַיִם יִתְהַלְּכוּ־לָמוֹ יִדְרֹךְ חִצּוֹ כְּמוֹ יִתְמֹלָלוּ: כְּמוֹ
י שַׁבְּלוּל תֶּמֶס יַהֲלֹךְ נֵפֶל אֵשֶׁת בַּל־חָזוּ שָׁמֶשׁ: בְּטֶרֶם ׀ יָבִינוּ סִּירֹתֵיכֶם
יא אָטָד כְּמוֹ־חַי כְּמוֹ־חָרוֹן יִשְׂעָרֶנּוּ: יִשְׂמַח צַדִּיק כִּי־חָזָה נָקָם פְּעָמָיו
יב יִרְחַץ בְּדַם הָרָשָׁע: וְיֹאמַר אָדָם אַךְ־פְּרִי לַצַּדִּיק אַךְ יֵשׁ־אֱלֹהִים שֹׁפְטִים
בָּאָרֶץ:

נט

א לַמְנַצֵּחַ אַל־תַּשְׁחֵת לְדָוִד מִכְתָּם בִּשְׁלֹחַ שָׁאוּל וַיִּשְׁמְרוּ אֶת־הַבַּיִת
ב-ג לַהֲמִיתוֹ: הַצִּילֵנִי מֵאֹיְבַי ׀ אֱלֹהָי מִמִּתְקוֹמְמַי תְּשַׂגְּבֵנִי: הַצִּילֵנִי מִפֹּעֲלֵי אָוֶן
ד וּמֵאַנְשֵׁי דָמִים הוֹשִׁיעֵנִי: כִּי הִנֵּה אָרְבוּ לְנַפְשִׁי יָגוּרוּ עָלַי עַזִּים לֹא־פִשְׁעִי
ה-ו וְלֹא־חַטָּאתִי יְהוָה: בְּלִי־עָוֹן יְרֻצוּן וְיִכּוֹנָנוּ עוּרָה לִקְרָאתִי וּרְאֵה: וְאַתָּה
יְהוָה־אֱלֹהִים ׀ צְבָאוֹת אֱלֹהֵי יִשְׂרָאֵל הָקִיצָה לִפְקֹד כָּל־הַגּוֹיִם אַל־תָּחֹן
ז-ח כָּל־בֹּגְדֵי אָוֶן סֶלָה: יָשׁוּבוּ לָעֶרֶב יֶהֱמוּ כַכָּלֶב וִיסוֹבְבוּ עִיר: הִנֵּה ׀ יַבִּיעוּן
ט בְּפִיהֶם חֲרָבוֹת בְּשִׂפְתוֹתֵיהֶם כִּי־מִי שֹׁמֵעַ: וְאַתָּה יְהוָה תִּשְׂחַק־לָמוֹ
י-יא תִּלְעַג לְכָל־גּוֹיִם: עֻזּוֹ אֵלֶיךָ אֶשְׁמֹרָה כִּי־אֱלֹהִים מִשְׂגַּבִּי: אֱלֹהֵי °חסדו
יב [°חַסְדִּי ק] יְקַדְּמֵנִי אֱלֹהִים יַרְאֵנִי בְשֹׁרְרָי: אַל־תַּהַרְגֵם ׀ פֶּן־יִשְׁכְּחוּ עַמִּי

57:1. See I Samuel Chapter 24.

57:7. David sees prophetically that his enemies will be
ensnared in their own traps (Radak).

58:1. See I Samuel Chapter 26.

58:3. Not only do you not defend me, you even devise
schemes against me (Rashi; Metzudos).

59:1. See I Samuel 19:11-18.

59:5. I have never harmed them; they have no reason to

hate me (Rashi).

59:6. David prays not only for himself, but for all
persecuted people.

59:7. They slander me by day and "return at evening" to
keep watch on my house, to prevent my escape (Rashi).

59:8. They do not fear Divine retribution for their slander.

59:10. Saul's power.

57

Hotly
pursued,
his life
in dire peril,
David affirms
his absolute
faith in God.

¹ For the conductor, a plea to be spared from destruction, by David, a mich-tam, when he fled from Saul, in the cave. * ² Favor me, O God, favor me, for in You has my soul taken refuge; and in the shelter of Your wings I shall take refuge until devastation shall pass. ³ I will call upon God, Most High, to the God Who fulfills for me. ⁴ He will dispatch from heaven and save me from the disgrace of the one who yearns to swallow me, Selah; God will dispatch His mercy and His truth. ⁵ My soul is among lions, I lie with men who are aflame; people whose teeth are spears and arrows, and whose tongue is a sharp sword. ⁶ Be exalted above the heavens, O God, above all the earth be Your glory. ⁷ They prepared a snare for my footsteps, my soul is bent over; they dug a pit before me; they fell into it, * Selah. ⁸ My heart is steadfast, O God, my heart is steadfast; I will sing and I will make music. ⁹ Awake, my soul, awake, O psalter and harp, I shall awaken the dawn. ¹⁰ I will thank You among the peoples, O Lord; I will sing to You among the regimes. ¹¹ For great until the very heavens is Your kindness, and until the upper heights is Your truth. ¹² Be exalted above the heavens, O God; above all the earth be Your glory.

58

A prayer
for the
destruction
of the violent
oppressors in
order that all
may say,
"God is the
true judge in
the land"

¹ For the conductor, a plea to be spared from destruction, * by David, a michtam. ² Is there indeed silence when you should be speaking righteous-ness? When you should be judging people with fairness? ³ Even in [your] heart you do wrongs, * you weigh out the violence of your hands in the land. ⁴ The wicked are estranged from the womb, the speakers of falsehood went astray from birth. ⁵ They have venom like the venom of a snake, like a deaf viper that closes its ear; ⁶ so as not to hearken to the voice of charmers, of the most skillful caster of spells. ⁷ O God, smash their teeth in their mouth; shatter the molars of the young lions, O HASHEM. ⁸ May they melt like water that flows away; when each one draws his arrows, may they be as if crumbled to pieces. ⁹ Like the snail that melts and slithers away; [like] a stillbirth or a mole, who did not see the sun. ¹⁰ Before your tender briars develop into hardened thorns, with vigor, with wrath, He will stormily sweep them away. ¹¹ The righteous one will rejoice when he sees vengeance, he shall bathe his feet in the blood of the wicked one. ¹² And mankind shall say, "There is, indeed, fruit for the righteous; there is, indeed, a God Who judges in the land."

59

Surrounded
by Saul's
men who
were ordered
to murder
him, David
prays that
God rescue
him, so that
he may sing
His praises.

¹ For the conductor, a plea to be spared from destruction, by David, a michtam; when Saul dispatched, and they guarded the house to kill him. * ² Rescue me from my foes, O my God; over those who rise against me raise me high. ³ Rescue me from evildoers; and from bloodthirsty men save me. ⁴ For behold, they lie in ambush for my soul, brazen ones gather around me — not for my transgression and not for my sin, O HASHEM! ⁵ Without iniquity, * they run and prepare. Awaken [Yourself] towards me and see. ⁶ And You, HASHEM, God, Master of Legions, God of Israel, arouse Yourself to remember all the nations, * do not show favor to any faithless men of violence, Selah. ⁷ They return towards evening, * they howl like the dog, and they go round about the city. ⁸ Behold, they spew with their mouths, swords are in their lips; for [they say], "Who listens?" * ⁹ But You, HASHEM — You will laugh at them, You will mock all nations. ¹⁰ [In the face of] his * power, for You do I wait; for God is my stronghold. ¹¹ The God of my kindness will anticipate me; God will show me [what will befall] my watchful foes. ¹² Do not slay them, lest my people forget;

יג הַנִיעֵמוֹ בְחֵילְךָ וְהוֹרִידֵמוֹ מָגִנֵּנוּ אֲדֹנָי: חַטַּאת־פִּימוֹ דְּבַר־שְׂפָתֵימוֹ
יד וְיִלָּכְדוּ בִגְאוֹנָם וּמֵאָלָה וּמִכַּחַשׁ יְסַפֵּרוּ: כַּלֵּה בְחֵמָה כַּלֵּה וְאֵינֵמוֹ וְיֵדְעוּ
טו כִּי־אֱלֹהִים מֹשֵׁל בְּיַעֲקֹב לְאַפְסֵי הָאָרֶץ סֶלָה: וְיָשׁוּבוּ לָעֶרֶב יֶהֱמוּ כַכָּלֶב
טז וִיסוֹבְבוּ עִיר: הֵמָּה °יְנִיעוּן [יְנִיעוֹן ק] לֶאֱכֹל אִם־לֹא יִשְׂבְּעוּ וַיָּלִינוּ:
יז וַאֲנִי ׀ אָשִׁיר עֻזֶּךָ וַאֲרַנֵּן לַבֹּקֶר חַסְדֶּךָ כִּי־הָיִיתָ מִשְׂגָּב לִי וּמָנוֹס בְּיוֹם צַר־
יח לִי: עֻזִּי אֵלֶיךָ אֲזַמֵּרָה כִּי־אֱלֹהִים מִשְׂגַּבִּי אֱלֹהֵי חַסְדִּי:

ס
יום יא לחדש
א־ב לַמְנַצֵּחַ עַל־שׁוּשַׁן עֵדוּת מִכְתָּם לְדָוִד לְלַמֵּד: בְּהַצּוֹתוֹ ׀ אֶת אֲרַם נַהֲרַיִם
וְאֶת־אֲרַם צוֹבָה וַיָּשָׁב יוֹאָב וַיַּךְ אֶת־אֱדוֹם בְּגֵיא־מֶלַח שְׁנֵים עָשָׂר אָלֶף:
ג אֱלֹהִים זְנַחְתָּנוּ פְרַצְתָּנוּ אָנַפְתָּ תְּשׁוֹבֵב לָנוּ: הִרְעַשְׁתָּה אֶרֶץ פְּצַמְתָּהּ
ד־ה רְפָה שְׁבָרֶיהָ כִי־מָטָה: הִרְאִיתָה עַמְּךָ קָשָׁה הִשְׁקִיתָנוּ יַיִן תַּרְעֵלָה: נָתַתָּה
ו־ז לִּירֵאֶיךָ נֵּס לְהִתְנוֹסֵס מִפְּנֵי קֹשֶׁט סֶלָה: לְמַעַן יֵחָלְצוּן יְדִידֶיךָ הוֹשִׁיעָה
ח יְמִינְךָ °וַעֲנֵנוּ [וַעֲנֵנִי ק]: אֱלֹהִים ׀ דִּבֶּר בְּקָדְשׁוֹ אֶעְלֹזָה אֲחַלְּקָה שְׁכֶם
ט וְעֵמֶק סֻכּוֹת אֲמַדֵּד: לִי גִלְעָד ׀ וְלִי מְנַשֶּׁה וְאֶפְרַיִם מָעוֹז רֹאשִׁי יְהוּדָה
י מְחֹקְקִי: מוֹאָב ׀ סִיר רַחְצִי עַל־אֱדוֹם אַשְׁלִיךְ נַעֲלִי עָלַי פְּלֶשֶׁת הִתְרוֹעָעִי:
יא־יב מִי יֹבִלֵנִי עִיר מָצוֹר מִי נָחַנִי עַד־אֱדוֹם: הֲלֹא־אַתָּה אֱלֹהִים זְנַחְתָּנוּ וְלֹא־
יג תֵצֵא אֱלֹהִים בְּצִבְאוֹתֵינוּ: הָבָה־לָּנוּ עֶזְרָת מִצָּר וְשָׁוְא תְּשׁוּעַת אָדָם:
יד בֵּאלֹהִים נַעֲשֶׂה־חָיִל וְהוּא יָבוּס צָרֵינוּ:

סא
א־ב לַמְנַצֵּחַ ׀ עַל־נְגִינַת לְדָוִד: שִׁמְעָה אֱלֹהִים רִנָּתִי הַקְשִׁיבָה תְּפִלָּתִי: מִקְצֵה
ד הָאָרֶץ ׀ אֵלֶיךָ אֶקְרָא בַּעֲטֹף לִבִּי בְּצוּר־יָרוּם מִמֶּנִּי תַנְחֵנִי: כִּי־הָיִיתָ
ה מַחְסֶה לִי מִגְדַּל־עֹז מִפְּנֵי אוֹיֵב: אָגוּרָה בְאָהָלְךָ עוֹלָמִים אֶחֱסֶה בְסֵתֶר
ו־ז כְּנָפֶיךָ סֶּלָה: כִּי־אַתָּה אֱלֹהִים שָׁמַעְתָּ לִנְדָרָי נָתַתָּ יְרֻשַּׁת יִרְאֵי שְׁמֶךָ: יָמִים
ח עַל־יְמֵי־מֶלֶךְ תּוֹסִיף שְׁנוֹתָיו כְּמוֹ־דֹר וָדֹר: יֵשֵׁב עוֹלָם לִפְנֵי אֱלֹהִים חֶסֶד
ט וֶאֱמֶת מַן יִנְצְרֻהוּ: כֵּן אֲזַמְּרָה שִׁמְךָ לָעַד לְשַׁלְּמִי נְדָרַי יוֹם ׀ יוֹם:

סב
א־ב לַמְנַצֵּחַ עַל־יְדוּתוּן מִזְמוֹר לְדָוִד: אַךְ אֶל־אֱלֹהִים דּוּמִיָּה נַפְשִׁי מִמֶּנּוּ
ג־ד יְשׁוּעָתִי: אַךְ־הוּא צוּרִי וִישׁוּעָתִי מִשְׂגַּבִּי לֹא־אֶמּוֹט רַבָּה: עַד־
ה אָנָה ׀ תְּהוֹתְתוּ עַל־אִישׁ תְּרָצְּחוּ כֻלְּכֶם כְּקִיר נָטוּי גָּדֵר הַדְּחוּיָה: אַךְ
מִשְּׂאֵתוֹ ׀ יָעֲצוּ לְהַדִּיחַ יִרְצוּ כָזָב בְּפִיו יְבָרֵכוּ וּבְקִרְבָּם יְקַלְלוּ־סֶלָה:
ו־ז אַךְ לֵאלֹהִים דּוֹמִּי נַפְשִׁי כִּי־מִמֶּנּוּ תִּקְוָתִי: אַךְ־הוּא צוּרִי וִישׁוּעָתִי
ח מִשְׂגַּבִּי לֹא אֶמּוֹט: עַל־אֱלֹהִים יִשְׁעִי וּכְבוֹדִי צוּר־עֻזִּי מַחְסִי בֵּאלֹהִים:

59:12. If You kill them, the example will soon be forgotten. Instead, make them beg for their food, so that they will be constant reminders of Your punishment.

59:15. May they return from their day's labor hungry and empty-handed and need to "go around the city" seeking food. Their punishment is measure for measure for their offense related to verse 7 (*Meiri*).

60:1. A musical instrument (*Ibn Ezra*).

60:2. Joab left his campaign against Aram to attack Edom, which was en route to assist Aram, and killed twelve thousand of the enemy (*Metzudos*; see *Radak*).

61:1. A musical instrument.

61:6. In his distress, David vowed even greater devotion to God if He should save him from danger and return him safely to the Holy Land.

by Your might make them wander and cast them down, * O our Shield, O Lord — ¹³ because of the sin of their mouth, the word of their lips; and may they be ensnared by their own arrogance; and because of the curse and falsehood that they recount. ¹⁴ Destroy in wrath, destroy until they are no more! And then [men] shall know that God rules in Jacob, to the ends of the earth, Selah. ¹⁵ May they return towards evening, and howl like the dog, going around the city. * ¹⁶ They will wander about to eat, without being sated they will sleep. ¹⁷ But I will sing of Your might, and rejoice towards morning in Your kindness; for You have been a stronghold to me, and a refuge in the day of my distress. ¹⁸ My Power, to You shall I sing; for God is my stronghold, the God of my kindness.

60

At the outset of his campaign against Israel's enemies, David expresses his faith in God's assurance that his reign would be consolidated from within and feared from without.

¹ For the conductor, on the shushan eidus, * a michtam by David, to instruct. ² When he made war against Aram-naharaim and Aram-tzobah, and Joab returned and smote Edom* in the Valley of Salt, twelve thousand [men]. ³ O God, You forsook us, You breached us, You were angry with us, O restore us! ⁴ You have made the land quake, You have cleft it; heal its fragments, for it totters. ⁵ You have shown Your nation harshness, You made us drink wine of bewilderment. ⁶ To those who fear You, You gave a banner to be raised high, for truth's sake, Selah! ⁷ So that Your beloved ones may be released — save with Your right hand and answer me. ⁸ God spoke through His holy one so that I would exult; I would divide Shechem and measure out the Valley of Succoth. ⁹ Mine is Gilead, and mine is Manasseh, and Ephraim is the stronghold of my head; Judah is my lawgiver. ¹⁰ Moab is my washbasin; upon Edom will I cast my shoe; Philistia, will you shout triumphantly over me? ¹¹ Who will bring me to the fortified city? Who has led me unto Edom? ¹² Is it not You, O God, Who has [until now] forsaken us, and You do not go forth, O God, with our legions? ¹³ Give us help against the oppressor; human salvation is futile. ¹⁴ Through God we shall act valiantly, and He will trample our oppressors.

61

David's personal experiences while fleeing into exile from his enemies parallel Israel's national experience.

¹ For the conductor, on the neginas, by David. ² Hear, O God, my cry, listen to my prayer. ³ From the end of the land I call unto You, when my heart grows faint. Lead me to a rock that is too high for me [to climb alone]. ⁴ For You have been a refuge for me, a tower of strength in the face of the enemy. ⁵ May I dwell in Your tent forever, may I take refuge in the shelter of Your wings, Selah. ⁶ For You, O God, have heard my vows, * You have granted the inheritance of those who fear Your Name. ⁷ May You add days onto the days of the king, may his years be like all generations. ⁸ May he sit forever before God; appoint kindness and truth, that they may preserve him. ⁹ Thus shall I praise Your Name forever, to fulfill my vows day after day.

62

One must never allow the power and ill-gotten wealth of the oppressor to erode one's trust in God and faith in His justice.

¹ For the conductor, on Jeduthun, a song by David. ² For God alone my soul waits silently, from Him comes my salvation. ³ He alone is my Rock and my Salvation; my Stronghold, I shall not falter greatly. ⁴ Until when will you plot treacherously against a man?* May you all be slain — like a leaning wall, a toppled fence. ⁵ Only because of his loftiness have they plotted to topple [him], * they delight in deceit; with his mouth each one blesses, but inwardly they curse, Selah! ⁶ For God alone, wait silently, my soul, because my hope is from Him. ⁷ He alone is my Rock and my Salvation; my Stronghold, I shall not falter. ⁸ Upon God rests my salvation and my glory, the Rock of my strength, my Refuge, is in God.

62:4. The psalmist directly addresses the wicked, murderous schemers.

62:5. They plot against him because they fear that his rise to eminence will threaten their own position.

ט בִּטְח֬וּ ב֨וֹ בְכָל־עֵ֤ת ׀ עָ֗ם שִׁפְכֽוּ־לְפָנָ֥יו לְבַבְכֶ֑ם אֱלֹהִ֖ים מַחֲסֶה־לָּ֣נוּ סֶֽלָה:

י אַ֤ךְ ׀ הֶ֥בֶל בְּנֵֽי־אָדָם֮ כָּזָ֪ב בְּנֵ֫י־אִ֥ישׁ בְּמֹאזְנַ֥יִם לַעֲל֑וֹת הֵ֝֗מָּה מֵהֶ֥בֶל יָֽחַד:

יא אַל־תִּבְטְח֥וּ בְעֹשֶׁק֮ וּבְגָזֵ֪ל אַל־תֶּ֫הְבָּ֥לוּ חַ֤יִל ׀ כִּֽי־יָנ֑וּב אַל־תָּשִׁ֥יתוּ לֵֽב:

יב־יג אַחַ֤ת ׀ דִּבֶּ֬ר אֱלֹהִ֗ים שְׁתַּֽיִם־ז֥וּ שָׁמָ֑עְתִּי כִּ֥י עֹ֝֗ז לֵֽאלֹהִֽים: וּלְךָֽ־אֲדֹנָ֥י חָ֑סֶד כִּֽי־אַתָּ֨ה תְשַׁלֵּ֖ם לְאִ֣ישׁ כְּֽמַעֲשֵֽׂהוּ:

סג א־ב מִזְמ֥וֹר לְדָוִ֑ד בִּ֝הְיוֹת֗וֹ בְּמִדְבַּ֥ר יְהוּדָֽה: אֱלֹהִ֤ים ׀ אֵלִ֥י אַתָּ֗ה אֲֽשַׁחֲ֫רֶ֥ךָּ צָמְאָ֬ה

ג לְךָ֨ ׀ נַפְשִׁ֡י כָּמַ֬הּ לְךָ֣ בְשָׂרִ֑י בְּאֶֽרֶץ־צִיָּ֖ה וְעָיֵ֣ף בְּלִי־מָֽיִם: כֵּ֭ן בַּקֹּ֣דֶשׁ חֲזִיתִ֑יךָ

ד־ה לִרְא֥וֹת עֻ֝זְּךָ֗ וּכְבוֹדֶֽךָ: כִּי־ט֣וֹב חַ֭סְדְּךָ מֵֽחַיִּ֗ים שְׂפָתַ֥י יְשַׁבְּחֽוּנְךָ: כֵּ֭ן אֲבָרֶכְךָ֣

ו בְחַיָּ֑י בְּ֝שִׁמְךָ֗ אֶשָּׂ֥א כַפָּֽי: כְּמ֤וֹ חֵ֣לֶב וָ֭דֶשֶׁן תִּשְׂבַּ֣ע נַפְשִׁ֑י וְשִׂפְתֵ֥י רְ֝נָנ֗וֹת

ז־ח יְהַלֶּל־פִּֽי: אִם־זְכַרְתִּ֥יךָ עַל־יְצוּעָ֑י בְּ֝אַשְׁמֻר֗וֹת אֶהְגֶּה־בָּֽךְ: כִּֽי־הָיִ֣יתָ

ט עֶזְרָ֣תָה לִּ֑י וּבְצֵ֖ל כְּנָפֶ֣יךָ אֲרַנֵּֽן: דָּבְקָ֣ה נַפְשִׁ֣י אַחֲרֶ֑יךָ בִּ֝֗י תָּמְכָ֥ה יְמִינֶֽךָ:

י־יא וְהֵ֗מָּה לְ֭שׁוֹאָה יְבַקְשׁ֣וּ נַפְשִׁ֑י יָ֝בֹ֗אוּ בְּתַחְתִּיּ֥וֹת הָאָֽרֶץ: יַגִּירֻ֥הוּ עַל־יְדֵי־

יב חָ֑רֶב מְנָ֖ת שֻֽׁעָלִ֣ים יִהְיֽוּ: וְהַמֶּלֶךְ֮ יִשְׂמַ֪ח בֵּֽאלֹ֫הִ֥ים יִ֭תְהַלֵּל כָּל־הַנִּשְׁבָּ֣ע בּ֑וֹ כִּ֥י יִ֝סָּכֵ֗ר פִּ֣י דֽוֹבְרֵי־שָֽׁקֶר:

סד א־ב לַמְנַצֵּ֗חַ מִזְמ֥וֹר לְדָוִֽד: שְׁמַע־אֱלֹהִ֣ים קוֹלִ֣י בְשִׂיחִ֑י מִפַּ֥חַד א֝וֹיֵ֗ב תִּצֹּ֥ר חַיָּֽי:

ג־ד תַּ֭סְתִּירֵנִי מִסּ֣וֹד מְרֵעִ֑ים מֵ֝רִגְשַׁ֗ת פֹּ֣עֲלֵי אָֽוֶן: אֲשֶׁ֤ר שָׁנְנ֣וּ כַחֶ֣רֶב לְשׁוֹנָ֑ם

ה דָּרְכ֥וּ חִ֝צָּ֗ם דָּבָ֥ר מָֽר: לִיר֣וֹת בַּמִּסְתָּרִ֣ים תָּ֑ם פִּתְאֹ֥ם יֹ֝רֻ֗הוּ וְלֹ֣א יִירָֽאוּ:

ו יְחַזְּקוּ־לָ֨מוֹ ׀ דָּבָ֥ר רָ֗ע יְֽ֭סַפְּרוּ לִטְמ֣וֹן מוֹקְשִׁ֑ים אָ֝מְר֗וּ מִ֣י יִרְאֶה־לָּֽמוֹ:

ז־ח יַֽחְפְּֽשׂוּ־ע֗וֹלֹת תַּ֭מְנוּ חֵ֣פֶשׂ מְחֻפָּ֑שׂ וְקֶ֥רֶב אִ֝֗ישׁ וְלֵ֣ב עָמֹֽק: וַיֹּרֵ֗ם אֱלֹ֫הִ֥ים חֵ֥ץ

ט פִּתְא֑וֹם הָ֝י֗וּ מַכּוֹתָֽם: וַיַּכְשִׁיל֣וּהוּ עָלֵ֣ימוֹ לְשׁוֹנָ֑ם יִ֝תְנֹֽדֲד֗וּ כָּל־רֹ֥אֵה בָֽם:

י־יא וַיִּֽירְא֗וּ כָּל־אָ֫דָ֥ם וַ֭יַּגִּידוּ פֹּ֥עַל אֱלֹהִ֗ים וּֽמַעֲשֵׂ֥הוּ הִשְׂכִּֽילוּ: יִשְׂמַ֬ח צַדִּ֨יק

בַּיהֹוָה֮ וְחָ֪סָה ב֥וֹ וְ֝יִתְהַֽלְל֗וּ כָּל־יִשְׁרֵי־לֵֽב:

סה א־ב לַמְנַצֵּ֥חַ מִזְמ֗וֹר לְדָוִ֥ד שִֽׁיר: לְךָ֤ דֻֽמִיָּ֬ה תְהִלָּ֓ה אֱלֹ֘הִ֤ים בְּצִיּ֑וֹן וּ֝לְךָ֗ יְשֻׁלַּם־

ג־ד נֶֽדֶר: שֹׁמֵ֥עַ תְּפִלָּ֑ה עָ֝דֶ֗יךָ כָּל־בָּשָׂ֥ר יָבֹֽאוּ: דִּבְרֵ֣י עֲ֭וֺנֹת גָּ֣בְרוּ מֶ֑נִּי פְּ֝שָׁעֵ֗ינוּ

ה אַתָּ֥ה תְכַפְּרֵֽם: אַשְׁרֵ֤י ׀ תִּבְחַ֣ר וּתְקָרֵב֮ יִשְׁכֹּ֪ן חֲצֵ֫רֶ֥יךָ נִ֭שְׂבְּעָה בְּט֣וּב בֵּיתֶ֑ךָ

ו קְ֝דֹ֗שׁ הֵיכָלֶֽךָ: נֽוֹרָא֨וֹת ׀ בְּצֶ֡דֶק תַּעֲנֵנוּ֮ אֱלֹהֵ֪י יִשְׁ֫עֵ֥נוּ מִבְטָ֥ח כָּל־קַצְוֵי־אֶ֑רֶץ

ז־ח וְיָ֖ם רְחֹקִֽים: מֵכִ֣ין הָרִ֣ים בְּכֹח֑וֹ נֶ֝אְזָ֗ר בִּגְבוּרָֽה: מַשְׁבִּ֤יחַ ׀ שְׁא֣וֹן יַ֭מִּים שְׁא֥וֹן

ט גַּלֵּיהֶ֗ם וַהֲמ֥וֹן לְאֻמִּֽים: וַיִּ֤ירְא֨וּ ׀ יֹשְׁבֵ֣י קְ֭צָוֺת מֵאֽוֹתֹתֶ֑יךָ מ֤וֹצָֽאֵי־בֹ֖קֶר וָעֶ֣רֶב

י תַּרְנִֽין: פָּקַ֥דְתָּ הָאָ֨רֶץ ׀ וַתְּשֹׁ֪קְקֶ֡הָ רַבַּ֬ת תַּעְשְׁרֶ֗נָּה פֶּ֣לֶג אֱ֭לֹהִים מָ֣לֵא מָ֑יִם

62:12-13. Although we experience "two" different things — the strictness of God's "strength" and the bounty of His "kindness" — they are both manifestations of the "one thing that God has spoken," to improve each man according to his deeds.

63:3. My yearning "to have beheld You in the Sanctuary" is as intense as physical thirst in this desert.

63:5. In prayer and praise (*Rashi*).

63:12. David, who had already been anointed, refers to himself (*Rashi*).

64:8. From here until the end of the psalm, David prophesies — mixing the past and future tenses — regarding the eventual downfall of his enemies.

65:2. The praises of infinite God can never be exhausted. Silence is His most eloquent praise, since elaboration must leave glaring omissions (*Rashi*).

⁹ Trust in Him at every moment, O people! Pour out your hearts before Him; God is a refuge for us, Selah! ¹⁰ Common people are but vanity! Distinguished people are but deceit! Were they to be lifted up on the scales, together they would be lighter than vanity. ¹¹ Trust not in oppression, and in robbery place not vain hope; though wealth flourishes, set not your heart on it. ¹² One thing has God spoken, these two have I heard:* that strength belongs to God; ¹³ and Yours, O Lord, is kindness, for You repay each man according to his deeds.

63

Though a victim of malicious slander, exiled from nation, family, and home, alone in a desolate wilderness, David never wavers in his love for God.

¹ A psalm by David, when he was in the wilderness of Judah. ² O God: You are my God, I seek You. My soul thirsts for You, my flesh longs for You; in a parched and thirsty land with no water. ³ Thus* to have beheld You in the Sanctuary, to see Your might and Your glory. ⁴ For Your kindness is better than life, my lips shall praise You. ⁵ Thus shall I bless You all my life; in Your Name I shall lift my hands. * ⁶ It is as if my desire is sated with fat and abundance, when my mouth gives praise with joyous language. ⁷ When I remember You upon my couch, in night watches I meditate upon You. ⁸ For You have been a help for me; in the shelter of your wings I joyously sing. ⁹ My soul cleaves after You; Your right arm has supported me. ¹⁰ But they seek my soul for destruction; may they come to the depths of the earth. ¹¹ [The enemies] shall drag each one by the sword, the portion of foxes shall they be. ¹² The king* shall rejoice in God; glorified will be everyone who swears by Him, when the mouth of the liars will be stopped.

64

When the enemy plots evil, sharpens its attack, and lays traps, one should take refuge in God.

¹ For the conductor, a psalm by David. ² Hear, O God, my voice in my prayer, from the dread of the foe preserve my life. ³ Hide me from the counsel of the wicked, from the assembly of evildoers, ⁴ who have sharpened their tongue like the sword, and drawn their arrow — a bitter word — ⁵ to shoot in stealth at the innocent; suddenly they shoot him and they are unafraid. ⁶ They encourage themselves in an evil matter, they speak in order to conceal snares; they say, "Who will see them?" ⁷ They search out pretexts, they have completed a diligent search, and every inner thought of man and deep counsel. ⁸ Then God shot* at them; their wounds were [like] a sudden arrow. ⁹ Their own tongue made them stumble; all who see them will shudder. ¹⁰ Then all men came to fear; and they declared the work of God, and they comprehended His deed. ¹¹ The righteous one will rejoice in Hashem and take refuge in Him; and all who are upright in heart will be glorified.

65

Calamities such as drought should spur mankind to repentance. God Who subdues the mightiest forces can revitalize the most parched land and withered nation.

¹ For the conductor, a psalm; a song, by David. ² To You, silence is praise, * O God in Zion; and unto You shall the vow be fulfilled. ³ O Heeder of prayer, unto You does all flesh come. ⁴ Matters of iniquities have over-whelmed me; our transgressions, You will pardon them. ⁵ Praises to the one whom You choose and draw near to dwell in Your courts; may we be sated with the goodness of Your House, the holiest part of Your Sanctuary. ⁶ With awesome deeds in righteousness You will answer us, O God of our salvation; O Security of all [who inhabit] the ends of the earth and those far off at sea, * ⁷ Who sets mountains with His strength, Who is girded with might, ⁸ Who calms the roar of the seas, the roar of their waves and the multitude of regimes. ⁹ Inhabitants of the furthest ends are awed by Your signs; with the outgoings of morning and evening You cause joyful praise. ¹⁰ You paid heed to the earth and watered it, You enriched it abundantly from God's stream filled with water;

65:6. The scattered flock of Israel.

תָּכִין דְּגָנָם כִּי־כֵן תְּכִינֶהָ: תְּלָמֶיהָ רַוֵּה נַחֵת גְּדוּדֶיהָ בִּרְבִיבִים תְּמֹגְגֶנָה יא

צִמְחָהּ תְּבָרֵךְ: עִטַּרְתָּ שְׁנַת טוֹבָתֶךָ וּמַעְגָּלֶיךָ יִרְעֲפוּן דָּשֶׁן: יִרְעֲפוּ נְאוֹת יב-יג

מִדְבָּר וְגִיל גְּבָעוֹת תַּחְגֹּרְנָה: לָבְשׁוּ כָרִים ׀ הַצֹּאן וַעֲמָקִים יַעַטְפוּ־בָר יד

יִתְרוֹעֲעוּ אַף־יָשִׁירוּ:

סו א-ב לַמְנַצֵּחַ שִׁיר מִזְמוֹר הָרִיעוּ לֵאלֹהִים כָּל־הָאָרֶץ: זַמְּרוּ כְבוֹד־שְׁמוֹ שִׂימוּ

יום יב לחדש כָבוֹד תְּהִלָּתוֹ: אִמְרוּ לֵאלֹהִים מַה־נּוֹרָא מַעֲשֶׂיךָ בְּרֹב עֻזְּךָ יְכַחֲשׁוּ לְךָ ג

אֹיְבֶיךָ: כָּל־הָאָרֶץ ׀ יִשְׁתַּחֲווּ לְךָ וִיזַמְּרוּ־לָךְ יְזַמְּרוּ שִׁמְךָ סֶלָה: לְכוּ וּרְאוּ ד-ה

מִפְעֲלוֹת אֱלֹהִים נוֹרָא עֲלִילָה עַל־בְּנֵי אָדָם: הָפַךְ יָם ׀ לְיַבָּשָׁה בַּנָּהָר ו

יַעַבְרוּ בְרָגֶל שָׁם נִשְׂמְחָה־בּוֹ: מֹשֵׁל בִּגְבוּרָתוֹ ׀ עוֹלָם עֵינָיו בַּגּוֹיִם ז

תִּצְפֶּינָה הַסּוֹרְרִים ׀ אַל־°יָרִימוּ [°יָרוּמוּ ק] לָמוֹ סֶלָה: בָּרְכוּ עַמִּים ׀ ח

אֱלֹהֵינוּ וְהַשְׁמִיעוּ קוֹל תְּהִלָּתוֹ: הַשָּׂם נַפְשֵׁנוּ בַּחַיִּים וְלֹא־נָתַן לַמּוֹט ט

רַגְלֵנוּ: כִּי־בְחַנְתָּנוּ אֱלֹהִים צְרַפְתָּנוּ כִּצְרָף־כָּסֶף: הֲבֵאתָנוּ בַמְּצוּדָה י-יא

שַׂמְתָּ מוּעָקָה בְמָתְנֵינוּ: הִרְכַּבְתָּ אֱנוֹשׁ לְרֹאשֵׁנוּ בָּאנוּ־בָאֵשׁ וּבַמַּיִם יב

וַתּוֹצִיאֵנוּ לָרְוָיָה: אָבוֹא בֵיתְךָ בְעוֹלוֹת אֲשַׁלֵּם לְךָ נְדָרָי: אֲשֶׁר־פָּצוּ יג-יד

שְׂפָתָי וְדִבֶּר־פִּי בַּצַּר־לִי: עֹלוֹת מֵחִים אַעֲלֶה־לָּךְ עִם־קְטֹרֶת אֵילִים טו

אֶעֱשֶׂה בָקָר עִם־עַתּוּדִים סֶלָה: לְכוּ־שִׁמְעוּ וַאֲסַפְּרָה כָּל־יִרְאֵי אֱלֹהִים טז

אֲשֶׁר עָשָׂה לְנַפְשִׁי: אֵלָיו פִּי־קָרָאתִי וְרוֹמַם תַּחַת לְשׁוֹנִי: אָוֶן אִם־ יז-יח

רָאִיתִי בְלִבִּי לֹא יִשְׁמַע ׀ אֲדֹנָי: אָכֵן שָׁמַע אֱלֹהִים הִקְשִׁיב בְּקוֹל תְּפִלָּתִי: יט

בָּרוּךְ אֱלֹהִים אֲשֶׁר לֹא־הֵסִיר תְּפִלָּתִי וְחַסְדּוֹ מֵאִתִּי: כ

סז א-ב לַמְנַצֵּחַ בִּנְגִינֹת מִזְמוֹר שִׁיר: אֱלֹהִים יְחָנֵּנוּ וִיבָרְכֵנוּ יָאֵר פָּנָיו אִתָּנוּ סֶלָה:

לָדַעַת בָּאָרֶץ דַּרְכֶּךָ בְּכָל־גּוֹיִם יְשׁוּעָתֶךָ: יוֹדוּךָ עַמִּים ׀ אֱלֹהִים יוֹדוּךָ ג-ד

עַמִּים כֻּלָּם: יִשְׂמְחוּ וִירַנְּנוּ לְאֻמִּים כִּי־תִשְׁפֹּט עַמִּים מִישׁוֹר וּלְאֻמִּים ׀ ה

בָּאָרֶץ תַּנְחֵם סֶלָה: יוֹדוּךָ עַמִּים ׀ אֱלֹהִים יוֹדוּךָ עַמִּים כֻּלָּם: אֶרֶץ ו-ז

נָתְנָה יְבוּלָהּ יְבָרְכֵנוּ אֱלֹהִים אֱלֹהֵינוּ: יְבָרְכֵנוּ אֱלֹהִים וְיִירְאוּ אֹתוֹ כָּל־ ח

אַפְסֵי־אָרֶץ:

סח א-ב לַמְנַצֵּחַ לְדָוִד מִזְמוֹר שִׁיר: יָקוּם אֱלֹהִים יָפוּצוּ אוֹיְבָיו וְיָנוּסוּ מְשַׂנְאָיו

מִפָּנָיו: כְּהִנְדֹּף עָשָׁן תִּנְדֹּף כְּהִמֵּס דּוֹנַג מִפְּנֵי־אֵשׁ יֹאבְדוּ רְשָׁעִים מִפְּנֵי ג

אֱלֹהִים: וְצַדִּיקִים יִשְׂמְחוּ יַעַלְצוּ לִפְנֵי אֱלֹהִים וְיָשִׂישׂוּ בְשִׂמְחָה: שִׁירוּ ׀ ד-ה

לֵאלֹהִים זַמְּרוּ שְׁמוֹ סֹלּוּ לָרֹכֵב בָּעֲרָבוֹת בְּיָהּ שְׁמוֹ וְעִלְזוּ לְפָנָיו:

אֲבִי יְתוֹמִים וְדַיַּן אַלְמָנוֹת אֱלֹהִים בִּמְעוֹן קָדְשׁוֹ: אֱלֹהִים ׀ מוֹשִׁיב ו-ז

יְחִידִים ׀ בַּיְתָה מוֹצִיא אֲסִירִים בַּכּוֹשָׁרוֹת אַךְ סוֹרְרִים שָׁכְנוּ צְחִיחָה:

אֱלֹהִים בְּצֵאתְךָ לִפְנֵי עַמֶּךָ בְּצַעְדְּךָ בִישִׁימוֹן סֶלָה: אֶרֶץ רָעָשָׁה ׀ ח-ט

66:3. God's enemies will stand in such fear of Him that they will try to deny that they ever sinned against Him (*Rashi*).

68:5. He guides and directs the heavens as the rider on His steed. Praise Him with His Name *"YAH,"* which denotes Him as the Creator and Sustainer of the universe (*Radak*).

You prepare their grain, for thus do You prepare it, [11] *to abundantly water its ridges, settle its furrows; with showers You soften it, You bless its growth.* [12] *You crown the year of Your goodness, and Your paths drip with abundance.* [13] *They drip onto desert pastures and the hills gird themselves with joy.* [14] *The meadows don sheep and the valleys cloak themselves with fodder, they shout joyfully, they even sing!*

66

God's inter-
vention in
the affairs of
man is not
mere
speculation;
it is attested
to by history,
physically,
perceptibly
and
irrefutably.

[1] *For the conductor, a song, a psalm. Shout joyfully to God all the earth!* [2] *Sing the glory of His Name, make glorious His praise.* [3] *Say unto God, "How awesome are Your works!" Because of Your abundant power Your enemies will lie to You.* * [4] *All the earth will bow to You and they will sing to You, they will sing [to] Your Name, Selah.* [5] *Go and see the works of God, He is awesome in deed toward mankind.* [6] *He changed the sea into dry land, they passed through the river on foot; there we rejoiced in Him.* [7] *He rules in His might forever, His eyes oversee the nations; let not the rebellious exalt themselves, Selah.* [8] *Bless our God, O peoples, and make heard the sound of His praise;* [9] *He Who set our soul in life and did not allow our foot to falter.* [10] *For You examined us, O God, You refined us as if refining silver.* [11] *You brought us into the prison, You placed constraint upon our loins,* [12] *You mounted a mortal over our head; we entered fire and water and You brought us out into abundance.* [13] *I will enter Your House with burnt-offerings; I will fulfill to You my vows,* [14] *that my lips uttered and my mouth spoke in my distress.* [15] *Burnt-offerings of fat animals will I offer up to You, with the smoke of rams, I will prepare cattle with goats, Selah.* [16] *Go, all you who fear God, and hearken so that I may relate what He did for my soul.* [17] *Unto Him my mouth called, and [His] exaltation was under my tongue.* [18] *Had I perceived iniquity in my heart, the Lord would not have listened.* [19] *In truth, God has heard, He has hearkened to the sound of my prayer.* [20] *Blessed is God, Who has not turned away my prayer or His lovingkindness from me.*

67

A prayer for
the arrival of
the Messianic
era, when all
mankind will
worship God
and earn His
blessing

[1] *For the conductor with the neginos, a psalm, a song.* [2] *May God favor us and bless us, may He illuminate His countenance with us, Selah.* [3] *To make known Your way on earth, among all nations Your salvation.* [4] *The peoples will acknowledge You, O God; the peoples will acknowledge You — all of them.* [5] *Regimes will be glad and sing for joy, because You will judge the peoples fairly and guide with fairness the regimes on earth, Selah.* [6] *The peoples will acknowledge You, O God; the peoples will acknowledge You — all of them.* [7] *The earth will then have yielded its produce; may God, our God, bless us.* [8] *May God bless us, and may all the ends of the earth fear Him.*

68

Israel's
triumph over
the mightiest
empires has
been played
out many
times
throughout
history.

[1] *For the conductor, by David, a psalm, a song.* [2] *May God arise, let His enemies be scattered, and His foes will flee from before Him.* [3] *As smoke is dispersed, so disperse [them]; as wax melts before fire, so may the wicked perish from before God.* [4] *And the righteous will be glad, they will exult before God; they will rejoice with gladness.* [5] *Sing to God, make music [to] His Name; extol He Who rides upon the highest heavens, with His Name YAH,* * *and exult before Him.* [6] *Father of orphans and Defender of widows is God in the abode of His holiness.* [7] *God settles the solitary into a family, He releases those bound in fetters; only the rebellious dwell in the thirsty land.* [8] *O God, when You went forth before Your nation, when You marched through the wilderness, Selah;* [9] *the earth quaked,*

י אַף־שָׁמַ֫יִם נָטְפ֥וּ מִפְּנֵ֣י אֱלֹהִ֑ים זֶ֥ה סִינַ֑י מִפְּנֵ֥י אֱלֹ֝הִ֗ים אֱלֹהֵ֥י יִשְׂרָאֵֽל: גֶּ֤שֶׁם

יא נְדָב֣וֹת תָּנִ֣יף אֱלֹהִ֑ים נַחֲלָתְךָ֣ וְ֝נִלְאָ֗ה אַתָּ֥ה כֽוֹנַנְתָּֽהּ: חַיָּתְךָ֥ יֵ֥שְׁבוּ־בָ֑הּ

יב-יג תָּכִ֥ין בְּטֽוֹבָתְךָ֖ לֶֽעָנִ֣י אֱלֹהִֽים: אֲדֹנָ֥י יִתֶּן־אֹ֑מֶר הַֽ֝מְבַשְּׂר֗וֹת צָבָ֥א רָֽב: מַלְכֵ֣י

יד צְבָא֣וֹת יִדֹּד֣וּן יִדֹּד֑וּן וּנְוַת־בַּ֝֗יִת תְּחַלֵּ֥ק שָׁלָֽל: אִֽם־תִּשְׁכְּבוּן֘ בֵּ֤ין שְׁפַ֫תָּ֥יִם

טו כַּנְפֵ֣י י֭וֹנָה נֶחְפָּ֣ה בַכֶּ֑סֶף וְ֝אֶבְרוֹתֶ֗יהָ בִּֽירַקְרַ֥ק חָרֽוּץ: בְּפָרֵ֣שׂ שַׁדַּ֣י מְלָכִ֥ים

טז-יז בָּ֗הּ תַּשְׁלֵ֥ג בְּצַלְמֽוֹן: הַר־אֱ֭לֹהִים הַר־בָּשָׁ֑ן הַ֥ר גַּ֝בְנֻנִּ֗ים הַר־בָּשָֽׁן: לָ֤מָּה ׀ תְּֽרַצְּדוּן֘ הָרִ֪ים גַּבְנֻ֫נִּ֥ים הָהָ֗ר חָמַ֣ד אֱלֹהִ֣ים לְשִׁבְתּ֑וֹ אַף־יְ֝הֹוָ֗ה יִשְׁכֹּ֥ן לָנֶֽצַח:

יח-יט רֶ֖כֶב אֱלֹהִ֗ים רִבֹּתַ֣יִם אַלְפֵ֣י שִׁנְאָ֑ן אֲדֹנָ֥י בָ֝֗ם סִינַ֥י בַּקֹּֽדֶשׁ: עָלִ֤יתָ לַמָּר֗וֹם ׀ שָׁבִ֥יתָ שֶּׁ֗בִי לָקַ֣חְתָּ מַ֭תָּנוֹת בָּֽאָדָ֑ם וְאַ֥ף ס֝וֹרְרִ֗ים לִשְׁכֹּ֤ן ׀ יָ֬הּ אֱלֹהִֽים: בָּר֥וּךְ

כ אֲדֹנָ֥י י֨וֹם ׀ י֤וֹם יַֽעֲמָס־לָ֗נוּ הָ֘אֵ֤ל יְֽשׁוּעָתֵ֥נוּ סֶֽלָה: הָאֵ֤ל ׀ לָ֨נוּ אֵ֣ל לְֽמוֹשָׁע֑וֹת

כא וְלֵֽיהֹוִ֥ה אֲדֹנָ֑י לַ֝מָּ֗וֶת תֹּצָאֽוֹת: אַךְ־אֱלֹהִ֗ים יִמְחַץ֮ רֹ֤אשׁ אֹ֫יְבָ֥יו קׇדְקֹ֥ד

כב שֵׂעָ֑ר מִ֝תְהַלֵּ֗ךְ בַּֽאֲשָׁמָֽיו: אָמַ֣ר אֲ֭דֹנָי מִבָּשָׁ֣ן אָשִׁ֑יב אָ֝שִׁ֗יב מִֽמְּצֻל֥וֹת יָֽם:

כג-כד-כה לְמַ֤עַן ׀ תִּֽמְחַ֥ץ רַגְלְךָ֗ בְּ֫דָ֥ם לְשׁ֥וֹן כְּלָבֶ֑יךָ מֵאֹֽיְבִ֥ים מִנֵּֽהוּ: רָא֣וּ הֲלִיכוֹתֶ֣יךָ

כו אֱלֹהִ֑ים הֲלִ֘יכ֤וֹת אֵלִ֣י מַלְכִּ֣י בַקֹּֽדֶשׁ: קִדְּמ֣וּ שָׁ֭רִים אַחַ֣ר נֹֽגְנִ֑ים בְּת֥וֹךְ

כז-כח עֲ֝לָמ֗וֹת תּֽוֹפֵפֽוֹת: בְּֽ֭מַקְהֵלוֹת בָּרְכ֣וּ אֱלֹהִ֑ים אֲ֝דֹנָ֗י מִמְּק֥וֹר יִשְׂרָאֵֽל: שָׁ֤ם

כט בִּנְיָמִ֨ן ׀ צָעִ֡יר רֹ֫דֵ֥ם שָׂרֵ֣י יְ֭הוּדָה רִגְמָתָ֑ם שָׂרֵ֥י זְ֝בֻל֗וּן שָׂרֵ֥י נַפְתָּלִֽי: צִוָּ֥ה

ל אֱלֹהֶ֗יךָ עֻ֫זֶּ֥ךָ עוּזָּ֥ה אֱלֹהִ֑ים ז֥וּ פָּעַ֥לְתָּ לָּֽנוּ: מֵֽ֭הֵיכָלֶ֗ךָ עַל־יְרֽוּשָׁלָ֑͏ִם לְךָ֤

לא יוֹבִ֖ילוּ מְלָכִ֣ים שָֽׁי: גְּעַ֨ר חַיַּ֪ת קָנֶ֡ה עֲדַ֤ת אַבִּירִ֨ים ׀ בְּעֶגְלֵ֬י עַמִּ֗ים מִתְרַפֵּ֣ס

לב בְּרַצֵּי־כָ֑סֶף בִּזַּ֥ר עַ֝מִּ֗ים קְרָב֥וֹת יֶחְפָּֽצוּ: יֶֽאֱתָ֣יוּ חַ֭שְׁמַנִּים מִנִּ֣י מִצְרָ֑יִם כּ֥וּשׁ

לג תָּרִ֥יץ יָ֝דָ֗יו לֵֽאלֹהִֽים: מַמְלְכ֣וֹת הָ֭אָרֶץ שִׁ֣ירוּ לֵֽאלֹהִ֑ים זַמְּר֖וּ אֲדֹנָ֣י סֶֽלָה:

לד-לה לָ֭רֹכֵב בִּשְׁמֵ֥י שְׁמֵי־קֶ֗דֶם הֵ֤ן יִתֵּ֣ן בְּ֭קוֹלוֹ ק֣וֹל עֹֽז: תְּנ֥וּ עֹ֗ז לֵֽאלֹהִ֥ים עַֽל־

לו יִשְׂרָאֵ֥ל גַּֽאֲוָת֑וֹ וְ֝עֻזּ֗וֹ בַּשְּׁחָקִֽים: נוֹרָ֤א אֱלֹהִ֗ים מִֽמִּקְדָּ֫שֶׁ֥יךָ אֵ֤ל יִשְׂרָאֵ֗ל ה֤וּא נֹתֵ֨ן ׀ עֹ֖ז וְתַֽעֲצֻמ֥וֹת לָעָ֗ם בָּר֥וּךְ אֱלֹהִֽים:

סט יום יג לחדש

א-ב לַמְנַצֵּ֬חַ עַל־שֽׁוֹשַׁנִּ֬ים לְדָוִֽד: הוֹשִׁיעֵ֥נִי אֱלֹהִ֑ים כִּ֤י בָ֖אוּ מַ֣יִם עַד־נָֽפֶשׁ:

ג טָבַ֤עְתִּי ׀ בִּיוֵ֣ן מְ֭צוּלָה וְאֵ֣ין מׇֽעֳמָ֑ד בָּ֥אתִי בְמַֽעֲמַקֵּי־מַ֝֗יִם וְשִׁבֹּ֥לֶת שְׁטָפָֽתְנִי:

ד-ה יָגַ֣עְתִּי בְקׇרְאִי֮ נִחַ֢ר גְּר֫וֹנִ֥י כָּל֥וּ עֵינַ֑י מְ֝יַחֵ֗ל לֵאלֹהָֽי: רַבּ֤וּ ׀ מִשַּֽׂעֲר֣וֹת רֹאשִׁי֮ שֹֽׂנְאַ֢י חִ֫נָּ֥ם עָצְמ֣וּ מַ֭צְמִיתַי אֹֽיְבַ֣י שֶׁ֑קֶר אֲשֶׁ֥ר לֹֽא־גָ֝זַ֗לְתִּי אָ֣ז אָשִֽׁיב:

ו-ז אֱֽלֹהִ֗ים אַתָּ֣ה יָ֭דַעְתָּ לְאִוַּלְתִּ֑י וְ֝אַשְׁמוֹתַ֗י מִמְּךָ֥ לֹֽא־נִכְחָֽדוּ: אַל־יֵ֘בֹ֤שׁוּ בִ֨י ׀ קֹוֶ֗יךָ אֲדֹנָ֣י יֱהֹוִ֣ה צְבָא֑וֹת אַל־יִכָּ֘לְמ֤וּ בִ֥י מְ֝בַקְשֶׁ֗יךָ אֱלֹהֵ֥י יִשְׂרָאֵֽל:

68:13. Invading kings will flee ... and Israel, which dwells within the land, will divide their abandoned wealth (*Rashi*).

68:14. In the degradation of exile and persecution.

68:15. The Land of Israel (*Metzudos*).

68:17. The highest mountains have no cause for pride because God chose Mt. Zion over them for His abode on earth (*Radak*).

68:20. With the weight of His bounty and kindness (*Ibn Ezra*).

68:21. See *Genesis* 15:2.

68:22. A reference to the Edomite empire, descendants of hairy Esau [see *Genesis* 25:25] (*Rashi*).

68:24. Of your enemies whom God will decimate before you (*Rashi*).

68:36. The Sanctuary in Jerusalem and its correspond-

The
phenomenon
of Israel's
triumph will
be repeated
for the last
time with
the Final
Redemption,
when God
will be
universally
worshiped.
even the heavens dripped before the Presence of God; even Sinai, before the Presence of God, the God of Israel. ¹⁰ A generous rain did You lavish, O God, when Your heritage was weary You established it firmly. ¹¹ Your flock settled there; You prepared for the poor in Your goodness, O God. ¹² The Lord made a declaration, the heralds are a mighty host: ¹³ Kings of legions flee, they flee, and the dweller within apportions booty. * ¹⁴ Even if you lie among the cooking pots, * [you will be like] the wings of a dove that is coated with silver and her pinions with brilliant gold. ¹⁵ When the Almighty scatters kings, in it * shall those in shadowy darkness be whitened. ¹⁶ The mountain of God is a choice mountain, the mountain of majestic peaks is a choice mountain. ¹⁷ Why do you prance, O you mountains of majestic peaks? * The mountain that God desired for His abode — HASHEM will even dwell there forever! ¹⁸ God's entourage is twice ten thousand, thousands of angels; the Lord is among them, at Sinai in holiness. ¹⁹ You ascended on high, You have taken captives, You took gifts of man and even of rebels, to dwell with YAH, God. ²⁰ Blessed is the Lord, day by day He burdens us, * the God of our salvation, Selah. ²¹ God is for us a God of salvations; and though HASHEM/ELOHIM, * the Lord, has many avenues toward death, ²² God will cleave only the head of His foes, the hairy skull * of him who saunters with his guilt. ²³ The Lord promised, "I will bring back from Bashan, I will bring back from the depths of the sea; ²⁴ that your foot may wade through blood; * the tongue of your dogs may have its food portion from the enemies." ²⁵ They saw Your ways, O God, the ways of my God, my King, in holiness. ²⁶ First went singers, then musicians, in the midst of timbrel-playing maidens. ²⁷ In congregations bless God; [bless] my Lord, all who descend from Israel. ²⁸ There Benjamin, the youngest, rules them, the princes of Judah stoned them; the princes of Zebulun, the princes of Naphtali. ²⁹ Your God decreed your might; display Your strength, O God, Who has wrought [this] for us. ³⁰ Because of Your Sanctuary upon Jerusalem, to You the kings shall deliver tribute. ³¹ Rebuke the flock of spears, the assembly of bulls among the calves of nations, [until] each prostrates himself with pieces of silver; He [God] scatters nations who desire battles. ³² Nobles shall come from Egypt, Cush shall hasten its hands to God. ³³ O Kingdoms of the earth, sing to God, make music to the Lord, Selah — ³⁴ to the One Who rides upon the loftiest of primeval heavens: Behold, He shouts with His voice, a voice of might. ³⁵ Acknowledge invincible might to God, Whose grandeur is upon Israel as His might is in the skies. ³⁶ You are awesome, O God, from Your Sanctuaries; * God of Israel — it is He Who grants might and power to the people, blessed is God.

69

A vivid
prophetic
portrayal of
Israel's plight
in its long
and bitter
exile, and an
impassioned
plea for its
speedy
deliverance
¹ For the conductor, on the shoshanim, by David. ² Save me, O God, for the waters have reached until the soul! ³ I am sunk in the mire of the shadowy depths, and there is no foothold; I have entered watery depths, and a rushing current sweeps me away. ⁴ I am wearied by my outcry, my throat is parched; my eyes pined, waiting for my God. ⁵ More abundant than the hairs of my head are those who hate me without cause. Mighty are those who would cut me off, those who are unjustly my foes; what I never stole I must then restore. * ⁶ O God, You know my folly, and my guilty acts are not hidden from You. ⁷ Let those who wait for You not be shamed through me, O Lord HASHEM/ELOHIM, Master of Legions; let those who seek You not be humiliated through me, O God of Israel.

---

ing spiritual heavenly Sanctuary (*Radak*).
69:5. Israel's exile is replete with instances in which

charges were trumped up against Jews so that their wealth could be seized (*R' Hirsch*).

ח־ט   כִּי־עָלֶיךָ נָשָׂאתִי חֶרְפָּה כִּסְּתָה כְלִמָּה פָנָי: מוּזָר הָיִיתִי לְאֶחָי וְנָכְרִי

י־יא   לִבְנֵי אִמִּי: כִּי־קִנְאַת בֵּיתְךָ אֲכָלָתְנִי וְחֶרְפּוֹת חוֹרְפֶיךָ נָפְלוּ עָלָי: וָאֶבְכֶּה

יב   בַצּוֹם נַפְשִׁי וַתְּהִי לַחֲרָפוֹת לִי: וָאֶתְּנָה לְבוּשִׁי שָׂק וָאֱהִי לָהֶם לְמָשָׁל:

יג־יד   יָשִׂיחוּ בִי יֹשְׁבֵי שָׁעַר וּנְגִינוֹת שׁוֹתֵי שֵׁכָר: וַאֲנִי תְפִלָּתִי־לְךָ | יהוה עֵת

טו   רָצוֹן אֱלֹהִים בְּרָב־חַסְדֶּךָ עֲנֵנִי בֶּאֱמֶת יִשְׁעֶךָ: הַצִּילֵנִי מִטִּיט וְאַל־

טז   אֶטְבָּעָה אִנָּצְלָה מִשֹּׂנְאַי וּמִמַּעֲמַקֵּי מָיִם: אַל־תִּשְׁטְפֵנִי | שִׁבֹּלֶת מַיִם

יז   וְאַל־תִּבְלָעֵנִי מְצוּלָה וְאַל־תֶּאְטַר־עָלַי בְּאֵר פִּיהָ: עֲנֵנִי יהוה כִּי־טוֹב

יח   חַסְדֶּךָ כְּרֹב רַחֲמֶיךָ פְּנֵה אֵלָי: וְאַל־תַּסְתֵּר פָּנֶיךָ מֵעַבְדֶּךָ כִּי־צַר־לִי מַהֵר

יט־כ   עֲנֵנִי: קָרְבָה אֶל־נַפְשִׁי גְאָלָהּ לְמַעַן אֹיְבַי פְּדֵנִי: אַתָּה יָדַעְתָּ חֶרְפָּתִי

כא   וּבָשְׁתִּי וּכְלִמָּתִי נֶגְדְּךָ כָּל־צוֹרְרָי: חֶרְפָּה | שָׁבְרָה לִבִּי וָאָנוּשָׁה וָאֲקַוֶּה

כב   לָנוּד וָאַיִן וְלַמְנַחֲמִים וְלֹא מָצָאתִי: וַיִּתְּנוּ בְּבָרוּתִי רֹאשׁ וְלִצְמָאִי יַשְׁקוּנִי

כג־כד   חֹמֶץ: יְהִי־שֻׁלְחָנָם לִפְנֵיהֶם לְפָח וְלִשְׁלוֹמִים לְמוֹקֵשׁ: תֶּחְשַׁכְנָה עֵינֵיהֶם

כה   מֵרְאוֹת וּמָתְנֵיהֶם תָּמִיד הַמְעַד: שְׁפָךְ־עֲלֵיהֶם זַעְמֶךָ וַחֲרוֹן אַפְּךָ יַשִּׂיגֵם:

כו־כז   תְּהִי־טִירָתָם נְשַׁמָּה בְּאָהֳלֵיהֶם אַל־יְהִי יֹשֵׁב: כִּי־אַתָּה אֲשֶׁר־הִכִּיתָ

כח   רָדָפוּ וְאֶל־מַכְאוֹב חֲלָלֶיךָ יְסַפֵּרוּ: תְּנָה־עָוֹן עַל־עֲוֹנָם וְאַל־יָבֹאוּ

כט־ל   בְּצִדְקָתֶךָ: יִמָּחוּ מִסֵּפֶר חַיִּים וְעִם צַדִּיקִים אַל־יִכָּתֵבוּ: וַאֲנִי עָנִי וְכוֹאֵב

לא   יְשׁוּעָתְךָ אֱלֹהִים תְּשַׂגְּבֵנִי: אֲהַלְלָה שֵׁם־אֱלֹהִים בְּשִׁיר וַאֲגַדְּלֶנּוּ בְתוֹדָה:

לב־לג   וְתִיטַב לַיהוה מִשּׁוֹר פָּר מַקְרִן מַפְרִיס: רָאוּ עֲנָוִים יִשְׂמָחוּ דֹּרְשֵׁי אֱלֹהִים

לד   וִיחִי לְבַבְכֶם: כִּי־שֹׁמֵעַ אֶל־אֶבְיוֹנִים יהוה וְאֶת־אֲסִירָיו לֹא בָזָה:

לה־לו   יְהַלְלוּהוּ שָׁמַיִם וָאָרֶץ יַמִּים וְכָל־רֹמֵשׂ בָּם: כִּי אֱלֹהִים | יוֹשִׁיעַ צִיּוֹן

לז   וְיִבְנֶה עָרֵי יְהוּדָה וְיָשְׁבוּ שָׁם וִירֵשׁוּהָ: וְזֶרַע עֲבָדָיו יִנְחָלוּהָ וְאֹהֲבֵי שְׁמוֹ

  יִשְׁכְּנוּ־בָהּ:

ע   א־ג   לַמְנַצֵּחַ לְדָוִד לְהַזְכִּיר: אֱלֹהִים לְהַצִּילֵנִי יהוה לְעֶזְרָתִי חוּשָׁה: יֵבֹשׁוּ

ד   וְיַחְפְּרוּ מְבַקְשֵׁי נַפְשִׁי יִסֹּגוּ אָחוֹר וְיִכָּלְמוּ חֲפֵצֵי רָעָתִי: יָשׁוּבוּ עַל־עֵקֶב

ה   בָּשְׁתָּם הָאֹמְרִים הֶאָח | הֶאָח: יָשִׂישׂוּ וְיִשְׂמְחוּ | בְּךָ כָּל־מְבַקְשֶׁיךָ וְיֹאמְרוּ

ו   תָמִיד יִגְדַּל אֱלֹהִים אֹהֲבֵי יְשׁוּעָתֶךָ: וַאֲנִי | עָנִי וְאֶבְיוֹן אֱלֹהִים חוּשָׁה־לִּי

  עֶזְרִי וּמְפַלְטִי אַתָּה יהוה אַל־תְּאַחַר:

עא   א־ב   בְּךָ־יהוה חָסִיתִי אַל־אֵבוֹשָׁה לְעוֹלָם: בְּצִדְקָתְךָ תַּצִּילֵנִי וּתְפַלְּטֵנִי

ג   הַטֵּה־אֵלַי אָזְנְךָ וְהוֹשִׁיעֵנִי: הֱיֵה לִי | לְצוּר מָעוֹן לָבוֹא תָּמִיד צִוִּיתָ

ד   לְהוֹשִׁיעֵנִי כִּי־סַלְעִי וּמְצוּדָתִי אָתָּה: אֱלֹהַי פַּלְּטֵנִי מִיַּד רָשָׁע מִכַּף מְעַוֵּל

ה־ו   וְחוֹמֵץ: כִּי־אַתָּה תִקְוָתִי אֲדֹנָי יהוה מִבְטַחִי מִנְּעוּרָי: עָלֶיךָ | נִסְמַכְתִּי

69:8. Instead of abandoning their religion, Jews remained loyal to God, through mockery and disgrace (*Radak*).

69:9. Ishmael and Esau and their descendants (*Radak*).

69:19. Rescue me so that my enemies should not say that You are powerless.

69:27. They persecuted Jews far more than necessary and with savage delight (*Rashi*).

[8] *Because for Your sake* I have borne disgrace; humiliation covered my face. [9] I became a stranger to my brothers, and an alien to my mother's sons. * [10] For the envy of Your House devoured me, and the disgraces of those who scorn You have fallen upon me. [11] And I wept while my soul was fasting, and it was disgraceful to me. [12] I made sackcloth my garment, I became for them a byword. [13] Those who sit by the gate talk about me and make up drinking songs of drunkards. [14] As for me, may my prayer to You, HASHEM, be at an opportune time; O God, in Your abundant kindness, answer me with the truth of Your salvation. [15] Rescue me from the mire so that I will not sink; let me be rescued from my enemies and from the deep waters. [16] Let not the rushing current sweep me away, nor let the shadowy depths swallow me; and do not let the pit close its mouth over me. [17] Answer me, HASHEM, for Your kindness is good; according to the abundance of Your mercy turn toward me. [18] Hide not Your face from Your servant; because I am distressed, answer me quickly. [19] Draw near to my soul, redeem it; because of my foes, deliver me.* [20] You know of my disgrace, my shame, and my humiliation; all my tormentors are before You. [21] Disgrace has broken my heart and I am deathly sick. I longed for sympathy but there was none, and for consolers, but I found none. [22] But they put gall in my meal, and for my thirst they gave me vinegar to drink. [23] May their table become a snare before them, and a trap to their peacefulness. [24] Let their eyes be darkened so that they cannot see, and let their loins falter continually. [25] Pour Your fury upon them, and let the fierceness of Your anger overtake them. [26] Let their palace be desolate, in their tents let there be no dweller. [27] For the one whom You smote they persecuted, * and they tell about the pain of Your mortally wounded. [28] Add iniquity to their iniquity, and let them not have access to Your righteousness. [29] May they be erased from the Book of Life, and let them not be inscribed with the righteous. [30] But I am afflicted and in pain; Your salvation, O God, shall raise me high. [31] I shall praise the Name of God with song, and I shall magnify it with thanksgiving; [32] and it shall please HASHEM more than a full-grown bull, possessed of horns and hoofs. [33] The humble have seen [it] and will be glad — you who seek God — and your hearts will revive. [34] For HASHEM hearkens to the destitute, and has not despised His prisoners. [35] Heaven and earth shall praise Him, the seas and all that moves within them. [36] For God shall save Zion and build the cities of Judah, and they shall settle there and possess it. [37] The offspring of His servants shall inherit it, and those who love His Name shall dwell in it.

70

An appeal
to God
for rescue
from one's
enemies

[1] For the conductor, by David, for remembrance. [2] O God, to rescue me; O HASHEM, to my assistance — hasten! [3] Shamed and disgraced be those who seek my soul; repulsed and humiliated be those who desire my harm. [4] Let them be turned back in consequence of their shaming [me], those who say, "Aha! Aha!" [5] Let all who seek You rejoice and be glad in You; and let those who love Your salvation always say, "May God be magnified." [6] As for me, I am poor and destitute, O God, hasten to me! You are my assistance and my deliverance; HASHEM, do not delay!

71

[1] In You, HASHEM, I have taken refuge, let me not be shamed, ever. [2] In Your righteousness rescue me and deliver me; incline Your ear to me and save me. [3] Be for me a sheltering rock to which to come always; [in the past] You commanded my salvation, for my Rock and my Fortress are You. [4] My God, deliver me from the wicked one's hand, from the palm of the schemer and the violent one. [5] For You are my hope; O Lord HASHEM/ELOHIM, my security since my youth. [6] I relied

מִבֶּטֶן מִמְּעֵי אִמִּי אַתָּה גוֹזִי בְּךָ תְהִלָּתִי תָמִיד: כְּמוֹפֵת הָיִיתִי לְרַבִּים ז

וְאַתָּה מַחֲסִי־עֹז: יִמָּלֵא פִי תְּהִלָּתֶךָ כָּל־הַיּוֹם תִּפְאַרְתֶּךָ: אַל־תַּשְׁלִיכֵנִי ח-ט

לְעֵת זִקְנָה כִּכְלוֹת כֹּחִי אַל־תַּעַזְבֵנִי: כִּי־אָמְרוּ אוֹיְבַי לִי וְשֹׁמְרֵי נַפְשִׁי י

נוֹעֲצוּ יַחְדָּו: לֵאמֹר אֱלֹהִים עֲזָבוֹ רִדְפוּ וְתִפְשׂוּהוּ כִּי־אֵין מַצִּיל: אֱלֹהִים יא-יב

אַל־תִּרְחַק מִמֶּנִּי אֱלֹהַי לְעֶזְרָתִי °חִישָׁה [°חוּשָׁה ק]: יֵבֹשׁוּ יִכְלוּ שֹׂטְנֵי יג

נַפְשִׁי יַעֲטוּ חֶרְפָּה וּכְלִמָּה מְבַקְשֵׁי רָעָתִי: וַאֲנִי תָּמִיד אֲיַחֵל וְהוֹסַפְתִּי יד

עַל־כָּל־תְּהִלָּתֶךָ: פִּי | יְסַפֵּר צִדְקָתֶךָ כָּל־הַיּוֹם תְּשׁוּעָתֶךָ כִּי לֹא יָדַעְתִּי טו

סְפֹרוֹת: אָבוֹא בִּגְבֻרוֹת אֲדֹנָי יֱהֹוִה אַזְכִּיר צִדְקָתְךָ לְבַדֶּךָ: אֱלֹהִים טז-יז

לִמַּדְתַּנִי מִנְּעוּרָי וְעַד־הֵנָּה אַגִּיד נִפְלְאוֹתֶיךָ: וְגַם עַד־זִקְנָה | וְשֵׂיבָה

אֱלֹהִים אַל־תַּעַזְבֵנִי עַד־אַגִּיד זְרוֹעֲךָ לְדוֹר לְכָל־יָבוֹא גְּבוּרָתֶךָ: וְצִדְקָתְךָ יח-יט

אֱלֹהִים עַד־מָרוֹם אֲשֶׁר־עָשִׂיתָ גְדֹלוֹת אֱלֹהִים מִי כָמוֹךָ: אֲשֶׁר כ

°הִרְאִיתַנוּ [°הִרְאִיתַנִי ק] | צָרוֹת רַבּוֹת וְרָעוֹת תָּשׁוּב °תְּחַיֵּינוּ [°תְּחַיֵּינִי ק]

°וּמִתְּהֹמוֹת הָאָרֶץ תָּשׁוּב תַּעֲלֵנִי: תֶּרֶב | גְּדֻלָּתִי וְתִסֹּב תְּנַחֲמֵנִי: גַּם־אֲנִי כא-כב

[ק °וּמִתְּהֹמוֹת]

אוֹדְךָ בִכְלִי־נֶבֶל אֲמִתְּךָ אֱלֹהָי אֲזַמְּרָה לְךָ בְכִנּוֹר קְדוֹשׁ יִשְׂרָאֵל: תְּרַנֵּנָּה כג

שְׂפָתַי כִּי אֲזַמְּרָה־לָּךְ וְנַפְשִׁי אֲשֶׁר פָּדִיתָ: גַּם־לְשׁוֹנִי כָּל־הַיּוֹם תֶּהְגֶּה כד

צִדְקָתֶךָ כִּי־בֹשׁוּ כִי־חָפְרוּ מְבַקְשֵׁי רָעָתִי:

עב   לִשְׁלֹמֹה | אֱלֹהִים מִשְׁפָּטֶיךָ לְמֶלֶךְ תֵּן וְצִדְקָתְךָ לְבֶן־מֶלֶךְ: יָדִין עַמְּךָ א-ב

יום יד לחדש

בְצֶדֶק וַעֲנִיֶּיךָ בְמִשְׁפָּט: יִשְׂאוּ הָרִים שָׁלוֹם לָעָם וּגְבָעוֹת בִּצְדָקָה: יִשְׁפֹּט | ג-ד

עֲנִיֵּי־עָם יוֹשִׁיעַ לִבְנֵי אֶבְיוֹן וִידַכֵּא עוֹשֵׁק: יִירָאוּךָ עִם־שָׁמֶשׁ וְלִפְנֵי יָרֵחַ ה

דּוֹר דּוֹרִים: יֵרֵד כְּמָטָר עַל־גֵּז כִּרְבִיבִים זַרְזִיף אָרֶץ: יִפְרַח־בְּיָמָיו צַדִּיק ו-ז

וְרֹב שָׁלוֹם עַד־בְּלִי יָרֵחַ: וְיֵרְדְּ מִיָּם עַד־יָם וּמִנָּהָר עַד־אַפְסֵי־אָרֶץ: ח

לְפָנָיו יִכְרְעוּ צִיִּים וְאֹיְבָיו עָפָר יְלַחֵכוּ: מַלְכֵי תַרְשִׁישׁ וְאִיִּים מִנְחָה ט

יָשִׁיבוּ מַלְכֵי שְׁבָא וּסְבָא אֶשְׁכָּר יַקְרִיבוּ: וְיִשְׁתַּחֲווּ־לוֹ כָל־מְלָכִים כָּל־ יא

גּוֹיִם יַעַבְדוּהוּ: כִּי־יַצִּיל אֶבְיוֹן מְשַׁוֵּעַ וְעָנִי וְאֵין־עֹזֵר לוֹ: יָחֹס עַל־דַּל יב-יג

וְאֶבְיוֹן וְנַפְשׁוֹת אֶבְיוֹנִים יוֹשִׁיעַ: מִתּוֹךְ וּמֵחָמָס יִגְאַל נַפְשָׁם וְיֵיקַר דָּמָם יד

בְּעֵינָיו: וִיחִי וְיִתֶּן־לוֹ מִזְּהַב שְׁבָא וְיִתְפַּלֵּל בַּעֲדוֹ תָמִיד כָּל־הַיּוֹם יְבָרְכֶנְהוּ: טו

יְהִי פִסַּת־בַּר | בָּאָרֶץ בְּרֹאשׁ הָרִים יִרְעַשׁ כַּלְּבָנוֹן פִּרְיוֹ וְיָצִיצוּ מֵעִיר טז

כְּעֵשֶׂב הָאָרֶץ: יְהִי שְׁמוֹ | לְעוֹלָם לִפְנֵי־שֶׁמֶשׁ °יָנִין [°יִנּוֹן ק] שְׁמוֹ וְיִתְבָּרְכוּ יז

בוֹ כָּל־גּוֹיִם יְאַשְּׁרוּהוּ: בָּרוּךְ | יְהוָה אֱלֹהִים אֱלֹהֵי יִשְׂרָאֵל עֹשֵׂה נִפְלָאוֹת יח

לְבַדּוֹ: וּבָרוּךְ | שֵׁם כְּבוֹדוֹ לְעוֹלָם וְיִמָּלֵא כְבוֹדוֹ אֶת־כֹּל הָאָרֶץ אָמֵן | יט

וְאָמֵן: כָּלּוּ תְפִלּוֹת דָּוִד בֶּן־יִשָׁי: כ

71:18. Old age affords the opportunity to transmit the knowledge of God accumulated throughout a lifetime.

71:24. The hopes of my enemies (verses 10-13) will be dashed because God will accept my prayer (verses 14-24).

72:3. A metaphor for the world's mighty nations. They

will be at peace with Israel because they will recognize her "righteousness."

72:20. Possibly, this was David's final psalm, composed at the end of his life, as suggested by its dedication to his successor, Solomon. However, David placed it here since

Even in old age, when one's normal resources for contending with difficulty are diminished, one should turn to God Whose comfort never fails.

on You from my birth, You withdrew me from the innards of my mother; of You is my praise always. [7] When I became an example to the multitude, You were my mighty refuge. [8] My mouth was filled with Your praise, all day long with Your splendor. [9] Do not cast me off in time of old age; when my strength fails, forsake me not. [10] For my foes speak of me, and those who watch for my life consult together, [11] saying, "God has forsaken him, pursue and catch him, for there is no rescuer." [12] O God, be not far from me; O my God, hasten to my assistance. [13] Let the adversaries of my soul be shamed and consumed; let those who seek my harm be enwrapped in disgrace and humiliation. [14] As for me, I shall always hope, and I will yet add to all Your praise. [15] My mouth shall recount Your righteousness, all day long Your salvation, though I know not [their] numbers. [16] I shall come with the mighty deeds of the Lord, HASHEM/ELOHIM, I will mention Your righteousness, Yours alone. [17] O God, You have taught me from my youth, and until this moment I declare Your wonders. [18] And even until old age and hoariness, O God, forsake me not; until I proclaim Your strength to the generation, Your might to all who will yet come. * [19] And Your righteousness, O God, is unto the high heavens; You, Who have done great things, O God, who is like You? [20] You, Who have shown me many and grievous troubles; revive me again, and from the depths of the earth raise me again. [21] Increase my greatness, and turn back to comfort me. [22] I shall also thank You on the stringed instrument for Your faithfulness, my God; I shall sing to You on the harp, O Holy One of Israel. [23] My lips shall rejoice when I sing to You, as well as my soul that You have redeemed. [24] My tongue, too, shall utter Your righteousness all day long; for they are shamed, for they are humiliated, those who seek my harm. *

72

An aged King David turns over his unfinished work to his son and prays for his success.

[1] For Solomon. O God, give Your judgments to the king and Your righteousness to the king's son. [2] May he judge Your nation with righteousness, and Your poor with justice. [3] May mountains* bear peace to the nation; and hills, through righteousness. [4] May he judge the nation's poor, save the children of the destitute, and crush the oppressor. [5] They will fear You as long as the sun and moon endure, generation after generation. [6] May [his words] descend like rain upon cut vegetation, like showers, waterer of the earth. [7] May the righteous flourish in his days with abundant peace beyond the days of the moon. [8] May he dominate from sea to sea, and from river to the ends of the earth. [9] May nobles kneel before him, and may his foes lick the dust. [10] May the kings of Tarshish and the isles return tribute, the kings of Sheba and Seba offer gifts. [11] May all the kings prostrate themselves before him; all the nations serve him. [12] For he will deliver the destitute person who cries out, and the poor one with none to help him. [13] He will pity the impoverished and destitute, and save the souls of the destitute. [14] From fraud and from violence he will redeem their soul, and their blood will be precious in his eyes. [15] And he will live, and he will give him of the gold of Sheba; and he will pray for him continually and bless him every day. [16] May there be abundant grain on the earth of the mountaintops, may its fruit rustle like the [cedars of] Lebanon; may [people] blossom from the city like the grass of the earth. [17] May his name endure forever, may his name connote mastery as long as the sun endures; and all nations will bless themselves by him; they will praise him. [18] Blessed is HASHEM, God, the God of Israel, Who alone does wondrous things. [19] Blessed is His glorious Name forever; and may all the earth be filled with His glory. Amen and Amen. [20] The prayers of David, the son of Jesse, are ended. *

Scripture often follows topical, rather than chronological, arrangement (*Rashi*).

ספר שלישי

עג   א־ב מִזְמוֹר לְאָסָף אַךְ טוֹב לְיִשְׂרָאֵל אֱלֹהִים לְבָרֵי לֵבָב: וַאֲנִי כִּמְעַט °נָטוּי

יום רביעי   ג [נָטָיוּ ק] רַגְלָי כְּאַיִן °שֻׁפְּכָה [°שֻׁפְּכוּ ק] אֲשֻׁרָי: כִּי־קִנֵּאתִי בַּהוֹלְלִים

ד־ה שְׁלוֹם רְשָׁעִים אֶרְאֶה: כִּי אֵין חַרְצֻבּוֹת לְמוֹתָם וּבָרִיא אוּלָם: בַּעֲמַל

ו אֱנוֹשׁ אֵינֵמוֹ וְעִם־אָדָם לֹא יְנֻגָּעוּ: לָכֵן עֲנָקַתְמוֹ גַאֲוָה יַעֲטָף־שִׁית חָמָס

ז־ח לָמוֹ: יָצָא מֵחֵלֶב עֵינֵמוֹ עָבְרוּ מַשְׂכִּיּוֹת לֵבָב: יָמִיקוּ ׀ וִידַבְּרוּ בְרָע עֹשֶׁק

ט מִמָּרוֹם יְדַבֵּרוּ: שַׁתּוּ בַשָּׁמַיִם פִּיהֶם וּלְשׁוֹנָם תִּהֲלַךְ בָּאָרֶץ: °יָשִׁיב

י־יא [°יָשׁוּב ק] עַמּוֹ הֲלֹם וּמֵי מָלֵא יִמָּצוּ לָמוֹ: וְאָמְרוּ אֵיכָה יָדַע־אֵל וְיֵשׁ דֵּעָה

יב־יג בְעֶלְיוֹן: הִנֵּה־אֵלֶּה רְשָׁעִים וְשַׁלְוֵי עוֹלָם הִשְׂגּוּ־חָיִל: אַךְ־רִיק זִכִּיתִי לְבָבִי

יד־טו וָאֶרְחַץ בְּנִקָּיוֹן כַּפָּי: וָאֱהִי נָגוּעַ כָּל־הַיּוֹם וְתוֹכַחְתִּי לַבְּקָרִים: אִם־אָמַרְתִּי

טז אֲסַפְּרָה כְמוֹ הִנֵּה דוֹר בָּנֶיךָ בָגָדְתִּי: וָאֲחַשְּׁבָה לָדַעַת זֹאת עָמָל °הִיא

יז־יח [°הוּא ק] בְעֵינָי: עַד־אָבוֹא אֶל־מִקְדְּשֵׁי־אֵל אָבִינָה לְאַחֲרִיתָם: אַךְ

יט בַּחֲלָקוֹת תָּשִׁית לָמוֹ הִפַּלְתָּם לְמַשּׁוּאוֹת: אֵיךְ הָיוּ לְשַׁמָּה כְרָגַע סָפוּ תַמּוּ

כ־כא מִן־בַּלָּהוֹת: כַּחֲלוֹם מֵהָקִיץ אֲדֹנָי בָּעִיר ׀ צַלְמָם תִּבְזֶה: כִּי יִתְחַמֵּץ לְבָבִי

כב־כג וְכִלְיוֹתַי אֶשְׁתּוֹנָן: וַאֲנִי־בַעַר וְלֹא אֵדָע בְּהֵמוֹת הָיִיתִי עִמָּךְ: וַאֲנִי תָמִיד

כד־כה עִמָּךְ אָחַזְתָּ בְּיַד־יְמִינִי: בַּעֲצָתְךָ תַנְחֵנִי וְאַחַר כָּבוֹד תִּקָּחֵנִי: מִי־לִי בַשָּׁמַיִם

כו וְעִמְּךָ לֹא־חָפַצְתִּי בָאָרֶץ: כָּלָה שְׁאֵרִי וּלְבָבִי צוּר־לְבָבִי וְחֶלְקִי אֱלֹהִים

כז־כח לְעוֹלָם: כִּי־הִנֵּה רְחֵקֶיךָ יֹאבֵדוּ הִצְמַתָּה כָּל־זוֹנֶה מִמֶּךָּ: וַאֲנִי ׀ קִרְבַת

אֱלֹהִים לִי טוֹב שַׁתִּי ׀ בַּאדֹנָי יֱהֹוִה מַחְסִי לְסַפֵּר כָּל־מַלְאֲכוֹתֶיךָ:

עד   א מַשְׂכִּיל לְאָסָף לָמָה אֱלֹהִים זָנַחְתָּ לָנֶצַח יֶעְשַׁן אַפְּךָ בְּצֹאן מַרְעִיתֶךָ:

ב זְכֹר עֲדָתְךָ ׀ קָנִיתָ קֶּדֶם גָּאַלְתָּ שֵׁבֶט נַחֲלָתֶךָ הַר־צִיּוֹן זֶה ׀ שָׁכַנְתָּ בּוֹ:

ג־ד הָרִימָה פְעָמֶיךָ לְמַשֻּׁאוֹת נֶצַח כָּל־הֵרַע אוֹיֵב בַּקֹּדֶשׁ: שָׁאֲגוּ צֹרְרֶיךָ בְּקֶרֶב

ה מוֹעֲדֶךָ שָׂמוּ אוֹתֹתָם אֹתוֹת: יִוָּדַע כְּמֵבִיא לְמָעְלָה בִּסְבָךְ־עֵץ קַרְדֻּמּוֹת:

ו־ז °וְעֵת [°וְעַתָּה ק] פִּתּוּחֶיהָ יָּחַד בְּכַשִּׁיל וְכֵילַפּוֹת יַהֲלֹמוּן: שִׁלְחוּ בָאֵשׁ

ח מִקְדָּשֶׁךָ לָאָרֶץ חִלְּלוּ מִשְׁכַּן־שְׁמֶךָ: אָמְרוּ בְלִבָּם נִינָם יָחַד שָׂרְפוּ כָל־

ט מוֹעֲדֵי־אֵל בָּאָרֶץ: אוֹתֹתֵינוּ לֹא רָאִינוּ אֵין־עוֹד נָבִיא וְלֹא־אִתָּנוּ יֹדֵעַ

י־יא עַד־מָה: עַד־מָתַי אֱלֹהִים יְחָרֶף צָר יְנָאֵץ אוֹיֵב שִׁמְךָ לָנֶצַח: לָמָה תָשִׁיב

יב יָדְךָ וִימִינֶךָ מִקֶּרֶב °חוֹקְךָ [°חֵיקְךָ ק] כַלֵּה: וֵאלֹהִים מַלְכִּי מִקֶּדֶם פֹּעֵל

73:12. This question regarding Divine justice is a recurrent and perplexing problem.

73:17. *I was vexed by this until I thought of God's "sanctuaries,"* the eternal World to Come where the righteous receive true reward. By comparison, the fleeting pleasures of This World are insignificant (*Radak*).

74:4. When they prevailed over the Holy Temple in Jerusalem, they construed their success as a "sign" that their cause was just.

74:5-6. The Temple had been constructed with such religious joy that the very act of bringing the axe to a forest to chop the necessary wood was regarded as an offering to God. "And now" the enemies demolish that glorious Temple.

74:8. The enemies believed that by destroying the Sanctuary they destroyed the future of Judaism. But they failed to realize that God's Torah is not limited to a Temple or a land, but guides Jewish life everywhere.

BOOK THREE

73

*It may seem
that the
wicked
prosper,
exempt from
Divine
punishment.
However, a
deeper and
broader
perspective
reveals the
emptiness
and futility
of their
glamorous
lives.*

¹ A song of Asaph. Truly God is good to Israel, to the pure of heart. ² But as for
me, my feet were almost turned astray; my steps were very nearly washed
aside. ³ For I envied the roisterers, when I saw the peace of the wicked. ⁴ Because
there are no fetters to their death, and their vitality is sound. ⁵ They are excluded
from the toil of frail humans, and they are not plagued as are other men.
⁶ Therefore arrogance is their necklace; their violence wraps their hips [with fat].
⁷ Their eye bulges from fat, they have exceeded the fantasies of [their] heart.
⁸ They consume, and speak evilly about oppression, from on high do they speak.
⁹ They set their mouth against Heaven, and their tongue struts on earth.
¹⁰ Therefore His people return here, and the [bitter] waters of the full [cup] are
sucked out by them. ¹¹ And they say, "How can God know? Is there knowledge
in the Most High?" ¹² Behold these are the wicked, but they are always tranquil,
they have attained great wealth. * ¹³ Surely in vain have I purified my heart, and
washed my hands in cleanliness. ¹⁴ For I was plagued all day long, and I was
chastised every morning. ¹⁵ Were I to say, "I will tell how it is," behold I would
cause the generation of Your children to rebel. ¹⁶ And when I reflected to understand this, it was iniquity in my eyes, ¹⁷ until I came to the sanctuaries of God; I
contemplated their end. * ¹⁸ Only on slippery places do You set them, You cast
them down into destruction. ¹⁹ How have they become desolate in an instant!
They came to an end, they were consumed through bewildering terrors. ²⁰ Like a
dream upon awakening, so, the Lord, in the city You will render their appearance
despicable. ²¹ When my heart was in ferment, though my mind was sharpened,
²² and I was senseless and unknowing, like [mindless] beasts was I with You;
²³ still, I was always with You, You grasped my right hand. ²⁴ May You guide me
in Your counsel; and afterwards, You will take [my] soul unto You. ²⁵ Whom [else]
do I have in heaven? And when I am with You I do not desire [anything] on earth.
²⁶ My flesh and my heart yearn — God is the rock of my heart and my portion
forever. ²⁷ For behold, those removed from You shall perish, You cut down all who
stray from You. ²⁸ But as for me, God's nearness is my good; I have placed my
trust in the Lord HASHEM/ELOHIM, to recount all of Your works.

74

*From the
agony of
exile, the
Jew prays
that God will
deliver His
nation,
thereby
causing His
sovereignty
to be
acknowl-
edged
by the
entire world.*

¹ A maskil by Asaph. Why, O God, have You abandoned [us] for an eternity?
[Why] does Your wrath smolder against the sheep of Your pasture?
² Remember Your congregation, which You acquired long ago, You redeemed the
tribe of Your heritage; the mountain of Zion, the one where You rested Your
Presence. ³ Lift Your footsteps to wreak eternal ruin, [to avenge] everything that
the enemy has harmed in the Sanctuary. ⁴ Your enemies have roared amidst Your
meeting place, they made their signs for signs. * ⁵ It had been regarded as bringing
[a gift] to the One Above, the axes in the thicket of trees;* ⁶ and now all its
ornaments together, they beat down with hammer and chisels. ⁷ They have sent
Your Sanctuary up in flames; to the ground have they desecrated the Abode of
Your Name. ⁸ In their heart, they said — their rulers all together — they have
burned all of God's meeting places on earth. * ⁹ Our signs we have not seen; there
is no longer a prophet, and there is none among us who knows for how long.
¹⁰ Until when, O God, will the tormentor revile, will the foe blaspheme Your Name
forever? ¹¹ Why do You withdraw Your hand, even Your right hand? Remove
[it] from within Your bosom! ¹² For God is my King from days of old, working

יג יְשׁוּעוֹת בְּקֶרֶב הָאָרֶץ: אַתָּה פוֹרַרְתָּ בְעָזְּךָ יָם שִׁבַּרְתָּ רָאשֵׁי תַנִּינִים עַל־

יד-טו הַמָּיִם: אַתָּה רִצַּצְתָּ רָאשֵׁי לִוְיָתָן תִּתְּנֶנּוּ מַאֲכָל לְעָם לְצִיִּים: אַתָּה בָקַעְתָּ

טז מַעְיָן וָנָחַל אַתָּה הוֹבַשְׁתָּ נַהֲרוֹת אֵיתָן: לְךָ יוֹם אַף־לְךָ לָיְלָה אַתָּה

יז הֲכִינוֹתָ מָאוֹר וָשָׁמֶשׁ: אַתָּה הִצַּבְתָּ כָּל־גְּבוּלוֹת אָרֶץ קַיִץ וָחֹרֶף אַתָּה

יח-יט יְצַרְתָּם: זְכָר־זֹאת אוֹיֵב חֵרֵף | יהוה וְעַם נָבָל נִאֲצוּ שְׁמֶךָ: אַל־תִּתֵּן לְחַיַּת

כ נֶפֶשׁ תּוֹרֶךָ חַיַּת עֲנִיֶּיךָ אַל־תִּשְׁכַּח לָנֶצַח: הַבֵּט לַבְּרִית כִּי מָלְאוּ מַחֲשַׁכֵּי־

כא-כב אֶרֶץ נְאוֹת חָמָס: אַל־יָשֹׁב דַּךְ נִכְלָם עָנִי וְאֶבְיוֹן יְהַלְלוּ שְׁמֶךָ: קוּמָה

כג אֱלֹהִים רִיבָה רִיבֶךָ זְכֹר חֶרְפָּתְךָ מִנִּי־נָבָל כָּל־הַיּוֹם: אַל־תִּשְׁכַּח קוֹל

צֹרְרֶיךָ שְׁאוֹן קָמֶיךָ עֹלֶה תָמִיד:

עה א-ב לַמְנַצֵּחַ אַל־תַּשְׁחֵת מִזְמוֹר לְאָסָף שִׁיר: הוֹדִינוּ לְּךָ | אֱלֹהִים הוֹדִינוּ

ג-ד וְקָרוֹב שְׁמֶךָ סִפְּרוּ נִפְלְאוֹתֶיךָ: כִּי אֶקַּח מוֹעֵד אֲנִי מֵישָׁרִים אֶשְׁפֹּט: נְמֹגִים

ה אֶרֶץ וְכָל־יֹשְׁבֶיהָ אָנֹכִי תִכַּנְתִּי עַמּוּדֶיהָ סֶּלָה: אָמַרְתִּי לַהוֹלְלִים אַל־

ו תָּהֹלּוּ וְלָרְשָׁעִים אַל־תָּרִימוּ קָרֶן: אַל־תָּרִימוּ לַמָּרוֹם קַרְנְכֶם תְּדַבְּרוּ

ז-ח בְצַוָּאר עָתָק: כִּי לֹא מִמּוֹצָא וּמִמַּעֲרָב וְלֹא מִמִּדְבַּר הָרִים: כִּי־אֱלֹהִים

ט שֹׁפֵט זֶה יַשְׁפִּיל וְזֶה יָרִים: כִּי כוֹס בְּיַד־יהוה וְיַיִן חָמַר | מָלֵא מֶסֶךְ וַיַּגֵּר

י מִזֶּה אַךְ־שְׁמָרֶיהָ יִמְצוּ יִשְׁתּוּ כֹּל רִשְׁעֵי־אָרֶץ: וַאֲנִי אַגִּיד לְעֹלָם אֲזַמְּרָה

יא לֵאלֹהֵי יַעֲקֹב: וְכָל־קַרְנֵי רְשָׁעִים אֲגַדֵּעַ תְּרוֹמַמְנָה קַרְנוֹת צַדִּיק:

עו א-ב לַמְנַצֵּחַ בִּנְגִינֹת מִזְמוֹר לְאָסָף שִׁיר: נוֹדָע בִּיהוּדָה אֱלֹהִים בְּיִשְׂרָאֵל גָּדוֹל

ג שְׁמוֹ: וַיְהִי בְשָׁלֵם סֻכּוֹ וּמְעוֹנָתוֹ בְצִיּוֹן: שָׁמָּה שִׁבַּר רִשְׁפֵי־קָשֶׁת מָגֵן וְחֶרֶב

ה וּמִלְחָמָה סֶּלָה: נָאוֹר אַתָּה אַדִּיר מֵהַרְרֵי־טָרֶף: אֶשְׁתּוֹלְלוּ | אַבִּירֵי לֵב

ו נָמוּ שְׁנָתָם וְלֹא־מָצְאוּ כָל־אַנְשֵׁי־חַיִל יְדֵיהֶם: מִגַּעֲרָתְךָ אֱלֹהֵי יַעֲקֹב

ח-ט נִרְדָּם וְרֶכֶב וָסוּס: אַתָּה | נוֹרָא אַתָּה וּמִי־יַעֲמֹד לְפָנֶיךָ מֵאָז אַפֶּךָ:

י מִשָּׁמַיִם הִשְׁמַעְתָּ דִּין אֶרֶץ יָרְאָה וְשָׁקָטָה: בְּקוּם־לַמִּשְׁפָּט אֱלֹהִים

יא-יב לְהוֹשִׁיעַ כָּל־עַנְוֵי־אֶרֶץ סֶלָה: כִּי־חֲמַת אָדָם תּוֹדֶךָּ שְׁאֵרִית חֵמֹת תַּחְגֹּר:

יג נִדְרוּ וְשַׁלְּמוּ לַיהוה אֱלֹהֵיכֶם כָּל־סְבִיבָיו יוֹבִילוּ שַׁי לַמּוֹרָא: יִבְצֹר רוּחַ

נְגִידִים נוֹרָא לְמַלְכֵי־אָרֶץ:

עז א-ב לַמְנַצֵּחַ עַל־יְדִיתוּן [°יְדוּתוּן ק] לְאָסָף מִזְמוֹר: קוֹלִי אֶל־אֱלֹהִים

יום טו לחדש

ג וְאֶצְעָקָה קוֹלִי אֶל־אֱלֹהִים וְהַאֲזִין אֵלָי: בְּיוֹם צָרָתִי אֲדֹנָי דָּרָשְׁתִּי יָדִי |

ד לַיְלָה נִגְּרָה וְלֹא תָפוּג מֵאֲנָה הִנָּחֵם נַפְשִׁי: אֶזְכְּרָה אֱלֹהִים וְאֶהֱמָיָה

74:21. Do not reject his prayer, and turn him away from You empty-handed.

75:4. Even if the moral fiber of the entire world will have melted, God's moral absolutes will remain applicable and relevant, and they will ultimately prevail (R' Hirsch).

75:10. The story of God's vengeance.

76:3. The Holy Temple *will* be rebuilt. The psalmist uses the past tense to emphasize the inevitable fulfillment of this prophecy.

76:4. All instruments of war and defense will become obsolete (see *Isaiah 2:4*; *Micah 4:3*).

76:9. From its war against Israel.

76:11. Reports of God's intervention will instill fear in the nations and cause them to suppress their anger against Israel.

77:3. The long night of exile.

salvations in the midst of the earth. ¹³ You shattered the sea with Your might; You smashed the heads of sea serpents upon the water. ¹⁴ You crushed the head of Leviathan; You will serve him as food to the people destined for the desolate wilderness. ¹⁵ You split open fountain and stream; You dried the mighty rivers. ¹⁶ Yours is the day, Yours is the night; You prepared the luminary and the sun. ¹⁷ You established all the boundaries of earth; summer and winter, You fashioned them. ¹⁸ Remember this: The foe reviled HASHEM, and the degenerate people blasphemed Your Name. ¹⁹ Do not deliver the soul of Your turtledove to the wild beast, do not forget the life of Your poor forever. ²⁰ Look upon the covenant, for the earth's dark places [of Israel's exile] are filled with habitations of violence. ²¹ Let not the oppressed turn back in shame;* let the poor and destitute praise Your Name. ²² Arise, O God, champion Your cause! Remember Your disgrace from the degenerate all day long. ²³ Forget not the voice of your enemies, the tumult of Your opponents which always rises.

75

A prayer for the ultimate Redemption, when God will bring about the collapse of evil, and the lasting elevation of Israel

¹ For the conductor, a plea to be spared from destruction, a psalm by Asaph, a song. ² We have acknowledged You, O God, we have acknowledged, and Your Name is near; Your wonders have declared [this]: ³ "When I shall seize the appointed time, I shall judge with fairness. ⁴ The earth and all its inhabitants are melted, I have firmly established its pillars,* Selah." ⁵ I said to the roisterers, "Be not profligate"; and to the wicked, "Raise not your pride." ⁶ Raise not your pride, heavenward, [nor] speak insolence with a haughty neck. ⁷ For neither from sunrise nor from sunset, nor from the wilderness comes greatness. ⁸ For God is the Judge — He lowers this one and raises that one. ⁹ For there is a cup [of punishment] in HASHEM's hand, with strong wine of full mixture, which overflows from it; [until] all the wicked of the earth will drain and drink only its dregs. ¹⁰ But as for me, I shall recount [it]* forever; I shall sing to the God of Jacob! ¹¹ And I shall cut down all the pride of the wicked; the pride of the righteous shall be exalted!

76

A prayer for the time when people will realize the futility of rebelling against God, and will completely accept His mastery

¹ For the conductor, with the neginos, a psalm of Asaph, a song. ² God is recognized in Judah; in Israel His Name is great. ³ Then His Tabernacle was in Jerusalem,* and His Dwelling in Zion. ⁴ There He broke the flying bows, shield, sword, and battle,* Selah. ⁵ Illuminated are You, more powerful than the towering predators. ⁶ Bereft of reason were the stout-hearted, they slept their sleep, and all the warriors could not find their strength. ⁷ At Your rebuke, O God of Jacob, chariot and horse were stunned. ⁸ You, awesome are You! And who can stand before You when You are wrathful. ⁹ From heaven You made judgment heard; the earth feared, and subsided,* ¹⁰ when God arose to pass judgment, to save all the earth's humble, Selah. ¹¹ For the rage of man will acknowledge You; You will restrain the remnant of anger.* ¹² Make vows and fulfill them to HASHEM, your God; all who surround Him will present gifts to the Awesome One. ¹³ He will cut down the arrogance of the nobles; He is awesome to the kings of the earth.

77

¹ For the conductor, on Jeduthun, by Asaph, a psalm. ² My voice is to God when I cry out; My voice is to God, that He give ear to me. ³ On the day of my distress, I sought the Lord. My wound oozes through the night* and does not cease; my soul refuses to be comforted. ⁴ I remember God and I moan;

ה אָשִׂיחָה ׀ וְתִתְעַטֵּף רוּחִי סֶלָה: אָחַזְתָּ שְׁמֻרוֹת עֵינָי נִפְעַמְתִּי וְלֹא אֲדַבֵּר:

ו-ז חִשַּׁבְתִּי יָמִים מִקֶּדֶם שְׁנוֹת עוֹלָמִים: אֶזְכְּרָה נְגִינָתִי בַּלָּיְלָה עִם־לְבָבִי

ח אָשִׂיחָה וַיְחַפֵּשׂ רוּחִי: הַלְעוֹלָמִים יִזְנַח ׀ אֲדֹנָי וְלֹא־יֹסִיף לִרְצוֹת עוֹד:

ט-י הֶאָפֵס לָנֶצַח חַסְדּוֹ גָּמַר אֹמֶר לְדֹר וָדֹר: הֲשָׁכַח חַנּוֹת אֵל אִם־קָפַץ בְּאַף

יא-יב רַחֲמָיו סֶלָה: וָאֹמַר חַלּוֹתִי הִיא שְׁנוֹת יְמִין עֶלְיוֹן: °אזכיר [°אֶזְכּוֹר ק]

יג מַעַלְלֵי־יָהּ כִּי־אֶזְכְּרָה מִקֶּדֶם פִּלְאֶךָ: וְהָגִיתִי בְכָל־פָּעֳלֶךָ וּבַעֲלִילוֹתֶיךָ

יד-טו אָשִׂיחָה: אֱלֹהִים בַּקֹּדֶשׁ דַּרְכֶּךָ מִי־אֵל גָּדוֹל כֵּאלֹהִים: אַתָּה הָאֵל עֹשֵׂה

טז פֶלֶא הוֹדַעְתָּ בָעַמִּים עֻזֶּךָ: גָּאַלְתָּ בִּזְרוֹעַ עַמֶּךָ בְּנֵי־יַעֲקֹב וְיוֹסֵף סֶלָה: רָאוּךָ

יז מַיִם ׀ אֱלֹהִים רָאוּךָ מַיִם יָחִילוּ אַף יִרְגְּזוּ תְהֹמוֹת: זֹרְמוּ מַיִם ׀ עָבוֹת קוֹל

יח נָתְנוּ שְׁחָקִים אַף־חֲצָצֶיךָ יִתְהַלָּכוּ: קוֹל רַעַמְךָ ׀ בַּגַּלְגַּל הֵאִירוּ בְרָקִים תֵּבֵל

כ רָגְזָה וַתִּרְעַשׁ הָאָרֶץ: בַּיָּם דַּרְכֶּךָ °ושבילי [°וּשְׁבִילְךָ ק] בְּמַיִם רַבִּים

כא וְעִקְּבוֹתֶיךָ לֹא נֹדָעוּ: נָחִיתָ כַצֹּאן עַמֶּךָ בְּיַד־מֹשֶׁה וְאַהֲרֹן:

עח א-ב מַשְׂכִּיל לְאָסָף הַאֲזִינָה עַמִּי תּוֹרָתִי הַטּוּ אָזְנְכֶם לְאִמְרֵי־פִי: אֶפְתְּחָה

ג בְמָשָׁל פִּי אַבִּיעָה חִידוֹת מִנִּי־קֶדֶם: אֲשֶׁר שָׁמַעְנוּ וַנֵּדָעֵם וַאֲבוֹתֵינוּ סִפְּרוּ־

ד לָנוּ: לֹא נְכַחֵד ׀ מִבְּנֵיהֶם לְדוֹר אַחֲרוֹן מְסַפְּרִים תְּהִלּוֹת יְהוָה וֶעֱזוּזוֹ

ה וְנִפְלְאֹתָיו אֲשֶׁר עָשָׂה: וַיָּקֶם עֵדוּת ׀ בְּיַעֲקֹב וְתוֹרָה שָׂם בְּיִשְׂרָאֵל אֲשֶׁר

ו צִוָּה אֶת־אֲבוֹתֵינוּ לְהוֹדִיעָם לִבְנֵיהֶם: לְמַעַן יֵדְעוּ ׀ דּוֹר אַחֲרוֹן בָּנִים יִוָּלֵדוּ

ז יָקֻמוּ וִיסַפְּרוּ לִבְנֵיהֶם: וְיָשִׂימוּ בֵאלֹהִים כִּסְלָם וְלֹא יִשְׁכְּחוּ מַעַלְלֵי־אֵל

ח וּמִצְוֹתָיו יִנְצֹרוּ: וְלֹא יִהְיוּ ׀ כַּאֲבוֹתָם דּוֹר סוֹרֵר וּמֹרֶה דּוֹר לֹא־הֵכִין לִבּוֹ

ט וְלֹא־נֶאֶמְנָה אֶת־אֵל רוּחוֹ: בְּנֵי־אֶפְרַיִם נוֹשְׁקֵי רוֹמֵי־קָשֶׁת הָפְכוּ בְּיוֹם

י-יא קְרָב: לֹא שָׁמְרוּ בְּרִית אֱלֹהִים וּבְתוֹרָתוֹ מֵאֲנוּ לָלֶכֶת: וַיִּשְׁכְּחוּ עֲלִילוֹתָיו

יב וְנִפְלְאוֹתָיו אֲשֶׁר הֶרְאָם: נֶגֶד אֲבוֹתָם עָשָׂה פֶלֶא בְּאֶרֶץ מִצְרַיִם שְׂדֵה־

יג-יד צֹעַן: בָּקַע יָם וַיַּעֲבִירֵם וַיַּצֶּב־מַיִם כְּמוֹ־נֵד: וַיַּנְחֵם בֶּעָנָן יוֹמָם וְכָל־הַלַּיְלָה

טו-טז בְּאוֹר אֵשׁ: יְבַקַּע צֻרִים בַּמִּדְבָּר וַיַּשְׁקְ כִּתְהֹמוֹת רַבָּה: וַיּוֹצִא נוֹזְלִים

יז מִסָּלַע וַיּוֹרֶד כַּנְּהָרוֹת מָיִם: וַיּוֹסִיפוּ עוֹד לַחֲטֹא־לוֹ לַמְרוֹת עֶלְיוֹן בַּצִּיָּה:

יח-יט וַיְנַסּוּ־אֵל בִּלְבָבָם לִשְׁאָל־אֹכֶל לְנַפְשָׁם: וַיְדַבְּרוּ בֵּאלֹהִים אָמְרוּ הֲיוּכַל

כ אֵל לַעֲרֹךְ שֻׁלְחָן בַּמִּדְבָּר: הֵן הִכָּה־צוּר ׀ וַיָּזוּבוּ מַיִם וּנְחָלִים יִשְׁטֹפוּ

כא הֲגַם־לֶחֶם יוּכַל תֵּת אִם־יָכִין שְׁאֵר לְעַמּוֹ: לָכֵן ׀ שָׁמַע יְהוָה וַיִּתְעַבָּר

כב וְאֵשׁ נִשְּׂקָה בְיַעֲקֹב וְגַם־אַף עָלָה בְיִשְׂרָאֵל: כִּי לֹא הֶאֱמִינוּ בֵּאלֹהִים

77:5. The suffering of exile was so intense that sleep was impossible.

77:11. I realized that God withdrew His might from me to chasten me, so that I would repent.

77:20. The waters reverted to their natural course leaving no imprint behind. Those who experienced God's presence must overcome their natural tendency to let it recede from their consciousness.

78:2. Rather than "parables" and "riddles" in the usual sense, the psalm reviews events of Jewish history. The events of Israel's history are parables in the sense that they are object lessons for all time (*R' Hirsch*).

78:12. Zoan was a major Egyptian city.

78:13. See *Exodus* 14:21-22.

78:14. See *Exodus* 13:21.

78:15. See *Exodus* 17:17.

When the chastisement of exile has fully purified His nation, God will again intervene as He did when He redeemed Israel from Egypt.

I speak and my spirit swoons, Selah. [5] You held fast my eyelids; * I was agitated and could not speak. [6] [Then] I pondered olden days, ancient years. [7] I recall my [Temple] music in the night; in my heart I meditate, and my spirit searches: [8] Is it for eternity that the Lord rejects me, nevermore to be appeased? [9] Is His kindness ended forever? Has He sealed the decree for all generations? [10] Has God forgotten graciousness? Has He shut off His mercy in anger? Selah. [11] And I said, "It is to make me infirm — this change of the Most High One's right hand."* [12] I recall the works of God, when I remember Your ancient wonders. [13] I shall meditate upon all Your deeds and speak about Your works. [14] O God, Your way is in sanctity, what power is as great as God? [15] You are the God Who works wonders, You manifested Your might among the nations. [16] With Your powerful arm You redeemed Your nation, the sons of Jacob and Joseph, Selah. [17] The waters saw You, O God, the waters saw You and were terrified; even the depths trembled. [18] Clouds streamed water, heavens sounded forth, even Your arrows [of lightning] went forth. [19] The rumble of Your thunder was in the rolling wind; lightning bolts lit the world, the earth trembled and roared. [20] In the sea was Your way, and Your path went through the mighty waters; and Your footsteps were not known.* [21] You led Your nation like a flock, by the hand of Moses and Aaron.

78

God's love and concern for Israel are ever present. Failure to keep that memory alive is a major cause of sin, while remembering it brings solace in difficult times.

[1] A maskil by Asaph. Listen, my people, to my teaching, incline your ear to the words of my mouth. [2] I will open my mouth with a parable, I will utter [and explain] riddles* from antiquity. [3] That which we have heard and know and our fathers told us, [4] we shall not withhold from their sons, recounting unto the final generation the praises of HASHEM, His might and His wonders that He has wrought. [5] He established a testimony in Jacob and set down a Torah in Israel, which He commanded our fathers, to make them known to their sons. [6] So that the final generation may know; children yet to be born will arise and tell their own children; [7] so that they may place their trust in God, and not forget the works of God, and they will safeguard His commandments. [8] That they not become like their fathers, a wayward and rebellious generation; a generation that did not dedicate its heart aright, and whose spirit was not steadfast with God. [9] The sons of Ephraim, though armed archers, retreated on the day of battle, [10] [because] they did not guard the covenant of God, and they refused to follow His Torah. [11] They forgot His works, and His wonders that He had shown them. [12] In the presence of their fathers He did marvels, in the land of Egypt, in the field of Zoan. * [13] He split the sea and brought them across, and He stood the water like a wall. * [14] He led them with a cloud by day, and all night long with a fiery light. * [15] He split rocks in the wilderness, and provided drink like the abundant depths. * [16] He brought forth flowing waters from the rock, and caused waters to descend like rivers. [17] But they continued further to sin against Him, to rebel against the Most High in the thirsty desert. * [18] And they tested God in their hearts, by requesting food for their craving. * [19] And they spoke against God. They said, "Can God prepare a table in the wilderness? [20] True, He struck a rock and water flowed and streams flooded forth — [but] can He give bread also? Can He supply meat for His people?" [21] Therefore HASHEM heard and was enraged; and a fire was kindled against Jacob, and also anger flared against Israel. [22] For they did not have faith in God,

---

78:17. See *Numbers* 20:1-6.
78:18. See *Numbers* 11:1-6. People have a right to pray

for their needs, but the complaining, testy manner in which the Jews demanded meat was sinful.

כג-כד וְלֹא בָטְחוּ בִּישׁוּעָתוֹ: וַיְצַו שְׁחָקִים מִמָּעַל וְדַלְתֵי שָׁמַיִם פָּתָח: וַיַּמְטֵר

כה עֲלֵיהֶם מָן לֶאֱכֹל וּדְגַן־שָׁמַיִם נָתַן לָמוֹ: לֶחֶם אַבִּירִים אָכַל אִישׁ צֵידָה

כו-כז שָׁלַח לָהֶם לָשֹׂבַע: יַסַּע קָדִים בַּשָּׁמָיִם וַיְנַהֵג בְּעֻזּוֹ תֵימָן: וַיַּמְטֵר עֲלֵיהֶם

כח כֶּעָפָר שְׁאֵר וּכְחוֹל יַמִּים עוֹף כָּנָף: וַיַּפֵּל בְּקֶרֶב מַחֲנֵהוּ סָבִיב לְמִשְׁכְּנֹתָיו:

כט-ל וַיֹּאכְלוּ וַיִּשְׂבְּעוּ מְאֹד וְתַאֲוָתָם יָבִא לָהֶם: לֹא־זָרוּ מִתַּאֲוָתָם עוֹד אָכְלָם

לא בְּפִיהֶם: וְאַף אֱלֹהִים ׀ עָלָה בָהֶם וַיַּהֲרֹג בְּמִשְׁמַנֵּיהֶם וּבַחוּרֵי יִשְׂרָאֵל

לב-לג הִכְרִיעַ: בְּכָל־זֹאת חָטְאוּ־עוֹד וְלֹא־הֶאֱמִינוּ בְּנִפְלְאוֹתָיו: וַיְכַל־בַּהֶבֶל

לד-לה יְמֵיהֶם וּשְׁנוֹתָם בַּבֶּהָלָה: אִם־הֲרָגָם וּדְרָשׁוּהוּ וְשָׁבוּ וְשִׁחֲרוּ־אֵל: וַיִּזְכְּרוּ

לו כִּי־אֱלֹהִים צוּרָם וְאֵל עֶלְיוֹן גֹּאֲלָם: וַיְפַתּוּהוּ בְּפִיהֶם וּבִלְשׁוֹנָם יְכַזְּבוּ־לוֹ:

לז-לח וְלִבָּם לֹא־נָכוֹן עִמּוֹ וְלֹא נֶאֶמְנוּ בִּבְרִיתוֹ: וְהוּא רַחוּם ׀ יְכַפֵּר עָוֹן וְלֹא־

לט יַשְׁחִית וְהִרְבָּה לְהָשִׁיב אַפּוֹ וְלֹא־יָעִיר כָּל־חֲמָתוֹ: וַיִּזְכֹּר כִּי־בָשָׂר הֵמָּה

מ-מא רוּחַ הוֹלֵךְ וְלֹא יָשׁוּב: כַּמָּה יַמְרוּהוּ בַמִּדְבָּר יַעֲצִיבוּהוּ בִּישִׁימוֹן: וַיָּשׁוּבוּ

מב וַיְנַסּוּ אֵל וּקְדוֹשׁ יִשְׂרָאֵל הִתְווּ: לֹא־זָכְרוּ אֶת־יָדוֹ יוֹם אֲשֶׁר־פָּדָם מִנִּי־

מג-מד צָר: אֲשֶׁר־שָׂם בְּמִצְרַיִם אֹתוֹתָיו וּמוֹפְתָיו בִּשְׂדֵה־צֹעַן: וַיַּהֲפֹךְ לְדָם

מה יְאֹרֵיהֶם וְנֹזְלֵיהֶם בַּל־יִשְׁתָּיוּן: יְשַׁלַּח בָּהֶם עָרֹב וַיֹּאכְלֵם וּצְפַרְדֵּעַ

מו-מז וַתַּשְׁחִיתֵם: וַיִּתֵּן לֶחָסִיל יְבוּלָם וִיגִיעָם לָאַרְבֶּה: יַהֲרֹג בַּבָּרָד גַּפְנָם

מח-מט וְשִׁקְמוֹתָם בַּחֲנָמַל: וַיַּסְגֵּר לַבָּרָד בְּעִירָם וּמִקְנֵיהֶם לָרְשָׁפִים: יְשַׁלַּח־בָּם ׀

נ חֲרוֹן אַפּוֹ עֶבְרָה וָזַעַם וְצָרָה מִשְׁלַחַת מַלְאֲכֵי רָעִים: יְפַלֵּס נָתִיב לְאַפּוֹ

נא לֹא־חָשַׂךְ מִמָּוֶת נַפְשָׁם וְחַיָּתָם לַדֶּבֶר הִסְגִּיר: וַיַּךְ כָּל־בְּכוֹר בְּמִצְרָיִם

נב רֵאשִׁית אוֹנִים בְּאָהֳלֵי־חָם: וַיַּסַּע כַּצֹּאן עַמּוֹ וַיְנַהֲגֵם כַּעֵדֶר בַּמִּדְבָּר:

נג-נד וַיַּנְחֵם לָבֶטַח וְלֹא פָחָדוּ וְאֶת־אוֹיְבֵיהֶם כִּסָּה הַיָּם: וַיְבִיאֵם אֶל־גְּבוּל

נה קָדְשׁוֹ הַר־זֶה קָנְתָה יְמִינוֹ: וַיְגָרֶשׁ מִפְּנֵיהֶם ׀ גּוֹיִם וַיַּפִּילֵם בְּחֶבֶל נַחֲלָה

נו וַיַּשְׁכֵּן בְּאָהֳלֵיהֶם שִׁבְטֵי יִשְׂרָאֵל: וַיְנַסּוּ וַיַּמְרוּ אֶת־אֱלֹהִים עֶלְיוֹן וְעֵדוֹתָיו

נז-נח לֹא שָׁמָרוּ: וַיִּסֹּגוּ וַיִּבְגְּדוּ כַּאֲבוֹתָם נֶהְפְּכוּ כְּקֶשֶׁת רְמִיָּה: וַיַּכְעִיסוּהוּ

נט בְּבָמוֹתָם וּבִפְסִילֵיהֶם יַקְנִיאוּהוּ: שָׁמַע אֱלֹהִים וַיִּתְעַבָּר וַיִּמְאַס מְאֹד

ס-סא בְּיִשְׂרָאֵל: וַיִּטֹּשׁ מִשְׁכַּן שִׁלוֹ אֹהֶל שִׁכֵּן בָּאָדָם: וַיִּתֵּן לַשְּׁבִי עֻזּוֹ וְתִפְאַרְתּוֹ

סב-סג בְּיַד־צָר: וַיַּסְגֵּר לַחֶרֶב עַמּוֹ וּבְנַחֲלָתוֹ הִתְעַבָּר: בַּחוּרָיו אָכְלָה־אֵשׁ

סד-סה וּבְתוּלֹתָיו לֹא הוּלָּלוּ: כֹּהֲנָיו בַּחֶרֶב נָפָלוּ וְאַלְמְנֹתָיו לֹא תִבְכֶּינָה: וַיִּקַץ

סו כְּיָשֵׁן ׀ אֲדֹנָי כְּגִבּוֹר מִתְרוֹנֵן מִיָּיִן: וַיַּךְ־צָרָיו אָחוֹר חֶרְפַּת עוֹלָם נָתַן לָמוֹ:

78:24. See *Exodus* Chapter 16.

78:27. See *Numbers* 11:31-34.

78:36. Their repentance was insincere.

78:38. He forgives in some measure even when the repentance is incomplete.

78:44. *Exodus* 7:19-24.

78:45. See *Exodus* 8:16-28; 7:26-11.

78:46. See *Exodus* 10:1-20.

78:47-48. See *Exodus* 9:13-35.

78:51. Mizraim, the progenitor of the Egyptians, was a son of Ham the son of Noah (*Genesis* 10:6).

78:60. Where it had stood for 369 years, until the Ark was captured by the Philistines (see *I Samuel* Ch. 4).

78:61. The Ark of the Covenant, the symbol of God's "strength and splendor."

and trusted not in His salvation, [23] *[even though] He had already commanded the skies above, and opened the doors of heaven,* [24] *and rained upon them manna * to eat, and gave them heavenly grain.* [25] *Humans ate the bread of angels; He sent them food for satisfaction.* [26] *He made the east [wind] blow in the heavens and He steered the south [wind] with His strength,* [27] *and He rained upon them meat like dust, and winged birds like the sand of seas, * [28] and He dropped it amid His camp, around His dwellings.* [29] *Then they ate and were very sated, for He brought them their craving.* [30] *They had not yet been estranged from their craving; their food was still in their mouth,* [31] *when the anger of God flared against them and slew their fattest, and He bent over the chosen of Israel.* [32] *Nevertheless, they sinned further and did not believe in His wonders.* [33] *So He ended their days in vanity, and their years in bewildering terror.* [34] *When He slew them, then they would seek Him; they would repent and pray to God.* [35] *They would remember that God was their Rock, and the Most High God their Redeemer.* [36] *But they sought to beguile him with their mouth, * and they deceived Him with their tongues.* [37] *Their heart was not constant with Him, and they were not steadfast in His covenant.* [38] *Nevertheless, He, the Merciful One, * is forgiving of iniquity and does not destroy; frequently He withdraws His anger, not arousing His entire wrath.* [39] *For He remembered that they were but flesh, a fleeting breath, not returning.* [40] *How often did they defy Him in the wilderness, did they grieve Him in the wasteland!* [41] *Again and again they tested God, and they set limits to the Holy One of Israel.* [42] *They did not remember His hand, the day He redeemed them from the oppressor;* [43] *how he set His signs in Egypt, and His wonders in the field of Zoan,* [44] *and changed their rivers into blood and made their flowing waters undrinkable. * [45] He sent against them a mixture of beasts that devoured them, and frogs that brought them ruin. * [46] He gave the grasshopper their produce, and their wearying labor to the locust. * [47] He killed their grapevines with hail, and their fig-trees with biting frost. * [48] He delivered their cattle to the hail, and their flocks to the fiery bolts.* [49] *He sent upon them His fierce anger, fury and wrath and trouble, a band of emissaries of evil.* [50] *He leveled a path for His anger; He did not spare their soul from death, and He delivered their lives to pestilence.* [51] *He smote every firstborn in Egypt, the first fruit of their strength in the tents of Ham. * [52] Then He caused His nation to journey like sheep, and guided them like a flock in the wilderness.* [53] *He led them with security so they had no fear, for the sea had covered their foes.* [54] *And He brought them to His sacred boundary, this mountain that His right hand acquired.* [55] *Then He drove away nations from before them and apportioned them a measured inheritance, and settled the tribes of Israel in their tents.* [56] *Yet they tested and rebelled against the Supreme God, and did not observe His testimonies.* [57] *They drew back and betrayed like their fathers, they shifted like a treacherous bow.* [58] *They angered Him with their high altars, and they aroused His jealousy with their idols.* [59] *God heard and His anger overflowed, and He greatly rejected Israel.* [60] *He abandoned the Tabernacle of Shiloh, * the tent where He dwelled among men.* [61] *He placed His strength into captivity, and His splendor into the oppressor's hand. * [62] And He delivered His people to the sword, and His anger overflowed against His inheritance.* [63] *Fire consumed His young men, and His maidens had no marriage celebration.* [64] *His priests fell by the sword, and His widows did not weep.* [65] *Then the Lord awoke like one who had been sleeping, like a warrior rousing himself from wine.* [66] *He struck His enemies into retreat, He gave them eternal disgrace.*

סז־סח	וַיִּמְאַס בְּאֹהֶל יוֹסֵף וּבְשֵׁבֶט אֶפְרַיִם לֹא בָחָר: וַיִּבְחַר אֶת־שֵׁבֶט
סט	יְהוּדָה אֶת־הַר־צִיּוֹן אֲשֶׁר אָהֵב: וַיִּבֶן כְּמוֹ־רָמִים מִקְדָּשׁוֹ כְּאֶרֶץ יְסָדָהּ
ע־עא	לְעוֹלָם: וַיִּבְחַר בְּדָוִד עַבְדּוֹ וַיִּקָּחֵהוּ מִמִּכְלְאֹת צֹאן: מֵאַחַר עָלוֹת הֱבִיאוֹ
עב	לִרְעוֹת בְּיַעֲקֹב עַמּוֹ וּבְיִשְׂרָאֵל נַחֲלָתוֹ: וַיִּרְעֵם כְּתֹם לְבָבוֹ וּבִתְבוּנוֹת
	כַּפָּיו יַנְחֵם:

עט
יוֹם טֹב לַחֹדֶשׁ

א	מִזְמוֹר לְאָסָף אֱלֹהִים בָּאוּ גוֹיִם בְּנַחֲלָתֶךָ טִמְּאוּ אֶת־הֵיכַל קָדְשֶׁךָ שָׂמוּ
ב	אֶת־יְרוּשָׁלַ͏ִם לְעִיִּים: נָתְנוּ אֶת־נִבְלַת עֲבָדֶיךָ מַאֲכָל לְעוֹף הַשָּׁמָיִם בְּשַׂר
ג	חֲסִידֶיךָ לְחַיְתוֹ־אָרֶץ: שָׁפְכוּ דָמָם כַּמַּיִם סְבִיבוֹת יְרוּשָׁלָ͏ִם וְאֵין קוֹבֵר:
ד־ה	הָיִינוּ חֶרְפָּה לִשְׁכֵנֵינוּ לַעַג וָקֶלֶס לִסְבִיבוֹתֵינוּ: עַד־מָה יְהוָה תֶּאֱנַף לָנֶצַח
ו	תִּבְעַר כְּמוֹ־אֵשׁ קִנְאָתֶךָ: שְׁפֹךְ חֲמָתְךָ אֶל־הַגּוֹיִם אֲשֶׁר לֹא־יְדָעוּךָ וְעַל
ז	מַמְלָכוֹת אֲשֶׁר בְּשִׁמְךָ לֹא קָרָאוּ: כִּי אָכַל אֶת־יַעֲקֹב וְאֶת־נָוֵהוּ הֵשַׁמּוּ:
ח	אַל־תִּזְכָּר־לָנוּ עֲוֺנֹת רִאשֹׁנִים מַהֵר יְקַדְּמוּנוּ רַחֲמֶיךָ כִּי דַלּוֹנוּ מְאֹד:
ט	עָזְרֵנוּ אֱלֹהֵי יִשְׁעֵנוּ עַל־דְּבַר כְּבוֹד־שְׁמֶךָ וְהַצִּילֵנוּ וְכַפֵּר עַל־חַטֹּאתֵינוּ
י	לְמַעַן שְׁמֶךָ: לָמָּה יֹאמְרוּ הַגּוֹיִם אַיֵּה אֱלֹהֵיהֶם יִוָּדַע °בַּגֹּיִם [°בַּגּוֹיִם ק]
יא	לְעֵינֵינוּ נִקְמַת דַּם־עֲבָדֶיךָ הַשָּׁפוּךְ: תָּבוֹא לְפָנֶיךָ אֶנְקַת אָסִיר כְּגֹדֶל
יב	זְרוֹעֲךָ הוֹתֵר בְּנֵי תְמוּתָה: וְהָשֵׁב לִשְׁכֵנֵינוּ שִׁבְעָתַיִם אֶל־חֵיקָם חֶרְפָּתָם
יג	אֲשֶׁר חֵרְפוּךָ אֲדֹנָי: וַאֲנַחְנוּ עַמְּךָ וְצֹאן מַרְעִיתֶךָ נוֹדֶה לְּךָ לְעוֹלָם לְדֹר
	וָדֹר נְסַפֵּר תְּהִלָּתֶךָ:

פ

א־ב	לַמְנַצֵּחַ אֶל־שֹׁשַׁנִּים עֵדוּת לְאָסָף מִזְמוֹר: רֹעֵה יִשְׂרָאֵל הַאֲזִינָה נֹהֵג
ג	כַּצֹּאן יוֹסֵף יֹשֵׁב הַכְּרוּבִים הוֹפִיעָה: לִפְנֵי אֶפְרַיִם וּבִנְיָמִן וּמְנַשֶּׁה עוֹרְרָה
ד	אֶת־גְּבוּרָתֶךָ וּלְכָה לִישֻׁעָתָה לָּנוּ: אֱלֹהִים הֲשִׁיבֵנוּ וְהָאֵר פָּנֶיךָ וְנִוָּשֵׁעָה:
ה־ו	יְהוָה אֱלֹהִים צְבָאוֹת עַד־מָתַי עָשַׁנְתָּ בִּתְפִלַּת עַמֶּךָ: הֶאֱכַלְתָּם לֶחֶם
ז	דִּמְעָה וַתַּשְׁקֵמוֹ בִּדְמָעוֹת שָׁלִישׁ: תְּשִׂימֵנוּ מָדוֹן לִשְׁכֵנֵינוּ וְאֹיְבֵינוּ יִלְעֲגוּ
ח־ט	לָמוֹ: אֱלֹהִים צְבָאוֹת הֲשִׁיבֵנוּ וְהָאֵר פָּנֶיךָ וְנִוָּשֵׁעָה: גֶּפֶן מִמִּצְרַיִם תַּסִּיעַ
י־יא	תְּגָרֵשׁ גּוֹיִם וַתִּטָּעֶהָ: פִּנִּיתָ לְפָנֶיהָ וַתַּשְׁרֵשׁ שָׁרָשֶׁיהָ וַתְּמַלֵּא־אָרֶץ: כָּסּוּ
יב	הָרִים צִלָּהּ וַעֲנָפֶיהָ אַרְזֵי־אֵל: תְּשַׁלַּח קְצִירֶהָ עַד־יָם וְאֶל־נָהָר יוֹנְקוֹתֶיהָ:
יג־יד	לָמָּה פָּרַצְתָּ גְדֵרֶיהָ וְאָרוּהָ כָּל־עֹבְרֵי דָרֶךְ: יְכַרְסְמֶנָּה חֲזִיר *מִיָּעַר וְזִיז
טו	שָׂדַי יִרְעֶנָּה: אֱלֹהִים צְבָאוֹת שׁוּב־נָא הַבֵּט מִשָּׁמַיִם וּרְאֵה וּפְקֹד גֶּפֶן זֹאת:
טז־יז	וְכַנָּה אֲשֶׁר־נָטְעָה יְמִינֶךָ וְעַל־בֵּן אִמַּצְתָּה לָּךְ: שְׂרֻפָה בָאֵשׁ כְּסוּחָה
יח	מִגַּעֲרַת פָּנֶיךָ יֹאבֵדוּ: תְּהִי־יָדְךָ עַל־אִישׁ יְמִינֶךָ עַל־בֶּן־אָדָם אִמַּצְתָּ לָּךְ:

*עֵין תליה

78:70. See *I Samuel* 16:11. The true Jewish leader displays the character and qualities of a shepherd, who is devoted to the welfare of his flock.

79:2. Once a person is punished for his sins, he reverts to his status as God's devout servant (*Rashi*).

80:2. The entire Jewish nation is called by Joseph's name because he sustained them in Egypt during the famine (*Rashi*).

80:7. A euphemism for mocking God (*Ibn Ezra*).

80:13. Some of the Children of Israel's finest products are plucked from its vineyard to espouse alien cultures.

80:14. The nations of the world.

67 He rejected the tent of Joseph and did not choose the tribe of Ephraim; 68 He chose the tribe of Judah, Mount Zion, which He loves. 69 And He built His Temple like the high heavens; like the earth He established it forever. 70 And He chose David, His servant, and took him from the sheep corrals. * 71 From behind the nursing ewes He brought him; to tend to Jacob, His nation, and to Israel, His inheritance. 72 And he tended them according to the integrity of his heart, and by the skill of his hands he led them.

79

A prayer that Israel be restored to its land, so that God's honor will be restored in the eyes of a doubting world

1 A psalm of Asaph: O God! The nations have entered into Your inheritance, they have defiled the Sanctuary of Your holiness, they have turned Jerusalem into heaps of rubble. 2 They have given the corpse of Your servants * as food for the birds of the sky, the flesh of Your devout ones to the beasts of the earth. 3 They have shed their blood like water round about Jerusalem, and there is none who buries. 4 We became an object of disgrace to our neighbors, of mockery and scorn to those around us. 5 Until when, HASHEM, will You be ceaselessly angry, will Your jealousy burn like fire? 6 Pour Your wrath upon the nations that do not recognize You, and upon the kingdoms that do not invoke Your Name. 7 For they have devoured Jacob, and destroyed His habitation. 8 Recall not against us the sins of the ancients; may Your mercies meet us swiftly, for we have become exceedingly impoverished. 9 Assist us, O God of our salvation, for the sake of Your Name's glory, rescue us and atone for our sins for Your Name's sake. 10 Why should the nations say, "Where is their God?" Let there be known among the nations, before our eyes, revenge for Your servants' spilled blood. 11 Let the groan of the prisoner come before You; as befits the greatness of Your might, spare those condemned to die. 12 And repay our neighbors sevenfold into their bosom, their disgrace with which they have disgraced You, O Lord. 13 As for us, Your nation and the sheep of Your pasture, we shall thank You forever; for generation after generation we shall relate Your praise.

80

Recalling its earlier glorious relationship with God, Israel pleads for its restoration.

1 For the conductor, for the shoshannim, a testimony, a psalm of Asaph. 2 Give ear, O Shepherd of Israel, You Who leads Joseph * like a flock; appear, O You Who is enthroned upon the Cherubim. 3 Before Ephraim and Benjamin and Manasseh, arouse Your might, it is for You to save us. 4 O God, return us, and illuminate Your face that we may be saved. 5 HASHEM, God, Master of Legions, how long will You fume at the prayers of Your people? 6 You fed them bread of tears, You made them drink tears in great measure. 7 You made us an object of strife to our neighbors, and our enemies mock themselves. * 8 O God, Master of Legions, return us, and illuminate Your face that we may be saved. 9 You caused a grapevine to journey out of Egypt; You expelled nations and implanted it. 10 You cleared a space before it; it struck its roots and filled the land. 11 Mountains were covered with its shadow, and its branches became mighty cedars. 12 It stretched its boughs until the sea, and its tender shoots until the river. 13 Why have You breached its fences, so that all who pass by the way pluck its fruit? * 14 The boar of the forest ravages it, and the crawler of the field * feeds on it. 15 O God, Master of Legions, please return; look down from heaven and see, and be mindful of this vine. 16 And the foundation that Your right hand has planted, and the son whom You strengthened for Yourself. 17 [He is now] consumed by fire, razed; they perish before Your angry shout. 18 Let Your strong hand protect the man acquired by Your right hand, the son of man whom You strengthened for Yourself.

יט־כ וְלֹא־נָסוֹג מִמֶּךָ תְּחַיֵּנוּ וּבְשִׁמְךָ נִקְרָא: יְהֹוָה אֱלֹהִים צְבָאוֹת הֲשִׁיבֵנוּ הָאֵר פָּנֶיךָ וְנִוָּשֵׁעָה:

פא א־ב לַמְנַצֵּחַ ׀ עַל־הַגִּתִּית לְאָסָף: הַרְנִינוּ לֵאלֹהִים עוּזֵּנוּ הָרִיעוּ לֵאלֹהֵי
ג יַעֲקֹב: שְׂאוּ־זִמְרָה וּתְנוּ־תֹף כִּנּוֹר נָעִים עִם־נָבֶל: תִּקְעוּ בַחֹדֶשׁ שׁוֹפָר
ד־ה בַּכֵּסֶה לְיוֹם חַגֵּנוּ: כִּי חֹק לְיִשְׂרָאֵל הוּא מִשְׁפָּט לֵאלֹהֵי יַעֲקֹב: עֵדוּת ׀
בִּיהוֹסֵף שָׂמוֹ בְּצֵאתוֹ עַל־אֶרֶץ מִצְרָיִם שְׂפַת לֹא־יָדַעְתִּי אֶשְׁמָע:
ו־ח הֲסִירוֹתִי מִסֵּבֶל שִׁכְמוֹ כַּפָּיו מִדּוּד תַּעֲבֹרְנָה: בַּצָּרָה קָרָאתָ וָאֲחַלְּצֶךָּ
אֶעֶנְךָ בְּסֵתֶר רַעַם אֶבְחָנְךָ עַל־מֵי מְרִיבָה סֶלָה: שְׁמַע עַמִּי וְאָעִידָה בָּךְ
ט־י יִשְׂרָאֵל אִם־תִּשְׁמַע־לִי: לֹא־יִהְיֶה בְךָ אֵל זָר וְלֹא תִשְׁתַּחֲוֶה לְאֵל נֵכָר:
יא אָנֹכִי ׀ יְהֹוָה אֱלֹהֶיךָ הַמַּעַלְךָ מֵאֶרֶץ מִצְרָיִם הַרְחֶב־פִּיךָ וַאֲמַלְאֵהוּ:
יב־יג וְלֹא־שָׁמַע עַמִּי לְקוֹלִי וְיִשְׂרָאֵל לֹא־אָבָה לִי: וָאֲשַׁלְּחֵהוּ בִּשְׁרִירוּת
יד־טו לִבָּם יֵלְכוּ בְּמוֹעֲצוֹתֵיהֶם: לוּ עַמִּי שֹׁמֵעַ לִי יִשְׂרָאֵל בִּדְרָכַי יְהַלֵּכוּ: כִּמְעַט
טז אוֹיְבֵיהֶם אַכְנִיעַ וְעַל צָרֵיהֶם אָשִׁיב יָדִי: מְשַׂנְאֵי יְהֹוָה יְכַחֲשׁוּ־לוֹ וִיהִי
עִתָּם לְעוֹלָם: וַיַּאֲכִילֵהוּ מֵחֵלֶב חִטָּה וּמִצּוּר דְּבַשׁ אַשְׂבִּיעֶךָ:

פב א־ב מִזְמוֹר לְאָסָף אֱלֹהִים נִצָּב בַּעֲדַת־אֵל בְּקֶרֶב אֱלֹהִים יִשְׁפֹּט: עַד־מָתַי
ג תִּשְׁפְּטוּ־עָוֶל וּפְנֵי רְשָׁעִים תִּשְׂאוּ־סֶלָה: שִׁפְטוּ־דָל וְיָתוֹם עָנִי וָרָשׁ
ד־ה הַצְדִּיקוּ: פַּלְּטוּ־דַל וְאֶבְיוֹן מִיַּד רְשָׁעִים הַצִּילוּ: לֹא יָדְעוּ ׀ וְלֹא יָבִינוּ
ו בַּחֲשֵׁכָה יִתְהַלָּכוּ יִמּוֹטוּ כָּל־מוֹסְדֵי אָרֶץ: אֲנִי־אָמַרְתִּי אֱלֹהִים אַתֶּם וּבְנֵי
ז־ח עֶלְיוֹן כֻּלְּכֶם: אָכֵן כְּאָדָם תְּמוּתוּן וּכְאַחַד הַשָּׂרִים תִּפֹּלוּ: קוּמָה אֱלֹהִים
שָׁפְטָה הָאָרֶץ כִּי־אַתָּה תִנְחַל בְּכָל־הַגּוֹיִם:

פג א־ב שִׁיר מִזְמוֹר לְאָסָף: אֱלֹהִים אַל־דֳּמִי־לָךְ אַל־תֶּחֱרַשׁ וְאַל־תִּשְׁקֹט
ג־ד אֵל: כִּי־הִנֵּה אוֹיְבֶיךָ יֶהֱמָיוּן וּמְשַׂנְאֶיךָ נָשְׂאוּ רֹאשׁ: עַל־עַמְּךָ יַעֲרִימוּ
ה סוֹד וְיִתְיָעֲצוּ עַל־צְפוּנֶיךָ: אָמְרוּ לְכוּ וְנַכְחִידֵם מִגּוֹי וְלֹא־יִזָּכֵר שֵׁם־
ו־ז יִשְׂרָאֵל עוֹד: כִּי נוֹעֲצוּ לֵב יַחְדָּו עָלֶיךָ בְּרִית יִכְרֹתוּ: אָהֳלֵי אֱדוֹם
וְיִשְׁמְעֵאלִים מוֹאָב וְהַגְרִים: גְּבָל וְעַמּוֹן וַעֲמָלֵק פְּלֶשֶׁת עִם־יֹשְׁבֵי צוֹר:
ח־ט גַּם־אַשּׁוּר נִלְוָה עִמָּם הָיוּ זְרוֹעַ לִבְנֵי־לוֹט סֶלָה: עֲשֵׂה־לָהֶם כְּמִדְיָן
י־יא כְּסִיסְרָא כְיָבִין בְּנַחַל קִישׁוֹן: נִשְׁמְדוּ בְעֵין־דֹּאר הָיוּ דֹּמֶן לָאֲדָמָה:
יב־יג שִׁיתֵמוֹ נְדִיבֵמוֹ כְּעֹרֵב וְכִזְאֵב וּכְזֶבַח וּכְצַלְמֻנָּע כָּל־נְסִיכֵמוֹ: אֲשֶׁר אָמְרוּ
יד נִירֲשָׁה לָּנוּ אֵת נְאוֹת אֱלֹהִים: אֱלֹהַי שִׁיתֵמוֹ כַגַּלְגַּל כְּקַשׁ לִפְנֵי־
טו־טז רוּחַ: כְּאֵשׁ תִּבְעַר־יָעַר וּכְלֶהָבָה תְּלַהֵט הָרִים: כֵּן תִּרְדְּפֵם בְּסַעֲרֶךָ

81:8. See *Numbers* 20:1-13.

81:11. With requests.

81:16. Israel's time.

82:2-4. These verses are addressed directly to judges who fail to carry out their responsibilities.

82:5. Many judges are unaware of their awesome responsibility; they walk in darkness, blinded by prejudice and selfishness.

82:8. Since human judges are corrupt, You must see to it that justice prevails in the world.

83:9. Ammon and Moab.

83:10-11. See *Judges* Chapter 4.

(פג margin note) יום יז לחדש

¹⁹ *Then we shall not draw back from You; revive us and we shall proclaim Your Name.* ²⁰ HASHEM, *God, Master of Legions, return us; illuminate Your face that we may be saved.*

81

No matter how low one has sunk, a firm resolve to heed God's word will cause Him to loosen the fetters and send Redemption.

¹ **F**or the conductor, on the gittis, by Asaph. ² *Sing joyously to the God of our strength, call out to the God of Jacob —* ³ *Raise up a song and sound the drum, the sweet harp with the lyre.* ⁴ *Blow the shofar at the moon's renewal, at the time appointed for our festive day.* ⁵ *Because it is a decree for Israel, a judgment [day] for the God of Jacob.* ⁶ *He appointed it as a testimony for Joseph when He went out over the land of Egypt, when I heard a language unknown to me.* ⁷ *[Says God:] "I removed his shoulder from the burden, his hands passed from the kettle.* ⁸ *In distress you called out, and I released you; I answered you when you called privately with a thunderous reply, I tested you at the Waters of Strife,* * Selah. ⁹ *Listen, My people, and I will attest to you; O Israel, if you would but listen to Me.* ¹⁰ *There shall be no strange god within you, nor shall you bow before an alien god.* ¹¹ *I am* HASHEM, *your God, Who raised you from the land of Egypt; open wide your mouth** and I will fill it."* ¹² *But My people did not heed My voice; Israel did not desire Me.* ¹³ *So I let them follow their heart's fantasies, that they might follow their own counsels.* ¹⁴ *If only My people would heed Me, if Israel would walk in My ways.* ¹⁵ *In an instant I would subdue their foes, and against their tormentors I would turn My hand.* ¹⁶ *Those who hate* HASHEM *would lie to him; but their** time would be forever.* ¹⁷ *And He would feed him with the cream of the wheat, and from a rock I would sate you with honey.*

82

The maintenance of equity and justice is a prerequisite for the continued existence of the world.

¹ **A** psalm of Asaph: God stands in the Divine assembly, in the midst of judges shall He judge. ² *Until when will you** judge lawlessly and favor the presence of the wicked, Selah?* ³ *Dispense justice for the needy and the orphan; vindicate the poor and impoverished.* ⁴ *Rescue the needy and destitute, and deliver them from the hand of the wicked.* ⁵ *They do not know nor do they understand,** they walk in darkness; all the foundations of the earth collapse.* ⁶ *I said, "You are angelic, sons of the Most High are you all."* ⁷ *But like men you shall die, and like one of the princes you shall fall.* ⁸ *Arise, O God,** judge the earth, for You shall seek Your inheritance among all the nations.*

83

The historical enmity of the nations against Israel is an outgrowth of hatred for that which Israel stands for: the complete subordination of all human striving to God's will.

¹ **A** song, a psalm of Asaph. ² *O God, do not hold Yourself silent; be not deaf and be not still, O God.* ³ *For behold, Your foes are in uproar and those who hate You have raised their head.* ⁴ *Against Your people they plot deviously, they take counsel against those sheltered by You.* ⁵ *They said, "Come, let us cut them off from nationhood, so Israel's name will not be remembered any longer!"* ⁶ *For they take counsel together unanimously, they strike a covenant against You:* ⁷ *The tents of Edom and Ishmaelites; Moab and Hagrites;* ⁸ *Gebal and Ammon, and Amalek; Philistia, with the inhabitants of Tyre.* ⁹ *Even Assyria joined with them, they became the strong arm of Lot's sons,** Selah.* ¹⁰ *Do to them as to Midian, as to Sisera and as to Jabin at Kishon Brook,* ¹¹ *who were destroyed at Ein-dor;** they became dung for the earth.* ¹² *Make their nobles like Oreb and Zeeb; and all their princes like Zebah and Zalmunna.** ¹³ *Who** said, "We will conquer for ourselves the pleasant habitations of God."* ¹⁴ *O my God, make them like the whirling chaff, like stubble before the wind;* ¹⁵ *like a fire burning the forest, and like a flame that sets mountains ablaze.* ¹⁶ *So pursue them with Your tempest*

83:12. See *Judges* 7:25; 8:12,21.   **83:13.** The nations enumerated in verses 7-9.

יז-יח וּבְסוּפָתְךָ תְבַהֲלֵם: מַלֵּא פְנֵיהֶם קָלוֹן וִיבַקְשׁוּ שִׁמְךָ יְהוָה: יֵבֹשׁוּ וְיִבָּהֲלוּ
יט עֲדֵי־עַד וְיַחְפְּרוּ וְיֹאבֵדוּ: וְיֵדְעוּ כִּי־אַתָּה שִׁמְךָ יְהוָה לְבַדֶּךָ עֶלְיוֹן עַל־
כָּל־הָאָרֶץ:
פד א-ב לַמְנַצֵּחַ עַל־הַגִּתִּית לִבְנֵי־קֹרַח מִזְמוֹר: מַה־יְּדִידוֹת מִשְׁכְּנוֹתֶיךָ יְהוָה
ג צְבָאוֹת: נִכְסְפָה וְגַם־כָּלְתָה | נַפְשִׁי לְחַצְרוֹת יְהוָה לִבִּי וּבְשָׂרִי יְרַנְּנוּ אֶל
*ק׳ רבתי ד אֵל־חָי: גַּם־צִפּוֹר | מָצְאָה בַיִת וּדְרוֹר | *קֵן לָהּ אֲשֶׁר־שָׁתָה אֶפְרֹחֶיהָ
ה אֶת־מִזְבְּחוֹתֶיךָ יְהוָה צְבָאוֹת מַלְכִּי וֵאלֹהָי: אַשְׁרֵי יוֹשְׁבֵי בֵיתֶךָ עוֹד
ו-ז יְהַלְלוּךָ סֶּלָה: אַשְׁרֵי אָדָם עוֹז־לוֹ בָךְ מְסִלּוֹת בִּלְבָבָם: עֹבְרֵי | בְּעֵמֶק
ח הַבָּכָא מַעְיָן יְשִׁיתוּהוּ גַּם־בְּרָכוֹת יַעְטֶה מוֹרֶה: יֵלְכוּ מֵחַיִל אֶל־חָיִל
ט יֵרָאֶה אֶל־אֱלֹהִים בְּצִיּוֹן: יְהוָה אֱלֹהִים צְבָאוֹת שִׁמְעָה תְפִלָּתִי הַאֲזִינָה
י-יא אֱלֹהֵי יַעֲקֹב סֶלָה: מָגִנֵּנוּ רְאֵה אֱלֹהִים וְהַבֵּט פְּנֵי מְשִׁיחֶךָ: כִּי טוֹב־יוֹם
יב בַּחֲצֵרֶיךָ מֵאָלֶף בָּחַרְתִּי הִסְתּוֹפֵף בְּבֵית אֱלֹהַי מִדּוּר בְּאָהֳלֵי־רֶשַׁע: כִּי
שֶׁמֶשׁ | וּמָגֵן יְהוָה אֱלֹהִים חֵן וְכָבוֹד יִתֵּן יְהוָה לֹא יִמְנַע־טוֹב לַהֹלְכִים
יג בְּתָמִים: יְהוָה צְבָאוֹת אַשְׁרֵי אָדָם בֹּטֵחַ בָּךְ:
פה א-ב לַמְנַצֵּחַ | לִבְנֵי־קֹרַח מִזְמוֹר: רָצִיתָ יְהוָה אַרְצֶךָ שַׁבְתָּ °שבות [°שְׁבִית ק]
ג-ד יַעֲקֹב: נָשָׂאתָ עֲוֹן עַמֶּךָ כִּסִּיתָ כָל־חַטָּאתָם סֶלָה: אָסַפְתָּ כָל־עֶבְרָתֶךָ
ה-ו הֱשִׁיבוֹתָ מֵחֲרוֹן אַפֶּךָ: שׁוּבֵנוּ אֱלֹהֵי יִשְׁעֵנוּ וְהָפֵר כַּעַסְךָ עִמָּנוּ: הַלְעוֹלָם
ז תֶּאֱנַף־בָּנוּ תִּמְשֹׁךְ אַפְּךָ לְדֹר וָדֹר: הֲלֹא־אַתָּה תָּשׁוּב תְּחַיֵּנוּ וְעַמְּךָ
ח-ט יִשְׂמְחוּ־בָךְ: הַרְאֵנוּ יְהוָה חַסְדֶּךָ וְיֶשְׁעֲךָ תִּתֶּן־לָנוּ: אֶשְׁמְעָה מַה־יְדַבֵּר
הָאֵל | יְהוָה כִּי | יְדַבֵּר שָׁלוֹם אֶל־עַמּוֹ וְאֶל־חֲסִידָיו וְאַל־יָשׁוּבוּ לְכִסְלָה:
י-יא אַךְ | קָרוֹב לִירֵאָיו יִשְׁעוֹ לִשְׁכֹּן כָּבוֹד בְּאַרְצֵנוּ: חֶסֶד־וֶאֱמֶת נִפְגָּשׁוּ צֶדֶק
יב-יג וְשָׁלוֹם נָשָׁקוּ: אֱמֶת מֵאֶרֶץ תִּצְמָח וְצֶדֶק מִשָּׁמַיִם נִשְׁקָף: גַּם־יְהוָה יִתֵּן
יד הַטּוֹב וְאַרְצֵנוּ תִּתֵּן יְבוּלָהּ: צֶדֶק לְפָנָיו יְהַלֵּךְ וְיָשֵׂם לְדֶרֶךְ פְּעָמָיו:
פו א-ב תְּפִלָּה לְדָוִד הַטֵּה־יְהוָה אָזְנְךָ עֲנֵנִי כִּי־עָנִי וְאֶבְיוֹן אָנִי: שָׁמְרָה נַפְשִׁי
ג כִּי־חָסִיד אָנִי הוֹשַׁע עַבְדְּךָ אַתָּה אֱלֹהַי הַבּוֹטֵחַ אֵלֶיךָ: חָנֵּנִי אֲדֹנָי כִּי
ד אֵלֶיךָ אֶקְרָא כָּל־הַיּוֹם: שַׂמֵּחַ נֶפֶשׁ עַבְדֶּךָ כִּי אֵלֶיךָ אֲדֹנָי נַפְשִׁי
ה-ו אֶשָּׂא: כִּי־אַתָּה אֲדֹנָי טוֹב וְסַלָּח וְרַב־חֶסֶד לְכָל־קֹרְאֶיךָ: הַאֲזִינָה
ז יְהוָה תְּפִלָּתִי וְהַקְשִׁיבָה בְּקוֹל תַּחֲנוּנוֹתָי: בְּיוֹם צָרָתִי אֶקְרָאֶךָּ כִּי תַעֲנֵנִי:
ח-ט אֵין־כָּמוֹךָ בָאֱלֹהִים | אֲדֹנָי וְאֵין כְּמַעֲשֶׂיךָ: כָּל־גּוֹיִם | אֲשֶׁר עָשִׂיתָ
י יָבוֹאוּ | וְיִשְׁתַּחֲווּ לְפָנֶיךָ אֲדֹנָי וִיכַבְּדוּ לִשְׁמֶךָ: כִּי־גָדוֹל אַתָּה וְעֹשֵׂה
יא נִפְלָאוֹת אַתָּה אֱלֹהִים לְבַדֶּךָ: הוֹרֵנִי יְהוָה | דַּרְכֶּךָ אֲהַלֵּךְ בַּאֲמִתֶּךָ

84:4. A bird will unerringly seek its nest where it has nurtured the most precious treasures of its life. So too, the exiled Jew yearns to return to God's service (*R' Hirsch*).

84:7. A play on words: בָּכָא, "thorns," is similar to בָּכָה, "weeping," or "tears."

86:4. Lifting one's soul to God has several connotations: wholehearted supplication, complete dedication, and awaiting His kindness with hope and trust (*Radak*).

and terrify them with Your storm. ¹⁷ Fill their faces with shame, then they will seek Your Name, HASHEM. ¹⁸ Let them be shamed and terrified forever, then they will be disgraced and they will perish. ¹⁹ Then they will know that You — Whose Name is HASHEM — are alone, Most High over all the earth.

84

Neither crushing persecution nor the blandishments of alien prosperity should deflect one from striving to attain closeness with God.

¹ For the conductor, on the gittis, by the sons of Korah, a psalm. ² How beloved are Your dwelling places, HASHEM, Master of Legions! ³ My soul yearns, indeed it pines, for the courtyards of HASHEM; my heart and my flesh pray fervently to the Living God. ⁴ Even the bird finds its home and the free bird her nest where she laid her young; O, [to be] at Your altars, * HASHEM, Master of Legions, my King and my God. ⁵ Praiseworthy are those who dwell in Your house, continually they will praise You, Selah. ⁶ Praiseworthy is the man whose strength is in You, those whose hearts focus on upward paths. ⁷ Those who pass through the Valley of Thorns, * they transform it into a wellspring; also the rain will cloak [it] with blessings. ⁸ They advance from strength to strength; each one will appear before God in Zion. ⁹ HASHEM, God, Master of Legions, hear my prayer; listen, O God of Jacob, Selah. ¹⁰ Look upon our shield, O God, and gaze at Your anointed one's face. ¹¹ For one day in Your courtyards is better than a thousand [elsewhere]; I prefer to stand exposed at the threshold of my God's house than to dwell securely in the tents of wickedness. ¹² For a sun and a shield is HASHEM, God; favor and glory does HASHEM bestow; He withholds no goodness from those who walk in perfect innocence. ¹³ HASHEM, Master of Legions, praiseworthy is the man who trusts in You.

85

As He had restored Israel and the Temple after the first Destruction, so may He again restore them, this time permanently.

¹ For the conductor, by the sons of Korah, a psalm. ² HASHEM, You have favored Your land, You have returned the captivity of Jacob. ³ You have forgiven the iniquity of Your people; You have covered up their entire sin, Selah. ⁴ You have withheld Your entire fury; You have retreated from the fierceness of Your anger. ⁵ Return us, O God of our salvation, and annul Your anger with us. ⁶ Will You forever be angry with us, allowing Your wrath to endure for generation to generation? ⁷ Will You not revive us again, that Your people may rejoice in You? ⁸ Show us Your kindness, HASHEM, and grant us Your salvation. ⁹ I can hear what the Almighty, HASHEM, will speak; for He speaks peace to His people and to His devout ones, and they will not revert to folly. ¹⁰ Surely His salvation is close to those who fear Him, that [His] glory may again dwell in our land. ¹¹ Kindness and Truth have met, Righteousness and Peace have kissed; ¹² Truth will sprout from earth, and Righteousness will peer from heaven. ¹³ HASHEM, too, will provide what is good, and our land will yield its produce. ¹⁴ [The man of] righteousness will walk before Him, and set his footsteps on the way.

86

Wholehearted supplication, complete dedication, and awareness of God's closeness lift one's soul and bring it closer to God.

¹ A prayer of David; HASHEM, incline Your ear, answer me, for I am poor and destitute. ² Guard my soul, for I am devout; save Your servant who trusts You, O You, my God. ³ Show me favor, O Lord, for to You do I call all the day. ⁴ Gladden the soul of Your servant, for to You, O Lord, I lift up my soul. * ⁵ For You, O Lord, are good and forgiving and abundantly kind to all who call upon You. ⁶ Give ear, HASHEM, to my prayer, and heed the sound of my supplications. ⁷ On the day of my distress I call upon You, for You will answer me. ⁸ There is none like You among the powers, O Lord, and there is nothing like Your works. ⁹ All the nations that You have made will come and bow down before You, O Lord, and will give glory to Your Name. ¹⁰ For You are great and work wonders; You alone are God. ¹¹ Teach me, O HASHEM, Your way, that I may travel in Your truth,

יב יַחֵד לְבָבִי לְיִרְאָה שְׁמֶךָ: אוֹדְךָ | אֲדֹנָי אֱלֹהַי בְּכָל־לְבָבִי וַאֲכַבְּדָה שִׁמְךָ

יג-יד לְעוֹלָם: כִּי־חַסְדְּךָ גָּדוֹל עָלָי וְהִצַּלְתָּ נַפְשִׁי מִשְּׁאוֹל תַּחְתִּיָּה: אֱלֹהִים |

זֵדִים קָמוּ־עָלַי וַעֲדַת עָרִיצִים בִּקְשׁוּ נַפְשִׁי וְלֹא שָׂמוּךָ לְנֶגְדָּם: וְאַתָּה

טו אֲדֹנָי אֵל־רַחוּם וְחַנּוּן אֶרֶךְ אַפַּיִם וְרַב־חֶסֶד וֶאֱמֶת: פְּנֵה אֵלַי וְחָנֵּנִי

טז תְּנָה־עֻזְּךָ לְעַבְדֶּךָ וְהוֹשִׁיעָה לְבֶן־אֲמָתֶךָ: עֲשֵׂה־עִמִּי אוֹת לְטוֹבָה וְיִרְאוּ

שֹׂנְאַי וְיֵבֹשׁוּ כִּי־אַתָּה יְהוָה עֲזַרְתַּנִי וְנִחַמְתָּנִי:

פז א לִבְנֵי־קֹרַח מִזְמוֹר שִׁיר יְסוּדָתוֹ בְּהַרְרֵי־קֹדֶשׁ: אֹהֵב יְהוָה שַׁעֲרֵי צִיּוֹן

ג-ד מִכֹּל מִשְׁכְּנוֹת יַעֲקֹב: נִכְבָּדוֹת מְדֻבָּר בָּךְ עִיר הָאֱלֹהִים סֶלָה: אַזְכִּיר |

ה רַהַב וּבָבֶל לְיֹדְעָי הִנֵּה פְלֶשֶׁת וְצוֹר עִם־כּוּשׁ זֶה יֻלַּד־שָׁם: וּלְצִיּוֹן | יֵאָמַר

ו אִישׁ וְאִישׁ יֻלַּד־בָּהּ וְהוּא יְכוֹנְנֶהָ עֶלְיוֹן: יְהוָה יִסְפֹּר בִּכְתוֹב עַמִּים זֶה

ז יֻלַּד־שָׁם סֶלָה: וְשָׁרִים כְּחֹלְלִים כָּל־מַעְיָנַי בָּךְ:

פח א שִׁיר מִזְמוֹר לִבְנֵי קֹרַח לַמְנַצֵּחַ עַל־מָחֲלַת לְעַנּוֹת מַשְׂכִּיל לְהֵימָן

יום יח לחדש

ב-ג הָאֶזְרָחִי: יְהוָה אֱלֹהֵי יְשׁוּעָתִי יוֹם־צָעַקְתִּי בַלַּיְלָה נֶגְדֶּךָ: תָּבוֹא לְפָנֶיךָ

ד תְּפִלָּתִי הַטֵּה־אָזְנְךָ לְרִנָּתִי: כִּי־שָׂבְעָה בְרָעוֹת נַפְשִׁי וְחַיַּי לִשְׁאוֹל הִגִּיעוּ:

ה-ו נֶחְשַׁבְתִּי עִם־יוֹרְדֵי בוֹר הָיִיתִי כְּגֶבֶר אֵין־אֱיָל: בַּמֵּתִים חָפְשִׁי כְּמוֹ

ז חֲלָלִים | שֹׁכְבֵי קֶבֶר אֲשֶׁר לֹא זְכַרְתָּם עוֹד וְהֵמָּה מִיָּדְךָ נִגְזָרוּ: שַׁתַּנִי

ח בְּבוֹר תַּחְתִּיּוֹת בְּמַחֲשַׁכִּים בִּמְצֹלוֹת: עָלַי סָמְכָה חֲמָתֶךָ וְכָל־מִשְׁבָּרֶיךָ

ט עִנִּיתָ סֶּלָה: הִרְחַקְתָּ מְיֻדָּעַי מִמֶּנִּי שַׁתַּנִי תוֹעֵבוֹת לָמוֹ כָּלֻא וְלֹא אֵצֵא:

י עֵינִי דָאֲבָה מִנִּי עֹנִי קְרָאתִיךָ יְהוָה בְּכָל־יוֹם שִׁטַּחְתִּי אֵלֶיךָ כַפָּי:

יא-יב הֲלַמֵּתִים תַּעֲשֶׂה־פֶּלֶא אִם־רְפָאִים יָקוּמוּ | יוֹדוּךָ סֶּלָה: הַיְסֻפַּר בַּקֶּבֶר

יג חַסְדֶּךָ אֱמוּנָתְךָ בָּאֲבַדּוֹן: הֲיִוָּדַע בַּחֹשֶׁךְ פִּלְאֶךָ וְצִדְקָתְךָ בְּאֶרֶץ נְשִׁיָּה:

יד-טו וַאֲנִי | אֵלֶיךָ יְהוָה שִׁוַּעְתִּי וּבַבֹּקֶר תְּפִלָּתִי תְקַדְּמֶךָּ: לָמָה יְהוָה תִּזְנַח נַפְשִׁי

תַּסְתִּיר פָּנֶיךָ מִמֶּנִּי: עָנִי אֲנִי וְגֹוֵעַ מִנֹּעַר נָשָׂאתִי אֵמֶיךָ אָפוּנָה: עָלַי עָבְרוּ

יח חֲרוֹנֶיךָ בִּעוּתֶיךָ צִמְּתוּתֻנִי: סַבּוּנִי כַמַּיִם כָּל־הַיּוֹם הִקִּיפוּ עָלַי יָחַד:

יט הִרְחַקְתָּ מִמֶּנִּי אֹהֵב וָרֵעַ מְיֻדָּעַי מַחְשָׁךְ:

פט א-ב מַשְׂכִּיל לְאֵיתָן הָאֶזְרָחִי: חַסְדֵי יְהוָה עוֹלָם אָשִׁירָה לְדֹר וָדֹר | אוֹדִיעַ

ג אֱמוּנָתְךָ בְּפִי: כִּי־אָמַרְתִּי עוֹלָם חֶסֶד יִבָּנֶה שָׁמַיִם | תָּכִן אֱמוּנָתְךָ בָהֶם:

ד-ה כָּרַתִּי בְרִית לִבְחִירִי נִשְׁבַּעְתִּי לְדָוִד עַבְדִּי: עַד־עוֹלָם אָכִין זַרְעֶךָ וּבָנִיתִי

ו לְדֹר־וָדוֹר כִּסְאֲךָ סֶלָה: וְיוֹדוּ שָׁמַיִם פִּלְאֲךָ יְהוָה אַף־אֱמוּנָתְךָ בִּקְהַל

87:1. Mount Sinai and Mount Zion (*Shocher Tov*). All the greatness described in this psalm stems from the Torah revealed at Sinai, which finds fulfillment around the Holy Temple in Jerusalem (*R' Hirsch*).

87:4-5. Each great nation has occasionally produced great men. Israel, on the other hand, has consistently produced many men of greatness (*Radak*).

87:7. Zion is a "wellspring" that produces an endless supply of people who glorify God (*Ibn Ezra*; *R' Hirsch*).

88:1. *Machalas le'annos* is a musical instrument.

88:6. To sustain them with life; rather, You decreed that they should perish.

89:1. See *I Chronicles* 2:6. The Talmud identifies him as the Patriarch Abraham (*Bava Basra* 14b).

89:4. God is the speaker from here through verse 38.

unite my heart to fear Your Name. [12] I will thank You, O Lord, my God, with all my heart, and I will give honor to Your Name forever. [13] For Your kindness toward me is great, and You have rescued my soul from the nethermost depth. [14] O God, transgressors have risen up against me, a company of ruthless men has sought my soul; and they have not set You before themselves. [15] But You, O Lord, are the Merciful and Compassionate God, Slow to Anger, Abundant in Kindness and Truth. [16] Turn to me and show me favor; give Your strength to Your servant, and save the son of Your handmaid. [17] Display for me a sign for good; so that my enemies may see it and be ashamed, for You, HASHEM, will have helped and consoled me.

87

Greatness and nobility emanate from Jerusalem, Israel's spiritual center.

[1] By the sons of Korah, a psalm, a song, whose foundation is in the holy mountains. * [2] HASHEM loves the gates of Zion more than all the dwellings of Jacob. [3] The most glorious things are spoken of you, O city of God, Selah. [4] I mention Rahab and Babylon to those who know me, behold there are Philistia and Tyre, with Cush, "This one was born there." * [5] But of Zion it can be said, "Man after man was born in her," and He, the Most High, maintains her thus. [6] HASHEM will count, when He records nations, "This one was born there," Selah. [7] But singers as well as flute players, all my wellsprings are in you [O Zion]. *

88

An impassioned plea for deliverance from Israel's long, almost unbearable, exile

[1] A song, a psalm, by the sons of Korah, for the conductor, on the machalas le'annos, * a maskil by Heman the Ezrahite. [2] HASHEM, God of my salvation, I cried out by day — [and] by night before You. [3] Let my prayer come before You, incline Your ear to my supplication. [4] For my soul is sated with troubles, and my life has reached the grave. [5] I was reckoned with those who descend to the pit, I was like a man without strength — [6] among the dead who are free; like the corpses lying in the grave, whom You remember no more, * for they were cut off by Your hand. [7] You placed me in the lowest of pits, into utter darkness, into shadowy depths. [8] Upon me Your wrath weighed down, and You have afflicted [me] with all Your crashing waves, Selah. [9] You have estranged my acquaintances from me; You made me abominable to them; I am imprisoned and cannot leave. [10] My eye is grieved by affliction; I have called upon You, O HASHEM, every day; I have stretched out my hands to You. [11] Will You work wonders for the dead? Will the lifeless arise and offer You thanks? Selah. [12] Will Your kindness be recounted in the grave, or Your faithfulness in utter ruin? [13] Will Your wonders become known in the dark, or Your righteousness in the land of oblivion? [14] As for me, to You, HASHEM, have I cried, and in the morning my prayer will greet You. [15] Why, HASHEM, should You abandon my soul, should You conceal Your face from me? [16] Afflicted am I, and close to death since youth; I have borne Your frightening judgment and feel constant dread. [17] Your rages have gone over me; Your terrors have flayed me. [18] They surround me like water all day long; they encircle me in unison. [19] You have estranged friend and companion from me; my acquaintances have hidden in darkness.

89

Throughout its exile, Israel is sure that God will fulfill His promises to David.

[1] A maskil by Ethan* the Ezrahite. [2] Of HASHEM's kindness I will sing forever; I will make Your faithfulness known to every generation with my mouth. [3] For I said, "Forever will [Your] kindness be built; the heavens, You establish Your faithfulness in them." [4] "I* made a covenant with My chosen one, I have sworn to David, My servant: [5] For all eternity I will establish your seed; and I will build your throne for generation after generation," Selah. [6] Then the heavens will acknowledge Your wonders, HASHEM, Your faithfulness, too, in the assembly of

ד-ח קְדֹשִׁים: כִּי מִי בַשַּׁחַק יַעֲרֹךְ לַיהוָה יִדְמֶה לַיהוָה בִּבְנֵי אֵלִים: אֵל נַעֲרָץ

ט בְּסוֹד־קְדֹשִׁים רַבָּה וְנוֹרָא עַל־כָּל־סְבִיבָיו: יְהוָה ׀ אֱלֹהֵי צְבָאוֹת מִי־

י כָמוֹךָ חֲסִין ׀ יָהּ וֶאֱמוּנָתְךָ סְבִיבוֹתֶיךָ: אַתָּה מוֹשֵׁל בְּגֵאוּת הַיָּם בְּשׂוֹא

יא גַלָּיו אַתָּה תְשַׁבְּחֵם: אַתָּה דִכִּאתָ כֶחָלָל רָהַב בִּזְרוֹעַ עֻזְּךָ פִּזַּרְתָּ אוֹיְבֶיךָ:

יב-יג לְךָ שָׁמַיִם אַף־לְךָ אָרֶץ תֵּבֵל וּמְלֹאָהּ אַתָּה יְסַדְתָּם: צָפוֹן וְיָמִין אַתָּה

יד בְרָאתָם תָּבוֹר וְחֶרְמוֹן בְּשִׁמְךָ יְרַנֵּנוּ: לְךָ זְרוֹעַ עִם־גְּבוּרָה תָּעֹז יָדְךָ

טו-טז תָּרוּם יְמִינֶךָ: צֶדֶק וּמִשְׁפָּט מְכוֹן כִּסְאֶךָ חֶסֶד וֶאֱמֶת יְקַדְּמוּ פָנֶיךָ: אַשְׁרֵי

יז הָעָם יוֹדְעֵי תְרוּעָה יְהוָה בְּאוֹר־פָּנֶיךָ יְהַלֵּכוּן: בְּשִׁמְךָ יְגִילוּן כָּל־הַיּוֹם

יח וּבְצִדְקָתְךָ יָרוּמוּ: כִּי־תִפְאֶרֶת עֻזָּמוֹ אָתָּה וּבִרְצֹנְךָ °תָּרֵים ׳תָּרוּם [°תָּרִים ק]

יט-כ קַרְנֵנוּ: כִּי לַיהוָה מָגִנֵּנוּ וְלִקְדוֹשׁ יִשְׂרָאֵל מַלְכֵּנוּ: אָז דִּבַּרְתָּ בְחָזוֹן

כא לַחֲסִידֶיךָ וַתֹּאמֶר שִׁוִּיתִי עֵזֶר עַל־גִּבּוֹר הֲרִימוֹתִי בָחוּר מֵעָם: מָצָאתִי

כב דָּוִד עַבְדִּי בְּשֶׁמֶן קָדְשִׁי מְשַׁחְתִּיו: אֲשֶׁר יָדִי תִּכּוֹן עִמּוֹ אַף־זְרוֹעִי

כג-כד תְאַמְּצֶנּוּ: לֹא־יַשִּׁא אוֹיֵב בּוֹ וּבֶן־עַוְלָה לֹא יְעַנֶּנּוּ: וְכַתּוֹתִי מִפָּנָיו צָרָיו

כה וּמְשַׂנְאָיו אֶגּוֹף: וֶאֱמוּנָתִי וְחַסְדִּי עִמּוֹ וּבִשְׁמִי תָּרוּם קַרְנוֹ: וְשַׂמְתִּי בַיָּם

כו-כז יָדוֹ וּבַנְּהָרוֹת יְמִינוֹ: הוּא יִקְרָאֵנִי אָבִי אָתָּה אֵלִי וְצוּר יְשׁוּעָתִי: אַף־אָנִי

כט-ל בְּכוֹר אֶתְּנֵהוּ עֶלְיוֹן לְמַלְכֵי־אָרֶץ: לְעוֹלָם °אשמור ׳אֶשְׁמָר [°אֶשְׁמוֹר ק] לוֹ

לא חַסְדִּי וּבְרִיתִי נֶאֱמֶנֶת לוֹ: וְשַׂמְתִּי לָעַד זַרְעוֹ וְכִסְאוֹ כִּימֵי שָׁמָיִם: אִם־

לב יַעַזְבוּ בָנָיו תּוֹרָתִי וּבְמִשְׁפָּטַי לֹא יֵלֵכוּן: אִם־חֻקֹּתַי יְחַלֵּלוּ וּמִצְוֹתַי לֹא

לג-לד יִשְׁמֹרוּ: וּפָקַדְתִּי בְשֵׁבֶט פִּשְׁעָם וּבִנְגָעִים עֲוֹנָם: וְחַסְדִּי לֹא־אָפִיר מֵעִמּוֹ

לה וְלֹא־אֲשַׁקֵּר בֶּאֱמוּנָתִי: לֹא־אֲחַלֵּל בְּרִיתִי וּמוֹצָא שְׂפָתַי לֹא אֲשַׁנֶּה:

לו-לז אַחַת נִשְׁבַּעְתִּי בְקָדְשִׁי אִם־לְדָוִד אֲכַזֵּב: זַרְעוֹ לְעוֹלָם יִהְיֶה וְכִסְאוֹ

לח-לט כַשֶּׁמֶשׁ נֶגְדִּי: כְּיָרֵחַ יִכּוֹן עוֹלָם וְעֵד בַּשַּׁחַק נֶאֱמָן סֶלָה: וְאַתָּה זָנַחְתָּ

מ וַתִּמְאָס הִתְעַבַּרְתָּ עִם־מְשִׁיחֶךָ: נֵאַרְתָּה בְּרִית עַבְדֶּךָ חִלַּלְתָּ לָאָרֶץ

מא-מב נִזְרוֹ: פָּרַצְתָּ כָל־גְּדֵרֹתָיו שַׂמְתָּ מִבְצָרָיו מְחִתָּה: שַׁסֻּהוּ כָּל־עֹבְרֵי

מג דָרֶךְ הָיָה חֶרְפָּה לִשְׁכֵנָיו: הֲרִימוֹתָ יְמִין צָרָיו הִשְׂמַחְתָּ כָּל־אוֹיְבָיו:

מד-מה אַף־תָּשִׁיב צוּר חַרְבּוֹ וְלֹא הֲקֵימֹתוֹ בַּמִּלְחָמָה: הִשְׁבַּתָּ מִטְּהָרוֹ וְכִסְאוֹ

מו-מז לָאָרֶץ מִגַּרְתָּה: הִקְצַרְתָּ יְמֵי עֲלוּמָיו הֶעֱטִיתָ עָלָיו בּוּשָׁה סֶלָה: עַד־

מח מָה יְהוָה תִּסָּתֵר לָנֶצַח תִּבְעַר כְּמוֹ־אֵשׁ חֲמָתֶךָ: זְכָר־אֲנִי מֶה־חָלֶד

מט עַל־מַה־שָּׁוְא בָּרָאתָ כָל־בְּנֵי־אָדָם: מִי גֶבֶר יִחְיֶה וְלֹא יִרְאֶה־מָּוֶת

נ יְמַלֵּט נַפְשׁוֹ מִיַּד־שְׁאוֹל סֶלָה: אַיֵּה ׀ חֲסָדֶיךָ הָרִאשֹׁנִים ׀ אֲדֹנָי נִשְׁבַּעְתָּ

89:11. Egypt.

89:15. Though God is omnipotent, His reign is characterized by "righteousness, justice, kindness, and truth" (*Ibn Ezra*). Unlike human governments, whose ethical and moral standards are based on pragmatic consider-

ations of mutual protection and survival, God's standards are absolute.

89:39. Those of David's royal descendants who abandoned the righteous ways of their ancestor.

holy ones. [7] *For who in the sky can be compared to HASHEM; be likened to HASHEM among the angels?* [8] *God is dreaded in the great counsel of the holy [angels], and is awesome over all who surround Him.* [9] *HASHEM, God of Legions, who is like You, O Strong One, God? Your surrounding angels [attest to] Your faithfulness.* [10] *You rule the grandeur of the sea; when its waves rise, You calm them.* [11] *You crushed arrogant Rahab* like a corpse, with the arm of Your might You scattered Your foes.* [12] *Yours are the heavens, Yours, too, is the earth; the world and its fullness, You founded them.* [13] *North and south — You created them; Tabor and Hermon sing joyously in Your Name.* [14] *Yours is the arm with power; Your hand is strengthened, Your right hand uplifted.* [15] *Righteousness and justice are Your throne's foundation, kindness and truth precede Your countenance.** [16] *Praises to the people who know the shofar's cry; HASHEM, by the illumination of Your countenance they walk.* [17] *In Your Name they rejoice all day long, and through Your righteousness they are exalted.* [18] *For You are the splendor of their power, and through Your favor our pride will be exalted.* [19] *For to HASHEM belongs our shield, and to the Holy One of Israel our king.* [20] *Then You spoke in a vision to Your devout [prophets], and said, "I have placed [My] assistance upon the mighty one, I have exalted the one chosen from among the people.* [21] *I have found David, My servant; with My holy oil I have anointed him;* [22] *with whom My hand shall be established [to assist him], My arm also shall strengthen him.* [23] *The enemy shall not exact from him, nor shall the iniquitous person afflict him.* [24] *And I will smash his tormentors from before him, and smite those who hate him.* [25] *And My faithfulness and My kindness shall be with him, and through My Name his power shall be exalted.* [26] *And I will set his hand upon the sea, and his right hand upon the rivers.* [27] *He will call to Me, 'You are my Father, my God and the Rock of my salvation!'* [28] *I, too, will make him a firstborn, supreme over the earth's kings.* [29] *Forever shall I preserve My kindness for him, and My covenant shall remain true to him.* [30] *And I shall establish his seed eternally, and his throne like the days of the heavens.* [31] *If his sons should forsake My Torah and not walk in My judgments;* [32] *if they should profane My statutes, and not observe My commandments,* [33] *then I will punish their transgression with the rod, and their iniquity with plagues;* [34] *but I shall not utterly remove My kindness from him, and I will not be false to My faithfulness.* [35] *I shall not profane My covenant, and I shall not alter the utterance of My lips.* [36] *One thing have I sworn by My holiness — that I would not be deceitful to David.* [37] *His seed will endure forever, and his throne shall be like the sun before Me.* [38] *Like the moon, it shall be established forever — a faithful witness in the sky, Selah."* [39] *But You have abandoned and rejected; You have been angry with Your anointed one.** [40] *You have destroyed the covenant of Your servant; You have profaned his crown to the ground.* [41] *You have breached all his fences; You have made his strongholds into debris.* [42] *All wayfarers have plundered him; he has become a disgrace to his neighbors.* [43] *You have exalted the right hand of his tormentors; You have gladdened all his foes.* [44] *You even turn back the edge of his sword; and You did not uphold him in battle.* [45] *You brought an end to his splendor, and toppled his throne to the ground.* [46] *You shortened the days of his youth; You shrouded him in shame, Selah.* [47] *Until when, HASHEM, will You constantly hide Yourself, will Your wrath burn like fire?* [48] *I am mindful of how short is my lifetime, for what worthlessness You have created all the sons of man.* [49] *What man lives and will never see death, and will rescue his soul from the grasp of the grave? Selah.* [50] *Where are Your former acts of kindness, O Lord, those You pledged*

נא לְדָוִד בֶּאֱמוּנָתֶךָ: זְכֹר אֲדֹנָי חֶרְפַּת עֲבָדֶיךָ שְׂאֵתִי בְחֵיקִי כָּל־רַבִּים

נב־נג עַמִּים: אֲשֶׁר חֵרְפוּ אוֹיְבֶיךָ | יהוה אֲשֶׁר חֵרְפוּ עִקְּבוֹת מְשִׁיחֶךָ: בָּרוּךְ

יהוה לְעוֹלָם אָמֵן | וְאָמֵן:

סֵפֶר רְבִיעִי

צ
יום חמישי
יום יט לחדש

א תְּפִלָּה לְמֹשֶׁה אִישׁ־הָאֱלֹהִים אֲדֹנָי מָעוֹן אַתָּה הָיִיתָ לָּנוּ בְּדֹר וָדֹר:

ב בְּטֶרֶם | הָרִים יֻלָּדוּ וַתְּחוֹלֵל אֶרֶץ וְתֵבֵל וּמֵעוֹלָם עַד־עוֹלָם אַתָּה אֵל:

ג־ד תָּשֵׁב אֱנוֹשׁ עַד־דַּכָּא וַתֹּאמֶר שׁוּבוּ בְנֵי־אָדָם: כִּי אֶלֶף שָׁנִים בְּעֵינֶיךָ

ה כְּיוֹם אֶתְמוֹל כִּי יַעֲבֹר וְאַשְׁמוּרָה בַלָּיְלָה: זְרַמְתָּם שֵׁנָה יִהְיוּ בַּבֹּקֶר

ו־ז כֶּחָצִיר יַחֲלֹף: בַּבֹּקֶר יָצִיץ וְחָלָף לָעֶרֶב יְמוֹלֵל וְיָבֵשׁ: כִּי־כָלִינוּ בְאַפֶּךָ

ח־ט וּבַחֲמָתְךָ נִבְהָלְנוּ: °שַׁת [°שַׁתָּה ק] עֲוֹנֹתֵינוּ לְנֶגְדֶּךָ עֲלֻמֵנוּ לִמְאוֹר פָּנֶיךָ:

י כִּי כָל־יָמֵינוּ פָּנוּ בְעֶבְרָתֶךָ כִּלִּינוּ שָׁנֵינוּ כְמוֹ־הֶגֶה: יְמֵי־שְׁנוֹתֵינוּ בָהֶם

שִׁבְעִים שָׁנָה וְאִם בִּגְבוּרֹת | שְׁמוֹנִים שָׁנָה וְרָהְבָּם עָמָל וָאָוֶן כִּי־גָז

יא־יב חִישׁ וַנָּעֻפָה: מִי־יוֹדֵעַ עֹז אַפֶּךָ וּכְיִרְאָתְךָ עֶבְרָתֶךָ: לִמְנוֹת יָמֵינוּ כֵּן

יג הוֹדַע וְנָבִא לְבַב חָכְמָה: שׁוּבָה יהוה עַד־מָתָי וְהִנָּחֵם עַל־עֲבָדֶיךָ:

יד־טו שַׂבְּעֵנוּ בַבֹּקֶר חַסְדֶּךָ וּנְרַנְּנָה וְנִשְׂמְחָה בְּכָל־יָמֵינוּ: שַׂמְּחֵנוּ כִּימוֹת

טז עִנִּיתָנוּ שְׁנוֹת רָאִינוּ רָעָה: יֵרָאֶה אֶל־עֲבָדֶיךָ פָעֳלֶךָ וַהֲדָרְךָ עַל־בְּנֵיהֶם:

יז וִיהִי | נֹעַם אֲדֹנָי אֱלֹהֵינוּ עָלֵינוּ וּמַעֲשֵׂה יָדֵינוּ כּוֹנְנָה עָלֵינוּ וּמַעֲשֵׂה יָדֵינוּ

כּוֹנְנֵהוּ:

צא
א־ב יֹשֵׁב בְּסֵתֶר עֶלְיוֹן בְּצֵל שַׁדַּי יִתְלוֹנָן: אֹמַר לַיהוה מַחְסִי וּמְצוּדָתִי אֱלֹהַי

ג־ד אֶבְטַח־בּוֹ: כִּי הוּא יַצִּילְךָ מִפַּח יָקוּשׁ מִדֶּבֶר הַוּוֹת: בְּאֶבְרָתוֹ | יָסֶךְ לָךְ

ה וְתַחַת־כְּנָפָיו תֶּחְסֶה צִנָּה וְסֹחֵרָה אֲמִתּוֹ: לֹא־תִירָא מִפַּחַד לָיְלָה מֵחֵץ

ו־ז יָעוּף יוֹמָם: מִדֶּבֶר בָּאֹפֶל יַהֲלֹךְ מִקֶּטֶב יָשׁוּד צָהֳרָיִם: יִפֹּל מִצִּדְּךָ | אֶלֶף

ח וּרְבָבָה מִימִינֶךָ אֵלֶיךָ לֹא יִגָּשׁ: רַק בְּעֵינֶיךָ תַבִּיט וְשִׁלֻּמַת רְשָׁעִים

ט תִּרְאֶה: כִּי־אַתָּה יהוה מַחְסִי עֶלְיוֹן שַׂמְתָּ מְעוֹנֶךָ: לֹא־תְאֻנֶּה אֵלֶיךָ רָעָה

יא וְנֶגַע לֹא־יִקְרַב בְּאָהֳלֶךָ: כִּי מַלְאָכָיו יְצַוֶּה־לָּךְ לִשְׁמָרְךָ בְּכָל־דְּרָכֶיךָ:

יב־יג עַל־כַּפַּיִם יִשָּׂאוּנְךָ פֶּן־תִּגֹּף בָּאֶבֶן רַגְלֶךָ: עַל־שַׁחַל וָפֶתֶן תִּדְרֹךְ תִּרְמֹס

יד־טו כְּפִיר וְתַנִּין: כִּי בִי חָשַׁק וַאֲפַלְּטֵהוּ אֲשַׂגְּבֵהוּ כִּי־יָדַע שְׁמִי: יִקְרָאֵנִי |

טז וְאֶעֱנֵהוּ עִמּוֹ־אָנֹכִי בְצָרָה אֲחַלְּצֵהוּ וַאֲכַבְּדֵהוּ: אֹרֶךְ יָמִים אַשְׂבִּיעֵהוּ

וְאַרְאֵהוּ בִּישׁוּעָתִי:

90:1. Psalms 90-100 were written by Moses and incorporated by David into *Psalms* (Rashi; *Bava Basra* 14b).

90:3. You crush the pride of arrogant people *(Rashi)*.

90:8. Man may forget his sins, but God's memory is eternal *(Radak)*.

90:9. Because we incurred God's wrath, our days passed by unproductively *(Rashi)*.

90:10. Although Moses, who composed this psalm, lived to one hundred and twenty years, this verse speaks of the average lifespan of people *(Radak)*.

90:12. Help us be mindful of our limited time so that we use it wisely and productively *(Ibn Ezra)*.

90:13. How long will You abandon us? *(Radak)*.

91:14. From here to the end of the psalm, God is the speaker.

to David in Your faithfulness? [51] Remember, O Lord, the taunt of Your servant —
borne in my bosom from the entire multitude of nations — [52] that Your enemies
have taunted, O HASHEM, that they have taunted the footsteps of Your Messiah.
[53] Blessed is HASHEM forever, Amen and Amen.

BOOK FOUR

90

*After
portraying
the brevity
and fragility
of man's
existence on
earth, Moses
beseeches
God to help
man use his
finite time
properly and
productively.*

[1] A prayer by Moses, * the man of God: O Lord, You have been an abode for
us in all generations; [2] before the mountains were born and You had not
yet fashioned the earth and the inhabited land, and from the remotest past and to
the most distant future, You are God. [3] You reduce man to pulp* and You say,
"Repent, O sons of man." [4] For even a thousand years in Your eyes are but a
bygone yesterday, and like a watch in the night. [5] You flood them away, they
become sleeplike; by morning they are like grass that withers. [6] In the morning it
blossoms and is rejuvenated; by evening it is cut down and brittle. [7] For we are
consumed by Your anger; and we are confounded by Your wrath. [8] You have set
our iniquities before Yourself, * our immaturity before the light of Your countenance. [9] For all our days passed by because of Your fury,* we consumed our
years like a fleeting thought. [10] The days of our years among them are seventy
years, * and if with might, eighty years; their proudest success is but toil and
pain, for it is cut off swiftly and we fly away. [11] Who knows the power of Your
anger? As You are feared, so is Your fury. [12] Teach us to count our days, * then
we shall acquire a heart of wisdom. [13] Return, HASHEM, until when?* Relent
concerning Your servants. [14] Satisfy us in the morning with Your kindness, then
we shall sing out and rejoice throughout our days. [15] Gladden us according to the
days You afflicted us, the years when we saw evil. [16] May Your works be visible
to Your servants, and Your majesty upon their children. [17] May the pleasantness
of the Lord, our God, be upon us; our handiwork, establish for us; our handiwork, establish it.

91

*By scorning
conventional
forms of
protection
and seeking
refuge only
in the Most
High, the
believer can
live without
fear of those
who would
harm him.*

[1] Whoever sits in the refuge of the Most High, he shall dwell in the [protective]
shade of the Almighty. [2] I will say of HASHEM, "[He is] my refuge and my
fortress, my God, I will trust in Him." [3] For He will deliver you from the ensnaring
trap, from devastating pestilence. [4] With His pinion He will cover you, and
beneath His wings you will be protected; His truth is shield and armor. [5] You shall
not fear the terror of night; nor of the arrow that flies by day; [6] nor the pestilence
that walks in gloom; nor the destroyer who lays waste at noon. [7] A thousand
may fall victim at your side and a myriad at your right hand, but to you it shall
not approach. [8] You will merely peer with your eyes and you will see the
retribution of the wicked. [9] Because [you said], "You, HASHEM, are my refuge,"
you have made the Most High your abode. [10] No evil will befall you, nor will
any plague come near your tent. [11] He will charge His angels for you, to protect
you in all your ways. [12] On [their] palms they will carry you, lest you strike your
foot against a stone. [13] Upon the lion and the viper you will tread; you will
trample the young lion and the serpent. [14] For he has yearned for Me* and I will
deliver him; I will elevate him because he knows My Name. [15] He will call upon
Me and I will answer him, I am with him in distress; I will release him and I will
bring him honor. [16] With long life will I satisfy him, and I will show him My
salvation.

צב   א-ב מִזְמוֹר שִׁיר לְיוֹם הַשַּׁבָּת: טוֹב לְהֹדוֹת לַיהוָה וּלְזַמֵּר לְשִׁמְךָ עֶלְיוֹן:

ג-ד לְהַגִּיד בַּבֹּקֶר חַסְדֶּךָ וֶאֱמוּנָתְךָ בַּלֵּילוֹת: עֲלֵי-עָשׂוֹר וַעֲלֵי-נָבֶל עֲלֵי הִגָּיוֹן

ה-ו בְּכִנּוֹר: כִּי שִׂמַּחְתַּנִי יהוה בְּפָעֳלֶךָ בְּמַעֲשֵׂי יָדֶיךָ אֲרַנֵּן: מַה-גָּדְלוּ מַעֲשֶׂיךָ

ז יהוה מְאֹד עָמְקוּ מַחְשְׁבֹתֶיךָ: אִישׁ-בַּעַר לֹא יֵדָע וּכְסִיל לֹא-יָבִין אֶת-

ח זֹאת: בִּפְרֹחַ רְשָׁעִים ׀ כְּמוֹ עֵשֶׂב וַיָּצִיצוּ כָּל-פֹּעֲלֵי אָוֶן לְהִשָּׁמְדָם עֲדֵי-

ט-י עַד: וְאַתָּה מָרוֹם לְעֹלָם יהוה: כִּי הִנֵּה אֹיְבֶיךָ ׀ יהוה כִּי-הִנֵּה אֹיְבֶיךָ יֹאבֵדוּ

יא-יב יִתְפָּרְדוּ כָּל-פֹּעֲלֵי אָוֶן: וַתָּרֶם כִּרְאֵים קַרְנִי בַּלֹּתִי בְּשֶׁמֶן רַעֲנָן: וַתַּבֵּט

יג עֵינִי בְּשׁוּרָי בַּקָּמִים עָלַי מְרֵעִים תִּשְׁמַעְנָה אָזְנָי: צַדִּיק כַּתָּמָר יִפְרָח

יד כְּאֶרֶז בַּלְּבָנוֹן יִשְׂגֶּה: שְׁתוּלִים בְּבֵית יהוה בְּחַצְרוֹת אֱלֹהֵינוּ יַפְרִיחוּ:

טו-טז עוֹד יְנוּבוּן בְּשֵׂיבָה דְּשֵׁנִים וְרַעֲנַנִּים יִהְיוּ: לְהַגִּיד כִּי-יָשָׁר יהוה צוּרִי

וְלֹא-°עלתה [עַוְלָתָה ק׳] בּוֹ:

צג   א יהוה מָלָךְ גֵּאוּת לָבֵשׁ לָבֵשׁ יהוה עֹז הִתְאַזָּר אַף-תִּכּוֹן תֵּבֵל בַּל-תִּמּוֹט:

ב-ג נָכוֹן כִּסְאֲךָ מֵאָז מֵעוֹלָם אָתָּה: נָשְׂאוּ נְהָרוֹת ׀ יהוה נָשְׂאוּ נְהָרוֹת קוֹלָם

ד יִשְׂאוּ נְהָרוֹת דָּכְיָם: מִקֹּלוֹת ׀ מַיִם רַבִּים אַדִּירִים מִשְׁבְּרֵי-יָם אַדִּיר

ה בַּמָּרוֹם יהוה: עֵדֹתֶיךָ ׀ נֶאֶמְנוּ מְאֹד לְבֵיתְךָ נָאֲוָה-קֹּדֶשׁ יהוה לְאֹרֶךְ

יָמִים:

צד   א-ב אֵל-נְקָמוֹת יהוה אֵל נְקָמוֹת הוֹפִיעַ: הִנָּשֵׂא שֹׁפֵט הָאָרֶץ הָשֵׁב גְּמוּל עַל-

ג-ד גֵּאִים: עַד-מָתַי רְשָׁעִים ׀ יהוה עַד-מָתַי רְשָׁעִים יַעֲלֹזוּ: יַבִּיעוּ יְדַבְּרוּ עָתָק

ה-ו יִתְאַמְּרוּ כָּל-פֹּעֲלֵי אָוֶן: עַמְּךָ יהוה יְדַכְּאוּ וְנַחֲלָתְךָ יְעַנּוּ: אַלְמָנָה וְגֵר

ז יַהֲרֹגוּ וִיתוֹמִים יְרַצֵּחוּ: וַיֹּאמְרוּ לֹא יִרְאֶה-יָּהּ וְלֹא-יָבִין אֱלֹהֵי יַעֲקֹב:

ח-ט בִּינוּ בֹּעֲרִים בָּעָם וּכְסִילִים מָתַי תַּשְׂכִּילוּ: הֲנֹטַע אֹזֶן הֲלֹא יִשְׁמָע אִם-

י-יא יֹצֵר עַיִן הֲלֹא יַבִּיט: הֲיֹסֵר גּוֹיִם הֲלֹא יוֹכִיחַ הַמְלַמֵּד אָדָם דָּעַת: יהוה

יב יֹדֵעַ מַחְשְׁבוֹת אָדָם כִּי-הֵמָּה הָבֶל: אַשְׁרֵי ׀ הַגֶּבֶר אֲשֶׁר-תְּיַסְּרֶנּוּ יָּהּ

יג-יד וּמִתּוֹרָתְךָ תְלַמְּדֶנּוּ: לְהַשְׁקִיט לוֹ מִימֵי רָע עַד יִכָּרֶה לָרָשָׁע שָׁחַת: כִּי ׀

טו לֹא-יִטֹּשׁ יהוה עַמּוֹ וְנַחֲלָתוֹ לֹא יַעֲזֹב: כִּי-עַד-צֶדֶק יָשׁוּב מִשְׁפָּט וְאַחֲרָיו

טז כָּל-יִשְׁרֵי-לֵב: מִי-יָקוּם לִי עִם-מְרֵעִים מִי-יִתְיַצֵּב לִי עִם-פֹּעֲלֵי אָוֶן: לוּלֵי

יז-יח יהוה עֶזְרָתָה לִּי כִּמְעַט ׀ שָׁכְנָה דוּמָה נַפְשִׁי: אִם-אָמַרְתִּי מָטָה רַגְלִי

יט חַסְדְּךָ יהוה יִסְעָדֵנִי: בְּרֹב שַׂרְעַפַּי בְּקִרְבִּי תַּנְחוּמֶיךָ יְשַׁעַשְׁעוּ נַפְשִׁי:

כ-כא הַיְחָבְרְךָ כִּסֵּא הַוּוֹת יֹצֵר עָמָל עֲלֵי-חֹק: יָגוֹדּוּ עַל-נֶפֶשׁ צַדִּיק וְדָם

92:3. Dawn alludes to redemption; night symbolizes exile. Even though there are times when God makes one suffer, those, too, are manifestations of His "kindness," because He does it for one's ultimate benefit.

92:8. Why do the wicked prosper? God gives temporal success and happiness to the wicked as reward for whatever good deeds they have done. Having been recompensed, they will sink to destruction, while the righteous gain eternal reward (Rashi).

92:11. See 22:22.

93:1. This psalm speaks of Messianic times, but it is couched in the past tense, as if spoken by those of Messiah's generation. The past tense implies that God *has always* reigned, it is only we who failed to perceive it.

93:3. The enemies of Israel will roar against them like raging rivers at flood stage (Radak).

93:5. The assurances of Your prophets regarding the eventual rebuilding of the Temple (Rashi).

92

On the Sabbath, free from the weekday struggle for a livelihood, the Jew can turn heart and mind to the perception of God's ways.

¹ A psalm, a song for the Sabbath day. ² It is good to thank HASHEM and to sing praise to Your Name, O Exalted One; ³ to relate Your kindness in the dawn and Your faith in the nights. * ⁴ Upon a ten-stringed instrument and upon lyre, with singing accompanied by a harp. ⁵ For You have gladdened me, HASHEM, with Your deeds; at the works of Your hands I sing glad song. ⁶ How great are Your deeds, HASHEM; exceedingly profound are Your thoughts. ⁷ A boor cannot know, nor can a fool understand this: ⁸ When the wicked bloom like grass and all the doers of iniquity blossom, * it is to destroy them till eternity. ⁹ But You remain exalted forever, HASHEM. ¹⁰ For behold Your enemies, O HASHEM, for behold, Your enemies shall perish; dispersed shall be all doers of iniquity. ¹¹ You raised my pride as a re'eim's, * I was saturated with ever-fresh oil. ¹² My eyes have seen my vigilant foes; when those who would harm me rise up against me, my ears have heard. ¹³ A righteous man will flourish like a date palm, like a cedar in the Lebanon he will grow tall. ¹⁴ Planted in the house of HASHEM, in the courtyards of our God they will flourish. ¹⁵ They will still be fruitful in old age, vigorous and fresh they will be, ¹⁶ to declare that HASHEM is just, my Rock in Whom there is no wrong.

93

In Messianic times, God's majesty and grandeur will be recognized by all.

¹ HASHEM has reigned, * He has donned grandeur; HASHEM has donned strength and girded Himself; even the world of men is firm, it shall not falter. ² Your throne is established from of old; eternal are You. ³ [Like] rivers they raised, O HASHEM, [like] rivers they raised their voice; * [like] rivers they shall raise their destructiveness. ⁴ More than the roars of many waters, mightier than the waves of the sea, You are mighty on high, HASHEM. ⁵ Your testimonies * about Your House, the Sacred Dwelling, are exceedingly trustworthy; O HASHEM, may it be for lengthy days.

94

Goodness will prevail and evil will be punished. God will champion Israel's cause and deliver it from its enemies.

¹ O God of vengeance, HASHEM; O God of vengeance, appear! ² Arise, O Judge of the earth, render recompense to the haughty. ³ Until when will the wicked, O HASHEM, until when will the wicked exult? ⁴ They speak freely, they utter malicious falsehood, they glorify themselves, all doers of iniquity. ⁵ Your nation, HASHEM, they crush, and they afflict Your heritage. ⁶ The widow and the stranger they slay, and the orphans they murder. ⁷ And they say, "God will not see, nor will the God of Jacob understand." ⁸ Understand, you boors among the people; and you fools, when will you gain wisdom? ⁹ He Who implants the ear, will He not hear? Will He Who fashions the eye not see? ¹⁰ He Who chastises nations, will He not rebuke? It is He Who teaches man knowledge. ¹¹ HASHEM knows the thoughts of man, that they are futile. ¹² Praiseworthy is the man whom God disciplines, * and whom You teach from Your Torah, ¹³ to give him rest from the days of evil, while a pit is dug for the wicked. ¹⁴ For HASHEM will not cast off His people, nor will He forsake His heritage. ¹⁵ For justice shall revert to righteousness, and following it will be all of upright heart. ¹⁶ Who will rise up for me against evildoers? Who will stand up for me against the doers of iniquity? ¹⁷ Had HASHEM not been a help to me, my soul would soon have dwelt in silence. ¹⁸ If I said, "My foot falters," Your kindness, HASHEM, supported me. ¹⁹ When my forebodings were abundant within me, Your comforts cheered my soul. ²⁰ Can the throne of destruction be associated with You? — those who fashion evil into a statute. ²¹ They join together against the soul of the righteous, and the blood of the

---

94:12-13. The wicked ask why the righteous suffer, if God truly controls everything. The psalmist answers that God afflicts the righteous only when it is to their benefit: to make them correct their ways, to make them realize the futility of physical pleasures, or to atone for their sins *(Radak; Meiri).*

כב־כג נָקִי יַרְשִׁיעוּ: וַיְהִי יְהֹוָה לִי לְמִשְׂגָּב וֵאלֹהַי לְצוּר מַחְסִי: וַיָּשֶׁב עֲלֵיהֶם ׀
אֶת־אוֹנָם וּבְרָעָתָם יַצְמִיתֵם יַצְמִיתֵם יְהֹוָה אֱלֹהֵינוּ:

צה א־ב לְכוּ נְרַנְּנָה לַיהֹוָה נָרִיעָה לְצוּר יִשְׁעֵנוּ: נְקַדְּמָה פָנָיו בְּתוֹדָה בִּזְמִרוֹת
ג־ד נָרִיעַ לוֹ: כִּי אֵל גָּדוֹל יְהֹוָה וּמֶלֶךְ גָּדוֹל עַל־כָּל־אֱלֹהִים: אֲשֶׁר בְּיָדוֹ
ה מֶחְקְרֵי־אָרֶץ וְתוֹעֲפוֹת הָרִים לוֹ: אֲשֶׁר־לוֹ הַיָּם וְהוּא עָשָׂהוּ וְיַבֶּשֶׁת יָדָיו
ו־ז יָצָרוּ: בֹּאוּ נִשְׁתַּחֲוֶה וְנִכְרָעָה נִבְרְכָה לִפְנֵי־יְהֹוָה עֹשֵׂנוּ: כִּי הוּא אֱלֹהֵינוּ
ח וַאֲנַחְנוּ עַם מַרְעִיתוֹ וְצֹאן יָדוֹ הַיּוֹם אִם־בְּקֹלוֹ תִשְׁמָעוּ: אַל־תַּקְשׁוּ
ט לְבַבְכֶם כִּמְרִיבָה כְּיוֹם מַסָּה בַּמִּדְבָּר: אֲשֶׁר נִסּוּנִי אֲבוֹתֵיכֶם בְּחָנוּנִי גַּם־
י רָאוּ פָעֳלִי: אַרְבָּעִים שָׁנָה ׀ אָקוּט בְּדוֹר וָאֹמַר עַם תֹּעֵי לֵבָב הֵם וְהֵם
יא לֹא־יָדְעוּ דְרָכָי: אֲשֶׁר־נִשְׁבַּעְתִּי בְאַפִּי אִם־יְבֹאוּן אֶל־מְנוּחָתִי:

צו א־ב שִׁירוּ לַיהֹוָה שִׁיר חָדָשׁ שִׁירוּ לַיהֹוָה כָּל־הָאָרֶץ: שִׁירוּ לַיהֹוָה בָּרְכוּ
ג שְׁמוֹ בַּשְּׂרוּ מִיּוֹם־לְיוֹם יְשׁוּעָתוֹ: סַפְּרוּ בַגּוֹיִם כְּבוֹדוֹ בְּכָל־הָעַמִּים
ד־ה נִפְלְאוֹתָיו: כִּי גָדוֹל יְהֹוָה וּמְהֻלָּל מְאֹד נוֹרָא הוּא עַל־כָּל־אֱלֹהִים: כִּי ׀
ו כָּל־אֱלֹהֵי הָעַמִּים אֱלִילִים וַיהֹוָה שָׁמַיִם עָשָׂה: הוֹד־וְהָדָר לְפָנָיו עֹז
ז וְתִפְאֶרֶת בְּמִקְדָּשׁוֹ: הָבוּ לַיהֹוָה מִשְׁפְּחוֹת עַמִּים הָבוּ לַיהֹוָה כָּבוֹד וָעֹז:
ח־ט הָבוּ לַיהֹוָה כְּבוֹד שְׁמוֹ שְׂאוּ־מִנְחָה וּבֹאוּ לְחַצְרוֹתָיו: הִשְׁתַּחֲווּ לַיהֹוָה
י בְּהַדְרַת־קֹדֶשׁ חִילוּ מִפָּנָיו כָּל־הָאָרֶץ: אִמְרוּ בַגּוֹיִם ׀ יְהֹוָה מָלָךְ אַף־
יא תִּכּוֹן תֵּבֵל בַּל־תִּמּוֹט יָדִין עַמִּים בְּמֵישָׁרִים: יִשְׂמְחוּ הַשָּׁמַיִם וְתָגֵל
יב הָאָרֶץ יִרְעַם הַיָּם וּמְלֹאוֹ: יַעֲלֹז שָׂדַי וְכָל־אֲשֶׁר־בּוֹ אָז יְרַנְּנוּ כָּל־
יג עֲצֵי־יָעַר: לִפְנֵי יְהֹוָה ׀ כִּי בָא כִּי בָא לִשְׁפֹּט הָאָרֶץ יִשְׁפֹּט־תֵּבֵל בְּצֶדֶק
וְעַמִּים בֶּאֱמוּנָתוֹ:

צז א־ב יְהֹוָה מָלָךְ תָּגֵל הָאָרֶץ יִשְׂמְחוּ אִיִּים רַבִּים: עָנָן וַעֲרָפֶל סְבִיבָיו צֶדֶק
יום כ לחדש ג־ד וּמִשְׁפָּט מְכוֹן כִּסְאוֹ: אֵשׁ לְפָנָיו תֵּלֵךְ וּתְלַהֵט סָבִיב צָרָיו: הֵאִירוּ בְרָקָיו
ה תֵּבֵל רָאֲתָה וַתָּחֵל הָאָרֶץ: הָרִים כַּדּוֹנַג נָמַסּוּ מִלִּפְנֵי יְהֹוָה מִלִּפְנֵי אֲדוֹן
ו־ז כָּל־הָאָרֶץ: הִגִּידוּ הַשָּׁמַיִם צִדְקוֹ וְרָאוּ כָל־הָעַמִּים כְּבוֹדוֹ: יֵבֹשׁוּ ׀ כָּל־
ח עֹבְדֵי פֶסֶל הַמִּתְהַלְלִים בָּאֱלִילִים הִשְׁתַּחֲווּ־לוֹ כָּל־אֱלֹהִים: שָׁמְעָה
ט וַתִּשְׂמַח ׀ צִיּוֹן וַתָּגֵלְנָה בְּנוֹת יְהוּדָה לְמַעַן מִשְׁפָּטֶיךָ יְהֹוָה: כִּי־אַתָּה
י יְהֹוָה עֶלְיוֹן עַל־כָּל־הָאָרֶץ מְאֹד נַעֲלֵיתָ עַל־כָּל־אֱלֹהִים: אֹהֲבֵי יְהֹוָה
יא שִׂנְאוּ רָע שֹׁמֵר נַפְשׁוֹת חֲסִידָיו מִיַּד רְשָׁעִים יַצִּילֵם: אוֹר זָרֻעַ לַצַּדִּיק
יב וּלְיִשְׁרֵי־לֵב שִׂמְחָה: שִׂמְחוּ צַדִּיקִים בַּיהֹוָה וְהוֹדוּ לְזֵכֶר קָדְשׁוֹ:

95:7. If we only heed God's call, He will end our travail and suffering even today.

95:8. *Meribah* means "strife"; *Massah* means "testing." See *Exodus* 17:1-7.

96:11. The components of nature exult in carrying out their assigned functions. The heavens give abundant rain, the earth gives generous crops, and so on *(Ibn Ezra)*.

97:1. See 93:1.

97:2. The justice of God's ways is often masked by "cloud and darkness." In reality, however, everything He does is for a reason.

97:5. A metaphor for great and towering leaders.

innocent they condemn. [22] Then HASHEM became a stronghold for me, and my God, the Rock of my refuge. [23] He turned upon them their own violence, and with their own evil He will cut them off; HASHEM, our God, will cut them off.

95

Come acknowledge God as Creator and guiding force of the universe. Do not emulate your ances- tors who strayed after falsehood.

[1] **C**ome! Let us sing to HASHEM, let us call out to the Rock of our salvation. [2] Let us greet Him with thanksgiving, with praiseful songs let us call out to Him. [3] For a great God is HASHEM, and a great King above all heavenly powers. [4] For in His power are the hidden mysteries of earth, and the mountain summits are His. [5] For His is the sea and He perfected it, and the dry land — His hands fashioned it. [6] Come! Let us prostrate ourselves and bow, let us kneel before HASHEM, our Maker. [7] For He is our God and we can be the flock He pastures, and the sheep in His charge — even today, if we but heed His call!* [8] Do not harden your heart as at Meribah, * as on the day of Massah* in the Wilderness; [9] when your ancestors tried Me; they tested Me, though they had seen My deed. [10] For forty years I was angry with the generation; then I said, "An errant-hearted people are they, and they know not My ways." [11] Therefore, I have sworn in My anger that they shall not enter My land of contentment.

96

When all the nations on earth will recognize God's sovereignty, they will join in a new song ac- knowledging Him.

[1] **S**ing to HASHEM a new song; sing to HASHEM, everyone on earth. [2] Sing to HASHEM, bless His Name; announce His salvation daily. [3] Relate His glory among the nations; among all peoples, His wonders: [4] That HASHEM is great and exceedingly lauded; awesome is He above all heavenly powers. [5] For all the gods of the peoples are nothings — but HASHEM made heaven! [6] Glory and majesty are before Him, might and splendor in His Sanctuary. [7] Render unto HASHEM, O families of the peoples, render unto HASHEM honor and might. [8] Render unto HASHEM honor worthy of His Name; take an offering and come to His courtyards. [9] Prostrate yourselves before HASHEM in His intensely holy place; tremble before Him, everyone on earth. [10] Declare among the nations, "HASHEM has reigned!" Indeed, the world is fixed so that it cannot falter. He will judge the peoples with fairness. [11] The heavens will be glad and the earth will rejoice, * the sea and its fullness will roar; [12] the field and everything in it will exult; then all the trees of the forest will sing with joy — [13] before HASHEM, for He will have arrived, He will have arrived to judge the earth. He will judge the world with righteousness, and peoples with His truth.

97

After the upheavals that will precede the Messiah's coming, the world will recognize its folly, and God will reign supreme over the entire earth.

[1] **H**ASHEM has reigned, * let the world rejoice; let the numerous islands be glad. [2] Cloud and thick cloud surround Him;* righteousness and justice are His throne's foundation. [3] Fire goes before Him and consumes His enemies all around. [4] His lightning bolts lit up the world, [the inhabitants of] the earth saw and tremble. [5] Mountains* melted like wax before HASHEM, before the Lord of all the earth. [6] The heavens declare His righteousness, and all the peoples saw His glory. [7] Humiliated will be all who worship idols, who pride them- selves in worthless gods; bow to Him, all you powers. [8] Zion heard and was glad, and the daughters of Judah exulted, because of Your judgments, HASHEM. [9] For You, HASHEM, are supreme above all the earth; exceedingly exalted above all powers. [10] O lovers of HASHEM, despise evil! He guards the lives of His devout ones, from the hand of the wicked He rescues them. [11] Light is sown for the righteous; and for the upright of heart, gladness. [12] Be glad, O righteous, in HASHEM, and give grateful praise at the mention of His Holy [Name].

צח

א מִזְמוֹר שִׁירוּ לַיהוה ׀ שִׁיר חָדָשׁ כִּי־נִפְלָאוֹת עָשָׂה הוֹשִׁיעָה־לּוֹ יְמִינוֹ
ב־ג וּזְרוֹעַ קָדְשׁוֹ: הוֹדִיעַ יהוה יְשׁוּעָתוֹ לְעֵינֵי הַגּוֹיִם גִּלָּה צִדְקָתוֹ: זָכַר חַסְדּוֹ ׀
ד וֶאֱמוּנָתוֹ לְבֵית יִשְׂרָאֵל רָאוּ כָל־אַפְסֵי־אָרֶץ אֵת יְשׁוּעַת אֱלֹהֵינוּ: הָרִיעוּ
ה לַיהוה כָּל־הָאָרֶץ פִּצְחוּ וְרַנְּנוּ וְזַמֵּרוּ: זַמְּרוּ לַיהוה בְּכִנּוֹר בְּכִנּוֹר וְקוֹל
ו־ז זִמְרָה: בַּחֲצֹצְרוֹת וְקוֹל שׁוֹפָר הָרִיעוּ לִפְנֵי ׀ הַמֶּלֶךְ יהוה: יִרְעַם הַיָּם
ח־ט וּמְלֹאוֹ תֵּבֵל וְיֹשְׁבֵי בָהּ: נְהָרוֹת יִמְחֲאוּ־כָף יַחַד הָרִים יְרַנֵּנוּ: לִפְנֵי־יהוה
כִּי בָא לִשְׁפֹּט הָאָרֶץ יִשְׁפֹּט־תֵּבֵל בְּצֶדֶק וְעַמִּים בְּמֵישָׁרִים:

צט

א־ב יהוה מָלָךְ יִרְגְּזוּ עַמִּים יֹשֵׁב כְּרוּבִים תָּנוּט הָאָרֶץ: יהוה בְּצִיּוֹן גָּדוֹל וְרָם
ג־ד הוּא עַל־כָּל־הָעַמִּים: יוֹדוּ שִׁמְךָ גָּדוֹל וְנוֹרָא קָדוֹשׁ הוּא: וְעֹז מֶלֶךְ מִשְׁפָּט
אָהֵב אַתָּה כּוֹנַנְתָּ מֵישָׁרִים מִשְׁפָּט וּצְדָקָה בְּיַעֲקֹב ׀ אַתָּה עָשִׂיתָ: רוֹמְמוּ
ו יהוה אֱלֹהֵינוּ וְהִשְׁתַּחֲווּ לַהֲדֹם רַגְלָיו קָדוֹשׁ הוּא: מֹשֶׁה וְאַהֲרֹן ׀ בְּכֹהֲנָיו
ז וּשְׁמוּאֵל בְּקֹרְאֵי שְׁמוֹ קֹרִאים אֶל־יהוה וְהוּא יַעֲנֵם: בְּעַמּוּד עָנָן יְדַבֵּר
ח אֲלֵיהֶם שָׁמְרוּ עֵדֹתָיו וְחֹק נָתַן־לָמוֹ: יהוה אֱלֹהֵינוּ אַתָּה עֲנִיתָם אֵל נֹשֵׂא
ט הָיִיתָ לָהֶם וְנֹקֵם עַל־עֲלִילוֹתָם: רוֹמְמוּ יהוה אֱלֹהֵינוּ וְהִשְׁתַּחֲווּ לְהַר
קָדְשׁוֹ כִּי־קָדוֹשׁ יהוה אֱלֹהֵינוּ:

ק

א־ב מִזְמוֹר לְתוֹדָה הָרִיעוּ לַיהוה כָּל־הָאָרֶץ: עִבְדוּ אֶת־יהוה בְּשִׂמְחָה בֹּאוּ
ג לְפָנָיו בִּרְנָנָה: דְּעוּ כִּי־יהוה הוּא אֱלֹהִים הוּא־עָשָׂנוּ °וְלֹא [וְלוֹ ק]
ד אֲנַחְנוּ עַמּוֹ וְצֹאן מַרְעִיתוֹ: בֹּאוּ שְׁעָרָיו ׀ בְּתוֹדָה חֲצֵרֹתָיו בִּתְהִלָּה הוֹדוּ־
ה לוֹ בָּרֲכוּ שְׁמוֹ: כִּי־טוֹב יהוה לְעוֹלָם חַסְדּוֹ וְעַד־דֹּר וָדֹר אֱמוּנָתוֹ:

קא

א־ב לְדָוִד מִזְמוֹר חֶסֶד־וּמִשְׁפָּט אָשִׁירָה לְךָ יהוה אֲזַמֵּרָה: אַשְׂכִּילָה ׀ בְּדֶרֶךְ
ג תָּמִים מָתַי תָּבוֹא אֵלָי אֶתְהַלֵּךְ בְּתָם־לְבָבִי בְּקֶרֶב בֵּיתִי: לֹא־אָשִׁית ׀
ד לְנֶגֶד עֵינַי דְּבַר־בְּלִיָּעַל עֲשֹׂה־סֵטִים שָׂנֵאתִי לֹא יִדְבַּק בִּי: לֵבָב עִקֵּשׁ
ה יָסוּר מִמֶּנִּי רָע לֹא אֵדָע: °מְלוֹשְׁנִי [°מְלָשְׁנִי ק] בַסֵּתֶר ׀ רֵעֵהוּ אוֹתוֹ
ו אַצְמִית גְּבַהּ־עֵינַיִם וּרְחַב לֵבָב אֹתוֹ לֹא אוּכָל: עֵינַי ׀ בְּנֶאֶמְנֵי־אֶרֶץ
ז לָשֶׁבֶת עִמָּדִי הֹלֵךְ בְּדֶרֶךְ תָּמִים הוּא יְשָׁרְתֵנִי: לֹא־יֵשֵׁב ׀ בְּקֶרֶב בֵּיתִי
ח עֹשֵׂה רְמִיָּה דֹּבֵר שְׁקָרִים לֹא־יִכּוֹן לְנֶגֶד עֵינָי: לַבְּקָרִים אַצְמִית כָּל־
רִשְׁעֵי־אָרֶץ לְהַכְרִית מֵעִיר־יהוה כָּל־פֹּעֲלֵי אָוֶן:

קב

א־ב תְּפִלָּה לְעָנִי כִי־יַעֲטֹף וְלִפְנֵי יהוה יִשְׁפֹּךְ שִׂיחוֹ: יהוה שִׁמְעָה תְפִלָּתִי
ג וְשַׁוְעָתִי אֵלֶיךָ תָבוֹא: אַל־תַּסְתֵּר פָּנֶיךָ ׀ מִמֶּנִּי בְּיוֹם צַר לִי הַטֵּה־אֵלַי אָזְנֶךָ
ד־ה בְּיוֹם אֶקְרָא מַהֵר עֲנֵנִי: כִּי־כָלוּ בְעָשָׁן יָמָי וְעַצְמוֹתַי כְּמוֹקֵד נִחָרוּ: הוּכָּה־

98:1. God requires no assistance. He acts through His "right hand," a term symbolic of power (*Radak*).

99:1. See 93:1.

99:6. During the inauguration of the Tabernacle, Moses served as *Kohen Gadol* (High Priest) for a seven-day period (see *Leviticus,* Chapter 8).

100:2. But in 2:11 we are told to "serve HASHEM with awe" — how can we reconcile gladness with awe? To feel fear, respect, and awe for God is essential to spiritual growth. Once a person realizes that his fear is the beginning of a process that leads to personal greatness and bliss, even the difficulties along the way can be accepted with gladness (*Ikkarim*).

98

A song of praise for the revelation of the final Redemption

¹ **A** psalm! Sing to HASHEM a new song for He has done wonders; His own right hand and holy arm have helped Him. * ² HASHEM has made known His salvation; in the sight of the nations He revealed His righteousness. ³ He recalled His kindness and his faithfulness to the House of Israel; all ends of the earth have seen the salvation of our God. ⁴ Call out to HASHEM, all the earth; open your mouths in joyous songs and play music. ⁵ Play music to HASHEM on a harp, with harp and sound of chanted praise. ⁶ With trumpets and shofar sound, call out before the King, HASHEM. ⁷ The sea and its fullness will roar, the inhabited land and those who dwell therein; ⁸ rivers will clap hands, mountains will exult together ⁹ before HASHEM, for He will have arrived to judge the earth. He will judge the world with righteousness and peoples with fairness.

99

Once the nations acknowledge His sovereignty, they will follow the dictates of righteousness that Israel has safeguarded throughout its history.

¹ **H** ASHEM has reigned: * Let peoples tremble; before Him Who is enthroned on Cherubim, let the earth quake. ² Before HASHEM Who is great in Zion and Who is exalted above all peoples. ³ Let them gratefully praise Your great and awesome Name; it is holy! ⁴ Mighty is the King, Who loves justice. You founded fairness. The justice and righteousness of Jacob, You have made. ⁵ Exalt HASHEM, our God, and bow at His footstool; He is holy! ⁶ Moses and Aaron were among His priests, * and Samuel among those who invoke His Name; they called upon HASHEM and He answered them. ⁷ In a pillar of cloud He spoke to them; they obeyed His testimonies and whatever decree He gave them. ⁸ HASHEM, our God, You answered them. A forgiving God were You because of them, yet an Avenger for their iniquities. ⁹ Exalt HASHEM, our God, and bow at His holy mountain; for holy is HASHEM, our God.

100

A psalm to accompany the thanksgiving-offering

¹ **A** psalm of thanksgiving, call out to HASHEM, all the earth. ² Serve HASHEM with gladness, * come before Him with joyous song. ³ Know that HASHEM, He is God; He made us and we are His, His people and the sheep of His pasture. ⁴ Enter His gates with thanksgiving, His courts with praise; give thanks to Him, bless His Name. ⁵ For HASHEM is good, His kindness endures forever, and from generation to generation is His faithfulness.

101

The traits of purity and truth enable an individual to utilize his abilities for their intended purpose.

¹ **B** y David, a psalm. Of kindness and justice do I sing; to You, HASHEM, do I sing praise. ² I contemplate the way of perfect innocence, O when will You come to me? I walk constantly with innocence of heart within my house. ³ I do not place before my eyes any lawless thing; I despise doing wayward deeds, it does not cling to me. ⁴ A perverted heart shall remain removed from me; I shall not know evil. ⁵ He who slanders his neighbor in secret — him will I cut down [with rebuke]; one with haughty eyes and an expansive heart, him I cannot bear. ⁶ My eyes are upon the faithful of the land, that they may dwell with me; he who walks the way of perfect innocence, he shall serve me. ⁷ In the midst of my house shall not dwell a practitioner of deceit; one who tells lies shall not be established before my eyes. ⁸ Every morning I will cut down all the wicked of the land, to excise from the city of HASHEM all doers of evil.

102

A prayer for anyone beset by any misfortune

¹ **A** prayer of the afflicted man when he swoons, and pours forth his supplications before HASHEM: ² "HASHEM, hear my prayer, and let my cry reach You! ³ Hide not Your face from me on the day of my distress; incline Your ear to me, on the day that I call, answer me speedily. ⁴ For my days are consumed in smoke, and my bones are charred as a hearth. ⁵ Smitten

ו כְּעֵשֶׂב וַיִּבַשׁ לִבִּי כִּי־שָׁכַחְתִּי מֵאֲכֹל לַחְמִי: מִקּוֹל אַנְחָתִי דָּבְקָה עַצְמִי

ז-ח לִבְשָׂרִי: דָּמִיתִי לִקְאַת מִדְבָּר הָיִיתִי כְּכוֹס חֳרָבוֹת: שָׁקַדְתִּי וָאֶהְיֶה

ט-י כְּצִפּוֹר בּוֹדֵד עַל־גָּג: כָּל־הַיּוֹם חֵרְפוּנִי אוֹיְבָי מְהוֹלָלַי בִּי נִשְׁבָּעוּ: כִּי־

יא אֵפֶר כַּלֶּחֶם אָכָלְתִּי וְשִׁקֻּוַי בִּבְכִי מָסָכְתִּי: מִפְּנֵי־זַעַמְךָ וְקִצְפֶּךָ כִּי נְשָׂאתַנִי

יב-יג וַתַּשְׁלִיכֵנִי: יָמַי כְּצֵל נָטוּי וַאֲנִי כָּעֵשֶׂב אִיבָשׁ: וְאַתָּה יהוה לְעוֹלָם תֵּשֵׁב

יד וְזִכְרְךָ לְדֹר וָדֹר: אַתָּה תָקוּם תְּרַחֵם צִיּוֹן כִּי־עֵת לְחֶנְנָהּ כִּי־בָא מוֹעֵד:

טו-טז כִּי־רָצוּ עֲבָדֶיךָ אֶת־אֲבָנֶיהָ וְאֶת־עֲפָרָהּ יְחֹנֵנוּ: וְיִירְאוּ גוֹיִם אֶת־שֵׁם יהוה

יז-יח וְכָל־מַלְכֵי הָאָרֶץ אֶת־כְּבוֹדֶךָ: כִּי־בָנָה יהוה צִיּוֹן נִרְאָה בִּכְבוֹדוֹ: פָּנָה

יט אֶל־תְּפִלַּת הָעַרְעָר וְלֹא־בָזָה אֶת־תְּפִלָּתָם: תִּכָּתֶב זֹאת לְדוֹר אַחֲרוֹן

כ וְעַם נִבְרָא יְהַלֶּל־יָהּ: כִּי־הִשְׁקִיף מִמְּרוֹם קָדְשׁוֹ יהוה מִשָּׁמַיִם ׀ אֶל־אֶרֶץ

כא-כב הִבִּיט: לִשְׁמֹעַ אֶנְקַת אָסִיר לְפַתֵּחַ בְּנֵי תְמוּתָה: לְסַפֵּר בְּצִיּוֹן שֵׁם יהוה

כג-כד וּתְהִלָּתוֹ בִּירוּשָׁלָ͏ִם: בְּהִקָּבֵץ עַמִּים יַחְדָּו וּמַמְלָכוֹת לַעֲבֹד אֶת־יהוה: עִנָּה

כה בַדֶּרֶךְ °כֹּחוֹ [°כֹחִי ק] קִצַּר יָמָי: אֹמַר אֵלִי אַל־תַּעֲלֵנִי בַּחֲצִי יָמָי בְּדוֹר

כו-כז דּוֹרִים שְׁנוֹתֶיךָ: לְפָנִים הָאָרֶץ יָסַדְתָּ וּמַעֲשֵׂה יָדֶיךָ שָׁמָיִם: הֵמָּה ׀ יֹאבֵדוּ

כח וְאַתָּה תַעֲמֹד וְכֻלָּם כַּבֶּגֶד יִבְלוּ כַּלְּבוּשׁ תַּחֲלִיפֵם וְיַחֲלֹפוּ: וְאַתָּה־הוּא

כט וּשְׁנוֹתֶיךָ לֹא יִתָּמּוּ: בְּנֵי־עֲבָדֶיךָ יִשְׁכּוֹנוּ וְזַרְעָם לְפָנֶיךָ יִכּוֹן:

קג א לְדָוִד ׀ בָּרְכִי נַפְשִׁי אֶת־יהוה וְכָל־קְרָבַי אֶת־שֵׁם קָדְשׁוֹ: בָּרְכִי נַפְשִׁי אֶת־

ב-ג יהוה וְאַל־תִּשְׁכְּחִי כָּל־גְּמוּלָיו: הַסֹּלֵחַ לְכָל־עֲוֹנֵכִי הָרֹפֵא לְכָל־

ד-ה תַּחֲלֻאָיְכִי: הַגּוֹאֵל מִשַּׁחַת חַיָּיְכִי הַמְעַטְּרֵכִי חֶסֶד וְרַחֲמִים: הַמַּשְׂבִּיעַ

ו בַּטּוֹב עֶדְיֵךְ תִּתְחַדֵּשׁ כַּנֶּשֶׁר נְעוּרָיְכִי: עֹשֵׂה צְדָקוֹת יהוה וּמִשְׁפָּטִים לְכָל־

ז-ח עֲשׁוּקִים: יוֹדִיעַ דְּרָכָיו לְמֹשֶׁה לִבְנֵי יִשְׂרָאֵל עֲלִילוֹתָיו: רַחוּם וְחַנּוּן יהוה

ט-י אֶרֶךְ אַפַּיִם וְרַב־חָסֶד: לֹא־לָנֶצַח יָרִיב וְלֹא לְעוֹלָם יִטּוֹר: לֹא כַחֲטָאֵינוּ

יא עָשָׂה לָנוּ וְלֹא כַעֲוֹנֹתֵינוּ גָּמַל עָלֵינוּ: כִּי כִגְבֹהַּ שָׁמַיִם עַל־הָאָרֶץ גָּבַר

יב חַסְדּוֹ עַל־יְרֵאָיו: כִּרְחֹק מִזְרָח מִמַּעֲרָב הִרְחִיק מִמֶּנּוּ אֶת־פְּשָׁעֵינוּ:

יג-יד כְּרַחֵם אָב עַל־בָּנִים רִחַם יהוה עַל־יְרֵאָיו: כִּי־הוּא יָדַע יִצְרֵנוּ זָכוּר כִּי־

טו-טז עָפָר אֲנָחְנוּ: אֱנוֹשׁ כֶּחָצִיר יָמָיו כְּצִיץ הַשָּׂדֶה כֵּן יָצִיץ: כִּי רוּחַ עָבְרָה־בּוֹ

יז וְאֵינֶנּוּ וְלֹא־יַכִּירֶנּוּ עוֹד מְקוֹמוֹ: וְחֶסֶד יהוה ׀ מֵעוֹלָם וְעַד־עוֹלָם עַל־

יח-יט יְרֵאָיו וְצִדְקָתוֹ לִבְנֵי בָנִים: לְשֹׁמְרֵי בְרִיתוֹ וּלְזֹכְרֵי פִקֻּדָיו לַעֲשׂוֹתָם: יהוה

כ בַּשָּׁמַיִם הֵכִין כִּסְאוֹ וּמַלְכוּתוֹ בַּכֹּל מָשָׁלָה: בָּרְכוּ יהוה מַלְאָכָיו גִּבֹּרֵי כֹחַ

102:5. God does not remove the sources of revival. It is the despair of the afflicted that makes them ignore the spiritual nourishment through which they could bear their troubles (*R' Hirsch*).

102:6. I have become emaciated.

102:15. Throughout their exile, Jews have never stopped yearning to return to their Land.

102:19. Jews born after the final redemption will praise God for the miracles he wrought for their forefathers.

103:5. Who annually renews his feathers.

103:7. This refers to the Thirteen Attributes of Mercy (*Exodus 34:6-7*), some of which are described in the ensuing verses.

103:14. God allows for the fact that the material side of man's dual nature beckons him to sin.

like grass [by the sun] until my heart is withered, for I have forgotten to eat my food. * ⁶ From the sound of my sigh my bone has clung to my skin. * ⁷ I am like a wilderness bird, I have become like the owl of the wasteland. ⁸ I have been diligent, yet I have become like a lonely bird upon a rooftop. ⁹ All day long my enemies revile me; those who boisterously ridicule me curse by me. ¹⁰ For I have eaten ashes like bread, and mixed my drink with tears, ¹¹ because of Your fury and Your wrath, for You have raised me high and hurled me down. ¹² My days are like a lengthened shadow, and I wither away like grass. ¹³ But You, HASHEM, will be enthroned forever, and Your memory endures from generation to generation. ¹⁴ You will arise and show Zion mercy, for [there will come] the time to favor her, for the appointed time will have come. ¹⁵ For Your servants have cherished her stones, and favored her dust. * ¹⁶ Then the nations will fear the Name of HASHEM, and all the kings of the earth Your glory. ¹⁷ For HASHEM will have built Zion, He will have appeared in His glory. ¹⁸ He will have turned to the prayer of each devastated one and not have despised their prayer." ¹⁹ Let this be recorded for the final generation, so that the newborn people* will praise God. ²⁰ For He gazed from His exalted Sanctuary; HASHEM looked down from heaven to earth, ²¹ to hear the groaning of the prisoner, to liberate those doomed to die, ²² to declare in Zion the Name of HASHEM, and His praise in Jerusalem, ²³ when peoples gather together, and kingdoms, to serve HASHEM. ²⁴ He has afflicted my strength on the way; He has shortened my days. ²⁵ I say, "O my God, do not remove me in the midst of my days; Your years endure through all generations. ²⁶ Of old, You laid the earth's foundation, and the heavens are Your handiwork. ²⁷ They will perish, but You will endure; all of them will wear out like a garment, You will exchange them like a cloak and they will pass on. ²⁸ But You remain the same, and Your years will never end. ²⁹ Your servants' children shall be settled and their children will be established before You."

103

The soul in turmoil is calmed by recounting God's infinite kindness.

¹ **B**y David, bless HASHEM, O my soul; and all that is within me [bless] His Holy Name. ² Bless HASHEM, O my soul, and forget not all His kindnesses; ³ Who forgives all your sins; Who heals all your diseases; ⁴ Who redeems your life from the pit; Who crowns you with kindness and mercy; ⁵ Who satisfies your mouth with goodness, so that your youth is renewed like the eagle. * ⁶ HASHEM is the doer of righteous deeds, and judgments for all the oppressed. ⁷ He made known His ways to Moses, * His actions to the Children of Israel: ⁸ Compassionate and Gracious is HASHEM, Slow to Anger and Abundant of Kindness. ⁹ He will not quarrel for eternity, nor will He forever bear a grudge. ¹⁰ He has not treated us according to our sins, nor repaid us according to our iniquities. ¹¹ For as high as heaven is above the earth, has His kindness overwhelmed those who fear Him. ¹² As far as east from west, has He distanced our transgressions from us. ¹³ As a father is merciful towards his children, so has HASHEM shown mercy to those who fear Him. ¹⁴ For He knew our nature; * He is mindful that we are dust. ¹⁵ Frail man, his days are like grass; like a sprout of the field, so he sprouts. ¹⁶ When a wind passes over it, it is gone, and its place recognizes it no more. ¹⁷ But the kindness of HASHEM is forever and ever upon those who fear Him, and His righteousness is upon children's children, ¹⁸ to those who keep His covenant, and to those who remember His commands to fulfill them. ¹⁹ HASHEM has established His throne in heaven, and His kingdom reigns over all. ²⁰ Bless HASHEM, O His angels; the strong warriors

כא עֹשֵׂי דְבָרוֹ לִשְׁמֹעַ בְּקוֹל דְּבָרוֹ: בָּרְכוּ יְהוָה כָּל־צְבָאָיו מְשָׁרְתָיו עֹשֵׂי
כב רְצוֹנוֹ: בָּרְכוּ יְהוָה ׀ כָּל־מַעֲשָׂיו בְּכָל־מְקֹמוֹת מֶמְשַׁלְתּוֹ בָּרְכִי נַפְשִׁי אֶת־
יְהוָה:

קד
יום כא לחדש

א-ב בָּרְכִי נַפְשִׁי אֶת־יְהוָה יְהוָה אֱלֹהַי גָּדַלְתָּ מְּאֹד הוֹד וְהָדָר לָבָשְׁתָּ: עֹטֶה־
ג אוֹר כַּשַּׂלְמָה נוֹטֶה שָׁמַיִם כַּיְרִיעָה: הַמְקָרֶה בַמַּיִם עֲלִיּוֹתָיו הַשָּׂם־עָבִים
ד רְכוּבוֹ הַמְהַלֵּךְ עַל־כַּנְפֵי־רוּחַ: עֹשֶׂה מַלְאָכָיו רוּחוֹת מְשָׁרְתָיו אֵשׁ לֹהֵט:
ה-ו יָסַד־אֶרֶץ עַל־מְכוֹנֶיהָ בַּל־תִּמּוֹט עוֹלָם וָעֶד: תְּהוֹם כַּלְּבוּשׁ כִּסִּיתוֹ עַל־
ז-ח הָרִים יַעַמְדוּ־מָיִם: מִן־גַּעֲרָתְךָ יְנוּסוּן מִן־קוֹל רַעַמְךָ יֵחָפֵזוּן: יַעֲלוּ הָרִים
ט יֵרְדוּ בְקָעוֹת אֶל־מְקוֹם זֶה ׀ יָסַדְתָּ לָהֶם: גְּבוּל־שַׂמְתָּ בַּל־יַעֲבֹרוּן בַּל־
י-יא יְשׁוּבוּן לְכַסּוֹת הָאָרֶץ: הַמְשַׁלֵּחַ מַעְיָנִים בַּנְּחָלִים בֵּין הָרִים יְהַלֵּכוּן:
יב יַשְׁקוּ כָּל־חַיְתוֹ שָׂדָי יִשְׁבְּרוּ פְרָאִים צְמָאָם: עֲלֵיהֶם עוֹף־הַשָּׁמַיִם יִשְׁכּוֹן
יג מִבֵּין עֳפָאיִם יִתְּנוּ־קוֹל: מַשְׁקֶה הָרִים מֵעֲלִיּוֹתָיו מִפְּרִי מַעֲשֶׂיךָ תִּשְׂבַּע
יד הָאָרֶץ: מַצְמִיחַ חָצִיר ׀ לַבְּהֵמָה וְעֵשֶׂב לַעֲבֹדַת הָאָדָם לְהוֹצִיא לֶחֶם מִן־
טו הָאָרֶץ: וְיַיִן ׀ יְשַׂמַּח לְבַב־אֱנוֹשׁ לְהַצְהִיל פָּנִים מִשָּׁמֶן וְלֶחֶם לְבַב־אֱנוֹשׁ
טז-יז יִסְעָד: יִשְׂבְּעוּ עֲצֵי יְהוָה אַרְזֵי לְבָנוֹן אֲשֶׁר נָטָע: אֲשֶׁר־שָׁם צִפֳּרִים יְקַנֵּנוּ
יח-יט חֲסִידָה בְּרוֹשִׁים בֵּיתָהּ: הָרִים הַגְּבֹהִים לַיְּעֵלִים סְלָעִים מַחְסֶה לַשְׁפַנִּים:
כ עָשָׂה יָרֵחַ לְמוֹעֲדִים שֶׁמֶשׁ יָדַע מְבוֹאוֹ: תָּשֶׁת־חֹשֶׁךְ וִיהִי לָיְלָה בּוֹ־
כא-כב תִרְמֹשׂ כָּל־חַיְתוֹ־יָעַר: הַכְּפִירִים שֹׁאֲגִים לַטָּרֶף וּלְבַקֵּשׁ מֵאֵל אָכְלָם:
כג תִּזְרַח הַשֶּׁמֶשׁ יֵאָסֵפוּן וְאֶל־מְעוֹנֹתָם יִרְבָּצוּן: יֵצֵא אָדָם לְפָעֳלוֹ וְלַעֲבֹדָתוֹ
כד-כה עֲדֵי־עָרֶב: מָה־רַבּוּ מַעֲשֶׂיךָ ׀ יְהוָה כֻּלָּם בְּחָכְמָה עָשִׂיתָ מָלְאָה הָאָרֶץ
קִנְיָנֶךָ: זֶה ׀ הַיָּם גָּדוֹל וּרְחַב יָדָיִם שָׁם־רֶמֶשׂ וְאֵין מִסְפָּר חַיּוֹת קְטַנּוֹת עִם־
כו-כז גְּדֹלוֹת: שָׁם אֳנִיּוֹת יְהַלֵּכוּן לִוְיָתָן זֶה־יָצַרְתָּ לְשַׂחֶק־בּוֹ: כֻּלָּם אֵלֶיךָ
כח-כט יְשַׂבֵּרוּן לָתֵת אָכְלָם בְּעִתּוֹ: תִּתֵּן לָהֶם יִלְקֹטוּן תִּפְתַּח יָדְךָ יִשְׂבְּעוּן טוֹב:
ל תַּסְתִּיר פָּנֶיךָ יִבָּהֵלוּן תֹּסֵף רוּחָם יִגְוָעוּן וְאֶל־עֲפָרָם יְשׁוּבוּן: תְּשַׁלַּח רוּחֲךָ
לא-לב יִבָּרֵאוּן וּתְחַדֵּשׁ פְּנֵי אֲדָמָה: יְהִי כְבוֹד יְהוָה לְעוֹלָם יִשְׂמַח יְהוָה בְּמַעֲשָׂיו:
לג הַמַּבִּיט לָאָרֶץ וַתִּרְעָד יִגַּע בֶּהָרִים וְיֶעֱשָׁנוּ: אָשִׁירָה לַיהוָה בְּחַיָּי אֲזַמְּרָה
לד-לה לֵאלֹהַי בְּעוֹדִי: יֶעֱרַב עָלָיו שִׂיחִי אָנֹכִי אֶשְׂמַח בַּיהוָה: יִתַּמּוּ חַטָּאִים ׀ מִן־
הָאָרֶץ וּרְשָׁעִים ׀ עוֹד אֵינָם בָּרְכִי נַפְשִׁי אֶת־יְהוָה הַלְלוּ־יָהּ:

קה
א-ב הוֹדוּ לַיהוָה קִרְאוּ בִשְׁמוֹ הוֹדִיעוּ בָעַמִּים עֲלִילוֹתָיו: שִׁירוּ־לוֹ
ג זַמְּרוּ־לוֹ שִׂיחוּ בְּכָל־נִפְלְאוֹתָיו: הִתְהַלְלוּ בְּשֵׁם קָדְשׁוֹ יִשְׂמַח לֵב
ד-ה מְבַקְשֵׁי יְהוָה: דִּרְשׁוּ יְהוָה וְעֻזּוֹ בַּקְּשׁוּ פָנָיו תָּמִיד: זִכְרוּ נִפְלְאוֹתָיו אֲשֶׁר־

104:17-18. God created the setting to suit the needs of the species.

104:19. The moon and its cycles were made to facilitate the lunar calendar, upon which the Torah bases the

dating of the festivals.

104:24. No creature evolved by chance; every one was designed by God in His wisdom *(Sforno).*

104:35. "Praise God."

who do His bidding, to obey the voice of His word. ²¹ Bless HASHEM, all His legions, His servants who do His will. ²² Bless HASHEM, all His works, in all the places of His dominion. Bless HASHEM, O my soul.

104

A tribute to God for the wondrous world He has created and continuously sustains; a depiction of His unmistakable hand in nature

¹ Bless HASHEM, O my soul. HASHEM, my God, You are very great; You have donned glory and majesty; ² covering with light as with a garment, stretching out the heavens like a curtain. ³ He Who roofs His upper chambers with water; He Who makes clouds His chariot; He Who walks on winged wind; ⁴ He makes the winds His messengers, the flaming fire His attendants. ⁵ He established the earth upon its foundations, that it not falter forever and ever. ⁶ The watery deep, as with a garment You covered it; upon the mountains, water would stand. ⁷ From Your rebuke they flee; from the sound of Your thunder they rush away. ⁸ They ascend mountains, they descend to valleys, to the special place You founded for them. ⁹ You set a boundary they cannot overstep, they cannot return to cover the earth. ¹⁰ He sends the springs into the streams, they flow between the mountains. ¹¹ They water every beast of the field, they quench the wild creatures' thirst. ¹² Near them dwell the heaven's birds, from among the branches they give forth song. ¹³ He waters the mountains from His upper chambers, from the fruit of Your works the earth is sated. ¹⁴ He causes vegetation to sprout for the animal, and plants through man's labor, to bring forth bread from the earth; ¹⁵ and wine that gladdens man's heart, to make the face glow from oil, and bread that sustains the heart of man. ¹⁶ The trees of HASHEM are sated, the cedars of Lebanon that He has planted; ¹⁷ there where the birds nest, the stork with its home among cypresses; ¹⁸ high mountains for the wild goats, rocks as refuge for the gophers. * ¹⁹ He made the moon for festivals, * the sun knows its destination. ²⁰ You make darkness and it is night, in which every forest beast stirs. ²¹ The young lions roar after their prey, and to seek their food from God. ²² The sun rises and they are gathered in, and in their dens they crouch. ²³ Man goes forth to his work, and to his labor until evening. ²⁴ How abundant are Your works, HASHEM; with wisdom You made them all; * the earth is full of Your possessions. ²⁵ Behold this sea, great and of broad measure; creeping things are there without number, creatures small and great. ²⁶ There ships travel, this Leviathan You fashioned to sport with. ²⁷ All of them look to You with hope, to provide their food in its proper time. ²⁸ You give to them, they gather it in; You open Your hand, they are sated with good. ²⁹ When You hide Your face, they are dismayed; when You retrieve their spirit, they perish, and to their dust they return. ³⁰ When You send forth Your breath, they are created, and You renew the surface of the earth. ³¹ May the glory of HASHEM endure forever; let HASHEM rejoice in His works. ³² He looks toward the earth and it trembles; He touches the mountains and they smoke. ³³ I will sing to HASHEM while I live; I will sing praises to my God while I endure. ³⁴ May my words be sweet to Him — I will rejoice in HASHEM. ³⁵ Sinners will cease from the earth, and the wicked will be no more; Bless HASHEM, O my soul. Halleluyah! *

105

¹ Give thanks to HASHEM, declare His Name, make His acts known among the peoples. ² Sing to Him, make music to Him, speak of all His wonders. ³ Glory in His Holy Name, may the heart of those who seek HASHEM be glad. ⁴ Search out HASHEM and His might, seek His Presence always. ⁵ Remember His wonders that

עָשָׂה מִפְּתָיו וּמִשְׁפְּטֵי־פִיו: זֶרַע אַבְרָהָם עַבְדּוֹ בְּנֵי יַעֲקֹב בְּחִירָיו: הוּא ‎ ו

יהוה אֱלֹהֵינוּ בְּכָל־הָאָרֶץ מִשְׁפָּטָיו: זָכַר לְעוֹלָם בְּרִיתוֹ דָּבָר צִוָּה לְאֶלֶף ‎ ח

דּוֹר: אֲשֶׁר כָּרַת אֶת־אַבְרָהָם וּשְׁבוּעָתוֹ לְיִשְׂחָק: וַיַּעֲמִידֶהָ לְיַעֲקֹב לְחֹק ‎ ט

לְיִשְׂרָאֵל בְּרִית עוֹלָם: לֵאמֹר לְךָ אֶתֵּן אֶת־אֶרֶץ־כְּנָעַן חֶבֶל נַחֲלַתְכֶם: ‎ יא

בִּהְיוֹתָם מְתֵי מִסְפָּר כִּמְעַט וְגָרִים בָּהּ: וַיִּתְהַלְּכוּ מִגּוֹי אֶל־גּוֹי מִמַּמְלָכָה ‎ יב-יג

אֶל־עַם אַחֵר: לֹא־הִנִּיחַ אָדָם לְעָשְׁקָם וַיּוֹכַח עֲלֵיהֶם מְלָכִים: אַל־ ‎ יד-טו

תִּגְּעוּ בִמְשִׁיחָי וְלִנְבִיאַי אַל־תָּרֵעוּ: וַיִּקְרָא רָעָב עַל־הָאָרֶץ כָּל־מַטֵּה־ ‎ טז

לֶחֶם שָׁבָר: שָׁלַח לִפְנֵיהֶם אִישׁ לְעֶבֶד נִמְכַּר יוֹסֵף: עִנּוּ בַכֶּבֶל °רַגְלָיו ‎ יז-יח

[רַגְלוֹ ק] בַּרְזֶל בָּאָה נַפְשׁוֹ: עַד־עֵת בֹּא־דְבָרוֹ אִמְרַת יהוה צְרָפָתְהוּ: ‎ יט

שָׁלַח מֶלֶךְ וַיַּתִּירֵהוּ מֹשֵׁל עַמִּים וַיְפַתְּחֵהוּ: שָׂמוֹ אָדוֹן לְבֵיתוֹ וּמֹשֵׁל ‎ כ-כא

בְּכָל־קִנְיָנוֹ: לֶאְסֹר שָׂרָיו בְּנַפְשׁוֹ וּזְקֵנָיו יְחַכֵּם: וַיָּבֹא יִשְׂרָאֵל מִצְרָיִם ‎ כב-כג

וְיַעֲקֹב גָּר בְּאֶרֶץ־חָם: וַיֶּפֶר אֶת־עַמּוֹ מְאֹד וַיַּעֲצִמֵהוּ מִצָּרָיו: הָפַךְ לִבָּם ‎ כד-כה

לִשְׂנֹא עַמּוֹ לְהִתְנַכֵּל בַּעֲבָדָיו: שָׁלַח מֹשֶׁה עַבְדּוֹ אַהֲרֹן אֲשֶׁר בָּחַר־בּוֹ: ‎ כו

שָׂמוּ־בָם דִּבְרֵי אֹתוֹתָיו וּמֹפְתִים בְּאֶרֶץ חָם: שָׁלַח חֹשֶׁךְ וַיַּחְשִׁךְ וְלֹא־ ‎ כז-כח

מָרוּ אֶת־°דְּבָרָיו [דְּבָרוֹ ק]: הָפַךְ אֶת־מֵימֵיהֶם לְדָם וַיָּמֶת אֶת־דְּגָתָם: ‎ כט

שָׁרַץ אַרְצָם צְפַרְדְּעִים בְּחַדְרֵי מַלְכֵיהֶם: אָמַר וַיָּבֹא עָרֹב כִּנִּים בְּכָל־ ‎ ל-לא

גְּבוּלָם: נָתַן גִּשְׁמֵיהֶם בָּרָד אֵשׁ לֶהָבוֹת בְּאַרְצָם: וַיַּךְ גַּפְנָם וּתְאֵנָתָם ‎ לב-לג

וַיְשַׁבֵּר עֵץ גְּבוּלָם: אָמַר וַיָּבֹא אַרְבֶּה וְיֶלֶק וְאֵין מִסְפָּר: וַיֹּאכַל כָּל־עֵשֶׂב ‎ לד-לה

בְּאַרְצָם וַיֹּאכַל פְּרִי אַדְמָתָם: וַיַּךְ כָּל־בְּכוֹר בְּאַרְצָם רֵאשִׁית לְכָל־אוֹנָם: ‎ לו

וַיּוֹצִיאֵם בְּכֶסֶף וְזָהָב וְאֵין בִּשְׁבָטָיו כּוֹשֵׁל: שָׂמַח מִצְרַיִם בְּצֵאתָם כִּי־ ‎ לז-לח

נָפַל פַּחְדָּם עֲלֵיהֶם: פָּרַשׂ עָנָן לְמָסָךְ וְאֵשׁ לְהָאִיר לָיְלָה: שָׁאַל וַיָּבֵא שְׂלָו ‎ לט-מ

וְלֶחֶם שָׁמַיִם יַשְׂבִּיעֵם: פָּתַח צוּר וַיָּזוּבוּ מָיִם הָלְכוּ בַּצִּיּוֹת נָהָר: כִּי־זָכַר ‎ מא-מב

אֶת־דְּבַר קָדְשׁוֹ אֶת־אַבְרָהָם עַבְדּוֹ: וַיּוֹצִא עַמּוֹ בְשָׂשׂוֹן בְּרִנָּה אֶת־ ‎ מג

בְּחִירָיו: וַיִּתֵּן לָהֶם אַרְצוֹת גּוֹיִם וַעֲמַל לְאֻמִּים יִירָשׁוּ: בַּעֲבוּר ׀ יִשְׁמְרוּ ‎ מד-מה

חֻקָּיו וְתוֹרֹתָיו יִנְצֹרוּ הַלְלוּ־יָהּ:

הַלְלוּ יָהּ ׀ הוֹדוּ לַיהוה כִּי־טוֹב כִּי לְעוֹלָם חַסְדּוֹ: מִי יְמַלֵּל גְּבוּרוֹת יהוה ‎ א-ב   **קו**

יוֹם כב לחדש

יַשְׁמִיעַ כָּל־תְּהִלָּתוֹ: אַשְׁרֵי שֹׁמְרֵי מִשְׁפָּט עֹשֵׂה צְדָקָה בְכָל־עֵת: זָכְרֵנִי ‎ ג-ד

יהוה בִּרְצוֹן עַמֶּךָ פָּקְדֵנִי בִּישׁוּעָתֶךָ: לִרְאוֹת ׀ בְּטוֹבַת בְּחִירֶיךָ לִשְׂמֹחַ ‎ ה

בְּשִׂמְחַת גּוֹיֶךָ לְהִתְהַלֵּל עִם־נַחֲלָתֶךָ: חָטָאנוּ עִם־אֲבוֹתֵינוּ הֶעֱוִינוּ ‎ ו

הִרְשָׁעְנוּ: אֲבוֹתֵינוּ בְמִצְרַיִם ׀ לֹא־הִשְׂכִּילוּ נִפְלְאוֹתֶיךָ לֹא זָכְרוּ אֶת־ ‎ ז

105:17. *Genesis 37:13-36.*

105:20-21. *Genesis 41:1-44.*

105:24-25. *Exodus 1:7-10.*

105:28. *Exodus 10:21-29.* The ten plagues, through which God changed nature, "did not defy His word," but issued forth as He commanded.

105:37. *Exodus 12:35-36.*

105:39. *Exodus 13:21-22.*

105:40. *Exodus Ch. 16 and Numbers Ch. 11.*

105:41. *Exodus 17:1-7 and Numbers 20:1-13.*

105:42. *Genesis 15:13-14.*

106:1-2. Literally, "Praise God!"

God guides the course of history; seemingly unrelated events were tied together to bring about a society of all mankind governed by God's holy Torah.

He wrought, His marvels and the judgments of His mouth. ⁶ O seed of Abraham, His servant; O children of Jacob, His chosen ones, ⁷ He is HASHEM, our God; over all the earth are His judgments. ⁸ He remembered His covenant forever — the Word He commanded for a thousand generations — ⁹ that He made with Abraham and His vow to Isaac. ¹⁰ Then He established it for Jacob as a statute, for Israel as an everlasting covenant, ¹¹ saying, "To you I shall give the land of Canaan, the lot of your inheritance." ¹² When they were but few in number, hardly dwelling there; ¹³ and they wandered from nation to nation, from one kingdom to another people — ¹⁴ He allowed no man to rob them, and He rebuked kings for their sake: ¹⁵ "Dare not touch My anointed ones, and to My prophets do no harm." ¹⁶ He declared a famine upon the land, every staff of bread He broke. ¹⁷ He sent a man before them, Joseph was sold as a slave. * ¹⁸ They afflicted his leg with fetters; his soul came into irons. ¹⁹ Until the time that His word came to pass, the decree of HASHEM had purified him. ²⁰ He sent a king who released him, * a ruler of peoples who freed him. ²¹ He appointed him master of his palace, and ruler of all his wealth. ²² To imprison his princes at his whim, and to make his elders wise. ²³ Thus Israel came to Egypt and Jacob sojourned in the land of Ham. ²⁴ And He made His nation exceedingly fruitful, and made it mightier than its oppressors. * ²⁵ He turned their hearts to hate His nation, to plot against His servants. ²⁶ He sent Moses, His servant, Aaron whom He had chosen. ²⁷ They placed among them the words of His signs, and wonders in the land of Ham. ²⁸ He sent darkness and made it dark, and they did not defy His word. * ²⁹ He turned their waters into blood, and He killed their fish. ³⁰ Their land swarmed with frogs, in the chambers of their kings. ³¹ He spoke and hordes of beasts arrived, and lice throughout their borders. ³² He made their rains into hail, flaming fires in their land. ³³ It struck their vine and fig tree, and it broke the tree of their territory. ³⁴ He spoke and the locust came, and grasshoppers without number. ³⁵ And it consumed all grass in their land, and consumed the fruit of their soil. ³⁶ Then He smote every firstborn in their land, the first of all their strength. ³⁷ And He took them out with silver and gold, and there was no pauper among His tribes. * ³⁸ Egypt was glad at their departure, for their fear had fallen upon them. ³⁹ He spread out a cloud for shelter, and a fire to illuminate the night. ⁴⁰ [Israel] asked and He brought quail, and bread from heaven sated them. * ⁴¹ He opened a rock and waters gushed, * and ran like a river through dry places. ⁴² For He remembered His holy promise, to Abraham, His servant, * ⁴³ and He led out His nation with joy, His chosen ones with joyous song. ⁴⁴ And He gave them the lands of nations, and they inherited the toil of regimes. ⁴⁵ So that they might safeguard His statutes and observe His teachings. Halleluyah!

106 ¹ **H**alleluyah! * Give thanks to HASHEM for He is good; for His kindness is eternal. ² Who can express the mighty acts of HASHEM, [who] can make all of His praise heard? ³ Praiseworthy are those who maintain justice, who perform righteousness in every time. ⁴ Remember me, HASHEM, when You show Your people favor; recall me with Your salvation: ⁵ to see the good of Your chosen ones; to rejoice in the gladness of Your nation; to glory with Your inheritance. ⁶ We have sinned like our fathers, we have committed iniquity and wickedness. ⁷ Our fathers in Egypt did not contemplate Your wonders, they were not mindful of

ח רֹב חֲסָדֶיךָ וַיַּמְרוּ עַל־יָם בְּיַם־סוּף: וַיּוֹשִׁיעֵם לְמַעַן שְׁמוֹ לְהוֹדִיעַ אֶת־
ט־י גְּבוּרָתוֹ: וַיִּגְעַר בְּיַם־סוּף וַיֶּחֱרָב וַיּוֹלִיכֵם בַּתְּהֹמוֹת כַּמִּדְבָּר: וַיּוֹשִׁיעֵם
יא מִיַּד שׂוֹנֵא וַיִּגְאָלֵם מִיַּד אוֹיֵב: וַיְכַסּוּ־מַיִם צָרֵיהֶם אֶחָד מֵהֶם לֹא
יב־יג נוֹתָר: וַיַּאֲמִינוּ בִדְבָרָיו יָשִׁירוּ תְּהִלָּתוֹ: מִהֲרוּ שָׁכְחוּ מַעֲשָׂיו לֹא־
יד־טו חִכּוּ לַעֲצָתוֹ: וַיִּתְאַוּוּ תַאֲוָה בַּמִּדְבָּר וַיְנַסּוּ־אֵל בִּישִׁימוֹן: וַיִּתֵּן לָהֶם
טז שֶׁאֱלָתָם וַיְשַׁלַּח רָזוֹן בְּנַפְשָׁם: וַיְקַנְאוּ לְמֹשֶׁה בַּמַּחֲנֶה לְאַהֲרֹן קְדוֹשׁ
יז־יח יְהוָה: תִּפְתַּח־אֶרֶץ וַתִּבְלַע דָּתָן וַתְּכַס עַל־עֲדַת אֲבִירָם: וַתִּבְעַר־אֵשׁ
יט בַּעֲדָתָם לֶהָבָה תְּלַהֵט רְשָׁעִים: יַעֲשׂוּ־עֵגֶל בְּחֹרֵב וַיִּשְׁתַּחֲווּ לְמַסֵּכָה:
כ־כא וַיָּמִירוּ אֶת־כְּבוֹדָם בְּתַבְנִית שׁוֹר אֹכֵל עֵשֶׂב: שָׁכְחוּ אֵל מוֹשִׁיעָם
כב־כג עֹשֶׂה גְדֹלוֹת בְּמִצְרָיִם: נִפְלָאוֹת בְּאֶרֶץ חָם נוֹרָאוֹת עַל־יַם־סוּף: וַיֹּאמֶר
לְהַשְׁמִידָם לוּלֵי מֹשֶׁה בְחִירוֹ עָמַד בַּפֶּרֶץ לְפָנָיו לְהָשִׁיב חֲמָתוֹ
כד־כה מֵהַשְׁחִית: וַיִּמְאֲסוּ בְּאֶרֶץ חֶמְדָּה לֹא־הֶאֱמִינוּ לִדְבָרוֹ: וַיֵּרָגְנוּ בְאָהֳלֵיהֶם
כו לֹא שָׁמְעוּ בְּקוֹל יְהוָה: וַיִּשָּׂא יָדוֹ לָהֶם לְהַפִּיל אוֹתָם בַּמִּדְבָּר:
כז־כח וּלְהַפִּיל זַרְעָם בַּגּוֹיִם וּלְזָרוֹתָם בָּאֲרָצוֹת: וַיִּצָּמְדוּ לְבַעַל פְּעוֹר וַיֹּאכְלוּ
כט זִבְחֵי מֵתִים: וַיַּכְעִיסוּ בְּמַעַלְלֵיהֶם וַתִּפְרָץ־בָּם מַגֵּפָה: וַיַּעֲמֹד פִּינְחָס
לא וַיְפַלֵּל וַתֵּעָצַר הַמַּגֵּפָה: וַתֵּחָשֶׁב לוֹ לִצְדָקָה לְדֹר וָדֹר עַד־עוֹלָם:
לב־לג וַיַּקְצִיפוּ עַל־מֵי מְרִיבָה וַיֵּרַע לְמֹשֶׁה בַּעֲבוּרָם: כִּי־הִמְרוּ אֶת־רוּחוֹ
לד וַיְבַטֵּא בִּשְׂפָתָיו: לֹא־הִשְׁמִידוּ אֶת־הָעַמִּים אֲשֶׁר אָמַר יְהוָה לָהֶם:
לה־לו וַיִּתְעָרְבוּ בַגּוֹיִם וַיִּלְמְדוּ מַעֲשֵׂיהֶם: וַיַּעַבְדוּ אֶת־עֲצַבֵּיהֶם וַיִּהְיוּ לָהֶם
לז־לח לְמוֹקֵשׁ: וַיִּזְבְּחוּ אֶת־בְּנֵיהֶם וְאֶת־בְּנוֹתֵיהֶם לַשֵּׁדִים: וַיִּשְׁפְּכוּ דָם נָקִי דַּם־
בְּנֵיהֶם וּבְנוֹתֵיהֶם אֲשֶׁר זִבְּחוּ לַעֲצַבֵּי כְנָעַן וַתֶּחֱנַף הָאָרֶץ בַּדָּמִים:
לט־מ וַיִּטְמְאוּ בְמַעֲשֵׂיהֶם וַיִּזְנוּ בְּמַעַלְלֵיהֶם: וַיִּחַר־אַף יְהוָה בְּעַמּוֹ וַיְתָעֵב אֶת־
מא־מב נַחֲלָתוֹ: וַיִּתְּנֵם בְּיַד־גּוֹיִם וַיִּמְשְׁלוּ בָהֶם שֹׂנְאֵיהֶם: וַיִּלְחָצוּם אוֹיְבֵיהֶם וַיִּכָּנְעוּ
מג תַּחַת יָדָם: פְּעָמִים רַבּוֹת יַצִּילֵם וְהֵמָּה יַמְרוּ בַעֲצָתָם וַיָּמֹכּוּ
מד־מה בַּעֲוֹנָם: וַיַּרְא בַּצַּר לָהֶם בְּשָׁמְעוֹ אֶת־רִנָּתָם: וַיִּזְכֹּר לָהֶם בְּרִיתוֹ וַיִּנָּחֵם
מו־מז כְּרֹב חֲסָדָיו: וַיִּתֵּן אוֹתָם לְרַחֲמִים לִפְנֵי כָּל־שׁוֹבֵיהֶם: הוֹשִׁיעֵנוּ ׀ יְהוָה
אֱלֹהֵינוּ וְקַבְּצֵנוּ מִן־הַגּוֹיִם לְהֹדוֹת לְשֵׁם קָדְשֶׁךָ לְהִשְׁתַּבֵּחַ בִּתְהִלָּתֶךָ:
מח בָּרוּךְ יְהוָה אֱלֹהֵי יִשְׂרָאֵל מִן־הָעוֹלָם ׀ וְעַד הָעוֹלָם וְאָמַר כָּל־הָעָם אָמֵן
הַלְלוּ־יָהּ:

106:7. *Exodus* 14:10-12.

106:9-11. *Exodus* 14:15-31.

106:12. *Exodus* 15:1-21.

106:14-15. *Exodus* Ch. 16; *Numbers* Ch. 11.

106:16-18. *Numbers* Chs. 16-17.

106:19-23. *Exodus* Chs. 32-33.

106:24-27. *Numbers* 13:1-14:25.

106:27. On Tishah B'Av, Israel mourned over the report of the Spies, and God made it a day of misfortune. On that day, both Temples would be destroyed and the Jews would be exiled and thrown "down among the nations."

106:28-31. *Numbers* Ch. 25.

106:28. Idols, who have no more power than the dead.

106:32-33. *Numbers* 20:1-13.

106:34-35. *Deuteronomy* 20:16; *Joshua* 16:10.

God's
presence and
lovingkind-
ness are
always near;
one need but
have open
eyes and an
open heart to
see them.

Your abundant kindnesses, and they rebelled by the sea, at the Sea of Reeds. * ⁸ But He saved them for His Name's sake, to make known His might. ⁹ He roared at the Sea of Reeds and it became dry, and He led them through the depths as through a desert. * ¹⁰ And He saved them from the hand of the enemy, and redeemed them from the hand of the foe. ¹¹ And the waters covered their tormentors, not one of them was left. ¹² Then they believed His words, they sang His praise. * ¹³ Swiftly they forgot His deeds, they did not await His counsel. ¹⁴ And they craved a lust in the wilderness, and tested God in the desert. * ¹⁵ And He gave them their request, but dispatched emaciation to their soul. ¹⁶ They were jealous of Moses in the camp, of Aaron, HASHEM's holy one. * ¹⁷ The earth opened and swallowed Dathan, and covered over the company of Abiram. ¹⁸ And a fire burned amid their company, a flame set the wicked ablaze. ¹⁹ They made a calf* in Horeb, and prostrated themselves before a molten image. ²⁰ They exchanged their Glory for the likeness of a grass-eating ox. ²¹ They forgot God, their Savior, Who had done great things in Egypt, ²² wondrous works in the Land of Ham, awesome things by the Sea of Reeds. ²³ He said He would destroy them — had not Moses, His chosen one, stood in the breach before Him to turn away His wrath from destroying. ²⁴ And they despised the desirable land, * they had no faith in His Word. ²⁵ They murmured in their tents, they did not heed the voice of HASHEM. ²⁶ Then He lifted up His hand [in an oath] against them, to cast them down in the wilderness, ²⁷ and to cast down their descendants among the nations, * and to scatter them among the lands. ²⁸ Then they attached themselves to Baal Peor, * and ate the sacrifices of the dead. * ²⁹ And they angered [Him] with their behavior, and a plague broke out among them. ³⁰ And Phinehas arose and executed judgment, and the plague was halted. ³¹ It was accounted to him as a righteous deed, for all generations, forever. ³² They provoked at the Waters of Strife, * and Moses suffered because of them, ³³ because they acted contrary to His spirit, and He pronounced with His lips. ³⁴ They did not destroy the peoples as HASHEM had told them. ³⁵ But they mingled with the nations and learned their deeds, ³⁶ and served their idols, * which became a snare for them. ³⁷ And they sacrificed their sons and daughters to the demons. ³⁸ They spilled innocent blood, the blood of their sons and daughters whom they sacrificed to the Canaanite idols; and the land was polluted by the blood-guilt. ³⁹ Thus were they defiled by their deeds, and went astray through their actions. ⁴⁰ And HASHEM's anger was kindled against His people, and He abhorred His inheritance. ⁴¹ So He delivered them to the hands of the nations, and their enemies ruled over them. ⁴² Their foes oppressed them, and they were humbled under their power. ⁴³ Many times did He rescue them; yet they were defiant in their counsel and were impoverished by their iniquity. ⁴⁴ But He took note when they were in distress, when He heard their outcry. ⁴⁵ He remembered His covenant for them and relented in accordance with His abundant kindness. ⁴⁶ He caused them to be pitied by all their captors. ⁴⁷ Save us HASHEM, our God, and gather us from among the nations, to thank Your Holy Name, and to glory in Your praise! ⁴⁸ Blessed is HASHEM, the God of Israel, from This World to the World to Come, and let all the people say, "Amen!" Halleluyah!

106:36-46. Intermittently, throughout the periods of the Judges and the Kings.

ספר חמישי

קז

הֹדוּ לַיהוָה כִּי־טוֹב כִּי לְעוֹלָם חַסְדּוֹ: יֹאמְרוּ גְּאוּלֵי יְהוָה אֲשֶׁר גְּאָלָם אב

מִיַּד־צָר: וּמֵאֲרָצוֹת קִבְּצָם מִמִּזְרָח וּמִמַּעֲרָב מִצָּפוֹן וּמִיָּם: תָּעוּ בַמִּדְבָּר גד

בִּישִׁימוֹן דָּרֶךְ עִיר מוֹשָׁב לֹא מָצָאוּ: רְעֵבִים גַּם־צְמֵאִים נַפְשָׁם בָּהֶם ה

תִּתְעַטָּף: וַיִּצְעֲקוּ אֶל־יְהוָה בַּצַּר לָהֶם מִמְּצוּקוֹתֵיהֶם יַצִּילֵם: וַיַּדְרִיכֵם וז

בְּדֶרֶךְ יְשָׁרָה לָלֶכֶת אֶל־עִיר מוֹשָׁב: יוֹדוּ לַיהוָה חַסְדּוֹ וְנִפְלְאוֹתָיו לִבְנֵי ח

אָדָם: כִּי־הִשְׂבִּיעַ נֶפֶשׁ שֹׁקֵקָה וְנֶפֶשׁ רְעֵבָה מִלֵּא־טוֹב: יֹשְׁבֵי חֹשֶׁךְ ט

וְצַלְמָוֶת אֲסִירֵי עֳנִי וּבַרְזֶל: כִּי־הִמְרוּ אִמְרֵי־אֵל וַעֲצַת עֶלְיוֹן נָאָצוּ: וַיַּכְנַע יא-יב

בֶּעָמָל לִבָּם כָּשְׁלוּ וְאֵין עֹזֵר: וַיִּזְעֲקוּ אֶל־יְהוָה בַּצַּר לָהֶם מִמְּצֻקוֹתֵיהֶם יג

יוֹשִׁיעֵם: יוֹצִיאֵם מֵחֹשֶׁךְ וְצַלְמָוֶת וּמוֹסְרוֹתֵיהֶם יְנַתֵּק: יוֹדוּ לַיהוָה חַסְדּוֹ יד-טו

וְנִפְלְאוֹתָיו לִבְנֵי אָדָם: כִּי־שִׁבַּר דַּלְתוֹת נְחֹשֶׁת וּבְרִיחֵי בַרְזֶל גִּדֵּעַ: טז

אֱוִילִים מִדֶּרֶךְ פִּשְׁעָם וּמֵעֲוֹנֹתֵיהֶם יִתְעַנּוּ: כָּל־אֹכֶל תְּתַעֵב נַפְשָׁם וַיַּגִּיעוּ יז-יח

עַד־שַׁעֲרֵי מָוֶת: וַיִּזְעֲקוּ אֶל־יְהוָה בַּצַּר לָהֶם מִמְּצֻקוֹתֵיהֶם יוֹשִׁיעֵם: יִשְׁלַח יט-כ

דְּבָרוֹ וְיִרְפָּאֵם וִימַלֵּט מִשְּׁחִיתוֹתָם: יוֹדוּ לַיהוָה חַסְדּוֹ וְנִפְלְאוֹתָיו לִבְנֵי כא

אָדָם: וְיִזְבְּחוּ זִבְחֵי תוֹדָה וִיסַפְּרוּ מַעֲשָׂיו בְּרִנָּה: ¶ יוֹרְדֵי הַיָּם בָּאֳנִיּוֹת כב-כג

עֹשֵׂי מְלָאכָה בְּמַיִם רַבִּים: ¶ הֵמָּה רָאוּ מַעֲשֵׂי יְהוָה וְנִפְלְאוֹתָיו כד

בִּמְצוּלָה: ¶ וַיֹּאמֶר וַיַּעֲמֵד רוּחַ סְעָרָה וַתְּרוֹמֵם גַּלָּיו: ¶ יַעֲלוּ כה-כו

שָׁמַיִם יֵרְדוּ תְהוֹמוֹת נַפְשָׁם בְּרָעָה תִתְמוֹגָג: ¶ יָחוֹגּוּ וְיָנוּעוּ כז

כַּשִּׁכּוֹר וְכָל־חָכְמָתָם תִּתְבַּלָּע: ¶ וַיִּצְעֲקוּ אֶל־יְהוָה בַּצַּר לָהֶם כח

וּמִמְּצוּקֹתֵיהֶם יוֹצִיאֵם: יָקֵם סְעָרָה לִדְמָמָה וַיֶּחֱשׁוּ גַּלֵּיהֶם: וַיִּשְׂמְחוּ כִי־ כט-ל

יִשְׁתֹּקוּ וַיַּנְחֵם אֶל־מְחוֹז חֶפְצָם: יוֹדוּ לַיהוָה חַסְדּוֹ וְנִפְלְאוֹתָיו לִבְנֵי אָדָם: לא

וִירֹמְמוּהוּ בִּקְהַל־עָם וּבְמוֹשַׁב זְקֵנִים יְהַלְלוּהוּ: יָשֵׂם נְהָרוֹת לְמִדְבָּר לב-לג

וּמֹצָאֵי מַיִם לְצִמָּאוֹן: אֶרֶץ פְּרִי לִמְלֵחָה מֵרָעַת יֹשְׁבֵי בָהּ: יָשֵׂם מִדְבָּר לד-לה

לַאֲגַם־מַיִם וְאֶרֶץ צִיָּה לְמֹצָאֵי מָיִם: וַיּוֹשֶׁב שָׁם רְעֵבִים וַיְכוֹנְנוּ עִיר מוֹשָׁב: לו

וַיִּזְרְעוּ שָׂדוֹת וַיִּטְּעוּ כְרָמִים וַיַּעֲשׂוּ פְּרִי תְבוּאָה: וַיְבָרֲכֵם וַיִּרְבּוּ מְאֹד לז-לח

וּבְהֶמְתָּם לֹא יַמְעִיט: וַיִּמְעֲטוּ וַיָּשֹׁחוּ מֵעֹצֶר רָעָה וְיָגוֹן: ¶ שֹׁפֵךְ לט-מ

בּוּז עַל־נְדִיבִים וַיַּתְעֵם בְּתֹהוּ לֹא־דָרֶךְ: וַיְשַׂגֵּב אֶבְיוֹן מֵעוֹנִי וַיָּשֶׂם כַּצֹּאן מא

מִשְׁפָּחוֹת: יִרְאוּ יְשָׁרִים וְיִשְׂמָחוּ וְכָל־עַוְלָה קָפְצָה פִּיהָ: מִי־חָכָם וְיִשְׁמָר־ מב-מג

אֵלֶּה וְיִתְבּוֹנְנוּ חַסְדֵי יְהוָה:

107:1. This psalm of thanksgiving describes the peril and deliverance of four groups of people: a desert traveler (vv. 3-6); a prisoner (vv. 10-16); a sick person (vv. 17-22); and a seafarer (vv. 27-32).

107:8. One should publicize his personal experience of God's kindness so that others, too, may gain increased awareness of His Providence.

107:30. The seafarers rejoiced because the waves had calmed down.

107:39. They, whom God showered with His bounty, became arrogant in their affluence, so He diminished them by withholding their prosperity and bringing trouble upon them.

107:40. Those who rely on their own wealth become hopelessly lost in futility.

BOOK FIVE

107

Those who experience God's deliverance — from desolation, from captivity, from sickness, from the sea — must publicly proclaim their gratitude for God's enduring kindness.

¹ Give thanks to HASHEM, * for He is good, for His kindness endures forever! ² Those redeemed by HASHEM will say [it], those whom He redeemed from the hand of distress, ³ and whom He gathered from the lands: from east and from west, from north and from the sea. ⁴ They wandered in the wilderness, in the desolation of the path; they found no inhabited city. ⁵ Hungry as well as thirsty, their soul grew faint within them. ⁶ Then they cried out to HASHEM in their distress, He would rescue them from their straits. ⁷ And He led them upon a straight path, to go to an inhabited city. ⁸ Let them give thanks to HASHEM for His kindness, and His wonders to the children of man. * ⁹ For He sated the yearning soul, and filled the hungry soul with good.

¹⁰ Those who sat in darkness and the shadow of death, shackled in affliction and iron, ¹¹ because they rebelled against the words of God, and scorned the counsel of the Supreme One. ¹² So He humbled their heart with hard labor; they stumbled, and there was none to help. ¹³ Then they cried out to HASHEM in their distress, He would save them from their straits. ¹⁴ He would take them out of darkness and the shadow of death, and break open their shackles. ¹⁵ Let them give thanks to HASHEM for His kindness, and His wonders to the children of man. ¹⁶ For He smashed copper gates, and cut asunder iron bolts.

¹⁷ Fools, because of their sinful path and because of their iniquities, were afflicted. ¹⁸ Their soul abhorred all food, and they reached until the portals of death. ¹⁹ Then they cried out to HASHEM in their distress, He would save them from their straits. ²⁰ He would dispatch His word and cure them, and let them escape their destruction. ²¹ Let them give thanks to HASHEM for His kindness, and His wonders to the children of man. ²² And let them slaughter thanksgiving offerings, and relate His works with joyful song.

²³ Those who go down to the sea in ships, who do their work in great waters. ²⁴ They have seen the deeds of HASHEM, and His wonders in the watery deep. ²⁵ He spoke and raised the stormy wind and lifted its waves. ²⁶ They rise heavenward, they descend to the depths, their soul melts with trouble. ²⁷ They reel, they stagger like a drunkard, and all their wisdom is swallowed up. ²⁸ Then they cried out to HASHEM in their distress, and He would take them out from their straits. ²⁹ He would halt the storm to restore calmness, and their waves were stilled. ³⁰ And they rejoiced because they were quiet, * and He guided them to their desired boundary. ³¹ Let them give thanks to HASHEM for His kindness, and His wonders to the children of man. ³² Let them exalt Him in the assembly of people, and praise Him in the session of the elders.

³³ He turns rivers into a desert, and springs of water into drought; ³⁴ a fruitful land into a salty waste, because of the evil of its inhabitants. ³⁵ He turns a desert into a pool of water, and an arid land into springs of water. ³⁶ There He settled the hungry, and they established an inhabited city. ³⁷ And they sowed fields and planted vineyards that yielded a fruitful harvest. ³⁸ And He blessed them and they multiplied greatly, and He did not decrease their livestock. * ³⁹ But they became few and they sank down, from lingering trouble and agony. * ⁴⁰ He pours contempt upon the affluent, and He made them wander in a pathless wasteland. * ⁴¹ But He strengthened the destitute from poverty, and makes [his] families like the flock. ⁴² The upright shall see and be glad, while all iniquity will have shut its mouth. ⁴³ Whoever is wise let him note these things, and they will comprehend the kindnesses of HASHEM.

קח
א-ג שִׁיר מִזְמוֹר לְדָוִד: נָכוֹן לִבִּי אֱלֹהִים אָשִׁירָה וַאֲזַמְּרָה אַף־כְּבוֹדִי: עוּרָה
יום כג לחדש
ד-ה הַנֵּבֶל וְכִנּוֹר אָעִירָה שָּׁחַר: אוֹדְךָ בָעַמִּים ׀ יְהֹוָה וַאֲזַמֶּרְךָ בַּלְאֻמִּים: כִּי־
ו גָדוֹל מֵעַל־שָׁמַיִם חַסְדֶּךָ וְעַד־שְׁחָקִים אֲמִתֶּךָ: רוּמָה עַל־שָׁמַיִם אֱלֹהִים
ז וְעַל כָּל־הָאָרֶץ כְּבוֹדֶךָ: לְמַעַן יֵחָלְצוּן יְדִידֶיךָ הוֹשִׁיעָה יְמִינְךָ וַעֲנֵנִי:
ח-ט אֱלֹהִים ׀ דִּבֶּר בְּקָדְשׁוֹ אֶעְלֹזָה אֲחַלְּקָה שְׁכֶם וְעֵמֶק סֻכּוֹת אֲמַדֵּד: לִי
י גִלְעָד ׀ לִי מְנַשֶּׁה וְאֶפְרַיִם מָעוֹז רֹאשִׁי יְהוּדָה מְחֹקְקִי: מוֹאָב ׀ סִיר רַחְצִי
יא עַל־אֱדוֹם אַשְׁלִיךְ נַעֲלִי עֲלֵי־פְלֶשֶׁת אֶתְרוֹעָע: מִי יֹבִלֵנִי עִיר מִבְצָר מִי
יב נָחַנִי עַד־אֱדוֹם: הֲלֹא־אֱלֹהִים זְנַחְתָּנוּ וְלֹא־תֵצֵא אֱלֹהִים בְּצִבְאֹתֵינוּ:
יג-יד הָבָה־לָּנוּ עֶזְרָת מִצָּר וְשָׁוְא תְּשׁוּעַת אָדָם: בֵּאלֹהִים נַעֲשֶׂה־חָיִל וְהוּא
יָבוּס צָרֵינוּ:

קט
א-ב לַמְנַצֵּחַ לְדָוִד מִזְמוֹר אֱלֹהֵי תְהִלָּתִי אַל־תֶּחֱרַשׁ: כִּי פִי רָשָׁע וּפִי־מִרְמָה
ג עָלַי פָּתָחוּ דִּבְּרוּ אִתִּי לְשׁוֹן שָׁקֶר: וְדִבְרֵי שִׂנְאָה סְבָבוּנִי וַיִּלָּחֲמוּנִי חִנָּם:
ד-ה תַּחַת־אַהֲבָתִי יִשְׂטְנוּנִי וַאֲנִי תְפִלָּה: וַיָּשִׂימוּ עָלַי רָעָה תַּחַת טוֹבָה וְשִׂנְאָה
ו-ז תַּחַת אַהֲבָתִי: הַפְקֵד עָלָיו רָשָׁע וְשָׂטָן יַעֲמֹד עַל־יְמִינוֹ: בְּהִשָּׁפְטוֹ יֵצֵא
ח-ט רָשָׁע וּתְפִלָּתוֹ תִּהְיֶה לַחֲטָאָה: יִהְיוּ־יָמָיו מְעַטִּים פְּקֻדָּתוֹ יִקַּח אַחֵר: יִהְיוּ־
י בָנָיו יְתוֹמִים וְאִשְׁתּוֹ אַלְמָנָה: וְנוֹעַ יָנוּעוּ בָנָיו וְשִׁאֵלוּ וְדָרְשׁוּ מֵחָרְבוֹתֵיהֶם:
יא-יב יְנַקֵּשׁ נוֹשֶׁה לְכָל־אֲשֶׁר־לוֹ וְיָבֹזּוּ זָרִים יְגִיעוֹ: אַל־יְהִי־לוֹ מֹשֵׁךְ חָסֶד וְאַל־
יג-יד יְהִי חוֹנֵן לִיתוֹמָיו: יְהִי־אַחֲרִיתוֹ לְהַכְרִית בְּדוֹר אַחֵר יִמַּח שְׁמָם: יִזָּכֵר ׀
טו עֲוֹן אֲבֹתָיו אֶל־יְהֹוָה וְחַטַּאת אִמּוֹ אַל־תִּמָּח: יִהְיוּ נֶגֶד־יְהֹוָה תָּמִיד
טז וְיַכְרֵת מֵאֶרֶץ זִכְרָם: יַעַן אֲשֶׁר ׀ לֹא זָכַר עֲשׂוֹת חָסֶד וַיִּרְדֹּף אִישׁ־עָנִי
יז וְאֶבְיוֹן וְנִכְאֵה לֵבָב לְמוֹתֵת: וַיֶּאֱהַב קְלָלָה וַתְּבוֹאֵהוּ וְלֹא־חָפֵץ בִּבְרָכָה
יח וַתִּרְחַק מִמֶּנּוּ: וַיִּלְבַּשׁ קְלָלָה כְּמַדּוֹ וַתָּבֹא כַמַּיִם בְּקִרְבּוֹ וְכַשֶּׁמֶן
יט-כ בְּעַצְמוֹתָיו: תְּהִי־לוֹ כְּבֶגֶד יַעְטֶה וּלְמֵזַח תָּמִיד יַחְגְּרֶהָ: זֹאת פְּעֻלַּת שֹׂטְנַי
כא מֵאֵת יְהֹוָה וְהַדֹּבְרִים רָע עַל־נַפְשִׁי: וְאַתָּה ׀ יֱהֹוִה אֲדֹנָי עֲשֵׂה־אִתִּי לְמַעַן
כב שְׁמֶךָ כִּי־טוֹב חַסְדְּךָ הַצִּילֵנִי: כִּי־עָנִי וְאֶבְיוֹן אָנֹכִי וְלִבִּי חָלַל בְּקִרְבִּי:
כג-כד כְּצֵל־כִּנְטוֹתוֹ נֶהֱלָכְתִּי נִנְעַרְתִּי כָּאַרְבֶּה: בִּרְכַּי כָּשְׁלוּ מִצּוֹם וּבְשָׂרִי
כה-כו כָּחַשׁ מִשָּׁמֶן: וַאֲנִי ׀ הָיִיתִי חֶרְפָּה לָהֶם יִרְאוּנִי יְנִיעוּן רֹאשָׁם: עָזְרֵנִי יְהֹוָה
כז-כח אֱלֹהָי הוֹשִׁיעֵנִי כְחַסְדֶּךָ: וְיֵדְעוּ כִּי־יָדְךָ זֹּאת אַתָּה יְהֹוָה עֲשִׂיתָהּ: יְקַלְלוּ־
כט הֵמָּה וְאַתָּה תְבָרֵךְ קָמוּ ׀ וַיֵּבֹשׁוּ וְעַבְדְּךָ יִשְׂמָח: יִלְבְּשׁוּ שׂוֹטְנַי כְּלִמָּה
ל וְיַעֲטוּ כַמְעִיל בָּשְׁתָּם: אוֹדֶה יְהֹוָה מְאֹד בְּפִי וּבְתוֹךְ רַבִּים אֲהַלְלֶנּוּ:

109:4. My love for them was genuine, as I would pray on their behalf (*Ibn Ezra*).

109:6-19. David asks that his treacherous enemies be punished. The abrupt shift from plural to singular indicates a reference to the leader of these enemies, Doeg the Edomite [see *I Samuel* Chs. 21-22] (*Ibn Ezra; Radak*).

109:21. See *Genesis* 15:2.

108

A prophetic psalm about the consolidation of the Messiah's reign

¹ **A** song, a psalm by David. ² My heart is steadfast, O God. I will sing and make music even with my soul. ³ Awake, O psalter and harp, I shall awaken the dawn. ⁴ I will thank You among the peoples, HASHEM, and I will sing to You among the regimes. ⁵ For great above the very heavens is Your kindness, and until the upper heights is Your truth. ⁶ Be exalted above heaven, O God, and above all the earth, Your glory. ⁷ So that Your beloved ones may be released, let Your right hand save and respond to me. ⁸ God spoke through His holy one that I would exult, that I would divide Shechem and measure out the Valley of Succoth. ⁹ Mine is Gilead, mine is Manasseh, and Ephraim is the stronghold of my head; Judah is my lawgiver. ¹⁰ Moab is my washbasin; upon Edom I will cast my shoe; over Philistia I will shout. ¹¹ Who will bring me to the fortified city? Who has led me unto Edom? ¹² Is it not [You, O] God, Who has [until now] forsaken us, and does not go forth, O God, with our legions? ¹³ Give us help against the oppressor; man's salvation is futile. ¹⁴ Through God we shall perform valiantly; and He will trample our oppressors.

109

A plea to God for deliverance from scheming maligners who arise against the individual or the nation

¹ **F**or the conductor, by David, a psalm; O God of my praise, be not silent. ² For the mouth of the wicked and the mouth of the deceitful have opened against me, they have spoken to me the language of falsehood. ³ And with words of hatred they have encircled me, and attacked me without cause. ⁴ In return for my love they accuse me, but I was prayer. * ⁵ They placed upon me evil in return for good, and hatred in return for my love.

⁶ Appoint a wicked man over him, * and let an adversary stand at his right; ⁷ when he is judged may he go out condemned, and may his prayer be turned into sin; ⁸ may his days be few; may another take his position; ⁹ may his children be orphans and his wife a widow; ¹⁰ may his children constantly wander and beg, and may they seek charity from amid their ruins; ¹¹ may the creditor seize all that he has, and may strangers despoil his labor; ¹² may he have no one who extends him kindness; and may no one be merciful to his orphans; ¹³ may his posterity be cut off, in a later generation let their name be erased; ¹⁴ may the iniquity of his fathers be remembered before HASHEM, and the sin of his mother not be erased; ¹⁵ may they be before HASHEM at all times, and may He cut off their memory from the earth. ¹⁶ [All this] because he never remembered to do kindness, and he pursued the poor and destitute man, and the brokenhearted to kill [him]. ¹⁷ He loved the curse, so it has come upon him; he desired not blessing, so it has stayed far from him. ¹⁸ He donned curse like his garment; it has come like water into his innards, and like oil into his bones. ¹⁹ May it be to him like a garment in which he wraps himself, and a belt with which he constantly girds himself.

²⁰ This is the reward of my adversaries from HASHEM, and those who speak evil against my soul. ²¹ But You, HASHEM/ELOHIM, * O Lord, deal with me for Your Name's sake; because Your kindness is good, rescue me! ²² For poor and destitute am I, and my heart has died within me. ²³ Like a vanishing shadow, I am gone; I am tossed about like a locust. ²⁴ My knees totter from fasting, and my flesh has become lean without fat. ²⁵ And I have become a disgrace to them; they see me and shake their heads. ²⁶ Help me, HASHEM, my God, save me according to Your kindness! ²⁷ Let them know that this is Your hand, that You, HASHEM, have made it happen. ²⁸ Let them curse, but You will bless; they rose up, but they will be shamed — and Your servant will rejoice! ²⁹ May my adversaries be clothed in humiliation, and may they wrap themselves in their shame as in a cloak. ³⁰ I will thank HASHEM exceedingly with my mouth, and amid the multitude I will praise

לא כִּי־יַעֲמֹד לִימִין אֶבְיֻוֹן לְהוֹשִׁיעַ מִשֹּׁפְטֵי נַפְשׁוֹ:

קי א לְדָוִד מִזְמוֹר נְאֻם יהוה ׀ לַאדֹנִי שֵׁב לִימִינִי עַד־אָשִׁית אֹיְבֶיךָ הֲדֹם
ב-ג לְרַגְלֶיךָ: מַטֵּה־עֻזְּךָ יִשְׁלַח יהוה מִצִּיּוֹן רְדֵה בְּקֶרֶב אֹיְבֶיךָ: עַמְּךָ נְדָבֹת
ד בְּיוֹם חֵילֶךָ בְּהַדְרֵי־קֹדֶשׁ מֵרֶחֶם מִשְׁחָר לְךָ טַל יַלְדֻתֶיךָ: נִשְׁבַּע יהוה ׀
ה וְלֹא יִנָּחֵם אַתָּה־כֹהֵן לְעוֹלָם עַל־דִּבְרָתִי מַלְכִּי־צֶדֶק: אֲדֹנָי עַל־יְמִינְךָ
ו מָחַץ בְּיוֹם־אַפּוֹ מְלָכִים: יָדִין בַּגּוֹיִם מָלֵא גְוִיּוֹת מָחַץ רֹאשׁ עַל־אֶרֶץ
ז רַבָּה: מִנַּחַל בַּדֶּרֶךְ יִשְׁתֶּה עַל־כֵּן יָרִים רֹאשׁ:

קיא א-ב הַלְלוּ־יָהּ ׀ אוֹדֶה יהוה בְּכָל־לֵבָב בְּסוֹד יְשָׁרִים וְעֵדָה: גְּדֹלִים מַעֲשֵׂי יהוה
ג-ד דְּרוּשִׁים לְכָל־חֶפְצֵיהֶם: הוֹד־וְהָדָר פָּעֳלוֹ וְצִדְקָתוֹ עֹמֶדֶת לָעַד: זֵכֶר
ה עָשָׂה לְנִפְלְאֹתָיו חַנּוּן וְרַחוּם יהוה: טֶרֶף נָתַן לִירֵאָיו יִזְכֹּר לְעוֹלָם
ו-ז בְּרִיתוֹ: כֹּחַ מַעֲשָׂיו הִגִּיד לְעַמּוֹ לָתֵת לָהֶם נַחֲלַת גּוֹיִם: מַעֲשֵׂי יָדָיו אֱמֶת
ח וּמִשְׁפָּט נֶאֱמָנִים כָּל־פִּקּוּדָיו: סְמוּכִים לָעַד לְעוֹלָם עֲשׂוּיִם בֶּאֱמֶת וְיָשָׁר:
ט פְּדוּת ׀ שָׁלַח לְעַמּוֹ צִוָּה־לְעוֹלָם בְּרִיתוֹ קָדוֹשׁ וְנוֹרָא שְׁמוֹ: רֵאשִׁית
י חָכְמָה ׀ יִרְאַת יהוה שֵׂכֶל טוֹב לְכָל־עֹשֵׂיהֶם תְּהִלָּתוֹ עֹמֶדֶת לָעַד:

קיב א-ב הַלְלוּ־יָהּ ׀ אַשְׁרֵי־אִישׁ יָרֵא אֶת־יהוה בְּמִצְוֹתָיו חָפֵץ מְאֹד: גִּבּוֹר בָּאָרֶץ
ג יִהְיֶה זַרְעוֹ דּוֹר יְשָׁרִים יְבֹרָךְ: הוֹן־וָעֹשֶׁר בְּבֵיתוֹ וְצִדְקָתוֹ עֹמֶדֶת לָעַד:
ד-ה זָרַח בַּחֹשֶׁךְ אוֹר לַיְשָׁרִים חַנּוּן וְרַחוּם וְצַדִּיק: טוֹב־אִישׁ חוֹנֵן וּמַלְוֶה
ו יְכַלְכֵּל דְּבָרָיו בְּמִשְׁפָּט: כִּי־לְעוֹלָם לֹא־יִמּוֹט לְזֵכֶר עוֹלָם יִהְיֶה צַדִּיק:
ז-ח מִשְּׁמוּעָה רָעָה לֹא יִירָא נָכוֹן לִבּוֹ בָּטֻחַ בַּיהוה: סָמוּךְ לִבּוֹ לֹא יִירָא עַד
ט אֲשֶׁר־יִרְאֶה בְצָרָיו: פִּזַּר ׀ נָתַן לָאֶבְיוֹנִים צִדְקָתוֹ עֹמֶדֶת לָעַד קַרְנוֹ תָּרוּם
י בְּכָבוֹד: רָשָׁע יִרְאֶה ׀ וְכָעָס שִׁנָּיו יַחֲרֹק וְנָמָס תַּאֲוַת רְשָׁעִים תֹּאבֵד:

קיג א-ב הַלְלוּ־יָהּ ׀ הַלְלוּ עַבְדֵי יהוה הַלְלוּ אֶת־שֵׁם יהוה: יְהִי שֵׁם יהוה מְבֹרָךְ
יום כד לחדש
ג-ד מֵעַתָּה וְעַד־עוֹלָם: מִמִּזְרַח־שֶׁמֶשׁ עַד־מְבוֹאוֹ מְהֻלָּל שֵׁם יהוה: רָם עַל־
ה כָּל־גּוֹיִם ׀ יהוה עַל הַשָּׁמַיִם כְּבוֹדוֹ: מִי כַּיהוה אֱלֹהֵינוּ הַמַּגְבִּיהִי לָשָׁבֶת:
ו-ז הַמַּשְׁפִּילִי לִרְאוֹת בַּשָּׁמַיִם וּבָאָרֶץ: מְקִימִי מֵעָפָר דָּל מֵאַשְׁפֹּת יָרִים
ח-ט אֶבְיוֹן: לְהוֹשִׁיבִי עִם־נְדִיבִים עִם נְדִיבֵי עַמּוֹ: מוֹשִׁיבִי ׀ עֲקֶרֶת הַבַּיִת אֵם־
הַבָּנִים שְׂמֵחָה הַלְלוּ־יָהּ:

110:1. An unnamed psalmist, possibly one of David's soldiers, composed this psalm about his king (*Ibn Ezra; Radak*).

110:3. When you do battle, your nation will be loyal to you, because you retained the pure, unselfish character of your humble shepherd youth (*Meiri*).

110:4. A Jewish king should be like a priest, drawing God's people closer to His service.

111:1. Praise God. This psalm's alphabetical arrangement indicates the encompassing nature of its theme.

111:8. They are as binding and relevant today as they were when God revealed them at Sinai thirty-three centuries ago.

112:1. Not only when he is weak and old, but while he is a "man" (*Avodah Zarah* 19a). His greatest desire is the fulfillment of God's will. The reward which he will assuredly receive in return is only secondary in his thinking and not his primary motivation.

112:5. The true philanthropist is sensitive to others. Realizing that some needy people are too proud to accept charity, he compassionately offers the poor man an opportunity for financial rehabilitation by lending him

Him. ³¹ For He stands at the right of the destitute, to save [him] from the condemners of his soul.

110

David's legendary power came through Divine favor earned through his righteousness.

¹ Regarding David,* a psalm. The word of HASHEM to my master, "Wait at My right, until I make your enemies a stool for your feet." ² HASHEM will dispatch the staff of your strength from Zion; rule amid your enemies! ³ Your people volunteer on the day of your campaign; because of your majestic sanctity from the inception of [your reign], you retain the dewlike freshness of your youth.* ⁴ HASHEM has sworn and will not relent, "You shall be a priest* forever, because you are a king of righteousness." ⁵ The Lord is at your right; He crushes kings on the day of His anger. ⁶ He will judge the corpse-filled nations, He will crush the leader of the mighty land. ⁷ From a river along the way he shall drink — therefore he may proudly lift his head.

111

God created man with all that he needs, in body and mind, to perform God's will; but man must choose to embark on this path.

¹ Halleluyah!* א I shall thank HASHEM wholeheartedly, ב in the counsel of the upright and the congregation. ² ג Great are the deeds of HASHEM, ד accessible to all who want them. ³ ה Glory and majesty are His work, ו and His righteousness endures forever. ⁴ ז He made a memorial for His wonders, ח gracious and compassionate is HASHEM. ⁵ ט He provided food for those who fear Him, י He eternally remembers His covenant. ⁶ כ The strength of His deeds He declared to His people, ל to give them the heritage of the nations. ⁷ מ His handwork is truth and justice, נ faithful are all his orders. ⁸ ס They are steadfast forever, ע for eternity,* accomplished in truth and fairness. ⁹ פ He sent redemption to His people, צ He commanded His covenant for eternity; ק holy and awesome is His Name. ¹⁰ ר The beginning of wisdom is fear of HASHEM, ש good understanding to all their practitioners. ת His praise endures forever.

112

One who truly fears God will fear no misfortune; he will be safe and secure in God's Providence.

¹ Halleluyah! א Praiseworthy is the man* who fears HASHEM, ב who greatly desires His commandments. ² ג Mighty in the land will his offspring be, ד a generation of the upright who shall be blessed. ³ ה Wealth and riches are in his house, ו and his righteousness endures forever. ⁴ ז Even in darkness a light shines for the upright; ח He is gracious, compassionate, and righteous. ⁵ ט Good is the man who is gracious and lends;* י who conducts his affairs with justice. ⁶ כ Surely he will never falter; ל an everlasting remembrance will the righteous man remain. ⁷ מ Of evil tidings he will have no fear; נ his heart is firm, confident in HASHEM. ⁸ ס His heart is steadfast, he shall not fear, ע until he can look calmly upon his tormentors. ⁹ פ He distributed widely to the destitute, צ his righteousness endures forever; ק his pride will be exalted with glory. ¹⁰ ר The wicked man will see this and be angered, ש he will gnash his teeth and melt away; ת the ambition of the wicked shall perish.

113

A psalm to God's control of creation and to His kindness to all creatures

¹ Halleluyah! Give praise, you servants of HASHEM; praise the Name of HASHEM! ² Blessed be the Name of HASHEM, from this time and forever. ³ From the rising of the sun to its setting, HASHEM's Name is praised. ⁴ High above all nations is HASHEM, above the heavens is His glory. ⁵ Who is like HASHEM, our God, Who is enthroned on high — ⁶ yet deigns to look upon the heavens and the earth? ⁷ He raises the needy from the dust, from the trash heaps He lifts the destitute, ⁸ to seat them with nobles, with the nobles of His people. ⁹ He transforms the barren wife into a glad mother of children. Halleluyah!

---

funds. **Rambam** rules that the highest level of philanthropy is to lend a poor person money so that he can avoid becoming a public charge (*Matnos Aniyim* 10:7).

קיד בְּצֵאת יִשְׂרָאֵל מִמִּצְרָיִם בֵּית יַעֲקֹב מֵעַם לֹעֵז: הָיְתָה יְהוּדָה לְקָדְשׁוֹ יִשְׂרָאֵל מַמְשְׁלוֹתָיו: הַיָּם רָאָה וַיָּנֹס הַיַּרְדֵּן יִסֹּב לְאָחוֹר: הֶהָרִים רָקְדוּ כְאֵילִים גְּבָעוֹת כִּבְנֵי־צֹאן: מַה־לְּךָ הַיָּם כִּי תָנוּס הַיַּרְדֵּן תִּסֹּב לְאָחוֹר: הֶהָרִים תִּרְקְדוּ כְאֵילִים גְּבָעוֹת כִּבְנֵי־צֹאן: מִלִּפְנֵי אָדוֹן חוּלִי אָרֶץ מִלִּפְנֵי אֱלוֹהַּ יַעֲקֹב: הַהֹפְכִי הַצּוּר אֲגַם־מָיִם חַלָּמִישׁ לְמַעְיְנוֹ־מָיִם:

קטו לֹא לָנוּ יְהוָה לֹא לָנוּ כִּי־לְשִׁמְךָ תֵּן כָּבוֹד עַל־חַסְדְּךָ עַל־אֲמִתֶּךָ: לָמָּה יֹאמְרוּ הַגּוֹיִם אַיֵּה־נָא אֱלֹהֵיהֶם: וֵאלֹהֵינוּ בַשָּׁמָיִם כֹּל אֲשֶׁר־חָפֵץ עָשָׂה: עֲצַבֵּיהֶם כֶּסֶף וְזָהָב מַעֲשֵׂה יְדֵי אָדָם: פֶּה־לָהֶם וְלֹא יְדַבֵּרוּ עֵינַיִם לָהֶם וְלֹא יִרְאוּ: אָזְנַיִם לָהֶם וְלֹא יִשְׁמָעוּ אַף לָהֶם וְלֹא יְרִיחוּן: יְדֵיהֶם וְלֹא יְמִישׁוּן רַגְלֵיהֶם וְלֹא יְהַלֵּכוּ לֹא־יֶהְגּוּ בִּגְרוֹנָם: כְּמוֹהֶם יִהְיוּ עֹשֵׂיהֶם כֹּל אֲשֶׁר־בֹּטֵחַ בָּהֶם: יִשְׂרָאֵל בְּטַח בַּיהוָה עֶזְרָם וּמָגִנָּם הוּא: בֵּית אַהֲרֹן בִּטְחוּ בַיהוָה עֶזְרָם וּמָגִנָּם הוּא: יִרְאֵי יְהוָה בִּטְחוּ בַיהוָה עֶזְרָם וּמָגִנָּם הוּא: יְהוָה זְכָרָנוּ יְבָרֵךְ יְבָרֵךְ אֶת־בֵּית יִשְׂרָאֵל יְבָרֵךְ אֶת־בֵּית אַהֲרֹן: יְבָרֵךְ יִרְאֵי יְהוָה הַקְּטַנִּים עִם־הַגְּדֹלִים: יֹסֵף יְהוָה עֲלֵיכֶם עֲלֵיכֶם וְעַל־בְּנֵיכֶם: בְּרוּכִים אַתֶּם לַיהוָה עֹשֵׂה שָׁמַיִם וָאָרֶץ: הַשָּׁמַיִם שָׁמַיִם לַיהוָה וְהָאָרֶץ נָתַן לִבְנֵי־אָדָם: לֹא הַמֵּתִים יְהַלְלוּ־יָהּ וְלֹא כָּל־יֹרְדֵי דוּמָה: וַאֲנַחְנוּ נְבָרֵךְ יָהּ מֵעַתָּה וְעַד־עוֹלָם הַלְלוּ־יָהּ:

קטז אָהַבְתִּי כִּי־יִשְׁמַע יְהוָה אֶת־קוֹלִי תַּחֲנוּנָי: כִּי־הִטָּה אָזְנוֹ לִי וּבְיָמַי אֶקְרָא: אֲפָפוּנִי חֶבְלֵי־מָוֶת וּמְצָרֵי שְׁאוֹל מְצָאוּנִי צָרָה וְיָגוֹן אֶמְצָא: וּבְשֵׁם־יְהוָה אֶקְרָא אָנָּה יְהוָה מַלְּטָה נַפְשִׁי: חַנּוּן יְהוָה וְצַדִּיק וֵאלֹהֵינוּ מְרַחֵם: שֹׁמֵר פְּתָאיִם יְהוָה דַּלּוֹתִי וְלִי יְהוֹשִׁיעַ: שׁוּבִי נַפְשִׁי לִמְנוּחָיְכִי כִּי־יְהוָה גָּמַל עָלָיְכִי: כִּי חִלַּצְתָּ נַפְשִׁי מִמָּוֶת אֶת־עֵינִי מִן־דִּמְעָה אֶת־רַגְלִי מִדֶּחִי: אֶתְהַלֵּךְ לִפְנֵי יְהוָה בְּאַרְצוֹת הַחַיִּים: הֶאֱמַנְתִּי כִּי אֲדַבֵּר אֲנִי עָנִיתִי מְאֹד: אֲנִי אָמַרְתִּי בְחָפְזִי כָּל־הָאָדָם כֹּזֵב: מָה־אָשִׁיב לַיהוָה כָּל־תַּגְמוּלוֹהִי עָלָי: כּוֹס־יְשׁוּעוֹת אֶשָּׂא וּבְשֵׁם יְהוָה אֶקְרָא: נְדָרַי לַיהוָה אֲשַׁלֵּם נֶגְדָה־נָּא לְכָל־עַמּוֹ: יָקָר בְּעֵינֵי יְהוָה הַמָּוְתָה לַחֲסִידָיו: אָנָּה יְהוָה כִּי־אֲנִי עַבְדֶּךָ אֲנִי־עַבְדְּךָ בֶּן־אֲמָתֶךָ פִּתַּחְתָּ לְמוֹסֵרָי: לְךָ־אֶזְבַּח זֶבַח תּוֹדָה וּבְשֵׁם יְהוָה אֶקְרָא: נְדָרַי לַיהוָה אֲשַׁלֵּם נֶגְדָה־נָּא לְכָל־עַמּוֹ: בְּחַצְרוֹת בֵּית יְהוָה בְּתוֹכֵכִי יְרוּשָׁלִַם הַלְלוּ־יָהּ:

קיז הַלְלוּ אֶת־יְהוָה כָּל־גּוֹיִם שַׁבְּחוּהוּ כָּל־הָאֻמִּים: כִּי גָבַר עָלֵינוּ חַסְדּוֹ וֶאֱמֶת־יְהוָה לְעוֹלָם הַלְלוּ־יָהּ:

114:1. The Jews in Egypt persisted in speaking Hebrew with one another. Thus, Egyptian was an "alien tongue."
114:3. See *Exodus* 14:15-15:21 and *Joshua* 3:7-4:14.
114:8. *Exodus* 17:1-7.
115:16. Man need not perfect heaven because it is al-

ready dedicated to the holiness of God. But the earth is man's province, and he is bidden to perfect it. Indeed, mankind was created to elevate the earth to a heavenly state.

116:14. As I was fleeing in exile, I vowed that were

114

Israel was elevated upon leaving Egypt; all of nature was overwhelmed by God's intervention.

[1] **W**hen Israel went out of Egypt, Jacob's household from a people of alien tongue, * [2] Judah became His sanctuary, Israel His dominions. [3] The sea saw and fled; * the Jordan turned backward. [4] The mountains skipped like rams; the hills like young lambs. [5] What ails you, O sea, that you flee? O Jordan, that you turn backward? [6] O mountains, that you skip like rams? O hills, like young lambs? [7] Before the Lord's Presence did I, the earth, tremble, before the presence of the God of Jacob, [8] Who turns the rock into a pond of water, the flint into a flowing fountain. *

115

May God once again intervene in the affairs of man, so that the idolaters may know Him and become as imbued with Israel with faith in the true God.

[1] **N**ot for our sake, HASHEM, not for our sake, but for Your Name's sake give glory, for Your kindness and for Your truth! [2] Why should the nations say, "Where now is their God?" [3] Our God is in the heavens; whatever He pleases, He does! [4] Their idols are silver and gold, the handiwork of man. [5] They have a mouth, but cannot speak; they have eyes, but cannot see; [6] they have ears, but cannot hear; they have a nose, but cannot smell. [7] Their hands — they cannot feel; their feet — they cannot walk; they cannot utter a sound from their throat. [8] Those who make them should become like them, whoever trusts in them! [9] O Israel, trust in HASHEM; their help and their shield is He! [10] House of Aaron, trust in HASHEM; their help and their shield is He! [11] You who fear HASHEM, trust in HASHEM; their help and their shield is He! [12] HASHEM Who has remembered us will bless: He will bless the House of Israel, He will bless the House of Aaron; [13] He will bless those who fear HASHEM, the small as well as the great. [14] May HASHEM increase upon you, upon you and upon your children! [15] You are blessed of HASHEM, Maker of heaven and earth. [16] As for the heavens, the heavens are HASHEM's; but the earth He has given to mankind. * [17] Neither the dead can praise God, nor any who descend into silence; [18] but we will bless God from this time and forever. Halleluyah!

116

Israel declares its love for God despite its lowly state among the nations, and prays for the Redemption.

[1] **I** love [Him], for HASHEM hears my voice, my supplications. [2] As He has inclined His ear to me, so in my days shall I call. [3] The pains of death encircled me; the confines of the grave have found me; distress and grief I would find. [4] Then I would invoke the Name of HASHEM, "Please, HASHEM, save my soul." [5] Gracious is HASHEM and righteous, our God is merciful. [6] HASHEM protects the simple; I was brought low, but He saved me. [7] Return, my soul, to your rest; for HASHEM has been kind to you. [8] For You have delivered my soul from death, my eyes from tears, my feet from stumbling. [9] I shall walk before HASHEM in the lands of the living. [10] I have kept faith although I say, "I suffer exceedingly." [11] I said in my haste, "All mankind is deceitful." [12] How can I repay HASHEM for all His bounty to me? [13] I will raise the cup of salvations and the Name of HASHEM I will invoke. [14] My vows to HASHEM I will pay, * in the presence, now, of His entire people. [15] Difficult in the eyes of HASHEM is the death of His devout ones. [16] Please, HASHEM, for I am Your servant, I am Your servant, son of Your handmaid; You have released my bonds. [17] To You I will sacrifice a thanksgiving offering, and the Name of HASHEM I will invoke. [18] My vows to HASHEM I will pay, in the presence, now, of His entire people, [19] in the courtyards of the House of HASHEM, in your midst, O Jerusalem, Halleluyah!

117

[1] **P**raise HASHEM, all nations; praise Him, all the states! [2] For His kindness has overwhelmed us, * and the truth of HASHEM is eternal, Halleluyah!

God to return me safely to the Land of Israel, I would bring thanksgiving offerings to His Name (*Radak*).

117:2. The enemies of Israel are the ones who are best equipped to praise God, for they know better than anyone how He has thwarted their anti-Semitic designs (*Netziv*).

קיח

א־ב הוֹדוּ לַיהוָה כִּי־טוֹב כִּי לְעוֹלָם חַסְדּוֹ: יֹאמַר־נָא יִשְׂרָאֵל כִּי לְעוֹלָם
ג־ד חַסְדּוֹ: יֹאמְרוּ־נָא בֵית־אַהֲרֹן כִּי לְעוֹלָם חַסְדּוֹ: יֹאמְרוּ־נָא יִרְאֵי יְהוָה כִּי
ה־ו לְעוֹלָם חַסְדּוֹ: מִן־הַמֵּצַר קָרָאתִי יָּהּ עָנָנִי בַמֶּרְחָב יָהּ: יְהוָה לִי לֹא אִירָא
ז־ח מַה־יַּעֲשֶׂה לִי אָדָם: יְהוָה לִי בְּעֹזְרָי וַאֲנִי אֶרְאֶה בְשֹׂנְאָי: טוֹב לַחֲסוֹת
ט בַּיהוָה מִבְּטֹחַ בָּאָדָם: טוֹב לַחֲסוֹת בַּיהוָה מִבְּטֹחַ בִּנְדִיבִים: כָּל־גּוֹיִם
יא סְבָבוּנִי בְשֵׁם יְהוָה כִּי אֲמִילַם: סַבּוּנִי גַם־סְבָבוּנִי בְּשֵׁם יְהוָה כִּי אֲמִילַם:
יב־יג סַבּוּנִי כִדְבוֹרִים דֹּעֲכוּ כְּאֵשׁ קוֹצִים בְּשֵׁם יְהוָה כִּי אֲמִילַם: דָּחֹה דְחִיתַנִי
יד־טו לִנְפֹּל וַיהוָה עֲזָרָנִי: עָזִּי וְזִמְרָת יָהּ וַיְהִי־לִי לִישׁוּעָה: קוֹל | רִנָּה וִישׁוּעָה
טז בְּאָהֳלֵי צַדִּיקִים יְמִין יְהוָה עֹשָׂה חָיִל: יְמִין יְהוָה רוֹמֵמָה יְמִין יְהוָה עֹשָׂה
יז־יח חָיִל: לֹא־אָמוּת כִּי־אֶחְיֶה וַאֲסַפֵּר מַעֲשֵׂי יָהּ: יַסֹּר יִסְּרַנִּי יָּהּ וְלַמָּוֶת לֹא
יט נְתָנָנִי: פִּתְחוּ־לִי שַׁעֲרֵי־צֶדֶק אָבֹא־בָם אוֹדֶה יָהּ: זֶה־הַשַּׁעַר לַיהוָה
כ־כב צַדִּיקִים יָבֹאוּ בוֹ: אוֹדְךָ כִּי עֲנִיתָנִי וַתְּהִי־לִי לִישׁוּעָה: אֶבֶן מָאֲסוּ
כג הַבּוֹנִים הָיְתָה לְרֹאשׁ פִּנָּה: מֵאֵת יְהוָה הָיְתָה זֹּאת הִיא נִפְלָאת בְּעֵינֵינוּ:
כד־כה זֶה־הַיּוֹם עָשָׂה יְהוָה נָגִילָה וְנִשְׂמְחָה בוֹ: אָנָּא יְהוָה הוֹשִׁיעָה נָּא אָנָּא
כו־כז יְהוָה הַצְלִיחָה נָּא: בָּרוּךְ הַבָּא בְּשֵׁם יְהוָה בֵּרַכְנוּכֶם מִבֵּית יְהוָה: אֵל |
כח יְהוָה וַיָּאֶר לָנוּ אִסְרוּ־חַג בַּעֲבֹתִים עַד־קַרְנוֹת הַמִּזְבֵּחַ: אֵלִי אַתָּה וְאוֹדֶךָּ
כט אֱלֹהַי אֲרוֹמְמֶךָּ: הוֹדוּ לַיהוָה כִּי־טוֹב כִּי לְעוֹלָם חַסְדּוֹ:

קיט

יוֹם כה לחדש

א־ב אַשְׁרֵי תְמִימֵי־דָרֶךְ הַהֹלְכִים בְּתוֹרַת יְהוָה: אַשְׁרֵי נֹצְרֵי עֵדֹתָיו בְּכָל־לֵב
ג־ד יִדְרְשׁוּהוּ: אַף לֹא־פָעֲלוּ עַוְלָה בִּדְרָכָיו הָלָכוּ: אַתָּה צִוִּיתָה פִקֻּדֶיךָ
ה־ו לִשְׁמֹר מְאֹד: אַחֲלַי יִכֹּנוּ דְרָכָי לִשְׁמֹר חֻקֶּיךָ: אָז לֹא־אֵבוֹשׁ בְּהַבִּיטִי
ז־ח אֶל־כָּל־מִצְוֹתֶיךָ: אוֹדְךָ בְּיֹשֶׁר לֵבָב בְּלָמְדִי מִשְׁפְּטֵי צִדְקֶךָ: אֶת־חֻקֶּיךָ
אֶשְׁמֹר אַל־תַּעַזְבֵנִי עַד־מְאֹד:
ט בַּמֶּה יְזַכֶּה־נַּעַר אֶת־אָרְחוֹ לִשְׁמֹר כִּדְבָרֶךָ: בְּכָל־לִבִּי דְרַשְׁתִּיךָ אַל־
יא־יב תַּשְׁגֵּנִי מִמִּצְוֹתֶיךָ: בְּלִבִּי צָפַנְתִּי אִמְרָתֶךָ לְמַעַן לֹא אֶחֱטָא־לָךְ: בָּרוּךְ
יג־יד אַתָּה יְהוָה לַמְּדֵנִי חֻקֶּיךָ: בִּשְׂפָתַי סִפַּרְתִּי כֹּל מִשְׁפְּטֵי־פִיךָ: בְּדֶרֶךְ
טו עֵדְוֹתֶיךָ שַׂשְׂתִּי כְּעַל כָּל־הוֹן: בְּפִקֻּדֶיךָ אָשִׂיחָה וְאַבִּיטָה אֹרְחֹתֶיךָ:
טז בְּחֻקֹּתֶיךָ אֶשְׁתַּעֲשָׁע לֹא אֶשְׁכַּח דְּבָרֶךָ:
יז־יח גְּמֹל עַל־עַבְדְּךָ אֶחְיֶה וְאֶשְׁמְרָה דְבָרֶךָ: גַּל־עֵינַי וְאַבִּיטָה נִפְלָאוֹת
יט מִתּוֹרָתֶךָ: גֵּר אָנֹכִי בָאָרֶץ אַל־תַּסְתֵּר מִמֶּנִּי מִצְוֹתֶיךָ: גָּרְסָה נַפְשִׁי
כא לְתַאֲבָה אֶל־מִשְׁפָּטֶיךָ בְכָל־עֵת: גָּעַרְתָּ זֵדִים אֲרוּרִים הַשֹּׁגִים

118:7. If my helpers were not granted strength by God, their assistance would be futile *(Ibn Ezra; Radak)*.

118:13. The psalmist addresses the foe directly.

118:18. I survived because whatever suffering God decreed was only to atone for my sins *(Rashi)*.

118:22. David was rejected by his own father and brothers. When the prophet Samuel announced that one

of Jesse's sons was to be anointed king, not one of them even thought of summoning David, who was with the sheep (see *I Samuel* 16:4-13).

118:23. When David was crowned, all were amazed. David said, "This has emanated from God!"

119:2. Throughout this psalm, "testimonies" refers to the Torah and mitzvos, which bear testimony to God's

118

Israel expresses gratitude and confidence as it looks forward to Divine Redemption from the straits of exile and oppression.

¹ **G**ive thanks to HASHEM for He is good; for His kindness endures forever! ² Let Israel say now, "For His kindness endures forever!" ³ Let the House of Aaron say now, "For His kindness endures forever!" ⁴ Let those who fear HASHEM say now, "For His kindness endures forever!" ⁵ From the straits did I call upon God; God answered me with expansiveness. ⁶ HASHEM is with me, I have no fear; how can man affect me? ⁷ HASHEM is with me through my helpers; * therefore I can face my foes. ⁸ It is better to take refuge in HASHEM than to rely on man. ⁹ It is better to take refuge in HASHEM than to rely on nobles. ¹⁰ All the nations surround me; in the Name of HASHEM, I cut them down! ¹¹ They encircle me, they also surround me; in the Name of HASHEM, I cut them down! ¹² They encircle me like bees, but they are extinguished as a fire does thorns; in the Name of HASHEM, I cut them down! ¹³ You * pushed me hard that I might fall, but HASHEM assisted me. ¹⁴ God is my might and my praise, and He was a salvation for me. ¹⁵ The sound of rejoicing and salvation is in the tents of the righteous, "HASHEM's right hand does valiantly. ¹⁶ HASHEM's right hand is raised triumphantly; HASHEM's right hand does valiantly!" ¹⁷ I shall not die! But I shall live and relate the deeds of God. ¹⁸ God has chastened me exceedingly, but He did not give me over to death. * ¹⁹ Open for me the gates of righteousness; I will enter them and thank God. ²⁰ This is the gate of HASHEM; the righteous shall enter through it. ²¹ I thank You for You have answered me and become my salvation. ²² The stone the builders despised has become the cornerstone. * ²³ This emanated from HASHEM; * it is wondrous in our eyes. ²⁴ This is the day HASHEM has made; let us rejoice and be glad on it. ²⁵ Please, HASHEM, save now! Please, HASHEM, bring success now! ²⁶ Blessed is he who comes in the Name of HASHEM; we bless you from the House of HASHEM. ²⁷ HASHEM is God. He illuminated for us; bind the festival offering with cords until the corners of the Altar. ²⁸ You are my God, and I will thank You; my God, I will exalt You. ²⁹ Give thanks to HASHEM, for He is good; for His kindness endures forever.

119

An alphabetical arrangement — eight verses for each letter — that describes the ceaseless striving to faithfully live a Torah-true life regardless of time, place, circumstance or social environment

א ¹ **P**raiseworthy are those whose way is perfect, who walk with the Torah of HASHEM. ² Praiseworthy are those who guard His testimonies, * they seek Him wholeheartedly. ³ They have also done no iniquity, for they have walked in His ways. ⁴ You have issued Your precepts to be kept diligently. ⁵ My prayers: May my ways be firmly guided to keep Your statutes. ⁶ Then I will not be ashamed, when I gaze at all Your commandments. ⁷ I will give thanks to You with upright heart, when I study Your righteous ordinances. ⁸ I will keep Your statutes, O, do not forsake me utterly.

ב ⁹ How can a youngster purify his path? By observing Your word. ¹⁰ With all my heart I sought You, do not let me stray from Your commandments. ¹¹ In my heart I have stored Your word, so that I would not sin against You. ¹² Blessed are You, HASHEM, teach me Your statutes. ¹³ With my lips I recounted all the ordinances of Your mouth. ¹⁴ I rejoiced over the way of Your testimonies as much as in all riches. ¹⁵ Of Your precepts I speak and I look at Your paths. ¹⁶ I occupy myself with Your statutes, I will not forget Your word.

ג ¹⁷ Bestow upon Your servant that I should live, that I may keep Your word. ¹⁸ Unveil my eyes that I may perceive wonders from Your Torah. ¹⁹ I am a sojourner in the world, * hide not Your commandments from me. ²⁰ My soul is shattered with yearning for Your ordinances always. ²¹ You rebuked the accursed willful sinners

relationship with the Jewish nation.
119:19. Man must not fritter away his brief opportunity

to infuse meaning into his existence through adherence to God's commandments.

כב־כג מִמְּצוֹתֶיךָ: גַּל מֵעָלַי חֶרְפָּה וָבוּז כִּי עֵדֹתֶיךָ נָצָרְתִּי: גַּם יָשְׁבוּ שָׂרִים בִּי

כד נִדְבָּרוּ עַבְדְּךָ יָשִׂיחַ בְּחֻקֶּיךָ: גַּם־עֵדֹתֶיךָ שַׁעֲשֻׁעָי אַנְשֵׁי עֲצָתִי:

כה־כו דָּבְקָה לֶעָפָר נַפְשִׁי חַיֵּנִי כִּדְבָרֶךָ: דְּרָכַי סִפַּרְתִּי וַתַּעֲנֵנִי לַמְּדֵנִי חֻקֶּיךָ:

כז־כח דֶּרֶךְ־פִּקּוּדֶיךָ הֲבִינֵנִי וְאָשִׂיחָה בְּנִפְלְאוֹתֶיךָ: דָּלְפָה נַפְשִׁי מִתּוּגָה קַיְּמֵנִי

כט־ל כִּדְבָרֶךָ: דֶּרֶךְ־שֶׁקֶר הָסֵר מִמֶּנִּי וְתוֹרָתְךָ חָנֵּנִי: דֶּרֶךְ־אֱמוּנָה בָחָרְתִּי

לא־לב מִשְׁפָּטֶיךָ שִׁוִּיתִי: דָּבַקְתִּי בְעֵדְוֺתֶיךָ יהוה אַל־תְּבִישֵׁנִי: דֶּרֶךְ־מִצְוֺתֶיךָ

אָרוּץ כִּי תַרְחִיב לִבִּי:

לג־לד הוֹרֵנִי יהוה דֶּרֶךְ חֻקֶּיךָ וְאֶצְּרֶנָּה עֵקֶב: הֲבִינֵנִי וְאֶצְּרָה תוֹרָתֶךָ וְאֶשְׁמְרֶנָּה

לה־לו בְכָל־לֵב: הַדְרִיכֵנִי בִּנְתִיב מִצְוֺתֶיךָ כִּי־בוֹ חָפָצְתִּי: הַט־לִבִּי אֶל־עֵדְוֺתֶיךָ

לז־לח וְאַל אֶל־בָּצַע: הַעֲבֵר עֵינַי מֵרְאוֹת שָׁוְא בִּדְרָכֶךָ חַיֵּנִי: הָקֵם לְעַבְדְּךָ

לט אִמְרָתֶךָ אֲשֶׁר לְיִרְאָתֶךָ: הַעֲבֵר חֶרְפָּתִי אֲשֶׁר יָגֹרְתִּי כִּי מִשְׁפָּטֶיךָ טוֹבִים:

מ הִנֵּה תָּאַבְתִּי לְפִקֻּדֶיךָ בְּצִדְקָתְךָ חַיֵּנִי:

מא־מב וִיבֹאֻנִי חֲסָדֶךָ יהוה תְּשׁוּעָתְךָ כְּאִמְרָתֶךָ: וְאֶעֱנֶה חֹרְפִי דָבָר כִּי־בָטַחְתִּי

מג בִּדְבָרֶךָ: וְאַל־תַּצֵּל מִפִּי דְבַר־אֱמֶת עַד־מְאֹד כִּי לְמִשְׁפָּטֶךָ יִחָלְתִּי:

מד־מה וְאֶשְׁמְרָה תוֹרָתְךָ תָמִיד לְעוֹלָם וָעֶד: וְאֶתְהַלְּכָה בָרְחָבָה כִּי פִקֻּדֶיךָ

מו־מז דָרָשְׁתִּי: וַאֲדַבְּרָה בְעֵדֹתֶיךָ נֶגֶד מְלָכִים וְלֹא אֵבוֹשׁ: וְאֶשְׁתַּעֲשַׁע

מח בְּמִצְוֺתֶיךָ אֲשֶׁר אָהָבְתִּי: וְאֶשָּׂא־כַפַּי אֶל־מִצְוֺתֶיךָ אֲשֶׁר אָהָבְתִּי וְאָשִׂיחָה

בְחֻקֶּיךָ:

מט־נ זְכֹר־דָּבָר לְעַבְדֶּךָ עַל אֲשֶׁר יִחַלְתָּנִי: זֹאת נֶחָמָתִי בְעָנְיִי כִּי אִמְרָתְךָ

נא־נב חִיָּתְנִי: זֵדִים הֱלִיצֻנִי עַד־מְאֹד מִתּוֹרָתְךָ לֹא נָטִיתִי: זָכַרְתִּי מִשְׁפָּטֶיךָ

נג־נד מֵעוֹלָם ׀ יהוה וָאֶתְנֶחָם: זַלְעָפָה אֲחָזַתְנִי מֵרְשָׁעִים עֹזְבֵי תּוֹרָתֶךָ: זְמִרוֹת

נה הָיוּ־לִי חֻקֶּיךָ בְּבֵית מְגוּרָי: זָכַרְתִּי בַלַּיְלָה שִׁמְךָ יהוה וָאֶשְׁמְרָה תּוֹרָתֶךָ:

נו זֹאת הָיְתָה־לִּי כִּי פִקֻּדֶיךָ נָצָרְתִּי:

נז־נח חֶלְקִי יהוה אָמַרְתִּי לִשְׁמֹר דְּבָרֶיךָ: חִלִּיתִי פָנֶיךָ בְכָל־לֵב חָנֵּנִי כְּאִמְרָתֶךָ:

נט־ס חִשַּׁבְתִּי דְרָכָי וָאָשִׁיבָה רַגְלַי אֶל־עֵדֹתֶיךָ: חַשְׁתִּי וְלֹא הִתְמַהְמָהְתִּי

סא־סב לִשְׁמֹר מִצְוֺתֶיךָ: חֶבְלֵי רְשָׁעִים עִוְּדֻנִי תּוֹרָתְךָ לֹא שָׁכָחְתִּי: חֲצוֹת־לַיְלָה

סג אָקוּם לְהוֹדוֹת לָךְ עַל מִשְׁפְּטֵי צִדְקֶךָ: חָבֵר אָנִי לְכָל־אֲשֶׁר יְרֵאוּךָ

סד וּלְשֹׁמְרֵי פִּקּוּדֶיךָ: חַסְדְּךָ יהוה מָלְאָה הָאָרֶץ חֻקֶּיךָ לַמְּדֵנִי:

סה־סו טוֹב עָשִׂיתָ עִם־עַבְדְּךָ יהוה כִּדְבָרֶךָ: טוּב טַעַם וָדַעַת לַמְּדֵנִי כִּי בְמִצְוֺתֶיךָ

סז־סח הֶאֱמָנְתִּי: טֶרֶם אֶעֱנֶה אֲנִי שֹׁגֵג וְעַתָּה אִמְרָתְךָ שָׁמָרְתִּי: טוֹב־אַתָּה

סט וּמֵטִיב לַמְּדֵנִי חֻקֶּיךָ: טָפְלוּ עָלַי שֶׁקֶר זֵדִים אֲנִי בְּכָל־לֵב ׀ אֶצֹּר פִּקּוּדֶיךָ:

119:24. God's testimonies, not the fashionable trends of the rich and powerful, should guide a person through life.
119:48. I will practice Your commandments in addition to meditating upon them. Only through fusion of thought and deed can one draw near to God and perfect himself.

119:53. There is no comfort for the tragedy of those who have abandoned God's Torah in the tribulations of exile (*Maharam Arama*).
119:59. David constantly reevaluated his ways to ensure that he did not veer off course.

who stray from Your commandments. ²² Remove from upon me disgrace and contempt, for I have guarded Your testimonies. ²³ Though princes sat and spoke against me, Your servant discusses Your statutes. ²⁴ Indeed, Your testimonies are my preoccupation, they are my counselors. *

ד ²⁵ My soul has clung to the dust, revive me in accordance with Your word. ²⁶ I have recounted my ways and You answered me, teach me Your statutes. ²⁷ Let me understand the way of Your precepts, that I may discuss Your wonders. ²⁸ My soul drips away from sorrow, sustain me in accordance with Your word. ²⁹ Remove from me the way of falsehood, and graciously endow me with Your Torah. ³⁰ I have chosen the way of faithfulness; I have placed Your ordinances [before me]. ³¹ I have clung to Your testimonies, O HASHEM, put me not to shame. ³² I will run in the way of Your commandments, for You will broaden my heart.

ה ³³ Teach me, O HASHEM, the way of Your statutes, and I will cherish it to the utmost. ³⁴ Grant me understanding so that I may cherish Your Torah, and keep it with [my] whole heart. ³⁵ Lead me on the path of Your commandments, for that is my desire. ³⁶ Incline my heart toward Your testimonies and not to greed. ³⁷ Avert my eyes from seeing futility; through Your ways preserve me. ³⁸ Fulfill Your word to Your servant regarding fear of You. ³⁹ Remove my disgrace, which I dreaded, for Your ordinances are good. ⁴⁰ Behold, I yearn for Your precepts; preserve me through Your righteousness.

ו ⁴¹ May Your kindness come to me, O HASHEM, Your salvation, according to Your word. ⁴² I shall offer a response to those who scorn me, for I have trusted in Your word. ⁴³ Do not remove from my mouth the word of utmost truth, because I have yearned for Your ordinances. ⁴⁴ I will safeguard Your Torah constantly, forever and ever. ⁴⁵ And I will walk in broad pathways, for I have sought Your precepts. ⁴⁶ I will speak of Your testimonies before kings, and I will not be ashamed. ⁴⁷ I will be preoccupied with Your commandments that I love, ⁴⁸ and I will lift my hands * to Your commandments, which I love, and I will discuss Your statutes.

ז ⁴⁹ Remember the assurance to Your servant, by which You gave me hope. ⁵⁰ This is my comfort in my affliction, for Your word preserved me. ⁵¹ Willful sinners taunted me exceedingly, but I did not swerve from Your Torah. ⁵² I remembered Your judgments of old, O HASHEM, and I was comforted. ⁵³ Trembling seized me because of the wicked who forsake Your Torah. * ⁵⁴ Your statutes were music to me, in my dwelling place. ⁵⁵ In the night I remembered Your Name, O HASHEM, and I kept Your Torah. ⁵⁶ All this came to me because I guarded Your precepts.

ח ⁵⁷ My portion is HASHEM; I have pledged to keep Your words. ⁵⁸ I pleaded before You with all [my] heart; favor me according to Your promise. ⁵⁹ I considered my ways * and returned my feet to Your testimonies. ⁶⁰ I hastened and I did not delay to keep Your commandments. ⁶¹ Bands of wicked men plundered me, but I did not forget Your Torah. ⁶² At midnight I arise to thank You for Your righteous ordinances. ⁶³ I am a friend to all who fear You, and to those who keep Your precepts. ⁶⁴ Your kindness, HASHEM, fills the earth, teach me Your statutes.

ט ⁶⁵ You have done good to Your servant, O HASHEM, according to Your word. ⁶⁶ Teach me good reasoning and knowledge, for I have been faithful to Your commandments. ⁶⁷ Before I was afflicted I erred; but now I keep Your word. ⁶⁸ You are good and beneficent, teach me Your statutes. ⁶⁹ Willful sinners have piled false accusations upon me, but I guard Your precepts with all [my] heart.

ע-עא   טָפַשׁ כַּחֵלֶב לִבָּם אֲנִי תּוֹרָתְךָ שִׁעֲשָׁעְתִּי: טוֹב־לִי כִי־עֻנֵּיתִי לְמַעַן אֶלְמַד

עב   חֻקֶּיךָ: טוֹב־לִי תוֹרַת־פִּיךָ מֵאַלְפֵי זָהָב וָכָסֶף:

עג-עד   יָדֶיךָ עָשׂוּנִי וַיְכוֹנְנוּנִי הֲבִינֵנִי וְאֶלְמְדָה מִצְוֺתֶיךָ: יְרֵאֶיךָ יִרְאוּנִי וְיִשְׂמָחוּ

עה-עו   כִּי לִדְבָרְךָ יִחָלְתִּי: יָדַעְתִּי יְהוָה כִּי־צֶדֶק מִשְׁפָּטֶיךָ וֶאֱמוּנָה עִנִּיתָנִי: יְהִי־

עז   נָא חַסְדְּךָ לְנַחֲמֵנִי כְּאִמְרָתְךָ לְעַבְדֶּךָ: יְבֹאוּנִי רַחֲמֶיךָ וְאֶחְיֶה כִּי־תוֹרָתְךָ

עח-עט   שַׁעֲשֻׁעָי: יֵבֹשׁוּ זֵדִים כִּי־שֶׁקֶר עִוְּתוּנִי אֲנִי אָשִׂיחַ בְּפִקּוּדֶיךָ: יָשׁוּבוּ לִי

פ   יְרֵאֶיךָ °וידעו [°וְיֹדְעֵי ק] עֵדֹתֶיךָ: יְהִי־לִבִּי תָמִים בְּחֻקֶּיךָ לְמַעַן לֹא

  אֵבוֹשׁ:

פא-פב   כָּלְתָה לִתְשׁוּעָתְךָ נַפְשִׁי לִדְבָרְךָ יִחָלְתִּי: כָּלוּ עֵינַי לְאִמְרָתֶךָ לֵאמֹר מָתַי

פג-פד   תְּנַחֲמֵנִי: כִּי־הָיִיתִי כְּנֹאד בְּקִיטוֹר חֻקֶּיךָ לֹא שָׁכָחְתִּי: כַּמָּה יְמֵי־עַבְדֶּךָ

פה   מָתַי תַּעֲשֶׂה בְרֹדְפַי מִשְׁפָּט: כָּרוּ־לִי זֵדִים שִׁיחוֹת אֲשֶׁר לֹא כְתוֹרָתֶךָ:

פו-פז   כָּל־מִצְוֺתֶיךָ אֱמוּנָה שֶׁקֶר רְדָפוּנִי עָזְרֵנִי: כִּמְעַט כִּלּוּנִי בָאָרֶץ וַאֲנִי לֹא־

פח   עָזַבְתִּי פִקּוּדֶיךָ: כְּחַסְדְּךָ חַיֵּנִי וְאֶשְׁמְרָה עֵדוּת פִּיךָ:

פט-צ   לְעוֹלָם יְהוָה דְּבָרְךָ נִצָּב בַּשָּׁמָיִם: לְדֹר וָדֹר אֱמוּנָתֶךָ כּוֹנַנְתָּ אֶרֶץ וַתַּעֲמֹד:

צא-צב   לְמִשְׁפָּטֶיךָ עָמְדוּ הַיּוֹם כִּי הַכֹּל עֲבָדֶיךָ: לוּלֵי תוֹרָתְךָ שַׁעֲשֻׁעָי אָז אָבַדְתִּי

צג-צד   בְעָנְיִי: לְעוֹלָם לֹא־אֶשְׁכַּח פִּקּוּדֶיךָ כִּי בָם חִיִּיתָנִי: לְךָ־אֲנִי הוֹשִׁיעֵנִי כִּי

צה-צו   פִקּוּדֶיךָ דָרָשְׁתִּי: לִי קִוּוּ רְשָׁעִים לְאַבְּדֵנִי עֵדֹתֶיךָ אֶתְבּוֹנָן: לְכָל־תִּכְלָה

  רָאִיתִי קֵץ רְחָבָה מִצְוָתְךָ מְאֹד:

צז-צח   מָה־אָהַבְתִּי תוֹרָתֶךָ כָּל־הַיּוֹם הִיא שִׂיחָתִי: מֵאֹיְבַי תְּחַכְּמֵנִי מִצְוֺתֶךָ

צט   כִּי לְעוֹלָם הִיא־לִי: מִכָּל־מְלַמְּדַי הִשְׂכַּלְתִּי כִּי עֵדְוֺתֶיךָ שִׂיחָה לִי:

ק-קא   מִזְּקֵנִים אֶתְבּוֹנָן כִּי פִקּוּדֶיךָ נָצָרְתִּי: מִכָּל־אֹרַח רָע כָּלִאתִי רַגְלָי לְמַעַן

קב-קג   אֶשְׁמֹר דְּבָרֶךָ: מִמִּשְׁפָּטֶיךָ לֹא־סָרְתִּי כִּי־אַתָּה הוֹרֵתָנִי: מַה־נִּמְלְצוּ

קד   לְחִכִּי אִמְרָתֶךָ מִדְּבַשׁ לְפִי: מִפִּקּוּדֶיךָ אֶתְבּוֹנָן עַל־כֵּן שָׂנֵאתִי | כָּל־

  אֹרַח שָׁקֶר:

קה-קו   נֵר־לְרַגְלִי דְבָרֶךָ וְאוֹר לִנְתִיבָתִי: נִשְׁבַּעְתִּי וָאֲקַיֵּמָה לִשְׁמֹר מִשְׁפְּטֵי

קז-קח   צִדְקֶךָ: נַעֲנֵיתִי עַד־מְאֹד יְהוָה חַיֵּנִי כִדְבָרֶךָ: נִדְבוֹת פִּי רְצֵה־נָא יְהוָה

קט-קי   וּמִשְׁפָּטֶיךָ לַמְּדֵנִי: נַפְשִׁי בְכַפִּי תָמִיד וְתוֹרָתְךָ לֹא שָׁכָחְתִּי: נָתְנוּ רְשָׁעִים

קיא   פַּח לִי וּמִפִּקּוּדֶיךָ לֹא תָעִיתִי: נָחַלְתִּי עֵדְוֺתֶיךָ לְעוֹלָם כִּי־שְׂשׂוֹן לִבִּי

קיב   הֵמָּה: נָטִיתִי לִבִּי לַעֲשׂוֹת חֻקֶּיךָ לְעוֹלָם עֵקֶב:

יום כו
לחדש

119:85. My Jewish enemies, though they profess loyalty to Your Torah, resort to means which violate its precepts of love, truth, and justice in order to persecute me.

119:91. The heavens and the earth.

119:100. If one adheres to the Torah's precepts even when he does not yet understand them, he becomes familiar with them and may eventually be enlightened by the elders to comprehend them. However, one who makes his observance conditional on his comprehension will never attain either.

119:108. The prayers and praises that I have uttered in a spirit of devotion.

119:109. My life is always at risk.

[70] *Their heart grew thick as fat; but for me, Your Torah is my preoccupation.* [71] *It is good for me that I was afflicted, so that I might learn Your statutes.* [72] *The Torah of Your mouth is better for me than thousands in gold and silver.*

ר [73] *Your hands made me and prepared me; grant me understanding so that I may learn Your commandments.* [74] *Those who revere You shall see me and they will rejoice, because I hoped in Your word.* [75] *I know, HASHEM, that Your judgment is righteous, and that You afflicted me in faithfulness.* [76] *May Your kindness comfort me, according to your word to Your servant.* [77] *May Your mercies come upon me so that I may live, for Your Torah is my preoccupation.* [78] *May the willful sinners be shamed, for they have maligned me with lies; but I will discuss Your precepts.* [79] *May they return to me — those who fear You, and who know Your testimonies.* [80] *May my heart be perfect in Your statutes, so that I be not shamed.*

כ [81] *My soul pines for Your salvation; for Your word I hope.* [82] *My eyes pine for Your promise, saying, "When will You comfort me?"* [83] *Though I have been like a wineskin [dried] in smoke, I did not forget Your statutes.* [84] *How many are Your servant's days? When will You execute judgment upon my pursuers?* [85] *Willful sinners dug pits for me, which is not in accordance with Your Torah. ** [86] *All Your commandments are faithful; they pursue me with lies: Help me!* [87] *They had almost destroyed me on earth, but I did not forsake Your precepts.* [88] *In accordance with Your kindness preserve me, and I will keep the testimony of Your mouth.*

ל [89] *Forever, HASHEM, Your word stands firm in the heavens.* [90] *Your faithfulness is from generation to generation, You established the earth and it endures.* [91] *To fulfill Your decree they * stand until this day, for all are Your servants.* [92] *Had your Torah not been my preoccupation, then I would have perished in my affliction.* [93] *I will never forget Your precepts, for through them You have preserved me.* [94] *I am Yours, save me, for I have sought Your precepts.* [95] *The wicked hoped to destroy me, but I contemplate Your testimonies.* [96] *To every goal I have seen an end, but Your commandment is exceedingly broad.*

מ [97] *O how I love Your Torah! All day long it is my conversation.* [98] *[Each of] Your commandments makes me wiser than my enemies, for it is ever with me.* [99] *From all my teachers I grew wise, for Your testimonies are a conversation for me.* [100] *From wise elders I gain understanding, because I have guarded Your precepts. ** [101] *From every evil path I restrained my feet, so that I might keep Your word.* [102] *From Your ordinances I did not turn aside, for You have taught me.* [103] *How sweet to my palate is Your word, more than honey to my mouth.* [104] *From Your precepts I acquire understanding, therefore I hate every path of falsehood.*

נ [105] *Your word is a lamp for my feet and a light for my path.* [106] *I have sworn, and I will fulfill, to keep Your righteous ordinances.* [107] *I am exceedingly afflicted; O HASHEM, preserve me in accordance with Your word.* [108] *Please accept with favor the offerings of my mouth, * O HASHEM, and teach me Your ordinances.* [109] *My life is constantly in my hand, * but I did not forget Your Torah.* [110] *The wicked laid a snare for me, but I did not stray from Your precepts.* [111] *I have taken Your testimonies as my eternal heritage, for they are the joy of my heart.* [112] *I have inclined my heart to perform Your statutes, forever, to the utmost.*

קיג־קטו סֵעֲפִים שָׂנֵאתִי וְתוֹרָתְךָ אָהָבְתִּי: סִתְרִי וּמָגִנִּי אָתָּה לִדְבָרְךָ יִחָלְתִּי: סוּרוּ־
קטז מִמֶּנִּי מְרֵעִים וְאֶצְּרָה מִצְוֹת אֱלֹהָי: סָמְכֵנִי כְאִמְרָתְךָ וְאֶחְיֶה וְאַל־
קיז־קיח תְּבִישֵׁנִי מִשִּׂבְרִי: סְעָדֵנִי וְאִוָּשֵׁעָה וְאֶשְׁעָה בְחֻקֶּיךָ תָמִיד: סָלִיתָ כָּל־
קיט שׁוֹגִים מֵחֻקֶּיךָ כִּי־שֶׁקֶר תַּרְמִיתָם: סִגִים הִשְׁבַּתָּ כָל־רִשְׁעֵי־אָרֶץ לָכֵן
קכ אָהַבְתִּי עֵדֹתֶיךָ: סָמַר מִפַּחְדְּךָ בְשָׂרִי וּמִמִּשְׁפָּטֶיךָ יָרֵאתִי:
קכא־קכב עָשִׂיתִי מִשְׁפָּט וָצֶדֶק בַּל־תַּנִּיחֵנִי לְעֹשְׁקָי: עֲרֹב עַבְדְּךָ לְטוֹב אַל־יַעַשְׁקֻנִי
קכג־קכד זֵדִים: עֵינַי כָּלוּ לִישׁוּעָתֶךָ וּלְאִמְרַת צִדְקֶךָ: עֲשֵׂה עִם־עַבְדְּךָ כְחַסְדֶּךָ
קכה־קכו וְחֻקֶּיךָ לַמְּדֵנִי: עַבְדְּךָ־אָנִי הֲבִינֵנִי וְאֵדְעָה עֵדֹתֶיךָ: עֵת לַעֲשׂוֹת לַיהֹוָה
קכז־קכח הֵפֵרוּ תּוֹרָתֶךָ: עַל־כֵּן אָהַבְתִּי מִצְוֹתֶיךָ מִזָּהָב וּמִפָּז: עַל־כֵּן ׀ כָּל־פִּקּוּדֵי
כֹל יִשָּׁרְתִּי כָּל־אֹרַח שֶׁקֶר שָׂנֵאתִי:
קכט־קלא פְּלָאוֹת עֵדְוֹתֶיךָ עַל־כֵּן נְצָרָתַם נַפְשִׁי: פֵּתַח דְּבָרֶיךָ יָאִיר מֵבִין פְּתָיִים:
קלב פִּי־פָעַרְתִּי וָאֶשְׁאָפָה כִּי לְמִצְוֹתֶיךָ יָאָבְתִּי: פְּנֵה־אֵלַי וְחָנֵּנִי כְּמִשְׁפָּט
קלג־קלד לְאֹהֲבֵי שְׁמֶךָ: פְּעָמַי הָכֵן בְּאִמְרָתֶךָ וְאַל־תַּשְׁלֶט־בִּי כָל־אָוֶן: פְּדֵנִי
קלה־קלו מֵעֹשֶׁק אָדָם וְאֶשְׁמְרָה פִּקּוּדֶיךָ: פָּנֶיךָ הָאֵר בְּעַבְדֶּךָ וְלַמְּדֵנִי אֶת־חֻקֶּיךָ:
פַּלְגֵי־מַיִם יָרְדוּ עֵינָי עַל לֹא־שָׁמְרוּ תוֹרָתֶךָ:
קלז־קלח צַדִּיק אַתָּה יְהֹוָה וְיָשָׁר מִשְׁפָּטֶיךָ: צִוִּיתָ צֶדֶק עֵדֹתֶיךָ וֶאֱמוּנָה מְאֹד:
קלט־קמ צִמְּתַתְנִי קִנְאָתִי כִּי־שָׁכְחוּ דְבָרֶיךָ צָרָי: צְרוּפָה אִמְרָתְךָ מְאֹד וְעַבְדְּךָ
קמא־קמב אֲהֵבָהּ: צָעִיר אָנֹכִי וְנִבְזֶה פִּקֻּדֶיךָ לֹא שָׁכָחְתִּי: צִדְקָתְךָ צֶדֶק לְעוֹלָם
קמג־קמד וְתוֹרָתְךָ אֱמֶת: צַר־וּמָצוֹק מְצָאוּנִי מִצְוֹתֶיךָ שַׁעֲשֻׁעָי: צֶדֶק עֵדְוֹתֶיךָ
לְעוֹלָם הֲבִינֵנִי וְאֶחְיֶה:
קמה־קמו קָרָאתִי בְכָל־לֵב עֲנֵנִי יְהֹוָה חֻקֶּיךָ אֶצֹּרָה: קְרָאתִיךָ הוֹשִׁיעֵנִי וְאֶשְׁמְרָה
קמז־קמח עֵדֹתֶיךָ: קִדַּמְתִּי בַנֶּשֶׁף וָאֲשַׁוֵּעָה °לִדְבָרְךָ [לִדְבָרְךָ ק] יִחָלְתִּי: קִדְּמוּ
קמט עֵינַי אַשְׁמֻרוֹת לָשִׂיחַ בְּאִמְרָתֶךָ: קוֹלִי שִׁמְעָה כְחַסְדֶּךָ יְהֹוָה כְּמִשְׁפָּטֶךָ
קנ־קנא חַיֵּנִי: קָרְבוּ רֹדְפֵי זִמָּה מִתּוֹרָתְךָ רָחָקוּ: קָרוֹב אַתָּה יְהֹוָה וְכָל־מִצְוֹתֶיךָ
קנב אֱמֶת: קֶדֶם יָדַעְתִּי מֵעֵדֹתֶיךָ כִּי לְעוֹלָם יְסַדְתָּם:
קנג־קנד רְאֵה־עָנְיִי וְחַלְּצֵנִי כִּי־תוֹרָתְךָ לֹא שָׁכָחְתִּי: רִיבָה רִיבִי וּגְאָלֵנִי
קנה־קנו לְאִמְרָתְךָ חַיֵּנִי: רָחוֹק מֵרְשָׁעִים יְשׁוּעָה כִּי־חֻקֶּיךָ לֹא דָרָשׁוּ: רַחֲמֶיךָ
קנז רַבִּים ׀ יְהֹוָה כְּמִשְׁפָּטֶיךָ חַיֵּנִי: רַבִּים רֹדְפַי וְצָרָי מֵעֵדְוֹתֶיךָ לֹא
קנח־קנט נָטִיתִי: רָאִיתִי בֹגְדִים וָאֶתְקוֹטָטָה אֲשֶׁר אִמְרָתְךָ לֹא שָׁמָרוּ: רְאֵה

119:115. David interrupts his prayer to address those whom he is denouncing before God.

119:118. Those who stray from the Torah way try to deceive the world into thinking that their defection was based upon philosophical or scientific considerations or new insights into the Torah. But their contention is utterly false. It is merely a rationalization for their desire to cast off the yoke of Torah (R' Hirsch).

119:126. At a time when many have abandoned God's Torah, those who remain loyal must intensify their own knowledge of the Torah (Radak).

119:127. At such times, I value God's commandments far more than the material wealth for which the defectors sold themselves.

119:136. "They" refers to "my eyes," which caused sins by looking at things that arouse one to sin.

ס ¹¹³ *I hate the plotters of evil, but I love Your Torah.* ¹¹⁴ *You are my concealment and my shield, I put hope in Your word.* ¹¹⁵ *Depart from me, you evildoers,* * and I will guard the commandments of my God.* ¹¹⁶ *Support me according to Your promise that I may live, disgrace me not in my hope.* ¹¹⁷ *Sustain me that I may be saved, and I will always be engrossed in Your statutes.* ¹¹⁸ *You trampled all who stray from Your statutes, for their deceit is false.* * ¹¹⁹ *Like dross, You purged all the wicked of the earth, therefore I have loved Your testimonies.* ¹²⁰ *My flesh shuddered from dread of You, and I feared Your judgments.*

ע ¹²¹ *I practiced justice and righteousness, abandon me not to those who exploit me.* ¹²² *Be Your servant's guarantor for good, let not willful sinners exploit me.* ¹²³ *My eyes pine for Your salvation, and for Your promised righteousness.* ¹²⁴ *Treat Your servant according to Your kindness, and teach me Your statutes.* ¹²⁵ *I am Your servant, grant me understanding, so that I may know Your testimonies.* ¹²⁶ *For it is a time to act for HASHEM; they have voided Your Torah.* * ¹²⁷ *Therefore I have loved Your commandments more than gold,* * even more than fine gold.* ¹²⁸ *Therefore I have declared the fairness of every precept regarding everything! I have hated every path of falsehood.*

פ ¹²⁹ *Your testimonies are wonders, therefore my soul has guarded them.* ¹³⁰ *The introduction of Your words illuminates, making simpletons understand.* ¹³¹ *I opened my mouth and swallowed deeply, because I crave for Your command-ments.* ¹³² *Turn to me and favor me, as is Your practice to those who love Your Name.* ¹³³ *Ready my steps in Your word, and do not let any iniquity dominate me.* ¹³⁴ *Redeem me from human exploitation, and I will keep Your precepts.* ¹³⁵ *Cause Your countenance to shine upon Your servant, and teach me Your statutes.* ¹³⁶ *My eyes shed streams of water, because they* * did not keep Your Torah.*

צ ¹³⁷ *Righteous are You, HASHEM, and each of Your ordinances is fair.* ¹³⁸ *You commanded the righteousness of Your testimonies, and great faithfulness.* ¹³⁹ *My zeal has consumed me, for my oppressors have forgotten Your words.* ¹⁴⁰ *Your word is very pure, and Your servant loves it.* ¹⁴¹ *I am young and despised, yet I do not forget Your precepts.* ¹⁴² *Your righteousness is an everlasting righteous-ness, and Your Torah is truth.* ¹⁴³ *Distress and anguish have overtaken me, Your commandments are my preoccupation.* ¹⁴⁴ *Your testimonies are righteous forever, grant me understanding so that I may live.*

ק ¹⁴⁵ *I called with all my heart, answer me, O HASHEM; I will guard Your statutes.* ¹⁴⁶ *I called You, save me, and I will keep Your testimonies.* ¹⁴⁷ *I arose before dawn and I cried out; I hoped for Your word.* ¹⁴⁸ *My eyes preceded the night watches, to discuss Your word.* ¹⁴⁹ *Hear my voice in accordance with Your kindness; O HASHEM, preserve me in accordance with Your practice.* ¹⁵⁰ *The pursuers of sinful counsel draw near; they are far from Your Torah.* ¹⁵¹ *Yet You are nearby,* * O HASHEM, and all Your commandments are true.* ¹⁵² *From the start I gained knowledge from Your testimonies, because You established them forever.*

ר ¹⁵³ *See my affliction and release me, for I have not forgotten Your Torah.* ¹⁵⁴ *Champion my cause and redeem me; for Your word's sake, preserve me.* ¹⁵⁵ *Salvation is far from the wicked, for they sought not Your statutes.* ¹⁵⁶ *Your mercies, HASHEM, are abundant; preserve me as is Your practice.* ¹⁵⁷ *Many were my pursuers and my tormentors, but I did not swerve from Your testimonies.* ¹⁵⁸ *I saw traitors and I quarreled [with them], because they kept not Your word.* ¹⁵⁹ *See*

119:151. Though the sinners have distanced them-selves from You, You are near to them, ready to   accept their repentance.

קס כִּי־פִקּוּדֶיךָ אָהָבְתִּי כְּחַסְדְּךָ יְהוָה חַיֵּנִי: רֹאשׁ־דְּבָרְךָ אֱמֶת וּלְעוֹלָם כָּל־
מִשְׁפַּט צִדְקֶךָ:

קסא־קסב שָׂרִים רְדָפוּנִי חִנָּם °וּמִדְּבָרֶיךָ [°וּמִדְּבָרְךָ ק] פָּחַד לִבִּי: שָׂשׂ אָנֹכִי עַל־

קסג־קסד אִמְרָתֶךָ כְּמוֹצֵא שָׁלָל רָב: שֶׁקֶר שָׂנֵאתִי וַאֲתַעֵבָה תּוֹרָתְךָ אָהָבְתִּי: שֶׁבַע

קסה בַּיּוֹם הִלַּלְתִּיךָ עַל מִשְׁפְּטֵי צִדְקֶךָ: שָׁלוֹם רָב לְאֹהֲבֵי תוֹרָתֶךָ וְאֵין־לָמוֹ

קסו־קסז מִכְשׁוֹל: שִׂבַּרְתִּי לִישׁוּעָתְךָ יְהוָה וּמִצְוֺתֶיךָ עָשִׂיתִי: שָׁמְרָה נַפְשִׁי עֵדֹתֶיךָ

קסח וָאֹהֲבֵם מְאֹד: שָׁמַרְתִּי פִקּוּדֶיךָ וְעֵדֹתֶיךָ כִּי כָל־דְּרָכַי נֶגְדֶּךָ:

קסט־קע תִּקְרַב רִנָּתִי לְפָנֶיךָ יְהוָה כִּדְבָרְךָ הֲבִינֵנִי: תָּבוֹא תְּחִנָּתִי לְפָנֶיךָ כְּאִמְרָתְךָ

קעא־קעב הַצִּילֵנִי: תַּבַּעְנָה שְׂפָתַי תְּהִלָּה כִּי תְלַמְּדֵנִי חֻקֶּיךָ: תַּעַן לְשׁוֹנִי אִמְרָתֶךָ כִּי

קעג־קעד כָל־מִצְוֺתֶיךָ צֶּדֶק: תְּהִי־יָדְךָ לְעָזְרֵנִי כִּי פִקּוּדֶיךָ בָחָרְתִּי: תָּאַבְתִּי

קעה לִישׁוּעָתְךָ יְהוָה וְתוֹרָתְךָ שַׁעֲשֻׁעָי: תְּחִי־נַפְשִׁי וּתְהַלְלֶךָּ וּמִשְׁפָּטֶךָ יַעְזְרֻנִי:

קעו תָּעִיתִי כְּשֶׂה אֹבֵד בַּקֵּשׁ עַבְדֶּךָ כִּי מִצְוֺתֶיךָ לֹא שָׁכָחְתִּי:

קכ
יום השבת
יום כו
לחדש

א־ב שִׁיר הַמַּעֲלוֹת אֶל־יְהוָה בַּצָּרָתָה לִּי קָרָאתִי וַיַּעֲנֵנִי: יְהוָה הַצִּילָה נַפְשִׁי

ג־ד מִשְּׂפַת־שֶׁקֶר מִלָּשׁוֹן רְמִיָּה: מַה־יִּתֵּן לְךָ וּמַה־יֹּסִיף לָךְ לָשׁוֹן רְמִיָּה: חִצֵּי

ה גִבּוֹר שְׁנוּנִים עִם גַּחֲלֵי רְתָמִים: אוֹיָה־לִי כִּי־גַרְתִּי מֶשֶׁךְ שָׁכַנְתִּי עִם־

ו־ז אָהֳלֵי קֵדָר: רַבַּת שָׁכְנָה־לָּהּ נַפְשִׁי עִם שׂוֹנֵא שָׁלוֹם: אֲנִי־שָׁלוֹם וְכִי

אֲדַבֵּר הֵמָּה לַמִּלְחָמָה:

קכא
א־ב שִׁיר לַמַּעֲלוֹת אֶשָּׂא עֵינַי אֶל־הֶהָרִים מֵאַיִן יָבֹא עֶזְרִי: עֶזְרִי מֵעִם יְהוָה

ג־ד עֹשֵׂה שָׁמַיִם וָאָרֶץ: אַל־יִתֵּן לַמּוֹט רַגְלֶךָ אַל־יָנוּם שֹׁמְרֶךָ: הִנֵּה לֹא־יָנוּם

ה־ו וְלֹא יִישָׁן שׁוֹמֵר יִשְׂרָאֵל: יְהוָה שֹׁמְרֶךָ יְהוָה צִלְּךָ עַל־יַד יְמִינֶךָ: יוֹמָם

ז הַשֶּׁמֶשׁ לֹא־יַכֶּכָּה וְיָרֵחַ בַּלָּיְלָה: יְהוָה יִשְׁמָרְךָ מִכָּל־רָע יִשְׁמֹר אֶת־

ח נַפְשֶׁךָ: יְהוָה יִשְׁמָר־צֵאתְךָ וּבוֹאֶךָ מֵעַתָּה וְעַד־עוֹלָם:

קכב
א־ב שִׁיר הַמַּעֲלוֹת לְדָוִד שָׂמַחְתִּי בְּאֹמְרִים לִי בֵּית יְהוָה נֵלֵךְ: עֹמְדוֹת

ג הָיוּ רַגְלֵינוּ בִּשְׁעָרַיִךְ יְרוּשָׁלָ͏ִם: יְרוּשָׁלַ͏ִם הַבְּנוּיָה כְּעִיר שֶׁחֻבְּרָה־לָּהּ

ד יַחְדָּו: שֶׁשָּׁם עָלוּ שְׁבָטִים שִׁבְטֵי־יָהּ עֵדוּת לְיִשְׂרָאֵל לְהֹדוֹת לְשֵׁם יְהוָה:

ה־ו כִּי שָׁמָּה | יָשְׁבוּ כִסְאוֹת לְמִשְׁפָּט כִּסְאוֹת לְבֵית דָּוִיד: שַׁאֲלוּ שְׁלוֹם

ז־ח יְרוּשָׁלָ͏ִם יִשְׁלָיוּ אֹהֲבָיִךְ: יְהִי־שָׁלוֹם בְּחֵילֵךְ שַׁלְוָה בְּאַרְמְנוֹתָיִךְ: לְמַעַן

ט אַחַי וְרֵעָי אֲדַבְּרָה־נָּא שָׁלוֹם בָּךְ: לְמַעַן בֵּית־יְהוָה אֱלֹהֵינוּ אֲבַקְשָׁה
טוֹב לָךְ:

119:165. They are content with their material lot in this world, and serene amid the turbulent seas of life (see *Radak*).

120:1. There were fifteen steps leading from the Lower Courtyard of the Temple to the Upper Courtyard. Psalms 120-134 — the fifteen "Songs of Ascents" — correspond to the steps. On Succos, as a procession brought water to the Temple for use in the service, the Levite singers and musicians would perform one of these psalms on each of the steps as the procession advanced upward.

120:3. The psalmist addresses the tongue: What can the Almighty do, tongue, to restrain you from doing further damage? (*Rashi*).

120:4. These charcoals are especially dangerous, because long after they appear to be extinguished on the surface, they continue to burn within (*Rashi*).

that I have loved Your precepts; O HASHEM, preserve me in accordance with Your kindness. [160] *Your very first utterance is truth, and Your every righteous ordinance is for all time.*

ש [161] *Princes have pursued me without cause, but my heart has feared Your word.* [162] *I rejoice over Your word, like one who finds abundant spoils.* [163] *I have hated falsehood and abhorred it; Your Torah I love.* [164] *Seven times a day I have praised You for Your righteous ordinances.* [165] *There is abundant peace to the lovers of Your Torah,* * *and there is no stumbling block for them.* [166] *I hoped for Your salvation, O HASHEM, and I performed Your commandments.* [167] *My soul kept Your testimonies, and I loved them very much.* [168] *I have kept Your precepts and Your testimonies, because all my ways are before You.*

ת [169] *May my prayerful song approach Your Presence, HASHEM, that You grant me understanding in accordance with Your word.* [170] *May my supplication come before You, rescue me in accordance with Your word.* [171] *My lips will speak praise when You teach me Your statutes.* [172] *My tongue shall proclaim Your word, because all Your commandments are righteous.* [173] *Let Your hand be ready to assist me, for I have chosen Your precepts.* [174] *I crave Your salvation, O HASHEM, and Your Torah is my preoccupation.* [175] *Let my soul live and it shall praise You, and Your ordinances will assist me.* [176] *I have strayed like a lost sheep; seek out Your servant, for I have not forgotten Your commandments.*

120

The first of fifteen "Songs of Ascents"

[1] A *song of ascents.* * *To HASHEM, in my distress I cried and He answered me.* [2] *HASHEM, rescue my soul from lying lips, from a deceitful tongue.* [3] *What can He give you,* * *and what can He add to you, O deceitful tongue?* [4] *[You are like] the sharp arrows of the mighty; with coals of rotem-wood.* * [5] *Woe unto me, for my drawn-out sojourn; I dwelled with [those who inhabit] the tents of Kedar.* [6] *Long has my soul dwelt with those who hate peace.* [7] *I am peace; but when I speak, they are for war.* *

121

A declaration of faith and a prayer for God's constant protection

[1] A *song to the ascents. I raise my eyes upon the mountains; whence will come my help?* [2] *My help is from HASHEM, Maker of heaven and earth.* [3] *He will not allow your foot to falter; your Guardian will not slumber.* [4] *Behold, He neither slumbers nor sleeps, the Guardian of Israel.* [5] *HASHEM is your Guardian; HASHEM is your protective Shade at your right hand.* [6] *By day the sun will not harm you, nor the moon by night.* [7] *HASHEM will protect you from every evil; He will guard your soul.* [8] *HASHEM will guard your departure and your arrival, from this time and forever.*

122

A hymn to Jerusalem, the city where every visitor experiences an encounter with holiness

[1] A *song of ascents, by David. I rejoiced when they said to me, "Let us go to the House of HASHEM."* [2] *Our feet stood firm within your gates, O Jerusalem.* [3] *The built-up Jerusalem is like a city that is united together.* [4] *For there the tribes ascended, the tribes of God, a testimony for Israel, to give thanks to the Name of HASHEM.* [5] *For there sat thrones of judgment, thrones for the house of David.* [6] *Pray for the peace of Jerusalem; those who love you will be serene.* [7] *May there be peace within your wall, serenity within your palaces.* [8] *For the sake of my brethren and my comrades, I shall speak of peace in your midst.* [9] *For the sake of the House of HASHEM, our God, I will request good for you.*

120:5. The exiles among the Roman empire and its present-day successors, Kedar, the Arab empire of Ishmael *(Radak; Ibn Ezra).*

120:7. They clamor for war, because they view my appeal for peace as a sign of weakness and vulnerability.

קכג אב שִׁ֗יר הַֽמַּ֫עֲל֥וֹת אֵלֶ֣יךָ נָשָׂ֣אתִי אֶת־עֵינַ֑י הַ֝יֹּשְׁבִ֗י בַּשָּׁמָֽיִם׃ הִנֵּ֨ה כְעֵינֵ֪י עֲבָדִ֡ים אֶל־יַ֤ד אֲֽדוֹנֵיהֶ֗ם כְּעֵינֵ֣י שִׁפְחָה֮ אֶל־יַ֪ד גְּבִ֫רְתָּ֥הּ כֵּ֣ן עֵ֭ינֵינוּ אֶל־יְהֹוָ֣ה אֱלֹהֵ֑ינוּ

גד עַ֝֗ד שֶׁיְּחׇנֵּֽנוּ׃ חׇנֵּ֣נוּ יְהֹוָ֣ה חׇנֵּ֑נוּ כִּֽי־רַ֝֗ב שָׂבַ֥עְנוּ בֽוּז׃ רַבַּת֮ שָֽׂבְעָה־לָּ֢הּ נַ֫פְשֵׁ֥נוּ הַלַּ֥עַג הַשַּׁאֲנַנִּ֑ים הַ֝בּ֗וּז °לִגְאֵיוֹנִ֥ים [°לִגְאֵ֥י יוֹנִֽים ק]׃

קכד אב שִׁ֥יר הַֽמַּעֲל֗וֹת לְדָ֫וִ֥ד לוּלֵ֣י יְ֭הֹוָה שֶׁהָ֣יָה לָ֑נוּ יֹֽאמַר־נָ֝֗א יִשְׂרָאֵֽל׃ לוּלֵ֣י יְ֭הֹוָה

גד שֶׁהָ֣יָה לָ֑נוּ בְּק֖וּם עָלֵ֣ינוּ אָדָֽם׃ אֲ֭זַי חַיִּ֣ים בְּלָע֑וּנוּ בַּחֲר֖וֹת אַפָּ֣ם בָּֽנוּ׃ אֲ֭זַי

ה הַמַּ֣יִם שְׁטָפ֑וּנוּ נַ֝֗חְלָה עָבַ֥ר עַל־נַפְשֵֽׁנוּ׃ אֲ֭זַי עָבַ֣ר עַל־נַפְשֵׁ֑נוּ הַ֝מַּ֗יִם

וז הַזֵּידוֹנִֽים׃ בָּר֥וּךְ יְהֹוָ֑ה שֶׁלֹּ֥א נְתָנָ֥נוּ טֶ֝֗רֶף לְשִׁנֵּיהֶֽם׃ נַפְשֵׁ֗נוּ כְּצִפּ֥וֹר נִמְלְטָה֮

ח מִפַּ֢ח י֫וֹקְשִׁ֥ים הַפַּ֥ח נִשְׁבָּ֗ר וַאֲנַ֥חְנוּ נִמְלָֽטְנוּ׃ עֶ֭זְרֵנוּ בְּשֵׁ֣ם יְהֹוָ֑ה עֹ֝שֵׂ֗ה שָׁמַ֥יִם וָאָֽרֶץ׃

קכה א שִׁ֗יר הַֽמַּ֫עֲל֥וֹת הַבֹּטְחִ֥ים בַּיהֹוָ֑ה כְּֽהַר־צִיּ֥וֹן לֹא־יִ֝מּ֗וֹט לְעוֹלָ֥ם יֵשֵֽׁב׃

בג יְֽרוּשָׁלַ֗͏ִם הָרִים֮ סָבִ֢יב לָ֥הּ וַ֝יהֹוָ֗ה סָבִ֥יב לְעַמּ֑וֹ מֵ֝עַתָּ֗ה וְעַד־עוֹלָֽם׃ כִּ֤י לֹ֪א יָנ֡וּחַ שֵׁ֤בֶט הָרֶ֗שַׁע עַל֮ גּוֹרַ֢ל הַֽצַּדִּ֫יקִ֥ים לְמַ֡עַן לֹא־יִשְׁלְח֖וּ הַצַּדִּיקִ֛ים

דה בְּעַוְלָ֖תָה יְדֵיהֶֽם׃ הֵיטִ֣יבָה יְ֭הֹוָה לַטּוֹבִ֑ים וְ֝לִ֣ישָׁרִ֗ים בְּלִבּוֹתָֽם׃ וְהַמַּטִּ֤ים עֲ֭קַלְקַלּוֹתָם יוֹלִיכֵ֣ם יְהֹוָה֮ אֶת־פֹּעֲלֵ֪י הָ֫אָ֥וֶן שָׁ֝ל֗וֹם עַל־יִשְׂרָאֵֽל׃

קכו אב שִׁ֗יר הַֽמַּ֫עֲל֥וֹת בְּשׁ֣וּב יְ֭הֹוָה אֶת־שִׁיבַ֣ת צִיּ֑וֹן הָ֝יִ֗ינוּ כְּחֹלְמִֽים׃ אָ֤ז יִמָּלֵ֪א שְׂח֡וֹק פִּינוּ֮ וּלְשׁוֹנֵ֢נוּ רִ֫נָּ֥ה אָ֭ז יֹאמְר֣וּ בַגּוֹיִ֑ם הִגְדִּ֥יל יְ֝הֹוָ֗ה לַעֲשׂ֥וֹת עִם־אֵֽלֶּה׃

גד הִגְדִּ֣יל יְ֭הֹוָה לַעֲשׂ֣וֹת עִמָּ֑נוּ הָ֝יִ֗ינוּ שְׂמֵחִֽים׃ שׁוּבָ֣ה יְ֭הֹוָה אֶת־°שְׁבִיתֵ֑נוּ

הו [°שְׁבוּתֵ֑נוּ ק] כַּאֲפִיקִ֥ים בַּנֶּֽגֶב׃ הַזֹּרְעִ֥ים בְּדִמְעָ֗ה בְּרִנָּ֥ה יִקְצֹֽרוּ׃ הָ֘ל֤וֹךְ יֵלֵ֨ךְ ׀ וּבָכֹה֮ נֹשֵׂ֢א מֶֽשֶׁךְ־הַ֫זָּ֥רַע בֹּֽא־יָב֥וֹא בְרִנָּ֑ה נֹ֝שֵׂ֗א אֲלֻמֹּתָֽיו׃

קכז א שִׁ֥יר הַֽמַּעֲל֗וֹת לִשְׁלֹ֫מֹ֥ה אִם־יְהֹוָ֤ה ׀ לֹא־יִבְנֶ֬ה בַ֗יִת שָׁ֤וְא ׀ עָמְל֣וּ בוֹנָ֣יו בּ֑וֹ אִם־

ב יְהֹוָ֥ה לֹא־יִשְׁמׇר־עִ֝֗יר שָׁ֤וְא ׀ שָׁקַ֬ד שׁוֹמֵֽר׃ שָׁ֤וְא לָכֶ֨ם ׀ מַשְׁכִּ֪ימֵי ק֡וּם מְאַֽחֲרֵי־

ג שֶׁ֗בֶת אֹ֭כְלֵי לֶ֣חֶם הָעֲצָבִ֑ים כֵּ֤ן יִתֵּ֖ן לִֽידִיד֣וֹ שֵׁנָֽא׃ הִנֵּ֤ה נַחֲלַ֣ת יְהֹוָ֣ה בָּנִ֑ים

דה שָׂ֝כָ֗ר פְּרִ֣י הַבָּֽטֶן׃ כְּחִצִּ֥ים בְּיַד־גִּבּ֑וֹר כֵּ֝֗ן בְּנֵ֣י הַנְּעוּרִֽים׃ אַשְׁרֵ֤י הַגֶּ֗בֶר אֲשֶׁ֤ר

מִלֵּ֥א אֶת־אַשְׁפָּת֗וֹ מֵ֫הֶ֥ם לֹא־יֵבֹ֑שׁוּ כִּֽי־יְדַבְּר֖וּ אֶת־אוֹיְבִ֣ים בַּשָּֽׁעַר׃

קכח אב שִׁ֗יר הַֽמַּ֫עֲל֥וֹת אַ֭שְׁרֵי כׇּל־יְרֵ֣א יְהֹוָ֑ה הַ֝הֹלֵ֗ךְ בִּדְרָכָֽיו׃ יְגִ֣יעַ כַּ֭פֶּיךָ כִּ֣י תֹאכֵ֑ל

ג אַ֝שְׁרֶ֗יךָ וְט֣וֹב לָֽךְ׃ אֶשְׁתְּךָ֤ ׀ כְּגֶ֥פֶן פֹּרִיָּה֮ בְּיַרְכְּתֵ֢י בֵ֫יתֶ֥ךָ בָּ֭נֶיךָ כִּשְׁתִלֵ֣י זֵיתִ֑ים

דה סָ֝בִ֗יב לְשֻׁלְחָנֶֽךָ׃ הִנֵּ֣ה כִי־כֵ֭ן יְבֹ֥רַךְ גָּ֑בֶר יְרֵ֣א יְהֹוָֽה׃ יְבָרֶכְךָ֥ יְהֹוָ֗ה מִצִּ֫יּ֥וֹן

ו וּ֭רְאֵה בְּט֣וּב יְרֽוּשָׁלָ֑͏ִם כֹּ֝֗ל יְמֵ֣י חַיֶּֽיךָ׃ וּרְאֵ֥ה בָנִ֥ים לְבָנֶ֑יךָ שָׁ֝ל֗וֹם עַל־יִשְׂרָאֵֽל׃

125:5. When corruption is removed from Israel, no one will disturb the internal harmony of the nation (Radak).

126:1. When the long-awaited return to Zion finally comes to pass, the recollection of the past oppression of the exile will swiftly fade away and seem like a bad dream (Radak).

126:6. A poor person weeps in fear that some of his seeds will go to waste, but God will bless him with a bountiful crop.

127:1. David dedicated this psalm to Solomon, who was to build the Temple.

127:3. Wise parents realize that each newborn infant is a precious gift from God, which enables them to participate in the process of creation (R' Hirsch).

127:4. Young parents have the patience and energy to

123

A Jew in exile yearns for God's succor.

¹ **A** song of ascents. To You I raised my eyes, O You Who dwell in the heavens. ² Behold! Like the eyes of servants unto their masters' hand, like the eyes of a maid unto her mistress's hand, so are our eyes unto HASHEM, our God, until He will favor us. ³ Favor us, HASHEM, favor us, for we are fully sated with contempt. ⁴ Our soul is fully sated with the mockery of the complacent ones, with the contempt of the arrogant.

124

It is only God's care and protection that has saved Israel from extinction.

¹ **A** song of ascents, by David. Had not HASHEM been with us — let Israel declare it now! ² Had not HASHEM been with us when men rose up against us, ³ then they would have swallowed us alive, when their anger was kindled against us. ⁴ Then the waters would have inundated us; the current would have surged across our soul. ⁵ Then they would have surged across our soul — the treacherous waters. ⁶ Blessed is HASHEM, Who did not present us as prey for their teeth. ⁷ Our soul escaped like a bird from the hunters' snare; the snare broke and we escaped. ⁸ Our help is through the Name of HASHEM, Maker of heaven and earth.

125

Those who trust in God will be secure in His protection.

¹ **A** song of ascents. Those who trust in HASHEM are like Mount Zion that falters not, but abides forever. ² Jerusalem, mountains enwrap it, and HASHEM enwraps His people, from this time and forever. ³ For the rod of wickedness shall not rest upon the lot of the righteous, so that the righteous shall not stretch their hands into iniquity. ⁴ Do good, HASHEM, to good people, and to the upright in their hearts. ⁵ But those who turn to their perverseness, HASHEM will lead them with the doers of iniquity; peace upon Israel. *

126

Eventually God will return Israel to its land, rejuvenated in body and spirit.

¹ **A** song of ascents. When HASHEM will return the captivity of Zion, we will be like dreamers. * ² Then our mouth will be filled with laughter and our tongue with glad song. Then will they declare among the nations, "HASHEM has done greatly with these." ³ HASHEM has done greatly with us, we were gladdened. ⁴ O HASHEM, return our captivity like springs in the desert. ⁵ Those who tearfully sow will reap in glad song. ⁶ He who bears the measure of seeds walks along weeping, * but will return in exultation, a bearer of his sheaves.

127

When God crowns man's efforts with success, he can raise his children to serve God.

¹ **A** song of ascents for Solomon. * If HASHEM will not build the house, in vain do its builders labor on it; if HASHEM will not guard the city, in vain is the watchman vigilant. ² It is vain for you who rise early, who sit up late, who eat the bread of sorrows; for indeed, He gives His beloved ones restful sleep. ³ Behold! The heritage of HASHEM is children; * a reward is the fruit of the womb. ⁴ Like arrows in the hand of a warrior, so are the children of youth. * ⁵ Praiseworthy is the man who fills his quiver with them; they shall not be shamed, when they speak with enemies in the gate.

128

Only the righteous person and his family experience true bliss in both worlds.

¹ **A** song of ascents. Praiseworthy is each person who fears HASHEM, who walks in His ways. ² When you eat the labor of your hands, you are praiseworthy, * and it is well with you. ³ Your wife will be like a fruitful vine in the inner chambers of your home; your children will be like olive shoots surrounding your table. ⁴ Behold, for so is blessed the man who fears HASHEM. ⁵ May HASHEM bless you from Zion, and may you gaze upon the goodness of Jerusalem, all the days of your life. ⁶ And may you see children [born] to your children, peace upon Israel.

---

develop their child's personality. The child becomes a weapon in the legions of the Lord to fight the enemies of our faith (Sforno).

128:2. Man must toil to produce results with his own two hands. Only then does God send His blessing (Tanchuma, Vayeitzei).

קכט א-ב שִׁיר הַמַּעֲלוֹת רַבַּת צְרָרוּנִי מִנְּעוּרַי יֹאמַר־נָא יִשְׂרָאֵל: רַבַּת צְרָרוּנִי
ג מִנְּעוּרָי גַּם לֹא־יָכְלוּ לִי: עַל־גַּבִּי חָרְשׁוּ חֹרְשִׁים הֶאֱרִיכוּ °לְמַעֲנוֹתָם
ד-ה [°לְמַעֲנִיתָם ק]: יְהוָה צַדִּיק קִצֵּץ עֲבוֹת רְשָׁעִים: יֵבֹשׁוּ וְיִסֹּגוּ אָחוֹר כֹּל
ו-ז שֹׂנְאֵי צִיּוֹן: יִהְיוּ כַּחֲצִיר גַּגּוֹת שֶׁקַּדְמַת שָׁלַף יָבֵשׁ: שֶׁלֹּא מִלֵּא כַפּוֹ קוֹצֵר
ח וְחִצְנוֹ מְעַמֵּר: וְלֹא אָמְרוּ ׀ הָעֹבְרִים בִּרְכַּת־יְהוָה אֲלֵיכֶם בֵּרַכְנוּ אֶתְכֶם
בְּשֵׁם יְהוָה:

קל א-ב שִׁיר הַמַּעֲלוֹת מִמַּעֲמַקִּים קְרָאתִיךָ יְהוָה: אֲדֹנָי שִׁמְעָה בְקוֹלִי תִּהְיֶינָה
ג-ד אָזְנֶיךָ קַשֻּׁבוֹת לְקוֹל תַּחֲנוּנָי: אִם־עֲוֹנוֹת תִּשְׁמָר־יָהּ אֲדֹנָי מִי יַעֲמֹד: כִּי־
ה עִמְּךָ הַסְּלִיחָה לְמַעַן תִּוָּרֵא: קִוִּיתִי יְהוָה קִוְּתָה נַפְשִׁי וְלִדְבָרוֹ הוֹחָלְתִּי:
ו-ז נַפְשִׁי לַאדֹנָי מִשֹּׁמְרִים לַבֹּקֶר שֹׁמְרִים לַבֹּקֶר: יַחֵל יִשְׂרָאֵל אֶל־יְהוָה כִּי־
ח עִם־יְהוָה הַחֶסֶד וְהַרְבֵּה עִמּוֹ פְדוּת: וְהוּא יִפְדֶּה אֶת־יִשְׂרָאֵל מִכֹּל
עֲוֹנֹתָיו:

קלא א שִׁיר הַמַּעֲלוֹת לְדָוִד יְהוָה ׀ לֹא־גָבַהּ לִבִּי וְלֹא־רָמוּ עֵינַי וְלֹא־הִלַּכְתִּי ׀
ב בִּגְדֹלוֹת וּבְנִפְלָאוֹת מִמֶּנִּי: אִם־לֹא שִׁוִּיתִי ׀ וְדוֹמַמְתִּי נַפְשִׁי כְּגָמֻל עֲלֵי
ג אִמּוֹ כַּגָּמֻל עָלַי נַפְשִׁי: יַחֵל יִשְׂרָאֵל אֶל־יְהוָה מֵעַתָּה וְעַד־עוֹלָם:

קלב א-ב שִׁיר הַמַּעֲלוֹת זְכוֹר־יְהוָה לְדָוִד אֵת כָּל־עֻנּוֹתוֹ: אֲשֶׁר נִשְׁבַּע לַיהוָה נָדַר
ג לַאֲבִיר יַעֲקֹב: אִם־אָבֹא בְּאֹהֶל בֵּיתִי אִם־אֶעֱלֶה עַל־עֶרֶשׂ יְצוּעָי: אִם־
ד-ה אֶתֵּן שְׁנַת לְעֵינָי לְעַפְעַפַּי תְּנוּמָה: עַד־אֶמְצָא מָקוֹם לַיהוָה מִשְׁכָּנוֹת
ו לַאֲבִיר יַעֲקֹב: הִנֵּה־שְׁמַעֲנוּהָ בְאֶפְרָתָה מְצָאנוּהָ בִּשְׂדֵי־יָעַר: נָבוֹאָה
ז-ח לְמִשְׁכְּנוֹתָיו נִשְׁתַּחֲוֶה לַהֲדֹם רַגְלָיו: קוּמָה יְהוָה לִמְנוּחָתֶךָ אַתָּה וַאֲרוֹן
ט עֻזֶּךָ: כֹּהֲנֶיךָ יִלְבְּשׁוּ־צֶדֶק וַחֲסִידֶיךָ יְרַנֵּנוּ: בַּעֲבוּר דָּוִד עַבְדֶּךָ אַל־תָּשֵׁב
יא פְּנֵי מְשִׁיחֶךָ: נִשְׁבַּע־יְהוָה ׀ לְדָוִד אֱמֶת לֹא־יָשׁוּב מִמֶּנָּה מִפְּרִי בִטְנְךָ
יב אָשִׁית לְכִסֵּא־לָךְ: אִם־יִשְׁמְרוּ בָנֶיךָ ׀ בְּרִיתִי וְעֵדֹתִי זוֹ אֲלַמְּדֵם גַּם־
יג-יד בְּנֵיהֶם עֲדֵי־עַד יֵשְׁבוּ לְכִסֵּא־לָךְ: כִּי־בָחַר יְהוָה בְּצִיּוֹן אִוָּהּ לְמוֹשָׁב לוֹ:
טו זֹאת־מְנוּחָתִי עֲדֵי־עַד פֹּה־אֵשֵׁב כִּי אִוִּתִיהָ: צֵידָהּ בָּרֵךְ אֲבָרֵךְ אֶבְיוֹנֶיהָ
טז-יז אַשְׂבִּיעַ לָחֶם: וְכֹהֲנֶיהָ אַלְבִּישׁ יֶשַׁע וַחֲסִידֶיהָ רַנֵּן יְרַנֵּנוּ: שָׁם אַצְמִיחַ קֶרֶן
יח לְדָוִד עָרַכְתִּי נֵר לִמְשִׁיחִי: אוֹיְבָיו אַלְבִּישׁ בֹּשֶׁת וְעָלָיו יָצִיץ נִזְרוֹ:

קלג א שִׁיר הַמַּעֲלוֹת לְדָוִד הִנֵּה מַה־טּוֹב וּמַה־נָּעִים שֶׁבֶת אַחִים גַּם־יָחַד:
ב כַּשֶּׁמֶן הַטּוֹב ׀ עַל־הָרֹאשׁ יֹרֵד עַל־הַזָּקָן זְקַן־אַהֲרֹן שֶׁיֹּרֵד עַל־פִּי מִדּוֹתָיו:
ג כְּטַל־חֶרְמוֹן שֶׁיֹּרֵד עַל־הַרְרֵי צִיּוֹן כִּי שָׁם ׀ צִוָּה יְהוָה אֶת־הַבְּרָכָה חַיִּים
עַד־הָעוֹלָם:

130:6. The phrase is repeated to emphasize that the psalmist never gave up hope, despite many disappointments (Rashi).

131:2. Like a suckling child who desires nothing more than what his mother has provided him, I have complete faith in God (Metzudos).

132:3-5. David vowed not to enjoy the comforts of his own home until he built a Temple for God.

132:17. The power of kingship (Targum).

129

Israel's survival against all odds attests to God's providential control of its destiny.

¹ **A** song of ascents. "Much have they distressed me since my youth," let Israel declare now, ² "much have they distressed me since my youth, but they never conquered me. ³ On my back the plowers plowed, they lengthened their furrow. ⁴ HASHEM is righteous, He cut the ropes of the wicked." ⁵ Let them be ashamed and turned back, all who hate Zion. ⁶ Let them be like the grass on rooftops, which, even before it is plucked, withers; ⁷ with which the reaper cannot fill his hand, nor the binder of sheaves his arm; ⁸ and of which passersby have never said, "HASHEM's blessing to you; we bless you in the Name of HASHEM."

130

A person in distress prays to God from the depths of his heart.

¹ **A** song of ascents. From the depths I called You, HASHEM. ² O Lord, hear my voice, may Your ears be attentive to the sound of my pleas. ³ If You preserve iniquities, O God, O Lord, who could survive? ⁴ For with You is forgiveness, that You may be feared. ⁵ I put confidence in HASHEM, my soul put confidence, and I hoped for His word. ⁶ My soul [yearns] for the Lord, among those longing for the dawn, those longing for the dawn. * ⁷ Let Israel hope for HASHEM, for with HASHEM is kindness, and with Him is abundant redemption. ⁸ And He shall redeem Israel from all its iniquities.

131

A righteous person is not arrogant.

¹ **A** song of ascents, by David. HASHEM, my heart was not proud, and my eyes were not haughty, nor did I pursue matters too great and too wondrous for me. ² I swear that I stilled and silenced my soul, like a suckling child at his mother's side, like the suckling child is my soul. * ³ Let Israel hope to HASHEM, from this time and forever.

132

If one cannot complete a task, yet faithfully lays the groundwork, the final goal will be achieved in his merit.

¹ **A** song of ascents. O HASHEM, remember unto David all his suffering. ² How he swore to HASHEM, and vowed to the Strong One of Jacob, ³ "If I enter the tent of my home;* if I go upon the bed that is spread for me; ⁴ if I allow sleep to my eyes, slumber to my eyelids; ⁵ before I find a place for HASHEM, resting places for the Strong One of Jacob." ⁶ Behold! We heard of it in Ephrath, we found it in the forested field. ⁷ We will arrive at His Tabernacles, we will prostrate ourselves at His footstool. ⁸ Arise, HASHEM, to Your resting place, You and the Ark of Your strength. ⁹ Let Your priests be clothed in righteousness, and Your devout ones will sing joyously. ¹⁰ For the sake of David, Your servant, turn not away the face of Your anointed. ¹¹ HASHEM has sworn to David, a truth from which He will never retreat, "From the fruit of your issue I will place upon your throne. ¹² If your sons keep My covenant, and this, My testament, that I shall teach them, then their sons, too, forever and ever, shall sit upon your throne." ¹³ For HASHEM has chosen Zion; He has desired it for His habitation. ¹⁴ This is My resting place forever and ever, here I will dwell, for I have desired it. ¹⁵ Her sustenance I will bless abundantly; her needy I will satisfy with food. ¹⁶ I will clothe her priests with salvation; her devout ones will always sing joyously. ¹⁷ There I shall cause pride * to sprout for David; I have prepared a lamp for My anointed. ¹⁸ His enemies I will clothe with shame, but upon him, his crown will shine.

133

The idyllic unity among brothers brings God's blessings.

¹ **A** song of ascents, by David. Behold, how good and how pleasant is the dwelling of brothers, moreover, in unity. ² Like the precious oil* upon the head running down upon the beard, the beard of Aaron, running down over his garments, ³ so the dew of Hermon descends upon the mountains of Zion, for there HASHEM has commanded the blessing. May there be life forever!

133:2-3. The psalmist likens the flow of heavenly blessing to the precious oil with which High Priests   and kings were anointed.

קלד א שִׁיר הַמַּעֲלוֹת הִנֵּה ׀ בָּרְכוּ אֶת־יהוה כָּל־עַבְדֵי יהוה הָעֹמְדִים בְּבֵית־
ב־ג יהוה בַּלֵּילוֹת: שְׂאוּ־יְדֵכֶם קֹדֶשׁ וּבָרְכוּ אֶת־יהוה: יְבָרֶכְךָ יהוה מִצִּיּוֹן
עֹשֵׂה שָׁמַיִם וָאָרֶץ:

קלה א־ב הַלְלוּ יָהּ ׀ הַלְלוּ אֶת־שֵׁם יהוה הַלְלוּ עַבְדֵי יהוה: שֶׁעֹמְדִים בְּבֵית יהוה
ג־ד בְּחַצְרוֹת בֵּית אֱלֹהֵינוּ: הַלְלוּ־יָהּ כִּי־טוֹב יהוה זַמְּרוּ לִשְׁמוֹ כִּי נָעִים:
ה כִּי־יַעֲקֹב בָּחַר לוֹ יָהּ יִשְׂרָאֵל לִסְגֻלָּתוֹ: כִּי אֲנִי יָדַעְתִּי כִּי־גָדוֹל יהוה
ו וַאֲדֹנֵינוּ מִכָּל־אֱלֹהִים: כֹּל אֲשֶׁר־חָפֵץ יהוה עָשָׂה בַּשָּׁמַיִם וּבָאָרֶץ
ז בַּיַּמִּים וְכָל־תְּהֹמוֹת: מַעֲלֶה נְשִׂאִים מִקְצֵה הָאָרֶץ בְּרָקִים לַמָּטָר עָשָׂה
ח־ט מוֹצֵא־רוּחַ מֵאוֹצְרוֹתָיו: שֶׁהִכָּה בְּכוֹרֵי מִצְרָיִם מֵאָדָם עַד־בְּהֵמָה: שָׁלַח
י אֹתוֹת וּמֹפְתִים בְּתוֹכֵכִי מִצְרָיִם בְּפַרְעֹה וּבְכָל־עֲבָדָיו: שֶׁהִכָּה גּוֹיִם
יא רַבִּים וְהָרַג מְלָכִים עֲצוּמִים: לְסִיחוֹן ׀ מֶלֶךְ הָאֱמֹרִי וּלְעוֹג מֶלֶךְ הַבָּשָׁן
יב־יג וּלְכֹל מַמְלְכוֹת כְּנָעַן: וְנָתַן אַרְצָם נַחֲלָה נַחֲלָה לְיִשְׂרָאֵל עַמּוֹ: יהוה
יד שִׁמְךָ לְעוֹלָם יהוה זִכְרְךָ לְדֹר־וָדֹר: כִּי־יָדִין יהוה עַמּוֹ וְעַל־עֲבָדָיו
טו־טז יִתְנֶחָם: עֲצַבֵּי הַגּוֹיִם כֶּסֶף וְזָהָב מַעֲשֵׂה יְדֵי אָדָם: פֶּה־לָהֶם וְלֹא יְדַבֵּרוּ
יז עֵינַיִם לָהֶם וְלֹא יִרְאוּ: אָזְנַיִם לָהֶם וְלֹא יַאֲזִינוּ אַף אֵין־יֶשׁ־רוּחַ בְּפִיהֶם:
יח־יט כְּמוֹהֶם יִהְיוּ עֹשֵׂיהֶם כֹּל אֲשֶׁר־בֹּטֵחַ בָּהֶם: בֵּית יִשְׂרָאֵל בָּרְכוּ אֶת־יהוה
כ בֵּית אַהֲרֹן בָּרְכוּ אֶת־יהוה: בֵּית הַלֵּוִי בָּרְכוּ אֶת־יהוה יִרְאֵי יהוה בָּרְכוּ
כא אֶת־יהוה: בָּרוּךְ יהוה ׀ מִצִּיּוֹן שֹׁכֵן יְרוּשָׁלִָם הַלְלוּ־יָהּ:

קלו א־ב הוֹדוּ לַיהוה כִּי־טוֹב כִּי לְעוֹלָם חַסְדּוֹ: הוֹדוּ לֵאלֹהֵי הָאֱלֹהִים כִּי לְעוֹלָם
ג־ד חַסְדּוֹ: הוֹדוּ לַאֲדֹנֵי הָאֲדֹנִים כִּי לְעוֹלָם חַסְדּוֹ: לְעֹשֵׂה נִפְלָאוֹת גְּדֹלוֹת
ה־ו לְבַדּוֹ כִּי לְעוֹלָם חַסְדּוֹ: לְעֹשֵׂה הַשָּׁמַיִם בִּתְבוּנָה כִּי לְעוֹלָם חַסְדּוֹ: לְרֹקַע
ז הָאָרֶץ עַל־הַמָּיִם כִּי לְעוֹלָם חַסְדּוֹ: לְעֹשֵׂה אוֹרִים גְּדֹלִים כִּי לְעוֹלָם
ח־ט חַסְדּוֹ: אֶת־הַשֶּׁמֶשׁ לְמֶמְשֶׁלֶת בַּיּוֹם כִּי לְעוֹלָם חַסְדּוֹ: אֶת־הַיָּרֵחַ
י וְכוֹכָבִים לְמֶמְשְׁלוֹת בַּלָּיְלָה כִּי לְעוֹלָם חַסְדּוֹ: לְמַכֵּה מִצְרַיִם בִּבְכוֹרֵיהֶם
יא־יב כִּי לְעוֹלָם חַסְדּוֹ: וַיּוֹצֵא יִשְׂרָאֵל מִתּוֹכָם כִּי לְעוֹלָם חַסְדּוֹ: בְּיָד חֲזָקָה
יג וּבִזְרוֹעַ נְטוּיָה כִּי לְעוֹלָם חַסְדּוֹ: לְגֹזֵר יַם־סוּף לִגְזָרִים כִּי לְעוֹלָם חַסְדּוֹ:
יד־טו וְהֶעֱבִיר יִשְׂרָאֵל בְּתוֹכוֹ כִּי לְעוֹלָם חַסְדּוֹ: וְנִעֵר פַּרְעֹה וְחֵילוֹ בְיַם־סוּף כִּי
טז לְעוֹלָם חַסְדּוֹ: לְמוֹלִיךְ עַמּוֹ בַּמִּדְבָּר כִּי לְעוֹלָם חַסְדּוֹ: לְמַכֵּה מְלָכִים
יז־יח גְּדֹלִים כִּי לְעוֹלָם חַסְדּוֹ: וַיַּהֲרֹג מְלָכִים אַדִּירִים כִּי לְעוֹלָם חַסְדּוֹ:
יט־כ לְסִיחוֹן מֶלֶךְ הָאֱמֹרִי כִּי לְעוֹלָם חַסְדּוֹ: וּלְעוֹג מֶלֶךְ הַבָּשָׁן כִּי לְעוֹלָם
כא־כב חַסְדּוֹ: וְנָתַן אַרְצָם לְנַחֲלָה כִּי לְעוֹלָם חַסְדּוֹ: נַחֲלָה לְיִשְׂרָאֵל עַבְדּוֹ כִּי
כג־כד לְעוֹלָם חַסְדּוֹ: שֶׁבְּשִׁפְלֵנוּ זָכַר לָנוּ כִּי לְעוֹלָם חַסְדּוֹ: וַיִּפְרְקֵנוּ מִצָּרֵינוּ כִּי

134:1. The servant of Hashem never abandons his position; even in "nights" of adversity and gloom, he remains at his post (*Malbim*).

135:11. See *Numbers* 21:21-35. These two kings are symbolic of all the rulers whom Israel defeated. They are singled out because of their unusual might (*Radak*).

134

Even in exile, Israel blesses God.

¹ **A** song of ascents. Behold, bless HASHEM, all you servants of HASHEM, who stand in the House of HASHEM in the nights. * ² Lift your hands in the Sanctuary and bless HASHEM. ³ May HASHEM bless you from Zion, Maker of heaven and earth.

135

God's continuing role in supervising and guiding history leads to the conclusion that all is futile except to serve Him.

¹ **H**alleluyah! Praise the Name of HASHEM! Praise, O you servants of HASHEM; ² you who stand in the House of HASHEM, in the courtyards of the House of our God, ³ praise God, for HASHEM is good. Sing to His Name, for It is pleasant. ⁴ For God selected Jacob for His own, Israel as His treasure. ⁵ For I know that HASHEM is greater — our Lord — than all heavenly powers. ⁶ Whatever HASHEM wished, He did, in heaven and on earth; in the seas and all the depths. ⁷ He raises clouds from the end of the earth; He made lightning bolts for the rain; He brings forth wind from His treasuries. ⁸ It was He Who smote the firstborn of Egypt, from man to beast. ⁹ He sent signs and wonders into your midst, O Egypt, upon Pharaoh and upon all of his servants. ¹⁰ It was He Who smote many nations, and slew mighty kings — ¹¹ Sihon, King of the Amorite, Og, King of Bashan; * and all the kingdoms of Canaan — ¹² and presented their land as a heritage, a heritage for Israel, His people. ¹³ HASHEM, Your Name is forever; HASHEM, Your memorial is throughout the generations. ¹⁴ When HASHEM will judge His people, He will relent concerning His servants. ¹⁵ The idols of the nations are silver and gold, human handiwork. ¹⁶ They have mouths, but they speak not; they have eyes, but they see not; ¹⁷ they have ears, but they hear not; neither is there any breath in their mouths. ¹⁸ Like them shall their makers become, everyone who trusts in them. ¹⁹ O House of Israel, bless HASHEM; O House of Aaron, bless HASHEM. ²⁰ O House of Levi, bless HASHEM; O those who fear HASHEM, bless HASHEM. ²¹ Blessed is HASHEM from Zion, He Who dwells in Jerusalem. Halleluyah!

136

A song of God's creation and rulership of the world in general and Israel in particular

¹ **G**ive thanks to HASHEM for He is good, for His kindness endures forever. ² Give thanks to the God of the heavenly powers, for His kindness endures forever. ³ Give thanks to the Lord of the lords, for His kindness endures forever. ⁴ To Him Who alone performs great wonders, for His kindness endures forever. ⁵ To Him Who made the heavens with understanding, for His kindness endures forever. ⁶ To Him Who spread out the earth upon the waters, for His kindness endures forever. ⁷ To Him Who made great lights, for His kindness endures forever; ⁸ the sun for the reign of the day, for His kindness endures forever; ⁹ the moon and the stars for the reign of the night, for His kindness endures forever. ¹⁰ To Him Who smote Egypt through their firstborn, for His kindness endures forever; ¹¹ and brought Israel forth from their midst, for His kindness endures forever; ¹² with strong hand and outstretched arm, for His kindness endures forever. ¹³ To Him Who divided the Sea of Reeds into parts, for His kindness endures forever; ¹⁴ and caused Israel to pass through it, for His kindness endures forever; ¹⁵ and threw Pharaoh and his army into the Sea of Reeds, for His kindness endures forever. ¹⁶ To Him Who led His people through the wilderness, for His kindness endures forever. ¹⁷ To Him Who smote great kings, for His kindness endures forever; ¹⁸ and slew mighty kings, for His kindness endures forever; ¹⁹ Sihon, king of the Amorite, for His kindness endures forever; ²⁰ and Og, king of Bashan, for His kindness endures forever; ²¹ and presented their land as a heritage, for His kindness endures forever; ²² a heritage for Israel, His servant, for His kindness endures forever. ²³ In our lowliness He remembered us, for His kindness endures forever; ²⁴ and He released us from our tormentors, for

כה-כו לְעוֹלָם חַסְדּֽוֹ: נֹתֵן לֶחֶם לְכָל־בָּשָׂר כִּי לְעוֹלָם חַסְדּֽוֹ: הוֹדוּ לְאֵל הַשָּׁמָיִם כִּי לְעוֹלָם חַסְדּֽוֹ:

קלז א-ב עַל נַהֲרוֹת ׀ בָּבֶל שָׁם יָשַׁבְנוּ גַּם־בָּכִינוּ בְּזָכְרֵנוּ אֶת־צִיּֽוֹן: עַל־עֲרָבִים
ג בְּתוֹכָהּ תָּלִינוּ כִּנֹּרוֹתֵֽינוּ: כִּי שָׁם שְׁאֵלוּנוּ שׁוֹבֵינוּ דִּבְרֵי־שִׁיר וְתוֹלָלֵינוּ
ד שִׂמְחָה שִׁירוּ לָנוּ מִשִּׁיר צִיּֽוֹן: אֵיךְ נָשִׁיר אֶת־שִׁיר־יְהוָה עַל אַדְמַת נֵכָֽר:
ה-ו אִם־אֶשְׁכָּחֵךְ יְרוּשָׁלָ͏ִם תִּשְׁכַּח יְמִינִֽי: תִּדְבַּק־לְשׁוֹנִי ׀ לְחִכִּי אִם־לֹא
ז אֶזְכְּרֵכִי אִם־לֹא אַעֲלֶה אֶת־יְרוּשָׁלַ͏ִם עַל רֹאשׁ שִׂמְחָתִֽי: זְכֹר יְהוָה ׀
ח לִבְנֵי אֱדוֹם אֵת יוֹם יְרוּשָׁלָ͏ִם הָאֹמְרִים עָרוּ ׀ עָרוּ עַד הַיְסוֹד בָּֽהּ: בַּת־בָּבֶל
ט הַשְּׁדוּדָה אַשְׁרֵי שֶׁיְשַׁלֶּם־לָךְ אֶת־גְּמוּלֵךְ שֶׁגָּמַלְתְּ לָֽנוּ: אַשְׁרֵי ׀ שֶׁיֹּאחֵז וְנִפֵּץ אֶת־עֹלָלַיִךְ אֶל־הַסָּֽלַע:

קלח א-ב לְדָוִד ׀ אוֹדְךָ בְכָל־לִבִּי נֶגֶד אֱלֹהִים אֲזַמְּרֶֽךָ: אֶשְׁתַּחֲוֶה אֶל־הֵיכַל קָדְשְׁךָ֒ וְאוֹדֶה אֶת־שְׁמֶךָ עַל־חַסְדְּךָ וְעַל־אֲמִתֶּךָ כִּי־הִגְדַּלְתָּ עַל־כָּל־שִׁמְךָ
ג-ד אִמְרָתֶֽךָ: בְּיוֹם קָרָאתִי וַתַּעֲנֵֽנִי תַּרְהִבֵֽנִי בְנַפְשִׁי עֹֽז: יוֹדֽוּךָ יְהוָה כָּל־מַלְכֵי־
ה-ו אָרֶץ כִּי שָׁמְעוּ אִמְרֵי־פִֽיךָ: וְיָשִׁירוּ בְּדַרְכֵי יְהוָה כִּי־גָדוֹל כְּבוֹד יְהוָֽה: כִּי־
ז רָם יְהוָה וְשָׁפָל יִרְאֶה וְגָבֹהַּ מִמֶּרְחָק יְיֵדָֽע: אִם־אֵלֵךְ ׀ בְּקֶרֶב צָרָה תְּחַיֵּֽנִי
ח עַל אַף אֹיְבַי תִּשְׁלַח יָדֶךָ וְתוֹשִׁיעֵנִי יְמִינֶֽךָ: יְהוָה יִגְמֹר בַּעֲדִי יְהוָה חַסְדְּךָ לְעוֹלָם מַעֲשֵׂי יָדֶיךָ אַל־תֶּֽרֶף:

קלט א-ב לַמְנַצֵּחַ לְדָוִד מִזְמוֹר יְהוָה חֲקַרְתַּנִי וַתֵּדָֽע: אַתָּה יָדַעְתָּ שִׁבְתִּי וְקוּמִי
ג-ד בַּנְתָּה לְרֵעִי מֵרָחֽוֹק: אָרְחִי וְרִבְעִי זֵרִיתָ וְכָל־דְּרָכַי הִסְכַּֽנְתָּה: כִּי אֵין
ה מִלָּה בִּלְשׁוֹנִי הֵן יְהוָה יָדַעְתָּ כֻלָּֽהּ: אָחוֹר וָקֶדֶם צַרְתָּנִי וַתָּשֶׁת עָלַי
ו-ז כַּפֶּֽכָה: °פְּלִאיָה [פְּלִיאָה ק] דַעַת מִמֶּנִּי נִשְׂגְּבָה לֹא־אוּכַל לָֽהּ: אָנָה
ח אֵלֵךְ מֵרוּחֶךָ וְאָנָה מִפָּנֶיךָ אֶבְרָֽח: אִם־אֶסַּק שָׁמַיִם שָׁם אָתָּה וְאַצִּיעָה
ט-י שְּׁאוֹל הִנֶּֽךָּ: אֶשָּׂא כַנְפֵי־שָׁחַר אֶשְׁכְּנָה בְּאַחֲרִית יָֽם: גַּם־שָׁם יָדְךָ תַנְחֵנִי
יא-יב וְתֹאחֲזֵנִי יְמִינֶֽךָ: וָאֹמַר אַךְ־חֹשֶׁךְ יְשׁוּפֵנִי וְלַיְלָה אוֹר בַּעֲדֵֽנִי: גַּם־חֹשֶׁךְ
יג לֹא־יַחְשִׁיךְ מִמֶּךָ וְלַיְלָה כַּיּוֹם יָאִיר כַּחֲשֵׁיכָה כָּאוֹרָֽה: כִּי־אַתָּה קָנִיתָ
יד כִלְיֹתָי תְּסֻכֵּנִי בְּבֶטֶן אִמִּֽי: אֽוֹדְךָ עַל כִּי נוֹרָאוֹת נִפְלֵיתִי נִפְלָאִים מַעֲשֶׂיךָ
טו וְנַפְשִׁי יֹדַעַת מְאֹֽד: לֹא־נִכְחַד עָצְמִי מִמֶּךָּ אֲשֶׁר־עֻשֵּׂיתִי בַסֵּתֶר רֻקַּמְתִּי
טז בְּתַחְתִּיּוֹת אָֽרֶץ: גָּלְמִי ׀ רָאוּ עֵינֶיךָ וְעַל־סִפְרְךָ כֻּלָּם יִכָּתֵבוּ יָמִים יֻצָּֽרוּ
יז °וְלֹא [וְלוֹ ק] אֶחָד בָּהֶֽם: וְלִי מַה־יָּקְרוּ רֵעֶיךָ אֵל מֶה עָצְמוּ רָאשֵׁיהֶֽם:

137:5-6. No matter what the occasion of personal joy, the memory of Jerusalem must come first *(Ibn Ezra)*. From this verse stems the custom that a bridegroom places ashes on his head before the marriage ceremony, and the custom that a glass is broken after the ceremony in memory of Jerusalem *(Rama)*.

137:8-9. Darius the Mede, Babylon's conqueror, will hate and torment her cruelly exactly as she hated and tormented Israel *(Malbim)*.

138:4. God's prophetic assurances regarding the future ascendancy of David and Israel were given when their situations seemed hopeless and irreversible. The world considered them fanciful, but when they will be fulfilled, the world will acknowledge God's Providence.

139:15. In the lowest chamber of my mother's innards.

139:17. The general categories of Divine power and wisdom evident in Creation would overwhelm the most brilliant mind, even ignoring the countless, exacting

His kindness endures forever. ²⁵ He gives nourishment to all flesh, for His kindness endures forever. ²⁶ Give thanks to God of the heavens, for His kindness endures forever.

137

A prophetic lament over the exiles, and a charge to them to never remove Jerusalem from their hearts and minds

¹ By the rivers of Babylon, there we sat and also wept when we remembered Zion. ² On the willows within it we hung our lyres. ³ For there our captors requested words of song from us, with our lyres [playing] joyous music, "Sing for us from Zion's song!" ⁴ "How can we sing the song of HASHEM upon the alien's soil?" ⁵ If I forget you, O Jerusalem, * let my right hand forget its skill. ⁶ Let my tongue adhere to my palate, if I fail to recall you, if I fail to elevate Jerusalem above my foremost joy. ⁷ Remember, HASHEM, for the offspring of Edom, the day of Jerusalem; for those who say, "Destroy! Destroy! to its very foundation." ⁸ O violated daughter of Babylon, praiseworthy is he who repays you * in accordance with the manner that you treated us. ⁹ Praiseworthy is he who will clutch and dash your infants against the rock.

138

One must live with profound awareness that God is omnipotent and intimately close to those who seek Him.

¹ By David. I will acknowledge You with all my heart, in the presence of princes I will sing to You. ² I will prostrate myself toward Your Holy Sanctuary, and I will acknowledge Your Name, for Your kindness and Your truth; for You have exalted Your promise even beyond Your Name. ³ On the day I cried You answered me, You emboldened me, there is strength in my soul. ⁴ All the kings of earth will acknowledge You, HASHEM, because they heard the words of Your mouth. * ⁵ And they will sing of the ways of HASHEM, for great is the glory of HASHEM. ⁶ For, though HASHEM is exalted, He notes the lowly; and the High One makes Himself known from afar. ⁷ Though I walk amid distress, You preserve me; to counter the wrath of my enemies You extend Your hand, and Your right hand saves me. ⁸ May HASHEM complete on my behalf; HASHEM, Your kindness is eternal, do not let go of the creatures of Your hand.

139

God's omniscience and omnipotence are absolute; He is aware of a person's innermost thoughts.

¹ For the conductor, by David, a psalm. O HASHEM, You have scrutinized me and You know. ² You know my sitting down and my rising up; You understand my thought from afar. ³ You encompass my path and my repose, You are familiar with all my ways. ⁴ For the word is not yet on my tongue, behold, HASHEM, You knew it all. ⁵ Back and front You have restricted me, and You have laid Your hand upon me. ⁶ Knowledge is beyond me; exalted, I am incapable of it. ⁷ Where can I go from Your spirit? And where can I flee from Your Presence? ⁸ If I ascend to heaven, You are there; if I make my bed in the lowest depths, behold, You are there; ⁹ were I to take up wings of dawn, were I to dwell in the distant west, ¹⁰ there, too, Your hand would guide me, and Your right hand would grasp me. ¹¹ Would I say, "Surely darkness will shadow me," then the night would become as light around me. ¹² Even darkness obscures not from You; and night shines like the day; darkness and light are the same. ¹³ For You have created my mind; You have covered me in my mother's womb. ¹⁴ I acknowledge You, for I am awesomely, wondrously fashioned; wondrous are Your works, and my soul knows it well. ¹⁵ My frame was not hidden from You; that which I was made in concealment, which I was knit together in the lowest parts of the earth. * ¹⁶ Your eyes saw my unshaped form, and in Your book all were recorded; though they will be fashioned through many days, to Him they are one. ¹⁷ To me — how glorious are Your thoughts, O God! How very great are their headings! *

---

details of each and every one of those categories.

יח-יט   אֶסְפְּרֵם מֵחוֹל יִרְבּוּן הֱקִיצֹתִי וְעוֹדִי עִמָּךְ: אִם-תִּקְטֹל אֱלוֹהַּ ׀ רָשָׁע

כ-כא   וְאַנְשֵׁי דָמִים סוּרוּ מֶנִּי: אֲשֶׁר יֹאמְרֻךָ לִמְזִמָּה נָשֻׂא לַשָּׁוְא עָרֶיךָ: הֲלוֹא-

כב   מְשַׂנְאֶיךָ יְהוָה ׀ אֶשְׂנָא וּבִתְקוֹמְמֶיךָ אֶתְקוֹטָט: תַּכְלִית שִׂנְאָה שְׂנֵאתִים

כג-כד   לְאוֹיְבִים הָיוּ לִי: חׇקְרֵנִי אֵל וְדַע לְבָבִי בְּחָנֵנִי וְדַע שַׂרְעַפָּי: וּרְאֵה אִם-

  דֶּרֶךְ-עֹצֶב בִּי וּנְחֵנִי בְּדֶרֶךְ עוֹלָם:

קמ   א-ב   לַמְנַצֵּחַ מִזְמוֹר לְדָוִד: חַלְּצֵנִי יְהוָה מֵאָדָם רָע מֵאִישׁ חֲמָסִים תִּנְצְרֵנִי:

יום כט לחדש   ג-ד   אֲשֶׁר חָשְׁבוּ רָעוֹת בְּלֵב כָּל-יוֹם יָגוּרוּ מִלְחָמוֹת: שָׁנְנוּ לְשׁוֹנָם כְּמוֹ-נָחָשׁ

ה   חֲמַת עַכְשׁוּב תַּחַת שְׂפָתֵימוֹ סֶלָה: שָׁמְרֵנִי יְהוָה ׀ מִידֵי רָשָׁע מֵאִישׁ

ו   חֲמָסִים תִּנְצְרֵנִי אֲשֶׁר חָשְׁבוּ לִדְחוֹת פְּעָמָי: טָמְנוּ-גֵאִים ׀ פַּח לִי

ז   וַחֲבָלִים פָּרְשׂוּ רֶשֶׁת לְיַד-מַעְגָּל מֹקְשִׁים שָׁתוּ-לִי סֶלָה: אָמַרְתִּי לַיהוָה

ח   אֵלִי אָתָּה הַאֲזִינָה יְהוָה קוֹל תַּחֲנוּנָי: יְהוִה אֲדֹנָי עֹז יְשׁוּעָתִי סַכֹּתָה

ט   לְרֹאשִׁי בְּיוֹם נָשֶׁק: אַל-תִּתֵּן יְהוָה מַאֲוַיֵּי רָשָׁע זְמָמוֹ אַל-תָּפֵק יָרוּמוּ

יא-יב   סֶלָה: רֹאשׁ מְסִבָּי עֲמַל שְׂפָתֵימוֹ [יְכַסֵּמוֹ ק] יכסומו: [יִמּוֹטוּ ק] ימיטו:

יב   ק] עֲלֵיהֶם גֶּחָלִים בָּאֵשׁ יַפִּלֵם בְּמַהֲמֹרוֹת בַּל-יָקוּמוּ: אִישׁ לָשׁוֹן בַּל-יִכּוֹן

יג   בָּאָרֶץ אִישׁ-חָמָס רָע יְצוּדֶנּוּ לְמַדְחֵפֹת: [יָדַעְתִּי ק] ידעת כִּי-יַעֲשֶׂה

יד   יְהוָה דִּין עָנִי מִשְׁפַּט אֶבְיֹנִים: אַךְ צַדִּיקִים יוֹדוּ לִשְׁמֶךָ יֵשְׁבוּ יְשָׁרִים אֶת-

  פָּנֶיךָ:

קמא   א-ב   מִזְמוֹר לְדָוִד יְהוָה קְרָאתִיךָ חוּשָׁה לִי הַאֲזִינָה קוֹלִי בְּקָרְאִי-לָךְ: תִּכּוֹן

ג   תְּפִלָּתִי קְטֹרֶת לְפָנֶיךָ מַשְׂאַת כַּפַּי מִנְחַת-עָרֶב: שִׁיתָה יְהוָה שָׁמְרָה לְפִי

ד   נִצְּרָה עַל-דַּל שְׂפָתָי: אַל-תַּט-לִבִּי לְדָבָר ׀ רָע לְהִתְעוֹלֵל עֲלִלוֹת ׀

ה   בְּרֶשַׁע אֶת-אִישִׁים פֹּעֲלֵי-אָוֶן וּבַל-אֶלְחַם בְּמַנְעַמֵּיהֶם: יֶהֶלְמֵנִי-צַדִּיק ׀

ו   חֶסֶד וְיוֹכִיחֵנִי שֶׁמֶן רֹאשׁ אַל-יָנִי רֹאשִׁי כִּי-עוֹד וּתְפִלָּתִי בְּרָעוֹתֵיהֶם:

ז   נִשְׁמְטוּ בִידֵי-סֶלַע שֹׁפְטֵיהֶם וְשָׁמְעוּ אֲמָרַי כִּי נָעֵמוּ: כְּמוֹ פֹלֵחַ וּבֹקֵעַ

ח   בָּאָרֶץ נִפְזְרוּ עֲצָמֵינוּ לְפִי שְׁאוֹל: כִּי אֵלֶיךָ ׀ יְהוִה אֲדֹנָי עֵינָי בְּכָה חָסִיתִי

ט-י   אַל-תְּעַר נַפְשִׁי: שָׁמְרֵנִי מִידֵי פַח יָקְשׁוּ לִי וּמֹקְשׁוֹת פֹּעֲלֵי אָוֶן: יִפְּלוּ

  בְמַכְמֹרָיו רְשָׁעִים יַחַד אָנֹכִי עַד-אֶעֱבוֹר:

קמב   א-ב   מַשְׂכִּיל לְדָוִד בִּהְיוֹתוֹ בַמְּעָרָה תְפִלָּה: קוֹלִי אֶל-יְהוָה אֶזְעָק קוֹלִי אֶל-

ג   יְהוָה אֶתְחַנָּן: אֶשְׁפֹּךְ לְפָנָיו שִׂיחִי צָרָתִי לְפָנָיו אַגִּיד: בְּהִתְעַטֵּף עָלַי ׀

ד   רוּחִי וְאַתָּה יָדַעְתָּ נְתִיבָתִי בְּאֹרַח-זוּ אֲהַלֵּךְ טָמְנוּ פַח לִי: הַבֵּיט יָמִין ׀

ה   וּרְאֵה וְאֵין-לִי מַכִּיר אָבַד מָנוֹס מִמֶּנִּי אֵין דּוֹרֵשׁ לְנַפְשִׁי: זָעַקְתִּי אֵלֶיךָ

ו   יְהוָה אָמַרְתִּי אַתָּה מַחְסִי חֶלְקִי בְּאֶרֶץ הַחַיִּים: הַקְשִׁיבָה ׀ אֶל-רִנָּתִי כִּי-

---

¹⁸ *Were I to count them, they would outnumber the grains of sand, even if I were to be constantly awake and always with You.* ¹⁹ *O that You would slay the wicked, O God, and men of blood [to whom I say,] "Depart from me!"* ²⁰ *Those who pronounce Your Name for wicked schemes, it is taken in vain by Your enemies.* ²¹ *For indeed those who hate You, O HASHEM, I hate them, and I quarrel with those who rise up against You!* ²² *With the utmost hatred, I hate them; they have become enemies unto me.* ²³ *Examine me, O God, and know my heart; test me and know my thoughts.* ²⁴ *And see if I have a vexing way; and lead me in the way of eternity.*

140

A person who feels powerless to combat the working of deceit must place his trust in God.

¹ **F**or the conductor, a psalm of David. ² *Free me, HASHEM, from the wicked man; from the man of violence preserve me,* ³ *who devise evil schemes in [their] heart, who assemble daily for wars.* ⁴ *They have sharpened their tongue like a serpent, a spider's venom* is under their lips, Selah.* ⁵ *Guard me, HASHEM, from the hands of the wicked one, from the man of violence preserve me, those who have contrived to cause my steps to slip.* ⁶ *The arrogant have hidden a snare for me and ropes, they spread a net near [my] footpath, they set traps for me, Selah.* ⁷ *I said to HASHEM, "You are my God! Give ear, O HASHEM, to the sound of my pleading."* ⁸ *HASHEM/ELOHIM, * O Lord, Might of my salvation, You protected my head on the day of armed battle.* ⁹ *Grant not, HASHEM, the desires of the wicked one; do not grant his conspiracy fruition, for them to be exalted, Selah.* ¹⁰ *As for the head of my besiegers, let the mischief of their own lips bury them.* ¹¹ *Let fiery coals descend upon them; may it* cast them down into the fire, into deep pits, never to rise again.* ¹² *Let not the slanderous man be established on earth — the evil man of violence — may it hunt him until he is overthrown.* ¹³ *I know that HASHEM will champion the cause of the poor, the rights of those who are destitute.* ¹⁴ *Only the righteous will give thanks to Your Name; the upright will dwell in Your Presence.*

141

Even in crisis, one must pray not only for physical deliverance, but also for God's help in avoiding the slightest trace of sin.

¹ **A** psalm by David. O HASHEM, I have called You; hasten to me, give ear to my voice when I call to You. ² *Let my prayer stand as incense before You; the lifting of my hands as an afternoon offering.* ³ *Post a sentry for my mouth, O HASHEM; guard the door of my lips.* ⁴ *Let not my heart incline toward an evil thing, to perform evil acts with men who are doers of iniquity, and let me not break bread in their pleasure-feasts.* ⁵ *Let the righteous one strike me with kindness and let him rebuke me, like the finest oil, let my head not refuse it; for my prayer is eternally against their evils.* ⁶ *Their judges have gone astray through [their hearts of] stone, though they heard my words so pleasant.* ⁷ *Like one who chops and splinters [wood] on the ground, so have our bones been scattered to the mouth of the pit.* ⁸ *For to You, HASHEM/ELOHIM, O Lord, are my eyes turned, I have sought refuge in You, do not cause my soul to be poured out.* ⁹ *Protect me from the hands of the snare they laid for me, and from the traps of the doers of iniquity.* ¹⁰ *The wicked will fall into its nets, all of them together, until I pass through.*

142

Utterly trapped, one places oneself completely at God's mercy.

¹ **A** maskil by David, when he was in the cave* — a prayer. ² *With my voice I cry out to HASHEM, with my voice I plead with HASHEM.* ³ *I pour out my plaint before Him; I declare my distress before Him.* ⁴ *When my spirit faints within me, then You know my [perilous] path; on this road that I walk they have laid a snare for me.* ⁵ *Look to the right and see that I have no friend; escape is lost to me, no one seeks to save my life.* ⁶ *I have cried out to You, HASHEM; I have said, "You are my refuge, my portion in the land of the living."* ⁷ *Attend to my cry, for*

ח דַּלּוֹתִי מְאֹד הַצִּילֵנִי מֵרֹדְפַי כִּי אָמְצוּ מִמֶּנִּי: הוֹצִיאָה מִמַּסְגֵּר ׀ נַפְשִׁי
לְהוֹדוֹת אֶת־שְׁמֶךָ בִּי יַכְתִּרוּ צַדִּיקִים כִּי תִגְמֹל עָלָי:

קמג א מִזְמוֹר לְדָוִד יְהוָה ׀ שְׁמַע תְּפִלָּתִי הַאֲזִינָה אֶל־תַּחֲנוּנַי בֶּאֱמֻנָתְךָ עֲנֵנִי
ב בְּצִדְקָתֶךָ: וְאַל־תָּבוֹא בְמִשְׁפָּט אֶת־עַבְדֶּךָ כִּי לֹא־יִצְדַּק לְפָנֶיךָ כָל־חָי: כִּי
ג רָדַף אוֹיֵב ׀ נַפְשִׁי דִּכָּא לָאָרֶץ חַיָּתִי הוֹשִׁיבַנִי בְמַחֲשַׁכִּים כְּמֵתֵי עוֹלָם:
דה וַתִּתְעַטֵּף עָלַי רוּחִי בְּתוֹכִי יִשְׁתּוֹמֵם לִבִּי: זָכַרְתִּי יָמִים ׀ מִקֶּדֶם הָגִיתִי
ו בְכָל־פָּעֳלֶךָ בְּמַעֲשֵׂה יָדֶיךָ אֲשׂוֹחֵחַ: פֵּרַשְׂתִּי יָדַי אֵלֶיךָ נַפְשִׁי ׀ כְּאֶרֶץ־
ז עֲיֵפָה לְךָ סֶלָה: מַהֵר עֲנֵנִי ׀ יְהוָה כָּלְתָה רוּחִי אַל־תַּסְתֵּר פָּנֶיךָ מִמֶּנִּי
ח וְנִמְשַׁלְתִּי עִם־יֹרְדֵי בוֹר: הַשְׁמִיעֵנִי בַבֹּקֶר ׀ חַסְדֶּךָ כִּי־בְךָ בָטָחְתִּי
ט הוֹדִיעֵנִי דֶּרֶךְ־זוּ אֵלֵךְ כִּי־אֵלֶיךָ נָשָׂאתִי נַפְשִׁי: הַצִּילֵנִי מֵאֹיְבַי ׀ יְהוָה אֵלֶיךָ
י כִסִּתִי: לַמְּדֵנִי ׀ לַעֲשׂוֹת רְצוֹנֶךָ כִּי־אַתָּה אֱלוֹהָי רוּחֲךָ טוֹבָה תַּנְחֵנִי בְּאֶרֶץ
יא מִישׁוֹר: לְמַעַן־שִׁמְךָ יְהוָה תְּחַיֵּנִי בְּצִדְקָתְךָ ׀ תוֹצִיא מִצָּרָה נַפְשִׁי:
יב וּבְחַסְדְּךָ תַּצְמִית אֹיְבָי וְהַאֲבַדְתָּ כָּל־צֹרֲרֵי נַפְשִׁי כִּי אֲנִי עַבְדֶּךָ:

קמד אב לְדָוִד ׀ בָּרוּךְ יְהוָה ׀ צוּרִי הַמְלַמֵּד יָדַי לַקְרָב אֶצְבְּעוֹתַי לַמִּלְחָמָה: חַסְדִּי
ג וּמְצוּדָתִי מִשְׂגַּבִּי וּמְפַלְטִי לִי מָגִנִּי וּבוֹ חָסִיתִי הָרוֹדֵד עַמִּי תַחְתָּי: יְהוָה
ד מָה־אָדָם וַתֵּדָעֵהוּ בֶּן־אֱנוֹשׁ וַתְּחַשְּׁבֵהוּ: אָדָם לַהֶבֶל דָּמָה יָמָיו כְּצֵל
הו עוֹבֵר: יְהוָה הַט־שָׁמֶיךָ וְתֵרֵד גַּע בֶּהָרִים וְיֶעֱשָׁנוּ: בְּרוֹק בָּרָק וּתְפִיצֵם
ז שְׁלַח חִצֶּיךָ וּתְהֻמֵּם: שְׁלַח יָדֶיךָ מִמָּרוֹם פְּצֵנִי וְהַצִּילֵנִי מִמַּיִם רַבִּים מִיַּד
חט בְּנֵי נֵכָר: אֲשֶׁר פִּיהֶם דִּבֶּר־שָׁוְא וִימִינָם יְמִין שָׁקֶר: אֱלֹהִים שִׁיר חָדָשׁ
י אָשִׁירָה לָּךְ בְּנֵבֶל עָשׂוֹר אֲזַמְּרָה־לָּךְ: הַנּוֹתֵן תְּשׁוּעָה לַמְּלָכִים הַפּוֹצֶה
יא אֶת־דָּוִד עַבְדּוֹ מֵחֶרֶב רָעָה: פְּצֵנִי וְהַצִּילֵנִי מִיַּד בְּנֵי־נֵכָר אֲשֶׁר פִּיהֶם
יב דִּבֶּר־שָׁוְא וִימִינָם יְמִין שָׁקֶר: אֲשֶׁר בָּנֵינוּ ׀ כִּנְטִעִים מְגֻדָּלִים בִּנְעוּרֵיהֶם
יג בְּנוֹתֵינוּ כְזָוִיֹּת מְחֻטָּבוֹת תַּבְנִית הֵיכָל: מְזָוֵינוּ מְלֵאִים מְפִיקִים מִזַּן אֶל־זַן
יד צֹאונֵנוּ מַאֲלִיפוֹת מְרֻבָּבוֹת בְּחוּצוֹתֵינוּ: אַלּוּפֵינוּ מְסֻבָּלִים אֵין־פֶּרֶץ וְאֵין
טו יוֹצֵאת וְאֵין צְוָחָה בִּרְחֹבֹתֵינוּ: אַשְׁרֵי הָעָם שֶׁכָּכָה לּוֹ אַשְׁרֵי הָעָם שֶׁיְהוָה
אֱלֹהָיו:

קמה א תְּהִלָּה לְדָוִד אֲרוֹמִמְךָ אֱלוֹהַי הַמֶּלֶךְ וַאֲבָרְכָה שִׁמְךָ לְעוֹלָם וָעֶד:
יום ל׳ לחדש
בג בְּכָל־יוֹם אֲבָרְכֶךָּ וַאֲהַלְלָה שִׁמְךָ לְעוֹלָם וָעֶד: גָּדוֹל יְהוָה וּמְהֻלָּל
דה מְאֹד וְלִגְדֻלָּתוֹ אֵין חֵקֶר: דּוֹר לְדוֹר יְשַׁבַּח מַעֲשֶׂיךָ וּגְבוּרֹתֶיךָ יַגִּידוּ: הֲדַר
ו כְּבוֹד הוֹדֶךָ וְדִבְרֵי נִפְלְאֹתֶיךָ אָשִׂיחָה: וֶעֱזוּז נוֹרְאֹתֶיךָ יֹאמֵרוּ
ז °וּגְדוּלָּתְךָ [וּגְדֻלָּתְךָ ק] אֲסַפְּרֶנָּה: זֵכֶר רַב־טוּבְךָ יַבִּיעוּ וְצִדְקָתְךָ יְרַנֵּנוּ:

143:8. At the dawn of my deliverance.   144:8. Their boastful predictions of victory are vain;
144:5. A metaphor for God's becoming openly involved   their celebrated might is in fact impotent, because You,
in the earthly affairs of man.   God, are on my side.

I have been brought very low; rescue me from my pursuers, for they are stronger than I. [8] *Release my soul from confinement to acknowledge Your Name; the righteous will crown themselves with me, when You bestow kindness upon me.*

143

Sorely pained by persecution and suffering, one can be pulled from the abyss by recalling God's past miracles.

[1] **A** psalm of David. HASHEM, hear my prayer, give ear to my supplications, answer me in Your faithfulness, in Your righteousness. [2] *And do not enter into strict judgment with Your servant, for no living creature would be vindicated before You.* [3] *For the enemy pursued my soul, he ground my life into the dirt, he sat me in utter darkness, like those who are long dead.* [4] *When my spirit grew faint upon me, within me my heart was appalled.* [5] *I recalled days of old, I pondered over all Your deeds, I spoke about Your handiwork.* [6] *I spread out my hands to You, my soul longs for You like the thirsty land. Selah.* [7] *Answer me soon, O HASHEM, my spirit is spent; conceal not Your face from me, lest I be like those who descend into the pit.* [8] *Let me hear Your kindness at dawn,* * *for in You have I placed my trust; let me know the way I should walk, for to You have I lifted my soul.* [9] *Rescue me from my enemies, O HASHEM, I have hidden my plight from all but You.* [10] *Teach me to do Your will, for You are my God. May Your good spirit guide me over level ground.* [11] *For Your Name's sake, HASHEM, revive me; with Your righteousness remove my soul from distress.* [12] *And with Your kindness cut off my enemies; and destroy all who oppress my soul, for I am Your servant.*

144

David, the quintessential Jewish monarch, attributes all his accomplishments to God alone.

[1] **B**y David. Blessed is HASHEM, my Rock, Who trains my hands for battle, my fingers for war. [2] *My Benefactor, my Fortress, my Stronghold, my own Rescuer; my Shield, in Him I take refuge, He Who subjugates my nation to me.* [3] *HASHEM, what is man that You recognize him; the son of a frail human that You reckon with him?* [4] *Man is like a breath; his days are like a passing shadow.* [5] *HASHEM! Bend Your heavens and descend;* * *touch the mountains and they will go up in smoke.* [6] *Flash a lightning bolt and scatter them; shoot Your arrows and panic them.* [7] *Stretch out Your hands from above; release me and rescue me from great waters, from the hand of strangers.* [8] *Their mouth speaks vanity, and their right hand is a right hand of falsehood.* * [9] *O God, a new song will I sing to You, on a ten-stringed harp will I play to You.* [10] *He Who grants salvation to the kings, He Who releases David, His servant, from the evil sword,* [11] *release me and rescue me from the hand of strangers. Their mouth speaks vanity and their right hand is a right hand of falsehood.* [12] *For our sons are like saplings, nurtured from their youth; our daughters are like cornerstones, crafted in palatial form.* [13] *Our storehouses overflow to their very corners, providing from harvest to harvest; our sheep increase by the thousands, by the myriads in our open spaces.* [14] *Our oxen are laden; there is neither breach, nor outburst, nor wailing in our streets.* [15] *Praiseworthy is the people for whom this is so; praiseworthy is the people whose God is HASHEM.*

145

Man is obligated to praise God's providential provision of the needs of every living creature.

[1] **A** psalm of praise by David: א *I will exalt You, my God the King, and I will bless Your Name forever and ever.* [2] ב *Every day I will bless You, and I will laud Your Name forever and ever.* [3] ג *HASHEM is great and exceedingly lauded, and His greatness is beyond investigation.* [4] ד *Each generation will praise Your deeds to the next and of Your mighty deeds they will tell;* [5] ה *the splendrous glory of Your power and Your wondrous deeds I shall discuss.* [6] ו *And of the might of Your awesome deeds they will speak, and Your greatness I shall relate.* [7] ז *A recollection of Your abundant goodness they will utter, and of Your righteousness they will sing exultantly.*

ח-ט   חַנּוּן וְרַחוּם יְהוָה אֶרֶךְ אַפַּיִם וּגְדָל־חָסֶד: טוֹב־יְהוָה לַכֹּל וְרַחֲמָיו עַל־

כָּל־מַעֲשָׂיו: יוֹדוּךָ יְהוָה כָּל־מַעֲשֶׂיךָ וַחֲסִידֶיךָ יְבָרְכוּכָה: כְּבוֹד מַלְכוּתְךָ

יא-יב   יֹאמֵרוּ וּגְבוּרָתְךָ יְדַבֵּרוּ: לְהוֹדִיעַ ׀ לִבְנֵי הָאָדָם גְּבוּרֹתָיו וּכְבוֹד הֲדַר

יג   מַלְכוּתוֹ: מַלְכוּתְךָ מַלְכוּת כָּל־עֹלָמִים וּמֶמְשַׁלְתְּךָ בְּכָל־דּוֹר וָדוֹר: סוֹמֵךְ

יד-טו   יְהוָה לְכָל־הַנֹּפְלִים וְזוֹקֵף לְכָל־הַכְּפוּפִים: עֵינֵי־כֹל אֵלֶיךָ יְשַׂבֵּרוּ וְאַתָּה

טז   נוֹתֵן־לָהֶם אֶת־אָכְלָם בְּעִתּוֹ: פּוֹתֵחַ אֶת־יָדֶךָ וּמַשְׂבִּיעַ לְכָל־חַי רָצוֹן:

יז-יח   צַדִּיק יְהוָה בְּכָל־דְּרָכָיו וְחָסִיד בְּכָל־מַעֲשָׂיו: קָרוֹב יְהוָה לְכָל־קֹרְאָיו

יט   לְכֹל אֲשֶׁר יִקְרָאֻהוּ בֶאֱמֶת: רְצוֹן־יְרֵאָיו יַעֲשֶׂה וְאֶת־שַׁוְעָתָם יִשְׁמַע

כ   וְיוֹשִׁיעֵם: שׁוֹמֵר יְהוָה אֶת־כָּל־אֹהֲבָיו וְאֵת כָּל־הָרְשָׁעִים יַשְׁמִיד: תְּהִלַּת

כא   יְהוָה יְדַבֶּר פִּי וִיבָרֵךְ כָּל־בָּשָׂר שֵׁם קָדְשׁוֹ לְעוֹלָם וָעֶד:

קמו   א-ב   הַלְלוּ־יָהּ הַלְלִי נַפְשִׁי אֶת־יְהוָה: אֲהַלְלָה יְהוָה בְּחַיָּי אֲזַמְּרָה לֵאלֹהַי

ג-ד   בְּעוֹדִי: אַל־תִּבְטְחוּ בִנְדִיבִים בְּבֶן־אָדָם ׀ שֶׁאֵין לוֹ תְשׁוּעָה: תֵּצֵא רוּחוֹ

ה   יָשֻׁב לְאַדְמָתוֹ בַּיּוֹם הַהוּא אָבְדוּ עֶשְׁתֹּנֹתָיו: אַשְׁרֵי שֶׁאֵל יַעֲקֹב בְּעֶזְרוֹ

ו   שִׂבְרוֹ עַל־יְהוָה אֱלֹהָיו: עֹשֶׂה ׀ שָׁמַיִם וָאָרֶץ אֶת־הַיָּם וְאֶת־כָּל־אֲשֶׁר־

ז   בָּם הַשֹּׁמֵר אֱמֶת לְעוֹלָם: עֹשֶׂה מִשְׁפָּט ׀ לַעֲשׁוּקִים נֹתֵן לֶחֶם לָרְעֵבִים

ח   יְהוָה מַתִּיר אֲסוּרִים: יְהוָה ׀ פֹּקֵחַ עִוְרִים יְהוָה זֹקֵף כְּפוּפִים יְהוָה אֹהֵב

ט   צַדִּיקִים: יְהוָה ׀ שֹׁמֵר אֶת־גֵּרִים יָתוֹם וְאַלְמָנָה יְעוֹדֵד וְדֶרֶךְ רְשָׁעִים יְעַוֵּת:

י   יִמְלֹךְ יְהוָה ׀ לְעוֹלָם אֱלֹהַיִךְ צִיּוֹן לְדֹר וָדֹר הַלְלוּ־יָהּ:

קמז   א-ב   הַלְלוּ יָהּ ׀ כִּי־טוֹב זַמְּרָה אֱלֹהֵינוּ כִּי־נָעִים נָאוָה תְהִלָּה: בּוֹנֵה יְרוּשָׁלַ͏ִם

ג-ד   יְהוָה נִדְחֵי יִשְׂרָאֵל יְכַנֵּס: הָרֹפֵא לִשְׁבוּרֵי לֵב וּמְחַבֵּשׁ לְעַצְּבוֹתָם: מוֹנֶה

ה   מִסְפָּר לַכּוֹכָבִים לְכֻלָּם שֵׁמוֹת יִקְרָא: גָּדוֹל אֲדוֹנֵינוּ וְרַב־כֹּחַ לִתְבוּנָתוֹ

ו-ז   אֵין מִסְפָּר: מְעוֹדֵד עֲנָוִים יְהוָה מַשְׁפִּיל רְשָׁעִים עֲדֵי־אָרֶץ: עֱנוּ לַיהוָה

ח   בְּתוֹדָה זַמְּרוּ לֵאלֹהֵינוּ בְכִנּוֹר: הַמְכַסֶּה שָׁמַיִם ׀ בְּעָבִים הַמֵּכִין לָאָרֶץ

ט   מָטָר הַמַּצְמִיחַ הָרִים חָצִיר: נוֹתֵן לִבְהֵמָה לַחְמָהּ לִבְנֵי עֹרֵב אֲשֶׁר יִקְרָאוּ:

יא   לֹא בִגְבוּרַת הַסּוּס יֶחְפָּץ לֹא־בְשׁוֹקֵי הָאִישׁ יִרְצֶה: רוֹצֶה יְהוָה אֶת־יְרֵאָיו

יב-יג   אֶת־הַמְיַחֲלִים לְחַסְדּוֹ: שַׁבְּחִי יְרוּשָׁלַ͏ִם אֶת־יְהוָה הַלְלִי אֱלֹהַיִךְ צִיּוֹן: כִּי־

יד   חִזַּק בְּרִיחֵי שְׁעָרָיִךְ בֵּרַךְ בָּנַיִךְ בְּקִרְבֵּךְ: הַשָּׂם־גְּבוּלֵךְ שָׁלוֹם חֵלֶב חִטִּים

טו-טז   יַשְׂבִּיעֵךְ: הַשֹּׁלֵחַ אִמְרָתוֹ אָרֶץ עַד־מְהֵרָה יָרוּץ דְּבָרוֹ: הַנֹּתֵן שֶׁלֶג כַּצָּמֶר

יז-יח   כְּפוֹר כָּאֵפֶר יְפַזֵּר: מַשְׁלִיךְ קַרְחוֹ כְפִתִּים לִפְנֵי קָרָתוֹ מִי יַעֲמֹד: יִשְׁלַח

יט   דְּבָרוֹ וְיַמְסֵם יַשֵּׁב רוּחוֹ יִזְּלוּ־מָיִם: מַגִּיד דְּבָרָו לְיַעֲקֹב חֻקָּיו וּמִשְׁפָּטָיו

כ   לְיִשְׂרָאֵל: לֹא עָשָׂה כֵן ׀ לְכָל־גּוֹי וּמִשְׁפָּטִים בַּל־יְדָעוּם הַלְלוּ־יָהּ:

145:14. Although the first letters of the verses follow the *aleph-beis*, the letter נ is omitted, since it can be taken as an allusion to נְפִילָה, "downfall." Nevertheless, knowing that downfalls would take place, the psalmist comforted Israel by saying, "God supports all the fallen ones."

146:1. "Praise God!"

147:4. The stars number in the billions, but God is aware of each one and gives it a "name" that denotes its purpose in the universe. Thus, nothing goes unnoticed or unprovided for. (See *Isaiah* 40:26.)

⁸ ח Gracious and merciful is HASHEM, slow to anger, and great in [bestowing] kindness. ⁹ ט HASHEM is good to all; His mercies are on all His works. ¹⁰ י All Your works shall thank You, HASHEM, and Your devout ones will bless You. ¹¹ כ Of the glory of Your kingdom they will speak, and of Your power they will tell. ¹² ל To inform human beings of His mighty deeds, and the glorious splendor of His kingdom. ¹³ מ Your kingdom is a kingdom spanning all eternities, and Your dominion is throughout every generation. ¹⁴ ס* HASHEM supports all the fallen ones and straightens all the bent. ¹⁵ ע The eyes of all look to You with hope and You give them their food in its proper time; ¹⁶ פ You open Your hand, and satisfy the desire of every living thing. ¹⁷ צ Righteous is HASHEM in all His ways and magnanimous in all His deeds. ¹⁸ ק HASHEM is close to all who call upon Him, to all who call upon Him sincerely. ¹⁹ ר The will of those who fear Him He will do; and their cry He will hear, and He will save them. ²⁰ ש HASHEM protects all who love Him; but all the wicked He will destroy. ²¹ ת May my mouth declare the praise of HASHEM, and may all flesh bless His Holy Name forever and ever.

146

God is the One Who cares for the underprivileged and oppressed, despite the current ascendancy of our enemies.

¹ Halleluyah!* Praise HASHEM, O my Soul! ² I will praise HASHEM while I live, I will make music to my God while I exist. ³ Do not rely on nobles, nor on a human being, for he holds no salvation. ⁴ When his spirit departs he returns to his earth, on that day his plans all perish. ⁵ Praiseworthy is one whose help is Jacob's God, whose hope is in HASHEM, his God. ⁶ He is the Maker of heaven and earth, the sea and all that is in them; He safeguards truth forever; ⁷ He does justice for the exploited, He gives bread to the hungry. HASHEM releases the bound; ⁸ HASHEM gives sight to the blind; HASHEM straightens the bent; HASHEM loves the righteous. ⁹ HASHEM protects strangers, orphan and widow He encourages; but the way of the wicked He contorts. ¹⁰ HASHEM shall reign forever; your God, O Zion; from generation to generation. Halleluyah!

147

The Creator of the universe and all it contains will redeem and rebuild Jerusalem, from whence holiness and Torah emanate.

¹ Halleluyah! For it is good to make music to our God, for praise is pleasant and befitting. ² The Builder of Jerusalem is HASHEM; the outcast of Israel He will gather in. ³ He is the Healer of the brokenhearted, and the One Who binds up their sorrows. ⁴ He counts the number of the stars, to all of them He assigns names.* ⁵ Great is our Lord and abundant in strength; His understanding is beyond calculation. ⁶ HASHEM encourages the humble; He lowers the wicked down to the ground. ⁷ Call out to HASHEM with thanks, with the harp sing to our God — ⁸ Who covers the heavens with clouds, Who prepares rain for the earth, Who makes mountains sprout with grass. ⁹ He gives to an animal its food, to young ravens that cry out. ¹⁰ Not in the strength of the horse does He desire, and not in the legs of man does He favor. ¹¹ HASHEM favors those who fear Him, those who hope for His kindness. ¹² Praise HASHEM, O Jerusalem, laud your God, O Zion, ¹³ for He has strengthened the bars of your gates,* and blessed your children in your midst. ¹⁴ It is He Who makes your borders peaceful, and with the cream of the wheat He sates you; ¹⁵ He Who dispatches His utterance earthward; His word runs swiftly; ¹⁶ He Who gives snow like fleece, He scatters frost like ashes. ¹⁷ He hurls His ice like crumbs — who can stand before His cold? ¹⁸ He issues His command and it melts them; He blows His wind, the waters flow. ¹⁹ He relates His Words to Jacob, His statutes and His judgments to Israel. ²⁰ He did not do so for any other nation; such judgments — they know them not. Halleluyah!

147:13. The verse is figurative. The Jerusalem of the future will need no bars on its gates. The people will feel secure because God will protect their city (Radak).

קמח א-ב הַלְלוּ יָהּ ׀ הַלְלוּ אֶת־יהוה מִן־הַשָּׁמַיִם הַלְלוּהוּ בַּמְּרוֹמִים: הַלְלוּהוּ כָל־
ג מַלְאָכָיו הַלְלוּהוּ כָּל־צְבָאָו: הַלְלוּהוּ שֶׁמֶשׁ וְיָרֵחַ הַלְלוּהוּ כָּל־כּוֹכְבֵי
ד-ה אוֹר: הַלְלוּהוּ שְׁמֵי הַשָּׁמָיִם וְהַמַּיִם אֲשֶׁר ׀ מֵעַל הַשָּׁמָיִם: יְהַלְלוּ אֶת־שֵׁם
ו יהוה כִּי הוּא צִוָּה וְנִבְרָאוּ: וַיַּעֲמִידֵם לָעַד לְעוֹלָם חָק־נָתַן וְלֹא יַעֲבוֹר:
ז-ח הַלְלוּ אֶת־יהוה מִן־הָאָרֶץ תַּנִּינִים וְכָל־תְּהֹמוֹת: אֵשׁ וּבָרָד שֶׁלֶג וְקִיטוֹר
ט-י רוּחַ סְעָרָה עֹשָׂה דְבָרוֹ: הֶהָרִים וְכָל־גְּבָעוֹת עֵץ פְּרִי וְכָל־אֲרָזִים: הַחַיָּה
יא וְכָל־בְּהֵמָה רֶמֶשׂ וְצִפּוֹר כָּנָף: מַלְכֵי־אֶרֶץ וְכָל־לְאֻמִּים שָׂרִים וְכָל־
יב-יג שֹׁפְטֵי אָרֶץ: בַּחוּרִים וְגַם־בְּתוּלוֹת זְקֵנִים עִם־נְעָרִים: יְהַלְלוּ ׀ אֶת־שֵׁם
יד יהוה כִּי־נִשְׂגָּב שְׁמוֹ לְבַדּוֹ הוֹדוֹ עַל־אֶרֶץ וְשָׁמָיִם: וַיָּרֶם קֶרֶן ׀ לְעַמּוֹ
תְּהִלָּה לְכָל־חֲסִידָיו לִבְנֵי יִשְׂרָאֵל עַם־קְרֹבוֹ הַלְלוּ־יָהּ:

קמט א-ב הַלְלוּ יָהּ ׀ שִׁירוּ לַיהוה שִׁיר חָדָשׁ תְּהִלָּתוֹ בִּקְהַל חֲסִידִים: יִשְׂמַח
ג יִשְׂרָאֵל בְּעֹשָׂיו בְּנֵי־צִיּוֹן יָגִילוּ בְמַלְכָּם: יְהַלְלוּ שְׁמוֹ בְמָחוֹל בְּתֹף וְכִנּוֹר
ד-ה יְזַמְּרוּ־לוֹ: כִּי־רוֹצֶה יהוה בְּעַמּוֹ יְפָאֵר עֲנָוִים בִּישׁוּעָה: יַעְלְזוּ חֲסִידִים
ו בְּכָבוֹד יְרַנְּנוּ עַל־מִשְׁכְּבוֹתָם: רוֹמְמוֹת אֵל בִּגְרוֹנָם וְחֶרֶב פִּיפִיּוֹת בְּיָדָם:
ז-ח לַעֲשׂוֹת נְקָמָה בַּגּוֹיִם תּוֹכֵחֹת בַּלְאֻמִּים: לֶאְסֹר מַלְכֵיהֶם בְּזִקִּים
ט וְנִכְבְּדֵיהֶם בְּכַבְלֵי בַרְזֶל: לַעֲשׂוֹת בָּהֶם ׀ מִשְׁפָּט כָּתוּב הָדָר הוּא לְכָל־
חֲסִידָיו הַלְלוּ־יָהּ:

קנ א-ב הַלְלוּ יָהּ ׀ הַלְלוּ אֵל בְּקָדְשׁוֹ הַלְלוּהוּ בִּרְקִיעַ עֻזּוֹ: הַלְלוּהוּ בִגְבוּרֹתָיו
ג-ד הַלְלוּהוּ כְּרֹב גֻּדְלוֹ: הַלְלוּהוּ בְּתֵקַע שׁוֹפָר הַלְלוּהוּ בְּנֵבֶל וְכִנּוֹר:
ה הַלְלוּהוּ בְּתֹף וּמָחוֹל הַלְלוּהוּ בְּמִנִּים וְעֻגָב: הַלְלוּהוּ בְצִלְצְלֵי־שָׁמַע
ו הַלְלוּהוּ בְּצִלְצְלֵי תְרוּעָה: כֹּל הַנְּשָׁמָה תְּהַלֵּל יָהּ הַלְלוּ־יָהּ:

סכום פסוקי דספר תהלים אלפים וחמש מאות ועשרים ושבעה.
וסימנו ה' אהבתי מעון ביתך ומקום משכן כבודך. וסימנו בך אכבד.

149:5. The righteous will thank God for allowing them to go to bed without fear of danger and attack (Eitz Yosef).
149:7. Israel's primary goal is that the nations accept moral rebuke and mend their ways.

149:9. The future judgment upon the nations, which has already been described in Prophets.
150:6. Far greater than the most sublime instrumental songs of praise is the song of the human soul that utilizes its full potential in His service (Radak).

148

All of nature — celestial and terrestrial — joins in a grand symphony of joyous songs of praise to God.

[1] Halleluyah! Praise HASHEM from the heavens; praise Him in the heights: [2] Praise Him, all His angels; praise Him, all His legions. [3] Praise Him, sun and moon; praise Him, all bright stars. [4] Praise Him, the most exalted of the heavens and the waters that are above the heavens. [5] Let them praise the Name of HASHEM, for He commanded and they were created. [6] And He established them forever and ever, He issued a decree that will not change.

[7] Praise HASHEM from the earth: sea giants and all watery depths; [8] fire and hail, snow and vapor, stormy wind fulfilling His word; [9] mountains and all hills; fruitful trees and all cedars; [10] beasts and all cattle, crawling things and winged fowl; [11] kings of the earth and all regimes, princes and all judges on earth; [12] young men and also maidens, old men together with youths. [13] Let them praise the Name of HASHEM, for His Name alone is exalted; His glory is above earth and heaven. [14] And He will have exalted the pride of His nation, causing praise for all His devout ones, for the Children of Israel, His intimate people. Halleluyah!

149

The lofty praises uttered in honor of God will cut down the wicked and bring forward the glory of the righteous.

[1] Halleluyah! Sing to HASHEM a new song; His praise is in the congregation of the devout. [2] Let Israel exult in its Maker; let the Children of Zion rejoice in their King. [3] Let them praise His Name with dancing; with drums and harp let them make music to Him. [4] For HASHEM favors His people; He adorns the humble with salvation. [5] Let the devout exult in glory, let them sing joyously upon their beds. * [6] The lofty praises of God are in their throats, and a double-edged sword is in their hand — [7] to execute vengeance among the nations, rebukes* among the regimes; [8] to bind their kings with chains, and their nobles with fetters of iron; [9] to execute upon them written judgment* — that will be the splendor of all His devout ones. Halleluyah!

150

Praise God in every way possible for all the manifestations of His greatness.

[1] Halleluyah! Praise God in His Sanctuary; praise Him in the firmament of His power; [2] praise Him for His mighty acts; praise Him as befits His abundant greatness; [3] praise Him with the blast of the shofar; praise Him with lyre and harp; [4] praise Him with drum and dance; praise Him with organ and flute; [5] praise Him with clanging cymbals; praise Him with resonant trumpets. [6] Let all souls praise God, * Halleluyah!

148

1 Halleluyah! Praise Hashem from the heavens, praise Him in the heights. 2 Praise Him, all His angels; praise Him, all His legions. 3 Praise Him, sun and moon; praise Him, all bright stars. 4 Praise Him, the most exalted of the heavens, and the waters that are above the heavens. 5 Let them praise the Name of Hashem, for He commanded and they were created. 6 And He established them forever and ever; He issued a decree that will not change.

7 Praise Hashem from the earth, sea giants and all watery depths; 8 fire and hail, snow and vapor, storm wind fulfilling His word; 9 mountains and all hills, fruitful trees and all cedars; 10 beasts and all cattle, creeping things and winged fowl; 11 kings of the earth and all governments, princes and all judges on earth; 12 young men and also maidens, old men together with youths. 13 Let them praise the Name of Hashem, for His Name alone is exalted; His glory is above earth and heaven. 14 And He will have exalted the pride of His nation, causing praise for all His devout ones, for the Children of Israel, His intimate people. Halleluyah!

149

1 Halleluyah! Sing to Hashem a new song; His praise is in the congregation of the devout. 2 Let Israel exult in its Maker; let the Children of Zion rejoice in their King. 3 Let them praise His Name with dancing; with drums and harp let them make music to Him. 4 For Hashem favors His people; He adorns the humble with salvation. 5 Let the devout exult in glory; let them sing joyously upon their beds. 6 The lofty praises of God are in their throats, and a double-edged sword is in their hand — 7 to execute vengeance among the nations, rebukes among the regimes; 8 to bind their kings with chains, and their nobles with fetters of iron; 9 to execute upon them written judgment — that will be the splendor of all His devout ones. Halleluyah!

150

1 Halleluyah! Praise God in His Sanctuary; praise Him in the firmament of His power. 2 Praise Him for His mighty acts; praise Him as befits His abundant greatness. 3 Praise Him with the blast of the shofar; praise Him with lyre and harp. 4 Praise Him with drum and dance; praise Him with organ and flute. 5 Praise Him with clanging cymbals; praise Him with resonant trumpets. 6 Let all souls praise God, Halleluyah!

Proverbs משלי

When the wisest of all people shares his wisdom, one would expect his teachings to have more than one layer of meaning. Though they can be understood in their simplest, literal sense, they may also allude to much deeper ideas. So it is with King Solomon's Book of Proverbs. Few Books of Scripture are as widely quoted as Proverbs, for its wise and pithy aphorisms are so readily applicable to many areas of life. Nevertheless, both the Sages of the Talmud and the classic commentators say that the true meaning of these proverbs is allegorical, and that when we plumb their depths they allude to much more than their simple meaning. Rashi begins his commentary by saying that all Solomon's words are allusions and parables. For example, when Solomon speaks of a good woman he is alluding to the Torah; and when he speaks of a promiscuous woman, he is alluding to idolatry.

The last twenty-two verses of the Book of Proverbs — the beautiful Eishes Chayil paean to an accomplished and righteous woman — are surely its most familiar portion. There, too, although the simple meaning of the words is undoubtedly true, the passage is also interpreted as a song of praise to the Torah, to the Sabbath, and to the Matriarch Sarah, among others.

It is to be expected that Solomon would praise Torah, wisdom, and understanding throughout the Book. But there is another constant theme: fear of God. And not merely because Solomon himself was pious and demanded piety of others. He states very clearly at the outset that "the beginning of wisdom is fear of God" (1:7). Wisdom itself loses its meaning without fear of God — a lesson that is all too clear from the dismal achievements of some of history's brightest intellectuals.

Even a superficial reading of Proverbs yields countless nuggets of wisdom. Over and over, Solomon suggests, as we all know, that wealth brings popularity, but he goes on to insist that ill-gotten gains have no value. In other words, it is the quality of a bank account that matters, not its size. Solomon urges that with wealth comes responsibility to the poor and the obligation to heed their cries. Thus, the Book of Proverbs is a collection of lessons for life, and it contains formulas that give life the only meaning that truly matters.

א

א-ב מִשְׁלֵי שְׁלֹמֹה בֶן־דָּוִד מֶלֶךְ יִשְׂרָאֵל: לָדַעַת חָכְמָה וּמוּסָר לְהָבִין אִמְרֵי

ג-ד בִינָה: לָקַחַת מוּסַר הַשְׂכֵּל צֶדֶק וּמִשְׁפָּט וּמֵישָׁרִים: לָתֵת לִפְתָאיִם עָרְמָה

ה-ו לְנַעַר דַּעַת וּמְזִמָּה: יִשְׁמַע חָכָם וְיוֹסֶף לֶקַח וְנָבוֹן תַּחְבֻּלוֹת יִקְנֶה: לְהָבִין

ז מָשָׁל וּמְלִיצָה דִּבְרֵי חֲכָמִים וְחִידֹתָם: יִרְאַת יהוה רֵאשִׁית דָּעַת חָכְמָה
וּמוּסָר אֱוִילִים בָּזוּ:

ח-ט שְׁמַע בְּנִי מוּסַר אָבִיךָ וְאַל־תִּטֹּשׁ תּוֹרַת אִמֶּךָ: כִּי ׀ לִוְיַת חֵן הֵם לְרֹאשֶׁךָ

י-יא וַעֲנָקִים לְגַרְגְּרֹתֶיךָ: בְּנִי אִם־יְפַתּוּךָ חַטָּאִים אַל־תֹּבֵא: אִם־יֹאמְרוּ לְכָה

יב אִתָּנוּ נֶאֶרְבָה לְדָם נִצְפְּנָה לְנָקִי חִנָּם: נִבְלָעֵם כִּשְׁאוֹל חַיִּים וּתְמִימִים

יג-יד כְּיוֹרְדֵי בוֹר: כָּל־הוֹן יָקָר נִמְצָא נְמַלֵּא בָתֵּינוּ שָׁלָל: גּוֹרָלְךָ תַּפִּיל בְּתוֹכֵנוּ

טו כִּיס אֶחָד יִהְיֶה לְכֻלָּנוּ: בְּנִי אַל־תֵּלֵךְ בְּדֶרֶךְ אִתָּם מְנַע רַגְלְךָ מִנְּתִיבָתָם:

טז-יז כִּי רַגְלֵיהֶם לָרַע יָרוּצוּ וִימַהֲרוּ לִשְׁפָּךְ־דָּם: כִּי־חִנָּם מְזֹרָה הָרָשֶׁת בְּעֵינֵי

יח-יט כָל־בַּעַל כָּנָף: וְהֵם לְדָמָם יֶאֱרֹבוּ יִצְפְּנוּ לְנַפְשֹׁתָם: כֵּן אָרְחוֹת כָּל־בֹּצֵעַ
בָּצַע אֶת־נֶפֶשׁ בְּעָלָיו יִקָּח:

כ-כא חָכְמוֹת בַּחוּץ תָּרֹנָּה בָּרְחֹבוֹת תִּתֵּן קוֹלָהּ: בְּרֹאשׁ הֹמִיּוֹת תִּקְרָא בְּפִתְחֵי

כב שְׁעָרִים בָּעִיר אֲמָרֶיהָ תֹאמֵר: עַד־מָתַי ׀ פְּתָיִם תְּאֵהֲבוּ פֶתִי וְלֵצִים לָצוֹן

כג חָמְדוּ לָהֶם וּכְסִילִים יִשְׂנְאוּ־דָעַת: תָּשׁוּבוּ לְתוֹכַחְתִּי הִנֵּה אַבִּיעָה לָכֶם

כד רוּחִי אוֹדִיעָה דְבָרַי אֶתְכֶם: יַעַן קָרָאתִי וַתְּמָאֵנוּ נָטִיתִי יָדִי וְאֵין מַקְשִׁיב:

כה-כו וַתִּפְרְעוּ כָל־עֲצָתִי וְתוֹכַחְתִּי לֹא אֲבִיתֶם: גַּם־אֲנִי בְּאֵידְכֶם אֶשְׂחָק אֶלְעַג

כז בְּבֹא פַחְדְּכֶם: בְּבֹא °כְשׁוֹאָה [כְּשׁוֹאָה ק] ׀ פַּחְדְּכֶם וְאֵידְכֶם כְּסוּפָה

כח יֶאֱתֶה בְּבֹא עֲלֵיכֶם צָרָה וְצוּקָה: אָז יִקְרָאֻנְנִי וְלֹא אֶעֱנֶה יְשַׁחֲרֻנְנִי וְלֹא

כט-ל יִמְצָאֻנְנִי: תַּחַת כִּי־שָׂנְאוּ דָעַת וְיִרְאַת יהוה לֹא בָחָרוּ: לֹא־אָבוּ לַעֲצָתִי

לא-לב נָאֲצוּ כָּל־תּוֹכַחְתִּי: וְיֹאכְלוּ מִפְּרִי דַרְכָּם וּמִמֹּעֲצֹתֵיהֶם יִשְׂבָּעוּ: כִּי

לג מְשׁוּבַת פְּתָיִם תַּהַרְגֵם וְשַׁלְוַת כְּסִילִים תְּאַבְּדֵם: וְשֹׁמֵעַ לִי יִשְׁכָּן־בֶּטַח
וְשַׁאֲנַן מִפַּחַד רָעָה:

ב

א-ב בְּנִי אִם־תִּקַּח אֲמָרָי וּמִצְוֹתַי תִּצְפֹּן אִתָּךְ: לְהַקְשִׁיב לַחָכְמָה אָזְנֶךָ תַּטֶּה

ג-ד לִבְּךָ לַתְּבוּנָה: כִּי אִם לַבִּינָה תִקְרָא לַתְּבוּנָה תִּתֵּן קוֹלֶךָ: אִם־תְּבַקְשֶׁנָּה

ה כַכָּסֶף וְכַמַּטְמוֹנִים תַּחְפְּשֶׂנָּה: אָז תָּבִין יִרְאַת יהוה וְדַעַת אֱלֹהִים תִּמְצָא:

ו-ז כִּי־יהוה יִתֵּן חָכְמָה מִפִּיו דַּעַת וּתְבוּנָה: °וצפן [יִצְפֹּן ק] ׀ לַיְשָׁרִים תּוּשִׁיָּה

1:1. The Hebrew word מִשְׁלֵי, *mishlei*, here translated "proverbs," refers to various literary devices — allegories, aphorisms, maxims, metaphors, parables, proverbs — used to make the subject matter comprehensible (*Rabbeinu Bachya*); and to illustrate and clarify the intent of important teachings (*Ralbag*); and to clothe abstract concepts in concrete terms (*Malbim*).

1:4-5. These proverbs will benefit everyone, from the unlearned youth to the erudite elder (*Metzudos*).

1:7. Fear of God and subordination to Him, foster a thirst for wisdom and knowledge (*Rashi*).

1:12. We will trap them while they are still "whole," i.e., with all their wealth, for us to loot (*Ralbag*).

1:17. The blandishments of seducers is like the appetizing bait that hunters put in their nets. Unsuspecting birds partake as if it were a free feast (*Rashi*).

1:20. The wisdom of God's teaching is not limited to the synagogue and study hall; it appeals to people in the midst of human life and strivings (*R' Hirsch*).

1:32. Mistakenly interpreting their success, the wicked continue their ways, thinking that retribution

1 ¹ **T**he proverbs * of Solomon, son of David, king of Israel: ² [In order] to make
known words of wisdom and discipline; to make words of understanding
discernible; ³ to accept wise discipline, righteousness, justice, and fairness; ⁴ to
provide simpletons with cleverness, a youth with knowledge and design; * ⁵ that
a wise one may hear and increase [his] learning, and a discerning one may
acquire strategies; ⁶ to understand parable and epigram, the words of the wise
and their enigmas.

Solomon's purpose

⁷ The fear of HASHEM is the beginning of knowledge; foolish ones scorn wisdom
and discipline. * ⁸ Hear, my child, the discipline of your father, and do not forsake
the teaching of your mother. ⁹ For they are an adornment of grace for your head
and a chain for your neck.

Let God and your parents be your adornment

¹⁰ My child, if sinners seduce you, do not be enticed. ¹¹ If they say, "Come with
us; let us wait in ambush for bloodshed; let us lurk for an innocent one, without
cause. ¹² Like the grave, let us swallow them alive — whole, * like those descending to the pit. ¹³ All precious wealth is found [with them]; we will fill our houses
with booty. ¹⁴ Cast your lot among us; there will be one pouch for all of us!" ¹⁵ My
child, do not walk on the way with them; withhold your feet from their pathways.
¹⁶ For their feet run to evil and they hasten to spill blood. ¹⁷ For the net seems
spread out with free [bait], * in the eyes of every winged creature, ¹⁸ but they wait
in ambush for their blood and lurk for their souls. ¹⁹ Such are the ways of all
despoilers; they take the souls of [wealth's] owners.

*The blandish-
ments of the
wicked . . .*

*. . . are a
dangerous
trap*

*God's
message is
everywhere
— if you
care to see it*

²⁰ Wisdom sings out in the street; it gives forth its voice in the squares. * ²¹ It
cries out at the head of noisy throngs, at the entrances of the gates, in the city, it
speaks its words: ²² How long, O simpletons, will you love folly? Scoffers covet
mockery for themselves, and fools hate knowledge. ²³ Return to my reproof!
Behold, I will express my spirit to you; I will make my words known to you. ²⁴ But
because I have called you and you refused; because I stretched forth my hand and
no one listened; ²⁵ and you rejected my every counsel, and desired not my
reproof, ²⁶ I, too, will laugh at your misfortune and mock when your dread arrives.
²⁷ When your fear arrives as sudden darkness, and misfortune comes like a storm;
when affliction and oppression come upon you, ²⁸ then they will call me, but I will
not answer; they will search for me, but they will not find me. ²⁹ Because they
hated knowledge and did not choose fear of HASHEM, ³⁰ they did not desire my
counsel, they spurned all my reproof. ³¹ They will eat of the fruit of their way and
will be sated with their own schemes. ³² For the tranquility of the simpletons will
kill them, and the contentment of fools will destroy them. * ³³ But he who listens
to me will dwell securely, and will be undisturbed by fear of evil.

*But if you
refuse to
heed it,
retribution is
inevitable*

2 *Only if
you treasure
wisdom will
you acquire
it . . . for
then God will
grant it to
you*

¹ My child: If you accept My words and treasure my commandments with yourself, ² to make your ears attentive to wisdom, incline your heart to understanding
³ — [for] only if you call out to understanding [and] give forth your voice to discernment, ⁴ if you seek it as [if it were] silver, if you search for it as [if it were] hidden treasures — ⁵ then you will understand the fear of HASHEM, and discover the
knowledge of God. * ⁶ For HASHEM grants wisdom; from His mouth [come] knowledge and understanding. ⁷ He has secured the eternal Torah for the upright; *

---

will never come.

2:3-5. Hard work and single-minded pursuit can lead to
financial success; the identical efforts can lead to piety
and wisdom (*Malbim*).

2:7. The literal meaning of תּוּשִׁיָּה is "something substan-

tive, of independent existence." It is usually translated
"wise counsel" and is a reference to the wisdom of the
Torah, which is independent and eternal (see *Ibn Ezra*).
Rashi renders *The eternal Torah was hidden;* i.e., God hid
the Torah from mankind for twenty-six generations, until
He presented it to Israel.

ח מָגֵן לְהֹלְכֵי תֹם: לִנְצֹר אָרְחוֹת מִשְׁפָּט וְדֶרֶךְ °חסידו [°חֲסִידָיו ק]

ט יִשְׁמֹר: אָז תָּבִין צֶדֶק וּמִשְׁפָּט וּמֵישָׁרִים כָּל־מַעְגַּל־טוֹב: כִּי־תָבוֹא חָכְמָה

יא בְלִבֶּךָ וְדַעַת לְנַפְשְׁךָ יִנְעָם: מְזִמָּה תִּשְׁמֹר עָלֶיךָ תְּבוּנָה תִנְצְרֶכָּה:

יב-יג לְהַצִּילְךָ מִדֶּרֶךְ רָע מֵאִישׁ מְדַבֵּר תַּהְפֻּכוֹת: הַעֹזְבִים אָרְחוֹת יֹשֶׁר

יד לָלֶכֶת בְּדַרְכֵי־חֹשֶׁךְ: הַשְּׂמֵחִים לַעֲשׂוֹת רָע יָגִילוּ בְּתַהְפֻּכוֹת רָע: אֲשֶׁר

טו-טז אָרְחֹתֵיהֶם עִקְּשִׁים וּנְלוֹזִים בְּמַעְגְּלוֹתָם: לְהַצִּילְךָ מֵאִשָּׁה זָרָה מִנָּכְרִיָּה

יז אֲמָרֶיהָ הֶחֱלִיקָה: הַעֹזֶבֶת אַלּוּף נְעוּרֶיהָ וְאֶת־בְּרִית אֱלֹהֶיהָ שָׁכֵחָה: כִּי

יח-יט שָׁחָה אֶל־מָוֶת בֵּיתָהּ וְאֶל־רְפָאִים מַעְגְּלֹתֶיהָ: כָּל־בָּאֶיהָ לֹא יְשׁוּבוּן

כ וְלֹא־יַשִּׂיגוּ אָרְחוֹת חַיִּים: לְמַעַן תֵּלֵךְ בְּדֶרֶךְ טוֹבִים וְאָרְחוֹת צַדִּיקִים

כא-כב תִּשְׁמֹר: כִּי־יְשָׁרִים יִשְׁכְּנוּ־אָרֶץ וּתְמִימִים יִוָּתְרוּ בָהּ: וּרְשָׁעִים מֵאֶרֶץ

יִכָּרֵתוּ וּבוֹגְדִים יִסְּחוּ מִמֶּנָּה:

ג א-ב בְּנִי תּוֹרָתִי אַל־תִּשְׁכָּח וּמִצְוֹתַי יִצֹּר לִבֶּךָ: כִּי אֹרֶךְ יָמִים וּשְׁנוֹת חַיִּים

ג וְשָׁלוֹם יוֹסִיפוּ לָךְ: חֶסֶד וֶאֱמֶת אַל־יַעַזְבֻךָ קָשְׁרֵם עַל־גַּרְגְּרוֹתֶיךָ כָּתְבֵם

ד עַל־לוּחַ לִבֶּךָ: וּמְצָא־חֵן וְשֵׂכֶל־טוֹב בְּעֵינֵי אֱלֹהִים וְאָדָם:

ה-ו בְּטַח אֶל־יְהוָה בְּכָל־לִבֶּךָ וְאֶל־בִּינָתְךָ אַל־תִּשָּׁעֵן: בְּכָל־דְּרָכֶיךָ דָעֵהוּ

ז וְהוּא יְיַשֵּׁר אֹרְחֹתֶיךָ: אַל־תְּהִי חָכָם בְּעֵינֶיךָ יְרָא אֶת־יְהוָה וְסוּר מֵרָע:

ח-ט רִפְאוּת תְּהִי לְשָׁרֶּךָ וְשִׁקּוּי לְעַצְמוֹתֶיךָ: כַּבֵּד אֶת־יְהוָה מֵהוֹנֶךָ וּמֵרֵאשִׁית

כָּל־תְּבוּאָתֶךָ: וְיִמָּלְאוּ אֲסָמֶיךָ שָׂבָע וְתִירוֹשׁ יְקָבֶיךָ יִפְרֹצוּ:

יא-יב מוּסַר יְהוָה בְּנִי אַל־תִּמְאָס וְאַל־תָּקֹץ בְּתוֹכַחְתּוֹ: כִּי אֶת אֲשֶׁר יֶאֱהַב

יג יְהוָה יוֹכִיחַ וּכְאָב אֶת־בֵּן יִרְצֶה: אַשְׁרֵי אָדָם מָצָא חָכְמָה וְאָדָם יָפִיק

יד-טו תְּבוּנָה: כִּי טוֹב סַחְרָהּ מִסְּחַר־כָּסֶף וּמֵחָרוּץ תְּבוּאָתָהּ: יְקָרָה הִיא

טז °מפניים [°מִפְּנִינִים ק] וְכָל־חֲפָצֶיךָ לֹא יִשְׁווּ־בָהּ: אֹרֶךְ יָמִים בִּימִינָהּ

יז-יח בִּשְׂמֹאולָהּ עֹשֶׁר וְכָבוֹד: דְּרָכֶיהָ דַרְכֵי־נֹעַם וְכָל־נְתִיבוֹתֶיהָ שָׁלוֹם: עֵץ־

חַיִּים הִיא לַמַּחֲזִיקִים בָּהּ וְתֹמְכֶיהָ מְאֻשָּׁר:

יט יְהוָה בְּחָכְמָה יָסַד־אָרֶץ כּוֹנֵן שָׁמַיִם בִּתְבוּנָה: בְּדַעְתּוֹ תְּהוֹמוֹת נִבְקָעוּ

כא-כב וּשְׁחָקִים יִרְעֲפוּ־טָל: בְּנִי אַל־יָלֻזוּ מֵעֵינֶיךָ נְצֹר תֻּשִׁיָּה וּמְזִמָּה: וְיִהְיוּ

כג חַיִּים לְנַפְשֶׁךָ וְחֵן לְגַרְגְּרֹתֶיךָ: אָז תֵּלֵךְ לָבֶטַח דַּרְכֶּךָ וְרַגְלְךָ לֹא תִגּוֹף:

כד-כה אִם־תִּשְׁכַּב לֹא־תִפְחָד וְשָׁכַבְתָּ וְעָרְבָה שְׁנָתֶךָ: אַל־תִּירָא מִפַּחַד פִּתְאֹם

כו וּמִשֹּׁאַת רְשָׁעִים כִּי תָבֹא: כִּי־יְהוָה יִהְיֶה בְכִסְלֶךָ וְשָׁמַר רַגְלְךָ מִלָּכֶד:

2:12-15. Good character, righteous deeds, and Torah study will protect a person against mishap (*Vilna Gaon*).

2:16-19. Heresy is like a temptress. Once someone succumbs to either, it is difficult to detach oneself and repent (*Rashi*).

3:7. Do not think you can disregard those who reprimand or reprove you (*Rashi*).

3:8. Just as an adequate supply of blood — in a fetus, through the navel; later, by the new cells produced in the marrow — is vital to one's physical health, so is an adequate supply of Torah vital to one's spiritual health, whether a neophyte or an accomplished scholar (*Ralbag*).

3:11-12. Just as physical pain helps a person by warning him of the underlying cause of the symptom, so too it should be regarded as a loving Father's message that His child must correct his behavior. In that sense, physical suffering should be welcomed as proof of God's regard.

it is a shield for those who walk in innocence, [8] *to safeguard the paths of justice, for He protects the way of His devout ones.*

The Torah will save you from perverse ideas . . . . . . from evildoers . . .

[9] *Then you will understand righteousness and justice, fairness and every good course,* [10] *when wisdom enters your heart and knowledge becomes pleasant to your soul.* [11] *[A wise] design will watch over you [and] understanding will safeguard you —* [12] *to rescue you* * *from the way of evil, from a person who speaks duplicities,* [13] *[from those] who forsake paths of uprightness to walk in ways of darkness,* [14] *who are glad to do evil, who rejoice in the duplicities of evil,* [15] *whose*

. . . and from purveyors of temptation

ways are crooked and who go astray in their courses; [16] *to save you from the strange woman,* * *from the foreign woman, whose words are glib,* [17] *who forsakes the husband of her youth and forgets the covenant of her God,* [18] *for her house declines toward death, and her course toward the lifeless,* [19] *and all who*

For in the end, the just will prevail

come to her do not return, nor do they attain the paths of life — [20] *in order that you may walk in the way of the good and keep the paths of the righteous.* [21] *For the upright will dwell in the land [forever], and the wholehearted will remain in it;* [22] *but the wicked will be cut off from the land, and the faithless uprooted from it.*

3

Cleave to the Torah

[1] **M**y *child, do not forget My Torah, and let your heart guard My commandments,* [2] *for they add to you length of days and years of life and peace.* [3] *Kindness and truth will not forsake you. Bind them upon your neck; inscribe them on the tablet of your heart,* [4] *and you will find favor and goodly wisdom in the eyes of God and man.*

Trust in God will bring you success

[5] *Trust in* HASHEM *with all your heart and do not rely upon your own understanding.* [6] *In all your ways know Him, and He will smooth your paths.* [7] *Do not be wise in your own eyes;* * *fear* HASHEM *and turn away from evil.* [8] *It will be health to your navel* * *and marrow to your bones.* [9] *Honor* HASHEM *with your wealth, and with the first of all your produce,* [10] *then your storehouses will be filled with plenty, and the wine of your vats will burst forth.*

Seek discipline and wisdom

[11] *My child, do not despise* HASHEM'S *discipline,* * *and do not despise His reproof,* [12] *for* HASHEM *admonishes the one He loves, and like a father He mollifies the child.* [13] *Praiseworthy is a person who has found wisdom, a person who can derive understanding [from it],* * [14] *for its commerce is better than the commerce of silver, and its produce [is better] than fine gold.* [15] *It is more precious than pearls, and all your desires cannot compare to it.* [16] *Length of days is at its right; at its left, wealth and honor.* [17] *Its ways are ways of pleasantness and all its pathways are peace.* [18] *It is a tree of life to those who grasp it, and its supporters are praiseworthy.*

The Torah and its wisdom are your guarantors for a good life

[19] HASHEM *founded the earth with wisdom; He established the heavens with understanding;* [20] *through His knowledge,* * *the depths were cleaved, and the heavens dripped dew.* [21] *My child, do not let them stray from your eyes; safeguard the eternal Torah* * *and [its]wise design.* [22] *They will be life to your soul and a graceful [ornament] for your neck.* [23] *Then you will walk on your way securely, and your foot will not stumble.* [24] *When you lie down you will not fear; you will lie down and your sleep will be pleasant.* [25] *You will not fear sudden terror, nor the holocaust of the wicked when it comes.* [26] *For* HASHEM *will be your security, and He will guard your feet from entrapment.*

3:13. "Wisdom," an accumulation of facts, is the raw material from which one can "understand," i.e., derive new knowledge through clear comprehension of information.

3:19-20. God created the universe with the wisdom, understanding, and knowledge of His Torah (*Rashi*). **3:21.** See 2:7.

כז-כח אַל־תִּמְנַע־טוֹב מִבְּעָלָיו בִּהְיוֹת לְאֵל °יָדֶיךָ [°יָדְךָ ק] לַעֲשׂוֹת: אַל־תֹּאמַר
°לְרֵעֲךָ [°לְרֵעֶךָ ק] לֵךְ וָשׁוּב וּמָחָר אֶתֵּן וְיֵשׁ אִתָּךְ: אַל־תַּחֲרֹשׁ עַל־
כט-ל רֵעֲךָ רָעָה וְהוּא־יוֹשֵׁב לָבֶטַח אִתָּךְ: אַל־°תרוב [°תָּרִיב ק] עִם־אָדָם חִנָּם
לא-לב אִם־לֹא גְמָלְךָ רָעָה: אַל־תְּקַנֵּא בְּאִישׁ חָמָס וְאַל־תִּבְחַר בְּכָל־דְּרָכָיו: כִּי
לג תוֹעֲבַת יהוה נָלוֹז וְאֶת־יְשָׁרִים סוֹדוֹ: מְאֵרַת יהוה בְּבֵית רָשָׁע וּנְוֵה
לד צַדִּיקִים יְבָרֵךְ: אִם־לַלֵּצִים הוּא־יָלִיץ °ולעניים [°וְלַעֲנָוִים ק] יִתֶּן־חֵן:
לה כָּבוֹד חֲכָמִים יִנְחָלוּ וּכְסִילִים מֵרִים קָלוֹן:

ד א-ב שִׁמְעוּ בָנִים מוּסַר אָב וְהַקְשִׁיבוּ לָדַעַת בִּינָה: כִּי לֶקַח טוֹב נָתַתִּי לָכֶם
ג תּוֹרָתִי אַל־תַּעֲזֹבוּ: כִּי־בֵן הָיִיתִי לְאָבִי רַךְ וְיָחִיד לִפְנֵי אִמִּי: וַיֹּרֵנִי וַיֹּאמֶר
ד-ה לִי יִתְמָךְ־דְּבָרַי לִבֶּךָ שְׁמֹר מִצְוֺתַי וֶחְיֵה: קְנֵה חָכְמָה קְנֵה בִינָה אַל־
ו תִּשְׁכַּח וְאַל־תֵּט מֵאִמְרֵי־פִי: אַל־תַּעַזְבֶהָ וְתִשְׁמְרֶךָּ אֱהָבֶהָ וְתִצְּרֶךָּ:
ז-ח רֵאשִׁית חָכְמָה קְנֵה חָכְמָה וּבְכָל־קִנְיָנְךָ קְנֵה בִינָה: סַלְסְלֶהָ וּתְרוֹמְמֶךָּ
ט תְּכַבֵּדְךָ כִּי תְחַבְּקֶנָּה: תִּתֵּן לְרֹאשְׁךָ לִוְיַת־חֵן עֲטֶרֶת תִּפְאֶרֶת תְּמַגְּנֶךָּ:
י-יא שְׁמַע בְּנִי וְקַח אֲמָרָי וְיִרְבּוּ לְךָ שְׁנוֹת חַיִּים: בְּדֶרֶךְ חָכְמָה הֹרֵתִיךָ
יב הִדְרַכְתִּיךָ בְּמַעְגְּלֵי־יֹשֶׁר: בְּלֶכְתְּךָ לֹא־יֵצַר צַעֲדֶךָ וְאִם־תָּרוּץ לֹא תִכָּשֵׁל:
יג-יד הַחֲזֵק בַּמּוּסָר אַל־תֶּרֶף נִצְּרֶהָ כִּי־הִיא חַיֶּיךָ: בְּאֹרַח רְשָׁעִים אַל־תָּבֹא
טו וְאַל־תְּאַשֵּׁר בְּדֶרֶךְ רָעִים: פְּרָעֵהוּ אַל־תַּעֲבָר־בּוֹ שְׂטֵה מֵעָלָיו וַעֲבוֹר: כִּי
טז-יז לֹא יִשְׁנוּ אִם־לֹא יָרֵעוּ וְנִגְזְלָה שְׁנָתָם אִם־לֹא °יכשולו [°יַכְשִׁילוּ ק]: כִּי
יח לָחֲמוּ לֶחֶם רֶשַׁע וְיֵין חֲמָסִים יִשְׁתּוּ: וְאֹרַח צַדִּיקִים כְּאוֹר נֹגַהּ הוֹלֵךְ וָאוֹר
יט עַד־נְכוֹן הַיּוֹם: דֶּרֶךְ רְשָׁעִים כָּאֲפֵלָה לֹא יָדְעוּ בַּמֶּה יִכָּשֵׁלוּ: בְּנִי
כ-כא לִדְבָרַי הַקְשִׁיבָה לַאֲמָרַי הַט־אָזְנֶךָ: אַל־יַלִּיזוּ מֵעֵינֶיךָ שָׁמְרֵם בְּתוֹךְ לְבָבֶךָ:
כב-כג כִּי־חַיִּים הֵם לְמֹצְאֵיהֶם וּלְכָל־בְּשָׂרוֹ מַרְפֵּא: מִכָּל־מִשְׁמָר נְצֹר לִבֶּךָ כִּי־
כד מִמֶּנּוּ תּוֹצְאוֹת חַיִּים: הָסֵר מִמְּךָ עִקְּשׁוּת פֶּה וּלְזוּת שְׂפָתַיִם הַרְחֵק מִמֶּךָּ:
כה-כו עֵינֶיךָ לְנֹכַח יַבִּיטוּ וְעַפְעַפֶּיךָ יַיְשִׁרוּ נֶגְדֶּךָ: פַּלֵּס מַעְגַּל רַגְלֶךָ וְכָל־דְּרָכֶיךָ
כז יִכֹּנוּ: אַל־תֵּט־יָמִין וּשְׂמֹאול הָסֵר רַגְלְךָ מֵרָע:

ה א-ב בְּנִי לְחָכְמָתִי הַקְשִׁיבָה לִתְבוּנָתִי הַט־אָזְנֶךָ: לִשְׁמֹר מְזִמּוֹת וְדַעַת שְׂפָתֶיךָ
ג-ד יִנְצֹרוּ: כִּי נֹפֶת תִּטֹּפְנָה שִׂפְתֵי זָרָה וְחָלָק מִשֶּׁמֶן חִכָּהּ: וְאַחֲרִיתָהּ מָרָה
ה-ו כַלַּעֲנָה חַדָּה כְּחֶרֶב פִּיּוֹת: רַגְלֶיהָ יֹרְדוֹת מָוֶת שְׁאוֹל צְעָדֶיהָ יִתְמֹכוּ: אֹרַח

3:27-28. Do not be reluctant or slow to help others. Even unwarranted delay is a form of refusal.

3:34. One is readily influenced by the company one keeps (*Rashi*).

4:1. The Father is God (*Rashi*), and His discipline is the Torah (*Ralbag*).

4:3. Solomon assures his listeners that his criticism of their conduct does not indicate ill-will on his part. To the contrary, he was treated tenderly by his parents, and absorbed their feelings of love and tenderness (*Rashi*).

4:7. Wisdom must be acquired, not invented. Then true understanding is gained by probing the implications of wisdom (*R' Hirsch*).

4:23. More than anything, a person must guard his heart, which is pivotal in focusing thoughts and desires away from the negative and toward the positive (*Rabbeinu Yonah*).

5:3. The forbidden woman is a metaphor for heresy (*Rashi*).

5:4. Falling prey to heresy leads to a double death: loss

Be kind and thought-ful . . .   ²⁷ Do not withhold good from its rightful recipients, when you have the power to do it. * ²⁸ Do not tell your neighbor, "Leave and come back; tomorrow I will give it," when it is [already] by you. ²⁹ Do not devise evil against your neighbor, one who dwells securely near you. ³⁰ Do not quarrel with any man without cause, if he has done you no evil. ³¹ Do not envy the man of violence, and do not choose any of his ways, ³² for one who deviates is an abomination to HASHEM; and His counsel is with the upright. ³³ HASHEM's blight is upon the house of the wicked; He blesses the abode of the righteous. ³⁴ If [one is drawn] to the scoffers, he will scoff; but [if one is drawn] to the humble, he will find favor. * ³⁵ The wise inherit honor and fools generate disgrace.

. . . avoid strife, violence, and scoffing

4

A loving chastisement

¹ **H**ear, children, the Father's discipline, * and be attentive to know understand-ing: ² "For I have given you a good teaching, do not forsake My Torah." ³ For I was a son to my father, a tender and only son before my mother. * ⁴ He taught me, and said to me, "Let my words sustain your heart; observe my commandments and live. ⁵ Acquire wisdom; acquire understanding. Do not forget and do not stray from the words of my mouth. ⁶ Do not forsake [the Torah], and it will guard you; love it and it will protect you."

Appreciate the value of wisdom

⁷ The beginning of wisdom is to acquire wisdom; from your every acquisition acquire understanding. * ⁸ Caress it and it will uplift you; it will honor you when you embrace it. ⁹ It will set an adornment of grace upon your head; it will bestow a crown of splendor upon you.

The Torah guarantees meaningful life

¹⁰ Hear, my child, take my words; and they will add years of life to you. ¹¹ I instruct you in the way of wisdom; I lead you in courses of fairness. ¹² When you walk, your steps will not be constricted, and when you run, you will not stumble. ¹³ Hold fast to discipline; do not let go. Guard it, for it is your life. ¹⁴ Do not come to the path of the wicked, and do not walk in the way of evildoers. ¹⁵ Reject it; do not pass on it; veer away from it and pass on. ¹⁶ For [the wicked] cannot sleep if they do not do evil; their sleep will be robbed if they do not cause others to stumble. ¹⁷ For their bread is the bread of wickedness, and they drink the wine of violence.

Evil people are worse than one can imagine

Righteous and wicked; light and darkness

¹⁸ The path of the righteous is like the glow of sunlight, growing brighter until high noon, ¹⁹ [but] the way of the wicked is like darkness, they know not upon what they stumble.

²⁰ My child, be attentive to my speech; incline your ear to my words. ²¹ Let them not depart from your eyes; guard them within your heart. ²² For they are life to he who finds them, and healing for all his flesh. ²³ More than you guard anything, safeguard your heart, * for from it are the sources of life. ²⁴ Remove from yourself distortion of the mouth, and distance perversity of lips from yourself. ²⁵ Let your eyes look ahead, and your eyelids will direct your path. ²⁶ Weigh the course of your foot, and all your ways will be established. ²⁷ Do not deviate right or left; remove your foot from evil.

Safeguard that which matters most

Consider your deeds carefully

5

Beware of enticement; it leads to doom

¹ **M**y child, be attentive to my wisdom, give ear to my understanding, ² to heed [wise] designs and let your lips guard wisdom. ³ For the lips of a forbidden woman* drip honey, and her palate is smoother than oil, ⁴ but her end is as bitter as wormwood, as sharp as a double-edged sword. * ⁵ Her feet lead to death; her footsteps support her to the grave. ⁶ Lest you liken the path

of both This World and the World to Come (*Midrash Mishlei*).

חַיִּים פֶּן־תְּפַלֵּס נָעוּ מַעְגְּלֹתֶיהָ לֹא תֵדָע:

ז־ח וְעַתָּה בָנִים שִׁמְעוּ־לִי וְאַל־תָּסוּרוּ מֵאִמְרֵי־פִי: הַרְחֵק מֵעָלֶיהָ דַרְכֶּךָ

ט וְאַל־תִּקְרַב אֶל־פֶּתַח בֵּיתָהּ: פֶּן־תִּתֵּן לַאֲחֵרִים הוֹדֶךָ וּשְׁנֹתֶיךָ לְאַכְזָרִי:

י־יא פֶּן־יִשְׂבְּעוּ זָרִים כֹּחֶךָ וַעֲצָבֶיךָ בְּבֵית נָכְרִי: וְנָהַמְתָּ בְאַחֲרִיתֶךָ בִּכְלוֹת

יב בְּשָׂרְךָ וּשְׁאֵרֶךָ: וְאָמַרְתָּ אֵיךְ שָׂנֵאתִי מוּסָר וְתוֹכַחַת נָאַץ לִבִּי: וְלֹא־

יד שָׁמַעְתִּי בְּקוֹל מוֹרָי וְלִמְלַמְּדַי לֹא־הִטִּיתִי אָזְנִי: כִּמְעַט הָיִיתִי בְכָל־רָע

טו־טז בְּתוֹךְ קָהָל וְעֵדָה: שְׁתֵה־מַיִם מִבּוֹרֶךָ וְנֹזְלִים מִתּוֹךְ בְּאֵרֶךָ: יָפוּצוּ

יז מַעְיְנֹתֶיךָ חוּצָה בָּרְחֹבוֹת פַּלְגֵי־מָיִם: יִהְיוּ־לְךָ לְבַדֶּךָ וְאֵין לְזָרִים אִתָּךְ:

יח־יט יְהִי־מְקוֹרְךָ בָרוּךְ וּשְׂמַח מֵאֵשֶׁת נְעוּרֶךָ: אַיֶּלֶת אֲהָבִים וְיַעֲלַת חֵן דַּדֶּיהָ

כ יְרַוֻּךָ בְכָל־עֵת בְּאַהֲבָתָהּ תִּשְׁגֶּה תָמִיד: וְלָמָּה תִשְׁגֶּה בְנִי בְזָרָה וּתְחַבֵּק

כא חֵק נָכְרִיָּה: כִּי נֹכַח ו עֵינֵי יְהוָה דַּרְכֵי־אִישׁ וְכָל־מַעְגְּלֹתָיו מְפַלֵּס:

כב־כג עֲווֹנוֹתָיו יִלְכְּדֻנוֹ אֶת־הָרָשָׁע וּבְחַבְלֵי חַטָּאתוֹ יִתָּמֵךְ: הוּא יָמוּת בְּאֵין

ו א מוּסָר וּבְרֹב אִוַּלְתּוֹ יִשְׁגֶּה: בְּנִי אִם־עָרַבְתָּ לְרֵעֶךָ תָּקַעְתָּ לַזָּר כַּפֶּיךָ:

ב־ג נוֹקַשְׁתָּ בְאִמְרֵי־פִיךָ נִלְכַּדְתָּ בְּאִמְרֵי־פִיךָ: עֲשֵׂה זֹאת אֵפוֹא ו בְּנִי וְהִנָּצֵל כִּי

ד בָאתָ בְכַף־רֵעֶךָ לֵךְ הִתְרַפֵּס וּרְהַב רֵעֶיךָ: אַל־תִּתֵּן שֵׁנָה לְעֵינֶיךָ וּתְנוּמָה

ה לְעַפְעַפֶּיךָ: הִנָּצֵל כִּצְבִי מִיָּד וּכְצִפּוֹר מִיַּד יָקוּשׁ:

ו־ז לֵךְ־אֶל־נְמָלָה עָצֵל רְאֵה דְרָכֶיהָ וַחֲכָם: אֲשֶׁר אֵין־לָהּ קָצִין שֹׁטֵר וּמֹשֵׁל:

ח־ט תָּכִין בַּקַּיִץ לַחְמָהּ אָגְרָה בַקָּצִיר מַאֲכָלָהּ: עַד־מָתַי עָצֵל ו תִּשְׁכָּב מָתַי

י־יא תָּקוּם מִשְּׁנָתֶךָ: מְעַט שֵׁנוֹת מְעַט תְּנוּמוֹת מְעַט ו חִבֻּק יָדַיִם לִשְׁכָּב: וּבָא־

כִמְהַלֵּךְ רֵאשֶׁךָ וּמַחְסֹרְךָ כְּאִישׁ מָגֵן:

יב־יג אָדָם בְּלִיַּעַל אִישׁ אָוֶן הוֹלֵךְ עִקְּשׁוּת פֶּה: קֹרֵץ בְּעֵינָיו מֹלֵל °בְּרַגְלוֹ

יד [בְּרַגְלָיו ק] °מֹרֶה בְּאֶצְבְּעֹתָיו: תַּהְפֻּכוֹת ו בְּלִבּוֹ חֹרֵשׁ רָע בְּכָל־עֵת

טו °מְדָנִים [מִדְיָנִים ק] יְשַׁלֵּחַ: עַל־כֵּן פִּתְאֹם יָבוֹא אֵידוֹ פֶּתַע יִשָּׁבֵר וְאֵין

מַרְפֵּא:

טז־יז שֶׁשׁ־הֵנָּה שָׂנֵא יְהוָה וְשֶׁבַע °תּוֹעֲבַת [תּוֹעֲבוֹת ק] נַפְשׁוֹ: עֵינַיִם רָמוֹת

יח לְשׁוֹן שָׁקֶר וְיָדַיִם שֹׁפְכוֹת דָּם־נָקִי: לֵב חֹרֵשׁ מַחְשְׁבוֹת אָוֶן רַגְלַיִם

יט מְמַהֲרוֹת לָרוּץ לָרָעָה: יָפִיחַ כְּזָבִים עֵד שָׁקֶר וּמְשַׁלֵּחַ מְדָנִים בֵּין

כ אַחִים: נְצֹר בְּנִי מִצְוַת אָבִיךָ וְאַל־תִּטֹּשׁ תּוֹרַת

5:9. The master of *Gehinnom* (*Rashi*), who will exact punishment from sinners.

5:11-14. At life's end you will recognize the truth and the error of your life. Too late, you will regret your blind stubbornness.

5:15-23. Instead of seeking happiness with forbidden women, i.e., heresy, remain with your own cistern, i.e., your wife and your Torah, and enjoy the reward of springs, i.e., children.

5:19. Just as a hind remains beloved to her mate, the Torah is most beloved by those who study it (*Rashi*).

5:21. God knows man's actions and weighs his sins and merits (*Rashi*).

6:1-2. Even when performing good deeds, consider all possible consequences before obligating yourself to others (*R' Hirsch*).

6:3-5. Since you are in the lender's power, hasten to implore him to extend the time of repayment (*R' Saadiah Gaon*). Then, continue to keep after the borrower to repay what he can.

6:6-8. Learn diligence from the ant. It lives just six months, but industriously gathers much more food than *of life [to hers] — her courses wander [astray]; you cannot know.*

Her wiles come at a prohibitive price

⁷ And now, [my] children, listen to me, and do not stray from the words of my mouth. ⁸ Distance your way from her, and do not come near the door of her house, ⁹ lest you give your glory to others, and your [remaining] years to the cruel one.* ¹⁰ Lest strangers be sated with your strength, and your painfully earned

Too late, you will regret your horrendous error

wealth [be] in a stranger's house. ¹¹ You will groan at your [life's] end when your flesh and your body perish.* ¹² Then you will say, "How could I have hated discipline, and my heart spurned rebuke? ¹³ I have not listened to the voice of my masters, and have not inclined my ear to my teachers. ¹⁴ For a pittance [of enjoyment] I was into everything evil, in the presence of congregation and assembly!"

Remain loyal to your wife and your Torah

¹⁵ Drink water from your own cistern and flowing water from your own well.* ¹⁶ [Then] your springs will spread outwards, streams of water in the thoroughfares. ¹⁷ They will be yours alone, strangers not sharing them with you. ¹⁸ Your source will be blessed, and you will rejoice with the wife of your youth, ¹⁹ a beloved hind inspiring favor;* her breasts will sate you at all times; you will always be intoxicated with her love.

The wicked will be trapped by their own sins

²⁰ Why then, my son, should you err with a strange woman and embrace an alien bosom? ²¹ For a man's ways are opposite HASHEM's eyes, and He weighs all his courses.* ²² The iniquities of the wicked one will trap him, and he will be suspended in the cords of his sins. ²³ He will die for refusing discipline, and for the abundant foolishness with which he strayed.

6

Avoid commitments that are beyond your abilities

¹ **M**y child, if you have been a guarantor for your friend,* if you have given your handshake for a stranger, ² you have been trapped by the words of your mouth, snared by the words of your mouth. ³ Do this, therefore, my child, and be rescued; for you have come into your fellow's hand. Go humble yourself [before him], and placate your fellow.* ⁴ Give not sleep to your eyes, nor slumber to your eyelids; ⁵ be rescued like a deer from the [hunter's] hand, and like a bird from the fowler.

From an ant learn to be industrious

⁶ Go to the ant, you sluggard; see its ways and grow wise. ⁷ Though there is neither officer nor guard nor ruler over her, ⁸ she prepares her food in the summer and stores up her food in the harvest time.* ⁹ How long will you recline, O sluggard? When will you arise from your sleep? ¹⁰ A little sleep,* a little slumber, a little folding of the hands to recline, ¹¹ and your poverty will come like a traveler, and your lacking like an armed man.

Dishonest people will get their undoing

¹² The lawless man is a man of iniquity: He goes forth with distortion of the mouth; ¹³ he winks with his eyes, shuffles with his feet, points with his fingers; ¹⁴ duplicity in his heart, he plots evil all the time; he stirs up strife. ¹⁵ Therefore, his undoing will come suddenly; he will be broken in an instant, without healing.

God hates those who incite strife

¹⁶ HASHEM hates these six, but the seventh* is the abomination of His soul: ¹⁷ haughty eyes, a false tongue, and hands spilling innocent blood, ¹⁸ a heart plotting iniquitous thoughts, feet hastening to run to evil, ¹⁹ a false witness spouting lies; and one who stirs up strife among brothers.

²⁰ Heed, my son, the command of your father, and do not forsake the teaching

---

it needs. So too, man must also perform good deeds in This World so his soul will have merit in the World to Come (*Devarim Rabbah*).

6:10-11. With a minimum of sleep and relaxation, your

periods of poverty and want will soon pass, like a traveler or a soldier girded for battle, who spends but a night and then continues on his way (*Ralbag*).

6:16. The seventh is the one who stirs up strife (v. 19).

כא־כב אִמֶּךָ: קָשְׁרֵם עַל־לִבְּךָ תָמִיד עָנְדֵם עַל־גַּרְגְּרֹתֶךָ: בְּהִתְהַלֶּכְךָ ׀ תַּנְחֶה

כג אֹתָךְ בְּשָׁכְבְּךָ תִּשְׁמֹר עָלֶיךָ וַהֲקִיצוֹתָ הִיא תְשִׂיחֶךָ: כִּי נֵר מִצְוָה וְתוֹרָה

כד אוֹר וְדֶרֶךְ חַיִּים תּוֹכְחוֹת מוּסָר: לִשְׁמָרְךָ מֵאֵשֶׁת רָע מֵחֶלְקַת לָשׁוֹן

כה־כו נָכְרִיָּה: אַל־תַּחְמֹד יָפְיָהּ בִּלְבָבֶךָ וְאַל־תִּקָּחֲךָ בְּעַפְעַפֶּיהָ: כִּי בְעַד־אִשָּׁה

כו זוֹנָה עַד־כִּכַּר לָחֶם וְאֵשֶׁת אִישׁ נֶפֶשׁ יְקָרָה תָצוּד: הֲיַחְתֶּה אִישׁ אֵשׁ

כח בְּחֵיקוֹ וּבְגָדָיו לֹא תִשָּׂרַפְנָה: אִם־יְהַלֵּךְ אִישׁ עַל־הַגֶּחָלִים וְרַגְלָיו לֹא

כט־ל תִּכָּוֶינָה: כֵּן הַבָּא אֶל־אֵשֶׁת רֵעֵהוּ לֹא יִנָּקֶה כָּל־הַנֹּגֵעַ בָּהּ: לֹא־יָבוּזוּ לַגַּנָּב

ל כִּי יִגְנוֹב לְמַלֵּא נַפְשׁוֹ כִּי יִרְעָב: וְנִמְצָא יְשַׁלֵּם שִׁבְעָתָיִם אֶת־כָּל־הוֹן

לב־לג בֵּיתוֹ יִתֵּן: נֹאֵף אִשָּׁה חֲסַר־לֵב מַשְׁחִית נַפְשׁוֹ הוּא יַעֲשֶׂנָּה: נֶגַע־וְקָלוֹן

לד יִמְצָא וְחֶרְפָּתוֹ לֹא תִמָּחֶה: כִּי־קִנְאָה חֲמַת־גָּבֶר וְלֹא־יַחְמוֹל בְּיוֹם נָקָם:

ז לה־א לֹא־יִשָּׂא פְּנֵי כָל־כֹּפֶר וְלֹא־יֹאבֶה כִּי תַרְבֶּה־שֹׁחַד: בְּנִי שְׁמֹר

ב אֲמָרָי וּמִצְוֹתַי תִּצְפֹּן אִתָּךְ: שְׁמֹר מִצְוֹתַי וֶחְיֵה וְתוֹרָתִי כְּאִישׁוֹן עֵינֶיךָ:

ג־ד קָשְׁרֵם עַל־אֶצְבְּעֹתֶיךָ כָּתְבֵם עַל־לוּחַ לִבֶּךָ: אֱמֹר לַחָכְמָה אֲחֹתִי אָתְּ

ה־ו וּמֹדָע לַבִּינָה תִקְרָא: לִשְׁמָרְךָ מֵאִשָּׁה זָרָה מִנָּכְרִיָּה אֲמָרֶיהָ הֶחֱלִיקָה: כִּי

ז בְּחַלּוֹן בֵּיתִי בְּעַד אֶשְׁנַבִּי נִשְׁקָפְתִּי: וָאֵרֶא בַפְּתָאיִם אָבִינָה בַבָּנִים נַעַר

ח־ט חֲסַר־לֵב: עֹבֵר בַּשּׁוּק אֵצֶל פִּנָּהּ וְדֶרֶךְ בֵּיתָהּ יִצְעָד: בְּנֶשֶׁף־בְּעֶרֶב יוֹם

י־יא בְּאִישׁוֹן לַיְלָה וַאֲפֵלָה: וְהִנֵּה אִשָּׁה לִקְרָאתוֹ שִׁית זוֹנָה וּנְצֻרַת לֵב: הֹמִיָּה

יב הִיא וְסֹרָרֶת בְּבֵיתָהּ לֹא־יִשְׁכְּנוּ רַגְלֶיהָ: פַּעַם ׀ בַּחוּץ פַּעַם בָּרְחֹבוֹת וְאֵצֶל

יג־יד כָּל־פִּנָּה תֶאֱרֹב: וְהֶחֱזִיקָה בּוֹ וְנָשְׁקָה לּוֹ הֵעֵזָה פָנֶיהָ וַתֹּאמַר לוֹ: זִבְחֵי

טו שְׁלָמִים עָלָי הַיּוֹם שִׁלַּמְתִּי נְדָרָי: עַל־כֵּן יָצָאתִי לִקְרָאתֶךָ לְשַׁחֵר פָּנֶיךָ

טז־יז וָאֶמְצָאֶךָּ: מַרְבַדִּים רָבַדְתִּי עַרְשִׂי חֲטֻבוֹת אֵטוּן מִצְרָיִם: נַפְתִּי מִשְׁכָּבִי

יח־יט מֹר אֲהָלִים וְקִנָּמוֹן: לְכָה נִרְוֶה דֹדִים עַד־הַבֹּקֶר נִתְעַלְּסָה בָּאֳהָבִים: כִּי אֵין

כ הָאִישׁ בְּבֵיתוֹ הָלַךְ בְּדֶרֶךְ מֵרָחוֹק: צְרוֹר־הַכֶּסֶף לָקַח בְּיָדוֹ לְיוֹם הַכֵּסֶא

כא־כב יָבֹא בֵיתוֹ: הִטַּתּוּ בְּרֹב לִקְחָהּ בְּחֵלֶק שְׂפָתֶיהָ תַּדִּיחֶנּוּ: הוֹלֵךְ אַחֲרֶיהָ

כג פִּתְאֹם כְּשׁוֹר אֶל־טֶבַח יָבוֹא וּכְעֶכֶס אֶל־מוּסַר אֱוִיל: עַד יְפַלַּח חֵץ כְּבֵדוֹ

כד־כה כְּמַהֵר צִפּוֹר אֶל־פָּח וְלֹא־יָדַע כִּי־בְנַפְשׁוֹ הוּא: וְעַתָּה בָנִים שִׁמְעוּ־לִי וְהַקְשִׁיבוּ לְאִמְרֵי־פִי: אַל־יֵשְׂטְ אֶל־דְּרָכֶיהָ לִבֶּךָ אַל־

כו־כו תֵּתַע בִּנְתִיבוֹתֶיהָ: כִּי־רַבִּים חֲלָלִים הִפִּילָה וַעֲצֻמִים כָּל־הֲרֻגֶיהָ: דַּרְכֵי

6:24-26. The alluring woman is a metaphor for physical gratification or heretical ideas. Only Torah and chastisement can protect one from these dangers.

6:31-32. An apprehended thief will pay whatever he must, but he will not surrender his soul. Someone who commits adultery, however, forfeits his soul.

7:5. The forbidden woman is the Evil Inclination personified.

7:7-13. Heresy, the harlot, bides its time and begins casually. Someone slowly goes astray, distancing himself from the Torah's moral values, until he becomes the harlot's guest. He becomes accustomed to going to her, until she controls him (*Vilna Gaon*).

7:14-15. Deceitfully, she implies that she is inviting him to perform the good deed of enjoying sacrificial meat (*Ibn Ezra*).

7:22. A fool lunges toward his undoing with the speed of a serpent lunging to poison its victim (*Rashi*).

Seek ways to keep the commandments of your mother. ²¹ Tie them to your heart always; entwine them upon your neck. ²² As you go forth, it will guide you; as you recline, it will guard you; and when you awake, it will converse with you. ²³ For a commandment is a lamp and the Torah is light; and reproving discipline is the way of life, ²⁴ to guard you from an *Passion is a consuming fire* evil woman,* from the smoothness of the foreign woman's tongue. ²⁵ Do not desire her beauty in your heart, and do not let her captivate you with her eyelids, ²⁶ because, for the sake of a licentious woman, [one may beg] for a loaf of bread; an adulterous woman can ensnare a precious soul. ²⁷ Can a man draw fire into his bosom without his clothes being burned? ²⁸ Can a man walk on coals without his feet being scorched? ²⁹ So is one who consorts with his friend's wife; anyone who touches her will not be exonerated.

It is worse and more unforgivable than theft ³⁰ A thief is not [overly] scorned if he steals to satisfy his soul when he is hungry. ³¹ When he is found, he would even pay sevenfold, even give all the wealth of his house!* ³² But he who commits adultery with a woman is lacking an [understanding] heart; a destroyer of his soul will do this. ³³ Plague and shame will he find, and his disgrace will not be erased. ³⁴ For jealousy ignites a husband's wrath, and he will not have mercy on the day of revenge. ³⁵ He will not be appeased by any ransom, and will not relent, though the bribe be made great.

7

Do not let my advice slip away ¹ My child, heed my words and store up my commandments with yourself. ² Heed my commandments and live, and [heed] my Torah as the apple of your eyes. ³ Bind them on your fingers; inscribe them on the tablet of your heart. ⁴ Say to wisdom, "You are my sister," and call understanding a friend, ⁵ that they may safeguard you from a forbidden woman,* from a strange woman who *A naive youth lurches toward temptation,* makes her words glib. ⁶ For I have looked out from the window of my house, through my lattice, ⁷ and I saw among the fools, I discerned among the youths, a lad who lacked [an understanding] heart* ⁸ passing through the marketplace near her corner, and he strode toward her house, ⁹ in the twilight, as daylight wanes, in the blackness of night and darkness. ¹⁰ Then behold, a woman approached him, bedecked as a harlot and with siege in [her] heart. ¹¹ She coos and she entices, her feet do not dwell at home. ¹² Sometimes in the courtyard, sometimes in the streets, she lurks at every corner. ¹³ She seized him and kissed him; she thrust forth her face and said to him: ¹⁴ "I had vowed to bring peace-offerings, and today I have fulfilled my vow.*

and is approached by a harlot who tempts him with promises of pleasure . . .

¹⁵ "That is why I went out toward you, to seek your countenance, and I have found you! ¹⁶ I have decked my bed with spreads; carved bed poles are hung with Egyptian linen. ¹⁷ I have perfumed my bed with myrrh, aloes, and cinna-*. . . and convinces him that he has nothing to fear* mon. ¹⁸ Come, let us sate ourselves with love until the morning; let us rejoice with acts of love, ¹⁹ for [my] husband is not at home; he has gone on a distant journey. ²⁰ He has taken the money-pouch with him; he will come home at the appointed time."

He rushes to his doom ²¹ She sways him with her abundant sophistication; she thrusts him with the glibness of her lips. ²² He follows her unsuspectingly, like an ox to the slaughter; rushing like a venomous snake to discipline the foolish one,* ²³ until the arrow splits his liver; he is like a bird hurrying to the trap, unaware that its life will be lost.

Listen to me and avoid her wiles ²⁴ So now, children, listen to me, and heed the words of my mouth. ²⁵ Do not incline your heart to her ways; do not stray in her pathways. ²⁶ For she has felled many victims; the number of her slain is huge. ²⁷ Her house is the way to

ח   א שְׁאוֹל בֵּיתֶהָ יְרֹדוֹת אֶל־חַדְרֵי־מָוֶת: הֲלֹא־חָכְמָה תִקְרָא וּתְבוּנָה תִּתֵּן

ב־ג קוֹלָהּ: בְּרֹאשׁ־מְרוֹמִים עֲלֵי־דָרֶךְ בֵּית נְתִיבוֹת נִצָּבָה: לְיַד־שְׁעָרִים לְפִי־

ד קָרֶת מְבוֹא פְתָחִים תָּרֹנָּה: אֲלֵיכֶם אִישִׁים אֶקְרָא וְקוֹלִי אֶל־בְּנֵי אָדָם:

ה־ו הָבִינוּ פְתָאיִם עָרְמָה וּכְסִילִים הָבִינוּ לֵב: שִׁמְעוּ כִּי־נְגִידִים אֲדַבֵּר

ז־ח וּמִפְתַּח שְׂפָתַי מֵישָׁרִים: כִּי־אֱמֶת יֶהְגֶּה חִכִּי וְתוֹעֲבַת שְׂפָתַי רֶשַׁע: בְּצֶדֶק

ט כָּל־אִמְרֵי־פִי אֵין בָּהֶם נִפְתָּל וְעִקֵּשׁ: כֻּלָּם נְכֹחִים לַמֵּבִין וִישָׁרִים לְמֹצְאֵי

י־יא דָעַת: קְחוּ־מוּסָרִי וְאַל־כָּסֶף וְדַעַת מֵחָרוּץ נִבְחָר: כִּי־טוֹבָה חָכְמָה

יב מִפְּנִינִים וְכָל־חֲפָצִים לֹא יִשְׁווּ־בָהּ: אֲנִי־חָכְמָה שָׁכַנְתִּי עָרְמָה וְדַעַת

יג מְזִמּוֹת אֶמְצָא: יִרְאַת יהוה שְׂנֹאת רָע גֵּאָה וְגָאוֹן וְדֶרֶךְ רָע וּפִי תַהְפֻּכוֹת

יד־טו שָׂנֵאתִי: לִי־עֵצָה וְתוּשִׁיָּה אֲנִי בִינָה לִי גְבוּרָה: בִּי מְלָכִים יִמְלֹכוּ וְרוֹזְנִים

טז יְחֹקְקוּ צֶדֶק: בִּי שָׂרִים יָשֹׂרוּ וּנְדִיבִים כָּל־שֹׁפְטֵי צֶדֶק: אֲנִי °אֹהֲבֶיהָ

יז [אֹהֲבַי ק] אֵהָב וּמְשַׁחֲרַי יִמְצָאֻנְנִי: עֹשֶׁר־וְכָבוֹד אִתִּי הוֹן עָתֵק וּצְדָקָה:

יט־כ טוֹב פִּרְיִי מֵחָרוּץ וּמִפָּז וּתְבוּאָתִי מִכֶּסֶף נִבְחָר: בְּאֹרַח־צְדָקָה אֲהַלֵּךְ

כא בְּתוֹךְ נְתִיבוֹת מִשְׁפָּט: לְהַנְחִיל אֹהֲבַי ׀ יֵשׁ וְאֹצְרֹתֵיהֶם אֲמַלֵּא:

כב־כג יהוה קָנָנִי רֵאשִׁית דַּרְכּוֹ קֶדֶם מִפְעָלָיו מֵאָז: מֵעוֹלָם נִסַּכְתִּי מֵרֹאשׁ

כד־כה מִקַּדְמֵי־אָרֶץ: בְּאֵין־תְּהֹמוֹת חוֹלָלְתִּי בְּאֵין מַעְיָנוֹת נִכְבַּדֵּי־מָיִם: בְּטֶרֶם

כו הָרִים הָטְבָּעוּ לִפְנֵי גְבָעוֹת חוֹלָלְתִּי: עַד־לֹא עָשָׂה אֶרֶץ וְחוּצוֹת

כז וְרֹאשׁ עַפְרוֹת תֵּבֵל: בַּהֲכִינוֹ שָׁמַיִם שָׁם אָנִי בְּחוּקוֹ חוּג עַל־פְּנֵי תְהוֹם:

כח־כט בְּאַמְּצוֹ שְׁחָקִים מִמָּעַל בַּעֲזוֹז עִינוֹת תְּהוֹם: בְּשׂוּמוֹ לַיָּם ׀ חֻקּוֹ וּמַיִם לֹא

ל יַעַבְרוּ־פִיו בְּחוּקוֹ מוֹסְדֵי אָרֶץ: וָאֶהְיֶה אֶצְלוֹ אָמוֹן וָאֶהְיֶה שַׁעֲשֻׁעִים

לא יוֹם ׀ יוֹם מְשַׂחֶקֶת לְפָנָיו בְּכָל־עֵת: מְשַׂחֶקֶת בְּתֵבֵל אַרְצוֹ וְשַׁעֲשֻׁעַי אֶת־

בְּנֵי אָדָם:

לב־לג וְעַתָּה בָנִים שִׁמְעוּ־לִי וְאַשְׁרֵי דְּרָכַי יִשְׁמֹרוּ: שִׁמְעוּ מוּסָר וַחֲכָמוּ וְאַל־

לד תִּפְרָעוּ: אַשְׁרֵי אָדָם שֹׁמֵעַ לִי לִשְׁקֹד עַל־דַּלְתֹתַי יוֹם ׀ יוֹם לִשְׁמֹר מְזוּזֹת

לה־לו פְּתָחָי: כִּי מֹצְאִי °מֹצְאֵי [מָצָא ק] חַיִּים וַיָּפֶק רָצוֹן מֵיהוה: וְחֹטְאִי חֹמֵס

נַפְשׁוֹ כָּל־מְשַׂנְאַי אָהֲבוּ מָוֶת:

ט   א־ב חָכְמוֹת בָּנְתָה בֵיתָהּ חָצְבָה עַמּוּדֶיהָ שִׁבְעָה: טָבְחָה טִבְחָהּ מָסְכָה יֵינָהּ

ג־ד אַף עָרְכָה שֻׁלְחָנָהּ: שָׁלְחָה נַעֲרֹתֶיהָ תִקְרָא עַל־גַּפֵּי מְרֹמֵי קָרֶת: מִי־

8:1-3. Unlike the harlot, heresy, lurking in the darkness to trap and destroy her prey (Ch. 7), wisdom proclaims the delights of Torah, which brings happiness and life (*Vilna Gaon*).

8:12-21. The Torah now speaks on her own behalf.

8:13. This is the discipline that wisdom proclaims (*Rashi*). Only the humble and truthful are allowed to discover her treasures and truth (*R' Hirsch*).

8:15-16. By imbuing themselves with the Torah's wisdom, kings become righteous sovereigns, leaders mani-

fest leadership, princes gain authority, and judges remain dedicated to truth and justice (*Maharal*).

8:22-31. Torah was the blueprint of the universe (*Bereishis Rabbah* 1:2). God created the Torah before the universe; it is manifest in Creation, preserves the world, and is a guide to all mankind (*Maimonides*).

8:32-36. Only one path can lead to fulfillment: "Harken unto discipline and grow wise." Only by unswerving obedience to the Torah can we succeed (*Vilna Gaon*).

the grave, descending to the chambers of death.

8

Wisdom invites all to learn from her

¹ **S**urely wisdom will call out, * and understanding will raise her voice. ² Atop the heights along the way, at the place where pathways diverge, she stands. Near the gateways of the city, at the approach to its entrances, she cries out: ⁴ "To you, O men, do I call, and my voice is to the sons of man. ⁵ Simpletons, understand cleverness; fools, understand [in your] heart. ⁶ Listen, for I will speak noble thoughts; the opinion of my lips will be fair words. ⁷ For my palate will utter truth; wickedness is an abomination to my lips. ⁸ All the words of my mouth are with righteousness; they contain no twisting or perversion. ⁹ They are all correct

It is superior to all earthly riches

to one who understands, and upright to those who find knowledge. ¹⁰ Accept my discipline and not silver, [for] knowledge is choicer than fine gold, ¹¹ for wisdom is better than pearls, and all desires cannot compare to it."

Torah is the source of the truest success

¹² I am wisdom;* I dwell in cleverness; I provide knowledge of designs. ¹³ Fear of HASHEM is hatred of evil. * I hate pride and haughtiness, the way of evil, and a duplicitous mouth. ¹⁴ With me there is counsel and wisdom; I am understanding; with me is might. ¹⁵ Through me,* kings will reign, and nobles will decree righteousness; ¹⁶ through me officials will rule, and nobles, all who judge righ-

The Torah is generous to those who love it

teously. ¹⁷ I love those who love me, and those who search for me shall find me. ¹⁸ Wealth and honor are with me, great fortune and righteousness. ¹⁹ My fruits are better than fine gold, even choice gold, and my produce is choicer than silver. ²⁰ I lead in the path of righteousness, amid the pathways of justice. ²¹ I have what to bequeath [to] those who love me, and I shall fill their storehouses.

The Torah preceded everything; it is the blueprint of Creation

²² HASHEM made me as the beginning of His way, * before His deeds of yore. ²³ I have reigned for all time: from the beginning, from before [there was] the earth. ²⁴ When there were no depths, I was formed; when there were no pools rich with water, ²⁵ before the mountains were settled, before the hills, I was formed; ²⁶ when He had not yet made the earth and its environs or the first dust of the inhabited world. ²⁷ When He prepared the heavens, I was there; when He etched out the globe upon the face of the depths; ²⁸ when He strengthened the heavens above; when he fortified the wellsprings of the depths; ²⁹ when He set for the sea its limit and the waters would not transgress His word; when He forged the foundations of the earth; ³⁰ I was then His nursling, I was then His delight every day, playing before Him at all times, ³¹ playing in the inhabited areas of His earth, my delights are with the sons of man.

Be wise: Follow the Torah and its teachings

³² And now, children, listen to me;* praiseworthy are those who heed my ways. ³³ Harken unto discipline and grow wise and you will not reject [wisdom]. ³⁴ Praiseworthy is the person who listens to me, to hasten to my doors every day, to guard the doorposts of my entranceways. ³⁵ For one who finds me finds life and elicits favor from HASHEM. ³⁶ But one who sins against me despoils his soul; all who hate me love death.

9

The wise woman prepares

¹ **W**ith all forms of wisdom did she build her house; she carved out its seven* pillars. ² She prepared her meat, mixed her wine and also set her table. * ³ She has sent out her maidens to announce upon the city heights: ⁴ "Whoever is

---

9:1-18. This chapter contrasts the benefit to those who follow the wisdom of Torah with the harm to those who are lured by the enticements of idol worship (*Rabbeinu Bachya*).

9:1. In Scripture, the number seven is idiomatic for "many" (*Ralbag*).

9:2. Her lessons are prepared and she is ready to teach (*Rashi*).

ה   פְּתִי יָסֻר הֵנָּה חֲסַר־לֵב אָמְרָה לּוֹ: לְכוּ לַחֲמוּ בְלַחֲמִי וּשְׁתוּ בְּיַיִן מָסָכְתִּי:

ו-ז   עִזְבוּ פְתָאיִם וִחְיוּ וְאִשְׁרוּ בְּדֶרֶךְ בִּינָה: יֹסֵר ׀ לֵץ לֹקֵחַ לוֹ קָלוֹן וּמוֹכִיחַ

ח-ט   לְרָשָׁע מוּמוֹ: אַל־תּוֹכַח לֵץ פֶּן־יִשְׂנָאֶךָּ הוֹכַח לְחָכָם וְיֶאֱהָבֶךָּ: תֵּן לְחָכָם

י   וְיֶחְכַּם־עוֹד הוֹדַע לְצַדִּיק וְיוֹסֶף לֶקַח: תְּחִלַּת חָכְמָה יִרְאַת יהוה וְדַעַת

יא-יב   קְדֹשִׁים בִּינָה: כִּי־בִי יִרְבּוּ יָמֶיךָ וְיוֹסִיפוּ לְךָ שְׁנוֹת חַיִּים: אִם־חָכַמְתָּ

יג   חָכַמְתָּ לָּךְ וְלַצְתָּ לְבַדְּךָ תִשָּׂא: אֵשֶׁת כְּסִילוּת הֹמִיָּה פְּתַיּוּת וּבַל־יָדְעָה

יד-טו   מָּה: וְיָשְׁבָה לְפֶתַח בֵּיתָהּ עַל־כִּסֵּא מְרֹמֵי קָרֶת: לִקְרֹא לְעֹבְרֵי־דָרֶךְ

טז   הַמְיַשְּׁרִים אֹרְחוֹתָם: מִי־פֶתִי יָסֻר הֵנָּה וַחֲסַר־לֵב וְאָמְרָה לּוֹ: מַיִם־

יז-יח   גְּנוּבִים יִמְתָּקוּ וְלֶחֶם סְתָרִים יִנְעָם: וְלֹא־יָדַע כִּי־רְפָאִים שָׁם בְּעִמְקֵי שְׁאוֹל קְרֻאֶיהָ:

י   א-ב   מִשְׁלֵי שְׁלֹמֹה בֵּן חָכָם יְשַׂמַּח־אָב וּבֵן כְּסִיל תּוּגַת אִמּוֹ: לֹא־יוֹעִילוּ

ג   אוֹצְרוֹת רֶשַׁע וּצְדָקָה תַּצִּיל מִמָּוֶת: לֹא־יַרְעִיב יהוה נֶפֶשׁ צַדִּיק וְהַוַּת

ד-ה   רְשָׁעִים יֶהְדֹּף: רָאשׁ עֹשֶׂה כַף־רְמִיָּה וְיַד חָרוּצִים תַּעֲשִׁיר: אֹגֵר בַּקַּיִץ בֵּן

ו   מַשְׂכִּיל נִרְדָּם בַּקָּצִיר בֵּן מֵבִישׁ: בְּרָכוֹת לְרֹאשׁ צַדִּיק וּפִי רְשָׁעִים יְכַסֶּה

ז-ח   חָמָס: זֵכֶר צַדִּיק לִבְרָכָה וְשֵׁם רְשָׁעִים יִרְקָב: חֲכַם־לֵב יִקַּח מִצְוֹת וֶאֱוִיל

ט   שְׂפָתַיִם יִלָּבֵט: הוֹלֵךְ בַּתֹּם יֵלֶךְ בֶּטַח וּמְעַקֵּשׁ דְּרָכָיו יִוָּדֵעַ: קֹרֵץ עַיִן יִתֵּן

יא   עַצָּבֶת וֶאֱוִיל שְׂפָתַיִם יִלָּבֵט: מְקוֹר חַיִּים פִּי צַדִּיק וּפִי רְשָׁעִים יְכַסֶּה חָמָס:

יב-יג   שִׂנְאָה תְּעֹרֵר מְדָנִים וְעַל כָּל־פְּשָׁעִים תְּכַסֶּה אַהֲבָה: בְּשִׂפְתֵי נָבוֹן

יד   תִּמָּצֵא חָכְמָה וְשֵׁבֶט לְגֵו חֲסַר־לֵב: חֲכָמִים יִצְפְּנוּ־דָעַת וּפִי־אֱוִיל מְחִתָּה

טו-טז   קְרֹבָה: הוֹן עָשִׁיר קִרְיַת עֻזּוֹ מְחִתַּת דַּלִּים רֵישָׁם: פְּעֻלַּת צַדִּיק לְחַיִּים

יז   תְּבוּאַת רָשָׁע לְחַטָּאת: אֹרַח לְחַיִּים שׁוֹמֵר מוּסָר וְעוֹזֵב תּוֹכַחַת מַתְעֶה:

יח-יט   מְכַסֶּה שִׂנְאָה שִׂפְתֵי־שָׁקֶר וּמוֹצִא דִבָּה הוּא כְסִיל: בְּרֹב דְּבָרִים לֹא יֶחְדַּל־

כ   פָּשַׁע וְחֹשֵׂךְ שְׂפָתָיו מַשְׂכִּיל: כֶּסֶף נִבְחָר לְשׁוֹן צַדִּיק לֵב רְשָׁעִים כִּמְעָט:

9:4. To acquire the wisdom that he lacks.

9:7-8. Although it is proper to teach a simpleton, teaching the scoffer and the wicked is worse than futile.

9:13-15. Like wisdom, the woman of foolishness seeks attention while remaining idle and destructive, but the wise woman builds and strengthens.

9:18. The simpleton she attracts does not realize that she leads not to life, but to death.

∽§ Chapters 10-24

These chapters comprise the second section of *Proverbs*. It consists of ethical maxims, rules of conduct, lessons from experience, and moral teachings. Most of the verses postulate individual points. The verses fall into four general categories: (1) antithetical couplets, where the two halves of the verse describe opposite behavioral patterns (the wise and the foolish, love and hatred, industry and sloth); (2) single cohesive thoughts; (3) parallelism in which the second clause reinforces the first

clause; and (4) parallel denigrations of base traits and actions (*Meiri*).

Since each verse is a separate thought, this section of *Proverbs* does not lend itself to marginal notes.

10:1. The industrious wise son will spend his time in the study hall with his father, while the lazy foolish son will loll around the house to his mother's anguish (*Ibn Ezra*). A mother will often suffer more from her foolish son's antics, because most boys are afraid to misbehave in their fathers' presence (*Ralbag*).

10:2. See 11:4.

10:4. One who uses false weights and measures will eventually become impoverished (*Ibn Ezra*).

10:6. As the righteous person always blesses others, God will bless him in return (*Vilna Gaon*); and he will be blessed by all who know him (*Malbim*).

10:7. When people hear the righteous one's name, they will bless him, but the name of the wicked will "rot" from disuse; people will refrain even from mention-

She wants to share with others a simpleton, let him turn here!"* As for the one who lacks [an understanding] heart, she says to him: ⁵ "Come and partake of my food and drink of the wine that I mixed. ⁶ Leave [your paths], O simpletons, and live, and stride in the way of *Avoid the evil; cultivate good people* understanding."⁷ But one who chastises the scoffer* acquires shame for himself, and he who rebukes the wicked [acquires] a blemish. ⁸ Do not rebuke a scoffer, lest he hate you; rebuke a wise man, and he will love you. ⁹ Give the wise man and he will become even wiser; make known to the righteous and he will add [to *Fear of God is the road to blessing* his] learning. ¹⁰ The beginning of wisdom is fear of HASHEM, and [the beginning of] understanding is knowledge of the sacred. ¹¹ For through me your days will be increased, and they will increase years of life for you. ¹² If you have become wise, you have become wise for your own good, and if you have scoffed, you alone will bear [responsibility].

The temptress is alluring ¹³ The woman of foolishness croons; [the woman] of simpleness, who does not know anything. * ¹⁴ She sits at the door of her house, on a chair at the city heights, ¹⁵ to call out to the passersby, who make their ways upright: ¹⁶ "Whoever is a simpleton, let him turn here." As for the one who lacks [an understanding] heart, *But it is the bait of death* she says to him: ¹⁷ "Stolen waters are sweet, and bread [eaten] in secret places is pleasing."¹⁸ But he does not know* that dead men are there, that those she invites are in the deepest grave.

10 ¹ The Proverbs of Solomon:
A wise son gladdens his father, but a foolish son is his mother's sorrow. *
² Treasures of wickedness will not avail, but charity rescues from death. *
³ HASHEM will not bring hunger upon the souls of the righteous, but the destructiveness of the wicked shall batter them. ⁴ A deceitful scale makes a pauper, * but the hand of the diligent brings prosperity. ⁵ A wise son harvests in the summer, but the shameful son is fast asleep at harvest time. ⁶ Blessings [will descend] upon the head of the righteous one, * but [their] violence will smother the mouth of the wicked. ⁷ Remembrance of a righteous one brings blessing, but the name of the wicked will rot. * ⁸ The wise of heart will seize good deeds, but the foolish one's lips will become weary. * ⁹ He who walks in innocence will walk securely, but one who perverts his ways will be broken. ¹⁰ He who winks his eye instills trepidation, * but the foolish one's lips will become weary. ¹¹ The mouth of the righteous one is a source of life, but the mouth of the wicked conceals their [intended] violence. ¹² Hatred arouses strife, but love covers all offenses. ¹³ In the lips of an understanding one will be found wisdom, but a rod [must be used] on the back of one who lacks [an understanding] heart. ¹⁴ The wise conceal knowledge, but the mouth of the fool brings ruin near. * ¹⁵ A rich man's wealth is his citadel of strength, but poverty is the ruin of the impoverished. ¹⁶ The deed of a righteous person brings life, but the produce of a wicked one brings lacking. ¹⁷ To heed discipline is a path to life, but one who abandons reproof goes astray. ¹⁸ One who conceals hatred has lying lips, * but one who utters slander is a fool. ¹⁹ In an abundance of words offense will not be lacking, but one who restrains his lips is wise. ²⁰ The tongue of a righteous person is choice silver, but the heart of the wicked is minute.

---

ing him (*Rashi*).

10:8. A wise person actively pursues good deeds, but a fool merely talks, without following through.

10:10. A powerful person can frighten others with a threatening flicker of an eyelid.

10:14. Fools have no discretion; they reveal potentially harmful information.

10:18. He hides his hatred behind dishonest flattery.

כא־כב שִׂפְתֵי צַדִּיק יִרְעוּ רַבִּים וֶאֱוִילִים בַּחֲסַר־לֵב יָמוּתוּ: בִּרְכַּת יהוה הִיא

כג תַעֲשִׁיר וְלֹא־יוֹסִף עֶצֶב עִמָּהּ: כִּשְׂחוֹק לִכְסִיל עֲשׂוֹת זִמָּה וְחָכְמָה לְאִישׁ

כד־כה תְבוּנָה: מְגֹרַת רָשָׁע הִיא תְבוֹאֶנּוּ וְתַאֲוַת צַדִּיקִים יִתֵּן: כַּעֲבוֹר סוּפָה וְאֵין

כו רָשָׁע וְצַדִּיק יְסוֹד עוֹלָם: כַּחֹמֶץ | לַשִּׁנַּיִם וְכֶעָשָׁן לָעֵינָיִם כֵּן הֶעָצֵל

כז־כח לְשֹׁלְחָיו: יִרְאַת יהוה תּוֹסִיף יָמִים וּשְׁנוֹת רְשָׁעִים תִּקְצֹרְנָה: תּוֹחֶלֶת

כט צַדִּיקִים שִׂמְחָה וְתִקְוַת רְשָׁעִים תֹּאבֵד: מָעוֹז לַתֹּם דֶּרֶךְ יהוה וּמְחִתָּה

ל־לא לְפֹעֲלֵי אָוֶן: צַדִּיק לְעוֹלָם בַּל־יִמּוֹט וּרְשָׁעִים לֹא יִשְׁכְּנוּ־אָרֶץ: פִּי־צַדִּיק

לב יָנוּב חָכְמָה וּלְשׁוֹן תַּהְפֻּכוֹת תִּכָּרֵת: שִׂפְתֵי צַדִּיק יֵדְעוּן רָצוֹן וּפִי רְשָׁעִים

יא א־ב תַּהְפֻּכוֹת: מֹאזְנֵי מִרְמָה תּוֹעֲבַת יהוה וְאֶבֶן שְׁלֵמָה רְצוֹנוֹ: בָּא־זָדוֹן וַיָּבֹא

ג קָלוֹן וְאֶת־צְנוּעִים חָכְמָה: תֻּמַּת יְשָׁרִים תַּנְחֵם וְסֶלֶף בּוֹגְדִים °ושדם

ד־ה [יְשָׁדֵּם ק]: לֹא־יוֹעִיל הוֹן בְּיוֹם עֶבְרָה וּצְדָקָה תַּצִּיל מִמָּוֶת: צִדְקַת תָּמִים

ו תְּיַשֵּׁר דַּרְכּוֹ וּבְרִשְׁעָתוֹ יִפֹּל רָשָׁע: צִדְקַת יְשָׁרִים תַּצִּילֵם וּבְהַוַּת בֹּגְדִים

ז־ח יִלָּכֵדוּ: בְּמוֹת אָדָם רָשָׁע תֹּאבַד תִּקְוָה וְתוֹחֶלֶת אוֹנִים אָבָדָה: צַדִּיק

ט מִצָּרָה נֶחֱלָץ וַיָּבֹא רָשָׁע תַּחְתָּיו: בְּפֶה חָנֵף יַשְׁחִת רֵעֵהוּ וּבְדַעַת צַדִּיקִים

י־יא יֵחָלֵצוּ: בְּטוּב צַדִּיקִים תַּעֲלֹץ קִרְיָה וּבַאֲבֹד רְשָׁעִים רִנָּה: בְּבִרְכַּת יְשָׁרִים

יב תָּרוּם קָרֶת וּבְפִי רְשָׁעִים תֵּהָרֵס: בָּז־לְרֵעֵהוּ חֲסַר־לֵב וְאִישׁ תְּבוּנוֹת

יג־יד יַחֲרִישׁ: הוֹלֵךְ רָכִיל מְגַלֶּה־סּוֹד וְנֶאֱמַן־רוּחַ מְכַסֶּה דָבָר: בְּאֵין תַּחְבֻּלוֹת

טו יִפָּל־עָם וּתְשׁוּעָה בְּרֹב יוֹעֵץ: רַע־יֵרוֹעַ כִּי־עָרַב זָר וְשֹׂנֵא תֹקְעִים בּוֹטֵחַ:

טז־יז אֵשֶׁת־חֵן תִּתְמֹךְ כָּבוֹד וְעָרִיצִים יִתְמְכוּ־עֹשֶׁר: גֹּמֵל נַפְשׁוֹ אִישׁ חָסֶד

יח־יט וְעֹכֵר שְׁאֵרוֹ אַכְזָרִי: רָשָׁע עֹשֶׂה פְעֻלַּת־שָׁקֶר וְזֹרֵעַ צְדָקָה שֶׂכֶר אֱמֶת: כֵּן־

כ צְדָקָה לְחַיִּים וּמְרַדֵּף רָעָה לְמוֹתוֹ: תּוֹעֲבַת יהוה עִקְּשֵׁי־לֵב וּרְצוֹנוֹ תְּמִימֵי

כא־כב דָרֶךְ: יָד לְיָד לֹא־יִנָּקֶה רָּע וְזֶרַע צַדִּיקִים נִמְלָט: נֶזֶם זָהָב בְּאַף חֲזִיר אִשָּׁה

כג־כד יָפָה וְסָרַת טָעַם: תַּאֲוַת צַדִּיקִים אַךְ־טוֹב תִּקְוַת רְשָׁעִים עֶבְרָה: יֵשׁ

כה מְפַזֵּר וְנוֹסָף עוֹד וְחוֹשֵׂךְ מִיֹּשֶׁר אַךְ־לְמַחְסוֹר: נֶפֶשׁ־בְּרָכָה תְדֻשָּׁן

כו וּמַרְוֶה גַּם־הוּא יוֹרֶא: מֹנֵעַ בָּר יִקְּבֻהוּ לְאוֹם וּבְרָכָה לְרֹאשׁ מַשְׁבִּיר:

כז־כח שֹׁחֵר טוֹב יְבַקֵּשׁ רָצוֹן וְדֹרֵשׁ רָעָה תְבוֹאֶנּוּ: בּוֹטֵחַ בְּעָשְׁרוֹ הוּא יִפֹּל

10:21. Multitudes benefit from the prayers and blessings of the righteous.

10:25. Even after death, the merits of the righteous protect the world (*Vilna Gaon*).

11:4. This identical teaching is found in 10:2. Here it speaks of saving a person from the punishment of *Gehinnom* in the afterlife; there it speaks of saving him from an unusual death (*Bava Basra* 10a).

11:12. A discerning person does not respond to one who belittles him, for to do so would put him on par with that person (*Rabbeinu Yonah*).

11:14. Just as a city must use every possible means to overcome attack, so too a person must devise plans and seek advice in his war against sin (*Chevel Nachalah*).

11:16. A woman of grace upholds both her dignity and that of others; an insolent person respects only wealth.

11:18. He thinks his deeds will stand forever, but, in truth, his actions betray him (*Rashi*).

11:21. Recompense comes from God's hand to the sinner's hand and the sinner cannot exonerate himself from it (*Rashi*); nevertheless, the merit of his righteous forebears may save him (*Metzudos*).

11:22. Adornment adds beauty only to something essentially beautiful; otherwise, the adornment itself is a precious gem in an ugly setting.

11:24. Money spent on doing God's will brings additional wealth, but a refusal to contribute for worthy causes brings a loss.

21 *The lips of the righteous one will nourish many, * but the foolish will die through lack of [an understanding] heart.* 22 *It is the blessing of HASHEM that enriches, and one need not add toil with it.* 23 *It is like sport to a fool to carry out [his] evil design; wisdom [is like sport] to a man of understanding.* 24 *What a wicked one fears will come upon him, and [God] will fulfill the desire of the righteous.* 25 *When the storm passes a wicked one is no more, but a righteous one is the foundation of the world. ** 26 *Like vinegar to the teeth and like smoke to the eyes, so is a sluggard to those who send him.* 27 *The fear of HASHEM will increase days, but the years of the wicked will be shortened.* 28 *The expectation of the righteous is gladness, but the hope of the wicked will go lost.* 29 *The way of HASHEM is a stronghold to the innocent, but a ruin to the workers of iniquity.* 30 *A righteous one will never falter, but the wicked will not dwell [tranquilly] in the land.* 31 *The mouth of a righteous one speaks wisdom, but a duplicitous tongue will be cut off.* 32 *The lips of a righteous one know how to appease [God], but the mouth of the wicked is duplicitous.*

11 1 Deceitful scales are an abomination of HASHEM, but a perfect weight is His desire. 2 *When a willful sinner comes shame comes, but with modest ones [comes] wisdom.* 3 *The innocence of the just will guide them, but the corruption of the faithless will despoil them.* 4 *Wealth will not avail in the day of wrath, but charity will rescue from death. ** 5 *The righteousness of the innocent one straightens his path, but the wicked one shall fall in his wickedness.* 6 *The righteousness of the just will rescue them, but the faithless will be trapped in the destruction [they plotted].* 7 *When a wicked man dies, hope is lost, and the expectation of his offspring perishes.* 8 *The righteous one is removed from affliction, but the wicked one comes in his place.* 9 *With a flattering mouth one corrupts his friend, but the righteous are delivered through knowledge.* 10 *The city exults in the good of the righteous, and when the wicked perish there is glad song.* 11 *Through the blessing of the upright a city is exalted, but through the mouth of the wicked it is torn down.* 12 *He who shames his friend lacks a heart, but a man of understanding will be silent. ** 13 *He who reveals a secret is a talebearer, but the faithful of spirit conceals a matter.* 14 *Without strategies a nation will fall, but salvation [lies] in much counsel. ** 15 *One will be utterly broken by co-signing for a stranger; but a hater of handshakes will be secure.* 16 *The woman of grace upholds honor; but the insolent uphold wealth. ** 17 *A man of kindness brings good upon himself, but a cruel person troubles his flesh.* 18 *The wicked one does false deeds, * but one who sows righteousness has a true reward.* 19 *[One who gives] sincere charity [is consigned] to life; but the pursuer of evil [is consigned] to his death.* 20 *The perverse of heart are an abomination unto HASHEM, but His desire is for those whose way is wholehearted.* 21 *[From] hand to hand — evil will not be exonerated, but the offspring of the righteous will escape. ** 22 *[Like] a golden ring in the snout of a pig, [so] is a beautiful woman whose good sense has departed. ** 23 *The lust of the righteous is only for good; the hope of the wicked is wrath.* 24 *There is one who scatters and gathers more, and one who refrains from what is proper, only for a loss. ** 25 *The soul that blesses will grow fat, and one who sates [others] will himself be sated.* 26 *One who withholds produce* will be cursed by the nation, but blessing will be on the head of the provider.* 27 *He who seeks good [for others] seeks [God's] favor, but he who searches out evil [for others], it will come upon him.* 28 *He who trusts in his wealth — he will fall,*

11:26. Spiritual produce, as well as field crops (*Rashi; Ralbag*).

כט וְכֶעָלֶה צַדִּיקִים יִפְרָחוּ: עוֹכֵר בֵּיתוֹ יִנְחַל־רוּחַ וְעֶבֶד אֱוִיל לַחֲכַם־לֵב:
ל-לא פְּרִי־צַדִּיק עֵץ חַיִּים וְלֹקֵחַ נְפָשׁוֹת חָכָם: הֵן צַדִּיק בָּאָרֶץ יְשֻׁלָּם אַף כִּי־

יב א-ב רָשָׁע וְחוֹטֵא: אֹהֵב מוּסָר אֹהֵב דָּעַת וְשֹׂנֵא תוֹכַחַת בָּעַר: טוֹב יָפִיק רָצוֹן
ג מֵיהוָה וְאִישׁ מְזִמּוֹת יַרְשִׁיעַ: לֹא־יִכּוֹן אָדָם בְּרֶשַׁע וְשֹׁרֶשׁ צַדִּיקִים בַּל־
ד-ה יִמּוֹט: אֵשֶׁת־חַיִל עֲטֶרֶת בַּעְלָהּ וּכְרָקָב בְּעַצְמוֹתָיו מְבִישָׁה: מַחְשְׁבוֹת
ו צַדִּיקִים מִשְׁפָּט תַּחְבֻּלוֹת רְשָׁעִים מִרְמָה: דִּבְרֵי רְשָׁעִים אֱרָב־דָּם וּפִי
ז-ח יְשָׁרִים יַצִּילֵם: הָפוֹךְ רְשָׁעִים וְאֵינָם וּבֵית צַדִּיקִים יַעֲמֹד: לְפִי־שִׂכְלוֹ
ט יְהֻלַּל־אִישׁ וְנַעֲוֵה־לֵב יִהְיֶה לָבוּז: טוֹב נִקְלֶה וְעֶבֶד לוֹ מִמְּתַכַּבֵּד וַחֲסַר־
י-יא לָחֶם: יוֹדֵעַ צַדִּיק נֶפֶשׁ בְּהֶמְתּוֹ וְרַחֲמֵי רְשָׁעִים אַכְזָרִי: עֹבֵד אַדְמָתוֹ
יב יִשְׂבַּע־לָחֶם וּמְרַדֵּף רֵיקִים חֲסַר־לֵב: חָמַד רָשָׁע מְצוֹד רָעִים וְשֹׁרֶשׁ
יג-יד צַדִּיקִים יִתֵּן: בְּפֶשַׁע שְׂפָתַיִם מוֹקֵשׁ רָע וַיֵּצֵא מִצָּרָה צַדִּיק: מִפְּרִי פִי־אִישׁ
טו יִשְׂבַּע־טוֹב וּגְמוּל יְדֵי־אָדָם °יָשׁוּב [יָשִׁיב ק] לוֹ: דֶּרֶךְ אֱוִיל יָשָׁר בְּעֵינָיו
טז-יז וְשֹׁמֵעַ לְעֵצָה חָכָם: אֱוִיל בַּיּוֹם יִוָּדַע כַּעְסוֹ וְכֹסֶה קָלוֹן עָרוּם: יָפִיחַ
יח אֱמוּנָה יַגִּיד צֶדֶק וְעֵד שְׁקָרִים מִרְמָה: יֵשׁ בּוֹטֶה כְּמַדְקְרוֹת חָרֶב וּלְשׁוֹן
יט-כ חֲכָמִים מַרְפֵּא: שְׂפַת־אֱמֶת תִּכּוֹן לָעַד וְעַד־אַרְגִּיעָה לְשׁוֹן שָׁקֶר: מִרְמָה
כא בְּלֶב־חֹרְשֵׁי רָע וּלְיֹעֲצֵי שָׁלוֹם שִׂמְחָה: לֹא־יְאֻנֶּה לַצַּדִּיק כָּל־אָוֶן
כב-כג וּרְשָׁעִים מָלְאוּ רָע: תּוֹעֲבַת יהוה שִׂפְתֵי־שָׁקֶר וְעֹשֵׂי אֱמוּנָה רְצוֹנוֹ: אָדָם
כד עָרוּם כֹּסֶה דָּעַת וְלֵב כְּסִילִים יִקְרָא אִוֶּלֶת: יַד־חָרוּצִים תִּמְשׁוֹל וּרְמִיָּה
כה-כו תִּהְיֶה לָמַס: דְּאָגָה בְלֶב־אִישׁ יַשְׁחֶנָּה וְדָבָר טוֹב יְשַׂמְּחֶנָּה: יָתֵר מֵרֵעֵהוּ
כז צַדִּיק וְדֶרֶךְ רְשָׁעִים תַּתְעֵם: לֹא־יַחֲרֹךְ רְמִיָּה צֵידוֹ וְהוֹן־אָדָם יָקָר חָרוּץ:
כח בְּאֹרַח־צְדָקָה חַיִּים וְדֶרֶךְ נְתִיבָה אַל־מָוֶת:

יג א-ב בֵּן חָכָם מוּסַר אָב וְלֵץ לֹא־שָׁמַע גְּעָרָה: מִפְּרִי פִי־אִישׁ יֹאכַל טוֹב
ג וְנֶפֶשׁ בֹּגְדִים חָמָס: נֹצֵר פִּיו שֹׁמֵר נַפְשׁוֹ פֹּשֵׂק שְׂפָתָיו מְחִתָּה־לוֹ:
ד-ה מִתְאַוָּה וָאַיִן נַפְשׁוֹ עָצֵל וְנֶפֶשׁ חָרֻצִים תְּדֻשָּׁן: דְּבַר־שֶׁקֶר יִשְׂנָא צַדִּיק
ו וְרָשָׁע יַבְאִישׁ וְיַחְפִּיר: צְדָקָה תִּצֹּר תָּם־דָּרֶךְ וְרִשְׁעָה תְּסַלֵּף חַטָּאת:

11:30. A wise man who teaches others gets credit for their good deeds, as if he had acquired the people he taught (*Rashi*).

12:6. The wicked conspire to testify falsely, but upright people will act to save the intended victim (*Rashi*).

12:9. A person should hold himself in low esteem and do even menial work, rather than hold himself high and go hungry (*Vilna Gaon*).

12:10. Divine law teaches one to be mindful even of the animals that depend on him. But one whose pity derives from his own inclination can just as easily become cruel as compassionate, depending on the mood or the current set of values (*R' Hirsch*).

12:12. The wicked crave the spoils of those who rob others, but the righteous are content with whatever they produce honestly, on their own (*Rashi*).

12:13. Slander, falsehood, offensive language, gossip, ridicule, etc.

12:16. A fool does not have the sense or self-control to rein in his anger; he reacts quickly and vociferously.

12:23. A wise person conceals knowledge until the proper time to reveal it, but a fool says whatever foolishness enters his mind (*Ibn Nachmias*).

12:25. A person who trusts in God should not worry about things that are not in his power to change. Rather he should dwell on good things that will gladden him.

12:26. Though the righteous suffer hardships and the wicked prosper, one should recognize the superiority of the former (*Meiri*).

but the righteous will sprout like foliage. ²⁹ *One who troubles his household will inherit wind, and the foolish one will become a servant of the wise of heart.* ³⁰ *The fruit of a righteous one is a tree of life, and a wise man acquires souls.* * ³¹ *If a righteous person is punished on earth, surely a wicked one and a sinner.*

12 ¹ **O**ne who loves knowledge loves discipline, but he who hates rebuke is a boor.* ² *A good man draws forth favor from* HASHEM, *but a scheming man causes wickedness.* ³ *A man will not become established through wickedness, but the root of the righteous will not falter.* ⁴ *An accomplished woman is the crown of her husband, but a shameful one is like rot in his bones.* ⁵ *The thoughts of the righteous are just, but the schemes of the wicked are deceit.* ⁶ *The words of the wicked lie in ambush for blood, but the mouth of the upright will rescue them.* * ⁷ *The wicked are overturned and are no more, but the house of the righteous will endure.* ⁸ *According to a man's wisdom will he be praised, but the distorted of heart will be put to shame.* ⁹ *Better off is the lowly one who serves for his keep than the pompous one who lacks bread.* * ¹⁰ *The righteous one knows [the needs of] his animal's soul, but the mercies of the wicked are cruel.* * ¹¹ *He who works his soil will be sated with bread, but he who pursues vanities lacks an [understanding] heart.* ¹² *A wicked person craves spoils of evildoers, but the root of the righteous will provide for them.* * ¹³ *In the sin of the lips* * *lies a snare of evil, but a righteous person escapes travail.* ¹⁴ *From the fruit of a man's mouth he will be sated with good, for the recompense of a man's handiwork will be returned to him!* ¹⁵ *The way of the foolish one is upright in his eyes, but the wise man heeds counsel.* ¹⁶ *The foolish one's anger will become known on that very day,* * *but a clever man conceals his shame.* ¹⁷ *One who [always] spouts the truth will give righteous testimony, but a witness saying falsehoods [personifies] deceit.* ¹⁸ *There is one who speaks [harshly] like piercings of a sword, but the tongue of the wise heals.* ¹⁹ *True speech is established forever, but a false tongue is only for a moment.* ²⁰ *Deceit lurks in the heart of those who plot evil, but for those who counsel peace there is gladness.* ²¹ *There will not befall a righteous man any iniquity, but the wicked are filled with evil.* ²² *False lips are an abomination to* HASHEM, *but those who act in faith are His desire.* ²³ *A clever person conceals knowledge, but the heart of fools proclaims foolishness.* * ²⁴ *The hand of the diligent will rule, but deceit will melt.* ²⁵ *When there is worry in a man's heart, he should suppress it, let a good thing convert it to gladness.* * ²⁶ *A righteous one has an advantage over his fellow, but the [successful] way of the wicked leads them astray.* * ²⁷ *A deceitful person will not get to roast his catch, but the wealth of the diligent person is precious.* ²⁸ *In the pathway of charity there is life; in the pathway it leads there is no death.*

13 ¹ **A** wise son [desires] a father's discipline, but a scoffer has not heard chastisement.* ² *From the fruits of man's speech he will eat good [reward],* * *but the soul of the faithless [will eat] violence.* ³ *One who guards his mouth protects his soul; [but] one who opens wide his lips, that is his ruin.* ⁴ *The soul of the sluggard lusts and has nothing, but the soul of the diligent will be fattened.* ⁵ *A righteous person despises a false matter, but a wicked person sullies and insults.* * ⁶ *Charity will guard he who is upright of way, but evil will corrupt the sinner.*

13:2. If someone's words are kind, he will enjoy a good and peaceful life (*Yalkut Shimoni*).

13:5. A wicked person accepts every slander and uses it against his innocent victim.

יֵ֣שׁ מִ֭תְעַשֵּׁר וְאֵ֣ין כֹּ֑ל מִ֝תְרוֹשֵׁ֗שׁ וְה֣וֹן רָֽב: כֹּ֣פֶר נֶֽפֶשׁ־אִ֣ישׁ עָשְׁר֑וֹ וְ֝רָ֗שׁ לֹא־ ז–ח

שָׁמַ֥ע גְּעָרָֽה: אֽוֹר־צַדִּיקִ֥ים יִשְׂמָ֑ח וְנֵ֖ר רְשָׁעִ֣ים יִדְעָֽךְ: רַק־בְּ֭זָדוֹן יִתֵּ֣ן מַצָּ֑ה ט–י

וְאֶת־נ֖וֹעָצִ֣ים חָכְמָֽה: ה֭וֹן מֵהֶ֣בֶל יִמְעָ֑ט וְקֹבֵ֖ץ עַל־יָ֣ד יַרְבֶּֽה: תּוֹחֶ֣לֶת יא–יב

מְ֭מֻשָּׁכָה מַחֲלָה־לֵ֑ב וְעֵ֥ץ חַ֝יִּ֗ים תַּאֲוָ֥ה בָאָֽה: בָּ֣ז לְ֭דָבָר יֵחָ֣בֶל ל֑וֹ וְיִרֵ֥א יג

מִ֝צְוָ֗ה ה֣וּא יְשֻׁלָּֽם: תּוֹרַ֣ת חָ֭כָם מְק֣וֹר חַיִּ֑ים לָ֝ס֗וּר מִמֹּ֥קְשֵׁי מָֽוֶת: שֵֽׂכֶל־ט֭וֹב יד–טו

יִתֶּן־חֵ֑ן וְדֶ֖רֶךְ בֹּגְדִ֣ים אֵיתָֽן: כָּל־עָ֭רוּם יַעֲשֶׂ֣ה בְדָ֑עַת וּ֝כְסִ֗יל יִפְרֹ֥שׂ אִוֶּֽלֶת: טז

מַלְאָ֣ךְ רָ֭שָׁע יִפֹּ֣ל בְּרָ֑ע וְצִ֖יר אֱמוּנִ֣ים מַרְפֵּֽא: רֵ֣ישׁ וְ֭קָלוֹן פּוֹרֵ֣עַ מוּסָ֑ר יז–יח

וְשׁוֹמֵ֖ר תּוֹכַ֣חַת יְכֻבָּֽד: תַּאֲוָ֣ה נִ֭הְיָה תֶּעֱרַ֣ב לְנָ֑פֶשׁ וְתוֹעֲבַ֥ת כְּ֝סִילִ֗ים ס֥וּר יט

מֵרָֽע: °הַלוֹךְ [הוֹלֵ֣ךְ ק] אֶת־חֲכָמִ֣ים °וחכם [יֶחְכָּ֑ם ק] וְרֹעֶ֖ה כְסִילִ֣ים כ

יֵר֣וֹעַ: חַ֭טָּאִים תְּרַדֵּ֣ף רָעָ֑ה וְאֶת־צַ֝דִּיקִ֗ים יְשַׁלֶּם־טֽוֹב: ט֗וֹב יַנְחִ֥יל בְּנֵֽי־ כא–כב

בָנִ֑ים וְצָפ֥וּן לַ֝צַּדִּ֗יק חֵ֣יל חוֹטֵֽא: רָב־אֹ֭כֶל נִ֣יר רָאשִׁ֑ים וְיֵ֥שׁ נִ֝סְפֶּ֗ה בְּלֹ֣א כג

מִשְׁפָּֽט: חוֹשֵׂ֣ךְ שִׁ֭בְטוֹ שׂוֹנֵ֣א בְנ֑וֹ וְ֝אֹהֲב֗וֹ שִֽׁחֲר֥וֹ מוּסָֽר: צַדִּ֗יק אֹ֭כֵל לְשֹׂ֣בַע כד–כה

נַפְשׁ֑וֹ וּבֶ֖טֶן רְשָׁעִ֣ים תֶּחְסָֽר: חַכְמ֣וֹת נָ֭שִׁים בָּֽנְתָ֣ה בֵיתָ֑הּ וְ֝אִוֶּ֗לֶת בְּיָדֶ֥יהָ א

תֶהֶרְסֶֽנּוּ: הוֹלֵ֣ךְ בְּ֭יָשְׁרוֹ יְרֵ֣א יְהֹוָ֑ה וּנְל֖וֹז דְּרָכָ֣יו בּוֹזֵֽהוּ: בְּֽפִי־אֱ֭וִיל חֹ֣טֶר ב–ג

גַּאֲוָ֑ה וְשִׂפְתֵ֥י חֲ֝כָמִ֗ים תִּשְׁמוּרֵֽם: בְּאֵ֣ין אֲ֭לָפִים אֵב֣וּס בָּ֑ר וְרָב־תְּ֝בוּא֗וֹת ד

בְּכֹ֣חַ שֽׁוֹר: עֵ֣ד אֱ֭מוּנִים לֹ֣א יְכַזֵּ֑ב וְיָפִ֥יחַ כְּ֝זָבִ֗ים עֵ֣ד שָֽׁקֶר: בִּקֶּשׁ־לֵ֣ץ חָכְמָ֣ה ה–ו

וָאָ֑יִן וְדַ֖עַת לְנָב֣וֹן נָקָֽל: לֵ֣ךְ מִ֭נֶּגֶד לְאִ֣ישׁ כְּסִ֑יל וּבַל־יָ֝דַ֗עְתָּ שִׂפְתֵי־דָֽעַת: ז

חָכְמַ֣ת עָ֭רוּם הָבִ֣ין דַּרְכּ֑וֹ וְאִוֶּ֖לֶת כְּסִילִ֣ים מִרְמָֽה: אֱ֭וִלִים יָלִ֣יץ אָשָׁ֑ם וּבֵ֖ין ח–ט

יְשָׁרִ֣ים רָצֽוֹן: לֵ֗ב י֭וֹדֵעַ מָרַ֣ת נַפְשׁ֑וֹ וּ֝בְשִׂמְחָת֗וֹ לֹא־יִתְעָ֥רַב זָֽר: בֵּ֤ית י–יא

רְשָׁעִ֥ים יִשָּׁמֵ֑ד וְאֹ֖הֶל יְשָׁרִ֣ים יַפְרִֽיחַ: יֵ֤שׁ דֶּ֣רֶךְ יָ֭שָׁר לִפְנֵי־אִ֑ישׁ וְ֝אַחֲרִיתָ֗הּ יב

דַּרְכֵי־מָֽוֶת: גַּם־בִּשְׂח֥וֹק יִכְאַב־לֵ֑ב וְאַחֲרִיתָ֖הּ שִׂמְחָ֣ה תוּגָֽה: מִדְּרָכָ֣יו יג–יד

יִ֭שְׂבַּע ס֣וּג לֵ֑ב וּ֝מֵעָלָ֗יו אִ֣ישׁ טֽוֹב: פֶּ֭תִי יַאֲמִ֣ין לְכָל־דָּבָ֑ר וְ֝עָר֗וּם יָבִ֥ין טו

לַאֲשֻׁרֽוֹ: חָכָ֣ם יָ֭רֵא וְסָ֣ר מֵרָ֑ע וּ֝כְסִ֗יל מִתְעַבֵּ֥ר וּבוֹטֵֽחַ: קְֽצַר־אַ֭פַּיִם יַעֲשֶׂ֣ה טז–יז

אִוֶּ֑לֶת וְאִ֥ישׁ מְ֝זִמּ֗וֹת יִשָּׂנֵֽא: נָחֲל֣וּ פְתָאיִ֣ם אִוֶּ֑לֶת וַ֝עֲרוּמִ֗ים יַכְתִּ֥רוּ דָֽעַת: יח

13:7. Both of these courses should be avoided. If a person feigns wealth he will impoverish himself by incurring needless expenses. If he feigns poverty, he will not fulfill his charitable obligations (*Meiri*).

13:8. A person's generous charities can atone for his sins, but only if he does not rebuke or insult the poor when he gives to them (*Rashi*).

13:11. Wealth gained dishonestly will not last; but if it is accumulated gradually through hard work, it will grow (*Ibn Ezra*).

13:15. Traitors are too set in their ways to respond to the arguments of reasonable people (*Ibn Ezra*).

13:17. Someone who becomes the agent of evil people will himself be dragged down, but one who serves the righteous will be a source of goodness (*Ralbag*).

13:19. Fools detest the very idea that they should give up their wickedness.

13:20. One who walks with the wise is compared to someone who enters a perfumery; the pleasant scent will linger on his clothing. Likewise one who associates with the wicked is like one who enters a tannery; the foul odor will accompany him all day (*Yalkut Shimoni*).

13:21. A person's own deeds will pursue him: The sinners will be pursued by their evil; the righteous by their good (*Rashi; Metzudos*).

13:23. Poor laborers work hard for the landowners who enjoy the fruits of their workers' efforts, but if the rich do not provide for the poor, their wealth will be swept away (*Yalkut HaMachiri*).

13:24. One who truly loves his child disciplines him promptly (*Rabbeinu Yonah*).

13:25. The righteous feel satisfied with what they have, but the wicked always want more.

7 Some pretend to be rich and have nothing, but others act poor and have great wealth. * 8 A man's wealth may redeem his soul, but only if the poor hear no chastisement. * 9 The light of the righteous will rejoice, but the lamp of the wicked shall die out. 10 Only by willfulness is strife fomented; but wisdom is with those who take counsel. 11 Wealth gained by vanity will diminish, but that gathered by hand will increase. * 12 A drawn-out hope brings sickness of heart, but desire attained is a tree of life. 13 He who scorns a word will cause himself injury, but he who reveres a commandment will be rewarded. 14 The teaching of the wise man is a source of life, to turn [him] away from the snares of death. 15 Good sense provides grace, but the way of the faithless is hard. * 16 Every clever person acts with knowledge, but the fool broadcasts his foolishness. 17 The agent of a wicked person will fall into evil, but the emissary of the faithful will bring healing. * 18 Poverty and shame befall one who rejects discipline, but he who heeds rebuke will be honored. 19 Lust broken is sweet to the soul, but turning from evil is an abomination to fools. * 20 One who walks with the wise will grow wise, * but the companion of fools will be broken. 21 Evil pursues sinners, but the righteous will be rewarded with good. * 22 A good person will bequeath to grandchildren, but wealth of a sinner is secreted for a righteous person. 23 Much food grows from the furrows of the poor, and substance may be swept away for lack of justice. * 24 One who spares his rod hates his child, but he who loves him disciplines him in his youth. * 25 A righteous person eats to satisfy his soul, but the stomach of the wicked will [always] lack. *

14 1 The wise among women, each built her house, * but the foolish one tears it down with her hands. 2 One who walks in his uprightness fears HASHEM; the perverse one, his ways shame Him. 3 In the mouth of the foolish one is the staff of pride, but the lips of the wise will guard them. 4 Where there are no oxen, the trough is clean; but many crops come [through] the power of the ox. 5 One who will not deceive is a trustworthy witness, but the spouter of deceptions is a false witness. 6 The scoffer seeks wisdom yet there is none, but wisdom will come easily to the understanding one. 7 Go far away from a man who is a fool, lest you not know the lips of knowledge. 8 The wisdom of the clever is to understand his way; the folly of fools is deceit. 9 A guilt-offering will interpose for foolish ones, but [HASHEM's] favor is among the upright. 10 The heart knows its own bitterness, and no stranger will share in its joy. 11 The house of the wicked will be destroyed, but the tent of the just will blossom. 12 There is a way that seems right to a man, but at its end are the ways of death; 13 even in sporting the heart may ache, and the end of gladness may be sorrow. * 14 A wayward heart will be satisfied with its ways, but a good man will take leave of him. 15 A fool believes anything, but a clever person understands it correctly. 16 A wise man fears and turns away from evil, but a fool becomes enraged and is confident. * 17 A short-tempered person acts foolishly, and a person who designs [evil] is hated. 18 Fools have inherited folly, but the clever are crowned with knowledge.

14:1. The wise woman is industrious and her power proves itself in private, communal and public life. Through her wisdom she knows what to avoid, what is destructive to her home (R' Hirsch).

14:13. Innocent sporting may seem enjoyable, but it will be punished if it prevents productive activity (Ralbag).

14:16-18. Careful scrutiny and meticulous self-evaluation are characteristic of the righteous. Impulsive actions and superficiality are the mark of fools.

שַׁחוּ רָעִים לִפְנֵי טוֹבִים וּרְשָׁעִים עַל־שַׁעֲרֵי צַדִּיק: גַּם־לְרֵעֵהוּ יִשָּׂנֵא רָשׁ

יט-כ

וְאֹהֲבֵי עָשִׁיר רַבִּים: בָּז־לְרֵעֵהוּ חוֹטֵא וּמְחוֹנֵן °עֲנָיִים [°עֲנָוִים ק] אַשְׁרָיו:

כא

הֲלוֹא־יִתְעוּ חֹרְשֵׁי רָע וְחֶסֶד וֶאֱמֶת חֹרְשֵׁי טוֹב: בְּכָל־עֶצֶב יִהְיֶה מוֹתָר

כב-כג

וּדְבַר־שְׂפָתַיִם אַךְ־לְמַחְסוֹר: עֲטֶרֶת חֲכָמִים עָשְׁרָם אִוֶּלֶת כְּסִילִים

כד

אִוֶּלֶת: מַצִּיל נְפָשׁוֹת עֵד אֱמֶת וְיָפִחַ כְּזָבִים מִרְמָה: בְּיִרְאַת יְהוָה מִבְטַח

כה-כו

עֹז וּלְבָנָיו יִהְיֶה מַחְסֶה: יִרְאַת יְהוָה מְקוֹר חַיִּים לָסוּר מִמֹּקְשֵׁי מָוֶת: בְּרָב־

כז-כח

עָם הַדְרַת־מֶלֶךְ וּבְאֶפֶס לְאֹם מְחִתַּת רָזוֹן: אֶרֶךְ אַפַּיִם רַב־תְּבוּנָה וּקְצַר־

כט

רוּחַ מֵרִים אִוֶּלֶת: חַיֵּי בְשָׂרִים לֵב מַרְפֵּא וּרְקַב עֲצָמוֹת קִנְאָה: עֹשֵׁק

ל-לא

דָּל חֵרֵף עֹשֵׂהוּ וּמְכַבְּדוֹ חֹנֵן אֶבְיוֹן: בְּרָעָתוֹ יִדָּחֶה רָשָׁע וְחֹסֶה בְמוֹתוֹ

לב

צַדִּיק: בְּלֵב נָבוֹן תָּנוּחַ חָכְמָה וּבְקֶרֶב כְּסִילִים תִּוָּדֵעַ: צְדָקָה תְּרוֹמֵם־גּוֹי

לג-לד

וְחֶסֶד לְאֻמִּים חַטָּאת: רְצוֹן־מֶלֶךְ לְעֶבֶד מַשְׂכִּיל וְעֶבְרָתוֹ תִּהְיֶה מֵבִישׁ:

לה

מַעֲנֶה־רַּךְ יָשִׁיב חֵמָה וּדְבַר־עֶצֶב יַעֲלֶה־אָף: לְשׁוֹן חֲכָמִים תֵּיטִיב דָּעַת

טו א-ב

וּפִי כְסִילִים יַבִּיעַ אִוֶּלֶת: בְּכָל־מָקוֹם עֵינֵי יְהוָה צֹפוֹת רָעִים וְטוֹבִים:

ג

מַרְפֵּא לָשׁוֹן עֵץ חַיִּים וְסֶלֶף בָּהּ שֶׁבֶר בְּרוּחַ: אֱוִיל יִנְאַץ מוּסַר אָבִיו

ד-ה

וְשֹׁמֵר תּוֹכַחַת יַעְרִם: בֵּית צַדִּיק חֹסֶן רָב וּבִתְבוּאַת רָשָׁע נֶעְכָּרֶת: שִׂפְתֵי

ו-ז

חֲכָמִים יְזָרוּ דָעַת וְלֵב כְּסִילִים לֹא־כֵן: זֶבַח רְשָׁעִים תּוֹעֲבַת יְהוָה

ח

וּתְפִלַּת יְשָׁרִים רְצוֹנוֹ: תּוֹעֲבַת יְהוָה דֶּרֶךְ רָשָׁע וּמְרַדֵּף צְדָקָה יֶאֱהָב: מוּסָר

ט-י

רָע לְעֹזֵב אֹרַח שׂוֹנֵא תוֹכַחַת יָמוּת: שְׁאוֹל וַאֲבַדּוֹן נֶגֶד יְהוָה אַף כִּי־

יא

לִבּוֹת בְּנֵי־אָדָם: לֹא יֶאֱהַב־לֵץ הוֹכֵחַ לוֹ אֶל־חֲכָמִים לֹא יֵלֵךְ: לֵב שָׂמֵחַ

יב-יג

יֵיטִב פָּנִים וּבְעַצְּבַת־לֵב רוּחַ נְכֵאָה: לֵב נָבוֹן יְבַקֶּשׁ־דָּעַת °וּפְנֵי [°וּפִי ק]

יד

כְּסִילִים יִרְעֶה אִוֶּלֶת: כָּל־יְמֵי עָנִי רָעִים וְטוֹב־לֵב מִשְׁתֶּה תָמִיד: טוֹב־

טו-טז

מְעַט בְּיִרְאַת יְהוָה מֵאוֹצָר רָב וּמְהוּמָה בוֹ: טוֹב אֲרֻחַת יָרָק וְאַהֲבָה־שָׁם

יז

מִשּׁוֹר אָבוּס וְשִׂנְאָה־בוֹ: אִישׁ חֵמָה יְגָרֶה מָדוֹן וְאֶרֶךְ אַפַּיִם יַשְׁקִיט רִיב:

יח-יט

דֶּרֶךְ עָצֵל כִּמְשֻׂכַת חָדֶק וְאֹרַח יְשָׁרִים סְלֻלָה:

בֵּן חָכָם יְשַׂמַּח־אָב וּכְסִיל אָדָם בּוֹזֶה אִמּוֹ: אִוֶּלֶת שִׂמְחָה לַחֲסַר־

כ-כא

לֵב וְאִישׁ תְּבוּנָה יְיַשֶּׁר־לָכֶת: הָפֵר מַחֲשָׁבוֹת בְּאֵין סוֹד וּבְרֹב יוֹעֲצִים

כב

תָּקוּם: שִׂמְחָה לָאִישׁ בְּמַעֲנֵה־פִיו וְדָבָר בְּעִתּוֹ מַה־טּוֹב: אֹרַח חַיִּים

כג-כד

לְמַעְלָה לְמַשְׂכִּיל לְמַעַן סוּר מִשְּׁאוֹל מָטָּה: בֵּית גֵּאִים יִסַּח | יְהוָה

כה

14:25. If an honest witness testifies against a murderer, he prevents him from killing other people; if he testifies for the defense, he saves the defendant. A liar saves only the guilty party (*Metzudos*).

14:26-27. Fear of God is a life-giving spring, for it keeps one from sinning and falling into death's snares (*Ibn Ezra*).

14:32. One who always puts his trust in God will receive the reward of the righteous in the World to Come (*Rashi*).

14:33. Wise men keep their virtues private, but fools rush to publicize whatever little bit of wisdom they may possess (*Rashi*).

14:34. Regimes that rob from one group in order to dispense "kindness" to others (*Rashi*).

15:6. It is fortified with the merit of the owner's righteousness, and with the Divine Providence that rests upon this righteous individual (*Ralbag*).

15:7. Fools do not spread wisdom (*Ibn Ezra*).

¹⁹ *Evildoers will grovel before good people, and the wicked at the gates of a righteous one.* ²⁰ *A poor person will be hated even by his companion, but the lovers of the rich [will be] many.* ²¹ *He who shames his friend is a sinner, but praiseworthy is one who is gracious to the humble.* ²² *Have the plotters of evil not gone astray? But those who plan goodness [will reap] kindness and truth.* ²³ *In all toil there will be gain, but talk of the lips brings only loss.* ²⁴ *The crown of the wise is their wealth; but the foolishness of fools is but foolishness.* ²⁵ *A true witness saves lives, but a spouter of deceptions [saves only a man of] deceit.* * ²⁶ *In fear of HASHEM is a powerful stronghold, and for his children it will be a shelter;* ²⁷ *fear of HASHEM is the source of life, to turn one away from the snares of death.* * ²⁸ *A multitude of people is a king's glory, but without a regime, rulership is broken.* ²⁹ *Slowness to anger [shows] much understanding, but a short-spirited person elevates foolishness.* ³⁰ *A tender heart [brings] healing of the flesh, but envy [brings] rotting of the bones.* ³¹ *One who robs the poor man disgraces his Maker, but he who is gracious to the destitute honors Him.* ³² *In his trouble the wicked one is cast off [from God], but he who takes shelter [in Him] remains righteous in death.* * ³³ *Wisdom will reside in an understanding heart, but within fools it will be publicized.* * ³⁴ *Charity will uplift a nation, but the kindness of regimes* *is a sin.* ³⁵ *The favor of the king will be upon the wise servant, but his wrath will be [upon] the shameful one.*

15 ¹ A gentle reply turns away wrath, but a galling word incites anger. ² *The tongue of the wise will enhance wisdom, but the mouth of fools will spout foolishness.* ³ *The eyes of HASHEM are everywhere, seeing the evil and the good.* ⁴ *A soothing tongue is a tree of life, but corruption of it is damage of the spirit.* ⁵ *A foolish one despises his father's discipline, but he who harbors reproof will become clever.* ⁶ *The house of the righteous one is greatly fortified,* * *but with the arrival of a wicked one it becomes sullied.* ⁷ *The lips of the wise spread knowledge, but not so the heart of fools.* * ⁸ *The offering of the wicked is an abomination to HASHEM, but His desire is the prayer of the upright.* ⁹ *The way of a wicked person is an abomination to HASHEM, but He loves a pursuer of righteousness.* ¹⁰ *Stern discipline [awaits] for one who forsakes the path; one who hates reproof will die.* ¹¹ *The grave and perdition are exposed to HASHEM, surely the hearts of men.* * ¹² *A scoffer does not like his being reproved; he will not go to the wise.* ¹³ *A glad heart cheers the face, but a despondent heart [causes] a broken spirit.* ¹⁴ *An understanding heart will seek wisdom, and the mouth of fools will befriend folly.* ¹⁵ *All the days of a poor man are bad, but a good-hearted person feasts perpetually.* ¹⁶ *Better a little [gained] through fear of HASHEM than a great treasure accompanied by turmoil.* ¹⁷ *Better a meal of greens where there is love than a fattened ox where there is hatred.* ¹⁸ *The wrathful man incites strife, but the slow to anger calms a quarrel.* ¹⁹ *The way of the sluggard is fenced with thorns, but the path of the upright is paved.* ²⁰ *A wise son gladdens his father, and the foolish man shames his mother.* ²¹ *Foolishness is joy to one who lacks [an understanding] heart, but a man of understanding [will rejoice] when he walks uprightly.* ²² *Thoughts are frustrated when there is no counsel, but through an abundance of counsel they will be established.* ²³ *A man has joy through the reply of his mouth, and how good is a word in its time.* ²⁴ *A path of life [waits] above for the intelligent one, so that his soul will turn away from the grave below.* ²⁵ *HASHEM will uproot the house of the arrogant,*

15:11. Nothing escapes God's view. If the netherworld and perdition — places of the greatest impurity — are before Him, surely He sees the hearts of mankind (*Vilna Gaon*).

כו־כז   יִסַּ֤ע גְּב֣וּל אַלְמָנָֽה׃ תּוֹעֲבַ֣ת יְ֭הוָה מַחְשְׁב֣וֹת רָ֑ע וּ֝טְהֹרִ֗ים אִמְרֵי־נֹֽעַם׃ עֹכֵ֣ר

כח   בֵּ֭יתוֹ בּוֹצֵ֣עַ בָּ֑צַע וְשׂוֹנֵ֖א מַתָּנֹ֣ת יִחְיֶֽה׃ לֵ֣ב צַ֭דִּיק יֶהְגֶּ֣ה לַעֲנ֑וֹת וּפִ֥י רְ֝שָׁעִ֗ים

כט־ל   יַבִּ֥יעַ רָעֽוֹת׃ רָח֣וֹק יְ֭הוָה מֵרְשָׁעִ֑ים וּתְפִלַּ֖ת צַדִּיקִ֣ים יִשְׁמָֽע׃ מְאוֹר־עֵ֭ינַיִם

לא   יְשַׂמַּֽח־לֵ֑ב שְׁמוּעָ֥ה ט֝וֹבָ֗ה תְּדַשֶּׁן־עָֽצֶם׃ אֹ֣זֶן שֹׁ֭מַעַת תּוֹכַ֣חַת חַיִּ֑ים בְּקֶ֥רֶב

לב־לג   חֲכָמִ֣ים תָּלִֽין׃ פּוֹרֵ֣עַ מ֭וּסָר מוֹאֵ֣ס נַפְשׁ֑וֹ וְשׁוֹמֵ֥עַ תּ֝וֹכַ֗חַת ק֣וֹנֶה לֵּֽב׃ יִרְאַ֣ת

טז   א   יְהוָ֣ה מוּסַ֣ר חָכְמָ֑ה וְלִפְנֵ֖י כָב֣וֹד עֲנָוָֽה׃ לְאָדָ֥ם מַֽעַרְכֵי־לֵ֑ב וּ֝מֵיְהוָ֗ה מַעֲנֵ֥ה

ב־ג   לָשֽׁוֹן׃ כָּֽל־דַּרְכֵי־אִ֭ישׁ זַ֣ךְ בְּעֵינָ֑יו וְתֹכֵ֖ן רוּח֣וֹת יְהוָֽה׃ גֹּ֣ל אֶל־יְהוָ֣ה מַעֲשֶׂ֑יךָ

ד־ה   וְ֝יִכֹּ֗נוּ מַחְשְׁבֹתֶֽיךָ׃ כֹּ֤ל פָּעַ֣ל יְ֭הוָה לַֽמַּעֲנֵ֑הוּ וְגַם־רָ֝שָׁ֗ע לְי֣וֹם רָעָֽה׃ תּוֹעֲבַ֣ת

ו   יְ֭הוָה כָּל־גְּבַהּ־לֵ֑ב יָ֥ד לְ֝יָ֗ד לֹ֣א יִנָּקֶֽה׃ בְּחֶ֣סֶד וֶ֭אֱמֶת יְכֻפַּ֣ר עָוֺ֑ן וּבְיִרְאַ֥ת

ז   יְ֝הוָ֗ה ס֣וּר מֵרָֽע׃ בִּרְצ֣וֹת יְ֭הוָה דַּרְכֵי־אִ֑ישׁ גַּם־א֝וֹיְבָ֗יו יַשְׁלִ֥ם אִתּֽוֹ׃ טֽוֹב־

ט   מְ֭עַט בִּצְדָקָ֑ה מֵרֹ֥ב תְּ֝בוּא֗וֹת בְּלֹ֣א מִשְׁפָּֽט׃ לֵ֣ב אָ֭דָם יְחַשֵּׁ֣ב דַּרְכּ֑וֹ וַֽיהוָ֗ה

י־יא   יָכִ֥ין צַעֲדֽוֹ׃ קֶ֤סֶם ׀ עַֽל־שִׂפְתֵי־מֶ֗לֶךְ בְּ֭מִשְׁפָּט לֹ֣א יִמְעַל־פִּֽיו׃ פֶּ֤לֶס ׀ וּמֹאזְנֵ֣י

יב   מִ֭שְׁפָּט לַֽיהוָ֑ה מַ֝עֲשֵׂ֗הוּ כָּל־אַבְנֵי־כִֽיס׃ תּוֹעֲבַ֣ת מְ֭לָכִים עֲשׂ֣וֹת רֶ֑שַׁע כִּ֥י

יג־יד   בִ֝צְדָקָ֗ה יִכּ֥וֹן כִּסֵּֽא׃ רְצ֣וֹן מְ֭לָכִים שִׂפְתֵי־צֶ֑דֶק וְדֹבֵ֖ר יְשָׁרִ֣ים יֶאֱהָֽב׃ חֲמַת־

טו   מֶ֥לֶךְ מַלְאֲכֵי־מָ֑וֶת וְאִ֖ישׁ חָכָ֣ם יְכַפְּרֶֽנָּה׃ בְּאוֹר־פְּנֵי־מֶ֥לֶךְ חַיִּ֑ים וּ֝רְצוֹנ֗וֹ

טז   כְּעָ֥ב מַלְקֽוֹשׁ׃ קְנֹֽה־חָכְמָ֗ה מַה־טּ֥וֹב מֵחָר֑וּץ וּקְנ֥וֹת בִּ֝ינָ֗ה נִבְחָ֥ר מִכָּֽסֶף׃

יז־יח   מְסִלַּ֣ת יְ֭שָׁרִים ס֣וּר מֵרָ֑ע שֹׁמֵ֥ר נַ֝פְשׁ֗וֹ נֹצֵ֥ר דַּרְכּֽוֹ׃ לִפְנֵי־שֶׁ֥בֶר גָּא֑וֹן וְלִפְנֵ֥י

יט   כִ֝שָּׁל֗וֹן גֹּ֣בַהּ רֽוּחַ׃ ט֣וֹב שְׁפַל־ר֭וּחַ אֶת־°עניים [עֲנָוִ֑ים ק] מֵֽחַלֵּ֥ק שָׁלָ֗ל

כ־כא   אֶת־גֵּאִֽים׃ מַשְׂכִּ֣יל עַל־דָּ֭בָר יִמְצָא־ט֑וֹב וּבוֹטֵ֖חַ בַּֽיהוָ֣ה אַשְׁרָֽיו׃ לַחֲכַם־

כב   לֵ֭ב יִקָּרֵ֣א נָב֑וֹן וּמֶ֥תֶק שְׂ֝פָתַ֗יִם יֹסִ֥יף לֶֽקַח׃ מְק֣וֹר חַ֭יִּים שֵׂ֣כֶל בְּעָלָ֑יו וּמוּסַ֖ר

כג־כד   אֱוִלִ֣ים אִוֶּֽלֶת׃ לֵ֣ב חָ֭כָם יַשְׂכִּ֣יל פִּ֑יהוּ וְעַל־שְׂ֝פָתָ֗יו יֹסִ֥יף לֶֽקַח׃ צוּף־דְּבַ֥שׁ

כה   אִמְרֵי־נֹ֑עַם מָת֥וֹק לַ֝נֶּ֗פֶשׁ וּמַרְפֵּ֥א לָעָֽצֶם׃ יֵ֤שׁ דֶּ֣רֶךְ יָ֭שָׁר לִפְנֵי־אִ֑ישׁ

כו־כז   וְ֝אַחֲרִיתָ֗הּ דַּרְכֵי־מָֽוֶת׃ נֶ֣פֶשׁ עָ֭מֵל עָ֣מְלָה לּ֑וֹ כִּֽי־אָכַ֖ף עָלָ֣יו פִּֽיהוּ׃ אִ֣ישׁ

כח   בְּ֭לִיַּעַל כֹּרֶ֣ה רָעָ֑ה וְעַל־°שפתיו [שְׂפָת֗וֹ ק] כְּאֵ֣שׁ צָרָֽבֶת׃ אִ֣ישׁ תַּ֭הְפֻּכוֹת

כט   °ין זעירא   יְשַׁלַּ֣ח מָד֑וֹן וְ֝נִרְגָּ֗ן מַפְרִ֥יד אַלּֽוּף׃ אִ֣ישׁ חָ֭מָס יְפַתֶּ֣ה רֵעֵ֑הוּ וְ֝הוֹלִיכ֗וֹ בְּדֶ֖רֶךְ

ל־לא   לֹא־טֽוֹב׃ עֹצֶ֣ה עֵ֭ינָיו לַחְשֹׁ֣ב תַּהְפֻּכ֑וֹת קֹרֵ֥ץ שְׂ֝פָתָ֗יו כִּלָּ֥ה רָעָֽה׃ עֲטֶ֣רֶת

15:25. Divine Providence levels the edifices of those whose proud fortunes have misled them. But He establishes a humble, forsaken widow in a position of self-sufficient independence (R' Hirsch).

15:26. God abhors those who clothe evil ideas in mellow language (Metzudos).

15:28. Righteousness requires deliberation before deciding whether to speak and what to say. But the wicked spout slander and heresy without any control (Malbim).

15:30. The eyes are enlightened when doubts are resolved.

15:33. Fear of God will lead a person to accept chastisement wisely, and thus live honorably (Ralbag).

16:1. Man has ideas, but God gives speech, which will either cause him to stumble with his words or speak eloquently (Rashi).

16:5. See 11:21 above.

16:9. When a righteous person plans his way, God will help him, for "One who comes to purify is assisted from on High" (Shabbos 104a).

16:11. Just as each item weighed on a balance scale offsets a different combination of weights, depending on its mass, so God deals with everyone individually, depending on their deeds (Rashi).

16:20. If one's analysis of a subject shows that performance of a particular commandment may involve danger or financial loss, yet he trusts in God and does it, he is praiseworthy (Rashi).

but He upholds the boundary of a widow. * ²⁶ The abomination of HASHEM is thoughts of evil; words of pleasantness should be pure. * ²⁷ One who gains through greed sullies his home, but one who hates gifts will live. ²⁸ The heart of a righteous person will consider what to answer, but the mouth of the wicked will spout evil. * ²⁹ HASHEM is far from the wicked, but He hears the prayer of the righteous. ³⁰ Enlightened eyes * will gladden the heart; good news will fatten a bone. ³¹ The ear that hears life-giving reproof will abide in the midst of the wise. ³² He who negates discipline despises his soul, but one who listens to reproof acquires [an understanding] heart. ³³ Fear of HASHEM is the discipline of wisdom, * and humility precedes honor.

16

¹ To man belongs the arrangements of [thoughts in] his heart, but from HASHEM comes the tongue's reply. * ² All of man's ways are pure in his own eyes, but HASHEM is in the midst of spirits. ³ Turn your deeds towards HASHEM and your thoughts will be set aright. ⁴ Everything HASHEM made [He made] for His sake, even the evildoer for the day of retribution. ⁵ Every haughty heart is the abomination of HASHEM, [from] hand to hand — he will not be exonerated. * ⁶ Through kindness and truth iniquity will be forgiven, if through fear of HASHEM one turns from evil. ⁷ When HASHEM favors a man's ways, even his foes will make peace with him. ⁸ Better a little through righteousness than much produce without justice. ⁹ A man's heart will plot his way, and HASHEM will set his steps aright. * ¹⁰ There is a charm on the lips of a king; in judgment his mouth will not deceive. ¹¹ A scale and just balances are HASHEM's; His deeds are like weights in a pouch. * ¹² To do evil is an abomination for kings, for a throne is established through righteousness. ¹³ The desire of kings is righteous lips, and he will love one who speaks upright [words]. ¹⁴ The king's wrath is [like] angels of death, but a wise man will appease it. ¹⁵ In the light of the king's countenance is life, and his favor is like a rain cloud. ¹⁶ How much better than fine gold is the acquisition of wisdom, and the acquisition of understanding is choicer than silver! ¹⁷ The paved road of the upright is turning from evil; one who keeps his way guards his soul. ¹⁸ Pride precedes destruction, and arrogance comes before failure. ¹⁹ Better [to be] lowly of spirit with the humble than [to be] sharing spoils with the proud. ²⁰ One who undertakes a matter intelligently will find good [success]; and praiseworthy is he who trusts in HASHEM. * ²¹ The wise of heart will be called an understanding person, and one whose speech is sweet will gain learning. * ²² Intelligence is a source of life to its possessor, but the discipline of foolish ones foolishness. * ²³ The heart of a wise man places intelligence into his mouth, and increases learning on his lips. ²⁴ Words of pleasantness are a honeycomb, sweet to the soul and healing to the bone. ²⁵ There is a way that seems right to man, but at its end are the ways of death. ²⁶ The working spirit works for itself, when its mouth humbles itself to it. * ²⁷ The lawless man digs up evil, as if a fire burns on his lip. ²⁸ A duplicitous man incites strife, and a complainer estranges a ruler. ²⁹ The man of violence entices his companion and leads him in a way that is not good. ³⁰ One who shuts his eyes to think of duplicity [and] signals with his lips has consummated evil. * ³¹ The crown of

---

16:21. There is a progression: The wise student will gain understanding (*Metzudos*); and the teacher who makes his words appealing to his students will himself grow in learning (*Rashi*).

16:22. It is folly to chastise fools.

16:26. When a mouth forgoes its desire for food and

goads the spirit to labor in pursuit of knowledge, benefits accrue to the person (*Ralbag*).

16:30. He closes his eyes to concentrate on his evil designs and then signals to his co-conspirators, thus carrying out his plan (*Metzudos*).

לב תִּפְאֶרֶת שֵׂיבָה בְּדֶרֶךְ צְדָקָה תִּמָּצֵא: טוֹב אֶרֶךְ אַפַּיִם מִגִּבּוֹר וּמֹשֵׁל

יז לג‑א בְּרוּחוֹ מִלֹּכֵד עִיר: בַּחֵיק יוּטַל אֶת־הַגּוֹרָל וּמֵיהוָֹה כָּל־מִשְׁפָּטוֹ: טוֹב פַּת

ב חֲרֵבָה וְשַׁלְוָה־בָהּ מִבַּיִת מָלֵא זִבְחֵי־רִיב: עֶבֶד־מַשְׂכִּיל יִמְשֹׁל בְּבֵן

ג מֵבִישׁ וּבְתוֹךְ אַחִים יַחֲלֹק נַחֲלָה: מַצְרֵף לַכֶּסֶף וְכוּר לַזָּהָב וּבֹחֵן לִבּוֹת

ד יְהוָֹה: מֵרַע מַקְשִׁיב עַל־שְׂפַת־אָוֶן שֶׁקֶר מֵזִין עַל־לְשׁוֹן הַוֹּת: לֹעֵג לָרָשׁ

ו חֵרֵף עֹשֵׂהוּ שָׂמֵחַ לְאֵיד לֹא יִנָּקֶה: עֲטֶרֶת זְקֵנִים בְּנֵי בָנִים וְתִפְאֶרֶת בָּנִים

ז‑ח אֲבוֹתָם: לֹא־נָאוָה לְנָבָל שְׂפַת־יֶתֶר אַף כִּי־לְנָדִיב שְׂפַת־שָׁקֶר: אֶבֶן־חֵן

ט הַשֹּׁחַד בְּעֵינֵי בְעָלָיו אֶל־כָּל־אֲשֶׁר יִפְנֶה יַשְׂכִּיל: מְכַסֶּה־פֶּשַׁע מְבַקֵּשׁ

י אַהֲבָה וְשֹׁנֶה בְדָבָר מַפְרִיד אַלּוּף: תֵּחַת גְּעָרָה בְמֵבִין מֵהַכּוֹת כְּסִיל מֵאָה

יא‑יב אַךְ־מְרִי יְבַקֶּשׁ־רָע וּמַלְאָךְ אַכְזָרִי יְשֻׁלַּח־בּוֹ: פָּגוֹשׁ דֹּב שַׁכּוּל בְּאִישׁ וְאַל־

יג כְּסִיל בְּאִוַּלְתּוֹ: מֵשִׁיב רָעָה תַּחַת טוֹבָה לֹא־°תמיש [תָּמוּשׁ ק] רָעָה

יד‑טו מִבֵּיתוֹ: פּוֹטֵר מַיִם רֵאשִׁית מָדוֹן וְלִפְנֵי הִתְגַּלַּע הָרִיב נְטוֹשׁ: מַצְדִּיק רָשָׁע

טז וּמַרְשִׁיעַ צַדִּיק תּוֹעֲבַת יְהוָֹה גַּם־שְׁנֵיהֶם: לָמָּה־זֶּה מְחִיר בְּיַד־כְּסִיל

יז‑יח לִקְנוֹת חָכְמָה וְלֶב־אָיִן: בְּכָל־עֵת אֹהֵב הָרֵעַ וְאָח לְצָרָה יִוָּלֵד: אָדָם חֲסַר־

יט לֵב תּוֹקֵעַ כָּף עֹרֵב עֲרֻבָּה לִפְנֵי רֵעֵהוּ: אֹהֵב פֶּשַׁע אֹהֵב מַצָּה מַגְבִּיהַּ

כ‑כא פִּתְחוֹ מְבַקֶּשׁ־שָׁבֶר: עִקֶּשׁ־לֵב לֹא יִמְצָא־טוֹב וְנֶהְפָּךְ בִּלְשׁוֹנוֹ יִפּוֹל

כב בְּרָעָה: יֵלֵד כְּסִיל לְתוּגָה לוֹ וְלֹא־יִשְׂמַח אֲבִי נָבָל: לֵב שָׂמֵחַ יֵיטִב גֵּהָה

כג וְרוּחַ נְכֵאָה תְּיַבֶּשׁ־גָּרֶם: שֹׁחַד מֵחֵק רָשָׁע יִקָּח לְהַטּוֹת אָרְחוֹת מִשְׁפָּט:

כד‑כה אֶת־פְּנֵי מֵבִין חָכְמָה וְעֵינֵי כְסִיל בִּקְצֵה־אָרֶץ: כַּעַס לְאָבִיו בֵּן כְּסִיל וּמֶמֶר

כו לְיוֹלַדְתּוֹ: גַּם עֲנוֹשׁ לַצַּדִּיק לֹא־טוֹב לְהַכּוֹת נְדִיבִים עַל־יֹשֶׁר: חוֹשֵׂךְ

כח אֲמָרָיו יוֹדֵעַ דָּעַת °וקר [וִיקַר ק] רוּחַ אִישׁ תְּבוּנָה: גַּם אֱוִיל מַחֲרִישׁ

יח א חָכָם יֵחָשֵׁב אֹטֵם שְׂפָתָיו נָבוֹן: לְתַאֲוָה יְבַקֵּשׁ נִפְרָד בְּכָל־תּוּשִׁיָּה יִתְגַּלָּע:

ב‑ג לֹא־יַחְפֹּץ כְּסִיל בִּתְבוּנָה כִּי אִם־בְּהִתְגַּלּוֹת לִבּוֹ: בְּבוֹא־רָשָׁע בָּא

ד גַם־בּוּז וְעִם־קָלוֹן חֶרְפָּה: מַיִם עֲמֻקִּים דִּבְרֵי פִי־אִישׁ נַחַל נֹבֵעַ מְקוֹר

ה‑ו חָכְמָה: שְׂאֵת פְּנֵי־רָשָׁע לֹא־טוֹב לְהַטּוֹת צַדִּיק בַּמִּשְׁפָּט: שִׂפְתֵי כְסִיל

16:33. While people cast lots, customarily putting the lots in their laps for privacy, God has already decided the outcome (*Ralbag*).

17:1. Worldly success may be an illusion. A pauper with a tranquil home is more fortunate than a magnate whose home is filled with strife (*Malbim*).

17:2. A shameful son of his master.

17:3. With the proper tools, anyone can test the purity of precious metals, but only God can examine a person's heart (*Ralbag*).

17:5. One who rejoices in someone else's misfortune will suffer misfortune himself.

17:8. Just as a precious stone gains favor for its wearer, someone who bribes a judge expects to succeed in whatever he does (*Ibn Ezra*).

17:9. A victim of an offense who chooses to ignore it wins love, but if he keeps complaining about it, the result will be ill will and alienation of important people (*Ralbag*).

17:12. A raging fool can be more dangerous than a furious animal. A steel blade may penetrate a bear's fur, but a conceited fool's heart is armored against truth and sensible arguments (*R' Hirsch*).

17:14. Whoever commences a quarrel is like one who opens a hole in a dam. Just as the opening becomes progressively wider, so a quarrel escalates (*Rashi*).

17:16. A fool may have money in hand to hire a teacher, but it will be of no avail if he lacks will and an appreciation of the importance of knowledge.

17:17. A brother may not always show his love, but he can be counted on in times of adversity.

splendor is old age; it will be found in the path of righteousness. [32] He who is slow to anger is better than a strong man, and a master of his passions [is better] than a conqueror of a city. [33] [When] the lot is cast in the lap, its entire judgment has been decided by HASHEM. *

17   [1] **B**etter a dry piece of bread with peace in it than a house full of contentious celebrations. * [2] An intelligent servant will rule over a shameful son, * and will share the inheritance among the brothers. [3] A refining pot is for silver and a crucible for gold, but HASHEM tests hearts. * [4] An evildoer is attentive to iniquitous speech; a false person listens to a destructive tongue. [5] One who mocks a pauper insults his Maker; one who rejoices in [another's] misfortune will not be exonerated. * [6] The crown of elders is grandchildren, and the glory of children is their parents. [7] Lofty speech is unbecoming in a degraded person; and surely lying speech in a noble person. [8] To its giver, a bribe is like a charming gem; wherever he turns he will succeed. * [9] One who covers an offense seeks love; but one who harps on the matter alienates a ruler [from himself]. * [10] Chastisement frightens an understanding one more than smiting a fool a hundred times. [11] The rebellious one seeks only evil, and a cruel emissary will be sent against him. [12] Better for a man to be confronted by a bear bereft of its whelps than by a fool in his foolishness. * [13] [If] one repays good with evil, evil will not depart from his house. [14] The beginning of a quarrel is like releasing water; * before the argument is revealed, abandon it! [15] Justifying an evildoer and condemning a righteous person, both are abominations of HASHEM. [16] Why is there money in the hand of a fool to purchase wisdom, though he has not an [understanding] heart? * [17] A friend's love is for all times, and a brother is born for [times of] affliction. * [18] A man who lacks [an understanding] heart will give his handshake to be a co-signer for his friend. [19] One who loves betrayal loves contention; one who opens his mouth arrogantly is asking to be broken. [20] The perverse of heart will not find good, and one duplicitous in his tongue will fall into evil. [21] One who begets a fool has done so to his sorrow, and the father of a degraded one will not rejoice. [22] A glad heart is as beneficial as a cure, but a broken spirit will desiccate the bone. [23] An evildoer will take a bribe from the lap [of the giver], to pervert the paths of justice. [24] Wisdom lies before an understanding person, but a fool's eyes are in the ends of the earth. * [25] The foolish son is an annoyance to his father and a rebellion to the one who bore him. [26] One who is not good will punish even the righteous, and will smite generous people for integrity. [27] One who is sparing with his words knows knowledge, and a man of understanding speaks sparingly. [28] Even a fool will be considered wise if he is silent; when he seals his lips [he will be considered] understanding.

18   [1] **O**ne who removes himself to court lust will be exposed in every Torah conclave. * [2] The fool does not desire understanding, except when his essence is revealed. * [3] With the arrival of an evildoer, scorn arrives; and with [a man of] disgrace, there comes insult. [4] The words of man's mouth are deep waters; the source of wisdom is like a flowing stream. [5] To show favor to an evildoer is not good, it turns astray the judgment of a righteous person. [6] The lips of the fool

---

17:24. A wise man learns from every situation, but a fool always imagines success is somewhere out of reach.

18:1. A Torah scholar who leaves the group to pursue his passions will be disgraced among those who overcame

such desire (Rashi).

18:2. Only when he is shown up publicly as a fool does he wish he were a wise man, but then he reverts to his former way of life (Ralbag).

ז יָבֹאוּ בְרִיב וּפִיו לְמַהֲלֻמוֹת יִקְרָא: פִּי־כְסִיל מְחִתָּה־לוֹ וּשְׂפָתָיו מוֹקֵשׁ

ח-ט נַפְשׁוֹ: דִּבְרֵי נִרְגָּן כְּמִתְלַהֲמִים וְהֵם יָרְדוּ חַדְרֵי־בָטֶן: גַּם מִתְרַפֶּה

י בִמְלַאכְתּוֹ אָח הוּא לְבַעַל מַשְׁחִית: מִגְדַּל־עֹז שֵׁם יהוה בּוֹ־יָרוּץ צַדִּיק

יא-יב וְנִשְׂגָּב: הוֹן עָשִׁיר קִרְיַת עֻזּוֹ וּכְחוֹמָה נִשְׂגָּבָה בְּמַשְׂכִּיתוֹ: לִפְנֵי־שֶׁבֶר יִגְבַּהּ

יג לֶב־אִישׁ וְלִפְנֵי כָבוֹד עֲנָוָה: מֵשִׁיב דָּבָר בְּטֶרֶם יִשְׁמָע אִוֶּלֶת הִיא־לוֹ

יד-טו וּכְלִמָּה: רוּחַ־אִישׁ יְכַלְכֵּל מַחֲלֵהוּ וְרוּחַ נְכֵאָה מִי יִשָּׂאֶנָּה: לֵב נָבוֹן

טז יִקְנֶה־דָּעַת וְאֹזֶן חֲכָמִים תְּבַקֶּשׁ־דָּעַת: מַתָּן אָדָם יַרְחִיב לוֹ וְלִפְנֵי גְדֹלִים

יז-יח יַנְחֶנּוּ: צַדִּיק הָרִאשׁוֹן בְּרִיבוֹ יבא [°וּבָא ק] רֵעֵהוּ וַחֲקָרוֹ: מִדְיָנִים

יט יַשְׁבִּית הַגּוֹרָל וּבֵין עֲצוּמִים יַפְרִיד: אָח נִפְשָׁע מִקִּרְיַת־עֹז °וּמִדוֹנִים

כ [°וּמִדְיָנִים ק] כִּבְרִיחַ אַרְמוֹן: מִפְּרִי פִי־אִישׁ תִּשְׂבַּע בִּטְנוֹ תְּבוּאַת שְׂפָתָיו

כא-כב יִשְׂבָּע: מָוֶת וְחַיִּים בְּיַד־לָשׁוֹן וְאֹהֲבֶיהָ יֹאכַל פִּרְיָהּ: מָצָא אִשָּׁה מָצָא טוֹב

כג-כד וַיָּפֶק רָצוֹן מֵיהוה: תַּחֲנוּנִים יְדַבֶּר־רָשׁ וְעָשִׁיר יַעֲנֶה עַזּוֹת: אִישׁ רֵעִים

יט א לְהִתְרֹעֵעַ וְיֵשׁ אֹהֵב דָּבֵק מֵאָח: טוֹב־רָשׁ הוֹלֵךְ בְּתֻמּוֹ מֵעִקֵּשׁ שְׂפָתָיו וְהוּא

ב-ג כְסִיל: גַּם בְּלֹא־דַעַת נֶפֶשׁ לֹא־טוֹב וְאָץ בְּרַגְלַיִם חוֹטֵא: אִוֶּלֶת אָדָם

ד תְּסַלֵּף דַּרְכּוֹ וְעַל־יהוה יִזְעַף לִבּוֹ: הוֹן יֹסִיף רֵעִים רַבִּים וְדָל מֵרֵעֵהוּ יִפָּרֵד:

ה-ו עֵד שְׁקָרִים לֹא יִנָּקֶה וְיָפִיחַ כְּזָבִים לֹא יִמָּלֵט: רַבִּים יְחַלּוּ פְנֵי־נָדִיב וְכָל־

ז הָרֵעַ לְאִישׁ מַתָּן: כָּל אֲחֵי־רָשׁ שְׂנֵאֻהוּ אַף כִּי מְרֵעֵהוּ רָחֲקוּ מִמֶּנּוּ מְרַדֵּף

ח אֲמָרִים °לֹא [°לוֹ ק] הֵמָּה: קֹנֶה־לֵּב אֹהֵב נַפְשׁוֹ שֹׁמֵר תְּבוּנָה לִמְצֹא־

ט טוֹב: עֵד שְׁקָרִים לֹא יִנָּקֶה וְיָפִיחַ כְּזָבִים יֹאבֵד:

י-יא לֹא־נָאוֶה לִכְסִיל תַּעֲנוּג אַף כִּי־לְעֶבֶד ׀ מְשֹׁל בְּשָׂרִים: שֵׂכֶל אָדָם הֶאֱרִיךְ

יב אַפּוֹ וְתִפְאַרְתּוֹ עֲבֹר עַל־פָּשַׁע: נַהַם כַּכְּפִיר זַעַף מֶלֶךְ וּכְטַל עַל־עֵשֶׂב

יג-יד רְצוֹנוֹ: הַוֹּת לְאָבִיו בֵּן כְּסִיל וְדֶלֶף טֹרֵד מִדְיְנֵי אִשָּׁה: בַּיִת וָהוֹן נַחֲלַת אָבוֹת

טו וּמֵיהוה אִשָּׁה מַשְׂכָּלֶת: עַצְלָה תַּפִּיל תַּרְדֵּמָה וְנֶפֶשׁ רְמִיָּה תִרְעָב: שֹׁמֵר

טז-יז מִצְוָה שֹׁמֵר נַפְשׁוֹ בּוֹזֵה דְרָכָיו °יוּמָת [°יָמוּת ק]: מַלְוֵה יהוה

יח חוֹנֵן דָּל וּגְמֻלוֹ יְשַׁלֶּם־לוֹ: יַסֵּר בִּנְךָ כִּי־יֵשׁ תִּקְוָה וְאֶל־הֲמִיתוֹ אַל־

יט תִּשָּׂא נַפְשֶׁךָ: °גְרָל [°גְּדָל ק] חֵמָה נֹשֵׂא עֹנֶשׁ כִּי אִם־תַּצִּיל וְעוֹד תּוֹסִף:

18:8. A habitually irascible complainer offends his adversary with insults that penetrate into the depths of his being. Instead of protecting himself, he destroys the other (*Yalkut HaMachiri*).

18:10. One who trusts in God rejects the lure of enticement and gains tremendous strength and protection (*Rabbeinu Bachya*).

18:11. A rich man's wealth gives him a sense of security, which he can rely on in time of crisis.

18:15. Understanding will enable someone to derive more knowledge on his own, but someone who lacks such understanding must rely on the wisdom he gathers from others (*Ralbag*).

18:19. Though brothers quarrel bitterly, their underlying loyalty is such that when one is in danger the other will spring to his defense (*Ralbag*).

18:23. But even though a wealthy person may answer impudently, the poor one should speak with supplications. The same applies to teacher and pupil (*Rashi*).

18:24. At times friends become more deeply attached than brothers, because friendship is founded on choice; the hearts and minds of friends have come to know and esteem one another (*R' Hirsch*).

19:6. When someone becomes known for giving to the poor, even great people seek his friendship and assistance (*Ibn Ezra*).

19:10. Being cleverer than their foolish masters, servants may exploit their folly so well as to become will come forth in contention, and his mouth will invite blows [upon himself]. [7] *The mouth of a fool brings destruction to himself, and his lips are a stumbling block to his soul.* [8] *The words of a complainer are like blows and they descend to the chambers of one's innards.* * [9] *One who grows lax in his work is also a brother to the master of destruction.* [10] *The Name of HASHEM is a tower of strength; through it a righteous person will race and be strong.* * [11] *The treasure of a wealthy person is his city of strength, and like a high wall in his chambers.* * [12] *Prior to [his] destruction a man's heart grows haughty; but prior to honor there is humility.* [13] *He who answers before he has heard, it will be foolishness and humiliation for him.* [14] *A man's spirit will sustain [him in] his sickness; but who can support a broken spirit?* [15] *An understanding heart will acquire knowledge, but the ear of the wise must seek wisdom.* * [16] *A man's gift broadens [access] for him and leads him before the great.* [17] *The first [to present his case] seems righteous in his grievance; then his fellow arrives and he is interrogated.* [18] *The lottery can put quarrels to rest and cause the contentious to move apart.* [19] *Better a wronged brother than a fortified city; and though they quarrel, they are like a palace bolt.* * [20] *A man's stomach will be sated with the fruits of his mouth; he will be sated with the produce of his lips.* [21] *Death and life are in the power of the tongue; those who love [to use] it will eat its fruit.* [22] *One who has found a wife has found goodness, and has brought forth favor from HASHEM.* [23] *A pauper utters supplications, but a rich one responds with brazen words.* * [24] *A man with friends is befriended; sometimes a friend is closer than a brother.* *

19 [1] **B**etter a pauper who walks in his innocence than one who perverts his lips and is a fool. [2] *Also, for the soul to be without knowledge is not good, and he who quickens his feet [without reflection] is a sinner.* [3] *A man's foolishness corrupts his way, and his heart rages against HASHEM.* [4] *Wealth adds many friends, but the poor man is parted from his fellow.* [5] *A witness saying falsehoods will not be exonerated, and a spouter of lies will not escape.* [6] *Many court the presence of a patron, and all befriend a man with gifts.* * [7] *All a pauper's brothers hate him, surely his friends withdraw from him. Though he pursues [them] with words, [the words] remain his.* [8] *One who acquires understanding loves his soul, guarding understanding to find good.* [9] *A witness saying falsehoods will not be exonerated, and the spouter of lies will go lost.* [10] *Pleasure does not befit a fool; surely [it is not fitting for] a servant to rule over dignitaries.* * [11] *It is intelligent of a person to be slow to anger, and his splendor to ignore an offense.* [12] *Like the roar of a young lion, so is the wrath of a king; and like dew upon grass is his favor.* [13] *A foolish son is a father's heartbreak, and a contentious woman is like an irksome dripping.* * [14] *A house and wealth are an inheritance from fathers, but an intelligent woman comes from HASHEM.* [15] *Laziness casts one into slumber, and the deceptive soul will go hungry.* [16] *He who observes a commandment safeguards his soul; one who scorns his [proper] ways will die.* [17] *One who is gracious to the poor has lent to HASHEM, and He will pay him his reward.* [18] *Discipline your son, for there is hope; let your soul not be swayed by his protest.* [19] *A person of great wrath will bear punishment; for if you rescue him, his wrath will only grow.* *

---

indispensable to them and to completely dominate them (R' Hirsch).

19:13. A contentious wife's quarrels drive her husband from the house, while the foolish son does not (Ibn Ezra; see also 27:15-16 below).

19:19. A person with an uncontrollable temper can only come to grief, for even if someone restrains him, his anger will only intensify.

כ-כא שְׁמַע עֵצָה וְקַבֵּל מוּסָר לְמַעַן תֶּחְכַּם בְּאַחֲרִיתֶךָ: רַבּוֹת מַחֲשָׁבוֹת בְּלֶב־
כב אִישׁ וַעֲצַת יְהוָה הִיא תָקוּם: תַּאֲוַת אָדָם חַסְדּוֹ וְטוֹב־רָשׁ מֵאִישׁ כָּזָב:
כג-כד יִרְאַת יְהוָה לְחַיִּים וְשָׂבֵעַ יָלִין בַּל־יִפָּקֶד רָע: טָמַן עָצֵל יָדוֹ בַּצַּלָּחַת גַּם־
כה אֶל־פִּיהוּ לֹא יְשִׁיבֶנָּה: לֵץ תַּכֶּה וּפֶתִי יַעְרִם וְהוֹכִיחַ לְנָבוֹן יָבִין דָּעַת:
כו-כז מְשַׁדֶּד־אָב יַבְרִיחַ אֵם בֵּן מֵבִישׁ וּמַחְפִּיר: חֲדַל־בְּנִי לִשְׁמֹעַ מוּסָר לִשְׁגוֹת
כח-כט מֵאִמְרֵי־דָעַת: עֵד בְּלִיַּעַל יָלִיץ מִשְׁפָּט וּפִי רְשָׁעִים יְבַלַּע־אָוֶן: נָכוֹנוּ לַלֵּצִים
א שְׁפָטִים וּמַהֲלֻמוֹת לְגֵו כְּסִילִים: לֵץ הַיַּיִן הֹמֶה שֵׁכָר וְכָל־שֹׁגֶה בּוֹ לֹא
ב-ג יֶחְכָּם: נַהַם כַּכְּפִיר אֵימַת מֶלֶךְ מִתְעַבְּרוֹ חוֹטֵא נַפְשׁוֹ: כָּבוֹד לָאִישׁ שֶׁבֶת
ד מֵרִיב וְכָל־אֱוִיל יִתְגַּלָּע: מֵחֹרֶף עָצֵל לֹא־יַחֲרֹשׁ °יִשְׁאַל [°וְשָׁאַל ק]
ה בַּקָּצִיר וָאָיִן: מַיִם עֲמֻקִּים עֵצָה בְלֶב־אִישׁ וְאִישׁ תְּבוּנָה יִדְלֶנָּה: רָב־
ז אָדָם יִקְרָא אִישׁ חַסְדּוֹ וְאִישׁ אֱמוּנִים מִי יִמְצָא: מִתְהַלֵּךְ בְּתֻמּוֹ צַדִּיק
ח-ט אַשְׁרֵי בָנָיו אַחֲרָיו: מֶלֶךְ יוֹשֵׁב עַל־כִּסֵּא־דִין מְזָרֶה בְעֵינָיו כָּל־רָע: מִי־
י יֹאמַר זִכִּיתִי לִבִּי טָהַרְתִּי מֵחַטָּאתִי: אֶבֶן וָאֶבֶן אֵיפָה וְאֵיפָה תּוֹעֲבַת יְהוָה
יא-יב גַּם־שְׁנֵיהֶם: גַּם בְּמַעֲלָלָיו יִתְנַכֶּר־נָעַר אִם־זַךְ וְאִם־יָשָׁר פָּעֳלוֹ: אֹזֶן
יג שֹׁמַעַת וְעַיִן רֹאָה יְהוָה עָשָׂה גַּם־שְׁנֵיהֶם: אַל־תֶּאֱהַב שֵׁנָה פֶּן־תִּוָּרֵשׁ
יד-טו פְּקַח עֵינֶיךָ שְׂבַע־לָחֶם: רַע רַע יֹאמַר הַקּוֹנֶה וְאֹזֵל לוֹ אָז יִתְהַלָּל: יֵשׁ זָהָב
טז וְרָב־פְּנִינִים וּכְלִי יְקָר שִׂפְתֵי־דָעַת: לְקַח־בִּגְדוֹ כִּי־עָרַב זָר וּבְעַד °נָכְרִים
יז [°נָכְרִיָּה ק] חַבְלֵהוּ: עָרֵב לָאִישׁ לֶחֶם שָׁקֶר וְאַחַר יִמָּלֵא־פִיהוּ חָצָץ:
יח-יט מַחֲשָׁבוֹת בְּעֵצָה תִכּוֹן וּבְתַחְבֻּלוֹת עֲשֵׂה מִלְחָמָה: גּוֹלֶה־סּוֹד הוֹלֵךְ רָכִיל
כ וּלְפֹתֶה שְׂפָתָיו לֹא תִתְעָרָב: מְקַלֵּל אָבִיו וְאִמּוֹ יִדְעַךְ נֵרוֹ °בֶּאֱשׁוּן
כא [°בֶּאֱשׁוֹן ק] חֹשֶׁךְ: נַחֲלָה °מְבֹחֶלֶת [°מְבֹהֶלֶת ק] בָּרִאשֹׁנָה וְאַחֲרִיתָהּ
כב-כג לֹא תְבֹרָךְ: אַל־תֹּאמַר אֲשַׁלְּמָה־רָע קַוֵּה לַיהוָה וְיֹשַׁע לָךְ: תּוֹעֲבַת יְהוָה
כד אֶבֶן וָאָבֶן וּמֹאזְנֵי מִרְמָה לֹא־טוֹב: מֵיְהוָה מִצְעֲדֵי־גָבֶר וְאָדָם מַה־יָּבִין
כה-כו דַּרְכּוֹ: מוֹקֵשׁ אָדָם יָלַע קֹדֶשׁ וְאַחַר נְדָרִים לְבַקֵּר: מְזָרֶה רְשָׁעִים מֶלֶךְ
כז חָכָם וַיָּשֶׁב עֲלֵיהֶם אוֹפָן: נֵר יְהוָה נִשְׁמַת אָדָם חֹפֵשׂ כָּל־חַדְרֵי־בָטֶן: חֶסֶד
כח-כט וֶאֱמֶת יִצְּרוּ־מֶלֶךְ וְסָעַד בַּחֶסֶד כִּסְאוֹ: תִּפְאֶרֶת בַּחוּרִים כֹּחָם וַהֲדַר
ל זְקֵנִים שֵׂיבָה: חַבֻּרוֹת פֶּצַע °תַּמְרִיק [°תַּמְרוּק ק] בְּרָע וּמַכּוֹת חַדְרֵי־בָטֶן:

כ

19:22. People seek the friendship of someone who promises generosity, but it is better to be poor and promise nothing than to be rich and promise falsely.

19:26. A misbehaving child makes his father feel destitute and his mother feel homeless.

19:28. He will swallow his words so that his deception will go unnoticed (*Metzudos*).

20:1. A small quantity of wine is beneficial, but excess is harmful (*Vilna Gaon*).

20:10. See *Deuteronomy* 25:13-16.

20:18. Even the wisest person needs counsel, for others are more objective and can better advise him (*Meiri*).

20:20. Generally, "A commandment is a lamp, and the Torah is light" (also 6:23), and the merit of one's mitzvah observance will illuminate one's way through difficult times. However, if one desecrates the very commandment that has warranted this merit, the merit will flicker and die like a lamp in the deepest, darkest part of a tunnel. For example, a person who curses his parents will lose the merits he has earned by honoring and serving them on previous occasions (*Rabbeinu Yonah*).

20:23. See *Deuteronomy* 25:13-16.

²⁰ Hear counsel and accept discipline in order that you grow wise in your later days. ²¹ Many designs are in a man's heart, but the counsel of HASHEM, only it will prevail. ²² Longing for a person is for his kindness, but a pauper is better than a [rich] man who deceives. * ²³ The fear of HASHEM brings life; such a person will rest sated and not be remembered for evil. ²⁴ The lazy one buries his hand in the dish; he will not even return it to his mouth. ²⁵ Strike the scoffer and the simpleton grows clever; chastise an understanding person and he will understand [even more] knowledge. ²⁶ He despoils his father and drives out his mother — the son who shames and humiliates. * ²⁷ To obey discipline, my son, is to cease to stray from words of knowledge. ²⁸ The lawless witness will mock judgment, and the mouth of the wicked will swallow [his words of] iniquity. * ²⁹ Judgments are readied for the scoffers, and blows for the backs of fools.

20

¹ Wine makes a scoffer; strong drink makes one cry out; and whoever errs after it will not grow wise. * ² Like the roar of a young lion, so is the terror of a king; one who angers him forfeits his soul. ³ Abstention from quarrel is a man's honor, but every foolish one reveals himself [in it]. ⁴ Because of the winter [cold] a sluggard will not plow; he will desire [a crop] at harvest time, but it will not be there. ⁵ Counsel is like deep water in the heart of man; and the man of understanding will draw them forth. ⁶ Among most people, each man proclaims his kindness; but who can find an honest man? ⁷ One who walks in his innocence is a righteous man; fortunate are his sons after him. ⁸ When the king sits on the seat of judgment, he scatters all who are evil in his eyes. ⁹ Who can say, "I have cleansed my heart. I have purified myself from my sin"? ¹⁰ A weight and a weight, a measure and a measure, * both of them are an abomination of HASHEM. ¹¹ Even a youth can be recognized by his deeds, whether his acts are pure or just. ¹² A hearing ear and a seeing eye, HASHEM made both of them. ¹³ Do not love sleep lest you become impoverished; open your eyes, [then] you will be sated with food. ¹⁴ "Bad, bad," the buyer says, but when he goes his way, then he boasts. ¹⁵ There is gold and many pearls, but lips of wisdom are a precious vessel. ¹⁶ Take the garment of one who co-signs for a stranger, or offers collateral for an alien woman. ¹⁷ The bread of falsehood is sweet to man; but afterwards his mouth will be filled with gravel. ¹⁸ Thoughts conceived in counsel will be firm; * wage war with strategies. ¹⁹ With a revealer of secrets, a bearer of tales, or a simpleton of lips, do not mingle. ²⁰ One who curses his father or mother, his light [soul] will flicker out in the deepening darkness. * ²¹ If an inheritance is seized hastily in the beginning, its end will not be blessed. ²² Do not say, "I will pay retribution for evil!" Hope to HASHEM and He will help you. ²³ Having one weight and a [different] weight is an abomination of HASHEM, * and scales of deceit are not good. ²⁴ A man's steps are from HASHEM; but what does a man understand of his way? ²⁵ A man's stumbling [in sin] undermines [his] sanctity, and his remedy is to seek vows [of atonement]. ²⁶ A wise king scatters the wicked and turns the wheel [measure for measure] upon them. ²⁷ A man's soul is the lamp of HASHEM, which searches the chambers of one's innards. * ²⁸ Kindness and truth protect a king; he sustains his throne in kindness. ²⁹ The splendor of youth is their strength, and the glory of the old is their hoariness. ³⁰ Bruises and wounds purge evil, as do blows to the chambers of one's innards. *

20:27. By means of the soul, God searches man's innermost thoughts and scrutinizes him (*Rabbeinu Yonah*).

20:30. Afflictions can force a person to reconsider and desist from his evil ways.

כא א-ב פַּלְגֵי־מַיִם לֶב־מֶלֶךְ בְּיַד־יְהֹוָה עַל־כָּל־אֲשֶׁר יַחְפֹּץ יַטֶּנּוּ: כָּל־דֶּרֶךְ־אִישׁ
ג יָשָׁר בְּעֵינָיו וְתֹכֵן לִבּוֹת יְהֹוָה: עֲשֹׂה צְדָקָה וּמִשְׁפָּט נִבְחָר לַיהֹוָה מִזָּבַח:
ד-ה רוּם־עֵינַיִם וּרְחַב־לֵב נִר רְשָׁעִים חַטָּאת: מַחְשְׁבוֹת חָרוּץ אַךְ־לְמוֹתָר
ו וְכָל־אָץ אַךְ־לְמַחְסוֹר: פֹּעַל אוֹצָרוֹת בִּלְשׁוֹן שָׁקֶר הֶבֶל נִדָּף מְבַקְשֵׁי־
ז-ח מָוֶת: שֹׁד־רְשָׁעִים יְגוֹרֵם כִּי מֵאֲנוּ לַעֲשׂוֹת מִשְׁפָּט: הֲפַכְפַּךְ דֶּרֶךְ אִישׁ וָזָר
ט-י וְזַךְ יָשָׁר פָּעֳלוֹ: טוֹב לָשֶׁבֶת עַל־פִּנַּת־גָּג מֵאֵשֶׁת מִדְיָנִים וּבֵית חָבֶר: נֶפֶשׁ
יא רָשָׁע אִוְּתָה־רָע לֹא־יֻחַן בְּעֵינָיו רֵעֵהוּ: בַּעֲנָשׁ־לֵץ יֶחְכַּם־פֶּתִי וּבְהַשְׂכִּיל
יב-יג לְחָכָם יִקַּח־דָּעַת: מַשְׂכִּיל צַדִּיק לְבֵית רָשָׁע מְסַלֵּף רְשָׁעִים לָרָע: אֹטֵם
יד אָזְנוֹ מִזַּעֲקַת־דָּל גַּם־הוּא יִקְרָא וְלֹא יֵעָנֶה: מַתָּן בַּסֵּתֶר יִכְפֶּה־אָף וְשֹׁחַד
טו-טז בַּחֵק חֵמָה עַזָּה: שִׂמְחָה לַצַּדִּיק עֲשׂוֹת מִשְׁפָּט וּמְחִתָּה לְפֹעֲלֵי אָוֶן: אָדָם
יז תּוֹעֶה מִדֶּרֶךְ הַשְׂכֵּל בִּקְהַל רְפָאִים יָנוּחַ: אִישׁ מַחְסוֹר אֹהֵב שִׂמְחָה אֹהֵב
יח-יט יַיִן־וָשֶׁמֶן לֹא יַעֲשִׁיר: כֹּפֶר לַצַּדִּיק רָשָׁע וְתַחַת יְשָׁרִים בּוֹגֵד: טוֹב שֶׁבֶת
כ בְּאֶרֶץ־מִדְבָּר מֵאֵשֶׁת °מִדוֹנִים [°מִדְיָנִים ק]: אוֹצָר ׀ נֶחְמָד וָשֶׁמֶן
כא בִּנְוֵה חָכָם וּכְסִיל אָדָם יְבַלְּעֶנּוּ: רֹדֵף צְדָקָה וָחָסֶד יִמְצָא חַיִּים צְדָקָה
כב-כג וְכָבוֹד: עִיר גִּבֹּרִים עָלָה חָכָם וַיֹּרֶד עֹז מִבְטֶחָה: שֹׁמֵר פִּיו וּלְשׁוֹנוֹ שֹׁמֵר
כד-כה מִצָּרוֹת נַפְשׁוֹ: זֵד יָהִיר לֵץ שְׁמוֹ עוֹשֶׂה בְּעֶבְרַת זָדוֹן: תַּאֲוַת עָצֵל תְּמִיתֶנּוּ
כו כִּי־מֵאֲנוּ יָדָיו לַעֲשׂוֹת: כָּל־הַיּוֹם הִתְאַוָּה תַאֲוָה וְצַדִּיק יִתֵּן וְלֹא יַחְשֹׂךְ:
כז-כח זֶבַח רְשָׁעִים תּוֹעֵבָה אַף כִּי־בְזִמָּה יְבִיאֶנּוּ: עֵד־כְּזָבִים יֹאבֵד וְאִישׁ שׁוֹמֵעַ
כט לָנֶצַח יְדַבֵּר: הֵעֵז אִישׁ רָשָׁע בְּפָנָיו וְיָשָׁר הוּא ׀ °יָכִין דרכיו [°יָבִין ק
ל-לא דַּרְכּוֹ ק]: אֵין חָכְמָה וְאֵין תְּבוּנָה וְאֵין עֵצָה לְנֶגֶד יְהֹוָה: סוּס
כב א מוּכָן לְיוֹם מִלְחָמָה וְלַיהֹוָה הַתְּשׁוּעָה: נִבְחָר שֵׁם מֵעֹשֶׁר רָב מִכֶּסֶף
ב-ג וּמִזָּהָב חֵן טוֹב: עָשִׁיר וָרָשׁ נִפְגָּשׁוּ עֹשֵׂה כֻלָּם יְהֹוָה: עָרוּם ׀ רָאָה רָעָה
ד °ויסתר [°וְנִסְתָּר ק] וּפְתָאיִם עָבְרוּ וְנֶעֱנָשׁוּ: עֵקֶב עֲנָוָה יִרְאַת יְהֹוָה עֹשֶׁר
ה-ו וְכָבוֹד וְחַיִּים: צִנִּים פַּחִים בְּדֶרֶךְ עִקֵּשׁ שׁוֹמֵר נַפְשׁוֹ יִרְחַק מֵהֶם: חֲנֹךְ
ז לַנַּעַר עַל־פִּי דַרְכּוֹ גַּם כִּי־יַזְקִין לֹא־יָסוּר מִמֶּנָּה: עָשִׁיר בְּרָשִׁים יִמְשׁוֹל

21:1. Because a king's choices affect so many people, God may intervene to direct them, as a farmer might direct the flow of a stream to irrigate his fields.

21:2. Since it is natural for one to justify his traits and deeds, God may intervene to inspire people to rectify their mistakes (*Rabbeinu Yonah*).

21:10. An evildoer desires only evil and is never concerned with his companions unless he can benefit from them (*Rabbeinu Yonah*).

21:12. God brings general blessing in the merit of the righteous, but wicked people misinterpret it as justification for their way of life (*Metzudos*).

21:14. One who seeks out the poor and helps them secretly will be saved from God's anger, even if a decree has been cast against him (*Sfas Emes*).

21:18. A righteous man is rescued and a wicked man comes in his stead, such as with Mordechai and Haman (*Rashi*).

21:20. Wise people store their provisions to use as needed, but foolish people squander them wastefully (*Ralbag*).

21:22. Wisdom overcame strength, and righteousness became the protector of the city.

21:25-26. A lazy one has only desire, but no accomplishment. A righteous man, however, accomplishes for himself and teaches others, as well (*Vilna Gaon*).

21:29. A wicked man shows his brazenness when he is angry, without shame, but the just person controls his behavior.

21:30. Nothing avails to nullify God's will (*Rabbeinu Bachya*).

21 ¹ L ike streams of water is the heart of a king in the hand of HASHEM, wherever He wishes, so He directs it. * ² A man's every way is upright in his eyes; but HASHEM resides inside his heart. * ³ Doing what is right and just is preferable to HASHEM than an offering. ⁴ Haughty eyes and a proud heart are the plotting of the wicked, a sin. ⁵ The thoughts of the zealous are purely beneficial, but all hastiness is only for loss. ⁶ The accumulation of treasures through a false tongue is a smitten vapor; they seek death. ⁷ The robbery of the wicked will cause them to fear, for they refuse to execute justice. ⁸ The way of a man is [sometimes] inconsistent and strange, but a pure one's every deed is upright. ⁹ Better to dwell on a corner of a roof than [to dwell with] a contentious wife in a house of friends. ¹⁰ The soul of the evildoer desires evil; his companion [in evil] will not find favor in his eyes. * ¹¹ When the scoffer is punished, the simpleton gains wisdom; and when the wise one receives instruction, he gains knowledge. ¹² A righteous person brings success to the house of the evildoer, which corrupts the wicked toward evil. * ¹³ One who shuts his ear to the cry of the pauper, he too will call out and not be answered. ¹⁴ An anonymous gift will cover up anger, and a bribe in the bosom [will appease] strong wrath. * ¹⁵ Performance of justice is a joy to the righteous, and destruction to workers of iniquity. ¹⁶ A person who wanders from the intelligent way will rest in the congregation of the dead. ¹⁷ The lover of pleasure will be a man who lacks; the lover of wine and oil will not grow rich. ¹⁸ The evildoer will be an atonement for the righteous one, and the faithless one for the upright. * ¹⁹ Better to dwell in a wasteland than [with] a woman of contention and anger. ²⁰ A desirable treasure and oil endures in the abode of the wise, but the fool of a man swallows it up. * ²¹ One who pursues righteousness and kindness will find life, righteousness, and honor. ²² The wise one went up to the city of the strong, and brought down the strength of its trust. * ²³ One who guards his mouth and his tongue guards his soul from troubles. ²⁴ The boastful, willful man, scoffer is his name; the arrogant evildoer, he is a willful man. ²⁵ The lust of the sluggard will kill him; for his hands refuse to work. ²⁶ All day long he will court lust, and the righteous one will give to him and not hold back. * ²⁷ The offering of the wicked is an abomination; and surely when they bring it with [impure] design. ²⁸ The testimony of falsehoods will be lost, but the man who hears it will speak of it eternally. ²⁹ A wicked person shows his audacity on his face, but the upright one considers his way. * ³⁰ There is neither wisdom nor understanding nor counsel against HASHEM. * ³¹ The horse is readied for the day of battle, but salvation is HASHEM's.

22 ¹ A [good] name is preferred to wealth, and goodly favor than silver and gold. ² The rich man and the pauper meet; HASHEM is the Maker of them all. * ³ A clever person sees evil and hides, but simpletons pass on and are punished. ⁴ The result of humility is fear of HASHEM, wealth, honor, and life. * ⁵ Thorns and snares are in the path of the perverse; he who guards his soul will distance himself from them. ⁶ Train the youth according to his way; even when he grows old, he will not swerve from it. * ⁷ A rich man dominates paupers, *

22:2. Having lauded a good name over wealth, Solomon explains that the rich are not to be praised for their wealth and the poor are not to be condemned for their poverty. Their circumstances were decreed by God, and He can make them converge or even reverse their positions, for He made them all (*Rashi; Metzudos*).

22:4. Recognition of his own insignificance leads a

person to humility and fear of God. In turn, God will reward him with success.

22:6. The effect of a proper upbringing is lifelong, but in raising a child, parents and teachers must take careful account of his ability and personality.

22:7. The unlearned are indebted to the wise person who teaches and guides them (*Rashi*).

ח וְעֹבֵד לֹֽזֶה לְאִישׁ מַלְוֶה: זוֹרֵעַ עַוְלָה °יִקְצוֹר־ [°יִקְצָר־ ק] אָֽוֶן וְשֵׁ֥בֶט

ט עֶבְרָת֥וֹ יִכְלֶֽה: טֽוֹב־עַ֭יִן ה֣וּא יְבֹרָ֑ךְ כִּֽי־נָתַ֖ן מִלַּחְמ֣וֹ לַדָּֽל: גָּ֣רֶשׁ לֵ֭ץ וְיֵצֵ֣א

י מָד֑וֹן וְ֝יִשְׁבֹּ֗ת דִּ֣ין וְקָלֽוֹן: אֹהֵ֥ב °טְהוֹר־ [°טְהָר־ ק] לֵ֑ב חֵ֥ן שְׂ֝פָתָ֗יו רֵעֵ֥הוּ

יב-יג מֶֽלֶךְ: עֵינֵ֣י יְ֭הוה נָ֣צְרוּ דָ֑עַת וַ֝יְסַלֵּ֗ף דִּבְרֵ֥י בֹגֵֽד: אָמַ֣ר עָ֭צֵל אֲרִ֣י בַח֑וּץ בְּת֥וֹךְ

יד רְ֝חֹב֗וֹת אֵֽרָצֵֽחַ: שׁוּחָ֣ה עֲ֭מֻקָּה פִּ֣י זָר֑וֹת זְע֥וּם יְ֝הוה °יִפּוֹל־ [°יִפָּל־ ק] שָֽׁם:

טו-טז אִ֭וֶּלֶת קְשׁוּרָ֣ה בְלֶב־נָ֑עַר שֵׁ֥בֶט מ֝וּסָ֗ר יַרְחִיקֶ֥נָּה מִמֶּֽנּוּ: עֹ֣שֵֽׁק דָּ֭ל לְהַרְבּ֣וֹת

יז ל֑וֹ נֹתֵ֥ן לְ֝עָשִׁ֗יר אַךְ־לְמַחְסֽוֹר: הַ֣ט אָ֭זְנְךָ וּֽשְׁמַ֗ע דִּבְרֵ֣י חֲכָמִ֑ים וְ֝לִבְּךָ֗ תָּשִׁ֥ית

יח-יט לְדַעְתִּֽי: כִּֽי־נָ֭עִים כִּֽי־תִשְׁמְרֵ֣ם בְּבִטְנֶ֑ךָ יִכֹּ֥נוּ יַ֝חְדָּ֗ו עַל־שְׂפָתֶֽיךָ: לִהְי֣וֹת

כ בַּ֭יהוה מִבְטַחֶ֑ךָ הוֹדַעְתִּ֖יךָ הַיּ֣וֹם אַף־אָֽתָּה: הֲלֹ֤א כָתַ֣בְתִּי לְ֭ךָ °שָׁלִשׁוֹם [°שָׁלִשִׁ֗ים ק]

כא בְּמֽוֹעֵצ֥וֹת וָדָֽעַת: לְהוֹדִֽיעֲךָ֗ קֹ֭שְׁטְ אִמְרֵ֣י אֱמֶ֑ת לְהָשִׁ֥יב

כב אֲמָרִ֥ים אֱ֝מֶ֗ת לְשֹׁלְחֶֽיךָ: אַֽל־תִּגְזָל־דָּ֭ל כִּ֣י דַל־ה֑וּא וְאַל־תְּדַכֵּ֖א

כג-כד עָנִ֣י בַשָּֽׁעַר: כִּֽי־יְ֭הוה יָרִ֣יב רִיבָ֑ם וְקָבַ֖ע אֶת־קֹבְעֵיהֶ֣ם נָֽפֶשׁ: אַל־תִּ֭תְרַע

כה אֶת־בַּ֣עַל אָ֑ף וְאֶת־אִ֥ישׁ חֵ֝מ֗וֹת לֹ֣א תָבֽוֹא: פֶּן־תֶּאֱלַ֥ף °אֹרְחֹתָו [°אֹֽרְחֹתָ֑יו ק]

כו-כז וְלָקַחְתָּ֖ מוֹקֵ֣שׁ לְנַפְשֶֽׁךָ: אַל־תְּהִ֥י בְתֹֽקְעֵי־כָ֑ף בַּ֝עֹֽרְבִ֗ים מַשָּׁאֽוֹת: אִם־

כח אֵֽין־לְךָ֥ לְשַׁלֵּ֑ם לָ֥מָּה יִקַּ֥ח מִ֝שְׁכָּבְךָ֗ מִתַּחְתֶּֽיךָ: אַל־תַּ֭סֵּג גְּב֣וּל עוֹלָ֑ם אֲשֶׁ֖ר

כט עָשׂ֣וּ אֲבוֹתֶֽיךָ: חָזִ֡יתָ אִ֤ישׁ ׀ מָ֘הִ֤יר בִּמְלַאכְתּ֗וֹ לִֽפְנֵֽי־מְלָכִ֥ים יִתְיַצָּ֑ב בַּל־

כג א יִ֝תְיַצֵּ֗ב לִפְנֵ֥י חֲשֻׁכִּֽים: כִּֽי־תֵ֭שֵׁב לִלְח֣וֹם אֶת־מוֹשֵׁ֑ל בִּ֥ין תָּ֝בִ֗ין אֶת־אֲשֶׁ֥ר

ב-ג לְפָנֶֽיךָ: וְשַׂמְתָּ֣ שַׂכִּ֣ין בְּלֹעֶ֑ךָ אִם־בַּ֖עַל נֶ֣פֶשׁ אָֽתָּה: אַל־תִּ֭תְאָו לְמַטְעַמּוֹתָ֑יו

ד-ה וְ֝ה֗וּא לֶ֣חֶם כְּזָבִֽים: אַל־תִּיגַ֥ע לְֽהַעֲשִׁ֑יר מִֽבִּינָתְךָ֥ חֲדָֽל: °הֲתָעוּף [°הֲתָעִ֥יף ק] עֵינֶ֨יךָ ׀ ב֘וֹ וְֽאֵינֶ֥נּוּ כִּ֤י עָשֹׂ֣ה יַעֲשֶׂה־לּ֣וֹ כְנָפַ֑יִם כְּ֝נֶ֗שֶׁר °וְעֵיף

ו °[וְיָע֥וּף ק] הַשָּׁמָֽיִם: אַל־תִּ֭לְחַם אֶת־לֶ֣חֶם רַ֣ע עָ֑יִן וְאַל־°תִּתְאָ֗ו לְמַטְעַמֹּתָֽיו:

ז-ח כִּ֤י ׀ כְּמוֹ־שָׁעַ֥ר בְּנַפְשׁ֗וֹ כֶּ֫ן־ה֥וּא אֱכֹ֣ל וּ֭שְׁתֵה יֹ֣אמַר לָ֑ךְ וְ֝לִבּ֗וֹ בַּל־עִמָּֽךְ: פִּֽתְּךָ֥

ט אָכַ֗לְתָּ תְקִיאֶ֥נָּה וְ֝שִׁחַ֗תָּ דְּבָרֶ֥יךָ הַנְּעִימִֽים: בְּאָזְנֵ֣י כְ֭סִיל אַל־תְּדַבֵּ֑ר כִּֽי־יָ֝ב֗וּז

י-יא לְשֵׂ֥כֶל מִלֶּֽיךָ: אַל־תַּ֭סֵּג גְּב֣וּל עוֹלָ֑ם וּבִשְׂדֵ֥י יְ֝תוֹמִ֗ים אַל־תָּבֹֽא: כִּֽי־גֹאֲלָ֥ם

יב חָזָ֑ק הֽוּא־יָרִ֖יב אֶת־רִיבָ֣ם אִתָּֽךְ: הָבִ֣יאָה לַמּוּסָ֣ר לִבֶּ֑ךָ וְ֝אָזְנֶ֗ךָ לְאִמְרֵי־דָֽעַת:

יג-יד אַל־תִּמְנַ֣ע מִנַּ֣עַר מוּסָ֑ר כִּֽי־תַכֶּ֥נּוּ בַ֝שֵּׁ֗בֶט לֹ֣א יָמֽוּת: אַ֭תָּה בַּשֵּׁ֣בֶט תַּכֶּ֑נּוּ

טו וְ֝נַפְשׁ֗וֹ מִשְּׁא֥וֹל תַּצִּֽיל: בְּ֭נִי אִם־חָכַ֣ם לִבֶּ֑ךָ יִשְׂמַ֖ח לִבִּ֣י גַם־אָֽנִי:

22:8. The power he amassed by his injustice will be destroyed by God's wrath (*Ibn Ezra*).

22:9. A good eye refers to someone who not only gives, but does so willingly and without resentment; he enjoys helping others.

22:11. God Himself is the friend of one who loves good people (*Rashi*).

22:13. He fabricates tales of danger to excuse his failure to act.

22:16. But one who aids the poor fulfills God's will and will receive reward.

22:18. Habitual repetition and recitation enable one to remember what he has learned (*Rabbeinu Yonah*).

22:20-21. The Torah was not written merely for theoretical knowledge, but to give us a concrete basis upon which to shape our thoughts and feelings (*R' Hirsch*).

22:22-23. It is particularly heinous to rob or crush the indigent just because they are defenseless (*Malbim*).

22:25. The trait of anger will no longer be repugnant to you, and you will become accustomed to it.

22:28. This stich is repeated in 23:10 below. Here it refers figuratively to the customs instituted by your ancestors (*Yalkut Shimoni*); there it is literal.

and a debtor is a servant to the creditor. ⁸ One who sows injustice will reap iniquity, and the rod of His fury will destroy it. * ⁹ One with a good eye* will be blessed, for he has given of his bread to the poor. ¹⁰ Drive away the scoffer and strife will depart, and judgment and shame will cease. ¹¹ He who loves purity of heart, [and] whose lips are gracious — the King is his friend.* ¹² The eyes of HASHEM protect knowledge, and He perverts the words of the faithless one. ¹³ A lazy person says, "There is a lion outside; I will be killed in the midst of the streets!"* ¹⁴ The mouth of heresy is a deep pit; the scorned of HASHEM will fall there. ¹⁵ Foolishness is bound in the heart of a youth; the rod of discipline will distance it from him. ¹⁶ He who oppresses the destitute to increase for himself or who makes gifts to the rich, it is only for a loss. * ¹⁷ Incline your ear and hear the words of the wise; set your heart to My knowledge. ¹⁸ For it is pleasant if you guard them in your innards and establish all of them upon your lips.* ¹⁹ Let your trust remain with HASHEM, I have made this known to you today, you also. ²⁰ Surely, I have written for you [in the Torah] extremely noble things, with counsel and knowledge, * ²¹ to teach you the veracity of true words, so that you may answer words of truth to those who send word to you. ²² Do not rob the destitute because he is destitute, * and do not oppress the poor man in the gate [of judgment]. ²³ For HASHEM will take up their grievance; He will steal the soul of those who would steal from them. ²⁴ Do not befriend an angry man, and do not come [together] with a man of wrath. ²⁵ Lest you learn his ways and take a snare for your soul. * ²⁶ Do not be among those who shake hands, among the guarantors for loans. ²⁷ If you have no money to pay, why should he take your bedding from beneath you? ²⁸ Do not move back the long-standing boundary marker* that your forefathers established. ²⁹ Have you seen a man with alacrity in his work? He will stand before kings. He will not stand before [men of] darkness.

23 ¹ **W**hen you sit down to dine with a ruler, know well what lies before you,* ² and put a knife to your throat if you are master of [your] soul. ³ Do not lust for his delicacies, for it is deceitful bread. ⁴ Do not weary yourself to become rich; forbear from your own understanding. ⁵ You cast your eyes upon [wealth] and it is gone, for it makes itself wings for itself [and], like an eagle, it soars to the heavens. ⁶ Do not eat the bread of the miserly, and do not lust for his delicacies. * ⁷ For as one who fantasizes in his soul, so is he. "Eat and drink," he will tell you, but his heart will not be with you. ⁸ The loaf you have eaten you will regurgitate, and you will have wasted your pleasant words. ⁹ Speak not in the ears of a fool, for he will scorn the intelligence of your words. ¹⁰ Do not move back the long-standing boundary marker, and do not enter into orphans' fields, * ¹¹ for their Redeemer is strong, and He will take up their grievance against you. ¹² Present your heart for discipline and your ears for words of knowledge. ¹³ Do not withhold discipline from the youth. If you strike him with the rod, he will not die. ¹⁴ You should strike him with the rod and you will rescue his soul from the grave. ¹⁵ My child, when your heart becomes wise, then my heart, too, will rejoice,

---

23:1-3. Before dining with an absolute ruler, or anyone with considerable power, one should consider the consequences of incurring the host's displeasure, or the moral harm that can come from being subservient to an unscrupulous person.

23:6-8. The generous host gives unstintingly, but a miser does not. When a guest senses this, the food grows nauseating, and he regrets his pleasantries and compliments (Rav Sa'adiah Gaon).

23:10. See 22:28.

טז‑יז וְתַעְלֹזְנָה כִלְיוֹתָי בְּדַבֵּר שְׂפָתֶיךָ מֵישָׁרִים: אַל‑יְקַנֵּא לִבְּךָ בַּחַטָּאִים כִּי
יח אִם‑בְּיִרְאַת‑יְהוָה כָּל‑הַיּוֹם: כִּי אִם‑יֵשׁ אַחֲרִית וְתִקְוָתְךָ לֹא תִכָּרֵת:
יט‑כ שְׁמַע‑אַתָּה בְנִי וַחֲכָם וְאַשֵּׁר בַּדֶּרֶךְ לִבֶּךָ: אַל‑תְּהִי בְסֹבְאֵי‑יַיִן בְּזֹלֲלֵי
כא‑כב בָשָׂר לָמוֹ: כִּי‑סֹבֵא וְזוֹלֵל יִוָּרֵשׁ וּקְרָעִים תַּלְבִּישׁ נוּמָה: שְׁמַע לְאָבִיךָ זֶה
כג יְלָדֶךָ וְאַל‑תָּבוּז כִּי‑זָקְנָה אִמֶּךָ: אֱמֶת קְנֵה וְאַל‑תִּמְכֹּר חָכְמָה וּמוּסָר
כד וּבִינָה: °גּוֹל יָגוֹל [°גִּיל יָגִיל ק] אֲבִי צַדִּיק °יוֹלֵד [°וְיוֹלֵד ק] חָכָם
כה‑כו וְיִשְׂמַח [°יִשְׂמַח ק] בּוֹ: יִשְׂמַח‑אָבִיךָ וְאִמֶּךָ וְתָגֵל יוֹלַדְתֶּךָ: תְּנָה‑בְנִי
כז לִבְּךָ לִי וְעֵינֶיךָ דְּרָכַי °תִּרֹצְנָה [°תִּצֹּרְנָה ק]: כִּי‑שׁוּחָה עֲמֻקָּה זוֹנָה וּבְאֵר
כח‑כט צָרָה נָכְרִיָּה: אַף‑הִיא כְּחֶתֶף תֶּאֱרֹב וּבוֹגְדִים בְּאָדָם תּוֹסִף: לְמִי אוֹי לְמִי
אֲבוֹי לְמִי °מִדוֹנִים [°מִדְיָנִים ק] | לְמִי שִׂיחַ לְמִי פְּצָעִים חִנָּם לְמִי
ל‑לא חַכְלִלוּת עֵינָיִם: לַמְאַחֲרִים עַל‑הַיַּיִן לַבָּאִים לַחְקֹר מִמְסָךְ: אַל‑תֵּרֶא יַיִן
לב כִּי יִתְאַדָּם כִּי‑יִתֵּן °בַּכִּיס [°בַּכּוֹס ק] עֵינוֹ יִתְהַלֵּךְ בְּמֵישָׁרִים: אַחֲרִיתוֹ
לג כְּנָחָשׁ יִשָּׁךְ וּכְצִפְעֹנִי יַפְרִשׁ: עֵינֶיךָ יִרְאוּ זָרוֹת וְלִבְּךָ יְדַבֵּר תַּהְפֻּכוֹת:
לד‑לה וְהָיִיתָ כְּשֹׁכֵב בְּלֶב‑יָם וּכְשֹׁכֵב בְּרֹאשׁ חִבֵּל: הִכּוּנִי בַל‑חָלִיתִי הֲלָמוּנִי

כד
א בַּל‑יָדָעְתִּי מָתַי אָקִיץ אוֹסִיף אֲבַקְשֶׁנּוּ עוֹד: אַל‑תְּקַנֵּא בְּאַנְשֵׁי רָעָה
ב וְאַל‑תִּתְאָו לִהְיוֹת אִתָּם: כִּי‑שֹׁד יֶהְגֶּה לִבָּם וְעָמָל שִׂפְתֵיהֶם תְּדַבֵּרְנָה:
ג‑ד בְּחָכְמָה יִבָּנֶה בָּיִת וּבִתְבוּנָה יִתְכּוֹנָן: וּבְדַעַת חֲדָרִים יִמָּלְאוּ כָּל‑הוֹן יָקָר
ה‑ו וְנָעִים: גֶּבֶר‑חָכָם בַּעוֹז וְאִישׁ‑דַּעַת מְאַמֶּץ‑כֹּחַ: כִּי בְתַחְבֻּלוֹת תַּעֲשֶׂה
ז לְּךָ מִלְחָמָה וּתְשׁוּעָה בְּרֹב יוֹעֵץ: רָאמוֹת לֶאֱוִיל חָכְמוֹת בַּשַּׁעַר לֹא
ח‑ט יִפְתַּח‑פִּיהוּ: מְחַשֵּׁב לְהָרֵעַ לוֹ בַּעַל‑מְזִמּוֹת יִקְרָאוּ: זִמַּת אִוֶּלֶת חַטָּאת
יא‑יב וְתוֹעֲבַת לְאָדָם לֵץ: הִתְרַפִּיתָ בְּיוֹם צָרָה צַר כֹּחֶכָה: הַצֵּל לְקֻחִים לַמָּוֶת
יב וּמָטִים לַהֶרֶג אִם‑תַּחְשׂוֹךְ: כִּי‑תֹאמַר הֵן לֹא‑יָדַעְנוּ זֶה הֲלֹא‑תֹכֵן
יג לִבּוֹת | הוּא‑יָבִין וְנֹצֵר נַפְשְׁךָ הוּא יֵדָע וְהֵשִׁיב לְאָדָם כְּפָעֳלוֹ: אֱכָל‑בְּנִי
יד דְבַשׁ כִּי‑טוֹב וְנֹפֶת מָתוֹק עַל‑חִכֶּךָ: כֵּן | דְּעֵה חָכְמָה לְנַפְשֶׁךָ אִם‑מָצָאתָ
טו וְיֵשׁ אַחֲרִית וְתִקְוָתְךָ לֹא תִכָּרֵת: אַל‑תֶּאֱרֹב רָשָׁע לִנְוֵה צַדִּיק אַל‑
טז‑יז תְּשַׁדֵּד רִבְצוֹ: כִּי שֶׁבַע | יִפּוֹל צַדִּיק וָקָם וּרְשָׁעִים יִכָּשְׁלוּ בְרָעָה: בִּנְפֹל
יח °אוֹיִבְךָ [°אוֹיִבֶיךָ ק] אַל‑תִּשְׂמָח וּבִכָּשְׁלוֹ אַל‑יָגֵל לִבֶּךָ: פֶּן‑יִרְאֶה יְהוָה
וְרַע בְּעֵינָיו וְהֵשִׁיב מֵעָלָיו אַפּוֹ:

23:17-18. One should envy the person who truly fears God, learn from him and emulate his deeds (Ibn Nachmias). Only this is lasting; wealth and sinful pleasures are ephemeral.

23:20-21. Such excesses lead to spiritual and intellectual impoverishment (Rabbeinu Bachya).

23:23. Hire a teacher, if necessary (Rashi). Buy books of truth and do not sell them (Ibn Ezra).

23:27. Once entrapped in sin, it is hard for one to escape.

23:29-36. Base desires and wine lead to lewdness and

quarrel and ultimately affect our behavior, causing us to ridicule and degrade basic values (R' Hirsch).

23:34. Infatuation with sin will make you as dizzy and incoherent as someone seasick from tossing about on a boat or balancing atop a mast.

23:35. When he becomes sober, he is oblivious to the ill-effects that overcame him and he drinks again (Rashi).

24:3-4. After warning against envying the wicked, King Solomon teaches that if one engages in wisdom, understanding, and knowledge, he will achieve tranquility and

 [16] and my yearnings will exult when your lips speak righteous words. [17] Let your heart not envy sinners, rather those who revere HASHEM all the day. * [18] For it shall endure and your hope will not be cut off. [19] Hear, you my child, and grow wise, and stride in the way of your heart. [20] Do not be among the guzzlers of wine, among the gorgers of meat for themselves. * [21] For the guzzler and the gorger will be poor, and slumber will clothe [you] in tatters. [22] Give ear to your father, who begot you, and though your mother may be old, do not scorn [her]. [23] Purchase truth, do not sell it — wisdom, discipline, and understanding. * [24] The father of a righteous person will be mirthful; one who begets a wise child will rejoice in him. [25] Your father and mother will be glad, and the one who bore you will rejoice. [26] My child, give your heart to me, and your eyes will desire my ways. [27] For the harlot is a deep pit, and the strange woman is a narrow well. * [28] She, too, lurks to snatch and multiplies the faithless among men. [29] Who cries, "Alas!"? Who cries, "Woe!"? Who is contentious? Who prattles? Who is wounded for naught? Whose eyes are red? * [30] Those who linger over wine; those who come to inquire over mixed drinks. [31] Do not look at wine becoming red, for to one who fixes his eyes on the goblet all paths are upright. [32] His end is like that of one bitten by a snake, like one dispatched by a serpent. [33] Your eyes will see strange things and your heart will speak duplicities. [34] And you will be like one who sleeps in the heart of the sea, like one who lies on the top of a mast. * [35] [In your drunkenness you will say:] "They struck me, but I did not become ill; they beat me, but I was unaware. When will I awaken? I will continue asking for more [wine]!" *

24   [1] Do not envy men of evil, and do not desire to be with them, [2] for their hearts contemplate spoils and their lips speak mischief. [3] Through wisdom a house is built, and it is established through understanding; [4] and through knowledge, its chambers become filled with all dear and pleasant treasures. * [5] The wise man remains steadfast, and the man of knowledge grows stronger. * [6] For through [wise] strategies, you can wage war for your benefit; and salvation is in abundant counsel. [7] [But] to a foolish one, wisdom is an unattainable gem; he will not open his mouth at the gate. [8] One who thinks of doing evil will be called a master of wicked designs. [9] Foolish designs are a sin, and scoffing makes a man abominable. [10] If you were weak in [another's] day of affliction, your strength will become limited. * [11] If you desist from rescuing those being put to death, and those on the way to be murdered, [12] yet you say, "Surely we did not know this!" But the One Who resides in hearts, He understands; and the Protector of your soul, He knows; and He recompenses a man according to his deeds. * [13] Eat honey, my child, for it is good, and drippings of the honeycomb are sweet on your palate; [14] so is knowledge of wisdom to your soul, if you have found it, for it has a lasting outcome, and your hope will not be cut off. [15] Do not lurk, O wicked one, near the habitation of the righteous one; do not plunder his resting place. [16] For though the righteous one may fall seven times, he will arise, but the wicked ones will stumble through evil. [17] When your foe falls, be not glad, and when he stumbles, let your heart not be joyous, [18] lest HASHEM see and it be displeasing in His eyes, and He turn His anger from him [to you].

---

riches (*Rabbeinu Yonah*).

24:5-7. Wisdom is an indispensable ally for the attainment of success, but the fool will fail to achieve such goals.

24:10. If you are slack in helping others in their time of need, you will grow too weak to help yourself.

24:12. Someone may excuse his apathy saying he was unaware of the other person's need — but God knows the truth, and will deal with him in kind (*Malbim*).

כד־יט   אַל־תִּתְחַר בַּמְּרֵעִים אַל־תְּקַנֵּא בָּרְשָׁעִים: כִּי | לֹא־תִהְיֶה אַחֲרִית לָרָע

כא־כב   נֵר רְשָׁעִים יִדְעָךְ: יְרָא־אֶת־יהוה בְּנִי וָמֶלֶךְ עִם־שׁוֹנִים אַל־תִּתְעָרָב: כִּי־פִּתְאֹם יָקוּם אֵידָם וּפִיד שְׁנֵיהֶם מִי יוֹדֵעַ:

כג־כד   גַּם־אֵלֶּה לַחֲכָמִים הַכֵּר־פָּנִים בְּמִשְׁפָּט בַּל־טוֹב: אֹמֵר | לְרָשָׁע צַדִּיק אַתָּה יִקְּבֻהוּ עַמִּים יִזְעָמוּהוּ לְאֻמִּים: וְלַמּוֹכִיחִים יִנְעָם וַעֲלֵיהֶם תָּבוֹא

כה־כו   בִרְכַּת־טוֹב: שְׂפָתַיִם יִשָּׁק מֵשִׁיב דְּבָרִים נְכֹחִים: הָכֵן בַּחוּץ | מְלַאכְתֶּךָ וְעַתְּדָהּ בַּשָּׂדֶה לָךְ אַחַר וּבָנִיתָ בֵיתֶךָ:

כח־כט   אַל־תְּהִי עֵד־חִנָּם בְּרֵעֶךָ וַהֲפִתִּיתָ בִּשְׂפָתֶיךָ: אַל־תֹּאמַר כַּאֲשֶׁר עָשָׂה־לִי כֵּן אֶעֱשֶׂה־לּוֹ אָשִׁיב לָאִישׁ כְּפָעֳלוֹ:

ל־לא   עַל־שְׂדֵה אִישׁ־עָצֵל עָבַרְתִּי וְעַל־כֶּרֶם אָדָם חֲסַר־לֵב: וְהִנֵּה עָלָה כֻלּוֹ | קִמְּשֹׂנִים כָּסּוּ פָנָיו חֲרֻלִּים וְגֶדֶר אֲבָנָיו נֶהֱרָסָה: וָאֶחֱזֶה אָנֹכִי אָשִׁית לִבִּי

לב־לג   רָאִיתִי לָקַחְתִּי מוּסָר: מְעַט שֵׁנוֹת מְעַט תְּנוּמוֹת מְעַט | חִבֻּק יָדַיִם

לד   לִשְׁכָּב: וּבָא־מִתְהַלֵּךְ רֵישֶׁךָ וּמַחְסֹרֶיךָ כְּאִישׁ מָגֵן:

כה   א   גַּם־אֵלֶּה מִשְׁלֵי שְׁלֹמֹה אֲשֶׁר הֶעְתִּיקוּ אַנְשֵׁי | חִזְקִיָּה מֶלֶךְ־יְהוּדָה: כְּבֹד

ג   אֱלֹהִים הַסְתֵּר דָּבָר וּכְבֹד מְלָכִים חֲקֹר דָּבָר: שָׁמַיִם לָרוּם וָאָרֶץ לָעֹמֶק

ד־ה   וְלֵב מְלָכִים אֵין חֵקֶר: הָגוֹ סִיגִים מִכָּסֶף וַיֵּצֵא לַצֹּרֵף כֶּלִי: הָגוֹ רָשָׁע

ו   לִפְנֵי־מֶלֶךְ וְיִכּוֹן בַּצֶּדֶק כִּסְאוֹ: אַל־תִּתְהַדַּר לִפְנֵי־מֶלֶךְ וּבִמְקוֹם גְּדֹלִים

ז   אַל־תַּעֲמֹד: כִּי טוֹב אֲמָר־לְךָ עֲלֵה הֵנָּה מֵהַשְׁפִּילְךָ לִפְנֵי נָדִיב אֲשֶׁר רָאוּ

ח   עֵינֶיךָ: אַל־תֵּצֵא לָרִב מַהֵר פֶּן מַה־תַּעֲשֶׂה בְּאַחֲרִיתָהּ בְּהַכְלִים אֹתְךָ

ט־י   רֵעֶךָ: רִיבְךָ רִיב אֶת־רֵעֶךָ וְסוֹד אַחֵר אַל־תְּגָל: פֶּן־יְחַסֶּדְךָ שֹׁמֵעַ וְדִבָּתְךָ

יא־יב   לֹא תָשׁוּב: תַּפּוּחֵי זָהָב בְּמַשְׂכִּיּוֹת כָּסֶף דָּבָר דָּבֻר עַל־אָפְנָיו: נֶזֶם זָהָב וַחֲלִי־כָתֶם מוֹכִיחַ חָכָם עַל־אֹזֶן שֹׁמָעַת:

יג   כְּצִנַּת־שֶׁלֶג | בְּיוֹם קָצִיר צִיר נֶאֱמָן לְשֹׁלְחָיו וְנֶפֶשׁ אֲדֹנָיו יָשִׁיב:

יד־טו   נְשִׂיאִים וְרוּחַ וְגֶשֶׁם אָיִן אִישׁ מִתְהַלֵּל בְּמַתַּת־שָׁקֶר: בְּאֹרֶךְ אַפַּיִם יְפֻתֶּה

טז   קָצִין וְלָשׁוֹן רַכָּה תִּשְׁבָּר־גָּרֶם: דְּבַשׁ מָצָאתָ אֱכֹל דַּיֶּךָּ פֶּן־תִּשְׂבָּעֶנּוּ

יז־יח   וַהֲקֵאתוֹ: הֹקַר רַגְלְךָ מִבֵּית רֵעֶךָ פֶּן־יִשְׂבָּעֲךָ וּשְׂנֵאֶךָ: מֵפִיץ וְחֶרֶב וְחֵץ

24:21-22. Fear God and your mortal king, but fear of God comes first. Avoid the friendship of someone who wavers between God and king, because he will be punished, but you cannot know whose punishment will be greater, God's or the king's.

24:23. The following statements are addressed to the wise who sit in judgment (*Rashi*).

24:25. When admonishing, it is proper to begin with praise, because such sensitivity will help influence the wicked to repent (*Meiri*).

24:27. First establish yourself financially and then start a family (*Rashi*).

24:28-29. Do not testify falsely or misleadingly to please a friend, or to repay a similar favor (*Ralbag*).

24:33-34. See 6:10-11.

◈§ **Chapter 25**

With this chapter, the third and final section of *Proverbs* begins. Its teachings, as indicated by verse 1, were culled and consolidated from various sources left by King Solomon. When Hezekiah became king, he expounded Solomon's proverbs and placed disciples in every city (*Sanhedrin* 94b). Thus, *Ralbag* suggests that the previous chapters in their final form were found in Solomon's own writings, but those from Chapter 25 to the end of the Book were gathered by Hezekiah and his men (*Bava Basra* 15a) and redacted in this collection.

A few of the verses in this section have appeared earlier, either with the identical wording or with minor variations

¹⁹ *Do not assimilate among evildoers; do not envy the wicked.* ²⁰ *For there will be no lasting outcome to evil; but the lamp of the wicked shall die out.* ²¹ *Fear* HASHEM, *my child, and the king. Do not mix with inconsistent people,* * ²² *for their disaster will arise suddenly, and who knows the punishment of both?*

²³ *These things, too, are for the wise [to consider]:* * *Showing favoritism in judgment is not good;* ²⁴ *one who tells a wicked person, "You are righteous," —* *the peoples will curse him, the nations will anathemize him.* ²⁵ *The reprovers should be pleasant,* * *and a good blessing will come upon them.* ²⁶ *The lips of one who responds with proper words should be kissed.* ²⁷ *Prepare your work outside and provide for yourself in the field; then build your house.* *

²⁸ *Do not offer vain testimony against your fellow, to endear yourself with your lips.* * ²⁹ *Do not say, "As he has done for me, so will I do for him; I will reward the man according to his acts."*

³⁰ *I passed by the field of a lazy man, and by the vineyard of a man lacking [an understanding] heart,* ³¹ *and, behold, it was all overgrown with thorns; nettles had covered its surface; and its stone wall was broken down.* ³² *When I saw this, I set my heart [to understand]; I saw and accepted discipline:* ³³ *A little sleep; a little slumber; a little folding of the hands to recline,* ³⁴ *then, your poverty will come like a traveler, and your lacking like an armed man.* *

25

Rulers should be straightforward and avoid evildoers

¹ **T**hese, too, are the proverbs of King Solomon, which were copied by the men of Hezekiah, king of Judah.* ² *It is the honor of God to conceal a matter; but it is the honor of kings to search out a matter.* * ³ *The heavens for height, the earth for depth, and the heart of kings cannot be fathomed.* ⁴ *When dross is removed from silver, a vessel can emerge for the refiner;* ⁵ *when an evildoer is removed from the king, his throne is established in righteousness.* ⁶ *Do not glorify yourself in the presence of the king, and do not stand in the place of the great,* ⁷ *for it is better that it should be said to you, "Come up here," than that you be demoted*

Be careful where you glorify yourself and beware of what you say

before the prince, as your eyes have seen [happen to others]. ⁸ *Do not be quick to enter into strife, unless you know what you will do in the end, when your fellow humiliates you.* * ⁹ *Pursue your quarrel with your friend, but do not reveal another's confidence,* * ¹⁰ *lest a listener disgrace you and you be unable to retract your slander.* ¹¹ *[Like] golden apples carved on silver plates, [so is] a word spoken in its proper place.* ¹² *[Like] a golden nose ring and an ornament of fine gold, [so is] the reproof of the wise upon a heedful ear.*

¹³ *Like a cooling snow on a harvest day, [so is] a faithful emissary to his sender; he refreshes his master's soul.*

Be sincere, but do not make yourself a burden to others

¹⁴ *[Like] clouds and wind without rain, [so is] one who lauds himself for a false gift.* ¹⁵ *By forbearance a ruler is mollified, and a soft tongue breaks strong anger.* ¹⁶ *When you find honey, eat what is sufficient for you, lest you be satiated and vomit it up.* ¹⁷ *Let your feet be scarce in your fellow's house, lest he be satiated with you and come to hate you.* * ¹⁸ *A maul, a sword, and a sharp arrow*

(e.g., 2:19 and 25:24; 19:24 and 26:15; 20:16 and 27:13). However, it is not always clear why they were repeated.

25:2. Regarding the mysteries of the Torah and Creation, many of which are beyond human intelligence, the prophets and Sages spoke indirectly and figuratively, using symbols and metaphors. In matters of state, however, openness and clarity are virtues (*Malbim*).

25:8. Do not become involved in an argument unless you have thought through how it may end.

25:9-10. If you must litigate, do not divulge confidences, for if you do, even if you regret it, you will be unable to rectify it.

25:16-17. Do not burden even good friends with too many visits; one can become weary of too much of a good thing.

יט שָׁנּוּן אִישׁ עֹנֶה בְרֵעֵהוּ עֵד שָׁקֶר: שֵׁן רֹעָה וְרֶגֶל מוּעָדֶת מִבְטָח בּוֹגֵד
כ בְּיוֹם צָרָה: מַעֲדֶה בֶּגֶד ׀ בְּיוֹם קָרָה חֹמֶץ עַל־נָתֶר וְשָׁר בַּשִּׁרִים עַל לֵב־
כא-כב רָע: אִם־רָעֵב שֹׂנַאֲךָ הַאֲכִלֵהוּ לָחֶם וְאִם־צָמֵא הַשְׁקֵהוּ מָיִם: כִּי גֶחָלִים
כג אַתָּה חֹתֶה עַל־רֹאשׁוֹ וַיהוֹה יְשַׁלֶּם־לָךְ: רוּחַ צָפוֹן תְּחוֹלֵל גָּשֶׁם וּפָנִים
כד נִזְעָמִים לְשׁוֹן סָתֶר: טוֹב שֶׁבֶת עַל־פִּנַּת־גָּג מֵאֵשֶׁת °מדונים [°מִדְיָנִים
ק] וּבֵית חָבֶר:
כה-כו מַיִם קָרִים עַל־נֶפֶשׁ עֲיֵפָה וּשְׁמוּעָה טוֹבָה מֵאֶרֶץ מֶרְחָק: מַעְיָן נִרְפָּשׂ
כז וּמָקוֹר מָשְׁחָת צַדִּיק מָט לִפְנֵי־רָשָׁע: אָכֹל דְּבַשׁ הַרְבּוֹת לֹא־טוֹב וְחֵקֶר
כח כְּבֹדָם כָּבוֹד: עִיר פְּרוּצָה אֵין חוֹמָה אִישׁ אֲשֶׁר אֵין מַעְצָר לְרוּחוֹ:

כו א-ב כַּשֶּׁלֶג ׀ בַּקַּיִץ וְכַמָּטָר בַּקָּצִיר כֵּן לֹא־נָאוֶה לִכְסִיל כָּבוֹד: כַּצִּפּוֹר לָנוּד
ג כַּדְּרוֹר לָעוּף כֵּן קִלְלַת חִנָּם °לא [°לוֹ ק] תָּבֹא: שׁוֹט לַסּוּס מֶתֶג לַחֲמוֹר
ד-ה וְשֵׁבֶט לְגֵו כְּסִילִים: אַל־תַּעַן כְּסִיל כְּאִוַּלְתּוֹ פֶּן־תִּשְׁוֶה־לּוֹ גַם־אָתָּה: עֲנֵה
ו כְסִיל כְּאִוַּלְתּוֹ פֶּן־יִהְיֶה חָכָם בְּעֵינָיו: מְקַצֶּה רַגְלַיִם חָמָס שֹׁתֶה שֹׁלֵחַ
ז-ח דְּבָרִים בְּיַד־כְּסִיל: דַּלְיוּ שֹׁקַיִם מִפִּסֵּחַ וּמָשָׁל בְּפִי כְסִילִים: כִּצְרוֹר אֶבֶן
ט בְּמַרְגֵּמָה כֵּן־נוֹתֵן לִכְסִיל כָּבוֹד: חוֹחַ עָלָה בְיַד־שִׁכּוֹר וּמָשָׁל בְּפִי
י-יא כְסִילִים: רַב מְחוֹלֵל־כֹּל וְשֹׂכֵר כְּסִיל וְשֹׂכֵר עֹבְרִים: כְּכֶלֶב
יב שָׁב עַל־קֵאוֹ כְּסִיל שׁוֹנֶה בְאִוַּלְתּוֹ: רָאִיתָ אִישׁ חָכָם בְּעֵינָיו תִּקְוָה לִכְסִיל
יג מִמֶּנּוּ: אָמַר עָצֵל שַׁחַל בַּדָּרֶךְ אֲרִי בֵּין הָרְחֹבוֹת: הַדֶּלֶת תִּסּוֹב עַל־צִירָהּ
יד-טו וְעָצֵל עַל־מִטָּתוֹ: טָמַן עָצֵל יָדוֹ בַּצַּלָּחַת נִלְאָה לַהֲשִׁיבָהּ אֶל־פִּיו: חָכָם
יז עָצֵל בְּעֵינָיו מִשִּׁבְעָה מְשִׁיבֵי טָעַם: מַחֲזִיק בְּאָזְנֵי־כָלֶב עֹבֵר מִתְעַבֵּר
יח-יט עַל־רִיב לֹּא־לוֹ: כְּמִתְלַהְלֵהַּ הַיֹּרֶה זִקִּים חִצִּים וָמָוֶת: כֵּן־אִישׁ רִמָּה אֶת־
כ רֵעֵהוּ וְאָמַר הֲלֹא־מְשַׂחֵק אָנִי: בְּאֶפֶס עֵצִים תִּכְבֶּה־אֵשׁ וּבְאֵין נִרְגָּן
כא יִשְׁתֹּק מָדוֹן: פֶּחָם לְגֶחָלִים וְעֵצִים לְאֵשׁ וְאִישׁ °מדונים [°מִדְיָנִים ק]
לְחַרְחַר־רִיב:
כב-כג דִּבְרֵי נִרְגָּן כְּמִתְלַהֲמִים וְהֵם יָרְדוּ חַדְרֵי־בָטֶן: כֶּסֶף סִיגִים מְצֻפֶּה עַל־
כד חָרֶשׂ שְׂפָתַיִם דֹּלְקִים וְלֶב־רָע: °בשפתו [°בִּשְׂפָתָיו ק] יִנָּכֵר שׂוֹנֵא וּבְקִרְבּוֹ
כה יָשִׁית מִרְמָה: כִּי־יְחַנֵּן קוֹלוֹ אַל־תַּאֲמֶן־בּוֹ כִּי שֶׁבַע תּוֹעֵבוֹת בְּלִבּוֹ:

25:18. False testimony is a maul, destroying relationships; a sword, cutting those nearby; and a sharp arrow, killing even those who are far away (*Vilna Gaon*).

25:20. Something that is beautiful and pleasant at the right time can be totally inappropriate at the wrong time.

25:21-22. If you are good to your enemy, he will be ashamed of his behavior toward you.

25:26. When a righteous person fails to stand up for a principle, he is like a polluted water supply.

26:1. Just as rain and snow are harmful at the wrong time of the year, so honor is harmful to a fool, for it only

confirms his attitudes (*Malbim*).

26:2. Birds always return to their nests; so too, an unjustified curse will rest upon the head of the one who uttered it.

26:4-5. The two verses are in apparent contradiction. The Talmud explains that one should not be drawn into vain arguments with a fool in worldly or inconsequential matters. However, if he disputes or errs regarding the Torah, it is essential that he be corrected (*Shabbos* 30b).

26:6. A fool will misinterpret his mission and deliver the wrong message; the sender will then weary his feet when he rushes to correct the error and cope with the anger of

Never betray a friend . . . is someone who bears false witness against his fellow. * ¹⁹ [Like] a broken tooth and a slipping foot, [so is] a trust betrayed in a day of distress. ²⁰ [Like] an ornamental garment on a cold day, [like] vinegar upon natron, [so is] one who sings songs upon a sorrowful heart. * ²¹ If your foe is hungry, feed him bread; and if he is thirsty, give him water to drink, * ²² for you will be scooping coals [to heap] on his head, and HASHEM will reward you. ²³ [As] the north wind brings forth rain, [so does] stealthy slander brings forth an angry face. ²⁴ Better is dwelling on a corner of a roof than [dwelling with] a contentious wife [even] in a house of friends.

be generous to your foe . . .

and never speak slander

Be principled and avoid excess ²⁵ [Like] cold water on a weary soul, [so is] good news from a distant land. ²⁶ Like a muddied spring and a ruined fountain, [so is] a righteous one who bows before the evildoer. * ²⁷ Eating too much honey is not good, but searching out the honor [of the righteous] is honorable. ²⁸ [Like] a breached city without a wall, [so is] a man with no constraint to his spirit.

26

Everything in its proper time ¹ Like snow in the summer and rain at the harvest, so does honor not befit a fool. * ² Like a bird that wanders off, like a swallow that flies off, so an unwarranted curse comes [back] to he [who utters it]. * ³ A whip for the horse, a bridle for the donkey, and a rod for the back of fools. ⁴ Do not answer a fool according to his foolishness, lest you also be considered like him. * ⁵ Answer a fool according to his foolishness, lest he be wise in his own eyes. ⁶ One will cut off [his own] feet and drink rancor if one sends messages with a fool. * ⁷ [Like] the limp-hanging thighs of the cripple, [so is] a parable in the mouth of fools. ⁸ Like one who loads a stone into a sling, so is one who gives honor to a fool. ⁹ [Like] a thorn in the hand of a drunkard, [so is] a parable in the mouth of fools.

To deal with fools requires judgment

Fools ruin good things

Avoid contentious and foolish people ¹⁰ A contentious person may cause many deaths; he hires the fool, and he hires adventurers. ¹¹ Like a dog that returns to his vomit, [so is] a fool who repeats his foolishness. ¹² Have you seen a man who is wise in his own eyes? There is more hope for a fool than for him. * ¹³ A lazy person * says, "There is a young lion on the path, a lion between the streets." ¹⁴ The door turns on its hinges, and a lazy person on his bed. ¹⁵ The lazy one buries his hand in the dish; he is too weary to return it to his mouth. ¹⁶ The lazy one is wiser in his own eyes than seven who answer sensibly. ¹⁷ [Like] one who seizes a dog's ears, [so is] one who grows wrathful over a dispute that is not his. ¹⁸ Like someone who wears himself out throwing firebrands, arrows and lethal objects, * ¹⁹ so is a man who deceives his fellow and says, "Surely, I was joking." ²⁰ [Just as] when there is no wood the fire goes out, [so] when no one complains, strife is silenced. ²¹ [Like] kindling to coals, and twigs to a fire, [so is] the contentious man to kindling strife.

Lazy people harm themselves

Avoid disputes . . .

. . . it takes two to argue

Insincere compliments camouflage evil . . . ²² The words of the complainer are like blows, and they descend to the chambers of the stomach. ²³ [Like] silver dross coating earthenware, [so are] hotly pursuing lips above an evil heart. * ²⁴ With his lips the foe acts estranged [from hatred], but within himself he casts deceit. ²⁵ Though his voice is ingratiating, do not trust him, for there are seven abominations in his heart.

---

the misinformed recipient.

26:12. Someone who considers himself a fool is less dangerous than someone with an overblown opinion of himself.

26:13. A lazy person creates excuses not to work (*Ibn Ezra*).

26:18-19. One practices by throwing firebrands that will be extinguished in midair, so that when he gets the range, he will switch to lethal projectiles.

26:23. Like shining silver camouflaging a cheap utensil are lips overflowing with bogus love, concealing a venomous heart (*Rashi*).

כו-כז תִּכַּסֶּה שִׂנְאָה בְּמַשָּׁאוֹן תִּגָּלֶה רָעָתוֹ בְקָהָל: כֹּרֶה־שַּׁחַת בָּהּ יִפֹּל וְגֹלֵל אֶבֶן

כז כח-א אֵלָיו תָּשׁוּב: לָשׁוֹן־שֶׁקֶר יִשְׂנָא דַכָּיו וּפֶה חָלָק יַעֲשֶׂה מִדְחֶה: אַל־תִּתְהַלֵּל

ב בְּיוֹם מָחָר כִּי לֹא־תֵדַע מַה־יֵּלֶד יוֹם: יְהַלֶּלְךָ זָר וְלֹא־פִיךָ נָכְרִי וְאַל־

ג-ד שְׂפָתֶיךָ: כֹּבֶד־אֶבֶן וְנֵטֶל הַחוֹל וְכַעַס אֱוִיל כָּבֵד מִשְּׁנֵיהֶם: אַכְזְרִיּוּת חֵמָה

ה וְשֶׁטֶף אָף וּמִי יַעֲמֹד לִפְנֵי קִנְאָה: טוֹבָה תּוֹכַחַת מְגֻלָּה מֵאַהֲבָה מְסֻתָּרֶת:

ו-ז נֶאֱמָנִים פִּצְעֵי אוֹהֵב וְנַעְתָּרוֹת נְשִׁיקוֹת שׂוֹנֵא: נֶפֶשׁ שְׂבֵעָה תָּבוּס נֹפֶת

ח וְנֶפֶשׁ רְעֵבָה כָּל־מַר מָתוֹק: כְּצִפּוֹר נוֹדֶדֶת מִן־קִנָּהּ כֵּן־אִישׁ נוֹדֵד

ט מִמְּקוֹמוֹ: שֶׁמֶן וּקְטֹרֶת יְשַׂמַּח־לֵב וּמֶתֶק רֵעֵהוּ מֵעֲצַת־נָפֶשׁ: רֵעֲךָ °וְרֵעַה

[ק °וְרֵעַ] אָבִיךָ אַל־תַּעֲזֹב וּבֵית אָחִיךָ אַל־תָּבוֹא בְּיוֹם אֵידֶךָ טוֹב שָׁכֵן

יא-יב קָרוֹב מֵאָח רָחוֹק: חֲכַם בְּנִי וְשַׂמַּח לִבִּי וְאָשִׁיבָה חֹרְפִי דָבָר: עָרוּם רָאָה

יג רָעָה נִסְתָּר פְּתָאִים עָבְרוּ נֶעֱנָשׁוּ: קַח־בִּגְדוֹ כִּי־עָרַב זָר וּבְעַד נָכְרִיָּה

יד-טו חַבְלֵהוּ: מְבָרֵךְ רֵעֵהוּ ׀ בְּקוֹל גָּדוֹל בַּבֹּקֶר הַשְׁכֵּים קְלָלָה תֵּחָשֶׁב לוֹ: דֶּלֶף

טז טוֹרֵד בְּיוֹם סַגְרִיר וְאֵשֶׁת °מדונים וְאֵשֶׁת °מדונים [ק °מִדְיָנִים] נִשְׁתָּוָה: צֹפְנֶיהָ צָפַן־רוּחַ

יז-יח וְשֶׁמֶן יְמִינוֹ יִקְרָא: בַּרְזֶל בְּבַרְזֶל יָחַד וְאִישׁ יַחַד פְּנֵי־רֵעֵהוּ: נֹצֵר תְּאֵנָה

יט יֹאכַל פִּרְיָהּ וְשֹׁמֵר אֲדֹנָיו יְכֻבָּד: כַּמַּיִם הַפָּנִים לַפָּנִים כֵּן לֵב־הָאָדָם

כ לָאָדָם: שְׁאוֹל וַאֲבַדֹּה לֹא תִשְׂבַּעְנָה וְעֵינֵי הָאָדָם לֹא תִשְׂבַּעְנָה:

כא-כב מַצְרֵף לַכֶּסֶף וְכוּר לַזָּהָב וְאִישׁ לְפִי מַהֲלָלוֹ: אִם תִּכְתּוֹשׁ־אֶת־הָאֱוִיל ׀

בַּמַּכְתֵּשׁ בְּתוֹךְ הָרִיפוֹת בַּעֱלִי לֹא־תָסוּר מֵעָלָיו אִוַּלְתּוֹ:

כג-כד יָדֹעַ תֵּדַע פְּנֵי צֹאנֶךָ שִׁית לִבְּךָ לַעֲדָרִים: כִּי לֹא לְעוֹלָם חֹסֶן וְאִם־נֵזֶר

כה לְדוֹר °דור [ק °וָדוֹר]: גָּלָה חָצִיר וְנִרְאָה־דֶשֶׁא וְנֶאֶסְפוּ עִשְּׂבוֹת הָרִים:

כו-כז כְּבָשִׂים לִלְבוּשֶׁךָ וּמְחִיר שָׂדֶה עַתּוּדִים: וְדֵי ׀ חֲלֵב עִזִּים לְלַחְמְךָ לְלֶחֶם

כח א בֵּיתֶךָ וְחַיִּים לְנַעֲרוֹתֶיךָ: נָסוּ וְאֵין־רֹדֵף רָשָׁע וְצַדִּיקִים כִּכְפִיר יִבְטָח:

ב-ג בְּפֶשַׁע אֶרֶץ רַבִּים שָׂרֶיהָ וּבְאָדָם מֵבִין יֹדֵעַ כֵּן יַאֲרִיךְ: גֶּבֶר רָשׁ וְעֹשֵׁק

ד דַּלִּים מָטָר סֹחֵף וְאֵין לָחֶם: עֹזְבֵי תוֹרָה יְהַלְלוּ רָשָׁע וְשֹׁמְרֵי תוֹרָה

ה יִתְגָּרוּ בָם: אַנְשֵׁי־רָע לֹא־יָבִינוּ מִשְׁפָּט וּמְבַקְשֵׁי יהוה יָבִינוּ כֹל:

ו-ז טוֹב־רָשׁ הוֹלֵךְ בְּתֻמּוֹ מֵעִקֵּשׁ דְּרָכַיִם וְהוּא עָשִׁיר: נוֹצֵר תּוֹרָה בֵּן מֵבִין

26:27. God punishes a sinner "measure for measure" (*Ibn Nachmias*).

26:28. An oppressor is sure of his victims' hatred, but if the victim speaks soothingly, he deflects it (*Ralbag*).

27:4. Envy is worse than wrath and anger.

27:7. A satisfied person does not pursue wealth, even through "honeyed" means. To the greedy, even sin is sweet, if it brings profits (*Ralbag*).

27:8. Birds remain home unless they must migrate, so a person should not migrate without good reason (*Ralbag*).

27:11. When children make their parents proud, they shrug off those who try to shame them.

27:13. As a lender, you are entitled to foreclose on a co-signer, for he knowingly risked his possessions.

27:14. One who ostentatiously blesses someone's generosity is harming his benefactor, because others will try to take advantage of him (*Rashi*).

27:15-16. The annoyance of a constantly nagging, quarrelsome wife is like a steadily dripping leak: One cannot escape it. Just as it is impossible to hide the wind, or conceal the aroma of a perfumed hand, so is it impossible to hide a spouse's contentious presence (*Meiri*).

27:19. Kindred hearts find their sentiments, feelings and convictions reflected in one another (*R' Hirsch*).

27:21. One's character can be seen in the things he considers important enough to praise (*Rabbeinu Yonah*).

27:23. Pay close attention to your business affairs. Only if you know others well, face to face, can you delegate

. . . it will
boomerang

26 [Though] his hatred is covered by darkness, his evil will be revealed in public. 27 He who digs a pit will fall into it, and he who rolls a stone will have it turn back upon him. * 28 A lying tongue hates those it oppresses, but a smooth mouth will turn [the hatred] back. *

27

Do not boast

1 **D**o not boast about tomorrow, for you know not what a day may bring. 2 Let another praise you, not your own mouth; a stranger, not your own lips. 3 A stone has weight and sand has mass, but the anger of a fool is heavier than both.

Envy is
worse than
wrath

4 Wrath is cruelty, and anger is torrential, but who can withstand envy?* 5 Open rebuke is good, if it stems from hidden love. 6 Faithful are the wounds inflicted by a lover; but superfluous are the kisses of a foe. 7 The sated soul will trample a honeycomb; but to the hungry soul, all bitter is sweet. * 8 Like a bird wandering

Loving
rebuke is
good

from its nest — so is a man who wanders from his place. * 9 Oil and incense gladden the heart, so does the sweetness of one's friend from his sincere counsel.

Be loyal

10 Do not forsake your friend and the friend of your father. Do not come to your brother's house in the day of your misfortune; a close neighbor is better than a distant brother. 11 Grow wise, my child, and gladden my heart; then I will have an answer for those who humiliate me. * 12 A shrewd person recognizes evil and hides; but simpletons go on and are punished. 13 Take the garment of one who co-signs for a stranger;* or offers collateral for an alien woman. 14 If one blesses his friend loudly from early in the morning, it will be considered a curse to him. *

Good
children
gladden
parents

Excess
praise and
excess
nagging
are bad

15 An irksome dripping on a day of [rainy] confinement and a contentious wife are alike. * 16 He who would hide her would hide the wind, as one's right hand proclaims the oil [with which it was anointed]. 17 As iron sharpens iron, so a man sharpens his fellow. 18 The protector of a fig tree will eat its fruit, and the guardian of his master will be honored. 19 As water reflects a face back to a face, so one's heart is reflected back to him by another. * 20 [As] the grave and Gehinnom are not sated, [so] the eyes of man are not sated. 21 A refining pot is for silver and a crucible for gold, and a man according to his praises. *

Friendly
competition
and diligence
are good

A fool
refuses to
learn

22 If you crush a foolish person in a mortar with softened grain and pound him with a pestle you will not remove his foolishness from him. 23 Know well the faces of your sheep; set your heart to the flocks. * 24 For strength endures not forever. Does the crown [of wealth] last from generation to generation? 25 [Sometimes] grass sprouts and vegetation is seen; but [sometimes] the herbage of the mountains is depleted. 26 Let the lambs be your clothing, and let he-goats be as valuable as a field to you. 27 And let the milk of goats be sufficient for your food, and for the food of your household, and give life to your maidens.

Tend to your
business and
prepare for
the future

28

Injustice has
far-reaching
conse-
quences

1 **T**he wicked flee though none pursue, but the righteous are confident as a young lion. 2 Through the perfidy of the land its officers increase, but through an understanding, knowing man, it will prolong [its days]. 3 A pauper who robs the destitute is like a torrential rain, which leaves no food. * 4 Those who forsake the Torah praise the wicked, * but the keepers of Torah contend with them. 5 Men of evil will not discern [the inevitable] judgment, but those who seek HASHEM will understand all.

Better
naïvete than
perversion

6 Better a poor man who walks in his innocence than a rich man who perverts [his] ways. 7 One who preserves the Torah is an understanding son,

---

responsibility to them (*Malbim*).

27:25-27. Prepare your land and tend your livestock; they can provide clothing and nutrition if the crops fail (*Yalkut HaMachiri*).

28:3. The judge whose decisions are inappropriate and

impoverish the wrong party destroys justice in the same way as a torrential downpour floods a field and destroys whatever crops would have grown there (*Ralbag*).

28:4. He who once learned but has abandoned his learning is the worst one of all (*Pesachim* 49).

ח וְרֹעֶה זוֹלְלִים יַכְלִים אָבִיו: מַרְבֶּה הוֹנוֹ בְּנֶשֶׁךְ °וּבְתַרְבִּית [°וְתַרְבִּית ק]

ט לְחוֹנֵן דַּלִּים יִקְבְּצֶנּוּ: מֵסִיר אָזְנוֹ מִשְּׁמֹעַ תּוֹרָה גַּם תְּפִלָּתוֹ תּוֹעֵבָה: מַשְׁגֶּה

י יְשָׁרִים | בְּדֶרֶךְ רָע בִּשְׁחוּתוֹ הוּא יִפּוֹל וּתְמִימִים יִנְחֲלוּ טוֹב: חָכָם בְּעֵינָיו

יא אִישׁ עָשִׁיר וְדַל מֵבִין יַחְקְרֶנּוּ: בַּעֲלֹץ צַדִּיקִים רַבָּה תִפְאָרֶת וּבְקוּם רְשָׁעִים

יב יְחֻפַּשׂ אָדָם: מְכַסֶּה פְשָׁעָיו לֹא יַצְלִיחַ וּמוֹדֶה וְעֹזֵב יְרֻחָם: אַשְׁרֵי אָדָם

יג מְפַחֵד תָּמִיד וּמַקְשֶׁה לִבּוֹ יִפּוֹל בְּרָעָה: אֲרִי־נֹהֵם וְדֹב שׁוֹקֵק מֹשֵׁל רָשָׁע עַל

יד עַם־דָּל:

טו נָגִיד חֲסַר תְּבוּנוֹת וְרַב מַעֲשַׁקּוֹת °שֹׂנְאֵי [°שֹׂנֵא ק] בֶצַע יַאֲרִיךְ יָמִים:

טז אָדָם עָשֻׁק בְּדַם־נָפֶשׁ עַד־בּוֹר יָנוּס אַל־יִתְמְכוּ־בוֹ: הוֹלֵךְ תָּמִים יִוָּשֵׁעַ

יז־יח וְנֶעְקַשׁ דְּרָכַיִם יִפּוֹל בְּאֶחָת: עֹבֵד אַדְמָתוֹ יִשְׂבַּע־לָחֶם וּמְרַדֵּף רֵקִים יִשְׂבַּע־

יט רִישׁ: אִישׁ אֱמוּנוֹת רַב־בְּרָכוֹת וְאָץ לְהַעֲשִׁיר לֹא יִנָּקֶה: הַכֵּר־פָּנִים לֹא־טוֹב

כ־כא וְעַל־פַּת־לֶחֶם יִפְשַׁע־גָּבֶר: נִבְהָל לַהוֹן אִישׁ רַע עָיִן וְלֹא־יֵדַע כִּי־חֶסֶר

כב יְבֹאֶנּוּ: מוֹכִיחַ אָדָם אַחֲרַי חֵן יִמְצָא מִמַּחֲלִיק לָשׁוֹן: גּוֹזֵל | אָבִיו וְאִמּוֹ וְאֹמֵר

כג־כד אֵין־פָּשַׁע חָבֵר הוּא לְאִישׁ מַשְׁחִית: רְחַב־נֶפֶשׁ יְגָרֶה מָדוֹן וּבוֹטֵחַ עַל־יְהֹוָה

כה יְדֻשָּׁן: בּוֹטֵחַ בְּלִבּוֹ הוּא כְסִיל וְהוֹלֵךְ בְּחָכְמָה הוּא יִמָּלֵט: נוֹתֵן לָרָשׁ אֵין

כו־כז מַחְסוֹר וּמַעְלִים עֵינָיו רַב־מְאֵרוֹת: בְּקוּם רְשָׁעִים יִסָּתֵר אָדָם וּבְאָבְדָם יִרְבּוּ

כח צַדִּיקִים: אִישׁ תּוֹכָחוֹת מַקְשֶׁה־עֹרֶף פֶּתַע יִשָּׁבֵר וְאֵין מַרְפֵּא: בִּרְבוֹת

כט
א־ג צַדִּיקִים יִשְׂמַח הָעָם וּבִמְשֹׁל רָשָׁע יֵאָנַח עָם: אִישׁ־אֹהֵב חָכְמָה יְשַׂמַּח

ד אָבִיו וְרֹעֶה זוֹנוֹת יְאַבֶּד־הוֹן: מֶלֶךְ בְּמִשְׁפָּט יַעֲמִיד אָרֶץ וְאִישׁ תְּרוּמוֹת

ה יֶהֶרְסֶנָּה: גֶּבֶר מַחֲלִיק עַל־רֵעֵהוּ רֶשֶׁת פּוֹרֵשׂ עַל־פְּעָמָיו: בְּפֶשַׁע אִישׁ רָע

ו־ז מוֹקֵשׁ וְצַדִּיק יָרוּן וְשָׂמֵחַ: יֹדֵעַ צַדִּיק דִּין דַּלִּים רָשָׁע לֹא־יָבִין דָּעַת: אַנְשֵׁי

ח־ט לָצוֹן יָפִיחוּ קִרְיָה וַחֲכָמִים יָשִׁיבוּ אָף: אִישׁ־חָכָם נִשְׁפָּט אֶת־אִישׁ אֱוִיל וְרָגַז

י וְשָׂחַק וְאֵין נָחַת: אַנְשֵׁי דָמִים יִשְׂנְאוּ־תָם וִישָׁרִים יְבַקְשׁוּ נַפְשׁוֹ: כָּל־רוּחוֹ

יא־יב יוֹצִיא כְסִיל וְחָכָם בְּאָחוֹר יְשַׁבְּחֶנָּה: מֹשֵׁל מַקְשִׁיב עַל־דְּבַר־שָׁקֶר כָּל־

יג מְשָׁרְתָיו רְשָׁעִים: רָשׁ וְאִישׁ תְּכָכִים נִפְגָּשׁוּ מֵאִיר־עֵינֵי שְׁנֵיהֶם יְהֹוָה:

יד־טו שׁוֹפֵט בֶּאֱמֶת דַּלִּים כִּסְאוֹ לָעַד יִכּוֹן: שֵׁבֶט וְתוֹכַחַת יִתֵּן חָכְמָה וְנַעַר מְשֻׁלָּח

טז מֵבִישׁ אִמּוֹ: בִּרְבוֹת רְשָׁעִים יִרְבֶּה־פָּשַׁע וְצַדִּיקִים בְּמַפַּלְתָּם יִרְאוּ: יַסֵּר בִּנְךָ

יז וִינִיחֶךָ וְיִתֵּן מַעֲדַנִּים לְנַפְשֶׁךָ:

יח־יט בְּאֵין חָזוֹן יִפָּרַע עָם וְשֹׁמֵר תּוֹרָה אַשְׁרֵהוּ: בִּדְבָרִים לֹא־יִוָּסֶר עָבֶד

28:8. God will transfer his wrongful profits to generous people (*Ibn Ezra*).

28:14. One fearful of real danger devises precautions to protect himself, but the overconfident suffers misfortune.

28:22. Greedy people think that if they give charity to the poor, it will diminish their fortune (*Ralbag*).

28:23. An intelligent person eventually realizes that the one who corrects his faults sincerely is his true friend.

28:24. By rationalizing that he will inherit the money anyway, such a thief habituates dishonesty and his theft will almost certainly escalate to steal from others (*Ralbag*).

29:4. A king who demands a share of all transactions for himself will destroy his country's economy.

29:6. Glad that he did not follow the ways of the wicked.

29:11. After a fool displays his anger loudly and disruptively, a wise man replies with wisdom and discretion.

29:12. When a ruler is eager to hear gossip, all his servants vie for his favor with scandalous stories.

Dishonest
profits
will be lost

but the companion of swillers humiliates his father. ⁸ One who multiplies his wealth through interest and increase gathers it for the patron of the poor. * ⁹ If one turns aside his ear from hearing the Torah, his prayer, too, will be [considered] an abomination. ¹⁰ One who causes the upright to stray on an evil way will fall into his own pit, but the innocent will inherit goodness. ¹¹ A rich man is wise in his own eyes, but a destitute person with understanding can search out more. ¹² When the righteous exult, there is much splendor, but when the wicked rise, victims are sought. ¹³ One who conceals his sins will not succeed, but he who confesses and forsakes them will be granted mercy. ¹⁴ Praiseworthy is the man who always fears, but he who is stubborn of heart will fall into misfortune. * ¹⁵ [Like] a roaring lion and a growling bear, [so is] a wicked ruler over a destitute people.

Innocence,
understand-
ing and
honesty are
keys to
success

Rulers must
not be
greedy

¹⁶ A prince who lacks understanding will increase plunder, but one who hates spoil will prolong [his] days.

¹⁷ A man guilty of bloodshed will flee until the grave; no one will support him.

Evildoers will
pay; good
people will
succeed

¹⁸ One who walks in innocence will be saved, but one who perverts his ways will fall in one [of the ways]. ¹⁹ One who works his land will be sated with bread, but one who chases vain pursuits will be sated with poverty. ²⁰ A man of integrity will increase blessings, but one impatient to be rich will not be exonerated. ²¹ To show favoritism in judgment is not good; for a loaf of bread [as a bribe] man will have become a sinner. ²² One overeager for wealth has an evil eye; * he does not know that want may befall him. ²³ One who reproves a person will later find favor, more than one with a flattering tongue. * ²⁴ He who steals from his father and mother and says there is no sin, he is a companion to a destructive person. * ²⁵ A greedy person stirs up strife, but one who trusts HASHEM will have abundance. ²⁶ One who trusts his heart is a fool, but one who walks with wisdom will escape. ²⁷ One who gives to a pauper will not lack, but one who averts his eyes will suffer many curses. ²⁸ When the wicked rise, men hide; but when they perish, the righteous increase.

Greed brings
destruction

Generosity is
rewarded;
wickedness
is hated

29

Stubborn
people do
not improve

¹ A man deserving rebukes stiffens his neck, he will be broken suddenly, with none to heal him. ² When the righteous are ascendant, the people will be glad; but in the rule of the wicked, the people will groan. ³ A man who loves wisdom gladdens his father, but the companion of harlots will lose a fortune.

Dishonest
rulers ruin
their country

⁴ Through justice a king establishes a land, but a man of graft tears it down. * ⁵ One who deceives his fellow through flattery is spreading a net for his own footsteps. ⁶ The offense of a wicked person is a snare, but a righteous person will sing and be glad. * ⁷ A righteous person knows the oppression of the poor, [but] an evil person will not understand such knowledge. ⁸ Scoffing men will inflame a city, but the wise will turn back anger. ⁹ When a wise man contends with a foolish one, [the wise man] may rage or laugh, but will have no satisfaction. ¹⁰ Bloody men hate an innocent person, but the upright seek [to cleave to] his soul. ¹¹ The fool vents all his anger, but the wise man comes afterwards and assuages it. * ¹² If a ruler hearkens to falsehood, all his servants are wicked. * ¹³ The poor man and the broken man have had [their fate] ordained, but HASHEM will enlighten the eyes of both. ¹⁴ If a king judges the destitute honestly, his throne will be established forever. ¹⁵ The rod and rebuke provide wisdom, but a self-indulgent youth brings shame to his mother. ¹⁶ When wicked people increase, offense increases, but the righteous will see their downfall. ¹⁷ Discipline your son and he will give you peace, and he will give pleasures to your soul.

Good and
wise people
are incom-
parably
better for
the world

Discipline
is an
investment
in happiness

The Torah
is the best
restraint

¹⁸ When there is no prophecy the people become unrestrained, but one who keeps the Torah is praiseworthy. ¹⁹ With words the servant will not be disciplined;

ל

כ־כא   כִּי־יָבִין וְאֵין מַעֲנֶה: חָזִיתָ אִישׁ אָץ בִּדְבָרָיו תִּקְוָה לִכְסִיל מִמֶּנּוּ: מְפַנֵּק

כב   מִנַּעַר עַבְדּוֹ וְאַחֲרִיתוֹ יִהְיֶה מָנוֹן: אִישׁ־אַף יְגָרֶה מָדוֹן וּבַעַל חֵמָה רַב־

כג־כד   פָּשַׁע: גַּאֲוַת אָדָם תַּשְׁפִּילֶנּוּ וּשְׁפַל־רוּחַ יִתְמֹךְ כָּבוֹד: חוֹלֵק עִם־גַּנָּב שׂוֹנֵא

כה   נַפְשׁוֹ אָלָה יִשְׁמַע וְלֹא יַגִּיד: חֶרְדַּת אָדָם יִתֵּן מוֹקֵשׁ וּבוֹטֵחַ בַּיהֹוָה יְשֻׂגָּב:

כו־כז   רַבִּים מְבַקְשִׁים פְּנֵי־מוֹשֵׁל וּמֵיהֹוָה מִשְׁפַּט־אִישׁ: תּוֹעֲבַת צַדִּיקִים אִישׁ

     עָוֶל וְתוֹעֲבַת רָשָׁע יְשַׁר־דָּרֶךְ:

א־ב   דִּבְרֵי ׀ אָגוּר בִּן־יָקֶה הַמַּשָּׂא נְאֻם הַגֶּבֶר לְאִיתִיאֵל לְאִיתִיאֵל וְאֻכָל: כִּי

ג   בַעַר אָנֹכִי מֵאִישׁ וְלֹא־בִינַת אָדָם לִי: וְלֹא־לָמַדְתִּי חָכְמָה וְדַעַת קְדֹשִׁים

ד   אֵדָע: מִי עָלָה־שָׁמַיִם ׀ וַיֵּרַד מִי אָסַף־רוּחַ ׀ בְּחָפְנָיו מִי צָרַר־מַיִם ׀ בַּשִּׂמְלָה

ה   מִי הֵקִים כָּל־אַפְסֵי־אָרֶץ מַה־שְּׁמוֹ וּמַה־שֶּׁם־בְּנוֹ כִּי תֵדָע: כָּל־אִמְרַת

ו   אֱלוֹהַּ צְרוּפָה מָגֵן הוּא לַחֹסִים בּוֹ: אַל־תּוֹסְףְּ עַל־דְּבָרָיו פֶּן־יוֹכִיחַ בְּךָ

ז   וְנִכְזָבְתָּ: שְׁתַּיִם שָׁאַלְתִּי מֵאִתָּךְ אַל־תִּמְנַע מִמֶּנִּי בְּטֶרֶם

ח   אָמוּת: שָׁוְא ׀ וּדְבַר־כָּזָב הַרְחֵק מִמֶּנִּי רֵאשׁ וָעֹשֶׁר אַל־תִּתֶּן־לִי הַטְרִיפֵנִי

ט   לֶחֶם חֻקִּי: פֶּן אֶשְׂבַּע ׀ וְכִחַשְׁתִּי וְאָמַרְתִּי מִי יְהֹוָה וּפֶן־אִוָּרֵשׁ וְגָנַבְתִּי

י   וְתָפַשְׂתִּי שֵׁם אֱלֹהָי: אַל־תַּלְשֵׁן עֶבֶד אֶל־°אדנו [°אֲדֹנָיו ק]

יא־יב   פֶּן־יְקַלֶּלְךָ וְאָשָׁמְתָּ: דּוֹר אָבִיו יְקַלֵּל וְאֶת־אִמּוֹ לֹא יְבָרֵךְ: דּוֹר טָהוֹר

יג   בְּעֵינָיו וּמִצֹּאָתוֹ לֹא רֻחָץ: דּוֹר מָה־רָמוּ עֵינָיו וְעַפְעַפָּיו יִנָּשֵׂאוּ: דּוֹר ׀

     חֲרָבוֹת שִׁנָּיו וּמַאֲכָלוֹת מְתַלְּעֹתָיו לֶאֱכֹל עֲנִיִּים מֵאֶרֶץ וְאֶבְיוֹנִים מֵאָדָם:

טו   לַעֲלוּקָה ׀ שְׁתֵּי בָנוֹת הַב ׀ הַב הֵנָּה שָׁלוֹשׁ לֹא תִשְׂבַּעְנָה אַרְבַּע לֹא־אָמְרוּ

     *כ"ב וזעירא

טז־יז   הוֹן: שְׁאוֹל וְעֹצֶר רָחַם אֶרֶץ לֹא־שָׂבְעָה מַּיִם וְאֵשׁ לֹא־אָמְרָה הוֹן: עַיִן ׀

     תִּלְעַג לְאָב וְתָבֻז לִיקֲּהַת אֵם יִקְּרוּהָ עֹרְבֵי־נַחַל וְיֹאכְלוּהָ בְנֵי־

יח   נָשֶׁר: שְׁלֹשָׁה הֵמָּה נִפְלְאוּ מִמֶּנִּי °וארבע [°וְאַרְבָּעָה ק] לֹא

יט   יְדַעְתִּים: דֶּרֶךְ הַנֶּשֶׁר ׀ בַּשָּׁמַיִם דֶּרֶךְ נָחָשׁ עֲלֵי צוּר דֶּרֶךְ־אֳנִיָּה בְלֶב־יָם

כ   וְדֶרֶךְ גֶּבֶר בְּעַלְמָה: כֵּן ׀ דֶּרֶךְ אִשָּׁה מְנָאָפֶת אָכְלָה וּמָחֲתָה פִיהָ וְאָמְרָה

     לֹא־פָעַלְתִּי אָוֶן:

כא־כב   תַּחַת שָׁלוֹשׁ רָגְזָה אֶרֶץ וְתַחַת אַרְבַּע לֹא־תוּכַל שְׂאֵת: תַּחַת־עֶבֶד כִּי

כג   יִמְלוֹךְ וְנָבָל כִּי יִשְׂבַּע־לָחֶם: תַּחַת שְׂנוּאָה כִּי תִבָּעֵל וְשִׁפְחָה כִּי־תִירַשׁ

     גְּבִרְתָּהּ:

29:24. When the court imposes an oath on a witness to tell what he knows, the thief's accomplice will violate it by refusing to testify, and thereby be punished (*Ralbag*).

30:1. Most commentators interpret the names in this verse as poetic references to Solomon:

     These are the words of אָגוּר, the "collector" of understanding, בִּן־יָקֶה, who "spewed out," הַמַּשָּׂא, "the prophecy." This man said: Because אִיתִיאֵל, "God is with me," וְאֻכָל, "I am capable."

30:2-4. Solomon realized that he should not consider himself greater than Moses: Moses ascended to heaven to

receive the Torah and bring it down to earth for Israel (*Exodus* 19:3,20-25; 24:12-18, 31:18, 32:15-16; 34:1-4; *Deuteronomy* 9:7ff); Moses controlled the winds (*Exodus* 10:13, 18-19; 14:20); Moses restricted the waters of the sea (*Exodus* 14:15ff); Moses erected the Tabernacle (*Exodus* 40:17-18), and, as the Talmud (*Megillah* 31a) explains, "If not for the service [of the Tabernacle and Torah] the foundations of heaven and earth would not have been established" (*Rashi*).

30:10-14. Do not slander even the extremely evil.

30:15-16. *Gan Eden* (Paradise) never ceases saying,

Impetuosity, though he understands, there is no response. [20] Have you seen a man who is
injudicious hasty in his affairs? There is more hope for the fool than for him. [21] If one indulges
kindness, his servant from youth, he will end up being ruled by him. [22] A man of anger will
anger and incite strife, and a man of wrath is full of offense. [23] A man's pride will bring him
dishonesty low, but a lowly spirit will support [his] honor. [24] He who shares with a thief hates
are a cancer his own soul; he will hear an oath but will not testify. * [25] Fear of man will add a
Fear God, snare, but one who trusts in HASHEM will be encouraged. [26] Many solicit a ruler's
not people favor, but a man's judgment is from HASHEM. [27] A man of iniquity is the abomination of the righteous, and one who walks an upright path is the abomination of the
wicked.

30

Human [1] These are the words of Agur son of Jakeh, the prophecy, the words of this
wisdom is man to Ithiel, to Ithiel and Ucal: * [2] Surely I am a boor of a man and do not
extremely have human understanding. * [3] I have not learned wisdom, nor known sacred
limited; knowledge. [4] Who [but Moses] ascended to heaven and descended? Who else
trust in gathered the wind in his palm? Who else tied the waters in a cloak? Who estab-
God's word lished all the ends of the earth? What is his name, and what is his son's name, if
you know? [5] Every word of God is refined; He is a shield to those who trust in
Him. [6] Do not add to His words, lest He test you and find that you deceived.

A request [7] I ask two things of You. Do not withhold them from me before I die: [8] Keep
of God vanity and falseness far from me; give me neither poverty nor wealth, but allot me
my daily bread, [9] lest I be sated and deny [You], and say, "Who is HASHEM?" and
lest I become impoverished and steal, and take the Name of my God [in a vain
oath of innocence]!

Avoid every [10] Do not slander: [not even] a servant to his master, lest he curse you and you
form of be made desolate; * [11] [nor] a generation that curses its father and does not bless
slander its mother; [12] [nor] a generation that is pure in its own eyes, and does not cleanse
itself of its filth; [13] [nor] a generation whose eyes are very haughty and whose
eyelids are arched; [14] [nor] a generation whose teeth are swords and whose molars are knives, to devour the poor from the land and the destitute from mankind.

Some are [15] The grave has two daughters [that say,] "Give me, give me." There are three
never sated that are never sated, [indeed] four that never say, "Enough!": * [16] the grave, the
sealed womb, the land unsated with water, and the fire which never says,
"Enough!" [17] The eye that mocks a father and scorns a mother's accumulated lore
— the ravens of the stream will gouge it out and the young eagles will eat it!

Some things [18] There are three that are beyond me and a fourth that I do not know: [19] the
are unknow- way of an eagle in the heavens; the way of a snake upon a rock; the way of a ship
able . . . in the heart of the sea; and the way of a man with a young woman. [20] Such is the
. . . denial of way of the adulterous woman: She eats and wipes her mouth and says, "I have
sin is done no wrong." *
incompre-
hensible [21] Because of three things the earth trembles, and because of a fourth she
cannot bear it: [22] because of a slave who reigns; [because of] a scoundrel who is
sated with bread; [23] because of a hateful woman * when she is married; and
[because of] a maidservant who inherits [the place of] her mistress.

"Give me the righteous," and *Gehinnom* (Purgatory) never
ceases saying, "Give me the sinners." The next verse lists
the three that are never sated: the grave, i.e., death is
constant; there are always women who cannot conceive;
and the earth never has enough rain. The fourth is the fire
of *Gehinnom*, which is never extinguished.

30:18-20. Just as the eagle, snake and ship leave no
obvious trail, so the adulterers wipe their mouths to
destroy any telltale signs of their feast (*Ibn Ezra*).

30:23. When the harlot weds, she continues to be promiscuous, but when conceives she will insist that her
husband is the true father.

כד-כה אַרְבָּעָה הֵם קְטַנֵּי־אָרֶץ וְהֵמָּה חֲכָמִים מְחֻכָּמִים: הַנְּמָלִים עַם לֹא־עָז

כו וַיָּכִינוּ בַקַּיִץ לַחְמָם: שְׁפַנִּים עַם לֹא־עָצוּם וַיָּשִׂימוּ בַסֶּלַע בֵּיתָם: מֶלֶךְ אֵין

כז-כח לָאַרְבֶּה וַיֵּצֵא חֹצֵץ כֻּלּוֹ: שְׂמָמִית בְּיָדַיִם תְּתַפֵּשׂ וְהִיא בְּהֵיכְלֵי מֶלֶךְ:

כט-ל שְׁלֹשָׁה הֵמָּה מֵיטִיבֵי צָעַד וְאַרְבָּעָה מֵיטִבֵי לָכֶת: לַיִשׁ גִּבּוֹר בַּבְּהֵמָה וְלֹא־

לא-לב יָשׁוּב מִפְּנֵי־כֹל: זַרְזִיר מָתְנַיִם אוֹ־תָיִשׁ וּמֶלֶךְ אַלְקוּם עִמּוֹ: אִם־נָבַלְתָּ

לג בְהִתְנַשֵּׂא וְאִם־זַמּוֹתָ יָד לְפֶה: כִּי מִיץ חָלָב יוֹצִיא חֶמְאָה וּמִיץ־אַף יוֹצִיא

א דָם וּמִיץ אַפַּיִם יוֹצִיא רִיב: **לא** דִּבְרֵי לְמוּאֵל

ב מֶלֶךְ מַשָּׂא אֲשֶׁר־יִסְּרַתּוּ אִמּוֹ: מַה־בְּרִי וּמַה־בַּר־בִּטְנִי וּמֶה בַּר־נְדָרָי: אַל־

ג-ד תִּתֵּן לַנָּשִׁים חֵילֶךָ וּדְרָכֶיךָ לַמְחוֹת מְלָכִין: אַל לַמְלָכִים ׀ לְמוֹאֵל אַל

ה לַמְלָכִים שְׁתוֹ־יָיִן וּלְרוֹזְנִים °אוֹ [°אֵי ק] שֵׁכָר: פֶּן־יִשְׁתֶּה וְיִשְׁכַּח מְחֻקָּק

ו-ז וִישַׁנֶּה דִּין כָּל־בְּנֵי־עֹנִי: תְּנוּ־שֵׁכָר לְאוֹבֵד וְיַיִן לְמָרֵי נָפֶשׁ: יִשְׁתֶּה וְיִשְׁכַּח

ח רִישׁוֹ וַעֲמָלוֹ לֹא יִזְכָּר־עוֹד: פְּתַח־פִּיךָ לְאִלֵּם אֶל־דִּין כָּל־בְּנֵי חֲלוֹף: פְּתַח־

ט פִּיךָ שְׁפָט־צֶדֶק וְדִין עָנִי וְאֶבְיוֹן:

י-יא אֵשֶׁת־חַיִל מִי יִמְצָא וְרָחֹק מִפְּנִינִים מִכְרָהּ: בָּטַח בָּהּ לֵב בַּעְלָהּ וְשָׁלָל לֹא

יב-יג יֶחְסָר: גְּמָלַתְהוּ טוֹב וְלֹא־רָע כֹּל יְמֵי חַיֶּיהָ: דָּרְשָׁה צֶמֶר וּפִשְׁתִּים וַתַּעַשׂ

יד בְּחֵפֶץ כַּפֶּיהָ: הָיְתָה כָּאֳנִיּוֹת סוֹחֵר מִמֶּרְחָק תָּבִיא לַחְמָהּ:

טו-טז וַתָּקָם ׀ בְּעוֹד לַיְלָה וַתִּתֵּן טֶרֶף לְבֵיתָהּ וְחֹק לְנַעֲרֹתֶיהָ: זָמְמָה שָׂדֶה

יז וַתִּקָּחֵהוּ מִפְּרִי כַפֶּיהָ °נטע [°נָטְעָה ק] כָּרֶם: חָגְרָה בְעוֹז מָתְנֶיהָ וַתְּאַמֵּץ

יח זְרוֹעֹתֶיהָ: טָעֲמָה כִּי־טוֹב סַחְרָהּ לֹא־יִכְבֶּה °בליל [°בַלַּיְלָה ק] נֵרָהּ: יָדֶיהָ

יט-כ שִׁלְּחָה בַכִּישׁוֹר וְכַפֶּיהָ תָּמְכוּ פָלֶךְ: כַּפָּהּ פָּרְשָׂה לֶעָנִי וְיָדֶיהָ שִׁלְּחָה

כא-כב לָאֶבְיוֹן: לֹא־תִירָא לְבֵיתָהּ מִשָּׁלֶג כִּי כָל־בֵּיתָהּ לָבֻשׁ שָׁנִים: מַרְבַדִּים

כג עָשְׂתָה־לָּהּ שֵׁשׁ וְאַרְגָּמָן לְבוּשָׁהּ: נוֹדָע בַּשְּׁעָרִים בַּעְלָהּ בְּשִׁבְתּוֹ עִם־זִקְנֵי־

כד-כה אָרֶץ: סָדִין עָשְׂתָה וַתִּמְכֹּר וַחֲגוֹר נָתְנָה לַכְּנַעֲנִי: עֹז־וְהָדָר לְבוּשָׁהּ

כו וַתִּשְׂחַק לְיוֹם אַחֲרוֹן: פִּיהָ פָּתְחָה בְחָכְמָה וְתוֹרַת־חֶסֶד עַל־לְשׁוֹנָהּ:

30:24-28. The instincts of these four creatures reveal significant God-given wisdom.

30:28. Though a spider may dwell in a delicacy-laden palace, it makes a web to catch its food (cf. *Psalms* 128:2).

31:1. Solomon was called Lemuel, a compound of למו, אל, "[belonging] to God" (see v. 4).

31:2. I raised you, I bore you, and I loved you so much that all my vows were dedicated to you.

31:8. A king must speak up for the mute because they cannot defend themselves.

31:10. The concluding verses of *Proverbs* are the famous paean to the righteous woman, which is chanted in Jewish homes at the beginning of the first Sabbath

meal. The word חַיִל as used in Scripture implies more than just valor; it includes the possession of whatever attributes are needed to carry out the task at hand. The hymn contains an alphabetical acrostic as a further allusion to her all-encompassing virtues. This passage has been interpreted as a metaphor for the *Shechinah* (Divine Presence), the Sabbath, the Torah, and the soul.

31:12. According to *Metzudos*, when her husband is kind, she reacts accordingly, but when he falls short, she is not petty and vindictive.

31:19. These are parts of a spinning wheel.

31:23. Thanks to her care, her husband stands out as well dressed and well groomed when he sits in the councils of the elders.

Four weak
creatures;
four lessons

²⁴ *There are four among the small [creatures] of earth who are wise, having been made wise [by the Creator]:* * ²⁵ *The ants are a nation that is not strong, yet they prepare their food in the summer;* ²⁶ *rabbits are a nation that is not powerful, yet they make their abode in the rock;* ²⁷ *there is no king of the locusts, and yet they all go out in a single swarm;* ²⁸ *the spider seizes [its prey] with its handiwork, though it dwells in the king's palace.* *

Four strong
creatures

²⁹ *There are three that step securely, and a fourth that walks with confidence:* ³⁰ *The lion is the strongest of the animals, and does not turn back from anything;* ³¹ *the thigh-belted greyhound, the he-goat, and the king against whom none can stand.* ³² *If you have been abused, remain aloof; and if you have thoughts [of responding in kind], put your hand to your mouth;* ³³ *for the squeezing of milk produces butter; the squeezing of the nose produces blood; and the squeezing of anger produces strife.*

31

The
queen-
mother's
advice:
Rule with
dignity and
justice

¹ T*he words of Lemuel the king,* * *the prophecy with which his mother disci-plined him:* ² *What is it, my son? And what is it, O son of my womb? And what is it, O son of my vows?* * ³ *Give not your strength to women, and let your conduct not destroy the protocol of kings.* ⁴ *It is not proper for kings who belong to God, it is not proper for kings to drink [much] wine, and for princes to imbibe strong drink.* ⁵ *Lest he drink and forget the statute [of the Torah] and pervert the judgment of all the children of the poor.* ⁶ *Give strong drink to the woebegone and wine to those of embittered soul.* ⁷ *Let him drink and forget his poverty, and not remember his travail any more.* ⁸ *Open your mouth on behalf of the mute, in the judgment of all confused children.* * ⁹ *Open your mouth, judge righteously, and obtain justice for the poor and destitute.*

Paean to the
woman of
accomplish-
ment

א ¹⁰ *An accomplished woman* * *who can find? Far beyond pearls is her value.*

ב ¹¹ *Her husband's heart relies on her, and he shall lack no fortune.*

ג ¹² *She bestows goodness upon him, never evil,* * *all the days of her life.*

ד ¹³ *She seeks wool and flax, and her hands work willingly.*

ה ¹⁴ *She is like a merchant's ships; from afar she brings her sustenance.*

She has
judgment
and diligence

ו ¹⁵ *She arises while it is yet night,*
     and gives food to her household and a portion to her maidens.

ז ¹⁶ *She envisions a field and buys it;*
     from the fruit of her handiwork she plants a vineyard.

ח ¹⁷ *With strength she girds her loins, and invigorates her arms.*

ט ¹⁸ *She discerns that her enterprise is good; her lamp is not snuffed out by night.*

She cares for
the poor
and for her
household

י ¹⁹ *She stretches out her hands to the distaff,*
     and her palms support the spindle. *

כ ²⁰ *She spreads out her palm to the poor, and extends her hands to the destitute.*

ל ²¹ *She fears not snow for her household,*
     for all her household is clothed in scarlet wool.

מ ²² *She made for herself luxurious bedspreads;*
     linen and purple wool are her clothing.

נ ²³ *Her husband is distinctive in the councils,*
     when he sits with the elders of the land. *

ס ²⁴ *She makes a cloak and sells [it], and delivers a belt to the peddler.*

She speaks
wisely
and kindly

ע ²⁵*Strength and majesty are her raiment, and she joyfully awaits the last day.*

פ ²⁶*She opens her mouth with wisdom,*
     and the teaching of kindness is on her tongue.

צוֹפִיָּה °הילכות [°הֲלִיכוֹת ק] בֵּיתָהּ וְלֶחֶם עַצְלוּת לֹא תֹאכֵל: קָמוּ
בָנֶיהָ וַיְאַשְּׁרוּהָ בַּעְלָהּ וַיְהַלְלָהּ: רַבּוֹת בָּנוֹת עָשׂוּ חָיִל וְאַתְּ עָלִית עַל־
כֻּלָּנָה: שֶׁקֶר הַחֵן וְהֶבֶל הַיֹּפִי אִשָּׁה יִרְאַת־יהוה הִיא תִתְהַלָּל: תְּנוּ־לָהּ
מִפְּרִי יָדֶיהָ וִיהַלְלוּהָ בַשְּׁעָרִים מַעֲשֶׂיהָ:

סכום פסוקים של ספר משלי תשע מאות וחמשה עשר. ותשר דבורה סימן.

31:31. She needs no praise. Her deeds are the most eloquent testimony to her greatness.

All praise her ‫א‬   ²⁷ *She anticipates the ways of her household,*
— but her   *and does not eat the bread of laziness.*
greatest ‫ק‬   ²⁸ *Her children have risen and praised her; her husband, and he extolled her:*
praise is
her deeds ‫ר‬   ²⁹ *"Many women have amassed achievement, but you surpassed them all."*

‫ש‬   ³⁰ *Grace is false, and beauty vain;*
                a woman who fears HASHEM, she should be praised.

‫ת‬   ³¹ *Give her the fruits of her hands;*
                and let her be praised in the gates by her very own deeds. *

Job אִיּוֹב

*T*he Book of Job and the anguished attempts of Job and his comrades to understand the ways of God have perplexed, stimulated, and inspired thinkers and philosophers for thousands of years. The ideas in this Book are at the heart of the age-old question: Why do bad people prosper while good people suffer?

There is another question about the Book that may shed some light on how we are to understand it. When did Job live? Unlike other narratives in Scripture, we are not told when or in what context the events took place. Indeed, the Talmud notes eight different opinions regarding when he lived — and there is even a ninth opinion that the story of Job is a parable, that he never lived at all! (Bava Basra 15a-b).

Maharal explains that the theme of suffering is universal and cannot be isolated to any particular period. Job could only have lived — if he ever did — in a time of crisis, when God judges people strictly. That is when people must be concerned that their deeds may be subject to rigorous and painful scrutiny. The Satan of the Book of Job was sent to test its protagonist to let him prove that he was worthy of God's blessing. Job's ordeal, therefore, is recorded because it is a paradigm for anyone who suffers and seeks to know why. Just as Job's suffering can be understood in the context of various historical periods, so each individual's ordeal must be interpreted within the context of his own period of history. In discussing when the story happened, the Sages differ only regarding what is the most fitting setting for such a test.

The many messages of the Book are wrapped in enigmas. Job's friends do not convince him. His arguments seem to overpower theirs. One wonders why they do not show him more sympathy. In the end, God Himself comes to blunt Job's challenge. Job accepts, not because of logic, but because he realizes that he is mortal and cannot understand Divine wisdom or Divine justice. At times when we are at a loss to understand the rigors of life, that must be our response as well — that there is a plan, and that man must trust the Planner.

א אִישׁ הָיָה בְאֶרֶץ־עוּץ אִיּוֹב שְׁמוֹ וְהָיָה ׀ הָאִישׁ הַהוּא תָּם וְיָשָׁר וִירֵא

ב-ג אֱלֹהִים וְסָר מֵרָע: וַיִּוָּלְדוּ לוֹ שִׁבְעָה בָנִים וְשָׁלוֹשׁ בָּנוֹת: וַיְהִי מִקְנֵהוּ

שִׁבְעַת אַלְפֵי־צֹאן וּשְׁלֹשֶׁת אַלְפֵי גְמַלִּים וַחֲמֵשׁ מֵאוֹת צֶמֶד־בָּקָר

וַחֲמֵשׁ מֵאוֹת אֲתוֹנוֹת וַעֲבֻדָּה רַבָּה מְאֹד וַיְהִי הָאִישׁ הַהוּא גָּדוֹל מִכָּל־

ד בְּנֵי־קֶדֶם: וְהָלְכוּ בָנָיו וְעָשׂוּ מִשְׁתֶּה בֵּית אִישׁ יוֹמוֹ וְשָׁלְחוּ וְקָרְאוּ

ה לִשְׁלֹשֶׁת אַחְיֹתֵיהֶם לֶאֱכֹל וְלִשְׁתּוֹת עִמָּהֶם: וַיְהִי כִּי הִקִּיפוּ יְמֵי

הַמִּשְׁתֶּה וַיִּשְׁלַח אִיּוֹב וַיְקַדְּשֵׁם וְהִשְׁכִּים בַּבֹּקֶר וְהֶעֱלָה עֹלוֹת מִסְפַּר

כֻּלָּם כִּי אָמַר אִיּוֹב אוּלַי חָטְאוּ בָנַי וּבֵרְכוּ אֱלֹהִים בִּלְבָבָם כָּכָה

ו יַעֲשֶׂה אִיּוֹב כָּל־הַיָּמִים: וַיְהִי הַיּוֹם וַיָּבֹאוּ בְּנֵי

הָאֱלֹהִים לְהִתְיַצֵּב עַל־יְהוָה וַיָּבוֹא גַם־הַשָּׂטָן בְּתוֹכָם: וַיֹּאמֶר יְהוָה אֶל־

ז הַשָּׂטָן מֵאַיִן תָּבֹא וַיַּעַן הַשָּׂטָן אֶת־יְהוָה וַיֹּאמַר מִשּׁוּט בָּאָרֶץ וּמֵהִתְהַלֵּךְ

ח בָּהּ: וַיֹּאמֶר יְהוָה אֶל־הַשָּׂטָן הֲשַׂמְתָּ לִבְּךָ עַל־עַבְדִּי אִיּוֹב כִּי אֵין כָּמֹהוּ

ט בָּאָרֶץ אִישׁ תָּם וְיָשָׁר יְרֵא אֱלֹהִים וְסָר מֵרָע: וַיַּעַן הַשָּׂטָן אֶת־יְהוָה

י וַיֹּאמַר הַחִנָּם יָרֵא אִיּוֹב אֱלֹהִים: הֲלֹא־°אַת [°אַתָּה ק] שַׂכְתָּ בַעֲדוֹ

וּבְעַד־בֵּיתוֹ וּבְעַד כָּל־אֲשֶׁר־לוֹ מִסָּבִיב מַעֲשֵׂה יָדָיו בֵּרַכְתָּ וּמִקְנֵהוּ פָּרַץ

יא בָּאָרֶץ: וְאוּלָם שְׁלַח־נָא יָדְךָ וְגַע בְּכָל־אֲשֶׁר־לוֹ אִם־לֹא עַל־פָּנֶיךָ

יב יְבָרְכֶךָּ: וַיֹּאמֶר יְהוָה אֶל־הַשָּׂטָן הִנֵּה כָל־אֲשֶׁר־לוֹ בְּיָדֶךָ רַק אֵלָיו אַל־

יג תִּשְׁלַח יָדֶךָ וַיֵּצֵא הַשָּׂטָן מֵעִם פְּנֵי יְהוָה: וַיְהִי הַיּוֹם וּבָנָיו וּבְנֹתָיו אֹכְלִים

יד וְשֹׁתִים יַיִן בְּבֵית אֲחִיהֶם הַבְּכוֹר: וּמַלְאָךְ בָּא אֶל־אִיּוֹב וַיֹּאמַר הַבָּקָר הָיוּ

טו חֹרְשׁוֹת וְהָאֲתֹנוֹת רֹעוֹת עַל־יְדֵיהֶם: וַתִּפֹּל שְׁבָא וַתִּקָּחֵם וְאֶת־הַנְּעָרִים

טז הִכּוּ לְפִי־חָרֶב וָאִמָּלְטָה רַק־אֲנִי לְבַדִּי לְהַגִּיד לָךְ: עוֹד ׀ זֶה מְדַבֵּר וְזֶה

בָּא וַיֹּאמַר אֵשׁ אֱלֹהִים נָפְלָה מִן־הַשָּׁמַיִם וַתִּבְעַר בַּצֹּאן וּבַנְּעָרִים

יז וַתֹּאכְלֵם וָאִמָּלְטָה רַק־אֲנִי לְבַדִּי לְהַגִּיד לָךְ: עוֹד ׀ זֶה מְדַבֵּר וְזֶה בָּא

וַיֹּאמַר כַּשְׂדִּים שָׂמוּ ׀ שְׁלֹשָׁה רָאשִׁים וַיִּפְשְׁטוּ עַל־הַגְּמַלִּים וַיִּקָּחוּם

יח וְאֶת־הַנְּעָרִים הִכּוּ לְפִי־חָרֶב וָאִמָּלְטָה רַק־אֲנִי לְבַדִּי לְהַגִּיד לָךְ: עַד זֶה

מְדַבֵּר וְזֶה בָּא וַיֹּאמַר בָּנֶיךָ וּבְנוֹתֶיךָ אֹכְלִים וְשֹׁתִים יַיִן בְּבֵית אֲחִיהֶם

יט הַבְּכוֹר: וְהִנֵּה רוּחַ גְּדוֹלָה בָּאָה ׀ מֵעֵבֶר הַמִּדְבָּר וַיִּגַּע בְּאַרְבַּע

פִּנּוֹת הַבַּיִת וַיִּפֹּל עַל־הַנְּעָרִים וַיָּמוּתוּ וָאִמָּלְטָה רַק־אֲנִי לְבַדִּי לְהַגִּיד לָךְ:

כ וַיָּקָם אִיּוֹב וַיִּקְרַע אֶת־מְעִלוֹ וַיָּגָז אֶת־רֹאשׁוֹ וַיִּפֹּל אַרְצָה וַיִּשְׁתָּחוּ:

כא וַיֹּאמֶר עָרֹם °יָצָתִי [°יָצָאתִי ק] מִבֶּטֶן אִמִּי וְעָרֹם אָשׁוּב שָׁמָּה יְהוָה נָתַן

1:1. The Talmud (*Bava Basra* 15a-b) cites no less than eight opinions about when Job lived, ranging from the time of Jacob to that of the Babylonian exiles' return to the Holy Land. There is also an opinion (ibid.) that Job did not actually exist at all, and the story is a parable.

1:6. That is, the Adversary.

1:7. Satan circulated through the earth evaluating the deeds of Mankind (*Rashi*). This dialogue took place on Rosh Hashanah, the Day of Judgment (*Ibn Ezra*).

1:16. That is, an extraordinarily great fire.

1:21. "My mother's womb" is a metaphor for the earth from which man was originally made [see *Genesis* 3:19] (*Rashi*; *Ibn Ezra*).

1 TRIBULA-
TIONS
OF THE
RIGHTEOUS
JOB
1:1-2:14

¹ There was a man in the land of Uz whose name was Job; * that man was wholesome and upright, he feared God and shunned evil. ² Seven sons and three daughters were born to him. ³ His possessions consisted of seven thousand sheep and goats, three thousand camels, five hundred pairs of cattle, five hundred she-donkeys, and very many enterprises. That man was the wealthiest man of all the people in the East.

The feasts
of Job's
children

⁴ His sons would go and make a feast, at each one's home each on his set day; and they would send word and invite their three sisters to eat and drink with them. ⁵ When each cycle of feast-days had ended, Job would send to summon them. He would rise early in the morning and bring as many burnt-offerings as the number of them all, for Job said [to himself], "Perhaps my children have sinned and blasphemed HASHEM in their hearts." Thus would Job do all the days.

The Satan's
challenge

⁶ It happened one day: The angels came to stand before HASHEM, and the Satan, * too, came among them. ⁷ HASHEM said to the Satan, "From where have you come?"

The Satan answered HASHEM, and said, "From wandering and walking about the earth."*

⁸ HASHEM said to the Satan, "Did you set your heart to [take note of] My servant Job? For there is no one like him on earth; a wholesome and upright man, who fears God and shuns evil."

⁹ The Satan answered HASHEM, and said, "Is it for nothing that Job fears God? ¹⁰ Have You not set a protective wall about him, about his household, and about everything he owns from all around? You have blessed his handiwork, and his livestock have spread throughout the land. ¹¹ But send forth Your hand and touch everything that is his, [and see] if he does not blaspheme You to Your face!"

¹² So HASHEM said to the Satan, "Behold, everything that is his is hereby in your hand. But do not send forth your hand against his [person]!" The Satan then departed from the presence of HASHEM.

The evil
decree

¹³ It happened one day, when his sons and daughters were eating and drinking wine in the home of their eldest brother, ¹⁴ that a messenger came to Job and said, "The oxen were plowing and the she-donkeys were grazing alongside them, ¹⁵ when Sabeans befell and seized them. They struck down the servants by the edge of the sword. Only I, by myself, escaped to tell you!"

¹⁶ This one was still speaking, when this [other] one came and said, "A fire of God* fell from the heavens. It burned among the sheep and the servants and consumed them. Only I, by myself, escaped to tell you!"

¹⁷ This one was still speaking, when this [other] one came and said, "The Chaldeans formed three divisions and deployed around the camels and seized them. They struck down the servants by the edge of the sword. Only I, by myself, escaped to tell you!"

¹⁸ This one was still speaking, when this [other] one came and said, "Your sons and your daughters were eating and drinking wine in the home of their eldest brother, ¹⁹ when behold, a great wind came from across the desert. It struck the four corners of the house, it collapsed upon the young men and killed them. Only I, by myself, escaped to tell you!"

Job's
reaction

²⁰ Job stood up and ripped his shirt, and he tore [the hair of] his head. He threw himself upon the ground and prostrated himself. ²¹ He said, "Naked did I emerge from my mother's womb, and naked shall I return there. * HASHEM has given,

כב וַיהוָה לָקַח יְהִי שֵׁם יְהוָה מְבֹרָךְ: בְּכָל־זֹאת לֹא־חָטָא אִיּוֹב וְלֹא־נָתַן
תִּפְלָה לֵאלֹהִים: **ב** א וַיְהִי הַיּוֹם וַיָּבֹאוּ בְּנֵי הָאֱלֹהִים לְהִתְיַצֵּב עַל־יְהוָה

ב וַיָּבוֹא גַם־הַשָּׂטָן בְּתֹכָם לְהִתְיַצֵּב עַל־יְהוָה: וַיֹּאמֶר יְהוָה אֶל־הַשָּׂטָן אֵי
מִזֶּה תָּבֹא וַיַּעַן הַשָּׂטָן אֶת־יְהוָה וַיֹּאמַר מִשֻּׁט בָּאָרֶץ וּמֵהִתְהַלֵּךְ בָּהּ:

ג וַיֹּאמֶר יְהוָה אֶל־הַשָּׂטָן הֲשַׂמְתָּ לִבְּךָ אֶל־עַבְדִּי אִיּוֹב כִּי אֵין כָּמֹהוּ בָּאָרֶץ
אִישׁ תָּם וְיָשָׁר יְרֵא אֱלֹהִים וְסָר מֵרָע וְעֹדֶנּוּ מַחֲזִיק בְּתֻמָּתוֹ וַתְּסִיתֵנִי בוֹ

ד לְבַלְּעוֹ חִנָּם: וַיַּעַן הַשָּׂטָן אֶת־יְהוָה וַיֹּאמַר עוֹר בְּעַד־עוֹר וְכֹל אֲשֶׁר
ה לָאִישׁ יִתֵּן בְּעַד נַפְשׁוֹ: אוּלָם שְׁלַח־נָא יָדְךָ וְגַע אֶל־עַצְמוֹ וְאֶל־בְּשָׂרוֹ

ו אִם־לֹא אֶל־פָּנֶיךָ יְבָרֲכֶךָּ: וַיֹּאמֶר יְהוָה אֶל־הַשָּׂטָן הִנּוֹ בְיָדֶךָ אַךְ אֶת־
ז נַפְשׁוֹ שְׁמֹר: וַיֵּצֵא הַשָּׂטָן מֵאֵת פְּנֵי יְהוָה וַיַּךְ אֶת־אִיּוֹב בִּשְׁחִין רָע מִכַּף

ח רַגְלוֹ °וְעַד [°עַד ק] קָדְקֳדוֹ: וַיִּקַּח־לוֹ חֶרֶשׂ לְהִתְגָּרֵד בּוֹ וְהוּא יֹשֵׁב
ט בְּתוֹךְ־הָאֵפֶר: וַתֹּאמֶר לוֹ אִשְׁתּוֹ עֹדְךָ מַחֲזִיק בְּתֻמָּתֶךָ בָּרֵךְ אֱלֹהִים וָמֻת:

י וַיֹּאמֶר אֵלֶיהָ כְּדַבֵּר אַחַת הַנְּבָלוֹת תְּדַבֵּרִי גַּם אֶת־הַטּוֹב נְקַבֵּל מֵאֵת
הָאֱלֹהִים וְאֶת־הָרָע לֹא נְקַבֵּל בְּכָל־זֹאת לֹא־חָטָא אִיּוֹב בִּשְׂפָתָיו:

יא וַיִּשְׁמְעוּ שְׁלֹשֶׁת | רֵעֵי אִיּוֹב אֵת כָּל־הָרָעָה הַזֹּאת הַבָּאָה עָלָיו וַיָּבֹאוּ
אִישׁ מִמְּקֹמוֹ אֱלִיפַז הַתֵּימָנִי וּבִלְדַּד הַשּׁוּחִי וְצוֹפַר הַנַּעֲמָתִי וַיִּוָּעֲדוּ יַחְדָּו

יב לָבוֹא לָנוּד־לוֹ וּלְנַחֲמוֹ: וַיִּשְׂאוּ אֶת־עֵינֵיהֶם מֵרָחוֹק וְלֹא הִכִּירֻהוּ וַיִּשְׂאוּ
קוֹלָם וַיִּבְכּוּ וַיִּקְרְעוּ אִישׁ מְעִלוֹ וַיִּזְרְקוּ עָפָר עַל־רָאשֵׁיהֶם הַשָּׁמָיְמָה:

יג וַיֵּשְׁבוּ אִתּוֹ לָאָרֶץ שִׁבְעַת יָמִים וְשִׁבְעַת לֵילוֹת וְאֵין־דֹּבֵר אֵלָיו דָּבָר כִּי
רָאוּ כִּי־גָדַל הַכְּאֵב מְאֹד: **ג** א אַחֲרֵי־כֵן פָּתַח אִיּוֹב אֶת־פִּיהוּ וַיְקַלֵּל אֶת־
יוֹמוֹ:

ב–ג וַיַּעַן אִיּוֹב וַיֹּאמַר: יֹאבַד יוֹם אִוָּלֶד בּוֹ וְהַלַּיְלָה אָמַר הֹרָה גָבֶר: הַיּוֹם
הַהוּא יְהִי חֹשֶׁךְ אַל־יִדְרְשֵׁהוּ אֱלוֹהַּ מִמָּעַל וְאַל־תּוֹפַע עָלָיו נְהָרָה:

ד–ה יִגְאָלֻהוּ חֹשֶׁךְ וְצַלְמָוֶת תִּשְׁכָּן־עָלָיו עֲנָנָה יְבַעֲתֻהוּ כִּמְרִירֵי יוֹם: הַלַּיְלָה
הַהוּא יִקָּחֵהוּ אֹפֶל אַל־יִחַדְּ בִּימֵי שָׁנָה בְּמִסְפַּר יְרָחִים אַל־יָבֹא:

ו–ז הִנֵּה הַלַּיְלָה הַהוּא יְהִי גַלְמוּד אַל־תָּבֹא רְנָנָה בוֹ: יִקְּבֻהוּ אֹרְרֵי־יוֹם
הָעֲתִידִים עֹרֵר לִוְיָתָן: יֶחְשְׁכוּ כּוֹכְבֵי נִשְׁפּוֹ יְקַו־לְאוֹר וָאַיִן וְאַל־יִרְאֶה

ח–ט בְּעַפְעַפֵּי־שָׁחַר: כִּי לֹא סָגַר דַּלְתֵי בִטְנִי וַיַּסְתֵּר עָמָל מֵעֵינָי: לָמָּה לֹא
יא מֵרֶחֶם אָמוּת מִבֶּטֶן יָצָאתִי וְאֶגְוָע: מַדּוּעַ קִדְּמוּנִי בִרְכָּיִם וּמַה־שָּׁדַיִם כִּי

2:4. The Satan belittled Job's righteous acceptance of calamity by claiming that Job had expected to die for his sins, and thus was relieved by his comparatively "light" punishment. As an analogy, the Satan compared Job to a person who sees a sword approaching his head and instinctively blocks it with his arm — he willingly sacrifices the skin of his arm for the sake of his life (*Rashi*).
2:8. Either as a sign of mourning (*Ibn Ezra*), or to soothe the pain of his wounds (*Metzudos*).

2:9. You may as well blaspheme God even if you die for it, since even death is preferable to your agony (*Ramban*).
2:12. To show that they shared in his mourning (*Rashi*).
2:14. The day of his birth (*Ibn Ezra*).
3:3. That is, each year on the anniversary of my birth.
3:7. Professional mourners, who are brought to funerals to stir up emotions (see *Ibn Ezra*).
3:9. The womb from which I emerged (*Rashi*).

and HASHEM *has taken away, blessed be the Name of* HASHEM." ²² *Despite all this, Job did not sin nor ascribe impropriety to God.*

2

The Satan's second challenge

¹ It *happened one day: The angels came to stand before* HASHEM, *and the Satan, too, came among them to stand before* HASHEM. ² HASHEM *said to the Satan, "Where is it that you are coming from?"*

The Satan answered God, and said, "From wandering and walking about the earth."

³ HASHEM *asked the Satan, "Did you set your heart to [take note of] My servant Job? For there is no one like him on earth; a wholesome and upright man, who fears God and shuns evil, and he still maintains his wholesomeness. You incited Me against him, to destroy him, for no reason!"*

⁴ *The Satan answered* HASHEM, *and said, "Skin for the sake of skin! Whatever a man has he would give up for his life!** ⁵ *But send forth Your hand and touch his bone and his flesh, and surely he will blaspheme You to Your face!"*

⁶ HASHEM *said to the Satan, "Behold, he is in your hand, but preserve his soul [from death]!"*

Job himself is afflicted

⁷ *The Satan departed from the presence of* HASHEM *and afflicted Job with severe boils, from the soles of his feet to the top of his head.* ⁸ *He took a potsherd to scratch himself with, and he sat amid the ashes.**

⁹ *His wife said to him, "Do you still maintain your wholesomeness? Blaspheme God and die!"**

¹⁰ *Job said to her, "You talk as any impious woman might talk. Furthermore, shall we accept the good from God and not accept the bad?" Despite everything, Job did not sin with his lips.*

Job's three friends

¹¹ *Job's three friends heard about this total calamity that had befallen him, and each one of them came from his place: Eliphaz the Temanite, Bildad the Shuhite and Zophar the Naamathite. They gathered together to go and mourn with him and comfort him.* ¹² *They raised their eyes from a distance, but did not recognize him. They raised their voices and wept, each man rent his coat, and they threw dust over their heads toward heaven.** ¹³ *They sat with him on the ground for a period of seven days and seven nights. No one said a word to him, for they saw that his pain was very great.* ¹⁴ *After that, Job opened his mouth and cursed his day.**

3

THE FIRST ROUND OF DISCUSSION 3:1-14:22

Job curses the day of his birth . . .

¹ Job *then spoke up and said:*

² *Lost be the day when I was born, and the night when it was announced: 'A man has been born.'* ³ *May that day** become dark; may God pay it no heed from above; may light never shine upon it;* ⁴ *may darkness and the shadow of death sully it; may a cloud rest upon it; may it be terrified by the demons of day.* ⁵ *May thick darkness snatch that night; may it not have joy among the days of the year; may it not come among the count of the months;* ⁶ *may that night be desolate; may no joyful song come into it;* ⁷ *may those who curse the day curse it, [and so too] those who arouse others in their mourning;** ⁸ *may its twilight stars be dimmed; may it crave light but have none; may it not see the glimmer of dawn.* ⁹ *For no one closed the portals of my womb,** to hide misery from my eyes.*

. . . questions his birth . . .

¹⁰ *Why did I not die from the womb, [not] expire as I came forth from the belly?* ¹¹ *Why did the knees come to meet me? Why were breasts there for*

יב־יג אֵינָק: כִּי־עַתָּה שָׁכַבְתִּי וְאֶשְׁקוֹט יָשַׁנְתִּי אָז ׀ יָנוּחַ לִי: עִם־מְלָכִים וְיֹעֲצֵי

יד אֶרֶץ הַבֹּנִים חֳרָבוֹת לָמוֹ: אוֹ עִם־שָׂרִים זָהָב לָהֶם הַמְמַלְאִים בָּתֵּיהֶם כָּסֶף:

טו־טז אוֹ כְנֵפֶל טָמוּן לֹא אֶהְיֶה כְּעֹלְלִים לֹא־רָאוּ אוֹר: שָׁם רְשָׁעִים חָדְלוּ רֹגֶז

יז־יח וְשָׁם יָנוּחוּ יְגִיעֵי כֹחַ: יַחַד אֲסִירִים שַׁאֲנָנוּ לֹא שָׁמְעוּ קוֹל נֹגֵשׂ: קָטֹן וְגָדוֹל

יט שָׁם הוּא וְעֶבֶד חָפְשִׁי מֵאֲדֹנָיו: לָמָּה יִתֵּן לְעָמֵל אוֹר וְחַיִּים לְמָרֵי נָפֶשׁ:

כ־כא הַמְחַכִּים לַמָּוֶת וְאֵינֶנּוּ וַיַּחְפְּרֻהוּ מִמַּטְמוֹנִים: הַשְּׂמֵחִים אֱלֵי־גִיל יָשִׂישׂוּ

כב־כג כִּי יִמְצְאוּ־קָבֶר: לְגֶבֶר אֲשֶׁר־דַּרְכּוֹ נִסְתָּרָה וַיָּסֶךְ אֱלוֹהַּ בַּעֲדוֹ: כִּי־לִפְנֵי

כד לַחְמִי אַנְחָתִי תָבֹא וַיִּתְּכוּ כַמַּיִם שַׁאֲגֹתָי: כִּי פַחַד פָּחַדְתִּי וַיֶּאֱתָיֵנִי וַאֲשֶׁר

כה יָגֹרְתִּי יָבֹא לִי: לֹא שָׁלַוְתִּי וְלֹא שָׁקַטְתִּי וְלֹא־נָחְתִּי וַיָּבֹא רֹגֶז:

ד

א־ב וַיַּעַן אֱלִיפַז הַתֵּימָנִי וַיֹּאמַר: הֲנִסָּה דָבָר אֵלֶיךָ תִּלְאֶה וַעְצֹר בְּמִלִּין מִי

ג־ד יוּכָל: הִנֵּה יִסַּרְתָּ רַבִּים וְיָדַיִם רָפוֹת תְּחַזֵּק: כּוֹשֵׁל יְקִימוּן מִלֶּיךָ וּבִרְכַּיִם

ה־ו כֹּרְעוֹת תְּאַמֵּץ: כִּי עַתָּה ׀ תָּבוֹא אֵלֶיךָ וַתֵּלֶא תִּגַּע עָדֶיךָ וַתִּבָּהֵל: הֲלֹא

ז יִרְאָתְךָ כִּסְלָתֶךָ תִּקְוָתְךָ וְתֹם דְּרָכֶיךָ: זְכָר־נָא מִי הוּא נָקִי אָבָד וְאֵיפֹה

ח־ט יְשָׁרִים נִכְחָדוּ: כַּאֲשֶׁר רָאִיתִי חֹרְשֵׁי אָוֶן וְזֹרְעֵי עָמָל יִקְצְרֻהוּ: מִנִּשְׁמַת

י אֱלוֹהַּ יֹאבֵדוּ וּמֵרוּחַ אַפּוֹ יִכְלוּ: שַׁאֲגַת אַרְיֵה וְקוֹל שָׁחַל וְשִׁנֵּי כְפִירִים

יא־יב נִתָּעוּ: לַיִשׁ אֹבֵד מִבְּלִי־טָרֶף וּבְנֵי לָבִיא יִתְפָּרָדוּ: וְאֵלַי דָּבָר יְגֻנָּב

יג וַתִּקַּח אָזְנִי שֵׁמֶץ מֶנְהוּ: בִּשְׂעִפִּים מֵחֶזְיֹנוֹת לָיְלָה בִּנְפֹל תַּרְדֵּמָה

יד־טו עַל־אֲנָשִׁים: פַּחַד קְרָאַנִי וּרְעָדָה וְרֹב עַצְמוֹתַי הִפְחִיד: וְרוּחַ עַל־פָּנַי

טז יַחֲלֹף תְּסַמֵּר שַׂעֲרַת בְּשָׂרִי: יַעֲמֹד ׀ וְלֹא־אַכִּיר מַרְאֵהוּ תְּמוּנָה לְנֶגֶד

יז עֵינָי דְּמָמָה וָקוֹל אֶשְׁמָע: הַאֱנוֹשׁ מֵאֱלוֹהַּ יִצְדָּק אִם מֵעֹשֵׂהוּ יִטְהַר־גָּבֶר:

יח־יט הֵן בַּעֲבָדָיו לֹא יַאֲמִין וּבְמַלְאָכָיו יָשִׂים תָּהֳלָה: אַף ׀ שֹׁכְנֵי בָתֵּי־חֹמֶר

כ אֲשֶׁר־בֶּעָפָר יְסוֹדָם יְדַכְּאוּם לִפְנֵי־עָשׁ: מִבֹּקֶר לָעֶרֶב יֻכַּתּוּ מִבְּלִי מֵשִׂים

כא לָנֶצַח יֹאבֵדוּ: הֲלֹא־נִסַּע יִתְרָם בָּם יָמוּתוּ וְלֹא בְחָכְמָה:

ה

א קְרָא־נָא

ב הֲיֵשׁ עוֹנֶךָּ וְאֶל־מִי מִקְּדֹשִׁים תִּפְנֶה: כִּי־לֶאֱוִיל יַהֲרָג־כָּעַשׂ וּפֹתֶה תָּמִית

ג־ד קִנְאָה: אֲנִי־רָאִיתִי אֱוִיל מַשְׁרִישׁ וָאֶקּוֹב נָוֵהוּ פִתְאֹם: יִרְחֲקוּ בָנָיו מִיֶּשַׁע

3:22. Job complains that his worthy deeds seem to have been ignored by God, as if a wall had been erected between him and the Creator (*Rashi*).

3:25. I was always concerned that misfortune would befall me (*Rashi*).

4:1. Eliphaz is the first of the friends to respond to Job's plaint. He contends that suffering is not haphazard. Rather than railing about his fate, Job should examine his deeds and try to discover why God punished him.

4:2. I feel compelled to respond to your statements.

4:3. Before his personal tragedy, Job would console individuals who had suffered hardship and strengthen those whose faith was weak (*Rashi*).

4:6. Since you, who encouraged others, are so quick to lose heart when you are afflicted, it would seem that your professed piety was not genuine (*Rashi*).

4:10-11. Five Hebrew terms are used for "lion" in these verses. They represent wicked people with various levels of power. Despite their great might, they will be stunned by the force of God's punishment (*Rashi*).

4:20. During their entire life, they do not contemplate repentance (*Rashi*) or self-perfection (*Ralbag*).

4:21. Their proud accomplishments do them no good (*Rashi*).

5:1. Eliphaz continues his rebuke of Job for having cried out against God (*Rashi*).

5:2. Eliphaz said, in essence, "Had you overcome your anger and remained silent, God may have had mercy on you" (*Rashi*).

5:3. This word is used here with the connotation of "wicked person" (*Ramban*).

me to suckle? ¹² So now I would be lying calmly [in my grave], I would be asleep; then I would be at rest, ¹³ together with kings and counselors of the world who rebuild ruins for themselves, ¹⁴ or with ministers who have gold and fill their houses with silver; ¹⁵ or had I, like a concealed stillborn, never been [alive], like infants who never saw light. ¹⁶ There the wicked cease from agitation; and there exhausted ones repose; ¹⁷ the captives, all together, are tranquil; they do not hear the taskmaster's voice. ¹⁸ Small and great are [equal] there, and the slave is freed from his master.

. . . and complains of his suffering

¹⁹ Why does [He] give light to the sufferer and life to those bitter of soul; ²⁰ [to] those who crave death but it is not there, who seek it more eagerly than hidden treasure; ²¹ [to] those who exult at a joyous occasion, who rejoice when they find the grave; ²² to a man whose deeds are concealed, before whom God has raised a barrier?*

²³ For my sigh ushers in my meal, my groan pours forth like water. ²⁴ Because I feared a fright, and it has overtaken me; what I dreaded has come upon me. ²⁵ I was not secure, I was not quiet, I was not at rest; and torment has come. *

4

ELIPHAZ' FIRST SPEECH AND JOB'S RESPONSE
4:1-7:21

¹ Eliphaz the Temanite then spoke up* and said:

² If He tests you with one thing, will you become wearied? Who can withhold his words now?* ³ Behold, you have rebuked many, and have strengthened weak hands. * ⁴ Your words would stand up one who stumbles; you would brace buckling knees. ⁵ And now, when it befalls you, you become weary? It touches you, and you are bewildered! ⁶ Behold, was your fear [of God] not your foolishness, and so too your hope and the wholesomeness of your ways?*

The harvest of the iniquitous

⁷ Remember, please, which innocent person ever perished? Where have upright people ever been obliterated? ⁸ As I have seen, those who plow iniquity and sow injustice harvest them. ⁹ By the breath of God, they perish; by the wind of His anger, they expire. ¹⁰ The [adult] lion's roar, the whelp's cry and the cubs' teeth — [all] are lost. * ¹¹ The mature lion perishes for lack of prey, and the lioness' children are dispersed.

A vision about God's way with man

¹² A message surreptitiously reached me, of which my ear absorbed a small portion. ¹³ When thoughts are filled with nocturnal visions, when slumber falls upon men, ¹⁴ fear came upon me, and trembling, it caused most of my bones to shudder. ¹⁵ A spirit brushed my face; it made the hair on my flesh stand on end. ¹⁶ It stood still, but I could not recognize its features; an image was before my eyes. I heard a faint whisper: ¹⁷ "Can a mortal man be more righteous than God? Can a man be purer than his Maker? ¹⁸ If He cannot have faith even in His servants and finds fault with His angels, ¹⁹ then surely [He does the same with] those who dwell in clay houses, whose foundation is in the dust, who are crushed before maggots! ²⁰ They are ground down from morning to evening; without contemplation, they are lost forever. * ²¹ Behold, the pride within them departs, * and they die without wisdom."

5

Eliphaz' curse

¹ Cry out now! Is there anyone who will answer you?* To which of the holy beings will you turn? ² For anger kills the fool; envy slays the naive. * ³ I saw a fool* strike roots, but I cursed his dwelling with sudden [destruction] — ⁴ that his children be far from salvation and

ה וְיִקָּחֵהוּ וְאֶל־מִצִּנִּים וְאֶל־יֹאכֵל רָעֵב ׀ קְצִירוֹ אֲשֶׁר מַצִּיל וְאֵין בַּשַּׁעַר וִיְדַכְּאוּ

ו עָמָל לֹא־יִצְמַח וּמֵאֲדָמָה אָוֶן מֵעָפָר יֵצֵא לֹא ׀ כִּי חֵילָם צַמִּים שָׁאַף

ז-ח אֶל־אֵל אֶדְרֹשׁ אֲנִי אוּלָם עוּף יַגְבִּיהוּ וּבְנֵי־רֶשֶׁף יוּלָּד לְעָמָל אָדָם־כִּי

ט לָשׂוּם חוּצוֹת פְּנֵי עַל־מַיִם וְשֹׁלֵחַ אָרֶץ פְּנֵי עַל־מָטָר הַנֹּתֵן מִסְפָּר: עַד־אֵין נִפְלָאוֹת חֵקֶר וְאֵין גְּדֹלוֹת עֹשֶׂה דִבְרָתִי אֲשִׂים אֱלֹהִים וְאֶל־

יא-יב וְלֹא־ עֲרוּמִים מַחְשְׁבוֹת מֵפֵר יֶשַׁע: שָׂגְבוּ וְקֹדְרִים לְמָרוֹם שְׁפָלִים

יג נִמְהָרָה: נִפְתָּלִים וַעֲצַת בְּעָרְמָם חֲכָמִים לֹכֵד תּוּשִׁיָּה: יְדֵיהֶם תַּעֲשֶׂינָה

יד-טו וּמִיַּד מִפִּיהֶם מֵחֶרֶב וַיֹּשַׁע בַּצָּהֳרָיִם: יְמַשְׁשׁוּ וְכַלַּיְלָה חֹשֶׁךְ יְפַגְּשׁוּ־יוֹמָם

טז-יז אֱנוֹשׁ אַשְׁרֵי הִנֵּה פִּיהָ: קָפְצָה וְעֹלָתָה תִּקְוָה לַדָּל וַתְּהִי תִקְוָה: חָזַק אֶבְיוֹן

יח וְיָדָיו יִמְחָץ יַכְאִיב הוּא כִּי אַל־תִּמְאָס: שַׁדַּי וּמוּסַר אֱלוֹהַּ יוֹכִיחֶנּוּ

יט-כ בְּרָעָב רָע: בְּךָ לֹא־יִגַּע וּבְשֶׁבַע יַצִּילֶךָּ צָרוֹת בְּשֵׁשׁ תִּרְפֶּנָּה:

כא כִּי מִשֹּׁד לֹא־תִירָא וְלֹא תֵחָבֵא לָשׁוֹן בְּשׁוֹט חָרֶב: מִידֵי וּבְמִלְחָמָה מִמָּוֶת

כב-כג הַשָּׂדֶה אַבְנֵי־עִם כִּי אַל־תִּירָא: הָאָרֶץ וּמֵחַיַּת תִּשְׂחָק וּלְכָפָן לְשֹׁד יָבוֹא:

כד נָוְךָ וּפָקַדְתָּ אָהֳלֶךָ שָׁלוֹם כִּי־וְיָדַעְתָּ לָךְ: הַשָּׂדֶה וְחַיַּת בְרִיתֶךָ

כה-כו בְלָח תָּבוֹא הָאָרֶץ כְּעֵשֶׂב וְצֶאֱצָאֶיךָ זַרְעֶךָ כִּי־רָב וְיָדַעְתָּ תֶחְטָא: וְלֹא

כז שְׁמָעֶנָּה הִיא־כֶן חֲקָרְנוּהָ זֹאת־הִנֵּה בְעִתּוֹ: גָדִישׁ כַּעֲלוֹת בְּכֶלַח אֱלֵי־קֶבֶר

א-ב יִשָּׁקֵל שָׁקוֹל לוּ וַיֹּאמַר: אִיּוֹב וַיַּעַן לָךְ: וְאַתָּה דַע־ ו

ג יַמִּים מֵחוֹל מֵעַתָּה כִּי־ יָחַד: יִשָּׂאוּ בְּמֹאזְנַיִם [ק׳ וְהַוָּתִי °] ׀ [וְהַיָּתִי] כַּעְשִׂי

ד רוּחִי שֹׁתָה חֲמָתָם אֲשֶׁר עִמָּדִי שַׁדַּי חִצֵּי כִּי לָעוּ: דְבָרַי עַל־כֵּן יִכְבָּד

ה עַל־שׁוֹר יִגְעֶה אִם עֲלֵי־דֶשֶׁא פֶּרֶא הֲיִנְהַק־ יַעַרְכוּנִי: אֱלוֹהַּ בִּעוּתֵי

ו-ז מֵאֲנָה הַלָּמוּת: בְּרִיר טַעַם אִם־יֶשׁ־מֶלַח מִבְּלִי תָּפֵל הֲיֵאָכֵל בְּלִילוֹ:

ח אֱלוֹהַּ: יִתֵּן וְתִקְוָתִי שֶׁאֱלָתִי תָבוֹא מִי־יִתֵּן לַחְמִי: כִּדְוֵי הֵמָּה נַפְשִׁי לִנְגּוֹעַ

ט וַאֲסַלְּדָה וְנֶחָמָתִי ׀ עוֹד וּתְהִי וִיבַצְּעֵנִי יָדוֹ יַתֵּר וִידַכְּאֵנִי אֱלוֹהַּ וְיֹאֵל

יא-יב אֲיַחֵל כִּי־מַה־קִּצִּי אֲיַחֵל: כִּי־מַה־כֹּחִי אִמְרֵי קָדוֹשׁ: כִחַדְתִּי כִּי־לֹא יַחְמוֹל לֹא בְחִילָה

יב נָחוּשׁ: אִם־בְּשָׂרִי כֹּחַ אֲבָנִים אִם־כֹּחַ כִּי־אַאֲרִיךְ נַפְשִׁי: וּמַה־קִּצִּי

5:4. That is, in public (*Ibn Ezra*).

5:5. The hungry and thirsty are those who were wronged or despoiled by the wicked (*Rashi*).

5:6. Suffering befalls a person as a consequence of his own sins (*Metzudos*).

5:7. Unlike the angels, man will sin, and consequently incur Divine punishment (*Rashi*).

5:11. Referring to the somber appearance of individuals who have undergone personal tragedy (*Ralbag*), or, to the dark skin color characteristic of famine victims (*Rashi*).

5:14. These planners of evil.

5:15. Foul mouths are the sword of the wicked; God protects the destitute from being devoured by them (*Rashi*).

5:17. Hardship atones for and expunges one's transgressions, bringing blessings and good fortune in its

5:19. The number seven is often used to denote totality; i.e., God will prevent you from being overwhelmed by evil (*Ramban*).

5:23. So that you will not be harmed by stumbling on them (*Ibn Ezra*).

6:2. If Job's twin suffering could be weighed — his broken body and shattered spirit . . .

6:4. In essence, Job told his friends that they could not understand his plight. "If I were living your life of peace and contentment, I, too, would not cry out in pain" (*Ibn Ezra*).

6:5-6. Job complains that his friends mollify him with empty, senseless statements (*Rashi*).

6:7. Before I became afflicted, this disease disgusted me, that they be crushed at the gate* with no one to save them; [5] that the hungry devour his harvest and take it from amid the thorns, and that the thirsty gulp their possessions. * [6] For destruction does not emerge from dust, nor does misery grow from earth. * [7] For man is born to weariness, while spiritual beings soar in flight. *

Be confident of God's help

[8] However, I would beseech the Almighty and direct my words to God, [9] Who performs great deeds that are beyond comprehension, [and] wonders beyond number; [10] Who gives rain upon the face of the earth and sends water over the outlying fields, [11] so as to place the lowly on high, and uplift the blackened* with salvation; [12] Who thwarts the plottings of the cunning so that their hands will not produce results; [13] Who traps the shrewd with their trickery, and causes the plans of the devious to turn to folly. [14] By day they* encounter darkness, and at midday they grope as in the night. [15] He delivers [their victims] from the sword, their mouths, * and the destitute from the hand of the mighty. [16] Thus there is hope for the poor, and iniquity shuts its mouth.

Eliphaz' advice to Job

[17] Behold, fortunate is the man whom God rebukes!* Do not despise the Almighty's discipline: [18] For He inflicts pain and bandages; He crushes, and His hands heal. [19] From six travails He will save you, and in the seventh* no harm will reach you; [20] in famine He will deliver you from death, and in war, from the power of the sword. [21] You will be concealed from the prowling tongue, and you will not need to be frightened of destruction when it comes. [22] You will laugh at robbery and famine, and have no fear of the beasts of the land. [23] For you will have a treaty with the stones in the field, * and the beasts of the field will be at peace with you. [24] You will know that your tent is at peace, and you will visit your home and find nothing amiss. [25] You will know that your offspring are abundant and your descendants like the grass of the earth. [26] You will go to the grave in ripe old age, just as a sheaf is brought in, in its season. [27] Behold, we have investigated this, and it is so. Hear it, and you will know!

6

Job's response

[1] Job then spoke up and said:

The scales of suffering

[2] If only my anger were to be weighed, or my trauma placed on a scale, both lifted together, * [3] it would now be heavier than the sand of the seas; therefore my words are confused. [4] For the arrows of the Almighty are with me; my spirit drinks their poison. God's horrors are arrayed against me. * [5] Does a wild ass bray over grass? Does an ox low over its fodder?* [6] Is bland food eaten without salt? Does the white of an egg have taste? [7] What my soul had refused to touch is now the cloth for my food. *

Job cannot wait for deliverance

[8] Who would grant that my request be realized, that God would grant my hope, [9] and God would be willing to crush me, to let loose His hand and cut me off! [10] Moreover, that would be my consolation! I tremble with the plea that He show no mercy, for I have never disregarded the words of the Holy One. [11] What strength have I that I should wait?* What is my end, that I should extend my life? [12] Is my strength the strength of rocks? Is my flesh made of copper?

---

yet now that I am afflicted, the disease comes in contact with my food (*Rashi*). Alternatively: Job said, "You expect me to eat bland and tasteless declarations that I would never have thought of touching" (*Ramban*).

6:11-12. In response to Eliphaz' comforting assurance that God will yet give him life and health (5:17-27), Job says that he will not live long enough to have a full recovery. Better that he should die immediately.

יג-יד הַאִם אֵין עֶזְרָתִי בִי וְתֻשִׁיָּה נִדְּחָה מִמֶּנִּי: לַמָּס מֵרֵעֵהוּ חָסֶד וְיִרְאַת שַׁדַּי

טו-טז יַעֲזוֹב: אַחַי בָּגְדוּ כְמוֹ־נָחַל כַּאֲפִיק נְחָלִים יַעֲבֹרוּ: הַקֹּדְרִים מִנִּי־קָרַח

יז-יח עָלֵימוֹ יִתְעַלֶּם־שָׁלֶג: בְּעֵת יְזֹרְבוּ נִצְמָתוּ בְּחֻמּוֹ נִדְעֲכוּ מִמְּקוֹמָם: יִלָּפְתוּ

יט אָרְחוֹת דַּרְכָּם יַעֲלוּ בַתֹּהוּ וְיֹאבֵדוּ: הִבִּיטוּ אָרְחוֹת תֵּמָא הֲלִיכֹת שְׁבָא

כ-כא קִוּוּ־לָמוֹ: בֹּשׁוּ כִּי־בָטָח בָּאוּ עָדֶיהָ וַיֶּחְפָּרוּ: כִּי־עַתָּה הֱיִיתֶם לֹא תִּרְאוּ

כב-כג חֲתַת וַתִּירָאוּ: הֲכִי־אָמַרְתִּי הָבוּ לִי וּמִכֹּחֲכֶם שִׁחֲדוּ בַעֲדִי: וּמַלְּטוּנִי מִיַּד־

כד צָר וּמִיַּד עָרִיצִים תִּפְדּוּנִי: הוֹרוּנִי וַאֲנִי אַחֲרִישׁ וּמַה־שָּׁגִיתִי הָבִינוּ לִי:

כה-כו מַה־נִּמְרְצוּ אִמְרֵי־יֹשֶׁר וּמַה־יּוֹכִיחַ הוֹכֵחַ מִכֶּם: הַלְהוֹכַח מִלִּים תַּחְשֹׁבוּ

כז-כח וּלְרוּחַ אִמְרֵי נֹאָשׁ: אַף־עַל־יָתוֹם תַּפִּילוּ וְתִכְרוּ עַל־רֵיעֲכֶם: וְעַתָּה

כט הוֹאִילוּ פְנוּ־בִי וְעַל־פְּנֵיכֶם אִם־אֲכַזֵּב: שֻׁבוּ־נָא אַל־תְּהִי עַוְלָה °עוּלָה ושבי

ל [°וְשֻׁבוּ ק׳] עוֹד צִדְקִי־בָהּ: הֲיֵשׁ־בִּלְשׁוֹנִי עַוְלָה אִם־חִכִּי לֹא־יָבִין הַוּוֹת:

ז

א-ב הֲלֹא־צָבָא לֶאֱנוֹשׁ °על [°עֲלֵי ק׳] אֶרֶץ וְכִימֵי שָׂכִיר יָמָיו: כְּעֶבֶד יִשְׁאַף־

ג צֵל וּכְשָׂכִיר יְקַוֶּה פָעֳלוֹ: כֵּן הָנְחַלְתִּי לִי יַרְחֵי־שָׁוְא וְלֵילוֹת עָמָל מִנּוּ־לִי:

ד אִם־שָׁכַבְתִּי וְאָמַרְתִּי מָתַי אָקוּם וּמִדַּד־עָרֶב וְשָׂבַעְתִּי נְדֻדִים עֲדֵי־נָשֶׁף:

ה-ו לָבַשׁ בְּשָׂרִי רִמָּה °וגיש [°וְגוּשׁ ק׳] עָפָר עוֹרִי רָגַע וַיִּמָּאֵס: יָמַי קַלּוּ מִנִּי־

ז אָרֶג וַיִּכְלוּ בְּאֶפֶס תִּקְוָה: זְכֹר כִּי־רוּחַ חַיָּי לֹא־תָשׁוּב עֵינִי לִרְאוֹת טוֹב:

ח-ט לֹא־תְשׁוּרֵנִי עֵין רֹאִי עֵינֶיךָ בִּי וְאֵינֶנִּי: כָּלָה עָנָן וַיֵּלַךְ כֵּן יוֹרֵד שְׁאוֹל לֹא

י-יא יַעֲלֶה: לֹא־יָשׁוּב עוֹד לְבֵיתוֹ וְלֹא־יַכִּירֶנּוּ עוֹד מְקֹמוֹ: גַּם־אֲנִי לֹא אֶחֱשָׂךְ

יב פִּי אֲדַבְּרָה בְּצַר רוּחִי אָשִׂיחָה בְּמַר נַפְשִׁי: הֲיָם־אָנִי אִם־תַּנִּין כִּי־

יג תָשִׂים עָלַי מִשְׁמָר: כִּי־אָמַרְתִּי תְּנַחֲמֵנִי עַרְשִׂי יִשָּׂא בְשִׂיחִי מִשְׁכָּבִי:

יד-טו וְחִתַּתַּנִי בַחֲלֹמוֹת וּמֵחֶזְיֹנוֹת תְּבַעֲתַנִּי: וַתִּבְחַר מַחֲנָק נַפְשִׁי מָוֶת

טז-יז מֵעַצְמוֹתָי: מָאַסְתִּי לֹא־לְעֹלָם אֶחְיֶה חֲדַל מִמֶּנִּי כִּי־הֶבֶל יָמָי: מָה־

יח אֱנוֹשׁ כִּי תְגַדְּלֶנּוּ וְכִי־תָשִׁית אֵלָיו לִבֶּךָ: וַתִּפְקְדֶנּוּ לִבְקָרִים לִרְגָעִים

יט-כ תִּבְחָנֶנּוּ: כַּמָּה לֹא־תִשְׁעֶה מִמֶּנִּי עַד־תַּרְפֵּנִי עַד־בִּלְעִי רֻקִּי: חָטָאתִי

מָה אֶפְעַל לָךְ נֹצֵר הָאָדָם לָמָה שַׂמְתַּנִי לְמִפְגָּע לָךְ וָאֶהְיֶה עָלַי לְמַשָּׂא:

6:13. Job bewails the inability of his loyal friends to console him or give him practical advice (*Rashi*).

6:15-17. Seasonal watercourses are dry except in the rainy season. The waters of such streams change constantly, "betraying" those who need water. In the winter the water is concealed, and in the summer it evaporates (*Rashi*).

6:19. Low-lying plains into which much water flows (*Rashi*).

6:20-21. People feel ashamed when they fail to find water where they had confidently expected it. So too, Job accuses his friends of lacking the courage to admit that an injustice had been done him for fear that God would punish them in the same manner (*Rashi*).

6:23. I do not ask you for monetary aid, but for moral assistance (*Ramban*).

6:27. Job calls himself an orphan due to his unfortunate, pitiable situation.

7:1. Like the hired hand's term of employment, everyone's life will eventually end (*Rashi*).

7:7. How long will my ordeal continue? Since my life passes by as swiftly as the wind, I will die if You wait much longer (*Metzudos*).

7:12. As the sea is bounded by the sand, and a fish is confined in the water, so have I been prevented from dying (*Rashi*).

7:16. Since my days are numbered and of no worth, why don't You let me die?

¹³ *Is my own help not with me? Is counsel to be withheld from me,* * ¹⁴ *by one who withholds kindness from his friend and forsakes the fear of the Almighty?*

Empty talk is not moral support

¹⁵ *My brothers have betrayed [me] like a [seasonal] watercourse; they shift like the flow of streams,* ¹⁶ *tucking themselves under ice, hidden under concealing snow.* * ¹⁷ *When they are scorched, they shrivel up; in the heat they depart abruptly from their place.* ¹⁸ *They determine their own courses, enter the wastes and are lost.* ¹⁹ *They set their eyes on the path to Tema, and draw a line toward the direction of Sheba.* * ²⁰ *People become ashamed for having trusted [them]; they approached it and were humiliated.* * ²¹ *And now, that is how you have been — you saw disaster and became frightened.*

"Show me where I went wrong."

²² *Did I say, 'Give me [money],' or, 'Use your power to pay a bribe for me,* ²³ *and save me from an oppressor, redeeming me from fierce men'?* * ²⁴ *Instruct me, and I shall be silent. Make me understand where I have erred.* ²⁵ *How eloquent is upright talk; but what result have any of you proven?* ²⁶ *Do you believe that [mere] words can convince? Empty talk is so much wind!* ²⁷ *You cast anger upon an orphan;* * *you dig [a trap] against your friend!*

Can they deny that Job is right?

²⁸ *Now, be so good as to turn to me; [see] if I speak falsely before you.* ²⁹ *Please reconsider, and [see] that there is no dishonesty. Reconsider again — I am right.* ³⁰ *Is there dishonesty upon my tongue? Can my palate not discern folly?*

7

Job loses hope

¹ Behold, *man has an allotted time upon the earth; his days are like those of a hired hand.* * ² *Like a slave he awaits the [evening] shade; like a hired hand longs for his wages,* ³ *so was I allotted months of frustration, and nights of misery were assigned to me.* ⁴ *When I lie down, I say, 'When will I arise, and the night depart?' and I had my fill of tossing and turning until dawn.* ⁵ *My flesh is clothed with maggots and clumps of dirt; my skin is cracked and dissolved.* ⁶ *My days fly faster than a weaver's shuttle, and have ended in hopelessness.*

Job addresses God

⁷ *Remember that my life is like the wind, and my eyes will never again see goodness!* * ⁸ *The eyes of my observers will not see me; Your eyes are upon me, but I am no more.* ⁹ *[As] a cloud disperses and is gone, so does one who descends to the grave not rise.* ¹⁰ *He will not return again to his home, nevermore will his community know him.* ¹¹ *As for me, I will not muzzle my mouth, I will speak in the anguish of my spirit; I will express myself in the bitterness of my soul!*

"Why do You force me to live?"

¹² *Am I the sea, or a sea-giant, that You put me under guard?* * ¹³ *If I say, 'My bed will console me; my couch will ease my pain,'* ¹⁴ *You shatter me with dreams, and terrify me with visions.* ¹⁵ *My soul would prefer strangulation, death over [survival of] my bones.* ¹⁶ *I am disgusted; I shall not live forever, leave me alone, for my days are as nothing!* *

"Why am I worthy of Your attention?"

¹⁷ *What is man, that You exalt him, that You turn Your attention to him,* ¹⁸ *that you inspect him every morning and observe him every moment?* ¹⁹ *It is so long since You ignored me? You do not leave me alone long enough to swallow my own spittle!* ²⁰ *[If] I sin, how have I affected You, O Guardian of man? Why make me Your target, so that I have become a burden to*

כא וּמֶה | לֹא־תִשָּׂא פִשְׁעִי וְתַעֲבִיר אֶת־עֲוֹנִי כִּי־עַתָּה לֶעָפָר אֶשְׁכָּב

א־ב וְשִׁחֲרְתַּנִי וְאֵינֶנִּי: וַיַּעַן בִּלְדַּד הַשּׁוּחִי וַיֹּאמַר: עַד־אָן **ח**

ג תְּמַלֶּל־אֵלֶּה וְרוּחַ כַּבִּיר אִמְרֵי־פִיךָ: הַאֵל יְעַוֵּת מִשְׁפָּט וְאִם־שַׁדַּי יְעַוֵּת־

ד־ה צֶדֶק: אִם־בָּנֶיךָ חָטְאוּ־לוֹ וַיְשַׁלְּחֵם בְּיַד־פִּשְׁעָם: אִם־אַתָּה תְּשַׁחֵר אֶל־

ו אֵל וְאֶל־שַׁדַּי תִּתְחַנָּן: אִם־זַךְ וְיָשָׁר אָתָּה כִּי־עַתָּה יָעִיר עָלֶיךָ וְשִׁלַּם נְוַת

ז־ח צִדְקֶךָ: וְהָיָה רֵאשִׁיתְךָ מִצְעָר וְאַחֲרִיתְךָ יִשְׂגֶּה מְאֹד: כִּי־שְׁאַל־נָא לְדֹר

ט רִישׁוֹן וְכוֹנֵן לְחֵקֶר אֲבוֹתָם: כִּי־תְמוֹל אֲנַחְנוּ וְלֹא נֵדָע כִּי צֵל יָמֵינוּ עֲלֵי־

י־יא אָרֶץ: הֲלֹא־הֵם יוֹרוּךָ יֹאמְרוּ לָךְ וּמִלִּבָּם יוֹצִאוּ מִלִּים: הֲיִגְאֶה־גֹּמֶא בְּלֹא

יב בִצָּה יִשְׂגֶּה־אָחוּ בְלִי־מָיִם: עֹדֶנּוּ בְאִבּוֹ לֹא יִקָּטֵף וְלִפְנֵי כָל־חָצִיר יִיבָשׁ:

יג־יד כֵּן אָרְחוֹת כָּל־שֹׁכְחֵי אֵל וְתִקְוַת חָנֵף תֹּאבֵד: אֲשֶׁר־יָקוֹט כִּסְלוֹ וּבֵית

טו־טז עַכָּבִישׁ מִבְטַחוֹ: יִשָּׁעֵן עַל־בֵּיתוֹ וְלֹא יַעֲמֹד יַחֲזִיק בּוֹ וְלֹא יָקוּם: רָטֹב

יז הוּא לִפְנֵי־שָׁמֶשׁ וְעַל גַּנָּתוֹ יֹנַקְתּוֹ תֵצֵא: עַל־גַּל שָׁרָשָׁיו יְסֻבָּכוּ בֵּית

יח־יט אֲבָנִים יֶחֱזֶה: אִם־יְבַלְּעֶנּוּ מִמְּקוֹמוֹ וְכִחֶשׁ בּוֹ לֹא רְאִיתִיךָ: הֶן־הוּא מְשׂוֹשׂ

כ דַּרְכּוֹ וּמֵעָפָר אַחֵר יִצְמָחוּ: הֶן־אֵל לֹא יִמְאַס־תָּם וְלֹא־יַחֲזִיק בְּיַד־

כא־כב מְרֵעִים: עַד־יְמַלֶּה שְׂחוֹק פִּיךָ וּשְׂפָתֶיךָ תְרוּעָה: שֹׂנְאֶיךָ יִלְבְּשׁוּ־בֹשֶׁת

א־ב וְאֹהֶל רְשָׁעִים אֵינֶנּוּ: וַיַּעַן אִיּוֹב וַיֹּאמַר: אָמְנָם **ט**

ג יָדַעְתִּי כִי־כֵן וּמַה־יִּצְדַּק אֱנוֹשׁ עִם־אֵל: אִם־יַחְפֹּץ לָרִיב עִמּוֹ לֹא־

ד יַעֲנֶנּוּ אַחַת מִנִּי־אָלֶף: חֲכַם לֵבָב וְאַמִּיץ כֹּחַ מִי־הִקְשָׁה אֵלָיו וַיִּשְׁלָם:

ה־ו הַמַּעְתִּיק הָרִים וְלֹא יָדָעוּ אֲשֶׁר הֲפָכָם בְּאַפּוֹ: הַמַּרְגִּיז אֶרֶץ מִמְּקוֹמָהּ

ז וְעַמּוּדֶיהָ יִתְפַלָּצוּן: הָאֹמֵר לַחֶרֶס וְלֹא יִזְרָח וּבְעַד כּוֹכָבִים יַחְתֹּם:

ח־ט נֹטֶה שָׁמַיִם לְבַדּוֹ וְדוֹרֵךְ עַל־בָּמֳתֵי יָם: עֹשֶׂה־עָשׁ כְּסִיל וְכִימָה וְחַדְרֵי

י־יא תֵמָן: עֹשֶׂה גְדֹלוֹת עַד־אֵין חֵקֶר וְנִפְלָאוֹת עַד־אֵין מִסְפָּר: הֵן יַעֲבֹר

יב עָלַי וְלֹא אֶרְאֶה וְיַחֲלֹף וְלֹא־אָבִין לוֹ: הֵן יַחְתֹּף מִי יְשִׁיבֶנּוּ מִי־יֹאמַר

יג אֵלָיו מַה־תַּעֲשֶׂה: אֱלוֹהַּ לֹא־יָשִׁיב אַפּוֹ תַּחַת [תַחְתָּיו ק] שָׁחֲחוּ

יד־טו עֹזְרֵי רָהַב: אַף כִּי־אָנֹכִי אֶעֱנֶנּוּ אֶבְחֲרָה דְבָרַי עִמּוֹ: אֲשֶׁר אִם־צָדַקְתִּי

טז לֹא אֶעֱנֶה לִמְשֹׁפְטִי אֶתְחַנָּן: אִם־קָרָאתִי וַיַּעֲנֵנִי לֹא־אַאֲמִין כִּי־יַאֲזִין

7:20. According to tradition, the word "myself" is a euphemistic substitution for the irreverent "You."

8:7. If you would repent, the blessings He would bestow upon you would overshadow even those of the past (*Ramban*).

8:9. Our lives are so short that we cannot understand the long-range patterns of events (*Kara*).

8:17. He establishes himself firmly in his place (*Rashi*).

8:18. No trace of him will remain (*Rashi*).

8:19. The success of the wicked is transitory. They will fade and others will rise to take their place (*Rashi*).

9:2. Job will argue that he sees no difference between the fates of the righteous and the wicked. And even the wicked should not suffer because man's inevitable decline and death should be punishment enough (*Ramban*).

9:5. So suddenly does God make upheavals that people do not even realize what had happened.

9:9. These star clusters are identified by *Ibn Ezra* (to *Amos* 5:8).

myself? * [21] *Why do You not forgive my sin and pardon my iniquity? For soon I will lie down in the dust; You will search for me, but I will be no more.*

8

BILDAD'S FIRST SPEECH AND JOB'S RESPONSE
8:1-10:22

[1] **B**ildad the Shuhite then spoke up and said:

[2] *How long will you say such things? The words of your mouth are a powerful wind!* [3] *Would God pervert justice? Would the Almighty pervert righteousness?* [4] *When your sons sinned against Him, He delivered them into the hand of their own transgression.* [5] *If you would beseech God and implore to the Almighty,* [6] *if you would be pure and upright, He would even now recall [your merits] for you, and make whole the abode of your righteousness.* [7] *Then, though your beginning was insignificant, your end will flourish exceedingly.* *

Testimony of earlier times

[8] *Inquire, now, of an earlier generation, and prepare yourself for the investigation of their fathers.* [9] *For we are but since yesterday, so we do not know;* * *our days upon the earth are but a shadow.* [10] *Behold, they will instruct you, they will tell you, and extract words from their heart.*

Destruction of the wicked

[11] *Can reeds grow without a swamp? [Can] a marshland thrive without water?* [12] *While it is still fresh, it will not snap, yet it withers before any other grass.* [13] *So with the ways of all who forget God; the hope of the hypocrite is doomed.* [14] *His reliance is cut down, his trust is a spider web.* [15] *He leans on his house, but it does not stand; he holds onto it, but it does not remain.* [16] *He is moist before the sun's heat, and his shoots spread out in his garden.* [17] *His roots are thickly entangled on a mound; he searches out a house of stone.* * [18] *[But] when he is uprooted from his place, it denies him, [saying,] 'I never saw you.'* * [19] *Such is the 'joy' of his way; and from the earth, others will sprout.* * [20] *For God does not detest the wholesome nor support the hand of evildoers.* [21] *Until He will fill your mouth with laughter and your lips with shouting [for joy].* [22] *Your enemies will be covered with disgrace, and the tents of the wicked will be no more.*

9

Job's response to Bildad

[1] **J**ob then spoke up and said:

[2] *Truly, I know that it is so. How can man be righteous with God?* * [3] *If he would want to contend with Him, He would not reply even once in a thousand.* [4] *He is wise of heart and immensely strong. Who ever stubbornly opposed Him and remained whole?* [5] *It is He Who uproots mountains and [people] do not know, when He overturns them in His anger;* * [6] *Who shakes the earth from its place, and its pillars tremble;* [7] *Who gives the command to the sun, and it does not shine; and seals up the stars;* [8] *Who alone stretches out the heavens, and treads upon the crests of the sea;* [9] *Who made Ursa Minor, Orion and Pleiades, and the southern constellations;* * [10] *Who performs great deeds that are beyond comprehension, and wonders beyond number.* [11] *If He would pass before me, I would not see [Him]; He would move across and I would not perceive Him.* [12] *If He would suddenly strike, who could restrain Him? Who could say to Him, 'What are You doing?'* [13] *God does not turn back His anger; bent underneath Him are those who assist the arrogant.*

It is futile to contend with God

[14] *Could I, then, answer Him, or choose to argue with Him?* [15] *Even if I were right, I would not speak up, nor would I implore my Judge.* [16] *If I would cry out and He would answer me, I would not believe that He would hear*

יז־יח   קוֹלִי: אֲשֶׁר־בִּשְׂעָרָה יְשׁוּפֵנִי וְהִרְבָּה פְצָעַי חִנָּם: לֹא־יִתְּנֵנִי הָשֵׁב רוּחִי כִּי

יט־כ   יַשְׂבִּעַנִי מַמְּרֹרִים: אִם־לְכֹחַ אַמִּיץ הִנֵּה וְאִם־לְמִשְׁפָּט מִי יוֹעִידֵנִי: אִם־

כא   אֶצְדָּק פִּי יַרְשִׁיעֵנִי תָם־אָנִי וַיַּעְקְשֵׁנִי: תָּם־אָנִי לֹא־אֵדַע נַפְשִׁי אֶמְאַס חַיָּי:

כב־כג   אַחַת הִיא עַל־כֵּן אָמַרְתִּי תָּם וְרָשָׁע הוּא מְכַלֶּה: אִם־שׁוֹט יָמִית פִּתְאֹם

כד   לְמַסַּת נְקִיִּם יִלְעָג: אֶרֶץ | נִתְּנָה בְיַד־רָשָׁע פְּנֵי־שֹׁפְטֶיהָ יְכַסֶּה אִם־לֹא

כה־כו   אֵפוֹא מִי־הוּא: וְיָמַי קַלּוּ מִנִּי־רָץ בָּרְחוּ לֹא־רָאוּ טוֹבָה: חָלְפוּ עִם־אֳנִיּוֹת

כז   אֵבֶה כְּנֶשֶׁר יָטוּשׂ עֲלֵי־אֹכֶל: אִם־אָמְרִי אֶשְׁכְּחָה שִׂיחִי אֶעֶזְבָה פָנַי

כח־כט   וְאַבְלִיגָה: יָגֹרְתִּי כָל־עַצְּבֹתָי יָדַעְתִּי כִּי־לֹא תְנַקֵּנִי: אָנֹכִי אֶרְשָׁע לָמָּה־זֶּה

ל   הֶבֶל אִיגָע: אִם־הִתְרָחַצְתִּי במו־[בְמֵי־ ק] שָׁלֶג וַהֲזִכּוֹתִי בְּבֹר כַּפָּי:

לא־לב   אָז בַּשַּׁחַת תִּטְבְּלֵנִי וְתִעֲבוּנִי שַׂלְמוֹתָי: כִּי־לֹא־אִישׁ כָּמֹנִי אֶעֱנֶנּוּ נָבוֹא

לג־לד   יַחְדָּו בַּמִּשְׁפָּט: לֹא יֵשׁ־בֵּינֵינוּ מוֹכִיחַ יָשֵׁת יָדוֹ עַל־שְׁנֵינוּ: יָסֵר מֵעָלַי

לה   שִׁבְטוֹ וְאֵמָתוֹ אַל־תְּבַעֲתַנִּי: אֲדַבְּרָה וְלֹא אִירָאֶנּוּ כִּי לֹא־כֵן אָנֹכִי עִמָּדִי:

א־ב   **י** נָקְטָה נַפְשִׁי בְּחַיָּי אֶעֶזְבָה עָלַי שִׂיחִי אֲדַבְּרָה בְּמַר נַפְשִׁי: אֹמַר אֶל־

ג   אֱלוֹהַּ אַל־תַּרְשִׁיעֵנִי הוֹדִיעֵנִי עַל מַה־תְּרִיבֵנִי: הֲטוֹב לְךָ | כִּי־תַעֲשֹׁק

ד   כִּי־תִמְאַס יְגִיעַ כַּפֶּיךָ וְעַל־עֲצַת רְשָׁעִים הוֹפָעְתָּ: הַעֵינֵי בָשָׂר לָךְ אִם־

ה־ו   כִּרְאוֹת אֱנוֹשׁ תִּרְאֶה: הֲכִימֵי אֱנוֹשׁ יָמֶיךָ אִם־שְׁנוֹתֶיךָ כִּימֵי גָבֶר: כִּי־

ז   תְבַקֵּשׁ לַעֲוֹנִי וּלְחַטָּאתִי תִדְרוֹשׁ: עַל־דַּעְתְּךָ כִּי־לֹא אֶרְשָׁע וְאֵין מִיָּדְךָ

ח־ט   מַצִּיל: יָדֶיךָ עִצְּבוּנִי וַיַּעֲשׂוּנִי יַחַד סָבִיב וַתְּבַלְּעֵנִי: זְכָר־נָא כִּי־כַחֹמֶר

י־יא   עֲשִׂיתָנִי וְאֶל־עָפָר תְּשִׁיבֵנִי: הֲלֹא כֶחָלָב תַּתִּיכֵנִי וְכַגְּבִנָּה תַּקְפִּיאֵנִי: עוֹר

יב   וּבָשָׂר תַּלְבִּישֵׁנִי וּבַעֲצָמוֹת וְגִידִים תְּשֹׂכְכֵנִי: חַיִּים וָחֶסֶד עָשִׂיתָ עִמָּדִי

יג־יד   וּפְקֻדָּתְךָ שָׁמְרָה רוּחִי: וְאֵלֶּה צָפַנְתָּ בִלְבָבֶךָ יָדַעְתִּי כִּי־זֹאת עִמָּךְ: אִם־

טו   חָטָאתִי וּשְׁמַרְתָּנִי וּמֵעֲוֹנִי לֹא תְנַקֵּנִי: אִם־רָשַׁעְתִּי אַלְלַי לִי וְצָדַקְתִּי לֹא־

טז   אֶשָּׂא רֹאשִׁי שְׂבַע קָלוֹן וּרְאֵה עָנְיִי: וְיִגְאֶה כַּשַּׁחַל תְּצוּדֵנִי וְתָשֹׁב

יז   תִּתְפַּלָּא־בִי: תְּחַדֵּשׁ עֵדֶיךָ | נֶגְדִּי וְתֶרֶב כַּעַשְׂךָ עִמָּדִי חֲלִיפוֹת וְצָבָא עִמִּי:

9:19. How can I contend with Him? If I come with force, He is mightier than I; and if I come with justice, who can plead for me? (*Rashi*).

9:20. The terror I would feel when speaking before Him would prevent me from pleading my case (*Rashi*).

9:23. If it is as you, Bildad, claim, that the wicked are smitten, then the wicked would be happy with his speedy death and laugh at the lengthy suffering of the righteous whose righteousness keeps them from the peace of death (*Ralbag*).

9:24. Satan has the power to instigate evil, and then confuses the judges so that they will absolve the guilty (*Rashi*).

9:25-10:22. As he did in his response to Eliphaz, Job ends his response to Bildad with a plaint addressed directly to God.

9:26. The name of a fast-flowing river (*Rashi*), or a warship (*Ramban*).

9:31. Even if I tried to cleanse myself from sin, You would find me soiled.

9:34-10:1. Job here interrupts his words to God with an aside to Bildad.

9:35. I am convinced of my innocence (*Rashi*).

10:3. I.e., strip a righteous person of his integrity (*Rashi*).

10:5-6. Job said to God, "You are not like a human being who is driven to avenge himself before he dies. Why, therefore, do You send hardships upon me in such quick succession? (*Metzudos*).

10:12. A reference to the miraculous laws of nature that are crucial to human survival (*Malbim*).

10:13. "Your actions imply that, in Your resolve to destroy me, You have forgotten Your kindnesses towards me; but I know that You still remember them!" (*Rashi*).

10:15. So there is no difference whether I am guilty or innocent.

my voice. [17] He shattered me in a tempest; He multiplied my wounds without cause. [18] He does not let me refresh my spirit, but satiates me with bitterness.

[19] If it is for strength, behold He is mighty! But if it is for justice, who can plead on my behalf? * [20] Even if I am righteous, my mouth would condemn me. [If] I am innocent, it would pronounce me crooked. * [21] I am innocent, yet I cannot know rest! I am disgusted with my life!

The wicked dead laugh

[22] It is all the same; therefore I say, 'He destroys the blameless with the wicked.' [23] When the rod would slay [the wicked one] suddenly, he would mock the tribulation of the innocent. * [24] The earth is delivered into the hands of the wicked one, who covers the faces of its judges. * If this is not so, then who [does this]?

"Whatever I say, I will be found guilty."

[25] * My days passed more swiftly than a runner; they have run away without seeing goodness. [26] They have passed by with the ships of Ebeh, * like an eagle swooping after prey. [27] Even if I would say, 'I will forget my grieving; I will renounce my anger and show fortitude,' [28] I fear all my sorrows; I know that You will not acquit me. [29] I will be found guilty, so why should I weary myself for nothing? [30] Though I would wash myself in melted snow and I would cleanse my hands with soap, [31] You would immerse me in the pit; my very clothes would loathe me. * [32] For You are not a mortal as I am, whom I could answer, so that we could go together for judgment. [33] There is no arbiter between us who might impose his authority upon us both.

"If I could only speak without fear!"

[34] * Were He to remove His rod from me, and His terror not frighten me, [35] I would speak out and not fear Him, for this is not how I perceive myself. *

10

"Why are You so vindictive?"

[1] My soul is disgusted with my life. I will load my grief upon myself and I speak out in the bitterness of my soul. [2] I say to God:

Do not condemn me. Tell me why You contend with me. [3] Does it befit You to plunder, * that You despise the labor of Your hands, but glow upon the schemes of the wicked? [4] Do You have eyes of flesh? Do You see as a man sees? [5] Are Your days like a person's days, are Your years like a man's days, [6] that You search out my iniquity and seek my transgression? * [7] You know that I will not be found guilty, yet none can save from Your hand.

Have compassion on Your handiwork

[8] Your hands made me and fashioned me; altogether, all around, yet You devour me! [9] Remember, please, that You molded me like clay, and that You will return me to the dust. [10] Behold, You poured me out like milk, and curdled me like cheese. [11] You clothed me with skin and flesh; You covered me with bones and sinews. [12] You granted me life and were kind to me, and Your ordinances * protected my spirit. [13] Although You have hidden this in Your heart, I know that this is [still] with You. *

You are preoccupied with me

[14] If I have sinned and You scrutinize me, then do not cleanse me of my transgression. [15] If I have been guilty, woe to me! And if I am innocent, I should not raise my head, * [for I am] satiated with disgrace, and see my misery. [16] It has become important [to You]: You hunt me as if I were a lion's whelp, and You repeatedly judge me severely. [17] You always bring new witnesses * against me, and You magnify Your anger against me. The legion takes turns with me.

10:17. Job refers to the diverse aches and pains that continually plagued him. The legion of suffering takes turns in revisiting him (*Rashi*).

וְלָמָּה מֵרֶחֶם הֹצֵאתָנִי אֶגְוַע וְעַיִן לֹא־תִרְאֵנִי: כַּאֲשֶׁר לֹא־הָיִיתִי אֶהְיֶה יח־יט

מִבֶּטֶן לַקֶּבֶר אוּבָל: הֲלֹא־מְעַט יָמַי °יֶחְדָּל ישׁית [וַחֲדָל וְשִׁית ק] כ

מִמֶּנִּי וְאַבְלִיגָה מְעָט: בְּטֶרֶם אֵלֵךְ וְלֹא אָשׁוּב אֶל־אֶרֶץ חֹשֶׁךְ כא

וְצַלְמָוֶת: אֶרֶץ עֵפָתָה ׀ כְּמוֹ אֹפֶל צַלְמָוֶת וְלֹא סְדָרִים וַתֹּפַע כב

כְּמוֹ־אֹפֶל: וַיַּעַן צֹפַר הַנַּעֲמָתִי וַיֹּאמַר: הֲרֹב דְּבָרִים לֹא **יא** א־ב

יֵעָנֶה וְאִם־אִישׁ שְׂפָתַיִם יִצְדָּק: בַּדֶּיךָ מְתִים יַחֲרִישׁוּ וַתִּלְעַג וְאֵין מַכְלִם: ג

וַתֹּאמֶר זַךְ לִקְחִי וּבַר הָיִיתִי בְעֵינֶיךָ: וְאוּלָם מִי־יִתֵּן אֱלוֹהַּ דַּבֵּר וְיִפְתַּח ד־ה

שְׂפָתָיו עִמָּךְ: וְיַגֶּד־לְךָ ׀ תַּעֲלֻמוֹת חָכְמָה כִּי־כִפְלַיִם לְתוּשִׁיָּה וְדַע ו

כִּי־יַשֶּׁה לְךָ אֱלוֹהַּ מֵעֲוֺנֶךָ: הַחֵקֶר אֱלוֹהַּ תִּמְצָא אִם עַד־תַּכְלִית שַׁדַּי ז

תִּמְצָא: גָּבְהֵי שָׁמַיִם מַה־תִּפְעָל עֲמֻקָּה מִשְּׁאוֹל מַה־תֵּדָע: אֲרֻכָּה ח־ט

מֵאֶרֶץ מִדָּהּ וּרְחָבָה מִנִּי־יָם: אִם־יַחֲלֹף וְיַסְגִּיר וְיַקְהִיל וּמִי יְשִׁיבֶנּוּ: כִּי־ י־יא

הוּא יָדַע מְתֵי־שָׁוְא וַיַּרְא־אָוֶן וְלֹא יִתְבּוֹנָן: וְאִישׁ נָבוּב יִלָּבֵב וְעַיִר פֶּרֶא יב

אָדָם יִוָּלֵד: אִם־אַתָּה הֲכִינוֹתָ לִבֶּךָ וּפָרַשְׂתָּ אֵלָיו כַּפֶּךָ: אִם־אָוֶן בְּיָדְךָ יג־יד

הַרְחִיקֵהוּ וְאַל־תַּשְׁכֵּן בְּאֹהָלֶיךָ עַוְלָה: כִּי־אָז ׀ תִּשָּׂא פָנֶיךָ מִמּוּם וְהָיִיתָ טו

מֻצָק וְלֹא תִירָא: כִּי־אַתָּה עָמָל תִּשְׁכָּח כְּמַיִם עָבְרוּ תִזְכֹּר: וּמִצָּהֳרַיִם טז־יז

יָקוּם חָלֶד תָּעֻפָה כַּבֹּקֶר תִּהְיֶה: וּבָטַחְתָּ כִּי־יֵשׁ תִּקְוָה וְחָפַרְתָּ יח

לָבֶטַח תִּשְׁכָּב: וְרָבַצְתָּ וְאֵין מַחֲרִיד וְחִלּוּ פָנֶיךָ רַבִּים: וְעֵינֵי רְשָׁעִים יט־כ

תִּכְלֶינָה וּמָנוֹס אָבַד מִנְהֶם וְתִקְוָתָם מַפַּח־נָפֶשׁ:   **יב** א

אִיּוֹב וַיֹּאמַר: אׇמְנָם כִּי אַתֶּם־עָם וְעִמָּכֶם תָּמוּת חׇכְמָה: גַּם־לִי ב־ג

לֵבָב ׀ כְּמוֹכֶם לֹא־נֹפֵל אָנֹכִי מִכֶּם וְאֶת־מִי־אֵין כְּמוֹ־אֵלֶּה: שְׂחֹק ד

לְרֵעֵהוּ ׀ אֶהְיֶה קֹרֵא לֶאֱלוֹהַּ וַיַּעֲנֵהוּ שְׂחוֹק צַדִּיק תָּמִים: לַפִּיד בּוּז ה

לְעַשְׁתּוּת שַׁאֲנָן נָכוֹן לְמוֹעֲדֵי רָגֶל: יִשְׁלָיוּ אֹהָלִים ׀ לְשֹׁדְדִים וּבַטֻּחוֹת ו

לְמַרְגִּיזֵי אֵל לַאֲשֶׁר הֵבִיא אֱלוֹהַּ בְּיָדוֹ: וְאוּלָם שְׁאַל־נָא בְהֵמוֹת וְתֹרֶךָּ ז

וְעוֹף הַשָּׁמַיִם וְיַגֶּד־לָךְ: אוֹ שִׂיחַ לָאָרֶץ וְתֹרֶךָּ וִיסַפְּרוּ לְךָ דְּגֵי הַיָּם: מִי־ ח־ט

לֹא־יָדַע בְּכׇל־אֵלֶּה כִּי יַד־יְהֹוָה עָשְׂתָה זֹּאת: אֲשֶׁר בְּיָדוֹ נֶפֶשׁ כׇּל־ י

חָי וְרוּחַ כׇּל־בְּשַׂר־אִישׁ: הֲלֹא־אֹזֶן מִלִּין תִּבְחָן וְחֵךְ אֹכֶל יִטְעַם־לוֹ: יא

10:22. Unlike this world where day follows night (*Kara*).

11:6. Zophar berates Job for thinking himself "virtuous in God's eyes," since no mortal can fully fathom God's doctrine (*Ibn Ezra*). If all were known, Job would realize that he deserved to be punished even more.

11:12. Since God does not react immediately to sin (v. 11), man should be intelligent enough to repent.

12:2. Sardonically and with exaggerated reverence, Job addresses his friends, whom he sees as having claimed a monopoly on wisdom.

12:4. Job rebukes Zophar. He describes himself as a

righteous person whom God answers, but whose friends make him the butt of their scorn.

12:6. Job maintains that God grants tranquility indiscriminately to both the righteous and the wicked (*Rashi*).

12:7. See below 40:15.

12:7-8. Although Job had complained that fate is haphazard, he nevertheless says that the complexity and magnificence of the world and its creatures testify to the guiding hand of God (*Ralbag*).

12:11. Recognition of God's omnipotence should be as self-evident as the taste of food is to the palate (*Rashi*).

Tranquility
before death

¹⁸ Why did You remove me from the womb? [If only] I had expired and no eye had ever seen me; ¹⁹ as though I had never existed, I would have been brought from the womb to the grave. ²⁰ Behold, my days are few — so desist! Remove Yourself from me and I will regain my strength for a while, ²¹ before I go — and never return — to the land of darkness and the shadow of death, ²² the land whose darkness is like pitch-blackness, a shadow of death and without order, * whose very light is like pitch-blackness.

11

ZOPHAR'S
FIRST
SPEECH
AND JOB'S
RESPONSE
11:1-14:22

¹ Zophar the Naamathite then spoke up and said:

² Should an effusive speaker not be answered? Is an eloquent orator correct? ³ Your fabrications strike men dumb; you scoff, and no one ridicules you. ⁴ You say, 'My teaching is pure; I am virtuous in Your eyes.' ⁵ But if God would speak and open His lips to you, ⁶ He would relate to you hidden recesses of wisdom, for His sagacity is manifold. * Know, then, that God exacts from you less than your iniquities!

Man cannot
fathom
God's ways

⁷ Can you achieve an understanding of God? Can you fathom the extent of the Almighty? ⁸ It is like the heights of heaven; what can you do [to understand]? It is deeper than the Pit; what can you know? ⁹ Its measure is longer than the earth and wider than the sea. ¹⁰ If He were to cause death or to aggrieve, and then convene [the heavenly beings], who could challenge Him? ¹¹ For He discerns deceitful people; He sees iniquity, though He seems not to notice.

If Job
would accept
and repent,
all would
be well

¹² Let the hollow man acquire a heart! Let one who is [like] a wild ass be reborn as a man! * ¹³ If you would focus your heart, and spread forth your hands to Him! ¹⁴ If there is iniquity in your hand, put it far away; and let not sin dwell in your tent. ¹⁵ Then you would lift your face without blemish; you would be steadfast and never fear. ¹⁶ Then you would forget misery; you would remember it as water flowed by. ¹⁷ [Your] fate would be brighter than the noon; it would glimmer like the morning. ¹⁸ You would be confident, for there would be hope; you would lie down entrenched in security. ¹⁹ You would repose with none to make you afraid, and many people would seek your favor. ²⁰ The eyes of the wicked would look with longing, haven would be denied them. Their hope would become despair.

12

Job's
response
to Zophar

Job rebukes
Zophar

¹ Job then spoke up and said:

² Truly, you are the many, but will wisdom expire with you? * ³ I, like you, also possess an [understanding] heart. I am not inferior to you. Who does not know such things?

⁴ I have become [like one who is] a laughingstock to his fellow; [I am one] who calls out to God and He answers him, the wholesome righteous one is a laughingstock! * ⁵ A torch of scorn to the one who is complacent in his thoughts! He is destined to be among those whose feet slip. ⁶ The tents of robbers are tranquil, and there is security for those who anger God, into whomever's hand God brings it. *

God's
mastery is
obvious . . .

⁷ Please ask the Behemoth, * however, and it will teach you; the bird of the heavens, and it will tell you. ⁸ Or speak to the earth, and it will teach you; the fish of the sea will report to you. * ⁹ Who cannot know from all these things that the hand of God made this? ¹⁰ That in His hand is the soul of every living thing and the spirit of all mankind? ¹¹ Can the ear not discern words, as the palate tastes food? *

בִּישִׁישִׁים חָכְמָה וְאֹרֶךְ יָמִים תְּבוּנָה: עִמּוֹ חָכְמָה וּגְבוּרָה לוֹ עֵצָה יב-יג

וּתְבוּנָה: הֵן יַהֲרוֹס וְלֹא יִבָּנֶה יִסְגֹּר עַל־אִישׁ וְלֹא יִפָּתֵחַ: הֵן יַעְצֹר בַּמַּיִם יד-טו

וְיִבָשׁוּ וִישַׁלְּחֵם וְיַהַפְכוּ אָרֶץ: עִמּוֹ עֹז וְתוּשִׁיָּה לוֹ שֹׁגֵג וּמַשְׁגֶּה: מוֹלִיךְ טז-יז

יוֹעֲצִים שׁוֹלָל וְשֹׁפְטִים יְהוֹלֵל: מוּסַר מְלָכִים פִּתֵּחַ וַיֶּאְסֹר אֵזוֹר יח

בְּמָתְנֵיהֶם: מוֹלִיךְ כֹּהֲנִים שׁוֹלָל וְאֵתָנִים יְסַלֵּף: מֵסִיר שָׂפָה לְנֶאֱמָנִים יט-כ

וְטַעַם זְקֵנִים יִקָּח: שׁוֹפֵךְ בּוּז עַל־נְדִיבִים וּמְזִיחַ אֲפִיקִים רִפָּה: מְגַלֶּה כא-כב

עֲמֻקוֹת מִנִּי־חֹשֶׁךְ וַיֹּצֵא לָאוֹר צַלְמָוֶת: מַשְׂגִּיא לַגּוֹיִם וַיְאַבְּדֵם שֹׁטֵחַ כג

לַגּוֹיִם וַיַּנְחֵם: מֵסִיר לֵב רָאשֵׁי עַם־הָאָרֶץ וַיַּתְעֵם בְּתֹהוּ לֹא־דָרֶךְ: יְמַשְׁשׁוּ־ כד-כה

חֹשֶׁךְ וְלֹא־אוֹר וַיַּתְעֵם כַּשִּׁכּוֹר: הֶן־כֹּל רָאֲתָה עֵינִי שָׁמְעָה אָזְנִי וַתָּבֶן לָהּ: **יג** א

כְּדַעְתְּכֶם יָדַעְתִּי גַם־אָנִי לֹא־נֹפֵל אָנֹכִי מִכֶּם: אוּלָם אֲנִי אֶל־שַׁדַּי אֲדַבֵּר ב-ג

וְהוֹכֵחַ אֶל־אֵל אֶחְפָּץ: וְאוּלָם אַתֶּם טֹפְלֵי־שָׁקֶר רֹפְאֵי אֱלִל כֻּלְּכֶם: מִי־ ד-ה

יִתֵּן הַחֲרֵשׁ תַּחֲרִישׁוּן וּתְהִי לָכֶם לְחָכְמָה: שִׁמְעוּ־נָא תוֹכַחְתִּי וְרִבוֹת ו

שְׂפָתַי הַקְשִׁיבוּ: הַלְאֵל תְּדַבְּרוּ עַוְלָה וְלוֹ תְּדַבְּרוּ רְמִיָּה: הֲפָנָיו תִּשָּׂאוּן ז-ח

אִם־לָאֵל תְּרִיבוּן: הֲטוֹב כִּי־יַחְקֹר אֶתְכֶם אִם־כְּהָתֵל בֶּאֱנוֹשׁ תְּהָתֵלּוּ בוֹ: ט

הוֹכֵחַ יוֹכִיחַ אֶתְכֶם אִם־בַּסֵּתֶר פָּנִים תִּשָּׂאוּן: הֲלֹא שְׂאֵתוֹ תְּבַעֵת אֶתְכֶם י-יא

וּפַחְדּוֹ יִפֹּל עֲלֵיכֶם: זִכְרֹנֵיכֶם מִשְׁלֵי־אֵפֶר לְגַבֵּי־חֹמֶר גַּבֵּיכֶם: הַחֲרִישׁוּ יב-יג

מִמֶּנִּי וַאֲדַבְּרָה־אָנִי וְיַעֲבֹר עָלַי מָה: עַל־מָה ׀ אֶשָּׂא בְשָׂרִי בְשִׁנָּי וְנַפְשִׁי יד

אָשִׂים בְּכַפִּי: הֵן יִקְטְלֵנִי °לֹא [°לוֹ ק] אֲיַחֵל אַךְ־דְּרָכַי אֶל־פָּנָיו אוֹכִיחַ: טו

גַּם־הוּא־לִי לִישׁוּעָה כִּי־לֹא לְפָנָיו חָנֵף יָבוֹא: שִׁמְעוּ שָׁמוֹעַ מִלָּתִי טז

וְאַחֲוָתִי בְּאָזְנֵיכֶם: הִנֵּה־נָא עָרַכְתִּי מִשְׁפָּט יָדַעְתִּי כִּי־אֲנִי אֶצְדָּק: מִי־הוּא יז-יח

יָרִיב עִמָּדִי כִּי־עַתָּה אַחֲרִישׁ וְאֶגְוָע: אַךְ־שְׁתַּיִם אַל־תַּעַשׂ עִמָּדִי אָז יט-כ

מִפָּנֶיךָ לֹא אֶסָּתֵר: כַּפְּךָ מֵעָלַי הַרְחַק וְאֵמָתְךָ אַל־תְּבַעֲתַנִּי: וּקְרָא וְאָנֹכִי כא-כב

אֶעֱנֶה אוֹ־אֲדַבֵּר וַהֲשִׁיבֵנִי: כַּמָּה לִי עֲוֹנוֹת וְחַטָּאוֹת פִּשְׁעִי וְחַטָּאתִי כג

הֹדִיעֵנִי: לָמָּה־פָנֶיךָ תַסְתִּיר וְתַחְשְׁבֵנִי לְאוֹיֵב לָךְ: הֶעָלֶה נִדָּף תַּעֲרוֹץ כד-כה

וְאֶת־קַשׁ יָבֵשׁ תִּרְדֹּף: כִּי־תִכְתֹּב עָלַי מְרֹרוֹת וְתוֹרִישֵׁנִי עֲוֹנוֹת נְעוּרָי: כו

וְתָשֵׂם בַּסַּד ׀ רַגְלַי וְתִשְׁמֹר כָּל־אָרְחוֹתָי עַל־שָׁרְשֵׁי רַגְלַי תִּתְחַקֶּה: כז

12:16. This refers to man who is deceived by the archdeceiver, Satan (*Rashi*); or to the innocent person who is deceived by his wily fellow (*Metzudos*).

12:18. God controls the rulers of the world: When they please Him He fastens strength and leadership about their loins, but when they incur His wrath He weakens their authority (*Rashi*).

13:9. In essence, Job told his friends, "When God assesses your deeds, He will find you guilty of lying to me. And what will you say in your defense? That you lied on His behalf? Fools! You cannot make jest of God as you would make jest of a man!" (*Rashi*).

13:10. When you stand before Him for judgment, will you excuse your lies by saying you were trying to silence

me on His behalf? (*Rashi*).

13:14. It would be unbearable for me to bite my lip and be silent; I must speak up against the injustice to me (*Rashi*).

13:15. Though his love for God is unwavering, Job is driven to defend his actions (*Rashi*).

13:16. Job is sure that his honesty will gain him God's favor. This, in addition to his many merits, will acquit him of guilt (*Metzudos*).

13:17-14:22. Once again, as in his responses to Eliphaz (7:7-21) and Bildad (9:25-10:22), Job ends his rebuttal of Zophar's argument by addressing his words directly to God.

13:22. Job calls for a direct dialogue with God: "Either

. . . and He is
all-powerful

¹² *In the aged is wisdom, and [in] length of days understanding* ¹³ *[that] with Him are wisdom and might; His are counsel and understanding.* ¹⁴ *Behold! He demolishes, and it cannot be rebuilt; He locks [the door] on a man, and it cannot be opened.* ¹⁵ *Behold! He holds back the waters, and they dry up; He sends them forth, and they overturn the land.* ¹⁶ *With Him are might and sagacity; His are the deceived one and the deceiver.* * ¹⁷ *He leads counselors to folly and makes judges irrational;* ¹⁸ *He loosens the yoke of kings, and fastens a belt about their loins;* * ¹⁹ *He leads ministers to folly, and subverts the mighty;* ²⁰ *He distorts the utterances of the trustworthy, and takes reason away from the elders;* ²¹ *He pours scorn upon nobles, and loosens the girdle of the strong;* ²² *He reveals deep mysteries from the darkness, and brings the shadow of death out into the light;* ²³ *He exalts nations and [then] destroys them; He spreads out nations and then leads them away;* ²⁴ *He removes wisdom from the leaders of common people, and causes them to wander in a pathless wasteland.* ²⁵ *They grope [in] darkness and not [in] light; He makes them stagger like a drunkard.*

13

Job lashes
out at his
friends'
empty
arguments

¹ **B**ehold, my eye has seen everything; my ear has heard and understood *it.* ² *What you know, I know, as well; I am not inferior to you.* ³ *However, I shall speak to the Almighty; I desire to argue with God.* ⁴ *But you are concocters of falsehood; worthless healers, all of you!* ⁵ *Who would grant that you fall utterly silent; that would be a wise thing for you!*

⁶ *Hear my argument, if you will, and harken to the contentions of my lips:* ⁷ *Will you speak dishonestly on God's behalf? Will you speak deceitfully for His sake?* ⁸ *Will you flatter Him? Will you contend on God's behalf?* ⁹ *Will all be well when He scrutinizes you? Will you make jest of Him as you would make jest of a man?* * ¹⁰ *He will surely admonish you! Will you venerate Him when you are in [His] private chamber?* * ¹¹ *Surely His exaltedness will terrify you; His fear will fall upon you!* ¹² *Your remembrance will be likened to ashes; your stature to lumps of clay.* ¹³ *So be silent toward me, and I shall speak; let anything [that comes] pass over me!* ¹⁴ *Why should I carry my flesh with my teeth,* * *and put my life in my hand?*

Loyalty to
God

¹⁵ *Were He to kill me, I would still yearn for Him, but I will justify my ways before Him.* * ¹⁶ *He will also be my salvation,* * *but a hypocrite will not come before Him.*

Job pleads
that God let
him speak

¹⁷ * *Hear well my words, and let my expression [be] in Your ears.* ¹⁸ *Behold, I have arranged [my] argument; I know that I will be vindicated.* ¹⁹ *Who is he that would contend with me? Were I to keep silent now, I would expire.* ²⁰ *Just do not do these two things to me, and I will not conceal myself from Your presence:* ²¹ *Remove Your hand from upon me, and let not fear of You terrify me.* ²² *Call out and I will answer; or else let me speak, and You respond.* * ²³ *How many iniquities and sins have I? Apprise me of my transgression and my sin!* ²⁴ *Why do You hide Your face* * *and consider me as an enemy unto You?*

²⁵ *Do You frighten a driven leaf, or chase dry straw,* ²⁶ *that You record re-belliousness about me and ascribe to me the sins of my youth,* ²⁷ *[that] You place my feet in fetters, scrutinize all my ways, and inscribe my very foot-*

You begin by accusing me and I'll defend myself, or
I'll begin by proving my righteousness and You refute

my claims."
13:24. From seeing my righteousness (*Rashi*).

יד כח־א וְהוּא כְּרָקָב יִבְלֶה כְּבֶגֶד אֲכָלוֹ עָשׁ: אָדָם יְלוּד אִשָּׁה קְצַר יָמִים
ב־ג וּשְׂבַע־רֹגֶז: כְּצִיץ יָצָא וַיִּמָּל וַיִּבְרַח כַּצֵּל וְלֹא יַעֲמוֹד: אַף־עַל־זֶה
ד פָּקַחְתָּ עֵינֶךָ וְאֹתִי תָבִיא בְמִשְׁפָּט עִמָּךְ: מִי־יִתֵּן טָהוֹר מִטָּמֵא לֹא אֶחָד:
ה אִם חֲרוּצִים | יָמָיו מִסְפַּר־חֳדָשָׁיו אִתָּךְ °חקו [°חֻקָּיו קׂ] עָשִׂיתָ
ו־ז וְלֹא יַעֲבוֹר: שְׁעֵה מֵעָלָיו וְיֶחְדָּל עַד־יִרְצֶה כְּשָׂכִיר יוֹמוֹ: כִּי יֵשׁ לָעֵץ
ח תִּקְוָה אִם־יִכָּרֵת וְעוֹד יַחֲלִיף וְיֹנַקְתּוֹ לֹא תֶחְדָּל: אִם־יַזְקִין בָּאָרֶץ
ט שָׁרְשׁוֹ וּבֶעָפָר יָמוּת גִּזְעוֹ: מֵרֵיחַ מַיִם יַפְרִחַ וְעָשָׂה קָצִיר כְּמוֹ־נָטַע:
י־יא וְגֶבֶר יָמוּת וַיֶּחֱלָשׁ וַיִּגְוַע אָדָם וְאַיּוֹ: אָזְלוּ־מַיִם מִנִּי־יָם וְנָהָר יֶחֱרַב
יב וְיָבֵשׁ: וְאִישׁ שָׁכַב וְלֹא־יָקוּם עַד־בִּלְתִּי שָׁמַיִם לֹא יָקִיצוּ וְלֹא־
יג יֵעֹרוּ מִשְּׁנָתָם: מִי יִתֵּן | בִּשְׁאוֹל תַּצְפִּנֵנִי תַּסְתִּירֵנִי עַד־שׁוּב אַפֶּךָ
יד תָּשִׁית לִי חֹק וְתִזְכְּרֵנִי: אִם־יָמוּת גֶּבֶר הֲיִחְיֶה כָּל־יְמֵי צְבָאִי אֲיַחֵל
טו־טז עַד־בּוֹא חֲלִיפָתִי: תִּקְרָא וְאָנֹכִי אֶעֱנֶךָּ לְמַעֲשֵׂה יָדֶיךָ תִכְסֹף: כִּי־
 עַתָּה צְעָדַי תִּסְפּוֹר לֹא־תִשְׁמוֹר עַל־חַטָּאתִי: חָתֻם בִּצְרוֹר פִּשְׁעִי
יז־יח וַתִּטְפֹּל עַל־עֲוֹנִי: וְאוּלָם הַר־נוֹפֵל יִבּוֹל וְצוּר יֶעְתַּק מִמְּקֹמוֹ | אֲבָנִים |
יט שָׁחֲקוּ מַיִם תִּשְׁטֹף־סְפִיחֶיהָ עֲפַר־אָרֶץ וְתִקְוַת אֱנוֹשׁ הֶאֱבַדְתָּ:
כ־כא תִּתְקְפֵהוּ לָנֶצַח וַיַּהֲלֹךְ מְשַׁנֶּה פָנָיו וַתְּשַׁלְּחֵהוּ: יִכְבְּדוּ בָנָיו וְלֹא
כב יֵדָע וְיִצְעֲרוּ וְלֹא־יָבִין לָמוֹ: אַךְ־בְּשָׂרוֹ עָלָיו יִכְאָב וְנַפְשׁוֹ עָלָיו
טו ח־א תֶּאֱבָל: וַיַּעַן אֱלִיפַז הַתֵּימָנִי
ב־ג וַיֹּאמַר: הֶחָכָם יַעֲנֶה דַעַת־רוּחַ וִימַלֵּא קָדִים בִּטְנוֹ: הוֹכֵחַ בְּדָבָר
ד לֹא יִסְכּוֹן וּמִלִּים לֹא־יוֹעִיל בָּם: אַף־אַתָּה תָּפֵר יִרְאָה וְתִגְרַע שִׂיחָה
ה־ו לִפְנֵי־אֵל: כִּי יְאַלֵּף עֲוֹנְךָ פִּיךָ וְתִבְחַר לְשׁוֹן עֲרוּמִים: יַרְשִׁיעֲךָ פִּיךָ
ז וְלֹא־אָנִי וּשְׂפָתֶיךָ יַעֲנוּ־בָךְ: הֲרִאישׁוֹן אָדָם תִּוָּלֵד וְלִפְנֵי גְבָעוֹת
ח־ט חוֹלָלְתָּ: הַבְסוֹד אֱלוֹהַּ תִּשְׁמָע וְתִגְרַע אֵלֶיךָ חָכְמָה: מַה־יָּדַעְתָּ
י וְלֹא נֵדָע תָּבִין וְלֹא־עִמָּנוּ הוּא: גַּם־שָׂב גַּם־יָשִׁישׁ בָּנוּ כַּבִּיר מֵאָבִיךָ
יא־יב יָמִים: הַמְעַט מִמְּךָ תַּנְחֻמוֹת אֵל וְדָבָר לָאַט עִמָּךְ: מַה־יִּקָּחֲךָ לִבֶּךָ
יג וּמַה־יִּרְזְמוּן עֵינֶיךָ: כִּי־תָשִׁיב אֶל־אֵל רוּחֶךָ וְהֹצֵאתָ מִפִּיךָ מִלִּין:

13:28. Job refers to his body (*Rashi*). He is too insignificant for such scrutiny on God's part.

14:1-4. Resuming an earlier theme, Job in essence asks, "Why do you judge so severely the sins of such a lowly creature as man?" (*Rashi*).

14:4. In light of the manner in which a human being is conceived, can he really be expected to be completely pure and free from sin? (*Rashi*).

14:5-6. Is the human condition itself not sufficient punishment for man's sins? (*Rashi*).

14:13. If it were possible to go to the grave temporarily, and then be revived at a later date (*Kara*).

14:15. Job asks again for an opportunity to plead his case with God (*Rashi*).

14:18-19. Mountains and stones can be worn into dirt from which the produce of previously dropped seeds will emerge, but when a man's end comes, nothing is left of him (*Rashi*).

15:6. Your own response to the arguments I am about to present will demonstrate how wrong you are (*Rashi*).

15:7-11. Is Job so all-knowing that he can derogate everyone so easily? Why did he not appreciate all the gifts God gave him before his fall?

15:12. The look in your eyes adds to your pronouncements of indignation (*Kara*).

steps? ²⁸ When, after all, it* will wear out like rot, like a garment that a moth has consumed!

14

Man's mortality

¹ A man,* born of woman, has a short life span, and is sated with anxiety. ² He emerges like a blossom, and is then cut down; he flees like a shadow, and does not endure. ³ Do You fix Your eyes even upon such [a being], that You bring me to judgment with You?⁴ Who can produce purity from impurity? No one!*

⁵ If His days are predetermined and the number of his months is with You, and You have made his limits which he cannot surpass, * ⁶ then turn away from him, and let [his pain] be relieved, until, like a hired hand, he craves [the end of] his day.

A felled tree grows back; man's end is final

⁷ For there is hope for a tree: [Even] if it is felled it can still renew itself, and its branching will not cease; ⁸ were its root to become old in the ground and its trunk to die in the dirt, ⁹ with [but] a whiff of water it would blossom and generate branches like a sapling. ¹⁰ But a man dies; he becomes feeble; a person perishes, and then where is he? ¹¹ [As] water flows from a sea, [as] the river becomes arid and dry, ¹² [so] a man lies down and does not rise. They do not awaken until the heavens are no more; they will not be roused from their slumber.

An afterlife for man

¹³ If only You would hide me in the pit, conceal me until Your anger subsides, set a fixed time for me, and then remember me. * ¹⁴ When a man dies, will he live [again]? Throughout the days of my life span I long [for life], until the time of my passing comes.

¹⁵ Call out, and I will answer You!* Cherish Your handiwork! ¹⁶ For now You count my steps; You have no patience for my sins. ¹⁷ My transgressions are sealed in a pouch, and You cling to my iniquity.

Irrevocable death

¹⁸ In truth, a collapsing mountain will produce grain, so too, a rock torn from its place. * ¹⁹ Stones are worn away by water, it washes them into dirt that produces its own aftergrowth; but You have destroyed man's hope. ²⁰ You overwhelm him forever, and he passes away; You change his countenance and then send him away. ²¹ Then, when his sons attain honor he will not know it; when they suffer he will not discern them. ²² He feels only the pain of his flesh, and his soul will mourn over him.

15

THE SECOND
ROUND OF
DISCUSSION
15:1-21:34

ELIPHAZ'
SECOND
SPEECH
AND JOB'S
RESPONSE
15:1-17:16

¹ Eliphaz the Temanite then spoke up and said:

² Should a wise man respond with blustery knowledge, or fill his belly with the east wind? ³ Should he argue with unavailing expressions, or with words that do no good? ⁴ So too, you have undermined awe and have diminished prayer before God.

⁵ For your sinfulness teaches your mouth; you should have chosen the language of the clever! ⁶ Let your own mouth condemn you, not I; let your own lips testify against you. *

⁷ Were you born before Adam, or created before the hills?* ⁸ Are you privy to God's council; have you diminished wisdom [from everyone else and taken it all] for yourself? ⁹ What do you know that we do not know? [What do] you understand that is beyond us? ¹⁰ Even the white-haired, even the aged are among us, more advanced in age than your father. ¹¹ Do you deem inadequate God's consolations, the bounty He had graciously granted you?

Man cannot question God

¹² What does your heart teach you; what do your eyes intimate, * ¹³ that you turn your bluster toward God and bring such words out of your mouth?

יד-טו מָה־אֱנוֹשׁ כִּי־יִזְכֶּה וְכִי־יִצְדַּק יְלוּד אִשָּׁה: הֵן °בקדשו [בִּקְדֹשָׁיו ק]

טו לֹא יַאֲמִין וְשָׁמַיִם לֹא־זַכּוּ בְעֵינָיו: אַף כִּי־נִתְעָב וְנֶאֱלָח אִישׁ־שֹׁתֶה

יז-יח כַמַּיִם עַוְלָה: אֲחַוְךָ שְׁמַע־לִי וְזֶה־חָזִיתִי וַאֲסַפֵּרָה: אֲשֶׁר־חֲכָמִים

יט יַגִּידוּ וְלֹא כִחֲדוּ מֵאֲבוֹתָם: לָהֶם לְבַדָּם נִתְּנָה הָאָרֶץ וְלֹא־עָבַר זָר

כ-כא בְּתוֹכָם: כָּל־יְמֵי רָשָׁע הוּא מִתְחוֹלֵל וּמִסְפַּר שָׁנִים נִצְפְּנוּ לֶעָרִיץ: קוֹל־

כב פְּחָדִים בְּאָזְנָיו בַּשָּׁלוֹם שׁוֹדֵד יְבוֹאֶנּוּ: לֹא־יַאֲמִין שׁוּב מִנִּי־חֹשֶׁךְ °וצפו

כג [וְצָפוּי ק] הוּא אֱלֵי־חָרֶב: נֹדֵד הוּא לַלֶּחֶם אַיֵּה יָדַע כִּי־נָכוֹן בְּיָדוֹ יוֹם־

כד-כה חֹשֶׁךְ: יְבַעֲתֻהוּ צַר וּמְצוּקָה תִּתְקְפֵהוּ כְּמֶלֶךְ עָתִיד לַכִּידוֹר: כִּי־נָטָה

כו-כז אֶל־אֵל יָדוֹ וְאֶל־שַׁדַּי יִתְגַּבָּר: יָרוּץ אֵלָיו בְּצַוָּאר בַּעֲבִי גַּבֵּי מָגִנָּיו: כִּי־

כח כִסָּה פָנָיו בְּחֶלְבּוֹ וַיַּעַשׂ פִּימָה עֲלֵי־כָסֶל: וַיִּשְׁכּוֹן עָרִים נִכְחָדוֹת בָּתִּים

כט לֹא־יֵשְׁבוּ לָמוֹ אֲשֶׁר הִתְעַתְּדוּ לְגַלִּים: לֹא־יֶעְשַׁר וְלֹא־יָקוּם חֵילוֹ וְלֹא־

ל יִטֶּה לָאָרֶץ מִנְלָם: לֹא־יָסוּר ׀ מִנִּי־חֹשֶׁךְ יֹנַקְתּוֹ תְּיַבֵּשׁ שַׁלְהָבֶת וְיָסוּר

לא-לב בְּרוּחַ פִּיו: אַל־יַאֲמֵן בַּשָּׁו נִתְעָה כִּי־שָׁוְא תִּהְיֶה תְמוּרָתוֹ: בְּלֹא־יוֹמוֹ

לג-לד תִּמָּלֵא וְכִפָּתוֹ לֹא רַעֲנָנָה: יַחְמֹס כַּגֶּפֶן בִּסְרוֹ וְיַשְׁלֵךְ כַּזַּיִת נִצָּתוֹ: כִּי־עֲדַת

לה חָנֵף גַּלְמוּד וְאֵשׁ אָכְלָה אָהֳלֵי־שֹׁחַד: הָרֹה עָמָל וְיָלֹד אָוֶן וּבִטְנָם תָּכִין

א-ב מִרְמָה: וַיַּעַן אִיּוֹב וַיֹּאמַר: שָׁמַעְתִּי כְאֵלֶּה רַבּוֹת מְנַחֲמֵי עָמָל **טז**

ג-ד כֻּלְּכֶם: הֲקֵץ לְדִבְרֵי־רוּחַ אוֹ מַה־יַּמְרִיצְךָ כִּי תַעֲנֶה: גַּם ׀ אָנֹכִי כָּכֶם

אֲדַבֵּרָה לוּ יֵשׁ נַפְשְׁכֶם תַּחַת נַפְשִׁי אַחְבִּירָה עֲלֵיכֶם בְּמִלִּים וְאָנִיעָה

ה-ו עֲלֵיכֶם בְּמוֹ רֹאשִׁי: אֲאַמִּצְכֶם בְּמוֹ־פִי וְנִיד שְׂפָתַי יַחְשֹׂךְ: אִם־אֲדַבְּרָה

ז לֹא־יֵחָשֵׂךְ כְּאֵבִי וְאַחְדְּלָה מַה־מִנִּי יַהֲלֹךְ: אַךְ־עַתָּה הֶלְאָנִי הֲשִׁמּוֹתָ

ח-ט כָּל־עֲדָתִי: וַתִּקְמְטֵנִי לְעֵד הָיָה וַיָּקָם בִּי כַחֲשִׁי בְּפָנַי יַעֲנֶה: אַפּוֹ טָרַף ׀

י וַיִּשְׂטְמֵנִי חָרַק עָלַי בְּשִׁנָּיו צָרִי יִלְטוֹשׁ עֵינָיו לִי: פָּעֲרוּ עָלַי ׀ בְּפִיהֶם

יא בְּחֶרְפָּה הִכּוּ לְחָיָי יַחַד עָלַי יִתְמַלָּאוּן: יַסְגִּירֵנִי אֵל אֶל עֲוִיל וְעַל־יְדֵי

יב רְשָׁעִים יִרְטֵנִי: שָׁלֵו הָיִיתִי ׀ וַיְפַרְפְּרֵנִי וְאָחַז בְּעָרְפִּי וַיְפַצְפְּצֵנִי וַיְקִימֵנִי לוֹ

יג לְמַטָּרָה: יָסֹבּוּ עָלַי ׀ רַבָּיו יְפַלַּח כִּלְיוֹתַי וְלֹא יַחְמוֹל יִשְׁפֹּךְ לָאָרֶץ מְרֵרָתִי:

יד-טו יִפְרְצֵנִי פֶרֶץ עַל־פְּנֵי־פָרֶץ יָרֻץ עָלַי כְּגִבּוֹר: שַׂק תָּפַרְתִּי עֲלֵי גִלְדִּי

15:19. I am referring to people who were so wise that they were given exclusive dominion over the land (*Ramban*).

15:20. Though he may prosper, the wicked person always fears heavenly punishment (*Rashi*).

15:27. That is, when he luxuriates in his ill-gotten wealth.

15:28. It appeals to the wicked man's conceit to rebuild ruined cities with his fabulous wealth (*Rashi*).

15:30. The offspring of the wicked will die prematurely (*Ramban*).

15:35. People bear "offspring" according to what they conceive. Those who do evil are responsible for their eventual punishments (*Rashi*).

16:5. If you were suffering instead of me, I would console you and stop my own complaints (*Rashi*).

16:6. Dismissing Eliphaz, Job says that his situation will not be improved by arguing or by silence. In the next verse, he turns from his friends and begins to speak of his own plight.

16:7-8. Job alternates between second and third person as he speaks to and about his pain-racked body (*Ibn Ezra*).

16:9. The Satan (*Rashi*).

16:10. Job accuses his friends of turning against him (*Metzudos*).

¹⁴ *What is a human being that he might be vindicated? Can one born of woman ever be considered righteous?* ¹⁵ *Behold, He cannot have faith even in His holy beings, and the [hosts of] heaven are not pure in His eyes,* ¹⁶ *surely it is so for the loathsome and tainted one, man, who drinks iniquity like water!*

The wicked
are doomed
to fear

¹⁷ *Let me tell you something. Listen to me. I will recount what I have seen.* ¹⁸ *Wise men say it; it was not withheld from their fathers.* ¹⁹ *To them alone the land was given; no stranger passed among them:* *

²⁰ *All the days of the wicked he is anguished,* * the number of years allotted the oppressor.* ²¹ *Sounds of terror are in his ears; when he is at peace, the robber befalls him.* ²² *He should not believe that he will return from the darkness, for he is destined for the sword.* ²³ *He wanders about for food — where is it? — he realizes that the day of darkness is ready, at hand.* ²⁴ *Distress and travail terrify him; they surround him like a king destined for the flames [of Gehinnom].* ²⁵ *For he turned his hand against God, and tried to overpower the Almighty;* ²⁶ *he charges at Him with an [upright] neck within the massive bulk of his shield.* ²⁷ *When he covers his face with his fat and forms rolls of blubber on his loins,* * ²⁸ *when he dwells in destroyed cities, in deserted houses that had been destined to become heaps,* * ²⁹ *he will not be rich, his wealth will not endure, and their aspirations will not touch the ground.* ³⁰ *He will not shake off darkness; a flame will dry up his tender branches,* * and it will be gone by the breath of His mouth.* ³¹ *He who is misled by nothingness does not believe that nothingness will be his [final] reward!* ³² *He will be stunted before his time, and his canopy will not flourish.* ³³ *He will scatter his unripe fruit like a vine, and shed his blossoms like an olive tree.* ³⁴ *For the hypocrite's clan will be forlorn, fire will consume the tents of bribery.* ³⁵ *Conceiving iniquity and bearing destruction, their belly prepares deceit.* *

... for they
dared defy
God

They and
their
offspring will
reap the
seeds they
planted

16

Job's
response to
Eliphaz

It is futile to
engage in
sterile debate

Job depicts
his plight

¹ **J**ob then spoke up and said:

² *I have heard many such things; you are all worthless consolers!* ³ *Is there an end to words of bluster? What compels you to answer?* ⁴ *I am as able to speak as you; were you in my place, I would compose words over you, and shake my head over you.* ⁵ *I would encourage you with my mouth, and the movement of my lips would stop.* * ⁶ *If I speak, my pain will not cease, and if I keep silent, what will leave me?* *

⁷ *Oh, how it* * has wearied me! You shocked my entire clan into silence!* ⁸ *You wizened me; it has become a witness [against me]. My weakened [body] has stood up against me and has given testimony to my face.* ⁹ *His anger has torn at [me]; he has despised me; he has gnashed his teeth at me; my foe* * casts barbed glances at me.* ¹⁰ *They* * opened their mouths against me; they contemptuously struck my cheeks; they joined in thronging against me.*

¹¹ *God has handed me over to an evildoer, and He consoles me through the wicked.* ¹² *I was once serene, but he broke me into pieces; he grasped me by my neck and mangled me, and he stood me up as a target.* ¹³ *His archers surrounded me; he sliced open my kidneys without mercy; he spilled my bile to the ground.* ¹⁴ *He attacked me with one attack upon another. He charged at me like a warrior.* ¹⁵ *I have sewn sackcloth for my scabs*

טז וְעַלַלְתִּי בֶעָפָר קַרְנִי: פָּנַי °חמרמרה [°חֳמַרְמְרוּ ק] מִנִּי־בֶכִי וְעַל עַפְעַפַּי
יז-יח צַלְמָוֶת: עַל לֹא־חָמָס בְּכַפָּי וּתְפִלָּתִי זַכָּה: אֶרֶץ אַל־תְּכַסִּי דָמִי וְאַל־יְהִי
יט-כ מָקוֹם לְזַעֲקָתִי: גַּם־עַתָּה הִנֵּה־בַשָּׁמַיִם עֵדִי וְשָׂהֲדִי בַּמְּרוֹמִים: מְלִיצַי רֵעָי
כא-כב אֶל־אֱלוֹהַּ דָּלְפָה עֵינִי: וְיוֹכַח לְגֶבֶר עִם־אֱלוֹהַּ וּבֶן־אָדָם לְרֵעֵהוּ: כִּי־
יז א שְׁנוֹת מִסְפָּר יֶאֱתָיוּ וְאֹרַח לֹא־אָשׁוּב אֶהֱלֹךְ: רוּחִי חֻבָּלָה יָמַי נִזְעָכוּ
ב-ג קְבָרִים לִי: אִם־לֹא הֲתֻלִים עִמָּדִי וּבְהַמְּרוֹתָם תָּלַן עֵינִי: שִׂימָה־נָּא
ד עָרְבֵנִי עִמָּךְ מִי הוּא לְיָדִי יִתָּקֵעַ: כִּי־לִבָּם צָפַנְתָּ מִּשָּׂכֶל עַל־כֵּן לֹא תְרֹמֵם
ה-ו לְחֵלֶק יַגִּיד רֵעִים וְעֵינֵי בָנָיו תִּכְלֶנָה: וְהִצִּגַנִי לִמְשֹׁל עַמִּים וְתֹפֶת לְפָנִים
ז-ח אֶהְיֶה: וַתֵּכַהּ מִכַּעַשׂ עֵינִי וִיצֻרַי כַּצֵּל כֻּלָּם: יָשֹׁמּוּ יְשָׁרִים עַל־זֹאת וְנָקִי
ט עַל־חָנֵף יִתְעֹרָר: וְיֹאחֵז צַדִּיק דַּרְכּוֹ וּטְהָר־יָדַיִם יֹסִיף אֹמֶץ: וְאוּלָם כֻּלָּם
יא תָּשֻׁבוּ וּבֹאוּ נָא וְלֹא־אֶמְצָא בָכֶם חָכָם: יָמַי עָבְרוּ זִמֹּתַי נִתְּקוּ מוֹרָשֵׁי
יב-יג לְבָבִי: לַיְלָה לְיוֹם יָשִׂימוּ אוֹר קָרוֹב מִפְּנֵי־חֹשֶׁךְ: אִם־אֲקַוֶּה שְׁאוֹל בֵּיתִי
יד בַּחֹשֶׁךְ רִפַּדְתִּי יְצוּעָי: לַשַּׁחַת קָרָאתִי אָבִי אָתָּה אִמִּי וַאֲחֹתִי לָרִמָּה:
טו-טז וְאַיֵּה אֵפוֹ תִקְוָתִי וְתִקְוָתִי מִי יְשׁוּרֶנָּה: בַּדֵּי שְׁאֹל תֵּרַדְנָה אִם־יַחַד עַל־
יח א-ב עָפָר נָחַת: וַיַּעַן בִּלְדַּד הַשֻּׁחִי וַיֹּאמַר: עַד־אָנָה ׀ תְּשִׂימוּן
ג קִנְצֵי לְמִלִּין תָּבִינוּ וְאַחַר נְדַבֵּר: מַדּוּעַ נֶחְשַׁבְנוּ כַבְּהֵמָה נִטְמִינוּ
ד-ה בְעֵינֵיכֶם: טֹרֵף נַפְשׁוֹ בְּאַפּוֹ הַלְמַעַנְךָ תֵּעָזַב אָרֶץ וְיֶעְתַּק־צוּר מִמְּקֹמוֹ: גַּם
ו אוֹר רְשָׁעִים יִדְעָךְ וְלֹא־יִגַּהּ שְׁבִיב אִשּׁוֹ: אוֹר חָשַׁךְ בְּאָהֳלוֹ וְנֵרוֹ עָלָיו
ז-ח יִדְעָךְ: יֵצְרוּ צַעֲדֵי אוֹנוֹ וְתַשְׁלִיכֵהוּ עֲצָתוֹ: כִּי־שֻׁלַּח בְּרֶשֶׁת בְּרַגְלָיו וְעַל־
ט שְׂבָכָה יִתְהַלָּךְ: יֹאחֵז בְּעָקֵב פָּח יַחֲזֵק עָלָיו צַמִּים: טָמוּן בָּאָרֶץ חַבְלוֹ
יא-יב וּמַלְכֻּדְתּוֹ עֲלֵי נָתִיב: סָבִיב בִּעֲתֻהוּ בַלָּהוֹת וֶהֱפִיצֻהוּ לְרַגְלָיו: יְהִי־רָעֵב
יג-יד אֹנוֹ וְאֵיד נָכוֹן לְצַלְעוֹ: יֹאכַל בַּדֵּי עוֹרוֹ יֹאכַל בַּדָּיו בְּכוֹר מָוֶת: יִנָּתֵק
טו מֵאָהֳלוֹ מִבְטַחוֹ וְתַצְעִדֵהוּ לְמֶלֶךְ בַּלָּהוֹת: תִּשְׁכּוֹן בְּאָהֳלוֹ מִבְּלִי־לוֹ יְזֹרֶה
טז-יז עַל־נָוֵהוּ גָפְרִית: מִתַּחַת שָׁרָשָׁיו יִבָשׁוּ וּמִמַּעַל יִמַּל קְצִירוֹ: זִכְרוֹ־אָבַד

16:17. I always prayed for the welfare of others; I never hoped that anyone else would be harmed.

16:18. Let the earth not swallow up my outcries; let them ascend directly to heaven (*Rashi*).

16:19. Despite his friends' opinion that adversity befalls only the wicked, Job is confident that God testifies to his righteousness.

17:3. Job begs God to engage in direct dialogue with him at some point, for none of his friends are coming to his aid (*Rashi*).

17:5. Job wishes this punishment on his friends (*Rashi*), measure for measure for their empty cliches to him.

17:8. And reprimand him for his empty accusations against me (*Rashi*).

17:9. With indignation against these hypocrites (*Rashi*).

17:10. Though he has expressed his disappointment in them, Job invites a response from his friends.

17:12. His friends' (*Ibn Ezra*) senseless comments kept Job awake at night as if it were day, but the daylight hours seem so short because of the intensity of his suffering at night (*Rashi*).

17:13. That is, in the grave (*Rashi*).

17:15. My wish to die (*Rashi*).

17:16. Job speaks of his limbs which are destined for the grave (*Rashi*).

18:3. Bildad addressed his colleagues, demanding that they not allow Job to cut them short, as if they were fools. They should all have their say and not let him interrupt (*Rambam*).

18:4. Addressing Job, Bildad asks sarcastically whether Job expects God ("the Rock") and the world to change as a consequence of his complaints (*Rashi*).

18:13. A person's children are his branches (*Rashi*).

18:14. That is, to Death.

and sullied my countenance with dirt. [16] My face is wrinkled from weeping; death's shadows are upon my eyelids — [17] but for no iniquity in my hands; and my prayers were virtuous. * [18] O earth, do not conceal my blood! Let there not be a place for my screams!*

Only God knows the truth

[19] Even now, my Witness is in heaven, my Attester is on high. * [20] O, my orators, my friends: It is to God that my eyes shed tears. [21] If only a man could argue with God, as a human being with his fellow! [22] For [my] allotted years will come, and then I will embark on a path from which I will never return.

17

Job contrasts God with his friends

[1] My spirit is devastated, my days have rushed by; graves await me, [2] except that these mocking men accompany me, and my eyes are constantly on their provocations. [3] Give me [Your hand], be my Guarantor!* Who then will shake my hand? [4] For You have blocked their hearts from intelligence, so You will not be exalted [by them]. [5] Glibly each talks with his fellows. May the eyes of his children look on with longing!*

He decries the hypocrites

[6] He has made me a byword for nations; I have become [the embodiment] of hell to people. [7] My eye has dimmed from anger; all my limbs have become like a shadow. [8] Let the upright be appalled at this; let the pure bestir themselves against the hypocrite. * [9] Let the righteous man hold fast to his path; let the one with clean hands strengthen himself. *

Nevertheless, he invites his friends back to the fray

[10] Nevertheless, let them all reconsider; come here, please, for I cannot find any wise man among you. * [11] My days have passed by; my thoughts, the legacies of my heart, have been cut down. [12] They turn night into day; daylight seems shortened before darkness. *

[13] Since I crave that the grave be my home, I have made my bed in the darkness;* [14] I call out to the pit, 'You are my father,' and to the maggots, 'My mother and sister!' [15] Where, then, is my hope?* Who can discern my hope? [16] Let [my] grave's limbs* descend, that they might rest together upon the dust!

18

BILDAD'S SECOND SPEECH AND JOB'S RESPONSE
18:1-19:29

[1] Bildad the Shuhite then spoke up and said:

[2] Until when? Put an end to words. [First] understand, and then we will talk. [3] Why are we considered as a beast, and obtuse in your eyes?*

[4] You who tears himself apart in his anger, will the earth be abandoned for your sake? Will the Rock be dislodged from His place?* [5] Indeed, the light of the wicked flickers out; the sparks of his fire will not shine. [6] Light becomes darkness in his tent; his lamp will flicker out in his presence. [7] His powerful strides will be constrained; his schemes will throw him down. [8] For he is sent by his own feet into a net; he walks upon a snare. [9] A trap will seize him by the heel; [blood]thirsty men will overpower him. [10] Hidden in the ground is his rope, his snare is on the path. [11] Demons terrify him on all sides, they will beat him to [the ground under] his feet.

Job's fate will be an object of astonishment

[12] His offspring will go hungry; calamity awaits his wife. [13] The Prince of Death will devour the limbs of his skin, he will devour his branches. * [14] He will be torn from his wife, who had depended on him; she will march him off to the king of demons;* [15] she will dwell in his tent without him. Sulfur will be strewn upon his home. [16] From below, his roots will dry up; and from above, his sproutings will be lopped off. [17] His memory will be lost

יח   מִנִּי־אֶרֶץ וְלֹא־שֵׁם ל֫וֹ עַל־פְּנֵי־חֽוּץ: יֶהְדְּפֻהוּ מֵא֥וֹר אֶל־חֹ֑שֶׁךְ וּֽמִתֵּבֵ֥ל

יט-כ   יְנִדֻּֽהוּ: לֹ֤א נִ֥ין ל֣וֹ וְלֹא־נֶ֣כֶד בְּעַמּ֑וֹ וְאֵ֥ין שָׂ֝רִ֗יד בִּמְגוּרָֽיו: עַל־י֭וֹמוֹ נָשַׁ֣מּוּ

כא   אַחֲרֹנִ֑ים וְ֝קַדְמֹנִ֗ים אָ֣חֲזוּ שָֽׂעַר: אַךְ־אֵ֭לֶּה מִשְׁכְּנ֣וֹת עַוָּ֑ל וְ֝זֶ֗ה מְק֣וֹם

יט   לֹא־יָדַֽע־אֵֽל: וַיַּ֥עַן אִיּ֗וֹב וַיֹּאמַֽר: עַד־אָ֭נָה תּוֹגְי֣וּן

ב-ג   נַפְשִׁ֑י וּֽתְדַכְּאוּנַ֥נִי בְמִלִּֽים: זֶ֤ה עֶ֣שֶׂר פְּ֭עָמִים תַּכְלִימ֑וּנִי לֹֽא־תֵ֝בֹ֗שׁוּ

ד-ה   תַּהְכְּרוּ־לִֽי: וְאַף־אׇמְנָ֣ם שָׁגִ֑יתִי אִ֝תִּ֗י תָּלִ֥ין מְשׁוּגָתִֽי: אִם־אׇמְנָם֮ עָלַ֢י

ו   תַּגְדִּ֥ילוּ וְתוֹכִ֖יחוּ עָלַ֣י חֶרְפָּתִֽי: דְּעֽוּ־אֵ֭פוֹ כִּֽי־אֱל֣וֹהַּ עִוְּתָ֑נִי וּ֝מְצוּד֗וֹ עָלַ֥י

ז-ח   הִקִּֽיף: הֵ֤ן אֶצְעַ֣ק חָ֭מָס וְלֹ֣א אֵעָנֶ֑ה אֲ֝שַׁוַּ֗ע וְאֵ֣ין מִשְׁפָּֽט: אׇרְחִ֣י גָ֭דַר וְלֹ֣א

ט   אֶעֱב֑וֹר וְעַ֥ל נְ֝תִיבוֹתַ֗י חֹ֣שֶׁךְ יָשִֽׂים: כְּ֭בוֹדִי מֵעָלַ֣י הִפְשִׁ֑יט וַ֝יָּ֗סַר עֲטֶ֥רֶת

י-יא   רֹאשִֽׁי: יִתְּצֵ֣נִי סָ֭בִיב וָאֵלַ֑ךְ וַיַּסַּ֥ע כָּ֝עֵ֗ץ תִּקְוָתִֽי: וַיַּ֣חַר עָלַ֣י אַפּ֑וֹ וַיַּחְשְׁבֵ֖נִי ל֥וֹ

יב-יג   כְצָרָֽיו: יַ֤חַד ׀ יָ֘בֹ֤אוּ גְדוּדָ֗יו וַיָּסֹ֣לּוּ עָלַ֣י דַּרְכָּ֑ם וַיַּחֲנ֖וּ סָבִ֣יב לְאׇהֳלִֽי: אַחַ֗י

יד-טו   מֵעָלַ֣י הִרְחִ֑יק וְ֝יֹדְעַ֗י אַךְ־זָ֥רוּ מִמֶּֽנִּי: חָדְל֣וּ קְרוֹבַ֑י וּֽמְיֻדָּעַ֥י שְׁכֵחֽוּנִי: גָּ֘רֵ֤י בֵיתִ֣י וְ֭אַמְהֹתַי לְזָ֣ר תַּחְשְׁבֻ֑נִי נׇ֝כְרִ֗י הָיִ֥יתִי בְעֵינֵיהֶֽם: לְעַבְדִּ֣י קָ֭רָאתִי

טז-יז   וְלֹ֣א יַעֲנֶ֑ה בְּמוֹ־פִ֝֗י אֶתְחַנֶּן־לֽוֹ: ר֭וּחִי זָ֣רָה לְאִשְׁתִּ֑י וְ֝חַנֹּתִ֗י לִבְנֵ֥י בִטְנִֽי:

יח-יט   גַּם־עֲ֭וִילִים מָ֣אֲסוּ בִ֑י אָ֝ק֗וּמָה וַיְדַבְּרוּ־בִֽי: תִּֽ֭עֲבוּנִי כׇּל־מְתֵ֣י סוֹדִ֑י וְזֶֽה־

כ   אָ֝הַ֗בְתִּי נֶהְפְּכוּ־בִֽי: בְּעוֹרִ֣י וּ֭בִבְשָׂרִי דָּבְקָ֣ה עַצְמִ֑י וָ֝אֶתְמַלְּטָ֗ה בְּע֣וֹר שִׁנָּֽי:

כא-כב   חׇנֻּ֬נִי חׇנֻּ֣נִי אַתֶּ֣ם רֵעָ֑י כִּ֥י יַד־אֱ֝ל֗וֹהַּ נָ֣גְעָה בִּֽי: לָ֭מָּה תִּרְדְּפֻ֣נִי כְמוֹ־אֵ֑ל

כג   וּ֝מִבְּשָׂרִ֗י לֹ֣א תִשְׂבָּֽעוּ: מִֽי־יִתֵּ֣ן אֵ֭פוֹ וְיִכָּתְב֣וּן מִלָּ֑י מִֽי־יִתֵּ֖ן בַּסֵּ֣פֶר וְיֻחָֽקוּ:

כד-כה   בְּעֵט־בַּרְזֶ֥ל וְעֹפָ֑רֶת לָ֝עַ֗ד בַּצּ֥וּר יֵחָצְבֽוּן: וַאֲנִ֣י יָ֭דַעְתִּי גֹּ֣אֲלִי חָ֑י וְ֝אַחֲר֗וֹן

כו-כז   עַל־עָפָ֥ר יָקֽוּם: וְאַחַ֣ר ע֭וֹרִי נִקְּפוּ־זֹ֑את וּ֝מִבְּשָׂרִ֗י אֶחֱזֶ֥ה אֱלֽוֹהַּ: אֲשֶׁ֤ר

כח   אֲנִ֨י ׀ אֶֽחֱזֶה־לִּ֗י וְעֵינַ֣י רָא֣וּ וְלֹא־זָ֑ר כָּל֖וּ כִלְיֹתַ֣י בְּחֵקִֽי: כִּ֣י תֹ֭אמְרוּ מַה־

כט   נִּרְדׇּף־ל֑וֹ וְשֹׁ֥רֶשׁ דָּ֝בָ֗ר נִמְצָא־בִֽי: גּ֤וּרוּ לָכֶ֨ם ׀ מִפְּנֵי־חֶ֗רֶב כִּֽי־חֵ֭מָה עֲוֺנ֣וֹת

כ   חָ֑רֶב לְמַ֖עַן תֵּדְע֣וּן °שַׁדּֽוּן° [שַׁדּֽוּן ק]: וַיַּ֗עַן

ב-ג   צֹפַ֣ר הַנַּעֲמָתִ֗י וַיֹּאמַֽר: לָ֭כֵן שְׂעִפַּ֣י יְשִׁיב֑וּנִי וּ֝בַעֲב֗וּר ח֥וּשִׁי בִֽי: מוּסַ֣ר

ד-ה   כְּלִמָּתִ֣י אֶשְׁמָ֑ע וְר֥וּחַ מִ֝בִּֽינָתִ֗י יַעֲנֵֽנִי: הֲזֹ֣את יָ֭דַעְתָּ מִנִּי־עַ֑ד מִנִּ֖י שִׂ֣ים

ו-ז   אָדָ֣ם עֲלֵי־אָֽרֶץ: כִּ֤י רִנְנַ֣ת רְ֭שָׁעִים מִקָּר֑וֹב וְשִׂמְחַ֖ת חָנֵ֣ף עֲדֵי־רָֽגַע: אִם־

ז   יַעֲלֶ֣ה לַשָּׁמַ֣יִם שִׂיא֑וֹ וְ֝רֹאשׁ֗וֹ לָעָ֥ב יַגִּֽיעַ: כְּֽגֶלְל֗וֹ לָנֶ֥צַח יֹאבֵ֑ד רֹ֝אָ֗יו יֹאמְר֥וּ

19:3. The friends had ignored Job's five speeches, and had made five of their own (*Ibn Ezra*, from *Sa'adia Gaon*).

19:4. I, not you, am suffering for my sins — so why do you humiliate me? (*Rashi*).

19:17. Job's disease made even his wife and children avoid him. Although his children were all dead (1:18-19), he referred to grandchildren as his children (*Ramban*).

19:20. Job's gums were the only areas of skin that were not inflamed (*Rashi*).

19:24. Engravers would carve words into rock with an iron tool, then fill the carvings with molten lead (*Rashi*).

19:26. Job accuses his friends of mercilessly tormenting

him with their harsh words of reproof despite the obvious suffering he is experiencing as a result of his skin inflammation. The condition of his skin testifies to God's judgment (*Rashi*).

19:28. Why don't you show me sympathy? Why don't you wonder what underlying cause could have made me deserve such suffering?

19:29. Job warns his friends that their sinful speech will surely incur God's wrath, and lead to their destruction (*Rashi*).

20:4. Are you so all-knowing that you can judge whether or not your situation is fair?

from the land; he will remain without fame abroad. [18] They will drive him from light to darkness and banish him from the inhabited world. [19] He will have neither child nor grandchild among his people, no survivor in his habitations. [20] The latter [generations] will be astounded at his fate, and the earlier [generations] will be seized by turmoil. [21] Such is [the fate] of evildoer's dwellings; such is a place that does not know God.

19

Job's response to Bildad

[1] Job then spoke up and said:

[2] Until when will you sadden my spirit and crush me with words? [3] These ten times you have humiliated me!* Are you not ashamed of acting like strangers toward me? [4] Even if I have erred, my error lodges within me. *

He protests that God has wronged him, that God treats him as an enemy

[5] Although you try to overwhelm me, by reproving me with my disgrace, [6] know that God has wronged me, for He has encircled me with His net. [7] In truth, were I to protest against unfairness I would not be answered; were I to plead there would be no justice. [8] He has fenced in my way and I cannot pass; He has set darkness upon my pathway. [9] He has stripped my honor from me and removed the crown of my head. [10] He has smashed me from all sides and I have gone away; He has uprooted my hope like a tree. [11] He has kindled His anger against me and regarded me like His foes. [12] Together His legions advance; they pave their way towards me and encamp around my tent.

He is isolated and reviled by family and friend

[13] He alienated my brothers from me; those who knew me estranged themselves from me. [14] My close ones stay away; my friends have forgotten me. [15] Those who live in my house and my maidservants regard me as a stranger; I have become an alien in their eyes. [16] I call out to my servant but he does not answer, though I beg him with my own mouth. [17] My breath is repulsive to my wife; I must ingratiate myself to my offspring. * [18] Even the youth despise me; when I rise, they talk about me. [19] All my confidants detest me, those I loved have turned against me. [20] My bones cling to my skin and flesh; I have escaped with the skin of my teeth. *

Job pleads for pity

[21] Pity me, pity me, O you, my friends, for the hand of God has afflicted me! [22] Why do you pursue me, as does God? Have you not been sated with my flesh? [23] If only my words would be written down! If only they would be inscribed in a book, [24] with an iron stylus and lead* engraved forever on rock! [25] But I know that my Redeemer lives, and that He will be the final one remaining upon the earth.

He needs no chastisement, his condition is its own rebuke

[26] After my skin [was stricken] they pierced me with this [bombast], * and I see [the judgment of] God from my flesh. [27] I see it for myself; my eyes have seen it, and not a stranger's. My kidneys have been destroyed within me. [28] Perhaps you should say, 'Why do we beleaguer him?' What is the root of the matter within me?* [29] You should fear the sword, for wrath against sin [brings] the sword, that you may know that there is punishment!*

20

ZOPHAR'S SECOND SPEECH AND JOB'S RESPONSE
20:1-21:34

[1] Zophar the Naamathite then spoke up and said:

[2] Therefore my thoughts compel me to answer, because my silence is within me. [3] I have been listening to insulting reproofs, and a spirit of my understanding prods me to answer. [4] Do you know [everything] since time began, from when Adam was placed on the earth?* [5] For the exultation of the wicked is but recent; the happiness of the hypocrite lasts but a moment. [6] Though his eminence ascends to heaven and his head touches the clouds, [7] he will perish forever like his own dung; those who had seen him will ask,

ח-ט אֵינּוּ: כַּחֲלוֹם יָעוּף וְלֹא יִמְצָאוּהוּ וְיֻדַּד כְּחֶזְיוֹן לָיְלָה: עַיִן שְׁזָפַתּוּ וְלֹא

י תוֹסִיף וְלֹא־עוֹד תְּשׁוּרֶנּוּ מְקוֹמוֹ: בָּנָיו יְרַצּוּ דַלִּים וְיָדָיו תָּשֵׁבְנָה אוֹנוֹ:

יא-יב עַצְמוֹתָיו מָלְאוּ °עֲלוּמוֹ [°עֲלוּמָיו ק] וְעִמּוֹ עַל־עָפָר תִּשְׁכָּב: אִם־

יג תַּמְתִּיק בְּפִיו רָעָה יַכְחִידֶנָּה תַּחַת לְשׁוֹנוֹ: יַחְמֹל עָלֶיהָ וְלֹא יַעַזְבֶנָּה

יד-טו וְיִמְנָעֶנָּה בְּתוֹךְ חִכּוֹ: לַחְמוֹ בְּמֵעָיו נֶהְפָּךְ מְרוֹרַת פְּתָנִים בְּקִרְבּוֹ: חַיִל

טז בָּלַע וַיְקִאֶנּוּ מִבִּטְנוֹ יוֹרִשֶׁנּוּ אֵל: רֹאשׁ־פְּתָנִים יִינָק תַּהַרְגֵהוּ לְשׁוֹן אֶפְעֶה:

יז-יח אַל־יֵרֶא בִפְלַגּוֹת נַהֲרֵי נַחֲלֵי דְּבַשׁ וְחֶמְאָה: מֵשִׁיב יָגָע וְלֹא יִבְלָע כְּחֵיל

יט-כ תְּמוּרָתוֹ וְלֹא יַעֲלֹס: כִּי־רִצַּץ עָזַב דַּלִּים בַּיִת גָּזַל וְלֹא יִבְנֵהוּ: כִּי ׀ לֹא־

כא יָדַע שָׁלֵו בְּבִטְנוֹ בַּחֲמוּדוֹ לֹא יְמַלֵּט: אֵין־שָׂרִיד לְאָכְלוֹ עַל־כֵּן לֹא־

כב-כג יָחִיל טוּבוֹ: בִּמְלֹאות שִׂפְקוֹ יֵצֶר לוֹ כָּל־יַד עָמֵל תְּבוֹאֶנּוּ: יְהִי ׀ לְמַלֵּא

כד בִטְנוֹ יְשַׁלַּח־בּוֹ חֲרוֹן אַפּוֹ וְיַמְטֵר עָלֵימוֹ בִּלְחוּמוֹ: יִבְרַח מִנֵּשֶׁק

כה בַּרְזֶל תַּחְלְפֵהוּ קֶשֶׁת נְחוּשָׁה: שָׁלַף וַיֵּצֵא מִגֵּוָה וּבָרָק מִמְּרֹרָתוֹ יַהֲלֹךְ

כו עָלָיו אֵמִים: כָּל־חֹשֶׁךְ טָמוּן לִצְפּוּנָיו תְּאָכְלֵהוּ אֵשׁ לֹא־נֻפָּח יֵרַע

כז-כח שָׂרִיד בְּאָהֳלוֹ: יְגַלּוּ שָׁמַיִם עֲוֹנוֹ וְאֶרֶץ מִתְקוֹמָמָה לוֹ: יִגֶל יְבוּל בֵּיתוֹ

כט נִגָּרוֹת בְּיוֹם אַפּוֹ: זֶה ׀ חֵלֶק־אָדָם רָשָׁע מֵאֱלֹהִים וְנַחֲלַת אִמְרוֹ

כא א-ב מֵאֵל: וַיַּעַן אִיּוֹב וַיֹּאמַר: שִׁמְעוּ

ג שָׁמוֹעַ מִלָּתִי וּתְהִי־זֹאת תַּנְחוּמֹתֵיכֶם: שָׂאוּנִי וְאָנֹכִי אֲדַבֵּר וְאַחַר

ד דַּבְּרִי תַלְעִיג: הֶאָנֹכִי לְאָדָם שִׂיחִי וְאִם־מַדּוּעַ לֹא־תִקְצַר רוּחִי:

ה-ו פְּנוּ־אֵלַי וְהָשַׁמּוּ וְשִׂימוּ יָד עַל־פֶּה: וְאִם־זָכַרְתִּי וְנִבְהָלְתִּי וְאָחַז

ז-ח בְּשָׂרִי פַּלָּצוּת: מַדּוּעַ רְשָׁעִים יִחְיוּ עָתְקוּ גַּם־גָּבְרוּ חָיִל: זַרְעָם נָכוֹן

ט לִפְנֵיהֶם עִמָּם וְצֶאֱצָאֵיהֶם לְעֵינֵיהֶם: בָּתֵּיהֶם שָׁלוֹם מִפָּחַד וְלֹא

י שֵׁבֶט אֱלוֹהַּ עֲלֵיהֶם: שׁוֹרוֹ עִבַּר וְלֹא יַגְעִל תְּפַלֵּט פָּרָתוֹ וְלֹא תְשַׁכֵּל:

יא-יב יְשַׁלְּחוּ כַצֹּאן עֲוִילֵיהֶם וְיַלְדֵיהֶם יְרַקֵּדוּן: יִשְׂאוּ כְּתֹף וְכִנּוֹר וְיִשְׂמְחוּ

יג לְקוֹל עוּגָב: °יְבַלּוּ [°יְכַלּוּ ק] בַטּוֹב יְמֵיהֶם וּבְרֶגַע שְׁאוֹל יֵחָתּוּ:

יד-טו וַיֹּאמְרוּ לָאֵל סוּר מִמֶּנּוּ וְדַעַת דְּרָכֶיךָ לֹא חָפָצְנוּ: מַה־שַׁדַּי כִּי־נַעַבְדֶנּוּ

טז וּמַה־נּוֹעִיל כִּי נִפְגַּע־בּוֹ: הֵן לֹא בְיָדָם טוּבָם עֲצַת רְשָׁעִים רָחֲקָה

יז מֶנִּי: כַּמָּה ׀ נֵר־רְשָׁעִים יִדְעָךְ וְיָבֹא עָלֵימוֹ אֵידָם חֲבָלִים יְחַלֵּק בְּאַפּוֹ:

יח-יט יִהְיוּ כְּתֶבֶן לִפְנֵי־רוּחַ וּכְמֹץ גְּנָבַתּוּ סוּפָה: אֱלוֹהַּ יִצְפֹּן־לְבָנָיו אוֹנוֹ

20:12. When he hatches one of his evil plans he "savors it in his mouth" until the time is ripe to implement it (*Rashi*).

20:17. A metaphor for the pleasures of Paradise (*Rashi*).

20:20. His constant hunger for additional wealth allowed him no tranquility (*Rashi*).

20:21. He took everything for himself and never shared of his wealth with the poor (*Rashi*).

20:26. The fire will be so fierce that it will not need to be fanned (*Kara*).

21:2. I would feel somewhat consoled if you would but listen to my words! (*Rashi*).

21:4. It is not to man, but to God, that I direct my complaint; so I have the right to expect a fair hearing (*Rashi*).

21:13. They die without any suffering (*Rashi*).

21:16. Since I do not let myself be swayed by the good fortune of the wicked, why do I suffer so? (*Rashi*).

'Where is he?' [8] He will fly away like a dream and they will not find him; he will be hustled away like a nighttime vision. [9] The eye that beheld him will not [see him] again; [the people of] his place will not observe him again.

His illegal gains will leave him

[10] His children must appease the poor, and his hands must make restitution for his robbery. [11] His power filled his youth, but it will all lie with him in the dirt. [12] When an evil [idea] becomes sweet in his mouth he hides it under his tongue. * [13] He will cherish it, never abandoning it; he will keep it inside his palate. [14] But his food will twist in his innards; the bitter venom of asps is inside him. [15] He devoured wealth, but will disgorge it; God will purge it from his gut. [16] He will suck the poison of asps; a cobra's tongue will kill him. [17] He will not see the streams, the rivers, the brooks of honey and cream. * [18] He returns [his victims'] toil and does not devour it; in exchange for his [dishonest] wealth, he will have no exultation. [19] Because he smashed the poor and laid them waste; he has stolen a house, but he did not build it. [20] Because he

His greed is his undoing

never knew tranquility in his stomach, * he will not escape with his desire. [21] There was nothing left of his food; * therefore he will not achieve his prosperity. [22] After his satiety has been gained, misfortune will strike him; the hand of all the weary will overtake him. [23] [God] will dispatch His burning

God will punish his evil

wrath against him; it will fill his stomach, He will shower His warfare upon him. [24] He may flee from weapons of iron, but a bow of brass will pierce him. [25] He has drawn [His weapon], it leaves its sheath; the flash of its bitter [terror] overwhelms him with fright. [26] Total darkness lies in wait for his hidden treasures; an unfanned fire will consume him; * misfortune will befall the survivor in his tent. [27] The heavens will reveal his sin; the land will rise up against him. [28] The produce of his house will be exiled, swept away on the day of His anger. [29] This is the wicked man's portion from God, and the legacy assigned him by God.

21 [1] Then Job spoke up and said:

Job's response to Zophar

[2] Listen carefully to my word, and let this be your consolation [for me]. * [3] Bear with me and I will speak; after I have spoken, you may mock. [4] Is my complaint directed to a man? So why should I not be impatient? * [5] Turn your attention to me and be astonished; set [your] hand on [your] mouth.

Why do the wicked deserve undiluted good fortune?

[6] When I recall [this matter] I am confounded, trembling grips my flesh: [7] Why do the wicked live, become powerful and even amass fortunes? [8] Their offspring are well-established before them, with them, and their descendants are before their eyes. [9] Their homes are peaceful, [safe] from fear; the rod of God is not against them. [10] His bull impregnates without fail; his cow gives birth and does not miscarry. [11] They send out their young ones [carefree] as sheep; their children prance about. [12] They raise [their voices] like a drum and a harp; they rejoice at the sound of the flute. [13] They spend their days with good fortune, and they descend to the grave in a moment. * [14] They said to God, "Go away from us! We have no desire to know Your ways! [15] What is the Almighty that we should serve Him? What will we gain if we pray to Him?"

Punishment should befall them, not their children

[16] Behold! Is not their good fortune in their hand? Yet the counsel of the wicked was far from me. * [17] How long! But the lamp of the wicked shall die out, and their downfall come upon them! May [God] apportion their due in His anger! [18] May they be like straw before the wind and like chaff snatched by a tempest! [19] Should God store away his affliction for his children?

כ-כא יְשַׁלֵּם אֵלָיו וְיֵדָע: יִרְאוּ °עֵינָו [°עֵינָיו ק] כִּידֹו וּמֵחֲמַת שַׁדַּי יִשְׁתֶּה: כִּי

כב מַה־חֶפְצוֹ בְּבֵיתוֹ אַחֲרָיו וּמִסְפַּר חֳדָשָׁיו חֻצָּצוּ: הַלְאֵל יְלַמֶּד־דָּעַת

כג-כד וְהוּא רָמִים יִשְׁפּוֹט: זֶה יָמוּת בְּעֶצֶם תֻּמּוֹ כֻּלּוֹ שַׁלְאֲנַן וְשָׁלֵיו: עֲטִינָיו

כה מָלְאוּ חָלָב וּמֹחַ עַצְמוֹתָיו יְשֻׁקֶּה: וְזֶה יָמוּת בְּנֶפֶשׁ מָרָה וְלֹא־אָכַל

כו-כז בַּטּוֹבָה: יַחַד עַל־עָפָר יִשְׁכָּבוּ וְרִמָּה תְּכַסֶּה עֲלֵיהֶם: הֵן יָדַעְתִּי

כח מַחְשְׁבוֹתֵיכֶם וּמְזִמּוֹת עָלַי תַּחְמֹסוּ: כִּי תֹאמְרוּ אַיֵּה בֵית־נָדִיב וְאַיֵּה

כט אֹהֶל ׀ מִשְׁכְּנוֹת רְשָׁעִים: הֲלֹא שְׁאֶלְתֶּם עוֹבְרֵי דָרֶךְ וְאֹתֹתָם לֹא

ל-לא תְנַכֵּרוּ: כִּי לְיוֹם אֵיד יֵחָשֶׂךְ רָע לְיוֹם עֲבָרוֹת יוּבָלוּ: מִי־יַגִּיד עַל־פָּנָיו

לב דַּרְכּוֹ וְהוּא־עָשָׂה מִי יְשַׁלֶּם־לוֹ: וְהוּא לִקְבָרוֹת יוּבָל וְעַל־גָּדִישׁ יִשְׁקוֹד:

לג-לד מָתְקוּ־לוֹ רִגְבֵי נָחַל וְאַחֲרָיו כָּל־אָדָם יִמְשׁוֹךְ וּלְפָנָיו אֵין מִסְפָּר: וְאֵיךְ

א תְּנַחֲמוּנִי הָבֶל וּתְשׁוּבֹתֵיכֶם נִשְׁאַר־מָעַל:

כב

ב-ג וַיַּעַן אֱלִיפַז הַתֵּמָנִי וַיֹּאמַר: הַלְאֵל יִסְכָּן־גָּבֶר כִּי־יִסְכֹּן עָלֵימוֹ מַשְׂכִּיל: הַחֵפֶץ

ד לְשַׁדַּי כִּי תִצְדָּק וְאִם־בֶּצַע כִּי־תַתֵּם דְּרָכֶיךָ: הֲמִיִּרְאָתְךָ יְכִיחֶךָ יָבוֹא

ה עִמְּךָ בַּמִּשְׁפָּט: הֲלֹא רָעָתְךָ רַבָּה וְאֵין־קֵץ לַעֲוֹנֹתֶיךָ: כִּי־תַחְבֹּל אַחֶיךָ

ז חִנָּם וּבִגְדֵי עֲרוּמִּים תַּפְשִׁיט: לֹא־מַיִם עָיֵף תַּשְׁקֶה וּמֵרָעֵב תִּמְנַע־לָחֶם:

ח-ט וְאִישׁ זְרוֹעַ לוֹ הָאָרֶץ וּנְשׂוּא פָנִים יֵשֶׁב בָּהּ: אַלְמָנוֹת שִׁלַּחְתָּ רֵיקָם

י-יא וּזְרֹעוֹת יְתֹמִים יְדֻכָּא: עַל־כֵּן סְבִיבוֹתֶיךָ פַּחִים וִיבַהֶלְךָ פַּחַד פִּתְאֹם: אוֹ־

יב חֹשֶׁךְ לֹא־תִרְאֶה וְשִׁפְעַת־מַיִם תְּכַסֶּךָּ: הֲלֹא־אֱלוֹהַּ גֹּבַהּ שָׁמָיִם וּרְאֵה

יג-יד רֹאשׁ כּוֹכָבִים כִּי־רָמּוּ: וְאָמַרְתָּ מַה־יָּדַע אֵל הַבְעַד עֲרָפֶל יִשְׁפּוֹט: עָבִים

טו סֵתֶר־לוֹ וְלֹא יִרְאֶה וְחוּג שָׁמַיִם יִתְהַלָּךְ: הַאֹרַח עוֹלָם תִּשְׁמֹר אֲשֶׁר דָּרְכוּ

טז-יז מְתֵי־אָוֶן: אֲשֶׁר־קֻמְּטוּ וְלֹא־עֵת נָהָר יוּצַק יְסוֹדָם: הָאֹמְרִים לָאֵל סוּר

יח מִמֶּנּוּ וּמַה־יִּפְעַל שַׁדַּי לָמוֹ: וְהוּא מִלֵּא בָתֵּיהֶם טוֹב וַעֲצַת רְשָׁעִים רָחֲקָה

יט-כ מֶנִּי: יִרְאוּ צַדִּיקִים וְיִשְׂמָחוּ וְנָקִי יִלְעַג־לָמוֹ: אִם־לֹא נִכְחַד קִימָנוּ וְיִתְרָם

כא-כב אָכְלָה אֵשׁ: הַסְכֶּן־נָא עִמּוֹ וּשְׁלָם בָּהֶם תְּבוֹאַתְךָ טוֹבָה: קַח־נָא מִפִּיו

כג תּוֹרָה וְשִׂים אֲמָרָיו בִּלְבָבֶךָ: אִם־תָּשׁוּב עַד־שַׁדַּי תִּבָּנֶה תַּרְחִיק עַוְלָה

כד-כה מֵאָהֳלֶךָ: וְשִׁית־עַל־עָפָר בָּצֶר וּבְצוּר נְחָלִים אוֹפִיר: וְהָיָה שַׁדַּי בְּצָרֶיךָ

21:19-21. It is not fair for the wicked to be punished through the suffering of their children; let the sinners themselves experience the suffering they deserve (*Rashi*).

21:24. A metaphor for youthfulness and the ability to provide for one's family.

21:31. Without shuddering in fear (*Rashi*).

21:33. Many men preceded him to the grave.

22:8. Should Job prevail merely because he had power and prestige? (*Rashi*).

22:12. You say that God is too lofty to bother with earthly affairs (*Rashi*).

22:16. The reference is to the wicked men of the generation of the Flood (*Rashi*).

22:20. The righteous mentioned above are encouraged that their world will survive, while the wicked will be consumed (*Ramban*).

Let Him pay it to him himself, that he should know [his punishment]! * ²⁰ Let his own eyes see his ruination, and let him drink of the Almighty's wrath! ²¹ For what is his interest in his household after he [dies], when the number of his months has been cut off?

Good and evil people fare the same

²² Can one teach knowledge to God, He Who judges the lofty? ²³ One person dies in unimpaired perfection, completely peaceful and serene, ²⁴ his breasts full of milk * and the marrow of his bones moist; ²⁵ while someone else dies with a bitter soul, not having tasted good fortune. ²⁶ Together they will lie in the dirt, and maggots will cover them.

Deceitfully, you say that only the wicked suffer

²⁷ Behold! I know your thoughts, the schemes that you wrongfully plot! ²⁸ For you say, "Where is the house of this generous one, and where is the tent of wicked people's dwellings? ²⁹ Did you not inquire of wayfarers? Do not ignore their testimonies! ³⁰ For evil is withheld until the day of calamity, until the day when [sinners] are brought to [face God's] fury. ³¹ Who is it who can be told to his face about [God's] ways, * [about all] He has done, [about] the One Who will requite his deeds? ³² He is brought to the grave, and lies forever upon a mound [of dirt]. ³³ The clumps of dirt in the valley become sweet to him; all men are drawn after him, and before him, without number. '* ³⁴ How can you console me with meaningless words? Your responses remain a betrayal!

22

THE THIRD
ROUND OF
DISCUSSION
22:1-32:1

ELIPHAZ'
THIRD
SPEECH
AND JOB'S
RESPONSE
22:1-24:25

¹ **E**liphaz the Temanite then spoke up and said:

² Does man benefit God when he learns wisdom from people? ³ Does the Almighty care if you are right, or does He gain if you perfect your ways? ⁴ Would fear of you make Him contend with you [or] enter into judgment with you? ⁵ Is your evil not great and is there is no end to your sins? ⁶ For you exacted collateral from your brethren without due cause, and stripped off the garments of the ill-clad; ⁷ you did not give drinking water to the exhausted, and you withheld bread from the hungry. ⁸ Should the land belong to a strong-armed man or should prestigious people settle in it?* ⁹ You drove away widows empty-handed and crushed the arms of orphans, ¹⁰ therefore you are surrounded by snares, and sudden fear confounds you.

Job's delusion that God is unaware

¹¹ Perhaps you cannot see [in] darkness, or a torrent of water covers you, ¹² [that you say,] 'Is not God in the heights of the heavens!' You look to the tops of the stars, which are lofty, * ¹³ and you say, 'What does God know? Can He judge through thick cloud? ¹⁴ The clouds block Him so He cannot see; He walks about in the Heavenly orbit!'

Heresy is not new

¹⁵ Will you keep the traditional path, where walked men of falsehood ¹⁶ who were cut down before [their] time, whose foundation was swept away by a river, * ¹⁷ who said to God, 'Go away from us!' and 'What can God do to them?' ¹⁸ Yet it was He Who filled their houses with bounty! But the counsel of the wicked is far from me! ¹⁹ Let the righteous see this and rejoice; let the innocent man scoff at them! ²⁰ Has not their stature been destroyed and their pride consumed by fire?!*

The best hope is repentance

²¹ Learn now to go with Him and you will stay whole; through [these words] goodness will come to you. ²² Accept guidance, if you will, from His mouth, and place His utterances in your heart. ²³ If you would return to the Almighty, you would be built up, if you would drive iniquity from your tent. ²⁴ Then you would have a stronghold on the earth, and Ophir [gold] among the rocks of the brooks. ²⁵ Your stronghold would be powerful, and you

כו וָכֶ֥סֶף תּוֹעָפֹ֖ות לָ֑ךְ: כִּי־אָ֤ז עַל־שַׁדַּ֣י תִּתְעַנָּ֑ג וְתִשָּׂ֖א אֶל־אֱל֣וֹהַּ פָּנֶֽיךָ:

כז-כח תַּעְתִּ֣יר אֵ֭לָיו וְיִשְׁמָעֶ֑ךָּ וּנְדָרֶ֥יךָ תְשַׁלֵּֽם: וְתִגְזַר־א֭וֹמֶר וְיָ֣קָם לָ֑ךְ וְעַל־דְּרָכֶ֗יךָ

כט-ל נָ֣גַהּ אֽוֹר: כִּֽי־הִ֭שְׁפִּילוּ וַתֹּ֣אמֶר גֵּוָ֑ה וְשַׁ֖ח עֵינַ֣יִם יוֹשִֽׁעַ: יְמַלֵּ֥ט אִֽי־נָקִ֑י וְ֝נִמְלַ֗ט בְּבֹ֣ר כַּפֶּֽיךָ:

כג א-ב וַיַּ֥עַן אִיּ֗וֹב וַיֹּאמַֽר: גַּם־הַ֭יּוֹם מְרִ֣י שִׂחִ֑י יָדִ֗י

ג-ד כָּ֝בְדָ֥ה עַל־אַנְחָתִֽי: מִֽי־יִתֵּ֣ן יָ֭דַעְתִּי וְאֶמְצָאֵ֑הוּ אָ֝ב֗וֹא עַד־תְּכוּנָתֽוֹ: אֶעֶרְכָ֣ה

ה לְפָנָ֣יו מִשְׁפָּ֑ט וּ֝פִ֗י אֲמַלֵּ֥א תוֹכָחֽוֹת: אֵ֭דְעָה מִלִּ֣ים יַעֲנֵ֑נִי וְ֝אָבִ֗ינָה מַה־יֹּ֥אמַר

ו-ז לִֽי: הַבְּרָב־כֹּ֭חַ יָרִ֣יב עִמָּדִ֑י לֹ֥א אַךְ־ה֝֗וּא יָשִׂ֥ם בִּֽי: שָׁ֗ם יָ֭שָׁר נוֹכָ֣ח עִמּֽוֹ

ח וַ֝אֲפַלְּטָ֗ה לָנֶ֥צַח מִשֹּׁפְטִֽי: הֵ֤ן קֶ֣דֶם אֶהֱלֹ֣ךְ וְאֵינֶ֑נּוּ וְ֝אָח֗וֹר וְלֹֽא־אָבִ֥ין לֽוֹ:

ט-י שְׂמֹ֣אול בַּעֲשׂתֹ֣ו וְלֹא־אָ֑חַז יַעְטֹ֥ף יָ֝מִ֗ין וְלֹ֣א אֶרְאֶֽה: כִּֽי־יָ֭דַע דֶּ֣רֶךְ עִמָּדִ֑י

יא-יב בְּ֝חָנַ֗נִי כַּזָּהָ֥ב אֵצֵֽא: בַּ֭אֲשֻׁרוֹ אָחֲזָ֣ה רַגְלִ֑י דַּרְכּ֖וֹ שָׁמַ֣רְתִּי וְלֹא־אָֽט: מִצְוַ֣ת

יג שְׂ֭פָתָיו וְלֹ֣א אָמִ֑ישׁ מֵ֝חֻקִּ֗י צָפַ֥נְתִּי אִמְרֵי־פִֽיו: וְה֣וּא בְ֭אֶחָד וּמִ֣י יְשִׁיבֶ֑נּוּ

יד-טו וְנַפְשׁ֖וֹ אִוְּתָ֣ה וַיָּֽעַשׂ: כִּ֭י יַשְׁלִ֣ים חֻקִּ֑י וְכָהֵ֖נָּה רַבּ֣וֹת עִמּֽוֹ: עַל־כֵּ֭ן מִפָּנָ֣יו

טז-יז אֶבָּהֵ֑ל אֶ֝תְבּוֹנֵ֗ן וְאֶפְחַ֥ד מִמֶּֽנּוּ: וְ֭אֵל הֵרַ֣ךְ לִבִּ֑י וְ֝שַׁדַּ֗י הִבְהִילָֽנִי: כִּֽי־לֹ֣א

כד א נִ֭צְמַתִּי מִפְּנֵי־חֹ֑שֶׁךְ וּ֝מִפָּנַ֗י כִּסָּה־אֹֽפֶל: מַדּ֗וּעַ מִ֭שַּׁדַּי לֹ֣א־

ב נִצְפְּנ֣וּ עִתִּ֑ים °וְידעו [°וְיֹ֥דְעָ֗יו ק] לֹא־חָ֥זוּ יָמָֽיו: גְּבֻל֥וֹת יַשִּׂ֑יגוּ עֵ֥דֶר גָּ֝זְל֗וּ

ג-ד וַיִּרְעֽוּ: חֲמ֣וֹר יְתוֹמִ֣ים יִנְהָ֑גוּ יַ֝חְבְּל֗וּ שׁ֣וֹר אַלְמָנָֽה: יַטּ֣וּ אֶבְיוֹנִ֣ים מִדָּ֑רֶךְ יַ֥חַד

ה חֻ֝בְּא֗וּ עֲנִיֵּי־אָֽרֶץ: הֵ֤ן פְּרָאִ֨ים ׀ בַּֽמִּדְבָּ֗ר יָצְא֣וּ בְּ֭פָעֳלָם מְשַׁחֲרֵ֣י לַטָּ֑רֶף

ו עֲרָבָ֥ה ל֥וֹ לֶ֝֗חֶם לַנְּעָרִֽים: בַּ֭שָּׂדֶה בְּלִיל֣וֹ °יקצירו [°יִקְצ֑וֹרוּ ק] וְכֶ֖רֶם רָשָׁ֣ע

ז-ח יְלַקֵּֽשׁוּ: עָר֣וֹם יָ֭לִינוּ מִבְּלִ֣י לְב֑וּשׁ וְאֵ֥ין כְּ֝ס֗וּת בַּקָּרָֽה: מִזֶּ֣רֶם הָרִ֣ים יִרְטָ֑בוּ

ט וּֽמִבְּלִ֥י מַ֝חְסֶ֗ה חִבְּקוּ־צֽוּר: יִ֭גְזְל֣וּ מִשֹּׁ֣ד יָת֑וֹם וְֽעַל־עָנִ֥י יַחְבֹּֽלוּ: עָר֣וֹם הִלְּכ֣וּ

י-יא בְּלִ֣י לְב֑וּשׁ וּ֝רְעֵבִ֗ים נָ֣שְׂאוּ עֹֽמֶר: בֵּין־שׁוּרֹתָ֥ם יַצְהִ֑ירוּ יְקָבִ֥ים דָּ֝רְכ֗וּ וַיִּצְמָֽאוּ:

יב מֵ֘עִ֤יר מְתִ֨ים ׀ יִנְאָ֗קוּ וְנֶֽפֶשׁ־חֲלָלִ֥ים תְּשַׁוֵּ֑עַ וֶ֝אֱל֗וֹהַּ לֹא־יָשִׂ֥ים תִּפְלָֽה:

יג הֵ֤מָּה ׀ הָיוּ֮ בְּֽמֹרְדֵ֫י־א֥וֹר לֹֽא־הִכִּ֥ירוּ דְרָכָ֑יו וְלֹ֥א יָ֝שְׁב֗וּ בִּנְתִֽיבֹתָֽיו:

יד-טו לָא֡וֹר יָ֘ק֤וּם רוֹצֵ֗חַ יִֽקְטָל־עָנִ֥י וְאֶבְי֑וֹן וּ֝בַלַּ֗יְלָה יְהִ֣י כַגַּנָּֽב: וְעֵ֤ין נֹאֵ֨ף ׀ שָׁ֤מְרָ֣ה

טז נֶ֗שֶׁף לֵאמֹר֮ לֹא־תְשׁוּרֵ֪נִי עָ֥יִן וְסֵ֖תֶר פָּנִ֣ים יָשִׂ֑ים: חָ֖תַר בַּחֹ֣שֶׁךְ בָּתִּ֑ים

22:26. You would not be embarrassed to beseech God for all your needs (*Kara*).

23:2. That is, the hand that afflicts me. Job replied, "Your attempts to console me have failed. I have suffered even more than my groans would indicate" (*Rashi*).

23:6. God will not intimidate me through His superior strength; He will hear me out and respond according to what I have done (*Ramban*).

23:13. Nothing can prevent Him from carrying out His will.

23:14. He will continue to chastise me until my full portion of punishment is complete; there have been many other such cases in the past (*Rashi*).

23:17. I was confounded because I remained alive to suffer the gloom of these disasters, instead of my life ending quickly and relatively painlessly (*Rashi*).

24:1. Job asks two questions: (a) Why are people's life spans not hidden from God? If He did not know when each person would die, He may postpone someone's punishment until he has died. (b) Why are those who are close to God not able to understand the way in which He conducts His days? (*Rashi*).

24:2. Job resumes his theme that the wicked perpetrate all sorts of crimes, yet seem to flourish, without Divine intervention.

24:5. Through robbery of wayfarers (*Rashi*).

24:11. The poor people work hard to produce oil and wine, but never enjoy it, because the wicked steal it from them (*Rashi*).

24:13. The wicked rebel against God, the Source of light.

would have an abundance of money. ²⁶ Then you would delight in the Almighty, and you would raise your face to God; * ²⁷ you would entreat Him and He would hear you, and you would fulfill your vows. ²⁸ You would utter a decree and it would be done, and light would shine upon your ways. ²⁹ When people are downtrodden you would say, 'Arise'; and He will save those with downcast eyes. ³⁰ Those who are not innocent will be saved through the pureness of your hands.

The righteous can even help the wicked

23

Job's response to Eliphaz

¹ Job then spoke up and said:

² Still today my speech is bitter; my hand* is worse than my sigh. ³ If only I knew how to find Him, I would approach His seat; ⁴ I would set out my case before Him; I would fill my mouth with arguments! ⁵ I would know what words He would answer me and I would understand what He would say to me. ⁶ Would He contend with me through superior power? No! He would only direct Himself to me. * ⁷ There [my] uprightness would be proven before Him, and I would be forever released from my Judge!

God is everywhere, but cannot be found

⁸ Behold, I go to the east, He is not there; to the west, I cannot discern Him; ⁹ though He created the north, I do not see Him [there]; He cloaked the south so I cannot see Him.

Again Job protests his innocence

But who can contend with God?

¹⁰ For He knows the way that is mine; He has scrutinized me, and I have emerged like gold. ¹¹ My feet have held fast in His footsteps; I have kept His way and have not strayed. ¹² I do not move away from the commandments of His lips; I have cherished the words of His mouth more than my sustenance. ¹³ He is unique, and who can contradict Him? His soul desires and He does!* ¹⁴ For He will complete my just allotment; and with Him are many such things. * ¹⁵ Therefore I am confounded by His presence; when I contemplate [this], I am terrified of Him. ¹⁶ God has made my heart faint; the Almighty has confounded me, ¹⁷ because I was not cut off before this darkness, and because He did not cover the blackness from before me!*

24

The cruelty and brazenness of the wicked

¹ Why could not time spans have been hidden from the Almighty. And why do those who know Him not comprehend His days?* ² People move boundary markers; they rob a flock and graze it [for themselves]. * ³ They carry off the donkey of orphans; they exact the ox of a widow as collateral. ⁴ They steer the needy off the road; together, the poor of the land go into hiding. ⁵ Behold, like wild asses in the wilderness they go out for their labor, searching for prey; the desert provides him food for his lads. * ⁶ They reap produce in the field; the wicked denude the vineyard. ⁷ They let the naked spend the night unclothed, without a garment against the cold; ⁸ they become drenched from the mountain's flow; clinging to a rock for lack of shelter. ⁹ The [wicked] tear an orphan from the breast; they take collateral from off [the backs of] the poor. ¹⁰ They let the naked go without clothing; they carry away a sheaf from the hungry. ¹¹ Between the rows [of olives] they produce oil and they trample vintages, yet they go thirsty. * ¹² From the city the populace groans and the souls of the slain cry out, but God does not lay guilt!

They are preoccupied with dishonesty and immorality

¹³ They were among those who rebel against daylight;* not recognizing His ways nor settling in His pathways. ¹⁴ At the light the murderer arises to kill the poor and destitute, and at night he acts as a thief. ¹⁵ The adulterer's eye awaits the night, saying, 'No eye will see me!' and he applies himself [to sin] in concealment. ¹⁶ In darkness burrowing into houses,

יז יוֹמָם חִתְּמוּ־לָמוֹ לֹא־יָדְעוּ אוֹר: כִּי יַחְדָּו ׀ בֹּקֶר לָמוֹ צַלְמָוֶת כִּי־יַכִּיר

יח בַּלְהוֹת צַלְמָוֶת: קַל־הוּא ׀ עַל־פְּנֵי־מַיִם תְּקֻלַּל חֶלְקָתָם בָּאָרֶץ לֹא־יִפְנֶה

יט־כ דֶּרֶךְ כְּרָמִים: צִיָּה גַם־חֹם יִגְזְלוּ מֵימֵי־שֶׁלֶג שְׁאוֹל חָטָאוּ: יִשְׁכָּחֵהוּ

כא רֶחֶם ׀ מְתָקוֹ רִמָּה עוֹד לֹא־יִזָּכֵר וַתִּשָּׁבֵר כָּעֵץ עַוְלָה: רֹעֶה עֲקָרָה

כב לֹא תֵלֵד וְאַלְמָנָה לֹא יְיֵטִיב: וּמָשַׁךְ אַבִּירִים בְּכֹחוֹ יָקוּם וְלֹא־יַאֲמִין

כג־כד בַּחַיִּין: יִתֶּן־לוֹ לָבֶטַח וְיִשָּׁעֵן וְעֵינֵיהוּ עַל־דַּרְכֵיהֶם: רוֹמּוּ מְּעַט ׀ וְאֵינֶנּוּ

כה וְהֻמְּכוּ כַּכֹּל יִקָּפְצוּן וּכְרֹאשׁ שִׁבֹּלֶת יִמָּלוּ: וְאִם־לֹא אֵפוֹ מִי יַכְזִיבֵנִי

כה א־ב וְיָשֵׂם לְאַל מִלָּתִי: וַיַּעַן בִּלְדַּד הַשֻּׁחִי וַיֹּאמַר: הַמְשֵׁל וָפַחַד

ג עִמּוֹ עֹשֶׂה שָׁלוֹם בִּמְרוֹמָיו: הֲיֵשׁ מִסְפָּר לִגְדוּדָיו וְעַל־מִי לֹא־יָקוּם

ד־ה אוֹרֵהוּ: וּמַה־יִּצְדַּק אֱנוֹשׁ עִם־אֵל וּמַה־יִּזְכֶּה יְלוּד אִשָּׁה: הֶן עַד־יָרֵחַ

ו וְלֹא יַאֲהִיל וְכוֹכָבִים לֹא־זַכּוּ בְעֵינָיו: אַף כִּי־אֱנוֹשׁ רִמָּה וּבֶן־אָדָם

כו א־ב תּוֹלֵעָה: וַיַּעַן אִיּוֹב וַיֹּאמַר: מֶה־עָזַרְתָּ לְלֹא־כֹחַ הוֹשַׁעְתָּ זְרוֹעַ

ג־ד לֹא־עֹז: מַה־יָּעַצְתָּ לְלֹא חָכְמָה וְתוּשִׁיָּה לָרֹב הוֹדָעְתָּ: אֶת־מִי הִגַּדְתָּ

ה מִלִּין וְנִשְׁמַת־מִי יָצְאָה מִמֶּךָּ: הָרְפָאִים יְחוֹלָלוּ מִתַּחַת מַיִם וְשֹׁכְנֵיהֶם:

ו־ז עָרוֹם שְׁאוֹל נֶגְדּוֹ וְאֵין כְּסוּת לָאֲבַדּוֹן: נֹטֶה צָפוֹן עַל־תֹּהוּ תֹּלֶה אֶרֶץ

ח־ט עַל־בְּלִי־מָה: צֹרֵר־מַיִם בְּעָבָיו וְלֹא־נִבְקַע עָנָן תַּחְתָּם: מְאַחֵז פְּנֵי־כִסֵּה

י פַּרְשֵׁז עָלָיו עֲנָנוֹ: חֹק־חָג עַל־פְּנֵי־מָיִם עַד־תַּכְלִית אוֹר עִם־חֹשֶׁךְ:

יא־יב עַמּוּדֵי שָׁמַיִם יְרוֹפָפוּ וְיִתְמְהוּ מִגַּעֲרָתוֹ: בְּכֹחוֹ רָגַע הַיָּם °וּבִתְבוּנָתוֹ

יג [°וּבִתְבוּנָתוֹ ק] מָחַץ רָהַב: בְּרוּחוֹ שָׁמַיִם שִׁפְרָה חֹלֲלָה יָדוֹ נָחָשׁ בָּרִיחַ:

יד הֶן־אֵלֶּה ׀ קְצוֹת °דרכו [°דְּרָכָיו ק] וּמַה־שֵּׁמֶץ דָּבָר נִשְׁמַע־בּוֹ וְרַעַם

כז א גְּבוּרוֹתָיו מִי יִתְבּוֹנָן: וַיֹּסֶף אִיּוֹב שְׂאֵת מְשָׁלוֹ

ב־ג וַיֹּאמַר: חַי־אֵל הֵסִיר מִשְׁפָּטִי וְשַׁדַּי הֵמַר נַפְשִׁי: כִּי־כָל־עוֹד נִשְׁמָתִי

ד בִי וְרוּחַ אֱלוֹהַּ בְּאַפִּי: אִם־תְּדַבֵּרְנָה שְׂפָתַי עַוְלָה וּלְשׁוֹנִי אִם־יֶהְגֶּה

ה רְמִיָּה: חָלִילָה לִּי אִם־אַצְדִּיק אֶתְכֶם עַד־אֶגְוָע לֹא־אָסִיר תֻּמָּתִי מִמֶּנִּי:

24:17. Both the adulterer and the robber dread daylight, when their victims might recognize them.

24:18. Always in flight from possible apprehension, they do not work their fields; they prefer to steal from others (*Ramban*).

24:19-20. Why should the wicked die a swift death while I, Job, must suffer?

24:24. They die like all other men, without any particularly difficult suffering (*Ramban*).

25:2. Despite God's absolute power, He rules through peace. Why, then, should you insist that He has judged you unfairly? (*Kara*).

25:5. God, at His discretion, can send clouds to block the light of the heavenly bodies from reaching earth.

25:6. Bildad does not criticize Job; he asks his suffering friend to accept human helplessness before God's might.

26:4-5. Neither the living nor the dead are stirred by your wisdom (*Ramban*).

26:7. The northern hemisphere holds the vast majority of mankind and therefore is a metaphor for the inhabited world. The stable, stationary earth is suspended in space, not resting on foundations (*Ibn Ezra*).

26:9. His celestial Throne of Glory (*Rashi*); the heavens as a whole (*Ramban*).

26:11. A poetic description of the phenomenon of thunder (*Ramban*).

26:12. At times, God causes parts of the sea to recede and become dry land (*Ramban*), thereby subduing the sea's power (*Kara*).

26:13. Identified variously as the Leviathan (*Rashi*; see 40:25-41:26); the constellation Draco (*Ibn Ezra*); or the Milky Way (*Ralbag*).

by day they seal themselves shut, they do not know daylight. [17] For both, the morning is the shadow of death for them; for they recognize the shadow of death. * [18] He glides swiftly, as on the water's surface; their portion in the land is forsaken; he does not turn to the way of the vineyards. *

Why do the wicked die a quick and easy death?

[19] As drought and heat snatch melting snow, so the grave [snatches] sinners. * [20] The womb [that bore him] will forget him; he will be sweet to maggots, nevermore to be remembered. Wickedness will be broken like a tree. [21] He oppresses the barren woman who cannot give birth; and will not benefit the widow. [22] Therefore [God] will sweep away [each of] the powerful ones with His might; he will arise one day and not believe that he will live. [23] [God] grants him security, and he relies on it, but His eyes are fixed on their ways. [24] They are exalted briefly, and then they are gone. They are crushed, like all who are swept away, * and they are snapped off like the top of a stalk.

[25] If this is not so, then who can prove me false and make my words into nothing?

25

BILDAD'S THIRD SPEECH AND JOB'S RESPONSE
25:1-26:14

[1] Bildad the Shuhite then spoke up and said:

[2] Dominion and dread are with Him; He makes peace in His heights. * [3] Is there a number for His legions? Upon whom does His light not shine? [4] How can man be considered righteous before God? How can one born of woman be considered pure? [5] Behold! the moon passed by and cast no light and the stars are not pure in His eyes, * [6] how much more so man, [who is like] a maggot, and a mortal, [who is like] a worm! *

26

Job's response to Bildad

[1] Job then spoke up and said:

[2] How have you helped the one who has no strength? How have you saved the arm that has no power? [3] What have you advised the one who has no wisdom? Yet you have dispensed counsel so liberally! [4] To whom have you told [new] words? Whose breath has gone out from you? [5] Will the dead spirits, who are underneath the water, be stirred, or those who dwell there? *

Job himself depicts God's unparalleled might

[6] The grave is naked before Him, and there is no covering for doom; [7] He spreads out the North over a void; He suspends the earth upon nothingness; * [8] He bundles water in His clouds, yet the cloud does not burst under them; [9] He put walls around the Throne; * He spread out His cloud over it; [10] He drew a boundary around the water's edge, until light and darkness come to an end. [11] The pillars of the heavens shudder and are astounded by His rebuke. * [12] With His strength He divides the ocean, and with His understanding He crushes [its] pride. * [13] By His breath the heavens were spread; His hand fashioned the [earth-]girdling serpent. *

[14] Behold, these are but the tip of His ways. What is the least we can understand about Him? Who can fathom the thunder of His mighty deeds?

27

JOB'S FIRST SOLILOQUY
27:1-28:28

[1] Job continued declaiming his parable, and said:

[2] As God lives, [I swear that] He has removed justice from me, and the Almighty has embittered my soul. [3] But as long as my soul is within me and the spirit of God is in my nostrils, [4] my lips shall not speak iniquity and my tongue shall not utter deceit. [5] Far be it from me — until I perish — to say you are right! I will not renounce my [claim of] innocence from myself!

ז־ו   בְּצִדְקָתִי הֶחֱזַקְתִּי וְלֹא אַרְפֶּהָ לֹא־יֶחֱרַף לְבָבִי מִיָּמָי: יְהִי כְרָשָׁע אֹיְבִי

ח   וּמִתְקוֹמְמִי כְעַוָּל: כִּי מַה־תִּקְוַת חָנֵף כִּי יִבְצָע כִּי יֵשֶׁל אֱלוֹהַּ נַפְשׁוֹ:

ט־י   הַצַּעֲקָתוֹ יִשְׁמַע ׀ אֵל כִּי־תָבוֹא עָלָיו צָרָה: אִם־עַל־שַׁדַּי יִתְעַנָּג יִקְרָא

יא   אֱלוֹהַּ בְּכָל־עֵת: אוֹרֶה אֶתְכֶם בְּיַד־אֵל אֲשֶׁר עִם־שַׁדַּי לֹא אֲכַחֵד:

יב־יג   הֵן־אַתֶּם כֻּלְּכֶם חֲזִיתֶם וְלָמָּה־זֶּה הֶבֶל תֶּהְבָּלוּ: זֶה ׀ חֵלֶק־אָדָם רָשָׁע ׀

יד   עִם־אֵל וְנַחֲלַת עָרִיצִים מִשַּׁדַּי יִקָּחוּ: אִם־יִרְבּוּ בָנָיו לְמוֹ־חָרֶב

טו   וְצֶאֱצָאָיו לֹא יִשְׂבְּעוּ־לָחֶם: שְׂרִידָו [שְׂרִידָיו ק] בַּמָּוֶת יִקָּבֵרוּ

טז   וְאַלְמְנֹתָיו לֹא תִבְכֶּינָה: אִם־יִצְבֹּר כֶּעָפָר כָּסֶף וְכַחֹמֶר יָכִין מַלְבּוּשׁ:

יז־יח   יָכִין וְצַדִּיק יִלְבָּשׁ וְכֶסֶף נָקִי יַחֲלֹק: בָּנָה כָעָשׁ בֵּיתוֹ וּכְסֻכָּה עָשָׂה

יט   נֹצֵר: עָשִׁיר יִשְׁכַּב וְלֹא יֵאָסֵף עֵינָיו פָּקַח וְאֵינֶנּוּ: תַּשִּׂיגֵהוּ כַמַּיִם בַּלָּהוֹת

כא־כב   לַיְלָה גְּנָבַתּוּ סוּפָה: יִשָּׂאֵהוּ קָדִים וְיֵלַךְ וִישָׂעֲרֵהוּ מִמְּקֹמוֹ: וְיַשְׁלֵךְ עָלָיו

כג   וְלֹא יַחְמֹל מִיָּדוֹ בָּרוֹחַ יִבְרָח: יִשְׂפֹּק עָלֵימוֹ כַפֵּימוֹ וְיִשְׁרֹק עָלָיו

כח א־ב   מִמְּקֹמוֹ: כִּי יֵשׁ לַכֶּסֶף מוֹצָא וּמָקוֹם לַזָּהָב יָזֹקּוּ: בַּרְזֶל מֵעָפָר יֻקָּח

ג   וְאֶבֶן יָצוּק נְחוּשָׁה: קֵץ ׀ שָׂם לַחֹשֶׁךְ וּלְכָל־תַּכְלִית הוּא חוֹקֵר אֶבֶן

ד   אֹפֶל וְצַלְמָוֶת: פָּרַץ נַחַל ׀ מֵעִם־גָּר הַנִּשְׁכָּחִים מִנִּי־רָגֶל דַּלּוּ מֵאֱנוֹשׁ

ה־ו   נָעוּ: אֶרֶץ מִמֶּנָּה יֵצֵא־לָחֶם וְתַחְתֶּיהָ נֶהְפַּךְ כְּמוֹ־אֵשׁ: מְקוֹם־סַפִּיר

ז   אֲבָנֶיהָ וְעַפְרֹת זָהָב לוֹ: נָתִיב לֹא־יְדָעוֹ עָיִט וְלֹא שְׁזָפַתּוּ עֵין אַיָּה:

ח־ט   לֹא־הִדְרִיכֻהוּ בְנֵי־שָׁחַץ לֹא־עָדָה עָלָיו שָׁחַל: בַּחַלָּמִישׁ שָׁלַח יָדוֹ

י־יא   הָפַךְ מִשֹּׁרֶשׁ הָרִים: בַּצּוּרוֹת יְאֹרִים בִּקֵּעַ וְכָל־יְקָר רָאֲתָה עֵינוֹ: מִבְּכִי

יב   נְהָרוֹת חִבֵּשׁ וְתַעֲלֻמָהּ יֹצִא אוֹר: וְהַחָכְמָה

יג   מֵאַיִן תִּמָּצֵא וְאֵי זֶה מְקוֹם בִּינָה: לֹא־יָדַע אֱנוֹשׁ עֶרְכָּהּ וְלֹא

יד־טו   תִּמָּצֵא בְּאֶרֶץ הַחַיִּים: תְּהוֹם אָמַר לֹא בִי־הִיא וְיָם אָמַר אֵין עִמָּדִי:

טו־טז   לֹא־יֻתַּן סְגוֹר תַּחְתֶּיהָ וְלֹא יִשָּׁקֵל כֶּסֶף מְחִירָהּ: לֹא־תְסֻלֶּה בְּכֶתֶם

יז   אוֹפִיר בְּשֹׁהַם יָקָר וְסַפִּיר: לֹא־יַעַרְכֶנָּה זָהָב וּזְכוֹכִית וּתְמוּרָתָהּ כְּלִי־פָז:

27:8. Knowing this, I always avoided doing evil (Rashi).

27:11. The way He conducts the world (Rashi).

27:12. You have all seen the lot of the wicked, as described in the following verses (Rashi).

27:15. There will be so many deaths that the pain of his widows will be dulled (Kara).

27:18. It is fragile and will not last.

27:19. He will be lying at death's door but will recuperate to find that his wealth is gone (Metzudos).

27:23. Clapping and whistling were gestures of astonishment over great destruction.

28:1-12. Despite the many things that God has revealed to man (vv. 1-11), He did not reveal His wisdom (Ramban).

28:4. So that "human feet" are unable to ford it (Ramban).

28:5. The once-fertile soil of Sodom (see Genesis 13:10) became sulfur and salt (Rashi, Kara).

28:10. New river channels were formed by the cataclysm.

28:11. He knows many secrets that are hidden from mankind (Kara).

28:14. Even the vastness of the oceans cannot contain God's wisdom (Kara).

He
condemns
those who
blame him

⁶ I have held fast to my righteousness and I will not release [it]; my heart has never embarrassed me. ⁷ May my enemy [be treated] like the wicked, and those who rise up against me like the iniquitous. ⁸ For what is the hypocrite's hope though he gains a profit, for surely God will cast away his soul?* ⁹ Will God heed his cry when misfortune befalls him? ¹⁰ Can he delight in the Almighty, calling on God at all times?

The futility of
the wicked

¹¹ I will teach you what is in God's hand; * I will not withhold from you that which is with the Almighty. ¹² Behold, all of you have seen it, * so why is it that you embrace folly? ¹³ This is the wicked man's portion with God, and the legacy that the brutal men will take from the Almighty: ¹⁴ If his children multiply, it is for the sword; his offspring will not be sated with food. ¹⁵ Those who survive him will be buried in death, and his widows will not weep. *

Nothing will
be left of
their wealth

¹⁶ Though he may amass money like dirt and prepare a wardrobe as [abundant as] clay, ¹⁷ he may prepare, but a righteous man will wear it, and a virtuous man will apportion his money. ¹⁸ He builds his home like [that of] a moth, * like the booth a watchman makes. ¹⁹ A rich man may be bedridden but not gathered in; * [when] he opens his eyes, it is gone. ²⁰ Fright overcomes him like flooding water; a tempest abducts him by night. ²¹ An east wind carries him and he goes away; it blows him from his place. ²² He casts misfortune upon him, and will not show mercy; from His hand he desperately flees. ²³ [People] from his place will clap their hands over him and whistle* over him.

28

**JOB'S
PAEAN TO
WISDOM**
28:1-28

God's
mastery over
earth

¹ * For there is a source for silver, and a place where gold is refined.

² Iron is taken from the soil, and copper is smelted from stone.

³ He sets a limit to the darkness, and He investigates the end of everything: the source of gloom and the shadow of death.

⁴ A river bursts forth from its normal flow, to where it is unknown to human feet; it rises and surges over people. *

⁵ There is a land where food once grew; but its place was transformed, resembling fire. *

⁶ It was a place whose stones were sapphires, and it had dust of gold; ⁷ [on] a route not known to the buzzard, [that] the vulture's eye has not seen.

⁸ Lions' whelps did not traverse it and lions did not pass over it.

⁹ [But God] stretched out His hand to the flint and overturned mountains from the root.

¹⁰ He split open river channels in the rocks. * His eye saw every precious thing.

¹¹ From the waters of the deep He fashioned rivers; He brings secret things out into the light. *

His wisdom
is
incalculable

¹² [But as for] wisdom: Where can it be found? Which is the place of understanding?

¹³ Mankind does not know its worth; it cannot be found in the land of the living.

¹⁴ The depth says, 'It is not in me!' and the sea says, 'It is not with me!'*

¹⁵ Precious gold cannot be exchanged for it and its price cannot be weighed in silver.

¹⁶ It cannot be compared to Ophir gold or to precious shoham or sapphire.

¹⁷ Gold and glass cannot approximate it, nor can its exchange be [in] golden articles.

יח-יט רָאמ֣וֹת וְ֭גָבִישׁ לֹ֣א יִזָּכֵ֑ר וּמֶ֥שֶׁךְ חָ֝כְמָ֗ה מִפְּנִינִֽים׃ לֹֽא־יַ֭עַרְכֶנָּה פִּטְדַת־

כ כּ֑וּשׁ בְּכֶ֥תֶם טָ֝ה֗וֹר לֹ֣א תְסֻלֶּֽה׃ וְֽהַחָכְמָ֗ה

כא מֵאַ֥יִן תָּב֑וֹא וְאֵ֥י זֶ֝֗ה מְק֣וֹם בִּינָֽה׃ וְֽ֭נֶעֶלְמָה מֵעֵינֵ֣י כָל־חָ֑י וּמֵע֖וֹף

כב-כג הַשָּׁמַ֣יִם נִסְתָּֽרָה׃ אֲבַדּ֣וֹן וָ֭מָוֶת אָמְר֑וּ בְּ֝אָזְנֵ֗ינוּ שָׁמַ֥עְנוּ שִׁמְעָֽהּ׃ אֱ֭לֹהִים

כד הֵבִ֣ין דַּרְכָּ֑הּ וְ֝ה֗וּא יָדַ֥ע אֶת־מְקוֹמָֽהּ׃ כִּי־ה֭וּא לִקְצוֹת־הָאָ֣רֶץ יַבִּ֑יט

כה תַּ֖חַת כָּל־הַשָּׁמַ֣יִם יִרְאֶֽה׃ לַעֲשׂ֣וֹת לָר֣וּחַ מִשְׁקָ֑ל וּ֝מַ֗יִם תִּכֵּ֥ן בְּמִדָּֽה׃

כו-כז בַּעֲשֹׂת֣וֹ לַמָּטָ֣ר חֹ֑ק וְ֝דֶ֗רֶךְ לַחֲזִ֥יז קֹלֽוֹת׃ אָ֤ז רָאָ֣הּ וַֽיְסַפְּרָ֑הּ הֱ֝כִינָ֗הּ

כח וְגַם־חֲקָרָֽהּ׃ וַיֹּ֤אמֶר ׀ לָֽאָדָ֗ם הֵ֤ן יִרְאַ֣ת אֲ֭דֹנָי הִ֣יא חָכְמָ֑ה וְס֖וּר מֵרָ֣ע

כט   א בִּינָֽה׃ וַיֹּ֣סֶף אִ֭יּוֹב שְׂאֵ֥ת מְשָׁל֗וֹ וַיֹּאמַֽר׃

ב-ג מִֽי־יִתְּנֵ֥נִי כְיַרְחֵי־קֶ֑דֶם כִּ֝ימֵ֗י אֱל֥וֹהַּ יִשְׁמְרֵֽנִי׃ בְּהִלּ֣וֹ נֵ֭רוֹ עֲלֵ֣י רֹאשִׁ֑י

ד לְ֝אוֹר֗וֹ אֵ֣לֶךְ חֹֽשֶׁךְ׃ כַּאֲשֶׁ֣ר הָ֭יִיתִי בִּימֵ֣י חׇרְפִּ֑י בְּס֥וֹד אֱ֝ל֗וֹהַּ עֲלֵ֣י אׇהֳלִֽי׃

ה-ו בְּע֣וֹד שַׁ֭דַּי עִמָּדִ֑י סְבִ֖יבוֹתַ֣י נְעָרָֽי׃ בִּרְחֹ֣ץ הֲלִיכַ֣י בְּחֵמָ֑ה וְצ֥וּר יָצ֥וּק

ז עִ֝מָּדִ֗י פַּלְגֵי־שָֽׁמֶן׃ בְּצֵ֣אתִי שַׁ֣עַר עֲלֵי־קָ֑רֶת בָּ֝רְח֗וֹב אָכִ֥ין מוֹשָׁבִֽי׃

ח-ט רָא֣וּנִי נְ֭עָרִים וְנֶחְבָּ֑אוּ וִ֝ישִׁישִׁ֗ים קָ֣מוּ עָמָֽדוּ׃ שָׂ֭רִים עָצְר֣וּ בְמִלִּ֑ים

י-יא וְ֝כַ֗ף יָשִׂ֥ימוּ לְפִיהֶֽם׃ קוֹל־נְגִידִ֥ים נֶחְבָּ֑אוּ וּ֝לְשׁוֹנָ֗ם לְחִכָּ֥ם דָּבֵֽקָה׃ כִּ֤י

יב אֹ֣זֶן שָׁ֭מְעָה וַֽתְּאַשְּׁרֵ֑נִי וְעַ֥יִן רָ֝אֲתָ֗ה וַתְּעִידֵֽנִי׃ כִּֽי־אֲ֭מַלֵּט עָנִ֣י מְשַׁוֵּ֑עַ

יג-יד וְ֝יָת֗וֹם וְֽלֹא־עֹזֵ֥ר לֽוֹ׃ בִּרְכַּ֣ת אֹ֭בֵד עָלַ֣י תָּבֹ֑א וְלֵ֖ב אַלְמָנָ֣ה אַרְנִֽן׃ צֶ֣דֶק

טו לָ֭בַשְׁתִּי וַיִּלְבָּשֵׁ֑נִי כִּֽמְעִ֥יל וְ֝צָנִ֗יף מִשְׁפָּטִֽי׃ עֵינַ֣יִם הָ֭יִיתִי לַֽעִוֵּ֑ר וְרַגְלַ֖יִם

טז-יז לַפִּסֵּ֣חַ אָֽנִי׃ אָ֣ב אָ֭נֹכִי לָֽאֶבְיוֹנִ֑ים וְרִ֖ב לֹא־יָדַ֣עְתִּי אֶחְקְרֵֽהוּ׃ וָֽאֲשַׁבְּרָ֗ה

יח מְֽתַלְּע֣וֹת עַוָּ֑ל וּ֝מִשִּׁנָּ֗יו אַשְׁלִ֥יךְ טָֽרֶף׃ וָ֭אֹמַר עִם־קִנִּ֣י אֶגְוָ֑ע וְ֝כַח֗וֹל

יט-כ אַרְבֶּ֥ה יָמִֽים׃ שׇׁרְשִׁ֣י פָת֣וּחַ אֱלֵי־מָ֑יִם וְ֝טַ֗ל יָלִ֥ין בִּקְצִירִֽי׃ כְּ֭בוֹדִי חָדָ֣שׁ

כא-כב עִמָּדִ֑י וְ֝קַשְׁתִּ֗י בְּיָדִ֥י תַחֲלִֽיף׃ לִֽי־שָׁמְע֥וּ וְיִחֵ֑לּוּ וְ֝יִדְּמ֗וּ לְמ֣וֹ עֲצָתִֽי׃ אַחֲרֵ֣י

כג דְ֭בָרִי לֹ֣א יִשְׁנ֑וּ וְ֝עָלֵ֗ימוֹ תִּטֹּ֥ף מִלָּתִֽי׃ וְיִחֲל֣וּ כַמָּטָ֣ר לִ֑י וּ֝פִיהֶ֗ם פָּ֝עֲר֗וּ

כד-כה לְמַלְקֽוֹשׁ׃ אֶשְׂחַ֣ק אֲ֭לֵהֶם לֹ֣א יַאֲמִ֑ינוּ וְא֥וֹר פָּ֝נַ֗י לֹ֣א יַפִּילֽוּן׃ אֶֽבְחַ֣ר

דַּרְכָּ֗ם וְאֵשֵׁ֥ב רֹ֑אשׁ וְ֝אֶשְׁכּ֗וֹן כְּמֶ֣לֶךְ בַּגְּד֑וּד כַּאֲשֶׁ֖ר אֲבֵלִ֣ים יְנַחֵֽם׃

28:27. God looked at wisdom.

29:7. The elders and judges would convene at the city gate (Rashi).

29:8. Job recalled how his very appearance would evoke respect and awe (Rashi).

29:11. People knew that I was honest and trustworthy.

29:21. People held me in such high esteem that they awaited my counsel and accepted it unquestioningly.

29:24. Such was their reverence for me that they would not allow themselves to develop an intimate friendship with me (Rashi).

29:25. Like mourners thirsty for words of comfort, people would gather around to drink up my words. Job recalls how greatly he was respected and how it seemed that his status could only grow ever more exalted (Metzudos).

¹⁸ *Corals and crystal cannot be considered; the pursuit of wisdom [is more precious] than pearls.*

¹⁹ *The pitdah of Cush cannot approximate it; the purest gold cannot be compared to it.*

Where can wisdom be found?

²⁰ *Wisdom: From where does it come? Which is the place of understanding?*

²¹ *It is hidden from the eyes of all living things and is concealed from the bird of the heavens.*

²² *Doom and Death say, 'With our ears we have heard of its reputation.'*

Only God can know

²³ *[Only] God understands its way, and He knows its place.*

²⁴ *For He peers to the ends of the world; He sees what is under the entire heavens,*

²⁵ *making a prescribed weight for the wind, apportioning water with a measure,*

²⁶ *when He makes a set allotment for the rain and a path for clouds of thunder.*

²⁷ *Then He looked and recorded it;* * *He prepared it and perfected it;*

Wisdom's essence is piety

²⁸ *and He said to man, 'Behold, the fear of the Lord is wisdom, and refraining from evil is understanding!'*

29 JOB'S SECOND SOLILOQUY
29:1-31:40
Longing for bygone days of comfort, of respect . . .

¹ **J**ob continued declaiming his parable, and said:

² *If only I could be as in the earlier months, as in the days when God would watch over me;* ³ *when His lamp would shine over my head, and I would walk [in] darkness by His light;* ⁴ *when I was in the days of my prime; when God's mystery was above my tent;* ⁵ *when the Almighty was still with me, with my attendants all around me;* ⁶ *when my steps were bathed in cream and the rocks would pour out pools of oil for me.* ⁷ *When I would go out to the city gate atop a platform,* * *and set my seat in the town square,* ⁸ *youths would see me and conceal themselves; the aged would rise and stand;* * ⁹ *ministers would withhold [their] words, and place [their] hand to their mouth;* ¹⁰ *the voice of leaders would be hidden, their tongue would cleave to their palate.* ¹¹ *When an ear would hear [me], it would praise me; [when] an eye would see [me], it would vouch for me.* * ¹² *For I would rescue a pauper*

. . . of righteous charity . . .

from [his] wailing and an orphan who had no one to help him. ¹³ *The blessings of the forlorn would be upon me, and I would bring joyous song to a widow's heart.* ¹⁴ *I donned righteousness, and it suited me; my justice was like a cloak and a headdress.* ¹⁵ *I was eyes to the blind and feet to the lame;* ¹⁶ *I was a father to the destitute; if I was ignorant of their grievance I would investigate;* ¹⁷ *I smashed the fangs of injustice and caused prey to be cast from its teeth.* ¹⁸ *I said [to myself], 'I will expire with my nest [intact]; I*

. . . of security . . .

will live as long as the phoenix; ¹⁹ *my roots will be open to water and dew will always dwell on my branches;* ²⁰ *my honor will always renew itself and my bow will refresh itself in my hand.'*

. . . and of prestige

²¹ *People would hear me with anticipation; await my counsel silently.* * ²² *After my word, nothing more was said; my speech would be pleasing to them.* ²³ *They would long for me as for rain, opening their mouth wide for the late rain.* ²⁴ *If I would joke with them they would not believe it; they would not let my radiant face be diminished.* * ²⁵ *I would choose their way. I would sit at the head, I would rest like a king among his troops, as one who consoles mourners.* *

ל

א וְעַתָּה ׀ שָׂחֲק֣וּ עָלַי֮ צְעִירִ֥ים מִמֶּ֗נִּי לְיָ֫מִ֥ים אֲשֶׁר־מָאַ֥סְתִּי אֲבוֹתָ֑ם לָ֝שִׁ֗ית

ב-ג עִם־כַּלְבֵ֥י צֹאנִֽי: גַּם־כֹּ֣חַ יְ֭דֵיהֶם לָ֣מָּה לִּ֑י עָ֝לֵ֗ימוֹ אָ֣בַד כָּֽלַח: בְּחֶ֥סֶר וּבְכָפָ֗ן

ד גַּֽלְמ֗וּד הַֽעֹרְקִ֥ים צִיָּ֑ה אֶ֝֗מֶשׁ שׁוֹאָ֥ה וּמְשֹׁאָֽה: הַקֹּטְפִ֣ים מַלּ֣וּחַ עֲלֵי־שִׂ֑יחַ

ה-ו וְשֹׁ֖רֶשׁ רְתָמִ֣ים לַחְמָֽם: מִן־גֵּ֥ו יְגֹרָ֑שׁוּ יָרִ֥יעוּ עָ֝לֵ֗ימוֹ כַּגַּנָּֽב: בַּעֲר֣וּץ נְחָלִ֣ים

ז-ח לִ֭שְׁכֹּן חֹרֵ֣י עָפָ֣ר וְכֵפִֽים: בֵּֽין־שִׂיחִ֥ים יִנְהָ֑קוּ תַּ֖חַת חָר֣וּל יְסֻפָּֽחוּ: בְּֽנֵי־נָ֭בָל

ט גַּם־בְּנֵ֣י בְלִי־שֵׁ֑ם נִ֝כְּא֗וּ מִן־הָאָֽרֶץ: וְ֭עַתָּה נְגִינָתָ֣ם הָיִ֑יתִי וָֽאֱהִ֖י לָהֶ֣ם לְמִלָּֽה:

יא תִּֽעֲב֣וּנִי רָ֣חֲקוּ מֶ֑נִּי וּ֝מִפָּנַ֗י לֹא־חָ֥שְׂכוּ רֹֽק: כִּֽי־°יִתְרוֹ [יִתְרִ֣י ק] פִּ֭תַּח

יב וַיְעַנֵּ֗נִי וְרֶ֥סֶן מִפָּנַ֥י שִׁלֵּֽחוּ: עַל־יָמִין֮ פִּרְחַ֪ח יָ֫ק֥וּמוּ רַגְלַ֥י שִׁלֵּ֑חוּ וַיָּסֹ֥לּוּ עָ֝לַ֗י

יג-יד אָרְח֣וֹת אֵידָֽם: נָ֭תְסוּ נְֽתִיבָתִ֗י לְהַוָּתִ֥י יֹעִ֑ילוּ לֹ֖א עֹזֵ֣ר לָֽמוֹ: כְּפֶ֣רֶץ רָחָ֣ב

טו יֶֽאֱתָ֑יוּ תַּ֥חַת שֹׁ֝אָ֗ה הִתְגַּלְגָּֽלוּ: הָהְפַּ֥ךְ עָלַ֗י בַּלָּ֫ה֥וֹת תִּרְדֹּ֣ף כָּ֭רוּחַ נְדִבָתִ֑י

טז וּ֝כְעָ֗ב עָֽבְרָ֥ה יְשֻֽׁעָתִֽי: וְעַתָּ֗ה עָ֭לַי תִּשְׁתַּפֵּ֣ךְ נַפְשִׁ֑י יֹ֭אחֲז֣וּנִי יְמֵי־עֹֽנִי: לַ֗יְלָה

יז-יח עֲ֭צָמַי נִקַּ֣ר מֵֽעָלָ֑י וְ֝עֹרְקַ֗י לֹ֣א יִשְׁכָּבֽוּן: בְּרָב־כֹּ֭חַ יִתְחַפֵּ֣שׂ לְבוּשִׁ֑י כְּפִ֖י

יט כֻתָּנְתִּ֣י יַֽאַזְרֵֽנִי: הֹרָ֥נִי לַחֹ֑מֶר וָ֝אֶתְמַשֵּׁ֗ל כֶּעָפָ֥ר וָאֵֽפֶר: אֲשַׁוַּ֣ע אֵ֭לֶיךָ וְלֹ֣א

כ-כב תַעֲנֵ֑נִי עָ֝מַ֗דְתִּי וַתִּתְבֹּ֥נֶן בִּֽי: תֵּהָפֵ֣ךְ לְאַכְזָ֣ר לִ֑י בְּעֹ֖צֶם יָדְךָ֣ תִשְׂטְמֵֽנִי: תִּשָּׂאֵ֣נִי

כג אֶל־ר֭וּחַ תַּרְכִּיבֵ֑נִי וּ֝תְמֹגְגֵ֗נִי °תֻּשִׁיָּֽה [תּוּשִׁיָּֽה ק]: כִּֽי־יָדַ֗עְתִּי מָ֥וֶת תְּשִׁיבֵ֑נִי

כד-כה וּבֵ֖ית מוֹעֵ֣ד לְכָל־חָֽי: אַ֣ךְ לֹא־בְ֭עִי יִשְׁלַח־יָ֑ד אִם־בְּ֝פִיד֗וֹ לָהֶ֥ן שֽׁוּעַ: אִם־

כו לֹ֣א בָ֭כִיתִי לִקְשֵׁה־י֑וֹם עָגְמָ֥ה נַ֝פְשִׁ֗י לָאֶבְיֽוֹן: כִּ֤י ט֣וֹב קִ֭וִּיתִי וַיָּ֣בֹא רָ֑ע

כז-כח וַאֲיַֽחֲלָ֥ה לְ֝א֗וֹר וַיָּ֥בֹא אֹֽפֶל: מֵעַ֥י רֻתְּח֥וּ וְלֹא־דָ֑מּוּ קִדְּמֻ֥נִי יְמֵי־עֹֽנִי: קֹדֵ֥ר

כט הִ֭לַּכְתִּי בְּלֹ֣א חַמָּ֑ה קַ֖מְתִּי בַקָּהָ֣ל אֲשַׁוֵּֽעַ: אָ֭ח הָיִ֣יתִי לְתַנִּ֑ים וְ֝רֵ֗עַ לִבְנ֥וֹת

ל-לא יַֽעֲנָֽה: ע֭וֹרִי שָׁחַ֣ר מֵעָלָ֑י וְעַצְמִי־חָ֝֗רָה מִנִּי־חֹֽרֶב: וַיְהִ֣י לְ֭אֵבֶל כִּנֹּרִ֑י וְ֝עֻגָבִ֗י

לא

א לְק֣וֹל בֹּכִֽים: בְּ֭רִית כָּרַ֣תִּי לְעֵינָ֑י וּמָ֥ה אֶ֝תְבּוֹנֵ֗ן עַל־בְּתוּלָֽה: וּמֶ֤ה ׀ חֵ֨לֶק

ג אֱל֣וֹהַּ מִמָּ֑עַל וְֽנַחֲלַ֥ת שַׁ֝דַּ֗י מִמְּרֹמִֽים: הֲלֹא־אֵ֥יד לְעַוָּ֑ל וְ֝נֵ֗כֶר לְפֹ֣עֲלֵי אָֽוֶן:

ד-ה הֲלֹא־ה֭וּא יִרְאֶ֣ה דְרָכָ֑י וְֽכָל־צְעָדַ֥י יִסְפּֽוֹר: אִם־הָלַ֥כְתִּי עִם־שָׁ֑וְא וַתַּ֖חַשׁ

ו-ז עַל־מִרְמָ֣ה רַגְלִֽי: יִשְׁקְלֵ֥נִי בְמֹאזְנֵי־צֶ֑דֶק וְיֵדַ֥ע אֱ֝ל֗וֹהַּ תֻּמָּתִֽי: אִ֥ם תִּטֶּ֣ה

ח אַשֻּׁרִ֗י מִנִּ֪י הַ֫דָּ֥רֶךְ וְאַחַ֣ר עֵ֭ינַי הָלַ֣ךְ לִבִּ֑י וּ֝בְכַפַּ֗י דָּ֣בַק מאוּם [מֻאֽוּם ק]: אֶ֭זְרְעָה וְאַחֵ֣ר

ט יֹאכֵ֑ל וְֽצֶאֱצָאַ֥י יְשֹׁרָֽשׁוּ: אִם־נִפְתָּ֣ה לִ֭בִּי עַל־אִשָּׁ֑ה וְעַל־פֶּ֖תַח רֵעִ֣י אָרָֽבְתִּי:

30:2. Job describes at length the lowliness of [the fathers of] these young scoffers. They did not gain the maturity and wisdom that usually come with age (*Ramban*).

30:3. Their base character made them unwelcome in the towns (see v. 5).

30:9. The lowly people Job described in such scathing terms have now become his tormentors, as he has become the degraded, scorned one.

30:11. Once God weakened me, my opponents threw off all restraint.

30:12. When I get in their way (*Rashi*).

30:17-19. Job's illness ravaged his skin, causing him extreme discomfort, forcing him to change his clothing constantly because of filth, oozing, and perspiration; and

causing him to seek relief by covering himself with clay.

30:20. To decide how to worsen my condition (*Rashi*).

30:22. A reference to God's handing over of Job's fate to the Satan (*Kara*).

30:25. Shouldn't I, who was merciful to others, deserve mercy for myself? (*Rashi*).

30:29. Jackals and owls make mournful sounds.

31:1. Job concludes his long argument. In contrast to Chapter 29 where he spoke of his prestige and his kindness to others, here he concentrates on his personal piety: "I always acted with the utmost propriety and modesty. Although I would have been permitted to marry a maiden, I still avoided immodest gazes."

31:4. Surely God is aware of my innocence (*Rashi*).

30

Knaves now
scoff at Job

Their fathers
were
degraded
people . . .

¹ *But now, they scoff at me, people younger in age than I, whose fathers I rejected from serving with my sheep dogs.* ² *Of what use was the strength of their hands to me? Their old age was utterly lost for them.* * ³ *They were lonely in privation and hunger; they would flee to the wilderness,* * *a place of darkness, destruction and desolation.* ⁴ *They would scrape moss from trees, and juniper roots would be their food.* ⁵ *They would be driven from the inside [of cities], pursued like thieves by tumultuous cries,* ⁶ *to dwell in the clefts of valleys, [in] holes [in the] dirt and rocks.* ⁷ *They would bray among the trees; huddling among the brambles.* ⁸ *Churlish people, people without names; too debased to have standing in the land.*

⁹ *But now I have become their refrain; I have become a byword for them.* * ¹⁰ *They have despised me, distanced themselves from me; have not withheld spittle from my face.* ¹¹ *[God] has loosened my bowstring and afflicted me; they have thrown off their harness from my presence.* * ¹² *On my right, youngsters rise up; they push my feet away;* * *they pave their destructive paths beside me.* ¹³ *They have repudiated my [virtuous] pathways, they have helped with my downfall — these people whom no one has ever helped.* ¹⁴ *They come as through a wide breach; they roll under the ruins.* ¹⁵ *Demons turn against me; [evil] chases away my nobility like the wind; my salvation has drifted away like a cloud.*

¹⁶ *So now my soul pours itself out upon me; my days of affliction seize me.* ¹⁷ *By night my bones are pecked from upon me and my sinews have no rest.* * ¹⁸ *Its intensity makes me change my garments; girdling me like my robe's collar.* ¹⁹ *It has taught me [to sit] in clay; I am likened to dust and ashes.* ²⁰ *I cry out to You, but You do not answer me; when I stop, You scrutinize me.* * ²¹ *You turned to be cruel to me; with the might of Your hand, You despise me.* ²² *You have cast me off to the [evil] spirits and have suppressed me [under them];* * *weakness melts me.*

. . . but not
total
destruction

But didn't
Job deserve
some mercy?

²³ *For I knew that You would bring me to Death, to the destination of all life.* ²⁴ *But let Him not stretch out His hand in total fury; though destruction is their lot, there is some relief.* ²⁵ *Did I not weep for the heavily burdened, did I not sorrow for the destitute?* * ²⁶ *I had hoped for goodness, but evil came; I had looked forward to light, but darkness came.* ²⁷ *My innards boiled and did not cease; days of oppression came toward me.* ²⁸ *I go about darkened, though not from the sun. I rise up in public and scream.* ²⁹ *I have become a brother to jackals, a friend to owls.* * ³⁰ *My skin has become blackened upon me, and my bones have dried out from heat.* ³¹ *My harp has turned for mourning, my flute to the sound of weepers.*

31

¹ I *forged a covenant for my eyes, and I would not gaze at a maiden.* * ² *Why, then, is [this my] portion from God above and the legacy of the Almighty from on high?* ³ *Behold, calamity is for a perverse person; disaster for those who commit iniquity.* ⁴ *Does He not see my ways and count all my footsteps,* * ⁵ *whether I went with falsehood or if my feet hurried to deceit?* ⁶ *Let Him weigh me in the scales of righteousness; then God would know of my integrity.*

⁷ *If my steps [ever] veered from the [proper] way or if my heart [ever] went after my eyes, or if anything [ever] clung to my hand,* ⁸ *then may I sow and let another eat, and may my produce be uprooted!* ⁹ *If my heart was [ever] seduced over a woman, or if I ever lay in wait at my neighbor's*

יא־יא תִּטְחַ֣ן לְאַחֵ֣ר אִשְׁתִּ֑י וְ֝עָלֶ֗יהָ יִכְרְע֥וּן אֲחֵרִֽין: כִּי־°ה֣וּא [°הִ֣יא ק] זִמָּ֑ה °וְהִיא [°וְה֣וּא ק] עָוֺ֣ן פְּלִילִֽים: כִּ֤י אֵ֣שׁ הִ֭יא עַד־אֲבַדּ֣וֹן תֹּאכֵ֑ל וּֽבְכׇל־תְּב֖וּאָתִ֣י

יב תְשָׁרֵֽשׁ: אִם־אֶמְאַ֗ס מִשְׁפַּ֣ט עַ֭בְדִּי וַאֲמָתִ֑י בְּ֝רִבָ֗ם עִמָּדִֽי: וּמָ֣ה אֶֽעֱשֶׂה֮ כִּֽי־

יג־יד יָק֣וּם אֵ֑ל וְכִֽי־יִ֝פְקֹ֗ד מָ֣ה אֲשִׁיבֶֽנּוּ: הֲֽלֹא־בַ֭בֶּטֶן עֹשֵׂ֣נִי עָשָׂ֑הוּ וַ֝יְכֻנֶ֗נּוּ בָּרֶ֥חֶם

טו־טז אֶחָֽד: אִם־אֶ֭מְנַע מֵחֵ֣פֶץ דַּלִּ֑ים וְעֵינֵ֖י אַלְמָנָ֣ה אֲכַלֶּֽה: וְאֹכַ֣ל פִּתִּ֣י לְבַדִּ֑י וְלֹא־

יז־יח אָכַ֖ל יָת֣וֹם מִמֶּֽנָּה: כִּ֣י מִ֭נְּעוּרַי גְּדֵלַ֣נִי כְאָ֑ב וּמִבֶּ֖טֶן אִמִּ֣י אַנְחֶֽנָּה: אִם־אֶרְאֶ֣ה

יט־כ א֭וֹבֵד מִבְּלִ֣י לְב֑וּשׁ וְאֵ֥ין כְּ֝ס֗וּת לָֽאֶבְיֽוֹן: אִם־לֹ֣א בֵרְכ֣וּנִי °חֲלָצָ֑ו [°חֲלָצָֽיו ק]

כא וּמִגֵּ֥ז כְּ֝בָשַׂ֗י יִתְחַמָּֽם: אִם־הֲנִיפ֣וֹתִי עַל־יָת֣וֹם יָדִ֑י כִּֽי־אֶרְאֶ֥ה בַ֝שַּׁ֗עַר

כב־כג עֶזְרָתִֽי: כְּ֭תֵפִי מִשִּׁכְמָ֣ה תִפּ֑וֹל וְ֝אֶזְרֹעִ֗י מִקָּנָ֥ה תִשָּׁבֵֽר: כִּ֤י פַ֣חַד אֵ֭לַי אֵ֣יד אֵ֑ל

כד וּ֝מִשְּׂאֵת֗וֹ לֹ֣א אוּכָֽל: אִם־שַׂ֣מְתִּי זָהָ֣ב כִּסְלִ֑י וְ֝לַכֶּ֗תֶם אָמַ֥רְתִּי מִבְטַחִֽי: אִם־

כה־כו אֶ֭שְׂמַח כִּי־רַ֣ב חֵילִ֑י וְכִֽי־כַ֝בִּ֗יר מָצְאָ֥ה יָדִֽי: אִם־אֶרְאֶ֣ה א֭וֹר כִּ֣י יָהֵ֑ל וְ֝יָרֵ֗חַ

כז־כח יָקָ֣ר הֹלֵֽךְ: וַיִּ֣פְתְּ בַּסֵּ֣תֶר לִבִּ֑י וַתִּשַּׁ֖ק יָדִ֣י לְפִֽי: גַּם־ה֭וּא עָוֺ֣ן פְּלִילִ֑י כִּֽי־כִחַ֖שְׁתִּי

כט לָאֵ֣ל מִמָּֽעַל: אִם־אֶ֭שְׂמַח בְּפִ֣יד מְשַׂנְאִ֑י וְ֝הִֽתְעֹרַ֗רְתִּי כִּֽי־מְצָ֥א֥וֹ רָֽע: וְלֹא־

ל־לא נָתַ֣תִּי לַחֲטֹ֣א חִכִּ֑י לִשְׁאֹ֖ל בְּאָלָ֣ה נַפְשֽׁוֹ: אִם־לֹ֣א אָ֭מְרוּ מְתֵ֣י אׇהֳלִ֑י מִֽי־יִתֵּ֥ן

לב מִ֝בְּשָׂר֗וֹ לֹ֣א נִשְׂבָּֽע: בַּ֭חוּץ לֹא־יָלִ֣ין גֵּ֑ר דְּ֝לָתַ֗י לָאֹ֥רַח אֶפְתָּֽח: אִם־כִּסִּ֣יתִי

לג־לד כְאָדָ֣ם פְּשָׁעָ֑י לִטְמ֖וֹן בְּחֻבִּ֣י עֲוֺנִֽי: כִּ֤י אֶ֘עֱר֤וֹץ ׀ הָמ֣וֹן רַבָּ֗ה וּבוּז־מִשְׁפָּח֥וֹת

לה יְ֭חִתֵּנִי וָ֝אֶדֹּ֗ם לֹא־אֵ֣צֵא פָֽתַח: מִ֤י יִתֶּן־לִ֨י ׀ שֹׁמֵ֬עַֽ לִ֗י הֶן־תָּ֭וִֽי שַׁדַּ֣י יַעֲנֵ֑נִי וְסֵ֥פֶר

לו כָּ֝תַ֗ב אִ֣ישׁ רִיבִֽי: אִם־לֹ֣א עַל־שִׁ֭כְמִי אֶשָּׂאֶ֑נּוּ אֶֽעֶנְדֶ֖נּוּ עֲטָר֣וֹת לִֽי: מִסְפַּ֣ר

לז־לח צְ֭עָדַי אַגִּידֶ֑נּוּ כְּמוֹ־נָ֝גִ֗יד אֲקׇרֲבֶֽנּוּ: אִם־עָ֭לַי אַדְמָתִ֣י תִזְעָ֑ק וְ֝יַ֗חַד תְּלָמֶ֥יהָ

לט־מ יִבְכָּיֽוּן: אִם־כֹּ֭חָהּ אָכַ֣לְתִּי בְלִי־כָ֑סֶף וְנֶ֖פֶשׁ בְּעָלֶ֣יהָ הִפָּֽחְתִּי: תַּ֤חַת חִטָּ֨ה ׀

יֵ֘צֵ֤א ח֗וֹחַ וְתַֽחַת־שְׂעֹרָ֥ה בׇאְשָׁ֑ה תַּ֝֗מּוּ דִּבְרֵ֥י אִיּֽוֹב:

לב

א וַֽיִּשְׁבְּת֡וּ שְׁלֹ֤שֶׁת הָאֲנָשִׁ֣ים הָ֭אֵלֶּה מֵעֲנ֣וֹת אֶת־אִיּ֑וֹב כִּ֤י ה֖וּא צַדִּ֣יק

ב בְּעֵינָֽיו: וַיִּ֤חַר אַ֨ף ׀ אֱלִיה֣וּא בֶן־בַּרַכְאֵ֣ל הַבּוּזִי֮ מִמִּשְׁפַּ֢חַ֫ת

רָ֥ם בְּאִיּ֗וֹב חָרָ֣ה אַפּ֑וֹ עַֽל־צַדְּק֥וֹ נַ֝פְשׁ֗וֹ מֵאֱלֹהִֽים: וּבִשְׁלֹ֤שֶׁת רֵעָ֨יו ׀ חָ֘רָ֤ה

ג־ד אַפּ֗וֹ עַ֤ל אֲשֶׁ֣ר לֹא־מָצְא֣וּ מַעֲנֶ֑ה וַ֝יַּרְשִׁ֗יעוּ אֶת־אִיּֽוֹב: וֶֽאֱלִיה֗וּ חִכָּ֣ה

ה אֶת־אִ֭יּוֹב בִּדְבָרִ֑ים כִּ֤י זְֽקֵנִ֖ים הֵ֣מָּה מִמֶּ֣נּוּ לְיָמִֽים: וַיַּ֤רְא אֱלִיה֗וּא כִּ֤י אֵ֤ין

31:9-10. Job says that if he had ever engaged in immoral conduct, then he would deserve to have his wife be disloyal to him.

31:15. God made both me and my servant (v. 13); we are both entitled to dignity and justice.

31:18. The trait of being charitable has guided me through life like a father leading and training his son.

31:21. Did I ever take advantage of an orphan, even if the court at the gate would have ruled that I was justified? (*Metzudos*).

31:25. I never flaunted my wealth in the presence of the poor (*Rashi*).

31:26-27. I never deified the sun and moon, secretly attributing my wealth to them (*Ramban*).

31:31. My household was furious with me for the extent of my hospitality to all passersby, because my servants were forced to work hard to provide hospitality (*Rashi*).

31:35-37. Let my worst enemy write a book with all the accusations against me. So confident am I of my innocence that I would proudly display the book publicly.

31:37. I would honor my antagonist like a prince, hiding nothing from him, because I know he will find nothing negative to write (*Ralbag*).

31:38-39. If I did not pay my laborers (*Kara*), or if I did not give my sharecroppers their rightful portion of the yield (*Rashi*).

door,* ¹⁰ then may my wife grind for another man, and may strangers kneel over her! ¹¹ For that is licentiousness; that is an iniquity for the judges [to punish]! ¹² For it is a fire; it consumes unto doom, and it would uproot all my produce.

¹³ If I ever spurned justice for my servants and maidservants when they contended with me, ¹⁴ then what could I do when God would rise up? When He would attend to me, what could I answer Him? ¹⁵ Did not the One Who made me in the belly make him too?* Was it not the One Who prepared us in the womb? ¹⁶ Never did I withhold the needs of the destitute, nor did I let a widow's eyes long in vain, ¹⁷ nor did I eat my bread in solitude, so that an orphan could not eat from it. ¹⁸ For it* raised me since my youth as [if it were] a father, and I have practiced it from my mother's womb. ¹⁹ Did I ever see a forlorn person without a garment, or was there ever a destitute person without clothing, ²⁰ whose loins would not bless me, who would [not] warm himself by the shearings of my sheep? ²¹ If I ever raised my hand against an orphan, though I saw that I would be supported at the gate,* ²² then let my shoulder fall from [its] blade and let my forearm be broken off from [my] upper arm. ²³ For the fear of God's punishment was upon me, and I could not bear His burden. ²⁴ If I ever put my trust in gold, or ever said of jewels, '[This] is my security!'; ²⁵ if I ever rejoiced because my wealth was great or that my hand had attained much;* ²⁶ if I ever saw the sun as it shone or the moon as growing glorious ²⁷ and my heart was seduced in secret, my hand pressed against my lips* — ²⁸ that would also be an iniquity for a judge [to punish], for I would have denied the God above. ²⁹ Or, if I ever rejoiced at the downfall of my enemy or enthused when misfortune befell him, ³⁰ for I did not let my palate sin, to request his life with a curse. ³¹ Or, if the people of my household did not say, 'If only we could get his flesh, we would never be sated!'* ³² No sojourner ever slept outside; I opened my doors to the street. ³³ Or, if I ever covered my sins as man does, hiding my transgression in my heart. ³⁴ For I used to strike a great multitude with awe, but [now] the basest of families frightens me; I am silenced, unable to go out the door.

³⁵ Who will grant that someone would hear me; my desire is for the Almighty to answer me! Let whoever contends with me write a book* — ³⁶ I would carry it on my shoulder, bind it as crowns upon myself! ³⁷ I would tell him the number of my steps; I would draw him close to me like a prince.* ³⁸ If my land would shout out against me* or its furrows would weep in unison, ³⁹ if I have ever eaten its yield without payment or embittered the soul of its owner — ⁴⁰ then in place of wheat may thorns emerge, and in place of barley, weeds.

Job's words have ended.

32

¹ These three men then stopped responding to Job, for [they saw that] he was righteous in his own eyes.

² The wrath of Elihu son of Barachel the Buzite of the family of Ram flared up: His wrath flared up against Job for judging himself more righteous than God; ³ and his wrath flared up against his three friends because they had not found a proper response and had condemned Job. ⁴ Elihu waited before addressing Job, for they were older in years than he. ⁵ But when Elihu saw that there was no

Margin notes:

"I always treated people respectfully."

"I was always charitable."

"I never trusted in wealth or in idols."

"I never neglected others."

"But now I have fallen so low!"

No one can challenge Job's rectitude

Job's friends give up

ELIHU THE BUZITE
32:2-37:24

וַיַּעַן ׀ אֱלִיהוּא בֶן־ מַעֲנֶה בְּפִי שְׁלֹשֶׁת הָאֲנָשִׁים וַיִּחַר אַפּוֹ: ו

בַּרַכְאֵל הַבּוּזִי וַיֹּאמַר צָעִיר אֲנִי לְיָמִים וְאַתֶּם יְשִׁישִׁים עַל־כֵּן זָחַלְתִּי

וָאִירָא ׀ מֵחַוֹּת דֵּעִי אֶתְכֶם: אָמַרְתִּי יָמִים יְדַבֵּרוּ וְרֹב שָׁנִים יֹדִיעוּ ז

חָכְמָה: אָכֵן רוּחַ־הִיא בֶאֱנוֹשׁ וְנִשְׁמַת שַׁדַּי תְּבִינֵם: לֹא־רַבִּים יֶחְכָּמוּ ח-ט

וּזְקֵנִים יָבִינוּ מִשְׁפָּט: לָכֵן אָמַרְתִּי שִׁמְעָה־לִּי אֲחַוֶּה דֵּעִי אַף־אָנִי: הֵן יא-י

הוֹחַלְתִּי לְדִבְרֵיכֶם אָזִין עַד־תְּבוּנֹתֵיכֶם עַד־תַּחְקְרוּן מִלִּין: וְעָדֵיכֶם יב

אֶתְבּוֹנָן וְהִנֵּה אֵין לְאִיּוֹב מוֹכִיחַ עוֹנֶה אֲמָרָיו מִכֶּם: פֶּן־תֹּאמְרוּ מָצָאנוּ יג

חָכְמָה אֵל יִדְּפֶנּוּ לֹא־אִישׁ: וְלֹא־עָרַךְ אֵלַי מִלִּין וּבְאִמְרֵיכֶם לֹא יד

אֲשִׁיבֶנּוּ: חַתּוּ לֹא־עָנוּ עוֹד הֶעְתִּיקוּ מֵהֶם מִלִּים: וְהוֹחַלְתִּי כִּי־לֹא טו-טז

יְדַבֵּרוּ כִּי עָמְדוּ לֹא־עָנוּ עוֹד: אַעֲנֶה אַף־אֲנִי חֶלְקִי אֲחַוֶּה דֵּעִי אַף־אָנִי: יז

כִּי מָלֵתִי מִלִּים הֱצִיקַתְנִי רוּחַ בִּטְנִי: הִנֵּה־בִטְנִי כְּיַיִן לֹא־יִפָּתֵחַ כְּאֹבוֹת יח-יט

חֲדָשִׁים יִבָּקֵעַ: אֲדַבְּרָה וְיִרְוַח־לִי אֶפְתַּח שְׂפָתַי וְאֶעֱנֶה: אַל־נָא אֶשָּׂא כ-כא

פְנֵי־אִישׁ וְאֶל־אָדָם לֹא אֲכַנֶּה: כִּי לֹא יָדַעְתִּי אֲכַנֶּה כִּמְעַט יִשָּׂאֵנִי עֹשֵׂנִי: כב

וְאוּלָם שְׁמַע־נָא אִיּוֹב מִלָּי וְכָל־דְּבָרַי הַאֲזִינָה: הִנֵּה־נָא פָּתַחְתִּי פִי א-ב לג

דִּבְּרָה לְשׁוֹנִי בְחִכִּי: יֹשֶׁר־לִבִּי אֲמָרָי וְדַעַת שְׂפָתַי בָּרוּר מִלֵּלוּ: רוּחַ־אֵל ג-ד

עָשָׂתְנִי וְנִשְׁמַת שַׁדַּי תְּחַיֵּנִי: אִם־תּוּכַל הֲשִׁיבֵנִי עֶרְכָה לְפָנַי הִתְיַצָּבָה: ה

הֵן־אֲנִי כְפִיךָ לָאֵל מֵחֹמֶר קֹרַצְתִּי גַם־אָנִי: הִנֵּה אֵמָתִי לֹא תְבַעֲתֶךָּ ו-ז

וְאַכְפִּי עָלֶיךָ לֹא־יִכְבָּד: אַךְ אָמַרְתָּ בְאָזְנָי וְקוֹל מִלִּין אֶשְׁמָע: זַךְ אֲנִי בְּלִי ח-ט

פֶשַׁע חַף אָנֹכִי וְלֹא עָוֹן לִי: הֵן תְּנוּאוֹת עָלַי יִמְצָא יַחְשְׁבֵנִי לְאוֹיֵב לוֹ: י *ח׳ זעירא

יָשֵׂם בַּסַּד רַגְלָי יִשְׁמֹר כָּל־אָרְחֹתָי: הֶן־זֹאת לֹא־צָדַקְתָּ אֶעֱנֶךָּ כִּי־יִרְבֶּה יא-יב

אֱלוֹהַּ מֵאֱנוֹשׁ: מַדּוּעַ אֵלָיו רִיבוֹתָ כִּי כָל־דְּבָרָיו לֹא־יַעֲנֶה: כִּי־בְאַחַת יג-יד

יְדַבֶּר־אֵל וּבִשְׁתַּיִם לֹא יְשׁוּרֶנָּה: בַּחֲלוֹם ׀ חֶזְיוֹן לַיְלָה בִּנְפֹל תַּרְדֵּמָה עַל־ טו

אֲנָשִׁים בִּתְנוּמוֹת עֲלֵי מִשְׁכָּב: אָז יִגְלֶה אֹזֶן אֲנָשִׁים וּבְמֹסָרָם יַחְתֹּם: טז

לְהָסִיר אָדָם מַעֲשֶׂה וְגֵוָה מִגֶּבֶר יְכַסֶּה: יַחְשֹׂךְ נַפְשׁוֹ מִנִּי־שָׁחַת וְחַיָּתוֹ יז-יח

מֵעֲבֹר בַּשָּׁלַח: וְהוּכַח בְּמַכְאוֹב עַל־מִשְׁכָּבוֹ °וְרִיב °רוֹב [°וְרוֹב ק] עֲצָמָיו יט

אֵתָן [°וְשָׁפוּ ק]: וְזִהֲמַתּוּ חַיָּתוֹ לָחֶם וְנַפְשׁוֹ מַאֲכַל תַּאֲוָה: יִכֶל בְּשָׂרוֹ מֵרֹאִי °וְשֻׁפּוּ כ-כא

[°וְשֻׁפּוּ ק] עַצְמוֹתָיו לֹא רֻאּוּ: וַתִּקְרַב לַשַּׁחַת נַפְשׁוֹ וְחַיָּתוֹ לַמְמִתִים: כב

אִם־יֵשׁ עָלָיו ׀ מַלְאָךְ מֵלִיץ אֶחָד מִנִּי־אָלֶף לְהַגִּיד לְאָדָם יָשְׁרוֹ: וַיְחֻנֶּנּוּ כג-כד

32:8. I see that wisdom is a Divine gift from above, and does not necessarily come with age (*Rashi*).

32:13. Do not claim that you decided to be silent because further argument would be useless. Since God has punished Job, your silence implies that Job's harangues against his fate are justified and that God was wrong.

32:18-20. Elihu likens himself to a container filled with fermenting wine. It emits fermentation gasses that can cause the container to burst, unless the pressure is relieved (*Rashi*). So too, Elihu says, "I have repressed my words for so long I feel as if I am about to explode."

32:21. I will not "mince any words."

32:22. God will not forgive me if I do not speak up.

33:4. I, like you, am mere flesh and blood (*Rashi*).

33:6. You demanded that God respond to your complaints (see above 13:3, 16:21, 23:3-4).

33:12. Even if you are righteous, God would not have treated you as an enemy without good reason (*Ramban*).

33:18. God inflicts illness to make the victim consider his mortality and mend his ways, thereby saving his life in the process (*Rashi*).

response in the mouths of the three men, his wrath flared.

⁶ *Elihu son of Barachel the Buzite then spoke up and said:*

God, not age, is the source of wisdom

I am young in years and you are elderly; therefore, I trembled and feared to express my opinion to you. ⁷ *I had thought, "Let days speak out; let abundant years teach wisdom."* ⁸ *But [in truth,] it is a spirit in man, and it is the soul from the Almighty that gives them understanding;* * ⁹ *it is not that great men are [always] wise, or that elders understand justice.* ¹⁰ *Therefore, I say, "Hear*

Elihu criticizes the friends' tactics

me. I, too, will express my opinion." ¹¹ *Behold, I waited for your words, I gave ear to your wisdom, until you had searched for [proper] words.* ¹² *I contemplated you and behold, there is no one to clarify for Job, no one among you to refute his statements.* ¹³ *Do not say, "We have found wisdom!" — for God, not man, has smitten him!* * ¹⁴ *He did not direct his words to me, but I would not have answered him with your statements.*

. . . then takes up the challenge

¹⁵ *They have become confounded and do not speak up any more; words have escaped them.* ¹⁶ *So I waited, for they did not speak; they stood still, and did not respond any more.* ¹⁷ *I, too, will speak up my portion; I, too, will express my opinion.* ¹⁸ *For I am filled with words; the spirit inside of my belly oppresses me.* * ¹⁹ *Behold, my belly is like unopened wine, like new flagons about to split.* ²⁰ *Let me speak and I will feel relieved; I shall open my lips and speak up!* ²¹ *Let me not show favor to any man, nor dissemble for any person.* * ²² *For I know not how to dissemble; for then my Maker would consume me.* *

33

Elihu asks leave to speak

¹ *However, I beg you, Job, listen to my words; give ear to all my statements.* ² *Behold, I have opened my mouth now; my tongue speaks with my palate.* ³ *My pronouncements express the uprightness of my heart, and the knowledge of my lips speaks clearly.* ⁴ *The spirit of God has made me, and a soul from the Almighty gives me life.* * ⁵ *If you can, answer me; state your case before me and stand firm.* ⁶ *Behold, I represent God, as you requested,* * *though I, too, am fashioned from clay.* ⁷ *Behold, fear of me should not intimidate you; let my authority not overwhelm you.*

ELIHU'S FIRST THEME: PAIN AND SUFFERING 33:8-33

Suffering can spare man from worse travail

⁸ *Indeed, you said in my ears, and I heard the sound of [those] words:* ⁹ *'I am innocent, without sin; I am pure and there is no transgression in me.* ¹⁰ *Behold, He seeks pretexts against me; He considers me His enemy.* ¹¹ *He places my feet in fetters, scrutinizes all my paths.'* ¹² *Behold, I will answer you that in this you are incorrect; for God is greater than man.* * ¹³ *Why do you complain against Him that He does not answer all of [man's] statements?* ¹⁴ *For God speaks once, and sees no need for twice.* ¹⁵ *In a dream, a vision of the night, when a deep sleep falls over people, during slumbers upon the bed,* ¹⁶ *then He uncovers people's ears and seals their affliction,* ¹⁷ *in order to divert a person from his [planned] action, and to suppress pride from man,* ¹⁸ *thus sparing his soul from the grave, and his life from perishing by the sword.* *

A small amount of good can save man

¹⁹ *And so he is afflicted with pain upon his bed, and upon the multitude of his strong bones.* ²⁰ *His being finds food loathsome,* * *and his soul [rejects] enticing foods.* ²¹ *His flesh is consumed from sight; his bulging bones become unseen.* ²² *His soul approaches the grave, and his being the killers.* * ²³ *If there will be for someone but a single defending angel out of a thousand* * *to declare a man's uprightness on his behalf,* ²⁴ *then [God] will be gracious to him*

33:20. His illness causes him a loss of appetite.
33:22. The angels of death (*Ibn Ezra*).

33:23-24. Even if only one angel defends him against a thousand accusers, God will spare him (*Rashi; Kara*).

כה	וַיֶּאֱמַר פְּדָעֵהוּ מֵרֶדֶת שָׁחַת מָצָאתִי כֹפֶר: רֻטֲפַשׁ בְּשָׂרוֹ מִנֹּעַר יָשׁוּב
כו	לִימֵי עֲלוּמָיו: יֶעְתַּר אֶל־אֱלוֹהַּ וַיִּרְצֵהוּ וַיַּרְא פָּנָיו בִּתְרוּעָה וַיָּשֶׁב
כז	לֶאֱנוֹשׁ צִדְקָתוֹ: יָשֹׁר ׀ עַל־אֲנָשִׁים וַיֹּאמֶר חָטָאתִי וְיָשָׁר הֶעֱוֵיתִי וְלֹא־
כח	שָׁוָה לִי: פָּדָה °נַפְשִׁי °נַפְשׁוֹ ק] מֵעֲבָר בַּשָּׁחַת °וְחַיָּתִי °וְחַיָּתוֹ ק]
כט־ל	בָּאוֹר תִּרְאֶה: הֶן־כָּל־אֵלֶּה יִפְעַל־אֵל פַּעֲמַיִם שָׁלוֹשׁ עִם־גָּבֶר: לְהָשִׁיב
לא	נַפְשׁוֹ מִנִּי־שָׁחַת לֵאוֹר בְּאוֹר הַחַיִּים: הַקְשֵׁב אִיּוֹב שְׁמַע־לִי הַחֲרֵשׁ
לב־לג	וְאָנֹכִי אֲדַבֵּר: אִם־יֵשׁ־מִלִּין הֲשִׁיבֵנִי דַּבֵּר כִּי־חָפַצְתִּי צַדְּקֶךָּ: אִם־אַיִן
א	אַתָּה שְׁמַע־לִי הַחֲרֵשׁ וַאֲאַלֶּפְךָ חָכְמָה:
לד	
ב־ג	וַיַּעַן אֱלִיהוּא וַיֹּאמַר: שִׁמְעוּ חֲכָמִים מִלָּי וְיֹדְעִים הַאֲזִינוּ לִי: כִּי־אֹזֶן מִלִּין
ד	תִּבְחָן וְחֵךְ יִטְעַם לֶאֱכֹל: מִשְׁפָּט נִבְחֲרָה־לָּנוּ נֵדְעָה בֵינֵינוּ מַה־טּוֹב:
ה־ו	כִּי־אָמַר אִיּוֹב צָדַקְתִּי וְאֵל הֵסִיר מִשְׁפָּטִי: עַל־מִשְׁפָּטִי אֲכַזֵּב אָנוּשׁ
ז־ח	חִצִּי בְלִי־פָשַׁע: מִי־גֶבֶר כְּאִיּוֹב יִשְׁתֶּה־לַּעַג כַּמָּיִם: וְאָרַח לְחֶבְרָה
ט	עִם־פֹּעֲלֵי אָוֶן וְלָלֶכֶת עִם־אַנְשֵׁי־רֶשַׁע: כִּי־אָמַר לֹא יִסְכָּן־גָּבֶר בִּרְצֹתוֹ
י	עִם־אֱלֹהִים: לָכֵן ׀ אַנְשֵׁי לֵבָב שִׁמְעוּ לִי חָלִלָה לָאֵל מֵרֶשַׁע וְשַׁדַּי
יא־יב	מֵעָוֶל: כִּי פֹעַל אָדָם יְשַׁלֶּם־לוֹ וּכְאֹרַח אִישׁ יַמְצִאֶנּוּ: אַף־אָמְנָם אֵל
יג	לֹא־יַרְשִׁיעַ וְשַׁדַּי לֹא־יְעַוֵּת מִשְׁפָּט: מִי־פָקַד עָלָיו אָרְצָה וּמִי שָׂם
יד־טו	תֵּבֵל כֻּלָּהּ: אִם־יָשִׂים אֵלָיו לִבּוֹ רוּחוֹ וְנִשְׁמָתוֹ אֵלָיו יֶאֱסֹף: יִגְוַע כָּל־
טז	בָּשָׂר יָחַד וְאָדָם עַל־עָפָר יָשׁוּב: וְאִם־בִּינָה שִׁמְעָה־זֹּאת הַאֲזִינָה
יז	לְקוֹל מִלָּי: הַאַף שׂוֹנֵא מִשְׁפָּט יַחֲבוֹשׁ וְאִם־צַדִּיק כַּבִּיר תַּרְשִׁיעַ:
יח־יט	הַאֲמֹר לְמֶלֶךְ בְּלִיָּעַל רָשָׁע אֶל־נְדִיבִים: אֲשֶׁר לֹא־נָשָׂא ׀ פְּנֵי שָׂרִים
כ	וְלֹא נִכַּר־שׁוֹעַ לִפְנֵי־דָל כִּי־מַעֲשֵׂה יָדָיו כֻּלָּם: רֶגַע ׀ יָמֻתוּ וַחֲצוֹת
כא	לַיְלָה יְגֹעֲשׁוּ עָם וְיַעֲבֹרוּ וְיָסִירוּ אַבִּיר לֹא בְיָד: כִּי־עֵינָיו עַל־
כב	דַּרְכֵי־אִישׁ וְכָל־צְעָדָיו יִרְאֶה: אֵין־חֹשֶׁךְ וְאֵין צַלְמָוֶת לְהִסָּתֶר שָׁם
כג־כד	פֹּעֲלֵי אָוֶן: כִּי לֹא עַל־אִישׁ יָשִׂים עוֹד לַהֲלֹךְ אֶל־אֵל בַּמִּשְׁפָּט: יָרֹעַ
כה	כַבִּירִים לֹא־חֵקֶר וַיַּעֲמֵד אֲחֵרִים תַּחְתָּם: לָכֵן יַכִּיר מַעְבָּדֵיהֶם
כו־כז	וְהָפַךְ לַיְלָה וְיִדַּכָּאוּ: תַּחַת־רְשָׁעִים סְפָקָם בִּמְקוֹם רֹאִים: אֲשֶׁר עַל־
כח	כֵּן סָרוּ מֵאַחֲרָיו וְכָל־דְּרָכָיו לֹא הִשְׂכִּילוּ: לְהָבִיא עָלָיו צַעֲקַת־
כט	דָּל וְצַעֲקַת עֲנִיִּים יִשְׁמָע: וְהוּא יַשְׁקִט ׀ וּמִי יַרְשִׁעַ וְיַסְתֵּר פָּנִים
ל	וּמִי יְשׁוּרֶנּוּ וְעַל־גּוֹי וְעַל־אָדָם יָחַד: מִמְּלֹךְ אָדָם חָנֵף מִמֹּקְשֵׁי עָם

33:27. He comprehends the message that his illness was meant to convey to him, and he announces his feelings of gratitude to God in public (*Rashi*).

34:7. Job utters words of scorn as copiously as other people drink water, with an unlimited supply (*Ralbag*).

34:8. As evidenced by his statements in the next verse (*Ralbag*).

34:13-15. God is not responsible to a Higher Authority and has no need to pervert justice to destroy a man. Why should God deal with man unjustly? He could simply take back the soul that He granted man (*Rashi*).

34:28. God punishes those who ignore the pleas of the needy.

and say, 'Redeem him from going down to the grave. I have found [him] atonement.' ²⁵ His flesh has revived from its trembling, and he will return to his days of youthfulness. ²⁶ He entreats God, and He accepts him; he appears before Him in prayer, and He recompenses man for his righteousness. ²⁷ He then goes around to people and says, * 'I have sinned; I have made crooked that which was straight; but to no avail.' ²⁸ For [God] absolved him from passing into the grave; so that his being might see the light. ²⁹ Behold, God does all these things with man two or three times, ³⁰ to bring back his soul from the grave, to bask in the light of the living.

³¹ Hearken, Job, and listen to me; be still and I will speak. ³² If there are words, answer me; speak, for I wish to vindicate you. ³³ If there are not, you listen to me; be still and I will teach you wisdom!

34   ¹ **E**lihu then spoke up and said:

² Hear my words, O wise men; men of knowledge give ear to me! ³ For an ear can discern words as a palate can taste for eating. ⁴ Let us choose judgment for ourselves; let us decide among ourselves what is good. ⁵ For Job has said, 'I was righteous and God has taken away my justice! ⁶ I claim my judgment was deceitful; my wound was grave without guilt!' ⁷ Who is a man like Job, who drinks scorn like water; * ⁸ who goes toward a company of workers of iniquity, * to walk with men of wickedness; ⁹ and who has said, 'A man has nothing to gain by pleasing God.'

¹⁰ Therefore, you men with [understanding] hearts, listen to me! To do evil is sacrilegious to God, and iniquity to the Almighty! ¹¹ For He repays the deeds of man, and causes man to find according to his conduct. ¹² Surely God will not act wickedly, and the Almighty will not pervert justice. ¹³ Who gave Him command over the earth, and who placed the entire inhabited world [under Him]? * ¹⁴ If He were to set his heart against someone, He would [simply] gather in his spirit and his soul to Himself; ¹⁵ all flesh would expire together, and man would return to the dust.

¹⁶ But if [you seek] understanding, listen to this; give ear to the sound of my words. ¹⁷ Would [God] heal someone who despises justice? Would you declare the mighty Righteous One to be wicked? ¹⁸ Can one say to a king, '[You are] lawless!' or to princes, 'Wicked one!'? ¹⁹ [Surely not of] the One Who does not favor leaders, nor lets a noble be given recognition over a pauper, for they are all His handiwork! ²⁰ In one moment they die; in [the] middle of the night the people fall into turmoil and pass away; and the mighty are removed without physical force. ²¹ For [His] eyes are upon man's ways, and He sees all his steps; ²² there is no darkness and no shadow of death where evildoers can be hidden. ²³ For He does not impose too much upon man, so that they could come before God for justice. ²⁴ He smashes mighty men without calculation and sets up others in their place; ²⁵ because He knows their works, He turns over the night and crushes them. ²⁶ He strikes the wicked in their places, in a place of witnesses, ²⁷ because they turned away from following Him, and did not contemplate all His ways, ²⁸ causing the cry of the needy to come before Him, and He hears the cry of the poor. * ²⁹ When He grants [a person] serenity, who can cause [that person] turmoil? And when He hides [His] face [from a person], who can take note of him? Upon a nation or upon an individual — all are alike. ³⁰ [He removes] the hypocrite from kingship, that the people not become ensnared. ³¹ For can

Prayerful repentance is the cure

ELIHU'S SECOND THEME: GOD'S WAY IS JUST
34:1-37

Man suffers only if he deserves to

God has no reason to pervert justice

He is impartial

Man is helpless against Him

לא-לב   כִּי־אֶל־אֵל הֶאָמַר נָשָׂאתִי לֹא אֶחְבֹּל: בִּלְעֲדֵי אֶחֱזֶה אַתָּה הֹרֵנִי

לג   אִם־עָוֶל פָּעַלְתִּי לֹא אֹסִיף: הֲמֵעִמְּךָ יְשַׁלְמֶנָּה כִּי־מָאַסְתָּ כִּי־אַתָּה

לד   תִבְחַר וְלֹא־אָנִי וּמַה־יָדַעְתָּ דַבֵּר: אַנְשֵׁי לֵבָב יֹאמְרוּ לִי וְגֶבֶר חָכָם

לה-לו   שֹׁמֵעַ לִי: אִיּוֹב לֹא־בְדַעַת יְדַבֵּר וּדְבָרָיו לֹא בְּהַשְׂכֵּיל: אָבִי יִבָּחֵן

לו   אִיּוֹב עַד־נֶצַח עַל־תְּשֻׁבֹת בְּאַנְשֵׁי־אָוֶן: כִּי יֹסִיף עַל־חַטָּאתוֹ פֶשַׁע

א   **לה**   בֵּינֵינוּ יִסְפּוֹק וְיֶרֶב אֲמָרָיו לָאֵל: וַיַּעַן אֱלִיהוּ

ב-ג   וַיֹּאמַר: הֲזֹאת חָשַׁבְתָּ לְמִשְׁפָּט אָמַרְתָּ צִדְקִי מֵאֵל: כִּי־תֹאמַר מַה־

ד   יִּסְכָּן־לָךְ מָה־אֹעִיל מֵחַטָּאתִי: אֲנִי אֲשִׁיבְךָ מִלִּין וְאֶת־רֵעֶיךָ עִמָּךְ:

ה-ו   הַבֵּט שָׁמַיִם וּרְאֵה וְשׁוּר שְׁחָקִים גָּבְהוּ מִמֶּךָּ: אִם־חָטָאתָ מַה־תִּפְעָל־

ז   בּוֹ וְרַבּוּ פְשָׁעֶיךָ מַה־תַּעֲשֶׂה־לּוֹ: אִם־צָדַקְתָּ מַה־תִּתֶּן־לוֹ אוֹ מַה־

ח-ט   מִיָּדְךָ יִקָּח: לְאִישׁ־כָּמוֹךָ רִשְׁעֶךָ וּלְבֶן־אָדָם צִדְקָתֶךָ: מֵרֹב עֲשׁוּקִים

י   יַזְעִיקוּ יְשַׁוְּעוּ מִזְּרוֹעַ רַבִּים: וְלֹא־אָמַר אַיֵּה אֱלוֹהַּ עֹשָׂי נֹתֵן זְמִרוֹת

יא-יב   בַּלָּיְלָה: מַלְּפֵנוּ מִבַּהֲמוֹת אָרֶץ וּמֵעוֹף הַשָּׁמַיִם יְחַכְּמֵנוּ: שָׁם יִצְעֲקוּ

יג   וְלֹא יַעֲנֶה מִפְּנֵי גְּאוֹן רָעִים: אַךְ־שָׁוְא לֹא־יִשְׁמַע אֵל וְשַׁדַּי לֹא יְשׁוּרֶנָּה:

יד-טו   אַף כִּי־תֹאמַר לֹא תְשׁוּרֶנּוּ דִּין לְפָנָיו וּתְחוֹלֵל לוֹ: וְעַתָּה כִּי־אַיִן פָּקַד

טו   אַפּוֹ וְלֹא־יָדַע בַּפַּשׁ מְאֹד: וְאִיּוֹב הֶבֶל יִפְצֶה־פִּיהוּ בִּבְלִי־דַעַת מִלִּין

א-ב   **לו**   יַכְבִּר: וַיֹּסֶף אֱלִיהוּא וַיֹּאמַר: כַּתַּר־לִי זְעֵיר

ג   וַאֲחַוֶּךָּ כִּי עוֹד לֶאֱלוֹהַּ מִלִּים: אֶשָּׂא דֵעִי לְמֵרָחוֹק וּלְפֹעֲלִי אֶתֵּן־

ד-ה   צֶדֶק: כִּי־אָמְנָם לֹא־שֶׁקֶר מִלָּי תְּמִים דֵּעוֹת עִמָּךְ: הֶן־אֵל כַּבִּיר וְלֹא

ו-ז   יִמְאָס כַּבִּיר כֹּחַ לֵב: לֹא־יְחַיֶּה רָשָׁע וּמִשְׁפַּט עֲנִיִּים יִתֵּן: לֹא־יִגְרַע

ח   מִצַּדִּיק עֵינָיו וְאֶת־מְלָכִים לַכִּסֵּא וַיֹּשִׁיבֵם לָנֶצַח וַיִּגְבָּהוּ: וְאִם־אֲסוּרִים

ט   בַּזִּקִּים יִלָּכְדוּן בְּחַבְלֵי־עֹנִי: וַיַּגֵּד לָהֶם פָּעֳלָם וּפִשְׁעֵיהֶם כִּי יִתְגַּבָּרוּ: וַיִּגֶל

יא   אָזְנָם לַמּוּסָר וַיֹּאמֶר כִּי־יְשֻׁבוּן מֵאָוֶן: אִם־יִשְׁמְעוּ וְיַעֲבֹדוּ יְכַלּוּ יְמֵיהֶם

יב   בַּטּוֹב וּשְׁנֵיהֶם בַּנְּעִימִים: וְאִם־לֹא יִשְׁמְעוּ בְּשֶׁלַח יַעֲבֹרוּ וְיִגְוְעוּ בִּבְלִי־

יג-יד   דָעַת: וְחַנְפֵי־לֵב יָשִׂימוּ אָף לֹא יְשַׁוְּעוּ כִּי אֲסָרָם: תָּמֹת בַּנֹּעַר נַפְשָׁם

טו   וְחַיָּתָם בַּקְּדֵשִׁים: יְחַלֵּץ עָנִי בְעָנְיוֹ וְיִגֶל בַּלַּחַץ אָזְנָם: וְאַף הֱסִיתְךָ |

35:5. That will show you how inconsequential you are as compared to God.

35:10. The spectacle of myriad stars in the nighttime sky should instill in anyone a sense of awe. But these people were not inspired even by this majestic display of God's might (*Ramban*).

35:11. Why would God give intelligence to us, but not to other life forms, if not to form a just society in which, unlike the animal kingdom, strong people do not devour the weak (*Ramban*).

35:12-13. The time will come when the wicked oppressors will themselves cry out for help, but God will ignore them, because they are men of deception (*Kara*).

36:3. When I contemplate events all the way to the distant past, I recognize that God is righteous (*Kara*). Alternatively: I will raise my voice in knowledge, that my words may be heard from afar (*Metzudos*).

36:4. Everything He has brought upon you is with a precise, deliberate purpose (*Ramban*).

36:5. God's mercy is so strong that He does not neglect the poor; and He is also strong in His heartfelt indignation, to punish the wicked (*Rashi*).

36:15. Those who are essentially righteous, but "poor" in good deeds, will be spared from the terrors of *Gehinnom* by the suffering they endure in this world (*Rashi*).

one say to God, 'I have suffered enough; I wish no more harm. ³² Besides what I see — you teach me! If I have done wrong, I will not continue.'

Job must stop his rebellious criticism

³³ Must [God] have your [consent] to punish, that you can reject it? [God says,] 'Will you choose and not I?' Say now whatever you know!

³⁴ People of [understanding] heart say this to me, and the wise man listens to me: ³⁵ 'Job does not speak with knowledge, and his words are without intelligence!' ³⁶ My desire is that Job be disproven forever, as a rebuttal for men of wrongdoing — ³⁷ for he adds rebellion to his error, by speaking so profusely among us, and utters too many pronouncements against God.

35

¹ **E**lihu then spoke up and said:

ELIHU'S THIRD THEME: GOD VIS-A-VIS MAN 35:2-16

Virtue benefits man, not God

² Do you consider this — [when] you say, 'My righteousness is greater than God's' — to be just? ³ [And] when you say, 'What benefit is there for You [in my righteousness]? What does it avail me more than my sinfulness?' ⁴ I will reply with words to you and to your friends with you.

⁵ Look at the heavens and see; gaze at the skies that tower above you. *

The wicked do not reflect on God's purpose . . .

⁶ If you have sinned, how have you affected Him? If your transgressions multiply, what have you done to Him? ⁷ If you were righteous, what have you given Him, or what has He taken from your hand? ⁸ Your wickedness [is of concern] to a man like yourself, and your righteousness to a human being. ⁹ [The wicked] cause many victims to scream; they cry out because of the strong-armed oppressors. ¹⁰ And none of them said, 'Where is the God Who made me, Who gives songs at night, ¹¹ Who makes us more knowing than the beasts of the land, * and makes us wiser than the birds of the sky?'"

. . . and He will ignore their cries

¹² There they * will cry out, but He will not answer, because of the pride of the evil ones. ¹³ It will be only for naught! For God will not listen, and the Almighty will not look. ¹⁴ Although you may say that you cannot see Him, yet there is judgment before Him, and you should place your hope in Him. ¹⁵ So now — [know] that His anger against you is [comparatively] nothing, as if He did not know the vastness [of your guilt]. ¹⁶ Job opens his mouth with nonsense; he multiplies verbiage without knowledge.

His judgments are never haphazard

36

¹ **E**lihu continued and said:

ELIHU'S FOURTH THEME: METHOD-OLOGY OF DIVINE DISCIPLINE 36:1-22

² Wait for me a bit and I will tell you; for there are more words on God's behalf. ³ I will raise my knowledge from afar, I will ascribe righteousness to my Maker. * ⁴ For in truth, my words are not false; [God] is perfect in His knowledge of you. * ⁵ Behold, God is mighty and does not despise; and He is mighty in the strength of his heart. * ⁶ He will not keep the wicked alive; He will grant justice to the poor. ⁷ He will not remove His eyes from a righteous man until he is on the throne with kings; He will seat them [there] forever and they will become exalted. ⁸ And if they are shackled in fetters, trapped in ropes of affliction, ⁹ He [thus] informs them of their [errant] deeds and their transgressions, for they have become overpowering. ¹⁰ He opened their ears to discipline, and said that they should turn back from wrongdoing. ¹¹ If they will listen and serve [Him], then they will finish their days in goodness and their years in pleasantness. ¹² But if they will not listen, they will pass away by the sword and expire for lack of knowledge. ¹³ And those with insincere hearts will bring on [God's] anger; they should not cry out [to Him] when He afflicts them. ¹⁴ Their soul will die amid turmoil, and their life among the promiscuous. ¹⁵ But He will extricate a poor man [from his sins] through his poverty, and open their ears through oppression. * ¹⁶ He has led you out,

The fate of the wicked encourages the righteous

יז מִפִּי־צָ֗ר רַ֖חַב לֹא־מוּצָ֣ק תַּחְתֶּ֑יהָ וְנַ֥חַת שֻׁ֝לְחָנְךָ֗ מָ֣לֵא דָֽשֶׁן׃ וְדִין־רָשָׁ֥ע

יח מָלֵ֥אתָ דִּ֖ין וּמִשְׁפָּ֣ט יִתְמֹ֑כוּ׃ כִּֽי־חֵ֭מָה פֶּן־יְסִֽיתְךָ֣ בְסָ֑פֶק וְרָב־כֹּ֝פֶר אַל־

יט יַטֶּֽךָ׃ הֲיַעֲרֹ֣ךְ שׁ֭וּעֲךָ לֹ֣א בְצָ֑ר וְ֝כֹ֗ל מַאֲמַצֵּי־כֹֽחַ׃ אַל־תִּשְׁאַ֥ף הַלָּ֑יְלָה

כא לַעֲל֥וֹת עַמִּ֣ים תַּחְתָּֽם׃ הִ֭שָּׁמֶר אַל־תֵּ֣פֶן אֶל־אָ֑וֶן כִּֽי־עַל־זֶ֝֗ה בָּחַ֥רְתָּ מֵעֹֽנִי׃

כב-כג הֶן־אֵ֭ל יַשְׂגִּ֣יב בְּכֹח֑וֹ מִ֖י כָמֹ֣הוּ מוֹרֶֽה׃ מִֽי־פָקַ֣ד עָלָ֣יו דַּרְכּ֑וֹ וּמִֽי־אָ֝מַ֗ר

כד-כה פָּעַ֥לְתָּ עַוְלָֽה׃ זְ֭כֹר כִּֽי־תַשְׂגִּ֣יא פׇעֳל֑וֹ אֲשֶׁ֖ר שֹׁרְר֣וּ אֲנָשִֽׁים׃ כׇּל־אָדָ֥ם חָֽזוּ־

כו ב֑וֹ אֱנ֖וֹשׁ יַבִּ֣יט מֵרָחֽוֹק׃ הֶן־אֵ֣ל שַׂ֭גִּיא וְלֹ֣א נֵדָ֑ע מִסְפַּ֖ר שָׁנָ֣יו וְלֹא־חֵֽקֶר׃

כז-כח כִּ֭י יְגָרַ֣ע נִטְפֵי־מָ֑יִם יָזֹ֖קּוּ מָטָ֣ר לְאֵדֽוֹ׃ אֲשֶֽׁר־יִזְּל֥וּ שְׁחָקִ֑ים יִרְעֲפ֖וּ עֲלֵ֣י ׀

כט אָדָ֥ם רָֽב׃ אַ֣ף אִם־יָ֭בִין מִפְרְשֵׂי־עָ֑ב תְּ֝שֻׁא֗וֹת סֻכָּתֽוֹ׃ הֵן־פָּרַ֣שׂ עָלָ֣יו אוֹר֑וֹ

לא-לב וְשׇׁרְשֵׁ֖י הַיָּ֣ם כִּסָּֽה׃ כִּי־בָ֭ם יָדִ֣ין עַמִּ֑ים יִֽתֶּן־אֹ֥כֶל לְמַכְבִּֽיר׃ עַל־כַּפַּ֥יִם כִּסָּה־

לג-לו:א א֑וֹר וַיְצַ֥ו עָלֶ֗יהָ בְמַפְגִּֽיעַ׃ יַגִּ֣יד עָלָ֣יו רֵע֑וֹ מִ֝קְנֶ֗ה אַ֣ף עַל־עוֹלֶֽה׃ אַף־לְזֹ֗את

ב-ג יֶחֱרַ֣ד לִבִּ֑י וְ֝יִתַּ֗ר מִמְּקוֹמֽוֹ׃ שִׁמְע֤וּ שָׁמ֣וֹעַ בְּרֹ֣גֶז קֹל֑וֹ וְ֝הֶ֗גֶה מִפִּ֥יו יֵצֵֽא׃ תַּחַת־

ד כׇּל־הַשָּׁמַ֥יִם יִשְׁרֵ֑הוּ וְ֝אוֹר֗וֹ עַל־כַּנְפ֥וֹת הָאָֽרֶץ׃ אַחֲרָ֤יו ׀ יִשְׁאַג־ק֗וֹל יַרְעֵ֤ם

ה בְּק֣וֹל גְּאוֹנ֑וֹ וְלֹ֥א יְ֝עַקְּבֵ֗ם כִּֽי־יִשָּׁמַ֥ע קוֹלֽוֹ׃ יַרְעֵ֤ם אֵ֣ל בְּ֭קוֹלוֹ נִפְלָא֑וֹת עֹשֶׂ֥ה

ו גְ֝דֹל֗וֹת וְלֹ֣א נֵדָֽע׃ כִּ֤י לַשֶּׁ֨לַג ׀ יֹאמַ֗ר הֱוֵ֫א אָ֥רֶץ וְגֶ֥שֶׁם מָטָ֑ר וְ֝גֶ֗שֶׁם מִטְר֥וֹת

ז-ח עֻזּֽוֹ׃ בְּיַד־כׇּל־אָדָ֥ם יַחְתּ֑וֹם לָ֝דַ֗עַת כׇּל־אַנְשֵׁ֥י מַעֲשֵֽׂהוּ׃ וַתָּבֹ֣א חַיָּ֣ה בְמוֹ־

ט אָ֑רֶב וּבִמְע֖וֹנֹתֶ֣יהָ תִשְׁכֹּֽן׃ מִן־הַ֭חֶדֶר תָּב֣וֹא סוּפָ֑ה וּֽמִמְּזָרִ֥ים קָרָֽה׃

י-יא מִנִּשְׁמַת־אֵ֥ל יִתֶּן־קָ֑רַח וְרֹ֖חַב מַ֣יִם בְּמוּצָֽק׃ אַף־בְּ֭רִי יַטְרִ֣יחַ עָ֑ב יָ֝פִ֗יץ עֲנַ֥ן

יב אוֹרֽוֹ׃ וְה֤וּא מְסִבּ֨וֹת ׀ מִתְהַפֵּ֣ךְ °בְּתַחְבּוּלֹתָו [°בְּתַחְבּֽוּלֹתָ֗יו ק] לְפׇעֳלָ֥ם

יג כֹּ֖ל אֲשֶׁ֣ר יְצַוֵּ֑ם עַל־פְּנֵ֖י תֵבֵ֣ל אָֽרְצָה׃ אִם־לְשֵׁ֥בֶט אִם־לְאַרְצ֑וֹ אִם־לְ֝חֶ֗סֶד

יד-טו יַמְצִאֵֽהוּ׃ הַאֲזִ֣ינָה זֹּ֣את אִיּ֑וֹב עֲ֝מֹ֗ד וְהִתְבּוֹנֵ֨ן ׀ נִפְלְא֬וֹת אֵֽל׃ הֲ֭תֵדַע בְּשׂוּם־

טז אֱל֣וֹהַּ עֲלֵיהֶ֑ם וְ֝הוֹפִ֗יעַ א֣וֹר עֲנָנֽוֹ׃ הֲ֭תֵדַע עַל־מִפְלְשֵׂי־עָ֑ב מִ֝פְלְא֗וֹת תְּמִ֥ים

יז-יח דֵּעִֽים׃ אֲשֶׁר־בְּגָדֶ֥יךָ חַמִּ֑ים בְּהַשְׁקִ֥ט אֶ֝֗רֶץ מִדָּרֽוֹם׃ תַּרְקִ֣יעַ עִ֭מּוֹ לִשְׁחָקִ֑ים

יט חֲ֝זָקִ֗ים כִּרְאִ֥י מוּצָֽק׃ ה֭וֹדִיעֵנוּ מַה־נֹּ֣אמַר ל֑וֹ לֹ֥א נַ֝עֲרֹ֗ךְ מִפְּנֵי־חֹֽשֶׁךְ׃

36:16. You, too, have experienced suffering only in order to be saved from a worse fate in the future, as described above 33:15-30 and again here, 36:8-10 (*Ramban*).

36:20. "Night" symbolizes catastrophe, as when a nation is suddenly defeated in war on its own ground.

36:21. Elihu pleads with Job to submit to God's judgment and stop blaming Him for his plight (*Metzudos*).

36:22. God is unequaled in His use of illness or other suffering as a means to instruct a person and awaken him to the necessity to repent.

36:23-25. No one has the authority to command God or to criticize Him for His actions (*Kara*). Instead, focus on His Omnipotence and praise Him.

36:30-32. God seeds His heavenly canopy with rain, which pours down and covers the earth, as reward for those whose prayers earn it.

36:33. Animals, particularly pregnant or nursing fe-males, sense an impending storm before humans do, and the animals' behavior "announces" the rain (*Ibn Ezra*).

37:1. The thunder and lightning described in the following verses (*Kara*).

37:4. Lightning is always followed by thunder (*Ralbag*).

37:7. Since God uses rainfall to reward and punish, when a particular region has rainfall or drought, the rains are a public affirmation of men's deeds (*Kara*).

37:9. The place where storm winds are "stored."

37:12-13. God sends clouds from place to place to bring rain, depending on what people deserve — sometimes a severe storm, sometimes to water the land, and some-times, out of Divine mercy, even when it is not deserved (*Rashi, Kara*).

37:17. The very weather is an expression of God's power. Thus, winter clothing feels too warm when the cold north wind is replaced by the warm, calm, south wind.

as well, from a constricted entrance, into a broad place with no narrowness at its bottom, so that your table might be full of rich foods. * ¹⁷ So if you have been filled with the fate of a wicked man, [this] sentence and judgment will sustain [you], ¹⁸ lest [God's] wrath lead you out, along with your affluence, and even a large ransom would not return you. ¹⁹ Would your wealth avail you? Not in adversity! Nor would all the power of [your] strength. ²⁰ Do not desire the night, * when peoples are cut down in their places. ²¹ Be careful, do not turn to wrongdoing; for this is what you have chosen over submission. * ²² Behold, in His omnipotence God will raise up. Who can instruct as He does? *

SONG OF
THE RAIN:
TESTIMONY
TO THE
OMNIPO-
TENCE OF
GOD
36:23-37:24

²³ Who could have designated His course for Him, * and who could have said, 'You have committed iniquity?' ²⁴ Remember so that you will extol His works, of which men sing. ²⁵ All men have seen them, a person views [it] from afar. ²⁶ Behold, God is mightier than we can know; the number of His years is beyond calculation. ²⁷ For He proliferates water-droplets, rain is distilled [to form] its clouds, ²⁸ so that the heavens may drip water, pouring it out over a multitude of people. ²⁹ Can a person even understand the spreading out of the thick cloud, or the dark clouds of His canopy? ³⁰ Behold, He spreads His rain over it, and covers over the roots of the sea. * ³¹ For through them he judges peoples, and he gives food to people with abundance. ³² He covers the clouds with rain; and commands it upon those who entreat Him. ³³ Its thunder announces it, as does the herd [and] even the dam. *

37 *God's "voice" is heard through His control of nature*

Harmful rain, beneficial rain: God's recompense to man

¹ **B**ecause of this* my heart trembles and jumps from its place: ² Listen well as, in fury, He gives voice, speech emanates from His mouth. ³ Under all the heavens He sends it forth, its flash unto the ends of the earth. ⁴ After that a sound roars out, and thunders in its majestic voice; He does not hold them back, for its sound is heard. * ⁵ God thunders marvelously with His voice; He does wonders that we do not comprehend. ⁶ For He says to the snow, 'Be upon the ground!' — and [also says this] to showers of [light] rain and showers of his mighty rains. ⁷ He seals [a judgment] with the hand of every man, * so that all people He has made may know. ⁸ The beast then enters [its] lair, and rests in its dens. ⁹ A tempest emerges from the inner chamber, * and cold weather from the constellations. ¹⁰ By God's breath He makes ice, and an expanse of water becomes solidified. ¹¹ Even when it is clear, He troubles thick clouds [to form]; He spreads out His rain clouds. ¹² Good reasons direct its movements, cunningly it pursues its tasks, according to [man's] deeds; * however He commands them, upon the inhabited surface of the earth. ¹³ Whether for punishment or for [the benefit of] His land, or for kindness, He may supply it.

God's ways: beyond human comprehension

¹⁴ Give ear to this, Job; stop and contemplate the wonders of God. ¹⁵ Do you know how God imposes upon [the clouds], and how He makes His rain-cloud appear? ¹⁶ Do you understand the spreading out of the clouds or the wonders of the One of Perfect Knowledge, ¹⁷ or why your clothes feel warm when the land is becalmed from the South? * ¹⁸ Did you stretch out the heavens with Him, to be as strong as a molten mirror? * ¹⁹ Let us know what we can say to Him; we cannot prepare our case because of darkness. *

37:18. Mirrors used to be made of hard, strong burnished metal (*Rashi*).

37:19. We cannot formulate our contention before God

because of the mystery that surrounds Him (*Rashi*). But if you can answer the questions posed earlier (vv. 15-18), perhaps you can help us confront God! (*Ramban*).

הַיְסֻפַּר־לוֹ כִּי אֲדַבֵּר אִם־אָמַר אִישׁ כִּי יְבֻלָּע: וְעַתָּה ׀ לֹא רָאוּ אוֹר בָּהִיר   כ-כא

הוּא בַּשְּׁחָקִים וְרוּחַ עָבְרָה וַתְּטַהֲרֵם: מִצָּפוֹן זָהָב יֶאֱתֶה עַל־אֱלוֹהַּ נוֹרָא   כב

הוֹד: שַׁדַּי לֹא־מְצָאנֻהוּ שַׂגִּיא־כֹחַ וּמִשְׁפָּט וְרֹב־צְדָקָה לֹא יְעַנֶּה: לָכֵן   כג-כד

יְרֵאוּהוּ אֲנָשִׁים לֹא־יִרְאֶה כָּל־חַכְמֵי־לֵב: וַיַּעַן־יְהֹוָה אֶת־אִיּוֹב   א | לח

°מנהסערה [°מִן ׀ הַסְּעָרָה ק] וַיֹּאמַר: מִי זֶה ׀ מַחְשִׁיךְ עֵצָה בְמִלִּין בְּלִי־   ב

דָעַת: אֱזָר־נָא כְגֶבֶר חֲלָצֶיךָ וְאֶשְׁאָלְךָ וְהוֹדִיעֵנִי: אֵיפֹה הָיִיתָ בְּיָסְדִי־אָרֶץ   ג-ד

הַגֵּד אִם־יָדַעְתָּ בִינָה: מִי־שָׂם מְמַדֶּיהָ כִּי תֵדָע אוֹ מִי־נָטָה עָלֶיהָ קָּו: עַל־   ה-ו

מָה אֲדָנֶיהָ הָטְבָּעוּ אוֹ מִי־יָרָה אֶבֶן פִּנָּתָהּ: בְּרָן־יַחַד כּוֹכְבֵי בֹקֶר וַיָּרִיעוּ   ז-ח

כָּל־בְּנֵי אֱלֹהִים: וַיָּסֶךְ בִּדְלָתַיִם יָם בְּגִיחוֹ מֵרֶחֶם יֵצֵא: בְּשׂוּמִי עָנָן לְבֻשׁוֹ   ט

וַעֲרָפֶל חֲתֻלָּתוֹ: וָאֶשְׁבֹּר עָלָיו חֻקִּי וָאָשִׂים בְּרִיחַ וּדְלָתָיִם: וָאֹמַר עַד־פֹּה   י-יא

תָבוֹא וְלֹא תֹסִיף וּפֹא־יָשִׁית בִּגְאוֹן גַּלֶּיךָ: הַמִיָּמֶיךָ צִוִּיתָ בֹּקֶר °ידעתה   יב

שחר [°יִדַּעְתָּ הַשַּׁחַר ק] מְקֹמוֹ: לֶאֱחֹז בְּכַנְפוֹת הָאָרֶץ וְיִנָּעֲרוּ רְשָׁעִים   יג   *עי"ן תלויה

מִמֶּנָּה: תִּתְהַפֵּךְ כְּחֹמֶר חוֹתָם וְיִתְיַצְּבוּ כְּמוֹ לְבֻשׁ: וְיִמָּנַע מֵרְשָׁעִים אוֹרָם   יד-טו   *עי"ן תלויה

וּזְרוֹעַ רָמָה תִּשָּׁבֵר: הֲבָאתָ עַד־נִבְכֵי־יָם וּבְחֵקֶר תְּהוֹם הִתְהַלָּכְתָּ: הֲנִגְלוּ   טז-יז

לְךָ שַׁעֲרֵי־מָוֶת וְשַׁעֲרֵי צַלְמָוֶת תִּרְאֶה: הִתְבֹּנַנְתָּ עַד־רַחֲבֵי־אָרֶץ הַגֵּד   יח

אִם־יָדַעְתָּ כֻלָּהּ: אֵי־זֶה הַדֶּרֶךְ יִשְׁכָּן־אוֹר וְחֹשֶׁךְ אֵי־זֶה מְקֹמוֹ: כִּי תִקָּחֶנּוּ   יט-כ

אֶל־גְּבוּלוֹ וְכִי־תָבִין נְתִיבוֹת בֵּיתוֹ: יָדַעְתָּ כִּי־אָז תִּוָּלֵד וּמִסְפַּר יָמֶיךָ   כא

רַבִּים: הֲבָאתָ אֶל־אֹצְרוֹת שָׁלֶג וְאֹצְרוֹת בָּרָד תִּרְאֶה: אֲשֶׁר־חָשַׂכְתִּי   כב-כג

לְעֶת־צָר לְיוֹם קְרָב וּמִלְחָמָה: אֵי־זֶה הַדֶּרֶךְ יֵחָלֶק אוֹר יָפֵץ קָדִים עֲלֵי־   כד

אָרֶץ: מִי־פִלַּג לַשֶּׁטֶף תְּעָלָה וְדֶרֶךְ לַחֲזִיז קֹלוֹת: לְהַמְטִיר עַל־אֶרֶץ   כה-כו

לֹא־אִישׁ מִדְבָּר לֹא־אָדָם בּוֹ: לְהַשְׂבִּיעַ שֹׁאָה וּמְשֹׁאָה וּלְהַצְמִיחַ   כז

מֹצָא דֶשֶׁא: הֲיֵשׁ־לַמָּטָר אָב אוֹ מִי־הוֹלִיד אֶגְלֵי־טָל: מִבֶּטֶן מִי יָצָא   כח-כט

הַקָּרַח וּכְפֹר שָׁמַיִם מִי יְלָדוֹ: כָּאֶבֶן מַיִם יִתְחַבָּאוּ וּפְנֵי תְהוֹם יִתְלַכָּדוּ:   ל

37:20. God knows everything we say, even if we do not confront Him (*Rashi*).

37:21. Elihu dismisses Job and his friends, each of whom put forth erroneous arguments (*Rashi*). Like clouds that appear to hold rain, only to be blown away, the friends came to refute Job's assertions, only to fail completely.

37:22. Like someone who does not see the light even after a north wind has blown away all the clouds (*Rashi*).

37:23. With all His awesome power, he does not mete out justice without compassion (*Rashi*).

37:24. People are afraid to contend with God because their understanding and wisdom is nothing compared to His (*Rashi*).

Elihu's speech is over and he does not appear again — nor does Job respond with anger and resentment, as he had to the other friends. Apparently Job was impressed with Elihu's theme: God and His ways are beyond human comprehension, and His inscrutable ways are filled with underlying compassion — like the creation of rain, which is the major theme of Elihu's final argument.

38:1. God now speaks directly to Job, for the first time.

38:8. God created the sands of the shore, as a border to enclose the seas.

38:13. The sunlight is depicted as the instrument through which God purges the wicked (*Ibn Ezra*).

38:14. As people are constantly replaced by others, the earth is depicted as changing its appearance and putting on a new garment (*Ibn Ezra*).

38:17. Do you understand all the different ways in which God brings death to man? (*Kara*).

38:20. Can you cause the morning or even the evening to come about by consigning the darkness to its resting place or taking it out of its abode? (*Kara*).

38:23. I set aside the hail to be used as a punishment against wicked nations.

38:25-30. Rain is solely in God's control. That He lets it fall on uninhabited places proves that His compassion extends even to animals, and certainly to people (*Ramban; Kara*).

²⁰ *Must He be told when I speak? When a person says something, need it be revealed?* *

²¹ *Thus, they have never seen the light; they are [like] spots of cloud in the sky, which a wind comes and clears away.* * ²² *The golden [sunshine] has come because of the north [wind]; it is an awesome magnificence from God.* *

²³ *We do not find the Almighty to be overbearing in His strength;* * *with justice and an abundance of kindness, he does not deal harshly.* ²⁴ *Therefore people fear Him — for He is not impressed with those who are wise of heart.* *

38

GOD SPEAKS
FROM OUT
OF THE
WHIRLWIND
38:1-41:26

¹ H ASHEM *then responded to Job* * *from out of the whirlwind, and said:*

² *Who is this who gives murky counsel, with words without knowledge?* ³ *Gird your loins like a warrior, and I will ask you, and you will inform Me.*

Was Job
present when
God created
the earth?
. . . the sea?
. . . day and
night?

⁴ *Where were you when I laid the earth's foundation? Tell, if you know understanding!* ⁵ *Who set its dimensions? — if you know — or who stretched a [surveyor's] line over it?* ⁶ *Into what are its bases sunken, or who laid its cornerstone?* ⁷ *When the morning stars sang in unison and all the heavenly beings shouted,* ⁸ *as He dammed in the sea with bolted doors as its flow emerged from the womb,* * ⁹ *when I put a cloud on it as its garment and a thick cloud as its swaddling,* ¹⁰ *and I constrained it with My limits, and I emplaced a bar and bolted doors,* ¹¹ *and said, 'Until here shall you go, and no further, and only here shall your waves flaunt their majesty!'?*

¹² *Did you ever in your life command the morning, or teach the dawn its place,* ¹³ *to grasp the edges of the earth and shake the wicked from it;* * ¹⁴ *as it changes itself,* * *as a seal does to clay, as [people] come into being like [the earth's] garment,* ¹⁵ *as light is withheld from the wicked, and their raised arm is broken?*

Does Job
realize the
limits of his
experience
and
knowledge?

¹⁶ *Have you penetrated the hidden depths of the sea, or gone to plumb the deep?*

¹⁷ *Were the gates of death revealed to you? Have you seen the gates of the shadow of death?* *

¹⁸ *Have you contemplated up to the wide expanses of the world? Tell, if you know it all!* ¹⁹ *What is the path where the light dwells? And darkness, where is its place,* ²⁰ *that you may take it to its boundary, that you may understand the paths of its home?* * ²¹ *Do you know, because then you were already born and the number of your days is so great?*

²² *Have you come upon the storehouses of snow, or seen the storehouses of hail,* ²³ *which I have kept for times of travail, for a day of battle and war?* *

²⁴ *Which is the way where light is dispersed, which the eastern [sun] spreads upon the land?*

God created
and controls
the rain,
the dew,
the ice . . .

²⁵ *Who fashioned a channel for the torrent,* * *or a path for thunder clouds,* ²⁶ *that it may rain upon a land without man, and in a wilderness in which there is no person,* ²⁷ *to sate desolation and wasteland, to make vegetation sprout forth?* ²⁸ *Does rain have a father?* * *Who begot the dewdrops?* ²⁹ *From whose belly did the ice come forth? Who gave birth to the frost of heaven?* ³⁰ *Like a [submerged] stone, the waters are concealed, the very depths are imprisoned.* *

38:28. Raindrops come into existence only through the hand of God (*Ramban*).

38:30. When bodies of water are covered by ice, the water is as invisible as a stone that fell into the sea.

לא-לב   הַתְקַשֵּׁר מַעֲדַנּוֹת כִּימָה אוֹ־מֹשְׁכוֹת כְּסִיל תְּפַתֵּחַ: הֲתֹצִיא מַזָּרוֹת
לב   בְּעִתּוֹ וְעַיִשׁ עַל־בָּנֶיהָ תַנְחֵם: הֲיָדַעְתָּ חֻקּוֹת שָׁמָיִם אִם־תָּשִׂים מִשְׁטָרוֹ
לד-לה   בָּאָרֶץ: הֲתָרִים לָעָב קוֹלֶךָ וְשִׁפְעַת־מַיִם תְּכַסֶּךָּ: הַתְשַׁלַּח בְּרָקִים וְיֵלֵכוּ
לו   וְיֹאמְרוּ לְךָ הִנֵּנוּ: מִי־שָׁת בַּטֻּחוֹת חָכְמָה אוֹ מִי־נָתַן לַשֶּׂכְוִי בִינָה:
לז-לח   מִי־יְסַפֵּר שְׁחָקִים בְּחָכְמָה וְנִבְלֵי שָׁמַיִם מִי יַשְׁכִּיב: בְּצֶקֶת עָפָר
לט   לַמּוּצָק וּרְגָבִים יְדֻבָּקוּ: הֲתָצוּד לְלָבִיא טָרֶף וְחַיַּת כְּפִירִים תְּמַלֵּא:
מ-מא   כִּי־יָשֹׁחוּ בַּמְּעוֹנוֹת יֵשְׁבוּ בַסֻּכָּה לְמוֹ־אָרֶב: מִי יָכִין לָעֹרֵב צֵידוֹ

לט
א   כִּי ﹖יֵלְדוּ [יְלָדָיו ק] אֶל־אֵל יְשַׁוֵּעוּ יִתְעוּ לִבְלִי־אֹכֶל: הֲיָדַעְתָּ
ב   עֵת לֶדֶת יַעֲלֵי־סָלַע חֹלֵל אַיָּלוֹת תִּשְׁמֹר: תִּסְפֹּר יְרָחִים תְּמַלֶּאנָה
ג   וְיָדַעְתָּ עֵת לִדְתָּנָה: תִּכְרַעְנָה יַלְדֵיהֶן תְּפַלַּחְנָה חֶבְלֵיהֶם תְּשַׁלַּחְנָה:
ה   יַחְלְמוּ בְנֵיהֶם יִרְבּוּ בַבָּר יָצְאוּ וְלֹא־שָׁבוּ לָמוֹ: מִי־שִׁלַּח פֶּרֶא חָפְשִׁי
ו-ז   וּמֹסְרוֹת עָרוֹד מִי פִתֵּחַ: אֲשֶׁר־שַׂמְתִּי עֲרָבָה בֵיתוֹ וּמִשְׁכְּנוֹתָיו מְלֵחָה:
ח   יִשְׂחַק לַהֲמוֹן קִרְיָה תְּשֻׁאוֹת נוֹגֵשׂ לֹא יִשְׁמָע: יְתוּר הָרִים מִרְעֵהוּ וְאַחַר
ט-י   כָּל־יָרוֹק יִדְרוֹשׁ: הֲיֹאבֶה רֵּים עָבְדֶךָ אִם־יָלִין עַל־אֲבוּסֶךָ: הֲתִקְשָׁר
יא   רֵים בְּתֶלֶם עֲבֹתוֹ אִם־יְשַׂדֵּד עֲמָקִים אַחֲרֶיךָ: הֲתִבְטַח־בּוֹ כִּי־רַב כֹּחוֹ
יב   וְתַעֲזֹב אֵלָיו יְגִיעֶךָ: הֲתַאֲמִין בּוֹ כִּי־ ﹖יָשׁוּב [יָשִׁיב ק] זַרְעֶךָ וְגָרְנְךָ
יג-יד   יֶאֱסֹף: כְּנַף־רְנָנִים נֶעֱלָסָה אִם־אֶבְרָה חֲסִידָה וְנֹצָה: כִּי־תַעֲזֹב לָאָרֶץ
טו   בֵּצֶיהָ וְעַל־עָפָר תְּחַמֵּם: וַתִּשְׁכַּח כִּי־רֶגֶל תְּזוּרֶהָ וְחַיַּת הַשָּׂדֶה
טז-יז   תְּדוּשֶׁהָ: הִקְשִׁיחַ בָּנֶיהָ לְּלֹא־לָהּ לְרִיק יְגִיעָהּ בְּלִי־פָחַד: כִּי־הִשָּׁהּ אֱלוֹהַּ
יח   חָכְמָה וְלֹא־חָלַק לָהּ בַּבִּינָה: כָּעֵת בַּמָּרוֹם תַּמְרִיא תִּשְׂחַק לַסּוּס
יט-כ   וּלְרֹכְבוֹ: הֲתִתֵּן לַסּוּס גְּבוּרָה הֲתַלְבִּישׁ צַוָּארוֹ רַעְמָה: הְַתַרְעִישֶׁנּוּ
כא   כָּאַרְבֶּה הוֹד נַחְרוֹ אֵימָה: יַחְפְּרוּ בָעֵמֶק וְיָשִׂישׂ בְּכֹחַ יֵצֵא לִקְרַאת־
כב-כג   נָשֶׁק: יִשְׂחַק לְפַחַד וְלֹא יֵחָת וְלֹא־יָשׁוּב מִפְּנֵי־חָרֶב: עָלָיו תִּרְנֶה
כד   אַשְׁפָּה לַהַב חֲנִית וְכִידוֹן: בְּרַעַשׁ וְרֹגֶז יְגַמֶּא־אָרֶץ וְלֹא־יַאֲמִין כִּי־קוֹל
כה   שׁוֹפָר: בְּדֵי שֹׁפָר | יֹאמַר הֶאָח וּמֵרָחוֹק יָרִיחַ מִלְחָמָה רַעַם שָׂרִים
כו-כז   וּתְרוּעָה: הֲמִבִּינָתְךָ יַאֲבֶר־נֵץ יִפְרֹשׂ ﹖כְנָפוֹ [כְּנָפָיו ק] לְתֵימָן: אִם־
כח   עַל־פִּיךָ יַגְבִּיהַּ נָשֶׁר וְכִי יָרִים קִנּוֹ: סֶלַע יִשְׁכֹּן וְיִתְלֹנָן עַל־שֶׁן־סָלַע

38:31. The seven stars of Pleiades are clustered together, as if "tied up"; the stars in Orion are spaced far apart, as if unbound (see *Ramban*).

38:38. Heavy rain loosens the soil, and when the sun comes out it forms clumps (*Ramban*).

39:1. The offspring of these animals could not survive their harsh environment without God's benevolence.

39:18. Though it cannot fly, an ostrich can readily outrun a horse.

39:20. That is, his galloping hooves.

39:24. He gallops swiftly, as if swallowing the land. He is so anxious for the battle that he "cannot believe it" when the trumpet signals the beginning of the fray (*Rashi*).

*. . . the
constellations
. . .*

*. . . the
clouds, the
lightning . . .*

*God cares
for all
creatures: the
lion, the
raven . . .*

39

*. . . the
goats
and the
gazelles . . .*

*. . . the wild
donkey and
the wild ox
. . .*

*. . . the wild
birds . . .*

*. . . the
horses . . .*

*. . . the hawk
and the eagle*

³¹ *Did you tie up the bond of Pleiades, or unbind the cords of Orion?* * ³² *Did you ever take out the constellations in their times, or lead Ursa together with her children?* ³³ *Do you know the laws of heaven; did you place its rule upon the land?*

³⁴ *Did you raise your voice to the clouds, so that a multitude of water should drench you?* ³⁵ *Did you dispatch lightning bolts, so that they would go forth, and then say to you, 'Here we are!'?*

³⁶ *[Do you know] who placed wisdom in the innards? Or who imbued the heart with understanding?*

³⁷ *Who, with wisdom, makes the heavens glisten, and Who pours from the flagons of heaven,* ³⁸ *when dirt flows with the poured-out [rain], and clumps are stuck together?* *

³⁹ *Will you trap prey for a lion, or fill the needs of lion whelps,* ⁴⁰ *when they hunch over in [their] lairs, lie low in their den in wait?* ⁴¹ *Who prepares nourishment for the raven, when its young ones call out to God, helpless without food?*

¹ **D**o *you know the time when the mountain goats give birth, or anticipate the labor pains of the gazelle?* * ² *Did you count the months as they came to term, to know the moment of their birth?* ³ *They crouch and expel their offspring, they rid themselves of their agonies.* ⁴ *Their young become hardy and grow up in the wild; they go off, and do not return to them.*

⁵ *Who set the wild ass free and who loosened the bonds of the wild donkey,* ⁶ *for whom I designated the desert as his home, his habitats in arid land?* ⁷ *He scoffs at the city's tumult; he does not hear a driver's shouts.* ⁸ *He searches out mountains for his pasture, and seeks every greenery.* ⁹ *Would a wild ox be willing to serve you? Would he lodge by your feeding trough?* ¹⁰ *Can you hitch a wild ox to the plow with its rope? Would he hoe valleys behind you?* ¹¹ *Could you trust him, though his strength is great, and leave your labor to him?* ¹² *Could you rely on him to bring back your seed and gather your threshed grain?*

¹³ *The wing of the ostriches is a delight; the stork with [its] pinion and feathers.* ¹⁴ *She abandons her eggs on the ground and they are warmed in the dust,* ¹⁵ *but she forgets that feet might crush her egg and the beast of the field might trample it,* ¹⁶ *becoming hardened against her offspring as if they were not hers, her toil being in vain, without fear,* ¹⁷ *for God has denied her wisdom, and He did not apportion to her understanding.* ¹⁸ *At the opportune time she flies off on high; she laughs at the horse and his rider.* *

¹⁹ *Did you give the horse his strength? Did you adorn his throat with fearsomeness?* ²⁰ *Did you make him louder* * *than locusts; his majestic snort so fearful?* ²¹ *He lies in ambush in the valleys and rejoices in [his] strength, he goes out to face weapons.* ²² *He laughs at fear and never trembles; he does not recoil before the sword.* ²³ *Let the quiver rattle against him, the flash of spear and lance.* ²⁴ *With noise and trembling he drinks up the land; he cannot believe it when the horn sounds.* * ²⁵ *As the [blasts of the] horn increase, he says, 'Hurrah!' From the distance he smells battle, the thunder of officers and shouting!*

²⁶ *Is it by your wisdom that the hawk hovers, spreads its wings toward the south?* ²⁷ *Is it by your command that the eagle soars, or makes his nest on high,* ²⁸ *dwelling and lodging in the clefts of rocks, upon rocky cliff*

כט־ל וּמִצּוּדָה: מִשָּׁם חָפַר־אֹכֶל לְמֵרָחוֹק עֵינָיו יַבִּיטוּ: °וְאֶפְרֹחָו [°וְאֶפְרֹחָיו ק]

מ   א וַיַּעֲלוּ־דָם וּבַאֲשֶׁר חֲלָלִים שָׁם הוּא: וַיַּעַן יהוה אֶת־אִיּוֹב

ב־ג וַיֹּאמַר: הֲרֹב עִם־שַׁדַּי יִסּוֹר מוֹכִיחַ אֱלוֹהַּ יַעֲנֶנָּה: וַיַּעַן אִיּוֹב

ד־ה אֶת־יהוה וַיֹּאמַר: הֵן קַלֹּתִי מָה אֲשִׁיבֶךָּ יָדִי שַׂמְתִּי לְמוֹ־פִי: אַחַת דִּבַּרְתִּי

ו וְלֹא אֶעֱנֶה וּשְׁתַּיִם וְלֹא אוֹסִיף: וַיַּעַן־יהוה אֶת־אִיּוֹב

ז °מִנסערה [°מִן ק] °סְעָרָה ק] וַיֹּאמַר: אֱזָר־נָא כְגֶבֶר חֲלָצֶיךָ אֶשְׁאָלְךָ

ח־ט וְהוֹדִיעֵנִי: הַאַף תָּפֵר מִשְׁפָּטִי תַּרְשִׁיעֵנִי לְמַעַן תִּצְדָּק: וְאִם־זְרוֹעַ כָּאֵל |

י־יא לָךְ וּבְקוֹל כָּמֹהוּ תַרְעֵם: עֲדֵה נָא גָאוֹן וָגֹבַהּ וְהוֹד וְהָדָר תִּלְבָּשׁ: הָפֵץ

יב עֶבְרוֹת אַפֶּךָ וּרְאֵה כָל־גֵּאֶה וְהַשְׁפִּילֵהוּ: רְאֵה כָל־גֵּאֶה הַכְנִיעֵהוּ וַהֲדֹךְ

יג־יד רְשָׁעִים תַּחְתָּם: טָמְנֵם בֶּעָפָר יָחַד פְּנֵיהֶם חֲבֹשׁ בַּטָּמוּן: וְגַם־אֲנִי אוֹדֶךָּ כִּי

טו תוֹשִׁעַ לְךָ יְמִינֶךָ: הִנֵּה־נָא בְהֵמוֹת אֲשֶׁר־עָשִׂיתִי עִמָּךְ חָצִיר כַּבָּקָר יֹאכֵל:

טז־יז הִנֵּה־נָא כֹחוֹ בְמָתְנָיו וְאֹנוֹ בִּשְׁרִירֵי בִטְנוֹ: יַחְפֹּץ זְנָבוֹ כְמוֹ־אָרֶז גִּידֵי

יח °פחדו [°פַחֲדָיו ק] יְשֹׂרָגוּ: עֲצָמָיו אֲפִיקֵי נְחוּשָׁה גְּרָמָיו כִּמְטִיל בַּרְזֶל:

יט הוּא רֵאשִׁית דַּרְכֵי־אֵל הָעֹשׂוֹ יַגֵּשׁ חַרְבּוֹ: כִּי־בוּל הָרִים יִשְׂאוּ־לוֹ וְכָל־

כ־כב חַיַּת הַשָּׂדֶה יְשַׂחֲקוּ־שָׁם: תַּחַת־צֶאֱלִים יִשְׁכָּב בְּסֵתֶר קָנֶה וּבִצָּה: יְסֻכֻּהוּ

כג צֶאֱלִים צִלֲלוֹ יְסֻבּוּהוּ עַרְבֵי־נָחַל: הֵן יַעֲשֹׁק נָהָר לֹא יַחְפּוֹז יִבְטַח |

כד־כה כִּי־יָגִיחַ יַרְדֵּן אֶל־פִּיהוּ: בְּעֵינָיו יִקָּחֶנּוּ בְּמוֹקְשִׁים יִנְקָב־אָף: תִּמְשֹׁךְ לִוְיָתָן

כו בְּחַכָּה וּבְחֶבֶל תַּשְׁקִיעַ לְשֹׁנוֹ: הֲתָשִׂים אַגְמוֹן בְּאַפּוֹ וּבְחוֹחַ תִּקּוֹב לֶחֱיוֹ:

כז־כח הֲיַרְבֶּה אֵלֶיךָ תַּחֲנוּנִים אִם־יְדַבֵּר אֵלֶיךָ רַכּוֹת: הֲיִכְרֹת בְּרִית עִמָּךְ תִּקָּחֶנּוּ

כט־ל לְעֶבֶד עוֹלָם: הַתְשַׂחֶק־בּוֹ כַּצִּפּוֹר וְתִקְשְׁרֶנּוּ לְנַעֲרוֹתֶיךָ: יִכְרוּ עָלָיו

לא חַבָּרִים יֶחֱצוּהוּ בֵּין כְּנַעֲנִים: הַתְמַלֵּא בְשֻׂכּוֹת עוֹרוֹ וּבְצִלְצַל דָּגִים רֹאשׁוֹ:

מא   לב־א שִׂים־עָלָיו כַּפֶּךָ זְכֹר מִלְחָמָה אַל־תּוֹסַף: הֵן־תֹּחַלְתּוֹ נִכְזָבָה הֲגַם אֶל־

ב־ג מַרְאָיו יֻטָל: לֹא־אַכְזָר כִּי יְעוּרֶנּוּ וּמִי הוּא לְפָנַי יִתְיַצָּב: מִי הִקְדִּימַנִי

ד וַאֲשַׁלֵּם תַּחַת כָּל־הַשָּׁמַיִם לִי־הוּא: °לֹא [°לוֹ ק] אַחֲרִישׁ בַּדָּיו

40:4-5. Job acknowledges that he has no right to dispute God and he will henceforth remain silent. He says that his first question — Why do the righteous suffer? — has been answered by Elihu: God's ways are good, though we do not understand them. But his second question — Why should the wicked prosper? — remains (*Ralbag*).

40:10. God invites Job to try to assume His role as Judge of the world.

40:15. The Behemoth is a gigantic animal, the "Wild Ox" mentioned in Aggadic literature (*Ramban*). God is telling Job: If you cannot subdue proud and wicked people, perhaps you will fare better with a dumb animal (*Ramban*) that lives on dry land with you (*Ibn Ezra*).

Scripture goes into great length to describe the huge Behemoth and the even larger and fearsomely ferocious Leviathan in order to show Job that he dare not presume to make demands of the God Who can create such

awesome creatures in His world. In a deeper sense, God wanted to make Job understand that everything has a role in the universe and that the comforts of the wicked, to which Job took such exception, cannot be understood in a vacuum. Infinite calculations are involved and only God's wisdom is adequate to know why they are here and what would be lost if they were removed.

40:17. An allusion to virility and ferocity.

40:19. Of all the species of land animals, the Behemoth was the first one created (*Metzudos*).

40:20. Though he needs a mountainful of produce to satisfy his appetite, animals frolic near him without fear, for he is not a carnivore (*Ramban*).

40:23. He gulps huge amounts of water, but does not fear attack while he drinks, because of his great strength (*Ibn Ezra*).

40:25. A great sea creature.

and tower, ^{29} from there he searches for food, his eyes look out to the distance? ^{30} His eaglets gulp up blood, and where there are corpses, there he is [found].

40
God rebukes Job

^{1} **H**ASHEM then responded to Job and said:
^{2} "Can one who contends with the Almighty be arrogant? One who argues with God must answer [His words]!"

Job admits his error

^{3} Job then responded to HASHEM and said: ^{4} "Behold, I am deficient; what can I answer You?* I place my hand against my mouth! ^{5} I spoke once and I will not speak up again; as for the second, I will say no more."

^{6} HASHEM then responded to Job from out of the whirlwind and said:

Dare Job think that he is God's equal?

^{7} Gird your loins like a warrior! I will ask, and you answer Me! ^{8} Will you also discredit My judgment? Will you declare Me wrong in order to make yourself right?! ^{9} Do you have power like God; can you, like Him, produce a thunder clap? ^{10} Adorn yourself, if you will, with majesty and exaltedness;* don

Let him vent his rage against the wicked and haughty

glory and majesty. ^{11} Spew forth the furies of your anger; see every haughty one and lower him. ^{12} See every haughty one and humble him; crush the wicked in their places. ^{13} Hide them all together in the dirt; confine their faces into a hidden place. ^{14} Then I, too, will praise you, when your right hand triumphs for you!

The Behemoth

^{15} Behold now the Behemoth that I have created with you;* he eats grass like cattle. ^{16} Behold, now, his strength is in his loins and his might is in the navel of his abdomen. ^{17} When he wishes, his tail is like a cedar; the sinews of his stones become entangled. * ^{18} His bones have the strength of copper; his limbs are like an iron weight. ^{19} He is the first of God's ways;* [only] his Maker can direct His sword up close. ^{20} For the mountains present him their crops, yet all the beasts of the field frolic there. * ^{21} He lies under shady trees, in the seclusion of reed and marsh. ^{22} Shady trees cover him with shade; the willows of the stream surround him. ^{23} Behold he plunders the river and is not anxious;* he feels secure that he can gulp the Jordan into his mouth. ^{24} [God] will subdue it with His eyes, perforate its nose with snares.

The Leviathan

^{25} Can you pull the Leviathan* with a hook, can you embed a line in his tongue? ^{26} Can you put a curved hook in his nose, or pierce his cheek with a barbed hook? ^{27} Will he beset you with entreaties, or speak ingratiatingly to you?* ^{28} Would he forge a covenant with you? Could you take him as a lifetime servant? ^{29} Could you sport with him as with a bird, or tether him for your maidens?* ^{30} Can friends make a feast of him, can they divide him among the merchants? ^{31} Can you riddle his skin with barbs, or put his head in a fish bucket? ^{32} If you put your hand on him, you will no more remember warfare!*

41
The Leviathan's intimidating appearance . . .

^{1} How disillusioned his ambition must be; he is felled by its very appearance!* ^{2} No person is rash enough to stir him up. Who, then, would dare stand up to Me? ^{3} Whoever anticipated Me, I can reward him,* for whatever is under all the heavens is mine! ^{4} I would not suppress his boastings,

---

40:27. Can you ever get him to be at your mercy?

40:29. Can you make him a pet?

40:32. You will surely be killed if you dare place a hand on him (*Ramban*).

41:1. If one thinks he can overpower the Leviathan, he

will be disillusioned. So fearsome is the Leviathan that any hope of defeating it is doomed; the mere sight of it is enough to make people swoon.

41:3. If anyone would try to battle the Leviathan even before God challenged him, God will reward him (*Ramban*).

ה וּדְבַר־גְּבוּרוֹת וְחִין עֶרְכּוֹ: מִי־גִלָּה פְּנֵי לְבוּשׁוֹ בְּכֶפֶל רִסְנוֹ מִי יָבוֹא:

ו-ז דַּלְתֵי פָנָיו מִי פִתֵּחַ סְבִיבוֹת שִׁנָּיו אֵימָה: גַּאֲוָה אֲפִיקֵי מָגִנִּים סָגוּר

ח-ט חוֹתָם צָר: אֶחָד בְּאֶחָד יִגַּשׁוּ וְרוּחַ לֹא־יָבוֹא בֵינֵיהֶם: אִישׁ־בְּאָחִיהוּ

י יְדֻבָּקוּ יִתְלַכְּדוּ וְלֹא יִתְפָּרָדוּ: עֲטִישֹׁתָיו תָּהֶל אוֹר וְעֵינָיו כְּעַפְעַפֵּי־שָׁחַר:

יא-יב מִפִּיו לַפִּידִים יַהֲלֹכוּ כִּידוֹדֵי אֵשׁ יִתְמַלָּטוּ: מִנְּחִירָיו יֵצֵא עָשָׁן כְּדוּד

יג-יד נָפוּחַ וְאַגְמֹן: נַפְשׁוֹ גֶּחָלִים תְּלַהֵט וְלַהַב מִפִּיו יֵצֵא: בְּצַוָּארוֹ יָלִין עֹז

טו-טז וּלְפָנָיו תָּדוּץ דְּאָבָה: מַפְּלֵי בְשָׂרוֹ דָבֵקוּ יָצוּק עָלָיו בַּל־יִמּוֹט: לִבּוֹ יָצוּק

יז כְּמוֹ־אָבֶן וְיָצוּק כְּפֶלַח תַּחְתִּית: מִשֵּׂתוֹ יָגוּרוּ אֵלִים מִשְּׁבָרִים יִתְחַטָּאוּ:

יח-יט מַשִּׂיגֵהוּ חֶרֶב בְּלִי תָקוּם חֲנִית מַסָּע וְשִׁרְיָה: יַחְשֹׁב לְתֶבֶן בַּרְזֶל לְעֵץ

כ-כא רִקָּבוֹן נְחוּשָׁה: לֹא־יַבְרִיחֶנּוּ בֶן־קָשֶׁת לְקַשׁ נֶהְפְּכוּ־לוֹ אַבְנֵי־קָלַע: כְּקַשׁ

כב נֶחְשְׁבוּ תוֹתָח וְיִשְׂחַק לְרַעַשׁ כִּידוֹן: תַּחְתָּיו חַדּוּדֵי חָרֶשׂ יִרְפַּד חָרוּץ

כג-כד עֲלֵי־טִיט: יַרְתִּיחַ כַּסִּיר מְצוּלָה יָם יָשִׂים כַּמֶּרְקָחָה: אַחֲרָיו יָאִיר נָתִיב

כה-כו יַחְשֹׁב תְּהוֹם לְשֵׂיבָה: אֵין־עַל־עָפָר מָשְׁלוֹ הֶעָשׂוּ לִבְלִי־חָת: אֶת־כָּל־

א גָּבֹהַּ יִרְאֶה הוּא מֶלֶךְ עַל־כָּל־בְּנֵי־שָׁחַץ: וַיַּעַן אִיּוֹב אֶת־ **מב**

ב יְהֹוָה וַיֹּאמַר: °יָדַעְתִּי [יָדַעְתָּ ק] כִּי־כֹל תּוּכָל וְלֹא־יִבָּצֵר מִמְּךָ מְזִמָּה:

ג מִי זֶה | מַעְלִים עֵצָה בְּלִי דָעַת לָכֵן הִגַּדְתִּי וְלֹא אָבִין נִפְלָאוֹת מִמֶּנִּי וְלֹא

ד-ה אֵדָע: שְׁמַע־נָא וְאָנֹכִי אֲדַבֵּר אֶשְׁאָלְךָ וְהוֹדִיעֵנִי: לְשֵׁמַע־אֹזֶן שְׁמַעְתִּיךָ

ו וְעַתָּה עֵינִי רָאָתְךָ: עַל־כֵּן אֶמְאַס וְנִחַמְתִּי עַל־עָפָר וָאֵפֶר:

ז וַיְהִי אַחַר דִּבֶּר יְהֹוָה אֶת־הַדְּבָרִים הָאֵלֶּה אֶל־אִיּוֹב וַיֹּאמֶר יְהֹוָה אֶל־

אֱלִיפַז הַתֵּימָנִי חָרָה אַפִּי בְךָ וּבִשְׁנֵי רֵעֶיךָ כִּי לֹא דִבַּרְתֶּם אֵלַי נְכוֹנָה

ח כְּעַבְדִּי אִיּוֹב: וְעַתָּה קְחוּ־לָכֶם שִׁבְעָה־פָרִים וְשִׁבְעָה אֵילִים וּלְכוּ | אֶל־

עַבְדִּי אִיּוֹב וְהַעֲלִיתֶם עוֹלָה בַּעַדְכֶם וְאִיּוֹב עַבְדִּי יִתְפַּלֵּל עֲלֵיכֶם כִּי אִם־

פָּנָיו אֶשָּׂא לְבִלְתִּי עֲשׂוֹת עִמָּכֶם נְבָלָה כִּי לֹא דִבַּרְתֶּם אֵלַי נְכוֹנָה כְּעַבְדִּי

ט אִיּוֹב: וַיֵּלְכוּ אֱלִיפַז הַתֵּימָנִי וּבִלְדַּד הַשּׁוּחִי צֹפַר הַנַּעֲמָתִי וַיַּעֲשׂוּ כַּאֲשֶׁר

י דִּבֶּר אֲלֵיהֶם יְהֹוָה וַיִּשָּׂא יְהֹוָה אֶת־פְּנֵי אִיּוֹב: וַיהֹוָה שָׁב אֶת־°שְׁבִית

[שְׁבוּת ק] אִיּוֹב בְּהִתְפַּלְלוֹ בְּעַד רֵעֵהוּ וַיֹּסֶף יְהֹוָה אֶת־כָּל־אֲשֶׁר לְאִיּוֹב

יא לְמִשְׁנֶה: וַיָּבֹאוּ אֵלָיו כָּל־אֶחָיו וְכָל־אַחְיוֹתָיו וְכָל־יֹדְעָיו לְפָנִים וַיֹּאכְלוּ

41:5. The sea is the Leviathan's garment. Even if he were tied to a double cord, who would be able to pull him from the sea? (*Ramban*).

41:6. His jaws (*Ramban*).

41:7. His scales (*Kara*).

41:10. Because the waters of the sea part from his mighty sneeze, until his sparkling eyes are visible (*Ramban*).

41:14. To the Leviathan, any dangerous or worrisome situation is an invigorating challenge.

41:15. The layers of the Leviathan's flesh are firmly packed together, an indication of his strength (*Kara*).

41:22. He sleeps on sharp shards; his hide is so thick that they do not disturb him in the least (*Ramban*).

41:23. So violently is the water pounded by his movements.

41:24. As he glides through the sea, he leaves a white wake of frothing water (*Ibn Ezra*).

41:26. Because of his immense strength and size, he is not impressed with the dimensions of any other creature, no matter how lofty and haughty it may be (*Ramban*).

42:6. Having glimpsed the majesty of God, Job relents. He has no further need to comprehend what is beyond

. . .
impregna-
bility . . .

. . .
awesome
destructive
power . . .

the story of his might, nor the stateliness of his standing! ⁵ Who has uncovered the surface of his garment? Who can undertake his double bridle?* ⁶ Who could open the portals of his face?* Surrounding his teeth is terror! ⁷ His pride is in the strength of his shields;* their seal is closed tightly. ⁸ One [scale] touches the next; even air cannot come between them. ⁹ Each is attached to the other; they are interlocked, and cannot be separated. ¹⁰ His sneezes flash light;* his eyes are like the glimmer of the dawn. ¹¹ Flames go forth from his mouth; sparks of fire escape from it. ¹² Smoke belches from his nostrils, like a seething pot or cauldron. ¹³ His breath ignites coals and a flame shoots from his mouth. ¹⁴ Power resides in his neck; before him worry turns to delight. * ¹⁵ The layers of his flesh are stuck together;* firmly upon one another, immovable. ¹⁶ His heart is firm as rock, firm as the lower millstone. ¹⁷ When he ascends, the mighty become frightened; the very waves are found wanting. ¹⁸ If someone would apprehend him, a sword would not prevail, nor would a spear, a slingshot, or armor. ¹⁹ He treats iron as straw and copper as rotten wood. ²⁰ A bow's arrow cannot chase him away; sling stones become straw for him. ²¹ A catapult is considered like straw, he laughs at the swish of a javelin. ²² Under him are pointed shards; he spreads [himself] on jagged rocks as if on the mud. * ²³ He bubbles up the deep sea like a [seething] pot; he ferments the sea like a boiling concoction. * ²⁴ In his wake a path shines; he makes the deep sea look like an old man. *

. . . and
disdain for
everything

²⁵ Nothing on earth can compare to him; he was made to be without fear. ²⁶ He looks down on everything elevated;* he is the king over all the haughty.

42

JOB'S
REPEN-
TANCE AND
RESTORA-
TION
42:1-17

¹ Job then responded to HASHEM, and said: ² "I knew that You can do everything, and that nothing can impede [Your] purpose from You. ³ Who is it that would deny [Your] counsel without knowledge? Therefore I declared, yet I understand nothing. It is beyond me. I shall not know! ⁴ Listen, please, and I will speak; I will ask You, and You inform me. ⁵ I had heard of You through hearsay, but now my eye has beheld You! ⁶ Therefore, I renounce [my words] and relent, for [I am but] dust and ashes."*

Job is
superior to
his friends

⁷ It was after HASHEM had spoken these words to Job that HASHEM said to Eliphaz the Temanite, "My wrath anger burns against you and against your two friends, for you did not speak properly about Me as My servant Job did. * ⁸ And now, take yourselves seven bulls and seven rams, and go to My servant Job, and bring them up as a burnt-offering for yourselves, and My servant Job will pray for you. * For his sake I will show consideration, not to do anything vile to you, for you did not speak properly about Me, as My servant Job did."

⁹ So Eliphaz the Temanite and Bildad the Shuhite [and] Zophar the Naamathite went and did as HASHEM had spoken to them, and HASHEM showed consideration for Job.

Job's wealth
restored

¹⁰ HASHEM returned Job's captivity* after he had prayed for his friend, and HASHEM added on to all that Job had had, until there was double. ¹¹ All his brothers and all his sisters and all his former acquaintances came to him and ate

---

human comprehension.
42:7. Although Job also said things that were improper, he did so out of his suffering (Kara), and at any rate he has now recanted (Ibn Ezra).

42:8. Because of his righteousness Job will officiate at the offering (Ramban).

42:10. Job's stolen livestock (see 1:13-17) was returned to him (Ramban).

עִמּוֹ לֶחֶם בְּבֵיתוֹ וַיָּנֻדוּ לוֹ וַיְנַחֲמוּ אֹתוֹ עַל כָּל־הָרָעָה אֲשֶׁר־הֵבִיא יהוה

יב עָלָיו וַיִּתְּנוּ־לוֹ אִישׁ קְשִׂיטָה אֶחָת וְאִישׁ נֶזֶם זָהָב אֶחָד: וַיהוֹה בֵּרַךְ אֶת־
אַחֲרִית אִיּוֹב מֵרֵאשִׁתוֹ וַיְהִי־לוֹ אַרְבָּעָה עָשָׂר אֶלֶף צֹאן וְשֵׁשֶׁת אֲלָפִים

יג גְּמַלִּים וְאֶלֶף־צֶמֶד בָּקָר וְאֶלֶף אֲתוֹנוֹת: וַיְהִי־לוֹ שִׁבְעָנָה בָנִים וְשָׁלוֹשׁ

יד בָּנוֹת: וַיִּקְרָא שֵׁם־הָאַחַת יְמִימָה וְשֵׁם הַשֵּׁנִית קְצִיעָה וְשֵׁם הַשְּׁלִישִׁית

טו קֶרֶן הַפּוּךְ: וְלֹא נִמְצָא נָשִׁים יָפוֹת כִּבְנוֹת אִיּוֹב בְּכָל־הָאָרֶץ וַיִּתֵּן לָהֶם

טז אֲבִיהֶם נַחֲלָה בְּתוֹךְ אֲחֵיהֶם: וַיְחִי אִיּוֹב אַחֲרֵי־זֹאת מֵאָה וְאַרְבָּעִים

יז שָׁנָה °וַיִּרְא [°וַיִּרְאֶה ק] אֶת־בָּנָיו וְאֶת־בְּנֵי בָנָיו אַרְבָּעָה דֹרוֹת: וַיָּמָת
אִיּוֹב זָקֵן וּשְׂבַע יָמִים:

סכום פסוקי איוב אלף ושבעים. וסימנו וגליתי להם **עטרת** שלום.

42:13. Alternatively: "double-seven," i.e. fourteen (*Targum*; *Rashi*).
42:14-15. Job named his daughters in accordance with their attractiveness: Jemimah means "day," for

her beauty shone forth like the sunlight; Keziah was as redolent as the spice "cassia"; and Keren-happuch's countenance radiated with the "sparkle of an emerald" (*Targum*).

bread with him in his house. They recalled his mourning and consoled him for all the misfortune that HASHEM had brought upon him, and each [of them] gave him a sheep and each a golden ring.

 ^12^ HASHEM blessed Job's end more than [He had blessed] his beginning. He had fourteen thousand sheep, six thousand camels, a thousand pairs of cattle and a thousand she-asses. ^13^ He had seven* sons and three daughters. ^14^ He called the first one's name Jemimah, the second one's name Keziah and the third one's name Keren-happuch. * ^15^ There were not found any women as beautiful as the daughters of Job anywhere in the land. Their father gave them an inheritance among their brothers.

A new and fruitful family

^16^ After this, Job lived a hundred and forty years; he saw his children and his children's children, to four generations. ^17^ Then Job died, old and satiated with years.

Song of Songs שיר השירים

Rabbi Akiva, one of the greatest Sages of the Talmud, said, "All the songs of Scripture are holy, but the Song of Songs is holy of holies." What is it about this song that raises it to so lofty a plane? The question is especially perplexing if Song of Songs is taken literally, for it appears to be a song of uncommon passion; it seems out of place among Scripture's Books of prophecy and sacred spirit. Moreover, although some of the Sages wondered whether Ecclesiastes should be included among the Books of Scripture, there was never a question about Song of Songs.

To both the Sages of the Talmud and the classic commentators, it was clear that Song of Songs is an allegory, a duet of longing between God and Israel. That is why it is read publicly during Passover, the time when Israel became God's people. Its verses are so saturated with meaning that every commentator finds new themes in its beautiful and cryptic words. All agree, however, that the truth of the Song is to be found only in its allegory.

That is why, in the interest of accuracy, our translation of the Song is different from that of any other ArtScroll translation of Scripture. Although we provide the literal meaning as part of our commentary, we translate the Song according to Rashi's allegorical translation. As he explains in his introduction:

> Solomon foresaw through the Holy Spirit that Israel is destined to suffer a series of exiles and will lament, nostalgically recalling her former status as God's chosen beloved ... And they will recall the goodness He promised for the End of Days.
>
> The prophets frequently likened the relationship between God and Israel to that of a loving husband angered by his straying wife who had betrayed him. Solomon composed the Song of Songs in the form of that same allegory. It is a passionate dialogue between the husband [God] who still loves his estranged exiled wife [Israel], and the wife who longs for her husband and seeks to endear herself to him again, as she recalls her youthful love for him and admits her guilt.
>
> God too ... recalls the kindness of [Israel's] youth, her beauty, and her skillful deeds for which He loved her so. He proclaims that ... she is still His wife and He her husband, and He will yet return to her.

א   א־ב   שִׁיר הַשִּׁירִים אֲשֶׁר לִשְׁלֹמֹה: יִשָּׁקֵנִי מִנְּשִׁיקוֹת פִּיהוּ כִּי־טוֹבִים דֹּדֶיךָ

ג   מִיָּיִן: לְרֵיחַ שְׁמָנֶיךָ טוֹבִים שֶׁמֶן תּוּרַק שְׁמֶךָ עַל־כֵּן עֲלָמוֹת אֲהֵבוּךָ:

ד   מָשְׁכֵנִי אַחֲרֶיךָ נָּרוּצָה הֱבִיאַנִי הַמֶּלֶךְ חֲדָרָיו נָגִילָה וְנִשְׂמְחָה בָּךְ נַזְכִּירָה

ה   דֹדֶיךָ מִיַּיִן מֵישָׁרִים אֲהֵבוּךָ:   שְׁחוֹרָה אֲנִי וְנָאוָה בְּנוֹת

ו   יְרוּשָׁלַ͏ִם כְּאָהֳלֵי קֵדָר כִּירִיעוֹת שְׁלֹמֹה: אַל־תִּרְאֻנִי שֶׁאֲנִי שְׁחַרְחֹרֶת

        שֶׁשֱּׁזָפַתְנִי הַשָּׁמֶשׁ בְּנֵי אִמִּי נִחֲרוּ־בִי שָׂמֻנִי נֹטֵרָה אֶת־הַכְּרָמִים כַּרְמִי

ז   שֶׁלִּי לֹא נָטָרְתִּי: הַגִּידָה לִּי שֶׁאָהֲבָה נַפְשִׁי אֵיכָה תִרְעֶה אֵיכָה תַּרְבִּיץ

ח   בַּצָּהֳרָיִם שַׁלָּמָה אֶהְיֶה כְּעֹטְיָה עַל עֶדְרֵי חֲבֵרֶיךָ: אִם־לֹא תֵדְעִי לָךְ

        הַיָּפָה בַּנָּשִׁים צְאִי־לָךְ בְּעִקְבֵי הַצֹּאן וּרְעִי אֶת־גְּדִיֹּתַיִךְ עַל מִשְׁכְּנוֹת

ט   הָרֹעִים: לְסֻסָתִי בְּרִכְבֵי פַרְעֹה דִּמִּיתִיךְ רַעְיָתִי: נָאווּ

יא   לְחָיַיִךְ בַּתֹּרִים צַוָּארֵךְ בַּחֲרוּזִים: תּוֹרֵי זָהָב נַעֲשֶׂה־לָּךְ עִם נְקֻדּוֹת הַכָּסֶף:

1:1. שִׁיר הַשִּׁירִים — *The song that excels all songs* [lit., *The song of songs*]. The greatest song uttered to God by Israel.

אֲשֶׁר לִשְׁלֹמֹה — *dedicated to God, Him to Whom peace belongs* [lit., *which is Solomon's*]. In Proverbs and Ecclesiastes, Solomon is identified as the "son of David." The omission of David's name here implies that there is a second שְׁלֹמֹה, namely מֶּלֶךְ שֶׁהַשָׁלוֹם שֶׁלּוֹ, "the King to Whom peace belongs," i.e., God, the Source of peace.

1:2. יִשָּׁקֵנִי מִנְּשִׁיקוֹת פִּיהוּ — *Communicate Your innermost wisdom to me again in loving closeness* [lit., *May He kiss me with the kisses of His mouth*]. Exiled Israel longs for God to teach the Torah, "mouth to mouth," as at Sinai.

כִּי טוֹבִים דֹדֶיךָ מִיַּיִן — *for Your love is dearer to me than all earthly delights* [lit., *for Your love is better than wine*]. The love You showed when You redeemed us from Egypt and gave us the Torah is dearer to us than wine or any other earthly pleasure.

1:3. לְרֵיחַ שְׁמָנֶיךָ טוֹבִים — *Like the scent of goodly oils is the spreading fame of Your great deeds* [lit., *For fragrance Your oils are good*]. The "fragrance" of God's miracles in Egypt was felt everywhere.

שֶׁמֶן תּוּרַק שְׁמֶךָ — *Your very name is "Flowing Oil"* [lit., *Your name is oil poured forth*]. Your reputation is like fine oil; the more it is poured, the more its fragrance spreads.

עַל כֵּן עֲלָמוֹת אֲהֵבוּךָ — *therefore have nations loved You* [lit., *therefore do young maidens love You*]. "Maidens" refers to the nations of the world.

1:4. מָשְׁכֵנִי אַחֲרֶיךָ נָּרוּצָה — *Upon perceiving a mere hint that You wished to draw me [near], we rushed with perfect faith after You into the wilderness* [lit., *Draw me, we will run after You!*]. We followed God faithfully, without food or drink (see Jeremiah 2:2,6).

הֱבִיאַנִי הַמֶּלֶךְ חֲדָרָיו — *The King brought me into His cloud-pillared chamber* [lit., *the King has brought me into His chambers*]. God protected us with His clouds of glory (see Exodus 13:21-22).

נָגִילָה וְנִשְׂמְחָה בָּךְ — *whatever our travail, we shall always be glad and rejoice in Your Torah* [lit., *we will rejoice and be glad in You*]. We take delight in Your Torah.

נַזְכִּירָה דֹדֶיךָ מִיַּיִן — *We recall Your love more than earthly delights* [lit., *we will commemorate Your love (better) than wine*]. We recall Your former love as the finest of all pleasures.

מֵישָׁרִים אֲהֵבוּךָ — *unrestrainedly do they love You* [lit., *sincerely do they love You*].

1:5. שְׁחוֹרָה אֲנִי וְנָאוָה — *Though I am black with sin, I am comely with virtue* [lit., *I am black, yet comely*]. Though my Husband left me because my sins blackened me, I am comely by virtue of my forefathers' deeds.

בְּנוֹת יְרוּשָׁלַ͏ִם — *O nations destined to ascend to Jerusalem* [lit., *O daughters of Jerusalem*]. Ultimately, all peoples will stream to honor Jerusalem, and you nations, earlier called "maidens" (v. 3), will become "her daughters."

כְּאָהֳלֵי קֵדָר כִּירִיעוֹת שְׁלֹמֹה — *though sullied as the tents of Kedar, I will be immaculate as the draperies of Him to whom peace belongs* [lit., *as the tents of Kedar, as the curtains of Solomon*].

1:6. אַל תִּרְאֻנִי שֶׁאֲנִי שְׁחַרְחֹרֶת — *Do not view me with contempt despite my swarthiness* [lit., *Do not look upon me that I am swarthy*].

שֶׁשֱּׁזָפַתְנִי הַשָּׁמֶשׁ — *for it is but the sun which has glared upon me* [lit., *because the sun has gazed upon me*]. My darkness, i.e., sinfulness, is not genetic; it will go away when I avoid the sun.

בְּנֵי אִמִּי נִחֲרוּ בִי — *The alien children of my mother incited me* [lit., *my mother's sons kindled in me*]. The mixed multitude of Egyptians and other aliens who accompanied us at the Exodus incited us to worship idols.

שָׂמֻנִי נֹטֵרָה אֶת־הַכְּרָמִים — *and made me a keeper of the vineyards of idols* [lit., *they made me keeper of the vineyards*]. . .

כַּרְמִי שֶׁלִּי לֹא נָטָרְתִּי — *but the vineyard of my own true God I did not keep* [lit., *my own vineyard I did not guard*]. I served strange gods, but not the God of my fathers.

ALLEGORICAL RENDERING FOLLOWING RASHI

1 *Prologue* ¹ The song that excels all songs dedicated to God, Him to Whom peace belongs:

Israel in exile ² Communicate Your innermost wisdom to me again in loving closeness, for
to God Your love is dearer to me than all earthly delights. ³ Like the scent of goodly oils is the spreading fame of Your great deeds; Your very name is "Flowing Oil," therefore have nations loved You. ⁴ Upon perceiving a mere hint that You wished to draw me [near], we rushed with perfect faith after You into the wilderness. The King brought me into His cloud-pillared chamber; whatever our travail, we shall always be glad and rejoice in Your Torah. We recall Your love more than earthly delights, unrestrainedly do they love You.

Israel to ⁵ Though I am black with sin, I am comely with virtue, O nations destined to
the nations ascend to Jerusalem; though sullied as the tents of Kedar, I will be immaculate as the draperies of Him to Whom peace belongs. ⁶ Do not view me with contempt despite my swarthiness, for it is but the sun which has glared upon me. The alien children of my mother incited me and made me a keeper of the vineyards of idols, but the vineyard of my own true God I did not keep.

Israel ⁷ Tell me, O You Whom my soul loves: Where will You graze Your flock? Where
to God will You rest them under the fiercest sun of harshest exile? Why shall I be like one veiled in mourning among the flocks of Your fellow shepherds?

God ⁸ If you know not where to graze, O fairest of nations, follow the footsteps of the
responds sheep, your forefathers, who traced a straight, unswerving path after My Torah.
to Israel Then you can graze your tender kids even among the dwellings of foreign shepherds. ⁹ With My mighty steeds who battled Pharaoh's chariots I revealed that you are My beloved. ¹⁰ Your cheeks are lovely with rows of gems, your neck with necklaces, My gifts to you from the splitting sea, ¹¹ by inducing Pharaoh to engage in pursuit, to add circlets of gold to your spangles of silver.

NOTES INCLUDING PHRASE-BY-PHRASE LITERAL TRANSLATION

1:7. Israel addresses God as a woman addressing her beloved Husband, and compares herself to sheep, as she contends that the exile is too difficult for her and unbecoming to Him.

הַגִּידָה לִּי שֶׁאָהֲבָה נַפְשִׁי — *Tell me, O You Whom my soul loves . . .*

אֵיכָה תִרְעֶה אֵיכָה תַּרְבִּיץ בַּצָּהֳרָיִם — *Where will You graze your flock? Where will You rest them under the fiercest sun of harshest exile?* [lit., *Where will You graze (Your flock), where will You rest (them) at noon?*]. Where will You graze us, Your flock, among the seventy wolflike nations? Where will You give us rest in the fierce lands of our exile?

שַׁלָּמָה אֶהְיֶה כְּעֹטְיָה — *Why shall I be like one veiled in mourning* [lit., *for what reason should I be as one veiled*]. It is unbecoming to You that I display grief.

עַל עֶדְרֵי חֲבֵרֶיךָ — *among the flocks of Your fellow shepherds* [lit., *by the flocks of Your colleagues*]? The other nations, who are "shepherded" by their rulers.

1:8. אִם לֹא תֵדְעִי לָךְ הַיָּפָה בַּנָּשִׁים — *If you know not where to graze, O fairest of nations* [lit., *If you do not know, O fairest of women*] . . .

צְאִי לָךְ בְּעִקְבֵי הַצֹּאן — *follow the footsteps of the sheep, your forefathers, who traced a straight, unswerving path after*

My Torah [lit., *go out in the tracks of the sheep*]. If you do not know how to safeguard your children from alien cultures, follow the example of your ancestors who observed My commandments.

וּרְעִי אֶת גְּדִיֹּתַיִךְ עַל מִשְׁכְּנוֹת הָרֹעִים — *Then you can graze your tender kids even among the dwellings of foreign shepherds* [lit., *and graze your kids by the shepherds' tents*]. Then you will be able to raise your children among the nations.

1:9. לְסֻסָתִי בְּרִכְבֵי פַרְעֹה — *With My mighty steeds who battled Pharaoh's chariots* [lit., *To a steed in Pharaoh's chariot*]. God saved the Jews from Pharaoh's army at the Sea of Reeds (*Exodus* Chs. 14-15).

דִּמִּיתִיךְ רַעְיָתִי — *I revealed that you are My beloved* [lit., *I have compared you, My beloved*].

1:10. נָאווּ לְחָיַיִךְ בַּתֹּרִים צַוָּארֵךְ בַּחֲרוּזִים — *Your cheeks are lovely with rows of gems, your neck with necklaces, My gifts to you from the splitting sea* [lit., *your cheeks are comely with circlets, your neck with strings of jewels*] . . .

1:11. תּוֹרֵי זָהָב נַעֲשֶׂה לָּךְ עִם נְקֻדּוֹת הַכָּסֶף — *by inducing Pharaoh to engage in pursuit, to add circlets of gold to your spangles of silver* [lit., *circlets of gold will We make for you and points of silver*]. God influenced the pursuing Egyptians to wear their treasures, so that, upon their defeat, Israel could claim the booty.

יב-יג עַד־שֶׁהַמֶּ֙לֶךְ֙ בִּמְסִבּ֔וֹ נִרְדִּ֖י נָתַ֥ן רֵיחֽוֹ: צְר֨וֹר הַמֹּ֤ר ׀ דּוֹדִי֙ לִ֔י בֵּ֥ין שָׁדַ֖י יָלִֽין:

יד-טו אֶשְׁכֹּ֨ל הַכֹּ֤פֶר ׀ דּוֹדִי֙ לִ֔י בְּכַרְמֵ֖י עֵ֥ין גֶּֽדִי: הִנָּ֤ךְ יָפָה֙ רַעְיָתִ֔י הִנָּ֖ךְ

טז-א יָפָ֑ה עֵינַ֖יִךְ יוֹנִֽים: הִנְּךָ֙ יָפֶ֤ה דוֹדִי֙ אַ֣ף נָעִ֔ים אַף־עַרְשֵׂ֖נוּ רַֽעֲנָנָֽה: קֹר֤וֹת בָּתֵּ֙ינוּ֙ אֲרָזִ֔ים °רַחִיטֵ֖נוּ [רַהִיטֵ֖נוּ ק׳] בְּרוֹתִֽים: אֲנִי֙ חֲבַצֶּ֣לֶת הַשָּׁר֔וֹן שֽׁוֹשַׁנַּ֖ת

ב ‖

ב-ג הָֽעֲמָקִֽים: כְּשֽׁוֹשַׁנָּה֙ בֵּ֣ין הַחוֹחִ֔ים כֵּ֥ן רַעְיָתִ֖י בֵּ֥ין הַבָּנֽוֹת: כְּתַפּ֙וּחַ֙ בַּֽעֲצֵ֣י הַיַּ֔עַר כֵּ֥ן דּוֹדִ֖י בֵּ֣ין הַבָּנִ֑ים בְּצִלּוֹ֙ חִמַּ֣דְתִּי וְיָשַׁ֔בְתִּי וּפִרְי֖וֹ מָת֥וֹק לְחִכִּֽי:

ד-ה הֱבִיאַ֙נִי֙ אֶל־בֵּ֣ית הַיַּ֔יִן וְדִגְל֥וֹ עָלַ֖י אַֽהֲבָֽה: סַמְּכ֙וּנִי֙ בָּֽאֲשִׁישׁ֔וֹת רַפְּד֖וּנִי

ו בַּתַּפּוּחִ֑ים כִּֽי־חוֹלַ֥ת אַֽהֲבָ֖ה אָֽנִי: שְׂמֹאלוֹ֙ תַּ֣חַת לְרֹאשִׁ֔י וִֽימִינ֖וֹ תְּחַבְּקֵֽנִי:

ז הִשְׁבַּ֣עְתִּי אֶתְכֶ֞ם בְּנ֤וֹת יְרֽוּשָׁלִַ֙ם֙ בִּצְבָא֔וֹת א֖וֹ בְּאַיְל֣וֹת הַשָּׂדֶ֑ה אִם־תָּעִ֧ירוּ ׀

ח וְאִם־תְּעֽוֹרְר֛וּ אֶת־הָאַֽהֲבָ֖ה עַ֥ד שֶׁתֶּחְפָּֽץ: ק֣וֹל דּוֹדִ֔י הִנֵּה־זֶ֖ה בָּ֑א

ט מְדַלֵּג֙ עַל־הֶ֣הָרִ֔ים מְקַפֵּ֖ץ עַל־הַגְּבָעֽוֹת: דּוֹמֶ֤ה דוֹדִי֙ לִצְבִ֔י א֖וֹ לְעֹ֣פֶר הָֽאַיָּלִ֑ים הִנֵּה־זֶ֤ה עוֹמֵד֙ אַחַ֣ר כָּתְלֵ֔נוּ מַשְׁגִּ֙יחַ֙ מִן־הַֽחַלֹּנ֔וֹת מֵצִ֖יץ מִן־הַֽחֲרַכִּֽים:

NOTES INCLUDING PHRASE-BY-PHRASE LITERAL TRANSLATION

1:12. עַד שֶׁהַמֶּלֶךְ בִּמְסִבּוֹ נִרְדִּי נָתַן רֵיחוֹ — *While the King was yet at Sinai my malodorous deed gave forth its scent as my Golden Calf defiled the covenant* [lit., *While the King was (still) at His table, my nard gave forth its fragrance*]. Nard is a fragrant herb, but is used here as a euphemism for the bad odor of idolatry.

1:13. צְרוֹר הַמֹּר דּוֹדִי לִי — *But my Beloved responded with a bundle of myrrh, the fragrant atonement of erecting a Tabernacle* [lit., *A bag of myrrh is my Beloved to me*]. After the disaster of the Golden Calf, God offered me a new fragrance. "Contribute toward the construction of the Tabernacle to atone for the gold you gave to make the Calf."

בֵּין שָׁדַי יָלִין — *where His Presence would dwell between the Holy Ark's staves* [lit., *lodged between my breasts*], i.e., the Shechinah (God's immanent Presence) dwelled between the two staves of the Ark. The long staves of the Ark pressed against the curtain that separated between it and the other appurtenances of the Tabernacle, causing breastlike protrusions on the other side of the curtain (Yoma 54a; Menachos 98a).

1:14. אֶשְׁכֹּל הַכֹּפֶר דּוֹדִי לִי בְּכַרְמֵי עֵין גֶּדִי — *Like a cluster of henna in En-gedi vineyards has my Beloved multiplied His forgiveness to me* [lit., *A cluster of henna is my Beloved to me, in the vineyards of En-gedi*]. The word כֹּפֶר, "henna," is linguistically related to כַּפָּרָה, "atonement."

1:15. הִנָּךְ יָפָה רַעְיָתִי הִנָּךְ יָפָה עֵינַיִךְ יוֹנִים — *He said, "I forgive you, My friend, for you are lovely in deed and lovely in resolve"* [lit., *Behold, you are beautiful, My beloved; behold, you are beautiful, your eyes are doves*]. Your righteous leaders — the "eyes" of the generation — have cleaved to Me like doves, who are faithful to their mates.

1:16. הִנְּךָ יָפֶה דוֹדִי אַף נָעִים — *It is You Who are lovely, my Beloved, so pleasant that You pardoned my sin* [lit., *You are handsome, my Beloved, indeed pleasant*]. The beauty is Yours, for having forgiven us.

אַף עַרְשֵׂנוּ רַעֲנָנָה — *enabling our Temple to make me ever fresh* [lit., *even our couch is full of vigor*]. "Couch" refers to

---

the Tabernacle, whose existence led to flourishing growth of the Jewish population.

1:17. קֹרוֹת בָּתֵּינוּ אֲרָזִים רַהִיטֵנוּ בְּרוֹתִים — *The beams of our houses are cedar, our panels are cypress.*

2:1. אֲנִי חֲבַצֶּלֶת הַשָּׁרוֹן שׁוֹשַׁנַּת הָעֲמָקִים — *I am but a rose of Sharon, even an ever-fresh rose of the valleys* [lit., *I am a rose of the Sharon, a rose of the valleys*].

2:2. כְּשׁוֹשַׁנָּה בֵּין הַחוֹחִים כֵּן רַעְיָתִי בֵּין הַבָּנוֹת — *Like the rose maintaining its beauty among the thorns, so is My faithful beloved among the nations* [lit., *As a rose among thorns, so is My beloved among the daughters*]. Just as the rose retains its beauty though surrounded by thorns, so My beloved people maintains her faith despite the torments of her neighbors.

2:3. כְּתַפּוּחַ בַּעֲצֵי הַיַּעַר כֵּן דּוֹדִי בֵּין הַבָּנִים — *Like the fruitful, fragrant apple among the barren trees of the forest, so is my Beloved among the gods* [lit., *As an apple tree among the trees of the forest, so is my Beloved among the sons*]. God is superior to all the fruitless idols of the nations.

בְּצִלּוֹ חִמַּדְתִּי וְיָשַׁבְתִּי — *In His shade I delighted and [there] I sat . . .*

וּפִרְיוֹ מָתוֹק לְחִכִּי — *and the fruit of His Torah was sweet to my palate* [lit., *and His fruit is sweet to my palate*]. We spent twelve months at Mount Sinai enjoying the sweetness of His Torah.

2:4. הֱבִיאַנִי אֶל בֵּית הַיַּיִן — *He brought me to the chamber of Torah delights* [lit., *He has brought me to the house of wine*]; an allusion to the Tent of the Meeting, where Moses expounded the Torah's commandments.

וְדִגְלוֹ עָלַי אַהֲבָה — *and clustered my encampments about Him in love* [lit., *and His banner upon me is love*]. He gathered the tribes about His Tabernacle.

2:5. סַמְּכוּנִי בָּאֲשִׁישׁוֹת רַפְּדוּנִי בַּתַּפּוּחִים — *I say to Him, "Sustain me in exile with dainty cakes, spread fragrant apples about me to comfort my dispersion* [lit., *Sustain me with dainties, spread out apples around me*] . . .

כִּי חוֹלַת אַהֲבָה אָנִי — *for, bereft of Your Presence, I am sick with love"* [lit., *for I am sick with love*]. In exile, I am sick for

ALLEGORICAL RENDERING FOLLOWING RASHI

Israel about God ¹² *While the King was yet at Sinai my malodorous deed gave forth its scent as my Golden Calf defiled the covenant.* ¹³ *But my Beloved responded with a bundle of myrrh, the fragrant atonement of erecting a Tabernacle where His Presence would dwell between the Holy Ark's staves.* ¹⁴ *Like a cluster of henna in En-gedi vineyards has my Beloved multiplied His forgiveness to me.* ¹⁵ *He said, "I forgive you, My friend, for you are lovely in deed and lovely in resolve. The righteous among you are loyal as a dove."*

Israel to God ¹⁶ *It is You Who are lovely, my Beloved, so pleasant that You pardoned my sin, enabling our Temple to make me ever fresh.* ¹⁷ *The beams of our houses are cedar, our panels are cypress.* ¹ *I am but a rose of Sharon, even an ever-fresh rose of the valleys.*

2

God to Israel ² *Like the rose maintaining its beauty among the thorns, so is My faithful beloved among the nations.*

Israel reminisces · · · ³ *Like the fruitful, fragrant apple among the barren trees of the forest, so is my Beloved among the gods. In His shade I delighted and [there] I sat, and the fruit of His Torah was sweet to my palate.* ⁴ *He brought me to the chamber of Torah delights and clustered my encampments about Him in love.* ⁵ *I say to Him, "Sustain me in exile with dainty cakes, spread fragrant apples about me to comfort my dispersion, for, bereft of Your Presence, I am sick with love."* ⁶ *With memories of His loving support in the desert, of His left hand under my head, of His right hand enveloping me.*

· · · turns to the nations · · · ⁷ *I adjure you, O nations destined to ascend to Jerusalem, for if you violate your oath, you will become as defenseless as gazelles or hinds of the field, if you dare provoke God to hate me or disturb His love for me while He still desires it.*

· · · then reminisces further ⁸ *The voice of my Beloved! Behold, it came suddenly to redeem me, as if leaping over mountains, skipping over hills.* ⁹ *In His swiftness to redeem me, my Beloved is like a gazelle or a young hart. I thought I would be forever alone, but behold! He was standing behind our wall, observing through the windows, peering through the lattices.*

NOTES INCLUDING PHRASE-BY-PHRASE LITERAL TRANSLATION

want of His love; I thirst for Him here in exile.

2:6. שְׂמֹאלוֹ תַּחַת לְרֹאשִׁי וִימִינוֹ תְּחַבְּקֵנִי — *With memories of His loving support in the desert, of His left hand under my head, of His right hand enveloping me* [lit., *His left hand is under my head and His right arm embraces me*]. Ecstatically, I recall how I was accompanied by God's Ark, enveloped in His cloud, eating His manna.

2:7. הִשְׁבַּעְתִּי אֶתְכֶם בְּנוֹת יְרוּשָׁלָ͏ִם — *I adjure you, O nations destined to ascend to Jerusalem* [lit., *I have adjured you, O daughters of Jerusalem*]. See 1:5.

בִּצְבָאוֹת אוֹ בְּאַיְלוֹת הַשָּׂדֶה — *for if you violate your oath, you will become as defenseless as gazelles or hinds of the field* [lit., *by gazelles or by hinds of the field*] . . .

אִם תָּעִירוּ וְאִם תְּעוֹרְרוּ אֶת הָאַהֲבָה עַד שֶׁתֶּחְפָּץ — *if you dare provoke God to hate me or disturb His love for me while He still desires it* [lit., *should you wake or rouse the love until it pleases*].

2:8. With this verse, Israel begins a recapitulation of God's remembrance of His people in Egypt.

קוֹל דּוֹדִי הִנֵּה זֶה בָּא — *The voice of my Beloved! Behold it came suddenly to redeem me* [lit., *The voice of my Beloved! Behold He comes*] . . .

מְדַלֵּג עַל הֶהָרִים מְקַפֵּץ עַל הַגְּבָעוֹת — *as if leaping over mountains, skipping over hills* [lit., *leaping upon the mountains skipping upon the hills*]. God leaped and skipped, so to speak, redeeming the Jews one hundred and ninety years before the completion of the prophecy of four hundred years of bondage.

2:9. דּוֹמֶה דוֹדִי לִצְבִי אוֹ לְעֹפֶר הָאַיָּלִים — *In His swiftness to redeem me, my Beloved is like a gazelle or a young hart* [lit., *My Beloved is like a gazelle or a young hart*].

I — הִנֵּה זֶה עוֹמֵד אַחַר כָּתְלֵנוּ מַשְׁגִּיחַ מִן הַחַלֹּנוֹת מֵצִיץ מִן הַחֲרַכִּים — *thought I would be forever alone, but behold! He was standing behind our wall, observing through the windows, peering through the lattices* [lit., *behold He stands behind our wall looking through the windows, peering through the lattices*]. I was like a woman resigned to being an *agunah* (bereft of husband, yet legally bound to him), for a still undetermined period of time. Then, suddenly, He came to tell me that He is peering through the windows of the heavens taking notice of my plight (see *Exodus* 3:7), reassuring me that whatever my travail, He will never fail to keep the closest watch over me.

יא עָנָה דוֹדִי וְאָמַר לִי קוּמִי לָךְ רַעְיָתִי יָפָתִי וּלְכִי־לָךְ: כִּי־הִנֵּה הַסְּתָו עָבָר

יב הַגֶּשֶׁם חָלַף הָלַךְ לוֹ: הַנִּצָּנִים נִרְאוּ בָאָרֶץ עֵת הַזָּמִיר הִגִּיעַ וְקוֹל

יג הַתּוֹר נִשְׁמַע בְּאַרְצֵנוּ: הַתְּאֵנָה חָנְטָה פַגֶּיהָ וְהַגְּפָנִים ׀ סְמָדַר נָתְנוּ
רֵיחַ קוּמִי °לכי [לָךְ קּ] רַעְיָתִי יָפָתִי וּלְכִי־לָךְ: יוֹנָתִי

יד בְּחַגְוֵי הַסֶּלַע בְּסֵתֶר הַמַּדְרֵגָה הַרְאִינִי אֶת־מַרְאַיִךְ הַשְׁמִיעִנִי אֶת־
קוֹלֵךְ כִּי־קוֹלֵךְ עָרֵב וּמַרְאֵיךְ נָאוֶה: אֶחֱזוּ־לָנוּ שֻׁעָלִים

טו שֻׁעָלִים קְטַנִּים מְחַבְּלִים כְּרָמִים וּכְרָמֵינוּ סְמָדַר: דּוֹדִי לִי וַאֲנִי לוֹ

טז הָרֹעֶה בַּשּׁוֹשַׁנִּים: עַד שֶׁיָּפוּחַ הַיּוֹם וְנָסוּ הַצְּלָלִים סֹב דְּמֵה־לְךָ דוֹדִי

יז לִצְבִי אוֹ לְעֹפֶר הָאַיָּלִים עַל־הָרֵי בָתֶר: עַל־מִשְׁכָּבִי

ג א בַּלֵּילוֹת בִּקַּשְׁתִּי אֵת שֶׁאָהֲבָה נַפְשִׁי בִּקַּשְׁתִּיו וְלֹא מְצָאתִיו: אָקוּמָה

ב נָּא וַאֲסוֹבְבָה בָעִיר בַּשְּׁוָקִים וּבָרְחֹבוֹת אֲבַקְשָׁה אֵת שֶׁאָהֲבָה נַפְשִׁי

ג בִּקַּשְׁתִּיו וְלֹא מְצָאתִיו: מְצָאוּנִי הַשֹּׁמְרִים הַסֹּבְבִים בָּעִיר אֵת שֶׁאָהֲבָה

ד נַפְשִׁי רְאִיתֶם: כִּמְעַט שֶׁעָבַרְתִּי מֵהֶם עַד שֶׁמָּצָאתִי אֵת שֶׁאָהֲבָה נַפְשִׁי

NOTES INCLUDING PHRASE-BY-PHRASE LITERAL TRANSLATION

2:10. עָנָה דוֹדִי וְאָמַר לִי — *When He redeemed me from Egypt, my Beloved called out and said to me,* [lit., *My Beloved lifted His voice and said to me,*] . . .

קוּמִי לָךְ רַעְיָתִי יָפָתִי וּלְכִי לָךְ — *"Arise My love, My fair one, and go forth* [lit., *Arise My love, My fair one, and go forth for yourself*]. "Carry out My precepts, and I will bring you up out of the affliction of Egypt" (*Exodus* 3:17).

2:11-13. A poetic picture describing the season of Redemption. Metaphorically, the verses conjure up an image of the worst being over, of redemption being at hand.

2:11. כִּי הִנֵּה הַסְּתָו עָבָר — *For the winter of bondage has passed* [lit., *For, behold, the winter is past*]. The years of bondage are over. It is time to travel forth.

הַגֶּשֶׁם חָלַף הָלַךְ לוֹ — *the deluge of suffering is over and gone* [lit., *the rain is over and gone*].

2:12. הַנִּצָּנִים נִרְאוּ בָאָרֶץ — *The righteous blossoms are seen in the land* [lit., *The blossoms have appeared in the land*]. The "blossoms" are Moses and Aaron who blossomed in response to Israel's needs.

עֵת הַזָּמִיר הִגִּיעַ — *The time of your song has arrived* [lit., *the time of singing has come*], to praise God, by singing the Song of the Sea (*Exodus* Ch. 15).

וְקוֹל הַתּוֹר נִשְׁמַע בְּאַרְצֵנוּ — *and the voice of your guide is heard in the land* [lit., *and the voice of the turtledove is heard in the land*]. The word תּוֹר, "turtledove," is linguistically related to תַּיָּר, "guide," an allusion to Moses.

2:13. הַתְּאֵנָה חָנְטָה פַגֶּיהָ וְהַגְּפָנִים סְמָדַר נָתְנוּ רֵיחַ — *The fig tree has formed its first small figs, ready for ascent to the Temple; the vines are in blossom, their fragrance declaring they are ready for libation* [lit., *The fig tree has formed its first figs, and the vines in blossom give forth fragrance*]. The time is drawing near for you to bring the first fruits and the wine libations in the Temple.

קוּמִי לָךְ רַעְיָתִי יָפָתִי וּלְכִי לָךְ — *Arise, My beloved, My fair one, and go forth"* [lit., *Arise, My beloved, My fair one, and go forth for yourself*].

2:14. יוֹנָתִי בְּחַגְוֵי הַסֶּלַע בְּסֵתֶר הַמַּדְרֵגָה — *At the sea, He said to me, "O My dove, trapped at the sea as if in the clefts of the rock, the concealment of the terrace* [lit., *O My dove, in the crannies of the rock, in the covert of the step*]. When the Jews were trapped between the sea and the Egyptian army, they were like a dove fleeing a hawk. It flew into the cleft of a rock, and found a serpent lurking there. It could neither enter, because of the snake, nor turn back, because of the hawk.

הַרְאִינִי אֶת מַרְאַיִךְ — *Show Me your prayerful gaze* [lit., *show Me your countenance*]. Show Me to whom you turn when you are in trouble.

הַשְׁמִיעִנִי אֶת קוֹלֵךְ — *let Me hear your supplicating voice* [lit., *let Me hear your voice*] . . .

כִּי קוֹלֵךְ עָרֵב וּמַרְאֵיךְ נָאוֶה — *for your voice is sweet and your countenance comely."*

2:15. אֶחֱזוּ לָנוּ שֻׁעָלִים שֻׁעָלִים קְטַנִּים מְחַבְּלִים כְּרָמִים וּכְרָמֵינוּ סְמָדַר — *Then He told the sea, "Seize for us the Egyptian foxes, even the small foxes who spoiled Israel's vineyards while our vineyards had just begun to blossom"* [lit., *The foxes have seized us, the little foxes that ruin the vineyard, and our vineyards are in blossom*].

2:16. דּוֹדִי לִי וַאֲנִי לוֹ — *My Beloved is mine, He fills all my needs and I seek from Him and none other* [lit., *My Beloved is mine, and I am His*]. He makes demands upon us and we rely on none other but Him.

הָרֹעֶה בַּשּׁוֹשַׁנִּים — *He grazes me in roselike bounty* [lit., *Who grazes (others) among the roses*]. God grazes us, His flock, in pastures of tranquil beauty.

2:17. עַד שֶׁיָּפוּחַ הַיּוֹם וְנָסוּ הַצְּלָלִים — *Until my sin blows His friendship away and sears me like the midday sun and His protection departs* [lit., *until the day blows and the shadows flee*]. The condition of "My Beloved is mine, and I am His" was dispelled when the sins of the Golden Calf (*Exodus* Ch. 32) and the Spies (*Numbers* Chs. 13-14) blackened us with the ferocity of the noontime sun.

ALLEGORICAL RENDERING FOLLOWING RASHI

¹⁰ *When He redeemed me from Egypt, my Beloved called out and said to me, "Arise, My love, My fair one, and go forth.* ¹¹ *For the winter of bondage has passed, the deluge of suffering is over and gone.* ¹² *The righteous blossoms are seen in the land, the time of your song has arrived, and the voice of your guide is heard in the land.* ¹³ *The fig tree has formed its first small figs, ready for ascent to the Temple; the vines are in blossom, their fragrance declaring they are ready for libation. Arise, My beloved, My fair one, and go forth!"*

¹⁴ *At the sea, He said to me, "O My dove, trapped at the sea as if in the clefts of the rock, the concealment of the terrace. Show Me your prayerful gaze, let Me hear your supplicating voice, for your voice is sweet and your countenance comely."* ¹⁵ *Then He told the sea, "Seize for us the Egyptian foxes, even the small foxes who spoiled Israel's vineyards while our vineyards had just begun to blossom."*

¹⁶ *My Beloved is mine, He fills all my needs and I seek from Him and none other. He grazes me in roselike bounty.* ¹⁷ *Until my sin blows His friendship away and sears me like the midday sun and His protection departs. My sin caused Him to turn away.*

I say to him, "My Beloved, You became like a gazelle or like a young hart on the distant mountains."

3 Israel to the nations ¹ *As I lay on my bed in the night of my desert travail, I sought Him Whom my soul loves. I sought Him but I found Him not, for He maintained His aloofness.* ² *I resolved to arise then, and roam through the city, in the streets and squares; that through Moses I would seek Him Whom my soul loved. I sought Him, but I found Him not.* ³ *They, Moses and Aaron, the watchmen patrolling the city, found me. "You have seen Him Whom my soul loves; what has He said?"* ⁴ *Scarcely had I departed from them, when, in the days of Joshua, I found Him Whom my soul loves.*

NOTES INCLUDING PHRASE-BY-PHRASE LITERAL TRANSLATION

סב — *My sin caused Him to turn away* [lit., *turn*].

דְּמֵה לְךָ דוֹדִי לִצְבִי אוֹ לְעֹפֶר הָאַיָּלִים — *I say to him, "My Beloved, You became like a gazelle or like a young hart* [lit., *My Beloved, and be like a gazelle or a young hart*]. Through my sins I caused Him to depart from me, as swiftly as a gazelle. . .

עַל הָרֵי בָתֶר — *on the distant mountains"* [lit., *upon the mountains of separation*], out of reach.

3:1. עַל מִשְׁכָּבִי בַּלֵּילוֹת בִּקַּשְׁתִּי אֵת שֶׁאָהֲבָה נַפְשִׁי — *As I lay on my bed in the night of my desert travail, I sought Him Whom my soul loves* [lit., *Upon my bed during the nights I sought the One my soul loves*]. After the sin of the Spies, God did not speak directly to Moses for thirty-eight years (see *Deuteronomy* 2:14-17), a period depicted as "during the nights." This chapter depicts the anguish of Israel, bereft of its former uninhibited relationship with God, longing for a resumption of His love.

בִּקַּשְׁתִּיו וְלֹא מְצָאתִיו — *I sought Him, but I found Him not, for He maintained His aloofness* [lit., *I sought Him, but I found Him not*]. As He warned, "For I will not go up in your midst" (*Exodus* 33:3); "For I am not among you" (*Deuteronomy* 1:42).

3:2. אָקוּמָה נָּא וַאֲסוֹבְבָה בָעִיר בַּשְּׁוָקִים וּבָרְחֹבוֹת — *I resolved to arise then, and roam through the city, in the streets and*

squares [lit., *I will rise now and roam about the city, through the streets and through the squares*]. We were determined to seek God by every possible avenue.

אֲבַקְשָׁה אֵת שֶׁאָהֲבָה נַפְשִׁי — *that through Moses I would seek Him Whom my soul loved* [lit., *I will seek the One I love*]. As Moses said, "I will go up to HASHEM; perhaps I can win atonement for your sins" (*Exodus* 32:30).

בִּקַּשְׁתִּיו וְלֹא מְצָאתִיו — *I sought Him, but I found Him not.*

3:3. מְצָאוּנִי הַשֹּׁמְרִים הַסֹּבְבִים בָּעִיר — *They, Moses and Aaron, the watchmen patrolling the city, found me* [lit., *The watchmen who circle the city found me*]. Moses and Aaron went among us to instill us with the love of God. They guided us, and inspired us to be patient, for Redemption was at hand.

אֵת שֶׁאָהֲבָה נַפְשִׁי רְאִיתֶם — *"You have seen Him Whom my soul loves; what has He said?"* [lit., *Have you seen Him Whom my soul loves?*].

3:4. כִּמְעַט שֶׁעָבַרְתִּי מֵהֶם עַד שֶׁמָּצָאתִי אֵת שֶׁאָהֲבָה נַפְשִׁי — *Scarcely had I departed from them, when, in the days of Joshua, I found Him Whom my soul loves* [lit., *Scarcely had I passed them, when I found Him Whom my soul loves*]. When Moses and Aaron died, God remained with Joshua, helping him to conquer the thirty-one kings of Canaan.

אֲחַזְתִּיו וְלֹא אַרְפֶּנּוּ עַד־שֶׁהֲבֵיאתִיו אֶל־בֵּית אִמִּי וְאֶל־חֶדֶר הוֹרָתִי:

ה   הִשְׁבַּעְתִּי אֶתְכֶם בְּנוֹת יְרוּשָׁלַ͏ִם בִּצְבָאוֹת אוֹ בְּאַיְלוֹת הַשָּׂדֶה אִם־תָּעִירוּ ׀

ו   וְאִם־תְּעוֹרְרוּ אֶת־הָאַהֲבָה עַד שֶׁתֶּחְפָּץ: מִי זֹאת עֹלָה

ז   מִן־הַמִּדְבָּר כְּתִימְרוֹת עָשָׁן מְקֻטֶּרֶת מוֹר וּלְבוֹנָה מִכֹּל אַבְקַת רוֹכֵל: הִנֵּה

ח   מִטָּתוֹ שֶׁלִּשְׁלֹמֹה שִׁשִּׁים גִּבֹּרִים סָבִיב לָהּ מִגִּבֹּרֵי יִשְׂרָאֵל: כֻּלָּם אֲחֻזֵי חֶרֶב

ט   מְלֻמְּדֵי מִלְחָמָה אִישׁ חַרְבּוֹ עַל־יְרֵכוֹ מִפַּחַד בַּלֵּילוֹת:

י   עָשָׂה לוֹ הַמֶּלֶךְ שְׁלֹמֹה מֵעֲצֵי הַלְּבָנוֹן: עַמּוּדָיו עָשָׂה כֶסֶף רְפִידָתוֹ

יא   זָהָב מֶרְכָּבוֹ אַרְגָּמָן תּוֹכוֹ רָצוּף אַהֲבָה מִבְּנוֹת יְרוּשָׁלָ͏ִם ׀ צְאֶינָה ׀

וּרְאֶינָה בְּנוֹת צִיּוֹן בַּמֶּלֶךְ שְׁלֹמֹה בָּעֲטָרָה שֶׁעִטְּרָה־לּוֹ אִמּוֹ בְּיוֹם

ד   א   חֲתֻנָּתוֹ וּבְיוֹם שִׂמְחַת לִבּוֹ:   הִנָּךְ יָפָה רַעְיָתִי הִנָּךְ יָפָה עֵינַיִךְ

ב   יוֹנִים מִבַּעַד לְצַמָּתֵךְ שַׂעְרֵךְ כְּעֵדֶר הָעִזִּים שֶׁגָּלְשׁוּ מֵהַר גִּלְעָד: שִׁנַּיִךְ

כְּעֵדֶר הַקְּצוּבוֹת שֶׁעָלוּ מִן־הָרַחְצָה שֶׁכֻּלָּם מַתְאִימוֹת וְשַׁכֻּלָה אֵין בָּהֶם:

אֲחַזְתִּיו וְלֹא אַרְפֶּנּוּ — *I grasped Him, determined that my deeds would never again cause me to lose hold of Him* [lit., *I have grasped Him and I would not let Him go*] . . .

עַד שֶׁהֲבֵיאתִיו אֶל בֵּית אִמִּי וְאֶל חֶדֶר הוֹרָתִי — *until I brought His Presence to the Tabernacle of my mother and to the chamber of the one who conceived me* [lit., *until I brought Him to my mother's house, and to the chamber of the one who conceived me*]. I built the Tabernacle at Shiloh, in return for all that He wrought for me.

3:5. הִשְׁבַּעְתִּי אֶתְכֶם בְּנוֹת יְרוּשָׁלַ͏ִם — *I adjure you, O nations destined to ascend to Jerusalem* [lit., *I have adjured you, O daughters of Jerusalem*]. See 1:5.

בִּצְבָאוֹת אוֹ בְּאַיְלוֹת הַשָּׂדֶה — *for if you violate your oath, you will become as defenseless as gazelles or hinds of the field* [lit., *by gazelles or by hinds of the field*] . . .

אִם תָּעִירוּ וְאִם תְּעוֹרְרוּ אֶת הָאַהֲבָה עַד שֶׁתֶּחְפָּץ — *if you dare provoke God to hate me or disturb His love for me while He still desires it* [lit., *if you will wake or rouse the love until it pleases*].

3:6. מִי זֹאת עֹלָה מִן הַמִּדְבָּר — *You nations have asked, "Who is this that is ascending from the wilderness* [lit., *Who is it that rises up from the wilderness*]. In the wilderness, Israel was led by the pillar of fire and the pillar of cloud (*Exodus* 13:21 ff), which killed snakes and scorpions, and burned thorns and thistles to clear the way. The nations exclaimed: "Who is this [i.e., How great is this spectacle] that comes up from the wilderness?"

כְּתִימְרוֹת עָשָׁן — *its way secured and smoothed by palmlike pillars of smoke* [lit., *like columns of smoke*]. The word תִּימְרָה, "column," is linguistically related to תָּמָר, "date-palm." The pillar of clouds that accompanied Israel through the wilderness was tall and erect as a palm tree . . .

מְקֻטֶּרֶת מוֹר וּלְבוֹנָה מִכֹּל אַבְקַת רוֹכֵל — *burning fragrant myrrh and frankincense, of all the perfumer's powders?"* [lit., *perfumed with myrrh and frankincense, with every powder of the merchant*] . . . like the "cloud of the incense" (*Leviticus* 16:13) that ascended from the Altar in the Tabernacle.

3:7. הִנֵּה מִטָּתוֹ שֶׁלִּשְׁלֹמֹה — *Behold the resting place of Him to Whom peace belongs* [lit., *Behold, it is the couch of Solomon*], i.e., the Tent of Meeting and the Ark . . .

שִׁשִּׁים גִּבֹּרִים סָבִיב לָהּ מִגִּבֹּרֵי יִשְׂרָאֵל — *with sixty myriads of Israel's mighty encircling it* [lit., *sixty mighty men round about it, of the mighty men of Israel*]. Sixty times ten thousand men were eligible to fight in the Israelite army (see *Numbers* 1:45-46).

3:8. כֻּלָּם אֲחֻזֵי חֶרֶב מְלֻמְּדֵי מִלְחָמָה — *All of them gripping the sword of tradition, skilled in the battle of Torah* [lit., *They all handle the sword, learned in warfare*].

אִישׁ חַרְבּוֹ עַל יְרֵכוֹ מִפַּחַד בַּלֵּילוֹת — *each with his sword ready at his side, lest he succumb in the nights of exile* [lit., *each with his sword on his thigh, because of terror in the nights*]. "Sword" refers to the means by which to transmit the Torah intact from one generation to the next.

3:9. אַפִּרְיוֹן עָשָׂה לוֹ הַמֶּלֶךְ שְׁלֹמֹה מֵעֲצֵי הַלְּבָנוֹן — *A Tabernacle for His Presence has the King whose peace belongs made of the wood of Lebanon* [lit., *A sedan chair has King Solomon made unto Him, of the wood of Lebanon*], a metaphor for a private chamber for His glory.

3:10. עַמּוּדָיו עָשָׂה כֶסֶף — *Its pillars He made of silver.* A reference to the silver hooks of the Tabernacle's courtyard pillars (see *Exodus* 27:10).

רְפִידָתוֹ זָהָב — *His resting place was gold* [lit., *its covering was gold*]. God's Presence rested upon the golden Cover of the Ark, from which He spoke to Moses (see *Exodus* 27:17,22).

מֶרְכָּבוֹ אַרְגָּמָן — *Its suspended curtain was purple wool* [lit., *its seat was purple wool*]. The dominant color of the *Paroches* (Curtain) between the Holy and the Holy of Holies was purple (see *Exodus* 26:31-33).

תּוֹכוֹ רָצוּף אַהֲבָה — *Its midst was decked with implements bespeaking love* [lit., *its inner side was decked with love*]. The Ark, its Cover, its Cherubim and Tablets were all symbolic of the love between God and Israel.

מִבְּנוֹת יְרוּשָׁלַ͏ִם — *by the daughters of Jerusalem.* Throughout the rest of the Book (see, e.g., 1:5) "daughters of

ALLEGORICAL RENDERING FOLLOWING RASHI

I grasped Him, determined that my deeds would never again cause me to lose hold of Him, until I brought His Presence to the Tabernacle of my mother and to the chamber of the one who conceived me. [5] *I adjure you, O nations destined to ascend to Jerusalem, for if you violate your oath, you will become as defenseless as gazelles or hinds of the field, if you dare provoke God to hate me or disturb His love for me while He still desires it.*

Quoting the nations
[6] *You nations have asked, "Who is this ascending from the wilderness, its way secured and smoothed by palmlike pillars of smoke, burning fragrant myrrh and frankincense, of all the perfumer's powders?"* [7] *Behold the resting place of Him to Whom peace belongs, with sixty myriads of Israel's mighty encircling it.* [8] *All of them gripping the sword of tradition, skilled in the battle of Torah, each with his sword ready at his side, lest he succumb in the nights of exile.*

[9] *A Tabernacle for His presence has the King to Whom peace belongs made of the wood of Lebanon:* [10] *Its pillars He made of silver; His resting place was gold; its suspended curtain was purple wool, its midst was decked with implements bespeaking love by the daughters of Jerusalem.* [11] *Go forth and gaze, O daughters distinguished by loyalty to God, upon the King to Whom peace belongs adorned with the crown His nation made for Him, on the day His Law was given and He became one with Israel, and on the day His heart was gladdened by His Tabernacle's consecration.*

4
God to Israel
[1] **B**ehold, *you are lovely, My beloved, behold you are lovely, your very appearance radiates dovelike constancy. The most common sons within your encampments are as dearly beloved as the children of Jacob in the goatlike procession descending the slopes of Mount Gilead.* [2] *Accountable in deed are your mighty leaders like a well-numbered flock come up from the washing, all of them unblemished with no miscarriage of action in them.*

NOTES INCLUDING PHRASE-BY-PHRASE LITERAL TRANSLATION

Jerusalem" refers to the heathen nations who will flock to Jerusalem in the future; here it refers to the Jews.

3:11. צְאֶינָה וּרְאֶינָה בְּנוֹת צִיּוֹן בַּמֶּלֶךְ שְׁלֹמֹה — *Go forth and gaze, O daughters distinguished by loyalty to God, upon the King to Whom peace belongs* [lit., *Go forth and gaze, O daughters of Zion, upon King Solomon*]. צִיּוֹן, "Zion," is linguistically related to צִיּוּן, "distinguishing mark." The daughters of Zion, Israel, are distinguished in their loyalty to God and to His commandments.

בָּעֲטָרָה שֶׁעִטְּרָה לּוֹ אִמּוֹ — *adorned with the crown His nation made for Him* [lit., *with the crown with which his mother crowned him*]. The Tabernacle was "crowned" with coverings of colored skins; of blue, purple and scarlet wool, and fine linen; and of goat's hair (*Exodus* 26:1,7,14).

בְּיוֹם חֲתֻנָתוֹ — *on the day His Law was given and He became one with Israel* [lit., *on His wedding day*]; the day the Torah was given.

וּבְיוֹם שִׂמְחַת לִבּוֹ — *and on the day His heart was gladdened by His Tabernacle's consecration* [lit., *and on the day of His heart's bliss*]. The dedication day of the Tabernacle in the wilderness.

4:1. הִנָּךְ יָפָה רַעְיָתִי הִנָּךְ יָפָה עֵינַיִךְ יוֹנִים — *Behold, you are lovely, My beloved, behold you are lovely, your very appearance radiates dovelike constancy* [lit., *Behold, you*

are beautiful, My beloved; behold, you are beautiful, your eyes are doves]. You are like the dove which is loyal to its mate.

מִבַּעַד לְצַמָּתֵךְ שַׂעְרֵךְ כְּעֵדֶר הָעִזִּים שֶׁגָּלְשׁוּ מֵהַר גִּלְעָד — *The most common sons within your encampments are as dearly beloved as the children of Jacob in the goatlike procession descending the slopes of Mount Gilead* [lit., *Within your kerchief, your hair is like a flock of goats streaming down from Mount Gilead*]. Even your common people, whose merits are hidden by veils, are as dear to Me as Jacob and his sons who streamed down Mount Gilead when Laban pursued them (see *Genesis* 31:23ff).

4:2. שִׁנַּיִךְ כְּעֵדֶר הַקְּצוּבוֹת שֶׁעָלוּ מִן הָרַחְצָה — *Accountable in deed are your mighty leaders like a well-numbered flock come up from the washing* [lit., *Your teeth are like a flock well counted, which have come up from the washing*]. Israel's warriors who "tear apart and consume" their enemies are allegorized as teeth. By refraining from plunder and lewdness, the warriors remain untainted by sin, as if they "came up from the washing."

שֶׁכֻּלָּם מַתְאִימוֹת וְשַׁכֻּלָה אֵין בָּהֶם — *all of them unblemished with no miscarriage of action in them* [lit., *all of them are perfect and there is none blemished among them*].

ג כְּחוּט הַשָּׁנִי שִׂפְתוֹתַיִךְ וּמִדְבָּרֵךְ נָאוֶה כְּפֶלַח הָרִמּוֹן רַקָּתֵךְ מִבַּעַד
ד לְצַמָּתֵךְ: כְּמִגְדַּל דָּוִיד צַוָּארֵךְ בָּנוּי לְתַלְפִּיּוֹת אֶלֶף הַמָּגֵן תָּלוּי עָלָיו
ה כֹּל שִׁלְטֵי הַגִּבֹּרִים: שְׁנֵי שָׁדַיִךְ כִּשְׁנֵי עֳפָרִים תְּאוֹמֵי צְבִיָּה הָרֹעִים
ו בַּשּׁוֹשַׁנִּים: עַד שֶׁיָּפוּחַ הַיּוֹם וְנָסוּ הַצְּלָלִים אֵלֶךְ לִי אֶל־הַר הַמּוֹר וְאֶל־
ז־ח גִּבְעַת הַלְּבוֹנָה: כֻּלָּךְ יָפָה רַעְיָתִי וּמוּם אֵין בָּךְ: אִתִּי
מִלְּבָנוֹן כַּלָּה אִתִּי מִלְּבָנוֹן תָּבוֹאִי תָּשׁוּרִי ׀ מֵרֹאשׁ אֲמָנָה מֵרֹאשׁ
ט שְׂנִיר וְחֶרְמוֹן מִמְּעֹנוֹת אֲרָיוֹת מֵהַרְרֵי נְמֵרִים: לִבַּבְתִּנִי אֲחֹתִי כַלָּה
י לִבַּבְתִּנִי °בְּאַחַד [בְּאַחַת ק] מֵעֵינַיִךְ בְּאַחַד עֲנָק מִצַּוְּרֹנָיִךְ: מַה־יָּפוּ
דֹדַיִךְ אֲחֹתִי כַלָּה מַה־טֹּבוּ דֹדַיִךְ מִיַּיִן וְרֵיחַ שְׁמָנַיִךְ מִכָּל־בְּשָׂמִים:
יא נֹפֶת תִּטֹּפְנָה שִׂפְתוֹתַיִךְ כַּלָּה דְּבַשׁ וְחָלָב תַּחַת לְשׁוֹנֵךְ וְרֵיחַ שַׂלְמֹתַיִךְ
יב כְּרֵיחַ לְבָנוֹן: גַּן ׀ נָעוּל אֲחֹתִי כַלָּה גַּל נָעוּל מַעְיָן חָתוּם:
יג־יד שְׁלָחַיִךְ פַּרְדֵּס רִמּוֹנִים עִם פְּרִי מְגָדִים כְּפָרִים עִם־נְרָדִים: נֵרְדְּ ׀ וְכַרְכֹּם
קָנֶה וְקִנָּמוֹן עִם כָּל־עֲצֵי לְבוֹנָה מֹר וַאֲהָלוֹת עִם כָּל־רָאשֵׁי בְשָׂמִים:

NOTES INCLUDING PHRASE-BY-PHRASE LITERAL TRANSLATION

4:3. כְּחוּט הַשָּׁנִי שִׂפְתוֹתַיִךְ — *Like the scarlet thread, guarantor of Rahab's safety, is the sincerity of your lips* [lit., *Your lips are like a thread of scarlet*]. This refers to the sincere pledge that Joshua's spies made to Rahab in Jericho. They guaranteed her safety if she would display a scarlet thread as a signal to the conquering Jews (see *Joshua* Ch. 2).

וּמִדְבָּרֵךְ נָאוֶה — *and your word is unfeigned* [lit., *and your speech is comely*].

כְּפֶלַח הָרִמּוֹן רַקָּתֵךְ מִבַּעַד לְצַמָּתֵךְ — *As many as a pomegranate's seeds are the merits of your unworthiest within your modest veil* [lit., *Your cheeks are like a slice of pomegranate, from behind your veil*]. The word רַקָּה, "cheeks," is linguistically related to רֵק, "empty," and is a metaphor for those who are relatively empty of mitzvos; rosy cheeks also resemble a pomegranate. Even the comparatively few merits of the lowest among you are as numerous as a pomegranate's seeds.

4:4. כְּמִגְדַּל דָּוִיד צַוָּארֵךְ בָּנוּי לְתַלְפִּיּוֹת — *As stately as the Tower of David is the site of your Sanhedrin built as a model to emulate* [lit., *Your neck is the Tower of David, built as an ornament*]. The verse alludes to the Stronghold of Zion, a beautiful, stately fortification, and to the chamber of the Sanhedrin, the spiritual stronghold of Israel.

אֶלֶף הַמָּגֵן תָּלוּי עָלָיו — *with a thousand shields of Torah armor hung upon it, all the disciple-filled quivers of the mighty* [lit., *a thousand shields are hung upon it; all the quivers of the mighty men*]. Students are likened to arrows (see *Psalms* 127:4-5).

4:5. שְׁנֵי שָׁדַיִךְ כִּשְׁנֵי עֳפָרִים תְּאוֹמֵי צְבִיָּה — *Moses and Aaron, your two sustainers, are like two fawns, twins of the gazelle* [lit., *Your breasts are like two fawns, twins of a gazelle*]. Moses and Aaron are like the breasts that nurtured Israel. They are called "twins" because they were of equal stature.

הָרֹעִים בַּשּׁוֹשַׁנִּים — *who graze their sheep in roselike bounty*

[lit., *who feed among the roses*]. Like shepherds, Moses and Aaron guided their nation along tranquil paths.

4:6. עַד שֶׁיָּפוּחַ הַיּוֹם וְנָסוּ הַצְּלָלִים — *Until My sunny benevolence was withdrawn from Shiloh and the protective shadows were dispersed by your sin* [lit., *Until the day breathes and the shadows flee*]. God had been Israel's protective shade, until they sinned.

אֵלֶךְ לִי אֶל־הַר הַמּוֹר וְאֶל גִּבְעַת הַלְּבוֹנָה — *I will go to Mount Moriah and the hill of frankincense* [lit., *I will get me to the mountain of myrrh, and to the hill of frankincense*]. After His anger abated, He chose Mount Moriah as the site of the Temple, where incense would be offered.

4:7. כֻּלָּךְ יָפָה רַעְיָתִי וּמוּם אֵין בָּךְ — *where [on Mount Moriah] you will be completely fair, My beloved, and no blemish will be in you* [lit., *You are entirely fair, My beloved, and there is no blemish in you*].

4:8. אִתִּי מִלְּבָנוֹן כַּלָּה אִתִּי מִלְּבָנוֹן תָּבוֹאִי — *With Me will you be exiled from the Temple, O bride, with Me from the Temple until you return* [lit., *With Me from Lebanon, O bride! With Me from Lebanon shall you come*]. The Temple is called Lebanon (לְבָנוֹן, lit., "whitener") because it whitens the sins of Israel (Talmud, *Yoma* 39b). You will be exiled "with Me," says God, "for in all your afflictions, I, too, am afflicted" (see *Isaiah* 63:9).

תָּשׁוּרִי מֵרֹאשׁ אֲמָנָה — *then to contemplate the fruits of your faith from its earliest beginnings* [lit., *Look from the peak of Amanah*]. The word ראש means both "head (or, peak)" and "beginning"; אֲמָנָה means "covenant of faith" and is the name of a mountain on the northern border of the Land of Israel.

מֵרֹאשׁ שְׂנִיר וְחֶרְמוֹן מִמְּעֹנוֹת אֲרָיוֹת מֵהַרְרֵי נְמֵרִים — *from your first arrival at the summits of Senir and Hermon, the lands of mighty Sihon and Og, as impregnable as dens of lions, and as mountains of leopards* [lit., *from the peak of Senir and Hermon, from the dens of lions, from the mountains of leopards*].

ALLEGORICAL RENDERING FOLLOWING RASHI

³ *Like the scarlet thread, guarantor of Rahab's safety, is the sincerity of your lips, and your word is unfeigned. As many as a pomegranate's seeds are the merits of your unworthiest within your modest veil.* ⁴ *As stately as the Tower of David is the site of your Sanhedrin built as a model to emulate, with a thousand shields of Torah armor hung upon it, all the disciple-filled quivers of the mighty.* ⁵ *Moses and Aaron, your two sustainers, are like two fawns, twins of the gazelle, who graze their sheep in roselike bounty.*

⁶ *Until My sunny benevolence was withdrawn from Shiloh and the protective shadows were dispersed by your sin. I will go to Mount Moriah and the hill of frankincense —* ⁷ *where you will be completely fair, My beloved, and no blemish will be in you.*

⁸ *With Me will you be exiled from the Temple, O bride, with Me from the Temple until you return; then to contemplate the fruits of your faith from its earliest beginnings, from your first arrival at the summits of Senir and Hermon, the lands of mighty Sihon and Og, as impregnable as dens of lions, and as mountains of leopards.*

⁹ *You have captured My heart, My sister, O bride; you have captured My heart with but one of your virtues, with but one of the precepts that adorn you like beads of a necklace resplendent.* ¹⁰ *How fair was your love in so many settings, My sister, O bride; so superior is your love to wine and your spreading fame to all perfumes.*

¹¹ *The sweetness of Torah drips from your lips, like honey and milk it lies under your tongue; your very garments are scented with precepts like the scent of Lebanon.* ¹² *As chaste as a garden locked, My sister, O bride; a spring locked up, a fountain sealed.* ¹³ *Your least gifted ones are a pomegranate orchard with luscious fruit; henna with nard;* ¹⁴ *nard and saffron, calamus and cinnamon, with all trees of frankincense, myrrh and aloes with all the chief spices;*

NOTES INCLUDING PHRASE-BY-PHRASE LITERAL TRANSLATION

4:9. לִבַּבְתִּנִי אֲחֹתִי כַלָּה — *You have captured My heart, My sister, O bride.*

לִבַּבְתִּנִי בְּאַחַת מֵעֵינַיִךְ בְּאַחַד עֲנָק מִצַּוְּרֹנָיִךְ — *you have captured My heart with but one of your virtues, with but one of the precepts that adorn you like beads of a necklace resplendent* [lit., *You have captured my heart with one of your eyes, with one bead of your necklace*]. I would have loved you even had you possessed only one of your endearing qualities; how much more so since you possess so many!

4:10. מַה יָּפוּ דֹדַיִךְ אֲחֹתִי כַלָּה — *How fair was your love in so many settings, My sister, O bride* [lit., *How fair was your love, My sister O bride!*]. Your love is pleasing everywhere, whether in the Tabernacle or in the Temple.

מַה טֹּבוּ דֹדַיִךְ מִיַּיִן וְרֵיחַ שְׁמָנַיִךְ מִכָּל בְּשָׂמִים — *so superior is your love to wine and your spreading fame to all perfumes* [lit., *how much better your love than wine, and the fragrance of your oils than all spices!*].

4:11. נֹפֶת תִּטֹּפְנָה שִׂפְתוֹתַיִךְ כַלָּה דְּבַשׁ וְחָלָב תַּחַת לְשׁוֹנֵךְ — *The sweetness of Torah drips from your lips, like honey and milk it lies under your tongue* [lit., *Honey drops from your lips, O bride, honey and milk are under your tongue*].

וְרֵיחַ שַׂלְמֹתַיִךְ כְּרֵיחַ לְבָנוֹן — *your very garments are scented with precepts like the scent of Lebanon* [lit., *and the scent of your garments is like the scent of Lebanon*]. This refers to the precepts associated with clothing, such as the commandment of wearing *tzitzis* and the prohibition against wearing *shaatnez* (see *Deuteronomy* 22:11).

4:12. גַּן נָעוּל אֲחֹתִי כַלָּה גַּל נָעוּל מַעְיָן חָתוּם — *As chaste as a garden locked, My sister, O bride; a spring locked up, a fountain sealed* [lit., *A garden locked up is my sister, the bride, a spring locked up, a fountain sealed*]. The beauty and charm of the daughters of Israel are guided by modesty and purity.

4:13. שְׁלָחַיִךְ פַּרְדֵּס רִמּוֹנִים עִם פְּרִי מְגָדִים — *Your least gifted ones are a pomegranate orchard with luscious fruit* [lit., *Your arid areas are an orchard of pomegranates with precious fruits*]. Like a field in need of irrigation, your youngsters strive to be "moistened" with Torah and good deeds.

כְּפָרִים עִם נְרָדִים — *henna with nard.* Types of spices (see 1:14).

4:14. נֵרְדְּ וְכַרְכֹּם קָנֶה וְקִנָּמוֹן עִם כָּל עֲצֵי לְבוֹנָה מֹר וַאֲהָלוֹת עִם כָּל רָאשֵׁי בְשָׂמִים — *Nard and saffron, calamus and cinnamon, with all trees of frankincense, myrrh, and aloes, with all the chief spices.*

ה

טו-טז מַעְיַן גַּנִּים בְּאֵר מַיִם חַיִּים וְנֹזְלִים מִן־לְבָנוֹן: עוּרִי צָפוֹן וּבוֹאִי תֵימָן

א הָפִיחִי גַנִּי יִזְּלוּ בְשָׂמָיו יָבֹא דוֹדִי לְגַנּוֹ וְיֹאכַל פְּרִי מְגָדָיו: בָּאתִי לְגַנִּי

אֲחֹתִי כַלָּה אָרִיתִי מוֹרִי עִם־בְּשָׂמִי אָכַלְתִּי יַעְרִי עִם־דִּבְשִׁי שָׁתִיתִי יֵינִי

ב עִם־חֲלָבִי אִכְלוּ רֵעִים שְׁתוּ וְשִׁכְרוּ דּוֹדִים: אֲנִי יְשֵׁנָה

וְלִבִּי עֵר קוֹל | דּוֹדִי דוֹפֵק פִּתְחִי־לִי אֲחֹתִי רַעְיָתִי יוֹנָתִי תַמָּתִי שֶׁרֹאשִׁי

ג נִמְלָא־טָל קְוֻצּוֹתַי רְסִיסֵי לָיְלָה: פָּשַׁטְתִּי אֶת־כֻּתָּנְתִּי אֵיכָכָה אֶלְבָּשֶׁנָּה

ד רָחַצְתִּי אֶת־רַגְלַי אֵיכָכָה אֲטַנְּפֵם: דּוֹדִי שָׁלַח יָדוֹ מִן־הַחֹר וּמֵעַי הָמוּ

ה עָלָיו: קַמְתִּי אֲנִי לִפְתֹּחַ לְדוֹדִי וְיָדַי נָטְפוּ־מוֹר וְאֶצְבְּעֹתַי מוֹר עֹבֵר עַל

ו כַּפּוֹת הַמַּנְעוּל: פָּתַחְתִּי אֲנִי לְדוֹדִי וְדוֹדִי חָמַק עָבָר נַפְשִׁי יָצְאָה

ז בְדַבְּרוֹ בִּקַּשְׁתִּיהוּ וְלֹא מְצָאתִיהוּ קְרָאתִיו וְלֹא עָנָנִי: מְצָאֻנִי הַשֹּׁמְרִים

הַסֹּבְבִים בָּעִיר הִכּוּנִי פְצָעוּנִי נָשְׂאוּ אֶת־רְדִידִי מֵעָלַי שֹׁמְרֵי הַחֹמוֹת:

NOTES INCLUDING PHRASE-BY-PHRASE LITERAL TRANSLATION

4:15. מַעְיַן גַּנִּים בְּאֵר מַיִם חַיִּים וְנֹזְלִים מִן לְבָנוֹן — *purified in a garden spring, a well of waters alive and flowing clean from Lebanon* [lit., (You are) a garden spring; a well of living waters streams from Lebanon]. God praises the women of Israel whose ritual immersion is like a spring enabling the fields to be fruitful.

4:16. עוּרִי צָפוֹן וּבוֹאִי תֵימָן הָפִיחִי גַנִּי יִזְּלוּ בְשָׂמָיו — *Awake from the north and come from the south! Like the winds let My exiles return to My garden, let their fragrant goodness flow in Jerusalem* [lit., Awake, O north (wind), and come, O south! Blow (upon) my garden, let its spices flow out]. Having found delight in you, command the winds to waft your fragrance afar. Allegorically, Israel's host nations will be so overwhelmed by the miracles preceding the Redemption that they will bring the Jews to Eretz Yisrael (see *Isaiah* 66:20). In the Temple, the Jews will say to God . . .

יָבֹא דוֹדִי לְגַנּוֹ וְיֹאכַל פְּרִי מְגָדָיו — *Let but my Beloved come to His garden and enjoy His precious people* [lit., Let my Beloved come to His garden and eat its precious fruit]. If You are there, all is there.

5:1. בָּאתִי לְגַנִּי אֲחֹתִי כַלָּה — *To your Tabernacle Dedication, My sister, O bride, I came as if to My garden* [lit., I have come into My garden, My sister, O bride]. When the Tabernacle was set up, God's glory filled it (*Exodus* 40:33,34).

אָרִיתִי מוֹרִי עִם בְּשָׂמִי — *I gathered My myrrh with My spice from your princely incense* [lit., I have gathered My myrrh with My spice]. The princes of the tribes offered incense at the Dedication of the Tabernacle (*Numbers* Ch. 7).

אָכַלְתִּי יַעְרִי עִם דִּבְשִׁי — *I accepted your unbidden as well as your bidden offerings to Me* [lit., I have eaten My honeycomb with My honey]. After its sweetness has been sucked, the comb is discarded. However, God's love of Israel was such that, during the inauguration of the Tabernacle, He accepted even offerings that would have otherwise been inappropriate. The tribal princes brought not only incense, but also sin-offerings, even though sin-offerings are not appropriate to be brought voluntarily.

שָׁתִיתִי יֵינִי עִם חֲלָבִי — *I drank your libations pure as milk* [lit., I have drunk My wine with My milk].

אִכְלוּ רֵעִים שְׁתוּ וְשִׁכְרוּ דּוֹדִים — *Eat, My beloved priests! Drink and become God-intoxicated, O friends* [lit., Eat, friends; drink and become intoxicated, O beloved ones], you who partook of the flesh of the peace-offerings.

5:2. [The following verses allegorize the period of the First Temple and its destruction, Israel's sins, God's pleas for repentance, and Israel's recalcitrance — until it was too late.]

אֲנִי יְשֵׁנָה וְלִבִּי עֵר — *I let my devotion slumber, but the God of my heart was awake* [lit., I (was) asleep but my heart (was) awake]. Secure in the peaceful period of feeling secure, Israel neglected the service of God, as if asleep, but, "my heart," i.e., God, was wakeful to guard me and grant me goodness.

קוֹל דּוֹדִי דוֹפֵק — *A sound! My Beloved knocks* [lit., The sound of my Beloved knocking!]. Throughout my slumber, He issued daily warnings through the prophets (see *Jeremiah* 7:25).

פִּתְחִי לִי אֲחֹתִי רַעְיָתִי יוֹנָתִי תַמָּתִי — *He said, "Open your heart to Me, My sister, My love, My dove, My perfection* [lit., Open to Me (i.e., Let Me in), My sister, My love, My dove, My perfect one]. Do not cause Me to depart from you.

שֶׁרֹאשִׁי נִמְלָא טָל — *admit Me and My head is filled with dewlike memories of Abraham* [lit., for My head is filled with dew]. Through His prophets, He said to me, "Abraham's deeds were pleasing to Me as dew, and I will shower you with blessings if you will but return to Me."

קְוֻצּוֹתַי רְסִיסֵי לָיְלָה — *spurn Me and I bear collections of punishing rains in exile-nights"* [lit., My locks (with) the rains of the night].

5:3. פָּשַׁטְתִּי אֶת כֻּתָּנְתִּי אֵיכָכָה אֶלְבָּשֶׁנָּה רָחַצְתִּי אֶת רַגְלַי אֵיכָכָה אֲטַנְּפֵם — *And I responded, "I have doffed my robe of devotion; how can I don it? I have washed my feet that trod Your path; how can I soil them?"* [lit., I have taken off my robe, how shall I don it? I have washed my feet, how shall I soil them?]. In reaction to God's knock on the door, we thought, "We have accustomed ourselves to serve other gods — how can we return to our God?"

ALLEGORICAL RENDERING FOLLOWING RASHI

¹⁵ *purified in a garden spring, a well of waters alive and flowing clean from Lebanon.*

¹⁶ *Awake from the north and come from the south! Like the winds let My exiles*

Israel responds *return to My garden, let their fragrant goodness flow in Jerusalem.*
Let but my Beloved come to His garden and enjoy His precious people.

5

God replies ¹T*o your Tabernacle Dedication, My sister, O bride, I came as if to My garden. I gathered My myrrh with My spice from your princely incense; I accepted your unbidden as well as your bidden offerings to Me; I drank your libations pure as milk. Eat, My beloved priests! Drink and become God-intoxicated, O friends!*

Israel reminisces regretfully ² *I let my devotion slumber, but the God of my heart was awake! A sound! My Beloved knocks!*

He said, "Open your heart to Me, My sister, My love, My dove, My perfection; admit Me and My head is filled with dewlike memories of Abraham; spurn Me and I bear collections of punishing rains in exile-nights."

³ *And I responded, "I have doffed my robe of devotion; how can I don it? I have washed my feet that trod Your path; how can I soil them?"*

⁴ *In anger at my recalcitrance, my Beloved sent forth His hand from the portal in wrath, and my intestines churned with longing for Him.* ⁵ *I arose to open for my Beloved and my hands dripped myrrh of repentant devotion to Torah and God, and my fingers flowing with myrrh to remove the traces of my foolish rebuke from the handles of the lock.* ⁶ *I opened for my Beloved; but, alas, my Beloved had turned His back on my plea and was gone. My soul departed at His decree! I sought His closeness, but could not find it; I beseeched Him, but He would not answer.*

⁷ *They found me, the enemy watchmen patrolling the city; they struck me, they bloodied me wreaking God's revenge on me. They stripped my mantle of holiness from me, the angelic watchmen of the wall.*

NOTES INCLUDING PHRASE-BY-PHRASE LITERAL TRANSLATION

5:4. דּוֹדִי שָׁלַח יָדוֹ מִן הַחוֹר — *In anger at my recalcitrance, my Beloved sent forth His hand from the portal in wrath* [lit., *My Beloved sent forth His hand from the portal*]. When we spurned Him, God brought Aram upon us and our king, Ahaz (see *II Chronicles* 28:5,6).

וּמֵעַי הָמוּ עָלָיו — *and my intestines churned with longing for Him* [lit., *and my intestines stirred for Him*]. We changed our ways, and became righteous in the service of God.

5:5. קַמְתִּי אֲנִי לִפְתֹּחַ לְדוֹדִי וְיָדַי נָטְפוּ מוֹר — *I arose to open for my Beloved and my hands dripped myrrh of repentant devotion to Torah and God* [lit., *I rose to open for my Beloved and my hands dripped with myrrh*]. Hezekiah, Ahaz's son, became a model of piety. His entire generation was perfect; and there never arose another generation like it (*Talmud, Sanhedrin* 94b).

וְאֶצְבְּעֹתַי מוֹר עֹבֵר עַל כַּפּוֹת הַמַּנְעוּל — *and my fingers flowing with myrrh to remove the traces of my foolish rebuke from the handles of the lock* [lit., *and my fingers flowing with myrrh upon the handles of the lock*].

5:6. But, His Decree was to be enforced.

פָּתַחְתִּי אֲנִי לְדוֹדִי וְדוֹדִי חָמַק עָבָר — *I opened for my Beloved; but, alas, my Beloved had turned His back on my plea and was gone* [lit., *I opened for my Beloved, but my Beloved*

had turned and gone]. Belatedly, I responded to my Beloved, but, alas, He did not annul His decree.

נַפְשִׁי יָצְאָה בְדַבְּרוֹ — *My soul departed at His decree* [lit., *my soul departed* (i.e., I became faint) *as He spoke*]. In effect, He said, "I will not enter, since at first you had refused to let Me in."

בִּקַּשְׁתִּיהוּ וְלֹא מְצָאתִיהוּ — *I sought His closeness, but could not find it* [lit., *I sought Him, but did not find Him*].

קְרָאתִיו וְלֹא עָנָנִי — *I beseeched Him, but He would not answer* [lit., *I called Him, but He did not answer me*].

5:7. מְצָאֻנִי הַשֹּׁמְרִים הַסֹּבְבִים בָּעִיר — *They found me, the enemy watchmen patrolling the city* [lit., *The watchmen who circle the city found me*]. Nebuchadnezzar's forces lay siege to Jerusalem . . .

הִכּוּנִי פְצָעוּנִי — *they struck me, they bloodied me, wreaking God's revenge on me* [lit., *they struck me, they wounded me*]. The Destruction of the First Temple was beginning.

נָשְׂאוּ אֶת רְדִידִי מֵעָלַי שֹׁמְרֵי הַחֹמוֹת — *They stripped my mantle of holiness from me, the angelic watchmen of the wall* [lit., *the guards of the walls stripped my mantle from me*]. Even the angels that had formerly been assigned to protect the city now took part in the destruction (see *Lamentations* 1:13).

ח הִשְׁבַּעְתִּי אֶתְכֶם בְּנוֹת יְרוּשָׁלָ͏ִם אִם־תִּמְצְאוּ אֶת־דּוֹדִי מַה־תַּגִּידוּ לוֹ

ט שֶׁחוֹלַת אַהֲבָה אָנִי: מַה־דּוֹדֵךְ מִדּוֹד הַיָּפָה בַּנָּשִׁים מַה־דּוֹדֵךְ מִדּוֹד

יא ·יא שֶׁכָּכָה הִשְׁבַּעְתָּנוּ: דּוֹדִי צַח וְאָדוֹם דָּגוּל מֵרְבָבָה: רֹאשׁוֹ כֶּתֶם פָּז

יב קְוֻצּוֹתָיו תַּלְתַּלִּים שְׁחֹרוֹת כָּעוֹרֵב: עֵינָיו כְּיוֹנִים עַל־אֲפִיקֵי מָיִם

יג רֹחֲצוֹת בֶּחָלָב יֹשְׁבוֹת עַל־מִלֵּאת: לְחָיָו כַּעֲרוּגַת הַבֹּשֶׂם מִגְדְּלוֹת

יד מֶרְקָחִים שִׂפְתוֹתָיו שׁוֹשַׁנִּים נֹטְפוֹת מוֹר עֹבֵר: יָדָיו גְּלִילֵי זָהָב מְמֻלָּאִים

טו בַּתַּרְשִׁישׁ מֵעָיו עֶשֶׁת שֵׁן מְעֻלֶּפֶת סַפִּירִים: שׁוֹקָיו עַמּוּדֵי שֵׁשׁ

טז מְיֻסָּדִים עַל־אַדְנֵי־פָז מַרְאֵהוּ כַּלְּבָנוֹן בָּחוּר כָּאֲרָזִים: חִכּוֹ מַמְתַקִּים

א וְכֻלּוֹ מַחֲמַדִּים זֶה דוֹדִי וְזֶה רֵעִי בְּנוֹת יְרוּשָׁלָ͏ִם: אָנָה הָלַךְ דּוֹדֵךְ

ו

ב הַיָּפָה בַּנָּשִׁים אָנָה פָּנָה דוֹדֵךְ וּנְבַקְשֶׁנּוּ עִמָּךְ: דּוֹדִי יָרַד לְגַנּוֹ לַעֲרֻגוֹת

ג הַבֹּשֶׂם לִרְעוֹת בַּגַּנִּים וְלִלְקֹט שׁוֹשַׁנִּים: אֲנִי לְדוֹדִי וְדוֹדִי לִי הָרֹעֶה

בַּשּׁוֹשַׁנִּים:

NOTES INCLUDING PHRASE-BY-PHRASE LITERAL TRANSLATION

5:8. הִשְׁבַּעְתִּי אֶתְכֶם בְּנוֹת יְרוּשָׁלָ͏ִם — *I adjure you, O nations destined to ascend to Jerusalem* [lit., *I adjure you, O daughters of Jerusalem*]. You, our oppressors, should testify that we remained loyal to our God.

אִם־תִּמְצְאוּ אֶת־דּוֹדִי — *when you see my Beloved on the future Day of Judgment* [lit., *If you find my Beloved*], when the nations will be called upon to bear witness for Israel . . .

מַה־תַּגִּידוּ לוֹ שֶׁחוֹלַת אַהֲבָה אָנִי — *will you not tell Him that I bore all travails for love of Him?* [lit., *What shall you tell him? That I am sick with love*]. Tell Him that only for love of Him were we afflicted with harsh suffering.

5:9. מַה־דּוֹדֵךְ מִדּוֹד הַיָּפָה בַּנָּשִׁים — *With what does your beloved God excel all others that you suffer for His Name, O fairest of nations?* [lit., *What (makes) your Beloved (better) than (another) beloved, O fairest among women?*]. How is your God so superior to other gods that you are ready to be burned and tortured for Him? You are handsome, you are mighty; come intermingle with us!

מַה־דּוֹדֵךְ מִדּוֹד שֶׁכָּכָה הִשְׁבַּעְתָּנוּ — *With what does your beloved God excel all others that you dare to adjure us?* [lit., *What (makes) your Beloved (better) than (another) beloved, that you so adjure us?*].

5:10. דּוֹדִי צַח וְאָדוֹם — *My Beloved is pure and purifies sin, and is ruddy with vengeance to punish betrayers* [lit., *My Beloved is white, yet ruddy*]. Even when He sits in judgment, He is anxious to purify your deeds. But when exacting retribution from His enemies, He is depicted as clad in blood-red vestments (see *Isaiah* 63:2).

דָּגוּל מֵרְבָבָה — *surrounded with myriad angels* [lit., *pre-eminent above ten thousand*].

5:11. רֹאשׁוֹ כֶּתֶם פָּז — *His opening words were finest gold* [lit., *His head is finest gold*]. When He gave us the Ten Commandments, His words were like fine gold.

קְוֻצּוֹתָיו תַּלְתַּלִּים — *His crowns hold mounds of statutes* [lit., *His locks are wavy*]. From every one of the scribal crowns that adorn the tops of many letters in the Torah script, mounds and mounds of laws can be derived (*Eruvin* 21b).

שְׁחֹרוֹת כָּעוֹרֵב — *written in raven-black flame* [lit., *black as the raven*]. In Heaven, the Torah is written in black fire upon white fire.

5:12. עֵינָיו כְּיוֹנִים עַל אֲפִיקֵי מָיִם — *Like the gaze of doves toward their cotes, His eyes are fixed on the waters of Torah* [lit., *His eyes are like doves besides brooks of water*].

רֹחֲצוֹת בֶּחָלָב — *bathing all things in clarity* [lit., *bathing in milk*]. God's "eyes" see clearly, rewarding the righteous, and condemning the wicked.

יֹשְׁבוֹת עַל מִלֵּאת — *established upon Creation's fullness* [lit., *sitting upon the fullness*]. His judgment is upon the fullness of the earth.

5:13. לְחָיָו כַּעֲרוּגַת הַבֹּשֶׂם מִגְדְּלוֹת מֶרְקָחִים — *Like a bed of spices are His words at Sinai, like towers of perfume* [lit., *His cheeks are like a bed of spices, towers of perfume*]. God's utterances at Mount Sinai during which He displayed a friendly, smiling demeanor were like beds of spices and mounds of sweet herbs to be processed into perfumes.

שִׂפְתוֹתָיו שׁוֹשַׁנִּים נֹטְפוֹת מוֹר עֹבֵר — *His comforting words from the Tabernacle are roses dripping flowing myrrh* [lit., *His lips are like roses; they drip flowing myrrh*]. In the Tabernacle, God taught us about the offerings that atone for sin.

5:14. יָדָיו גְּלִילֵי זָהָב — *The Tablets, His handiwork, are desirable above even rolls of gold* [lit., *His arms are rods of gold*]. The Tablets of the Ten Commandments, written by the "finger" of God (*Exodus* 31:18), "are more desirable than gold, than even much fine gold" (*Psalms* 19:11).

מְמֻלָּאִים בַּתַּרְשִׁישׁ — *they are studded with commandments precious as gems* [lit., *studded with crystal*].

מֵעָיו עֶשֶׁת שֵׁן מְעֻלֶּפֶת סַפִּירִים — *the Torah's innards are sparkling as ivory intricately inlaid with precious stone* [lit., *his innards are as shiny as ivory inlaid with sapphires*].

5:15. שׁוֹקָיו עַמּוּדֵי שֵׁשׁ מְיֻסָּדִים עַל אַדְנֵי פָז — *The Torah's columns are marble set in contexts of finest gold* [lit., *His legs are pillars of marble set upon sockets of fine gold*] . . .

ALLEGORICAL RENDERING FOLLOWING RASHI

Israel to the
nations
8 *I adjure you, O nations destined to ascend to Jerusalem, when you see my Beloved on the future Day of Judgment, will you not tell Him that I bore all travails for love of Him?*

The nations
ask Israel
9 *With what does your beloved God excel all others that you suffer for His Name, O fairest of nations? With what does your beloved God excel all others that you dare to adjure us?*

Israel
responds
10 *My Beloved is pure and purifies sin, and is ruddy with vengeance to punish betrayers, surrounded with myriad angels.* **11** *His opening words were finest gold, His crowns hold mounds of statutes written in raven-black flame.*

12 *Like the gaze of doves toward their cotes, His eyes are fixed on the waters of Torah, bathing all things in clarity, established upon Creation's fullness.* **13** *Like a bed of spices are His words at Sinai, like towers of perfume. His comforting words from the Tabernacle are roses dripping flowing myrrh.* **14** *The Tablets, His handiwork, are desirable above even rolls of gold; they are studded with commandments precious as gems, the Torah's innards are sparkling as ivory intricately inlaid with precious stone.* **15** *The Torah's columns are marble set in contexts of finest gold, its contemplation flowers like Lebanon, it is sturdy as cedars.* **16** *The words of His palate are sweet and He is all delight.*

This is my Beloved and this is my Friend, O nations destined to ascend to Jerusalem.

6
The
nations,
derisively,
to Israel
1 *Where has your Beloved gone, O fairest among women? Where has your Beloved turned to rejoin you? Let us seek Him with you and build His Temple with you.*

Israel
responds
2 *My Beloved has descended to His Temple garden, to His Incense Altar, yet still He grazes my brethren remaining in gardens of exile to gather the roseate fragrance of their words of Torah.* **3** *I alone am my Beloved's and my Beloved is mine, He Who grazes His sheep in roselike pastures.*

NOTES INCLUDING PHRASE-BY-PHRASE LITERAL TRANSLATION

מַרְאֵהוּ כַּלְּבָנוֹן בָּחוּר כָּאֲרָזִים — *its contemplation flowers like Lebanon, it is sturdy as cedars* [lit., *its appearance is like (the forest of) Lebanon, choicest among cedars*]. Just as one sees beautiful flowers and lofty trees in a forest, so one discovers limitless wisdom in the Torah.

5:16. חִכּוֹ מַמְתַקִּים וְכֻלּוֹ מַחֲמַדִּים — *The words of His palate are sweet and all of him is a delight* [lit., *His palate is most sweet; and all of him is a delight*].

זֶה דוֹדִי וְזֶה רֵעִי בְּנוֹת יְרוּשָׁלָ‏ם — *This is my Beloved and this is my Friend, O nations destined to ascend to Jerusalem* [lit., *this is my Beloved, and this is my Friend, O daughters of Jerusalem*].

6:1. The nations continue to taunt Israel:

אָנָה הָלַךְ דּוֹדֵךְ הַיָּפָה בַּנָּשִׁים — *Where has your Beloved gone, O fairest among women?* Why has He left you alone, widowed?

אָנָה פָּנָה דוֹדֵךְ וּנְבַקְשֶׁנּוּ עִמָּךְ — *Where has your Beloved turned to rejoin you? Let us seek Him with you and build His Temple with you* [lit., *Where has your Beloved turned, that we may seek Him with you?*]. When King Cyrus permitted the rebuilding of the Temple, the heathens tried to undermine the work by joining the builders and sabotaging the construction (see *Ezra* 4:1-2).

6:2. דוֹדִי יָרַד לְגַנּוֹ לַעֲרֻגוֹת הַבֹּשֶׂם — *My Beloved has descended to His Temple garden, to His Incense Altar* [lit., *My Beloved has gone down to His garden, to the beds of spices*]. He commanded us to build His Temple, and He will surely be there with us.

לִרְעוֹת בַּגַּנִּים וְלִלְקֹט שׁוֹשַׁנִּים — *yet still He grazes my brethren remaining in gardens of exile to gather the roseate fragrance of their words of Torah* [lit., *to graze in the gardens and to pick roses*]. God did not neglect those of His children who chose not to return to the land. He manifested His Presence in their synagogues and study halls.

6:3. In reply to the nations' insincere offer to help Israel:

אֲנִי לְדוֹדִי — *I alone am my Beloved's* [lit., *I am My Beloved's*]. I, alone, am my Beloved's. You are not His, and you will not assist us in the construction (see *Ezra* 4:3).

וְדוֹדִי לִי — *and my Beloved is mine*.

הָרֹעֶה בַּשׁוֹשַׁנִּים — *He Who grazes His sheep in roselike pastures* [lit., *Who feeds (others) among the roses*].

ד-ה יָפָה אַתְּ רַעְיָתִי כְּתִרְצָה נָאוָה כִּירוּשָׁלָםִ אֲיֻמָּה כַּנִּדְגָּלוֹת: הָסֵבִּי עֵינַיִךְ

ו מִנֶּגְדִּי שֶׁהֵם הִרְהִיבֻנִי שַׂעְרֵךְ כְּעֵדֶר הָעִזִּים שֶׁגָּלְשׁוּ מִן־הַגִּלְעָד: שִׁנַּיִךְ

כְּעֵדֶר הָרְחֵלִים שֶׁעָלוּ מִן־הָרַחְצָה שֶׁכֻּלָּם מַתְאִימוֹת וְשַׁכֻּלָה אֵין

ז-ח בָּהֶם: כְּפֶלַח הָרִמּוֹן רַקָּתֵךְ מִבַּעַד לְצַמָּתֵךְ: שִׁשִּׁים הֵמָּה מְלָכוֹת

ט וּשְׁמֹנִים פִּילַגְשִׁים וַעֲלָמוֹת אֵין מִסְפָּר: אַחַת הִיא יוֹנָתִי תַמָּתִי אַחַת הִיא

לְאִמָּהּ בָּרָה הִיא לְיוֹלַדְתָּהּ רָאוּהָ בָנוֹת וַיְאַשְּׁרוּהָ מְלָכוֹת וּפִילַגְשִׁים

י וַיְהַלְלוּהָ: מִי־זֹאת הַנִּשְׁקָפָה כְּמוֹ־שָׁחַר יָפָה כַלְּבָנָה

יא בָּרָה כַּחַמָּה אֲיֻמָּה כַּנִּדְגָּלוֹת: אֶל־גִּנַּת אֱגוֹז יָרַדְתִּי לִרְאוֹת בְּאִבֵּי

יב הַנָּחַל לִרְאוֹת הֲפָרְחָה הַגֶּפֶן הֵנֵצוּ הָרִמֹּנִים: לֹא יָדַעְתִּי נַפְשִׁי שָׂמַתְנִי

ז א מַרְכְּבוֹת עַמִּי נָדִיב: שׁוּבִי שׁוּבִי הַשּׁוּלַמִּית שׁוּבִי שׁוּבִי וְנֶחֱזֶה־בָּךְ

ב מַה־תֶּחֱזוּ בַּשּׁוּלַמִּית כִּמְחֹלַת הַמַּחֲנָיִם: מַה־יָּפוּ פְעָמַיִךְ בַּנְּעָלִים בַּת־

NOTES INCLUDING PHRASE-BY-PHRASE LITERAL TRANSLATION

6:4. יָפָה אַתְּ רַעְיָתִי כְּתִרְצָה — *You are beautiful, My love, when your deeds are pleasing* [lit., *You are beautiful, My love, as Tirzah*]. Tirzah was a beautiful city that was the capital for a succession of kings of the Northern Kingdom of Israel (see *I Kings* 15:33; 16:8-9,15,23).

נָאוָה כִּירוּשָׁלָםִ — *as comely now as you once were in Jerusalem of old* [lit., *comely as Jerusalem*].

אֲיֻמָּה כַּנִּדְגָּלוֹת — *the nations stand in awe of you as of hosts of angels* [lit., *awe inspiring as an army with banners*]. See *Ezra* Ch. 5.

6:5. הָסֵבִּי עֵינַיִךְ מִנֶּגְדִּי שֶׁהֵם הִרְהִיבֻנִי — *Turn your pleading eyes from Me lest I be tempted to bestow upon you holiness more than you can bear* [lit., *Turn your eyes away from Me, for they overwhelm Me*]. As the Second Temple was being built, God said figuratively, "You are as beautiful to Me now as you were before, but in this Temple I will not return the Ark, the Cherubim and the *Paroches* Curtain that you had in the First Temple. They invoke special love in Me that you cannot have now that you have sinned. But in every other way you have maintained the former virtues that endeared you to Me."

שַׂעְרֵךְ כְּעֵדֶר הָעִזִּים שֶׁגָּלְשׁוּ מִן־הַגִּלְעָד — *But with all your flaws, your most common sons are as dearly beloved as the children of Jacob in the goatlike procession descending the slopes of Mount Gilead* [lit., *your hair is like a flock of goats streaming down from Gilead*]. Even the young, tender and insignificant among you are praiseworthy.

6:6. שִׁנַּיִךְ כְּעֵדֶר הָרְחֵלִים שֶׁעָלוּ מִן־הָרַחְצָה שֶׁכֻּלָּם מַתְאִימוֹת וְשַׁכֻּלָה אֵין בָּהֶם — *Your mighty leaders are perfect, as a flock of ewes come up from the washing, all of them unblemished with no miscarriage of action in them* [lit., *Your teeth are like a flock of ewes which have come up from the washing, all of them are perfect and there is none blemished among them*] (see 4:2).

6:7. כְּפֶלַח הָרִמּוֹן רַקָּתֵךְ מִבַּעַד לְצַמָּתֵךְ — *As many as a pomegranate's seeds are the merits of your unworthiest within your modest veil* [lit., *Your cheeks are like a slice of pomegranate, from behind your veil*] (see 4:3).

6:8. שִׁשִּׁים הֵמָּה מְלָכוֹת — *The queenly offspring of Abraham are sixty* [lit., *There are sixty queens*]. Abraham's male

descendants through the children of Jacob (*Genesis* 25:1-4, 12-15; 35:23-36:19) numbered sixty (see Appendix B, charts 2 and 4).

וּשְׁמֹנִים פִּילַגְשִׁים וַעֲלָמוֹת אֵין מִסְפָּר — *compared to whom the eighty Noachides and all their countless nations are like mere concubines* [lit., *and eighty concubines and maidens without number*]. Noah's descendants, until Abraham (*Genesis* Chs. 10-11), numbered eighty (See Appendix B, chart 1). Each of them branched out into many families.

6:9. אַחַת הִיא יוֹנָתִי תַמָּתִי — *Unique is she, My constant dove, My perfect one* [lit., *One is My dove, My perfect one*]. Israel is My chosen nation, like a perfect dove, loyal to her mate.

אַחַת הִיא לְאִמָּהּ — *Unique is she, this nation striving for the truth* [lit., *one is she to her mother*]. To comprehend Torah in its fundamentals and its truth.

בָּרָה הִיא לְיוֹלַדְתָּהּ — *pure is she to Jacob who begot her* [lit., *she is pure to the one that begot her*]. All of Jacob's sons were righteous.

רָאוּהָ בָנוֹת וַיְאַשְּׁרוּהָ מְלָכוֹת וּפִילַגְשִׁים וַיְהַלְלוּהָ — Nations [lit., *maidens*] *saw her and they extolled her; queens and concubines, and they praised her* (see *Malachi* 3:12).

6:10. God now quotes to Israel how the nations will extol and praise her:

מִי־זֹאת הַנִּשְׁקָפָה כְּמוֹ־שָׁחַר — *"Who is this that gazes down from atop the Temple Mount, brightening like the dawn* [lit., *Who is that gazing down like dawn?*]. Like a steadily brightening dawn, Israel began the Second Temple era in subjugation, but later became independent under the Hasmonean dynasty.

יָפָה כַלְּבָנָה בָּרָה כַּחַמָּה — *beautiful as the moon, brilliant as the sun* [lit., *beautiful as the moon, pure as the sun*]. At first, Israel was like the moon, because it could only reflect the power permitted it by King Cyrus.

אֲיֻמָּה כַּנִּדְגָּלוֹת — *awesome as the bannered hosts of kings?"* [lit., *awe inspiring as an army with banners*].

6:11. אֶל־גִּנַּת אֱגוֹז יָרַדְתִּי — *I descended upon the deceptively simple holiness of the Second Temple* [lit., *I went down to the garden of nuts*]. Israel is modest and unpretentious; her scholars are not conspicuous, but they are full of wisdom.

ALLEGORICAL RENDERING FOLLOWING RASHI

God to Israel   **4** *You are beautiful, My love, when your deeds are pleasing, as comely now as you once were in Jerusalem of old, the nations stand in awe of you as of hosts of angels.* **5** *Turn your pleading eyes from Me lest I be tempted to bestow upon you holiness more than you can bear. But with all your flaws, your most common sons are as dearly beloved as the children of Jacob in the goatlike procession descending the slopes of Mount Gilead.* **6** *Your mighty leaders are perfect, as a flock of ewes come up from the washing, all of them unblemished with no miscarriage of action in them.* **7** *As many as a pomegranate's seeds are the merits of your unworthiest within your modest veil.* **8** *The queenly offspring of Abraham are sixty, compared to whom the eighty Noachides and all their countless nations are like mere concubines.*

9 *Unique is she, My constant dove, My perfect one. Unique is she, this nation striving for the truth; pure is she to Jacob who begot her. Nations saw her and they extolled her; queens and concubines, and they praised her:* **10** *"Who is this that gazes down from atop the Temple Mount, brightening like the dawn, beautiful as the moon, brilliant as the sun, awesome as the bannered hosts of kings?"*

11 *I descended upon the deceptively simple holiness of the Second Temple to see your moisture-laden deeds in the river beds; to see whether your Torah scholars had budded on the vine, whether your merit-laden righteous had flowered like the pomegranates filled with seeds.*

Israel re-   **12** *Alas, I knew not how to guard myself from sin! My own devices harnessed sponds sadly*   *me, like chariots subject to a foreign nation's mercies.*

7   **1** *The nations have said to me, "Turn away, turn away from God, O nation whose faith in Him is perfect, turn away, turn away, and we shall choose nobility from you."*

     But I replied to them, "What can you bestow upon a nation of perfect faith The nations   *commensurate even with the desert camps encircling?"*

to Israel   **2** *But your footsteps were so lovely when shod in pilgrim's sandals, O daughter*

NOTES INCLUDING PHRASE-BY-PHRASE LITERAL TRANSLATION

לִרְאוֹת בְּאִבֵּי הַנָּחַל — *to see your moisture-laden deeds in the river beds* [lit., *to look at the green plants of the streams*], to examine the good deeds that I could find in you . . .

לִרְאוֹת הֲפָרְחָה הַגֶּפֶן — *to see whether your Torah scholars had budded on the vine* [lit., *to see whether the vine has budded*] . . .

הֵנֵצוּ הָרִמֹּנִים — *whether your merit-laden righteous had flowered like the pomegranates filled with seeds* [lit., *if the pomegranates were in flower*].

6:12. Hearing God's praise of her glorious past, Israel reflects on her current plight and responds sadly:

לֹא יָדַעְתִּי נַפְשִׁי שָׂמַתְנִי מַרְכְּבוֹת עַמִּי נָדִיב — *Alas, I knew not how to guard myself from sin! My own devices harnessed me, like chariots subject to a foreign nation's mercies* [lit., *I did not know; my soul set me (as) chariots of a noble nation*]. Instead of avoiding sin, I stumbled into the sin of hatred and controversy, which caused Jews to invite Rome into the land and take control. From that point, I became a chariot driven by foreign nations.

7:1. שׁוּבִי שׁוּבִי הַשּׁוּלַמִּית — *The nations have said to me, "Turn away, turn away from God, O nation whose faith in*

Him is perfect [lit., *Turn, turn, O Shulammite*]. The word שׁוּלַמִּית, "Shulammite," is linguistically related to שָׁלֵם, "whole, perfect."

שׁוּבִי שׁוּבִי וְנֶחֱזֶה בָּךְ — *turn away, turn away, and we shall choose nobility from you"* [lit., *turn, turn, that we may see you*]. Join us and we will discern what greatness to bestow upon you.

מַה תֶּחֱזוּ בַּשׁוּלַמִּית כִּמְחֹלַת הַמַּחֲנָיִם — *But I replied to them, "What can you bestow upon a nation of perfect faith commensurate even with the desert camps encircling?"* [lit., *What will you see in the Shulammite like a dance of the camps?*]. Your highest honors are not equal even to the greatness of the encircling encampments in the desert. See *Numbers* Ch. 2.

7:2. מַה יָּפוּ פְעָמַיִךְ בַּנְּעָלִים בַּת נָדִיב — *But your footsteps were so lovely when shod in pilgrim's sandals, O daughter of nobles* [lit., *How lovely are your steps in sandals, O daughter of nobility!*]. The word פְּעָמִים means both "footsteps," (hence, "pilgrimage") and "times, repeated occasions." The nations were impressed by Israel's pilgrimages to the Temple three times each year to celebrate the festivals.

ג נָדִיב חַמּוּקֵי יְרֵכַיִךְ כְּמוֹ חֲלָאִים מַעֲשֵׂה יְדֵי אָמָּן: שָׁרְרֵךְ אַגַּן הַסַּהַר

ד אַל־יֶחְסַר הַמָּזֶג בִּטְנֵךְ עֲרֵמַת חִטִּים סוּגָה בַּשּׁוֹשַׁנִּים: שְׁנֵי שָׁדַיִךְ

ה כִּשְׁנֵי עֳפָרִים תָּאֳמֵי צְבִיָּה: צַוָּארֵךְ כְּמִגְדַּל הַשֵּׁן עֵינַיִךְ בְּרֵכוֹת בְּחֶשְׁבּוֹן

ו עַל־שַׁעַר בַּת־רַבִּים אַפֵּךְ כְּמִגְדַּל הַלְּבָנוֹן צוֹפֶה פְּנֵי דַמָּשֶׂק: רֹאשֵׁךְ

ז עָלַיִךְ כַּכַּרְמֶל וְדַלַּת רֹאשֵׁךְ כָּאַרְגָּמָן מֶלֶךְ אָסוּר בָּרְהָטִים: מַה־יָּפִית

ח וּמַה־נָּעַמְתְּ אַהֲבָה בַּתַּעֲנוּגִים: זֹאת קוֹמָתֵךְ דָּמְתָה לְתָמָר וְשָׁדַיִךְ

ט לְאַשְׁכֹּלוֹת: אָמַרְתִּי אֶעֱלֶה בְתָמָר אֹחֲזָה בְּסַנְסִנָּיו וְיִהְיוּ־נָא שָׁדַיִךְ

י כְּאֶשְׁכְּלוֹת הַגֶּפֶן וְרֵיחַ אַפֵּךְ כַּתַּפּוּחִים: וְחִכֵּךְ כְּיֵין הַטּוֹב הוֹלֵךְ

יא לְדוֹדִי לְמֵישָׁרִים דּוֹבֵב שִׂפְתֵי יְשֵׁנִים: אֲנִי לְדוֹדִי וְעָלַי תְּשׁוּקָתוֹ:

יב-יג לְכָה דוֹדִי נֵצֵא הַשָּׂדֶה נָלִינָה בַּכְּפָרִים: נַשְׁכִּימָה לַכְּרָמִים נִרְאֶה אִם־
פָּרְחָה הַגֶּפֶן פִּתַּח הַסְּמָדַר הֵנֵצוּ הָרִמּוֹנִים שָׁם אֶתֵּן אֶת־דֹּדַי לָךְ:

NOTES INCLUDING PHRASE-BY-PHRASE LITERAL TRANSLATION

חַמּוּקֵי יְרֵכַיִךְ כְּמוֹ חֲלָאִים מַעֲשֵׂה יְדֵי אָמָּן — *The rounded shafts for your libations' abysslike trenches, handiwork of the Master Craftsman* [lit., *The roundness of your flanks are like jewels, the work of a master's hand*]. The wine libations, poured onto the top of the Temple's Courtyard Altar, flowed through pipes into deep pits under the Altar. Those pits had been placed there by God Himself during the Six Days of Creation. They were rounded like a thigh and descended into the abyss.

7:3. שָׁרְרֵךְ אַגַּן הַסַּהַר — *At earth's very center your Sanhedrin site is a crescent basin* [lit., *Your umbilicus is like a moon-shaped basin*]. The seat of the Sanhedrin (high court) was in the Temple complex, at the center of the world. Its members were seated in a semicircle, like the crescent moon, so they could see each other and speak face to face.

אַל־יֶחְסַר הַמָּזֶג — *of ceaseless, flowing teaching* [lit., *wherein no mixed wine is lacking*]. The Sanhedrin was an endless source of wisdom.

בִּטְנֵךְ עֲרֵמַת חִטִּים — *your national center an indispensable heap of nourishing knowledge* [lit., *your stomach is like a heap of wheat*]. Wheat is an indispensable staple.

סוּגָה בַּשּׁוֹשַׁנִּים — *Hedged about with roses.* Just as a hedge of roses is hardly an imposing barrier, similarly, the sanctions of the Torah are gentle reminders to refrain from trespass against the handiwork of God.

7:4. שְׁנֵי שָׁדַיִךְ כִּשְׁנֵי עֳפָרִים תָּאֳמֵי צְבִיָּה — *Your twin sustainers, the Tablets of the Law, are like two fawns, twins of the gazelle* [lit., *Your two breasts are like two fawns, twins of a gazelle*]. This refers to the twin Tablets of the Covenant (see also 4:5).

7:5. צַוָּארֵךְ כְּמִגְדַּל הַשֵּׁן — *Your Altar and Temple, erect and stately as an ivory tower* [lit., *Your neck is like a tower of ivory*]. The Sanctuary and Altar, which stood erect and tall, provided spiritual strength and protection like an ivory tower.

עֵינַיִךְ בְּרֵכוֹת בְּחֶשְׁבּוֹן עַל שַׁעַר בַּת רַבִּים — *your wise men aflow with springs of complex wisdom at the gate of the many-peopled city* [lit., *your eyes are (like the) pools in Heshbon by the gate of Bath-rabbim*]. Your wise men (the "eyes" of

the nation) sit at the gates of Jerusalem (Bath-rabbim, lit., "of great population") where they are involved in the complex calculations of the Hebrew calendar.

אַפֵּךְ כְּמִגְדַּל הַלְּבָנוֹן צוֹפֶה פְּנֵי דַמָּשֶׂק — *your face, like the tower of Lebanon, looks to your future boundary as far as Damascus* [lit., *your face is like the tower of Lebanon facing toward Damascus*]. An allusion to the prophetic vision (see *Zechariah* 9:1) that in the future the gates of Jerusalem will stretch forth until Damascus.

7:6. רֹאשֵׁךְ עָלַיִךְ כַּכַּרְמֶל — *The Godly name on your head is as mighty as Carmel* [lit., *Your head upon you is like (Mount) Carmel*]. This refers to the *tefillin* of the head, of which the verse says, "Then all the peoples of the earth will see that the Name of HASHEM is proclaimed over you, and they will revere you" (*Deuteronomy* 28:10). The *tefillin* are Israel's strength; they are as awe inspiring as the lofty cliffs of Mount Carmel.

וְדַלַּת רֹאשֵׁךְ כָּאַרְגָּמָן — *your crowning braid is royal purple* [lit., *and the locks of your head are like purple*]. The locks of your Nazirites are as comely as garments of royal purple.

מֶלֶךְ אָסוּר בָּרְהָטִים — *your King is bound in Nazirite tresses* [lit., *a king bound in tresses*]. The crown of the King (God) is associated with the Nazirite's hair (see *Numbers* 6:7).

7:7. מַה יָּפִית וּמַה נָּעַמְתְּ אַהֲבָה בַּתַּעֲנוּגִים — *How beautiful and pleasant are you, befitting the pleasures of spiritual love* [lit., *How beautiful you are, and how pleasant, love in delights*]. The nations now praise Israel's lofty spiritual ideals.

7:8. זֹאת קוֹמָתֵךְ דָּמְתָה לְתָמָר — *Such is your stature, likened to a towering palm tree* [lit., *This is your stature, like unto a palm tree*]. We witnessed your lovely stature in the days of Nebuchadnezzar, when all the nations bowed down to the statue (see *Daniel* Ch. 3).

וְשָׁדַיִךְ לְאַשְׁכֹּלוֹת — *from your teachers flow sustenance like wine-filled clusters* [lit., *and your breasts are like clusters*]. "Your breasts," your sources of spiritual nourishment, i.e., Daniel and his companions Hananiah, Mishael, and Azariah, nurtured everyone with the knowledge that there is no fear of God like yours.

7:9. אָמַרְתִּי אֶעֱלֶה בְתָמָר — *I boast on High that your deeds cause Me to ascend on your palm tree* [lit., *I said: I will*

ALLEGORICAL RENDERING FOLLOWING RASHI

of nobles. The rounded shafts for your libations' abysslike trenches, handiwork of the Master Craftsman. ³ *At earth's very center your Sanhedrin site is a crescent basin of ceaseless, flowing teaching; your national center an indispensable heap of nourishing knowledge hedged about with roses.* ⁴ *Your twin sustainers, the Tablets of the Law, are like two fawns, twins of the gazelle.* ⁵ *Your Altar and Temple, erect and stately as an ivory tower; your wise men aflow with springs of complex wisdom at the gate of the many-peopled city; your face, like the tower of Lebanon, looks to your future boundary as far as Damascus.*

⁶ *The Godly name on your head is as mighty as Carmel; your crowning braid is royal purple, your King is bound in Naziritic tresses.* ⁷ *How beautiful and pleasant are you, befitting the pleasures of spiritual love.* ⁸ *Such is your stature, likened to a towering palm tree, from your teachers flow sustenance like wine-filled clusters.*

God to Israel ⁹ *I boast on High that your deeds cause Me to ascend on your palm tree, I grasp onto your branches. I beg now your teachers that they may remain like clusters of grapes from which flow strength to your weakest ones, and the fragrance of your countenance like apples,* ¹⁰ *and may your utterance be like finest wine.*

Israel to *I shall heed Your plea to uphold my faith before my Beloved in love so upright*
God . . . *and honest that my slumbering fathers will move their lips in approval.*
. . . to the
nations . . . ¹¹ *I am my Beloved's and He longs for my perfection.*
. . . to God ¹² *Come, my Beloved, let us go to the fields where Your children serve You in want, there let us lodge with Esau's children who are blessed with plenty yet still deny.*

¹³ *Let us wake at dawn in vineyards of prayer and study. Let us see if students of Writ have budded, if students of Oral Law have blossomed, if ripened scholars have bloomed; there I will display my finest products to You.*

NOTES INCLUDING PHRASE-BY-PHRASE LITERAL TRANSLATION

ascend in the palm tree]. I boast about you among the Celestial Hosts, that I am elevated through your actions on earth.

אֶחֱזָה בְּסַנְסִנָּיו — *I grasp onto your branches* [lit., *I will take hold of its branches*]. I cleave to the branches, i.e., the children, of this palm tree, Israel.

וְיִהְיוּ נָא שָׁדַיִךְ כְּאֶשְׁכְּלוֹת הַגֶּפֶן וְרֵיחַ אַפֵּךְ כַּתַּפּוּחִים — *I beg now your teachers that they may remain like clusters of grapes from which flow strength to your weakest ones, and the fragrance of your countenance like apples* [lit., *and let your breasts be like clusters of the vine, and the fragrance of your countenance like apples*]. May the righteous and wise inspire the young to withstand the taunts of their heathen neighbors who wish to lead Israel astray.

7:10. וְחִכֵּךְ כְּיֵין הַטּוֹב — *and may your utterance be like finest wine* [lit., *your palate is like choice wine*]. May your response to the taunts of the heathens be as clear and potent as fine wine.

הוֹלֵךְ לְדוֹדִי לְמֵישָׁרִים — *I shall heed Your plea to uphold my faith before my Beloved in love so upright and honest* [lit., *it goes to my Beloved in righteousness*].

דּוֹבֵב שִׂפְתֵי יְשֵׁנִים — *that my slumbering fathers will move their lips in approval* [lit., *causing the lips of sleepers to speak*]. My love is so intense that even my departed ancestors will rejoice in me and be thankful for their lot.

7:11. אֲנִי לְדוֹדִי וְעָלַי תְּשׁוּקָתוֹ — *I am my Beloved's and He*

longs for my perfection [lit., *I am my Beloved's and His longing is upon me*].

7:12. לְכָה דוֹדִי נֵצֵא הַשָּׂדֶה — *Come, my Beloved, let us go to the fields where Your children serve You in want* [lit., *Come, my Beloved, let us go forth into the field*]. Do not judge me by the affluent people who indulge in robbery and immorality; come, let me show You scholars who study the Torah in poverty.

נָלִינָה בַּכְּפָרִים — *there let us lodge with Esau's children who are blessed with plenty yet still deny* [lit., *let us lodge in the villages*]. I will show You the children of Esau, upon whom You have bestowed much bounty, yet they do not believe in You.

7:13. נַשְׁכִּימָה לַכְּרָמִים — *Let us wake at dawn in vineyards of prayer and study* [lit., *Let us rise early for the vineyards*].

נִרְאֶה אִם פָּרְחָה הַגֶּפֶן פִּתַּח הַסְּמָדַר הֵנֵצוּ הָרִמּוֹנִים — *Let us see if students of Writ have budded, if students of Oral Law have blossomed, if ripened scholars have bloomed* [lit., *Let us see if the vine has budded, if the blossom has opened, if the pomegranates are in bloom*]. The stages of the ripening grape — budding, flowering, fruiting — symbolize the progress of the developing Torah scholars, from Scripture to Mishnah to Talmud.

שָׁם אֶתֵּן אֶת דֹּדַי לָךְ — *there I will display my finest products to You* [lit., *there I will give my love to You*]. I will show You my glory and my greatness, my sons and my daughters.

ח

יד הַֽדּוּדָאִ֣ים נָֽתְנוּ־רֵ֗יחַ וְעַל־פְּתָחֵ֨ינוּ֙ כָּל־מְגָדִ֔ים חֲדָשִׁ֖ים גַּם־יְשָׁנִ֑ים דּוֹדִ֖י

א צָפַ֥נְתִּי לָֽךְ: מִ֤י יִתֶּנְךָ֙ כְּאָ֣ח לִ֔י יוֹנֵ֖ק שְׁדֵ֣י אִמִּ֑י אֶֽמְצָֽאֲךָ֤ בַחוּץ֙ אֶשָּׁ֣קְךָ֔

ב גַּ֖ם לֹֽא־יָב֥וּזוּ לִֽי: אֶנְהָֽגְךָ֗ אֲבִֽיאֲךָ֛ אֶל־בֵּ֥ית אִמִּ֖י תְּלַמְּדֵ֑נִי אַשְׁקְךָ֙ מִיַּ֣יִן

ג-ד הָרֶ֔קַח מֵֽעֲסִ֖יס רִמֹּנִֽי: שְׂמֹאלוֹ֙ תַּ֣חַת רֹאשִׁ֔י וִֽימִינ֖וֹ תְּחַבְּקֵֽנִי: הִשְׁבַּ֤עְתִּי

אֶתְכֶם֙ בְּנ֣וֹת יְרֽוּשָׁלִַ֔ם מַה־תָּעִ֧ירוּ ׀ וּֽמַה־תְּעֹֽרֲר֛וּ אֶת־הָֽאַהֲבָ֖ה עַ֥ד

ה שֶׁתֶּחְפָּֽץ: מִ֣י זֹ֗את עֹלָה֙ מִן־הַמִּדְבָּ֔ר מִתְרַפֶּ֖קֶת עַל־דּוֹדָ֑הּ תַּ֤חַת

ו הַתַּפּ֨וּחַ֙ עֽוֹרַרְתִּ֔יךָ שָׁ֚מָּה חִבְּלַ֣תְךָ֣ אִמֶּ֔ךָ שָׁ֖מָּה חִבְּלָ֥ה יְלָדַֽתְךָ: שִׂימֵ֨נִי

כַחוֹתָ֜ם עַל־לִבֶּ֗ךָ כַּֽחוֹתָם֙ עַל־זְרוֹעֶ֔ךָ כִּֽי־עַזָּ֤ה כַמָּ֨וֶת֙ אַֽהֲבָ֔ה קָשָׁ֥ה כִשְׁא֖וֹל

ז קִנְאָ֑ה רְשָׁפֶ֕יהָ רִשְׁפֵּ֕י אֵ֖שׁ שַׁלְהֶ֥בֶתְיָֽה: מַ֣יִם רַבִּ֗ים לֹ֤א יֽוּכְלוּ֙ לְכַבּ֣וֹת אֶת־

הָֽאַהֲבָ֔ה וּנְהָר֖וֹת לֹ֣א יִשְׁטְפ֑וּהָ אִם־יִתֵּ֨ן אִ֜ישׁ אֶת־כָּל־ה֤וֹן בֵּיתוֹ֙ בָּֽאַהֲבָ֔ה

ח בּ֖וֹז יָב֥וּזוּ לֽוֹ:   אָח֥וֹת לָ֨נוּ֙ קְטַנָּ֔ה וְשָׁדַ֖יִם אֵ֣ין לָ֑הּ מַֽה־נַּֽעֲשֶׂה֙

ט לַֽאֲחֹתֵ֔נוּ בַּיּ֖וֹם שֶׁיְּדֻבַּר־בָּֽהּ: אִם־חוֹמָ֣ה הִ֔יא נִבְנֶ֥ה עָלֶ֖יהָ טִ֣ירַת כָּ֑סֶף

NOTES INCLUDING PHRASE-BY-PHRASE LITERAL TRANSLATION

7:14. הַדּוּדָאִים נָתְנוּ רֵיחַ — *All my baskets, good and bad, emit a fragrance* [lit., *The baskets yield fragrance*]. "Good figs" are an allusion to the righteous; "bad figs," to the wicked. In time, even the wicked will seek out God.

וְעַל פְּתָחֵינוּ כָּל מְגָדִים חֲדָשִׁים גַּם יְשָׁנִים — *all at our doors have the precious fruits of comely deeds, both the Scribes' new ordinances and the Torah's timeless wisdom* [lit., *and at our door are all precious fruits, both new and old*].

דּוֹדִי צָפַנְתִּי לָךְ — *for You, my Beloved, has my heart stored them* [lit., *I have hidden for You, my Beloved*]. Your commandments are in the depths of my heart.

8:1. מִי יִתֶּנְךָ כְּאָח לִי יוֹנֵק שְׁדֵי אִמִּי — *If only, despite my wrongs, You could comfort me as Joseph did, like a brother nurtured at my mother's breasts* [lit., *If only You were as a brother to me, who had nursed at my mother's breasts!*]. If only You would comfort me as Joseph comforted his brothers (see *Genesis* 50:21).

אֶמְצָאֲךָ בַחוּץ אֶשָּׁקְךָ גַּם לֹא יָבוּזוּ לִי — *if in the streets I found Your prophets I would kiss and embrace You through them, nor could anyone despise me for it* [lit., *(when) I would find You in the street I would kiss You and no one would scorn me*]. I would find Your prophets speaking in Your Name and I would embrace and kiss them.

8:2. אֶנְהָגְךָ אֲבִיאֲךָ אֶל בֵּית אִמִּי תְּלַמְּדֵנִי — *I would lead You, I would bring You to my mother's Temple for You to teach me as You did in Moses' Tent* [lit., *I would lead You, I would bring You to my mother's house that You should instruct me*].

אַשְׁקְךָ מִיַּיִן הָרֶקַח מֵעֲסִיס רִמֹּנִי — *to drink I would give You spiced libations, wines like pomegranate nectar* [lit., *I would give You spiced wine to drink, of the juice of my pomegranate*].

8:3. שְׂמֹאלוֹ תַּחַת רֹאשִׁי וִימִינוֹ תְּחַבְּקֵנִי — *Despite my laments in exile, His left hand supports my head and His right hand embraces me in support* [lit., *His left hand is under my head and His right arm embraces me*].

8:4. הִשְׁבַּעְתִּי אֶתְכֶם בְּנוֹת יְרוּשָׁלִַם מַה תָּעִירוּ וּמַה תְּעֹרֲרוּ אֶת הָאַהֲבָה עַד שֶׁתֶּחְפָּץ — *I adjure you, O nations who are destined to ascend to Jerusalem, if you dare provoke God to hate me or disturb His love for me while He still desires it* [lit., *I have adjured you O daughters of Jerusalem: should you wake or rouse the love until it pleases*]. Your efforts will be of no avail! (see 2:6-7).

8:5. מִי זֹאת עֹלָה מִן הַמִּדְבָּר מִתְרַפֶּקֶת עַל דּוֹדָהּ — *How worthy she is ascending from the wilderness bearing Torah and His Presence, clinging to her Beloved!* [lit., *Who is she that rises up from the wilderness leaning upon her Beloved?*]. Israel ascended from the desert bearing wonderful gifts from God; there she rose spiritually by cleaving to the Divine Presence.

תַּחַת הַתַּפּוּחַ עוֹרַרְתִּיךָ — *Under Sinai suspended above me, there I roused Your love* [lit., *Under the apple tree I roused You*]. Remember, how, beneath Mount Sinai, which was suspended over my head like an apple ["and they stood beneath the mountain" (*Deuteronomy* 4:11)], I manifested my love for You.

שָׁמָּה חִבְּלַתְךָ אִמֶּךָ שָׁמָּה חִבְּלָה יְלָדַתְךָ — *there was Your people born; a mother to other nations, there she endured the travail of her birth* [lit., *there Your mother was in travail for You; she who bore You was in travail*].

8:6. שִׂימֵנִי כַחוֹתָם עַל לִבֶּךָ כַּחוֹתָם עַל זְרוֹעֶךָ — *For the sake of my love, place me like a seal on Your heart, like a seal to dedicate Your strength for me* [lit., *Set me as a seal upon Your heart, as a seal upon Your arm*]. And because of that love, seal me upon Your heart so that You do not forget me.

כִּי עַזָּה כַמָּוֶת אַהֲבָה — *for strong till the death is my love* [lit., *that love is strong as death*].

קָשָׁה כִשְׁאוֹל קִנְאָה — *though their zeal for vengeance is hard as the grave* [lit., *jealousy is hard as the grave*], i.e., the unjust complaints, rivalries and jealousies that the nations provoked against me because of You.

רְשָׁפֶיהָ רִשְׁפֵּי אֵשׁ שַׁלְהֶבֶתְיָה — *its flashes are flashes of fire, the flame of God*. Its flashes are of a fierce fire emanating from the flames of Gehinnom.

8:7. מַיִם רַבִּים לֹא יוּכְלוּ לְכַבּוֹת אֶת הָאַהֲבָה — *Many waters of*

ALLEGORICAL RENDERING FOLLOWING RASHI

---

¹⁴ *All my baskets, good and bad, emit a fragrance; all at our doors have the precious fruits of comely deeds, both the Scribes' new ordinances and the Torah's timeless wisdom; for You, my Beloved, has my heart stored them.*

8

¹ *If only, despite my wrongs, You could comfort me as Joseph did, like a brother nurtured at my mother's breasts, if in the streets I found Your prophets I would kiss You and embrace You through them, nor could anyone despise me for it.* ² *I would lead You, I would bring You to my mother's Temple for You to teach me as You did in Moses' Tent; to drink I would give You spiced libations, wines like pomegranate nectar.*

Israel to the nations

³ *Despite my laments in exile, His left hand supports my head and His right hand embraces me in support.* ⁴ *I adjure you, O nations who are destined to ascend to Jerusalem, if you dare provoke God to hate me or disturb His love for me while He still desires it.*

God and the Heavenly Tribunal

⁵ *How worthy she is ascending from the wilderness bearing Torah and His Presence, clinging to her Beloved!*

Israel interjects

Under Sinai suspended above me, there I roused Your love, there was Your people born; a mother to other nations, there she endured the travail of her birth. ⁶ *For the sake of my love, place me like a seal on Your heart, like a seal to dedicate Your strength for me, for strong till the death is my love; though their zeal for vengeance is hard as the grave, its flashes are flashes of fire, the flame of God.* ⁷ *Many waters of heathen tribulation cannot extinguish the fire of this love, nor rivers of royal seduction or torture wash it away.*

God replies to Israel

Were any man to offer all the treasure of his home to entice you away from your love, they would scorn him to extreme.

The Heavenly Tribunal reflects

⁸ *Israel desires to cleave to us, the small and humble one, but her time of spiritual maturity has not come. What shall we do for our cleaving one on the day the nations plot against her?*

⁹ *If her faith and belief are strong as a wall withstanding incursions from without, we shall become her fortress and beauty, building her city and Holy Temple;*

NOTES INCLUDING PHRASE-BY-PHRASE LITERAL TRANSLATION

---

heathen tribulation cannot extinguish the fire of this love [lit., *Many waters cannot extinguish the love*]. "Many waters" refers to the heathen nations (see *Isaiah* 17:12,13).

וּנְהָרוֹת לֹא יִשְׁטְפוּהָ — *nor rivers of royal seduction or torture wash it away* [lit., *and rivers cannot drown it*]. Their leaders and kings cannot drown it, neither by force, nor by terror, nor by seductive enticement.

אִם יִתֵּן אִישׁ אֶת כָּל הוֹן בֵּיתוֹ בָּאַהֲבָה בּוֹז יָבוּזוּ לוֹ — *Were any man to offer all the treasure of his home to entice you away from your love, they would scorn him to extreme* [lit., *If a man would give all the substance of his house in exchange for love, he would be laughed to scorn*]. God and His Tribunal bear witness to Israel's love for her Beloved.

8:8. אָחוֹת לָנוּ קְטַנָּה — *Israel desires to cleave to us, the small and humble one* [lit., *We have a little sister*]. The words אָח, "brother," and אָחוֹת, "sister," are linguistically related to the verb אחה, "to join together." The Heavenly Tribunal said, "One small, humble nation

longs to join with us."

וְשָׁדַיִם אֵין לָהּ — *but her time of spiritual maturity has not come* [lit., *but she has no breasts*]. She is not yet ripe for Redemption (see *Ezekiel* 16:7).

מַה נַּעֲשֶׂה לַאֲחוֹתֵנוּ בַּיּוֹם שֶׁיְּדֻבַּר בָּהּ — *What shall we do for our cleaving one on the day the nations plot against her?* [lit., *What shall we do for our sister on the day she is spoken for?*]. How will we treat her when she seeks our protection?

8:9. אִם חוֹמָה הִיא נִבְנֶה עָלֶיהָ טִירַת כָּסֶף — *If her faith and belief are strong as a wall withstanding incursions from without, we shall become her fortress and beauty, building her city and Holy Temple* [lit., *If she be a wall, we will build upon her a turret of silver*]. Our response depends upon how she conducts herself in exile: If Israel will gird herself with faith and act toward the nations as if fortified with impenetrable "walls of copper" (*Jeremiah* 1:18), i.e., if she will neither intermarry nor intermingle with them, then we will rebuild the Holy City and Temple.

יְ וְאִם־דֶּלֶת הִיא נָצוּר עָלֶיהָ לוּחַ אָרֶז: אֲנִי חוֹמָה וְשָׁדַי כַּמִּגְדָּלוֹת אָז

יא הָיִיתִי בְעֵינָיו כְּמוֹצְאֵת שָׁלוֹם: כֶּרֶם הָיָה לִשְׁלֹמֹה בְּבַעַל הָמוֹן נָתַן אֶת

יב הַכֶּרֶם לַנֹּטְרִים אִישׁ יָבִא בְּפִרְיוֹ אֶלֶף כָּסֶף: כַּרְמִי שֶׁלִּי לְפָנָי הָאֶלֶף לְךָ

יג שְׁלֹמֹה וּמָאתַיִם לְנֹטְרִים אֶת־פִּרְיוֹ: הַיּוֹשֶׁבֶת בַּגַּנִּים חֲבֵרִים מַקְשִׁיבִים

יד לְקוֹלֵךְ הַשְׁמִיעִנִי: בְּרַח דּוֹדִי וְדְמֵה־לְךָ לִצְבִי אוֹ לְעֹפֶר הָאַיָּלִים עַל הָרֵי

בְשָׂמִים:

סכום פסוקי דשיר השירים מאה ושבעה עשר.

וסימנו וחכך **כיין הטוב** הולך לדודי. וסימנא אשר דבר **טוב על** המלך.

NOTES INCLUDING PHRASE-BY-PHRASE LITERAL TRANSLATION

וְאִם־דֶּלֶת הִיא נָצוּר עָלֶיהָ לוּחַ אָרֶז — *but if she wavers like a door, succumbing to every alien knock, with fragile cedar panels shall we then enclose her* [lit., *But if she be a door we will enclose her with cedar panel*]. If she is open to all blandishments, like a door that always swings open, then we will line her doors with wooden panels that will rot, thus exposing her to danger.

8:10. אֲנִי חוֹמָה וְשָׁדַי כַּמִּגְדָּלוֹת — *My faith is firm as a wall, and my nourishing synagogues and study halls are strong as towers!* [lit., *I am a wall, and my breasts are like towers!*]. I comport myself like a wall, strong in the love of my Beloved. My synagogues and study halls nurture Israel with words of Torah; they "are like towers."

אָז הָיִיתִי בְעֵינָיו כְּמוֹצְאֵת שָׁלוֹם — *Then, having said so, I become in His eyes like a bride found perfect* [lit., *Then I am in His eyes like one who found peace*].

8:11. כֶּרֶם הָיָה לִשְׁלֹמֹה בְּבַעַל הָמוֹן — *Israel was the vineyard of Him to Whom peace belongs in populous Jerusalem* [lit., *Solomon had a vineyard in Baal-hamon*]. "Solomon" refers to God (see 1:1); "vineyard" to Israel (see Isaiah 5:7); "Baal-hamon" [lit., "the owner of the multitude"] to Jerusalem, the greatly populated city.

נָתַן אֶת הַכֶּרֶם לַנֹּטְרִים — *He gave His vineyard to harsh, cruel guardians* [lit., *He gave over the vineyard to guardians*]. He handed over His people to harsh rulers: Babylon, Media, Greece and Rome.

אִישׁ יָבִא בְּפִרְיוֹ אֶלֶף כָּסֶף — *each one came to extort his fruit, even a thousand silver pieces* [lit., *everyone would bring for its fruit a thousand silver pieces*]. The "guardians" would impose exorbitant levies and taxes to feed their lusts.

8:12. כַּרְמִי שֶׁלִּי לְפָנָי — *The vineyard is Mine! Your iniquities are before Me!* [lit., *My vineyard, which is Mine, is before*

ALLEGORICAL RENDERING FOLLOWING RASHI

but if she wavers like a door, succumbing to every alien knock, with fragile cedar panels shall we then enclose her.

Israel replies proudly . . . [10] *My faith is firm as a wall, and my nourishing synagogues and study halls are strong as towers! Then, having said so, I become in His eyes like a bride found perfect.*

. . . and reminisces [11] *Israel was the vineyard of Him to Whom peace belongs in populous Jerusalem. He gave His vineyard to harsh, cruel guardians; each one came to extort his fruit, even a thousand silver pieces.*

God to the nations, on judgment day [12] *The vineyard is Mine! Your iniquities are before Me!*

The nations will reply *The thousand silver pieces are Yours, You to Whom peace belongs, and two hundred more to the Sages who guarded the fruit of Torah from our designs.*

God to Israel [13] *O My beloved, dwelling in far-flung gardens, your fellows, the angels, hearken to your voice of Torah and prayer. Let Me hear it, that they may then sanctify Me.*

Israel to God [14] *Flee, my Beloved, from our common exile and be like a gazelle or a young hart in Your swiftness to redeem and rest Your Presence among us on the fragrant Mount Moriah, site of Your Temple.*

NOTES INCLUDING PHRASE-BY-PHRASE LITERAL TRANSLATION

Me!] Although I transferred My vineyard to you, I am still the sole owner. All your injustices against Israel are before Me; nothing eludes Me.

הָאֶלֶף לְךָ שְׁלֹמֹה — *The thousand silver pieces are Yours, You to Whom peace belongs* [lit., *You, Solomon, can have Your thousand*]. Whatever we stole from them will all be returned to You.

וּמָאתַיִם לְנֹטְרִים אֶת פִּרְיוֹ — *and two hundred more to the Sages who guarded the fruit of Torah from our designs* [lit., *and two hundred to the tenders of its fruit*]. We will recompense Israel's leaders and Sages (see *Isaiah* 60:17).

8:13. הַיּוֹשֶׁבֶת בַּגַּנִּים חֲבֵרִים מַקְשִׁיבִים לְקוֹלֵךְ — *O My beloved, dwelling in far-flung gardens, your fellows, the angels, hearken to your voice of Torah and prayer* [lit., *O you who dwell in the gardens, companions are attentive to your voice*]. The angels listen to the prayers of Israel in the Diaspora, tending the gardens of others, and who dwell in

the synagogues and study halls.

הַשְׁמִיעִנִי — *Let Me hear it, that they may then sanctify Me* [lit., *let Me hear it*]. Let Me hear your voice, for after you are finished, the ministering angels will commence to sanctify Me.

8:14. בְּרַח דּוֹדִי — *Flee, my Beloved, from our common exile* [lit., *Flee, my Beloved*]. Flee away with us, O God Who has accompanied us throughout every exile! And let us leave this exile together.

וּדְמֵה לְךָ לִצְבִי אוֹ לְעֹפֶר הָאַיָּלִים — *and be like a gazelle or a young hart in Your swiftness to redeem and rest Your Presence among us* [lit., *and be like a gazelle or a young hart*]. Hasten the Redemption.

עַל הָרֵי בְשָׂמִים — *on the fragrant Mount Moriah, site of Your Temple* [lit., *upon the mountains of spices*], may it be rebuilt speedily in our days. Amen.

Ruth רוּת

The Book of Ruth relates the story of a Moabite woman who left
her homeland and came to the Land of Israel as a convert to Judaism.
There she lived in abject poverty, searching for food for herself and
her widowed, elderly mother-in-law. Subsequently she became the
wife of Boaz, which, according to the Talmudic tradition, was another
name for Ibzan, one of the Judges of Israel. Ruth and Boaz were an
unlikely match. She was a Moabite princess who had fallen from honor
and wealth to contempt and poverty. He was the Judge, the leader of
the Jewish nation, venerable, wealthy, and revered. Much more than a
hostile border separated Ruth from Boaz. He was two generations her
senior. In background they were even further apart. Yet the two came
together under the most implausible circumstances, to become the
forebears of the royal family of Israel. The Talmud calls Ruth the mother
of royalty, because her progeny includes David, Solomon, and the future
King Messiah.

There are various reasons why the Book of Ruth is read on the festival
of Shavuos. One of them is instructive and inspiring in our everyday
lives. No one had more right to feel that she was a failure than Ruth,
scrounging in the fields for her next meal. Boaz could not have attached
much significance to his attempts to make her life easier. But God
viewed them differently; He attached such importance to their deeds that
He incorporated them into the sacred Scriptures.

As the Midrash puts it, had Boaz only known that the Holy One,
Blessed is He, would consider his generosity to Ruth important enough
to inscribe in Scripture, he would have given her a sumptuous banquet
meal of stuffed calves!

It is true that in times past, a person would perform a commandment
and a prophet would inscribe it for eternity in Scripture, but now that
the sacred Books are written and sealed, how will our worthy deeds
be inscribed and remembered? The Midrash responds that the prophet
Elijah inscribes them and the King Messiah and the Holy One, Blessed is
He, affix their signatures to them, as it is written: "Then those who fear
HASHEM spoke to one another, and HASHEM listened and heard" (Malachi
3:16).

What a remarkable and inspiring teaching! No deed is ignored. No act
is forgotten. This is the lesson of the Book of Ruth. Just as God gave His
Torah on Shavuos, so He wants us to know that the deeds of mortals
can become part of His plan. Ruth's story of triumph over adversity
remains a historic teaching of man's potential for greatness.

א וַיְהִ֗י בִּימֵי֙ שְׁפֹ֣ט הַשֹּׁפְטִ֔ים וַיְהִ֥י רָעָ֖ב בָּאָ֑רֶץ וַיֵּ֨לֶךְ אִ֜ישׁ מִבֵּ֧ית לֶ֣חֶם יְהוּדָ֗ה

ב לָגוּר֙ בִּשְׂדֵ֣י מוֹאָ֔ב ה֥וּא וְאִשְׁתּ֖וֹ וּשְׁנֵ֣י בָנָֽיו: וְשֵׁ֣ם הָאִ֣ישׁ אֱ‍ֽלִימֶ֡לֶךְ וְשֵׁם֩ אִשְׁתּ֨וֹ
נׇעֳמִ֜י וְשֵׁ֣ם שְׁנֵֽי־בָנָ֣יו ׀ מַחְל֤וֹן וְכִלְיוֹן֙ אֶפְרָתִ֔ים מִבֵּ֥ית לֶ֖חֶם יְהוּדָ֑ה וַיָּבֹ֥אוּ

ג שְׂדֵי־מוֹאָ֖ב וַיִּֽהְיוּ־שָֽׁם: וַיָּ֥מׇת אֱלִימֶ֖לֶךְ אִ֣ישׁ נָעֳמִ֑י וַתִּשָּׁאֵ֥ר הִ֖יא וּשְׁנֵ֥י בָנֶֽיהָ:

ד וַיִּשְׂא֣וּ לָהֶ֗ם נָשִׁים֙ מֹ֣אֲבִיּ֔וֹת שֵׁ֤ם הָֽאַחַת֙ עׇרְפָּ֔ה וְשֵׁ֥ם הַשֵּׁנִ֖ית ר֑וּת וַיֵּ֥שְׁב֖וּ שָׁ֖ם

ה כְּעֶ֥שֶׂר שָׁנִֽים: וַיָּמֻ֥תוּ גַם־שְׁנֵיהֶ֖ם מַחְל֣וֹן וְכִלְי֑וֹן וַתִּשָּׁאֵר֙ הָֽאִשָּׁ֔ה מִשְּׁנֵ֥י יְלָדֶ֖יהָ

ו וּמֵֽאִישָֽׁהּ: וַתָּ֤קׇם הִיא֙ וְכַלֹּתֶ֔יהָ וַתָּ֖שׇׁב מִשְּׂדֵ֣י מוֹאָ֑ב כִּ֤י שָֽׁמְעָה֙ בִּשְׂדֵ֣ה מוֹאָ֔ב

ז כִּֽי־פָקַ֤ד יְהֹוָה֙ אֶת־עַמּ֔וֹ לָתֵ֥ת לָהֶ֖ם לָֽחֶם: וַתֵּצֵ֗א מִן־הַמָּקוֹם֙ אֲשֶׁ֣ר הָֽיְתָה־
שָּׁ֔מָּה וּשְׁתֵּ֥י כַלֹּתֶ֖יהָ עִמָּ֑הּ וַתֵּלַ֣כְנָה בַדֶּ֔רֶךְ לָשׁ֖וּב אֶל־אֶ֥רֶץ יְהוּדָֽה: וַתֹּ֤אמֶר

ח נָעֳמִי֙ לִשְׁתֵּ֣י כַלֹּתֶ֔יהָ לֵ֣כְנָה שֹּׁ֔בְנָה אִשָּׁ֖ה לְבֵ֣ית אִמָּ֑הּ °[יַ֣עַשׂ ק] יהוה [°יעשה]
יְהֹוָ֤ה

ט עִמָּכֶם֙ חֶ֔סֶד כַּֽאֲשֶׁ֧ר עֲשִׂיתֶ֛ם עִם־הַמֵּתִ֖ים וְעִמָּדִֽי: יִתֵּ֤ן יְהֹוָה֙ לָכֶ֔ם וּמְצֶ֣אןָ
מְנוּחָ֔ה אִשָּׁ֖ה בֵּ֣ית אִישָׁ֑הּ וַתִּשַּׁ֣ק לָהֶ֔ן וַתִּשֶּׂ֥אנָה קוֹלָ֖ן וַתִּבְכֶּֽינָה: וַתֹּאמַ֖רְנָה־

יא לָּ֑הּ כִּֽי־אִתָּ֥ךְ נָשׁ֖וּב לְעַמֵּֽךְ: וַתֹּ֤אמֶר נָעֳמִי֙ שֹׁ֣בְנָה בְנֹתַ֔י לָ֥מָּה תֵלַ֖כְנָה עִמִּ֑י

יב הַ‍ֽעֽוֹד־לִ֤י בָנִים֙ בְּֽמֵעַ֔י וְהָי֥וּ לָכֶ֖ם לַֽאֲנָשִֽׁים: שֹׁ֤בְנָה בְנֹתַי֙ לֵ֔כְןָ כִּ֥י זָקַ֖נְתִּי מִֽהְי֣וֹת
לְאִ֑ישׁ כִּ֤י אָמַ֨רְתִּי֙ יֶשׁ־לִ֣י תִקְוָ֔ה גַּ֣ם הָיִ֤יתִי הַלַּ֨יְלָה֙ לְאִ֔ישׁ וְגַ֖ם יָלַ֥דְתִּי בָנִֽים:

יג הֲלָהֵ֣ן ׀ תְּשַׂבֵּ֗רְנָה עַ֚ד אֲשֶׁ֣ר יִגְדָּ֔לוּ הֲלָהֵן֙ תֵּֽעָגֵ֔נָה לְבִלְתִּ֖י הֱי֣וֹת לְאִ֑ישׁ אַ֣ל

יד בְּנֹתַ֗י כִּי־מַר־לִ֤י מְאֹד֙ מִכֶּ֔ם כִּֽי־יָצְאָ֥ה בִ֖י יַד־יְהֹוָֽה: וַתִּשֶּׂ֣נָה קוֹלָ֔ן וַתִּבְכֶּ֖ינָה
ע֑וֹד וַתִּשַּׁ֤ק עׇרְפָּה֙ לַֽחֲמוֹתָ֔הּ וְר֖וּת דָּ֥בְקָה בָּֽהּ: וַתֹּ֗אמֶר הִנֵּה֙ שָׁ֣בָה יְבִמְתֵּ֔ךְ אֶל־

טו
עַמָּ֖הּ וְאֶל־אֱלֹהֶ֑יהָ שׁ֖וּבִי אַֽחֲרֵ֥י יְבִמְתֵּֽךְ: וַתֹּ֤אמֶר רוּת֙ אַל־תִּפְגְּעִי־בִ֔י לְעׇזְבֵ֖ךְ

טז
לָשׁ֣וּב מֵאַֽחֲרָ֑יִךְ כִּ֠י אֶל־אֲשֶׁ֨ר תֵּלְכִ֜י אֵלֵ֗ךְ וּבַֽאֲשֶׁ֤ר תָּלִ֨ינִי֙ אָלִ֔ין עַמֵּ֣ךְ עַמִּ֔י

יז
וֵֽאלֹהַ֖יִךְ אֱלֹהָֽי: בַּֽאֲשֶׁ֤ר תָּמ֨וּתִי֙ אָמ֔וּת וְשָׁ֖ם אֶקָּבֵ֑ר כֹּה֩ יַֽעֲשֶׂ֨ה יְהֹוָ֥ה לִי֙ וְכֹ֣ה
יֹסִ֔יף כִּ֣י הַמָּ֔וֶת יַפְרִ֖יד בֵּינִ֥י וּבֵינֵֽךְ: וַתֵּ֕רֶא כִּֽי־מִתְאַמֶּ֥צֶת הִ֖יא לָלֶ֣כֶת אִתָּ֑הּ

יח
וַתֶּחְדַּ֖ל לְדַבֵּ֥ר אֵלֶֽיהָ: וַתֵּלַ֣כְנָה שְׁתֵּיהֶ֔ם עַד־בֹּאָ֖נָה בֵּ֣ית לָ֑חֶם וַיְהִ֗י כְּבֹאָ֨נָה֙

יט
בֵּ֣ית לֶ֔חֶם וַתֵּהֹ֤ם כׇּל־הָעִיר֙ עֲלֵיהֶ֔ן וַתֹּאמַ֖רְנָה הֲזֹ֣את נׇעֳמִֽי: וַתֹּ֣אמֶר אֲלֵיהֶ֗ן

כ
אַל־תִּקְרֶ֥אןָ לִ֖י נׇעֳמִ֑י קְרֶ֤אןָ לִי֙ מָרָ֔א כִּֽי־הֵמַ֥ר שַׁדַּ֛י לִ֖י מְאֹֽד: אֲנִי֙ מְלֵאָ֣ה

כא
הָלַ֔כְתִּי וְרֵיקָ֖ם הֱשִׁיבַ֣נִי יְהֹוָ֑ה לָ֣מָּה תִקְרֶ֤אנָה לִי֙ נׇעֳמִ֔י וַֽיהֹוָה֙ עָ֣נָה בִ֔י וְשַׁדַּ֖י

כב
הֵ֥רַֽע לִֽי: וַתָּ֣שׇׁב נׇעֳמִ֗י וְר֨וּת הַמּֽוֹאֲבִיָּ֤ה כַלָּתָהּ֙ עִמָּ֔הּ

1:1. The Talmud identifies Boaz (see 2:1) as Ibzan (*Judges* 12:8-10) who succeeded Jephthah as Judge (*Bava Basra* 91a).

1:2.. Elimelech was very wealthy and did not want every impoverished person to knock at his door for help. For this he was punished (*Rashi*).

1:3. Naomi is mentioned here in conjunction with Elimelech's death, because the death of a man is felt by no one as keenly and as deeply as by his wife (*Sanhedrin* 22b).

1:8. That Naomi encouraged the young widows to return to their idolatrous families suggests that they had never converted to Judaism; otherwise, how could she have sent them to, in effect, renounce their Jewish faith?

Indeed, according to Rabbi Meir, they had not converted (*Ruth Rabbah* 1:4).

According to *Zohar Chadash*, they *did* convert when they married the brothers. Such conversions, however, involved a degree of coercion, since the parents of the brides had arranged the marriages, and the women of that society would not be free to refuse. Therefore, it would be only future fidelity to Judaism that could prove the conversions to have been sincere. Orpah, by leaving Naomi, showed that her conversion had never been valid. Ruth, however, gave the most eloquent proof that she was a Jewess of the highest order.

1:13. Realizing that they wanted to go with her, Naomi

1 *Famine* ¹ **A**nd it happened in the days when the judges* judged, that there was a famine in the land, and a man went from Beth-lehem in Judah to sojourn in the fields of Moab, he, his wife, and his two sons. ² The name of the man was Elimelech, * the name of his wife Naomi, and the name of his two sons Mahlon and Chilion, Ephrathites of Beth-lehem in Judah. They came to the field of Moab and there they remained.

Untimely ³ Elimelech, Naomi's husband, * died; and she was left with her two sons.
deaths ⁴ They married Moabite women, the name of the one was Orpah, and the name of the second Ruth, and they lived there about ten years. ⁵ The two of them, Mahlon and Chilion, also died; and the woman was left of her two children and of her husband.

⁶ She then arose along with her daughters-in-law to return from the fields of Moab, for she had heard in the fields of Moab that HASHEM had remembered His people by giving them food. ⁷ She left the place where she had been, her two daughters-in-law with her, and they set out on the road to return to the land of Judah.

⁸ Then Naomi said to her two daughters-in-law, "Go, return, each of you to her
Three mother's house. * May HASHEM deal kindly with you, as you have dealt kindly
widows with the dead and with me! ⁹ May HASHEM grant that you may find security, each in the home of her husband." She kissed them, and they raised their voice and wept. ¹⁰ And they said to her, "No, we will return with you to your people." ¹¹ But Naomi said, "Turn back, my daughters. Why should you come with me? Have I more sons in my womb who could become husbands to you? ¹² Turn back, my daughters, go, for I am too old to have a husband. Even if I were to say, 'There
Dissuasion is hope for me!' and even if I were to have a husband tonight — and even bear sons — ¹³ would you wait for them until they were grown up? Would you tie yourselves down for them, not to marry anyone else? No, my daughters! I am very embittered on account of you, for the hand of HASHEM has gone forth against me."*

¹⁴ They raised their voice and wept again. Orpah kissed her mother-in-law, but Ruth clung to her. * ¹⁵ So she said, "Look, your sister-in-law has returned to her
Sincerity people and to her gods; return after your sister-in-law." ¹⁶ But Ruth said, "Do not urge me to leave you, to turn back from following you. For where you go, I will go; where you lodge, I will lodge; your people are my people, and your God is my God; ¹⁷ where you die, I will die, and there I will be buried. Thus may HASHEM do to me, and so may He do more, if anything but death separates me from you."

¹⁸ When she saw that she was determined to go with her, she stopped arguing with her, * ¹⁹ and the two of them went on until they came to Beth-lehem.

And it came to pass, when they arrived in Beth-lehem, the entire city was
Naomi tumultuous over them, and the women said, "Could this be Naomi?" ²⁰ She said
returns; to them, "Do not call me Naomi [pleasant one], call me Mara [embittered one],
Beth-lehem for the Almighty has dealt very bitterly with me. ²¹ I was full when I went away,
is astounded but HASHEM has brought me back empty. Why shall you call me Naomi; HASHEM has testified against me, the Almighty has brought misfortune upon me!"

²² And so Naomi returned, and Ruth the Moabite, her daughter-in-law, with her

---

said, "I cannot bear to see you suffer on my account, for you are sinless; it was for my sins that God has been punishing me."

1:14. In Ruth's clinging to her, Naomi felt a spirit of

holiness (*Alshich*).

1:18. From this verse the Talmud (*Yevamos* 47b) deduces that a convert is neither to be overly persuaded to nor overly dissuaded from accepting Judaism (*Rashi*).

הַשָּׁבָה מִשְּׂדֵי מוֹאָב וְהֵמָּה בָּאוּ בֵּית לֶחֶם בִּתְחִלַּת קְצִיר שְׂעֹרִים:

ב   א וּלְנָעֳמִי [°מוֹדַע מֵידָע ק] לְאִישָׁהּ אִישׁ גִּבּוֹר חַיִל מִמִּשְׁפַּחַת אֱלִימֶלֶךְ
ב וּשְׁמוֹ בֹּעַז: וַתֹּאמֶר רוּת הַמּוֹאֲבִיָּה אֶל־נָעֳמִי אֵלְכָה־נָּא הַשָּׂדֶה וַאֲלַקֳּטָה
ג בַשִּׁבֳּלִים אַחַר אֲשֶׁר אֶמְצָא־חֵן בְּעֵינָיו וַתֹּאמֶר לָהּ לְכִי בִתִּי: וַתֵּלֶךְ
וַתָּבוֹא וַתְּלַקֵּט בַּשָּׂדֶה אַחֲרֵי הַקֹּצְרִים וַיִּקֶר מִקְרֶהָ חֶלְקַת הַשָּׂדֶה לְבֹעַז
ד אֲשֶׁר מִמִּשְׁפַּחַת אֱלִימֶלֶךְ: וְהִנֵּה־בֹעַז בָּא מִבֵּית לֶחֶם וַיֹּאמֶר לַקּוֹצְרִים
ה יְהֹוָה עִמָּכֶם וַיֹּאמְרוּ לוֹ יְבָרֶכְךָ יְהֹוָה: וַיֹּאמֶר בֹּעַז לְנַעֲרוֹ הַנִּצָּב עַל־
ו הַקּוֹצְרִים לְמִי הַנַּעֲרָה הַזֹּאת: וַיַּעַן הַנַּעַר הַנִּצָּב עַל־הַקּוֹצְרִים וַיֹּאמַר
ז נַעֲרָה מוֹאֲבִיָּה הִיא הַשָּׁבָה עִם־נָעֳמִי מִשְּׂדֵה מוֹאָב: וַתֹּאמֶר אֲלַקֳטָה־נָּא
וְאָסַפְתִּי בָעֳמָרִים אַחֲרֵי הַקּוֹצְרִים וַתָּבוֹא וַתַּעֲמוֹד מֵאָז הַבֹּקֶר וְעַד־
ח עַתָּה זֶה שִׁבְתָּהּ הַבַּיִת מְעָט: וַיֹּאמֶר בֹּעַז אֶל־רוּת הֲלוֹא שָׁמַעַתְּ בִּתִּי אַל־
תֵּלְכִי לִלְקֹט בְּשָׂדֶה אַחֵר וְגַם לֹא תַעֲבוּרִי מִזֶּה וְכֹה תִדְבָּקִין עִם־נַעֲרֹתָי:
ט עֵינַיִךְ בַּשָּׂדֶה אֲשֶׁר־יִקְצֹרוּן וְהָלַכְתְּ אַחֲרֵיהֶן הֲלוֹא צִוִּיתִי אֶת־הַנְּעָרִים
לְבִלְתִּי נָגְעֵךְ וְצָמִת וְהָלַכְתְּ אֶל־הַכֵּלִים וְשָׁתִית מֵאֲשֶׁר יִשְׁאֲבוּן הַנְּעָרִים:
י וַתִּפֹּל עַל־פָּנֶיהָ וַתִּשְׁתַּחוּ אָרְצָה וַתֹּאמֶר אֵלָיו מַדּוּעַ מָצָאתִי חֵן בְּעֵינֶיךָ
יא לְהַכִּירֵנִי וְאָנֹכִי נָכְרִיָּה: וַיַּעַן בֹּעַז וַיֹּאמֶר לָהּ הֻגֵּד הֻגַּד לִי כֹּל אֲשֶׁר־
עָשִׂית אֶת־חֲמוֹתֵךְ אַחֲרֵי מוֹת אִישֵׁךְ וַתַּעַזְבִי אָבִיךְ וְאִמֵּךְ וְאֶרֶץ
יב מוֹלַדְתֵּךְ וַתֵּלְכִי אֶל־עַם אֲשֶׁר לֹא־יָדַעַתְּ תְּמוֹל שִׁלְשׁוֹם: יְשַׁלֵּם יְהֹוָה
פָּעֳלֵךְ וּתְהִי מַשְׂכֻּרְתֵּךְ שְׁלֵמָה מֵעִם יְהֹוָה אֱלֹהֵי יִשְׂרָאֵל אֲשֶׁר־בָּאת
יג לַחֲסוֹת תַּחַת־כְּנָפָיו: וַתֹּאמֶר אֶמְצָא־חֵן בְּעֵינֶיךָ אֲדֹנִי כִּי נִחַמְתָּנִי וְכִי
יד דִבַּרְתָּ עַל־לֵב שִׁפְחָתֶךָ וְאָנֹכִי לֹא אֶהְיֶה כְּאַחַת שִׁפְחֹתֶיךָ: וַיֹּאמֶר לָה
בֹעַז לְעֵת הָאֹכֶל גֹּשִׁי הֲלֹם וְאָכַלְתְּ מִן־הַלֶּחֶם וְטָבַלְתְּ פִּתֵּךְ בַּחֹמֶץ
וַתֵּשֶׁב מִצַּד הַקֹּצְרִים וַיִּצְבָּט־לָהּ קָלִי וַתֹּאכַל וַתִּשְׂבַּע וַתֹּתַר: וַתָּקָם
טו לְלַקֵּט וַיְצַו בֹּעַז אֶת־נְעָרָיו לֵאמֹר גַּם בֵּין הָעֳמָרִים תְּלַקֵּט וְלֹא
טז תַכְלִימוּהָ: וְגַם שֹׁל־תָּשֹׁלּוּ לָהּ מִן־הַצְּבָתִים וַעֲזַבְתֶּם וְלִקְּטָה וְלֹא
יז תִגְעֲרוּ־בָהּ: וַתְּלַקֵּט בַּשָּׂדֶה עַד־הָעָרֶב וַתַּחְבֹּט אֵת אֲשֶׁר־לִקֵּטָה וַיְהִי
יח כְּאֵיפָה שְׂעֹרִים: וַתִּשָּׂא וַתָּבוֹא הָעִיר וַתֵּרֶא חֲמוֹתָהּ אֵת אֲשֶׁר־לִקֵּטָה
יט וַתּוֹצֵא וַתִּתֶּן־לָהּ אֵת אֲשֶׁר־הוֹתִרָה מִשָּׂבְעָהּ: וַתֹּאמֶר לָהּ חֲמוֹתָהּ
אֵיפֹה לִקַּטְתְּ הַיּוֹם וְאָנָה עָשִׂית יְהִי מַכִּירֵךְ בָּרוּךְ וַתַּגֵּד לַחֲמוֹתָהּ אֵת
אֲשֶׁר־עָשְׂתָה עִמּוֹ וַתֹּאמֶר שֵׁם הָאִישׁ אֲשֶׁר עָשִׂיתִי עִמּוֹ הַיּוֹם בֹּעַז:

2:1. Boaz was the son of one of Elimelech's brothers (Rashi). Naomi did not ask him for support because she still felt shame at having deserted her people during the famine, while Boaz stayed on and supported them (Alshich).

2:5. When Boaz noticed her modesty, he inquired about

her (Midrash).

2:17. The verse stresses "gleaned" because, although Boaz had ordered his harvesters to drop large amounts for her, Ruth limited herself to the "gleanings" she was entitled to by law [i.e., a maximum of two stalks at a time], and did not avail herself of Boaz' charity (Iggeres Shmuel).

— who returned from the fields of Moab. They came to Beth-lehem at the beginning of the barley harvest.

2

Boaz of Beth-lehem; cousin to Elimelech

¹ Naomi had a relative through her husband, a man of substance, from the family of Elimelech; his name was Boaz. *

² Ruth the Moabite said to Naomi, "Let me go out to the field and glean among the ears of grain behind someone in whose eyes I shall find favor."

She said to her, "Go, my daughter." ³ So she went. She came and gleaned in the field behind the harvesters, and her fate made her happen upon a parcel of land belonging to Boaz, who was of the family of Elimelech.

⁴ Behold, Boaz arrived from Beth-lehem. He said to the harvesters, "HASHEM be with you!" And they answered him, "May HASHEM bless you!" ⁵ Boaz then said to his servant who was overseeing the harvesters, "To whom does that young woman belong?" * ⁶ The servant who was overseeing the harvesters replied, "She is a Moabite girl, the one who returned with Naomi from the fields of Moab; ⁷ and she had said, 'Please let me glean and gather among the sheaves behind the harvesters.' So she came, and has stood since the morning until now; [except for] her resting a little in the hut."

"Do not go to glean in another field!"

⁸ Then Boaz said to Ruth, "Hear me well, my daughter. Do not go to glean in another field, and don't leave here, but stay close to my maidens. ⁹ Keep your eyes on the field which they are harvesting and follow after them. I have ordered the servants not to molest you. Should you become thirsty, go to the jugs and drink from that which the servants have drawn."

¹⁰ Then she fell on her face, bowing down to the ground, and said to him, "Why have I found favor in your eyes that you should take special note of me though I am a foreigner?"

¹¹ Boaz replied and said to her, "I have been fully informed of all that you have done for your mother-in-law after the death of your husband — how you left your father and mother and the land of your birth and went to a people you had not known yesterday or earlier. ¹² May HASHEM reward your deed, and may your payment be full from HASHEM, the God of Israel, under Whose wings you have come to seek refuge."

¹³ Then she said, "May I continue to find favor in your eyes, my lord, because you have comforted me, and because you have spoken to the heart of your maidservant, though I am not even [as worthy] as one of your maidservants."

¹⁴ At mealtime, Boaz said to her, "Come over here and partake of the bread, and dip your morsel in the vinegar." So she sat beside the harvesters. He handed her parched grain, and she ate and was satisfied, and had some left over.

¹⁵ Then she got up to glean, and Boaz ordered his servants, saying, "Let her glean even among the sheaves; do not embarrass her. ¹⁶ And even deliberately pull out some for her from the heaps and leave them for her to glean; don't rebuke her."

Ruth returns to Naomi

¹⁷ So she gleaned* in the field until evening, and she beat out what she had gleaned; it was about an ephah of barley. ¹⁸ She carried it and came to the city. Her mother-in-law saw what she had gleaned, and she took out and gave her what she had left over after eating her fill.

¹⁹ "Where did you glean today?" her mother-in-law asked her. "Where did you work? May the one that took [such generous] notice of you be blessed." So she told her mother-in-law by whom she had worked, and said, "The name of the man by whom I worked today is Boaz."

כ וַתֹּאמֶר נָעֳמִי לְכַלָּתָהּ בָּרוּךְ הוּא לַיהוָה אֲשֶׁר לֹא־עָזַב חַסְדּוֹ אֶת־
הַחַיִּים וְאֶת־הַמֵּתִים וַתֹּאמֶר לָהּ נָעֳמִי קָרוֹב לָנוּ הָאִישׁ מִגֹּאֲלֵנוּ הוּא:
כא וַתֹּאמֶר רוּת הַמּוֹאֲבִיָּה גַּם ׀ כִּי־אָמַר אֵלַי עִם־הַנְּעָרִים אֲשֶׁר־לִי תִּדְבָּקִין
כב עַד אִם־כִּלּוּ אֵת כָּל־הַקָּצִיר אֲשֶׁר־לִי: וַתֹּאמֶר נָעֳמִי אֶל־רוּת כַּלָּתָהּ טוֹב
כג בִּתִּי כִּי תֵצְאִי עִם־נַעֲרוֹתָיו וְלֹא יִפְגְּעוּ־בָךְ בְּשָׂדֶה אַחֵר: וַתִּדְבַּק בְּנַעֲרוֹת
בֹּעַז לְלַקֵּט עַד־כְּלוֹת קְצִיר־הַשְּׂעֹרִים וּקְצִיר הַחִטִּים וַתֵּשֶׁב אֶת־חֲמוֹתָהּ:

ג א וַתֹּאמֶר לָהּ נָעֳמִי חֲמוֹתָהּ בִּתִּי הֲלֹא אֲבַקֶּשׁ־לָךְ מָנוֹחַ אֲשֶׁר יִיטַב־לָךְ:
ב וְעַתָּה הֲלֹא בֹעַז מֹדַעְתָּנוּ אֲשֶׁר הָיִית אֶת־נַעֲרוֹתָיו הִנֵּה־הוּא זֹרֶה אֶת־גֹּרֶן
ג הַשְּׂעֹרִים הַלָּיְלָה: וְרָחַצְתְּ ׀ וָסַכְתְּ וְשַׂמְתְּ °שִׂמְלֹתַיִךְ [שִׂמְלֹתֵךְ ק] עָלַיִךְ
°וְיָרַדְתִּי [וְיָרַדְתְּ ק] הַגֹּרֶן אַל־תִּוָּדְעִי לָאִישׁ עַד כַּלֹּתוֹ לֶאֱכֹל וְלִשְׁתּוֹת:
ד וִיהִי בְשָׁכְבוֹ וְיָדַעַתְּ אֶת־הַמָּקוֹם אֲשֶׁר יִשְׁכַּב־שָׁם וּבָאת וְגִלִּית מַרְגְּלֹתָיו
ה °וּשְׁכָבְתִּי [וְשָׁכָבְתְּ ק] וְהוּא יַגִּיד לָךְ אֵת אֲשֶׁר תַּעֲשִׂין: וַתֹּאמֶר אֵלֶיהָ
ו כֹּל אֲשֶׁר־תֹּאמְרִי [°אֵלַי קרי ולא כתיב] אֶעֱשֶׂה: וַתֵּרֶד הַגֹּרֶן וַתַּעַשׂ כְּכֹל
ז אֲשֶׁר־צִוַּתָּה חֲמוֹתָהּ: וַיֹּאכַל בֹּעַז וַיֵּשְׁתְּ וַיִּיטַב לִבּוֹ וַיָּבֹא לִשְׁכַּב בִּקְצֵה
הָעֲרֵמָה וַתָּבֹא בַלָּט וַתְּגַל מַרְגְּלֹתָיו וַתִּשְׁכָּב: וַיְהִי בַּחֲצִי הַלַּיְלָה וַיֶּחֱרַד
ח הָאִישׁ וַיִּלָּפֵת וְהִנֵּה אִשָּׁה שֹׁכֶבֶת מַרְגְּלֹתָיו: וַיֹּאמֶר מִי־אָתְּ וַתֹּאמֶר אָנֹכִי
ט רוּת אֲמָתֶךָ וּפָרַשְׂתָּ כְנָפֶךָ עַל־אֲמָתְךָ כִּי גֹאֵל אָתָּה: וַיֹּאמֶר בְּרוּכָה אַתְּ
י לַיהוָה בִּתִּי הֵיטַבְתְּ חַסְדֵּךְ הָאַחֲרוֹן מִן־הָרִאשׁוֹן לְבִלְתִּי־לֶכֶת אַחֲרֵי
יא הַבַּחוּרִים אִם־דַּל וְאִם־עָשִׁיר: וְעַתָּה בִּתִּי אַל־תִּירְאִי כֹּל אֲשֶׁר־תֹּאמְרִי
יב אֶעֱשֶׂה־לָּךְ כִּי יוֹדֵעַ כָּל־שַׁעַר עַמִּי כִּי אֵשֶׁת חַיִל אָתְּ: וְעַתָּה כִּי אָמְנָם
יג כִּי °אִם [כתיב ולא קרי] גֹאֵל אָנֹכִי וְגַם יֵשׁ גֹּאֵל קָרוֹב מִמֶּנִּי: לִינִי ׀ הַלַּיְלָה
וְהָיָה בַבֹּקֶר אִם־יִגְאָלֵךְ טוֹב יִגְאָל וְאִם־לֹא יַחְפֹּץ לְגָאֳלֵךְ וּגְאַלְתִּיךְ
יד אָנֹכִי חַי־יְהוָה שִׁכְבִי עַד־הַבֹּקֶר: וַתִּשְׁכַּב °מַרְגְּלוֹתוֹ [מַרְגְּלוֹתָיו ק]
עַד־הַבֹּקֶר וַתָּקָם °בטרום [בְּטֶרֶם ק] יַכִּיר אִישׁ אֶת־רֵעֵהוּ וַיֹּאמֶר
טו אַל־יִוָּדַע כִּי־בָאָה הָאִשָּׁה הַגֹּרֶן: וַיֹּאמֶר הָבִי הַמִּטְפַּחַת אֲשֶׁר־עָלַיִךְ
וְאֶחֳזִי־בָהּ וַתֹּאחֶז בָּהּ וַיָּמָד שֵׁשׁ־שְׂעֹרִים וַיָּשֶׁת עָלֶיהָ וַיָּבֹא הָעִיר:
טז וַתָּבוֹא אֶל־חֲמוֹתָהּ וַתֹּאמֶר מִי־אַתְּ בִּתִּי וַתַּגֶּד־לָהּ אֵת כָּל־אֲשֶׁר
יז עָשָׂה־לָהּ הָאִישׁ: וַתֹּאמֶר שֵׁשׁ־הַשְּׂעֹרִים הָאֵלֶּה נָתַן לִי כִּי אָמַר
יח [°אֵלַי קרי ולא כתיב] אַל־תָּבוֹאִי רֵיקָם אֶל־חֲמוֹתֵךְ: וַתֹּאמֶר שְׁבִי בִתִּי עַד
אֲשֶׁר תֵּדְעִין אֵיךְ יִפֹּל דָּבָר כִּי לֹא יִשְׁקֹט הָאִישׁ כִּי־אִם־כִּלָּה הַדָּבָר הַיּוֹם:

3:4. The Sages understood Ruth's conduct as being fully for the sake of Heaven. Two women, Tamar and Ruth, sacrificed themselves for the sake of the tribe of Judah.

Naomi decided that the best course of action — however daring and unconventional — was for Ruth herself to approach Boaz under the most intimate circumstances and remind him of his responsibility to his uncle's family. (See 3:9.) Then, convinced of her sincerity, his compassion for her bitter plight might be evoked (*R' Meir Zlotowitz*).

3:5. אֵלַי, *to me*, is read but not written. Although the advice seemed improper *to her*, nevertheless, Ruth would obey because Naomi had given it (*Akeidas Yitzchak*).

Naomi's ²⁰ Naomi said to her daughter-in-law, "Blessed is he to HASHEM, Who has not
approval failed in His kindness to the living or to the dead!" Naomi then said to her, "The
man is closely related to us; he is one of our redeeming kinsmen."

²¹ And Ruth the Moabite said, "What's more, he even said to me, 'Stay close to
my servants, until they have finished all my harvest.' " ²² Naomi said to her
daughter-in-law Ruth, "It is fine, my daughter, that you go out with his maidens,
so that you will not be annoyed in another field."

²³ So she stayed close to Boaz' maidens to glean, until the end of the barley
harvest and of the wheat harvest. Then she stayed [at home] with her mother-
in-law.

3 ¹ N aomi, her mother-in-law, said to her, "My daughter, I must seek security
Naomi's for you, that it may go well with you. ² Now, Boaz, our relative, with whose
plan maidens you have been, will be winnowing barley tonight on the threshing floor.
³ Therefore, bathe and anoint yourself, don your finery, and go down to the
threshing floor, but do not make yourself known to the man until he has finished
eating and drinking. ⁴ And when he lies down, note the place where he lies, and
go over, uncover his feet, and lie down. He will tell you what you are to do."*
⁵ She replied "All that you say to me* I will do."

⁶ So she went down to the threshing floor and did everything as her
mother-in-law instructed her. ⁷ Boaz ate and drank and his heart was merry. He
went to lie down at the end of the grain pile, and she came stealthily, uncovered
his feet, and lay down. ⁸ In the middle of the night the man was startled, and
turned about — and behold! there was a woman lying at his feet!

Conversation ⁹ He said, "Who are you?" And she answered, "I am your handmaid, Ruth.
at midnight Spread your robe over your handmaid, for you are a redeemer."*

¹⁰ And he said, "You are blessed of HASHEM, my daughter; you have made your
latest act of kindness greater than the first, in that you have not gone after the
younger men, be they poor or rich. ¹¹ And now, my daughter, do not fear; whatever you say, I will do for you; for all the men in the gate of my people know that
you are a worthy woman. ¹² Now while it is true that I am a redeemer, there is also
another redeemer closer than I. * ¹³ Stay the night, then in the morning, if he will
redeem you, fine! Let him redeem. But if he does not want to redeem you, then
[I swear that] as HASHEM lives, I will redeem you! Lie down until the morning."

¹⁴ So she lay at his feet until the morning and she arose before one man could
recognize another, for he said, "Let it not be known that the woman came to the
threshing floor." ¹⁵ And he said, "Hold out the shawl that is upon you and grasp
it." She held it, and he measured out six measures of barley, and set it on her; then
he went to the city.

¹⁶ She came to her mother-in-law who said, "Who are you, my daughter?" So
she told her all that the man had done for her, ¹⁷ and she said, "He gave me these
six measures of barley for he said to me, 'Do not go empty-handed to your
mother-in-law.' "

¹⁸ Then she said, "Sit [patiently], my daughter, until you know how the matter
will turn out, for the man will not rest unless he settles the matter today."

3:9. "As a close relative, you are obligated to redeem the
estate of my husband in accordance with *Leviticus* 25:25,
otherwise Naomi will be forced to sell it." Ruth added,
"Take me, too, so that the name of the deceased will be
perpetuated on his property" (*Rashi*).

3:12. Boaz agreed, but said that the privilege of redemption should be offered first to Elimelech's brother, a
closer relative (*Rashi*).

ד א וּבֹעַז עָלָה הַשַּׁעַר וַיֵּשֶׁב שָׁם וְהִנֵּה הַגֹּאֵל עֹבֵר אֲשֶׁר דִּבֶּר־בֹּעַז וַיֹּאמֶר סוּרָה
ב שְׁבָה־פֹּה פְּלֹנִי אַלְמֹנִי וַיָּסַר וַיֵּשֵׁב: וַיִּקַּח עֲשָׂרָה אֲנָשִׁים מִזִּקְנֵי הָעִיר וַיֹּאמֶר
ג שְׁבוּ־פֹה וַיֵּשֵׁבוּ: וַיֹּאמֶר לַגֹּאֵל חֶלְקַת הַשָּׂדֶה אֲשֶׁר לְאָחִינוּ לֶאֱלִימֶלֶךְ
ד מָכְרָה נָעֳמִי הַשָּׁבָה מִשְּׂדֵה מוֹאָב: וַאֲנִי אָמַרְתִּי אֶגְלֶה אָזְנְךָ לֵאמֹר קְנֵה
      נֶגֶד הַיֹּשְׁבִים וְנֶגֶד זִקְנֵי עַמִּי אִם־תִּגְאַל גְּאָל וְאִם־לֹא יִגְאַל הַגִּידָה לִּי
      וְאֵדַע [וְאֵדְעָה ק'] כִּי אֵין זוּלָתְךָ לִגְאוֹל וְאָנֹכִי אַחֲרֶיךָ וַיֹּאמֶר אָנֹכִי
ה אֶגְאָל: וַיֹּאמֶר בֹּעַז בְּיוֹם־קְנוֹתְךָ הַשָּׂדֶה מִיַּד נָעֳמִי וּמֵאֵת רוּת הַמּוֹאֲבִיָּה
ו אֵשֶׁת־הַמֵּת קָנִיתִי [קָנִיתָה ק'] לְהָקִים שֵׁם־הַמֵּת עַל־נַחֲלָתוֹ: וַיֹּאמֶר
      הַגֹּאֵל לֹא אוּכַל לִגְאוֹל־ [לִגְאָל־ ק'] לִי פֶּן־אַשְׁחִית אֶת־נַחֲלָתִי גְּאַל־
ז לְךָ אַתָּה אֶת־גְּאֻלָּתִי כִּי לֹא־אוּכַל לִגְאֹל: וְזֹאת לְפָנִים בְּיִשְׂרָאֵל עַל־
      הַגְּאֻלָּה וְעַל־הַתְּמוּרָה לְקַיֵּם כָּל־דָּבָר שָׁלַף אִישׁ נַעֲלוֹ וְנָתַן לְרֵעֵהוּ וְזֹאת
ח הַתְּעוּדָה בְּיִשְׂרָאֵל: וַיֹּאמֶר הַגֹּאֵל לְבֹעַז קְנֵה־לָךְ וַיִּשְׁלֹף נַעֲלוֹ: וַיֹּאמֶר בֹּעַז
ט לַזְּקֵנִים וְכָל־הָעָם עֵדִים אַתֶּם הַיּוֹם כִּי קָנִיתִי אֶת־כָּל־אֲשֶׁר לֶאֱלִימֶלֶךְ
י וְאֵת כָּל־אֲשֶׁר לְכִלְיוֹן וּמַחְלוֹן מִיַּד נָעֳמִי: וְגַם אֶת־רוּת הַמֹּאֲבִיָּה אֵשֶׁת
      מַחְלוֹן קָנִיתִי לִי לְאִשָּׁה לְהָקִים שֵׁם־הַמֵּת עַל־נַחֲלָתוֹ וְלֹא־יִכָּרֵת שֵׁם־
יא הַמֵּת מֵעִם אֶחָיו וּמִשַּׁעַר מְקוֹמוֹ עֵדִים אַתֶּם הַיּוֹם: וַיֹּאמְרוּ כָּל־הָעָם
      אֲשֶׁר־בַּשַּׁעַר וְהַזְּקֵנִים עֵדִים יִתֵּן יְהוָה אֶת־הָאִשָּׁה הַבָּאָה אֶל־בֵּיתֶךָ
      כְּרָחֵל וּכְלֵאָה אֲשֶׁר בָּנוּ שְׁתֵּיהֶם אֶת־בֵּית יִשְׂרָאֵל וַעֲשֵׂה־חַיִל בְּאֶפְרָתָה
יב וּקְרָא־שֵׁם בְּבֵית לָחֶם: וִיהִי בֵיתְךָ כְּבֵית פֶּרֶץ אֲשֶׁר־יָלְדָה תָמָר לִיהוּדָה
יג מִן־הַזֶּרַע אֲשֶׁר יִתֵּן יְהוָה לְךָ מִן־הַנַּעֲרָה הַזֹּאת: וַיִּקַּח בֹּעַז אֶת־רוּת וַתְּהִי־
יד לוֹ לְאִשָּׁה וַיָּבֹא אֵלֶיהָ וַיִּתֵּן יְהוָה לָהּ הֵרָיוֹן וַתֵּלֶד בֵּן: וַתֹּאמַרְנָה הַנָּשִׁים
      אֶל־נָעֳמִי בָּרוּךְ יְהוָה אֲשֶׁר לֹא הִשְׁבִּית לָךְ גֹּאֵל הַיּוֹם וְיִקָּרֵא שְׁמוֹ
טו בְּיִשְׂרָאֵל: וְהָיָה לָךְ לְמֵשִׁיב נֶפֶשׁ וּלְכַלְכֵּל אֶת־שֵׂיבָתֵךְ כִּי כַלָּתֵךְ אֲשֶׁר־
טז אֲהֵבָתֶךְ יְלָדַתּוּ אֲשֶׁר־הִיא טוֹבָה לָךְ מִשִּׁבְעָה בָּנִים: וַתִּקַּח נָעֳמִי אֶת־
יז הַיֶּלֶד וַתְּשִׁתֵהוּ בְחֵיקָהּ וַתְּהִי־לוֹ לְאֹמֶנֶת: וַתִּקְרֶאנָה לוֹ הַשְּׁכֵנוֹת שֵׁם
      לֵאמֹר יֻלַּד־בֵּן לְנָעֳמִי וַתִּקְרֶאנָה שְׁמוֹ עוֹבֵד הוּא אֲבִי־יִשַׁי אֲבִי דָוִד:
יח-יט וְאֵלֶּה תּוֹלְדוֹת פָּרֶץ פֶּרֶץ הוֹלִיד אֶת־חֶצְרוֹן: וְחֶצְרוֹן הוֹלִיד אֶת־רָם וְרָם
כ הוֹלִיד אֶת־עַמִּינָדָב: וְעַמִּינָדָב הוֹלִיד אֶת־נַחְשׁוֹן וְנַחְשׁוֹן הוֹלִיד אֶת־
כא-כב שַׂלְמָה: וְשַׂלְמוֹן הוֹלִיד אֶת־בֹּעַז וּבֹעַז הוֹלִיד אֶת־עוֹבֵד: וְעֹבֵד הוֹלִיד
      אֶת־יִשַׁי וְיִשַׁי הוֹלִיד אֶת־דָּוִד:

סכום הפסוקים של ספר רות שמונים וחמשה. וסימנו **ובעז** הוליד את עובד. וסימנו סורה שבה **פה** פלני אלמני.

4:1.Literally, "Unnamed, anonymous one." Since he did not fulfill his familial duty by marrying Ruth, Scripture hides his name.
4:3. Ploni Almoni was a brother; Boaz, a nephew.
4:5. Delicately, Boaz implied that the redeemer should marry Ruth, to which he replied, "Mahlon and Chilion died only because they married Moabite women; shall I then go and take her?" (Midrash).
4:7-8. The transfer of a shoe [or, "glove" (Targum)] symbolizes and finalizes the legal transfer of ownership [קִנְיָן].

4

Boaz acts

¹ Boaz, meanwhile, had gone up to the gate, and sat down there. Just then, the redeemer of whom Boaz had spoken passed by. He said, "Come over, sit down here, Ploni Almoni,"* and he came over and sat down. ² He then took ten men of the elders of the city, and said, "Sit here," and they sat down.

³ Then he said to the redeemer, "The parcel of land which belonged to our brother,* Elimelech, is being offered for sale by Naomi who has returned from the fields of Moab. ⁴ I resolved that I should inform you to this effect: Buy it in the presence of those sitting here and in the presence of the elders of my people. If you are willing to redeem, redeem! But if it will not be redeemed, tell me, that I may know; for there is no one else to redeem it but you, and I am after you." And he said, "I am willing to redeem."

⁵ Then Boaz said, "The day you buy the field from the hand of Naomi, you must also buy it from Ruth the Moabite, wife of the deceased, to perpetuate the name of the deceased* on his inheritance." ⁶ The redeemer said, "Then I cannot redeem it for myself, lest I imperil my own inheritance. Take over my redemption responsibility on yourself for I am unable to redeem."

The transaction

⁷ Formerly this was done in Israel in cases of redemption and exchange transactions to validate any matter: One would draw off his shoe, and give it to the other. This was the process of ratification in Israel.* ⁸ So when the redeemer said to Boaz, "Buy it for yourself," he drew off his shoe.

⁹ And Boaz said to the elders, and to all the people, "You are witness this day, that I have bought all that was Elimelech's and all that was Chilion's and Mahlon's from the hand of Naomi. ¹⁰ And, what is more, I have also acquired Ruth the Moabite, the wife of Mahlon, as my wife,* to perpetuate the name of the deceased on his inheritance, that the name of the deceased not be cut off from among his brethren, and from the gate of his place. You are witnesses today."

¹¹ Then all the people who were at the gate, and the elders, said, "[We are] witnesses! May HASHEM make the woman who is coming into your house like Rachel and like Leah, both of whom built up the House of Israel. May you prosper in Ephrath and be famous in Beth-lehem; ¹² and may your house be like the house of Perez whom Tamar bore to Judah, through the offspring which HASHEM will give you by this young woman."

Boaz takes Ruth

¹³ And so, Boaz took Ruth and she became his wife; and he came to her. HASHEM let her conceive, and she bore a son. ¹⁴ And the women said to Naomi, "Blessed is HASHEM who has not left you without a redeemer today! May his name be famous in Israel. ¹⁵ He will become your life-restorer, to sustain your old age; for your daughter-in-law, who loves you, has borne him, and she is better to you than seven sons."

¹⁶ Naomi took the child, and held it in her bosom, and she became his nurse. ¹⁷ The neighborhood women gave him a name, saying, "A son is born to Naomi."* They named him Obed; he was the father of Jesse, the father of David.

The lineage of King David

¹⁸ Now these are the generations of Perez: Perez begot Hezron; ¹⁹ and Hezron begot Ram, and Ram begot Amminadab; ²⁰ and Amminadab begot Nahshon, and Nahshon begot Salmah; ²¹ and Salman begot Boaz, and Boaz begot Obed; ²² and Obed begot Jesse, and Jesse begot David.

4:10. Boaz mentions his marriage separately and does not include Ruth with his newly acquired land. A wife is not a piece of property, but a beloved partner in the sacred task of building a home (*R' Meir Zlotowitz*).

4:17. Naomi brought him up; hence he was called after Naomi's name (*Sanhedrin* 19b).

Lamentations איכה

Jeremiah was a young prophet to whom God assigned a heartbreaking task. He was to tell Israel over and over again that destruction and exile were impending. Warnings of destruction and pleas for repentance — these were Jeremiah's message, but to no avail. Prophets of doom are not popular, and no one was more unpopular than Jeremiah. His written prophecies were burned, he was accused as a false prophet and a charlatan, and finally he was thrown into a dungeon.

Someone else might have become consumed with hatred for the people that spurned and humiliated him, but not Jeremiah. At the orders of King Nebuchadnezzar, the conquering Babylonian general Nebuzaradan released Jeremiah and treated him graciously, but he was not comforted by his vindication or his freedom. Jeremiah sought his suffering brothers. He found their bloody footprints and weepingly knelt to kiss the bloodstained ground. When he caught up with their famished, brutalized ranks, he embraced and kissed them. He tried to put his own head into their heavy, abrasive chains, but Nebuzaradan forced him away.

To his brethren, he cried out, "If only you had wept once [in remorse over your sins] when you were still in Zion, you would not have been exiled!" Alas, they had not wept, but he did — before, during, and after his personal and national ordeals. The Book of Lamentations is Jeremiah's personal elegy, his lament for his people, and it alludes to Jewish woe throughout history.

The Book is read on Tishah B'Av, the ninth day of the Hebrew month of Av, the quintessential day of Jewish tragedy. It was the day when the Jews in the Wilderness believed the libel of the Spies, and that generation lost its chance to enter the Land of Israel. Among other national calamities, both Temples were destroyed on Tishah B'Av. Nor was the catalogue of woe limited to ancient times. During the time of the Spanish Inquisition, Tishah B'Av 1492 was the deadline for the Jews to leave the country or face death. And in 1914, Tishah B'Av was the day when World War I was declared, thus ushering in the political and economic collapse that resulted in the Bolshevik Revolution and the Holocaust.

The Sages teach that the Messiah will be born on Tishah B'Av, meaning that a proper understanding of and reflection upon the causes of destruction reveal that contained within it are the seeds of redemption. We do not forget our tragedies; rather we retain our optimism, because "Had I not fallen, I could not have arisen; had I not sat in the darkness, God would not have been a light for me" (Midrash Tehillim Ch. 22).

א אֵיכָה ׀ יָשְׁבָה בָדָד הָעִיר רַבָּתִי עָם הָיְתָה כְּאַלְמָנָה רַבָּתִי בַגּוֹיִם שָׂרָתִי
בַּמְּדִינוֹת הָיְתָה לָמַס: בָּכוֹ תִבְכֶּה בַּלַּיְלָה וְדִמְעָתָהּ עַל לֶחֱיָהּ אֵין־לָהּ
ב מְנַחֵם מִכָּל־אֹהֲבֶיהָ כָּל־רֵעֶיהָ בָּגְדוּ בָהּ הָיוּ לָהּ לְאֹיְבִים: גָּלְתָה יְהוּדָה
מֵעֹנִי וּמֵרֹב עֲבֹדָה הִיא יָשְׁבָה בַגּוֹיִם לֹא מָצְאָה מָנוֹחַ כָּל־רֹדְפֶיהָ
ג הִשִּׂיגוּהָ בֵּין הַמְּצָרִים: דַּרְכֵי צִיּוֹן אֲבֵלוֹת מִבְּלִי בָּאֵי מוֹעֵד כָּל־שְׁעָרֶיהָ
ד שׁוֹמֵמִין כֹּהֲנֶיהָ נֶאֱנָחִים בְּתוּלֹתֶיהָ נּוּגוֹת וְהִיא מַר־לָהּ: הָיוּ צָרֶיהָ לְרֹאשׁ
ה אֹיְבֶיהָ שָׁלוּ כִּי־יהוה הוֹגָהּ עַל־רֹב פְּשָׁעֶיהָ עוֹלָלֶיהָ הָלְכוּ שְׁבִי לִפְנֵי־צָר:
ו וַיֵּצֵא °מִן־בַּת [°מִבַּת־ ק] צִיּוֹן כָּל־הֲדָרָהּ הָיוּ שָׂרֶיהָ כְּאַיָּלִים לֹא־מָצְאוּ
ז מִרְעֶה וַיֵּלְכוּ בְלֹא־כֹחַ לִפְנֵי רוֹדֵף: זָכְרָה יְרוּשָׁלַ͏ִם יְמֵי עָנְיָהּ וּמְרוּדֶיהָ כֹּל
מַחֲמֻדֶיהָ אֲשֶׁר הָיוּ מִימֵי קֶדֶם בִּנְפֹל עַמָּהּ בְּיַד־צָר וְאֵין עוֹזֵר לָהּ רָאוּהָ
ח צָרִים שָׂחֲקוּ עַל־מִשְׁבַּתֶּהָ: חֵטְא חָטְאָה יְרוּשָׁלַ͏ִם עַל־כֵּן לְנִידָה הָיָתָה
כָּל־מְכַבְּדֶיהָ הִזִּילוּהָ כִּי־רָאוּ עֶרְוָתָהּ גַּם־הִיא נֶאֶנְחָה וַתָּשָׁב אָחוֹר:
ט טֻמְאָתָהּ בְּשׁוּלֶיהָ לֹא זָכְרָה אַחֲרִיתָהּ וַתֵּרֶד פְּלָאִים אֵין מְנַחֵם לָהּ רְאֵה
י יהוה אֶת־עָנְיִי כִּי הִגְדִּיל אוֹיֵב: יָדוֹ פָּרַשׂ צָר עַל כָּל־מַחֲמַדֶּיהָ כִּי־רָאֲתָה
יא גוֹיִם בָּאוּ מִקְדָּשָׁהּ אֲשֶׁר צִוִּיתָה לֹא־יָבֹאוּ בַקָּהָל לָךְ: כָּל־עַמָּהּ נֶאֱנָחִים
מְבַקְשִׁים לֶחֶם נָתְנוּ °מַחֲמוֹדֵיהֶם [°מַחֲמַדֵּיהֶם ק] בְּאֹכֶל לְהָשִׁיב נָפֶשׁ
יב רְאֵה יהוה וְהַבִּיטָה כִּי הָיִיתִי זוֹלֵלָה: לוֹא אֲלֵיכֶם כָּל־עֹבְרֵי דֶרֶךְ הַבִּיטוּ
וּרְאוּ אִם־יֵשׁ מַכְאוֹב כְּמַכְאֹבִי אֲשֶׁר עוֹלַל לִי אֲשֶׁר הוֹגָה יהוה בְּיוֹם
יג חֲרוֹן אַפּוֹ: מִמָּרוֹם שָׁלַח־אֵשׁ בְּעַצְמֹתַי וַיִּרְדֶּנָּה פָּרַשׂ רֶשֶׁת לְרַגְלַי
יד הֱשִׁיבַנִי אָחוֹר נְתָנַנִי שֹׁמֵמָה כָּל־הַיּוֹם דָּוָה: נִשְׂקַד עֹל פְּשָׁעַי בְּיָדוֹ
יִשְׂתָּרְגוּ עָלוּ עַל־צַוָּארִי הִכְשִׁיל כֹּחִי נְתָנַנִי אֲדֹנָי בִּידֵי לֹא־אוּכַל קוּם:
טו סִלָּה כָל־אַבִּירַי ׀ אֲדֹנָי בְּקִרְבִּי קָרָא עָלַי מוֹעֵד לִשְׁבֹּר בַּחוּרָי גַּת דָּרַךְ
טז אֲדֹנָי לִבְתוּלַת בַּת־יְהוּדָה: עַל־אֵלֶּה ׀ אֲנִי בוֹכִיָּה עֵינִי ׀ עֵינִי יֹרְדָה
מַּיִם כִּי־רָחַק מִמֶּנִּי מְנַחֵם מֵשִׁיב נַפְשִׁי הָיוּ בָנַי שׁוֹמֵמִים כִּי גָבַר אוֹיֵב:

1:1. Jeremiah originally wrote the first, second and fourth chapters of Lamentations on a scroll that was subsequently burnt by Jehoiakim (see *Jeremiah* 36:23). When he rewrote the Book, he added the third and fifth chapters (*Rashi; Moed Katan* 26a).

The Talmud explains that Jeremiah wrote the verses of the first four chapters in alphabetical order because the Jews transgressed the Torah from *alef* to *tav*, i.e., from the first to the last letter of the alphabet (*Sanhedrin* 104b).

The Talmud stresses that Jerusalem was only like a widow, because her bereavement would be temporary. She is like a woman whose husband went to a foreign country, albeit with the intention of returning to her (*Sanhedrin* 104b).

1:2. The "night" alludes to the night of Tishah B'Av (the Ninth of Av), when the Jewish people wept upon hearing

the slanderous report of the spies (*Numbers* 14:1). God said to Israel: "You have wept without cause; therefore I will appoint [this date as a time of] weeping for you in future generations" (*Sanhedrin* 104b).

The paramours are those nations that feigned friendship (*Rashi*), i.e., the neighboring countries — Egypt, Moab, Ammon — with whom Judah had hoped to form an alliance.

1:8. Jeremiah attributes all of the suffering described above to Divine retribution for Jerusalem's grievous sins.

1:10. When the Babylonian conquerors entered the Temple, Ammonites and Moabites entered among them. While the others ran to plunder the silver and gold, the Ammonites and Moabites ran to plunder the Torah itself to expurge the verse "An Ammonite or Moabite shall not enter the congregation of Hashem" (*Deuteronomy* 23:4; *Midrash*).

1

¹ א **A** las — she sits in solitude! * The city that was great with people has become like a widow. * The greatest among nations, the princess among provinces, has become a tributary.

² ב She weeps bitterly in the night * and her tear is on her cheek. She has no comforter from all her paramours; * all her friends have betrayed her, they have become her enemies.

³ ג Judah has gone into exile because of suffering and great servitude. She dwelled among the nations, but found no rest; all her pursuers overtook her in dire straits.

⁴ ד The roads of Zion are mourning for lack of festival pilgrims. All her gates are desolate, her priests sigh; her maidens are afflicted and she herself is embittered.

⁵ ה Her adversaries have become [her] master, her enemies are at ease, for HASHEM has afflicted her for her abundant transgressions. Her young children have gone into captivity before the enemy.

⁶ ו Gone from the daughter of Zion is all her splendor. Her leaders were like harts that found no pasture; they walked on without strength before the pursuer.

⁷ ז Jerusalem recalled the days of her suffering and sorrow, all the treasures that were hers in the days of old. With the fall of her people into the enemy's hand and none to help her, her enemies saw her and gloated at her downfall.

⁸ ח Jerusalem sinned greatly, she has therefore become a wanderer. * All who once respected her disparage her, for they have seen her disgrace. She herself sighs and turns away.

⁹ ט Her impurity is on her hems, she was heedless of her end. She has descended astonishingly, there is no one to comfort her. "See, O HASHEM, my suffering, for the enemy has acted prodigiously!"

¹⁰ י The enemy spread out his hand on all her treasures; indeed, she saw nations invade her Sanctuary, [nations] about whom You had commanded that they should not enter Your congregation. *

¹¹ כ All her people are sighing, searching for bread. They traded with their enemies for food to restore the soul. "See, O HASHEM, and behold what a glutton I have become!"

¹² ל May it not befall you, * all who pass by this road. Behold and see, if there is any pain like my pain which befell me; which HASHEM has afflicted me on the day of His burning wrath.

¹³ מ From on high He sent a fire into my bones, and it overcame them. He spread a net for my feet; He hurled me backward. He made me desolate; sick throughout the day.

¹⁴ נ The burden of my transgressions was accumulated in His hand; they were knit together and thrust upon my neck; He sapped my strength. * The Lord has delivered me into the hands of those I cannot withstand.

¹⁵ ס The Lord has trampled all my heroes in my midst; He proclaimed a set time against me to crush my young men. As in a winepress the Lord has trodden the maiden daughter of Judah.

¹⁶ ע Over these do I weep; my eye continuously runs with water because a comforter to restore my soul is far from me. My children have become forlorn, because the enemy has prevailed.

1:12. Jerusalem addresses the nations of the world.
1:14. Instead of constantly doling out a punishment whenever Zion transgressed, God was patient. Metaphor-

ically, He knit her accumulated transgressions together into a heavy garment that He thrust upon her neck, weighing her down and sapping her strength.

יז פֵּרְשָׂה צִיּוֹן בְּיָדֶ֔יהָ אֵ֤ין מְנַחֵם֙ לָ֔הּ צִוָּ֨ה יְהוָ֤ה לְיַֽעֲקֹב֙ סְבִיבָ֣יו צָרָ֔יו
יח הָֽיְתָ֧ה יְרֽוּשָׁלַ֛͏ִם לְנִדָּ֖ה בֵּֽינֵיהֶֽם: צַדִּ֥יק ה֛וּא יְהוָ֖ה כִּ֣י פִ֣יהוּ מָרִ֑יתִי
שִׁמְעוּ־נָ֣א כָל־ °עמים [°הָֽעַמִּ֖ים ק] וּרְאוּ֙ מַכְאֹבִ֔י בְּתֽוּלֹתַ֥י וּבַֽחוּרַ֖י
הָֽלְכ֥וּ בַשֶּֽׁבִי: יט קָרָ֤אתִי לַֽמְאַֽהֲבַי֙ הֵ֣מָּה רִמּ֔וּנִי כֹּֽהֲנַ֥י וּזְקֵנַ֖י בָּעִ֣יר גָּוָ֑עוּ
כ כִּֽי־בִקְשׁ֥וּ אֹ֨כֶל֙ לָ֔מוֹ וְיָשִׁ֖יבוּ אֶת־נַפְשָֽׁם: רְאֵ֨ה יְהוָ֤ה כִּֽי־צַר־לִ֨י מֵעַ֣י
חֳמַרְמָ֔רוּ נֶהְפַּ֤ךְ לִבִּי֙ בְּקִרְבִּ֔י כִּ֥י מָר֖וֹ מָרִ֑יתִי מִח֥וּץ שִׁכְּלָה־חֶ֖רֶב בַּבַּ֥יִת
כַּמָּֽוֶת: כא שָֽׁמְע֗וּ כִּ֤י נֶֽאֱנָחָה֙ אָ֔נִי אֵ֥ין מְנַחֵ֖ם לִ֑י כָּל־אֹֽיְבַ֞י שָֽׁמְע֤וּ רָֽעָתִי֙
כב שָׂ֗שׂוּ כִּ֤י אַתָּה֙ עָשִׂ֔יתָ הֵבֵ֥אתָ יוֹם־קָרָ֖אתָ וְיִֽהְי֣וּ כָמֹ֑נִי תָּבֹ֣א כָל־
רָֽעָתָ֣ם לְפָנֶ֗יךָ וְעוֹלֵ֤ל לָמוֹ֙ כַּֽאֲשֶׁ֤ר עוֹלַ֨לְתָּ֙ לִ֔י עַ֖ל כָּל־פְּשָׁעָ֑י כִּֽי־רַבּ֥וֹת
אַנְחֹתַ֖י וְלִבִּ֥י דַוָּֽי:

א אֵיכָה֩ יָעִ֨יב בְּאַפּ֤וֹ ׀ אֲדֹנָי֙ אֶת־בַּת־צִיּ֔וֹן הִשְׁלִ֤יךְ מִשָּׁמַ֨יִם֙ אֶ֔רֶץ תִּפְאֶ֖רֶת
יִשְׂרָאֵ֑ל וְלֹֽא־זָכַ֥ר הֲדֹם־רַגְלָ֖יו בְּי֥וֹם אַפּֽוֹ: ב בִּלַּ֨ע אֲדֹנָ֜י °לא [°וְלֹ֣א ק]
חָמַ֗ל אֵ֚ת כָּל־נְא֣וֹת יַֽעֲקֹ֔ב הָרַ֧ס בְּעֶבְרָת֛וֹ מִבְצְרֵ֥י בַת־יְהוּדָ֖ה הִגִּ֣יעַ
לָאָ֑רֶץ חִלֵּ֥ל מַמְלָכָ֖ה וְשָׂרֶֽיהָ: ג גָּדַ֣ע בָּֽחֳרִי־אַ֗ף כֹּ֚ל קֶ֣רֶן יִשְׂרָאֵ֔ל הֵשִׁ֥יב
אָח֛וֹר יְמִינ֖וֹ מִפְּנֵ֣י אוֹיֵ֑ב וַיִּבְעַ֤ר בְּיַֽעֲקֹב֙ כְּאֵ֣שׁ לֶֽהָבָ֔ה אָֽכְלָ֖ה סָבִֽיב:
ד דָּרַ֨ךְ קַשְׁתּ֜וֹ כְּאוֹיֵ֗ב נִצָּ֤ב יְמִינוֹ֙ כְּצָ֔ר וַֽיַּֽהֲרֹ֔ג כֹּ֖ל מַֽחֲמַדֵּי־עָ֑יִן בְּאֹ֨הֶל֙
בַּת־צִיּ֔וֹן שָׁפַ֥ךְ כָּאֵ֖שׁ חֲמָתֽוֹ: ה הָיָ֨ה אֲדֹנָ֤י ׀ כְּאוֹיֵב֙ בִּלַּ֣ע יִשְׂרָאֵ֔ל בִּלַּע֙
כָּל־אַרְמְנוֹתֶ֔יהָ שִׁחֵ֖ת מִבְצָרָ֑יו וַיֶּ֨רֶב֙ בְּבַת־יְהוּדָ֔ה תַּֽאֲנִיָּ֖ה וַֽאֲנִיָּֽה:
ו וַיַּחְמֹ֤ס כַּגַּן֙ שֻׂכּ֔וֹ שִׁחֵ֖ת מֹֽעֲד֑וֹ שִׁכַּ֨ח יְהוָ֤ה ׀ בְּצִיּוֹן֙ מוֹעֵ֣ד וְשַׁבָּ֔ת וַיִּנְאַ֥ץ
בְּזַֽעַם־אַפּ֖וֹ מֶ֥לֶךְ וְכֹהֵֽן: ז זָנַ֨ח אֲדֹנָ֤י ׀ מִזְבְּחוֹ֙ נִאֵ֣ר מִקְדָּשׁ֔וֹ הִסְגִּ֛יר בְּיַד־
אוֹיֵ֔ב חוֹמֹ֖ת אַרְמְנוֹתֶ֑יהָ ק֛וֹל נָֽתְנ֥וּ בְּבֵית־יְהוָ֖ה כְּי֥וֹם מוֹעֵֽד: ח חָשַׁ֨ב
יְהוָ֤ה ׀ לְהַשְׁחִית֙ חוֹמַ֣ת בַּת־צִיּ֔וֹן נָ֣טָה קָ֔ו לֹֽא־הֵשִׁ֥יב יָד֖וֹ מִבַּלֵּ֑עַ
ט וַיַּֽאֲבֶל־חֵ֥ל וְחוֹמָ֖ה יַחְדָּ֣ו אֻמְלָ֑לוּ טָֽבְע֤וּ בָאָ֨רֶץ֙ שְׁעָרֶ֔יהָ אִבַּ֥ד וְשִׁבַּ֖ר
בְּרִיחֶ֑יהָ מַלְכָּ֨הּ וְשָׂרֶ֤יהָ בַגּוֹיִם֙ אֵ֣ין תּוֹרָ֔ה גַּם־נְבִיאֶ֕יהָ לֹֽא־מָֽצְא֥וּ חָז֖וֹן
מֵֽיהוָֽה: י יֵֽשְׁב֨וּ לָאָ֤רֶץ יִדְּמוּ֙ זִקְנֵ֣י בַת־צִיּ֔וֹן הֶֽעֱל֤וּ עָפָר֙ עַל־רֹאשָׁ֔ם
חָֽגְר֣וּ שַׂקִּ֑ים הוֹרִ֤ידוּ לָאָ֨רֶץ֙ רֹאשָׁ֔ן בְּתוּלֹ֖ת יְרֽוּשָׁלָֽ͏ִם: יא כָּל֤וּ בַדְּמָעוֹת֙
עֵינַ֔י חֳמַרְמְר֣וּ מֵעַ֔י נִשְׁפַּ֤ךְ לָאָ֨רֶץ֙ כְּבֵדִ֔י עַל־שֶׁ֖בֶר בַּת־עַמִּ֑י בֵּֽעָטֵ֤ף
עוֹלֵל֙ וְיוֹנֵ֔ק בִּרְחֹב֖וֹת קִרְיָֽה: יב לְאִמֹּתָם֙ יֹ֣אמְר֔וּ אַיֵּ֖ה דָּגָ֣ן וָיָ֑יִן בְּהִֽתְעַטְּפָ֤ם

1:18. Zion acknowledges that God is righteous and justified in what He has done.

2:1. "Daughter of Zion" refers to Jerusalem's populace. "His footstool" is the Holy Temple (Rashi).

2:6. "His booth" is His Temple; "His place of assembly," the Holy of Holies; "king and Kohen" are Zedekiah —

whose children were slaughtered in his presence, and who was then blinded, bound in chains and led off to Babylon — and Seraiah, who were killed by Nebuchadnezzar himself [see II Kings 25:16,18-21] (Rashi).

2:9. There is no one to provide religious instruction (Rashi).

¹⁷ פ *Zion spreads out her hands; there is none to comfort her. H*ASHEM *commanded against Jacob that his enemies should surround him; Jerusalem has become as one unclean in their midst.*

¹⁸ צ H*ASHEM *is righteous, for I disobeyed His utterance.* * Listen, now, all you peoples and see my pain: My maidens and my youths have gone into captivity.*

¹⁹ ק *I called for my paramours but they deceived me. My priests and my elders perished in the city as they sought food for themselves to restore their souls.*

²⁰ ר *See, H*ASHEM, *for I am in distress; my innards burn! My heart is turned over inside me for I rebelled grievously. Outside the sword bereaved, inside was deathlike.*

²¹ ש *They heard how I sighed, there was none to comfort me. All my enemies heard of my plight and rejoiced, for it was You Who did it. O bring on the day You proclaimed and let them be like me!*

²² ת *Let all their wickedness come before You, and inflict them as You inflicted me for all my transgressions. For my groans are many, and my heart is sick.*

2

¹ א $\mathbf{A}$*las — the Lord in His anger has clouded the daughter of Zion.* * He cast down from heaven to earth the glory of Israel. He did not remember His footstool* * on the day of His wrath.*

² ב *The Lord consumed without pity all the dwellings of Jacob; in His anger He razed the fortresses of the daughter of Judah down to the ground; He profaned the kingdom and its leaders.*

³ ג *He cut down, in burning anger, all the dignity of Israel; He drew back His right hand in the presence of the enemy. He burned through Jacob like a flaming fire, consuming on all sides.*

⁴ ד *He bent His bow like an enemy; His right hand poised like a foe, He slew all who were pleasant to the eye. In the tent of the daughter of Zion He poured out His wrath like fire.*

⁵ ה *The Lord became like an enemy. He consumed Israel; He consumed all her citadels; He destroyed its fortresses. He increased within the daughter of Judah agony and grief.*

⁶ ו *He stripped His booth like a garden, He destroyed His place of assembly.* * H*ASHEM *made Zion oblivious of festival and Sabbath, and in His fierce anger He spurned king and Kohen.* *

⁷ ז *The Lord rejected His Altar, abolished His Sanctuary; He handed over to the hand of the enemy the walls of her citadels. They raised a clamor in the Temple of H*ASHEM *as though it were a festival.*

⁸ ח H*ASHEM *resolved to destroy the wall of the daughter of Zion. He stretched out the line and did not draw back His hand from consuming. Indeed, He made rampart and wall mourn; together they languished.*

⁹ ט *Her gates have sunk into the earth, He has destroyed and broken her bars; her king and her officers are among the nations, there is no Torah;* * her prophets, too, find no vision from H*ASHEM.

¹⁰ י *They sit on the ground, they are silent, the elders of the daughter of Zion; they have strewn ashes on their heads, they have girded themselves in sackcloth. The maidens of Jerusalem have bowed their heads to the ground.*

¹¹ כ *My eyes fail with tears, my innards burn; my liver spills on the ground at the ruination of the daughter of my people, while babes and sucklings swoon in the streets of the city.*

¹² ל *They say to their mothers, "Where is grain and wine?" as they swoon*

יג כֶּחָלָל֙ בִּרְחֹב֣וֹת עִ֔יר בְּהִשְׁתַּפֵּ֤ךְ נַפְשָׁם֙ אֶל־חֵ֣יק אִמֹּתָֽם: מָֽה־ °אֲעוֹדֵךְ [°אֲעִידֵךְ ק'] מָ֣ה אֲדַמֶּה־לָּ֗ךְ הַבַּת֙ יְר֣וּשָׁלַ֔ם מָ֤ה אַשְׁוֶה־לָּךְ֙ וַאֲנַֽחֲמֵ֔ךְ

יד בְּתוּלַ֖ת בַּת־צִיּ֑וֹן כִּֽי־גָד֥וֹל כַּיָּ֛ם שִׁבְרֵ֖ךְ מִ֥י יִרְפָּא־לָֽךְ: נְבִיאַ֗יִךְ חָ֤זוּ לָךְ֙ שָׁ֣וְא וְתָפֵ֔ל וְלֹֽא־גִלּ֥וּ עַל־עֲוֺנֵ֖ךְ לְהָשִׁ֣יב °שְׁבִיתֵ֑ךְ [°שְׁבוּתֵ֑ךְ ק'] וַיֶּ֣חֱזוּ לָ֔ךְ

טו מַשְׂא֥וֹת שָׁ֖וְא וּמַדּוּחִֽים: סָֽפְק֨וּ עָלַ֤יִךְ כַּפַּ֙יִם֙ כָּל־עֹ֣בְרֵי דֶ֔רֶךְ שָֽׁרְקוּ֙ וַיָּנִ֣עוּ רֹאשָׁ֔ם עַל־בַּ֖ת יְרוּשָׁלָ֑ם הֲזֹ֣את הָעִ֗יר שֶׁיֹּֽאמְרוּ֙ כְּלִ֣ילַת יֹ֔פִי מָשׂ֖וֹשׂ לְכָל־

טז הָאָֽרֶץ: פָּצ֨וּ עָלַ֤יִךְ פִּיהֶם֙ כָּל־אֹ֣יְבַ֔יִךְ שָֽׁרְקוּ֙ וַיַּֽחַרְקוּ־שֵׁ֔ן אָֽמְר֖וּ בִּלָּ֑עְנוּ אַ֣ךְ

יז זֶ֥ה הַיּ֛וֹם שֶׁקִּוִּינֻ֖הוּ מָצָ֣אנוּ רָאִֽינוּ: עָשָׂ֨ה יְהֹוָ֜ה אֲשֶׁ֣ר זָמָ֗ם בִּצַּ֤ע אֶמְרָתוֹ֙ אֲשֶׁ֣ר צִוָּ֣ה מִֽימֵי־קֶ֔דֶם הָרַ֖ס וְלֹ֣א חָמָ֑ל וַיְשַׂמַּ֤ח עָלַ֙יִךְ֙ אוֹיֵ֔ב הֵרִ֖ים קֶ֥רֶן

יח צָרָֽיִךְ: צָעַ֥ק לִבָּ֖ם אֶל־אֲדֹנָ֑י חוֹמַ֣ת בַּת־צִ֠יּ֠וֹן הוֹרִ֨ידִי כַנַּ֤חַל דִּמְעָה֙ יוֹמָ֣ם

יט וָלַ֔יְלָה אַל־תִּתְּנִ֤י פוּגַת֙ לָ֔ךְ אַל־תִּדֹּ֖ם בַּת־עֵינֵֽךְ: ק֣וּמִי ׀ רֹ֣נִּי °בַלַּ֗יְלָה [°בַלַּ֗יְלָ ק'] לְרֹאשׁ֙ אַשְׁמֻר֔וֹת שִׁפְכִ֤י כַמַּ֙יִם֙ לִבֵּ֔ךְ נֹ֖כַח פְּנֵ֣י אֲדֹנָ֑י שְׂאִ֧י

כ אֵלָ֣יו כַּפַּ֗יִךְ עַל־נֶ֙פֶשׁ֙ עֽוֹלָלַ֔יִךְ הָעֲטוּפִ֥ים בְּרָעָ֖ב בְּרֹ֣אשׁ כָּל־חוּצֽוֹת: רְאֵ֤ה יְהֹוָה֙ וְֽהַבִּ֔יטָה לְמִ֥י עוֹלַ֖לְתָּ כֹּ֑ה אִם־תֹּאכַ֨לְנָה נָשִׁ֤ים פִּרְיָם֙ עֹֽלֲלֵ֣י טִפֻּחִ֔ים

כא אִם־יֵֽהָרֵ֛ג בְּמִקְדַּ֥שׁ אֲדֹנָ֖י כֹּהֵ֥ן וְנָבִֽיא: שָֽׁכְב֨וּ לָאָ֤רֶץ חוּצוֹת֙ נַ֣עַר וְזָקֵ֔ן

כב בְּתֽוּלֹתַ֥י וּבַחוּרַ֖י נָֽפְל֣וּ בֶחָ֑רֶב הָרַ֙גְתָּ֙ בְּי֣וֹם אַפֶּ֔ךָ טָבַ֖חְתָּ לֹ֥א חָמָֽלְתָּ: תִּקְרָ֤א כְיוֹם֙ מוֹעֵד֙ מְגוּרַ֣י מִסָּבִ֔יב וְלֹ֥א הָיָ֛ה בְּי֥וֹם אַף־יְהֹוָ֖ה פָּלִ֣יט וְשָׂרִ֑יד אֲשֶׁר־טִפַּ֥חְתִּי וְרִבִּ֖יתִי אֹֽיְבִ֥י כִלָּֽם:

ג

א אֲנִ֤י הַגֶּ֙בֶר֙ רָאָ֣ה עֳנִ֔י בְּשֵׁ֖בֶט עֶבְרָתֽוֹ: אוֹתִ֥י נָהַ֛ג וַיֹּלַ֖ךְ חֹ֥שֶׁךְ וְלֹא־אֽוֹר:

ג אַ֣ךְ בִּ֥י יָשֻׁ֛ב יַהֲפֹ֥ךְ יָד֖וֹ כָּל־הַיּֽוֹם: בִּלָּ֤ה בְשָׂרִי֙ וְעוֹרִ֔י שִׁבַּ֖ר עַצְמוֹתָֽי: בָּנָ֥ה

ו עָלַ֛י וַיַּקַּ֖ף רֹ֣אשׁ וּתְלָאָֽה: בְּמַחֲשַׁכִּ֥ים הוֹשִׁיבַ֖נִי כְּמֵתֵ֥י עוֹלָֽם: גָּדַ֧ר בַּעֲדִ֛י

ח וְלֹ֥א אֵצֵ֖א הִכְבִּ֣יד נְחָשְׁתִּֽי: גַּ֣ם כִּ֤י אֶזְעַק֙ וַאֲשַׁוֵּ֔עַ שָׂתַ֖ם תְּפִלָּתִֽי: גָּדַ֤ר

י דְּרָכַי֙ בְּגָזִ֔ית נְתִיבֹתַ֖י עִוָּֽה: דֹּ֣ב אֹרֵ֥ב הוּא֙ לִ֔י °אֲרִיֵ֖ה [°אֲרִ֖י ק']

יא בְּמִסְתָּרִֽים: דְּרָכַ֥י סוֹרֵ֛ר וַֽיְפַשְּׁחֵ֖נִי שָׂמַ֣נִי שֹׁמֵֽם: דָּרַ֤ךְ קַשְׁתּוֹ֙ וַיַּצִּיבֵ֔נִי

יג כַּמַּטָּרָ֖א לַחֵֽץ: הֵבִיא֙ בְּכִלְיוֹתָ֔י בְּנֵ֖י אַשְׁפָּתֽוֹ: הָיִ֤יתִי שְּׂחֹק֙ לְכָל־עַמִּ֔י

טו נְגִינָתָ֖ם כָּל־הַיּֽוֹם: הִשְׂבִּיעַ֥נִי בַמְּרוֹרִ֖ים הִרְוַ֥נִי לַעֲנָֽה: וַיַּגְרֵ֤ס בֶּֽחָצָץ֙

יז שִׁנָּ֔י הִכְפִּישַׁ֖נִי בָּאֵֽפֶר: וַתִּזְנַ֧ח מִשָּׁל֛וֹם נַפְשִׁ֖י נָשִׁ֥יתִי טוֹבָֽה: וָאֹמַר֙ אָבַ֣ד

2:13. In times of trouble one finds comfort in hearing of others who experienced similar tribulations, but Israel's suffering is beyond comparison (*Rashi*).

2:15. People will show astonishment at the disaster that befell the once-glorious city.

2:16. In the *aleph-beis*, the letter ע precedes the letter פ; nevertheless, in the *aleph-beis* acrostic of Chapters 2,3 and 4, the פ precedes the ע. The Talmud explains this as an allusion to the spies (see 1:2), who placed their פֶּה, "mouth," before their עַיִן, "eye," by reporting things they

had not actually seen (*Sanhedrin* 104b).

2:20. A reference to Zechariah son of Jehoiada the Kohen who prophesied against King Joash and was stoned to death in the Temple Courtyard (*II Chronicles* 24:20-22).

3:1. The initials of the verses of this chapter form a threefold alphabet.

In a personal statement, Jeremiah laments that of all the prophets who foretold the Destruction of the Temple, it was he who actually saw it (*Rashi*).

like a dying man in the streets of the town; as their soul ebbs away in their mothers' laps.

¹³ מ With what shall I bear witness for you? To what can I compare you, O daughter of Jerusalem? To what can I liken you that I may comfort you, * O maiden daughter of Zion? — Your ruin is as vast as the sea; who can heal you?

¹⁴ נ Your prophets envisioned for you vanity and foolishness, and they did not expose your iniquity to bring you back in repentance; they envisioned for you oracles of vanity and deception.

¹⁵ ס All who pass along the way clap hands at you; they whistle and wag their head at the daughter of Jerusalem, "Could this be the city that was called Perfect in Beauty, Joy of All the Earth?"*

¹⁶ פ* All your enemies opened their mouths wide at you; they whistle and gnash their teeth. They say, "We have devoured her! Indeed, this is the day we longed for; we have found it, we have seen it!"

¹⁷ ע HASHEM has done what He has planned; He carried out His decree which He ordained from days of old; He devastated, and did not pity. He let the enemy rejoice over you; He raised the pride of your foes.

¹⁸ צ Their heart cried out to the Lord. O wall of the daughter of Zion, shed tears like a river, day and night; give yourself no respite, do not let the apple of your eye be still.

¹⁹ ק Arise, cry out at night in the beginning of the watches! Pour out your heart like water in the presence of the Lord; lift up your hands to Him for the life of your young children, who swoon from hunger at every street corner.

²⁰ ר See, O HASHEM, and behold whom You have treated so. Should women eat their own offspring, the babes of their care? Should Kohen and prophet* be slain in the Sanctuary of the Lord?

²¹ ש Out on the ground, in the streets they lie, young and old; my maidens and my young men have fallen by the sword. You slew them on the day of Your wrath; You slaughtered them; You showed no mercy.

²² ת You invited, as on a festival time, my evil neighbors round about. So that, at the day of HASHEM's wrath, there was no survivor or escapee. Those I cherished and brought up, my enemy has wiped out.

3 ¹ א I am the man who has seen affliction* by the rod of His anger. ² He has led me and driven me into darkness and not light. ³ Only against me did He turn His hand all day long.

⁴ ב He has worn away my flesh and skin; He has broken my bones. ⁵ He has besieged me and encircled [me] with bitterness and travail. ⁶ He has placed me in darkness like the eternally dead.

⁷ ג He has walled me in so I cannot escape; He has weighted down my chain. ⁸ Though I would cry out and plead, He shut out my prayer. ⁹ He has walled up my roads with hewn stones; He distorted my paths.

¹⁰ ד He is a lurking bear to me, a lion in hiding. ¹¹ He has strewn my paths with thorns and made me tread carefully; He made me desolate. ¹² He bent his bow and set me up as a target for the arrow.

¹³ ה He shot into my vitals the arrows of His quiver. ¹⁴ I have become a laughingstock to all my people; object of their jibes all day long. ¹⁵ He filled me with bitterness, sated me with wormwood.

¹⁶ ו He ground my teeth on gravel, He made me cower in ashes. ¹⁷ My soul despaired of having peace, I have forgotten goodness. ¹⁸ And I said, "Lost is

יט־כ נִצְחִי וְתוֹחַלְתִּי מֵיהוֹה: זְכׇר־עׇנְיִי וּמְרוּדִי לַעֲנָה וָרֹאשׁ: זָכוֹר תִּזְכּוֹר

כא °וְתָשִׁיחַ [°וְתָשׁוֹחַ ק] עָלַי נַפְשִׁי: זֹאת אָשִׁיב אֶל־לִבִּי עַל־כֵּן אוֹחִיל:

כב־כג חַסְדֵי יהוה כִּי לֹא־תָמְנוּ כִּי לֹא־כָלוּ רַחֲמָיו: חֲדָשִׁים לַבְּקָרִים רַבָּה

כד־כה אֱמוּנָתֶךָ: חֶלְקִי יהוה אָמְרָה נַפְשִׁי עַל־כֵּן אוֹחִיל לוֹ: טוֹב יהוה לְקֹוָו

כו־כז לְנֶפֶשׁ תִּדְרְשֶׁנּוּ: טוֹב וְיָחִיל וְדוּמָם לִתְשׁוּעַת יהוה: טוֹב לַגֶּבֶר כִּי־יִשָּׂא

כח־כט עֹל בִּנְעוּרָיו: יֵשֵׁב בָּדָד וְיִדֹּם כִּי נָטַל עָלָיו: יִתֵּן בֶּעָפָר פִּיהוּ אוּלַי יֵשׁ

ל־לב תִּקְוָה: יִתֵּן לְמַכֵּהוּ לֶחִי יִשְׂבַּע בְּחֶרְפָּה: כִּי לֹא יִזְנַח לְעוֹלָם אֲדֹנָי: כִּי

לג אִם־הוֹגָה וְרִחַם כְּרֹב °חסדו [°חֲסָדָיו ק]: כִּי לֹא עִנָּה מִלִּבּוֹ וַיַּגֶּה בְּנֵי־

לד־לה אִישׁ: לְדַכֵּא תַּחַת רַגְלָיו כֹּל אֲסִירֵי אָרֶץ: לְהַטּוֹת מִשְׁפַּט־גָּבֶר נֶגֶד פְּנֵי

לו־לז עֶלְיוֹן: לְעַוֵּת אָדָם בְּרִיבוֹ אֲדֹנָי לֹא רָאָה: מִי זֶה אָמַר וַתֶּהִי אֲדֹנָי לֹא

לח־לט צִוָּה: מִפִּי עֶלְיוֹן לֹא תֵצֵא הָרָעוֹת וְהַטּוֹב: מַה־יִּתְאוֹנֵן אָדָם חָי גֶּבֶר

מ עַל־°חטאו [°חֲטָאָיו ק]: נַחְפְּשָׂה דְרָכֵינוּ וְנַחְקֹרָה וְנָשׁוּבָה עַד־יהוה:

מא־מב נִשָּׂא לְבָבֵנוּ אֶל־כַּפָּיִם אֶל־אֵל בַּשָּׁמָיִם: נַחְנוּ פָשַׁעְנוּ וּמָרִינוּ אַתָּה לֹא

מג־מד סָלָחְתָּ: סַכֹּתָה בָאַף וַתִּרְדְּפֵנוּ הָרַגְתָּ לֹא חָמָלְתָּ: סַכּוֹתָה בֶעָנָן לָךְ

מה־מו מֵעֲבוֹר תְּפִלָּה: סְחִי וּמָאוֹס תְּשִׂימֵנוּ בְּקֶרֶב הָעַמִּים: פָּצוּ עָלֵינוּ פִּיהֶם

מז־מח כׇּל־אֹיְבֵינוּ: פַּחַד וָפַחַת הָיָה לָנוּ הַשֵּׁאת וְהַשָּׁבֶר: פַּלְגֵי־מַיִם תֵּרַד עֵינִי

מט־נ עַל־שֶׁבֶר בַּת־עַמִּי: עֵינִי נִגְּרָה וְלֹא תִדְמֶה מֵאֵין הֲפֻגוֹת: עַד־יַשְׁקִיף

נא־נב וְיֵרֶא יהוה מִשָּׁמָיִם: עֵינִי עוֹלְלָה לְנַפְשִׁי מִכֹּל בְּנוֹת עִירִי: צוֹד צָדוּנִי

נג־נד כַּצִּפּוֹר אֹיְבַי חִנָּם: צָמְתוּ בַבּוֹר חַיָּי וַיַּדּוּ־אֶבֶן בִּי: צָפוּ־מַיִם עַל־רֹאשִׁי

נה־נו אָמַרְתִּי נִגְזָרְתִּי: קָרָאתִי שִׁמְךָ יהוה מִבּוֹר תַּחְתִּיּוֹת: קוֹלִי שָׁמָעְתָּ אַל־

נז תַּעְלֵם אׇזְנְךָ לְרַוְחָתִי לְשַׁוְעָתִי: קָרַבְתָּ בְּיוֹם אֶקְרָאֶךָּ אָמַרְתָּ אַל־

נח־נט תִּירָא: רַבְתָּ אֲדֹנָי רִיבֵי נַפְשִׁי גָּאַלְתָּ חַיָּי: רָאִיתָה יהוה עַוָּתָתִי שָׁפְטָה

ס־סא מִשְׁפָּטִי: רָאִיתָה כׇּל־נִקְמָתָם כׇּל־מַחְשְׁבֹתָם לִי: שָׁמַעְתָּ חֶרְפָּתָם יהוה

סב־סג כׇּל־מַחְשְׁבֹתָם עָלָי: שִׂפְתֵי קָמַי וְהֶגְיוֹנָם עָלַי כׇּל־הַיּוֹם: שִׁבְתָּם וְקִימָתָם

סד־סה הַבִּיטָה אֲנִי מַנְגִּינָתָם: תָּשִׁיב לָהֶם גְּמוּל יהוה כְּמַעֲשֵׂה יְדֵיהֶם: תִּתֵּן

סו לָהֶם מְגִנַּת־לֵב תַּאֲלָתְךָ לָהֶם: תִּרְדֹּף בְּאַף וְתַשְׁמִידֵם מִתַּחַת שְׁמֵי

יהוה:

3:22. Jeremiah's expression of faith and hope continues until verse 39.

3:23. Your kindnesses are renewed from day to day (Rashi).

3:26-27. Since it is certain that God will not neglect His people eternally, it is prudent to accept His yoke in quiet resignation and silent anticipation for His ulti-

mate salvation.

3:37-42. One should never ascribe his suffering to chance. Rather than complain, everyone should investigate his own sins and repent.

3:46. See 2:16.

3:64-66. May God mete out retribution to Israel's enemies, in kind, for all their evil.

my strength and my expectation from HASHEM."

¹⁹ ז *Remember my afflictions and my sorrow; the wormwood and bitterness.* ²⁰ *My soul remembers well, and makes me despondent.* ²¹ *Yet, this I bear in mind; therefore I still hope:*

²² ח *HASHEM's kindness surely has not ended,* * *nor are His mercies exhausted.* ²³ *They are new every morning;* * *great is Your faithfulness!* ²⁴ *"HASHEM is my portion," says my soul, "therefore I have hope in Him."*

²⁵ ט *HASHEM is good to those who trust in Him; to the soul that seeks Him.* ²⁶ *It is good to hope silently for HASHEM's salvation.* ²⁷ *It is good for a man that he bear a yoke in his youth.* *

²⁸ י *Let one sit in solitude and be submissive, for He has laid it upon him.* ²⁹ *Let him put his mouth to the dust — there may yet be hope.* ³⁰ *Let one offer his cheek to his smiter, let him be filled with disgrace;*

³¹ כ *For the Lord does not reject forever;* ³² *He first afflicts, then pities, according to His abundant kindness.* ³³ *For He does not torment capriciously, nor afflict man;*

³⁴ ל *To crush under His feet all the prisoners of the earth;* ³⁵ *to deny a man justice in the presence of the Most High;* ³⁶ *to wrong a man in his conflict; the Lord does not approve.*

³⁷ מ *Whose decree was ever fulfilled, if the Lord did not ordain it?* ³⁸ *Is it not from the mouth of the Most High that evil and good emanate?* ³⁹ *Of what shall a living man complain? A man for his sins!*

⁴⁰ נ *Let us search and examine our ways and return to HASHEM.* ⁴¹ *Let us lift our hearts with our hands to God in heaven.* ⁴² *We have transgressed and rebelled; You have not forgiven.* *

⁴³ ס *You have enveloped Yourself in anger and pursued us; You have slain, You have not shown mercy.* ⁴⁴ *You wrapped Yourself in a cloud that prayer cannot pierce.* ⁴⁵ *You made us filth and refuse among the nations.*

⁴⁶ פ* *All our enemies opened their* * *mouths wide at us;* ⁴⁷ *panic and pitifulness were ours, ravage and ruin.* ⁴⁸ *My eye runs with streams of water at the ruination of my people.*

⁴⁹ ע *My eye will flow and will not cease — without relief —* ⁵⁰ *until HASHEM looks down and takes notice from heaven.* ⁵¹ *My eyes have brought me grief over all the daughters of my city.*

⁵² צ *I have been constantly ensnared like a bird by my enemies without cause.* ⁵³ *They cut off my life in a pit and threw stones at me.* ⁵⁴ *Waters flowed over my head; I said, "I am doomed!"*

⁵⁵ ק *I called on Your name, HASHEM, from the depths of the pit.* ⁵⁶ *You have heard my voice; do not shut Your ear to (my prayer for) my relief, to my cry.* ⁵⁷ *You drew near on the day I would call You; You said, "Fear not!"*

⁵⁸ ר *You championed my cause, O Lord, You redeemed my life.* ⁵⁹ *You have seen, HASHEM, the injustices I suffer; judge my cause.* ⁶⁰ *You have seen all their vengeance, all their designs regarding me.*

⁶¹ ש *You have heard their insults, HASHEM; all their designs against me.* ⁶² *The speech of my enemies and their thoughts are against me all day long.* ⁶³ *Look at their sitting and their rising; I am the butt of their taunts.*

⁶⁴ ת *Pay them back their due, HASHEM,* * *as they have done.* ⁶⁵ *Give them a broken heart; may Your curse be upon them!* ⁶⁶ *Pursue them in anger and destroy them from under the heavens of HASHEM.*

א אֵיכָה֙ יוּעַם֙ זָהָ֔ב יִשְׁנֶ֖א הַכֶּ֣תֶם הַטּ֑וֹב תִּשְׁתַּפֵּ֙כְנָה֙ אַבְנֵי־קֹ֔דֶשׁ בְּרֹ֖אשׁ כָּל־
ב חוּצֽוֹת: בְּנֵ֤י צִיּוֹן֙ הַיְקָרִ֔ים הַמְסֻלָּאִ֖ים בַּפָּ֑ז אֵיכָ֤ה נֶחְשְׁבוּ֙ לְנִבְלֵי־חֶ֔רֶשׂ
ג מַעֲשֵׂ֖ה יְדֵ֥י יוֹצֵֽר: גַּם־ °תַּנִּין֙ [°תַּנִּ֣ים ק] חָ֣לְצוּ שַׁ֔ד הֵינִ֖יקוּ גּֽוּרֵיהֶ֑ן בַּת־
ד עַמִּ֣י לְאַכְזָ֔ר °כִּי עֵנִ֖ים [°כַּיְעֵנִ֖ים ק] בַּמִּדְבָּֽר: דָּבַ֨ק לְשׁ֤וֹן יוֹנֵק֙ אֶל־חִכּ֔וֹ
ה בַּצָּמָ֑א עֽוֹלָלִים֙ שָׁ֣אֲלוּ לֶ֔חֶם פֹּרֵ֖שׂ אֵ֥ין לָהֶֽם: הָאֹֽכְלִים֙ לְמַעֲדַנִּ֔ים נָשַׁ֖מּוּ
ו בַּחוּצ֑וֹת הָאֱמֻנִים֙ עֲלֵ֣י תוֹלָ֔ע חִבְּק֖וּ אַשְׁפַּתּֽוֹת: וַיִּגְדַּל֙ עֲוֺ֣ן בַּת־עַמִּ֔י
ז מֵֽחַטַּ֖את סְדֹ֑ם הַהֲפוּכָ֣ה כְמוֹ־רָ֔גַע וְלֹא־חָ֥לוּ בָ֖הּ יָדָֽיִם: זַכּ֤וּ נְזִירֶ֙יהָ֙ מִשֶּׁ֔לֶג
ח צַח֖וּ מֵחָלָ֑ב אָ֣דְמוּ עֶ֞צֶם מִפְּנִינִ֗ים סַפִּ֖יר גִּזְרָתָֽם: חָשַׁ֤ךְ מִשְּׁחוֹר֙ תָּֽאֳרָ֔ם לֹ֥א
ט נִכְּר֖וּ בַּחוּצ֑וֹת צָפַ֤ד עוֹרָם֙ עַל־עַצְמָ֔ם יָבֵ֖שׁ הָיָ֥ה כָעֵֽץ: טוֹבִ֤ים הָיוּ֙ חַלְלֵי־
י חֶ֔רֶב מֵֽחַלְלֵ֖י רָעָ֑ב שֶׁ֣הֵ֤ם יָזֻ֙בוּ֙ מְדֻקָּרִ֔ים מִתְּנוּבֹ֖ת שָׂדָֽי: יְדֵ֗י נָשִׁים֙
יא רַחֲמָ֣נִיּ֔וֹת בִּשְּׁל֖וּ יַלְדֵיהֶ֑ן הָי֤וּ לְבָרוֹת֙ לָ֔מוֹ בְּשֶׁ֖בֶר בַּת־עַמִּֽי: כִּלָּ֤ה יהוה֙
יב אֶת־חֲמָת֔וֹ שָׁפַ֖ךְ חֲר֣וֹן אַפּ֑וֹ וַיַּצֶּת־אֵשׁ֙ בְּצִיּ֔וֹן וַתֹּ֖אכַל יְסֹדֹתֶֽיהָ: לֹ֤א
    הֶאֱמִ֙ינוּ֙ מַלְכֵי־אֶ֔רֶץ °וּכֹל [°כֹּ֖ל ק] יֹשְׁבֵ֣י תֵבֵ֑ל כִּ֤י יָבֹא֙ צַ֣ר וְאוֹיֵ֔ב בְּשַׁעֲרֵ֖י
יג יְרֽוּשָׁלָֽ͏ִם: מֵֽחַטֹּ֣את נְבִיאֶ֔יהָ עֲוֺנֹ֖ת כֹּהֲנֶ֑יהָ הַשֹּׁפְכִ֥ים בְּקִרְבָּ֖הּ דַּ֥ם צַדִּיקִֽים:
יד־טו נָע֤וּ עִוְרִים֙ בַּֽחוּצ֔וֹת נְגֹֽאֲל֖וּ בַּדָּ֑ם בְּלֹ֣א יֽוּכְל֔וּ יִגְּע֖וּ בִּלְבֻשֵׁיהֶֽם: ס֣וּרוּ טָמֵ֞א
    קָ֣רְאוּ לָ֗מוֹ ס֤וּרוּ ס֙וּרוּ֙ אַל־תִּגָּ֔עוּ כִּ֥י נָצ֖וּ גַּם־נָ֑עוּ אָֽמְרוּ֙ בַּגּוֹיִ֔ם לֹ֥א יוֹסִ֖פוּ
טז לָגֽוּר: פְּנֵ֤י יהוה֙ חִלְּקָ֔ם לֹ֥א יוֹסִ֖יף לְהַבִּיטָ֑ם פְּנֵ֤י כֹֽהֲנִים֙ לֹ֣א נָשָׂ֔אוּ °זְקֵנִ֖ים
יז [°וּזְקֵנִ֖ים ק] לֹ֥א חָנָֽנוּ: °עוֹדֵֽינוּ [°עוֹדֵ֙ינוּ֙ ק] תִּכְלֶ֣ינָה עֵינֵ֔ינוּ אֶל־עֶזְרָתֵ֖נוּ
יח הָ֑בֶל בְּצִפִּיָּתֵ֙נוּ֙ צִפִּ֔ינוּ אֶל־גּ֖וֹי לֹ֥א יוֹשִֽׁעַ: צָד֣וּ צְעָדֵ֔ינוּ מִלֶּ֖כֶת בִּרְחֹֽבֹתֵ֑ינוּ
יט קָרַ֣ב קִצֵּ֔נוּ מָֽלְא֥וּ יָמֵ֖ינוּ כִּי־בָ֥א קִצֵּֽנוּ: קַלִּ֤ים הָיוּ֙ רֹֽדְפֵ֔ינוּ מִנִּשְׁרֵ֖י שָׁמָ֑יִם עַל־
כ הֶהָרִ֣ים דְּלָקֻ֔נוּ בַּמִּדְבָּ֖ר אָ֥רְבוּ לָֽנוּ: ר֤וּחַ אַפֵּ֙ינוּ֙ מְשִׁ֣יחַ יהוה֔ נִלְכַּ֖ד
כא בִּשְׁחִית֑וֹתָם אֲשֶׁ֣ר אָמַ֔רְנוּ בְּצִלּ֖וֹ נִֽחְיֶ֥ה בַגּוֹיִֽם: שִׂ֤ישִׂי וְשִׂמְחִי֙ בַּת־אֱד֔וֹם
    °יוֹשַׁבְתִּי [°יוֹשֶׁ֖בֶת ק] בְּאֶ֣רֶץ ע֑וּץ גַּם־עָלַ֙יִךְ֙ תַּֽעֲבָר־כּ֔וֹס תִּשְׁכְּרִ֖י
כב וְתִתְעָרִֽי: תַּם־עֲוֺנֵךְ֙ בַּת־צִיּ֔וֹן לֹ֥א יוֹסִ֖יף לְהַגְלוֹתֵ֑ךְ פָּקַ֤ד עֲוֺנֵךְ֙ בַּת־אֱד֔וֹם
    גִּלָּ֖ה עַל־חַטֹּאתָֽיִךְ:

4:1. The "gold" figuratively refers to the people of Jerusalem. Its external appearance and brilliance has become dimmed, but its essence is still pure (*Midrash; Rashi; Ibn Yachya*).

This elegy is the one spoken of in *II Chronicles* 35:25, as Jeremiah's lament for King Josiah.

4:3. Although jackals are vicious, they are warm and kind to their young. Jeremiah laments how compassionate Jewish mothers consumed whatever food was available while letting their children go hungry (*Rashi*).

4:6. Since the punishment of Zion was greater than that of Sodom, its iniquity must have been greater as well (*Rashi*).

4:9. A swift death is preferable to the slow agony of famine (*Alshich*).

4:13. She became vulnerable to such calamity because

of the sins of her false prophets (*Rashi*) and idolatrous priests (*Targum*).

4:16. See 2:16.

4:17. In the last days of the siege, nearly everyone still hoped that outside help would arrive. The advancing Egyptian army caused the Babylonians to retreat from Jerusalem, but the relief was only temporary. The Egyptians never came to save them, and the Babylonians returned (*Jeremiah* 37:5-11).

4:20. This refers to King Josiah, who was killed by Egyptian archers [see *II Chronicles* 35:23-25] (*Taanis* 22b; *Rashi*).

4:21. Sarcastically, Jeremiah tells the enemy, rejoice while you can, because you too will drink from the cup of punishment (*Midrash Lekach Tov*).

4

¹ א **A** las — the gold is dimmed! * The finest gold is changed! Sacred stones are scattered at the head of every street!

² ב *The precious children of Zion, who are comparable to fine gold — alas, they are now treated like earthen jugs, work of a potter.*

³ ג *Even jackals will offer the breast and suckle their young; * the daughter of my people has become cruel, like ostriches in the desert.*

⁴ ד *The tongue of the suckling cleaves to its palate for thirst; young children plead for bread, no one extends it to them.*

⁵ ה *Those who feasted extravagantly lie desolate in the streets; those who were brought up in scarlet clothing embrace garbage heaps.*

⁶ ו *The iniquity of the daughter of my people is greater than the sin of Sodom, which was overturned in a moment, though no [mortal] hands were laid on her. **

⁷ ז *Her crowned ones who were purer than snow, whiter than milk, whose complexion was ruddier than rubies, whose build was [solid like] sapphire,*

⁸ ח *Their appearance has become blacker than soot, they are not recognized in the streets; their skin has shriveled on their bones, it became dry as wood.*

⁹ ט *More fortunate were those slain by the sword than those slain by famine, * for they pine away, stricken, lacking the fruits of the field.*

¹⁰ י *The hands of compassionate women have boiled their own children; they became their food in the ruination of the daughter of my people.*

¹¹ כ *HASHEM vented His fury, He poured out His burning anger; He kindled a fire in Zion which consumed its foundations.*

¹² ל *The kings of the earth did not believe, nor did any of the world's inhabitants, that the adversary or enemy could enter the gates of Jerusalem.*

¹³ מ *It was for the sins of her prophets, the iniquities of her priests, * who had shed in her midst the blood of the righteous.*

¹⁴ נ *The blind wandered through the streets, defiled with blood, so that none could touch their garments.*

¹⁵ ס *"Away, unclean one!" people shouted at them; "Away! Away! Don't touch! For they are loathsome and wander about." The nations had said, "They will no longer sojourn [here]."*

¹⁶ פ* *The anger of HASHEM has divided them, caring for them no longer; they showed no regard for the Kohanim nor did they favor the elders.*

¹⁷ ע *Our eyes still strained in vain for our deliverance; in our expectations we watched for a nation that could not save. **

¹⁸ צ *They dogged our steps so we could not walk in our streets; our end drew near, our days are filled, for our end has come.*

¹⁹ ק *Our pursuers were swifter than eagles of the sky; they chased us in the mountains, ambushed us in the desert.*

²⁰ ר *The breath of our nostrils, HASHEM's anointed, * was caught in their traps; he, under whose protection, we had said, we would live among the nations.*

²¹ ש *Rejoice and exult, O daughter of Edom, who dwells in the land of Uz; to you, too, will the cup pass, you will become drunk and you will vomit. **

²² ת *Your iniquity is expiated, O daughter of Zion, He will not exile you again; He remembers your iniquity, daughter of Edom, He will uncover your sins.*

ה   א-ב זְכֹר יהוה מֶה־הָיָה לָנוּ °הביט [°הַבִּיטָה ק] וּרְאֵה אֶת־חֶרְפָּתֵנוּ: נַחֲלָתֵנוּ
נֶהֶפְכָה לְזָרִים בָּתֵּינוּ לְנָכְרִים: ג יְתוֹמִים הָיִינוּ °אין [°וְאֵין ק] אָב אִמֹּתֵינוּ
ד-ה כְּאַלְמָנוֹת: מֵימֵינוּ בְּכֶסֶף שָׁתִינוּ עֵצֵינוּ בִּמְחִיר יָבֹאוּ: עַל צַוָּארֵנוּ נִרְדָּפְנוּ
ו יָגַעְנוּ °לא [°וְלֹא ק] הוּנַח־לָנוּ: מִצְרַיִם נָתַנּוּ יָד אַשּׁוּר לִשְׂבֹּעַ לָחֶם:
ז אֲבֹתֵינוּ חָטְאוּ °אינם [°וְאֵינָם ק] °אנחנו [°וַאֲנַחְנוּ ק] עֲוֹנֹתֵיהֶם סָבָלְנוּ:
ח-ט עֲבָדִים מָשְׁלוּ בָנוּ פֹּרֵק אֵין מִיָּדָם: בְּנַפְשֵׁנוּ נָבִיא לַחְמֵנוּ מִפְּנֵי חֶרֶב
י-יא הַמִּדְבָּר: עוֹרֵנוּ כְּתַנּוּר נִכְמָרוּ מִפְּנֵי זַלְעֲפוֹת רָעָב: נָשִׁים בְּצִיּוֹן עִנּוּ
יב-יג בְּתֻלֹת בְּעָרֵי יְהוּדָה: שָׂרִים בְּיָדָם נִתְלוּ פְּנֵי זְקֵנִים לֹא נֶהְדָּרוּ: בַּחוּרִים
יד טְחוֹן נָשָׂאוּ וּנְעָרִים בָּעֵץ כָּשָׁלוּ: זְקֵנִים מִשַּׁעַר שָׁבָתוּ בַּחוּרִים מִנְּגִינָתָם:
טו-טז שָׁבַת מְשׂוֹשׂ לִבֵּנוּ נֶהְפַּךְ לְאֵבֶל מְחֹלֵנוּ: נָפְלָה עֲטֶרֶת רֹאשֵׁנוּ אוֹי־נָא
יז-יח לָנוּ כִּי חָטָאנוּ: עַל־זֶה הָיָה דָוֶה לִבֵּנוּ עַל־אֵלֶּה חָשְׁכוּ עֵינֵינוּ: עַל הַר־
יט צִיּוֹן שֶׁשָּׁמֵם שׁוּעָלִים הִלְּכוּ־בוֹ: אַתָּה יהוה לְעוֹלָם תֵּשֵׁב כִּסְאֲךָ לְדֹר
כ-כא וָדוֹר: לָמָּה לָנֶצַח תִּשְׁכָּחֵנוּ תַּעַזְבֵנוּ לְאֹרֶךְ יָמִים: הֲשִׁיבֵנוּ יהוה ׀ אֵלֶיךָ
כב °ונשוב [°וְנָשׁוּבָה ק] חַדֵּשׁ יָמֵינוּ כְּקֶדֶם: כִּי אִם־מָאֹס מְאַסְתָּנוּ קָצַפְתָּ
עָלֵינוּ עַד־מְאֹד:

הֲשִׁיבֵנוּ יהוה ׀ אֵלֶיךָ וְנָשׁוּבָה חַדֵּשׁ יָמֵינוּ כְּקֶדֶם:

סכום פסוקי איכה מאה וחמשים וארבעה. וסימן טוב וְיִחֵל וְדוּמָם לתשועת ה'. וסימנו יסע קָדִים בשמים.

5:1. Chapter 5 differs from the previous four chapters in that it is not arranged alphabetically.

5:3. Fatherless orphans are often supported to some degree by their father's family. Even that possibility is not available to us (Ibn Ezra).

5:4. Afraid to fetch water from the river, we were forced to buy it at an inflated price from the enemy (Rashi).

5:7. We were punished because we persisted in committing the sins of our ancestors (Ibn Ezra).

5   ¹ Remember, * HASHEM, what has befallen us; look and see our disgrace. ² Our inheritance has been turned over to strangers; our houses to foreigners. ³ We have become [like] orphans, and there is no father; * our mothers are like widows. ⁴ We pay money to drink our own water, * obtain our wood at a price. ⁵ Upon our necks we are pursued; we toil, but nothing is left us. ⁶ We stretched out a hand to Egypt, and to Assyria to be satisfied with bread. ⁷ Our fathers have sinned and are no more, and we have suffered for their iniquities. * ⁸ Slaves ruled us, there is no redeemer from their hands. ⁹ In mortal danger we bring our bread, because of the sword of the wilderness. ¹⁰ Our skin was scorched like an oven, with the fever of famine. ¹¹ They ravaged women in Zion; maidens in the towns of Judah. ¹² Leaders were hanged by their hand, elders were shown no respect. ¹³ Young men drag the millstone, and youths stumble under the wood. ¹⁴ The elders are gone from the gate, the young men from their music. ¹⁵ Gone is the joy of our hearts, our dancing has turned into mourning. ¹⁶ The crown of our head has fallen; woe to us, for we have sinned. ¹⁷ For this our heart was ill, for these our eyes were dimmed: ¹⁸ for Mount Zion which lies desolate, foxes prowl over it. ¹⁹ Yet You, HASHEM, are enthroned forever, Your throne is ageless. ²⁰ Why do You ignore us eternally, forsake us for so long? ²¹ Bring us back to You, HASHEM, and we shall return, renew our days as of old. * ²² For even if You had utterly rejected us, You have already raged sufficiently against us.

> Bring us back to You, HASHEM, and we shall return,
> renew our days as of old. *

5:21. Israel beseeches God: take the initiative and draw us near; then we will repent our sins and return to You wholeheartedly (*Lechem Dim'ah*).

It is customary, during the public readings of *Lamenta-* *tions*, to repeat the *penultimate* verse. This is done to end the reading on a positive note. The same custom is also followed at the conclusion of *Isaiah, Malachi* and *Ecclesiastes (Rashi).*

Ecclesiastes קֹהֶלֶת

T
*he Book of Ecclesiastes begins on a note of gloom: "Futility of
futilities ... All is futile! What profit does man have for all his labor
which he toils beneath the sun?" (1:2-3). The Sages of the Talmud
were so troubled by this blanket condemnation that — even though
the author of the Book was King Solomon — they doubted that it should
be included in the sacred works of Scripture. What tipped the scales in
favor of Ecclesiastes was its concluding verse: "The sum of the matter
when all has been considered: Fear God and keep His commandments,
for that is man's whole duty" (12:13). The climax of the Book, the Sages
recognized, proved that the treatise — all of it — was intended to lead
people to the ultimate goal of fearing and serving God (Shabbos 30b).*

*What then of its gloomy passages? The Talmud explains that man's
striving is futile only if his goal is for success in matters that are under
the sun, but if he strives to advance in Torah and affairs of the spirit —
which preceded and surpass the sun — then his activities are hardly
futile. The Book of Ecclesiastes teaches that man should not be deceived
by the dazzling splendor that blinds so many people to what really
matters in life. Rather, one must maintain one's sense of values and
always recognize that man, as the only creature with a Godly soul, must
aspire to higher goals.*

*Ramban sets forth three themes of Ecclesiastes: (1) Solomon, the
very wealthy king who knew what opulence was, proclaimed that the
pleasures and allures of this world are fleeting and valueless.
(2) Spirituality is eternal; man must recognize that his health and
prosperity should be used to enable him to better serve God. (3) We are
faced with the troubling question of why good people suffer and bad
people prosper. We can know the answer only when we know and
understand all the elements upon which God bases His decisions. Such
intelligence is beyond our capacity, so our incomplete knowledge cannot
be used as a basis to doubt God's justice. That level of understanding
will come only when the Messiah leads the world to its future state of
perfection. Until then, our faith must remain strong.*

*Because Ecclesiastes focuses man's aspirations on what is truly
important, it is read publicly during the Succos festival, the time of joy
and the prosperity of the harvest season, when man's purpose can easily
be swamped by the thrill of success.*

א   א-ב דִּבְרֵי֙ קֹהֶ֣לֶת בֶּן־דָּוִ֔ד מֶ֖לֶךְ בִּירֽוּשָׁלָֽ͏ִם: הֲבֵ֤ל הֲבָלִים֙ אָמַ֣ר קֹהֶ֔לֶת הֲבֵ֥ל

ג הֲבָלִ֖ים הַכֹּ֥ל הָֽבֶל: מַה־יִּתְר֖וֹן לָֽאָדָ֑ם בְּכָל־עֲמָל֔וֹ שֶֽׁיַּעֲמֹ֖ל תַּ֥חַת הַשָּֽׁמֶשׁ:

ד-ה דּ֤וֹר הֹלֵךְ֙ וְד֣וֹר בָּ֔א וְהָאָ֖רֶץ לְעוֹלָ֥ם עֹמָֽדֶת: וְזָרַ֤ח הַשֶּׁ֙מֶשׁ֙ וּבָ֣א הַשָּׁ֔מֶשׁ

ו וְאֶ֨ל־מְקוֹמ֔וֹ שׁוֹאֵ֛ף זוֹרֵ֥חַ ה֖וּא שָֽׁם: הוֹלֵךְ֙ אֶל־דָּר֔וֹם וְסוֹבֵ֖ב אֶל־צָפ֑וֹן

ז סוֹבֵ֣ב ׀ סֹבֵב֮ הוֹלֵ֣ךְ הָר֒וּחַ֒ וְעַל־סְבִיבֹתָ֖יו שָׁ֥ב הָרֽוּחַ: כָּל־הַנְּחָלִים֙ הֹלְכִ֣ים

אֶל־הַיָּ֔ם וְהַיָּ֖ם אֵינֶ֣נּוּ מָלֵ֑א אֶל־מְק֗וֹם שֶׁ֤הַנְּחָלִים֙ הֹֽלְכִ֔ים שָׁ֛ם הֵ֥ם שָׁבִ֖ים

ח לָלָֽכֶת: כָּל־הַדְּבָרִ֣ים יְגֵעִ֔ים לֹא־יוּכַ֥ל אִ֖ישׁ לְדַבֵּ֑ר לֹא־תִשְׂבַּ֥ע עַ֙יִן֙ לִרְא֔וֹת

ט וְלֹא־תִמָּלֵ֥א אֹ֖זֶן מִשְּׁמֹֽעַ: מַה־שֶּֽׁהָיָה֙ ה֣וּא שֶׁיִּֽהְיֶ֔ה וּמַה־שֶּׁנַּֽעֲשָׂ֔ה ה֖וּא

י שֶׁיֵּעָשֶׂ֑ה וְאֵ֥ין כָּל־חָדָ֖שׁ תַּ֥חַת הַשָּֽׁמֶשׁ: יֵ֥שׁ דָּבָ֛ר שֶׁיֹּאמַ֥ר רְאֵה־זֶ֖ה חָדָ֣שׁ

יא ה֑וּא כְּבָר֙ הָיָ֣ה לְעֹֽלָמִ֔ים אֲשֶׁ֥ר הָיָ֖ה מִלְּפָנֵֽנוּ: אֵ֥ין זִכְר֖וֹן לָרִֽאשֹׁנִ֑ים וְגַ֣ם

לָאַחֲרֹנִ֗ים שֶׁיִּֽהְיוּ֙ לֹֽא־יִהְיֶ֤ה לָהֶם֙ זִכָּר֔וֹן עִ֥ם שֶׁיִּֽהְי֖וּ לָאַחֲרֹנָֽה:

יב-יג אֲנִ֣י קֹהֶ֗לֶת הָיִ֥יתִי מֶ֛לֶךְ עַל־יִשְׂרָאֵ֖ל בִּירֽוּשָׁלָֽ͏ִם: וְנָתַ֣תִּי אֶת־לִבִּ֗י לִדְר֤וֹשׁ

וְלָתוּר֙ בַּֽחָכְמָ֔ה עַ֛ל כָּל־אֲשֶׁ֥ר נַעֲשָׂ֖ה תַּ֣חַת הַשָּׁמָ֑יִם ה֣וּא ׀ עִנְיַ֣ן רָ֗ע נָתַ֧ן

יד אֱלֹהִ֛ים לִבְנֵ֥י הָאָדָ֖ם לַעֲנ֥וֹת בּֽוֹ: רָאִ֙יתִי֙ אֶת־כָּל־הַֽמַּעֲשִׂ֔ים שֶֽׁנַּעֲשׂ֖וּ

טו תַּ֣חַת הַשָּׁ֑מֶשׁ וְהִנֵּ֥ה הַכֹּ֛ל הֶ֖בֶל וּרְע֥וּת רֽוּחַ: מְעֻוָּ֖ת לֹא־יוּכַ֣ל לִתְקֹ֑ן וְחֶסְר֖וֹן

טז לֹא־יוּכַ֥ל לְהִמָּנֽוֹת: דִּבַּ֨רְתִּי אֲנִ֤י עִם־לִבִּי֙ לֵאמֹ֔ר אֲנִ֗י הִנֵּ֨ה הִגְדַּ֤לְתִּי

וְהוֹסַ֙פְתִּי֙ חָכְמָ֔ה עַ֛ל כָּל־אֲשֶׁר־הָיָ֥ה לְפָנַ֖י עַל־יְרֽוּשָׁלָ֑͏ִם וְלִבִּ֛י רָאָ֥ה

יז הַרְבֵּ֖ה חָכְמָ֥ה וָדָֽעַת: וָאֶתְּנָ֤ה לִבִּי֙ לָדַ֣עַת חָכְמָ֔ה וְדַ֥עַת הֹלֵל֖וֹת וְשִׂכְל֑וֹת

יח יָדַ֕עְתִּי שֶׁגַּם־זֶ֖ה ה֣וּא רַעְי֣וֹן רֽוּחַ: כִּ֛י בְּרֹ֥ב חָכְמָ֖ה רָב־כָּ֑עַס וְיוֹסִ֥יף

ב א יוֹסִ֥יף מַכְאֽוֹב: אָמַ֤רְתִּי אֲנִי֙ בְּלִבִּ֔י לְכָה־נָּ֛א אֲנַסְּכָ֥ה בְשִׂמְחָ֖ה וּרְאֵ֣ה בְט֑וֹב

ב וְהִנֵּ֥ה גַם־ה֖וּא הָֽבֶל: לִשְׂח֖וֹק אָמַ֣רְתִּי מְהוֹלָ֑ל וּלְשִׂמְחָ֖ה מַה־זֹּ֥ה עֹשָֽׂה:

ג תַּ֣רְתִּי בְלִבִּ֗י לִמְשׁ֤וֹךְ בַּיַּ֙יִן֙ אֶת־בְּשָׂרִ֔י וְלִבִּ֖י נֹהֵ֣ג בַּֽחָכְמָ֑ה וְלֶאֱחֹ֣ז בְּסִכְל֗וּת

עַ֣ד ׀ אֲשֶׁ֣ר אֶרְאֶ֗ה אֵי־זֶ֨ה ט֜וֹב לִבְנֵ֤י הָאָדָם֙ אֲשֶׁ֤ר יַעֲשׂוּ֙ תַּ֣חַת הַשָּׁמַ֔יִם

ד מִסְפַּ֖ר יְמֵ֥י חַיֵּיהֶֽם: הִגְדַּ֖לְתִּי מַעֲשָׂ֑י בָּנִ֤יתִי לִי֙ בָּתִּ֔ים נָטַ֥עְתִּי לִ֖י כְּרָמִֽים:

ה-ו עָשִׂ֣יתִי לִ֔י גַּנּ֖וֹת וּפַרְדֵּסִ֑ים וְנָטַ֥עְתִּי בָהֶ֖ם עֵ֥ץ כָּל־פֶּֽרִי: עָשִׂ֥יתִי לִ֖י בְּרֵכ֣וֹת

ז מָ֑יִם לְהַשְׁק֣וֹת מֵהֶ֔ם יַ֖עַר צוֹמֵ֥חַ עֵצִֽים: קָנִ֙יתִי֙ עֲבָדִ֣ים וּשְׁפָח֔וֹת וּבְנֵי־

בַ֖יִת הָ֣יָה לִ֑י גַּם֩ מִקְנֶ֨ה בָקָ֤ר וָצֹאן֙ הַרְבֵּ֣ה הָ֣יָה לִ֔י מִכֹּ֛ל שֶֽׁהָי֥וּ לְפָנַ֖י

ח בִּירֽוּשָׁלָֽ͏ִם: כָּנַ֤סְתִּי לִי֙ גַּם־כֶּ֣סֶף וְזָהָ֔ב וּסְגֻלַּ֥ת מְלָכִ֖ים וְהַמְּדִינ֑וֹת עָשִׂ֤יתִי לִי֙

1:1. The author of this Book was King Solomon, who was also called "Koheles," because of the wisdom שֶׁנִּקְהֲלָה בּוֹ, "which was assembled within him" (*Ibn Ezra*), or because שֶׁקִּהֵל חָכְמוֹת הַרְבֵּה, "he assembled many branches of wisdom" (*Rashi*).

1:2. Something empty of substance, utterly futile.

1:5. This verse refers allegorically to the wicked. Although the "sun" of wicked people shines and they prosper, ultimately their "sun" will set (*Rashi*).

1:7. The elements are unable to break away from their monotonous course. Since there is no lasting value to toil in this world, why should man strive aimlessly for material gain? (*Ibn Ezra*).

1:8. If one gives up Torah study to engage in idle talk, visual indulgence or aural gratification, he will find them "wearying" and unsatisfying (*Rashi*).

1:9. Whatever we view as new has already been provided for in God's infinite wisdom. He created the resources, conditions and concepts for all discoveries and inventions until the end of time.

1

¹ The words of Koheles son of David, king in Jerusalem: *
² *Futility of futilities!* * — said Koheles — *futility of futilities! All is futile!*
³ What profit does man have for all his labor which he toils beneath the sun?
⁴ A generation goes and a generation comes, but the earth endures forever.
⁵ And the sun rises and the sun sets * — then to its place it rushes; there it rises again. ⁶ It goes toward the south and veers toward the north; the wind goes round and round, and on its rounds the wind returns. ⁷ All the rivers flow into the sea, yet the sea is not full; to the place where the rivers flow, there they flow once more. *

⁸ All words are wearying, one becomes speechless; the eye is never sated with seeing, nor the ear filled with hearing. * ⁹ Whatever has been is what will be, and whatever has been done is what will be done. There is nothing new beneath the sun! * ¹⁰ Sometimes there is something of which one says: "Look, this is new!" — it has already existed in the ages before us. ¹¹ As there is no recollection of the former ones, so too, of the latter ones that are yet to be, there will be no recollection among those of a still later time.

¹² I, Koheles, was king over Israel in Jerusalem. ¹³ I applied my mind to seek and probe by wisdom all that happens beneath the sky — it is a sorry task that God has given to the sons of man with which to be concerned. ¹⁴ I have seen all the deeds done beneath the sun, and behold all is futile and a vexation of the spirit. ¹⁵ A twisted thing cannot be made straight; * and what is not there cannot be numbered.

¹⁶ I said to myself: Here I have acquired great wisdom, more than any of my predecessors over Jerusalem, and my mind has had much experience with wisdom and knowledge. ¹⁷ I applied my mind to know wisdom and to know madness and folly. I perceived that this, too, is a vexation of the spirit. ¹⁸ For with much wisdom comes much grief, and he who increases knowledge increases pain. *

2

¹ I said to myself: Come, I will experiment with joy and enjoy pleasure. That, too, turned out to be futile. * ² I said of laughter, "It is mad!" and of joy, "what does it accomplish!"

³ I ventured to stimulate my body with wine — while my heart is involved with wisdom * — and to grasp folly, until I can discern which is best for mankind to do under the heavens during the brief span of their lives. ⁴ I acted in grand style: * I built myself houses, I planted vineyards; ⁵ I made for myself gardens and orchards and planted in them every kind of fruit tree; ⁶ I constructed pools from which to irrigate a grove of young trees; ⁷ I bought slaves — male and female — and I acquired stewards; I also owned more possessions, both cattle and sheep, than all of my predecessors in Jerusalem; ⁸ I amassed even silver and gold for myself, and the treasure of kings and the provinces; I provided myself

---

1:15. If one had illicit relations and begot a *mamzer*, the result of his sin lives on, unlike one who steals and can always return the stolen item. Alternatively, the verse refers to a sage who abandoned the Torah — from a good beginning he became crooked (*Rashi*).

1:18. Increased knowledge of the futility of strivings will only increase the wise man's pain at this realization (*Metzudos*).

2:1. Because much evil is caused by light-hearted frivolity (*Rashi*), this obsession with worldly pleasure is itself futility (*Sforno*).

2:3. Having found pure wisdom a source of pain [1:18] and merriment futile [2:1], he resolves to combine pleasure with wisdom (*Ibn Ezra*).

2:4-10. Solomon relates his experiment with self-indulgence, only to conclude that "it was all futile" (v. 11).

ט שָׁרִים וְשָׁרוֹת וְתַעֲנֻגֹת בְּנֵי הָאָדָם שִׁדָּה וְשִׁדּוֹת: וְגָדַלְתִּי וְהוֹסַפְתִּי מִכֹּל

י שֶׁהָיָה לְפָנַי בִּירוּשָׁלָ͏ִם אַף חָכְמָתִי עָמְדָה לִּי: וְכֹל אֲשֶׁר שָׁאֲלוּ עֵינַי לֹא אָצַלְתִּי מֵהֶם לֹא־מָנַעְתִּי אֶת־לִבִּי מִכָּל־שִׂמְחָה כִּי־לִבִּי שָׂמֵחַ מִכָּל־

יא עֲמָלִי וְזֶה־הָיָה חֶלְקִי מִכָּל־עֲמָלִי: וּפָנִיתִי אֲנִי בְּכָל־מַעֲשַׂי שֶׁעָשׂוּ יָדַי וּבֶעָמָל שֶׁעָמַלְתִּי לַעֲשׂוֹת וְהִנֵּה הַכֹּל הֶבֶל וּרְעוּת רוּחַ וְאֵין יִתְרוֹן תַּחַת

יב הַשָּׁמֶשׁ: וּפָנִיתִי אֲנִי לִרְאוֹת חָכְמָה וְהוֹלֵלוֹת וְסִכְלוּת כִּי ׀ מֶה הָאָדָם

יג שֶׁיָּבוֹא אַחֲרֵי הַמֶּלֶךְ אֵת אֲשֶׁר־כְּבָר עָשׂוּהוּ: וְרָאִיתִי אָנִי שֶׁיֵּשׁ יִתְרוֹן

יד לַחָכְמָה מִן־הַסִּכְלוּת כִּיתְרוֹן הָאוֹר מִן־הַחֹשֶׁךְ: הֶחָכָם עֵינָיו בְּרֹאשׁוֹ וְהַכְּסִיל בַּחֹשֶׁךְ הוֹלֵךְ וְיָדַעְתִּי גַם־אָנִי שֶׁמִּקְרֶה אֶחָד יִקְרֶה אֶת־כֻּלָּם:

טו וְאָמַרְתִּי אֲנִי בְּלִבִּי כְּמִקְרֵה הַכְּסִיל גַּם־אֲנִי יִקְרֵנִי וְלָמָּה חָכַמְתִּי אֲנִי אָז

טז יוֹתֵר וְדִבַּרְתִּי בְלִבִּי שֶׁגַּם־זֶה הָבֶל: כִּי אֵין זִכְרוֹן לֶחָכָם עִם־הַכְּסִיל לְעוֹלָם בְּשֶׁכְּבָר הַיָּמִים הַבָּאִים הַכֹּל נִשְׁכָּח וְאֵיךְ יָמוּת הֶחָכָם עִם־הַכְּסִיל:

יז וְשָׂנֵאתִי אֶת־הַחַיִּים כִּי רַע עָלַי הַמַּעֲשֶׂה שֶׁנַּעֲשָׂה תַּחַת הַשָּׁמֶשׁ כִּי־הַכֹּל

יח הֶבֶל וּרְעוּת רוּחַ: וְשָׂנֵאתִי אֲנִי אֶת־כָּל־עֲמָלִי שֶׁאֲנִי עָמֵל תַּחַת הַשָּׁמֶשׁ

יט שֶׁאַנִּיחֶנּוּ לָאָדָם שֶׁיִּהְיֶה אַחֲרָי: וּמִי יוֹדֵעַ הֶחָכָם יִהְיֶה אוֹ סָכָל וְיִשְׁלַט

כ בְּכָל־עֲמָלִי שֶׁעָמַלְתִּי וְשֶׁחָכַמְתִּי תַּחַת הַשָּׁמֶשׁ גַּם־זֶה הָבֶל: וְסַבּוֹתִי אֲנִי

כא לְיַאֵשׁ אֶת־לִבִּי עַל כָּל־הֶעָמָל שֶׁעָמַלְתִּי תַּחַת הַשָּׁמֶשׁ: כִּי־יֵשׁ אָדָם שֶׁעֲמָלוֹ בְּחָכְמָה וּבְדַעַת וּבְכִשְׁרוֹן וּלְאָדָם שֶׁלֹּא עָמַל־בּוֹ יִתְּנֶנּוּ חֶלְקוֹ

כב גַּם־זֶה הֶבֶל וְרָעָה רַבָּה: כִּי מֶה־הֹוֶה לָאָדָם בְּכָל־עֲמָלוֹ וּבְרַעְיוֹן לִבּוֹ

כג שֶׁהוּא עָמֵל תַּחַת הַשָּׁמֶשׁ: כִּי כָל־יָמָיו מַכְאֹבִים וָכַעַס עִנְיָנוֹ גַּם־בַּלַּיְלָה

כד לֹא־שָׁכַב לִבּוֹ גַּם־זֶה הֶבֶל הוּא: אֵין־טוֹב בָּאָדָם שֶׁיֹּאכַל וְשָׁתָה וְהֶרְאָה אֶת־נַפְשׁוֹ טוֹב בַּעֲמָלוֹ גַּם־זֹה רָאִיתִי אָנִי כִּי מִיַּד הָאֱלֹהִים הִיא: כִּי מִי

כה

כו יֹאכַל וּמִי יָחוּשׁ חוּץ מִמֶּנִּי: כִּי לְאָדָם שֶׁטּוֹב לְפָנָיו נָתַן חָכְמָה וְדַעַת וְשִׂמְחָה וְלַחוֹטֶא נָתַן עִנְיָן לֶאֱסֹף וְלִכְנוֹס לָתֵת לְטוֹב לִפְנֵי הָאֱלֹהִים

ג א גַּם־זֶה הֶבֶל וּרְעוּת רוּחַ: לַכֹּל זְמָן וְעֵת לְכָל־חֵפֶץ תַּחַת הַשָּׁמָיִם:

ב עֵת לָלֶדֶת   וְעֵת לָמוּת
עֵת לָטַעַת   וְעֵת לַעֲקוֹר נָטוּעַ:

ג עֵת לַהֲרוֹג   וְעֵת לִרְפּוֹא
עֵת לִפְרוֹץ   וְעֵת לִבְנוֹת:

ד עֵת לִבְכּוֹת   וְעֵת לִשְׂחוֹק

2:10. My only reward for all my endeavors was fleeting satisfaction (*Ibn Ezra*).

2:12. Since the king's personal experience qualifies him to evaluate the difference between wisdom and folly, there is no need for anyone to repeat the experiment.

2:13. Just as one can appreciate light only by comparison with darkness, so folly helps one cherish wisdom.

2:16. How can one even suggest that the deaths of the wise man and the fool are similar! [The former's fame lives on; the latter leaves nothing worth remembering.] (*Metzudos, Alshich*).

2:18-23. Koheles is further distressed because man's strenuously acquired wealth will go to heirs, whose prudence and wisdom are questionable.

with various musical instruments, and with every human luxury — chests and chests of them. ⁹ *Thus, I grew and surpassed any of my predecessors in Jerusalem; still, my wisdom stayed with me.* ¹⁰ *Whatever my eyes desired I did not deny them; I did not deprive myself of any kind of joy. Indeed, my heart drew joy from all my activities, and this was my reward for all my endeavors.* *

¹¹ *Then I looked at all the things that I had done and the energy I had expended in doing them; it was clear that it was all futile and a vexation of the spirit — and there is no real profit under the sun.*

¹² *Then I turned my attention to appraising wisdom with madness and folly — for what can man who comes after the king do? It has already been done.* * ¹³*And I perceived that wisdom excels folly as light excels darkness.* * ¹⁴*The wise man has his eyes in his head, whereas a fool walks in darkness. But I also realized that the same fate awaits them all.* ¹⁵ *So I said to myself: The fate of the fool will befall me also; to what advantage, then, have I become wise? But I concluded that this, too, was futility,* ¹⁶ *for there is no comparison between the remembrance of the wise man and of the fool at all, for as the succeeding days roll by, is all forgotten? How can the wise man die like the fool?* *

¹⁷ *So I hated life, for I was depressed by all that goes on under the sun, because everything is futile and a vexation of the spirit.*

¹⁸ *Thus I hated all my achievements laboring under the sun, for I must leave it to the man who succeeds me* * ¹⁹ *— and who knows whether he will be wise or foolish? — and he will have control of all my possessions for which I toiled and have shown myself wise beneath the sun. This, too, is futility.* ²⁰ *So I turned my heart to despair of all that I had achieved by laboring under the sun,* ²¹ *for there is a man who labored with wisdom, knowledge and skill, yet he must give over his portion to one who has not toiled for it. This, too, is futility and a great evil.* ²² *For what has a man of all his toil and his stress in which he labors beneath the sun?* ²³ *For all his days are painful, and his business is a vexation; even at night his mind has no rest. This, too, is futility!*

²⁴ *Is it not good for man that he eats and drinks and shows his soul satisfaction in his labor? And even that, I perceived, is from the hand of God. —* ²⁵ *For who should eat and who should make haste except me?* * ²⁶*To the man who pleases Him He has given wisdom, knowledge and joy; but to the sinner He has given the urge to gather and amass — that he may give it over to one who is pleasing to God. That, too, is futility and a vexation of the spirit.*

3 ¹ *E**verything has its season, and there is a time for everything under the heaven:*

²*A time to be born*   *and a time to die;* *
    a time to plant   *and a time to uproot the planted.*
³*A time to kill* *   *and a time to heal;*
    a time to wreck   *and a time to build.*
⁴*A time to weep*   *and a time to laugh;*

2:25. If all my property will eventually pass on to others, I should view my possessions as a Divine gift and perform lofty spiritual deeds with them while I am still alive.

3:2. Just as he was pure in the hour of his birth, so should he be pure in the hour of his death (*Midrash*).

3:3. In wartime (*Midrash*), or in the legal execution of criminals (*Michlol Yofi*).

וְעֵת רְקוֹד: עֵת סְפוֹד

וְעֵת כְּנוֹס אֲבָנִים ה עֵת לְהַשְׁלִיךְ אֲבָנִים

וְעֵת לִרְחֹק מֵחַבֵּק: עֵת לַחֲבוֹק

וְעֵת לְאַבֵּד ו עֵת לְבַקֵּשׁ

וְעֵת לְהַשְׁלִיךְ: עֵת לִשְׁמוֹר

וְעֵת לִתְפּוֹר ז עֵת לִקְרוֹעַ

וְעֵת לְדַבֵּר: עֵת לַחֲשׁוֹת

וְעֵת לִשְׂנֹא ח עֵת לֶאֱהֹב

וְעֵת שָׁלוֹם: עֵת מִלְחָמָה

ט-י מַה־יִּתְרוֹן הָעוֹשֶׂה בַּאֲשֶׁר הוּא עָמֵל: רָאִיתִי אֶת־הָעִנְיָן אֲשֶׁר נָתַן אֱלֹהִים

יא לִבְנֵי הָאָדָם לַעֲנוֹת בּוֹ: אֶת־הַכֹּל עָשָׂה יָפֶה בְעִתּוֹ גַּם אֶת־הָעֹלָם נָתַן בְּלִבָּם מִבְּלִי אֲשֶׁר לֹא־יִמְצָא הָאָדָם אֶת־הַמַּעֲשֶׂה אֲשֶׁר־עָשָׂה הָאֱלֹהִים

יב מֵרֹאשׁ וְעַד־סוֹף: יָדַעְתִּי כִּי אֵין טוֹב בָּם כִּי אִם־לִשְׂמוֹחַ וְלַעֲשׂוֹת טוֹב

יג בְּחַיָּיו: וְגַם כָּל־הָאָדָם שֶׁיֹּאכַל וְשָׁתָה וְרָאָה טוֹב בְּכָל־עֲמָלוֹ מַתַּת

יד אֱלֹהִים הִיא: יָדַעְתִּי כִּי כָּל־אֲשֶׁר יַעֲשֶׂה הָאֱלֹהִים הוּא יִהְיֶה לְעוֹלָם עָלָיו

טו אֵין לְהוֹסִיף וּמִמֶּנּוּ אֵין לִגְרֹעַ וְהָאֱלֹהִים עָשָׂה שֶׁיִּרְאוּ מִלְּפָנָיו: מַה־שֶּׁהָיָה

טז כְּבָר הוּא וַאֲשֶׁר לִהְיוֹת כְּבָר הָיָה וְהָאֱלֹהִים יְבַקֵּשׁ אֶת־נִרְדָּף: וְעוֹד רָאִיתִי תַּחַת הַשָּׁמֶשׁ מְקוֹם הַמִּשְׁפָּט שָׁמָּה הָרֶשַׁע וּמְקוֹם הַצֶּדֶק שָׁמָּה

יז הָרָשַׁע: אָמַרְתִּי אֲנִי בְּלִבִּי אֶת־הַצַּדִּיק וְאֶת־הָרָשָׁע יִשְׁפֹּט הָאֱלֹהִים כִּי־

יח עֵת לְכָל־חֵפֶץ וְעַל כָּל־הַמַּעֲשֶׂה שָׁם: אָמַרְתִּי אֲנִי בְּלִבִּי עַל־דִּבְרַת בְּנֵי

יט הָאָדָם לְבָרָם הָאֱלֹהִים וְלִרְאוֹת שְׁהֶם־בְּהֵמָה הֵמָּה לָהֶם: כִּי מִקְרֶה בְנֵי־ הָאָדָם וּמִקְרֶה הַבְּהֵמָה וּמִקְרֶה אֶחָד לָהֶם כְּמוֹת זֶה כֵּן מוֹת זֶה וְרוּחַ אֶחָד

כ לַכֹּל וּמוֹתַר הָאָדָם מִן־הַבְּהֵמָה אָיִן כִּי הַכֹּל הָבֶל: הַכֹּל הוֹלֵךְ אֶל־מָקוֹם

כא אֶחָד הַכֹּל הָיָה מִן־הֶעָפָר וְהַכֹּל שָׁב אֶל־הֶעָפָר: מִי יוֹדֵעַ רוּחַ בְּנֵי הָאָדָם

כב הָעֹלָה הִיא לְמָעְלָה וְרוּחַ הַבְּהֵמָה הַיֹּרֶדֶת הִיא לְמַטָּה לָאָרֶץ: וְרָאִיתִי כִּי אֵין טוֹב מֵאֲשֶׁר יִשְׂמַח הָאָדָם בְּמַעֲשָׂיו כִּי־הוּא חֶלְקוֹ כִּי מִי יְבִיאֶנּוּ

ד א לִרְאוֹת בְּמֶה שֶׁיִּהְיֶה אַחֲרָיו: וְשַׁבְתִּי אֲנִי וָאֶרְאֶה אֶת־כָּל־הָעֲשֻׁקִים אֲשֶׁר נַעֲשִׂים תַּחַת הַשָּׁמֶשׁ וְהִנֵּה ׀ דִּמְעַת הָעֲשׁוּקִים וְאֵין לָהֶם מְנַחֵם וּמִיַּד

ב עֹשְׁקֵיהֶם כֹּחַ וְאֵין לָהֶם מְנַחֵם: וְשַׁבֵּחַ אֲנִי אֶת־הַמֵּתִים שֶׁכְּבָר מֵתוּ

ג מִן־הַחַיִּים אֲשֶׁר הֵמָּה חַיִּים עֲדֶנָה: וְטוֹב מִשְּׁנֵיהֶם אֵת אֲשֶׁר־עֲדֶן לֹא הָיָה אֲשֶׁר לֹא־רָאָה אֶת־הַמַּעֲשֶׂה הָרָע אֲשֶׁר נַעֲשָׂה תַּחַת הַשָּׁמֶשׁ:

ד וְרָאִיתִי אֲנִי אֶת־כָּל־עָמָל וְאֵת כָּל־כִּשְׁרוֹן הַמַּעֲשֶׂה כִּי הִיא קִנְאַת־אִישׁ

3:7. "To rend" garments over the dead; "to mend" new clothes for a wedding (*R' Saadiah Gaon*).

3:10. I perceive that God caused man to toil in order to keep him subservient lest he rebel against Him (*Sforno*).

3:12. There is nothing better for people than to rejoice in their lot and do what is right in God's eyes while they

                                    a time to wail   and a time to dance.
⁵ A time to scatter stones   and a time to gather stones;
                                    a time to embrace   and a time to shun embraces.
⁶ A time to seek   and a time to lose;
                                    a time to keep   and a time to discard.
⁷ A time to rend   and a time to mend; *
                                    a time to be silent   and a time to speak.
⁸ A time to love   and a time to hate;
                                    a time for war   and a time for peace.

⁹ What gain, then, has the worker by his toil?

¹⁰ I have observed the task which God has given the sons of man to be concerned with: * ¹¹ He made everything beautiful in its time; He has also put an enigma into their minds so that man cannot comprehend what God has done from beginning to end.

¹² Thus I perceived that there is nothing better for them than to rejoice and do good in his life. * ¹³ Indeed every man who eats and drinks and finds satisfaction in all his labor — this is a gift of God.

¹⁴ I realized that whatever God does will endure forever: Nothing can be added to it and nothing can be subtracted from it, and God has acted so that [man] should stand in awe of Him. ¹⁵ What has been, already exists, and what is still to be, has already been, and God always seeks the pursued. *

¹⁶ Furthermore, I have observed beneath the sun: * In the place of justice there is wickedness, and in the place of righteousness there is wickedness. ¹⁷ I mused: God will judge the righteous and the wicked, for there is a time for everything and for every deed there.

¹⁸ Then I said to myself concerning men: "God has chosen them, but only to see that they themselves are as beasts."* ¹⁹ For the fate of men and the fate of beast — they have one and the same fate: As one dies, so dies the other, and they all have the same spirit. Man has no superiority over beast, for all is futile. ²⁰ All go to the same place; all originate from dust and all return to dust. ²¹ Who perceives that the spirit of man is the one that ascends on high while the spirit of the beast is the one that descends down into the earth? ²² I therefore observed that there is nothing better for man than to be happy in what he is doing, for that is his lot. For who can enable him to see what will be after him?

4   ¹ I returned and contemplated all the acts of oppression that are committed beneath the sun: Behold! Tears of the oppressed with none to comfort them, and their oppressors have the power — with none to comfort them. ² So I consider more fortunate the dead who have already died than the living who are still alive; ³ but better than either of them is he who has not yet been, and has never witnessed the evil that is committed beneath the sun.

⁴ And I saw that all labor and all skillful enterprise spring from man's rivalry

---

are yet alive (Rashi).

3:15. History repeats itself. "And God always seeks [i.e., to be on the side of] the pursued," and to exact retribution from the pursuer. Ultimately man will be held to account for his deeds (Rashi).

3:16-22. Koheles now discusses corruption in the administration of justice, eventual Divine retribution

against the wicked, and the seeming similarity between man and beast.

3:18. Although men are vain about their supposed superiority, God has selected the most eminent among them — kings and officers — to demonstrate that they can be as selfish and shortsighted as any other animal or beast.

ה מְרֵעֵהוּ גַּם־זֶה הֶבֶל וּרְעוּת רוּחַ: הַכְּסִיל חֹבֵק אֶת־יָדָיו וְאֹכֵל אֶת־בְּשָׂרוֹ:

ו־ז טוֹב מְלֹא כַף נָחַת מִמְּלֹא חָפְנַיִם עָמָל וּרְעוּת רוּחַ: וְשַׁבְתִּי אֲנִי וָאֶרְאֶה

ח הֶבֶל תַּחַת הַשָּׁמֶשׁ: יֵשׁ אֶחָד וְאֵין שֵׁנִי גַּם בֵּן וָאָח אֵין־לוֹ וְאֵין קֵץ לְכָל־ עֲמָלוֹ גַּם־°עֵינָיו [°עֵינוֹ ק] לֹא־תִשְׂבַּע עֹשֶׁר וּלְמִי ׀ אֲנִי עָמֵל וּמְחַסֵּר

ט אֶת־נַפְשִׁי מִטּוֹבָה גַּם־זֶה הֶבֶל וְעִנְיַן רָע הוּא: טוֹבִים הַשְּׁנַיִם מִן־הָאֶחָד

י אֲשֶׁר יֵשׁ־לָהֶם שָׂכָר טוֹב בַּעֲמָלָם: כִּי אִם־יִפֹּלוּ הָאֶחָד יָקִים אֶת־חֲבֵרוֹ

יא וְאִילוֹ הָאֶחָד שֶׁיִּפּוֹל וְאֵין שֵׁנִי לַהֲקִימוֹ: גַּם אִם־יִשְׁכְּבוּ שְׁנַיִם וְחַם לָהֶם

יב וּלְאֶחָד אֵיךְ יֵחָם: וְאִם־יִתְקְפוֹ הָאֶחָד הַשְּׁנַיִם יַעַמְדוּ נֶגְדּוֹ וְהַחוּט

יג הַמְשֻׁלָּשׁ לֹא בִמְהֵרָה יִנָּתֵק: טוֹב יֶלֶד מִסְכֵּן וְחָכָם מִמֶּלֶךְ זָקֵן וּכְסִיל

יד אֲשֶׁר לֹא־יָדַע לְהִזָּהֵר עוֹד: כִּי־מִבֵּית הָסוּרִים יָצָא לִמְלֹךְ כִּי גַּם

טו בְּמַלְכוּתוֹ נוֹלַד רָשׁ: רָאִיתִי אֶת־כָּל־הַחַיִּים הַמְהַלְּכִים תַּחַת הַשָּׁמֶשׁ עִם

טז הַיֶּלֶד הַשֵּׁנִי אֲשֶׁר יַעֲמֹד תַּחְתָּיו: אֵין־קֵץ לְכָל־הָעָם לְכֹל אֲשֶׁר־הָיָה לִפְנֵיהֶם גַּם הָאַחֲרוֹנִים לֹא יִשְׂמְחוּ־בוֹ כִּי־גַם־זֶה הֶבֶל וְרַעְיוֹן רוּחַ:

יז שְׁמֹר °רַגְלֶיךָ [°רַגְלְךָ ק] כַּאֲשֶׁר תֵּלֵךְ אֶל־בֵּית הָאֱלֹהִים וְקָרוֹב לִשְׁמֹעַ

ה

א מִתֵּת הַכְּסִילִים זָבַח כִּי־אֵינָם יוֹדְעִים לַעֲשׂוֹת רָע: אַל־תְּבַהֵל עַל־פִּיךָ וְלִבְּךָ אַל־יְמַהֵר לְהוֹצִיא דָבָר לִפְנֵי הָאֱלֹהִים כִּי הָאֱלֹהִים בַּשָּׁמַיִם וְאַתָּה

ב עַל־הָאָרֶץ עַל־כֵּן יִהְיוּ דְבָרֶיךָ מְעַטִּים: כִּי בָּא הַחֲלוֹם בְּרֹב עִנְיָן וְקוֹל

ג כְּסִיל בְּרֹב דְּבָרִים: כַּאֲשֶׁר תִּדֹּר נֶדֶר לֵאלֹהִים אַל־תְּאַחֵר לְשַׁלְּמוֹ

ד כִּי אֵין חֵפֶץ בַּכְּסִילִים אֵת אֲשֶׁר־תִּדֹּר שַׁלֵּם: טוֹב אֲשֶׁר לֹא־תִדֹּר

ה מִשֶּׁתִּדּוֹר וְלֹא תְשַׁלֵּם: אַל־תִּתֵּן אֶת־פִּיךָ לַחֲטִיא אֶת־בְּשָׂרֶךָ וְאַל־ תֹּאמַר לִפְנֵי הַמַּלְאָךְ כִּי שְׁגָגָה הִיא לָמָּה יִקְצֹף הָאֱלֹהִים עַל־קוֹלֶךָ

ו וְחִבֵּל אֶת־מַעֲשֵׂה יָדֶיךָ: כִּי בְרֹב חֲלֹמוֹת וַהֲבָלִים וּדְבָרִים הַרְבֵּה כִּי אֶת־

ז הָאֱלֹהִים יְרָא: אִם־עֹשֶׁק רָשׁ וְגֵזֶל מִשְׁפָּט וָצֶדֶק תִּרְאֶה בַמְּדִינָה אַל־

ח תִּתְמַהּ עַל־הַחֵפֶץ כִּי גָבֹהַּ מֵעַל גָּבֹהַּ שֹׁמֵר וּגְבֹהִים עֲלֵיהֶם: וְיִתְרוֹן אֶרֶץ

ט בַּכֹּל °הִיא [°הוּא ק] מֶלֶךְ לְשָׂדֶה נֶעֱבָד: אֹהֵב כֶּסֶף לֹא־יִשְׂבַּע כֶּסֶף וּמִי־

י אֹהֵב בֶּהָמוֹן לֹא תְבוּאָה גַּם־זֶה הָבֶל: בִּרְבוֹת הַטּוֹבָה רַבּוּ אוֹכְלֶיהָ וּמַה־

יא כִּשְׁרוֹן לִבְעָלֶיהָ כִּי אִם־°רְאִית [°רְאוּת ק] עֵינָיו: מְתוּקָה שְׁנַת הָעֹבֵד אִם־מְעַט וְאִם־הַרְבֵּה יֹאכֵל וְהַשָּׂבָע לֶעָשִׁיר אֵינֶנּוּ מַנִּיחַ לוֹ לִישׁוֹן:

4:5. I.e., the fool destroys himself (Ibn Ezra).

4:6. It is better for man to earn less, but with tranquility and quiet, than to earn much more through difficult labor and aggravation (Metzudos).

4:9. One should seek out companions with whom to toil and share (Ibn Ezra).

4:13. Solomon proceeds to extol the reign of wisdom, but concludes that it, too, is impermanent and ultimately futile.

4:15-16. Although people flocked around this new young king, he ultimately fell into disfavor because popularity is short-lived.

5:2. Dreams reflect an overabundance of thoughts during the day. Similarly, excessive chatter betrays the fool (Rashi).

5:8. Having discoursed on the fear of God, Solomon reverts to the theme of which occupation is best and most sin-free. Agriculture yields the most reward, for even a king is sustained by the soil.

with his neighbor. This, too, is futility and a vexation of the spirit! ⁵ The fool folds his hands and eats his own flesh. * ⁶ Better is one handful of pleasantness than two fistfuls of labor and vexation of the spirit. *

⁷ Then I returned and contemplated [another] futility beneath the sun: ⁸ a lone and solitary man who has neither son nor brother, yet there is no end to his toil, nor is his eye ever sated with riches, [nor does he ask himself,] "For whom am I toiling and depriving myself of goodness?" This, too, is futility; indeed, it is a sorry task.

⁹ Two are better than one, for they get a greater return for their labor. * ¹⁰ For should they fall, one can lift the other; but woe to him who is alone when he falls and there is no one to lift him! ¹¹ Also, if two sleep together they keep warm, but how can one be warm alone? ¹² Where one can be overpowered, two can resist attack: A three-ply cord is not easily severed!

¹³ Better is a poor but wise youth than an old and foolish king who no longer knows how to take care of himself; * ¹⁴ because from the prison he emerged to reign, while even in his reign he was born poor. ¹⁵ I saw all the living that wander beneath the sun throng to the succeeding youth who steps into his place. * ¹⁶ There is no end to the entire nation, to all that was before them; similarly, the ones that come later will not rejoice in him. For this, too, is futility and a vexation of the spirit.

¹⁷ Guard your foot when you go to the House of God; better to draw near and hearken than to offer the sacrifices of fools, for they do not consider that they do evil.

5 ¹ Be not rash with your mouth, and let not your heart be hasty to utter a word before God; for God is in heaven and you are on earth, so let your words be few. ² For a dream comes from much concern, * and foolish talk from many words.

³ When you make a vow to God, do not delay paying it, for He has no liking for fools; what you vow, pay. ⁴ Better that you do not vow at all than that you vow and not pay. ⁵ Let not your mouth bring guilt on your flesh, and do not tell the messenger that it was an error. Why should God be angered by your speech and destroy the work of your hands? ⁶ In spite of all dreams, futility and idle chatter, rather: Fear God!

⁷ If you see oppression of the poor, and the suppression of justice and right in the State, do not be astonished at the fact, for there is One higher than high Who watches and there are high ones above them.

⁸ The advantage of land is supreme; even a king is indebted to the soil. *

⁹ A lover of money will never be satisfied with money; * a lover of abundance has no wheat. This, too, is futility! ¹⁰ As goods increase, so do those who consume them; * what advantage, then, has the owner except what his eyes see? ¹¹ Sweet is the sleep of the laborer, whether he eats little or much; the satiety of the rich does not let him sleep. *

5:9. Money will never still a rich man's hunger, for who can eat money? (*Akeidas Yitzchak*).

5:10. A wealthier household with its larger stock of supplies attracts more relatives, friends and paupers (*Rav Yosef Kara*).

5:11. A man who tills the ground to support his family has no large fortunes over which to worry constantly. He can sleep undisturbed by business worries (*Rav Yosef Kara*).

יב יֵ֣שׁ רָעָ֣ה חוֹלָ֔ה רָאִ֖יתִי תַּ֣חַת הַשָּׁ֑מֶשׁ עֹ֛שֶׁר שָׁמ֥וּר לִבְעָלָ֖יו לְרָעָתֽוֹ:

יג־יד וְאָבַ֛ד הָעֹ֥שֶׁר הַה֖וּא בְּעִנְיַ֣ן רָ֑ע וְהוֹלִ֣יד בֵּ֔ן וְאֵ֥ין בְּיָד֖וֹ מְאֽוּמָה: כַּאֲשֶׁ֤ר יָצָא֙ מִבֶּ֣טֶן אִמּ֔וֹ עָר֛וֹם יָשׁ֥וּב לָלֶ֖כֶת כְּשֶׁבָּ֑א וּמְא֗וּמָה לֹא־יִשָּׂ֧א בַעֲמָל֛וֹ שֶׁיֹּלֵ֖ךְ

טו בְּיָדֽוֹ: וְגַם־זֹה֙ רָעָ֣ה חוֹלָ֔ה כָּל־עֻמַּ֥ת שֶׁבָּ֖א כֵּ֣ן יֵלֵ֑ךְ וּמַה־יִּתְר֣וֹן ל֔וֹ שֶׁיַּעֲמֹ֖ל

טז־יז לָרֽוּחַ: גַּ֧ם כָּל־יָמָ֛יו בַּחֹ֥שֶׁךְ יֹאכֵ֖ל וְכָעַ֣ס הַרְבֵּ֑ה וְחָלְי֖וֹ וָקָֽצֶף: הִנֵּ֞ה אֲשֶׁר־ רָאִ֣יתִי אָ֗נִי ט֣וֹב אֲשֶׁר־יָפֶ֣ה לֶאֱכֽוֹל־וְ֠לִשְׁתּוֹת וְלִרְא֨וֹת טוֹבָ֜ה בְּכָל־עֲמָל֣וֹ ׀ שֶׁיַּעֲמֹ֣ל תַּֽחַת־הַשֶּׁ֗מֶשׁ מִסְפַּ֧ר יְמֵי־חַיָּ֛ו אֲשֶׁר־נָֽתַן־ל֥וֹ הָאֱלֹהִ֖ים כִּי־ה֥וּא

יח חֶלְקֽוֹ: גַּ֣ם כָּֽל־הָאָדָ֡ם אֲשֶׁ֣ר נָֽתַן־ל֣וֹ הָאֱלֹהִים֩ עֹ֨שֶׁר וּנְכָסִ֜ים וְהִשְׁלִיט֣וֹ לֶאֱכֹ֤ל מִמֶּ֨נּוּ֙ וְלָשֵׂ֣את אֶת־חֶלְק֔וֹ וְלִשְׂמֹ֖חַ בַּעֲמָל֑וֹ זֹ֕ה מַתַּ֥ת אֱלֹהִ֖ים הִֽיא:

יט כִּ֚י לֹ֣א הַרְבֵּ֔ה יִזְכֹּ֖ר אֶת־יְמֵ֣י חַיָּ֑יו כִּ֚י הָֽאֱלֹהִ֣ים מַעֲנֶ֔ה בְּשִׂמְחַ֖ת לִבּֽוֹ:

ו א יֵ֣שׁ רָעָ֔ה אֲשֶׁ֥ר רָאִ֖יתִי תַּ֣חַת הַשָּׁ֑מֶשׁ וְרַבָּ֥ה הִ֖יא עַל־הָאָדָֽם: אִ֣ישׁ אֲשֶׁ֣ר

ב יִתֶּן־ל֣וֹ הָאֱלֹהִ֡ים עֹשֶׁר֩ וּנְכָסִ֨ים וְכָב֜וֹד וְֽאֵינֶ֨נּוּ חָסֵ֪ר לְנַפְשׁ֣וֹ ׀ מִכֹּ֣ל אֲשֶׁר־ יִתְאַוֶּ֗ה וְלֹֽא־יַשְׁלִיטֶ֤נּוּ הָֽאֱלֹהִים֙ לֶאֱכֹ֣ל מִמֶּ֔נּוּ כִּ֛י אִ֥ישׁ נָכְרִ֖י יֹֽאכְלֶ֑נּוּ זֶ֥ה

ג הֶ֛בֶל וָחֳלִ֥י רָ֖ע הֽוּא: אִם־יוֹלִ֣יד אִ֣ישׁ מֵאָ֡ה וְשָׁנִים֩ רַבּ֨וֹת יִֽחְיֶ֜ה וְרַ֣ב ׀ שֶׁיִּהְי֣וּ יְמֵֽי־שָׁנָ֗יו וְנַפְשׁוֹ֙ לֹֽא־תִשְׂבַּ֣ע מִן־הַטּוֹבָ֔ה וְגַם־קְבוּרָ֖ה לֹא־הָ֣יְתָה לּ֑וֹ

ד אָמַ֕רְתִּי ט֥וֹב מִמֶּ֖נּוּ הַנָּֽפֶל: כִּֽי־בַהֶ֥בֶל בָּ֖א וּבַחֹ֣שֶׁךְ יֵלֵ֑ךְ וּבַחֹ֖שֶׁךְ שְׁמ֥וֹ

ה־ו יְכֻסֶּֽה: גַּם־שֶׁ֥מֶשׁ לֹא־רָאָ֖ה וְלֹ֣א יָדָ֑ע נַ֥חַת לָזֶ֖ה מִזֶּֽה: וְאִלּ֣וּ חָיָ֗ה אֶ֤לֶף שָׁנִים֙ פַּעֲמַ֔יִם וְטוֹבָ֖ה לֹ֣א רָאָ֑ה הֲלֹ֛א אֶל־מָק֥וֹם אֶחָ֖ד הַכֹּ֥ל הוֹלֵֽךְ: כָּל־

ז־ח עֲמַ֥ל הָאָדָ֖ם לְפִ֑יהוּ וְגַם־הַנֶּ֖פֶשׁ לֹ֥א תִמָּלֵֽא: כִּ֛י מַה־יּוֹתֵ֥ר לֶחָכָ֖ם מִן־

ט הַכְּסִ֑יל מַה־לֶּעָנִ֣י יוֹדֵ֔עַ לַהֲלֹ֖ךְ נֶ֥גֶד הַֽחַיִּֽים: ט֛וֹב מַרְאֵ֥ה עֵינַ֖יִם מֵֽהֲלָךְ־

י נָ֑פֶשׁ גַּם־זֶ֥ה הֶ֖בֶל וּרְע֥וּת רֽוּחַ: מַה־שֶּֽׁהָיָ֗ה כְּבָר֙ נִקְרָ֣א שְׁמ֔וֹ וְנוֹדָ֖ע אֲשֶׁר־ה֣וּא אָדָ֑ם וְלֹא־יוּכַ֣ל לָדִ֔ין עִ֖ם °שֶׁהַתְּקִ֥יף [°שֶׁתַּקִּ֥יף ק] מִמֶּֽנּוּ:

יא־יב כִּ֛י יֵשׁ־דְּבָרִ֥ים הַרְבֵּ֖ה מַרְבִּ֣ים הָ֑בֶל מַה־יֹּתֵ֖ר לָאָדָֽם: כִּ֣י מִֽי־יוֹדֵ֩עַ֩ מַה־ טּ֨וֹב לָֽאָדָ֜ם בַּֽחַיִּ֗ים מִסְפַּ֛ר יְמֵי־חַיֵּ֥י הֶבְל֖וֹ וְיַעֲשֵׂ֣ם כַּצֵּ֑ל אֲשֶׁר֙ מִֽי־

ז א יַגִּ֣יד לָֽאָדָ֔ם מַה־יִּהְיֶ֥ה אַחֲרָ֖יו תַּ֥חַת הַשָּֽׁמֶשׁ: **ט֥וֹב שֵׁם**

ב מִשֶּׁ֣מֶן ט֑וֹב וְי֣וֹם הַמָּ֔וֶת מִיּ֖וֹם הִוָּֽלְדֽוֹ: ט֞וֹב לָלֶ֣כֶת אֶל־בֵּֽית־אֵ֗בֶל מִלֶּ֨כֶת֙ אֶל־בֵּ֣ית מִשְׁתֶּ֔ה בַּאֲשֶׁ֕ר ה֖וּא ס֣וֹף כָּל־הָאָדָ֑ם וְהַחַ֖י יִתֵּ֥ן אֶל־לִבּֽוֹ:

ג־ד ט֥וֹב כַּ֖עַס מִשְּׂח֑וֹק כִּֽי־בְרֹ֥עַ פָּנִ֖ים יִ֥יטַב לֵֽב: לֵ֤ב חֲכָמִים֙ בְּבֵ֣ית אֵ֔בֶל

ה וְלֵ֥ב כְּסִילִ֖ים בְּבֵ֥ית שִׂמְחָֽה: ט֕וֹב לִשְׁמֹ֖עַ גַּעֲרַ֣ת חָכָ֑ם מֵאִ֕ישׁ שֹׁמֵ֖עַ

5:17-18. Since man must depart exactly as he came, let him involve himself in Torah pursuits (*Rashi*), and let him eat of God's bounty and be content (*Ibn Yachya; Ibn Ezra*).

According to the *Midrash*, the eating and drinking mentioned in this Book refer to Torah and good deeds. See 8:15.

6:8. Both the wise man and the fool must toil for what they achieve. The difference lies in how they utilize and appreciate the fruits of their labor.

6:12. Can anyone guarantee that unjustly gained fortune will endure for his children on this world? (*Rashi*).

The best course, therefore, is to store up spiritual fortunes which will definitely live on beyond him (*Alshich*) — as the next verse teaches, "a good name is better than good oil" (*Midrash*).

7:1. A fine reputation will preserve a deceased person's memory more effectively than precious oils will preserve

¹² There is a sickening evil which I have seen under the sun: riches hoarded by their owner to his misfortune, ¹³ and he loses those riches in some bad venture. If he begets a son, he has nothing in his hand. ¹⁴ As he emerged from his mother's womb, naked, will he return, as he had come; he can salvage nothing from his labor to take with him. ¹⁵ This, too, is a sickening evil: Exactly as he came he must depart, and what did he gain by toiling for the wind? ¹⁶ Indeed, all his life he eats in darkness; he is greatly grieved, and has illness and anger.

¹⁷ So what I have seen to be good is that it is suitable to eat and drink and enjoy pleasure with all one's labor that he toils beneath the sun during the brief span of his life that God has given him, for that is his lot. * ¹⁸ Furthermore, every man to whom God has given riches and possessions and has given him the power to enjoy them, possess his share and be happy in his work — this is the gift of God. ¹⁹ For he shall remember that the days of his life are not many, while God provides him with the joy of his heart.

6 ¹ There is an evil I have observed beneath the sun, and it is prevalent among mankind: ² a man to whom God has given riches, wealth and honor, and he lacks nothing that the heart could desire, yet God did not give him the power to enjoy it; instead, a stranger will enjoy it. This is futility and an evil disease. ³ If a man begets a hundred children and lives many years — great being the days of his life — and his soul is not content with the good — and he is even deprived of burial, I say: The stillborn is better off than he. ⁴ Though its coming is futile and it departs in darkness, though its very name is enveloped in darkness, ⁵ though it never saw the sun nor knew it, it has more satisfaction than he. ⁶ Even if he should live a thousand years twice over, but find no contentment — do not all go to the same place?

⁷ All man's toil is for his mouth, yet his wants are never satisfied. ⁸ What advantage, then, has the wise man over the fool? * What [less] has the pauper who knows how to conduct himself among the living? ⁹ Better is what the eyes see than what is imagined. That, too, is futility and a vexation of the spirit.

¹⁰ What has been was already named, and it is known that he is but a man. He cannot contend with one who is mightier than he. ¹¹ There are many things that increase futility; how does it benefit man? ¹² Who can possibly know what is good for man in life, * during the short span of his futile existence which he should consider like a shadow; who can tell a man what will be after him beneath the sun?

7 ¹ A good name is better than good oil, * and the day of death than the day of birth.

² It is better to go to the house of mourning than to go to a house of feasting, * for that is the end of all man, and the living should take it to heart.

³ Grief is better than gaiety — for through a sad countenance the heart is improved. ⁴ The thoughts of the wise turn to the house of mourning, but the thoughts of a fool to the house of feasting.

⁵ It is better to listen to the rebuke of a wise man than for one to listen to the

---

his body (*Alshich*).
7:2. Eulogies will stimulate one to think about the

beauty of life, and inspire one to repent and realize that only a good reputation has lasting value.

ו שִׁיר כְּסִילִים: כִּי כְקוֹל הַסִּירִים תַּחַת הַסִּיר כֵּן שְׂחֹק הַכְּסִיל וְגַם־זֶה הָבֶל:

ז-ח כִּי הָעֹשֶׁק יְהוֹלֵל חָכָם וִיאַבֵּד אֶת־לֵב מַתָּנָה: טוֹב אַחֲרִית דָּבָר מֵרֵאשִׁיתוֹ

ט טוֹב אֶרֶךְ־רוּחַ מִגְּבַהּ־רוּחַ: אַל־תְּבַהֵל בְּרוּחֲךָ לִכְעוֹס כִּי כַעַס בְּחֵיק

י כְּסִילִים יָנוּחַ: אַל־תֹּאמַר מֶה הָיָה שֶׁהַיָּמִים הָרִאשֹׁנִים הָיוּ טוֹבִים מֵאֵלֶּה

יא כִּי לֹא מֵחָכְמָה שָׁאַלְתָּ עַל־זֶה: טוֹבָה חָכְמָה עִם־נַחֲלָה וְיֹתֵר לְרֹאֵי

יב הַשָּׁמֶשׁ: כִּי בְּצֵל הַחָכְמָה בְּצֵל הַכָּסֶף וְיִתְרוֹן דַּעַת הַחָכְמָה תְּחַיֶּה בְעָלֶיהָ:

יג-יד רְאֵה אֶת־מַעֲשֵׂה הָאֱלֹהִים כִּי מִי יוּכַל לְתַקֵּן אֵת אֲשֶׁר עִוְּתוֹ: בְּיוֹם טוֹבָה הֱיֵה בְטוֹב וּבְיוֹם רָעָה רְאֵה גַּם אֶת־זֶה לְעֻמַּת־זֶה עָשָׂה הָאֱלֹהִים עַל־

טו דִּבְרַת שֶׁלֹּא יִמְצָא הָאָדָם אַחֲרָיו מְאוּמָה: אֶת־הַכֹּל רָאִיתִי בִּימֵי הֶבְלִי

טז יֵשׁ צַדִּיק אֹבֵד בְּצִדְקוֹ וְיֵשׁ רָשָׁע מַאֲרִיךְ בְּרָעָתוֹ: אַל־תְּהִי צַדִּיק הַרְבֵּה

יז וְאַל־תִּתְחַכַּם יוֹתֵר לָמָּה תִּשּׁוֹמֵם: אַל־תִּרְשַׁע הַרְבֵּה וְאַל־תְּהִי סָכָל

יח לָמָּה תָמוּת בְּלֹא עִתֶּךָ: טוֹב אֲשֶׁר תֶּאֱחֹז בָּזֶה וְגַם־מִזֶּה אַל־תַּנַּח אֶת־

יט יָדֶךָ כִּי־יְרֵא אֱלֹהִים יֵצֵא אֶת־כֻּלָּם: הַחָכְמָה תָּעֹז לֶחָכָם מֵעֲשָׂרָה

כ שַׁלִּיטִים אֲשֶׁר הָיוּ בָּעִיר: כִּי אָדָם אֵין צַדִּיק בָּאָרֶץ אֲשֶׁר יַעֲשֶׂה־טּוֹב וְלֹא

כא יֶחֱטָא: גַּם לְכָל־הַדְּבָרִים אֲשֶׁר יְדַבֵּרוּ אַל־תִּתֵּן לִבֶּךָ אֲשֶׁר לֹא־תִשְׁמַע

כב אֶת־עַבְדְּךָ מְקַלְלֶךָ: כִּי גַּם־פְּעָמִים רַבּוֹת יָדַע לִבֶּךָ אֲשֶׁר גַּם־אַתְּ קִלַּלְתָּ

כג אֲחֵרִים: כָּל־זֹה נִסִּיתִי בַחָכְמָה אָמַרְתִּי אֶחְכָּמָה וְהִיא רְחוֹקָה מִמֶּנִּי:

כד-כה רָחוֹק מַה־שֶּׁהָיָה וְעָמֹק עָמֹק מִי יִמְצָאֶנּוּ: סַבּוֹתִי אֲנִי וְלִבִּי לָדַעַת וְלָתוּר

כו וּבַקֵּשׁ חָכְמָה וְחֶשְׁבּוֹן וְלָדַעַת רֶשַׁע כֶּסֶל וְהַסִּכְלוּת הוֹלֵלוֹת: וּמוֹצֶא אֲנִי מַר מִמָּוֶת אֶת־הָאִשָּׁה אֲשֶׁר־הִיא מְצוֹדִים וַחֲרָמִים לִבָּהּ אֲסוּרִים יָדֶיהָ

כז טוֹב לִפְנֵי הָאֱלֹהִים יִמָּלֵט מִמֶּנָּה וְחוֹטֵא יִלָּכֶד בָּהּ: רְאֵה זֶה מָצָאתִי

כח אָמְרָה קֹהֶלֶת אַחַת לְאַחַת לִמְצֹא חֶשְׁבּוֹן: אֲשֶׁר עוֹד־בִּקְשָׁה נַפְשִׁי וְלֹא

כט מָצָאתִי אָדָם אֶחָד מֵאֶלֶף מָצָאתִי וְאִשָּׁה בְכָל־אֵלֶּה לֹא מָצָאתִי: לְבַד רְאֵה־זֶה מָצָאתִי אֲשֶׁר עָשָׂה הָאֱלֹהִים אֶת־הָאָדָם יָשָׁר וְהֵמָּה בִקְשׁוּ

ח א חֶשְׁבֹּנוֹת רַבִּים: מִי כְּהֶחָכָם וּמִי יוֹדֵעַ פֵּשֶׁר דָּבָר חָכְמַת אָדָם תָּאִיר פָּנָיו

ב-ג וְעֹז פָּנָיו יְשֻׁנֶּא: אֲנִי פִּי־מֶלֶךְ שְׁמֹר וְעַל דִּבְרַת שְׁבוּעַת אֱלֹהִים: אַל־תִּבָּהֵל

ד מִפָּנָיו תֵּלֵךְ אַל־תַּעֲמֹד בְּדָבָר רָע כִּי כָּל־אֲשֶׁר יַחְפֹּץ יַעֲשֶׂה: בַּאֲשֶׁר דְּבַר־

ה מֶלֶךְ שִׁלְטוֹן וּמִי יֹאמַר־לוֹ מַה־תַּעֲשֶׂה: שׁוֹמֵר מִצְוָה לֹא יֵדַע דָּבָר רָע

ו וְעֵת וּמִשְׁפָּט יֵדַע לֵב חָכָם: כִּי לְכָל־חֵפֶץ יֵשׁ עֵת וּמִשְׁפָּט כִּי־רָעַת הָאָדָם

ז רַבָּה עָלָיו: כִּי־אֵינֶנּוּ יֹדֵעַ מַה־שֶּׁיִּהְיֶה כִּי כַּאֲשֶׁר יִהְיֶה מִי יַגִּיד לוֹ:

7:11. If a scholar is self-supporting, he can immerse himself in his studies (*Alshich*).

7:13. God gave man life so that he can act righteously — for who can right his wrongs after death? (*Tuv Taam*).

7:14. I.e., all punishment is clearly in response to man's deeds (*Rashi*).

7:15. God deals strictly with the righteous to atone for their sins, so that they will not require punishment in the Hereafter. He defers punishment of the wicked because He is waiting for them to repent, or He may be rewarding their good deeds in This World so that song of fools, [6] for like the crackling of thorns under a pot, so is the laughter of the fool; and this, too, is futility; [7] for oppression makes the wise foolish, and a gift corrupts the heart.

[8] The end of a matter is better than its beginning; patience is better than pride. [9] Do not be hastily upset, for anger lingers in the bosom of fools.

[10] Do not say, "How was it that former times were better than these?" For that is not a question prompted by wisdom.

[11] Wisdom is good with an inheritance, * and a boon to those who see the sun, [12] for to sit in the shelter of wisdom is to sit in the shelter of money, and the advantage of knowledge is that wisdom preserves the life of its possessors. [13] Observe God's doing! For who can straighten what He has twisted? * [14] Be pleased when things go well, but in a time of misfortune reflect: God has made the one as well as the other so that man should find nothing after Him. *

[15] I have seen everything during my futile existence: Sometimes a righteous man perishes for all his righteousness, and sometimes a wicked man endures for all his wickedness. * [16] Do not be overly righteous or excessively wise. Why be left desolate? [17] Be not overly wicked nor be a fool. Why die before your time? [18] It is best to grasp the one and not let go of the other; he who fears God performs them all. [19] Wisdom strengthens the wise more than ten rulers who are in the city. [20] For there is no man so wholly righteous on earth that he [always] does good and never sins.

[21] Moreover, pay no attention to everything men say, lest you hear your own servant disparaging you, [22] for your own conscience knows that many times you yourself disparaged others.

[23] All this I tested with wisdom; I thought I could become wise, but it is beyond me. [24] What existed is elusive and so very deep. Who can fathom it? [25] So I turned my attention to study and probe and seek wisdom and reckoning, and to know the wickedness of folly, and the foolishness which is madness:

[26] And I have discovered more bitter than death: the woman who is snares, whose heart is nets, whose arms are chains. * He who is pleasing to God escapes her but the sinner is caught by her.

[27] See, this is what I found, said Koheles, adding one to another to reach a conclusion, [28] which yet my soul seeks but I have not found. One man in a thousand I have found, but one woman among them * I have not found. [29] But, see, this I did find: God has made man simple, but they sought many intrigues.

8 [1] Who is like the wise man? And who knows what things mean? A man's wisdom lights up his face, and the boldness of his face is transformed. [2] I counsel you: Obey the king's command, and that in the manner of an oath of God. [3] Do not hasten to leave his presence, do not persist in an evil thing; for he can do whatever he pleases. [4] Since a king's word is law, who would dare say to him, "What are you doing?" [5] He who obeys the commandment will know no evil; and a wise mind will know time and justice. [6] For everything has its time and justice, for man's evil overwhelms him. [7] Indeed, he does not know what will happen, for when it happens, who will tell him?

---

they will not enjoy the bliss of the World to Come (*Alshich*).

7:26. Solomon gives lavish praise to God-fearing women in *Proverbs* 31:10-32. Here he refers only to licentious women, who entice men to evil.

7:28. Solomon regrets that his own thousand wives [700 wives, 300 concubines (*I Kings* 11:3)] led him into sin (*Ibn Yachya*).

ח אֵין אָדָם שַׁלִּיט בָּרוּחַ לִכְלוֹא אֶת־הָרוּחַ וְאֵין שִׁלְטוֹן בְּיוֹם הַמָּוֶת וְאֵין
ט מִשְׁלַחַת בַּמִּלְחָמָה וְלֹא־יְמַלֵּט רֶשַׁע אֶת־בְּעָלָיו: אֶת־כָּל־זֶה רָאִיתִי
וְנָתוֹן אֶת־לִבִּי לְכָל־מַעֲשֶׂה אֲשֶׁר נַעֲשָׂה תַּחַת הַשָּׁמֶשׁ עֵת אֲשֶׁר
י שָׁלַט הָאָדָם בְּאָדָם לְרַע לוֹ: וּבְכֵן רָאִיתִי רְשָׁעִים קְבֻרִים וָבָאוּ וּמִמְּקוֹם
יא קָדוֹשׁ יְהַלֵּכוּ וְיִשְׁתַּכְּחוּ בָעִיר אֲשֶׁר כֵּן־עָשׂוּ גַּם־זֶה הָבֶל: אֲשֶׁר אֵין־
נַעֲשָׂה פִתְגָם מַעֲשֵׂה הָרָעָה מְהֵרָה עַל־כֵּן מָלֵא לֵב בְּנֵי־הָאָדָם בָּהֶם
יב לַעֲשׂוֹת רָע: אֲשֶׁר חֹטֶא עֹשֶׂה רָע מְאַת וּמַאֲרִיךְ לוֹ כִּי גַּם־יוֹדֵעַ אָנִי
יג אֲשֶׁר יִהְיֶה־טּוֹב לְיִרְאֵי הָאֱלֹהִים אֲשֶׁר יִירְאוּ מִלְּפָנָיו: וְטוֹב לֹא־יִהְיֶה
יד לָרָשָׁע וְלֹא־יַאֲרִיךְ יָמִים כַּצֵּל אֲשֶׁר אֵינֶנּוּ יָרֵא מִלִּפְנֵי אֱלֹהִים: יֶשׁ־
הֶבֶל אֲשֶׁר נַעֲשָׂה עַל־הָאָרֶץ אֲשֶׁר | יֵשׁ צַדִּיקִים אֲשֶׁר מַגִּיעַ אֲלֵהֶם
כְּמַעֲשֵׂה הָרְשָׁעִים וְיֵשׁ רְשָׁעִים שֶׁמַּגִּיעַ אֲלֵהֶם כְּמַעֲשֵׂה הַצַּדִּיקִים
טו אָמַרְתִּי שֶׁגַּם־זֶה הָבֶל: וְשִׁבַּחְתִּי אֲנִי אֶת־הַשִּׂמְחָה אֲשֶׁר אֵין־טוֹב
לָאָדָם תַּחַת הַשֶּׁמֶשׁ כִּי אִם־לֶאֱכוֹל וְלִשְׁתּוֹת וְלִשְׂמוֹחַ וְהוּא יִלְוֶנּוּ
טז בַעֲמָלוֹ יְמֵי חַיָּיו אֲשֶׁר־נָתַן־לוֹ הָאֱלֹהִים תַּחַת הַשָּׁמֶשׁ: כַּאֲשֶׁר נָתַתִּי
אֶת־לִבִּי לָדַעַת חָכְמָה וְלִרְאוֹת אֶת־הָעִנְיָן אֲשֶׁר נַעֲשָׂה עַל־הָאָרֶץ כִּי
יז גַם בַּיּוֹם וּבַלַּיְלָה שֵׁנָה בְּעֵינָיו אֵינֶנּוּ רֹאֶה: וְרָאִיתִי אֶת־כָּל־מַעֲשֵׂה
הָאֱלֹהִים כִּי לֹא יוּכַל הָאָדָם לִמְצוֹא אֶת־הַמַּעֲשֶׂה אֲשֶׁר נַעֲשָׂה תַחַת־
הַשֶּׁמֶשׁ בְּשֶׁל אֲשֶׁר יַעֲמֹל הָאָדָם לְבַקֵּשׁ וְלֹא יִמְצָא וְגַם אִם־יֹאמַר
ט א הֶחָכָם לָדַעַת לֹא יוּכַל לִמְצֹא: כִּי אֶת־כָּל־זֶה נָתַתִּי אֶל־לִבִּי וְלָבוּר
אֶת־כָּל־זֶה אֲשֶׁר הַצַּדִּיקִים וְהַחֲכָמִים וַעֲבָדֵיהֶם בְּיַד הָאֱלֹהִים גַּם־
ב אַהֲבָה גַם־שִׂנְאָה אֵין יוֹדֵעַ הָאָדָם הַכֹּל לִפְנֵיהֶם: הַכֹּל כַּאֲשֶׁר לַכֹּל
מִקְרֶה אֶחָד לַצַּדִּיק וְלָרָשָׁע לַטּוֹב וְלַטָּהוֹר וְלַטָּמֵא וְלַזֹּבֵחַ וְלַאֲשֶׁר אֵינֶנּוּ
ג זֹבֵחַ כַּטּוֹב כַּחֹטֶא הַנִּשְׁבָּע כַּאֲשֶׁר שְׁבוּעָה יָרֵא: זֶה | רָע בְּכֹל אֲשֶׁר־
נַעֲשָׂה תַּחַת הַשֶּׁמֶשׁ כִּי־מִקְרֶה אֶחָד לַכֹּל וְגַם לֵב בְּנֵי־הָאָדָם מָלֵא־רָע
ד וְהוֹלֵלוֹת בִּלְבָבָם בְּחַיֵּיהֶם וְאַחֲרָיו אֶל־הַמֵּתִים: כִּי־מִי אֲשֶׁר °יבחר
[°יְחֻבַּר ק׳] אֶל כָּל־הַחַיִּים יֵשׁ בִּטָּחוֹן כִּי־לְכֶלֶב חַי הוּא טוֹב מִן־הָאַרְיֵה
ה הַמֵּת: כִּי הַחַיִּים יוֹדְעִים שֶׁיָּמֻתוּ וְהַמֵּתִים אֵינָם יוֹדְעִים מְאוּמָה וְאֵין־עוֹד
ו לָהֶם שָׂכָר כִּי נִשְׁכַּח זִכְרָם: גַּם אַהֲבָתָם גַּם־שִׂנְאָתָם גַּם־קִנְאָתָם כְּבָר
אָבָדָה וְחֵלֶק אֵין־לָהֶם עוֹד לְעוֹלָם בְּכֹל אֲשֶׁר־נַעֲשָׂה תַּחַת הַשָּׁמֶשׁ:

8:8. Evildoers will not escape punishment for their deeds — their "wickedness" will not be their salvation (*Kara*).

8:10. The wicked are buried peacefully and they come into the world a second time (i.e., their children live on after them) . . . But the righteous who die without children become forgotten . . . (*Ibn Ezra*).

The "futility" is that the good deeds of the righteous are forgotten, but the wicked die peacefully and leave a legacy of evil.

8:11-13. Although a delay in retribution tends to strengthen the tendency toward evil, Koheles affirms his faith in God, Who rewards the righteous and punishes the sinner.

8:14. The following verses until 9:12 form a cohesive unit discussing the dilemma presented by the prosperity

⁸ Man is powerless over the spirit — to restrain the spirit; nor is there authority over the day of death; nor discharge in war; and wickedness cannot save the wrongdoer. *

⁹ All this have I seen; and I applied my mind to every deed that is done under the sun: There is a time when one man rules over another to his detriment.

¹⁰ And then I saw the wicked buried and newly come* while those who had done right were gone from the holy place and were forgotten in the city. This, too, is futility! ¹¹ Because the sentence for wrongdoing is not executed quickly — that is why men are encouraged to do evil, * ¹² because a sinner does what is wrong a hundred times and He is patient with him, yet nevertheless I am aware that it will be well with those who fear God, those that show fear before Him, ¹³ and that it will not be well with the wicked, and he will not long endure — like a shadow — because he does not fear God.

¹⁴ There is a futility that takes place on earth: * Sometimes there are righteous men who are treated as [if they had done] the deeds of the wicked; and there are wicked men who are treated as [if they had done] the deeds of the righteous. I declared: This, too, is vanity.

¹⁵ So I praised enjoyment, for man has no other goal under the sun but to eat, drink and be joyful; and this will accompany him in his toil* during the days of his life which God has given him beneath the sun.

¹⁶ When I set my mind to know wisdom and to observe the activity which takes place on earth — for even day or night its eyes see no sleep — ¹⁷ and I perceived all the work of God. Indeed, man cannot fathom the events that occur under the sun, inasmuch as man tries strenuously to search, but cannot fathom it. And even though a wise man should presume to know, he cannot fathom it.

9

¹ For all this I noted and I sought to ascertain all this: that the righteous and the wise together with their actions are in the hand of God; whether love or hate man does not know; all preceded them.

² All things come alike to all; the same fate awaits the righteous and the wicked, the good and the clean and the unclean, the one who brings a sacrifice and the one who does not. * As is the good man, so is the sinner; as is the one who swears, so is the one who fears an oath.

³ This is an evil about all things that go on under the sun: that the same fate awaits all. Therefore, the heart of man is full of evil; and madness is in their heart while they live; and after that, they go to the dead.

⁴ For he who is attached to all the living has hope, a live dog being better than a dead lion. ⁵ For the living know that they will die, but the dead know nothing at all; there is no more reward for them, * their memory is forgotten. ⁶ Their love, their hate, their jealousy have already perished — nor will they ever again have a share in whatever is done beneath the sun.

---

of the wicked and the suffering of the righteous.

8:15. The *Midrash* notes that all "eating and drinking" mentioned in this Book signify Torah and good deeds, which sustain the soul. Obviously, food and drink do not accompany one to the grave.

9:2. Though death awaits all men in this world, intelligent people realize that there is a distinction between good and evil people in the Hereafter (*Rashi*).

9:5. The dead can no longer perform *mitzvos*.

ז לֵךְ אֱכֹל בְּשִׂמְחָה לַחְמֶךָ וּשְׁתֵה בְלֶב־טוֹב יֵינֶךָ כִּי כְבָר רָצָה הָאֱלֹהִים

ח אֶת־מַעֲשֶׂיךָ: בְּכָל־עֵת יִהְיוּ בְגָדֶיךָ לְבָנִים וְשֶׁמֶן עַל־רֹאשְׁךָ אַל־יֶחְסָר:

ט רְאֵה חַיִּים עִם־אִשָּׁה אֲשֶׁר־אָהַבְתָּ כָּל־יְמֵי חַיֵּי הֶבְלֶךָ אֲשֶׁר נָתַן־לְךָ
תַּחַת הַשֶּׁמֶשׁ כֹּל יְמֵי הֶבְלֶךָ כִּי הוּא חֶלְקְךָ בַּחַיִּים וּבַעֲמָלְךָ אֲשֶׁר־אַתָּה

י עָמֵל תַּחַת הַשָּׁמֶשׁ: כֹּל אֲשֶׁר תִּמְצָא יָדְךָ לַעֲשׂוֹת בְּכֹחֲךָ עֲשֵׂה כִּי אֵין

יא מַעֲשֶׂה וְחֶשְׁבּוֹן וְדַעַת וְחָכְמָה בִּשְׁאוֹל אֲשֶׁר אַתָּה הֹלֵךְ שָׁמָּה: שַׁבְתִּי
וְרָאֹה תַחַת־הַשֶּׁמֶשׁ כִּי לֹא לַקַּלִּים הַמֵּרוֹץ וְלֹא לַגִּבּוֹרִים הַמִּלְחָמָה וְגַם
לֹא לַחֲכָמִים לֶחֶם וְגַם לֹא לַנְּבֹנִים עֹשֶׁר וְגַם לֹא לַיֹּדְעִים חֵן כִּי־עֵת

יב וָפֶגַע יִקְרֶה אֶת־כֻּלָּם: כִּי גַּם לֹא־יֵדַע הָאָדָם אֶת־עִתּוֹ כַּדָּגִים שֶׁנֶּאֱחָזִים
בִּמְצוֹדָה רָעָה וְכַצִּפֳּרִים הָאֲחֻזוֹת בַּפָּח כָּהֵם יוּקָשִׁים בְּנֵי הָאָדָם לְעֵת

יג רָעָה כְּשֶׁתִּפּוֹל עֲלֵיהֶם פִּתְאֹם: גַּם־זֹה רָאִיתִי חָכְמָה תַּחַת הַשָּׁמֶשׁ

יד וּגְדוֹלָה הִיא אֵלָי: עִיר קְטַנָּה וַאֲנָשִׁים בָּהּ מְעָט וּבָא־אֵלֶיהָ מֶלֶךְ גָּדוֹל

טו וְסָבַב אֹתָהּ וּבָנָה עָלֶיהָ מְצוֹדִים גְּדֹלִים: וּמָצָא בָהּ אִישׁ מִסְכֵּן חָכָם
וּמִלַּט־הוּא אֶת־הָעִיר בְּחָכְמָתוֹ וְאָדָם לֹא זָכַר אֶת־הָאִישׁ הַמִּסְכֵּן

טז הַהוּא: וְאָמַרְתִּי אָנִי טוֹבָה חָכְמָה מִגְּבוּרָה וְחָכְמַת הַמִּסְכֵּן בְּזוּיָה וּדְבָרָיו

יז אֵינָם נִשְׁמָעִים: דִּבְרֵי חֲכָמִים בְּנַחַת נִשְׁמָעִים מִזַּעֲקַת מוֹשֵׁל בַּכְּסִילִים:

י יח-א טוֹבָה חָכְמָה מִכְּלֵי קְרָב וְחוֹטֶא אֶחָד יְאַבֵּד טוֹבָה הַרְבֵּה: זְבוּבֵי

ב מָוֶת יַבְאִישׁ יַבִּיעַ שֶׁמֶן רוֹקֵחַ יָקָר מֵחָכְמָה מִכָּבוֹד סִכְלוּת מְעָט: לֵב

ג חָכָם לִימִינוֹ וְלֵב כְּסִיל לִשְׂמֹאלוֹ: וְגַם־בַּדֶּרֶךְ ‏°כְּשֶׁהַסָּכָל [כְּשֶׁסָּכָל ק]

ד הֹלֵךְ לִבּוֹ חָסֵר וְאָמַר לַכֹּל סָכָל הוּא: אִם־רוּחַ הַמּוֹשֵׁל תַּעֲלֶה עָלֶיךָ

ה מְקוֹמְךָ אַל־תַּנַּח כִּי מַרְפֵּא יַנִּיחַ חֲטָאִים גְּדוֹלִים: יֵשׁ רָעָה רָאִיתִי תַּחַת

ו הַשָּׁמֶשׁ כִּשְׁגָגָה שֶׁיֹּצָא מִלִּפְנֵי הַשַּׁלִּיט: נִתַּן הַסֶּכֶל בַּמְּרוֹמִים רַבִּים

ז וַעֲשִׁירִים בַּשֵּׁפֶל יֵשֵׁבוּ: רָאִיתִי עֲבָדִים עַל־סוּסִים וְשָׂרִים הֹלְכִים

ח-ט כַּעֲבָדִים עַל־הָאָרֶץ: חֹפֵר גּוּמָץ בּוֹ יִפּוֹל וּפֹרֵץ גָּדֵר יִשְּׁכֶנּוּ נָחָשׁ: מַסִּיעַ

י אֲבָנִים יֵעָצֵב בָּהֶם בּוֹקֵעַ עֵצִים יִסָּכֶן בָּם: אִם־קֵהָה הַבַּרְזֶל וְהוּא לֹא־

יא פָנִים קִלְקַל וַחֲיָלִים יְגַבֵּר וְיִתְרוֹן הַכְשֵׁיר חָכְמָה: אִם־יִשֹּׁךְ הַנָּחָשׁ בְּלוֹא־

יב לָחַשׁ וְאֵין יִתְרוֹן לְבַעַל הַלָּשׁוֹן: דִּבְרֵי פִי־חָכָם חֵן וְשִׂפְתוֹת כְּסִיל

יג תְּבַלְּעֶנּוּ: תְּחִלַּת דִּבְרֵי־פִיהוּ סִכְלוּת וְאַחֲרִית פִּיהוּ הוֹלֵלוּת רָעָה:

יד וְהַסָּכָל יַרְבֶּה דְבָרִים לֹא־יֵדַע הָאָדָם מַה־שֶּׁיִּהְיֶה וַאֲשֶׁר יִהְיֶה מֵאַחֲרָיו

טו מִי יַגִּיד לוֹ: עֲמַל הַכְּסִילִים תְּיַגְּעֶנּוּ אֲשֶׁר לֹא־יָדַע לָלֶכֶת אֶל־עִיר:

9:8. I.e., one should always be in a state of spiritual preparedness.

9:11. Solomon affirms his principle that this world is transitory and man is governed by God (*Rashi*).

9:14-15. According to the Talmud [*Nedarim* 32b] and *Midrash*, the story is an allegory: The puny human body is like a small town conquered by a mighty king, the Evil Inclination. Then the usually disparaged Good Inclination saves the town, but is often discarded (*Nedarim* 32b).

10:2. There follows a series of one-sentence proverbs.

10:8-9. A fool will place himself in danger, while a wise man will guard himself. Also, nothing in this world is acquired without toil and some inherent danger (*Ibn Ezra*).

⁷ *Go, eat your bread with joy and drink your wine with a glad heart, for God has already approved your deeds.* ⁸ *Let your garments always be white,* * *and your head never lack oil.*

⁹ *Enjoy life with the wife you love through all the fleeting days of your life that He has granted you beneath the sun, all of your futile existence; for that is your compensation in life and in your toil which you exert beneath the sun.* ¹⁰ *Whatever you are able to do with your might, do it. For there is neither doing nor reckoning nor knowledge nor wisdom in the grave where you are going.*

¹¹ *Once more I saw under the sun that the race is not won by the swift,* * *nor the battle by the strong, nor does bread come to the wise, riches to the intelligent, nor favor to the learned; but time and death will happen to them all.* ¹² *For man does not even know his hour: Like fish caught in a fatal net, like birds seized in a snare, so are men caught in the moment of disaster when it falls upon them suddenly.*

¹³ *This, too, have I observed [about] wisdom beneath the sun, and it affected me profoundly:*

¹⁴ *There was a small town with only a few inhabitants;* * *and a mighty king came upon it and surrounded it, and built great siege works over it.* ¹⁵ *Present in the city was a poor wise man who by his wisdom saved the town. Yet no one remembered that poor man.* ¹⁶ *So I said: Wisdom is better than might, although a poor man's wisdom is despised and his words go unheeded.*

¹⁷ *The gentle words of the wise are heard above the shouts of a king over fools,* ¹⁸ *and wisdom is better than weapons, but a single rogue can ruin a great deal of good.*

10   ¹ *Dead flies putrefy the perfumer's oil; a little folly outweighs wisdom and honor.*

² *A wise man's mind [tends] to his right, while a fool's mind [tends] to his left.* *
³ *Even on the road as the fool walks, he lacks sense, and proclaims to all that he is a fool.*

⁴ *If the anger of a ruler flares up against you, do not leave your place, for deference appeases great offenses.*

⁵ *There is an evil which I have observed beneath the sun as if it were an error proceeding from the ruler:* ⁶ *Folly is placed on lofty heights, while rich men sit in low places.* ⁷ *I have seen slaves on horses and nobles walking on foot like slaves.*

⁸ *He who digs a pit will fall into it, and he who breaks down a wall will be bitten by a snake.* * ⁹ *He who moves about stones will be hurt by them; he who splits logs will be endangered by them.*

¹⁰ *If an axe is blunt and one has not honed the edge, nevertheless it strengthens the warriors. Wisdom is a more powerful skill.*

¹¹ *If the snake bites because it was not charmed, then there is no advantage to the charmer's art.*

¹² *The words of a wise man's mouth win favor, but a fool's lips devour him.* ¹³ *His talk begins as foolishness and ends as evil madness.* ¹⁴ *The fool prattles on and on, but man does not know what will be; and who can tell what will happen after him?*

¹⁵ *The toil of fools exhaust them, as one who does not know the way to town.* *

10:15. A wise traveler asks directions, but a fool persists onward to the point of exhaustion.

טז אִי־לָךְ אֶרֶץ שֶׁמַּלְכֵּךְ נָעַר וְשָׂרַיִךְ בַּבֹּקֶר יֹאכֵלוּ: אַשְׁרֵיךְ אֶרֶץ שֶׁמַּלְכֵּךְ
יז בֶּן־חוֹרִים וְשָׂרַיִךְ בָּעֵת יֹאכֵלוּ בִּגְבוּרָה וְלֹא בַשְּׁתִי: בַּעֲצַלְתַּיִם יִמַּךְ
יח הַמְּקָרֶה וּבְשִׁפְלוּת יָדַיִם יִדְלֹף הַבָּיִת: לִשְׂחוֹק עֹשִׂים לֶחֶם וְיַיִן יְשַׂמַּח
כ חַיִּים וְהַכֶּסֶף יַעֲנֶה אֶת־הַכֹּל: גַּם בְּמַדָּעֲךָ מֶלֶךְ אַל־תְּקַלֵּל וּבְחַדְרֵי
מִשְׁכָּבְךָ אַל־תְּקַלֵּל עָשִׁיר כִּי עוֹף הַשָּׁמַיִם יוֹלִיךְ אֶת־הַקּוֹל וּבַעַל

יא
א °הכנפים [ֹכְּנָפַיִם ק] יַגֵּיד דָּבָר: שַׁלַּח לַחְמְךָ עַל־פְּנֵי הַמָּיִם כִּי־בְרֹב
ב הַיָּמִים תִּמְצָאֶנּוּ: תֶּן־חֵלֶק לְשִׁבְעָה וְגַם לִשְׁמוֹנָה כִּי לֹא תֵדַע מַה־יִּהְיֶה
ג רָעָה עַל־הָאָרֶץ: אִם־יִמָּלְאוּ הֶעָבִים גֶּשֶׁם עַל־הָאָרֶץ יָרִיקוּ וְאִם־יִפּוֹל
ד עֵץ בַּדָּרוֹם וְאִם בַּצָּפוֹן מְקוֹם שֶׁיִּפּוֹל הָעֵץ שָׁם יְהוּא: שֹׁמֵר רוּחַ לֹא יִזְרָע
ה וְרֹאֶה בֶעָבִים לֹא יִקְצוֹר: כַּאֲשֶׁר אֵינְךָ יוֹדֵעַ מַה־דֶּרֶךְ הָרוּחַ כַּעֲצָמִים
בְּבֶטֶן הַמְּלֵאָה כָּכָה לֹא תֵדַע אֶת־מַעֲשֵׂה הָאֱלֹהִים אֲשֶׁר יַעֲשֶׂה אֶת־
ו הַכֹּל: בַּבֹּקֶר זְרַע אֶת־זַרְעֶךָ וְלָעֶרֶב אַל־תַּנַּח יָדֶךָ כִּי אֵינְךָ יוֹדֵעַ אֵי זֶה
ז יִכְשָׁר הֲזֶה אוֹ־זֶה וְאִם־שְׁנֵיהֶם כְּאֶחָד טוֹבִים: וּמָתוֹק הָאוֹר וְטוֹב לַעֵינַיִם
ח לִרְאוֹת אֶת־הַשָּׁמֶשׁ: כִּי אִם־שָׁנִים הַרְבֵּה יִחְיֶה הָאָדָם בְּכֻלָּם יִשְׂמָח
ט וְיִזְכֹּר אֶת־יְמֵי הַחֹשֶׁךְ כִּי־הַרְבֵּה יִהְיוּ כָּל־שֶׁבָּא הָבֶל: שְׂמַח בָּחוּר
בְּיַלְדוּתֶךָ וִיטִיבְךָ לִבְּךָ בִּימֵי בְחוּרוֹתֶיךָ וְהַלֵּךְ בְּדַרְכֵי לִבְּךָ °ובמראי
[ֹוּבְמַרְאֵה ק] עֵינֶיךָ וְדָע כִּי עַל־כָּל־אֵלֶּה יְבִיאֲךָ הָאֱלֹהִים בַּמִּשְׁפָּט:
י וְהָסֵר כַּעַס מִלִּבֶּךָ וְהַעֲבֵר רָעָה מִבְּשָׂרֶךָ כִּי־הַיַּלְדוּת וְהַשַּׁחֲרוּת הָבֶל:

יב
א וּזְכֹר אֶת־בּוֹרְאֶיךָ בִּימֵי בְּחוּרֹתֶיךָ עַד אֲשֶׁר לֹא־יָבֹאוּ יְמֵי הָרָעָה וְהִגִּיעוּ
ב שָׁנִים אֲשֶׁר תֹּאמַר אֵין־לִי בָהֶם חֵפֶץ: עַד אֲשֶׁר לֹא־תֶחְשַׁךְ הַשֶּׁמֶשׁ
ג וְהָאוֹר וְהַיָּרֵחַ וְהַכּוֹכָבִים וְשָׁבוּ הֶעָבִים אַחַר הַגָּשֶׁם: בַּיּוֹם שֶׁיָּזֻעוּ
שֹׁמְרֵי הַבַּיִת וְהִתְעַוְּתוּ אַנְשֵׁי הֶחָיִל וּבָטְלוּ הַטֹּחֲנוֹת כִּי מִעֵטוּ וְחָשְׁכוּ
ד הָרֹאוֹת בָּאֲרֻבּוֹת: וְסֻגְּרוּ דְלָתַיִם בַּשּׁוּק בִּשְׁפַל קוֹל הַטַּחֲנָה וְיָקוּם לְקוֹל
ה הַצִּפּוֹר וְיִשַּׁחוּ כָּל־בְּנוֹת הַשִּׁיר: גַּם מִגָּבֹהַּ יִרָאוּ וְחַתְחַתִּים בַּדֶּרֶךְ וְיָנֵאץ
הַשָּׁקֵד וְיִסְתַּבֵּל הֶחָגָב וְתָפֵר הָאֲבִיּוֹנָה כִּי־הֹלֵךְ הָאָדָם אֶל־בֵּית עוֹלָמוֹ
ו וְסָבְבוּ בַשּׁוּק הַסֹּפְדִים: עַד אֲשֶׁר לֹא־°ירחק [ֹיֵרָתֵק ק] חֶבֶל הַכֶּסֶף
ז וְתָרֻץ גֻּלַּת הַזָּהָב וְתִשָּׁבֶר כַּד עַל־הַמַּבּוּעַ וְנָרֹץ הַגַּלְגַּל אֶל־הַבּוֹר: וְיָשֹׁב

10:16. Unconcerned with the welfare of the state, irresponsible leaders indulge in revelry when they should attend to the needs of the people (*Ibn Latif*).

10:19. Money is necessary and makes everything possible. The previous verse condemns slothfulness; this one encourages industry. Lazy people do not earn a living (*Rashi*).

Yalkut HaGershuni comments that יַעֲנֶה can be related to עִנּוּי, *affliction:* "money afflicts all." Its abundance as well as its absence causes suffering.

11:1. Charity should be given even to strangers; generosity will not go unrewarded.

11:4. One who forever waits for ideal conditions will never get his work done (*Ibn Latif*). Similarly in matters of dispensing charity, one should not be too suspicious or prudent (*Nachal Eshkol*).

11:7. I.e., life, while man can still enjoy the light of day!

11:9. Solomon warns rebellious, pleasure-seeking youths: I know that fools tend to sin in their youth, but beware! Judgment is forthcoming (*Midrash Lekach Tov*).

12:1-7. Warning that people should use their youthful years wisely, Solomon metaphorically conjures the ravages of old age and physical decline.

¹⁶ Woe to you, O land, whose king acts as an adolescent, and whose ministers dine in the morning. * ¹⁷ Happy are you, O land, whose king is a man of dignity, and whose ministers dine at the proper time — in strength and not in drunkenness.

¹⁸ Through slothfulness the ceiling sags, and through idleness of the hands the house leaks.

¹⁹ A feast is made for laughter, and wine gladdens life, but money answers everything. *

²⁰ Even in your thoughts do not curse a king, and in your bedchamber do not curse the rich, for a bird of the skies may carry the sound, and some winged creature may betray the matter.

11 ¹ Send your bread upon the waters, for after many days you will find it. * ² Distribute portions to seven, or even to eight, for you never know what calamity will strike the land.

³ If the clouds are filled they will pour down rain on the earth; if a tree falls down in the south or in the north, wherever the tree falls, there it remains. ⁴ One who watches the wind will never sow, * and one who keeps his eyes on the clouds will never reap. ⁵ Just as you do not know the way of the wind, nor the nature of the embryo in a pregnant stomach, so can you never know the work of God Who makes everything. ⁶ In the morning sow your seed and in the evening do not be idle, for you cannot know which will succeed — this or that — or whether both are equally good.

⁷ Sweet is the light, * and it is good for the eyes to behold the sun! ⁸ Even if a man lives many years, let him rejoice in all of them, but let him remember that the days of darkness will be many. All that comes is futility. ⁹ Rejoice, young man, in your childhood; let your heart cheer you in the days of your youth; follow the path of your heart and the sight of your eyes — but be aware that for all these things God will call you to account. * ¹⁰ Rather, banish anger from your heart and remove evil from your flesh — for childhood and youth are futile.

12 ¹ So remember your Creator in the days of your youth, before the evil days come, * and those years arrive of which you will say, "I have no pleasure in them"; ² before the sun, the light, the moon and the stars grow dark, and the clouds return after the rain; ³ in the day when the guards of the house will tremble, and the powerful men will stoop, and the grinders are idle because they are few, and the gazers through windows are dimmed; ⁴ when the doors in the street are shut; when the sound of the grinding is low; when one rises up at the voice of the bird, and all the daughters of song grow dim; ⁵ when they even fear a height and terror in the road; and the almond tree blossoms and the grasshopper becomes a burden and the desire fails — so man goes to his eternal home, while the mourners go about the streets.

⁶ Before the silver cord snaps, * and the golden bowl is shattered, and the pitcher is broken at the fountain, and the wheel is smashed at the pit. ⁷ Thus the

---

12:6. The body — near death — is likened to the malfunctioning machinery of a well. The cord (spine) snaps; the skull shatters; the stomach breaks; and the body is smashed.

הֶעָפָר עַל־הָאָרֶץ כְּשֶׁהָיָה וְהָרוּחַ תָּשׁוּב אֶל־הָאֱלֹהִים אֲשֶׁר נְתָנָהּ:

ח-ט הֲבֵל הֲבָלִים אָמַר הַקּוֹהֶלֶת הַכֹּל הָבֶל: וְיֹתֵר שֶׁהָיָה קֹהֶלֶת חָכָם עוֹד

י לִמַּד־דַּעַת אֶת־הָעָם וְאִזֵּן וְחִקֵּר תִּקֵּן מְשָׁלִים הַרְבֵּה: בִּקֵּשׁ קֹהֶלֶת

יא לִמְצֹא דִּבְרֵי־חֵפֶץ וְכָתוּב יֹשֶׁר דִּבְרֵי אֱמֶת: דִּבְרֵי חֲכָמִים כַּדָּרְבֹנוֹת

יב וּכְמַשְׂמְרוֹת נְטוּעִים בַּעֲלֵי אֲסֻפּוֹת נִתְּנוּ מֵרֹעֶה אֶחָד: וְיֹתֵר מֵהֵמָּה בְּנִי

יג הִזָּהֵר עֲשׂוֹת סְפָרִים הַרְבֵּה אֵין קֵץ וְלַהַג הַרְבֵּה יְגִעַת בָּשָׂר: סוֹף דָּבָר

הַכֹּל נִשְׁמָע אֶת־הָאֱלֹהִים יְרָא וְאֶת־מִצְוֹתָיו שְׁמוֹר כִּי־זֶה כָּל־

יד הָאָדָם: כִּי אֶת־כָּל־מַעֲשֶׂה הָאֱלֹהִים יָבִא בְמִשְׁפָּט עַל כָּל־נֶעְלָם אִם־

טוֹב וְאִם־רָע:

סוֹף דָּבָר הַכֹּל נִשְׁמָע אֶת־הָאֱלֹהִים יְרָא וְאֶת־מִצְוֹתָיו שְׁמוֹר כִּי־זֶה כָּל־הָאָדָם:

סכום פסוקי ספר קהלת מאתים ועשרים ושנים. וסימנו מה שהיה **כבר** נקרא שמו.

12:8. Epilogue. Having discoursed on the life and trials of man, Koheles reiterates the recurring refrain of his conclusions: "All is futile" (*Rashbam*).

12:10. Solomon discovered that all his thoughts were already alluded to in the Word of Truth, i.e., the Torah (*Rashi*).

12:12. Lest you say, "If it is necessary to obey wise men, why are their words not published?" The answer is that it is not possible to commit everything to writing (*Rashi*).

12:13. Solomon sums up: Although I have expounded upon many concepts in this Book, nevertheless the

dust returns to the ground, as it was, and the spirit returns to God Who gave it.
⁸ *Futility of futilities — said Koheles — all is futile!* *

⁹ *And besides being wise, Koheles also imparted knowledge to the people; he listened, and sought out, and arranged many proverbs.*

¹⁰ *Koheles sought to find words of delight and words of truth* * recorded properly.* ¹¹ *The words of the wise are like goads, and the nails well driven are the sayings of the masters of collections, coming from one Shepherd.*

¹² *Beyond these, my son, beware: The making of many books is without limit,* * and much study is weariness of the flesh.*

¹³ *The sum of the matter, when all has been considered:* * Fear God and keep His commandments, for that is man's whole duty.* ¹⁴ *For God will judge every deed — even everything hidden — whether good or evil.*

The sum of the matter, * when all has been considered:*
Fear God and keep His commandments, for that is man's whole duty.

---

conclusion is obvious to all and unquestionable: "Fear God" with your every limb and organ, "for that is man's whole duty" (*Derech Chaim*). This is the essence of man (*Ibn Ezra*); and "the entire world was created only for such a person" (*Shabbos* 30b).

It is customary, during public readings of *Ecclesiastes*, to repeat the *penultimate* verse. This is done to end the reading on a positive note. The same custom is also followed at the conclusion of *Isaiah, Malachi* and *Lamentations* (*Rashi*).

BLESSINGS RECITED BEFORE
READING MEGILLAS ESTHER

Before reading *Megillas Esther* on Purim [both at night and again in the morning], the reader recites the following three blessings. The congregation should answer *Amen* only [not בָּרוּךְ הוּא וּבָרוּךְ שְׁמוֹ] after each blessing, and have in mind that they thereby fulfill the obligation of reciting the blessings themselves. During the morning reading, they should also have in mind that the third blessing applies to the other mitzvos of Purim — *shalach manos*, gifts to the poor, and the festive Purim meal — as well as to the *Megillah* reading. [These blessings are recited whether or not a *minyan* is present for the reading.]

Blessed are You, HASHEM, our God, King of the universe, Who has sanctified us with His commandments and has commanded us regarding the reading of the Megillah. *(Cong. — Amen.)*

בָּרוּךְ אַתָּה יהוה אֱלֹהֵינוּ מֶלֶךְ הָעוֹלָם, אֲשֶׁר קִדְּשָׁנוּ בְּמִצְוֹתָיו, וְצִוָּנוּ עַל מִקְרָא מְגִלָּה. (קהל – אָמֵן.)

Blessed are You, HASHEM, our God, King of the universe, Who has wrought miracles for our forefathers, in those days at this season.

(Cong. — Amen.)

בָּרוּךְ אַתָּה יהוה אֱלֹהֵינוּ מֶלֶךְ הָעוֹלָם, שֶׁעָשָׂה נִסִּים לַאֲבוֹתֵינוּ, בַּיָּמִים הָהֵם, בַּזְּמַן הַזֶּה. (קהל – אָמֵן.)

Blessed are You, HASHEM, our God, King of the universe, Who has kept us alive, sustained us and brought us to this season. *(Cong. — Amen.)*

בָּרוּךְ אַתָּה יהוה אֱלֹהֵינוּ מֶלֶךְ הָעוֹלָם, שֶׁהֶחֱיָנוּ, וְקִיְּמָנוּ, וְהִגִּיעָנוּ לַזְּמַן הַזֶּה. (קהל – אָמֵן.)

[The Megillah is read.]

Esther אֶסְתֵּר

*T*he Talmudic Sages describe the events recorded in the Book of Esther as the last of the miracles to be written and canonized as part of Scripture. Clearly, the Prophets and Sages determined that this first attempt at genocide and the way it was thwarted were relevant to the Jewish people throughout the ages. The story of Esther is deceptively simple. If one were to hear it for the first time as an adult, it would be exciting and suspenseful, but it would seem to be without religious significance, for its plot seems to be a string of coincidences that come together to produce a happy ending. In fact, it is the only Book of Scripture where God's Name is never mentioned.

Precisely that phenomenon is what gives it profound significance, especially for Jews mired in an existence where God's hand seems to be absent. For that is the predicament in which Esther and her people found themselves. She was an unwilling queen to an anti-Semitic king; her husband was the same Ahasuerus who, as recorded in the Book of Ezra, had put a halt to the construction of the Second Temple. And she lived during the years of the Babylonian exile, a time when Jews feared that God had rejected them and they were no longer His Chosen People.

Into this time when God was concealed, Mordechai entered and convinced the doubting, fearful nation that God was indeed cognizant and concerned, and that repentance and reignited fervor for God's service were the keys to their salvation. And Mordechai prevailed upon Esther to throw reason to the wind and risk her life in order to turn her king away from Haman.

One can interpret events as coincidences — until they fit a pattern too well to be anything but part of a well-conceived plan. So it was in the Book of Esther. All the pieces fit, and the Jewish people suddenly realized that nothing had been left to chance, that God had been watchful all along, and that all that was wanting for their salvation was for them to recognize the Source of their existence. What Book could be more necessary for a nation in exile, a nation that would have to endure more exiles before the final Redemption would come? So the Book of Esther is the last one to be recorded — and one of the first that should come to mind when everything seems hopeless.

א   וַיְהִי בִּימֵי אֲחַשְׁוֵרוֹשׁ הוּא אֲחַשְׁוֵרוֹשׁ הַמֹּלֵךְ מֵהֹדּוּ וְעַד־כּוּשׁ שֶׁבַע וְעֶשְׂרִים

ב וּמֵאָה מְדִינָה: בַּיָּמִים הָהֵם כְּשֶׁבֶת | הַמֶּלֶךְ אֲחַשְׁוֵרוֹשׁ עַל כִּסֵּא מַלְכוּתוֹ

ג אֲשֶׁר בְּשׁוּשַׁן הַבִּירָה: בִּשְׁנַת שָׁלוֹשׁ לְמָלְכוֹ עָשָׂה מִשְׁתֶּה לְכָל־שָׂרָיו

ד וַעֲבָדָיו חֵיל | פָּרַס וּמָדַי הַפַּרְתְּמִים וְשָׂרֵי הַמְּדִינוֹת לְפָנָיו: בְּהַרְאֹתוֹ אֶת־

עֹשֶׁר כְּבוֹד מַלְכוּתוֹ וְאֶת־יְקָר תִּפְאֶרֶת גְּדוּלָּתוֹ יָמִים רַבִּים שְׁמוֹנִים וּמְאַת

ה יוֹם: וּבִמְלוֹאת | הַיָּמִים הָאֵלֶּה עָשָׂה הַמֶּלֶךְ לְכָל־הָעָם הַנִּמְצְאִים בְּשׁוּשַׁן

הַבִּירָה לְמִגָּדוֹל וְעַד־קָטָן מִשְׁתֶּה שִׁבְעַת יָמִים בַּחֲצַר גִּנַּת בִּיתַן הַמֶּלֶךְ:

ו חוּר | כַּרְפַּס וּתְכֵלֶת אָחוּז בְּחַבְלֵי־בוּץ וְאַרְגָּמָן עַל־גְּלִילֵי כֶסֶף וְעַמּוּדֵי

ז שֵׁשׁ מִטּוֹת | זָהָב וָכֶסֶף עַל רִצְפַת בַּהַט־וָשֵׁשׁ וְדַר וְסֹחָרֶת: וְהַשְׁקוֹת בִּכְלֵי

ח זָהָב וְכֵלִים מִכֵּלִים שׁוֹנִים וְיֵין מַלְכוּת רָב כְּיַד הַמֶּלֶךְ: וְהַשְּׁתִיָּה

כַדָּת אֵין אֹנֵס כִּי־כֵן | יִסַּד הַמֶּלֶךְ עַל כָּל־רַב בֵּיתוֹ לַעֲשׂוֹת כִּרְצוֹן אִישׁ־

ט וָאִישׁ: גַּם וַשְׁתִּי הַמַּלְכָּה עָשְׂתָה מִשְׁתֵּה נָשִׁים בֵּית הַמַּלְכוּת

י אֲשֶׁר לַמֶּלֶךְ אֲחַשְׁוֵרוֹשׁ: בַּיּוֹם הַשְּׁבִיעִי כְּטוֹב לֵב־הַמֶּלֶךְ בַּיָּיִן אָמַר לִמְהוּמָן

בִּזְּתָא חַרְבוֹנָא בִּגְתָא וַאֲבַגְתָא זֵתַר וְכַרְכַּס שִׁבְעַת הַסָּרִיסִים הַמְשָׁרְתִים

יא אֶת־פְּנֵי הַמֶּלֶךְ אֲחַשְׁוֵרוֹשׁ: לְהָבִיא אֶת־וַשְׁתִּי הַמַּלְכָּה לִפְנֵי הַמֶּלֶךְ בְּכֶתֶר

מַלְכוּת לְהַרְאוֹת הָעַמִּים וְהַשָּׂרִים אֶת־יָפְיָהּ כִּי־טוֹבַת מַרְאֶה הִיא: וַתְּמָאֵן

יב הַמַּלְכָּה וַשְׁתִּי לָבוֹא בִּדְבַר הַמֶּלֶךְ אֲשֶׁר בְּיַד הַסָּרִיסִים וַיִּקְצֹף הַמֶּלֶךְ מְאֹד

יג וַחֲמָתוֹ בָּעֲרָה בוֹ: וַיֹּאמֶר הַמֶּלֶךְ

לַחֲכָמִים יֹדְעֵי הָעִתִּים כִּי־כֵן דְּבַר הַמֶּלֶךְ לִפְנֵי כָּל־יֹדְעֵי דָּת וָדִין: וְהַקָּרֹב

יד אֵלָיו כַּרְשְׁנָא שֵׁתָר אַדְמָתָא תַרְשִׁישׁ מֶרֶס מַרְסְנָא מְמוּכָן שִׁבְעַת שָׂרֵי |

טו פָּרַס וּמָדַי רֹאֵי פְּנֵי הַמֶּלֶךְ הַיֹּשְׁבִים רִאשֹׁנָה בַּמַּלְכוּת: כְּדָת מַה־לַעֲשׂוֹת

בַּמַּלְכָּה וַשְׁתִּי עַל | אֲשֶׁר לֹא־עָשְׂתָה אֶת־מַאֲמַר הַמֶּלֶךְ אֲחַשְׁוֵרוֹשׁ בְּיַד

טז הַסָּרִיסִים: וַיֹּאמֶר °מוּמְכָן [°מְמוּכָן ק] לִפְנֵי הַמֶּלֶךְ וְהַשָּׂרִים

לֹא עַל־הַמֶּלֶךְ לְבַדּוֹ עָוְתָה וַשְׁתִּי הַמַּלְכָּה כִּי עַל־כָּל־הַשָּׂרִים וְעַל־כָּל־

יז הָעַמִּים אֲשֶׁר בְּכָל־מְדִינוֹת הַמֶּלֶךְ אֲחַשְׁוֵרוֹשׁ: כִּי־יֵצֵא דְבַר־הַמַּלְכָּה עַל־

כָּל־הַנָּשִׁים לְהַבְזוֹת בַּעְלֵיהֶן בְּעֵינֵיהֶן בְּאָמְרָם הַמֶּלֶךְ אֲחַשְׁוֵרוֹשׁ אָמַר

יח לְהָבִיא אֶת־וַשְׁתִּי הַמַּלְכָּה לְפָנָיו וְלֹא־בָאָה: וְהַיּוֹם הַזֶּה תֹּאמַרְנָה | שָׂרוֹת

פָּרַס־וּמָדַי אֲשֶׁר שָׁמְעוּ אֶת־דְּבַר הַמַּלְכָּה לְכֹל שָׂרֵי הַמֶּלֶךְ וּכְדַי בִּזָּיוֹן

יט וָקָצֶף: אִם־עַל־הַמֶּלֶךְ טוֹב יֵצֵא דְבַר־מַלְכוּת מִלְּפָנָיו וְיִכָּתֵב בְּדָתֵי פָרַס־

וּמָדַי וְלֹא יַעֲבוֹר אֲשֶׁר לֹא־תָבוֹא וַשְׁתִּי לִפְנֵי הַמֶּלֶךְ אֲחַשְׁוֵרוֹשׁ

א

°ח' רבתי

1:1. Ahasuerus was the successor to Cyrus, near the end of the seventy years of the Babylonian exile (*Rashi*).

Hodu and Cush are usually identified as India and Ethiopia, respectively.

1:3. According to the king's calculations, the prophetic seventy-year deadline for the end of the Jewish exile (*Jeremiah* 25:11-12; see Appendix A, timeline 5) had

passed, yet Babylonia and its successors, Persia and Media, had not been desolated, and the Jews had not been returned to their land. Therefore, convinced that his throne was secure, he made this lavish feast (*Megillah* 11b).

1:10. See verse 5.

1:12. Vashti did not refuse out of modesty; she refused

1

**THE ROYAL
BANQUET**

¹ **A** nd it came to pass in the days of Ahasuerus* — he is the Ahasuerus who
reigned from Hodu to Cush,* a hundred and twenty-seven provinces —
² in those days, when King Ahasuerus sat on his royal throne which was in
Shushan the capital, ³ in the third year of his reign, he made a feast for all his
officials and his servants;* the army of Persia and Media; the nobles and
officials of the provinces being present; ⁴ when he displayed the riches of his
glorious kingdom and the honor of his splendrous majesty for many days, a

*The king's
lavish
celebration*
hundred and eighty days. ⁵ And when these days were fulfilled, the king made
a seven-day feast for all the people who were present in Shushan the capital,
great and small alike, in the courtyard of the garden of the king's palace. ⁶ There
were [hangings of] white, fine cotton, and turquoise wool, held with cords of
fine linen and purple wool, upon silver rods and marble pillars; the couches of
gold and silver were on a pavement of variegated marble. ⁷ The drinks were
served in golden vessels — vessels of diverse form — and royal wine in
abundance, in accordance with the king's wealth. ⁸ And the drinking was
according to the law, there was no coercion, for so the king had established for
every officer of his house to do according to each man's pleasure.

*Queen
Vashti's
feast . . .*
⁹ Queen Vashti also made a feast for the women in the royal house of King
Ahasuerus. ¹⁰ On the seventh day,* when the heart of the king was merry with
wine, he told Mehuman, Bizzetha, Harbona, Bigtha and Abagtha, Zethar and
Carcas, the seven chamberlains who attended King Ahasuerus, ¹¹ to bring
Queen Vashti before the king [adorned] with the royal crown, to show off to the
people and the officials her beauty, for she was beautiful of appearance. ¹² But

*. . . and her
defiance of
the king*
Queen Vashti refused to come* at the king's command [conveyed] by the hand
of the chamberlains; the king therefore became very enraged and his wrath
burned in him.

*The king
consults . . .*
¹³ Then the king spoke to the wise men, those who knew the times (for such
was the king's procedure [to turn] to all who knew law and judgment), ¹⁴ those
closest to him — Carshena, Shethar, Admatha, Tarshish, Meres, Marsena and
Memucan, the seven officers of Persia and Media, who had access to the king,
who sat first in the kingdom: ¹⁵ "By the law, what should be done to Queen
Vashti for not having obeyed the bidding of the King Ahasuerus [conveyed] by
the hand of the chamberlains?"

*. . . and his
advisers call
for her
death . . .*
¹⁶ Memucan declared before the king and the officials, "Not only against the
king has Queen Vashti done wrong, but against all the officials and all the
people in all the provinces of King Ahasuerus. ¹⁷ For the queen's deed will go
forth to all women, making their husbands contemptible in their eyes, when
they will say, 'King Ahasuerus said to bring Queen Vashti before him, but
she did not come!'* ¹⁸ And this day the princesses of Persia and Media who
have heard of the queen's deed will speak of it to all the king's officials, and
there will be much contempt and rage. ¹⁹ If it pleases the king, let there go forth
a royal edict from him, and let it be written into the laws of Persia and Media,
that it not be revoked, that Vashti never again appear before King Ahasuerus;*

---

because God caused her to break out with leprosy. Thus
was the way paved for her downfall (*Megillah* 12b).

1:17. When the word gets out that the queen acted
contemptibly to the king, every woman will consider this
as license to act likewise to her own husband (*Rashi*).

1:19. Well aware of Ahasuerus' vacillating moods,
Memucan [whom the Talmud identifies as Haman
(*Megillah* 12b)] was concerned that he would one day
face the vengeance of a re-instated Vashti. Therefore he
requested that the decree be irrevocable (*Me'am Loez*).

וּמַלְכוּתָהּ יִתֵּן הַמֶּלֶךְ לִרְעוּתָהּ הַטּוֹבָה מִמֶּנָּה: וְנִשְׁמַע פִּתְגָם הַמֶּלֶךְ כ
אֲשֶׁר־יַעֲשֶׂה בְּכָל־מַלְכוּתוֹ כִּי רַבָּה הִיא וְכָל־הַנָּשִׁים יִתְּנוּ יְקָר לְבַעְלֵיהֶן
לְמִגָּדוֹל וְעַד־קָטָן: וַיִּיטַב הַדָּבָר בְּעֵינֵי הַמֶּלֶךְ וְהַשָּׂרִים וַיַּעַשׂ הַמֶּלֶךְ כא
כִּדְבַר מְמוּכָן: וַיִּשְׁלַח סְפָרִים אֶל־כָּל־מְדִינוֹת הַמֶּלֶךְ אֶל־מְדִינָה כב
וּמְדִינָה כִּכְתָבָהּ וְאֶל־עַם וָעָם כִּלְשׁוֹנוֹ לִהְיוֹת כָּל־אִישׁ שֹׂרֵר בְּבֵיתוֹ
וּמְדַבֵּר כִּלְשׁוֹן עַמּוֹ: אַחַר הַדְּבָרִים הָאֵלֶּה כְּשֹׁךְ חֲמַת ב א
הַמֶּלֶךְ אֲחַשְׁוֵרוֹשׁ זָכַר אֶת־וַשְׁתִּי וְאֵת אֲשֶׁר־עָשָׂתָה וְאֵת אֲשֶׁר־נִגְזַר
עָלֶיהָ: וַיֹּאמְרוּ נַעֲרֵי־הַמֶּלֶךְ מְשָׁרְתָיו יְבַקְשׁוּ לַמֶּלֶךְ נְעָרוֹת בְּתוּלוֹת ב
טוֹבוֹת מַרְאֶה: וְיַפְקֵד הַמֶּלֶךְ פְּקִידִים בְּכָל־מְדִינוֹת מַלְכוּתוֹ וְיִקְבְּצוּ ג
אֶת־כָּל־נַעֲרָה־בְתוּלָה טוֹבַת מַרְאֶה אֶל־שׁוּשַׁן הַבִּירָה אֶל־בֵּית הַנָּשִׁים
אֶל־יַד הֵגֶא סְרִיס הַמֶּלֶךְ שֹׁמֵר הַנָּשִׁים וְנָתוֹן תַּמְרוּקֵיהֶן: וְהַנַּעֲרָה אֲשֶׁר ד
תִּיטַב בְּעֵינֵי הַמֶּלֶךְ תִּמְלֹךְ תַּחַת וַשְׁתִּי וַיִּיטַב הַדָּבָר בְּעֵינֵי הַמֶּלֶךְ
וַיַּעַשׂ כֵּן: אִישׁ יְהוּדִי הָיָה בְּשׁוּשַׁן הַבִּירָה וּשְׁמוֹ מָרְדֳּכַי ה
בֶּן יָאִיר בֶּן־שִׁמְעִי בֶּן־קִישׁ אִישׁ יְמִינִי: אֲשֶׁר הָגְלָה מִירוּשָׁלַיִם עִם־ ו
הַגֹּלָה אֲשֶׁר הָגְלְתָה עִם יְכָנְיָה מֶלֶךְ־יְהוּדָה אֲשֶׁר הֶגְלָה נְבוּכַדְנֶאצַּר
מֶלֶךְ בָּבֶל: וַיְהִי אֹמֵן אֶת־הֲדַסָּה הִיא אֶסְתֵּר בַּת־דֹּדוֹ כִּי אֵין לָהּ אָב וָאֵם ז
וְהַנַּעֲרָה יְפַת־תֹּאַר וְטוֹבַת מַרְאֶה וּבְמוֹת אָבִיהָ וְאִמָּהּ לְקָחָהּ מָרְדֳּכַי לוֹ
לְבַת: וַיְהִי בְּהִשָּׁמַע דְּבַר־הַמֶּלֶךְ וְדָתוֹ וּבְהִקָּבֵץ נְעָרוֹת רַבּוֹת אֶל־שׁוּשַׁן ח
הַבִּירָה אֶל־יַד הֵגָי וַתִּלָּקַח אֶסְתֵּר אֶל־בֵּית הַמֶּלֶךְ אֶל־יַד הֵגַי שֹׁמֵר
הַנָּשִׁים: וַתִּיטַב הַנַּעֲרָה בְעֵינָיו וַתִּשָּׂא חֶסֶד לְפָנָיו וַיְבַהֵל אֶת־תַּמְרוּקֶיהָ ט
וְאֶת־מָנוֹתֶהָ לָתֵת לָהּ וְאֵת שֶׁבַע הַנְּעָרוֹת הָרְאֻיוֹת לָתֶת־לָהּ מִבֵּית
הַמֶּלֶךְ וַיְשַׁנֶּהָ וְאֶת־נַעֲרוֹתֶיהָ לְטוֹב בֵּית הַנָּשִׁים: לֹא־הִגִּידָה אֶסְתֵּר אֶת־ י
עַמָּהּ וְאֶת־מוֹלַדְתָּהּ כִּי מָרְדֳּכַי צִוָּה עָלֶיהָ אֲשֶׁר לֹא־תַגִּיד: וּבְכָל־יוֹם יא
וָיוֹם מָרְדֳּכַי מִתְהַלֵּךְ לִפְנֵי חֲצַר בֵּית־הַנָּשִׁים לָדַעַת אֶת־שְׁלוֹם אֶסְתֵּר
וּמַה־יֵּעָשֶׂה בָּהּ: וּבְהַגִּיעַ תֹּר נַעֲרָה וְנַעֲרָה לָבוֹא | אֶל־הַמֶּלֶךְ אֲחַשְׁוֵרוֹשׁ יב
מִקֵּץ הֱיוֹת לָהּ כְּדָת הַנָּשִׁים שְׁנֵים עָשָׂר חֹדֶשׁ כִּי כֵּן יִמְלְאוּ יְמֵי מְרוּקֵיהֶן
שִׁשָּׁה חֳדָשִׁים בְּשֶׁמֶן הַמֹּר וְשִׁשָּׁה חֳדָשִׁים בַּבְּשָׂמִים וּבְתַמְרוּקֵי הַנָּשִׁים:
וּבָזֶה הַנַּעֲרָה בָּאָה אֶל־הַמֶּלֶךְ אֵת כָּל־אֲשֶׁר תֹּאמַר יִנָּתֵן לָהּ לָבוֹא עִמָּהּ יג
מִבֵּית הַנָּשִׁים עַד־בֵּית הַמֶּלֶךְ: בָּעֶרֶב | הִיא בָאָה וּבַבֹּקֶר הִיא שָׁבָה יד
אֶל־בֵּית הַנָּשִׁים שֵׁנִי אֶל־יַד שַׁעֲשְׁגַז סְרִיס הַמֶּלֶךְ שֹׁמֵר הַפִּילַגְשִׁים
לֹא־תָבוֹא עוֹד אֶל־הַמֶּלֶךְ כִּי אִם־חָפֵץ בָּהּ הַמֶּלֶךְ וְנִקְרְאָה בְשֵׁם:

2:5. During the public reading of *Megillas Esther* on Purim, this verse is first recited aloud by the congregation, then repeated by the reader.

2:6. See *II Kings* 24:8ff.

2:10. Esther, a descendant of King Saul, did not declare her *royal lineage*. She had hoped the king would think that she was of humble origin and send her away (*Rashi*). Alternatively: She feared that had she declared her faith, she would have been forced to transgress the dictates of her religion (*Ibn Ezra*).

and let the king confer her royal estate upon another who is better than she.

. . . and a decree that wives be subservient

[20] Then, the king's decree which he will proclaim shall be heard throughout all his kingdom — great though it be — and all the wives will show respect to their husbands, great and small alike." [21] This proposal was favorable in the eyes of the king and the officials, and the king did according to the word of Memucan; [22] and he sent letters into all the king's provinces, to each province in its own script, and to each people in its own language, [to the effect that] every man should rule in his own home, and speak the language of his own people.

2

THE SEARCH FOR A QUEEN

[1] After these things, when the wrath of King Ahasuerus subsided, he remembered Vashti, and what she had done, and what had been decreed against her. [2] Then the king's attendants said, "Let there be sought for the king young maidens of beautiful appearance; [3] and let the king appoint commissioners in all the provinces of his kingdom, that they gather together every young maiden of beautiful appearance to Shushan the capital, to the harem, under the charge of Hegai the king's chamberlain, guardian of the women; and let their cosmetics be given them. [4] Then, let the girl who pleases the king reign in place of Vashti." The matter pleased the king, and he did so.

Mordechai and Esther

[5] *There was a Jewish man in Shushan the capital whose name was Mordechai son of Jair son of Shimei son of Kish, a Benjamite, [6] who had been exiled from Jerusalem along with the exiles who had been exiled with Jeconiah king of Judah, whom Nebuchadnezzar king of Babylon had exiled. * [7] And he had reared Hadassah, she is Esther, his uncle's daughter; for she had neither father nor mother. The maiden was finely featured and beautiful of appearance, and when her father and mother had died, Mordechai adopted her as [his] daughter. [8] So it came to pass, when the king's bidding and decree were announced, and when many young maidens were being brought together to Shushan the capital, under the charge of Hegai, that Esther was taken to the

Esther is brought to the competition . . .

king's palace, under the charge of Hegai, guardian of the women. [9] The girl was pleasing in his eyes, and she found favor before him; he hurriedly prepared her cosmetics and her allowance of delicacies to present [to] her, along with the seven attendants from the king's palace, and he transferred her and her maidens

. . . but keeps her identity secret

to the best [quarters] in the harem. [10] Esther had not told of her people or her kindred, for Mordechai had instructed her not to tell.* [11] Day after day Mordechai would walk about in front of the courtyard of the harem to learn about Esther's well-being and what would become of her.

The procession of candidates

[12] Now when each maiden's turn arrived to come to King Ahasuerus, after having been treated according to the law prescribed for women for twelve months (for so was the prescribed length of their anointing accomplished: six months with oil of myrrh, and six months with perfumes and feminine cosmetics) — [13] and when the girl came in this manner to the king, she was given whatever she requested to accompany her from the harem to the king's palace. [14] In the evening she would come, and in the morning she would return to the second harem in the charge of Shaashgaz, the king's chamberlain, guardian of the concubines.* She would never again come to the king unless the king desired her, and she was summoned by name.

2:14. There were two harems: one for the maidens being groomed for the king, the other for those who already had their turn with the king (*Rashi*).

טו וּבְהַגִּיעַ תֹּר־אֶסְתֵּר בַּת־אֲבִיחַיִל ׀ דֹּד מָרְדֳּכַי אֲשֶׁר לָקַח־לוֹ לְבַת לָבוֹא אֶל־הַמֶּלֶךְ לֹא בִקְשָׁה דָּבָר כִּי אִם אֶת־אֲשֶׁר יֹאמַר הֵגַי סְרִיס־הַמֶּלֶךְ

טז שֹׁמֵר הַנָּשִׁים וַתְּהִי אֶסְתֵּר נֹשֵׂאת חֵן בְּעֵינֵי כָּל־רֹאֶיהָ: וַתִּלָּקַח אֶסְתֵּר אֶל־הַמֶּלֶךְ אֲחַשְׁוֵרוֹשׁ אֶל־בֵּית מַלְכוּתוֹ בַּחֹדֶשׁ הָעֲשִׂירִי הוּא־חֹדֶשׁ טֵבֵת

יז בִּשְׁנַת־שֶׁבַע לְמַלְכוּתוֹ: וַיֶּאֱהַב הַמֶּלֶךְ אֶת־אֶסְתֵּר מִכָּל־הַנָּשִׁים וַתִּשָּׂא־חֵן וָחֶסֶד לְפָנָיו מִכָּל־הַבְּתוּלֹת וַיָּשֶׂם כֶּתֶר־מַלְכוּת בְּרֹאשָׁהּ וַיַּמְלִיכֶהָ תַּחַת

יח וַשְׁתִּי: וַיַּעַשׂ הַמֶּלֶךְ מִשְׁתֶּה גָדוֹל לְכָל־שָׂרָיו וַעֲבָדָיו אֵת מִשְׁתֵּה אֶסְתֵּר

יט וַהֲנָחָה לַמְּדִינוֹת עָשָׂה וַיִּתֵּן מַשְׂאֵת כְּיַד הַמֶּלֶךְ: וּבְהִקָּבֵץ בְּתוּלוֹת שֵׁנִית

כ וּמָרְדֳּכַי יֹשֵׁב בְּשַׁעַר־הַמֶּלֶךְ: אֵין אֶסְתֵּר מַגֶּדֶת מוֹלַדְתָּהּ וְאֶת־עַמָּהּ כַּאֲשֶׁר צִוָּה עָלֶיהָ מָרְדֳּכָי וְאֶת־מַאֲמַר מָרְדֳּכַי אֶסְתֵּר עֹשָׂה כַּאֲשֶׁר הָיְתָה בְאָמְנָה

כא אִתּוֹ: בַּיָּמִים הָהֵם וּמָרְדֳּכַי יֹשֵׁב בְּשַׁעַר־הַמֶּלֶךְ קָצַף בִּגְתָן וָתֶרֶשׁ שְׁנֵי־סָרִיסֵי הַמֶּלֶךְ מִשֹּׁמְרֵי הַסַּף וַיְבַקְשׁוּ לִשְׁלֹחַ

כב יָד בַּמֶּלֶךְ אֲחַשְׁוֵרֹשׁ: וַיִּוָּדַע הַדָּבָר לְמָרְדֳּכַי וַיַּגֵּד לְאֶסְתֵּר הַמַּלְכָּה וַתֹּאמֶר

כג אֶסְתֵּר לַמֶּלֶךְ בְּשֵׁם מָרְדֳּכָי: וַיְבֻקַּשׁ הַדָּבָר וַיִּמָּצֵא וַיִּתָּלוּ שְׁנֵיהֶם עַל־עֵץ וַיִּכָּתֵב בְּסֵפֶר דִּבְרֵי הַיָּמִים לִפְנֵי הַמֶּלֶךְ:

ג

א אַחַר ׀ הַדְּבָרִים הָאֵלֶּה גִּדַּל הַמֶּלֶךְ אֲחַשְׁוֵרוֹשׁ אֶת־הָמָן בֶּן־הַמְּדָתָא הָאֲגָגִי

ב וַיְנַשְּׂאֵהוּ וַיָּשֶׂם אֶת־כִּסְאוֹ מֵעַל כָּל־הַשָּׂרִים אֲשֶׁר אִתּוֹ: וְכָל־עַבְדֵי הַמֶּלֶךְ אֲשֶׁר־בְּשַׁעַר הַמֶּלֶךְ כֹּרְעִים וּמִשְׁתַּחֲוִים לְהָמָן כִּי־כֵן צִוָּה־לוֹ הַמֶּלֶךְ

ג וּמָרְדֳּכַי לֹא יִכְרַע וְלֹא יִשְׁתַּחֲוֶה: וַיֹּאמְרוּ עַבְדֵי הַמֶּלֶךְ אֲשֶׁר־בְּשַׁעַר

ד הַמֶּלֶךְ לְמָרְדֳּכָי מַדּוּעַ אַתָּה עוֹבֵר אֵת מִצְוַת הַמֶּלֶךְ: וַיְהִי °בְּאמְרָם [כְּאָמְרָם ק] אֵלָיו יוֹם וָיוֹם וְלֹא שָׁמַע אֲלֵיהֶם וַיַּגִּידוּ לְהָמָן לִרְאוֹת

ה הֲיַעַמְדוּ דִּבְרֵי מָרְדֳּכַי כִּי־הִגִּיד לָהֶם אֲשֶׁר־הוּא יְהוּדִי: וַיַּרְא

ו הָמָן כִּי־אֵין מָרְדֳּכַי כֹּרֵעַ וּמִשְׁתַּחֲוֶה לוֹ וַיִּמָּלֵא הָמָן חֵמָה: וַיִּבֶז בְּעֵינָיו לִשְׁלֹחַ יָד בְּמָרְדֳּכַי לְבַדּוֹ כִּי־הִגִּידוּ לוֹ אֶת־עַם מָרְדֳּכָי וַיְבַקֵּשׁ הָמָן לְהַשְׁמִיד אֶת־כָּל־הַיְּהוּדִים אֲשֶׁר בְּכָל־מַלְכוּת אֲחַשְׁוֵרוֹשׁ עַם מָרְדֳּכָי:

ז בַּחֹדֶשׁ הָרִאשׁוֹן הוּא־חֹדֶשׁ נִיסָן בִּשְׁנַת שְׁתֵּים עֶשְׂרֵה לַמֶּלֶךְ אֲחַשְׁוֵרוֹשׁ הִפִּיל פּוּר הוּא הַגּוֹרָל לִפְנֵי הָמָן מִיּוֹם ׀ לְיוֹם וּמֵחֹדֶשׁ לְחֹדֶשׁ שְׁנֵים־

ח עָשָׂר הוּא־חֹדֶשׁ אֲדָר: וַיֹּאמֶר הָמָן לַמֶּלֶךְ אֲחַשְׁוֵרוֹשׁ יֶשְׁנוֹ עַם־אֶחָד מְפֻזָּר וּמְפֹרָד בֵּין הָעַמִּים בְּכֹל מְדִינוֹת מַלְכוּתֶךָ וְדָתֵיהֶם שֹׁנוֹת מִכָּל־עָם וְאֶת־דָּתֵי הַמֶּלֶךְ אֵינָם עֹשִׂים וְלַמֶּלֶךְ אֵין־שֹׁוֶה לְהַנִּיחָם:

2:17. The Talmud explains that Esther was taken by Ahasuerus against her will and was never an active participant in their marital relations (*Sanhedrin* 74b).

2:22. The plotters spoke in their native Tarsian tongue, not expecting Mordechai the Jew to understand them (*Megillah* 13b).

2:23. This is not the Scriptural Book of Chronicles;

rather it is the annals of Persia and Media spoken of in 10:2.

3:1. Haman was a descendant of Agag, the Amalekite king conquered by King Saul (*I Samuel* 15:9).

3:2. Normally, Mordechai would have bowed in accordance with the king's instructions, for bowing to a king or his official is not forbidden by Torah law. Mordechai

¹⁵ *Now when the turn came for Esther daughter of Abihail uncle of Mordechai (who had adopted her as [his] daughter) to come to the king, she requested nothing except that which Hegai, the king's chamberlain, guardian of the women, had advised. Esther would find favor in the eyes of all who saw her.*

Esther pleases Ahasuerus . . .

¹⁶ *Esther was taken to King Ahasuerus into his royal palace in the tenth month, which is the month of Teves, in the seventh year of his reign.* ¹⁷ *The king loved Esther more than all the women, and she found more favor and kindness before him than all the other maidens; so that he set the royal crown upon her head, and made her queen in place of Vashti.* *

. . . and becomes the queen

¹⁸ *Then the king made a great banquet for all his officers and his servants — it was Esther's banquet — and he proclaimed an amnesty for the provinces, and gave gifts worthy of the king's hand.*

¹⁹ *And when the maidens were gathered together the second time, and Mordechai sat at the king's gate,* ²⁰ *Esther still told nothing of her kindred or her people as Mordechai had instructed her; for Esther continued to obey Mordechai, just as when she was reared by him.*

²¹ *In those days, while Mordechai was sitting at the king's gate, Bigthan and Teresh, two of the king's chamberlains of the guardians of the threshold, became enraged and sought to send [their] hand against King Ahasuerus.* ²² *The matter became known to Mordechai,* * *who told it to Queen Esther, and Esther informed the king in Mordechai's name.* ²³ *The matter was investigated and found [to be true], and they were both hanged on a gallows. It was recorded in the book of chronicles* * *in the king's presence.*

Mordechai saves the king's life

3

HAMAN'S RISE

¹ *A*fter these things King Ahasuerus promoted Haman son of Hammedatha the Agagite* and elevated him; he set his seat above all the officers who were with him.* ² *All the king's servants at the king's gate would bow down and prostrate themselves before Haman, for so had the king commanded concerning him. But Mordechai would not bow and would not prostrate himself.* *

Mordechai defies Haman . . .

³ *So the king's servants who were at the king's gate said to Mordechai, "Why do you disobey the king's command?"* ⁴ *Now it happened when they said this to him day after day and he did not heed them, they told Haman, to see whether Mordechai's words would prevail; for he had told them that he was a Jew.* ⁵ *When Haman, himself, saw that Mordechai did not bow down and prostrate himself before him, Haman was filled with wrath.* ⁶ *However, it seemed contemptible to him to send [his] hand against Mordechai alone, for they had told him of the people of Mordechai.* *

. . . who decides to kill all Jews

So Haman sought to destroy all the Jews who were throughout the entire kingdom of Ahasuerus — the people of Mordechai. ⁷ *In the first month, which is the month of Nissan, in the twelfth year of King Ahasuerus, pur* (that is, the lot) was cast in the presence of Haman from day to day, and from month to month, to the twelfth month, which is the month of Adar.*

Haman persuades the king . . .

⁸ *Then Haman said to King Ahasuerus, "There is a certain people scattered abroad and dispersed among the peoples in all the provinces of your realm. Their laws are different from every other people's and they do not observe the king's laws; therefore it is not befitting the king to tolerate them.*

---

refused to bow either because Haman had declared himself divine (*Rashi*) or because Haman's robes were decorated with idols (*Ibn Ezra*). In either of these cases, bowing to him would be an act of idolatry.

3:6. When Haman learned that Mordechai did not bow before him on religious grounds, he wished to take revenge upon all Jews.

3:7. The Persian word for "lottery" (*Ibn Ezra*).

ט אִם־עַל־הַמֶּלֶךְ טוֹב יִכָּתֵב לְאַבְּדָם וַעֲשֶׂרֶת אֲלָפִים כִּכַּר־כֶּסֶף אֶשְׁקוֹל
י עַל־יְדֵי עֹשֵׂי הַמְּלָאכָה לְהָבִיא אֶל־גִּנְזֵי הַמֶּלֶךְ: וַיָּסַר הַמֶּלֶךְ אֶת־
יא טַבַּעְתּוֹ מֵעַל יָדוֹ וַיִּתְּנָהּ לְהָמָן בֶּן־הַמְּדָתָא הָאֲגָגִי צֹרֵר הַיְּהוּדִים: וַיֹּאמֶר
יב הַמֶּלֶךְ לְהָמָן הַכֶּסֶף נָתוּן לָךְ וְהָעָם לַעֲשׂוֹת בּוֹ כַּטּוֹב בְּעֵינֶיךָ: וַיִּקָּרְאוּ
סֹפְרֵי הַמֶּלֶךְ בַּחֹדֶשׁ הָרִאשׁוֹן בִּשְׁלוֹשָׁה עָשָׂר יוֹם בּוֹ וַיִּכָּתֵב כְּכָל־אֲשֶׁר־
צִוָּה הָמָן אֶל אֲחַשְׁדַּרְפְּנֵי־הַמֶּלֶךְ וְאֶל־הַפַּחוֹת אֲשֶׁר | עַל־מְדִינָה
וּמְדִינָה וְאֶל־שָׂרֵי עַם וָעָם מְדִינָה וּמְדִינָה כִּכְתָבָהּ וְעַם וָעָם כִּלְשׁוֹנוֹ
יג בְּשֵׁם הַמֶּלֶךְ אֲחַשְׁוֵרֹשׁ נִכְתָּב וְנֶחְתָּם בְּטַבַּעַת הַמֶּלֶךְ: וְנִשְׁלוֹחַ סְפָרִים
בְּיַד הָרָצִים אֶל־כָּל־מְדִינוֹת הַמֶּלֶךְ לְהַשְׁמִיד לַהֲרֹג וּלְאַבֵּד אֶת־כָּל־
הַיְּהוּדִים מִנַּעַר וְעַד־זָקֵן טַף וְנָשִׁים בְּיוֹם אֶחָד בִּשְׁלוֹשָׁה עָשָׂר לְחֹדֶשׁ
יד שְׁנֵים־עָשָׂר הוּא־חֹדֶשׁ אֲדָר וּשְׁלָלָם לָבוֹז: פַּתְשֶׁגֶן הַכְּתָב לְהִנָּתֵן דָּת
בְּכָל־מְדִינָה וּמְדִינָה גָּלוּי לְכָל־הָעַמִּים לִהְיוֹת עֲתִדִים לַיּוֹם הַזֶּה: הָרָצִים
טו יָצְאוּ דְחוּפִים בִּדְבַר הַמֶּלֶךְ וְהַדָּת נִתְּנָה בְּשׁוּשַׁן הַבִּירָה וְהַמֶּלֶךְ וְהָמָן

ד יָשְׁבוּ לִשְׁתּוֹת וְהָעִיר שׁוּשָׁן נָבוֹכָה: וּמָרְדֳּכַי יָדַע אֶת־כָּל־
א אֲשֶׁר נַעֲשָׂה וַיִּקְרַע מָרְדֳּכַי אֶת־בְּגָדָיו וַיִּלְבַּשׁ שַׂק וָאֵפֶר וַיֵּצֵא בְּתוֹךְ
ב הָעִיר וַיִּזְעַק זְעָקָה גְדֹלָה וּמָרָה: וַיָּבוֹא עַד לִפְנֵי שַׁעַר־הַמֶּלֶךְ כִּי אֵין
ג לָבוֹא אֶל־שַׁעַר הַמֶּלֶךְ בִּלְבוּשׁ שָׂק: וּבְכָל־מְדִינָה וּמְדִינָה מְקוֹם אֲשֶׁר
דְּבַר־הַמֶּלֶךְ וְדָתוֹ מַגִּיעַ אֵבֶל גָּדוֹל לַיְּהוּדִים וְצוֹם וּבְכִי וּמִסְפֵּד שַׂק וָאֵפֶר
ד יֻצַּע לָרַבִּים: ◦וַתְּבוֹאֶינָה [◦וַתָּבוֹאנָה ק׳] נַעֲרוֹת אֶסְתֵּר וְסָרִיסֶיהָ וַיַּגִּידוּ
לָהּ וַתִּתְחַלְחַל הַמַּלְכָּה מְאֹד וַתִּשְׁלַח בְּגָדִים לְהַלְבִּישׁ אֶת־מָרְדֳּכַי
ה וּלְהָסִיר שַׂקּוֹ מֵעָלָיו וְלֹא קִבֵּל: וַתִּקְרָא אֶסְתֵּר לַהֲתָךְ מִסָּרִיסֵי הַמֶּלֶךְ
אֲשֶׁר הֶעֱמִיד לְפָנֶיהָ וַתְּצַוֵּהוּ עַל־מָרְדֳּכָי לָדַעַת מַה־זֶּה וְעַל־מַה־זֶּה:
ו וַיֵּצֵא הֲתָךְ אֶל־מָרְדֳּכָי אֶל־רְחוֹב הָעִיר אֲשֶׁר לִפְנֵי שַׁעַר־הַמֶּלֶךְ: וַיַּגֶּד־
ז לוֹ מָרְדֳּכַי אֵת כָּל־אֲשֶׁר קָרָהוּ וְאֵת | פָּרָשַׁת הַכֶּסֶף אֲשֶׁר אָמַר הָמָן
לִשְׁקוֹל עַל־גִּנְזֵי הַמֶּלֶךְ ◦בַּיְּהוּדִיים [◦בַּיְּהוּדִים ק׳] לְאַבְּדָם: וְאֶת־פַּתְשֶׁגֶן
ח כְּתָב־הַדָּת אֲשֶׁר־נִתַּן בְּשׁוּשָׁן לְהַשְׁמִידָם נָתַן לוֹ לְהַרְאוֹת אֶת־אֶסְתֵּר
וּלְהַגִּיד לָהּ וּלְצַוּוֹת עָלֶיהָ לָבוֹא אֶל־הַמֶּלֶךְ לְהִתְחַנֶּן־לוֹ וּלְבַקֵּשׁ מִלְּפָנָיו
ט עַל־עַמָּהּ: וַיָּבוֹא הֲתָךְ וַיַּגֵּד לְאֶסְתֵּר אֵת דִּבְרֵי מָרְדֳּכָי: וַתֹּאמֶר אֶסְתֵּר
י לַהֲתָךְ וַתְּצַוֵּהוּ אֶל־מָרְדֳּכָי: כָּל־עַבְדֵי הַמֶּלֶךְ וְעַם מְדִינוֹת הַמֶּלֶךְ יֹדְעִים
יא אֲשֶׁר כָּל־אִישׁ וְאִשָּׁה אֲשֶׁר יָבוֹא־אֶל־הַמֶּלֶךְ אֶל־הֶחָצֵר הַפְּנִימִית
אֲשֶׁר לֹא־יִקָּרֵא אַחַת דָּתוֹ לְהָמִית לְבַד מֵאֲשֶׁר יוֹשִׁיט־לוֹ הַמֶּלֶךְ אֶת־
שַׁרְבִיט הַזָּהָב וְחָיָה וַאֲנִי לֹא נִקְרֵאתִי לָבוֹא אֶל־הַמֶּלֶךְ זֶה שְׁלוֹשִׁים יוֹם:

3:10. The king's signet ring symbolized that Haman had full authority to act (*Rashi*).

3:15. The Jews within the city, that is (*Rashi*).

4:8. The time had come for Esther to reveal her identity and thus gain the king's mercy (*Alshich*).

9 If it pleases the king, let it be recorded that they be destroyed; and I will pay ten thousand silver talents into the hands of those who perform the duties, for deposit in the king's treasuries."

... receives the royal signet ...

10 So the king removed his signet ring from his hand, and gave it to Haman son of Hammedatha the Agagite, enemy of the Jews. * 11 Then the king said to Haman, "The silver is given to you, the people also, to do with as you see fit."

... and issues the decree of genocide

12 The king's scribes were summoned on the thirteenth day of the first month, and everything was written exactly as Haman had dictated, to the king's satraps, to the governors who were over every province, and to the officials of every people; [to] each province in its own script, and [to] each people in its own language; it was written in the name of King Ahasuerus, and it was sealed with the king's signet ring. 13 Letters were sent by courier to all the provinces of the king, to destroy, to slay and to exterminate all the Jews, from young to old, children and women, in one day, on the thirteenth of the twelfth month, which is the month of Adar, and to plunder their possessions. 14 Copies of the document were to be promulgated in every province, and be published to all peoples, for them to be prepared for that day. 15 The couriers went forth hur- riedly by order of the king, and the edict was distributed in Shushan the capital. The king and Haman sat down to drink, but the city of Shushan * was bewildered.

4

Mordechai's lament

1 Mordechai learned of all that had been done; and Mordechai tore his clothes and donned sackcloth and ashes. He went out into the midst of the city, and cried a loud and bitter cry. 2 He came until the front of the king's gate for it was forbidden to enter the king's gate in a garment of sackcloth. 3 And in every province, any place the king's command and his decree extended, there was great mourning among the Jews, and fasting and weeping and lament; sack- cloth and ashes were spread out for the masses.

Esther is informed ...

4 And Esther's maidens came, as well as her chamberlains, and told her about it, and the queen was greatly distressed; she sent garments to clothe Mordechai, and to remove his sackcloth from upon him, but he would not accept [them].

5 Then Esther summoned Hathach, one of the king's chamberlains whom he had stationed before her, and ordered him [to go] to Mordechai, to learn what this was about and why. 6 So Hathach went out to Mordechai to the city square, which was in front of the king's gate. 7 And Mordechai told him of all that had happened to him, and all about the sum of money that Haman had promised to pay to the royal treasuries for the annihilation of the Jews. 8 He also gave him a copy of the text of the decree that was distributed in Shushan

... and urged to help

for their destruction, so that he might show it to Esther and inform her, and bid her to go to the king, to implore of him, and to plead with him for her people. *

She demurs ...

9 Hathach came and told Esther the words of Mordechai. 10 Then Esther told Hathach, and ordered him [to return] to Mordechai, [saying]: 11 "All the king's servants and the people of the king's provinces know that any man or woman who approaches the king in the inner court, who is not summoned, his law is one — to be put to death; except for the one to whom the king shall extend the gold scepter so that he may live. Now I, I have not been summoned to come to the king for these [past] thirty days."

יב-יג וַיַּגִּ֖ידוּ לְמָרְדֳּכָ֑י אֵ֖ת דִּבְרֵ֥י אֶסְתֵּֽר: וַיֹּ֧אמֶר מָרְדֳּכַ֛י לְהָשִׁ֥יב אֶל־אֶסְתֵּ֖ר אַל־

יד תְּדַמִּ֣י בְנַפְשֵׁ֔ךְ לְהִמָּלֵ֥ט בֵּית־הַמֶּ֖לֶךְ מִכָּל־הַיְּהוּדִֽים: כִּ֣י אִם־הַחֲרֵ֣שׁ

תַּחֲרִ֘ישִׁי֮ בָּעֵ֣ת הַזֹּאת֒ רֶ֣וַח וְהַצָּלָ֞ה יַעֲמ֤וֹד לַיְּהוּדִים֙ מִמָּק֣וֹם אַחֵ֔ר וְאַ֥תְּ

טו וּבֵית־אָבִ֖יךְ תֹּאבֵ֑דוּ וּמִ֣י יוֹדֵ֔עַ אִם־לְעֵ֣ת כָּזֹ֔את הִגַּ֖עַתְּ לַמַּלְכֽוּת: וַתֹּ֥אמֶר

טז אֶסְתֵּ֖ר לְהָשִׁ֥יב אֶֽל־מָרְדֳּכָֽי: לֵךְ֩ כְּנ֨וֹס אֶת־כָּל־הַיְּהוּדִ֜ים הַֽנִּמְצְאִ֣ים

בְּשׁוּשָׁ֗ן וְצ֣וּמוּ עָ֠לַי וְאַל־תֹּֽאכְל֨וּ וְאַל־תִּשְׁתּ֜וּ שְׁלֹ֤שֶׁת יָמִים֙ לַ֣יְלָה וָי֔וֹם

גַּם־אֲנִ֥י וְנַעֲרֹתַ֖י אָצ֣וּם כֵּ֑ן וּבְכֵ֞ן אָב֤וֹא אֶל־הַמֶּ֨לֶךְ֙ אֲשֶׁ֣ר לֹֽא־כַדָּ֔ת וְכַאֲשֶׁ֥ר

יז אָבַ֖דְתִּי אָבָֽדְתִּי: וַֽיַּעֲבֹ֖ר מָרְדֳּכָ֑י וַיַּ֨עַשׂ֙ כְּכֹ֛ל אֲשֶׁר־צִוְּתָ֥ה עָלָ֖יו אֶסְתֵּֽר:

ה א וַיְהִ֣י ׀ בַּיּ֣וֹם הַשְּׁלִישִׁ֗י וַתִּלְבַּ֤שׁ אֶסְתֵּר֙ מַלְכ֔וּת וַֽתַּעֲמֹ֞ד בַּחֲצַ֣ר בֵּית־הַמֶּ֤לֶךְ

הַפְּנִימִ֔ית נֹ֖כַח בֵּ֣ית הַמֶּ֑לֶךְ וְהַמֶּ֗לֶךְ יוֹשֵׁ֞ב עַל־כִּסֵּ֤א מַלְכוּתוֹ֙ בְּבֵ֣ית

ב הַמַּלְכ֔וּת נֹ֖כַח פֶּ֥תַח הַבָּֽיִת: וַיְהִי֩ כִרְא֨וֹת הַמֶּ֜לֶךְ אֶת־אֶסְתֵּ֣ר הַמַּלְכָּ֗ה

עֹמֶ֨דֶת֙ בֶּֽחָצֵ֔ר נָשְׂאָ֥ה חֵ֖ן בְּעֵינָ֑יו וַיּ֨וֹשֶׁט הַמֶּ֜לֶךְ לְאֶסְתֵּ֗ר אֶת־שַׁרְבִ֤יט

ג הַזָּהָב֙ אֲשֶׁ֣ר בְּיָד֔וֹ וַתִּקְרַ֣ב אֶסְתֵּ֔ר וַתִּגַּ֖ע בְּרֹ֥אשׁ הַשַּׁרְבִֽיט: וַיֹּ֤אמֶר לָהּ֙

הַמֶּ֔לֶךְ מַה־לָּ֖ךְ אֶסְתֵּ֣ר הַמַּלְכָּ֑ה וּמַה־בַּקָּשָׁתֵ֛ךְ עַד־חֲצִ֥י הַמַּלְכ֖וּת וְיִנָּ֥תֵֽן

ד לָֽךְ: וַתֹּ֣אמֶר אֶסְתֵּ֔ר אִם־עַל־הַמֶּ֖לֶךְ ט֑וֹב יָב֨וֹא הַמֶּ֤לֶךְ וְהָמָן֙ הַיּ֔וֹם אֶל־

ה הַמִּשְׁתֶּ֖ה אֲשֶׁר־עָשִׂ֥יתִי לֽוֹ: וַיֹּ֣אמֶר הַמֶּ֔לֶךְ מַהֲר֣וּ אֶת־הָמָ֔ן לַעֲשׂ֖וֹת אֶת־

דְּבַ֣ר אֶסְתֵּ֑ר וַיָּבֹ֤א הַמֶּ֨לֶךְ֙ וְהָמָ֔ן אֶל־הַמִּשְׁתֶּ֖ה אֲשֶׁר־עָשְׂתָ֥ה אֶסְתֵּֽר:

ו וַיֹּ֨אמֶר הַמֶּ֤לֶךְ לְאֶסְתֵּר֙ בְּמִשְׁתֵּ֣ה הַיַּ֔יִן מַה־שְּׁאֵלָתֵ֖ךְ וְיִנָּ֣תֵֽן לָ֑ךְ וּמַה־

ז בַּקָּשָׁתֵ֛ךְ עַד־חֲצִ֥י הַמַּלְכ֖וּת וְתֵעָֽשׂ: וַתַּ֥עַן אֶסְתֵּ֖ר וַתֹּאמַ֑ר שְׁאֵלָתִ֖י

ח וּבַקָּשָׁתִֽי: אִם־מָצָ֨אתִי חֵ֜ן בְּעֵינֵ֣י הַמֶּ֗לֶךְ וְאִם־עַל־הַמֶּ֨לֶךְ֙ ט֔וֹב לָתֵת֙ אֶת־

שְׁאֵ֣לָתִ֔י וְלַעֲשׂ֖וֹת אֶת־בַּקָּשָׁתִ֑י יָב֧וֹא הַמֶּ֣לֶךְ וְהָמָ֗ן אֶל־הַמִּשְׁתֶּה֙ אֲשֶׁ֣ר

ט אֶעֱשֶׂ֣ה לָהֶ֔ם וּמָחָ֥ר אֶעֱשֶׂ֖ה כִּדְבַ֥ר הַמֶּֽלֶךְ: וַיֵּצֵ֨א הָמָ֜ן בַּיּ֤וֹם הַהוּא֙ שָׂמֵ֣חַ

וְט֣וֹב לֵ֔ב וְכִרְא֨וֹת הָמָ֜ן אֶֽת־מָרְדֳּכַ֣י בְּשַׁ֣עַר הַמֶּ֗לֶךְ וְלֹא־קָם֙ וְלֹא־זָ֣ע מִמֶּ֔נּוּ

י וַיִּמָּלֵ֥א הָמָ֛ן עַֽל־מָרְדֳּכַ֖י חֵמָֽה: וַיִּתְאַפַּ֣ק הָמָ֔ן וַיָּב֖וֹא אֶל־בֵּית֑וֹ וַיִּשְׁלַ֛ח

יא וַיָּבֵ֧א אֶת־אֹהֲבָ֛יו וְאֶת־זֶ֥רֶשׁ אִשְׁתּֽוֹ: וַיְסַפֵּ֨ר לָהֶ֤ם הָמָן֙ אֶת־כְּב֣וֹד עָשְׁר֔וֹ

וְרֹ֖ב בָּנָ֑יו וְאֵת֩ כָּל־אֲשֶׁ֨ר גִּדְּל֤וֹ הַמֶּ֨לֶךְ֙ וְאֵ֣ת אֲשֶׁ֣ר נִשְּׂא֔וֹ עַל־הַשָּׂרִ֖ים

יב וְעַבְדֵ֥י הַמֶּֽלֶךְ: וַיֹּ֨אמֶר֙ הָמָ֔ן אַ֣ף לֹא־הֵבִ֩יאָה֩ אֶסְתֵּ֨ר הַמַּלְכָּ֧ה עִם־הַמֶּ֛לֶךְ

אֶל־הַמִּשְׁתֶּ֥ה אֲשֶׁר־עָשָׂ֖תָה כִּ֣י אִם־אוֹתִ֑י וְגַם־לְמָחָ֛ר אֲנִ֥י קָֽרוּא־לָ֖הּ

יג עִם־הַמֶּֽלֶךְ: וְכָל־זֶ֕ה אֵינֶ֥נּוּ שֹׁוֶ֖ה לִ֑י בְּכָל־עֵ֗ת אֲשֶׁ֨ר אֲנִ֤י רֹאֶה֙ אֶֽת־

יד מָרְדֳּכַ֣י הַיְּהוּדִ֔י יוֹשֵׁ֖ב בְּשַׁ֥עַר הַמֶּֽלֶךְ: וַתֹּ֣אמֶר לוֹ֩ זֶ֨רֶשׁ אִשְׁתּ֜וֹ וְכָל־אֹֽהֲבָ֗יו

יַֽעֲשׂוּ־עֵץ֮ גָּבֹ֣הַּ חֲמִשִּׁ֣ים אַמָּה֒ וּבַבֹּ֣קֶר ׀ אֱמֹ֣ר לַמֶּ֗לֶךְ וְיִתְל֤וּ אֶֽת־מָרְדֳּכַי֙

עָלָ֔יו וּבֹֽא־עִם־הַמֶּ֥לֶךְ אֶל־הַמִּשְׁתֶּ֖ה שָׂמֵ֑חַ וַיִּיטַ֧ב הַדָּבָ֛ר לִפְנֵ֥י הָמָ֖ן וַיַּ֥עַשׂ

5:1. The third day of the fast, which was the first day of Passover (*Rashi*).

5:4. To show that God protects Israel in hidden ways,

His Name is not mentioned explicitly in this Book. However, in this verse it is alluded to, since the first Hebrew letters of the words יָבוֹא הַמֶּלֶךְ וְהָמָן הַיּוֹם, *let the king*

. . . but Mordechai demands action

^{12} *They related Esther's words to Mordechai.* ^{13} *Then Mordechai said to reply to Esther, "Do not imagine in your soul that you will be able to escape in the king's palace any more than the rest of the Jews.* ^{14} *For if you persist in keeping silent at a time like this, relief and deliverance will come to the Jews from another place, while you and your father's house will perish. And who knows whether it was just for such a time as this that you attained the royal position!"*

Esther asks for a fast

^{15} *Then Esther said to reply to Mordechai:* ^{16} *"Go, assemble all the Jews that are to be found in Shushan, and fast for me; do not eat or drink for three days, night or day; and I, with my maids, will fast also. Thus I will come to the king though it is unlawful; and if I perish, I perish."* ^{17} *Mordechai then left and did exactly as Esther had commanded him.*

5

Esther risks her life

^{1} **N**ow *it came to pass on the third day,* * *Esther donned royalty and stood in the inner courtyard of the king's palace facing the king's palace, while the king was sitting on his royal throne in the royal palace facing the entrance of the palace.* ^{2} *When the king noticed Queen Esther standing in the courtyard, she found favor in his eyes. The king extended to Esther the gold scepter that was in his hand, and Esther approached and touched the tip of the scepter.*

The king is gracious

^{3} *The king said to her, "What is it for you, O Queen Esther? And what is your petition? [Even if it be] until half the kingdom, it shall be granted you."*

Esther's invitation

^{4} *Esther said, "If it please the king, let the king and Haman come today* * *to the banquet that I have prepared for him."*

^{5} *Then the king commanded, "Hasten Haman to fulfill Esther's word." So the king and Haman came to the banquet that Esther had prepared.*

What is your request?

^{6} *The king said to Esther during the wine feast, "What is your request? It shall be granted you. And what is your petition? [Even if it be] until half the kingdom, it shall be fulfilled."*

Another invitation

^{7} *So Esther responded and said, "My request and my petition:* ^{8} *If I have found favor in the king's eyes, and if it pleases the king to grant my request and to fulfill my petition, let the king and Haman come to the banquet that I shall prepare for them, and tomorrow I shall fulfill the king's word."* *

Haman's anger and arrogance

^{9} *That day Haman went out joyful and exuberant. But when Haman noticed Mordechai in the king's gate and that he did not stand up and did not stir before him, Haman was filled with wrath at Mordechai.* ^{10} *[Nevertheless,] Haman restrained himself and went home. He sent and summoned his friends and his wife, Zeresh.* ^{11} *Haman recounted to them the glory of his wealth and of his many sons, and all [the ways] in which the king had promoted him and elevated him above the officials and royal servants.* ^{12} *Haman said, "Moreover, Queen Esther brought no one but myself to accompany the king to the banquet that she had prepared, and tomorrow, too, I am invited by her along with the king.* ^{13} *Yet all this is worth nothing to me so long as I see Mordechai the Jew sitting at the king's gate."*

The gallows

^{14} *So his wife, Zeresh, as well as all his friends, said to him, "Let them make a gallows, fifty cubits high; and in the morning speak to the king and have them hang Mordechai on it. Then, accompany the king to the banquet in good spirits." This suggestion pleased Haman, and he had the gallows made.*

---

and Haman come today, spell the Holy Name of God
(*Rabbeinu Bachya*).

5:8. Esther promised to reveal her origins as the king
had repeatedly requested (*Rashi*).

ו   בַּלַּיְלָה הַהוּא נָדְדָה שְׁנַת הַמֶּלֶךְ וַיֹּאמֶר לְהָבִיא   א   הָעֵץ:
אֶת־סֵפֶר הַזִּכְרֹנוֹת דִּבְרֵי הַיָּמִים וַיִּהְיוּ נִקְרָאִים לִפְנֵי הַמֶּלֶךְ: וַיִּמָּצֵא   ב
כָתוּב אֲשֶׁר הִגִּיד מָרְדֳּכַי עַל־בִּגְתָנָא וָתֶרֶשׁ שְׁנֵי סָרִיסֵי הַמֶּלֶךְ מִשֹּׁמְרֵי
הַסַּף אֲשֶׁר בִּקְשׁוּ לִשְׁלֹחַ יָד בַּמֶּלֶךְ אֲחַשְׁוֵרוֹשׁ: וַיֹּאמֶר הַמֶּלֶךְ מַה־נַּעֲשָׂה   ג
יְקָר וּגְדוּלָּה לְמָרְדֳּכַי עַל־זֶה וַיֹּאמְרוּ נַעֲרֵי הַמֶּלֶךְ מְשָׁרְתָיו לֹא־נַעֲשָׂה
עִמּוֹ דָּבָר: וַיֹּאמֶר הַמֶּלֶךְ מִי בֶחָצֵר וְהָמָן בָּא לַחֲצַר בֵּית־הַמֶּלֶךְ   ד
הַחִיצוֹנָה לֵאמֹר לַמֶּלֶךְ לִתְלוֹת אֶת־מָרְדֳּכַי עַל־הָעֵץ אֲשֶׁר־הֵכִין לוֹ:
וַיֹּאמְרוּ נַעֲרֵי הַמֶּלֶךְ אֵלָיו הִנֵּה הָמָן עֹמֵד בֶּחָצֵר וַיֹּאמֶר הַמֶּלֶךְ יָבוֹא: ה
וַיָּבוֹא הָמָן וַיֹּאמֶר לוֹ הַמֶּלֶךְ מַה־לַעֲשׂוֹת בָּאִישׁ אֲשֶׁר הַמֶּלֶךְ חָפֵץ   ו
בִּיקָרוֹ וַיֹּאמֶר הָמָן בְּלִבּוֹ לְמִי יַחְפֹּץ הַמֶּלֶךְ לַעֲשׂוֹת יְקָר יוֹתֵר מִמֶּנִּי:
וַיֹּאמֶר הָמָן אֶל־הַמֶּלֶךְ אִישׁ אֲשֶׁר הַמֶּלֶךְ חָפֵץ בִּיקָרוֹ: יָבִיאוּ לְבוּשׁ   ז ח
מַלְכוּת אֲשֶׁר לָבַשׁ־בּוֹ הַמֶּלֶךְ וְסוּס אֲשֶׁר רָכַב עָלָיו הַמֶּלֶךְ וַאֲשֶׁר נִתַּן
כֶּתֶר מַלְכוּת בְּרֹאשׁוֹ: וְנָתוֹן הַלְּבוּשׁ וְהַסּוּס עַל־יַד־אִישׁ מִשָּׂרֵי הַמֶּלֶךְ   ט
הַפַּרְתְּמִים וְהִלְבִּישׁוּ אֶת־הָאִישׁ אֲשֶׁר הַמֶּלֶךְ חָפֵץ בִּיקָרוֹ וְהִרְכִּיבֻהוּ
עַל־הַסּוּס בִּרְחוֹב הָעִיר וְקָרְאוּ לְפָנָיו כָּכָה יֵעָשֶׂה לָאִישׁ אֲשֶׁר הַמֶּלֶךְ
חָפֵץ בִּיקָרוֹ: וַיֹּאמֶר הַמֶּלֶךְ לְהָמָן מַהֵר קַח אֶת־הַלְּבוּשׁ וְאֶת־הַסּוּס   י
כַּאֲשֶׁר דִּבַּרְתָּ וַעֲשֵׂה־כֵן לְמָרְדֳּכַי הַיְּהוּדִי הַיּוֹשֵׁב בְּשַׁעַר הַמֶּלֶךְ אַל־תַּפֵּל
דָּבָר מִכֹּל אֲשֶׁר דִּבַּרְתָּ: וַיִּקַּח הָמָן אֶת־הַלְּבוּשׁ וְאֶת־הַסּוּס וַיַּלְבֵּשׁ אֶת־   יא
מָרְדֳּכָי וַיַּרְכִּיבֵהוּ בִּרְחוֹב הָעִיר וַיִּקְרָא לְפָנָיו כָּכָה יֵעָשֶׂה לָאִישׁ אֲשֶׁר
הַמֶּלֶךְ חָפֵץ בִּיקָרוֹ: וַיָּשָׁב מָרְדֳּכַי אֶל־שַׁעַר הַמֶּלֶךְ וְהָמָן נִדְחַף אֶל־בֵּיתוֹ   יב
אָבֵל וַחֲפוּי רֹאשׁ: וַיְסַפֵּר הָמָן לְזֶרֶשׁ אִשְׁתּוֹ וּלְכָל־אֹהֲבָיו אֵת כָּל־אֲשֶׁר   יג
קָרָהוּ וַיֹּאמְרוּ לוֹ חֲכָמָיו וְזֶרֶשׁ אִשְׁתּוֹ אִם מִזֶּרַע הַיְּהוּדִים מָרְדֳּכַי אֲשֶׁר
הַחִלּוֹתָ לִנְפֹּל לְפָנָיו לֹא־תוּכַל לוֹ כִּי־נָפוֹל תִּפּוֹל לְפָנָיו: עוֹדָם מְדַבְּרִים   יד
עִמּוֹ וְסָרִיסֵי הַמֶּלֶךְ הִגִּיעוּ וַיַּבְהִלוּ לְהָבִיא אֶת־הָמָן אֶל־הַמִּשְׁתֶּה אֲשֶׁר־
עָשְׂתָה אֶסְתֵּר: וַיָּבֹא הַמֶּלֶךְ וְהָמָן לִשְׁתּוֹת עִם־אֶסְתֵּר הַמַּלְכָּה: וַיֹּאמֶר   א   **ז**
הַמֶּלֶךְ לְאֶסְתֵּר גַּם בַּיּוֹם הַשֵּׁנִי בְּמִשְׁתֵּה הַיַּיִן מַה־שְּׁאֵלָתֵךְ אֶסְתֵּר
הַמַּלְכָּה וְתִנָּתֵן לָךְ וּמַה־בַּקָּשָׁתֵךְ עַד־חֲצִי הַמַּלְכוּת וְתֵעָשׂ: וַתַּעַן אֶסְתֵּר   ב
הַמַּלְכָּה וַתֹּאמַר אִם־מָצָאתִי חֵן בְּעֵינֶיךָ הַמֶּלֶךְ וְאִם־עַל־הַמֶּלֶךְ טוֹב   ג
תִּנָּתֶן־לִי נַפְשִׁי בִּשְׁאֵלָתִי וְעַמִּי בְּבַקָּשָׁתִי: כִּי נִמְכַּרְנוּ אֲנִי וְעַמִּי לְהַשְׁמִיד
לַהֲרוֹג וּלְאַבֵּד וְאִלּוּ לַעֲבָדִים וְלִשְׁפָחוֹת נִמְכַּרְנוּ הֶחֱרַשְׁתִּי כִּי אֵין הַצָּר   ד
שֹׁוֶה בְּנֵזֶק הַמֶּלֶךְ: וַיֹּאמֶר הַמֶּלֶךְ אֲחַשְׁוֵרוֹשׁ וַיֹּאמֶר   ה
לְאֶסְתֵּר הַמַּלְכָּה מִי הוּא זֶה וְאֵי־זֶה הוּא אֲשֶׁר־מְלָאוֹ לִבּוֹ לַעֲשׂוֹת כֵּן:

6:1. Allegorically the *Midrash* comments that the distress of the Jews caused God's Heavenly throne to be shaken.

6:2. See 2:21-23.

6:13. Zeresh and the advisers were sure the king's command to honor Mordechai was not coincidental; it

6

THE WHEEL TURNS

¹ That night the king's sleep was disturbed* so he commanded to bring the book of records, the chronicles, and that they be read before the king. ² And it was found written [there] that Mordechai had denounced Bigthana and Teresh,* two of the king's chamberlains of the guardians of the threshold, who had sought to send [their] hand against King Ahasuerus. ³ The king said, "What honor or majesty has been done for Mordechai for this?"

Was Mordechai honored?

The king's attendants, his ministrants, said, "Nothing has been done for him."

⁴ The king said, "Who is in the courtyard?" (Now Haman was [just] coming into the outer courtyard of the royal palace to speak to the king about hanging Mordechai on the gallows that he had prepared for him.)

Haman's arrival . . .

⁵ So the king's attendants said to him, "Behold! Haman stands in the courtyard."

And the king said, "Let him enter." ⁶ Haman entered and the king said to him, "What should be done for the man whom the king desires to honor?"

. . . and prescription for honor

Now Haman said in his heart, "Whom would the king especially want to honor more than me?" ⁷ So Haman said to the king, "For the man whom the king desires to honor, ⁸ have them bring royal attire that the king has worn and a horse upon which the king has ridden, one with a royal crown placed on his head. ⁹ Then let the attire and the horse be given over into the hand of one of the king's most noble officials, and let them dress the man whom the king desires to honor, and have him ride on the horse through the city square, and let them proclaim before him, 'This is what shall be done for the man whom the king desires to honor.' "

Do so for Mordechai the Jew!

¹⁰ Then the king said to Haman, "Hurry, take the attire and the horse as you have said, and do all this for Mordechai the Jew, who sits at the king's gate. Do not omit a single detail of all that you have suggested!"

¹¹ So Haman took the garment and the horse and dressed Mordechai, and had him ride through the city square, and proclaimed before him, "This is what shall be done for the man whom the king desires to honor."

Despondent and doomed

¹² Mordechai returned to the king's gate; but Haman hurried home, despondent and with his head covered. ¹³ Haman told his wife, Zeresh, and all his friends everything that had happened to him, and his wise men and his wife, Zeresh, said to him, "If Mordechai, before whom you have begun to fall, is of Jewish descent, you will not prevail against him, but will undoubtedly fall before him."* ¹⁴ While they were still talking with him, the king's chamberlains arrived, and they hurried to bring Haman to the banquet which Esther had prepared.

7

The second banquet

¹ So the king and Haman came to feast with Queen Esther. ² The king asked Esther again on the second day at the wine feast, "What is your request, Queen Esther? — it shall be granted you. And what is your petition? [Even if it be] until half the kingdom, it shall be fulfilled."

Esther's plea

³ So Queen Esther responded and said, "If I have found favor in your eyes, O king, and if it pleases the king, let my life be granted to me as my request and my people as my petition. ⁴ For we have been sold, I and my people, to be destroyed, to be slain and to be exterminated. Had we been sold as slaves and maidservants, I would have kept quiet, for the adversary is not worthy of the king's damage."

⁵ Thereupon, King Ahasuerus exclaimed and said to Queen Esther, "Who is this? Where is this one who dared to do so?"

---

signified the beginning of the Jews' rise — and of Haman's downfall (*Yosef Lekach*; *Malbim*).

ו וַתֹּאמֶר אֶסְתֵּר אִישׁ צַר וְאוֹיֵב הָמָן הָרָע הַזֶּה וְהָמָן נִבְעַת מִלִּפְנֵי הַמֶּלֶךְ
ז וְהַמַּלְכָּה: וְהַמֶּלֶךְ קָם בַּחֲמָתוֹ מִמִּשְׁתֵּה הַיַּיִן אֶל־גִּנַּת הַבִּיתָן וְהָמָן עָמַד
לְבַקֵּשׁ עַל־נַפְשׁוֹ מֵאֶסְתֵּר הַמַּלְכָּה כִּי רָאָה כִּי־כָלְתָה אֵלָיו הָרָעָה מֵאֵת
ח הַמֶּלֶךְ: וְהַמֶּלֶךְ שָׁב מִגִּנַּת הַבִּיתָן אֶל־בֵּית | מִשְׁתֵּה הַיַּיִן וְהָמָן נֹפֵל עַל־
הַמִּטָּה אֲשֶׁר אֶסְתֵּר עָלֶיהָ וַיֹּאמֶר הַמֶּלֶךְ הֲגַם לִכְבּוֹשׁ אֶת־הַמַּלְכָּה עִמִּי
ט בַּבָּיִת הַדָּבָר יָצָא מִפִּי הַמֶּלֶךְ וּפְנֵי הָמָן חָפוּ: וַיֹּאמֶר חַרְבוֹנָה אֶחָד מִן־
הַסָּרִיסִים לִפְנֵי הַמֶּלֶךְ גַּם הִנֵּה־הָעֵץ אֲשֶׁר־עָשָׂה הָמָן לְמָרְדֳּכַי אֲשֶׁר
דִּבֶּר־טוֹב עַל־הַמֶּלֶךְ עֹמֵד בְּבֵית הָמָן גָּבֹהַּ חֲמִשִּׁים אַמָּה וַיֹּאמֶר הַמֶּלֶךְ
י תְּלֻהוּ עָלָיו: וַיִּתְלוּ אֶת־הָמָן עַל־הָעֵץ אֲשֶׁר־הֵכִין לְמָרְדֳּכַי וַחֲמַת הַמֶּלֶךְ

ח

א שָׁכָכָה: בַּיּוֹם הַהוּא נָתַן הַמֶּלֶךְ אֲחַשְׁוֵרוֹשׁ לְאֶסְתֵּר הַמַּלְכָּה
אֶת־בֵּית הָמָן צֹרֵר °הַיְּהוּדִיִּים [°הַיְּהוּדִים ק] וּמָרְדֳּכַי בָּא לִפְנֵי הַמֶּלֶךְ
ב כִּי־הִגִּידָה אֶסְתֵּר מַה הוּא־לָהּ: וַיָּסַר הַמֶּלֶךְ אֶת־טַבַּעְתּוֹ אֲשֶׁר הֶעֱבִיר
מֵהָמָן וַיִּתְּנָהּ לְמָרְדֳּכָי וַתָּשֶׂם אֶסְתֵּר אֶת־מָרְדֳּכַי עַל־בֵּית הָמָן:
ג וַתּוֹסֶף אֶסְתֵּר וַתְּדַבֵּר לִפְנֵי הַמֶּלֶךְ וַתִּפֹּל לִפְנֵי רַגְלָיו וַתֵּבְךְּ וַתִּתְחַנֶּן־לוֹ לְהַעֲבִיר
ד אֶת־רָעַת הָמָן הָאֲגָגִי וְאֵת מַחֲשַׁבְתּוֹ אֲשֶׁר חָשַׁב עַל־הַיְּהוּדִים: וַיּוֹשֶׁט
הַמֶּלֶךְ לְאֶסְתֵּר אֵת שַׁרְבִט הַזָּהָב וַתָּקָם אֶסְתֵּר וַתַּעֲמֹד לִפְנֵי הַמֶּלֶךְ:
ה וַתֹּאמֶר אִם־עַל־הַמֶּלֶךְ טוֹב וְאִם־מָצָאתִי חֵן לְפָנָיו וְכָשֵׁר הַדָּבָר לִפְנֵי
הַמֶּלֶךְ וְטוֹבָה אֲנִי בְּעֵינָיו יִכָּתֵב לְהָשִׁיב אֶת־הַסְּפָרִים מַחֲשֶׁבֶת הָמָן בֶּן־
הַמְּדָתָא הָאֲגָגִי אֲשֶׁר כָּתַב לְאַבֵּד אֶת־הַיְּהוּדִים אֲשֶׁר בְּכָל־מְדִינוֹת
ו הַמֶּלֶךְ: כִּי אֵיכָכָה אוּכַל וְרָאִיתִי בָּרָעָה אֲשֶׁר־יִמְצָא אֶת־עַמִּי וְאֵיכָכָה
ז אוּכַל וְרָאִיתִי בְּאָבְדַן מוֹלַדְתִּי: וַיֹּאמֶר הַמֶּלֶךְ אֲחַשְׁוֵרֹשׁ
לְאֶסְתֵּר הַמַּלְכָּה וּלְמָרְדֳּכַי הַיְּהוּדִי הִנֵּה בֵית־הָמָן נָתַתִּי לְאֶסְתֵּר
וְאֹתוֹ תָּלוּ עַל־הָעֵץ עַל אֲשֶׁר־שָׁלַח יָדוֹ °בַּיְּהוּדִיִּים [°בַּיְּהוּדִים ק]: וְאַתֶּם
ח כִּתְבוּ עַל־הַיְּהוּדִים כַּטּוֹב בְּעֵינֵיכֶם בְּשֵׁם הַמֶּלֶךְ וְחִתְמוּ בְּטַבַּעַת
הַמֶּלֶךְ כִּי־כְתָב אֲשֶׁר־נִכְתָּב בְּשֵׁם־הַמֶּלֶךְ וְנַחְתּוֹם בְּטַבַּעַת הַמֶּלֶךְ
ט אֵין לְהָשִׁיב: וַיִּקָּרְאוּ סֹפְרֵי־הַמֶּלֶךְ בָּעֵת־הַהִיא בַּחֹדֶשׁ הַשְּׁלִישִׁי הוּא־
חֹדֶשׁ סִיוָן בִּשְׁלוֹשָׁה וְעֶשְׂרִים בּוֹ וַיִּכָּתֵב כְּכָל־אֲשֶׁר־צִוָּה מָרְדֳּכַי אֶל־
הַיְּהוּדִים וְאֶל הָאֲחַשְׁדַּרְפְּנִים־וְהַפַּחוֹת וְשָׂרֵי הַמְּדִינוֹת אֲשֶׁר | מֵהֹדּוּ
וְעַד־כּוּשׁ שֶׁבַע וְעֶשְׂרִים וּמֵאָה מְדִינָה מְדִינָה וּמְדִינָה כִּכְתָבָהּ וְעַם
י וָעָם כִּלְשֹׁנוֹ וְאֶל־הַיְּהוּדִים כִּכְתָבָם וְכִלְשׁוֹנָם: וַיִּכְתֹּב בְּשֵׁם הַמֶּלֶךְ
אֲחַשְׁוֵרֹשׁ וַיַּחְתֹּם בְּטַבַּעַת הַמֶּלֶךְ וַיִּשְׁלַח סְפָרִים בְּיַד הָרָצִים בַּסּוּסִים
יא רֹכְבֵי הָרֶכֶשׁ הָאֲחַשְׁתְּרָנִים בְּנֵי הָרַמָּכִים: אֲשֶׁר נָתַן הַמֶּלֶךְ לַיְּהוּדִים |
אֲשֶׁר | בְּכָל־עִיר־וָעִיר לְהִקָּהֵל וְלַעֲמֹד עַל־נַפְשָׁם לְהַשְׁמִיד וְלַהֲרֹג
וּלְאַבֵּד אֶת־כָּל־חֵיל עַם וּמְדִינָה הַצָּרִים אֹתָם טַף וְנָשִׁים וּשְׁלָלָם לָבוֹז:

Esther accuses Haman

⁶ And Esther said, "A man who is an adversary and an enemy! This wicked Haman!" Haman trembled in terror before the king and queen.

⁷ The king rose in his wrath from the wine feast and went into the palace garden while Haman remained to beg Queen Esther for his soul, for he saw that evil had been determined against him by the king. ⁸ When the king returned from the palace garden to the hall of the wine feast, Haman had fallen onto the couch upon which Esther was; so the king exclaimed, "Would he actually assault the queen while I'm in the house?" As soon as the king uttered this, they covered Haman's face.

The king's fury

⁹ Then Harbonah, one of the chamberlains [in attendance] before the king, said, "Furthermore, the gallows which Haman made for Mordechai — who spoke good for the king — is standing in Haman's house; it is fifty cubits high." * And the king said, "Hang him on it." ¹⁰ So they hanged Haman on the gallows that he had prepared for Mordechai, and the king's anger abated.

"Hang him on it"

8

Mordechai becomes viceroy

¹ That very day, King Ahasuerus gave the estate of Haman, the enemy of the Jews, to Queen Esther. Mordechai came before the king, for Esther had told [the king] what he was to her. ² The king removed his signet ring, which he had taken away from Haman, and gave it to Mordechai; and Esther put Mordechai in charge of Haman's estate.

Esther's new plea

³ Esther yet again spoke to the king, she fell at his feet, and wept and implored him to avert the evil [intention] of Haman the Agagite, and his scheme that he had plotted against the Jews. ⁴ The king extended the gold scepter to Esther, and Esther arose and stood before the king. ⁵ She said, "If it pleases the king, and if I have found favor before him, and the proposal seems proper before the king, and I be pleasing in his eyes, let it be written to countermand those dispatches, the scheme of Haman the son of Hammedatha the Agagite, [in] which he had written to exterminate the Jews who are in all the king's provinces. * ⁶ For how can I bear to witness the disaster which will befall my people?! How can I bear to witness the extermination of my kindred?!"

Permission to write

⁷ Then King Ahasuerus said to Queen Esther and to Mordechai the Jew, "Behold, I have given Haman's estate to Esther, and they have hanged him on the gallows because he sent [his] hand against the Jews. ⁸ You may write concerning the Jews whatever is favorable in your eyes, in the name of the king, and seal it with the king's signet, for an edict which is written in the king's name and sealed with the king's signet may not be revoked."

The revised decree

⁹ So they summoned the king's scribes at that time, in the third month, which is the month of Sivan, on its twenty-third [day], and it was written as Mordechai had dictated to the Jews and to the satraps, the governors and officials of the provinces from Hodu to Cush, a hundred and twenty-seven provinces, to each province in its own script, and each people in its own language, and to the Jews in their own script and language. ¹⁰ He wrote in the name of King Ahasuerus and sealed it with the king's signet. He sent dispatches by couriers on horseback, riders of swift mules bred of mares, ¹¹ [to the effect] that the king had given [permission] to the Jews of every city to organize and to defend themselves; to destroy, to slay and to exterminate every armed force of any people or province that threaten them, [along with their] children and women, and to plunder their possessions,

Jewish self-defense

7:9. Harbonah's swift advice prevented Haman from bribing his way back into the king's good graces.

8:5. Since Haman's decree was still in effect, Esther proposed the recall of the sealed letters.

יב בְּיוֹם אֶחָד בְּכָל־מְדִינוֹת הַמֶּלֶךְ אֲחַשְׁוֵרוֹשׁ בִּשְׁלוֹשָׁה עָשָׂר לְחֹדֶשׁ שְׁנֵים־

יג עָשָׂר הוּא־חֹדֶשׁ אֲדָר: פַּתְשֶׁגֶן הַכְּתָב לְהִנָּתֵן דָּת בְּכָל־מְדִינָה וּמְדִינָה גָּלוּי לְכָל־הָעַמִּים וְלִהְיוֹת °הַיְּהוּדִים עתודים [°הַיְּהוּדִים עֲתִידִים ק] לַיּוֹם הַזֶּה

יד לְהִנָּקֵם מֵאֹיְבֵיהֶם: הָרָצִים רֹכְבֵי הָרֶכֶשׁ הָאֲחַשְׁתְּרָנִים יָצְאוּ מְבֹהָלִים

טו וּדְחוּפִים בִּדְבַר הַמֶּלֶךְ וְהַדָּת נִתְּנָה בְּשׁוּשַׁן הַבִּירָה: וּמָרְדֳּכַי יָצָא | מִלִּפְנֵי הַמֶּלֶךְ בִּלְבוּשׁ מַלְכוּת תְּכֵלֶת וָחוּר וַעֲטֶרֶת זָהָב גְּדוֹלָה

טז וְתַכְרִיךְ בּוּץ וְאַרְגָּמָן וְהָעִיר שׁוּשָׁן צָהֲלָה וְשָׂמֵחָה: לַיְּהוּדִים הָיְתָה אוֹרָה

יז וְשִׂמְחָה וְשָׂשֹׂן וִיקָר: וּבְכָל־מְדִינָה וּמְדִינָה וּבְכָל־עִיר וָעִיר מְקוֹם אֲשֶׁר דְּבַר־הַמֶּלֶךְ וְדָתוֹ מַגִּיעַ שִׂמְחָה וְשָׂשׂוֹן לַיְּהוּדִים מִשְׁתֶּה וְיוֹם טוֹב וְרַבִּים מֵעַמֵּי הָאָרֶץ מִתְיַהֲדִים כִּי־נָפַל פַּחַד־הַיְּהוּדִים עֲלֵיהֶם: וּבִשְׁנֵים עָשָׂר חֹדֶשׁ

ט:א הוּא־חֹדֶשׁ אֲדָר בִּשְׁלוֹשָׁה עָשָׂר יוֹם בּוֹ אֲשֶׁר הִגִּיעַ דְּבַר־הַמֶּלֶךְ וְדָתוֹ לְהֵעָשׂוֹת בַּיּוֹם אֲשֶׁר שִׂבְּרוּ אֹיְבֵי הַיְּהוּדִים לִשְׁלוֹט בָּהֶם וְנַהֲפוֹךְ

ב הוּא אֲשֶׁר יִשְׁלְטוּ הַיְּהוּדִים הֵמָּה בְּשֹׂנְאֵיהֶם: נִקְהֲלוּ הַיְּהוּדִים בְּעָרֵיהֶם בְּכָל־מְדִינוֹת הַמֶּלֶךְ אֲחַשְׁוֵרוֹשׁ לִשְׁלֹחַ יָד בִּמְבַקְשֵׁי רָעָתָם וְאִישׁ לֹא־עָמַד

ג לִפְנֵיהֶם כִּי־נָפַל פַּחְדָּם עַל־כָּל־הָעַמִּים: וְכָל־שָׂרֵי הַמְּדִינוֹת וְהָאֲחַשְׁדַּרְפְּנִים וְהַפַּחוֹת וְעֹשֵׂי הַמְּלָאכָה אֲשֶׁר לַמֶּלֶךְ מְנַשְּׂאִים אֶת־

ד הַיְּהוּדִים כִּי־נָפַל פַּחַד־מָרְדֳּכַי עֲלֵיהֶם: כִּי־גָדוֹל מָרְדֳּכַי בְּבֵית הַמֶּלֶךְ וְשָׁמְעוֹ הוֹלֵךְ בְּכָל־הַמְּדִינוֹת כִּי־הָאִישׁ מָרְדֳּכַי הוֹלֵךְ וְגָדוֹל: וַיַּכּוּ הַיְּהוּדִים

ה בְּכָל־אֹיְבֵיהֶם מַכַּת־חֶרֶב וְהֶרֶג וְאַבְדָן וַיַּעֲשׂוּ בְשֹׂנְאֵיהֶם כִּרְצוֹנָם: וּבְשׁוּשַׁן

ו־ז הַבִּירָה הָרְגוּ הַיְּהוּדִים וְאַבֵּד חֲמֵשׁ מֵאוֹת אִישׁ: וְאֵת | פַּרְשַׁנְדָּתָא וְאֵת |

דַּלְפוֹן וְאֵת |

ח אַסְפָּתָא: וְאֵת | פּוֹרָתָא וְאֵת | אֲדַלְיָא וְאֵת |

ט אֲרִידָתָא: וְאֵת | פַּרְמַשְׁתָּא וְאֵת | אֲרִיסַי וְאֵת | אֲרִדַי וְאֵת | וַיְזָתָא:

י עֲשֶׂרֶת בְּנֵי הָמָן בֶּן־הַמְּדָתָא צֹרֵר הַיְּהוּדִים הָרָגוּ וּבַבִּזָּה לֹא שָׁלְחוּ אֶת־יָדָם:

יא בַּיּוֹם הַהוּא בָּא מִסְפַּר הַהֲרוּגִים בְּשׁוּשַׁן הַבִּירָה לִפְנֵי הַמֶּלֶךְ: וַיֹּאמֶר הַמֶּלֶךְ

יב לְאֶסְתֵּר הַמַּלְכָּה בְּשׁוּשַׁן הַבִּירָה הָרְגוּ הַיְּהוּדִים וְאַבֵּד חֲמֵשׁ מֵאוֹת אִישׁ וְאֵת עֲשֶׂרֶת בְּנֵי־הָמָן בִּשְׁאָר מְדִינוֹת הַמֶּלֶךְ מֶה עָשׂוּ וּמַה־שְּׁאֵלָתֵךְ

¹² *on one day in all the provinces of King Ahasuerus, namely, upon the thirteenth day of the twelfth month, that is, the month of Adar.* ¹³ *Copies of the document were to be promulgated in every province, and be published to all peoples, for the Jews to be prepared for that day to avenge themselves on their enemies.* ¹⁴ *The couriers, riders of swift mules, went forth in urgent haste by word of the king, and the edict was distributed in Shushan the capital.*

The decree is promulgated

¹⁵ *Mordechai* left the king's presence clad in royal apparel of turquoise and white with a large gold crown and a robe of fine linen and purple; then the city of Shushan was cheerful and glad.* ¹⁶ *The Jews had light and gladness and joy and honor.* ¹⁷ *And in every province, and in every city, every place where the king's word and his decree reached, the Jews had gladness and joy, a feast and a holiday. Moreover, many from among the people of the land professed themselves Jews, for the fear of the Jews had fallen upon them.*

9

¹*Then, in the twelfth month, which is the month of Adar, on its thirteenth day, when the king's command and edict were about to be enforced, on the day that the enemies of the Jews expected to prevail over them, and it was turned about: The Jews prevailed over their adversaries.* ² *The Jews organized themselves in their cities in all the provinces of King Ahasuerus, to send forth [their] hand against those who sought their hurt; and no man could stand before them, for fear of them had fallen upon all the peoples.* ³ *And all the officials of the provinces, the satraps and the governors and those that conduct the king's affairs, exalted the Jews for the fear of Mordechai had fallen upon them.* ⁴ *For Mordechai was now pre-eminent in the royal palace and his fame was spreading throughout all the provinces, for the man Mordechai grew increasingly greater.* ⁵ *And the Jews struck at all their enemies with the stroke of the sword, slaughtering and annihilating; they treated their enemies as they pleased.* ⁶ *In Shushan the capital, the Jews slew and annihilated five hundred men.* ⁷ *and*

Jews organize against their enemies

The Jews are exalted

Parshandatha	*and*
Dalphon	*and*
Aspatha	⁸ *and*
Poratha	*and*
Adalia	*and*
Aridatha	⁹ *and*
Parmashta	*and*
Arisai	*and*
Aridai	*and*
Vaizatha	¹⁰ *the ten*

Haman's ten sons

sons of Haman son of Hammedatha, the Jews' enemy; but they did not lay their hand on the spoils.*

¹¹ *That same day the number of those killed in Shushan the capital was reported to the king.* ¹² *The king said to Queen Esther, "In Shushan the capital the Jews have slain and annihilated five hundred men, as well as the ten sons of Haman; what have they done in the rest of the king's provinces?! What is your request now?*

What now?

8:15-16. During the public reading of *Megillas Esther* on Purim, each of these verses is first recited aloud by the congregation, then repeated by the reader.

9:10. Spontaneously, the Jews decided not to take the spoils, to make it clear that they did not act for mercenary reasons.

יג וַיִּנָּתֶן לָךְ וּמַה־בַּקָּשָׁתֵךְ עוֹד וְתֵעָשׂ: וַתֹּאמֶר אֶסְתֵּר אִם־עַל־הַמֶּלֶךְ טוֹב יִנָּתֵן גַּם־מָחָר לַיְּהוּדִים אֲשֶׁר בְּשׁוּשָׁן לַעֲשׂוֹת כְּדָת הַיּוֹם וְאֵת עֲשֶׂרֶת

יד בְּנֵי־הָמָן יִתְלוּ עַל־הָעֵץ: וַיֹּאמֶר הַמֶּלֶךְ לְהֵעָשׂוֹת כֵּן וַתִּנָּתֵן דָּת בְּשׁוּשָׁן

טו וְאֵת עֲשֶׂרֶת בְּנֵי־הָמָן תָּלוּ: וַיִּקָּהֲלוּ °הַיְּהוּדִיִּים [הַיְּהוּדִים ק] אֲשֶׁר־ בְּשׁוּשָׁן גַּם בְּיוֹם אַרְבָּעָה עָשָׂר לְחֹדֶשׁ אֲדָר וַיַּהַרְגוּ בְשׁוּשָׁן שְׁלֹשׁ מֵאוֹת

טז אִישׁ וּבַבִּזָּה לֹא שָׁלְחוּ אֶת־יָדָם: וּשְׁאָר הַיְּהוּדִים אֲשֶׁר בִּמְדִינוֹת הַמֶּלֶךְ נִקְהֲלוּ ׀ וְעָמֹד עַל־נַפְשָׁם וְנוֹחַ מֵאֹיְבֵיהֶם וְהָרוֹג בְּשֹׂנְאֵיהֶם חֲמִשָּׁה

יז וְשִׁבְעִים אָלֶף וּבַבִּזָּה לֹא שָׁלְחוּ אֶת־יָדָם: בְּיוֹם־שְׁלֹשָׁה עָשָׂר לְחֹדֶשׁ אֲדָר וְנוֹחַ בְּאַרְבָּעָה עָשָׂר בּוֹ וְעָשֹׂה אֹתוֹ יוֹם מִשְׁתֶּה וְשִׂמְחָה:

יח °וְהַיְּהוּדִיִּים [וְהַיְּהוּדִים ק] אֲשֶׁר־בְּשׁוּשָׁן נִקְהֲלוּ בִּשְׁלֹשָׁה עָשָׂר בּוֹ וּבְאַרְבָּעָה עָשָׂר בּוֹ וְנוֹחַ בַּחֲמִשָּׁה עָשָׂר בּוֹ וְעָשֹׂה אֹתוֹ יוֹם מִשְׁתֶּה

יט וְשִׂמְחָה: עַל־כֵּן הַיְּהוּדִים °הַפְּרוֹזִים [הַפְּרָזִים ק] הַיֹּשְׁבִים בְּעָרֵי הַפְּרָזוֹת עֹשִׂים אֵת יוֹם אַרְבָּעָה עָשָׂר לְחֹדֶשׁ אֲדָר שִׂמְחָה וּמִשְׁתֶּה וְיוֹם

כ טוֹב וּמִשְׁלֹחַ מָנוֹת אִישׁ לְרֵעֵהוּ: וַיִּכְתֹּב מָרְדֳּכַי אֶת־הַדְּבָרִים הָאֵלֶּה וַיִּשְׁלַח סְפָרִים אֶל־כָּל־הַיְּהוּדִים אֲשֶׁר בְּכָל־מְדִינוֹת הַמֶּלֶךְ אֲחַשְׁוֵרוֹשׁ

כא הַקְּרוֹבִים וְהָרְחוֹקִים: לְקַיֵּם עֲלֵיהֶם לִהְיוֹת עֹשִׂים אֵת יוֹם אַרְבָּעָה עָשָׂר

כב לְחֹדֶשׁ אֲדָר וְאֵת יוֹם־חֲמִשָּׁה עָשָׂר בּוֹ בְּכָל־שָׁנָה וְשָׁנָה: כַּיָּמִים אֲשֶׁר־ נָחוּ בָהֶם הַיְּהוּדִים מֵאֹיְבֵיהֶם וְהַחֹדֶשׁ אֲשֶׁר נֶהְפַּךְ לָהֶם מִיָּגוֹן לְשִׂמְחָה וּמֵאֵבֶל לְיוֹם טוֹב לַעֲשׂוֹת אוֹתָם יְמֵי מִשְׁתֶּה וְשִׂמְחָה וּמִשְׁלֹחַ מָנוֹת אִישׁ

כג לְרֵעֵהוּ וּמַתָּנוֹת לָאֶבְיֹנִים: וְקִבֵּל הַיְּהוּדִים אֵת אֲשֶׁר־הֵחֵלּוּ לַעֲשׂוֹת וְאֵת

כד אֲשֶׁר־כָּתַב מָרְדֳּכַי אֲלֵיהֶם: כִּי הָמָן בֶּן־הַמְּדָתָא הָאֲגָגִי צֹרֵר כָּל־ הַיְּהוּדִים חָשַׁב עַל־הַיְּהוּדִים לְאַבְּדָם וְהִפִּל פּוּר הוּא הַגּוֹרָל לְהֻמָּם

כה וּלְאַבְּדָם: וּבְבֹאָהּ לִפְנֵי הַמֶּלֶךְ אָמַר עִם־הַסֵּפֶר יָשׁוּב מַחֲשַׁבְתּוֹ הָרָעָה

כו אֲשֶׁר־חָשַׁב עַל־הַיְּהוּדִים עַל־רֹאשׁוֹ וְתָלוּ אֹתוֹ וְאֶת־בָּנָיו עַל־הָעֵץ: עַל־ כֵּן קָרְאוּ לַיָּמִים הָאֵלֶּה פוּרִים עַל־שֵׁם הַפּוּר עַל־כֵּן עַל־כָּל־דִּבְרֵי

כז הָאִגֶּרֶת הַזֹּאת וּמָה־רָאוּ עַל־כָּכָה וּמָה הִגִּיעַ אֲלֵיהֶם: קִיְּמוּ °וְקִבֵּל [וְקִבְּלוּ ק] הַיְּהוּדִים ׀ עֲלֵיהֶם ׀ וְעַל־זַרְעָם וְעַל כָּל־הַנִּלְוִים עֲלֵיהֶם וְלֹא יַעֲבוֹר לִהְיוֹת עֹשִׂים אֵת שְׁנֵי הַיָּמִים הָאֵלֶּה כִּכְתָבָם וְכִזְמַנָּם בְּכָל־שָׁנָה

כח וְשָׁנָה: וְהַיָּמִים הָאֵלֶּה נִזְכָּרִים וְנַעֲשִׂים בְּכָל־דּוֹר וָדוֹר מִשְׁפָּחָה וּמִשְׁפָּחָה מְדִינָה וּמְדִינָה וְעִיר וָעִיר וִימֵי הַפּוּרִים הָאֵלֶּה לֹא יַעַבְרוּ מִתּוֹךְ הַיְּהוּדִים

כט וְזִכְרָם לֹא־יָסוּף מִזַּרְעָם: וַתִּכְתֹּב אֶסְתֵּר הַמַּלְכָּה בַת־ אֲבִיחַיִל וּמָרְדֳּכַי הַיְּהוּדִי אֶת־כָּל־תֹּקֶף לְקַיֵּם אֵת אִגֶּרֶת הַפֻּרִים הַזֹּאת

ל הַשֵּׁנִית: וַיִּשְׁלַח סְפָרִים אֶל־כָּל־הַיְּהוּדִים אֶל־שֶׁבַע וְעֶשְׂרִים וּמֵאָה מְדִינָה

לא מַלְכוּת אֲחַשְׁוֵרוֹשׁ דִּבְרֵי שָׁלוֹם וֶאֱמֶת: לְקַיֵּם אֶת־יְמֵי הַפֻּרִים הָאֵלֶּה

It shall be granted you. What is your petition further? It shall be fulfilled."

Another day in Shushan   ¹³ Esther replied, "If it pleases the king, let tomorrow also be given to the Jews who are in Shushan to act as they did today, and let Haman's ten sons be hanged on the gallows." ¹⁴ The king ordered that this be done, and a decree was distributed in Shushan; and they hanged Haman's ten sons. ¹⁵ The Jews that were in Shushan assembled again on the fourteenth day of the month of Adar and slew three hundred men in Shushan; but they did not lay their hand on the spoils.

Destruction of foes — but no loot   ¹⁶ The rest of the Jews that were in the king's provinces assembled and defended themselves gaining relief from their foes, slaying seventy-five thousand of their enemies, but they did not lay their hand on the spoils, ¹⁷ on the thirteenth day of the month of Adar. And they gained relief on its fourteenth [day], making it a day of feasting and gladness. ¹⁸ But the Jews that were in Shushan assembled on both its thirteenth [day] and its fourteenth, and they gained relief on its fifteenth, making it a day of feasting and gladness. ¹⁹ Therefore, Jewish villagers who live in unwalled towns celebrate the fourteenth day of the month of Adar as an occasion of gladness, feasting and festival, and for sending delicacies to one another.

Purim is proclaimed   ²⁰ Mordechai recorded these events and sent letters to all the Jews who were in all the provinces of King Ahasuerus, the near ones and the distant ones, ²¹ [charging them] to observe annually the fourteenth day of the month of Adar and its fifteenth day, ²² as the days on which the Jews gained relief from their enemies, and the month which had been turned about for them from one of sorrow to gladness, and from mourning to festival; to observe them as days of feasting and gladness, and sending delicacies to one another, and gifts to the poor. * ²³ The Jews undertook [to continue] that which they had begun, * just as Mordechai had prescribed to them.

Feasts and gifts

²⁴ For Haman son of Hammedatha the Agagite, enemy of all the Jews, had plotted to annihilate the Jews and had cast a pur (that is, the lot) to terrify and to annihilate them. ²⁵ But when she appeared before the king, he commanded by means of letters that [Haman's] wicked scheme, which he had devised against the Jews, should recoil on his own head; and they hanged him and his sons on the gallows. ²⁶ Therefore, they called these days "Purim" from the word "pur."* Therefore, because of all that was written in this letter, and because of what they had seen concerning this, and what has happened to them, ²⁷ the Jews confirmed and undertook upon themselves, and their posterity, and upon all who might join them, without fail, to observe these two days, in their prescribed manner, and in their proper time each year. ²⁸ And these days should be remembered and celebrated by every generation, every family, every province, and every city; and these days of Purim should never cease from among the Jews, nor shall their remembrance perish from their descendants.

In every generation

The second letter of Purim   ²⁹ Then Queen Esther daughter of Abihail wrote, along with Mordechai the Jew, with full authority to ratify this second letter of Purim. ³⁰ Dispatches were sent to all the Jews, to the hundred and twenty-seven provinces of the kingdom of Ahasuerus — [with] words of peace and truth — ³¹ to establish these days of Purim

---

9:22. Eating and drinking and merry-making was instituted on Purim because the miracles occurred through feasting: the royal feast that led to the death of Vashti; the feast of Esther's coronation; and Esther's two feasts that led to Haman's downfall.

9:23. The laws and customs associated with Purim.

9:26. See 3:7.

בִּזְמַנֵּיהֶם כַּאֲשֶׁר קִיַּם עֲלֵיהֶם מָרְדֳּכַי הַיְּהוּדִי וְאֶסְתֵּר הַמַּלְכָּה וְכַאֲשֶׁר

לב קִיְּמוּ עַל־נַפְשָׁם וְעַל־זַרְעָם דִּבְרֵי הַצּוֹמוֹת וְזַעֲקָתָם: וּמַאֲמַר אֶסְתֵּר קִיַּם

א דִּבְרֵי הַפֻּרִים הָאֵלֶּה וְנִכְתָּב בַּסֵּפֶר: וַיָּשֶׂם הַמֶּלֶךְ

ב °אחשרש [°אֲחַשְׁוֵרוֹשׁ ק] ׀ מַס עַל־הָאָרֶץ וְאִיֵּי הַיָּם: וְכָל־מַעֲשֵׂה תָקְפּוֹ

וּגְבוּרָתוֹ וּפָרָשַׁת גְּדֻלַּת מָרְדֳּכַי אֲשֶׁר גִּדְּלוֹ הַמֶּלֶךְ הֲלוֹא־הֵם כְּתוּבִים

ג עַל־סֵפֶר דִּבְרֵי הַיָּמִים לְמַלְכֵי מָדַי וּפָרָס: כִּי ׀ מָרְדֳּכַי הַיְּהוּדִי מִשְׁנֶה

לַמֶּלֶךְ אֲחַשְׁוֵרוֹשׁ וְגָדוֹל לַיְּהוּדִים וְרָצוּי לְרֹב אֶחָיו דֹּרֵשׁ טוֹב לְעַמּוֹ

וְדֹבֵר שָׁלוֹם לְכָל־זַרְעוֹ:

סכום פסוקי מגלת אסתר מאה וששים וששה.
וסימן על כן קראו **לימים האלה** פורים. וסימנו כבדני נגד **זקני** עמי.

10:3. During the public reading of *Megillas Esther* on
Purim, this seminal verse is first recited aloud by the
congregation, then repeated by the reader.

on their [proper] dates just as Mordechai the Jew and Queen Esther had enjoined them, and as they had confirmed upon themselves and their posterity the matter of the fasts and their lamentations. ³² Esther's ordinance confirmed these regulations for Purim; and it was recorded in the book.

10

The great-ness of the king . . .

. . . and Mordechai his viceroy

¹ **K**ing Ahasuerus levied a tax on the mainland and the islands of the sea. ² All his mighty and powerful acts, and the account of the greatness of Mordechai, whom the king had promoted, are recorded in the book of chronicles of the kings of Media and Persia. ³ For Mordechai* the Jew was viceroy to King Ahasuerus; he was a great man among the Jews, and found favor with the multitude of his brethren; he sought the good of his people and spoke for the welfare of all his seed.

After the *Megillah* reading, each member of the congregation recites the following blessing.
[This blessing is not recited unless a *minyan* is present for the reading.]

Blessed are You, HASHEM, our God, King of the universe, (the God) Who takes up our grievance, judges our claim, avenges our wrong; Who brings just retribution upon all enemies of our soul and exacts vengeance for us from our foes. Blessed are You, HASHEM, Who exacts vengeance for His people Israel from all their foes, the God Who brings salvation.

בָּרוּךְ אַתָּה יהוה אֱלֹהֵינוּ מֶלֶךְ הָעוֹלָם, (הָאֵל) הָרָב אֶת רִיבֵנוּ, וְהַדָּן אֶת דִּינֵנוּ, וְהַנּוֹקֵם אֶת נִקְמָתֵנוּ, וְהַמְשַׁלֵּם גְּמוּל לְכָל אֹיְבֵי נַפְשֵׁנוּ, וְהַנִּפְרָע לָנוּ מִצָּרֵינוּ. בָּרוּךְ אַתָּה יהוה, הַנִּפְרָע לְעַמּוֹ יִשְׂרָאֵל מִכָּל צָרֵיהֶם, הָאֵל הַמּוֹשִׁיעַ.

After the nighttime *Megillah* reading, the following two paragraphs are recited.
After the daytime reading, only the second paragraph is recited.

אֲשֶׁר הֵנִיא עֲצַת גּוֹיִם, וַיֵּפֶר מַחְשְׁבוֹת עֲרוּמִים.

א Who balked the counsel of the nations
   and annulled the designs of the cunning,

ב When a wicked man stood up against us,
   a wantonly evil branch of Amalek's offspring.

בְּקוּם עָלֵינוּ אָדָם רָשָׁע, נֵצֶר זָדוֹן, מִזֶּרַע עֲמָלֵק.

ג Haughty with his wealth he dug himself a grave,
   and his very greatness snared him in a trap.

גָּאָה בְעָשְׁרוֹ, וְכָרָה לוֹ בּוֹר, וּגְדֻלָּתוֹ יָקְשָׁה לוֹ לֶכֶד.

ד Fancying to trap, he became entrapped;
   attempting to destroy, he was swiftly destroyed.

דִּמָּה בְנַפְשׁוֹ לִלְכֹּד, וְנִלְכַּד,
בִּקֵּשׁ לְהַשְׁמִיד, וְנִשְׁמַד מְהֵרָה.

ה Haman showed his forebears' enmity,
   and aroused the brotherly hate of Esau on the children.

הָמָן הוֹדִיעַ אֵיבַת אֲבוֹתָיו,
וְעוֹרֵר שִׂנְאַת אַחִים לַבָּנִים.

ו He would not remember Saul's compassion,
   that through his pity of Agag the foe was born.

וְלֹא זָכַר רַחֲמֵי שָׁאוּל,
כִּי בְחֶמְלָתוֹ עַל אֲגַג נוֹלַד אוֹיֵב.

ז The wicked one conspired to cut away the righteous,
   but the impure was trapped in the pure one's hands.

זָמַם רָשָׁע לְהַכְרִית צַדִּיק, וְנִלְכַּד טָמֵא, בִּידֵי טָהוֹר.

ח Kindness overcame the father's error,
   and the wicked one piled sin on sins.

חֶסֶד גָּבַר עַל שִׁגְגַת אָב,
וְרָשָׁע הוֹסִיף חֵטְא עַל חֲטָאָיו.

ט In his heart he hid his cunning thoughts,
   and devoted himself to evildoing.

טָמַן בְּלִבּוֹ מַחְשְׁבוֹת עֲרוּמָיו, וַיִּתְמַכֵּר לַעֲשׂוֹת רָעָה.

י He stretched his hand against God's holy ones,
   he spent his silver to destroy their memory.

יָדוֹ שָׁלַח בִּקְדוֹשֵׁי אֵל, כַּסְפּוֹ נָתַן לְהַכְרִית זִכְרָם.

כ When Mordechai saw the wrath commence,
   and Haman's decrees be issued in Shushan,

כִּרְאוֹת מָרְדְּכַי, כִּי יָצָא קֶצֶף, וְדָתֵי הָמָן נִתְּנוּ בְשׁוּשָׁן.

ל He put on sackcloth and bound himself in mourning,
   decreed a fast and sat on ashes.

לָבַשׁ שַׂק וְקָשַׁר מִסְפֵּד, וְגָזַר צוֹם, וַיֵּשֶׁב עַל הָאֵפֶר.

מ 'Who would arise to atone for error,
   to gain forgiveness for our ancestors' sins?'

מִי זֶה יַעֲמֹד לְכַפֵּר שְׁגָגָה,
וְלִמְחֹל חַטַּאת עֲוֹן אֲבוֹתֵינוּ.

נ A blossom bloomed from a lulav branch — behold!
   Hadassah stood up to arouse the sleeping.

נֵץ פָּרַח מִלּוּלָב, הֵן הֲדַסָּה עָמְדָה לְעוֹרֵר יְשֵׁנִים.

ס His servants hastened Haman,
   to serve him wine of serpent's poison.

סָרִיסֶיהָ הִבְהִילוּ לְהָמָן, לְהַשְׁקוֹתוֹ יֵין חֲמַת תַּנִּינִים.

ע He stood tall through his wealth
   and toppled through his evil —
   he built the gallows on which he was hung.

עָמַד בְּעָשְׁרוֹ, וְנָפַל בְּרִשְׁעוֹ,
עָשָׂה לוֹ עֵץ, וְנִתְלָה עָלָיו.

פ The earth's inhabitants opened their mouths,
   for Haman's lot became our Purim.

פִּיהֶם פָּתְחוּ, כָּל יוֹשְׁבֵי תֵבֵל,
כִּי פוּר הָמָן נֶהְפַּךְ לְפוּרֵנוּ.

צ The righteous man was saved from the wicked's hand;
   the foe was substituted for him.

צַדִּיק נֶחֱלַץ מִיַּד רָשָׁע, אוֹיֵב נִתַּן תַּחַת נַפְשׁוֹ.

ק They undertook to establish Purim,
   to rejoice in every single year.

קִימּוּ עֲלֵיהֶם, לַעֲשׂוֹת פוּרִים, וְלִשְׂמֹחַ בְּכָל שָׁנָה וְשָׁנָה.

ר You noted the prayer of Mordechai and Esther;
   Haman and his sons You hung on the gallows.

רָאִיתָ אֶת תְּפִלַּת מָרְדְּכַי וְאֶסְתֵּר, הָמָן וּבָנָיו עַל הָעֵץ תָּלִיתָ.

The following is recited after both *Megillah* readings.

שׁ The rose of Jacob was cheerful and glad,
   when they jointly saw Mordechai robed in royal blue.

ת You have been their eternal salvation,
   and their hope throughout generations.
   To make known that all who hope in You will not be shamed; nor ever be humiliated, those taking refuge in You. Accursed be Haman who sought to destroy me, blessed be Mordechai the Yehudi. Accursed be Zeresh the wife of my terrorizer, blessed be Esther [who sacrificed] for me — and Charvonah, too, be remembered for good.

שׁוֹשַׁנַּת יַעֲקֹב צָהֲלָה וְשָׂמֵחָה, בִּרְאוֹתָם יַחַד תְּכֵלֶת מָרְדְּכָי. תְּשׁוּעָתָם הָיִיתָ לָנֶצַח, וְתִקְוָתָם בְּכָל דּוֹר וָדוֹר. לְהוֹדִיעַ, שֶׁכָּל קֹוֶיךָ לֹא יֵבֹשׁוּ, וְלֹא יִכָּלְמוּ לָנֶצַח כָּל הַחוֹסִים בָּךְ. אָרוּר הָמָן, אֲשֶׁר בִּקֵּשׁ לְאַבְּדִי, בָּרוּךְ מָרְדְּכַי הַיְּהוּדִי. אֲרוּרָה זֶרֶשׁ, אֵשֶׁת מַפְחִידִי, בְּרוּכָה אֶסְתֵּר בַּעֲדִי, וְגַם חַרְבוֹנָה זָכוּר לַטּוֹב.

Daniel דָּנִיֵּאל

*T*he ways of God are mysterious. When it seems that He is plowing under His treasures, He may be planting seeds that are undiscernible, until they take root and blossom, sometimes decades or even centuries later. So it was when King Nebuchadnezzar planned diabolically to enrich his own court while impoverishing Judah and assuring that it would have no rebirth. He picked the finest, most promising young men of Jerusalem, and carted them off to Babylon (442 B.C.E.), there to serve in his court and make him the beneficiary of their brilliance.

Among these young captives was Daniel. There, in a land of spiritual poverty, the young captives sanctified God's Name so undeniably that even Nebuchadnezzar had to acknowledge His greatness; and there they built the foundations of the flourishing Torah community that would eventually return to its land and build the Second Temple. Daniel was the leader of that generation, the inspiration of his peers, and the one who brought God's message to the heathen kings of Babylon.

Daniel became one of the leading figures in the royal court. Kings tried to intimidate him to follow their ways, but he refused and prevailed. His companions Hananiah, Mishael, and Azariah were thrown into a flaming furnace, but they emerged unscathed. Daniel himself was flung into a lions' den, but he too came out unharmed. They proved that Israel remains loyal to God and that He remains its Protector. The kings of Babylon had no choice but to turn to Daniel to explain God's cryptic messages, and he brought them terrifying truths. When Belshazzar saw the "handwriting on the wall," only Daniel could interpret its frightening message for him.

In the concluding chapters of the book, Daniel saw visions that remain the subject of intense speculation, for he was shown prophetic scenes of the "Four Beasts" representing the "Four Monarchies" that will dominate Israel during its long series of exiles. And he was shown the calculations of the "End of Days," when Israel will be redeemed and the world will finally achieve the Divine goal for which it was created. What did the numbers mean? When and how will the events come about? These visions remain clothed in mysteries that will not be stripped away until the time of the final Redemption is at hand. Then we will know how God's seeds will sprout into the glorious fulfillment of the Scriptural prophecies.

א

א בִּשְׁנַ֣ת שָׁל֔וֹשׁ לְמַלְכ֖וּת יְהוֹיָקִ֣ים מֶֽלֶךְ־יְהוּדָ֑ה בָּ֣א נְבֽוּכַדְנֶאצַּ֧ר מֶֽלֶךְ־בָּבֶ֛ל
ב יְרוּשָׁלַ֖͏ִם וַיָּ֣צַר עָלֶֽיהָ: וַיִּתֵּן֩ אֲדֹנָ֨י בְּיָד֜וֹ אֶת־יְהוֹיָקִ֣ים מֶֽלֶךְ־יְהוּדָ֗ה וּמִקְצָת֙
כְּלֵ֣י בֵית־הָֽאֱלֹהִ֔ים וַיְבִיאֵ֥ם אֶֽרֶץ־שִׁנְעָ֖ר בֵּ֣ית אֱלֹהָ֑יו וְאֶת־הַכֵּלִ֣ים הֵבִ֔יא
ג בֵּ֖ית אוֹצַ֥ר אֱלֹהָֽיו: וַיֹּ֣אמֶר הַמֶּ֔לֶךְ לְאַשְׁפְּנַ֖ז רַ֣ב סָרִיסָ֑יו לְהָבִ֞יא מִבְּנֵ֧י
ד יִשְׂרָאֵ֛ל וּמִזֶּ֥רַע הַמְּלוּכָ֖ה וּמִן־הַֽפַּרְתְּמִֽים: יְלָדִ֣ים אֲשֶׁ֣ר אֵֽין־בָּהֶ֣ם כׇּל־
°מאום [°מוּם ק] וְטוֹבֵ֨י מַרְאֶ֜ה וּמַשְׂכִּילִ֣ים בְּכׇל־חׇכְמָ֗ה וְיֹ֤דְעֵי דַ֙עַת֙
וּמְבִינֵ֣י מַדָּ֔ע וַֽאֲשֶׁר֙ כֹּ֣חַ בָּהֶ֔ם לַֽעֲמֹ֖ד בְּהֵיכַ֣ל הַמֶּ֑לֶךְ וּֽלְלַמְּדָ֥ם סֵ֖פֶר וּלְשׁ֥וֹן
ה כַּשְׂדִּֽים: וַיְמַן֩ לָהֶ֨ם הַמֶּ֜לֶךְ דְּבַר־י֣וֹם בְּיוֹמ֗וֹ מִפַּת־בַּ֤ג הַמֶּ֙לֶךְ֙ וּמִיֵּ֣ין מִשְׁתָּ֔יו
ו וּֽלְגַדְּלָ֖ם שָׁנִ֣ים שָׁל֑וֹשׁ וּמִ֨קְצָתָ֔ם יַעַמְד֖וּ לִפְנֵ֥י הַמֶּֽלֶךְ: וַיְהִ֣י בָהֶ֔ם מִבְּנֵ֖י יְהוּדָ֑ה
ז דָּֽנִיֵּ֣אל חֲנַנְיָ֔ה מִֽישָׁאֵ֖ל וַֽעֲזַרְיָֽה: וַיָּ֧שֶׂם לָהֶ֛ם שַׂ֥ר הַסָּֽרִיסִ֖ים שֵׁמ֑וֹת וַיָּ֨שֶׂם
לְדָֽנִיֵּ֜אל בֵּ֣לְטְשַׁאצַּ֗ר וְלַֽחֲנַנְיָה֙ שַׁדְרַ֔ךְ וּֽלְמִֽישָׁאֵ֣ל מֵישַׁ֔ךְ וְלַֽעֲזַרְיָ֖ה עֲבֵ֥ד נְגֽוֹ:
ח וַיָּ֤שֶׂם דָּֽנִיֵּאל֙ עַל־לִבּ֔וֹ אֲשֶׁ֛ר לֹ֥א יִתְגָּאַ֖ל בְּפַת־בַּ֣ג הַמֶּ֑לֶךְ וּבְיֵ֣ין מִשְׁתָּ֔יו
ט וַיְבַקֵּשׁ֙ מִשַּׂ֣ר הַסָּֽרִיסִ֔ים אֲשֶׁ֖ר לֹ֥א יִתְגָּאָֽל: וַיִּתֵּ֤ן הָֽאֱלֹהִים֙ אֶת־דָּ֣נִיֵּ֔אל
י לְחֶ֖סֶד וּֽלְרַֽחֲמִ֑ים לִפְנֵ֖י שַׂ֥ר הַסָּֽרִיסִֽים: וַיֹּ֜אמֶר שַׂ֤ר הַסָּֽרִיסִים֙ לְדָ֣נִיֵּ֔אל יָרֵ֤א
אֲנִי֙ אֶת־אֲדֹנִ֣י הַמֶּ֔לֶךְ אֲשֶׁ֣ר מִנָּ֔ה אֶת־מַֽאֲכַלְכֶ֖ם וְאֶת־מִשְׁתֵּיכֶ֑ם אֲשֶׁ֡ר
לָ֣מָּה יִרְאֶה֩ אֶת־פְּנֵיכֶ֨ם זֹֽעֲפִ֜ים מִן־הַיְלָדִים֙ אֲשֶׁ֣ר כְּגִֽילְכֶ֔ם וְחִיַּבְתֶּ֥ם אֶת־
יא רֹאשִׁ֖י לַמֶּֽלֶךְ: וַיֹּ֥אמֶר דָּֽנִיֵּ֖אל אֶל־הַמֶּלְצַ֑ר אֲשֶׁ֤ר מִנָּה֙ שַׂ֣ר הַסָּֽרִיסִ֔ים עַל־
יב דָּֽנִיֵּ֣אל חֲנַנְיָ֔ה מִֽישָׁאֵ֖ל וַֽעֲזַרְיָֽה: נַ֥ס־נָ֛א אֶת־עֲבָדֶ֖יךָ יָמִ֣ים עֲשָׂרָ֑ה וְיִתְּנוּ־לָ֜נוּ
יג מִן־הַזֵּֽרֹעִ֛ים וְנֹֽאכְלָ֖ה וּמַ֥יִם וְנִשְׁתֶּֽה: וְיֵֽרָא֤וּ לְפָנֶ֙יךָ֙ מַרְאֵ֔ינוּ וּמַרְאֵה֙ הַיְלָדִ֔ים
יד הָאֹ֣כְלִ֔ים אֵ֖ת פַּת־בַּ֣ג הַמֶּ֑לֶךְ וְכַֽאֲשֶׁ֣ר תִּרְאֵ֔ה עֲשֵׂ֖ה עִם־עֲבָדֶֽיךָ: וַיִּשְׁמַ֥ע
טו לָהֶ֛ם לַדָּבָ֥ר הַזֶּ֖ה וַיְנַסֵּ֑ם יָמִ֥ים עֲשָׂרָֽה: וּמִקְצָת֙ יָמִ֣ים עֲשָׂרָ֔ה נִרְאָ֤ה מַרְאֵיהֶם֙
טז ט֣וֹב וּבְרִיאֵ֣י בָשָׂ֔ר מִן־כׇּ֨ל־הַיְלָדִ֔ים הָ֣אֹ֣כְלִ֔ים אֵ֖ת פַּת־בַּ֥ג הַמֶּֽלֶךְ: וַיְהִ֣י
יז הַמֶּלְצַ֗ר נֹשֵׂא֙ אֶת־פַּת־בָּגָ֔ם וְיֵ֖ין מִשְׁתֵּיהֶ֑ם וְנֹתֵ֥ן לָהֶ֖ם זֵֽרֹעֽנִים: וְהַיְלָדִ֣ים
הָאֵ֡לֶּה אַרְבַּעְתָּ֡ם נָתַן֩ לָהֶ֨ם הָֽאֱלֹהִ֜ים מַדָּ֧ע וְהַשְׂכֵּ֛ל בְּכׇל־סֵ֖פֶר וְחׇכְמָ֑ה
יח וְדָ֣נִיֵּ֔אל הֵבִ֕ין בְּכׇל־חָז֖וֹן וַֽחֲלֹמֽוֹת: וּלְמִקְצָ֣ת הַיָּמִ֔ים אֲשֶׁר־אָמַ֥ר הַמֶּ֖לֶךְ
יט לַֽהֲבִיאָ֑ם וַיְבִיאֵם֙ שַׂ֣ר הַסָּֽרִיסִ֔ים לִפְנֵ֖י נְבֻֽכַדְנֶצַּֽר: וַיְדַבֵּ֣ר אִתָּם֮ הַמֶּלֶךְ֒ וְלֹ֣א
נִמְצָ֣א מִכֻּלָּ֗ם כְּדָֽנִיֵּאל֙ חֲנַנְיָ֔ה מִֽישָׁאֵ֖ל וַֽעֲזַרְיָ֑ה וַיַּֽעַמְד֖וּ לִפְנֵ֥י הַמֶּֽלֶךְ: וְכֹ֗ל
כ דְּבַ֨ר חׇכְמַ֣ת בִּינָ֔ה אֲשֶׁר־בִּקֵּ֥שׁ מֵהֶ֖ם הַמֶּ֑לֶךְ וַיִּמְצָאֵ֞ם עֶ֣שֶׂר יָד֗וֹת עַ֤ל כׇּל־
כא הַֽחַרְטֻמִּים֙ הָֽאַשָּׁפִ֔ים אֲשֶׁ֖ר בְּכׇל־מַלְכוּתֽוֹ: וַֽיְהִי֙ דָּ֣נִיֵּ֔אל עַד־שְׁנַ֥ת אַחַ֖ת
לְכ֥וֹרֶשׁ הַמֶּֽלֶךְ:   **ב** א וּבִשְׁנַ֣ת שְׁתַּ֗יִם לְמַלְכוּת֙ נְבֻֽכַדְנֶצַּ֔ר חָלַ֥ם נְבֻֽכַדְנֶצַּ֖ר

1:1. According to *Jeremiah* (25:1), Nebuchadnezzar came to power in the fourth year of Jehoiakim. (*Seder Olam* therefore explains that our verse refers to the third year following Jehoiakim's rebellion against Nebuchadnezzar; see *II Kings* 24:1. [See Appendix A, timelines 4-5.])

1:2. See *Genesis* 11:2,9.

1:8. Daniel refrained from eating to avoid forming a social bond with his gentile masters, lest they lead him astray (see *Avodah Zarah* 36a).

1:21. When King Cyrus encouraged the Jews to return to Jerusalem (*Ezra* 1:3), Daniel did so (*Ralbag*).

According to *Seder Olam*, the chronology of the kings is as follows: Nebuchadnezzar of Babylonia; his son Evil-merodach; his son Belshazzar (see 5:1); Darius the Mede

1

(See Appendix A, timelines 4-5)

¹ In the third year of the reign of Jehoiakim* king of Judah, Nebuchadnezzar king of Babylonia came to Jerusalem and laid siege to it. ² The Lord delivered Jehoiakim, king of Judah, into his hand, with some of the vessels of the Temple of God. He brought them to the land of Shinar* to the temple of his god, and the vessels he brought into the treasure-house of his god.

Quest for courtiers ³ The king told Ashpenaz, the chief of his officers, to bring from the children of Israel, from the royal seed and from the nobles, ⁴ youths in whom there was no blemish, who were good looking, skillful in all wisdom, discerning in knowledge and perceptive in learning, and who have the stamina to stand [and serve] in the king's palace, and to teach them the script and language of the Chaldeans.

⁵ The king provided for them a daily portion from the king's food and from his drinking-wine to nurture them for three years, at the conclusion of which they *New names* would stand [and serve] before the king. ⁶ Among them were, from the children of Judah: Daniel, Hananiah, Mishael and Azariah. ⁷ The chief officer gave them names: to Daniel he gave [the name] Belteshazzar; to Hananiah, Shadrach; to Mishael, Meshach; and to Azariah, Abed-nego.

Daniel's ⁸ Daniel set [the resolve] in his heart not to be defiled by the king's food* nor by *resolve* his drinking-wine, so he requested of the chief officer that he not be defiled. ⁹ God granted Daniel favor and mercy before the chief officer, ¹⁰ and the chief officer said to Daniel, "I fear my lord the king, who has provided your food and your drinks, lest he see your faces more ill at ease than the other youths in your situation, and you will forfeit my head to the king!"

Daniel's ¹¹ So Daniel said to the steward whom the chief officer had assigned to Daniel, *proposal* Hananiah, Mishael and Azariah, ¹² "Please test your servants for ten days, and let them give us of the pulse and we will eat, and [give us] water and we will drink. ¹³ Then let our appearance and the appearance of the youths who eat the king's food be seen by you, and act toward your servants in accordance with what you see."

The test ¹⁴ He heeded them in this matter, and tested them for ten days. ¹⁵ At the end of ten days their appearance seemed better and they were of healthier flesh than all the youths eating the king's food. ¹⁶ Thereafter the steward would take away their food and their drinking-wine and give them pulse.

¹⁷ As for these youths, the four of them, God gave them learning and skill in every script and wisdom; and Daniel understood every kind of vision and dreams.

¹⁸ At the end of the years after which the king had said to bring them, the chief *Incomparable* officer brought them before Nebuchadnezzar. ¹⁹ The king spoke with them, and *foursome* there was not found among them all [anyone] like Daniel, Hananiah, Mishael and Azariah; so they stood [and served] before the king. ²⁰ In every matter of the art of reasoning that the king asked of them, he found them ten times better than all the necromancers and astrologers that were in his entire kingdom.

²¹ Daniel was [there] until the first year of King Cyrus.*

2

¹ In the second year of Nebuchadnezzar's reign,* Nebuchadnezzar dreamt

---

(see 6:1 and 9:1); Cyrus the Persian (see 6:29 and 10:1); Ahasuerus (husband of Esther); their son, Darius the Persian (353-318 B.C.E.). [See Appendix A, timeline 5.]

2:1. Since Daniel was in training for three years before serving Nebuchadnezzar (see 1:5,18), this dating cannot

be taken literally. Accordingly, it means the second year after Nebuchadnezzar destroyed the Temple (*Seder Olam*). Alternatively: Nebuchadnezzar's dream had been recurring since his second year and now he was sufficiently alarmed to seek an interpretation (*R' Saadiah Gaon*).

ג חֲלֹמוֹת וַתִּתְפָּעֶם רוּחוֹ וּשְׁנָתוֹ נִהְיְתָה עָלָיו: וַיֹּאמֶר הַמֶּלֶךְ לִקְרֹא
לַחַרְטֻמִּים וְלָאַשָּׁפִים וְלַמְכַשְּׁפִים וְלַכַּשְׂדִּים לְהַגִּיד לַמֶּלֶךְ חֲלֹמֹתָיו

ג וַיָּבֹאוּ וַיַּעַמְדוּ לִפְנֵי הַמֶּלֶךְ: וַיֹּאמֶר לָהֶם הַמֶּלֶךְ חֲלוֹם חָלָמְתִּי וַתִּפָּעֶם

ד רוּחִי לָדַעַת אֶת־הַחֲלוֹם: וַיְדַבְּרוּ הַכַּשְׂדִּים לַמֶּלֶךְ אֲרָמִית מַלְכָּא לְעָלְמִין

ה חֱיִי אֱמַר חֶלְמָא °לְעַבְדָיִךְ [°לְעַבְדָךְ ק] וּפִשְׁרָא נְחַוֵּא: עָנֵה מַלְכָּא וְאָמַר
°לְכַשְׂדָּיֵא [°לְכַשְׂדָּאֵי ק] מִלְּתָא מִנִּי אַזְדָּא הֵן לָא תְהוֹדְעוּנַּנִי חֶלְמָא

ו וּפִשְׁרֵהּ הַדָּמִין תִּתְעַבְדוּן וּבָתֵּיכוֹן נְוָלִי יִתְּשָׂמוּן: וְהֵן חֶלְמָא וּפִשְׁרֵהּ
תְּהַחֲוֹן מַתְּנָן וּנְבִזְבָּה וִיקָר שַׂגִּיא תְּקַבְּלוּן מִן־קֳדָמָי לָהֵן חֶלְמָא וּפִשְׁרֵהּ

ז הַחֲוֹנִי: עֲנוֹ תִנְיָנוּת וְאָמְרִין מַלְכָּא חֶלְמָא יֵאמַר לְעַבְדוֹהִי וּפִשְׁרָה נְהַחֲוֵה:

ח עָנֵה מַלְכָּא וְאָמַר מִן־יַצִּיב יָדַע אֲנָה דִּי עִדָּנָא אַנְתּוּן זָבְנִין כָּל־קֳבֵל דִּי

ט חֲזֵיתוֹן דִּי אַזְדָּא מִנִּי מִלְּתָא: דִּי הֵן־חֶלְמָא לָא תְהוֹדְעֻנַּנִי חֲדָה־הִיא
דָתְכוֹן וּמִלָּה כִדְבָה וּשְׁחִיתָה °הַזְמַנְתּוּן [°הִזְדְּמִנְתּוּן ק] לְמֵאמַר קֳדָמַי עַד

י דִּי עִדָּנָא יִשְׁתַּנֵּא לָהֵן חֶלְמָא אֱמַרוּ לִי וְאִנְדַּע דִּי פִשְׁרֵהּ תְּהַחֲוֻנַּנִי: עֲנוֹ
°כַשְׂדָיֵא [°כַשְׂדָּאֵי ק] קֳדָם־מַלְכָּא וְאָמְרִין לָא־אִיתַי אֱנָשׁ עַל־יַבֶּשְׁתָּא

יא דִּי מִלַּת מַלְכָּא יוּכַל לְהַחֲוָיָה כָּל־קֳבֵל דִּי כָּל־מֶלֶךְ רַב וְשַׁלִּיט מִלָּה
כִדְנָה לָא שְׁאֵל לְכָל־חַרְטֹם וְאָשַׁף וְכַשְׂדָּי: וּמִלְּתָא דִּי־מַלְכָּה שָׁאֵל

יב יַקִּירָה וְאָחֳרָן לָא אִיתַי דִּי יְחַוִּנַּהּ קֳדָם מַלְכָּא לָהֵן אֱלָהִין דִּי מְדָרְהוֹן עִם־
בִּשְׂרָא לָא אִיתוֹהִי: כָּל־קֳבֵל דְּנָה מַלְכָּא בְּנַס וּקְצַף שַׂגִּיא וַאֲמַר לְהוֹבָדָה

יג לְכֹל חַכִּימֵי בָבֶל: וְדָתָא נֶפְקַת וְחַכִּימַיָּא מִתְקַטְּלִין וּבְעוֹ דָּנִיֵּאל וְחַבְרוֹהִי

יד לְהִתְקְטָלָה: בֵּאדַיִן דָּנִיֵּאל הֲתִיב עֵטָא וּטְעֵם לְאַרְיוֹךְ רַב־

טו טַבָּחַיָּא דִּי מַלְכָּא דִּי נְפַק לְקַטָּלָה לְחַכִּימֵי בָבֶל: עָנֵה וְאָמַר לְאַרְיוֹךְ
שַׁלִּיטָא דִּי־מַלְכָּא עַל־מָה דָתָא מְהַחְצְפָה מִן־קֳדָם מַלְכָּא אֱדַיִן מִלְּתָא

טז הוֹדַע אַרְיוֹךְ לְדָנִיֵּאל: וְדָנִיֵּאל עַל וּבְעָה מִן־מַלְכָּא דִּי זְמָן יִנְתֶּן־לֵהּ

יז וּפִשְׁרָא לְהַחֲוָיָה לְמַלְכָּא: אֱדַיִן דָּנִיֵּאל לְבַיְתֵהּ אֲזַל וְלַחֲנַנְיָה

יח מִישָׁאֵל וַעֲזַרְיָה חַבְרוֹהִי מִלְּתָא הוֹדַע: וְרַחֲמִין לְמִבְעֵא מִן־קֳדָם אֱלָהּ
שְׁמַיָּא עַל־רָזָה דְּנָה דִּי לָא יְהֹבְדוּן דָּנִיֵּאל וְחַבְרוֹהִי עִם־שְׁאָר חַכִּימֵי

יט בָבֶל: אֱדַיִן לְדָנִיֵּאל בְּחֶזְוָא דִי־לֵילְיָא רָזָה גֲלִי אֱדַיִן דָּנִיֵּאל בָּרִךְ לֶאֱלָהּ

כ שְׁמַיָּא: עָנֵה דָנִיֵּאל וְאָמַר לֶהֱוֵא שְׁמֵהּ דִּי־אֱלָהָא מְבָרַךְ מִן־עָלְמָא וְעַד־

כא עָלְמָא דִּי חָכְמְתָא וּגְבוּרְתָא דִּי לֵהּ־הִיא: וְהוּא מְהַשְׁנֵא עִדָּנַיָּא וְזִמְנַיָּא
מְהַעְדֵּה מַלְכִין וּמְהָקֵים מַלְכִין יָהֵב חָכְמְתָא לְחַכִּימִין וּמַנְדְּעָא לְיָדְעֵי

כב בִינָה: הוּא גָּלֵא עַמִּיקָתָא וּמְסַתְּרָתָא יָדַע מָה בַחֲשׁוֹכָא °וּנְהִירָא
[°וּנְהוֹרָא ק] עִמֵּהּ שְׁרֵא: לָךְ אֱלָהּ אֲבָהָתִי מְהוֹדֵא וּמְשַׁבַּח אֲנָה דִּי

כג חָכְמְתָא וּגְבוּרְתָא יְהַבְתְּ לִי וּכְעַן הוֹדַעְתַּנִי דִּי־בְעֵינָא מִנָּךְ דִּי־מִלַּת

כד מַלְכָּא הוֹדַעְתֶּנָא: כָּל־קֳבֵל דְּנָה דָּנִיֵּאל עַל עַל־אַרְיוֹךְ דִּי מַנִּי מַלְכָּא

The king's dreams; his spirit was agitated and his sleep was interrupted. [2] *The king said to*
dreams call the necromancers, the astrologers, the sorcerers and the Chaldean [stargaz-
ers], * *to tell the king his dreams. They came and stood before the king.* [3] *The king*
said to them, "I have dreamt a dream and my spirit is agitated to know the dream."

[4] *The Chaldeans spoke to the king in Aramaic,* * *"May the king live forever! Tell*
your servants the dream and we will relate the interpretation."

[5] *The king responded and said to the Chaldeans, "The thing has escaped me!*
The If you do not make the dream and its interpretation known to me, you will be cut
forgotten to bits, and your homes will be made a dunghill! [6] *But if you do tell the dream and*
dream its interpretation, you will receive from me gifts, rewards and great honor; just tell
me the dream and its interpretation!"

[7] *They answered a second time and said, "Let the king tell his servants the*
dream, and we will relate the interpretation."

"Just tell [8] *The king responded and said, "I know for a certainty that you are buying time,*
me the because you have seen that the matter is firmly established by me [9] *that if you do*
dream" not make the dream known to me your sentence is unequivocal; thus you have
arranged lying and corrupt words to speak before me, until the time changes! Just
tell me the dream, and then I will know that you can relate its interpretation to
me."

[10] *The Chaldeans responded before the king and said, "There is no man on*
earth who can relate the king's matter; that is why no king, leader or ruler has ever
requested such a thing of any necromancer or astrologer or Chaldean. [11] *The*
king's request is difficult, and there is no other who can relate it before the king,
except the angels, whose dwelling is not with human beings!"

[12] *As a result of this the king grew upset and very angry, and he commanded*
The king to destroy all the sages of Babylonia. [13] *As the decree was being implemented and*
orders the the wise men slain, Daniel and his companions were sought to be slain.
sages killed

[14] *Then Daniel gave counsel and advice to Arioch, the king's chief executioner,*
who had gone to slay the wise men of Babylonia. [15] *He exclaimed and said to*
Arioch, the king's official, "Why is the king's decree so peremptory?" Then Arioch
told Daniel the story. [16] *Daniel went and requested of the king that he give him*
time to relate the interpretation to the king.

[17] *Then Daniel went to his house and made the matter known to his com-*
Revelation panions, Hananiah, Mishael, and Azariah, [18] *and to pray for mercy from before*
to Daniel the God of Heaven concerning this secret, so that Daniel and his companions
should not be destroyed with the rest of the sages of Babylonia. [19] *Then, in a*
nocturnal vision, the secret was revealed to Daniel. Daniel then blessed the God
of Heaven.

[20] *Daniel exclaimed and said, "May the Name of God be blessed forever and*
Daniel ever, for wisdom and might are His! [21] *He alters times and seasons; He deposes*
thanks God kings and establishes kings; He gives wisdom to the wise and knowledge to those
who know how to reason. [22] *He reveals the deep and the mysterious; He knows*
what is in the darkness, and light dwells with Him. [23] *To You, O God of my*
forefathers, I give thanks and praise, for You have given me wisdom and might,
and now You have made known to me what we requested of You, for You have
made known to us the matter of the king."

[24] *Consequently, Daniel came to Arioch, whom the king had appointed to*

2:2. Alternatively translated as the demonists (*R' Saa-*   **2:4.** From this point until the end of Chapter 7 the text
diah Gaon).   switches from Hebrew to Aramaic.

לְהוֹבָדָה לְחַכִּימֵי בָבֶל אֲזַל ׀ וְכֵן אֲמַר־לֵהּ לְחַכִּימֵי בָבֶל אַל־תְּהוֹבֵד הַעֵלְנִי קֳדָם מַלְכָּא וּפִשְׁרָא לְמַלְכָּא אֲחַוֵּא:

כה אֱדַיִן אַרְיוֹךְ בְּהִתְבְּהָלָה הַנְעֵל לְדָנִיֵּאל קֳדָם מַלְכָּא וְכֵן אֲמַר־לֵהּ דִּי־

כו הַשְׁכַּחַת גְּבַר מִן־בְּנֵי גָלוּתָא דִּי יְהוּד דִּי פִשְׁרָא לְמַלְכָּא יְהוֹדַע: עָנֵה מַלְכָּא וְאָמַר לְדָנִיֵּאל דִּי שְׁמֵהּ בֵּלְטְשַׁאצַּר °הַאִיתַיִךְ ק [°הַאִיתָךְ] כָּהֵל

כז לְהוֹדָעֻתַנִי חֶלְמָא דִי־חֲזֵית וּפִשְׁרֵהּ: עָנֵה דָנִיֵּאל קֳדָם מַלְכָּא וְאָמַר רָזָה דִּי־מַלְכָּא שָׁאֵל לָא חַכִּימִין אָשְׁפִין חַרְטֻמִּין גָּזְרִין יָכְלִין לְהַחֲוָיָה

כח לְמַלְכָּא: בְּרַם אִיתַי אֱלָהּ בִּשְׁמַיָּא גָּלֵא רָזִין וְהוֹדַע לְמַלְכָּא נְבוּכַדְנֶצַּר מָה דִּי לֶהֱוֵא בְּאַחֲרִית יוֹמַיָּא חֶלְמָךְ וְחֶזְוֵי רֵאשָׁךְ עַל־מִשְׁכְּבָךְ דְּנָה

כט הוּא: °אנתה [°אַנְתְּ ק] מַלְכָּא °רַעְיוֹנָיִךְ [°רַעְיוֹנָךְ ק] עַל־ מִשְׁכְּבָךְ סְלִקוּ מָה דִּי לֶהֱוֵא אַחֲרֵי דְנָה וְגָלֵא רָזַיָּא הוֹדְעָךְ מָה־דִּי לֶהֱוֵא:

ל וַאֲנָה לָא בְחָכְמָה דִּי־אִיתַי בִּי מִן־כָּל־חַיַּיָּא רָזָא דְנָה גֱּלִי לִי לָהֵן עַל־ דִּבְרַת דִּי פִשְׁרָא לְמַלְכָּא יְהוֹדְעוּן וְרַעְיוֹנֵי לִבְבָךְ תִּנְדַּע: °אנתה

לא [°אַנְתְּ ק] מַלְכָּא חָזֵה הֲוַיְתָ וַאֲלוּ צְלֵם חַד שַׂגִּיא צַלְמָא דִּכֵּן רַב וְזִיוֵהּ

לב יַתִּיר קָאֵם לְקָבְלָךְ וְרֵוֵהּ דְּחִיל: הוּא צַלְמָא רֵאשֵׁהּ דִּי־דְהַב טָב חֲדוֹהִי

לג וּדְרָעוֹהִי דִּי כְסַף מְעוֹהִי וְיַרְכָתֵהּ דִּי נְחָשׁ: שָׁקוֹהִי דִּי פַרְזֶל רַגְלוֹהִי °מנהון

לד [°מִנְּהֵן ק] דִּי פַרְזֶל °וּמִנְּהֹן [°וּמִנְּהֵן ק] דִּי חֲסַף: חָזֵה הֲוַיְתָ עַד דִּי הִתְגְּזֶרֶת אֶבֶן דִּי־לָא בִידַיִן וּמְחָת לְצַלְמָא עַל־רַגְלוֹהִי דִּי פַרְזְלָא וְחַסְפָּא

לה וְהַדֵּקֶת הִמּוֹן: בֵּאדַיִן דָּקוּ כַחֲדָה פַּרְזְלָא חַסְפָּא נְחָשָׁא כַּסְפָּא וְדַהֲבָא וַהֲווֹ כְּעוּר מִן־אִדְּרֵי־קַיִט וּנְשָׂא הִמּוֹן רוּחָא וְכָל־אֲתַר לָא־הִשְׁתֲּכַח

לו לְהוֹן וְאַבְנָא ׀ דִּי־מְחָת לְצַלְמָא הֲוָת לְטוּר רַב וּמְלָת כָּל־אַרְעָא: דְּנָה חֶלְמָא וּפִשְׁרֵהּ נֵאמַר קֳדָם־מַלְכָּא: °אנתה [°אַנְתְּ ק]

לז מַלְכָּא מֶלֶךְ מַלְכַיָּא דִּי אֱלָהּ שְׁמַיָּא מַלְכוּתָא חִסְנָא וְתָקְפָּא וִיקָרָא

לח יְהַב־לָךְ: וּבְכָל־דִּי °דאריִן [°דָיְרִין ק] בְּנֵי־אֲנָשָׁא חֵיוַת בָּרָא וְעוֹף שְׁמַיָּא יְהַב בִּידָךְ וְהַשְׁלְטָךְ בְּכָלְּהוֹן °אנתה [°אַנְתְּ ק] הוּא רֵאשָׁה דִּי

לט דַהֲבָא: וּבָתְרָךְ תְּקוּם מַלְכוּ אָחֳרִי °ארעי [°אֲרַע ק] מִנָּךְ וּמַלְכוּ °תליתיא [°תְלִיתָאָה ק] אָחֳרִי דִּי נְחָשָׁא דִּי תִשְׁלַט בְּכָל־אַרְעָא: וּמַלְכוּ

מ °רביעיה [°רְבִיעָאָה ק] תֶּהֱוֵא תַקִּיפָה כְּפַרְזְלָא כָּל־קֳבֵל דִּי פַרְזְלָא מְהַדֵּק וְחָשֵׁל כֹּלָּא וּכְפַרְזְלָא דִּי־מְרָעַע כָּל־אִלֵּין תַּדִּק וְתֵרֹעַ: וְדִי־חֲזַיְתָה

מא רַגְלַיָּא וְאֶצְבְּעָתָא °מנהון [°מִנְּהֵן ק] חֲסַף דִּי־פֶחָר °וּמִנְּהוֹן [°וּמִנְּהֵן ק] פַּרְזֶל מַלְכוּ פְלִיגָה תֶּהֱוֵה וּמִן־נִצְבְּתָא דִי־פַרְזְלָא לֶהֱוֵא־בַהּ כָּל־קֳבֵל דִּי

מב חֲזַיְתָה פַּרְזְלָא מְעָרַב בַּחֲסַף טִינָא: וְאֶצְבְּעָת רַגְלַיָּא °מנהון [°וּמִנְּהֵן ק] פַּרְזֶל °וּמִנְּהוֹן [°וּמִנְּהֵן ק] חֲסַף מִן־קְצָת מַלְכוּתָא תֶּהֱוֵה תַקִּיפָה

מג וּמִנַּהּ תֶּהֱוֵה תְבִירָה: °די [°וְדִי ק] חֲזַיְתָ פַּרְזְלָא מְעָרַב בַּחֲסַף טִינָא

destroy the sages of Babylonia; he went and said thus to him, "Do not annihilate the wise men of Babylonia. Bring me before the king, and I will tell the interpretation to the king!"

Daniel
before the
king ²⁵ *Then Arioch brought Daniel before the king in haste, and said thus to him, "I have found a man from the people of the exile of Judah who will make known the interpretation to the king."*

²⁶ *The king responded and said to Daniel, whose name was Belteshazzar, "Are you capable of making known to me the dream that I saw and its interpretation?"*

²⁷ *Daniel answered before the king, and said, "The secret the king requests, no wise men, astrologers, necromancers or demonists are able to tell the king.* ²⁸ *But there is a God in Heaven Who reveals secrets, and He has informed King Nebuchadnezzar what will be at the End of Days. Your dream, and the visions in your head on your bed, are these:*

²⁹ *"You, O king, your thoughts came while you were on your bed about what would happen in the future, and the Revealer of secrets informed you what will be.* ³⁰ *As for me, it is not because I possess more wisdom than any other being that this secret was revealed to me, but rather to make the interpretation known to the king, so that you may know what has occupied your thoughts.*

This is the
dream ³¹ *"You, O king, were watching and behold! a huge statue; this statue, which was immense, and whose brightness was extraordinary, stood opposite you, and its appearance was fearsome.* ³² *This statue: its head of fine gold; its breast and arms of silver; its belly and thighs of copper;* ³³ *its legs of iron; and its feet, partly of iron and partly of earthenware.* ³⁴ *As you watched, a stone was hewn without hands and struck the statue on its feet of iron and earthenware, and crumbled them.* ³⁵ *Then they crumbled together: the iron, the earthenware, the copper, the silver and the gold. They became like chaff from summer threshing floors, and the wind carried them away and no trace was found of them. And the stone that struck the statue became a great mountain and filled the entire earth.* ³⁶ *This is the dream, and we will tell its interpretation before the king.*

The Four
Kingdoms ³⁷ *"You, O king — to whom the King of kings, Who is the God of Heaven, has given a strong kingdom, power, and honor,* ³⁸ *and wherever people, beasts of the field and birds of the sky dwell, He has given them into your hand and made you ruler over them all — you are the head of gold.* ³⁹ *And after you will arise another kingdom inferior to you,* * *and [then] another, a third kingdom, of copper, which will rule the whole earth.* ⁴⁰ *The fourth kingdom* * *will be as strong as iron: Just as iron crumbles and flattens everything, and as iron shatters all these, it will crumble and shatter.* ⁴¹ *The feet and the toes that you saw, partly of potter's earthenware and partly of iron: It will be a divided kingdom* * *and will have some of the firmness of iron, just as you saw iron mixed with clay-like earthenware.* ⁴² *As for the toes, partly of iron and partly of earthenware: Part of the kingdom will be powerful and part of it will be broken.* ⁴³ *That you saw iron mixed with clay-like earthenware:*

2:39. Just as silver is inferior to gold, and the chest lower than the head, so will the kingdom that follows yours, that of the Persians and Medes, be inferior to yours.

Then will come the "copper kingdom," the Greek empire of Alexander the Great and his successors (*Rashi*).

2:40. The Roman empire.

2:41. The lands of the Roman empire came to be dominated by Edom and Ishmael, represented by Christianity and Islam. Both — one as strong as iron, the other as weak as pottery — comprise the latter day "fourth kingdom" (*Abarbanel*).

מִתְעָרְבִין לֶהֱוֺן בִּזְרַע אֲנָשָׁא וְלָא־לֶהֱוֺן דָּבְקִין דְּנָה עִם־דְּנָה הֵא־כְּדִי
מד פַרְזְלָא לָא מִתְעָרַב עִם־חַסְפָּא: וּבְיוֹמֵיהוֹן דִּי מַלְכַיָּא אִנּוּן יְקִים אֱלָהּ
שְׁמַיָּא מַלְכוּ דִּי לְעָלְמִין לָא תִתְחַבַּל וּמַלְכוּתָה לְעַם אָחֳרָן לָא תִשְׁתְּבִק
מה תַּדִּק וְתָסֵיף כָּל־אִלֵּין מַלְכְוָתָא וְהִיא תְּקוּם לְעָלְמַיָּא: כָּל־קֳבֵל דִּי־חֲזַיְתָ
דִּי מִטּוּרָא אִתְגְּזֶרֶת אֶבֶן דִּי־לָא בִידַיִן וְהַדֵּקֶת פַּרְזְלָא נְחָשָׁא חַסְפָּא
כַּסְפָּא וְדַהֲבָא אֱלָהּ רַב הוֹדַע לְמַלְכָּא מָה דִּי לֶהֱוֵא אַחֲרֵי דְנָה וְיַצִּיב
מו חֶלְמָא וּמְהֵימַן פִּשְׁרֵהּ: בֵּאדַיִן מַלְכָּא נְבוּכַדְנֶצַּר נְפַל עַל־
מז אַנְפּוֹהִי וּלְדָנִיֵּאל סְגִד וּמִנְחָה וְנִיחֹחִין אֲמַר לְנַסָּכָה לֵהּ: עָנֵה מַלְכָּא
לְדָנִיֵּאל וְאָמַר מִן־קְשֹׁט דִּי אֱלָהֲכוֹן הוּא אֱלָהּ אֱלָהִין וּמָרֵא מַלְכִין וְגָלֵה
מח רָזִין דִּי יְכֵלְתָּ לְמִגְלֵא רָזָה דְנָה: אֱדַיִן מַלְכָּא לְדָנִיֵּאל רַבִּי וּמַתְּנָן רַבְרְבָן
שַׂגִּיאָן יְהַב־לֵהּ וְהַשְׁלְטֵהּ עַל כָּל־מְדִינַת בָּבֶל וְרַב־סִגְנִין עַל כָּל־חַכִּימֵי
מט בָבֶל: וְדָנִיֵּאל בְּעָא מִן־מַלְכָּא וּמַנִּי עַל עֲבִידְתָּא דִּי מְדִינַת בָּבֶל לְשַׁדְרַךְ
ג א מֵישַׁךְ וַעֲבֵד נְגוֹ וְדָנִיֵּאל בִּתְרַע מַלְכָּא: נְבוּכַדְנֶצַּר מַלְכָּא
עֲבַד צְלֵם דִּי־דְהַב רוּמֵהּ אַמִּין שִׁתִּין פְּתָיֵהּ אַמִּין שֵׁת אֲקִימֵהּ בְּבִקְעַת
ב דּוּרָא בִּמְדִינַת בָּבֶל: וּנְבוּכַדְנֶצַּר מַלְכָּא שְׁלַח לְמִכְנַשׁ ׀ לַאֲחַשְׁדַּרְפְּנַיָּא
סִגְנַיָּא וּפַחֲוָתָא אֲדַרְגָּזְרַיָּא גְדָבְרַיָּא דְּתָבְרַיָּא תִּפְתָּיֵא וְכֹל שִׁלְטֹנֵי
ג מְדִינָתָא לְמֵתֵא לַחֲנֻכַּת צַלְמָא דִּי הֲקֵים נְבוּכַדְנֶצַּר מַלְכָּא: בֵּאדַיִן
מִתְכַּנְּשִׁין אֲחַשְׁדַּרְפְּנַיָּא סִגְנַיָּא וּפַחֲוָתָא אֲדַרְגָּזְרַיָּא גְדָבְרַיָּא דְּתָבְרַיָּא
תִּפְתָּיֵא וְכֹל שִׁלְטֹנֵי מְדִינָתָא לַחֲנֻכַּת צַלְמָא דִּי הֲקֵים נְבוּכַדְנֶצַּר מַלְכָּא
ד °וְקָאמִין [°וְקָיְמִין ק] לָקֳבֵל צַלְמָא דִּי הֲקֵים נְבוּכַדְנֶצַּר: וְכָרוֹזָא קָרֵא
ה בְחָיִל לְכוֹן אָמְרִין עַמְמַיָּא אֻמַּיָּא וְלִשָּׁנַיָּא: בְּעִדָּנָא דִּי־תִשְׁמְעוּן קָל קַרְנָא
°מַשְׁרוֹקִיתָא °קִיתֹרֹס [°קַתְרֹס ק] סַבְּכָא פְּסַנְתֵּרִין סוּמְפֹּנְיָה וְכֹל זְנֵי
ו זְמָרָא תִּפְּלוּן וְתִסְגְּדוּן לְצֶלֶם דַּהֲבָא דִּי הֲקֵים נְבוּכַדְנֶצַּר מַלְכָּא: וּמַן־
ז דִּי־לָא יִפֵּל וְיִסְגֻּד בַּהּ־שַׁעֲתָא יִתְרְמֵא לְגוֹא־אַתּוּן נוּרָא יָקִדְתָּא: כָּל־
קֳבֵל דְּנָה בֵּהּ־זִמְנָא כְּדִי שָׁמְעִין כָּל־עַמְמַיָּא קָל קַרְנָא °מַשְׁרוֹקִיתָא
°קִיתֹרֹס [°קַתְרֹס ק] שַׂבְּכָא פְּסַנְטֵרִין וְכֹל זְנֵי זְמָרָא נָפְלִין כָּל־עַמְמַיָּא
ח אֻמַיָּא וְלִשָּׁנַיָּא סָגְדִין לְצֶלֶם דַּהֲבָא דִּי הֲקֵים נְבוּכַדְנֶצַּר מַלְכָּא: כָּל־קֳבֵל
ט דְּנָה בֵּהּ־זִמְנָא קְרִבוּ גֻּבְרִין כַּשְׂדָּאִין וַאֲכַלוּ קַרְצֵיהוֹן דִּי יְהוּדָיֵא: עֲנוֹ
י וְאָמְרִין לִנְבוּכַדְנֶצַּר מַלְכָּא מַלְכָּא לְעָלְמִין חֱיִי: °אַנְתָּה [°אַנְתְּ ק] מַלְכָּא
שָׂמְתָּ טְעֵם דִּי כָל־אֱנָשׁ דִּי־יִשְׁמַע קָל קַרְנָא מַשְׁרוֹקִיתָא °קִיתֹרֹס
[°קַתְרֹס ק] שַׂבְּכָא פְסַנְתֵּרִין °וְסוּפֹנְיָה [°וְסוּמְפֹּנְיָה ק] וְכֹל זְנֵי זְמָרָא יִפֵּל
יא וְיִסְגֻּד לְצֶלֶם דַּהֲבָא: וּמַן דִּי־לָא יִפֵּל וְיִסְגֻּד יִתְרְמֵא לְגוֹא־אַתּוּן
יב נוּרָא יָקִדְתָּא: אִיתַי גֻּבְרִין יְהוּדָאִין דִּי־מַנִּיתָ יָתְהוֹן עַל־עֲבִידַת מְדִינַת

2:46. Nebuchadnezzar believed Daniel to be a Divine being.

3:1. Nebuchadnezzar's golden statue (and his command that all his subjects bow to it) was in reaction to Daniel's

They will mix with the offspring of men, but they will not cling to one another, just as iron does not mix with earthenware. [44] *Then, in the days of these kingdoms, the God of Heaven will establish a kingdom that will never be destroyed nor will its sovereignty be left to another people; it will crumble and consume all these kingdoms, and it will stand forever.* [45] *Just as you saw that a stone was hewn from the mountain, not by human hands, and it crumbled the iron, the copper, the earthenware, the silver and the gold, so has the great God made known to the king what will happen in the future. The dream is true and its interpretation is reliable."*

Nebuchad-
nezzar
exalts Daniel [46] *Then King Nebuchadnezzar fell upon his face and prostrated himself to Daniel; and with offering and incense he wished to exalt him.* * [47] *The king exclaimed to Daniel and said, "In truth I know that your God is the God over gods, Lord of kings and the Revealer of secrets, since you were able to reveal this secret."* [48] *Then the king promoted Daniel and gave him many great gifts. He empowered him as ruler over the entire land of Babylon and chief official over all the sages of Babylonia.* [49] *Daniel requested of the king, and he appointed Shadrach, Meshach and Abed-nego over the affairs of the land of Babylonia; and Daniel was at the king's gate.*

3

Nebuchad-
nezzar's
golden statue [1] **K**ing Nebuchadnezzar made a statue of gold, its height sixty cubits and its width six cubits; he stood it in the plain of Dura, in the province of Babylon. * [2] *Then King Nebuchadnezzar sent to assemble the satraps, the nobles, the governors, the judges, the treasurers, the advisers, the guards and all the provincial officials to come to the dedication of the statue that King Nebuchadnezzar had set up.*

The king's
command [3] *Thereupon the rulers, the nobles, the governors, the judges, the treasurers, the advisers, the guards and all the provincial officials gathered together for the dedication of the statue that King Nebuchadnezzar had set up, and they stood facing the statue that Nebuchadnezzar had set up.* [4] *A herald cried aloud, "It is commanded to you, O peoples, nations, and languages:* [5] *When you hear the sound of the horn, the whistle, the tambourine, the drum, the cymbals, the flute and all kinds of music, you shall fall and prostrate yourselves to the golden statue that King Nebuchadnezzar has set up.* [6] *Whoever does not fall and prostrate himself will immediately be thrown into a fiery, burning furnace."*

[7] *Therefore, as soon as all the peoples heard the sound of the horn, the whistle, the tambourine, the drum, the cymbals and all kinds of music, all the peoples, the nations and the languages fell and prostrated themselves to the golden statue that King Nebuchadnezzar had set up.*

Slander [8] *Thereupon, at that very time, some Chaldean men came forth and defamed the Jews.* [9] *They exclaimed and said to King Nebuchadnezzar, "May the king live forever!* [10] *You, O king, issued a decree that every person who hears the sound of the horn, the whistle, the tambourine, the drum, the cymbals, the flute and all kinds of music is to fall and prostrate himself to the golden statue,* [11] *and whoever does not fall and prostrate himself is to be thrown into a fiery, burning furnace.* [12] *There are Jewish men whom you have appointed over the affairs of the province*

---

interpretation of the dream. Nebuchadnezzar was sure that if he could coerce the Jewish people to engage in idolatry, the climax of the prophecy of the Four Kingdoms, Israel's dominance, would not be fulfilled (*R' Saadiah Gaon*). Alternatively: The king reasoned that since the golden head in the dream symbolized Babylonia, if the entire statue were made of gold rather than other metals and clay, his kingdom could never be toppled, and Babylonia would remain triumphant forever (*Rabbeinu Tam; Abarbanel*).

בָּבֶ֔ל שַׁדְרַ֥ךְ מֵישַׁ֖ךְ וַעֲבֵ֣ד נְג֑וֹ גֻּבְרַיָּ֣א אִלֵּ֗ךְ לָא־שָׂ֨מוּ °עֲלַ֜יךְ [°עֲלָ֛ךְ ק] מַלְכָּא֩
טְעֵ֨ם °לֵאלָהָיךְ [°לֵֽאלָהָ֜ךְ ק] לָ֣א פָֽלְחִ֗ין וּלְצֶ֧לֶם דַּהֲבָ֛א דִּ֥י הֲקֵ֖ימְתָּ לָ֥א
סָגְדִֽין: בֵּאדַ֤יִן נְבֽוּכַדְנֶצַּר֙ בִּרְגַ֣ז וַחֲמָ֔ה אֲמַר֙ לְהַיְתָיָ֔ה לְשַׁדְרַ֥ךְ מֵישַׁ֖ךְ

וַעֲבֵ֣ד נְג֑וֹ בֵּאדַ֕יִן גֻּבְרַיָּ֣א אִלֵּ֔ךְ הֵיתָ֖יוּ קֳדָ֥ם מַלְכָּֽא: עָנֵ֤ה נְבֽוּכַדְנֶצַּר֙ וְאָמַ֣ר לְה֔וֹן
הַצְדָּ֕א שַׁדְרַ֥ךְ מֵישַׁ֖ךְ וַעֲבֵ֣ד נְג֑וֹ לֵֽאלָהַ֗י לָ֤א אִֽיתֵיכוֹן֙ פָּ֣לְחִ֔ין וּלְצֶ֧לֶם דַּהֲבָ֛א
דִּ֥י הֲקֵ֖ימֶת לָ֥א סָֽגְדִֽין: כְּעַ֞ן הֵ֧ן אִֽיתֵיכ֣וֹן עֲתִידִ֗ין דִּ֣י בְעִדָּנָ֡א דִּֽי־תִשְׁמְע֡וּן קָ֣ל
קַרְנָ֣א מַ֠שְׁרוֹקִיתָ֤א °קיתרס [°קַתְר֤וֹס ק] שַׂבְּכָ֣א פְּסַנְתֵּרִין֙ וְסֽוּמְפֹּ֣נְיָ֔ה וְכֹ֣ל ׀
זְנֵ֣י זְמָרָ֔א תִּפְּל֤וּן וְתִסְגְּדוּן֙ לְצַלְמָ֣א דִֽי־עַבְדֵ֔ת וְהֵ֣ן לָ֣א תִסְגְּד֗וּן בַּהּ־שַׁעֲתָ֤ה

תִּתְרְמ֗וֹן לְגֽוֹא־אַתּ֥וּן נוּרָ֖א יָקִֽדְתָּ֑א וּמַן־ה֣וּא אֱלָ֔הּ דִּ֥י יְשֵֽׁיזְבִנְכ֖וֹן מִן־יְדָֽי: עֲנ֨וֹ
שַׁדְרַ֤ךְ מֵישַׁךְ֙ וַעֲבֵ֣ד נְג֔וֹ וְאָמְרִ֖ין לְמַלְכָּ֑א נְבֽוּכַדְנֶצַּ֔ר לָֽא־חַשְׁחִ֧ין אֲנַ֛חְנָא
עַל־דְּנָ֖ה פִּתְגָ֥ם לַהֲתָבוּתָֽךְ: הֵ֣ן אִיתַ֗י אֱלָהַ֙נָא֙ דִּֽי־אֲנַ֣חְנָא פָֽלְחִ֔ין יָכִ֖ל
לְשֵׁיזָבוּתַ֑נָא מִן־אַתּ֨וּן נוּרָ֧א יָקִֽדְתָּ֛א וּמִן־יְדָ֥ךְ מַלְכָּ֖א יְשֵׁיזִֽב: וְהֵ֣ן לָ֔א יְדִ֥יעַ
לֶהֱוֵא־לָ֖ךְ מַלְכָּ֑א דִּ֤י °לאלהיך [°לֵֽאלָהָךְ֙ ק] לָ֣א °איתינא [°אִיתַ֔נָא ק] פָֽלְחִ֔ין

וּלְצֶ֧לֶם דַּהֲבָ֛א דִּ֥י הֲקֵ֖ימְתָּ לָ֥א נִסְגֻּֽד: בֵּאדַ֨יִן נְבֽוּכַדְנֶצַּ֜ר הִתְמְלִ֣י
חֱמָ֗א וּצְלֵ֤ם אַנְפּ֙וֹהִי֙ °אשתנו [°אֶשְׁתַּנִּ֔י ק] עַל־שַׁדְרַ֥ךְ מֵישַׁ֖ךְ וַעֲבֵ֣ד נְג֑וֹ עָנֵ֤ה
וְאָמַר֙ לְמֵזֵ֣א לְאַתּוּנָ֔א חַד־שִׁבְעָ֕ה עַ֛ל דִּ֥י חֲזֵ֖ה לְמֵזְיֵֽהּ: וּלְגֻבְרִ֣ין גִּבָּֽרֵי־חַ֗יִל
דִּ֣י בְחַיְלֵ֔הּ אֲמַר֙ לְכַפָּתָ֔ה לְשַׁדְרַ֥ךְ מֵישַׁ֖ךְ וַעֲבֵ֣ד נְג֑וֹ לְמִרְמֵ֕א לְאַתּ֥וּן נוּרָ֖א

יָקִֽדְתָּֽא: בֵּאדַ֜יִן גֻּבְרַיָּ֣א אִלֵּ֗ךְ כְּפִ֙תוּ֙ בְּסַרְבָּ֣לֵיה֔וֹן °פטישיהון [°פַּטְּשֵׁיה֗וֹן ק]
וְכַרְבְּלָתְה֖וֹן וּלְבֻשֵׁיה֑וֹן וּרְמִ֕יו לְגֽוֹא־אַתּ֥וּן נוּרָ֖א יָקִֽדְתָּ֑א כָּל־קֳבֵ֣ל דְּנָ֗ה מִן־
דִּ֞י מִלַּ֤ת מַלְכָּא֙ מַחְצְפָ֔ה וְאַתּוּנָ֖א אֵזֵ֣ה יַתִּ֑ירָא גֻּבְרַיָּ֣א אִלֵּ֗ךְ דִּ֤י הַסִּ֙קוּ֙ לְשַׁדְרַ֤ךְ

מֵישַׁךְ֙ וַעֲבֵ֣ד נְג֔וֹ קַטִּ֣ל הִמּ֔וֹן שְׁבִיבָ֖א דִּ֥י נוּרָֽא: וְגֻבְרַיָּ֤א אִלֵּךְ֙ תְּלָ֣תֵּה֔וֹן שַׁדְרַ֥ךְ
מֵישַׁ֖ךְ וַעֲבֵ֣ד נְג֑וֹ נְפַ֛לוּ לְגֽוֹא־אַתּוּן־נוּרָ֥א יָקִֽדְתָּ֖א מְכַפְּתִֽין: אֱדַ֙יִן֙
נְבֽוּכַדְנֶצַּ֣ר מַלְכָּ֔א תְּוַ֖הּ וְקָ֣ם בְּהִתְבְּהָלָ֑ה עָנֵ֨ה וְאָמַ֜ר לְהַדָּֽבְר֗וֹהִי הֲלָ֨א גֻבְרִ֤ין
תְּלָתָא֙ רְמֵ֤ינָא לְגֽוֹא־נוּרָא֙ מְכַפְּתִ֔ין עָנַ֤יִן וְאָמְרִין֙ לְמַלְכָּ֔א יַצִּיבָ֖א

מַלְכָּֽא: עָנֵ֣ה וְאָמַ֗ר הָֽא־אֲנָ֨ה חָזֵ֜ה גֻּבְרִ֣ין אַרְבְּעָ֗ה שְׁרַ֙יִן֙ מַהְלְכִ֣ין בְּגֽוֹא־
נוּרָ֔א וַחֲבָ֖ל לָֽא־אִיתַ֣י בְּה֑וֹן וְרֵוֵהּ֙ דִּ֣י °רביעיא [°רְֽבִיעָאָ֔ה ק] דָּמֵ֖ה לְבַר־
אֱלָהִֽין: בֵּאדַ֜יִן קְרֵ֣ב נְבֽוּכַדְנֶצַּ֗ר לִתְרַע֮ אַתּ֣וּן נוּרָ֣א יָקִֽדְתָּא֒ עָנֵ֣ה
וְאָמַ֗ר שַׁדְרַ֥ךְ מֵישַׁ֛ךְ וַעֲבֵד־נְג֛וֹ עַבְד֛וֹהִי דִּֽי־אֱלָהָ֥א °עליא [°עִלָּאָ֖ה ק]

פֻּ֣קוּ וֶאֱת֑וֹ בֵּאדַ֣יִן נָֽפְקִ֗ין שַׁדְרַ֥ךְ מֵישַׁ֛ךְ וַעֲבֵ֥ד נְג֖וֹ מִן־גּ֥וֹא נוּרָֽא: °וּמִֽתְכַּנְּשִׁ֞ין
אֲחַשְׁדַּרְפְּנַיָּ֣א סִגְנַיָּ֣א וּפַחֲוָתָא֮ וְהַדָּֽבְרֵ֣י מַלְכָּא֒ חָזַ֣יִן לְגֻבְרַיָּ֣א אִלֵּ֗ךְ דִּי֩ לָֽא־
שְׁלֵ֨ט נוּרָ֜א בְּגֶשְׁמְה֗וֹן וּשְׂעַ֤ר רֵֽאשְׁהוֹן֙ לָ֣א הִתְחָרַ֔ךְ וְסָרְבָּלֵיה֖וֹן לָ֣א שְׁנ֑וֹ
וְרֵ֣יחַ נ֔וּר לָ֥א עֲדָ֖ת בְּהֽוֹן: עָנֵ֨ה נְבֽוּכַדְנֶצַּ֜ר וְאָמַ֗ר בְּרִ֤יךְ אֱלָֽהֲהוֹן֙ דִּֽי־שַׁדְרַ֤ךְ
מֵישַׁךְ֙ וַעֲבֵ֣ד נְג֔וֹ דִּֽי־שְׁלַ֤ח מַלְאֲכֵהּ֙ וְשֵׁיזִ֣ב לְעַבְד֔וֹהִי דִּ֥י הִתְרְחִ֖צֽוּ
עֲל֑וֹהִי וּמִלַּ֤ת מַלְכָּא֙ שַׁנִּ֔יו וִיהַ֣בוּ °גשמיהון [°גֶשְׁמְה֗וֹן ק] דִּ֣י לָֽא־

of Babylon, Shadrach, Meshach and Abed-nego. These men have not accepted your decree upon themselves, O king; your god they do not worship; and to the golden statue that you have set up they do not prostrate themselves."

Nebuchadnezzar's fury

¹³ Then King Nebuchadnezzar, in anger and fury, commanded to bring Shadrach, Meshach and Abed-nego; these men were then brought before the king. ¹⁴ Nebuchadnezzar exclaimed and said to them, "Is it true, Shadrach, Meshach and Abed-Nego, that you do not worship my god and that you do not prostrate yourselves to the golden statue that I have set up? ¹⁵ Now, behold, you must be prepared when you hear the sound of the horn, the whistle, the tambourine, the drum, the cymbals, the flute and all kinds of music, to fall and prostrate yourselves to the statue I have made; but if you do not prostrate yourselves, you will immediately be thrown into a fiery, burning furnace; and who is the god who can save you from my hands?"

"He is able to save us"

¹⁶ Shadrach, Meshach and Abed-nego responded and said to the king, "Nebuchadnezzar, we are not worried about replying to you about this matter. ¹⁷ Behold, our God Whom we worship is able to save us; He will rescue from the fiery, burning furnace and from your hand, O king. ¹⁸ But if [He does] not, let it be known to you, O king, that we do not worship your god, and to the golden statue that you have set up we shall not prostrate ourselves."

Into the flaming furnace

¹⁹ Then Nebuchadnezzar was filled with fury and the form of his face became contorted at Shadrach, Meshach and Abed-nego. He exclaimed and commanded [his men] to heat the furnace to seven times more than it was normally heated. ²⁰ Then he commanded the strong men of his guard to bind Shadrach, Meshach and Abed-nego, to throw them into the fiery, burning furnace. ²¹ Then these men were bound in their cloaks, their pants, their robes and their [other] clothing, and were thrown into the fiery, burning furnace. ²² Thereupon, because of the king's peremptory command and because the furnace was so overheated, those men who carried up Shadrach, Meshach and Abed-nego were killed by a flame of fire. ²³ And these three men, Shadrach, Meshach and Abed-nego, fell bound into the fiery, burning furnace.

Four unbound men

²⁴ Then King Nebuchadnezzar, bewildered, stood up in haste. He exclaimed to his ministers and said, "Did we not throw three bound men into the fire?"

They replied and said to the king, "True, O King!"

²⁵ He exclaimed and said, "Behold, I see four unbound men walking in the fire, and there is no wound on them; and the appearance of the fourth [one] is like an angel's."

Ineffective fire

²⁶ Then Nebuchadnezzar approached the opening of the fiery, burning furnace. He exclaimed and said, "Shadrach, Meshach and Abed-nego, servants of the Supreme God, step out and come here!" Thereupon Shadrach, Meshach and Abed-nego stepped out of the fire. ²⁷ The satraps, the nobles, the governors and the ministers of the king assembled and saw these men over whose bodies the fire had no effect, the hair of whose heads was not singed, whose cloaks were unaltered and who had not absorbed the smell of fire.

²⁸ Nebuchadnezzar exclaimed and said, "Blessed is the God of Shadrach, Meshach and Abed-nego, Who sent His angel and saved His servants who relied on Him and disobeyed the king's order and offered their bodies in order not to

כט יִפְלְחוּן וְלָא־יִסְגְּדוּן לְכָל־אֱלָהּ לָהֵן לֵאלָהֲהוֹן: וּמִנִּי שִׂים טְעֵם דִּי כָל־
עַם אֻמָּה וְלִשָּׁן דִּי־יֵאמַר °שלה° [ק׳ °שָׁלוּ] עַל אֱלָהֲהוֹן דִּי־שַׁדְרַךְ מֵישַׁךְ
וַעֲבֵד נְגוֹא הַדָּמִין יִתְעֲבֵד וּבַיְתֵהּ נְוָלִי יִשְׁתַּוֵּה כָּל־קֳבֵל דִּי לָא אִיתַי אֱלָהּ
ל אָחֳרָן דִּי־יִכֻּל לְהַצָּלָה כִּדְנָה: בֵּאדַיִן מַלְכָּא הַצְלַח לְשַׁדְרַךְ מֵישַׁךְ וַעֲבֵד
לא נְגוֹ בִּמְדִינַת בָּבֶל: נְבוּכַדְנֶצַּר מַלְכָּא לְכָל־עַמְמַיָּא
אֻמַּיָּא וְלִשָּׁנַיָּא דִּי־°דארין° [°דָּיְרִין ק׳] בְּכָל־אַרְעָא שְׁלָמְכוֹן יִשְׂגֵּא:
לב אָתַיָּא וְתִמְהַיָּא דִּי עֲבַד עִמִּי אֱלָהָא °עליא° [°עִלָּאָה ק׳] שְׁפַר קָדָמַי
לג לְהַחֲוָיָה: אָתוֹהִי כְּמָה רַבְרְבִין וְתִמְהוֹהִי כְּמָה תַקִּיפִין מַלְכוּתֵהּ מַלְכוּת
ד עָלַם וְשָׁלְטָנֵהּ עִם־דָּר וְדָר: אֲנָה נְבוּכַדְנֶצַּר שְׁלֵה הֲוֵית בְּבֵיתִי וְרַעְנַן
ב בְּהֵיכְלִי: חֵלֶם חֲזֵית וִידַחֲלִנַּנִי וְהַרְהֹרִין עַל־מִשְׁכְּבִי וְחֶזְוֵי רֵאשִׁי
ג יְבַהֲלֻנַּנִי: וּמִנִּי שִׂים טְעֵם לְהַנְעָלָה קָדָמַי לְכֹל חַכִּימֵי בָבֶל דִּי־פְשַׁר
ד חֶלְמָא יְהוֹדְעֻנַּנִי: בֵּאדַיִן °עללין° [°עָלִּין ק׳] חַרְטֻמַיָּא אָשְׁפַיָּא °כשדיא
[°כַּשְׂדָּאֵי ק׳] וְגָזְרַיָּא וְחֶלְמָא אָמַר אֲנָה קֳדָמֵיהוֹן וּפִשְׁרֵהּ לָא־מְהוֹדְעִין
ה לִי: וְעַד אָחֳרֵין עַל קָדָמַי דָּנִיֵּאל דִּי־שְׁמֵהּ בֵּלְטְשַׁאצַּר כְּשֻׁם אֱלָהִי וְדִי
ו רוּחַ־אֱלָהִין קַדִּישִׁין בֵּהּ וְחֶלְמָא קָדָמוֹהִי אַמְרֵת: בֵּלְטְשַׁאצַּר רַב
חַרְטֻמַיָּא דִּי | אֲנָה יִדְעֵת דִּי רוּחַ אֱלָהִין קַדִּישִׁין בָּךְ וְכָל־רָז לָא־אָנֵס
ז לָךְ חֶזְוֵי חֶלְמִי דִי־חֲזֵית וּפִשְׁרֵהּ אֱמַר: וְחֶזְוֵי רֵאשִׁי עַל־מִשְׁכְּבִי חָזֵה
ח הֲוֵית וַאֲלוּ אִילָן בְּגוֹא אַרְעָא וְרוּמֵהּ שַׂגִּיא: רְבָה אִילָנָא וּתְקִף וְרוּמֵהּ
ט יִמְטֵא לִשְׁמַיָּא וַחֲזוֹתֵהּ לְסוֹף כָּל־אַרְעָא: עָפְיֵהּ שַׁפִּיר וְאִנְבֵּהּ שַׂגִּיא וּמָזוֹן
לְכֹלָּא־בֵהּ תְּחֹתוֹהִי תַּטְלֵל | חֵיוַת בָּרָא וּבְעַנְפוֹהִי °ידרון° [°יְדוּרָן ק׳]
י צִפֲּרֵי שְׁמַיָּא וּמִנֵּהּ יִתְּזִין כָּל־בִּשְׂרָא: חָזֵה הֲוֵית בְּחֶזְוֵי רֵאשִׁי עַל־מִשְׁכְּבִי
יא וַאֲלוּ עִיר וְקַדִּישׁ מִן־שְׁמַיָּא נָחִת: קָרֵא בְחַיִל וְכֵן אָמַר גֹּדּוּ אִילָנָא וְקַצִּצוּ
עַנְפוֹהִי אַתַּרוּ עָפְיֵהּ וּבַדַּרוּ אִנְבֵּהּ תְּנֻד חֵיוְתָא מִן־תַּחְתּוֹהִי וְצִפֲּרַיָּא מִן־
יב עַנְפוֹהִי: בְּרַם עִקַּר שָׁרְשׁוֹהִי בְּאַרְעָא שְׁבֻקוּ וּבֶאֱסוּר דִּי־פַרְזֶל וּנְחָשׁ
בְּדִתְאָא דִּי בָרָא וּבְטַל שְׁמַיָּא יִצְטַבַּע וְעִם־חֵיוְתָא חֲלָקֵהּ בַּעֲשַׂב אַרְעָא:
יג לִבְבֵהּ מִן־°אנושא° [°אֲנָשָׁא ק׳] יְשַׁנּוֹן וּלְבַב חֵיוָה יִתְיְהִב לֵהּ וְשִׁבְעָה
יד עִדָּנִין יַחְלְפוּן עֲלוֹהִי: בִּגְזֵרַת עִירִין פִּתְגָמָא וּמֵאמַר קַדִּישִׁין שְׁאֵלְתָא
עַד־דִּבְרַת דִּי יִנְדְּעוּן חַיַּיָּא דִּי־שַׁלִּיט °עליא° [°עִלָּאָה ק׳] בְּמַלְכוּת
°אנושא° [°אֲנָשָׁא ק׳] וּלְמַן־דִּי יִצְבֵּא יִתְּנִנַּהּ וּשְׁפַל אֲנָשִׁים יְקִים °עליה
טו °עֲלַהּ ק׳]: דְּנָה חֶלְמָא חֲזֵית אֲנָה מַלְכָּא נְבוּכַדְנֶצַּר °ואנתה° [°וְאַנְתְּ ק׳]
בֵּלְטְשַׁאצַּר פִּשְׁרֵא אֱמַר | כָּל־קֳבֵל דִּי | כָּל־חַכִּימֵי מַלְכוּתִי לָא־יָכְלִין
פִּשְׁרָא לְהוֹדָעֻתַנִי °ואנתה° [°וְאַנְתְּ ק׳] כָּהֵל דִּי רוּחַ־אֱלָהִין קַדִּישִׁין בָּךְ:
טז אֱדַיִן דָּנִיֵּאל דִּי־שְׁמֵהּ בֵּלְטְשַׁאצַּר אֶשְׁתּוֹמַם כְּשָׁעָה חֲדָה וְרַעְיֹנֹהִי
יְבַהֲלֻנֵּהּ עָנֵה מַלְכָּא וְאָמַר בֵּלְטְשַׁאצַּר חֶלְמָא וּפִשְׁרֵא אַל־יְבַהֲלָךְ

"There is no other god able to rescue so" worship or prostrate themselves to any god other than their God! [29] I issue a decree that any people, nation, or language who will speak amiss about the God of Shadrach, Meshach, and Abed-Nego shall be cut to bits, and his house will be turned into a dunghill; for there is no other god able to rescue in this manner." [30] Then the king promoted Shadrach, Meshach and Abed-nego in the province of Babylon.

Nebuchadnezzar's letter [31] [From] King Nebuchadnezzar, to all the peoples, nations and languages that dwell throughout the earth: May your peace be abundant!

[32] It behooves me to relate the signs and the wonders that the Supreme God has performed for me. [33] How great are His signs and how mighty are His wonders! His kingdom is an everlasting kingdom, and His dominion for all generations!

4

A frightening dream [1] I, Nebuchadnezzar, was tranquil in my house and vigorous in my palace. [2] I saw a dream that frightened me, and my thoughts upon my bed and the visions of my head bewildered me. [3] I issued a command to bring before me all the sages of Babylonia, so that they should make known to me the interpretation of the dream. [4] Then the necromancers, the astrologers, the Chaldean [stargazers] and the demonists came; I related the dream before them, but they could not make known its interpretation to me. [5] At last there came before me Daniel, whose name is Belteshazzar after the name of my god, and in whom is the spirit of the Holy God, and I related the dream before him:

[6] 'Belteshazzar, chief of the necromancers, since I know that the spirit of the Holy God is in you, and no secret is hidden from you, this is the vision of the dream that I saw; tell its interpretation. [7] [These were] the visions of my head upon my bed: I was watching and behold, a tree in the midst of the earth, the height of it was great. [8] The tree grew and became strong, its height reached to the heavens; it was visible to the end of the entire earth; [9] its foliage was beautiful and its fruit plentiful, and there was food for all in it; under it beasts of the field took shade, and the birds of heaven nested in its branches, and all flesh was fed from it. [10] In the visions of my head upon my bed, I was watching and behold! a holy angel came down from heaven. [11] He cried out loudly, and said thus, "Chop down the tree and cut off its branches; cast down its foliage and scatter its fruit; let the animals move away from under it, and the birds from its branches! [12] However, leave its major roots in the ground, [secured] with a band of iron and copper in the herbage of the field; let it be washed by the dew of heaven, and let its lot be together with the beasts, in the grass of the earth. [13] They will change its heart from that of a man, and a beast's heart will be given to it, and seven periods will pass over it. [14] The matter is by decree of the angels, and the sentence is by word of the holy ones; so that all living beings may know that the Supreme One rules over the kingdom of man, giving it to whomever He wishes and appointing the lowest of men over it."

[15] 'This dream I saw, I, King Nebuchadnezzar. And you, Belteshazzar, tell its interpretation, because all the sages of my kingdom are unable to make the interpretation known to me; but you can, for the spirit of the Holy God is in you.'

Daniel interprets and advises [16] Then Daniel, whose name is Belteshazzar, was silent for a while, and his thoughts confounded him. The king exclaimed and said, 'Belteshazzar! Let the dream and its interpretation not bewilder you!'

The dream of the tree

A holy angel speaks

עָנֵה בֵלְטְשַׁאצַּר וְאָמַר מָרִאי חֶלְמָא °לְשַׂנְאָיךְ [°לְשָׂנְאָךְ ק׳] וּפִשְׁרֵהּ

°לְעֲרָךְ [°לְעָרָךְ ק׳]: אִילָנָא דִּי חֲזַיְתָ דִּי רְבָה וּתְקִף וְרוּמֵהּ יִמְטֵא לִשְׁמַיָּא יז

וַחֲזוֹתֵהּ לְכָל־אַרְעָא: וְעָפְיֵהּ שַׁפִּיר וְאִנְבֵּהּ שַׂגִּיא וּמָזוֹן לְכֹלָּא־בֵהּ יח

תְּחֹתוֹהִי תְּדוּר חֵיוַת בָּרָא וּבְעַנְפוֹהִי יִשְׁכְּנָן צִפֳּרֵי שְׁמַיָּא: °אַנְתָּה־ יט

[°אַנְתְּ־ ק׳] הוּא מַלְכָּא דִּי °רְבִית [°רְבַת ק׳] וּתְקֵפְתְּ וּרְבוּתָךְ רְבָת וּמְטָת

לִשְׁמַיָּא וְשָׁלְטָנָךְ לְסוֹף אַרְעָא: וְדִי חֲזָה מַלְכָּא עִיר וְקַדִּישׁ נָחִת ׀ מִן־ כ

שְׁמַיָּא וְאָמַר גֹּדּוּ אִילָנָא וְחַבְּלוּהִי בְּרַם עִקַּר שָׁרְשׁוֹהִי בְּאַרְעָא שְׁבֻקוּ

וּבֶאֱסוּר דִּי־פַרְזֶל וּנְחָשׁ בְּדִתְאָא דִּי בָרָא וּבְטַל שְׁמַיָּא יִצְטַבַּע וְעִם־חֵיוַת

בָּרָא חֲלָקֵהּ עַד דִּי־שִׁבְעָה עִדָּנִין יַחְלְפוּן עֲלוֹהִי: דְּנָה פִשְׁרָא מַלְכָּא כא

וּגְזֵרַת °עִלָּיָא [°עִלָּאָה ק׳] הִיא דִּי מְטָת עַל־מָרִאי מַלְכָּא: וְלָךְ טָרְדִין כב

מִן־אֲנָשָׁא וְעִם־חֵיוַת בָּרָא לֶהֱוֵה מְדֹרָךְ וְעִשְׂבָּא כְתוֹרִין ׀ לָךְ יְטַעֲמוּן

וּמִטַּל שְׁמַיָּא לָךְ מְצַבְּעִין וְשִׁבְעָה עִדָּנִין יַחְלְפוּן °עֲלַיִךְ [°עֲלָךְ ק׳] עַד דִּי־

תִנְדַּע דִּי־שַׁלִּיט °עִלָּיָא [°עִלָּאָה ק׳] בְּמַלְכוּת אֲנָשָׁא וּלְמַן־דִּי יִצְבֵּא כג

יִתְּנִנַּהּ: וְדִי אֲמַרוּ לְמִשְׁבַּק עִקַּר שָׁרְשׁוֹהִי דִּי אִילָנָא מַלְכוּתָךְ לָךְ קַיָּמָה

מִן־דִּי תִנְדַּע דִּי שַׁלִּטִן שְׁמַיָּא: לָהֵן מַלְכָּא מִלְכִּי יִשְׁפַּר °עֲלַיִךְ [°עֲלָךְ ק׳] כד

°וַחֲטָאָיךְ [°וַחֲטָאָךְ ק׳] בְּצִדְקָה פְרֻק וַעֲוָיָתָךְ בְּמִחַן עֲנָיִן הֵן תֶּהֱוֵא אַרְכָה

לִשְׁלֵוְתָךְ: כֹּלָּא מְטָא עַל־נְבוּכַדְנֶצַּר מַלְכָּא: כה-כו לִקְצָת יַרְחִין תְּרֵי־

עֲשַׂר עַל־הֵיכַל מַלְכוּתָא דִּי בָבֶל מְהַלֵּךְ הֲוָה: עָנֵה מַלְכָּא וְאָמַר הֲלָא כז

דָא־הִיא בָּבֶל רַבְּתָא דִּי־אֲנָה בֱנַיְתַהּ לְבֵית מַלְכוּ בִּתְקַף חִסְנִי וְלִיקָר

הַדְרִי: עוֹד מִלְּתָא בְּפֻם מַלְכָּא קָל מִן־שְׁמַיָּא נְפַל לָךְ אָמְרִין נְבוּכַדְנֶצַּר כח

מַלְכָּא מַלְכוּתָה עֲדָת מִנָּךְ: וּמִן־אֲנָשָׁא לָךְ טָרְדִין וְעִם־חֵיוַת בָּרָא מְדֹרָךְ כט

עִשְׂבָּא כְתוֹרִין לָךְ יְטַעֲמוּן וְשִׁבְעָה עִדָּנִין יַחְלְפוּן °עֲלַיִךְ [°עֲלָךְ ק׳] עַד

דִּי־תִנְדַּע דִּי־שַׁלִּיט °עִלָּיָא [°עִלָּאָה ק׳] בְּמַלְכוּת אֲנָשָׁא וּלְמַן־דִּי יִצְבֵּא

יִתְּנִנַּהּ: בַּהּ־שַׁעֲתָא מִלְּתָא סָפַת עַל־נְבוּכַדְנֶצַּר וּמִן־אֲנָשָׁא טְרִיד ל

וְעִשְׂבָּא כְתוֹרִין יֵאכֻל וּמִטַּל שְׁמַיָּא גִּשְׁמֵהּ יִצְטַבַּע עַד דִּי שַׂעְרֵהּ כְּנִשְׁרִין

רְבָה וְטִפְרוֹהִי כְצִפְּרִין: וְלִקְצָת יוֹמַיָּה אֲנָה נְבוּכַדְנֶצַּר עַיְנַי ׀ לִשְׁמַיָּא לא

נִטְלֵת וּמַנְדְּעִי עֲלַי יְתוּב °וְלְעִלָּיָא [°וּלְעִלָּאָה ק׳] בָּרְכֵת וּלְחַי עָלְמָא

שַׁבְּחֵת וְהַדְּרֵת דִּי שָׁלְטָנֵהּ שָׁלְטָן עָלַם וּמַלְכוּתֵהּ עִם־דָּר וְדָר: וְכָל־ לב

°דָּארִי [°דָּיְרֵי ק׳] אַרְעָא כְּלָה חֲשִׁיבִין וּכְמִצְבְּיֵהּ עָבֵד בְּחֵיל שְׁמַיָּא

°וְדָארִי [°וְדָיְרֵי ק׳] אַרְעָא וְלָא אִיתַי דִּי־יְמַחֵא בִידֵהּ וְיֵאמַר לֵהּ מָה

עֲבַדְתְּ: בֵּהּ־זִמְנָא מַנְדְּעִי ׀ יְתוּב עֲלַי וְלִיקַר מַלְכוּתִי הַדְרִי וְזִוִי יְתוּב עֲלַי לג

וְלִי הַדָּבְרַי וְרַבְרְבָנַי יְבַעוֹן וְעַל־מַלְכוּתִי הָתְקְנֵת וּרְבוּ יַתִּירָה הוּסְפַת לִי:

כְּעַן אֲנָה נְבוּכַדְנֶצַּר מְשַׁבַּח וּמְרוֹמֵם וּמְהַדַּר לְמֶלֶךְ שְׁמַיָּא דִּי כָל־ לד

מַעֲבָדוֹהִי קְשֹׁט וְאֹרְחָתֵהּ דִּין וְדִי מַהְלְכִין בְּגֵוָה יָכִל לְהַשְׁפָּלָה:

Belteshazzar replied and said, 'My lord, may this dream be upon your foes, and its interpretation upon your enemies! [17] *The tree that you saw, which grew and became strong, whose height reached the heavens and which was visible to the entire earth,* [18] *whose foliage was beautiful and whose fruit plentiful, with food for all in it, under which dwelled the beasts of the field, and in whose branches nested the birds of the heaven —* [19] *it is you, O king, who have grown and become powerful; your greatness has grown and reached the sky, and your dominion to the end of the earth.* [20] *And that which the king saw — a holy angel came down from heaven and said, "Chop down the tree and destroy it, but leave its major roots in the ground, [secured] with a band of iron and copper in the herbage of the field; it will be washed by the dew of heaven and its lot will be with the beasts of the field, until seven periods pass over it" —* [21] *this is the interpretation, O king: It is the decree of the Supreme One that befalls my lord the king.* [22] *They will drive you from mankind, and your dwelling will be among the beasts of the field; they will feed you grass like oxen, and wash you with the dew of heaven, and seven periods will pass over you, until you recognize that the Supreme One rules over the kingdom of man, and He gives it to whomever He wishes.* [23] *As to that which they said to leave the major roots of the tree: Your kingdom will remain for you, after you recognize that Heaven rules.* [24] *Nevertheless, O king, let my advice be acceptable to you: Redeem your sin through righteousness and your iniquities through kindness to the poor; perhaps there will be an extension to your tranquility.'*

A historical aside: The dream is fulfilled

([25] *All this befell King Nebuchadnezzar.* [26] *At the end of twelve months he was walking atop the royal palace of Babylon.* [27] *The king exclaimed and said, "Is this not the great Babylon, which I have built up into a royal house with my powerful strength for glorification of my splendor!"*

[28] *While the words were still in the king's mouth, a voice fell from heaven, "To you, King Nebuchadnezzar, we say: The kingdom has departed from you!* [29] *We are driving you from mankind, and your dwelling will be with the beasts of the field; they will feed you grass like oxen; and seven periods will pass over you, until you recognize that the Supreme One rules over the kingdom of man and He gives it to whomever He wishes."* [30] *At that moment the decree befell Nebuchadnezzar. He was driven from mankind, he ate grass like oxen, and his body was washed by the dew of heaven, until his hair grew like eagles' [feathers] and his nails like birds' [talons].)*

More of the letter: "My senses returned to me"

[31] *At the end of the [seven periods of] years, I, Nebuchadnezzar, raised my eyes to Heaven, and my senses returned to me. I blessed the Supreme One and I praised and glorified the Eternal One, Whose rule is an eternal rule and Whose kingship is for all generations.* [32] *All the inhabitants of the earth are reckoned as nothing; and He acts according to His will with the host of heaven and the inhabitants of the earth; there is no one who can stay His hand or say to Him, 'What have You done?'*

[33] *At that time, my senses returned to me and I returned to the glory of my kingdom; my appearance came back to me, and my ministers and nobles sought me; I was reestablished over my kingdom, and additional greatness was given to me.*

[34] *Now, I, Nebuchadnezzar, praise, extol and glorify the King of Heaven, Whose actions are all in truth, and Whose paths are in justice, and Who is able to humble those who walk proudly!*

ה א בֵּלְשַׁאצַּר מַלְכָּא עֲבַד לְחֶם רַב לְרַבְרְבָנוֹהִי אֲלַף וְלָקֳבֵל אַלְפָּא חַמְרָא
   שָׁתֵה: ב בֵּלְשַׁאצַּר אֲמַר ׀ בִּטְעֵם חַמְרָא לְהַיְתָיָה לְמָאנֵי דַּהֲבָא וְכַסְפָּא דִּי
   הַנְפֵּק נְבוּכַדְנֶצַּר אֲבוּהִי מִן־הֵיכְלָא דִּי בִירוּשְׁלֶם וְיִשְׁתּוֹן בְּהוֹן מַלְכָּא
   ג וְרַבְרְבָנוֹהִי שֵׁגְלָתֵהּ וּלְחֵנָתֵהּ: בֵּאדַיִן הַיְתִיו מָאנֵי דַהֲבָא דִּי הַנְפִּקוּ מִן־
   הֵיכְלָא דִּי־בֵית אֱלָהָא דִּי בִירוּשְׁלֶם וְאִשְׁתִּיו בְּהוֹן מַלְכָּא וְרַבְרְבָנוֹהִי
   שֵׁגְלָתֵהּ וּלְחֵנָתֵהּ: ד אִשְׁתִּיו חַמְרָא וְשַׁבַּחוּ לֵאלָהֵי דַּהֲבָא וְכַסְפָּא נְחָשָׁא
   ה פַרְזְלָא אָעָא וְאַבְנָא: בַּהּ־שַׁעֲתָה °נפקו ⁿנְפַקו ק [°נְפַקָה ק] אֶצְבְּעָן דִּי יַד־אֱנָשׁ
   וְכָתְבָן לָקֳבֵל נֶבְרַשְׁתָּא עַל־גִּירָא דִּי־כְתַל הֵיכְלָא דִּי מַלְכָּא וּמַלְכָּא חָזֵה
   פַּס יְדָה דִּי כָתְבָה: ו אֱדַיִן מַלְכָּא זִיוֺהִי שְׁנוֹהִי וְרַעְיֹנֹהִי יְבַהֲלוּנֵּהּ וְקִטְרֵי
   ז חַרְצֵהּ מִשְׁתָּרַיִן וְאַרְכֻבָּתֵהּ דָּא לְדָא נָקְשָׁן: קָרֵא מַלְכָּא בְּחַיִל לְהֶעָלָה
   לְאָשְׁפַיָּא °כשדיא [°כַּשְׂדָּאֵי ק] וְגָזְרַיָּא עָנֵה מַלְכָּא וְאָמַר ׀ לְחַכִּימֵי בָבֶל
   דִּי כָל־אֱנָשׁ דִּי־יִקְרֵה כְּתָבָה דְנָה וּפִשְׁרֵהּ יְחַוִּנַּנִי אַרְגְּוָנָא יִלְבַּשׁ
   °והמונכא [°וְהַמְנִיכָא ק] דִּי־דַהֲבָא עַל־צַוְּארֵהּ וְתַלְתִּי בְמַלְכוּתָא
   ח יִשְׁלַט: אֱדַיִן °עללין [°עָלֲלִין ק] °עָלִין ק] כֹּל חַכִּימֵי מַלְכָּא וְלָא־כָהֲלִין
   ט כְּתָבָא לְמִקְרֵא °ופשרא [°וּפִשְׁרֵהּ ק] לְהוֹדָעָה לְמַלְכָּא: אֱדַיִן מַלְכָּא
   בֵּלְשַׁאצַּר שַׂגִּיא מִתְבָּהַל וְזִיוֺהִי שָׁנַיִן עֲלוֹהִי וְרַבְרְבָנוֹהִי מִשְׁתַּבְּשִׁין:
   י מַלְכְּתָא לָקֳבֵל מִלֵּי מַלְכָּא וְרַבְרְבָנוֹהִי לְבֵית מִשְׁתְּיָא °עללת [°עַלַּת ק]
   עֲנָת מַלְכְּתָא וַאֲמֶרֶת מַלְכָּא לְעָלְמִין חֱיִי אַל־יְבַהֲלוּךְ רַעְיוֹנָךְ °וזיויך
   יא [°וְזִיוָךְ ק] אַל־יִשְׁתַּנּוֹ: אִיתַי גְּבַר בְּמַלְכוּתָךְ דִּי רוּחַ אֱלָהִין קַדִּישִׁין בֵּהּ
   וּבְיוֹמֵי אֲבוּךְ נַהִירוּ וְשָׂכְלְתָנוּ וְחָכְמָה כְּחָכְמַת־אֱלָהִין הִשְׁתְּכַחַת בֵּהּ
   וּמַלְכָּא נְבֻכַדְנֶצַּר אֲבוּךְ רַב חַרְטֻמִּין אָשְׁפִין כַּשְׂדָּאִין גָּזְרִין הֲקִימֵהּ אֲבוּךְ
   יב מַלְכָּא: כָּל־קֳבֵל דִּי רוּחַ ׀ יַתִּירָה וּמַנְדַּע וְשָׂכְלְתָנוּ מְפַשַּׁר חֶלְמִין וַאַחֲוָיַת
   אֲחִידָן וּמְשָׁרֵא קִטְרִין הִשְׁתְּכַחַת בֵּהּ בְּדָנִיֵּאל דִּי־מַלְכָּא שָׂם־שְׁמֵהּ
   יג בֵּלְטְשַׁאצַּר כְּעַן דָּנִיֵּאל יִתְקְרֵי וּפִשְׁרָה יְהַחֲוֵה: בֵּאדַיִן דָּנִיֵּאל
   הֻעַל קֳדָם מַלְכָּא עָנֵה מַלְכָּא וְאָמַר לְדָנִיֵּאל °אנתה ⁿאַנְתָּה ק [°אַנְתְּ ק] °הוּא
   יד דָּנִיֵּאל דִּי־מִן־בְּנֵי גָלוּתָא דִּי יְהוּד דִּי הַיְתִי מַלְכָּא אַבִי מִן־יְהוּד: וְשִׁמְעֵת
   °עליך [°עֲלָךְ ק] דִּי רוּחַ אֱלָהִין בָּךְ וְנַהִירוּ וְשָׂכְלְתָנוּ וְחָכְמָה יַתִּירָה
   טו הִשְׁתְּכַחַת בָּךְ: וּכְעַן הֻעַלּוּ קָדָמַי חַכִּימַיָּא אָשְׁפַיָּא דִּי־כְתָבָה דְנָה יִקְרוֹן
   טז וּפִשְׁרֵהּ לְהוֹדָעֻתַנִי וְלָא־כָהֲלִין פְּשַׁר־מִלְּתָא לְהַחֲוָיָה: וַאֲנָה שִׁמְעֵת °עליך
   [°עֲלָךְ ק] דִּי־°תוכל [°תוּכַל ק] °תְּכוּל ק] פִּשְׁרִין לְמִפְשַׁר וְקִטְרִין לְמִשְׁרֵא כְּעַן הֵן
   תּוּכַל °תכול [°תְּכוּל ק] כְּתָבָא לְמִקְרֵא וּפִשְׁרֵהּ לְהוֹדָעֻתַנִי אַרְגְּוָנָא תִלְבַּשׁ
   °והמונכא [°וְהַמְנִיכָא ק] דִּי־דַהֲבָא עַל־צַוְּארָךְ וְתַלְתָּא בְמַלְכוּתָא
   יז תִשְׁלַט: בֵּאדַיִן עָנֵה דָנִיֵּאל וְאָמַר קֳדָם מַלְכָּא מַתְּנָתָךְ לָךְ לֶהֶוְיָן
   וּנְבָזְבְּיָתָךְ לְאָחֳרָן הַב בְּרַם כְּתָבָא אֶקְרֵא לְמַלְכָּא וּפִשְׁרָא אֲהוֹדְעִנֵּהּ:

5

Belshazzar's great feast

[1] **K**ing Belshazzar* made a great feast for a thousand of his nobles and drank wine before the thousand [guests]. [2] While under the influence of wine, Belshazzar gave an order to bring the golden and silver vessels that Nebuchadnezzar, his [grand]father, had removed from the Sanctuary that was in Jerusalem, for the king and his nobles, his consorts and his concubines to drink from them. [3] So they brought the golden vessels that they had removed from the Sanctuary of the Temple of God in Jerusalem, and the king, his nobles, his consorts and his concubines drank from them. [4] They drank wine and praised the gods of gold and silver, copper, iron, wood and stone.

The handwriting on the wall

[5] Just then fingers of a human hand came forth and wrote on the plaster of the wall of the king's palace, facing the candelabrum; and the king saw the palm of the hand that was writing. [6] The king's appearance thereupon changed and his thoughts bewildered him; the belt around his waist opened and his knees knocked one against the other. [7] The king cried aloud to bring in the astrologers, the Chaldean [stargazers] and the demonists. The king exclaimed to the sages of Babylonia that any person who would read this writing and tell its interpretation would wear royal purple with a chain of gold on his neck, and would rule one third of the kingdom.

Bewilderment and consternation

[8] Then all the king's sages came in, but they could not read the writing and make its interpretation known to the king. [9] Then King Belshazzar was greatly bewildered and his appearance changed upon him, and his nobles were confounded.

"Let Daniel be called"

[10] As a consequence of the words of the king and his nobles, the queen came into the banquet hall. The queen exclaimed and said, "May the king live forever! Do not be bewildered nor let your appearance be changed. [11] There is a man in your kingdom in whom is the spirit of the Holy God; and in your [grand]father's days, brilliance, understanding and wisdom like the wisdom of God were found in him; and King Nebuchadnezzar, your [grand]father, made him chief of the necromancers, astrologers, Chaldean [stargazers] and demonists. [12] Since extraordinary spirit, intelligence, understanding, interpreting of dreams, solving of riddles and resolving of difficulties have been found in Daniel, whom the king named Belteshazzar, let Daniel now be called and he will relate the interpretation."

"Read, interpret, and rule"

[13] Then Daniel was brought before the king. The king spoke up and said to Daniel, "You are Daniel, from among the people of the exile of Judah, whom the king, my [grand]father, brought from Judah. [14] I have heard about you that the spirit of God is in you, and that brilliance, understanding and extraordinary wisdom are found in you. [15] The sages, the astrologers, were now brought before me to read this writing and make its interpretation known to me, but they could not tell the interpretation of the matter. [16] But I have heard about you that you are able to provide interpretations and to resolve difficulties. Now, if you will be able to read the writing and make its interpretation known to me, you will wear royal purple with a chain of gold on your neck, and you will rule one third of the kingdom."

"Keep your gifts"

[17] Daniel then replied and said before the king, "Let your gifts remain yours, and give your rewards to others. But I will read the writing for the king and make its interpretation known to him.

5:1. Nebuchadnezzar was succeeded by his son Evil-merodach (*II Kings* 25:27), who reigned for twenty-three years. Evil-merodach was succeeded by his son Belshazzar, who reigned for three years (see note to 1:21; see Appendix A, timeline 5). The narrative thus skips at least twenty-five years at this point.

יח °אנתה [°אַ֣נְתְּ ק׳] מַלְכָּ֑א אֱלָהָ֗א °עליא [°עִלָּאָ֞ה ק׳] מַלְכוּתָ֧א וּרְבוּתָ֛א
יט וִיקָרָ֥א וְהַדְרָ֖ה יְהַ֣ב לִנְבֻכַדְנֶצַּ֣ר אֲב֑וּךְ: וּמִן־רְבוּתָא֙ דִּ֣י יְהַב־לֵ֔הּ כֹּ֣ל עַֽמְמַיָּ֗א
אֻמַּיָּא֙ וְלִשָּׁ֣נַיָּ֔א הֲו֤וֹ °זאעין [°זָיְעִ֣ין ק׳] וְדָ֣חֲלִ֔ין מִן־קֳדָמ֑וֹהִי דִּֽי־הֲוָ֤ה צָבֵא֙ הֲוָ֣ה צָבֵ֥א
הֲוָ֣א קָטֵ֔ל וְדִֽי־הֲוָ֤ה צָבֵא֙ הֲוָ֣ה מַחֵ֔א וְדִֽי־הֲוָ֤ה צָבֵא֙ הֲוָ֣ה מָרִ֔ים וְדִֽי־הֲוָ֥ה
צָבֵ֖א הֲוָ֥ה מַשְׁפִּֽיל: כ וּכְדִ֤י רִם לִבְבֵהּ֙ וְרוּחֵ֣הּ תִּקְפַ֣ת לַהֲזָדָ֔ה הָנְחַת֙ מִן־כָּרְסֵ֣א
כא מַלְכוּתֵ֔הּ וִֽיקָרָ֖ה הֶעְדִּ֣יו מִנֵּֽהּ: וּמִן־בְּנֵי֩ אֲנָשָׁ֨א טְרִ֜יד וְלִבְבֵ֣הּ ׀ עִם־חֵיוְתָ֣א
°שוי [°שַׁוִּ֗יו ק׳] וְעִם־עֲרָֽדַיָּא֙ מְדֹרֵ֔הּ עִשְׂבָּ֤א כְתוֹרִין֙ יְטַֽעֲמוּנֵּ֔הּ וּמִטַּ֥ל
שְׁמַיָּ֖א גִּשְׁמֵ֣הּ יִצְטַבַּ֑ע עַ֣ד דִּֽי־יְדַ֗ע דִּֽי־שַׁלִּ֞יט אֱלָהָ֤א °עליא [°עִלָּאָה֙ ק׳]
כב בְּמַלְכ֣וּת אֲנָשָׁ֔א וּלְמַן־דִּ֥י יִצְבֵּ֖ה יְהָקֵ֥ים °עליה [°עֲלַֽהּ ק׳]: °ואנתה [°וְאַ֤נְתְּ
כג בְּרֵהּ֙ בֵּלְשַׁאצַּ֔ר לָ֥א הַשְׁפֵּ֖לְתְּ לִבְבָ֑ךְ כָּל־קֳבֵ֕ל דִּ֥י כָל־דְּנָ֖ה יְדַֽעְתָּ: וְעַ֣ל
מָרֵֽא־שְׁמַיָּ֣א ׀ הִתְרוֹמַ֗מְתָּ וּלְמָֽאנַיָּ֤א דִֽי־בַיְתֵהּ֙ הַיְתִ֣יו °קדמיך [°קָֽדָמָ֔ךְ ק׳]
°ואנתה [°וְאַ֣נְתְּ ק׳] °ורברבניך [°וְרַבְרְבָנָ֗ךְ ק׳] שֵֽׁגְלָתָךְ֙ וּלְחֵ֣נָתָ֔ךְ חַמְרָא֮
שָׁתַ֣יִן בְּהוֹן֒ וְלֵֽאלָהֵ֣י כַסְפָּֽא־וְ֠דַהֲבָא נְחָשָׁ֨א פַרְזְלָ֜א אָעָ֣א וְאַבְנָ֗א דִּ֤י לָֽא־
חָזַ֙יִן֙ וְלָ֣א־שָֽׁמְעִ֔ין וְלָ֣א יָֽדְעִ֔ין שַׁבַּ֑חְתָּ וְלֵֽאלָהָ֞א דִּֽי־נִשְׁמְתָ֥ךְ בִּידֵ֛הּ וְכָל־
כד אֹרְחָתָ֥ךְ לֵ֖הּ לָ֣א הַדַּֽרְתָּ: בֵּאדַ֙יִן֙ מִן־קֳדָמ֔וֹהִי שְׁלִ֖יחַ פַּסָּ֣א דִֽי־יְדָ֑א וּכְתָבָ֥א
כה-כו דְנָ֖ה רְשִֽׁים: וּדְנָ֥ה כְתָבָ֖א דִּ֣י רְשִׁ֑ים מְנֵ֥א מְנֵ֖א תְּקֵ֥ל וּפַרְסִֽין: דְּנָ֖ה פְּשַֽׁר־
כז מִלְּתָ֑א מְנֵ֕א מְנָֽה־אֱלָהָ֥א מַלְכוּתָ֖ךְ וְהַשְׁלְמַֽהּ: תְּקֵ֑ל תְּקִ֥ילְתָּה בְמֹֽאזַנְיָ֖א
כח-כט וְהִשְׁתְּכַ֥חַתְּ חַסִּֽיר: פְּרֵ֑ס פְּרִיסַת֙ מַלְכוּתָ֔ךְ וִיהִיבַ֖ת לְמָדַ֥י וּפָרָֽס: בֵּאדַ֣יִן ׀
אֲמַ֣ר בֵּלְשַׁאצַּ֗ר וְהַלְבִּ֤ישׁוּ לְדָֽנִיֵּאל֙ אַרְגְּוָנָ֔א °והמונכא [°וְהַֽמְנִיכָ֤א ק׳] דִֽי־
דַהֲבָא֙ עַֽל־צַוְּארֵ֔הּ וְהַכְרִ֣זֽוּ עֲל֔וֹהִי דִּֽי־לֶהֱוֵ֥א שַׁלִּ֛יט תַּלְתָּ֖א בְּמַלְכוּתָֽא:
ל בֵּ֚הּ בְּלֵ֣ילְיָ֔א קְטִ֕יל בֵּלְאשַׁצַּ֖ר מַלְכָּ֥א °כשדיא °כַשְׂדָּאָֽה [°כַשְׂדָּאָֽה ק׳]:

ו א וְדָרְיָ֥וֶשׁ °מדיא [°מָֽדָאָ֖ה ק׳] קַבֵּ֣ל מַלְכוּתָ֑א כְּבַ֥ר שְׁנִ֖ין שִׁתִּ֥ין וְתַרְתֵּֽין:
ב שְׁפַ֣ר קֳדָ֣ם דָּֽרְיָ֗וֶשׁ וַהֲקִ֤ים עַל־מַלְכוּתָא֙ לַֽאֲחַשְׁדַּרְפְּנַיָּ֔א מְאָ֖ה וְעֶשְׂרִ֑ין
ג דִּ֥י לֶהֱוֺ֖ן בְּכָל־מַלְכוּתָֽא: וְעֵ֤לָּא מִנְּהוֹן֙ סָֽרְכִ֣ין תְּלָתָ֔א דִּ֥י דָֽנִיֵּ֖אל חַ֣ד־
מִנְּה֑וֹן דִּֽי־לֶהֱוֺ֞ן אֲחַשְׁדַּרְפְּנַיָּ֣א אִלֵּ֗ין יָהֲבִ֤ין לְהוֹן֙ טַעְמָ֔א וּמַלְכָּ֖א לָא־
ד לֶהֱוֵ֥א נָזִֽק: אֱדַ֙יִן֙ דָּנִיֵּ֣אל דְּנָ֔ה הֲוָ֣א מִתְנַצַּ֔ח עַל־סָֽרְכַיָּ֖א וַֽאֲחַשְׁדַּרְפְּנַיָּ֑א
כָּל־קֳבֵ֗ל דִּ֣י ר֤וּחַ יַתִּירָא֙ בֵּ֔הּ וּמַלְכָּ֣א עֲשִׁ֔ית לַהֲקָמוּתֵ֖הּ עַל־כָּל־מַלְכוּתָֽא:
ה אֱדַ֨יִן סָֽרְכַיָּ֜א וַֽאֲחַשְׁדַּרְפְּנַיָּ֗א הֲו֤וֹ בָעַ֨יִן֙ עִלָּ֣ה לְהַשְׁכָּחָ֤ה לְדָֽנִיֵּאל֙ מִצַּ֣ד
מַלְכוּתָ֔א וְכָל־עִלָּ֤ה וּשְׁחִיתָה֙ לָ֣א־יָֽכְלִ֣ין לְהַשְׁכָּחָ֔ה כָּל־קֳבֵ֖ל דִּֽי־מְהֵימַ֣ן
ו ה֔וּא וְכָל־שָׁלוּ֙ וּשְׁחִיתָ֔ה לָ֥א הִשְׁתְּכַ֖חַת עֲל֑וֹהִי: אֱדַ֙יִן֙ גֻּבְרַיָּ֤א אִלֵּךְ֙ אָֽמְרִ֔ין
דִּ֣י לָ֤א נְהַשְׁכַּח֙ לְדָנִיֵּ֣אל דְּנָ֔ה כָּל־עִלָּ֑א לָהֵ֕ן הַשְׁכַּ֥חְנָֽה עֲל֖וֹהִי בְּדָ֥ת
ז אֱלָהֵֽהּ: אֱדַ֨יִן סָֽרְכַיָּ֜א וַֽאֲחַשְׁדַּרְפְּנַיָּ֤א אִלֵּן֙ הַרְגִּ֣שׁוּ עַל־
ח מַלְכָּ֑א וְכֵ֣ן אָֽמְרִ֣ין לֵ֗הּ דָּֽרְיָ֤וֶשׁ מַלְכָּא֙ לְעָלְמִ֣ין חֱיִֽי: אִתְיָעַ֜טוּ כֹּ֣ל ׀ סָֽרְכֵ֣י
מַלְכוּתָ֗א סִגְנַיָּ֤א וַֽאֲחַשְׁדַּרְפְּנַיָּא֙ הַדָּֽבְרַיָּ֣א וּפַֽחֲוָתָ֔א לְקַיָּמָ֥ה קְיָ֣ם מַלְכָּ֖א

18 *"You, O king! The Supreme God gave kingship, greatness, honor and majesty to Nebuchadnezzar, your [grand]father.* 19 *And because of the greatness that He gave him, all the peoples, nations and languages used to tremble and be frightened before him; whomever he wished he would kill, and whomever he wished he would keep alive; whomever he wished he would raise up, and* whomever he wished he would put down. 20 *But when his heart grew proud and his spirit was hardened to rebel, he was deposed from his royal throne, and honor was taken from him.* 21 *He was driven from mankind, and his heart was made like a beast's; his dwelling was with wild asses, and they fed him grass like oxen, and his body was washed with the dew of heaven, until he recognized that the Supreme God rules over the kingdom of men, and that whomever He wishes He appoints over it.*

Nebuchad-nezzar knew that God rules

22 *"But you, his [grand]son Belshazzar, did not humble your heart, although you knew all this.* 23 *You exalted yourself against the Lord of Heaven, and the vessels of His House were brought before you, and you, your nobles, your consorts and your concubines drank wine from them, and you praised the gods of silver and gold, copper, iron, wood and stone, which do not see nor hear nor know; but the God in Whose hand is your soul, and to Whom all your ways belong, you did not glorify.* 24 *Thus the palm of a hand was sent from before Him, and it inscribed this writing.*

"But you exalted yourself"

25 *This is the writing that was inscribed: 'MENE MENE TEKEL UPHARSIN.'* 26 *This is the interpretation of the matter: 'MENE' (counted) — God has counted [the years of] your kingship and terminated it.* 27 *'TEKEL' (weighed) — you have been weighed in the scales and found wanting.* 28 *'PERES'* (broken up) — your kingdom has been broken and given to Media and Persia."*

"Your kingship is broken"

29 *Then Belshazzar gave the command and they clothed Daniel in royal purple with a chain of gold on his neck, and they proclaimed about him that he would rule one third of the kingdom.* 30 *That very night Belshazzar, the Chaldean king, was slain.*

6 1 **T**hen Darius the Mede received the kingship at the age of sixty-two years. 2 *It pleased Darius to appoint over the kingdom one hundred and twenty satraps to be throughout the kingdom,* 3 *and over them three viziers — of whom Daniel was one — to whom these satraps would give advice, so that the king should suffer no harm.* 4 *Then this Daniel oversaw the viziers and satraps, because of the extraordinary spirit in him; and the king thought to appoint him over the whole kingdom.*

Daniel appointed vizier

5 *Thereupon the viziers and the satraps tried to find a libel against Daniel with regard to the kingdom, but they could find neither fault nor corruption, because he was faithful and nor could error or corruption be found in him.* 6 *Then these men said, "We will not find any fault with this Daniel, unless we find it in him through the law of his God."*

Quest for a libel

7 *Thereupon these viziers and satraps assembled about the king, and said thus to him, "May King Darius live forever!* 8 *All the viziers of the kingdom, the nobles and the satraps, the advisers and the governors have conferred to affirm the king's*

The king's prohibition

5:28. Daniel interpreted וּפַרְסִין (upharsin) as the plural of פְּרַס (peres), as if the word פרס were written twice. The first פרס is a verb meaning "break up" or "divide"; the

second, the name of the nation פָּרַס, "Persia." Thus the Babylonian rule will be broken and given over to a Persian conqueror (*Rashi*).

וּלְתַקָּפָה אֱסָר דִּי כָל־דִּי־יִבְעֵה בָעוּ מִן־כָּל־אֱלָהּ וֶאֱנָשׁ עַד־יוֹמִין תְּלָתִין

ט לָהֵן מִנָּךְ מַלְכָּא יִתְרְמֵא לְגֹב אַרְיָוָתָא: כְּעַן מַלְכָּא תְּקִים אֱסָרָא וְתִרְשֻׁם

י כְּתָבָא דִּי לָא לְהַשְׁנָיָה כְּדָת־מָדַי וּפָרַס דִּי־לָא תֶעְדֵּא: כָּל־קָבֵל דְּנָה

יא מַלְכָּא דָּרְיָוֶשׁ רְשַׁם כְּתָבָא וֶאֱסָרָא: ◌וְדָנִיֵּאל כְּדִי יְדַע דִּי־רְשִׁים כְּתָבָא

עַל לְבַיְתֵהּ וְכַוִּין פְּתִיחָן לֵהּ בְּעִלִּיתֵהּ נֶגֶד יְרוּשְׁלֶם וְזִמְנִין תְּלָתָה בְיוֹמָא

הוּא ׀ בָּרֵךְ עַל־בִּרְכוֹהִי וּמְצַלֵּא וּמוֹדֵא קֳדָם אֱלָהֵהּ כָּל־קֳבֵל דִּי־הֲוָא

יב עָבֵד מִן־קַדְמַת דְּנָה: ◌אֱדַיִן גֻּבְרַיָּא אִלֵּךְ הַרְגִּשׁוּ וְהַשְׁכַּחוּ לְדָנִיֵּאל בָּעֵא

יג וּמִתְחַנַּן קֳדָם אֱלָהֵהּ: ◌בֵּאדַיִן קְרִיבוּ וְאָמְרִין קֳדָם־מַלְכָּא עַל־אֱסָר מַלְכָּא

הֲלָא אֱסָר רְשַׁמְתָּ דִּי כָל־אֱנָשׁ דִּי־יִבְעֵה מִן־כָּל־אֱלָהּ וֶאֱנָשׁ עַד־יוֹמִין

תְּלָתִין לָהֵן מִנָּךְ מַלְכָּא יִתְרְמֵא לְגוֹב אַרְיָוָתָא עָנֵה מַלְכָּא וְאָמַר יַצִּיבָא

יד מִלְּתָא כְּדָת־מָדַי וּפָרַס דִּי־לָא תֶעְדֵּא: ◌בֵּאדַיִן עֲנוֹ וְאָמְרִין קֳדָם מַלְכָּא דִּי

דָנִיֵּאל דִּי מִן־בְּנֵי גָלוּתָא דִּי יְהוּד לָא־שָׂם עֲ[°עֲלָיךְ] עֲלַיךְ [°עֲלָךְ] מַלְכָּא טְעֵם

טו וְעַל־אֱסָרָא דִּי רְשַׁמְתָּ וְזִמְנִין תְּלָתָה בְּיוֹמָא בָעֵא בָּעוּתֵהּ: אֱדַיִן מַלְכָּא

כְּדִי מִלְּתָא שְׁמַע שַׂגִּיא בְּאֵשׁ עֲלוֹהִי וְעַל דָּנִיֵּאל שָׂם בָּל לְשֵׁיזָבוּתֵהּ וְעַד

טז מֶעָלֵי שִׁמְשָׁא הֲוָא מִשְׁתַּדַּר לְהַצָּלוּתֵהּ: בֵּאדַיִן גֻּבְרַיָּא אִלֵּךְ הַרְגִּשׁוּ עַל־

מַלְכָּא וְאָמְרִין לְמַלְכָּא דַּע מַלְכָּא דִּי־דָת לְמָדַי וּפָרַס דִּי־כָל־אֱסָר וּקְיָם

יז דִּי־מַלְכָּא יְהָקֵים לָא לְהַשְׁנָיָה: בֵּאדַיִן מַלְכָּא אֲמַר וְהַיְתִיו לְדָנִיֵּאל וּרְמוֹ

לְגֻבָּא דִּי אַרְיָוָתָא עָנֵה מַלְכָּא וְאָמַר לְדָנִיֵּאל אֱלָהָךְ דִּי °אנתה [°אַנְתְּ]

יח פָּלַח־לֵהּ בִּתְדִירָא הוּא יְשֵׁיזְבִנָּךְ: וְהֵיתָיִת אֶבֶן חֲדָה וְשֻׂמַת עַל־פֻּם גֻּבָּא

וְחַתְמַהּ מַלְכָּא בְּעִזְקְתֵהּ וּבְעִזְקָת רַבְרְבָנוֹהִי דִּי לָא־תִשְׁנֵא צְבוּ בְּדָנִיֵּאל:

יט אֱדַיִן אֲזַל מַלְכָּא לְהֵיכְלֵהּ וּבָת טְוָת וְדַחֲוָן לָא־הַנְעֵל קֳדָמוֹהִי וְשִׁנְתֵּהּ

כ נַדַּת עֲלוֹהִי: בֵּאדַיִן מַלְכָּא בִּשְׁפַּרְפָּרָא יְקוּם בְּנָגְהָא וּבְהִתְבְּהָלָה לְגֻבָּא

כא דִּי־אַרְיָוָתָא אֲזַל: וּכְמִקְרְבֵהּ לְגֻבָּא לְדָנִיֵּאל בְּקָל עֲצִיב זְעִק עָנֵה מַלְכָּא

וְאָמַר לְדָנִיֵּאל דָּנִיֵּאל עֲבֵד אֱלָהָא חַיָּא אֱלָהָךְ דִּי °אנתה [°אַנְתְּ]

כב פָּלַח־לֵהּ בִּתְדִירָא הַיְכֵל לְשֵׁיזָבוּתָךְ מִן־אַרְיָוָתָא: אֱדַיִן דָּנִיֵּאל עִם־

כג מַלְכָּא מַלִּל מַלְכָּא לְעָלְמִין חֱיִי: אֱלָהִי שְׁלַח מַלְאֲכֵהּ וּסֲגַר פֻּם אַרְיָוָתָא

וְלָא חַבְּלוּנִי כָּל־קָבֵל דִּי קָדָמוֹהִי זָכוּ הִשְׁתְּכַחַת לִי וְאַף °קדמיך [°קָדָמָךְ]

כד מַלְכָּא חֲבוּלָה לָא עַבְדֵת: בֵּאדַיִן מַלְכָּא שַׂגִּיא טְאֵב עֲלוֹהִי וּלְדָנִיֵּאל

אֲמַר לְהַנְסָקָה מִן־גֻּבָּא וְהֻסַּק דָּנִיֵּאל מִן־גֻּבָּא וְכָל־חֲבָל לָא־הִשְׁתְּכַח בֵּהּ

כה דִּי הֵימִן בֵּאלָהֵהּ: וַאֲמַר מַלְכָּא וְהַיְתִיו גֻּבְרַיָּא אִלֵּךְ דִּי־אֲכַלוּ קַרְצוֹהִי דִּי

דָנִיֵּאל וּלְגֹב אַרְיָוָתָא רְמוֹ אִנּוּן בְּנֵיהוֹן וּנְשֵׁיהוֹן וְלָא־מְטוֹ לְאַרְעִית גֻּבָּא

כו עַד דִּי־שְׁלִטוּ בְהוֹן אַרְיָוָתָא וְכָל־גַּרְמֵיהוֹן הַדִּקוּ: בֵּאדַיִן דָּרְיָוֶשׁ מַלְכָּא

כְּתַב לְכָל־עַמְמַיָּא אֻמַיָּא וְלִשָּׁנַיָּא דִּי־°דארין [°דָּיְרִין] בְּכָל־אַרְעָא

6:18. So that no one would try to rescue him — or harm him — by removing the stone.

law, and to strengthen his prohibition — that whoever will make a request of any god or man for thirty days, other than of you, O king, shall be thrown into the lions' pit. ⁹ Now, O king, approve the prohibition and inscribe the writing so that it cannot be abrogated, according to the law of Media and Persia, which shall never lapse." ¹⁰ As a result of this, King Darius inscribed the writing and the prohibition.

Daniel prays as usual

¹¹ *When Daniel learned that the writing had been inscribed, he went home. He had windows open in his upper story, facing Jerusalem, and three times a day he fell to his knees and prayed and gave thanks before his God, exactly as he used to do before this. ¹² Then these men assembled and found Daniel praying and supplicating before his God.*

¹³ *So they approached and spoke before the king concerning the king's prohibition, "Did you not inscribe a prohibition that any person who would make a request of any god or person for thirty days, other than of you, O king, would be thrown into the lions' pit?"*

The king replied and said, "The matter is true, according to the law of Media and Persia, which shall never lapse."

¹⁴ *Then they exclaimed and said before the king, "That Daniel, who is one of the people of the exile of Judah, has not paid attention to you, O king, and to the prohibition that you have inscribed. Three times a day he prays his prayer!"*

Darius struggles to save Daniel

¹⁵ *Then the king, when he heard this statement, was deeply grieved, and he set his heart on Daniel to save him, and until sundown he strove to rescue him.* ¹⁶ *Then these men assembled around the king and said to the king, "Know, O king, that the law of Media and Persia is that any prohibition or statute that the king establishes cannot be altered."*

Daniel in the lions' pit

¹⁷ *Then the king commanded and they brought Daniel and threw him into the lions' pit. The king exclaimed to Daniel, "May your God, Whom you serve continually, save you!"* ¹⁸ *A stone was brought and was placed over the opening of the pit, and the king sealed it with his signet ring and with the signet rings of his nobles, so that his will regarding Daniel could not be changed. **

The king's concern

¹⁹ *Then the king went to his palace and went to bed fasting, and had no table brought before him; and his sleep wandered from him.* ²⁰ *The king arose in the darkness before dawn, and went in haste to the lions' pit.* ²¹ *When he drew near to the pit, to Daniel, he cried out in a sad voice; the king called out and said to Daniel, "Daniel, servant of the living God! Was your God, Whom you serve continually, able to save you from the lions?"*

"They did not wound me"

²² *Then Daniel spoke to the king: "May the king live forever!* ²³ *My God sent His angel and shut the lions' mouths, and they did not wound me, because merit was found for me before Him. Also before you, O king, I have done no harm."*

²⁴ *Then the king was very pleased, and he commanded that Daniel be brought up from the pit. Daniel was brought up from the pit, and no wound was found on him, for he had trusted in his God.* ²⁵ *The king gave the command and they brought those men who had slandered Daniel, and they threw them into the lions' pit, them, their children and their wives. They had not reached the floor of the pit when the lions overpowered them and crushed all their bones.*

The defamers' end

²⁶ *Then King Darius wrote:*

Darius' letter

To all the peoples, nations and languages who dwell in the entire earth:

כג שָׁלְמְכוֹן יִשְׁגֵּא: מִן־קֳדָמַי שִׂים טְעֵם דִּי ׀ בְּכָל־שָׁלְטָן מַלְכוּתִי לֶהֱוֹן
°זָאֲעִין [°זָיְעִין ק] וְדָחֲלִין מִן־קֳדָם אֱלָהֵהּ דִּי־דָנִיֵּאל דִּי־הוּא ׀ אֱלָהָא
חַיָּא וְקַיָּם לְעָלְמִין וּמַלְכוּתֵהּ דִּי־לָא תִתְחַבַּל וְשָׁלְטָנֵהּ עַד־סוֹפָא:
כד מְשֵׁיזִב וּמַצִּל וְעָבֵד אָתִין וְתִמְהִין בִּשְׁמַיָּא וּבְאַרְעָא דִּי שֵׁיזִב לְדָנִיֵּאל
כה מִן־יַד אַרְיָוָתָא: וְדָנִיֵּאל דְּנָה הַצְלַח בְּמַלְכוּת דָּרְיָוֶשׁ וּבְמַלְכוּת כּוֹרֶשׁ
°פָּרְסִיא [°פָּרְסָאָה ק]:

ז

א בִּשְׁנַת חֲדָה לְבֵלְאשַׁצַּר מֶלֶךְ בָּבֶל דָּנִיֵּאל חֵלֶם חֲזָה וְחֶזְוֵי רֵאשֵׁהּ עַל־
ב מִשְׁכְּבֵהּ בֵּאדַיִן חֶלְמָא כְתַב רֵאשׁ מִלִּין אֲמַר: עָנֵה דָנִיֵּאל וְאָמַר חָזֵה
הֲוֵית בְּחֶזְוִי עִם־לֵילְיָא וַאֲרוּ אַרְבַּע רוּחֵי שְׁמַיָּא מְגִיחָן לְיַמָּא רַבָּא:
ג וְאַרְבַּע חֵיוָן רַבְרְבָן סָלְקָן מִן־יַמָּא שָׁנְיָן דָּא מִן־דָּא: קַדְמָיְתָא כְאַרְיֵה
וְגַפִּין דִּי־נְשַׁר לַהּ חָזֵה הֲוֵית עַד דִּי־מְּרִיטוּ °גפיה [°גַפַּהּ ק] וּנְטִילַת מִן־
ה אַרְעָא וְעַל־רַגְלַיִן כֶּאֱנָשׁ הֳקִימַת וּלְבַב אֱנָשׁ יְהִיב לַהּ: וַאֲרוּ חֵיוָה אָחֳרִי
תִנְיָנָה דָּמְיָה לְדֹב וְלִשְׂטַר־חַד הֳקִמַת וּתְלָת עִלְעִין בְּפֻמַּהּ בֵּין °שניה
[°שִׁנַּהּ ק] וְכֵן אָמְרִין לַהּ קוּמִי אֲכֻלִי בְּשַׂר שַׂגִּיא: בָּאתַר דְּנָה חָזֵה הֲוֵית
ו וַאֲרוּ אָחֳרִי כִּנְמַר וְלַהּ גַּפִּין אַרְבַּע דִּי־°עוֹף עַל־°גַּבַּיהּ [°גַּבַּהּ ק]
ז וְאַרְבְּעָה רֵאשִׁין לְחֵיוְתָא וְשָׁלְטָן יְהִיב לַהּ: בָּאתַר דְּנָה חָזֵה הֲוֵית בְּחֶזְוֵי
לֵילְיָא וַאֲרוּ חֵיוָה °רביעיה [°רְבִיעָאָה ק] דְּחִילָה וְאֵימְתָנִי וְתַקִּיפָא
יַתִּירָא וְשִׁנַּיִן דִּי־פַרְזֶל לַהּ רַבְרְבָן אָכְלָה וּמַדֱּקָה וּשְׁאָרָא °בְרַגְלַיהּ
[°בְּרַגְלַהּ ק] רָפְסָה וְהִיא מְשַׁנְּיָה מִן־כָּל־חֵיוָתָא דִּי °קדמיה [°קָדָמַהּ ק]
ח וְקַרְנַיִן עֲשַׂר לַהּ: מִשְׂתַּכַּל הֲוֵית בְּקַרְנַיָּא וַאֲלוּ קֶרֶן אָחֳרִי זְעֵירָה סִלְקָת
°בֵּינֵיהוֹן [°בֵּינֵיהֵן ק] וּתְלָת מִן־קַרְנַיָּא קַדְמָיָתָא °אתעקרו [°אֶתְעֲקַרָה ק]
מִן־°קדמיה [°קֳדָמַהּ ק] וַאֲלוּ עַיְנִין כְּעַיְנֵי אֲנָשָׁא בְּקַרְנָא־דָא וּפֻם
ט מְמַלִּל רַבְרְבָן: חָזֵה הֲוֵית עַד דִּי כָרְסָוָן °רְמִיו וְעַתִּיק יוֹמִין יְתִב לְבוּשֵׁהּ ׀
כִּתְלַג חִוָּר וּשְׂעַר רֵאשֵׁהּ כַּעֲמַר נְקֵא כָּרְסְיֵהּ שְׁבִיבִין דִּי־נוּר גַּלְגִּלּוֹהִי
י נוּר דָּלִק: נְהַר דִּי־נוּר נָגֵד וְנָפֵק מִן־קֳדָמוֹהִי אֶלֶף °אלפים [°אַלְפִין ק]
יְשַׁמְּשׁוּנֵהּ וְרִבּוֹ °רבון [°רִבְבָן ק] קָדָמוֹהִי יְקוּמוּן דִּינָא יְתִב וְסִפְרִין
יא פְּתִיחוּ: חָזֵה הֲוֵית בֵּאדַיִן מִן־קָל מִלַּיָּא רַבְרְבָתָא דִּי קַרְנָא מְמַלֱּלָה
חָזֵה הֲוֵית עַד דִּי קְטִילַת חֵיוְתָא וְהוּבַד גִּשְׁמַהּ וִיהִיבַת לִיקֵדַת אֶשָּׁא:
יב וּשְׁאָר חֵיוָתָא הֶעְדִּיו שָׁלְטָנְהוֹן וְאַרְכָה בְחַיִּין יְהִיבַת לְהוֹן עַד־זְמַן וְעִדָּן:

6:29. Cyrus succeeded Darius.

7:1. This occurred a year or two *before* the events in Chapters 5 and 6. Until this point, the "events" of Daniel's life were presented in chronological sequence; from this point on, Daniel's "visions" are presented, also in chronological order.

7:4. The lion represents the great power of the Babylonian empire (see *Jeremiah* 4:7). The high-flying eagle's

wings symbolize its arrogance.

7:5. The bear represents the Persian empire (see *Megillah* 11a) — powerful and corpulent, but not speedy. It lacked the "eagle's wings" and the regal power of the lion (*Abarbanel*). The three ribs symbolized the three Persian kings: Cyrus, Ahasuerus and Darius (*Rashi*).

7:6. The ferocious, impudent leopard represents the Greek empire founded by Alexander, who conquered

May your peace be abundant! [27] *An order is hereby issued by me that in all the dominion of my kingdom people shall tremble and be in fear before the God of Daniel, Who is the living God and endures forever, Whose kingdom will not be destroyed and Whose dominion is until the End,* [28] *Who saves and rescues and performs signs and wonders in heaven and on earth, Who has saved Daniel from the clutches of the lions.*

[29] *This Daniel met with success in the reign of Darius and in the reign of Cyrus the Persian.* *

7

Daniel's vision of the four beasts

[1] **I**n *the first year of Belshazzar* * *king of Babylonia, Daniel saw a dream and visions in his head upon his bed; he then wrote down the dream, and told the major parts.* [2] *Daniel began and exclaimed:*

I saw in my vision at night that behold! the four winds of heaven were stirring up the Great Sea. [3] *Four immense beasts came up from the sea, each different from the other.*

The Babylonian lion

[4] *The first was like a lion, and it had eagle's wings.* * *I was watching as its wings were plucked, and it was removed from the earth and stood upon two feet like a man, and it was given a human heart.*

The Persian bear

[5] *Then behold! another beast, a second one, similar to a bear;* * *it was placed on one side, and there were three ribs in its mouth between its teeth; and this is what they said to it, 'Arise, devour much flesh!'*

The Greek leopard

[6] *After this I was watching and behold! another [beast], like a leopard,* * *with four bird's wings on its back; the beast had four heads, and it was given dominion.*

The fourth beast

[7] *After this I was watching in night visions, and behold! a fourth beast,* * *exceedingly terrifying, awesome and strong. It had immense iron teeth, and it was devouring and crumbling, and trampling with its feet what remained. It was different from all the beasts that had preceded it, and it had ten horns.* [8] *As I was contemplating the horns, behold! another horn, a small one, came up among them, and three of the previous horns were uprooted before it. There were eyes like human eyes in this horn, and a mouth speaking haughty words.*

The judgment

[9] *I watched as thrones were set up, and the One of Ancient Days sat.* * *His garment was white as snow, and the hair of His head like clean wool; His throne was of fiery flames, its wheels blazing fire.* [10] *A stream of fire was flowing forth from before Him, a thousand thousands were serving Him and myriad myriads were standing before Him. The judgment was set, and the books were opened.*

[11] *I saw that after this, because of the sound of the haughty words which the horn spoke, I watched until the beast was slain and its body destroyed and consigned to a flame of fire.* [12] *As for the rest of the beasts, their dominion was taken away, yet an extension of life was given them until a season and a time.*

---

most of Asia in one continuous advance; the wings symbolize his speedy conquests in all four directions, and the four heads allude to the four generals who divided the empire after Alexander's death (*Abarbanel*).

7:7-8. The fourth kingdom is the Roman empire, including its successor powers in the long exile. This exile, the current one, is called the exile of Edom, because, as the Sages taught, Edom was the progenitor of the ancient Romans. Although the individual symbols such as the horns are variously interpreted as particular historical events or personalities, the general picture is one of a far more terrifying and enduring exile than any of the previous three.

7:9-12. "The Ancient of Days," i.e., God, will set up two thrones, one of strict justice, and the other of mercy (*Rashi*). He will judge Edom/Esau at the "season and time," i.e., when the Messianic era arrives.

יג חָזֵה הֲוֵית בְּחֶזְוֵי לֵילְיָא וַאֲרוּ עִם־עֲנָנֵי שְׁמַיָּא כְּבַר אֱנָשׁ אָתֵה הֲוָה וְעַד־

יד עַתִּיק יוֹמַיָּא מְטָה וּקְדָמוֹהִי הַקְרְבוּהִי: וְלֵהּ יְהִיב שָׁלְטָן וִיקָר וּמַלְכוּ וְכֹל עַמְמַיָּא אֻמַיָּא וְלִשָּׁנַיָּא לֵהּ יִפְלְחוּן שָׁלְטָנֵהּ שָׁלְטָן עָלַם דִּי־לָא יֶעְדֵּה

טו וּמַלְכוּתֵהּ דִּי־לָא תִתְחַבַּל: אֶתְכְּרִיַּת רוּחִי אֲנָה דָנִיֵּאל בְּגוֹא נִדְנֶה

טז וְחֶזְוֵי רֵאשִׁי יְבַהֲלֻנַּנִי: קִרְבֵת עַל־חַד מִן־קָאֲמַיָּא וְיַצִּיבָא אֶבְעֵא־מִנֵּהּ

יז עַל־כָּל־דְּנָה וַאֲמַר־לִי וּפְשַׁר מִלַּיָּא יְהוֹדְעִנַּנִי: אִלֵּין חֵיוָתָא רַבְרְבָתָא דִּי

יח אִנִּין אַרְבַּע אַרְבְּעָה מַלְכִין יְקוּמוּן מִן־אַרְעָא: וִיקַבְּלוּן מַלְכוּתָא קַדִּישֵׁי

יט עֶלְיוֹנִין וְיַחְסְנוּן מַלְכוּתָא עַד־עָלְמָא וְעַד עָלַם עָלְמַיָּא: אֱדַיִן צְבִית לְיַצָּבָא עַל־חֵיוְתָא רְבִיעָיְתָא דִּי־הֲוָת שָׁנְיָה מִן־כלהון [°כָּלְּהֵין ק] דְּחִילָה יַתִּירָה שִׁניה [°שִׁנַּהּ ק] דִּי־פַרְזֶל וטפריה [°וְטִפְרַהּ ק] דִּי־

כ נְחָשׁ אָכְלָה מַדְּקָה וּשְׁאָרָא ברגליה [°בְּרַגְלַהּ ק] רָפְסָה: וְעַל־קַרְנַיָּא עֲשַׂר דִּי בְרֵאשַׁהּ וְאָחֳרִי דִּי סִלְקַת ונפלו [°וּנְפַלָה ק] מִן־קדמיה [°קֳדָמַיהּ ק]

כא תְּלָת וְקַרְנָא דִכֵּן וְעַיְנִין לַהּ וּפֻם מְמַלִּל רַבְרְבָן וְחֶזְוַהּ רַב מִן־חַבְרָתַהּ: חָזֵה הֲוֵית וְקַרְנָא דִכֵּן עָבְדָה קְרָב עִם־קַדִּישִׁין וְיָכְלָה לְהוֹן: עַד

כב דִּי־אֲתָה עַתִּיק יוֹמַיָּא וְדִינָא יְהִב לְקַדִּישֵׁי עֶלְיוֹנִין וְזִמְנָא מְטָה וּמַלְכוּתָא

כג הֶחֱסִנוּ קַדִּישִׁין: כֵּן אֲמַר חֵיוְתָא רְבִיעָיְתָא מַלְכוּ רביעיה [°רְבִיעָאָה ק] תֶּהֱוֵא בְאַרְעָא דִּי תִשְׁנֵא מִן־כָּל־מַלְכְוָתָא וְתֵאכֻל כָּל־אַרְעָא וּתְדוּשִׁנַּהּ

כד וְתַדְּקִנַּהּ: וְקַרְנַיָּא עֲשַׂר מִנַּהּ מַלְכוּתָה עַשְׂרָה מַלְכִין יְקֻמוּן וְאָחֳרָן יְקוּם אַחֲרֵיהוֹן וְהוּא יִשְׁנֵא מִן־קַדְמָיֵא וּתְלָתָה מַלְכִין יְהַשְׁפִּל: וּמִלִּין לְצַד

כה °עִלָּיָא [°עִלָּאָה ק] יְמַלִּל וּלְקַדִּישֵׁי עֶלְיוֹנִין יְבַלֵּא וְיִסְבַּר לְהַשְׁנָיָה זִמְנִין וְדָת וְיִתְיַהֲבוּן בִּידֵהּ עַד־עִדָּן וְעִדָּנִין וּפְלַג עִדָּן: וְדִינָא יִתִּב וְשָׁלְטָנֵהּ

כו יְהַעְדּוֹן לְהַשְׁמָדָה וּלְהוֹבָדָה עַד־סוֹפָא: וּמַלְכוּתָה וְשָׁלְטָנָא וּרְבוּתָא דִּי

כז מַלְכְוָת תְּחוֹת כָּל־שְׁמַיָּא יְהִיבַת לְעַם קַדִּישֵׁי עֶלְיוֹנִין מַלְכוּתֵהּ מַלְכוּת עָלַם וְכֹל שָׁלְטָנַיָּא לֵהּ יִפְלְחוּן וְיִשְׁתַּמְּעוּן: עַד־כָּה סוֹפָא דִי־מִלְּתָא אֲנָה

כח דָנִיֵּאל שַׂגִּיא | רַעְיוֹנַי יְבַהֲלֻנַּנִי וְזִיוַי יִשְׁתַּנּוֹן עֲלַי וּמִלְּתָא בְּלִבִּי נִטְרֵת:

ח א בִּשְׁנַת שָׁלוֹשׁ לְמַלְכוּת בֵּלְאשַׁצַּר הַמֶּלֶךְ חָזוֹן נִרְאָה אֵלַי אֲנִי דָנִיֵּאל

ב אַחֲרֵי הַנִּרְאָה אֵלַי בַּתְּחִלָּה: וָאֶרְאֶה בֶּחָזוֹן וַיְהִי בִּרְאֹתִי וַאֲנִי בְּשׁוּשַׁן הַבִּירָה אֲשֶׁר בְּעֵילָם הַמְּדִינָה וָאֶרְאֶה בֶּחָזוֹן וַאֲנִי הָיִיתִי עַל־אוּבַל

ג אוּלָי: וָאֶשָּׂא עֵינַי וָאֶרְאֶה וְהִנֵּה | אַיִל אֶחָד עֹמֵד לִפְנֵי הָאֻבָל וְלוֹ קְרָנָיִם וְהַקְּרָנַיִם גְּבֹהוֹת וְהָאַחַת גְּבֹהָה מִן־הַשֵּׁנִית וְהַגְּבֹהָה עֹלָה

ד בָּאַחֲרֹנָה: רָאִיתִי אֶת־הָאַיִל מְנַגֵּחַ יָמָּה וְצָפוֹנָה וָנֶגְבָּה וְכָל־חַיּוֹת לֹא־יַעַמְדוּ לְפָנָיו וְאֵין מַצִּיל מִיָּדוֹ וְעָשָׂה כִרְצֹנוֹ וְהִגְדִּיל:

7:13. This is the King Messiah (*Rashi*).
7:15. The body is the receptacle for the spirit, just as a sheath is the receptacle for a sword.

7:18. Israel.
7:25. The meaning of this cryptic allusion to the time of the End [קֵץ], i.e., the Messianic era at the End of Days, is

One like a
man

¹³ I was watching in night visions and behold! with the clouds of heaven, one like a man came; * he came up to the One of Ancient Days, and they brought him before Him. ¹⁴ He was given dominion, honor and kingship, so that all peoples, nations and languages would serve him; his dominion would be an everlasting dominion that would never pass, and his kingship would never be destroyed.

An angel
interprets

¹⁵ As for me, Daniel, my spirit became uneasy in its sheath, * and the visions of my head bewildered me. ¹⁶ I approached one of the standing ones, and I asked him for the truth concerning all this. So he spoke to me, making the interpretation of the matters known to me: ¹⁷ 'These immense beasts, which are four: Four kingdoms will arise from the earth. ¹⁸ But the holy supreme ones * will receive the kingship, and they will inherit the kingship forever, forever and ever.'

More about
the fourth
beast

¹⁹ Then I desired to know the truth about the fourth beast, which was different from them all — exceedingly terrifying, with teeth of iron and claws of copper, it devoured and crumbled, and trampled what remained with its feet — ²⁰ and about the ten horns that were on its head, and the other one that came up as three fell before it, that horn had eyes and a mouth speaking haughty words, and an appearance greater than that of its fellows. ²¹ I had watched as that horn waged war with the holy ones and was prevailing over them, ²² until the One of Ancient Days came and the holy supreme ones were granted justice; and the time came, and the holy ones inherited the kingship.

²³ This is what he said, 'The fourth beast: There will be a fourth kingdom on the earth which will be different from all kingdoms; it will devour the entire earth, and trample and crumble it. ²⁴ And the ten horns: From that kingdom

The End —
Daniel's
prophetic
allusion to
the final
Redemption

ten kings will arise, and another one will rise up after these, who will be different from the former ones, and he will humble three kings. ²⁵ He will speak words against the Supreme One, and he will exhaust the holy supreme ones, and he will plan to alter the seasons and the law; and they will be given over into his hand until a time, and times, and half a time. * ²⁶ But judgment will be set, and they will take away his dominion to be

The
everlasting
kingdom

annihilated and to be destroyed completely. ²⁷ And the kingship, the dominion and the grandeur of the kingdoms under all the heavens will be given to the holy supreme nation. Its kingdom will be an everlasting kingdom, and all rulers will serve and obey it.'

²⁸ Until here is the end of the description. I, Daniel — my thoughts frightened me greatly and my countenance changed; but I guarded the matter in my heart.

8

Another
vision

¹ In the third year of King Belshazzar's reign, a vision appeared to me — I, Daniel — after that which had appeared to me at first. ² I saw in the vision (when I saw it I was in Shushan, the capital, which is in the province of Elam):

I saw in the vision that I was at the Ulai Stream. ³ I raised my eyes and looked, and behold! a ram is standing before the stream, and it has horns. The horns are high, but one is higher than the other, and the higher one is coming up last. ⁴ I saw the ram goring westward, northward and southward; and no beasts could stand before it, nor could anyone rescue from its hand. It did as it pleased, and it grew.

---

veiled in mystery. Indeed, the angel commanded Daniel to "obscure the matters and seal the book" (12:4), and the

Sages warned against attempts to foretell the End (*Sanhedrin* 97b).

ה וַאֲנִי ן הָיִיתִי מֵבִין וְהִנֵּה צְפִיר־הָעִזִּים בָּא מִן־הַמַּעֲרָב עַל־פְּנֵי כָל־הָאָרֶץ
ו וְאֵין נוֹגֵעַ בָּאָרֶץ וְהַצָּפִיר קֶרֶן חָזוּת בֵּין עֵינָיו: וַיָּבֹא עַד־הָאַיִל בַּעַל
הַקְּרָנַיִם אֲשֶׁר רָאִיתִי עֹמֵד לִפְנֵי הָאֻבָל וַיָּרָץ אֵלָיו בַּחֲמַת כֹּחוֹ: וּרְאִיתִיו
ז מַגִּיעַ ן אֵצֶל הָאַיִל וַיִּתְמַרְמַר אֵלָיו וַיַּךְ אֶת־הָאַיִל וַיְשַׁבֵּר אֶת־שְׁתֵּי קְרָנָיו
וְלֹא־הָיָה כֹחַ בָּאַיִל לַעֲמֹד לְפָנָיו וַיַּשְׁלִיכֵהוּ אַרְצָה וַיִּרְמְסֵהוּ וְלֹא־הָיָה
ח מַצִּיל לָאַיִל מִיָּדוֹ: וּצְפִיר הָעִזִּים הִגְדִּיל עַד־מְאֹד וּכְעָצְמוֹ נִשְׁבְּרָה הַקֶּרֶן
ט הַגְּדוֹלָה וַתַּעֲלֶנָה חָזוּת אַרְבַּע תַּחְתֶּיהָ לְאַרְבַּע רוּחוֹת הַשָּׁמָיִם: וּמִן־
הָאַחַת מֵהֶם יָצָא קֶרֶן־אַחַת מִצְּעִירָה וַתִּגְדַּל־יֶתֶר אֶל־הַנֶּגֶב וְאֶל־
י הַמִּזְרָח וְאֶל־הַצֶּבִי: וַתִּגְדַּל עַד־צְבָא הַשָּׁמָיִם וַתַּפֵּל אַרְצָה מִן־הַצָּבָא
יא וּמִן־הַכּוֹכָבִים וַתִּרְמְסֵם: וְעַד שַׂר־הַצָּבָא הִגְדִּיל וּמִמֶּנּוּ °הרים [°הוּרַם
יב ק׳] הַתָּמִיד וְהֻשְׁלַךְ מְכוֹן מִקְדָּשׁוֹ: וְצָבָא תִּנָּתֵן עַל־הַתָּמִיד בְּפָשַׁע וְתַשְׁלֵךְ
יג אֱמֶת אַרְצָה וְעָשְׂתָה וְהִצְלִיחָה: וָאֶשְׁמְעָה אֶחָד־קָדוֹשׁ מְדַבֵּר וַיֹּאמֶר
אֶחָד קָדוֹשׁ לַפַּלְמוֹנִי הַמְדַבֵּר עַד־מָתַי הֶחָזוֹן הַתָּמִיד וְהַפֶּשַׁע שֹׁמֵם תֵּת
יד וְקֹדֶשׁ וְצָבָא מִרְמָס: וַיֹּאמֶר אֵלַי עַד עֶרֶב בֹּקֶר אַלְפַּיִם וּשְׁלֹשׁ מֵאוֹת
טו וְנִצְדַּק קֹדֶשׁ: וַיְהִי בִּרְאֹתִי אֲנִי דָנִיֵּאל אֶת־הֶחָזוֹן וָאֲבַקְשָׁה בִינָה וְהִנֵּה
טז עֹמֵד לְנֶגְדִּי כְּמַרְאֵה־גָבֶר: וָאֶשְׁמַע קוֹל־אָדָם בֵּין אוּלָי וַיִּקְרָא וַיֹּאמַר
יז גַּבְרִיאֵל הָבֵן לְהַלָּז אֶת־הַמַּרְאֶה: וַיָּבֹא אֵצֶל עָמְדִי וּבְבֹאוֹ נִבְעַתִּי וָאֶפְּלָה
יח עַל־פָּנָי וַיֹּאמֶר אֵלַי הָבֵן בֶּן־אָדָם כִּי לְעֶת־קֵץ הֶחָזוֹן: וּבְדַבְּרוֹ עִמִּי
יט נִרְדַּמְתִּי עַל־פָּנַי אָרְצָה וַיִּגַּע־בִּי וַיַּעֲמִידֵנִי עַל־עָמְדִי: וַיֹּאמֶר הִנְנִי
כ מוֹדִיעֲךָ אֵת אֲשֶׁר־יִהְיֶה בְּאַחֲרִית הַזָּעַם כִּי לְמוֹעֵד קֵץ: הָאַיִל אֲשֶׁר־
כא רָאִיתָ בַּעַל הַקְּרָנָיִם מַלְכֵי מָדַי וּפָרָס: וְהַצָּפִיר הַשָּׂעִיר מֶלֶךְ יָוָן וְהַקֶּרֶן
כב הַגְּדוֹלָה אֲשֶׁר בֵּין־עֵינָיו הוּא הַמֶּלֶךְ הָרִאשׁוֹן: וְהַנִּשְׁבֶּרֶת וַתַּעֲמֹדְנָה
כג אַרְבַּע תַּחְתֶּיהָ אַרְבַּע מַלְכֻיּוֹת מִגּוֹי יַעֲמֹדְנָה וְלֹא בְכֹחוֹ: וּבְאַחֲרִית
כד מַלְכוּתָם כְּהָתֵם הַפֹּשְׁעִים יַעֲמֹד מֶלֶךְ עַז־פָּנִים וּמֵבִין חִידוֹת: וְעָצַם
כה כֹּחוֹ וְלֹא בְכֹחוֹ וְנִפְלָאוֹת יַשְׁחִית וְהִצְלִיחַ וְעָשָׂה וְהִשְׁחִית עֲצוּמִים וְעַם־
קְדֹשִׁים: וְעַל־שִׂכְלוֹ וְהִצְלִיחַ מִרְמָה בְּיָדוֹ וּבִלְבָבוֹ יַגְדִּיל וּבְשַׁלְוָה יַשְׁחִית
כו רַבִּים וְעַל־שַׂר־שָׂרִים יַעֲמֹד וּבְאֶפֶס יָד יִשָּׁבֵר: וּמַרְאֵה הָעֶרֶב וְהַבֹּקֶר
אֲשֶׁר נֶאֱמַר אֱמֶת הוּא וְאַתָּה סְתֹם הֶחָזוֹן כִּי לְיָמִים רַבִּים:

8:9. Most commentators interpret this vision as an allusion to the persecutions of King Antiochus, whose Seleucid Kingdom emerged from one of Alexander's four successors. He advanced to the south and invaded Egypt and conquered the Land of Israel, where he was eventually defeated by the Maccabees. Others relate the vision to Rome, Titus and Vespasian.

8:12. Israel's enemies will succeed in ending the daily Temple offerings and in denigrating the honor of the Torah.

8:13. A mute idol with which the conqueror will replace the daily Temple offering (Rashi).

8:14. Another cryptic allusion to the End of Days.

8:21. Alexander the Great, who conquered the Persians.

8:22. Four kingdoms will be carved out of Alexander's empire.

8:23. A reference to Antiochus (Ibn Ezra) or to Titus, who destroyed the Temple (Rashi).

8:25. The enemy will treacherously attack peoples with whom he had peace treaties. In the end, however, both Titus (Rashi) and Antiochus (Ibn Ezra) died through miraculous illnesses.

It smote
the ram

⁵ I was contemplating [this] and behold! a he-goat comes from the west, across the surface of the entire earth, but not touching the ground; and the he-goat had a conspicuous horn between its eyes. ⁶ It came up to the two-horned ram that I had seen standing before the stream, and ran at it with the fury of its might. ⁷ I saw it reach the ram; it fought bitterly with it, and smote the ram and broke its two horns. The ram had no strength to stand before it; [the goat] threw it to the ground and trampled it, and there was no one to rescue the ram from its hand.

⁸ Then the he-goat grew greatly. At its mightiest the great horn was broken, and a semblance of four [horns] came up in its place, [pointing] toward the four directions of the heavens. ⁹ Out of one of them came forth one little horn, which grew exceedingly southward and eastward and to-ward the [coveted] land. * ¹⁰ It grew up to the host of the heavens, and it threw some of the host and some of the stars to the ground and trampled them. ¹¹ It exalted itself even up to the Master of the host; because of it the daily offering was removed and the foundation of His Sanctuary was thrown down. ¹² A set time will be allotted for [the discontinuation of] the daily offering because of sin. It will throw truth to the ground, * and it will achieve and prosper.

One
little horn

¹³ I heard a holy one speaking; and the holy one said to the anonymous one who was speaking, 'Until when, this vision concerning the daily offering and the mute abomination, * allowing the trampling of the holy one and the host?' ¹⁴ And he said to me, 'Until nightfall, morning, two thousand and three hundred; and then the holy one will be rectified.' *

"Gabriel,
explain the
vision"

¹⁵ When I, Daniel, saw the vision I sought understanding, then, behold! there stood before me the likeness of a man. ¹⁶ I heard a human voice in the middle of the Ulai; he called out and said, 'Gabriel, explain the vision to that [man].'

¹⁷ So he came to where I was standing. When he came I was terrified, and I fell face down. He said to me, 'Understand, Son of Man, that the vision concerns the time of the End.' ¹⁸ As he spoke to me I fell into a deep sleep with my face to the ground; but he touched me and stood me up in my place. ¹⁹ He said, 'I am ready to inform you what will be after the fury, for at the appointed time will be the End. ²⁰ The two-horned ram that you saw [symbolizes] the kings of Media and Persia. ²¹ The he-goat, the kingdom of Greece, and the large horn that is between its eyes is its first king. * ²² As for the broken one, in whose place four arose, four kingdoms will arise from one nation, * but lacking its strength.

A brazen-
faced king

²³ 'At the end of their kingdom, when the sinners are annihilated, a brazen-faced king, * an understander of mysteries, will arise. ²⁴ His power will grow, but not through his [own] power, and he will destroy mightily; he will succeed and accomplish, and will destroy mighty ones and the nation of holy ones, ²⁵ because of his cunning, and [because] he will proceed with deceit in his hand, he will grow proud in his heart. He will destroy many in peace; but he will stand up against the Master of masters and he will be broken, not through a [human] hand. * ²⁶ The vision of the nightfall and the morning which has been spoken is true. As for you, obscure the vision, for it [belongs] to many days hence.'

כז וַאֲנִ֣י דָנִיֵּ֗אל נִהְיֵ֤יתִי֙ וְנֶֽחֱלֵ֙יתִי֙ יָמִ֔ים וָאָק֕וּם וָאֶֽעֱשֶׂ֖ה אֶת־מְלֶ֣אכֶת הַמֶּ֑לֶךְ וָאֶשְׁתּוֹמֵ֥ם עַל־הַמַּרְאֶ֖ה וְאֵ֥ין מֵבִֽין׃

ט

א בִּשְׁנַ֣ת אַחַ֗ת לְדָרְיָ֛וֶשׁ בֶּן־אֲחַשְׁוֵר֖וֹשׁ מִזֶּ֣רַע מָדָ֑י אֲשֶׁ֣ר הָמְלַ֔ךְ עַ֖ל מַלְכ֥וּת כַּשְׂדִּֽים׃

ב בִּשְׁנַ֤ת אַחַת֙ לְמָלְכ֔וֹ אֲנִי֙ דָּֽנִיֵּ֔אל בִּינֹ֖תִי בַּסְּפָרִ֑ים מִסְפַּ֣ר הַשָּׁנִ֗ים אֲשֶׁ֨ר הָיָ֤ה דְבַר־יְהֹוָה֙ אֶל־יִרְמְיָ֣ה הַנָּבִ֔יא לְמַלֹּ֛אות לְחׇרְב֥וֹת יְרוּשָׁלַ֖͏ִם שִׁבְעִ֥ים שָׁנָֽה׃

ג וָאֶתְּנָ֣ה אֶת־פָּנַ֗י אֶל־אֲדֹנָי֙ הָֽאֱלֹהִ֔ים לְבַקֵּ֥שׁ תְּפִלָּ֖ה וְתַחֲנוּנִ֑ים בְּצ֖וֹם וְשַׂ֥ק וָאֵֽפֶר׃

ד וָֽאֶתְפַּֽלְלָ֛ה לַיהֹוָ֥ה אֱלֹהַ֖י וָאֶתְוַדֶּ֑ה וָאֹ֣מְרָ֗ה אָֽנָּ֤א אֲדֹנָי֙ הָאֵ֤ל הַגָּדוֹל֙ וְהַנּוֹרָ֔א שֹׁמֵ֤ר הַבְּרִית֙ וְהַחֶ֔סֶד לְאֹהֲבָ֖יו וּלְשֹׁמְרֵ֥י מִצְוֺתָֽיו׃

ה חָטָ֥אנוּ וְעָוִ֖ינוּ ⁰והרשענו [°הִרְשַׁ֣עְנוּ ק] וּמָרָ֑דְנוּ וְס֥וֹר מִמִּצְוֺתֶ֖ךָ וּמִמִּשְׁפָּטֶֽיךָ׃

ו וְלֹ֣א שָׁמַ֗עְנוּ אֶל־עֲבָדֶ֙יךָ֙ הַנְּבִיאִ֔ים אֲשֶׁ֤ר דִּבְּרוּ֙ בְּשִׁמְךָ֔ אֶל־מְלָכֵ֥ינוּ שָׂרֵ֖ינוּ וַאֲבֹתֵ֑ינוּ וְאֶ֖ל כׇּל־עַ֥ם הָאָֽרֶץ׃

ז לְךָ֤ אֲדֹנָי֙ הַצְּדָקָ֔ה וְלָ֛נוּ בֹּ֥שֶׁת הַפָּנִ֖ים כַּיּ֣וֹם הַזֶּ֑ה לְאִ֤ישׁ יְהוּדָה֙ וּלְיֹשְׁבֵ֣י יְרֽוּשָׁלַ֔͏ִם וּֽלְכׇל־יִשְׂרָאֵ֞ל הַקְּרֹבִ֣ים וְהָרְחֹקִ֗ים בְּכׇל־הָֽאֲרָצוֹת֙ אֲשֶׁ֣ר הִדַּחְתָּ֣ם שָׁ֔ם בְּמַעֲלָ֖ם אֲשֶׁ֥ר מָֽעֲלוּ־בָֽךְ׃

ח יְהֹוָ֗ה לָ֚נוּ בֹּ֣שֶׁת הַפָּנִ֔ים לִמְלָכֵ֥ינוּ לְשָׂרֵ֖ינוּ וְלַאֲבֹתֵ֑ינוּ אֲשֶׁ֥ר חָטָ֖אנוּ לָֽךְ׃

ט לַֽאדֹנָ֣י אֱלֹהֵ֔ינוּ הָרַחֲמִ֖ים וְהַסְּלִח֑וֹת כִּ֥י מָרַ֖דְנוּ בּֽוֹ׃ וְלֹ֣א שָׁמַ֔עְנוּ בְּק֖וֹל יְהֹוָ֣ה

יא אֱלֹהֵ֑ינוּ לָלֶ֤כֶת בְּתֽוֹרֹתָיו֙ אֲשֶׁ֣ר נָתַ֣ן לְפָנֵ֔ינוּ בְּיַ֖ד עֲבָדָ֥יו הַנְּבִיאִֽים׃ וְכׇל־יִשְׂרָאֵ֗ל עָֽבְרוּ֙ אֶת־תּ֣וֹרָתֶ֔ךָ וְס֕וֹר לְבִלְתִּ֖י שְׁמ֣וֹעַ בְּקֹלֶ֑ךָ וַתִּתַּ֨ךְ עָלֵ֜ינוּ הָאָלָ֣ה

יב וְהַשְּׁבֻעָ֗ה אֲשֶׁ֤ר כְּתוּבָה֙ בְּתוֹרַת֙ מֹשֶׁ֣ה עֶֽבֶד־הָֽאֱלֹהִ֔ים כִּ֥י חָטָ֖אנוּ לֽוֹ׃ וַיָּ֜קֶם אֶת־⁰דבריו [°דְּבָר֣וֹ ק] ׀ אֲשֶׁר־דִּבֶּ֣ר עָלֵ֗ינוּ וְעַ֤ל שֹׁפְטֵ֙ינוּ֙ אֲשֶׁ֣ר שְׁפָט֔וּנוּ לְהָבִ֥יא עָלֵ֖ינוּ רָעָ֣ה גְדֹלָ֑ה אֲשֶׁ֣ר לֹֽא־נֶעֶשְׂתָ֗ה תַּ֚חַת כׇּל־הַשָּׁמַ֔יִם כַּאֲשֶׁ֥ר

יג נֶעֶשְׂתָ֖ה בִּירֽוּשָׁלָֽ͏ִם׃ כַּאֲשֶׁ֤ר כָּתוּב֙ בְּתוֹרַ֣ת מֹשֶׁ֔ה אֵ֛ת כׇּל־הָרָעָ֥ה הַזֹּ֖את בָּ֣אָה עָלֵ֑ינוּ וְלֹֽא־חִלִּ֜ינוּ אֶת־פְּנֵ֣י ׀ יְהֹוָ֣ה אֱלֹהֵ֗ינוּ לָשׁוּב֙ מֵֽעֲוֺנֵ֔נוּ וּלְהַשְׂכִּ֖יל

יד בַּאֲמִתֶּֽךָ׃ וַיִּשְׁקֹ֤ד יְהֹוָה֙ עַל־הָ֣רָעָ֔ה וַיְבִיאֶ֖הָ עָלֵ֑ינוּ כִּֽי־צַדִּ֞יק יְהֹוָ֣ה אֱלֹהֵ֗ינוּ

טו עַל־כׇּל־מַעֲשָׂיו֙ אֲשֶׁ֣ר עָשָׂ֔ה וְלֹ֥א שָׁמַ֖עְנוּ בְּקֹלֽוֹ׃ וְעַתָּ֣ה ׀ אֲדֹנָ֣י אֱלֹהֵ֗ינוּ אֲשֶׁר֩ הוֹצֵ֨אתָ אֶֽת־עַמְּךָ֜ מֵאֶ֤רֶץ מִצְרַ֙יִם֙ בְּיָ֣ד חֲזָקָ֔ה וַתַּֽעַשׂ־לְךָ֥ שֵׁ֖ם כַּיּ֣וֹם

טז הַזֶּ֑ה חָטָ֖אנוּ רָשָֽׁעְנוּ׃ אֲדֹנָ֗י כְּכׇל־צִדְקֹתֶ֙ךָ֙ יָֽשׇׁב־נָ֤א אַפְּךָ֙ וַחֲמָ֣תְךָ֔ מֵעִֽירְךָ֥ יְרוּשָׁלַ֖͏ִם הַר־קׇדְשֶׁ֑ךָ כִּ֤י בַחֲטָאֵ֙ינוּ֙ וּבַעֲוֺנ֣וֹת אֲבֹתֵ֔ינוּ יְרוּשָׁלַ֧͏ִם וְעַמְּךָ֛ לְחֶרְפָּ֖ה

יז לְכׇל־סְבִיבֹתֵֽינוּ׃ וְעַתָּ֣ה ׀ שְׁמַ֣ע אֱלֹהֵ֗ינוּ אֶל־תְּפִלַּ֤ת עַבְדְּךָ֙ וְאֶל־תַּ֣חֲנוּנָ֔יו וְהָאֵ֣ר פָּנֶ֔יךָ עַל־מִקְדָּשְׁךָ֖ הַשָּׁמֵ֑ם לְמַ֖עַן אֲדֹנָֽי׃

יח הַטֵּ֨ה אֱלֹהַ֤י ׀ אׇזְנְךָ֙ וּֽשְׁמָ֔ע ⁰פקחה [°פְּקַ֣ח ק] עֵינֶ֗יךָ וּרְאֵה֙ שֹֽׁמְמֹתֵ֔ינוּ וְהָעִ֕יר אֲשֶׁר־נִקְרָ֥א שִׁמְךָ֖ עָלֶ֑יהָ כִּ֣י ׀ לֹ֣א עַל־צִדְקֹתֵ֗ינוּ אֲנַ֨חְנוּ מַפִּילִ֤ים תַּחֲנוּנֵ֙ינוּ֙ לְפָנֶ֔יךָ כִּ֖י עַל־רַחֲמֶ֥יךָ

8:27. He attended to his official government duties.
9:1. This is Darius the Mede (see note to 1:21), not Darius the Persian whose parents were King Ahasuerus and Queen Esther. According to the Talmud, this vision took place in the seventieth year after Nebuchadnezzar's sub- jugation of Jehoiakim, eighteen years before the destruction of the Temple. [See Appendix A, timeline 5.]

9:2. See *Jeremiah* 29:10.

9:9. And He has not punished us accordingly.

²⁷ I, Daniel, became disturbed and ill for days; then I arose and attended to the king's business. * I was upset by the vision, but no one perceived it.

9

Daniel prays for redemption

¹ In the first year of Darius son of Ahasuerus of the offspring of Media, * who was made king over the kingdom of the Chaldeans, ² in the first year of his reign, I, Daniel, contemplated the calculations, the number of years about which the word of HASHEM had come to the prophet Jeremiah, to complete the seventy years since the ruin of Jerusalem. * ³ I set my face toward the Lord, God, to beseech [with] prayer and supplication, with fasting, sackcloth, and ashes.

Ours is the shamefaced-ness

⁴ I prayed to HASHEM, my God, and I confessed; I said:

I beg of You, O Lord, the Great and Awesome God, Who keeps the covenant and kindness for those who love Him and for those who keep His command-ments: ⁵ We have sinned; we have been iniquitous; we have done evil; we have rebelled; and we have deviated from Your commandments and Your ordinances. ⁶ We did not heed Your servants the prophets, who spoke in Your Name to our kings, our officers and our forefathers, and to all the populace of the land. ⁷ To You, O Lord, is the righteousness, and to us is the shamefacedness, as of this very day — to the men of Judah and to the inhabitants of Jerusalem and to all of Israel, those near and those far, in all the lands to which You have driven them, because of their betrayal by which they have betrayed You. ⁸ HASHEM, to us is the shamefacedness — to our kings, to our officers and to our forefathers — for we have sinned against You.

God hastened the calamity

⁹ To the Lord our God [belong] compassion and forgiveness, for we have rebelled against Him, * ¹⁰ and we did not heed the voice of HASHEM our God, to follow His teachings which He put before us through the hand of His servants the prophets. ¹¹ All Israel has transgressed Your Torah and has deviated, not heeding Your voice; so the curse and the oath that are written in the Torah of Moses, servant of God, have been poured out upon us, for we have sinned against Him. ¹² He upheld His word that He spoke about us and about our judges who judged us, to bring upon us a great calamity; for under the entire heaven there has never been done as has been done in Jerusalem. ¹³ Just as it is written in the Torah of Moses, all this calamity has come upon us; yet we have not entreated the countenance of HASHEM our God, to repent from our iniquities and to comprehend Your truth. ¹⁴ HASHEM hastened the calamity and brought it upon us; for HASHEM our God is just in all His deeds that He has done, for we have not heeded His voice. ¹⁵ And

For Your sake, O God

now, O Lord our God, Who took Your people out of the land of Egypt with a strong hand, and gained Yourself renown as of this day — we have sinned and we have been wicked. ¹⁶ O Lord, [in keeping] with all Your righteous-ness, please let Your anger and Your wrath turn away from Your city Jerusalem, Your holy mountain; for because of our sins and the iniquities of our forefathers, Jerusalem and Your people have become the scorn of all those around us. ¹⁷ And now, pay heed, our God, to the prayer of Your servant and to his supplications, and let Your countenance shine upon Your desolate Sanctuary, for the Lord's sake. ¹⁸ Incline Your ear, my God, and listen; open Your eyes and see our desolations, and the city upon which Your Name is proclaimed; for not because of our righteousness do we pour out our supplications before You, but because of Your great compassion.

הָרַבִּים: אֲדֹנָי ׀ שְׁמָעָה אֲדֹנָי ׀ סְלָחָה אֲדֹנָי הַקְשִׁיבָה וַעֲשֵׂה אַל־תְּאַחַ֫ר

כ לְמַעַנְךָ֣ אֱלֹהַ֔י כִּי־שִׁמְךָ֣ נִקְרָ֔א עַל־עִירְךָ֖ וְעַל־עַמֶּ֑ךָ: וְע֣וֹד אֲנִי֮ מְדַבֵּ֣ר
וּמִתְפַּלֵּל֒ וּמִתְוַדֶּה֙ חַטָּאתִ֔י וְחַטַּ֖את עַמִּ֣י יִשְׂרָאֵ֑ל וּמַפִּ֣יל תְּחִנָּתִ֗י לִפְנֵ֛י יהוה

כא אֱלֹהַ֖י עַל־הַר־קֹ֥דֶשׁ אֱלֹהָֽי: וְע֛וֹד אֲנִ֥י מְדַבֵּ֖ר בַּתְּפִלָּ֑ה וְהָאִ֣ישׁ גַּבְרִיאֵ֡ל

כב אֲשֶׁר֩ רָאִ֨יתִי בֶחָז֤וֹן בַּתְּחִלָּה֙ מֻעָ֣ף בִּיעָ֔ף נֹגֵ֣עַ אֵלַ֔י כְּעֵ֖ת מִנְחַת־עָֽרֶב: וַיָּ֖בֶן

כג וַיְדַבֵּ֣ר עִמִּ֔י וַיֹּאמַ֑ר דָּנִיֵּ֕אל עַתָּ֥ה יָצָ֖אתִי לְהַשְׂכִּילְךָ֣ בִינָ֑ה בִּתְחִלַּ֨ת
תַּחֲנוּנֶ֜יךָ יָצָ֣א דָבָ֗ר וַאֲנִי֙ בָּ֣אתִי לְהַגִּ֔יד כִּ֥י חֲמוּד֖וֹת אָ֑תָּה וּבִין֙ בַּדָּבָ֔ר וְהָבֵ֖ן

כד בַּמַּרְאֶֽה: שָׁבֻעִ֨ים שִׁבְעִ֜ים נֶחְתַּ֣ךְ עַֽל־עַמְּךָ֣ ׀ וְעַל־עִ֣יר קָדְשֶׁ֗ךָ לְכַלֵּ֨א
הַפֶּ֜שַׁע °וּלַחְתֵּם [°וּלְהָתֵם ק] °חטאות [°חַטָּ֤את ק] וּלְכַפֵּ֣ר עָוֹ֔ן וּלְהָבִ֤יא

כה צֶ֣דֶק עֹֽלָמִ֗ים וְלַחְתֹּם֙ חָז֣וֹן וְנָבִ֔יא וְלִמְשֹׁ֖חַ קֹ֣דֶשׁ קָֽדָשִֽׁים: וְתֵדַ֣ע וְתַשְׂכֵּ֗ל
מִן־מֹצָ֣א דָבָ֗ר לְהָשִׁיב֙ וְלִבְנ֤וֹת יְרֽוּשָׁלִַ֙ם֙ עַד־מָשִׁ֣יחַ נָגִ֔יד שָׁבֻעִ֖ים שִׁבְעָ֑ה
וְשָׁבֻעִ֞ים שִׁשִּׁ֣ים וּשְׁנַ֗יִם תָּשׁוּב֙ וְנִבְנְתָ֤ה רְחוֹב֙ וְחָר֔וּץ וּבְצ֖וֹק הָעִתִּֽים:

כו וְאַחֲרֵ֤י הַשָּׁבֻעִים֙ שִׁשִּׁ֣ים וּשְׁנַ֔יִם יִכָּרֵ֥ת מָשִׁ֖יחַ וְאֵ֣ין ל֑וֹ וְהָעִ֣יר וְהַקֹּ֡דֶשׁ
יַ֠שְׁחִ֠ית עַ֣ם נָגִ֤יד הַבָּא֙ וְקִצּ֣וֹ בַשֶּׁ֔טֶף וְעַד֙ קֵ֣ץ מִלְחָמָ֔ה נֶחֱרֶ֖צֶת שֹׁמֵמֽוֹת:

כז וְהִגְבִּ֥יר בְּרִ֛ית לָֽרַבִּ֖ים שָׁב֣וּעַ אֶחָ֑ד וַחֲצִ֨י הַשָּׁב֜וּעַ יַשְׁבִּ֣ית ׀ זֶ֣בַח וּמִנְחָ֗ה וְעַ֨ל
כְּנַ֤ף שִׁקּוּצִים֙ מְשֹׁמֵ֔ם וְעַד־כָּלָה֙ וְנֶ֣חֱרָצָ֔ה תִּתַּ֖ךְ עַל־שֹׁמֵֽם:

י א בִּשְׁנַ֣ת שָׁל֗וֹשׁ לְכ֙וֹרֶשׁ֙ מֶ֣לֶךְ פָּרַ֔ס דָּבָר֙ נִגְלָ֣ה לְדָֽנִיֵּ֔אל אֲשֶׁר־נִקְרָ֥א שְׁמ֖וֹ
בֵּלְטְשַׁאצַּ֑ר וֶאֱמֶ֤ת הַדָּבָר֙ וְצָבָ֣א גָד֔וֹל וּבִין֙ אֶת־הַדָּבָ֔ר וּבִ֥ינָה ל֖וֹ בַּמַּרְאֶֽה:

ב-ג בַּיָּמִ֣ים הָהֵ֗ם אֲנִ֤י דָֽנִיֵּאל֙ הָיִ֣יתִי מִתְאַבֵּ֔ל שְׁלֹשָׁ֥ה שָׁבֻעִ֖ים יָמִֽים: לֶ֣חֶם
חֲמֻד֞וֹת לֹ֣א אָכַ֗לְתִּי וּבָשָׂ֥ר וָיַ֛יִן לֹא־בָ֥א אֶל־פִּ֖י וְס֣וֹךְ לֹא־סָ֑כְתִּי עַד־
מְלֹ֕את שְׁלֹ֥שֶׁת שָׁבֻעִ֖ים יָמִֽים:

ד וּבְי֣וֹם עֶשְׂרִ֤ים וְאַרְבָּעָה֙ לַחֹ֣דֶשׁ הָֽרִאשׁ֔וֹן וַאֲנִ֣י הָיִ֔יתִי עַ֖ל יַ֣ד הַנָּהָ֣ר הַגָּד֑וֹל

ה ה֖וּא חִדָּֽקֶל: וָאֶשָּׂ֤א אֶת־עֵינַי֙ וָאֵ֔רֶא וְהִנֵּ֥ה אִישׁ־אֶחָ֖ד לָב֣וּשׁ בַּדִּ֑ים וּמָתְנָ֥יו

ו חֲגֻרִ֖ים בְּכֶ֥תֶם אוּפָֽז: וּגְוִיָּת֣וֹ כְתַרְשִׁ֗ישׁ וּפָנָ֞יו כְּמַרְאֵ֤ה בָרָק֙ וְעֵינָיו֙ כְּלַפִּ֣ידֵי
אֵ֔שׁ וּזְרֹֽעֹתָיו֙ וּמַרְגְּלֹתָ֔יו כְּעֵ֖ין נְחֹ֣שֶׁת קָלָ֑ל וְק֥וֹל דְּבָרָ֖יו כְּק֥וֹל הָמֽוֹן:

ז וְרָאִיתִי֩ אֲנִ֨י דָנִיֵּ֤אל לְבַדִּי֙ אֶת־הַמַּרְאָ֔ה וְהָֽאֲנָשִׁ֗ים אֲשֶׁ֤ר הָיוּ֙ עִמִּ֔י לֹ֥א
רָא֖וּ אֶת־הַמַּרְאָ֑ה אֲבָ֗ל חֲרָדָ֤ה גְדֹלָה֙ נָפְלָ֣ה עֲלֵיהֶ֔ם וַֽיִּבְרְח֖וּ בְּהֵחָבֵֽא:

ח וַאֲנִי֙ נִשְׁאַ֣רְתִּי לְבַדִּ֔י וָֽאֶרְאֶ֗ה אֶת־הַמַּרְאָ֤ה הַגְּדֹלָה֙ הַזֹּ֔את וְלֹ֥א נִשְׁאַר־

ט בִּ֖י כֹּ֑חַ וְהוֹדִ֗י נֶהְפַּ֤ךְ עָלַי֙ לְמַשְׁחִ֔ית וְלֹ֥א עָצַ֖רְתִּי כֹּֽחַ: וָאֶשְׁמַ֖ע אֶת־

9:24. Lit., "seventy weeks," this phrase refers to seventy times seven years, or 490 years. This refers to the seventy years of exile that have passed from the Destruction of the First Temple until this vision, and the entire 420 year period of the Second Temple (*Rashi*).

9:25. The "septets" refer to full seven-year periods. The prince of this verse is Cyrus, who gave permission to rebuild Jerusalem and the Temple. He ascended to the throne fifty-two years (seven full septets plus three years) after the exile had begun. From then until the second destruction of Jerusalem was 438 years, or sixty-two septets and four years (*Rashi*).

9:26. I.e., Agrippa, the last Jewish king, at the end of the Second Temple Era. After his death, the prince of this verse, the Roman Titus, would command the destruction of the Temple, which will not be rebuilt until after the War

¹⁹ O Lord, heed; O Lord, forgive; O Lord, be attentive and act, do not delay; for Your sake, my God, for Your Name is proclaimed upon Your city and Your people.

²⁰ I was still speaking, praying and confessing my sin and the sin of my people Israel, and pouring out my supplication before HASHEM my God, for my God's holy mountain: ²¹ I was still speaking in prayer, when the man Gabriel, whom I had seen in the earlier vision, was lifted in flight approaching me, at about the time of the afternoon offering.

Gabriel clarifies   ²² He made me understand and spoke with me. He said:

Daniel, I have gone forth now to teach you understanding. ²³ At the beginning of your supplications a word went forth, and I have come to relate it, for you are beloved. Contemplate this matter and gain understanding in the vision. ²⁴ Seventy septets * have been decreed upon your people and upon your holy city to terminate transgression, to end sin, to wipe away iniquity, to bring everlasting righteousness, to confirm the visions and prophets, and to anoint the Holy of Holies. ²⁵ Know and comprehend: From the emergence of the word to return and to build Jerusalem until the anointment of the prince will be seven septets, * and for sixty-two septets it will be rebuilt, street and moat, but in troubled times. ²⁶ Then, after the sixty-two septets, the anointed one * will be cut off and will exist no longer; the people of the prince will come will destroy the city and the Sanctuary; but his end will be [to be swept away as] in a flood. Then, until the end of the war, desolation is decreed. ²⁷ He will forge a strong covenant with the great ones for one septet; * but for half of that septet he will abolish sacrifice and meal-offering, and the mute abominations will be upon soaring heights, until extermination as decreed will pour down upon the mute [abomination].

10

Daniel's fast   ¹ In the third year of Cyrus, king of Persia, * a matter was revealed to Daniel, who was named Belteshazzar — the matter was true, but for a long time off — to understand the matter, and to explain it to him through a vision. ² In those days, I, Daniel, had been mourning for three weeks of days. ³ I ate no desirable bread; meat or wine did not enter my mouth, and I did not anoint myself, until the completion of three weeks of days.

The angel   ⁴ Then, on the twenty-fourth day of the first month, I was next to the great river, which is Hiddekel. * ⁵ I raised my eyes and saw, behold! one man clothed in linen, * his loins girded with fine gold. ⁶ His body was like tarshish, * his face like the appearance of lightning, his eyes like flaming torches, and his arms and legs like the color of burnished copper; the sound of his words [loud] as the sound of a multitude. ⁷ I, Daniel, alone saw the vision; the people who were with me did not see the vision, but a great fear fell upon them and they fled into hiding.

A great vision is revealed   ⁸ So I remained alone. I saw this great vision. No strength remained in me; my robustness changed to pallor, and I could retain no strength. ⁹ I heard the

---

of Gog and Magog, in Messianic times (*Rashi*).

9:27. The Roman emperor would make a treaty with the Jewish nation for seven years; but for the second half of that term the Romans would violate that covenant and impede the Temple service. The "mute abomination," i.e., a temple of idolatry, was erected by the emperor

Hadrian on the Temple Mount (*Rashi*).

10:1. See note to 1:21.

10:4. Usually identified as the Tigris.

10:5. Most commentators identify this "man" as Gabriel, who had spoken to Daniel previously (see 8:16 and 9:21).

10:6. Rock crystal or beryl.

קוֹל דְּבָרָיו וּכְשָׁמְעִי אֶת־קוֹל דְּבָרָיו וַאֲנִי הָיִיתִי נִרְדָּם עַל־פָּנַי וּפָנַי אָרְצָה:

י־יא וְהִנֵּה־יָד נָגְעָה בִּי וַתְּנִיעֵנִי עַל־בִּרְכַּי וְכַפּוֹת יָדָי: וַיֹּאמֶר אֵלַי דָּנִיֵּאל אִישׁ־חֲמֻדוֹת הָבֵן בַּדְּבָרִים אֲשֶׁר אָנֹכִי דֹבֵר אֵלֶיךָ וַעֲמֹד עַל־עָמְדֶךָ כִּי עַתָּה

יב שֻׁלַּחְתִּי אֵלֶיךָ וּבְדַבְּרוֹ עִמִּי אֶת־הַדָּבָר הַזֶּה עָמַדְתִּי מַרְעִיד: וַיֹּאמֶר אֵלַי אַל־תִּירָא דָנִיֵּאל כִּי מִן־הַיּוֹם הָרִאשׁוֹן אֲשֶׁר נָתַתָּ אֶת־לִבְּךָ לְהָבִין

יג וּלְהִתְעַנּוֹת לִפְנֵי אֱלֹהֶיךָ נִשְׁמְעוּ דְבָרֶיךָ וַאֲנִי־בָאתִי בִּדְבָרֶיךָ: וְשַׂר מַלְכוּת פָּרַס עֹמֵד לְנֶגְדִּי עֶשְׂרִים וְאֶחָד יוֹם וְהִנֵּה מִיכָאֵל אַחַד הַשָּׂרִים

יד הָרִאשֹׁנִים בָּא לְעָזְרֵנִי וַאֲנִי נוֹתַרְתִּי שָׁם אֵצֶל מַלְכֵי פָרָס: וּבָאתִי לַהֲבִינְךָ

טו אֵת אֲשֶׁר־יִקְרָה לְעַמְּךָ בְּאַחֲרִית הַיָּמִים כִּי־עוֹד חָזוֹן לַיָּמִים: וּבְדַבְּרוֹ

טז עִמִּי כַּדְּבָרִים הָאֵלֶּה נָתַתִּי פָנַי אַרְצָה וְנֶאֱלָמְתִּי: וְהִנֵּה כִּדְמוּת בְּנֵי אָדָם נֹגֵעַ עַל־שְׂפָתָי וָאֶפְתַּח־פִּי וָאֲדַבְּרָה וָאֹמְרָה אֶל־הָעֹמֵד לְנֶגְדִּי אֲדֹנִי

יז בַּמַּרְאָה נֶהֶפְכוּ צִירַי עָלַי וְלֹא עָצַרְתִּי כֹּחַ: וְהֵיךְ יוּכַל עֶבֶד אֲדֹנִי זֶה לְדַבֵּר

יח עִם־אֲדֹנִי זֶה וַאֲנִי מֵעַתָּה לֹא־יַעֲמָד־בִּי כֹחַ וּנְשָׁמָה לֹא נִשְׁאֲרָה־בִי: וַיֹּסֶף

יט וַיִּגַּע־בִּי כְּמַרְאֵה אָדָם וַיְחַזְּקֵנִי: וַיֹּאמֶר אַל־תִּירָא אִישׁ־חֲמֻדוֹת שָׁלוֹם לָךְ חֲזַק וַחֲזָק וּכְדַבְּרוֹ עִמִּי הִתְחַזַּקְתִּי וָאֹמְרָה יְדַבֵּר אֲדֹנִי כִּי חִזַּקְתָּנִי: וַיֹּאמֶר

כ הֲיָדַעְתָּ לָמָּה־בָּאתִי אֵלֶיךָ וְעַתָּה אָשׁוּב לְהִלָּחֵם עִם־שַׂר פָּרָס וַאֲנִי יוֹצֵא

כא וְהִנֵּה שַׂר־יָוָן בָּא: אֲבָל אַגִּיד לְךָ אֶת־הָרָשׁוּם בִּכְתָב אֱמֶת וְאֵין אֶחָד

יא א מִתְחַזֵּק עִמִּי עַל־אֵלֶּה כִּי אִם־מִיכָאֵל שַׂרְכֶם: וַאֲנִי בִּשְׁנַת

ב אַחַת לְדָרְיָוֶשׁ הַמָּדִי עָמְדִי לְמַחֲזִיק וּלְמָעוֹז לוֹ: וְעַתָּה אֱמֶת אַגִּיד לָךְ הִנֵּה־עוֹד שְׁלֹשָׁה מְלָכִים עֹמְדִים לְפָרַס וְהָרְבִיעִי יַעֲשִׁיר עֹשֶׁר־גָּדוֹל

ג מִכֹּל וּכְחֶזְקָתוֹ בְעָשְׁרוֹ יָעִיר הַכֹּל אֵת מַלְכוּת יָוָן: וְעָמַד מֶלֶךְ גִּבּוֹר וּמָשַׁל

ד מִמְשָׁל רַב וְעָשָׂה כִּרְצוֹנוֹ: וּכְעָמְדוֹ תִּשָּׁבֵר מַלְכוּתוֹ וְתֵחָץ לְאַרְבַּע רוּחוֹת הַשָּׁמָיִם וְלֹא לְאַחֲרִיתוֹ וְלֹא כְמָשְׁלוֹ אֲשֶׁר מָשָׁל כִּי תִנָּתֵשׁ מַלְכוּתוֹ

ה וְלַאֲחֵרִים מִלְּבַד־אֵלֶּה: וְיֶחֱזַק מֶלֶךְ־הַנֶּגֶב וּמִן־שָׂרָיו וְיֶחֱזַק עָלָיו וּמָשָׁל

ו מִמְשָׁל רַב מֶמְשַׁלְתּוֹ: וּלְקֵץ שָׁנִים יִתְחַבָּרוּ וּבַת מֶלֶךְ־הַנֶּגֶב תָּבוֹא אֶל־מֶלֶךְ הַצָּפוֹן לַעֲשׂוֹת מֵישָׁרִים וְלֹא־תַעְצֹר כּוֹחַ הַזְּרוֹעַ וְלֹא יַעֲמֹד וּזְרֹעוֹ

ז וְתִנָּתֵן הִיא וּמְבִיאֶיהָ וְהַיַּלְדָהּ וּמַחֲזִקָהּ בָּעִתִּים: וְעָמַד מִנֵּצֶר שָׁרָשֶׁיהָ כַּנּוֹ

10:13. That is, the angel that guides the destiny of Persia (*Rashi*).

10:17. How can I, a human being, speak with you, an angel?

10:20. After thwarting the designs of Persia, I must depart; Greek domination over Israel will then commence.

10:21. The angel Gabriel is the "heavenly prince" of Israel. Now, the angel was about to tell Daniel of the impending decree.

11:1. Gabriel (see 10:5) says that he stood up for Michael (see 10:21).

11:2. The three kings after Darius the Mede were Cyrus, Ahasuerus and Darius the Persian. The latter would be the fourth Median-Persian king (*Rashi*, from *Seder Olam*; see note to 1:21).

11:3. Alexander the Great, of Macedonia, Greece (ibid.).

11:4. After Alexander's death at an early age, his empire was divided among four of his generals, but they would not have his authority, and parts of the empire were split off and controlled by other rulers.

11:5. The classic commentators give widely varying interpretations of the historical personalities and events foretold in this vision. Unless otherwise noted, the remainder of this chapter has been interpreted acsound of his words, and when I heard the sound of his words I was in a deep sleep upon my face, with my face towards the ground. [10] Behold! a hand touched me and moved me onto my knees and the palms of my hands.

The angel has been delayed

[11] He said to me, "Daniel, greatly beloved man, understand the words that I speak to you, and stand in your place, for I have been sent to you now." As he spoke these words to me, I stood atremble. [12] He said to me, "Do not fear, Daniel, for from the first day that you set your heart to understand and to fast before your God, your words have been heard; and I have come because of your words. [13] But the [heavenly] prince* of the Persian kingdom stood opposed to me for twenty-one days, until Michael, one of the foremost [heavenly] princes, came to help me, for I had remained there [alone] beside the kings of Persia. [14] I have come to make you understand what will befall your people in the End of Days, for there is yet a vision for [those] days."

Daniel's fright

[15] As he spoke these words to me I set my face toward the ground, and was dumbfounded. [16] Then behold! [one] with the likeness of a human being touched my lips; I opened my mouth and spoke, and I said to the one standing opposite me, "My lord, during the vision my joints shuddered and I could retain no strength; [17] how can this servant of my lord speak with this lord of mine?* From now on no strength will remain in me, and there is no breath left in me!"

The angel strengthens Daniel

[18] Then he — the likeness of a human being — touched me again and strengthened me. [19] He said, "Fear not, greatly beloved man. Peace to you! Grow stronger and stronger!"

As he spoke to me I strengthened myself, and I said, "Speak, my lord, for you have strengthened me."

[20] He said:

Do you know why I came to you? Now I will return to do battle with the [heavenly] prince of Persia; then I will depart. But behold — the [heavenly] prince of Greece approaches. * [21] However, I will tell you what is inscribed in truthful writing. * No one reinforces me against these, except your [heavenly] prince, Michael; [1] and I, in the first year of Darius the Mede, stood up as a support and stronghold for him. *

11

[2] Now, I will tell you the truth. Behold, three more kings will arise for Persia. * The fourth will acquire the greatest wealth of them all; and when he grows strong with his riches he will arouse all [of his kingdom] against the kingdom of Greece. [3] A mighty king* will then arise; he will rule with great domination, and he will do as he pleases. [4] But after he has arisen, his kingdom will be broken and will be divided into the four directions of the heaven — but not to his posterity; * nor will it be like his dominion with which he ruled, for his kingdom will be uprooted, and for others besides these. [5] The king of the South* will grow stronger [than his enemy] and his nobles, and he will overpower him and rule; his dominion will be a great dominion. [6] At the end of [many] years they will join together, * and the daughter of the king of the South will come to the king of the North to establish uprightness, but she will not restrain the power of the [strong] arm, nor will [the king] nor his arm withstand; so she and those who brought her will be surrendered, as well as the one who fathered her and he who supported her in times [of need]. [7] A scion from her roots will stand [firmly] on his foundation.

cording to Rashi.
11:6. An attempt will be made to unite the two kingdoms   through a royal marriage, but it will end in failure, and the Southerners will be defeated.

ח וַיָּבֹא אֶל־הַחַיִל וַיָּבֹא בְּמָעוֹז מֶלֶךְ הַצָּפוֹן וְעָשָׂה בָהֶם וְהֶחֱזִיק: וְגַם אֱלֹהֵיהֶם עִם־נְסִכֵיהֶם עִם־כְּלֵי חֶמְדָּתָם כֶּסֶף וְזָהָב בַּשְּׁבִי יָבִא מִצְרָיִם

ט וְהוּא שָׁנִים יַעֲמֹד מִמֶּלֶךְ הַצָּפוֹן: וּבָא בְּמַלְכוּת מֶלֶךְ הַנֶּגֶב וְשָׁב אֶל־אַדְמָתוֹ: °וּבְנוֹ [°וּבָנָיו ק] יִתְגָּרוּ וְאָסְפוּ הֲמוֹן חֲיָלִים רַבִּים וּבָא בוֹא וְשָׁטַף

י וְעָבַר וְיָשֹׁב °וְיִתְגָּרוּ [°וְיִתְגָּרֶה ק] עַד־°מָעֻזֹה [°מָעֻזּוֹ ק]: וְיִתְמַרְמַר מֶלֶךְ הַנֶּגֶב וְיָצָא וְנִלְחַם עִמּוֹ עִם־מֶלֶךְ הַצָּפוֹן וְהֶעֱמִיד הָמוֹן רָב וְנִתַּן הֶהָמוֹן

יא-יג בְּיָדוֹ: וְנִשָּׂא הֶהָמוֹן °יָרוּם [°וְרָם ק] לְבָבוֹ וְהִפִּיל רִבֹּאוֹת וְלֹא יָעוֹז: וְשָׁב מֶלֶךְ הַצָּפוֹן וְהֶעֱמִיד הָמוֹן רַב מִן־הָרִאשׁוֹן וּלְקֵץ הָעִתִּים שָׁנִים יָבוֹא

יד בוֹא בְּחַיִל גָּדוֹל וּבִרְכוּשׁ רָב: וּבָעִתִּים הָהֵם רַבִּים יַעַמְדוּ עַל־מֶלֶךְ הַנֶּגֶב

טו וּבְנֵי ׀ פָּרִיצֵי עַמְּךָ יִנַּשְׂאוּ לְהַעֲמִיד חָזוֹן וְנִכְשָׁלוּ: וְיָבֹא מֶלֶךְ הַצָּפוֹן וְיִשְׁפֹּךְ סוֹלְלָה וְלָכַד עִיר מִבְצָרוֹת וּזְרֹעוֹת הַנֶּגֶב לֹא יַעֲמֹדוּ וְעַם מִבְחָרָיו וְאֵין

טז כֹּחַ לַעֲמֹד: וְיַעַשׂ הַבָּא אֵלָיו כִּרְצוֹנוֹ וְאֵין עוֹמֵד לְפָנָיו וְיַעֲמֹד בְּאֶרֶץ־הַצְּבִי

יז וְכָלָה בְיָדוֹ: וְיָשֵׂם ׀ פָּנָיו לָבוֹא בְּתֹקֶף כָּל־מַלְכוּתוֹ וִישָׁרִים עִמּוֹ וְעָשָׂה וּבַת הַנָּשִׁים יִתֶּן־לוֹ לְהַשְׁחִיתָהּ וְלֹא תַעֲמֹד וְלֹא־לוֹ תִהְיֶה: °וְיָשֵׁב [°וְיָשֹׁב ק] ׀

יח פָּנָיו לְאִיִּים וְלָכַד רַבִּים וְהִשְׁבִּית קָצִין חֶרְפָּתוֹ לוֹ בִּלְתִּי חֶרְפָּתוֹ יָשִׁיב לוֹ:

יט וְיָשֵׁב פָּנָיו לְמָעוּזֵּי אַרְצוֹ וְנִכְשַׁל וְנָפַל וְלֹא יִמָּצֵא: וְעָמַד עַל־כַּנּוֹ מַעֲבִיר נוֹגֵשׂ הֶדֶר מַלְכוּת וּבְיָמִים אֲחָדִים יִשָּׁבֵר וְלֹא בְאַפַּיִם וְלֹא בְמִלְחָמָה:

כא וְעָמַד עַל־כַּנּוֹ נִבְזֶה וְלֹא־נָתְנוּ עָלָיו הוֹד מַלְכוּת וּבָא בְשַׁלְוָה וְהֶחֱזִיק

כב מַלְכוּת בַּחֲלַקְלַקּוֹת: וּזְרֹעוֹת הַשֶּׁטֶף יִשָּׁטְפוּ מִלְּפָנָיו וְיִשָּׁבֵרוּ וְגַם נְגִיד

כג בְּרִית: וּמִן־הִתְחַבְּרוּת אֵלָיו יַעֲשֶׂה מִרְמָה וְעָלָה וְעָצַם בִּמְעַט־גּוֹי:

כד בְּשַׁלְוָה וּבְמִשְׁמַנֵּי מְדִינָה יָבוֹא וְעָשָׂה אֲשֶׁר לֹא־עָשׂוּ אֲבֹתָיו וַאֲבוֹת אֲבֹתָיו בִּזָּה וְשָׁלָל וּרְכוּשׁ לָהֶם יִבְזוֹר וְעַל מִבְצָרִים יְחַשֵּׁב מַחְשְׁבֹתָיו

כה וְעַד־עֵת: וְיָעֵר כֹּחוֹ וּלְבָבוֹ עַל־מֶלֶךְ הַנֶּגֶב בְּחַיִל גָּדוֹל וּמֶלֶךְ הַנֶּגֶב יִתְגָּרֶה לַמִּלְחָמָה בְּחַיִל־גָּדוֹל וְעָצוּם עַד־מְאֹד וְלֹא יַעֲמֹד כִּי־יַחְשְׁבוּ עָלָיו

כו מַחֲשָׁבוֹת: וְאֹכְלֵי פַת־בָּגוֹ יִשְׁבְּרוּהוּ וְחֵילוֹ יִשְׁטוֹף וְנָפְלוּ חֲלָלִים רַבִּים:

11:14. *Rashi* and *Rambam* take this as an allusion to the Nazarene and his disciples. "For is there a greater stumbling block than this? All the prophets foretold that the Messiah would redeem the Jews, help them, gather in the exiles and support their observance of the commandments. But he caused Jewry to be put to the sword, to be scattered and to be degraded; he tampered with the Torah and its laws; and he misled most of the world to serve something other than God" (*Hil. Melachim* 11:4).

11:15. In order to penetrate a walled city, the invaders would build a huge mound of dirt in front of the wall, which the soldiers would climb.

11:17. An epithet for the people of Israel (see v. 37). The king of the North will order his commanders to slaughter the defeated Jews. Verses 16-19 prophesy the persecutions of Antiochus IV and the Hasmonean revolt.

11:18-19. God (the Commander) will punish Antiochus, causing him to retreat in disgrace and to die on the way.

11:20. The Hasmonean dynasty will succeed Antiochus in Jerusalem, but it will eventually fall as a result of a battle of succession between the two brothers, Aristobulus and Hyrcanus.

11:21. The Roman empire.

11:22. The Jews, who had forged a covenant with the Romans, will also be crushed by them (see *Avodah Zarah* 8b).

11:23. By signing a "holy covenant" of friendship (see vv. 28,30) with the Hasmoneans, Rome will be able to conquer the countries surrounding the Land of Israel without fear of Hasmonean intervention.

11:24. Until the time would come when he would turn against them and conquer them.

He will confront the army of, and enter the stronghold of, the king of the North; he will succeed against them and overpower. ⁸ Also he will bring their gods and their princes, with their precious vessels of silver and gold, in captivity to Egypt; and he will stand [secure] for years against the king of the North. ⁹ He will enter the kingdom of the king of the South, but he will return to his soil. ¹⁰ Then [the Northern king's] sons will stir themselves up and gather a multitude of great armies; he will then launch an attack, inundate, and pass through. Then he will once again stir himself up, right up to [the South's] stronghold. ¹¹ The king of the South will become embittered, and go out and battle with him, with the king of the North; he will raise a great multitude, but that multitude will be delivered into [the South's] hand. ¹² Then the multitude will feel uplifted and their hearts will be proud; but, although they will cut down myriads [of their enemies], they will not prevail.

¹³ The king of the North will once again raise a multitude greater than the first; at the end of the times, [several] years, he will launch an attack with a great army and with vast resources. ¹⁴ In those times, many will rise up against the king of the South; and sons of the lawless men of your people will exalt themselves to establish a vision, * but they will stumble. ¹⁵ The king of the North will come and pour out a mound* and conquer a fortified city; the arms of the South will not hold out; his chosen warriors will have no strength to withstand [it].

¹⁶ The invader will then do to [the Southern king] as he pleases, and none will stand in his way; he will also stand in the Coveted Land with annihilation in his hand. ¹⁷ He will set his face to penetrate the strength of [the Southern king's] whole kingdom — and the upright ones who are with him — and he will succeed. He will give over to him the Daughter-among-women* to destroy her, but it will not succeed, and she will not be his. ¹⁸ Then he will turn his attention toward isles, and he will conquer many, but the Commander* will cause his insolence to cease; for his insolence alone He will punish him. ¹⁹ Then he will direct himself toward the strongholds of his homeland, and he will stumble and fall, and not be found.

²⁰ There will arise in his place one whose glory of kingship is the overthrow of the oppressor, * yet in a few years it will be broken, but neither through [an enemy's] wrath nor through war.

²¹ Then in its place will stand a contemptible one, * upon whom they did not confer the glory of kingship; he will come in peace, attaining kingship through treachery. ²² The powers that had swept away [others] will themselves be swept away before him and will be broken, as well as the prince of the covenant. * ²³ Through alliance with him* he will act with deceit, and he will come up and gain power with a small nation. ²⁴ He will come in peace, into the richest parts of the province will he come, and he will do what his fathers and forefathers did not do; [among his allies] he will distribute booty, spoils and wealth, and he will devise his plans against [their] fortresses until the time. * ²⁵ He will stir up his strength and his heart against the king of the South with a great army. The king of the South will confront him in war with an exceedingly great and powerful army, but he will not withstand, for they will devise plans against him, ²⁶ for those who eat of his food will break him; he will then sweep away his army, * and many slain will fall.

11:26. Rome will sweep away the leaderless army of the slain king of the South.

כז וּשְׁנֵיהֶם הַמְּלָכִים לְבָבָם לְמֵרָע וְעַל־שֻׁלְחָן אֶחָד כָּזָב יְדַבֵּרוּ וְלֹא תִצְלָח

כח כִּי־עוֹד קֵץ לַמּוֹעֵד: וְיָשֹׁב אַרְצוֹ בִּרְכוּשׁ גָּדוֹל וּלְבָבוֹ עַל־בְּרִית קֹדֶשׁ

כט וְעָשָׂה וְשָׁב לְאַרְצוֹ: לַמּוֹעֵד יָשׁוּב וּבָא בַנֶּגֶב וְלֹא־תִהְיֶה כָרִאשֹׁנָה

ל וְכָאַחֲרֹנָה: וּבָאוּ בוֹ צִיִּים כִּתִּים וְנִכְאָה וְשָׁב וְזָעַם עַל־בְּרִית־קוֹדֶשׁ וְעָשָׂה

לא וְשָׁב וְיָבֵן עַל־עֹזְבֵי בְּרִית קֹדֶשׁ: וּזְרֹעִים מִמֶּנּוּ יַעֲמֹדוּ וְחִלְּלוּ הַמִּקְדָּשׁ

לב הַמָּעוֹז וְהֵסִירוּ הַתָּמִיד וְנָתְנוּ הַשִּׁקּוּץ מְשֹׁמֵם: וּמַרְשִׁיעֵי בְרִית יַחֲנִיף

לג בַּחֲלַקּוֹת וְעַם יֹדְעֵי אֱלֹהָיו יַחֲזִקוּ וְעָשׂוּ: וּמַשְׂכִּילֵי עָם יָבִינוּ לָרַבִּים

לד וְנִכְשְׁלוּ בְּחֶרֶב וּבְלֶהָבָה בִּשְׁבִי וּבְבִזָּה יָמִים: וּבְהִכָּשְׁלָם יֵעָזְרוּ עֵזֶר מְעָט

לה וְנִלְווּ עֲלֵיהֶם רַבִּים בַּחֲלַקְלַקּוֹת: וּמִן־הַמַּשְׂכִּילִים יִכָּשְׁלוּ לִצְרוֹף בָּהֶם

לו וּלְבָרֵר וְלַלְבֵּן עַד־עֵת קֵץ כִּי־עוֹד לַמּוֹעֵד: וְעָשָׂה כִרְצוֹנוֹ הַמֶּלֶךְ
וְיִתְרוֹמֵם וְיִתְגַּדֵּל עַל־כָּל־אֵל וְעַל אֵל אֵלִים יְדַבֵּר נִפְלָאוֹת וְהִצְלִיחַ עַד־

לז כָּלָה זַעַם כִּי נֶחֱרָצָה נֶעֱשָׂתָה: וְעַל־אֱלֹהֵי אֲבֹתָיו לֹא יָבִין וְעַל־חֶמְדַּת

לח נָשִׁים וְעַל־כָּל־אֱלוֹהַּ לֹא יָבִין כִּי עַל־כֹּל יִתְגַּדָּל: וְלֶאֱלֹהַּ מָעֻזִּים עַל־כַּנּוֹ
יְכַבֵּד וְלֶאֱלוֹהַּ אֲשֶׁר לֹא־יְדָעֻהוּ אֲבֹתָיו יְכַבֵּד בְּזָהָב וּבְכֶסֶף וּבְאֶבֶן יְקָרָה

לט וּבַחֲמֻדוֹת: וְעָשָׂה לְמִבְצְרֵי מָעֻזִּים עִם־אֱלוֹהַּ נֵכָר אֲשֶׁר ["הַכִּיר ק] [°יַכִּיר ק]

מ יַרְבֶּה כָבוֹד וְהִמְשִׁילָם בָּרַבִּים וַאֲדָמָה יְחַלֵּק בִּמְחִיר: וּבְעֵת קֵץ יִתְנַגַּח
עִמּוֹ מֶלֶךְ הַנֶּגֶב וְיִשְׂתָּעֵר עָלָיו מֶלֶךְ הַצָּפוֹן בְּרֶכֶב וּבְפָרָשִׁים וּבָאֳנִיּוֹת

מא רַבּוֹת וּבָא בַאֲרָצוֹת וְשָׁטַף וְעָבָר: וּבָא בְּאֶרֶץ הַצְּבִי וְרַבּוֹת יִכָּשֵׁלוּ וְאֵלֶּה

מב יִמָּלְטוּ מִיָּדוֹ אֱדוֹם וּמוֹאָב וְרֵאשִׁית בְּנֵי עַמּוֹן: וְיִשְׁלַח יָדוֹ בַּאֲרָצוֹת וְאֶרֶץ

מג מִצְרַיִם לֹא תִהְיֶה לִפְלֵיטָה: וּמָשַׁל בְּמִכְמַנֵּי הַזָּהָב וְהַכֶּסֶף וּבְכֹל חֲמֻדוֹת

מד מִצְרָיִם וְלֻבִים וְכֻשִׁים בְּמִצְעָדָיו: וּשְׁמֻעוֹת יְבַהֲלֻהוּ מִמִּזְרָח וּמִצָּפוֹן וְיָצָא

מה בְּחֵמָא גְדֹלָה לְהַשְׁמִיד וּלְהַחֲרִים רַבִּים: וְיִטַּע אָהֳלֵי אַפַּדְנוֹ בֵּין יַמִּים

יב א לְהַר־צְבִי־קֹדֶשׁ וּבָא עַד־קִצּוֹ וְאֵין עוֹזֵר לוֹ: וּבָעֵת הַהִיא יַעֲמֹד מִיכָאֵל
הַשַּׂר הַגָּדוֹל הָעֹמֵד עַל־בְּנֵי עַמֶּךָ וְהָיְתָה עֵת צָרָה אֲשֶׁר לֹא־נִהְיְתָה
מִהְיוֹת גּוֹי עַד הָעֵת הַהִיא וּבָעֵת הַהִיא יִמָּלֵט עַמְּךָ כָּל־הַנִּמְצָא

ב כָּתוּב בַּסֵּפֶר: וְרַבִּים מִיְּשֵׁנֵי אַדְמַת־עָפָר יָקִיצוּ אֵלֶּה לְחַיֵּי עוֹלָם וְאֵלֶּה

11:27. Erstwhile enemies will conspire against Israel, but they will not succeed because the time of the exile has not yet come.

11:28. The king of Rome will head back to his homeland, enriched by the spoils of his successful campaign against the Southern king, and with no intention of keeping the pact he had made with the Hasmoneans.

11:30. Kittim is another name for the Romans. Rome will ignore its prior pact with the Hasmoneans (v. 23), and nullify the treaty. It will realize that Jewish disunity, brought about by their forsaking the Torah, "the Covenant of Sanctity," provides Rome the opportunity to conquer.

11:33. These sages will be subjected to severe persecution.

11:34. They will be able to bribe their enemies and thus help themselves.

11:35. They will err in their attempts to predict the End of the exile based on this prophecy.

11:37. An epithet for Israel (see v. 17 above and *Song of Songs* 5:9).

11:38. He will feign veneration for the gods of the fortified cities in his realm in order to cajole the people into submission (*Metzudos*).

12:1. Michael, the guardian angel of Israel, will stand in defense of his people at this time of catastrophe.

²⁷ As for the two kings, their hearts will be to do harm; * at one table they conspire deceitfully, but it will not succeed, for there is yet an end for the appointed time. ²⁸ He will return to his land with great wealth, with his heart opposed to the holy covenant; having succeeded, he will return to his land. *
²⁹ At a set time he will come once again to the South; but he will not be [as successful] as the first [time], nor as the last [time]; ³⁰ ships of Kittim will come against [the South] and he will be weakened; he will then return. Then he will be upset at the holy covenant, and act [accordingly]. Then he will return and contemplate those who have forsaken the Covenant of Sanctity. *
³¹ Arms will arise from him and will profane the fortified Sanctuary; they will abolish the daily offering and will install the mute abomination. ³² He will glibly flatter those who corrupt the Covenant, but the people who recognize their God will persevere and accomplish.

³³ Wise men among the people will give understanding to the multitudes. They will stumble by the sword and by flame, through captivity and through plunder for years. * ³⁴ But when they stumble they will be helped with a little help, * for many will come to their aid through glibness. ³⁵ Some of the wise men will stumble in clarifying [these words], * and in elucidating and interpreting when the time of the End will be, for it is not yet the designated time.

³⁶ The king will do as he pleases, and he will glorify and exalt himself over every god; and he will utter fantastic things against the God of the mighty. Yet he will succeed until [God's] fury is terminated, for that which was decreed will have been executed. ³⁷ He will not give consideration to the God of [Israel's] ancestors nor to the Desirable-among-women; * nor will he give consideration to any god, for he will aggrandize himself above everything.
³⁸ But he will honor the god of the fortresses when in his place; * and he will honor a god whom his ancestors did not know, with gold, with silver, with precious stones and with desirable objects; ³⁹ and he will build strong fortresses in honor of a strange god. He will accord great honor to whomever he acknowledges; he will empower them over the multitudes, and he will apportion land at a price.

⁴⁰ Then, at the time of the End, the king of the South will clash with him, and the king of the North will storm against him with chariot, horsemen and many ships; he will invade countries, flood [them] and pass through. ⁴¹ Then he will invade the coveted land. Many will stumble, but these will be saved from his hand: Edom, Moab and the choice parts of the Children of Ammon. ⁴² He will stretch forth his hand against lands, and the land of Egypt will not be a survivor. ⁴³ He will gain control of the caches of gold and silver and all the desirables of Egypt, with Lubians and Cushites [crushed] in his footsteps. ⁴⁴ But news from the east and the north will alarm him, and he will set out in great anger to destroy and annihilate many. ⁴⁵ He will pitch the tents of his palace between the seas and the holy, coveted mountain; there he will come to his end, and none will help him. ¹ At that time Michael will stand, the great [heavenly] prince who stands in support of the members of your people, * and there will be a time of trouble such as there had never been since there was a nation until that time. But at that time your people will escape; everything that is found written in this book [will occur]. ² Many of those who sleep in the dusty earth will awaken: these for everlasting life

12

ג לַחֲרָפוֹת לְדִרְאוֹן עוֹלָם: וְהַמַּשְׂכִּלִים יַזְהִרוּ כְּזֹהַר הָרָקִיעַ וּמַצְדִּיקֵי
ד הָרַבִּים כַּכּוֹכָבִים לְעוֹלָם וָעֶד: וְאַתָּה דָנִיֵּאל סְתֹם הַדְּבָרִים
ה וַחֲתֹם הַסֵּפֶר עַד־עֵת קֵץ יְשֹׁטְטוּ רַבִּים וְתִרְבֶּה הַדָּעַת: וְרָאִיתִי אֲנִי
   דָנִיֵּאל וְהִנֵּה שְׁנַיִם אֲחֵרִים עֹמְדִים אֶחָד הֵנָּה לִשְׂפַת הַיְאֹר וְאֶחָד הֵנָּה
ו לִשְׂפַת הַיְאֹר: וַיֹּאמֶר לָאִישׁ לְבוּשׁ הַבַּדִּים אֲשֶׁר מִמַּעַל לְמֵימֵי הַיְאֹר
ז עַד־מָתַי קֵץ הַפְּלָאוֹת: וָאֶשְׁמַע אֶת־הָאִישׁ ׀ לְבוּשׁ הַבַּדִּים אֲשֶׁר מִמַּעַל
   לְמֵימֵי הַיְאֹר וַיָּרֶם יְמִינוֹ וּשְׂמֹאלוֹ אֶל־הַשָּׁמַיִם וַיִּשָּׁבַע בְּחֵי הָעוֹלָם כִּי
ח לְמוֹעֵד מוֹעֲדִים וָחֵצִי וּכְכַלּוֹת נַפֵּץ יַד־עַם־קֹדֶשׁ תִּכְלֶינָה כָל־אֵלֶּה: וַאֲנִי
ט שָׁמַעְתִּי וְלֹא אָבִין וָאֹמְרָה אֲדֹנִי מָה אַחֲרִית אֵלֶּה: וַיֹּאמֶר לֵךְ דָּנִיֵּאל כִּי־
י סְתֻמִים וַחֲתֻמִים הַדְּבָרִים עַד־עֵת קֵץ: יִתְבָּרֲרוּ וְיִתְלַבְּנוּ וְיִצָּרְפוּ רַבִּים
יא וְהִרְשִׁיעוּ רְשָׁעִים וְלֹא יָבִינוּ כָּל־רְשָׁעִים וְהַמַּשְׂכִּלִים יָבִינוּ: וּמֵעֵת הוּסַר
יב הַתָּמִיד וְלָתֵת שִׁקּוּץ שֹׁמֵם יָמִים אֶלֶף מָאתַיִם וְתִשְׁעִים: אַשְׁרֵי הַמְחַכֶּה
יג וְיַגִּיעַ לְיָמִים אֶלֶף שְׁלֹשׁ מֵאוֹת שְׁלֹשִׁים וַחֲמִשָּׁה: וְאַתָּה לֵךְ לַקֵּץ וְתָנוּחַ
   וְתַעֲמֹד לְגֹרָלְךָ לְקֵץ הַיָּמִין:

סכום פסוקי דספר דניאל שלש מאות וחמשים ושבעה. וסימנך כי רוח ה׳ **נשבה** בו.

12:4. Write the prophecies in an obscure manner so that their exact meaning remains unclear. People will have to investigate thoroughly and search hard to discern the true intent of these prophecies.

12:6. The angel who had been speaking to Daniel.

12:7. This mysterious time frame for the End is predicted above, 7:25.

12:10. Many people will succeed in understanding the true meaning of these prophecies (*Abarbanel*).

12:13. You will die before these events occur.

and these for shame, for everlasting abhorrence. [3] The wise will shine like the radiance of the firmament, and those who teach righteousness to the multitudes [will shine] like the stars, forever and ever.

[4] As for you, Daniel, obscure the matters and seal the book until the time of the End; let many muse and let knowledge increase. *

[5] Then I, Daniel, looked and behold! two others are standing, one on this side of the riverbank and one on that side of the riverbank. [6] [One] said to the man clothed in linen, * who was above the waters of the river, "How long until the concealed End?" [7] I heard the man clothed in linen, who was above the waters of the river, as he lifted his right hand and his left hand to the heavens and swore by the Life Source of the World that after a period, periods, and a half, * upon the completion of the fragmenting of the hand of the holy people, all these would be finished.

[8] I heard [this] but I did not comprehend [it], so I said, "My lord, what is the end of these [matters]?"

[9] He said, "Go, Daniel! For the matters are obscured and sealed until the time of the End. [10] They will be elucidated and clarified and refined by many [people]; * the wicked will act wickedly, and none of the wicked will understand; but the wise will understand. [11] From the time the daily offering was removed and the mute abomination put in place, one thousand two hundred and ninety years. [12] Praiseworthy is he who awaits and reaches one thousand three hundred and thirty-five years. [13] As for you, go to [your] end; * you will rest — then arise for your portion at the End of Days."

Ezra/ Nehemiah עזרא/ נחמיה

*T*he Book of Ezra / Nehemiah brings us to a pivotal turning point in
Jewish history. It begins an epoch that, in a sense, is still with us,
because the glories of David and Solomon were never regained. Even
after the Second Temple was rebuilt (349 B.C.E.), the level of holiness
of the First Temple era did not return. The Jews were still under the
domination of a foreign power, and so it was to remain during most of
the years that the Second Temple stood. It was only due to the kindness
and generosity of King Cyrus that the Temple could be built at all.

That the return to the land took place at all was thanks to the
leadership of Ezra and Nehemiah. Ezra was so great that the Talmud
describes him as worthy of having received the Torah, had not Moses
preceded him. Nehemiah gave up a prominent position as a royal
courtier for the sake of coming to the Land of Israel and rescuing the
miniscule settlement from demoralization.

The nation was not worthy of a total redemption; that will come only
at the end of the current exile. Even when the royal edict was issued
allowing the Jews to return to their land, only 43,000 accepted the offer
— a tiny fraction of the nation. Shocking? Most certainly. This was an
indication of the sorry state of the nation under foreign domination.

But there was a blaze of greatness unrelated to temporal sovereignty.
Ezra and Nehemiah were members of the Anshei Knesses HaGedolah,
the Men of the Great Assembly, a council of one hundred and twenty
men, many of whom were prophets, which functioned over several
generations and rejuvenated the nation. They prayed, successfully,
that the craving for idolatry be abolished (which is why the idea of
such worship seems so outlandish to modern man); they composed the
standard prayers; and — most important of all — brought about the
dramatic flowering of the Oral Law, which was and remains the primary
repository of Divine wisdom.

Ezra was one of the supreme teachers in Jewish history. He and
the Men of the Great Assembly returned the crown of God's greatness
to its former splendor by teaching successive generations to seek
His beneficent hand behind the mists of history and the ephemeral
ascendancy of the wicked. That teaching will illuminate the universe
when the final Redemption is at hand.

א

א וּבִשְׁנַת אַחַת לְכוֹרֶשׁ מֶלֶךְ פָּרַס לִכְלוֹת דְּבַר־יהוה מִפִּי יִרְמְיָה הֵעִיר יהוה אֶת־רוּחַ כֹּרֶשׁ מֶלֶךְ־פָּרַס וַיַּעֲבֶר־קוֹל בְּכָל־מַלְכוּתוֹ וְגַם־בְּמִכְתָּב

ב לֵאמֹר: כֹּה אָמַר כֹּרֶשׁ מֶלֶךְ פָּרַס כֹּל מַמְלְכוֹת הָאָרֶץ נָתַן לִי יהוה אֱלֹהֵי הַשָּׁמַיִם וְהוּא־פָקַד עָלַי לִבְנוֹת־לוֹ בַיִת בִּירוּשָׁלִַם אֲשֶׁר בִּיהוּדָה: מִי־

ג בָכֶם מִכָּל־עַמּוֹ יְהִי אֱלֹהָיו עִמּוֹ וְיַעַל לִירוּשָׁלִַם אֲשֶׁר בִּיהוּדָה וְיִבֶן אֶת־

ד בֵּית יהוה אֱלֹהֵי יִשְׂרָאֵל הוּא הָאֱלֹהִים אֲשֶׁר בִּירוּשָׁלִָם: וְכָל־הַנִּשְׁאָר מִכָּל־הַמְּקֹמוֹת אֲשֶׁר הוּא גָר־שָׁם יְנַשְּׂאוּהוּ אַנְשֵׁי מְקֹמוֹ בְּכֶסֶף וּבְזָהָב

ה וּבִרְכוּשׁ וּבִבְהֵמָה עִם־הַנְּדָבָה לְבֵית הָאֱלֹהִים אֲשֶׁר בִּירוּשָׁלִָם: וַיָּקוּמוּ רָאשֵׁי הָאָבוֹת לִיהוּדָה וּבִנְיָמִן וְהַכֹּהֲנִים וְהַלְוִיִּם לְכֹל הֵעִיר הָאֱלֹהִים

ו אֶת־רוּחוֹ לַעֲלוֹת לִבְנוֹת אֶת־בֵּית יהוה אֲשֶׁר בִּירוּשָׁלִָם: וְכָל־סְבִיבֹתֵיהֶם חִזְּקוּ בִידֵיהֶם בִּכְלֵי־כֶסֶף בַּזָּהָב בָּרְכוּשׁ וּבַבְּהֵמָה וּבַמִּגְדָּנוֹת לְבַד עַל־כָּל־הִתְנַדֵּב:

ז וְהַמֶּלֶךְ כּוֹרֶשׁ הוֹצִיא אֶת־כְּלֵי בֵית־יהוה אֲשֶׁר הוֹצִיא נְבוּכַדְנֶצַּר

ח מִירוּשָׁלִַם וַיִּתְּנֵם בְּבֵית אֱלֹהָיו: וַיּוֹצִיאֵם כּוֹרֶשׁ מֶלֶךְ פָּרַס עַל־יַד מִתְרְדָת

ט הַגִּזְבָּר וַיִּסְפְּרֵם לְשֵׁשְׁבַּצַּר הַנָּשִׂיא לִיהוּדָה: וְאֵלֶּה מִסְפָּרָם אֲגַרְטְלֵי זָהָב שְׁלֹשִׁים אֲגַרְטְלֵי־כֶסֶף אָלֶף מַחֲלָפִים תִּשְׁעָה וְעֶשְׂרִים:

י כְּפוֹרֵי זָהָב שְׁלֹשִׁים כְּפוֹרֵי כֶסֶף מִשְׁנִים אַרְבַּע מֵאוֹת וַעֲשָׂרָה כֵּלִים

יא אֲחֵרִים אָלֶף: כָּל־כֵּלִים לַזָּהָב וְלַכֶּסֶף חֲמֵשֶׁת אֲלָפִים וְאַרְבַּע מֵאוֹת הַכֹּל הֶעֱלָה שֵׁשְׁבַּצַּר עִם הֵעָלוֹת הַגּוֹלָה מִבָּבֶל לִירוּשָׁלִָם:

ב

א וְאֵלֶּה | בְּנֵי הַמְּדִינָה הָעֹלִים מִשְּׁבִי הַגּוֹלָה אֲשֶׁר הֶגְלָה °נבוכדנצור [נְבוּכַדְנֶצַּר ק] מֶלֶךְ־בָּבֶל לְבָבֶל וַיָּשׁוּבוּ לִירוּשָׁלִַם וִיהוּדָה אִישׁ לְעִירוֹ:

ב אֲשֶׁר־בָּאוּ עִם־זְרֻבָּבֶל יֵשׁוּעַ נְחֶמְיָה שְׂרָיָה רְעֵלָיָה מָרְדֳּכַי בִּלְשָׁן מִסְפָּר

ג בִּגְוַי רְחוּם בַּעֲנָה מִסְפַּר אַנְשֵׁי עַם יִשְׂרָאֵל: בְּנֵי פַרְעֹשׁ אַלְפַּיִם מֵאָה

ד-ה שִׁבְעִים וּשְׁנָיִם: בְּנֵי שְׁפַטְיָה שְׁלֹשׁ מֵאוֹת שִׁבְעִים וּשְׁנָיִם: בְּנֵי אָרַח שְׁבַע

ו מֵאוֹת חֲמִשָּׁה וְשִׁבְעִים: בְּנֵי־פַחַת מוֹאָב לִבְנֵי יֵשׁוּעַ יוֹאָב אַלְפַּיִם שְׁמֹנֶה

ז-ח מֵאוֹת וּשְׁנֵים עָשָׂר: בְּנֵי עֵילָם אֶלֶף מָאתַיִם חֲמִשִּׁים וְאַרְבָּעָה: בְּנֵי זַתּוּא

ט-י תְּשַׁע מֵאוֹת וְאַרְבָּעִים וַחֲמִשָּׁה: בְּנֵי זַכָּי שְׁבַע מֵאוֹת וְשִׁשִּׁים: בְּנֵי בָנִי שֵׁשׁ

יא-יב מֵאוֹת אַרְבָּעִים וּשְׁנָיִם: בְּנֵי בֵבָי שֵׁשׁ מֵאוֹת עֶשְׂרִים וּשְׁלֹשָׁה: בְּנֵי עַזְגָּד

יג-יד אֶלֶף מָאתַיִם עֶשְׂרִים וּשְׁנָיִם: בְּנֵי אֲדֹנִיקָם שֵׁשׁ מֵאוֹת שִׁשִּׁים וְשִׁשָּׁה: בְּנֵי

טו בִגְוָי אַלְפַּיִם חֲמִשִּׁים וְשִׁשָּׁה: בְּנֵי עָדִין אַרְבַּע מֵאוֹת חֲמִשִּׁים וְאַרְבָּעָה:

1:1. The chronology of the kings of the Eastern Empires is as follows: Nebuchadnezzar of Babylonia; his son Evil-merodach; and his son Belshazzar. The Babylonian Empire was conquered by Darius the Mede (see *Daniel* 6:1, 9:1) and his son-in-law Cyrus the Persian of our verse; they were succeeded by Ahasuerus husband of Esther and his son, Darius the Persian (see 4:5-6 below).

This Book begins at the conclusion of the seventy-year period foretold in *Jeremiah* 29:10. The first two verses are almost identical with the last two verses of Chronicles.

1:4. Should any Jew be prevented by poverty from going to Jerusalem, let his gentile neighbors supply whatever he needs, so that he may go (*Rashi*).

1:8. A pseudonym either for Daniel (*Rashi; Midrash*) or

1

RETURN TO THE LAND
1:1-2:70

Cyrus'
proclamation
(See Appendix A,
timeline 5)

¹ In the first year of Cyrus king of Persia, * upon the conclusion of HASHEM's prophecy by the mouth of Jeremiah, HASHEM aroused the spirit of Cyrus king of Persia, and he issued a proclamation throughout his kingdom — and in writing as well, saying: ² "Thus said Cyrus king of Persia: All the kingdoms of the earth has HASHEM, God of heaven, given to me and He has commanded me to build Him a Temple in Jerusalem, which is in Judah. ³ Whoever is among you of His entire people — may his God be with him — and let him go up to Jerusalem which is in Judah and build the Temple of HASHEM, God of Israel — He is the God! — which is in Jerusalem. ⁴ And whoever remains, * in whatever place he dwells, let the inhabitants of that place bestow upon him gifts of silver and gold, of valuables and of animals; together with the contribution for the Temple of God which is in Jerusalem."

The
response

⁵ So the heads of the families of Judah and Benjamin and the Kohanim and the Levites — with all those whose spirits God had aroused — got up to ascend and build the Temple of HASHEM which is in Jerusalem. ⁶ And all the people around them strengthened their hands with silver utensils, with gold, with valuables and with animals and with fine goods, besides all that was contributed [for the Temple].

The Temple
vessels

⁷ King Cyrus removed the vessels of the Temple of HASHEM that Nebuchadnezzar had removed from Jerusalem and placed in the temple of his gods. ⁸ Cyrus king of Persia removed them by the hand of Mithredath the treasurer, who then counted them [over] to Sheshbazzar, * the leader of Judah. ⁹ This was their number: thirty golden utensils, one thousand silver utensils, twenty-nine slaughtering knives, ¹⁰ thirty golden bowls, four hundred and ten secondary silver bowls and one thousand other vessels; ¹¹ all the vessels of gold and silver, five thousand four hundred. * Sheshbazzar brought them all up with the ascension of the exile from Babylonia to Jerusalem.

2

Returning
Israelites by
family . . .

¹ These are the people of the country * who ascended from the captivity of the exile that Nebuchadnezzar king of Babylonia had exiled to Babylonia, who returned to Jerusalem and Judah, each man to his city, ² who came with Zerubbabel, Jeshua, Nehemiah, Seraiah, Reelaiah, Mordechai-bilshan, * Mispar-bigvai, Rehum and Baanah, [who comprised] the sum of the dignitaries of the people of Israel:

³ The children of Parosh, two thousand one hundred seventy-two; ⁴ the children of Shephatiah, three hundred seventy-two; ⁵ the children of Arah, seven hundred seventy-five; ⁶ the children of the Governor of Moab * — of the children of Jeshua and Joab — two thousand eight hundred twelve; ⁷ the children of Elam, one thousand two hundred fifty-four; ⁸ the children of Zattu, nine hundred forty-five; ⁹ the children of Zaccai, seven hundred sixty; ¹⁰ the children of Bani, six hundred forty-two; ¹¹ the children of Bebai, six hundred twenty-three; ¹² the children of Azgad, one thousand two hundred twenty-two; ¹³ the children of Adonikam, six hundred sixty-six; ¹⁴ the children of Bigvai, two thousand fifty-six; ¹⁵ the children of Adin, four hundred fifty-four;

Zerubbabel (*Ibn Ezra*).

1:11. Including many that were not enumerated in previous verses.

2:1. That is, the Land of Israel (*Rashi*).

2:2. This was the Mordechai of the Book of *Esther*. The Talmud states that the appellation "Bilshan" [from לשון,

language] was added to his name because of his unusual mastery of many languages (*Menachos* 65a).

2:6. This family was descended from King David, or from his general and nephew, Joab (*Taanis* 28a). Both David and Joab were descendants of the Moabite princess Ruth, hence the family name "Governor of Moab" (*Tosafos*).

טז בְּנֵי־אָטֵר לִיחִזְקִיָּה תִּשְׁעִים וּשְׁמֹנָה: בְּנֵי בֵצָי שְׁלֹשׁ מֵאוֹת עֶשְׂרִים
יח-יט וּשְׁלֹשָׁה: בְּנֵי יוֹרָה מֵאָה וּשְׁנֵים עָשָׂר: בְּנֵי חָשֻׁם מָאתַיִם עֶשְׂרִים וּשְׁלֹשָׁה:
כ-כב בְּנֵי גִבָּר תִּשְׁעִים וַחֲמִשָּׁה: בְּנֵי בֵית־לָחֶם מֵאָה עֶשְׂרִים וּשְׁלֹשָׁה: אַנְשֵׁי
כג-כד נְטֹפָה חֲמִשִּׁים וְשִׁשָּׁה: אַנְשֵׁי עֲנָתוֹת מֵאָה עֶשְׂרִים וּשְׁמֹנָה: בְּנֵי עַזְמָוֶת
כה אַרְבָּעִים וּשְׁנָיִם: בְּנֵי קִרְיַת עָרִים כְּפִירָה וּבְאֵרוֹת שְׁבַע מֵאוֹת וְאַרְבָּעִים
כו-כז וּשְׁלֹשָׁה: בְּנֵי הָרָמָה וָגָבַע שֵׁשׁ מֵאוֹת עֶשְׂרִים וְאֶחָד: אַנְשֵׁי מִכְמָס מֵאָה
כח-כט עֶשְׂרִים וּשְׁנָיִם: אַנְשֵׁי בֵית־אֵל וְהָעָי מָאתַיִם עֶשְׂרִים וּשְׁלֹשָׁה: בְּנֵי נְבוֹ
ל-לא חֲמִשִּׁים וּשְׁנָיִם: בְּנֵי מַגְבִּישׁ מֵאָה חֲמִשִּׁים וְשִׁשָּׁה: בְּנֵי עֵילָם אַחֵר
לב-לג אֶלֶף מָאתַיִם חֲמִשִּׁים וְאַרְבָּעָה: בְּנֵי חָרִם שְׁלֹשׁ מֵאוֹת וְעֶשְׂרִים: בְּנֵי־לֹד
לד חָדִיד וְאוֹנוֹ שְׁבַע מֵאוֹת עֶשְׂרִים וַחֲמִשָּׁה: בְּנֵי יְרֵחוֹ שְׁלֹשׁ מֵאוֹת
לה אַרְבָּעִים וַחֲמִשָּׁה: בְּנֵי סְנָאָה שְׁלֹשֶׁת אֲלָפִים וְשֵׁשׁ מֵאוֹת וּשְׁלֹשִׁים:
לו-לז הַכֹּהֲנִים בְּנֵי יְדַעְיָה לְבֵית יֵשׁוּעַ תְּשַׁע מֵאוֹת שִׁבְעִים וּשְׁלֹשָׁה: בְּנֵי אִמֵּר
לח-לט אֶלֶף חֲמִשִּׁים וּשְׁנָיִם: בְּנֵי פַשְׁחוּר אֶלֶף מָאתַיִם אַרְבָּעִים וְשִׁבְעָה: בְּנֵי
מ חָרִם אֶלֶף וְשִׁבְעָה עָשָׂר: הַלְוִיִּם בְּנֵי־יֵשׁוּעַ וְקַדְמִיאֵל לִבְנֵי הוֹדַוְיָה
מא-מב שִׁבְעִים וְאַרְבָּעָה: הַמְשֹׁרְרִים בְּנֵי אָסָף מֵאָה עֶשְׂרִים וּשְׁמֹנָה: בְּנֵי
הַשֹּׁעֲרִים בְּנֵי־שַׁלּוּם בְּנֵי־אָטֵר בְּנֵי־טַלְמֹן בְּנֵי־עַקּוּב בְּנֵי חֲטִיטָא בְּנֵי
מג שֹׁבָי הַכֹּל מֵאָה שְׁלֹשִׁים וְתִשְׁעָה: הַנְּתִינִים בְּנֵי־צִיחָא בְנֵי־חֲשׂוּפָא בְּנֵי
מד-מה טַבָּעוֹת: בְּנֵי־קֵרֹס בְּנֵי־סִיעֲהָא בְּנֵי פָדוֹן: בְּנֵי־לְבָנָה בְנֵי־חֲגָבָה בְּנֵי
מו-מז עַקּוּב: בְּנֵי־חָגָב בְּנֵי־°שַׁמְלַי [°שַׁלְמַי ק] בְּנֵי חָנָן: בְּנֵי־גִדֵּל בְּנֵי־גַחַר בְּנֵי
מח רְאָיָה: בְּנֵי־רְצִין בְּנֵי־נְקוֹדָא בְּנֵי גַזָּם: בְּנֵי־עֻזָּא בְנֵי־פָסֵחַ בְּנֵי בֵסָי: בְּנֵי־
נא אַסְנָה בְנֵי־°מְעִינִים [°מְעוּנִים ק] בְּנֵי °נְפִיסִים [°נְפוּסִים ק]: בְּנֵי־בַקְבּוּק
נב-נג בְּנֵי־חֲקוּפָא בְּנֵי חַרְחוּר: בְּנֵי־בַצְלוּת בְּנֵי־מְחִידָא בְּנֵי חַרְשָׁא: בְּנֵי־
נד-נה בַרְקוֹס בְּנֵי־סִיסְרָא בְּנֵי־תָמַח: בְּנֵי נְצִיחַ בְּנֵי חֲטִיפָא: בְּנֵי עַבְדֵי שְׁלֹמֹה
נו-נז בְּנֵי־סֹטַי בְּנֵי־הַסֹּפֶרֶת בְּנֵי פְרוּדָא: בְּנֵי־יַעְלָה בְנֵי־דַרְקוֹן בְּנֵי גִדֵּל: בְּנֵי
נח שְׁפַטְיָה בְנֵי־חַטִּיל בְּנֵי פֹכֶרֶת הַצְּבָיִים בְּנֵי אָמִי: כָּל־הַנְּתִינִים וּבְנֵי עַבְדֵי
נט שְׁלֹמֹה שְׁלֹשׁ מֵאוֹת תִּשְׁעִים וּשְׁנָיִם: וְאֵלֶּה הָעֹלִים
מִתֵּל מֶלַח תֵּל חַרְשָׁא כְּרוּב אַדָּן אִמֵּר וְלֹא יָכְלוּ לְהַגִּיד בֵּית־אֲבוֹתָם
ס וְזַרְעָם אִם מִיִּשְׂרָאֵל הֵם: בְּנֵי־דְלָיָה בְנֵי־טוֹבִיָּה בְּנֵי נְקוֹדָא שֵׁשׁ מֵאוֹת
סא חֲמִשִּׁים וּשְׁנָיִם: וּמִבְּנֵי הַכֹּהֲנִים בְּנֵי חֳבַיָּה בְּנֵי
הַקּוֹץ בְּנֵי בַרְזִלַּי אֲשֶׁר לָקַח מִבְּנוֹת בַּרְזִלַּי הַגִּלְעָדִי אִשָּׁה וַיִּקָּרֵא עַל־
סב שְׁמָם: אֵלֶּה בִּקְשׁוּ כְתָבָם הַמִּתְיַחְשִׂים וְלֹא נִמְצָאוּ וַיְגֹאֲלוּ מִן־הַכְּהֻנָּה:

2:31. This Elam is a city; the one mentioned in verse 7 is a family. Nevertheless, the number of people is the same.

2:43. Descendants of the Gibeonites who were assigned menial tasks (woodcutting, water drawing) for the Temple. They were permitted to live among the Jews but not to intermarry with them (see *Joshua* Ch. 9).

2:55. The descendants of Solomon's slaves lived among the Jews, but never converted (see *Rambam*, *Melachim* 6:1).

2:61. See *II Samuel* 17:27 and 19:32-39. The family

¹⁶ the children of Ater — of Hezekiah — ninety-eight; ¹⁷ the children of Bezai, three hundred twenty-three; ¹⁸ the children of Jorah, one hundred twelve; ¹⁹ the children of Hashum, two hundred twenty-three; ²⁰ the children of Gibbar, ninety-five.

²¹ The people of Beth-lehem, one hundred twenty-three; ²² the people of Netophah, fifty-six; ²³ the people of Anathoth, one hundred twenty-eight; ²⁴ the people of Azmaveth, forty-two; ²⁵ the people of Kiriath-arim, Chephirah and Beeroth, seven hundred forty-three; ²⁶ the people of the Ramah and Geba, six hundred twenty-one; ²⁷ the people of Michmas, one hundred twenty-two; ²⁸ the people of Beth-el and Ai, two hundred twenty-three; ²⁹ the people of Nebo, fifty-two; ³⁰ the people of Magbish, one hundred fifty-six; ³¹ the people of a different Elam,* one thousand two hundred fifty-four; ³² the people of Harim, three hundred twenty; ³³ the people of Lod, Hadid and Ono, seven hundred twenty-five; ³⁴ the people of Jericho, three hundred forty-five; ³⁵ the people of Senaah, three thousand six hundred thirty.

³⁶ The Kohanim: The children of Jedaiah, of the house of Jeshua, nine hundred seventy-three; ³⁷ the children of Immer, one thousand fifty-two; ³⁸ the children of Pashhur, one thousand two hundred forty-seven; ³⁹ the children of Harim, one thousand seventeen.

⁴⁰ The Levites: The children of Jeshua and Kadmiel, of the children of Hodaviah, seventy-four; ⁴¹ the singers — the children of Asaph — one hundred twenty-eight; ⁴² the children of the gatekeepers — the children of Shallum, the children of Ater, the children of Talmon, the children of Akkub, the children of Hatita and the children of Shobai — altogether one hundred thirty-nine.

⁴³ The Nethinim:* The children of Ziha, the children of Hasupha, the children of Tabbaoth, ⁴⁴ the children of Keros, the children of Siaha, the children of Padon, ⁴⁵ the children of Lebanah, the children of Hagabah, the children of Akkub, ⁴⁶ the children of Hagab, the children of Salmai, the children of Hanan, ⁴⁷ the children of Giddel, the children of Gahar, the children of Reaiah, ⁴⁸ the children of Rezin, the children of Nekoda, the children of Gazzam, ⁴⁹ the children of Uzza, the children of Paseah, the children of Besai, ⁵⁰ the children of Asnah, the children of Meunim, the children of Nephusim, ⁵¹ the children of Bakbuk, the children of Hakupha, the children of Harhur, ⁵² the children of Bazluth, the children of Mehida, the children of Harsha, ⁵³ the children of Barkos, the children of Sisera, the children of Tamah, ⁵⁴ the children of Neziah, the children of Hatipha. ⁵⁵ The children of Solomon's slaves:* The children of Sotai, the children of Hassophereth, the children of Peruda, ⁵⁶ the children of Jaalah, the children of Darkon, the children of Giddel, ⁵⁷ the children of Shephatiah, the children of Hattil, the children of Pochereth-hazzebaim, the children of Ami. ⁵⁸ All of the Nethinim and the children of Solomon's slaves numbered three hundred ninety-two.

⁵⁹ These are the ones who went up from Tel-melah, Tel-harsha, Cherub, Addan and Immer, and could not declare their fathers' families and their descent, whether they were from Israel: ⁶⁰ The children of Delaiah, the children of Tobiah and the children of Nekoda, six hundred fifty-two.

⁶¹ Of the children of the Kohanim: The children of Habaiah, the children of Hakkoz and the children of Barzillai, who took wives from the daughters of Barzillai of Gilead* and were called by their name. ⁶² These sought their genealogical records, but they could not be found, so they were disqualified from the priesthood.

... and by city

The Temple ministrants: Kohanim

... Levites ...

... Nethinim and the descendants of Solomon's slaves

Those of dubious descent

---

known as "the children of Barzillai" was actually descended from Barzillai's daughters. They claimed to be   Kohanim but could produce no genealogical evidence to support that claim.

סג   וַיֹּ֤אמֶר הַתִּרְשָׁ֙תָא֙ לָהֶ֔ם אֲשֶׁ֥ר לֹא־יֹאכְל֖וּ מִקֹּ֣דֶשׁ הַקֳּדָשִׁ֑ים עַ֛ד עֲמֹ֥ד כֹּהֵ֖ן

סד   לְאוּרִ֥ים וּלְתֻמִּֽים: כָּל־הַקָּהָ֖ל כְּאֶחָ֑ד אַרְבַּ֣ע רִבּ֔וֹא אַלְפַּ֖יִם שְׁלֹשׁ־מֵא֥וֹת

סה   שִׁשִּֽׁים: מִ֠לְּבַד עַבְדֵיהֶ֤ם וְאַמְהֹֽתֵיהֶם֙ אֵ֔לֶּה שִׁבְעַ֣ת אֲלָפִ֔ים שְׁלֹ֥שׁ מֵא֖וֹת

סו   שְׁלֹשִׁ֣ים וְשִׁבְעָ֑ה וְלָהֶ֛ם מְשֹׁרְרִ֥ים וּֽמְשֹׁרְר֖וֹת מָאתָֽיִם: סוּסֵיהֶ֕ם שְׁבַ֥ע

סז   מֵא֖וֹת שְׁלֹשִׁ֣ים וְשִׁשָּׁ֑ה פִּרְדֵיהֶ֕ם מָאתַ֖יִם אַרְבָּעִ֥ים וַחֲמִשָּֽׁה: גְּמַלֵּיהֶ֕ם אַרְבַּ֣ע מֵא֔וֹת שְׁלֹשִׁ֖ים וַחֲמִשָּׁ֑ה חֲמֹרִ֕ים שֵׁ֣שֶׁת אֲלָפִ֔ים שְׁבַ֥ע מֵא֖וֹת

סח   וְעֶשְׂרִֽים: וּמֵרָאשֵׁ֣י הָֽאָב֗וֹת בְּבוֹאָ֞ם לְבֵ֤ית יְהֹוָה֙ אֲשֶׁ֣ר בִּירֽוּשָׁלִָ֔ם

סט   הִֽתְנַדְּבוּ֙ לְבֵ֣ית הָֽאֱלֹהִ֔ים לְהַעֲמִיד֖וֹ עַל־מְכוֹנֽוֹ: כְּכֹחָ֗ם נָתְנוּ֙ לְאוֹצַ֣ר הַמְּלָאכָ֔ה זָהָ֗ב דַּרְכְּמוֹנִים֙ שֵׁשׁ־רִבֹּ֣אות וָאֶ֔לֶף   וְכֶ֕סֶף מָנִ֖ים חֲמֵ֣שֶׁת אֲלָפִ֑ים

ע   וְכָתְנֹ֥ת כֹּהֲנִ֖ים מֵאָֽה: וַיֵּֽשְׁב֣וּ הַכֹּהֲנִ֣ים וְהַלְוִיִּ֡ם וּמִן־הָעָם֩ וְהַמְשֹׁרְרִ֨ים וְהַשּֽׁוֹעֲרִ֜ים וְהַנְּתִינִ֛ים בְּעָרֵיהֶ֖ם וְכָל־יִשְׂרָאֵ֥ל בְּעָרֵיהֶֽם:

ג   א   וַיִּגַּע֙ הַחֹ֣דֶשׁ הַשְּׁבִיעִ֔י וּבְנֵ֥י יִשְׂרָאֵ֖ל בֶּֽעָרִ֑ים   וַיֵּאָסְפ֥וּ הָעָ֛ם כְּאִ֥ישׁ אֶחָ֖ד אֶל־יְרוּשָׁלִָֽם:

ב   וַיָּקָם֩ יֵשׁ֨וּעַ בֶּן־יֽוֹצָדָ֜ק וְאֶחָ֣יו הַכֹּהֲנִ֗ים וּזְרֻבָּבֶ֤ל בֶּן־שְׁאַלְתִּיאֵל֙ וְאֶחָ֔יו וַיִּבְנ֕וּ אֶת־מִזְבַּ֖ח אֱלֹהֵ֣י יִשְׂרָאֵ֑ל לְהַעֲל֤וֹת עָלָיו֙ עֹל֔וֹת כַּכָּת֕וּב בְּתוֹרַ֖ת מֹשֶׁ֥ה

ג   אִישׁ־הָאֱלֹהִֽים: וַיָּכִ֤ינוּ הַמִּזְבֵּ֙חַ֙ עַל־מְכ֣וֹנֹתָ֔יו כִּ֚י בְּאֵימָ֣ה עֲלֵיהֶ֔ם מֵֽעַמֵּ֖י

ד   הָֽאֲרָצ֑וֹת ◦וַיַּ֙עַל֙ [°וַיַּעֲל֤וּ ק] עָלָיו֙ עֹלוֹת֙ לַֽיהֹוָ֔ה עֹל֖וֹת לַבֹּ֥קֶר וְלָעָֽרֶב: וַיַּֽעֲשׂ֛וּ אֶת־חַ֥ג הַסֻּכּ֖וֹת כַּכָּת֑וּב וְעֹלַ֨ת י֤וֹם בְּיוֹם֙ בְּמִסְפָּ֔ר כְּמִשְׁפַּ֖ט דְּבַר־י֥וֹם

ה   בְּיוֹמֽוֹ: וְאַחֲרֵי־כֵ֞ן עֹלַ֤ת תָּמִיד֙ וְלֶ֣חֳדָשִׁ֔ים וּלְכָל־מוֹעֲדֵ֥י יְהֹוָ֖ה הַמְקֻדָּשִׁ֑ים

ו   וּלְכֹ֛ל מִתְנַדֵּ֥ב נְדָבָ֖ה לַֽיהֹוָֽה: מִיּ֤וֹם אֶחָד֙ לַחֹ֣דֶשׁ הַשְּׁבִיעִ֔י הֵחֵ֕לּוּ לְהַעֲל֖וֹת עֹל֣וֹת לַֽיהֹוָ֑ה וְהֵיכַ֥ל יְהֹוָ֖ה לֹ֥א יֻסָּֽד:

ז   וַיִּ֨תְּנוּ־כֶ֔סֶף לַחֹצְבִ֖ים וְלֶחָרָשִׁ֑ים וּמַֽאֲכָ֨ל וּמִשְׁתֶּ֜ה וָשֶׁ֗מֶן לַצִּֽדֹנִים֙ וְלַצֹּרִ֔ים לְהָבִיא֩ עֲצֵ֨י אֲרָזִ֤ים מִן־הַלְּבָנוֹן֙

ח   אֶל־יָ֣ם יָפ֔וֹא כְּרִשְׁי֛וֹן כּ֥וֹרֶשׁ מֶֽלֶךְ־פָּרַ֖ס עֲלֵיהֶֽם: וּבַשָּׁנָ֣ה הַשֵּׁנִ֗ית לְבוֹאָ֞ם אֶל־בֵּ֤ית הָֽאֱלֹהִים֙ לִיר֣וּשָׁלַ֔͏ִם בַּחֹ֖דֶשׁ הַשֵּׁנִ֑י הֵחֵ֡לּוּ זְרֻבָּבֶ֣ל בֶּן־שְׁ֠אַלְתִּיאֵ֠ל וְיֵשׁ֨וּעַ בֶּן־יֽוֹצָדָ֜ק וּשְׁאָ֥ר אֲחֵיהֶ֣ם ׀ הַכֹּהֲנִ֣ים וְהַלְוִיִּ֗ם וְכָל־הַבָּאִים֙ מֵֽהַשְּׁבִ֣י יְרֽוּשָׁלַ֔͏ִם וַיַּעֲמִ֜ידוּ אֶת־הַלְוִיִּ֗ם מִבֶּ֨ן עֶשְׂרִ֤ים שָׁנָה֙

ט   וָמַ֔עְלָה לְנַצֵּ֖חַ עַל־מְלֶ֣אכֶת בֵּית־יְהֹוָֽה: וַיַּעֲמֹ֣ד יֵשׁ֡וּעַ בָּנָ֣יו וְ֠אֶחָ֠יו קַדְמִיאֵ֨ל וּבָנָ֤יו בְּנֵֽי־יְהוּדָה֙ כְּאֶחָ֔ד לְנַצֵּ֖חַ עַל־עֹשֵׂ֣ה הַמְּלָאכָ֑ה בְּבֵ֖ית הָאֱלֹהִ֑ים בְּנֵי֙

י   חֵֽנָדָ֔ד בְּנֵיהֶ֥ם וַאֲחֵיהֶ֖ם הַלְוִיִּֽם: וְיִסְּד֥וּ הַבֹּנִ֖ים אֶת־הֵיכַ֣ל יְהֹוָ֑ה וַיַּֽעֲמִ֩ידוּ֩ הַכֹּהֲנִ֨ים מְלֻבָּשִׁ֜ים בַּחֲצֹֽצְר֗וֹת וְהַלְוִיִּ֤ם בְּנֵֽי־אָסָף֙ בַּֽמְצִלְתַּ֔יִם לְהַלֵּל֙ אֶת־

יא   יְהֹוָ֔ה עַל־יְדֵ֖י דָּוִ֥יד מֶֽלֶךְ־יִשְׂרָאֵֽל: וַֽ֠יַּעֲנ֠וּ בְּהַלֵּ֨ל וּבְהוֹדֹ֤ת לַֽיהֹוָה֙ כִּ֣י ט֔וֹב

2:63. In *Nehemiah* 8:9 this name, or title, is identified with Nehemiah. As a leader of the people, he had the authority to prohibit these *Kohanim* whose genealogy was suspect from eating the meat of offerings that was limited to *Kohanim*. The way to clarify their status would have been through the *Urim VeTumim* of the *Kohen Gadol* (see *Exodus* 28:30).

2:65. Marching choirs accompanied the returnees leading them in songs of praise, thanksgiving and joy.

3:1. The month of Tishrei.

3:2. The *Kohen Gadol* (*Haggai* 1:1).

3:3. They hoped that the daily continual sacrificial service (see *Numbers* 28:1-8) would help protect them from

⁶³ Hattirshatha* told them that they should not eat of the most-holy offerings until there would arise a Kohen to [inquire of] the Urim and the Tumim.

The total   ⁶⁴ The entire congregation together numbered forty-two thousand three hundred sixty, ⁶⁵ besides their male slaves and female slaves, of which there were seven thousand three hundred thirty-seven. They also had two hundred male singers and female singers. * ⁶⁶ Their horses [numbered] seven hundred thirty-six; their mules, two hundred forty-five; ⁶⁷ their camels, four hundred thirty-five; [their] donkeys, six thousand seven hundred twenty.

The leaders   ⁶⁸ Some of the heads of the families, when they came to [the site of] the Temple
contribute   of HASHEM that is in Jerusalem, made contributions to the Temple of God, to establish it on its foundation. ⁶⁹ They gave according to their means to the work fund: of gold, sixty-one thousand darkemons; of silver, five thousand manehs; and one hundred priestly tunics. ⁷⁰ The Kohanim and the Levites and some of the people, and the singers and the gatekeepers and the Nethinim, settled in their cities; and all of Israel in their cities.

3   ¹ The seventh month* arrived and the children of Israel were [settled] in the
BUILDING   cities. The people then assembled as one man to Jerusalem. ² Then Jeshua
THE SECOND   son of Jozadak* arose, along with his brethren the Kohanim and Zerubbabel son
TEMPLE   of Shealtiel and his brethren, and they built the Altar of the God of Israel, to offer
3:1-6:22   burnt-offerings upon it, as is written in the Torah of Moses, the man of God. ³ They
The Altar   established the Altar on its foundations, for the fear of the peoples of the land was
and its   upon them, so they offered burnt-offerings upon it to HASHEM — burnt-offerings
offerings   for the morning and the evening. * ⁴ They then observed the festival of Succos as it is written, with the burnt-offerings of each day in its day according to the [required] amount, according to the law of each day in its day. * ⁵ Afterwards [they offered] daily burnt-offerings as well as those of the New Moons and of all the sanctified festivals of HASHEM; and [offerings] from anyone who dedicated a voluntary offering to HASHEM. ⁶ From the first day of the seventh month they commenced offering burnt-offerings to HASHEM, but the foundation of the Sanctuary of HASHEM had not yet been laid. ⁷ They gave money to the quarriers and carpenters, and food, drink and oil to the Sidonians and to the Tyrians, to transport cedar wood from Lebanon to the Sea of Jaffa, as authorized for them by Cyrus, king of Persia.

Construction   ⁸ In the second year of their arrival at the [site of the] Temple of God, to
of the   Jerusalem, in the second month, Zerubbabel son of Shealtiel and Jeshua son of
Temple's   Jozadak and the rest of their brethren, the Kohanim and the Levites and all those
foundation   who came back from the captivity to Jerusalem commenced, and they stationed
begins   the Levites aged twenty years and older to direct the work of the Temple of HASHEM. ⁹ Then Jeshua, his sons and kinsmen, Kadmiel and his sons, [of] the children of Judah, arose as one, to direct the workers in the Temple of God; [as well as] the sons of Henadad, their sons and their brother Levites. ¹⁰ When the builders had laid the foundation of the Sanctuary of HASHEM they stationed the Kohanim, [elegantly] attired, with trumpets, and the Levites, the sons of Asaph, with cymbals, to praise HASHEM through [the psalms of] David, king of Israel. ¹¹ They sang responsively with praise and thanksgiving to HASHEM, for it is good

---

their enemies (Ibn Ezra). Alternatively, their prompt   populace that they had royal backing (Rashi).
construction of the Altar demonstrated to the hostile   **3:4.** See Numbers 29:12-38.

כִּי־לְעוֹלָם חַסְדּוֹ עַל־יִשְׂרָאֵל וְכָל־הָעָם הֵרִ֫יעוּ תְרוּעָה גְדוֹלָה בְהַלֵּל

יב לַֽיהוָה עַל הוּסַד בֵּית־יְהוָה: וְרַבִּים מֵהַכֹּהֲנִים וְהַלְוִיִּם וְרָאשֵׁי הָאָבוֹת

הַזְּקֵנִים אֲשֶׁר רָאוּ אֶת־הַבַּיִת הָרִאשׁוֹן בְּיָסְדוֹ זֶה הַבַּיִת בְּעֵינֵיהֶם בֹּכִים

יג בְּקוֹל גָּדוֹל וְרַבִּים בִּתְרוּעָה בְשִׂמְחָה לְהָרִים קוֹל: וְאֵין הָעָם מַכִּירִים קוֹל

תְּרוּעַת הַשִּׂמְחָה לְקוֹל בְּכִי הָעָם כִּי הָעָם מְרִיעִים תְּרוּעָה גְדוֹלָה וְהַקּוֹל

נִשְׁמַע עַד־לְמֵרָחֽוֹק:

ד א וַֽיִּשְׁמְעוּ צָרֵי יְהוּדָה וּבִנְיָמִן כִּי־בְנֵי הַגּוֹלָה בּוֹנִים הֵיכָל לַיהוָה אֱלֹהֵי

ב יִשְׂרָאֵל: וַיִּגְּשׁוּ אֶל־זְרֻבָּבֶל וְאֶל־רָאשֵׁי הָאָבוֹת וַיֹּאמְרוּ לָהֶם נִבְנֶה עִמָּכֶם

כִּי כָכֶם נִדְרוֹשׁ לֵאלֹהֵיכֶם וְלֹא ׀ [°וְלוֹ ק] אֲנַחְנוּ זֹבְחִים מִימֵי אֵסַר חַדֹּן

ג מֶלֶךְ אַשּׁוּר הַמַּעֲלֶה אֹתָנוּ פֹּה: וַיֹּאמֶר לָהֶם זְרֻבָּבֶל וְיֵשׁוּעַ וּשְׁאָר רָאשֵׁי

הָאָבוֹת לְיִשְׂרָאֵל לֹא־לָכֶם וָלָנוּ לִבְנוֹת בַּיִת לֵאלֹהֵינוּ כִּי אֲנַחְנוּ יַחַד נִבְנֶה

ד לַֽיהוָה אֱלֹהֵי יִשְׂרָאֵל כַּאֲשֶׁר צִוָּנוּ הַמֶּלֶךְ כּוֹרֶשׁ מֶֽלֶךְ־פָּרָס: וַיְהִי עַם־הָאָרֶץ

מְרַפִּים יְדֵי עַם־יְהוּדָה °וּמבלהים [°וּמְבַהֲלִים ק] אוֹתָם לִבְנוֹת: וְסֹכְרִים

ה עֲלֵיהֶם יֽוֹעֲצִים לְהָפֵר עֲצָתָם כָּל־יְמֵי כּוֹרֶשׁ מֶלֶךְ פָּרָס וְעַד־מַלְכוּת דָּֽרְיָוֶשׁ

ו מֶֽלֶךְ־פָּרָס: וּבְמַלְכוּת אֲחַשְׁוֵרוֹשׁ בִּתְחִלַּת מַלְכוּתוֹ כָּתְבוּ שִׂטְנָה עַל־יֹֽשְׁבֵי

ז יְהוּדָה וִירוּשָׁלָֽ͏ִם: וּבִימֵי

אַרְתַּחְשַׁשְׂתָּא כָּתַב בִּשְׁלָם מִתְרְדָת טָֽבְאֵל וּשְׁאָר °כנותו [°כְּנָוֺתָיו ק] עַל־

אַרְתַּחְשַׁשְׂתָּא מֶלֶךְ פָּרָס וּכְתָב הַנִּשְׁתְּוָן כָּתוּב אֲרָמִית וּמְתֻרְגָּם

ח אֲרָמִֽית: רְחוּם בְּעֵל־טְעֵם וְשִׁמְשַׁי סָֽפְרָא כְּתַבוּ

ט אִגְּרָה חֲדָה עַל־יְרוּשְׁלֶם לְאַרְתַּחְשַׁשְׂתְּא מַלְכָּא כְּנֵֽמָא: אֱדַיִן רְחוּם בְּעֵל־

טְעֵם וְשִׁמְשַׁי סָֽפְרָא וּשְׁאָר כְּנָוָתְהוֹן דִּינָיֵא וַאֲפַרְסַתְכָיֵא טַרְפְּלָיֵא אֲפָֽרְסָיֵא

°ארכוי [°אַרְכְּוָיֵא ק] בָבְלָיֵא שֽׁוּשַׁנְכָיֵא °דהוא [°דֶּהָיֵא ק] עֵֽלְמָיֵא: וּשְׁאָר

י אֻמַּיָּא דִּי הַגְלִי אָסְנַפַּר רַבָּא וְיַקִּירָא וְהוֹתֵב הִמּוֹ בְּקִרְיָה דִּי שָׁמְרָיִן וּשְׁאָר

עֲבַֽר־נַהֲרָה וּכְעֶֽנֶת: דְּנָה פַּרְשֶׁגֶן

יא אִגַּרְתָּא דִּי שְׁלַחוּ עֲלוֹהִי עַל־אַרְתַּחְשַׁשְׂתְּא מַלְכָּא °עבדיך [°עַבְדָּךְ ק]

אֱנָשׁ עֲבַֽר־נַהֲרָה וּכְעֶֽנֶת: יְדִיעַ לֶהֱוֵא לְמַלְכָּא דִּי

יב יְהוּדָיֵא דִּי סְלִקוּ מִן־לְוָתָךְ עֲלֶינָא אֲתוֹ לִירוּשְׁלֶם קִרְיְתָא מָֽרָדְתָּא

וּבְאִ֯ישְׁתָּא בָּנַיִן °ושורי אשכללו [°וְשׁוּרַיָּא שַׁכְלִלוּ ק] וְאֻשַּׁיָּא יַחִֽיטוּ: כְּעַן

יג יְדִיעַ לֶהֱוֵא לְמַלְכָּא דִּי הֵן קִרְיְתָא דָךְ תִּתְבְּנֵא וְשׁוּרַיָּה יִֽשְׁתַּכְלְלוּן מִנְדָּה־

יד בְלוֹ וַהֲלָךְ לָא יִנְתְּנוּן וְאַפְּתֹם מַלְכִים תְּהַנְזִק: כְּעַן כָּל־קֳבֵל דִּֽי־

    * יתיר א׳

3:11. Their words of praise are not recorded here (*Rashi; Metzudos*). Alternatively, the verse reads, 'They sang responsively with praise and thanksgiving: 'To HASHEM, for He is good, for His benevolence towards Israel is eternal' ' (*Malbim*).

3:12. Although the younger people justifiably rejoiced, the older ones were saddened, because the new Temple

was of lesser magnitude in comparison with the Temple of Solomon (*Haggai* 2:3).

4:1. The foreign tribes installed in Samaria by Sennacherib (see *II Kings* 17:24-41). These newcomers adopted a distorted version of the Jewish religion, sacrificing to the God of Israel as well as to their own idols.

4:2. Sennacherib's son and successor (*II Kings* 19:37).

[to praise Him], * *for His benevolence towards Israel is eternal. All the people burst into a great shout of praise to* HASHEM, *upon the laying of the foundation of the*

Joy and
grief

Temple of HASHEM. [12] *But many of the elder Kohanim, Levites and heads of families, who had beheld the First Temple on its foundation, wept loudly [when] this Temple was before their eyes;* * *while many [who had not seen the First Temple] raised their voices in shouting for joy.* [13] *The people did not notice the sound of the joyful shouting because of the sound of the people's weeping, although the people shouted with a great shout and the noise was heard from afar.*

4

The enemies
offer
assistance

[1] T*he enemies of Judah and Benjamin* * *heard that the people of the exile were building a Sanctuary for* HASHEM, *God of Israel.* [2] *They approached Zerubbabel and the heads of families and said to them, "Let us build with you, for, like you, we will seek your God; it is to Him that we have been sacrificing since the days of Esar-haddon,* * *king of Assyria, who brought us up here."*

[3] *But Zerubbabel, along with Jeshua and the rest of the family heads of Israel, said to them, "It is not for you together with us to build a Temple for our God; rather we, by ourselves, will build [it]* * *for* HASHEM, *God of Israel, as King Cyrus* *

Disruption

king of Persia has commanded us." [4] *Then, people of the land weakened the hands of the people of Judah and frightened them [from] building.* [5] *They hired advisers against them to disrupt their plans, all the days of Cyrus king of Persia, until the reign of Darius king of Persia.* [6] *During the reign of Ahasuerus, at the beginning of his reign, they wrote a calumny against the inhabitants of Judah and Jerusalem.*

[7] *In the days of Artaxerxes,* * *Mithredath-tabeel and the rest of his cohorts wrote a greeting to Artaxerxes king of Persia. The text of the letter was written in Aramaic script and in the Aramaic language.*

[8]* *Rehum the counselor and Shimshai the scribe wrote a letter concerning Jerusalem to King Artaxerxes, as we will state.* [9] *Then Rehum the spokesman and Shimshai the scribe and the rest of their cohorts — the Dinites, the Apharesattechites, the Tarpelites, the Apharesites, the Archevites, the Babylonians, the Shusanchites, the Dehites, the Elamites,* [10] *and the rest of the nations whom the great and venerated Asenappar* * *had exiled and settled in the cities of Samaria, along with the rest of the [residents of] the Trans-Euphrates region and [the city*

The
enemies'
letter to
King
Artaxerxes

of] Cheeneth — [wrote this letter]. [11] *This is the text of the letter that they dispatched to him, to King Artaxerxes:*

[From] your servants the people of the Trans-Euphrates region on this date: [12] *Let it be known to the king that the Jews who went up from you to us have arrived in Jerusalem. They are constructing a rebellious and villainous city; they have laid the foundations for the ramparts and are linking the walls.* [13] *Now let it be known to the king that should this city be built and the ramparts established they will no longer pay levy, tax and duty, and you will [thus] cause damage to the royal revenue.* [14] *Now, inasmuch as we are*

4:3. They suspected that the Samaritans would try to sabotage their work.

4:3-6. For the chronology of the kings, see note to 1:1. King Cyrus was the first to give permission to rebuild the Temple, and Ahasuerus revoked it.

4:7. Artaxerxes was Cyrus; Artaxerxes was a generic term for "king" in Persian, like "Pharaoh" in Egyptian

(Rosh Hashanah 3b).

4:8. The disputes, discussions and correspondence of the Jewish leaders, their gentile neighbors and the Persian monarch were carried out in Aramaic. Thus, from this verse through 6:18, the text uses that language instead of Hebrew.

4:10. King Sennacherib (Rashi etc.).

מְלַח הֵיכְלָא מְלַחְנָא וְעַרְוַת מַלְכָּא לָא אֲרִיךְ־לַנָא לְמֶחֱזֵא עַל־דְּנָה
שְׁלַחְנָא וְהוֹדַעְנָא לְמַלְכָּא: דִּי יְבַקַּר בִּסְפַר־דָּכְרָנַיָּא דִּי אֲבָהָתָךְ טו
וּתְהַשְׁכַּח בִּסְפַר דָּכְרָנַיָּא וְתִנְדַּע דִּי קִרְיְתָא דָךְ קִרְיָא מָרָדָא וּמְהַנְזִקַת
מַלְכִין וּמְדִנָן וְאֶשְׁתַּדּוּר עָבְדִין בְּגַוַּהּ מִן־יוֹמָת עָלְמָא עַל־דְּנָה קִרְיְתָא דָךְ
הָחָרְבַת: מְהוֹדְעִין אֲנַחְנָה לְמַלְכָּא דִּי הֵן קִרְיְתָא דָךְ תִּתְבְּנֵא וְשׁוּרַיָּה טז
יִשְׁתַּכְלְלוּן לָקֳבֵל דְּנָה חֲלָק בַּעֲבַר נַהֲרָא לָא אִיתַי לָךְ: פִּתְגָמָא יז
שְׁלַח מַלְכָּא עַל־רְחוּם בְּעֵל־טְעֵם וְשִׁמְשַׁי סָפְרָא וּשְׁאָר כְּנָוָתְהוֹן דִּי
יָתְבִין בְּשָׁמְרָיִן וּשְׁאָר עֲבַר־נַהֲרָה שְׁלָם וּכְעֶת: נִשְׁתְּוָנָא דִּי שְׁלַחְתּוּן יח
עֲלֶינָא מְפָרַשׁ קֱרִי קָדָמָי: וּמִנִּי שִׂים טְעֵם וּבַקַּרוּ וְהַשְׁכַּחוּ דִּי קִרְיְתָא דָךְ יט
מִן־יוֹמָת עָלְמָא עַל־מַלְכִין מִתְנַשְּׂאָה וּמְרַד וְאֶשְׁתַּדּוּר מִתְעֲבֶד־בַּהּ:
וּמַלְכִין תַּקִּיפִין הֲווֹ עַל־יְרוּשְׁלֶם וְשַׁלִּיטִין בְּכֹל עֲבַר נַהֲרָה וּמִדָּה בְלוֹ כ
וַהֲלָךְ מִתְיְהֵב לְהוֹן: כְּעַן שִׂימוּ טְעֵם לְבַטָּלָא גֻּבְרַיָּא אִלֵּךְ וְקִרְיְתָא דָךְ לָא כא
תִתְבְּנֵא עַד־מִנִּי טַעְמָא יִתְּשָׂם: וּזְהִירִין הֱווֹ שָׁלוּ לְמֶעְבַּד עַל־דְּנָה לְמָה כב
יִשְׂגֵּא חֲבָלָא לְהַנְזָקַת מַלְכִין: אֱדַיִן מִן־דִּי פַּרְשֶׁגֶן נִשְׁתְּוָנָא דִּי כג
אַרְתַּחְשַׁשְׂתְּא מַלְכָּא קֱרִי קֳדָם־רְחוּם וְשִׁמְשַׁי סָפְרָא וּכְנָוָתְהוֹן אֲזַלוּ
בִבְהִילוּ לִירוּשְׁלֶם עַל־יְהוּדָיֵא וּבַטִּלוּ הִמּוֹ בְּאֶדְרָע וְחָיִל: בֵּאדַיִן כד
בְּטֵלַת עֲבִידַת בֵּית־אֱלָהָא דִּי בִּירוּשְׁלֶם וַהֲוָת בָּטְלָא עַד שְׁנַת תַּרְתֵּין
לְמַלְכוּת דָּרְיָוֶשׁ מֶלֶךְ־פָּרָס:

ה וְהִתְנַבִּי חַגַּי נְבִיָּאה [°נְבִיָּא ק׳] וּזְכַרְיָה בַר־עִדּוֹא נְבִיַּאיָּא עַל־יְהוּדָיֵא דִּי א
בִיהוּד וּבִירוּשְׁלֶם בְּשֻׁם אֱלָהּ יִשְׂרָאֵל עֲלֵיהוֹן: בֵּאדַיִן קָמוּ זְרֻבָּבֶל בַּר־ ב
שְׁאַלְתִּיאֵל וְיֵשׁוּעַ בַּר־יוֹצָדָק וְשָׁרִיו לְמִבְנֵא בֵּית אֱלָהָא דִּי בִּירוּשְׁלֶם
וְעִמְּהוֹן נְבִיַּאיָּא דִי־אֱלָהָא מְסָעֲדִין לְהוֹן: בֵּהּ־זִמְנָא אֲתָא עֲלֵיהוֹן תַּתְּנַי פַּחַת עֲבַר־נַהֲרָה וּשְׁתַר בּוֹזְנַי וּכְנָוָתְהוֹן וְכֵן ג
אָמְרִין לְהֹם מַן־שָׂם לְכֹם טְעֵם בַּיְתָא דְנָה לִבְּנֵא וְאֻשַּׁרְנָא דְנָה לְשַׁכְלָלָה:
אֱדַיִן כְּנֵמָא אֲמַרְנָא לְהֹם מַן־אִנּוּן שְׁמָהָת גֻּבְרַיָּא דִּי־דְנָה בִנְיָנָא בָּנַיִן: ד
וְעֵין אֱלָהֲהֹם הֲוָת עַל־שָׂבֵי יְהוּדָיֵא וְלָא־בַטִּלוּ הִמּוֹ עַד־טַעְמָא לְדָרְיָוֶשׁ ה
יְהָךְ וֶאֱדַיִן יְתִיבוּן נִשְׁתְּוָנָא עַל־דְּנָה: פַּרְשֶׁגֶן אִגַּרְתָּא דִּי־שְׁלַח ו
תַּתְּנַי ׀ פַּחַת עֲבַר־נַהֲרָה וּשְׁתַר בּוֹזְנַי וּכְנָוָתֵהּ אֲפַרְסְכָיֵא דִּי בַּעֲבַר נַהֲרָה
עַל־דָּרְיָוֶשׁ מַלְכָּא: פִּתְגָמָא שְׁלַחוּ עֲלוֹהִי וְכִדְנָה כְּתִיב בְּגַוֵּהּ לְדָרְיָוֶשׁ ז
מַלְכָּא שְׁלָמָא כֹלָּא: יְדִיעַ ׀ לֶהֱוֵא לְמַלְכָּא דִּי־אֲזַלְנָא לִיהוּד מְדִינְתָּא ח
לְבֵית אֱלָהָא רַבָּא וְהוּא מִתְבְּנֵא אֶבֶן גְּלָל וְאָע מִתְּשָׂם בְּכֻתְלַיָּא
וַעֲבִידְתָּא דָךְ אָסְפַּרְנָא מִתְעַבְדָא וּמַצְלַח בְּיֶדְהֹם: אֱדַיִן שְׁאֵלְנָא לְשָׂבַיָּא ט

4:14. Alternatively, "of preserving the [king's] palace," i.e., we have the king's interest in mind.   **4:24.** A hiatus of eighteen years (*Seder Olam*).   **5:1.** At the end of the time period mentioned in the desirous of destroying the Sanctuary, * for it is not proper for us to witness the king's disgrace — therefore, we have dispatched and notified the king ¹⁵ that he should examine the book of records of his ancestors, and he will find in the book of records and become aware, that this city is a rebellious city, and damaging to kings and provinces, and they have made insurrection in it since ancient days; that is why this city was destroyed. ¹⁶ We notify the king that if this city is built and the foundations for its ramparts laid, in consequence of this you will have no part of the Trans-Euphrates region.

The king's reply ¹⁷ The king sent a message to Rehum the counselor and Shimshai the scribe and the rest of their cohorts living in Samaria and to the rest of the Trans-Euphrates region, [and the cities of] Shelam and Che[en]eth:

¹⁸ The letter that you dispatched to us has been read explicitly before me. ¹⁹ An order was given by me, and [my officials] investigated and discovered that this city has risen up against its kings since ancient days, and rebellion and insurrection have perpetrated in it. ²⁰ Mighty kings once reigned over Jerusalem, who ruled over all of the Trans-Euphrates region, and levy, tax and duty were paid to them. ²¹ Now, issue a decree to halt these people; this city shall not be built until a decree is issued by me. ²² Take care not to be remiss in doing this, why should destruction increase, to the harm of kings.

The Temple construction is halted ²³ Then, as soon as the text of King Artaxerxes' letter was read before Rehum, Shimshai the scribe and their cohorts, they went in haste to Jerusalem to the Jews and halted them with force and power.

²⁴ The work of the Temple of God in Jerusalem was thus halted, and remained halted until the second year of the reign of Darius king of Persia. *

5

(See Appendix A, timeline 5)

Haggai and Zechariah prophesy

¹ Haggai the prophet and Zechariah son of Iddo the prophets prophesied* to the Jews who were in Judah and in Jerusalem, in the name of the God of Israel, about them. ² Then Zerubbabel son of Shealtiel and Jeshua son of Jozadak arose and began to build the Temple of God that was in Jerusalem, and with them were the prophets of God, assisting them.

Tattenai investigates . . . ³ At that time, Tattenai, governor of the Trans-Euphrates region, approached them, along with Shethar-bozenai and their accomplices. They said this to them, "Who issued you a decree to construct this building and to lay the foundation for these ramparts?" ⁴ Then they said the following to them, "What are the names of the persons constructing this building?" ⁵ But the eye of their God watched over the elders of the Jews, and [Tattenai and his accomplices] did not halt them until the matter could be brought before Darius, when [Darius and his officials] would write a reply about it.

. . . and informs the king ⁶ [This is] the text of the letter which Tattenai, governor of the Trans-Euphrates region, along with Shethar-bozenai and his cohorts, the Apharesachites who were in the Trans-Euphrates region, sent to King Darius. ⁷ They sent a message to him, and this was written therein:

To King Darius, all peace! ⁸ Let it be known to the king that we have gone to the province of Judah, to the Temple of the great God; it is being built of marble stone, with wood reinforcing the walls. This work is proceeding rapidly and is succeeding in their hands. ⁹ Then we questioned these elders,

---

previous verse — during the second year of Darius — Haggai and Zechariah prophesied that the Jews should resume the building of the Temple, even in the absence of official permission.

אֱלָךְ כְּנֵמָא אֲמַרְנָא לְהֹם מַן־שָׂם לְכֹם טְעֵם בַּיְתָא דְנָה לְמִבְנְיָה וְאֻשַּׁרְנָא

דְנָה לְשַׁכְלָלָה: וְאַף שְׁמָהָתְהֹם שְׁאֵלְנָא לְּהֹם לְהוֹדָעוּתָךְ דִּי נִכְתֻּב שֻׁם ׳

גֻּבְרַיָּא דִּי בְרָאשֵׁיהֹם: וּכְנֵמָא פִתְגָמָא הֲתִיבוּנָא לְמֵמַר אֲנַחְנָא הִמּוֹ יא

עַבְדוֹהִי דִּי־אֱלָהּ שְׁמַיָּא וְאַרְעָא וּבָנַיִן בַּיְתָא דִּי־הֲוָא בְנֵה מִקַּדְמַת דְּנָה

שְׁנִין שַׂגִּיאָן וּמֶלֶךְ לְיִשְׂרָאֵל רַב בְּנָהִי וְשַׁכְלְלֵהּ: לָהֵן מִן־דִּי הַרְגִּזוּ יב

אֲבָהָתַנָא לֶאֱלָהּ שְׁמַיָּא יְהַב הִמּוֹ בְּיַד נְבוּכַדְנֶצַּר מֶלֶךְ־בָּבֶל °כַּסְדִּיא

[°כַּסְדָּאָה ק] וּבַיְתָה דְנָה סַתְרֵהּ וְעַמָּה הַגְלִי לְבָבֶל: בְּרַם בִּשְׁנַת יג

חֲדָה לְכוֹרֶשׁ מַלְכָּא דִּי בָבֶל כּוֹרֶשׁ מַלְכָּא שָׂם טְעֵם בֵּית־אֱלָהָא דְנָה

לְבְּנֵא: וְאַף מָאנַיָּא דִי־בֵית־אֱלָהָא דִּי דַהֲבָה וְכַסְפָּא דִּי נְבוּכַדְנֶצַּר הַנְפֵּק יד

מִן־הֵיכְלָא דִּי בִירוּשְׁלֶם וְהֵיבֵל הִמּוֹ לְהֵיכְלָא דִּי בָבֶל הַנְפֵּק הִמּוֹ כּוֹרֶשׁ

מַלְכָּא מִן־הֵיכְלָא דִּי בָבֶל וִיהִיבוּ לְשֵׁשְׁבַּצַּר שְׁמֵהּ דִּי פֶחָה שָׂמֵהּ: וַאֲמַר־ טו

לֵהּ ׀ °אלה [°אֵל ק] מָאנַיָּא שֵׂא אֵזֶל־אֲחֵת הִמּוֹ בְּהֵיכְלָא דִּי בִירוּשְׁלֶם

וּבֵית אֱלָהָא יִתְבְּנֵא עַל־אַתְרֵהּ:   אֱדַיִן שֵׁשְׁבַּצַּר דֵּךְ אֲתָא יְהַב טז

אֻשַּׁיָּא דִּי־בֵית אֱלָהָא דִּי בִירוּשְׁלֶם וּמִן־אֱדַיִן וְעַד־כְּעַן מִתְבְּנֵא וְלָא

שְׁלִם: וּכְעַן הֵן עַל־מַלְכָּא טָב יִתְבַּקַּר בְּבֵית גִּנְזַיָּא דִּי־מַלְכָּא תַמָּה דִּי יז

בְּבָבֶל הֵן אִיתַי דִּי־מִן־כּוֹרֶשׁ מַלְכָּא שִׂים טְעֵם לְמִבְנֵא בֵּית־אֱלָהָא דֵךְ

בִּירוּשְׁלֶם וּרְעוּת מַלְכָּא עַל־דְּנָה יִשְׁלַח עֲלֶינָא: בֵּאדַיִן דָּרְיָוֶשׁ ו א

מַלְכָּא שָׂם טְעֵם וּבַקַּרוּ ׀ בְּבֵית סָפְרַיָּא דִּי גִנְזַיָּא מְהַחֲתִין תַּמָּה בְּבָבֶל:

וְהִשְׁתְּכַח בְּאַחְמְתָא בְּבִירְתָא דִּי בְּמָדַי מְדִינְתָּה מְגִלָּה חֲדָה וְכֵן־כְּתִיב ב

בְּגַוַּהּ דִּכְרוֹנָה: בִּשְׁנַת חֲדָה לְכוֹרֶשׁ מַלְכָּא כּוֹרֶשׁ מַלְכָּא שָׂם ג

טְעֵם בֵּית־אֱלָהָא בִירוּשְׁלֶם בַּיְתָא יִתְבְּנֵא אֲתַר דִּי־דָבְחִין דִּבְחִין

וְאֻשּׁוֹהִי מְסוֹבְלִין רוּמֵהּ אַמִּין שִׁתִּין פְּתָיֵהּ אַמִּין שִׁתִּין: נִדְבָּכִין דִּי־אֶבֶן ד

גְּלָל תְּלָתָא וְנִדְבָּךְ דִּי־אָע חֲדַת וְנִפְקְתָא מִן־בֵּית מַלְכָּא תִּתְיְהִב: וְאַף ה

מָאנֵי בֵית־אֱלָהָא דִּי דַהֲבָה וְכַסְפָּא דִּי נְבוּכַדְנֶצַּר הַנְפֵּק מִן־הֵיכְלָא דִּי־

בִירוּשְׁלֶם וְהֵיבֵל לְבָבֶל יַהֲתִיבוּן וִיהָךְ לְהֵיכְלָא דִּי־בִירוּשְׁלֶם לְאַתְרֵהּ

וְתַחֵת בְּבֵית אֱלָהָא: כְּעַן תַּתְּנַי פַּחַת עֲבַר־נַהֲרָה שְׁתַר בּוֹזְנַי ו

וּכְנָוָתְהוֹן אֲפַרְסְכָיֵא דִּי בַּעֲבַר נַהֲרָה רַחִיקִין הֲווֹ מִן־תַּמָּה: שְׁבֻקוּ ז

לַעֲבִידַת בֵּית־אֱלָהָא דֵךְ פַּחַת יְהוּדָיֵא וּלְשָׂבֵי יְהוּדָיֵא בֵּית־אֱלָהָא דֵךְ

יִבְנוֹן עַל־אַתְרֵהּ: וּמִנִּי שִׂים טְעֵם לְמָא דִי־תַעַבְדוּן עִם־שָׂבֵי יְהוּדָיֵא אִלֵּךְ ח

לְמִבְנֵא בֵּית־אֱלָהָא דֵךְ וּמִנִּכְסֵי מַלְכָּא דִּי מִדַּת עֲבַר נַהֲרָה אָסְפַּרְנָא

נִפְקְתָא תֶּהֱוֵא מִתְיַהֲבָא לְגֻבְרַיָּא אִלֵּךְ דִּי־לָא לְבַטָּלָא: וּמָה חַשְׁחָן וּבְנֵי ט

תוֹרִין וְדִכְרִין וְאִמְּרִין ׀ לַעֲלָוָן ׀ לֶאֱלָהּ שְׁמַיָּא חִנְטִין מְלַח ׀ חֲמַר וּמְשַׁח

5:13-15. See Chapter 1.

6:6. Although this verse contains no introductory phrase, it is obviously not a continuation of the scroll text. Rather, it is Darius' reply to Tattenai.

saying thus to them: 'Who issued you a decree to construct this building and to lay the foundation for these ramparts?' ¹⁰ We also asked them for their names, in order to inform you, so that we could record the names of the men at their head. ¹¹ This is the answer they replied to us, saying: 'We are the servants of the God of heaven and earth, and we are rebuilding a Temple that had been built these many years ago; a great king of Israel built it and laid its foundation. ¹² However, because our ancestors had angered the God of heaven, He delivered them into the hand of Nebuchadnezzar king of Babylonia, the Chaldean, who destroyed this Temple and exiled the people to Babylonia. ¹³ However, * in the first year of Cyrus king of Babylonia, King Cyrus gave an order to have this Temple of God rebuilt. ¹⁴ In addition, the vessels of gold and silver of the Temple of God which Nebuchadnezzar had removed from the Sanctuary in Jerusalem and brought to the temple in Babylon, King Cyrus removed them from the temple in Babylon and they were given to the one named Sheshbazzar, whom he had appointed governor. ¹⁵ And he said to him, "Take these vessels and go and put them in the Sanctuary that is in Jerusalem, and let the Temple of God be built on its place." ¹⁶ Then this Sheshbazzar came and set in place the walls of the Temple of God which is in Jerusalem. From then until now it has been under construction, but has not been completed.' ¹⁷ And now, if it pleases the king, let a search be made of the royal archives that are there in Babylon if it is true that a decree was issued by King Cyrus to build this Temple of God in Jerusalem; and let the king convey to us his will in this matter.

6 ¹ Then King Darius issued a decree, and they searched in the library where the archives were stored in Babylonia. ² A scroll was discovered in a pouch in the palace in the province of Media, and this was the record that was written in it:

³ In the first year of King Cyrus, King Cyrus issued a decree [concerning] the Temple of God in Jerusalem: The Temple shall be built, a place for the offering of sacrifices, with its walls strongly founded, its height sixty cubits and its width sixty cubits. ⁴ [There shall be] three rows of marble and one row of new wood, with the expenses provided for by the royal palace. ⁵ Also, the golden and silver vessels of the Temple of God, which Nebuchadnezzar removed from the Sanctuary in Jerusalem and brought to Babylon, shall be returned and shall go to the Sanctuary that is in Jerusalem, to their place, and they shall be placed in the Temple of God.

⁶ *So now, Tattenai, governor of the Trans-Euphrates region, Shethar-bozenai and their cohorts, the Apharesachites of the Trans-Euphrates region — keep a distance from that place. ⁷ Leave the work of this Temple of God alone; the governor of the Jews and the elders of the Jews shall rebuild this Temple of God in its place. ⁸ A decree is hereby issued by me that you should cooperate with these elders of the Jews to rebuild this Temple of God; and the expenses should be provided immediately to these people from the royal estate, from the Trans-Euphrates Region's taxes, so that [their work] not be halted. ⁹ And whatever they require — young bulls, rams, and sheep for burnt-offerings to the God of heaven, wheat, salt, wine and oil,

Recollection of Cyrus' decree

The king's reply to Tattenai

The king's directive

כְּמֵאמַ֣ר כַּהֲנַיָּ֣א דִּֽי־בִירֽוּשְׁלֶ֗ם לֶֽהֱוֵ֨א מִתְיְהֵ֤ב לְהֹם֙ יֽוֹם ׀ בְּי֔וֹם דִּי־לָ֖א שָׁלֽוּ:

י דִּֽי־לֶהֱוֺ֧ן מְהַקְרְבִ֛ין נִיחוֹחִ֖ין לֶאֱלָ֣הּ שְׁמַיָּ֑א וּמְצַלַּ֕יִן לְחַיֵּ֥י מַלְכָּ֖א וּבְנֽוֹהִי:

יא וּמִנִּי֮ שִׂ֣ים טְעֵם֒ דִּ֣י כָל־אֱנָ֗שׁ דִּ֤י יְהַשְׁנֵא֙ פִּתְגָמָ֣א דְנָ֔ה יִתְנְסַ֥ח אָע֙ מִן־בַּיְתֵ֔הּ

יב וּזְקִ֖יף יִתְמְחֵ֣א עֲל֑וֹהִי וּבַיְתֵ֛הּ נְוָל֥וּ יִתְעֲבֵ֖ד עַל־דְּנָֽה: וֵֽאלָהָ֞א דִּ֣י שַׁכִּ֧ן שְׁמֵ֣הּ תַּמָּ֗ה יְמַגַּ֞ר כָּל־מֶ֤לֶךְ וְעַם֙ דִּ֣י ׀ יִשְׁלַ֣ח יְדֵ֗הּ לְהַשְׁנָיָ֛ה לְחַבָּלָ֛ה בֵּית־אֱלָהָ֥א

יג דֵ֖ךְ דִּ֣י בִירֽוּשְׁלֶ֑ם אֲנָ֤ה דָרְיָ֙וֶשׁ֙ שָׂ֣מֶת טְעֵ֔ם אָסְפַּ֥רְנָא יִתְעֲבִֽד: אֱדַ֡יִן תַּתְּנַ֣י פַּחַ֣ת עֲבַֽר־נַהֲרָ֗ה שְׁתַ֤ר בּֽוֹזְנַי֙ וּכְנָוָ֣תְה֔וֹן לָקֳבֵ֗ל דִּֽי־שְׁלַ֞ח דָּרְיָ֥וֶשׁ

יד מַלְכָּ֖א כְּנֵ֑מָא אָסְפַּ֥רְנָא עֲבַֽדוּ: וְשָׂבֵ֤י יְהוּדָיֵא֙ בָּנַ֣יִן וּמַצְלְחִ֔ין בִּנְבוּאַת֙ חַגַּ֣י °נְבִיאה [נְבִיָּ֔א ק] וּזְכַרְיָ֖ה בַּר־עִדּ֑וֹא וּבְנ֣וֹ וְשַׁכְלִ֗לוּ מִן־טַ֣עַם אֱלָ֣הּ

טו יִשְׂרָאֵ֔ל וּמִטְּעֵם֙ כּ֣וֹרֶשׁ וְדָרְיָ֔וֶשׁ וְאַרְתַּחְשַׁ֖שְׂתְּא מֶ֣לֶךְ פָּרָֽס: וְשֵׁיצִ֣יא בַּיְתָ֣ה דְנָ֔ה עַ֛ד י֥וֹם תְּלָתָ֖ה לִירַ֣ח אֲדָ֑ר דִּי־הִ֣יא שְׁנַת־שֵׁ֔ת לְמַלְכ֖וּת דָּרְיָ֥וֶשׁ

טז מַלְכָּֽא: וַעֲבַ֣דוּ בְנֵֽי־יִ֠שְׂרָאֵל כָּהֲנַיָּ֨א וְלֵוָיֵ֜א וּשְׁאָ֣ר בְּנֵֽי־גָלוּתָ֗א

יז חֲנֻכַּ֛ת בֵּית־אֱלָהָ֥א דְנָ֖ה בְּחֶדְוָֽה: וְהַקְרִ֗בוּ לַחֲנֻכַּת֙ בֵּית־אֱלָהָ֣א דְנָ֔ה תּוֹרִ֣ין מְאָ֗ה דִּכְרִ֤ין מָאתַ֙יִן֙ אִמְּרִ֣ין אַרְבַּ֣ע מְאָ֔ה וּצְפִירֵ֥י עִזִּ֖ין °לחטיא

יח [°לְחַטָּאָ֣ה ק] עַֽל־כָּל־יִשְׂרָאֵ֔ל תְּרֵֽי־עֲשַׂ֖ר לְמִנְיָ֥ן שִׁבְטֵ֥י יִשְׂרָאֵֽל: וַהֲקִ֨ימוּ כָהֲנַיָּ֜א בִּפְלֻגָּתְה֗וֹן וְלֵוָיֵא֙ בְּמַחְלְקָ֣תְה֔וֹן עַל־עֲבִידַ֥ת אֱלָהָ֖א דִּ֣י בִירֽוּשְׁלֶ֑ם

יט כִּכְתָ֖ב סְפַ֥ר מֹשֶֽׁה: וַיַּעֲשׂ֥וּ בְנֵי־הַגּוֹלָ֖ה אֶת־הַפָּ֑סַח בְּאַרְבָּעָ֥ה

כ עָשָׂ֛ר לַחֹ֖דֶשׁ הָרִאשֽׁוֹן: כִּ֣י הִֽטַּהֲר֞וּ הַכֹּהֲנִ֧ים וְהַלְוִיִּ֛ם כְּאֶחָ֖ד כֻּלָּ֣ם טְהוֹרִ֑ים

כא וַיִּשְׁחֲט֤וּ הַפֶּ֙סַח֙ לְכָל־בְּנֵ֣י הַגּוֹלָ֔ה וְלַאֲחֵיהֶ֥ם הַכֹּהֲנִ֖ים וְלָהֶֽם: וַיֹּאכְל֣וּ בְנֵֽי־יִשְׂרָאֵ֗ל הַשָּׁבִים֙ מֵהַגּוֹלָ֔ה וְכֹ֗ל הַנִּבְדָּ֛ל מִטֻּמְאַ֥ת גּוֹיֵֽי־הָאָ֖רֶץ אֲלֵהֶ֑ם לִדְרֹ֕שׁ

כב לַֽיהֹוָ֖ה אֱלֹהֵ֥י יִשְׂרָאֵֽל: וַיַּֽעֲשׂ֧וּ חַג־מַצּ֛וֹת שִׁבְעַ֥ת יָמִ֖ים בְּשִׂמְחָ֑ה כִּ֣י ׀ שִׂמְּחָ֣ם יְהֹוָ֗ה וְֽהֵסֵ֞ב לֵ֤ב מֶֽלֶךְ־אַשּׁוּר֙ עֲלֵיהֶ֔ם לְחַזֵּ֣ק יְדֵיהֶ֔ם בִּמְלֶ֥אכֶת בֵּית־

ז א הָאֱלֹהִ֖ים אֱלֹהֵ֥י יִשְׂרָאֵֽל: וְאַחַר֙ הַדְּבָרִ֣ים הָאֵ֔לֶּה בְּמַלְכ֖וּת

ב אַרְתַּחְשַׁ֣סְתְּא מֶֽלֶךְ־פָּרָ֑ס עֶזְרָא֙ בֶּן־שְׂרָיָ֔ה בֶּן־עֲזַרְיָ֖ה בֶּן־חִלְקִיָּֽה: בֶּן־

ג-ד שַׁלּ֥וּם בֶּן־צָד֖וֹק בֶּן־אֲחִיטֽוּב: בֶּן־אֲמַרְיָ֥ה בֶן־עֲזַרְיָ֖ה בֶּן־מְרָי֑וֹת: בֶּן־

ה זְרַֽחְיָ֥ה בֶן־עֻזִּ֖י בֶּן־בֻּקִּֽי: בֶּן־אֲבִישׁ֗וּעַ בֶּן־פִּֽינְחָס֙ בֶּן־אֶלְעָזָ֔ר בֶּן־אַהֲרֹ֖ן

ו הַכֹּהֵ֣ן הָרֹֽאשׁ: ה֤וּא עֶזְרָא֙ עָלָ֣ה מִבָּבֶ֔ל וְהֽוּא־סֹפֵ֤ר מָהִיר֙ בְּתוֹרַ֣ת מֹשֶׁ֔ה אֲשֶׁר־נָתַ֖ן יְהֹוָ֣ה אֱלֹהֵ֣י יִשְׂרָאֵ֑ל וַיִּתֶּן־ל֣וֹ הַמֶּ֗לֶךְ כְּיַד־יְהֹוָ֤ה אֱלֹהָיו֙ עָלָ֔יו כֹּ֖ל

ז בַּקָּשָׁתֽוֹ: וַיַּֽעֲל֣וּ מִבְּנֵֽי־יִ֠שְׂרָאֵל וּמִן־הַכֹּהֲנִ֨ים וְהַלְוִיִּ֜ם וְהַמְשֹׁרְרִ֧ים

ח וְהַשֹּׁעֲרִ֛ים וְהַנְּתִינִ֖ים אֶל־יְרוּשָׁלָ֑͏ִם בִּשְׁנַת־שֶׁ֖בַע לְאַרְתַּחְשַׁ֥סְתְּא הַמֶּֽלֶךְ:

ח-ט וַיָּבֹ֥א יְרוּשָׁלַ֖͏ִם בַּחֹ֣דֶשׁ הַחֲמִישִׁ֑י הִ֛יא שְׁנַ֥ת הַשְּׁבִיעִ֖ית לַמֶּֽלֶךְ: כִּ֣י בְּאֶחָד֩

6:19. The text here reverts to Hebrew.
On the fourteenth of Nissan, they resumed bringing the *pesach*-offering in the Temple (see *Exodus* 12:3-10; *Deuteronomy* 16:1-3).

6:21. I.e., those who had converted to Judaism (*Rashi*).

7:6. Literally, "hand." Darius granted every request that God commanded Ezra to make (*Rashi*).

7:7. See 2:43.

7:8. The month of Av.

according to the specifications of the Kohanim who are in Jerusalem — shall be supplied to them day by day, without fail, ¹⁰ so that they may offer pleasing offerings to the God of heaven and pray for the lives of the king and his children. ¹¹ And a decree is hereby issued by me that any person who will deviate from this matter shall have a beam torn out of his house, upon which he shall be hanged, and his house shall be designated a dunghill for this. ¹² And may the God Who has caused His Name to dwell there topple any king or people who may stretch out his hand to disobey [this decree], to damage this Temple of God that is in Jerusalem. I, Darius, have issued a decree; let it be implemented expeditiously!

¹³ Then Tattenai, governor of the Trans-Euphrates region, Shethar-bozenai and their cohorts, in consideration of King Darius' dispatch, acted expeditiously according to what was stated. ¹⁴ The elders of the Jews built and were *Successful* successful, through the prophecy of Haggai the prophet and Zechariah son of *construction* Iddo; they built and they established the foundations [of the Temple] by the decree of the God of Israel and by the decree of Cyrus, Darius and Artaxerxes king of Persia.

¹⁵ This Temple was completed by the third day of the month of Adar, during *The* the sixth year of the reign of King Darius. ¹⁶ The Children of Israel, the Kohanim *inauguration* and the Levites and the remainder of the people of the exile celebrated the *celebration* inauguration of this Temple of God with joy. ¹⁷ They offered for the inauguration of this Temple of God: one hundred bulls, two hundred rams and four hundred sheep, and twelve young goats as sin-offerings for all of Israel, corresponding to the number of the tribes of Israel. ¹⁸ They established the Kohanim in their groups and the Levites in their divisions for the service of God in Jerusalem, as written in the Book of Moses.

The pesach- ¹⁹ The people of the exile brought the pesach-offering on the fourteenth day of *offering* the first month. * ²⁰ For the Kohanim and the Levites had purified themselves as one; all of them were pure. They slaughtered the pesach-offering for all the people of the exile, and for their brethren the Kohanim, and for themselves. ²¹ The Children of Israel who had returned from the exile ate it, together with all those who had separated themselves from the defilement of the nations of the land to join them* and to seek HASHEM, God of Israel. ²² They celebrated the Festival of Matzos joyfully for a seven-day period, for HASHEM had brought them joy, for He turned the heart of the king of Assyria toward them, to strengthen their hands in the labor for the Temple of God, the God of Israel.

7

EZRA TAKES CHARGE

7:1-10:44

¹ After these things, during the reign of Artaxerxes king of Persia, Ezra son of Seraiah son of Azariah son of Hilkiah ² son of Shallum son of Zadok son of Ahitub ³ son of Amariah son of Azariah son of Meraioth ⁴ son of Zerahiah son of Uzzi son of Bukki ⁵ son of Abishua son of Phinehas son of Elazar son of Aaron, the first Kohen — ⁶ this Ezra ascended from Babylonia; he was a brilliant scholar of the Torah of Moses, which HASHEM, God of Israel, had given. The king granted him his every request, according to the command* of HASHEM, His God, to him. ⁷ And some of the Children of Israel and the Kohanim and the Levites, singers and gatekeepers, and the Nethinim, * ascended to Jerusalem during the seventh year of King Artaxerxes. ⁸ He arrived in Jerusalem in the fifth month* of the seventh year of the king. ⁹ For the first day

לַחֹדֶשׁ הָרִאשׁוֹן הוּא יְסֻד הַמַּעֲלָה מִבָּבֶל וּבְאֶחָד לַחֹדֶשׁ הַחֲמִישִׁי בָּא

ט   אֶל־יְרוּשָׁלִַם כְּיַד־אֱלֹהָיו הַטּוֹבָה עָלָיו: כִּי עֶזְרָא הֵכִין לְבָבוֹ לִדְרוֹשׁ

יא   אֶת־תּוֹרַת יְהוָה וְלַעֲשֹׂת וּלְלַמֵּד בְּיִשְׂרָאֵל חֹק וּמִשְׁפָּט: וְזֶה |

פַּרְשֶׁגֶן הַנִּשְׁתְּוָן אֲשֶׁר נָתַן הַמֶּלֶךְ אַרְתַּחְשַׁסְתְּא לְעֶזְרָא הַכֹּהֵן הַסֹּפֵר

יב   סֹפֵר דִּבְרֵי מִצְוֹת־יְהוָה וְחֻקָּיו עַל־יִשְׂרָאֵל: אַרְתַּחְשַׁסְתְּא

מֶלֶךְ מַלְכַיָּא לְעֶזְרָא כָהֲנָא סָפַר דָּתָא דִּי־אֱלָהּ שְׁמַיָּא גְּמִיר וּכְעֶנֶת:

יג   מִנִּי שִׂים טְעֵם דִּי כָל־מִתְנַדַּב בְּמַלְכוּתִי מִן־עַמָּה יִשְׂרָאֵל וְכָהֲנוֹהִי

יד   וְלֵוָיֵא לִמְהָךְ לִירוּשְׁלֶם עִמָּךְ יְהָךְ: כָּל־קֳבֵל דִּי מִן־קֳדָם מַלְכָּא וְשִׁבְעַת

יָעֲטֹהִי שְׁלִיחַ לְבַקָּרָא עַל־יְהוּד וְלִירוּשְׁלֶם בְּדָת אֱלָהָךְ דִּי בִידָךְ:

טו   וּלְהֵיבָלָה כְּסַף וּדְהַב דִּי־מַלְכָּא וְיָעֲטוֹהִי הִתְנַדַּבוּ לֶאֱלָהּ יִשְׂרָאֵל דִּי

טז   בִירוּשְׁלֶם מִשְׁכְּנֵהּ: וְכֹל כְּסַף וּדְהַב דִּי תְהַשְׁכַּח בְּכֹל מְדִינַת בָּבֶל עִם

הִתְנַדָּבוּת עַמָּא וְכָהֲנַיָּא מִתְנַדְּבִין לְבֵית אֱלָהֲהֹם דִּי בִירוּשְׁלֶם: כָּל־קֳבֵל

יז   דְּנָה אָסְפַּרְנָא תִקְנֵא בְּכַסְפָּא דְנָה תּוֹרִין | דִּכְרִין אִמְּרִין וּמִנְחָתְהוֹן

וְנִסְכֵּיהוֹן וּתְקָרֵב הִמּוֹ עַל־מַדְבְּחָה דִּי בֵּית אֱלָהֲכֹם דִּי בִירוּשְׁלֶם: וּמָה

יח   דִי °עֲלָיִךְ [°עֲלָךְ ק] וְעַל־°אֶחָיִךְ [°אֶחָךְ ק] יֵיטַב בִּשְׁאָר כַּסְפָּא וְדַהֲבָה

לְמֶעְבַּד כִּרְעוּת אֱלָהֲכֹם תַּעַבְדוּן: וּמָאנַיָּא דִּי־מִתְיַהֲבִין לָךְ לְפָלְחָן

יט   בֵּית אֱלָהָךְ הַשְׁלֵם קֳדָם אֱלָהּ יְרוּשְׁלֶם: וּשְׁאָר חַשְׁחוּת בֵּית אֱלָהָךְ דִּי

כ   יִפֶּל־לָךְ לְמִנְתַּן תִּנְתֵּן מִן־בֵּית גִּנְזֵי מַלְכָּא: וּמִנִּי אֲנָה אַרְתַּחְשַׁסְתְּא

כא   מַלְכָּא שִׂים טְעֵם לְכֹל גִּזַּבְרַיָּא דִּי בַּעֲבַר נַהֲרָה דִּי כָל־דִּי יִשְׁאֲלֶנְכוֹן

עֶזְרָא כָהֲנָא סָפַר דָּתָא דִּי־אֱלָהּ שְׁמַיָּא אָסְפַּרְנָא יִתְעֲבִד: עַד־כְּסַף

כב   כַּכְּרִין מְאָה וְעַד־חִנְטִין כֹּרִין מְאָה וְעַד־חֲמַר בַּתִּין מְאָה וְעַד־בַּתִּין

מְשַׁח מְאָה וּמְלַח דִּי־לָא כְתָב: כָּל־דִּי מִן־טַעַם אֱלָהּ שְׁמַיָּא יִתְעֲבֵד

כג   אַדְרַזְדָּא לְבֵית אֱלָהּ שְׁמַיָּא דִּי־לְמָה לֶהֱוֵא קְצַף עַל־מַלְכוּת מַלְכָּא

כד   וּבְנוֹהִי: וּלְכֹם מְהוֹדְעִין דִּי כָל־כָּהֲנַיָּא וְלֵוָיֵא זַמָּרַיָּא תָרָעַיָּא נְתִינַיָּא

וּפָלְחֵי בֵּית אֱלָהָא דְנָה מִנְדָּה בְלוֹ וַהֲלָךְ לָא שַׁלִּיט לְמִרְמֵא עֲלֵיהֹם:

כה   וְאַנְתְּ עֶזְרָא כְּחָכְמַת אֱלָהָךְ דִּי־בִידָךְ מֶנִּי שָׁפְטִין וְדַיָּנִין דִּי־לֶהֱוֹן °דָּאנִין

[°דָּאיְנִין ק] לְכָל־עַמָּה דִּי בַּעֲבַר נַהֲרָה לְכָל־יָדְעֵי דָּתֵי אֱלָהָךְ וְדִי לָא

כו   יָדַע תְּהוֹדְעוּן: וְכָל־דִּי־לָא לֶהֱוֵא עָבֵד דָּתָא דִי־אֱלָהָךְ וְדָתָא דִּי מַלְכָּא

אָסְפַּרְנָא דִּינָה לֶהֱוֵא מִתְעֲבֵד מִנֵּהּ הֵן לְמוֹת הֵן °לִשְׁרֹשִׁו [°לִשְׁרֹשִׁי ק]

כז   הֵן לַעֲנָשׁ נִכְסִין וְלֶאֱסוּרִין: בָּרוּךְ יְהוָה אֱלֹהֵי אֲבֹתֵינוּ

אֲשֶׁר נָתַן כָּזֹאת בְּלֵב הַמֶּלֶךְ לְפָאֵר אֶת־בֵּית יְהוָה אֲשֶׁר בִּירוּשָׁלִָם:

כח   וְעָלַי הִטָּה־חֶסֶד לִפְנֵי הַמֶּלֶךְ וְיוֹעֲצָיו וּלְכָל־שָׂרֵי הַמֶּלֶךְ הַגִּבֹּרִים

7:9. The month of Nissan.

7:12. The text again turns to Aramaic in recording the king's letter.

7:16. From donations.

7:22. The *kor* and the *bath* are measures of volume.

7:25. The judges you appoint should be well versed in your laws, either from previous knowledge or from instruction that you will provide for them.

of the first month* was the beginning of the ascent from Babylonia, and on the first day of the fifth month he arrived in Jerusalem, by the benevolence of the hand of his God upon him. ¹⁰ For Ezra set his heart to expound the Torah of HASHEM and to fulfill and to teach [its] statute and law in Israel.

The king's letter ¹¹ This is the text of the letter that King Artaxerxes gave to Ezra the Kohen, the scholar of the commandments of HASHEM and His statutes to Israel:

¹² *Artaxerxes, king of kings, to Ezra the Kohen, scholar of the Law of the *Permission to return* God of heaven and master of it, on this date: ¹³ A decree is hereby issued by me that anyone in my kingdom among the people of Israel and their Kohanim and the Levites who volunteers to journey to Jerusalem with you may go. ¹⁴ Because you have been dispatched by the king and his seven counselors to investigate Judah and Jerusalem concerning the Torah of *Contributions for the Temple* your God, which is in your hand, ¹⁵ and to transport the silver and gold that the king and his counselors have contributed to the God of Israel, whose dwelling place is in Jerusalem, ¹⁶ and all the silver and gold that you may find* in the entire province of Babylonia, together with contributions that the people and the Kohanim contribute to the Temple of their God that is in Jerusalem — ¹⁷ by means of this you shall immediately purchase with this money bulls, rams, sheep, and their meal-offerings and their libations, and offer them on the Altar of the Temple of your God that is in Jerusalem. ¹⁸ You may do with the remaining silver and gold whatever seems proper to you and your brethren, [and is] in accordance with the will of your God, you may do. ¹⁹ Furthermore, deliver the vessels that were given to you for the service *The king finances the Temple services* of the Temple of your God before God in Jerusalem. ²⁰ And any other needs of the Temple of your God that may arise for you to provide, you may provide from the king's treasury. ²¹ Furthermore, a decree is hereby issued by me — I, King Artaxerxes — to all the treasurers in the Trans-Euphrates region, that whatever Ezra the Kohen, scholar of the Law of the God of heaven, shall request of you, shall be granted expeditiously, ²² up to one hundred talents of silver, up to one hundred kors* of wheat, up to one hundred baths* of wine, up to one hundred baths of oil and unlimited salt. ²³ Whatever is decreed by the God of Heaven shall be done by the [king's] seal for the Temple of God; lest [His] rage befall the king's realm and his *Temple personnel exempted from taxes* children. ²⁴ We also declare to you that concerning all the Kohanim and the Levites, the singers and gatekeepers, the Nethinim and whoever serves in this Temple of God — it shall not be lawful to impose upon them any levy, tax or duty. ²⁵ And you, Ezra, in accordance with the Divine wisdom that *Enforcement of Torah law* you possess, shall appoint judges and magistrates who will judge all the people who are in the Trans-Euphrates region; [appoint] men who know the Law of your God, or teach those who do not know.* ²⁶ Anyone who does not fulfill the Law of your God and the law of the king, judgment shall be swiftly executed against him, whether to be put to death or to be uprooted or to be punished with loss of property or with imprisonment.

²⁷ "Blessed is HASHEM,* God of our forefathers, Who has put such [thoughts] *Ezra's* in the heart of the king, to glorify the Temple of HASHEM that is in Jerusalem, *thanksgiving* ²⁸ Who extended kindness to me from before the king and his counselors and all *praise* of the king's powerful officers!"

7:27. Once again the text reverts to Hebrew. Ezra thanked God for causing the king to give such unstinting support to him and to the holy work in Jerusalem.

וַאֲנִי הִתְחַזַּקְתִּי כְּיַד־יְהֹוָה אֱלֹהַי עָלָי וָאֶקְבְּצָה מִיִּשְׂרָאֵל רָאשִׁים לַעֲלוֹת
עִמִּי:

ח א וְאֵלֶּה רָאשֵׁי אֲבֹתֵיהֶם וְהִתְיַחְשָׂם הָעֹלִים עִמִּי בְּמַלְכוּת אַרְתַּחְשַׁסְתְּא
ב הַמֶּלֶךְ מִבָּבֶל: מִבְּנֵי פִינְחָס גֵּרְשֹׁם מִבְּנֵי אִיתָמָר דָּנִיֵּאל מִבְּנֵי דָוִיד חַטּוּשׁ:
ג מִבְּנֵי שְׁכַנְיָה מִבְּנֵי פַרְעֹשׁ זְכַרְיָה וְעִמּוֹ הִתְיַחֵשׂ לִזְכָרִים מֵאָה וַחֲמִשִּׁים:
ד-ה מִבְּנֵי פַחַת מוֹאָב אֶלְיְהוֹעֵינַי בֶּן־זְרַחְיָה וְעִמּוֹ מָאתַיִם הַזְּכָרִים: מִבְּנֵי
ו שְׁכַנְיָה בֶּן־יַחֲזִיאֵל וְעִמּוֹ שְׁלֹשׁ מֵאוֹת הַזְּכָרִים: וּמִבְּנֵי עָדִין עֶבֶד בֶּן־יוֹנָתָן
ז וְעִמּוֹ חֲמִשִּׁים הַזְּכָרִים: וּמִבְּנֵי עֵילָם יְשַׁעְיָה בֶּן־עֲתַלְיָה וְעִמּוֹ שִׁבְעִים
ח-ט הַזְּכָרִים: וּמִבְּנֵי שְׁפַטְיָה זְבַדְיָה בֶּן־מִיכָאֵל וְעִמּוֹ שְׁמֹנִים הַזְּכָרִים: מִבְּנֵי
י יוֹאָב עֹבַדְיָה בֶּן־יְחִיאֵל וְעִמּוֹ מָאתַיִם וּשְׁמֹנָה עָשָׂר הַזְּכָרִים: וּמִבְּנֵי
יא שְׁלוֹמִית בֶּן־יוֹסִפְיָה וְעִמּוֹ מֵאָה וְשִׁשִּׁים הַזְּכָרִים: וּמִבְּנֵי בֵבַי זְכַרְיָה בֶּן־
יב בֵּבַי וְעִמּוֹ עֶשְׂרִים וּשְׁמֹנָה הַזְּכָרִים: וּמִבְּנֵי עַזְגָּד יוֹחָנָן בֶּן־הַקָּטָן וְעִמּוֹ
יג מֵאָה וַעֲשָׂרָה הַזְּכָרִים: וּמִבְּנֵי אֲדֹנִיקָם אַחֲרֹנִים וְאֵלֶּה שְׁמוֹתָם אֱלִיפֶלֶט
יד יְעִיאֵל וּשְׁמַעְיָה וְעִמָּהֶם שִׁשִּׁים הַזְּכָרִים: וּמִבְּנֵי בִגְוַי עוּתַי °וְזָבוּד
[°וְזַכּוּר ק] וְעִמּוֹ שִׁבְעִים הַזְּכָרִים:

טו וָאֶקְבְּצֵם אֶל־הַנָּהָר הַבָּא אֶל־אַהֲוָא וַנַּחֲנֶה שָׁם יָמִים שְׁלֹשָׁה וָאָבִינָה
טז בָעָם וּבַכֹּהֲנִים וּמִבְּנֵי לֵוִי לֹא־מָצָאתִי שָׁם: וָאֶשְׁלְחָה לֶאֱלִיעֶזֶר לַאֲרִיאֵל
לִשְׁמַעְיָה וּלְאֶלְנָתָן וּלְיָרִיב וּלְאֶלְנָתָן וּלְנָתָן וְלִזְכַרְיָה וְלִמְשֻׁלָּם רָאשִׁים
יז וּלְיוֹיָרִיב וּלְאֶלְנָתָן מְבִינִים: °וָאוֹצִאָה [°וָאֲצַוֶּה ק] אוֹתָם עַל־אִדּוֹ הָרֹאשׁ
בְּכָסִפְיָא הַמָּקוֹם וָאָשִׂימָה בְּפִיהֶם דְּבָרִים לְדַבֵּר אֶל־אִדּוֹ אָחִיו °הַנְּתוּנִים
[°הַנְּתִינִים ק] בְּכָסִפְיָא הַמָּקוֹם לְהָבִיא־לָנוּ מְשָׁרְתִים לְבֵית אֱלֹהֵינוּ:
יח וַיָּבִיאוּ לָנוּ כְּיַד־אֱלֹהֵינוּ הַטּוֹבָה עָלֵינוּ אִישׁ שֶׂכֶל מִבְּנֵי מַחְלִי בֶּן־לֵוִי בֶּן־
יט יִשְׂרָאֵל וְשֵׁרֵבְיָה וּבָנָיו וְאֶחָיו שְׁמֹנָה עָשָׂר: וְאֶת־חֲשַׁבְיָה וְאִתּוֹ יְשַׁעְיָה
כ מִבְּנֵי מְרָרִי אֶחָיו וּבְנֵיהֶם עֶשְׂרִים: וּמִן־הַנְּתִינִים שֶׁנָּתַן דָּוִיד
וְהַשָּׂרִים לַעֲבֹדַת הַלְוִיִּם נְתִינִים מָאתַיִם וְעֶשְׂרִים כֻּלָּם נִקְּבוּ בְשֵׁמוֹת:
כא וָאֶקְרָא שָׁם צוֹם עַל־הַנָּהָר אַהֲוָא לְהִתְעַנּוֹת לִפְנֵי אֱלֹהֵינוּ לְבַקֵּשׁ מִמֶּנּוּ
כב דֶּרֶךְ יְשָׁרָה לָנוּ וּלְטַפֵּנוּ וּלְכָל־רְכוּשֵׁנוּ: כִּי בֹשְׁתִּי לִשְׁאוֹל מִן־הַמֶּלֶךְ חַיִל
וּפָרָשִׁים לְעָזְרֵנוּ מֵאוֹיֵב בַּדָּרֶךְ כִּי־אָמַרְנוּ לַמֶּלֶךְ לֵאמֹר יַד־אֱלֹהֵינוּ עַל־
כג כָּל־מְבַקְשָׁיו לְטוֹבָה וְעֻזּוֹ וְאַפּוֹ עַל כָּל־עֹזְבָיו: וַנָּצוּמָה וַנְּבַקְשָׁה מֵאֱלֹהֵינוּ
כד עַל־זֹאת וַיֵּעָתֵר לָנוּ: וָאַבְדִּילָה מִשָּׂרֵי הַכֹּהֲנִים שְׁנֵים עָשָׂר לְשֵׁרֵבְיָה
כה חֲשַׁבְיָה וְעִמָּהֶם מֵאֲחֵיהֶם עֲשָׂרָה: °וָאֶשְׁקוֹלָה [°וָאֶשְׁקֲלָה ק] לָהֶם אֶת־
הַכֶּסֶף וְאֶת־הַזָּהָב וְאֶת־הַכֵּלִים תְּרוּמַת בֵּית־אֱלֹהֵינוּ הַהֵרִימוּ הַמֶּלֶךְ

8:4. See 2:6.

8:16. Ezra wanted them to help find Levites and Nethinim who would join him in the journey to the Land of Israel.

8:17. The town of Casiphia, as opposed to the province of the same name (*Malbim*).

I then strengthened myself, in accordance with whatever the hand of HASHEM, my God, gave me the ability to do, and I assembled leaders from Israel to ascend with me.

8

The family heads

¹ **T**hese are the heads of families and the genealogies of those who ascended *with me from Babylon during the reign of King Artaxerxes:* ² *Of the sons of Phinehas — Gershom; of the sons of Ithamar — Daniel; of the sons of David — Hattush;* ³ *of the sons of Shecaniah, of the sons of Pharosh — Zechariah, and with him one hundred fifty males traced their lineage;* ⁴ *of the sons of the Governor of Moab* — Eliehoenai son of Zerahiah, and with him two hundred males;* ⁵ *of the sons of Shecaniah — the son of Jahaziel, and with him three hundred males;* ⁶ *of the sons of Adin — Ebed son of Jonathan, and with him fifty males;* ⁷ *of the sons of Elam — Jeshaiah son of Athaliah, and with him seventy males;* ⁸ *of the sons of Shephatiah — Zebadiah son of Michael, and with him eighty males;* ⁹ *of the sons of Joab — Obadiah son of Jehiel, and with him two hundred eighteen males;* ¹⁰ *of the sons of Shelomith — the son of Josiphiah, and with him one hundred sixty males;* ¹¹ *of the sons of Bebai — Zechariah son of Bebai, and with him twenty-eight males;* ¹² *of the sons of Azgad — Johanan the son of Hakkatan, and with him one hundred ten males;* ¹³ *of the sons of Adonikam, the last ones, and these were their names — Eliphelet, Jeiel and Shemaiah, and with them sixty males;* ¹⁴ *and of the sons of Bigvai — Uthai and Zaccur, and with him seventy males.*

The missing Levites

¹⁵ *I assembled them at the flowing river, at the Ahava, and we encamped there for three days. I then scrutinized the people and the Kohanim, but I could find no Levites there.* ¹⁶ *So I dispatched the leaders* Eliezer, Ariel, Shemaiah, Elnathan, Jarib, Elnathan, Nathan, Zechariah and Meshullam, and the sages Joiarib and Elnathan.* ¹⁷ *I directed them to the leader Iddo, in the place* Casiphia, and I gave them a message to convey to Iddo [and] his brother, who were settled in the place* Casiphia, to bring us ministers for the*

The Levites

Temple of our God. ¹⁸ *By the benevolence of the hand of our God to us, they brought to us a wise man of the descendants of Mahli [grand]son of Levi son of Israel; and Sherebiah and eighteen of his sons and kinsmen;* ¹⁹ *and Hashabiah, and with him Isaiah of the sons of Merari, and twenty of his kinsmen and their sons;* ²⁰ *and of the Nethinim, whom David and his officers had designated for the service of the Levites,* two hundred twenty Nethinim, all of them designated by name.*

Ezra's fast

²¹ *I proclaimed a fast [there], on the River Ahava, to afflict ourselves before our God and beseech Him for favorable passage for us, for our young children and for all our possessions.* ²² *For I was embarrassed to request troops and horsemen of the king to assist us against an adversary along the way, since we had told the king that the hand of our God is benevolent to all who seek Him, and His might and anger befall all who forsake Him.* ²³ *So we fasted and beseeched our God for this, and He granted our prayers.* ²⁴ *I then set aside*

Guardians for the valuables

twelve of the chiefs of the Kohanim: Sherebiah, Hashabiah and ten of their brethren with them. ²⁵ *I weighed out to them the silver and the gold and the vessels — contributions for the Temple of our God that were donated by the king*

8:20. Originally, Joshua had set the Gibeonites up as servants (*Joshua* 9:21), and David confirmed and ex-   tended this status (see *Yevamos* 79a).

כו וָיַּעֲצָיו וְשָׂרָיו וְכָל־יִשְׂרָאֵל הַנִּמְצָאִים: וָאֶשְׁקֲלָה עַל־יָדָם כֶּסֶף כִּכָּרִים
כז שֵׁשׁ־מֵאוֹת וַחֲמִשִּׁים וּכְלֵי־כֶסֶף מֵאָה לְכִכָּרִים זָהָב מֵאָה כִכָּר: וּכְפֹרֵי זָהָב
עֶשְׂרִים לַאֲדַרְכֹנִים אָלֶף וּכְלֵי נְחֹשֶׁת מֻצְהָב טוֹבָה שְׁנַיִם חֲמוּדֹת כַּזָּהָב:
כח וָאֹמְרָה אֲלֵהֶם אַתֶּם קֹדֶשׁ לַיהוָה וְהַכֵּלִים קֹדֶשׁ וְהַכֶּסֶף וְהַזָּהָב נְדָבָה
כט לַיהוָה אֱלֹהֵי אֲבֹתֵיכֶם: שִׁקְדוּ וְשִׁמְרוּ עַד־תִּשְׁקְלוּ לִפְנֵי שָׂרֵי הַכֹּהֲנִים
ל וְהַלְוִיִּם וְשָׂרֵי־הָאָבוֹת לְיִשְׂרָאֵל בִּירוּשָׁלִָם הַלִּשְׁכוֹת בֵּית יְהוָה: וְקִבְּלוּ
הַכֹּהֲנִים וְהַלְוִיִּם מִשְׁקַל הַכֶּסֶף וְהַזָּהָב וְהַכֵּלִים לְהָבִיא לִירוּשָׁלִַם לְבֵית
לא אֱלֹהֵינוּ:   וַנִּסְעָה מִנְּהַר אַהֲוָא בִּשְׁנֵים עָשָׂר לַחֹדֶשׁ הָרִאשׁוֹן לָלֶכֶת
יְרוּשָׁלִָם וְיַד־אֱלֹהֵינוּ הָיְתָה עָלֵינוּ וַיַּצִּילֵנוּ מִכַּף אוֹיֵב וְאוֹרֵב עַל־הַדָּרֶךְ:
לב-לג וַנָּבוֹא יְרוּשָׁלִָם וַנֵּשֶׁב שָׁם יָמִים שְׁלֹשָׁה: וּבַיּוֹם הָרְבִיעִי נִשְׁקַל הַכֶּסֶף וְהַזָּהָב
וְהַכֵּלִים בְּבֵית אֱלֹהֵינוּ עַל יַד־מְרֵמוֹת בֶּן־אוּרִיָּה הַכֹּהֵן וְעִמּוֹ אֶלְעָזָר בֶּן־
לד פִּינְחָס וְעִמָּהֶם יוֹזָבָד בֶּן־יֵשׁוּעַ וְנוֹעַדְיָה בֶן־בִּנּוּי הַלְוִיִּם: בְּמִסְפָּר בְּמִשְׁקָל
לה לַכֹּל וַיִּכָּתֵב כָּל־הַמִּשְׁקָל בָּעֵת הַהִיא: הַבָּאִים מֵהַשְּׁבִי בְנֵי־
הַגּוֹלָה הִקְרִיבוּ עֹלוֹת ׀ לֵאלֹהֵי יִשְׂרָאֵל פָּרִים שְׁנֵים־עָשָׂר עַל־כָּל־יִשְׂרָאֵל
אֵילִים ׀ תִּשְׁעִים וְשִׁשָּׁה כְּבָשִׂים שִׁבְעִים וְשִׁבְעָה צְפִירֵי חַטָּאת שְׁנֵים עָשָׂר
לו הַכֹּל עוֹלָה לַיהוָה: וַיִּתְּנוּ ׀ אֶת־דָּתֵי הַמֶּלֶךְ לַאֲחַשְׁדַּרְפְּנֵי הַמֶּלֶךְ וּפַחֲווֹת
עֵבֶר הַנָּהָר וְנִשְּׂאוּ אֶת־הָעָם וְאֶת־בֵּית־הָאֱלֹהִים:

ט

א וּכְכַלּוֹת אֵלֶּה נִגְּשׁוּ אֵלַי הַשָּׂרִים לֵאמֹר לֹא־נִבְדְּלוּ הָעָם יִשְׂרָאֵל וְהַכֹּהֲנִים וְהַלְוִיִּם
מֵעַמֵּי הָאֲרָצוֹת כְּתוֹעֲבֹתֵיהֶם לַכְּנַעֲנִי הַחִתִּי הַפְּרִזִּי הַיְבוּסִי הָעַמֹּנִי
ב הַמֹּאָבִי הַמִּצְרִי וְהָאֱמֹרִי: כִּי־נָשְׂאוּ מִבְּנֹתֵיהֶם לָהֶם וְלִבְנֵיהֶם וְהִתְעָרְבוּ
זֶרַע הַקֹּדֶשׁ בְּעַמֵּי הָאֲרָצוֹת וְיַד הַשָּׂרִים וְהַסְּגָנִים הָיְתָה בַּמַּעַל הַזֶּה
ג רִאשׁוֹנָה: וּכְשָׁמְעִי אֶת־הַדָּבָר הַזֶּה קָרַעְתִּי אֶת־בִּגְדִי וּמְעִילִי וָאֶמְרְטָה
ד מִשְּׂעַר רֹאשִׁי וּזְקָנִי וָאֵשְׁבָה מְשׁוֹמֵם: וְאֵלַי יֵאָסְפוּ כֹּל חָרֵד בְּדִבְרֵי אֱלֹהֵי־
ה יִשְׂרָאֵל עַל מַעַל הַגּוֹלָה וַאֲנִי יֹשֵׁב מְשׁוֹמֵם עַד לְמִנְחַת הָעָרֶב: וּבְמִנְחַת
הָעֶרֶב קַמְתִּי מִתַּעֲנִיתִי וּבְקָרְעִי בִגְדִי וּמְעִילִי וָאֶכְרְעָה עַל־בִּרְכַּי
ו וָאֶפְרְשָׂה כַפַּי אֶל־יהוה אֱלֹהָי: וָאֹמְרָה אֱלֹהַי בֹּשְׁתִּי וְנִכְלַמְתִּי לְהָרִים
אֱלֹהַי פָּנַי אֵלֶיךָ כִּי עֲוֹנֹתֵינוּ רָבוּ לְמַעְלָה רֹּאשׁ וְאַשְׁמָתֵנוּ גָדְלָה עַד
ז לַשָּׁמָיִם: מִימֵי אֲבֹתֵינוּ אֲנַחְנוּ בְּאַשְׁמָה גְדֹלָה עַד הַיּוֹם הַזֶּה וּבַעֲוֹנֹתֵינוּ
נִתַּנּוּ אֲנַחְנוּ מְלָכֵינוּ כֹהֲנֵינוּ בְּיַד ׀ מַלְכֵי הָאֲרָצוֹת בַּחֶרֶב בַּשְּׁבִי
ח וּבַבִּזָּה וּבְבֹשֶׁת פָּנִים כְּהַיּוֹם הַזֶּה: וְעַתָּה כִּמְעַט־רֶגַע הָיְתָה תְחִנָּה מֵאֵת ׀
יהוה אֱלֹהֵינוּ לְהַשְׁאִיר לָנוּ פְּלֵיטָה וְלָתֶת־לָנוּ יָתֵד בִּמְקוֹם קָדְשׁוֹ
ט לְהָאִיר עֵינֵינוּ אֱלֹהֵינוּ וּלְתִתֵּנוּ מִחְיָה מְעַט בְּעַבְדֻתֵנוּ: כִּי־עֲבָדִים אֲנַחְנוּ

9:1. These are the ranking Jewish officials, not the foreign officers of the preceding verse or the lower echelon functionaries of the next verse.

9:9. We are still totally subservient to the powers in Persia.

and his counselors and his officers and all of Israel who were present. ²⁶ I weighed out into their hand six hundred fifty talents of silver; one hundred silver vessels, each a talent; one hundred talents of gold; ²⁷ twenty golden bowls, weighing one thousand darkons; and two vessels of fine golden-colored copper, as splendid as gold. ²⁸ I said to them, "You are sacred to HASHEM, and the vessels are sacred; and the silver and the gold are contributions to HASHEM, God of your forefathers. ²⁹ Be diligent and guard [them] until you weigh [them over] before the chiefs of the Kohanim and Levites and the heads of the families of Israel in Jerusalem for the chambers of the Temple of HASHEM." ³⁰ The Kohanim and the Levites thus accepted the weight of the silver and the gold and the vessels, to bring to Jerusalem for the Temple of God.

³¹ We departed from the River Ahava on the twelfth of the first month to go to Jerusalem; and the hand of our God assisted us, and He saved us from the hand of [any] enemy and ambush along the way. ³² We arrived in Jerusalem, and

The remained there for three days. ³³ On the fourth day, the silver and the gold and the
valuables vessels were weighed over at the Temple of our God by the hand of Meremoth son
delivered of Uriah the Kohen, along with Elazar son of Phinehas, and with them Jozabad
and weighed son of Jeshua and Noadiah son of Binnui, the Levites, ³⁴ with a count and with
a weight for everything; and all the weight was recorded at that time.

Burnt- ³⁵ The people of the exile returning from the captivity brought as burnt-offerings
offerings to the God of Israel, twelve bulls for all [the tribes of] Israel, ninety-six rams,
seventy-seven sheep; twelve goats as sin-offerings; brought up [on the Altar] in
The royal their entirety as offerings to HASHEM. ³⁶ They delivered the royal decrees to the
decrees king's satraps and the governors of the Trans-Euphrates region, who then showed
transmitted respect for the people and the Temple of God.

9 ¹ When these [matters] were concluded, the officers * approached me, saying,
INTER- "The people of Israel, the Kohanim and the Levites have not kept them-
MARRIAGE selves apart from the peoples of the lands; [doing] like the abominations of the
9:1-10:44 Canaanite, the Hittite, the Perizzite, the Jebusite, the Ammonite, the Moabite, the
Egyptian and the Amorite. ² For they have taken of their daughters in marriage for
themselves and for their sons, and the sacred offspring [of Israel] have intermingled with the peoples of the land. And the hand of the officers and the chiefs
has been foremost in this transgression!"

Ezra's ³ When I heard this thing I tore my garment and my cloak; tore hair from my
anguish head and my beard, and I sat down in silence. ⁴ Everyone who hastened at the
word of the God of Israel then gathered around me concerning the transgression
Ezra's of the exile, while I sat in silence until [the time of] the afternoon offering. ⁵ At the
public afternoon offering I arose from my fast, with my garment and my cloak torn, and
prayer I fell upon my knees and spread out my palms to HASHEM, my God. ⁶ I said, "My
God, I am embarrassed and ashamed to lift my face to You, my God; for our
iniquities have multiplied over [our] head, and our sins extend up to the heavens!
⁷ From the days of our forefathers we have been in great guilt, until this day; and
because of our iniquities we have been delivered — we, our kings and our
Kohanim — into the hand of the kings of the lands, to the sword, to captivity and
to plunder and to shamefacedness, as of this very day. ⁸ And now, for a
fleeting moment, favor has been bestowed by HASHEM, our God, to leave us a
remnant and to grant us a stake in His sacred place for our God to enlighten our
eyes, and to give us a slight revival in our servitude. ⁹ For we are slaves, *

וּבְעַבְדֻתֵ֙נוּ֙ לֹ֣א עֲזָבָ֣נוּ אֱלֹהֵ֔ינוּ וַיַּט־עָלֵ֣ינוּ חֶ֡סֶד לִפְנֵי֩ מַלְכֵ֨י פָרַ֜ס לָֽתֶת־לָ֣נוּ מִֽחְיָ֗ה לְרוֹמֵ֞ם אֶת־בֵּ֤ית אֱלֹהֵ֙ינוּ֙ וּֽלְהַעֲמִ֣יד אֶת־חָרְבֹתָ֔יו וְלָֽתֶת־לָ֣נוּ גָדֵ֔ר

י בִּֽיהוּדָ֖ה וּבִירֽוּשָׁלָֽ͏ִם: וְעַתָּ֛ה מַה־נֹּאמַ֥ר אֱלֹהֵ֖ינוּ אַֽחֲרֵי־זֹ֑את כִּ֥י עֲזַ֖בְנוּ

יא מִצְוֹתֶֽיךָ: אֲשֶׁ֣ר צִוִּ֗יתָ בְּיַ֤ד עֲבָדֶ֨יךָ֙ הַנְּבִיאִ֣ים לֵאמֹ֔ר הָאָ֗רֶץ אֲשֶׁ֤ר אַתֶּם֙ בָּאִ֣ים לְרִשְׁתָּ֔הּ אֶ֤רֶץ נִדָּה֙ הִ֔יא בְּנִדַּ֖ת עַמֵּ֣י הָֽאֲרָצ֑וֹת בְּתֽוֹעֲבֹֽתֵיהֶם֙ אֲשֶׁ֣ר

יב מִלְא֔וּהָ מִפֶּ֥ה אֶל־פֶּ֖ה בְּטֻמְאָתָֽם: וְ֠עַתָּ֠ה בְּנֽוֹתֵיכֶ֞ם אַל־תִּתְּנ֣וּ לִבְנֵיהֶ֗ם וּבְנֹֽתֵיהֶם֙ אַל־תִּשְׂא֣וּ לִבְנֵיכֶ֔ם וְלֹֽא־תִדְרְשׁ֧וּ שְׁלֹמָ֛ם וְטֽוֹבָתָ֖ם עַד־עוֹלָ֑ם לְמַ֣עַן תֶּֽחֶזְק֗וּ וַֽאֲכַלְתֶּם֙ אֶת־ט֣וּב הָאָ֔רֶץ וְהֽוֹרַשְׁתֶּ֥ם לִבְנֵיכֶ֖ם עַד־עוֹלָֽם:

יג וְאַֽחֲרֵי֙ כָּל־הַבָּ֣א עָלֵ֔ינוּ בְּמַֽעֲשֵׂ֖ינוּ הָֽרָעִ֑ים וּבְאַשְׁמָתֵ֖נוּ הַגְּדֹלָ֑ה כִּ֣י ׀ אַתָּ֣ה

יד אֱלֹהֵ֗ינוּ חָשַׂ֤כְתָּ לְמַ֨טָּה֙ מֵֽעֲוֺנֵ֔נוּ וְנָתַ֥תָּה לָּ֛נוּ פְּלֵיטָ֖ה כָּזֹ֑את: הֲנָשׁ֞וּב לְהָפֵ֣ר מִצְוֺתֶ֗יךָ וּֽלְהִתְחַתֵּ֞ן בְּעַמֵּ֤י הַתֹּֽעֵבוֹת֙ הָאֵ֔לֶּה הֲל֤וֹא תֶֽאֱנַף־בָּ֨נוּ֙ עַד־כַּלֵּ֔ה

טו לְאֵ֥ין שְׁאֵרִ֖ית וּפְלֵיטָֽה: יְהֹוָ֞ה אֱלֹהֵ֤י יִשְׂרָאֵל֙ צַדִּ֣יק אַ֔תָּה כִּֽי־ נִשְׁאַ֥רְנוּ פְלֵיטָ֖ה כְּהַיּ֣וֹם הַזֶּ֑ה הִנְנ֤וּ לְפָנֶ֨יךָ֙ בְּאַשְׁמָתֵ֔ינוּ כִּ֣י אֵ֥ין לַֽעֲמ֖וֹד

י א לְפָנֶ֖יךָ עַל־זֹֽאת: וּכְהִתְפַּלֵּ֤ל עֶזְרָא֙ וּכְהִ֨תְוַדֹּת֔וֹ בֹּכֶ֖ה וּמִתְנַפֵּ֔ל לִפְנֵ֖י בֵּ֣ית הָֽאֱלֹהִ֑ים נִקְבְּצוּ֩ אֵלָ֨יו מִיִּשְׂרָאֵ֜ל קָהָ֣ל רַב־מְאֹ֗ד אֲנָשִׁ֤ים וְנָשִׁים֙ וִֽילָדִ֔ים כִּֽי־בָכ֥וּ הָעָ֖ם הַרְבֵּֽה־בֶֽכֶה:

ב וַיַּ֩עַן֩ שְׁכַנְיָ֨ה בֶן־יְחִיאֵ֜ל מִבְּנֵ֣י °עוֹלָ֗ם [°עֵילָ֗ם ק] וַיֹּ֙אמֶר֙ לְעֶזְרָ֔א אֲנַ֗חְנוּ מָעַ֣לְנוּ בֵּֽאלֹהֵ֔ינוּ וַנֹּ֛שֶׁב נָשִׁ֥ים נָכְרִיּ֖וֹת מֵֽעַמֵּ֣י הָאָ֑רֶץ וְעַתָּ֛ה יֵשׁ־מִקְוֶ֥ה

ג לְיִשְׂרָאֵ֖ל עַל־זֹֽאת: וְעַתָּ֣ה נִֽכְרָת־בְּרִ֣ית לֵֽאלֹהֵ֗ינוּ לְהוֹצִ֤יא כָל־נָשִׁים֙

ד וְהַנּוֹלָ֣ד מֵהֶ֔ם בַּֽעֲצַ֣ת אֲדֹנָ֔י וְהַֽחֲרֵדִ֖ים בְּמִצְוַ֣ת אֱלֹהֵ֑ינוּ וְכַתּוֹרָ֖ה יֵֽעָשֶֽׂה: ק֛וּם

ה כִּֽי־עָלֶ֥יךָ הַדָּבָ֖ר וַֽאֲנַ֣חְנוּ עִמָּ֑ךְ חֲזַ֖ק וַֽעֲשֵֽׂה: וַיָּ֣קָם עֶזְרָ֗א וַיַּשְׁבַּ֣ע

ו אֶת־שָׂרֵ֨י הַכֹּֽהֲנִ֜ים הַֽלְוִיִּ֗ם וְכָל־יִשְׂרָאֵ֛ל לַֽעֲשׂ֖וֹת כַּדָּבָ֣ר הַזֶּ֑ה וַיִּשָּׁבֵֽעוּ: וַיָּ֣קָם עֶזְרָ֗א מִלִּפְנֵי֙ בֵּ֣ית הָֽאֱלֹהִ֔ים וַיֵּ֕לֶךְ אֶל־לִשְׁכַּ֖ת יְהֽוֹחָנָ֣ן בֶּן־אֶלְיָשִׁ֑יב וַיֵּ֣לֶךְ שָׁ֗ם לֶ֤חֶם לֹֽא־אָכַל֙ וּמַ֣יִם לֹֽא־שָׁתָ֔ה כִּ֥י מִתְאַבֵּ֖ל עַל־מַ֥עַל הַגּוֹלָֽה:

ז־ח וַיַּֽעֲבִ֨ירוּ ק֜וֹל בִּֽיהוּדָ֣ה וִֽירֽוּשָׁלַ֗͏ִם לְכֹל֙ בְּנֵ֣י הַגּוֹלָ֔ה לְהִקָּבֵ֖ץ יְרֽוּשָׁלָֽ͏ִם: וְכֹ֣ל אֲשֶׁ֣ר לֹֽא־יָב֡וֹא לִשְׁלֹ֣שֶׁת הַיָּמִים֩ כַּֽעֲצַ֨ת הַשָּׂרִ֜ים וְהַזְּקֵנִ֗ים יׇֽחֳרַם֙ כָּל־ רְכוּשׁ֔וֹ וְה֥וּא יִבָּדֵ֖ל מִקְּהַ֥ל הַגּוֹלָֽה:

ט וַיִּקָּֽבְצ֣וּ כָל־אַנְשֵֽׁי־יְהוּדָ֣ה וּבִנְיָמִ֣ן ׀ יְרֽוּשָׁלַ֗͏ִם לִשְׁלֹ֤שֶׁת הַיָּמִים֙ ה֣וּא חֹ֣דֶשׁ הַתְּשִׁיעִ֔י בְּעֶשְׂרִ֖ים בַּחֹ֑דֶשׁ וַיֵּֽשְׁב֣וּ כָל־הָעָ֗ם בִּרְחוֹב֙ בֵּ֣ית הָֽאֱלֹהִ֔ים

י מַרְעִידִ֥ים עַל־הַדָּבָ֖ר וּמֵֽהַגְּשָׁמִֽים: וַיָּ֩קׇם֩ עֶזְרָ֨א הַכֹּהֵ֜ן וַיֹּ֣אמֶר אֲלֵהֶ֗ם אַתֶּ֤ם

יא מְעַלְתֶּם֙ וַתֹּשִׁ֙יבוּ֙ נָשִׁ֣ים נָכְרִיּ֔וֹת לְהוֹסִ֖יף עַל־אַשְׁמַ֣ת יִשְׂרָאֵֽל: וְעַתָּ֗ה תְּנ֥וּ תוֹדָ֛ה לַֽיהֹוָ֥ה אֱלֹהֵֽי־אֲבֹֽתֵיכֶ֖ם וַֽעֲשׂ֣וּ רְצוֹנ֑וֹ וְהִבָּֽדְלוּ֙ מֵֽעַמֵּ֣י הָאָ֔רֶץ וּמִן־

10:2. Although only a small fraction of the people married alien wives [the list contains only one hundred twelve names], and Shecaniah was certainly not among them, he nevertheless said "we have transgressed." He included himself to minimize the embarrassment of the true culprits who would later confess (*Talmud, Sanhedrin* 116a).

but our God has not forsaken us in our servitude; and he has extended kindness over us before the kings of Persia to grant us a revival, to raise up the Temple of our God and to restore its ruins and to provide us with a fence in Judah and in

Confession *Jerusalem.* [10] *So now, what can we say, O our God, after this? For we have forsaken Your commandments* [11] *which You have commanded through Your servants the prophets, saying, 'The land that you are approaching to inherit is a land of repulsiveness, because of the repulsiveness of the peoples of the lands, because of their abominations with which they have filled it from end to end, with their defilement.* [12] *So now, do not give your daughters to their sons, and do not wed their daughters to your sons, and do not seek after their peace and their well-being forever, so that you may possess and eat of the goodness of the land, and bequeath it to your sons forever.'* [13] *After all that has befallen us for our evil deeds and great guilt — yet You, our God, have withheld [retribution] to less than our iniquities [deserve], and have granted us this remnant —* [14] *shall we again violate Your commandments and intermarry with the peoples of these abominations? Surely You would become enraged at us, until [our] destruction without remnant or survivor!*

[15] *"HASHEM, God of Israel, You are charitable, for we have survived as a remnant to this very day. Behold, we are before You in our guilt, for we are unworthy to stand before You because of this."*

10

Assembly
and remorse

[1] *A*s Ezra prayed and as he confessed, weeping and prostrating himself before the Temple of God, there gathered near him an exceedingly large congregation from Israel — men, women and children — for the people wept profusely.* [2] *Then, Shecaniah son of Jehiel of the sons of Elam spoke up and said to Ezra, "We* * *have transgressed against our God and have taken in alien women of the*

Covenant
and oath

peoples of the land! But now there is hope for Israel concerning this. [3] *So now let us seal a covenant with our God to send away all of the women and those born from them, according to the counsel of the Lord and those who hasten at the commandment of our God; let it be done according to the Torah.* [4] *Arise, for the matter rests upon you and we are with you; be strong and act!"*

Ezra's grief

[5] *So Ezra arose and administered an oath to the chiefs of the Kohanim, the Levites, and all of Israel to carry out this matter, and they swore.* [6] *Ezra then arose from before the Temple of God and went to the chamber of Johanan son of Eliashib; he went there, but he did not eat any bread and did not drink any water, for he was mourning over the faithlessness of the exiles.*

Public
assembly in
Jerusalem

[7] *A proclamation was issued in Judah and Jerusalem to all of the people of the exile to assemble in Jerusalem,* [8] *and that if anyone failed to come within three days, in accordance with the counsel of the officers and the elders, all his property would be destroyed, and he would be isolated from the congregation of the exile.*

[9] *All the men of Judah and Benjamin assembled in Jerusalem within three days, which was in the ninth month,* * *on the twentieth of the month; all the people sat in the plaza of the Temple of God trembling because of the matter*

Ezra's
charge to the
people

and from the rains. [10] *Ezra the Kohen arose and said to them, "You have been unfaithful and have taken in alien wives, adding to Israel's guilt.* [11] *So now, make confession before HASHEM, God of your forefathers, and perform His will, and separate yourselves from the peoples of the land and from*

10:9. The month of Kislev, in the beginning of the winter. The people trembled because of the sin of rampant intermarriage and because of the chill winter rains.

יב הַנָּשִׁים הַנָּכְרִיּֽוֹת: וַיַּעֲנ֣וּ כָֽל־הַקָּהָ֗ל וַיֹּאמְר֖וּ ק֣וֹל גָּד֑וֹל כֵּ֖ן °כדבריך

יג [°כִּדְבָרְךָ֥ ק] עָלֵ֖ינוּ לַעֲשֽׂוֹת: אֲבָ֣ל הָעָ֣ם רָ֗ב וְהָעֵ֤ת גְּשָׁמִים֙ וְאֵ֣ין כֹּ֣חַ לַעֲמ֣וֹד בַּח֔וּץ וְהַמְּלָאכָ֛ה לֹֽא־לְי֥וֹם אֶחָ֖ד וְלֹ֣א לִשְׁנָ֑יִם כִּֽי־הִרְבִּ֥ינוּ לִפְשֹׁ֖עַ בַּדָּבָ֥ר

יד הַזֶּֽה: יַעֲמְדוּ־נָ֣א שָׂרֵ֣ינוּ לְֽכָל־הַקָּהָ֗ל וְכֹ֣ל ׀ אֲשֶׁ֣ר בֶּעָרֵ֗ינוּ הַהֹשִׁ֞יב נָשִׁ֤ים נָכְרִיּוֹת֙ יָבֹא֙ לְעִתִּ֣ים מְזֻמָּנִ֔ים וְעִמָּהֶ֛ם זִקְנֵי־עִ֥יר וָעִ֖יר וְשֹׁפְטֶ֑יהָ עַ֠ד לְהָשִׁ֞יב

טו חֲר֤וֹן אַף־אֱלֹהֵ֙ינוּ֙ מִמֶּ֔נּוּ עַ֖ד לַדָּבָ֥ר הַזֶּֽה: אַ֣ךְ יוֹנָתָ֧ן בֶּן־עֲשָׂהאֵ֛ל וְיַחְזְיָ֥ה בֶן־

טז תִּקְוָ֖ה עָ֣מְד֣וּ עַל־זֹ֑את וּמְשֻׁלָּ֛ם וְשַׁבְּתַ֥י הַלֵּוִ֖י עֲזָרֻֽם: וַיַּֽעֲשׂוּ־כֵן֮ בְּנֵ֣י הַגּוֹלָה֒ וַיִּבָּֽדְלוּ֩ עֶזְרָ֨א הַכֹּהֵ֜ן אֲנָשִׁ֗ים רָאשֵׁ֧י הָאָב֛וֹת לְבֵ֥ית אֲבֹתָ֖ם וְכֻלָּ֣ם בְּשֵׁמ֑וֹת

יז וַיֵּשְׁב֗וּ בְּי֤וֹם אֶחָד֙ לַחֹ֣דֶשׁ הָעֲשִׂירִ֔י לְדַרְי֖וֹשׁ הַדָּבָֽר: וַיְכַלּ֣וּ בַכֹּ֗ל אֲנָשִׁים֙ הַהֹשִׁ֙יבוּ֙ נָשִׁ֣ים נָכְרִיּ֔וֹת עַ֖ד י֣וֹם אֶחָ֑ד לַחֹ֖דֶשׁ הָרִאשֽׁוֹן:

יח וַיִּמָּצֵא֙ מִבְּנֵ֣י הַכֹּהֲנִ֔ים אֲשֶׁ֥ר הֹשִׁ֖יבוּ נָשִׁ֣ים נָכְרִיּ֑וֹת מִבְּנֵ֤י יֵשׁ֙וּעַ֙ בֶּן־יֽוֹצָדָ֣ק וְאֶחָ֔יו

יט מַעֲשֵׂיָה֙ וֶֽאֱלִיעֶ֔זֶר וְיָרִ֖יב וּגְדַלְיָֽה: וַיִּתְּנ֥וּ יָדָ֖ם לְהוֹצִ֣יא נְשֵׁיהֶ֑ם וַאֲשֵׁמִ֥ים

כ-כא אֵֽיל־צֹ֖אן עַל־אַשְׁמָתָֽם: וּמִבְּנֵ֖י אִמֵּ֑ר חֲנָ֖נִי וּזְבַדְיָֽה: וּמִבְּנֵ֖י חָרִ֑ם מַעֲשֵׂיָ֤ה

כב וְאֵֽלִיָּה֙ וּֽשְׁמַֽעְיָ֔ה וִיחִיאֵ֖ל וְעֻזִּיָּֽה: וּמִבְּנֵ֖י פַּשְׁח֑וּר אֶלְיוֹעֵינַ֤י מַֽעֲשֵׂיָה֙

כג יִשְׁמָעֵ֣אל נְתַנְאֵ֔ל יוֹזָבָ֖ד וְאֶלְעָשָֽׂה: וּמִן־הַלְוִיִּ֑ם יוֹזָבָ֣ד וְשִׁמְעִ֗י וְקֵֽלָיָה֙ ה֣וּא

כד קְלִיטָ֔א פְּתַֽחְיָ֥ה יְהוּדָ֖ה וֶאֱלִיעֶֽזֶר: וּמִן־הַמְשֹׁרְרִ֖ים אֶלְיָשִׁ֑יב וּמִן־הַשֹּׁעֲרִ֔ים

כה שַׁלֻּ֥ם וָטֶ֖לֶם וְאוּרִֽי: וּמִיִּשְׂרָאֵ֑ל מִבְּנֵ֣י פַרְעֹ֡שׁ רַ֠מְיָ֤ה וְיִזִּיָּה֙ וּמַלְכִּיָּ֣ה וּמִיָּמִ֔ן

כו וְאֶלְעָזָ֖ר וּמַלְכִּיָּ֥ה וּבְנָיָֽה: וּמִבְּנֵ֣י עֵילָ֑ם מַתַּנְיָ֤ה זְכַרְיָה֙ וִיחִיאֵ֣ל וְעַבְדִּ֔י

כז וִירֵמ֖וֹת וְאֵֽלִיָּֽה: וּמִבְּנֵ֖י זַתּ֑וּא אֶלְיוֹעֵנַ֤י אֶלְיָשִׁיב֙ מַתַּנְיָ֣ה וִֽירֵמ֔וֹת וְזָבָ֖ד

כח-כט וַעֲזִיזָֽא: וּמִבְּנֵ֖י בֵּבָ֑י יְהֽוֹחָנָ֥ן חֲנַנְיָ֖ה זַבַּ֥י עַתְלָֽי: וּמִבְּנֵ֖י בָּנִ֑י מְשֻׁלָּ֣ם מַלּ֣וּךְ

ל וַעֲדָיָ֗ה יָשׁ֧וּב וּשְׁאָ֛ל °ירמות [°וְרָמ֖וֹת ק]: וּמִבְּנֵ֖י פַּחַ֣ת מוֹאָ֑ב עַדְנָ֤א וּכְלָל֙

לא בְּנָיָ֔ה מַעֲשֵׂיָ֧ה מַתַּנְיָ֛ה בְצַלְאֵ֖ל וּבִנּ֣וּי וּמְנַשֶּֽׁה: וּבְנֵ֖י חָרִ֑ם אֱלִיעֶ֖זֶר יִשִּׁיָּ֥ה

לב-לג מַלְכִּיָּ֖ה שְׁמַֽעְיָ֥ה שִׁמְעֽוֹן: בְּנְיָמִ֥ן מַלּ֖וּךְ שְׁמַרְיָֽה: מִבְּנֵ֖י חָשֻׁ֑ם מַתְּנַ֤י מַתַּתָּה֙

לד-לה זָבָ֣ד אֱלִיפֶ֔לֶט יְרֵמַ֥י מְנַשֶּׁ֖ה שִׁמְעִֽי: מִבְּנֵ֣י בָנִ֑י מַעֲדַ֤י עַמְרָם֙ וְאוּאֵֽל: בְּנָיָ֥ה

לו-לז בֵדְיָ֖ה °כלוהי [°כְּלֽוּהוּ ק]: וַנְיָ֥ה מְרֵמ֖וֹת אֶלְיָשִֽׁיב: מַתַּנְיָ֥ה מַתְּנַ֖י °ויעשו

לח-מ [°וְיַעֲשָׂ֥י ק]: וּבָנִ֥י וּבִנּ֖וּי שִׁמְעִֽי: וְשֶׁלֶמְיָ֥ה וְנָתָ֖ן וַעֲדָיָֽה: מַכְנַדְבַ֥י שָׁשַׁ֖י שָׁרָֽי:

מא-מג עֲזַרְאֵ֥ל וְשֶֽׁלֶמְיָ֖הוּ שְׁמַרְיָֽה: שַׁלּ֥וּם אֲמַרְיָ֖ה יוֹסֵֽף: מִבְּנֵ֖י נְב֑וֹ יְעִיאֵ֤ל מַתִּתְיָה֙

מד זָבָ֣ד זְבִינָ֔א °ידו [°יַדַּ֖י ק] וְיוֹאֵ֣ל בְּנָיָֽה: כָּל־אֵ֕לֶּה °נשאי [°נָשְׂא֖וּ ק] נָשִׁ֣ים

נָכְרִיּ֑וֹת וְיֵ֣שׁ מֵהֶ֣ם נָשִׁ֔ים וַיָּשִׂ֖ימוּ בָּנִֽים:

נחמיה

א דִּבְרֵ֖י נְחֶמְיָ֥ה בֶן־חֲכַלְיָ֑ה

ב וַיְהִ֤י בְחֹֽדֶשׁ־כִּסְלֵיו֙ שְׁנַ֣ת עֶשְׂרִ֔ים וַאֲנִ֥י הָיִ֖יתִי בְּשׁוּשַׁ֥ן הַבִּירָֽה: וַיָּבֹ֨א חֲנָ֜נִי אֶחָ֧ד מֵאַחַ֛י ה֖וּא וַאֲנָשִׁ֣ים מִֽיהוּדָ֑ה וָאֶשְׁאָלֵ֗ם עַל־הַיְּהוּדִ֤ים הַפְּלֵיטָה֙ אֲשֶׁ֣ר

10:16. The month of Teves.

◁§ **Nehemiah**
   Like the divisions of *Samuel, Kings* and *Chronicles* into two Books, the division of *Ezra* into the two Books of *Ezra* and *Nehemiah* is a Christian invention. It was introduced into Jewish Bibles by Italian printers early in the sixteenth century when Jews were not permitted to own printing presses. Like the chapter numbers, also a non-Jewish innovation, this usage has no halachic implications, and has been retained in virtually all editions of Scripture as

the alien wives!"

The congregation's response

12 The entire congregation then called out and exclaimed in a loud voice, "It is true! We must do as you say! 13 But there are many people, and it is the rainy season and there is no strength to remain outdoors. This is not a task for one day or for two days, for we have sinned abundantly in this matter. 14 Let our chiefs now remain with the entire congregation, and let all those in our cities who have taken in alien wives appear at designated times, accompanied by the elders and judges of each city, until we cause the burning wrath of our God to recede from us, until

Minuscule opposition

this matter [is resolved]." 15 Only Jonathan son of Asahel and Jahzeiah son of Tikvah stood against this, and Meshullam and Shabbethai the Levite supported them.

Compliance of the assembled

16 The people of the exile did so. Ezra the Kohen and the distinguished men who were the heads of the families — all of them renowned — separated themselves and convened on the first day of the tenth month * to investigate the matter. 17 They finished dealing with all the men who had taken in alien wives, by the first day of the first month.

The repentant transgressors

18 Among the sons of the Kohanim who were found to have taken in alien wives were: of the sons of Jeshua son of Jozadak and his brethren — Maaseiah, Eliezer, Jarib and Gedaliah — 19 they gave their hand [in oath] to send away their wives and to offer a guilt-offering of a ram from the flock for their guilt; 20 and of the sons of Immer: Hanani and Zebadiah; 21 and of the sons of Harim — Maaseiah, Elijah, Shemaiah, Jehiel and Uzziah; 22 and of the sons of Pashhur — Elioenai, Maaseiah, Ishmael, Nethanel, Jozabad and Elasah; 23 and from the Levites — Jozabad, Shimei, Kelaiah (he is Kelita), Pethahiah, Judah and Eliezer; 24 and from the singers — Eliashib; and from the gatekeepers — Shallum, Telem and Uri. 25 And of Israel: of the sons of Parosh — Ramiah, Izziah, Malchijah, Miamin, Eleazar, Malchijah and Benaiah; 26 and of the sons of Elam — Mattaniah, Zechariah, Jehiel, Abdi, Jeremoth and Elijah; 27 and of the sons of Zattu — Elioenai, Eliashib, Mattaniah, Jeremoth, Zabad and Aziza; 28 and of the sons of Bebai — Jehohanan, Hananiah, Zabbai and Athlai; 29 and of the sons of Bani — Meshullam, Malluch, Adaiah, Jashub, Sheal and Ramoth; 30 and of the sons of the governor of Moab — Adna, Chelal, Benaiah, Maaseiah, Mattaniah, Bezalel, Binnui and Manasseh; 31 and the sons of Harim: Eliezer, Isshijah, Malchijah, Shemaiah, Shimeon, 32 Benjamin, Malluch and Shemariah; 33 of the sons of Hashum — Mattenai, Mattattah, Zabad, Eliphelet, Jeremai, Manasseh and Shimei; 34 of the sons of Bani — Maadai, Amram, Uel, 35 Benaiah, Bedeiah, Cheluhu, 36 Vaniah, Meremoth, Eliashib, 37 Mattaniah, Mattenai, Jaasai, 38 Bani, Binnui, Shimei, 39 Shelemiah, Nathan, Adaiah, 40 Machnadebai, Shashai, Sharai, 41 Azarel, Shelemiah, Shemariah, 42 Shallum, Amariah and Joseph; 43 of the sons of Nebo — Jeiel, Mattithiah, Zabad, Zebina, Jaddai, Joel and Benaiah. 44 All these had married alien wives, some of them wives by whom they had had children.

NEHEMIAH
1

News of Jerusalem

1 The words of Nehemiah son of Hacaliah:

It was during the month of Kislev of the twentieth year, * and I was in the capital city of Shushan. 2 Hanani, one of my brethren, came, he and men from Judah, and I inquired of them about the Jews who had survived, who

---

a matter of convenience.

The events in this Book took place fourteen years after the completion of the Second Temple (*Ezra* 6:15). Although the Temple now stood, the Jews in Jerusalem suffered from privation and the threat of attack (see Ch.

4). Nehemiah left his position in the Persian royal court to rejuvenate the Jerusalem community.

1:1. That is, the twentieth year of the reign of Artaxerxes (see 2:1), who is identified as Darius of Persia, the son of Ahasuerus and Esther (*Rashi*).

ג נִשְׁאֲרוּ מִן־הַשְּׁבִי וְעַל־יְרוּשָׁלָ͏ִם: וַיֹּאמְרוּ לִי הַנִּשְׁאָרִים אֲשֶׁר־נִשְׁאֲרוּ מִן־
הַשְּׁבִי שָׁם בַּמְּדִינָה בְּרָעָה גְדֹלָה וּבְחֶרְפָּה וְחוֹמַת יְרוּשָׁלַ͏ִם מְפֹרָצֶת
ד וּשְׁעָרֶיהָ נִצְּתוּ בָאֵשׁ: וַיְהִי כְּשָׁמְעִי ׀ אֶת־הַדְּבָרִים הָאֵלֶּה יָשַׁבְתִּי וָאֶבְכֶּה
ה וָאֶתְאַבְּלָה יָמִים וָאֱהִי צָם וּמִתְפַּלֵּל לִפְנֵי אֱלֹהֵי הַשָּׁמָיִם: וָאֹמַר אָנָּא יְהוָה
אֱלֹהֵי הַשָּׁמַיִם הָאֵל הַגָּדוֹל וְהַנּוֹרָא שֹׁמֵר הַבְּרִית וָחֶסֶד לְאֹהֲבָיו וּלְשֹׁמְרֵי
ו מִצְוֺתָיו: תְּהִי נָא אָזְנְךָ־קַשֶּׁבֶת וְעֵינֶיךָ פְתֻחוֹת לִשְׁמֹעַ אֶל־תְּפִלַּת עַבְדְּךָ
אֲשֶׁר אָנֹכִי מִתְפַּלֵּל לְפָנֶיךָ הַיּוֹם יוֹמָם וָלַיְלָה עַל־בְּנֵי יִשְׂרָאֵל עֲבָדֶיךָ
וּמִתְוַדֶּה עַל־חַטֹּאות בְּנֵי־יִשְׂרָאֵל אֲשֶׁר חָטָאנוּ לָךְ וַאֲנִי וּבֵית־אָבִי
ז חָטָאנוּ: חֲבֹל חָבַלְנוּ לָךְ וְלֹא־שָׁמַרְנוּ אֶת־הַמִּצְוֺת וְאֶת־הַחֻקִּים וְאֶת־
ח הַמִּשְׁפָּטִים אֲשֶׁר צִוִּיתָ אֶת־מֹשֶׁה עַבְדֶּךָ: זְכָר־נָא אֶת־הַדָּבָר אֲשֶׁר צִוִּיתָ
ט אֶת־מֹשֶׁה עַבְדְּךָ לֵאמֹר אַתֶּם תִּמְעָלוּ אֲנִי אָפִיץ אֶתְכֶם בָּעַמִּים: וְשַׁבְתֶּם
אֵלַי וּשְׁמַרְתֶּם מִצְוֺתַי וַעֲשִׂיתֶם אֹתָם אִם־יִהְיֶה נִדַּחֲכֶם בִּקְצֵה הַשָּׁמַיִם
מִשָּׁם אֲקַבְּצֵם °וַהֲבוֹתִים [°וַהֲבִיאוֹתִים ק] אֶל־הַמָּקוֹם אֲשֶׁר בָּחַרְתִּי
י לְשַׁכֵּן אֶת־שְׁמִי שָׁם: וְהֵם עֲבָדֶיךָ וְעַמֶּךָ אֲשֶׁר פָּדִיתָ בְּכֹחֲךָ הַגָּדוֹל וּבְיָדְךָ
יא הַחֲזָקָה: אָנָּא אֲדֹנָי תְּהִי נָא אָזְנְךָ־קַשֶּׁבֶת אֶל־תְּפִלַּת עַבְדְּךָ וְאֶל־תְּפִלַּת
עֲבָדֶיךָ הַחֲפֵצִים לְיִרְאָה אֶת־שְׁמֶךָ וְהַצְלִיחָה־נָּא לְעַבְדְּךָ הַיּוֹם וּתְנֵהוּ
לְרַחֲמִים לִפְנֵי הָאִישׁ הַזֶּה וַאֲנִי הָיִיתִי מַשְׁקֶה לַמֶּלֶךְ:

ב א וַיְהִי ׀
בְּחֹדֶשׁ נִיסָן שְׁנַת עֶשְׂרִים לְאַרְתַּחְשַׁסְתְּא הַמֶּלֶךְ יַיִן לְפָנָיו וָאֶשָּׂא אֶת־
ב הַיַּיִן וָאֶתְּנָה לַמֶּלֶךְ וְלֹא־הָיִיתִי רַע לְפָנָיו: וַיֹּאמֶר לִי הַמֶּלֶךְ מַדּוּעַ ׀ פָּנֶיךָ
ג רָעִים וְאַתָּה אֵינְךָ חוֹלֶה אֵין זֶה כִּי־אִם רֹעַ לֵב וָאִירָא הַרְבֵּה מְאֹד: וָאֹמַר
לַמֶּלֶךְ הַמֶּלֶךְ לְעוֹלָם יִחְיֶה מַדּוּעַ לֹא־יֵרְעוּ פָנַי אֲשֶׁר הָעִיר בֵּית־קִבְרוֹת
ד אֲבֹתַי חֲרֵבָה וּשְׁעָרֶיהָ אֻכְּלוּ בָאֵשׁ: וַיֹּאמֶר לִי הַמֶּלֶךְ עַל־מַה־
ה זֶּה אַתָּה מְבַקֵּשׁ וָאֶתְפַּלֵּל אֶל־אֱלֹהֵי הַשָּׁמָיִם: וָאֹמַר לַמֶּלֶךְ אִם־עַל־
הַמֶּלֶךְ טוֹב וְאִם־יִיטַב עַבְדְּךָ לְפָנֶיךָ אֲשֶׁר תִּשְׁלָחֵנִי אֶל־יְהוּדָה אֶל־עִיר
ו קִבְרוֹת אֲבֹתַי וְאֶבְנֶנָּה: וַיֹּאמֶר לִי הַמֶּלֶךְ וְהַשֵּׁגַל ׀ יוֹשֶׁבֶת אֶצְלוֹ עַד־מָתַי
יִהְיֶה מַהֲלָכְךָ וּמָתַי תָּשׁוּב וַיִּיטַב לִפְנֵי־הַמֶּלֶךְ וַיִּשְׁלָחֵנִי וָאֶתְּנָה לוֹ זְמָן:
ז וָאוֹמַר לַמֶּלֶךְ אִם־עַל־הַמֶּלֶךְ טוֹב אִגְּרוֹת יִתְּנוּ־לִי עַל־פַּחֲווֹת עֵבֶר
ח הַנָּהָר אֲשֶׁר יַעֲבִירוּנִי עַד אֲשֶׁר־אָבוֹא אֶל־יְהוּדָה: וְאִגֶּרֶת אֶל־אָסָף שֹׁמֵר
הַפַּרְדֵּס אֲשֶׁר לַמֶּלֶךְ אֲשֶׁר יִתֶּן־לִי עֵצִים לְקָרוֹת אֶת־שַׁעֲרֵי הַבִּירָה
אֲשֶׁר־לַבַּיִת וּלְחוֹמַת הָעִיר וְלַבַּיִת אֲשֶׁר־אָבוֹא אֵלָיו וַיִּתֶּן־לִי הַמֶּלֶךְ
ט כְּיַד־אֱלֹהַי הַטּוֹבָה עָלָי: וָאָבוֹא אֶל־פַּחֲווֹת עֵבֶר הַנָּהָר וָאֶתְּנָה לָהֶם אֵת
י אִגְּרוֹת הַמֶּלֶךְ וַיִּשְׁלַח עִמִּי הַמֶּלֶךְ שָׂרֵי חַיִל וּפָרָשִׁים: וַיִּשְׁמַע

1:2. The Jews who left Babylonian captivity to return to the Land of Israel with Ezra (*Metzudos*).

1:8-9. See *Deuteronomy* 28:64 and 30:1-5.

1:11. King Darius.

2:4. Nehemiah prayed inwardly that his request be accepted by the king.

remained of the captivity, * and about Jerusalem.

³ They said to me, "The remaining ones, who remained of the captivity there in the province, are in great misery and humiliation; the wall of Jerusalem is breached, and its gates have been set afire."

Nehemiah's distress and prayer

⁴ It was when I heard these words that I sat and wept and grieved for days, and I fasted and prayed before the God of the heavens. ⁵ I said, "I beseech You, HASHEM, God of the heavens, the great and awesome God, Keeper of the covenant and of kindness for those who love Him and for those who observe His commandments. ⁶ Please, may Your ear be attentive and Your eyes open to listen to Your servant's prayer, which I pray before You today, day and night, for the Children of Israel, Your servants. I confess to the sins of the Children of Israel that we have sinned against You; I and my father's household have sinned. ⁷ We have been destructive toward You; we have not observed the commandments, the precepts and the laws that You commanded Your servant Moses. ⁸ Remember, please, the word that You commanded Your servant Moses, saying, 'If you will act with treachery, I will disperse you among the nations, ⁹ but when you return to Me and observe My commandments and perform them, even if the banished among you reach the ends of the heavens, I shall gather them from there and bring them to the place that I have chosen to rest My Name there.'* ¹⁰ For they are Your servants and Your people whom You redeemed with Your great strength and with Your powerful hand. ¹¹ I beseech You, my Lord, please let Your ear be attentive to the prayer of Your servant, and to the prayer of Your servants who desire to fear Your Name, and grant Your servant success this day, and make him the object of compassion before this man."* I was the king's cupbearer.

2

Nehemiah before the king

¹ It happened in the month of Nissan of the twentieth year of King Artaxerxes, that wine [was brought] before him. I carried the wine and gave it to the king. I had never before appeared downcast in his presence. ² So the king said to me, "Why is your face downcast? You are not ill. This can only signify [that there is] evil [in your] heart!" I became very frightened.

³ I said to the king, "May the king live forever! Why should my face not be downcast, when the city of my ancestors' graves is in ruin, and its gates are consumed by fire?"

⁴ The king said to me, "What is it that you request?"

I then prayed to the God of Heaven;* ⁵ and I said to the king, "If it please the king, and if your servant is worthy before you, then send me to Judah, to the city of my ancestors' graves, that I may rebuild it."

⁶ The king said to me, with the queen sitting beside him, "When will you depart and when will you return?" It pleased the king and he gave me leave; and I gave him a time.

⁷ Then I said to the king, "If it please the king, let them give me letters for the governors of the Trans-Euphrates region, so that they will grant me passage until I arrive in Judah, ⁸ and a letter for Asaph, the keeper of the king's forest, that he should give me timber to roof the gates of the Temple complex, and for the walls of the city, and for the home into which I will enter." The king granted me [this], by the hand of my God which was benevolent to me.

⁹ I came to the governors of the Trans-Euphrates region and gave them the king's letters. The king had sent army officers and horsemen with me.

סַנְבַלַּט הַחֹרֹנִי וְטוֹבִיָּה הָעֶבֶד הָעַמּוֹנִי וַיֵּרַע לָהֶם רָעָה גְדֹלָה אֲשֶׁר־בָּא

יא אָדָם לְבַקֵּשׁ טוֹבָה לִבְנֵי יִשְׂרָאֵל: וָאָבוֹא אֶל־יְרוּשָׁלַ֫ם וָאֱהִי־שָׁם יָמִים

יב שְׁלֹשָׁה: וָאָקוּם | לַיְלָה אֲנִי | וַאֲנָשִׁים ׀ מְעַט עִמִּי וְלֹא־הִגַּדְתִּי לְאָדָם מָה

אֱלֹהַי נֹתֵן אֶל־לִבִּי לַעֲשׂוֹת לִירוּשָׁלָ֑ם וּבְהֵמָה אֵין עִמִּי כִּי אִם־הַבְּהֵמָה

יג אֲשֶׁר אֲנִי רֹכֵב בָּהּ: וָאֵצְאָה בְשַֽׁעַר־הַגַּיְא לַיְלָה וְאֶל־פְּנֵי עֵין הַתַּנִּין וְאֶל־

שַֽׁעַר הָאַשְׁפֹּת וָאֱהִי *שֹׁבֵר בְּחוֹמֹת יְרוּשָׁלַ֫ם אֲשֶׁר־°הַמְפֹרָצִים [°הֵם ׀

יד פְּרוּצִים ק] וּשְׁעָרֶיהָ אֻכְּלוּ בָאֵשׁ: וָאֶעֱבֹר אֶל־שַֽׁעַר הָעַ֫יִן וְאֶל־בְּרֵכַת

טו הַמֶּלֶךְ וְאֵין־מָקוֹם לַבְּהֵמָה לַעֲבֹר תַּחְתָּי: וָאֱהִי עֹלֶה בַנַּ֫חַל לַיְלָה וָאֱהִי

טז *שֹׁבֵר בַּחוֹמָה וָאָשׁוּב וָאָבוֹא בְּשַֽׁעַר הַגַּיְא וָאָשׁוּב: וְהַסְּגָנִים לֹא יָדְעוּ

אָנָה הָלַ֫כְתִּי וּמָה אֲנִי עֹשֶׂה וְלַיְּהוּדִים וְלַכֹּהֲנִים וְלַחֹרִים וְלַסְּגָנִים וּלְיֶ֫תֶר

יז עֹשֵׂה הַמְּלָאכָה עַד־כֵּן לֹא הִגַּדְתִּי: וָאוֹמַר אֲלֵהֶם אַתֶּם רֹאִים הָרָעָה

אֲשֶׁר אֲנַחְנוּ בָהּ אֲשֶׁר יְרוּשָׁלַ֫ם חֲרֵבָה וּשְׁעָרֶיהָ נִצְּתוּ בָאֵשׁ לְכוּ וְנִבְנֶה

יח אֶת־חוֹמַת יְרוּשָׁלַ֫ם וְלֹא־נִהְיֶה עוֹד חֶרְפָּה: וָאַגִּיד לָהֶם אֶת־יַד אֱלֹהַי

אֲשֶׁר־הִיא טוֹבָה עָלַי וְאַף־דִּבְרֵי הַמֶּלֶךְ אֲשֶׁר אָמַר־לִי וַיֹּאמְרוּ נָקוּם ׀

יט וּבָנִינוּ וַיְחַזְּקוּ יְדֵיהֶם לַטּוֹבָה: וַיִּשְׁמַע סַנְבַלַּט הַחֹרֹנִי וְטֹבִיָּה ׀

הָעֶבֶד הָעַמּוֹנִי וְגֶ֫שֶׁם הָעַרְבִי וַיַּלְעִגוּ לָנוּ וַיִּבְזוּ עָלֵינוּ וַיֹּאמְרוּ מָה־הַדָּבָר

כ הַזֶּה אֲשֶׁר אַתֶּם עֹשִׂים הַעַל הַמֶּלֶךְ אַתֶּם מֹרְדִים: וָאָשִׁיב אוֹתָם דָּבָר

וָאוֹמַר לָהֶם אֱלֹהֵי הַשָּׁמַ֫יִם הוּא יַצְלִיחַ לָנוּ וַאֲנַחְנוּ עֲבָדָיו נָקוּם וּבָנִינוּ

וְלָכֶם אֵין־חֵלֶק וּצְדָקָה וְזִכָּרוֹן בִּירוּשָׁלָ֑ם:

ג א וַיָּ֫קָם אֶלְיָשִׁיב הַכֹּהֵן הַגָּדוֹל וְאֶחָיו הַכֹּהֲנִים וַיִּבְנוּ אֶת־שַֽׁעַר הַצֹּאן

הֵמָּה קִדְּשׁוּהוּ וַיַּעֲמִידוּ דַּלְתֹתָיו וְעַד־מִגְדַּל הַמֵּאָה קִדְּשׁוּהוּ עַד מִגְדַּל

ב־ג חֲנַנְאֵל: וְעַל־יָדוֹ בָנוּ אַנְשֵׁי יְרֵחוֹ וְעַל־יָדוֹ בָנָה זַכּוּר בֶּן־אִמְרִי: וְאֵת

שַֽׁעַר הַדָּגִים בָּנוּ בְּנֵי הַסְּנָאָה הֵמָּה קֵרוּהוּ וַיַּעֲמִידוּ דַּלְתֹתָיו מַנְעוּלָיו

ד וּבְרִיחָיו: וְעַל־יָדָם הֶחֱזִיק מְרֵמוֹת בֶּן־אוּרִיָּה בֶּן־הַקּוֹץ וְעַל־יָדָם הֶחֱזִיק

מְשֻׁלָּם בֶּן־בֶּרֶכְיָה בֶּן־מְשֵׁיזַבְאֵל וְעַל־יָדָם הֶחֱזִיק צָדוֹק בֶּן־בַּעֲנָא:

ה וְעַל־יָדָם הֶחֱזִיקוּ הַתְּקוֹעִים וְאַדִּירֵיהֶם לֹא־הֵבִיאוּ צַוָּרָם בַּעֲבֹדַת

ו אֲדֹנֵיהֶם: וְאֵת שַֽׁעַר הַיְשָׁנָה הֶחֱזִיקוּ יוֹיָדָע בֶּן־פָּסֵחַ וּמְשֻׁלָּם בֶּן־

בְּסוֹדְיָה הֵמָּה קֵרוּהוּ וַיַּעֲמִידוּ דַּלְתֹתָיו וּמַנְעֻלָיו וּבְרִיחָיו: וְעַל־יָדָם

ז הֶחֱזִיק מְלַטְיָה הַגִּבְעֹנִי וְיָדוֹן הַמֵּרֹנֹתִי אַנְשֵׁי גִבְעוֹן וְהַמִּצְפָּה לְכִסֵּא

פַּחַת עֵבֶר הַנָּהָר: עַל־יָדוֹ הֶחֱזִיק עֻזִּיאֵל בֶּן־חַרְהֲיָה צוֹרְפִים וְעַל־

ח יָדוֹ הֶחֱזִיק חֲנַנְיָה בֶּן־הָרַקָּחִים וַיַּעַזְבוּ יְרוּשָׁלַ֫ם עַד הַחוֹמָה הָרְחָבָה:

ט וְעַל־יָדָם הֶחֱזִיק רְפָיָה בֶן־חוּר שַׂר חֲצִי פֶּלֶךְ יְרוּשָׁלָ֑ם: וְעַל־יָדָם

2:10. Sanballat the Horonite, an apostate Jew, was numbered among the adversaries of the Jews (*Ri Mitrani*).

2:12. The men who accompanied me walked on foot.

2:13. The translation follows *Ibn Ezra* and *Ralbag*. *Rashi*

renders, "I broke the wall," i.e., Nehemiah made additional breaches to the already breached wall, in order to arouse the citizenry to rebuild it.

2:14. Because of all the debris from the wall at that point.

Enemies of ¹⁰ Sanballat the Horonite* and Tobiah, the Ammonite slave, heard and they
Judah and were extremely disturbed that someone had come to seek the welfare of the
Benjamin Children of Israel.

¹¹ I arrived in Jerusalem, and was there for three days. ¹² I arose during the
night, I and a few people with me but I did not tell anyone what my God had set
in my heart to do for Jerusalem. I had no animal with me, except the animal upon
Nehemiah's which I was riding. * ¹³ I went out at night through the Gate of the Valley, towards
nighttime the direction of the Serpent's Spring, to the Dung Gate; I contemplated* the walls
excursion of Jerusalem which had been breached, and its gates consumed by fire. ¹⁴ I then
passed on to the Spring Gate and the King's Pool, but there was no room for the
animal under me to pass. * ¹⁵ I went up the valley in the night, and I contemplated
the wall; then I turned back and I entered by the Gate of the Valley and returned.

¹⁶ The nobles did not know where I had gone nor what I was doing; for I had
not as yet informed the Jews and the Kohanim and the aristocrats and the nobles
The people and the others who did the work. ¹⁷ So I said to them, "You see the bad situation
accept we are in, that Jerusalem is in ruin and its gates have been burned in fire. Come,
Nehemiah's let us build the wall of Jerusalem, so that we will no longer be a [source of]
plan humiliation!" ¹⁸ I told them of the hand of my God which was benevolent to me, *
and also of the king's words that he had said to me.

They said, "Let us get up and build!" and they strengthened their hands [in
resolve] for the benefit [of the city].

The ¹⁹ Sanballat the Horonite, Tobiah the Ammonite slave, and Geshem the Arab
enemies' heard; they ridiculed us and were contemptuous of us and said, "What is this
ridicule and thing you are doing? Are you rebelling against the king?"
Nehemiah's
reply ²⁰ I answered them a word; I said to them, "The God of Heaven will grant us
success, and we, His servants, will arise and build — but you have no portion nor
merit nor remembrance in Jerusalem!"

3

BUILDING
JERUSALEM'S
WALL
3:1-4:17;
6:1-6:19

The
eastern wall

The
northern wall

¹ Eliashib the Kohen Gadol arose, along with his brethren the Kohanim, and
they rebuilt the Sheep Gate. They sanctified it* and erected its doors; they
sanctified [the wall] up to the Tower of Hammeah [and] up to the Tower of
Hananel. ² Next to him, * the men of Jericho built [the wall]; and next to him,
Zaccur son of Imri built. * ³ The children of Hassenaah built the Fish Gate; they
roofed it and erected its doors, its locks and its bars. ⁴ Next to them, Meremoth son
of Uriah son of Hakkoz reinforced [the wall]; next to them, Meshullam son of
Berechiah son of Meshezabel reinforced; next to them, Zadok son of Baana
reinforced. ⁵ Next to them, the Tekoites reinforced, but their dignitaries did not put
their necks to the labor of their Lord. ⁶ Joiada son of Paseah and Meshullam son
of Besodeiah reinforced the Old Gate; they roofed it and erected its doors, its locks
and its bars. ⁷ Next to them, Melatiah the Gibeonite, Jadon the Meronothite [and]
the men of Gibeon and Mizpah reinforced up to the seat of the governor of
the Trans-Euphrates region. ⁸ Next to him, Uzziel son of Harhaiah [of the] gold-
smiths reinforced; next to him, Hananiah son of the perfumers reinforced;
they fortified Jerusalem up to the Broad Wall. ⁹ Next to them, Rephaiah son of
Hur, the officer over half the district of Jerusalem, reinforced. ¹⁰ Next to them,

---

2:18. For God had granted me grace in the eyes of the
king.
3:1. They invested this area with the sanctity of the Holy
City (*Rashi*).

3:2. Each person or group of people was assigned to
build a section of the wall. The men of Jericho stood and
built next to the last Kohen; Zaccur stood and built next
to the last Jerichoite.

הֶחֱזִיק יְדָיָה בֶן־חֲרוּמַף וְנֶגֶד בֵּיתֽוֹ וְעַל־יָדֽוֹ הֶחֱזִיק חַטּוּשׁ בֶּן־חֲשַׁבְנְיָֽה:

יא מִדָּה שֵׁנִית הֶחֱזִיק מַלְכִּיָּה בֶן־חָרִם וְחַשּׁוּב בֶּן־פַּחַת מוֹאָב וְאֵת מִגְדַּל

הַתַּנּוּרִֽים: וְעַל־יָדוֹ הֶחֱזִיק שַׁלּוּם בֶּן־הַלּוֹחֵשׁ שַׂר חֲצִי פֶּלֶךְ יְרוּשָׁלָ‍ִם הוּא

יב וּבְנוֹתָֽיו: אֵת שַׁעַר הַגַּיְא הֶחֱזִיק חָנוּן וְיֹשְׁבֵי זָנ֫וֹחַ הֵמָּה בָנ֫וּהוּ וַיַּעֲמִ֫ידוּ

יג דַּלְתֹתָיו מַנְעֻלָיו וּבְרִיחָיו וְאֶלֶף אַמָּה בַּחוֹמָה עַד שַׁעַר הָשֲׁפֽוֹת: וְאֵת ׀

יד שַׁעַר הָאַשְׁפּוֹת הֶחֱזִיק מַלְכִּיָּה בֶן־רֵכָב שַׂר פֶּלֶךְ בֵּית־הַכָּרֶם הוּא יִבְנֶ֫נּוּ

וַיַּעֲמִיד דַּלְתֹתָיו מַנְעֻלָיו וּבְרִיחָֽיו: וְאֵת שַׁעַר הָעַיִן הֶחֱזִיק שַׁלּוּן בֶּן־כָּל־

טו חֹזֶה שַׂר פֶּלֶךְ הַמִּצְפָּה הוּא יִבְנֶ֫נּוּ וִיטַלְלֶ֫נּוּ [וִיעַמִּידוּ ק] וִיעַמִּיד [וְיַעֲמִיד ק] דַּלְתֹתָ֫יו

מַנְעֻלָיו וּבְרִיחָיו וְאֵת חוֹמַת בְּרֵכַת הַשֶּׁלַח לְגַן־הַמֶּלֶךְ וְעַד־הַמַּעֲלוֹת

טז הַיּוֹרְדוֹת מֵעִיר דָּוִֽיד: אַחֲרָיו הֶחֱזִיק נְחֶמְיָה בֶן־עַזְבּ֫וּק שַׂר חֲצִי פֶּלֶךְ בֵּית־

יז צ֫וּר עַד־נֶגֶד קִבְרֵי דָוִיד וְעַד־הַבְּרֵכָה הָעֲשׂ֫וּיָה וְעַד בֵּית הַגִּבֹּרִֽים: אַחֲרָיו

הֶחֱזִיקוּ הַלְוִיִּם רְחוּם בֶּן־בָּנִי עַל־יָדוֹ הֶחֱזִיק חֲשַׁבְיָה שַׂר־חֲצִי־פֶלֶךְ קְעִילָה

יח לְפִלְכּֽוֹ: אַחֲרָיו הֶחֱזִיקוּ אֲחֵיהֶם בַּוַּי בֶּן־חֵנָדָד שַׂר חֲצִי פֶּלֶךְ קְעִילָה: וַיְחַזֵּק

יט עַל־יָדוֹ עֵזֶר בֶּן־יֵשׁוּעַ שַׂר הַמִּצְפָּה מִדָּה שֵׁנִית מִנֶּגֶד עֲלֹת הַנֶּשֶׁק הַמִּקְצֹֽעַ:

כ אַחֲרָיו הֶחֱרָה הֶחֱזִיק בָּרוּךְ בֶּן־זוֹבִי [זַכַּי ק] מִדָּה שֵׁנִית מִן־הַמִּקְצֹועַ

כא עַד־פֶּתַח בֵּית אֶלְיָשִׁיב הַכֹּהֵן הַגָּדֽוֹל: אַחֲרָיו הֶחֱזִיק מְרֵמוֹת בֶּן־אוּרִיָּה

כב בֶּן־הַקּ֫וֹץ מִדָּה שֵׁנִית מִפֶּתַח בֵּית אֶלְיָשִׁיב וְעַד־תַּכְלִית בֵּית אֶלְיָשִֽׁיב:

כג וְאַחֲרָיו הֶחֱזִיקוּ הַכֹּהֲנִים אַנְשֵׁי הַכִּכָּֽר: אַחֲרָיו הֶחֱזִיק בִּנְיָמִן וְחַשּׁוּב נֶגֶד

כד בֵּיתָם אַחֲרָיו הֶחֱזִיק עֲזַרְיָה בֶן־מַעֲשֵׂיָה בֶּן־עֲנָנְיָה אֵצֶל בֵּיתֽוֹ: אַחֲרָיו

כה הֶחֱזִיק בִּנּוּי בֶּן־חֵנָדָד מִדָּה שֵׁנִית מִבֵּית עֲזַרְיָה עַד־הַמִּקְצֹועַ וְעַד־הַפִּנָּֽה:

פָּלָל בֶּן־אוּזַי מִנֶּגֶד הַמִּקְצֹועַ וְהַמִּגְדָּל הַיּוֹצֵא מִבֵּית הַמֶּלֶךְ הָעֶלְיוֹן אֲשֶׁר

כו לַחֲצַר הַמַּטָּרָה אַחֲרָיו פְּדָיָה בֶן־פַּרְעֹֽשׁ: וְהַנְּתִינִים הָיוּ יֹשְׁבִים בָּעֹפֶל עַד

כז נֶגֶד שַׁעַר הַמַּיִם לַמִּזְרָח וְהַמִּגְדָּל הַיּוֹצֵֽא: אַחֲרָיו הֶחֱזִיקוּ הַתְּקֹעִים מִדָּה

כח שֵׁנִית מִנֶּגֶד הַמִּגְדָּל הַגָּדוֹל הַיּוֹצֵא וְעַד חוֹמַת הָעֹֽפֶל: מֵעַל ׀ שַׁעַר הַסּוּסִים

כט הֶחֱזִיקוּ הַכֹּהֲנִים אִישׁ לְנֶגֶד בֵּיתֽוֹ: אַחֲרָיו הֶחֱזִיק צָד֫וֹק בֶּן־אִמֵּר נֶגֶד בֵּיתֽוֹ

ל וְאַחֲרָיו הֶחֱזִיק שְׁמַעְיָה בֶן־שְׁכַנְיָה שֹׁמֵר שַׁעַר הַמִּזְרָֽח: אַחֲרֵי [אַחֲרָיו ק]

הֶחֱזִיק חֲנַנְיָה בֶּן־שֶׁלֶמְיָה וְחָנוּן בֶּן־צָלָף הַשִּׁשִּׁי מִדָּה שֵׁנִי אַחֲרָיו

לא הֶחֱזִיק מְשֻׁלָּם בֶּן־בֶּרֶכְיָה נֶגֶד נִשְׁכָּתֽוֹ: אַחֲרֵי [אַחֲרָיו ק] הֶחֱזִיק מַלְכִּיָּה

בֶּן־הַצֹּרְפִי עַד־בֵּית הַנְּתִינִים וְהָרֹכְלִים נֶגֶד שַׁעַר הַמִּפְקָד וְעַד עֲלִיַּת

לב־לג הַפִּנָּֽה: וּבֵין עֲלִיַּת הַפִּנָּה לְשַׁעַר הַצֹּאן הֶחֱזִיקוּ הַצֹּרְפִים וְהָרֹכְלִֽים: וַיְהִי

כַּאֲשֶׁר שָׁמַע סַנְבַלַּט כִּי־אֲנַחְנוּ בוֹנִים אֶת־הַחוֹמָה וַיִּחַר לוֹ וַיִּכְעַס

לד הַרְבֵּה וַיַּלְעֵג עַל־הַיְּהוּדִֽים: וַיֹּאמֶר ׀ לִפְנֵי אֶחָיו וְחֵיל שֹׁמְרוֹן וַיֹּאמֶר מָה

3:11. They reinforced a section equal in measure to the section mentioned in the previous verse (Rashi).

3:17. That is, together with the constituents of his district (Metzudos).

3:26. See Ezra 2:43 and Joshua Ch. 9. The Ophel was a district in Jerusalem.

opposite his house, Jedaiah son of Harumaph reinforced; next to him, Hattush son of Hashabneiah reinforced. [11] Malchijah son of Harim and Hasshub son of the governor of Moab reinforced a similar measure, * and the Tower of the

The western wall Ovens. [12] Next to him, Shallum son of Hallohesh, the officer over half the district of Jerusalem, reinforced, he together with his daughters. [13] Hanun and the inhabitants of Zanoah reinforced the Gate of the Valley; they built it and erected its doors, its locks and its bars, along with one thousand cubits of the wall, up to the Dung Gate. [14] Malchijah son of Rechab, officer of the district of Beth-cherem, reinforced the Dung Gate; he built it and erected its doors, its locks and its bars; [15] Shallun son of Col-hozeh, officer of the district of Mizpah, reinforced the Spring Gate — he built it, covered it and erected its doors, its locks and its bars — [and also] the wall of the Pool of Shelah up to the King's Garden and up to the steps descending from the City of David. [16] Beyond this, Nehemiah son of Azbuk, the officer of half the district of Beth-zur, reinforced up to opposite the graves of David and up to the man-made pool and up to the House of the Warriors. [17] Beyond this the Levites reinforced: Rehum son of Bani; next to him, Hashabiah, officer of half the district of Keilah, and his district, * reinforced. [18] After him, their brothers, [under] Bavvai son of Henadad, officer of

The southern wall half the district of Keilah, reinforced. [19] Next to him, Ezer son of Jeshua, officer of Mizpah, reinforced a similar measure, opposite the ascent to the armory, at the corner. [20] After him, Baruch son of Zaccai enthusiastically reinforced a similar measure, from the corner up to the entrance of the house of Eliashib the Kohen Gadol. [21] After him, Meremoth son of Uriah son of Hakkoz reinforced a similar measure, from the entrance of Eliashib's house up to the end of Eliashib's house. [22] After him, the Kohanim, men of the Plain, reinforced. [23] After him, Benjamin and Hasshub, opposite their houses; after him, Azariah son of Maaseiah son of Ananiah reinforced near his house. [24] After him, Binnui son of Henadad reinforced a similar measure, from the house of Azariah up to the corner and up to the tower; [25] Palal son of Uzai, opposite the corner and the

The remainder of the eastern wall tower that extends from the king's upper house, which is [adjacent] to the prison courtyard; after him, Pedaiah son of Parosh; [26] the Nethinim, * [who] dwelt in Ophel, * up to opposite the Water Gate on the east, and also the extending tower. [27] After him, the Tekoites reinforced a similar measure, from opposite the Great Extending Tower up to the wall of the Ophel. [28] The Kohanim reinforced above the Horses' Gate, each one opposite his home. [29] After him, Zadok son of Immer reinforced opposite his house; after him, Shemaiah son of Shecaniah, guard of the Eastern Gate, reinforced. [30] After him, Hananiah son of Shelemiah and Hanun, the sixth son of Zalaph, reinforced a similar measure; after him, Meshullam son of Berechiah, reinforced opposite his chamber. [31] After him, Malchijah, the son of the goldsmith, reinforced up to the house of the Nethinim and the merchants, opposite Hammiphkad Gate, up to the tower ascent. [32] The smiths and merchants reinforced between the tower ascent and the Sheep Gate.

Sanballat's threat [33] It happened when Sanballat heard that we were building the wall that he became enraged and he grew extremely angry, and he ridiculed the Jews. [34] He spoke before his compatriots and the populace of Samaria and said, "What are

הַיְּהוּדִים הָאֲמֵלָלִים עֹשִׂים הֲיַעַזְבוּ לָהֶם הֲיִזְבָּחוּ הַיְכַלּוּ בַיּוֹם הַיְחַיּוּ
לה אֶת־הָאֲבָנִים מֵעֲרֵמוֹת הֶעָפָר וְהֵמָּה שְׂרוּפוֹת: וְטוֹבִיָּה הָעַמֹּנִי אֶצְלוֹ
לו וַיֹּאמֶר גַּם אֲשֶׁר־הֵם בּוֹנִים אִם־יַעֲלֶה שׁוּעָל וּפָרַץ חוֹמַת אַבְנֵיהֶם: שְׁמַע
אֱלֹהֵינוּ כִּי־הָיִינוּ בוּזָה וְהָשֵׁב חֶרְפָּתָם אֶל־רֹאשָׁם וּתְנֵם לְבִזָּה בְּאֶרֶץ
לז שִׁבְיָה: וְאַל־תְּכַס עַל־עֲוֹנָם וְחַטָּאתָם מִלְּפָנֶיךָ אַל־תִּמָּחֶה כִּי הִכְעִיסוּ
לח לְנֶגֶד הַבּוֹנִים: וַנִּבְנֶה אֶת־הַחוֹמָה וַתִּקָּשֵׁר כָּל־הַחוֹמָה עַד־חֶצְיָהּ וַיְהִי לֵב
לָעָם לַעֲשׂוֹת:

ד א וַיְהִי כַאֲשֶׁר שָׁמַע סַנְבַלַּט וְטוֹבִיָּה וְהָעַרְבִים וְהָעַמֹּנִים וְהָאַשְׁדּוֹדִים כִּי־
עָלְתָה אֲרוּכָה לְחֹמוֹת יְרוּשָׁלִַם כִּי־הֵחֵלּוּ הַפְּרֻצִים לְהִסָּתֵם וַיִּחַר לָהֶם
ב מְאֹד: וַיִּקְשְׁרוּ כֻלָּם יַחְדָּו לָבוֹא לְהִלָּחֵם בִּירוּשָׁלִָם וְלַעֲשׂוֹת לוֹ תּוֹעָה:
ג־ד וַנִּתְפַּלֵּל אֶל־אֱלֹהֵינוּ וַנַּעֲמִיד מִשְׁמָר עֲלֵיהֶם יוֹמָם וָלַיְלָה מִפְּנֵיהֶם: וַיֹּאמֶר
יְהוּדָה כָּשַׁל כֹּחַ הַסַּבָּל וְהֶעָפָר הַרְבֵּה וַאֲנַחְנוּ לֹא נוּכַל לִבְנוֹת בַּחוֹמָה:
ה וַיֹּאמְרוּ צָרֵינוּ לֹא יֵדְעוּ וְלֹא יִרְאוּ עַד אֲשֶׁר־נָבוֹא אֶל־תּוֹכָם וַהֲרַגְנוּם
ו וְהִשְׁבַּתְנוּ אֶת־הַמְּלָאכָה: וַיְהִי כַּאֲשֶׁר־בָּאוּ הַיְּהוּדִים הַיֹּשְׁבִים אֶצְלָם
ז וַיֹּאמְרוּ לָנוּ עֶשֶׂר פְּעָמִים מִכָּל־הַמְּקֹמוֹת אֲשֶׁר־תָּשׁוּבוּ עָלֵינוּ: וָאַעֲמִיד
מִתַּחְתִּיּוֹת לַמָּקוֹם מֵאַחֲרֵי לַחוֹמָה בְּצִחֲחִים [°בַּצְּחִחִים ק] וָאַעֲמִיד
ח אֶת־הָעָם לְמִשְׁפָּחוֹת עִם־חַרְבֹתֵיהֶם רָמְחֵיהֶם וְקַשְּׁתֹתֵיהֶם: וָאֵרֶא וָאָקוּם
וָאֹמַר אֶל־הַחֹרִים וְאֶל־הַסְּגָנִים וְאֶל־יֶתֶר הָעָם אַל־תִּירְאוּ מִפְּנֵיהֶם אֶת־
אֲדֹנָי הַגָּדוֹל וְהַנּוֹרָא זְכֹרוּ וְהִלָּחֲמוּ עַל־אֲחֵיכֶם בְּנֵיכֶם וּבְנֹתֵיכֶם נְשֵׁיכֶם
ט וּבָתֵּיכֶם: וַיְהִי כַּאֲשֶׁר־שָׁמְעוּ אוֹיְבֵינוּ כִּי־נוֹדַע לָנוּ וַיָּפֶר הָאֱלֹהִים
אֶת־עֲצָתָם °וַנָּשׁוּב [°וַנָּשָׁב ק] כֻּלָּנוּ אֶל־הַחוֹמָה אִישׁ אֶל־מְלַאכְתּוֹ:
י וַיְהִי ׀ מִן־הַיּוֹם הַהוּא חֲצִי נְעָרַי עֹשִׂים בַּמְּלָאכָה וְחֶצְיָם מַחֲזִיקִים
וְהָרְמָחִים הַמָּגִנִּים וְהַקְּשָׁתוֹת וְהַשִּׁרְיֹנִים וְהַשָּׂרִים אַחֲרֵי כָּל־בֵּית יְהוּדָה:
יא הַבּוֹנִים בַּחוֹמָה וְהַנֹּשְׂאִים בַּסֶּבֶל עֹמְשִׂים בְּאַחַת יָדוֹ עֹשֶׂה בַמְּלָאכָה
יב וְאַחַת מַחֲזֶקֶת הַשָּׁלַח: וְהַבּוֹנִים אִישׁ חַרְבּוֹ אֲסוּרִים עַל־מָתְנָיו וּבוֹנִים
יג וְהַתּוֹקֵעַ בַּשּׁוֹפָר אֶצְלִי: וָאֹמַר אֶל־הַחֹרִים וְאֶל־הַסְּגָנִים וְאֶל־יֶתֶר הָעָם
הַמְּלָאכָה הַרְבֵּה וּרְחָבָה וַאֲנַחְנוּ נִפְרָדִים עַל־הַחוֹמָה רְחוֹקִים אִישׁ
יד מֵאָחִיו: בִּמְקוֹם אֲשֶׁר תִּשְׁמְעוּ אֶת־קוֹל הַשּׁוֹפָר שָׁמָּה תִּקָּבְצוּ
אֵלֵינוּ אֱלֹהֵינוּ יִלָּחֶם לָנוּ: וַאֲנַחְנוּ עֹשִׂים בַּמְּלָאכָה וְחֶצְיָם מַחֲזִיקִים
טו בָּרְמָחִים מֵעֲלוֹת הַשַּׁחַר עַד צֵאת הַכּוֹכָבִים: גַּם בָּעֵת הַהִיא אָמַרְתִּי
טז לָעָם אִישׁ וְנַעֲרוֹ יָלִינוּ בְּתוֹךְ יְרוּשָׁלִָם וְהָיוּ־לָנוּ הַלַּיְלָה מִשְׁמָר וְהַיּוֹם
יז מְלָאכָה: וְאֵין אֲנִי וְאַחַי וּנְעָרַי וְאַנְשֵׁי הַמִּשְׁמָר אֲשֶׁר אַחֲרַי אֵין־אֲנַחְנוּ

3:34. Can they finish it so quickly that we will not be able to disrupt the work? (*Rashi*).

4:4. The workers are exhausted and there is so much still to do! The work was beginning to overwhelm the people.

4:5. They planned a surprise attack.

these Jewish weaklings doing? Will they reinforce [the wall]? Will they bring offerings? Can they finish in a day?* Can they restore the stones out of the mounds of dirt, when they have been charred?"

³⁵ Tobiah the Ammonite was next to him, and he said, "Even that which they build, if [even] a fox were to go up, he would breach their stone wall!"

Nehemiah's prayer ³⁶ "Hear, our God, that we are an object of scorn! Return their humiliation upon their own heads! Make them despoiled in a land of captivity! ³⁷ Do not cover up their sins, nor let their transgressions be eradicated from before You, for they have reviled the builders."

³⁸ Yet we built the wall. When the entire wall was joined halfway, the people were heartened to accomplish!

4

Jerusalem's enemies conspire ¹ It happened when Sanballat and Tobiah, and the Arabs and the Ammonites and the Ashdodites heard that the walls of Jerusalem were being healed, that the breaches had begun to be sealed, they grew extremely angry. ² So they all banded together to come and do battle in Jerusalem, and to bring ruin upon it. ³ So we prayed to our God, and we set up a guard over [the workers], by day and by night against them.

⁴ Then [the men of] Judah said, "The strength of the bearer is failing and the earth is abundant;* we are not able to build the wall! ⁵ And our enemies said, 'They will not know [of us] nor see [us] before we come among them and kill them;* and we halt the work!' "

⁶ But then, when Jews who lived near them came and told us ten times, "From all the places to which you return [they will come] against us!"*

Defensive measures ⁷ I set up [defenders] beneath the site, behind the wall, on the cliffs; I set up the people by families with their swords, their spears, and their bows. ⁸ When I saw, I got up and said to the aristocrats and to the nobles, and to the rest of the people, "Do not fear them! Remember the great and awesome Lord, and fight for your brothers, your sons and daughters, your wives and your homes!"

⁹ It happened when our enemies heard that it had became known to us, that God annulled their scheme. We all then returned to the wall, each man to his *Workers and warriors* work. ¹⁰ It happened from that day onward, that half of my youths did the work and half of them held the spears, the shields and the bows, and the armor, and the officers backed the entire House of Judah. ¹¹ Those who built the walls and those who lifted and carried the burdens would do their work with one hand, while one [hand] held a weapon. ¹² As for the builders, each man's sword was girded at his side as they built. The one who sounded the shofar* was next to me. ¹³ I said to the aristocrats and to the nobles, and to the rest of the people, "The work is great and extensive, and we are dispersed along the wall, distant from one another; ¹⁴ to the place where you hear the sound of the shofar, there you are to gather yourselves to us. Our God will fight for us!"

A full day's work ¹⁵ So we did the work, with half of them grasping the spears, from the rising of the dawn until the emergence of the stars. ¹⁶ Also, at that time I said to the people, "Let each man and his attendant spend the night in Jerusalem."* Thus, the night was a watch for us and the day was [for] work. ¹⁷ Thus, neither I nor my brethren nor my servants nor the men of the watch who were under me, none of us

---

4:6. They are planning to attack the workers as they return from work in the evening (*Ibn Ezra*).

4:12. To sound the alarm in event of emergency.
4:16. To help keep guard (*Rashi*).

פְּשָׁטִים בִּגְדֵינוּ אִישׁ שְׁלָחוּ הַמָּיִם:

ה א-ב וַתְּהִי צַעֲקַת הָעָם וּנְשֵׁיהֶם גְּדוֹלָה אֶל־אֲחֵיהֶם הַיְּהוּדִים: וְיֵשׁ אֲשֶׁר
ג אֹמְרִים בָּנֵינוּ וּבְנֹתֵינוּ אֲנַחְנוּ רַבִּים וְנִקְחָה דָגָן וְנֹאכְלָה וְנִחְיֶה: וְיֵשׁ אֲשֶׁר
ד אֹמְרִים שְׂדֹתֵינוּ וּכְרָמֵינוּ וּבָתֵּינוּ אֲנַחְנוּ עֹרְבִים וְנִקְחָה דָגָן בָּרָעָב: וְיֵשׁ
ה אֲשֶׁר אֹמְרִים לָוִינוּ כֶסֶף לְמִדַּת הַמֶּלֶךְ שְׂדֹתֵינוּ וּכְרָמֵינוּ: וְעַתָּה כִּבְשַׂר
אַחֵינוּ בְּשָׂרֵנוּ כִּבְנֵיהֶם בָּנֵינוּ וְהִנֵּה אֲנַחְנוּ כֹבְשִׁים אֶת־בָּנֵינוּ וְאֶת־בְּנֹתֵינוּ
לַעֲבָדִים וְיֵשׁ מִבְּנֹתֵינוּ נִכְבָּשׁוֹת וְאֵין לְאֵל יָדֵנוּ וּשְׂדֹתֵינוּ וּכְרָמֵינוּ
ו לַאֲחֵרִים: וַיִּחַר לִי מְאֹד כַּאֲשֶׁר שָׁמַעְתִּי אֶת־זַעֲקָתָם וְאֵת הַדְּבָרִים
ז הָאֵלֶּה: וַיִּמָּלֵךְ לִבִּי עָלַי וָאָרִיבָה אֶת־הַחֹרִים וְאֶת־הַסְּגָנִים וָאֹמְרָה לָהֶם
מַשָּׁא אִישׁ־בְּאָחִיו אַתֶּם °נֹשִׁאים [°נֹשִׁים ק] וָאֶתֵּן עֲלֵיהֶם קְהִלָּה גְדוֹלָה:
ח וָאֹמְרָה לָהֶם אֲנַחְנוּ קָנִינוּ אֶת־אַחֵינוּ הַיְּהוּדִים הַנִּמְכָּרִים לַגּוֹיִם כְּדֵי בָנוּ
וְגַם־אַתֶּם תִּמְכְּרוּ אֶת־אֲחֵיכֶם וְנִמְכְּרוּ־לָנוּ וַיַּחֲרִישׁוּ וְלֹא מָצְאוּ דָּבָר:
ט °וַיֹּאמֶר [°וָאֹמַר ק] לֹא־טוֹב הַדָּבָר אֲשֶׁר אַתֶּם עֹשִׂים הֲלוֹא בְּיִרְאַת
י אֱלֹהֵינוּ תֵּלֵכוּ מֵחֶרְפַּת הַגּוֹיִם אוֹיְבֵינוּ: וְגַם־אֲנִי אַחַי וּנְעָרַי נֹשִׁים בָּהֶם
יא כֶּסֶף וְדָגָן נַעַזְבָה־נָּא אֶת־הַמַּשָּׁא הַזֶּה: הָשִׁיבוּ נָא לָהֶם כְּהַיּוֹם שְׂדֹתֵיהֶם
כַּרְמֵיהֶם זֵיתֵיהֶם וּבָתֵּיהֶם וּמְאַת הַכֶּסֶף וְהַדָּגָן הַתִּירוֹשׁ וְהַיִּצְהָר אֲשֶׁר
יב אַתֶּם נֹשִׁים בָּהֶם: וַיֹּאמְרוּ נָשִׁיב וּמֵהֶם לֹא נְבַקֵּשׁ כֵּן נַעֲשֶׂה כַּאֲשֶׁר אַתָּה
אוֹמֵר וָאֶקְרָא אֶת־הַכֹּהֲנִים וָאַשְׁבִּיעֵם לַעֲשׂוֹת כַּדָּבָר הַזֶּה: גַּם־חָצְנִי
יג נָעַרְתִּי וָאֹמְרָה כָּכָה יְנַעֵר הָאֱלֹהִים אֶת־כָּל־הָאִישׁ אֲשֶׁר לֹא־יָקִים אֶת־
הַדָּבָר הַזֶּה מִבֵּיתוֹ וּמִיגִיעוֹ וְכָכָה יִהְיֶה נָעוּר וָרֵק וַיֹּאמְרוּ כָל־הַקָּהָל אָמֵן
יד וַיְהַלְלוּ אֶת־יְהֹוָה וַיַּעַשׂ הָעָם כַּדָּבָר הַזֶּה: גַּם מִיּוֹם | אֲשֶׁר־צִוָּה אֹתִי
לִהְיוֹת פֶּחָם בְּאֶרֶץ יְהוּדָה מִשְּׁנַת עֶשְׂרִים וְעַד שְׁנַת שְׁלֹשִׁים וּשְׁתַּיִם
לְאַרְתַּחְשַׁסְתְּא הַמֶּלֶךְ שָׁנִים שְׁתֵּים עֶשְׂרֵה אֲנִי וְאַחַי לֶחֶם הַפֶּחָה לֹא
טו אָכַלְתִּי: וְהַפַּחוֹת הָרִאשֹׁנִים אֲשֶׁר־לְפָנַי הִכְבִּידוּ עַל־הָעָם וַיִּקְחוּ מֵהֶם
בְּלֶחֶם וָיַיִן אַחַר כֶּסֶף־שְׁקָלִים אַרְבָּעִים גַּם נַעֲרֵיהֶם שָׁלְטוּ עַל־הָעָם וַאֲנִי
טז לֹא־עָשִׂיתִי כֵן מִפְּנֵי יִרְאַת אֱלֹהִים: וְגַם בִּמְלֶאכֶת הַחוֹמָה הַזֹּאת
הֶחֱזַקְתִּי וְשָׂדֶה לֹא קָנִינוּ וְכָל־נְעָרַי קְבוּצִים שָׁם עַל־הַמְּלָאכָה:
יז וְהַיְּהוּדִים וְהַסְּגָנִים מֵאָה וַחֲמִשִּׁים אִישׁ וְהַבָּאִים אֵלֵינוּ מִן־הַגּוֹיִם
יח אֲשֶׁר־סְבִיבֹתֵינוּ עַל־שֻׁלְחָנִי: וַאֲשֶׁר הָיָה נַעֲשֶׂה לְיוֹם אֶחָד שׁוֹר אֶחָד
צֹאן שֵׁשׁ־בְּרֻרוֹת וְצִפֳּרִים נַעֲשׂוּ־לִי וּבֵין עֲשֶׂרֶת יָמִים בְּכָל־יַיִן לְהַרְבֵּה
וְעִם־זֶה לֶחֶם הַפֶּחָה לֹא בִקַּשְׁתִּי כִּי־כָבְדָה הָעֲבֹדָה עַל־הָעָם הַזֶּה:

5:2. "We do not have enough money to support our large families" (*Metzudos*).

5:8. If you sell them to collect your debts, we will only have to redeem them again! (*Rashi*).

5:9. If you do not act for the sake of righteousness, at least be sensitive to the humiliation that this situation causes us in the eyes of our enemies (*Metzudos*).

5:12. Nehemiah wanted the *Kohanim* to witness the oath, thus adding to its solemnity (*Ibn Ezra*).

5:14. As the next verse explains, a levy had been

removed our garments; no one disrobed [even to launder] in water.

5

ECONOMIC
INEQUITY
AND
INIQUITY
5:1-5:19

¹ **N**ow, the outcry of the people and their wives concerning their Jewish brethren was great. ² There were those who said, "[With] our sons and our daughters, we are numerous, and we must buy grain that we may eat and remain alive."* ³ And there were those who said, "We are mortgaging our fields and our vineyards and our homes to buy grain during the famine." ⁴ And there were those who said, "We have borrowed money [against] our fields and our vineyards for the king's tax. ⁵ Now, our flesh is as worthy as the flesh of our brethren and our sons are as worthy as their sons, yet we must press our sons and our daughters into being servants! Some of our daughters have been pressed into servitude, and our hands do not have the means [to redeem them]; and our fields and our vineyards are [held] by others!"

Nehemiah
confronts
the lords
and sets
the example

⁶ I became very angry when I heard their outcry and these matters. ⁷ Then my heart moved me and I confronted the aristocrats and the nobles and said to them, "Are you creditors of loans against your brothers?" and I gathered a large crowd around them. ⁸ I said to them, "We have ransomed our brother Jews who were sold to gentiles for as much as we could afford. Now will you sell your brothers again, only to be resold to us?"* They were silent; they could not find a response. ⁹ Then I said, "The thing you are doing is not good; surely you should walk with the fear of our God, because of the scorn of the nations, our enemies!* ¹⁰ I and my brethren and my servants, as well, have lent them money and grain; let us all now relinquish this debt. ¹¹ Return to them now, this very day, their fields, their vineyards, their olive orchards and their homes, as well as the hundreds in money, and the grain, the wine, and the oil that you hold against them."

¹² They replied, "We shall return [it all]; and we will make no demands of them. We shall do as you say."

Then I summoned the Kohanim,* and I administered an oath upon them to act in accordance with this matter. ¹³ I also shook the hem of my garment and said, "So may God shake out from his home and from his toil any man who does not fulfill this matter, and so may he remain, shaken out and empty!" The entire congregation said, "Amen," and they praised HASHEM; and the people acted in accordance with this matter.

¹⁴ Moreover, from the day that [the king] appointed me as governor of the land of Judah, from the twentieth year until the thirty-second year of King Artaxerxes — twelve years — I and my brethren did not eat of the governor's food. * ¹⁵ The former governors who were before me had imposed burdens upon the people and taken bread and wine from them, in addition to forty silver shekels, and also their servants domineered over the people; but I did not do so, because of [my] fear of God. ¹⁶ Also, I supported the work of this wall, so we did not buy any field, and

Nehemiah's
expenditure

all of my servants were gathered there for work. * ¹⁷ [Ordinary] Jews and nobles, a hundred and fifty men, in addition to those [proselytes] who came to us from the nations around us, were at my table. ¹⁸ That which was prepared for each day was one bull, six selected sheep and fowl prepared for me, and every ten days a multitude of all sorts of wine. Yet, despite this, I did not request the governor's food, for the labor weighed heavily upon this people.

---

imposed by previous governors upon the local populace to provide the governor's food, but Nehemiah refused to make use of it.

5:16. I put all the manpower at my disposal towards the building of the wall, rather than applying them toward farming and my own personal income (*Malbim*).

ו

יט-א זָכְרָה־לִּי אֱלֹהַי לְטוֹבָה כֹּל אֲשֶׁר־עָשִׂיתִי עַל־הָעָם הַזֶּה: וַיְהִי
כַאֲשֶׁר נִשְׁמַע לְסַנְבַלַּט וְטוֹבִיָּה וּלְגֶשֶׁם הָעַרְבִי וּלְיֶתֶר אֹיְבֵינוּ כִּי בָנִיתִי
אֶת־הַחוֹמָה וְלֹא־נוֹתַר בָּהּ פָּרֶץ גַּם עַד־הָעֵת הַהִיא דְּלָתוֹת לֹא־
ב הֶעֱמַדְתִּי בַשְּׁעָרִים: וַיִּשְׁלַח סַנְבַלַּט וְגֶשֶׁם אֵלַי לֵאמֹר לְכָה וְנִוָּעֲדָה יַחְדָּו
ג בַּכְּפִירִים בְּבִקְעַת אוֹנוֹ וְהֵמָּה חֹשְׁבִים לַעֲשׂוֹת לִי רָעָה: וָאֶשְׁלְחָה עֲלֵיהֶם
מַלְאָכִים לֵאמֹר מְלָאכָה גְדוֹלָה אֲנִי עֹשֶׂה וְלֹא אוּכַל לָרֶדֶת לָמָּה תִשְׁבַּת
ד הַמְּלָאכָה כַּאֲשֶׁר אַרְפֶּהָ וְיָרַדְתִּי אֲלֵיכֶם: וַיִּשְׁלְחוּ אֵלַי כַּדָּבָר הַזֶּה אַרְבַּע
ה פְּעָמִים וָאָשִׁיב אוֹתָם כַּדָּבָר הַזֶּה: וַיִּשְׁלַח אֵלַי סַנְבַלַּט כַּדָּבָר הַזֶּה פַּעַם
ו חֲמִישִׁית אֶת־נַעֲרוֹ וְאִגֶּרֶת פְּתוּחָה בְּיָדוֹ: כָּתוּב בָּהּ בַּגּוֹיִם נִשְׁמָע וְגַשְׁמוּ
אֹמֵר אַתָּה וְהַיְּהוּדִים חֹשְׁבִים לִמְרוֹד עַל־כֵּן אַתָּה בוֹנֶה הַחוֹמָה וְאַתָּה
ז הֹוֶה לָהֶם לְמֶלֶךְ כַּדְּבָרִים הָאֵלֶּה: וְגַם־נְבִיאִים הֶעֱמַדְתָּ לִקְרֹא עָלֶיךָ
בִירוּשָׁלַ͏ִם לֵאמֹר מֶלֶךְ בִּיהוּדָה וְעַתָּה יִשָּׁמַע לַמֶּלֶךְ כַּדְּבָרִים הָאֵלֶּה
ח וְעַתָּה לְכָה וְנִוָּעֲצָה יַחְדָּו: וָאֶשְׁלְחָה אֵלָיו לֵאמֹר לֹא נִהְיָה כַּדְּבָרִים
ט הָאֵלֶּה אֲשֶׁר אַתָּה אוֹמֵר כִּי מִלִּבְּךָ אַתָּה בוֹדָאָם: כִּי כֻלָּם מְיָרְאִים אוֹתָנוּ
י לֵאמֹר יִרְפּוּ יְדֵיהֶם מִן־הַמְּלָאכָה וְלֹא תֵעָשֶׂה וְעַתָּה חַזֵּק אֶת־יָדָי: וַאֲנִי־
בָאתִי בֵּית שְׁמַעְיָה בֶן־דְּלָיָה בֶּן־מְהֵיטַבְאֵל וְהוּא עָצוּר וַיֹּאמֶר נִוָּעֵד אֶל־
בֵּית הָאֱלֹהִים אֶל־תּוֹךְ הַהֵיכָל וְנִסְגְּרָה דַּלְתוֹת הַהֵיכָל כִּי בָּאִים לְהָרְגֶךָ
יא וְלַיְלָה בָּאִים לְהָרְגֶךָ: וָאֹמְרָה הַאִישׁ כָּמוֹנִי יִבְרָח וּמִי כָמוֹנִי אֲשֶׁר־יָבוֹא
יב אֶל־הַהֵיכָל וָחָי לֹא אָבוֹא: וָאַכִּירָה וְהִנֵּה לֹא־אֱלֹהִים שְׁלָחוֹ כִּי הַנְּבוּאָה
יג דִּבֶּר עָלַי וְטוֹבִיָּה וְסַנְבַלַּט שְׂכָרוֹ: לְמַעַן שָׂכוּר הוּא לְמַעַן־אִירָא וְאֶעֱשֶׂה
יד כֵּן וְחָטָאתִי וְהָיָה לָהֶם לְשֵׁם רָע לְמַעַן יְחָרְפוּנִי: זָכְרָה אֱלֹהַי
לְטוֹבִיָּה וּלְסַנְבַלַּט כְּמַעֲשָׂיו אֵלֶּה וְגַם לְנוֹעַדְיָה הַנְּבִיאָה וּלְיֶתֶר הַנְּבִיאִים
טו אֲשֶׁר הָיוּ מְיָרְאִים אוֹתִי: וַתִּשְׁלַם הַחוֹמָה בְּעֶשְׂרִים וַחֲמִשָּׁה לֶאֱלוּל
טז לַחֲמִשִּׁים וּשְׁנַיִם יוֹם: וַיְהִי כַּאֲשֶׁר שָׁמְעוּ כָּל־אוֹיְבֵינוּ וַיִּרְאוּ
כָּל־הַגּוֹיִם אֲשֶׁר סְבִיבֹתֵינוּ וַיִּפְּלוּ מְאֹד בְּעֵינֵיהֶם וַיֵּדְעוּ כִּי מֵאֵת אֱלֹהֵינוּ
יז נֶעֶשְׂתָה הַמְּלָאכָה הַזֹּאת: גַּם ׀ בַּיָּמִים הָהֵם מַרְבִּים חֹרֵי יְהוּדָה אִגְּרֹתֵיהֶם
יח הוֹלְכוֹת עַל־טוֹבִיָּה וַאֲשֶׁר לְטוֹבִיָּה בָּאוֹת אֲלֵיהֶם: כִּי־רַבִּים בִּיהוּדָה
בַּעֲלֵי שְׁבוּעָה לוֹ כִּי־חָתָן הוּא לִשְׁכַנְיָה בֶן־אָרַח וִיהוֹחָנָן בְּנוֹ לָקַח אֶת־
יט בַּת־מְשֻׁלָּם בֶּן בֶּרֶכְיָה: גַּם טוֹבֹתָיו הָיוּ אֹמְרִים לְפָנַי וּדְבָרַי הָיוּ מוֹצִיאִים
לוֹ אִגְּרוֹת שָׁלַח טוֹבִיָּה לְיָרְאֵנִי:

6:5. Sanballat wanted his message to become public to frighten the people.

6:7. Let us plan how to conceal this matter from the king (*Metzudos*).

6:9. Your constant attempts to weaken our resolve have only achieved the opposite result (*Ralbag*).

6:10. Shemaiah was a false prophet who lived as an ascetic hermit. In an attempt to frame Nehemiah, Sanballat and Tobiah had hired Shemaiah to prophesy, "There is a king in Judah!" (v. 7). Nehemiah, who did not know whether Shemaiah was a true prophet, now went to question him about his statement.

6:11. Nehemiah gave two reasons for refusing the invitation: It is wrong for the leader of the people to go into

¹⁹ *"Remember in my favor, O my God, all that I did for this people!"*

6

Sanballat's
devious
invitation

¹ **N**ow, *when it was reported to Sanballat and Tobiah, and to Geshem the Arab and to the rest of our enemies that I had built the wall and no breach remained in it, and also that as of that time I had not [yet] erected doors in the gateways,* ² *Sanballat and Geshem sent [word] to me, saying, "Come, let us meet at Chephirim in the valley of Ono." But [I understood that] they were planning to harm me.*

³ *I sent envoys to them, saying, "I am involved in a great work, and I am unable to come down; why should the work be halted when I leave it and come down to you?"*

⁴ *They sent me this message four times, and I replied to them the same way.*

Sanballat's
charge and
Nehemiah's
reply

⁵ *Then Sanballat sent me the same message a fifth time with his servant, with an open letter in his hand.* * ⁶ *In it was written these words: "It has been heard among the nations, and Geshem confirms it, [that] you and the Jews plan to rebel, and that is why you are building the wall; and [that] you are becoming their king, and similar things;* ⁷ *and [that] you have also set up prophets to proclaim about you in Jerusalem, saying, 'There is a king in Judah!' Now these things will be heard by the king! So now, come and let us take counsel together!"* *

⁸ *I sent [word] to him, saying, "These things that you say have never happened; you have fabricated them from your heart!* ⁹ *For you all try to frighten us, saying, 'Let [the resolve of] their hands for doing the work be weakened, so that it will not be done.' But now, you strengthen my hand!"* *

False
prophet
detected

¹⁰ *I then came to the home of Shemaiah son of Delaiah son of Mehetabel who was confined indoors.* * *He said, "Let us meet at the Temple of God, inside the Sanctuary, and let us close the Sanctuary doors, for they are coming to kill you. Tonight they are coming to kill you!"*

¹¹ *But I said, "Can a man like me run away? And who, being like me, may enter the Sanctuary and live?* * *I will not come!"* ¹² *Then I realized that, behold! God had not sent him, for he had spoken as if it was a prophecy for me!* * *Rather, Tobiah or Sanballat had hired him!* ¹³ *It was because he was a hireling, so that I would be frightened, comply, and sin — so that they would have a scandal with which to humiliate me.*

¹⁴ *"My God, recall for Tobiah or Sanballat these deeds of his; and also for Noadiah the prophetess and the rest of the [false] prophets who [tried to] intimidate me!"*

Completion
of the wall

¹⁵ *The wall was completed on the twenty-fifth of Elul, after fifty-two days.* ¹⁶ *It happened when all our enemies heard [this], and all the nations around us saw, they fell greatly in their own eyes, for they realized that this work was accomplished by our God.* ¹⁷ *But even in those days the aristocrats of Judah wrote many*

Tobiah's
Jewish
friends

letters addressed to Tobiah, and Tobiah's came to them, ¹⁸ *for many people in Judah had sworn allegiance to him, because he was the son-in-law of Shecaniah son of Arah, and his son Jehohanan had married the daughter of Meshullam son of Berechiah.* ¹⁹ *They also would recite his merits before me* * *and passed along my remarks to him, and Tobiah sent letters to intimidate me.*

---

hiding; and, since he was not a *Kohen,* he was forbidden to enter the Sanctuary.

6:12. A wise counselor may, on occasion, advise a person to transgress a commandment in order to save his life; but a true prophet, particularly an unproven one, would never prophesy to transgress a prohibition stated in the Torah (*Rashi, Metzudos*).

6:19. To justify their support for him.

א וַיְהִ֗י כַּאֲשֶׁ֤ר נִבְנְתָה֙ הַ֣חוֹמָ֔ה וָאַעֲמִ֖יד הַדְּלָת֑וֹת וַיִּפָּ֣קְד֔וּ הַשּֽׁוֹעֲרִ֖ים

ב וְהַֽמְשֹׁרְרִ֖ים וְהַלְוִיִּֽם: וָאֲצַוֶּ֞ה אֶת־חֲנָ֣נִי אָחִ֗י וְאֶת־חֲנַנְיָ֛ה שַׂ֥ר הַבִּירָ֖ה עַל־

ג יְרוּשָׁלָ֑͏ִם כִּי־ה֤וּא כְּאִ֣ישׁ אֱמֶ֔ת וְיָרֵ֥א אֶת־הָאֱלֹהִ֖ים מֵרַבִּֽים: °וַיֹּ֣אמֶר

[וָאֹמַ֣ר ק] לָהֶ֗ם לֹ֣א יִפָּֽתְח֞וּ שַֽׁעֲרֵ֤י יְרֽוּשָׁלַ֙͏ִם֙ עַד־חֹ֣ם הַשֶּׁ֔מֶשׁ וְעַ֨ד הֵ֤ם

עֹֽמְדִים֙ יָגִ֣יפוּ הַדְּלָת֔וֹת וֶאֱחֹ֑זוּ וְהַעֲמֵ֗יד מִשְׁמְרוֹת֙ יֹשְׁבֵ֣י יְרֽוּשָׁלַ֔͏ִם אִ֚ישׁ

ד בְּמִשְׁמָר֔וֹ וְאִ֖ישׁ נֶ֥גֶד בֵּיתֽוֹ: וְהָעִ֞יר רַחֲבַ֤ת יָדַ֙יִם֙ וּגְדוֹלָ֔ה וְהָעָ֥ם מְעַ֖ט בְּתוֹכָ֑הּ

ה וְאֵ֥ין בָּתִּ֖ים בְּנוּיִֽם: וַיִּתֵּ֤ן אֱלֹהַי֙ אֶל־לִבִּ֔י וָאֶקְבְּצָ֞ה אֶת־הַחֹרִ֤ים וְאֶת־

הַסְּגָנִ֛ים וְאֶת־הָעָ֖ם לְהִתְיַחֵ֑שׂ וָֽאֶמְצָ֗א סֵ֤פֶר הַיַּ֙חַשׂ֙ הָעוֹלִ֣ים בָּרִאשׁוֹנָ֔ה

ו וָאֶמְצָ֖א כָּת֥וּב בּֽוֹ: אֵ֣לֶּה | בְּנֵ֣י הַמְּדִינָ֗ה הָעֹלִים֙ מִשְּׁבִ֣י הַגּוֹלָ֔ה

אֲשֶׁ֣ר הֶגְלָ֔ה נְבֽוּכַדְנֶצַּ֖ר מֶ֣לֶךְ בָּבֶ֑ל וַיָּשׁ֧וּבוּ לִירֽוּשָׁלַ֛͏ִם וְלִיהוּדָ֖ה אִ֥ישׁ לְעִירֽוֹ:

ז הַבָּאִ֣ים עִם־זְרֻבָּבֶ֗ל יֵשׁ֡וּעַ נְ֠חֶמְיָ֠ה עֲזַרְיָ֨ה רַֽעַמְיָ֜ה נַחֲמָ֗נִי מָרְדֳּכַ֤י בִּלְשָׁן֙

ח מִסְפֶּ֣רֶת בִּגְוַ֔י נְח֖וּם בַּֽעֲנָ֑ה מִסְפַּ֕ר אַנְשֵׁ֖י עַ֥ם יִשְׂרָאֵֽל: בְּנֵ֣י פַרְעֹ֔שׁ אַלְפַּ֕יִם

ט-י מֵאָ֖ה וְשִׁבְעִ֥ים וּשְׁנָֽיִם: בְּנֵ֣י שְׁפַטְיָ֔ה שְׁלֹ֥שׁ מֵא֖וֹת שִׁבְעִ֥ים וּשְׁנָֽיִם: בְּנֵ֣י אָרַ֔ח

יא שֵׁ֥שׁ מֵא֖וֹת חֲמִשִּׁ֥ים וּשְׁנָֽיִם: בְּנֵֽי־פַחַ֥ת מוֹאָ֛ב לִבְנֵ֥י יֵשׁ֖וּעַ וְיוֹאָ֑ב אַלְפַּ֕יִם

יב-יג וּשְׁמֹנֶ֥ה מֵא֖וֹת שְׁמֹנָ֥ה עָשָֽׂר: בְּנֵ֣י עֵילָ֔ם אֶ֕לֶף מָאתַ֖יִם חֲמִשִּׁ֥ים וְאַרְבָּעָֽה: בְּנֵ֣י

יד-טו זַתּ֔וּא שְׁמֹנֶ֥ה מֵא֖וֹת אַרְבָּעִ֥ים וַחֲמִשָּֽׁה: בְּנֵ֣י זַכָּ֔י שְׁבַ֥ע מֵא֖וֹת וְשִׁשִּֽׁים: בְּנֵ֣י

טז-יז בִנּ֔וּי שֵׁ֥שׁ מֵא֖וֹת אַרְבָּעִ֥ים וּשְׁמֹנָֽה: בְּנֵ֣י בֵבָ֔י שֵׁ֥שׁ מֵא֖וֹת עֶשְׂרִ֥ים וּשְׁמֹנָֽה: בְּנֵ֣י

יח עַזְגָּ֔ד אַלְפַּ֕יִם שְׁלֹ֥שׁ מֵא֖וֹת עֶשְׂרִ֥ים וּשְׁנָֽיִם: בְּנֵ֣י אֲדֹנִיקָ֔ם שֵׁ֥שׁ מֵא֖וֹת שִׁשִּׁ֥ים

יט וְשִׁבְעָֽה: בְּנֵ֣י בִגְוָ֔י אַלְפַּ֕יִם שִׁשִּׁ֥ים וְשִׁבְעָֽה: בְּנֵ֣י עָדִ֔ין שֵׁ֥שׁ מֵא֖וֹת חֲמִשִּׁ֥ים

כא-כב וַחֲמִשָּֽׁה: בְּנֵֽי־אָטֵ֥ר לְחִזְקִיָּ֖ה תִּשְׁעִ֥ים וּשְׁמֹנָֽה: בְּנֵ֣י חָשֻׁ֔ם שְׁלֹ֥שׁ מֵא֖וֹת

כג-כד עֶשְׂרִ֥ים וּשְׁמֹנָֽה: בְּנֵ֣י בֵצָ֔י שְׁלֹ֥שׁ מֵא֖וֹת עֶשְׂרִ֥ים וְאַרְבָּעָֽה: בְּנֵ֣י חָרִ֔יף מֵאָ֥ה

כה-כו שְׁנֵ֥ים עָשָֽׂר: בְּנֵ֣י גִבְע֔וֹן תִּשְׁעִ֥ים וַחֲמִשָּֽׁה: אַנְשֵׁ֤י בֵֽית־לֶ֙חֶם֙ וּנְטֹפָ֔ה מֵאָ֥ה

כז-כח שְׁמֹנִ֥ים וּשְׁמֹנָֽה: אַנְשֵׁ֣י עֲנָת֔וֹת מֵאָ֥ה עֶשְׂרִ֥ים וּשְׁמֹנָֽה: אַנְשֵׁ֥י בֵית־עַזְמָ֖וֶת

כט אַרְבָּעִ֥ים וּשְׁנָֽיִם: אַנְשֵׁ֨י קִרְיַ֤ת יְעָרִים֙ כְּפִירָ֣ה וּבְאֵר֔וֹת שְׁבַ֥ע מֵא֖וֹת

ל-לא אַרְבָּעִ֥ים וּשְׁלֹשָֽׁה: אַנְשֵׁ֤י הָֽרָמָה֙ וָגָ֔בַע שֵׁ֥שׁ מֵא֖וֹת עֶשְׂרִ֥ים וְאֶחָֽד: אַנְשֵׁ֣י

לב מִכְמָ֔ס מֵאָ֖ה וְעֶשְׂרִ֥ים וּשְׁנָֽיִם: אַנְשֵׁ֤י בֵֽית־אֵל֙ וְהָעָ֔י מֵאָ֖ה עֶשְׂרִ֥ים וּשְׁלֹשָֽׁה:

לג-לד אַנְשֵׁ֥י נְב֖וֹ אַחֵ֑ר חֲמִשִּׁ֥ים וּשְׁנָֽיִם: בְּנֵ֣י עֵילָ֔ם אַחֵ֕ר אֶ֕לֶף מָאתַ֖יִם חֲמִשִּֽׁים

לה-לו וְאַרְבָּעָֽה: בְּנֵ֣י חָרִ֔ם שְׁלֹ֥שׁ מֵא֖וֹת וְעֶשְׂרִֽים: בְּנֵֽי־יְרֵח֔וֹ שְׁלֹ֥שׁ מֵא֖וֹת אַרְבָּעִ֥ים

לז-לח וַחֲמִשָּֽׁה: בְּנֵי־לֹ֣ד חָדִ֗יד וְאוֹנ֔וֹ שְׁבַ֥ע מֵא֖וֹת עֶשְׂרִ֥ים וְאֶחָֽד: בְּנֵ֣י סְנָאָ֔ה

לט שְׁלֹ֥שֶׁת אֲלָפִ֕ים תְּשַׁ֥ע מֵא֖וֹת וּשְׁלֹשִֽׁים: הַכֹּ֣הֲנִ֑ים בְּנֵ֤י יְדַֽעְיָה֙ לְבֵ֣ית יֵשׁ֔וּעַ

7:3. The doors would be opened only long enough to let people pass through. This drastic precaution was to prevent Sanballat's infiltrators from entering (*Rashi*).

7:4. Many of the old houses were still in ruins, providing excellent cover for hostile people (*Metzudos*).

7:5. In the days of Cyrus.

7:6. Although Nehemiah states that the document he found was written at the time of the original settlement, he updated the number of settlers to reflect the population of the Jewish community at the time of his writing, thirty-six years later. The sizes of the various families had changed through deaths and births. In general, the birth rate exceeded the death rate, so that the numbers in

7

¹ It happened after the wall was built and I had erected its doors, that the gatekeepers and the singers and the [other] Levites were designated. ² I then appointed Hanani my brother and Hananiah, officer of the palace, over Jerusalem, for [Hananiah] was a man of truth, and had long been God-fearing. ³ I said to them, "Let the gates of Jerusalem not be opened until the heat of the day, and while they are standing there let them shut the doors and secure them. * Also, establish watches by the inhabitants of Jerusalem, each man at his watch, and each man opposite his home." ⁴ For the city had wide open spaces and was large, but there were few people in it, and houses had not been built. *

⁵ Then my God inspired me and I assembled the aristocrats and the nobles, and the people to trace their lineage. I found the Book of Lineage of those who had ascended at first* and found written in it:

*The Book
of Lineage*

⁶ These* are the people of the country who ascended from the captivity of the exile that Nebuchadnezzar king of Babylonia had exiled, who returned to Jerusalem and Judah, each man to his city, ⁷ who came with Zerubbabel, Jeshua, Nehemiah, Azariah, Raamiah, Nahamani, Mordechai-bilshan, Mispereth-bigvai, Nehum and Baanah; [who comprised] the sum of the dignitaries of the people of Israel:

*Returnees
by family
. . .*

⁸ The children of Parosh, two thousand one hundred seventy-two; ⁹ the children of Shephatiah, three hundred seventy-two; ¹⁰ the children of Arah, six hundred fifty-two; ¹¹ the children of the governor of Moab — of the children of Jeshua and Joab — two thousand eight hundred eighteen; ¹² the children of Elam, one thousand two hundred fifty-four; ¹³ the children of Zattu, eight hundred forty-five; ¹⁴ the children of Zaccai, seven hundred sixty; ¹⁵ the children of Binnui, six hundred forty-eight; ¹⁶ the children of Bebai, six hundred twenty-eight; ¹⁷ the children of Azgad, two thousand three hundred twenty-two; ¹⁸ the children of Adonikam, six hundred sixty-seven; ¹⁹ the children of Bigvai, two thousand sixty-seven; ²⁰ the children of Adin, six hundred fifty-five; ²¹ the children of Ater of Hezekiah, ninety-eight; ²² the children of Hashum, three hundred twenty-eight; ²³ the children of Bezai, three hundred twenty-four; ²⁴ the children of Hariph, one hundred twelve.

*. . . and
by city*

²⁵ The people of Gibeon, ninety-five; ²⁶ the people of Bethlehem and Netophah, one hundred eighty-eight; ²⁷ the people of Anathoth, one hundred twenty-eight; ²⁸ the people of Beth-azmaveth, forty-two; ²⁹ the people of Kiriath-jearim, Chephirah and Beeroth, seven hundred forty-three; ³⁰ the people of Ramah and Geba, six hundred twenty-one; ³¹ the people of Michmas, one hundred twenty-two; ³² the people of Beth-el and Ai, one hundred twenty-three; ³³ the people of Nebo-aher, fifty-two; ³⁴ the people of a different Elam,* one thousand two hundred fifty-four; ³⁵ the people of Harim, three hundred twenty; ³⁶ the people of Jericho, three hundred forty-five; ³⁷ the people of Lod, Hadid and Ono, seven hundred twenty-one; ³⁸ the people of Senaah, three thousand nine hundred thirty.

³⁹ The Kohanim: The children of Jedaiah, of the house of Jeshua,

---

Nehemiah generally exceed those in *Ezra.* Nevertheless, Nehemiah was careful to give the original total in his account as well, in order to reflect accurately the condi-

tions of the original settlement (*Metzudos*).
7:34. This Elam is a city; in verse 12 it is a family. Nevertheless, the number of people is the same.

מ-מא   תֵּשַׁע מֵאוֹת שִׁבְעִים וּשְׁלֹשָׁה: בְּנֵי אִמֵּר אֶלֶף חֲמִשִּׁים וּשְׁנָיִם: בְּנֵי פַשְׁחוּר

מב-מג   אֶלֶף מָאתַיִם אַרְבָּעִים וְשִׁבְעָה: בְּנֵי חָרִם אֶלֶף שִׁבְעָה עָשָׂר: הַלְוִיִּם בְּנֵי־

מד   יֵשׁוּעַ לְקַדְמִיאֵל לִבְנֵי לְהוֹדְוָה שִׁבְעִים וְאַרְבָּעָה: הַמְשֹׁרְרִים בְּנֵי אָסָף

מה   מֵאָה אַרְבָּעִים וּשְׁמֹנָה: הַשֹּׁעֲרִים בְּנֵי־שַׁלּוּם בְּנֵי־אָטֵר בְּנֵי־טַלְמֹן בְּנֵי־

מו   עַקּוּב בְּנֵי חֲטִיטָא בְּנֵי שֹׁבָי מֵאָה שְׁלֹשִׁים וּשְׁמֹנָה: הַנְּתִינִים בְּנֵי־צִחָא

מז-מח   בְּנֵי־חֲשֻׂפָא בְּנֵי טַבָּעוֹת: בְּנֵי־קֵירֹס בְּנֵי־סִיעָא בְּנֵי פָדוֹן: בְּנֵי־לְבָנָה בְּנֵי־

מט-נ   חֲגָבָה בְּנֵי שַׁלְמָי: בְּנֵי־חָנָן בְּנֵי־גִדֵּל בְּנֵי־גָחַר: בְּנֵי־רְאָיָה בְּנֵי־רְצִין בְּנֵי

נא-נב   נְקוֹדָא: בְּנֵי־גַזָּם בְּנֵי עֻזָּא בְּנֵי פָסֵחַ: בְּנֵי־בֵסַי בְּנֵי־מְעוּנִים בְּנֵי °נְפוּשְׁסִים

נג-נד   [°נְפִישְׁסִים ק]: בְּנֵי־בַקְבּוּק בְּנֵי־חֲקוּפָא בְּנֵי חַרְחוּר: בְּנֵי־בַצְלִית בְּנֵי־

נה-נו   מְחִידָא בְּנֵי חַרְשָׁא: בְּנֵי־בַרְקוֹס בְּנֵי־סִיסְרָא בְּנֵי־תָמַח: בְּנֵי נְצִיחַ בְּנֵי

נז-נח   חֲטִיפָא: בְּנֵי עַבְדֵי שְׁלֹמֹה בְּנֵי־סוֹטַי בְּנֵי־סוֹפֶרֶת בְּנֵי פְרִידָא: בְּנֵי־יַעְלָא

נט   בְּנֵי־דַרְקוֹן בְּנֵי גִדֵּל: בְּנֵי שְׁפַטְיָה בְּנֵי־חַטִּיל בְּנֵי פֹּכֶרֶת הַצְּבָיִים בְּנֵי אָמוֹן:

ס-סא   כָּל־הַנְּתִינִים וּבְנֵי עַבְדֵי שְׁלֹמֹה שְׁלֹשׁ מֵאוֹת תִּשְׁעִים וּשְׁנָיִם: וְאֵלֶּה

הָעוֹלִים מִתֵּל מֶלַח תֵּל חַרְשָׁא כְּרוּב אַדּוֹן וְאִמֵּר וְלֹא יָכְלוּ לְהַגִּיד

סב   בֵּית־אֲבוֹתָם וְזַרְעָם אִם מִיִּשְׂרָאֵל הֵם: בְּנֵי־דְלָיָה בְּנֵי־טוֹבִיָּה בְּנֵי נְקוֹדָא

סג   שֵׁשׁ מֵאוֹת וְאַרְבָּעִים וּשְׁנָיִם: וּמִן־הַכֹּהֲנִים בְּנֵי חֲבַיָּה בְּנֵי הַקּוֹץ בְּנֵי

סד   בַּרְזִלַּי אֲשֶׁר לָקַח מִבְּנוֹת בַּרְזִלַּי הַגִּלְעָדִי אִשָּׁה וַיִּקָּרֵא עַל־שְׁמָם: אֵלֶּה

סה   בִּקְשׁוּ כְתָבָם הַמִּתְיַחְשִׂים וְלֹא נִמְצָא וַיִּגֹּאֲלוּ מִן־הַכְּהֻנָּה: וַיֹּאמֶר

הַתִּרְשָׁתָא לָהֶם אֲשֶׁר לֹא־יֹאכְלוּ מִקֹּדֶשׁ הַקֳּדָשִׁים עַד עֲמֹד הַכֹּהֵן

סו   לְאוּרִים וְתֻמִּים: כָּל־הַקָּהָל כְּאֶחָד אַרְבַּע רִבּוֹא אַלְפַּיִם שְׁלֹשׁ־מֵאוֹת

סז   וְשִׁשִּׁים: מִלְּבַד עַבְדֵיהֶם וְאַמְהֹתֵיהֶם אֵלֶּה שִׁבְעַת אֲלָפִים שְׁלֹשׁ מֵאוֹת

שְׁלֹשִׁים וְשִׁבְעָה וְלָהֶם מְשֹׁרְרִים וּמְשֹׁרְרוֹת מָאתַיִם וְאַרְבָּעִים וַחֲמִשָּׁה:°°

סח   גְּמַלִּים אַרְבַּע מֵאוֹת שְׁלֹשִׁים וַחֲמִשָּׁה חֲמֹרִים שֵׁשֶׁת אֲלָפִים שְׁבַע מֵאוֹת

סט   וְעֶשְׂרִים: וּמִקְצָת רָאשֵׁי הָאָבוֹת נָתְנוּ לַמְּלָאכָה הַתִּרְשָׁתָא נָתַן

לָאוֹצָר זָהָב דַּרְכְּמֹנִים אֶלֶף מִזְרָקוֹת חֲמִשִּׁים כָּתְנוֹת כֹּהֲנִים שְׁלֹשִׁים

ע   וַחֲמֵשׁ מֵאוֹת: וּמֵרָאשֵׁי הָאָבוֹת נָתְנוּ לְאוֹצַר הַמְּלָאכָה זָהָב דַּרְכְּמוֹנִים

עא   שְׁתֵּי רִבּוֹת וְכֶסֶף מָנִים אַלְפַּיִם וּמָאתָיִם: וַאֲשֶׁר נָתְנוּ שְׁאֵרִית הָעָם זָהָב

דַּרְכְּמוֹנִים שְׁתֵּי רִבּוֹא וְכֶסֶף מָנִים אַלְפַּיִם וְכָתְנֹת כֹּהֲנִים שִׁשִּׁים וְשִׁבְעָה:

°°בְּקְצָת סְפָרִים אַחֵר פָּסוּק סז:
סוּסֵיהֶם שְׁבַע מֵאוֹת שְׁלֹשִׁים וְשִׁשָּׁה פִּרְדֵיהֶם מָאתַיִם אַרְבָּעִים וַחֲמִשָּׁה:

7:63. See *II Samuel* 17:27 and 19:32-39, and *Ezra* 2:61.

7:65. See 8:9, where this name, or title, is identified with Nehemiah.

For *Urim VeTumim* see *Exodus* 28:30.

7:66-68. Unlike the earlier and later parts of this list, these totals were not updated by Nehemiah but taken directly from Ezra's record.

7:68. Some editions insert the following phrase at the beginning of verse 68: Their horses [numbered] seven hundred thirty-six; their mules, two hundred forty-five. However, various Masoretic notes indicate that, although that phrase appears in the parallel verse (2:66) in *Ezra*, it

The Temple
ministrants:
Kohanim . . .

nine hundred seventy-three; [40] the children of Immer, one thousand fifty-two; [41] the children of Passhur, one thousand two hundred forty-seven; [42] the children of Harim, one thousand seventeen.

The Levites

[43] The Levites: The children of Jeshua and Kadmiel, of the children of Hodevah, seventy-four; [44] the singers — the children of Asaph — one hundred forty-eight; [45] the gatekeepers — the children of Shallum, the children of Ater, the children of Talmon, the children of Akkub, the children of Hatita, the children of Shobai — one hundred thirty-eight.

The
Nethinim
and
descendants
of Solomon's
slaves

[46] The Nethinim: The children of Ziha, the children of Hasupha, the children of Tabbaoth, [47] the children of Keros, the children of Sia, the children of Padon, [48] the children of Lebanah, the children of Hagabah, the children of Salmai, [49] the children of Hanan, the children of Giddel, the children of Gahar, [50] the children of Reaiah, the children of Rezin, the children of Nekoda, [51] the children of Gazzam, the children of Uzza, the children of Paseah, [52] the children of Besai, the children of Meunim, the children of Nephishesim, [53] the children of Bakbuk, the children of Hakupha, the children of Harhur, [54] the children of Bazlith, the children of Mehida, the children of Harsha, [55] the children of Barkos, the children of Sisera, the children of Tamah, [56] the children of Neziah, the children of Hatipha. [57] The children of Solomon's slaves: The children of Sotai, the children of Sophereth, the children of Perida, [58] the children of Jaala, the children of Darkon, the children of Giddel, [59] the children of Shephatiah, the children of Hattil, the children of Pochereth-hazzebaim, the children of Amon. [60] All of the Nethinim and the children of Solomon's slaves were three hundred ninety-two.

Those of
dubious
descent

[61] These are the ones who went up from Tel-melah, Tel-harsha, Cherub, Addon and Immer, and could not declare their fathers' families and their descent, whether they were from Israel; [62] the children of Delaiah, the children of Tobiah, the children of Nekoda, six hundred forty-two.

[63] Of the Kohanim: The children of Habaiah, the children of Hakkoz, the children of Barzillai, who took wives from the daughters of Barzillai of Gilead* and were called by their name. [64] These sought their genealogical record but it could not be found, so they were disqualified from the priesthood. [65] Hattirshatha* told them that they should not eat of the most holy offerings until there would arise a Kohen to [inquire of] the Urim and the Tumim. *

The total

[66] The entire congregation together numbered forty-two thousand three hundred sixty, * [67] besides their male slaves and female slaves, of which there were seven thousand three hundred thirty-seven. They also had two hundred forty-five male singers and female singers. [68] *The camels [numbered] four hundred thirty-five; the donkeys, six thousand seven hundred twenty.

[69] Some of the family heads contributed* for the work. Hattirshatha contributed to the treasury: of gold, one thousand golden darkemons, [and] fifty basins; [and] priestly robes, five hundred thirty. [70] Some of the heads of the families contributed to the work fund: of gold, twenty thousand darkemons; and of silver, two thousand two hundred manehs. [71] What the rest of the people contributed was: of gold, twenty thousand darkemons; of silver, two thousand manehs; and sixty-seven priestly tunics.

The leaders
contribute

---

is nevertheless not part of the original Masoretic text of Nehemiah (Minchas Shai).

7:69-71. Nehemiah only recorded the contributions given during his term, not those of the earlier collections.

עב וַיֵּשְׁבוּ הַכֹּהֲנִים וְהַלְוִיִּם וְהַשּׁוֹעֲרִים וְהַמְשֹׁרְרִים וּמִן־הָעָם וְהַנְּתִינִים וְכָל־
יִשְׂרָאֵל בְּעָרֵיהֶם   וַיִּגַּע הַחֹדֶשׁ הַשְּׁבִיעִי וּבְנֵי יִשְׂרָאֵל בְּעָרֵיהֶם׃

ח א וַיֵּאָסְפוּ כָל־הָעָם כְּאִישׁ אֶחָד אֶל־הָרְחוֹב אֲשֶׁר לִפְנֵי שַׁעַר־הַמָּיִם וַיֹּאמְרוּ
לְעֶזְרָא הַסֹּפֵר לְהָבִיא אֶת־סֵפֶר תּוֹרַת מֹשֶׁה אֲשֶׁר־צִוָּה יְהוָה אֶת־יִשְׂרָאֵל׃
ב וַיָּבִיא עֶזְרָא הַכֹּהֵן אֶת־הַתּוֹרָה לִפְנֵי הַקָּהָל מֵאִישׁ וְעַד־אִשָּׁה וְכֹל מֵבִין
לִשְׁמֹעַ בְּיוֹם אֶחָד לַחֹדֶשׁ הַשְּׁבִיעִי׃ ג וַיִּקְרָא־בוֹ לִפְנֵי הָרְחוֹב אֲשֶׁר ׀ לִפְנֵי
שַׁעַר־הַמַּיִם מִן־הָאוֹר עַד־מַחֲצִית הַיּוֹם נֶגֶד הָאֲנָשִׁים וְהַנָּשִׁים וְהַמְּבִינִים
וְאָזְנֵי כָל־הָעָם אֶל־סֵפֶר הַתּוֹרָה׃ ד וַיַּעֲמֹד עֶזְרָא הַסֹּפֵר עַל־מִגְדַּל־עֵץ
אֲשֶׁר עָשׂוּ לַדָּבָר וַיַּעֲמֹד אֶצְלוֹ מַתִּתְיָה וְשֶׁמַע וַעֲנָיָה וְאוּרִיָּה וְחִלְקִיָּה
וּמַעֲשֵׂיָה עַל־יְמִינוֹ וּמִשְּׂמֹאלוֹ פְּדָיָה וּמִישָׁאֵל וּמַלְכִּיָּה וְחָשֻׁם וְחַשְׁבַּדָּנָה
זְכַרְיָה מְשֻׁלָּם׃ ה וַיִּפְתַּח עֶזְרָא הַסֵּפֶר לְעֵינֵי כָל־הָעָם כִּי־מֵעַל
כָּל־הָעָם הָיָה וּכְפִתְחוֹ עָמְדוּ כָל־הָעָם׃ ו וַיְבָרֶךְ עֶזְרָא אֶת־יְהוָה הָאֱלֹהִים
הַגָּדוֹל וַיַּעֲנוּ כָל־הָעָם אָמֵן ׀ אָמֵן בְּמֹעַל יְדֵיהֶם וַיִּקְּדוּ וַיִּשְׁתַּחֲוֻ °וַיִּשְׁתַּחוּ
ז [וַיִּשְׁתַּחֲוֻ ק] לַיהוָה אַפַּיִם אָרְצָה׃ וְיֵשׁוּעַ וּבָנִי וְשֵׁרֵבְיָה ׀ יָמִין עַקּוּב
שַׁבְּתַי ׀ הוֹדִיָּה מַעֲשֵׂיָה קְלִיטָא עֲזַרְיָה יוֹזָבָד חָנָן פְּלָאיָה וְהַלְוִיִּם מְבִינִים
ח אֶת־הָעָם לַתּוֹרָה וְהָעָם עַל־עָמְדָם׃ וַיִּקְרְאוּ בַסֵּפֶר בְּתוֹרַת הָאֱלֹהִים
מְפֹרָשׁ וְשׂוֹם שֶׂכֶל וַיָּבִינוּ בַּמִּקְרָא׃ ט וַיֹּאמֶר נְחֶמְיָה הוּא
הַתִּרְשָׁתָא וְעֶזְרָא הַכֹּהֵן ׀ הַסֹּפֵר וְהַלְוִיִּם הַמְּבִינִים אֶת־הָעָם לְכָל־
הָעָם הַיּוֹם קָדֹשׁ־הוּא לַיהוָה אֱלֹהֵיכֶם אַל־תִּתְאַבְּלוּ וְאַל־תִּבְכּוּ כִּי בוֹכִים
י כָל־הָעָם כְּשָׁמְעָם אֶת־דִּבְרֵי הַתּוֹרָה׃ וַיֹּאמֶר לָהֶם לְכוּ אִכְלוּ מַשְׁמַנִּים
וּשְׁתוּ מַמְתַקִּים וְשִׁלְחוּ מָנוֹת לְאֵין נָכוֹן לוֹ כִּי־קָדוֹשׁ הַיּוֹם לַאֲדֹנֵינוּ
יא וְאַל־תֵּעָצֵבוּ כִּי־חֶדְוַת יְהוָה הִיא מָעֻזְּכֶם׃ וְהַלְוִיִּם מַחְשִׁים לְכָל־הָעָם
יב לֵאמֹר הַסּוּ כִּי הַיּוֹם קָדֹשׁ וְאַל־תֵּעָצֵבוּ׃ וַיֵּלְכוּ כָל־הָעָם לֶאֱכֹל וְלִשְׁתּוֹת
וּלְשַׁלַּח מָנוֹת וְלַעֲשׂוֹת שִׂמְחָה גְדוֹלָה כִּי הֵבִינוּ בַּדְּבָרִים אֲשֶׁר הוֹדִיעוּ
יג לָהֶם׃ וּבַיּוֹם הַשֵּׁנִי נֶאֶסְפוּ רָאשֵׁי הָאָבוֹת לְכָל־
הָעָם הַכֹּהֲנִים וְהַלְוִיִּם אֶל־עֶזְרָא הַסֹּפֵר וּלְהַשְׂכִּיל אֶל־דִּבְרֵי הַתּוֹרָה׃
יד וַיִּמְצְאוּ כָּתוּב בַּתּוֹרָה אֲשֶׁר צִוָּה יְהוָה בְּיַד־מֹשֶׁה אֲשֶׁר יֵשְׁבוּ בְנֵי־יִשְׂרָאֵל
טו בַּסֻּכּוֹת בֶּחָג בַּחֹדֶשׁ הַשְּׁבִיעִי׃ וַאֲשֶׁר יַשְׁמִיעוּ וְיַעֲבִירוּ קוֹל בְּכָל־עָרֵיהֶם
וּבִירוּשָׁלַ͏ִם לֵאמֹר צְאוּ הָהָר וְהָבִיאוּ עֲלֵי־זַיִת וַעֲלֵי־עֵץ שֶׁמֶן וַעֲלֵי הֲדַס
טז וַעֲלֵי תְמָרִים וַעֲלֵי עֵץ עָבֹת לַעֲשֹׂת סֻכֹּת כַּכָּתוּב׃ וַיֵּצְאוּ הָעָם וַיָּבִיאוּ

7:72. The month of Tishrei.
8:2. These people helped explain the words of the Torah to the rest of the audience, the simple "men and women" (see v. 7).

This reading took place on the first of Tishrei, Rosh Hashanah.
8:9. Or, "who was *the* Tirshatha," that being a title of a Persian official (*Ibn Ezra*)

The listeners were weeping because they realized that they had been neglecting the laws of the Torah, but Ezra encouraged them, saying that they must not be sad on Rosh Hashanah. Rather, he insisted, fulfilling the commandments of the Torah with joy is more appropriate than mourning over past lapses.

⁷² *The Kohanim and the Levites and the gatekeepers and the singers and some of the people and the Nethinim, and all of Israel settled in their cities. The seventh month* arrived and the children of Israel were [settled] in their cities.*

8

The people request Torah

Ezra reads to them

¹ T*hen all the people gathered together as one man at the plaza before the Water Gate and they asked Ezra the scholar to bring the scroll of the Torah of Moses, which H*ASHEM *had commanded to Israel.* ² *So Ezra the Kohen brought the Torah before the congregation — men and women, and all those who could listen with understanding* — on the first day of the seventh month.** ³ *He read from it before the plaza that is before the Water Gate, from the [first] light until midday, in front of the [common] men and women and those who understood; and the ears of all the people were attentive to the Torah scroll.* ⁴ *Ezra the scholar stood on a wooden tower that they had made for the purpose; next to him stood Mattithiah, as well as Shema, Anaiah, Uriah, Hilkiah and Maaseiah on his right; and on his left, Pedaiah, Mishael, Malchijah, Hashum, Hashbaddanah, Zechariah and Meshullam.*

⁵ *Ezra opened the scroll before the eyes of all the people, for he was above all the people; and when he opened it, all the people stood silent.* ⁶ *Ezra blessed* H*ASHEM, the great God, and all the people answered, "Amen! Amen!" with their hands upraised; then they bowed and prostrated themselves before* H*ASHEM,*

The learned clarify for the un- learned

faces to the ground. ⁷ *Jeshua, Bani, Sherebiah, Jamin, Akkub, Shabbethai, Hodiah, Maaseiah, Kelita, Azariah, Jozabad, Hanan, Pelaiah and the Levites helped the people understand the Torah, while the people [stood] in their place.* ⁸ *They read in the scroll, in God's Torah, clearly, with the application of wisdom, and they helped [the people] understand the reading.*

⁹ *Then Nehemiah, who is Hattirshatha,* as well as Ezra the Kohen, the scholar, and the Levites who were helping the people understand, said to all the people, "Today is sacred to H*ASHEM *your God; do not mourn and do not weep." For all the people were weeping* as they heard the words of the Torah.* ¹⁰ *He said to them, "Go, eat rich foods and drink sweet beverages, and send portions to those who have nothing prepared, for today is sacred to our Lord. Do not be sad; the enjoyment of H*ASHEM *is your strength!"*

¹¹ *And the Levites quieted all the people saying, "Be silent, for this day is sacred; do not be sad."*

¹² *So all the people went to eat and to drink and to send portions [to the needy], and to engage in great rejoicing, for they had understood the matters of which they had informed them.*

The Succos festival

¹³ *On the second day, the heads of the families of all the people, the Kohanim and the Levites gathered together to Ezra the scholar, to delve into the words of the Torah.* ¹⁴ *They found written in the Torah that H*ASHEM *had commanded through the hand of Moses that the Children of Israel should dwell in succos during the festival [that is] in the seventh month.* ¹⁵ *[They commanded] that they should announce it and make a proclamation in all their cities and in Jerusalem, saying, "Go out to the mountain and get [branches with] olive leaves, pine needles, myrtle leaves, palm leaves and leaves of the braided tree,* to make succos, as written [in the Torah]."* ¹⁶ *So the people went out and brought [these items]*

8:15. The palm and myrtle branches were used with the esrog on the Succos festival (see *Leviticus* 23:40), irre- spective of the building of the *succos*-booths. The other branches were used as roofing for the *succos* (*Talmud*).

וַיַּעֲשׂ֣וּ לָהֶ֣ם סֻכּ֡וֹת אִישׁ֩ עַל־גַּגּ֨וֹ וּבְחַצְרֹֽתֵיהֶ֜ם וּבְחַצְר֣וֹת בֵּ֣ית הָאֱלֹהִ֗ים
יח וּבִרְח֙וֹב֙ שַׁ֣עַר הַמַּ֔יִם וּבִרְח֖וֹב שַׁ֣עַר אֶפְרָ֑יִם וַיַּעֲשׂ֣וּ כָֽל־הַ֠קָּהָל הַשָּׁבִ֨ים
מִן־הַשְּׁבִ֥י | סֻכּוֹת֮ וַיֵּשְׁב֣וּ בַסֻּכּוֹת֒ כִּ֣י לֹא־עָשׂ֡וּ מִימֵי֩ יֵשׁ֨וּעַ בִּן־נ֥וּן כֵּן֙ בְּנֵ֣י
יִשְׂרָאֵ֔ל עַ֖ד הַיּ֣וֹם הַה֑וּא וַתְּהִ֥י שִׂמְחָ֖ה גְּדוֹלָ֥ה מְאֹֽד: וַיִּקְרָ֞א בְּסֵ֤פֶר תּוֹרַת֙
הָאֱלֹהִ֔ים י֣וֹם | בְּי֗וֹם מִן־הַיּוֹם֙ הָֽרִאשׁ֔וֹן עַ֖ד הַיּ֣וֹם הָאַחֲר֑וֹן וַיַּֽעֲשׂוּ־חָ֣ג
שִׁבְעַ֣ת יָמִ֔ים וּבַיּ֧וֹם הַשְּׁמִינִ֛י עֲצֶ֖רֶת כַּמִּשְׁפָּֽט:

ט א וּבְי֣וֹם עֶשְׂרִים֩ וְאַרְבָּעָ֨ה לַחֹ֜דֶשׁ הַזֶּ֗ה נֶאֶסְפ֤וּ בְנֵֽי־יִשְׂרָאֵל֙ בְּצ֣וֹם וּבְשַׂקִּ֔ים
ב וַֽאֲדָמָ֖ה עֲלֵיהֶֽם: וַיִּבָּֽדְלוּ֙ זֶ֣רַע יִשְׂרָאֵ֔ל מִכֹּ֖ל בְּנֵ֣י נֵכָ֑ר וַיַּֽעַמְד֗וּ וַיִּתְוַדּוּ֙ עַל־
ג חַטֹּ֣אתֵיהֶ֔ם וַֽעֲוֺנ֖וֹת אֲבֹֽתֵיהֶֽם: וַיָּק֙וּמוּ֙ עַל־עׇמְדָ֔ם וַֽיִּקְרְא֗וּ בְּסֵ֨פֶר תּוֹרַ֧ת
יְהֹוָ֛ה אֱלֹֽהֵיהֶ֖ם רְבִעִ֣ית הַיּ֑וֹם וּרְבִעִית֙ מִתְוַדִּ֣ים וּמִֽשְׁתַּחֲוִ֔ים לַֽיהֹוָ֖ה
ד אֱלֹֽהֵיהֶֽם: וַיָּ֜קׇם עַֽל־מַעֲלֵ֣ה הַֽלְוִיִּ֗ם יֵשׁ֨וּעַ֙ וּבָנִ֣י קַדְמִיאֵ֔ל
שְׁבַנְיָ֖ה בֻּנִּ֣י שֵֽׁרֵבְיָ֑ה בָּנִ֣י כְנָ֔נִי וַיִּזְעֲקוּ֙ בְּק֣וֹל גָּד֔וֹל אֶל־יְהֹוָ֖ה אֱלֹֽהֵיהֶֽם:
ה וַיֹּאמְר֣וּ הַלְוִיִּ֡ם יֵשׁ֣וּעַ וְ֠קַדְמִיאֵ֨ל בָּנִ֜י חֲשַׁבְנְיָ֤ה שֵׁרֵֽבְיָה֙ הֽוֹדִיָּ֣ה שְׁבַנְיָ֔ה
פְּתַחְיָ֗ה ק֗וּמוּ בָּרְכוּ֙ אֶת־יְהֹוָ֣ה אֱלֹֽהֵיכֶ֔ם מִן־הָֽעוֹלָ֖ם עַד־הָֽעוֹלָ֑ם וִיבָרְכוּ֙
ו שֵׁ֣ם כְּבוֹדֶ֔ךָ וּמְרוֹמַ֥ם עַל־כׇּל־בְּרָכָ֖ה וּתְהִלָּֽה: אַתָּה־ה֣וּא יְהֹוָה֮ לְבַדֶּךָ֒
°אַתָּ֣ה קּ] °אַת [עָשִׂ֡יתָ אֶֽת־הַשָּׁמַ֩יִם֩ שְׁמֵ֨י הַשָּׁמַ֜יִם וְכׇל־צְבָאָ֗ם הָאָ֜רֶץ
וְכׇל־אֲשֶׁ֤ר עָלֶ֙יהָ֙ הַיַּמִּים֙ וְכׇל־אֲשֶׁ֣ר בָּהֶ֔ם וְאַתָּ֖ה מְחַיֶּ֣ה אֶת־כֻּלָּ֑ם וּצְבָ֥א
ז הַשָּׁמַ֖יִם לְךָ֥ מִשְׁתַּחֲוִֽים: אַתָּה־הוּא֙ יְהֹוָ֣ה הָֽאֱלֹהִ֔ים אֲשֶׁ֤ר בָּחַ֙רְתָּ֙ בְּאַבְרָ֔ם
ח וְהֽוֹצֵאת֖וֹ מֵא֣וּר כַּשְׂדִּ֑ים וְשַׂ֥מְתָּ שְּׁמ֖וֹ אַבְרָהָֽם: וּמָצָ֣אתָ אֶת־לְבָבוֹ֮ נֶֽאֱמָ֣ן
לְפָנֶיךָ֒ וְכָר֣וֹת עִמּ֣וֹ הַבְּרִ֡ית לָתֵ֡ת אֶת־אֶ֩רֶץ֩ הַכְּנַעֲנִ֨י הַחִתִּ֜י הָֽאֱמֹרִ֗י
וְהַפְּרִזִּ֤י וְהַיְבוּסִי֙ וְהַגִּרְגָּשִׁ֔י לָתֵ֖ת לְזַרְע֑וֹ וַתָּ֙קֶם֙ אֶת־דְּבָרֶ֔יךָ כִּ֥י צַדִּ֖יק אָֽתָּה:
ט וַתֵּ֛רֶא אֶת־עֳנִ֥י אֲבֹתֵ֖ינוּ בְּמִצְרָ֑יִם וְאֶת־זַֽעֲקָתָ֥ם שָׁמַ֖עְתָּ עַל־יַם־סֽוּף: וַתִּתֵּ֣ן
י אֹתֹ֣ת וּ֠מֹפְתִ֨ים בְּפַרְעֹ֤ה וּבְכׇל־עֲבָדָיו֙ וּבְכׇל־עַ֣ם אַרְצ֔וֹ כִּ֣י יָדַ֔עְתָּ כִּ֥י הֵזִ֖ידוּ
עֲלֵיהֶ֑ם וַתַּֽעַשׂ־לְךָ֥ שֵׁ֖ם כְּהַיּ֣וֹם הַזֶּֽה: וְהַיָּם֙ בָּקַ֣עְתָּ לִפְנֵיהֶ֔ם וַיַּֽעַבְר֥וּ בְתֽוֹךְ־
יא הַיָּ֖ם בַּיַּבָּשָׁ֑ה וְאֶת־רֹ֣דְפֵיהֶ֗ם הִשְׁלַ֧כְתָּ בִמְצוֹלֹ֛ת כְּמוֹ־אֶ֖בֶן בְּמַ֥יִם עַזִּֽים:
יב וּבְעַמּ֣וּד עָנָ֔ן הִנְחִיתָ֖ם יוֹמָ֑ם וּבְעַמּ֥וּד אֵשׁ֙ לַ֔יְלָה לְהָאִ֣יר לָהֶ֔ם אֶת־
הַדֶּ֖רֶךְ אֲשֶׁ֥ר יֵֽלְכוּ־בָֽהּ: וְעַ֤ל הַר־סִינַי֙ יָרַ֔דְתָּ וְדַבֵּ֥ר עִמָּהֶ֖ם מִשָּׁמָ֑יִם וַתִּתֵּ֨ן
יג לָהֶ֜ם מִשְׁפָּטִ֤ים יְשָׁרִים֙ וְתוֹר֣וֹת אֱמֶ֔ת חֻקִּ֥ים וּמִצְוֺ֖ת טוֹבִֽים: וְאֶת־שַׁבַּ֣ת
קׇדְשְׁךָ֮ הוֹדַ֣עְתָּ לָהֶם֒ וּמִצְו֤וֹת וְחֻקִּים֙ וְתוֹרָ֔ה צִוִּ֣יתָ לָהֶ֔ם בְּיַ֖ד מֹשֶׁ֥ה עַבְדֶּֽךָ:
יד וְ֠לֶ֨חֶם מִשָּׁמַ֜יִם נָתַ֤תָּה לָהֶם֙ לִרְעָבָ֔ם וּמַ֗יִם מִסֶּ֛לַע הוֹצֵ֥אתָ לָהֶ֖ם לִצְמָאָ֑ם
טו וַתֹּ֣אמֶר לָהֶ֗ם לָבוֹא֙ לָרֶ֣שֶׁת אֶת־הָאָ֔רֶץ אֲשֶׁר־נָשָׂ֥אתָ אֶת־יָֽדְךָ֖ לָתֵ֥ת לָהֶֽם:

8:17. They had not celebrated the Succos festival with such enthusiasm.

9:1. On the day after the Succos festival described above, a mass demonstration of repentance, an expression of national resolve not to repeat the shortcomings of the past, took place.

9:5. After instructing the masses to arise and bless God, the Levites turned to address God. They asked that he allow the people to compose and recite His praises even though He is exalted above anything they would say.

and made themselves succos, each man on his roof, and in their courtyards, in the courtyards of the Temple of God, in the plaza of the Water Gate and in the plaza of the Gate of Ephraim. [17] The entire congregation that had returned from the captivity made succos and dwelt in succos. The Children of Israel had not done so* from the days of Joshua son of Nun until that day, and there was very great joy. [18] [Ezra] read in the scroll of God's Torah day by day, from the first day until the last day. They observed the festival for seven days, and the assembly on the eighth day, according to the law.

9

Public penance

[1] On the twenty-fourth day of this month* the Children of Israel gathered together, in fasting and [wearing] sackcloth, with earth upon them. * [2] The offspring of Israel had separated themselves from all the alien people, and then they rose and confessed their sins and the iniquities of their fathers. [3] They stood in their place and read from the scroll of the Torah of HASHEM, their God, one quarter of the day, and [another] quarter they confessed and prostrated themselves before HASHEM their God.

[4] Then Jeshua stood upon the platform of the Levites, with Bani, Kadmiel, Shebaniah, Bunni, Sherebiah, Bani and Chenani, and they cried out in a loud voice to HASHEM their God. [5] The Levites Jeshua, Kadmiel, Bani, Hashabneiah, Sherebiah, Hodiah, Shebaniah and Pethahiah said, "Rise up and bless HASHEM your God, from This World to the World to Come!"

"Let them bless* Your glorious Name, which is exalted above every blessing and praise!"

**LEVITES'
SONG OF
PRAISE
9:6-10:1**

*Selection
and
covenant of
Abraham*

*Redemption
from Egypt*

*Revelation
at Sinai*

[6] You alone are HASHEM; You made the heavens, the most exalted heavens and all their legion, the earth and all that is upon it, the seas and all that is in them, and you give them all life; and the heavenly legion bows to You. [7] You are HASHEM the God, You selected Abram and brought him out of Ur of the Chaldees, and changed his name to Abraham. [8] You found his heart faithful before You, and You sealed the covenant with him to give the land of the Canaanite, the Hittite, the Amorite and the Perizzite and the Jebusite and the Girgashite — to give it to his offspring; and You affirmed Your word, for You are righteous. [9] You observed the suffering of our forefathers in Egypt, and You heard their outcry at the Sea of Reeds. * [10] You imposed signs and wonders upon Pharaoh and upon all his servants and upon all the people of his land, for you knew that they had sinned willfully against them; and You brought Yourself renown, as clear as this very day. [11] You split the sea before them and they crossed in the midst of the sea on dry land; but You hurled their pursuers into the depths, like a stone in turbulent waters. [12] You led them by day with a pillar of cloud and with a pillar of fire by night to illuminate for them the way they were to travel. * [13] You descended upon Mount Sinai* and spoke to them from heaven; You gave them righteous laws and true teachings, and beneficial decrees and commandments. [14] You made known Your sacred Sabbath to them; and You instructed them with commandments, decrees, and teaching through the hand of Your servant Moses. [15] You gave them bread from heaven for their hunger, and brought forth water from a rock for their thirst. * You told them to enter and inherit the land about which You had raised Your hand [in oath] to give to them.

9:9-11. See *Exodus* 14:9-35.   **9:13-14.** See *Exodus* Chs. 19-20.
9:12. See *Exodus* 13:21-22.   **9:15.** See *Exodus* Chs. 16-17.

טז וְהֵם וַאֲבֹתֵינוּ הֵזִידוּ וַיַּקְשׁוּ אֶת־עָרְפָּם וְלֹא שָׁמְעוּ אֶל־מִצְוֹתֶיךָ:

יז וַיְמָאֲנוּ לִשְׁמֹעַ וְלֹא־זָכְרוּ נִפְלְאֹתֶיךָ אֲשֶׁר עָשִׂיתָ עִמָּהֶם וַיַּקְשׁוּ אֶת־עָרְפָּם וַיִּתְּנוּ־רֹאשׁ לָשׁוּב לְעַבְדֻתָם בְּמִרְיָם וְאַתָּה אֱלוֹהַּ סְלִיחוֹת חַנּוּן וְרַחוּם אֶרֶךְ־אַפַּיִם וְרַב־◦ֹוחֶסֶד [°חֶסֶד ק] וְלֹא עֲזַבְתָּם: אַף כִּי־עָשׂוּ

יח לָהֶם עֵגֶל מַסֵּכָה וַיֹּאמְרוּ זֶה אֱלֹהֶיךָ אֲשֶׁר הֶעֶלְךָ מִמִּצְרָיִם וַיַּעֲשׂוּ נֶאָצוֹת גְּדֹלוֹת:

יט וְאַתָּה בְּרַחֲמֶיךָ הָרַבִּים לֹא עֲזַבְתָּם בַּמִּדְבָּר אֶת־עַמּוּד הֶעָנָן לֹא־סָר מֵעֲלֵיהֶם בְּיוֹמָם לְהַנְחֹתָם בְּהַדֶּרֶךְ וְאֶת־עַמּוּד הָאֵשׁ בְּלַיְלָה לְהָאִיר לָהֶם וְאֶת־הַדֶּרֶךְ אֲשֶׁר יֵלְכוּ־בָהּ: וְרוּחֲךָ הַטּוֹבָה נָתַתָּ

כ לְהַשְׂכִּילָם וּמַנְךָ לֹא־מָנַעְתָּ מִפִּיהֶם וּמַיִם נָתַתָּה לָהֶם לִצְמָאָם:

כא וְאַרְבָּעִים שָׁנָה כִּלְכַּלְתָּם בַּמִּדְבָּר לֹא חָסֵרוּ שַׂלְמֹתֵיהֶם לֹא בָלוּ וְרַגְלֵיהֶם לֹא בָצֵקוּ: וַתִּתֵּן לָהֶם מַמְלָכוֹת וַעֲמָמִים וַתַּחְלְקֵם לְפֵאָה

כב וַיִּירְשׁוּ אֶת־אֶרֶץ סִיחוֹן וְאֶת־אֶרֶץ מֶלֶךְ חֶשְׁבּוֹן וְאֶת־אֶרֶץ עוֹג מֶלֶךְ־

כג הַבָּשָׁן: וּבְנֵיהֶם הִרְבִּיתָ כְּכֹכְבֵי הַשָּׁמָיִם וַתְּבִיאֵם אֶל־הָאָרֶץ אֲשֶׁר־

כד אָמַרְתָּ לַאֲבֹתֵיהֶם לָבוֹא לָרָשֶׁת: וַיָּבֹאוּ הַבָּנִים וַיִּירְשׁוּ אֶת־הָאָרֶץ וַתַּכְנַע לִפְנֵיהֶם אֶת־יֹשְׁבֵי הָאָרֶץ הַכְּנַעֲנִים וַתִּתְּנֵם בְּיָדָם וְאֶת־מַלְכֵיהֶם

כה וְאֶת־עַמְמֵי הָאָרֶץ לַעֲשׂוֹת בָּהֶם כִּרְצוֹנָם: וַיִּלְכְּדוּ עָרִים בְּצֻרוֹת וַאֲדָמָה שְׁמֵנָה וַיִּירְשׁוּ בָּתִּים מְלֵאִים־כָּל־טוּב בֹּרוֹת חֲצוּבִים כְּרָמִים וְזֵיתִים וְעֵץ מַאֲכָל לָרֹב וַיֹּאכְלוּ וַיִּשְׂבְּעוּ וַיַּשְׁמִינוּ וַיִּתְעַדְּנוּ בְּטוּבְךָ הַגָּדוֹל:

כו וַיַּמְרוּ וַיִּמְרְדוּ בָּךְ וַיַּשְׁלִכוּ אֶת־תּוֹרָתְךָ אַחֲרֵי גַוָּם וְאֶת־נְבִיאֶיךָ הָרָגוּ אֲשֶׁר־הֵעִידוּ בָם לַהֲשִׁיבָם אֵלֶיךָ וַיַּעֲשׂוּ נֶאָצוֹת גְּדוֹלֹת: וַתִּתְּנֵם בְּיַד

כז צָרֵיהֶם וַיָּצֵרוּ לָהֶם וּבְעֵת צָרָתָם יִצְעֲקוּ אֵלֶיךָ וְאַתָּה מִשָּׁמַיִם תִּשְׁמָע וּכְרַחֲמֶיךָ הָרַבִּים תִּתֵּן לָהֶם מוֹשִׁיעִים וְיוֹשִׁיעוּם מִיַּד צָרֵיהֶם: וּכְנוֹחַ

כח לָהֶם יָשׁוּבוּ לַעֲשׂוֹת רַע לְפָנֶיךָ וַתַּעַזְבֵם בְּיַד אֹיְבֵיהֶם וַיִּרְדּוּ בָהֶם וַיָּשׁוּבוּ וַיִּזְעָקוּךָ וְאַתָּה מִשָּׁמַיִם תִּשְׁמַע וְתַצִּילֵם כְּרַחֲמֶיךָ רַבּוֹת עִתִּים: וַתָּעַד

כט בָּהֶם לַהֲשִׁיבָם אֶל־תּוֹרָתֶךָ וְהֵמָּה הֵזִידוּ וְלֹא־שָׁמְעוּ לְמִצְוֹתֶיךָ וּבְמִשְׁפָּטֶיךָ חָטְאוּ־בָם אֲשֶׁר־יַעֲשֶׂה אָדָם וְחָיָה בָהֶם וַיִּתְּנוּ כָתֵף

ל סוֹרֶרֶת וְעָרְפָּם הִקְשׁוּ וְלֹא שָׁמֵעוּ: וַתִּמְשֹׁךְ עֲלֵיהֶם שָׁנִים רַבּוֹת וַתָּעַד בָּם

לא בְּרוּחֲךָ בְּיַד־נְבִיאֶיךָ וְלֹא הֶאֱזִינוּ וַתִּתְּנֵם בְּיַד עַמֵּי הָאֲרָצֹת: וּבְרַחֲמֶיךָ הָרַבִּים לֹא־עֲשִׂיתָם כָּלָה וְלֹא עֲזַבְתָּם כִּי אֵל־חַנּוּן וְרַחוּם אָתָּה:

9:17. See Exodus 34:6-7.
9:18. Exodus 32:4.
9:21. See Deuteronomy 8:4.
9:22. You separated the Jews from the surrounding nations (Rashi).

9:26. See I Kings 18:4; II Chronicles 24:20-21.
9:29. Even when they ostensibly obeyed Your laws, they did so only when it suited their selfish purposes, so that even their good deeds were considered sinful.

Rebellious
nation:
Golden Calf

¹⁶ But they and our forefathers sinned willfully; they stiffened their necks and did not listen to your commandments. ¹⁷ They refused to listen, and they did not remember Your marvels that You had performed for them; they stiffened their necks and, in their rebelliousness, appointed a leader to return to their bondage. But You are the God of forgiveness, Gracious and Compassionate, Slow to anger and Abundant in kindness, * so You did not forsake them, ¹⁸ even when they made themselves a molten calf and said, 'This is your god who brought you up from Egypt,'* and they performed great provocations. ¹⁹ But You, in Your great compassion, did not forsake them in the Wilderness; the pillar of cloud did not turn away from them by day to lead them on the way, nor the pillar of fire by night to provide illumination upon them and upon the way they were to travel. ²⁰ You bestowed Your good spirit to make them understand. You did not withhold Your manna from their mouths, and You gave them water for their thirst. ²¹ For forty years You sustained them in the Wilderness and they lacked nothing; their clothing did not wear out and their feet did not swell. *

Nevertheless
, Divine
compassion

Conquest
of Canaan

²² Then You gave them kingdoms and nations, and separated them into a corner; * they took possession of the land of Sihon, the land of the king of Heshbon and the land of Og, king of Bashan. ²³ You multiplied their children like the stars of the heavens, and You brought them to the land about which You had spoken to their forefathers that they would come and take possession. ²⁴ The children came and took possession of the land, and You subdued inhabitants of the land, the Canaanites, before them, and delivered them into their hand, along with their kings and the peoples of the land, to do with them as they pleased. ²⁵ They captured fortified cities and a fertile land; they took possession of houses filled with every good thing, chiseled cisterns, vineyards and olive trees, and abundant fruit trees; so they ate and became satiated and fattened and took delight in Your great bounty.

Recurrent
rebellious-
ness

²⁶ Then they became recalcitrant and rebelled against You, casting Your Torah behind their backs. They killed Your prophets * who had warned them in order to make them return to You, and they committed great provocations. ²⁷ So You delivered them into the hands of their enemies and they afflicted them. But at the time of their affliction they would cry out to You and You would hear from Heaven; and in Your abundant compassion You would send them saviors who would save them from the hand of their enemies. ²⁸ But when it would ease for them they would revert to doing evil before You, so You would abandon them into the hand of their enemies, who would oppress them. Then they would once again cry out to You, and You would hear from Heaven and in Your compassion You would rescue them numerous times. ²⁹ You warned them, to return them to Your Torah, but they acted wickedly and did not listen to Your commandments and transgressed through Your laws, * which a man should do in order that he may live through them. They turned a rebellious shoulder away and stiffened their necks and did not listen. ³⁰ Yet You extended [grace] to them for many years, and You warned them by Your spirit, through the hand of Your prophets, but they did not give ear; so You delivered them into the hand of the peoples of the lands. ³¹ In Your abundant compassion You did not annihilate them and You did not abandon them, for You are a gracious and compassionate God.

לב וְעַתָּ֣ה אֱלֹהֵ֡ינוּ הָאֵל֩ הַגָּד֨וֹל הַגִּבּ֜וֹר וְהַנּוֹרָא֮ שׁוֹמֵ֣ר הַבְּרִ֣ית וְהַחֶ֒סֶד֒ אַל־יִמְעַ֣ט לְפָנֶ֡יךָ אֵ֣ת כָּל־הַתְּלָאָ֣ה אֲשֶׁר־מְצָאַ֣תְנוּ לִמְלָכֵ֣ינוּ לְשָׂרֵ֣ינוּ וּלְכֹהֲנֵ֣ינוּ וְלִנְבִיאֵ֣נוּ וְלַאֲבֹתֵ֣ינוּ וּלְכָל־עַמֶּ֑ךָ מִימֵי֙ מַלְכֵ֣י אַשּׁ֔וּר עַ֖ד הַיּ֥וֹם הַזֶּֽה:

לג וְאַתָּ֣ה צַדִּ֔יק עַ֖ל כָּל־הַבָּ֣א עָלֵ֑ינוּ כִּֽי־אֱמֶ֥ת עָשִׂ֖יתָ וַאֲנַ֥חְנוּ הִרְשָֽׁעְנוּ:

לד וְאֶת־מְלָכֵ֣ינוּ שָׂרֵ֣ינוּ כֹּהֲנֵ֣ינוּ וַאֲבֹתֵ֔ינוּ לֹ֥א עָשׂ֖וּ תּוֹרָתֶ֑ךָ וְלֹ֤א הִקְשִׁ֙יבוּ֙ אֶל־מִצְוֺתֶ֔יךָ וּלְעֵ֣דְוֺתֶ֔יךָ אֲשֶׁ֥ר הַעִידֹ֖תָ בָּהֶֽם:

לה וְהֵ֣ם בְּמַלְכוּתָם֩ וּבְטוּבְךָ֨ הָרָ֜ב אֲשֶׁר־נָתַ֣תָּ לָהֶ֗ם וּבְאֶ֨רֶץ הָרְחָבָ֧ה וְהַשְּׁמֵנָ֛ה אֲשֶׁר־נָתַ֥תָּ לִפְנֵיהֶ֖ם לֹ֣א עֲבָד֑וּךָ וְלֹא־שָׁ֙בוּ֙ מִמַּֽעַלְלֵיהֶ֖ם הָרָעִֽים:

לו הִנֵּ֛ה אֲנַ֥חְנוּ הַיּ֖וֹם עֲבָדִ֑ים וְהָאָ֗רֶץ אֲשֶׁר־נָתַ֤תָּה לַאֲבֹתֵ֙ינוּ֙ לֶאֱכֹ֣ל אֶת־פִּרְיָ֔הּ וְאֶת־טוּבָ֔הּ הִנֵּ֛ה אֲנַ֥חְנוּ עֲבָדִ֖ים עָלֶֽיהָ:

לז וּתְבוּאָתָ֣הּ מַרְבָּ֗ה לַמְּלָכִ֛ים אֲשֶׁר־נָתַ֥תָּה עָלֵ֖ינוּ בְּחַטֹּאותֵ֑ינוּ וְעַ֣ל גְּוִיֹּתֵ֗ינוּ מֹשְׁלִים֙ וּבִבְהֶמְתֵּ֣נוּ כִּרְצוֹנָ֔ם וּבְצָרָ֥ה גְדוֹלָ֖ה אֲנָֽחְנוּ:

י

א וּבְכָל־זֹ֗את אֲנַ֙חְנוּ֙ כֹּרְתִ֣ים אֲמָנָ֔ה וְכֹתְבִ֑ים וְעַל֙ הֶֽחָת֔וּם שָׂרֵ֥ינוּ לְוִיֵּ֖נוּ כֹּהֲנֵֽינוּ:

ב-ג וְעַ֖ל הַחֲתוּמִ֑ים נְחֶמְיָ֧ה הַתִּרְשָׁ֛תָא בֶּן־חֲכַלְיָ֖ה וְצִדְקִיָּֽה: שְׂרָיָ֥ה

ד-ה עֲזַרְיָ֖ה יִרְמְיָֽה: פַּשְׁח֥וּר אֲמַרְיָ֖ה מַלְכִּיָּֽה: חַטּ֥וּשׁ שְׁבַנְיָ֖ה מַלּֽוּךְ: חָרִ֛ם

ז-ט מְרֵמ֖וֹת עֹבַדְיָֽה: דָּנִיֵּ֥אל גִּנְּת֖וֹן בָּרֽוּךְ: מְשֻׁלָּ֥ם אֲבִיָּ֖ה מִיָּמִֽן: מַֽעַזְיָ֥ה בִלְגַּ֖י

י שְׁמַֽעְיָ֑ה אֵ֖לֶּה הַכֹּהֲנִֽים: וְהַ֨לְוִיִּ֔ם וְיֵשׁ֥וּעַ בֶּן־אֲזַנְיָ֛ה בִּנּ֥וּי מִבְּנֵ֖י חֵנָדָ֑ד

יא-יב קַדְמִיאֵֽל: וַאֲחֵיהֶ֗ם שְׁבַנְיָ֧ה הֽוֹדִיָּ֛ה קְלִיטָ֖א פְּלָאיָ֣ה חָנָֽן: מִיכָ֥א רְח֖וֹב

יג-טו חֲשַׁבְיָֽה: זַכּ֥וּר שֵׁרֵֽבְיָ֖ה שְׁבַנְיָֽה: הֽוֹדִיָּ֥ה בָנִ֖י בְּנִֽינוּ: רָאשֵׁ֣י הָעָ֑ם פַּרְעֹ֖שׁ

טז-יח פַּחַ֣ת מוֹאָ֔ב עֵילָ֖ם זַתּ֥וּא בָּנִֽי: בֻּנִּ֥י עַזְגָּ֖ד בֵּבָֽי: אֲדֹנִיָּ֥ה בִגְוַ֖י עָדִֽין: אָטֵ֤ר

יט-כא חִזְקִיָּ֣ה עַזּ֔וּר: הוֹדִיָּ֥ה חָשֻׁ֖ם בֵּצָֽי: חָרִ֥יף עֲנָת֖וֹת °נוֹבָֽי [°נֵיבָ֖י ק]: מַגְפִּיעָ֤שׁ

כב-כד מְשֻׁלָּ֣ם חֵזִ֔יר: מְשֵׁיזַבְאֵ֥ל צָד֖וֹק יַדּֽוּעַ: פְּלַטְיָ֥ה חָנָ֖ן עֲנָיָֽה: הוֹשֵׁ֥עַ חֲנַנְיָ֖ה

כה-כז חַשּֽׁוּב: הַלּוֹחֵ֥שׁ פִּלְחָ֖א שׁוֹבֵֽק: רְח֥וּם חֲשַׁבְנָ֖ה מַעֲשֵׂיָֽה: וַאֲחִיָּ֥ה חָנָ֖ן

כח-כט עָנָֽן: מַלּ֥וּךְ חָרִ֖ם בַּעֲנָֽה: וּשְׁאָ֣ר הָעָ֡ם הַכֹּהֲנִ֣ים הַ֠לְוִיִּ֠ם הַשּׁוֹעֲרִ֨ים הַמְשֹׁרְרִ֜ים הַנְּתִינִ֗ים וְכָל־הַנִּבְדָּ֞ל מֵעַמֵּ֤י הָאֲרָצוֹת֙ אֶל־תּוֹרַ֣ת הָאֱלֹהִ֔ים

ל נְשֵׁיהֶ֖ם בְּנֵיהֶ֣ם וּבְנֹתֵיהֶ֑ם כֹּ֖ל יוֹדֵ֥עַ מֵבִֽין: מַחֲזִיקִ֣ים עַל־אֲחֵיהֶם֮ אַדִּירֵיהֶם֒ וּבָאִ֞ים בְּאָלָ֣ה וּבִשְׁבוּעָ֗ה לָלֶ֙כֶת֙ בְּתוֹרַ֣ת הָאֱלֹהִ֔ים אֲשֶׁ֣ר נִתְּנָ֗ה בְּיַ֛ד מֹשֶׁ֥ה עֶֽבֶד־הָֽאֱלֹהִ֑ים וְלִשְׁמ֣וֹר וְלַעֲשׂ֗וֹת אֶת־כָּל־מִצְוֺת֙ יְהוָ֣ה אֲדֹנֵ֔ינוּ

לא וּמִשְׁפָּטָ֖יו וְחֻקָּֽיו: וַאֲשֶׁ֛ר לֹא־נִתֵּ֥ן בְּנֹתֵ֖ינוּ לְעַמֵּ֣י הָאָ֑רֶץ וְאֶת־בְּנֹתֵיהֶ֖ם לֹ֥א נִקַּ֥ח לְבָנֵֽינוּ:

לב וְעַמֵּ֣י הָאָ֡רֶץ הַֽמְבִיאִ֣ים אֶת־הַמַּקָּחוֹת֩ וְכָל־שֶׁ֨בֶר בְּי֤וֹם הַשַּׁבָּת֙ לִמְכּ֔וֹר לֹא־נִקַּ֥ח מֵהֶ֛ם בַּשַּׁבָּ֖ת וּבְי֣וֹם קֹ֑דֶשׁ וְנִטֹּ֛שׁ אֶת־

לג הַשָּׁנָ֥ה הַשְּׁבִיעִ֖ית וּמַשָּׁ֥א כָל־יָֽד: וְהֶעֱמַ֤דְנוּ עָלֵ֙ינוּ֙ מִצְוֺ֔ת לָתֵ֥ת עָלֵ֖ינוּ

לד שְׁלִשִׁ֥ית הַשֶּׁ֖קֶל בַּשָּׁנָ֑ה לַעֲבֹדַ֖ת בֵּ֣ית אֱלֹהֵֽינוּ: לְלֶ֣חֶם הַֽמַּעֲרֶ֗כֶת וּמִנְחַ֤ת

9:36. We are totally subservient to the Persian government.

10:1. Despite all the hardships described in the pre-

vious chapter.

10:10. Alternatively: Jeshua.

10:27. Alternatively: and Ahiah.

Plea for mercy

³² And now, our God — the great, powerful and awesome God, Who observes the covenant and the kindness — let all the travails that have befallen us, our kings, our rulers and our Kohanim and our prophets and our forefathers and all Your people, from the days of the kings of Assyria until this day, not be considered lightly before You. ³³ You are righteous in all that has come upon us, for You have acted truthfully, and we have been wicked, ³⁴ with our kings, our officers, our Kohanim and our forefathers who did not fulfill Your Torah and did not heed Your commandments and Your warnings with which You warned them. ³⁵ But they, in their kingdom — with Your abundant bounty that You granted them, and in the broad and fertile land that you placed before them — did not serve You, and they did not repent of their wicked deeds. ³⁶ Behold, today we are slaves; * and the land that You gave to our forefathers to eat of its fruit and its bounty, behold, we are slaves upon it. ³⁷ Its produce is abundant for [the benefit of] kings whom You have placed over us because of our sins; they rule over our bodies and over our animals as they please, and we are in great distress! ¹ But, despite all this, * we are establishing a lasting covenant and inscribing [it], and upon the sealed portion are our officers, our Levites, [and] our Kohanim.

10

THE LASTING COVENANT
10:1-40

The signers: Kohanim . . .

² [These are] the signatories: Nehemiah Hattirshatha son of Hacaliah and Zedekiah, ³ Seraiah, Azariah, Jeremiah, ⁴ Pashhur, Amariah, Malchijah, ⁵ Hattush, Shebaniah, Malluch, ⁶ Harim, Meremoth, Obadiah, ⁷ Daniel, Ginnethon, Baruch, ⁸ Meshullam, Abijah, Mijamin, ⁹ Maaziah, Bilgai [and] Shemaiah — these were the Kohanim [who signed].

. . . Levites . . .

¹⁰ And the Levites: Vejeshua * son of Azaniah, Binnui of the sons of Henadad, Kadmiel, ¹¹ and their brethren Shebaniah, Hodiah, Kelita, Pelaiah, Hanan, ¹² Mica, Rehob, Hashabiah, ¹³ Zaccur, Sherebiah, Shebaniah, ¹⁴ Hodiah, Bani and Beninu.

. . . others

¹⁵ The leaders of the people: Parosh the governor of Moab, Elam, Zattu, Bani, ¹⁶ Bunni, Azgad, Bebai, ¹⁷ Adonijah, Bigvai, Adin, ¹⁸ Ater, Hezekiah, Azzur, ¹⁹ Hodiah, Hashum, Bezai, ²⁰ Hariph, Anathoth, Nebai, ²¹ Magpiash, Meshullam, Hezir, ²² Meshezabel, Zadok, Jaddua, ²³ Pelatiah, Hanan, Anaiah, ²⁴ Hoshea, Hananiah, Hasshub, ²⁵ Hallohesh, Pilha, Shobek, ²⁶ Rehum, Hashabnah, Maaseiah, ²⁷ Vaahiah, * Hanan, Anan, ²⁸ Malluch, Harim and Baanah.

The oath of allegiance to the Torah and its laws

²⁹ The remainder of the people, the Kohanim, the Levites, the gatekeepers, the singers, the Nethinim and everyone who had separated themselves from the peoples of the lands to [accept] God's Torah, their wives, their sons and their daughters, all those who had knowledge [and] understanding, ³⁰ supported their brethren, their dignitaries, and entered into a curse and an oath to follow God's Torah, which was given through the hand of Moses, the servant of God, and to observe and fulfill all the commandments of HASHEM, our Lord, and His laws and His decrees; ³¹ and that we would not give our daughters [in marriage] to the peoples of the land, nor take their daughters for our sons; ³² and that regarding the peoples of the land who bring [their] wares and all kinds of produce to sell on the Sabbath day, we would not buy from them on the Sabbath and on holy days; and that we would relinquish [the land] and all loans during the seventh year. * ³³ We also instituted commandments upon ourselves to give one third of a shekel* yearly toward the service of the Temple of our God: ³⁴ for the arranged bread and* the meal-offering

Temple offerings

10:32. As commanded in *Exodus* 23:11; *Leviticus* Ch. 25, etc.
10:33. This amount was equal to the half-*shekel* com-

manded by the Torah in *Exodus* 30:13 (*Ralbag*).
10:34. As commanded in *Numbers* 15:2; *Exodus* 25:30; *Numbers* Chs. 28-29.

הַתָּמִיד וּלְעוֹלַת הַתָּמִיד הַשַּׁבָּתוֹת הֶחֳדָשִׁים לַמּוֹעֲדִים וְלַקֳּדָשִׁים

לה וְלַחַטָּאוֹת לְכַפֵּר עַל־יִשְׂרָאֵל וְכֹל מְלֶאכֶת בֵּית־אֱלֹהֵינוּ: וְהַגּוֹרָלוֹת הִפַּלְנוּ עַל־קֻרְבַּן הָעֵצִים הַכֹּהֲנִים הַלְוִיִּם וְהָעָם לְהָבִיא לְבֵית אֱלֹהֵינוּ לְבֵית־אֲבֹתֵינוּ לְעִתִּים מְזֻמָּנִים שָׁנָה בְשָׁנָה לְבַעֵר עַל־מִזְבַּח יהוה אֱלֹהֵינוּ

לו כַּכָּתוּב בַּתּוֹרָה: וּלְהָבִיא אֶת־בִּכּוּרֵי אַדְמָתֵנוּ וּבִכּוּרֵי כָל־פְּרִי כָל־עֵץ

לז שָׁנָה בְשָׁנָה לְבֵית יהוה: וְאֶת־בְּכֹרוֹת בָּנֵינוּ וּבְהֶמְתֵּנוּ כַּכָּתוּב בַּתּוֹרָה וְאֶת־בְּכוֹרֵי בְקָרֵינוּ וְצֹאנֵינוּ לְהָבִיא לְבֵית אֱלֹהֵינוּ לַכֹּהֲנִים הַמְשָׁרְתִים

לח בְּבֵית אֱלֹהֵינוּ: וְאֶת־רֵאשִׁית עֲרִיסֹתֵינוּ וּתְרוּמֹתֵינוּ וּפְרִי כָל־עֵץ תִּירוֹשׁ וְיִצְהָר נָבִיא לַכֹּהֲנִים אֶל־לִשְׁכוֹת בֵּית־אֱלֹהֵינוּ וּמַעְשַׂר אַדְמָתֵנוּ לַלְוִיִּם

לט וְהֵם הַלְוִיִּם הַמְעַשְּׂרִים בְּכֹל עָרֵי עֲבֹדָתֵנוּ: וְהָיָה הַכֹּהֵן בֶּן־אַהֲרֹן עִם־הַלְוִיִּם בַּעְשֵׂר הַלְוִיִּם וְהַלְוִיִּם יַעֲלוּ אֶת־מַעֲשַׂר הַמַּעֲשֵׂר לְבֵית אֱלֹהֵינוּ

מ אֶל־הַלְּשָׁכוֹת לְבֵית הָאוֹצָר: כִּי אֶל־הַלְּשָׁכוֹת יָבִיאוּ בְנֵי־יִשְׂרָאֵל וּבְנֵי הַלֵּוִי אֶת־תְּרוּמַת הַדָּגָן הַתִּירוֹשׁ וְהַיִּצְהָר וְשָׁם כְּלֵי הַמִּקְדָּשׁ וְהַכֹּהֲנִים

יא א הַמְשָׁרְתִים וְהַשּׁוֹעֲרִים וְהַמְשֹׁרְרִים וְלֹא נַעֲזֹב אֶת־בֵּית אֱלֹהֵינוּ: וַיֵּשְׁבוּ שָׂרֵי־הָעָם בִּירוּשָׁלָ͏ִם וּשְׁאָר הָעָם הִפִּילוּ גוֹרָלוֹת לְהָבִיא ׀ אֶחָד מִן־

ב הָעֲשָׂרָה לָשֶׁבֶת בִּירוּשָׁלַ͏ִם עִיר הַקֹּדֶשׁ וְתֵשַׁע הַיָּדוֹת בֶּעָרִים: וַיְבָרְכוּ הָעָם

ג לְכֹל הָאֲנָשִׁים הַמִּתְנַדְּבִים לָשֶׁבֶת בִּירוּשָׁלָ͏ִם: וְאֵלֶּה רָאשֵׁי הַמְּדִינָה אֲשֶׁר יָשְׁבוּ בִּירוּשָׁלָ͏ִם וּבְעָרֵי יְהוּדָה יָשְׁבוּ אִישׁ בַּאֲחֻזָּתוֹ

ד בְּעָרֵיהֶם יִשְׂרָאֵל הַכֹּהֲנִים וְהַלְוִיִּם וְהַנְּתִינִים וּבְנֵי עַבְדֵי שְׁלֹמֹה: וּבִירוּשָׁלַ͏ִם יָשְׁבוּ מִבְּנֵי יְהוּדָה וּמִבְּנֵי בִנְיָמִן מִבְּנֵי יְהוּדָה עֲתָיָה בֶן־עֻזִּיָּה בֶּן־זְכַרְיָה בֶן־

ה אֲמַרְיָה בֶּן־שְׁפַטְיָה בֶּן־מַהֲלַלְאֵל מִבְּנֵי־פָרֶץ: וּמַעֲשֵׂיָה בֶן־בָּרוּךְ בֶּן־כָּל־

ו חֹזֶה בֶן־חֲזָיָה בֶן־עֲדָיָה בֶן־יוֹיָרִיב בֶּן־זְכַרְיָה בֶּן־הַשִּׁלֹנִי: כָּל־בְּנֵי־פֶרֶץ

ז הַיֹּשְׁבִים בִּירוּשָׁלַ͏ִם אַרְבַּע מֵאוֹת שִׁשִּׁים וּשְׁמֹנָה אַנְשֵׁי־חָיִל: וְאֵלֶּה בְּנֵי בִנְיָמִן סַלֻּא בֶּן־מְשֻׁלָּם בֶּן־יוֹעֵד בֶּן־פְּדָיָה בֶן־קוֹלָיָה בֶן־מַעֲשֵׂיָה בֶּן־

ח-ט אִיתִיאֵל בֶּן־יְשַׁעְיָה: וְאַחֲרָיו גַּבַּי סַלָּי תְּשַׁע מֵאוֹת עֶשְׂרִים וּשְׁמֹנָה: וְיוֹאֵל

י בֶּן־זִכְרִי פָּקִיד עֲלֵיהֶם וִיהוּדָה בֶן־הַסְּנוּאָה עַל־הָעִיר מִשְׁנֶה:

יא הַכֹּהֲנִים יְדַעְיָה בֶן־יוֹיָרִיב יָכִין: שְׂרָיָה בֶן־חִלְקִיָּה בֶּן־מְשֻׁלָּם בֶּן־צָדוֹק בֶּן־

יב מְרָיוֹת בֶּן־אֲחִיטוּב נְגִד בֵּית הָאֱלֹהִים: וַאֲחֵיהֶם עֹשֵׂי הַמְּלָאכָה לַבַּיִת שְׁמֹנָה מֵאוֹת עֶשְׂרִים וּשְׁנָיִם וַעֲדָיָה בֶן־יְרֹחָם בֶּן־פְּלַלְיָה בֶן־אַמְצִי בֶן־

10:35. *Leviticus 6:6.*

10:36. See *Deuteronomy 26:2.*

10:37. "Animals" refers specifically to donkeys (*Ibn Ezra*); "cattle and flocks" to cows, sheep and goats (see *Exodus 13:12-13*).

10:38. Since there were many *Kohanim* who never left the Temple precincts, and they had to be guaranteed a share of the priestly offerings, the *Kohanim* would receive

their gifts from the storage houses. The Levites would receive them directly from the field.

For the portions to be offered the *Kohanim* and the Levites, see *Numbers 15:20* and *18:25-29*.

10:39. The Levites were required to set aside a tenth of their tithe for the *Kohanim* (*Numbers 18:26-28*). To ensure that they would do so, a *Kohen* would supervise the tithing (*Ralbag*), and bring it to the Temple, where the *Kohanim* would come to receive it.

of the [daily] continual offering and the continual burnt-offering, the Sabbath offerings, the New Moon offerings; [and] for the festival offerings and for the holy things, and for the sin-offerings to atone for Israel; and all the work in the Temple of our God. ³⁵ Then we cast lots for the wood-offering, [among] the Kohanim, the Levites and the people, to bring it to the Temple of our God, the Temple of our forefathers, at appointed times, year by year, to burn on the Altar of HASHEM our God,

Priestly as is written in the Torah. * ³⁶ And [we accepted upon ourselves] to bring the first
offering fruits of our ground and the first fruits of all the fruit of every required tree year by year to the Temple of HASHEM; * ³⁷ and [to redeem] the firstborn of our sons and our animals, * as written in the Torah; and to bring the firstborn of our cattle and our flocks * to the Temple of our God, to the Kohanim who serve in the Temple of our God; ³⁸ and that we would bring the first of our dough and our separated portions [of grain] and of the fruits of every tree, wine and olive oil, to the Kohanim, to the chambers of the Temple of our God; and a tithe of [the produce of] our land to the Levites, those Levites who receive the tithes being present in all the cities of our labor. * ³⁹ A Kohen, a descendant of Aaron, shall be with the Levites at the Levites' tithing, * and the Levites shall bring up the tithe of the tithe to the Temple of our God, to the chambers of the storage house; ⁴⁰ for the children of Israel and children of the Levites shall bring the separated portions of the grain, the wine and the oil to the chambers where the vessels of the Sanctuary and the ministering Kohanim and the gatekeepers and singers are, so that we not forsake the Temple of our God. *

11

Settlers of ¹ The officers of the people settled in Jerusalem, while the remainder of the
Jerusalem . . people cast lots to bring one tenth [of them] to settle in Jerusalem, the Holy
· City, with nine parts [remaining] in the [other] cities. * ² The people blessed all those who volunteered to settle in Jerusalem.

³ These are the heads of the provinces who settled in Jerusalem, while in the cities of Judah everyone settled on his ancestral property, in their cities — [the] Israel[ites], the Kohanim and the Levites and the Nethinim and the children of
. . . Judah Solomon's slaves. ⁴ In Jerusalem some of the children of Judah and some of the
and children of Benjamin settled.
Benjamin Of the children of Judah: Athaiah son of Uzziah son of Zechariah son of
· · · Amariah son of Shephatiah son of Mahalalel, of the sons of Perez;* ⁵ and Maaseiah son of Baruch son of Col-hozeh son of Hazaiah son of Adaiah son of Joiarib son of Zechariah son of Hashiloni. ⁶ All of the children of Perez who settled in Jerusalem [numbered] four hundred sixty-eight warriors.

⁷ And these are the sons of Benjamin: * Sallu son of Meshullam son of Joed son of Pedaiah son of Kolaiah son of Maaseiah son of Ithiel son of Jeshaiah; ⁸ after him Gabbai-sallai, nine hundred twenty-eight. ⁹ Joel son of Zichri was the appointed official over them, and Judah son of Hassenuah was assistant over the city.

¹⁰ Of the Kohanim: Jedaiah son of Joiarib, Jachin, ¹¹ Seraiah son of Hilkiah son
Kohanim . . . of Meshullam son of Zadok son of Meraioth son of Ahitub, the supervisor over the Temple of God, ¹² with eight hundred twenty-nine of their brethren who performed the Temple service; Adaiah son of Jeroham son of Pelaliah son of Amzi son of

---

10:40. If the *Kohanim* had to circulate throughout the country to receive their gifts, their Temple service would be disrupted (*Metzudos*).

11:1. In order to strengthen the underpopulated, vulnerable city (see 7:1-4).

11:4-6. Judah's sons were Perez, Zerah and Shelah (see *Genesis* 38:5,29,30). Some commentators identify Hashiloni with Shelah.

11:7. Who settled in Jerusalem.

יג זְכַרְיָה בֶן־פְּשַׁחְוּר בֶּן־מַלְכִּיָּה: וְאֶחָיו רָאשִׁים לְאָבוֹת מָאתַיִם אַרְבָּעִים

יד וּשְׁנָיִם וַעֲמַשְׁסַי בֶּן־עֲזַרְאֵל בֶּן־אַחְזַי בֶּן־מְשִׁלֵּמוֹת בֶּן־אִמֵּר: וַאֲחֵיהֶם

גִּבּוֹרֵי חַיִל מֵאָה עֶשְׂרִים וּשְׁמֹנָה וּפָקִיד עֲלֵיהֶם זַבְדִּיאֵל בֶּן־

טו הַגְּדוֹלִים: וּמִן־הַלְוִיִּם שְׁמַעְיָה בֶן־חַשּׁוּב בֶּן־עַזְרִיקָם בֶּן־

טז חֲשַׁבְיָה בֶּן־בֻּנִּי: וְשַׁבְּתַי וְיוֹזָבָד עַל־הַמְּלָאכָה הַחִיצֹנָה לְבֵית הָאֱלֹהִים

יז מֵרָאשֵׁי הַלְוִיִּם: וּמַתַּנְיָה בֶן־מִיכָא בֶּן־זַבְדִּי בֶן־אָסָף רֹאשׁ הַתְּחִלָּה

יְהוֹדֶה לַתְּפִלָּה וּבַקְבֻּקְיָה מִשְׁנֶה מֵאֶחָיו וְעַבְדָּא בֶּן־שַׁמּוּעַ בֶּן־גָּלָל בֶּן־

יח °יְדִיתוּן [°יְדוּתוּן ק]: כָּל־הַלְוִיִּם בְּעִיר הַקֹּדֶשׁ מָאתַיִם שְׁמֹנִים

יט וְאַרְבָּעָה: וְהַשּׁוֹעֲרִים עַקּוּב טַלְמוֹן וַאֲחֵיהֶם הַשֹּׁמְרִים

כ בַּשְּׁעָרִים מֵאָה שִׁבְעִים וּשְׁנָיִם: וּשְׁאָר יִשְׂרָאֵל הַכֹּהֲנִים הַלְוִיִּם בְּכָל־עָרֵי

כא יְהוּדָה אִישׁ בְּנַחֲלָתוֹ: וְהַנְּתִינִים יֹשְׁבִים בָּעֹפֶל וְצִיחָא וְגִשְׁפָּא עַל־

כב הַנְּתִינִים: וּפְקִיד הַלְוִיִּם בִּירוּשָׁלַם עֻזִּי בֶן־בָּנִי בֶּן־חֲשַׁבְיָה

בֶן־מַתַּנְיָה בֶּן־מִיכָא מִבְּנֵי אָסָף הַמְשֹׁרְרִים לְנֶגֶד מְלֶאכֶת בֵּית־

כג הָאֱלֹהִים: כִּי־מִצְוַת הַמֶּלֶךְ עֲלֵיהֶם וַאֲמָנָה עַל־הַמְשֹׁרְרִים דְּבַר־יוֹם

כד בְּיוֹמוֹ: וּפְתַחְיָה בֶּן־מְשֵׁיזַבְאֵל מִבְּנֵי־זֶרַח בֶּן־יְהוּדָה לְיַד

כה הַמֶּלֶךְ לְכָל־דָּבָר לָעָם: וְאֶל־הַחֲצֵרִים בִּשְׂדֹתָם מִבְּנֵי יְהוּדָה יָשְׁבוּ בְּקִרְיַת

כו הָאַרְבַּע וּבְנֹתֶיהָ וּבְדִיבֹן וּבְנֹתֶיהָ וּבִיקַבְצְאֵל וַחֲצֵרֶיהָ: וּבְיֵשׁוּעַ וּבְמוֹלָדָה וּבְבֵית

כז-כח פָּלֶט: וּבַחֲצַר שׁוּעָל וּבִבְאֵר שֶׁבַע וּבְנֹתֶיהָ: וּבְצִקְלַג וּבִמְכֹנָה

כט-ל וּבִבְנֹתֶיהָ: וּבְעֵין רִמּוֹן וּבְצָרְעָה וּבְיַרְמוּת: זָנֹחַ עֲדֻלָּם וְחַצְרֵיהֶם לָכִישׁ

לא וּשְׂדֹתֶיהָ עֲזֵקָה וּבְנֹתֶיהָ וַיַּחֲנוּ מִבְּאֵר־שֶׁבַע עַד־גֵּיא־הִנֹּם: וּבְנֵי בִנְיָמִן

לב-לג מִגֶּבַע מִכְמָשׂ וְעַיָּה וּבֵית־אֵל וּבְנֹתֶיהָ: עֲנָתוֹת נֹב עֲנָנְיָה: חָצוֹר ׀ רָמָה

לד-לה גִּתָּיִם: חָדִיד צְבֹעִים נְבַלָּט: לֹד וְאוֹנוֹ גֵּי הַחֲרָשִׁים: וּמִן־הַלְוִיִּם מַחְלְקוֹת

יב א יְהוּדָה לְבִנְיָמִן: וְאֵלֶּה הַכֹּהֲנִים וְהַלְוִיִּם אֲשֶׁר עָלוּ עִם־

ב זְרֻבָּבֶל בֶּן־שְׁאַלְתִּיאֵל וְיֵשׁוּעַ שְׂרָיָה יִרְמְיָה עֶזְרָא: אֲמַרְיָה מַלּוּךְ חַטּוּשׁ:

ג-ד שְׁכַנְיָה רְחֻם מְרֵמֹת: עִדּוֹא גִנְּתוֹי אֲבִיָּה: מִיָּמִין מַעַדְיָה בִּלְגָּה: שְׁמַעְיָה

ז וְיוֹיָרִיב יְדַעְיָה: סַלּוּ עָמוֹק חִלְקִיָּה יְדַעְיָה אֵלֶּה רָאשֵׁי הַכֹּהֲנִים וַאֲחֵיהֶם

ח בִּימֵי יֵשׁוּעַ: וְהַלְוִיִּם יֵשׁוּעַ בִּנּוּי קַדְמִיאֵל שֵׁרֵבְיָה יְהוּדָה מַתַּנְיָה עַל־

ט הֻיְדוֹת הוּא וְאֶחָיו: וּבַקְבֻּקְיָה °וְעֻנּוֹ [°וְעֻנִּי ק] אֲחֵיהֶם לְנֶגְדָּם לְמִשְׁמָרוֹת:

וְיֵשׁוּעַ הוֹלִיד אֶת־יוֹיָקִים וְיוֹיָקִים הוֹלִיד אֶת־אֶלְיָשִׁיב וְאֶלְיָשִׁיב אֶת־

יא-יב יוֹיָדָע: וְיוֹיָדָע הוֹלִיד אֶת־יוֹנָתָן וְיוֹנָתָן הוֹלִיד אֶת־יַדּוּעַ: וּבִימֵי יוֹיָקִים

יג הָיוּ כֹהֲנִים רָאשֵׁי הָאָבוֹת לִשְׂרָיָה מְרָיָה לְיִרְמְיָה חֲנַנְיָה לְעֶזְרָא

11:23. King Darius entrusted the Levite singers with responsibility for the finances he provided for the Temple and for the community of Jerusalem (*Rashi*).

11:30. That is, from the southernmost to the northernmost boundary of Judah.

12:1-7. The narrative reverts to the time recorded in *Ezra* 2:1. The first sixteen of the twenty-two *Kohanim* mentioned here are also listed (with some orthographic variation) in 10:2-9 as signers of the covenant. The remaining six on our list either died or had retired

Zechariah son of Pashhur son of Malchijah, [13] *with two hundred forty-two of his brethren, heads of families; and Amashsai son of Azarel son of Ahzai son of Meshillemoth son of Immer,* [14] *with one hundred twenty-eight of their brethren, mighty warriors. Appointed over them was Zabdiel, son of the great.*

Levites . . .   [15] *Of the Levites: Shemaiah son of Hasshub son of Azrikam son of Hashabiah son of Bunni;* [16] *and Shabbethai and Jozabad who were in charge of the outward work of the Temple of God from among the leaders of the Levites;* [17] *Mattaniah son of Micah son of Zabdi son of Asaph, who was the leader of beginning the thanksgiving at prayer; Bakbukiah, the assistant, from among his brethren; and Abda son of Shammua son of Galal son of Jeduthun.* [18] *All the Levites in the Holy City [numbered] two hundred eighty-four.*

[19] *The gatekeepers: Akkub, Talmon, and their brethren, who stood guard at the gates, one hundred seventy-two.*

. . . others   [20] *The remainder of Israel, the Kohanim and the Levites [settled] in all the cities of Judah, each in his ancestral property.* [21] *The Nethinim settled in Ophel; Ziha and Gishpa were over the Nethinim.*

[22] *The supervisor over the Levites in Jerusalem was Uzzi son of Bani son of Hashabiah son of Mattaniah son of Micah, of the children of Asaph, the singers, to supervise the work of the Temple of God.* [23] *For the king's commandment and trust was upon the singers,* * *each day's affair in its day.*

[24] *And Pethahiah son of Meshezabel, of the descendants of Zerah son of Judah,* Towns *was at the king's hand for every matter of the people.* [25] *Some of the children of Judah settled in the villages, in their open areas — in Kiriath-arba and its suburbs, in Dibon and its suburbs, in Jekabzeel and its villages,* [26] *in Jeshua, in Moladah, in Beth-pelet,* [27] *in Hazar-shual, in Beer-sheba and its suburbs,* [28] *in Ziklag, in Meconah and in its suburbs,* [29] *in En-rimmon, in Zorah, in Jarmuth,* [30] *Zanoah, Adullam and their villages, Lachish and its open areas and Azekah and its suburbs, they encamped from Beer-sheba until the Valley of Hinnom.* *

Benjamites   [31] *The children of Benjamin [lived in the area] from Geba, [in] Michmas, Aijah, Beth-el and its suburbs,* [32] *Anathoth, Nob, Ananiah,* [33] *Hazor, Ramah, Gittaim,* [34] *Hadid, Zeboim, Neballat,* [35] *Lod, Ono and Ge-harashim.* [36] *Some of the Levites [lived in] portions [from] Judah to Benjamin.*

12   [1] **T**hese are the Kohanim * *and the Levites who ascended with Zerubbabel son*
FAMILIES   *of Shealtiel and Jeshua: Seraiah, Jeremiah, Ezra,* [2] *Amariah, Malluch, Hat-*
OF THE   *tush,* [3] *Shecaniah, Rehum, Meremoth,* [4] *Iddo, Ginnethoi, Abijah,* [5] *Mijamin, Maa-*
KOHANIM   *diah, Bilgah,* [6] *Shemaiah; and Joiarib, Jedaiah,* [7] *Sallu, Amok, Hilkiah and Jeda-*
AND   *iah; these were the heads of the Kohanim and their brethren in the days of Jeshua.*
LEVITES   [8] *And the Levites:* * *Jeshua, Binnui, Kadmiel, Sherebiah, Judah, Mattaniah —*
12:1-26   *who was in charge of the thanksgiving — he and his brethren,* [9] *Bakbukiah and Unni; their kinsmen, like them, were divided into watches.*

Succession of   [10] *Jeshua [the Kohen Gadol] begot Joiakim; Joiakim begot Eliashib; Eliashib*
High Priests   *begot Joiada;* [11] *Joiada begot Jonathan; and Jonathan begot Jaddua.*

Family heads   [12] *In the days of Joiakim, the Kohanim who were heads of the families* * *were:*
of the   *over [the family of] Seraiah, Meraiaih; over Jeremiah, Hananiah;* [13] *over Ezra,*
Kohanim

---

from public life during the intervening years and were replaced as leaders by the six noted in 10:2-9 (Malbim).

12:8. The first five Levites on this list are identified with

the first five Levite signers of the covenant (10:10-11).

12:12. These families are descended from and named for the *Kohanim* mentioned in verses 1-7. Presumably, Hattush (v. 2) was still alive and the head of his family.

יד מְשֻׁלָּם לַאֲמַרְיָה יְהוֹחָנָן: °לִמְלוּכִי [לִמְלוּכִי ק] יוֹנָתָן לִשְׁבַנְיָה יוֹסֵף:

טו-טז לְחָרִם עַדְנָא לִמְרָיוֹת חֶלְקָי: °לְעִדָּא [לְעִדּוֹא ק] זְכַרְיָה לְגִנְּתוֹן מְשֻׁלָּם:

יז-יח לַאֲבִיָּה זִכְרִי לְמִנְיָמִין לְמוֹעַדְיָה פִּלְטָי: לְבִלְגָּה שַׁמּוּעַ לִשְׁמַעְיָה יְהוֹנָתָן:

יט-כא וּלְיוֹיָרִיב מַתְּנַי לִידַעְיָה עֻזִּי: לְסַלַּי קַלָּי לְעָמוֹק עֵבֶר: לְחִלְקִיָּה חֲשַׁבְיָה

כב לִידַעְיָה נְתַנְאֵל: הַלְוִיִּם בִּימֵי אֶלְיָשִׁיב יוֹיָדָע וְיוֹחָנָן וְיַדּוּעַ כְּתוּבִים רָאשֵׁי

כג אָבוֹת וְהַכֹּהֲנִים עַל־מַלְכוּת דָּרְיָוֶשׁ הַפָּרְסִי: בְּנֵי לֵוִי רָאשֵׁי הָאָבוֹת כְּתוּבִים עַל־סֵפֶר דִּבְרֵי הַיָּמִים וְעַד־יְמֵי יוֹחָנָן בֶּן־אֶלְיָשִׁיב:

כד וְרָאשֵׁי הַלְוִיִּם חֲשַׁבְיָה שֵׁרֵבְיָה וְיֵשׁוּעַ בֶּן־קַדְמִיאֵל וַאֲחֵיהֶם לְנֶגְדָּם לְהַלֵּל לְהוֹדוֹת בְּמִצְוַת דָּוִיד אִישׁ־הָאֱלֹהִים מִשְׁמָר לְעֻמַּת מִשְׁמָר:

כה מַתַּנְיָה וּבַקְבֻּקְיָה עֹבַדְיָה מְשֻׁלָּם טַלְמוֹן עַקּוּב שֹׁמְרִים שׁוֹעֲרִים מִשְׁמָר

כו בַּאֲסֻפֵּי הַשְּׁעָרִים: אֵלֶּה בִּימֵי יוֹיָקִים בֶּן־יֵשׁוּעַ בֶּן־יוֹצָדָק וּבִימֵי נְחֶמְיָה

כז הַפֶּחָה וְעֶזְרָא הַכֹּהֵן הַסּוֹפֵר: וּבַחֲנֻכַּת חוֹמַת יְרוּשָׁלַ͏ִם בִּקְשׁוּ אֶת־הַלְוִיִּם מִכָּל־מְקוֹמֹתָם לַהֲבִיאָם לִירוּשָׁלָ͏ִם לַעֲשֹׂת חֲנֻכָּה וְשִׂמְחָה

כח וּבְתוֹדוֹת וּבְשִׁיר מְצִלְתַּיִם נְבָלִים וּבְכִנֹּרוֹת: וַיֵּאָסְפוּ בְּנֵי הַמְשֹׁרְרִים וּמִן־

כט הַכִּכָּר סְבִיבוֹת יְרוּשָׁלַ͏ִם וּמִן־חַצְרֵי נְטֹפָתִי: וּמִבֵּית הַגִּלְגָּל וּמִשְּׂדוֹת גֶּבַע

ל וְעַזְמָוֶת כִּי חֲצֵרִים בָּנוּ לָהֶם הַמְשֹׁרְרִים סְבִיבוֹת יְרוּשָׁלָ͏ִם: וַיִּטַּהֲרוּ

לא הַכֹּהֲנִים וְהַלְוִיִּם וַיְטַהֲרוּ אֶת־הָעָם וְאֶת־הַשְּׁעָרִים וְאֶת־הַחוֹמָה: וָאַעֲלֶה אֶת־שָׂרֵי יְהוּדָה מֵעַל לַחוֹמָה וָאַעֲמִידָה שְׁתֵּי תוֹדֹת גְּדוֹלֹת וְתַהֲלֻכֹת

לב לַיָּמִין מֵעַל לַחוֹמָה לְשַׁעַר הָאַשְׁפֹּת: וַיֵּלֶךְ אַחֲרֵיהֶם הוֹשַׁעְיָה וַחֲצִי שָׂרֵי

לג-לד יְהוּדָה: וַעֲזַרְיָה עֶזְרָא וּמְשֻׁלָּם: יְהוּדָה וּבִנְיָמִן וּשְׁמַעְיָה וְיִרְמְיָה:

לה וּמִבְּנֵי הַכֹּהֲנִים בַּחֲצֹצְרוֹת זְכַרְיָה בֶן־יוֹנָתָן בֶּן־שְׁמַעְיָה בֶּן־מַתַּנְיָה בֶּן־

לו מִיכָיָה בֶּן־זַכּוּר בֶּן־אָסָף: וְאֶחָיו שְׁמַעְיָה וַעֲזַרְאֵל מִלֲלַי גִּלֲלַי מָעַי נְתַנְאֵל

לז וִיהוּדָה חֲנָנִי בִּכְלֵי־שִׁיר דָּוִיד אִישׁ הָאֱלֹהִים וְעֶזְרָא הַסּוֹפֵר לִפְנֵיהֶם: וְעַל שַׁעַר הָעַיִן וְנֶגְדָּם עָלוּ עַל־מַעֲלוֹת עִיר דָּוִיד בַּמַּעֲלֶה לַחוֹמָה מֵעַל

לח לְבֵית דָּוִיד וְעַד שַׁעַר הַמַּיִם מִזְרָח: וְהַתּוֹדָה הַשֵּׁנִית הַהוֹלֶכֶת לְמוֹאל וַאֲנִי אַחֲרֶיהָ וַחֲצִי הָעָם מֵעַל לְהַחוֹמָה מֵעַל לְמִגְדַּל הַתַּנּוּרִים וְעַד

לט הַחוֹמָה הָרְחָבָה: וּמֵעַל לְשַׁעַר־אֶפְרַיִם וְעַל־שַׁעַר הַיְשָׁנָה וְעַל־שַׁעַר הַדָּגִים וּמִגְדַּל חֲנַנְאֵל וּמִגְדַּל הַמֵּאָה וְעַד שַׁעַר הַצֹּאן וְעָמְדוּ בְּשַׁעַר

מ הַמַּטָּרָה: וַתַּעֲמֹדְנָה שְׁתֵּי הַתּוֹדֹת בְּבֵית הָאֱלֹהִים וַאֲנִי וַחֲצִי הַסְּגָנִים עִמִּי:

מא וְהַכֹּהֲנִים אֶלְיָקִים מַעֲשֵׂיָה מִנְיָמִין מִיכָיָה אֶלְיוֹעֵינַי זְכַרְיָה חֲנַנְיָה

מב בַּחֲצֹצְרוֹת: וּמַעֲשֵׂיָה וּשְׁמַעְיָה וְאֶלְעָזָר וְעֻזִּי וִיהוֹחָנָן וּמַלְכִּיָּה וְעֵילָם וָעָזֶר

12:23. He was also called Jonathan (v. 11).

12.24. They were divided into divisions of equal size and standing (*Metzudos*). [See Appendix B, chart 12.]

12:31. Two of the larger loaves of bread that accompany a thanksgiving-offering were carried around the city as part of the procession and the ritual of sanctification. The march proceeded to the right of one facing the city, i.e. counterclockwise (*Rashi, Shevuos* 15a).

12:38. Alternatively: to the left, i.e. clockwise.

12:39. The procession halted there.

Meshullam; over Amariah, Jehohanan; [14] over Melicu, Jonathan; over Sheba-niah, Joseph; [15] over Harim, Adna; over Meraioth, Helkai; [16] over Iddo, Zechariah; over Ginnethon, Meshullam; [17] over Abijah, Zichri; over Miniamin [and] over Moadiah, Piltai; [18] over Bilgah, Shammua; over Shemaiah, Jehonathan; [19] over Joiarib, Mattenai; over Jedaiah, Uzzi; [20] over Sallai, Kallai; over Amok, Eber; [21] over Hilkiah, Hashabiah; over Jedaiah, Nethanel.

Family heads of the Levites   [22] The Levites in the days of Eliashib, Joiada, Johanan and Jaddua were recorded as family heads, and the Kohanim [as well], during the reign of Darius the Persian. [23] The children of Levi who were the family heads were recorded in a book of chronicles down to the days of Johanan,* the [grand]son of Eliashib. [24] The heads of the Levites were: Hashabiah, Sherebiah and Jeshua son of Kadmiel, with their brethren opposite them, to praise and give thanks according to the command of David, the man of God, one watch parallel to the other watch;* [25] Mattaniah, Bakbukiah, Obadiah, Meshullam, Talmon and Akkub, who were guardians, gatekeepers at their watches at the gateposts. [26] These were in the days of Joiakim son of Jeshua son of Jozadak, and in the days of Nehemiah the governor and Ezra the Kohen, the scholar.

THE WALLS OF JERUSALEM DEDICATED
12:27-13:3
[27] At the dedication of the wall of Jerusalem the Levites were sought from all their places, to bring them to Jerusalem to celebrate the dedication with rejoicing and with thanksgiving-offerings, and with song, cymbals, lyres and harps. [28] The singers were gathered [from Jerusalem] and from the plain around Jerusalem, from the villages of the Netophatite, [29] from Beth-gilgal and from the open areas of Geba and Azmaveth; for the singers had built themselves villages around Jerusalem. [30] The Kohanim and the Levites purified themselves, and they purified the people, and the gates and the wall.

The march begins   [31] I then brought the officers of Judah alongside near the wall, and I emplaced two large thanksgiving loaves* there; then the march [set out] towards the right,* alongside the wall, towards the Dung Gate. [32] After them went Hoshaiah and half of the officers of Judah; [33] and Azariah, Ezra and Meshullam; [34] Judah and *The Kohanim* Benjamin and Shemaiah and Jeremiah. [35] Of the sons of the Kohanim, with trumpets: Zechariah son of Jonathan son of Shemaiah son of Mattaniah son of Micaiah son of Zaccur son of Asaph; [36] then his brethren Shemaiah and Azarel, Milalai, Gilalai, Maai, Nethanel and Judah [and] Hanani, with the musical instru-*The procession continues* ments of David, the man of God, with Ezra the scholar before them. [37] Then, near the Spring Gate and in front of them, ascending upon the steps of the City of David, on the stair to the wall, over the house of David, up to the Water Gate to the east.

[38] The second thanksgiving-offering went alongside,* and I followed with half the people alongside the wall, from near the Tower of the Ovens until the Broad Wall, [39] from near the Gate of Ephraim, near the Old Gate, near the Fish Gate and the Tower of Hananel and the Tower of the Hundred, up to the Sheep Gate; they stood still at the Prison Gate.*

[40] Then the two thanksgiving-offerings stopped at the Temple of God, and I, and half the leaders with me, [41] and the Kohanim Eliakim, Maaseiah, Miniamin, Mica-iah, Elioenai, Zechariah and Hananiah with trumpets; [42] and Maaseiah and She-maiah and Elazar and Uzzi and Jehohanan and Malchijah and Elam and Azer.

מג וַיִּשְׁמְעוּ הַמְשֹׁרְרִים וְיֶזְרַחְיָה הַפָּקִיד: וַיִּזְבְּחוּ בַיּוֹם־הַהוּא זְבָחִים גְּדוֹלִים וַיִּשְׂמָחוּ כִּי הָאֱלֹהִים שִׂמְּחָם שִׂמְחָה גְדוֹלָה וְגַם הַנָּשִׁים וְהַיְלָדִים

מד שָׂמֵחוּ וַתִּשָּׁמַע שִׂמְחַת יְרוּשָׁלַ͏ִם מֵרָחוֹק: וַיִּפָּקְדוּ בַיּוֹם הַהוּא אֲנָשִׁים עַל־הַנְּשָׁכוֹת לָאוֹצָרוֹת לַתְּרוּמוֹת לָרֵאשִׁית וְלַמַּעַשְׂרוֹת לִכְנוֹס בָּהֶם לִשְׂדֵי הֶעָרִים מְנָאוֹת הַתּוֹרָה לַכֹּהֲנִים וְלַלְוִיִּם כִּי שִׂמְחַת יְהוּדָה עַל־

מה הַכֹּהֲנִים וְעַל־הַלְוִיִּם הָעֹמְדִים: וַיִּשְׁמְרוּ מִשְׁמֶרֶת אֱלֹהֵיהֶם וּמִשְׁמֶרֶת

מו הַטָּהֳרָה וְהַמְשֹׁרְרִים וְהַשֹּׁעֲרִים כְּמִצְוַת דָּוִיד שְׁלֹמֹה בְנוֹ: כִּי־בִימֵי דָוִיד וְאָסָף מִקֶּדֶם °רֹאשׁ [°רָאשֵׁי ק] הַמְשֹׁרְרִים וְשִׁיר־תְּהִלָּה וְהֹדוֹת

מז לֵאלֹהִים: וְכָל־יִשְׂרָאֵל בִּימֵי זְרֻבָּבֶל וּבִימֵי נְחֶמְיָה נֹתְנִים מְנָיוֹת הַמְשֹׁרְרִים וְהַשֹּׁעֲרִים דְּבַר־יוֹם בְּיוֹמוֹ וּמַקְדִּשִׁים לַלְוִיִּם וְהַלְוִיִּם מַקְדִּשִׁים

יג א לִבְנֵי אַהֲרֹן: בַּיּוֹם הַהוּא נִקְרָא בְּסֵפֶר מֹשֶׁה בְּאָזְנֵי הָעָם וְנִמְצָא כָּתוּב בּוֹ אֲשֶׁר לֹא־יָבוֹא עַמֹּנִי וּמֹאָבִי בִּקְהַל הָאֱלֹהִים עַד־

ב עוֹלָם: כִּי לֹא קִדְּמוּ אֶת־בְּנֵי יִשְׂרָאֵל בַּלֶּחֶם וּבַמָּיִם וַיִּשְׂכֹּר עָלָיו אֶת־ בִּלְעָם לְקַלְלוֹ וַיַּהֲפֹךְ אֱלֹהֵינוּ הַקְּלָלָה לִבְרָכָה: וַיְהִי כְּשָׁמְעָם אֶת־

ג הַתּוֹרָה וַיַּבְדִּילוּ כָל־עֵרֶב מִיִּשְׂרָאֵל: וְלִפְנֵי מִזֶּה אֶלְיָשִׁיב הַכֹּהֵן נָתוּן

ד בְּלִשְׁכַּת בֵּית־אֱלֹהֵינוּ קָרוֹב לְטוֹבִיָּה: וַיַּעַשׂ לוֹ לִשְׁכָּה גְדוֹלָה וְשָׁם הָיוּ לְפָנִים נֹתְנִים אֶת־הַמִּנְחָה הַלְּבוֹנָה וְהַכֵּלִים וּמַעְשַׂר הַדָּגָן הַתִּירוֹשׁ

ה וְהַיִּצְהָר מִצְוַת הַלְוִיִּם וְהַמְשֹׁרְרִים וְהַשֹּׁעֲרִים וּתְרוּמַת הַכֹּהֲנִים: וּבְכָל־ זֶה לֹא הָיִיתִי בִּירוּשָׁלָ͏ִם כִּי בִּשְׁנַת שְׁלֹשִׁים וּשְׁתַּיִם לְאַרְתַּחְשַׁסְתְּא

ו מֶלֶךְ־בָּבֶל בָּאתִי אֶל־הַמֶּלֶךְ וּלְקֵץ יָמִים נִשְׁאַלְתִּי מִן־הַמֶּלֶךְ: וָאָבוֹא לִירוּשָׁלַ͏ִם וָאָבִינָה בָרָעָה אֲשֶׁר עָשָׂה אֶלְיָשִׁיב לְטוֹבִיָּה לַעֲשׂוֹת לוֹ נִשְׁכָּה

ז בְּחַצְרֵי בֵּית הָאֱלֹהִים: וַיֵּרַע לִי מְאֹד וָאַשְׁלִיכָה אֶת־כָּל־כְּלֵי בֵית־טוֹבִיָּה

ח הַחוּץ מִן־הַלִּשְׁכָּה: וָאֹמְרָה וַיְטַהֲרוּ הַלְּשָׁכוֹת וָאָשִׁיבָה שָׁם כְּלֵי בֵּית

ט הָאֱלֹהִים אֶת־הַמִּנְחָה וְהַלְּבוֹנָה: וָאֵדְעָה כִּי־מְנָיוֹת הַלְוִיִּם לֹא נִתָּנָה

י וַיִּבְרְחוּ אִישׁ־לְשָׂדֵהוּ הַלְוִיִּם וְהַמְשֹׁרְרִים עֹשֵׂי הַמְּלָאכָה: וָאָרִיבָה אֶת־

יא הַסְּגָנִים וָאֹמְרָה מַדּוּעַ נֶעֱזַב בֵּית־הָאֱלֹהִים וָאֶקְבְּצֵם וָאַעֲמִדֵם עַל־

יב עָמְדָם: וְכָל־יְהוּדָה הֵבִיאוּ מַעְשַׂר הַדָּגָן וְהַתִּירוֹשׁ וְהַיִּצְהָר לָאוֹצָרוֹת:

יג וָאוֹצְרָה עַל־אוֹצָרוֹת שֶׁלֶמְיָה הַכֹּהֵן וְצָדוֹק הַסּוֹפֵר וּפְדָיָה מִן־הַלְוִיִּם וְעַל־יָדָם חָנָן בֶּן־זַכּוּר בֶּן־מַתַּנְיָה כִּי נֶאֱמָנִים נֶחְשָׁבוּ וַעֲלֵיהֶם לַחֲלֹק

יד לַאֲחֵיהֶם: זָכְרָה־לִּי אֱלֹהַי עַל־זֹאת וְאַל־תֶּמַח חֲסָדַי אֲשֶׁר

12:44. The people wanted to insure that the *Kohanim* and Levites would be provided for in an organized manner.

12:45. Insuring that no impure thing or person entered the Temple grounds (*Metzudos*).

12:46. The ritual of Ezra and Nehemiah was patterned after those of David and Asaph.

13:1. *Deuteronomy* 23:4-6. The prohibition applies to Moabite and Ammonite men; women, however, may convert to Judaism, as did Ruth.

13:3. Alien men who had married Jewish women were removed from the nation.

13:4. See 2:10 and 13:28.

13:14. After recording each of his reforms, Nehemiah

The singers made their song heard with Jezrahiah, the supervisor. [43] They slaughtered a great number of sacrifices on that day, and they rejoiced; for God had caused them to rejoice, a great rejoicing; also the women and children rejoiced. The rejoicing of Jerusalem was heard from afar.

Portion of the Kohanim and Levites [44] On that day men were appointed over the chambers that were for the storage of the terumah-offerings, the first-fruits and the tithes, in which to gather from the fields around the cities the portions ordained by the Torah for the Kohanim and for the Levites. For there was rejoicing in Judah over the Kohanim and Levites who were stationed [in the Temple], * [45] who kept the watch of their God and the watch of purity, * and the singers and the gatekeepers, as the commandment of David [to] Solomon his son. [46] For in the days of David and Asaph, in former times, there were leaders of the singers and songs of praise and thanksgiving to God. * [47] All of Israel in the days of Zerubbabel and in the days of Nehemiah supplied portions of food for the singers and the gatekeepers, each day's need in its day. They also consecrated [the tithe] for the Levites, and the Levites consecrated [a portion] for the sons of Aaron.

13

NEHEMIAH'S REFORMS 13:1-31

Alien men [1] On that day the Book of Moses was read in the ears of the people, and it was found written in it that an Ammonite or Moabite shall not ever enter into the congregation of God, to eternity, * [2] because they did not greet the Children of Israel with bread and with water, and [the Moabite king] hired Balaam against [Israel] to curse [Israel], but our God reversed the curse into a blessing. [3] So it happened that when they heard the Torah, they separated all the assimilated ones from Israel. *

Eliashib and Tobiah [4] Before this, Eliashib the Kohen, a relative of Tobiah's, * had been stationed in a chamber of the Temple of our God. [5] He prepared a large chamber for [Tobiah], where they had formerly stored the meal-offering, the frankincense and the utensils and the tithe of the grain, the wine and the oil, which were ordained for the Levites and the singers and the gatekeepers, and the terumah-offerings for the Kohanim. [6] Now during all this, I was not in Jerusalem, for in the thirty-second year of Artaxerxes king of Babylonia, I had come to the king. Then, at the end of some time I requested [leave] of the king. [7] I arrived in Jerusalem and contemplated the evil that Eliashib had done for Tobiah, by preparing a chamber for him in the courtyards of the Temple of God. [8] This was extremely distressing to me, and I threw all of Tobiah's household articles out of the chamber. [9] Then I gave the order, and they purified the chambers; I returned to it the utensils of the Temple of God, the meal-offering and the frankincense.

Levite portions [10] I then became aware that the Levites' portions had not been given; and the Levites — the singers and those who performed the services — had fled, each to his own field. [11] So I contended with the nobles, and I said, "Why is the Temple of God forsaken?" I then gathered [the Levites] together and established them in their stations. [12] All of Judah then brought the tithe of the grain and the wine and the oil to the storehouses. [13] I appointed as treasurers of the storehouses Shelemiah the Kohen, Zadok the scholar, and Pedaiah of the Levites, and to assist them, Hanan son of Zaccur son of Mattaniah, for they were considered trustworthy; and it was their duty to apportion [the shares] to their brethren.

[14] "Remember me, * O my God, for this; do not disregard my kindnesses that

---

inserts a short prayer that his action should be remembered (see 5:19 and 13:22,29,31).

טו עָשִׂיתִי בְּבֵית אֱלֹהַי וּבְמִשְׁמָרָיו: בַּיָּמִים הָהֵמָּה רָאִיתִי בִיהוּדָה ׀ דֹּרְכִים־
גִּתּוֹת ׀ בַּשַּׁבָּת וּמְבִיאִים הָעֲרֵמוֹת וְעֹמְסִים עַל־הַחֲמֹרִים וְאַף־יַיִן עֲנָבִים
וּתְאֵנִים וְכָל־מַשָּׂא וּמְבִיאִים יְרוּשָׁלַ͏ִם בְּיוֹם הַשַּׁבָּת וָאָעִיד בְּיוֹם מִכְרָם
טז צָיִד: וְהַצֹּרִים יָשְׁבוּ בָהּ מְבִיאִים דָּאג וְכָל־מֶכֶר וּמֹכְרִים בַּשַּׁבָּת לִבְנֵי
יז יְהוּדָה וּבִירוּשָׁלָ͏ִם: וָאָרִיבָה אֵת חֹרֵי יְהוּדָה וָאֹמְרָה לָהֶם מָה־הַדָּבָר
הָרָע הַזֶּה אֲשֶׁר אַתֶּם עֹשִׂים וּמְחַלְּלִים אֶת־יוֹם הַשַּׁבָּת: הֲלוֹא כֹה עָשׂוּ
אֲבֹתֵיכֶם וַיָּבֵא אֱלֹהֵינוּ עָלֵינוּ אֵת כָּל־הָרָעָה הַזֹּאת וְעַל הָעִיר הַזֹּאת
יט וְאַתֶּם מוֹסִיפִים חָרוֹן עַל־יִשְׂרָאֵל לְחַלֵּל אֶת־הַשַּׁבָּת: וַיְהִי
כַּאֲשֶׁר צָלְלוּ שַׁעֲרֵי יְרוּשָׁלַ͏ִם לִפְנֵי הַשַּׁבָּת וָאֹמְרָה וַיִּסָּגְרוּ הַדְּלָתוֹת
וָאֹמְרָה אֲשֶׁר לֹא יִפְתָּחוּם עַד אַחַר הַשַּׁבָּת וּמִנְּעָרַי הֶעֱמַדְתִּי עַל־
כ הַשְּׁעָרִים לֹא־יָבוֹא מַשָּׂא בְּיוֹם הַשַּׁבָּת: וַיָּלִינוּ הָרֹכְלִים וּמֹכְרֵי כָל־
כא מִמְכָּר מִחוּץ לִירוּשָׁלָ͏ִם פַּעַם וּשְׁתָּיִם: וָאָעִידָה בָהֶם וָאֹמְרָה אֲלֵיהֶם
מַדּוּעַ אַתֶּם לֵנִים נֶגֶד הַחוֹמָה אִם־תִּשְׁנוּ יָד אֶשְׁלַח בָּכֶם מִן־הָעֵת הַהִיא
כב לֹא־בָאוּ בַּשַּׁבָּת: וָאֹמְרָה לַלְוִיִּם אֲשֶׁר יִהְיוּ מִטַּהֲרִים וּבָאִים שֹׁמְרִים
הַשְּׁעָרִים לְקַדֵּשׁ אֶת־יוֹם הַשַּׁבָּת גַּם־זֹאת זָכְרָה־לִּי אֱלֹהַי וְחוּסָה עָלַי
כג כְּרֹב חַסְדֶּךָ: גַּם ׀ בַּיָּמִים הָהֵם רָאִיתִי אֶת־הַיְּהוּדִים הֹשִׁיבוּ
נָשִׁים °אַשְׁדּוֹדִיּוֹת [°אַשְׁדֳּדִיּוֹת ק] °עַמֳּנִיּוֹת [°עַמּוֹנִיּוֹת ק] מוֹאֲבִיּוֹת:
כד וּבְנֵיהֶם חֲצִי מְדַבֵּר אַשְׁדּוֹדִית וְאֵינָם מַכִּירִים לְדַבֵּר יְהוּדִית וְכִלְשׁוֹן עַם
כה וָעָם: וָאָרִיב עִמָּם וָאֲקַלְלֵם וָאַכֶּה מֵהֶם אֲנָשִׁים וָאֶמְרְטֵם וָאַשְׁבִּיעֵם
בֵּאלֹהִים אִם־תִּתְּנוּ בְנֹתֵיכֶם לִבְנֵיהֶם וְאִם־תִּשְׂאוּ מִבְּנֹתֵיהֶם לִבְנֵיכֶם
כו וְלָכֶם: הֲלוֹא עַל־אֵלֶּה חָטָא־שְׁלֹמֹה מֶלֶךְ יִשְׂרָאֵל וּבַגּוֹיִם הָרַבִּים לֹא־
הָיָה מֶלֶךְ כָּמֹהוּ וְאָהוּב לֵאלֹהָיו הָיָה וַיִּתְּנֵהוּ אֱלֹהִים מֶלֶךְ עַל־כָּל־
כז יִשְׂרָאֵל גַּם־אוֹתוֹ הֶחֱטִיאוּ הַנָּשִׁים הַנָּכְרִיּוֹת: וְלָכֶם הֲנִשְׁמַע לַעֲשֹׂת אֵת
כח כָּל־הָרָעָה הַגְּדוֹלָה הַזֹּאת לִמְעֹל בֵּאלֹהֵינוּ לְהֹשִׁיב נָשִׁים נָכְרִיּוֹת: וּמִבְּנֵי
יוֹיָדָע בֶּן־אֶלְיָשִׁיב הַכֹּהֵן הַגָּדוֹל חָתָן לְסַנְבַלַּט הַחֹרֹנִי וָאַבְרִיחֵהוּ מֵעָלָי:
כט־ל זָכְרָה לָהֶם אֱלֹהָי עַל גָּאֳלֵי הַכְּהֻנָּה וּבְרִית הַכְּהֻנָּה וְהַלְוִיִּם: וְטִהַרְתִּים
לא מִכָּל־נֵכָר וָאַעֲמִידָה מִשְׁמָרוֹת לַכֹּהֲנִים וְלַלְוִיִּם אִישׁ בִּמְלַאכְתּוֹ: וּלְקֻרְבַּן
הָעֵצִים בְּעִתִּים מְזֻמָּנוֹת וְלַבִּכּוּרִים זָכְרָה־לִּי אֱלֹהַי לְטוֹבָה:

סכום פסוקי דעזרא ונחמיה שש מאות ושמונים ושמונה. וסימנו זכר ה' **חרפת** עבדך.

13:19. In the late afternoon, just before the onset of the Sabbath, as the sun was setting.

13:20. They hoped that some Jews would come outside to buy from them.

I did for the Temple of my God and for its watches!"

Sabbath
desecration ¹⁵ *In those days I observed in Judah [people] treading on winepresses on the Sabbath and [people] bringing sheaves and loading them on the donkeys, as well as wine, grapes and figs and every burden, bringing them to Jerusalem on the Sabbath day. I warned them on the day they sold their provisions.* ¹⁶ *[Also,] the Tyrians who dwelled there would bring fish and every merchandise and sell [them] on the Sabbath to the people of Judah — and in Jerusalem!* ¹⁷ *So I contended with the aristocrats of Judah, and I said to them, "What is this wicked thing that you are doing, desecrating the Sabbath day?* ¹⁸ *Did not your ancestors do this, and then our God brought all this evil upon us and upon this city? And now you bring additional wrath against Israel by desecrating the Sabbath!"*

¹⁹ *It happened when the gates of Jerusalem cast shadows before the Sabbath, * that I spoke [the order] and the doors were closed, and I spoke [the order] not to open them until after the Sabbath. I stationed some of my servants at the gates, [so that] no burden could come in on the Sabbath.* ²⁰ *So the merchants and the sellers of every merchandise lodged outside Jerusalem once and then a second time. ** ²¹ *I warned them, and said to them, "Why do you lodge across from the wall? If you repeat this, I will send a force against you!" From that time onward they did not come on the Sabbath.* ²² *Then I told the Levites that they should regularly purify themselves and come as guards of the gates, to sanctify the Sabbath day.*

"This, too, remember for me, O my God, and be compassionate towards me according to Your abundant kindness!"

Gentile
wives ²³ *Also in those days I observed the Jews who had married Ashdodite, Ammonite, and Moabite wives.* ²⁴ *Half their children spoke Ashdodian and did not know how to speak the language of the Jews; and likewise with the language of each nation.* ²⁵ *So I contended with them and I cursed them. I beat some of their men and tore their hair out. I made them swear by God, that "you not give your daughters over to their sons, nor marry their daughters to your sons or to yourselves."* ²⁶ *[I said,] "Did not Solomon, king of Israel, sin with such [women]? Among the many nations there was never a king like him; he was beloved by his God, and God appointed him king over all of Israel. Yet the alien wives caused even him to sin!* ²⁷ *Shall we then listen to you, to do all this great wickedness, to be unfaithful to our God by marrying alien wives?"* ²⁸ *One of the sons of Joiada son of Eliashib the Kohen Gadol was a son-in-law of Sanballat the Horonite, so I drove him away from me.*

²⁹ *"Remember them, O my God, for their desecrations of the priesthood and of the covenant of the priesthood and of the Levites!"*

³⁰ *And so I cleansed them from all that is alien; and I established the watches of the Kohanim and of the Levites, each one according to its task;* ³¹ *and for the wood-offering at scheduled times and for the first fruits.*

"Remember me, O my God, for good!"

13:31. Nehemiah had instituted both these services, as described in 10:35-36 (*Ibn Ezra*). Nehemiah emphasized his accomplishments so that others would learn from his example (*Ralbag*).

Chronicles דברי הימים

*T*he Book of Chronicles was composed by Ezra, and the Sages of the Talmud canonized it as part of Scripture (Bava Basra 14a). By definition, therefore, it was composed under the guidance of the Divine Spirit.

However, Chronicles seems to be little more than a combination of long lists of names and royal records of events, most of which have already been enumerated in the Books of Samuel and Kings — or so it seems on the surface. Upon closer examination, the Book is even more mystifying. Many of the names in the genealogical lists are different from those found in the other Books of Tanach. Not all the events of the earlier Books are recorded here; many that are found here do not appear earlier; and often details are different. It is beyond the scope of this work to deal specifically with these problems, but we offer a general view of Chronicles, as discussed at length in the full ArtScroll edition of this Book.

The focus of the Book of Chronicles is to serve as the prelude to the eventual kingdom of the Messiah, who will be a descendant of King David. As such, the Book deals primarily with the Davidic dynasty. Indeed, much of our information about such great Judean kings as Hezekiah and Josiah comes from Chronicles. This explains a striking difference between the respective endings of the Books of Kings and Chronicles. Kings culminates with the destruction of the First Temple and the exile from Jerusalem. Chronicles ends with the return of the Jews from exile. For the theme of this Book is return, and even though the Second Commonwealth was but a pale shadow of the future Redemption, it kept Jewish hopes alive and proved that the prophecies of an end to the Babylonian Exile were not in vain. And if those prophecies were fulfilled, then we can be sure that the fulfillment of the prophecies for the future still awaits us.

The unfamiliar names in Chronicles represent allusions to the inner essence of people. For example, in the Book of Ruth (1:2), the sons of Elimelech are called Mahlon and Chilion, but in I Chronicles (4:22) they are called Joash and Saraph, Hebrew words that allude to despair and burning — because those two men doomed themselves by their callous behavior.

We are about to begin a Book that is a harbinger of the future and of the final Redemption — may it soon unfold.

א-ד *אָדָם שֵׁת אֱנוֹשׁ: קֵינָן מַהֲלַלְאֵל יָרֶד: חֲנוֹךְ מְתוּשֶׁלַח לָמֶךְ: נֹחַ שֵׁם חָם

ה-ו וָיָפֶת: בְּנֵי יֶפֶת גֹּמֶר וּמָגוֹג וּמָדַי וְיָוָן וְתֻבָל וּמֶשֶׁךְ וְתִירָס: וּבְנֵי גֹּמֶר אַשְׁכְּנַז

ז-ח וְדִיפַת וְתוֹגַרְמָה: וּבְנֵי יָוָן אֱלִישָׁה וְתַרְשִׁישָׁה כִּתִּים וְרוֹדָנִים: בְּנֵי

ט חָם כּוּשׁ וּמִצְרַיִם פּוּט וּכְנָעַן: וּבְנֵי כוּשׁ סְבָא וַחֲוִילָה וְסַבְתָּא וְרַעְמָא

י וְסַבְתְּכָא וּבְנֵי רַעְמָא שְׁבָא וּדְדָן: וְכוּשׁ יָלַד אֶת־נִמְרוֹד הוּא הֵחֵל לִהְיוֹת

יא גִּבּוֹר בָּאָרֶץ: וּמִצְרַיִם יָלַד אֶת־°לוּדִיים [°לוּדִים ק] וְאֶת־עֲנָמִים

יב וְאֶת־לְהָבִים וְאֶת־נַפְתֻּחִים: וְאֶת־פַּתְרֻסִים וְאֶת־כַּסְלֻחִים אֲשֶׁר יָצְאוּ

יג מִשָּׁם פְּלִשְׁתִּים וְאֶת־כַּפְתֹּרִים: וּכְנַעַן יָלַד אֶת־צִידוֹן בְּכֹרוֹ

יד-טו וְאֶת־חֵת: וְאֶת־הַיְבוּסִי וְאֶת־הָאֱמֹרִי וְאֵת הַגִּרְגָּשִׁי: וְאֶת־הַחִוִּי וְאֶת־

טז הָעַרְקִי וְאֶת־הַסִּינִי: וְאֶת־הָאַרְוָדִי וְאֶת־הַצְּמָרִי וְאֶת־הַחֲמָתִי: בְּנֵי

יז שֵׁם עֵילָם וְאַשּׁוּר וְאַרְפַּכְשַׁד וְלוּד וַאֲרָם וְעוּץ וְחוּל וְגֶתֶר וָמֶשֶׁךְ:

יח-יט וְאַרְפַּכְשַׁד יָלַד אֶת־שָׁלַח וְשֶׁלַח יָלַד אֶת־עֵבֶר: וּלְעֵבֶר

יֻלַּד שְׁנֵי בָנִים שֵׁם הָאֶחָד פֶּלֶג כִּי בְיָמָיו נִפְלְגָה הָאָרֶץ וְשֵׁם אָחִיו יָקְטָן:

כ-כא וְיָקְטָן יָלַד אֶת־אַלְמוֹדָד וְאֶת־שָׁלֶף וְאֶת־חֲצַרְמָוֶת וְאֶת־יָרַח: וְאֶת־

כב הֲדוֹרָם וְאֶת־אוּזָל וְאֶת־דִּקְלָה: וְאֶת־עֵיבָל וְאֶת־אֲבִימָאֵל וְאֶת־שְׁבָא:

כג-כד וְאֶת־אוֹפִיר וְאֶת־חֲוִילָה וְאֶת־יוֹבָב כָּל־אֵלֶּה בְּנֵי יָקְטָן: שֵׁם ׀

כה-כו אַרְפַּכְשַׁד שָׁלַח: עֵבֶר פֶּלֶג רְעוּ: שְׂרוּג נָחוֹר תָּרַח: אַבְרָם הוּא

כז-כט אַבְרָהָם: בְּנֵי אַבְרָהָם יִצְחָק וְיִשְׁמָעֵאל: אֵלֶּה תֹּלְדוֹתָם

ל בְּכוֹר יִשְׁמָעֵאל נְבָיוֹת וְקֵדָר וְאַדְבְּאֵל וּמִבְשָׂם: מִשְׁמָע וְדוּמָה מַשָּׂא חֲדַד

לא-לב וְתֵימָא: יְטוּר נָפִישׁ וָקֵדְמָה אֵלֶּה הֵם בְּנֵי יִשְׁמָעֵאל: וּבְנֵי קְטוּרָה

פִּילֶגֶשׁ אַבְרָהָם יָלְדָה אֶת־זִמְרָן וְיָקְשָׁן וּמְדָן וּמִדְיָן וְיִשְׁבָּק וְשׁוּחַ וּבְנֵי

לג יָקְשָׁן שְׁבָא וּדְדָן: וּבְנֵי מִדְיָן עֵיפָה וָעֵפֶר וַחֲנוֹךְ וַאֲבִידָע וְאֶלְדָּעָה

לד כָּל־אֵלֶּה בְּנֵי קְטוּרָה: וַיּוֹלֶד אַבְרָהָם אֶת־יִצְחָק בְּנֵי יִצְחָק עֵשָׂו

לה-לו וְיִשְׂרָאֵל: בְּנֵי עֵשָׂו אֱלִיפַז רְעוּאֵל וִיעוּשׁ וְיַעְלָם וְקֹרַח: בְּנֵי

לז אֱלִיפַז תֵּימָן וְאוֹמָר צְפִי וְגַעְתָּם קְנַז וְתִמְנָע וַעֲמָלֵק: בְּנֵי רְעוּאֵל

לח נַחַת זֶרַח שַׁמָּה וּמִזָּה: וּבְנֵי שֵׂעִיר לוֹטָן וְשׁוֹבָל וְצִבְעוֹן וַעֲנָה

לט וְדִישׁוֹן וְאֵצֶר וְדִישָׁן: וּבְנֵי לוֹטָן חֹרִי וְהוֹמָם וַאֲחוֹת לוֹטָן

מ תִּמְנָע: בְּנֵי שׁוֹבָל עַלְיָן וּמָנַחַת וְעֵיבָל שְׁפִי וְאוֹנָם וּבְנֵי צִבְעוֹן

מא אַיָּה וַעֲנָה: בְּנֵי עֲנָה דִּישׁוֹן וּבְנֵי דִישׁוֹן חַמְרָן וְאֶשְׁבָּן וְיִתְרָן

מב-מג וּכְרָן: בְּנֵי־אֵצֶר בִּלְהָן וְזַעֲוָן יַעֲקָן בְּנֵי דִישׁוֹן עוּץ וַאֲרָן: וְאֵלֶּה

הַמְּלָכִים אֲשֶׁר מָלְכוּ בְּאֶרֶץ אֱדוֹם לִפְנֵי מְלָךְ־מֶלֶךְ לִבְנֵי יִשְׂרָאֵל

מד בֶּלַע בֶּן־בְּעוֹר וְשֵׁם עִירוֹ דִּנְהָבָה: וַיָּמָת בָּלַע וַיִּמְלֹךְ תַּחְתָּיו יוֹבָב

מה בֶּן־זֶרַח מִבָּצְרָה: וַיָּמָת יוֹבָב וַיִּמְלֹךְ תַּחְתָּיו חוּשָׁם מֵאֶרֶץ הַתֵּימָנִי:

1:1. Adam's son was Seth; Seth's son was Enosh, whose son was Kenan, and so on.

1:4. The verse lists Noah's three sons. Their own descendants are given in the following passages, begin-

1

GENEALOGY
OF THE
DAVIDIC
DYNASTY
1:1-3:24
(See Appendix A,
timeline 1;
Appendix B,
chart 1)

¹ **A**dam, Seth, Enosh, * ² Kenan, Mahalalel, Jared, ³ Enoch, Methuselah, Lamech. ⁴ Noah; * Shem, Ham and Japheth. ⁵ The sons of Japheth: Gomer, Magog, Madai, Javan, Tubal, Meshech and Tiras. ⁶ The sons of Gomer: Ashkenaz, Diphath and Togarmah. ⁷ The sons of Javan: Elishah, Tarshish, Kittim and Rodanim. ⁸ The sons of Ham: Cush, Mizraim, Put and Canaan. ⁹ The sons of Cush: Seba, Havilah, Sabta, Raamah and Sabtecha. The sons of Raamah: Sheba and Dedan. ¹⁰ And Cush begot Nimrod. He was the first to be a mighty man on earth. ¹¹ Mizraim begot Ludim, Anamim, Lehabim, Naphtuhim, ¹² Pathrusim, Casluhim, from whom the Philistines came forth, and Caphtorim. ¹³ Canaan begot Zidon his firstborn and Heth, ¹⁴ the Jebusite, the Amorite, the Girgashite, ¹⁵ the Hivite, the Arkite, the Sinite, ¹⁶ the Arvadite, the Zemarite and the Hamathite.

¹⁷ The sons of Shem: Elam, Asshur, Arphachshad, Lud and Aram; * Uz, Hul, Gether and Meshech. ¹⁸ Arphachshad begot Shelah, and Shelah begot Eber. ¹⁹ And to Eber were born two sons: The name of the [first] one was Peleg (Division), for in his days the earth was divided, and the name of his brother was Joktan. ²⁰ Joktan begot Almodad, Sheleph, Hazarmaveth, Jerah, ²¹ Hadoram, Uzal, Diklah, ²² Ebal, Abimael, Sheba, ²³ Ophir, Havilah and Jobab; all these were the sons of Joktan.

²⁴ Shem, Arphachshad, Shelah, * ²⁵ Eber, Peleg, Reu, ²⁶ Serug, Nahor, Terah, ²⁷ Abram, who is Abraham.

Abraham' seed

²⁸ The sons of Abraham: Isaac and Ishmael.

Ishmael
(See Appendix B,
chart 2)

²⁹ These are their generations: Ishmael's firstborn Nebaioth, Kedar, Adbeel, Mibsam, ³⁰ Mishma, Dumah, Massa, Hadad, Tema, ³¹ Jetur, Naphish, and Kedem. These are the sons of Ishmael.

Sons of Keturah

³² The sons of Keturah, Abraham's concubine: She bore Zimran, Jokshan, Medan, Midian, Ishbak and Shuah. The sons of Jokshan: Sheba and Dedan. ³³ The sons of Midian: Ephah, Epher, Enoch, Abida and Eldaah. All these were the descendants of Keturah.

Isaac
Esau
(See Appendix B,
chart 5)

³⁴ Abraham begot Isaac. The sons of Isaac: Esau and Israel. ³⁵ The sons of Esau: Eliphaz, Reuel, Jeush, Jalam and Korah. ³⁶ The sons of Eliphaz: Teman, Omar, Zephi, Gatam, Kenaz, Timna and Amalek. ³⁷ The sons of Reuel: Nahath, Zerah, Shammah and Mizzah.

Seir

³⁸ The sons of Seir: * Lotan, Shobal, Zibeon, Anah, Dishon, Ezer and Dishan. ³⁹ The sons of Lotan: Hori and Homam. Lotan's sister was Timna. ⁴⁰ The sons of Shobal: Alian, Manahath, Ebal, Shephi and Onam. The sons of Zibeon: Aiah and Anah. ⁴¹ The sons of Anah: Dishon. The sons of Dishon: * Hamran, Eshban, Ithran and Cheran. ⁴² The sons of Ezer: Bilhan, Zaavan and Jakan. The sons of Dishon: * Uz and Aran.

Edom's
early kings

⁴³ Now these are the kings who reigned in the land of Edom before a king reigned over the Children of Israel: Bela son of Beor, and the name of his city was Dinhabah. ⁴⁴ Bela died, and Jobab son of Zerah of Bozrah reigned in his place. ⁴⁵ Jobab died, and Husham of the land of the Temanites reigned in his place.

---

ning with Japheth.

1:17. The following are the sons of Aram (*Genesis* 10:23).

1:24. Shem's son was Arpachshad; Arpachshad's son was Shelah, and so on.

1:38. The progenitor of the original inhabitants of Mount Seir, whom Esau supplanted (ibid., 36:20).

1:41. The reference is to the Dishon of v. 38.

1:42. This man is called Dishan in v. 38.

מו וַיָּמָת חוּשָׁם וַיִּמְלֹךְ תַּחְתָּיו הֲדַד בֶּן־בְּדַד הַמַּכֶּה אֶת־מִדְיָן בִּשְׂדֵה מוֹאָב
מז וְשֵׁם עִירוֹ °עיות [°עֲוִית ק׳]: וַיָּמָת הֲדָד וַיִּמְלֹךְ תַּחְתָּיו שַׂמְלָה מִמַּשְׂרֵקָה:
מח-מט וַיָּמָת שַׂמְלָה וַיִּמְלֹךְ תַּחְתָּיו שָׁאוּל מֵרְחֹבוֹת הַנָּהָר: וַיָּמָת שָׁאוּל וַיִּמְלֹךְ
נ תַּחְתָּיו בַּעַל חָנָן בֶּן־עַכְבּוֹר: וַיָּמָת בַּעַל חָנָן וַיִּמְלֹךְ תַּחְתָּיו הֲדַד וְשֵׁם
נא עִירוֹ פָּעִי וְשֵׁם אִשְׁתּוֹ מְהֵיטַבְאֵל בַּת־מַטְרֵד בַּת מֵי זָהָב: וַיָּמָת הֲדַד וַיִּהְיוּ
נב אַלּוּפֵי אֱדוֹם אַלּוּף תִּמְנָע אַלּוּף °עליה [°עַלְוָה ק׳] אַלּוּף יְתֵת: אַלּוּף
נג אָהֳלִיבָמָה אַלּוּף אֵלָה אַלּוּף פִּינֹן: אַלּוּף קְנַז אַלּוּף תֵּימָן אַלּוּף מִבְצָר:
נד-א אַלּוּף מַגְדִּיאֵל אַלּוּף עִירָם אֵלֶּה אַלּוּפֵי אֱדוֹם: אֵלֶּה בְּנֵי יִשְׂרָאֵל   ב
ב רְאוּבֵן שִׁמְעוֹן לֵוִי וִיהוּדָה יִשָּׂשכָר וּזְבֻלוּן: דָּן יוֹסֵף וּבִנְיָמִן נַפְתָּלִי גָד
ג וְאָשֵׁר: בְּנֵי יְהוּדָה עֵר וְאוֹנָן וְשֵׁלָה שְׁלוֹשָׁה נוֹלַד לוֹ מִבַּת־שׁוּעַ
ד הַכְּנַעֲנִית וַיְהִי עֵר ׀ בְּכוֹר יְהוּדָה רַע בְּעֵינֵי יְהוָה וַיְמִיתֵהוּ: וְתָמָר
ה כַּלָּתוֹ יָלְדָה לּוֹ אֶת־פֶּרֶץ וְאֶת־זָרַח כָּל־בְּנֵי יְהוּדָה חֲמִשָּׁה: בְּנֵי־פֶרֶץ
ו חֶצְרוֹן וְחָמוּל: וּבְנֵי זֶרַח זִמְרִי וְאֵיתָן וְהֵימָן וְכַלְכֹּל וָדָרַע כֻּלָּם
ז-ח חֲמִשָּׁה: וּבְנֵי כַּרְמִי עָכָר עוֹכֵר יִשְׂרָאֵל אֲשֶׁר מָעַל בַּחֵרֶם: וּבְנֵי
ט אֵיתָן עֲזַרְיָה: וּבְנֵי חֶצְרוֹן אֲשֶׁר נוֹלַד־לוֹ אֶת־יְרַחְמְאֵל וְאֶת־רָם
י וְאֶת־כְּלוּבָי: וְרָם הוֹלִיד אֶת־עַמִּינָדָב וְעַמִּינָדָב הוֹלִיד אֶת־נַחְשׁוֹן נְשִׂיא
יא-יב בְנֵי יְהוּדָה: וְנַחְשׁוֹן הוֹלִיד אֶת־שַׂלְמָא וְשַׂלְמָא הוֹלִיד אֶת־בֹּעַז: וּבֹעַז
יג הוֹלִיד אֶת־עוֹבֵד וְעוֹבֵד הוֹלִיד אֶת־יִשָׁי: וְאִישַׁי הוֹלִיד אֶת־בְּכֹרוֹ אֶת־
יד אֱלִיאָב וַאֲבִינָדָב הַשֵּׁנִי וְשִׁמְעָא הַשְּׁלִישִׁי: נְתַנְאֵל הָרְבִיעִי רַדַּי הַחֲמִישִׁי:
טו-טז אֹצֶם הַשִּׁשִּׁי דָּוִיד הַשְּׁבִעִי: וְאַחְיֹתֵיהֶם צְרוּיָה וַאֲבִיגָיִל וּבְנֵי צְרוּיָה אַבְשַׁי
יז וְיוֹאָב וַעֲשָׂה־אֵל שְׁלֹשָׁה: וַאֲבִיגַיִל יָלְדָה אֶת־עֲמָשָׂא וַאֲבִי עֲמָשָׂא יֶתֶר
יח הַיִּשְׁמְעֵאלִי: וְכָלֵב בֶּן־חֶצְרוֹן הוֹלִיד אֶת־עֲזוּבָה אִשָּׁה וְאֶת־
יט יְרִיעוֹת וְאֵלֶּה בָנֶיהָ יֵשֶׁר וְשׁוֹבָב וְאַרְדּוֹן: וַתָּמָת עֲזוּבָה וַיִּקַּח־לוֹ כָלֵב אֶת־
כ אֶפְרָת וַתֵּלֶד לוֹ אֶת־חוּר: וְחוּר הוֹלִיד אֶת־אוּרִי וְאוּרִי הוֹלִיד אֶת־
כא בְּצַלְאֵל: וְאַחַר בָּא חֶצְרוֹן אֶל־בַּת־מָכִיר אֲבִי גִלְעָד וְהוּא לְקָחָהּ
כב וְהוּא בֶּן־שִׁשִּׁים שָׁנָה וַתֵּלֶד לוֹ אֶת־שְׂגוּב: וּשְׂגוּב הוֹלִיד אֶת־יָאִיר וַיְהִי־
כג לוֹ עֶשְׂרִים וְשָׁלוֹשׁ עָרִים בְּאֶרֶץ הַגִּלְעָד: וַיִּקַּח גְּשׁוּר־וַאֲרָם אֶת־
חַוֹּת יָאִיר מֵאִתָּם אֶת־קְנָת וְאֶת־בְּנֹתֶיהָ שִׁשִּׁים עִיר כָּל־אֵלֶּה בְּנֵי מָכִיר
כד אֲבִי־גִלְעָד: וְאַחַר מוֹת־חֶצְרוֹן בְּכָלֵב אֶפְרָתָה וְאֵשֶׁת חֶצְרוֹן אֲבִיָּה וַתֵּלֶד
כה לוֹ אֶת־אַשְׁחוּר אֲבִי תְקוֹעַ: וַיִּהְיוּ בְנֵי־יְרַחְמְאֵל בְּכוֹר חֶצְרוֹן הַבְּכוֹר ׀
כו רָם וּבוּנָה וָאֹרֶן וָאֹצֶם אֲחִיָּה: וַתְּהִי אִשָּׁה אַחֶרֶת לִירַחְמְאֵל וּשְׁמָהּ

2:7. Carmi was the son of Zimri (*Radak*). The entire story is related in *Joshua* Ch. 7, where Zimri is called Zabdi, and Achar is called Achan.

2:18. He is called Chelubai in v. 9.

2:19. According to the Sages, this was Caleb ben Je-

phunneh, a leader of the tribe of Judah in the Wilderness. His wife was Miriam, sister of Moses and Aaron (*Sotah* 11b). She was called Ephrath because Israel became fruitful [פרה, "to be fruitful"] through her (*Tanchuma*).

2:23. Although Segub's father Hezron was from the tribe

⁴⁶ *Husham died, and Hadad son of Bedad, who defeated Midian in the field of Moab, reigned in his place; and the name of his city was Avith.* ⁴⁷ *Hadad died, and Samlah of Masrekah reigned in his place.* ⁴⁸ *Samlah died, and Shaul of Rehoboth-nahar reigned in his place.* ⁴⁹ *Shaul died, and Baal-hanan son of Achbor reigned in his place.* ⁵⁰ *Baal-hanan died, and Hadad reigned in his place; and the name of his city was Pai. His wife's name was Mehetabel, the daughter of Matred, the daughter of Mei-zahab.*

⁵¹ *Hadad died. The chiefs of Edom were then: the chief of Timna, the chief of Alvah, the chief of Jetheth,* ⁵² *the chief of Oholibamah, the chief of Elah, the chief of Pinon,* ⁵³ *the chief of Kenaz, the chief of Teman, the chief of Mibzar,* ⁵⁴ *the chief of Magdiel and the chief of Iram. These were the chiefs of Edom.*

2

THE
GENEALOGY
OF JUDAH
2:1-4:23
(See Appendix B,
chart 4)

Perez to
David

Other
descendants
of Hezron

¹ *These were the sons of Israel: Reuben, Simeon, Levi, Judah, Issachar, Zebulun,* ² *Dan, Joseph, Benjamin, Naphtali, Gad and Asher.*

³ *The sons of Judah: Er, Onan and Shelah — the three who were born to him from the daughter of Shua the Canaanitess. Er, Judah's firstborn, was evil in the eyes of* HASHEM, *and He caused him to die.* ⁴ *Tamar, his daughter-in-law, bore [Judah] Perez and Zerah. All the sons of Judah [were thus] five.*

⁵ *The sons of Perez: Hezron and Hamul.*

⁶ *The sons of Zerah: Zimri, Ethan, Heman, Calcol and Dara — five in all.* ⁷ *And the sons of Carmi: Achar, the troubler of Israel, who transgressed the ban.* * ⁸ *The sons of Ethan: Azariah.*

⁹ *The sons of Hezron who were born to him: Jerahmeel, Ram and Chelubai.*

¹⁰ *Ram begot Amminadab; Amminadab begot Nahshon, the leader of the sons of Judah;* ¹¹ *Nahshon begot Salma; Salma begot Boaz;* ¹² *Boaz begot Obed; and Obed begot Jesse.* ¹³ *Jesse begot his firstborn Eliab, Abinadab the second, Shimea the third,* ¹⁴ *Nethanel the fourth, Raddai the fifth,* ¹⁵ *Ozem the sixth and David the seventh.* ¹⁶ *Their sisters were Zeruiah and Abigail. The sons of Zeruiah: Abishai, Joab and Asahel — three [in all].* ¹⁷ *Abigail bore Amasa; the father of Amasa was Jether the Ishmaelite.*

¹⁸ *Caleb* * *son of Hezron fathered children by Azubah [his] wife, and by Jerioth. These are her sons: Jesher, Shobab and Ardon.* ¹⁹ *When Azubah died, Caleb married Ephrath,* * *who bore him Hur.* ²⁰ *Hur begot Uri, and Uri begot Bezalel.*

²¹ *Afterwards Hezron consorted with the daughter of Machir, Gilead's father, whom he married when he was sixty years old, and she bore him Segub.* ²² *Segub begot Jair, who had twenty-three cities in the land of Gilead.* ²³ *But Geshur and Aram took Havvoth-jair from them — Kenath and its surrounding towns, sixty cities. All these [belonged to] the sons of Machir, Gilead's father.* *

²⁴ *After Hezron died, in Caleb-ephrathah, Hezron's wife bore him Ashhur, father* * *of Tekoa.*

²⁵ *The sons of Jerahmeel, Hezron's firstborn, were: Ram the firstborn, Bunah, Oren, Ozem and Ahijah.* ²⁶ *Jerahmeel had another wife, whose name was*

---

of Judah, Segub and his son Jair were counted as descendants of Machir, Manasseh's son; see *Numbers* 32:41. A person's lineage is traced through his father only if his parents are actually married, but since Segub's mother was a concubine to Hezron, his

lineage was traced through his mother, to Manasseh (*Malbim*).

2:24. In the context of *Chronicles*, the "father" of a town is the progenitor of the majority of the people who eventually settled there (*Radak*).

כז עֲטָרָה הִיא אֵם אוֹנָם: וַיִּהְיוּ בְנֵי־רָם בְּכוֹר יְרַחְמְאֵל מַעַץ וְיָמִין

כח־כט וָעֵקֶר: וַיִּהְיוּ בְנֵי־אוֹנָם שַׁמַּי וְיָדָע וּבְנֵי שַׁמַּי נָדָב וַאֲבִישׁוּר: וְשֵׁם אֵשֶׁת

ל אֲבִישׁוּר אֲבִיהָיִל וַתֵּלֶד לוֹ אֶת־אַחְבָּן וְאֶת־מוֹלִיד: וּבְנֵי נָדָב סֶלֶד וְאַפָּיִם

לא וַיָּמָת סֶלֶד לֹא בָנִים: וּבְנֵי אַפַּיִם יִשְׁעִי וּבְנֵי יִשְׁעִי שֵׁשָׁן וּבְנֵי

לב שֵׁשָׁן אַחְלָי: וּבְנֵי יָדָע אֲחִי שַׁמַּי יֶתֶר וְיוֹנָתָן וַיָּמָת יֶתֶר לֹא

לג־לד בָנִים: וּבְנֵי יוֹנָתָן פֶּלֶת וְזָזָא אֵלֶּה הָיוּ בְּנֵי יְרַחְמְאֵל: וְלֹא־הָיָה

לה לְשֵׁשָׁן בָּנִים כִּי אִם־בָּנוֹת וּלְשֵׁשָׁן עֶבֶד מִצְרִי וּשְׁמוֹ יַרְחָע: וַיִּתֵּן שֵׁשָׁן אֶת־

לו בִּתּוֹ לְיַרְחָע עַבְדּוֹ לְאִשָּׁה וַתֵּלֶד לוֹ אֶת־עַתָּי: וְעַתַּי הֹלִיד אֶת־נָתָן וְנָתָן

לז־לח הוֹלִיד אֶת־זָבָד: וְזָבָד הוֹלִיד אֶת־אֶפְלָל וְאֶפְלָל הוֹלִיד אֶת־עוֹבֵד: וְעוֹבֵד

לט הוֹלִיד אֶת־יֵהוּא וְיֵהוּא הוֹלִיד אֶת־עֲזַרְיָה: וַעֲזַרְיָה הֹלִיד אֶת־חָלֶץ וְחֶלֶץ

מ הֹלִיד אֶת־אֶלְעָשָׂה: וְאֶלְעָשָׂה הֹלִיד אֶת־סִסְמָי וְסִסְמַי הֹלִיד אֶת־שַׁלּוּם:

מא־מב וְשַׁלּוּם הוֹלִיד אֶת־יְקַמְיָה וִיקַמְיָה הֹלִיד אֶת־אֱלִישָׁמָע: וּבְנֵי כָלֵב

מג אֲחִי יְרַחְמְאֵל מֵישָׁע בְּכֹרוֹ הוּא אֲבִי־זִיף וּבְנֵי מָרֵשָׁה אֲבִי חֶבְרוֹן: וּבְנֵי

מד חֶבְרוֹן קֹרַח וְתַפֻּחַ וְרֶקֶם וָשָׁמַע: וְשֶׁמַע הוֹלִיד אֶת־רַחַם אֲבִי יָרְקֳעָם

מה־מו וְרֶקֶם הוֹלִיד אֶת־שַׁמָּי: וּבֶן־שַׁמַּי מָעוֹן וּמָעוֹן אֲבִי בֵית־צוּר: וְעֵיפָה

פִּילֶגֶשׁ כָּלֵב יָלְדָה אֶת־חָרָן וְאֶת־מוֹצָא וְאֶת־גָּזֵז וְחָרָן הֹלִיד אֶת־

מז־מח גָּזֵז: וּבְנֵי יָהְדָּי רֶגֶם וְיוֹתָם וְגֵישָׁן וָפֶלֶט וְעֵיפָה וָשָׁעַף: פִּלֶגֶשׁ

מט כָּלֵב מַעֲכָה יָלַד שֶׁבֶר וְאֶת־תִּרְחֲנָה: וַתֵּלֶד שַׁעַף אֲבִי מַדְמַנָּה אֶת־שְׁוָא

נ אֲבִי מַכְבֵּנָה וַאֲבִי גִבְעָא וּבַת־כָּלֵב עַכְסָה: אֵלֶּה הָיוּ בְּנֵי כָלֵב בֶּן־חוּר

נא בְּכוֹר אֶפְרָתָה שׁוֹבָל אֲבִי קִרְיַת יְעָרִים: שַׂלְמָא אֲבִי בֵית־לָחֶם חָרֵף אֲבִי

נב־נג בֵית־גָּדֵר: וַיִּהְיוּ בָנִים לְשׁוֹבָל אֲבִי קִרְיַת יְעָרִים הָרֹאֶה חֲצִי הַמְּנֻחוֹת: וּמִשְׁפְּחוֹת קִרְיַת יְעָרִים הַיִּתְרִי וְהַפּוּתִי וְהַשֻּׁמָתִי וְהַמִּשְׁרָעִי מֵאֵלֶּה יָצְאוּ

נד הַצָּרְעָתִי וְהָאֶשְׁתָּאֻלִי: בְּנֵי שַׂלְמָא בֵּית לֶחֶם וּנְטוֹפָתִי עַטְרוֹת

נה בֵּית יוֹאָב וַחֲצִי הַמָּנַחְתִּי הַצָּרְעִי: וּמִשְׁפְּחוֹת סֹפְרִים °ישבו [°יֹשְׁבֵי ק]

יַעְבֵּץ תִּרְעָתִים שִׁמְעָתִים שׂוּכָתִים הֵמָּה הַקִּינִים הַבָּאִים מֵחַמַּת אֲבִי

ג   א בֵית־רֵכָב: וְאֵלֶּה הָיוּ בְּנֵי דָוִיד אֲשֶׁר נוֹלַד־לוֹ בְּחֶבְרוֹן הַבְּכוֹר ׀

ב אַמְנֹן לַאֲחִינֹעַם הַיִּזְרְעֵאלִית שֵׁנִי דָנִיֵּאל לַאֲבִיגַיִל הַכַּרְמְלִית: הַשְּׁלִשִׁי

לְאַבְשָׁלוֹם בֶּן־מַעֲכָה בַּת־תַּלְמַי מֶלֶךְ גְּשׁוּר הָרְבִיעִי אֲדֹנִיָּה בֶן־חַגִּית:

ג־ד הַחֲמִישִׁי שְׁפַטְיָה לַאֲבִיטָל הַשִּׁשִּׁי יִתְרְעָם לְעֶגְלָה אִשְׁתּוֹ: שִׁשָּׁה נוֹלַד־לוֹ

בְחֶבְרוֹן וַיִּמְלָךְ־שָׁם שֶׁבַע שָׁנִים וְשִׁשָּׁה חֳדָשִׁים וּשְׁלֹשִׁים וְשָׁלוֹשׁ שָׁנָה

ה מָלַךְ בִּירוּשָׁלָ͏ִם: וְאֵלֶּה נוּלְּדוּ־לוֹ בִּירוּשָׁלָיִם שִׁמְעָא וְשׁוֹבָב

ו וְנָתָן וּשְׁלֹמֹה אַרְבָּעָה לְבַת־שׁוּעַ בַּת־עַמִּיאֵל: וְיִבְחָר וֶאֱלִישָׁמָע

2:34. His son Ahlai (v. 31) apparently died young.

2:47. Jahdai was apparently a descendant of Caleb, but his lineage is not clear.

3:6. This son is also called Elishua (*II Samuel* 5:15). *Malbim* suggests that he was originally named Elishama, but when a younger brother was born and given that name

Atarah; she was the mother of Onam. ²⁷ *The sons of Ram, Jerahmeel's firstborn, were Maaz, Jamin and Eker.*

²⁸ *The sons of Onam were Shammai and Jada. The sons of Shammai: Nadab and Abishur.* ²⁹ *The name of Abishur's wife was Abihail, and she bore him Ahban and Molid.* ³⁰ *The sons of Nadab: Seled and Appaim. Seled died childless.* ³¹ *The sons of Appaim: Ishi. The sons of Ishi: Sheshan. The sons of Sheshan: Ahlai.*

³² *The sons of Jada, Shammai's brother: Jether and Jonathan. Jether died childless.* ³³ *The sons of Jonathan: Peleth and Zaza. These were the sons of Jerahmeel.*

³⁴ *Sheshan had no sons,* * *but only daughters. Sheshan had an Egyptian servant, whose name was Jarha.* ³⁵ *Sheshan gave his daughter to his servant Jarha for a wife, and she bore him Attai.* ³⁶ *Attai begot Nathan, Nathan begot Zabad,* ³⁷ *Zabad begot Ephlal, Ephlal begot Obed,* ³⁸ *Obed begot Jehu, Jehu begot Azariah,* ³⁹ *Azariah begot Helez, Helez begot Eleasah,* ⁴⁰ *Eleasah begot Sisamai, Sisamai begot Shallum,* ⁴¹ *Shallum begot Jekamiah, and Jekamiah begot Elishama.*

Caleb son of Hezron ⁴² *The sons of Caleb, Jerahmeel's brother: Mesha his firstborn, who was the father of Ziph; and the sons of Mareshah the father of Hebron.* ⁴³ *The sons of Hebron: Korah, Tappuah, Rekem and Shema.* ⁴⁴ *Shema begot Raham, the father of Jorkeam, and Rekem begot Shammai.* ⁴⁵ *Shammai's son was Maon; Maon was the founder of Beth-zur.* ⁴⁶ *Ephah, Caleb's concubine, bore Haran, Moza and Gazez; and Haran begot Gazez.* ⁴⁷ *The sons of Jahdai:* * *Regem, Jotham, Gesham, Pelet, Ephah and Shaaph.*

⁴⁸ *Maachah, Caleb's concubine, bore Sheber and Tirhanah.* ⁴⁹ *She bore [also] Shaaph, the founder of Madmannah, and Sheva, the founder of Machbenah and the founder of Gibea. Caleb's daughter was Achsah.*

⁵⁰ *These were the descendants of Caleb the son of Hur, the firstborn of Ephrathah: Shobal, father of Kiriath-jearim,* ⁵¹ *Salma, the founder of Bethlehem; Hareph, the founder of Beth-gader.* ⁵² *Shobal, the father of Kiriath-jearim, had sons: Haroeh and Hazi-hamenuhoth.* ⁵³ *The families of Kiriath-jearim: the Ithrite, the Puthite, the Shumathite and the Mishraite; the Zorathite and the Eshtaolite were descended from them.*

⁵⁴ *The sons of Salma: [the people of] Beth-lehem, Netophathite, Atroth-beth-Joab, half of the Manahathite, and the Zorite;* ⁵⁵ *and the families of scribes who dwelt at Jabez — Tirathites, Shimeathites and Suchathites. These were the Kenites who descended from Hammath, the father of the house of Rechab.*

3

King David's children

¹ **T**hese *were the sons of David, who were born to him in Hebron: The first-born Amnon, by Ahinoam of Jezreel; the second, Daniel, by Abigail of Carmel;* ² *the third, Absalom, the son of Maachah daughter of Talmai, king of Geshur; the fourth, Adonijah the son of Haggith;* ³ *the fifth, Shephatiah, by Abital; the sixth, Ithream, by his wife Eglah.* ⁴ *[These] six were born to him in Hebron. He reigned there seven years and six months, and in Jerusalem he reigned thirty-three years.*

⁵ *These were born to him in Jerusalem: Shimea, Shobab, Nathan and Solomon — four [sons] by Bath-shua the daughter of Ammiel;* ⁶ *and Ibhar, Elishama,* *

(v. 8), his name was changed to Elishua, so as to distinguish between the two sons.

ז־ט וֶאֱלִיפֶלֶט: וְנֹגַהּ וְנֶפֶג וְיָפִיעַ: וֶאֱלִישָׁמָע וְאֶלְיָדָע וֶאֱלִיפָלֶט תִּשְׁעָה: כָּל־בְּנֵי

י דָוִיד מִלְּבַד בְּנֵי־פִילַגְשִׁים וְתָמָר אֲחוֹתָם: וּבֶן־שְׁלֹמֹה רְחַבְעָם

יא אֲבִיָּה בְנוֹ אָסָא בְנוֹ יְהוֹשָׁפָט בְּנוֹ: יוֹרָם בְּנוֹ אֲחַזְיָהוּ בְנוֹ יוֹאָשׁ בְּנוֹ

יב־יד אֲמַצְיָהוּ בְנוֹ עֲזַרְיָה בְנוֹ יוֹתָם בְּנוֹ: אָחָז בְּנוֹ חִזְקִיָּהוּ בְנוֹ מְנַשֶּׁה בְנוֹ: אָמוֹן

טו בְּנוֹ יֹאשִׁיָּהוּ בְנוֹ: וּבְנֵי יֹאשִׁיָּהוּ הַבְּכוֹר יוֹחָנָן הַשֵּׁנִי יְהוֹיָקִים הַשְּׁלִשִׁי

טז־יז צִדְקִיָּהוּ הָרְבִיעִי שַׁלּוּם: וּבְנֵי יְהוֹיָקִים יְכָנְיָה בְנוֹ צִדְקִיָּה בְנוֹ: וּבְנֵי יְכָנְיָה

יח אַסִּר שְׁאַלְתִּיאֵל בְּנוֹ: וּמַלְכִּירָם וּפְדָיָה וְשֶׁנְאַצַּר יְקַמְיָה הוֹשָׁמָע וּנְדַבְיָה:

יט וּבְנֵי פְדָיָה זְרֻבָּבֶל וְשִׁמְעִי וּבֶן־זְרֻבָּבֶל מְשֻׁלָּם וַחֲנַנְיָה וּשְׁלֹמִית אֲחוֹתָם:

כ־כא וַחֲשֻׁבָה וָאֹהֶל וּבֶרֶכְיָה וַחֲסַדְיָה יוּשַׁב חֶסֶד חָמֵשׁ: וּבֶן־חֲנַנְיָה פְּלַטְיָה וּבְנֵי

כב וִישַׁעְיָה בְּנֵי רְפָיָה בְּנֵי אַרְנָן בְּנֵי עֹבַדְיָה בְּנֵי שְׁכַנְיָה: וּבְנֵי

כג־כד שְׁכַנְיָה שְׁמַעְיָה וּבְנֵי שְׁמַעְיָה חַטּוּשׁ וְיִגְאָל וּבָרִיחַ וּנְעַרְיָה וְשָׁפָט שִׁשָּׁה: וּבֶן־נְעַרְיָה אֶלְיוֹעֵינַי וְחִזְקִיָּה וְעַזְרִיקָם שְׁלֹשָׁה: וּבְנֵי אֶלְיוֹעֵינַי °הוֹדַוְיָהוּ [°הוֹדַוְיָהוּ ק] וְאֶלְיָשִׁיב וּפְלָיָה וְעַקּוּב וְיוֹחָנָן וּדְלָיָה וַעֲנָנִי שִׁבְעָה:

ד

א־ב בְּנֵי יְהוּדָה פֶּרֶץ חֶצְרוֹן וְכַרְמִי וְחוּר וְשׁוֹבָל: וּרְאָיָה בֶן־שׁוֹבָל הוֹלִיד אֶת־יַחַת וְיַחַת הוֹלִיד אֶת־אֲחוּמַי וְאֶת־לָהַד אֵלֶּה מִשְׁפְּחוֹת הַצָּרְעָתִי:

ג וְאֵלֶּה אֲבִי עֵיטָם יִזְרְעֶאל וְיִשְׁמָא

ד וְיִדְבָּשׁ וְשֵׁם אֲחוֹתָם הַצְּלֶלְפּוֹנִי: וּפְנוּאֵל אֲבִי גְדֹר וְעֵזֶר אֲבִי חוּשָׁה אֵלֶּה

ה בְנֵי־חוּר בְּכוֹר אֶפְרָתָה אֲבִי בֵּית לָחֶם: וּלְאַשְׁחוּר אֲבִי תְקוֹעַ הָיוּ שְׁתֵּי

ו נָשִׁים חֶלְאָה וְנַעֲרָה: וַתֵּלֶד לוֹ נַעֲרָה אֶת־אֲחֻזָּם וְאֶת־חֵפֶר וְאֶת־תֵּימְנִי

ז וְאֶת־הָאֲחַשְׁתָּרִי אֵלֶּה בְּנֵי נַעֲרָה: וּבְנֵי חֶלְאָה צֶרֶת °יִצְחַר [°וְצֹחַר ק]

ח וְאֶתְנָן: וְקוֹץ הוֹלִיד אֶת־עָנוּב וְאֶת־הַצֹּבֵבָה וּמִשְׁפְּחוֹת אֲחַרְחֵל בֶּן־

ט הָרוּם: וַיְהִי יַעְבֵּץ נִכְבָּד מֵאֶחָיו וְאִמּוֹ קָרְאָה שְׁמוֹ יַעְבֵּץ לֵאמֹר כִּי יָלַדְתִּי

י בְּעֹצֶב: וַיִּקְרָא יַעְבֵּץ לֵאלֹהֵי יִשְׂרָאֵל לֵאמֹר אִם־בָּרֵךְ תְּבָרֲכֵנִי וְהִרְבִּיתָ אֶת־גְּבוּלִי וְהָיְתָה יָדְךָ עִמִּי וְעָשִׂיתָ מֵּרָעָה לְבִלְתִּי עָצְבִּי וַיָּבֵא אֱלֹהִים

יא אֵת אֲשֶׁר־שָׁאָל: וּכְלוּב אֲחִי־שׁוּחָה הוֹלִיד אֶת־

יב מְחִיר הוּא אֲבִי אֶשְׁתּוֹן: וְאֶשְׁתּוֹן הוֹלִיד אֶת־בֵּית רָפָא וְאֶת־פָּסֵחַ וְאֶת־

יג תְּחִנָּה אֲבִי עִיר נָחָשׁ אֵלֶּה אַנְשֵׁי רֵכָה: וּבְנֵי קְנַז עָתְנִיאֵל

יד וּשְׂרָיָה וּבְנֵי עָתְנִיאֵל חֲתַת: וּמְעוֹנֹתַי הוֹלִיד אֶת־עָפְרָה וּשְׂרָיָה

טו הוֹלִיד אֶת־יוֹאָב אֲבִי גֵּיא חֲרָשִׁים כִּי חֲרָשִׁים הָיוּ: וּבְנֵי

3:8. How could David have given the name Eliphelet to two boys? The commentators suggest that the first Eliphelet died, and the second was named after him.

3:15. According to the Talmud this Johanan is Jehoahaz, who reigned after Josiah (*II Kings* 23:30 ff.).

3:18. This verse lists the sons of Shealtiel (*Radak*).

4:1. These were succeeding generations: Judah was the father of Perez, who was the father of Hezron, and so on.

The *Vilna Gaon* identifies the Carmi of this verse as the Caleb of 2:19.

4:2-4. These verses are a repetition, with additional details, of the information given in 2:50 ff (*Vilna Gaon*), and Reaiah is identified with Haroeh of 2:52 (*Radak*).

4:9-10. The name Jabez [יַעְבֵּץ] contains the letters of עֶצֶב, meaning "pain" and "sadness." The Sages identify Jabez with the great judge Othniel, who succeeded

Eliphelet, [7] *Nogah, Nepheg, Japhia,* [8] *Elishama, Eliada and Eliphelet* * — *nine [in all].*

[9] *These were all the sons of David, besides the sons of the concubines, and Tamar their sister.*

King David's royal line (See Appendix A, timeline 4) [10] *Solomon's son was Rehoboam; Abijah was his son; Asa was his son; Jehoshaphat was his son;* [11] *Joram was his son; Ahaziah was his son; Joash was his son;* [12] *Amaziah was his son; Azariah was his son; Jotham was his son;* [13] *Ahaz was his son; Hezekiah was his son; Manasseh was his son;* [14] *Amon was his son; Josiah was his son.*

[15] *The sons of Josiah: the firstborn Johanan,* * *the second Jehoiakim, the third Zedekiah, the fourth Shallum.* [16] *The sons of Jehoiakim: Jeconiah his son and Zedekiah his son.*

[17] *The sons of Jeconiah: Assir, Shealtiel his son;* [18] *Malchiram,* * *Pedaiah, Shenazzar, Jekamiah, Hoshama and Nedabiah.* [19] *The sons of Pedaiah: Zerubbabel and Shimei. The sons of Zerubbabel: Meshullam and Hananiah, and Shelomith their sister;* [20] *and Hashubah, Ohel, Berechiah, Hasadiah, Jushab-hesed — five [in all].* [21] *The sons of Hananiah: Pelatiah and Jeshaiah. His son was Rephaiah; his son was Arnan; his son was Obadiah; his son was Shechaniah.* [22] *The children of Shechaniah: Shemaiah and the sons of Shemaiah: Hattush, Igal, Bariah, Neariah and Shaphat — six [in all].* [23] *The sons of Neariah: Elioenai, Hezekiah and Azrikam — three [in all].* [24] *The sons of Elioenai: Hodaviah, Eliashib, Pelaiah, Akkub, Johanan, Dalaiah and Anani — seven [in all].*

4 **Other descendants of Judah** [1] *The sons of Judah:* * *Perez, Hezron, Carmi, Hur and Shobal.* [2] *Reaiah* * *son of Shobal begot Jahath; and Jahath begot Ahumai and Lahad. These are the families of the Zorathites.*

[3] *These were the fathers of Etam: Jezreel, Ishma and Idbash; and the name of their sister was Hazlelponi.*

[4] *Penuel was the father of Gedor, and Ezer was the father of Hushah. These were [all] descendants of Hur, the firstborn of Ephrathah, the father of Bethlehem.*

[5] *Ashhur, the founder of Tekoa, had two wives, Helah and Naarah.* [6] *Naarah bore him Ahuzam, Hepher, Temeni and Haahashtari. These were the sons of Naarah.* [7] *The sons of Helah: Zereth, Zohar and Ethnan.* [8] *Koz begot Anub and Zobebah, and the families of Aharhel son of Harum.* [9] *Jabez was more honorable than his brothers. His mother called his name Jabez, saying, "because I bore him with pain."* * [10] *Jabez called out to the God of Israel, saying, "If You bless me and expand my borders, and Your hand is with me, and You keep me from harm, that I not be saddened . . ." And God granted him that which he requested.*

[11] *Chelub, the brother of Shuah, begot Mehir, who was the father of Eshton.* [12] *Eshton begot Beth-rapha, Paseah and Tehinnah, the father of the city of Nahash. These were the men of Rechah.* *

[13] *The sons of Kenaz: Othniel and Seraiah. The sons of Othniel: Hathath.*

[14] *Meonothai begot Ophrah. Seraiah begot Joab, the founder of Ge-harashim (Valley of Artisans), [so called] because they were artisans.*

Joshua (*Temurah* 16a). *Radak* suggests that the reason for Jabez' request was that he was concerned that his name (derived from "pain and sadness") would serve as a bad omen for him.

4:12. It is not known whether Rechah is the name of a place or a family.

טז כָּלֵב בֶּן־יְפֻנֶּה עִירוּ אֵלָה וָנָעַם וּבְנֵי אֵלָה וּקְנַז: וּבְנֵי יְהַלֶּלְאֵל זִיף וְזִיפָ֫ה

יז תִּירְיָא וַאֲשַׂרְאֵל: וּבֶן־עֶזְרָה יֶתֶר וּמֶרֶד וְעֵפֶר וְיָלֶון וַתַּהַר אֶת־מִרְיָם

יח וְאֶת־שַׁמַּי וְאֶת־יִשְׁבָּח אֲבִי אֶשְׁתְּמֹעַ: וְאִשְׁתּוֹ הַיְהֻדִיָּה יָלְדָה אֶת־יֶרֶד אֲבִי גְדוֹר וְאֶת־חֶבֶר אֲבִי שׂוֹכוֹ וְאֶת־יְקוּתִיאֵל אֲבִי זָנוֹחַ וְאֵלֶּה בְּנֵי בִּתְיָה בַת־פַּרְעֹה אֲשֶׁר לָקַח מָרֶד:

יט וּבְנֵי אֵשֶׁת הוֹדִיָּה אֲחוֹת נַחַם אֲבִי קְעִילָה הַגַּרְמִי וְאֶשְׁתְּמֹעַ הַמַּעֲכָתִי: וּבְנֵי שִׁמְעוֹן אַמְנוֹן וְרִנָּ֫ה

כ בֶּן־חָנָן °וְתוֹלוֹן [°וְתִילוֹן ק] וּבְנֵי יִשְׁעִי זוֹחֵת וּבֶן־זוֹחֵת: בְּנֵי שֵׁלָה בֶן־

כא יְהוּדָה עֵר אֲבִי לֵכָה וְלַעְדָּה אֲבִי מָרֵשָׁה וּמִשְׁפְּחוֹת בֵּית־עֲבֹדַת הַבֻּץ לְבֵית אַשְׁבֵּעַ:

כב וְיוֹקִים וְאַנְשֵׁי כֹזֵבָא וְיוֹאָשׁ וְשָׂרָף אֲשֶׁר־בָּעֲלוּ לְמוֹאָב וְיָשֻׁבִי לָחֶם וְהַדְּבָרִים עַתִּיקִים:

כג הֵמָּה הַיּוֹצְרִים וְיֹשְׁבֵי נְטָעִים וּגְדֵרָה עִם־הַמֶּלֶךְ בִּמְלַאכְתּוֹ יָשְׁבוּ שָׁם:

כד בְּנֵי שִׁמְעוֹן נְמוּאֵל וְיָמִין יָרִיב זֶרַח שָׁאוּל: שַׁלֻּם בְּנוֹ מִבְשָׂם בְּנוֹ מִשְׁמָע בְּנוֹ:

כה-כו וּבְנֵי מִשְׁמָע חַמּוּאֵל בְּנוֹ זַכּוּר בְּנוֹ שִׁמְעִי בְנוֹ:

כז וּלְשִׁמְעִי בָּנִים שִׁשָּׁה עָשָׂר וּבָנוֹת שֵׁשׁ וּלְאֶחָיו אֵין בָּנִים רַבִּים וְכֹל מִשְׁפַּחְתָּם לֹא הִרְבּוּ עַד־בְּנֵי יְהוּדָה:

כח וַיֵּשְׁבוּ בִּבְאֵר־ שֶׁבַע וּמוֹלָדָה וַחֲצַר שׁוּעָל: וּבְבִלְהָה וּבְעֶצֶם וּבְתוֹלָד: וּבִבְתוּאֵל

כט-ל וּבְחָרְמָה וּבְצִיקְלָג: וּבְבֵית מַרְכָּבוֹת וּבַחֲצַר סוּסִים וּבְבֵית בִּרְאִי

לא וּבְשַׁעֲרָיִם אֵלֶּה עָרֵיהֶם עַד־מְלָךְ דָּוִיד: וְחַצְרֵיהֶם עֵיטָם וָעַיִן רִמּוֹן וְתֹכֶן

לב וְעָשָׁן עָרִים חָמֵשׁ: וְכָל־חַצְרֵיהֶם אֲשֶׁר סְבִיבוֹת הֶעָרִים הָאֵלֶּה עַד־בַּעַל

לג זֹאת מוֹשְׁבֹתָם וְהִתְיַחְשָׂם לָהֶם: וּמְשׁוֹבָב וְיַמְלֵךְ וְיוֹשָׁה בֶּן־אֲמַצְיָה:

לד וְיוֹאֵל וְיֵהוּא בֶּן־יוֹשִׁבְיָה בֶּן־שְׂרָיָה בֶּן־עֲשִׂיאֵל: וְאֶלְיוֹעֵינַי וְיַעֲקֹבָה

לה-לו וִישׁוֹחָיָה וַעֲשָׂיָה וַעֲדִיאֵל וִישִׂימִאֵל וּבְנָיָה: וְזִיזָא בֶן־שִׁפְעִי בֶן־אַלּוֹן בֶּן־

לז יְדָיָה בֶן־שִׁמְרִי בֶּן־שְׁמַעְיָה: אֵלֶּה הַבָּאִים בְּשֵׁמוֹת נְשִׂיאִים בְּמִשְׁפְּחוֹתָם

לח וּבֵית אֲבוֹתֵיהֶם פָּרְצוּ לָרוֹב: וַיֵּלְכוּ לִמְבוֹא גְדֹר עַד לְמִזְרַח הַגָּיְא לְבַקֵּשׁ

לט מִרְעֶה לְצֹאנָם: וַיִּמְצְאוּ מִרְעֶה שָׁמֵן וָטוֹב וְהָאָרֶץ רַחֲבַת יָדַיִם וְשֹׁקֶטֶת

מ וּשְׁלֵוָה כִּי מִן־חָם הַיֹּשְׁבִים שָׁם לְפָנִים: וַיָּבֹאוּ אֵלֶּה הַכְּתוּבִים בְּשֵׁמוֹת בִּימֵי | יְחִזְקִיָּהוּ מֶלֶךְ־יְהוּדָה וַיַּכּוּ אֶת־אָהֳלֵיהֶם וְאֶת־°הַמְּעִינִים

מא [°הַמְּעוּנִים ק] אֲשֶׁר נִמְצְאוּ־שָׁמָּה וַיַּחֲרִימֻם עַד־הַיּוֹם הַזֶּה וַיֵּשְׁבוּ תַּחְתֵּיהֶם כִּי־מִרְעֶה לְצֹאנָם שָׁם: וּמֵהֶם | מִן־בְּנֵי שִׁמְעוֹן הָלְכוּ

מב לְהַר שֵׂעִיר אֲנָשִׁים חֲמֵשׁ מֵאוֹת וּפְלַטְיָה וּנְעַרְיָה וּרְפָיָה וְעֻזִּיאֵל בְּנֵי

מג יִשְׁעִי בְּרֹאשָׁם: וַיַּכּוּ אֶת־שְׁאֵרִית הַפְּלֵטָה לַעֲמָלֵק וַיֵּשְׁבוּ שָׁם עַד הַיּוֹם

4:17. Mered's wife Bithiah, as explained in the following verse (*Radak*).

4:18. As opposed to the first wife mentioned, Bithiah, an Egyptian.
Miriam, etc., mentioned in v. 17.

4:22. The personalities and events mentioned in the last several verses, although they are not found in other Books of Scripture, are based on reliable, ancient traditions.

4:25. Shallum's; and so on.

4:33. Each family group clustered around one of these cities, so that each family is associated with one of these places (*Malbim*).

¹⁵ The sons of Caleb son of Jephunneh: Iru, Elah and Naam. The sons of Elah: Kenaz.

¹⁶ The sons of Jehalleleel: Ziph, Ziphah, Tiria and Asareel.

¹⁷ The sons of Ezrah: Jether, Mered, Epher and Jalon. [His wife*] bore Miriam, Shammai and Ishbah, the father of Eshtemoa, ¹⁸ while his Jewish wife* bore Jered, the father of Gedor, and Heber, the father of Soco, and Jekuthiel, the father of Zanoah. These* are the sons of Bithiah the daughter of Pharaoh, whom Mered married.

¹⁹ The sons of Hodiah's wife, Naham's sister: The father of Keilah the Garmite, and Eshtemoa the Maachathite.

²⁰ The sons of Shimon: Amnon, Rinnah, Ben-hanan and Tilon. The sons of Ishi: Zoheth and Ben-zoheth.

²¹ The sons of Shelah son of Judah: Er, the father of Lecah, and Ladah, the father of Mareshah, the families of the linen factory of the house of Ashbea, ²² Jokim, the men of Cozeba, Joash, Saraph, who had dominion over Moab, and Jashubi-lehem. These are ancient traditions.* ²³ They were the potters, who dwelled in Netaim and Gederah; they resided there in the service of the king.

GENEALO-
GIES OF THE
OTHER
TRIBES
4:24-8:40

Simeon ²⁴ The sons of Simeon: Nemuel, Jamin, Jarib, Zerah and Shaul. ²⁵ [Shaul's] son was Shallum; Mibsam was his* son; Mishma was his son. ²⁶ The sons of Mishma: Hammuel his son, Zacchur his son and Shimei his son. ²⁷ Shimei had sixteen sons and six daughters; but his brothers did not have many children. Their whole family did not multiply as much as the children of Judah. ²⁸ They dwelt at Beer-sheba, Moladah, Hazar-shual, ²⁹ Bilhah, Ezem, Tolad, ³⁰ Bethuel, Hormah, Ziklag, ³¹ Beth-marcaboth, Hazar-susim, Beth-biri and Shaaraim. These were their cities until David reigned.

³² Their villages were: Etam, Ain, Rimmon, Tochen, Ashan — five cities, ³³ with all their villages that were around these cities, up to Baal. These were their habitations and their relationships to them.*

³⁴ Meshobab, Jamlech, Joshah son of Amaziah, ³⁵ Joel, Jehu son of Joshibiah, son of Seraiah, son of Asiel, ³⁶ Elioenai, Jaakobah, Jeshohaiah, Asaiah, Adiel, Jesimiel, Benaiah, ³⁷ Ziza son of Shiphi, son of Allon, son of Jedaiah, son of Shimri, son of Shemaiah — ³⁸ these mentioned by name were leaders in their families, and their fathers' houses increased greatly. ³⁹ So they went to the Approach of Gedor, to the east of the valley, to seek pasture for their flocks. ⁴⁰ They found rich and good pasture, and the land was wide open, quiet, and peaceful; because people of Ham had always lived there.* ⁴¹ Then these people who have been recorded by name came, in the days of Hezekiah king of Judah, and attacked their tents and the dwellings that were found there, annihilating them to this day, and settling in their place; for there was pasture there for their flocks.

⁴² Also, some of them — of the sons of Simeon — five hundred men, went to Mount Seir, with Pelatiah, Neariah, Rephaiah and Uzziel, the sons of Ishi, at their head. ⁴³ They smote the remnant of the Amalekites who had survived and dwelt there, up to this day.

4:40. They had never faced threats from any invaders (*Vilna Gaon*).

ה א וּבְנֵי רְאוּבֵן בְּכוֹר־יִשְׂרָאֵל כִּי הוּא הַבְּכוֹר וּבְחַלְּלוֹ יְצוּעֵי אָבִיו נִתְּנָה בְּכֹרָתוֹ לִבְנֵי יוֹסֵף בֶּן־יִשְׂרָאֵל וְלֹא לְהִתְיַחֵשׂ לַבְּכֹרָה: כִּי יְהוּדָה גָּבַר בְּאֶחָיו וּלְנָגִיד מִמֶּנּוּ וְהַבְּכֹרָה לְיוֹסֵף: בְּנֵי רְאוּבֵן בְּכוֹר יִשְׂרָאֵל חֲנוֹךְ וּפַלּוּא חֶצְרוֹן וְכַרְמִי: בְּנֵי יוֹאֵל שְׁמַעְיָה בְנוֹ גּוֹג בְּנוֹ שִׁמְעִי בְנוֹ: מִיכָה בְנוֹ רְאָיָה בְנוֹ בַּעַל בְּנוֹ: בְּאֵרָה בְנוֹ אֲשֶׁר הֶגְלָה תִּלְּגַת פִּלְנְאֶסֶר מֶלֶךְ אַשֻּׁר הוּא נָשִׂיא לָרֵאוּבֵנִי: וְאֶחָיו לְמִשְׁפְּחֹתָיו בְּהִתְיַחֵשׂ לְתֹלְדוֹתָם הָרֹאשׁ יְעִיאֵל וּזְכַרְיָהוּ: וּבֶלַע בֶּן־עָזָז בֶּן־שֶׁמַע בֶּן־יוֹאֵל הוּא יוֹשֵׁב בַּעֲרֹעֵר וְעַד־נְבוֹ וּבַעַל מְעוֹן: וְלַמִּזְרָח יָשַׁב עַד־לְבוֹא מִדְבָּרָה לְמִן־הַנָּהָר פְּרָת כִּי מִקְנֵיהֶם רָבוּ בְּאֶרֶץ גִּלְעָד: וּבִימֵי שָׁאוּל עָשׂוּ מִלְחָמָה עִם־הַהַגְרִיאִים וַיִּפְּלוּ בְּיָדָם וַיֵּשְׁבוּ בְּאָהֳלֵיהֶם עַל־כָּל־פְּנֵי מִזְרָח לַגִּלְעָד: וּבְנֵי־גָד לְנֶגְדָּם יָשְׁבוּ בְּאֶרֶץ הַבָּשָׁן עַד־סַלְכָה: יוֹאֵל הָרֹאשׁ וְשָׁפָם הַמִּשְׁנֶה וְיַעְנַי וְשָׁפָט בַּבָּשָׁן: וַאֲחֵיהֶם לְבֵית אֲבוֹתֵיהֶם מִיכָאֵל וּמְשֻׁלָּם וְשֶׁבַע וְיוֹרַי וְיַעְכָּן וְזִיעַ וָעֵבֶר שִׁבְעָה: אֵלֶּה בְּנֵי אֲבִיחַיִל בֶּן־חוּרִי בֶּן־יָרוֹחַ בֶּן־גִּלְעָד בֶּן־מִיכָאֵל בֶּן־יְשִׁישַׁי בֶּן־יַחְדּוֹ בֶּן־בּוּז: אֲחִי בֶּן־עַבְדִּיאֵל בֶּן־גּוּנִי רֹאשׁ לְבֵית אֲבוֹתָם: וַיֵּשְׁבוּ בַּגִּלְעָד בַּבָּשָׁן וּבִבְנֹתֶיהָ וּבְכָל־מִגְרְשֵׁי שָׁרוֹן עַל־תּוֹצְאוֹתָם: כֻּלָּם הִתְיַחְשׂוּ בִּימֵי יוֹתָם מֶלֶךְ־יְהוּדָה וּבִימֵי יָרָבְעָם מֶלֶךְ־יִשְׂרָאֵל: בְּנֵי־רְאוּבֵן וְגָדִי וַחֲצִי שֵׁבֶט־מְנַשֶּׁה מִן־בְּנֵי־חַיִל אֲנָשִׁים נֹשְׂאֵי מָגֵן וְחֶרֶב וְדֹרְכֵי קֶשֶׁת וּלְמוּדֵי מִלְחָמָה אַרְבָּעִים וְאַרְבָּעָה אֶלֶף וּשְׁבַע־מֵאוֹת וְשִׁשִּׁים יֹצְאֵי צָבָא: וַיַּעֲשׂוּ מִלְחָמָה עִם־הַהַגְרִיאִים וִיטוּר וְנָפִישׁ וְנוֹדָב: וַיֵּעָזְרוּ עֲלֵיהֶם וַיִּנָּתְנוּ בְיָדָם הַהַגְרִיאִים וְכֹל שֶׁעִמָּהֶם כִּי לֵאלֹהִים זָעֲקוּ בַּמִּלְחָמָה וְנַעְתּוֹר לָהֶם כִּי־בָטְחוּ בוֹ: וַיִּשְׁבּוּ מִקְנֵיהֶם גְּמַלֵּיהֶם חֲמִשִּׁים אֶלֶף וְצֹאן מָאתַיִם וַחֲמִשִּׁים אֶלֶף וַחֲמוֹרִים אַלְפָּיִם וְנֶפֶשׁ אָדָם מֵאָה אָלֶף: כִּי־חֲלָלִים רַבִּים נָפָלוּ כִּי מֵהָאֱלֹהִים הַמִּלְחָמָה וַיֵּשְׁבוּ תַחְתֵּיהֶם עַד־הַגֹּלָה: וּבְנֵי חֲצִי שֵׁבֶט מְנַשֶּׁה יָשְׁבוּ בָּאָרֶץ מִבָּשָׁן עַד־בַּעַל חֶרְמוֹן וּשְׂנִיר וְהַר־חֶרְמוֹן הֵמָּה רָבוּ: וְאֵלֶּה רָאשֵׁי בֵית־אֲבוֹתָם וְעֵפֶר וְיִשְׁעִי וֶאֱלִיאֵל וְעַזְרִיאֵל וְיִרְמְיָה וְהוֹדַוְיָה וְיַחְדִּיאֵל אֲנָשִׁים גִּבּוֹרֵי חַיִל אַנְשֵׁי שֵׁמוֹת רָאשִׁים לְבֵית אֲבוֹתָם: וַיִּמְעֲלוּ בֵּאלֹהֵי אֲבוֹתֵיהֶם וַיִּזְנוּ אַחֲרֵי אֱלֹהֵי עַמֵּי־הָאָרֶץ אֲשֶׁר־הִשְׁמִיד אֱלֹהִים מִפְּנֵיהֶם: וַיָּעַר אֱלֹהֵי יִשְׂרָאֵל אֶת־רוּחַ פּוּל מֶלֶךְ־אַשּׁוּר וְאֶת־רוּחַ תִּלְּגַת פִּלְנֶסֶר מֶלֶךְ אַשּׁוּר וַיַּגְלֵם לָראוּבֵנִי וְלַגָּדִי וְלַחֲצִי שֵׁבֶט מְנַשֶּׁה וַיְבִיאֵם לַחְלַח וְחָבוֹר וְהָרָא

ב
ג
ד
ה־ו
ז
ח
ט
י
יא־יב
יג
יד
טו־טז
יז
יח
יט־כ
כא
כב
כג
כד
כה
כו

5:1-2. The double portion of inheritance, which normally is the right of the firstborn son, was given to Joseph over Reuben, and his descendants were split into two independent tribes, Ephraim and Manasseh. The privilege of royalty, however, which should have gone to the first-born, was not conferred on Joseph. It was stripped from Reuben and given to Judah.

5:4-6. Joel was the son of Carmi, Shemaiah the son of Joel, and so on.

5:7. In the days of Jeroboam (v. 17).

5

Reuben

[1] The sons of Reuben, the firstborn of Israel. (He was the firstborn, but when he defiled his father's bed his birthright was given to the sons of Joseph son of Israel, although not to receive the hereditary right of the firstborn, * [2] for Judah prevailed over his brothers, and the ruler was to come from him; but the firstborn's portion was Joseph's.) [3] The sons of Reuben, the firstborn of Israel: Hanoch, Pallu, Hezron and Carmi. [4] The sons of Joel: * Shemaiah was his son; Gog was his son; Shimei was his son; [5] Micah was his son; Reaia was his son; Baal was his son; [6] Beerah was his son, whom Tillegath-pilneser king of Assyria exiled. He was the leader of the Reubenites.

(See Appendix D, map 1) [7] His brothers, by their families, when their genealogy was recorded according to their generations: * Jeiel the chief, Zechariah [8] and Bela son of Azaz son of Shema son of Joel, who settled around Aroer, up to Nebo and Baal-meon, [9] and settled eastward up to the approach of the wilderness from the Euphrates River. For their flocks had become numerous in the land of Gilead; [10] so in the days of Saul they waged war against the Hagrites, who fell into their hands; and they occupied their tents all across the eastern side of Gilead.

Gad

[11] And opposite them, the children of Gad settled in the land of Bashan, up to Salcah. [12] Joel was the leader, Shapham was second in command, and Jaanai and Shaphat [were] in Bashan. [13] Their kinsmen, of their fathers' families: Michael, Meshullam, Sheba, Jorai, Jacan, Zia and Eber — seven [in all]. [14] [All] these were the sons of Abihail son of Huri, son of Jaroah, son of Gilead, son of Michael, son of Jeshishai, son of Jahdo, son of Buz. [15] Ahi son of Abdiel, son of Guni, was the leader of their fathers' family. [16] They settled in Gilead, in Bashan and in its towns, and in all the open areas of Sharon, in their far-flung territory.

[17] All these had their genealogies recorded in the days of Jotham king of Judah, and in the days of Jeroboam* king of Israel.

[18] The sons of Reuben, the Gadites and half the tribe of Manasseh — forty-four thousand, seven hundred sixty brave men of their warriors, men bearing shield and sword, who were archers and skillful in war — [19] waged war against the Hagrites, against Jetur, Naphish and Nodab. [20] They were helped* against them, and the Hagrites and all those who were with them were delivered into their hand, for they cried out to God in the battle; and He heard their prayers, because they put their trust in Him. [21] They plundered their livestock — fifty thousand of their camels, two hundred fifty thousand sheep and two thousand donkeys — and one hundred thousand men. [22] For many were slain, because the war was from God. They then settled in their place, until the exile. *

Half of Manasseh

[23] The children of half the tribe of Manasseh lived in the land from Bashan up to Baal-hermon and Senir and Mount Hermon, for they were numerous. [24] These were the heads of their fathers' families: Epher, Ishi, Eliel, Azriel, Jeremiah, Hodaviah and Jahdiel — mighty warriors, men of fame, and heads of their fathers' families. [25] But they betrayed the God of their fathers and went astray after the gods of the peoples of the land whom God had destroyed before them. [26] So the God of Israel stirred up the spirit of Pul king of Assyria, and the spirit of Tillegath-pilneser king of Assyria, and he led away the Reubenites, the Gadites and half the tribe of Manasseh into exile, transporting them to Halah, Habor and Hara,

---

5:17. Jeroboam II, who was a contemporary of Jotham.
5:20. By their brethren from other tribes.

5:22. Until the tribes who lived on the East Bank were exiled by the Assyrians. See *II Kings* 17:7ff.

כז-כח	וְנֶהְדַּר גּוֹזָן עַד הַיּוֹם הַזֶּה: בְּנֵי לֵוִי גֵּרְשׁוֹן קְהָת וּמְרָרִי: וּבְנֵי קְהָת
כט	עַמְרָם יִצְהָר וְחֶבְרוֹן וְעֻזִּיאֵל: וּבְנֵי עַמְרָם אַהֲרֹן וּמֹשֶׁה וּמִרְיָם
ל	וּבְנֵי אַהֲרֹן נָדָב וַאֲבִיהוּא אֶלְעָזָר וְאִיתָמָר: אֶלְעָזָר הוֹלִיד אֶת־פִּינְחָס
לא	פִּינְחָס הוֹלִיד אֶת־אֲבִישׁוּעַ: וַאֲבִישׁוּעַ הוֹלִיד אֶת־בֻּקִּי וּבֻקִּי הוֹלִיד אֶת־
לב-לג	עֻזִּי: וְעֻזִּי הוֹלִיד אֶת־זְרַחְיָה וּזְרַחְיָה הוֹלִיד אֶת־מְרָיוֹת: מְרָיוֹת הוֹלִיד אֶת־
לד	אֲמַרְיָה וַאֲמַרְיָה הוֹלִיד אֶת־אֲחִיטוּב: וַאֲחִיטוּב הוֹלִיד אֶת־צָדוֹק וְצָדוֹק
לה	הוֹלִיד אֶת־אֲחִימָעַץ: וַאֲחִימַעַץ הוֹלִיד אֶת־עֲזַרְיָה וַעֲזַרְיָה הוֹלִיד אֶת־
לו	יוֹחָנָן: וְיוֹחָנָן הוֹלִיד אֶת־עֲזַרְיָה הוּא אֲשֶׁר כִּהֵן בַּבַּיִת אֲשֶׁר־בָּנָה שְׁלֹמֹה
לז	בִּירוּשָׁלָ͏ִם: וַיּוֹלֶד עֲזַרְיָה אֶת־אֲמַרְיָה וַאֲמַרְיָה הוֹלִיד אֶת־אֲחִיטוּב:
לח-לט	וַאֲחִיטוּב הוֹלִיד אֶת־צָדוֹק וְצָדוֹק הוֹלִיד אֶת־שַׁלּוּם: וְשַׁלּוּם הוֹלִיד אֶת־
מ	חִלְקִיָּה וְחִלְקִיָּה הוֹלִיד אֶת־עֲזַרְיָה: וַעֲזַרְיָה הוֹלִיד אֶת־שְׂרָיָה וּשְׂרָיָה
מא	הוֹלִיד אֶת־יְהוֹצָדָק: וִיהוֹצָדָק הָלַךְ בְּהַגְלוֹת יְהוָה אֶת־יְהוּדָה וִירוּשָׁלָ͏ִם

ו	א-ב	בְּיַד נְבֻכַדְנֶאצַּר: בְּנֵי לֵוִי גֵּרְשֹׁם קְהָת וּמְרָרִי: וְאֵלֶּה שְׁמוֹת בְּנֵי־

ג-ד	גֵרְשׁוֹם לִבְנִי וְשִׁמְעִי: וּבְנֵי קְהָת עַמְרָם וְיִצְהָר וְחֶבְרוֹן וְעֻזִּיאֵל: בְּנֵי מְרָרִי
ה	מַחְלִי וּמֻשִׁי וְאֵלֶּה מִשְׁפְּחוֹת הַלֵּוִי לַאֲבוֹתֵיהֶם: לְגֵרְשׁוֹם לִבְנִי בְנוֹ יַחַת
ו-ז	בְּנוֹ זִמָּה בְנוֹ: יוֹאָח בְּנוֹ עִדּוֹ בְנוֹ זֶרַח בְּנוֹ יְאָתְרַי בְּנוֹ: בְּנֵי קְהָת עַמִּינָדָב בְּנוֹ
ח-ט	קֹרַח בְּנוֹ אַסִּיר בְּנוֹ: אֶלְקָנָה בְנוֹ וְאֶבְיָסָף בְּנוֹ וְאַסִּיר בְּנוֹ: תַּחַת בְּנוֹ
י-יא	אוּרִיאֵל בְּנוֹ עֻזִּיָּה בְנוֹ וְשָׁאוּל בְּנוֹ: וּבְנֵי אֶלְקָנָה עֲמָשַׂי וַאֲחִימוֹת: אֶלְקָנָה
יב	°בנו [°בְּנֵי ק׳] אֶלְקָנָה צוֹפַי בְּנוֹ וְנַחַת בְּנוֹ: אֱלִיאָב בְּנוֹ יְרֹחָם בְּנוֹ אֶלְקָנָה
יג-יד	בְנוֹ: וּבְנֵי שְׁמוּאֵל הַבְּכֹר וַשְׁנִי וַאֲבִיָּה: בְּנֵי מְרָרִי מַחְלִי לִבְנִי בְנוֹ שִׁמְעִי בְנוֹ
טו-טז	עֻזָּה בְנוֹ: שִׁמְעָא בְנוֹ חַגִּיָּה בְנוֹ עֲשָׂיָה בְנוֹ: וְאֵלֶּה אֲשֶׁר הֶעֱמִיד דָּוִיד עַל־
יז	יְדֵי־שִׁיר בֵּית יְהוָה מִמְּנוֹחַ הָאָרוֹן: וַיִּהְיוּ מְשָׁרְתִים לִפְנֵי מִשְׁכַּן אֹהֶל־מוֹעֵד
יח	בַּשִּׁיר עַד־בְּנוֹת שְׁלֹמֹה אֶת־בֵּית יְהוָה בִּירוּשָׁלָ͏ִם וַיַּעַמְדוּ כְמִשְׁפָּטָם עַל־
	עֲבוֹדָתָם: וְאֵלֶּה הָעֹמְדִים וּבְנֵיהֶם מִבְּנֵי הַקְּהָתִי הֵימָן הַמְשׁוֹרֵר בֶּן־יוֹאֵל
יט	בֶּן־שְׁמוּאֵל: בֶּן־אֶלְקָנָה בֶּן־יְרֹחָם בֶּן־אֱלִיאֵל בֶּן־תּוֹחַ: בֶּן־°ציף [°צוּף ק׳]
כא	בֶּן־אֶלְקָנָה בֶּן־מַחַת בֶּן־עֲמָשָׂי: בֶּן־אֶלְקָנָה בֶּן־יוֹאֵל בֶּן־עֲזַרְיָה בֶּן־צְפַנְיָה:
כב-כג	בֶּן־תַּחַת בֶּן־אַסִּיר בֶּן־אֶבְיָסָף בֶּן־קֹרַח: בֶּן־יִצְהָר בֶּן־קְהָת בֶּן־לֵוִי בֶּן־
כד-כה	יִשְׂרָאֵל: וְאָחִיו אָסָף הָעֹמֵד עַל־יְמִינוֹ אָסָף בֶּן־בֶּרֶכְיָהוּ בֶּן־שִׁמְעָא: בֶּן־
כו-כז	מִיכָאֵל בֶּן־בַּעֲשֵׂיָה בֶּן־מַלְכִּיָּה: בֶּן־אֶתְנִי בֶן־זֶרַח בֶּן־עֲדָיָה: בֶּן־אֵיתָן בֶּן־
כח-כט	זִמָּה בֶּן־שִׁמְעִי: בֶּן־יַחַת בֶּן־גֵּרְשֹׁם בֶּן־לֵוִי: וּבְנֵי מְרָרִי
ל	אֲחֵיהֶם עַל־הַשְּׂמֹאול אֵיתָן בֶּן־קִישִׁי בֶּן־עַבְדִּי בֶּן־מַלּוּךְ: בֶּן־חֲשַׁבְיָה בֶן־
לא-לב	אֲמַצְיָה בֶּן־חִלְקִיָּה: בֶּן־אַמְצִי בֶן־בָּנִי בֶּן־שָׁמֶר: בֶּן־מַחְלִי בֶּן־מוּשִׁי בֶּן־

6:7. Another name of Izhar in v. 3.

6:13. Samuel son of Elkanah had two sons, Joel and Abiah (*I Samuel* 1:19-20; 8:2). Alternatively: "The sons of

Samuel were: the firstborn Vashi and Abiah."

6:16. In Jerusalem. See *II Samuel* Ch. 6.

6:17. Singing in the Temple (*Radak*).

and to the river Gozan, until this day.

The tribe
of Levi
Kohanim

²⁷ *The sons of Levi: Gershon, Kohath, and Merari.* ²⁸ *The sons of Kohath: Amram, Izhar, Hebron and Uzziel.* ²⁹ *The children of Amram: Aaron, Moses and Miriam. The sons of Aaron: Nadab, Abihu, Elazar and Ithamar.*

³⁰ *Elazar begot Phinehas; Phinehas begot Abishua;* ³¹ *Abishua begot Bukki; Bukki begot Uzzi;* ³² *Uzzi begot Zerahiah; Zerahiah begot Meraioth;* ³³ *Meraioth begot Amariah; Amariah begot Ahitub;* ³⁴ *Ahitub begot Zadok; Zadok begot Ahimaaz;* ³⁵ *Ahimaaz begot Azariah; Azariah begot Johanan;* ³⁶ *Johanan begot Azariah, he is the one who served as Kohen in the Temple that Solomon built in Jerusalem.* ³⁷ *Azariah begot Amariah; Amariah begot Ahitub;* ³⁸ *Ahitub begot Zadok; Zadok begot Shallum;* ³⁹ *Shallum begot Hilkiah; Hilkiah begot Azariah;* ⁴⁰ *Azariah begot Seraiah; and Seraiah begot Jehozadak.* ⁴¹ *Jehozadak left when* HASHEM *led Judah and Jerusalem into exile through the hand of Nebuchadnezzar.*

6

Levite
families

(See Appendix B,
chart 12)

¹ **T**he *sons of Levi: Gershom, Kohath and Merari.* ² *These are the names of the sons of Gershom: Libni and Shimei.* ³ *The sons of Kohath: Amram, Izhar, Hebron and Uzziel.* ⁴ *The sons of Merari: Mahli and Mushi.*

These are the families of the Levites according to their fathers. ⁵ *For Gershom: Libni was his son; Jahath was his son; Zimmah was his son;* ⁶ *Joah was his son; Iddo was his son; Zerah was his son; Jeatherai was his son.*

⁷ *The sons of Kohath: Amminadab* * *was his son; Korah was his son; Assir was his son;* ⁸ *Elkanah was his son and Ebiasaph was his son and Assir was [Ebiasaph's] son;* ⁹ *Tahath was his son; Uriel was his son; Uzziah was his son; and Shaul was his son.*

¹⁰ *The sons of Elkanah: Amasai, [whose son was] Ahimoth,* ¹¹ *[whose son was] Elkanah. The sons of Elkanah: Zophai was his son; Nahath was his son;* ¹² *Eliab was his son; Jeroham was his son; Elkanah was his son.* ¹³ *The sons of Samuel: the firstborn [Joel], and the second Abiah.* *

¹⁴ *The sons of Merari: Mahli. Libni was his son; Shimei was his son; Uzzah was his son;* ¹⁵ *Shimea was his son; Haggiah was his son; Asaiah was his son.*

The Temple
singers

¹⁶ *These are [the men] whom David appointed over the song in the Temple of* HASHEM, *after the Ark had come to rest.* * ¹⁷ *They ministered with song before the Tabernacle of the Tent of Meeting, until Solomon built the Temple of* HASHEM *in Jerusalem, when they carried on with their service,* * *according to their charge.*

¹⁸ *These are the ones who stood [in service], with their children: Of the sons of the Kohathites: Heman the singer, the son of Joel, son of Samuel;* ¹⁹ *son of Elkanah, son of Jeroham, son of Eliel, son of Toah;* ²⁰ *son of Zuph, son of Elkanah, son of Mahath, son of Amasai;* ²¹ *son of Elkanah, son of Joel, son of Azariah, son of Zephaniah;* ²² *son of Tahath, son of Assir, son of Ebiasaph, son of Korah;* ²³ *son of Izhar, son of Kohath, son of Levi, son of Israel.*

²⁴ *And his kinsman Asaph, who stood on his right — Asaph son of Berachiah son of Shimea;* ²⁵ *son of Michael, son of Baaseiah, son of Malchijah;* ²⁶ *son of Ethni, son of Zerah, son of Adaiah;* ²⁷ *son of Ethan, son of Zimmah, son of Shimei;* ²⁸ *son of Jahath, son of Gershom, son of Levi.*

²⁹ *And their kinsmen the sons of Merari stood on the left: Ethan son of Kishi, son of Abdi, son of Malluch;* ³⁰ *son of Hashabiah, son of Amaziah, son of Hilkiah;* ³¹ *son of Amzi, son of Bani, son of Shemer;* ³² *son of Mahli, son of Mushi, son of*

לג מְרָרִי בֶּן־לֵוִי: וַאֲחֵיהֶם הַלְוִיִּם נְתוּנִים לְכָל־עֲבוֹדַת מִשְׁכַּן בֵּית

לד הָאֱלֹהִים: וְאַהֲרֹן וּבָנָיו מַקְטִירִים עַל־מִזְבַּח הָעוֹלָה וְעַל־מִזְבַּח הַקְּטֹרֶת לְכֹל מְלֶאכֶת קֹדֶשׁ הַקֳּדָשִׁים וּלְכַפֵּר עַל־יִשְׂרָאֵל כְּכֹל אֲשֶׁר צִוָּה מֹשֶׁה

לה עֶבֶד הָאֱלֹהִים: וְאֵלֶּה בְּנֵי אַהֲרֹן אֶלְעָזָר בְּנוֹ פִּינְחָס בְּנוֹ אֲבִישׁוּעַ

לו-לח בְּנוֹ: בֻּקִּי בְנוֹ עֻזִּי בְנוֹ זְרַחְיָה בְנוֹ: מְרָיוֹת בְּנוֹ אֲמַרְיָה בְנוֹ אֲחִיטוּב בְּנוֹ:

לט צָדוֹק בְּנוֹ אֲחִימַעַץ בְּנוֹ: וְאֵלֶּה מוֹשְׁבוֹתָם לְטִירוֹתָם בִּגְבוּלָם לִבְנֵי

מ אַהֲרֹן לְמִשְׁפַּחַת הַקְּהָתִי כִּי לָהֶם הָיָה הַגּוֹרָל: וַיִּתְּנוּ לָהֶם אֶת־חֶבְרוֹן

מא בְּאֶרֶץ יְהוּדָה וְאֶת־מִגְרָשֶׁיהָ סְבִיבֹתֶיהָ: וְאֶת־שְׂדֵה הָעִיר וְאֶת־חֲצֵרֶיהָ

מב נָתְנוּ לְכָלֵב בֶּן־יְפֻנֶּה: וְלִבְנֵי אַהֲרֹן נָתְנוּ אֶת־עָרֵי הַמִּקְלָט אֶת־חֶבְרוֹן

מג וְאֶת־לִבְנָה וְאֶת־מִגְרָשֶׁיהָ וְאֶת־יַתִּר וְאֶת־אֶשְׁתְּמֹעַ וְאֶת־מִגְרָשֶׁיהָ: וְאֶת־

מד חִילֵז וְאֶת־מִגְרָשֶׁיהָ אֶת־דְּבִיר וְאֶת־מִגְרָשֶׁיהָ: וְאֶת־עָשָׁן וְאֶת־מִגְרָשֶׁיהָ °נ"א חִילָן

מה וְאֶת־בֵּית שֶׁמֶשׁ וְאֶת־מִגְרָשֶׁיהָ: וּמִמַּטֵּה בִנְיָמִן אֶת־גֶּבַע וְאֶת־מִגְרָשֶׁיהָ וְאֶת־עָלֶמֶת וְאֶת־מִגְרָשֶׁיהָ וְאֶת־עֲנָתוֹת וְאֶת־מִגְרָשֶׁיהָ כָּל־עָרֵיהֶם שְׁלֹשׁ־

מו עֶשְׂרֵה עִיר בְּמִשְׁפְּחוֹתֵיהֶם: וְלִבְנֵי קְהָת הַנּוֹתָרִים מִמִּשְׁפַּחַת

מז הַמַּטֶּה מִמַּחֲצִית מַטֵּה חֲצִי מְנַשֶּׁה בַּגּוֹרָל עָרִים עָשֶׂר: וְלִבְנֵי גֵרְשׁוֹם לְמִשְׁפְּחוֹתָם מִמַּטֵּה יִשָּׂשכָר וּמִמַּטֵּה אָשֵׁר וּמִמַּטֵּה נַפְתָּלִי

מח וּמִמַּטֵּה מְנַשֶּׁה בַּבָּשָׁן עָרִים שְׁלֹשׁ עֶשְׂרֵה: לִבְנֵי מְרָרִי לְמִשְׁפְּחוֹתָם מִמַּטֵּה רְאוּבֵן וּמִמַּטֵּה־גָד וּמִמַּטֵּה זְבוּלֻן בַּגּוֹרָל עָרִים שְׁתֵּים עֶשְׂרֵה:

מט-נ וַיִּתְּנוּ בְנֵי־יִשְׂרָאֵל לַלְוִיִּם אֶת־הֶעָרִים וְאֶת־מִגְרְשֵׁיהֶם: וַיִּתְּנוּ בַגּוֹרָל מִמַּטֵּה בְנֵי־יְהוּדָה וּמִמַּטֵּה בְנֵי־שִׁמְעוֹן וּמִמַּטֵּה בְּנֵי בִנְיָמִן אֵת

נא הֶעָרִים הָאֵלֶּה אֲשֶׁר־יִקְרְאוּ אֶתְהֶם בְּשֵׁמוֹת: וּמִמִּשְׁפְּחוֹת בְּנֵי

נב קְהָת וַיְהִי עָרֵי גְבוּלָם מִמַּטֵּה אֶפְרָיִם: וַיִּתְּנוּ לָהֶם אֶת־עָרֵי הַמִּקְלָט אֶת־

נג שְׁכֶם וְאֶת־מִגְרָשֶׁיהָ בְּהַר אֶפְרָיִם וְאֶת־גֶּזֶר וְאֶת־מִגְרָשֶׁיהָ: וְאֶת־יָקְמְעָם

נד וְאֶת־מִגְרָשֶׁיהָ וְאֶת־בֵּית חוֹרוֹן וְאֶת־מִגְרָשֶׁיהָ: וְאֶת־אַיָּלוֹן וְאֶת־

נה מִגְרָשֶׁיהָ וְאֶת־גַּת־רִמּוֹן וְאֶת־מִגְרָשֶׁיהָ: וּמִמַּחֲצִית מַטֵּה מְנַשֶּׁה אֶת־עָנֵר וְאֶת־מִגְרָשֶׁיהָ וְאֶת־בִּלְעָם וְאֶת־מִגְרָשֶׁיהָ לְמִשְׁפַּחַת לִבְנֵי־קְהָת

נו הַנּוֹתָרִים: לִבְנֵי גֵרְשׁוֹם מִמִּשְׁפַּחַת חֲצִי מַטֵּה מְנַשֶּׁה אֶת־גּוֹלָן בַּבָּשָׁן וְאֶת־מִגְרָשֶׁיהָ וְאֶת־עַשְׁתָּרוֹת וְאֶת־מִגְרָשֶׁיהָ: וּמִמַּטֵּה

נז יִשָּׂשכָר אֶת־קֶדֶשׁ וְאֶת־מִגְרָשֶׁיהָ אֶת־דָּבְרַת וְאֶת־מִגְרָשֶׁיהָ: וְאֶת־

נח רָאמוֹת וְאֶת־מִגְרָשֶׁיהָ וְאֶת־עָנֵם וְאֶת־מִגְרָשֶׁיהָ: וּמִמַּטֵּה אָשֵׁר

נט-ס אֶת־מָשָׁל וְאֶת־מִגְרָשֶׁיהָ וְאֶת־עַבְדּוֹן וְאֶת־מִגְרָשֶׁיהָ: וְאֶת־חוּקֹק

סא וְאֶת־מִגְרָשֶׁיהָ וְאֶת־רְחֹב וְאֶת־מִגְרָשֶׁיהָ: וּמִמַּטֵּה נַפְתָּלִי

6:35. The rest of the chapter deals with the towns that were apportioned by lottery (see *Joshua* Ch. 21) as the dwelling places of the Kohanim and the Levites. The first lottery was for the sons of Aaron mentioned here.

6:46. Those who were not descendants of Aaron, and were thus Levites.

Merari, son of Levi.

[33] *Their brother Levites were appointed over the entire service of the Tabernacle of the Temple of God.* [34] *Aaron and his sons offered sacrifices on the Altar of the Burnt-Offering, and on the Incense Altar, [caring] for all the labor of the Holy of Holies and atoning for Israel, according to all that Moses, the servant of God, had commanded.*

[35] *These are the sons of Aaron: Elazar was his son; Phinehas was his son; Abishua was his son;* [36] *Bukki was his son; Uzzi was his son; Zerahiah was his son;* [37] *Meraioth was his son; Amariah was his son; Ahitub was his son;* [38] *Zadok was his son; Ahimaaz was his son.*

Levite cities
(See Appendix D, map 5)

[39] **These are the dwelling places for the sons of Aaron of the Kohathite family, according to their towns throughout their borders; for the lottery fell upon them.* [40] *They gave them Hebron in the land of Judah, and the outlying areas around it;* [41] *but the fields of the city and its villages were given to Caleb son of Jephunneh.*

[42] *The sons of Aaron were given the cities of refuge: Hebron, Libnah with its outlying area, Jattir and Eshtemoa with their open areas,* [43] *Hilez with its open areas, Debir with its open areas,* [44] *Ashan with its open areas and Beth-shemesh with its open areas.*

[45] *And from the tribe of Benjamin [they were given] Geba with its open areas, Alemeth with its open areas and Anathoth with its open areas. All their cities for their families were thirteen cities.*

[46] *The remaining sons of Kohath,* of the family of that tribe, [were given] ten cities by lottery out of the half-portion of the half of the tribe of Manasseh.*

[47] *The sons of Gershom, according to their families: thirteen cities from the tribe of Issachar, the tribe of Asher, the tribe of Naphtali and the tribe of Manasseh in Bashan.*

[48] *The sons of Merari according to their families, from the tribe of Reuben, the tribe of Gad and the tribe of Zebulun, by lottery: twelve cities.*

[49] *The Children of Israel gave these cities to the Levites with their open areas.* [50] *They gave by lottery these cities, which have been mentioned by name, from the tribe of the children of Judah, the tribe of the children of Simeon and the tribe of the children of Benjamin.*

[51] *For some of the families of the sons of Kohath, the cities of their territory came from the tribe of Ephraim.* [52] *They gave them the cities of refuge Shechem in Mount Ephraim with its open areas and Gezer with its open areas;* [53] *and Jokmeam with its open areas, Beth-horon with its open areas,* [54] *Aijalon with its open areas and Gath-rimmon with its open areas.* [55] *And from half the tribe of Manasseh: Aner with its open areas and Bileam with its open areas for the remaining family of the sons of Kohath.*

[56] *To the sons of Gershom, from the family of half the tribe of Manasseh: Golan in Bashan with its open areas and Ashtaroth with its open areas.* [57] *And from the tribe of Issachar: Kedesh with its open areas, Daberath with its open areas,* [58] *Ramoth with its open areas and Anem with its open areas.* [59] *And from the tribe of Asher: Mashal with its open areas, Abdon with its open areas,* [60] *Hukok with its open areas and Rehob with its open areas.* [61] *And from the tribe of Naphtali:*

אֶת־קֶ֙דֶשׁ֙ בַּגָּלִיל֙ וְאֶת־מִגְרָשֶׁ֔יהָ וְאֶת־חַמּ֖וֹן וְאֶת־מִגְרָשֶׁ֑יהָ וְאֶת־קִרְיָתַ֖יִם

סב וְאֶת־מִגְרָשֶׁ֖יהָ: לִבְנֵ֣י מְרָרִי֮ הַנּֽוֹתָרִים֒ מִמַּטֵּ֣ה זְבוּלֻ֔ן אֶת־

סג רִמּוֹנוֹ֙ וְאֶת־מִגְרָשֶׁ֔יהָ אֶת־תָּב֖וֹר וְאֶת־מִגְרָשֶׁ֑יהָ וּמֵעֵ֨בֶר לְיַרְדֵּ֤ן יְרֵחוֹ֙ לְמִזְרַ֣ח הַיַּרְדֵּ֔ן מִמַּטֵּ֣ה רְאוּבֵ֔ן אֶת־בֶּ֥צֶר בַּמִּדְבָּ֖ר וְאֶת־מִגְרָשֶׁ֑יהָ וְאֶת־

סד יַ֙הְצָה֙ וְאֶת־מִגְרָשֶׁ֔יהָ: וְאֶת־קְדֵמוֹת֙ וְאֶת־מִגְרָשֶׁ֔יהָ וְאֶת־מֵיפַ֖עַת וְאֶת־

סה מִגְרָשֶֽׁיהָ: וּמִמַּטֵּה־גָ֗ד אֶת־רָאמ֤וֹת בַּגִּלְעָד֙ וְאֶת־מִגְרָשֶׁ֔יהָ

סו וְאֶת־מַֽחֲנַ֖יִם וְאֶת־מִגְרָשֶֽׁיהָ: וְאֶת־חֶשְׁבּוֹן֙ וְאֶת־מִגְרָשֶׁ֔יהָ וְאֶת־יַעְזֵ֖יר וְאֶת־מִגְרָשֶֽׁיהָ:

ז

א וְלִבְנֵ֣י יִשָּׂשכָ֗ר תּוֹלָ֧ע וּפוּאָ֛ה °יָשׁ֥וּב [יָשׁ֥יב ק] וְשִׁמְר֖וֹן אַרְבָּעָֽה:

ב וּבְנֵ֣י תוֹלָ֗ע עֻזִּ֤י וּרְפָיָה֙ וִירִיאֵ֣ל וְיַחְמַ֔י וְיִבְשָׂ֖ם וּשְׁמוּאֵ֑ל רָאשִׁ֣ים לְבֵית־אֲבוֹתָ֣ם לְתוֹלָ֗ע גִּבּ֤וֹרֵי חַ֙יִל֙ לְתֹלְדוֹתָ֔ם מִסְפָּרָם֙ בִּימֵ֣י דָוִ֔יד

ג עֶשְׂרִֽים־וּשְׁנַ֥יִם אֶ֖לֶף וְשֵׁ֥שׁ מֵאֽוֹת: וּבְנֵ֣י עֻזִּ֖י יִֽזְרַֽחְיָ֑ה וּבְנֵ֣י יִֽזְרַחְיָ֗ה מִיכָאֵ֤ל וְעֹבַדְיָה֙ וְיוֹאֵ֔ל יִשִּׁיָּ֖ה חֲמִשָּׁ֑ה רָאשִׁ֖ים כֻּלָּֽם:

ד וַעֲלֵיהֶ֨ם לְתֹלְדוֹתָ֜ם לְבֵ֣ית אֲבוֹתָ֗ם גְּדוּדֵי֙ צְבָ֣א מִלְחָמָ֔ה שְׁלֹשִׁ֥ים וְשִׁשָּׁ֖ה אָ֑לֶף כִּֽי־הִרְבּ֥וּ נָשִׁ֖ים וּבָנִֽים:

ה וַאֲחֵיהֶ֗ם לְכֹל֙ מִשְׁפְּח֣וֹת יִשָּׂשכָ֔ר גִּבּוֹרֵ֖י חֲיָלִ֑ים שְׁמוֹנִ֤ים וְשִׁבְעָה֙ אֶ֔לֶף הִתְיַחְשָׂ֖ם לַכֹּֽל:

ו בִּנְיָמִ֗ן בֶּ֧לַע וָבֶ֛כֶר

ז וִידִיעֲאֵ֖ל שְׁלֹשָֽׁה: וּבְנֵ֣י בֶ֗לַע אֶצְבּ֤וֹן וְעֻזִּי֙ וְעֻזִּיאֵ֔ל וִירִימ֥וֹת וְעִירִ֖י חֲמִשָּׁ֑ה רָאשֵׁי֙ בֵּ֣ית אָב֔וֹת גִּבּוֹרֵ֖י חֲיָלִ֑ים וְהִתְיַחְשָׂ֗ם עֶשְׂרִ֤ים וּשְׁנַ֙יִם֙ אֶ֔לֶף וּשְׁלֹשִׁ֖ים

ח וְאַרְבָּעָֽה: וּבְנֵ֣י בֶ֗כֶר זְמִירָ֤ה וְיוֹעָשׁ֙ וֶאֱלִיעֶ֙זֶר֙ וְאֶלְיוֹעֵינַ֣י וְעָמְרִ֔י

ט וִירֵמ֥וֹת וַאֲבִיָּ֖ה וַעֲנָת֣וֹת וְעָלָ֑מֶת כׇּל־אֵ֖לֶּה בְּנֵי־בָ֑כֶר: וְהִתְיַחְשָׂ֣ם לְתֹלְדוֹתָ֗ם

י רָאשֵׁי֙ בֵּ֣ית אֲבוֹתָ֔ם גִּבּוֹרֵ֖י חָ֑יִל עֶשְׂרִ֥ים אֶ֖לֶף וּמָאתָֽיִם: וּבְנֵ֣י יְדִיעֲאֵ֖ל בִּלְהָ֑ן וּבְנֵ֣י בִלְהָ֗ן °יעִ֥ושׁ [יְע֥וּשׁ ק] וּבִנְיָמִ֤ן וְאֵהוּד֙ וּכְנַעֲנָ֔ה וְזֵיתָ֖ן וְתַרְשִׁ֥ישׁ

יא וַאֲחִישָֽׁחַר: כׇּל־אֵ֜לֶּה בְּנֵ֤י יְדִֽיעֲאֵל֙ לְרָאשֵׁ֣י הָאָב֔וֹת גִּבּוֹרֵ֖י חֲיָלִ֑ים שִׁבְעָ֨ה

יב עָשָׂ֥ר אֶ֙לֶף֙ וּמָאתַ֔יִם יֹצְאֵ֥י צָבָ֖א לַמִּלְחָמָֽה: וְשֻׁפִּ֤ם וְחֻפִּם֙ בְּנֵ֣י עִ֔יר חֻשִׁ֖ם בְּנֵ֥י

יג-יד אַחֵֽר: בְּנֵ֣י נַפְתָּלִ֗י יַחֲצִיאֵ֧ל וְגוּנִ֛י וְיֵ֥צֶר וְשַׁלּ֖וּם בְּנֵ֥י בִלְהָֽה: בְּנֵ֣י מְנַשֶּׁ֗ה אַשְׂרִיאֵל֙ אֲשֶׁ֣ר יָלָ֔דָה פִּֽילַגְשׁוֹ֙ הָאֲרַמִּיָּ֔ה יָלְדָ֕ה אֶת־מָכִ֖יר אֲבִ֥י

טו גִלְעָֽד: וּמָכִ֞יר לָקַ֤ח אִשָּׁה֙ לְחֻפִּ֣ים וּלְשֻׁפִּ֔ים וְשֵׁ֤ם אֲחֹתוֹ֙ מַעֲכָ֔ה וְשֵׁ֥ם הַשֵּׁנִ֖י

טז צְלׇפְחָ֑ד וַתִּהְיֶ֥נָה לִצְלׇפְחָ֖ד בָּנֽוֹת: וַתֵּ֨לֶד מַעֲכָ֤ה אֵֽשֶׁת־מָכִיר֙ בֵּ֔ן וַתִּקְרָ֤א שְׁמוֹ֙ פֶּ֔רֶשׁ וְשֵׁ֥ם אָחִ֖יו שָׁ֑רֶשׁ וּבָנָ֖יו אוּלָ֥ם וָרָֽקֶם: וּבְנֵ֥י אוּלָ֖ם בְּדָ֑ן אֵ֚לֶּה

יז בְּנֵ֣י גִלְעָ֔ד בֶּן־מָכִ֖יר בֶּן־מְנַשֶּֽׁה: וַאֲחֹתוֹ֙ הַמֹּלֶ֔כֶת יָלְדָה֙ אֶת־אִישְׁה֔וֹד

יח וְאֶת־אֲבִיעֶ֖זֶר וְאֶת־מַחְלָֽה: וַיִּֽהְי֞וּ בְּנֵ֣י שְׁמִידָ֗ע אַחְיָ֥ן וָשֶׁ֖כֶם וְלִקְחִ֥י

יט

7:2. Besides the descendants of Uzzi, whose number is given in v. 4.

7:3. Izrahiah and his four sons (*Metzudos*).

7:4. This is why Uzzi's descendants so outnumbered those of his brothers.

7:12. Identified with Benjamin's grandson Iri of v. 7 (*Radak*).

Aher is Dan son of Jacob (see *Genesis* 46:23), who is otherwise not mentioned in these genealogical listings (*Malbim*).

7:13. Dan and Naphtali were sons of Bilhah, but the genealogy of Dan is not recorded here. Nor is Zebulun even mentioned in the lists.

7:14. Asriel was a great-grandson of Manasseh (see

Kedesh in Galilee with its open areas, Hammon with its open areas and Kiriathaim with its open areas.

⁶² The remaining sons of Merari, from the tribe of Zebulun: Rimmono with its open areas and Tabor with its open areas. ⁶³ And on the bank of the Jordan by Jericho east of the Jordan, from the tribe of Reuben: Bezer in the wilderness with its open areas, Jahzah with its open areas, ⁶⁴ Kedemoth with its open areas and Mephaath with its open areas. ⁶⁵ And from the tribe of Gad: Ramoth in Gilead with its open areas, Mahanaim with its open areas, ⁶⁶ Heshbon with its open areas and Jazer with its open areas.

7

Issachar

¹ The sons of Issachar: Tola, Puah, Jashub and Shimrom — four [in all]. ² The sons of Tola: Uzzi, Rephaiah, Jeriel, Jahmai, Ibsam and Shemuel — heads of their fathers' family, of Tola, mighty warriors throughout their generations — their number in the days of David was twenty-two thousand, six hundred. *

³ The sons of Uzzi: Izrahiah. The sons of Izrahiah: Michael, Obadiah, Joel and Isshiah — all five of them leaders. * ⁴ Among them, among their descendants, according to their fathers' families, were troops of an army for battle, thirty-six thousand men, for they had many wives and children. *

⁵ Their brothers, among all the families of Issachar, were mighty warriors, eighty-seven thousand; all had their genealogical lists.

Benjamin

⁶ Of Benjamin: Bela, Becher and Jediael — three [in all]. ⁷ The sons of Bela: Ezbon, Uzzi, Uzziel, Jerimoth and Iri — five [in all]; they were heads of their fathers' families, mighty warriors. Their genealogical lists showed twenty-two thousand, thirty-four.

⁸ The sons of Becher: Zemirah, Joash, Eliezer, Elioenai, Omri, Jerimoth, Abijah, Anathoth and Alameth. All these were the sons of Becher. ⁹ According to their genealogical lists of their descendants, there were twenty thousand, two hundred heads of fathers' families, mighty warriors.

¹⁰ The sons of Jediael: Bilhan. The sons of Bilhan: Jeush, Benjamin, Ehud, Chenaanah, Zethan, Tharshish and Ahishahar. ¹¹ All these were the sons of Jediael, by the heads of their fathers' [families], mighty warriors: seventeen thousand, two hundred soldiers for battle.

¹² Shuppim and Huppim were the sons of Ir. *

Naphtali

The other half of Manasseh

Hushim the sons of Aher. *

¹³ The sons of Naphtali: Jahziel, Guni, Jezer and Shallum; the sons of Bilhah. *

¹⁴ The descendants of Manasseh: Asriel, * whom [Gilead's wife] bore. His Aramean concubine bore Machir, the father of Gilead. ¹⁵ Machir took a wife [from the family] of Huppim and Shuppim, whose sister's name was Maacah. *

The name of a second descendant [of Manasseh] was Zelophehad. Zelophehad had [only] daughters. ¹⁶ Maacah, Machir's wife, bore a son, whom she called Peresh, and his brother's name was Sheresh. His sons were Ulam and Rakem. ¹⁷ The sons of Ulam: Bedan. These were the sons of Gilead son of Machir, son of Manasseh.

¹⁸ His sister, the governor, * bore Ish-hod, Abiezer and Mahlah.

¹⁹ The sons of Shemida * were: Ahian, Shechem, Likhi and Aniam.

Numbers 26:29-31). The "concubine" was Manasseh's.
7:15. Machir married Maacah, who was a sister of Shuppim (see next verse).
7:18. Gilead's sister ruled a part of the land of Gilead at

one time (*Radak*).
7:19. Shemida was another of Gilead's sons (*Numbers* 26:30-32).

כ וַאֲנִיעָם: וּבְנֵי אֶפְרַיִם שׁוּתָלַח וּבֶרֶד בְּנוֹ וְתַחַת בְּנוֹ וְאֶלְעָדָה

כא בְּנוֹ וְתַחַת בְּנוֹ: וְזָבָד בְּנוֹ וְשׁוּתֶלַח בְּנוֹ וְעֵזֶר וְאֶלְעָד וַהֲרָגוּם אַנְשֵׁי־גַת

כב הַנּוֹלָדִים בָּאָרֶץ כִּי יָרְדוּ לָקַחַת אֶת־מִקְנֵיהֶם: וַיִּתְאַבֵּל אֶפְרַיִם אֲבִיהֶם

כג יָמִים רַבִּים וַיָּבֹאוּ אֶחָיו לְנַחֲמוֹ: וַיָּבֹא אֶל־אִשְׁתּוֹ וַתַּהַר וַתֵּלֶד בֵּן וַיִּקְרָא

כד אֶת־שְׁמוֹ בְּרִיעָה כִּי בְרָעָה הָיְתָה בְּבֵיתוֹ: וּבִתּוֹ שֶׁאֱרָה וַתִּבֶן אֶת־

כה בֵּית־חוֹרוֹן הַתַּחְתּוֹן וְאֶת־הָעֶלְיוֹן וְאֵת אֻזֵּן שֶׁאֱרָה: וְרֶפַח בְּנוֹ וְרֶשֶׁף

כו-כז וְתֶלַח בְּנוֹ וְתַחַן בְּנוֹ: לַעְדָּן בְּנוֹ עַמִּיהוּד בְּנוֹ אֱלִישָׁמָע בְּנוֹ: נוֹן בְּנוֹ יְהוֹשֻׁעַ

כח בְּנוֹ:   וַאֲחֻזָּתָם וּמֹשְׁבוֹתָם בֵּית־אֵל וּבְנֹתֶיהָ וְלַמִּזְרָח נַעֲרָן

כט וְלַמַּעֲרָב גֶּזֶר וּבְנֹתֶיהָ וּשְׁכֶם וּבְנֹתֶיהָ עַד־עַיָּה וּבְנֹתֶיהָ: וְעַל־יְדֵי בְנֵי־

מְנַשֶּׁה בֵּית־שְׁאָן וּבְנֹתֶיהָ תַּעְנַךְ וּבְנֹתֶיהָ מְגִדּוֹ וּבְנוֹתֶיהָ דּוֹר וּבְנוֹתֶיהָ

ל בְּאֵלֶּה יָשְׁבוּ בְּנֵי יוֹסֵף בֶּן־יִשְׂרָאֵל: בְּנֵי אָשֵׁר יִמְנָה וְיִשְׁוָה

לא וְיִשְׁוִי וּבְרִיעָה וְשֶׂרַח אֲחוֹתָם: וּבְנֵי בְרִיעָה חֶבֶר וּמַלְכִּיאֵל הוּא אֲבִי

לב °בִרְזוֹת [°בִרְזָיִת ק]: וְחֶבֶר הוֹלִיד אֶת־יַפְלֵט וְאֶת־שׁוֹמֵר וְאֶת־חוֹתָם

לג-לד וְאֵת שׁוּעָא אֲחוֹתָם: וּבְנֵי יַפְלֵט פָּסַךְ וּבִמְהָל וְעַשְׂוָת אֵלֶּה בְּנֵי יַפְלֵט: וּבְנֵי

לה שָׁמֶר אֲחִי °ורוהגה יחבה [°וְרָהְגָּה וְחֻבָּה ק] וַאֲרָם: וּבֶן־הֵלֶם אָחִיו

לו צוֹפַח וְיִמְנָע וְשֵׁלֶשׁ וְעָמָל: בְּנֵי צוֹפַח סוּחַ וְחַרְנֶפֶר וְשׁוּעָל וּבֵרִי וְיִמְרָה:

לז-לח בֶּצֶר וָהוֹד וְשַׁמָּא וְשִׁלְשָׁה וְיִתְרָן וּבְאֵרָא: וּבְנֵי יֶתֶר יְפֻנֶּה וּפִסְפָּה וַאֲרָא:

לט-מ וּבְנֵי עֻלָּא אָרַח וְחַנִּיאֵל וְרִצְיָא: כָּל־אֵלֶּה בְנֵי־אָשֵׁר רָאשֵׁי בֵית־הָאָבוֹת

בְּרוּרִים גִּבּוֹרֵי חֲיָלִים רָאשֵׁי הַנְּשִׂיאִים וְהִתְיַחְשָׂם בַּצָּבָא בַּמִּלְחָמָה

מִסְפָּרָם אֲנָשִׁים עֶשְׂרִים וְשִׁשָּׁה אָלֶף:

ח

א-ב וּבִנְיָמִן הוֹלִיד אֶת־בֶּלַע בְּכֹרוֹ אַשְׁבֵּל הַשֵּׁנִי וְאַחְרַח הַשְּׁלִישִׁי: נוֹחָה

ג-ד הָרְבִיעִי וְרָפָא הַחֲמִישִׁי: וַיִּהְיוּ בָנִים לְבָלַע אַדָּר וְגֵרָא וַאֲבִיהוּד: וַאֲבִישׁוּעַ

ה-ו וְנַעֲמָן וַאֲחוֹחַ: וְגֵרָא וּשְׁפוּפָן וְחוּרָם: וְאֵלֶּה בְּנֵי אֵחוּד אֵלֶּה הֵם רָאשֵׁי

ז אָבוֹת לְיוֹשְׁבֵי גֶבַע וַיַּגְלוּם אֶל־מָנָחַת: וְנַעֲמָן וַאֲחִיָּה וְגֵרָא הוּא הֶגְלָם

ח וְהוֹלִיד אֶת־עֻזָּא וְאֶת־אֲחִיחֻד: וְשַׁחֲרַיִם הוֹלִיד בִּשְׂדֵה מוֹאָב מִן־שִׁלְחוֹ

ט אֹתָם חוּשִׁים וְאֶת־בַּעֲרָא נָשָׁיו: וַיּוֹלֶד מִן־חֹדֶשׁ אִשְׁתּוֹ אֶת־יוֹבָב וְאֶת־

י צִבְיָא וְאֶת־מֵישָׁא וְאֶת־מַלְכָּם: וְאֶת־יְעוּץ וְאֶת־שָׂכְיָה וְאֶת־מִרְמָה אֵלֶּה

יא-יב בָנָיו רָאשֵׁי אָבוֹת: וּמֵחֻשִׁים הוֹלִיד אֶת־אֲבִיטוּב וְאֶת־אֶלְפָּעַל: וּבְנֵי

יג אֶלְפַּעַל עֵבֶר וּמִשְׁעָם וָשָׁמֶד הוּא בָּנָה אֶת־אוֹנוֹ וְאֶת־לֹד וּבְנֹתֶיהָ: וּבְרִעָה

וָשֶׁמַע הֵמָּה רָאשֵׁי הָאָבוֹת לְיוֹשְׁבֵי אַיָּלוֹן הֵמָּה הִבְרִיחוּ אֶת־יוֹשְׁבֵי גַת:

7:20. Shuthelah, Bered and Tahath were sons of Ephraim. Eladah, Tahath, Zabad, etc. were sons of Bered (*Radak*).

7:21. During the Egyptian exile, large numbers of Ephraim's grandchildren escaped to the Land of Israel. They raided the area of Gath, where they were vanquished (*Pirkei d'Rabbi Eliezer*).

7:24. Beriah's (*Metzudos*).

7:25. They were Rephah's sons; Tahan was Telah's; and so on.

7:34. The Shomer of v. 32. Helem is identified with Hotham of v. 32 (*Vilna Gaon*).

7:38. To be identified with Ithran of v. 37 (*Metzudos*).

Ephraim   20 The sons of Ephraim: Shuthelah, his son Bered and his son Tahath; * Eleadah was his son, Tahath was his son, 21 Zabad was his son, Shuthelah was his son, as well as Ezer and Elead. The men of Gath, who were born in the Land, killed them, * because they had come down to take away their flocks. 22 Ephraim their father mourned [them] for many days, though his brothers came to comfort him. 23 He consorted with his wife, and she conceived and bore a son. He called his name Beriah (With Misfortune), because she was in his house at a time of misfortune.

24 His* daughter was Sheerah. She built Lower and Upper Beth-horon and Uzzen-sheerah.

25 Rephah was his son; Resheph and Telah were his* sons; Tahan was his son; 26 Ladan was his son; Ammihud was his son; Elishama was his son; 27 Non was his son; Joshua was his son.

28 Their homeland and dwelling places were: Beth-el and its towns, Naaran to the east, Gezer to the west and its towns, Shechem and its towns, up to Aiah and its towns — 29 adjacent to the children of Manasseh's [cities]: Beth-shean and its towns, Taanach and its towns, Megiddo and its towns and Dor and its towns. The children of Joseph son of Israel settled in them.

Asher   30 The sons of Asher: Imnah, Ishvah, Ishvi and Beriah, and Serah their sister.

31 The sons of Beriah: Heber and Malchiel, who was the founder of Birzaith.

32 Heber begot Japhlet, Shomer and Hotham, and Shua their sister. 33 The sons of Japhlet: Pasach, Bimhal and Asvath. These were the children of Japhlet. 34 The sons of Shamer:* Ahi, Rohgah, Hubbah and Aram. 35 The sons of his brother Helem: Zophah, Imna, Shelesh and Amal. 36 The sons of Zophah: Suah, Harnepher, Shual, Beri, Imrah, 37 Bezer, Hod, Shamma, Shilshah, Ithran and Beera. 38 The sons of Jether:* Jephunneh, Pispah and Ara. 39 The sons of Ulla:* Arah, Hanniel and Rizia.

40 All these were the children of Asher, heads of their fathers' families, select mighty warriors, chiefs of the princes. According to their genealogical lists, the number of soldiers for battle was twenty-six thousand.

8

Genealogy
of King Saul

1 **B**enjamin begot Bela his firstborn, Ashbel the second, Aharah the third, 2 Nohah the fourth and Rapha the fifth. 3 The sons of Bela were: Addar, Gera and Abihud; 4 Abishua,* Naaman, Ahoah, 5 Gera, Shephuphan and Huram. 6 Those were the sons of Ehud;* those were the heads of families who drove out the inhabitants of Geba to Manahath — 7 Naaman, Ahijah,* and Gera drove them out. He begot Uzza and Ahihud.

8 Shaharaim* begot children in the field of Moab, after he had divorced Hushim and Baara, his wives. 9 By his wife Hodesh he begot: Jobab, Zibia, Mesha, Malcam, 10 Jeuz, Sachiah and Mirmah. These were his sons, heads of families. 11 By Hushim he begot Abitub and Elpaal. 12 The sons of Elpaal: Eber; Misham; Shamed, who built Ono and Lod and their towns; 13 Beriah and Shema, who were heads of the families of the inhabitants of Aijalon, who drove away the inhabitants of Gath.

7:39. Apparently a descendant of Jether (Metzudos).

8:4. These were all sons of Abihud, as explained in v. 6 (Vilna Gaon).

8:6. To be identified with Abihud of v. 3 (Vilna Gaon).

8:7. Called Ahoah in v. 4 (Metzudos).

8:8. One of Benjamin's descendants (Radak), perhaps a son of Ahihud. After divorcing his wives, he remarried them and had children in Moab (Targum, Vilna Gaon).

יד-טו וְאַחְיוֹ שָׁשָׁק וִירֵמוֹת: וּזְבַדְיָה וַעֲרָד וָעָדֶר: וּמִיכָאֵל וְיִשְׁפָּה וְיוֹחָא בְּנֵי

טז-יח בְרִיעָה: וּזְבַדְיָה וּמְשֻׁלָּם וְחִזְקִי וָחָבֶר: וְיִשְׁמְרַי וְיִזְלִיאָה וְיוֹבָב בְּנֵי אֶלְפָּעַל:

יט-כא וְיָקִים וְזִכְרִי וְזַבְדִּי: וֶאֱלִיעֵנַי וְצִלְּתַי וֶאֱלִיאֵל: וַעֲדָיָה וּבְרָאיָה וְשִׁמְרָת בְּנֵי

כב-כד שִׁמְעִי: וְיִשְׁפָּן וָעֵבֶר וֶאֱלִיאֵל: וְעַבְדּוֹן וְזִכְרִי וְחָנָן: חֲנַנְיָה וְעֵילָם וְעַנְתֹתִיָּה:

כה-כו וְיִפְדְיָה °וּפְנוּאֵל [°וּפְנִיאֵל ק] בְּנֵי שָׁשָׁק: וְשַׁמְשְׁרַי וּשְׁחַרְיָה

כז-כח וַעֲתַלְיָה: וְיַעֲרֶשְׁיָה וְאֵלִיָּה וְזִכְרִי בְּנֵי יְרֹחָם: אֵלֶּה רָאשֵׁי אָבוֹת לְתֹלְדוֹתָם

כט רָאשִׁים אֵלֶּה יָשְׁבוּ בִירוּשָׁלָם: וּבְגִבְעוֹן יָשְׁבוּ אֲבִי גִבְעוֹן וְשֵׁם

ל-לא אִשְׁתּוֹ מַעֲכָה: וּבְנוֹ הַבְּכוֹר עַבְדּוֹן וְצוּר וְקִישׁ וּבַעַל וְנָדָב: וּגְדוֹר וְאַחְיוֹ

לב וָזָכֶר: וּמִקְלוֹת הוֹלִיד אֶת־שִׁמְאָה וְאַף־הֵמָּה נֶגֶד אֲחֵיהֶם יָשְׁבוּ בִירוּשָׁלַם

לג עִם־אֲחֵיהֶם: וְנֵר הוֹלִיד אֶת־קִישׁ וְקִישׁ הוֹלִיד אֶת־שָׁאוּל

וְשָׁאוּל הוֹלִיד אֶת־יְהוֹנָתָן וְאֶת־מַלְכִּי־שׁוּעַ וְאֶת־אֲבִינָדָב וְאֶת־אֶשְׁבָּעַל:

לד-לה וּבֶן־יְהוֹנָתָן מְרִיב בָּעַל וּמְרִיב בַּעַל הוֹלִיד אֶת־מִיכָה: וּבְנֵי מִיכָה פִּיתוֹן

לו וָמֶלֶךְ וְתַארֵעַ וְאָחָז: וְאָחָז הוֹלִיד אֶת־יְהוֹעַדָּה וִיהוֹעַדָּה הוֹלִיד אֶת־

לז עָלֶמֶת וְאֶת־עַזְמָוֶת וְאֶת־זִמְרִי וְזִמְרִי הוֹלִיד אֶת־מוֹצָא: וּמוֹצָא הוֹלִיד

לח אֶת־בִּנְעָא רָפָה בְנוֹ אֶלְעָשָׂה בְנוֹ אָצֵל בְּנוֹ: וּלְאָצֵל שִׁשָּׁה בָנִים וְאֵלֶּה

שְׁמוֹתָם עַזְרִיקָם ׀ בֹּכְרוּ וְיִשְׁמָעֵאל וּשְׁעַרְיָה וְעֹבַדְיָה וְחָנָן כָּל־אֵלֶּה בְּנֵי

לט-מ אָצֵל: וּבְנֵי עֵשֶׁק אָחִיו אוּלָם בְּכֹרוֹ יְעוּשׁ הַשֵּׁנִי וֶאֱלִיפֶלֶט הַשְּׁלִשִׁי: וַיִּהְיוּ

בְנֵי־אוּלָם אֲנָשִׁים גִּבּוֹרֵי־חַיִל דֹּרְכֵי קֶשֶׁת וּמַרְבִּים בָּנִים וּבְנֵי בָנִים מֵאָה

ט א וַחֲמִשִּׁים כָּל־אֵלֶּה מִבְּנֵי בִנְיָמִן: וְכָל־יִשְׂרָאֵל הִתְיַחְשׂוּ וְהִנָּם

ב כְּתוּבִים עַל־סֵפֶר מַלְכֵי יִשְׂרָאֵל וִיהוּדָה הָגְלוּ לְבָבֶל בְּמַעֲלָם: וְהַיּוֹשְׁבִים

הָרִאשֹׁנִים אֲשֶׁר בַּאֲחֻזָּתָם בְּעָרֵיהֶם יִשְׂרָאֵל הַכֹּהֲנִים הַלְוִיִּם וְהַנְּתִינִים:

ג וּבִירוּשָׁלַם יָשְׁבוּ מִן־בְּנֵי יְהוּדָה וּמִן־בְּנֵי בִנְיָמִן וּמִן־בְּנֵי אֶפְרַיִם וּמְנַשֶּׁה:

ד עוּתַי בֶּן־עַמִּיהוּד בֶּן־עָמְרִי בֶּן־אִמְרִי בֶן־°בנימן [°בָּנִי מִן ק] בְּנֵי־

ה-ו פֶרֶץ בֶּן־יְהוּדָה: וּמִן־הַשִּׁילוֹנִי עֲשָׂיָה הַבְּכוֹר וּבָנָיו: וּמִן־בְּנֵי זֶרַח יְעוּאֵל

ז וַאֲחֵיהֶם שֵׁשׁ־מֵאוֹת וְתִשְׁעִים: וּמִן־בְּנֵי בִּנְיָמִן סַלּוּא בֶּן־מְשֻׁלָּם בֶּן־

ח הוֹדַוְיָה בֶּן־הַסְּנֻאָה: וְיִבְנְיָה בֶּן־יְרֹחָם וְאֵלָה בֶן־עֻזִּי בֶּן־מִכְרִי וּמְשֻׁלָּם בֶּן־

ט שְׁפַטְיָה בֶּן־רְעוּאֵל בֶּן־יִבְנִיָּה: וַאֲחֵיהֶם לְתֹלְדוֹתָם תְּשַׁע מֵאוֹת וַחֲמִשִּׁים

י וְשִׁשָּׁה כָּל־אֵלֶּה אֲנָשִׁים רָאשֵׁי אָבוֹת לְבֵית אֲבֹתֵיהֶם: וּמִן־

יא הַכֹּהֲנִים יְדַעְיָה וִיהוֹיָרִיב וְיָכִין: וַעֲזַרְיָה בֶן־חִלְקִיָּה בֶּן־מְשֻׁלָּם בֶּן־צָדוֹק

יב בֶּן־מְרָיוֹת בֶּן־אֲחִיטוּב נְגִיד בֵּית הָאֱלֹהִים: וַעֲדָיָה בֶּן־יְרֹחָם

בֶּן־פַּשְׁחוּר בֶּן־מַלְכִּיָּה וּמַעְשַׂי בֶּן־עֲדִיאֵל בֶּן־יַחְזֵרָה בֶּן־מְשֻׁלָּם בֶּן־

8:21. To be identified with Shema of v. 13 (Vilna Gaon).

8:27. To be identified with Jeremoth of v. 14 (Vilna Gaon).

8:29. In 9:35, he is identified as Jeiel (Radak).

8:33. More commonly known as Ish Bosheth.

8:34. More commonly known as Mephibosheth.

9:1. This chapter explains why only some of the tribal genealogies were given at length in the preceding chap-

¹⁴ Ahio, Shashak, Jeremoth, ¹⁵ Zebadiah, Arad, Eder, ¹⁶ Michael, Ispah and Joha were the sons of Beriah. ¹⁷ Zebadiah, Meshullam, Hizki, Heber, ¹⁸ Ishmerai, Izliah and Jobab were [also] the sons of Elpaal.

¹⁹ Jakim, Zichri, Zabdi, ²⁰ Elienai, Zillethai, Eliel, ²¹ Adaiah, Beraiah and Shimrath were the sons of Shimei. *

²² Ishpan, Eber, Eliel, ²³ Abdon, Zichri, Hanan, ²⁴ Hananiah, Elam, Antotiah, ²⁵ Iphdeiah and Penuel were the sons of Shashak.

²⁶ Shamsherai, Shehariah, Athaliah, ²⁷ Jaaresiah, Eliah and Zichri were the sons of Jeroham. *

²⁸ These were heads of families, leaders, by their generations. They settled in Jerusalem.

²⁹ And in Gibeon settled the founder of Gibeon; * his wife's name was Maacah. ³⁰ His firstborn son was Abdon, then Zur, Kish, Baal, Nadab, ³¹ Gedor, Ahio, Zecher ³² and Mikloth, [who] begot Shimeah. They also settled across from their kinsmen in Jerusalem, with their kinsmen. ³³ Ner begot Kish. Kish begot Saul. Saul begot Jonathan, Malchi-shua, Abinadab and Eshbaal. * ³⁴ The son of Jonathan was Merib-baal; * Merib-baal begot Micah. ³⁵ The sons of Micah: Pithon, Melech, Tarea and Ahaz. ³⁶ Ahaz begot Jehoaddah; Jehoaddah begot Alemeth, Azmaveth and Zimri. Zimri begot Moza; ³⁷ Moza begot Binea. Raphah was his son; Eleasah was his son; Azel was his son. ³⁸ Azel had six sons, and these were their names: Azrikam, Bocheru, Ishmael, Sheariah, Obadiah and Hanan. All these were the sons of Azel.

³⁹ The sons of his brother Eshek: Ulam his firstborn, Jehush the second, and Eliphelet the third. ⁴⁰ The sons of Ulam were men who were mighty warriors, archers, and had many sons and grandsons — a hundred and fifty.

All these were among the sons of Benjamin.

The first royal family

9

THE RETURNING EXILES
9:1-38

¹ All of Israel registered their genealogies. They are recorded in the Book of the Kings of Israel. Judah was exiled to Babylonia for their treachery. * ² The first inhabitants to settle in [the lands of] their possession, * in their cities, were the Israelites, the Kohanim, the Levites and the Nethinim.

³ In Jerusalem there settled some of the children of Judah, some of the children of Benjamin and some of the children of Ephraim and Manasseh: ⁴ Uthai son of Ammihud, son of Omri, son of Imri, son of Bani, of the sons of Perez son of Judah. ⁵ Of the Shilonites: * Asaiah the firstborn and his sons. ⁶ Of the sons of Zerah: Jeuel, and six hundred ninety of their brethren.

⁷ Of the sons of Benjamin: Sallu son of Meshullam, son of Hodaviah, son of Hassenuah, ⁸ and Ibneiah son of Jeroham, and Elah son of Uzzi, son of Michri, and Meshullam son of Shephathiah, son of Reuel, son of Ibneiah, ⁹ and nine hundred fifty-six of their kinsmen according to their generations. All these men were heads of the family in their fathers' families.

¹⁰ Of the Kohanim: Jedaiah, Jehoiarib, Jachin, ¹¹ Azariah son of Hilkiah, son of Meshullam, son of Zadok, son of Meraioth, son of Ahitub, the supervisor of the Temple of God; ¹² Adaiah son of Jeroham, son of Pashur, son of Malchijah; and Maasiai son of Adiel, son of Jahzerah, son of Meshullam, son of

---

ters. They were the ones who lived among the people of Judah, and returned with them from the Babylonian exile. The genealogy of the other people, as this verse relates, can be found in the Book of the Chronicles of Kings of Israel, which was still extant in Ezra's days (*Ramban*).

9:2. After the return from Babylonian exile. For the *Nethinim*, see *Joshua* Ch. 9.

9:5. The descendants of Shelah.

יג מְשֻׁלֵּמִ֣ית בֶּן־אֹמֵ֑ר: וַאֲחֵיהֶ֡ם רָאשִׁים֙ לְבֵ֣ית אֲבוֹתָ֔ם אֶ֕לֶף וּשְׁבַ֥ע מֵא֖וֹת

יד וְשִׁשִּׁ֑ים גִּבּ֣וֹרֵי חֵ֔יל מְלֶ֖אכֶת עֲבוֹדַ֣ת בֵּית־הָאֱלֹהִֽים: וּמִן־הַלְוִיִּ֖ם שְׁמַֽעְיָ֥ה

טו בֶן־חַשּׁ֤וּב בֶּן־עַזְרִיקָם֙ בֶּן־חֲשַׁבְיָ֔ה מִן־בְּנֵ֖י מְרָרִ֑י: וּבַקְבַּקַּ֥ר חֶ֖רֶשׁ וְגָלָ֛ל

טז וּמַתַּנְיָ֥ה בֶן־מִיכָ֖א בֶּן־זִכְרִ֣י בֶּן־אָסָ֑ף: וְעֹבַדְיָ֥ה בֶּן־שְׁמַֽעְיָ֛ה בֶּן־גָּלָ֖ל בֶּן־

יז יְדוּת֑וּן וּבֶרֶכְיָ֧ה בֶן־אָסָ֛א בֶּן־אֶלְקָנָ֖ה הַיּוֹשֵׁ֥ב בְּחַצְרֵ֖י נְטוֹפָתִֽי: וְהַשֹּׁעֲרִים֙

יח שַׁלּ֤וּם וְעַקּוּב֙ וְטַלְמֹ֣ן וַאֲחִימָ֔ן וַאֲחִיהֶ֖ם שַׁלּ֣וּם הָרֹ֑אשׁ: וְעַד־הֵ֖נָּה בְּשַׁ֣עַר

יט הַמֶּ֣לֶךְ מִזְרָ֔חָה הֵ֖מָּה הַשֹּֽׁעֲרִ֑ים לְמַחֲנ֖וֹת בְּנֵ֣י לֵוִֽי: וְשַׁלּ֣וּם בֶּן־ק֠וֹרֵא בֶּן־

אֶבְיָסָ֨ף בֶּן־קֹ֜רַח וְאֶחָ֣יו לְבֵית־אָבִ֗יו הַקָּרְחִים֙ עַ֚ל מְלֶ֣אכֶת הָעֲבוֹדָ֔ה שֹׁמְרֵ֥י

כ הַסִּפִּ֖ים לָאֹ֑הֶל וַאֲבֹתֵיהֶ֛ם עַל־מַחֲנֵ֥ה יְהֹוָ֖ה שֹׁמְרֵ֥י הַמָּבֽוֹא: וּפִֽינְחָ֣ס בֶּן־

כא אֶלְעָזָ֗ר נָגִ֨יד הָיָ֧ה עֲלֵיהֶ֛ם לְפָנִ֖ים יְהֹוָ֣ה ׀ עִמּֽוֹ: זְכַרְיָה֙ בֶּ֣ן מְשֶֽׁלֶמְיָ֔ה שֹׁעֵ֕ר

כב פֶּ֖תַח לְאֹ֣הֶל מוֹעֵ֑ד כֻּלָּ֤ם הַבְּרוּרִים֙ לְשֹׁ֣עֲרִ֔ים בַּסִּפִּ֖ים מָאתַ֣יִם וּשְׁנֵ֣ים עָשָׂ֑ר

הֵ֥מָּה בְחַצְרֵיהֶ֖ם הִתְיַחְשָׂ֑ם הֵ֣מָּה יִסַּ֥ד דָּוִ֛יד וּשְׁמוּאֵ֥ל הָרֹאֶ֖ה בֶּאֱמוּנָתָֽם:

כג־כד וְהֵ֨ם וּבְנֵיהֶ֜ם עַל־הַשְּׁעָרִ֧ים לְבֵית־יְהֹוָ֛ה לְבֵ֥ית הָאֹ֖הֶל לְמִשְׁמָרֽוֹת: לְאַרְבַּ֣ע

כה רוּח֗וֹת יִהְי֣וּ הַשֹּֽׁעֲרִ֔ים מִזְרָ֥ח יָ֖מָּה צָפ֣וֹנָה וָנֶֽגְבָּה: וַאֲחֵיהֶ֥ם בְּחַצְרֵיהֶ֖ם לָב֑וֹא

כו לְשִׁבְעַ֥ת הַיָּמִ֖ים מֵעֵ֣ת אֶל־עֵ֑ת עִם־אֵֽלֶּה: כִּ֣י בֶאֱמוּנָ֞ה הֵ֗מָּה אַרְבַּ֨עַת֙ גִּבֹּרֵ֣י

הַשֹּׁעֲרִ֔ים הֵ֖ם הַלְוִיִּ֑ם וְהָיוּ֙ עַל־הַלְּשָׁכ֔וֹת וְעַ֥ל הָאֹצְר֖וֹת בֵּ֥ית הָאֱלֹהִֽים:

כז וּסְבִיב֥וֹת בֵּית־הָאֱלֹהִ֖ים יָלִ֑ינוּ כִּֽי־עֲלֵיהֶ֣ם מִשְׁמֶ֔רֶת וְהֵ֥ם עַל־הַמַּפְתֵּ֖חַ

כח וְלַבֹּ֥קֶר לַבֹּֽקֶר: וּמֵהֶ֕ם עַל־כְּלֵ֖י הָעֲבוֹדָ֑ה כִּֽי־בְמִסְפָּ֥ר יְבִיא֖וּם וּבְמִסְפָּ֥ר

כט יוֹצִיא֑וּם: וּמֵהֶ֗ם מְמֻנִּים֙ עַל־הַכֵּלִ֔ים וְעַ֖ל כָּל־כְּלֵ֣י הַקֹּ֑דֶשׁ וְעַל־הַסֹּ֙לֶת֙ וְהַיַּ֣יִן

ל וְהַשֶּׁ֔מֶן וְהַלְּבוֹנָ֖ה וְהַבְּשָׂמִֽים: וּמִן־בְּנֵי֙ הַכֹּ֣הֲנִ֔ים רֹקְחֵ֥י הַמִּרְקַ֖חַת לַבְּשָׂמִֽים:

לא וּמַתִּתְיָה֙ מִן־הַלְוִיִּ֔ם ה֥וּא הַבְּכ֖וֹר לְשַׁלֻּ֣ם הַקָּרְחִ֑י בֶּאֱמוּנָ֕ה עַ֖ל מַעֲשֵׂ֥ה

לב הַחֲבִתִּֽים: וּמִן־בְּנֵ֧י הַקְּהָתִ֛י מִן־אֲחֵיהֶ֖ם עַל־לֶ֣חֶם הַמַּעֲרָ֑כֶת לְהָכִ֖ין שַׁבַּ֥ת

לג שַׁבָּֽת: וְאֵ֣לֶּה הַמְשֹׁרְרִ֗ים רָאשֵׁ֤י אָבוֹת֙ לַלְוִיִּ֔ם בַּלְּשָׁכֹ֖ת

לד °פְּטִירִ֑ים [°פְּטוּרִ֖ים ק] כִּֽי־יוֹמָ֣ם וָלַ֔יְלָה עֲלֵיהֶ֖ם בַּמְּלָאכָֽה: אֵ֣לֶּה רָאשֵׁ֤י

הָאָבוֹת֙ לַלְוִיִּ֔ם לְתֹֽלְדוֹתָ֖ם רָאשִׁ֑ים אֵ֖לֶּה יָשְׁב֥וּ בִירוּשָׁלָֽ͏ִם:

לה וּבְגִבְע֛וֹן יָשְׁב֥וּ אֲבִֽי־גִבְע֖וֹן °יְעוּאֵ֑ל [°יְעִיאֵ֑ל ק] וְשֵׁ֥ם אִשְׁתּ֖וֹ מַעֲכָֽה:

לו־לז וּבְנ֤וֹ הַבְּכוֹר֙ עַבְדּ֔וֹן וְצ֥וּר וְקִ֖ישׁ וּבַ֣עַל וְנֵ֣ר וְנָדָֽב: וּגְד֣וֹר וְאַחְי֗וֹ וּזְכַרְיָ֖ה

לח וּמִקְלֽוֹת: וּמִקְל֖וֹת הוֹלִ֣יד אֶת־שִׁמְאָ֑ם וְאַף־הֵ֗ם נֶ֧גֶד אֲחֵיהֶ֛ם יָשְׁב֥וּ

לט בִירֽוּשָׁלַ֖͏ִם עִם־אֲחֵיהֶֽם: וְנֵר֙ הוֹלִ֣יד אֶת־קִ֔ישׁ וְקִ֖ישׁ הוֹלִ֣יד

אֶת־שָׁא֑וּל וְשָׁא֗וּל הוֹלִ֤יד אֶת־יְהֽוֹנָתָן֙ וְאֶת־מַלְכִּי־שׁ֔וּעַ וְאֶת־אֲבִֽינָדָ֖ב

מ וְאֶת־אֶשְׁבָּֽעַל: וּבֶן־יְהוֹנָתָ֖ן מְרִ֣יב בָּ֑עַל וּמְרִ֣יב בַּ֔עַל הוֹלִ֖יד אֶת־מִיכָֽה:

9:18. This same family had also stood guard at the King's Gate of Solomon's Temple (*Radak*).

9:19. The holiest area, the interior of the Temple building.

9:22. David and Samuel established which Levite families would be assigned to gatekeeping, which to singing, etc. (*Vilna Gaon*).

9:25. When their turn would come.

9:31. See *Leviticus* 6:13-15.

9:32. See ibid. 24:5-9.

Meshillemith son of Immer; [13] and one thousand seven hundred sixty of their kinsmen, heads of their fathers' families, accomplished experts in the work of the service of the Temple of God.

[14] Of the Levites: Shemaiah son of Hasshub, son of Azrikam, son of Hashabiah, of the sons of Merari; [15] Bakbakkar, Heresh, Galal, Mattaniah son of Mica, son of Zichri, son of Asaph; [16] Obadiah son of Shemaiah, son of Galal, son of Jeduthun; and Berechiah son of Asa, son of Elkanah, who dwelled in the villages of the Netophathite.

[17] The gatekeepers: Shallum, Akkub, Talmon, Ahiman and their kinsmen. Shallum was the chief. [18] As before, * at the King's Gate in the east, they were gatekeepers for the Levite camps. [19] Shallum son of Kore, son of Ebiasaph, son of Korah, and his kinsmen of his father's family, the Korahites, were in charge of the work of the service, guarding the doorways of the Tent [of Meeting]; as their fathers had been in charge of the camp of Hashem, * as guards of the entryway. [20] Phinehas son of Elazar had been the supervisor over them in former times, for Hashem was with him. [21] Zechariah son of Meshelemiah was gatekeeper of the entrance of the Tent of Meeting. [22] All those who were chosen to be gatekeepers at the doorways were two hundred twelve [men]. All these were registered by their genealogies in their villages. They were the ones whom David and Samuel the Seer established in their permanent positions. * [23] So they and their children were in charge of the gates of the Temple of Hashem, the house of the Tent [of Meeting], in shifts. [24] The gatekeepers were to be at the four directions — east, west, north and south. [25] Their kinsmen in their villages were [also] to come for seven days, from time to time, * with these. [26] For these Levites, the four principal gatekeepers, were permanently established. They were [also] in charge of the chambers and treasuries of the Temple of God. [27] They slept in the environs of the Temple of God, for they were responsible to guard it, and they were in charge of opening the doors every morning. [28] Some of them were in charge of the ministering vessels, for they would put them in by number and bring them out by number. [29] Some of them were appointed over the [other] vessels, all the articles of the Sanctuary, and of the fine flour, the wine, the oil, the frankincense and the spices. [30] But those who blended the mixture of the spices were from among the Kohanim. [31] Mattithiah, one of the Levites — he was the firstborn of Shallum the Korahite — had the permanent position over the offerings that were made in the pans. * [32] Others of their kinsmen of the sons of the Kohathites were in charge of the bread of array, * to prepare it every Sabbath.

[33] These were the singers, family heads of the Levites, in the Chambers of Peturim, for their work was upon them day and night. * [34] These were the family heads of the Levites, heads over their descendants; they lived in Jerusalem.

[35] Jeiel, the founder of Gibeon, settled in Gibeon. His wife's name was Maacah. [36] His firstborn son was Abdon, then Zur, Kish, Baal, Ner, Nadab, [37] Gedor, Ahio, Zechariah and Mikloth. [38] Mikloth begot Shimeam. They also settled across from their kinsmen in Jerusalem, with their kinsmen.

[39] Ner begot Kish. Kish begot Saul. Saul begot Jonathan, Malchi-shua, Abina-dab and Eshbaal. [40] The son of Jonathan was Merib-baal; Meri-baal begot Micah.

MORE
ABOUT
KING SAUL
9:39-10:14

9:32. I.e., the show-bread.
9:33. Their chamber was called Peturim, which means "exempt ones," because these Levites were excused from

other responsibilities, since their singing duties kept them occupied "day and night" (*Vilna Gaon*).

מא-מב וּבְנֵי מִיכָה פִּיתֹן וָמֶלֶךְ וְתַחְרֵעַ: וְאָחָז הוֹלִיד אֶת־יַעְרָה וְיַעְרָה הוֹלִיד

מג אֶת־עָלֶמֶת וְאֶת־עַזְמָוֶת וְאֶת־זִמְרִי וְזִמְרִי הוֹלִיד אֶת־מוֹצָא: וּמוֹצָא

מד הוֹלִיד אֶת־בִּנְעָא וּרְפָיָה בְנוֹ אֶלְעָשָׂה בְנוֹ אָצֵל בְּנוֹ: וּלְאָצֵל שִׁשָּׁה בָנִים

וְאֵלֶּה שְׁמוֹתָם עַזְרִיקָם ׀ בֹּכְרוּ וְיִשְׁמָעֵאל וּשְׁעַרְיָה וְעֹבַדְיָה וְחָנָן אֵלֶּה

בְּנֵי אָצַל:

י א וּפְלִשְׁתִּים נִלְחֲמוּ בְיִשְׂרָאֵל וַיָּנָס אִישׁ־יִשְׂרָאֵל מִפְּנֵי פְלִשְׁתִּים וַיִּפְּלוּ

ב חֲלָלִים בְּהַר גִּלְבֹּעַ: וַיַּדְבְּקוּ פְלִשְׁתִּים אַחֲרֵי שָׁאוּל וְאַחֲרֵי בָנָיו וַיַּכּוּ

ג פְלִשְׁתִּים אֶת־יוֹנָתָן וְאֶת־אֲבִינָדָב וְאֶת־מַלְכִּי־שׁוּעַ בְּנֵי שָׁאוּל: וַתִּכְבַּד

ד הַמִּלְחָמָה עַל־שָׁאוּל וַיִּמְצָאֻהוּ הַמּוֹרִים בַּקָּשֶׁת וַיָּחֶל מִן־הַיּוֹרִים: וַיֹּאמֶר

שָׁאוּל אֶל־נֹשֵׂא כֵלָיו שְׁלֹף חַרְבְּךָ ׀ וְדָקְרֵנִי בָהּ פֶּן־יָבֹאוּ הָעֲרֵלִים הָאֵלֶּה

וְהִתְעַלְּלוּ־בִי וְלֹא אָבָה נֹשֵׂא כֵלָיו כִּי יָרֵא מְאֹד וַיִּקַּח שָׁאוּל אֶת־הַחֶרֶב

ה וַיִּפֹּל עָלֶיהָ: וַיַּרְא נֹשֵׂא־כֵלָיו כִּי מֵת שָׁאוּל וַיִּפֹּל גַּם־הוּא עַל־הַחֶרֶב

ו-ז וַיָּמֹת: וַיָּמָת שָׁאוּל וּשְׁלֹשֶׁת בָּנָיו וְכָל־בֵּיתוֹ יַחְדָּו מֵתוּ: וַיִּרְאוּ כָּל־אִישׁ

יִשְׂרָאֵל אֲשֶׁר־בָּעֵמֶק כִּי נָסוּ וְכִי־מֵתוּ שָׁאוּל וּבָנָיו וַיַּעַזְבוּ עָרֵיהֶם וַיָּנֻסוּ

ח וַיָּבֹאוּ פְלִשְׁתִּים וַיֵּשְׁבוּ בָּהֶם: וַיְהִי מִמָּחֳרָת וַיָּבֹאוּ פְלִשְׁתִּים

לְפַשֵּׁט אֶת־הַחֲלָלִים וַיִּמְצְאוּ אֶת־שָׁאוּל וְאֶת־בָּנָיו נֹפְלִים בְּהַר גִּלְבֹּעַ:

ט וַיַּפְשִׁיטֻהוּ וַיִּשְׂאוּ אֶת־רֹאשׁוֹ וְאֶת־כֵּלָיו וַיְשַׁלְּחוּ בְאֶרֶץ־פְּלִשְׁתִּים סָבִיב

י לְבַשֵּׂר אֶת־עֲצַבֵּיהֶם וְאֶת־הָעָם: וַיָּשִׂימוּ אֶת־כֵּלָיו בֵּית אֱלֹהֵיהֶם וְאֶת־

יא גֻּלְגָּלְתּוֹ תָקְעוּ בֵּית דָּגוֹן: וַיִּשְׁמְעוּ כֹּל יָבֵישׁ גִּלְעָד אֵת כָּל־

יב אֲשֶׁר־עָשׂוּ פְלִשְׁתִּים לְשָׁאוּל: וַיָּקוּמוּ כָּל־אִישׁ חַיִל וַיִּשְׂאוּ אֶת־גּוּפַת

שָׁאוּל וְאֵת גּוּפֹת בָּנָיו וַיְבִיאוּם יָבֵישָׁה וַיִּקְבְּרוּ אֶת־עַצְמוֹתֵיהֶם תַּחַת

יג הָאֵלָה בְּיָבֵשׁ וַיָּצוּמוּ שִׁבְעַת יָמִים: וַיָּמָת שָׁאוּל בְּמַעֲלוֹ אֲשֶׁר מָעַל

בַּיהוה עַל־דְּבַר יהוה אֲשֶׁר לֹא־שָׁמָר וְגַם־לִשְׁאוֹל בָּאוֹב לִדְרוֹשׁ: וְלֹא־

יד דָרַשׁ בַּיהוה וַיְמִיתֵהוּ וַיַּסֵּב אֶת־הַמְּלוּכָה לְדָוִיד בֶּן־יִשָׁי:

יא א וַיִּקָּבְצוּ כָל־יִשְׂרָאֵל אֶל־דָּוִיד חֶבְרוֹנָה לֵאמֹר הִנֵּה עַצְמְךָ וּבְשָׂרְךָ אֲנָחְנוּ:

ב גַּם־תְּמוֹל גַּם־שִׁלְשׁוֹם גַּם בִּהְיוֹת שָׁאוּל מֶלֶךְ אַתָּה הַמּוֹצִיא וְהַמֵּבִיא

אֶת־יִשְׂרָאֵל וַיֹּאמֶר יהוה אֱלֹהֶיךָ לְךָ אַתָּה תִרְעֶה אֶת־עַמִּי אֶת־יִשְׂרָאֵל

ג וְאַתָּה תִּהְיֶה נָגִיד עַל עַמִּי יִשְׂרָאֵל: וַיָּבֹאוּ כָּל־זִקְנֵי יִשְׂרָאֵל אֶל־הַמֶּלֶךְ

חֶבְרוֹנָה וַיִּכְרֹת לָהֶם דָּוִיד בְּרִית בְּחֶבְרוֹן לִפְנֵי יהוה וַיִּמְשְׁחוּ אֶת־דָּוִיד

ד לְמֶלֶךְ עַל־יִשְׂרָאֵל כִּדְבַר יהוה בְּיַד־שְׁמוּאֵל: וַיֵּלֶךְ דָּוִיד

ה וְכָל־יִשְׂרָאֵל יְרוּשָׁלַ͏ִם הִיא יְבוּס וְשָׁם הַיְבוּסִי יֹשְׁבֵי הָאָרֶץ: וַיֹּאמְרוּ

יֹשְׁבֵי יְבוּס לְדָוִיד לֹא תָבוֹא הֵנָּה וַיִּלְכֹּד דָּוִיד אֶת־מְצֻדַת צִיּוֹן הִיא עִיר

9:43. Binea's; and so on.
10:4. See commentary to I Samuel 31:4.
10:13-14. Saul sinned in the matter of Amalek (I Samuel

Ch. 15), in not waiting for Samuel at Gilgal (ibid. Ch. 13),
and in consulting a necromancer (ibid. Ch. 28).
11:3. David promised that he would not punish the

[41] *The sons of Micah: Pithon, Melech, Taharea* [42] *and Ahaz, [who] begot Jarah. Jarah begot Alemeth, Azmaveth and Zimri. Zimri begot Moza;* [43] *Moza begot Binea. Rephaiah was his* * *son; Eleasah was his son; Azel was his son.* [44] *Azel had six sons, and these were their names: Azrikam, Bocru, Ishmael, Sheariah, Obadiah and Hanan. These were the sons of Azel.*

10

Death of King Saul

[1] *The Philistines battled with Israel. The men of Israel fled from before the Philistines and fell slain upon Mount Gilboa.* [2] *The Philistines then caught up with Saul and with his sons, and the Philistines slew Jonathan, Abinadab and Malchi-shua, Saul's sons.* [3] *The battle then grew fierce against Saul, and the archers found him; he was terrified of the archers.* [4] *Saul said to his armorbearer, "Draw your sword and stab me with it, lest these uncircumcised people come and make sport of me." But his armorbearer did not consent, for he was very frightened, so Saul took the sword and fell upon it.* * [5] *When the armorbearer saw that Saul was dying he, too, fell upon his sword and died.* [6] *So Saul and his three sons died, and his entire household died together.*

[7] *When all the men of Israel who were in the valley saw that they had fled and that Saul and his sons had died, they abandoned their cities and fled, and the Philistines came and settled in them.* [8] *It happened the next day, when the Philistines came to plunder the corpses, and they found [the bodies] of Saul and his sons, fallen on Mount Gilboa.* [9] *They stripped him and they removed his head and his gear, and sent [heralds] all about the land of the Philistines to inform [those in their temple of] their idols and the people.* [10] *They placed his gear in the temple of their gods, and they hung up his skull in Beth-dagon.* [11] *All [the inhabitants of] Yabesh-gilead heard about all that the Philistines had done to Saul,* [12] *and all the daring men arose, and they carried the remains of Saul and the remains of his sons and took them back to Yabesh. They then buried their bones under the terebinth tree in Yabesh, and they fasted seven days.*

[13] *Thus Saul died because of the betrayal by which he betrayed* HASHEM, *because of the command of* HASHEM *that he did not keep, and also for consulting necromancy to seek out,* [14] *and not seeking out* HASHEM, * *so that He caused him to die and He transferred the kingship to David son of Jesse.*

11

KING DAVID
11:1-29:30

[1] *All of Israel gathered together to David in Hebron, saying, "Behold, we are your bone and your flesh.* [2] *Even yesterday and before yesterday, even when Saul was king, you were the one who led Israel out and led them in; and* HASHEM *your God has said of you, 'You shall shepherd My people Israel and you shall be ruler over My people Israel.' "*

[3] *All the elders of Israel came to the king at Hebron, and David sealed a covenant with them* * *in Hebron. They anointed David as king of Israel, in accordance with the word of* HASHEM *through Samuel.*

[4] *David and all of Israel went to Jerusalem, which is Jebus; the Jebusite, the inhabitants of the land, were there.* [5] *The inhabitants of Jebus told David, "You shall not enter here. . .!"* * *But David captured the Zion Fortress, which is the City*

---

supporters of Saul's son Ish Bosheth (*Radak*); or, that he would protect all of Israel as faithfully as he would his own tribe of Judah (*Abarbanel*).

11:5. The rest of their taunt is recorded in *II Samuel* 5:6.

ו דָּוִיד: וַיֹּאמֶר דָּוִיד כָּל־מַכֵּה יְבוּסִי בָּרִאשׁוֹנָה יִהְיֶה לְרֹאשׁ וּלְשָׂר וַיַּעַל

ז בָרִאשׁוֹנָה יוֹאָב בֶּן־צְרוּיָה וַיְהִי לְרֹאשׁ: וַיֵּשֶׁב דָּוִיד בַּמְּצָד עַל־כֵּן קָרְאוּ־

ח לוֹ עִיר דָּוִיד: וַיִּבֶן הָעִיר מִסָּבִיב מִן־הַמִּלּוֹא וְעַד־הַסָּבִיב וְיוֹאָב יְחַיֶּה אֶת־

ט שְׁאָר הָעִיר: וַיֵּלֶךְ דָּוִיד הָלוֹךְ וְגָדוֹל וַיהוָה צְבָאוֹת עִמּוֹ:

י וְאֵלֶּה רָאשֵׁי הַגִּבּוֹרִים אֲשֶׁר לְדָוִיד הַמִּתְחַזְּקִים עִמּוֹ בְמַלְכוּתוֹ עִם־

יא כָל־יִשְׂרָאֵל לְהַמְלִיכוֹ כִּדְבַר יְהוָה עַל־יִשְׂרָאֵל: וְאֵלֶּה

מִסְפַּר הַגִּבֹּרִים אֲשֶׁר לְדָוִיד יָשָׁבְעָם בֶּן־חַכְמוֹנִי רֹאשׁ °הַשָּׁלוֹשִׁים

[°הַשָּׁלִישִׁים ק] הוּא־עוֹרֵר אֶת־חֲנִיתוֹ עַל־שְׁלֹשׁ־מֵאוֹת חָלָל בְּפַעַם

יב־יג אֶחָת: וְאַחֲרָיו אֶלְעָזָר בֶּן־דּוֹדוֹ הָאֲחוֹחִי הוּא בִּשְׁלוֹשָׁה הַגִּבֹּרִים: הוּא־

הָיָה עִם־דָּוִיד בַּפַּס דַּמִּים וְהַפְּלִשְׁתִּים נֶאֶסְפוּ־שָׁם לַמִּלְחָמָה וַתְּהִי חֶלְקַת

יד הַשָּׂדֶה מְלֵאָה שְׂעוֹרִים וְהָעָם נָסוּ מִפְּנֵי פְלִשְׁתִּים: וַיִּתְיַצְּבוּ בְתוֹךְ־

טו הַחֶלְקָה וַיַּצִּילוּהָ וַיַּכּוּ אֶת־פְּלִשְׁתִּים וַיּוֹשַׁע יְהוָה תְּשׁוּעָה גְדוֹלָה: וַיֵּרְדוּ

שְׁלוֹשָׁה מִן־הַשְּׁלוֹשִׁים רֹאשׁ עַל־הַצֻּר אֶל־דָּוִיד אֶל־מְעָרַת עֲדֻלָּם

טז וּמַחֲנֵה פְלִשְׁתִּים חֹנָה בְּעֵמֶק רְפָאִים: וְדָוִיד אָז בַּמְּצוּדָה וּנְצִיב פְּלִשְׁתִּים

יז אָז בְּבֵית לָחֶם: וַיִּתְאָו דָּוִיד וַיֹּאמַר מִי יַשְׁקֵנִי מַיִם מִבּוֹר בֵּית־לֶחֶם אֲשֶׁר

יח בַּשָּׁעַר: וַיִּבְקְעוּ הַשְּׁלֹשָׁה בְּמַחֲנֵה פְלִשְׁתִּים וַיִּשְׁאֲבוּ־מַיִם מִבּוֹר בֵּית־

לֶחֶם אֲשֶׁר בַּשַּׁעַר וַיִּשְׂאוּ וַיָּבִאוּ אֶל־דָּוִיד וְלֹא־אָבָה דָוִיד לִשְׁתּוֹתָם

יט וַיְנַסֵּךְ אֹתָם לַיהוָה: וַיֹּאמֶר חָלִילָה לִּי מֵאֱלֹהַי מֵעֲשׂוֹת זֹאת הֲדַם

הָאֲנָשִׁים הָאֵלֶּה אֶשְׁתֶּה בְנַפְשׁוֹתָם כִּי בְנַפְשׁוֹתָם הֱבִיאוּם וְלֹא אָבָה

כ לִשְׁתּוֹתָם אֵלֶּה עָשׂוּ שְׁלֹשֶׁת הַגִּבּוֹרִים: וְאַבְשַׁי אֲחִי־יוֹאָב

הוּא הָיָה רֹאשׁ הַשְּׁלוֹשָׁה וְהוּא עוֹרֵר אֶת־חֲנִיתוֹ עַל־שְׁלֹשׁ מֵאוֹת חָלָל

כא °וְלֹא־ [°וְלוֹ־ ק] שֵׁם בַּשְּׁלוֹשָׁה: מִן־הַשְּׁלוֹשָׁה בַשְּׁנַיִם נִכְבָּד וַיְהִי לָהֶם

לְשָׂר וְעַד־הַשְּׁלוֹשָׁה לֹא־בָא: בְּנָיָה בֶן־יְהוֹיָדָע בֶּן־

כב אִישׁ־חַיִל רַב־פְּעָלִים מִן־קַבְצְאֵל הוּא הִכָּה אֵת שְׁנֵי אֲרִיאֵל מוֹאָב וְהוּא

כג יָרַד וְהִכָּה אֶת־הָאֲרִי בְּתוֹךְ הַבּוֹר בְּיוֹם הַשָּׁלֶג: וְהוּא־הִכָּה אֶת־הָאִישׁ

הַמִּצְרִי אִישׁ מִדָּה ׀ חָמֵשׁ בָּאַמָּה וּבְיַד הַמִּצְרִי חֲנִית כִּמְנוֹר אֹרְגִים וַיֵּרֶד

כד אֵלָיו בַּשָּׁבֶט וַיִּגְזֹל אֶת־הַחֲנִית מִיַּד הַמִּצְרִי וַיַּהַרְגֵהוּ בַּחֲנִיתוֹ: אֵלֶּה עָשָׂה

כה בְּנָיָהוּ בֶן־יְהוֹיָדָע וְלוֹ־שֵׁם בִּשְׁלוֹשָׁה הַגִּבֹּרִים: מִן־הַשְּׁלוֹשִׁים הִנּוֹ נִכְבָּד

כו וְהוּא וְאֶל־הַשְּׁלוֹשָׁה לֹא־בָא וַיְשִׂימֵהוּ דָוִיד עַל־מִשְׁמַעְתּוֹ: וְגִבּוֹרֵי

הַחֲיָלִים עֲשָׂה־אֵל אֲחִי יוֹאָב אֶלְחָנָן בֶּן־דּוֹדוֹ מִבֵּית לָחֶם: שַׁמּוֹת

כח הַהֲרוֹרִי חֶלֶץ הַפְּלוֹנִי: עִירָא בֶן־עִקֵּשׁ הַתְּקוֹעִי אֲבִיעֶזֶר

כט־ל הָעַנְּתוֹתִי: סִבְּכַי הַחֻשָׁתִי עִילַי הָאֲחוֹחִי: מַהְרַי

11:8. For the meaning of *Millo*, see *II Samuel* 5:9. The "surrounding wall" of the fortress was inside the city (*Radak*).

11:11. This translation follows *Radak*, who equates this man with Adino the Eznite, described in *II Samuel* 23:8. Alternatively, the phrase should be translated "Jashobeam *of David.* ⁶ *David declared, "Whoever strikes the Jebusite first will become a chief and an officer." Joab son of Zeruiah was the first to go up, and he became a chief.* ⁷ *David settled in the fortress; therefore they called it the City of David.* ⁸ *He built up the city all around, from the Millo to the surrounding [wall],* * while Joab restored the rest of the city.* ⁹ *David grew continuously greater, and* HASHEM, *Master of Legions, was with him.*

David's leading warriors

¹⁰ *These are the chief warriors of David, who strove for him in his kingship, along with all of Israel, to crown him, in accordance with the word of* HASHEM *concerning Israel.* ¹¹ *This is the tally of David's warriors:*

The one who sat in the assembly, a sagacious man, * the head of the captains. He wielded his spear over three hundred slain men at one time.*

¹² *After him was Elazar son of Dodo the Ahohite. He was among the three mighty men.*

¹³ *One* * who was with David in Pas-dammim, where the Philistines had gathered for battle. There was a portion of the field full of barley, and the people had fled from before the Philistines.* ¹⁴ *They* * stood in the middle of the portion and saved it, and smote the Philistines; and* HASHEM *caused a great salvation.*

¹⁵ *Once three men* * of the thirty chiefs went down to the crag to David, to the cave of Adullam, and the Philistine camp was encamped in the Valley of Rephaim.* ¹⁶ *David was then in the stronghold, at that time, and there was a Philistine garrison in Beth-lehem.* ¹⁷ *David had a craving and said, "If only someone could give me water to drink from the well of Beth-lehem, which is in the city gate!"* ¹⁸ *So the three broke into the camp of the Philistines and drew water from the well of Beth-lehem, which is at the gate, and they carried it and brought it to David. But David refused to drink it, and he poured it out unto* HASHEM. * ¹⁹ *He said, "Far be it from me before my God to do this! Shall I drink [what is tantamount to] the blood of these men, by their lives? For they risked their lives to bring it!" and he refused to drink it. These are what the three mighty men did.*

²⁰ *Abishai, Joab's brother — he was the head of the three;* * he wielded his spear over three hundred slain men; he was well known among the three.* ²¹ *Of the three, he was more honored than the other two, and he became their leader, but he did not compare to the [first] three.*

²² *Benaiah son of Jehoiada was a valiant man of many achievements, from Kabzeel; he struck down the two commanders of Moab, and he [also] went down and slew a lion in the middle of a well on a snowy day.* ²³ *He also struck down the Egyptian man, a man of imposing size — five cubits tall. The Egyptian had a spear [as thick] as a weaver's beam. He came down upon him with a stick, stole the spear from out of the hand of the Egyptian, and killed him with his own spear.* ²⁴ *These are the things that Benaiah son of Jehoiada did; he was well known among the three mighty men.* ²⁵ *He was more honored than the thirty, but he did not compare to the [first] three; and David set him as his confidant.*

²⁶ *The mighty warriors: Joab's brother Asahel; Elhanan son of Dodo of Beth-lehem;* ²⁷ *Shammoth the Harorite; Helez the Pelonite;* ²⁸ *Ira son of Ikkesh Tekoite; Abiezer the Anathothite;* ²⁹ *Sibbecai the Hushathite; Ilai the Ahohite;* ³⁰ *Mahrai*

---

son of Hachmoni, the head of the captains . . ."

11:13. In *II Samuel* 23:11, he is identified as Shammah son of Age (*Radak*).

11:14. Shammah and Elazar (*Ralbag*).

11:15. See *II Samuel* 23:13.

11:18. See *II Samuel* 23:16.

11:20. This triad was not the same as the one described above.

לא הַנְּטֹפָתִי חֵלֶד בֶּן־בַּעֲנָה הַנְּטֹפָתִי ׃ אִתַּי בֶּן־רִיבַי מִגִּבְעַת בְּנֵי בִנְיָמִן

לב-לג בְּנָיָה הַפִּרְעָתֹנִי ׃ חוּרַי מִנַּחֲלֵי גָעַשׁ אֲבִיאֵל הָעַרְבָתִי ׃ עַזְמָוֶת

לד הַבַּחֲרוּמִי אֶלְיַחְבָּא הַשַּׁעַלְבֹנִי ׃ בְּנֵי הָשֵׁם הַגִּזוֹנִי יוֹנָתָן בֶּן־שָׁגֵה

לה-לו הַהֲרָרִי ׃ אֲחִיאָם בֶּן־שָׂכָר הַהֲרָרִי אֱלִיפַל בֶּן־אוּר ׃ חֵפֶר

לז-לח הַמְּכֵרָתִי אֲחִיָּה הַפְּלֹנִי ׃ חֶצְרוֹ הַכַּרְמְלִי נַעֲרַי בֶּן־אֶזְבָּי ׃ יוֹאֵל

לט אֲחִי נָתָן מִבְחָר בֶּן־הַגְרִי ׃ צֶלֶק הָעַמּוֹנִי נַחְרַי הַבֵּרֹתִי נֹשֵׂא כְּלֵי

מ-מא יוֹאָב בֶּן־צְרוּיָה ׃ עִירָא הַיִּתְרִי גָּרֵב הַיִּתְרִי ׃ אוּרִיָּה הַחִתִּי

מב זָבָד בֶּן־אַחְלָי ׃ עֲדִינָא בֶן־שִׁיזָא הָראוּבֵנִי רֹאשׁ לָראוּבֵנִי וְעָלָיו

מג-מד שְׁלוֹשִׁים ׃ חָנָן בֶּן־מַעֲכָה וְיוֹשָׁפָט הַמִּתְנִי ׃ עֻזִּיָּא הָעֶשְׁתְּרָתִי

מה שָׁמָע °ויעואל [°וִיעִיאֵל ק] בְּנֵי חוֹתָם הָעֲרֹעֵרִי ׃ יְדִיעֲאֵל בֶּן־

מו שִׁמְרִי וְיֹחָא אָחִיו הַתִּיצִי ׃ אֱלִיאֵל הַמַּחֲוִים וִירִיבַי וְיוֹשַׁוְיָה בְּנֵי

מז אֶלְנַעַם וְיִתְמָה הַמּוֹאָבִי ׃ אֱלִיאֵל וְעוֹבֵד וְיַעֲשִׂיאֵל הַמְּצֹבָיָה ׃

יב

א וְאֵלֶּה הַבָּאִים אֶל־דָּוִיד לְצִיקְלַג עוֹד עָצוּר מִפְּנֵי שָׁאוּל בֶּן־קִישׁ וְהֵמָּה

ב בַּגִּבּוֹרִים עֹזְרֵי הַמִּלְחָמָה ׃ נֹשְׁקֵי קֶשֶׁת מַיְמִינִים וּמַשְׂמִאלִים בָּאֲבָנִים

ג וּבַחִצִּים בַּקָּשֶׁת מֵאֲחֵי שָׁאוּל מִבִּנְיָמִן ׃ הָראשׁ אֲחִיעֶזֶר וְיוֹאָשׁ בְּנֵי

הַשְּׁמָעָה הַגִּבְעָתִי °ויזואל [°וִיזִיאֵל ק] וָפֶלֶט בְּנֵי עַזְמָוֶת וּבְרָכָה וְיֵהוּא

ד-ה הָעֲנְתֹתִי ׃ וְיִשְׁמַעְיָה הַגִּבְעוֹנִי גִּבּוֹר בַּשְּׁלֹשִׁים וְעַל־הַשְּׁלֹשִׁים ׃ וְיִרְמְיָה

ו וְיַחֲזִיאֵל וְיוֹחָנָן וְיוֹזָבָד הַגְּדֵרָתִי ׃ אֶלְעוּזַי וִירִימוֹת וּבְעַלְיָה וּשְׁמַרְיָהוּ

ז וּשְׁפַטְיָהוּ °החריפי [°הַחֲרוּפִי ק] ׃ אֶלְקָנָה וְיִשִּׁיָּהוּ וַעֲזַרְאֵל וְיוֹעֶזֶר וְיָשָׁבְעָם

ח-ט הַקָּרְחִים ׃ וְיוֹעֵאלָה וּזְבַדְיָה בְּנֵי יְרֹחָם מִן־הַגְּדוֹר ׃ וּמִן־הַגָּדִי נִבְדְּלוּ אֶל־

דָּוִיד לַמְּצַד מִדְבָּרָה גִּבֹּרֵי הַחַיִל אַנְשֵׁי צָבָא לַמִּלְחָמָה עֹרְכֵי צִנָּה וָרֹמַח

י וּפְנֵי אַרְיֵה פְּנֵיהֶם וְכִצְבָאיִם עַל־הֶהָרִים לְמַהֵר ׃ עֵזֶר הָראשׁ

יא-יב עֹבַדְיָה הַשֵּׁנִי אֱלִיאָב הַשְּׁלִשִׁי ׃ מִשְׁמַנָּה הָרְבִיעִי יִרְמְיָה הַחֲמִשִׁי ׃ עַתַּי

יג-יד הַשִּׁשִּׁי אֱלִיאֵל הַשְּׁבִעִי ׃ יוֹחָנָן הַשְּׁמִינִי אֶלְזָבָד הַתְּשִׁיעִי ׃ יִרְמְיָהוּ הָעֲשִׂירִי

טו מַכְבַּנַּי עַשְׁתֵּי עָשָׂר ׃ אֵלֶּה מִבְּנֵי־גָד רָאשֵׁי הַצָּבָא אֶחָד לְמֵאָה

טז הַקָּטָן וְהַגָּדוֹל לְאָלֶף ׃ אֵלֶּה הֵם אֲשֶׁר עָבְרוּ אֶת־הַיַּרְדֵּן בַּחֹדֶשׁ הָראשׁוֹן

וְהוּא מְמַלֵּא עַל־כָּל־°גדיתיו [°גְּדוֹתָיו ק] וַיַּבְרִיחוּ אֶת־כָּל־הָעֲמָקִים

יז לַמִּזְרָח וְלַמַּעֲרָב ׃ וַיָּבֹאוּ מִן־בְּנֵי בִנְיָמִן וִיהוּדָה עַד־לַמְצָד לְדָוִיד ׃

יח וַיֵּצֵא דָוִיד לִפְנֵיהֶם וַיַּעַן וַיֹּאמֶר לָהֶם אִם־לְשָׁלוֹם בָּאתֶם אֵלַי לְעָזְרֵנִי

יִהְיֶה־לִּי עֲלֵיכֶם לֵבָב לְיָחַד וְאִם־לְרַמּוֹתַנִי לְצָרַי בְּלֹא חָמָס בְּכַפַּי יֵרֶא

יט אֱלֹהֵי אֲבוֹתֵינוּ וְיוֹכַח ׃ וְרוּחַ לָבְשָׁה אֶת־עֲמָשַׂי ראשׁ °השלושים [°הַשָּׁלִשִׁים ק] לְךָ דָוִיד וְעִמְּךָ בֶן־יִשַׁי שָׁלוֹם ׀ שָׁלוֹם לְךָ וְשָׁלוֹם לְעֹזְרֶךָ

כ כִּי עֲזָרְךָ אֱלֹהֶיךָ וַיְקַבְּלֵם דָּוִיד וַיִּתְּנֵם בְּראשֵׁי הַגְּדוּד ׃ וּמִמְּנַשֶּׁה

נָפְלוּ עַל־דָּוִיד בְּבֹאוֹ עִם־פְּלִשְׁתִּים עַל־שָׁאוּל לַמִּלְחָמָה וְלֹא עֲזָרֻם כִּי

the Netophathite; Heled son of Baanah of Netophathite; [31] Ithai son of Ribai from Gibeah of the children of Benjamin; Benaiah the Pirathonite; [32] Hiteai from Nahalei-gaash; Abiel the Arbathite; [33] Azmaveth the Baharumite; Eliahba the Shaalbonite; [34] the sons of Hashem the Gizonite; Jonathan son of Shageh the Hararite; [35] Ahiam son of Sachar the Hararite; Eliphal son of Ur; [36] Hepher the Mecherathite; Ahijah the Pelonite; [37] Hezro the Carmelite; Naarai son of Ezbai; [38] Joel brother of Nathan; Mibhar son of Hagri; [39] Zelek the Ammonite; Nahrai the Berothite, who was Joab son of Zeruiah's armorbearer; [40] Ira the Ithrite; Gareb the Ithrite; [41] Uriah the Hittite; * Zabad son of Ahlai; [42] Adina son of Shiza the Reubenite, the head of the Reubenites, and with him thirty [men]; [43] Hanan son of Maacah; Joshaphat the Mithnite; [44] Uzzia the Ashterathite; Shama and Jeiel, the sons of Hotham the Aroerite; [45] Jediael son of Shimri; Joha his brother, the Tizite; [46] Eliel [of] the Mahavites; Jeribai and Joshaviah, the sons of Elnaam; Ithmah the Moabite; [47] Eliel; Obed; and Jaasiel the Mezobaite.

12

David's first loyalists

[1] These are [the men] who came to David at Ziklag, while he was still in hiding from Saul son of Kish. They were among the mighty men who helped in war, [2] armed with bows, both right-handed and left-handed in slinging stones or [shooting] arrows with a bow, of the kinsmen of Saul, from Benjamin:

[3] The chief was Ahiezer, and Joash, the sons of Shemaah the Gibeathite; Jeziel and Pelet, the sons of Azmaveth; Beraca; Jehu the Anathothite; [4] Ishmaiah the Gibeonite, who was [like] one of the thirty mighty [men], * and even superior to the thirty [men]; [5] Jeremiah; Jahaziel; Johanan; Jozabad; [6] Eluzai; Jerimoth; Bealiah; Shemariah; Shephatiah the Haruphite; [7] Elkanah, Isshiah, Azarel, Joezer and Jashobeam, the Korahites; [8] Joelah and Zebadiah, the sons of Jeroham of Gedud.

[9] Some men of the Gadites defected to David, to the stronghold in the wilderness — mighty warriors, soldiers, who wielded shields and bucklers; their faces were like the face of lion, and they were fleet as deer on the mountains:

[10] Ezer, the head; Obadiah, the second; Eliab, the third; [11] Mishmannah, the fourth; Jeremiah, the fifth; [12] Attai, the sixth; Eliel, the seventh; [13] Johanan, the eighth; Elzabad, the ninth; [14] Jeremiah, the tenth; Machbannai, the eleventh. [15] These were the heads of the army from the children of Gad, the least [was equal] to a hundred men and the greatest to a thousand men. [16] These were the ones who crossed the Jordan during the first month, when it was overflowing all of its banks, and they chased away all the [residents] of the valleys, to the east and to the west.

His camp grows

From Benjamin and Judah

[17] Some of the children of Benjamin and Judah came to David's stronghold. [18] David came out before them and spoke up, saying to them, "If you have come to me in peace, to assist me, then my will is to unite with you. But if you come to trick me for my enemies — though there is no injustice on my part — may the God of our fathers see it and pass judgment!" [19] A spirit then garbed Amasai, the head of the captains. "[We] are yours, David, and [we] are with you, son of Jesse! Peace! Peace unto you and peace unto those who assist you, for your God assists you!" David accepted them, and made them heads of troops.

From Manasseh

[20] Also, some [people] of Manasseh fell in with David, when he accompanied the Philistines to battle against Saul, * but he did not help [the Philistines], for the

---

12:4. Enumerated above, 11:26ff.   **12:20.** As related in I Samuel Chs. 28-29.

בְּעֵצָ֣ה שִׁלְּח֗וּהוּ סַרְנֵ֤י פְלִשְׁתִּים֙ לֵאמֹ֔ר בְּרָאשֵׁ֖ינוּ יִפּ֥וֹל אֶל־אֲדֹנָ֖יו

כא שָׁא֑וּל: בְּלֶכְתּ֣וֹ אֶל־צִֽיקְלַ֗ג נָפְל֣וּ עָלָ֣יו ׀ מִֽמְּנַשֶּׁ֡ה עַדְנַ֣ח וְיֽוֹזָבָ֣ד וִֽידִיֽעֲאֵ֡ל וּמִיכָאֵ֣ל וְיוֹזָבָד֩ וֶֽאֱלִיה֨וּא וְצִלְּתַ֜י רָאשֵׁ֧י הָאֲלָפִ֛ים אֲשֶׁ֖ר לִמְנַשֶּֽׁה:

כב וְהֵ֨מָּה עָזְר֤וּ עִם־דָּוִיד֙ עַל־הַגְּד֔וּד כִּֽי־גִבּ֥וֹרֵי חַ֖יִל כֻּלָּ֑ם וַיִּהְי֥וּ שָׂרִ֖ים בַּצָּבָֽא:

כג כִּ֚י לְעֶת־י֣וֹם בְּי֔וֹם יָבֹ֥אוּ עַל־דָּוִ֖יד לְעָזְר֑וֹ עַד־לְמַֽחֲנֶ֥ה גָד֖וֹל כְּמַֽחֲנֵ֥ה

כד אֱלֹהִֽים: וְ֠אֵלֶּה מִסְפְּרֵ֞י רָאשֵׁ֤י הֶֽחָלוּץ֙ לַצָּבָ֔א בָּ֥אוּ עַל־דָּוִ֖יד

כה חֶבְר֑וֹנָה לְהָסֵ֞ב מַלְכ֥וּת שָׁא֛וּל אֵלָ֖יו כְּפִ֥י יְהֹוָֽה: בְּנֵ֣י יְהוּדָ֗ה נֹֽשְׂאֵ֤י

כו צִנָּה֙ וָרֹ֔מַח שֵׁ֥שֶׁת אֲלָפִ֖ים וּשְׁמוֹנֶ֣ה מֵא֑וֹת חֲלוּצֵ֖י צָבָֽא: מִן־בְּנֵ֣י

כז שִׁמְע֔וֹן גִּבּ֥וֹרֵי חַ֖יִל לַצָּבָ֑א שִׁבְעַ֥ת אֲלָפִ֖ים וּמֵאָֽה: מִן־בְּנֵ֣י הַלֵּוִ֗י

כח אַרְבַּ֥עַת אֲלָפִ֖ים וְשֵׁ֥שׁ מֵאֽוֹת: וִיהֽוֹיָדָ֥ע הַנָּגִ֖יד לְאַֽהֲרֹ֑ן וְעִמּ֕וֹ

כט שְׁלֹ֥שֶׁת אֲלָפִ֖ים וּשְׁבַ֥ע מֵאֽוֹת: וְצָד֥וֹק נַ֖עַר גִּבּ֣וֹר חָ֑יִל וּבֵית־

ל אָבִ֛יו שָׂרִ֖ים עֶשְׂרִ֥ים וּשְׁנָֽיִם: וּמִן־בְּנֵ֣י בִנְיָמִ֗ן אֲחֵ֤י שָׁאוּל֙ שְׁלֹ֣שֶׁת

לא אֲלָפִ֑ים וְעַד־הֵ֨נָּה֙ מַרְבִּיתָ֔ם שֹֽׁמְרִ֕ים מִשְׁמֶ֖רֶת בֵּ֥ית שָׁאֽוּל: וּמִן־

בְּנֵ֣י אֶפְרַ֗יִם עֶשְׂרִ֥ים אֶ֨לֶף֙ וּשְׁמוֹנֶ֣ה מֵא֔וֹת גִּבּ֣וֹרֵי חַ֑יִל אַנְשֵׁ֥י שֵׁמ֖וֹת לְבֵ֥ית

לב אֲבוֹתָֽם: וּמֵֽחֲצִי֙ מַטֵּ֣ה מְנַשֶּׁ֔ה שְׁמוֹנָ֥ה עָשָׂ֖ר אָ֑לֶף אֲשֶׁ֤ר נִקְּבוּ֙

לג בְּשֵׁמ֔וֹת לָב֖וֹא לְהַמְלִ֥יךְ אֶת־דָּוִֽיד: וּמִבְּנֵ֣י יִשָּׂשכָ֗ר יֽוֹדְעֵ֤י

בִינָה֙ לַֽעִתִּ֔ים לָדַ֖עַת מַה־יַּֽעֲשֶׂ֣ה יִשְׂרָאֵ֑ל רָֽאשֵׁיהֶ֣ם מָאתַ֔יִם וְכָל־אֲחֵיהֶ֖ם

לד עַל־פִּיהֶֽם: מִזְּבֻל֞וּן יֽוֹצְאֵ֣י צָבָ֗א עֹ֥רְכֵ֤י מִלְחָמָה֙ בְּכָל־כְּלֵ֣י

לה מִלְחָמָ֖ה חֲמִשִּׁ֣ים אָ֑לֶף וְלַֽעֲדֹ֖ר בְּלֹֽא־לֵ֥ב וָלֵֽב: וּמִנַּפְתָּלִ֖י

לו שָׂרִ֣ים אָ֑לֶף וְעִמָּהֶם֙ בְּצִנָּ֣ה וַֽחֲנִ֔ית שְׁלֹשִׁ֥ים וְשִׁבְעָ֖ה אָֽלֶף: וּמִן־

לז הַדָּנִ֗י עֹֽרְכֵ֣י מִלְחָמָ֔ה עֶשְׂרִֽים־וּשְׁמוֹנָ֥ה אֶ֖לֶף וְשֵׁ֥שׁ מֵאֽוֹת: וּמֵֽעֵ֣בֶר לַיַּרְדֵּ֗ן

לח מִן־הָרֽאוּבֵנִ֤י וְהַגָּדִי֙ וַֽחֲצִ֣י ׀ שֵׁ֣בֶט מְנַשֶּׁ֔ה בְּכֹ֖ל כְּלֵ֣י צְבָ֣א מִלְחָמָ֑ה

לט מֵאָ֖ה וְעֶשְׂרִ֣ים אָֽלֶף: כָּל־אֵ֜לֶּה אַנְשֵׁ֣י מִלְחָמָה֮ עֹֽדְרֵ֣י מַֽעֲרָכָה֒ בְּלֵבָ֣ב

שָׁלֵ֗ם בָּ֚אוּ חֶבְר֔וֹנָה לְהַמְלִ֥יךְ אֶת־דָּוִ֖יד עַל־כָּל־יִשְׂרָאֵ֑ל וְ֠גַם כָּל־שֵׁרִ֨ית

מ יִשְׂרָאֵ֜ל לֵ֣ב אֶחָ֗ד לְהַמְלִ֖יךְ אֶת־דָּוִֽיד: וַיִּֽהְיוּ־שָׁ֤ם עִם־דָּוִיד֙ יָמִ֣ים שְׁלוֹשָׁ֔ה

מא אֹֽכְלִ֖ים וְשׁוֹתִ֑ים כִּֽי־הֵכִ֥ינוּ לָהֶ֖ם אֲחֵיהֶֽם: וְגַ֣ם הַקְּרֽוֹבִים־אֲלֵיהֶ֡ם עַד־

יִשָּׂשכָ֨ר וּזְבֻל֜וּן וְנַפְתָּלִ֗י מְבִיאִ֣ים לֶ֡חֶם בַּֽחֲמוֹרִ֣ים וּבַגְּמַלִּים֩ וּבַפְּרָדִ֨ים ׀

וּֽבַבָּקָ֜ר מַֽאֲכָ֣ל קֶ֗מַח דְּבֵלִ֣ים וְצִמּוּקִ֞ים וְיַ֧יִן וְשֶׁ֛מֶן וּבָקָ֥ר וְצֹ֖אן לָרֹ֑ב

יג א כִּ֥י שִׂמְחָ֖ה בְּיִשְׂרָאֵֽל: וַיִּוָּ֣עַץ דָּוִ֗יד עִם־שָׂרֵ֧י

ב הָֽאֲלָפִ֛ים וְהַמֵּא֖וֹת לְכָל־נָגִֽיד: וַיֹּ֨אמֶר דָּוִ֜יד לְכֹ֣ל ׀ קְהַ֣ל יִשְׂרָאֵ֗ל אִם־

עֲלֵיכֶ֨ם ט֜וֹב וּמִן־יְהֹוָ֤ה אֱלֹהֵ֨ינוּ֙ נִפְרְצָ֣ה נִשְׁלְחָ֗ה עַל־אַחֵ֨ינוּ֙ הַנִּשְׁאָרִ֔ים

12:22. They helped David attack the Amalekite marauders who had raided their camp (see ibid.).

12:23. An expression denoting an extremely large camp

(*Radak*).

12:34. Lit., "without a heart and [another] heart" — i.e., without duplicity.

Philistine governors advised to send him away, saying, "With our heads he will fall in with his master Saul!" ²¹ When he went to Ziklag, people of Manasseh defected to him: Adnah, Jozabad, Jediael, Michael, Jozabad, Elihu and Zillethai, who were captains of thousands from Manasseh. ²² They helped David against the troop, * for they were all mighty warriors, and they became officers in the army. ²³ For constantly, day after day, people came to David to assist him, until there was a large camp, like a camp of God. *

²⁴ This is the count of the leaders of those mobilized for the army, who came to David at Hebron to transfer Saul's kingship over to him, in accordance with the word of HASHEM.

²⁵ The children of Judah, bearers of shields and spears — six thousand eight hundred mobilized for the army.

²⁶ Of the children of Simeon — seven thousand one hundred mighty warriors for the army.

²⁷ Of the children of Levi — four thousand six hundred; ²⁸ and Jehoiada, the leader of Aaron's [descendants], and with him three thousand seven hundred; ²⁹ and Zadok, a young man who was a mighty warrior, with twenty-two officers of his father's family.

³⁰ Of the children of Benjamin, Saul's kinsmen — three thousand [men], most of whom had been maintaining their loyalty to the house of Saul.

³¹ Of the children of Ephraim — twenty thousand eight hundred mighty warriors, men of renown in their families.

³² Of half the tribe of Manasseh — eighteen thousand men [who] had been designated by name to come and crown David king.

³³ Of the children of Issachar, men with understanding for the times, to know what Israel should do — two hundred chiefs, with all of their kinsmen following their counsel.

³⁴ Of Zebulun — fifty thousand [men] going out in the army, who deployed themselves for war with all kinds of weapons of war, who arrayed themselves without hesitancy. *

³⁵ Of Naphtali — one thousand officers, and with them thirty-seven thousand [men] with shields and spears.

³⁶ Of the Danites — twenty-eight thousand six hundred [men] who deployed themselves for war.

³⁷ Of Asher — forty thousand [men] who went out to the army to deploy themselves for war.

³⁸ From the other side of the Jordan: of the Reubenite, the Gadite and half of the tribe of Manasseh — a hundred twenty thousand [men] with all the weapons of a fighting army.

³⁹ All of these were men of war, who were arrayed in formation. They came to Hebron wholeheartedly, to crown David king over all of Israel. Furthermore, all the remainder of Israel had a united heart to crown David king. ⁴⁰ They stayed there with David for three days, eating and drinking, for their kinsmen had prepared for them. ⁴¹ Furthermore, those close to them, up to Issachar and Zebulun and Naphtali, brought provisions by donkey, by camel, by mule and by ox — food of flour, dried figs, raisins, wine, oil and much cattle and sheep, for there was joy in Israel.

From the other tribes

David becomes king

13

Unity and the Ark

¹ David consulted with the officers of thousands and of hundreds — with every leader. ² David said to the entire congregation of Israel, "If it seems good to you and to HASHEM, our God, let us send out far and wide, to our remaining brethren

בְּכֹל אַרְצוֹת יִשְׂרָאֵל וְעִמָּהֶם הַכֹּהֲנִים וְהַלְוִיִּם בְּעָרֵי מִגְרְשֵׁיהֶם וְיִקָּבְצוּ

ג אֵלֵינוּ: וְנָסֵבָּה אֶת־אֲרוֹן אֱלֹהֵינוּ אֵלֵינוּ כִּי־לֹא דְרַשְׁנֻהוּ בִּימֵי שָׁאוּל:

ד־ה וַיֹּאמְרוּ כָל־הַקָּהָל לַעֲשׂוֹת כֵּן כִּי־יָשַׁר הַדָּבָר בְּעֵינֵי כָל־הָעָם: וַיַּקְהֵל

דָּוִיד אֶת־כָּל־יִשְׂרָאֵל מִן־שִׁיחוֹר מִצְרַיִם וְעַד־לְבוֹא חֲמָת לְהָבִיא אֶת־

ו אֲרוֹן הָאֱלֹהִים מִקִּרְיַת יְעָרִים: וַיַּעַל דָּוִיד וְכָל־יִשְׂרָאֵל בַּעֲלָתָה אֶל־

קִרְיַת יְעָרִים אֲשֶׁר לִיהוּדָה לְהַעֲלוֹת מִשָּׁם אֵת אֲרוֹן הָאֱלֹהִים ׀ יְהוָה

ז יוֹשֵׁב הַכְּרוּבִים אֲשֶׁר־נִקְרָא שָׁם: וַיַּרְכִּיבוּ אֶת־אֲרוֹן הָאֱלֹהִים עַל־עֲגָלָה

ח חֲדָשָׁה מִבֵּית אֲבִינָדָב וְעֻזָּא וְאַחְיוֹ נֹהֲגִים בָּעֲגָלָה: וְדָוִיד וְכָל־יִשְׂרָאֵל

מְשַׂחֲקִים לִפְנֵי הָאֱלֹהִים בְּכָל־עֹז וּבְשִׁירִים וּבְכִנֹּרוֹת וּבִנְבָלִים וּבְתֻפִּים

ט וּבִמְצִלְתַּיִם וּבַחֲצֹצְרוֹת: וַיָּבֹאוּ עַד־גֹּרֶן כִּידֹן וַיִּשְׁלַח עֻזָּא אֶת־יָדוֹ לֶאֱחֹז

י אֶת־הָאָרוֹן כִּי שָׁמְטוּ הַבָּקָר: וַיִּחַר־אַף יְהוָה בְּעֻזָּא וַיַּכֵּהוּ עַל אֲשֶׁר־שָׁלַח

יא יָדוֹ עַל־הָאָרוֹן וַיָּמָת שָׁם לִפְנֵי אֱלֹהִים: וַיִּחַר לְדָוִיד כִּי־פָרַץ יְהוָה פֶּרֶץ

יב בְּעֻזָּא וַיִּקְרָא לַמָּקוֹם הַהוּא פֶּרֶץ עֻזָּא עַד הַיּוֹם הַזֶּה: וַיִּירָא דָוִיד אֶת־

יג הָאֱלֹהִים בַּיּוֹם הַהוּא לֵאמֹר הֵיךְ אָבִיא אֵלַי אֵת אֲרוֹן הָאֱלֹהִים: וְלֹא־

הֵסִיר דָּוִיד אֶת־הָאָרוֹן אֵלָיו אֶל־עִיר דָּוִיד וַיַּטֵּהוּ אֶל־בֵּית עֹבֵד־אֱדֹם

יד הַגִּתִּי: וַיֵּשֶׁב אֲרוֹן הָאֱלֹהִים עִם־בֵּית עֹבֵד אֱדֹם בְּבֵיתוֹ שְׁלֹשָׁה חֳדָשִׁים

וַיְבָרֶךְ יְהוָה אֶת־בֵּית עֹבֵד־אֱדֹם וְאֶת־כָּל־אֲשֶׁר־לוֹ:

יד א וַיִּשְׁלַח °חִירָם [°חוּרָם ק] מֶלֶךְ־צֹר מַלְאָכִים אֶל־דָּוִיד וַעֲצֵי אֲרָזִים

ב וְחָרָשֵׁי קִיר וְחָרָשֵׁי עֵצִים לִבְנוֹת לוֹ בָּיִת: וַיֵּדַע דָּוִיד כִּי־הֱכִינוֹ

יְהוָה לְמֶלֶךְ עַל־יִשְׂרָאֵל כִּי־נִשֵּׂאת לְמַעְלָה מַלְכוּתוֹ בַּעֲבוּר עַמּוֹ

ג יִשְׂרָאֵל: וַיִּקַּח דָּוִיד עוֹד נָשִׁים בִּירוּשָׁלָ͏ִם וַיּוֹלֶד דָּוִיד עוֹד

ד בָּנִים וּבָנוֹת: וְאֵלֶּה שְׁמוֹת הַיְלוּדִים אֲשֶׁר הָיוּ־לוֹ בִּירוּשָׁלָ͏ִם שַׁמּוּעַ וְשׁוֹבָב

ה־ז נָתָן וּשְׁלֹמֹה: וְיִבְחָר וֶאֱלִישׁוּעַ וְאֶלְפָּלֶט: וְנֹגַהּ וְנֶפֶג וְיָפִיעַ: וֶאֱלִישָׁמָע

ח וּבְעֶלְיָדָע וֶאֱלִיפָלֶט: וַיִּשְׁמְעוּ פְלִשְׁתִּים כִּי־נִמְשַׁח דָּוִיד לְמֶלֶךְ עַל־כָּל־

יִשְׂרָאֵל וַיַּעֲלוּ כָל־פְּלִשְׁתִּים לְבַקֵּשׁ אֶת־דָּוִיד וַיִּשְׁמַע דָּוִיד וַיֵּצֵא לִפְנֵיהֶם:

ט וּפְלִשְׁתִּים בָּאוּ וַיִּפְשְׁטוּ בְּעֵמֶק רְפָאִים: וַיִּשְׁאַל דָּוִיד בֵּאלֹהִים לֵאמֹר

הַאֶעֱלֶה עַל־°פְּלִשְׁתִּיִּים [°פְּלִשְׁתִּים ק] וּנְתַתָּם בְּיָדִי וַיֹּאמֶר לוֹ יְהוָה

יא עֲלֵה וּנְתַתִּים בְּיָדֶךָ: וַיַּעֲלוּ בְּבַעַל־פְּרָצִים וַיַּכֵּם שָׁם דָּוִיד וַיֹּאמֶר דָּוִיד

פָּרַץ הָאֱלֹהִים אֶת־אוֹיְבַי בְּיָדִי כְּפֶרֶץ מָיִם עַל־כֵּן קָרְאוּ שֵׁם־הַמָּקוֹם

יב הַהוּא בַּעַל פְּרָצִים: וַיַּעַזְבוּ־שָׁם אֶת־אֱלֹהֵיהֶם וַיֹּאמֶר דָּוִיד וַיִּשָּׂרְפוּ

יג־יד בָּאֵשׁ: וַיֹּסִיפוּ עוֹד פְּלִשְׁתִּים וַיִּפְשְׁטוּ בָּעֵמֶק: וַיִּשְׁאַל עוֹד

דָּוִיד בֵּאלֹהִים וַיֹּאמֶר לוֹ הָאֱלֹהִים לֹא תַעֲלֶה אַחֲרֵיהֶם הָסֵב מֵעֲלֵיהֶם

13:3. The Ark had been in Kiriath-jearim since it was returned by the Philistines (*I Samuel* 7:1-2). David now wanted to bring it to Jerusalem.

13:5. That is, from the far north to the far south of Israel.

13:6 Another name for Kiryath-jearim (*Joshua* 15:9).

in all the lands of Israel, and with them to the Kohanim and Levites in their cities surrounded by their open areas, and let them gather together to us; ³ *and let us transfer the Ark of our God to us,* * *for we did not seek it out in the days of Saul."*

⁴ *The entire congregation said to do so, for the matter met with the approval of the entire people.*

⁵ *David gathered all of Israel, from the approach of Hamath to the Shihor [River] of Egypt,* * *to bring the Ark of God from Kiriath-jearim.* ⁶ *David and all of Israel went up to Baalah,* * *to Kiriath-jearim of Judah, to bring up from there the Ark of God — HASHEM, Who is enthroned upon the Cherubim — which is called by [His] Name.* ⁷ *They placed the Ark of God upon a new wagon, from the house of Abinadab. Uzza and Ahio* * *guided the wagon.* ⁸ *David and all of Israel were rejoicing before God with all their might, with songs and with harps, lyres, drums, cymbals and trumpets.*

⁹ *They came to the threshing-floor of Chidon, and Uzza sent out his hand to grasp the Ark, for the oxen had dislodged it.* ¹⁰ HASHEM *became angry at Uzza* * *and He struck him for sending out his hand to the Ark; and he died there before God.*

¹¹ *David was upset [with himself] because* HASHEM *had inflicted a breach against Uzza; he called that place Perez-uzza* * *(Breach of Uzzah), [which is its name] to this day.* ¹² *David feared God on that day, saying, "How can I bring the Ark of God to myself?"* ¹³ *So David did not move the Ark to himself to the City of David, and he diverted it to the house of Obed-edom the Gittite.* ¹⁴ *The Ark of God remained at the house of Obed-edom, in his house, for three months, and* HASHEM *blessed Obed-edom's household and all that was his.*

14

The monarchy is established

¹ **H**uram, king of Tyre, sent a delegation to David, with cedarwood, wall artisans* * *and carpenters, to build him a palace.* ² *David realized that* HASHEM *had established him as king over Israel — for his kingdom was greatly exalted — for the sake of His people Israel.* *

³ *David married additional wives in Jerusalem [after he came there from Hebron], and David begot more sons and daughters.* ⁴ *These are the names of those born to him in Jerusalem: Shammua, Shobab, Nathan, Solomon,* ⁵ *Ibhar, Elishua, Elpelet,* ⁶ *Nogah, Nepheg, Japhia,* ⁷ *Elishama, Beeliada and Eliphelet.*

David defeats the Philistines . . .

⁸ *The Philistines heard that David had been anointed as king of Israel, so all the Philistines came up to seek out David.* * *David heard, and he went out before them.* ⁹ *The Philistines came and spread out in the Valley of Rephaim.* * ¹⁰ *David inquired of God, saying, "Shall I go up against the Philistines; will You deliver them into my hands?" And* HASHEM *answered David, "Go up, and I shall deliver them into your hands."* ¹¹ *They came up to the Plain of Perazim, and David struck them there. David said, "God has broken down my enemies through my hand, as water breaches [a barrier]"; therefore that place is called the Plain of Perazim.* ¹² *[The Philistines] had left their gods behind there; David gave the command and they were burned in fire.*

. . . and does it again

¹³ *The Philistines once again spread out in the Valley.* ¹⁴ *David inquired of God again, and God said to him, "Do not go up after them, but circle around from*

13:7. Abinadab's sons (*II Samuel* 6:3).
13:10. See *II Samuel* 6:7.
14:1. Stonemasons (*II Samuel* 5:11).
14:2. See *II Samuel* 5:12.

14:8. The Philistines considered the newly united Kingdom of Israel as a direct threat to their hegemony over the area.
14:9. Just southwest of Jerusalem.

טו וּבְאֵ֥ת לָהֶ֖ם מִמּ֣וּל הַבְּכָאִ֑ים ׀ וִיהִ֗י כְּֽשָׁמְעֲךָ֙ אֶת־ק֤וֹל הַצְּעָדָה֙ בְּרָאשֵׁ֣י הַבְּכָאִ֔ים אָ֥ז תֵּצֵ֖א בַמִּלְחָמָ֑ה כִּֽי־יָצָ֤א הָֽאֱלֹהִים֙ לְפָנֶ֔יךָ לְהַכּ֖וֹת אֶת־מַחֲנֵ֥ה

טז פְלִשְׁתִּֽים: וַיַּ֣עַשׂ דָּוִ֔יד כַּאֲשֶׁ֥ר צִוָּ֖הוּ הָאֱלֹהִ֑ים וַיַּכּוּ֙ אֶת־מַחֲנֵ֣ה פְלִשְׁתִּ֔ים

יז מִגִּבְע֖וֹן וְעַד־גָּֽזְרָה: וַיֵּצֵ֤א שֵׁם־דָּוִיד֙ בְּכָל־הָֽאֲרָצ֔וֹת וַֽיהֹוָ֗ה נָתַ֥ן אֶת־פַּחְדּ֖וֹ

א עַל־כָּל־הַגּוֹיִֽם: וַיַּֽעַשׂ־ל֥וֹ בָתִּ֖ים בְּעִ֣יר דָּוִ֑יד וַיָּ֤כֶן מָקוֹם֙ לַֽאֲר֣וֹן הָֽאֱלֹהִ֔ים וַיֶּט־

ב ל֖וֹ אֹֽהֶל: אָ֚ז אָמַ֣ר דָּוִ֔יד לֹ֥א לָשֵׂ֛את אֶת־אֲר֥וֹן הָֽאֱלֹהִ֖ים כִּ֣י אִם־הַלְוִיִּ֑ם כִּי־

ג בָ֣ם ׀ בָּחַ֣ר יְהֹוָ֗ה לָשֵׂ֛את אֶת־אֲר֥וֹן יְהֹוָ֖ה וּֽלְשָׁרְת֥וֹ עַד־עוֹלָֽם: וַיַּקְהֵ֤ל דָּוִיד֙ אֶת־כָּל־יִשְׂרָאֵ֖ל אֶל־יְרֽוּשָׁלָ֑͏ִם לְהַעֲלוֹת֙ אֶת־אֲר֣וֹן יְהֹוָ֔ה אֶל־מְקוֹמ֖וֹ

ד-ה אֲשֶׁר־הֵכִ֥ין לֽוֹ: וַיֶּאֱסֹ֥ף דָּוִ֖יד אֶת־בְּנֵ֣י אַהֲרֹ֑ן וְאֶת־הַֽלְוִיִּֽם: לִבְנֵ֣י קְהָ֔ת

ו אֽוּרִיאֵ֣ל הַשָּׂ֔ר וְאֶחָ֖יו מֵאָ֥ה וְעֶשְׂרִֽים: לִבְנֵ֣י מְרָרִ֔י עֲשָׂיָ֖ה הַשָּׂ֑ר

ז וְאֶחָ֖יו מָאתַ֥יִם וְעֶשְׂרִֽים: לִבְנֵ֣י גֵּרְשׁ֔וֹם יוֹאֵ֖ל הַשָּׂ֑ר וְאֶחָ֖יו מֵאָ֥ה

ח-ט וּשְׁלֹשִֽׁים: לִבְנֵ֣י אֱלִ֣יצָפָ֔ן שְׁמַעְיָ֖ה הַשָּׂ֑ר וְאֶחָ֖יו מָאתָֽיִם: לִבְנֵ֣י

י חֶבְר֔וֹן אֱלִיאֵ֥ל הַשָּׂ֖ר וְאֶחָ֥יו שְׁמוֹנִֽים: לִבְנֵ֣י עֻזִּיאֵ֔ל עַמִּֽינָדָ֖ב הַשָּׂ֑ר

יא וְאֶחָ֖יו מֵאָ֥ה וּשְׁנֵ֥ים עָשָֽׂר: וַיִּקְרָ֣א דָוִ֔יד לְצָד֥וֹק וּלְאֶבְיָתָ֖ר הַכֹּהֲנִ֑ים

יב וְלַֽלְוִיִּ֡ם לְאֽוּרִיאֵ֡ל עֲשָׂיָ֡ה וְ֠יוֹאֵ֠ל שְׁמַעְיָ֧ה וֶֽאֱלִיאֵ֛ל וְעַמִּֽינָדָֽב: וַיֹּ֣אמֶר לָהֶ֔ם אַתֶּ֛ם רָאשֵׁ֥י הָֽאָב֖וֹת לַלְוִיִּ֑ם הִֽתְקַדְּשׁ֗וּ אַתֶּם֙ וַאֲחֵיכֶ֔ם וְהַֽעֲלִיתֶ֕ם אֵ֚ת אֲר֣וֹן

יג יְהֹוָ֔ה אֱלֹהֵ֖י יִשְׂרָאֵ֑ל אֶל־הֲכִֽינוֹתִי לֽוֹ: כִּ֛י לְמַבָּרִ֥אשׁוֹנָ֖ה לֹ֣א אַתֶּ֑ם פָּ֨רַ֜ץ יְהֹוָ֤ה אֱלֹהֵ֨ינוּ֙ בָּ֔נוּ כִּי־לֹ֥א דְרַשְׁנֻ֖הוּ כַּמִּשְׁפָּֽט: וַיִּֽתְקַדְּשׁ֔וּ הַכֹּֽהֲנִ֖ים וְהַֽלְוִיִּ֑ם לְהַֽעֲלֹ֕ות

יד-טו אֶת־אֲר֥וֹן יְהֹוָ֖ה אֱלֹהֵ֥י יִשְׂרָאֵֽל: וַיִּשְׂא֣וּ בְנֵֽי־הַלְוִיִּ֗ם אֵ֚ת אֲר֣וֹן הָֽאֱלֹהִ֔ים כַּאֲשֶׁ֛ר צִוָּ֥ה מֹשֶׁ֖ה כִּדְבַ֣ר יְהֹוָ֑ה בִּכְתֵפָ֛ם בַּמֹּט֖וֹת עֲלֵיהֶֽם: וַיֹּ֣אמֶר

טז דָּוִ֗יד לְשָׂרֵ֣י הַלְוִיִּ֔ם לְהַֽעֲמִ֗יד אֶת־אֲחֵיהֶ֤ם הַמְשֹׁרְרִים֙ בִּכְלֵי־שִׁ֔יר נְבָלִ֥ים וְכִנֹּר֖וֹת וּמְצִלְתָּ֑יִם מַשְׁמִעִ֥ים לְהָרִֽים־בְּקוֹל־לְשִׂמְחָֽה:

יז וַיַּֽעֲמִ֣ידוּ הַלְוִיִּ֗ם אֵ֚ת הֵימָ֣ן בֶּן־יוֹאֵ֔ל וּמִן־אֶחָ֖יו אָסָ֣ף בֶּן־בֶּֽרֶכְיָ֑הוּ וּמִן־

יח בְּנֵ֤י מְרָרִי֙ אֲחֵיהֶ֔ם אֵיתָ֖ן בֶּן־קֽוּשָׁיָֽהוּ: וְעִמָּהֶ֖ם אֲחֵיהֶ֣ם הַמִּשְׁנִ֑ים זְכַרְיָ֡הוּ בֵּ֡ן וְיַֽעֲזִיאֵ֡ל וּֽשְׁמִֽירָמ֡וֹת וִיחִיאֵ֡ל ׀ וְעֻנִּ֡י אֱלִיאָ֡ב וּבְנָיָ֡הוּ וּמַֽעֲשֵׂיָ֡הוּ

יט וּמַתִּתְיָ֡הוּ וֶאֱלִֽיפְלֵ֡הוּ וּמִקְנֵיָ֡הוּ וְעֹבֵ֥ד אֱדֹ֛ם וִֽיעִיאֵ֖ל הַשֹּֽׁעֲרִֽים: וְהַֽמְשֹׁרְרִ֗ים

כ הֵימָ֤ן אָסָף֙ וְאֵיתָ֔ן בִּמְצִלְתַּ֖יִם נְחֹ֑שֶׁת לְהַשְׁמִֽיעַ: וּזְכַרְיָ֨ה וַֽעֲזִיאֵ֜ל וּשְׁמִֽירָמ֣וֹת וִיחִיאֵ֣ל ׀ וְעֻנִּ֣י וֶאֱלִיאָ֗ב וּמַֽעֲשֵׂיָ֥הוּ וּבְנָיָ֛הוּ בִּנְבָלִ֖ים עַל־עֲלָמֽוֹת:

כא וּמַתִּתְיָ֣הוּ וֶאֱלִֽיפְלֵ֗הוּ וּמִקְנֵיָ֨הוּ֙ וְעֹבֵ֣ד אֱדֹ֔ם וִֽיעִיאֵ֖ל וַעֲזַזְיָ֑הוּ בְּכִנֹּר֥וֹת

כב עַל־הַשְּׁמִינִ֖ית לְנַצֵּֽחַ: וּכְנַנְיָ֥הוּ שַֽׂר־הַלְוִיִּ֖ם בְּמַשָּׂ֑א יָסֹר֙ בַּמַּשָּׂ֔א כִּ֥י מֵבִ֖ין

כג-כד הֽוּא: וּבֶֽרֶכְיָה֙ וְאֶלְקָנָ֔ה שֹׁעֲרִ֖ים לָֽאָר֑וֹן: וּֽשְׁבַנְיָ֡הוּ וְ֠יֽוֹשָׁפָ֠ט וּנְתַנְאֵ֨ל וַֽעֲמָשַׂ֜י וּזְכַרְיָ֗הוּ וּבְנָיָ֨הוּ֙ וֶֽאֱלִיעֶ֣זֶר הַכֹּֽהֲנִ֗ים °מחצצרים [°מַחְצְרִ֣ים ק] בַּֽחֲצֹֽצְרוֹת֙ לִפְנֵי֙ אֲר֣וֹן הָֽאֱלֹהִ֔ים וְעֹבֵ֥ד אֱדֹ֖ם וִֽיחִיָּ֑ה שֹֽׁעֲרִ֖ים לָֽאָרֽוֹן:

them, and approach them from opposite the mulberry trees. [15] And it shall be that when you hear a sound of marching at the tops of the mulberry trees, * then you shall go out to do battle, for HASHEM will have gone out before you to strike at the Philistine camp." [16] David did as God had commanded him, and he struck the Philistine camp from Gibeon until the approach to Gezer.

[17] David's fame spread throughout all the lands, and HASHEM placed his fear upon all the nations.

15

The Ark arrives

Preparations

[1] He built houses for himself in the City of David. He also prepared a place for the Ark of God, pitching a tent for it. [2] At that time David gave the command that no one but the Levites was to carry the Ark of God, for it was them whom HASHEM had chosen to carry the Ark of God and to minister before Him forever. [3] David assembled all of Israel to Jerusalem, to bring up the Ark of God to its place that he had prepared for it. [4] David gathered together the sons of Aaron and the Levites:

The Ark's Levite bearers

[5] Of the sons of Kohath: Uriel, the chief, and a hundred twenty of his kinsmen; [6] of the sons of Merari: Asaiah, the chief, and two hundred twenty of his kinsmen; [7] of the sons of Gershom: Joel, the chief, and a hundred thirty of his kinsmen; [8] of the sons of Elizaphan: Shemaiah, the chief, and two hundred of his kinsmen; [9] of the sons of Hebron: Eliel, the chief, and eighty of his kinsmen; [10] of the sons of Uzziel, Amminadab, the chief, and a hundred twelve of his kinsmen. [11] David called for Zadok and Ebiathar the Kohanim, and the Levites Uriel, Asaiah, Joel, Shemaiah, Eliel and Amminadab, [12] and he said to them, "You, the family heads of the Levites — you and your kinsmen — sanctify yourselves and bring up the Ark of HASHEM, God of Israel, to [the place] that I have prepared for it. [13] For the first time, * it was not you; HASHEM our God dealt harshly with us, for we did not seek Him out as was proper." [14] So the Kohanim and the Levites sanctified themselves to bring up the Ark of HASHEM, God of Israel. [15] The sons of the Levites carried the Ark of God, as Moses had commanded* in accordance with the word of HASHEM — on their shoulders, by staffs upon them.

The musical accompaniment

[16] David instructed the officers of the Levites to set up their kinsmen who made music with musical instruments — lyres, harps and cymbals — making themselves heard, to raise their voices in joy. [17] So the Levites appointed Heman son of Joel and one of his kinsmen, Asaph son of Berechiah; and of the sons of Merari their kinsmen, Ethan son of Kushaiah. [18] And with them were their kinsmen, next in rank: Zechariah, Ben, Jaaziel, Shemiramoth, Jehiel, Unni, Eliab, Benaiah, Maaseiah, Mattithiah, Eliphalehu, Mikneiah, Obed-edom and Jeiel, the gatekeepers. [19] The musicians Heman, Asaph and Ethan sounded the brass cymbals; [20] and Zechariah, Aziel, Shemiramoth, Jehiel, Unni, Eliab, Maaseiah and Benaiah played the lyre, upon Alamoth. * [21] Mattithiah, Eliphalehu, Mikneiah, Obed-edom, Jeiel and Azaziah led the music of the harps, upon the eight-stringed instrument. [22] Cheneniah was the officer over the Levites for the pitch of the singing; he oversaw the pitch, because he was an expert. [23] Berechiah and Elkanah were gatekeepers for the Ark. * [24] Shebaniah, Joshapahat, Nethanel, Amasai, Zechariah, Benaiah and Eliezer, the Kohanim, blew the trumpets before the Ark of God; and Obed-edom and Jehiah were gatekeepers for the Ark.

15:15. Cf. *Numbers* 7:6-9.
15:20. A musical instrument.

15:23. But on this occasion they also joined the singers (*Radak*).

כה וַיְהִי דָוִיד וְזִקְנֵי יִשְׂרָאֵל וְשָׂרֵי הָאֲלָפִים הַהֹלְכִים לְהַעֲלוֹת אֶת־אֲרוֹן
כו בְּרִית־יְהוָה מִן־בֵּית עֹבֵד־אֱדֹם בְּשִׂמְחָה: וַיְהִי בֶּעְזֹר הָאֱלֹהִים
אֶת־הַלְוִיִּם נֹשְׂאֵי אֲרוֹן בְּרִית־יְהוָה וַיִּזְבְּחוּ שִׁבְעָה־פָרִים וְשִׁבְעָה אֵילִים:
כז וְדָוִיד מְכֻרְבָּל ׀ בִּמְעִיל בּוּץ וְכָל־הַלְוִיִּם הַנֹּשְׂאִים אֶת־הָאָרוֹן וְהַמְשֹׁרְרִים
כח וּכְנַנְיָה הַשַּׂר הַמַּשָּׂא הַמְשֹׁרְרִים וְעַל־דָּוִיד אֵפוֹד בָּד: וְכָל־יִשְׂרָאֵל
מַעֲלִים אֶת־אֲרוֹן בְּרִית־יְהוָה בִּתְרוּעָה וּבְקוֹל שׁוֹפָר וּבַחֲצֹצְרוֹת
כט וּבִמְצִלְתַּיִם מַשְׁמִעִים בִּנְבָלִים וְכִנֹּרוֹת: וַיְהִי אֲרוֹן בְּרִית יְהוָה בָּא עַד־עִיר
דָּוִיד וּמִיכַל בַּת־שָׁאוּל נִשְׁקְפָה ׀ בְּעַד הַחַלּוֹן וַתֵּרֶא אֶת־הַמֶּלֶךְ דָּוִיד

טז א מְרַקֵּד וּמְשַׂחֵק וַתִּבֶז לוֹ בְּלִבָּהּ: וַיָּבִיאוּ אֶת־אֲרוֹן הָאֱלֹהִים וַיַּצִּיגוּ
אֹתוֹ בְּתוֹךְ הָאֹהֶל אֲשֶׁר נָטָה־לוֹ דָּוִיד וַיַּקְרִיבוּ עֹלוֹת וּשְׁלָמִים לִפְנֵי
ב הָאֱלֹהִים: וַיְכַל דָּוִיד מֵהַעֲלוֹת הָעֹלָה וְהַשְּׁלָמִים וַיְבָרֶךְ אֶת־הָעָם בְּשֵׁם
ג יְהוָה: וַיְחַלֵּק לְכָל־אִישׁ יִשְׂרָאֵל מֵאִישׁ וְעַד־אִשָּׁה לְאִישׁ כִּכַּר־לֶחֶם
ד וְאֶשְׁפָּר וַאֲשִׁישָׁה: וַיִּתֵּן לִפְנֵי אֲרוֹן יְהוָה מִן־הַלְוִיִּם מְשָׁרְתִים וּלְהַזְכִּיר
ה וּלְהוֹדוֹת וּלְהַלֵּל לַיהוָה אֱלֹהֵי יִשְׂרָאֵל: אָסָף הָרֹאשׁ וּמִשְׁנֵהוּ
זְכַרְיָה יְעִיאֵל וּשְׁמִירָמוֹת וִיחִיאֵל וּמַתִּתְיָה וֶאֱלִיאָב וּבְנָיָהוּ וְעֹבֵד אֱדֹם
ו וִיעִיאֵל בִּכְלֵי נְבָלִים וּבְכִנֹּרוֹת וְאָסָף בַּמְצִלְתַּיִם מַשְׁמִיעַ: וּבְנָיָהוּ וְיַחֲזִיאֵל
ז הַכֹּהֲנִים בַּחֲצֹצְרוֹת תָּמִיד לִפְנֵי אֲרוֹן בְּרִית־הָאֱלֹהִים: בַּיּוֹם הַהוּא אָז נָתַן
דָּוִיד בָּרֹאשׁ לְהֹדוֹת לַיהוָה בְּיַד־אָסָף וְאֶחָיו:

ח-ט הוֹדוּ לַיהוָה קִרְאוּ בִשְׁמוֹ הוֹדִיעוּ בָעַמִּים עֲלִילֹתָיו: שִׁירוּ לוֹ זַמְּרוּ־לוֹ
י שִׂיחוּ בְּכָל־נִפְלְאֹתָיו: הִתְהַלְלוּ בְּשֵׁם קָדְשׁוֹ יִשְׂמַח לֵב מְבַקְשֵׁי יְהוָה:
יא-יב דִּרְשׁוּ יְהוָה וְעֻזּוֹ בַּקְּשׁוּ פָנָיו תָּמִיד: זִכְרוּ נִפְלְאֹתָיו אֲשֶׁר עָשָׂה מֹפְתָיו
יג-יד וּמִשְׁפְּטֵי־פִיהוּ: זֶרַע יִשְׂרָאֵל עַבְדּוֹ בְּנֵי יַעֲקֹב בְּחִירָיו: הוּא יְהוָה אֱלֹהֵינוּ
טו-טז בְּכָל־הָאָרֶץ מִשְׁפָּטָיו: זִכְרוּ לְעוֹלָם בְּרִיתוֹ דָּבָר צִוָּה לְאֶלֶף דּוֹר: אֲשֶׁר
יז כָּרַת אֶת־אַבְרָהָם וּשְׁבוּעָתוֹ לְיִצְחָק: וַיַּעֲמִידֶהָ לְיַעֲקֹב לְחֹק לְיִשְׂרָאֵל
יח-יט בְּרִית עוֹלָם: לֵאמֹר לְךָ אֶתֵּן אֶרֶץ־כְּנָעַן חֶבֶל נַחֲלַתְכֶם: בִּהְיוֹתְכֶם מְתֵי
כ מִסְפָּר כִּמְעַט וְגָרִים בָּהּ: וַיִּתְהַלְּכוּ מִגּוֹי אֶל־גּוֹי וּמִמַּמְלָכָה אֶל־עַם אַחֵר:
כא-כב לֹא־הִנִּיחַ לְאִישׁ לְעָשְׁקָם וַיּוֹכַח עֲלֵיהֶם מְלָכִים: אַל־תִּגְּעוּ בִּמְשִׁיחָי
כג וּבִנְבִיאַי אַל־תָּרֵעוּ: שִׁירוּ לַיהוָה כָּל־הָאָרֶץ בַּשְּׂרוּ מִיּוֹם־אֶל־יוֹם
כד-כה יְשׁוּעָתוֹ: סַפְּרוּ בַגּוֹיִם אֶת־כְּבוֹדוֹ בְּכָל־הָעַמִּים נִפְלְאֹתָיו: כִּי גָדוֹל
כו יְהוָה וּמְהֻלָּל מְאֹד וְנוֹרָא הוּא עַל־כָּל־אֱלֹהִים: כִּי כָּל־אֱלֹהֵי הָעַמִּים
כז-כח אֱלִילִים וַיהוָה שָׁמַיִם עָשָׂה: הוֹד וְהָדָר לְפָנָיו עֹז וְחֶדְוָה בִּמְקֹמוֹ: הָבוּ
כט לַיהוָה מִשְׁפְּחוֹת עַמִּים הָבוּ לַיהוָה כָּבוֹד וָעֹז: הָבוּ לַיהוָה כְּבוֹד שְׁמוֹ

15:26. By granting them safe passage, without the calamity that had befallen Uzza (Radak).

15:29. See II Samuel 6:20-23.

16:4. Three types of psalms (Rashi).

16:8. David sang this psalm when he stationed the Ark in Jerusalem. The first section, vv. 8-22, is an abridgement of Psalm 105. The second section, vv. 23-36, is a slightly abbreviated version of Psalm 96, and ends with 106:1, 47,48.

Exuberant   ²⁵ David and the elders of Israel and the officers of thousands who went to bring
procession   up the Ark of the Covenant of HASHEM from Obed-edom's house were exuberant.
²⁶ It happened that because God helped the Levites* who were carrying the Ark
of the Covenant of HASHEM, they offered as sacrifices seven bulls and seven rams.
²⁷ David was clothed in a linen robe, as were all the Levites who carried the Ark,
and the musicians and Cheneniah, the officer over the pitch of the singers. David
had on him a linen tunic. ²⁸ All of Israel brought up the Ark of the Covenant of
HASHEM with joyous shouts and the sound of the shofar, with trumpets and
cymbals sounding among the lyres and harps.

Michal's   ²⁹ It happened as the Ark of HASHEM arrived at the City of David, Michal
dissonance   daughter of Saul peered out the window and saw King David dancing and
cavorting before HASHEM, and she became contemptuous of him in her heart. *

16   ¹ They brought the Ark of God and set it up inside the tent that David had
Celebration   pitched for it; and David offered burnt-offerings and peace-offerings before
and   God. ² When David had finished offering up the burnt-offering and the peace-offer-
thanksgiving   ing, he blessed the people with the Name of HASHEM. ³ He distributed to all the
people of Israel, to man and woman alike, a loaf of bread, a portion of beef and
a container of wine for each person.

⁴ He stationed some of the Levites before the Ark of HASHEM as ministers, and
to chant Remembrances, Thanksgivings and Praises* to HASHEM, God of Israel:
⁵ Asaph the chief, his second in command Zechariah, Jeiel, Shemiramoth, Jehiel,
Mattithiah, Eliab, Benaiah, Obed-edom and Jeiel, with instruments of lyres and
harps, with Asaph sounding the cymbals, ⁶ and Benaiah and Jahaziel, the
Kohanim, always being with the trumpets before the Ark of the Covenant of God.
⁷ Then, on that day, David placed the responsibility for thanksgiving to HASHEM
into the hands of Asaph and his kinsmen.

David's song   ⁸ Give thanks to HASHEM, declare His Name; make His acts known among
of praise   the nations. ⁹ Sing to Him, make music to Him, speak of all His wonders.
¹⁰ Glory in His holy Name; may the heart of those who seek HASHEM be glad.
¹¹ Search out HASHEM and His might, seek His Presence always. ¹² Remem-
ber His wonders that He wrought, His marvels and the judgments of His
mouth. ¹³ O seed of Israel His servant, O children of Jacob, His chosen ones,
Remembering   ¹⁴ He is HASHEM our God; over all the earth are His ordinances. ¹⁵ Remember
His covenant   His covenant forever, the word He commanded for a thousand generations
— ¹⁶ that He covenanted with Abraham, and His oath to Isaac. ¹⁷ Then He
established it for Jacob as a statute, for Israel as an everlasting covenant,
God's   ¹⁸ saying, 'To you I shall give the land of Canaan, the lot of your heritage.'
promise   ¹⁹ When you were but few in number, hardly dwelling there, ²⁰ and they
wandered from nation to nation, and from one kingdom to another people,
²¹ He allowed no man to rob them, and He rebuked kings for their sake:
²² 'Dare not touch My anointed ones, and to My prophets do no harm.'

Acknowledge   ²³ Sing to HASHEM, everyone on earth, announce His salvation daily. ²⁴ Re-
His salvation   late His glory among the nations, and His wonders among all the peoples —
²⁵ that HASHEM is great and exceedingly lauded, awesome is He above all
heavenly powers. ²⁶ For all the gods of the nations are nothings, but HASHEM
made the heavens. ²⁷ Glory and majesty are before Him; might and joy are
in His place. ²⁸ Render unto HASHEM, O families of peoples — render unto
HASHEM honor and might; ²⁹ render unto HASHEM honor worthy of His Name.

ל שְׂאוּ מִנְחָה וּבֹאוּ לְפָנָיו הִשְׁתַּחֲווּ לַיהוָה בְּהַדְרַת־קֹדֶשׁ: חִילוּ מִלְּפָנָיו

לא כָּל־הָאָרֶץ אַף־תִּכּוֹן תֵּבֵל בַּל־תִּמּוֹט: יִשְׂמְחוּ הַשָּׁמַיִם וְתָגֵל הָאָרֶץ

לב וְיֹאמְרוּ בַגּוֹיִם יְהוָה מָלָךְ: יִרְעַם הַיָּם וּמְלוֹאוֹ יַעֲלֹץ הַשָּׂדֶה וְכָל־אֲשֶׁר־בּוֹ:

לג-לד אָז יְרַנְּנוּ עֲצֵי הַיָּעַר מִלִּפְנֵי יְהוָה כִּי־בָא לִשְׁפּוֹט אֶת־הָאָרֶץ: הוֹדוּ לַיהוָה

לה כִּי טוֹב כִּי לְעוֹלָם חַסְדּוֹ: וְאִמְרוּ הוֹשִׁיעֵנוּ אֱלֹהֵי יִשְׁעֵנוּ וְקַבְּצֵנוּ

לו וְהַצִּילֵנוּ מִן־הַגּוֹיִם לְהֹדוֹת לְשֵׁם קָדְשֶׁךָ לְהִשְׁתַּבֵּחַ בִּתְהִלָּתֶךָ: בָּרוּךְ יְהוָה

אֱלֹהֵי יִשְׂרָאֵל מִן־הָעוֹלָם וְעַד הָעֹלָם וַיֹּאמְרוּ כָל־הָעָם אָמֵן וְהַלֵּל

לז לַיהוָה: וַיַּעֲזָב־שָׁם לִפְנֵי אֲרוֹן בְּרִית־יְהוָה לְאָסָף וּלְאֶחָיו לְשָׁרֵת

לח לִפְנֵי הָאָרוֹן תָּמִיד לִדְבַר־יוֹם בְּיוֹמוֹ: וְעֹבֵד אֱדֹם וַאֲחֵיהֶם שִׁשִּׁים וּשְׁמוֹנָה

וְעֹבֵד אֱדֹם בֶּן־יְדִיתוּן וְחֹסָה לְשֹׁעֲרִים: וְאֵת ׀ צָדוֹק הַכֹּהֵן וְאֶחָיו הַכֹּהֲנִים

לט לִפְנֵי מִשְׁכַּן יְהוָה בַּבָּמָה אֲשֶׁר בְּגִבְעוֹן: לְהַעֲלוֹת עֹלוֹת לַיהוָה עַל־מִזְבַּח

מ הָעֹלָה תָּמִיד לַבֹּקֶר וְלָעָרֶב וּלְכָל־הַכָּתוּב בְּתוֹרַת יְהוָה אֲשֶׁר צִוָּה עַל־

מא יִשְׂרָאֵל: וְעִמָּהֶם הֵימָן וִידוּתוּן וּשְׁאָר הַבְּרוּרִים אֲשֶׁר נִקְּבוּ בְּשֵׁמוֹת

מב לְהֹדוֹת לַיהוָה כִּי לְעוֹלָם חַסְדּוֹ: וְעִמָּהֶם הֵימָן וִידוּתוּן חֲצֹצְרוֹת

מג וּמְצִלְתַּיִם לְמַשְׁמִיעִים וּכְלֵי שִׁיר הָאֱלֹהִים וּבְנֵי יְדוּתוּן לַשָּׁעַר: וַיֵּלְכוּ כָל־

הָעָם אִישׁ לְבֵיתוֹ וַיִּסֹּב דָּוִיד לְבָרֵךְ אֶת־בֵּיתוֹ:   וַיְהִי כַּאֲשֶׁר יָשַׁב

יז   א דָּוִיד בְּבֵיתוֹ וַיֹּאמֶר דָּוִיד אֶל־נָתָן הַנָּבִיא הִנֵּה אָנֹכִי יוֹשֵׁב בְּבֵית הָאֲרָזִים

ב וַאֲרוֹן בְּרִית־יְהוָה תַּחַת יְרִיעוֹת: וַיֹּאמֶר נָתָן אֶל־דָּוִיד כֹּל אֲשֶׁר בִּלְבָבְךָ

ג עֲשֵׂה כִּי הָאֱלֹהִים עִמָּךְ:   וַיְהִי בַּלַּיְלָה הַהוּא וַיְהִי דְּבַר־אֱלֹהִים

ד אֶל־נָתָן לֵאמֹר: לֵךְ וְאָמַרְתָּ אֶל־דָּוִיד עַבְדִּי כֹּה אָמַר יְהוָה לֹא אַתָּה

ה תִבְנֶה־לִּי הַבַּיִת לָשָׁבֶת: כִּי לֹא יָשַׁבְתִּי בְּבַיִת מִן־הַיּוֹם אֲשֶׁר הֶעֱלֵיתִי

ו אֶת־יִשְׂרָאֵל עַד הַיּוֹם הַזֶּה וָאֶהְיֶה מֵאֹהֶל אֶל־אֹהֶל וּמִמִּשְׁכָּן: בְּכֹל אֲשֶׁר־

הִתְהַלַּכְתִּי בְּכָל־יִשְׂרָאֵל הֲדָבָר דִּבַּרְתִּי אֶת־אַחַד שֹׁפְטֵי יִשְׂרָאֵל אֲשֶׁר

ז צִוִּיתִי לִרְעוֹת אֶת־עַמִּי לֵאמֹר לָמָּה לֹא־בְנִיתֶם לִי בֵּית אֲרָזִים: וְעַתָּה

כֹּה־תֹאמַר לְעַבְדִּי לְדָוִיד כֹּה אָמַר יְהוָה צְבָאוֹת אֲנִי לְקַחְתִּיךָ מִן־הַנָּוֶה

ח מִן־אַחֲרֵי הַצֹּאן לִהְיוֹת נָגִיד עַל עַמִּי יִשְׂרָאֵל: וָאֶהְיֶה עִמְּךָ בְּכֹל אֲשֶׁר

הָלַכְתָּ וָאַכְרִית אֶת־כָּל־אוֹיְבֶיךָ מִפָּנֶיךָ וְעָשִׂיתִי לְךָ שֵׁם כְּשֵׁם הַגְּדוֹלִים

ט אֲשֶׁר בָּאָרֶץ: וְשַׂמְתִּי מָקוֹם לְעַמִּי יִשְׂרָאֵל וּנְטַעְתִּיהוּ וְשָׁכַן תַּחְתָּיו וְלֹא

י יִרְגַּז עוֹד וְלֹא־יוֹסִיפוּ בְנֵי־עַוְלָה לְבַלֹּתוֹ כַּאֲשֶׁר בָּרִאשׁוֹנָה: וּלְמִיָּמִים

אֲשֶׁר צִוִּיתִי שֹׁפְטִים עַל־עַמִּי יִשְׂרָאֵל וְהִכְנַעְתִּי אֶת־כָּל־אוֹיְבֶיךָ וָאַגִּד

יא לָךְ וּבַיִת יִבְנֶה־לְּךָ יְהוָה: וְהָיָה כִּי־מָלְאוּ יָמֶיךָ לָלֶכֶת עִם־אֲבֹתֶיךָ

16:30. If the people of the world would tremble in fear of God, calamities would not happen (*Ralbag*).

16:39. Even after the Ark was brought to Jerusalem, the communal offerings were still brought at the "High Place," i.e., the communal Altar in Gibeon.

17:11. Despite the above assurances to David, God now says that Israel had not yet achieved the absolute security and tranquility that are prerequisites to the building of the Temple (see *Deuteronomy* 12:10-11). That era would first arrive during the reign of Solomon (*Abarbanel*).

Take an offering and come before Him; prostrate yourselves before Hashem in His intensely holy place. ³⁰ Tremble before Him, everyone on earth; let the world be fixed so that it cannot falter* ³¹ The heavens will be glad and the earth will rejoice; let them declare among the peoples, 'Hashem reigns!' ³² The sea and its fullness will roar; the field and everything in it will exult; ³³ then all the trees of the forest will sing with joy — before Hashem, for He will have come to judge the earth.

Rejoice in His reign

³⁴ Give thanks to Hashem for He is good; for his kindness endures forever! ³⁵ Say, 'Save us, O God of our salvation; gather us and deliver us from the nations, to give thanks to Your holy Name, to glory in Your praise.' ³⁶ Blessed is Hashem, God of Israel, from This World to the World to Come!

Thankful prayer

And the entire nation said, "Amen" and "praise to Hashem!"

³⁷ [David] left Asaph and his kinsmen there before the Ark of the Covenant of Hashem to minister before the Ark permanently, each day according to what was appropriate on that day, ³⁸ along with Obed-edom and sixty-eight of their kinsmen; Obed-edom son of Jedithun and Hosah to be gatekeepers. ³⁹ Zadok the Kohen and his brethren the Kohanim served before the Tabernacle of Hashem, at the High Place that was in Gibeon, * ⁴⁰ to bring up burnt-offerings to Hashem upon the Altar of Burnt-Offerings continuously, morning and evening, according to all that is written in the Torah of Hashem, which He had commanded Israel. ⁴¹ With them were Heman and Jeduthun and the rest of the chosen ones who were specified by name, to give thanks to Hashem, for His mercy is forever. ⁴² With them, Heman and Jeduthun, were trumpets and cymbals for those who sounded them, and the musical instruments of God. Jeduthun's sons were in charge of the gate.

Jerusalem and Gibeon

⁴³ All the people then went back to their homes, and David turned to bless his [own] household.

17

¹ It happened after David was settled into his home that David said to Nathan the prophet, "Behold, I am living in a house of cedar while the Ark of the Covenant of Hashem dwells under curtains!"

David's rejected hope to build a Temple

² Nathan said to David, "Do whatever is in your heart, for God is with you."

³ It happened that night that the word of God came to Nathan, saying, ⁴ "Go and say to My servant David: Thus said Hashem: [It is] not you who will build a house for Me to dwell in. ⁵ For I have not dwelled in a house from the day I brought Israel up to this day; I have moved from tent to tent and from tabernacle [to tabernacle]. ⁶ Wherever I moved about among all of Israel, did I say a word to one of the judges of Israel, whom I have appointed to shepherd My people Israel, saying, 'Why have you not built Me a house of cedarwood?' ⁷ And now, thus shall you say to My servant David: So says Hashem, Master of Legions: I have taken you from the sheepfold, from following the flocks, to become ruler over My people, over Israel. ⁸ I was with you wherever you went — I cut down all your enemies before you and I gave you renown, like the renown of the great men of the land. ⁹ I shall yet secure a place for My people, for Israel; I shall plant it there and it shall dwell in its place so that it shall be disturbed no more; iniquitous people will no longer beleaguer it — as in early times, ¹⁰ and [also] from the day that I appointed judges over My people Israel — and I will subdue all your enemies. And I declare to you that Hashem will establish a dynasty for you. ¹¹ When your days are complete to go to your forefathers, *

וַהֲקִימוֹתִי אֶת־זַרְעֲךָ אַחֲרֶיךָ אֲשֶׁר יִהְיֶה מִבָּנֶיךָ וַהֲכִינוֹתִי אֶת־מַלְכוּתוֹ:

יב־יג הוּא יִבְנֶה־לִּי בַּיִת וְכֹנַנְתִּי אֶת־כִּסְאוֹ עַד־עוֹלָם: אֲנִי אֶהְיֶה־לּוֹ לְאָב וְהוּא יִהְיֶה־לִּי לְבֵן וְחַסְדִּי לֹא־אָסִיר מֵעִמּוֹ כַּאֲשֶׁר הֲסִירוֹתִי מֵאֲשֶׁר הָיָה

יד לְפָנֶיךָ: וְהַעֲמַדְתִּיהוּ בְּבֵיתִי וּבְמַלְכוּתִי עַד־הָעוֹלָם וְכִסְאוֹ יִהְיֶה נָכוֹן

טו עַד־עוֹלָם: כְּכֹל הַדְּבָרִים הָאֵלֶּה וּכְכֹל הֶחָזוֹן הַזֶּה כֵּן דִּבֶּר נָתָן אֶל־

טז דָּוִיד: וַיָּבֹא הַמֶּלֶךְ דָּוִיד וַיֵּשֶׁב לִפְנֵי יְהוָה וַיֹּאמֶר מִי־אֲנִי יְהוָה

יז אֱלֹהִים וּמִי בֵיתִי כִּי הֲבִיאֹתַנִי עַד־הֲלֹם: וַתִּקְטַן זֹאת בְּעֵינֶיךָ אֱלֹהִים וַתְּדַבֵּר עַל־בֵּית־עַבְדְּךָ לְמֵרָחוֹק וּרְאִיתַנִי כְּתוֹר הָאָדָם הַמַּעֲלָה יְהוָה

יח אֱלֹהִים: מַה־יּוֹסִיף עוֹד דָּוִיד אֵלֶיךָ לְכָבוֹד אֶת־עַבְדֶּךָ וְאַתָּה אֶת־עַבְדְּךָ

יט יָדָעְתָּ: יְהוָה בַּעֲבוּר עַבְדְּךָ וְכְלִבְּךָ עָשִׂיתָ אֵת כָּל־הַגְּדוּלָּה הַזֹּאת לְהֹדִיעַ

כ אֶת־כָּל־הַגְּדֻלוֹת: יְהוָה אֵין כָּמוֹךָ וְאֵין אֱלֹהִים זוּלָתֶךָ בְּכֹל אֲשֶׁר־שָׁמַעְנוּ

כא בְּאָזְנֵינוּ: וּמִי כְּעַמְּךָ יִשְׂרָאֵל גּוֹי אֶחָד בָּאָרֶץ אֲשֶׁר הָלַךְ הָאֱלֹהִים לִפְדּוֹת לוֹ עָם לָשׂוּם לְךָ שֵׁם גְּדֻלּוֹת וְנֹרָאוֹת לְגָרֵשׁ מִפְּנֵי עַמְּךָ אֲשֶׁר־פָּדִיתָ

כב מִמִּצְרַיִם גּוֹיִם: וַתִּתֵּן אֶת־עַמְּךָ יִשְׂרָאֵל לְךָ לְעָם עַד־עוֹלָם וְאַתָּה יְהוָה

כג הָיִיתָ לָהֶם לֵאלֹהִים: וְעַתָּה יְהוָה הַדָּבָר אֲשֶׁר דִּבַּרְתָּ עַל־עַבְדְּךָ וְעַל־

כד בֵּיתוֹ יֵאָמֵן עַד־עוֹלָם וַעֲשֵׂה כַּאֲשֶׁר דִּבַּרְתָּ: וְיֵאָמֵן וְיִגְדַּל שִׁמְךָ עַד־עוֹלָם לֵאמֹר יְהוָה צְבָאוֹת אֱלֹהֵי יִשְׂרָאֵל אֱלֹהִים לְיִשְׂרָאֵל וּבֵית־דָּוִיד עַבְדְּךָ

כה נָכוֹן לְפָנֶיךָ: כִּי אַתָּה אֱלֹהַי גָּלִיתָ אֶת־אֹזֶן עַבְדְּךָ לִבְנוֹת לוֹ בָּיִת עַל־כֵּן

כו מָצָא עַבְדְּךָ לְהִתְפַּלֵּל לְפָנֶיךָ: וְעַתָּה יְהוָה אַתָּה־הוּא הָאֱלֹהִים וַתְּדַבֵּר

כז עַל־עַבְדְּךָ הַטּוֹבָה הַזֹּאת: וְעַתָּה הוֹאַלְתָּ לְבָרֵךְ אֶת־בֵּית עַבְדְּךָ לִהְיוֹת

יח לְעוֹלָם לְפָנֶיךָ כִּי־אַתָּה יְהוָה בֵּרַכְתָּ וּמְבֹרָךְ לְעוֹלָם: א וַיְהִי אַחֲרֵי־כֵן וַיַּךְ דָּוִיד אֶת־פְּלִשְׁתִּים וַיַּכְנִיעֵם וַיִּקַּח אֶת־גַּת וּבְנֹתֶיהָ מִיַּד

ב־ג פְּלִשְׁתִּים: וַיַּךְ אֶת־מוֹאָב וַיִּהְיוּ מוֹאָב עֲבָדִים לְדָוִיד נֹשְׂאֵי מִנְחָה: וַיַּךְ דָּוִיד אֶת־הֲדַדְעֶזֶר מֶלֶךְ־צוֹבָה חֲמָתָה בְּלֶכְתּוֹ לְהַצִּיב יָדוֹ בִּנְהַר פְּרָת:

ד וַיִּלְכֹּד דָּוִיד מִמֶּנּוּ אֶלֶף רֶכֶב וְשִׁבְעַת אֲלָפִים פָּרָשִׁים וְעֶשְׂרִים אֶלֶף אִישׁ

ה רַגְלִי וַיְעַקֵּר דָּוִיד אֶת־כָּל־הָרֶכֶב וַיּוֹתֵר מִמֶּנּוּ מֵאָה רָכֶב: וַיָּבֹא אֲרַם דַּרְמֶשֶׂק לַעְזוֹר לַהֲדַדְעֶזֶר מֶלֶךְ צוֹבָה וַיַּךְ דָּוִיד בַּאֲרָם עֶשְׂרִים־וּשְׁנַיִם

ו אֶלֶף אִישׁ: וַיָּשֶׂם דָּוִיד בַּאֲרַם דַּרְמֶשֶׂק וַיְהִי אֲרָם לְדָוִיד עֲבָדִים נֹשְׂאֵי

ז מִנְחָה וַיּוֹשַׁע יְהוָה לְדָוִיד בְּכֹל אֲשֶׁר הָלָךְ: וַיִּקַּח דָּוִיד אֵת שִׁלְטֵי הַזָּהָב

17:18. "What more could David ask, for You have granted him all that he could possibly want" (*Targum*).

17:19. It is not due to my merit, but only the Divine will that has raised me to such lofty heights.

17:20. When we experience Your greatness, it confirms all the wonders of old of which we have heard from our forefathers.

17:21. Since You are the One and Only great God, how

fortunate is Your people Israel whom You have chosen to cling to You (*Metzudos*).

17:23. May there never be any reason, such as excessive sin, that might cause Your promise to be nullified.

17:25. Only because You have told me that You desire to create a dynasty from me have I dared pray that my house rule forever (*Kara*).

17:27. I and my house.

I will raise up after you your offspring who will be from among your sons, and I

Your son will build a Temple

shall make his kingdom firm. ¹² He shall build a Temple for Me, and I shall make his throne firm forever. ¹³ I shall be a Father unto him and he shall be a son unto Me, and I shall never remove My kindness from him, as I removed it from the one who preceded you. ¹⁴ I will establish him as My dynasty, as My kingdom, and his throne will be established forever."

¹⁵ *In accordance with all these words and this entire vision, so did Nathan speak to David.*

David's gratitude

¹⁶ *King David then came and settled before HASHEM, and said, "Who am I, O HASHEM, God, and who is my household, that You should have brought me this far? ¹⁷ And yet this was insufficient in Your eyes, O God, so You have spoken also of Your servant's household in the distant [future], and You have considered Me as befits a man of exalted stature, O HASHEM, God. ¹⁸ What more can David say to You to honor Your servant;* for You know Your servant. ¹⁹ O HASHEM, it is because of Your servant, and according to Your desire, that You have bestowed*

God and Israel incomparable

*all this greatness, * to make known all these great things. ²⁰ HASHEM, there is none like You and there is no god besides You, like all that we have heard with our ears. * ²¹ And who is like Your people Israel, a unique nation on earth, whom God went forth to redeem unto Himself for a people* — achieving for Yourself renown for great and marvelous wonders, driving out nations from before Your people, whom You had redeemed from Egypt. ²² You have made Your people Israel a*

May Your blessing come true

*people unto Yourself forever, and You, HASHEM, have been a God for them. ²³ And now, HASHEM, may the matter that You have spoken concerning Your servant and his house be fulfilled, and may You do as You have spoken. * ²⁴ And Your Name will thereby be recognized as true and glorified forever, when people say, 'HASHEM, Master of Legions, God of Israel, is God over Israel, and the house of Your servant David is established before You.' ²⁵ For You, my God, have revealed to the ear of Your servant, saying that [You] would create a dynasty for him — therefore Your servant has felt it proper to pray unto You. * ²⁶ And now, HASHEM, You are God, and You have spoken of this benevolence to Your servant. ²⁷ And now, You have consented to bless the house of Your servant, that it may remain forever before You. For You, O HASHEM, have blessed; may it* be blessed forever."*

18 **DAVID SUBDUES HIS ENEMIES**

18:1-20:8

Moab, Zobah and Aram

¹ *It happened after this that David struck the Philistines and subdued them. David took Gath and its suburbs from the hands of the Philistines. ² He struck Moab. The Moabites became servants, bearers of tribute,* to David. ³ David smote Hadadezer king of Zobah, * in Hamath, as he was on the way to assert his control over the Euphrates River. ⁴ David captured from him a thousand chariots, seven thousand [horse]men and twenty thousand foot soldiers. David hamstrung all the chariot [horses], * leaving over [enough for] one hundred chariots. ⁵ Aram of Damascus came to assist Hadarezer, king of Zobah, and David smote twenty-two thousand men of Aram. ⁶ David set up [authorities] in Aram of Damascus, and Aram became servants unto David, bearers of tribute. HASHEM caused salvation for David wherever he went. ⁷ David took the golden shields*

18:2. They were not actually enslaved to David, but were subjugated and had to pay taxes to him (*Radak*).
18:3. A Syrian kingdom. See *II Samuel* 8:3.

18:4. He did not kill the horses because it is forbidden to cause purposeless destruction (*Deuteronomy* 20:19); he removed their military potential (*Radak*).

ח אֲשֶׁר הָיוּ עַל עַבְדֵי הֲדַדְעֶזֶר וַיְבִיאֵם יְרוּשָׁלָ͏ִם: וּמִטִּבְחַת וּמִכּוּן עָרֵי
הֲדַדְעֶזֶר לָקַח דָּוִיד נְחֹשֶׁת רַבָּה מְאֹד בָּהּ ׀ עָשָׂה שְׁלֹמֹה אֶת־יָם הַנְּחֹשֶׁת
ט וְאֶת־הָעַמּוּדִים וְאֵת כְּלֵי הַנְּחֹשֶׁת: וַיִּשְׁמַע תֹּעוּ מֶלֶךְ חֲמָת כִּי

י הִכָּה דָוִיד אֶת־כָּל־חֵיל הֲדַדְעֶזֶר מֶלֶךְ־צוֹבָה: וַיִּשְׁלַח אֶת־הֲדוֹרָם־בְּנוֹ אֶל־
הַמֶּלֶךְ־דָּוִיד °לִשְׁאוֹל־ [°לִשְׁאָל־ ק] לוֹ לְשָׁלוֹם וּלְבָרֲכוֹ עַל אֲשֶׁר נִלְחַם
בַּהֲדַדְעֶזֶר וַיַּכֵּהוּ כִּי־אִישׁ מִלְחֲמוֹת תֹּעוּ הָיָה הֲדַדְעָזֶר וְכֹל כְּלֵי זָהָב וָכֶסֶף
יא וּנְחֹשֶׁת: גַּם־אֹתָם הִקְדִּישׁ הַמֶּלֶךְ דָּוִיד לַיהוָה עִם־הַכֶּסֶף וְהַזָּהָב אֲשֶׁר
נָשָׂא מִכָּל־הַגּוֹיִם מֵאֱדוֹם וּמִמּוֹאָב וּמִבְּנֵי עַמּוֹן וּמִפְּלִשְׁתִּים וּמֵעֲמָלֵק:
יב-יג וְאַבְשַׁי בֶּן־צְרוּיָה הִכָּה אֶת־אֱדוֹם בְּגֵיא הַמֶּלַח שְׁמוֹנָה עָשָׂר אָלֶף: וַיָּשֶׂם
בֶּאֱדוֹם נְצִיבִים וַיִּהְיוּ כָל־אֱדוֹם עֲבָדִים לְדָוִיד וַיּוֹשַׁע יהוה אֶת־דָּוִיד בְּכֹל
יד אֲשֶׁר הָלָךְ: וַיִּמְלֹךְ דָּוִיד עַל־כָּל־יִשְׂרָאֵל וַיְהִי עֹשֶׂה מִשְׁפָּט וּצְדָקָה לְכָל־
טו-טז עַמּוֹ: וְיוֹאָב בֶּן־צְרוּיָה עַל־הַצָּבָא וִיהוֹשָׁפָט בֶּן־אֲחִילוּד מַזְכִּיר: וְצָדוֹק
יז בֶּן־אֲחִיטוּב וַאֲבִימֶלֶךְ בֶּן־אֶבְיָתָר כֹּהֲנִים וְשַׁוְשָׁא סוֹפֵר: וּבְנָיָהוּ בֶּן־
יְהוֹיָדָע עַל־הַכְּרֵתִי וְהַפְּלֵתִי וּבְנֵי־דָוִיד הָרִאשֹׁנִים לְיַד הַמֶּלֶךְ:

יט א-ב וַיְהִי אַחֲרֵי־כֵן וַיָּמָת נָחָשׁ מֶלֶךְ בְּנֵי־עַמּוֹן וַיִּמְלֹךְ בְּנוֹ תַּחְתָּיו: וַיֹּאמֶר דָּוִיד
אֶעֱשֶׂה־חֶסֶד ׀ עִם־חָנוּן בֶּן־נָחָשׁ כִּי־עָשָׂה אָבִיו עִמִּי חֶסֶד וַיִּשְׁלַח דָּוִיד
מַלְאָכִים לְנַחֲמוֹ עַל־אָבִיו וַיָּבֹאוּ עַבְדֵי דָוִיד אֶל־אֶרֶץ בְּנֵי־עַמּוֹן אֶל־חָנוּן
ג לְנַחֲמוֹ: וַיֹּאמְרוּ שָׂרֵי בְנֵי־עַמּוֹן לְחָנוּן הַמְכַבֵּד דָּוִיד אֶת־אָבִיךָ בְּעֵינֶיךָ כִּי־
שָׁלַח לְךָ מְנַחֲמִים הֲלֹא בַּעֲבוּר לַחְקֹר וְלַהֲפֹךְ וּלְרַגֵּל הָאָרֶץ בָּאוּ עֲבָדָיו
ד אֵלֶיךָ: וַיִּקַּח חָנוּן אֶת־עַבְדֵי דָוִיד וַיְגַלְּחֵם וַיִּכְרֹת אֶת־מַדְוֵיהֶם בַּחֵצִי עַד־
ה הַמִּפְשָׂעָה וַיְשַׁלְּחֵם: וַיֵּלְכוּ וַיַּגִּידוּ לְדָוִיד עַל־הָאֲנָשִׁים וַיִּשְׁלַח לִקְרָאתָם
כִּי־הָיוּ הָאֲנָשִׁים נִכְלָמִים מְאֹד וַיֹּאמֶר הַמֶּלֶךְ שְׁבוּ בִירֵחוֹ עַד אֲשֶׁר־יְצַמַּח
ו זְקַנְכֶם וְשַׁבְתֶּם: וַיִּרְאוּ בְּנֵי עַמּוֹן כִּי הִתְבָּאֲשׁוּ עִם־דָּוִיד וַיִּשְׁלַח
חָנוּן וּבְנֵי עַמּוֹן אֶלֶף כִּכַּר־כֶּסֶף לִשְׂכֹּר לָהֶם מִן־אֲרַם נַהֲרַיִם וּמִן־אֲרַם
ז מַעֲכָה וּמִצּוֹבָה רֶכֶב וּפָרָשִׁים: וַיִּשְׂכְּרוּ לָהֶם שְׁנַיִם וּשְׁלֹשִׁים אֶלֶף רֶכֶב
וְאֶת־מֶלֶךְ מַעֲכָה וְאֶת־עַמּוֹ וַיָּבֹאוּ וַיַּחֲנוּ לִפְנֵי מֵידְבָא וּבְנֵי עַמּוֹן נֶאֶסְפוּ
ח מֵעָרֵיהֶם וַיָּבֹאוּ לַמִּלְחָמָה: וַיִּשְׁמַע דָּוִיד וַיִּשְׁלַח אֶת־יוֹאָב
ט וְאֵת כָּל־צָבָא הַגִּבּוֹרִים: וַיֵּצְאוּ בְּנֵי עַמּוֹן וַיַּעַרְכוּ מִלְחָמָה פֶּתַח הָעִיר
וְהַמְּלָכִים אֲשֶׁר־בָּאוּ לְבַדָּם בַּשָּׂדֶה: וַיַּרְא יוֹאָב כִּי־הָיְתָה פְנֵי־הַמִּלְחָמָה
אֵלָיו פָּנִים וְאָחוֹר וַיִּבְחַר מִכָּל־בָּחוּר בְּיִשְׂרָאֵל וַיַּעֲרֹךְ לִקְרַאת אֲרָם:
יא-יב וְאֵת יֶתֶר הָעָם נָתַן בְּיַד אַבְשַׁי אָחִיו וַיַּעַרְכוּ לִקְרַאת בְּנֵי עַמּוֹן: וַיֹּאמֶר
אִם־תֶּחֱזַק מִמֶּנִּי אֲרָם וְהָיִיתָ לִּי לִתְשׁוּעָה וְאִם־בְּנֵי עַמּוֹן יֶחֶזְקוּ מִמְּךָ

18:11. To be used for the construction of the Temple, in addition to that which was mentioned above in v. 8.

18:15. Or royal historian (*Targum*, *Radak*).

18:17. See *II Samuel* 8:18.

19:2. See *II Samuel* 8:2.

19:4. They shaved half their beards. See ibid. 10:5.

of Hadarezer's servants and brought them to Jerusalem. ⁸ And from Tibhath and Cun — cities of Hadarezer — David took a great deal of copper. From it, Solomon made the copper sea and the pillars and the copper vessels [of the Temple].

⁹ Tou, king of Hamath, heard that David had smitten the entire army of Hadarezer, king of Zobah. ¹⁰ So [Tou] sent his son Hadoram to King David to greet him and to wish him well for having fought and defeated Hadarezer, for Hadarezer was a battle foe of Tou; and [he brought] all kinds of silver and gold and copper articles. ¹¹ King David consecrated these [articles] also to HASHEM, * along with the silver and gold that he had taken from all the nations — from Edom and Moab, from the Children of Ammon and the Philistines and Amalek.

Edom   ¹² Abishai son of Zeruiah struck down eighteen thousand men of Edom in the Valley of Salt. ¹³ He appointed authorities in Edom, and all of Edom became subjects of David. HASHEM caused salvation for David wherever he went.

¹⁴ David reigned over all of Israel; he administered justice and kindness to all his people.

¹⁵ Joab son of Zeruiah was in command of the army. Jehoshaphat son of Ahilud was the secretary. * ¹⁶ Zadok son of Ahitub and Ahimelech son of Abiathar were Kohanim. Shavsha was the scribe. ¹⁷ Benaiah son of Jehoiada was in charge of the archers and slingers; * and David's sons were chief ministers at the king's side.

19   ¹ It happened after this that Nahash, the king of the Children of Ammon, died,
Ammonite   and his son reigned in his place. ² David thought, "I shall do an act of kindness
atrocity   for Hanun son of Nahash, for his father dealt kindly with me."* So David sent messengers to console him over his father. David's servants went to the land of the Children of Ammon, to Hanun, to console him. ³ The ministers of the Children of Ammon said to Hanun, "Do you think David is honoring your father by sending consolers to you? Surely it is in order to explore, overthrow and spy out the land that his servants have come to you!" ⁴ So Hanun took David's servants and shaved them, * and cut off half of their garments until their hips, and sent them off. ⁵ They went and sent word to David about the men, and he sent [messengers] to meet them, for the men were deeply humiliated. The king said, "Stay in Jericho until your beards grow back, and then return."

Ammon   ⁶ The Children of Ammon realized that they had made themselves repugnant to
hires   David, so Hanun and the children of Ammon sent a thousand talents of silver to
mercenaries   hire chariots and horsemen from Aram-naharaim, Aram-maacah and Zobah; ⁷ they also hired thirty-two thousand chariots, as well as the king of Maacah and his people. They went and encamped before Medeba; the Children of Ammon gathered together from their cities and went there for battle. ⁸ David heard and he dispatched Joab and all the mighty men of the army. ⁹ The Children of Ammon came out and deployed themselves for battle at the opening of the city, while the [foreign] kings who had come were in the field by themselves. ¹⁰ Joab saw that the battlefield faced him from the front and from the rear, so he selected from all the chosen ones of Israel, and he deployed them against Aram. ¹¹ He placed the rest of the people in the hand of his brother Abishai, and they deployed themselves against the Children of Ammon. ¹² He said, "If Aram will overpower me, then you will be my salvation; and if the Children of Ammon overpower you,

יג וְהוֹשַׁעְתָּיךְ: חֲזַק וְנִתְחַזְּקָה בְּעַד־עַמֵּנוּ וּבְעַד עָרֵי אֱלֹהֵינוּ וַיהוָה הַטּוֹב

בְּעֵינָיו יַעֲשֶׂה: וַיִּגַּשׁ יוֹאָב וְהָעָם אֲשֶׁר־עִמּוֹ לִפְנֵי אֲרָם לַמִּלְחָמָה וַיָּנוּסוּ יד

מִפָּנָיו: וּבְנֵי עַמּוֹן רָאוּ כִּי־נָס אֲרָם וַיָּנוּסוּ גַם־הֵם מִפְּנֵי אַבְשַׁי אָחִיו וַיָּבֹאוּ טו

הָעִירָה וַיָּבֹא יוֹאָב יְרוּשָׁלָ͏ִם: וַיַּרְא אֲרָם כִּי נִגְּפוּ לִפְנֵי יִשְׂרָאֵל טז

וַיִּשְׁלְחוּ מַלְאָכִים וַיּוֹצִיאוּ אֶת־אֲרָם אֲשֶׁר מֵעֵבֶר הַנָּהָר וְשׁוֹפַךְ שַׂר־צְבָא

הֲדַדְעֶזֶר לִפְנֵיהֶם: וַיֻּגַּד לְדָוִיד וַיֶּאֱסֹף אֶת־כָּל־יִשְׂרָאֵל וַיַּעֲבֹר הַיַּרְדֵּן וַיָּבֹא יז

אֲלֵהֶם וַיַּעֲרֹךְ אֲלֵהֶם וַיַּעֲרֹךְ דָּוִיד לִקְרַאת אֲרָם מִלְחָמָה וַיִּלָּחֲמוּ עִמּוֹ:

וַיָּנָס אֲרָם מִלִּפְנֵי יִשְׂרָאֵל וַיַּהֲרֹג דָּוִיד מֵאֲרָם שִׁבְעַת אֲלָפִים רֶכֶב יח

וְאַרְבָּעִים אֶלֶף אִישׁ רַגְלִי וְאֵת שׁוֹפַךְ שַׂר־הַצָּבָא הֵמִית: וַיִּרְאוּ עַבְדֵי יט

הֲדַדְעֶזֶר כִּי נִגְּפוּ לִפְנֵי יִשְׂרָאֵל וַיַּשְׁלִימוּ עִם־דָּוִיד וַיַּעַבְדֻהוּ וְלֹא־אָבָה

אֲרָם לְהוֹשִׁיעַ אֶת־בְּנֵי־עַמּוֹן עוֹד: וַיְהִי לְעֵת תְּשׁוּבַת הַשָּׁנָה **כ** א

לְעֵת ׀ צֵאת הַמְּלָכִים וַיִּנְהַג יוֹאָב אֶת־חֵיל הַצָּבָא וַיַּשְׁחֵת אֶת־אֶרֶץ בְּנֵי

עַמּוֹן וַיָּבֹא וַיָּצַר אֶת־רַבָּה וְדָוִיד יֹשֵׁב בִּירוּשָׁלָ͏ִם וַיַּךְ יוֹאָב אֶת־רַבָּה

וַיֶּהֶרְסֶהָ: וַיִּקַּח דָּוִיד אֶת־עֲטֶרֶת־מַלְכָּם מֵעַל רֹאשׁוֹ וַיִּמְצָאָהּ ׀ מִשְׁקָל ב

כִּכַּר־זָהָב וּבָהּ אֶבֶן יְקָרָה וַתְּהִי עַל־רֹאשׁ דָּוִיד וּשְׁלַל הָעִיר הוֹצִיא הַרְבֵּה

מְאֹד: וְאֶת־הָעָם אֲשֶׁר־בָּהּ הוֹצִיא וַיָּשַׂר בַּמְּגֵרָה וּבַחֲרִיצֵי הַבַּרְזֶל ג

וּבַמְּגֵרוֹת וְכֵן יַעֲשֶׂה דָוִיד לְכֹל עָרֵי בְנֵי־עַמּוֹן וַיָּשָׁב דָּוִיד וְכָל־הָעָם

יְרוּשָׁלָ͏ִם: וַיְהִי אַחֲרֵי־כֵן וַתַּעֲמֹד מִלְחָמָה בְּגֶזֶר עִם־פְּלִשְׁתִּים ד

אָז הִכָּה סִבְּכַי הַחֻשָׁתִי אֶת־סִפַּי מִילִדֵי הָרְפָאִים וַיִּכָּנֵעוּ: וַתְּהִי ה

עוֹד מִלְחָמָה אֶת־פְּלִשְׁתִּים וַיַּךְ אֶלְחָנָן בֶּן־°יָעוּר [קᵉ °יָעִיר] אֶת־לַחְמִי

אֲחִי גָּלְיָת הַגִּתִּי וְעֵץ חֲנִיתוֹ כִּמְנוֹר אֹרְגִים: וַתְּהִי־עוֹד מִלְחָמָה ו

בְּגַת וַיְהִי ׀ אִישׁ מִדָּה וְאֶצְבְּעֹתָיו שֵׁשׁ־וָשֵׁשׁ עֶשְׂרִים וְאַרְבַּע וְגַם־הוּא

נוֹלַד לְהָרָפָא: וַיְחָרֵף אֶת־יִשְׂרָאֵל וַיַּכֵּהוּ יְהוֹנָתָן בֶּן־שִׁמְעָא אֲחִי דָוִיד: אֵל ז

אֵל נוּלְדוּ לְהָרָפָא בְּגַת וַיִּפְּלוּ בְיַד־דָּוִיד וּבְיַד־עֲבָדָיו: וַיַּעֲמֹד שָׂטָן **כא** א

עַל־יִשְׂרָאֵל וַיָּסֶת אֶת־דָּוִיד לִמְנוֹת אֶת־יִשְׂרָאֵל: וַיֹּאמֶר דָּוִיד אֶל־יוֹאָב ב

וְאֶל־שָׂרֵי הָעָם לְכוּ סִפְרוּ אֶת־יִשְׂרָאֵל מִבְּאֵר שֶׁבַע וְעַד־דָּן וְהָבִיאוּ אֵלַי

וְאֵדְעָה אֶת־מִסְפָּרָם: וַיֹּאמֶר יוֹאָב יוֹסֵף יְהוָה עַל־עַמּוֹ ׀ כָּהֵם מֵאָה ג

פְעָמִים הֲלֹא אֲדֹנִי הַמֶּלֶךְ כֻּלָּם לַאדֹנִי לַעֲבָדִים לָמָּה יְבַקֵּשׁ זֹאת אֲדֹנִי

לָמָּה יִהְיֶה לְאַשְׁמָה לְיִשְׂרָאֵל: וּדְבַר־הַמֶּלֶךְ חָזַק עַל־יוֹאָב וַיֵּצֵא יוֹאָב ד

וַיִּתְהַלֵּךְ בְּכָל־יִשְׂרָאֵל וַיָּבֹא יְרוּשָׁלָ͏ִם: וַיִּתֵּן יוֹאָב אֶת־מִסְפַּר מִפְקַד־הָעָם ה

אֶל־דָּוִיד וַיְהִי כָל־יִשְׂרָאֵל אֶלֶף אֲלָפִים וּמֵאָה אֶלֶף אִישׁ שֹׁלֵף חֶרֶב

19:19. According to *II Samuel* 10:19, these *servants* were the other kings who had been hired by Hadarezer.

20:1. See *II Samuel* 11:1.

20:2. See *II Samuel* 12:30.

20:3. David punished the gratuitous cruelty of the Am-

monites publicly as a deterrent to others. There is an opinion that David did not torture the Ammonites but merely pressed them into forced labor — cutting and chopping wood and threshing grain — using these implements (*Daas Mikra*).

For the sake *I will save you.* ¹³ *Be strong and let us both be strong, for the sake of our people*
of God *and for the sake of the cities of our God; and* HASHEM *will do what is good in his*
and Israel *eyes."* ¹⁴ *Then Joab and the people who were with him approached to do battle*
against Aram, and they fled from him. ¹⁵ *When the Children of Ammon saw that*
Aram had fled, they also fled from before Abishai, [Joab's] brother, entering into
the city. Joab then returned to Jerusalem.

¹⁶ *Aram saw that they were beaten by Israel, so they sent messengers and*
brought over the Arameans from the other side of the [Euphrates] River, with
Shophach, the commander of Hadarezer's army, leading them. ¹⁷ *This was told*
to David and he gathered together all of Israel and crossed over the Jordan. He
came to them and deployed against them. David deployed for battle against
Aram, and they fought against him. ¹⁸ *Aram fled from before Israel, and David*
slew seven thousand charioteers and forty thousand foot soldiers; he also killed
Shophach, the commander of the army. ¹⁹ *When the servants of Hadarezer* * *saw*
that they were defeated by Israel, they surrendered to David and became sub-
servient to him. Aram was no longer willing to help the Children of Ammon.

20   ¹ I*t happened at the time of the turn of the year, at the time when kings go*
Joab   *forth,* * *that Joab led the battalions of the army. He destroyed the land of the*
smashes *Children of Ammon. Then he came and besieged Rabbah, while David was*
Ammon *settled in Jerusalem. Joab smote Rabbah and laid it waste.* ² *David removed their*
king's crown from his head. He found its weight to be a talent of gold, and in it was
a precious stone — and it remained over David's head. * *He also took out a great*
deal of booty from the city. ³ *He took out the people in it and cut them with saws,*
with iron threshing boards, and with axes; * *and this is what David would do to*
all the cities of the Children of Ammon.

⁴ *It happened after this that a war with the Philistines ensued, at Gezer. It was*
The *then that Sibbecai the Hushathite smote Sippai, who was one of the children of*
Philistines *the giants, and they were subdued.*

⁵ *There was another war with the Philistines, when Elhanan son of Jair smote*
Lahmi, the brother of Goliath the Gittite, who had a spear with a shaft like a
weaver's beam.

⁶ *There was another war, in Gath. There was a man of [huge] dimensions,*
whose digits were six for each [hand and foot], making twenty-four; he too was
born to the giant. ⁷ *He ridiculed Israel, and Jonathan, the son of David's brother*
Shimea, struck him down.

⁸ *These were born to the giant in Gath, and they fell by the hand of David and*
by the hand of his servants.

21   ¹ A*n adversary* * *stood against Israel, and enticed David to take a count of [the*
David's *people of] Israel.* * ² *So David said to Joab and to the officers of the people,*
ill-fated *"Go and make a tally of [the people of] Israel, from Beer-sheba to Dan, and bring*
census *it to me, so that I may know their number."* ³ *But Joab said, "May* HASHEM
increase the number of His people a hundred times over! Surely, my lord the king,
they are all servants to my lord! Why should my lord desire such a thing? Why
should this be a source of guilt for Israel?" ⁴ *But the word of the king prevailed over*
Joab; so Joab went and traveled through Israel, and returned to Jerusalem.

⁵ *Joab conveyed the sum of the tally of the people to David — all of Israel*
numbered one million one hundred thousand men — drawers of the sword; *

21:1. Literally, "Satan." See *II Samuel* 24:1.   **21:5.** That is, able-bodied fighters.

ו וְיהוּדָה אַרְבַּע מֵאוֹת וְשִׁבְעִים אֶלֶף אִישׁ שֹׁלֵף חָרֶב: וְלֵוִי וּבִנְיָמִן לֹא פָקַד

ז בְּתוֹכָם כִּי־נִתְעַב דְּבַר־הַמֶּלֶךְ אֶת־יוֹאָב: וַיֵּרַע בְּעֵינֵי הָאֱלֹהִים עַל־הַדָּבָר

ח הַזֶּה וַיַּךְ אֶת־יִשְׂרָאֵל: וַיֹּאמֶר דָּוִיד אֶל־הָאֱלֹהִים חָטָאתִי מְאֹד

אֲשֶׁר עָשִׂיתִי אֶת־הַדָּבָר הַזֶּה וְעַתָּה הַעֲבֶר־נָא אֶת־עֲווֹן עַבְדְּךָ כִּי נִסְכַּלְתִּי

ט מְאֹד: וַיְדַבֵּר יהוה אֶל־גָּד חֹזֵה דָוִיד לֵאמֹר: לֵךְ וְדִבַּרְתָּ אֶל־דָּוִיד

לֵאמֹר כֹּה אָמַר יהוה שָׁלוֹשׁ אֲנִי נֹטֶה עָלֶיךָ בְּחַר־לְךָ אַחַת מֵהֵנָּה וְאֶעֱשֶׂה

יא-יב לָךְ: וַיָּבֹא גָד אֶל־דָּוִיד וַיֹּאמֶר לוֹ כֹּה־אָמַר יהוה קַבֶּל־לָךְ: אִם־שָׁלוֹשׁ שָׁנִים

רָעָב וְאִם־שְׁלֹשָׁה חֳדָשִׁים נִסְפֶּה מִפְּנֵי־צָרֶיךָ וְחֶרֶב אוֹיְבֶיךָ לְמַשֶּׂגֶת וְאִם־

שְׁלֹשֶׁת יָמִים חֶרֶב יהוה וְדֶבֶר בָּאָרֶץ וּמַלְאַךְ יהוה מַשְׁחִית בְּכָל־גְּבוּל

יג יִשְׂרָאֵל וְעַתָּה רְאֵה מָה־אָשִׁיב אֶת־שֹׁלְחִי דָבָר: וַיֹּאמֶר

דָּוִיד אֶל־גָּד צַר־לִי מְאֹד אֶפְּלָה־נָּא בְיַד־יהוה כִּי־רַבִּים רַחֲמָיו מְאֹד

יד וּבְיַד־אָדָם אַל־אֶפֹּל: וַיִּתֵּן יהוה דֶּבֶר בְּיִשְׂרָאֵל וַיִּפֹּל מִיִּשְׂרָאֵל שִׁבְעִים

טו אֶלֶף אִישׁ: וַיִּשְׁלַח הָאֱלֹהִים מַלְאָךְ לִירוּשָׁלַםִ לְהַשְׁחִיתָהּ וּכְהַשְׁחִית

רָאָה יהוה וַיִּנָּחֶם עַל־הָרָעָה וַיֹּאמֶר לַמַּלְאָךְ הַמַּשְׁחִית רַב עַתָּה הֶרֶף יָדֶךָ

וּמַלְאַךְ יהוה עֹמֵד עִם־גֹּרֶן אָרְנָן הַיְבוּסִי: וַיִּשָּׂא דָוִיד אֶת־עֵינָיו

טז וַיַּרְא אֶת־מַלְאַךְ יהוה עֹמֵד בֵּין הָאָרֶץ וּבֵין הַשָּׁמַיִם וְחַרְבּוֹ שְׁלוּפָה בְּיָדוֹ

נְטוּיָה עַל־יְרוּשָׁלָםִ וַיִּפֹּל דָּוִיד וְהַזְּקֵנִים מְכֻסִּים בַּשַּׂקִּים עַל־פְּנֵיהֶם: וַיֹּאמֶר

יז דָּוִיד אֶל־הָאֱלֹהִים הֲלֹא אֲנִי אָמַרְתִּי לִמְנוֹת בָּעָם וַאֲנִי־הוּא אֲשֶׁר־חָטָאתִי

וְהָרֵעַ הֲרֵעוֹתִי וְאֵלֶּה הַצֹּאן מֶה עָשׂוּ יהוה אֱלֹהַי תְּהִי נָא יָדְךָ בִּי וּבְבֵית

יח אָבִי וּבְעַמְּךָ לֹא לְמַגֵּפָה: וּמַלְאַךְ יהוה אָמַר אֶל־גָּד לֵאמֹר

יט לְדָוִיד כִּי יַעֲלֶה דָוִיד לְהָקִים מִזְבֵּחַ לַיהוה בְּגֹרֶן אָרְנָן הַיְבֻסִי: וַיַּעַל דָּוִיד

כ בִּדְבַר־גָּד אֲשֶׁר דִּבֶּר בְּשֵׁם יהוה: וַיָּשָׁב אָרְנָן וַיַּרְא אֶת־הַמַּלְאָךְ וְאַרְבַּעַת

כא בָּנָיו עִמּוֹ מִתְחַבְּאִים וְאָרְנָן דָּשׁ חִטִּים: וַיָּבֹא דָוִיד עַד־אָרְנָן וַיַּבֵּט אָרְנָן

כב וַיַּרְא אֶת־דָּוִיד וַיֵּצֵא מִן־הַגֹּרֶן וַיִּשְׁתַּחוּ לְדָוִיד אַפַּיִם אָרְצָה: וַיֹּאמֶר דָּוִיד

אֶל־אָרְנָן תְּנָה־לִּי מְקוֹם הַגֹּרֶן וְאֶבְנֶה־בּוֹ מִזְבֵּחַ לַיהוה בְּכֶסֶף מָלֵא תְּנֵהוּ

כג לִי וְתֵעָצַר הַמַּגֵּפָה מֵעַל הָעָם: וַיֹּאמֶר אָרְנָן אֶל־דָּוִיד קַח־לָךְ וְיַעַשׂ אֲדֹנִי

הַמֶּלֶךְ הַטּוֹב בְּעֵינָיו רְאֵה נָתַתִּי הַבָּקָר לָעֹלוֹת וְהַמּוֹרִגִּים לָעֵצִים וְהַחִטִּים

כד לַמִּנְחָה הַכֹּל נָתָתִּי: וַיֹּאמֶר הַמֶּלֶךְ דָּוִיד לְאָרְנָן לֹא כִּי־קָנֹה אֶקְנֶה בְּכֶסֶף

כה מָלֵא כִּי לֹא־אֶשָּׂא אֲשֶׁר־לְךָ לַיהוה וְהַעֲלוֹת עוֹלָה חִנָּם: וַיִּתֵּן דָּוִיד לְאָרְנָן

כו בַּמָּקוֹם שִׁקְלֵי זָהָב מִשְׁקָל שֵׁשׁ מֵאוֹת: וַיִּבֶן שָׁם דָּוִיד מִזְבֵּחַ לַיהוה וַיַּעַל

עֹלוֹת וּשְׁלָמִים וַיִּקְרָא אֶל־יהוה וַיַּעֲנֵהוּ בָאֵשׁ מִן־הַשָּׁמַיִם עַל מִזְבַּח

כז-כח הָעֹלָה: וַיֹּאמֶר יהוה לַמַּלְאָךְ וַיָּשֶׁב חַרְבּוֹ אֶל־נְדָנָהּ: בָּעֵת

כט הַהִיא בִּרְאוֹת דָּוִיד כִּי־עָנָהוּ יהוה בְּגֹרֶן אָרְנָן הַיְבוּסִי וַיִּזְבַּח שָׁם: וּמִשְׁכַּן

21:15. See *II Samuel* 24:16. There he is called Araunah.   **21:28.** He began to use that site for offerings on a regular
21:25. See *II Samuel* 24:24.   basis (*Metzudos*).

and the men of Judah were four hundred seventy thousand men — drawers of the sword. ⁶ But [Joab] did not tally Levi and Benjamin among them, for the king's command was abhorrent to Joab.

David's
confession

⁷ This matter was bad in God's eyes, and He smote Israel. ⁸ David said to God, "I have sinned greatly in having done this thing. Now, please remove the sin of Your servant, for I have acted very foolishly."

David's
difficult
decision

⁹ HASHEM spoke to Gad, David's seer, saying, ¹⁰ "Go and speak to David, 'Thus said HASHEM: I am offering you three [things]; choose one of them and I will do it to you.' " ¹¹ So Gad came to David and said to him, "This is what HASHEM has said; accept [it] upon yourself: ¹² whether three years of famine; or three months during which you will be vanquished before your enemies, your enemies' sword gaining the upper hand; or three days of the sword of HASHEM, a pestilence in the land, with an angel of God bringing destruction throughout all the borders of Israel. Now consider, what answer should I return to the One Who has sent me!" ¹³ David said to Gad, "I am exceedingly distressed. Let me fall into HASHEM's hand, for His mercies are abundant; but let me not fall into the hand of man."

¹⁴ So HASHEM sent a pestilence in Israel, and seventy thousand men of Israel fell. ¹⁵ God sent an angel to Jerusalem to destroy it, but as he was destroying, HASHEM saw and reconsidered the evil. He told the destroying angel, "Enough! Now stay your hand!" The angel of HASHEM was standing at the threshing floor of Ornan the Jebusite. *

David's
penitence

¹⁶ David raised his eyes and saw the angel of HASHEM standing between the earth and heaven, with his sword drawn in his hand, stretched out over Jerusalem, and David and the elders, who were covered in sackcloth, fell on their faces. ¹⁷ David said to God, "Surely, I have said to take the count of the people, and I am the one who has sinned and acted wickedly; but these flock — what have they done? HASHEM, my God, let Your hand be against me and my father's house, but against Your people there should not be a plague!" ¹⁸ The angel of HASHEM told Gad to say to David, that David should go up and erect an altar to HASHEM in the threshing floor of Ornan the Jebusite. ¹⁹ So David went up as Gad had said, as HASHEM had commanded. ²⁰ Ornan had turned back and seen the angel, and his four sons were with him, hiding. Ornan had been threshing wheat. ²¹ David approached Ornan. Ornan looked out and saw David; he came out of the threshing floor and prostrated himself to David, with his face to the ground. ²² David said to Ornan, "Give me the site of the threshing floor, so that I may build an altar to HASHEM in it. Give it to me for the full price, so that the plague will cease from the people." ²³ But Ornan said to David, "Take [it] for yourself, and let my lord the king do whatever is proper in his eyes. See, I have given you the cattle for burnt-offerings, the threshing tools for firewood, and the wheat for a meal-offering — I have given everything!" ²⁴ But King David said to Ornan, "No; I shall buy it for the full price, for I shall not offer to HASHEM that which is yours, nor offer up a free burnt-offering!" ²⁵ So David gave Ornan for the place gold shekels weighing six hundred. * ²⁶ David then built an altar there to HASHEM, and he offered burnt-offerings and peace-offerings. He called out to HASHEM, and He responded to him with fire from heaven upon the Altar of burnt-offering. ²⁷ HASHEM then said [the command] to the angel, and he returned his sword to its sheath.

²⁸ At that time, when David saw that HASHEM had answered him at the threshing floor of Ornan the Jebusite, he brought offerings there. * ²⁹ The Tabernacle of

PREPARA-
TION FOR
THE TEMPLE
21:18-26:32

Purchasing
the site

יְהוָה אֲשֶׁר־עָשָׂה מֹשֶׁה בַּמִּדְבָּר וּמִזְבַּח הָעוֹלָה בָּעֵת הַהִיא בַּבָּמָה
בְּגִבְעוֹן: וְלֹא־יָכֹל דָּוִיד לָלֶכֶת לְפָנָיו לִדְרֹשׁ אֱלֹהִים כִּי נִבְעַת מִפְּנֵי חֶרֶב ל
מַלְאַךְ יְהוָה: וַיֹּאמֶר דָּוִיד זֶה הוּא בֵּית יְהוָה הָאֱלֹהִים וְזֶה־מִזְבֵּחַ לְעֹלָה א **כב**
לְיִשְׂרָאֵל: וַיֹּאמֶר דָּוִיד לִכְנוֹס אֶת־הַגֵּרִים אֲשֶׁר בְּאֶרֶץ יִשְׂרָאֵל ב
וַיַּעֲמֵד חֹצְבִים לַחְצוֹב אַבְנֵי גָזִית לִבְנוֹת בֵּית הָאֱלֹהִים: וּבַרְזֶל ׀ לָרֹב ג
לַמַּסְמְרִים לְדַלְתוֹת הַשְּׁעָרִים וְלַמְחַבְּרוֹת הֵכִין דָּוִיד וּנְחֹשֶׁת לָרֹב אֵין
מִשְׁקָל: וַעֲצֵי אֲרָזִים לְאֵין מִסְפָּר כִּי־הֵבִיאוּ הַצִּידֹנִים וְהַצֹּרִים עֲצֵי אֲרָזִים ד
לָרֹב לְדָוִיד: וַיֹּאמֶר דָּוִיד שְׁלֹמֹה בְנִי נַעַר וָרָךְ וְהַבַּיִת לִבְנוֹת ה
לַיהוָה לְהַגְדִּיל ׀ לְמַעְלָה לְשֵׁם וּלְתִפְאֶרֶת לְכָל־הָאֲרָצוֹת אָכִינָה נָּא לוֹ
וַיָּכֶן דָּוִיד לָרֹב לִפְנֵי מוֹתוֹ: וַיִּקְרָא לִשְׁלֹמֹה בְנוֹ וַיְצַוֵּהוּ לִבְנוֹת בַּיִת לַיהוָה ו
אֱלֹהֵי יִשְׂרָאֵל: וַיֹּאמֶר דָּוִיד לִשְׁלֹמֹה °בנו [°בְּנִי ק] אֲנִי הָיָה ז
עִם־לְבָבִי לִבְנוֹת בַּיִת לְשֵׁם יְהוָה אֱלֹהָי: וַיְהִי עָלַי דְּבַר־יְהוָה לֵאמֹר דָּם ח
לָרֹב שָׁפַכְתָּ וּמִלְחָמוֹת גְּדֹלוֹת עָשִׂיתָ לֹא־תִבְנֶה בַיִת לִשְׁמִי כִּי דָּמִים
רַבִּים שָׁפַכְתָּ אַרְצָה לְפָנָי: הִנֵּה־בֵן נוֹלָד לָךְ הוּא יִהְיֶה אִישׁ מְנוּחָה ט
וַהֲנִחוֹתִי לוֹ מִכָּל־אוֹיְבָיו מִסָּבִיב כִּי שְׁלֹמֹה יִהְיֶה שְׁמוֹ וְשָׁלוֹם וָשֶׁקֶט אֶתֵּן
עַל־יִשְׂרָאֵל בְּיָמָיו: הוּא־יִבְנֶה בַיִת לִשְׁמִי וְהוּא יִהְיֶה־לִּי לְבֵן וַאֲנִי־לוֹ י
לְאָב וַהֲכִינוֹתִי כִּסֵּא מַלְכוּתוֹ עַל־יִשְׂרָאֵל עַד־עוֹלָם: עַתָּה בְנִי יְהִי יְהוָה יא
עִמָּךְ וְהִצְלַחְתָּ וּבָנִיתָ בֵּית יְהוָה אֱלֹהֶיךָ כַּאֲשֶׁר דִּבֶּר עָלֶיךָ: אַךְ יִתֶּן־לְךָ יב
יְהוָה שֵׂכֶל וּבִינָה וִיצַוְּךָ עַל־יִשְׂרָאֵל וְלִשְׁמוֹר אֶת־תּוֹרַת יְהוָה אֱלֹהֶיךָ: אָז יג
תַּצְלִיחַ אִם־תִּשְׁמוֹר לַעֲשׂוֹת אֶת־הַחֻקִּים וְאֶת־הַמִּשְׁפָּטִים אֲשֶׁר צִוָּה
יְהוָה אֶת־מֹשֶׁה עַל־יִשְׂרָאֵל חֲזַק וֶאֱמָץ אַל־תִּירָא וְאַל־תֵּחָת: וְהִנֵּה יד
בְעָנְיִי הֲכִינוֹתִי לְבֵית־יְהוָה זָהָב כִּכָּרִים מֵאָה־אֶלֶף וְכֶסֶף אֶלֶף אֲלָפִים
כִּכָּרִים וְלַנְּחֹשֶׁת וְלַבַּרְזֶל אֵין מִשְׁקָל כִּי לָרֹב הָיָה וְעֵצִים וַאֲבָנִים הֲכִינוֹתִי
וַעֲלֵיהֶם תּוֹסִיף: וְעִמְּךָ לָרֹב עֹשֵׂי מְלָאכָה חֹצְבִים וְחָרָשֵׁי אֶבֶן וָעֵץ וְכָל־ טו
חָכָם בְּכָל־מְלָאכָה: לַזָּהָב לַכֶּסֶף וְלַנְּחֹשֶׁת וְלַבַּרְזֶל אֵין מִסְפָּר קוּם וַעֲשֵׂה טז
וִיהִי יְהוָה עִמָּךְ: וַיְצַו דָּוִיד לְכָל־שָׂרֵי יִשְׂרָאֵל לַעְזֹר לִשְׁלֹמֹה בְנוֹ: הֲלֹא יז-יח
יְהוָה אֱלֹהֵיכֶם עִמָּכֶם וְהֵנִיחַ לָכֶם מִסָּבִיב כִּי ׀ נָתַן בְּיָדִי אֵת יֹשְׁבֵי הָאָרֶץ
וְנִכְבְּשָׁה הָאָרֶץ לִפְנֵי יְהוָה וְלִפְנֵי עַמּוֹ: עַתָּה תְּנוּ לְבַבְכֶם וְנַפְשְׁכֶם לִדְרוֹשׁ יט
לַיהוָה אֱלֹהֵיכֶם וְקוּמוּ וּבְנוּ אֶת־מִקְדַּשׁ יְהוָה הָאֱלֹהִים לְהָבִיא אֶת־אֲרוֹן
בְּרִית־יְהוָה וּכְלֵי קֹדֶשׁ הָאֱלֹהִים לַבַּיִת הַנִּבְנֶה לְשֵׁם־יְהוָה:

21:30. Since the national altar was at Gibeon, it would
have been logical for David to go there to bring his offerings of thanksgiving, but he was afraid to attempt the trip
because of the sword-wielding angel. Once God responded to David's offering with the heavenly fire, David
instituted regular offerings at Ornan's threshing floor,
which later became the site of the Temple (*Vilna Gaon*).

22:1. This is the site where all of Israel should bring their
offerings from now on.

22:2. Although David had been told that he would not
build the Temple, he undertook all preparations for the
eventual construction. These "strangers" were gentiles
who had renounced idolatry (*Radak*), or the Gibeonites
[see *Joshua* Ch. 9], from whom David drafted workers.

22

HASHEM, which Moses had made in the Wilderness, and the Altar of Burnt-offerings, were at the High Place in Gibeon at that time, [30] but David could not go before it to seek God, for he was terrified before the sword of the angel of HASHEM. * [1] David said, "This is the House of HASHEM, God, and this is the Altar of Burnt-offering for Israel."*

[2] David commanded to gather in the strangers who were in the Land of Israel. He designated masons [from among them] to carve hewn stones [from which] to build the Temple of God. * [3] David prepared an abundance of iron for nails for the doors of the gateways and for joints, an abundance of copper beyond weighing, [4] and an abundance of cedarwood, for the Zidonians and the Tyrians had brought an abundance of cedarwood to David.

[5] David thought, "Solomon my son is young and tender, and the Temple that is to be built for HASHEM must be exceedingly grand, to be a source of fame and splendor throughout all the lands, so I will now prepare for him." So David prepared a great deal before his death.

David's charge to Solomon . . .

[6] He summoned his son Solomon and charged him to build a Temple for HASHEM, God of Israel. [7] David said to Solomon, "My son, I had in mind to build a Temple for the Name of HASHEM, my God, [8] but the word of HASHEM came to me, saying, 'You have shed much blood and have made great wars; you shall not build a Temple for My Name's sake, for you have shed much blood upon the ground before Me. [9] Behold, a son will be born to you; he will be a man of rest, and I shall grant him rest from all his enemies all around. His name will be Solomon, * and I will bestow peace and tranquility upon Israel in his days. [10] He will build a Temple for My Name's sake; he will be a son to Me and I will be a Father to him. And I will establish the throne of his kingdom over Israel forever.' [11] Now, my son, may HASHEM be with you; may you be successful and build the Temple of HASHEM your God, as He said about you. [12] Only may HASHEM give you wisdom and understanding, and give you command over Israel, to keep the Torah of HASHEM, your God. [13] Then you will succeed, if you are careful to follow the statutes and ordinances which HASHEM commanded Moses concerning Israel. Be strong and courageous! Do not fear and do not lose resolve. [14] Now, behold, despite my inadequacy, * I have prepared for the Temple of HASHEM a hundred thousand talents of gold, a million talents of silver, and an amount of copper and iron which is not weighed because of its abundance, and I have prepared timber and stones; you should add to this. [15] With you, there will be an abundance of workmen — quarry workers, artisans of stone and wood, and people skilled at every manner of work. [16] The gold, silver, copper and iron is beyond calculation. Therefore, arise and act, and may HASHEM be with you!"

. . . and to the people

[17] David commanded all the officers of Israel to help his son Solomon: [18] "Surely, HASHEM your God is with you; He will grant you rest all around you, for He has delivered the inhabitants of the land into my hand, and the land has been conquered before HASHEM and before his people. [19] Now apply your heart and soul to seek HASHEM, your God; get up and build the Sanctuary of HASHEM, God, to bring the Ark of the Covenant of HASHEM and the sacred vessels of God into the Temple that will be built for the sake of HASHEM."

22:9. The name Solomon, *Shelomoh*, is derived from the word *shalom*, peace.

22:14. Or "poverty." In comparison with God, every human being is poor and inadequate (*Yalkut*).

כג א-ב וְדָוִיד זָקֵן וְשָׂבַע יָמִים וַיַּמְלֵךְ אֶת־שְׁלֹמֹה בְנוֹ עַל־יִשְׂרָאֵל: וַיֶּאֱסֹף

ג אֶת־כָּל־שָׂרֵי יִשְׂרָאֵל וְהַכֹּהֲנִים וְהַלְוִיִּם: וַיִּסָּפְרוּ הַלְוִיִּם מִבֶּן שְׁלֹשִׁים שָׁנָה

ד וָמַעְלָה וַיְהִי מִסְפָּרָם לְגֻלְגְּלֹתָם לִגְבָרִים שְׁלֹשִׁים וּשְׁמוֹנָה אָלֶף: מֵאֵלֶּה

לְנַצֵּחַ עַל־מְלֶאכֶת בֵּית־יְהוָה עֶשְׂרִים וְאַרְבָּעָה אָלֶף וְשֹׁטְרִים וְשֹׁפְטִים

ה שֵׁשֶׁת אֲלָפִים: וְאַרְבַּעַת אֲלָפִים שֹׁעֲרִים וְאַרְבַּעַת אֲלָפִים מְהַלְלִים לַיהוָה

ו בַּכֵּלִים אֲשֶׁר עָשִׂיתִי לְהַלֵּל: וַיֶּחָלְקֵם דָּוִיד מַחְלְקוֹת   לִבְנֵי לֵוִי

ז-ח לְגֵרְשׁוֹן קְהָת וּמְרָרִי: לַגֵּרְשֻׁנִּי לַעְדָּן וְשִׁמְעִי: בְּנֵי לַעְדָּן הָרֹאשׁ

ט יְחִיאֵל וְזֵתָם וְיוֹאֵל שְׁלֹשָׁה: בְּנֵי שִׁמְעִי °שְׁלֹמוֹת [°שְׁלֹמִית ק]

י וַחֲזִיאֵל וְהָרָן שְׁלֹשָׁה אֵלֶּה רָאשֵׁי הָאָבוֹת לְלַעְדָּן: וּבְנֵי שִׁמְעִי

יא יַחַת זִינָא וִיעוּשׁ וּבְרִיעָה אֵלֶּה בְנֵי־שִׁמְעִי אַרְבָּעָה: וַיְהִי־יַחַת הָרֹאשׁ

וְזִיזָה הַשֵּׁנִי וִיעוּשׁ וּבְרִיעָה לֹא־הִרְבּוּ בָנִים וַיִּהְיוּ לְבֵית אָב לִפְקֻדָּה

יב-יג אֶחָת: בְּנֵי קְהָת עַמְרָם יִצְהָר חֶבְרוֹן וְעֻזִּיאֵל אַרְבָּעָה: בְּנֵי

עַמְרָם אַהֲרֹן וּמֹשֶׁה וַיִּבָּדֵל אַהֲרֹן לְהַקְדִּישׁוֹ קֹדֶשׁ קָדָשִׁים הוּא־וּבָנָיו עַד־

יד עוֹלָם לְהַקְטִיר לִפְנֵי יְהוָה לְשָׁרְתוֹ וּלְבָרֵךְ בִּשְׁמוֹ עַד־עוֹלָם: וּמֹשֶׁה אִישׁ

טו הָאֱלֹהִים בָּנָיו יִקָּרְאוּ עַל־שֵׁבֶט הַלֵּוִי: בְּנֵי מֹשֶׁה גֵּרְשֹׁם וֶאֱלִיעֶזֶר:

טז-יז בְּנֵי גֵרְשׁוֹם שְׁבוּאֵל הָרֹאשׁ: וַיִּהְיוּ בְנֵי־אֱלִיעֶזֶר רְחַבְיָה הָרֹאשׁ וְלֹא־הָיָה

יח לֶאֱלִיעֶזֶר בָּנִים אֲחֵרִים וּבְנֵי רְחַבְיָה רָבוּ לְמָעְלָה: בְּנֵי יִצְהָר

יט שְׁלֹמִית הָרֹאשׁ:   בְּנֵי חֶבְרוֹן יְרִיָּהוּ הָרֹאשׁ אֲמַרְיָה הַשֵּׁנִי יַחֲזִיאֵל

כ הַשְּׁלִישִׁי וִיקַמְעָם הָרְבִיעִי: בְּנֵי עֻזִּיאֵל מִיכָה הָרֹאשׁ וְיִשִּׁיָּה

כא-כב הַשֵּׁנִי: בְּנֵי מְרָרִי מַחְלִי וּמוּשִׁי בְּנֵי מַחְלִי אֶלְעָזָר וְקִישׁ: וַיָּמָת

כג אֶלְעָזָר וְלֹא־הָיוּ לוֹ בָּנִים כִּי אִם־בָּנוֹת וַיִּשָּׂאוּם בְּנֵי־קִישׁ אֲחֵיהֶם: בְּנֵי

כד מוּשִׁי מַחְלִי וְעֵדֶר וִירֵמוֹת שְׁלֹשָׁה: אֵלֶּה בְנֵי־לֵוִי לְבֵית אֲבֹתֵיהֶם רָאשֵׁי

הָאָבוֹת לִפְקוּדֵיהֶם בְּמִסְפַּר שֵׁמוֹת לְגֻלְגְּלֹתָם עֹשֵׂה הַמְּלָאכָה לַעֲבֹדַת

כה בֵּית יְהוָה מִבֶּן עֶשְׂרִים שָׁנָה וָמָעְלָה: כִּי אָמַר דָּוִיד הֵנִיחַ יְהוָה אֱלֹהֵי־

כו יִשְׂרָאֵל לְעַמּוֹ וַיִּשְׁכֹּן בִּירוּשָׁלִַם עַד־לְעוֹלָם: וְגַם לַלְוִיִּם אֵין־לָשֵׂאת

כז אֶת־הַמִּשְׁכָּן וְאֶת־כָּל־כֵּלָיו לַעֲבֹדָתוֹ: כִּי בְדִבְרֵי דָוִיד הָאַחֲרֹנִים הֵמָּה

כח מִסְפַּר בְּנֵי־לֵוִי מִבֶּן עֶשְׂרִים שָׁנָה וּלְמָעְלָה: כִּי מַעֲמָדָם לְיַד־בְּנֵי אַהֲרֹן

לַעֲבֹדַת בֵּית יְהוָה עַל־הַחֲצֵרוֹת וְעַל־הַלְּשָׁכוֹת וְעַל־טָהֳרַת לְכָל־קֹדֶשׁ

כט וּמַעֲשֵׂה עֲבֹדַת בֵּית הָאֱלֹהִים: וּלְלֶחֶם הַמַּעֲרֶכֶת וּלְסֹלֶת לְמִנְחָה

ל וְלִרְקִיקֵי הַמַּצּוֹת וְלַמַּחֲבַת וְלַמֻּרְבָּכֶת וּלְכָל־מְשׂוּרָה וּמִדָּה: וְלַעֲמֹד

23:1. He was satisfied with the days that God had given him, for the righteous are content with whatever God gives them.

23:5. The reference is to David.

23:7. More commonly known as Libni [Ch. 6; *Exodus* 6:17; *Numbers* 3:18] (*Radak*).

23:9. Not the Shimei of v. 7, but rather a son of Laadan (*Radak*).

23:10. This is the Shimei of v. 7 (*Radak*).

23:11. To be identified with Zina of v. 10.

23:27. Whereas the Levites had previously been counted from the age of thirty (v. 3), David reasoned that this was

23

Assignments of the Levites

(See Appendix B, chart 12)

¹ **W**hen David was old and fulfilled of days* he made his son Solomon king over Israel. ² He gathered together all the officers of Israel, as well as the Kohanim and the Levites. ³ The Levites were counted from the age of thirty years and above, and their number by the head count of their men was thirty-eight thousand. ⁴ Of these, twenty-four thousand were to oversee the work of the Temple of HASHEM, six thousand were marshals and judges, ⁵ four thousand were gatekeepers, and four thousand gave praise to HASHEM with the instruments that I* made for giving praise.

⁶ David divided them into divisions of Levites, according to [the families of] Gershon, Kohath and Merari.

Gershon

⁷ Of the Gershonites: Laadan* and Shimei. ⁸ The sons of Laadan: the chief, Jehiel, and Zetham and Joel — [altogether] three. ⁹ The sons of Shimei:* Shelomith, Haziel and Haran — [altogether] three. These were the family heads of Laadan. ¹⁰ The sons of Shimei:* Jahath, Zina, Jeush and Beriah. These were the four sons of Shimei. ¹¹ Jahath was the chief and Zizah* the second. Jeush and Beriah did not have many sons, so they became a single family, occupying one position.

Kohath

¹² The sons of Kohath: Amram, Izhar, Hebron and Uzziel — [altogether] four. ¹³ The sons of Amram: Aaron and Moses. Aaron was set apart, to sanctify him as holy of holies, he and his sons forever, to burn [offerings] before HASHEM, to minister before Him, and to bless in His Name forever. ¹⁴ [Concerning] Moses the man of God — his sons would be reckoned as the tribe of Levi. ¹⁵ The sons of Moses: Gershom and Eliezer. ¹⁶ Of the sons of Gershom: Shebuel, the chief. ¹⁷ The sons of Eliezer: Rehabiah, the chief. Eliezer had no other sons, but the sons of Rehabiah proliferated greatly. ¹⁸ Of the sons of Izhar: Shelomith, the chief. ¹⁹ Of the sons of Hebron: Jeriah, the chief; Amariah, the second; Jahaziel, the third; and Jekameam the fourth. ²⁰ Of the sons of Uzziel: Micah, the first; and Isshiah, the second.

Merari

²¹ The sons of Merari: Mahli and Mushi. The sons of Mahli: Elazar and Kish. ²² Elazar died having no sons but only daughters; their kinsmen, the sons of Kish, married them. ²³ The sons of Mushi: Mahli, Eder and Jeremoth — [altogether] three.

²⁴ These were the sons of Levi, according to their fathers' house, the heads of the fathers' [families], according to their counts, by the number of names, by their head count, who did the work for the service of the Temple of HASHEM, from the age of twenty years and above. ²⁵ For David said, "HASHEM, God of Israel, has granted rest to His people, and He has come to dwell in Jerusalem forever; ²⁶ thus the Levites need no longer carry the Tabernacle and all the vessels for its service."

To assist the Kohanim

²⁷ For the counting of the sons of Levi took place according to the latter words of David — from twenty years old and above. * ²⁸ For their position was to stand at the side of the sons of Aaron for the service of the Temple of HASHEM, to be in charge of the courts and the chambers and the purifying of all holy things, and the work of the service of the Temple of God, ²⁹ and of the bread of the stack and of the fine flour for meal-offerings and for the unleavened cakes, and of the pan-baked and scalded [meal-offerings], and for all matters of measures and sizes, ³⁰ and to stand

---

because the Levites had been the bearers of the heavy Ark, and a person's strength peaks from the age of twenty. From the time the Ark was placed permanently in Jerusalem, however, their tasks were limited to service in the Temple, so the minimum age was lowered (Metzudos).

לא בַּבֹּקֶר בַּבֹּקֶר לְהֹדוֹת וּלְהַלֵּל לַיהוה וְכֵן לָעָרֶב: וּלְכֹל הַעֲלוֹת עֹלוֹת
לַיהוה לַשַּׁבָּתוֹת לֶחֳדָשִׁים וְלַמֹּעֲדִים בְּמִסְפָּר כְּמִשְׁפָּט עֲלֵיהֶם תָּמִיד
לב לִפְנֵי יהוה: וְשָׁמְרוּ אֶת־מִשְׁמֶרֶת אֹהֶל־מוֹעֵד וְאֵת מִשְׁמֶרֶת הַקֹּדֶשׁ

כד א וּמִשְׁמֶרֶת בְּנֵי אַהֲרֹן אֲחֵיהֶם לַעֲבֹדַת בֵּית יהוה: וְלִבְנֵי אַהֲרֹן
ב מַחְלְקוֹתָם בְּנֵי אַהֲרֹן נָדָב וַאֲבִיהוּא אֶלְעָזָר וְאִיתָמָר: וַיָּמָת נָדָב וַאֲבִיהוּא
ג לִפְנֵי אֲבִיהֶם וּבָנִים לֹא־הָיוּ לָהֶם וַיְכַהֲנוּ אֶלְעָזָר וְאִיתָמָר: וַיֶּחָלְקֵם דָּוִיד
וְצָדוֹק מִן־בְּנֵי אֶלְעָזָר וַאֲחִימֶלֶךְ מִן־בְּנֵי אִיתָמָר לִפְקֻדָּתָם בַּעֲבֹדָתָם:
ד וַיִּמָּצְאוּ בְנֵי־אֶלְעָזָר רַבִּים לְרָאשֵׁי הַגְּבָרִים מִן־בְּנֵי אִיתָמָר וַיַּחְלְקוּם
לִבְנֵי אֶלְעָזָר רָאשִׁים לְבֵית־אָבוֹת שִׁשָּׁה עָשָׂר וְלִבְנֵי אִיתָמָר לְבֵית
ה אֲבוֹתָם שְׁמוֹנָה: וַיַּחְלְקוּם בְּגוֹרָלוֹת אֵלֶּה עִם־אֵלֶּה כִּי־הָיוּ שָׂרֵי־קֹדֶשׁ
ו וְשָׂרֵי הָאֱלֹהִים מִבְּנֵי אֶלְעָזָר וּבִבְנֵי אִיתָמָר: וַיִּכְתְּבֵם שְׁמַעְיָה
בֶן־נְתַנְאֵל הַסּוֹפֵר מִן־הַלֵּוִי לִפְנֵי הַמֶּלֶךְ וְהַשָּׂרִים וְצָדוֹק הַכֹּהֵן וַאֲחִימֶלֶךְ
בֶּן־אֶבְיָתָר וְרָאשֵׁי הָאָבוֹת לַכֹּהֲנִים וְלַלְוִיִּם בֵּית־אָב אֶחָד אָחֻז לְאֶלְעָזָר
ז וְאָחֻז ׀ אָחֻז לְאִיתָמָר: וַיֵּצֵא הַגּוֹרָל הָרִאשׁוֹן לִיהוֹיָרִיב לִידַעְיָה
ח-ט הַשֵּׁנִי: לְחָרִם הַשְּׁלִישִׁי לִשְׂעֹרִים הָרְבִעִי: לְמַלְכִּיָּה הַחֲמִישִׁי לְמִיָּמִן
י-יא הַשִּׁשִּׁי: לְהַקּוֹץ הַשְּׁבִעִי לַאֲבִיָּה הַשְּׁמִינִי: לְיֵשׁוּעַ הַתְּשִׁעִי לִשְׁכַנְיָהוּ
יב-יג הָעֲשִׂרִי: לְאֶלְיָשִׁיב עַשְׁתֵּי עָשָׂר לְיָקִים שְׁנֵים עָשָׂר: לְחֻפָּה שְׁלֹשָׁה עָשָׂר
יד-טו לְיֶשֶׁבְאָב אַרְבָּעָה עָשָׂר: לְבִלְגָּה חֲמִשָּׁה עָשָׂר לְאִמֵּר שִׁשָּׁה עָשָׂר: לַחֵזִיר
טז שִׁבְעָה עָשָׂר לְהַפִּצֵּץ שְׁמוֹנָה עָשָׂר: לִפְתַחְיָה תִּשְׁעָה עָשָׂר לִיחֶזְקֵאל
יז-יח הָעֶשְׂרִים: לְיָכִין אֶחָד וְעֶשְׂרִים לְגָמוּל שְׁנַיִם וְעֶשְׂרִים: לִדְלָיָהוּ שְׁלֹשָׁה
יט וְעֶשְׂרִים לְמַעַזְיָהוּ אַרְבָּעָה וְעֶשְׂרִים: אֵלֶּה פְקֻדָּתָם לַעֲבֹדָתָם
לָבוֹא לְבֵית־יהוה כְּמִשְׁפָּטָם בְּיַד אַהֲרֹן אֲבִיהֶם כַּאֲשֶׁר צִוָּהוּ יהוה אֱלֹהֵי
כ יִשְׂרָאֵל: וְלִבְנֵי לֵוִי הַנּוֹתָרִים לִבְנֵי עַמְרָם שׁוּבָאֵל לִבְנֵי שׁוּבָאֵל יֶחְדְּיָהוּ:
כא-כב לִרְחַבְיָהוּ לִבְנֵי רְחַבְיָהוּ הָרֹאשׁ יִשִּׁיָּה: לַיִּצְהָרִי שְׁלֹמוֹת לִבְנֵי שְׁלֹמוֹת
כג-כד יָחַת: וּבְנֵי יְרִיָּהוּ אֲמַרְיָהוּ הַשֵּׁנִי יַחֲזִיאֵל הַשְּׁלִישִׁי יְקַמְעָם הָרְבִיעִי: בְּנֵי
כה עֻזִּיאֵל מִיכָה לִבְנֵי מִיכָה *שמור [שָׁמִיר ק]: אֲחִי מִיכָה יִשִּׁיָּה לִבְנֵי
כו-כז יִשִּׁיָּה זְכַרְיָהוּ: בְּנֵי מְרָרִי מַחְלִי וּמוּשִׁי בְּנֵי יַעֲזִיָּהוּ בְנוֹ: בְּנֵי מְרָרִי לְיַעֲזִיָּהוּ
כח-כט בְנוֹ וְשֹׁהַם וְזַכּוּר וְעִבְרִי: לְמַחְלִי אֶלְעָזָר וְלֹא־הָיָה לוֹ בָּנִים: לְקִישׁ בְּנֵי־
ל קִישׁ יְרַחְמְאֵל: וּבְנֵי מוּשִׁי מַחְלִי וְעֵדֶר וִירִימוֹת אֵלֶּה בְּנֵי הַלְוִיִּם

23:32. Providing assistance to the *Kohanim* in the preparation and implementation of the sacrifices (*Metzudos*).

24:5. The men in charge of the Temple affairs, the descendants of Aaron through Elazar and Ithamar, drew lots to determine who would serve during which weeks of the year.

24:6. Originally, Elazar's and Ithamar's families had eight divisions each. Now, due to the discrepancy in their numbers; David expanded Elazar's family units into sixteen groups, while Ithamar's number of family units remained constant (*Taanis* 27a).

24:19. The concept of family units serving for a week at a time had been instituted by Aaron. David increased the number of shifts to twenty-four, so that each unit served approximately two weeks a year.

24:20. Scripture now lists the descendants of Levi

Praise and *every morning to give thanks and praise to* HASHEM, *and in the evening, as*
watch *well,* [31] *and over all the burnt-offerings that were offered to* HASHEM *on the*
Sabbaths, on the New Moons and on the Festivals, according to their number
ordained for them, continually, before HASHEM. [32] *And they would also maintain*
the watch over the Tent of Meeting and the watch over the holy place, and the
watch over their kinsmen the sons of Aaron, * *in the service of the Temple of*
HASHEM.

24   [1] For *the sons of Aaron, their divisions were:*

Assign-   *The sons of Aaron: Nadab, Abihu, Elazar and Ithamar.* [2] *Nadab and Abihu*
ments   *died in the presence of their father, and they had no children; but Elazar and*
of the   *Ithamar became the Kohanim.* [3] *David, together with Zadok, of the descendants*
Kohanim   *of Elazar, and Ahimelech, of the descendants of Ithamar, divided them according*
(See Appendix B,   *to their assignments in their service.* [4] *The chief men of the descendants of Elazar*
timeline 12)   *were found to be more numerous than those of the descendants of Ithamar, and*
they were divided accordingly: sixteen family heads for the sons of Elazar, and
eight for the sons of Ithamar according to their families. [5] *They divided [their*
shifts] by lots, with one another, for the officers of the Sanctuary and officers of
God were of the sons of Elazar and of the sons of Ithamar. * [6] *Shemaiah son of*
Nethanel the scribe, one of the Levites, recorded them before the king and the
officers and Zadok the Kohen and Ahimelech son of Abiathar, and the heads of
families of the Kohanim and Levites — one [extra] unit for [each of] Elazar's, but
one unit for one for Ithamar. *

The lots   [7] *The first lot fell upon Jehoiarib; the second upon Jedaiah,* [8] *the third upon*
Harim, the fourth upon Seorim, [9] *the fifth upon Malchijah, the sixth upon Mi-*
jamin, [10] *the seventh upon Hakkoz, the eighth upon Abijah,* [11] *the ninth upon*
Jeshua, the tenth upon Shecaniah, [12] *the eleventh upon Eliashib, the twelfth*
upon Jakim, [13] *the thirteenth upon Huppah, the fourteenth upon Jeshebeab,*
[14] *the fifteenth upon Bilgah, the sixteenth upon Immer,* [15] *the seventeenth*
upon Hezir, the eighteenth upon Happizzez, [16] *the nineteenth upon Pethahiah, the*
twentieth upon Jehezekel, [17] *the twenty-first upon Jachin, the twenty-second*
upon Gamul, [18] *the twenty-third upon Delaiah, and the twenty-fourth upon*
Maaziah.

[19] *These were their arrangements for their service, to come to the Temple of*
HASHEM, *according to the order set for them by Aaron their ancestor, as* HASHEM,
God of Israel, commanded him. *

The   [20] *As for the remaining sons of Levi:* * *Of the sons of Amram, Shubael; of*
remaining   *the sons of Shubael, Jehdeiah; for Rehabiah, of the sons of Rehabiah, Isshiah*
Levites   *the chief;* [22] *of the Izharites, Shelomoth; of the sons of Shelomoth, Jahath;*
[23] *of [the sons of Hebron,] Jeriah, Amariah the second, Jahaziel the third,*
Jekameam the fourth; [24] *of the sons of Uzziel, Micah; of the sons of Micah,*
Shamir; [25] *the brother of Micah was Isshiah; of the sons of Isshiah, Zechariah.*
[26] *The sons of Merari: Mahli and Mushi; the sons of Jaaziah,* * *Beno;* [27] *the*
sons of Merari through Jaaziah: Beno, Shoham, Zaccur and Ibri; [28] *of Mahli:*
Elazar, who had no sons; [29] *of Kish: the son of Kish was Jerahmeel;* [30] *the sons*
of Mushi: Mahli, Eder and Jerimoth. These were the sons of the Levites

---

who were not *Kohanim.* Altogether, the Levites were   twenty-four shifts of *Kohanim.*
divided into twenty-four shifts, corresponding to the   **24:26.** A descendant of Merari.

לא לְבֵית אֲבֹתֵיהֶם: וַיַּפִּילוּ גַּם־הֵם גּוֹרָלוֹת לְעֻמַּת ׀ אֲחֵיהֶם בְּנֵי־אַהֲרֹן לִפְנֵי
דָוִיד הַמֶּלֶךְ וְצָדוֹק וַאֲחִימֶלֶךְ וְרָאשֵׁי הָאָבוֹת לַכֹּהֲנִים וְלַלְוִיִּם אָבוֹת

כה א הָרֹאשׁ לְעֻמַּת אָחִיו הַקָּטָן: וַיַּבְדֵּל דָּוִיד וְשָׂרֵי הַצָּבָא לַעֲבֹדָה
לִבְנֵי אָסָף וְהֵימָן וְידוּתוּן °הַנְּבִיאִים [°הַנִּבְּאִים ק] בְּכִנֹּרוֹת בִּנְבָלִים
ב וּבִמְצִלְתָּיִם וַיְהִי מִסְפָּרָם אַנְשֵׁי מְלָאכָה לַעֲבֹדָתָם: לִבְנֵי אָסָף זַכּוּר וְיוֹסֵף
ג וּנְתַנְיָה וַאֲשַׂרְאֵלָה בְּנֵי אָסָף עַל יַד־אָסָף הַנִּבָּא עַל־יְדֵי הַמֶּלֶךְ: לִידוּתוּן
בְּנֵי יְדוּתוּן גְּדַלְיָהוּ וּצְרִי וִישַׁעְיָהוּ חֲשַׁבְיָהוּ וּמַתִּתְיָהוּ שִׁשָּׁה עַל יְדֵי
ד אֲבִיהֶם יְדוּתוּן בַּכִּנּוֹר הַנִּבָּא עַל־הֹדוֹת וְהַלֵּל לַיהוָה: לְהֵימָן בְּנֵי
הֵימָן בֻּקִּיָּהוּ מַתַּנְיָהוּ עֻזִּיאֵל שְׁבוּאֵל וִירִימוֹת חֲנַנְיָה חֲנָנִי אֱלִיאָתָה גִדַּלְתִּי
ה וְרֹמַמְתִּי עֶזֶר יָשָׁבְקָשָׁה מַלּוֹתִי הוֹתִיר מַחֲזִיאוֹת: כָּל־אֵלֶּה בָנִים לְהֵימָן
חֹזֵה הַמֶּלֶךְ בְּדִבְרֵי הָאֱלֹהִים לְהָרִים קָרֶן וַיִּתֵּן הָאֱלֹהִים לְהֵימָן בָּנִים
ו אַרְבָּעָה עָשָׂר וּבָנוֹת שָׁלוֹשׁ: כָּל־אֵלֶּה עַל־יְדֵי אֲבִיהֶם בַּשִּׁיר בֵּית יהוה
בִּמְצִלְתַּיִם נְבָלִים וְכִנֹּרוֹת לַעֲבֹדַת בֵּית הָאֱלֹהִים עַל יְדֵי הַמֶּלֶךְ
ז אָסָף וִידוּתוּן וְהֵימָן: וַיְהִי מִסְפָּרָם עִם־אֲחֵיהֶם מְלֻמְּדֵי־שִׁיר לַיהוָה כָּל־
ח הַמֵּבִין מָאתַיִם שְׁמוֹנִים וּשְׁמוֹנָה: וַיַּפִּילוּ גּוֹרָלוֹת מִשְׁמֶרֶת לְעֻמַּת כַּקָּטֹן
ט כַּגָּדוֹל מֵבִין עִם־תַּלְמִיד: וַיֵּצֵא הַגּוֹרָל הָרִאשׁוֹן לְאָסָף לְיוֹסֵף
י גְּדַלְיָהוּ הַשֵּׁנִי הוּא־וְאֶחָיו וּבָנָיו שְׁנֵים עָשָׂר: הַשְּׁלֹשִׁי זַכּוּר
יא בָּנָיו וְאֶחָיו שְׁנֵים עָשָׂר: הָרְבִיעִי לַיִּצְרִי
יב בָּנָיו וְאֶחָיו שְׁנֵים עָשָׂר: הַחֲמִישִׁי נְתַנְיָהוּ
יג בָּנָיו וְאֶחָיו שְׁנֵים עָשָׂר: הַשִּׁשִּׁי בֻקִּיָּהוּ
יד בָּנָיו וְאֶחָיו שְׁנֵים עָשָׂר: הַשְּׁבִיעִי יְשַׂרְאֵלָה
טו בָּנָיו וְאֶחָיו שְׁנֵים עָשָׂר: הַשְּׁמִינִי יְשַׁעְיָהוּ
טז בָּנָיו וְאֶחָיו שְׁנֵים עָשָׂר: הַתְּשִׁיעִי מַתַּנְיָהוּ
יז בָּנָיו וְאֶחָיו שְׁנֵים עָשָׂר: הָעֲשִׂירִי שִׁמְעִי
יח בָּנָיו וְאֶחָיו שְׁנֵים עָשָׂר: עַשְׁתֵּי־עָשָׂר עֲזַרְאֵל
יט בָּנָיו וְאֶחָיו שְׁנֵים עָשָׂר: הַשְּׁנֵים עָשָׂר לַחֲשַׁבְיָה
כ בָּנָיו וְאֶחָיו שְׁנֵים עָשָׂר: לִשְׁלֹשָׁה עָשָׂר שׁוּבָאֵל
כא בָּנָיו וְאֶחָיו שְׁנֵים עָשָׂר: לְאַרְבָּעָה עָשָׂר מַתִּתְיָהוּ
כב בָּנָיו וְאֶחָיו שְׁנֵים עָשָׂר: לַחֲמִשָּׁה עָשָׂר לִירֵמוֹת
כג בָּנָיו וְאֶחָיו שְׁנֵים עָשָׂר: לְשִׁשָּׁה עָשָׂר לַחֲנַנְיָהוּ
כד בָּנָיו וְאֶחָיו שְׁנֵים עָשָׂר: לְשִׁבְעָה עָשָׂר לְיָשְׁבְּקָשָׁה
כה בָּנָיו וְאֶחָיו שְׁנֵים עָשָׂר: לִשְׁמוֹנָה עָשָׂר לַחֲנָנִי
כו בָּנָיו וְאֶחָיו שְׁנֵים עָשָׂר: לְתִשְׁעָה עָשָׂר לְמַלּוֹתִי
כז בָּנָיו וְאֶחָיו שְׁנֵים עָשָׂר: לְעֶשְׂרִים לֶאֱלִיָּתָה

according to their fathers' houses. [31] *They also cast lots in conjunction with their kinsmen, the sons of Aaron, in the presence of King David, Zadok, Ahimelech and the heads of families of the Kohanim and Levites, the major families in conjunction with their lesser kinsmen.* *

25

Singers

[1] **D**avid and the officers of the service corps set aside the sons of Asaph, Heman and Jeduthun who prophesied while using harps, lyres, and cymbals. Their number, in accordance with the number of workmen required for their service, was:

[2] *Of the sons of Asaph: Zaccur, Joseph, Nethaniah and Asarelah, the sons of Asaph under the auspices of Asaph, who prophesied by authority of the king.*

[3] *Of Jeduthun: the sons of Jeduthun: Gedaliah, Zeri, Jeshaiah, Hashabiah and Mattithiah — [altogether] six,* * *under the auspices of their father Jeduthun, at the harp, prophesying while giving thanks and praise to* HASHEM.

[4] *Of Heman: The sons of Heman: Bukkiah, Mattaniah, Uzziel, Shebuel, Jerimoth, Hananiah, Hanani, Eliathah, Giddalti, Romamti-ezer, Joshbekashah, Mallothi, Hothir and Mahazioth.* [5] *All these were sons of Heman, the king's seer for the words of God, to exalt [David's] prestige.* * *God gave to Heman fourteen sons and three daughters.* [6] *All these were under the auspices of their father for song in the Temple of* HASHEM, *with cymbals, lyres, and harps for the service of the Temple of God, under the auspices of the king, Asaph, Jeduthun and Heman.* [7] *Their number, along with their kinsmen who were trained in the singing of songs for* HASHEM, *all of them with skill, was two hundred eighty-eight.* *

Twenty-four shifts by lot

[8] *The shifts cast lots with one another, minor and major alike, teacher as well as student.* * [9] *The first lot fell upon Asaph, upon Joseph; the second upon Gedaliah. He, his brothers and sons were twelve.* [10] *The third upon Zaccur; his sons and brothers were twelve.* [11] *The fourth upon Izri; his sons and brothers were twelve.* [12] *The fifth upon Nethaniah; his sons and brothers were twelve.* [13] *The sixth upon Bukkiah; his sons and brothers were twelve.* [14] *The seventh upon Jesarelah; his sons and brothers were twelve.* [15] *The eighth upon Jeshaiah; his sons and brothers were twelve.* [16] *The ninth upon Mattaniah; his sons and brothers were twelve.* [17] *The tenth upon Shimei; his sons and brothers were twelve.* [18] *The eleventh upon Azarel; his sons and brothers were twelve.* [19] *The twelfth upon Hashabiah; his sons and brothers were twelve.* [20] *The thirteenth upon Shubael; his sons and brothers were twelve.* [21] *The fourteenth upon Mattithiah; his sons and brothers were twelve.* [22] *The fifteenth upon Jeremoth; his sons and brothers were twelve.* [23] *The sixteenth upon Hananiah; his sons and brothers were twelve.* [24] *The seventeenth upon Joshbekashah; his sons and brothers were twelve.* [25] *The eighteenth upon Hanani; his sons and brothers were twelve.* [26] *The nineteenth upon Mallothi; his sons and brothers were twelve.* [27] *The twentieth upon Eliathah;*

24:31. All the various families joined equally in the lottery.

25:3. Only five are named. The missing son was Shimei, as indicated by v. 17.

25:5. Heman would sing Divinely inspired psalms beseeching God to grant David dominion and glory

(*Ralbag*).

25:7. Twelve members from each of the twenty-four divisions (*Rashi*).

25:8. Lots were cast to determine the order of the shifts and the individual assignments of each member. All shifts and Kohanim had equal opportunities in the lots.

כח לְאֶחָד וְעֶשְׂרִים שְׁנַיִם עָשָׂר: בָּנָיו וְאֶחָיו שְׁנֵים עָשָׂר

כט לִשְׁנַיִם וְעֶשְׂרִים שְׁנַיִם עָשָׂר: בָּנָיו וְאֶחָיו שְׁנֵים עָשָׂר לְגִדַּלְתִּי

ל לִשְׁלֹשָׁה וְעֶשְׂרִים שְׁנַיִם עָשָׂר: בָּנָיו וְאֶחָיו שְׁנֵים עָשָׂר לְמַחֲזִיאוֹת

לא לְאַרְבָּעָה וְעֶשְׂרִים שְׁנַיִם עָשָׂר: בָּנָיו וְאֶחָיו שְׁנֵים עָשָׂר לְרוֹמַמְתִּי עָזֶר

כו א לְמַחְלְקוֹת לְשֹׁעֲרִים לַקָּרְחִים בָּנָיו וְאֶחָיו שְׁנֵים עָשָׂר:

ב מְשֶׁלֶמְיָהוּ בֶן־קֹרֵא מִן־בְּנֵי אָסָף: וְלִמְשֶׁלֶמְיָהוּ בָּנִים זְכַרְיָהוּ הַבְּכוֹר

ג יְדִיעֲאֵל הַשֵּׁנִי זְבַדְיָהוּ הַשְּׁלִישִׁי יַתְנִיאֵל הָרְבִיעִי: עֵילָם הַחֲמִישִׁי יְהוֹחָנָן

ד הַשִּׁשִּׁי אֶלְיְהוֹעֵינַי הַשְּׁבִיעִי: וּלְעֹבֵד אֱדֹם בָּנִים שְׁמַעְיָה הַבְּכוֹר יְהוֹזָבָד

ה הַשֵּׁנִי יוֹאָח הַשְּׁלִישִׁי וְשָׂכָר הָרְבִיעִי וּנְתַנְאֵל הַחֲמִישִׁי: עַמִּיאֵל הַשִּׁשִּׁי

ו יִשָּׂשכָר הַשְּׁבִיעִי פְּעֻלְּתַי הַשְּׁמִינִי כִּי בֵרְכוֹ אֱלֹהִים: וְלִשְׁמַעְיָה

ז בְנוֹ נוֹלַד בָּנִים הַמִּמְשָׁלִים לְבֵית אֲבִיהֶם כִּי־גִבּוֹרֵי חַיִל הֵמָּה: בְּנֵי שְׁמַעְיָה עָתְנִי וּרְפָאֵל וְעוֹבֵד אֶלְזָבָד אֶחָיו בְּנֵי־חָיִל אֱלִיהוּ וּסְמַכְיָהוּ:

ח כָּל־אֵלֶּה מִבְּנֵי ׀ עֹבֵד אֱדֹם הֵמָּה וּבְנֵיהֶם וַאֲחֵיהֶם אִישׁ־חַיִל בַּכֹּחַ

ט לַעֲבֹדָה שִׁשִּׁים וּשְׁנַיִם לְעֹבֵד אֱדֹם: וְלִמְשֶׁלֶמְיָהוּ בָּנִים וְאַחִים בְּנֵי־חָיִל

י שְׁמוֹנָה עָשָׂר: וּלְחֹסָה מִן־בְּנֵי־מְרָרִי בָּנִים שִׁמְרִי הָרֹאשׁ כִּי

יא לֹא־הָיָה בְכוֹר וַיְשִׂימֵהוּ אָבִיהוּ לְרֹאשׁ: חִלְקִיָּהוּ הַשֵּׁנִי טְבַלְיָהוּ הַשְּׁלִשִׁי

יב זְכַרְיָהוּ הָרְבִעִי כָּל־בָּנִים וְאַחִים לְחֹסָה שְׁלֹשָׁה עָשָׂר: לְאֵלֶּה מַחְלְקוֹת הַשֹּׁעֲרִים לְרָאשֵׁי הַגְּבָרִים מִשְׁמָרוֹת לְעֻמַּת אֲחֵיהֶם לְשָׁרֵת בְּבֵית יְהוָה:

יג-יד וַיַּפִּילוּ גוֹרָלוֹת כַּקָּטֹן כַּגָּדוֹל לְבֵית אֲבוֹתָם לְשַׁעַר וָשָׁעַר: וַיִּפֹּל הַגּוֹרָל מִזְרָחָה לְשֶׁלֶמְיָהוּ וּזְכַרְיָהוּ בְנוֹ יוֹעֵץ ׀ בְּשֶׂכֶל הִפִּילוּ גוֹרָלוֹת וַיֵּצֵא

טו-טז גוֹרָלוֹ צָפוֹנָה: לְעֹבֵד אֱדֹם נֶגְבָּה וּלְבָנָיו בֵּית הָאֲסֻפִּים: לְשֻׁפִּים וּלְחֹסָה לַמַּעֲרָב עִם שַׁעַר שַׁלֶּכֶת בַּמְסִלָּה הָעוֹלָה מִשְׁמָר לְעֻמַּת מִשְׁמָר: לַמִּזְרָח

יז הַלְוִיִּם שִׁשָּׁה לַצָּפוֹנָה לַיּוֹם אַרְבָּעָה לַנֶּגְבָּה לַיּוֹם אַרְבָּעָה וְלָאֲסֻפִּים

יח-יט שְׁנַיִם שְׁנָיִם: לַפַּרְבָּר לַמַּעֲרָב אַרְבָּעָה לַמְסִלָּה שְׁנַיִם לַפַּרְבָּר: אֵלֶּה מַחְלְקוֹת הַשֹּׁעֲרִים לִבְנֵי הַקָּרְחִי וְלִבְנֵי מְרָרִי:

כ וְהַלְוִיִּם אֲחִיָּה עַל־אוֹצְרוֹת בֵּית הָאֱלֹהִים וּלְאֹצְרוֹת הַקֳּדָשִׁים:

כא בְּנֵי לַעְדָּן בְּנֵי הַגֵּרְשֻׁנִּי לְלַעְדָּן רָאשֵׁי הָאָבוֹת לְלַעְדָּן הַגֵּרְשֻׁנִּי יְחִיאֵלִי:

כב-כג בְּנֵי יְחִיאֵלִי זֵתָם וְיוֹאֵל אָחִיו עַל־אֹצְרוֹת בֵּית יְהוָה: לַעַמְרָמִי לַיִּצְהָרִי לַחֶבְרוֹנִי לָעָזִּיאֵלִי:

כד וּשְׁבֻאֵל בֶּן־גֵּרְשׁוֹם בֶּן־מֹשֶׁה נָגִיד עַל־

כה הָאֹצָרוֹת: וְאֶחָיו לֶאֱלִיעֶזֶר רְחַבְיָהוּ בְנוֹ וִישַׁעְיָהוּ בְנוֹ וְיֹרָם בְּנוֹ וְזִכְרִי

כו בְנוֹ °וּשְׁלֹמוֹת [וּשְׁלֹמִית ק] בְּנוֹ: הוּא שְׁלֹמוֹת וְאֶחָיו עַל כָּל־אֹצְרוֹת הַקֳּדָשִׁים אֲשֶׁר הִקְדִּישׁ דָּוִיד הַמֶּלֶךְ וְרָאשֵׁי הָאָבוֹת לְשָׂרֵי־הָאֲלָפִים

כז וְהַמֵּאוֹת וְשָׂרֵי הַצָּבָא: מִן־הַמִּלְחָמוֹת וּמִן־הַשָּׁלָל הִקְדִּישׁוּ לְחַזֵּק לְבֵית

כח יְהוָה: וְכֹל הַהִקְדִּישׁ שְׁמוּאֵל הָרֹאֶה וְשָׁאוּל בֶּן־קִישׁ וְאַבְנֵר בֶּן־נֵר וְיוֹאָב

his sons and brothers were twelve. ²⁸ The twenty-first upon Hothir; his sons and brothers were twelve. ²⁹ The twenty-second upon Giddalti; his sons and brothers were twelve. ³⁰ The twenty-third upon Mahazioth; his sons and brothers were twelve. ³¹ The twentieth-fourth upon Romamti-ezer; his sons and brothers were twelve.

26

Gatekeepers and their stations

¹ Concerning the divisions of the gatekeepers:

Of the Korahites: Meshelemiah the son of Kore, of the sons of Asaph. ² Meshelemiah had sons: Zechariah the firstborn, Jediael the second, Zebadiah the third, Jathniel the fourth, ³ Elam the fifth, Jehohanan the sixth and Eliehoenai the seventh.

⁴ Obed-edom had sons: Shemaiah the firstborn, Jehozabad the second, Joah the third, Sacar the fourth, Nethanel the fifth, ⁵ Ammiel the sixth, Issachar the seventh and Peullethai the eighth, for God blessed him. * ⁶ To Shemaiah his son were sons born who had dominion over their paternal family, for they were mighty warriors. ⁷ The sons of Shemaiah: Othni, with Rephael, Obed and Elzabad, his brothers were accomplished men, and Elihu and Semachiah. ⁸ All these [men] of the sons of Obed-edom — they and their sons and their brothers, accomplished men with strength for the service — were sixty-two for Obed-edom.

⁹ Meshelemiah had eighteen sons and brothers who were men of might.

¹⁰ Hosah, of the children of Merari, also had sons: Shimri the chief — although he was not the firstborn, his father made him the chief — ¹¹ Hilkiah the second, Tebaliah the third and Zechariah the fourth — all of Hosah's sons and brothers were thirteen.

¹² Among these were the divisions of the gatekeepers, among the chief men, who made groups opposite their kinsmen, to minister in the Temple of HASHEM. ¹³ They cast lots, minor ones and major ones alike, by their paternal families, for every gate. ¹⁴ The lot for the east fell upon Shelemiah. Then they cast lots for Zechariah his son, a wise counselor, and his lot came out for the north. ¹⁵ To Obed-edom [the lot] for the south, and to his sons the Asuppim House. ¹⁶ To Shuppim and Hosah [the lot] for the west, by the Shallecheth Gate, by the Path of Ascension, one watch opposite the other. ¹⁷ There were six Levites at the east, four each day at the north, four each day at the south, and two each for the Asuppim. ¹⁸ At the Parbar to the west: four at the path and two at the Parbar. ¹⁹ These were the divisions of the gatekeepers among the sons of Korah and among the sons of Merari.

Other assignments

²⁰ Concerning the Levites — Ahijah was in charge of the treasury of the Temple of God, and in charge of the treasury of the consecrated things. ²¹ The sons of Ladan — the sons of the Gershonites by Ladan, family heads of Ladan the Gershonite: Jehieli. ²² The sons of Jehieli: Zetham and his brother Joel, who were in charge of the treasury of the Temple of HASHEM.

²³ Of the Amramite, the Izharite, the Hebronite, the Uzzielite: ²⁴ Shebuel son of Gershom son of Moses was chairman of the treasury. ²⁵ His kinsmen by Eliezer: * Rehabiah his son, Jeshaiah his son, Joram his son, Zichri his son and Shelomith his son. ²⁶ He — Shelomoth — and his kinsmen were in charge of all the treasuries of the consecrated items which King David, the heads of families, the captains over thousands and hundreds, and the captains of the army had consecrated. ²⁷ They consecrated from the wars and the spoils, to maintain the Temple of HASHEM. ²⁸ Also, all that Samuel the seer, Saul son of Kish, Abner son of Ner and Joab

---

26:5. The father of this large family, Obed-edom, is the one who was host to the Ark and was profusely blessed by   God, as mentioned in 13:14.
26:25. Who was Gershon's uncle.

כט בֶּן־צְרוּיָ֖ה כֹּ֣ל הַמַּקְדִּ֑ישׁ עַ֣ל יַ֤ד־שְׁלֹמִית֙ וְאֶחָ֔יו: לַיִּצְהָרִ֖י כְּנַנְיָ֣הוּ

ל וּבָנָ֞יו לַמְּלָאכָ֤ה הַחִיצוֹנָה֙ עַל־יִשְׂרָאֵ֔ל לְשֹׁטְרִ֖ים וּלְשֹׁפְטִֽים: לַחֶבְרוֹנִ֗י חֲשַׁבְיָ֨הוּ֙ וְאֶחָ֜יו בְּנֵי־חַ֗יִל אֶ֤לֶף וּשְׁבַע־מֵאוֹת֙ עַ֚ל פְּקֻדַּ֣ת יִשְׂרָאֵ֔ל מֵעֵ֖בֶר

לא לַיַּרְדֵּ֥ן מַעְרָ֖בָה לְכֹ֤ל מְלֶ֣אכֶת יְהֹוָ֔ה וְלַעֲבֹדַ֖ת הַמֶּֽלֶךְ: לַחֶבְרוֹנִי֙ יְרִיָּ֣ה הָרֹ֔אשׁ לַֽחֶבְרוֹנִ֖י לְתֹלְדֹתָ֣יו לְאָב֑וֹת בִּשְׁנַ֤ת הָאַרְבָּעִים֙ לְמַלְכ֣וּת דָּוִ֔יד נִדְרָ֑שׁוּ

לב וַיִּמָּצֵ֥א בָהֶ֖ם גִּבּ֣וֹרֵי חַ֑יִל בְּיַעְזֵ֖יר גִּלְעָֽד: וְאֶחָ֣יו בְּנֵי־חַ֗יִל אַלְפַּ֙יִם֙ וּשְׁבַ֣ע מֵא֔וֹת רָאשֵׁ֖י הָאָב֑וֹת וַיַּפְקִידֵ֞ם דָּוִ֣יד הַמֶּ֗לֶךְ עַל־הָראוּבֵנִ֤י וְהַגָּדִי֙ וַחֲצִ֣י

כז א שֵׁ֣בֶט הַֽמְנַשִּׁ֔י לְכָל־דְּבַר־הָאֱלֹהִ֖ים וּדְבַ֥ר הַמֶּֽלֶךְ: וּבְנֵ֣י יִשְׂרָאֵ֣ל | לְמִסְפָּרָ֡ם רָאשֵׁ֣י הָאָב֣וֹת וְשָׂרֵ֣י הָאֲלָפִ֣ים | וְהַמֵּא֗וֹת וְשֹׁטְרֵיהֶם֙ הַמְשָׁרְתִ֣ים אֶת־הַמֶּ֔לֶךְ לְכֹ֣ל | דְּבַ֣ר הַֽמַּחְלְק֗וֹת הַבָּאָ֤ה וְהַיֹּצֵאת֙ חֹ֣דֶשׁ בְּחֹ֔דֶשׁ לְכֹ֖ל

ב חָדְשֵׁ֣י הַשָּׁנָ֑ה הַֽמַּחֲלֹ֙קֶת֙ הָֽאַחַ֔ת עֶשְׂרִ֥ים וְאַרְבָּעָ֖ה אָֽלֶף: עַ֚ל הַמַּחֲלֹ֣קֶת הָרִֽאשׁוֹנָה֙ לַחֹ֣דֶשׁ הָֽרִאשׁ֔וֹן יָשָׁבְעָ֖ם בֶּן־זַבְדִּיאֵ֑ל וְעַל֙ מַחֲלֻקְתּ֔וֹ

ג עֶשְׂרִ֥ים וְאַרְבָּעָ֖ה אָֽלֶף: מִן־בְּנֵי־פֶ֗רֶץ הָרֹ֛אשׁ לְכָל־שָׂרֵ֥י הַצְּבָא֖וֹת לַחֹ֥דֶשׁ

ד הָרִאשֽׁוֹן: וְעַ֞ל מַחֲלֹ֣קֶת | הַחֹ֣דֶשׁ הַשֵּׁנִ֗י דּוֹדַ֤י הָאֲחוֹחִי֙ וּמַֽחֲלֻקְתּ֔וֹ

ה וּמִקְל֖וֹת הַנָּגִ֑יד וְעַל֙ מַחֲלֻקְתּ֔וֹ עֶשְׂרִ֥ים וְאַרְבָּעָ֖ה אָֽלֶף: שַׂ֣ר הַצָּבָ֤א הַשְּׁלִישִׁי֙ לַחֹ֣דֶשׁ הַשְּׁלִישִׁ֔י בְּנָיָ֛הוּ בֶן־יְהוֹיָדָ֥ע הַכֹּהֵ֖ן רֹ֑אשׁ וְעַל֙ מַחֲלֻקְתּ֔וֹ

ו עֶשְׂרִ֥ים וְאַרְבָּעָ֖ה אָֽלֶף: ה֚וּא בְנָיָ֣הוּ גִּבּ֣וֹר הַשְּׁלֹשִׁ֔ים וְעַל־הַשְּׁלֹשִׁ֑ים

ז וּמַחֲלֻקְתּ֖וֹ עַמִּיזָבָ֣ד בְּנֽוֹ: הָרְבִיעִי֙ לַחֹ֣דֶשׁ הָֽרְבִיעִ֔י עֲשָׂהאֵ֣ל | אֲחִ֣י יוֹאָ֗ב וּזְבַדְיָ֤ה בְנוֹ֙ אַֽחֲרָ֔יו וְעַל֙ מַחֲלֻקְתּ֔וֹ עֶשְׂרִ֥ים וְאַרְבָּעָ֖ה

ח אָֽלֶף: הַֽחֲמִישִׁי֙ לַחֹ֣דֶשׁ הַֽחֲמִישִׁ֔י הַשַּׂ֖ר שַׁמְה֣וּת הַיִּזְרָ֑ח וְעַל֙

ט מַחֲלֻקְתּ֔וֹ עֶשְׂרִ֥ים וְאַרְבָּעָ֖ה אָֽלֶף: הַשִּׁשִּׁי֙ לַחֹ֣דֶשׁ הַשִּׁשִּׁ֔י עִירָ֖א

י בֶן־עִקֵּ֣שׁ הַתְּקוֹעִ֑י וְעַל֙ מַחֲלֻקְתּ֔וֹ עֶשְׂרִ֥ים וְאַרְבָּעָ֖ה אָֽלֶף: הַשְּׁבִיעִ֞י לַחֹ֣דֶשׁ הַשְּׁבִיעִ֗י חֶ֤לֶץ הַפְּלוֹנִי֙ מִן־בְּנֵ֣י אֶפְרָ֔יִם וְעַל֙ מַחֲלֻקְתּ֔וֹ עֶשְׂרִ֥ים

יא וְאַרְבָּעָ֖ה אָֽלֶף: הַשְּׁמִינִי֙ לַחֹ֣דֶשׁ הַשְּׁמִינִ֔י סִבְּכַ֥י הַחֻֽשָׁתִ֖י לַזַּרְחִ֑י

יב וְעַל֙ מַחֲלֻקְתּ֔וֹ עֶשְׂרִ֥ים וְאַרְבָּעָ֖ה אָֽלֶף: הַתְּשִׁיעִי֙ לַחֹ֣דֶשׁ הַתְּשִׁיעִ֔י אֲבִיעֶ֥זֶר הָעֲנְּתֹתִ֖י °לַבְּנִימִינִ֑י [°לַבֶּ֣ן | יְמִינִ֗י ק] וְעַל֙ מַחֲלֻקְתּ֔וֹ עֶשְׂרִ֥ים

יג וְאַרְבָּעָ֖ה אָֽלֶף: הָעֲשִׂירִי֙ לַחֹ֣דֶשׁ הָֽעֲשִׂירִ֔י מַהְרַ֥י הַנְּטֽוֹפָתִ֖י לַזַּרְחִ֑י

יד וְעַל֙ מַחֲלֻקְתּ֔וֹ עֶשְׂרִ֥ים וְאַרְבָּעָ֖ה אָֽלֶף: עַשְׁתֵּֽי־עָשָׂר֙ לְעַשְׁתֵּ֣י עָשָׂ֣ר הַחֹ֔דֶשׁ בְּנָיָ֖ה הַפִּרְעָתוֹנִ֑י מִן־בְּנֵ֣י אֶפְרָ֑יִם וְעַל֙ מַחֲלֻקְתּ֔וֹ עֶשְׂרִ֥ים

טו וְאַרְבָּעָ֖ה אָֽלֶף: הַשְּׁנֵ֤ים עָשָׂר֙ לִשְׁנֵ֣ים עָשָׂ֣ר הַחֹ֔דֶשׁ חֶלְדַּ֥י

טז הַנְּטוֹפָתִ֖י לְעָתְנִיאֵ֑ל וְעַל֙ מַחֲלֻקְתּ֔וֹ עֶשְׂרִ֥ים וְאַרְבָּעָ֖ה אָֽלֶף: וְעַ֖ל שִׁבְטֵ֣י יִשְׂרָאֵ֑ל לָרֽאוּבֵנִ֣י נָגִ֗יד אֱלִיעֶ֖זֶר בֶּן־זִכְרִ֑י לַשִּׁמְעוֹנִ֖י שְׁפַטְיָ֥הוּ בֶּן־

יז-יח מַעֲכָֽה: לְלֵוִ֖י חֲשַׁבְיָ֣ה בֶן־קְמוּאֵ֑ל לְאַֽהֲרֹ֖ן צָד֑וֹק: לִֽיהוּדָ֕ה

יט אֱלִיה֖וּ מֵֽאֲחֵ֣י דָוִ֑יד לְיִשָּׂשכָ֖ר עָמְרִ֥י בֶן־מִיכָאֵֽל: לִזְבוּלֻ֕ן יִֽשְׁמַֽעְיָ֖הוּ

the son of Zeruiah had consecrated — whoever had consecrated — was under the hand of Shelomith and of his kinsmen.

²⁹ Of the Izharite: Chenaniah and his sons were in charge of the outside labor* of Israel, as officers and judges.

³⁰ Of the Hebronite: Hashabiah and his kinsmen, one thousand seven hundred men of might, were in charge of Israel on the western side of the Jordan, for all the labor of HASHEM, and for the service of the king. ³¹ Of the Hebronite: Jerijah, the chief over the Hebronite, according to their generations by their families. In the fortieth year of the reign of David they were sought, and among them were found mighty warriors at Jazer of Gilead. ³² His kinsmen, men of might, [numbered] two thousand seven hundred heads of families; and King David appointed them over the Reubenite, the Gadite and half the tribe of the Manassites, for all matters of God and matters of the king.

27

Twenty-four monthly shifts

¹ **A**s for the Children of Israel by their number — the heads of families, the captains of thousands and hundreds, and their marshals who served the king in all the matters of the divisions, who entered [service] and left, month by month, throughout all the months of the year, each division consisting of twenty-four thousand [men]:

² Jashobeam son of Zabdiel was in charge of the first division for the first month, and in his division were twenty-four thousand [men]. ³ [Being] from the descendants of Perez, he was the chief of all the officers of the force for the first month. ⁴ Dodai the Ahohite and his division and Mikloth the leader were in charge of the division of the second month; and in his division were twenty-four thousand [men]. ⁵ The third officer of the force, for the third month, was Benaiah son of Jehoiada the Kohen, who was the chief; and in his division were twenty-four thousand [men]. ⁶ This is the same Benaiah who was the mighty man among the thirty,* and who was over the thirty; his son Ammizabad was in his division. ⁷ The fourth [chief], for the fourth month, was Asahel, the brother of Joab, with Zebadiah his son after him; and in his division were twenty-four thousand men. ⁸ The fifth, for the fifth month, was the officer Shamhuth the Izrahite; and in his division were twenty-four thousand [men]. ⁹ The sixth, for the sixth month, was Ira son of Ikkesh the Tekoite; and in his division were twenty-four thousand [men]. ¹⁰ The seventh, for the seventh month, was Helez the Pelonite of the children of Ephraim; and in his division were twenty-four thousand [men]. ¹¹ The eighth, for the eighth month, was Sibbecai the Hushathite, of the Zerahite; and in his division were twenty-four thousand [men]. ¹² The ninth, for the ninth month, was Abiezer the Anathothite, of the Benjamite; and in his division were twenty-four thousand [men]. ¹³ The tenth, for the tenth month, was Mahrai the Netophathite, of the Zerahite: and in his division were twenty-four thousand [men]. ¹⁴ The eleventh, for the eleventh month, was Benaiah the Pirathonite; of the children of Ephraim; and in his division were twenty-four thousand [men]. ¹⁵ The twelfth, for the twelfth month, was Heldai the Netophathite, of Othniel's [descendants]: and in his division were twenty-four thousand [men].

Tribal leaders

¹⁶ In charge of the tribes of Israel: The ruler of the Reubenite was Eliezer son of Zichri; of the Simeonite, Shephatiah son of Maachah; ¹⁷ of Levi, Hashabiah son of Kemuel: of Aaron's [descendants], Zadok; ¹⁸ of Judah, Elihu, one of David's kinsmen; of Issachar, Omri son of Michael; ¹⁹ of Zebulun, Ishmaiah

---

26:29. Work done outside the Temple precincts (*Radak*).   **27:6.** As described above in 11:25.

כ בֶּן־עֹבַדְיָהוּ לְנַפְתָּלִי יְרִימוֹת בֶּן־עַזְרִיאֵל: לִבְנֵי אֶפְרַיִם הוֹשֵׁעַ
כא בֶּן־עֲזַזְיָהוּ לַחֲצִי שֵׁבֶט מְנַשֶּׁה יוֹאֵל בֶּן־פְּדָיָהוּ: לַחֲצִי הַמְנַשֶּׁה
כב גִּלְעָדָה יִדּוֹ בֶּן־זְכַרְיָהוּ לְבִנְיָמִן יַעֲשִׂיאֵל בֶּן־אַבְנֵר: לְדָן עֲזַרְאֵל
כג בֶּן־יְרֹחָם אֵלֶּה שָׂרֵי שִׁבְטֵי יִשְׂרָאֵל: וְלֹא־נָשָׂא דָוִיד מִסְפָּרָם לְמִבֶּן
עֶשְׂרִים שָׁנָה וּלְמָטָּה כִּי אָמַר יְהוָה לְהַרְבּוֹת אֶת־יִשְׂרָאֵל כְּכוֹכְבֵי הַשָּׁמָיִם:
כד יוֹאָב בֶּן־צְרוּיָה הֵחֵל לִמְנוֹת וְלֹא כִלָּה וַיְהִי בָזֹאת קֶצֶף עַל־יִשְׂרָאֵל וְלֹא
כה עָלָה הַמִּסְפָּר בְּמִסְפַּר דִּבְרֵי־הַיָּמִים לַמֶּלֶךְ דָּוִיד: וְעַל
אֹצְרוֹת הַמֶּלֶךְ עַזְמָוֶת בֶּן־עֲדִיאֵל וְעַל הָאֹצָרוֹת בַּשָּׂדֶה בֶּעָרִים וּבַכְּפָרִים
כו וּבַמִּגְדָּלוֹת יְהוֹנָתָן בֶּן־עֻזִּיָּהוּ: וְעַל עֹשֵׂי מְלֶאכֶת הַשָּׂדֶה
כז לַעֲבֹדַת הָאֲדָמָה עֶזְרִי בֶּן־כְּלוּב: וְעַל־הַכְּרָמִים שִׁמְעִי
כח הָרָמָתִי וְעַל שֶׁבַּכְּרָמִים לְאֹצְרוֹת הַיַּיִן זַבְדִּי הַשִּׁפְמִי: וְעַל־
הַזֵּיתִים וְהַשִּׁקְמִים אֲשֶׁר בַּשְּׁפֵלָה בַּעַל חָנָן הַגְּדֵרִי וְעַל־אֹצְרוֹת הַשֶּׁמֶן
כט יוֹעָשׁ: וְעַל־הַבָּקָר הָרֹעִים בַּשָּׁרוֹן °שטרי [°שִׁרְטַי ק]
ל הַשָּׁרוֹנִי וְעַל־הַבָּקָר בָּעֲמָקִים שָׁפָט בֶּן־עַדְלָי: וְעַל־הַגְּמַלִּים
לא אוֹבִיל הַיִּשְׁמְעֵלִי וְעַל־הָאֲתֹנוֹת יֶחְדְּיָהוּ הַמֵּרֹנֹתִי: וְעַל־הַצֹּאן
לב יָזִיז הַהַגְרִי כָּל־אֵלֶּה שָׂרֵי הָרְכוּשׁ אֲשֶׁר לַמֶּלֶךְ דָּוִיד: וִיהוֹנָתָן
דּוֹד־דָּוִיד יוֹעֵץ אִישׁ־מֵבִין וְסוֹפֵר הוּא וִיחִיאֵל בֶּן־חַכְמוֹנִי עִם־בְּנֵי הַמֶּלֶךְ:
לג-לד וַאֲחִיתֹפֶל יוֹעֵץ לַמֶּלֶךְ וְחוּשַׁי הָאַרְכִּי רֵעַ הַמֶּלֶךְ: וְאַחֲרֵי אֲחִיתֹפֶל
כח א יְהוֹיָדָע בֶּן־בְּנָיָהוּ וְאֶבְיָתָר וְשַׂר־צָבָא לַמֶּלֶךְ יוֹאָב: וַיַּקְהֵל
דָּוִיד אֶת־כָּל־שָׂרֵי יִשְׂרָאֵל שָׂרֵי הַשְּׁבָטִים וְשָׂרֵי הַמַּחְלְקוֹת הַמְשָׁרְתִים
אֶת־הַמֶּלֶךְ וְשָׂרֵי הָאֲלָפִים וְשָׂרֵי הַמֵּאוֹת וְשָׂרֵי כָל־רְכוּשׁ־וּמִקְנֶה ׀
לַמֶּלֶךְ וּלְבָנָיו עִם־הַסָּרִיסִים וְהַגִּבּוֹרִים וּלְכָל־גִּבּוֹר חָיִל אֶל־יְרוּשָׁלָםִ:
ב וַיָּקָם דָּוִיד הַמֶּלֶךְ עַל־רַגְלָיו וַיֹּאמֶר שְׁמָעוּנִי אַחַי וְעַמִּי אֲנִי עִם־לְבָבִי
לִבְנוֹת בֵּית מְנוּחָה לַאֲרוֹן בְּרִית־יְהוָה וְלַהֲדֹם רַגְלֵי אֱלֹהֵינוּ וַהֲכִינוֹתִי
ג לִבְנוֹת: וְהָאֱלֹהִים אָמַר לִי לֹא־תִבְנֶה בַיִת לִשְׁמִי כִּי אִישׁ מִלְחָמוֹת
ד אַתָּה וְדָמִים שָׁפָכְתָּ: וַיִּבְחַר יְהוָה אֱלֹהֵי יִשְׂרָאֵל בִּי מִכֹּל בֵּית־אָבִי
לִהְיוֹת לְמֶלֶךְ עַל־יִשְׂרָאֵל לְעוֹלָם כִּי בִיהוּדָה בָּחַר לְנָגִיד וּבְבֵית
ה יְהוּדָה בֵּית אָבִי וּבִבְנֵי אָבִי בִּי רָצָה לְהַמְלִיךְ עַל־כָּל־יִשְׂרָאֵל: וּמִכָּל־
בָּנַי כִּי רַבִּים בָּנִים נָתַן לִי יְהוָה וַיִּבְחַר בִּשְׁלֹמֹה בְנִי לָשֶׁבֶת עַל־כִּסֵּא
ו מַלְכוּת יְהוָה עַל־יִשְׂרָאֵל: וַיֹּאמֶר לִי שְׁלֹמֹה בִנְךָ הוּא־יִבְנֶה בֵיתִי
ז וַחֲצֵרוֹתָי כִּי־בָחַרְתִּי בוֹ לִי לְבֵן וַאֲנִי אֶהְיֶה־לּוֹ לְאָב: וַהֲכִינוֹתִי אֶת־
מַלְכוּתוֹ עַד־לְעוֹלָם אִם־יֶחֱזַק לַעֲשׂוֹת מִצְוֺתַי וּמִשְׁפָּטַי כַּיּוֹם הַזֶּה:

27:23. God wished to increase the number of Jews so much that it would be impossible to count them, but there are times when this blessing was not fulfilled. To count the entire population would make it apparent that Israel had not been worthy of the blessing, and therefore David left all those under twenty years old uncounted. This extra son of Obadiah; of Naphtali, Jerimoth son of Azriel; [20] of the children of Ephraim, Hoshea son of Azaziah; of half the tribe of Manasseh, Joel son of Pedaiah; [21] of [half the tribe] of Manasseh in Gilead, Iddo son of Zechariah; of Benjamin, Jaasiel son of Abner; [22] of Dan, Azarel son of Jeroham. These were the leaders of the tribes of Israel.

[23] But David did not count tally of those from twenty years of age and below, because HASHEM had said he would increase Israel like the stars of the heavens. *

[24] Joab son of Zeruiah once began to count them, but he did not finish, because [God's] wrath came upon Israel for this, and the number was not entered among the numbers in King David's chronicles. *

Royal officers [25] In charge of the king's treasuries was Azmaveth son of Adiel; in charge of the storehouses in the fields, in the cities and in the villages and in the towers was Jehonathan the son of Uzziah. [26] In charge of those who did labor in the field, working the ground was Ezri son of Chelub. [27] In charge of the vineyards was Shimei the Ramathite; in charge of that which was in the vineyards, for the wine storehouses was Zabdi the Shiphmite. [28] In charge of the olive trees and the sycamore trees that were in the lowlands was Baal-hanan the Gederite. In charge of the storehouses of oil was Joash. [29] In charge of the cattle that grazed in Sharon was Shitrai the Sharonite; in charge of the cattle that were in the valleys was Shaphat son of Adlai. [30] In charge of the camels was Obil the Ishmaelite, and in charge of the she-donkeys was Jehdeiah the Meronothite. [31] In charge of the *Close* flocks Jaziz the Hagrite. All these were the managers of King David's property. *advisers* [32] David's uncle Jonathan was an adviser; he was a wise man and a scribe. Jehiel son of Hachmoni was with the king's sons. * [33] Ahithophel was an adviser to the king. Hushai the Archite was the king's companion. [34] Succeeding Ahithophel was Jehoiada son of Benaiah and Abiathar. The king's commander of the army was Joab.

28

DAVID'S LAST DAYS 28:1-29:30

[1] **D**avid assembled to Jerusalem all the leaders of Israel: the leaders of the tribes, the leaders of the divisions that serve the king, the leaders of the thousands and the leaders of the hundreds, and the officers in charge of all the possessions and livestock of the king and his sons, along with the officers, the mighty men and the men of valor. [2] King David stood up on his feet and said: "Hear me, my brothers and my people! I had in my heart to build a house of rest *David appoints Solomon as his successor* for the Ark of the Covenant of HASHEM, as a footstool for our God, and I prepared to build. [3] But God said to me, 'You shall not build a Temple for My Name, because you are a man of wars and have shed blood.' [4] HASHEM, God of Israel, chose me from all my father's family to be king over Israel forever. For He chose Judah to be the ruler, and of the House of Judah [He chose] my father's house, and of the sons of my father it was me that He saw fit to make king over all Israel. [5] And from all my sons — for many sons has HASHEM given me — He has chosen Solomon my son to sit upon the throne of the kingdom of HASHEM, over Israel. [6] He said to me, 'Your son Solomon — he shall build My Temple and My courtyards; for I have chosen him to be a son for Me, and I will be a Father for him. [7] And I will establish his kingdom forever — if he will be firm in fulfilling My commandments and My laws, as on this day.'

---

precaution was especially proper in light of the tragedy engendered by Joab's census.

27:24. See Chapter 21. Since the census incurred the wrath of God and became a source of tragedy for Israel, its results were omitted from King David's official chronicles.

27:32. He was their pedagogue.

ח וְעַתָּה לְעֵינֵי כָל־יִשְׂרָאֵל קְהַל־יהוה וּבְאָזְנֵי אֱלֹהֵינוּ שִׁמְרוּ וְדִרְשׁוּ כָּל־
מִצְוֹת יהוה אֱלֹהֵיכֶם לְמַעַן תִּירְשׁוּ אֶת־הָאָרֶץ הַטּוֹבָה וְהִנְחַלְתֶּם

ט לִבְנֵיכֶם אַחֲרֵיכֶם עַד־עוֹלָם: וְאַתָּה שְׁלֹמֹה־בְנִי דַּע אֶת־אֱלֹהֵי אָבִיךָ
וְעָבְדֵהוּ בְּלֵב שָׁלֵם וּבְנֶפֶשׁ חֲפֵצָה כִּי כָל־לְבָבוֹת דּוֹרֵשׁ יהוה
וְכָל־יֵצֶר מַחֲשָׁבוֹת מֵבִין אִם־תִּדְרְשֶׁנּוּ יִמָּצֵא לָךְ וְאִם־תַּעַזְבֶנּוּ יַזְנִיחֲךָ

י לָעַד: רְאֵה ׀ עַתָּה כִּי־יהוה בָּחַר בְּךָ לִבְנוֹת־בַּיִת לַמִּקְדָּשׁ חֲזַק

יא וַעֲשֵׂה: וַיִּתֵּן דָּוִיד לִשְׁלֹמֹה בְנוֹ אֶת־תַּבְנִית הָאוּלָם וְאֶת־
בָּתָּיו וְגַנְזַכָּיו וַעֲלִיֹּתָיו וַחֲדָרָיו הַפְּנִימִים וּבֵית הַכַּפֹּרֶת: וְתַבְנִית כֹּל אֲשֶׁר

יב הָיָה בָרוּחַ עִמּוֹ לְחַצְרוֹת בֵּית־יהוה וּלְכָל־הַלְּשָׁכוֹת סָבִיב לְאֹצְרוֹת בֵּית
הָאֱלֹהִים וּלְאֹצְרוֹת הַקֳּדָשִׁים: וּלְמַחְלְקוֹת הַכֹּהֲנִים וְהַלְוִיִּם וּלְכָל־

יג מְלֶאכֶת עֲבוֹדַת בֵּית־יהוה וּלְכָל־כְּלֵי עֲבוֹדַת בֵּית־יהוה: לַזָּהָב בַּמִּשְׁקָל
לַזָּהָב לְכָל־כְּלֵי עֲבוֹדָה וַעֲבוֹדָה לְכֹל כְּלֵי הַכֶּסֶף בְּמִשְׁקָל לְכָל־כְּלֵי

יד עֲבוֹדָה וַעֲבוֹדָה: וּמִשְׁקָל לִמְנֹרוֹת הַזָּהָב וְנֵרֹתֵיהֶם זָהָב בְּמִשְׁקַל־מְנוֹרָה
וּמְנוֹרָה וְנֵרֹתֶיהָ וְלִמְנֹרוֹת הַכֶּסֶף בְּמִשְׁקָל לִמְנוֹרָה וְנֵרֹתֶיהָ כַּעֲבוֹדַת

טו מְנוֹרָה וּמְנוֹרָה: וְאֶת־הַזָּהָב מִשְׁקָל לְשֻׁלְחֲנוֹת הַמַּעֲרֶכֶת לְשֻׁלְחָן וְשֻׁלְחָן

טז וְכֶסֶף לְשֻׁלְחֲנוֹת הַכָּסֶף: וְהַמִּזְלָגוֹת וְהַמִּזְרָקוֹת וְהַקְּשָׂוֹת זָהָב טָהוֹר

יז וְלִכְפוֹרֵי הַזָּהָב בְּמִשְׁקָל לִכְפוֹר וּכְפוֹר וְלִכְפוֹרֵי הַכֶּסֶף בְּמִשְׁקָל לִכְפוֹר

יח וּכְפוֹר: וּלְמִזְבַּח הַקְּטֹרֶת זָהָב מְזֻקָּק בַּמִּשְׁקָל וּלְתַבְנִית הַמֶּרְכָּבָה
הַכְּרוּבִים זָהָב לְפֹרְשִׂים וְסֹכְכִים עַל־אֲרוֹן בְּרִית־יהוה: הַכֹּל בִּכְתָב מִיַּד

יט יהוה עָלַי הִשְׂכִּיל כֹּל מַלְאֲכוֹת הַתַּבְנִית: וַיֹּאמֶר

כ דָּוִיד לִשְׁלֹמֹה בְנוֹ חֲזַק וֶאֱמַץ וַעֲשֵׂה אַל־תִּירָא וְאַל־תֵּחָת כִּי יהוה
אֱלֹהִים אֱלֹהַי עִמָּךְ לֹא יַרְפְּךָ וְלֹא יַעַזְבֶךָּ עַד־לִכְלוֹת כָּל־מְלֶאכֶת

כא עֲבוֹדַת בֵּית־יהוה: וְהִנֵּה מַחְלְקוֹת הַכֹּהֲנִים וְהַלְוִיִּם לְכָל־עֲבוֹדַת בֵּית
הָאֱלֹהִים וְעִמְּךָ בְכָל־מְלָאכָה לְכָל־נָדִיב בַּחָכְמָה לְכָל־עֲבוֹדָה
וְהַשָּׂרִים וְכָל־הָעָם לְכָל־דְּבָרֶיךָ:

כט א וַיֹּאמֶר דָּוִיד הַמֶּלֶךְ
לְכָל־הַקָּהָל שְׁלֹמֹה בְנִי אֶחָד בָּחַר־בּוֹ אֱלֹהִים נַעַר וָרָךְ וְהַמְּלָאכָה
גְדוֹלָה כִּי לֹא לְאָדָם הַבִּירָה כִּי לַיהוה אֱלֹהִים: וּבְכָל־כֹּחִי הֲכִינוֹתִי

ב לְבֵית־אֱלֹהַי הַזָּהָב ׀ לַזָּהָב וְהַכֶּסֶף לַכֶּסֶף וְהַנְּחֹשֶׁת לַנְּחֹשֶׁת הַבַּרְזֶל
לַבַּרְזֶל וְהָעֵצִים לָעֵצִים אַבְנֵי־שֹׁהַם וּמִלּוּאִים אַבְנֵי־פוּךְ וְרִקְמָה וְכֹל

28:10. That is the Holy Ark, the most sacred item in the Temple.

28:11. David had drawn up detailed plans for the building and administration of the Temple, which had come to him by Divine inspiration.

28:15. Silver candelabra are not mentioned elsewhere in Scripture, and it is not clear what function they served.

28:16. The gold tables were for the stacks of showbread. The silver tables are not mentioned elsewhere. However, *Radak* identifies them with the tables mentioned in *Ezekiel* 40:39-41.

28:17. Used as shelves for the tables of the show-bread (see *Exodus* 25:29).

28:18. The Cherubim represented the seat, or "Chariot" of God (*Ralbag*).

⁸ "So now, in the sight of all Israel, the congregation of HASHEM, and in the audience of our God: Observe and seek out all the commandments of HASHEM your God, so that you may possess the good land and bequeath it to your children after you forever.

David's charge to Solomon: Loyalty to God . . .

⁹ "And you, my son Solomon: Know the God of your father and serve Him with a perfect heart and with a willing soul, for HASHEM searches all hearts, and discerns every product of [one's] thoughts. If you seek Him, He will let Himself be found by you; but if you forsake Him, He will abandon you forever. ¹⁰ See now that HASHEM has chosen you to erect a building for the Holiness; * be strong, and act."

. . . the Temple plans . . .

¹¹ David then gave to his son Solomon the plans * for the Hall and its structures, storage rooms, upper chambers and inner rooms, and for the Chamber of the Ark-Cover, ¹² and the plans for all that he had with him by Divine inspiration — for the courtyards of the Temple of HASHEM, and for all the chambers all around, for the storage rooms of the Temple of God, and for the treasuries of the consecrated items, ¹³ as well as [the plan] for the divisions of the Kohanim and the Levites, and for all the work of the service of the Temple of HASHEM, and for all the vessels for the service of the Temple of HASHEM.

. . . and treasuries

¹⁴ Gold was by the weight of gold, for all the vessels of each kind of service; for all the silver vessels by weight, for all the vessels of each kind of service. ¹⁵ The weight of gold for the golden candelabra and their golden lamps was according to the weight for every candelabrum and its lamps; and so for the silver candelabra, * according to the weight for each candelabrum and its lamps, according to the function of each of the candelabra; ¹⁶ and gold by the weight for the tables of the stacks for each table, and likewise silver for the silver tables; * ¹⁷ and pure gold for the forks, the bowls and the tubes; * and for the golden basins according to the weight of each basin; and [silver] for the silver basins according to the weight of each basin; ¹⁸ and refined gold for the Altar of Incense by weight; and for the image of the Chariot, * the golden Cherubim that spread out [their wings] and covered the Ark of the Covenant of HASHEM. ¹⁹ Everything is in writing, by the hand of HASHEM, which He gave me * understanding to know — all the works of the plan.

Exhortation to Solomon

²⁰ David then said to his son Solomon, "Be strong and courageous — and act. Do not be afraid and do not be dismayed for HASHEM, God, my God, is with you; He will not release you nor will He forsake you, until the completion of all the labor of the work of the Temple of HASHEM. ²¹ Behold, here are the divisions of the Kohanim and the Levites, for all the service of the Temple of God. Assisting you in all the labor will be all those generous with their wisdom for all the work, the officers and all the people at your every word."

29

David's final charge to Israel

¹ **K**ing David said to the entire congregation, "Solomon my son is [but] lone; God has chosen him although he is young and tender; and the work is great, for this palace is not for a man, but for HASHEM, God. ² With all my might I have prepared for the Temple of my God — gold for golden things, silver for silver things, copper for copper things, iron for iron things and wood for wooden things; as well as shoham stones, [stones] for setting, emeralds, tapestries, and all kinds of

---

28:19. David announced to the throng that God had given him the understanding to know the Divine plan   for the Temple.

ג אֶבֶן יְקָרָה וַאֲבָנֵי־שַׁיִשׁ לָרֹב: וְעוֹד בִּרְצוֹתִי בְּבֵית אֱלֹהַי יֶשׁ־לִי סְגֻלָּה
זָהָב וָכָסֶף נָתַתִּי לְבֵית־אֱלֹהַי לְמַעְלָה מִכָּל־הֲכִינוֹתִי לְבֵית הַקֹּדֶשׁ:
ד שְׁלֹשֶׁת אֲלָפִים כִּכְּרֵי זָהָב מִזְּהַב אוֹפִיר וְשִׁבְעַת אֲלָפִים כִּכַּר־כֶּסֶף מְזֻקָּק
ה לָטוּחַ קִירוֹת הַבָּתִּים: לַזָּהָב לַזָּהָב וְלַכֶּסֶף לַכֶּסֶף וּלְכָל־מְלָאכָה בְּיַד
ו חָרָשִׁים וּמִי מִתְנַדֵּב לְמַלֹּאות יָדוֹ הַיּוֹם לַיהוָה: וַיִּתְנַדְּבוּ שָׂרֵי הָאָבוֹת
וְשָׂרֵי שִׁבְטֵי יִשְׂרָאֵל וְשָׂרֵי הָאֲלָפִים וְהַמֵּאוֹת וּלְשָׂרֵי מְלֶאכֶת
ז הַמֶּלֶךְ: וַיִּתְּנוּ לַעֲבוֹדַת בֵּית־הָאֱלֹהִים זָהָב כִּכָּרִים חֲמֵשֶׁת־אֲלָפִים
וַאֲדַרְכֹנִים רִבֹּו וְכֶסֶף כִּכָּרִים עֲשֶׂרֶת אֲלָפִים וּנְחֹשֶׁת רִבּוֹ וּשְׁמוֹנַת
ח אֲלָפִים כִּכָּרִים וּבַרְזֶל מֵאָה־אֶלֶף כִּכָּרִים: וְהַנִּמְצָא אִתּוֹ אֲבָנִים
ט נָתְנוּ לְאוֹצַר בֵּית־יְהוָה עַל יַד־יְחִיאֵל הַגֵּרְשֻׁנִּי: וַיִּשְׂמְחוּ הָעָם עַל־
הִתְנַדְּבָם כִּי בְּלֵב שָׁלֵם הִתְנַדְּבוּ לַיהוָה וְגַם דָּוִיד הַמֶּלֶךְ שָׂמַח שִׂמְחָה
י גְדוֹלָה: וַיְבָרֶךְ דָּוִיד אֶת־יְהוָה לְעֵינֵי כָּל־הַקָּהָל וַיֹּאמֶר
יא דָּוִיד בָּרוּךְ אַתָּה יְהוָה אֱלֹהֵי יִשְׂרָאֵל אָבִינוּ מֵעוֹלָם וְעַד־עוֹלָם: לְךָ
יְהוָה הַגְּדֻלָּה וְהַגְּבוּרָה וְהַתִּפְאֶרֶת וְהַנֵּצַח וְהַהוֹד כִּי־כֹל בַּשָּׁמַיִם וּבָאָרֶץ
יב לְךָ יְהוָה הַמַּמְלָכָה וְהַמִּתְנַשֵּׂא לְכֹל | לְרֹאשׁ: וְהָעֹשֶׁר וְהַכָּבוֹד מִלְּפָנֶיךָ
וְאַתָּה מוֹשֵׁל בַּכֹּל וּבְיָדְךָ כֹּחַ וּגְבוּרָה וּבְיָדְךָ לְגַדֵּל וּלְחַזֵּק לַכֹּל:
יג־יד וְעַתָּה אֱלֹהֵינוּ מוֹדִים אֲנַחְנוּ לָךְ וּמְהַלְלִים לְשֵׁם תִּפְאַרְתֶּךָ: וְכִי מִי
אֲנִי וּמִי עַמִּי כִּי־נַעְצֹר כֹּחַ לְהִתְנַדֵּב כָּזֹאת כִּי־מִמְּךָ הַכֹּל וּמִיָּדְךָ נָתַנּוּ
טו לָךְ: כִּי־גֵרִים אֲנַחְנוּ לְפָנֶיךָ וְתוֹשָׁבִים כְּכָל־אֲבֹתֵינוּ כַּצֵּל | יָמֵינוּ עַל־
טז הָאָרֶץ וְאֵין מִקְוֶה: יְהוָה אֱלֹהֵינוּ כֹּל הֶהָמוֹן הַזֶּה אֲשֶׁר הֲכִינֹנוּ לִבְנוֹת־
יז לְךָ בַיִת לְשֵׁם קָדְשֶׁךָ מִיָּדְךָ °הִיא [°הוּא ק] וּלְךָ הַכֹּל: וְיָדַעְתִּי אֱלֹהַי כִּי
אַתָּה בֹּחֵן לֵבָב וּמֵישָׁרִים תִּרְצֶה אֲנִי בְּיֹשֶׁר לְבָבִי הִתְנַדַּבְתִּי כָל־אֵלֶּה
יח וְעַתָּה עַמְּךָ הַנִּמְצְאוּ־פֹה רָאִיתִי בְשִׂמְחָה לְהִתְנַדֶּב־לָךְ: יְהוָה אֱלֹהֵי
אַבְרָהָם יִצְחָק וְיִשְׂרָאֵל אֲבֹתֵינוּ שָׁמְרָה־זֹּאת לְעוֹלָם לְיֵצֶר מַחְשְׁבוֹת
יט לְבַב עַמֶּךָ וְהָכֵן לְבָבָם אֵלֶיךָ: וְלִשְׁלֹמֹה בְנִי תֵּן לֵבָב שָׁלֵם לִשְׁמוֹר
מִצְוֹתֶיךָ עֵדְוֹתֶיךָ וְחֻקֶּיךָ וְלַעֲשׂוֹת הַכֹּל וְלִבְנוֹת הַבִּירָה אֲשֶׁר
כ הֲכִינוֹתִי: וַיֹּאמֶר דָּוִיד לְכָל־הַקָּהָל בָּרְכוּ־נָא אֶת־יְהוָה
אֱלֹהֵיכֶם וַיְבָרְכוּ כָל־הַקָּהָל לַיהוָה אֱלֹהֵי אֲבֹתֵיהֶם וַיִּקְּדוּ וַיִּשְׁתַּחֲווּ
כא לַיהוָה וְלַמֶּלֶךְ: וַיִּזְבְּחוּ לַיהוָה | זְבָחִים וַיַּעֲלוּ עֹלוֹת לַיהוָה לְמָחֳרַת הַיּוֹם
הַהוּא פָּרִים אֶלֶף אֵילִים אֶלֶף כְּבָשִׂים אֶלֶף וְנִסְכֵּיהֶם וּזְבָחִים לָרֹב
כב לְכָל־יִשְׂרָאֵל: וַיֹּאכְלוּ וַיִּשְׁתּוּ לִפְנֵי יְהוָה בַּיּוֹם הַהוּא בְּשִׂמְחָה גְדוֹלָה
וַיַּמְלִיכוּ שֵׁנִית לִשְׁלֹמֹה בֶן־דָּוִיד וַיִּמְשְׁחוּ לַיהוָה לְנָגִיד וּלְצָדוֹק לְכֹהֵן:

29:12. Whatever wealth and power we have accumulated is Yours (*Radak*).

29:18. May they always retain this nobility of purpose!

29:22. To reaffirm his original, hastily arranged coronation, which is described in *I Kings* 1:32ff.

precious stones and marble stones — in abundance. [3] Furthermore, because of my desire for a Temple of my God, I have treasures of gold and silver that I have given for the Temple of my God, beyond all that I had prepared for the Sacred House — [4] three thousand talents of gold, of Ophir gold, and seven thousand talents of refined silver, with which to overlay the walls of the buildings. [5] There is gold for gold[en things] and silver for silver [things], for all work done by artisans. Now who volunteers to consecrate himself for HASHEM today?"

The nation contributes   [6] Then the leaders of the fathers' houses, the leaders of the tribes of Israel, the leaders of thousands and of hundreds, and the officers of the king's property offered donations, [7] giving for the work of the Temple of God five thousand talents and ten thousand darkons of gold, ten thousand talents of silver, eighteen thousand talents of copper and one hundred thousand talents of iron. [8] Whoever had [precious] stones gave of them to the treasury of the Temple of HASHEM, under the auspices of Jehiel the Gershonite.

[9] The people rejoiced in their donations, for they donated wholeheartedly to HASHEM. King David also rejoiced with great gladness.

David's last blessing   [10] And David blessed HASHEM in the presence of the entire congregation. David said, "Blessed are You, HASHEM, God of Israel our forefather, from This World to the World to Come. [11] Yours, HASHEM, is the greatness, the strength, the splendor, the triumph and the glory, even everything in heaven and earth. Yours, HASHEM, is the kingdom, and the sovereignty over every leader. [12] Wealth and honor come from You and You rule everything — in Your hand is power and strength and it is in Your hand to make anyone great or strong. * [13] So now, our God, we thank You and praise Your splendrous Name.

Everything is from You   [14] "For who am I, and what is my people, that we should muster the strength to donate in this manner? For everything is from You, and from Your hand have we given to You. [15] For we are like sojourners before You, and like temporary residents, as were all our forefathers — our days on earth are like a shadow, and there is no hope [to escape death]. [16] HASHEM, our God, all this vast amount that we have prepared to build You a Temple for Your holy Name is from Your own hand, for everything is Yours. [17] I know [also], my God, that You examine the heart and desire integrity. I have offered all these donations in the uprightness of my heart, and now I see Your people, who are present here, to offer donations to You with gladness.

David's prayer   [18] "HASHEM, God of our forefathers Abraham, Isaac and Israel, preserve this forever* to be the product of the thoughts of the hearts of Your people, and set their hearts towards You! [19] [Also] grant to Solomon my son a perfect heart, to keep Your commandments, Your testimonies and Your statutes, to carry out everything and to build the palace for which I have prepared."

Joyous response   [20] David then said to the entire congregation, "Now bless HASHEM our God!" And all the congregation blessed HASHEM, the God of their forefathers, and they bowed down and prostrated themselves to HASHEM and to the king. [21] They slaughtered feast-offerings to HASHEM and offered burnt-offerings to HASHEM on the next day — a thousand bulls, a thousand rams and a thousand sheep, with their libations, an abundance of feast-offerings for all Israel. [22] They ate and drank before HASHEM on that day with great gladness. They crowned Solomon son of David as king a second time, * and anointed [him] to HASHEM to be the ruler, and Zadok to be the Kohen.

כג וַיֵּ֣שֶׁב שְׁלֹמֹ֗ה עַל־כִּסֵּ֧א יְהֹוָ֛ה ׀ לְמֶ֖לֶךְ תַּֽחַת־דָּוִ֣יד אָבִ֑יו וַיַּצְלַ֖ח וַיִּשְׁמְע֥וּ

כד אֵלָ֖יו כָּל־יִשְׂרָאֵ֑ל וְכָל־הַשָּׂרִים֙ וְהַגִּבֹּרִ֔ים וְגַ֕ם כָּל־בְּנֵ֖י הַמֶּ֣לֶךְ דָּוִ֑יד נָֽתְנ֛וּ

כה יָ֖ד תַּ֣חַת שְׁלֹמֹ֣ה הַמֶּֽלֶךְ׃ וַיְגַדֵּ֨ל יְהֹוָ֤ה אֶת־שְׁלֹמֹה֙ לְמַ֔עְלָה לְעֵינֵ֖י כָּל־

כו יִשְׂרָאֵ֑ל וַיִּתֵּ֤ן עָלָיו֙ ה֣וֹד מַלְכ֔וּת אֲֽשֶׁ֧ר לֹֽא־הָיָ֛ה עַל־כָּל־מֶ֖לֶךְ לְפָנָ֖יו עַל־

כו־כז יִשְׂרָאֵֽל׃   וְדָוִיד֙ בֶּן־יִשָׁ֔י מָלַ֖ךְ עַל־כָּל־יִשְׂרָאֵֽל׃ וְהַיָּמִ֗ים אֲשֶׁ֤ר

כז מָלַךְ֙ עַל־יִשְׂרָאֵ֔ל אַרְבָּעִ֖ים שָׁנָ֑ה בְּחֶבְר֤וֹן מָלַךְ֙ שֶׁ֣בַע שָׁנִ֔ים וּבִירוּשָׁלַ֖͏ִם

כח מָלַ֖ךְ שְׁלֹשִׁ֥ים וְשָׁלֽוֹשׁ׃ וַיָּ֨מׇת֙ בְּשֵׂיבָ֣ה טוֹבָ֔ה שְׂבַ֥ע יָמִ֖ים עֹ֣שֶׁר וְכָב֑וֹד וַיִּמְלֹ֛ךְ

כט שְׁלֹמֹ֥ה בְנ֖וֹ תַּחְתָּֽיו׃ וְדִבְרֵי֙ דָּוִ֣יד הַמֶּ֔לֶךְ הָרִֽאשֹׁנִ֖ים וְהָאַחֲרֹנִ֑ים הִנָּ֣ם

כתוּבִ֗ים עַל־דִּבְרֵי֙ שְׁמוּאֵ֣ל הָרֹאֶ֔ה וְעַל־דִּבְרֵי֙ נָתָ֣ן הַנָּבִ֔יא וְעַל־דִּבְרֵ֖י גָּ֥ד

דברי

הימים ב ל הַחֹזֶֽה׃ עִ֣ם כָּל־מַלְכוּת֞וֹ וּגְב֣וּרָת֗וֹ וְהָֽעִתִּ֛ים אֲשֶׁ֥ר עָֽבְר֖וּ עָלָ֑יו וְעַל־יִשְׂרָאֵ֖ל

א א וְעַ֖ל כָּל־מַמְלְכ֥וֹת הָאֲרָצֽוֹת׃   וַיִּתְחַזֵּ֛ק שְׁלֹמֹ֥ה בֶן־דָּוִ֖יד

ב עַל־מַלְכוּת֑וֹ וַֽיהֹוָ֤ה אֱלֹהָיו֙ עִמּ֔וֹ וַֽיְגַדְּלֵ֖הוּ לְמָֽעְלָה׃ וַיֹּ֣אמֶר שְׁלֹמֹ֗ה

לְכׇל־יִשְׂרָאֵ֔ל לְשָׂרֵ֥י הָֽאֲלָפִ֖ים וְהַמֵּא֑וֹת וְלַשֹּׁ֣פְטִ֔ים וּלְכֹ֖ל נָשִׂ֥יא לְכׇל־

ג יִשְׂרָאֵ֖ל רָאשֵׁ֣י הָֽאָב֑וֹת׃ וַיֵּ֣לְכ֡וּ שְׁלֹמֹה֩ וְכָל־הַקָּהָ֨ל עִמּ֜וֹ לַבָּמָ֣ה אֲשֶׁ֣ר

בְּגִבְע֗וֹן כִּי־שָׁ֣ם הָיָה֩ אֹ֨הֶל מוֹעֵ֤ד הָֽאֱלֹהִים֙ אֲשֶׁ֣ר עָשָׂ֔ה מֹשֶׁ֥ה עֶֽבֶד־יְהֹוָ֖ה

ד בַּמִּדְבָּֽר׃ אֲבָ֗ל אֲר֤וֹן הָֽאֱלֹהִים֙ הֶעֱלָ֤ה דָוִיד֙ מִקִּרְיַ֣ת יְעָרִ֔ים בַּֽהֵכִ֥ין ל֖וֹ דָּוִ֑יד

ה כִּֽי־נָ֤טָה־לוֹ֙ אֹ֔הֶל בִּירוּשָׁלָֽ͏ִם׃ וּמִזְבַּ֣ח הַנְּחֹ֗שֶׁת אֲשֶׁ֤ר עָשָׂה֙ בְּצַלְאֵל֙ בֶּן־אוּרִ֣י

ו בֶן־ח֔וּר שָׂ֕ם לִפְנֵ֖י מִשְׁכַּ֣ן יְהֹוָ֑ה וַיִּדְרְשֵׁ֥הוּ שְׁלֹמֹ֖ה וְהַקָּהָֽל׃ וַיַּ֧עַל שְׁלֹמֹ֣ה

שָׁ֗ם עַל־מִזְבַּ֤ח הַנְּחֹ֨שֶׁת֙ לִפְנֵ֣י יְהֹוָ֔ה אֲשֶׁ֖ר לְאֹ֣הֶל מוֹעֵ֑ד וַיַּ֧עַל עָלָ֛יו עֹל֖וֹת

ז אָֽלֶף׃   בַּלַּ֣יְלָה הַה֔וּא נִרְאָ֥ה אֱלֹהִ֖ים לִשְׁלֹמֹ֑ה וַיֹּ֣אמֶר ל֔וֹ שְׁאַ֖ל מָ֥ה

ח אֶתֶּן־לָֽךְ׃ וַיֹּ֤אמֶר שְׁלֹמֹה֙ לֵֽאלֹהִ֔ים אַתָּ֣ה עָשִׂ֗יתָ עִם־דָּוִ֥יד אָבִ֖י חֶ֣סֶד גָּד֑וֹל

ט וְהִמְלַכְתַּ֖נִי תַּחְתָּֽיו׃ עַתָּה֙ יְהֹוָ֣ה אֱלֹהִ֔ים יֵֽאָמֵן֙ דְּבָ֣רְךָ֔ עִ֖ם דָּוִ֣יד אָבִ֑י כִּ֣י אַתָּ֣ה

י הִמְלַכְתַּ֗נִי עַל־עַ֕ם רַ֖ב כַּעֲפַ֥ר הָאָֽרֶץ׃ עַתָּ֗ה חׇכְמָ֤ה וּמַדָּע֙ תֶּן־לִ֔י וְאֵֽצְאָ֛ה

לִפְנֵ֥י הָֽעָם־הַזֶּ֖ה וְאָב֑וֹאָה כִּֽי־מִ֣י יִשְׁפֹּ֔ט אֶת־עַמְּךָ֥ הַזֶּ֖ה הַגָּדֽוֹל׃

יא וַיֹּ֣אמֶר אֱלֹהִ֣ים ׀ לִשְׁלֹמֹ֗ה יַ֚עַן אֲשֶׁ֨ר הָֽיְתָ֪ה זֹ֣את עִם־לְבָבֶ֗ךָ וְלֹֽא־שָׁאַ֡לְתָּ

עֹ֩שֶׁר֩ נְכָסִ֨ים וְכָב֜וֹד וְאֵ֣ת ׀ נֶ֣פֶשׁ שֹׂנְאֶ֗יךָ וְגַם־יָמִ֤ים רַבִּים֙ לֹ֣א שָׁאָ֑לְתָּ

יב וַתִּֽשְׁאַל־לְךָ֙ חׇכְמָ֣ה וּמַדָּ֔ע אֲשֶׁ֤ר תִּשְׁפּוֹט֙ אֶת־עַמִּ֔י אֲשֶׁ֥ר הִמְלַכְתִּ֖יךָ עָלָֽיו׃

הַֽחׇכְמָ֥ה וְהַמַּדָּ֖ע נָת֣וּן לָ֑ךְ וְעֹ֨שֶׁר וּנְכָסִ֤ים וְכָבוֹד֙ אֶתֶּן־לָ֔ךְ אֲשֶׁ֣ר ׀ לֹא־הָ֣יָה

יג כֵּ֣ן לַמְּלָכִ֗ים אֲשֶׁ֤ר לְפָנֶ֨יךָ֙ וְאַֽחֲרֶ֔יךָ לֹ֥א יִֽהְיֶה־כֵּֽן׃ וַיָּבֹ֨א שְׁלֹמֹ֜ה לַבָּמָ֤ה

יד אֲשֶׁר־בְּגִבְעוֹן֙ יְר֣וּשָׁלַ֔͏ִם מִלִּפְנֵ֖י אֹ֣הֶל מוֹעֵ֑ד וַיִּמְלֹ֖ךְ עַל־יִשְׂרָאֵֽל׃ וַיֶּֽאֱסֹ֣ף

שְׁלֹמֹ֣ה רֶ֣כֶב וּפָרָשִׁ֗ים וַֽיְהִי־ל֞וֹ אֶ֤לֶף וְאַרְבַּע־מֵאוֹת֙ רֶ֔כֶב וּשְׁנֵים־עָשָׂ֥ר אֶ֖לֶף

טו פָּֽרָשִׁ֑ים וַיַּנִּיחֵם֙ בְּעָרֵ֣י הָרֶ֔כֶב וְעִם־הַמֶּ֖לֶךְ בִּירֽוּשָׁלָֽ͏ִם׃ וַיִּתֵּ֨ן הַמֶּ֧לֶךְ אֶת־

II Chronicles   According to the masoretic tradition, the "books" of *I Chronicles* and *II Chronicles* are actually *one* long book; their designation as two separate books is of non-Jewish origin. Thus, in the total of the twenty-four books of *Tanach,* all of *Chronicles* is counted as a single book. The

The mantle passes

²³ Solomon sat upon the throne of Hashem as king in place of his father David, and he was successful. All of Israel obeyed him. ²⁴ All the officers and the mighty men, as well as all of King David's sons, gave their support to King Solomon. ²⁵ Hashem greatly exalted Solomon in the eyes of all Israel, and He bestowed upon him royal majesty such as had not been upon any king before him in Israel.

²⁶ Thus, David son of Jesse reigned over all Israel. ²⁷ The time that he reigned over Israel was forty years — in Hebron he reigned for seven years, and in Jerusalem he reigned for thirty-three years. ²⁸ He died in a good old age, sated with years, wealth and honor; and Solomon his son reigned in his place.

²⁹ The earlier and later events of King David — behold, they are written in the records of Samuel the Seer, the records of Nathan the prophet and the records of Gad the Seer, ³⁰ with [details of] all his kingdom and his might, and the events that transpired with him and with Israel, and with all the kingdoms of the lands.

II CHRONICLES

1

KING SOLOMON
1:1-9:31

God is with Solomon

¹ Solomon son of David strengthened himself over his kingdom; Hashem his God was with him, and He made him very great. ² Solomon spoke to all of Israel* — to officers of the thousands and the hundreds, to judges, to every ruler in all of Israel, and to the heads of families — ³ and Solomon, along with the entire congregation, went to the High Place at Gibeon, for God's Tent of Meeting, which Moses the servant of Hashem had erected in the Wilderness, was there. ⁴ However, David had brought up the Ark of God from Kiriath-jearim to the [place] that David had prepared for it, for he had pitched a tent for it in Jerusalem. ⁵ But the Copper Altar that Bezalel son of Uri son of Hur had made was placed before the Tabernacle of Hashem, so Solomon and the congregation sought it out. ⁶ Solomon brought up offerings there before Hashem, on the Copper Altar that was before the Tent of Meeting — he brought upon it a thousand burnt-offerings.

Solomon requests wisdom

⁷ That night God appeared to Solomon and said to him, "Request what I should give to you." ⁸ Solomon said to God, "You have done a great kindness with David my father, and You have made me king in his place. ⁹ Now, Hashem, God, may Your words with my father David be fulfilled, for You have made me king over a nation as numerous as the dust of the earth. ¹⁰ Now, grant me wisdom and knowledge, so that I may go out and come in before this people, for who can judge this great people of Yours?"

¹¹ God said to Solomon, "Because this is what you had in your heart, and you did not request riches, property, honor or the life of your enemies, nor did you request a long life, but you requested wisdom and knowledge so that you can judge My people over whom I have made you king — ¹² the wisdom and knowledge are granted to you, and I will [even] grant you riches and property and honor, such as kings before you have never had, nor will there be such a thing after you."

¹³ Solomon, [who had gone] to the High Place in Gibeon, went to Jerusalem, from before the Tent of Meeting, and he began his reign over Israel.

Grandeur of his reign

¹⁴ Solomon assembled chariots and horsemen — he had one thousand four hundred chariots and twelve thousand riders; he kept them in chariot cities and [left some] with the king in Jerusalem. ¹⁵ And the king made

---

same applies to the "books" of *Samuel* and *Kings*. However, for the convenience of the reader, we refer to chapters and verses in the familiar way, e.g. *II Chronicles* 3:10.

1:2-3. He summoned them to accompany him to Gibeon.
1:9. That you establish me as king (see *I Chronicles* 17:11-14).

הַכֶּסֶף וְאֶת־הַזָּהָב בִּירוּשָׁלַ͏ִם כָּאֲבָנִים וְאֵת הָאֲרָזִים נָתַן כַּשִּׁקְמִים אֲשֶׁר

טז בַּשְּׁפֵלָה לָרֹב: וּמוֹצָא הַסּוּסִים אֲשֶׁר לִשְׁלֹמֹה מִמִּצְרָיִם וּמִקְוֵא סֹחֲרֵי

יז הַמֶּלֶךְ מִקְוֵא יִקְחוּ בִּמְחִיר: וַיַּעֲלוּ וַיּוֹצִיאוּ מִמִּצְרַיִם מֶרְכָּבָה בְּשֵׁשׁ מֵאוֹת
כֶּסֶף וְסוּס בַּחֲמִשִּׁים וּמֵאָה וְכֵן לְכָל־מַלְכֵי הַחִתִּים וּמַלְכֵי אֲרָם בְּיָדָם

ב יח-א יוֹצִיאוּ: וַיֹּאמֶר שְׁלֹמֹה לִבְנוֹת בַּיִת לְשֵׁם יהוה וּבַיִת לְמַלְכוּתוֹ: וַיִּסְפֹּר
שְׁלֹמֹה שִׁבְעִים אֶלֶף אִישׁ סַבָּל וּשְׁמוֹנִים אֶלֶף אִישׁ חֹצֵב בָּהָר וּמְנַצְּחִים
עֲלֵיהֶם שְׁלֹשֶׁת אֲלָפִים וְשֵׁשׁ מֵאוֹת:

ב וַיִּשְׁלַח שְׁלֹמֹה אֶל־חוּרָם מֶלֶךְ־צֹר לֵאמֹר כַּאֲשֶׁר עָשִׂיתָ עִם־דָּוִיד אָבִי

ג וַתִּשְׁלַח־לוֹ אֲרָזִים לִבְנוֹת־לוֹ בַיִת לָשֶׁבֶת בּוֹ: הִנֵּה אֲנִי בוֹנֶה־בַּיִת לְשֵׁם ׀
יהוה אֱלֹהָי לְהַקְדִּישׁ לוֹ לְהַקְטִיר לְפָנָיו קְטֹרֶת־סַמִּים וּמַעֲרֶכֶת תָּמִיד
וְעֹלוֹת לַבֹּקֶר וְלָעֶרֶב לַשַּׁבָּתוֹת וְלֶחֳדָשִׁים וּלְמוֹעֲדֵי יהוה אֱלֹהֵינוּ לְעוֹלָם

ד זֹאת עַל־יִשְׂרָאֵל: וְהַבַּיִת אֲשֶׁר־אֲנִי בוֹנֶה גָּדוֹל כִּי־גָדוֹל אֱלֹהֵינוּ מִכָּל־

ה הָאֱלֹהִים: וּמִי יַעֲצָר־כֹּחַ לִבְנוֹת־לוֹ בַיִת כִּי הַשָּׁמַיִם וּשְׁמֵי הַשָּׁמַיִם לֹא

ו יְכַלְכְּלֻהוּ וּמִי אֲנִי אֲשֶׁר אֶבְנֶה־לּוֹ בַיִת כִּי אִם־לְהַקְטִיר לְפָנָיו: וְעַתָּה
שְׁלַח־לִי אִישׁ־חָכָם לַעֲשׂוֹת בַּזָּהָב וּבַכֶּסֶף וּבַנְּחֹשֶׁת וּבַבַּרְזֶל וּבָאַרְגְּוָן
וְכַרְמִיל וּתְכֵלֶת וְיֹדֵעַ לְפַתֵּחַ פִּתּוּחִים עִם־הַחֲכָמִים אֲשֶׁר עִמִּי בִּיהוּדָה

ז וּבִירוּשָׁלַ͏ִם אֲשֶׁר הֵכִין דָּוִיד אָבִי: וּשְׁלַח־לִי עֲצֵי אֲרָזִים בְּרוֹשִׁים
וְאַלְגּוּמִּים מֵהַלְּבָנוֹן כִּי אֲנִי יָדַעְתִּי אֲשֶׁר עֲבָדֶיךָ יוֹדְעִים לִכְרוֹת עֲצֵי

ח לְבָנוֹן וְהִנֵּה עֲבָדַי עִם־עֲבָדֶיךָ: וּלְהָכִין לִי עֵצִים לָרֹב כִּי הַבַּיִת אֲשֶׁר־אֲנִי

ט בוֹנֶה גָּדוֹל וְהַפְלֵא: וְהִנֵּה לַחֹטְבִים לְכֹרְתֵי הָעֵצִים נָתַתִּי חִטִּים ׀ מַכּוֹת
לַעֲבָדֶיךָ כֹּרִים עֶשְׂרִים אֶלֶף וּשְׂעֹרִים כֹּרִים עֶשְׂרִים אָלֶף וְיַיִן בַּתִּים
עֶשְׂרִים אֶלֶף וְשֶׁמֶן בַּתִּים עֶשְׂרִים אָלֶף:

י וַיֹּאמֶר חוּרָם מֶלֶךְ־צֹר בִּכְתָב וַיִּשְׁלַח אֶל־שְׁלֹמֹה בְּאַהֲבַת יהוה אֶת־עַמּוֹ

יא נְתָנְךָ עֲלֵיהֶם מֶלֶךְ: וַיֹּאמֶר חוּרָם בָּרוּךְ יהוה אֱלֹהֵי יִשְׂרָאֵל אֲשֶׁר עָשָׂה
אֶת־הַשָּׁמַיִם וְאֶת־הָאָרֶץ אֲשֶׁר נָתַן לְדָוִיד הַמֶּלֶךְ בֵּן חָכָם יוֹדֵעַ שֵׂכֶל

יב וּבִינָה אֲשֶׁר יִבְנֶה־בַּיִת לַיהוה וּבַיִת לְמַלְכוּתוֹ: וְעַתָּה שָׁלַחְתִּי אִישׁ־חָכָם
יוֹדֵעַ בִּינָה לְחוּרָם אָבִי: בֶּן־אִשָּׁה מִן־בְּנוֹת דָּן וְאָבִיו אִישׁ־צֹרִי יוֹדֵעַ

יג לַעֲשׂוֹת בַּזָּהָב־וּבַכֶּסֶף בַּנְּחֹשֶׁת בַּבַּרְזֶל בָּאֲבָנִים וּבָעֵצִים בָּאַרְגָּמָן
בַּתְּכֵלֶת וּבַבּוּץ וּבַכַּרְמִיל וּלְפַתֵּחַ כָּל־פִּתּוּחַ וְלַחְשֹׁב כָּל־מַחֲשָׁבֶת אֲשֶׁר

יד יִנָּתֶן־לוֹ עִם־חֲכָמֶיךָ וְחַכְמֵי אֲדֹנִי דָּוִיד אָבִיךָ: וְעַתָּה הַחִטִּים וְהַשְּׂעֹרִים

טו הַשֶּׁמֶן וְהַיַּיִן אֲשֶׁר אָמַר אֲדֹנִי יִשְׁלַח לַעֲבָדָיו: וַאֲנַחְנוּ נִכְרֹת עֵצִים מִן־
הַלְּבָנוֹן כְּכָל־צָרְכֶּךָ וּנְבִיאֵם לְךָ רַפְסֹדוֹת עַל־יָם יָפוֹ וְאַתָּה תַּעֲלֶה אֹתָם

1:16-17. See *II Kings* 10:28-29.

2:3. Since the commandment of the Temple service is eternal, the structure must be large and sturdy (*Radak*).

2:7. Branching, treelike coral.

2:9. See *I Kings* 5:2. A *kor* is a dry measure; a *bath* is a liquid measure, which is one tenth of a *kor* (*Metzudos*).

silver and gold [as common] as stones in Jerusalem, and he made cedars as abundant as sycamores in the lowland. ¹⁶ The source of Solomon's horses was from Egypt and from Keve — the king's traders bought them from Keve for a [high] price. * ¹⁷ They went up and brought out a chariot from Egypt for six hundred [pieces of] silver and horses for a hundred and fifty; [Solomon's traders] would also export for all the kings of the Hittites and the kings of Aram.

¹⁸ Solomon then proposed to build a Temple for the Name of HASHEM, and a royal palace for himself.

2 ¹ **S**olomon counted out seventy thousand men [who carried] burdens and eighty thousand men who hewed stone in the mountain, with three thousand six hundred [people] overseeing them.

Alliance with Huram
² Solomon sent word to Huram king of Tyre, saying, "Just as you did for my father David, when you sent him cedars to build himself a house to live in — ³ behold, I am building a Temple for the Name of HASHEM, my God, in which to sanctify Him, to burn incense of spices before Him, to [set] a permanent stack [of show-bread] and [to bring] burnt-offerings each morning and evening, and on Sabbaths and on New Moons and on the festivals of HASHEM, our God — a permanent duty upon Israel. * ⁴ The Temple that I am building is large, for our God is greater than all gods, ⁵ and who can gather enough strength to build a Temple for Him? For the heavens and the highest heavens cannot contain Him, and who am I to build a Temple for Him, except to burn [offerings] before Him? ⁶ So now,

Request for Huram's help
send me a wise man to work with gold, silver, copper, and iron; and with purple, crimson and blue wool, and who knows how to cut engravings — along with the craftsmen who are with me in Judah and Jerusalem, whom my father David prepared. ⁷ Also, send me cedar trees, cypresses and almogs * from Lebanon — for I know that your servants know how to cut down the trees of Lebanon. Behold, my servants will be with your servants — ⁸ to prepare numerous trees for me, for the Temple that I am building will be great and extraordinary. ⁹ Behold, I have commissioned twenty thousand kors * of wheat as sustenance for the lumbermen — for those who cut down the trees — for your servants, and twenty thousand kors of barley, twenty thousand baths * of wine and twenty thousand baths of oil."

Huram's generous offer
¹⁰ Huram king of Tyre responded in writing, sending to Solomon: "In HASHEM's love for His people He has placed you as king over them!" ¹¹ Huram said, "Blessed is HASHEM, the God of Israel, Who made the heavens and the earth, Who gave King David a wise son who has intelligence and understanding, who will build a Temple for HASHEM and a royal palace!

¹² "Now, I have sent an artisan who understands wisdom, [who has worked] for Huram, [and for] my father. ¹³ He is the son of a woman of the daughters of Dan, whose father is a man of Tyre, who knows how to work with gold, silver, copper, iron, stones and wood; and with purple, blue, linen and crimson fabrics, and how to cut all kinds of engravings and make all kinds of designs that might be presented to him, with your artisan and the artisans of my master, your father David. ¹⁴ And now, the wheat and the barley, the oil and the wine that my master has mentioned — let him send them to his servants. ¹⁵ We will cut down trees from the Lebanon according to all your needs, and we will bring them to you by rafts on the Sea of Jaffa, and you will bring them up to Jerusalem."

טז וַיִּסְפֹּר שְׁלֹמֹה כָּל־הָאֲנָשִׁים הַגֵּירִים אֲשֶׁר בְּאֶרֶץ יְרוּשָׁלָ͏ִם:

יִשְׂרָאֵל אַחֲרֵי הַסְּפָר אֲשֶׁר סְפָרָם דָּוִיד אָבִיו וַיִּמָּצְאוּ מֵאָה וַחֲמִשִּׁים אֶלֶף

יז וּשְׁלֹשֶׁת אֲלָפִים וְשֵׁשׁ מֵאוֹת: וַיַּעַשׂ מֵהֶם שִׁבְעִים אֶלֶף סַבָּל וּשְׁמֹנִים אֶלֶף

ג א חֹצֵב בָּהָר וּשְׁלֹשֶׁת אֲלָפִים וְשֵׁשׁ מֵאוֹת מְנַצְּחִים לְהַעֲבִיד אֶת־הָעָם: וַיָּחֶל שְׁלֹמֹה לִבְנוֹת אֶת־בֵּית־יְהוָה בִּירוּשָׁלַ͏ִם בְּהַר הַמּוֹרִיָּה אֲשֶׁר נִרְאָה לְדָוִיד

ב אָבִיהוּ אֲשֶׁר הֵכִין בִּמְקוֹם דָּוִיד בְּגֹרֶן אָרְנָן הַיְבוּסִי: וַיָּחֶל לִבְנוֹת בַּחֹדֶשׁ

ג הַשֵּׁנִי בַּשֵּׁנִי בִּשְׁנַת אַרְבַּע לְמַלְכוּתוֹ: וְאֵלֶּה הוּסַד שְׁלֹמֹה לִבְנוֹת אֶת־ בֵּית הָאֱלֹהִים הָאֹרֶךְ אַמּוֹת בַּמִּדָּה הָרִאשׁוֹנָה אַמּוֹת שִׁשִּׁים וְרֹחַב

ד אַמּוֹת עֶשְׂרִים: וְהָאוּלָם אֲשֶׁר עַל־פְּנֵי הָאֹרֶךְ עַל־פְּנֵי רֹחַב־הַבַּיִת אַמּוֹת

ה עֶשְׂרִים וְהַגֹּבַהּ מֵאָה וְעֶשְׂרִים וַיְצַפֵּהוּ מִפְּנִימָה זָהָב טָהוֹר: וְאֵת הַבַּיִת הַגָּדוֹל חִפָּה עֵץ בְּרוֹשִׁים וַיְחַפֵּהוּ זָהָב טוֹב וַיַּעַל עָלָיו תִּמֹרִים וְשַׁרְשְׁרוֹת:

ו-ז וַיְצַף אֶת־הַבַּיִת אֶבֶן יְקָרָה לְתִפְאָרֶת וְהַזָּהָב זְהַב פַּרְוָיִם: וַיְחַף אֶת־ הַבַּיִת הַקֹּרוֹת הַסִּפִּים וְקִירוֹתָיו וְדַלְתוֹתָיו זָהָב וּפִתַּח כְּרוּבִים עַל־

ח הַקִּירוֹת: וַיַּעַשׂ אֶת־בֵּית־קֹדֶשׁ הַקֳּדָשִׁים אָרְכּוֹ עַל־פְּנֵי רֹחַב־ הַבַּיִת אַמּוֹת עֶשְׂרִים וְרָחְבּוֹ אַמּוֹת עֶשְׂרִים וַיְחַפֵּהוּ זָהָב טוֹב לְכִכָּרִים

ט שֵׁשׁ מֵאוֹת: וּמִשְׁקָל לְמִסְמְרוֹת לִשְׁקָלִים חֲמִשִּׁים זָהָב וְהָעֲלִיּוֹת חִפָּה

י זָהָב: וַיַּעַשׂ בְּבֵית־קֹדֶשׁ הַקֳּדָשִׁים כְּרוּבִים שְׁנַיִם מַעֲשֵׂה

יא צַעֲצֻעִים וַיְצַפּוּ אֹתָם זָהָב: וְכַנְפֵי הַכְּרוּבִים אָרְכָּם אַמּוֹת עֶשְׂרִים כְּנַף הָאֶחָד לְאַמּוֹת חָמֵשׁ מַגַּעַת לְקִיר הַבַּיִת וְהַכָּנָף הָאַחֶרֶת אַמּוֹת חָמֵשׁ

יב מַגִּיעַ לִכְנַף הַכְּרוּב הָאַחֵר: וּכְנַף הַכְּרוּב הָאֶחָד אַמּוֹת חָמֵשׁ מַגִּיעַ לְקִיר הַבַּיִת וְהַכָּנָף הָאַחֶרֶת אַמּוֹת חָמֵשׁ דְּבֵקָה לִכְנַף הַכְּרוּב הָאַחֵר: כַּנְפֵי

יג הַכְּרוּבִים הָאֵלֶּה פֹּרְשִׂים אַמּוֹת עֶשְׂרִים וְהֵם עֹמְדִים עַל־רַגְלֵיהֶם וּפְנֵיהֶם

יד לַבָּיִת: וַיַּעַשׂ אֶת־הַפָּרֹכֶת תְּכֵלֶת וְאַרְגָּמָן וְכַרְמִיל וּבוּץ וַיַּעַל עָלָיו

טו כְּרוּבִים: וַיַּעַשׂ לִפְנֵי הַבַּיִת עַמּוּדִים שְׁנַיִם אַמּוֹת שְׁלֹשִׁים וְחָמֵשׁ

טז אֹרֶךְ וְהַצֶּפֶת אֲשֶׁר־עַל־רֹאשׁוֹ אַמּוֹת חָמֵשׁ: וַיַּעַשׂ שַׁרְשְׁרוֹת בַּדְּבִיר

יז וַיִּתֵּן עַל־רֹאשׁ הָעַמֻּדִים וַיַּעַשׂ רִמּוֹנִים מֵאָה וַיִּתֵּן בַּשַּׁרְשְׁרוֹת: וַיָּקֶם אֶת־ הָעַמּוּדִים עַל־פְּנֵי הַהֵיכָל אֶחָד מִיָּמִין וְאֶחָד מֵהַשְּׂמֹאול וַיִּקְרָא שֵׁם

ד א הַיְמָנִי °[הַיְמִינִי ק] יָכִין וְשֵׁם הַשְּׂמָאלִי בֹּעַז: וַיַּעַשׂ מִזְבַּח נְחֹשֶׁת

ב עֶשְׂרִים אַמָּה אָרְכּוֹ וְעֶשְׂרִים אַמָּה רָחְבּוֹ וְעֶשֶׂר אַמּוֹת קוֹמָתוֹ: וַיַּעַשׂ אֶת־הַיָּם מוּצָק עֶשֶׂר בָּאַמָּה מִשְּׂפָתוֹ אֶל־שְׂפָתוֹ עָגוֹל סָבִיב וְחָמֵשׁ

ג בָּאַמָּה קוֹמָתוֹ וְקָו שְׁלֹשִׁים בָּאַמָּה יָסֹב אֹתוֹ סָבִיב: וּדְמוּת בְּקָרִים תַּחַת

2:16. This is perhaps a reference to *I Chronicles* 22:2 (*Radak*).

3:3. The dimensions are given in a cubit of the same length as that used by Moses in the construction of the Tabernacle (*Radak*).

3:5. The Sanctuary building.

3:6. An especially beautiful variety of gold.

3:9. Used to fasten the golden sheets to the wood on the walls (*Rashi*).

3:13. See *I Kings* 6:27.

The work force

¹⁶ Solomon counted all the foreign men who lived in the Land of Israel, besides the census with which his father David had counted them, * and they were found to be one hundred fifty-three thousand six hundred. ¹⁷ He made seventy thousand of them [carriers of] burden and eighty thousand of them hewers in the mountain, with three thousand six hundred overseers to direct the people's work.

3

SOLOMON BUILDS THE TEMPLE 3:1-7:22

¹ Solomon then began building the Temple of HASHEM in Jerusalem on Mount Moriah, where He had appeared to his father David. He established it at David's place, on the threshing floor of Ornan the Jebusite. ² He began to build on the second [day] of the second month, in the fourth year of his reign.

³ These are [the dimensions] of the foundations laid by Solomon for building the Temple of God: The length — in cubits like the original measurement* — was sixty cubits, and the width was twenty cubits. ⁴ The Hall, whose length ran along the width of the front of the Temple, was twenty cubits [long], and its height was a hundred and twenty [cubits]. He overlaid it inside with pure gold. ⁵ He covered over the large chamber* with cypress wood, which he then overlaid with fine gold, and he drew palm trees and chains on it. ⁶ He overlaid the Temple with precious stones for splendor. The gold was Parvaim gold.* ⁷ He covered the Temple — the beams, the sideposts, its walls and its doors — with gold, and he engraved cherubim on the walls.

Holy of Holies

⁸ He then made the chamber of the Holy of Holies. Its length, along the width of the building, was twenty cubits, and its width was twenty cubits. He overlaid it with fine gold, using six hundred talents. ⁹ The weight of the nails* was fifty golden shekels. He also overlaid the upper story with gold.

¹⁰ In the chamber of the Holy of Holies, he made two Cherubim, with the appearance of children, and they overlaid them with gold. ¹¹ The length of the Cherubim's wings was twenty cubits — the wing of one was five cubits, touching the wall of the Temple, with the other wing being five cubits, touching the wing of the other Cherub. ¹² The other Cherub's wing was five cubits, reaching the [opposite] wall of the Temple, with the other wing being five cubits, touching the wing of the other Cherub. ¹³ The wings of these Cherubim thus spread out over twenty cubits. They stood upon their feet, facing the Temple. *

¹⁴ He made the Curtain out of blue, purple, crimson and linen fabric, and he embroidered cherubim upon it.

The pillars

¹⁵ He made two pillars in front of the Temple, thirty-five [cubits] in length, and the cover for its top was five cubits.

¹⁶ He made chains for the Partition; * he also put them on the tops of the pillars, and he made a hundred pomegranates, which he placed on the chains.

¹⁷ He erected the pillars at the front of the Sanctuary, one on the right and one on the left; he called the right one "Jachin" and the left one "Boaz."*

4

The Altar

¹ He made a Copper Altar, its length twenty cubits, its width twenty cubits and its height ten cubits.

The "Sea"

² He made a "Sea" of cast [metal], * ten cubits in diameter, circular in shape, five cubits high; a thirty-cubit line could go around it. ³ It had figures of bulls * under

---

3:16. The Partition divided the Sanctuary from the Holy of Holies (see ibid. vv. 16-21).

3:17. The names mean "Establish" and "Strength in It," respectively. These names symbolized Solomon's prayer that the Temple be firmly established and be blessed

forever with Godly strength (*Radak*).

4:2. See *I Kings* 7:23.

4:3. In *I Kings* 7:24 these are described as "knobs under its lip." Apparently figures of bulls were etched into the oval-shaped decorations or knobs.

לוֹ סָבִיב ׀ סָבִיב סוֹבְבִים אֹתוֹ עֶשֶׂר בָּאַמָּה מַקִּיפִים אֶת־הַיָּם סָבִיב

ד סָבִיב: שְׁנַיִם טוּרִים הַבָּקָר יְצוּקִים בְּמֻצַקְתּוֹ: עוֹמֵד עַל־שְׁנֵים עָשָׂר בָּקָר שְׁלֹשָׁה פֹנִים ׀ צָפוֹנָה וּשְׁלֹשָׁה פֹנִים ׀ יָמָּה וּשְׁלֹשָׁה ׀ פֹּנִים נֶגְבָּה וּשְׁלֹשָׁה

ה פֹּנִים מִזְרָחָה וְהַיָּם עֲלֵיהֶם מִלְמָעְלָה וְכָל־אֲחֹרֵיהֶם בָּיְתָה: וְעָבְיוֹ טֶפַח וּשְׂפָתוֹ כְּמַעֲשֵׂה שְׂפַת־כּוֹס פֶּרַח שׁוֹשַׁנָּה מַחֲזִיק בַּתִּים שְׁלֹשֶׁת אֲלָפִים

יָכִיל: וַיַּעַשׂ כִּיּוֹרִים עֲשָׂרָה וַיִּתֵּן חֲמִשָּׁה מִיָּמִין וַחֲמִשָּׁה

ו מִשְּׂמֹאול לְרָחְצָה בָּהֶם אֶת־מַעֲשֵׂה הָעוֹלָה יָדִיחוּ בָם וְהַיָּם לְרָחְצָה

ז לַכֹּהֲנִים בּוֹ: וַיַּעַשׂ אֶת־מְנֹרוֹת הַזָּהָב עֶשֶׂר כְּמִשְׁפָּטָם וַיִּתֵּן

ח בַּהֵיכָל חָמֵשׁ מִיָּמִין וְחָמֵשׁ מִשְּׂמֹאול: וַיַּעַשׂ שֻׁלְחָנוֹת עֲשָׂרָה וַיַּנַּח בַּהֵיכָל חֲמִשָּׁה מִיָּמִין וַחֲמִשָּׁה מִשְּׂמֹאול וַיַּעַשׂ מִזְרְקֵי זָהָב

ט מֵאָה: וַיַּעַשׂ חֲצַר הַכֹּהֲנִים וְהָעֲזָרָה הַגְּדוֹלָה וּדְלָתוֹת

י לָעֲזָרָה וְדַלְתוֹתֵיהֶם צִפָּה נְחֹשֶׁת: וְאֶת־הַיָּם נָתַן מִכֶּתֶף הַיְמָנִית קֵדְמָה

יא מִמּוּל נֶגְבָּה: וַיַּעַשׂ חוּרָם אֶת־הַסִּירוֹת וְאֶת־הַיָּעִים וְאֶת־הַמִּזְרָקוֹת וַיְכַל [חוּרָם °חִירָם ק] לַעֲשׂוֹת אֶת־הַמְּלָאכָה אֲשֶׁר עָשָׂה

יב לַמֶּלֶךְ שְׁלֹמֹה בְּבֵית הָאֱלֹהִים: עַמּוּדִים שְׁנַיִם וְהַגֻּלּוֹת וְהַכֹּתָרוֹת עַל־רֹאשׁ הָעַמּוּדִים שְׁתָּיִם וְהַשְּׂבָכוֹת שְׁתַּיִם לְכַסּוֹת אֶת־שְׁתֵּי גֻּלּוֹת הַכֹּתָרוֹת

יג אֲשֶׁר עַל־רֹאשׁ הָעַמּוּדִים: וְאֶת־הָרִמּוֹנִים אַרְבַּע מֵאוֹת לִשְׁתֵּי הַשְּׂבָכוֹת שְׁנַיִם טוּרִים רִמּוֹנִים לַשְּׂבָכָה הָאֶחָת לְכַסּוֹת אֶת־שְׁתֵּי גֻּלּוֹת הַכֹּתָרוֹת

יד אֲשֶׁר עַל־פְּנֵי הָעַמּוּדִים: וְאֶת־הַמְּכֹנוֹת עָשָׂה וְאֶת־הַכִּיֹּרוֹת עָשָׂה עַל־

טו הַמְּכֹנוֹת: אֶת־הַיָּם אֶחָד וְאֶת־הַבָּקָר שְׁנֵים־עָשָׂר תַּחְתָּיו: וְאֶת־הַסִּירוֹת וְאֶת־הַיָּעִים וְאֶת־הַמִּזְלָגוֹת וְאֶת־כָּל־כְּלֵיהֶם עָשָׂה חוּרָם אָבִיו לַמֶּלֶךְ

יז שְׁלֹמֹה לְבֵית יְהוָה נְחֹשֶׁת מָרוּק: בְּכִכַּר הַיַּרְדֵּן יְצָקָם הַמֶּלֶךְ בַּעֲבִי

יח הָאֲדָמָה בֵּין סֻכּוֹת וּבֵין צְרֵדָתָה: וַיַּעַשׂ שְׁלֹמֹה כָּל־הַכֵּלִים הָאֵלֶּה לָרֹב

יט מְאֹד כִּי לֹא נֶחְקַר מִשְׁקַל הַנְּחֹשֶׁת: וַיַּעַשׂ שְׁלֹמֹה אֵת כָּל־הַכֵּלִים אֲשֶׁר בֵּית הָאֱלֹהִים וְאֵת מִזְבַּח הַזָּהָב וְאֶת־הַשֻּׁלְחָנוֹת וַעֲלֵיהֶם

כ לֶחֶם הַפָּנִים: וְאֶת־הַמְּנֹרוֹת וְנֵרֹתֵיהֶם לְבַעֲרָם כַּמִּשְׁפָּט לִפְנֵי הַדְּבִיר זָהָב

כא-כב סָגוּר: וְהַפֶּרַח וְהַנֵּרוֹת וְהַמֶּלְקַחַיִם זָהָב הוּא מִכְלוֹת זָהָב: וְהַמְזַמְּרוֹת וְהַמִּזְרָקוֹת וְהַכַּפּוֹת וְהַמַּחְתּוֹת זָהָב סָגוּר וּפֶתַח הַבַּיִת דַּלְתוֹתָיו הַפְּנִימִיּוֹת לְקֹדֶשׁ הַקֳּדָשִׁים וְדַלְתֵי הַבַּיִת לַהֵיכָל זָהָב:

ה א וַתִּשְׁלַם כָּל־הַמְּלָאכָה אֲשֶׁר עָשָׂה שְׁלֹמֹה לְבֵית יְהוָה וַיָּבֵא שְׁלֹמֹה אֶת־קָדְשֵׁי ׀ דָּוִיד אָבִיו וְאֶת־הַכֶּסֶף וְאֶת־הַזָּהָב וְאֶת־כָּל־הַכֵּלִים נָתַן בְּאֹצְרוֹת

ב בֵּית הָאֱלֹהִים: אָז יַקְהֵיל שְׁלֹמֹה אֶת־זִקְנֵי יִשְׂרָאֵל וְאֶת־כָּל־רָאשֵׁי

4:5. See I Kings 7:24.

4:7. The original Menorah of the Tabernacle was still in use, and these ten new candelabra were placed on its right and left, all along the southern wall of the Sanctuary. The same explanation is given concerning the ten tables of the following verse (Menachos 98b-99a).

it surrounding it all around, ten per cubit, circling the tank all around, two rows of bulls, which were cast with the casting [of the Sea]. ⁴ *It stood upon twelve oxen, three facing north, three facing west, three facing south and three facing east; the Sea was on top of them, and their haunches were toward the center [of the Sea].* ⁵ *Its thickness was a handbreadth; its lip was like the lip of a cup, with a rose-blossom design; its capacity was two thousand bath-measures.* *

Lavers   ⁶ *He then made ten lavers, placing five on the right [of the Temple] and five on the left, from which to wash. They would rinse the parts of the burnt-offerings from them, while the Sea was for the Kohanim to wash with.*

Candelabra   ⁷ *He then made the ten golden candelabra according to their specification, placing them in the Sanctuary, five on the right and five on the left.* *

Tables   ⁸ *He then made ten tables, setting them in the Sanctuary, five on the right and five on the left. He also made a hundred golden basins.*

Courtyards   ⁹ *He then made the Courtyard of the Kohanim and the Great Courtyard Area, with doors for the Courtyard Area, and he overlaid their doors with copper.* ¹⁰ *He placed the Sea at the right side [of the Temple], eastward, opposite the south.* *

¹¹ *Huram also made the pots, the shovels* *and the bowls; and Huram finished doing the work that he did for King Solomon for the Temple of God:* ¹² *two pillars, the two bases and capitals* *that were on top of the pillars, the two nettings to cover the two bases of the capitals that were on top of the pillars,* ¹³ *the pomegranates, four hundred for the two nettings, two rows of pomegranates for each netting to cover the two bases of the capitals that were on top of the pillars.* ¹⁴ *He made the stands, and he made the lavers upon the stands;* ¹⁵ *the one sea and the twelve bulls under it,* ¹⁶ *the pots, the shovels, the forks and all their vessels Huram made, [as] his father [would have], for King Solomon for the Temple of Hashem, from pure copper.* ¹⁷ *The king cast them in the Plain of the Jordan, in firm clay, between Succoth and Zeredah.* ¹⁸ *Solomon made all these articles in vast number; the weight of the copper could not be determined.*

Other utensils   ¹⁹ *Solomon made all the articles for the Temple of God; and the Golden Altar;* * *the tables with the show-bread upon them;* ²⁰ *the candelabra and their lamps of fine gold for kindling as required in front of the Inner Sanctum,* ²¹ *with their flowers, lamps and tongs of gold — the finest gold;* ²² *the musical instruments and the bowls, spoons and pans, all of fine gold; and the doorway of the Temple, its inner doors for the Holy of Holies, and the doors of the Temple — that is, the Sanctuary — of gold.*

5

The Temple is completed   ¹ **W**hen all the work that Solomon had done for the Temple of Hashem was completed, Solomon brought that which his father David had sanctified, and he placed the silver, the gold and all the articles in the treasuries of the Temple of God. *

² *Then Solomon gathered together the elders of Israel, all the heads of the*

4:10. That is, in the north.

4:11. The pots and shovels were used to remove accumulated ash from the surface of the Altar (*Rashi*).

4:12. The capitals were made up of two parts: the base (which was plain) and the main part (which was decorated, as described in *I Kings* 7:17).

4:19. See *Exodus* 30:1-10, 25:23-30.

5:1. David had prepared immense amounts of silver, gold, building materials, etc., to be used in the construction of the Temple (*I Chronicles* 22:2-19). Solomon did not use these materials, however, depositing them instead in the Temple storehouses. *Abarbanel* suggests that David interpreted Nathan's message (*II Samuel* 7:8-16) to mean that David should have no involvement at all, even indirect, in the building of the Temple.

הַמַּטּוֹת נְשִׂיאֵי הָאָבוֹת לִבְנֵי יִשְׂרָאֵל אֶל־יְרוּשָׁלֵָם לְהַעֲלוֹת אֶת־אֲרוֹן

ג בְּרִית־יְהוָה מֵעִיר דָּוִיד הִיא צִיּוֹן: וַיִּקָּהֲלוּ אֶל־הַמֶּלֶךְ כָּל־אִישׁ יִשְׂרָאֵל

ד בֶּחָג הוּא הַחֹדֶשׁ הַשְּׁבִעִי: וַיָּבֹאוּ כֹּל זִקְנֵי יִשְׂרָאֵל וַיִּשְׂאוּ הַלְוִיִּם אֶת־

ה הָאָרוֹן: וַיַּעֲלוּ אֶת־הָאָרוֹן וְאֶת־אֹהֶל מוֹעֵד וְאֶת־כָּל־כְּלֵי הַקֹּדֶשׁ אֲשֶׁר

ו בָּאֹהֶל הֶעֱלוּ אֹתָם הַכֹּהֲנִים הַלְוִיִּם: וְהַמֶּלֶךְ שְׁלֹמֹה וְכָל־עֲדַת יִשְׂרָאֵל

הַנּוֹעָדִים עָלָיו לִפְנֵי הָאָרוֹן מְזַבְּחִים צֹאן וּבָקָר אֲשֶׁר לֹא־יִסָּפְרוּ וְלֹא

ז יִמָּנוּ מֵרֹב: וַיָּבִיאוּ הַכֹּהֲנִים אֶת־אֲרוֹן בְּרִית־יְהוָה אֶל־מְקוֹמוֹ אֶל־דְּבִיר

ח הַבַּיִת אֶל־קֹדֶשׁ הַקֳּדָשִׁים אֶל־תַּחַת כַּנְפֵי הַכְּרוּבִים: וַיִּהְיוּ הַכְּרוּבִים

פֹּרְשִׂים כְּנָפַיִם עַל־מְקוֹם הָאָרוֹן וַיְכַסּוּ הַכְּרוּבִים עַל־הָאָרוֹן וְעַל־בַּדָּיו

ט מִלְמָעְלָה: וַיַּאֲרִיכוּ הַבַּדִּים וַיֵּרָאוּ רָאשֵׁי הַבַּדִּים מִן־הָאָרוֹן עַל־פְּנֵי

י הַדְּבִיר וְלֹא יֵרָאוּ הַחוּצָה וַיְהִי־שָׁם עַד הַיּוֹם הַזֶּה: אֵין בָּאָרוֹן רַק שְׁנֵי

הַלֻּחוֹת אֲשֶׁר־נָתַן מֹשֶׁה בְּחֹרֵב אֲשֶׁר כָּרַת יְהוָה עִם־בְּנֵי יִשְׂרָאֵל בְּצֵאתָם

יא מִמִּצְרָיִם: וַיְהִי בְּצֵאת הַכֹּהֲנִים מִן־הַקֹּדֶשׁ כִּי כָּל־הַכֹּהֲנִים

יב הַנִּמְצְאִים הִתְקַדָּשׁוּ אֵין לִשְׁמוֹר לְמַחְלְקוֹת: וְהַלְוִיִּם הַמְשֹׁרֲרִים לְכֻלָּם

לְאָסָף לְהֵימָן לִידֻתוּן וְלִבְנֵיהֶם וְלַאֲחֵיהֶם מְלֻבָּשִׁים בּוּץ בִּמְצִלְתַּיִם

וּבִנְבָלִים וְכִנֹּרוֹת עֹמְדִים מִזְרָח לַמִּזְבֵּחַ וְעִמָּהֶם כֹּהֲנִים לְמֵאָה וְעֶשְׂרִים

יג מַחְצְרִרִים [מַחְצְרִים ק] בַּחֲצֹצְרוֹת: וַיְהִי כְאֶחָד °לַמְחַצְצְרִים

[לַמְחַצְרִים ק] וְלַמְשֹׁרֲרִים לְהַשְׁמִיעַ קוֹל־אֶחָד לְהַלֵּל וּלְהֹדוֹת לַיהוָה

וּכְהָרִים קוֹל בַּחֲצֹצְרוֹת וּבִמְצִלְתַּיִם וּבִכְלֵי הַשִּׁיר וּבְהַלֵּל לַיהוָה כִּי טוֹב

יד כִּי לְעוֹלָם חַסְדּוֹ וְהַבַּיִת מָלֵא עָנָן בֵּית יְהוָה: וְלֹא־יָכְלוּ הַכֹּהֲנִים לַעֲמוֹד

ו   א לְשָׁרֵת מִפְּנֵי הֶעָנָן כִּי־מָלֵא כְבוֹד־יְהוָה אֶת־בֵּית הָאֱלֹהִים: אָז

ב אָמַר שְׁלֹמֹה יְהוָה אָמַר לִשְׁכּוֹן בָּעֲרָפֶל: וַאֲנִי בָּנִיתִי בֵית־זְבֻל לָךְ וּמָכוֹן

ג לְשִׁבְתְּךָ עוֹלָמִים: וַיַּסֵּב הַמֶּלֶךְ אֶת־פָּנָיו וַיְבָרֶךְ אֵת כָּל־קְהַל יִשְׂרָאֵל

ד וְכָל־קְהַל יִשְׂרָאֵל עוֹמֵד: וַיֹּאמֶר בָּרוּךְ יְהוָה אֱלֹהֵי יִשְׂרָאֵל אֲשֶׁר דִּבֶּר

ה בְּפִיו אֵת דָּוִיד אָבִי וּבְיָדָיו מִלֵּא לֵאמֹר: מִן־הַיּוֹם אֲשֶׁר הוֹצֵאתִי אֶת־עַמִּי

מֵאֶרֶץ מִצְרַיִם לֹא־בָחַרְתִּי בְעִיר מִכֹּל שִׁבְטֵי יִשְׂרָאֵל לִבְנוֹת בַּיִת לִהְיוֹת

ו שְׁמִי שָׁם וְלֹא־בָחַרְתִּי בְאִישׁ לִהְיוֹת נָגִיד עַל־עַמִּי יִשְׂרָאֵל: וָאֶבְחַר

ז בִּירוּשָׁלַם לִהְיוֹת שְׁמִי שָׁם וָאֶבְחַר בְּדָוִיד לִהְיוֹת עַל־עַמִּי יִשְׂרָאֵל: וַיְהִי

ח עִם־לְבַב דָּוִיד אָבִי לִבְנוֹת בַּיִת לְשֵׁם יְהוָה אֱלֹהֵי יִשְׂרָאֵל: וַיֹּאמֶר יְהוָה

אֶל־דָּוִיד אָבִי יַעַן אֲשֶׁר הָיָה עִם־לְבָבְךָ לִבְנוֹת בַּיִת לִשְׁמִי הֱטִיבוֹתָ

ט כִּי הָיָה עִם־לְבָבֶךָ: רַק אַתָּה לֹא תִבְנֶה הַבָּיִת כִּי בִנְךָ הַיּוֹצֵא מֵחֲלָצֶיךָ

י הוּא־יִבְנֶה הַבַּיִת לִשְׁמִי: וַיָּקֶם יְהוָה אֶת־דְּבָרוֹ אֲשֶׁר דִּבֵּר וָאָקוּם תַּחַת

5:3. Actually the celebration began a week before Succos; see 7:9-10.

5:5. Solomon brought Moses' Tabernacle to Jerusalem

and stored it in the Temple precincts (*Radak*).

5:9. See *II Kings* 8:8.

5:11-14. These verses are all parenthetical. Scripture

The nation gathers — tribes and the leaders of the ancestral families of the Children of Israel to Jerusalem, to bring up the Ark of the Covenant of HASHEM from the City of David, which is Zion. ³ All the men of Israel gathered before the king on the festival [of Succos], * which is [in] the seventh month. ⁴ All the elders of Israel came, and the Levites bore the Ark. ⁵ They brought up the Ark and the Tent of Meeting, * and all the sacred articles that were in that Tent; the Kohanim and the Levites brought them up. ⁶ King Solomon and the entire assembly of Israel who had assembled with him before the Ark offered up sheep and cattle, too abundant to be numbered or counted.

The Ark is emplaced — ⁷ The Kohanim brought the Ark of the Covenant of HASHEM to its place, to the Inner Sanctum of the Temple, to the Holy of Holies, to beneath the wings of the Cherubim. ⁸ For the Cherubim spread their wings over the place of the Ark; the Cherubim covered over the Ark and its staves from above. ⁹ They extended the staves so that the tips of the staves from the Ark were noticeable upon the Partition, but were not showing on the outside; * they remained there to this very day. ¹⁰ Nothing was in the Ark but the two [stone] Tablets that Moses placed there in Horeb, which HASHEM covenanted with the Children of Israel when they left Egypt. ¹¹ And it was as the Kohanim left the Sanctuary * (for all the Kohanim who were present had sanctified themselves; the divisions were not observed. ¹² The Levites, all of whom were singers: Asaph, Heman, Jeduthun and their sons and kinsmen were dressed in linen; with cymbals, lyres and harps, and stood to the east of the Altar. With them were a hundred twenty Kohanim blowing trumpets. ¹³ There was unison among the trumpeters and the singers, sounding out in one voice to praise and give thanksgiving to HASHEM, and when the sound of the trumpets and cymbals and other musical instruments sounded out, with praise of HASHEM "for He is good, for His kindness is forever,") and the cloud filled the House — the Temple of HASHEM — * ¹⁴ and the Kohanim could not stand and minister because of the cloud, for the glory of HASHEM filled the Temple of God.

6

SOLOMON'S PRAYER 6:1-41 — ¹ Then Solomon said, "HASHEM said that He would dwell in the thick cloud. ² I have built a house of habitation for You, and a foundation for Your dwelling forever."

Blessed is Hashem, Who was patient — ³ Then the king turned his face and blessed the entire congregation of Israel, while the entire congregation of Israel was standing. ⁴ He then said: "Blessed is HASHEM, God of Israel, Who spoke with His word to my father David — and fulfilled with power — saying: ⁵ 'From the day when I took My people Israel out of the land of Egypt, I did not choose a city from among all the tribes of Israel in which to build a Temple where My Name would be, nor did I choose a man to be a ruler over My people Israel, ⁶ but I chose Jerusalem for My Name to be there, and I chose David to rule over My people Israel.'

Solomon, not David — ⁷ "It was in the heart of my father David to build a Temple for the sake of HASHEM, God of Israel. ⁸ But HASHEM said to my father David, 'Inasmuch as it has been in your heart to build a Temple for My Name, you have done well by having this in your heart. ⁹ You, however, shall not build the Temple. Rather, your son, who will emerge from your loins — he will build the Temple for My Name.' ¹⁰ Now HASHEM has fulfilled His word that He spoke; for I have risen in place of

---

relates that because of the huge number of offerings brought during the inauguration of the Temple, all the Kohanim had to participate in the service, and the rotation of the twenty-four shifts of Kohanim was sus-

pended (Radak).

5:13. As soon as the Ark was set in place, the Shechinah, the Divine Presence, appeared in the Temple.

דָּוִיד אָבִי וָאֵשֵׁב ׀ עַל־כִּסֵּא יִשְׂרָאֵל כַּאֲשֶׁר דִּבֶּר יהוה וָאֶבְנֶה הַבַּיִת לְשֵׁם

יא יהוה אֱלֹהֵי יִשְׂרָאֵל: וָאָשִׂים שָׁם אֶת־הָאָרֹון אֲשֶׁר־שָׁם בְּרִית יהוה אֲשֶׁר

יב כָּרַת עִם־בְּנֵי יִשְׂרָאֵל: וַיַּעֲמֹד לִפְנֵי מִזְבַּח יהוה נֶגֶד כָּל־קְהַל יִשְׂרָאֵל

יג וַיִּפְרֹשׂ כַּפָּיו: כִּי־עָשָׂה שְׁלֹמֹה כִּיֹּור נְחֹשֶׁת וַיִּתְּנֵהוּ בְּתֹוךְ הָעֲזָרָה חָמֵשׁ

אַמֹּות אָרְכֹּו וְחָמֵשׁ אַמֹּות רָחְבֹּו וְאַמֹּות שָׁלֹושׁ קֹומָתֹו וַיַּעֲמֹד עָלָיו וַיִּבְרַךְ

יד עַל־בִּרְכָּיו נֶגֶד כָּל־קְהַל יִשְׂרָאֵל וַיִּפְרֹשׂ כַּפָּיו הַשָּׁמָיְמָה: וַיֹּאמַר יהוה

אֱלֹהֵי יִשְׂרָאֵל אֵין־כָּמֹוךָ אֱלֹהִים בַּשָּׁמַיִם וּבָאָרֶץ שֹׁמֵר הַבְּרִית וְהַחֶסֶד

טו לַעֲבָדֶיךָ הַהֹלְכִים לְפָנֶיךָ בְּכָל־לִבָּם: אֲשֶׁר שָׁמַרְתָּ לְעַבְדְּךָ דָּוִיד אָבִי אֵת

טז אֲשֶׁר־דִּבַּרְתָּ לֹו וַתְּדַבֵּר בְּפִיךָ וּבְיָדְךָ מִלֵּאתָ כַּיֹּום הַזֶּה: וְעַתָּה יהוה ׀ אֱלֹהֵי

יִשְׂרָאֵל שְׁמֹר לְעַבְדְּךָ דָוִיד אָבִי אֵת אֲשֶׁר דִּבַּרְתָּ לֹו לֵאמֹר לֹא־יִכָּרֵת לְךָ

אִישׁ מִלְּפָנַי יֹושֵׁב עַל־כִּסֵּא יִשְׂרָאֵל רַק אִם־יִשְׁמְרוּ בָנֶיךָ אֶת־דַּרְכָּם

יז לָלֶכֶת בְּתֹורָתִי כַּאֲשֶׁר הָלַכְתָּ לְפָנָי: וְעַתָּה יהוה אֱלֹהֵי יִשְׂרָאֵל יֵאָמֵן

יח דְּבָרְךָ אֲשֶׁר דִּבַּרְתָּ לְעַבְדְּךָ לְדָוִיד: כִּי הַאֻמְנָם יֵשֵׁב אֱלֹהִים אֶת־הָאָדָם

עַל־הָאָרֶץ הִנֵּה שָׁמַיִם וּשְׁמֵי הַשָּׁמַיִם לֹא יְכַלְכְּלוּךָ אַף כִּי־הַבַּיִת הַזֶּה

יט אֲשֶׁר בָּנִיתִי: וּפָנִיתָ אֶל־תְּפִלַּת עַבְדְּךָ וְאֶל־תְּחִנָּתֹו יהוה אֱלֹהָי לִשְׁמֹעַ

כ אֶל־הָרִנָּה וְאֶל־הַתְּפִלָּה אֲשֶׁר עַבְדְּךָ מִתְפַּלֵּל לְפָנֶיךָ: לִהְיֹות עֵינֶיךָ פְתֻחֹות

אֶל־הַבַּיִת הַזֶּה יֹומָם וָלַיְלָה אֶל־הַמָּקֹום אֲשֶׁר אָמַרְתָּ לָשׂוּם שִׁמְךָ שָׁם

כא לִשְׁמֹועַ אֶל־הַתְּפִלָּה אֲשֶׁר יִתְפַּלֵּל עַבְדְּךָ אֶל־הַמָּקֹום הַזֶּה: וְשָׁמַעְתָּ אֶל־

תַּחֲנוּנֵי עַבְדְּךָ וְעַמְּךָ יִשְׂרָאֵל אֲשֶׁר יִתְפַּלְלוּ אֶל־הַמָּקֹום הַזֶּה וְאַתָּה

כב תִּשְׁמַע מִמְּקֹום שִׁבְתְּךָ מִן־הַשָּׁמַיִם וְשָׁמַעְתָּ וְסָלָחְתָּ: אִם־יֶחֱטָא אִישׁ

לְרֵעֵהוּ וְנָשָׁא־בֹו אָלָה לְהַאֲלֹתֹו וּבָא אָלָה לִפְנֵי מִזְבַּחֲךָ בַּבַּיִת הַזֶּה:

כג וְאַתָּה ׀ תִּשְׁמַע מִן־הַשָּׁמַיִם וְעָשִׂיתָ וְשָׁפַטְתָּ אֶת־עֲבָדֶיךָ לְהָשִׁיב לְרָשָׁע

כד לָתֵת דַּרְכֹּו בְּרֹאשֹׁו וּלְהַצְדִּיק צַדִּיק לָתֶת לֹו כְּצִדְקָתֹו: וְאִם־

יִנָּגֵף עַמְּךָ יִשְׂרָאֵל לִפְנֵי אֹויֵב כִּי יֶחֶטְאוּ־לָךְ וְשָׁבוּ וְהֹודוּ אֶת־שְׁמֶךָ

כה וְהִתְפַּלְלוּ וְהִתְחַנְּנוּ לְפָנֶיךָ בַּבַּיִת הַזֶּה: וְאַתָּה תִּשְׁמַע מִן־הַשָּׁמַיִם וְסָלַחְתָּ

לְחַטַּאת עַמְּךָ יִשְׂרָאֵל וַהֲשֵׁיבֹותָם אֶל־הָאֲדָמָה אֲשֶׁר־נָתַתָּה לָהֶם

כו וְלַאֲבֹותֵיהֶם: בְּהֵעָצֵר הַשָּׁמַיִם וְלֹא־יִהְיֶה מָטָר כִּי יֶחֶטְאוּ־

לָךְ וְהִתְפַּלְלוּ אֶל־הַמָּקֹום הַזֶּה וְהֹודוּ אֶת־שְׁמֶךָ מֵחַטָּאתָם יְשׁוּבוּן כִּי

כז תַעֲנֵם: וְאַתָּה ׀ תִּשְׁמַע הַשָּׁמַיִם וְסָלַחְתָּ לְחַטַּאת עֲבָדֶיךָ וְעַמְּךָ יִשְׂרָאֵל כִּי

תֹורֵם אֶל־הַדֶּרֶךְ הַטֹּובָה אֲשֶׁר יֵלְכוּ־בָהּ וְנָתַתָּה מָטָר עַל־אַרְצְךָ אֲשֶׁר־

כח נָתַתָּה לְעַמְּךָ לְנַחֲלָה: רָעָב כִּי־יִהְיֶה בָאָרֶץ דֶּבֶר כִּי־

יִהְיֶה שִׁדָּפֹון וְיֵרָקֹון אַרְבֶּה וְחָסִיל כִּי יִהְיֶה כִּי יָצַר־לֹו אֹויְבָיו בְּאֶרֶץ

6:18-23. It would be absurd to think of this Temple as a "residence" for God; rather it is to be a conduit for the prayers of Israel — and all mankind.

6:21-22. See *I Kings* 8:31-32.

6:26. Even if they repent only in order to receive God's mercy, may You respond to their prayers (*Metzudos*).

my father David, and I sit on the throne of Israel as HASHEM spoke, and I have built the Temple for the sake of HASHEM, God of Israel's Name. ¹¹ And I have set there the Ark wherein is the covenant of HASHEM, which He made with the Children of Israel."

Solomon
stands
before God ¹² He stood before the Altar of HASHEM, in front of the entire congregation of Israel, and spread out his hands. ¹³ For Solomon had made a copper laver five cubits long, five cubits wide and three cubits tall, and placed it in the midst of the Courtyard, and he now stood on it. Then he knelt on his knees in front of the entire congregation of Israel, and spread out his hands towards Heaven. ¹⁴ He said,

His prayer "HASHEM, God of Israel, there is none like You, O God, in the heavens nor on the earth; Who preserves covenant and the kindness for Your servants who walk before You with all their heart, ¹⁵ for You have preserved for Your servant, my father David, all that You have spoken to him. You spoke with Your mouth and with Your power fulfilled this very day. ¹⁶ And now, O HASHEM, God of Israel, preserve [Your promise] to Your servant, my father David, that You spoke to him, saying, 'There shall not cease from you a man to sit before Me upon the throne of Israel — provided that your children preserve their way, to follow My Torah, as you have gone before Me.' ¹⁷ So now, HASHEM, God of Israel, cause Your word that You spoke to Your servant David to come true.

Please
accept our
prayers ¹⁸ "Would God truly dwell on earth with man? Behold, the heavens and the highest heavens cannot contain You, and surely not this Temple that I have built! ¹⁹ But, may You turn to the prayer of Your servant and to his supplication, O HASHEM my God, to hear the cry and the prayer that Your servant prays before You today: ²⁰ that Your eyes be open toward this Temple day and night, to the place of which You said that You would place Your Name there, to hear the prayer that Your servant shall pray in this place. ²¹ *And may You hear the supplications of Your servant and of Your people Israel, which they shall pray in this place; may You hear [it] from the place of Your habitation, from Heaven — may You hear and forgive.

Defend the
righteous ²² "If a man should wrong his fellow, who imposes an oath upon him and adjures him, and the oath comes before Your Altar in this Temple, ²³ may You hear from Heaven, may You act and judge Your servants, condemning the wicked party, to place the [consequences of] his way upon his head, and vindicating the righteous party, to give him according to his righteousness.

Forgive
Your people ²⁴ "If Your people are defeated by an enemy because they have sinned against You, and then they return [to You] and praise Your Name, and they pray and supplicate before You in this Temple, ²⁵ may You hear from Heaven and forgive the sin of Your people Israel, and return them to the land that You gave to them and their forefathers.

Give rain ²⁶ "If the heavens are restrained and there be no rain, for they have sinned against You, and they pray toward this place and praise Your Name, and they repent from their sin so that You will respond to them, * ²⁷ may You hear from Heaven and forgive the sin of Your servants and Your people Israel, when You teach them the proper path in which they should walk, and may You give rain upon Your land, which You gave to Your people as a heritage.

Banish
tragedy ²⁸ "If there be a famine in the land, if there be a pestilence, if there be windblast or withering or locust or grasshopper, if [Israel's] enemy oppresses it in the land

כט שְׁעָרָיו כָּל־נֶגַע וְכָל־מַחֲלָה: כָּל־תְּפִלָּה כָל־תְּחִנָּה אֲשֶׁר יִהְיֶה לְכָל־
הָאָדָם וּלְכֹל עַמְּךָ יִשְׂרָאֵל אֲשֶׁר יֵדְעוּ אִישׁ נִגְעוֹ וּמַכְאֹבוֹ וּפָרַשׂ כַּפָּיו אֶל־
ל הַבַּיִת הַזֶּה: וְאַתָּה תִּשְׁמַע מִן־הַשָּׁמַיִם מְכוֹן שִׁבְתֶּךָ וְסָלַחְתָּ וְנָתַתָּה
לָאִישׁ כְּכָל־דְּרָכָיו אֲשֶׁר תֵּדַע אֶת־לְבָבוֹ כִּי אַתָּה יָדַעְתָּ לְבַדְּךָ אֶת־לְבַב
לא בְּנֵי הָאָדָם: לְמַעַן יִרָאוּךָ לָלֶכֶת בִּדְרָכֶיךָ כָּל־הַיָּמִים אֲשֶׁר־הֵם חַיִּים עַל־
לב פְּנֵי הָאֲדָמָה אֲשֶׁר נָתַתָּה לַאֲבֹתֵינוּ: וְגַם אֶל־הַנָּכְרִי אֲשֶׁר
לֹא מֵעַמְּךָ יִשְׂרָאֵל הוּא וּבָא | מֵאֶרֶץ רְחוֹקָה לְמַעַן שִׁמְךָ הַגָּדוֹל וְיָדְךָ
לג הַחֲזָקָה וּזְרוֹעֲךָ הַנְּטוּיָה וּבָאוּ וְהִתְפַּלְלוּ אֶל־הַבַּיִת הַזֶּה: וְאַתָּה תִּשְׁמַע
מִן־הַשָּׁמַיִם מִמְּכוֹן שִׁבְתֶּךָ וְעָשִׂיתָ כְּכֹל אֲשֶׁר־יִקְרָא אֵלֶיךָ הַנָּכְרִי לְמַעַן
יֵדְעוּ כָל־עַמֵּי הָאָרֶץ אֶת־שְׁמֶךָ וּלְיִרְאָה אֹתְךָ כְּעַמְּךָ יִשְׂרָאֵל וְלָדַעַת
לד כִּי־שִׁמְךָ נִקְרָא עַל־הַבַּיִת הַזֶּה אֲשֶׁר בָּנִיתִי: כִּי־יֵצֵא עַמְּךָ
לַמִּלְחָמָה עַל־אוֹיְבָיו בַּדֶּרֶךְ אֲשֶׁר תִּשְׁלָחֵם וְהִתְפַּלְלוּ אֵלֶיךָ דֶּרֶךְ הָעִיר
לה הַזֹּאת אֲשֶׁר בָּחַרְתָּ בָּהּ וְהַבַּיִת אֲשֶׁר־בָּנִיתִי לִשְׁמֶךָ: וְשָׁמַעְתָּ מִן־הַשָּׁמַיִם
לו אֶת־תְּפִלָּתָם וְאֶת־תְּחִנָּתָם וְעָשִׂיתָ מִשְׁפָּטָם: כִּי יֶחֶטְאוּ־לָךְ כִּי אֵין אָדָם
אֲשֶׁר לֹא־יֶחֱטָא וְאָנַפְתָּ בָם וּנְתַתָּם לִפְנֵי אוֹיֵב וְשָׁבוּם שׁוֹבֵיהֶם אֶל־אֶרֶץ
לז רְחוֹקָה אוֹ קְרוֹבָה: וְהֵשִׁיבוּ אֶל־לְבָבָם בָּאָרֶץ אֲשֶׁר נִשְׁבּוּ־שָׁם וְשָׁבוּ |
לח וְהִתְחַנְּנוּ אֵלֶיךָ בְּאֶרֶץ שִׁבְיָם לֵאמֹר חָטָאנוּ הֶעֱוִינוּ וְרָשָׁעְנוּ: וְשָׁבוּ אֵלֶיךָ
בְּכָל־לִבָּם וּבְכָל־נַפְשָׁם בְּאֶרֶץ שִׁבְיָם אֲשֶׁר־שָׁבוּ אֹתָם וְהִתְפַּלְלוּ דֶּרֶךְ
אַרְצָם אֲשֶׁר נָתַתָּה לַאֲבוֹתָם וְהָעִיר אֲשֶׁר בָּחַרְתָּ וְלַבַּיִת אֲשֶׁר־בָּנִיתִי
לט לִשְׁמֶךָ: וְשָׁמַעְתָּ מִן־הַשָּׁמַיִם מִמְּכוֹן שִׁבְתְּךָ אֶת־תְּפִלָּתָם וְאֶת־תְּחִנֹּתֵיהֶם
מ וְעָשִׂיתָ מִשְׁפָּטָם וְסָלַחְתָּ לְעַמְּךָ אֲשֶׁר חָטְאוּ־לָךְ: עַתָּה אֱלֹהַי יִהְיוּ־נָא
מא עֵינֶיךָ פְּתֻחוֹת וְאָזְנֶיךָ קַשֻּׁבוֹת לִתְפִלַּת הַמָּקוֹם הַזֶּה: וְעַתָּה
קוּמָה יְהוָה אֱלֹהִים לְנוּחֶךָ אַתָּה וַאֲרוֹן עֻזֶּךָ כֹּהֲנֶיךָ יְהוָה אֱלֹהִים יִלְבְּשׁוּ
מב תְשׁוּעָה וַחֲסִידֶיךָ יִשְׂמְחוּ בַטּוֹב: יְהוָה אֱלֹהִים אַל־תָּשֵׁב פְּנֵי מְשִׁיחֶיךָ
א זָכְרָה לְחַסְדֵי דָּוִיד עַבְדֶּךָ: וּכְכַלּוֹת שְׁלֹמֹה לְהִתְפַּלֵּל וְהָאֵשׁ יָרְדָה ז

ב מֵהַשָּׁמַיִם וַתֹּאכַל הָעֹלָה וְהַזְּבָחִים וּכְבוֹד יְהוָה מָלֵא אֶת־הַבָּיִת: וְלֹא
יָכְלוּ הַכֹּהֲנִים לָבוֹא אֶל־בֵּית יְהוָה כִּי־מָלֵא כְבוֹד־יְהוָה אֶת־בֵּית יְהוָה:
ג וְכֹל | בְּנֵי יִשְׂרָאֵל רֹאִים בְּרֶדֶת הָאֵשׁ וּכְבוֹד יְהוָה עַל־הַבָּיִת וַיִּכְרְעוּ אַפַּיִם
אַרְצָה עַל־הָרִצְפָה וַיִּשְׁתַּחֲווּ וְהוֹדוֹת לַיהוָה כִּי טוֹב כִּי לְעוֹלָם חַסְדּוֹ:
ד־ה וְהַמֶּלֶךְ וְכָל־הָעָם זֹבְחִים זֶבַח לִפְנֵי יְהוָה: וַיִּזְבַּח הַמֶּלֶךְ שְׁלֹמֹה
אֶת־זֶבַח הַבָּקָר עֶשְׂרִים וּשְׁנַיִם אֶלֶף וְצֹאן מֵאָה וְעֶשְׂרִים אָלֶף וַיַּחְנְכוּ
ו אֶת־בֵּית הָאֱלֹהִים הַמֶּלֶךְ וְכָל־הָעָם: וְהַכֹּהֲנִים עַל־מִשְׁמְרוֹתָם עֹמְדִים

6:41. May You accept our wish that this place become Your permanent dwelling place. And may You always accept the offerings brought here by the *Kohanim* (*Radak*).

6:42. If not for our sake, dwell in this Temple for the sake of David, who planned its every detail.

of their cities — any plague, any disease — [29] for any prayer and any supplication that any person of Your entire people Israel may have — each man knowing his own afflictions and his own pain — when he spreads out his hands [in prayer] toward this Temple, [30] may You hear from Heaven, the foundation of Your abode, and forgive, and recompense every man according to his ways as You know his heart, for You alone know the hearts of people; [31] so that they may fear You, to follow Your ways, all the days that they live upon the land which You gave to our forefathers.

Hear the gentile [32] "Also a gentile who is not of Your people Israel, but will come from a distant land, for Your great Name's sake and Your strong hand and Your outstretched arm, and [they] come to pray in this Temple — [33] may You hear from Heaven, the foundation of Your abode, and act according to all that the gentile calls out to You, so that all the nations of the world may know Your Name, to fear You as [does] Your people Israel and to know that Your Name is proclaimed upon this Temple that I have built.

Help in war [34] "When Your people goes to war against their enemy, along the course on which You shall send them, and they direct their prayers to HASHEM by way of the city that You have chosen and the Temple that I have built for Your Name, [35] from heaven may You hear their prayer and their supplication, and carry out their judgment.

Release from captivity [36] "When they sin against You — for there is no man who never sins — and You become angry with them, and You deliver them to an enemy, and their captors take them away to a faraway or nearby land, [37] and they take it to heart in the land where they were taken captive, and they repent and supplicate to You in the land of their captivity, saying, 'We have sinned; we have been iniquitous; we have been wicked,' [38] and they return to You with all their heart and with all their soul in the land of their captivity — of those who had captured them — and they pray by way of their land that You gave to their forefathers, and [by way of] the city that You have chosen and through the Temple that I built for Your Name — [39] may You hear their prayer and their supplications from Heaven, the foundation of Your abode, and carry out their judgment, and forgive Your people who sinned against You. [40] Now, my God, may Your eyes be open and Your ears attentive to the prayers of this place!

Come to Your resting place [41] "Now, arise HASHEM, God, to Your resting place,* You and the Ark of Your might! May Your Kohanim, O HASHEM, God, be clothed in salvation, and may your righteous ones rejoice in goodness! [42] HASHEM, God, do not turn back the request of Your anointed one; remember the righteousness of Your servant David!"*

7

The inauguration

Heavenly fire

[1] When Solomon finished praying, the fire came down from heaven and consumed the burnt-offering and the feast-offerings, and the glory of HASHEM filled the Temple. [2] The Kohanim could not enter the Temple of HASHEM, for the glory of HASHEM filled the Temple of HASHEM. [3] All the Children of Israel were watching when the fire and the glory of HASHEM descended upon the Temple, and they bowed down with their faces to the ground, upon the floor, and they prostrated themselves and were giving praise to HASHEM: "For He is good, for His mercy endures forever."

Lavish offering [4] The king and the entire people were bringing an offering before HASHEM. [5] Solomon brought the cattle-offering of twenty-two thousand, and sheep of a hundred twenty thousand; and they dedicated the Temple of God — the king and all the people. [6] The Kohanim were standing at their watches,

וְהַלְוִיִּם בִּכְלֵי־שִׁיר יְהֹוָה אֲשֶׁר עָשָׂה דָּוִיד הַמֶּלֶךְ לְהֹדוֹת לַיהֹוָה כִּי־
לְעוֹלָם חַסְדּוֹ בְּהַלֵּל דָּוִיד בְּיָדָם וְהַכֹּהֲנִים °מַחֲצֹצְרִים [°מַחְצְרִים ק]
ז נֶגְדָּם וְכָל־יִשְׂרָאֵל עֹמְדִים: וַיְקַדֵּשׁ שְׁלֹמֹה אֶת־תּוֹךְ הֶחָצֵר
אֲשֶׁר לִפְנֵי בֵית־יְהֹוָה כִּי־עָשָׂה שָׁם הָעֹלוֹת וְאֵת חֶלְבֵי הַשְּׁלָמִים כִּי־
מִזְבַּח הַנְּחֹשֶׁת אֲשֶׁר עָשָׂה שְׁלֹמֹה לֹא יָכוֹל לְהָכִיל אֶת־הָעֹלָה וְאֶת־
ח הַמִּנְחָה וְאֶת־הַחֲלָבִים: וַיַּעַשׂ שְׁלֹמֹה אֶת־הֶחָג בָּעֵת הַהִיא שִׁבְעַת יָמִים
ט וְכָל־יִשְׂרָאֵל עִמּוֹ קָהָל גָּדוֹל מְאֹד מִלְּבוֹא חֲמָת עַד־נַחַל מִצְרָיִם: וַיַּעֲשׂוּ
בַּיּוֹם הַשְּׁמִינִי עֲצָרֶת כִּי ׀ חֲנֻכַּת הַמִּזְבֵּחַ עָשׂוּ שִׁבְעַת יָמִים וְהֶחָג שִׁבְעַת
י יָמִים: וּבְיוֹם עֶשְׂרִים וּשְׁלֹשָׁה לַחֹדֶשׁ הַשְּׁבִיעִי שִׁלַּח אֶת־הָעָם לְאָהֳלֵיהֶם
שְׂמֵחִים וְטוֹבֵי לֵב עַל־הַטּוֹבָה אֲשֶׁר עָשָׂה יְהֹוָה לְדָוִיד וְלִשְׁלֹמֹה
יא וּלְיִשְׂרָאֵל עַמּוֹ: וַיְכַל שְׁלֹמֹה אֶת־בֵּית־יְהֹוָה וְאֶת־בֵּית הַמֶּלֶךְ וְאֵת כָּל־
יב הַבָּא עַל־לֵב שְׁלֹמֹה לַעֲשׂוֹת בְּבֵית־יְהֹוָה וּבְבֵיתוֹ הִצְלִיחַ: וַיֵּרָא
יְהֹוָה אֶל־שְׁלֹמֹה בַּלָּיְלָה וַיֹּאמֶר לוֹ שָׁמַעְתִּי אֶת־תְּפִלָּתֶךָ וּבָחַרְתִּי
יג בַּמָּקוֹם הַזֶּה לִי לְבֵית זָבַח: הֵן אֶעֱצֹר הַשָּׁמַיִם וְלֹא־יִהְיֶה מָטָר וְהֵן־אֲצַוֶּה
יד עַל־חָגָב לֶאֱכוֹל הָאָרֶץ וְאִם־אֲשַׁלַּח דֶּבֶר בְּעַמִּי: וְיִכָּנְעוּ עַמִּי אֲשֶׁר
נִקְרָא־שְׁמִי עֲלֵיהֶם וְיִתְפַּלְלוּ וִיבַקְשׁוּ פָנַי וְיָשֻׁבוּ מִדַּרְכֵיהֶם הָרָעִים וַאֲנִי
טו אֶשְׁמַע מִן־הַשָּׁמַיִם וְאֶסְלַח לְחַטָּאתָם וְאֶרְפָּא אֶת־אַרְצָם: עַתָּה עֵינַי
טז יִהְיוּ פְתֻחוֹת וְאָזְנַי קַשֻּׁבוֹת לִתְפִלַּת הַמָּקוֹם הַזֶּה: וְעַתָּה בָּחַרְתִּי
וְהִקְדַּשְׁתִּי אֶת־הַבַּיִת הַזֶּה לִהְיוֹת־שְׁמִי שָׁם עַד־עוֹלָם וְהָיוּ עֵינַי וְלִבִּי שָׁם
יז כָּל־הַיָּמִים: וְאַתָּה אִם־תֵּלֵךְ לְפָנַי כַּאֲשֶׁר הָלַךְ דָּוִיד אָבִיךָ וְלַעֲשׂוֹת כְּכֹל
יח אֲשֶׁר צִוִּיתִיךָ וְחֻקַּי וּמִשְׁפָּטַי תִּשְׁמוֹר: וַהֲקִימוֹתִי אֵת כִּסֵּא מַלְכוּתֶךָ
כַּאֲשֶׁר כָּרַתִּי לְדָוִיד אָבִיךָ לֵאמֹר לֹא־יִכָּרֵת לְךָ אִישׁ מוֹשֵׁל בְּיִשְׂרָאֵל:
יט וְאִם־תְּשׁוּבוּן אַתֶּם וַעֲזַבְתֶּם חֻקּוֹתַי וּמִצְוֹתַי אֲשֶׁר נָתַתִּי לִפְנֵיכֶם וַהֲלַכְתֶּם
כ וַעֲבַדְתֶּם אֱלֹהִים אֲחֵרִים וְהִשְׁתַּחֲוִיתֶם לָהֶם: וּנְתַשְׁתִּים מֵעַל אַדְמָתִי
אֲשֶׁר נָתַתִּי לָהֶם וְאֶת־הַבַּיִת הַזֶּה אֲשֶׁר הִקְדַּשְׁתִּי לִשְׁמִי אַשְׁלִיךְ מֵעַל פָּנָי
כא וְאֶתְּנֶנּוּ לְמָשָׁל וְלִשְׁנִינָה בְּכָל־הָעַמִּים: וְהַבַּיִת הַזֶּה אֲשֶׁר הָיָה עֶלְיוֹן לְכָל־
עֹבֵר עָלָיו יִשֹּׁם וְאָמַר בַּמֶּה עָשָׂה יְהֹוָה כָּכָה לָאָרֶץ הַזֹּאת וְלַבַּיִת הַזֶּה:
כב וְאָמְרוּ עַל אֲשֶׁר עָזְבוּ אֶת־יְהֹוָה ׀ אֱלֹהֵי אֲבֹתֵיהֶם אֲשֶׁר הוֹצִיאָם מֵאֶרֶץ
מִצְרַיִם וַיַּחֲזִיקוּ בֵּאלֹהִים אֲחֵרִים וַיִּשְׁתַּחֲווּ לָהֶם וַיַּעַבְדוּם עַל־כֵּן הֵבִיא
עֲלֵיהֶם אֵת כָּל־הָרָעָה הַזֹּאת:
ח א וַיְהִי מִקֵּץ ׀ עֶשְׂרִים שָׁנָה אֲשֶׁר בָּנָה שְׁלֹמֹה אֶת־בֵּית יְהֹוָה וְאֶת־בֵּיתוֹ:
ב וְהֶעָרִים אֲשֶׁר נָתַן חוּרָם לִשְׁלֹמֹה בָּנָה שְׁלֹמֹה אֹתָם וַיּוֹשֶׁב שָׁם אֶת־בְּנֵי

7:7. The Altar could not accommodate all the offerings brought during the festivities, so Solomon temporarily sanctified the floor of the Courtyard as an altar (*Ralbag*).

7:9. Although Yom Kippur is one of the seven days preceding Succos, *Radak* suggests that they celebrated even though they were fasting. The Talmud, however, relates as well as the Levites, with HASHEM's musical instruments — which King David had made for giving "thanks to HASHEM for His mercy endures forever," for David's praises — in their hands, while the Kohanim were blowing trumpets opposite them, and all of Israel was standing. [7] Solomon sanctified the interior of the Courtyard that was before the Temple of HASHEM, * for there he performed the service of the burnt-offerings and the fats of the peace-offerings; for the Copper Altar that Solomon had made could not contain the burnt-offerings, the meal-offerings and the fats.

Joyous
climax

[8] At that time Solomon instituted the celebration for seven days, and all Israel was with him, a very huge congregation, from the Approach of Hamath until the Brook of Egypt. [9] On the eighth day they celebrated an assembly, for they celebrated the dedication of the Altar for seven days and the festival [of Succos] for seven days. * [10] On the twenty-third day of the seventh month [Solomon] sent the people off to their homes, joyous and good-hearted over the goodness that HASHEM had shown to David and to Solomon and to His people Israel.

God
assures
Solomon . . .

[11] When Solomon finished the Temple of HASHEM and the king's palace, and succeeded in all that had entered Solomon's mind to make in the Temple of HASHEM and in his own house, [12] HASHEM appeared to Solomon at night and said to him, "I have heard your prayer, and I have chosen this place to be a Temple of offering for Me. [13] If I ever restrain the heavens so that there will be no rain, or if I ever command locusts to devour the land, or if I ever send a pestilence among My people, [14] and My people, upon whom My Name is proclaimed, humble themselves and pray and seek My presence and repent of their evil ways — I will hear from Heaven and forgive their sin and heal their land. [15] Now, My eyes will be open and My ears attentive to the prayers of this place. [16] And now, I have chosen and sanctified this Temple, that My Name should remain there forever,

. . . but
with a
condition . . .

and My eyes and My heart should remain there all the days. [17] And as for you — if you walk before Me as your father David walked, and do all that I have commanded you, and observe My decrees and My statutes; [18] then I shall uphold the throne of your kingdom, as I promised your father David, saying, 'No man of

. . . warning
of exile and
destruction

yours will be cut off as a ruler of Israel.' [19] But if you turn away and forsake My decrees and commandments that I have placed before you, and you go and worship the gods of others and prostrate yourselves to them, [20] then I will uproot them from upon My land that I gave them; and this Temple that I have sanctified for My Name I will dismiss from My presence, and I will make [Israel] a parable and a conversation piece among all the nations. [21] And this Temple — which should be so exalted — all who pass by it will be appalled, and say, 'Why did HASHEM do such a thing to this land and to this Temple?' [22] And they will say, 'Because they forsook HASHEM the God of their fathers, Who brought them out of Egypt, and they grasped the gods of others, and prostrated themselves to them and worshiped them; therefore He brought all this evil upon them.' "

8   OTHER
DETAILS OF
SOLOMON'S
REIGN
8:1-9:31

[1] It happened at the end of the twenty years during which Solomon built the Temple of HASHEM and his own palace. [2] Solomon built up the cities that Huram had given him, * and he settled people of Israel there.

---

that the people ate on Yom Kippur that year; this was undoubtedly done by authority of Divinely ordained instruction, as conveyed by prophecy (*Abarbanel*).
8:2. *I Kings* 9:11 relates that King Solomon gave to

Huram twenty cities in the land of Galilee. The cities referred to here were given by Huram to Solomon. Apparently they exchanged gifts of cities to solidify the bond between them (*Radak*).

ג־ד יִשְׂרָאֵל: וַיֵּלֶךְ שְׁלֹמֹה חֲמָת צוֹבָה וַיֶּחֱזַק עָלֶיהָ: וַיִּבֶן אֶת־תַּדְמֹר בַּמִּדְבָּר

ה וְאֵת כָּל־עָרֵי הַמִּסְכְּנוֹת אֲשֶׁר בָּנָה בַּחֲמָת: וַיִּבֶן אֶת־בֵּית חוֹרוֹן הָעֶלְיוֹן

ו וְאֶת־בֵּית חוֹרוֹן הַתַּחְתּוֹן עָרֵי מָצוֹר חוֹמוֹת דְּלָתַיִם וּבְרִיחַ: וְאֶת־בַּעֲלָת

וְאֵת כָּל־עָרֵי הַמִּסְכְּנוֹת אֲשֶׁר הָיוּ לִשְׁלֹמֹה וְאֵת כָּל־עָרֵי הָרֶכֶב וְאֵת עָרֵי

הַפָּרָשִׁים וְאֵת ׀ כָּל־חֵשֶׁק שְׁלֹמֹה אֲשֶׁר חָשַׁק לִבְנוֹת בִּירוּשָׁלַ͏ִם וּבַלְּבָנוֹן

ז וּבְכֹל אֶרֶץ מֶמְשַׁלְתּוֹ: כָּל־הָעָם הַנּוֹתָר מִן־הַחִתִּי וְהָאֱמֹרִי וְהַפְּרִזִּי וְהַחִוִּי

ח וְהַיְבוּסִי אֲשֶׁר לֹא מִיִּשְׂרָאֵל הֵמָּה: מִן־בְּנֵיהֶם אֲשֶׁר נוֹתְרוּ אַחֲרֵיהֶם

בָּאָרֶץ אֲשֶׁר לֹא־כִלּוּם בְּנֵי יִשְׂרָאֵל וַיַּעֲלֵם שְׁלֹמֹה לְמַס עַד הַיּוֹם הַזֶּה:

ט וּמִן־בְּנֵי יִשְׂרָאֵל אֲשֶׁר לֹא־נָתַן שְׁלֹמֹה לַעֲבָדִים לִמְלַאכְתּוֹ כִּי־הֵמָּה

י אַנְשֵׁי מִלְחָמָה וְשָׂרֵי שָׁלִישָׁיו וְשָׂרֵי רִכְבּוֹ וּפָרָשָׁיו: וְאֵלֶּה שָׂרֵי °הַנִּצָּבִים

יא [°הַנִּצָּבִים ק] אֲשֶׁר־לַמֶּלֶךְ שְׁלֹמֹה חֲמִשִּׁים וּמָאתָיִם הָרֹדִים בָּעָם: וְאֶת־

בַּת־פַּרְעֹה הֶעֱלָה שְׁלֹמֹה מֵעִיר דָּוִיד לַבַּיִת אֲשֶׁר בָּנָה־לָהּ כִּי אָמַר לֹא־

תֵשֵׁב אִשָּׁה לִי בְּבֵית דָּוִיד מֶלֶךְ־יִשְׂרָאֵל כִּי־קֹדֶשׁ הֵמָּה אֲשֶׁר־בָּאָה

אֲלֵיהֶם אֲרוֹן יְהוָה:

יב אָז הֶעֱלָה שְׁלֹמֹה עֹלוֹת לַיהוָה עַל מִזְבַּח יְהוָה אֲשֶׁר בָּנָה לִפְנֵי הָאוּלָם:

יג וּבִדְבַר־יוֹם בְּיוֹם לְהַעֲלוֹת כְּמִצְוַת מֹשֶׁה לַשַּׁבָּתוֹת וְלֶחֳדָשִׁים וְלַמּוֹעֲדוֹת

יד שָׁלוֹשׁ פְּעָמִים בַּשָּׁנָה בְּחַג הַמַּצּוֹת וּבְחַג הַשָּׁבֻעוֹת וּבְחַג הַסֻּכּוֹת: וַיַּעֲמֵד

כְּמִשְׁפַּט דָּוִיד־אָבִיו אֶת־מַחְלְקוֹת הַכֹּהֲנִים עַל־עֲבֹדָתָם וְהַלְוִיִּם עַל־

°מִשְׁמְרוֹתָם לְהַלֵּל וּלְשָׁרֵת נֶגֶד הַכֹּהֲנִים לִדְבַר־יוֹם בְּיוֹמוֹ וְהַשּׁוֹעֲרִים

טו בְּמַחְלְקוֹתָם לְשַׁעַר וָשָׁעַר כִּי כֵן מִצְוַת דָּוִיד אִישׁ־הָאֱלֹהִים: וְלֹא סָרוּ

טז מִצְוַת הַמֶּלֶךְ עַל־הַכֹּהֲנִים וְהַלְוִיִּם לְכָל־דָּבָר וְלָאֹצָרוֹת: וַתִּכֹּן כָּל־

מְלֶאכֶת שְׁלֹמֹה עַד־הַיּוֹם מוּסַד בֵּית־יְהוָה וְעַד־כְּלֹתוֹ שָׁלֵם בֵּית

יז יְהוָה: אָז הָלַךְ שְׁלֹמֹה לְעֶצְיוֹן־גֶּבֶר וְאֶל־אֵילוֹת עַל־שְׂפַת

יח הַיָּם בְּאֶרֶץ אֱדוֹם: וַיִּשְׁלַח־לוֹ חוּרָם בְּיַד־עֲבָדָיו °אוֹנִיּוֹת [°אֳנִיּוֹת ק]

וַעֲבָדִים יוֹדְעֵי יָם וַיָּבֹאוּ עִם־עַבְדֵי שְׁלֹמֹה אוֹפִירָה וַיִּקְחוּ מִשָּׁם אַרְבַּע־

ט א מֵאוֹת וַחֲמִשִּׁים כִּכַּר זָהָב וַיָּבִיאוּ אֶל־הַמֶּלֶךְ שְׁלֹמֹה: וּמַלְכַּת־

שְׁבָא שָׁמְעָה אֶת־שֵׁמַע שְׁלֹמֹה וַתָּבוֹא לְנַסּוֹת אֶת־שְׁלֹמֹה בְחִידוֹת

בִּירוּשָׁלַ͏ִם בְּחַיִל כָּבֵד מְאֹד וּגְמַלִּים נֹשְׂאִים בְּשָׂמִים וְזָהָב לָרֹב וְאֶבֶן יְקָרָה

ב וַתָּבוֹא אֶל־שְׁלֹמֹה וַתְּדַבֵּר עִמּוֹ אֵת כָּל־אֲשֶׁר הָיָה עִם־לְבָבָהּ: וַיַּגֶּד־לָהּ

שְׁלֹמֹה אֶת־כָּל־דְּבָרֶיהָ וְלֹא־נֶעְלַם דָּבָר מִשְּׁלֹמֹה אֲשֶׁר לֹא הִגִּיד לָהּ:

ג־ד וַתֵּרֶא מַלְכַּת־שְׁבָא אֵת חָכְמַת שְׁלֹמֹה וְהַבַּיִת אֲשֶׁר בָּנָה: וּמַאֲכַל שֻׁלְחָנוֹ

וּמוֹשַׁב עֲבָדָיו וּמַעֲמַד מְשָׁרְתָיו וּמַלְבּוּשֵׁיהֶם וּמַשְׁקָיו וּמַלְבּוּשֵׁיהֶם

ה וַעֲלִיָּתוֹ אֲשֶׁר יַעֲלֶה בֵּית יְהוָה וְלֹא־הָיָה עוֹד בָּהּ רוּחַ: וַתֹּאמֶר אֶל־

8:11. Solomon had married Pharaoh's daughter (see *I Kings* 3:1).

8:17. More commonly known as Eilat or Elath (*Deuteronomy* 2:8).

New cities ³ Solomon went to Hamath-zobah, and he subdued it. ⁴ He built up Tadmor in the wilderness and all the storage cites that he built in Hamath. ⁵ He also built up Upper Beth-horon and Lower Beth-horon as fortified cities with walls, gates and bars, ⁶ as well as Baalath and all the storage cities which Solomon had, and all the chariot cities and all the cavalry cities; and every luxury of Solomon that he wished to build in Jerusalem and in the Lebanon and in all the land of his dominion. ⁷ All the people who were left of the Hittite, the Amorite, the Perizzite,

Labor conscripts the Hivite and the Jebusite, who were not of the Children of Israel — ⁸ of their descendants who were left after them in the land, whom the Children of Israel did not eliminate, Solomon conscripted them as laborers, until this day. ⁹ But Solomon did not enslave anyone of the Children of Israel for his labor, for they were men of war, and were commanders of his officers, and the commanders of his chariots and his riders. ¹⁰ And these were the commanders of the commissioners of King Solomon — two hundred and fifty [men] who directed the people.

Palace for the queen ¹¹ Solomon brought up Pharaoh's daughter* from the City of David, to her house that he had built for her, for he thought, "I should not have a wife dwell in the house of David, king of Israel, for they are holy [places], being that the Ark of HASHEM had been brought there."

In the Temple: ¹² At that time Solomon brought up burnt-offerings to HASHEM, upon the Altar of HASHEM that he had built before the Hall, ¹³ as well as what was required for each day on its day, to offer in accordance with the commandment of Moses, for Sabbaths and for New Moons and for the appointed festivals three times a year — the Festival of Matzos, the Festival of Shavuos and the Festival of

Divisions of Kohanim and Levites Succos. ¹⁴ He set up the divisions of Kohanim according to the instructions of his father David for their service, and the Levites in their watches to praise and to minister opposite the Kohanim for each day's needs in its day, and the gatekeepers in their divisions for each gate, for this was the commandment of David, the man of God, ¹⁵ and they did not deviate from the king's command concerning the Kohanim and the Levites, concerning all matters and concerning the treasuries.

Imported wealth ¹⁶ All of Solomon's labor was firmly established, from the day of the laying of the foundations of the Temple of HASHEM to its finish; the Temple of HASHEM was complete. ¹⁷ At that time Solomon went to Ezion-geber and to Eloth,* on the coast in the land of Edom. ¹⁸ Huram sent him, with his servants, ships and servants who knew the sea. They came to Ophir with Solomon's servants and took from there four hundred and fifty talents of gold, and brought them to King Solomon.

9

The Queen of Sheba ¹ The Queen of Sheba heard of Solomon's fame, and she came to test Solomon's [wisdom] with riddles in Jerusalem, with a very large entourage, and with camels bearing large amounts of spices and gold and precious stones. She came before Solomon, and she spoke with him about all that was in her heart. ² Solomon told her [the solutions to] all her questions; there was not a thing hidden from Solomon that he could not tell her. ³ The Queen of Sheba saw the wisdom of Solomon: the palace that he had erected; ⁴ the food [served] at his table and the seating of his servants, the station of his attendants and their uniforms, his cupbearers and their uniforms, and his passageway by which he ascended to the Temple of HASHEM — and she was overwhelmed. ⁵ She said to

ו הַמֶּלֶךְ אֱמֶת הַדָּבָר אֲשֶׁר שָׁמַעְתִּי בְּאַרְצִי עַל־דְּבָרֶיךָ וְעַל־חָכְמָתֶךָ׃ וְלֹא־
הֶאֱמַנְתִּי לְדִבְרֵיהֶם עַד אֲשֶׁר־בָּאתִי וַתִּרְאֶינָה עֵינַי וְהִנֵּה לֹא הֻגַּד־לִי
ז חֲצִי מַרְבִּית חָכְמָתֶךָ יָסַפְתָּ עַל־הַשְּׁמוּעָה אֲשֶׁר שָׁמָעְתִּי׃ אַשְׁרֵי אֲנָשֶׁיךָ
ח וְאַשְׁרֵי עֲבָדֶיךָ אֵלֶּה הָעֹמְדִים לְפָנֶיךָ תָּמִיד וְשֹׁמְעִים אֶת־חָכְמָתֶךָ׃ יְהִי
יְהוָה אֱלֹהֶיךָ בָּרוּךְ אֲשֶׁר ׀ חָפֵץ בְּךָ לְתִתְּךָ עַל־כִּסְאוֹ לְמֶלֶךְ לַיהוָה
אֱלֹהֶיךָ בְּאַהֲבַת אֱלֹהֶיךָ אֶת־יִשְׂרָאֵל לְהַעֲמִידוֹ לְעוֹלָם וַיִּתֶּנְךָ עֲלֵיהֶם
ט לְמֶלֶךְ לַעֲשׂוֹת מִשְׁפָּט וּצְדָקָה׃ וַתִּתֵּן לַמֶּלֶךְ מֵאָה וְעֶשְׂרִים ׀ כִּכַּר זָהָב
וּבְשָׂמִים לָרֹב מְאֹד וְאֶבֶן יְקָרָה וְלֹא הָיָה כַּבֹּשֶׂם הַהוּא אֲשֶׁר־נָתְנָה
י מַלְכַּת־שְׁבָא לַמֶּלֶךְ שְׁלֹמֹה׃ וְגַם־עַבְדֵי °חִירָם [°חוּרָם ק] וְעַבְדֵי שְׁלֹמֹה
יא אֲשֶׁר־הֵבִיאוּ זָהָב מֵאוֹפִיר הֵבִיאוּ עֲצֵי אַלְגּוּמִּים וְאֶבֶן יְקָרָה׃ וַיַּעַשׂ הַמֶּלֶךְ
אֶת־עֲצֵי הָאַלְגּוּמִּים מְסִלּוֹת לְבֵית־יְהוָה וּלְבֵית הַמֶּלֶךְ וְכִנֹּרוֹת וּנְבָלִים
יב לַשָּׁרִים וְלֹא־נִרְאוּ כָהֵם לְפָנִים בְּאֶרֶץ יְהוּדָה׃ וְהַמֶּלֶךְ שְׁלֹמֹה נָתַן
לְמַלְכַּת־שְׁבָא אֶת־כָּל־חֶפְצָהּ אֲשֶׁר שָׁאָלָה מִלְּבַד אֲשֶׁר־הֵבִיאָה אֶל־
יג הַמֶּלֶךְ וַתַּהֲפֹךְ וַתֵּלֶךְ לְאַרְצָהּ הִיא וַעֲבָדֶיהָ׃ וַיְהִי מִשְׁקַל הַזָּהָב
יד אֲשֶׁר־בָּא לִשְׁלֹמֹה בְּשָׁנָה אֶחָת שֵׁשׁ מֵאוֹת וְשִׁשִּׁים וָשֵׁשׁ כִּכְּרֵי זָהָב׃ לְבַד
מֵאַנְשֵׁי הַתָּרִים וְהַסֹּחֲרִים מְבִיאִים וְכָל־מַלְכֵי עֲרַב וּפַחוֹת הָאָרֶץ
טו מְבִיאִים זָהָב וָכֶסֶף לִשְׁלֹמֹה׃ וַיַּעַשׂ הַמֶּלֶךְ שְׁלֹמֹה מָאתַיִם צִנָּה זָהָב
שָׁחוּט שֵׁשׁ מֵאוֹת זָהָב שָׁחוּט יַעֲלֶה עַל־הַצִּנָּה הָאֶחָת׃ וּשְׁלֹשׁ־מֵאוֹת
טז מָגִנִּים זָהָב שָׁחוּט שְׁלֹשׁ מֵאוֹת זָהָב יַעֲלֶה עַל־הַמָּגֵן הָאֶחָת וַיִּתְּנֵם הַמֶּלֶךְ
יז בְּבֵית יַעַר הַלְּבָנוֹן׃ וַיַּעַשׂ הַמֶּלֶךְ כִּסֵּא־שֵׁן גָּדוֹל וַיְצַפֵּהוּ זָהָב
יח טָהוֹר׃ וְשֵׁשׁ מַעֲלוֹת לַכִּסֵּא וְכֶבֶשׁ בַּזָּהָב לַכִּסֵּא מָאֳחָזִים וְיָדוֹת מִזֶּה וּמִזֶּה
יט עַל־מְקוֹם הַשָּׁבֶת וּשְׁנַיִם אֲרָיוֹת עֹמְדִים אֵצֶל הַיָּדוֹת׃ וּשְׁנֵים עָשָׂר אֲרָיוֹת
עֹמְדִים שָׁם עַל־שֵׁשׁ הַמַּעֲלוֹת מִזֶּה וּמִזֶּה לֹא־נַעֲשָׂה כֵן לְכָל־מַמְלָכָה׃
כ וְכֹל כְּלֵי מַשְׁקֵה הַמֶּלֶךְ שְׁלֹמֹה זָהָב וְכֹל כְּלֵי בֵּית־יַעַר הַלְּבָנוֹן זָהָב סָגוּר
כא אֵין כֶּסֶף נֶחְשָׁב בִּימֵי שְׁלֹמֹה לִמְאוּמָה׃ כִּי־אֳנִיּוֹת לַמֶּלֶךְ הֹלְכוֹת תַּרְשִׁישׁ
עִם עַבְדֵי חוּרָם אַחַת לְשָׁלוֹשׁ שָׁנִים תָּבוֹאנָה ׀ אֳנִיּוֹת תַּרְשִׁישׁ נֹשְׂאוֹת
כב זָהָב וָכֶסֶף שֶׁנְהַבִּים וְקוֹפִים וְתוּכִּיִּים׃ וַיִּגְדַּל הַמֶּלֶךְ שְׁלֹמֹה מִכֹּל מַלְכֵי
כג הָאָרֶץ לְעֹשֶׁר וְחָכְמָה׃ וְכֹל מַלְכֵי הָאָרֶץ מְבַקְשִׁים אֶת־פְּנֵי שְׁלֹמֹה
כד לִשְׁמֹעַ אֶת־חָכְמָתוֹ אֲשֶׁר־נָתַן הָאֱלֹהִים בְּלִבּוֹ׃ וְהֵם מְבִיאִים אִישׁ מִנְחָתוֹ
כְּלֵי כֶסֶף וּכְלֵי זָהָב וּשְׂלָמוֹת נֵשֶׁק וּבְשָׂמִים סוּסִים וּפְרָדִים דְּבַר־שָׁנָה
כה בְּשָׁנָה׃ וַיְהִי לִשְׁלֹמֹה אַרְבַּעַת אֲלָפִים אֻרְיוֹת
סוּסִים וּמַרְכָּבוֹת וּשְׁנֵים־עָשָׂר אֶלֶף פָּרָשִׁים וַיַּנִּיחֵם בְּעָרֵי הָרֶכֶב וְעִם־

9:10. This account of the treasures brought by Huram's fleet is inserted in the middle of the story of the Queen of Sheba because it, too, involves a dazzling display of wealth. Alternatively, it provides a description of the passageway mentioned in v. 4, which so astounded the queen. Almog is branching, treelike coral (*Rashi; Radak*).

The queen is overwhelmed the king, "True was the word that I had heard in my country about your words and your wisdom! ⁶ I had not believed their words until I came and my own eyes saw; and behold — even half of your immense wisdom was not told to me! You have surpassed the report that I had heard! ⁷ Fortunate are your men — fortunate are these servants of yours — who stand before you constantly and hear your wisdom! ⁸ May HASHEM your God be blessed, Who has chosen you, to place you upon His throne as king, for HASHEM your God; because of your God's love for Israel, to establish it forever, He has made you king over them, to do justice and *Royal gifts* righteousness." ⁹ She then gave the king a hundred and twenty talents of gold and a large amount of spices and precious stones; there has never [again] been such a large quantity of spices as that which the Queen of Sheba gave to King Solomon. ¹⁰ (In addition, * Huram's servants and Solomon's servants, who had brought gold from Ophir, also brought almog trees* and precious stones from Ophir. ¹¹ The king made the almog wood into pathways for the Temple of HASHEM and the palace of the king, and into harps and lyres for the singers; such things had never been seen before in Judah.) ¹² King Solomon gave the Queen of Sheba whatever [answers] she desired to what she had asked, besides [reciprocating the gifts] that she had brought to the king. Then she turned around and went to her land, she and her servants.

Solomon's wealth ¹³ The amount of gold that came to Solomon in one year was six hundred sixty-six talents of gold, ¹⁴ besides [the tax income] that merchants and spice-peddlers brought in; all the vassal kings and the governors of the land also brought gold and silver to Solomon. ¹⁵ King Solomon made two hundred shields of beaten gold; he would put six hundred [measures] of beaten gold into each shield; ¹⁶ and three hundred bucklers of beaten gold; he would put three hundred [measures] of gold into each buckler; and the king placed them in the "House of the Forest of Lebanon."*

Solomon's throne ¹⁷ The king made a great throne of ivory, and overlaid it with pure gold. ¹⁸ The throne had six steps and a golden ramp attached to the throne. It had arms on either side, at the place of the seat, with two [figures of] lions standing next to the arms. ¹⁹ There were twelve [figures of] lions standing there, on the six steps on either side. Nothing like it had ever been made for any kingdom.

²⁰ All of King Solomon's drinking utensils were gold, and all the fixtures of the "House of the Forest of Lebanon" were pure gold; there was no silver, for [silver] was not considered of any worth in the days of Solomon. ²¹ For the king had ships that went to Tarshish with Huram's servants; once in three years the Tarshish ships would arrive, carrying gold, silver, ivory and monkeys and peacocks.

²² King Solomon became greater than all the kings of the land in wealth and wisdom. ²³ And all the kings of the world wanted to see Solomon, to hear his wisdom, which God had put in his heart. ²⁴ And each one of them would bring his gift — silver vessels, golden vessels, clothing, weapons, spices, horses and mules — each year's due in its year.

Solomon's stables ²⁵ Solomon had four thousand stables of horses and chariots and twelve thousand riders; he kept them in chariot cities,* and [left some] with

---

9:16. This building is described in *I Kings* 7:2ff. The shields were apparently used for ceremonial purposes

(see ibid 14:27-28).
9:25. Mentioned above in 8:6.

כו הַמֶּלֶךְ בִּירוּשָׁלִָם: וַיְהִי מוֹשֵׁל בְּכָל־הַמְּלָכִים מִן־הַנָּהָר וְעַד־אֶרֶץ פְּלִשְׁתִּים

כז וְעַד גְּבוּל מִצְרָיִם: וַיִּתֵּן הַמֶּלֶךְ אֶת־הַכֶּסֶף בִּירוּשָׁלִַם כָּאֲבָנִים וְאֵת

כח הָאֲרָזִים נָתַן כַּשִּׁקְמִים אֲשֶׁר־בַּשְּׁפֵלָה לָרֹב: וּמוֹצִיאִים סוּסִים מִמִּצְרַיִם

כט לִשְׁלֹמֹה וּמִכָּל־הָאֲרָצוֹת: וּשְׁאָר דִּבְרֵי שְׁלֹמֹה הָרִאשֹׁנִים וְהָאַחֲרוֹנִים הֲלֹא־הֵם כְּתוּבִים עַל־דִּבְרֵי נָתָן הַנָּבִיא וְעַל־נְבוּאַת אֲחִיָּה הַשִּׁילוֹנִי

ל וּבַחֲזוֹת [יֶעְדּוֹ ק׳] יֶעְדִּי הַחֹזֶה עַל־יָרָבְעָם בֶּן־נְבָט: וַיִּמְלֹךְ שְׁלֹמֹה

לא בִירוּשָׁלִַם עַל־כָּל־יִשְׂרָאֵל אַרְבָּעִים שָׁנָה: וַיִּשְׁכַּב שְׁלֹמֹה עִם־אֲבֹתָיו

א וַיִּקְבְּרֻהוּ בְּעִיר דָּוִיד אָבִיו וַיִּמְלֹךְ רְחַבְעָם בְּנוֹ תַּחְתָּיו: וַיֵּלֶךְ

י

ב רְחַבְעָם שְׁכֶמָה כִּי שְׁכֶם בָּאוּ כָל־יִשְׂרָאֵל לְהַמְלִיךְ אֹתוֹ: וַיְהִי כִּשְׁמֹעַ יָרָבְעָם בֶּן־נְבָט וְהוּא בְמִצְרַיִם אֲשֶׁר בָּרַח מִפְּנֵי שְׁלֹמֹה הַמֶּלֶךְ וַיָּשָׁב

ג יָרָבְעָם מִמִּצְרָיִם: וַיִּשְׁלְחוּ וַיִּקְרְאוּ־לוֹ וַיָּבֹא יָרָבְעָם וְכָל־יִשְׂרָאֵל וַיְדַבְּרוּ

ד אֶל־רְחַבְעָם לֵאמֹר: אָבִיךָ הִקְשָׁה אֶת־עֻלֵּנוּ וְעַתָּה הָקֵל מֵעֲבֹדַת אָבִיךָ

ה הַקָּשָׁה וּמֵעֻלּוֹ הַכָּבֵד אֲשֶׁר־נָתַן עָלֵינוּ וְנַעַבְדֶךָּ: וַיֹּאמֶר אֲלֵהֶם עוֹד שְׁלֹשֶׁת

ו יָמִים וְשׁוּבוּ אֵלָי וַיֵּלֶךְ הָעָם: וַיִּוָּעַץ הַמֶּלֶךְ רְחַבְעָם אֶת־הַזְּקֵנִים אֲשֶׁר־הָיוּ עֹמְדִים לִפְנֵי שְׁלֹמֹה אָבִיו בִּהְיֹתוֹ חַי לֵאמֹר אֵיךְ אַתֶּם נוֹעָצִים

ז לְהָשִׁיב לָעָם־הַזֶּה דָּבָר: וַיְדַבְּרוּ אֵלָיו לֵאמֹר אִם־תִּהְיֶה לְטוֹב לְהָעָם הַזֶּה

ח וּרְצִיתָם וְדִבַּרְתָּ אֲלֵהֶם דְּבָרִים טוֹבִים וְהָיוּ לְךָ עֲבָדִים כָּל־הַיָּמִים: וַיַּעֲזֹב אֶת־עֲצַת הַזְּקֵנִים אֲשֶׁר יְעָצֻהוּ וַיִּוָּעַץ אֶת־הַיְלָדִים אֲשֶׁר גָּדְלוּ אִתּוֹ

ט הָעֹמְדִים לְפָנָיו: וַיֹּאמֶר אֲלֵהֶם מָה אַתֶּם נוֹעָצִים וְנָשִׁיב דָּבָר אֶת־הָעָם

י הַזֶּה אֲשֶׁר דִּבְּרוּ אֵלַי לֵאמֹר הָקֵל מִן־הָעֹל אֲשֶׁר־נָתַן אָבִיךָ עָלֵינוּ: וַיְדַבְּרוּ אִתּוֹ הַיְלָדִים אֲשֶׁר גָּדְלוּ אִתּוֹ לֵאמֹר כֹּה־תֹאמַר לָעָם אֲשֶׁר־דִּבְּרוּ אֵלֶיךָ לֵאמֹר אָבִיךָ הִכְבִּיד אֶת־עֻלֵּנוּ וְאַתָּה הָקֵל מֵעָלֵינוּ כֹּה תֹּאמַר אֲלֵהֶם קָטָנִּי

יא עָבָה מִמָּתְנֵי אָבִי: וְעַתָּה אָבִי הֶעְמִיס עֲלֵיכֶם עֹל כָּבֵד וַאֲנִי אֹסִיף עַל־

יב עֻלְּכֶם אָבִי יִסַּר אֶתְכֶם בַּשּׁוֹטִים וַאֲנִי בָּעַקְרַבִּים: וַיָּבֹא יָרָבְעָם וְכָל־הָעָם אֶל־רְחַבְעָם בַּיּוֹם הַשְּׁלִשִׁי כַּאֲשֶׁר דִּבֶּר הַמֶּלֶךְ לֵאמֹר שׁוּבוּ

יג אֵלַי בַּיּוֹם הַשְּׁלִשִׁי: וַיַּעֲנֵם הַמֶּלֶךְ קָשָׁה וַיַּעֲזֹב הַמֶּלֶךְ רְחַבְעָם אֵת עֲצַת

יד הַזְּקֵנִים: וַיְדַבֵּר אֲלֵהֶם כַּעֲצַת הַיְלָדִים לֵאמֹר אַכְבִּיד אֶת־עֻלְּכֶם וַאֲנִי אֹסִיף עָלָיו אָבִי יִסַּר אֶתְכֶם בַּשּׁוֹטִים וַאֲנִי בָּעַקְרַבִּים: וְלֹא־שָׁמַע הַמֶּלֶךְ

טו אֶל־הָעָם כִּי־הָיְתָה נְסִבָּה מֵעִם הָאֱלֹהִים לְמַעַן הָקִים יְהוָה אֶת־דְּבָרוֹ

טז אֲשֶׁר דִּבֶּר בְּיַד אֲחִיָּהוּ הַשִּׁלוֹנִי אֶל־יָרָבְעָם בֶּן־נְבָט: וְכָל־יִשְׂרָאֵל כִּי לֹא־שָׁמַע הַמֶּלֶךְ לָהֶם וַיָּשִׁיבוּ הָעָם אֶת־הַמֶּלֶךְ ׀ לֵאמֹר מַה־לָּנוּ חֵלֶק בְּדָוִיד וְלֹא־נַחֲלָה בְּבֶן־יִשַׁי אִישׁ לְאֹהָלֶיךָ יִשְׂרָאֵל עַתָּה רְאֵה בֵיתְךָ דָוִיד

9:29. *Metzudos* suggests that these three prophets wrote works that are no longer extant.

10:1. Although the seat of government was Jerusalem, the coronation took place in Shechem, the "capi-the king in Jerusalem. ²⁶ He ruled over all the kings from the [Euphrates] River to the land of the Philistines, up to the border of Egypt. ²⁷ The king made silver in Jerusalem [as common] as stones, and he made cedars as abundant as sycamores in the lowland. ²⁸ They would export horses from Egypt to Solomon, and from all the lands.

²⁹ The rest of the events of Solomon — earlier and later — behold, they are written in the records of Nathan the Prophet and in the prophecies of Ahijah the Shilonite and in the visions of Jedo the Seer* concerning Jeroboam son of Nebat.

(See Appendix A, timeline 4)

³⁰ Solomon reigned over all of Israel in Jerusalem for forty years. ³¹ Solomon lay with his forefathers, and they buried him in the city of David his father. His son Rehoboam reigned in his place.

10

KING REHOBOAM
10:1-12:16

¹ Rehoboam went to Shechem, for all of Israel had come to Shechem to make him king. * ² When Jeroboam son of Nebat heard this while he was in Egypt, where he had fled from before King Solomon, * Jeroboam returned from Egypt,

Jeroboam confronts the new king

³ for [the people] sent for him and summoned him. Jeroboam came, along with all of Israel, and they spoke to Rehoboam, saying, ⁴ "Your father made our yoke [of taxation] difficult; now, you alleviate your father's difficult workload and his heavy yoke that he placed upon us, and we will serve you." ⁵ He said to them, "[Go away for] three more days and then come back to me." So the people left.

The elders' sound advice is ignored

⁶ King Rehoboam took counsel with the elders, who had stood before his father Solomon while he was alive, saying, "How would you advise what word to respond to this people?" ⁷ They spoke to him, saying, "If you are good to this people and show them favor, and speak kind words to them, they will be your servants all the days." ⁸ But he ignored the advice of the elders who had counseled him, and he took counsel with the youths who had grown up with him, who ministered before him. ⁹ He said to them, "What would you advise; what word shall we respond to this people who have spoken to me, saying, 'Alleviate the yoke that your father placed upon us'?" ¹⁰ The young men who had grown up with him spoke with him, saying, "This is what you should say to the people who have spoken to you, saying, 'Your father made our yoke heavy; you alleviate it for us' — this is what you should say to them: 'My little finger is thicker than my father's loins! ¹¹ So now, my father saddled you with a heavy yoke; I shall add to your yoke! My father chastised you with sticks; and I — with scorpions!' "

The king rebuffs his subjects . . .

¹² Jeroboam and all the people came to Rehoboam on the third day, as the king had spoken, saying, "Return to me on the third day." ¹³ The king responded harshly to them; King Rehoboam ignored the advice of the elders. ¹⁴ He spoke to them according to the counsel of the youths, saying, "I shall make your yoke heavy and I shall add to it! My father chastised you with sticks; and I — with scorpions!" ¹⁵ The king did not listen to the people, for it was caused from God, in order that HASHEM should fulfill His word that He had spoken through the hand

. . . and they respond in kind

of Ahijah the Shilonite to Jeroboam son of Nebat. ¹⁶ All of Israel [saw] that the king did not listen to them, and the people responded to the king, saying, "What share have we in [the house of] David? [We have] no heritage in the son of Jesse! Back to your homes, O Israel! Now see to your own house, O [Kingdom of] David!"*

---

tal" of Ephraim. *Radak* suggests that the northern tribes were seeking a pretext to rebel against Rehoboam and accept Jeroboam as the king, therefore they refused to

come to Jerusalem.
10:2. See *I Kings* 11:26-31.
10:16. See *I Kings* 12:16.

יז וּבְנֵי יִשְׂרָאֵל הַיֹּשְׁבִים בְּעָרֵי יְהוּדָה   וַיֵּלֶךְ כָּל־יִשְׂרָאֵל לְאֹהָלָיו:

יח וַיִּמְלֹךְ עֲלֵיהֶם רְחַבְעָם: וַיִּשְׁלַח הַמֶּלֶךְ רְחַבְעָם אֶת־הֲדֹרָם אֲשֶׁר עַל־הַמַּס וַיִּרְגְּמוּ־בוֹ בְנֵי־יִשְׂרָאֵל אֶבֶן וַיָּמֹת וְהַמֶּלֶךְ רְחַבְעָם הִתְאַמֵּץ לַעֲלוֹת

יט בַּמֶּרְכָּבָה לָנוּס יְרוּשָׁלָ͏ִם: וַיִּפְשְׁעוּ יִשְׂרָאֵל בְּבֵית דָּוִיד עַד הַיּוֹם הַזֶּה:

יא א וַיָּבֹא רְחַבְעָם יְרוּשָׁלַ͏ִם וַיַּקְהֵל אֶת־בֵּית יְהוּדָה וּבִנְיָמִן מֵאָה וּשְׁמוֹנִים אֶלֶף בָּחוּר עֹשֵׂה מִלְחָמָה לְהִלָּחֵם עִם־יִשְׂרָאֵל לְהָשִׁיב אֶת־

ב הַמַּמְלָכָה לִרְחַבְעָם: וַיְהִי דְּבַר־יְהוָה אֶל־שְׁמַעְיָהוּ אִישׁ־הָאֱלֹהִים

ג לֵאמֹר: אֱמֹר אֶל־רְחַבְעָם בֶּן־שְׁלֹמֹה מֶלֶךְ יְהוּדָה וְאֶל כָּל־יִשְׂרָאֵל

ד בִּיהוּדָה וּבִנְיָמִן לֵאמֹר: כֹּה אָמַר יְהוָה לֹא־תַעֲלוּ וְלֹא־תִלָּחֲמוּ עִם־אֲחֵיכֶם שׁוּבוּ אִישׁ לְבֵיתוֹ כִּי מֵאִתִּי נִהְיָה הַדָּבָר הַזֶּה וַיִּשְׁמְעוּ אֶת־דִּבְרֵי יְהוָה וַיָּשֻׁבוּ מִלֶּכֶת אֶל־יָרָבְעָם:

ה   וַיֵּשֶׁב רְחַבְעָם בִּירוּשָׁלָ͏ִם וַיִּבֶן

ו עָרִים לְמָצוֹר בִּיהוּדָה: וַיִּבֶן אֶת־בֵּית־לֶחֶם וְאֶת־עֵיטָם וְאֶת־תְּקוֹעַ: וְאֶת־

ז־ח בֵּית־צוּר וְאֶת־שׂוֹכוֹ וְאֶת־עֲדֻלָּם: וְאֶת־גַּת וְאֶת־מָרֵשָׁה וְאֶת־זִיף: וְאֶת־

ט־י אֲדוֹרַיִם וְאֶת־לָכִישׁ וְאֶת־עֲזֵקָה: וְאֶת־צָרְעָה וְאֶת־אַיָּלוֹן וְאֶת־חֶבְרוֹן

יא אֲשֶׁר בִּיהוּדָה וּבְבִנְיָמִן עָרֵי מְצֻרוֹת: וַיְחַזֵּק אֶת־הַמְּצֻרוֹת וַיִּתֵּן בָּהֶם

יב נְגִידִים וְאֹצְרוֹת מַאֲכָל וְשֶׁמֶן וָיָיִן: וּבְכָל־עִיר וָעִיר צִנּוֹת וּרְמָחִים וַיְחַזְּקֵם

יג לְהַרְבֵּה מְאֹד וַיְהִי־לוֹ יְהוּדָה וּבִנְיָמִן: וְהַכֹּהֲנִים וְהַלְוִיִּם אֲשֶׁר

יד בְּכָל־יִשְׂרָאֵל הִתְיַצְּבוּ עָלָיו מִכָּל־גְּבוּלָם: כִּי־עָזְבוּ הַלְוִיִּם אֶת־מִגְרְשֵׁיהֶם וַאֲחֻזָּתָם וַיֵּלְכוּ לִיהוּדָה וְלִירוּשָׁלָ͏ִם כִּי־הִזְנִיחָם יָרָבְעָם וּבָנָיו מִכַּהֵן

טו לַיהוָה: וַיַּעֲמֶד־לוֹ כֹּהֲנִים לַבָּמוֹת וְלַשְּׂעִירִים וְלָעֲגָלִים אֲשֶׁר עָשָׂה:

טז וְאַחֲרֵיהֶם מִכֹּל שִׁבְטֵי יִשְׂרָאֵל הַנֹּתְנִים אֶת־לְבָבָם לְבַקֵּשׁ אֶת־יְהוָה אֱלֹהֵי יִשְׂרָאֵל בָּאוּ יְרוּשָׁלַ͏ִם לִזְבּוֹחַ לַיהוָה אֱלֹהֵי אֲבוֹתֵיהֶם: וַיְחַזְּקוּ אֶת־

יז מַלְכוּת יְהוּדָה וַיְאַמְּצוּ אֶת־רְחַבְעָם בֶּן־שְׁלֹמֹה לְשָׁנִים שָׁלוֹשׁ כִּי הָלְכוּ בְּדֶרֶךְ דָּוִיד וּשְׁלֹמֹה לְשָׁנִים שָׁלוֹשׁ:   וַיִּקַּח־לוֹ רְחַבְעָם אִשָּׁה

יח אֶת־מָחֲלַת °בֶּן [°בַּת ק׳] יְרִימוֹת בֶּן־דָּוִיד אֲבִיהַיִל בַּת־אֱלִיאָב בֶּן־

יט־כ יִשָׁי: וַתֵּלֶד לוֹ בָּנִים אֶת־יְעוּשׁ וְאֶת־שְׁמַרְיָה וְאֶת־זָהַם: וְאַחֲרֶיהָ לָקַח אֶת־מַעֲכָה בַת־אַבְשָׁלוֹם וַתֵּלֶד לוֹ אֶת־אֲבִיָּה וְאֶת־עַתַּי וְאֶת־זִיזָא וְאֶת־

כא שְׁלֹמִית: וַיֶּאֱהַב רְחַבְעָם אֶת־מַעֲכָה בַת־אַבְשָׁלוֹם מִכָּל־נָשָׁיו וּפִילַגְשָׁיו כִּי נָשִׁים שְׁמוֹנֶה־עֶשְׂרֵה נָשָׂא וּפִילַגְשִׁים שִׁשִּׁים וַיּוֹלֶד עֶשְׂרִים וּשְׁמוֹנָה

כב בָנִים וְשִׁשִּׁים בָּנוֹת: וַיַּעֲמֵד לָרֹאשׁ רְחַבְעָם אֶת־אֲבִיָּה בֶן־מַעֲכָה

כג לְנָגִיד בְּאֶחָיו כִּי לְהַמְלִיכוֹ: וַיָּבֶן וַיִּפְרֹץ מִכָּל־בָּנָיו לְכָל־אַרְצוֹת יְהוּדָה וּבִנְיָמִן לְכֹל עָרֵי הַמְּצֻרוֹת וַיִּתֵּן לָהֶם הַמָּזוֹן לָרֹב וַיִּשְׁאַל הֲמוֹן נָשִׁים:

11:5. As a defense against the rebellious northern tribes, whom he felt might try to unseat him (*Rashi*).   11:17. Rehoboam and his officers (*Ralbag*).   11:19. It is unclear which wife gave birth. Apparently, the

All [the men of] Israel left for home.

Rebellion

¹⁷ As for the Children of Israel who lived in the cities of Judah — Rehoboam ruled over them. ¹⁸ King Rehoboam dispatched Hadoram, who was in charge of the tax, and the Children of Israel pelted him with stones and he died. King Rehoboam then hastened to mount his chariot to flee to Jerusalem.

¹⁹ Thus Israel rebelled against the House of David, to this day.

11

Rehoboam abandons the fight . . .

¹ **R**ehoboam came to Jerusalem, and gathered together the House of Judah and Benjamin, one hundred eighty thousand choice warriors, to fight against [the House of] Israel, to return the kingdom to Rehoboam.

² The word of HASHEM then came to Shemaiah, the man of God, saying, ³ "Speak to Rehoboam son of Solomon, king of Judah, and to all of Israel in Judah and Benjamin, saying, ⁴ Thus said HASHEM: Do not go up and fight with your brethren; let each man return to his home, for this matter was brought about by Me." They obeyed the words of HASHEM, and turned back from going to [fight] Jeroboam.

. . . and consolidates his rule

⁵ Rehoboam remained in Jerusalem. He built up cities for defense in Judah. * ⁶ He built up Beth-lehem, Etam, Tekoa, ⁷ Beth-zur, Soco, Adullam, ⁸ Gath, Mareshah, Ziph, ⁹ Adoraim, Lachish, Azekah, ¹⁰ Zorah, Aijalon and Hebron, which are in Judah and Benjamin, as fortified cities. ¹¹ He strengthened the fortified cities and in them he placed rulers and storehouses of food, oil and wine. ¹² In each city [he stored] shields and spears, and he fortified them very greatly. Thus Judah and Benjamin remained his.

God-fearing people rally to him

¹³ The Kohanim and Levites throughout Israel presented themselves to [Rehoboam] from all their territories, ¹⁴ for the Levites had abandoned their outlying areas and their property and went to Judah and Jerusalem, because Jeroboam and his sons had dismissed them from ministering to HASHEM, ¹⁵ for he had established priests for himself for the high places and demons and calves that he had made. ¹⁶ After them [people] from all the tribes of Israel who had dedicated their hearts to seek out HASHEM, the God of Israel, came to Jerusalem, to bring offerings to HASHEM, the God of their fathers. ¹⁷ They strengthened the kingdom of Judah, and they bolstered Rehoboam son of Solomon for three years, for they * followed the path of David and Solomon for three years.

Rehoboam's family

¹⁸ Rehoboam took Mahalath daughter of Jerimoth son of David for a wife, as well as Abihail daughter of Eliab son of Jesse. ¹⁹ She * bore him sons: Jeush, Shemariah and Zaham. ²⁰ After her he took Maacah daughter of Absalom, who bore him Abijah, Attai, Ziza and Shelomith. ²¹ Rehoboam loved Maacah daughter of Absalom more than his [other] wives and concubines (for he had married eighteen wives and sixty concubines, and he begot twenty-eight sons and sixty daughters), ²² so Rehoboam made Abijah son of Maacah as head, to be the ruler of his brothers, in order to make him king. ²³ He had insight, * and he dispersed some of his sons throughout all the lands of Judah and Benjamin, to all the fortified cities; he gave them abundant supplies of food and sought out many wives.

---

other one either died or did not have children (*Radak*).
11:23. Rehoboam had the insight to prevent jealousy on

the part of Abijah's older brothers by assigning them to various powerful posts throughout the country (*Malbim*).

יב א וַיְהִי כְּהָכִין מַלְכוּת רְחַבְעָם וּכְחֶזְקָתוֹ עָזַב אֶת־תּוֹרַת יהוה וְכָל־יִשְׂרָאֵל
ב עִמּוֹ:   וַיְהִי בַּשָּׁנָה הַחֲמִישִׁית לַמֶּלֶךְ רְחַבְעָם עָלָה שִׁישַׁק
ג מֶלֶךְ־מִצְרַיִם עַל־יְרוּשָׁלָ͏ִם כִּי מָעֲלוּ בַּיהוה: בְּאֶלֶף וּמָאתַיִם רֶכֶב
וּבְשִׁשִּׁים אֶלֶף פָּרָשִׁים וְאֵין מִסְפָּר לָעָם אֲשֶׁר־בָּאוּ עִמּוֹ מִמִּצְרַיִם לוּבִים
ד סֻכִּיִּים וְכוּשִׁים: וַיִּלְכֹּד אֶת־עָרֵי הַמְּצֻרוֹת אֲשֶׁר לִיהוּדָה וַיָּבֹא עַד־
ה יְרוּשָׁלָ͏ִם: וּשְׁמַעְיָה הַנָּבִיא בָּא אֶל־רְחַבְעָם וְשָׂרֵי יְהוּדָה אֲשֶׁר־
נֶאֶסְפוּ אֶל־יְרוּשָׁלַ͏ִם מִפְּנֵי שִׁישָׁק וַיֹּאמֶר לָהֶם כֹּה־אָמַר יהוה אַתֶּם עֲזַבְתֶּם
ו אֹתִי וְאַף־אֲנִי עָזַבְתִּי אֶתְכֶם בְּיַד־שִׁישָׁק: וַיִּכָּנְעוּ שָׂרֵי־יִשְׂרָאֵל וְהַמֶּלֶךְ
ז וַיֹּאמְרוּ צַדִּיק ׀ יהוה: וּבִרְאוֹת יהוה כִּי נִכְנָעוּ הָיָה דְבַר־יהוה אֶל־שְׁמַעְיָה ׀
לֵאמֹר נִכְנְעוּ לֹא אַשְׁחִיתֵם וְנָתַתִּי לָהֶם כִּמְעַט לִפְלֵיטָה וְלֹא־תִתַּךְ
ח חֲמָתִי בִּירוּשָׁלַ͏ִם בְּיַד־שִׁישָׁק: כִּי יִהְיוּ־לוֹ לַעֲבָדִים וְיֵדְעוּ עֲבוֹדָתִי וַעֲבוֹדַת
ט מַמְלְכוֹת הָאֲרָצוֹת: וַיַּעַל שִׁישַׁק מֶלֶךְ־מִצְרַיִם עַל־יְרוּשָׁלַ͏ִם
וַיִּקַּח אֶת־אֹצְרוֹת בֵּית־יהוה וְאֶת־אֹצְרוֹת בֵּית הַמֶּלֶךְ אֶת־הַכֹּל לָקָח
י וַיִּקַּח אֶת־מָגִנֵּי הַזָּהָב אֲשֶׁר עָשָׂה שְׁלֹמֹה: וַיַּעַשׂ הַמֶּלֶךְ רְחַבְעָם תַּחְתֵּיהֶם
יא מָגִנֵּי נְחֹשֶׁת וְהִפְקִיד עַל־יַד שָׂרֵי הָרָצִים הַשֹּׁמְרִים פֶּתַח בֵּית הַמֶּלֶךְ: וַיְהִי
מִדֵּי־בוֹא הַמֶּלֶךְ בֵּית יהוה בָּאוּ הָרָצִים וּנְשָׂאוּם וֶהֱשִׁבוּם אֶל־תָּא
יב הָרָצִים: וּבְהִכָּנְעוֹ שָׁב מִמֶּנּוּ אַף־יהוה וְלֹא לְהַשְׁחִית לְכָלָה וְגַם בִּיהוּדָה
יג הָיָה דְּבָרִים טוֹבִים: וַיִּתְחַזֵּק הַמֶּלֶךְ רְחַבְעָם בִּירוּשָׁלַ͏ִם וַיִּמְלֹךְ
כִּי בֶן־אַרְבָּעִים וְאַחַת שָׁנָה רְחַבְעָם בְּמָלְכוֹ וְשֶׁבַע עֶשְׂרֵה שָׁנָה ׀ מָלַךְ
בִּירוּשָׁלַ͏ִם הָעִיר אֲשֶׁר־בָּחַר יהוה לָשׂוּם אֶת־שְׁמוֹ שָׁם מִכֹּל שִׁבְטֵי
יד יִשְׂרָאֵל וְשֵׁם אִמּוֹ נַעֲמָה הָעַמֹּנִית: וַיַּעַשׂ הָרָע כִּי לֹא הֵכִין לִבּוֹ לִדְרוֹשׁ
טו אֶת־יהוה: וְדִבְרֵי רְחַבְעָם הָרִאשֹׁנִים וְהָאַחֲרוֹנִים הֲלֹא־הֵם
כְּתוּבִים בְּדִבְרֵי שְׁמַעְיָה הַנָּבִיא וְעִדּוֹ הַחֹזֶה לְהִתְיַחֵשׂ וּמִלְחֲמוֹת רְחַבְעָם
טז וְיָרָבְעָם כָּל־הַיָּמִים: וַיִּשְׁכַּב רְחַבְעָם עִם־אֲבֹתָיו וַיִּקָּבֵר בְּעִיר דָּוִיד וַיִּמְלֹךְ
יג א אֲבִיָּה בְנוֹ תַּחְתָּיו: בִּשְׁנַת שְׁמוֹנֶה עֶשְׂרֵה לַמֶּלֶךְ יָרָבְעָם וַיִּמְלֹךְ
ב אֲבִיָּה עַל־יְהוּדָה: שָׁלוֹשׁ שָׁנִים מָלַךְ בִּירוּשָׁלַ͏ִם וְשֵׁם אִמּוֹ מִיכָיָהוּ
ג בַת־אוּרִיאֵל מִן־גִּבְעָה וּמִלְחָמָה הָיְתָה בֵּין אֲבִיָּה וּבֵין יָרָבְעָם: וַיֶּאְסֹר
אֲבִיָּה אֶת־הַמִּלְחָמָה בְּחַיִל גִּבּוֹרֵי מִלְחָמָה אַרְבַּע־מֵאוֹת אֶלֶף אִישׁ
בָּחוּר   וְיָרָבְעָם עָרַךְ עִמּוֹ מִלְחָמָה בִּשְׁמוֹנֶה מֵאוֹת אֶלֶף אִישׁ
ד בָּחוּר גִּבּוֹר חָיִל: וַיָּקָם אֲבִיָּה מֵעַל לְהַר צְמָרַיִם אֲשֶׁר בְּהַר אֶפְרָיִם
ה וַיֹּאמֶר שְׁמָעוּנִי יָרָבְעָם וְכָל־יִשְׂרָאֵל: הֲלֹא לָכֶם לָדַעַת כִּי יהוה ׀ אֱלֹהֵי
יִשְׂרָאֵל נָתַן מַמְלָכָה לְדָוִיד עַל־יִשְׂרָאֵל לְעוֹלָם לוֹ וּלְבָנָיו בְּרִית מֶלַח:

12:9. Described in *I Kings* 10:16-17.

12:11. They would carry the shields in procession before the king (*Rashi*).

12:13. He had the maturity which enabled him to recover from his humiliation and have a reasonably long reign.

13:5. Lit. "a covenant of salt," i.e., permanent as salt.

12 Reho-
boam's
decline

Egypt
advances

1 It happened that as Rehoboam's kingdom became established and he became strong, he forsook the Torah of HASHEM, and all Israel with him.

2 It was in King Rehoboam's fifth year that Shishak king of Egypt ascended against Jerusalem — because they had betrayed HASHEM — **3** with twelve hundred chariots and sixty thousand horsemen, and countless people who came with him from Egypt — Lubim, Sukkiim and Ethiopians. **4** He captured Judah's fortified cities and he approached up to Jerusalem.

The
prophet's
warning

5 Shemaiah the prophet came to Rehoboam and the officers of Judah who had gathered together in Jerusalem because of Shishak, and he said to them, "Thus said HASHEM: You have abandoned Me; so I, too, have abandoned you into the hands of Shishak!"

Israel
repents;
God relents

6 The officers of Israel and the king thereupon humbled themselves, and they said, "HASHEM is the righteous One!" **7** When HASHEM saw that they had humbled themselves, the word of HASHEM came to Shemaiah, saying, "They have humbled themselves; I will not destroy them. I will grant them a small portion as a remnant, and my wrath will not be poured out upon Jerusalem through Shishak. **8** Rather, they will become slaves to him, and they will recognize [the difference between] serving Me and serving the kingdoms of the lands!"

Egypt
plunders

9 When Shishak had ascended against Jerusalem, he took away the treasures of the Temple of HASHEM and the treasures of the king's palace — he took everything. He also took the golden shields that Solomon had made. * **10** King Rehoboam made copper shields in their place, and he placed them in the charge of the captains of the runners, who guarded the entrance to the king's palace; **11** and it would be that whenever the king would come to the Temple of HASHEM, the runners would come and bear them * and then return them to the Chamber of the Runners.

Rehoboam
falls short

12 But when he humbled himself, the anger of HASHEM turned back from him, not destroying [Judah] completely. Furthermore, in Judah things went well. **13** King Rehoboam strengthened himself in Jerusalem and reigned, for he was forty-one years old when he became king, and he reigned for seventeen years * in Jerusalem, the city that HASHEM chose in which to place His Name, out of all the tribes of Israel. His mother's name was Naamah the Ammonite.

14 He did evil, for he did not set his heart to seek out HASHEM. **15** The earlier and later events of Rehoboam — behold, they are written in the words of Shemaiah the Prophet and Iddo the Seer, with the genealogy. The wars between Rehoboam and Jeroboam were constant.

(See Appendix A,
timeline 4)

16 Rehoboam lay with his forefathers and was buried in the City of David. His son Abijah reigned in his place.

13

KING
ABIJAH
13:1-23

1 In the eighteenth year of [the reign of] King Jeroboam, Abijah became king over Judah. **2** He reigned in Jerusalem for three years; his mother's name was Micaiah daughter of Uriel of Gibeah. There was a war between Abijah and Jeroboam. **3** Abijah led the battle with an army of mighty fighters — four hundred thousand chosen men, and Jeroboam set himself for war against him with eight hundred thousand chosen men, mighty warriors. **4** Abijah stood up on top of Mount Zemaraim which is in the hills of Ephraim and he said, "Hear me, Jeroboam and all of Israel! **5** Surely, you should know that HASHEM, God of Israel, gave kingship over Israel to David forever, to him and his children for an everlasting covenant. *

Abijah
challenges
Jeroboam

וז וַיָּ֙קָם֙ יָרָבְעָ֣ם בֶּן־נְבָ֔ט עֶ֖בֶד שְׁלֹמֹ֣ה בֶן־דָּוִ֑יד וַיִּמְרֹ֖ד עַל־אֲדֹנָֽיו: וַיִּקָּבְצ֣וּ
עָלָ֗יו אֲנָשִׁ֤ים רֵקִים֙ בְּנֵ֣י בְלִיַּ֔עַל וַיִּֽתְאַמְּצ֖וּ עַל־רְחַבְעָ֣ם בֶּן־שְׁלֹמֹ֑ה

ח וּרְחַבְעָ֤ם הָיָה֙ נַ֣עַר וְרַךְ־לֵבָ֔ב וְלֹ֥א הִתְחַזַּ֖ק לִפְנֵיהֶֽם: וְעַתָּ֣ה ׀ אַתֶּ֣ם אֹֽמְרִ֗ים
לְהִתְחַזֵּק֙ לִפְנֵי֙ מַמְלֶ֣כֶת יְהוָ֔ה בְּיַ֖ד בְּנֵ֣י דָוִ֑יד וְאַתֶּם֩ הָמ֙וֹן רָ֜ב וְעִמָּכֶ֗ם עֶגְלֵ֤י

ט זָהָב֙ אֲשֶׁ֨ר עָשָׂ֧ה לָכֶ֛ם יָרָבְעָ֖ם לֵאלֹהִֽים: הֲלֹ֤א הִדַּחְתֶּם֙ אֶת־כֹּהֲנֵ֣י יְהוָ֔ה
אֶת־בְּנֵ֥י אַהֲרֹ֖ן וְהַלְוִיִּ֑ם וַתַּעֲשׂ֨וּ לָכֶ֤ם כֹּֽהֲנִים֙ כְּעַמֵּ֣י הָֽאֲרָצ֔וֹת כָּל־הַבָּ֗א

י לְמַלֵּ֣א יָד֗וֹ בְּפַ֤ר בֶּן־בָּקָר֙ וְאֵילִ֣ם שִׁבְעָ֔ה וְהָיָ֥ה כֹהֵ֖ן לְלֹ֣א אֱלֹהִֽים: וַאֲנַ֙חְנוּ֙
יְהוָ֣ה אֱלֹהֵ֔ינוּ וְלֹ֖א עֲזַבְנֻ֑הוּ וְכֹהֲנִ֗ים מְשָׁרְתִ֤ים לַֽיהוָה֙ בְּנֵ֣י אַהֲרֹ֔ן וְהַלְוִיִּ֖ם

יא בַּמְּלָֽאכֶת: וּמַקְטִרִ֣ים לַיהוָ֡ה עֹל֣וֹת בַּבֹּֽקֶר־בַּבֹּ֣קֶר וּבָעֶֽרֶב־בָּעֶ֣רֶב וּקְטֹֽרֶת־
סַמִּים֙ וּמַעֲרֶ֤כֶת לֶ֙חֶם֙ עַל־הַשֻּׁלְחָ֣ן הַטָּה֔וֹר וּמְנוֹרַ֙ת הַזָּהָ֤ב וְנֵרֹתֶ֙יהָ֙ לְבָעֵ֣ר
בָּעֶֽרֶב־בָּעֶ֔רֶב כִּֽי־שֹׁמְרִ֣ים אֲנַ֔חְנוּ אֶת־מִשְׁמֶ֖רֶת יְהוָ֣ה אֱלֹהֵ֑ינוּ וְאַתֶּ֖ם

יב עֲזַבְתֶּ֥ם אֹתֽוֹ: וְהִנֵּה֩ עִמָּ֙נוּ בָרֹ֤אשׁ הָֽאֱלֹהִים֙ ׀ וְכֹהֲנָ֗יו וַחֲצֹצְר֤וֹת הַתְּרוּעָה֙
לְהָרִ֣יעַ עֲלֵיכֶ֔ם בְּנֵ֣י יִשְׂרָאֵ֗ל אַל־תִּלָּֽחֲמ֛וּ עִם־יְהוָ֥ה אֱלֹהֵֽי־אֲבֹתֵיכֶ֖ם כִּֽי־

יג לֹ֥א תַצְלִֽיחוּ: וְיָרָבְעָ֗ם הֵסֵב֙ אֶת־הַמַּאְרָ֔ב לָב֖וֹא מֵאַֽחֲרֵיהֶ֑ם וַיִּֽהְי֣וּ לִפְנֵ֣י
יְהוּדָ֔ה וְהַמַּאְרָ֖ב מֵאַֽחֲרֵיהֶֽם: וַיִּפְנ֣וּ יְהוּדָ֗ה וְהִנֵּ֨ה לָהֶ֤ם הַמִּלְחָמָה֙ פָּנִ֣ים

יד וְאָח֔וֹר וַֽיִּצְעֲקוּ֙ לַֽיהוָ֔ה וְהַכֹּהֲנִ֔ים °מחצרים [°מַחְצְרִ֖ים ק] בַּחֲצֹצְרֽוֹת:

טו וַיָּרִ֖יעוּ אִ֣ישׁ יְהוּדָ֑ה וַיְהִ֗י בְּהָרִ֙יעַ֙ אִ֣ישׁ יְהוּדָ֔ה וְהָ֣אֱלֹהִ֗ים נָגַ֤ף אֶת־יָֽרָבְעָם֙

טז וְכָל־יִשְׂרָאֵ֔ל לִפְנֵ֥י אֲבִיָּ֖ה וִֽיהוּדָֽה: וַיָּנ֥וּסוּ בְנֵֽי־יִשְׂרָאֵ֖ל מִפְּנֵ֣י יְהוּדָ֑ה וַיִּתְּנֵ֥ם

יז אֱלֹהִ֖ים בְּיָדָֽם: וַיַּכּ֙וּ בָהֶ֤ם אֲבִיָּה֙ וְעַמּ֔וֹ מַכָּ֖ה רַבָּ֑ה וַיִּפְּל֤וּ חֲלָלִים֙ מִיִּשְׂרָאֵ֔ל

יח חֲמֵשׁ־מֵא֥וֹת אֶ֖לֶף אִ֥ישׁ בָּחֽוּר: וַיִּכָּֽנְע֥וּ בְנֵֽי־יִשְׂרָאֵ֖ל בָּעֵ֣ת הַהִ֑יא וַיֶּֽאֶמְצוּ֙

יט בְּנֵ֣י יְהוּדָ֔ה כִּ֣י נִשְׁעֲנ֔וּ עַל־יְהוָ֖ה אֱלֹהֵ֣י אֲבֽוֹתֵיהֶֽם: וַיִּרְדֹּ֣ף אֲבִיָּ֗ה אַחֲרֵ֣י
יָרָבְעָ֔ם וַיִּלְכֹּ֤ד מִמֶּ֙נּוּ֙ עָרִ֔ים אֶת־בֵּֽית־אֵל֙ וְאֶת־בְּנוֹתֶ֔יהָ וְאֶת־יְשָׁנָ֖ה וְאֶת־

כ בְּנוֹתֶ֑יהָ וְאֶת־°עפרון [°עֶפְרַ֖יִן ק] וּבְנֹתֶֽיהָ: וְלֹֽא־עָצַ֧ר כֹּֽחַ־יָרָבְעָ֛ם ע֖וֹד

כא בִּימֵ֣י אֲבִיָּ֑הוּ וַיִּגְּפֵ֥הוּ יְהוָ֖ה וַיָּמֹֽת: וַיִּתְחַזֵּ֣ק אֲבִיָּ֔הוּ וַיִּ֙שָּׂא־ל֔וֹ

כב נָשִׁ֖ים אַרְבַּ֣ע עֶשְׂרֵ֑ה וַיּ֙וֹלֶד֙ עֶשְׂרִ֣ים וּשְׁנַ֔יִם בָּנִ֖ים וְשֵׁ֥שׁ עֶשְׂרֵ֖ה בָּנֽוֹת:

כג וְיֶ֨תֶר֙ דִּבְרֵ֣י אֲבִיָּ֔ה וּדְרָכָ֖יו וּדְבָרָ֑יו כְּתוּבִ֕ים בְּמִדְרַ֖שׁ הַנָּבִ֥יא עִדּֽוֹ: וַיִּשְׁכַּ֙ב
אֲבִיָּ֜ה עִם־אֲבֹתָ֗יו וַיִּקְבְּר֤וּ אֹתוֹ֙ בְּעִ֣יר דָּוִ֔יד וַיִּמְלֹ֛ךְ אָסָ֥א בְנ֖וֹ תַּחְתָּ֑יו

יד א בְּיָמָ֛יו שָׁקְטָ֥ה הָאָ֖רֶץ עֶ֥שֶׂר שָׁנִֽים: וַיַּ֥עַשׂ אָסָ֖א הַטּ֑וֹב

ב וְהַיָּשָׁ֔ר בְּעֵינֵ֖י יְהוָ֥ה אֱלֹהָֽיו: וַיָּ֛סַר אֶת־מִזְבְּח֥וֹת הַנֵּכָ֖ר וְהַבָּמ֑וֹת וַיְשַׁבֵּר֙

ג אֶת־הַמַּצֵּב֔וֹת וַיְגַדַּ֖ע אֶת־הָאֲשֵׁרִֽים: וַיֹּ֙אמֶר֙ לִֽיהוּדָ֔ה לִדְר֖וֹשׁ אֶת־יְהוָ֜ה

ד אֱלֹהֵ֣י אֲבוֹתֵיהֶ֑ם וְלַעֲשׂ֖וֹת הַתּוֹרָ֣ה וְהַמִּצְוָֽה: וַיָּ֙סַר֙ מִכָּל־עָרֵ֣י יְהוּדָ֔ה אֶת־

ה הַבָּמ֖וֹת וְאֶת־הַֽחַמָּנִ֑ים וַתִּשְׁקֹ֥ט הַמַּמְלָכָ֖ה לְפָנָֽיו: וַיִּ֛בֶן עָרֵ֥י מְצוּרָ֖ה
בִּיהוּדָ֑ה כִּֽי־שָׁקְטָ֣ה הָאָ֗רֶץ וְאֵין־עִמּ֤וֹ מִלְחָמָה֙ בַּשָּׁנִ֣ים הָאֵ֔לֶּה כִּֽי־

ו הֵנִ֥יחַ יְהוָ֖ה לֽוֹ: וַיֹּ֙אמֶר֙ לִֽיהוּדָ֔ה נִבְנֶ֣ה ׀ אֶת־הֶעָרִ֣ים הָאֵ֔לֶּה וְנָסֵ֙ב חוֹמָ֜ה

Jeroboam's   *⁶ But Jeroboam son of Nebat, a servant of Solomon son of David, got up and*
disloyalty . . .   *rebelled against his master. ⁷ Worthless, lawless people gathered around him and*
they set themselves resolutely against Rehoboam son of Solomon, when Re-
hoboam was young and weak-hearted, and did not stand up firmly against them.
⁸ And now you intend to stand defiantly before the kingdom of HASHEM that is in
the hands of David's descendants. You are a great multitude, and with you are the
golden calves that Jeroboam has made for you as gods. ⁹ Have you not dismissed
the Kohanim of HASHEM, the sons of Aaron, and the Levites, and made for
. . . and   *yourselves priests like the nations of the land? Anyone who comes forward to*
hypocrisy   *initiate himself with a young bull and seven rams becomes a priest to the non-god!*
¹⁰ But as for us — HASHEM is our God, and we have not forsaken Him; the priests
who minister to HASHEM are the sons of Aaron and the Levites do their work.
¹¹ Also, they burn burnt-offerings to HASHEM every morning and every evening, as
well as an incense of spices, and there is an array of bread upon the pure table,
and a golden candelabrum and its lamps to kindle every evening, for we observe
God is   *the charge of HASHEM, our God, while you have forsaken Him. ¹² Behold, with us,*
with us   *at our head, are God and His Kohanim and the blasting-trumpets to blast against*
you. Children of Israel, do not wage war against HASHEM, the God of your
forefathers, for you will not succeed!"

A miraculous   *¹³ Meanwhile, Jeroboam had moved an ambush party around, to approach*
victory for   *from their rear, so that they were in front of Judah and the ambush was behind*
Judah   *them. ¹⁴ Judah turned around and behold — the battle was in front and in the rear!*
They cried out to HASHEM, while the Kohanim sounded the trumpets. ¹⁵ The men
of Judah shouted, and it happened that as the men of Judah shouted, God struck
Jeroboam and all of Israel before Abijah and Judah. ¹⁶ The Children of Israel fled
before Judah, and God delivered them into their hand. ¹⁷ Abijah and his people
inflicted a very great blow against them, and five hundred thousand chosen men
of Israel fell slain.

Abijah   *¹⁸ The Children of Israel became humbled at that time, and the people of Judah*
is not   *gained strength, for they relied on HASHEM, the God of their fathers. ¹⁹ Abijah*
threatened   *pursued Jeroboam, and he captured several cities from him — Beth-el and its*
again   *villages, Jeshanah and its villages, and Ephrain and its villages. ²⁰ Jeroboam did*
not again muster strength in the days of Abijah; HASHEM struck him and he died.
²¹ Abijah established himself. He married fourteen wives, begetting twenty-two
sons and sixteen daughters. ²² The rest of the deeds of Abijah and his ways and
records are written in the Narration of the prophet Iddo. ²³ Abijah lay with his
(See Appendix A,   *forefathers, and they buried him in the City of David. Asa his son reigned in his*
timeline 4)   *place. In his days the land was tranquil for ten years.*

14

¹ A̲sa did what was good and proper in the eyes of HASHEM his God. ² He re-
KING   *moved the alien altars and the high places, shattered the [idolatrous] pillars,*
ASA   *and cut down the Asherah trees. ³ He told Judah to seek HASHEM, the God of their*
14:1-16:14   *forefathers, and to observe the Torah and the commandments. ⁴ He removed the*
Asa destroys   *high places and sun images from all the cities of Judah, and the kingdom was*
the idols   *tranquil before him. ⁵ He built fortified cities in Judah, for the land was tranquil* *
and he had no wars during these years, for HASHEM had granted him rest.
⁶ He said to Judah, "Let us build up these cities and surround them with walls

---

14:5. He took advantage of the years of tranquility to bolster his defenses.

וּמִגְדָּלִים֙ דְּלָתַ֣יִם וּבְרִיחִ֔ים עוֹדֶ֥נּוּ הָאָ֖רֶץ לְפָנֵ֑ינוּ כִּ֤י דָרַ֙שְׁנוּ֙ אֶת־יְהֹוָ֣ה

ז אֱלֹהֵ֔ינוּ דָּרַ֙שְׁנוּ֙ וַיָּ֧נַֽח לָ֛נוּ מִסָּבִ֖יב וַיִּבְנ֥וּ וַיַּצְלִֽיחוּ׃ וַיְהִ֣י לְאָסָ֗א חַ֙יִל֙

נֹשֵׂ֤א צִנָּה֙ וָרֹ֔מַח מִֽיהוּדָ֖ה שְׁלֹ֣שׁ מֵא֣וֹת אֶ֑לֶף וּמִבִּנְיָמִ֗ן נֹשְׂאֵ֤י מָגֵן֙ וְדֹ֣רְכֵי

ח קֶ֔שֶׁת מָאתַ֥יִם וּשְׁמוֹנִ֖ים אָ֑לֶף כׇּל־אֵ֖לֶּה גִּבּ֥וֹרֵי חָֽיִל׃ וַיֵּצֵ֨א אֲלֵיהֶ֜ם זֶ֣רַח

ט הַכּוּשִׁ֗י בְּחַ֙יִל֙ אֶ֣לֶף אֲלָפִ֔ים וּמַרְכָּב֖וֹת שְׁלֹ֣שׁ מֵא֑וֹת וַיָּבֹ֖א עַד־מָרֵשָֽׁה׃ וַיֵּצֵ֥א

י אָסָ֖א לְפָנָ֑יו וַיַּֽעַרְכ֥וּ מִלְחָמָ֖ה בְּגֵ֥יא צְפַ֖תָה לְמָרֵשָֽׁה׃ וַיִּקְרָ֨א אָסָ֜א אֶל־יְהֹוָ֣ה

אֱלֹהָיו֮ וַיֹּאמַר֒ יְהֹוָ֗ה אֵֽין־עִמְּךָ֤ לַעְזוֹר֙ בֵּ֥ין רַב֙ לְאֵ֣ין כֹּ֔חַ עׇזְרֵ֜נוּ יְהֹוָ֤ה

אֱלֹהֵ֙ינוּ֙ כִּֽי־עָלֶ֣יךָ נִשְׁעַ֔נּוּ וּבְשִׁמְךָ֣ בָ֔אנוּ עַל־הֶהָמ֖וֹן הַזֶּ֑ה יְהֹוָ֤ה אֱלֹהֵ֙ינוּ֙

יא אַתָּ֔ה אַֽל־יַעְצֹ֥ר עִמְּךָ֖ אֱנֽוֹשׁ׃ וַיִּגֹּ֤ף יְהֹוָה֙ אֶת־הַכּוּשִׁ֔ים לִפְנֵ֥י אָסָ֖א

יב וְלִפְנֵ֣י יְהוּדָ֑ה וַיָּנֻ֖סוּ הַכּוּשִֽׁים׃ וַיִּרְדְּפֵ֨ם אָסָ֜א וְהָעָ֣ם אֲשֶׁר־עִמּוֹ֮ עַד־לִגְרָר֒

וַיִּפֹּ֤ל מִכּוּשִׁים֙ לְאֵ֣ין לָהֶ֣ם מִֽחְיָ֔ה כִּֽי־נִשְׁבְּר֥וּ לִפְנֵֽי־יְהֹוָ֖ה וְלִפְנֵ֣י מַֽחֲנֵ֑הוּ

יג וַיִּשְׂא֥וּ שָׁלָ֖ל הַרְבֵּ֥ה מְאֹֽד׃ וַיַּכּ֗וּ אֵ֤ת כׇּל־הֶֽעָרִים֙ סְבִיב֣וֹת גְּרָ֔ר כִּֽי־הָיָ֥ה פַ֖חַד־

יהֹוָ֣ה עֲלֵיהֶ֑ם וַיָּבֹ֙זּוּ֙ אֶת־כׇּל־הֶ֣עָרִ֔ים כִּֽי־בִזָּ֥ה רַבָּ֖ה הָיְתָ֣ה בָהֶ֑ם וְגַם־אׇהֳלֵ֥י

יד מִקְנֶ֛ה הִכּ֖וּ וַיִּשְׁבּ֥וּ צֹ֣אן לָרֹ֗ב וּגְמַלִּ֖ים וַיָּשֻׁ֥בוּ יְרוּשָׁלָֽ͏ִם׃   וַעֲזַרְיָ֙הוּ֙

א בֶּן־עוֹדֵ֔ד הָיְתָ֥ה עָלָ֖יו ר֣וּחַ אֱלֹהִֽים׃ וַיֵּצֵא֮ לִפְנֵ֣י אָסָא֒ וַיֹּ֣אמֶר ל֔וֹ שְׁמָע֙וּנִי טו

אָסָ֔א וְכׇל־יְהוּדָ֖ה וּבִנְיָמִ֑ן יְהֹוָ֤ה עִמָּכֶם֙ בִּֽהְיֽוֹתְכֶ֣ם עִמּ֔וֹ וְאִם־תִּדְרְשֻׁ֙הוּ֙

ב יִמָּצֵ֣א לָכֶ֔ם וְאִם־תַּֽעַזְבֻ֖הוּ יַעֲזֹ֥ב אֶתְכֶֽם׃   וְיָמִ֤ים רַבִּים֙ לְיִשְׂרָאֵ֔ל

ג לְלֹ֣א ׀ אֱלֹהֵ֣י אֱמֶ֗ת וּלְלֹ֛א כֹּהֵ֥ן מוֹרֶ֖ה וּלְלֹ֥א תוֹרָֽה׃ וַיָּ֙שׇׁב֙ בַּצַּר־ל֔וֹ עַל־יְהֹוָ֖ה

ד אֱלֹהֵ֣י יִשְׂרָאֵ֑ל וַיְבַקְשֻׁ֖הוּ וַיִּמָּצֵ֥א לָהֶֽם׃ וּבָעִתִּ֣ים הָהֵ֔ם אֵ֥ין שָׁל֖וֹם לַיּוֹצֵ֣א

ה וְלַבָּ֑א כִּ֚י מְהוּמֹ֣ת רַבּ֔וֹת עַ֖ל כׇּל־יֹשְׁבֵ֥י הָאֲרָצֽוֹת׃ וְכֻתְּת֤וּ גוֹי־בְּגוֹי֙ וְעִ֣יר בְּעִ֔יר

ו כִּֽי־אֱלֹהִ֥ים הֲמָמָ֖ם בְּכׇל־צָרָֽה׃ וְאַתֶּ֣ם חִזְק֔וּ וְאַל־יִרְפּ֖וּ יְדֵיכֶ֑ם כִּ֛י יֵ֥שׁ

ז שָׂכָ֖ר לִפְעֻלַּתְכֶֽם׃ וְכִשְׁמֹ֙עַ אָסָ֜א הַדְּבָרִ֣ים הָאֵ֗לֶּה וְהַנְּבוּאָה֮

ח עֹדֵ֣ד הַנָּבִיא֒ הִתְחַזַּ֗ק וַיַּעֲבֵ֤ר הַשִּׁקּוּצִים֙ מִכׇּל־אֶ֤רֶץ יְהוּדָה֙ וּבִנְיָמִ֔ן וּמִן־

הֶ֣עָרִ֔ים אֲשֶׁ֥ר לָכַ֖ד מֵהַ֣ר אֶפְרָ֑יִם וַיְחַדֵּשׁ֙ אֶת־מִזְבַּ֣ח יְהֹוָ֔ה אֲשֶׁ֖ר לִפְנֵ֖י

ט אוּלָ֥ם יְהֹוָֽה׃ וַיִּקְבֹּ֗ץ אֶת־כׇּל־יְהוּדָה֙ וּבִנְיָמִ֔ן וְהַגָּרִ֣ים עִמָּהֶ֔ם מֵאֶפְרַ֙יִם֙

וּמְנַשֶּׁ֔ה וּמִשִּׁמְע֑וֹן כִּֽי־נָפְל֨וּ עָלָ֤יו מִיִּשְׂרָאֵל֙ לָרֹ֔ב בִּרְאֹתָ֕ם כִּֽי־יְהֹוָ֥ה אֱלֹהָ֖יו

י עִמּֽוֹ׃ וַיִּקָּבְצ֥וּ יְרוּשָׁלַ֖͏ִם בַּחֹ֣דֶשׁ הַשְּׁלִשִׁ֑י לִשְׁנַ֥ת חֲמֵשׁ־עֶשְׂרֵ֖ה

יא לְמַלְכ֥וּת אָסָֽא׃ וַיִּזְבְּח֤וּ לַֽיהֹוָה֙ בַּיּ֣וֹם הַה֔וּא מִן־הַשָּׁלָ֖ל הֵבִ֑יאוּ בָּקָ֣ר שְׁבַ֣ע

יב מֵא֔וֹת וְצֹ֖אן שִׁבְעַ֥ת אֲלָפִֽים׃ וַיָּבֹ֣אוּ בַבְּרִ֔ית לִדְר֕וֹשׁ אֶת־יְהֹוָ֖ה אֱלֹהֵ֣י

יג אֲבוֹתֵיהֶ֑ם בְּכׇל־לְבָבָ֖ם וּבְכׇל־נַפְשָֽׁם׃ וְכֹ֨ל אֲשֶׁ֧ר לֹֽא־יִדְרֹ֛שׁ לַיהֹוָ֥ה אֱלֹהֵֽי־

יד יִשְׂרָאֵ֖ל יוּמָ֑ת לְמִן־קָטֹן֙ וְעַד־גָּד֔וֹל לְמֵאִ֖ישׁ וְעַד־אִשָּֽׁה׃ וַיִּשָּׁבְע֥וּ לַיהֹוָ֖ה

טו בְּק֣וֹל גָּד֑וֹל וּבִתְרוּעָ֥ה וּבַחֲצֹצְר֖וֹת וּבַשּׁוֹפָרֽוֹת׃ וַיִּשְׂמְח֤וּ כׇל־יְהוּדָה֙ עַל־

14:13. The men of Judah inspired great fear wherever they went.

15:1. A prophet.

15:3. This is the condition of the nation when, because of its rejection of God, it is exiled or dominated by its enemies (*Radak*).

and towers, double doors and bolts. The land is still before us because we have sought out HASHEM, our God — we have sought [Him] out and he has granted us rest all around." So they built and they succeeded.

To battle with arms and prayer ⁷ *Asa had an army bearing shield and spear: from Judah three hundred thousand, and from Benjamin two hundred and eighty thousand who bore bucklers and drew bows, all these were mighty warriors.* ⁸ *Zerah the Ethiopian went out [to war] against them with an army of a million men and three hundred chariots, approaching up to Mareshah.* ⁹ *Asa went out before him, and they arrayed themselves for war in the Valley of Zephath, near Mareshah.* ¹⁰ *Asa called out to HASHEM, his God, saying, "HASHEM, there is none besides You to help [in battle] between the many and those with no strength. Help us, HASHEM, our God, for we depend on You, and we have come in Your Name against this great multitude! You are HASHEM, our God; let no human muster strength against You!"*

Victory and plunder ¹¹ *HASHEM struck the Ethiopians before Asa and before Judah, and the Ethiopians fled.* ¹² *Asa and the people with him pursued them to Gerar, and the Ethiopians fell, for lack of vitality, for they were crushed before HASHEM and before His camp. They carried off very much booty.* ¹³ *They struck all the cities around Gerar, for the dread of HASHEM was upon them, * and they plundered all the cities, for there was much plunder in them.* ¹⁴ *They also struck tents of livestock and captured sheep in abundance and camels, and then they returned to Jerusalem.*

15

¹ *A spirit of God came over Azariah son of Oded, * ² and he went out before Asa, saying to him, "Hear me, Asa and all of Judah and Benjamin! HASHEM is with you because you are with Him! If you seek Him He will make Himself accessible to you, but if you will abandon Him He will abandon you!*

Azariah exhorts Asa to repent ³ *"Many days passed by for Israel without a true God* and without a Kohen to teach and without Torah.* ⁴ *But they returned to HASHEM, the God of Israel, when they were in trouble, and He made Himself accessible to them.* ⁵ *In those times * there had been no peace for people coming and going, for many disturbances affected all the inhabitants of the lands.* ⁶ *One nation was battered by the other, and one city by the other, for God confounded them with all kinds of trouble.* ⁷ *But you be strong, and do not lose resolve, for there is reward for your actions!"*

Asa obeys ⁸ *When Asa heard these words and the prophecy of [the son of] Oded the prophet, he was encouraged, and he removed the detestable things from all of the land of Judah and Benjamin and from the cities which he had conquered from Mount Ephraim, and he renewed the Altar of HASHEM that was before the Hall of HASHEM.* ⁹ *He gathered together all of Judah and Benjamin, and those from Ephraim and Manasseh and Simeon who dwelled among them — for many people of Israel defected to him when they saw that HASHEM his God was with him.* ¹⁰ *They were gathered in Jerusalem in the third month of the fifteenth year of Asa's reign.* ¹¹ *They brought offerings to HASHEM on that day from the spoils that they had taken — seven hundred cattle and seven thousand sheep.* ¹² *They entered into a covenant to seek out HASHEM, the God of their forefathers, with all their heart and with all their soul;* ¹³ *and anyone who would not seek HASHEM, God of Israel, * would be put to death, whether small or great, man or woman.* ¹⁴ *They swore to HASHEM in a loud voice and with shouts, with trumpets and with shofars.* ¹⁵ *All of Judah rejoiced over*

Offerings and covenant

15:5. When the people was "without a true God, etc."   **15:13.** But would worship idols.

הַשְּׁבוּעָה כִּי בְכָל־לְבָבָם נִשְׁבָּעוּ וּבְכָל־רְצוֹנָם בִּקְשֻׁהוּ וַיִּמָּצֵא לָהֶם וַיָּנַח

טו יְהוָה לָהֶם מִסָּבִיב: וְגַם־מַעֲכָה אֵם ׀ אָסָא הַמֶּלֶךְ הֱסִירָהּ מִגְּבִירָה אֲשֶׁר־עָשְׂתָה לַאֲשֵׁרָה מִפְלָצֶת וַיִּכְרֹת אָסָא אֶת־מִפְלַצְתָּהּ וַיָּדֶק וַיִּשְׂרֹף בְּנַחַל

יז קִדְרוֹן: וְהַבָּמוֹת לֹא־סָרוּ מִיִּשְׂרָאֵל רַק לְבַב־אָסָא הָיָה שָׁלֵם כָּל־יָמָיו:

יח–יט וַיָּבֵא אֶת־קָדְשֵׁי אָבִיו וְקָדָשָׁיו בֵּית הָאֱלֹהִים כֶּסֶף וְזָהָב וְכֵלִים: וּמִלְחָמָה לֹא הָיָתָה עַד שְׁנַת־שְׁלֹשִׁים וְחָמֵשׁ לְמַלְכוּת אָסָא: בִּשְׁנַת

טז א שְׁלֹשִׁים וָשֵׁשׁ לְמַלְכוּת אָסָא עָלָה בַּעְשָׁא מֶלֶךְ־יִשְׂרָאֵל עַל־יְהוּדָה וַיִּבֶן

ב אֶת־הָרָמָה לְבִלְתִּי תֵּת יוֹצֵא וָבָא לְאָסָא מֶלֶךְ יְהוּדָה: וַיֹּצֵא אָסָא כֶּסֶף וְזָהָב מֵאֹצְרוֹת בֵּית יְהוָה וּבֵית הַמֶּלֶךְ וַיִּשְׁלַח אֶל־בֶּן־הֲדַד מֶלֶךְ אֲרָם

ג הַיּוֹשֵׁב בְּדַרְמֶשֶׂק לֵאמֹר: בְּרִית בֵּינִי וּבֵינֶךָ וּבֵין אָבִי וּבֵין אָבִיךָ הִנֵּה שָׁלַחְתִּי לְךָ כֶּסֶף וְזָהָב לֵךְ הָפֵר בְּרִיתְךָ אֶת־בַּעְשָׁא מֶלֶךְ יִשְׂרָאֵל וְיַעֲלֶה

ד מֵעָלָי: וַיִּשְׁמַע בֶּן־הֲדַד אֶל־הַמֶּלֶךְ אָסָא וַיִּשְׁלַח אֶת־שָׂרֵי הַחֲיָלִים אֲשֶׁר־לוֹ אֶל־עָרֵי יִשְׂרָאֵל וַיַּכּוּ אֶת־עִיּוֹן וְאֶת־דָּן וְאֵת אָבֵל מָיִם וְאֵת כָּל־

ה מִסְכְּנוֹת עָרֵי נַפְתָּלִי: וַיְהִי כִּשְׁמֹעַ בַּעְשָׁא וַיֶּחְדַּל מִבְּנוֹת אֶת־הָרָמָה

ו וַיַּשְׁבֵּת אֶת־מְלַאכְתּוֹ: וְאָסָא הַמֶּלֶךְ לָקַח אֶת־כָּל־יְהוּדָה וַיִּשְׂאוּ אֶת־אַבְנֵי הָרָמָה וְאֶת־עֵצֶיהָ אֲשֶׁר בָּנָה בַּעְשָׁא וַיִּבֶן בָּהֶם אֶת־גֶּבַע וְאֶת־

ז הַמִּצְפָּה: וּבָעֵת הַהִיא בָּא חֲנָנִי הָרֹאֶה אֶל־אָסָא מֶלֶךְ יְהוּדָה וַיֹּאמֶר אֵלָיו בְּהִשָּׁעֶנְךָ עַל־מֶלֶךְ אֲרָם וְלֹא נִשְׁעַנְתָּ עַל־יְהוָה אֱלֹהֶיךָ עַל־

ח כֵּן נִמְלַט חֵיל מֶלֶךְ־אֲרָם מִיָּדֶךָ: הֲלֹא הַכּוּשִׁים וְהַלּוּבִים הָיוּ לְחַיִל ׀ לָרֹב

ט לְרֶכֶב וּלְפָרָשִׁים לְהַרְבֵּה מְאֹד וּבְהִשָּׁעֶנְךָ עַל־יְהוָה נְתָנָם בְּיָדֶךָ: כִּי יְהוָה עֵינָיו מְשֹׁטְטוֹת בְּכָל־הָאָרֶץ לְהִתְחַזֵּק עִם־לְבָבָם שָׁלֵם אֵלָיו נִסְכַּלְתָּ עַל־

י זֹאת כִּי מֵעַתָּה יֵשׁ עִמְּךָ מִלְחָמוֹת: וַיִּכְעַס אָסָא אֶל־הָרֹאֶה וַיִּתְּנֵהוּ בֵּית הַמַּהְפֶּכֶת כִּי־בְזַעַף עִמּוֹ עַל־זֹאת וַיְרַצֵּץ אָסָא מִן־הָעָם בָּעֵת הַהִיא:

יא וְהִנֵּה דִּבְרֵי אָסָא הָרִאשׁוֹנִים וְהָאַחֲרוֹנִים הִנָּם כְּתוּבִים עַל־סֵפֶר הַמְּלָכִים

יב לִיהוּדָה וְיִשְׂרָאֵל: וַיֶּחֱלֶא אָסָא בִּשְׁנַת שְׁלוֹשִׁים וָתֵשַׁע לְמַלְכוּתוֹ בְּרַגְלָיו

יג עַד־לְמַעְלָה חָלְיוֹ וְגַם־בְּחָלְיוֹ לֹא־דָרַשׁ אֶת־יְהוָה כִּי בָּרֹפְאִים: וַיִּשְׁכַּב אָסָא עִם־אֲבֹתָיו וַיָּמָת בִּשְׁנַת אַרְבָּעִים וְאַחַת לְמָלְכוֹ: וַיִּקְבְּרֻהוּ בְקִבְרֹתָיו

יד אֲשֶׁר כָּרָה־לוֹ בְּעִיר דָּוִיד וַיַּשְׁכִּיבֻהוּ בַּמִּשְׁכָּב אֲשֶׁר מִלֵּא מְלֵא בְשָׂמִים וּזְנִים מְרֻקָּחִים בְּמִרְקַחַת מַעֲשֶׂה וַיִּשְׂרְפוּ־לוֹ שְׂרֵפָה גְדוֹלָה עַד־

יז א־ב לִמְאֹד: וַיִּמְלֹךְ יְהוֹשָׁפָט בְּנוֹ תַּחְתָּיו וַיִּתְחַזֵּק עַל־יִשְׂרָאֵל: וַיִּתֵּן חַיִל בְּכָל־עָרֵי יְהוּדָה הַבְּצֻרוֹת וַיִּתֵּן נְצִיבִים בְּאֶרֶץ יְהוּדָה וּבְעָרֵי אֶפְרַיִם

15:18. His father(s) had looted the Temple treasury, but Asa took this money, along with his own consecrated assets, and brought them to the Temple treasury (*Abarbanel*).

16:1. A city just north of Jerusalem.

16:3. Apparently Ben-hadad had peace treaties with both Israelite kingdoms.

16:7. The Arameans were apparently destined to be defeated by Asa at some time, but this would not occur now because of his sin (*Metzudos*).

the oath, for they had sworn with all their heart — they had sought Him with all their desire and He was accessible to them — and HASHEM had granted them rest all around them.

No favoritism [16] King Asa even deposed his [grand]mother Maacah from being a queen because she had made an abomination to asherah; Asa chopped up her abomination and ground it up and burned it in the Kidron Ravine. [17] The high places did not cease from Israel; nevertheless, Asa's heart was perfect all his days. [18] He brought in the consecrated goods of his father and his own consecrated goods to the Temple of HASHEM * — silver and gold and vessels.

16

[19] There was no war until the thirty-fifth year of Asa's reign. [1] In the thirty-sixth year of Asa's reign, Baasa king of Israel attacked Judah and built up Ramah, * in order to prevent Asa king of Judah from leaving or entering. [2] Asa removed silver and gold from the treasuries of the Temple of HASHEM and the king's palace and sent it to Ben-hadad, the king of Aram, who dwelled in Damascus, saying, [3] "[There is] a treaty between me and you, and between my father and your father. Behold I have sent you silver and gold; go, annul your treaty with Baasa king of Israel, * so that he will depart from me." [4] Ben-hadad heeded King Asa, and he sent the officers of his soldiers against cities of Israel. They struck at Ijon, Dan and Abel-maim, and all the storage cities among the cities of Naphtali. [5] When Baasa heard this he ceased his building of Ramah, and he halted his work. [6] And King Asa took all of Judah and they carried away the stones of Ramah and its wood, with which Baasa had built, and with them [King Asa] built up Geba and Mizpah.

The Seer's rebuke [7] At that time Hanani the Seer came to Asa king of Judah, and said to him, "Because you relied on the king of Aram and did not rely on HASHEM, your God — therefore the army of the king of Aram will slip out of your hands. * [8] Behold, the Ethiopians and the Lubim* constituted an immense army, with very many chariots and horsemen, yet when you relied on HASHEM He delivered them into your hand. [9] For HASHEM's eyes roam throughout the land, to strengthen those whose hearts are sincerely with Him. You have been foolish in this, for from now on you will have wars!"

The king's anger [10] Asa became angry with the seer, and he put him in prison, for he was furious with him for this. Asa began to oppress some of the people at that time.

[11] Behold, the earlier and latter events of Asa are recorded in the Book of Kings of Judah and Israel.

[12] Asa became ill in his legs in the thirty-ninth year of his reign, until his illness spread upwards. * Also in his illness he did not seek out HASHEM, but only doctors. [13] Asa lay with his forefathers. He died in the forty-first year of his reign. [14] They buried him in his grave that he had dug for himself in the City of David. They laid him down in a bed that he had filled with spices and perfumes, blended with an apothecary's art, and they made a very large pyre for him. * [1] His son Jehoshaphat reigned in his place, and he strengthened his reign over Israel. * [2] He placed forces in all the fortified cities of Judah, and he stationed garrisons in the land of Judah and in the cities of Ephraim

(See Appendix A, timeline 4)

17 KING JEHOSHA-PHAT
17:1-21:1

16:8. In the war described above, 14:8ff.

16:12. And affected his whole body.

16:14. It was customary to burn a king's personal effects at his funeral, to show that no commoner could use them (Avodah Zarah 11a).

17:1. Jehoshaphat's influence extended to parts of the Kingdom of Israel, as in the cities of Ephraim mentioned in verse 2.

ג אֲשֶׁר לָכַד אָסָא אָבִיו: וַיְהִי יְהוָה עִם־יְהוֹשָׁפָט כִּי הָלַךְ בְּדַרְכֵי דָּוִיד אָבִיו

ד הָרִאשֹׁנִים וְלֹא דָרַשׁ לַבְּעָלִים: כִּי לֵאלֹהֵי אָבִיו דָּרָשׁ וּבְמִצְוֺתָיו הָלָךְ

ה וְלֹא כְּמַעֲשֵׂה יִשְׂרָאֵל: וַיָּכֶן יְהוָה אֶת־הַמַּמְלָכָה בְּיָדוֹ וַיִּתְּנוּ כָל־יְהוּדָה

ו מִנְחָה לִיהוֹשָׁפָט וַיְהִי־לוֹ עֹשֶׁר־וְכָבוֹד לָרֹב: וַיִּגְבַּהּ לִבּוֹ בְּדַרְכֵי יְהוָה וְעוֹד

ז הֵסִיר אֶת־הַבָּמוֹת וְאֶת־הָאֲשֵׁרִים מִיהוּדָה:	וּבִשְׁנַת שָׁלוֹשׁ

לְמָלְכוֹ שָׁלַח לְשָׂרָיו לְבֶן־חַיִל וּלְעֹבַדְיָה וְלִזְכַרְיָה וְלִנְתַנְאֵל וּלְמִיכָיָהוּ

ח לְלַמֵּד בְּעָרֵי יְהוּדָה: וְעִמָּהֶם הַלְוִיִּם שְׁמַעְיָהוּ וּנְתַנְיָהוּ וּזְבַדְיָהוּ וַעֲשָׂהאֵל

יֹ וּשְׁמִירָמֹ[ת] וּשְׁמִירָמוֹת ק וִיהוֹנָתָן וַאֲדֹנִיָּהוּ וְטוֹבִיָּהוּ וְטוֹב אֲדוֹנִיָּה

ט הַלְוִיִּם וְעִמָּהֶם אֱלִישָׁמָע וִיהוֹרָם הַכֹּהֲנִים: וַיְלַמְּדוּ בִּיהוּדָה וְעִמָּהֶם סֵפֶר

י תּוֹרַת יְהוָה וַיָּסֹבּוּ בְּכָל־עָרֵי יְהוּדָה וַיְלַמְּדוּ בָּעָם: וַיְהִי פַּחַד יְהוָה עַל

כָּל־מַמְלְכוֹת הָאֲרָצוֹת אֲשֶׁר סְבִיבוֹת יְהוּדָה וְלֹא נִלְחֲמוּ עִם־יְהוֹשָׁפָט:

יא וּמִן־פְּלִשְׁתִּים מְבִיאִים לִיהוֹשָׁפָט מִנְחָה וְכֶסֶף מַשָּׂא גַּם הָעַרְבִיאִים

מְבִיאִים לוֹ צֹאן אֵילִים שִׁבְעַת אֲלָפִים וּשְׁבַע מֵאוֹת וּתְיָשִׁים שִׁבְעַת

יב אֲלָפִים וּשְׁבַע מֵאוֹת:	וַיְהִי יְהוֹשָׁפָט הֹלֵךְ וְגָדֵל עַד־לְמָעְלָה

יג וַיִּבֶן בִּיהוּדָה בִּירָנִיּוֹת וְעָרֵי מִסְכְּנוֹת: וּמְלָאכָה רַבָּה הָיָה לוֹ בְּעָרֵי יְהוּדָה

יד וְאַנְשֵׁי מִלְחָמָה גִּבּוֹרֵי חַיִל בִּירוּשָׁלָ͏ִם:	וְאֵלֶּה פְקֻדָּתָם לְבֵית

אֲבוֹתֵיהֶם לִיהוּדָה שָׂרֵי אֲלָפִים עַדְנָה הַשָּׂר וְעִמּוֹ גִּבּוֹרֵי חַיִל שְׁלֹשׁ

טו מֵאוֹת אָלֶף:	וְעַל־יָדוֹ יְהוֹחָנָן הַשָּׂר וְעִמּוֹ מָאתַיִם וּשְׁמוֹנִים

טז אָלֶף:	וְעַל־יָדוֹ עֲמַסְיָה בֶן־זִכְרִי הַמִּתְנַדֵּב לַיהוָה וְעִמּוֹ מָאתַיִם

יז אֶלֶף גִּבּוֹר חָיִל:	וּמִן־בִּנְיָמִן גִּבּוֹר חַיִל אֶלְיָדָע וְעִמּוֹ נֹשְׁקֵי־

יח קֶשֶׁת וּמָגֵן מָאתַיִם אָלֶף:	וְעַל־יָדוֹ יְהוֹזָבָד וְעִמּוֹ מֵאָה־וּשְׁמוֹנִים

יט אֶלֶף חֲלוּצֵי צָבָא:	אֵלֶּה הַמְשָׁרְתִים אֶת־הַמֶּלֶךְ מִלְּבַד אֲשֶׁר־

א נָתַן הַמֶּלֶךְ בְּעָרֵי הַמִּבְצָר בְּכָל־יְהוּדָה:	וַיְהִי לִיהוֹשָׁפָט	יח

ב עֹשֶׁר וְכָבוֹד לָרֹב וַיִּתְחַתֵּן לְאַחְאָב: וַיֵּרֶד לְקֵץ שָׁנִים אֶל־אַחְאָב

לְשֹׁמְרוֹן וַיִּזְבַּח־לוֹ אַחְאָב צֹאן וּבָקָר לָרֹב וְלָעָם אֲשֶׁר עִמּוֹ וַיְסִיתֵהוּ

ג לַעֲלוֹת אֶל־רָמוֹת גִּלְעָד: וַיֹּאמֶר אַחְאָב מֶלֶךְ־יִשְׂרָאֵל אֶל־יְהוֹשָׁפָט

מֶלֶךְ יְהוּדָה הֲתֵלֵךְ עִמִּי רָמֹת גִּלְעָד וַיֹּאמֶר לוֹ כָּמוֹנִי כָמוֹךָ וּכְעַמְּךָ

ד עַמִּי וְעִמְּךָ בַּמִּלְחָמָה: וַיֹּאמֶר יְהוֹשָׁפָט אֶל־מֶלֶךְ יִשְׂרָאֵל דְּרָשׁ־נָא כַיּוֹם

ה אֶת־דְּבַר יְהוָה: וַיִּקְבֹּץ מֶלֶךְ־יִשְׂרָאֵל אֶת־הַנְּבִאִים אַרְבַּע מֵאוֹת אִישׁ

וַיֹּאמֶר אֲלֵהֶם הֲנֵלֵךְ אֶל־רָמֹת גִּלְעָד לַמִּלְחָמָה אִם־אֶחְדָּל וַיֹּאמְרוּ עֲלֵה

ו וְיִתֵּן הָאֱלֹהִים בְּיַד הַמֶּלֶךְ: וַיֹּאמֶר יְהוֹשָׁפָט הַאֵין פֹּה נָבִיא לַיהוָה עוֹד

ז וְנִדְרְשָׁה מֵאֹתוֹ: וַיֹּאמֶר מֶלֶךְ־יִשְׂרָאֵל אֶל־יְהוֹשָׁפָט עוֹד אִישׁ־אֶחָד

לִדְרוֹשׁ אֶת־יְהוָה מֵאֹתוֹ וַאֲנִי שְׂנֵאתִיהוּ כִּי־אֵינֶנּוּ מִתְנַבֵּא עָלַי לְטוֹבָה

that his father Asa had captured.

God's approval ³ HASHEM was with Jehoshaphat, for he followed the original paths of his father David, and did not seek out the Baal idols, ⁴ but he sought out the God of his father and followed His commandments, unlike the deeds of [the Kingdom of] Israel. ⁵ So HASHEM established the kingdom in his hands and all of Judah brought tributes to Jehoshaphat, and he had much wealth and honor. ⁶ His heart was elevated in the ways of HASHEM; furthermore, he eliminated the high places and asherah-trees from Judah.

Teaching Torah ⁷ In the third year of his reign he sent his officers Ben-hail, Obadiah, Zechariah, Nethanel, and Micaiah to give instruction * in the cities of Judah. ⁸ With them were Levites — Shemaiah, Nethaniah, Zebadiah, Asahel, Shemiramoth, Jehonathan, Adonijah, Tobijah, and Tob-adonijah, the Levites; and with them were Elishama and Jehoram, the Kohanim. ⁹ They gave instruction in Judah, taking with them the Book of the Torah of HASHEM. They went around to all the cities of Judah, and they taught among the people.

Peace and respect ¹⁰ The dread of HASHEM was upon all the kingdoms of the lands that were around Judah; they did not make war against Jehoshaphat. ¹¹ Some of the Philistines would bring tribute and loads of silver to Jehoshaphat. Also the Arabs would bring him flocks — seven thousand seven hundred rams and seven thousand seven hundred goats. ¹² Jehoshaphat grew continuously ever greater. He built castles and storage cities in Judah.

Workers and warriors ¹³ He had a great work force in the cities of Judah, and soldiers — mighty warriors — in Jerusalem. ¹⁴ These were their number according to their families: officers of thousands were from Judah, with Adnah as the leader; and three hundred thousand mighty warriors with him. ¹⁵ At his side was the officer Jehohanan, and two hundred eighty thousand with him. ¹⁶ At his side was Amasiah son of Zichri, who volunteered to HASHEM, and two hundred thousand mighty warriors with him. ¹⁷ Of Benjamin: Eliada, a mighty warrior, and with him two hundred thousand men armed with bows and shields. ¹⁸ At his side was Jehozabad, and a hundred eighty thousand, armed for the legion, with him. ¹⁹ These were [the men] who ministered to the king, besides those whom the king stationed in the fortified cities in all of Judah.

18

Alliance with Ahab ¹ Jehoshaphat had much wealth and honor. He allied himself in marriage to Ahab. * ² After several years he went down to Ahab, at Samaria. Ahab slaughtered a great many sheep and cattle for him and the people accompanying him, and he incited him to go up for war against Ramoth-gilead. * ³ He said to Jehoshaphat, "Will you go [to do battle] with me for Ramoth-gilead?" He answered him, "I shall be like you, my people shall be like your people, with you in war!"

Ahab's false prophets ⁴ Jehoshaphat then said to the king of Israel, "Inquire, please, today, of the word of HASHEM." ⁵ The king of Israel gathered the prophets, four hundred men, and said to them, "Shall we go to war for Ramoth-gilead, or shall I refrain?" They answered, "Go up, for God will deliver it into the hand of the king!" ⁶ Jehoshaphat said, "Is there no longer here a prophet of HASHEM of whom we may inquire?" * ⁷ The king of Israel answered Jehoshaphat, "There is one more man through whom to inquire of HASHEM; but I hate him, for he does not prophesy good for me,

---

17:7. In the laws of the Torah.

18:1. The notoriously evil king of Israel (see *I Kings* 16:29ff). Jehoshaphat's son married Ahab's daughter

(*I Kings* 8:18).

18:2. See *I Kings* 22:3.

18:6. See *I Kings* 22:6.

כִּי כָל־יָמָיו לְרָעָה הוּא מִיכָיְהוּ בֶן־יִמְלָא וַיֹּאמֶר יְהוֹשָׁפָט אַל־יֹאמַר

ח הַמֶּלֶךְ כֵּן: וַיִּקְרָא מֶלֶךְ יִשְׂרָאֵל אֶל־סָרִיס אֶחָד וַיֹּאמֶר מַהֵר °מִיכהו

ט [°מִיכָיְהוּ ק] בֶן־יִמְלָא: וּמֶלֶךְ יִשְׂרָאֵל וִיהוֹשָׁפָט מֶלֶךְ־יְהוּדָה יוֹשְׁבִים

אִישׁ עַל־כִּסְאוֹ מְלֻבָּשִׁים בְּגָדִים וְיֹשְׁבִים בְּגֹרֶן פֶּתַח שַׁעַר שֹׁמְרוֹן וְכָל־

י הַנְּבִיאִים מִתְנַבְּאִים לִפְנֵיהֶם: וַיַּעַשׂ לוֹ צִדְקִיָּהוּ בֶן־כְּנַעֲנָה קַרְנֵי בַרְזֶל

יא וַיֹּאמֶר כֹּה־אָמַר יְהוָה בְּאֵלֶּה תְּנַגַּח אֶת־אֲרָם עַד־כַּלּוֹתָם: וְכָל־הַנְּבִאִים

נִבְּאִים כֵּן לֵאמֹר עֲלֵה רָמֹת גִּלְעָד וְהַצְלַח וְנָתַן יְהוָה בְּיַד הַמֶּלֶךְ:

יב וְהַמַּלְאָךְ אֲשֶׁר־הָלַךְ ׀ לִקְרֹא לְמִיכָיְהוּ דִּבֶּר אֵלָיו לֵאמֹר הִנֵּה דִּבְרֵי

הַנְּבִאִים פֶּה־אֶחָד טוֹב אֶל־הַמֶּלֶךְ וִיהִי־נָא דְבָרְךָ כְּאַחַד מֵהֶם וְדִבַּרְתָּ

יג טּוֹב: וַיֹּאמֶר מִיכָיְהוּ חַי־יְהוָה כִּי אֶת־אֲשֶׁר־יֹאמַר אֱלֹהַי אֹתוֹ אֲדַבֵּר:

יד וַיָּבֹא אֶל־הַמֶּלֶךְ וַיֹּאמֶר הַמֶּלֶךְ אֵלָיו מִיכָה הֲנֵלֵךְ אֶל־רָמֹת גִּלְעָד

לַמִּלְחָמָה אִם־אֶחְדָּל וַיֹּאמֶר עֲלוּ וְהַצְלִיחוּ וְיִנָּתְנוּ בְּיֶדְכֶם: וַיֹּאמֶר אֵלָיו

טו הַמֶּלֶךְ עַד־כַּמֶּה פְעָמִים אֲנִי מַשְׁבִּיעֶךָ אֲשֶׁר לֹא־תְדַבֵּר אֵלַי רַק־אֱמֶת

טז בְּשֵׁם יְהוָה: וַיֹּאמֶר רָאִיתִי אֶת־כָּל־יִשְׂרָאֵל נְפוֹצִים עַל־הֶהָרִים כַּצֹּאן

אֲשֶׁר אֵין־לָהֶן רֹעֶה וַיֹּאמֶר יְהוָה לֹא־אֲדֹנִים לָאֵלֶּה יָשׁוּבוּ אִישׁ־לְבֵיתוֹ

יז בְּשָׁלוֹם: וַיֹּאמֶר מֶלֶךְ־יִשְׂרָאֵל אֶל־יְהוֹשָׁפָט הֲלֹא אָמַרְתִּי אֵלֶיךָ לֹא־

יח יִתְנַבֵּא עָלַי טוֹב כִּי אִם־לְרָע: וַיֹּאמֶר לָכֵן שִׁמְעוּ דְבַר־יְהוָה

רָאִיתִי אֶת־יְהוָה יוֹשֵׁב עַל־כִּסְאוֹ וְכָל־צְבָא הַשָּׁמַיִם עֹמְדִים עַל־יְמִינוֹ

יט וּשְׂמֹאלוֹ: וַיֹּאמֶר יְהוָה מִי יְפַתֶּה אֶת־אַחְאָב מֶלֶךְ־יִשְׂרָאֵל וְיַעַל וְיִפֹּל

כ בְּרָמֹת גִּלְעָד וַיֹּאמֶר זֶה אֹמֵר כָּכָה וְזֶה אֹמֵר כָּכָה: וַיֵּצֵא הָרוּחַ וַיַּעֲמֹד

כא לִפְנֵי יְהוָה וַיֹּאמֶר אֲנִי אֲפַתֶּנּוּ וַיֹּאמֶר יְהוָה אֵלָיו בַּמָּה: וַיֹּאמֶר אֵצֵא

וְהָיִיתִי לְרוּחַ שֶׁקֶר בְּפִי כָּל־נְבִיאָיו וַיֹּאמֶר תְּפַתֶּה וְגַם־תּוּכָל צֵא וַעֲשֵׂה־

כב כֵן: וְעַתָּה הִנֵּה נָתַן יְהוָה רוּחַ שֶׁקֶר בְּפִי נְבִיאֶיךָ אֵלֶּה וַיהוָה דִּבֶּר עָלֶיךָ

כג רָעָה: וַיִּגַּשׁ צִדְקִיָּהוּ בֶן־כְּנַעֲנָה וַיַּךְ אֶת־מִיכָיְהוּ עַל־הַלֶּחִי

כד וַיֹּאמֶר אֵי זֶה הַדֶּרֶךְ עָבַר רוּחַ־יְהוָה מֵאִתִּי לְדַבֵּר אֹתָךְ: וַיֹּאמֶר מִיכָיְהוּ

כה הִנְּךָ רֹאֶה בַּיּוֹם הַהוּא אֲשֶׁר תָּבוֹא חֶדֶר בְּחֶדֶר לְהֵחָבֵא: וַיֹּאמֶר מֶלֶךְ

יִשְׂרָאֵל קְחוּ אֶת־מִיכָיְהוּ וַהֲשִׁיבֻהוּ אֶל־אָמוֹן שַׂר־הָעִיר וְאֶל־יוֹאָשׁ בֶּן־

כו הַמֶּלֶךְ: וַאֲמַרְתֶּם כֹּה אָמַר הַמֶּלֶךְ שִׂימוּ זֶה בֵּית הַכֶּלֶא וְהַאֲכִלֻהוּ לֶחֶם

כז לַחַץ וּמַיִם לַחַץ עַד שׁוּבִי בְשָׁלוֹם: וַיֹּאמֶר מִיכָיְהוּ אִם־שׁוֹב תָּשׁוּב

כח בְּשָׁלוֹם לֹא־דִבֶּר יְהוָה בִּי וַיֹּאמֶר שִׁמְעוּ עַמִּים כֻּלָּם: וַיַּעַל

כט מֶלֶךְ־יִשְׂרָאֵל וִיהוֹשָׁפָט מֶלֶךְ־יְהוּדָה אֶל־רָמֹת גִּלְעָד: וַיֹּאמֶר מֶלֶךְ

יִשְׂרָאֵל אֶל־יְהוֹשָׁפָט הִתְחַפֵּשׂ וָבוֹא בַמִּלְחָמָה וְאַתָּה לְבַשׁ בְּגָדֶיךָ

18:14. He said this in cynical mimicry of the false prophets, but Ahab insisted that he speak the truth.

18:16. Ahab would die in battle, but Israel would scatter and escape unharmed.

18:24. See *I Kings* 18:24.

18:27. All the tribes of Israel (*Metzudos*).

Micah is summoned but only bad all his life — that is Micaiah son of Imlah." Jehoshaphat said, "Let the king not speak this way!" ⁸ So the king of Israel summoned one officer and said, "Rush Micaiah son of Imlah [here]."

⁹ The king of Israel and Jehoshaphat king of Judah were sitting, each man on his throne, dressed in [royal] garb, sitting at the threshing floor at the gateway of *Zedekiah's* Samaria, and all the prophets were prophesying before them. ¹⁰ Zedekiah son of *charade* Chenaanah made himself iron horns and said, "Thus said HASHEM: With these you shall gore Aram, until they are obliterated!" ¹¹ All the prophets were prophesying similarly, saying, "Go up to Ramoth-gilead and triumph, for HASHEM will deliver it into the hand of the king." ¹² The messenger who had gone to summon Micaiah spoke to him, saying, "Behold, the words of the prophets are unanimously favorable towards the king; please let your words be like [those of] one of them, and speak favorably!" ¹³ But Micaiah said, "As HASHEM lives, [I swear] that whatever my God says to me, that shall I speak!"

Royal dis- ¹⁴ He came to the king and the king said to him, "Micah, shall we go to war *obedience* for Ramoth-Gilead or shall I refrain?" He said, "Go up and triumph, and they *and defeat* will be delivered into your hand."* ¹⁵ The king then said to him, "I adjure you many times over that you speak to me nothing but the truth in the Name *Micah's dire* of HASHEM!" ¹⁶ [Micaiah] then said, "I have seen all of Israel scattering to the *vision* mountains, like sheep that have no shepherd; and HASHEM saying, 'These have no master; let each man go to his house in peace!'"* ¹⁷ The king of Israel said to Jehoshaphat, "Did I not tell you that he never prophesies good for me, but only bad?" ¹⁸ [Micaiah] said [further], "Therefore listen to the word of HASHEM! I have seen HASHEM sitting upon His throne, with all the host of Heaven standing on His right and His left. ¹⁹ And HASHEM said, 'Who will lure Ahab king of Israel to go up [to war] that he may fall in Ramoth-gilead?' This one said, 'Like this' and this one said 'Like this.' ²⁰ Then the spirit came forward and stood before HASHEM and said, 'I shall lure him!' And HASHEM said, 'How?' ²¹ [The spirit] replied, 'I will go out and be a spirit of falsehood in the mouths of all his prophets.' And [HASHEM] said, 'You will lure him and you will succeed! Go forth and do so!' ²² And now, behold! HASHEM has put a spirit of falsehood in the mouths of these prophets of yours, for HASHEM has decreed evil upon *Violent* you." ²³ Zedekiah son of Chenaanah then approached and struck Micaiah on *reaction* the cheek, and said, "In what way did the spirit of HASHEM pass from me to *to truth* speak to you?" ²⁴ Micaiah said, "Behold, you will see for yourself on that day, when you go inside a room within a room to be hidden!"* ²⁵ The king of Israel then said, "Take Micaiah and turn him over to Amon, the minister of the city, and to Joash, the king's son, ²⁶ and say, 'Thus said the king: Put this one in the prison and feed him a minimum of food and a minimum of water, until I return in peace!' " ²⁷ Micaiah said, "If you indeed return in peace, then HASHEM did not speak through me!" And he said [further], "Hear this, all the peoples!"*

²⁸ The king of Israel and Jehoshaphat king of Judah then went up [to wage *The* war] at Ramoth-gilead. ²⁹ The king of Israel said to Jehoshaphat, "[I] will disguise *disguise* [myself] when [I] come to the battle, but you wear your royal garments."*

18:29. Ahab knew that the Arameans would kill him immediately if they recognized him, and that | Jehoshaphat was not in danger.

ל וַיִּתְחַפֵּשׂ מֶלֶךְ יִשְׂרָאֵל וַיָּבֹאוּ בַּמִּלְחָמָה: וּמֶלֶךְ אֲרָם צִוָּה אֶת־שָׂרֵי הָרֶכֶב
אֲשֶׁר־לוֹ לֵאמֹר לֹא תִּלָּחֲמוּ אֶת־הַקָּטֹן אֶת־הַגָּדוֹל כִּי אִם־אֶת־מֶלֶךְ

לא יִשְׂרָאֵל לְבַדּוֹ: וַיְהִי כִּרְאוֹת שָׂרֵי הָרֶכֶב אֶת־יְהוֹשָׁפָט וְהֵמָּה אָמְרוּ מֶלֶךְ
יִשְׂרָאֵל הוּא וַיָּסֹבּוּ עָלָיו לְהִלָּחֵם וַיִּזְעַק יְהוֹשָׁפָט וַיהוָה עֲזָרוֹ וַיְסִיתֵם

לב אֱלֹהִים מִמֶּנּוּ: וַיְהִי כִּרְאוֹת שָׂרֵי הָרֶכֶב כִּי לֹא־הָיָה מֶלֶךְ יִשְׂרָאֵל וַיָּשֻׁבוּ

לג מֵאַחֲרָיו: וְאִישׁ מָשַׁךְ בַּקֶּשֶׁת לְתֻמּוֹ וַיַּךְ אֶת־מֶלֶךְ יִשְׂרָאֵל בֵּין הַדְּבָקִים
וּבֵין הַשִּׁרְיָן וַיֹּאמֶר לָרַכָּב הֲפֹךְ °יָדֶיךָ ק [יָדְךָ כ] וְהוֹצֵאתַנִי מִן־הַמַּחֲנֶה כִּי

לד הָחֳלֵיתִי: וַתַּעַל הַמִּלְחָמָה בַּיּוֹם הַהוּא וּמֶלֶךְ יִשְׂרָאֵל הָיָה מַעֲמִיד

יט א בַּמֶּרְכָּבָה נֹכַח אֲרָם עַד־הָעָרֶב וַיָּמָת לְעֵת בּוֹא הַשָּׁמֶשׁ: וַיָּשָׁב

ב יְהוֹשָׁפָט מֶלֶךְ־יְהוּדָה אֶל־בֵּיתוֹ בְּשָׁלוֹם לִירוּשָׁלִָם: וַיֵּצֵא אֶל־פָּנָיו יֵהוּא
בֶן־חֲנָנִי הַחֹזֶה וַיֹּאמֶר אֶל־הַמֶּלֶךְ יְהוֹשָׁפָט הֲלָרָשָׁע לַעְזֹר וּלְשֹׂנְאֵי יְהוָה

ג תֶּאֱהָב וּבָזֹאת עָלֶיךָ קֶּצֶף מִלִּפְנֵי יְהוָה: אֲבָל דְּבָרִים טוֹבִים נִמְצְאוּ עִמָּךְ

ד כִּי־בִעַרְתָּ הָאֲשֵׁרוֹת מִן־הָאָרֶץ וַהֲכִינוֹתָ לְבָבְךָ לִדְרֹשׁ הָאֱלֹהִים: וַיֵּשֶׁב
יְהוֹשָׁפָט בִּירוּשָׁלִָם וַיָּשָׁב וַיֵּצֵא בָעָם מִבְּאֵר שֶׁבַע עַד־הַר אֶפְרַיִם וַיְשִׁיבֵם

ה אֶל־יְהוָה אֱלֹהֵי אֲבוֹתֵיהֶם: וַיַּעֲמֵד שֹׁפְטִים בָּאָרֶץ בְּכָל־עָרֵי יְהוּדָה
הַבְּצֻרוֹת לְעִיר וָעִיר: וַיֹּאמֶר אֶל־הַשֹּׁפְטִים רְאוּ מָה־אַתֶּם עֹשִׂים כִּי לֹא

ז לְאָדָם תִּשְׁפְּטוּ כִּי לַיהוָה וְעִמָּכֶם בִּדְבַר מִשְׁפָּט: וְעַתָּה יְהִי פַחַד־יְהוָה
עֲלֵיכֶם שִׁמְרוּ וַעֲשׂוּ כִּי־אֵין עִם־יְהוָה אֱלֹהֵינוּ עַוְלָה וּמַשֹּׂא פָנִים וּמִקַּח־

ח שֹׁחַד: וְגַם בִּירוּשָׁלִַם הֶעֱמִיד יְהוֹשָׁפָט מִן־הַלְוִיִּם וְהַכֹּהֲנִים וּמֵרָאשֵׁי
הָאָבוֹת לְיִשְׂרָאֵל לְמִשְׁפַּט יְהוָה וְלָרִיב וַיָּשֻׁבוּ יְרוּשָׁלִָם: וַיְצַו עֲלֵיהֶם

י לֵאמֹר כֹּה תַעֲשׂוּן בְּיִרְאַת יְהוָה בֶּאֱמוּנָה וּבְלֵבָב שָׁלֵם: וְכָל־רִיב אֲשֶׁר־
יָבוֹא עֲלֵיכֶם מֵאֲחֵיכֶם הַיֹּשְׁבִים בְּעָרֵיהֶם בֵּין־דָּם לְדָם בֵּין־תּוֹרָה לְמִצְוָה
לְחֻקִּים וּלְמִשְׁפָּטִים וְהִזְהַרְתֶּם אֹתָם וְלֹא יֶאְשְׁמוּ לַיהוָה וְהָיָה־קֶצֶף עֲלֵיכֶם

יא וְעַל־אֲחֵיכֶם כֹּה תַעֲשׂוּן וְלֹא תֶאְשָׁמוּ: וְהִנֵּה אֲמַרְיָהוּ כֹהֵן הָרֹאשׁ עֲלֵיכֶם
לְכֹל דְּבַר־יְהוָה וּזְבַדְיָהוּ בֶן־יִשְׁמָעֵאל הַנָּגִיד לְבֵית־יְהוּדָה לְכֹל דְּבַר־
הַמֶּלֶךְ וְשֹׁטְרִים הַלְוִיִּם לִפְנֵיכֶם חִזְקוּ וַעֲשׂוּ וִיהִי יְהוָה עִם־הַטּוֹב:

כ א וַיְהִי אַחֲרֵי־כֵן בָּאוּ בְנֵי־מוֹאָב וּבְנֵי עַמּוֹן וְעִמָּהֶם | מֵהָעַמּוֹנִים עַל־

ב יְהוֹשָׁפָט לַמִּלְחָמָה: וַיָּבֹאוּ וַיַּגִּידוּ לִיהוֹשָׁפָט לֵאמֹר בָּא עָלֶיךָ הָמוֹן רָב
מֵעֵבֶר לַיָּם מֵאֲרָם וְהִנָּם בְּחַצְצוֹן תָּמָר הִיא עֵין גֶּדִי: וַיִּרָא וַיִּתֵּן יְהוֹשָׁפָט

ד אֶת־פָּנָיו לִדְרוֹשׁ לַיהוָה וַיִּקְרָא־צוֹם עַל־כָּל־יְהוּדָה: וַיִּקָּבְצוּ יְהוּדָה לְבַקֵּשׁ

18:31-34. See I Kings 22:32-35.

19:4. He stopped pursuing political alliances with the Northern Kingdom.

19:8. This court was empowered to adjudicate cases beyond the capabilities of the lower courts in the other cities (*Malbim*).

19:10. That is, a case involving murder (*Rashi*).

19:11. Jehoshaphat appointed executives in charge of religious matters, temporal and political matters, and enforcement.

20:1. These were either foreigners who took up residence in Ammon, or Amelakites who disguised them-

So the king of Israel disguised himself and went out to battle. ³⁰ *The king of Aram commanded his chariot commanders, saying, "Do not wage war with anyone weak or strong, but only with the king of Israel himself."* ³¹ *It happened that when the chariot commanders saw Jehoshaphat, they said, "This is the king of Israel!" and they surrounded him to fight [him]. Jehoshaphat cried out, and HASHEM came to his aid; God induced them away from him.* ³² *When the chariot commanders realized that he was not the king of Israel,* * they turned away from him.* ³³ *One man drew his bow aimlessly, yet hit the king of Israel between the joints of his armor. [The king] said to the driver, "Reverse your hand and take me out of the camp, for I am wounded."* ³⁴ *The war intensified on that day, and the king forced himself to stand up in his chariot in the presence of Aram until the evening. He died at the time of the setting of the sun.* ¹ *But Jehoshaphat king of Judah returned safely to his house in Jerusalem.*

Jeho-
shaphat's
escape . . .

. . . and
Ahab's death

19

Jehu's
admonition

² *Jehu son of Hanani the Seer came out to greet him, and he said to King Jehoshaphat, "To aid the wicked? Will you love those who hate HASHEM?! Because of this, fury from before HASHEM is upon you!* ³ *However, good things are found in you, for you have destroyed the asherah-trees from the land and you have set your heart to seek out God."*

Justice and
peace

⁴ *Jehoshaphat stayed in Jerusalem.* * *He traveled back and forth among the people, from Beer-sheba to Mount Ephraim, and brought them back to HASHEM, God of their forefathers.* ⁵ *He stationed judges in the land, in all the fortified cities of Judah, for each city.* ⁶ *He said to the judges, "Take care in what you do, for it is not for man's sake that you judge, but for HASHEM's, and He is with you in the matter of judgment.* ⁷ *So now, let the fear of HASHEM be upon you; be careful when you act, for with HASHEM, our God, there is no corruption nor favoritism nor acceptance of bribes."*

Solving
quarrels

⁸ *Also in Jerusalem Jehoshaphat stationed some Levites and Kohanim and some of the family heads of Israel to [attend to] HASHEM's judgment and to quarrels,* * *and they returned to Jerusalem.* ⁹ *He commanded them saying, "Thus shall you act — with fear of HASHEM, with trust and with sincere hearts.* ¹⁰ *Any quarrel that may come before you from your kinsmen who dwell in your cities, whether it is between blood and blood,* * *or regarding instruction concerning a commandment or decrees and statutes, you shall warn them so that they do not incur guilt before HASHEM, which would bring fury upon you and your brethren. So shall you do not to incur guilt!* ¹¹ *Behold, Amariah the chief Kohen is over you concerning all matters of HASHEM,* * *and Zebadiah son of Ishmael, the ruler of the House of Judah, concerning all matters of the king, and the Levite officers are before you. Be strong and act; and may HASHEM be with him who does good!"*

20

God protects
Jehoshaphat

¹ *It happened after this that the Children of Moab and the Children of Ammon, along with some Ammonites,* * *went out to war against Jehoshaphat.* ² *[People] came and told Jehoshaphat, saying, "A great multitude is coming against you from the other side of the sea,* * *from Aram! Behold, they are already in Hazazon-tamar, which is En-gedi!"*

³ *He was afraid, so Jehoshaphat turned his attention to seek HASHEM, and he proclaimed a fast upon all of Judah.* ⁴ *Judah was gathered to beseech*

---

selves as Ammonites (*Radak*).   **20:2.** East of the Dead Sea.

ה מֵיהוָה גַּם מִכָּל־עָרֵי יְהוּדָה בָּאוּ לְבַקֵּשׁ אֶת־יְהוָה: וַיַּעֲמֹד יְהוֹשָׁפָט בִּקְהַל

ו יְהוּדָה וִירוּשָׁלִַם בְּבֵית יְהוָה לִפְנֵי הֶחָצֵר הַחֲדָשָׁה: וַיֹּאמַר יְהוָה אֱלֹהֵי אֲבֹתֵינוּ הֲלֹא אַתָּה־הוּא אֱלֹהִים בַּשָּׁמַיִם וְאַתָּה מוֹשֵׁל בְּכֹל מַמְלְכוֹת

ז הַגּוֹיִם וּבְיָדְךָ כֹּחַ וּגְבוּרָה וְאֵין עִמְּךָ לְהִתְיַצֵּב: הֲלֹא ׀ אַתָּה אֱלֹהֵינוּ הוֹרַשְׁתָּ אֶת־יֹשְׁבֵי הָאָרֶץ הַזֹּאת מִלִּפְנֵי עַמְּךָ יִשְׂרָאֵל וַתִּתְּנָהּ לְזֶרַע

ח אַבְרָהָם אֹהַבְךָ לְעוֹלָם: וַיֵּשְׁבוּ־בָהּ וַיִּבְנוּ לְךָ ׀ בָּהּ מִקְדָּשׁ לְשִׁמְךָ לֵאמֹר:

ט אִם־תָּבוֹא עָלֵינוּ רָעָה חֶרֶב שְׁפוֹט וְדֶבֶר וְרָעָב נַעַמְדָה לִפְנֵי הַבַּיִת הַזֶּה

י וּלְפָנֶיךָ כִּי שִׁמְךָ בַּבַּיִת הַזֶּה וְנִזְעַק אֵלֶיךָ מִצָּרָתֵנוּ וְתִשְׁמַע וְתוֹשִׁיעַ: וְעַתָּה הִנֵּה בְנֵי־עַמּוֹן וּמוֹאָב וְהַר־שֵׂעִיר אֲשֶׁר לֹא־נָתַתָּה לְיִשְׂרָאֵל לָבוֹא בָהֶם

יא בְּבֹאָם מֵאֶרֶץ מִצְרָיִם כִּי סָרוּ מֵעֲלֵיהֶם וְלֹא הִשְׁמִידוּם: וְהִנֵּה־הֵם גֹּמְלִים עָלֵינוּ לָבוֹא לְגָרְשֵׁנוּ מִיְּרֻשָּׁתְךָ אֲשֶׁר הוֹרַשְׁתָּנוּ: אֱלֹהֵינוּ הֲלֹא תִשְׁפָּט־בָּם

יב כִּי אֵין בָּנוּ כֹּחַ לִפְנֵי הֶהָמוֹן הָרָב הַזֶּה הַבָּא עָלֵינוּ וַאֲנַחְנוּ לֹא נֵדַע מַה־

יג נַּעֲשֶׂה כִּי עָלֶיךָ עֵינֵינוּ: וְכָל־יְהוּדָה עֹמְדִים לִפְנֵי יְהוָה גַּם־טַפָּם נְשֵׁיהֶם

יד וּבְנֵיהֶם: וִיחֲזִיאֵל בֶּן־זְכַרְיָהוּ בֶּן־בְּנָיָה בֶּן־יְעִיאֵל בֶּן־מַתַּנְיָה

טו הַלֵּוִי מִן־בְּנֵי אָסָף הָיְתָה עָלָיו רוּחַ יְהוָה בְּתוֹךְ הַקָּהָל: וַיֹּאמֶר הַקְשִׁיבוּ כָל־יְהוּדָה וְיֹשְׁבֵי יְרוּשָׁלִַם וְהַמֶּלֶךְ יְהוֹשָׁפָט כֹּה־אָמַר יְהוָה לָכֶם אַתֶּם אַל־תִּירְאוּ וְאַל־תֵּחַתּוּ מִפְּנֵי הֶהָמוֹן הָרָב הַזֶּה כִּי לֹא לָכֶם הַמִּלְחָמָה כִּי

טז לֵאלֹהִים: מָחָר רְדוּ עֲלֵיהֶם הִנָּם עֹלִים בְּמַעֲלֵה הַצִּיץ וּמְצָאתֶם אֹתָם

יז בְּסוֹף הַנַּחַל פְּנֵי מִדְבַּר יְרוּאֵל: לֹא לָכֶם לְהִלָּחֵם בָּזֹאת הִתְיַצְּבוּ עִמְדוּ וּרְאוּ אֶת־יְשׁוּעַת יְהוָה עִמָּכֶם יְהוּדָה וִירוּשָׁלִַם אַל־תִּירְאוּ וְאַל־תֵּחַתּוּ

יח מָחָר צְאוּ לִפְנֵיהֶם וַיהוָה עִמָּכֶם: וַיִּקֹּד יְהוֹשָׁפָט אַפַּיִם אָרְצָה וְכָל־יְהוּדָה

יט וְיֹשְׁבֵי יְרוּשָׁלִַם נָפְלוּ לִפְנֵי יְהוָה לְהִשְׁתַּחֲוֹת לַיהוָה: וַיָּקֻמוּ הַלְוִיִּם מִן־בְּנֵי הַקְּהָתִים וּמִן־בְּנֵי הַקָּרְחִים לְהַלֵּל לַיהוָה אֱלֹהֵי יִשְׂרָאֵל בְּקוֹל גָּדוֹל

כ לְמָעְלָה: וַיַּשְׁכִּימוּ בַבֹּקֶר וַיֵּצְאוּ לְמִדְבַּר תְּקוֹעַ וּבְצֵאתָם עָמַד יְהוֹשָׁפָט וַיֹּאמֶר שְׁמָעוּנִי יְהוּדָה וְיֹשְׁבֵי יְרוּשָׁלִַם הַאֲמִינוּ בַּיהוָה אֱלֹהֵיכֶם וְתֵאָמֵנוּ

כא הַאֲמִינוּ בִנְבִיאָיו וְהַצְלִיחוּ: וַיִּוָּעַץ אֶל־הָעָם וַיַּעֲמֵד מְשֹׁרְרִים לַיהוָה וּמְהַלְלִים לְהַדְרַת־קֹדֶשׁ בְּצֵאת לִפְנֵי הֶחָלוּץ וְאֹמְרִים הוֹדוּ לַיהוָה כִּי

כב לְעוֹלָם חַסְדּוֹ: וּבְעֵת הֵחֵלּוּ בְרִנָּה וּתְהִלָּה נָתַן יְהוָה ׀ מְאָרְבִים עַל־בְּנֵי

כג עַמּוֹן מוֹאָב וְהַר־שֵׂעִיר הַבָּאִים לִיהוּדָה וַיִּנָּגֵפוּ: וַיַּעַמְדוּ בְּנֵי עַמּוֹן וּמוֹאָב עַל־יֹשְׁבֵי הַר־שֵׂעִיר לְהַחֲרִים וּלְהַשְׁמִיד וּכְכַלּוֹתָם בְּיוֹשְׁבֵי שֵׂעִיר עָזְרוּ

כד אִישׁ־בְּרֵעֵהוּ לְמַשְׁחִית: וִיהוּדָה בָּא עַל־הַמִּצְפֶּה לַמִּדְבָּר וַיִּפְנוּ אֶל־

כה הֶהָמוֹן וְהִנָּם פְּגָרִים נֹפְלִים אַרְצָה וְאֵין פְּלֵיטָה: וַיָּבֹא יְהוֹשָׁפָט וְעַמּוֹ לָבֹז

20:10. See *Deuteronomy* 2:4-5, ibid. 2:9 and ibid. 2:19.   **20:23.** Believing that the ambush had come from the Seirites (*Metzudos*).

HASHEM; they came even from all the cities of Judah to beseech HASHEM.

The king's prayer ⁵ Jehoshaphat stood in the assembly of Judah and Jerusalem in the Temple of HASHEM, before the New Courtyard, ⁶ and he said, "O HASHEM, God of our fathers! Behold, You are God in Heaven, and You rule over all the kingdoms of the nations. In Your hand are power and might, and no one can stand up against You. ⁷ Surely, You are our God. You drove out the inhabitants of this land from before Your people Israel, and You gave it forever to the descendants of Abraham, who loved You. ⁸ They settled in it, and in it they built for You a Sanctuary for Your Name, saying, ⁹ 'If misfortune should come upon us — war, judgment, plague or famine — we will stand before this Temple and before You, for Your Name is in this Temple, and we will cry out to You in our affliction, and You will hear us and save us.' ¹⁰ Now, behold, the people of Ammon and Moab and Mount Seir — whom you did not allow Israel to invade when they came out of Egypt; * rather they turned away from them and did not destroy them. ¹¹ But behold they are repaying us — by coming to expel us from Your heritage that You have bequeathed to us! ¹² Our God, will You not perform justice against them? For we have no strength before this great multitude that is invading us. We do not know what we should do; rather, our eyes are upon You!" ¹³ All of Judah were standing before HASHEM, including their little children, their wives and their sons.

Prophecy and salvation ¹⁴ The spirit of HASHEM then came upon Jahaziel son of Zechariah son of Jeiel son of Mattaniah the Levite, of the descendants of Asaph, in the midst of the congregation. ¹⁵ He said, "Pay attention, all of Judah and the inhabitants of Jerusalem, and King Jehoshaphat! Thus said HASHEM concerning you: Do not fear and do not be intimidated before this great multitude, for the battle is not yours, but God's! ¹⁶ Tomorrow, go down against them; behold, they are advancing by the Ziz Ascent, and you will find them at the end of the ravine, facing the Wilderness of Jeruel. ¹⁷ It is not for you to do battle in this matter! Be erect, stand still and see the salvation of HASHEM for you, O Judah and Jerusalem! Do not fear and do not be broken! Tomorrow go out before them, and HASHEM will be with you!"

The nation's faith ¹⁸ Jehoshaphat bowed down with his face to the ground, and all [of] Judah and the inhabitants of Jerusalem fell down before HASHEM to prostrate themselves to HASHEM. ¹⁹ The Levites, of the children of the Kohathites and of the children of the Korahites, rose up to praise HASHEM, God of Israel, with an exceedingly loud voice.

The king exhorts his troops ²⁰ [The people] arose early in the morning, and they went out to the Wilderness of Tekoa. As they were leaving, Jehoshaphat stood up and said, "Hear me, O Judah and inhabitants of Jerusalem! Have faith in HASHEM your God, and show yourselves loyal; have faith in His prophets and be successful!" ²¹ He conferred with the people, and he set up men to sing to HASHEM and men to laud [His] majestic holiness; as they went out before the front-line troops, they said, "Give thanks to HASHEM, for His mercy endures forever!" ²² As soon as

God confuses the enemy they began their exuberant song and praise, HASHEM set up ambushers against the Children of Ammon, Moab and Mount Seir who were attacking Judah, and they were struck down. ²³ The people of Ammon and Moab then rose up against the inhabitants of Mount Seir* to destroy and annihilate them, and when they finished with the inhabitants of Seir they assisted in destroying one another. ²⁴ When Judah reached the lookout over the wilderness, they turned to look at the multitude and saw that they were all corpses, fallen upon the

Total victory ground, with no survivors. ²⁵ Jehoshaphat and his people then went to plunder

אֶת־שְׁלָלָם֩ וַיִּמְצְא֨וּ בָהֶ֜ם לָרֹ֗ב וּרְכ֤וּשׁ וּפְגָרִים֙ וּכְלֵ֣י חֲמֻד֔וֹת וַיְנַצְּל֥וּ לָהֶ֖ם

כו לְאֵ֣ין מַשָּׂ֑א וַיִּהְי֞וּ יָמִ֣ים שְׁלוֹשָׁ֗ה בֹּזְזִים֙ אֶת־הַשָּׁלָ֔ל כִּ֥י רַב־ה֖וּא: וּבַיּ֣וֹם הָרְבִעִ֗י נִקְהֲלוּ֙ לְעֵ֣מֶק בְּרָכָ֔ה כִּי־שָׁ֖ם בֵּרְכ֣וּ אֶת־יְהֹוָ֑ה עַל־כֵּ֗ן קָרְא֤וּ אֶת־

כז שֵׁ֞ם הַמָּק֤וֹם הַהוּא֙ עֵ֣מֶק בְּרָכָ֔ה עַד־הַיּֽוֹם: וַ֠יָּשֻׁ֠בוּ כָּל־אִ֨ישׁ יְהוּדָ֜ה וִירוּשָׁלַ֗͏ִם וִיהֽוֹשָׁפָט֙ בְּרֹאשָׁ֔ם לָשׁ֥וּב אֶל־יְרוּשָׁלַ֖͏ִם בְּשִׂמְחָ֑ה כִּי־שִׂמְּחָ֥ם

כח יְהֹוָ֖ה מֵאֽוֹיְבֵיהֶֽם: וַיָּבֹ֙אוּ֙ יְר֣וּשָׁלַ֔͏ִם בִּנְבָלִ֥ים וּבְכִנֹּר֖וֹת וּבַחֲצֹֽצְר֑וֹת אֶל־

כט בֵּ֖ית יְהֹוָֽה: וַיְהִי֙ פַּ֣חַד אֱלֹהִ֔ים עַ֖ל כָּל־מַמְלְכ֣וֹת הָאֲרָצ֑וֹת בְּשָׁמְעָ֔ם כִּ֚י

ל נִלְחַ֣ם יְהֹוָ֔ה עִ֖ם אוֹיְבֵ֥י יִשְׂרָאֵֽל: וַתִּשְׁקֹ֖ט מַלְכ֣וּת יְהֽוֹשָׁפָ֑ט וַיָּ֧נַֽח ל֦וֹ אֱלֹהָ֖יו

לא מִסָּבִֽיב: וַיִּמְלֹ֧ךְ יְהוֹשָׁפָ֛ט עַל־יְהוּדָ֑ה בֶּן־שְׁלֹשִׁ֨ים וְחָמֵ֤שׁ שָׁנָה֙ בְּמָלְכ֔וֹ וְעֶשְׂרִ֧ים וְחָמֵ֛שׁ שָׁנָ֖ה מָלַ֣ךְ בִּירֽוּשָׁלָ֑͏ִם וְשֵׁ֣ם אִמּ֔וֹ עֲזוּבָ֖ה בַּת־

לב שִׁלְחִֽי: וַיֵּ֗לֶךְ בְּדֶ֛רֶךְ אָבִ֥יו אָסָ֖א וְלֹא־סָ֣ר מִמֶּ֑נָּה לַעֲשׂ֥וֹת הַיָּשָׁ֖ר בְּעֵינֵ֥י

לג יְהֹוָֽה: אַ֥ךְ הַבָּמ֖וֹת לֹא־סָ֑רוּ וְע֤וֹד הָעָם֙ לֹא־הֵכִ֣ינוּ לְבָבָ֔ם לֵאלֹהֵ֖י

לד אֲבֹתֵיהֶֽם: וְיֶ֨תֶר֙ דִּבְרֵ֣י יְהֽוֹשָׁפָ֔ט הָרִאשֹׁנִ֖ים וְהָאַחֲרֹנִ֑ים הִנָּ֣ם כְּתוּבִ֗ים בְּדִבְרֵי֙ יֵה֣וּא בֶן־חֲנָ֔נִי אֲשֶׁ֣ר הֹעֲלָ֔ה עַל־סֵ֖פֶר מַלְכֵ֥י יִשְׂרָאֵֽל: וְאַחֲרֵי־כֵ֗ן

לה אֶתְחַבַּר֙ יְהוֹשָׁפָ֣ט מֶֽלֶךְ־יְהוּדָ֔ה עִ֖ם אֲחַזְיָ֣ה מֶֽלֶךְ־יִשְׂרָאֵ֑ל ה֖וּא הִרְשִׁ֥יעַ

לו לַעֲשֽׂוֹת: וַיְחַבְּרֵ֣הוּ עִמּ֔וֹ לַעֲשׂ֣וֹת אֳנִיּ֔וֹת לָלֶ֖כֶת תַּרְשִׁ֑ישׁ וַיַּעֲשׂ֥וּ אֳנִיּ֖וֹת

לז בְּעֶצְי֥וֹן גָּֽבֶר: וַיִּתְנַבֵּ֞א אֱלִיעֶ֤זֶר בֶּן־דֹּֽדָוָ֙הוּ֙ מִמָּ֣רֵשָׁ֔ה עַל־ יְהוֹשָׁפָ֖ט לֵאמֹ֑ר כְּהִֽתְחַבֶּרְךָ֣ עִם־אֲחַזְיָ֗הוּ פָּרַ֤ץ יְהֹוָה֙ אֶֽת־מַעֲשֶׂ֔יךָ וַיִּשָּׁבְר֣וּ

א אֳנִיּ֔וֹת וְלֹ֥א עָצְר֖וּ לָלֶ֥כֶת אֶל־תַּרְשִֽׁישׁ: וַיִּשְׁכַּ֤ב יְהֽוֹשָׁפָט֙ עִם־אֲבֹתָ֔יו

ב וַיִּקָּבֵ֥ר עִם־אֲבֹתָ֖יו בְּעִ֣יר דָּוִ֑יד וַיִּמְלֹ֛ךְ יְהוֹרָ֥ם בְּנ֖וֹ תַּחְתָּֽיו: וְלֽוֹ־אַחִ֣ים בְּנֵ֣י יְהֽוֹשָׁפָ֗ט עֲזַרְיָ֤ה וִֽיחִיאֵל֙ וּזְכַרְיָ֣הוּ וַעֲזַרְיָ֔הוּ וּמִיכָאֵ֖ל וּשְׁפַטְיָ֑הוּ כָּל־אֵ֕לֶּה בְּנֵ֖י

ג יְהוֹשָׁפָ֥ט מֶֽלֶךְ־יִשְׂרָאֵֽל: וַיִּתֵּ֣ן לָהֶ֣ם ׀ אֲ֠בִיהֶ֠ם מַתָּנ֨וֹת רַבּ֜וֹת לְכֶ֤סֶף וּלְזָהָב֙ וּלְמִגְדָּנ֔וֹת עִם־עָרֵ֥י מְצֻר֖וֹת בִּֽיהוּדָ֑ה וְאֶת־הַמַּמְלָכָ֛ה נָתַ֥ן לִיהוֹרָ֖ם כִּי־ה֥וּא

ד הַבְּכֽוֹר: וַיָּ֨קָם יְהוֹרָ֜ם עַל־מַמְלֶ֤כֶת אָבִיו֙ וַיִּתְחַזַּ֔ק וַיַּהֲרֹ֥ג

ה אֶת־כָּל־אֶחָ֖יו בֶּחָ֑רֶב וְגַ֖ם מִשָּׂרֵ֥י יִשְׂרָאֵֽל: בֶּן־שְׁלֹשִׁ֨ים וּשְׁתַּ֤יִם שָׁנָה֙

ו יְהוֹרָ֣ם בְּמָלְכ֔וֹ וּשְׁמוֹנֶ֣ה שָׁנִ֔ים מָלַ֖ךְ בִּירֽוּשָׁלָ֑͏ִם וַיֵּ֜לֶךְ בְּדֶ֣רֶךְ ׀ מַלְכֵ֣י יִשְׂרָאֵ֗ל כַּאֲשֶׁ֤ר עָשׂוּ֙ בֵּ֣ית אַחְאָ֔ב כִּ֚י בַּת־אַחְאָ֔ב הָ֥יְתָה לּ֖וֹ אִשָּׁ֑ה וַיַּ֥עַשׂ הָרַ֖ע בְּעֵינֵ֥י

ז יְהֹוָֽה: וְלֹא־אָבָ֣ה יְהֹוָ֗ה לְהַשְׁחִית֙ אֶת־בֵּ֣ית דָּוִ֔יד לְמַ֣עַן הַבְּרִ֔ית אֲשֶׁ֥ר כָּרַ֖ת

ח לְדָוִ֑יד וְכַאֲשֶׁ֣ר אָמַ֗ר לָתֵ֨ת ל֥וֹ נִ֛יר וּלְבָנָ֖יו כָּל־הַיָּמִֽים: בְּיָמָיו֙ פָּשַׁ֣ע אֱד֔וֹם

ט מִתַּ֖חַת יַד־יְהוּדָ֑ה וַיַּמְלִ֥יכוּ עֲלֵיהֶ֖ם מֶֽלֶךְ: וַיַּעֲבֹ֤ר יְהוֹרָם֙ עִם־שָׂרָ֔יו וְכָל־ הָרֶ֖כֶב עִמּ֑וֹ וַיְהִי֙ קָ֣ם לַ֔יְלָה וַיַּ֣ךְ אֶת־אֱד֗וֹם הַסּוֹבֵ֤ב אֵלָיו֙ וְאֵ֖ת שָׂרֵ֥י הָרָֽכֶב:

י וַיִּפְשַׁ֨ע אֱד֜וֹם מִתַּ֣חַת יַד־יְהוּדָ֗ה עַ֚ד הַיּ֣וֹם הַזֶּ֔ה אָ֣ז תִּפְשַׁ֥ע לִבְנָ֖ה בָּעֵ֣ת

יא הַהִ֑יא מִתַּ֣חַת יָד֑וֹ כִּ֣י עָזַ֔ב אֶת־יְהֹוָ֖ה אֱלֹהֵ֣י אֲבֹתָ֑יו: גַּם־ה֗וּא עָשָׂ֤ה בָמ֖וֹת־

---

their spoils, and they found an abundance among them, riches and corpses with luxurious items — and they removed [it] from them until it could not be carried. They spent three days plundering the spoils, so abundant was it. ²⁶ *On the fourth*

Valley of Blessing

day they gathered at Emek-berachah (Valley of Blessing) — for they blessed HASHEM there; hence they named that place Emek-berachah until this day.

²⁷ *All the men of Judah and Jerusalem, with Jehoshaphat at their head, turned back, to return to Jerusalem in joy, for HASHEM had given them joy from [the downfall of] their enemy.* ²⁸ *They came to Jerusalem with lyres and harps and trumpets, to the Temple of HASHEM.*

²⁹ *A dread of God came upon all the kingdoms of the lands when they heard that HASHEM was doing battle with the enemies of Israel.* ³⁰ *Jehoshaphat's reign was thus tranquil, for his God granted him respite from all around.*

Jeho-shaphat's successful reign

³¹ *So Jehoshaphat reigned over Judah. He was thirty-five years old when he became king, and he reigned for twenty-five years in Jerusalem. His mother's name was Azubah daughter of Shilhi.* ³² *He followed the way of his father Asa and did not deviate from it, doing what was proper in the eyes of HASHEM.* ³³ *However, the high places did not cease; the people still did not dedicate their hearts to the God of their forefathers.* ³⁴ *The rest of the earlier and the latter events of Jehoshaphat — behold they are recorded in the Words of Jehu son of Hanani, which was appended to the Book of the Kings of Israel.*

Improper alliance

(See Appendix A, timeline 4)

³⁵ *Afterwards Jehoshaphat, king of Judah, allied himself with Ahaziah, king of Israel, who had acted wickedly.* ³⁶ *He joined forces with him to make a fleet to go to Tarshish, and they built ships in Ezion-geber.* ³⁷ *Eliezer son of Dodavah of Mareshah prophesied about Jehoshaphat, saying, "Because you have allied yourself with Ahaziah, HASHEM has wrecked your undertakings!" The ships broke down and did not succeed in going to Tarshish.*

21

KING JEHORAM
21:1-20

¹ **J**ehoshaphat lay with his forefathers and was buried with his forefathers in the City of David; his son Jehoram reigned in his place.

² *He had brothers, the sons of Jehoshaphat — Azariah, Jehiel, Zechariah, Azariahu, Michael and Shephatiah. All these were the sons of Jehoshaphat king of Israel.* ³ *Their father gave them many gifts of silver and gold and luxurious things, along with fortified cities in Judah, but he gave the kingship to Jehoram, for he was the firstborn.* ⁴ *Jehoram rose up over the kingdom of his father, and he strengthened himself in it. He killed all of his brothers by the sword, as well as some of the officers of Israel.*

Jehoram sins

⁵ *Jehoram was thirty-two years old when he reigned, and he reigned for eight years in Jerusalem.* ⁶ *He went in the way of the kings of Israel, just as the house of Ahab had done, for Ahab's daughter had become his wife; he did what was evil in the eyes of HASHEM.* ⁷ *But HASHEM did not wish to destroy the house of David, because of the covenant He had sealed with David; in accordance with what He had said — that He would give dominion to him and to his descendants all the days.*

Edom's rebellion

⁸ *In his days Edom rebelled against the rule of Judah, and they appointed a king over themselves.* * ⁹ *So Jehoram went with his officers and with all his chariots; he arose in the night and smote Edom which had surrounded him, and the chariot captains.* ¹⁰ *But Edom rebelled against [being] under the hand of Judah to this day. Then Libnah rebelled against his rule at that time, for he had forsaken HASHEM, the God of his fathers.* ¹¹ *Furthermore, he erected high places*

יב בְּאַחֲרֵי יְהוּדָה וַיָּזֶן אֶת־יֹשְׁבֵי יְרוּשָׁלַ͏ִם וַיַּדַּח אֶת־יְהוּדָה: וַיָּבֹא
אֵלָיו מִכְתָּב מֵאֵלִיָּהוּ הַנָּבִיא לֵאמֹר כֹּה ׀ אָמַר יהוה אֱלֹהֵי דָּוִיד אָבִיךָ
תַּחַת אֲשֶׁר לֹא־הָלַכְתָּ בְּדַרְכֵי יְהוֹשָׁפָט אָבִיךָ וּבְדַרְכֵי אָסָא מֶלֶךְ־יְהוּדָה:
יג וַתֵּלֶךְ בְּדֶרֶךְ מַלְכֵי יִשְׂרָאֵל וַתַּזְנֶה אֶת־יְהוּדָה וְאֶת־יֹשְׁבֵי יְרוּשָׁלַ͏ִם כְּהַזְנוֹת
בֵּית אַחְאָב וְגַם אֶת־אַחֶיךָ בֵית־אָבִיךָ הַטּוֹבִים מִמְּךָ הָרָגְתָּ: הִנֵּה יהוה
יד נֹגֵף מַגֵּפָה גְדוֹלָה בְּעַמֶּךָ וּבְבָנֶיךָ וּבְנָשֶׁיךָ וּבְכָל־רְכוּשֶׁךָ: וְאַתָּה בׇּחֳלָיִים
טו רַבִּים בְּמַחֲלֵה מֵעֶיךָ עַד־יֵצְאוּ מֵעֶיךָ מִן־הַחֹלִי יָמִים עַל־יָמִים: וַיָּעַר
טז יהוה עַל־יְהוֹרָם אֵת רוּחַ הַפְּלִשְׁתִּים וְהָעַרְבִים אֲשֶׁר עַל־יַד כּוּשִׁים: וַיַּעֲלוּ
בִיהוּדָה וַיִּבְקָעוּהָ וַיִּשְׁבּוּ אֵת כׇּל־הָרְכוּשׁ הַנִּמְצָא לְבֵית־הַמֶּלֶךְ וְגַם־בָּנָיו
יז וְנָשָׁיו וְלֹא נִשְׁאַר־לוֹ בֵּן כִּי אִם־יְהוֹאָחָז קְטֹן בָּנָיו: וְאַחֲרֵי כׇּל־זֹאת נְגָפוֹ
יח יהוה ׀ בְּמֵעָיו לׇחֳלִי לְאֵין מַרְפֵּא: וַיְהִי לְיָמִים ׀ מִיָּמִים וּכְעֵת צֵאת הַקֵּץ
יט לְיָמִים שְׁנַיִם יָצְאוּ מֵעָיו עִם־חׇלְיוֹ וַיָּמׇת בְּתַחֲלֻאִים רָעִים וְלֹא־עָשׂוּ לוֹ
כ עַמּוֹ שְׂרֵפָה כִּשְׂרֵפַת אֲבֹתָיו: בֶּן־שְׁלֹשִׁים וּשְׁתַּיִם הָיָה בְמׇלְכוֹ וּשְׁמוֹנֶה
שָׁנִים מָלַךְ בִּירוּשָׁלָ͏ִם וַיֵּלֶךְ בְּלֹא חֶמְדָּה וַיִּקְבְּרֻהוּ בְּעִיר דָּוִיד וְלֹא בְּקִבְרוֹת

כב א הַמְּלָכִים: וַיַּמְלִיכוּ יוֹשְׁבֵי יְרוּשָׁלַ͏ִם אֶת־אֲחַזְיָהוּ בְנוֹ הַקָּטֹן תַּחְתָּיו כִּי כׇל־
הָרִאשֹׁנִים הָרַג הַגְּדוּד הַבָּא בַעֲרָבִים לַמַּחֲנֶה וַיִּמְלֹךְ אֲחַזְיָהוּ בֶן־יְהוֹרָם
ב מֶלֶךְ יְהוּדָה: בֶּן־אַרְבָּעִים וּשְׁתַּיִם שָׁנָה אֲחַזְיָהוּ בְמׇלְכוֹ
ג וְשָׁנָה אַחַת מָלַךְ בִּירוּשָׁלָ͏ִם וְשֵׁם אִמּוֹ עֲתַלְיָהוּ בַּת־עׇמְרִי: גַּם־הוּא הָלַךְ
ד בְּדַרְכֵי בֵּית אַחְאָב כִּי אִמּוֹ הָיְתָה יוֹעַצְתּוֹ לְהַרְשִׁיעַ: וַיַּעַשׂ הָרַע בְּעֵינֵי
יהוה כְּבֵית אַחְאָב כִּי־הֵמָּה הָיוּ־לוֹ יוֹעֲצִים אַחֲרֵי מוֹת אָבִיו לְמַשְׁחִית
ה לוֹ: גַּם בַּעֲצָתָם הָלַךְ וַיֵּלֶךְ אֶת־יְהוֹרָם בֶּן־אַחְאָב מֶלֶךְ יִשְׂרָאֵל לַמִּלְחָמָה
ו עַל־חֲזָאֵל מֶלֶךְ־אֲרָם בְּרָמוֹת גִּלְעָד וַיַּכּוּ הָרַמִּים אֶת־יוֹרָם: וַיָּשׇׁב
לְהִתְרַפֵּא בְיִזְרְעֶאל כִּי הַמַּכִּים אֲשֶׁר הִכֻּהוּ בְרָמָה בְּהִלָּחֲמוֹ אֶת־חֲזָהאֵל
מֶלֶךְ אֲרָם וַעֲזַרְיָהוּ בֶן־יְהוֹרָם מֶלֶךְ יְהוּדָה יָרַד לִרְאוֹת אֶת־יְהוֹרָם בֶּן־
ז אַחְאָב בְּיִזְרְעֶאל כִּי חֹלֶה הוּא: וּמֵאֱלֹהִים הָיְתָה תְּבוּסַת אֲחַזְיָהוּ לָבוֹא
אֶל־יוֹרָם וּבְבֹאוֹ יָצָא עִם־יְהוֹרָם אֶל־יֵהוּא בֶּן־נִמְשִׁי אֲשֶׁר מְשָׁחוֹ יהוה
ח לְהַכְרִית אֶת־בֵּית אַחְאָב: וַיְהִי כְּהִשָּׁפֵט יֵהוּא עִם־בֵּית אַחְאָב וַיִּמְצָא
ט אֶת־שָׂרֵי יְהוּדָה וּבְנֵי אֲחֵי אֲחַזְיָהוּ מְשָׁרְתִים לַאֲחַזְיָהוּ וַיַּהַרְגֵם: וַיְבַקֵּשׁ
אֶת־אֲחַזְיָהוּ וַיִּלְכְּדֻהוּ וְהוּא מִתְחַבֵּא בְשֹׁמְרוֹן וַיְבִאֻהוּ אֶל־יֵהוּא וַיְמִתֻהוּ
וַיִּקְבְּרֻהוּ כִּי אָמְרוּ בֶּן־יְהוֹשָׁפָט הוּא אֲשֶׁר־דָּרַשׁ אֶת־יהוה בְּכׇל־לְבָבוֹ

21:20. For his life was full of suffering.

22:1. See 21:16-17.

22:2. Athaliah was a *granddaughter* of Omri (see 21:6); it is common in Scripture for grandchildren to be referred to as children. According to *II Kings* 8:26, Ahaziah reigned at the age of twenty-two, not forty-two. The Sages (*Seder Olam Rabbah* Ch. 17) explain that it was now

forty-two years since Jehoshaphat, the future king of Judah, had married Omri's daughter. Thus our verse alludes to the decree that Omri's line would be annihilated. Now, because of Judah's sinfulness, that decree would be applied to the Davidic line, which was descended from Omri's daughter.

22:6. Ahaziah was also known by this name.

*in the mountains of Judah. He caused the inhabitants of Jerusalem to go astray,
and he induced Judah to sin.* ¹² *A letter came to him from Elijah the prophet,*

Elijah's
ominous
letter

*saying, "Thus said HASHEM, the God of your forefather David: Because you did
not follow the ways of your father Jehoshaphat and the ways of Asa, king of
Judah,* ¹³ *but you followed the way of the kings of Israel, and you caused Judah
and the inhabitants of Jerusalem to go astray as the house of Ahab caused
[people] to go astray, and you even murdered your brothers, your father's
household, who were superior to you —* ¹⁴ *behold, HASHEM is inflicting a great
plague upon your people, and upon your sons and your wives and all your
wealth.* ¹⁵ *You will suffer many diseases in an intestinal illness, until your innards
come out because of the illness, year after year."*

Disaster
strikes Judah

¹⁶ *HASHEM aroused against Jehoram the spirit of the Philistines and the Arabs
who were near the Ethiopians.* ¹⁷ *They attacked Judah and they breached its
defenses; they seized all the wealth that was found in the king's palace, as well
as his children and wives. There was no son left to him except Jehoahaz, the
youngest of his sons.* ¹⁸ *After all this HASHEM struck him in his intestines with an
incurable disease.* ¹⁹ *It plagued him for an entire year, and at the time when the
deadline arrived, after two years, his intestines came out because of his disease,
and he died of terrible illnesses. His people did not make a pyre for him like the
pyre of his forefathers.*

(See Appendix A,
timeline 4)

22

**KING
AHAZIAH**
22:1-12

²⁰ *He was thirty-two years old when he became king, and he ruled for eight
years in Jerusalem. He departed without enjoyment,* * *and they buried him in the
City of David, but not in the graves of the kings.* ¹ *The inhabitants of Jerusalem
proclaimed Ahaziah, his youngest son, king in his place, for all the older ones
were killed by the troops that came with the Arabs to the camp,* * *so Ahaziah son
of Jehoram reigned as king of Judah.*

² *Ahaziah was forty-two years old when he became king, and he reigned for
one year in Jerusalem. His mother's name was Athaliah, the [grand]daughter of*

His wicked
mother
dominates

Omri. * ³ *He, too, followed the way of the house of Ahab, for his mother would
advise him to act wickedly.* ⁴ *He did what was evil in the eyes of HASHEM, like the
house of Ahab, for they were his advisers after his father's death, toward his*

Misguided
wars

destruction. ⁵ *Moreover, upon their advice he went to war with Jehoram son of
Ahab, king of Israel, to war against Hazael, king of Aram, at Ramoth-gilead, and
the Arameans wounded Jehoram.* ⁶ *He returned to convalesce in Jezreel because
of the wounds that they had inflicted upon him at the Ramah as he battled against
Hazael king of Aram. Azariah* * *son of Jehoram, king of Judah, went down to visit
Jehoram son of Ahab in Jezreel, for he was ill.* ⁷ *It was God's decree for the
ruination of Ahaziah that he should come to Jehoram, for when he was there he
went out with Jehoram towards Jehu son of Nimshi,* * *whom HASHEM had
anointed to eliminate the house of Ahab.* ⁸ *It happened when Jehu executed*

Double
assassination

*judgment against the house of Ahab, that he found the officers of Judah and
Ahaziah's nephews attending to Ahaziah, and he killed them.* ⁹ *He looked for
Ahaziah, and [his men] apprehended him while he was hiding in Samaria. They
brought him to Jehu and they put him to death and buried him,* * *for they said, "He
is the [grand]son of Jehoshaphat, who sought out HASHEM with all his heart."*

22:7. For Jehu's story, see *II Kings* Ch. 9.
22:9. Contemptuously, Jehu had thrown Jehoram's

body into a field (*II Kings* 9:25), but out of respect for
Jehoshaphat, he allowed Ahaziah to be buried.

וְאֵין לְבֵית אֲחַזְיָהוּ לַעְצֹר כֹּחַ לְמַמְלָכָה: וַעֲתַלְיָהוּ אֵם אֲחַזְיָהוּ   י

רָאֲתָה כִּי מֵת בְּנָהּ וַתָּקָם וַתְּדַבֵּר אֶת־כָּל־זֶרַע הַמַּמְלָכָה לְבֵית יְהוּדָה:

וַתִּקַּח יְהוֹשַׁבְעַת בַּת־הַמֶּלֶךְ אֶת־יוֹאָשׁ בֶּן־אֲחַזְיָהוּ וַתִּגְנֹב אֹתוֹ מִתּוֹךְ   יא

בְּנֵי־הַמֶּלֶךְ הַמּוּמָתִים וַתִּתֵּן אֹתוֹ וְאֶת־מֵינִקְתּוֹ בַּחֲדַר הַמִּטּוֹת וַתַּסְתִּירֵהוּ

יְהוֹשַׁבְעַת בַּת־הַמֶּלֶךְ יְהוֹרָם אֵשֶׁת יְהוֹיָדָע הַכֹּהֵן כִּי הִיא הָיְתָה אֲחוֹת

אֲחַזְיָהוּ מִפְּנֵי עֲתַלְיָהוּ וְלֹא הֱמִיתָתְהוּ: וַיְהִי אִתָּם בְּבֵית הָאֱלֹהִים   יב

מִתְחַבֵּא שֵׁשׁ שָׁנִים וַעֲתַלְיָה מֹלֶכֶת עַל־הָאָרֶץ: וּבַשָּׁנָה   א   **כג**

הַשְּׁבִעִית הִתְחַזַּק יְהוֹיָדָע וַיִּקַּח אֶת־שָׂרֵי הַמֵּאוֹת לַעֲזַרְיָהוּ בֶן־יְרֹחָם

וּלְיִשְׁמָעֵאל בֶּן־יְהוֹחָנָן וְלַעֲזַרְיָהוּ בֶן־עוֹבֵד וְאֶת־מַעֲשֵׂיָהוּ בֶן־עֲדָיָהוּ

וְאֶת־אֱלִישָׁפָט בֶּן־זִכְרִי עִמּוֹ בַבְּרִית: וַיָּסֹבּוּ בִּיהוּדָה וַיִּקְבְּצוּ אֶת־הַלְוִיִּם   ב

מִכָּל־עָרֵי יְהוּדָה וְרָאשֵׁי הָאָבוֹת לְיִשְׂרָאֵל וַיָּבֹאוּ אֶל־יְרוּשָׁלִָם: וַיִּכְרֹת   ג

כָּל־הַקָּהָל בְּרִית בְּבֵית הָאֱלֹהִים עִם־הַמֶּלֶךְ וַיֹּאמֶר לָהֶם הִנֵּה בֶן־הַמֶּלֶךְ

יִמְלֹךְ כַּאֲשֶׁר דִּבֶּר יְהוָה עַל־בְּנֵי דָוִיד: זֶה הַדָּבָר אֲשֶׁר תַּעֲשׂוּ הַשְּׁלִשִׁית   ד

מִכֶּם בָּאֵי הַשַּׁבָּת לַכֹּהֲנִים וְלַלְוִיִּם לְשֹׁעֲרֵי הַסִּפִּים: וְהַשְּׁלִשִׁית בְּבֵית   ה

הַמֶּלֶךְ וְהַשְּׁלִשִׁית בְּשַׁעַר הַיְסוֹד וְכָל־הָעָם בְּחַצְרוֹת בֵּית יְהוָה: וְאַל־   ו

יָבוֹא בֵית־יְהוָה כִּי אִם־הַכֹּהֲנִים וְהַמְשָׁרְתִים לַלְוִיִּם הֵמָּה יָבֹאוּ כִּי־קֹדֶשׁ

הֵמָּה וְכָל־הָעָם יִשְׁמְרוּ מִשְׁמֶרֶת יְהוָה: וְהִקִּיפוּ הַלְוִיִּם אֶת־הַמֶּלֶךְ סָבִיב   ז

אִישׁ וְכֵלָיו בְּיָדוֹ וְהַבָּא אֶל־הַבַּיִת יוּמָת וִהְיוּ אֶת־הַמֶּלֶךְ בְּבֹאוֹ וּבְצֵאתוֹ:

וַיַּעֲשׂוּ הַלְוִיִּם וְכָל־יְהוּדָה כְּכֹל אֲשֶׁר־צִוָּה יְהוֹיָדָע הַכֹּהֵן וַיִּקְחוּ אִישׁ אֶת־   ח

אֲנָשָׁיו בָּאֵי הַשַּׁבָּת עִם יוֹצְאֵי הַשַּׁבָּת כִּי לֹא פָטַר יְהוֹיָדָע הַכֹּהֵן אֶת־

הַמַּחְלְקוֹת: וַיִּתֵּן יְהוֹיָדָע הַכֹּהֵן לְשָׂרֵי הַמֵּאוֹת אֶת־הַחֲנִיתִים   ט

וְאֶת־הַמָּגִנּוֹת וְאֶת־הַשְּׁלָטִים אֲשֶׁר לַמֶּלֶךְ דָּוִיד אֲשֶׁר בֵּית הָאֱלֹהִים:

וַיַּעֲמֵד אֶת־כָּל־הָעָם וְאִישׁ ׀ שִׁלְחוֹ בְיָדוֹ מִכֶּתֶף הַבַּיִת הַיְמָנִית עַד־כֶּתֶף   י

הַבַּיִת הַשְּׂמָאלִית לַמִּזְבֵּחַ וְלַבָּיִת עַל־הַמֶּלֶךְ סָבִיב: וַיּוֹצִיאוּ אֶת־בֶּן־הַמֶּלֶךְ   יא

וַיִּתְּנוּ עָלָיו אֶת־הַנֵּזֶר וְאֶת־הָעֵדוּת וַיַּמְלִיכוּ אֹתוֹ וַיִּמְשָׁחֻהוּ יְהוֹיָדָע וּבָנָיו

וַיֹּאמְרוּ יְחִי הַמֶּלֶךְ:   וַתִּשְׁמַע עֲתַלְיָהוּ אֶת־קוֹל הָעָם הָרָצִים   יב

וְהַמְהַלְלִים אֶת־הַמֶּלֶךְ וַתָּבוֹא אֶל־הָעָם בֵּית יְהוָה: וַתֵּרֶא וְהִנֵּה הַמֶּלֶךְ   יג

עֹמֵד עַל־עַמּוּדוֹ בַּמָּבוֹא וְהַשָּׂרִים וְהַחֲצֹצְרוֹת עַל־הַמֶּלֶךְ וְכָל־עַם הָאָרֶץ

שָׂמֵחַ וְתוֹקֵעַ בַּחֲצֹצְרוֹת וְהַמְשׁוֹרְרִים בִּכְלֵי הַשִּׁיר וּמוֹדִיעִים לְהַלֵּל

וַתִּקְרַע עֲתַלְיָהוּ אֶת־בְּגָדֶיהָ וַתֹּאמֶר קֶשֶׁר קָשֶׁר: וַיּוֹצֵא יְהוֹיָדָע   יד

הַכֹּהֵן אֶת־שָׂרֵי הַמֵּאוֹת ׀ פְּקוּדֵי הַחַיִל וַיֹּאמֶר אֲלֵהֶם הוֹצִיאוּהָ אֶל־מִבֵּית

הַשְּׂדֵרוֹת וְהַבָּא אַחֲרֶיהָ יוּמַת בֶּחָרֶב כִּי אָמַר הַכֹּהֵן לֹא תְמִיתוּהָ בֵּית

22:11. She was a daughter of Jehoram (II Kings 11:2).   **23:3.** That is, the child Joash.
23:1. He secured their support to reinstitute the Davidic   **23:4.** See II Kings 11:5.
dynasty and overthrow Athaliah.   **23:9.** See II Samuel 8:7 and I Kings 10:16-17.

There was no one in Ahaziah's household who could muster the power to reign.
Athaliah's ¹⁰ *When Athaliah, Ahaziah's mother, saw that her son had died, she arose and*
bloodshed *exterminated all the offspring of the royal family of Judah.* ¹¹ *But Jehoshabeath,*
*the king's daughter, * took Joash son of Ahaziah and smuggled him from the*
midst of the king's sons who were being killed, and put him and his nursemaid in
the bedchamber; Jehoshabeath, daughter of King Jehoram and wife of Jehoiada
the Kohen — because she was Ahaziah's sister — hid him from Athaliah so she
Sole survivor *could not put him to death.* ¹² *He remained with them in the Temple of God,*
hidden for six years, while Athaliah reigned over the land.

23   **KING**   ¹ *In the seventh year Jehoiada strengthened himself and took the captains of*
      JOASH   *hundreds — Azariah son of Jeroham, Ishmael son of Jehohanan, Azariah son*
  23:1-24:27 *of Obed, Maaseiah son of Adaiah and Elishaphat son of Zichri — into a covenant*
*with him. * ² They circulated in Judah and gathered the Levites from all the cities*
of Judah, and the family heads of Israel, and they came to Jerusalem. ³ *The entire*
*assembly sealed a covenant in the Temple of God with the king. * [Jehoiada] said*
to them, "Behold, the son of the king shall reign, as HASHEM spoke about the
descendants of David! ⁴ *This is what you are to do: a third of those of you, of the*
Kohanim and the Levites, who are arriving on the Sabbath will be gatekeepers*
of the doorways; ⁵ *a third will be stationed at the king's palace; and a third will be*
stationed at the Foundation Gate, while all the people will be in the Courtyards of
the Temple of HASHEM. ⁶ *No one is to enter the Temple of HASHEM except for the*
Kohanim and the ministers among the Levites; they may enter for they are holy.
Boy king *All the people are to keep the watch of HASHEM.* ⁷ *The Levites shall then encircle*
the king all around, each man with his weapons in his hand; anyone who enters
the Temple shall be put to death. You must remain with the king when he goes out
and when he comes in."

Marshaling ⁸ *So the Levites and all of Judah did according to all that Jehoiada the Kohen*
forces *had commanded them; each one took his men, those who were arriving on the*
Sabbath and those who were leaving on the Sabbath, for Jehoiada the Kohen had
not dismissed the [outgoing] shifts. ⁹ *Jehoiada the Kohen gave to the captains of*
*hundreds the spears and the shields and the shields of King David, * which were*
in the Temple of God. ¹⁰ *He stationed all the people, each man with his weapon*
(See Appendix A, *in his hand, from the right flank of the Temple to the left flank, near the Altar and*
timeline 4) *the Sanctuary, surrounding the king.* ¹¹ *They then brought out the king's son and*
Joash is *placed the crown and the Divine testimony* upon him; they declared him king*
crowned *and anointed him, and they said, "Long live the king!"*

¹² *Athaliah heard the sound of the people who were rushing and who were*
shouting praises to the king, and she came to the people in the Temple of HASHEM.
Athaliah is ¹³ *She looked, and there was the king standing at his position, * at the entryway,*
arrested ... *with the officers and the trumpets next to the king, and all the people of the land*
rejoicing and blowing trumpets, and the singers with their musical instruments
giving instructions to sing praises. Athaliah tore her garments and shouted, "A
Rebellion! A Rebellion!" ¹⁴ *Jehoiada the Kohen took aside the captains of hun-*
dreds, the officers of the force, and said to them, "Take her away, but keep her
within the ranks [of the guards], and anyone who comes after her shall be slain
by the sword!" For the Kohen said, "Do not put her to death in the Temple

---

23:11. A Torah scroll; see *II Kings* 11:12.   **23:13.** A place of honor reserved for the king.

טו יְהוָה: וַיָּשִׂימוּ לָהּ יָדַיִם וַתָּבוֹא אֶל־מְבוֹא שַׁעַר־הַסּוּסִים בֵּית הַמֶּלֶךְ וַיְמִיתוּהָ שָׁם:

טז וַיִּכְרֹת יְהוֹיָדָע בְּרִית בֵּינוֹ וּבֵין כָּל־הָעָם וּבֵין הַמֶּלֶךְ לִהְיוֹת לְעָם לַיהוָה:

יז וַיָּבֹאוּ כָל־הָעָם בֵּית־הַבַּעַל וַיִּתְּצֻהוּ וְאֶת־מִזְבְּחֹתָיו וְאֶת־צְלָמָיו שִׁבֵּרוּ וְאֵת מַתָּן כֹּהֵן הַבַּעַל הָרְגוּ לִפְנֵי הַמִּזְבְּחוֹת:

יח וַיָּשֶׂם יְהוֹיָדָע פְּקֻדֹּת בֵּית יְהוָה בְּיַד הַכֹּהֲנִים הַלְוִיִּם אֲשֶׁר חָלַק דָּוִיד עַל־בֵּית יְהוָה לְהַעֲלוֹת עֹלוֹת יְהוָה כַּכָּתוּב בְּתוֹרַת מֹשֶׁה בְּשִׂמְחָה וּבְשִׁיר עַל יְדֵי דָוִיד:

יט וַיַּעֲמֵד הַשּׁוֹעֲרִים עַל־שַׁעֲרֵי בֵּית יְהוָה וְלֹא־יָבֹא טָמֵא לְכָל־דָּבָר: וַיִּקַּח אֶת־שָׂרֵי הַמֵּאוֹת וְאֶת־הָאַדִּירִים וְאֶת־הַמּוֹשְׁלִים בָּעָם וְאֵת ׀ כָּל־עַם הָאָרֶץ וַיּוֹרֶד אֶת־הַמֶּלֶךְ מִבֵּית יְהוָה וַיָּבֹאוּ בְּתוֹךְ־שַׁעַר הָעֶלְיוֹן בֵּית הַמֶּלֶךְ

כא וַיּוֹשִׁיבוּ אֶת־הַמֶּלֶךְ עַל כִּסֵּא הַמַּמְלָכָה: וַיִּשְׂמְחוּ כָל־עַם־הָאָרֶץ וְהָעִיר שָׁקָטָה וְאֶת־עֲתַלְיָהוּ הֵמִיתוּ בֶחָרֶב: בֶּן־שֶׁבַע שָׁנִים יֹאָשׁ

כד א בְּמָלְכוֹ וְאַרְבָּעִים שָׁנָה מָלַךְ בִּירוּשָׁלָם וְשֵׁם אִמּוֹ צִבְיָה מִבְּאֵר שָׁבַע:

ב וַיַּעַשׂ יוֹאָשׁ הַיָּשָׁר בְּעֵינֵי יְהוָה כָּל־יְמֵי יְהוֹיָדָע הַכֹּהֵן:

ג-ד וַיִּשָּׂא־לוֹ יְהוֹיָדָע נָשִׁים שְׁתָּיִם וַיּוֹלֶד בָּנִים וּבָנוֹת: וַיְהִי אַחֲרֵי־כֵן הָיָה עִם־ לֵב יוֹאָשׁ לְחַדֵּשׁ אֶת־בֵּית יְהוָה: וַיִּקְבֹּץ אֶת־הַכֹּהֲנִים וְהַלְוִיִּם וַיֹּאמֶר לָהֶם צְאוּ לְעָרֵי יְהוּדָה וְקִבְצוּ מִכָּל־יִשְׂרָאֵל כֶּסֶף לְחַזֵּק ׀ אֶת־בֵּית אֱלֹהֵיכֶם

ו מִדֵּי שָׁנָה בְּשָׁנָה וְאַתֶּם תְּמַהֲרוּ לַדָּבָר וְלֹא מִהֲרוּ הַלְוִיִּם: וַיִּקְרָא הַמֶּלֶךְ לִיהוֹיָדָע הָרֹאשׁ וַיֹּאמֶר לוֹ מַדּוּעַ לֹא־דָרַשְׁתָּ עַל־הַלְוִיִּם לְהָבִיא מִיהוּדָה וּמִירוּשָׁלַם אֶת־מַשְׂאַת מֹשֶׁה עֶבֶד־יְהוָה וְהַקָּהָל לְיִשְׂרָאֵל לְאֹהֶל הָעֵדוּת:

ז כִּי עֲתַלְיָהוּ הַמִּרְשַׁעַת בָּנֶיהָ פָרְצוּ אֶת־בֵּית הָאֱלֹהִים וְגַם כָּל־קָדְשֵׁי בֵית־יְהוָה עָשׂוּ לַבְּעָלִים: וַיֹּאמֶר הַמֶּלֶךְ וַיַּעֲשׂוּ אֲרוֹן אֶחָד וַיִּתְּנֻהוּ בְּשַׁעַר בֵּית־יְהוָה חוּצָה: וַיִּתְּנוּ־קוֹל בִּיהוּדָה וּבִירוּשָׁלַם לְהָבִיא לַיהוָה מַשְׂאַת מֹשֶׁה עֶבֶד־הָאֱלֹהִים עַל־יִשְׂרָאֵל בַּמִּדְבָּר:

י וַיִּשְׂמְחוּ כָל־הַשָּׂרִים וְכָל־הָעָם וַיָּבִיאוּ וַיַּשְׁלִיכוּ לָאָרוֹן עַד־לְכַלֵּה:

יא וַיְהִי בְּעֵת יָבִיא אֶת־הָאָרוֹן אֶל־פְּקֻדַּת הַמֶּלֶךְ בְּיַד הַלְוִיִּם וְכִרְאוֹתָם כִּי־ רַב הַכֶּסֶף וּבָא סוֹפֵר הַמֶּלֶךְ וּפְקִיד כֹּהֵן הָרֹאשׁ וִיעָרוּ אֶת־הָאָרוֹן וְיִשָּׂאֻהוּ וִישִׁיבֻהוּ אֶל־מְקֹמוֹ כֹּה עָשׂוּ לְיוֹם ׀ בְּיוֹם וַיַּאַסְפוּ־כֶסֶף לָרֹב: וַיִּתְּנֵהוּ

יב הַמֶּלֶךְ וִיהוֹיָדָע אֶל־עוֹשֵׂה מְלֶאכֶת עֲבוֹדַת בֵּית־יְהוָה וַיִּהְיוּ שֹׂכְרִים חֹצְבִים וְחָרָשִׁים לְחַדֵּשׁ בֵּית יְהוָה וְגַם לְחָרָשֵׁי בַרְזֶל וּנְחֹשֶׁת לְחַזֵּק יג אֶת־בֵּית יְהוָה: וַיַּעֲשׂוּ עֹשֵׂי הַמְּלָאכָה וַתַּעַל אֲרוּכָה לַמְּלָאכָה בְּיָדָם יד וַיַּעֲמִידוּ אֶת־בֵּית הָאֱלֹהִים עַל־מַתְכֻּנְתּוֹ וַיְאַמְּצֻהוּ: וּכְכַלּוֹתָם הֵבִיאוּ

23:18. The Temple service had apparently fallen into disarray under Athaliah and had to be reinstated (*Rashi*).

24:6. See *Exodus* 30:12-16, where Moses commanded all the Israelites to donate a half-*shekel*.

24:7. Apparently she had sons from a previous marriage, because she had already murdered all the descendants of of HASHEM." ¹⁵ They made place for her and she came to the entrance of the Horses' Gate, to the palace of the king, and they put her to death there.

Jehoiadah's
covenant

¹⁶ Jehoiada then sealed a covenant between himself, between all the people and the king, to be the people of HASHEM. ¹⁷ All the people came to the temple of Baal and tore it down, they smashed its altars and images, and Mattan, priest of the Baal, they slew in front of the altars. ¹⁸ Jehoiada the Kohen established administrators over the Temple of HASHEM by the Kohanim and the Levites, * whom David had divided into divisions for the Temple of HASHEM, to offer up the burnt-offerings of HASHEM — as is written in the Torah of Moses — through joy and through songs, [made] by the hands of David. ¹⁹ He stationed the gatekeepers at the gates of the Temple of HASHEM, so that no impure person might enter for any purpose. ²⁰ He took the captains of hundreds, the nobles and the rulers of the people, and all the people of the land, and he escorted the king down from the Temple of HASHEM; they proceeded by way of the Upper Gate to the royal palace, and sat the king upon the royal throne.

²¹ The entire people of the land rejoiced and the city was tranquil, for Athaliah had been put to death by the sword.

24

¹ Joash was seven years old when he became king, and he reigned for forty years in Jerusalem; his mother's name was Zibiah of Beer-sheba. ² Joash did what was proper in the eyes of HASHEM all the days of Jehoiada the Kohen.

³ Jehoiada married two wives and fathered sons and daughters.

Joash
renovates
the Temple

⁴ It happened after this that it entered Joash's heart to renovate the Temple of HASHEM. ⁵ He gathered the Kohanim and the Levites and said to them, "Go out to the cities of Judah and collect money from all of Israel every year, to strengthen the Temple of your God. Now, you hurry in this matter." But the Levites did not hurry. ⁶ So the king summoned Jehoiada, the chief, and said to him, "Why have you not demanded of the Levites to bring from Judea and Jerusalem the levy ordained by Moses, servant of God, upon the congregation of Israel for the Tent of the Testimony?"* ⁷ (For Athaliah the evildoer [and] her sons* had made breaches in the Temple of God. They also used all the consecrated objects of the Temple of HASHEM for the Baal idols.)

The
collection
chest

⁸ The king issued an order, and they made a single chest and placed it at the gate of the Temple of HASHEM, on the outside. ⁹ They made an announcement throughout Judah and Jerusalem that people should bring to HASHEM the levy ordained by Moses, the servant of God, upon Israel in the Wilderness. ¹⁰ All the officers and all the people were glad; they brought [money] and dropped it into the chest until it was full. ¹¹ It happened that whenever they would bring the chest to the administration of the king, in the charge of the Levites, when they saw that there was much money, the king's scribe and an official of the chief Kohen would come, empty out the chest, lift it up and return it to its place. So they did every day, and

Expenditure

they collected a large amount of money. ¹² The king and Jehoiada gave it to the overseers of the labor for the work on the Temple of HASHEM, who hired with it hewers and craftsmen to renovate the Temple of HASHEM, and also to craftsmen of iron and copper, to strengthen the Temple of HASHEM. ¹³ The workmen acted and the work flourished in their hands. They restored the Temple of God to its proper status, and they strengthened it. ¹⁴ When they finished, they brought

---

her husband Jehoram (Radak).

לִפְנֵי הַמֶּלֶךְ וִיהוֹיָדָע אֶת־שְׁאָר הַכֶּסֶף וַיַּעֲשֵׂהוּ כֵלִים לְבֵית־יְהוָה כְּלֵי
שָׁרֵת וְהַעֲלוֹת וְכַפּוֹת וּכְלֵי זָהָב וָכָסֶף וַיִּהְיוּ מַעֲלִים עֹלוֹת בְּבֵית־יְהוָה

טו תָּמִיד כֹּל יְמֵי יְהוֹיָדָע: וַיִּזְקַן יְהוֹיָדָע וַיִּשְׂבַּע יָמִים וַיָּמׇת בֶּן־
טז מֵאָה וּשְׁלֹשִׁים שָׁנָה בְּמוֹתוֹ: וַיִּקְבְּרֻהוּ בְעִיר־דָּוִיד עִם־הַמְּלָכִים כִּי־עָשָׂה
יז טוֹבָה בְּיִשְׂרָאֵל וְעִם הָאֱלֹהִים וּבֵיתוֹ:   וְאַחֲרֵי מוֹת יְהוֹיָדָע
יח בָּאוּ שָׂרֵי יְהוּדָה וַיִּשְׁתַּחֲווּ לַמֶּלֶךְ אָז שָׁמַע הַמֶּלֶךְ אֲלֵיהֶם: וַיַּעַזְבוּ אֶת־
בֵּית יְהוָה אֱלֹהֵי אֲבוֹתֵיהֶם וַיַּעַבְדוּ אֶת־הָאֲשֵׁרִים וְאֶת־הָעֲצַבִּים וַיְהִי־
יט קֶצֶף עַל־יְהוּדָה וִירוּשָׁלִַם בְּאַשְׁמָתָם זֹאת: וַיִּשְׁלַח בָּהֶם נְבִאִים לַהֲשִׁיבָם
כ אֶל־יְהוָה וַיָּעִידוּ בָם וְלֹא הֶאֱזִינוּ:   וְרוּחַ אֱלֹהִים לָבְשָׁה אֶת־
זְכַרְיָה בֶּן־יְהוֹיָדָע הַכֹּהֵן וַיַּעֲמֹד מֵעַל לָעָם וַיֹּאמֶר לָהֶם כֹּה ׀ אָמַר
הָאֱלֹהִים לָמָה אַתֶּם עֹבְרִים אֶת־מִצְוֺת יְהוָה וְלֹא תַצְלִיחוּ כִּי־עֲזַבְתֶּם
כא אֶת־יְהוָה וַיַּעֲזֹב אֶתְכֶם: וַיִּקְשְׁרוּ עָלָיו וַיִּרְגְּמֻהוּ אֶבֶן בְּמִצְוַת הַמֶּלֶךְ
כב בַּחֲצַר בֵּית יְהוָה: וְלֹא־זָכַר יוֹאָשׁ הַמֶּלֶךְ הַחֶסֶד אֲשֶׁר עָשָׂה יְהוֹיָדָע אָבִיו
עִמּוֹ וַיַּהֲרֹג אֶת־בְּנוֹ וּכְמוֹתוֹ אָמַר יֵרֶא יְהוָה וְיִדְרֹשׁ:   וַיְהִי ׀
כג לִתְקוּפַת הַשָּׁנָה עָלָה עָלָיו חֵיל אֲרָם וַיָּבֹאוּ אֶל־יְהוּדָה וִירוּשָׁלִַם
כד וַיַּשְׁחִיתוּ אֶת־כָּל־שָׂרֵי הָעָם מֵעָם וְכָל־שְׁלָלָם שִׁלְּחוּ לְמֶלֶךְ דַּרְמָשֶׂק: כִּי
בְמִצְעַר אֲנָשִׁים בָּאוּ ׀ חֵיל אֲרָם וַיהוָה נָתַן בְּיָדָם חַיִל לָרֹב מְאֹד כִּי עָזְבוּ
כה אֶת־יְהוָה אֱלֹהֵי אֲבוֹתֵיהֶם וְאֶת־יוֹאָשׁ עָשׂוּ שְׁפָטִים: וּבְלֶכְתָּם מִמֶּנּוּ כִּי־
עָזְבוּ אֹתוֹ בְּמַחֲלֻיִים רַבִּים הִתְקַשְּׁרוּ עָלָיו עֲבָדָיו בִּדְמֵי בְּנֵי יְהוֹיָדָע הַכֹּהֵן
וַיַּהַרְגֻהוּ עַל־מִטָּתוֹ וַיָּמֹת וַיִּקְבְּרֻהוּ בְּעִיר דָּוִיד וְלֹא קְבָרֻהוּ בְּקִבְרוֹת
כו הַמְּלָכִים: וְאֵלֶּה הַמִּתְקַשְּׁרִים עָלָיו זָבָד בֶּן־שִׁמְעָת הָעַמּוֹנִית וִיהוֹזָבָד
כז בֶּן־שִׁמְרִית הַמּוֹאָבִית: וּבָנָיו °ורב [יֶרֶב ק] הַמַּשָּׂא עָלָיו וִיסוֹד בֵּית
הָאֱלֹהִים הִנָּם כְּתוּבִים עַל־מִדְרַשׁ סֵפֶר הַמְּלָכִים וַיִּמְלֹךְ אֲמַצְיָהוּ בְנוֹ
תַּחְתָּיו:

כה א בֶּן־עֶשְׂרִים וְחָמֵשׁ שָׁנָה מָלַךְ אֲמַצְיָהוּ וְעֶשְׂרִים
ב וָתֵשַׁע שָׁנָה מָלַךְ בִּירוּשָׁלִָם וְשֵׁם אִמּוֹ יְהוֹעַדָּן מִירוּשָׁלָיִם: וַיַּעַשׂ הַיָּשָׁר
ג בְּעֵינֵי יְהוָה רַק לֹא בְּלֵבָב שָׁלֵם: וַיְהִי כַּאֲשֶׁר חָזְקָה הַמַּמְלָכָה עָלָיו וַיַּהֲרֹג
ד אֶת־עֲבָדָיו הַמַּכִּים אֶת־הַמֶּלֶךְ אָבִיו: וְאֶת־בְּנֵיהֶם לֹא הֵמִית כִּי כַכָּתוּב
בַּתּוֹרָה בְּסֵפֶר מֹשֶׁה אֲשֶׁר־צִוָּה יְהוָה לֵאמֹר לֹא־יָמוּתוּ אָבוֹת עַל־בָּנִים
ה וּבָנִים לֹא־יָמוּתוּ עַל־אָבוֹת כִּי אִישׁ בְּחֶטְאוֹ יָמוּתוּ:   וַיִּקְבֹּץ
אֲמַצְיָהוּ אֶת־יְהוּדָה וַיַּעֲמִידֵם לְבֵית־אָבוֹת לְשָׂרֵי הָאֲלָפִים וּלְשָׂרֵי
הַמֵּאוֹת לְכָל־יְהוּדָה וּבִנְיָמִן וַיִּפְקְדֵם לְמִבֶּן עֶשְׂרִים שָׁנָה וָמַעְלָה

24:17. By ingratiating themselves to the king, the leaders influenced him to follow their advice and accept the idols of the neighboring peoples (*Radak*).

24:23. A year after Zechariah's murder.

24:25. The plural "sons" implies that after the murder of Zechariah, Joash ordered that Jehoiada's other sons be killed.

25:4. *Deuteronomy* 24:16.

25:5. To wage war against Edom.

the remaining money before the king and Jehoiada, who made it into utensils for the Temple of HASHEM — ministering vessels, mortars, pans, and golden and silver instruments. They continually offered burnt-offerings in the Temple of HASHEM all the days of Jehoiada.

15 Jehoiada grew old, sated with years, and he died. He was a hundred and thirty years old when he died. 16 They buried him in the City of David with the kings, for he had been benevolent towards Israel and towards God and His Temple.

Desertion of God
17 After Jehoiada died, the leaders of Judah came and prostrated themselves to the king; from then on the king listened to them. * 18 They forsook the Temple of HASHEM, the God of their fathers, and worshiped the asherah-trees and the idols; there was [Divine] fury against Judah and Jerusalem for this transgression of theirs. 19 He sent prophets among them to bring them back to HASHEM and they admonished them, but they did not listen.

Zechariah, Kohen and prophet, assassinated
20 A spirit of God came over Zechariah son of Jehoiada the Kohen. He stood above the people and said to them, "Thus said God: Why are you transgressing the commandments of HASHEM? You will not succeed, for you have forsaken HASHEM, so He has forsaken you!" 21 But they conspired against him and stoned him with rocks, by the command of the king, in the Courtyard of the Temple of HASHEM. 22 Thus King Joash did not remember the kindness that [Zechariah's] father Jehoiada had done for him, and he killed his son. As he was dying he said, "May God see this and demand redress!"

Aram invades
23 It happened at the turn of the year* that the army of Aram attacked [Joash]. They invaded Judah and Jerusalem and destroyed all the officers of the people from among the people, and they sent all their spoils to the king of Damascus. 24 For with a small force of men had the army of Aram come, but HASHEM delivered a great deal of wealth into their hands, for [Israel] had forsaken HASHEM, God of their fathers. They also executed judgment against Joash. 25 When they went away from him — for they left him with many wounds — his servants rebelled against him because of the blood of the sons* of Jehoiada the Kohen, and they killed him on his bed and he died. They buried him in the City of David, although they did not bury him in the tombs of the kings.

Joash assassinated
26 These are the men who rebelled against him: Zabad, son of Shimeath the Ammonite, and Jehozabad son of Shimrith the Moabite. 27 [The story of] his sons, the multitude of prophecies against him, and the establishment of the Temple of God — behold they are recorded in the Narration of the Book of Kings. His son Amaziah reigned in his place.

(See Appendix A, timeline 4)

25

KING AMAZIAH
25:1-28

1 At twenty-five years of age Amaziah became king, and he reigned for twenty-nine years in Jerusalem. His mother's name was Jehoaddan of Jerusalem. 2 He did what was proper in the eyes of HASHEM, but not with a perfect heart. 3 It happened that when the kingship became firmly established with him, he killed his servants who had assassinated his father, the king, 4 but he did not put their sons to death, as it is written in the Torah — in the Book of Moses — which HASHEM had commanded, saying, "Fathers shall not die because of sons, and sons shall not die because of fathers; rather a man should die for his own sin."*

Amaziah avenges his father's death

5 Amaziah gathered Judah together* and he organized them according to their paternal families, under officers of thousands and officers of hundreds, for all of Judah and Benjamin. He counted them from the age of twenty years and up,

וַיִּמְצָאֵם שְׁלֹשׁ־מֵאוֹת אֶלֶף בָּחוּר יוֹצֵא צָבָא צָבָא אֹחֵז רֹמַח וְצִנָּה: וַיִּשְׂכֹּר ו

מִיִּשְׂרָאֵל מֵאָה אֶלֶף גִּבּוֹר חָיִל בְּמֵאָה כִכַּר־כָּסֶף: וְאִישׁ הָאֱלֹהִים בָּא ז

אֵלָיו לֵאמֹר הַמֶּלֶךְ אַל־יָבֹא עִמְּךָ צְבָא יִשְׂרָאֵל כִּי אֵין יהוה עִם־יִשְׂרָאֵל

כֹּל בְּנֵי אֶפְרָיִם: כִּי אִם־בֹּא אַתָּה עֲשֵׂה חֲזַק לַמִּלְחָמָה יַכְשִׁילְךָ הָאֱלֹהִים ח

לִפְנֵי אוֹיֵב כִּי יֶשׁ־כֹּחַ בֵּאלֹהִים לַעְזוֹר וּלְהַכְשִׁיל: וַיֹּאמֶר אֲמַצְיָהוּ לְאִישׁ ט

הָאֱלֹהִים וּמַה־לַּעֲשׂוֹת לִמְאַת הַכִּכָּר אֲשֶׁר נָתַתִּי לִגְדוּד יִשְׂרָאֵל וַיֹּאמֶר

אִישׁ הָאֱלֹהִים יֵשׁ לַיהוה לָתֶת לְךָ הַרְבֵּה מִזֶּה: וַיַּבְדִּילֵם אֲמַצְיָהוּ י

לְהַגְּדוּד אֲשֶׁר־בָּא אֵלָיו מֵאֶפְרַיִם לָלֶכֶת לִמְקוֹמָם וַיִּחַר אַפָּם מְאֹד

בִּיהוּדָה וַיָּשׁוּבוּ לִמְקוֹמָם בׇּחֳרִי־אָף:　　　　וַאֲמַצְיָהוּ הִתְחַזַּק וַיִּנְהַג אֶת־ יא

עַמּוֹ וַיֵּלֶךְ גֵּיא הַמֶּלַח וַיַּךְ אֶת־בְּנֵי־שֵׂעִיר עֲשֶׂרֶת אֲלָפִים: וַעֲשֶׂרֶת אֲלָפִים יב

חַיִּים שָׁבוּ בְּנֵי יְהוּדָה וַיְבִיאוּם לְרֹאשׁ הַסָּלַע וַיַּשְׁלִיכוּם מֵרֹאשׁ הַסֶּלַע

וְכֻלָּם נִבְקָעוּ:　　וּבְנֵי הַגְּדוּד אֲשֶׁר הֵשִׁיב אֲמַצְיָהוּ מִלֶּכֶת עִמּוֹ לַמִּלְחָמָה יג

וַיִּפְשְׁטוּ בְּעָרֵי יְהוּדָה מִשֹּׁמְרוֹן וְעַד־בֵּית חוֹרוֹן וַיַּכּוּ מֵהֶם שְׁלֹשֶׁת אֲלָפִים

וַיָּבֹזּוּ בִּזָּה רַבָּה:　　　　וַיְהִי אַחֲרֵי בוֹא אֲמַצְיָהוּ מֵהַכּוֹת אֶת־אֲדוֹמִים יד

וַיָּבֵא אֶת־אֱלֹהֵי בְּנֵי שֵׂעִיר וַיַּעֲמִידֵם לוֹ לֵאלֹהִים וְלִפְנֵיהֶם יִשְׁתַּחֲוֶה

וְלָהֶם יְקַטֵּר: וַיִּחַר־אַף יהוה בַּאֲמַצְיָהוּ וַיִּשְׁלַח אֵלָיו נָבִיא וַיֹּאמֶר לוֹ לָמָה טו

דָרַשְׁתָּ אֶת־אֱלֹהֵי הָעָם אֲשֶׁר לֹא־הִצִּילוּ אֶת־עַמָּם מִיָּדֶךָ: וַיְהִי ׀ בְּדַבְּרוֹ טז

אֵלָיו וַיֹּאמֶר לוֹ הַלְיוֹעֵץ לַמֶּלֶךְ נְתַנּוּךָ חֲדַל־לְךָ לָמָה יַכּוּךָ וַיֶּחְדַּל הַנָּבִיא

וַיֹּאמֶר יָדַעְתִּי כִּי־יָעַץ אֱלֹהִים לְהַשְׁחִיתֶךָ כִּי־עָשִׂיתָ זֹּאת וְלֹא שָׁמַעְתָּ

לַעֲצָתִי:　　　　וַיִּוָּעַץ אֲמַצְיָהוּ מֶלֶךְ יְהוּדָה וַיִּשְׁלַח אֶל־יוֹאָשׁ בֶּן־יְהוֹאָחָז יז

בֶּן־יֵהוּא מֶלֶךְ יִשְׂרָאֵל לֵאמֹר °לך [לְכָה ק] נִתְרָאֶה פָנִים: וַיִּשְׁלַח יוֹאָשׁ יח

מֶלֶךְ־יִשְׂרָאֵל אֶל־אֲמַצְיָהוּ מֶלֶךְ־יְהוּדָה לֵאמֹר הַחוֹחַ אֲשֶׁר בַּלְּבָנוֹן שָׁלַח

אֶל־הָאֶרֶז אֲשֶׁר בַּלְּבָנוֹן לֵאמֹר תְּנָה־אֶת־בִּתְּךָ לִבְנִי לְאִשָּׁה וַתַּעֲבֹר חַיַּת

הַשָּׂדֶה אֲשֶׁר בַּלְּבָנוֹן וַתִּרְמֹס אֶת־הַחוֹחַ: אָמַרְתָּ הִנֵּה הִכִּיתָ אֶת־אֱדוֹם יט

וּנְשָׂאֲךָ לִבְּךָ לְהַכְבִּיד עַתָּה שְׁבָה בְּבֵיתֶךָ לָמָּה תִתְגָּרֶה בְּרָעָה וְנָפַלְתָּ

אַתָּה וִיהוּדָה עִמָּךְ: וְלֹא־שָׁמַע אֲמַצְיָהוּ כִּי מֵהָאֱלֹהִים הִיא לְמַעַן תִּתָּם כ

בְּיָד כִּי דָרְשׁוּ אֵת אֱלֹהֵי אֱדוֹם: וַיַּעַל יוֹאָשׁ מֶלֶךְ־יִשְׂרָאֵל וַיִּתְרָאוּ פָנִים כא

הוּא וַאֲמַצְיָהוּ מֶלֶךְ־יְהוּדָה בְּבֵית שֶׁמֶשׁ אֲשֶׁר לִיהוּדָה: וַיִּנָּגֶף יְהוּדָה לִפְנֵי כב

יִשְׂרָאֵל וַיָּנֻסוּ אִישׁ לְאֹהָלָיו: וְאֵת אֲמַצְיָהוּ מֶלֶךְ־יְהוּדָה בֶּן־יוֹאָשׁ בֶּן־ כג

יְהוֹאָחָז תָּפַשׂ יוֹאָשׁ מֶלֶךְ־יִשְׂרָאֵל בְּבֵית שָׁמֶשׁ וַיְבִיאֵהוּ יְרוּשָׁלִַם וַיִּפְרֹץ

25:7. Since the Northern Kingdom had been established by Jeroboam of Ephraim, it is often called "Ephraim."

25:12. It may be that this barbaric mass execution was intended to convey to Edom in the manner they could best understand that they must become subservient to Judah. However, the Sages teach that God was enraged by this impermissible savagery, and said, "What are these people doing here? Let them go into exile!" Thus, although the exile of Judah was still two hundred years in the future, Amaziah's act set it in motion (see ArtScroll edition of the Book of *Chronicles*).

25:14-15. It may be that Amaziah did not suddenly come to believe in the divinity of idols. Nor did the prophet castigate him for wickedness, only for foolishness (v. 15);

and found them to be three hundred thousand chosen men, ready to go out to war, bearing spear and shield. ⁶ He also hired a hundred thousand mighty warriors from Israel for a hundred talents of silver. ⁷ A man of God came to him

The prophet's warning saying, "O King, let the army of Israel not go with you, for HASHEM is not with Israel, all the children of Ephraim. * ⁸ For if you do go, readying yourself and strengthening yourself for war, God will cause you to fall before the enemy, for God has the power to aid or to bring defeat." ⁹ Amaziah said to the man of God, "What should I do about the hundred talents that I have given to the Israelite troop?" The man of God replied, "HASHEM can give you much more than that!"

Amaziah obeys and succeeds ¹⁰ So Amaziah separated the troop that had come to him from Ephraim, so that they could go to their place. Their wrath burned against Judah and they returned to their place in a rage. ¹¹ Amaziah strengthened himself and led his people, going out to the Valley of Salt, where he struck ten thousand men of the children of Seir. ¹² The children of Judah also captured ten thousand men alive. They brought them to the top of the cliff and threw them off from the top of the cliff, and they all burst open. *

¹³ Meanwhile, the people of the troop whom Amaziah had turned away from going to war with him spread out in the cities of Judah, from Samaria to Beth-horon, and struck down three thousand of them, plundering much booty.

Idolatry ¹⁴ It happened that when Amaziah came back after killing the Edomites, and brought the deities of Edom with him, that he set them up for himself as gods. He would bow down to them and burn incense to them. * ¹⁵ So God became angry with Amaziah. He sent a prophet to him, who said to him, "Why do you seek the gods of [another] nation, who did not save their people from your hands?!" ¹⁶ It happened that when he spoke to him, [Amaziah] said to him, "Did we appoint you as an adviser to the king? Desist, lest they strike you!" So the prophet desisted, but he said, "I know that God has made a plan to destroy you, for you have done this thing, and you have not heeded my counsel!"

Invitation to battle ¹⁷ Amaziah, king of Judah, took counsel and sent messengers to Joash son of Jehoahaz son of Jehu king of Israel saying, "Let us confront one another [in battle]."* ¹⁸ Joash king of Israel sent [word back] to Amaziah king of Judah saying, "The thornbush in Lebanon [once] sent [word] to the cedar of Lebanon, saying, 'Give your daughter to my son for a wife'; the wild beast of Lebanon then came by and trampled the thornbush. ¹⁹ You think, 'Behold, I have struck Edom!' and your heart became arrogant to seek honor. Now stay at home; why should you provoke evil against yourself and be defeated, you and Judah with you?!'

²⁰ But Amaziah did not listen, for it was [ordained] by God, in order to deliver them into [Israel's] hand, for they had sought out the gods of Edom. ²¹ So Joash king of Israel went up and they confronted each other — he and Amaziah king of Judah — in Beth-shemesh, which is in Judah. ²² Judah was defeated

Judah defeated before Israel and they fled, each man to his home. ²³ Joash king of Israel captured Amaziah king of Judah, the son of Joash son of Jehoahaz, * in Beth-shemesh; he then brought him to Jerusalem and he made a breach in

---

he is even described in 15:3 as having been righteous. Rather, Amaziah may have erred in thinking that the "idols" represented God's intermediaries in ruling the earth, a common mistake of the early idolaters (see ibid.).

25:17. Amaziah wanted to avenge that rampage of the Israelite mercenaries, described above, v. 13.

25:23. Jehoahaz was another name for Ahaziah. In Hebrew both names mean "One who holds fast to God."

כד בְּחוֹמַת יְרוּשָׁלִַם מִשַּׁעַר אֶפְרַיִם עַד־שַׁעַר הַפּוֹנֶה אַרְבַּע מֵאוֹת אַמָּה: וְכָל־
הַזָּהָב וְהַכֶּסֶף וְאֵת כָּל־הַכֵּלִים הַנִּמְצְאִים בְּבֵית־הָאֱלֹהִים עִם־עֹבֵד אֱדוֹם

כה וְאֶת־אֹצְרוֹת בֵּית הַמֶּלֶךְ וְאֵת בְּנֵי הַתַּעֲרֻבוֹת וַיָּשָׁב שֹׁמְרוֹן: וַיְחִי
אֲמַצְיָהוּ בֶן־יוֹאָשׁ מֶלֶךְ יְהוּדָה אַחֲרֵי מוֹת יוֹאָשׁ בֶּן־יְהוֹאָחָז מֶלֶךְ יִשְׂרָאֵל

כו חֲמֵשׁ עֶשְׂרֵה שָׁנָה: וְיֶתֶר דִּבְרֵי אֲמַצְיָהוּ הָרִאשֹׁנִים וְהָאַחֲרוֹנִים הֲלֹא הִנָּם

כז כְּתוּבִים עַל־סֵפֶר מַלְכֵי־יְהוּדָה וְיִשְׂרָאֵל: וּמֵעֵת אֲשֶׁר־סָר אֲמַצְיָהוּ
מֵאַחֲרֵי יְהוָה וַיִּקְשְׁרוּ עָלָיו קֶשֶׁר בִּירוּשָׁלִַם וַיָּנָס לָכִישָׁה וַיִּשְׁלְחוּ אַחֲרָיו

כח לָכִישָׁה וַיְמִיתֻהוּ שָׁם: וַיִּשָׂאֻהוּ עַל־הַסּוּסִים וַיִּקְבְּרוּ אֹתוֹ עִם־אֲבֹתָיו בְּעִיר

כו

א יְהוּדָה: וַיִּקְחוּ כָּל־עַם יְהוּדָה אֶת־עֻזִּיָּהוּ וְהוּא בֶּן־שֵׁשׁ עֶשְׂרֵה שָׁנָה

ב וַיַּמְלִיכוּ אֹתוֹ תַּחַת אָבִיו אֲמַצְיָהוּ: הוּא בָּנָה אֶת־אֵילוֹת וַיְשִׁיבֶהָ לִיהוּדָה
אַחֲרֵי שְׁכַב־הַמֶּלֶךְ עִם־אֲבֹתָיו:

ג בֶּן־שֵׁשׁ עֶשְׂרֵה שָׁנָה עֻזִּיָּהוּ בְמָלְכוֹ וַחֲמִשִּׁים וּשְׁתַּיִם שָׁנָה מָלַךְ בִּירוּשָׁלִָם

ד וְשֵׁם אִמּוֹ °יכילְיָה [°יְכָלְיָה ק] מִן־יְרוּשָׁלִָם: וַיַּעַשׂ הַיָּשָׁר בְּעֵינֵי יְהוָה כְּכֹל

ה אֲשֶׁר־עָשָׂה אֲמַצְיָהוּ אָבִיו: וַיְהִי לִדְרֹשׁ אֱלֹהִים בִּימֵי זְכַרְיָהוּ הַמֵּבִין

ו בִּרְאֹת הָאֱלֹהִים וּבִימֵי דָּרְשׁוֹ אֶת־יְהוָה הִצְלִיחוֹ הָאֱלֹהִים: וַיֵּצֵא וַיִּלָּחֶם
בַּפְּלִשְׁתִּים וַיִּפְרֹץ אֶת־חוֹמַת גַּת וְאֵת חוֹמַת יַבְנֵה וְאֵת חוֹמַת אַשְׁדּוֹד

ז וַיִּבְנֶה עָרִים בְּאַשְׁדּוֹד וּבַפְּלִשְׁתִּים: וַיַּעְזְרֵהוּ הָאֱלֹהִים עַל־פְּלִשְׁתִּים וְעַל־

ח °הערביים [°הָעַרְבִים ק] הַיֹּשְׁבִים בְּגוּר־בָּעַל וְהַמְּעוּנִים: וַיִּתְּנוּ הָעַמּוֹנִים

ט מִנְחָה לְעֻזִּיָּהוּ וַיֵּלֶךְ שְׁמוֹ עַד־לְבוֹא מִצְרַיִם כִּי הֶחֱזִיק עַד־לְמָעְלָה: וַיִּבֶן
עֻזִּיָּהוּ מִגְדָּלִים בִּירוּשָׁלִַם עַל־שַׁעַר הַפִּנָּה וְעַל־שַׁעַר הַגַּיְא וְעַל־הַמִּקְצוֹעַ

י וַיְחַזְּקֵם: וַיִּבֶן מִגְדָּלִים בַּמִּדְבָּר וַיַּחְצֹב בֹּרוֹת רַבִּים כִּי מִקְנֶה־רַּב הָיָה לוֹ
וּבַשְּׁפֵלָה וּבַמִּישׁוֹר אִכָּרִים וְכֹרְמִים בֶּהָרִים וּבַכַּרְמֶל כִּי־אֹהֵב אֲדָמָה

יא הָיָה: וַיְהִי לְעֻזִּיָּהוּ חַיִל עֹשֵׂה מִלְחָמָה יוֹצְאֵי צָבָא לִגְדוּד בְּמִסְפַּר
פְּקֻדָּתָם בְּיַד °יעואל [°יְעִיאֵל ק] הַסּוֹפֵר וּמַעֲשֵׂיָהוּ הַשּׁוֹטֵר עַל יַד־חֲנַנְיָהוּ

יב מִשָּׂרֵי הַמֶּלֶךְ: כֹּל מִסְפַּר רָאשֵׁי הָאָבוֹת לְגִבּוֹרֵי חָיִל אַלְפַּיִם וְשֵׁשׁ מֵאוֹת:

יג וְעַל־יָדָם חֵיל צָבָא שְׁלֹשׁ מֵאוֹת אֶלֶף וְשִׁבְעַת אֲלָפִים וַחֲמֵשׁ מֵאוֹת עוֹשֵׂי
מִלְחָמָה בְּכֹחַ חָיִל לַעְזֹר לַמֶּלֶךְ עַל־הָאוֹיֵב: וַיָּכֶן לָהֶם עֻזִּיָּהוּ לְכָל־הַצָּבָא

יד מָגִנִּים וּרְמָחִים וְכוֹבָעִים וְשִׁרְיֹנוֹת וּקְשָׁתוֹת וּלְאַבְנֵי קְלָעִים: וַיַּעַשׂ ׀

טו בִּירוּשָׁלִַם חִשְּׁבֹנוֹת מַחֲשֶׁבֶת חוֹשֵׁב לִהְיוֹת עַל־הַמִּגְדָּלִים וְעַל־הַפִּנּוֹת
לִירוֹא בַּחִצִּים וּבָאֲבָנִים גְּדֹלוֹת וַיֵּצֵא שְׁמוֹ עַד־לְמֵרָחוֹק כִּי־הִפְלִיא לְהֵעָזֵר

טז עַד כִּי־חָזָק: וּכְחֶזְקָתוֹ גָּבַהּ לִבּוֹ עַד־לְהַשְׁחִית וַיִּמְעַל בַּיהוָה אֱלֹהָיו וַיָּבֹא

יז אֶל־הֵיכַל יְהוָה לְהַקְטִיר עַל־מִזְבַּח הַקְּטֹרֶת: וַיָּבֹא אַחֲרָיו עֲזַרְיָהוּ הַכֹּהֵן

25:24. Obed-edom, an influential Levite family (see *I Chronicles* Ch. 26), was apparently in charge of the Temple treasury at the time. According to *Seder Olam*,   Joash died shortly after returning to Samaria, and Amaziah escaped (*Radak*). The "hostage children" were children of senior officers who were kept at the palace to the wall of Jerusalem, from the Ephraim Gate to the Corner Gate, [a distance of] four hundred cubits. ²⁴ And [he took] all the gold and silver and all the articles that were found in the Temple of God with Obed-edom, and the treasuries of the king's palace, along with the "hostage children" and he returned to Samaria. *

²⁵ Amaziah son of Joash king of Judah lived for fifteen years after the death of Joash son of Jehoahaz king of Israel. ²⁶ The rest of the earlier and later deeds of Amaziah — behold, they are recorded in the Book of the Kings of Judah and

Jerusalemites Israel. ²⁷ From the time that Amaziah turned away from HASHEM, they organized
loyal to God a revolt against him in Jerusalem, so he fled to Lachish; but they sent after him to Lachish and killed him there. ²⁸ They carried him with horses, and they buried him in Jerusalem, with his forefathers, in the City of Judah.

26   KING   ¹ All the people of Judah then took Uzziah, who was sixteen years old, and
UZZIAH   crowned him in place of his father Amaziah. ² He built up Eloth, after
26:1-23   having retrieved it for Judah* after King [Amaziah] lay with his fore-
(See Appendix A,
timeline 4)   fathers.

³ Uzziah was sixteen years old when he became king, and he reigned for fifty-two years in Jerusalem. His mother's name was Jecoliah of Jerusalem. ⁴ He did what was proper in the eyes of HASHEM, entirely as his father Amaziah had done. ⁵ He used to seek out God in the days of Zechariah, a man who had understanding in visions of God, and during the years that he sought out HASHEM,
Victory God granted him success. ⁶ He went out and did battle against the Philistines,
against breaching the wall of Gath, the wall of Jabneh and the wall of Ashdod; and he
Philistines built cities in Ashdod and among the Philistines. ⁷ God helped him against the Philistines, against the Arabs who dwelt in Gur-baal, and [against] the Meunim. ⁸ The Ammonites presented a tribute to Uzziah. His fame went as far as the approach to Egypt, for he became exceedingly powerful.

Uzziah's   ⁹ Uzziah built towers in Jerusalem, at the Corner Gate, at the Valley Gate and
towers at the Edge, and he fortified them. ¹⁰ He also built towers in the wilderness. He dug many wells, for he had much livestock in the lowlands and in the plains, as well as field workers and vine dressers in the hills and in the Carmel, for he was a lover of agriculture.

Offensive   ¹¹ Uzziah had an army of warriors, men going out to battle in troops, who were
and counted according to their number by Jeiel the scribe and Maaseiah the officer,
defensive through Hananiah, one of the king's officers. ¹² The total number of the heads of
weaponry families among the mighty warriors was two thousand six hundred. ¹³ Along with them was an army for battle of three hundred seven thousand five hundred, who would wage war with valiant strength, to help the king against the enemy. ¹⁴ Uzziah equipped all the army with shields, spears, helmets, armor, bows and catapults to sling stones. ¹⁵ He installed devices in Jerusalem, designed by creative people, to be stationed on the towers and on the corners [of the wall], to shoot arrows and large rocks. His fame spread far and wide, for he had fortified himself extraordinarily, until he was very strong.

Destructive   ¹⁶ But as he became strong, his heart became haughty to the point of destruc-
haughtiness tiveness, and he betrayed HASHEM his God — he entered the Sanctuary of HASHEM to burn incense upon the Incense Altar. ¹⁷ Azariah the Kohen went after him,

---

assure the loyalty of their parents.
26:2. From the Edomites, who apparently had taken the

city during their rebellion against Judah, as described
above (*Radak*).

יח וְעָמְד֣וּ כֹהֲנִ֣ים לַיהוָה֮ שְׁמוֹנִים֒ בְּנֵי־חָ֑יִל וַיַּעַמְד֞וּ עַל־עֻזִּיָּ֣הוּ הַמֶּ֗לֶךְ וַיֹּ֨אמְרוּ ל֜וֹ לֹא־לְךָ֣ עֻזִּיָּ֗הוּ לְהַקְטִ֣יר לַֽיהוָה֒ כִּ֣י לַכֹּהֲנִ֣ים בְּנֵֽי־אַהֲרֹ֮ן הַמְקֻדָּשִׁים֒ לְהַקְטִ֑יר צֵ֤א מִן־הַמִּקְדָּשׁ֙ כִּ֣י מָעַ֔לְתָּ וְלֹֽא־לְךָ֥ לְכָב֖וֹד מֵיְהוָ֥ה אֱלֹהִֽים:

יט וַיִּזְעַ֣ף עֻזִּיָּ֗הוּ וּבְיָד֤וֹ מִקְטֶ֙רֶת֙ לְהַקְטִ֔יר וּבְזַעְפּ֣וֹ עִם־הַכֹּהֲנִ֗ים וְ֠הַצָּרַעַת זָֽרְחָ֨ה בְמִצְחֹ֜ו לִפְנֵ֣י הַכֹּהֲנִ֗ים בְּבֵ֤ית יְהוָה֙ מֵעַ֣ל לְמִזְבַּ֣ח הַקְּטֹ֔רֶת: וַיִּ֣פֶן אֵלָ֡יו עֲזַרְיָ֩הוּ֩ כֹהֵ֨ן הָרֹ֜אשׁ וְכָל־הַכֹּהֲנִ֗ים וְהִנֵּה־ה֤וּא מְצֹרָע֙ בְּמִצְח֔וֹ וַיַּבְהִל֖וּהוּ

כא מִשָּׁ֑ם וְגַם־הוּא֙ נִדְחַ֣ף לָצֵ֔את כִּ֥י נִגְּע֖וֹ יְהוָֽה: וַיְהִי֩ עֻזִּיָּ֨הוּ הַמֶּ֜לֶךְ מְצֹרָ֣ע ׀ עַד־י֣וֹם מוֹת֗וֹ וַיֵּ֜שֶׁב בֵּ֤ית °הַחָפְשִׁית֙ [°הַֽחָפְשׁ֜וּת ק] מְצֹרָ֔ע כִּ֥י נִגְזַ֖ר מִבֵּ֣ית

כב יְהוָ֑ה וְיוֹתָ֤ם בְּנוֹ֙ עַל־בֵּ֣ית הַמֶּ֔לֶךְ שׁוֹפֵ֖ט אֶת־עַ֥ם הָאָֽרֶץ: וְיֶ֨תֶר֙ דִּבְרֵ֣י עֻזִּיָּ֔הוּ

כג הָרִֽאשֹׁנִ֖ים וְהָאַחֲרֹנִ֑ים כָּתַ֛ב יְשַֽׁעְיָ֥הוּ בֶן־אָמ֖וֹץ הַנָּבִֽיא: וַיִּשְׁכַּ֨ב עֻזִּיָּ֜הוּ עִם־אֲבֹתָ֗יו וַיִּקְבְּר֨וּ אֹת֤וֹ עִם־אֲבֹתָיו֙ בִּשְׂדֵ֤ה הַקְּבוּרָה֙ אֲשֶׁ֣ר לַמְּלָכִ֔ים כִּ֥י אָמְר֖וּ

כז מְצוֹרָ֣ע ה֑וּא וַיִּמְלֹ֛ךְ יוֹתָ֥ם בְּנ֖וֹ תַּחְתָּֽיו: בֶּן־עֶשְׂרִ֨ים וְחָמֵ֤שׁ שָׁנָה֙

א יוֹתָ֣ם בְּמָלְכ֔וֹ וְשֵׁשׁ־עֶשְׂרֵ֣ה שָׁנָ֔ה מָלַ֖ךְ בִּירֽוּשָׁלָ֑͏ִם וְשֵׁ֣ם אִמּ֔וֹ יְרוּשָׁ֖ה בַּת־

ב צָד֑וֹק וַיַּ֨עַשׂ הַיָּשָׁ֜ר בְּעֵינֵ֣י יְהוָ֗ה כְּכֹ֤ל אֲשֶׁר־עָשָׂה֙ עֻזִּיָּ֣הֽוּ אָבִ֔יו רַ֕ק לֹא־בָ֖א

ג אֶל־הֵיכַ֣ל יְהוָ֑ה וְע֥וֹד הָעָ֖ם מַשְׁחִיתִֽים: ה֗וּא בָּנָ֛ה אֶת־שַׁ֥עַר בֵּית־יְהוָ֖ה

ד הָעֶלְי֑וֹן וּבְחוֹמַ֥ת הָעֹ֖פֶל בָּנָ֥ה לָרֹֽב: וְעָרִ֥ים בָּנָ֖ה בְּהַר־יְהוּדָ֑ה וּבֶחֳרָשִׁ֖ים

ה בָּנָ֥ה בִּֽירָנִיּ֖וֹת וּמִגְדָּלִֽים: ֠וְהוּא נִלְחַ֞ם עִם־מֶ֣לֶךְ בְּנֵֽי־עַמּוֹן֮ וַיֶּחֱזַ֣ק עֲלֵיהֶם֒ וַיִּתְּנוּ־ל֨וֹ בְנֵֽי־עַמּ֜וֹן בַּשָּׁנָ֣ה הַהִ֗יא מֵאָה֙ כִּכַּר־כֶּ֔סֶף וַעֲשֶׂ֨רֶת אֲלָפִ֤ים כֹּרִים֙ חִטִּ֔ים וּשְׂעוֹרִ֖ים עֲשֶׂ֣רֶת אֲלָפִ֑ים זֹ֗את הֵשִׁ֤יבוּ לוֹ֙ בְּנֵ֣י עַמּ֔וֹן וּבַשָּׁנָ֥ה הַשֵּׁנִ֖ית

ו וְהַשְּׁלִשִֽׁית: וַיִּתְחַזֵּ֖ק יוֹתָ֑ם כִּ֚י הֵכִ֣ין דְּרָכָ֔יו לִפְנֵ֖י יְהוָ֥ה אֱלֹהָֽיו:

ז וְיֶ֨תֶר֙ דִּבְרֵ֣י יוֹתָ֔ם וְכָל־מִלְחֲמֹתָ֖יו וּדְרָכָ֑יו הִנָּ֣ם כְּתוּבִ֔ים עַל־סֵ֥פֶר מַלְכֵי־

ח יִשְׂרָאֵ֖ל וִיהוּדָֽה: בֶּן־עֶשְׂרִ֧ים וְחָמֵ֛שׁ שָׁנָ֖ה הָיָ֣ה בְמָלְכ֑וֹ וְשֵׁשׁ־עֶשְׂרֵ֣ה שָׁנָ֔ה

ט מָלַ֖ךְ בִּירֽוּשָׁלָֽ͏ִם: וַיִּשְׁכַּ֤ב יוֹתָם֙ עִם־אֲבֹתָ֔יו וַיִּקְבְּר֥וּ אֹת֖וֹ בְּעִ֣יר דָּוִ֑יד וַיִּמְלֹ֛ךְ

א אָחָ֥ז בְּנ֖וֹ תַּחְתָּֽיו: בֶּן־עֶשְׂרִ֤ים שָׁנָה֙ אָחָ֣ז בְּמָלְכ֔וֹ וְשֵׁשׁ־עֶשְׂרֵ֣ה שָׁנָ֔ה מָלַ֖ךְ כח

ב בִּירֽוּשָׁלָ֑͏ִם וְלֹא־עָשָׂ֧ה הַיָּשָׁ֛ר בְּעֵינֵ֥י יְהוָ֖ה כְּדָוִ֣יד אָבִֽיו: וַיֵּ֕לֶךְ בְּדַרְכֵ֖י מַלְכֵ֣י

ג יִשְׂרָאֵ֑ל וְגַ֧ם מַסֵּכ֛וֹת עָשָׂ֖ה לַבְּעָלִֽים: וְה֤וּא הִקְטִיר֙ בְּגֵ֣יא בֶן־הִנֹּ֔ם וַיַּבְעֵ֥ר אֶת־בָּנָ֖יו בָּאֵ֑שׁ כְּתֹֽעֲבוֹת֙ הַגּוֹיִ֔ם אֲשֶׁר֙ הֹרִ֣ישׁ יְהוָ֔ה מִפְּנֵ֖י בְּנֵ֥י יִשְׂרָאֵֽל:

ד וַיְזַבֵּ֧חַ וַיְקַטֵּ֛ר בַּבָּמ֖וֹת וְעַל־הַגְּבָע֑וֹת וְתַ֖חַת כָּל־עֵ֥ץ רַעֲנָֽן: וַֽיִּתְּנֵ֜הוּ יְהוָ֣ה ה

ה אֱלֹהָיו֮ בְּיַ֣ד מֶ֣לֶךְ אֲרָם֒ וַיַּ֨כּוּ־ב֔וֹ וַיִּשְׁבּ֤וּ מִמֶּ֙נּוּ֙ שִׁבְיָ֣ה גְדוֹלָ֔ה וַיָּבִ֖יאוּ דַּרְמָ֑שֶׂק וְ֠גַם בְּיַד־מֶ֤לֶךְ יִשְׂרָאֵל֙ נִתָּ֔ן וַיַּךְ־בּ֖וֹ מַכָּ֥ה גְדוֹלָֽה: וַיַּהֲרֹג֩

ו פֶּ֨קַח בֶּן־רְמַלְיָ֜הוּ בִּיהוּדָ֗ה מֵאָ֨ה וְעֶשְׂרִ֥ים אֶ֙לֶף֙ בְּי֣וֹם אֶחָ֔ד הַכֹּ֖ל בְּנֵי־חָ֑יִל בְּעָזְבָ֕ם

26:21. See *II Kings* 15:5.

26:23. Because of his leprosy, he was not interred with his ancestors *inside* the royal tombs, but was buried in the field where the tombs were located.

27:2. That is, "The high places did not cease; the people still sacrificed and burned incense upon the high places" (*II Kings* 15:35).

27:3. A fortified area of Jerusalem.

28:3. An idolatrous practice (*Deuteronomy* 18:10).

28:6. The king of Israel (*II Kings* 16:5).

The Kohanim remonstrate

along with eighty strong Kohanim of HASHEM. [18] They stood next to King Uzziah and said to him, "It is not for you, Uzziah, to burn incense to HASHEM, but it is for the Kohanim, the descendants of Aaron, who are consecrated, to burn incense. Leave the Temple, for you have been treacherous, and this will not bring you honor from HASHEM, God!" [19] Uzziah became enraged, and he already had a censer in his hand for burning incense. As he was becoming enraged with the

Uzziah's punishment: Leprosy

Kohanim, a leprous growth appeared on his forehead in the presence of the Kohanim in the Temple of HASHEM, near the Incense Altar. [20] Azariah, the chief Kohen, and all the other Kohanim turned to him, and behold he was leprous on his forehead! So they rushed him away from there; he, too, hastened to leave, for HASHEM had afflicted him. [21] King Uzziah was a leper until the day of his death. He dwelt in his leprosy in a place of asylum * for he was banished from the Temple of HASHEM. His son Jotham took charge of the royal house and judged the people of the land.

(See Appendix A, timeline 4)

[22] Isaiah son of Amoz the Prophet recorded the rest of the earlier and later deeds of Uzziah. [23] Uzziah lay with his forefathers and was buried with his forefathers in the burial field of the kings, for they said, "He is a leper." * His son Jotham ruled in his place.

27

KING JOTHAM 27:1-9

[1] Jotham was twenty-five years old when he became king, and he reigned for sixteen years in Jerusalem. His mother's name was Jerushah daughter of Zadok. [2] He did what was proper in the eyes of HASHEM, just as his father Uzziah had done, except that he did not enter the Sanctuary of HASHEM. The people were still acting corruptly. * [3] He built the Upper Gate of the Temple of HASHEM, and he built up the wall of the Ophel * a great deal. [4] He also built cities in the Judean Hills, and he built castles and towers in the forests.

Defeat Ammon

[5] He waged war with the king of the Children of Ammon and overpowered them. The Children of Ammon gave him a hundred talents of silver, ten thousand kors of wheat and ten thousand of barley that year. This is what the Children of Ammon paid him in the second and third year also.

[6] Jotham became strong, for he acted properly before HASHEM his God. [7] The rest of the deeds of Jotham and all his wars and actions — behold, they are recorded in the Book of the Kings of Israel and Judah. [8] He was twenty-five years old when he became king, and he reigned for sixteen years in Jerusalem. [9] Jotham lay with his forefathers and was buried in the City of David. His son Ahaz ruled in his place.

28

KING AHAZ 28:1-27

Baal worship

[1] Ahaz was twenty years old when he became king, and he reigned for sixteen years in Jerusalem. He did not do what is proper in the eyes of HASHEM as David had done. [2] He went in the ways of the kings of Israel; he even made molten idols for Baal. [3] He also burned incense in the Valley of Ben-hinnom and set his sons aflame, * like the abominations of the nations whom HASHEM had driven out before the Children of Israel. [4] He also sacrificed and burned incense at the high places and upon the hilltops and under every leafy tree.

Struck by kings of Aram and Israel

[5] HASHEM his God delivered him into the hand of the king of Aram; [the Aram- eans] struck him and took a large number of captives from him, taking them to Damascus. He was also delivered into the hand of the king of Israel, who delivered a great blow to him. [6] Pekah son of Remaliah * killed a hundred twenty thousand people in Judah in one day, all of them mighty men, for they had forsaken

ז אֶת־יְהֹוָה אֱלֹהֵי אֲבוֹתָם: וַיַּהֲרֹג זִכְרִי ׀ גִּבּוֹר אֶפְרַיִם אֶת־
מַעֲשֵׂיָהוּ בֶּן־הַמֶּלֶךְ וְאֶת־עַזְרִיקָם נְגִיד הַבָּיִת וְאֶת־אֶלְקָנָה מִשְׁנֵה
ח הַמֶּלֶךְ:   וַיִּשְׁבּוּ בְנֵי־יִשְׂרָאֵל מֵאֲחֵיהֶם מָאתַיִם אֶלֶף נָשִׁים בָּנִים
ט וּבָנוֹת וְגַם־שָׁלָל רַב בָּזְזוּ מֵהֶם וַיָּבִיאוּ אֶת־הַשָּׁלָל לְשֹׁמְרוֹן: וְשָׁם
הָיָה נָבִיא לַיהֹוָה עֹדֵד שְׁמוֹ וַיֵּצֵא לִפְנֵי הַצָּבָא הַבָּא לְשֹׁמְרוֹן וַיֹּאמֶר לָהֶם
הִנֵּה בַּחֲמַת יְהֹוָה אֱלֹהֵי־אֲבוֹתֵיכֶם עַל־יְהוּדָה נְתָנָם בְּיֶדְכֶם וַתַּהַרְגוּ־
י בָם בְּזַעַף עַד לַשָּׁמַיִם הִגִּיעַ:   וְעַתָּה בְּנֵי־יְהוּדָה וִירוּשָׁלִַם אַתֶּם אֹמְרִים
לִכְבֹּשׁ לַעֲבָדִים וְלִשְׁפָחוֹת לָכֶם הֲלֹא רַק־אַתֶּם עִמָּכֶם אֲשָׁמוֹת לַיהֹוָה
יא אֱלֹהֵיכֶם: וְעַתָּה שְׁמָעוּנִי וְהָשִׁיבוּ הַשִּׁבְיָה אֲשֶׁר שְׁבִיתֶם מֵאֲחֵיכֶם כִּי
יב חֲרוֹן אַף־יְהֹוָה עֲלֵיכֶם: וַיָּקֻמוּ אֲנָשִׁים מֵרָאשֵׁי בְנֵי־אֶפְרַיִם
עֲזַרְיָהוּ בֶן־יְהוֹחָנָן בֶּרֶכְיָהוּ בֶן־מְשִׁלֵּמוֹת וִיחִזְקִיָּהוּ בֶן־שַׁלֻּם וַעֲמָשָׂא בֶּן־
יג חַדְלָי עַל־הַבָּאִים מִן־הַצָּבָא: וַיֹּאמְרוּ לָהֶם לֹא־תָבִיאוּ אֶת־הַשִּׁבְיָה הֵנָּה
כִּי לְאַשְׁמַת יְהֹוָה עָלֵינוּ אַתֶּם אֹמְרִים לְהֹסִיף עַל־חַטֹּאתֵינוּ וְעַל־
יד אַשְׁמָתֵנוּ כִּי־רַבָּה אַשְׁמָה לָנוּ וַחֲרוֹן אָף עַל־יִשְׂרָאֵל: וַיַּעֲזֹב
טו הֶחָלוּץ אֶת־הַשִּׁבְיָה וְאֶת־הַבִּזָּה לִפְנֵי הַשָּׂרִים וְכָל־הַקָּהָל: וַיָּקֻמוּ
הָאֲנָשִׁים אֲשֶׁר־נִקְּבוּ בְשֵׁמוֹת וַיַּחֲזִיקוּ בַשִּׁבְיָה וְכָל־מַעֲרֻמֵּיהֶם הִלְבִּישׁוּ
מִן־הַשָּׁלָל וַיַּלְבִּשׁוּם וַיַּנְעִלוּם וַיַּאֲכִלוּם וַיַּשְׁקוּם וַיְסֻכוּם וַיְנַהֲלוּם
בַּחֲמֹרִים לְכָל־כּוֹשֵׁל וַיְבִיאוּם יְרֵחוֹ עִיר־הַתְּמָרִים אֵצֶל אֲחֵיהֶם
טז וַיָּשׁוּבוּ שֹׁמְרוֹן: בָּעֵת הַהִיא שָׁלַח הַמֶּלֶךְ אָחָז עַל־מַלְכֵי
יז–יח אַשּׁוּר לַעְזֹר לוֹ:   וְעוֹד אֲדוֹמִים בָּאוּ וַיַּכּוּ בִיהוּדָה וַיִּשְׁבּוּ־שֶׁבִי: וּפְלִשְׁתִּים
פָּשְׁטוּ בְּעָרֵי הַשְּׁפֵלָה וְהַנֶּגֶב לִיהוּדָה וַיִּלְכְּדוּ אֶת־בֵּית־שֶׁמֶשׁ וְאֶת־
אַיָּלוֹן וְאֶת־הַגְּדֵרוֹת וְאֶת־שׂוֹכוֹ וּבְנוֹתֶיהָ וְאֶת־תִּמְנָה וּבְנוֹתֶיהָ וְאֶת־גִּמְזוֹ
יט וְאֶת־בְּנֹתֶיהָ וַיֵּשְׁבוּ שָׁם: כִּי־הִכְנִיעַ יְהֹוָה אֶת־יְהוּדָה בַּעֲבוּר אָחָז מֶלֶךְ
כ יִשְׂרָאֵל כִּי הִפְרִיעַ בִּיהוּדָה וּמָעוֹל מַעַל בַּיהֹוָה: וַיָּבֹא עָלָיו תִּלְּגַת
כא פִּלְנְאֶסֶר מֶלֶךְ אַשּׁוּר וַיָּצַר לוֹ וְלֹא חֲזָקוֹ:   כִּי־חָלַק אָחָז אֶת־בֵּית יְהֹוָה
כב וְאֶת־בֵּית הַמֶּלֶךְ וְהַשָּׂרִים וַיִּתֵּן לְמֶלֶךְ אַשּׁוּר וְלֹא לְעֶזְרָה לוֹ:   וּבְעֵת
הָצֵר לוֹ וַיּוֹסֶף לִמְעוֹל בַּיהֹוָה הוּא הַמֶּלֶךְ אָחָז: וַיִּזְבַּח לֵאלֹהֵי דַרְמֶשֶׂק
כג הַמַּכִּים בּוֹ וַיֹּאמֶר כִּי אֱלֹהֵי מַלְכֵי־אֲרָם הֵם מַעְזְרִים אוֹתָם לָהֶם אֲזַבֵּחַ
כד וִיעְזְרוּנִי וְהֵם הָיוּ־לוֹ לְהַכְשִׁילוֹ וּלְכָל־יִשְׂרָאֵל: וַיֶּאֱסֹף אָחָז אֶת־כְּלֵי
בֵית־הָאֱלֹהִים וַיְקַצֵּץ אֶת־כְּלֵי בֵית־הָאֱלֹהִים וַיִּסְגֹּר אֶת־דַּלְתוֹת בֵּית־
כה יְהֹוָה וַיַּעַשׂ לוֹ מִזְבְּחוֹת בְּכָל־פִּנָּה בִּירוּשָׁלִָם: וּבְכָל־עִיר וָעִיר לִיהוּדָה
עָשָׂה בָמוֹת לְקַטֵּר לֵאלֹהִים אֲחֵרִים וַיַּכְעֵס אֶת־יְהֹוָה אֱלֹהֵי אֲבֹתָיו:

28:15. In v. 12.

28:15. Anointing one's skin with oil was an important facet of personal grooming in those days.

28:16. He sent a large bribe of gold and silver, which he confiscated from the Temple (*II Kings* 16:8).

28:21. His bribe was unsuccessful, because Assyria

HASHEM, God of their fathers. [7] Zichri, a warrior from Ephraim, killed Maaseiah, the king's son, Azrikam, the chamberlain of the palace, and Elkanah, the deputy to the king. [8] The Children of Israel also captured two hundred thousand women, boys and girls. They also plundered much booty from them, and brought the booty to Samaria.

A prophet warns Samaria

[9] There was a prophet of HASHEM there by the name of Oded. He went out before the army that was arriving in Samaria and said to them, "Behold, because of the wrath of HASHEM, God of your fathers, against Judah, He delivered them into your hands, and you killed among them with a rage that reached the very heavens. [10] And now you propose to subjugate the people of Judah and Jerusalem as slaves and maidservants for yourselves — behold, this will only bring guilt upon you to HASHEM, your God. [11] So now, listen to me and return the captives whom you have captured from your brothers, for the burning wrath of HASHEM is upon you!"

Ephraimites obey the prophet

[12] Some men of the heads of the children of Ephraim — Azariah son of Jehohanan, Berechiah son of Meshillemoth, Jehizkiah son of Shallum and Amasa son of Hadlai — stood up over those who had returned from the battle, [13] and they said to them, "Do not bring the captives here, for you are thus proposing to incur guilt from God upon us, to add onto our sins and our guilt, for we have much guilt, and burning wrath is against Israel." [14] Then the fighters released their captives and the spoils before the officers and the entire congregation. [15] The men who had been mentioned by name* then got up and gave assistance to the captives — they dressed all their unclothed people from the spoils. They dressed them, gave them shoes, fed them, gave them to drink, anointed them, * and led all the faint ones on donkeys. They brought them to Jericho, the city of palms, to their kinsmen, and then returned to Samaria.

Ahaz suffers at hands of Edomites, Philistines ...

[16] At that time King Ahaz sent* to the kings of Assyria to come to his aid. [17] Furthermore, the Edomites came and struck Judah and captured captives, [18] and the Philistines spread out in the cities of the lowland and the south of Judah and captured Beth-shemesh, Aijalon, Gederoth, Soco and its villages, Timnah and its villages, and Gimzo and its villages, and they settled there. [19] For HASHEM had humbled Judah because of Ahaz king of Israel, for he had led Judah to disgrace and betrayed HASHEM.

... and Assyria

[20] Tillegath-pilneser, king of Assyria, attacked him and besieged him, but he was not able to overcome him. [21] Although Ahaz had taken a portion from the Temple of HASHEM and from the palaces of the king and the officers, sending it to Assyria, it did not help him. *

Further idolatry

[22] In the midst of his misfortunes he — King Ahaz — added to his betrayal of HASHEM: [23] He sacrificed to the gods of Damascus, who were attacking him, saying, "The gods of the kings of Aram are helping them; I will sacrifice to them so they will help me." But they were a cause of downfall for him and for all of Israel. [24] Ahaz also gathered together the articles of the Temple of God; he cut up the articles of the Temple of God; he shut the doors of the Temple of HASHEM; and he made himself altars at every corner in Jerusalem. [25] In every city in Judah he made high places to burn incense to other gods, angering HASHEM, God of his fathers.

---

attacked him anyway.

כו וְיֶ֣תֶר דְּבָרָ֗יו וְכָל־דְּרָכָ֛יו הָרִאשֹׁנִ֥ים וְהָאַחֲרֹנִ֖ים הִנָּ֣ם כְּתוּבִ֑ים עַל־

כז סֵ֥פֶר מַלְכֵֽי־יְהוּדָ֖ה וְיִשְׂרָאֵֽל: וַיִּשְׁכַּ֨ב אָחָ֜ז עִם־אֲבֹתָ֗יו וַיִּקְבְּרֻ֨הוּ֙ בָעִ֣יר
בִּירוּשָׁלַ֔͏ִם כִּ֣י לֹ֤א הֱבִיאֻ֙הוּ֙ לְקִבְרֵ֖י מַלְכֵ֣י יִשְׂרָאֵ֑ל וַיִּמְלֹ֛ךְ יְחִזְקִיָּ֥הוּ בְנ֖וֹ

כט א תַּחְתָּֽיו: יְחִזְקִיָּ֣הוּ מָלַ֗ךְ בֶּן־עֶשְׂרִ֤ים וְחָמֵשׁ֙ שָׁנָ֔ה וְעֶשְׂרִ֤ים וָתֵ֙שַׁע֙

ב שָׁנָ֔ה מָלַ֖ךְ בִּירוּשָׁלָ֑͏ִם וְשֵׁ֣ם אִמּ֔וֹ אֲבִיָּ֖ה בַּת־זְכַרְיָֽהוּ: וַיַּ֥עַשׂ הַיָּשָׁ֖ר בְּעֵינֵ֣י

ג יְהוָ֑ה כְּכֹ֥ל אֲשֶׁר־עָשָׂ֖ה דָּוִ֥יד אָבִֽיו: ה֣וּא בַשָּׁנָ֣ה הָרִאשֹׁונָ֩ה לְמָלְכ֨וֹ בַּחֹ֤דֶשׁ

ד הָרִאשֹׁון֙ פָּתַ֗ח אֶת־דַּלְת֥וֹת בֵּית־יְהוָ֖ה וַֽיְחַזְּקֵֽם: וַיָּבֵ֥א אֶת־הַכֹּהֲנִ֖ים וְאֶת־

ה הַלְוִיִּ֑ם וַיַּֽאַסְפֵ֖ם לִרְח֥וֹב הַמִּזְרָֽח: וַיֹּ֣אמֶר לָהֶ֗ם שְׁמָע֖וּנִי הַלְוִיִּ֑ם עַתָּ֣ה
הִֽתְקַדְּשׁ֗וּ וְקַדְּשׁוּ֙ אֶת־בֵּ֣ית יְהוָ֔ה אֱלֹהֵ֖י אֲבֹֽתֵיכֶ֑ם וְהוֹצִ֥יאוּ אֶת־הַנִּדָּ֖ה מִן־

ו הַקֹּֽדֶשׁ: כִּֽי־מָעֲל֣וּ אֲבֹתֵ֗ינוּ וְעָשׂ֥וּ הָרַ֛ע בְּעֵינֵ֥י יְהוָֽה־אֱלֹהֵ֖ינוּ וַיַּֽעַזְבֻ֑הוּ וַיַּסֵּ֣בּוּ

ז פְנֵיהֶ֗ם מִמִּשְׁכַּ֤ן יְהוָה֙ וַיִּתְּנוּ־עֹֽרֶף: גַּ֣ם סָֽגְר֞וּ דַּלְת֣וֹת הָֽאוּלָ֗ם וַיְכַבּוּ֙ אֶת־

ח הַנֵּר֔וֹת וּקְטֹ֖רֶת לֹ֣א הִקְטִ֑ירוּ וְעֹלָה֙ לֹא־הֶעֱל֣וּ בַקֹּ֔דֶשׁ לֵֽאלֹהֵ֖י יִשְׂרָאֵֽל: וַיְהִ֤י
קֶ֙צֶף֙ יְהוָ֔ה עַל־יְהוּדָ֖ה וִירֽוּשָׁלָ֑͏ִם וַֽיִּתְּנֵ֤ם °לזועה °לְזַֽעֲוָה ק לְשַׁמָּ֣ה

ט וְלִשְׁרֵקָ֔ה כַּֽאֲשֶׁ֥ר אַתֶּ֖ם רֹאִ֥ים בְּעֵֽינֵיכֶֽם: וְהִנֵּ֛ה נָפְל֥וּ אֲבוֹתֵ֖ינוּ בֶּחָ֑רֶב וּבָנֵ֣ינוּ

י וּבְנוֹתֵ֥ינוּ וְנָשֵׁ֖ינוּ בַּשְּׁבִ֖י עַל־זֹֽאת: עַתָּה֙ עִם־לְבָבִ֔י לִכְר֣וֹת בְּרִ֔ית לַיהוָ֖ה

יא אֱלֹהֵ֣י יִשְׂרָאֵ֔ל וְיָשֹׁ֥ב מִמֶּ֖נּוּ חֲר֣וֹן אַפּֽוֹ: בָּנַ֕י עַתָּ֖ה אַל־תִּשָּׁל֑וּ כִּֽי־בָכֶ֞ם בָּחַ֣ר
יְהוָ֗ה לַֽעֲמֹ֤ד לְפָנָיו֙ לְשָֽׁרְת֔וֹ וְלִֽהְי֥וֹת ל֛וֹ מְשָֽׁרְתִ֖ים וּמַקְטִרִֽים: וַיָּקֻ֣מוּ

יב הַלְוִיִּ֡ם מַ֣חַת בֶּן־עֲ֠מָשַׂ֠י וְיוֹאֵ֨ל בֶּן־עֲזַרְיָ֜הוּ מִן־בְּנֵ֣י הַקְּהָתִ֗י וּמִן־בְּנֵ֣י מְרָרִ֞י
קִ֤ישׁ בֶּן־עַבְדִּי֙ וַֽעֲזַרְיָ֣הוּ בֶּן־יְהַלֶּלְאֵ֔ל וּמִן־הַגֵּֽרְשֻׁנִּ֕י יוֹאָ֖ח בֶּן־זִמָּ֑ה וְעֵ֖דֶן בֶּן־

יג יוֹאָֽח: וּמִן־בְּנֵ֤י אֱלִֽיצָפָן֙ שִׁמְרִ֣י °ויעואל °וִֽיעִיאֵ֔ל ק וּמִן־בְּנֵ֣י אָסָ֔ף זְכַרְיָ֖הוּ

יד וּמַתַּנְיָֽהוּ: וּמִן־בְּנֵ֤י הֵימָן֙ °יחואל °יְחִיאֵ֔ל ק וְשִׁמְעִ֖י וּמִן־בְּנֵ֣י

טו יְדוּת֔וּן שְׁמַֽעְיָ֖ה וְעֻזִּיאֵֽל: וַיַּֽאַסְפ֣וּ אֶת־אֲחֵיהֶ֗ם וַיִּֽתְקַדְּשׁ֛וּ וַיָּבֹ֥אוּ כְמִצְוַת־

טז הַמֶּ֖לֶךְ בְּדִבְרֵ֣י יְהוָ֑ה לְטַהֵ֖ר בֵּ֥ית יְהוָֽה: וַיָּבֹ֣אוּ הַ֠כֹּֽהֲנִ֠ים לִפְנִ֨ימָה בֵית־יְהוָה֮
לְטַהֵר֒ וַיּוֹצִ֗יאוּ אֵ֤ת כָּל־הַטֻּמְאָה֙ אֲשֶׁ֤ר מָֽצְאוּ֙ בְּהֵיכַ֣ל יְהוָ֔ה לַֽחֲצַ֖ר בֵּ֣ית

יז יְהוָ֑ה וַֽיְקַבְּלוּ֙ הַלְוִיִּ֔ם לְהוֹצִ֥יא לְנַֽחַל־קִדְר֖וֹן חֽוּצָה: וַ֠יָּחֵ֠לּוּ בְּאֶחָ֞ד
לַחֹ֣דֶשׁ הָֽרִאשׁ֗וֹן לְקַדֵּ֔שׁ וּבְי֧וֹם שְׁמוֹנָ֣ה לַחֹ֗דֶשׁ בָּ֚אוּ לְאוּלָ֣ם יְהוָ֔ה וַיְקַדְּשׁ֤וּ
אֶת־בֵּֽית־יְהוָה֙ לְיָמִ֣ים שְׁמוֹנָ֔ה וּבְי֛וֹם שִׁשָּׁ֥ה עָשָׂ֛ר לַחֹ֥דֶשׁ הָֽרִאשׁ֖וֹן

יח כִּלּֽוּ: וַיָּב֤וֹאוּ פְנִ֙ימָה֙ אֶל־חִזְקִיָּ֣הוּ הַמֶּ֔לֶךְ וַיֹּ֣אמְר֔וּ טִהַ֖רְנוּ אֶת־כָּל־
בֵּ֣ית יְהוָ֑ה אֶת־מִזְבַּ֤ח הָֽעוֹלָה֙ וְאֶת־כָּל־כֵּלָ֔יו וְאֶת־שֻׁלְחַ֥ן הַֽמַּֽעֲרֶ֖כֶת וְאֶת־

יט כָּל־כֵּלָֽיו: וְאֵ֣ת כָּל־הַכֵּלִ֗ים אֲשֶׁר֩ הִזְנִ֨יחַ הַמֶּ֧לֶךְ אָחָ֛ז בְּמַלְכוּת֖וֹ בְּמַֽעֲל֑וֹ הֵכַ֙נּוּ֙

כ וְהִקְדַּ֔שְׁנוּ וְהִנָּ֕ם לִפְנֵ֖י מִזְבַּ֥ח יְהוָֽה: וַיַּשְׁכֵּם֙ יְחִזְקִיָּ֣הוּ הַמֶּ֔לֶךְ וַיֶּֽאֱסֹ֕ף

כא אֵ֖ת שָׂרֵ֣י הָעִ֑יר וַיַּ֖עַל בֵּ֥ית יְהוָֽה: וַיָּבִ֣יאוּ פָרִֽים־שִׁבְעָה֩ וְאֵילִ֨ים שִׁבְעָ֜ה

28:27. Recognizing his wickedness, the people refused to bury him with such people as David and Solomon. **29:3.** Which had been sealed by his wicked father Ahaz

(28:24). **29:5.** The ritual objects of Ahaz' idolatrous cult. **29:8.** People who hear about us or see our desolation

²⁶ The rest of his deeds and all of his earlier and later ways — behold, they are recorded in the Book of the Kings of Judah and Israel. ²⁷ Ahaz lay with his fore-fathers and they buried him in the city, in Jerusalem, but they did not bring him into the tombs of the kings of Israel. * His son Hezekiah reigned in his place.

(See Appendix A, timeline 4)

29
KING HEZEKIAH
29:1-32:33

¹ Hezekiah was twenty-five years old when he became king, and he reigned for twenty-nine years in Jerusalem. His mother's name was Abijah daughter of Zechariah. ² He did what was proper in the eyes of HASHEM, just as his forefather David had done.

Hezekiah exhorts Kohanim and Levites to cleanse the Temple of idolatry

³ In the first year of his reign, in the first month, he opened up the doors of the Temple of HASHEM* and restored them. ⁴ He then brought the Kohanim and the Levites and assembled them in the eastern plaza. ⁵ He said to them, "Hear me, O Levites! Sanctify yourselves now, and sanctify the Temple of HASHEM, God of your fathers, removing all the contamination* from the Sanctuary. ⁶ For our fathers have been treacherous, doing evil in the eyes of HASHEM, our God, and they have forsaken Him; they turned their faces away from the Tabernacle of HASHEM and turned their backs [to it]. ⁷ They also shut the doors of the [Sanctuary's] Hall and extinguished the lamps; they did not burn incense, nor did they bring up burnt-offerings to the God of Israel in the Sanctuary. ⁸ And the rage of HASHEM was upon Judah and Jerusalem, and He caused them to be a horror, a desolation and a cause for whistling, * as you see with your own eyes. ⁹ Behold, our fathers have fallen by the sword, and our sons, our daughters and our wives are in captivity because of this! ¹⁰ Now it is in my heart to seal a covenant to HASHEM, the God of Israel, so that His burning wrath may recede from us. ¹¹ My sons, do not be negligent, for HASHEM has chosen you to stand before Him to serve Him and to be ministers and to burn incense." ¹² So the Levites* stood up — Mahath son of Amasai and Joel son of Azariah of the sons of the Kohathites; Kish son of Abdi and Azariah son of Jehallelel of the sons of Merari; Joah son of Zimmah and Eden son of Joah of Gershonites; ¹³ Shimri and Jeiel of the sons of Elizaphan; Zechariah and Mattaniah of the sons of Asaph; ¹⁴ Jehiel and Shimei of the sons of Heman, and Shemaiah and Uzziel of the sons of Jeduthun — ¹⁵ and gathered their kinsmen together, and they sanctified themselves. They then went, according to the command of the king, by the word of HASHEM, to purify the Temple of HASHEM. ¹⁶ The Kohanim went to the innermost part of the Temple of HASHEM to purify it; they moved out all the impure things that they found in the Sanctuary of HASHEM to the Courtyard of the Temple of HASHEM, where the Levites received them to take them outside to the Kidron Ravine.

The Levites obey

The consecration

¹⁷ They began to consecrate on the first [day] of the first month, and on the eighth day of the month they entered the Hall of HASHEM's [Temple] and sanctified the Temple of HASHEM for eight days; on the sixteenth day of the first month they finished.

¹⁸ They then came to the inner chamber to King Hezekiah and said, "We have purified the entire Temple of HASHEM, the Altar of Burnt-Offerings and all its utensils, and the Table of the Stacks and all its utensils; ¹⁹ we have also restored and sanctified all the articles that King Ahaz had caused to be abandoned during his reign, in his treachery, and behold, they are before the Altar of HASHEM."

²⁰ King Hezekiah arose early and gathered all the leaders of the city and ascended to the Temple of HASHEM. ²¹ They brought seven bulls, seven rams

---

whistle in amazement.   **29:12.** But not the Kohanim (see v. 34).

וּכְבָשִׂים שִׁבְעָה וּצְפִירֵי עִזִּים שִׁבְעָה לְחַטָּאת עַל־הַמַּמְלָכָה וְעַל־
הַמִּקְדָּשׁ וְעַל־יְהוּדָה וַיֹּאמֶר לִבְנֵי אַהֲרֹן הַכֹּהֲנִים לְהַעֲלוֹת עַל־מִזְבַּח
כב יְהוָה: וַיִּשְׁחֲטוּ הַבָּקָר וַיְקַבְּלוּ הַכֹּהֲנִים אֶת־הַדָּם וַיִּזְרְקוּ הַמִּזְבֵּחָה וַיִּשְׁחֲטוּ
הָאֵלִים וַיִּזְרְקוּ הַדָּם הַמִּזְבֵּחָה וַיִּשְׁחֲטוּ הַכְּבָשִׂים וַיִּזְרְקוּ הַדָּם הַמִּזְבֵּחָה:
כג וַיַּגִּישׁוּ אֶת־שְׂעִירֵי הַחַטָּאת לִפְנֵי הַמֶּלֶךְ וְהַקָּהָל וַיִּסְמְכוּ יְדֵיהֶם עֲלֵיהֶם:
כד וַיִּשְׁחָטוּם הַכֹּהֲנִים וַיְחַטְּאוּ אֶת־דָּמָם הַמִּזְבֵּחָה לְכַפֵּר עַל־כָּל־יִשְׂרָאֵל כִּי
כה לְכָל־יִשְׂרָאֵל אָמַר הַמֶּלֶךְ הָעוֹלָה וְהַחַטָּאת: וַיַּעֲמֵד אֶת־הַלְוִיִּם בֵּית
יְהוָה בִּמְצִלְתַּיִם בִּנְבָלִים וּבְכִנֹּרוֹת בְּמִצְוַת דָּוִיד וְגָד חֹזֵה־הַמֶּלֶךְ וְנָתָן
הַנָּבִיא כִּי בְיַד־יְהוָה הַמִּצְוָה בְּיַד־נְבִיאָיו:
כו־כז וַיַּעַמְדוּ הַלְוִיִּם בִּכְלֵי דָוִיד וְהַכֹּהֲנִים בַּחֲצֹצְרוֹת: וַיֹּאמֶר
חִזְקִיָּהוּ לְהַעֲלוֹת הָעֹלָה לְהַמִּזְבֵּחַ וּבְעֵת הֵחֵל הָעוֹלָה הֵחֵל שִׁיר־יְהוָה
כח וְהַחֲצֹצְרוֹת וְעַל־יְדֵי כְּלֵי דָּוִיד מֶלֶךְ־יִשְׂרָאֵל: וְכָל־הַקָּהָל מִשְׁתַּחֲוִים
וְהַשִּׁיר מְשׁוֹרֵר וְהַחֲצֹצְרוֹת °מַחְצְרִים [°מַחְצְרִים ק] הַכֹּל עַד לִכְלוֹת
כט הָעֹלָה: וּכְכַלּוֹת לְהַעֲלוֹת כָּרְעוּ הַמֶּלֶךְ וְכָל־הַנִּמְצְאִים אִתּוֹ וַיִּשְׁתַּחֲווּ:
ל וַיֹּאמֶר יְחִזְקִיָּהוּ הַמֶּלֶךְ וְהַשָּׂרִים לַלְוִיִּם לְהַלֵּל לַיהוָה בְּדִבְרֵי דָוִיד וְאָסָף
לא הַחֹזֶה וַיְהַלְלוּ עַד־לְשִׂמְחָה וַיִּקְּדוּ וַיִּשְׁתַּחֲווּ: וַיַּעַן יְחִזְקִיָּהוּ
וַיֹּאמֶר עַתָּה מִלֵּאתֶם יֶדְכֶם לַיהוָה גֹּשׁוּ וְהָבִיאוּ זְבָחִים וְתוֹדוֹת לְבֵית
לב יְהוָה וַיָּבִיאוּ הַקָּהָל זְבָחִים וְתוֹדוֹת וְכָל־נְדִיב לֵב עֹלוֹת: וַיְהִי מִסְפַּר
הָעֹלָה אֲשֶׁר הֵבִיאוּ הַקָּהָל בָּקָר שִׁבְעִים אֵילִים מֵאָה כְּבָשִׂים מָאתָיִם
לג לְעֹלָה לַיהוָה כָּל־אֵלֶּה: וְהַקֳּדָשִׁים בָּקָר שֵׁשׁ מֵאוֹת וְצֹאן שְׁלֹשֶׁת אֲלָפִים:
לד רַק הַכֹּהֲנִים הָיוּ לִמְעָט וְלֹא יָכְלוּ לְהַפְשִׁיט אֶת־כָּל־הָעֹלוֹת וַיְחַזְּקוּם
אֲחֵיהֶם הַלְוִיִּם עַד־כְּלוֹת הַמְּלָאכָה וְעַד יִתְקַדְּשׁוּ הַכֹּהֲנִים כִּי הַלְוִיִּם
לה יִשְׁרֵי לֵבָב לְהִתְקַדֵּשׁ מֵהַכֹּהֲנִים: וְגַם־עֹלָה לָרֹב בְּחֶלְבֵי הַשְּׁלָמִים
לו וּבַנְּסָכִים לָעֹלָה וַתִּכּוֹן עֲבוֹדַת בֵּית־יְהוָה: וַיִּשְׂמַח יְחִזְקִיָּהוּ וְכָל־הָעָם
א עַל הַהֵכִין הָאֱלֹהִים לָעָם כִּי בְּפִתְאֹם הָיָה הַדָּבָר: וַיִּשְׁלַח
יְחִזְקִיָּהוּ עַל־כָּל־יִשְׂרָאֵל וִיהוּדָה וְגַם־אִגְּרוֹת כָּתַב עַל־אֶפְרַיִם וּמְנַשֶּׁה
לָבוֹא לְבֵית־יְהוָה בִּירוּשָׁלַ͏ִם לַעֲשׂוֹת פֶּסַח לַיהוָה אֱלֹהֵי יִשְׂרָאֵל:
ב וַיִּוָּעַץ הַמֶּלֶךְ וְשָׂרָיו וְכָל־הַקָּהָל בִּירוּשָׁלַ͏ִם לַעֲשׂוֹת הַפֶּסַח בַּחֹדֶשׁ
ג הַשֵּׁנִי: כִּי לֹא יָכְלוּ לַעֲשֹׂתוֹ בָּעֵת הַהִיא כִּי הַכֹּהֲנִים לֹא־הִתְקַדְּשׁוּ לְמַדַּי

ל

29:25. The divisions of Levites into twenty-four family groups was ordained by David, in accordance with the dictates of these two prophets. See *I Chronicles* Chs. 24-25.

29:26. David designed special musical instruments for the Temple (see *I Chronicles* 23:5, and above 7:6).

29:31. It was only the people with "generous hearts" who brought burnt-offerings, which, unlike other offerings, are completely burned and not eaten.

29:35. This explains why the *Kohanim* needed so much help; everything mentioned here had to be brought to the top of the Altar, which only they could do (*Ralbag*).

29:36. All this was done at the start of Hezekiah's reign, and was possible only because God had assisted them.

30:2. That is, they decided to declare a leap year, so that the previous month would become Adar II of the previous year, and the current month would be Nissan of the new and seven sheep — and seven he-goats for a sin-offering for the kingdom, for the Temple and for Judah. He told the sons of Aaron, the Kohanim, to offer them up on the Altar of HASHEM. [22] So the bulls were slaughtered and the Kohanim collected the blood and threw it onto the Altar; the rams were slaughtered and they threw the blood upon the Altar; and the sheep were slaughtered and they threw the blood upon the Altar. [23] The goats of the sin-offering were then brought forth before the king and the congregation, and they leaned their hands upon them. [24] The Kohanim then slaughtered them and smeared their blood on the Altar, to atone for all of Israel, for the king said, "The burnt-offering and the sin-offering are for all of Israel." [25] He stationed the Levites in the Temple of HASHEM with cymbals, lyres and harps, according to the designations of David and Gad, the Seer of King [David], and Nathan the Prophet, * for it was from HASHEM that these designations were given, through His prophets. [26] The Levites stood with the [musical] instruments of David, * and the Kohanim with the trumpets. [27] Hezekiah gave the command to offer the burnt-offering upon the Altar, and as the offering of the burnt-offering began, the song to HASHEM began, with the trumpets and with the instruments of David, king of Israel. [28] All the congregation were bowing down, the song was being sung and the trumpets were blowing — all this until the burnt-offering was finished. [29] When it was finished being offered up, the king and all those who were with him knelt down and prostrated themselves. [30] King Hezekiah and the leaders then gave the command to the Levites to sing praises to HASHEM with the words of David and Asaph the Seer, so they sang praises until the point of exultation, and they bowed down and prostrated themselves.

[31] Hezekiah spoke up and said, "Now you have consecrated yourselves to HASHEM; approach and bring [peace-]offerings and thanksgiving-offerings to the Temple of HASHEM." So the congregation brought [peace-]offerings and thanksgiving-offerings, and all those with generous hearts brought burnt-offerings. * [32] The number of burnt-offerings that the congregation brought was: seventy bulls, a hundred rams and two hundred sheep — all these for a burnt-offering to HASHEM. [33] And the [other] sacrifices: Six hundred bulls and three thousand sheep. [34] However, the Kohanim were too few, and they could not flay all the burnt-offerings, so their kinsmen the Levites assisted them until the work was done, until the Kohanim could sanctify themselves, for the Levites had been more upright of heart about sanctifying themselves than the Kohanim were. [35] Also, there was an abundance of burnt-offerings, along with fats of peace-offerings and libations for offering up. *

The service in the Temple of HASHEM was thus re-established. [36] Hezekiah and all the people rejoiced that God had enabled the people to prepare, for the matter was undertaken suddenly. *

30

The pesach-offering

[1] **H**ezekiah then sent word to all of Israel and Judah, and also wrote letters to Ephraim and Manasseh to come to the Temple of HASHEM in Jerusalem to perform the pesach-offering to HASHEM, God of Israel. [2] For the king and his officers and all the congregation had conferred and decided to perform the pesach-offering in the second month, * [3] for they had not been able to perform it at its [proper] time, for the Kohanim had not yet sanctified themselves in sufficient numbers,

---

year. For the full halachic discussion, see *Sanhedrin* 12a-b.

ד וְהָעָם לֹא־נֶאֶסְפוּ לִירוּשָׁלָ͏ִם: וַיִּישַׁר הַדָּבָר בְּעֵינֵי הַמֶּלֶךְ וּבְעֵינֵי כָּל־
ה הַקָּהָל: וַיַּעֲמִידוּ דָבָר לְהַעֲבִיר קוֹל בְּכָל־יִשְׂרָאֵל מִבְּאֵר־שֶׁבַע וְעַד־דָּן לָבוֹא לַעֲשׂוֹת פֶּסַח לַיהוָה אֱלֹהֵי־יִשְׂרָאֵל בִּירוּשָׁלָ͏ִם כִּי לֹא לָרֹב עָשׂוּ
ו כַּכָּתוּב: וַיֵּלְכוּ הָרָצִים בָּאִגְּרוֹת מִיַּד הַמֶּלֶךְ וְשָׂרָיו בְּכָל־יִשְׂרָאֵל וִיהוּדָה וּכְמִצְוַת הַמֶּלֶךְ לֵאמֹר בְּנֵי יִשְׂרָאֵל שׁוּבוּ אֶל־יְהוָה אֱלֹהֵי אַבְרָהָם יִצְחָק
ז וְיִשְׂרָאֵל וְיָשֹׁב אֶל־הַפְּלֵיטָה הַנִּשְׁאֶרֶת לָכֶם מִכַּף מַלְכֵי אַשּׁוּר: וְאַל־תִּהְיוּ כַּאֲבוֹתֵיכֶם וְכַאֲחֵיכֶם אֲשֶׁר מָעֲלוּ בַּיהוָה אֱלֹהֵי אֲבוֹתֵיהֶם וַיִּתְּנֵם לְשַׁמָּה
ח כַּאֲשֶׁר אַתֶּם רֹאִים: עַתָּה אַל־תַּקְשׁוּ עָרְפְּכֶם כַּאֲבוֹתֵיכֶם תְּנוּ־יָד לַיהוָה וּבֹאוּ לְמִקְדָּשׁוֹ אֲשֶׁר הִקְדִּישׁ לְעוֹלָם וְעִבְדוּ אֶת־יְהוָה אֱלֹהֵיכֶם וְיָשֹׁב
ט מִכֶּם חֲרוֹן אַפּוֹ: כִּי בְשׁוּבְכֶם עַל־יְהוָה אֲחֵיכֶם וּבְנֵיכֶם לְרַחֲמִים לִפְנֵי שׁוֹבֵיהֶם וְלָשׁוּב לָאָרֶץ הַזֹּאת כִּי־חַנּוּן וְרַחוּם יְהוָה אֱלֹהֵיכֶם וְלֹא־יָסִיר
י פָּנִים מִכֶּם אִם־תָּשׁוּבוּ אֵלָיו: וַיִּהְיוּ הָרָצִים עֹבְרִים מֵעִיר ׀ לָעִיר בְּאֶרֶץ־אֶפְרַיִם וּמְנַשֶּׁה וְעַד־זְבֻלוּן וַיִּהְיוּ מַשְׂחִיקִים עֲלֵיהֶם וּמַלְעִגִים בָּם:
יא-יב אַךְ־אֲנָשִׁים מֵאָשֵׁר וּמְנַשֶּׁה וּמִזְּבֻלוּן נִכְנְעוּ וַיָּבֹאוּ לִירוּשָׁלָ͏ִם: גַּם בִּיהוּדָה הָיְתָה יַד הָאֱלֹהִים לָתֵת לָהֶם לֵב אֶחָד לַעֲשׂוֹת מִצְוַת הַמֶּלֶךְ וְהַשָּׂרִים
יג בִּדְבַר יְהוָה: וַיֵּאָסְפוּ יְרוּשָׁלַ͏ִם עַם־רָב לַעֲשׂוֹת אֶת־חַג הַמַּצּוֹת בַּחֹדֶשׁ
יד הַשֵּׁנִי קָהָל לָרֹב מְאֹד: וַיָּקֻמוּ וַיָּסִירוּ אֶת־הַמִּזְבְּחוֹת אֲשֶׁר בִּירוּשָׁלָ͏ִם וְאֵת
טו כָּל־הַמְקַטְּרוֹת הֵסִירוּ וַיַּשְׁלִיכוּ לְנַחַל קִדְרוֹן: וַיִּשְׁחֲטוּ הַפֶּסַח בְּאַרְבָּעָה עָשָׂר לַחֹדֶשׁ הַשֵּׁנִי וְהַכֹּהֲנִים וְהַלְוִיִּם נִכְלְמוּ וַיִּתְקַדְּשׁוּ וַיָּבִיאוּ עֹלוֹת בֵּית
טז יְהוָה: וַיַּעַמְדוּ עַל־עָמְדָם כְּמִשְׁפָּטָם כְּתוֹרַת מֹשֶׁה אִישׁ־הָאֱלֹהִים הַכֹּהֲנִים
יז זֹרְקִים אֶת־הַדָּם מִיַּד הַלְוִיִּם: כִּי־רַבַּת בַּקָּהָל אֲשֶׁר לֹא־הִתְקַדָּשׁוּ
יח וְהַלְוִיִּם עַל־שְׁחִיטַת הַפְּסָחִים לְכֹל לֹא טָהוֹר לְהַקְדִּישׁ לַיהוָה: כִּי מַרְבִּית הָעָם רַבַּת מֵאֶפְרַיִם וּמְנַשֶּׁה יִשָּׂשכָר וּזְבֻלוּן לֹא הִטֶּהָרוּ כִּי־אָכְלוּ אֶת־הַפֶּסַח בְּלֹא כַכָּתוּב כִּי הִתְפַּלֵּל יְחִזְקִיָּהוּ עֲלֵיהֶם לֵאמֹר יְהוָה
יט הַטּוֹב יְכַפֵּר בְּעַד: כָּל־לְבָבוֹ הֵכִין לִדְרוֹשׁ הָאֱלֹהִים ׀ יְהוָה אֱלֹהֵי אֲבוֹתָיו
כ וְלֹא כְּטָהֳרַת הַקֹּדֶשׁ: וַיִּשְׁמַע יְהוָה אֶל־יְחִזְקִיָּהוּ וַיִּרְפָּא אֶת־
כא הָעָם: וַיַּעֲשׂוּ בְנֵי־יִשְׂרָאֵל הַנִּמְצְאִים בִּירוּשָׁלַ͏ִם אֶת־חַג הַמַּצּוֹת שִׁבְעַת יָמִים בְּשִׂמְחָה גְדוֹלָה וּמְהַלְלִים לַיהוָה יוֹם ׀ בְּיוֹם
כב הַלְוִיִּם וְהַכֹּהֲנִים בִּכְלֵי־עֹז לַיהוָה: וַיְדַבֵּר יְחִזְקִיָּהוּ עַל־לֵב כָּל־הַלְוִיִּם הַמַּשְׂכִּילִים שֵׂכֶל־טוֹב לַיהוָה וַיֹּאכְלוּ אֶת־הַמּוֹעֵד שִׁבְעַת הַיָּמִים

30:5. It had been many years since they had fulfilled the Torah's commandment to bring the offering.

30:6. Although the Ten Tribes had not yet been exiled, they were under Assyrian dominion, and their overlords often took groups of people into exile.

30:15. Not believing that Hezekiah could transform the people so completely in such a short time, many Ko-hanim and Levites had not purified themselves until they saw the immense turnout at the Passover celebration.

30:16. The Levites slaughtered the offerings, since slaughter may be performed by a non-Kohen, and the Kohanim then performed the blood service.

30:18. The Torah forbids impure people to eat sacrificial meat (Leviticus 22:3).

and the people had not been gathered to Jerusalem by then. [4] *The matter was deemed proper by the king and all of the congregation.* [5] *They established the matter to make an announcement throughout all of Israel, from Beer-sheba to Dan, to come and perform the pesach-offering unto HASHEM, God of Israel, in Jerusalem, because for a long time they had not done in accordance with what was written.* *

Letters urging return . . .   [6] *The runners went throughout all of Israel and Judah with the letters from the hand of the king and his leaders, and by order of the king, saying, "Return to HASHEM, the God of Abraham, Isaac and Israel, and He will return to the remnant of you that still remains from the hands of the kings of Assyria.* * [7] *Do not be like your fathers and brothers who betrayed HASHEM, the God of their forefathers, so that He made them into a desolation, as you see.* [8] *Do not stiffen your necks now as your fathers did! Reach out to HASHEM and come to His Sanctuary, which He has sanctified forever, and worship HASHEM, your God, so that His burning wrath may turn away from you!* [9] *For when you return to HASHEM, your brothers and sons will be regarded with mercy by their captors, and [will be allowed] to return to this land, for HASHEM your God is gracious and merciful, and He will not turn His face away from you if you return to Him!"*

. . . are mocked by majority of Ephraim and Manasseh   [10] *The runners passed from city to city in the land of Ephraim and Manasseh, up to Zebulun, but people laughed at them and mocked them.* [11] *However, some people from Asher, Manasseh and Zebulun humbled themselves and came to Jerusalem.* [12] *Also in Judah the hand of God was upon them, instilling them all with a united heart to follow the commandment of the king and the leaders regarding the word of HASHEM.*

The Festival of Matzos   [13] *So a great crowd assembled in Jerusalem to observe the Festival of Matzos in the second month — a very large congregation.* [14] *They got up and removed the altars that were in Jerusalem; they also removed all the incense altars and threw them into the Kidron Ravine.* [15] *They slaughtered the pesach-offering on the fourteenth of the second month, and the Kohanim and Levites felt humiliated and sanctified themselves and brought burnt-offerings to the Temple of HASHEM.* * [16] *They stood at their ordained positions, in accordance with the Torah of Moses, the man of God — the Kohanim threw the blood [on the Altar], [taking it] from the hands of the Levites.* * [17] *For there were many in the congregation who had not sanctified themselves, and the Levites took charge of slaughtering the pesach-offering for anyone who was not pure, to sanctify it to HASHEM.* [18] *For many of the people — many from Ephraim, Manasseh, Issachar and Zebulun — had not purified themselves, and they ate the pesach-offering in accordance with that which is written;* * *but Hezekiah prayed for them, saying, "May the benevolent HASHEM grant atonement for* [19] *whoever sets his heart to seek out God, HASHEM, the God of his forefathers, though without the purity required for the sacred."* [20] *HASHEM listened to Hezekiah and absolved the people.*

[21] *The Children of Israel who were present in Jerusalem observed the Festival of Matzos for seven days with great joy, with the Levites and the Kohanim singing praises to HASHEM each day, playing their instruments with great fervor before HASHEM.* [22] *Hezekiah spoke words of encouragement to all the Levites who taught the good knowledge of HASHEM.* * *They ate the festival [offerings] for seven days,*

30:22. He encouraged them to continue instructing the huge congregation in the Torah throughout the holiday   period (*Ralbag*).

כג מְזַבְּחִים וְזֹבְחֵי שְׁלָמִים וּמִתְוַדִּים לַיהוָה אֱלֹהֵי אֲבוֹתֵיהֶם: וַיִּגְעֲצוּ
כד כָּל־הַקָּהָל לַעֲשׂוֹת שִׁבְעַת יָמִים אֲחֵרִים וַיַּעֲשׂוּ שִׁבְעַת־יָמִים שִׂמְחָה: כִּי
חִזְקִיָּהוּ מֶלֶךְ־יְהוּדָה הֵרִים לַקָּהָל אֶלֶף פָּרִים וְשִׁבְעַת אֲלָפִים צֹאן
וְהַשָּׂרִים הֵרִימוּ לַקָּהָל פָּרִים אֶלֶף וְצֹאן עֲשֶׂרֶת אֲלָפִים וַיִּתְקַדְּשׁוּ כֹהֲנִים
כה לָרֹב: וַיִּשְׂמְחוּ | כָּל־קְהַל יְהוּדָה וְהַכֹּהֲנִים וְהַלְוִיִּם וְכָל־הַקָּהָל הַבָּאִים
כו מִיִּשְׂרָאֵל וְהַגֵּרִים הַבָּאִים מֵאֶרֶץ יִשְׂרָאֵל וְהַיּוֹשְׁבִים בִּיהוּדָה: וַתְּהִי
שִׂמְחָה־גְדוֹלָה בִּירוּשָׁלִָם כִּי מִימֵי שְׁלֹמֹה בֶן־דָּוִיד מֶלֶךְ יִשְׂרָאֵל לֹא
כז כָזֹאת בִּירוּשָׁלִָם: וַיָּקֻמוּ הַכֹּהֲנִים הַלְוִיִּם וַיְבָרְכוּ אֶת־הָעָם

לא

א וַיִּשָּׁמַע בְּקוֹלָם וַתָּבוֹא תְפִלָּתָם לִמְעוֹן קָדְשׁוֹ לַשָּׁמָיִם: וּכְכַלּוֹת
כָּל־זֹאת יָצְאוּ כָל־יִשְׂרָאֵל הַנִּמְצְאִים לְעָרֵי יְהוּדָה וַיְשַׁבְּרוּ הַמַּצֵּבוֹת
וַיְגַדְּעוּ הָאֲשֵׁרִים וַיְנַתְּצוּ אֶת־הַבָּמוֹת וְאֶת־הַמִּזְבְּחֹת מִכָּל־יְהוּדָה וּבִנְיָמִן
וּבְאֶפְרַיִם וּמְנַשֶּׁה עַד־לְכַלֵּה וַיָּשׁוּבוּ כָל־בְּנֵי יִשְׂרָאֵל אִישׁ לַאֲחֻזָּתוֹ
ב לְעָרֵיהֶם: וַיַּעֲמֵד יְחִזְקִיָּהוּ אֶת־מַחְלְקוֹת הַכֹּהֲנִים וְהַלְוִיִּם עַל־
מַחְלְקוֹתָם אִישׁ | כְּפִי עֲבֹדָתוֹ לַכֹּהֲנִים וְלַלְוִיִּם לְעֹלָה וְלִשְׁלָמִים לְשָׁרֵת
ג וּלְהֹדוֹת וּלְהַלֵּל בְּשַׁעֲרֵי מַחֲנוֹת יְהוָה: וּמְנָת הַמֶּלֶךְ מִן־רְכוּשׁוֹ
לָעֹלוֹת לְעֹלוֹת הַבֹּקֶר וְהָעֶרֶב וְהָעֹלוֹת לַשַּׁבָּתוֹת וְלֶחֳדָשִׁים וְלַמֹּעֲדִים
ד כַּכָּתוּב בְּתוֹרַת יְהוָה: וַיֹּאמֶר לָעָם לְיוֹשְׁבֵי יְרוּשָׁלִַם לָתֵת מְנָת הַכֹּהֲנִים
ה וְהַלְוִיִּם לְמַעַן יֶחֶזְקוּ בְּתוֹרַת יְהוָה: וְכִפְרֹץ הַדָּבָר הִרְבּוּ בְנֵי־יִשְׂרָאֵל
רֵאשִׁית דָּגָן תִּירוֹשׁ וְיִצְהָר וּדְבַשׁ וְכֹל תְּבוּאַת שָׂדֶה וּמַעֲשַׂר הַכֹּל לָרֹב
ו הֵבִיאוּ: וּבְנֵי יִשְׂרָאֵל וִיהוּדָה הַיּוֹשְׁבִים בְּעָרֵי יְהוּדָה גַּם־הֵם מַעְשַׂר בָּקָר
וָצֹאן וּמַעְשַׂר קָדָשִׁים הַמְקֻדָּשִׁים לַיהוָה אֱלֹהֵיהֶם הֵבִיאוּ וַיִּתְּנוּ עֲרֵמוֹת
ז עֲרֵמוֹת: בַּחֹדֶשׁ הַשְּׁלִשִׁי הֵחֵלּוּ הָעֲרֵמוֹת לְיִסּוֹד וּבַחֹדֶשׁ הַשְּׁבִיעִי
ח כִּלּוּ: וַיָּבֹאוּ יְחִזְקִיָּהוּ וְהַשָּׂרִים וַיִּרְאוּ אֶת־הָעֲרֵמוֹת וַיְבָרְכוּ אֶת־
ט יְהוָה וְאֵת עַמּוֹ יִשְׂרָאֵל: וַיִּדְרֹשׁ יְחִזְקִיָּהוּ עַל־הַכֹּהֲנִים וְהַלְוִיִּם
י עַל־הָעֲרֵמוֹת: וַיֹּאמֶר אֵלָיו עֲזַרְיָהוּ הַכֹּהֵן הָרֹאשׁ לְבֵית צָדוֹק וַיֹּאמֶר
מֵהָחֵל הַתְּרוּמָה לָבִיא בֵית־יְהוָה אָכוֹל וְשָׂבוֹעַ וְהוֹתֵר עַד־לָרוֹב כִּי יְהוָה
יא בֵּרַךְ אֶת־עַמּוֹ וְהַנּוֹתָר אֶת־הֶהָמוֹן הַזֶּה: וַיֹּאמֶר יְחִזְקִיָּהוּ לְהָכִין
יב לְשָׁכוֹת בְּבֵית יְהוָה וַיָּכִינוּ: וַיָּבִיאוּ אֶת־הַתְּרוּמָה וְהַמַּעֲשֵׂר וְהַקֳּדָשִׁים
בֶּאֱמוּנָה וַעֲלֵיהֶם נָגִיד [כּוֹנַנְיָ֫הוּ °כָּנַנְיָהוּ ק] הַלֵּוִי וְשִׁמְעִי אָחִיהוּ מִשְׁנֶה:
יג וִיחִיאֵל וַעֲזַזְיָהוּ וְנַחַת וַעֲשָׂהאֵל וִירִימוֹת וְיוֹזָבָד וֶאֱלִיאֵל וְיִסְמַכְיָהוּ וּמַחַת

30:26. Such a display of unity had not been seen since the Ten Tribes had seceded after Solomon's death (*Malbim*).

31:4. By being scrupulous in giving tithes to the *Kohanim* and Levites, the people would enable them to devote themselves completely to their task of studying and disseminating the knowledge of the Torah through-

out the population (*Metzudos*).

31:6. Produce that belonged to the Temple treasury was exempt from tithes, but the people voluntarily made contributions equivalent to the tithes of whatever they had contributed to the Temple (*Radak*).

31:9. Seeing the immense size of the heaps, he suspected that the *Kohanim* and Levites were not taking brought peace offerings and confessed to Hashem, God of their fathers.

An added seven days ²³ The entire congregation conferred and decided to celebrate another seven days, so they made seven days of celebration. ²⁴ For Hezekiah, king of Judah, donated to the congregation a thousand bulls and seven thousand sheep, and the leaders donated to the congregation a thousand bulls and ten thousand sheep, and a great number of Kohanim sanctified themselves. ²⁵ The entire congregation of Judah rejoiced, along with the Kohanim and the Levites, and all the congregation who had come from Israel, and the proselytes who had come from the land of Israel and those who lived in Judah. ²⁶ There was great joy in Jerusalem, for such a thing had not taken place in Jerusalem since the days of Solomon son of David, king of Israel. *

²⁷ The Kohanim and the Levites got up and blessed the people, and He hearkened to their voice, and their prayers reached His holy abode in Heaven.

31

Destruction of idolatry ¹ When all this was finished all the people of Israel who were present went out to the cities of Judah and smashed the pillars, cut down the asherah-trees and dismantled the high places and the altars from out of all of Judah, Benjamin, Ephraim and Manasseh, until they were completely eradicated. Then all the Children of Israel returned, each man to his property, to their cities.

² Hezekiah stationed the groupings of the Kohanim and the Levites according to their divisions, each one according to its job, for the Kohanim and the Levites, for the burnt-offerings and peace-offerings, and to minister and to give thanks and praises [and stand guard] at the gates of the camps of Hashem.

³ A grant from the king, from his own possessions, paid for the burnt-offerings — for the burnt-offerings of the morning and the afternoon and the burnt-offerings of Sabbaths, New Moons and Festivals, as written in the Torah of Hashem.

The priestly and levitical portions ⁴ He told the people, the inhabitants of Jerusalem, to give the portion of the Kohanim and the Levites, so that they could strengthen themselves in the Torah of Hashem. * ⁵ As this observance became widespread, the Children of Israel brought an abundance of the first-portions of grain, oil, date-honey and all the produce of the field; they also brought tithes of everything, in abundance. ⁶ As for the Children of Israel and Judah who lived in the cities of Judah, they also brought tithes of cattle and sheep, as well as tithes of consecrated things that had been consecrated to Hashem their God. * Everything was piled into heaps. ⁷ In the third month they began to lay foundations for the heaps, and in the seventh month they were finished. ⁸ When Hezekiah and the leaders came and saw the heaps, they blessed Hashem and His people Israel. ⁹ Hezekiah questioned the Kohanim and the Levites about the heaps. * ¹⁰ Azariah, the chief Kohen, of the house of Zadok, said to him, "Since they began to bring the terumah-offering to the Temple of Hashem, there has been enough to eat and be satisfied and still leave over a great deal, for Hashem has blessed His people. What is left over is this great amount."

¹¹ Hezekiah then gave the command to prepare chambers in the Temple of Hashem, * and they were prepared. ¹² They brought the terumah-offerings, the tithes and the consecrated items faithfully; the supervisor who was over them was Cononiah the Levite, with his kinsman Shimei second in command. ¹³ Jehiel, Azaziah, Nahath, Asahel, Jerimoth, Jozabad, Eliel, Ismachiah, Mahath

---

their shares from them (*Rashi*).   **31:11.** To store these enormous quantities of food.

וּבְנֵיָהוּ פְּקִידִים מִיַּד °כּוֹנַנְיָהוּ [°כָּנַנְיָהוּ ק] וְשִׁמְעִי אָחִיו בְּמִפְקַד יְחִזְקִיָּהוּ
יד הַמֶּלֶךְ וַעֲזַרְיָהוּ נְגִיד בֵּית־הָאֱלֹהִים: וְקוֹרֵא בֶן־יִמְנָה הַלֵּוִי הַשּׁוֹעֵר
לַמִּזְרָחָה עַל נִדְבוֹת הָאֱלֹהִים לָתֵת תְּרוּמַת יהוה וְקָדְשֵׁי הַקֳּדָשִׁים: וְעַל־
טו יָדוֹ עֵדֶן וּמִנְיָמִן וְיֵשׁוּעַ וּשְׁמַעְיָהוּ אֲמַרְיָהוּ וּשְׁכַנְיָהוּ בְּעָרֵי הַכֹּהֲנִים
בֶּאֱמוּנָה לָתֵת לַאֲחֵיהֶם בַּמַּחְלְקוֹת כַּגָּדוֹל כַּקָּטָן: מִלְּבַד הִתְיַחְשָׂם
טז לִזְכָרִים מִבֶּן שָׁלוֹשׁ שָׁנִים וּלְמַעְלָה לְכָל־הַבָּא לְבֵית־יהוה לִדְבַר־יוֹם
יז בְּיוֹמוֹ לַעֲבוֹדָתָם בְּמִשְׁמְרוֹתָם כְּמַחְלְקוֹתֵיהֶם: וְאֵת הִתְיַחֵשׂ הַכֹּהֲנִים
לְבֵית אֲבוֹתֵיהֶם וְהַלְוִיִּם מִבֶּן עֶשְׂרִים שָׁנָה וּלְמָעְלָה בְּמִשְׁמְרוֹתֵיהֶם
יח בְּמַחְלְקוֹתֵיהֶם: וּלְהִתְיַחֵשׂ בְּכָל־טַפָּם נְשֵׁיהֶם וּבְנֵיהֶם וּבְנוֹתֵיהֶם לְכָל־
יט קָהָל כִּי בֶאֱמוּנָתָם יִתְקַדְּשׁוּ־קֹדֶשׁ: וְלִבְנֵי אַהֲרֹן הַכֹּהֲנִים בִּשְׂדֵי מִגְרַשׁ
עָרֵיהֶם בְּכָל־עִיר וָעִיר אֲנָשִׁים אֲשֶׁר נִקְּבוּ בְּשֵׁמוֹת לָתֵת מָנוֹת לְכָל־זָכָר
כ בַּכֹּהֲנִים וּלְכָל־הִתְיַחֵשׂ בַּלְוִיִּם: וַיַּעַשׂ כָּזֹאת יְחִזְקִיָּהוּ בְּכָל־יְהוּדָה וַיַּעַשׂ
כא הַטּוֹב וְהַיָּשָׁר וְהָאֱמֶת לִפְנֵי יהוה אֱלֹהָיו: וּבְכָל־מַעֲשֶׂה אֲשֶׁר־הֵחֵל |
בַּעֲבוֹדַת בֵּית־הָאֱלֹהִים וּבַתּוֹרָה וּבַמִּצְוָה לִדְרֹשׁ לֵאלֹהָיו בְּכָל־לְבָבוֹ
עָשָׂה וְהִצְלִיחַ:

לב א אַחֲרֵי הַדְּבָרִים וְהָאֱמֶת הָאֵלֶּה בָּא סַנְחֵרִיב מֶלֶךְ־אַשּׁוּר וַיָּבֹא בִיהוּדָה
ב וַיִּחַן עַל־הֶעָרִים הַבְּצֻרוֹת וַיֹּאמֶר לְבִקְעָם אֵלָיו: וַיַּרְא יְחִזְקִיָּהוּ כִּי־בָא
ג סַנְחֵרִיב וּפָנָיו לַמִּלְחָמָה עַל־יְרוּשָׁלִָם: וַיִּוָּעַץ עִם־שָׂרָיו וְגִבֹּרָיו לִסְתּוֹם
ד אֶת־מֵימֵי הָעֲיָנוֹת אֲשֶׁר מִחוּץ לָעִיר וַיַּעְזְרוּהוּ: וַיִּקָּבְצוּ עַם־רָב וַיִּסְתְּמוּ
אֶת־כָּל־הַמַּעְיָנוֹת וְאֶת־הַנַּחַל הַשּׁוֹטֵף בְּתוֹךְ־הָאָרֶץ לֵאמֹר לָמָּה יָבוֹאוּ
ה מַלְכֵי אַשּׁוּר וּמָצְאוּ מַיִם רַבִּים: וַיִּתְחַזַּק וַיִּבֶן אֶת־כָּל־הַחוֹמָה הַפְּרוּצָה
וַיַּעַל עַל־הַמִּגְדָּלוֹת וְלַחוּצָה הַחוֹמָה אַחֶרֶת וַיְחַזֵּק אֶת־הַמִּלּוֹא עִיר
ו דָּוִיד וַיַּעַשׂ שֶׁלַח לָרֹב וּמָגִנִּים: וַיִּתֵּן שָׂרֵי מִלְחָמוֹת עַל־הָעָם וַיִּקְבְּצֵם אֵלָיו
ז אֶל־רְחוֹב שַׁעַר הָעִיר וַיְדַבֵּר עַל־לְבָבָם לֵאמֹר: חִזְקוּ וְאִמְצוּ אַל־תִּירְאוּ
וְאַל־תֵּחַתּוּ מִפְּנֵי מֶלֶךְ אַשּׁוּר וּמִלִּפְנֵי כָּל־הֶהָמוֹן אֲשֶׁר־עִמּוֹ כִּי־עִמָּנוּ רַב
ח מֵעִמּוֹ: עִמּוֹ זְרוֹעַ בָּשָׂר וְעִמָּנוּ יהוה אֱלֹהֵינוּ לְעָזְרֵנוּ וּלְהִלָּחֵם מִלְחֲמֹתֵינוּ
ט וַיִּסָּמְכוּ הָעָם עַל־דִּבְרֵי יְחִזְקִיָּהוּ מֶלֶךְ־יְהוּדָה: אַחַר זֶה שָׁלַח
סַנְחֵרִיב מֶלֶךְ אַשּׁוּר עֲבָדָיו יְרוּשָׁלַיְמָה וְהוּא עַל־לָכִישׁ וְכָל־מֶמְשַׁלְתּוֹ
עִמּוֹ עַל־יְחִזְקִיָּהוּ מֶלֶךְ יְהוּדָה וְעַל־כָּל־יְהוּדָה אֲשֶׁר בִּירוּשָׁלַם לֵאמֹר:
י כֹּה אָמַר סַנְחֵרִיב מֶלֶךְ אַשּׁוּר עַל־מָה אַתֶּם בֹּטְחִים וְיֹשְׁבִים בְּמָצוֹר
יא בִּירוּשָׁלָ‍ִם: הֲלֹא יְחִזְקִיָּהוּ מַסִּית אֶתְכֶם לָתֵת אֶתְכֶם לָמוּת בְּרָעָב וּבְצָמָא
יב לֵאמֹר יהוה אֱלֹהֵינוּ יַצִּילֵנוּ מִכַּף מֶלֶךְ אַשּׁוּר: הֲלֹא־הוּא יְחִזְקִיָּהוּ הֵסִיר

31:16. The distribution of the priestly portions in their cities was in addition to the portions received by those who served in the Temple.

31:18. The families of the *Kohanim* were also given portions because they could be trusted to treat it with the required degree of sanctity (*Metzudos*).

and Benaiah were officials under Cononiah and his kinsman Shimei, by the command of King Hezekiah and Azariah, the director of the Temple of God.

¹⁴ Kore son of Imnah the Levite, the gatekeeper at the east, was in charge of the donations to God, to distribute the terumah-offerings of HASHEM and the most holy sacrificial portions. ¹⁵ With him faithfully were Eden, Miniamin, Jeshua, Shema- iah, Amariah and Shecaniah in the cities of the Kohanim, to distribute to their kinsmen according to their divisions, large and small alike. ¹⁶ This was besides* those males from the age of three years and up who gave their lineage — all those who came to the Temple of HASHEM for its daily functions, to do their service in their shifts according to their divisions — ¹⁷ when the Kohanim gave their lineage according to their fathers' families, as well as the Levites from the age of twenty years and up, in their shifts according to their divisions, ¹⁸ as this entire congrega- tion came with their young children, wives, sons and daughters to give their lineage, for they were trustworthy to keep the consecrated items holy. * ¹⁹ The men who were mentioned by name* gave portions to the sons of Aaron the Kohanim, to all the males among the Kohanim, as well as to all the Levites who gave their lineage, also in the fields of the open spaces around their cities, in each city — ²⁰ Hezekiah had this done in all of Judah. He did what was good and proper and truthful before HASHEM his God. ²¹ With all of his deeds that he undertook in the service of the Temple of God, in the Torah and the commandments, to seek out his God, he acted with all his heart, and he succeeded.

32

Preparations for war

¹ After these events and show of faith, Sennacherib king of Assyria came. He arrived in Judah and encamped against all the fortified cities of Judah, intending to breach them for himself. ² When Hezekiah saw that Sennacherib had come and was headed for battle against Jerusalem, ³ he conferred with his leaders and warriors and decided to stop up the waters of the springs that were outside the city, and they helped him — ⁴ a great crowd assembled and stopped all the wells and the brook that flowed in the midst of the land, * saying, "Why should the kings of Assyria come and find ample water?" ⁵ He also strengthened himself and rebuilt all the broken sections of the wall, raising it above the towers. [He erected] another wall outside of it, and he fortified the Millo, * in the City of David. He also prepared much weaponry and shields. ⁶ He appointed war officers over the people. He gathered them to himself to the plaza at the city gate, and he spoke encouragingly to them, saying, ⁷ "Be strong and courageous; do not be afraid and do not be dismayed in the face of the king of Assyria and in the face of the entire multitude that is with him, for we have more with us than he has with him. ⁸ With him is human might, but with us is HASHEM, our God, to help us and to fight our wars!" The people were reassured by the words of Hezekiah, king of Judah.

Sennacherib's blasphemous threats

⁹ After this Sennacherib king of Assyria sent his servants to Jerusalem, while he was besieging Lachish and his entire force was with him, saying, ¹⁰ "Thus said Sennacherib, king of Assyria: On what do you trust as you sit under siege in Jerusalem?* ¹¹ Behold, Hezekiah is enticing you, only to deliver you to death by hunger and thirst, saying, 'HASHEM, our God, will rescue us from the clutches of the king of Assyria!' ¹² Is this not the same Hezekiah who removed

---

31:19. In v. 15.
32:4. That is, the Gihon Spring just outside Jerusalem (see v. 30).

32:5. The plaza. See *I Chronicles* 11:8.
32:10. Ignoring Hezekiah, Sennacherib sarcastically de- mands from Jerusalem's inhabitants their surrender.

אֶת־בָּמֹתָיו וְאֶת־מִזְבְּחֹתָיו וַיֹּאמֶר לִיהוּדָה וְלִירוּשָׁלִַם לֵאמֹר לִפְנֵי מִזְבֵּחַ

יג אֶחָד תִּשְׁתַּחֲווּ וְעָלָיו תַּקְטִירוּ: הֲלֹא תֵדְעוּ מֶה עָשִׂיתִי אֲנִי וַאֲבוֹתַי לְכֹל

עַמֵּי הָאֲרָצוֹת הֲיָכוֹל יָכְלוּ אֱלֹהֵי גּוֹיֵ הָאֲרָצוֹת לְהַצִּיל אֶת־אַרְצָם מִיָּדִי:

יד מִי בְּכָל־אֱלֹהֵי הַגּוֹיִם הָאֵלֶּה אֲשֶׁר הֶחֱרִימוּ אֲבוֹתַי אֲשֶׁר יָכוֹל לְהַצִּיל

טו אֶת־עַמּוֹ מִיָּדִי כִּי יוּכַל אֱלֹהֵיכֶם לְהַצִּיל אֶתְכֶם מִיָּדִי: וְעַתָּה אַל־יַשִּׁיא

אֶתְכֶם חִזְקִיָּהוּ וְאַל־יַסִּית אֶתְכֶם כָּזֹאת וְאַל־תַּאֲמִינוּ לוֹ כִּי־לֹא יוּכַל

כָּל־אֱלוֹהַּ כָּל־גּוֹי וּמַמְלָכָה לְהַצִּיל עַמּוֹ מִיָּדִי וּמִיַּד אֲבוֹתָי אַף כִּי

טז אֱלֹהֵיכֶם לֹא־יַצִּילוּ אֶתְכֶם מִיָּדִי: וְעוֹד דִּבְּרוּ עֲבָדָיו עַל־יְהוָה הָאֱלֹהִים

יז וְעַל יְחִזְקִיָּהוּ עַבְדּוֹ: וּסְפָרִים כָּתַב לְחָרֵף לַיהוָה אֱלֹהֵי יִשְׂרָאֵל וְלֵאמֹר

עָלָיו לֵאמֹר כֵּאלֹהֵי גּוֹיֵ הָאֲרָצוֹת אֲשֶׁר לֹא־הִצִּילוּ עַמָּם מִיָּדִי כֵּן

יח לֹא־יַצִּיל אֱלֹהֵי יְחִזְקִיָּהוּ עַמּוֹ מִיָּדִי: וַיִּקְרְאוּ בְקוֹל־גָּדוֹל יְהוּדִית עַל־

עַם יְרוּשָׁלִַם אֲשֶׁר עַל־הַחוֹמָה לְיָרְאָם וּלְבַהֲלָם לְמַעַן יִלְכְּדוּ אֶת־

יט הָעִיר: וַיְדַבְּרוּ אֶל־אֱלֹהֵי יְרוּשָׁלִָם כְּעַל אֱלֹהֵי עַמֵּי הָאָרֶץ מַעֲשֵׂה יְדֵי

כ הָאָדָם: וַיִּתְפַּלֵּל יְחִזְקִיָּהוּ הַמֶּלֶךְ וִישַׁעְיָהוּ בֶן־אָמוֹץ הַנָּבִיא

כא עַל־זֹאת וַיִּזְעֲקוּ הַשָּׁמָיִם: וַיִּשְׁלַח יְהוָה מַלְאָךְ וַיַּכְחֵד כָּל־

גִּבּוֹר חַיִל וְנָגִיד וְשָׂר בְּמַחֲנֵה מֶלֶךְ אַשּׁוּר וַיָּשָׁב בְּבֹשֶׁת פָּנִים לְאַרְצוֹ וַיָּבֹא

כב בֵּית אֱלֹהָיו °וּמִיצִיאוֹ °[וּמִיצִיאֵי ק] מֵעָיו שָׁם הִפִּילֻהוּ בֶחָרֶב: וַיּוֹשַׁע

יְהוָה אֶת־יְחִזְקִיָּהוּ וְאֵת | יֹשְׁבֵי יְרוּשָׁלִַם מִיַּד סַנְחֵרִיב מֶלֶךְ־אַשּׁוּר וּמִיַּד־

כג כֹּל וַיְנַהֲלֵם מִסָּבִיב: וְרַבִּים מְבִיאִים מִנְחָה לַיהוָה לִירוּשָׁלִַם וּמִגְדָּנוֹת

לִיחִזְקִיָּהוּ מֶלֶךְ יְהוּדָה וַיִּנַּשֵּׂא לְעֵינֵי כָל־הַגּוֹיִם מֵאַחֲרֵי־כֵן:

כד בַּיָּמִים הָהֵם חָלָה יְחִזְקִיָּהוּ עַד־לָמוּת וַיִּתְפַּלֵּל אֶל־יְהוָה וַיֹּאמֶר לוֹ

כה וּמוֹפֵת נָתַן לוֹ: וְלֹא־כִגְמֻל עָלָיו הֵשִׁיב יְחִזְקִיָּהוּ כִּי גָבַהּ לִבּוֹ וַיְהִי עָלָיו

כו קֶצֶף וְעַל־יְהוּדָה וִירוּשָׁלִָם: וַיִּכָּנַע יְחִזְקִיָּהוּ בְּגֹבַהּ לִבּוֹ הוּא וְיֹשְׁבֵי יְרוּשָׁלִָם

כז וְלֹא־בָא עֲלֵיהֶם קֶצֶף יְהוָה בִּימֵי יְחִזְקִיָּהוּ: וַיְהִי לִיחִזְקִיָּהוּ עֹשֶׁר וְכָבוֹד

הַרְבֵּה מְאֹד וְאֹצָרוֹת עָשָׂה־לוֹ לְכֶסֶף וּלְזָהָב וּלְאֶבֶן יְקָרָה וְלִבְשָׂמִים

כח וּלְמָגִנִּים וּלְכֹל כְּלֵי חֶמְדָּה: וּמִסְכְּנוֹת לִתְבוּאַת דָּגָן וְתִירוֹשׁ וְיִצְהָר

כט וְאֻרָוֹת לְכָל־בְּהֵמָה וּבְהֵמָה וַעֲדָרִים לָאֲוֵרוֹת: וְעָרִים עָשָׂה לוֹ וּמִקְנֵה־

ל צֹאן וּבָקָר לָרֹב כִּי נָתַן־לוֹ אֱלֹהִים רְכוּשׁ רַב מְאֹד: וְהוּא יְחִזְקִיָּהוּ

סָתַם אֶת־מוֹצָא מֵימֵי גִיחוֹן הָעֶלְיוֹן °וַיִּשְׁרֵם °[וַיְיַשְּׁרֵם ק] לְמַטָּה־

לא מַעְרָבָה לְעִיר דָּוִיד וַיַּצְלַח יְחִזְקִיָּהוּ בְּכָל־מַעֲשֵׂהוּ: וְכֵן בִּמְלִיצֵי | שָׂרֵי

בָּבֶל הַמְשַׁלְּחִים עָלָיו לִדְרֹשׁ הַמּוֹפֵת אֲשֶׁר הָיָה בָאָרֶץ עֲזָבוֹ הָאֱלֹהִים

32:18. Instead of Aramaic, the diplomatic language of the time, the officers shouted their taunts in Hebrew, to frighten the common people (see *II Kings* 18:26-27).

32:24. The events described here happened just before

the abortive Assyrian invasion. See *II Kings* Ch. 20.

32:26. God's rage was postponed until later (see *II Kings* 20:16-19).

32:30. The Gihon Spring was east of Jerusalem. Hezekiah dug a long tunnel diverting the water westward,

[Hashem's] high places and altars, telling Judah and Jerusalem, 'You must prostrate yourselves before only one Altar and burn offerings upon it'? ¹³ *Do you not know what I and my fathers did to all the peoples of the lands? Were the gods of the nations of the lands at all able to save their countries from my hands?* ¹⁴ *Of all the gods of those nations whom my fathers annihilated, which was able to rescue his people from my hand, that your God should be able to rescue you from my hand?* ¹⁵ *So now, do not let Hezekiah delude you and entice you this way, and do not believe him, for no god of any nation or kingdom can save his people from my hand or the hand of my fathers, and neither will your God save you from my hand!"* ¹⁶ *And his servants continued to speak against Hashem, God, and against Hezekiah His servant.* ¹⁷ *He also wrote notes blaspheming Hashem, God of Israel, speaking against Him, saying: "Just as the gods of the nations of the lands did not rescue their people from my hand, so will the God of Hezekiah not save His people from my hand."* ¹⁸ *They called out in a loud voice in the language of the Jews* * *to the people of Jerusalem who were on the wall, in order to frighten them and terrify them, so that they would be able to capture the city.* ¹⁹ *They spoke about the God of Jerusalem as about the gods of the peoples of the land, which are the handiwork of man.*

Hezekiah and Isaiah pray and are answered   ²⁰ *King Hezekiah and the prophet Isaiah son of Amoz prayed about this, and they cried out to Heaven.* ²¹ *Then Hashem sent an angel who destroyed every mighty warrior, captain and officer in the camp of the king of Assyria. [Sennacherib] then returned in shame to his land, and he entered the temple of his god; there some of his own offspring struck him down by the sword.*

²² *Thus Hashem saved Hezekiah and the inhabitants of Jerusalem from the hand of Sennacherib king of Assyria and from the hand of everyone, and He guided them all around.* ²³ *Many [people] brought tributes to Hashem to Jerusalem, and luxurious gifts to Hezekiah. From then on he was exalted in the eyes of all the nations.*

Hezekiah's near-fatal illness   ²⁴ *In those days Hezekiah became deathly ill. He prayed to Hashem, and He answered Him and gave him a sign.* *

²⁵ *But Hezekiah did not reciprocate the benevolence that he was shown, for his heart became haughty. [God's] rage then came against him and against Judah and Jerusalem.* ²⁶ *But Hezekiah humbled himself from the haughtiness of his heart — he and the inhabitants of Jerusalem — so the rage of Hashem did not come against them in the days of Hezekiah.* *

Hezekiah's wealth   ²⁷ *Hezekiah had very many riches and honor. He made himself treasure houses for silver, gold, precious stones, spices, shields and all sorts of precious objects;* ²⁸ *silos for produce of grain, wine and oil; and stables for all sorts of various animals, and accommodations for herds.* ²⁹ *He made himself cities and he had an abundance of flocks of sheep and cattle, for God had granted him very much wealth.* ³⁰ *He, Hezekiah, stopped up the upper source of the waters of Gihon, diverting them underground westward, to the City of David.* * *Hezekiah was successful in all his endeavors.*

³¹ *So, too, in the matter of the emissaries of the Babylonian officers who were sent to him to inquire of the miracle that had happened in the land,* * *God left him*

---

into the city itself, so that the Assyrians would not have access to it.

32:31. The story of Hezekiah's inappropriate reaction to the emissaries is told in *II Kings* 20:12-19.

לב לְנַסּוֹתוֹ לָדַעַת כָּל־בִּלְבָבוֹ: וְיֶ֣תֶר דִּבְרֵ֤י יְחִזְקִיָּ֙הוּ֙ וַחֲסָדָ֔יו הִנָּ֣ם כְּתוּבִ֗ים בַּחֲז֞וֹן יְשַׁעְיָ֤הוּ בֶן־אָמוֹץ֙ הַנָּבִ֔יא עַל־סֵ֥פֶר מַלְכֵֽי־יְהוּדָ֖ה

לג וְיִשְׂרָאֵֽל: וַיִּשְׁכַּ֨ב יְחִזְקִיָּ֜הוּ עִם־אֲבֹתָ֗יו וַֽיִּקְבְּרֻ֙הוּ֙ בְּמַֽעֲלֵה֙ קִבְרֵי֙ בְנֵי־דָוִ֔יד וְכָבוֹד֙ עָשׂוּ־ל֣וֹ בְמוֹת֔וֹ כָּל־יְהוּדָה֙ וְיֹשְׁבֵ֣י יְרוּשָׁלִַ֔ם וַיִּמְלֹ֛ךְ מְנַשֶּׁ֥ה בְנ֖וֹ

א תַּחְתָּֽיו: בֶּן־שְׁתֵּ֧ים עֶשְׂרֵ֛ה שָׁנָ֖ה מְנַשֶּׁ֣ה בְמָלְכ֑וֹ וַחֲמִשִּׁ֤ים

ב וְחָמֵשׁ֙ שָׁנָ֔ה מָלַ֖ךְ בִּירוּשָׁלָֽם: וַיַּ֥עַשׂ הָרַ֖ע בְּעֵינֵ֣י יְהוָ֑ה כְּתֽוֹעֲבוֹת֙ הַגּוֹיִ֔ם

ג אֲשֶׁר֙ הוֹרִ֣ישׁ יְהוָ֔ה מִפְּנֵ֖י בְּנֵ֥י יִשְׂרָאֵֽל: וַיָּ֗שָׁב וַיִּ֙בֶן֙ אֶת־הַבָּמ֔וֹת אֲשֶׁ֥ר נִתַּ֖ץ יְחִזְקִיָּ֣הוּ אָבִ֑יו וַיָּ֨קֶם מִזְבְּח֤וֹת לַבְּעָלִים֙ וַיַּ֣עַשׂ אֲשֵׁר֔וֹת וַיִּשְׁתַּ֙חוּ֙ לְכָל־צְבָ֣א

ד הַשָּׁמַ֔יִם וַיַּעֲבֹ֖ד אֹתָֽם: וּבָנָ֥ה מִזְבְּח֖וֹת בְּבֵ֣ית יְהוָ֑ה אֲשֶׁר֙ אָמַ֣ר יְהוָ֔ה

ה בִּירוּשָׁלַ֥͏ִם יִהְיֶ֖ה שְׁמִ֥י לְעוֹלָֽם: וַיִּ֥בֶן מִזְבְּח֖וֹת לְכָל־צְבָ֣א הַשָּׁמָ֑יִם בִּשְׁתֵּ֖י

ו חַצְר֥וֹת בֵּית־יְהוָֽה: וְהוּא֩ הֶעֱבִ֨יר אֶת־בָּנָ֤יו בָּאֵשׁ֙ בְּגֵ֣י בֶן־הִנֹּ֔ם וְעוֹנֵ֤ן וְנִחֵשׁ֙ וְכִשֵּׁ֔ף וְעָ֥שָׂה א֖וֹב וְיִדְּעוֹנִ֑י הִרְבָּ֗ה לַעֲשׂ֤וֹת הָרַע֙ בְּעֵינֵ֣י יְהוָ֔ה לְהַכְעִיסֽוֹ:

ז וַיָּ֙שֶׂם֙ אֶת־פֶּ֣סֶל הַסֶּ֔מֶל אֲשֶׁ֖ר עָשָׂ֑ה בְּבֵ֣ית הָאֱלֹהִ֗ים אֲשֶׁ֨ר אָמַ֤ר אֱלֹהִים֙ אֶל־דָּוִ֗יד וְאֶל־שְׁלֹמֹ֣ה בְנ֔וֹ בַּבַּ֤יִת הַזֶּה֙ וּבִיר֣וּשָׁלַ֔͏ִם אֲשֶׁ֥ר בָּחַ֖רְתִּי מִכֹּל֙

ח שִׁבְטֵ֣י יִשְׂרָאֵ֔ל אָשִׂ֥ים אֶת־שְׁמִ֖י לְעֵילֽוֹם: וְלֹ֣א אוֹסִ֗יף לְהָסִיר֙ אֶת־רֶ֣גֶל יִשְׂרָאֵ֔ל מֵעַל֙ הָֽאֲדָמָ֔ה אֲשֶׁ֥ר הֶעֱמַ֖דְתִּי לַאֲבֹֽתֵיכֶ֑ם רַ֣ק ׀ אִם־יִשְׁמְר֣וּ לַעֲשׂ֗וֹת אֵ֤ת כָּל־אֲשֶׁ֙ר צִוִּיתִ֙ים֙ לְכָל־הַתּוֹרָ֔ה וְהַחֻקִּ֖ים וְהַמִּשְׁפָּטִ֑ים בְּיַד־

ט מֹשֶֽׁה: וַיֶּ֣תַע מְנַשֶּׁ֔ה אֶת־יְהוּדָ֖ה וְיֹשְׁבֵ֣י יְרוּשָׁלָ֑͏ִם לַעֲשׂ֣וֹת רָ֔ע מִן־הַגּוֹיִ֔ם

י אֲשֶׁר֙ הִשְׁמִ֣יד יְהוָ֔ה מִפְּנֵ֖י בְּנֵ֥י יִשְׂרָאֵֽל: וַיְדַבֵּ֧ר יְהוָ֛ה אֶל־

יא מְנַשֶּׁ֥ה וְאֶל־עַמּ֖וֹ וְלֹ֥א הִקְשִֽׁיבוּ: וַיָּבֵ֣א יְהוָ֣ה עֲלֵיהֶ֗ם אֶת־שָׂרֵ֤י הַצָּבָא֙ אֲשֶׁר֙ לְמֶ֣לֶךְ אַשּׁ֔וּר וַיִּלְכְּד֥וּ אֶת־מְנַשֶּׁ֖ה בַּחֹחִ֑ים וַיַּֽאַסְרֻ֙הוּ֙ בַּֽנְחֻשְׁתַּ֔יִם וַיּוֹלִיכֻ֖הוּ

יב בָּבֶֽלָה: וּכְהָצֵ֣ר ל֔וֹ חִלָּ֕ה אֶת־פְּנֵ֖י יְהוָ֣ה אֱלֹהָ֑יו וַיִּכָּנַ֣ע מְאֹ֔ד מִלִּפְנֵ֖י אֱלֹהֵ֥י

יג אֲבֹתָֽיו: וַיִּתְפַּלֵּ֣ל אֵלָ֗יו וַיֵּעָ֤תֶר לוֹ֙ וַיִּשְׁמַ֣ע תְּחִנָּת֔וֹ וַיְשִׁיבֵ֥הוּ יְרוּשָׁלַ֖͏ִם

יד לְמַלְכוּת֑וֹ וַיֵּ֣דַע מְנַשֶּׁ֔ה כִּ֥י יְהוָ֖ה ה֥וּא הָאֱלֹהִֽים: וְאַחֲרֵי־כֵ֡ן בָּנָ֣ה חוֹמָ֣ה חִֽיצוֹנָ֣ה ׀ לְעִיר־דָּוִ֡יד מַעְרָבָה֩ לְגִיח֨וֹן בַּנַּ֜חַל וְלָב֨וֹא בְשַׁ֤עַר הַדָּגִים֙ וְסָבַ֣ב לָעֹ֔פֶל וַיַּגְבִּיהֶ֖הָ מְאֹ֑ד וַיָּ֧שֶׂם שָֽׂרֵי־חַ֛יִל בְּכָל־הֶעָרִ֥ים הַבְּצֻר֖וֹת בִּיהוּדָֽה:

טו וַיָּ֡סַר אֶת־אֱלֹהֵ֣י הַנֵּכָר֩ וְאֶת־הַסֶּ֨מֶל מִבֵּ֣ית יְהוָ֗ה וְכָל־הַֽמִּזְבְּחוֹת֙ אֲשֶׁ֣ר בָּנָ֗ה בְּהַ֤ר בֵּית־יְהוָה֙ וּבִיר֣וּשָׁלָ֔͏ִם וַיַּשְׁלֵ֖ךְ ח֥וּצָה לָעִֽיר: °וייכן ⟨וַיִּ֙בֶן֙ ק'⟩

טז אֶת־מִזְבַּ֣ח יְהוָ֗ה וַיִּזְבַּ֤ח עָלָיו֙ זִבְחֵ֣י שְׁלָמִ֣ים וְתוֹדָ֔ה וַיֹּ֙אמֶר֙ לִֽיהוּדָ֔ה לַעֲב֕וֹד

יז אֶת־יְהוָ֖ה אֱלֹהֵ֣י יִשְׂרָאֵֽל: אֲבָ֤ל ע֣וֹד הָעָם֙ זֹבְחִ֣ים בַּבָּמ֔וֹת רַ֖ק לַיהוָ֥ה

יח אֱלֹהֵיהֶֽם: וְיֶ֣תֶר דִּבְרֵ֣י מְנַשֶּׁ֡ה וּתְפִלָּת֣וֹ אֶל־אֱלֹהָ֗יו וְדִבְרֵי֙ הַֽחֹזִ֔ים הַֽמְדַבְּרִ֤ים אֵלָיו֙ בְּשֵׁ֗ם יְהוָ֤ה אֱלֹהֵי֙ יִשְׂרָאֵ֔ל הִנָּ֕ם עַל־דִּבְרֵ֖י מַלְכֵ֥י יִשְׂרָאֵֽל:

יט וּתְפִלָּת֣וֹ וְהֵעָ֣תֶר לוֹ֮ וְכָל־חַטָּאת֣וֹ וּמַעְלוֹ֒ וְהַמְּקֹמ֗וֹת אֲשֶׁ֨ר בָּנָ֤ה בָהֶם֙

33:14. A fortified area of Jerusalem.

alone, to test him, to know all that was in his heart.

(See Appendix A, timeline 4) *32 The rest of the deeds of Hezekiah and his kindnesses — behold, they are recorded in The Visions of the Prophet Isaiah son of Amoz and in the Book of the Kings of Judah and Israel. 33 Hezekiah passed away and was buried in the choicest section of the tombs of the children of David. All of Judah and the inhabitants of Jerusalem paid tribute to him when he died. His son Manasseh reigned in his place.*

33

KING MANASSEH
33:1-20

Builder of idolatry

1 **M**enasseh was twelve years old when he became king, and he reigned for fifty-five years in Jerusalem. *2* He did what was evil in the eyes of HASHEM, like the abominations of the nations that HASHEM had driven out before the Children of Israel. *3* He rebuilt the high places that his father Hezekiah had broken down. He erected altars to Baal. He made asherah-trees; and he bowed down to the entire host of the heaven and worshiped them. *4* He built altars in the Temple of HASHEM — about which HASHEM had said, "My Name shall be in Jerusalem forever." *5* He built altars to the entire host of the heaven in the two Courtyards of the Temple of HASHEM. *6* He passed his sons through the fire in the Valley of Ben-(the son of) hinnom, practiced astrology, read omens, did sorcery, performed necromancy and conjured up spirits; he was profuse in doing what was evil in the eyes of HASHEM, to anger Him. *7* He placed the graven image that he had made in the Temple of God, concerning which God had said to David and his son Solomon, "In this Temple and in Jerusalem, which I have chosen from among all the tribes of Israel, I shall place My Name forever. *8* And I shall no longer remove Israel's feet from on the land that I have established for your forefathers, provided they are careful to act according to all that I have commanded them — all the*

Manasseh leads Judah astray

*Torah, statutes and ordinances — through Moses." *9* But Manasseh led Judah and the inhabitants of Jerusalem astray to do more evil than the nations that HASHEM had destroyed from before the Children of Israel.*

God sends Assyria; Manasseh repents

10 HASHEM spoke to Manasseh and his people, but they did not listen. *11* So HASHEM brought against them the officers of the king of Assyria's army, and they captured Manasseh with hunting hooks, bound him in chains and led him off to Babylonia. *12* But in his distress he beseeched HASHEM, His God, and he humbled himself greatly before the God of his fathers. *13* He prayed to Him, and He was entreated by him and heard his supplication, and He returned him to Jerusalem, to his kingship. Then Manasseh realized that HASHEM is God.

Manasseh fortifies Jerusalem, removes idols, and rebuilds God's Altar

14 After this he built an outer wall for the City of David, to the west of the Gihon Brook, approaching the Fish Gate, and going around to the Ophel, * and he raised it to a great height. He also placed army officers in all the fortified cities of Judah. *15* He removed the strange gods and the image from the Temple of HASHEM and all the altars that he had built on the Mountain of the Temple of HASHEM and in Jerusalem, discarding them outside the city. *16* He rebuilt the Altar of HASHEM and slaughtered peace-offerings and thanksgiving-offerings on it, and he commanded Judah to worship HASHEM, the God of Israel. *17* However, the people still brought offerings at the high places, albeit to HASHEM their God.

18 The rest of the deeds of Manasseh, his prayer to his God and the words of the seers who spoke to him in the name of HASHEM, God of Israel — behold, they are in the Chronicles of the Kings of Israel. *19* And his prayer and that [HASHEM] was entreated by him, and all his sins and his treachery, and the places in which he built*

בָּמוֹת וְהֶעֱמִיד הָאֲשֵׁרִים וְהַפְּסִלִים לִפְנֵי הַכְּנִעוֹ הֵנַם כְּתוּבִים עַל דִּבְרֵי

כ חוֹזָי: וַיִּשְׁכַּב מְנַשֶּׁה עִם־אֲבֹתָיו וַיִּקְבְּרֻהוּ בֵּיתוֹ וַיִּמְלֹךְ אָמוֹן בְּנוֹ תַּחְתָּיו:

כא־כב בֶּן־עֶשְׂרִים וּשְׁתַּיִם שָׁנָה אָמוֹן בְּמָלְכוֹ וּשְׁתַּיִם שָׁנִים מָלַךְ בִּירוּשָׁלָ͏ִם: וַיַּעַשׂ הָרַע בְּעֵינֵי יְהוָה כַּאֲשֶׁר עָשָׂה מְנַשֶּׁה אָבִיו וּלְכָל־הַפְּסִילִים אֲשֶׁר עָשָׂה

כג מְנַשֶּׁה אָבִיו זִבַּח אָמוֹן וַיַּעַבְדֵם: וְלֹא נִכְנַע מִלִּפְנֵי יְהוָה כְּהִכָּנַע מְנַשֶּׁה

כד אָבִיו כִּי הוּא אָמוֹן הִרְבָּה אַשְׁמָה: וַיִּקְשְׁרוּ עָלָיו עֲבָדָיו וַיְמִיתֻהוּ בְּבֵיתוֹ:

כה וַיַּכּוּ עַם־הָאָרֶץ אֵת כָּל־הַקֹּשְׁרִים עַל־הַמֶּלֶךְ אָמוֹן וַיַּמְלִיכוּ עַם־הָאָרֶץ אֶת־יֹאשִׁיָּהוּ בְנוֹ תַּחְתָּיו:

לד

א בֶּן־שְׁמוֹנֶה שָׁנִים יֹאשִׁיָּהוּ בְמָלְכוֹ וּשְׁלֹשִׁים וְאַחַת שָׁנָה מָלַךְ בִּירוּשָׁלָ͏ִם:

ב וַיַּעַשׂ הַיָּשָׁר בְּעֵינֵי יְהוָה וַיֵּלֶךְ בְּדַרְכֵי דָּוִיד אָבִיו וְלֹא־סָר יָמִין וּשְׂמֹאול:

ג וּבִשְׁמוֹנֶה שָׁנִים לְמָלְכוֹ וְהוּא עוֹדֶנּוּ נַעַר הֵחֵל לִדְרוֹשׁ לֵאלֹהֵי דָּוִיד אָבִיו וּבִשְׁתֵּים עֶשְׂרֵה שָׁנָה הֵחֵל לְטַהֵר אֶת־יְהוּדָה וִירוּשָׁלַ͏ִם מִן־הַבָּמוֹת

ד וְהָאֲשֵׁרִים וְהַפְּסִלִים וְהַמַּסֵּכוֹת: וַיְנַתְּצוּ לְפָנָיו אֵת מִזְבְּחוֹת הַבְּעָלִים וְהַחַמָּנִים אֲשֶׁר־לְמַעְלָה מֵעֲלֵיהֶם גִּדֵּעַ וְהָאֲשֵׁרִים וְהַפְּסִלִים וְהַמַּסֵּכוֹת

ה שִׁבַּר וְהֵדַק וַיִּזְרֹק עַל־פְּנֵי הַקְּבָרִים הַזֹּבְחִים לָהֶם: וְעַצְמוֹת כֹּהֲנִים שָׂרַף

ו עַל־ °מִזְבְּחוֹתִים [°מִזְבְּחוֹתָם ק] וַיְטַהֵר אֶת־יְהוּדָה וְאֶת־יְרוּשָׁלָ͏ִם: וּבְעָרֵי מְנַשֶּׁה וְאֶפְרַיִם וְשִׁמְעוֹן וְעַד־נַפְתָּלִי °בְּחַרְבֹתֵיהֶם [°בְּחַרְבֹתֵיהֶם ק]

ז סָבִיב: וַיְנַתֵּץ אֶת־הַמִּזְבְּחוֹת וְאֶת־הָאֲשֵׁרִים וְהַפְּסִלִים כִּתַּת לְהֵדַק וְכָל־

ח הַחַמָּנִים גִּדַּע בְּכָל־אֶרֶץ יִשְׂרָאֵל וַיָּשָׁב לִירוּשָׁלָ͏ִם: וּבִשְׁנַת שְׁמוֹנֶה עֶשְׂרֵה לְמָלְכוֹ לְטַהֵר הָאָרֶץ וְהַבָּיִת שָׁלַח אֶת־שָׁפָן בֶּן־אֲצַלְיָהוּ וְאֶת־מַעֲשֵׂיָהוּ שַׂר־הָעִיר וְאֵת יוֹאָח בֶּן־יוֹאָחָז הַמַּזְכִּיר לְחַזֵּק אֶת־בֵּית

ט יְהוָה אֱלֹהָיו: וַיָּבֹאוּ אֶל־חִלְקִיָּהוּ ׀ הַכֹּהֵן הַגָּדוֹל וַיִּתְּנוּ אֶת־הַכֶּסֶף הַמּוּבָא בֵית־אֱלֹהִים אֲשֶׁר אָסְפוּ־הַלְוִיִּם שֹׁמְרֵי הַסַּף מִיַּד מְנַשֶּׁה וְאֶפְרַיִם וּמִכֹּל שְׁאֵרִית יִשְׂרָאֵל וּמִכָּל־יְהוּדָה וּבִנְיָמִן °וַיָּשֻׁבוּ [°וַיֵּשְׁבוּ ק] יְרוּשָׁלָ͏ִם:

י וַיִּתְּנוּ עַל־יַד עֹשֵׂה הַמְּלָאכָה הַמֻּפְקָדִים בְּבֵית יְהוָה וַיִּתְּנוּ אֹתוֹ עוֹשֵׂי

יא הַמְּלָאכָה אֲשֶׁר עֹשִׂים בְּבֵית יְהוָה לִבְדּוֹק וּלְחַזֵּק הַבָּיִת: וַיִּתְּנוּ לֶחָרָשִׁים וְלַבֹּנִים לִקְנוֹת אַבְנֵי מַחְצֵב וְעֵצִים לַמְחַבְּרוֹת וּלְקָרוֹת אֶת־הַבָּתִּים

יב אֲשֶׁר הִשְׁחִיתוּ מַלְכֵי יְהוּדָה: וְהָאֲנָשִׁים עֹשִׂים בֶּאֱמוּנָה בַּמְּלָאכָה וַעֲלֵיהֶם ׀ מֻפְקָדִים יַחַת וְעֹבַדְיָהוּ הַלְוִיִּם מִן־בְּנֵי מְרָרִי וּזְכַרְיָה וּמְשֻׁלָּם מִן־בְּנֵי הַקְּהָתִים לְנַצֵּחַ וְהַלְוִיִּם כָּל־מֵבִין בִּכְלֵי־שִׁיר:

יג וְעַל הַסַּבָּלִים וּמְנַצְּחִים לְכֹל עֹשֵׂה מְלָאכָה לַעֲבוֹדָה וַעֲבוֹדָה

יד וּמֵהַלְוִיִּם סוֹפְרִים וְשֹׁטְרִים וְשׁוֹעֲרִים: וּבְהוֹצִיאָם אֶת־הַכֶּסֶף הַמּוּבָא בֵית

(See Appendix A, timeline 4) high places and erected asherah-trees and idols before he was humbled — behold, they are recorded in the words of the seers. ²⁰ Manasseh lay with his forefathers and was buried at his palace. His son Amon reigned in his place.

KING AMON
33:21-25

²¹ Amon was twenty-two years old when he became king, and he reigned for two years in Jerusalem. ²² He did what was evil in the eyes of HASHEM, as his father had done, and he sacrificed to all the idols that his father Manasseh had made, and he worshiped them. ²³ He did not humble himself before HASHEM as his father Manasseh had humbled himself, for he, Amon, incurred much guilt. ²⁴ His servants conspired against him and killed him in his palace. ²⁵ The people of the land struck down all the conspirators against King Amon; the people of the land crowned Josiah his son in his place.

34

KING JOSIAH
34:1-35:27

¹ Josiah was eight years old when he became king, and he reigned for thirty-one years in Jerusalem. ² He did what was proper in the eyes of HASHEM, following the ways of his forefather David; he did not veer right or left.

Seeker of God; destroyer of idols

³ In his eighth year, when he began to reign, while he was still a youngster, he began to seek out the God of his forefather David. In the twelfth year he began to purge Judah and Jerusalem of the high places and the asherah-trees, the idols and the molten images. ⁴ They broke down the altars of Baal before him, and he cut down the sun images that were on top of them. He smashed and ground up the asherah-trees, the idols and the molten images and threw them over the graves of the people who had sacrificed to them. ⁵ He burned the bones of priests upon their altars, and he cleansed Judah and Jerusalem, ⁶ and the cities of Manasseh and Ephraim and Simeon, up to Naphtali, with their hatchets all around. ⁷ He smashed the altars, he ground up the asherah-trees and the graven images into dust, and he cut down the sun images in all the Land of Israel, and then returned to Jerusalem.

⁸ In the eighteenth year of his reign, when he had purified the land and the Temple, he sent Shaphan son of Azaliah, Maaseiah the city officer, and Joah son of Joahaz the secretary to reinforce the Temple of HASHEM, his God.

The Temple is repaired

⁹ They went to Hilkiah, the Kohen Gadol, and delivered the money that had been brought for the Temple of God — which the Levite gatekeepers had collected from Manasseh and Ephraim and from the rest of the remnant of Israel, and from Judah and Benjamin, and then returned to Jerusalem — ¹⁰ they gave it over to the workmen who were in charge in the Temple of HASHEM, and they gave it to those who did the work, who acted in the Temple of HASHEM to repair and reinforce the Temple. * ¹¹ They gave it to the carpenters and the builders, to buy quarried stones and wood for joints and to lay beams for the buildings that the kings of Judah had destroyed. ¹² The men did their work with integrity. * The Levites Jahath and Obadiah of the children of Merari and Zechariah and Meshullam of the children of the Kohathites were appointed to oversee them. Of the Levites were all those who were experts in musical instruments, ¹³ those who were in charge of the porters and the overseers of every kind of work; and some of the Levites were also scribes, officers, and gatekeepers.

¹⁴ As they were removing the money that had been brought to the Temple of

---

34:10. The last extensive repairs had been carried out in the days of Joash (see *II Kings* Ch. 12), over two centuries earlier.

34:12. The honesty of the workers was such that no financial accounting was necessary.

טו יְהוָה מָצָא חִלְקִיָּהוּ הַכֹּהֵן אֶת־סֵפֶר תּוֹרַת־יְהוָה בְּיַד־מֹשֶׁה: וַיַּעַן חִלְקִיָּהוּ וַיֹּאמֶר אֶל־שָׁפָן הַסּוֹפֵר סֵפֶר הַתּוֹרָה מָצָאתִי בְּבֵית יְהוָה וַיִּתֵּן

טז חִלְקִיָּהוּ אֶת־הַסֵּפֶר אֶל־שָׁפָן: וַיָּבֵא שָׁפָן אֶת־הַסֵּפֶר אֶל־הַמֶּלֶךְ וַיָּשֶׁב עוֹד אֶת־הַמֶּלֶךְ דָּבָר לֵאמֹר כֹּל אֲשֶׁר־נִתַּן בְּיַד־עֲבָדֶיךָ הֵם עֹשִׂים:

יז וַיַּתִּיכוּ אֶת־הַכֶּסֶף הַנִּמְצָא בְּבֵית־יְהוָה וַיִּתְּנוּהוּ עַל־יַד הַמֻּפְקָדִים וְעַל־

יח יַד עוֹשֵׂי הַמְּלָאכָה: וַיַּגֵּד שָׁפָן הַסּוֹפֵר לַמֶּלֶךְ לֵאמֹר סֵפֶר נָתַן לִי חִלְקִיָּהוּ

יט הַכֹּהֵן וַיִּקְרָא־בוֹ שָׁפָן לִפְנֵי הַמֶּלֶךְ: וַיְהִי כִּשְׁמֹעַ הַמֶּלֶךְ אֵת דִּבְרֵי הַתּוֹרָה

כ וַיִּקְרַע אֶת־בְּגָדָיו: וַיְצַו הַמֶּלֶךְ אֶת־חִלְקִיָּהוּ וְאֶת־אֲחִיקָם בֶּן־שָׁפָן וְאֶת־

כא עַבְדּוֹן בֶּן־מִיכָה וְאֵת ׀ שָׁפָן הַסּוֹפֵר וְאֵת עֲשָׂיָה עֶבֶד־הַמֶּלֶךְ לֵאמֹר: לְכוּ דִרְשׁוּ אֶת־יְהוָה בַּעֲדִי וּבְעַד הַנִּשְׁאָר בְּיִשְׂרָאֵל וּבִיהוּדָה עַל־דִּבְרֵי הַסֵּפֶר אֲשֶׁר נִמְצָא כִּי־גְדוֹלָה חֲמַת־יְהוָה אֲשֶׁר נִתְּכָה בָנוּ עַל אֲשֶׁר לֹא־שָׁמְרוּ אֲבוֹתֵינוּ אֶת־דְּבַר יְהוָה לַעֲשׂוֹת כְּכָל־הַכָּתוּב עַל־הַסֵּפֶר

כב הַזֶּה: וַיֵּלֶךְ חִלְקִיָּהוּ וַאֲשֶׁר הַמֶּלֶךְ אֶל־חֻלְדָּה הַנְּבִיאָה אֵשֶׁת ׀ שַׁלֻּם בֶּן־°תּוֹקַהַת [תָּקְהַת ק] בֶּן־חַסְרָה שׁוֹמֵר הַבְּגָדִים וְהִיא יוֹשֶׁבֶת

כג בִּירוּשָׁלַ͏ִם בַּמִּשְׁנֶה וַיְדַבְּרוּ אֵלֶיהָ כָּזֹאת: וַתֹּאמֶר לָהֶם כֹּה־אָמַר יְהוָה אֱלֹהֵי יִשְׂרָאֵל אִמְרוּ לָאִישׁ אֲשֶׁר־שָׁלַח אֶתְכֶם אֵלָי:

כד כֹּה אָמַר יְהוָה הִנְנִי מֵבִיא רָעָה עַל־הַמָּקוֹם הַזֶּה וְעַל־יוֹשְׁבָיו אֵת כָּל־ הָאָלוֹת הַכְּתוּבוֹת עַל־הַסֵּפֶר אֲשֶׁר קָרְאוּ לִפְנֵי מֶלֶךְ יְהוּדָה: תַּחַת ׀ אֲשֶׁר

כה עֲזָבוּנִי °וַיְקַטִּירוּ [וַיְקַטְּרוּ ק] לֵאלֹהִים אֲחֵרִים לְמַעַן הַכְעִיסֵנִי בְּכֹל

כו מַעֲשֵׂי יְדֵיהֶם וְתִתַּךְ חֲמָתִי בַּמָּקוֹם הַזֶּה וְלֹא תִכְבֶּה: וְאֶל־מֶלֶךְ יְהוּדָה הַשֹּׁלֵחַ אֶתְכֶם לִדְרוֹשׁ בַּיהוָה כֹּה תֹאמְרוּ אֵלָיו   כֹּה־אָמַר יְהוָה

כז אֱלֹהֵי יִשְׂרָאֵל הַדְּבָרִים אֲשֶׁר שָׁמָעְתָּ: יַעַן רַךְ־לְבָבְךָ וַתִּכָּנַע ׀ מִלִּפְנֵי אֱלֹהִים בְּשָׁמְעֲךָ אֶת־דְּבָרָיו עַל־הַמָּקוֹם הַזֶּה וְעַל־יֹשְׁבָיו וַתִּכָּנַע לְפָנַי

כח וַתִּקְרַע אֶת־בְּגָדֶיךָ וַתֵּבְךְּ לְפָנָי וְגַם־אֲנִי שָׁמַעְתִּי נְאֻם־יְהוָה: הִנְנִי אֹסִפְךָ אֶל־אֲבֹתֶיךָ וְנֶאֱסַפְתָּ אֶל־קִבְרֹתֶיךָ בְּשָׁלוֹם וְלֹא־תִרְאֶינָה עֵינֶיךָ בְּכֹל הָרָעָה אֲשֶׁר אֲנִי מֵבִיא עַל־הַמָּקוֹם הַזֶּה וְעַל־יֹשְׁבָיו וַיָּשִׁיבוּ אֶת־הַמֶּלֶךְ

כט דָּבָר: וַיִּשְׁלַח הַמֶּלֶךְ וַיֶּאֱסֹף אֶת־כָּל־זִקְנֵי יְהוּדָה וִירוּשָׁלָ͏ִם:

ל וַיַּעַל הַמֶּלֶךְ בֵּית־יְהוָה וְכָל־אִישׁ יְהוּדָה וְיֹשְׁבֵי יְרוּשָׁלַ͏ִם וְהַכֹּהֲנִים וְהַלְוִיִּם וְכָל־הָעָם מִגָּדוֹל וְעַד־קָטָן וַיִּקְרָא בְאָזְנֵיהֶם אֶת־כָּל־דִּבְרֵי סֵפֶר

לא הַבְּרִית הַנִּמְצָא בֵּית יְהוָה: וַיַּעֲמֹד הַמֶּלֶךְ עַל־עָמְדוֹ וַיִּכְרֹת אֶת־הַבְּרִית לִפְנֵי יְהוָה לָלֶכֶת אַחֲרֵי יְהוָה וְלִשְׁמוֹר אֶת־מִצְוֺתָיו וְעֵדְוֺתָיו וְחֻקָּיו בְּכָל־ לְבָבוֹ וּבְכָל־נַפְשׁוֹ לַעֲשׂוֹת אֶת־דִּבְרֵי הַבְּרִית הַכְּתוּבִים עַל־הַסֵּפֶר הַזֶּה:

לב וַיַּעֲמֵד אֵת כָּל־הַנִּמְצָא בִירוּשָׁלַ͏ִם וּבִנְיָמִן וַיַּעֲשׂוּ יֹשְׁבֵי יְרוּשָׁלַ͏ִם כִּבְרִית

34:15. So thoroughly had Manasseh and Amon purged the Torah from national life that the people were unfamil- iar with its contents. Sixty-seven years had elapsed since the beginning of Manasseh's reign.

The newly-
found Torah
Scroll

HASHEM, Hilkiah the Kohen found the Book of the Torah of HASHEM by Moses.
15 So Hilkiah spoke up and said to Shaphan the scribe, "I have found a Book of
the Torah in the Temple of HASHEM."* Hilkiah gave the book to Shaphan.
16 Shaphan the scribe brought the book to the king and also brought back a report
to him, saying, "Your servants are fulfilling everything that they have been
charged with — 17 they have counted the silver that was found in the Temple of
HASHEM, and they have given it to those who are in charge and to the workers."

The Torah
is read
to the king

18 Shaphan the scribe then told the king, saying, "Hilkiah the Kohen has given
me a Scroll." Shaphan then read from it before the king. 19 It happened that when
the king heard the words of the Torah, he rent his garments.* 20 The king
commanded Hilkiah, Ahikam son of Shaphan, Abdon son of Micah, Shaphan the
scribe, and Asaiah, the king's servant, saying, 21 "Go and inquire of HASHEM on my
behalf and on behalf of the remnant of Israel and Judah concerning the words of
this Scroll that was found; for great is the wrath of HASHEM that is poured out
against us, because our fathers did not observe the word of HASHEM, to fulfill all
that was written in this Scroll."

Huldah the
prophetess

22 So Hilkiah and those [sent] by the king went to Huldah the prophetess — the
wife of Shallum son of Tokhath son of Hasrah, the keeper of the [royal] garments
— who dwelled in Jerusalem, in the study house, and they spoke to her accordingly. 23 She said to them, "Thus said HASHEM, God of Israel: Say to the man who

God's wrath
will not be
extinguished
. . .

sent you to me, 24 'Thus said HASHEM: Behold, I am bringing evil upon this place
and upon its inhabitants — [namely] all the curses written in the Scroll that they
read before the king of Judah — 25 because they have forsaken Me and burned
offerings to the gods of others, in order to anger Me with all their handiwork; My
wrath has been poured out against this place, and it will not be extinguished.'
26 And concerning the king of Judah who sent you to inquire of HASHEM, thus
should you say to him: 'Thus said HASHEM, God of Israel: [Regarding] the words
that you have just heard — 27 because your heart is soft and you humbled yourself
before God when you heard His words about this place and its inhabitants — you
humbled yourself before Me and rent your garments and cried before Me — and

. . . but you
will not
see the
destruction

I, too, have heard, the word of HASHEM. 28 Behold, I will gather you in to your
forefathers — you will be gathered to your grave in peace — and your eyes will
not see all the evil that I am bringing upon this place and upon its inhabitants.' "
They brought this report back to the king. 29 The king sent out and gathered
all the elders of Judah and Jerusalem. 30 The king went up to the Temple of
HASHEM, [with] all the men of Judah and the inhabitants of Jerusalem and the

The king
reads the
Scroll in
public

Kohanim and the Levites and all the people from great to small, and he read in their
ears all the words of the Book of the Covenant that had been found in the Temple
of HASHEM.
31 The king then stood at his place and sealed the Covenant before HASHEM, to
follow HASHEM and to observe His commandments and His testimonies and His
decrees with all his heart and with all his soul, to uphold the words of the Covenant
written in this book.
32 He made all those who were present in Jerusalem and Benjamin accept
it, and the inhabitants of Jerusalem acted in accordance with the Covenant of

---

34:19. A sign of deep distress. Verse 21 implies that
the selection dealt with the harsh punishments that
would come upon the people for not observing the
words of the Torah. There is a tradition in the Talmud
that the selection was from *Deuteronomy* Ch. 28 (especially v. 36).

לג אֱלֹהִים אֱלֹהֵי אֲבוֹתֵיהֶם: וַיָּסַר יֹאשִׁיָּהוּ אֶת־כָּל־הַתּוֹעֵבוֹת מִכָּל־הָאֲרָצוֹת אֲשֶׁר לִבְנֵי יִשְׂרָאֵל וַיַּעֲבֵד אֵת כָּל־הַנִּמְצָא בְּיִשְׂרָאֵל לַעֲבוֹד אֶת־יהוה

לה א אֱלֹהֵיהֶם כָּל־יָמָיו לֹא סָרוּ מֵאַחֲרֵי יהוה אֱלֹהֵי אֲבוֹתֵיהֶם: וַיַּעַשׂ יֹאשִׁיָּהוּ בִירוּשָׁלַ͏ִם פֶּסַח לַיהוה וַיִּשְׁחֲטוּ הַפֶּסַח בְּאַרְבָּעָה עָשָׂר לַחֹדֶשׁ

ב הָרִאשׁוֹן: וַיַּעֲמֵד הַכֹּהֲנִים עַל־מִשְׁמְרוֹתָם וַיְחַזְּקֵם לַעֲבוֹדַת בֵּית יהוה: ג וַיֹּאמֶר לַלְוִיִּם °הַמְּבוֹנִים [הַמְּבִינִים ק׳] לְכָל־יִשְׂרָאֵל הַקְּדוֹשִׁים לַיהוה תְּנוּ אֶת־אֲרוֹן־הַקֹּדֶשׁ בַּבַּיִת אֲשֶׁר בָּנָה שְׁלֹמֹה בֶן־דָּוִיד מֶלֶךְ יִשְׂרָאֵל אֵין־לָכֶם מַשָּׂא בַּכָּתֵף עַתָּה עִבְדוּ אֶת־יהוה אֱלֹהֵיכֶם וְאֵת עַמּוֹ יִשְׂרָאֵל:

ד °וְהַכּוֹנוּ [וְהָכִינוּ ק׳] לְבֵית־אֲבוֹתֵיכֶם כְּמַחְלְקוֹתֵיכֶם בִּכְתָב דָּוִיד מֶלֶךְ יִשְׂרָאֵל וּבְמִכְתַּב שְׁלֹמֹה בְנוֹ: ה וְעִמְדוּ בַקֹּדֶשׁ לִפְלֻגּוֹת בֵּית הָאָבוֹת לַאֲחֵיכֶם בְּנֵי הָעָם וַחֲלֻקַּת בֵּית־אָב לַלְוִיִּם: ו וְשַׁחֲטוּ הַפָּסַח וְהִתְקַדְּשׁוּ וְהָכִינוּ לַאֲחֵיכֶם לַעֲשׂוֹת כִּדְבַר־יהוה בְּיַד־מֹשֶׁה:

ז וַיָּרֶם יֹאשִׁיָּהוּ לִבְנֵי הָעָם צֹאן כְּבָשִׂים וּבְנֵי־עִזִּים הַכֹּל לַפְּסָחִים לְכָל־הַנִּמְצָא לְמִסְפַּר שְׁלֹשִׁים אֶלֶף וּבָקָר שְׁלֹשֶׁת אֲלָפִים אֵלֶּה מֵרְכוּשׁ הַמֶּלֶךְ: ח וְשָׂרָיו לִנְדָבָה לָעָם לַכֹּהֲנִים וְלַלְוִיִּם הֵרִימוּ חִלְקִיָּה וּזְכַרְיָהוּ וִיחִיאֵל נְגִידֵי בֵּית הָאֱלֹהִים לַכֹּהֲנִים נָתְנוּ לַפְּסָחִים אַלְפַּיִם וְשֵׁשׁ מֵאוֹת וּבָקָר שְׁלֹשׁ מֵאוֹת: ט °וְכוֹנַנְיָהוּ [וְכָנַנְיָהוּ ק׳] וּשְׁמַעְיָהוּ וּנְתַנְאֵל אֶחָיו וַחֲשַׁבְיָהוּ וִיעִיאֵל וְיוֹזָבָד שָׂרֵי הַלְוִיִּם הֵרִימוּ לַלְוִיִּם לַפְּסָחִים חֲמֵשֶׁת אֲלָפִים וּבָקָר חֲמֵשׁ מֵאוֹת:

י וַתִּכּוֹן הָעֲבוֹדָה וַיַּעַמְדוּ הַכֹּהֲנִים עַל־עָמְדָם וְהַלְוִיִּם עַל־מַחְלְקוֹתָם כְּמִצְוַת הַמֶּלֶךְ: יא וַיִּשְׁחֲטוּ הַפָּסַח וַיִּזְרְקוּ הַכֹּהֲנִים מִיָּדָם וְהַלְוִיִּם מַפְשִׁיטִים: יב וַיָּסִירוּ הָעֹלָה לְתִתָּם לְמִפְלַגּוֹת לְבֵית־אָבוֹת לִבְנֵי הָעָם לְהַקְרִיב לַיהוה כַּכָּתוּב בְּסֵפֶר מֹשֶׁה וְכֵן לַבָּקָר: יג וַיְבַשְּׁלוּ הַפֶּסַח בָּאֵשׁ כַּמִּשְׁפָּט וְהַקֳּדָשִׁים בִּשְּׁלוּ בַּסִּירוֹת וּבַדְּוָדִים וּבַצֵּלָחוֹת וַיָּרִיצוּ לְכָל־בְּנֵי הָעָם: יד וְאַחַר הֵכִינוּ לָהֶם וְלַכֹּהֲנִים כִּי הַכֹּהֲנִים בְּנֵי אַהֲרֹן בְּהַעֲלוֹת הָעוֹלָה וְהַחֲלָבִים עַד־לָיְלָה וְהַלְוִיִּם הֵכִינוּ לָהֶם וְלַכֹּהֲנִים בְּנֵי אַהֲרֹן: טו וְהַמְשֹׁרְרִים בְּנֵי־אָסָף עַל־מַעֲמָדָם כְּמִצְוַת דָּוִיד וְאָסָף וְהֵימָן וִידֻתוּן חוֹזֵה הַמֶּלֶךְ וְהַשֹּׁעֲרִים לְשַׁעַר וָשָׁעַר אֵין לָהֶם לָסוּר מֵעַל עֲבֹדָתָם כִּי־אֲחֵיהֶם הַלְוִיִּם הֵכִינוּ לָהֶם: טז וַתִּכּוֹן כָּל־עֲבוֹדַת יהוה בַּיּוֹם הַהוּא לַעֲשׂוֹת הַפֶּסַח וְהַעֲלוֹת עֹלוֹת עַל מִזְבַּח יהוה כְּמִצְוַת הַמֶּלֶךְ יֹאשִׁיָּהוּ:

35:3. Apparently Josiah's wicked predecessors had removed the Ark and replaced it with some form of idolatrous image, and Josiah now ordered it returned. After carrying the Ark on their shoulders (see *Numbers* 7:9), its designated bearers would return to their service as described below. According to the Talmud (and many commentators) our verse refers not to the Temple, but to a secret vault area that Solomon had prepared for hiding away the Ark in case of emergency. Based on Huldah's dire prophecy of 34:24-25, Josiah decided that that time had now come.

35:4. See *I Chronicles* 28:19.

35:5. Due to the huge numbers of Israelites who will be in the Temple to bring the *pesach*-offering, all the Levites were to be ready to assist them in addition to the Levites whose turn it was to be there that week (*Ralbag*).

35:7. For peace-offerings.

35:12. Not until the required parts were placed on the

God, the God of their fathers. [33] King Josiah removed all the abominations from all the lands that belonged to the Children of Israel, and he impressed all who were present in Israel to worship HASHEM, their God; all his days they did not veer from following HASHEM, the God of their fathers.

35

Josiah's pesach-offering

[1] Josiah made the pesach-offering to HASHEM. They slaughtered the pesach-offering on the fourteenth day of the first month.

[2] He set up the Kohanim according to their divisions, and he encouraged them in the service of the Temple of HASHEM. [3] He then said to the Levites, who taught all of Israel, who were consecrated to HASHEM, "Place the Holy Ark in the Temple * that Solomon son of David, the king of Israel, built. Then you will no longer have any carrying on your shoulder; so now serve HASHEM your God and His people Israel. [4] Organize yourselves by your fathers' families, according to your divisions, in accordance with the written instructions of David king of Israel and the written instructions of his son Solomon. * [5] Stand in the Sanctuary according to the groupings of your fathers' families near your kinsmen, the populace, and the Levites' fathers' family division. * [6] Slaughter the pesach-offering; sanctify yourselves and prepare your kinsmen to act in accordance with the word of HASHEM, through Moses."

The king supplies the animals

[7] Josiah donated animals of the flock — sheep and goats — to the populace, all of them for pesach-offerings for those who were present, in the amount of thirty thousand, in addition to three thousand [head of] cattle; * all this was from the personal property of the king. [8] His officers also contributed voluntarily to the populace, to the Kohanim and to the Levites. Hilkiah, Zechariah and Jehiel, the managers of the Temple of God, gave two thousand six hundred [sheep] to the Kohanim for pesach-offerings, and three hundred [head of] cattle. [9] Cononiah, together with his brethren Shemaiah and Nethanel, and Hashabiah, Jeiel and Jozabad, officers of the Levites, donated five thousand [sheep] for pesach-[offerings] for the Levites, and five hundred [head of] cattle.

The sacrificial service

[10] Thus the service was in order. The Kohanim were stationed at their positions and the Levites in their divisions, in accordance with the king's orders. [11] They slaughtered the pesach-offering, and the Kohanim threw [the blood, which they had taken] from their hands, while the Levites were flaying. [12] They removed the parts that were to be offered up — in order to give [flesh of the pesach-offering] to the family groups of the populace * — to offer them up before HASHEM, as is written in the Book of Moses; and similarly for the cattle. [13] They cooked the pesach-offering over the fire according to the law, and they cooked the [other] sacrificial meat in pots and cauldrons and pans, and distributed it quickly to all the populace. [14] Afterwards they prepared [the pesach-offering] for themselves and for the Kohanim, because the Kohanim — the descendants of Aaron — were busy burning burnt-offerings and fats until nighttime, so now the Levites prepared for themselves and for the Kohanim, the descendants of Aaron.

[15] The singers, the descendants of Asaph, stood at their positions — according to the decree of David, Asaph, Heman and Jeduthun the king's seer — with the gate-keepers at every gate; they did not have to leave their own tasks, for their brother Levites had prepared for them. [16] The entire service of HASHEM was thus well organized on that day, to perform the pesach-offering and to bring up burnt-offerings upon the Altar of HASHEM, in accordance with the command of King Josiah.

Altar were the people permitted to eat the meat of their offerings.

יז וַיַּעֲשׂוּ בְנֵי־יִשְׂרָאֵל הַנִּמְצְאִים אֶת־הַפֶּסַח בָּעֵת הַהִיא וְאֶת־חַג הַמַּצּוֹת
יח שִׁבְעַת יָמִים: וְלֹא־נַעֲשָׂה פֶסַח כָּמֹהוּ בְּיִשְׂרָאֵל מִימֵי שְׁמוּאֵל הַנָּבִיא וְכָל־
מַלְכֵי יִשְׂרָאֵל ׀ לֹא־עָשׂוּ כַּפֶּסַח אֲשֶׁר־עָשָׂה יֹאשִׁיָּהוּ וְהַכֹּהֲנִים וְהַלְוִיִּם
יט וְכָל־יְהוּדָה וְיִשְׂרָאֵל הַנִּמְצָא וְיוֹשְׁבֵי יְרוּשָׁלָ͏ִם: בִּשְׁמוֹנֶה עֶשְׂרֵה
כ שָׁנָה לְמַלְכוּת יֹאשִׁיָּהוּ נַעֲשָׂה הַפֶּסַח הַזֶּה: אַחֲרֵי כָל־זֹאת אֲשֶׁר הֵכִין
יֹאשִׁיָּהוּ אֶת־הַבַּיִת עָלָה נְכוֹ מֶלֶךְ־מִצְרַיִם לְהִלָּחֵם בְּכַרְכְּמִישׁ עַל־פְּרָת
כא וַיֵּצֵא לִקְרָאתוֹ יֹאשִׁיָּהוּ: וַיִּשְׁלַח אֵלָיו מַלְאָכִים ׀ לֵאמֹר ׀ מַה־לִּי וָלָךְ מֶלֶךְ
יְהוּדָה לֹא־עָלֶיךָ אַתָּה הַיּוֹם כִּי אֶל־בֵּית מִלְחַמְתִּי וֵאלֹהִים אָמַר לְבַהֲלֵנִי
כב חֲדַל־לְךָ מֵאֱלֹהִים אֲשֶׁר־עִמִּי וְאַל־יַשְׁחִיתֶךָ: וְלֹא־הֵסֵב יֹאשִׁיָּהוּ פָנָיו
מִמֶּנּוּ כִּי לְהִלָּחֵם־בּוֹ הִתְחַפֵּשׂ וְלֹא שָׁמַע אֶל־דִּבְרֵי נְכוֹ מִפִּי אֱלֹהִים וַיָּבֹא
כג לְהִלָּחֵם בְּבִקְעַת מְגִדּוֹ: וַיֹּרוּ הַיֹּרִים לַמֶּלֶךְ יֹאשִׁיָּהוּ וַיֹּאמֶר הַמֶּלֶךְ לַעֲבָדָיו
כד הַעֲבִירוּנִי כִּי הׇחֳלֵיתִי מְאֹד: וַיַּעֲבִירֻהוּ עֲבָדָיו מִן־הַמֶּרְכָּבָה וַיַּרְכִּיבֻהוּ עַל
רֶכֶב הַמִּשְׁנֶה אֲשֶׁר־לוֹ וַיּוֹלִיכֻהוּ יְרוּשָׁלַ͏ִם וַיָּמׇת וַיִּקָּבֵר בְּקִבְרוֹת אֲבֹתָיו
כה וְכָל־יְהוּדָה וִירוּשָׁלַ͏ִם מִתְאַבְּלִים עַל־יֹאשִׁיָּהוּ:   וַיְקוֹנֵן יִרְמְיָהוּ
עַל־יֹאשִׁיָּהוּ וַיֹּאמְרוּ כׇל־הַשָּׁרִים ׀ וְהַשָּׁרוֹת בְּקִינוֹתֵיהֶם עַל־יֹאשִׁיָּהוּ עַד־
כו הַיּוֹם וַיִּתְּנוּם לְחֹק עַל־יִשְׂרָאֵל וְהִנָּם כְּתוּבִים עַל־הַקִּינוֹת: וְיֶתֶר דִּבְרֵי
כז יֹאשִׁיָּהוּ וַחֲסָדָיו כַּכָּתוּב בְּתוֹרַת יְהֹוָה: וּדְבָרָיו הָרִאשֹׁנִים וְהָאַחֲרֹנִים הִנָּם
לו א כְּתוּבִים עַל־סֵפֶר מַלְכֵי־יִשְׂרָאֵל וִיהוּדָה: וַיִּקְחוּ עַם־
הָאָרֶץ אֶת־יְהוֹאָחָז בֶּן־יֹאשִׁיָּהוּ וַיַּמְלִיכֻהוּ תַחַת־אָבִיו בִּירוּשָׁלָ͏ִם: בֶּן־
ב שָׁלוֹשׁ וְעֶשְׂרִים שָׁנָה יוֹאָחָז בְּמׇלְכוֹ וּשְׁלֹשָׁה חֳדָשִׁים מָלַךְ בִּירוּשָׁלָ͏ִם:
ג וַיְסִירֵהוּ מֶלֶךְ־מִצְרַיִם בִּירוּשָׁלָ͏ִם וַיַּעֲנֹשׁ אֶת־הָאָרֶץ מֵאָה כִכַּר־
ד כֶּסֶף וְכִכַּר זָהָב: וַיַּמְלֵךְ מֶלֶךְ־מִצְרַיִם אֶת־אֶלְיָקִים אָחִיו עַל־יְהוּדָה
וִירוּשָׁלַ͏ִם וַיַּסֵּב אֶת־שְׁמוֹ יְהוֹיָקִים וְאֶת־יוֹאָחָז אָחִיו לָקַח נְכוֹ וַיְבִיאֵהוּ
ה מִצְרָיְמָה: בֶּן־עֶשְׂרִים וְחָמֵשׁ שָׁנָה יְהוֹיָקִים בְּמׇלְכוֹ וְאַחַת
עֶשְׂרֵה שָׁנָה מָלַךְ בִּירוּשָׁלָ͏ִם וַיַּעַשׂ הָרַע בְּעֵינֵי יְהֹוָה אֱלֹהָיו: עָלָיו עָלָה
ו נְבוּכַדְנֶאצַּר מֶלֶךְ בָּבֶל וַיַּאַסְרֵהוּ בַּנְחֻשְׁתַּיִם לְהֹלִיכוֹ בָּבֶלָה: וּמִכְּלֵי בֵּית
ז יְהֹוָה הֵבִיא נְבוּכַדְנֶאצַּר לְבָבֶל וַיִּתְּנֵם בְּהֵיכָלוֹ בְּבָבֶל: וְיֶתֶר דִּבְרֵי יְהוֹיָקִים
ח וְתֹעֲבֹתָיו אֲשֶׁר־עָשָׂה וְהַנִּמְצָא עָלָיו הִנָּם כְּתוּבִים עַל־סֵפֶר מַלְכֵי
יִשְׂרָאֵל וִיהוּדָה וַיִּמְלֹךְ יְהוֹיָכִין בְּנוֹ תַּחְתָּיו: בֶּן־שְׁמוֹנֶה שָׁנִים
ט יְהוֹיָכִין בְּמׇלְכוֹ וּשְׁלֹשָׁה חֳדָשִׁים וַעֲשֶׂרֶת יָמִים מָלַךְ בִּירוּשָׁלָ͏ִם וַיַּעַשׂ
י הָרַע בְּעֵינֵי יְהֹוָה: וְלִתְשׁוּבַת הַשָּׁנָה שָׁלַח הַמֶּלֶךְ נְבוּכַדְנֶאצַּר וַיְבִאֵהוּ

35:18. There had not been such a magnitude of participation by the people. One factor was that for centuries
the Israelites of the northern tribes had not observed the
pesach-offering in Jerusalem.

35:20. Against the Assyrians (*II Kings* 23:29).

35:21. *Radak* suggests that the prophet Jeremiah may
have conveyed God's word to Neco.

35:24. According to the Sages, the fourth chapter of the
Book of Lamentations is Jeremiah's dirge.

36:10. The anniversary of Jehoiakim's removal from the

¹⁷ *So the Children of Israel who were present performed the pesach-offering at that time, and then the Festival of Unleavened Bread for seven days.* ¹⁸ *Such a pesach-offering had not been celebrated since the days of Samuel the Prophet.* * *None of the kings of Israel performed like the pesach-offering that Josiah did with the Kohanim, the Levites, all of Judah and Israel who were present, and the inhabitants of Jerusalem.* ¹⁹ *It was in the eighteenth year of Josiah's reign that this pesach-offering was performed.*

Josiah confronts Neco king of Egypt . . .

²⁰ *After all this, when Josiah had set up the Temple, Neco king of Egypt went up to wage war at Carchemish on the Euphrates,* * *and King Josiah went to confront him.* ²¹ *[Neco] sent messengers to him saying, "What is there between me and you, O King of Judah? It is not against you [that I advance] but to the site of my war, and God* * *has told me to hurry. Refrain from [provoking] God Who is with me, so that He does not destroy you!"* ²² *But Josiah would not turn his attention away from him, but rather he disguised himself to go to war against him;*

. . . and is killed

he did not heed the words of Neco from God's mouth, and he came to make war in the Valley of Meggido. ²³ *The archers shot at King Josiah. The king said to his servants, "Remove me, for I am gravely wounded!"* ²⁴ *His servants moved him from the chariot and drove him in his second chariot and they brought him to Jerusalem. He died and was buried in the graves of his forefathers. All of Judah and Jerusalem mourned over Josiah.* ²⁵ *Jeremiah lamented over Josiah.* * *All the men and women singers mentioned Josiah in their lamentations until this day; they made these [dirges] a firm custom in Israel, and behold, they are inscribed in the lamentations.*

(See Appendix A, timelines 4-5)

²⁶ *The rest of the deeds of Josiah and his kindnesses in accordance with what is written in the Torah of HASHEM,* ²⁷ *and his earlier and later deeds — behold, they are recorded in the Book of the Kings of Israel and Judah.*

36

KING JEHOAHAZ 36:1-4

¹ **T**he common people then took Jehoahaz son of Josiah and crowned him in place of his father in Jerusalem.

² *Jehoahaz was twenty-three years old when he became king, and he reigned for three months in Jerusalem.* ³ *The king of Egypt deposed him in Jerusalem, and he levied a fine upon the land — a hundred talents of silver and a talent of gold.*

KING JEHOIAKIM 36:4-8

⁴ *The king of Egypt then enthroned [Jehoahaz's] brother Eliakim over Judah and Jerusalem, and he changed his name to Jehoiakim. As for his brother Joahaz, Neco took him and brought him to Egypt.*

⁵ *Jehoiakim was twenty-five years old when he became king, and he reigned for eleven years in Jerusalem. He did what was evil in the eyes of HASHEM his God.* ⁶ *Nebuchadnezzar, king of Babylonia, [came up and] invaded against him; bound him in chains, to take him away to Babylonia.* ⁷ *Nebuchadnezzar also brought some of the vessels of the Temple of HASHEM to Babylonia, placing them in his palace in Babylon.*

⁸ *The rest of the deeds of Jehoiakim and all the abominations that he committed and the [charges] that were discovered against him — behold, they are recorded in the Book of Chronicles of the Kings of Israel and Judah. His son Jehoiachin reigned in his place.*

KING JEHOIACHIN 36:9-10

⁹ *Jehoiachin was eight years old when he became king, and he reigned for three months and ten days in Jerusalem. He did what was evil in the eyes of HASHEM.* ¹⁰ *At the turn of the year,* * *King Nebuchadnezzar sent and had him brought*

throne (*Rashi*).

בָּבֶלָה עִם־כָּל־כְּלֵי חֶמְדַּת בֵּית־יְהֹוָה וַיַּמְלֵךְ אֶת־צִדְקִיָּהוּ אָחִיו עַל־יְהוּדָה
וִירוּשָׁלָֽםִ:   יא בֶּן־עֶשְׂרִים וְאַחַת שָׁנָה צִדְקִיָּהוּ בְמָלְכוֹ וְאַחַת

יב עֶשְׂרֵה שָׁנָה מָלַךְ בִּירוּשָׁלָֽםִ: וַיַּעַשׂ הָרַע בְּעֵינֵי יְהֹוָה אֱלֹהָיו לֹא נִכְנַע
מִלִּפְנֵי יִרְמְיָהוּ הַנָּבִיא מִפִּי יְהֹוָה: יג וְגַם בַּמֶּלֶךְ נְבוּכַדְנֶאצַּר מָרָד אֲשֶׁר
הִשְׁבִּיעוֹ בֵּאלֹהִים וַיֶּקֶשׁ אֶת־עָרְפּוֹ וַיְאַמֵּץ אֶת־לְבָבוֹ מִשּׁוּב אֶל־יְהֹוָה
אֱלֹהֵי יִשְׂרָאֵֽל: יד גַּם כָּל־שָׂרֵי הַכֹּהֲנִים וְהָעָם הִרְבּוּ ˚לִמְעֹול־ [°לִֽמְעָל־
ק] מַעַל כְּכֹל תֹּעֲבוֹת הַגּוֹיִם וַֽיְטַמְּאוּ אֶת־בֵּית יְהֹוָה אֲשֶׁר הִקְדִּישׁ
בִּירוּשָׁלָֽםִ: טו וַיִּשְׁלַח יְהֹוָה אֱלֹהֵי אֲבוֹתֵיהֶם עֲלֵיהֶם בְּיַד מַלְאָכָיו הַשְׁכֵּם
טז וְשָׁלוֹחַ כִּי־חָמַל עַל־עַמּוֹ וְעַל־מְעוֹנֽוֹ: וַיִּֽהְיוּ מַלְעִבִים בְּמַלְאֲכֵי הָאֱלֹהִים
וּבוֹזִים דְּבָרָיו וּמִֽתַּעְתְּעִים בִּנְבִאָיו עַד עֲלוֹת חֲמַת־יְהֹוָה בְּעַמּוֹ עַד־לְאֵין
מַרְפֵּֽא: יז וַיַּעַל עֲלֵיהֶם אֶת־מֶלֶךְ ˚כַּשְׂדִּיים [°כַּשְׂדִּים ק] וַיַּהֲרֹג בַּחוּרֵיהֶם
בַּחֶרֶב בְּבֵית מִקְדָּשָׁם וְלֹא חָמַל עַל־בָּחוּר וּבְתוּלָה זָקֵן וְיָשֵׁשׁ הַכֹּל נָתַן
בְּיָדֽוֹ: יח וְכֹל כְּלֵי בֵּית הָאֱלֹהִים הַגְּדֹלִים וְהַקְּטַנִּים וְאֹצְרוֹת בֵּית יְהֹוָה
וְאֹצְרוֹת הַמֶּלֶךְ וְשָׂרָיו הַכֹּל הֵבִיא בָבֶֽל: יט וַיִּשְׂרְפוּ אֶת־בֵּית הָאֱלֹהִים
וַֽיְנַתְּצוּ אֵת חוֹמַת יְרוּשָׁלָֽםִ וְכָל־אַרְמְנוֹתֶיהָ שָׂרְפוּ בָאֵשׁ וְכָל־כְּלֵי
כ מַחֲמַדֶּיהָ לְהַשְׁחִֽית: וַיֶּגֶל הַשְּׁאֵרִית מִן־הַחֶרֶב אֶל־בָּבֶל וַיִּהְיוּ־לוֹ וּלְבָנָיו
כא לַעֲבָדִים עַד־מְלֹךְ מַלְכוּת פָּרָֽס: לְמַלֹּאות דְּבַר־יְהֹוָה בְּפִי יִרְמְיָהוּ עַד־
רָצְתָה הָאָרֶץ אֶת־שַׁבְּתוֹתֶיהָ כָּל־יְמֵי הָשַּׁמָּה שָׁבָתָה לְמַלֹּאות שִׁבְעִים
כב שָׁנָֽה: וּבִשְׁנַת אַחַת לְכוֹרֶשׁ מֶלֶךְ פָּרַס לִכְלוֹת דְּבַר־יְהֹוָה
בְּפִי יִרְמְיָהוּ הֵעִיר יְהֹוָה אֶת־רוּחַ כֹּרֶשׁ מֶלֶךְ־פָּרַס וַיַּֽעֲבֶר־קוֹל בְּכָל־
כג מַלְכוּתֽוֹ וְגַם־בְּמִכְתָּב לֵאמֹֽר: כֹּה־אָמַר כֹּרֶשׁ ׀ מֶלֶךְ פָּרַס כָּל־מַמְלְכוֹת
הָאָרֶץ נָתַן לִי יְהֹוָה אֱלֹהֵי הַשָּׁמַיִם וְהֽוּא־פָקַד עָלַי לִבְנֽוֹת־לוֹ בַיִת
בִּירוּשָׁלַםִ אֲשֶׁר בִּֽיהוּדָה מִי־בָכֶם מִכָּל־עַמּוֹ יְהֹוָה אֱלֹהָיו עִמּוֹ וְיָֽעַל:

סכום הפסוקים של דברי הימים הם אלף וְשֵׁש מאות וחמשים וששה. ויראו **אֶת הָאָרֶן** וישמחו לראות סימן.

36:21. Most of *Jeremiah's* fifty-two chapters warned of the impending Destruction and Exile. *Leviticus* 26:34-35 foretells that in retribution for Israel's failure to observe the Sabbatical years properly, the land would rest be- cause its inhabitants would be banished. The Sages teach that seventy such years were violated, and this exile lasted for seventy years.

to Babylonia, together with the precious articles of the Temple of HASHEM, and he made Zedekiah, his brother, king over Judah and Jerusalem.

KING ZEDEKIAH
36:11-20
(See Appendix A, timelines 4-5)

[11] Zedekiah was twenty-one years old when he became king, and he reigned for eleven years in Jerusalem. [12] He did what was evil in the eyes of HASHEM his God, and he did not humble himself before Jeremiah the Prophet, who spoke for HASHEM. [13] He also rebelled against King Nebuchadnezzar, who had made him swear allegiance by God. He stiffened his neck and hardened his heart against repenting to HASHEM, God of Israel. [14] Also, all the officers among the Kohanim and the people were exceedingly treacherous, like all the abominations of the nations, and they contaminated the Temple of HASHEM, which He had sanctified, in Jerusalem. [15] HASHEM, God of their fathers, had addressed them through His messengers, sending them from early morning, for he had pity on His people and on His Abode. [16] But they only insulted the messengers of God and scorned His words and taunted His prophets, until the wrath of HASHEM rose up against His people beyond remedy.

[17] So He brought up against them the king of the Chaldeans, who killed their young men by the sword in their Sanctuary. He had no pity on lad or maiden, nor on elderly and aged men — [God] delivered everyone into his hand. [18] All the articles of the Temple of God, large and small, the treasures of the Temple of HASHEM and the treasures of the king and his officers — he brought everything to Babylonia. [19] They burned the Temple of God, broke down the wall of Jerusalem, and burned down all its palaces and destroyed all its precious articles. [20] Those who survived the sword he exiled to Babylonia, where they became slaves to him and his sons, until the kingdom of Persia began to reign. [21] This was in fulfillment of the word of HASHEM spoken by Jeremiah, until the land would be appeased of its Sabbatical years — all the years of its desolation it rested, to the completion of seventy years. *

Seventy years later

[22] In the first year of Cyrus king of Persia, upon the expiration of HASHEM's prophecy spoken by Jeremiah, * HASHEM aroused the spirit of Cyrus king of Persia, and he issued a proclamation throughout his kingdom — and in writing as well — saying:

[23] "Thus said Cyrus king of Persia: HASHEM, God of Heaven, has given to me all the kingdoms of the earth, and He has commanded me to build Him a Temple in Jerusalem, which is in Judah. Whoever there is among you of His entire people — may HASHEM his God be with him, and let him go up!"

36:22. *Jeremiah* 29:10: "Thus said HASHEM: After seventy years for Babylonia have passed I will attend to you and I will fulfill for you My favorable promise, to return you to this place."

Appendices

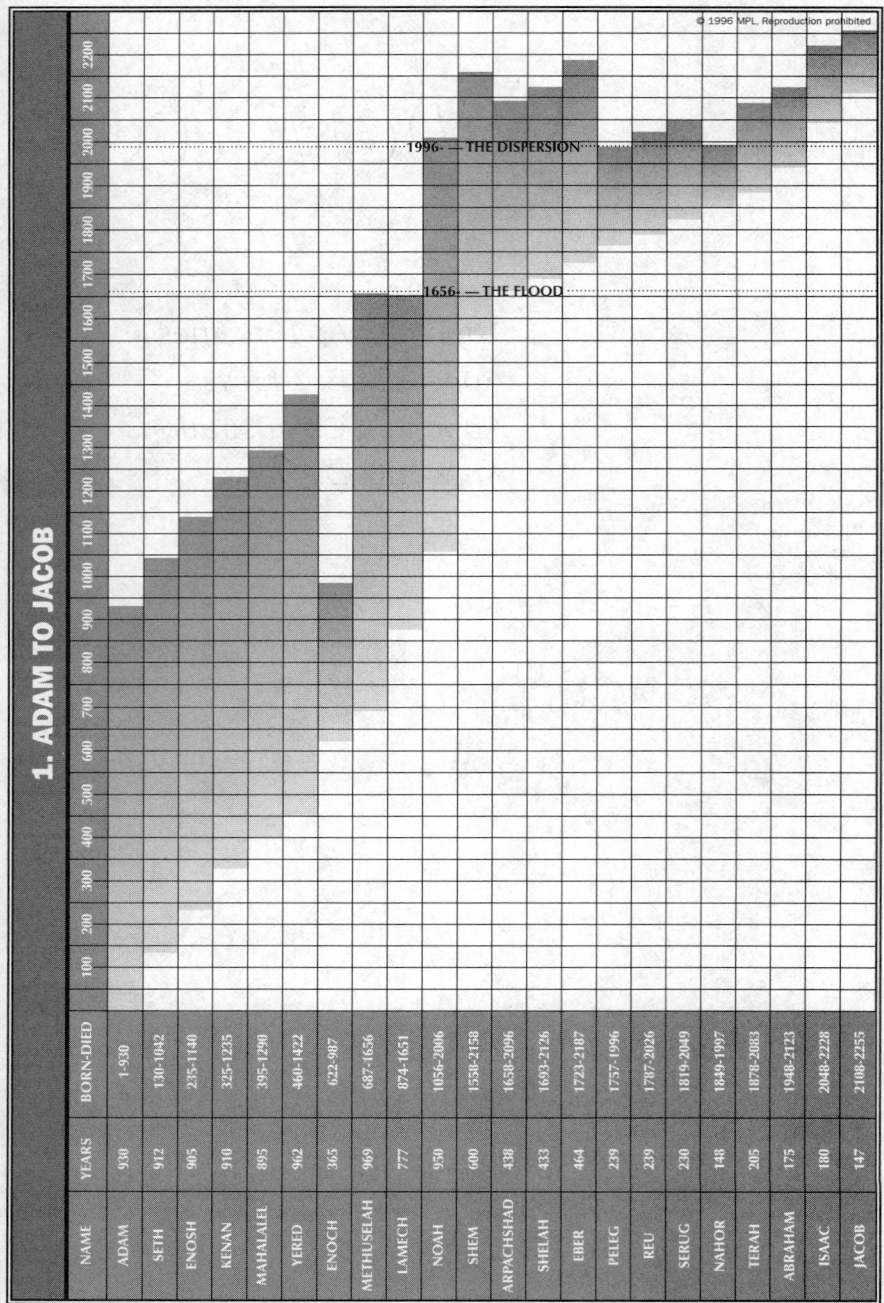

1. ADAM TO JACOB

1996 — THE DISPERSION

1656 — THE FLOOD

NAME	YEARS	BORN-DIED
ADAM	930	1-930
SETH	912	130-1042
ENOSH	905	235-1140
KENAN	910	325-1235
MAHALALEL	895	395-1290
YERED	962	460-1422
ENOCH	365	622-987
METHUSELAH	969	687-1656
LAMECH	777	874-1651
NOAH	950	1056-2006
SHEM	600	1558-2158
ARPACHSHAD	438	1658-2096
SHELAH	433	1693-2126
EBER	464	1723-2187
PELEG	239	1757-1996
REU	239	1787-2026
SERUG	230	1819-2049
NAHOR	148	1849-1997
TERAH	205	1878-2083
ABRAHAM	175	1948-2123
ISAAC	180	2048-2228
JACOB	147	2108-2255

2. THE FLOOD

[ACCORDING TO R' ELIEZER]

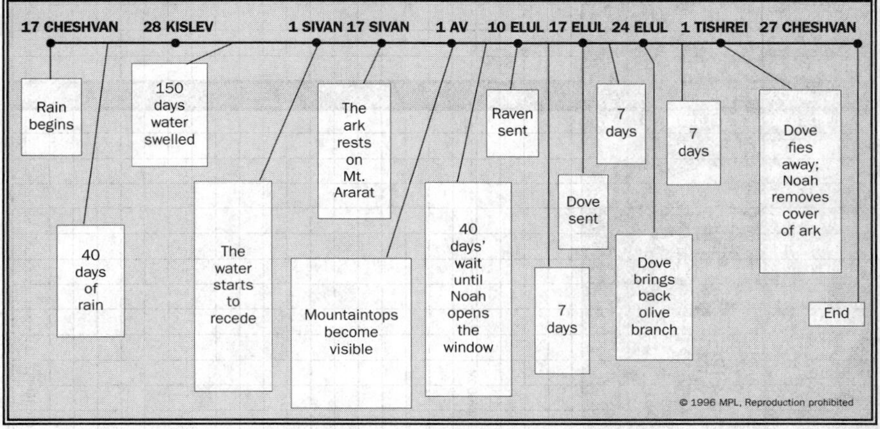
17 CHESHVAN
28 KISLEV
1 SIVAN
17 SIVAN
1 AV
10 ELUL
17 ELUL
24 ELUL
1 TISHREI
27 CHESHVAN
Rain begins
40 days of rain
150 days water swelled
The water starts to recede
The ark rests on Mt. Ararat
Mountaintops become visible
40 days' wait until Noah opens the window
Raven sent
7 days
Dove sent
7 days
Dove brings back olive branch
7 days
Dove fies away; Noah removes cover of ark
End

© 1996 MPL, Reproduction prohibited

3. THE ERA OF THE JUDGES

[ACCORDING TO THE GAON OF VILNA]

JOSHUA	28
OTHNIEL	40
EHUD	80
SHAMGAR	
DEBORAH & BARAK	40
GIDEON	40[1]
ABIMELECH	3
TOLA	23[2]
JAIR	22[2]
AMMONITE RULE	18
JEPHTHAH	6
IBZAN	7
ELON	10
ABDON	8
SAMSON	20
ELI	39[3]
SAMUEL	11

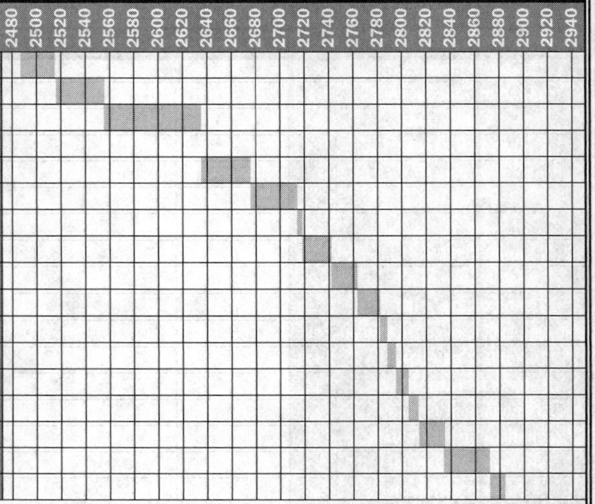
2480
2500
2520
2540
2560
2580
2600
2620
2640
2660
2680
2700
2720
2740
2760
2780
2800
2820
2840
2860
2880
2900
2920
2940

1. Includes 7 years of Midianite rule.
2. There is one year which counts for both Tola and Jair.
3. While the verse (*II Samuel* 4:18) refers to Eli having led Israel for 40 years, the last year was incomplete and is therefore not counted for the purposes of the chronology.

© 1996 MPL, Reproduction prohibited

4. THE JEWISH MONARCHY

KINGS OF ISRAEL	REIGN	2880	2900	2920	2940	2960	2980	3000	3020	3040	3060	3080	3100	3120	3140	3160	3180	3200	3220	3240	3260	3280	3300	3320	3340
SAUL BEN KISH	2																								
ISH-BOSHETH BEN SAUL	2																								
DAVID BEN JESSE	40																								
SOLOMON BEN DAVID	40																								
KINGS OF JUDAH																									
REHOBOAM BEN SOLOMON	17																								
ABIJAM BEN REHOBOAM	3																								
ASA BEN ABIJAM	41																								
JEHOSHAPHAT BEN ASA	25																								
JEHORAM BEN JEHOSHAPHAT	8																								
AHAZIAH BEN JEHORAM	1																								
ATHALIAH mother of AHAZIAH	6																								
JEHOASH BEN AHAZIAH	40																								
AMAZIAH BEN JEHOASH	29																								
UZZIAH[1] BEN AMAZIAH	52																								
JOTHAM BEN UZZIAH	16																								
AHAZ BEN JOTHAM	16																								
HEZEKIAH BEN AHAZ	29																								
MANASSEH BEN HEZEKIAH	55																								
AMON BEN MANASSEH	2																								
JOSIAH BEN AMON	31																								
JEHOAHAZ BEN JOSIAH	3*																								
JEHOIAKIM[2] BEN JOSIAH	11																								
JEHOIACHIN[3] BEN JEHOIAKIM	3*																								
ZEDEKIAH[4] BEN JOSIAH	11																								
KINGS OF ISRAEL (10 TRIBES)																									
JEROBOAM BEN NEBAT	22																								
NADAB BEN JEROBOAM	2																								
BAASA BEN AHIJAH	24																								
ELAH BEN BAASA	2																								
ZIMRI	7**																								
TIVNI	5																								
OMRI	12																								
AHAB BEN OMRI	22																								
AHAZIAH BEN AHAB	2																								
JEHORAM BEN AHAB	12																								
JEHU BEN JEHOSHAPHAT BEN NIMSHI	28																								
JEHOAHAZ BEN JEHU	17																								
JEHOASH BEN JEHOAHAZ	16																								
JEROBOAM BEN JEHOASH	41																								
ZECHARIAH BEN JEROBOAM	6*																								
SHALLUM BEN JABESH	1*																								
MENAHEM BEN GADI	10																								
PEKAHIAH BEN MENAHEM	2																								
PEKAH BEN REMALIAH	20																								
HOSHEA BEN ELAH	19																								

2964 — DIVISION OF THE KINGDOM

3338 — DESTRUCTION OF THE TEMPLE

3205 — EXILE OF THE TEN TRIBES

*months   **days   1. Also known as Azariah.   2. Also known as Eliakim.   3. Also known as Jeconiah.   4. Also known as Mattaniah.

5. THE BABYLONIAN EXILE

KING	COUNTRY	YEARS OF RULE*	COMMENT	3310	3320	3330	3340	3350	3360	3370	3380	3390	3400	3410	3420	3430	3440
		70 YEARS OF EXILE: 3338-3408															
NEBUCHADNEZZAR	BABYLON	3319-3363	Destroyed Jerusalem														
EVIL-MERODACH	BABYLON	3363-3386	Freed King Jehoiachin														
BELSHAZZAR	BABYLON	3386-3389	Last Babylonian king														
DARIUS THE MEDE	PERSIA-MEDIA	3389-3390	Defeated Belshazzar														
CYRUS	PERSIA-MEDIA	3390-3393	Authorized return of exiles and rebuilding of Temple														
AHASUERUS	PERSIA-MEDIA	3393-3407	Husband of Esther														
DARIUS THE PERSIAN	PERSIA-MEDIA	3407-3442	Esther's son; authorized Temple's completion														

3338 — DESTRUCTION OF THE TEMPLE

3408 — AUTHORIZATION TO COMPLETE THE TEMPLE

*Based on *Seder Olam* and *Talmud* (*Megillah* 11b-12a, according to *Rashi*).

1. THE SEVENTY NATIONS[1]

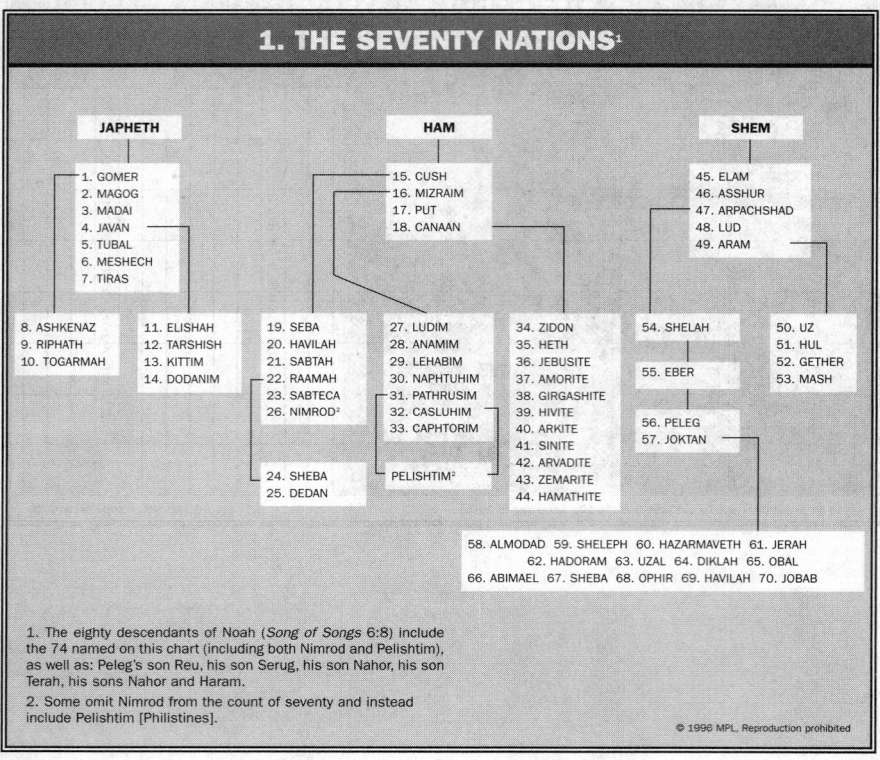

1. The eighty descendants of Noah (*Song of Songs* 6:8) include the 74 named on this chart (including both Nimrod and Pelishtim), as well as: Peleg's son Reu, his son Serug, his son Nahor, his son Terah, his sons Nahor and Haram.

2. Some omit Nimrod from the count of seventy and instead include Pelishtim [Philistines].

1a. THE SEVEN NOAHIDE LAWS[1]

1	IDOLATRY	עבודה זרה	א
2	"BLESSING" THE DIVINE NAME	ברכת השם	ב
3	MURDER	שפיכות דמים	ג
4	SEXUAL TRANSGRESSIONS	גלוי עריות	ד
5	THEFT (AND CIVIL LAW)	גזל	ה
6	COURTS SYSTEM	דינים	ו
7	EATING A LIMB TORN FROM A LIVE ANIMAL	אבר מן החי	ז

1. *Sanhedrin* 56a; *Rambam, Hil. Melachim* 9:1.

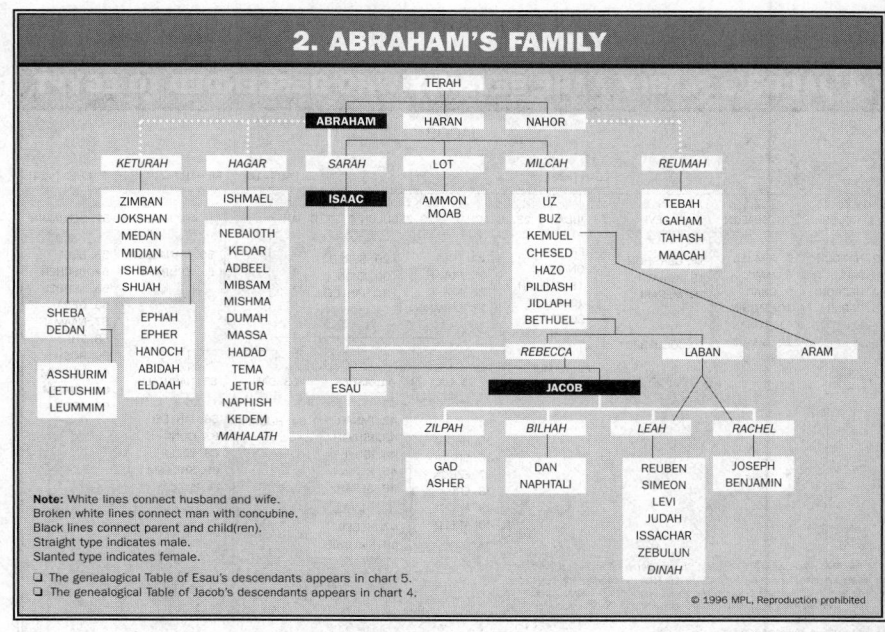

2. ABRAHAM'S FAMILY

Note: White lines connect husband and wife.
Broken white lines connect man with concubine.
Black lines connect parent and child(ren).
Straight type indicates male.
Slanted type indicates female.

❑ The genealogical Table of Esau's descendants appears in chart 5.
❑ The genealogical Table of Jacob's descendants appears in chart 4.

3. THE TEN TRIALS OF ABRAHAM

Although the Sages state clearly that Abraham was tested ten times (*Avos* 5:3), there are several versions of what the tests were. Following are the lists of tests given by *Rashi* and *Rambam* in their commentaries to the above Mishnah:

	RASHI	RAMBAM
1	Abraham hid underground for thirteen years from King Nimrod, who wanted to kill him.	Abraham's exile from his family and homeland.
2	Nimrod flung Abraham into a burning furnace.	The hunger in Canaan after God had assured him that he would become a great nation there.
3	Abraham was commanded to leave his family and homeland.	The corruption in Egypt that resulted in the abduction of Sarah.
4	Almost as soon as he arrived in Canaan, he was forced to leave to escape a famine.	The war with the four kings.
5	Sarah was kidnaped by Pharaoh's officials.	His marriage to Hagar after having despaired that Sarah would ever give birth.
6	The kings captured Lot, and Abraham was forced to go to war to rescue him.	The commandment of circumcision.
7	God told Abraham that his offspring would suffer under four monarchies.	Abimelech's abduction of Sarah.
8	At an advanced age, he was commanded to circumcise himself and his son.	Driving away Hagar after she had given brth.
9	He was commanded to drive away Ishmael and Hagar.	The very distasteful command to drive away Ishmael.
10	The binding of Isaac on the altar.	The binding of Isaac on the altar.

4. JACOB'S FAMILY / THE SEVENTY WHO DESCENDED TO EGYPT

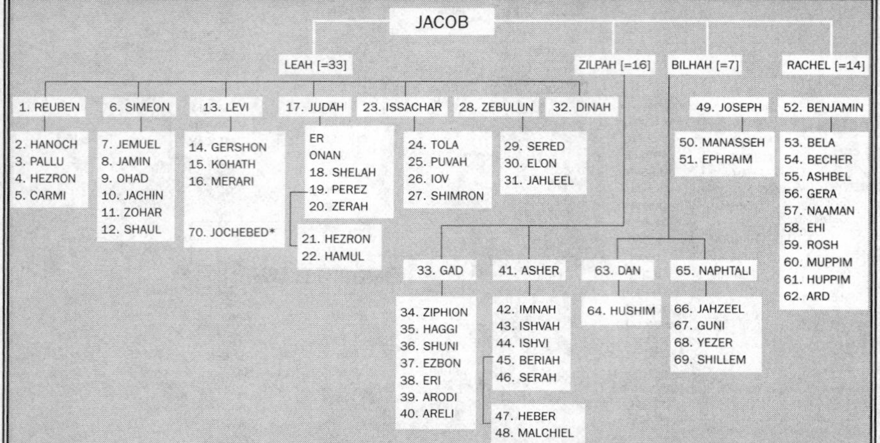

JACOB

LEAH [=33] ZILPAH [=16] BILHAH [=7] RACHEL [=14]

| 1. REUBEN | 6. SIMEON | 13. LEVI | 17. JUDAH | 23. ISSACHAR | 28. ZEBULUN | 32. DINAH | 49. JOSEPH | 52. BENJAMIN |

2. HANOCH	7. JEMUEL	14. GERSHON	ER	24. TOLA	29. SERED		50. MANASSEH	53. BELA
3. PALLU	8. JAMIN	15. KOHATH	ONAN	25. PUVAH	30. ELON		51. EPHRAIM	54. BECHER
4. HEZRON	9. OHAD	16. MERARI	18. SHELAH	26. IOV	31. JAHLEEL			55. ASHBEL
5. CARMI	10. JACHIN		19. PEREZ	27. SHIMRON				56. GERA
	11. ZOHAR		20. ZERAH					57. NAAMAN
	12. SHAUL	70. JOCHEBED*	21. HEZRON					58. EHI
			22. HAMUL					59. ROSH
								60. MUPPIM
								61. HUPPIM
								62. ARD

| 33. GAD | 41. ASHER | 63. DAN | 65. NAPHTALI |

34. ZIPHION	42. IMNAH	64. HUSHIM	66. JAHZEEL
35. HAGGI	43. ISHVAH		67. GUNI
36. SHUNI	44. ISHVI		68. YEZER
37. EZBON	45. BERIAH		69. SHILLEM
38. ERI	46. SERAH		
39. ARODI			
40. ARELI	47. HEBER		
	48. MALCHIEL		

*The Torah lists only 69 persons. The inclusion of Jochebed, who was born at the entrance to Egypt although she is not specifically listed in the Torah, follows the Midrash and Rashi. Others include Jacob himself in the count of 70. There is also a view that the Divine Presence, which accompanied the Israelites into Exile, is included in the count.

© 1996 MPL, Reproduction prohibited

5. ESAU'S FAMILY

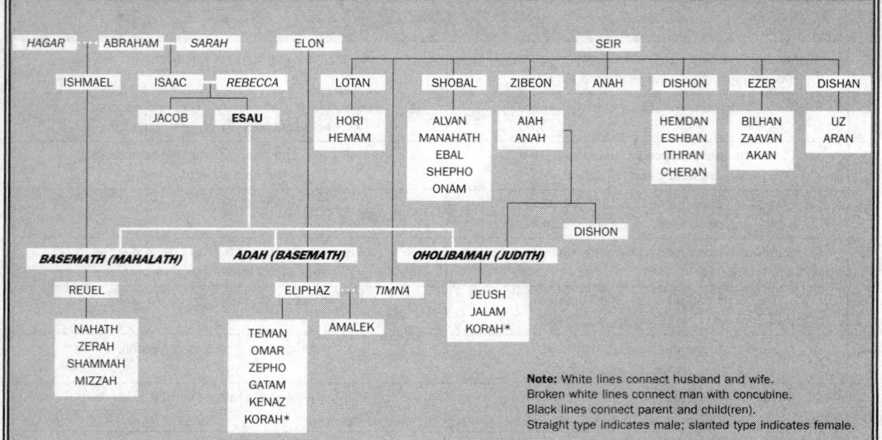

| HAGAR | ABRAHAM | SARAH | ELON | | | SEIR | | | |

| ISHMAEL | ISAAC | REBECCA | LOTAN | SHOBAL | ZIBEON | ANAH | DISHON | EZER | DISHAN |

	JACOB	ESAU	HORI	ALVAN	AIAH		HEMDAN	BILHAN	UZ
			HEMAM	MANAHATH	ANAH		ESHBAN	ZAAVAN	ARAN
				EBAL			ITHRAN	AKAN	
				SHEPHO			CHERAN		
				ONAM					

DISHON

| BASEMATH (MAHALATH) | ADAH (BASEMATH) | OHOLIBAMAH (JUDITH) |

REUEL	ELIPHAZ	TIMNA	JEUSH
			JALAM
NAHATH			KORAH*
ZERAH	TEMAN	AMALEK	
SHAMMAH	OMAR		
MIZZAH	ZEPHO		
	GATAM		
	KENAZ		
	KORAH*		

Note: White lines connect husband and wife.
Broken white lines connect man with concubine.
Black lines connect parent and child(ren).
Straight type indicates male; slanted type indicates female.

* Korah was the illegitimate son of Eliphaz and his father's wife Oholibamah.

© 1996 MPL, Reproduction prohibited

6. LISTING OF ALL THE ANIMAL OFFERINGS

The following chart lists all the circumstances that call for animal offerings, and details what type of animal is used for each, whether it is a male or female (M/F), communal or personal offering (C/P), and obligatory or voluntary (O/V). These are all grouped according to their general classifications, such as *chatas, olah,* etc.

lamb, כֶּבֶשׂ — from the eighth day[1] after birth until the first birthday

kid, שָׂעִיר עִזִּים — from the eighth day[1] after birth until the first birthday[2]

calf, עֵגֶל — from the eighth day[1] until the second birthday

ram, אַיִל — from the beginning of the fourteenth month until the second birthday

bull, פַּר בֶּן בָּקָר — from the first birthday until the third birthday

goat, עֵז — from the eighth day[1] after birth until the second birthday

cattle, בָּקָר — from the eighth day[1] after birth until the third birthday

1. But preferably after the thirtieth day.
2. See Mishnah *Parah* 1:4; *Sifra* to *Lev.* 4:28. As to *Rambam's* ruling on this matter, we have followed the view of *Kesef Mishneh* as per his emendation of *Rambam, Maaseh HaKorbanos* 1:4, and as interpreted by *Har HaMoriah* and *Aruch HaShulchan HeAssid* 63:24-25.

TYPE	OCCASION	C/P	TYPE OF ANIMAL	M/F	O/V
INNER CHATAS/ SIN-OFFERING	COMMUNAL YOM KIPPUR	C	KID	M	O
	KOHEN GADOL ON YOM KIPPUR	P	BULL	M	O
	BULL FOR A MATTER THAT WAS HIDDEN FROM CONGREGATION	C	BULL	M	O
	CHATAS FOR COMMUNAL IDOLATRY	C	KID	M	O
	BULL OF THE ANOINTED KOHEN	P	BULL	M	O
OUTER CHATAS/ SIN-OFFERING	MUSSAF ON ROSH CHODESH, THE THREE FESTIVALS, ROSH HASHANAH AND YOM KIPPUR	C	KID	M	O
	WITH TWO LOAVES OF SHAVUOS	C	KID	M	O
	PERSONAL SIN, VARIABLE *CHATAS*	P	KID OR LAMB	F	O
	CHATAS FOR INDIVIDUAL IDOLATRY	P	KID	F	O
	HE-GOAT OF A RULER	P	KID	M	O
	NAZIR TAHOR AND *METZORA*	P	LAMB	F	O
OLAH/ BURNT-OFFERING	*TAMID* (DAILY OFFERING)	C	1 LAMB A.M. /1 LAMB P.M.	M	O
	MUSSAF OF SHABBOS	C	2 LAMBS	M	O
	MUSSAF OF ROSH CHODESH, PESACH (7 DAYS), SHAVUOS	C	2 BULLS, 1 RAM, 7 LAMBS	M	O
	MUSSAF OF ROSH HASHANAH, YOM KIPPUR	C	1 BULL, 1 RAM, 7 LAMBS	M	O
	MUSSAF OF SUCCOS, DAYS 1-7	C	13-7 BULLS, 2 RAMS, 14 LAMBS	M	O
	MUSSAF OF SHEMINI ATZERES	C	1 BULL, 1 RAM, 7 LAMBS	M	O
	WITH *OMER* OFFERING	C	LAMB	M	O
	WITH TWO LOAVES OF SHAVUOS	C	1 BULL, 2 RAMS, 7 LAMBS	M	O
	KOHEN GADOL ON YOM KIPPUR	P	RAM	M	O
	OLAS RE'IYAH ON 3 FESTIVALS	P	SHEEP, GOAT OR CATTLE	M	O
	WOMAN AFTER CHILDBIRTH, *NAZIR TAHOR*, *METZORA*	P	LAMB	M	O
	COMMUNAL IDOLATRY	C	BULL	M	O
	CONVERT	P	SHEEP, GOAT OR CATTLE	M	O
	VOLUNTARY	P	SHEEP, GOAT OR CATTLE	M	V
	KAYITZ HAMIZBE'ACH (OFFERING WHEN ALTAR IS IDLE)	C	SHEEP, GOAT OR CATTLE	M	V
ASHAM/ GUILT-OFFERING	DOUBTFUL SIN, *ME'ILAH*, THEFT, BETROTHED MAIDSERVANT	P	RAM	M	O
	NAZIR TAMEI, *METZORA*	P	LAMB	M	O
SHELAMIM/ PEACE-OFFERING	WITH TWO LOAVES OF SHAVUOS	C	2 LAMBS	M	O
	CHAGIGAH AND *SIMCHAH* ON THE THREE FESTIVALS	P	SHEEP, GOAT OR CATTLE	M/F	O
	NAZIR TAHOR	P	RAM	M	O
	VOLUNTARY	P	SHEEP, GOAT OR CATTLE	M/F	V
	TODAH	P	SHEEP, GOAT OR CATTLE	M/F	V
OTHER OFFERINGS	*BECHOR*	P	SHEEP, GOAT OR CATTLE	M	O
	MAASER	P	SHEEP, GOAT OR CATTLE	M/F	O
	PESACH	P	LAMB OR KID	M	O

7. PROCEDURE FOR ANIMAL OFFERINGS

The category of זְבָחִים, *slaughtered offerings,* consists of animals slaughtered in the Temple and offered either partially or totally on the Altar. All such offerings share essential common features; the different types are distinguished from one another by certain details of their offering, such as where in the Courtyard the animal may be slaughtered, where and how its blood is applied to the Altar and in how many applications, whether or not it is eaten, by whom, and for how long. The following chart delineates these distinctions.

TYPE OF OFFERING	CLASSIFICATION	PLACE OF SLAUGHTER	BLOOD APPLICATION			DISPOSITION OF MEAT	EATING	
			SITE	TYPE	NUMBER		PLACE	TIME
חַטָּאוֹת פְּנִימִיּוֹת שֶׁל יוֹם הַכִּפּוּרִים **Inner Chataos of Yom Kippur** (Lev. ch. 16)	קָדְשֵׁי קָדָשִׁים Most-holy	Courtyard/north	Holy of Holies, Holy, Inner Altar	הַזָּאָה Sprinkling; מַתַּן אֶצְבַּע Daubing by finger	43[1]	Burned outside the camp[8]	Not eaten	Not eaten
שְׁאָר חַטָּאוֹת פְּנִימִיּוֹת **Other Inner Chataos** (Lev. ch. 4)	קָדְשֵׁי קָדָשִׁים Most-holy	Courtyard/north	Holy, Inner Altar	הַזָּאָה Sprinkling; מַתַּן אֶצְבַּע Daubing by finger	11	Burned outside the camp[8]	Not eaten	Not eaten
חַטַּאת הַחִיצוֹנָה **Outer Chatas**	קָדְשֵׁי קָדָשִׁים Most-holy	Courtyard/north	Horns of Outer Altar	Daubing by finger	4	Eaten by Kohanim	Courtyard	1 day 1 night
עוֹלָה **Burnt-offering** (Lev. ch. 1)	קָדְשֵׁי קָדָשִׁים Most-holy	Courtyard/north	N.E. and S.W. corners of outer Altar, lower part	זְרִיקָה Throwing	2 equivalent to 4	Burned on Outer Altar	Not eaten	Not eaten
אָשָׁם **Guilt-offering** (Lev. ch. 5)	קָדְשֵׁי קָדָשִׁים Most-holy	Courtyard/north	N.E. and S.W. corners of Outer Altar, lower part	זְרִיקָה Throwing	2 equivalent to 4	Eaten by male Kohanim	Courtyard	1 day 1 night
שַׁלְמֵי צִבּוּר[2] **Communal Peace-offering** (Lev. 23:19)	קָדְשֵׁי קָדָשִׁים Most-holy	Courtyard/north	N.E. and S.W. Corners of Outer Altar, lower part	זְרִיקָה Throwing	2 equivalent to 4	Eaten by male Kohanim	Courtyard	1 day 1 night
שַׁלְמֵי יָחִיד **Personal Peace-offering** (Lev. ch. 3)	קָדָשִׁים קַלִּים Lesser holiness	Courtyard/anywhere	N.E. and S.W. Corners of Outer Altar	זְרִיקָה Throwing	2 equivalent to 4	Breast and thigh: eaten by Kohanim and households/remainder: by anyone	Anywhere in the camp[3]	2 days 1 night
תּוֹדָה[4] **Thanksgiving-offering** (Lev. ch. 7)	קָדָשִׁים קַלִּים Lesser holiness	Courtyard/anywhere	Lower part of Corners of Outer Altar	זְרִיקָה Throwing	2 Equivalent to 4	Breast and thigh: eaten by Kohanim and households/remainder: by anyone	Anywhere in the camp[3]	1 day 1 night
בְּכוֹר[5] **First-born offering** (Num. 18:17,18)	קָדָשִׁים קַלִּים Lesser holiness	Courtyard/anywhere	Lower part of Altar wall[6]	שְׁפִיכָה Pouring	1	Eaten by Kohanim and households	Anywhere in the camp[3]	2 days 1 night
מַעֲשֵׂר **Tithe offering** (Lev. 27:32)	קָדָשִׁים קַלִּים Lesser holiness	Courtyard/anywhere	Lower part of Altar wall[6]	שְׁפִיכָה Pouring	1	Eaten by anyone	Anywhere in the camp[3]	2 days 1 night
פֶּסַח **Pesach-offering** (Ex. ch. 12)	קָדָשִׁים קַלִּים Lesser Holiness	Courtyard/anywhere	Lower part of Altar wall[6]	שְׁפִיכָה Pouring	1	Eaten by anyone who has registered	Anywhere in the camp[3,7]	1 night (until midnight)

1. This represents the combined total for both the bull and the he-goat of Yom Kippur. According to one opinion there were 47.
2. There is a question whether this offering was made in the Wilderness (see *Menachos* 4:3).
3. When the Temple was built, it could be eaten anywhere in Jerusalem.
4. The אֵיל נָזִיר, *nazir's ram,* is identical to the *todah* except that its right front leg [זְרוֹעַ] is also given to the Kohen (*Numbers* 6:19, 20).
5. There is a dispute whether the *bechor* offering was applied in the Wilderness (*Bechoros* 4b).
6. Any wall of the Altar which is above the יְסוֹד, *base,* is valid.
7. In the Wilderness, the *pesach* was offered only the first year.
8. When the Temple was built, it was burned outside of Jerusalem.

8. PROCEDURE FOR BIRD OFFERINGS

In contrast to the animal offerings, bird offerings are slaughtered by the procedure known as *melikah,* in which the Kohen punctures the back of the bird's neck with his thumbnail and cuts through to the front. In another departure, the blood is not caught in a vessel but is applied to the Altar directly from the bird's body. The following chart highlights the difference between the bird *chatas* and the bird *olah.*

	חַטָּאת — **CHATAS**	עוֹלָה — **OLAH**
CLASSIFICATION	קָדְשֵׁי קָדָשִׁים — MOST-HOLY	קָדְשֵׁי קָדָשִׁים — MOST-HOLY
PLACE OF *MELIKAH*	FLOOR OF THE COURTYARD NEAR SOUTHWEST CORNER OF ALTAR[1]	TOP OF THE ALTAR: SOUTHEAST OR SOUTHWEST CORNER
TYPE OF *MELIKAH*	EITHER WINDPIPE OR ESOPHAGUS[2]	BOTH WINDPIPE AND ESOPHAGUS
SITE OF BLOOD APPLICATIONS	LOWER PART OF SOUTHWEST CORNER OF ALTAR	UPPER WALL OF ALTAR
TYPE OF BLOOD APPLICATIONS	הַזָּאָה, SPRINKLING,[3] AND מִצּוּי, DRAINING[4]	מִצּוּי, DRAINING
DISPOSITION OF MEAT	EATEN BY KOHANIM	BURNED ON THE ALTAR
PLACE FOR EATING	COURTYARD	NOT EATEN
TIME FOR EATING	1 DAY AND NIGHT	NOT EATEN

1. However, it is valid even if he slaughters it near another area of the Altar.
2. Cutting both invalidates the bird *chatas*; by contrast, the bird *olah* is not valid unless both are cut.
3. The sprinkling is done directly from the neck of the bird, not by finger.
4. This is a procedure in which the neck of the bird is pressed against the Altar wall to drain the blood.

9. MINCHAH OFFERINGS

Minchah-offerings come in many forms, but they all share certain features. All consist primarily of flour, all have at least a part offered on the Altar, while some are burned in their entirety on the Altar. Of those not entirely burned, the part removed from the minchah and burned is known as the kometz; the remainder of the minchah is eaten by Kohanim. Most have added to them a measure of substance called levonah (frankincense) which is also burned on the Altar. Some minchah-offerings are fried or baked before being offered; the resulting loaves are then crumbled [פְּתִיתָה] and the kometz is taken from the pieces. A minchah may be either a communal or personal offering [C/P], voluntary or obligatory.

	TYPE OF MINCHAH	TYPE OF FLOUR	QUANTITY OF FLOUR	QUANTITY OF OIL	LEVONAH	PREPARATION	OFFERING	C/P
VOLUNTARY	סֹלֶת, FINE FLOUR	WHEAT	1-60 ISSARON [1]	1 LOG PER ISSARON [2]	YES	MIXED WITH OIL [3]	KOMETZ TO ALTAR, REMAINDER TO KOHEN	P
	מַחֲבַת, MACHAVAS	WHEAT	1-60 ISSARON [1]	1 LOG PER ISSARON [2]	YES	MIXED WITH OIL FRIED ON A GRIDDLE	KOMETZ TO ALTAR REMAINDER TO KOHEN	P
	מַרְחֶשֶׁת, MARCHESHES	WHEAT	1-60 ISSARON [1]	1 LOG PER ISSARON [2]	YES	MIXED WITH OIL, FRIED IN PAN	KOMETZ TO ALTAR REMAINDER TO KOHEN	P
	חַלּוֹת, CHALLOS	WHEAT	1-60 [1]	1 LOG PER ISSARON [2]	YES	MIXED WITH OIL BAKED IN OVEN	KOMETZ TO ALTAR REMAINDER TO KOHEN	P
	רְקִיקִים, REKIKIM	WHEAT	1-60 ISSARON [1]	1 LOG PER ISSARON [2]	YES	BAKED IN OVEN, OIL SMEARED ON, BAKED ON WAFERS	KOMETZ TO ALTAR REMAINDER TO KOHEN	P
	מִנְחַת כֹּהֵן, KOHEN'S MINCHAH	WHEAT	1-60 ISSARON [1]	1 LOG PER ISSARON [2]	YES	ANY OF THE ABOVE	BURNED ENTIRELY ON ALTAR	P
OBLIGATORY	חֲבִיתֵי כֹּהֵן גָּדוֹל (מִנְחַת כֹּהֵן מָשִׁיחַ), CHAVITIN OF THE KOHEN GADOL	WHEAT	1 ISSARON	3 LOG	YES	MIXED WITH OIL, SCALDED IN HOT WATER, BAKED AND FRIED	BURNED ENTIRELY ON ALTAR, ½ IN MORNING, ½ IN MORNING,	P
	מִנְחַת חִנּוּךְ, INDUCTION MINCHAH OF KOHEN	WHEAT	1 ISSARON	3 LOG	YES	MIXED WITH OIL, SCALDED IN HOT WATER, BAKED AND FRIED	BURNED ENTIRELY ON ALTAR,	P
	מִנְחַת חוֹטֵא, SINNER'S MINCHAH	WHEAT	1 ISSARON	NONE	NO	RAW FLOUR	KOMETZ TO ALTAR REMAINDER TO KOHEN	P
	מִנְחַת קְנָאוֹת, JEALOUSY MINCHAH/ SOTAH	BARLEY	1 ISSARON	NONE	NO	RAW FLOUR	KOMETZ TO ALTAR REMAINDER TO KOHEN	P
	מִנְחַת הָעֹמֶר, OMER MINCHAH	BARLEY	1 ISSARON	1 LOG	YES	MIXED WITH OIL [3]	KOMETZ TO ALTAR REMAINDER TO KOHEN	C
	מִנְחַת נְסָכִים, MINCHAS NESACHIM	WHEAT	3 ISSARON / BULL 2 ISSARON / RAM 1 ISSARON / LAMB	6 LOG / BULL 4 LOG / RAM 3 LOG / LAMB	NO	MIXED WITH OIL [3]	BURNED ENTIRELY ON ALTAR	C/P
	מִנְחַת נְסָכִים הַבָּא עִם הָעוֹמֶר, MINCHAS NESACHIM ACCOMPANYING THE OMER	WHEAT	2 ISSARON	3 LOG	NO	MIXED WITH OIL [3]	BURNED ENTIRELY ON ALTAR	C

1. A person donates as much flour for a voluntary minchah as he wants, but the quantity must always be in multiples of an issaron. A maximum of 60 issaron may be offered in one vessel as a single minchah-offering.
2. This is subject to a dispute of Tannaim: According to the Tanna Kamma, one log is required for each issaron; according to R' Eliezer ben Yaakov, up to 60 issaron receive only one log of oil.
3. The flour, however, was neither fried nor baked.

10. NON-ALTAR BAKED OFFERINGS

Of the regular *minchah*-offerings delinated in the previous chart, at least a part of them are burned on the Altar. There are also four kinds of baked products which figure in the sacrificial service of which *no* part is burned on the Altar. These are all joined to some other substance or offering, whose *avodah* serves for them as well, and permits them for consumption. All of these are made of wheat flour, but only one (לֶחֶם הַפָּנִים) has *levonah*, though this is kept separately from the breads. All are baked in an oven.

TYPE OF OFFERING	LOAVES		AMT. OF FLOUR		ASSOCIATED OFFERING	DISPOSITION OF BREAD
	TYPE	NUMBER	LOAF	TOTAL		
לֶחֶם הַפָּנִים **SHOW BREAD**	UNLEAVENED, SPECIALLY SHAPED	12	2 *ISSARON*	24 *ISSARON*	שְׁנֵי בָזִיכֵי לְבוֹנָה TWO SPOONFULS OF *LEVONAH*	EATEN BY KOHANIM
שְׁתֵּי הַלֶּחֶם **TWO LOAVES OF SHAVUOS**	LEAVENED, SPECIALLY SHAPED	2	1 *ISSARON*	2 *ISSARON*	כִּבְשֵׂי עֲצֶרֶת TWO *SHELAMIM* LAMBS OF SHAVUOS	EATEN BY KOHANIM
לַחְמֵי תוֹדָה **TODAH BREADS**	חָמֵץ/*CHAMETZ*, LEAVENED BREAD חַלּוֹת/*CHALLOS*, UNLEAVENED LOAVES רְקִיקִים/*REKIKIM*, UNLEAVENED WAFERS רְבוּכָה/*REVUCHAH*, SCALDED LOAVES	10 10 10 10	1 *ISSARON* ⅔ *ISSARON* ⅔ *ISSARON* ⅓ *ISSARON*	20 *ISSARON*	תּוֹדָה TODAH	4 BREADS (ONE OF EACH KIND) GIVEN TO KOHANIM REMAINDER EATEN BY OWNER AND GUESTS
לַחְמֵי אֵיל נָזִיר **BREAD ACCOMPANYING NAZIR'S RAM**	חַלּוֹת/*CHALLOS*, UNLEAVENED LOAVES רְקִיקִים/*REKIKIM*, UNLEAVENED WAFERS	10 10	⅓ *ISSARON* ⅓ *ISSARON*	6⅔ *ISSARON*	אֵיל נָזִיר NAZIR'S RAM	2 BREADS (ONE OF EACH KIND) GIVEN TO KOHANIM REMAINDER EATEN BY NAZIR AND GUESTS

For additional charts and a complete discussion of the laws of Temple Service, see ArtScroll *Vayikra/Leviticus* vol. I.

11. THE TRIBAL CENSUS

TRIBE	POPULATION NUMBERS CH. 1	POPULATION NUMBERS CH. 26	POPULATION CHANGE
Reuben	46,500	43,730	– 2,770
Simeon	59,300	22,200	– 37,100
Judah	74,600	76,500	+1,900
Issachar	54,400	64,300	+9,900
Zebulun	57,400	60,500	+3,100
Dan	62,700	64,400	+1,700
Naphtali	53,400	45,400	– 8,000
Gad	45,650	40,500	– 5,150
Asher	41,500	53,400	+11,900
Ephraim	40,500	32,500	– 8,000
Manasseh	32,200	52,700	+20,500
Benjamin	35,400	45,600	+10,200
TOTALS	**603,550**	**601,730**	**– 1,820**

12. THE FAMILIES OF LEVITES / THE 24 DIVISIONS[1]

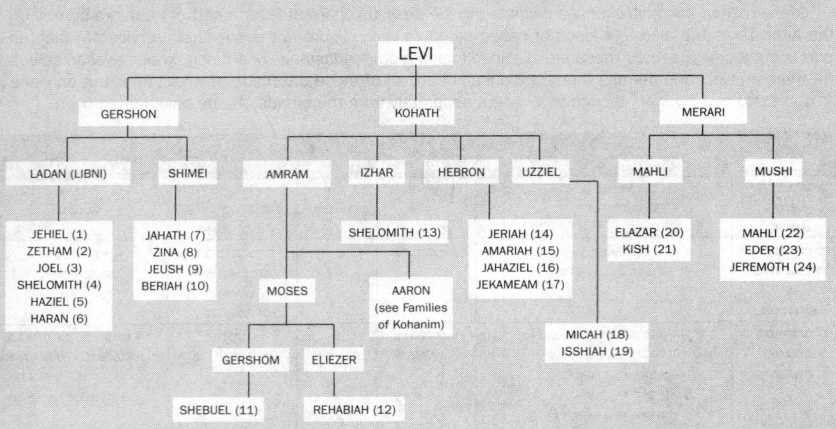

```
                              LEVI
        ┌──────────────────────┼──────────────────────┐
     GERSHON                 KOHATH                  MERARI
   ┌─────┴─────┐     ┌─────┬──────┬──────┬──────┐   ┌───┴────┐
LADAN (LIBNI) SHIMEI AMRAM IZHAR HEBRON UZZIEL   MAHLI    MUSHI
```

GERSHON		KOHATH				MERARI	
LADAN (LIBNI)	SHIMEI	AMRAM	IZHAR	HEBRON	UZZIEL	MAHLI	MUSHI
JEHIEL (1)	JAHATH (7)		SHELOMITH (13)		JERIAH (14)	ELAZAR (20)	MAHLI (22)
ZETHAM (2)	ZINA (8)				AMARIAH (15)	KISH (21)	EDER (23)
JOEL (3)	JEUSH (9)				JAHAZIEL (16)		JEREMOTH (24)
SHELOMITH (4)	BERIAH (10)	MOSES	AARON		JEKAMEAM (17)		
HAZIEL (5)			(see Families				
HARAN (6)			of Kohanim)				

GERSHON   ELIEZER

MICAH (18)
ISSHIAH (19)

SHEBUEL (11)   REHABIAH (12)

THE FAMILIES OF KOHANIM / THE 24 DIVISIONS[2]

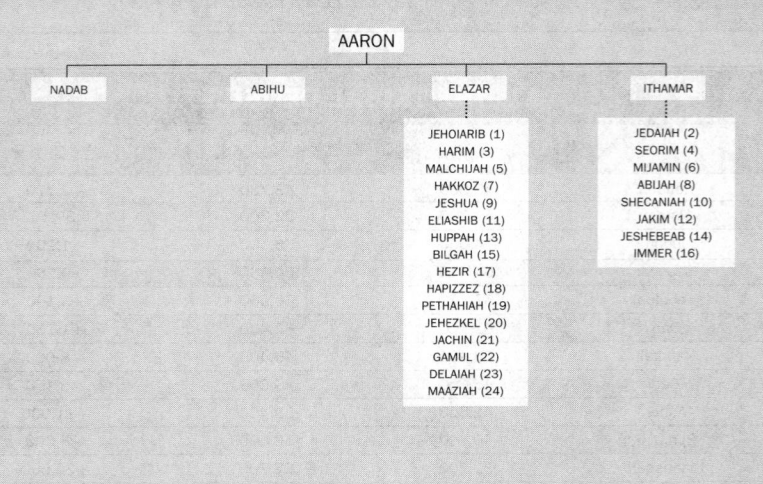

AARON			
NADAB	ABIHU	ELAZAR	ITHAMAR
		JEHOIARIB (1)	JEDAIAH (2)
		HARIM (3)	SEORIM (4)
		MALCHIJAH (5)	MIJAMIN (6)
		HAKKOZ (7)	ABIJAH (8)
		JESHUA (9)	SHECANIAH (10)
		ELIASHIB (11)	JAKIM (12)
		HUPPAH (13)	JESHEBEAB (14)
		BILGAH (15)	IMMER (16)
		HEZIR (17)	
		HAPIZZEZ (18)	
		PETHAHIAH (19)	
		JEHEZKEL (20)	
		JACHIN (21)	
		GAMUL (22)	
		DELAIAH (23)	
		MAAZIAH (24)	

1. According to the *Gaon* of Vilna.   2. According to *Malbim*.

13. THE MUSSAF OFFERINGS				
		OLAH/ BURNT-OFFERING		CHATAS SIN-OFFERING
VERSES	DAY	BULLS	RAMS	LAMBS	GOAT
28:9-10	SABBATH	0	0	2	0
28:11-15	ROSH CHODESH	2	1	7	1
28:16-25	PESACH (EACH DAY)	2	1	7	1
28:26-31	SHAVUOS[1]	2	1	7	1
29:1-6	ROSH HASHANAH[2]	1	1	7	1
29:7-11	YOM KIPPUR	1	1	7	1[3]
29:12-16	SUCCOS (DAY 1)	13	2	14	1
29:17-19	SUCCOS (DAY 2)	12	2	14	1
29:20-22	SUCCOS (DAY 3)	11	2	14	1
29:23-25	SUCCOS (DAY 4)	10	2	14	1
29:26-28	SUCCOS (DAY 5)	9	2	14	1
29:29-31	SUCCOS (DAY 6)	8	2	14	1
29:32-34	SUCCOS (DAY 7)	7	2	14	1
29:35-38	SHEMINI ATZERES	1	1	7	1

1. A second set of offerings is brought on Shavuos. It consists of: 2 loaves; an *olah* of 1 bull, 2 rams, 7 lambs, a *chatas* of 1 goat; and a *shelamim* of 2 lambs (see *Leviticus* 23:15-22).

2. The offerings of Rosh Chodesh are also brought on Rosh Hashanah

3. A second goat-*chatas* is also offered on Yom Kippur (see *Leviticus* 16:9).

The Kings of Judah and of Israel are listed in Timeline 4, page 2026
The Kings of Babylonia are listed in Timeline 5, page 2027

14. THE 48 PROPHETS*

1. Abraham / אַבְרָהָם	25. Micah the Morashtite / מִיכָה הַמּוֹרַשְׁתִּי
2. Isaac / יִצְחָק	26. Amoz / אָמוֹץ
3. Jacob / יַעֲקֹב	27. Elijah / אֵלִיָּהוּ
4. Moses / מֹשֶׁה	28. Elisha / אֱלִישָׁע
5. Aaron / אַהֲרֹן	29. Jonah ben Amittai / יוֹנָה בֶּן אֲמִתַּי
6. Joshua / יְהוֹשֻׁעַ	30. Isaiah / יְשַׁעְיָהוּ
7. Phinehas / פִּינְחָס	31. Joel / יוֹאֵל
8. Elkanah / אֶלְקָנָה	32. Nahum / נַחוּם
9. Eli / עֵלִי	33. Habakkuk / חֲבַקּוּק
10. Samuel / שְׁמוּאֵל	34. Zephaniah / צְפַנְיָה
11. Gad / גָּד	35. Urijah / אוּרִיָּה
12. Nathan / נָתָן	36. Jeremiah / יִרְמְיָהוּ
13. David / דָּוִד	37. Ezekiel / יְחֶזְקֵאל
14. Solomon / שְׁלֹמֹה	38. Shemaiah / שְׁמַעְיָה
15. Iddo / עִדּוֹ (עִדּוֹא)	39. Baruch / בָּרוּךְ
16. Michaiah son of Imlah / מִיכָיְהוּ בֶּן יִמְלָה	40. Neriah / נֵרִיָּה
17. Obadiah / עוֹבַדְיָה	41. Seraiah / שְׂרָיָה
18. Ahijah the Shilonite / אֲחִיָּה הַשִּׁילֹנִי	42. Mehseiah / מַחְסֵיָה
19. Jehu son of Hanani / יֵהוּא בֶּן חֲנָנִי	43. Haggai / חַגַּי
20. Azariah son of Oded / עֲזַרְיָהוּ בֶּן עוֹדֵד	44. Zechariah / זְכַרְיָה
21. Jahaziel the Levite / יַחֲזִיאֵל הַלֵּוִי	45. Malachi / מַלְאָכִי
22. Eliezer son of Dodavahu / אֱלִיעֶזֶר בֶּן דּוֹדָוָהוּ	46. Mordecai Bilshan / מָרְדְּכַי בִּלְשָׁן
23. Hosea / הוֹשֵׁעַ	47. Oded / עוֹדֵד
24. Amos / עָמוֹס	48. Hanani / חֲנָנִי

THE SEVEN PROPHETESSES

1. Sarah / שָׂרָה	4. Hannah / חַנָּה
2. Miriam / מִרְיָם	5. Abigail / אֲבִיגַיִל
3. Deborah / דְּבוֹרָה	6. Huldah / חֻלְדָּה

7. Esther / אֶסְתֵּר

*According to *Rashi*, *Megillah* 14a and glosses ad loc.

THE MISHKAN (TABERNACLE) AND ITS FURNISHINGS

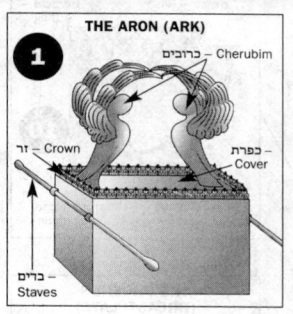

THE ARON (ARK)

1

כרובים – Cherubim

זר – Crown

כפרת – Cover

ברים – Staves

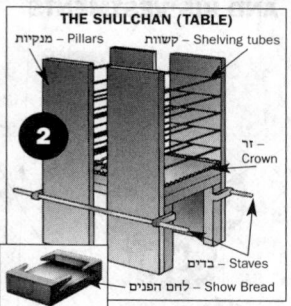

THE SHULCHAN (TABLE)

2

מנקיות – Pillars

קשוות – Shelving tubes

זר – Crown

ברים – Staves

לחם הפנים – Show Bread

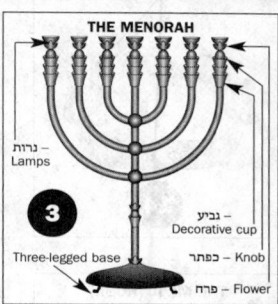

THE MENORAH

3

נרות – Lamps

גביע – Decorative cup

כפתר – Knob

פרח – Flower

Three-legged base

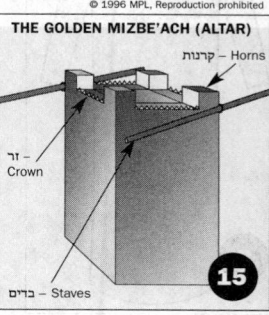

THE CHATZER (COURTYARD)
OF THE MISHKAN (TABERNACLE)
(not to scale)

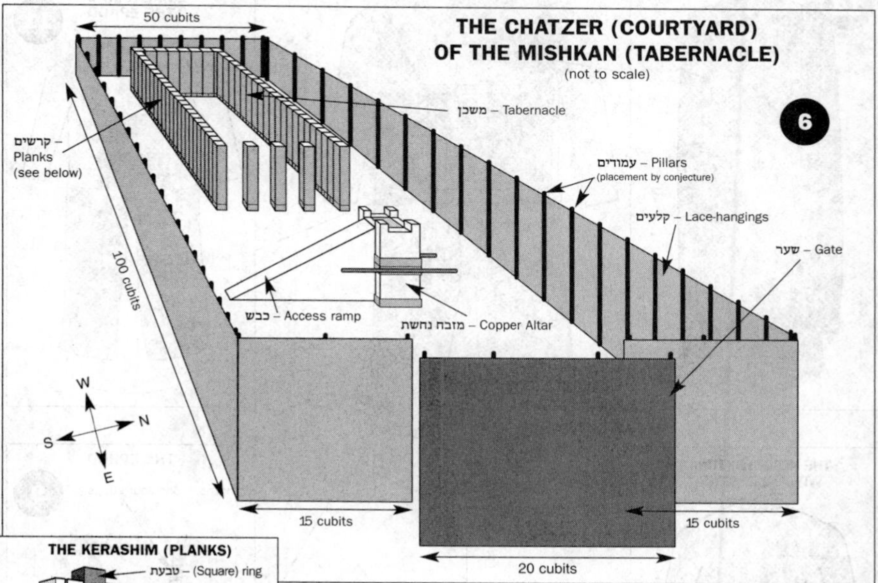

6

50 cubits

קרשים – Planks (see below)

100 cubits

משכן – Tabernacle

עמודים – Pillars (placement by conjecture)

קלעים – Lace-hangings

שער – Gate

כבש – Access ramp

מזבח נחשת – Copper Altar

W S N E

15 cubits

15 cubits

20 cubits

© 1996 MPL, Reproduction prohibited

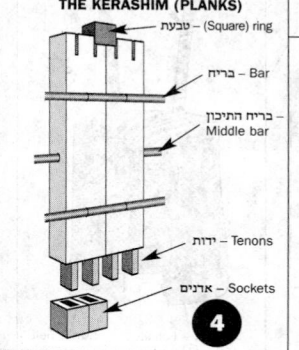

THE KERASHIM (PLANKS)

4

טבעת – (Square) ring

בריח – Bar

בריח התיכון – Middle bar

ידות – Tenons

אדנים – Sockets

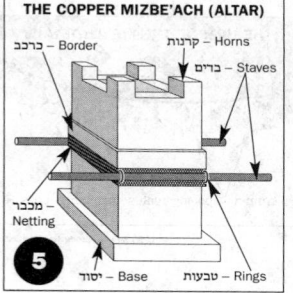

THE COPPER MIZBE'ACH (ALTAR)

5

כרכב – Border

קרנות – Horns

בדים – Staves

מכבר – Netting

יסוד – Base

טבעת – Rings

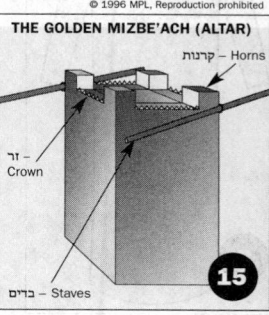

THE GOLDEN MIZBE'ACH (ALTAR)

15

קרנות – Horns

זר – Crown

בדים – Staves

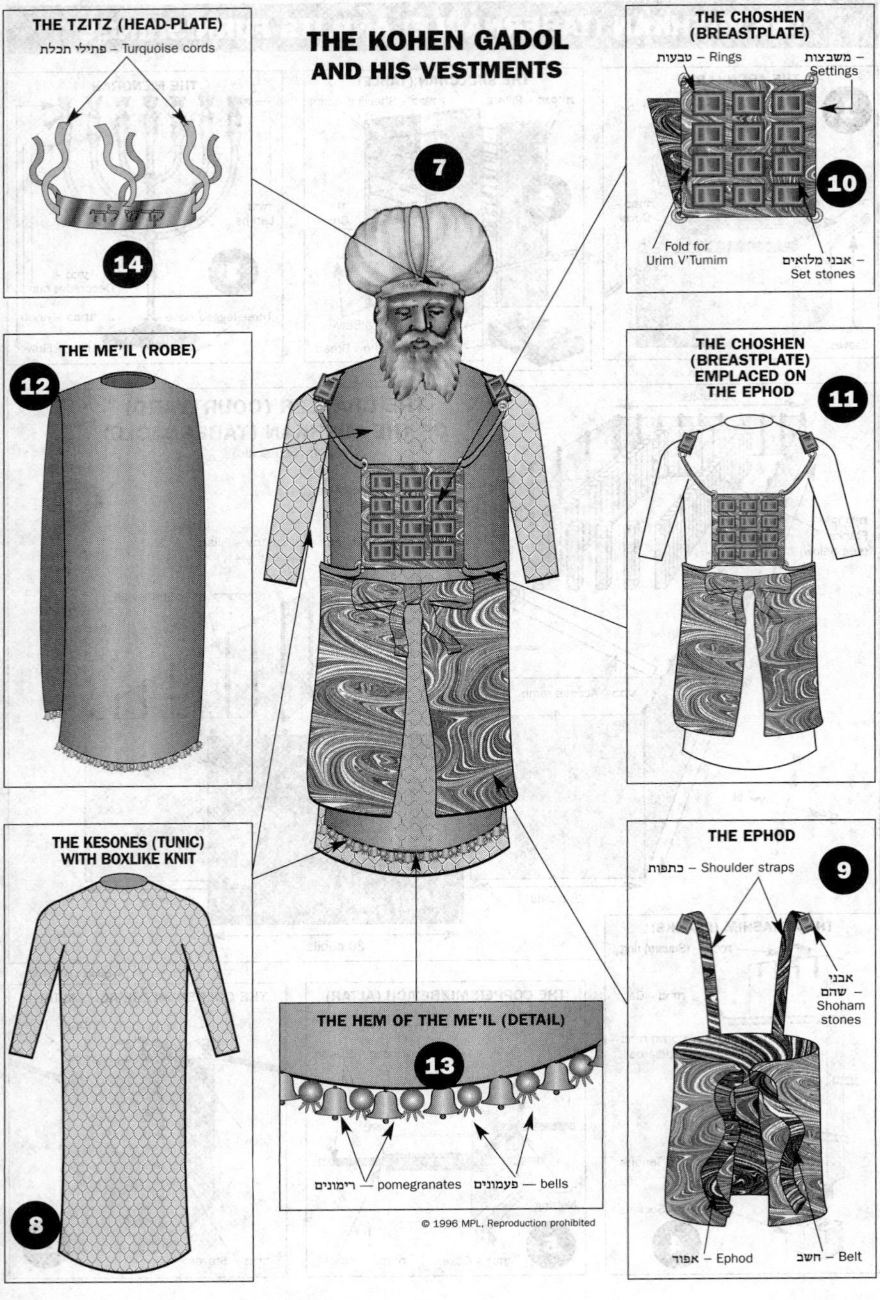

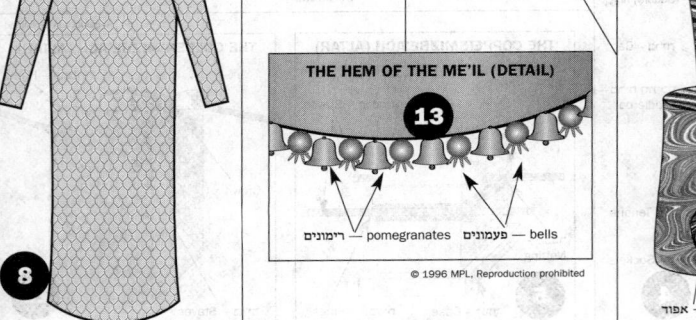

THE KOHEN GADOL AND HIS VESTMENTS

THE TZITZ (HEAD-PLATE)
פתילי תכלת – Turquoise cords
14

THE CHOSHEN (BREASTPLATE)
טבעות – Rings
משבצות – Settings
Fold for Urim V'Tumim
אבני מלואים – Set stones
10

THE ME'IL (ROBE)
12

THE CHOSHEN (BREASTPLATE) EMPLACED ON THE EPHOD
11

THE KESONES (TUNIC) WITH BOXLIKE KNIT
8

THE HEM OF THE ME'IL (DETAIL)
13
רימונים – pomegranates
פעמונים – bells

© 1996 MPL, Reproduction prohibited

THE EPHOD
כתפות – Shoulder straps
9
אבני שהם – Shoham stones
אפוד – Ephod
חשב – Belt

7

THE SIGNS OF KOSHER ANIMALS AND FISH

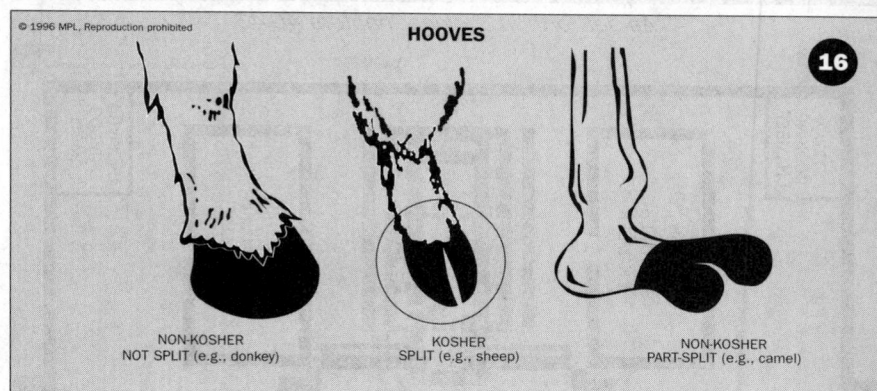

© 1996 MPL, Reproduction prohibited

HOOVES

16

NON-KOSHER
NOT SPLIT (e.g., donkey)

KOSHER
SPLIT (e.g., sheep)

NON-KOSHER
PART-SPLIT (e.g., camel)

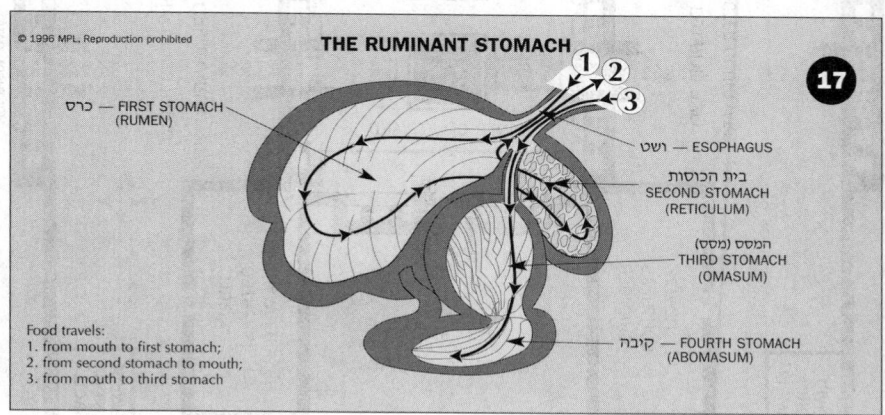

© 1996 MPL, Reproduction prohibited

THE RUMINANT STOMACH

17

כרס — FIRST STOMACH (RUMEN)

ושט — ESOPHAGUS

בית הכוסות
SECOND STOMACH (RETICULUM)

המסס (מסס)
THIRD STOMACH (OMASUM)

קיבה — FOURTH STOMACH (ABOMASUM)

Food travels:
1. from mouth to first stomach;
2. from second stomach to mouth;
3. from mouth to third stomach

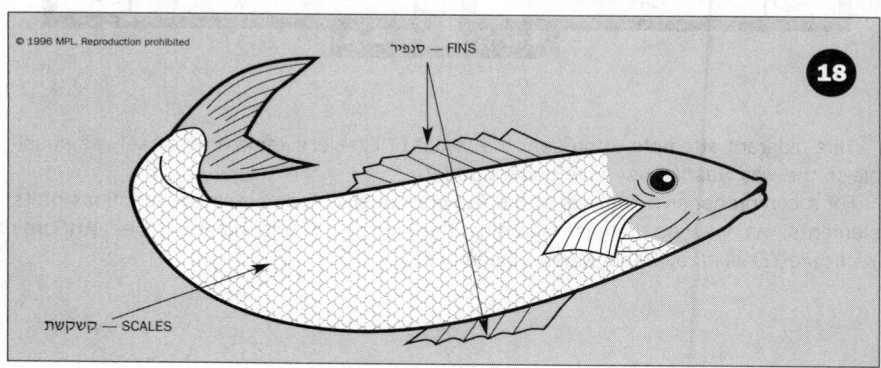

© 1996 MPL, Reproduction prohibited

סנפיר — FINS

18

קשקשת — SCALES

19. THE THIRD TEMPLE

As set forth in Ezekiel Chapters 40-43

This diagram attempts to present the layout of Ezekiel's Temple as closely as possible to the way *Rashi* must have understood it.

For a comprehensive analysis of the Temple's design and detailed descriptions of its elements, as well as details regarding the design of this diagram, see ArtScroll *Yechezkel/Ezekiel,* by Rabbi Moshe Eisemann.

LEGEND FOR THE DIAGRAM OF THE THIRD TEMPLE (facing page)

Numbers after each item refer to chapter and verse where mentioned (e.g. 1/1 is mentioned in chapter 40, verse 5).

1/x Outer Courtyard Gateway Complex
1/1 Wall surrounding the outer courtyard (40:5)
1/2 Steps leading to the outer courtyard (40:6)
1/3 Gateway to the outer courtyard (40:6, 16)
1/4 Cells (40:7,10,12,13)
1/5 Walls between the cells and their outer wall (40:7 and see *Metzudos*)
1/6 Walls of the hall (40:8-9)
1/7 Pillars (40:9,14,16)
1/8 Inner (hall) gate (40:11,16)
1/9 Vestibule (40:12)

2/x Inner Courtyard Gateway Complex
2/1 Wall surrounding the inner courtyard [Not explicated in text. See *Rashi* 42:5 and *Tzuras HaBayis* 22.]
2/2 Steps leading from the outer courtyard to the inner courtyard (40:31)
2/3 Gateway leading to the inner courtyard (40:28)
2/4 Cells (40:29)
2/5 Walls between the cells and the outer wall [implied in 40:29; see above at (1/5)]
2/6 Walls of the hall (40:29,31)
2/7 Pillars (40:29,31)
2/8 Outer hall gate (40:30)
2/9 Vestibule (40:39)
2/10 Chambers built into the walls of the inner courtyard (40:30)

3/x Inner Courtyard
3/1 Chamber for skinning and washing the sacrifices (40:38, 42-43)
3/2 Two chambers for the choristers (40:44)
3/3 Chamber for the Tzadokite *Kohanim* (40:44,46)
3/4 Platform (42:12)

4/x Temple Structure
4/1 Eastern wall of the Temple structure (40:48)
4/2 Steps leading from the inner courtyard to the Temple structure (40:49)
4/3 Gateway to the entrance hall of the Sanctuary (41:1-2)
4/4 Pillars in the entrance hall (40:49)
4/5 Walls creating gateway from hall to Sanctuary (41:1-2)
4/6 Gateway from the hall into the Sanctuary (41:1-2)
4/7 Walls between Sanctuary and Holy of Holies (41:5)
4/8 Western wall of the Holy of Holies (41:5)
4/9 Cell in the west, behind Holy of Holies (41:5)
4/10 Cells on the northern and southern sides (41:6,7,8,9,11;)
4/11 Northern and southern walls of the Temple [The width of these walls is not explicated in the text — although the text assumes the existence of these walls (41:6). *Middos* 4:7 assigns a width of 6 cubits and that is implied in the measurements given at 41:12 (see comm. there). The width of 6 cubits is assumed since these two walls are one with the western wall (4/8) to which 41:5 assigns a width of 6 cubits.]
4/12 Walls between cells [These walls are not explicated in the text.]

4/13 Northern, southern and western walls on the outside of the cells [The northern and southern walls are described in 41:8-9. The western wall is not explicated in the text but *Rashi* to 41:13 assumes it to have the same dimensions as the northern and southern walls.]
4/14 Access ramp leading upward from east to west [This ramp is not mentioned in the text but its existence is assumed at 41:12. It is mentioned in *Middos* 4:5.]
4/15 Western drainage ramp leading down from west to east [See 4/14 above.]
4/16 Outer walls of the Temple on northern and southern sides [See 4/14 above. *Middos* 4:7 assigns a thickness of 5 cubits to this wall. But 41:12 assumes a thickness of 6 cubits. The assumption is that it was 6 cubits at ground level but narrowed to 5 cubits above ground level and is therefore counted as 6 cubits.]
4/17 Open space (41:9,11)
4/18 The knife depository [This is not explicated in the text but assumed at 41:14 (see comm. there). It is mentioned in *Middos* 4:7.]
4/19 Wicket for entry into cells (4/10) and access ramp (4/14) (41:11)

5/x Western Chambers
5/1 Walls of the northwestern and southwestern chambers (42:1-3)
5/2 Gap in wall (42:4)
5/3 Walkway (42:4)
5/4 Space between chamber and Sanctuary (41:10)
5/5 Space between chamber and northern [or southern] wall of outer courtyard (42:2)
5/6 Space between chamber and western wall of outer courtyard (42:9)
5/7 Gate to the north [or south] (42:2,4)
5/8 Gate to the south [or north] [This gate is not explicated in the text but is assumed by *Rashi* to 46:19.]

6/x Eastern Chambers
According to *Rashi* (42:9) these chambers may not have existed.
6/1 Walls of northeastern and southeastern chambers (42:9)
6/2 Gateway into inner courtyard toward the platform (3/4), (42:12)
6/3 Space between chamber and eastern wall of outer courtyard (42:9)
6/4 Space between chamber and northern [or southern] wall of outer courtyard (42:9)
6/5 Gate to the north [or south] (see 5/8 above)

Altar (43:13-17)
Ramp (43:18)
Cooking Chambers (46:22-23)

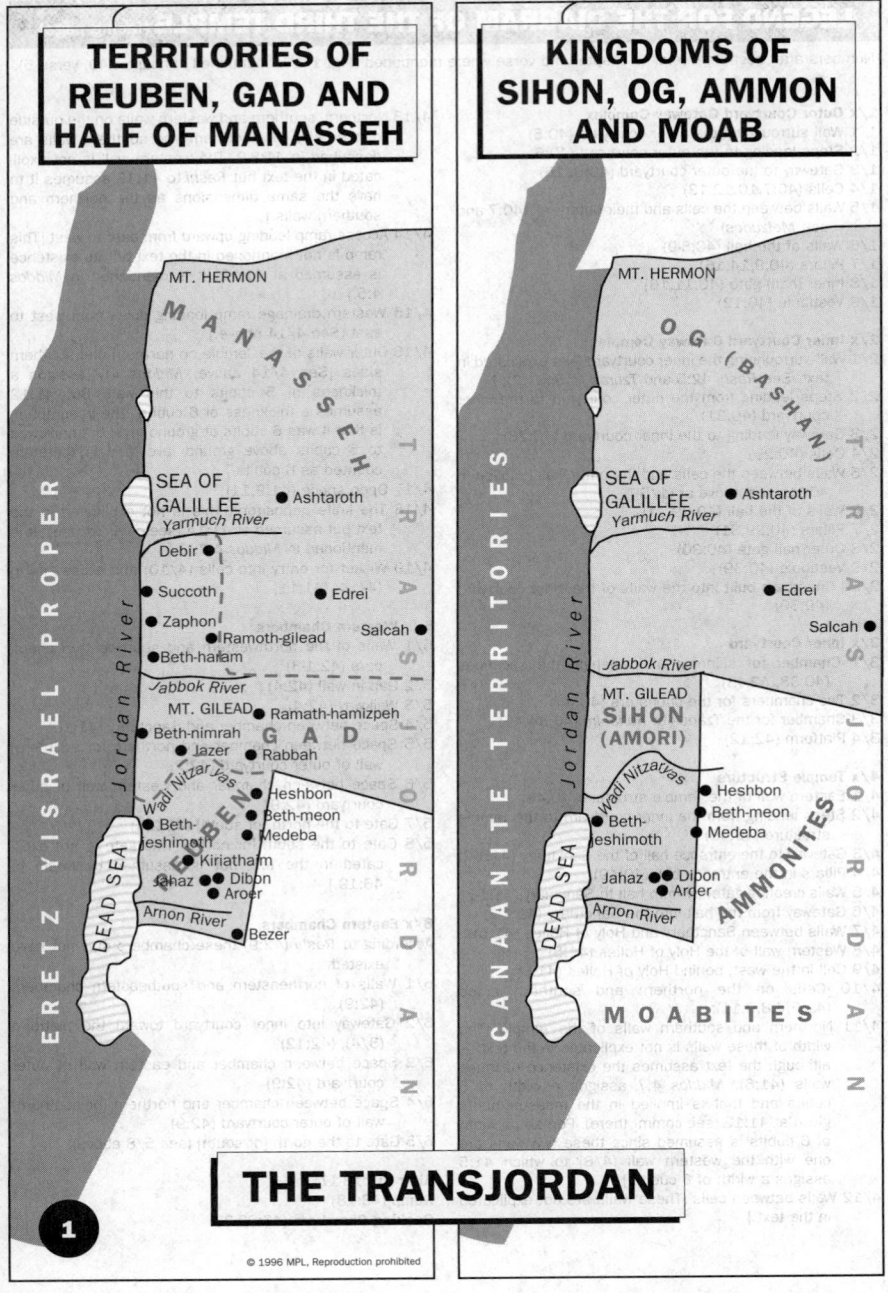

TERRITORIES OF REUBEN, GAD AND HALF OF MANASSEH

KINGDOMS OF SIHON, OG, AMMON AND MOAB

THE TRANSJORDAN

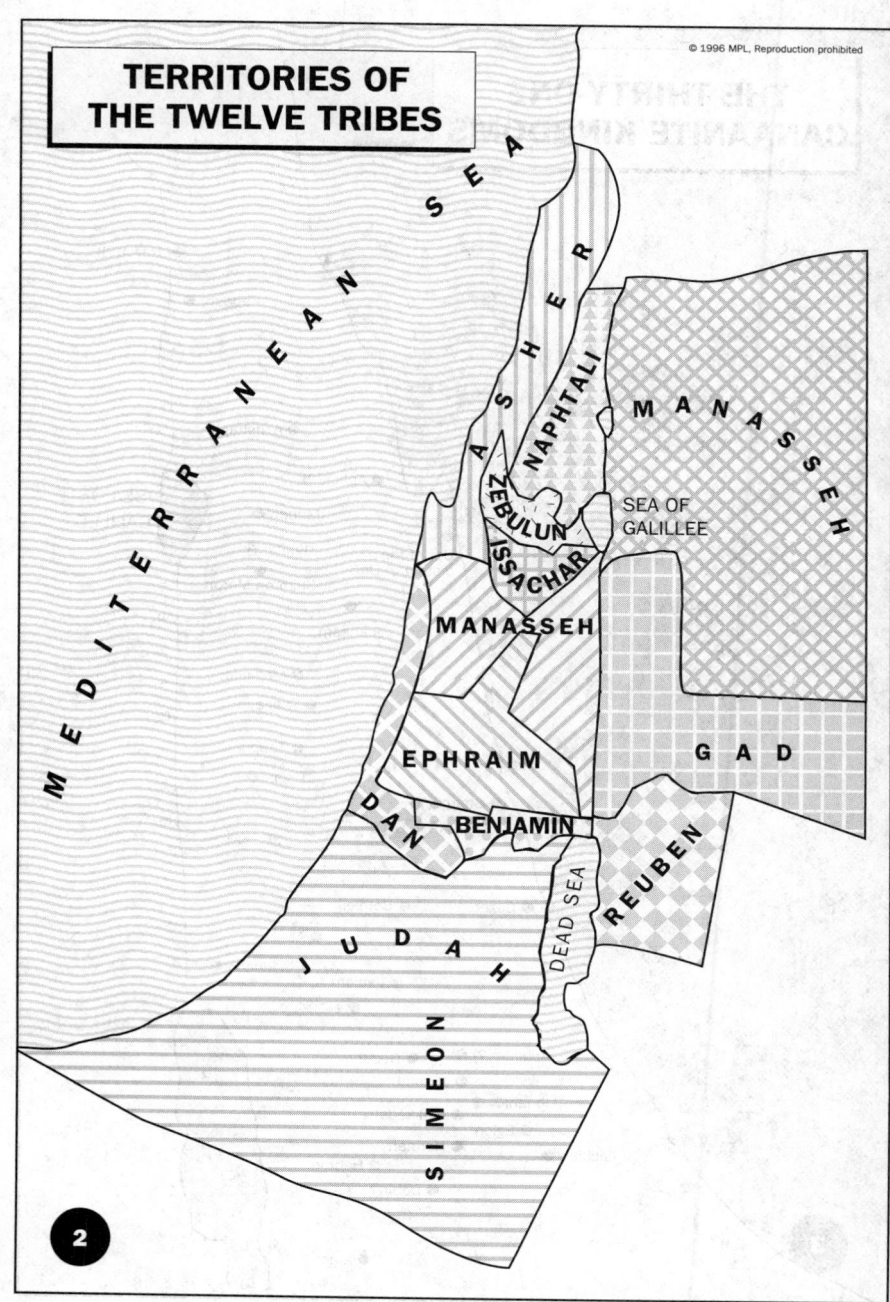

TERRITORIES OF
THE TWELVE TRIBES

MEDITERRANEAN SEA

ASHER

NAPHTALI

MANASSEH

ZEBULUN

ISSACHAR

SEA OF
GALILLEE

MANASSEH

EPHRAIM

GAD

DAN

BENJAMIN

REUBEN

DEAD SEA

JUDAH

SIMEON

2

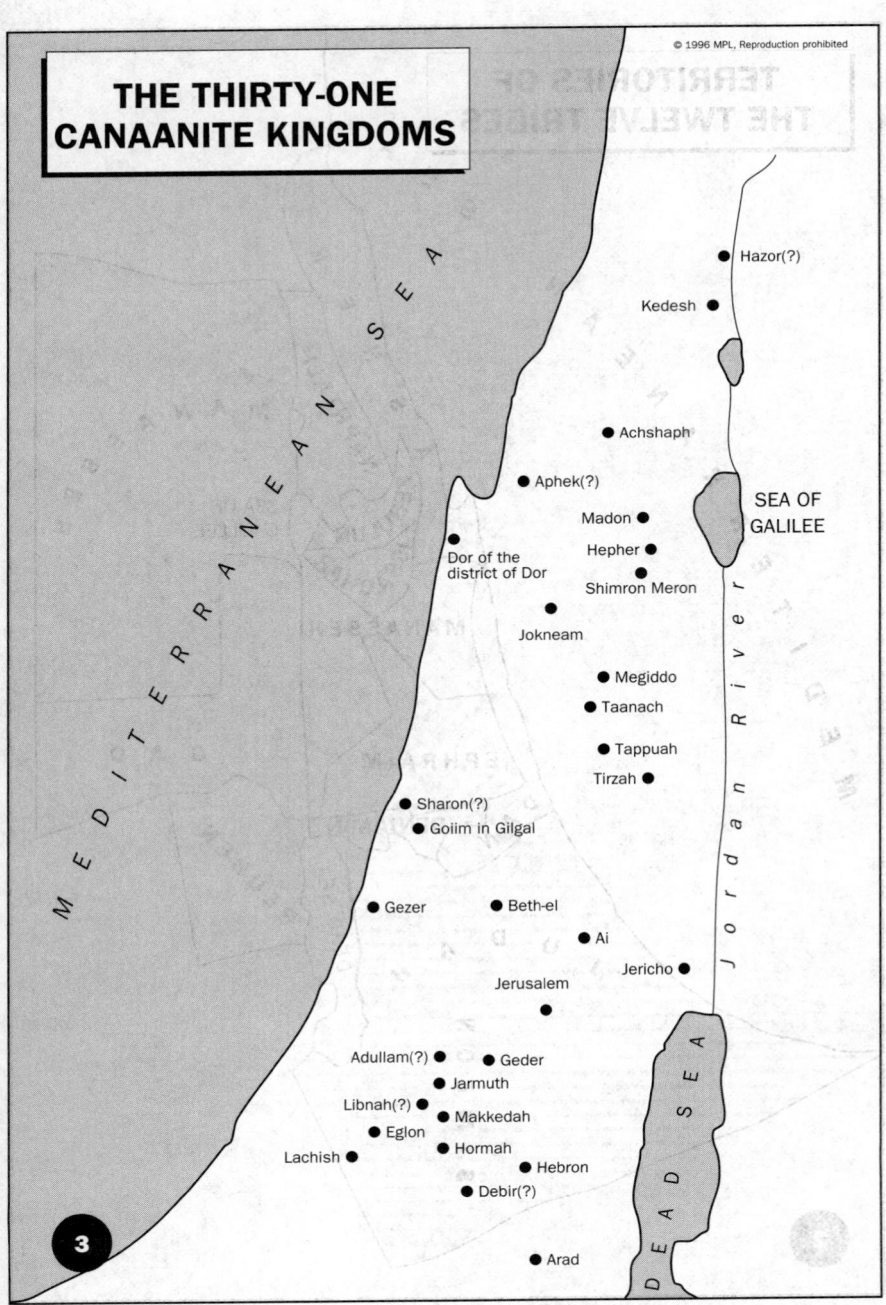

© 1996 MPL, Reproduction prohibited

THE THIRTY-ONE CANAANITE KINGDOMS

MEDITERRANEAN SEA

Hazor(?)

Kedesh

Achshaph

Aphek(?)

SEA OF GALILEE

Madon

Hepher

Dor of the district of Dor

Shimron Meron

Jordan River

Jokneam

Megiddo

Taanach

Tappuah

Tirzah

Sharon(?)

Goiim in Gilgal

Gezer

Beth-el

Ai

Jericho

Jerusalem

Adullam(?)

Geder

Jarmuth

Libnah(?)

Makkedah

Eglon

Lachish

Hormah

Hebron

Debir(?)

Arad

DEAD SEA

3

BORDERS OF ERETZ YISRAEL

— • —

The borders of Eretz Yisrael, according to the views of Kaftor VaFerach (broken line) and Tevuos HaAretz (solid).
Bold face type indicates agreement between Kaftor VaFerach and Tevuos HaAretz.
Italicized names follow the opinion of Tevuos HaAretz. Names in regular type follow Kaftor VaFerach.
Capitalized sites are for the reader's orientation. Shaded areas were not yet conquered at the time of the death of Joshua.

Mount Hor

Hamath

Zifron

Hazar-enan

Mount Hor

Hamath

Zedad

Gibal

Zifron

Sidon

Hazar-enan

Zur

Baal-gad

Riblah MOUNT HERMON

Sea of Galillee

LEBANON MOUNTAINS

ANTI-LEBANON MOUNTAINS

MEDITERRANEAN SEA

Jordan River

Gath

Ekron

JERUSALEM

Ashkelon

Gaza

Maaleh-akrabbim

Kadesh-barnea

Stream of Egypt

Azmon

4

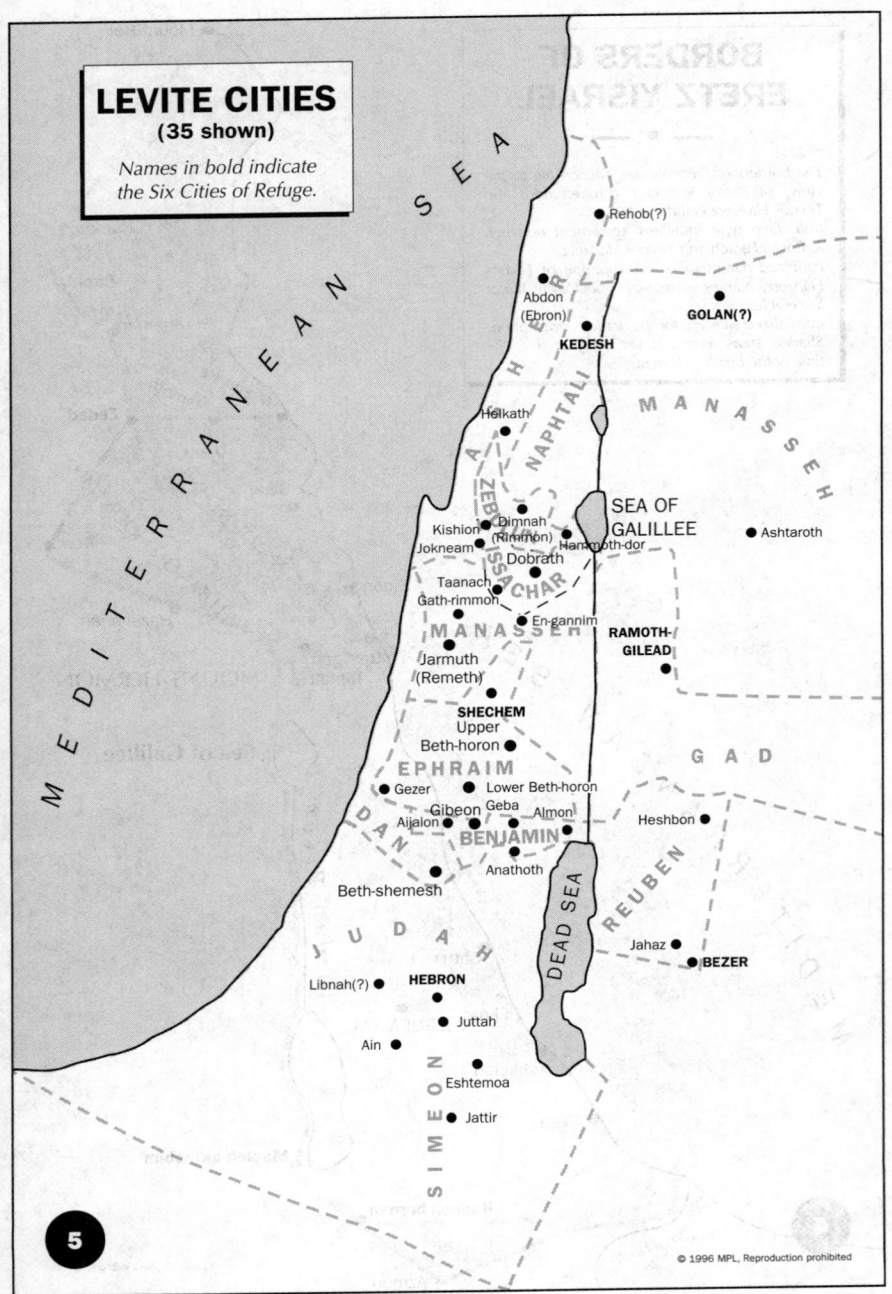

LEVITE CITIES
(35 shown)

*Names in bold indicate
the Six Cities of Refuge.*

MEDITERRANEAN SEA

Rehob(?)

Abdon
(Ebron)

GOLAN(?)

KEDESH

Helkath

NAPHTALI

ASHER

ZEBULUN

SEA OF
GALILEE

MANASSEH

Kishion
Jokneam

Dimnah
(Rimmon)

Dobrath

Hammoth-dor

Ashtaroth

ISSACHAR

Taanach
Gath-rimmon

En-gannim

**RAMOTH-
GILEAD**

MANASSEH

Jarmuth
(Remeth)

SHECHEM

Upper
Beth-horon

GAD

EPHRAIM

Gezer

Lower Beth-horon

Gibeon   Geba

Aijalon

Almon

Heshbon

DAN

BENJAMIN

Anathoth

DEAD SEA

REUBEN

Beth-shemesh

JUDAH

Jahaz

BEZER

Libnah(?)

HEBRON

Juttah

Ain

S
I
M
E
O
N

Eshtemoa

Jattir

5

© 1996 MPL, Reproduction prohibited

Translation of Names in Tanach

(IN HEBREW ALPHABETICAL ORDER)

		א
Boaz בּוֹעַז	Ahisar אֲחִישָׁר	Abigail אֲבִיגַיִל/אֲבִיגַיִל
Baladan בַּלְאֲדָן	Ahitophel אֲחִיתֹפֶל	Abi אֲבִי
Belshazzar בֵּלְאשַׁצַּר/בֵּלְשַׁאצַּר	Ahasuerus אֲחַשְׁוֵרוֹשׁ	Abijah אֲבִיָּה
Bildad בִּלְדַּד	Job אִיּוֹב	Abihail אֲבִי הַיִל
Bilhah בִּלְהָה	Jezebel אִיזֶבֶל	Abihail אֲבִיחַיִל
Belteshazzar בֵּלְטְשַׁאצַּר	Ichabod אִיכָבוֹד	Abihu אֲבִיהוּא
Balaam בִּלְעָם	Elon אֵילוֹן	Abijam אֲבִיָם
Balak בָּלָק	Ish-bosheth אִישׁ בֹּשֶׁת	Abimelech אֲבִימֶלֶךְ
Ben-hadad בֶּן־הֲדַד	Ithamar אִיתָמָר	Abinadab אֲבִינָדָב
Benaiah בְּנָיָהוּ	Achish אָכִישׁ	Abiner אֲבִינֵר
Benjamin בִּנְיָמִין	Elah אֵלָה	Abiram אֲבִירָם
Baanah בַּעֲנָא	Elhanan אֶלְחָנָן	Abishag אֲבִישַׁג
Baanah בַּעֲנָה	Eliab אֱלִיאָב	Abishai אֲבִישַׁי
Baasha בַּעְשָׁא	Elihoreph אֱלִיחֹרֶף	Abiathar אֶבְיָתָר
Bezalel בְּצַלְאֵל	Elijah אֵלִיָּהוּ	Abner אַבְנֵר
Berodach בְּראֹדַךְ	Elihu אֱלִיהוּא	Abraham אַבְרָהָם
Baruch בָּרוּךְ	Elimelech אֱלִימֶלֶךְ	Abram אַבְרָם
Barzillai בַּרְזִלַּי	Eliezer אֱלִיעֶזֶר	Absalom אַבְשָׁלוֹם
Bera בֶּרַע	Eliphaz אֱלִיפַז	Agag אֲגַג
Barak בָּרָק	Eliakim אֶלְיָקִים	Edom אֱדוֹם
Birsha בִּרְשַׁע	Eliashib אֶלְיָשִׁיב	Adalia אֲדַלְיָא
Bethuel בְּתוּאֵל	Elishama אֱלִישָׁמָע	Adam אָדָם
Bath-sheba בַּת־שֶׁבַע	Elisha אֱלִישָׁע	Adoni-bezek אֲדֹנִי־בֶזֶק
	Elazar אֶלְעָזָר	Adonijah אֲדֹנִיָּה
ג	Elkanah אֶלְקָנָה	Adoni-zedek אֲדֹנִי־צֶדֶק
Gabriel גַּבְרִיאֵל	Amon אָמוֹן	Adoram אֲדֹרָם
Gad גָּד	Amaziah אֲמַצְיָה	Adrammelech אַדְרַמֶּלֶךְ
Gedaliah גְּדַלְיָה	Amraphel אַמְרָפֶל	Ehud אֵהוּד
Gideon גִּדְעוֹן	Enosh אֱנוֹשׁ	Oholiab אָהֳלִיאָב
Gog גּוֹג	Asa אָסָא	Aaron אַהֲרֹן
Gehazi גֵּיחֲזִי	Asenath אָסְנַת	Evil-merodach אֱוִיל מְרֹדַךְ
Goliath גָּלְיָת	Asaph אָסָף	On אוֹן
Gomer גֹּמֶר	Esar-haddon אֵסַר חַדֹּן	Onan אוֹנָן
Gaal גַּעַל	Esther אֶסְתֵּר	Uri אוּרִי
Gershom גֵּרְשֹׁם	Ephraim אֶפְרַיִם	Uriah אוּרִיָה(וּ)
Gershon גֵּרְשׁוֹן	Ephrath אֶפְרָת	Urijah אוּרִיָּה (הַכֹּהֵן)
	Araunah אֲרַוְנָה	Ahab אַחְאָב
ד	Ornan אָרְנָן	Ahaz אָחָז
Deborah דְּבוֹרָה	Ashpenaz אַשְׁפְּנַז	Ahaziah אֲחַזְיָה
Doeg דּוֹאֵג	Asher אָשֵׁר	Ahijah אֲחִיָּה
David דָּוִד	Ittai אִתַּי	Ahimelech אֲחִימֶלֶךְ
Dinah דִּינָה		Ahinoam אֲחִינֹעַם
Delilah דְּלִילָה	ב	Ahiezer אֲחִיעֶזֶר
Dalphon דַּלְפוֹן	Bigthan בִּגְתָן	
	Bidkar בִּדְקַר	

Johanan	יוֹחָנָן	Hiram	חִירָם	Dan	דָּן
Joiada/	יוֹיָדָע/	Hilkiah	חִלְקִיָּהוּ/חִלְקִיָּה	Daniel	דָּנִיֵּאל
Jehoiada	יְהוֹיָדָע	Hamutal	חֲמוּטַל	Darius	דָּרְיָוֶשׁ
Jochebed	יוֹכֶבֶד	Hannah	חַנָּה	Dathan	דָּתָן
Jonadab	יוֹנָדָב	Enoch	חֲנוֹךְ		
Jonah	יוֹנָה	Hanani	חֲנָנִי	**ה**	
Joseph	יוֹסֵף	Hananiah	חֲנַנְיָה	Abel	הֶבֶל
Joram	יוֹרָם	Hophni	חָפְנִי	Hegai	הֵגַי
Jotham	יוֹתָם	Hefzibah	חֶפְצִי־בָהּ	Hagar	הָגָר
Jezreel	יִזְרְעֶאל	Hezron	חֶצְרוֹן	Hadad	הֲדַד
Jahaziel	יַחֲזִיאֵל	Harbonah	חַרְבוֹנָא	Hadadezer	הֲדַדְעֶזֶר
Jahzeiah	יַחְזְיָה	Haran	חָרָן	Hadassah	הֲדַסָּה
Ezekiel	יְחֶזְקֵאל			Hadoram	הֲדֹרָם
Jecoliah	יְכָלְיָה(וּ)	**ט**		Hoham	הֹהָם
Jabez	יַעְבֵּץ	Tob-adonijah	טוֹב אֲדוֹנִיָּה	Hosea	הוֹשֵׁעַ (הנביא)
Jedi the Seer	יֶעְדִּי/עִדּוֹ	Tobiah	טוֹבִיָּה	Hoshea	הוֹשֵׁעַ
Jael	יָעֵל	Tobijah	טוֹבִיָּהוּ	Heman	הֵימָן
Jacob	יַעֲקֹב			Haman	הָמָן
Japhia	יָפִיעַ	**י**		Horam	הֹרָם
Japheth	יֶפֶת	Jair	יָאִיר		
Jephthah	יִפְתָּח	Jaazaniah	יַאֲזַנְיָה	**ו**	
Isaac	יִצְחָק	Josiah	יֹאשִׁיָּהוּ	Vaizatha	וַיְזָתָא
Joktan	יָקְטָן	Jabin	יָבִין	Vashti	וַשְׁתִּי
Jerubaal	יְרֻבַּעַל	Jeduthun	יְדוּתוּן		
Jeroboam	יָרָבְעָם	Jedidah	יְדִידָה	**ז**	
Jerusah	יְרוּשָׁא/יְרוּשָׁה	Jehu	יֵהוּא	Zeeb	זְאֵב
Jeremiah	יִרְמְיָה(וּ)	Jehoahaz	יְהוֹאָחָז	Zabad	זָבָד
Ishvi	יִשְׁוִי	Jehoash	יְהוֹאָשׁ	Zebadiah	זְבַדְיָהוּ
Jeshua	יֵשׁוּעַ	Judah	יְהוּדָה	Zabud	זָבוּד
Jesse	יִשַׁי	Jehozabad	יְהוֹזָבָד	Zebudah	זְבוּדָה
Ishmael	יִשְׁמָעֵאל	Jehoiachin	יְהוֹיָכִין	Zebulun	זְבוּלֻן/זְבֻלוּן
Isaiah	יְשַׁעְיָה(וּ)	Jehoiakim	יְהוֹיָקִים	Zichri	זִכְרִי
Israel	יִשְׂרָאֵל	Jehonadab	יְהוֹנָדָב	Zechariah	זְכַרְיָה(וּ)
Issacher	יִשָׂשכָר	Jehonathan	יְהוֹנָתָן	Zilpah	זִלְפָּה
Jether	יֶתֶר	Jonathan	יְהוֹנָתָן/יוֹנָתָן	Zimri	זִמְרִי
Jethro	יִתְרוֹ		(בן שאול)	Zerubbabel	זְרֻבָּבֶל
Ithream	יִתְרְעָם	Jehoaddan	יְהוֹעַדָּן/יְהוֹעַדִּין	Zerah	זֶרַח
		Jehozadah	יְהוֹצָדָק	Zeresh	זֶרֶשׁ
כ		Jehoram	יְהוֹרָם		
Chedorlaomer	כְּדָרְלָעֹמֶר	Jehosheba	יְהוֹשֶׁבַע	**ח**	
Cyrus	כּוֹרֶשׁ	Jehoshabeath	יְהוֹשַׁבְעַת	Habakkuk	חֲבַקּוּק
Cush	כּוּשׁ	Joshua	יְהוֹשֻׁעַ	Haggai	חַגַּי
	כּוּשַׁן רִשְׁעָתַיִם	Jehoshaphat	יְהוֹשָׁפָט	Eve	חַוָּה
Cushan-rishathaim		Joab	יוֹאָב	Huldah	חֻלְדָּה
Cozbi	כָּזְבִּי	Joah	יוֹאָח	Huram	חוּרָם
Chileab	כִּלְאָב	Joel	יוֹאֵל	Hushai	חוּשַׁי
Caleb	כָּלֵב	Joash	יוֹאָשׁ	Hazael	חֲזָאֵל
Chilion	כִּלְיוֹן	Jobab	יוֹבָב	Hezekiah	חִזְקִיָּה
Cononiah	כָּנַנְיָהוּ	Jozacar	יוֹזָכָר	Hiel	חִיאֵל

Achan	עָכָן	Mattan	מַתָּן	Canaan	כְּנַעַן
Achsah	עַכְסָה	Mattaniah	מַתַּנְיָה		
Eli	עֵלִי	Mithredath	מִתְרְדָת	**ל**	
Amon	אָמוֹן				
Amos	עָמוֹס	**נ**		Leah	לֵאָה
Amminadab	עַמִּינָדָב			Lo-ammi	לֹא עַמִּי
Amalek	עֲמָלֵק	Nebuzaradan	נְבוּזַרְאֲדָן	Lo-ruhamah	לֹא רֻחָמָה
Omri	עָמְרִי	Nebuchadnezzar	נְבוּכַדְנֶאצַּר	Laban	לָבָן
Amram	עַמְרָם	Nebuchadrezzar	נְבוּכַדְרֶאצַּר	Labben	לַבֵּן
Amasa	עֲמָשָׂא	Naboth	נָבוֹת	Levi	לֵוִי
Ephron	עֶפְרוֹן	Nabal	נָבָל	Lemuel	לְמוּאֵל
Er	עֵר	Nadab	נָדָב	Lamech	לֶמֶךְ
Oreb	עֹרֵב	Noah	נֹחַ	Lappidoth	לַפִּידוֹת
Orpah	עָרְפָּה	Nahum	נַחוּם		
Asahel	עֲשָׂהאֵל	Nahor	נָחוֹר	**מ**	
Esau	עֵשָׂו	Nehemiah	נְחֶמְיָה		
Athaliah	עֲתַלְיָה	Nimrod	נִמְרֹד	Mehuman	מְהוּמָן
Othniel	עָתְנִיאֵל	Nahash	נָחָשׁ	Maher-shalal-hash-baz	מַהֵר שָׁלָל חָשׁ בַּז
		Nahshon	נַחְשׁוֹן	Moab	מוֹאָב
פ		Naamah	נַעֲמָה	Mahlon	מַחְלוֹן
		Naomi	נָעֳמִי	Michael	מִיכָאֵל
Potiphar	פּוֹטִיפַר	Naaman	נַעֲמָן	Micah	מִיכָה/מִיכָא
Poti-phera	פּוֹטִי־פֶרַע	Naphtali	נַפְתָּלִי	Micaiahu (הנביא)	מִיכָיְהוּ
Pul	פּוּל	Nathan	נָתָן	Micajehu (מהר אפרים)	מִיכָיְהוּ
Puah	פּוּעָה	Nethanel	נְתַנְאֵל	Michal	מִיכַל
Poratha	פּוֹרָתָא			Mishael	מִישָׁאֵל
Peleg	פֶּלֶג	**ס**		Meshach	מֵישַׁךְ
Palti	פַּלְטִי			Mesha	מֵישַׁע
Paltiel	פַּלְטִיאֵל	Sibbecai	סִבְּכַי	Malachi	מַלְאָכִי
Pelatiah	פְּלַטְיָהוּ	Sihon	סִיחוֹן	Malchizedek	מַלְכִּי־צֶדֶק
Ploni Almoni	פְּלֹנִי אַלְמֹנִי	Sisera	סִיסְרָא	Malchishua	מַלְכִּישׁוּעַ
Phinehas	פִּנְחָס	Sanballat	סַנְבַלַּט	Queen of Sheba	מַלְכַּת שְׁבָא
Peninnah	פְּנִנָּה	Sennacherib	סַנְחֵרִיב	Memucan	מְמוּכָן
Pekah	פֶּקַח	Saph	סַף	Manoah	מָנוֹחַ
Pekahiah	פְּקַחְיָה			Menahem	מְנַחֵם
Purah	פֻּרָה	**ע**		Manasseh	מְנַשֶּׁה
Parmashta	פַּרְמַשְׁתָּא			Mispar-begvai	מִסְפָּר־בִּגְוַי
Pharaoh	פַּרְעֹה	Obed-edom	עֹבֵד אֱדֹום/עֹבֵד אֱדֹם	Maacah	מַעֲכָה
Pharaoh-neco	פַּרְעֹה נְכֹו	Ebed-melech	עֶבֶד־מֶלֶךְ	Mephiboshet	מְפִיבֹשֶׁת
Perez	פֶּרֶץ	Eber	עֵבֶר	Merab	מֵרַב
Parshandatha	פַּרְשַׁנְדָתָא	Eglon	עֶגְלוֹן	Mordechai-bilshan	מָרְדְּכַי בִּלְשָׁן
Pashur	פַּשְׁחוּר	Oded	עֹדֵד	Mordechai	מָרְדְּכַי
		Iddo	עִדּוֹ	Merodach-baladan	מְרֹאדַךְ בַּלְאֲדָן
צ		Adriel	עַדְרִיאֵל	Miriam	מִרְיָם
		Obed	עוֹבֵד	Merari	מְרָרִי
Zibiah	צִבְיָה	Obadiah	עֹבַדְיָה	Moses	מֹשֶׁה
Zadok	צָדוֹק	Og	עוֹג	Meshullemeth	מְשֻׁלֶּמֶת
Zedekiah	צִדְקִיָה	Uzzah	עֻזָּא	Methusael	מְתוּשָׁאֵל
Zophar	צוֹפַר	Uzziah	עֻזִּיָה		
Ziba	צִיבָא	Ezra	עֶזְרָא		
Zelophehad	צְלָפְחָד	Azariah	עֲזַרְיָה		

English	Hebrew	English	Hebrew	English	Hebrew
Shemer	שֶׁמֶר	Rizpah	רִצְפָּה	Zemah	צֶמַח
Samson	שִׁמְשׁוֹן			Zephaniah	צְפַנְיָה
Shimshai	שִׁמְשַׁי	**שׁ**		Zipporah	צִפֹּרָה
Shinab	שִׁנְאָב			Zaphenath-paneah	צָפְנַת פַּעְנֵחַ
Seir	שֵׂעִיר	Saul	שָׁאוּל		
Shaashgaz	שַׁעַשְׁגַּז	Shearjashub	שְׁאָר יָשׁוּב	**ק**	
Shephatiah	שְׁפַטְיָה	Shebna	שֶׁבְנָא		
Shaphan	שָׁפָן	Sheba	שֶׁבַע	Kohath	קְהָת
Sarezer	שַׂרְאֶצֶר/שַׁרְאֶצֶר	Shadrach	שַׁדְרַךְ	Kore	קוֹרֵא
Sarah	שָׂרָה	Shavsha	שַׁוְשָׁא	Keturah	קְטוּרָה
Sarai	שָׂרַי	Shechem	שְׁכֶם/שְׁכֶם	Cain	קַיִן
Seraiah	שְׂרָיָה	Shecaniah	שְׁכַנְיָה	Kish	קִישׁ
Sheshbazzar	שֵׁשְׁבַּצַּר	Shelah	שֵׁלָה	Korah	קֹרַח
Seth	שֵׁת	Shallum	שַׁלּוּם		
Shethar-bozenai	שְׁתַר בּוֹזְנַאי	Solomon	שְׁלֹמֹה	**ר**	
		Salmah	שַׂלְמָה		
ת		Shelomith	שְׁלֹמִית	Reuben	רְאוּבֵן
		Shalmaneser	שַׁלְמַנְאֶסֶר	Rebecca	רִבְקָה
Tibni	תִּבְנִי	Shem	שֵׁם	Rabashakeh	רַב־שָׁקֵה
Tiglath-pileser	תִּגְלַת פִּלְאֶסֶר	Shemeber	שֶׁמְאֵבֶר	Regem-melech	רֶגֶם מֶלֶךְ
Tola	תּוֹלָע	Shamgar	שַׁמְגַּר	Ruth	רוּת
Tamar	תָּמָר	Shammah	שַׁמָּה	Rezon	רְזוֹן
Toi	תֹּעִי	Samuel	שְׁמוּאֵל	Rahab	רָחָב
Terah	תֶּרַח	Shemiramoth	שְׁמִירָמוֹת	Rehoboam	רְחַבְעָם
Tirzah	תִּרְצָה	Shimeah	שִׁמְעָא	Rachel	רָחֵל
Teresh	תֶּרֶשׁ	Simeon	שִׁמְעוֹן	Reuel	רְעוּאֵל
Tartan	תַּרְתָּן	Shimei	שִׁמְעִי	Reelaiah	רְעֵלָיָה
Tattenai	תַּתְּנַי	Shemaiah	שְׁמַעְיָה	Rezin	רְצִין

Tanach
at a Glance

Tanach at a Glance

The Jewish Bible is often referred to by the acronym תנ״ך, *Tanach*, derived from the first Hebrew letter of the word describing the content of each major division of the Jewish Scriptures — תורה, *Torah*; נביאים, *Neviim* (Prophets); and כתובים, *Kesuvim* (Writings). Following is a guide to themes and incidents seen in the Scriptures, with verse references. The verse number given indicates the beginning of a theme.

Torah / תורה

The word תורה, *Torah*, literally means *instruction*. In biblical terms, the Torah consists of חמשה חומשי תורה, the Five Books of Moses, also known as the *Chumash* [Pentateuch] (lit., "five books"): בראשית, *Genesis*; שמות, *Exodus*; ויקרא, *Leviticus*; במדבר, *Numbers*; and דברים, *Deuteronomy*. A portion of the Torah is read publicly in synagogues each week according to an annual reading cycle. This portion is called a "*parashah*" or "*sidrah*." Each *parashah* bears a name that is generally derived from a key Hebrew word in the first verse of the portion. There are 54 portions read throughout the Jewish calendar year, with some weeks including a double reading. The names of Torah portions read in the synagogue are transliterated from the Hebrew and provided as headings in **bold** font.

GENESIS / בראשית

PARASHAS BEREISHIS / פרשת בראשית

The beginning of Creation: First day — light & darkness	1:1
Second day — firmament and separation of waters	1:6
Third day — earth and seas	1:9
Fourth day — sun, moon, and stars	1:14
Fifth day — birds and fish	1:20
Sixth day — animals, insects, and Man	1:24
Seventh day: The Sabbath, day of rest	2:1
The Garden of Eden	2:8
Man in the garden	2:15
The Serpent's enticement	3:1
The first sin	3:6
The sinners are punished	3:14
Man's expulsion from Eden	3:23
Cain and Abel	4:1
The descendants of Cain	4:17
The genealogy of mankind	5:1
The ten generations from Adam to Noah	5:1
Prelude to the Flood	6:1

PARASHAS NOACH / פרשת נח

Noah	6:9
The decree of the Flood; dimensions of the Ark	6:13
The final call to enter the Ark	7:1
The animals enter the Ark, "two by two"	7:13
The Flood inundates the world	7:6
The waters recede	8:1
Noah sends forth the raven	8:6
Noah sends forth the dove three times	8:7
The earth dries	8:13
The command to leave the Ark	8:15
Noah brings an offering that pleases God	8:20
Rebuilding the world: God's covenant with Noah	9:1
The rainbow: An eternal covenant	9:12
The intoxication and shame of Noah	9:20
Noah foretells the destiny of his sons	9:25
The descendants of Noah	10:1
The seventy nations	10:2
Nimrod	10:8

The Tower of Babel and the dispersion	11:1
The ten generations from Noah to Abraham	11:10

PARASHAS LECH LECHA / פרשת לך לך

God's call to Abraham; the promise of greatness	12:1
Abraham comes to Canaan	12:4
Abraham and Sarah in Egypt	12:10
Sarah is kidnapped by the Egyptians	12:14
Abraham and Sarah return to the Land of Israel	13:1
Abraham and Lot part ways	13:5
The repetition of God's promise to Abraham	13:14
The war of the kings	14:1
Sodom is defeated	14:10
Lot is taken captive	14:12
Abraham saves Lot	14:13
Abraham shuns honors	14:22
God's reassurance to Abraham	15:1
The Covenant Between the Parts: The promise of the Land	15:7
God tells of future Egyptian exile and redemption	15:13
The ratification of the covenant	15:17
Hagar and Ishmael	16:3
The covenant: Father of a multitude of nations	17:1
New names and a new destiny	17:3
The covenant of circumcision	17:9
The promise to Sarah	17:16
Abraham circumcises all the males in his household	17:23

PARASHAS VAYEIRA / פרשת וירא

Visiting the sick and hospitality to strangers	18:1
The promise of a son is revealed to Sarah	18:10
God's love for Abraham	18:17
God reveals His plans for Sodom and Gommorah	18:20
Abraham intercedes for Sodom	18:23
Sodom is destroyed	19:1
Lot — a perplexing hero	19:4
Lot is saved	19:16
Lot begs for a concession	19:18

LEVITICUS / ויקרא

NUMBERS / במדבר

Prophets / נביאים

The middle section of the ך"נת, *Tanach*, is called נביאים, *Neviim*/Prophets. This section consists of the Books of יהושע, *Joshua*; שופטים, *Judges*; שמואל א-ב, *I & II Samuel*; מלכים א-ב, *I & II Kings*; ישעיה, *Isaiah*; ירמיה, *Jeremiah*; and יחזקאל, *Ezekiel*, as well as a grouping known as the Book of תרי עשר, *Trei Asar* — literally, *The Twelve* (Prophets). Although these are by no means the only prophets of Ancient Israel, as noted in the Overview, their prophetic books have been included in the canon of Jewish Scripture because of the timeless significance of the messages they contain. **Bold** entries indicate a new topic or note the reign of a new monarch.

JOSHUA / יהושע

JUDGES / שופטים

I SAMUEL / שמואל א

II SAMUEL / שמואל ב

I KINGS / מלכים א

II KINGS / מלכים ב

ISAIAH / ישעיה

JEREMIAH / ירמיה

EZEKIEL / יחזקאל

Writings / כתובים

The third major section of תנ"ך, *Tanach* is called כתובים, *Kesuvim*/Writings. It consists of the very familiar Books of תהלים, *Psalms* and משלי, *Proverbs*, as well as the Five Megillos (scrolls) of שיר השירים; *Song of Songs*; רות, *Ruth*; איכה, *Lamentations*; קהלת, *Ecclesiastes*; and אסתר, *Esther*. (These Megillos are read in conjunction with certain major Jewish holidays.) The remaining Books of the Writings include the Books of איוב, *Job*; דניאל, *Daniel*; עזרא־נחמיה, *Ezra-Nehemiah*; and דברי הימים א־ב, *I & II Chronicles*. **Bold** entries indicate a new topic or note the reign of a new monarch.

PSALMS / תהלים

Psalm 1. The Book of Psalms begins by asserting that the keys to good fortune are to shun evil influences and to study the Torah.

Psalm 2. No matter how powerful the force, nothing can thwart God's will. Rashi comments that the psalm alludes to the encounter between the nations and the Messiah.

Psalm 3. Despite the apparent hopelessness of one's situation, trust in God will bring peace and security.

Psalm 4. When sinners abandon the deceptiveness of temporary glory and recognize the truth, they will repent and find true happiness.

Psalm 5. When beset by enemies, pray for deliverance, not merely to alleviate physical suffering, but to be free to serve God without distraction.

Psalm 6. A prayer for when the community or individual suffers oppression and deprivation, sickness and distress.

Psalm 7. The righteous take heart in knowing that they will prevail over the wicked, while their enemies will fall victim to their own schemes.

Psalm 8. One with clarity of vision perceives God's handiwork everywhere and realizes that all man's accomplishments are His gifts.

Psalm 9. Despite their dazzling successes, the wicked will fade into oblivion; only the Godly will prevail.

Psalm 10. God punishes the wicked and champions the downtrodden.

Psalm 11. The righteous suffer to atone for sin, but are rewarded in the World to Come. Evildoers are rewarded in this world.

Psalm 12. Human friendship and loyalty are often suspect; but God's assurances are pure and enduring.

Psalm 13. Exile is like a long, dark, seemingly endless night.

Psalm 14. The entire world may have gone astray, but God will yet redeem His nation and Israel will rejoice.

Psalm 15. The way to come closer to God is to be generous and honest toward man.

Psalm 16. Talent and external forces are merely the Creator's tools in guiding history.

Psalm 17. The righteous person beseeches God to examine his deeds, to protect him from his enemies, and to allow him to enjoy God's glory.

Psalm 18. David earned the right to sing God's praises by perceiving the Divine hand in all the trials and triumphs of his long and varied career.

Psalm 19. Contemplation of nature and study of Torah will teach man to relate to God and to achieve spiritual fulfillment.

Psalm 20. God responds in times of distress.

Psalm 21. More than anyone else, kings and powerful people must set an example by acknowledging God's kindness.

Psalm 22. Speaking as an individual, the Jew prays for a final end to Israel's long exile from its land and its Temple.

Psalm 23. Whether in a verdant meadow or a parched desert, God provides man's every need.

Psalm 24. More than the land, brick, and mortar, only the personal qualities of the worshipers can build God's Temple.

Psalm 25. The righteous person seeks closeness to God and salvation from distress by repenting and extolling God's kindness to those who seek Him.

Psalm 26. A righteous person walks in purity and vigilance, and prays for Divine help in avoiding life's pitfalls.

Psalm 27. The House of God provides the sole island of constancy amid life's swirling waters of pain and disappointment. To dwell in it is David's constant goal.

Psalm 28. When He favors the righteous and rejects those unmindful of Him, God assists man in remaining on His chosen path.

Psalm 29. God's power and glory pervade all of creation. It functions solely according to His will, as has been manifested by His intervention in history.

Psalm 30. As darkness precedes dawn, so travail should be accepted as a prerequisite for success.

Psalm 31. David was relentlessly pursued, but always rescued. So too, we should entrust ourselves to God's mercy.

Psalm 32. God sends suffering and misfortune to help man reach the state of true repentance and its accompanying joy.

Psalm 33. Just as God created the physical world to function according to consistent laws, so His moral demands are constant and inviolable.

Psalm 34. David conquered despair by composing this hymn, in which the first verse begins with an *aleph* and each successive verse begins with the subsequent Hebrew letter, to show that our every faculty, from *aleph* to *tav*, should be dedicated to God.

Psalm 35. David appeals for help against friends turned traitors; so too, Israel in exile appeals against nations that repay Israel's contributions with oppression.

Psalm 36. Sin entices with false illusions; man can dispel them only with the objective light of truth.

Psalm 37. Do not be lured by the external trappings of

prosperity of the wicked, for it is God's blessed ones who will inherit the earth.

Psalm 38. Suffering must be recognized as chastisement for sin. One must repent and look to God for salvation.

Psalm 39. Suffering makes man aware of human frailty and transience. One should pray for the ability to devote oneself to Torah and *mitzvos*.

Psalm 40. A righteous person shows gratitude for God's help by affirming his allegiance to the Torah and proclaiming His wonders to the world.

Psalm 41. By contemplating the experiences of the poor and the sick, one becomes aware of God's loving closeness to man, even in the most hopeless circumstances.

Psalm 42. The exiled individual or nation calls longingly to God to be brought home.

Psalm 43. When God sends forth His light, the exiles will return to their land.

Psalm 44. Vividly portraying the recurring oppressions and persecutions of exile, Israel pleads for strength to endure until it is redeemed.

Psalm 45. A song of praise, describing the splendor and sovereignty of the king Messiah.

Psalm 46. In the upheavals of the Messianic era, God will shield Israel, as He shields all distraught people who seek His support.

Psalm 47. God's sovereignty will ultimately be recognized and accepted by all mankind.

Psalm 48. Jerusalem is eternally beautiful and glorious because God chose it for the abode of His Presence.

Psalm 49. Man should use his sojourn on earth to enhance his spiritual development and prepare for the World to Come.

Psalm 50. God desires not only external adherence to His commandments, but purity of spirit.

Psalm 51. David's psalm of remorse includes the principles of repentance. Thus, it is a fitting prayer for any penitent.

Psalm 52. Doeg's fate exemplifies the tragedy that results when one turns one's talents to evil.

Psalm 53. Alluding prophetically to the destruction of the Land and the Temple, this psalm also assures Israel's eventual restoration.

Psalm 54. Pursued by foes, one must pray for God's salvation.

Psalm 55. Despite the revolt of his son Absalom and the defection of his intimate friend and adviser Ahithophel, David was unwavering in his faith that God would enable him to prevail.

Psalm 56. Though his situation seemed hopeless, David's trust in God was unshaken, an attitude to be emulated by anyone in distress.

Psalm 57. Hotly pursued, his life in dire peril, David affirms his absolute faith in God.

Psalm 58. A prayer for the destruction of the violent oppressors in order that all may say, "God is the true judge in the land"

Psalm 59. Surrounded by Saul's men who were ordered to murder him, David prays that God rescue him, so that he may sing His praises.

Psalm 60. At the outset of his campaign against Israel's enemies, David expresses his faith in God's assurance that his reign would be consolidated from within and feared from without.

Psalm 61. David's personal experiences while fleeing into exile from his enemies parallel Israel's national experience.

Psalm 62. One must never allow the power and ill-gotten wealth of the oppressor to erode one's trust in God and faith in His justice.

Psalm 63. Though a victim of malicious slander; exiled from nation, family, and home; alone in a desolate wilderness, David never wavers in his love for God.

Psalm 64. When the enemy plots evil, sharpens its attack, and lays traps, one should take refuge in God.

Psalm 65. Calamities such as drought should spur mankind to repentance. God Who subdues the mightiest forces can revitalize the most parched land and withered nation.

Psalm 66. God's intervention in the affairs of man is not mere speculation; it is attested to by history, physically, perceptibly, and irrefutably.

Psalm 67. A prayer for the arrival of the Messianic era, when all mankind will worship God and earn His blessing

Psalm 68. Israel's triumph over the mightiest empires has been played out many times throughout history.

Psalm 68. The phenomenon of Israel's triumph will be repeated for the last time with the Final Redemption, when God will be universally worshiped.

Psalm 69. A vivid prophetic portrayal of Israel's plight in its long and bitter exile, and an impassioned plea for its speedy deliverance

Psalm 70. An appeal to God for rescue from one's enemies

Psalm 71. Even in old age, when one's normal resources for contending with difficulty are diminished, one should turn to God, Whose comfort never fails.

Psalm 72. An aged King David turns over his unfinished work to his son and prays for his success.

Psalm 73. It may seem that the wicked prosper, exempt from Divine punishment. However, a deeper and broader perspective reveals the emptiness and futility of their glamorous lives.

Psalm 74. From the agony of exile, the Jew prays that God will deliver His nation, thereby causing His sovereignty to be acknowledged by the entire world.

Psalm 75. A prayer for the ultimate Redemption, when God will bring about the collapse of evil, and the lasting elevation of Israel

Psalm 76. A prayer for the time when people will realize the futility of rebelling against God, and will completely accept His mastery

Psalm 77. When the chastisement of exile has fully purified His nation, God will again intervene as He did when He redeemed Israel from Egypt.

Psalm 78. God's love and concern for Israel are ever present. Failure to keep that memory alive is a major cause of sin, while remembering it brings solace in difficult times.

Psalm 79. A prayer that Israel be restored to its Land, so that God's honor will be restored in the eyes of a doubting world

Psalm 80. Recalling its earlier glorious relationship with God, Israel pleads for its restoration.

Psalm 81. No matter how low one has sunk, a firm resolve to heed God's word will cause Him to loosen the fetters and send Redemption.

Psalm 82. The maintenance of equity and justice is a prerequisite for the continued existence of the world.

Psalm 83. The historical enmity of the nations against Israel is an outgrowth of hatred for that which Israel stands for: the complete subordination of all human striving to God's will.

Psalm 84. Neither crushing persecution nor the blandishments of alien prosperity should deflect one from striving to attain closeness with God.

Psalm 85. As He had restored Israel and the Temple after the first Destruction, so may He again restore them, this time permanently.

Psalm 86. Wholehearted supplication, complete dedication, and awareness of God's closeness lift one's soul and bring it closer to God.

Psalm 87. Greatness and nobility emanate from Jerusalem, Israel's spiritual center.

Psalm 88. An impassioned plea for deliverance from Israel's long, almost unbearable, exile

Psalm 89. Throughout its exile, Israel is sure that God will fulfill His promises to David.

Psalm 90. After portraying the brevity and fragility of man's existence on earth, Moses beseeches God to help man use his finite time properly and productively.

Psalm 91. By scorning conventional forms of protection and seeking refuge only in the Most High, the believer can live without fear of those who would harm him.

Psalm 92. On the Sabbath, free from the weekday struggle for a livelihood, the Jew can turn heart and mind to the perception of God's ways.

Psalm 93. In Messianic times, God's majesty and grandeur will be recognized by all.

Psalm 94. Goodness will prevail and evil will be punished. God will champion Israel's cause and deliver it from its enemies.

Psalm 95. Come acknowledge God as Creator and guiding force of the universe. Do not emulate your ancestors who strayed after falsehood.

Psalm 96. When all the nations on earth will recognize God's sovereignty, they will join in a new song acknowledging Him.

Psalm 97. After the upheavals that will precede the Messiah's coming, the world will recognize its folly, and God will reign supreme over the entire earth.

Psalm 98. A song of praise for the revelation of the final Redemption

Psalm 99. Once the nations acknowledge His sovereignty, they will follow the dictates of righteousness that Israel has safeguarded throughout its history.

Psalm 100. A psalm to accompany the thanksgiving-offering

Psalm 101. The traits of purity and truth enable an individual to utilize his abilities for their intended purpose.

Psalm 102. A prayer for anyone beset by any misfortune.

Psalm 103. The soul in turmoil is calmed by recounting God's infinite kindness.

Psalm 104. A tribute to God for the wondrous world He has created and continuously sustains; a depiction of His unmistakable hand in nature

Psalm 105. God guides the course of history; seemingly unrelated events were tied together to bring about a society of all mankind governed by God's holy Torah.

Psalm 106. God's presence and loving-kindness are always near; one need but have open eyes and an open heart to see them.

Psalm 107. Those who experience God's deliverance — from desolation, from captivity, from sickness, from the sea — must publicly proclaim their gratitude for God's enduring kindness.

Psalm 108. A prophetic psalm about the consolidation of the Messiah's reign

Psalm 109. A plea to God for deliverance from scheming maligners who arise against the individual or the nation

Psalm 110. David's legendary power came through Divine favor earned through his righteousness.

Psalm 111. God created man with all that he needs, in body and mind, to perform God's will; but man must choose to embark on this path.

Psalm 112. One who truly fears God will fear no misfortune; he will be safe and secure in God's Providence.

Psalm 113. A psalm to God's control of creation and to His kindness to all creatures

Psalm 114. Israel was elevated upon leaving Egypt; all of nature was overwhelmed by God's intervention.

Psalm 115. May God once again intervene in the affairs of man, so that the idolaters may know Him and become as imbued as Israel with faith in the true God.

Psalm 116. Israel declares its love for God despite its lowly state among the nations, and prays for the Redemption.

Psalm 117. Praise God, all nations.

Psalm 118. Israel expresses gratitude and confidence as it looks forward to Divine Redemption from the straits of exile and oppression.

Psalm 119. In the Hebrew, an alphabetical arrangement — eight verses for each letter — describes the ceaseless striving to faithfully live a Torah-true life regardless of time, place, circumstance, or social environment

Psalm 120. The first of fifteen "Songs of Ascents"

Psalm 121. A declaration of faith and a prayer for God's constant protection

Psalm 122. A hymn to Jerusalem, the city where every visitor experiences an encounter with holiness

Psalm 123. A Jew in exile yearns for God's succor.

Psalm 124. It is only God's care and protection that have saved Israel from extinction.

Psalm 125. Those who trust in God will be secure in His protection.

Psalm 126. Eventually God will return Israel to its land, rejuvenated in body and spirit.

Psalm 127. When God crowns man's efforts with success, he can raise his children to serve God.

Psalm 128. Only the righteous person and his family experience true bliss in both worlds.

Psalm 129. Israel's survival against all odds attests to God's providential control of its destiny.

Psalm 130. A person in distress prays to God from the depths of his heart.

Psalm 131. A righteous person is not arrogant.

Psalm 132. If one cannot complete a task, yet faithfully lays the groundwork, the final goal will be achieved in his merit.

Psalm 133. The idyllic unity among brothers brings God's blessings.

Psalm 134. Even in exile, Israel blesses God.

Psalm 135. God's continuing role in supervising and guiding history leads to the conclusion that all is futile except to serve Him.

Psalm 136. A song of God's creation and rulership of the world in general and Israel in particular

Psalm 137. A prophetic lament over the exiles, and a charge to them to never remove Jerusalem from their hearts and minds

Psalm 138. One must live with profound awareness that God is omnipotent and intimately close to those who seek Him.

Psalm 139. God's omniscience and omnipotence

are absolute; He is aware of a person's innermost thoughts.

Psalm 140. A person who feels powerless to combat the working of deceit must place his trust in God.

Psalm 141. Even in crisis, one must pray not only for physical deliverance, but also for God's help in avoiding the slightest trace of sin.

Psalm 142. Utterly trapped, one places oneself completely at God's mercy.

Psalm 143. Sorely pained by persecution and suffering, one can be pulled from the abyss by recalling God's past miracles.

Psalm 144. David, the quintessential Jewish monarch, attributes all his accomplishments to God alone.

Psalm 145. Man is obligated to praise God's providential provision of the needs of every living creature.

Psalm 146. God is the One Who cares for the underprivileged and oppressed, despite the current ascendancy of our enemies.

Psalm 147. The Creator of the universe and all it contains will redeem and rebuild Jerusalem, from whence holiness and Torah emanate.

Psalm 148. All of nature — celestial and terrestrial — joins in a grand symphony of joyous songs of praise to God.

Psalm 149. The lofty praises uttered in honor of God will cut down the wicked and bring forward the glory of the righteous.

Psalm 150. Praise God in every way possible for all the manifestations of His greatness.

PROVERBS / משלי

Note: Chapters 10-24 contain one-or two-sentence aphorisms that have not been condensed into themes. See commentary at Chapter 10, p. 1580.

Solomon's purpose	1:1
Let God and your parents be your adornment	1:7
The blandishments of the wicked ...	1:10
... are a dangerous trap	1:17
God's message is everywhere —	
if you care to see it	1:20
But if you refuse to heed His message,	
retribution is inevitable	1:24
Only if you treasure wisdom will you	
acquire it ... for then God will grant it to you	2:1
The Torah will save you from perverse ideas ...	2:9
... from evildoers ...	2:12
... and from purveyors of temptation	2:16
For in the end, the just will prevail	2:20
Cleave to the Torah	3:1
Trust in God will bring you success	3:5
Seek discipline and wisdom	3:11
The Torah and its wisdom are	
your guarantors for a good life	3:19
Be kind and thoughtful ...	3:27
... avoid strife, violence, and scoffing	3:30
A loving chastisement	4:1
Appreciate the value of wisdom	4:7
The Torah guarantees meaningful life	4:10
Evil people are worse than one can imagine	4:16
Righteous and wicked; light and darkness	4:18

Safeguard that which matters most	4:20
Consider your deeds carefully	4:25
Beware of enticement; it leads to doom	5:1
The wicked woman's wiles	
come at a prohibitive price	5:7
Too late, you will regret your horrendous error	5:11
Remain loyal to your wife and your Torah	5:15
The wicked will be trapped by their own sins	5:20
Avoid commitments that are beyond your abilities	6:1
From an ant learn to be industrious	6:6
Dishonest people will get their undoing	6:12
God hates those who incite strife	6:16
Seek ways to keep the commandments	6:20
Passion is a consuming fire	6:25
Adultery is worse and more	
unforgivable than theft	6:30
Do not let my advice slip away	7:1
A naive youth lurches toward temptation,	
and is approached by a harlot who tempts	
him with promises of pleasure ...	7:7
... and convinces him that	
he has nothing to fear	7:18
He rushes to his doom	7:21
Listen to me and avoid her wiles	7:24
Wisdom invites all to learn from her	8:1
It is superior to all earthly riches	8:10

JOB / איוב

SONG OF SONGS / שיר השירים

RUTH / רות

LAMENTATIONS / איכה

ECCLESIASTES / קהלת

ESTHER / אסתר